A Biographical DIRECTORY OF LIBRARIANS in the United States and Canada

Sponsored by the
Council of National Library Associations

CNLA Advisory Committee

Gertrude L. Annan
Pauline Atherton
Joseph Becker
Harry Bitner
Robert H. Blackburn
David H. Clift
Jack Dalton
Luther Evans
Elizabeth Ferguson
John A. Humphry
Bill M. Woods

(formerly *Who's Who in Library Service*)

A Biographical DIRECTORY OF LIBRARIANS in the United States and Canada

Fifth Edition

LEE ASH, Editor
B. A. UHLENDORF, Associate editor

American Library Association
Chicago 1970

International Standard Book Number 0-8389-0084-4 (1970)
Library of Congress Catalog Card Number 79-118854

Printed in the United States of America

Dedicated to

John H. Ottemiller

Librarian, 1916–1968

who revived the series and who has been the inspiration for its continuation

Publisher's Foreword

With the publication of this fifth edition, the biographical directory formerly known as *Who's Who in Library Service* assumes a new name and a new publisher.

As the attentive reader may recognize, A BIOGRAPHICAL DIRECTORY OF LIBRARIANS IN THE UNITED STATES AND CANADA is really a modification of the subtitle that has been carried in the third and fourth editions. For some time the feeling has been that it is a more descriptive title of the contents, and so the Council of National Library Associations, sponsor of this and earlier editions, concurred in making the change now.

The Publishing Board of ALA has long been concerned with the continuation of this directory as a service to the profession. After thoughtful consideration, an agreement was reached with the Shoe String Press for ALA to become publisher of the fifth and succeeding editions.

The editorial and production work by the Shoe String Press for the fifth edition included using for the first time computers in the composition of the directory. This technological change will, it is hoped, make preparation of subsequent editions easier than it has been in the past and will enable ALA to issue revisions at more frequent intervals and increase the usefulness of the directory.

With the changes involved in publication of this edition, the Council of National Library Associations continues its concern with the directory through its Advisory Committee.

Editor's Preface

After many years of experimentation and a variety of mixed parentages stemming from an unstable and makeshift ancestry, *Who's Who in Library Service* at last comes into flower as a new species nurtured by the American Library Association and freshly called A BIOGRAPHICAL DIRECTORY OF LIBRARIANS IN THE UNITED STATES AND CANADA. This change in title reflects the reality of the book's inclusiveness. The change in publisher provides an opportunity for computerized updating at more frequent intervals under the supervision of our largest national library association with the continuing cooperation of all other library agencies, especially those represented among the sponsors of the present edition, the Council of National Library Associations.

The changeover from traditional composition to computer record and composition has caused what may appear to be unseemly delays in the production of a volume of this kind. It is our hope that the delays have not affected the usefulness of the book, and that the method that caused them will prove to have advantages that will justify the conversion to it.

For this fifth edition, all material in the fourth was computerized, and printouts were made for every name and mailed *first class* to addresses as of the record in 1966. Obviously a large number of these were not current because of relocations, marriages, retirements, and deaths. Printouts that were returned were kept in order and screened for name changes as requests for questionnaires or information came to us in response to our widely publicized notices of the new edition in preparation. The membership list of ALA (as of 1968) was compared with *Who's Who,* 1966, and all exact names with the new addresses were updated; all other entries were added, along with the membership lists of the Special Libraries Association and of the Canadian Library Association. Names not in the 1966 edition with either original addresses or updated addresses did not receive a printout but were sent a new blank questionnaire. We were all aware that we did not reach all practicing librarians and we made a special effort—through announcements at meetings and news notes sent to library journals and newsletters—to ask all active librarians who wished to be included in the new edition to write us for questionnaires if they had not received a printout for updating.

With indefatigable effort the associate editor, B. A. Uhlendorf, once again prepared a great part of the original copy for composition, and most of the typographical variances are due to the usual mechanical difficulties inherent in transfer from hard copy to computer exigencies. The same remarks about inconsistencies of entry that appeared in the previous edition apply to this one: the place of inclusion for some information may vary (for example, under which section of the questionnaire a biographee listed membership in an organization), or the hierarchical order of associations and their divisions and committees may be listed in varying arrangements. Furthermore, conversion to computer form may have created some still unrecognized complications besides changes in the alphabetization of the names of religious (Reverend, Sister, Brother, etc.), to say nothing of what *Mr., Mrs., Dr.,* and divorcees, especially, may have done. We have tried to be helpful by including as an appendix a list of all people who were in *Who's Who,* fourth edition, but from whom no replies or information was received. Readers are directed to the earlier edition for information valid as of that date.

Closely related to the "no reply" group are the individuals who did not update the printout sent to them. As a result, any incorrect information in the 1966 edition or any information wrong when copied by the transcribers will appear in incorrect form. The editors and publishers cannot take any responsibility for these errors.

Terms of eligibility were printed on the questionnaire: "Active members of the library profession, archivists, or information scientists associated with all types of libraries in the United States and Canada. . . . The norm of professional education is the bachelor's degree together with the bachelor's or master's degree from a library school, received prior to July 1, 1969. Five years of recognized and progressive professional experience may be substituted by those who do not possess one or both of these formal educational requirements."

Just as in the past, the editor's principal task was to evaluate each of the biographee's sketches within the confines of this statement. It has become apparent, over the past few years, that more and more persons are filling professional library positions whose professional preparation does not fall within the limits of the eligibility described above. We—the editor and his advisers—have felt that a number of the questionnaires reflected this trend and that *as a directory* the volume would be deficient if we limited ourselves to a strict interpretation of the terms of eligibility. Thus anyone is included who might conceivably be admitted to these pages with justification; for this reason we are especially grateful for the change in the name of the volume.

Some other conditions have, of course, affected judgment with regard to inclusion: the evaluation of education as against relative experience; lack of professional experience; foreign librarians not connected with United States or Canadian libraries (even though they may have graduated from an American library school); library friends or trustees who do not serve in any professional capacity; and persons who are inactive and who, on the basis of recorded information, do not seem likely to return to the profession. In the case of information specialists, programmers, and archivists, we relied upon data in the questionnaires, and only those individuals who specifically indicated a regular library position or assignment have been included. Retired persons were not included unless there was definite evidence in their questionnaires (or it was known to us) that they still work as paid consultants or are otherwise active in librarianship. Again, we can do no more than apologize for the omission of any such persons who are not included.

The tedium of the editorial process is not relieved by those who submit false, inaccurate, or incomplete entries. (Everyone knows about Nigel Molesworth of St. Custard's—who did not make it this time!) We are not equipped to follow through on unusual names, some of which are real. We continue to struggle with noteworthy recalcitrants but are powerless to include even the names and addresses of persons who request that they not be listed. And we still have flagitious feelings toward those who returned illegible questionnaires, who wrote entries that had to be rewritten, and who did not bother to fill in the form, referring us instead to previous editions or other reference books. There were also persons who left the questionnaire unsigned and thereby deprived us of one check on the accuracy of the name.

The questions asked of biographees are listed below, along with certain remarks concerning editorial form. For the most part, the editorial policy of previous editions was our guide. Specifically, we note the following problems that the copy editors faced and the additional rules that have been followed with general consistency. We did not, however, do more editing of content or arrangement than was considered necessary for the sake of clarity.

1. *Biographee's name*—With the change to computerized transcription and production there are some alterations in abbreviations, form, and alphabetization, which may not always be consistent. We hope, however, that our system of entry will be clear and that it will be perfected in subsequent editions. When persons who were listed in *Who's Who* IV filled out new questionnaires rather than update the printout, the copy editors added updated material and corrections to the printout, since it was necessarily the authoritative form. Unused parts of names are in parentheses and are ignored in alphabetization; titles do not influence alphabetization although they may appear in different positions. To follow this rule, considerable alteration of normal computer alphabetization has been required and some names (particularly religious) may still be found in incorrect order. Because of the prevalence of the name *Mary* among nuns, a nun's name has been alphabetized according to the last word of her religious name or to her surname. The editor went down in defeat to the uncompromising computer when its associates insisted on the "telephone book" instead of the library system of filing *M', Mac,* and *Mc.*

2. *Place of birth*—Only city and state are given. Except for major foreign cities, the country of birth is indicated if other than the United States.

3. *Date of birth*—Unless the year was given on the questionnaire, this item has been omitted. Editors took the dates as given by a biographee. The order requested was "day, month, year"; therefore, what was given as "3 8 04" is transcribed as "3 Ag 04."

4. *Name of spouse*—Deceased persons are not listed, nor are divorced or separated spouses.

5. *Education: Give colleges and universities only, with dates of attendance; degrees or certifications received, if any. List in order of attendance*—Colleges and universities are shown without city except where ambiguity exists; schools are listed only when years and/or major fields are shown; degrees are cited as listed by biographee.

6. *List languages read or spoken with facility*—All languages indicated by a biographee are included. English is listed only for French Canadians.

7. *List positions: All work in progressive order with present position last, including library and other. Include periods of service in the armed forces, showing branch of service, specialty, and rank attained*—Information appears as given (often incomplete and lacking place or dates). We cannot take responsibility for the indiscriminate use of the terms "Librarian," "Assistant Librarian," etc., for junior staff members. Part-time work is not indicated as "part time," though summer, temporary, and volunteer work are indicated as such. Only years are given for dates of employment.

8. *Activities: List other important career or special assignments (consultantships, advisory work, etc.) with title, place and dates*—Certain problems encountered here are described above. We can only hope that most information is current and reasonably correct insofar as citation of organizations is concerned.

9. *Organizations: Principal national, state, and regional professional associations and positions as officer or chairman; also special activities, etc.; a) National associations, b) State or regional associations*—The information supplied by some respondents demanded that editorial judgment be exercised and in those cases changes have been made.

10. *Other pertinent (professional/nonprofessional, community, or civic) organizations and clubs*—Information given is usually as supplied.

11. *Honors, awards, etc., of reference interest*—Only major honors are listed.

12. *Publications; major editorial contributions. (List books by title, giving dates of publication; list journals edited.)*—Only books, doctoral dissertations, major editorial contributions, and ACRL microcard publications are given; theses and articles are not.

13. *Contributions to other professional books or journals? Yes__No__*—A "yes" reply indicates articles published in professional journals (not necessarily library journals) and, occasionally, chapters or sections of books.

14. *Principal areas of professional interest (e.g. cataloging, reference, rare books, etc.)*—Listings are usually as given by biographee.

15. *Mailing address preferred*—The address of current employment is given if this question was not answered.

Above all, we must thank Frances Ottemiller, of The Shoe String Press, for her forbearance, good humor, and genial sense of balance in the face of innumerable mechanical problems. The associate editor, B. A. Uhlendorf, who continued his careful supervision of copy, must have our applause for his cheerful facing-up to the dreadful challenge of technical supervision. We particularly want to thank Jean Rovetti and Judith Talarczyk, of The Shoe String Press, and Alice Pickett, who picked up the pieces at the end, for many helpful services and their willingness to "go the extra mile."

The Shoe String Press wishes especially to thank William Rutter, Associate Executive Director of the American Library Association, and the ALA Publishing Services staff for their foresight, helpfulness, understanding, and cooperation in the transfer of this volume to ALA's publishing program from Shoe String's.

This fifth edition stands as a memorial to John H. Ottemiller to whom the book is dedicated. We have missed his guidance throughout the preparation of the volume, and we are sure that he would be relieved and pleased by the prospect of the series' continuation under the aegis of the American Library Association in cooperation with the Council of National Library Associations.

Abbreviations

This is a partial list of abbreviations since many in general use are not included.

AAAS—American Association for the Advancement of Science
AALL—American Association of Law Libraries
AALS—Association of American Library Schools
AASchL (ASchL)—American Association of School Librarians (Division of ALA)
AAStateL—American Association of State Libraries (Division of ALA)
AAUP—American Association of University Professors
AAUW—American Association of University Women
acad—academic, academy
access—accessions
ACA—Americans for Constitutional Action
ACEI—Association for Childhood Education International
ACLS—American Council of Learned Societies
ACLU—American Civil Liberties Union
acquis—acquisition, acquisitions
ACRL—Association of College & Research Libraries (Division of ALA)
ACS—American Chemical Society
act—acting
ADA—Americans for Democratic Action
admin—administration, administrative, administrator
adv—adviser, advisory
AEA—American Association for Adult Education
AEC—Atomic Energy Commission
AETH—American Educational Theatre Association
AFFS—American Federation of Film Societies
agcy—agency
agric—agricultural, agriculture
agt—agent
AHA—American Historical Association
AHIL—Association of Hospital & Institution Libraries (Division of ALA)
ALA—American Library Association
ALI—American Library Institute
ALTA—American Library Trustee Association (Division of ALA)
A&M—Agricultural & Mechanical College
Amer—America, American
AMA—American Medical Association
APLA—Atlantic Provinces Library Association
arch—architectural, architecture
archaeol—archaeological, archaeology
ARL—Association of Research Libraries
ARMA—American Records Management Association
ASA—American Standards Association
ASCAP—American Society of Composers, Authors & Publishers
ASCD—Association for Supervision & Curriculum Development
ASD—Adult Services Division (Division of ALA)
ASIS—American Society of Information Scientists

ASLIB—Association of Special Libraries and Information Bureaus
ASchL—Association of School Librarians or School Librarians Association
assn—association
assoc—associate
asst—assistant
ATA—American Teacher Association
a-v—audio-visual
bd—board
bibliog(r)—bibliographer, bibliography
bind—binding
biog—biographical, biography
biol—biological, biology
bk—book
bkmob—bookmobile
bot—botany
br—branch
BSA—Bibliographical Society of America
BWI—British West Indies
bur—bureau
bus—business
CACUL—Canadian Association of College & University Libraries
Can—Canada, Canadian
catlg—catalog, cataloging
catalgr (catlgr)—cataloger
ctr—center
certif—certificate, certification, certified
CFSTI—Clearinghouse for Federal Scientific & Technical Information
ch—church
chap—chapter
chem—chemical, chemist, chemistry
child—children, children's
chm—chairman
circ—circulating, circulation
CLR—Council of Library Resources
clr—classroom
clsf—classification, classified, classifying
clsfr—classifier
CNLA—Council of National Library Associations
C of C—Chamber of Commerce
Co, co—County, company
col—college
COLT—Council on Library Technology
com—commerce, commercial, committee
commsn—commission
commun—community
consul—consultant
contin—continuations
contrib—contributor
CORE—Congress of Racial Equality
corr—correspondence, correspondent, corresponding
coun—counselor, council, councilor
cpl—corporal
CSD—Children's Services Division (Division of ALA)
CURLS—College, University & Research Libraries Section of the California Library Association
DAR—Daughters of the American Revolution
DAVI—Department of Audio-Visual Instruction (Division of NEA)
DC—Decimal Classification, District of Columbia
DCW—Daughters of Colonial War
del—delegate
dept—department
descr—descriptive
devel—developing, development
dir—directing, director
dist—district
div—division
doc—document
DOD—U.S. Department of Defense
DOT—U.S. Department of Transportation
DR—Dominican Republic
dr—drive
E—East
EA—Education Association
East—Eastern
econ—economic(s), economical, economy
Ed—education—in degree
ed—edited, edition, editor, editorial
educ—education, educational
EFLA—Educational Film Library Association
elem—elementary
engr(g)—engineer, engineering
Eng—England, English
EOC—Economic Opportunities Council
eval—evaluating, evaluation
eve—evening
exec—executive
expt—experiment, experimental
ext—extension
fac—faculty
fed—federal, federated, federation
fin—finance, financial

Fr—French
FWA—Federal Works Agency
gen—general
geneal—genealogical, genealogy
geog—geography
geol—geology
Ger—German
Gk—Greek
gov—governor
govt—government
grad—graduate
gp—group
GSA—General Services Administration
Gt—Great
hd—head
hdqtrs—headquarters
hts—heights
hwy—highway
hist—historic, historical, history
histn—historian
hon—honorary
hosp—hospital
IAALD—International Association of Agricultural Librarians & Documentalists
ICOM—International Council of Museums
IFLA—International Federation of Library Associations
inc—incorporated
ind, indus—industrial, industry
info—information
ins—insurance
inst—institute, institution
instr—instructional, instructor
intermed—intermediate
intl—international
IRA—International Reading Association
ISAD—Information Science & Automation Division (Division of ALA)
Ital—Italian
jr—junior
jt—joint
LA—Library Association
lab—laboratory
LACONI—Library Administrators' Council of Northern Illinois
LACUNY—Library Association of City University of New York
LAD—Library Administration Division (Division of ALA)
lang—language
Lat—Latin
LC—Library of Congress
LED—Library Education Division (Division of ALA)
legis—legislation, legislative, legislature
LI—Long Island
lib—library
Lib Sci—Library Science
libn—librarian
libnship—librarianship
libs—libraries
lit—literary, literature
LOMS—Library Organization & Management Section of LAD
LPRC—Library Public Relations Council
LS—Library Science—in degree
LSU—Louisiana State University
LSCA—Library Service & Construction Act
Lt—Lieutenant
LWV—League of Women Voters
MARLC—Middle Atlantic Regional Library Conference
mech—mechanical, mechanics
med—medical, medicine
mem—member
memb—membership
Mex—Mexico
mfg—manufacturing
mfr—manufacturer
mgr—manager
mgt—management
mil—military
MPLA—Mountain Plains Library Association
ms(s)—manuscript, manuscripts
mt—mount, mountain
mun—municipal
mus—museum, music
N—North
NAACP—National Association for the Advancement of Colored People
NAS—National Academy of Science
NASA—National Aeronautics & Space Administration
nat—national
NCEA—National Catholic Education Association
NCSS—National Council for the Social Studies
NCTE—National Council of Teachers of English

NDEA—National Defense Education Act
NEA—National Education Association
NELA—New England Library Association
Nfld—Newfoundland
NIH—National Institutes of Health
NLM—National Library of Medicine
NLW—National Library Week
NMA—National Microfilm Association
No—Northern
NS—Nova Scotia
NSCD—National Society of Colonial Dames
NSF—National Science Foundation
NSPI—National Society for Programmed Instruction
NYA—National Youth Administration
OEO—Office of Economic Opportunity
off—office, officer
Ont—Ontario
org—organization, organized, organizer
period—periodical
philol—philological, philology
philos—philosophy
pfc—private first class
PHS—U.S. Public Health Service
phys—physical
PI—Philippine Islands
pk—park
pkwy—parkway
pl—place
PLA—Public Library Association (Division of ALA)
PNLA—Pacific Northwest Library Association
pol—political, politics
polytech—polytechnic
Portu—Portuguese
pos—position
PR—Puerto Rico
prep—preparation
Pres—President
prim—primary
prin—principal
prob—problem
proc—process, processes
prod—product, production
prof—professional, professor
proj—project
prov—province, provincial
psych—psychology
pt—point
pub—public
publ—publish, published, publishing
publn—publication
rec—recorder, recording
rectalgr—recataloger
ref—reference
reg—regional
rel—relations
relig—religion, religious
rep—representative
res—reserve, reserved
ret—retired
rd—road
rm—room
RN—Registered Nurse
RSD—Reference Services Division (Division of ALA)
RT—Round Table
Rte—Route
RTSD—Resources & Technical Services Division (Division of ALA)
S—South
SAA—Society of American Archivists
SAR—Sons of the American Revolution
SCD—Society for Childhood Development
sch—school
sci—science
SCLD—State College Library Division
sec—secretarial, secretary
sect—section
sel—selection
SELA—Southeastern Library Association
Sem—seminar, Seminary
sgt—sergeant
ser—serial, serials
serv—service, services
SI—Staten Island
SLA—Special Libraries Association
So—Southern
soc—social, society
sociol—sociological, sociology
Sp (Span)—Spanish
spec—special, specialization
Sq—Square
sr—senior
st—street
sta—station
Stat (statis, statist)—statistical, statistician, statistics
stud—student
sub—substitute
subs—subscriptions

subj—subject
SUC—State University College
SUNY—State University of New York
supt—superintendent
supv—supervising, supervisor, supervisory
SWLA—Southwest Library Association
syst—system
TA—Teachers Association
tchg—teaching
tchr—teacher
tech—technical, technician, technological, technology
temp—temporary
ter—terrace
TH—Territory of Hawaii
theol—theological, theology
twp—township
tr—translation, translator
train—training
travel—traveling
treas—treasurer, treasury
U (Univ)—University
UCLA—University of California (Los Angeles)
UDC—United Daughters of the Confederacy
USC—University of Southern California
USBE—United States Book Exchange
USIA, USIS—U.S. Information Agency
VA—Veterans Administration
VI—Virgin Islands
v-pres—vice-President
voc—vocational
W—West
West—Western
West Res—Western Reserve University
wk—work
wker—worker
wkshop—workshop
WNBA—Women's National Book Association
WPA—Works Progress Administration; Works Projects Administration
ya—young adult
YASD—Young Adult Services Division (Division of ALA)
yp—young people
zool—zoology, zoological

A Biographical DIRECTORY OF LIBRARIANS in the United States and Canada

A

AALDERS, CATHERINE A O. b Halifax NS Can 1 S 31. 4: Lewis E Aalders. 5: Dalhousie U 49-53 (Russian) BA. 6: Russian. 7: Asst to Ref Libn NS Provincial Lib 53-54; Physics libn Cornell U 54-57; Libn Canada Agric Research Station, Kentville NS 59-60; Hd Ref Dept Dartmouth Reg Lib 69-. 8: Free-lance Russ-Eng Trans 60-; Abstractor of Russian sci articles for Biological Abstracts 63-64. 9: ALA. 10: Alpha Gamma Delta; Nat Platform Assn. 14: Ref. 15: 299 Portland st, Dartmouth NS Can.

AAMODT, DAVID ARTHUR. b Salt Lake City Utah 7 My 37. 4: Christa Eisert. 5: UUtah 55-58, 61-62 (Ger) BA; UTubingen 59 (Ger); UMunchen 59-60 (Ger); UWash (Seattle) 64-65 (LS) ML. 6: Ger. 7: Supply clk PBO Offices, Salt Lake City Utah 55-56, 61-62, PBX operator 57-59; IBM operat Singer Co, Salt Lake City Utah 62-64; Catlg libn UIowa Lib 65-68; 1st asst catlg dept 68-. 9: ALA; AAUP. 14: Catlg, lib automation. 15: 1110 Downey dr, Iowa City Ia 52240.

AARON, ALFREDIA. b Mobile Ala 13 Ag 46. 5: Fla A&M 64-68 (LS) BA. 6: Sp. 7: Ref asst Mobile Pub Lib 68-. 10: Alpha Beta Alpha. 14: Ref. 15: 2010 Edwards st, Mobile Al 36617.

AASKOV, JUNE A. b Portland Me 18 Je 35. 5: Lutheran Bible Inst 53-55; Augsburg Col 55-59 (Eng) BA; Syracuse 62-66 MSLS. 7: Desk asst Portland Pub Lib, Portland Me 59-61; Circ libn 61-. 9: ALA; NELA; MeLA (Com on Certif 67-68). 15: 315 Blackstrap rd, Falmouth Me 04105.

ABAR, ELLEN LOUISE (JAHN). b Saginaw Mich 3 Je 43. 4: Anthony F Abar. 5: Delta Col 61-63; UMich 63-65 (Bio) BS, 67-68 AMLS. 6: Ger. 7: Research asst Mich State U zoology dept (E Lansing) 65-66; Lab tech Mich State U physiology dept (E Lansing) 66;Lab tech UMich Sch Pub Health industrial toxicology (Ann Arbor) 67-69; Asst ser libn UMd Health Sci Lib (Baltimore) 69-. 10: Alpha Gamma Delta. 14: R F. 15: 249 D Woodhill dr, Glen Burnie Md 21061.

ABARAY, MICHAEL JAMES. b Pittsburgh Penn 27 O 40. 5: St Vincent Col 60-64 (Philos) BA; UPittsburgh 65-66 MLS. 6: Fr, Lat. 7: Lib trainee UPittsburgh Grad Sch of Bus Lib 65-66; Catlgr ser libn UNotre Dame (Notre Dame Ind) 66-68; Docs libn BrandeisU 68-. 9: ASIS. 10: ACLU. 14: Automation, admin. 15: 43 Park Vale ave, Allston Ma 02134.

ABBEY, EUGENIA (HIGH). b Jacksonville Fla 26 Ag 41. 4: Leonard Broughton Abbey. 5: Emory Col 59-63 (Psych) BA; Emory U, Div Lib 63-66 (Libnship) MLn. 7: Stud asst Emory U Lib, Atlanta Ga 60-63; Lib trainee VA Hosp Lib, Atlanta Ga 63-66, Libn 66-. 9: SLA (memb chm & 1st v-pres S Atl chap). 14: Med ref, serv to hosp patients. 15: VA Hosp Lib PO Box 29457, Atlanta Ga 30329.

ABBOTT, CHARLOTTE (MACAULAY). b Stratford Ont Can 30 Ap 13. 5: Queen's U(Kingston Ont) 32-37 (Hist) BA; Toronto 58 BLS. 6: Fr. 7: Asst order libn Queen's U Lib (Kingston Ont) 48-49; Lib asst Lib of Geol Survey of Can, Ottawa 42-43; Women's Royal Can Naval Serv (Lt) 43-46; Libn Joint Intelligence Bur Defence Research Bd, Ottawa 46-50; Catlgr McLaughlin Pub Lib, Oshawa Ont 50-62; Libn Med Staff Lib Oshawa Gen Hosp, Oshawa Ont 63-; Curator Henry House Museum, Oshawa Ont 63-. 9: CanLA; OntLA; Inst Prof Libns, Ont. 10: Ont Hist Soc; Arctic Inst of N Amer; Can Museums Assn; NY State Hist Assn; Amer Assn State & Loc Hist. 14: Catlg. 15: 738 Simcoe st N, Oshawa Can.

ABBOTT, GEORGE LINDELL. b Rutland Vt 11 Jl 41. 4: Sandra Baker. 5: St Michael's Col, Winoosk Vt 59-63 (Math) BA; SyracuseU 64-66 (LS) MSLS; UIll 69 Certif. 7: Catlgr t mchaels Col, IOSKI Michaels Col, WinooskiVt 59-64; M DILIBN Sracuse U Libn 64-. 9: ALA; ASIS; NEA-DAVI; Math Assoc Amer. 10: Syracuse U Lib Sch Alum Assn. 14: Automation, a-v materials. 15: 722 University ave, Syracuse NY 13210.

ABBOTT, HELEN DANA. b Auburn Me 22 F 07. 5: Wheaton Col 25-29 (Hist) AB; Simmons 29-30 (LS) BS; Middlebury Col 33-36 (Eng) AM. 7: Asst catlgr Middlebury Col 30-36; Catlgr Dartmouth Col 36-43; Head catlgr UNH 43-. 9: ALA (NH State Memb Com 63-65); NELA; NHLA. 10: AAUP; AAUW. 14: Catlg. 15: Oyster River rd, Durham NH 03824.

ABBOTT, JOHN CUSHMAN. b Auburn Me 12 Ap 21. 4: Frances Noon. 5: Bowdoin 39-43 (Hist) AB; Syracuse 46-49 (Hist) MA; UMich 49-50 (LS) AMLS, 54-57 (LS) PhD. 6: Fr, Sp. 7: Aviation cadet USA 43-45, Navigator (2nd Lt) 45; Grad asst in hist Syracuse U 48-49; Spec recruit LC 50-51, Asst ed of subj headings 51-52, Hd Orientalia exchange sect 52-54; Libn Trinity U 55-60; Libn (dir Lovejoy Lib) So Ill U (Edwardsville) 60-. 8: Study of Lib Resources in Britain to suppot archaeol research summer 67. 9: ALA (life mem); Amer Anthrop Assn; SAA; SLA; BSA; IllLA (life mem). 13: Yes. 14: Coop lending. 15: 612 W High st, Edwardsville Il 62025.

ABEL, ARLENE RUTH. b York Pa 10 Ag 44. 5: Lake Erie Col 62-66 (Hist, Relig) AB; Simmons 66-67 MS. 7: Catlgr UNMex 67-68; Catlgr Penn StateU 68-. 14: Catlg. 15: 950 W Aaron dr C8, State College Pa 16801.

ABELL, J RICHARD. b Wilmington Ohio 7 Je 32. 5: Wilmington Col 50-54 (Eng) AB; West Res 54-55 MS in LS. 7: Stud asst Wilmington Col Lib 50-54; Stud asst Inst of Tech Lib 54-55; Clerk-typist US Army Infantry & Trans Corps (Spec-5) 55-57; Pub Lib of Cincinnati & Hamilton Co, Cincinnati: Prof asst hist & lit dept 57-60, Fiction spec 61-62, Head hist & lit dept 62-. 9: ALA; OhioLA (chm Jr mems Round Table 62). 10: Ohioana Lib Assn. 14: Ref. 15: Pub Lib of Cincinnati & Hamilton Co, Cincinnati Oh 45202.

ABELLA, ROSA M. b Habana Cuba. 5: UHabana 43 (Hist, Geog) DRA en Filosofia y Letras 58, Te3cnica Bibliotecaria 56. 6: Sp. 7: Libn Inst de la Habana 53-59; Head circ Biblioteca Nacional Jose3 Marti, Habana 59-61; Libn & Asst Prof of UMiami (Fla) Lib, Coral Gables 62-. 9: ALA; Fla State LA; Seminar on the Acquisition of Latin Amer Lib Materials; DadeCoLA. 10: Cuban Women's Club (Miami); The Truth about Cuba Com (Miami); Faculty Club. 13: Yes. 14: Acquis, ref. 15: 335 SW 47 ave, Miami Fla 33134.

ABELSON, ESTELLE R. b 1 S 20. 4: Nathan R Abelson. 5: Hunter Col 37-41 (Hist) AB; Columbia 41-42 (LS) BS. 6: Fr. 7: Libn Queensboro Pub Lib 42; Libn Answer Man Inc, NYC 43-44; Libn Jamaica High Sch, Jamaica NY 44; Libn Woodrow Wilson Voc High Sch, Jamaica NY 45; Libn Temple Israel, Lawrence NY 51-59; Libn G W Hewlett High Sch, Hewlett NY 59-. 9: NYStateLA; Nassau-Suffolk Co Sch LA. 10: Phi Beta Kappa. 14: Wk with young adults. 15: 534 Monroe st, Cedarhurst NY 11516.

ABER, JEANNE MARIE. b McConnelsville Ohio 26 O 15. 5: Col of Paola 36-44; Our Lady of the Lake 47-49 (Eng) BA; UTex 49-51 (LS); UOkla 56-58 MLS. 6: Fr, Sp, Lat. 7: Asst libn Ursuline Acad, Dallas 50-51; Libn NoOkla Jr Col 51-58; Asst libn Southwestern State Col 58-60; Ref libn Field Enterprises Educl Corp, Chicago 60-62; Asst libn Ill Tchrs Col, Chicago North 62- Asst dir Northeastern Ill State Col 67-. 9: ALA; IllLA; Chicago LibClub. 10: AAUP; Beta Phi Mu. 14: Acquis, catlg. 15: 1055 Hollywood, apt 1A, Chicago Il 60626.

ABETE, MARTA (FEHRMANN). b Havana Cuba 1 O 27. 4: Manuel A Abete. 5: Pfeiffer Jr Col 45-47 AA; Salem Col 47-49 (Fr Lit) AB; Columbia 49-50 MLS. 6: Sp, Fr. 7: Head Libn Biblioteca Publica "Ramon Guiteras," Matanzas Cuba 50-60; Libn Post Rd Sch, White Plains NY 65-69. 10: Sch Libns Southeast NY. 14: Tech serv, wk with child. 15: 342 Linda ave, Hawthorne NY 10532.

ABLE, ELLEN HANSCOM. b Philadelphia 1 Ag 07. 4: Augustus Henry Able 3rd. 5: UPenn 25-28 (Eng) BS in Ed, 30-33 (Eng Lit) MA; Drexel 58-61 MLS. 6: Fr. 7: Tchr Eng, hist Moravian Sem, Bethlehem Penn 28-30; Eng tchr Wm Penn Charter Sch, Phila 30-36; Tchr Deaf Classes Sch Dist, Phila 36-42; Elem tchr Newark Spec Sch Dist, Newark Del 52-55, Elem libn 55-62; Asst child serv NM State Lib 62-63, Head servs to child & schs 64-67; Travel Lib Bd of Educ, Phila 67-. 9: Assn State Lib Child Consultants; NEA (Life mem); ALA; DelSchLibns (pres 60-61). 10: AAUW. 14: Child bks, sch libs. 15: 523 Spruce st, Phila Pa 19106.

ABMAYR, REV GEORGE JOHN. b Pittsburgh 22 F 28. 5: UDayton 45-49 (Educ) BS; West Res 59-64 MS in LS. 6: Fr. 7: Tchr Chaminade High Sch, Mineola NY 49-53; Tchr Cathedral Latin Sch, Cleveland 58-59; Tchr-libn Chaminade High Sch, Dayton Ohio 59-61; Libn N Catholic High Sch, Pittsburgh 61-62; Libn Chaminade High Sch, Dayton Ohio 62-. 9: CathLA; ALA. 14: High sch libs. 15: 505 S Ludlow st, Dayton Oh 45402.

ABOLIN, ELIZABETH (KING). b Muskegan Mich 10 S 04. 5: Ward-Belmont 21-22; UWis 23; UMich 24-26 (Eng) 26. 7: Br libn NY Pub Lib; Exch libn Oxford City Lib, Oxford England;

Res libn & asst to pres Aircraft Owners & Pilots Assn, Wash DC; Films libn District of Columbia Pub Lib; Chief clsf & catlg sect, Nat Bur Standards Lib, Wash DC; Coord of adult serv P G Co Mem Lib, Hyattsville Md 56-. 8: Md State Exec Dir, Nat Lib Week 61-62. 9: AEAUSA; ALA (ALA-ASD Coord Com on Materials); Coun 68-72, columbiaLA; MdLA (chm Intel Freedom Com, Prog Com 66-67); Coun of Prince George's Co Md (Adv Com on Aging). 14: Public libs, materials & serv, films, wk with the disadvantaged, in-service train. 15: 6532 Adelphi rd, Hyattsville Md 20782.

ABOUTOK, ELIZABETH (CLARISSA) LAWRENCE. b Williamstown NY 19 Mr 20. 4: George John Aboutok. 5: Houghton Col 38-42 (Social studies) BA; Rutgers U 54-57 (Lib) MLS; UPenn 68 (Ed Media). 7: Eng tchr N Collins Bd of Ed, N Collins NY 43-44; Tchr & Security US Navy Sp(S)2/c 44-46; Soc wkr Dept of Welfare, Syracuse NY 46; High Sch Libn Bernardsville Bd of Ed NJ 55-66; High Sch Libn & A-V Coordinator Bridgewater-Raritan Bd of Ed, Raritan NJ 66-. 9: ALA-AASchL; BEA-DAVI; NJSchLA (Pub & Nom Com); NJEA; SomersetCoEA; Bridgewater-RaritanEA (bldg repr mem Exec Bd); Amer Field Serv. 14: Admin build & serv, readers serv. 15: Box 354 RD 1, Basking Ridge NJ 07920.

ABRAHAM, MILDRED (KOSCHES). b New York NY 28 N 30. 4: Henry Julian Abraham. 5: Russell Sage 48-52 (Engkish, Sec, Ed) BA; UPenn 52-54 (Eng lit) MA; Drexel 63-66 (LS) MS. 6: Fr, Sp. 7: Multiple Sclerosis Soc, Philadelphia: Pub rel asst 54-55, Field rep 55-56; Dir for Spec Projects, Soc for Crippled Children, Philadelphia 56-57; Shipley Sch, Bryn Mawr Pa: Asst libn 66-67, Libn 67-. 9: ALA; Amer Film Inst; Indep Sch Libns S East Penn. 14: Ref, sec schls. 15: 1243 Wyngate rd, Wynnewood Pa 19096.

ABRAHAMS, NORBERT S. b NYC 19 S 31. 5: Brooklyn Col -52 (Educ) BA; CCNY Grad Sch of Educ 52-5 3; Columbia 59-61 (LS) MS. 7: Staff Brooklyn Pub Lib 61-65; Sr libn New Rochelle Pub Lib, New Rochelle NY 65; Staff NY State Mental Hygiene Dept 66-67; Harcourt, Brace & World (part-time) 67-68; City U NY (Hunter Col, Bronx Community Col, part-ti me) 67-69. 15: 40 W 77 st, New York NY 10024.

ABRAHAMSON, AINA M. b Warren Minn 18 Ap 5. 5: Luther Jr Col 32-33; Gustavus Adolphus Col 31-32, 33-35 (Eng) BA; USoCal summers 48-55 MSLS. 6: Swedish. 7: High sch tchr Eng, lib, Isle Minn 35-36; High sch tchr Eng, lib, Grasston Minn 36-42; High sch tchr Eng, math, lib, Cambridge Minn 42-46; Libn Luth Jr Col & Acad (Wahoo Neb) 46-54; Elem sch libn Pub Schs, Long Beach Cal 54-58, 59-62; Tchr, libn Ashira Girls' Sch, Tanzania E Africa 58-59; Libn Marangu Tchr Train Col (Tanzania E Africa) summer 61; Pub serv libn Cal Lutheran Col 62-. 9: CalLA; CalASchL (Black Gold Dist, pres 66-67). 10: BetaPhi Mu; Delta Kappa Gamma. 13: Yes. 14: Period. 15: 3033 Hillcrest dr, Thousand Oaks Ca 91360.

ABRAHAMSON, JOAN S (SHAFER). b HARTFORD Conn 19 D 30. 4: Samuel W Abrahamson. 5: UConn 48-52 (Eng) BA; So Conn State Col 63 (LS). 6: Fr. 7: Libn Middletown 9conn) Bd of Educ 64-65; Libn Vinal Reg Tech Sch, Middletown Conn 66-. 9: ALA; -AASchL; ConnSchLA; So Conn LA. 10: Vocat Instr Org (Conn); Conn State Employees Assn. 14: Sch libs. 15: Lee st, Middletown Ct 06457.

ABRAITIS, SAUL, JUSTIN. b Kaunas Lithuania 26 Je 34. 5: Cleveland Col West Res 58-63 (Eng Lit) BA; Lib Sch of West Res 63-64 MSLS. 6: Lithuanian, Fr. 7: CPL USA, US & France 55-57; Ref libn Lakewood Pub Lib, Lakewood Ohio 64-67; Hd acquis dept Cleveland State U Lib 67-. 9: ALA; OhioLA (chm Jr mems member Exec Bd 65-66). 10: AAUP. 14: Tech serv, ref, admin. 15: 4279 Ardmore rd, South Euclid Oh 44121.

ABRAMOVITZ, MIRIAM. b Red Bank NJ 5 S 25. 5: Monmouth Col 48-49 (LS). 7: US Govt libs 43: Head libn, Tech Lib, Materiel Readiness Directorate, us army Electronics Command Ft Monmouth NJ. 8: Subst libn & consul to certain NJ colleges and spec libs. 9: SLA; NJLA; MonmouthCoLA. 10: Womens Auxiliary of Riverview Hosp, Red Bank NJ; Youth Commsn Adv, Bnai Israel Synagogue, Rumson NJ. 14: Ref, govt documents, catlg. 15: 45 Poplar ave, Fair Haven NJ 07702.

ABRAMS, FREDERICK II. b NYC 17 Jl 42. 5: UFla 61-65 (Eng) BA; Emory 65-67 MLS. 6: Sp. 7: Ref libn Reg Info & Communication Exch Fondren Lib RiceU 67-. 9: TexLA. 14: Ref. 15: 1832 W Main, Houston Tx 77006.

ABRAMS, MARY. b Okmulgee Okla 6 Je 30. 4: Norman R Abrams. 5: Conn Col 48-52 (Hist) BA; Syracuse U 65-69 (LS) MSLS. 7: Catlg libn SUNY Agric & Tech Col (Morrisville) 69-. 15: 83 Lincklaen st, Cazenovia NY 13035.

ABRAMS, NINA (MICHELE) DODGE. b Flint Mich 17 S 42. 4: Howard Barry Abrams. 5: UMiami (Oxford Ohio) 60-61 (Law); UMich 61-64 (Bus) BBA, 64-65 (LS) AMLS; UMich Grad Sch of Bus (Dearborn) 67-. 7: Libn Gelman Instruments, Ann Arbor 64-65; Libn Amer Soc of Tool and Manuf Engnrs, Dearborn 65-67; Adult asst Det Pub Lib Downtown Lib, Detroit 67-68, Y-a libn Ext dept & Utley br 68-. 9: ALA. 10: Friends of Detroit Pub Lib; Detroit Inst of Art. 14: Pub serv. 15: 5500 S Shore dr, Chicago Il 60637.

ABRAMS, WILLIAM STEPHEN. b Wilmington Del 23 S 34. 4: Martha Schade. 5: Syracuse 53-57 (Psych) BA, 60-61 MSLS. 6: Sp. 7: Interviewer US Army Quartermaster Research & Engnr Command, Ft Lee Va 57-59; Grad asst Syracuse U Lib 60-61; Asst ser-documents libn Fresno State Col 61-62; Ser catlgr Portland State U 62-. 9: ALA. 10: AAUP. 14: Catlg, ser, docs. 15: 2368 NW Lovejoy, Portland Or 97210.

ABRAMSON, DEBORA R(OSE). b Baton Rouge La 20 D 02. 5: La StateU 20-24 BA; ColumbiaU 28-29 (LS) BS. 7: Tchr Istrouma High Sch, Baton Rouge La 25-28; Libn University High Sch, Oxford Miss 29-30; Inst in Lib Sci, Tulane (summers) 30-31; Asst sec La Lib Commsn, Baton Rouge 30-46; Asst State libn La State Lib, Baton Rouge 46-69. 8: La State Bd of Lib Examiners 33-65. 9: ALA; (Memb Com, Lippincott Award Com); SWLA; LaLA; (pres 38-39, State Planning Com 60-64, Union Catlg Com 54-, Culver Distinguished Serv Award Com 63-); AAStateL (Nom Com 62, Legislation Liaison Com 63-66). 13: Yes. 14: State lib agencies. 15: 833 No 11th st, Baton Rouge La 70802.

ABRAMSON, GERTRUDE (KERNER). b NYC 13 D 05. 4: Dr Julius Abramson. 5: Wellesley 23-27 (Eng) BA; Columbia 27-29 (Art Hist) MA; Simmons 45 (LS) MS. 6: Fr, Ger. 7: Libn Ind Med Dept Mass Taxpayers' Assn, Boston; Consul MIT; Libn Sch of Nursing Lib Peter Bent Brigham Hosp, Boston 54-. 9: MedLA; MassLA. 10: LWV. 13: Yes. 14: Ref. 15: 393 Lee st, Brookline Mass 02146.

ABRASH, BARBARA (BLACKMAN). b Paterson NJ 23 Ap 33. 4: Merritt Abrash. 5: Ohio StateU 50-51; NYU 51-54 (Govt) BA; SUNY(Albany) 62-65 MLS. 7: Instructional specialist, Learning Technology Inc, Albany NY. 10: LWV; Rensselaer Co Exec Bd (publs chm); Phi Beta Kappa. 12: "Black African Literature in English Since 1952" (67). 13: Yes. 15: Van Winkle dr RD 1, Rensselaer NY.

ABSALOM, PHYLLIS LEVAUN. b Martins Ferry Ohio 14 J 37. 5: Pepperdine 55-59 (Ed) BA; USoCal 59-60 MS in LS. 7: Los Angeles Pub Lib: Messenger clk 55-59, Libn trainee 59-60, Libn 60-. 9: SLA. 14: Ref. 15: 5333 Granada st, Los Angeles Ca 90042.

ACETO, VINCENT JOHN. b Schenectady NY 5 F 32. 4: Jean Rasey. 5: SUNY(Albany) 49-53 (Hist) AB, 53-54 (Guidance) MA, 58-59 MLS. 6: Fr, Sp. 7: Radio chief (Cpl) USArmy, Alaska 54-56; Hist tchr Scotia-GlenvilleCentral Schs, Scotia NY 56-57; Houseparent-counselor Charlton Sch for Girls, BurntHills, NY 56-58; High sch libn, Burnt Hills-Ballston Lake Central Schs, Burnt Hills57-59; Lib dir Town of Ballston Commun Lib, Burnt Hills 58-60; Asst Prof Sch of LibSci, SUNY (Albany) 59-63; Assoc Prof 63-69, Prof 69-. 8: Fulbright lecturer inlib sci, U of Dacca, Dacca East Pakistan 64-65; Adv Com on sch lib standards NYState Educ dept 65-; Sch lib consul; Amsterdam Pub Sch 65, Albany Pub Sch 66, Mid-Hudson Sch Study Coun 66; Consul to Governor's Com on Lib Manpower, NY State EducDept 66. 9: ALA; ADI; NEA; Pakistan Lib Assn (Life mem); E Pakistan Lib Assn (Life mem); NYLA (chm Central Processing Com); NY State Tchrs Assn; Hudson-Mohawk' Lib Assn (pres). 10: Schenectady Citizen's League (Bd of Dirs); AAUP; Kappa Phi Kappa;Phi Delta Kappa; Friends of Schenectady Co Pub Lib Bd of Dirs. 11: US Off of Educresearch grant 67-68; Dir HEA Title II B Inst on Films & Libs 69-70. 13: Yes. 14: Admin,lib educ. 15: 2392 Rosendale rd, Schenectady NY 12309.

ACHAUER, LUCILLE. b Lock Spring Mo. 5: Central Mo State Col 26-29 (Eng) BS in Educ; USoCal summer 35 (LS); Wash U (St Louis) even 38 (Hist); UDenver summers 39-41 BS in LS. 6: Fr. 7: Tchr Higginsville (Mo) High Sch 30-37; Libn Wellston High Sch, St Louis Co Mo 37-42; Ref libn sub-br Dept of Agric, Kan City Mo 42-46; Ref libn Fed Power Commsn, Wash DC 46-51; Ref libn Bur of Ships Lib, Wash DC 51-69; Lib Naval Ship Systems Command 69-. 9: SLA (chm Mil Group Wash DC Chap 62); MoLA. 14: Ref. 15: 4007 Connecticut ave NW, Wash DC 20008.

ACHEE, NICHOLAS JR. b Belle Rose La 2 Ag 29. 4: Ingrid Claus. 5: LSU 55-58 (Geog) BA, 58-60 (Anthrop) MA, 60-63 (LS) MS. 6: Ger. 7: Radio (S/Sgt) US Army, USA & europe 47-52; Refrigeration Tech European Exchange Serv, Germany 52-54; Ref libn Parsons Col 63-64; Geol zool libn UNC (Chapel Hill) 64-68; Hd sci-tech div Auburn U Lib 68-. 9: ALA. 14: Ref, admin. 15: 415 N Gay, Auburn Al 36830.

ACKERMAN, CAROLYN S. b NYC 31 Mr 18. 4: Bruno J Ackerman. 5: Hunter Col 34-38 (Hist) BA; Columbia 38-40 (Hist) MA; LIU 64-66 (LS) MLS. 6: Fr, Ger. 7: High sch tchr NYC High Schs 40-43; Job analyst WD & VA, NYC 44-48; V-pres Am Finn Sauna of LI, Rockville Ctr NY 63-; Acquis libn Hofstra U Lib, 66-. 9: ALA; NYLA; NCLA; NYTSA. 10: Phi Beta Kappa. 14: Acquis, bibliog, admin. 15: 15 Bramshott st, Rockville Ctr NY 11570.

ACKERMAN, DOROTHY (ANNE PETERSEN). b Richmond Va 31 Jl 26. 4: Stephen H Ackerman. 5: McGill 43-47 (Hist) BA; Chicago 47-48 BLS; Northwestern 50-51 (Romance Lans) MA; Ohio State U 52-53 (Romance Langs); Bibliotheque Nationale & Archives Nationales 53-54 (LS) Diplome Superieur de Bibliothecaire. 6: Fr, Sp. 7: Asst catlgr Evanston Pub Lib, Evanston Ill 48-51; Libn modern lang Grad Lib Ohio State U 52-53, 54-55; Instr in Fr USCar 62-63, 64-65; Music libn Post Lib, Ft Jackson SC 55-. 9: ALA; SELA; SCLA. 11: Fulbright scholarship 53-54. 12: Comp "Catalogue of the Talfourd P Linn Collection of Cervantes Materials" (63). 14: Romance bibliog, ref. 15: 4141 Pinehaven ct, Columbia SC 29205.

ACKERMAN, PAGE. b Evanston Ill 30 Je 12. 5: UCLA 29-31; Agnes Scott Col 31-33 (Eng) AB; UNC 38-40 (LS) BS. 7: Sch libn Druid Hills Sch Emory U 39-42; Catlgr Columbia Theol Sem (Decatur Ga) 42-43; Post libn US Army Aberdeen Proving Ground 45; Asst libn Union Theol Sem (Richmond Va) 45-49; UCLA Lib: Ref libn 49-54, Asst u libn 54-65, Assoc u libn 65-. 9: ALA; (chm elect LAB/PAS); CalLA (coun mem). 10: Phi Beta Kappa; ACLU; Amer Mgt Assn. 11: Certif of Merit, AUS, 45, Aberdeen Proving Ground. 13: Yes. 14: Mgt, personnel, processing. 15: 310 20th st, Santa Monica Calif 90402.

ACKLEY, CORINNE B(ONDE). b Sheyenne ND 11 N 10. 4: Norman B Ackley. 5: Mont State U 37-41 (LS) BA; UWash 46-49 (LS) BS. 6: Fr, Ger. 7: Head Libn Carnegie Pub Lib, Lewistown Mont 41-45; Bind libn & ser libn UWash 45-51; Circ Seattle Pub Lib 51-52; Catlgr, ref, child libn, various 61-64; Documents coordinator Wash State Lib 65-. 9: ALA; PNLA; WashLA. 10: Ruth Sch for Girls; LWV. 13: Yes. 14: Docs. 15: 16923A Maplewild SW, Seattle Wa 98166.

ACOSTA, ESPERANZA. b El Paso Tex 23 D 32. 5: UTex (El Paso) 51-54 (Span) BA; UIll 54-55 (LS) MS; Youngstown U 55-56. 6: Sp, Fr. 7: Circ asst El Paso Pub Lib, El Paso Tex 51-54; Clerical asst UIll (Urbana) 54-55; Gen asst libn Pub Lib of Youngstown &Mahoning Co, Youngstown Ohio 55-58; Libn US Army Air Defense Human Research Unit, Ft Bliss Tex 58-64; Libn Hotel Dieu Sch of Nursing, El Paso Tex 64-67; Libn Hotel Dieu Medical Nursing Educational Media Center 67-. 8: Assisted in organizing Jesuit High Sch Lib, El Paso Tex 60-61; Lib consul, Father Yermo High Sch, El Paso Tex 64-; Program of Continuing Educ in Hosp Libnship by Carh Hosp Assn 65-. 9: ALA; SLA; MedLA; OhioLA; BorderRegLA (chm Scholarship Com). 10: Sigma Delta Pi; Confraternity of Christian Doctrine. 11: Libn of the Year, Border Reg LA 67. 14: Ref. 15: 511 N Raynor, El Paso Tx 79903.

ADAM, PHILIP. b NYC 12 Je 14. 4: Dorothy Messing. 5: Brooklyn Col 31-34 (Hist) BA; Columbia 34-35 BSLS. 7: US Army Infantry (T/Sgt) 43-46; brooklyn Pub Lib 38-; Ref asst, asst br libn, br libn, supt of lib ext, exec asst, personnel dir, reg libn, exec asst to dir. 8: NY State Pub Libns Certif Com (chm 60-61). 9: Assn NY Libs for Tech Serv (sec 68-). 14: Admin, adult serv. 15: Brooklyn Pub Lib Ingersoll Bldg Grand Army Plaza, Brooklyn NY 11238.

ADAMCZIK, JAN. b Prague 3 Ja 26. 5: Charles U (Prague) 46-50 (Mod Lang, Philos) BA; IndU (Bloomington) 60-61 (LS) MA. 6: Ger, Fr, Czech, Russian. 7: Libn I UCal (Berkeley) 61-62; Libn GS-9 US Army, Okinawa 62-64; Libn GS-9 USAF, Libya 64-66, Germany 66-. 9: ALA (European Armed Forces Libns Subsect). 15: APO NY 09012 POB 5876 26th CSGr.

ADAMO, ROSE M. b NYC 26 Ag 35. 5: Queens Col 53-58 (Psych, Sociol) BA; St John's U 58-60 MLS; Hunter Col 60-659hist, Educ, Guidance); LIU 65-66 (Data Processing & Programming). 6: Ital, Sp. 7: Queens Borough Pub Lib, NYC: Trainee 58-60, Asst br libn at several brs 60-63, Bkmob libn 63-64, Asst br libn 64-65, Asst head bkmob libn 65, Asst br libn 65-66, Br libn66-67; Dir Island Trees Pub Lib, Levittown NY 67-68; Adult consul Cooperative LibSyst, Bellport NY 68-. 8: Mem adv coun of Library Futures 68-69; Mem Exec Bd, StJohn's U LS 68-; Staff of Lib/USA, N Y World's Fair, 64. 9: ALA (Queens Memb chm74-67); NYLA; NY Lib Club; Nassau Co LA; Suffolk Co LA (mem Exec Bd, Directory chm69); Bksellers League Exhibits RT; Internat Rel RT; Lib Pub Rel Coun (treas 69-, Hospchm 67-69); NY Lib Club. 14: Admin, recr, personnel admin. 15: 86-75 Midland Pkwy,Jamaica NY 11432.

ADAMS, MRS ALBERTA (HOWARD). b Bellevue Penn 12 Je 14. 4: Ludwig Adams. 5: Wellesley 31-32 (Liberal Arts, Chem); Bryn Mawr 32-35 (Liberal Arts, Chem) BA in Chem; UPittsburgh 35-36 (Educ) M Ed, 37-38 (Chem). 6: Sp, Fr, Lat, Ger. 7: Tchr Pittsburgh Inst of Aeronautics 41-42; Abstractor lit & pat Gulf Res & Dev Co, Harmarville Penn 42-44; Tech rep Pittsburgh Plate Glass, Pittsburgh 44-47; Libn Vanadium Corp, Bridgeville Penn 47-52; Abstractor Ethyl Corp, Ferndale (Detroit) Mich 55-58; Abstractor Esso Development, Linden NJ 58-61; Libn Pittsburgh Chem Div of US Steel, Neville Island Penn 60-. 9: SLA; AIC. 10: Delta Delta Lambda. 13: Yes. 14: Tech, chem abstracting, surveys, bibliogs, ref. 15: 205 Thompson dr, Pittsburgh Pa 15229.

ADAMS, ALICE BENSON. b Seneca SC 6 Ag 03. 5: Greenville Woman's Col 19-23 (Hist) BA; UNC 38 (LS) BA; Columbia 50-51 (LS) MS. 7: Tchr High Schs, NC & SC 23-28; Libn High Sch, Rockingham NC 38-39; Libn Woman's Col Furman U 39-53; Asst libn Furman U 53-60, Assoc libn 60-. 9: ALA; SELA; SCLA. 10: AAUP. 15: Furman Univ Lib, Greenville SC 29690.

ADAMS, ANNETTE (CARROLL). b Owensboro Ky 20 Jl 10. 5: Newcomb Col Tulane 25-29 (Lat) BA; Jhons Hopkins 30-31 (Lat); UChicago 31-32 (Lat) MA; CatholicU 59-60 MSLS. 6: Fr, Lat, Gr. 7: Humanities libn CUA, Wash DC 60-62; Libn Our Lady of Grace, Beach Gorve Ind 62-63, 64-65; Hd libn Poly Prep Country Day Sch, Brooklyn NY 63-64L UCincinnati: Catlgr 68-69, Ref libn 69-. 10: Beta Phi Mu. 14: Ref. 15: 3346 Sherlock ave, Cincinnati Oh 45220.

ADAMS, BEATRICE ANN. b Owosso Mich 23 My 40. 5: Albion Col 58-62 (Sociol) AB; West Mich U 62-63 (LS) MA. 7: Child libn Niles Pub Lib, Niles Mich 63-65; Child libn Grosse Pointe Pub Lib (Central), Grosse Pointe Mich 65-. 9: ALA; MichLA. 10: Beta Phi Mu. 14: Child wk. 15: 26301 Jefferson, St Clair Shores Mi 48081.

ADAMS, CHARLES JAMES. b Clendenin WVa 20 Mr 27. 4: Jessie Coppage. 5: UChicago 47-48; IndU 50-53 (Sociol) AB, 62-66 (LS) MA. 7: Army (1st Army) Fort Jay, NYC 46-47; Var casewk positions in soc & rehabilitation agencies 52-61; Br libn Gary Pub Lib, Gary Ind 62-64; Hd tech serv dept Hammond Ind Pub Lib 64-66; Dir LaPorte City & Co Lib, LaPorte Ind 67-69; Dir Michigan City Pub Lib, Michigan City Ind 69-. 8: Exec dir, Nat Lib Week, Ind 69. 9: ALA; IndLA (var comassignments). 10: Ind Hist Soc; ACLU; LaPorte Co Human Rel Coun; Rotary Internat. 12: Co-ed spec issue on censorship of"FOCUS on Indiana Libraries" (vol 22, no 2, Je 68). 13: Yes. 14: Admin, coord pub & tech serv, censorship problems. 15: 1304 Jackson st, LaPorte In 46350.

ADAMS, CHARLES M. b La Moure ND 24 Ag 07. 4: Ellen Chase. 5: Carleton Col 25-26; Amherst 26-29 (Eng, Math) AB; Columbia 32-33 (LS) BS, 42 (Eng) MA. 7: Instr Athens Col, Athens Greece 29-32; Ref asst NY Pub Lib 34-37; Asst to the dir Columbia U 37-45; Libn UNC (Greensboro) 45-69; Dir Sinclair Lib & Prof of Lib Studies UHawaii 69-. 8: So Assn Lib Com on Standards Consul bldgs. 9: ALA-ACRL (pres 50-51, chm Col Sect 60-); NCLA; (Bd Dirs); SELA (Bd Dirs, chm-elect of Col & Univ Sect 66-68). 10: Piedmont Appalachian Trail Hikers; Appalachian Trail Ways; Campus Christian Life Com for Westminster Fellowship; Caxton Club (Chicago); Typophiles; Carolina Mountain Club; Alpine Club of Can. 12: Comp "Randall Jarrell, a Bibliography (58); ed "NC Libraries" (59-63). 13: Yes. 14: Bibliog, rare bks, admin. 15: 315 S Chapman st, Greensboro NC 27403.

ADAMS, CHARLES WALDRON. b Cambridge Mass 10 My 24. 4: Mary Bertolet. 5: Harvard 42-43, 46-49 (Am Govt) AB; Simmons Col Sch of LS 51 MSLS. 7: US Army amphibious eng Coxswain landing craft (Sgt tech 4th cl) 43-46; First asst Provicence PL, Prov RI 51-53; Hd cat ord proc dept Osterhout Lib, Wilkes-Barre Pa 53-55; Libn Cen Jr High Sch, Weymouth Mass 55-58, Libn Weymouth High Sch 58-62; Supv of S L Mass Bur of Lib Ext, Boston 62-65, Sr supv of S L dev, 66, Coord Title II ESEA 65-66; Dir of libs Cambridge sch dept,

Cambridge Mass 66-. 8: Testified on bill which became Public law 89-10 ESEA before House Subcom on Educ in behalf of NE states for ALA. 9: ALA-AASchL; NEA; NESchL; NEA; MassLA; MassSchLA; MassTA; CambridgeTA. 13: Yes. 15: 569 Main st, Hanover Ma 02339.

ADAMS, CHARLES WILLARD. b Des Moines Iowa 5 N 36. 4: Patricia (Snider). 5: U No Iowa 55-58; (Soc Sci, LS) BA; Drake U summer 59; UIowa summer 61; UDenver summers 62-64; (LS) MA. 7: Libn Ottumwa High Sch, Ottumwa Iowa 58-60; Head Libn Central High Sch, Davenport Iowa 60-63; Head Libn & dist catlgr Wheeling High Sch, High Sch Dist 214, Wheeling Ill 63-65; Libn Mayo High Sch, Rochester Minn 65-. 66; Instr Dept of L S U No Iowa. 8: Visiting Instr Ill State U summer 65 N Central Assn Eval Com 67-; Lib Extension, U No Iowa 67-. 9: ALA; IaStateEA; IaASchL; NEA; DAVI; AVEAIa. 14: Sch libnship, lib educ. 15: 1011 E Seerley blvd, Cedar Falls Ia 50613.

ADAMS, DOROTHY ELIZABETH. b Lancaster Penn 11 Ap 09. 5: State Col (Millersville Penn) 27-30 (Eng, LS) BS; UPenn 40 (Educ) MS; Cal State Col (Los Angeles) 62 (Admin) Cred. 7: Libn High Sch, Red Lion Penn 29-36; Sec YWCA, Bradford Penn 36-37; Libn High sch, Lampetyr Penn 37-44; Libn High Sch, Ambler Penn 44-45; Tchr-Eng High Sch, Swarthmore Penn 45-48; Libn Sec Schs, Los Angeles Cal 48-61; Supv (Sec Sch Lib Serv, Los Angeles Cal 61-. 8: Periodic short-term consul serv with var co sch districts in cal; consul Xerox Educ Serv. 9: CalSchLA (sec So Sec 56); Los Angeles SchLA (pres 56). 10: Sierra Club. 11: Ford Found grant (Tchr awatd) 55-56. 13: Yes. 14: Sch lib materials & mgt. 15: 468 Lewis st, Los Angeles Ca 90042.

ADAMS, E M JR. b Clarksville Tex 14 Ja 22. 5: Col of William & Mary 46; UTex 49, 50; E Tex State U 41-42, 55-56 MSLS. 7: Libn Pine Tree High Sch, Longview Tex 44-48; Libn Panola Col 48-57; Libn E Tex Baptist Col 57-67; Bibliographer Stephen F Austin State Col 67-68; Libn E Tex Baptist Col 68-. 9: Tex State LA (past chm Reg 6); Tex Jr Col Assn (past chm Lib Group). 14: Admin. 15: 504 E Houston, Marshall Tex.

ADAMS, EDWARDA M. b San Francisco 23 Ap 13. 5: UCal (Berkeley) 30-34 (Hist) BA, 34-35 Certif in Libnship. 6: Fr. 7: Libn Dept of Forestry UCal (Berkeley) 37-42; Libn US Army, Ft Ord Cal 43-47; Reflibn UN, Lake Success NY 47; Libn NY Pub Lib Central Circ 48; Act chief libn P2 USVAHosp, Oakland Cal 49; Libn I Educ Lib UCal (Berkeley) 50; Libn Langley PorterNeuropsychiatric Inst, San Francisco 50-. 8: Consul; Atascadlro State Hosp, Cal 60, Dewitt State Hosp, Cal 62, Colorado State Hosp, Pueblo Col 68. 9: MedLA; SLA (treas loc chap); CalLA. 14: Ref. 15: Lib Langley PorterInst, 401 Parnassus ave, San Francisco Ca 94122.

ADAMS, ELEANOR. b Haverhill Mass 26 Mr 24. 5: Simmons 42-46 (LS) BS; Boston U 53-54, 62-63; Columbia 63-64 (LS) MS. 6: Fr, Sp, Ger, Ital. 7: Catlgr Bryn Mawr Col Lib 46-48; Catlgr Wellesley Col Lib 48-56, Sr catlgr 56-. 9: ALA-DCC (Subcom on Recr 51-52, Com on Pub Rel & Recr 52-53, Boston Reg Group ofcatlgrs & Clsfrs sec-treas 52-54); MassLA (Memb Com 62-63); Bus mgr "Bay StateLibrarian" 66-68. 14: Catlg. 15: Wellesley Col Lib, Wellesley Ma 00181.

ADAMS, ELSIE DEE. b. Provo Utah. 5: Brigham Young U 43 (Elem Educ) BA; UDenver 54 (LS) MA. 7: Tchr Utah Pub Schs, Kamas, Salt Lake, Midvale Utah 44-54; Libn Salt Lake Co Lib, Midvale Utah 55; Libn Jordan Sch Dist, Sandy Utah 56-65; Libn Utah State Dept Pub Instr 65- Instr Lib Sci, Col of Ida, Caldwell Ida summers 64-65. 8: Chm Adv Com Title II, ESEA; Coordinator Title II, ESEA; Lib consul; Multi media demonstrations, Utah, Nev, Neb, Ind. 9: NEA; ALA; UtahEA; UtahLA. 10: Utah Congress Parents & Tchrs; Assn for Supervn & Curricm Development. 12: "John Edge Booth, 1847-1920." 14: Bk sel (elem & sec grades), instr media programs. 15: 445 N University ave, Provo Ut 84601.

ADAMS, FLORENCE NEWSOME. b Boston Mass 31 Ja 13. 4: George William Adams. 5: Simmons 31-35 (LS) BS; BostonU 38-42 (Eng Lit) MA; columbia 43-46 (LS). 6: Fr, Ger. 7: Gen asst NY Pub Lib 35; Ref asst Boston Pub Lib 36-42; Ref libn Newark Pub Lib, NJ 42-46; Libn Roselle Pub Lib, NJ 46-47; Br libn Hartford Pub Lib, Conn 49-. 9: ConnLA (Scholarship Com 51); Child Libns RT of Greater Hartford (chm Program Com 62); Greater Hartford Libns Club; NELA. 14: Ref. 15: 16 Brookfield dr, Glastonbury Ct 06033.

ADAMS, GENEVA (SHINN). b Benton Co Mo 14 N 16. 4: George H Adams. 5: Central Mo State Col 36-40, 54-57, 59-61 (Educ, LS) BS, MS; UKan City 56; Tex Woman's U 65 (LS). 7: Tchr pub schs, Benton Co Mo 36-40; Tchr pub schs, Belton Mo 64-60, Libn 60-64; Libn Pub Sch, Lee's Summit Mo 64-. 8: Lee S Summit Mo; Chm Dept of Libs, Libn Sr High Sch. 9: ALA; NEA; MoASchL (chm 64-65); Mo State Tchrs Assn. 10: AAUW. 14: Ref, bibliog, sel. 15: 316 Baldwin st, Benton Mo 64012.

ADAMS, GEORGE WM. b Peach Glenn Penn 23 Ja 10. 4: Florence Newsome. 5: Dickinson Col 27-31 (Eng, Hist) AB; Drexel 38-39 BS in LS. 6: Fr. 7: Visitor Phila Relief Bd Penn Dept of Pub Assistance 31-38; Ref asst Free Lib of Phila 39-40; Period libn Lincoln City Lib, Lincoln Neb 40-41; Ref & period libn UPenn Lib 41-43; MP USAAF, England 43-45; Lending & ref libn Newark Pub Lib, Newark NJ 46-48; Ref libn Trinity Col Lib (Conn) 48-59; Legis ref libn Conn State Lib 59-. 9: ALA; ConnLA. 10: Conn State Employees Assn. 14: Ref. 15: 16 Brookfield dr, Glastonbury Ct 06003.

ADAMS, GUSTAV C. b Cluster Springs Va 9 D 08. 5: Presbyterian Col 28-32 (Eng) AB; Stetson U 32-33 (Eng) MA; Columbia 46-47 BS in LS. 6: Fr. 7: Eng tchr Palatka High Sch, Fla 35-42; US Navy 42-45; Libn ref dept NY Pub Lib47-48; Libn Palatka High Sch, Fla 48-56; Libn Hialeah High Sch, Fla 56-60; LibnTchrs Prof Lib, Miami Fla 60-. 8: Chm Lib Eval Com, Clay Co (Fla) High Schs, 55. 9: ALA; AASchL; NEA; FlaLA; FlaEA; FlaASchL (chm Scholarship Com 58-60, chm Exhibit Com 59-61). 10: Pi Kappa Phi, Blue Key, Kiwanis. 11: Yes. 12: Ed "Bookcase," FlaASchL 64-69. 14: Ref. 15: 7600 NW 27th ave, Miami Fl 33147.

ADAMS, HARRIET (ARNOLD). b Garden Grove Iowa 25 Mr 05. 5: UIowa 22-26 (Eng, Ed) BA; UWash 33-34 BA in LS. 6: Fr. 7: Eng tchr Lynden Wash 26-33; Circ asst U Wash Lib, Seattle 34; Child Lib Wenatchee Wash 35-43; Army Libn Ephrata Army Air Base & Dibble Gen Hosp 43-46; Circ Libn Leominster (Mass) Pub Lib 50-55; YPLib Concord (NH) Pub Lib 55-60; Adult Serv Lib 60-66; Consul Sch Lib Serv, State Dept of Educ Concord NH 66-. 9: ALA; AASchL; NELA (sec 2 yrs); NHLA; NEStateLA; NEA-DAVI; NHEA; ASDC. 10: Commun Players; Appalachian Mtn Club; Zonta Club; Phi Beta Kappa. 14: Folkways; yp reading. 15: 25 Conant dr, Concord NH 03301.

ADAMS, JEAN ELIZABETH. b Rochester NY 23 Ap 24. 5: State Tchrs Col (Geneseo NY) 46-50 BS Lib Educ Prov Elem Tchrs Certif; Syracuse 60 (LS) Permanent Tchrs Certif. 7: Factory wker Bausch & Lomb Optical Co, Rochester NY 42-44; Hosp corps US Navy (WR) Hosp Apprentice 1st class 44-45; Off wker CS Sanitarium Med Records Lib, Clifton Springs NY 50-52; Off wker Ontario Co Lab, Canandaigua NY 53; Sub libn 99th St Elem Sch, Niagara Falls NY 55; High sch libn Port Byron Central Sch, Port Byron NY 55-62; Elem sch libn Phelps Central Sch, Phelps NY 62-. 9: NY State Tchrs Assn; NEA. 10: Nat Cong Parents & Tchrs; Delta Kappa Gamma; AAUW. 14: Catlg. 15: 29 Teft ave, Clifton Springs NY 14432.

ADAMS, JOAN MOYER. b Hamburg Penn. 4: Douglas R Adams. 5: Kutztown State Col 60-64 (LS) BS 65-69 (LS) MS. 7: Clerk Silco Cut Price Stores Inc, Hamburg Penn 58-64; Elem libn Hamburg Area Sch System, Hamburg Penn 64-. 9: NEA; PennEA. 10: Shoemakersville Jr Cof C Wives; Hamburg Area TA. 15: Hamburg Elem Schs Fourth and Sieber st, Shoemakersville Pa 19555.

ADAMS, JUNE (BOWEN). b Fresno Cal 12 N 26. 4: George F Adams. 5: UCal 45-48 (Psych); CCNY 55-57 (Psych) BA (SS); Rutgers 61-64 MLS; UGrenoble (France) 64-65 (Fr lang & lit). 6: Fr. 7: Psych aid; Med asst NYC; Ref & docs libn Hackensack Pub Lib, hackensack NJ 65-68; Dir Westwood Pub Lib, Westwood NJ 69-. 9: ALA-RSD (Conf Prog com); NJLA (Pub Rel Com & Recruit Com); Bergen-PassaicLA (v-pres 69). 10: LWV (pres Exec Bd). 14: Ref, adult serv, recruit. 15: 227 Vivien ct, Paramus NJ 07652.

ADAMS, LOUISE GESSNER. b Gambier Ohio 29 F 1896. 5: Col for Women West Res 14-16, 17-18 (Eng) BS; West Res 16-17 (LS). 7: Asst Lib of Cincinnati Walnut Hills Br 18-19; Asst Kenyon Col Lib 19-22; Libn Colburn Lib Beyley Hall, Gambier Ohio 25-34; Clerical wk Kenyon Col 34-36; Clerical wk Ministers Mutual Automobile Assn, Gambier Ohio 36-39; Asst Mt Vernon Pub Lib, Mt Vernon Ohio 42-46; Asst ed Antiques Journal, Mt Vernon Ohio 46-52; Catlgr Mt Vernon Pub Lib, Mt Vernon Ohio 52-66. 12: "St Luke's Church" (Granville Ohio) (27); "Harcourt Parish 1827-1967," (69). 13: Yes. 14: Catlg. 15: Colwill rd, Gambier Oh 43022.

ADAMS, MARGUERITE (LINDNER). b Milwaukee 18 My 21. 4: William C Adams. 5: Mt Mary Col 39-42 (Eng); Col of St Catherine 42-43 (LS) BS. 7: Libn VA, Wood Wis 50-56;

Tchr-libn St Agnes Sch, Butler Wis 56-. 67; Tchr-libn St Catherine Sch (Milwaukee) 67-. 9: CathLA (Wis Unit: sec 2 yrs, chm 3 yrs); Waukesha (Wis) LA. 15: W 147 N4956 Dolphin dr,Menomonee Falls Wi 53051.

ADAMS, MELBA (DAVIS). b Rocky Mount NC 29 Je 27. 4: Alphonso Rudolph Adams Jr. 5: Bennett Col 45-49 (Lib Arts) BA; NC Col at Durham 49-50 (LS) BLS. 6: Fr, Ger. 7: Tchr-libn Carver Sch, Mt Olive NC 50-53; Docs libn A&M U, Tallahasse Fla 53-56; Army libn US Army, Germany 56-58; Asst libn State Tchrs Col, Fayetteville NC 58-60; Descr catlgr LC Wash DC 60-66, Decimal clsf Spec 66-. 9: ALA; FlaLA (chm Exhib Com). 10: Delta Sigma Theta. 14: Tech proc. 15: 10001 Buena Vista ave, Lanham Md 20801.

ADAMS, MERLE S. b Minneapolis 23 Ja 06. 4: Doris (Huseby). 5: UMinn 25-28 (Music) BS, 50-51 BS in LS. 7: Violinist Minneapolis Symphony Orchestra 29-51; PA II Minneapolis Pub Lib 51-57, Br libn 57-60, Head music dept 60-. 9: MusLA. 10: Co-dir & org Metropolitan youth orchestra (Minneapolis); Minneapolis Musicians Assn; Lib Union Staff Assn; Evergreen Club. 14: Catlg music scores & records. 15: 4745 16 ave S, Minneapolis Mn 55407.

ADAMS, MILDRED (EHNI). b Somerville NJ 17 O12. 4: Wilbur I Adams. 5: Douglass Col Rutgers 30-34 (LS) BA. 7: Child libn Somerville Pub Lib, Somerville NJ 34-39; Adult catlgr Somerset Co Lib, Somerville NJ 57-62, Asst dir 62-68, Dir 68-. 9: ALA; NJLA (treas Tech Serv 65-66). 10: PTA. 15: 115 Middaugh st, Somerville NJ 08876.

ADAMS, SISTER MURIEL. b Ansonia Conn 15 N 13. 5: St Joseph Col 48 (Educ) BS; Catholic U 54 MS in LS. 7: Tchr parochial schs, Conn 34-48; Instr St Joseph Col, Conn 48-52; Tchr Catholic high schs, Conn 52-58; Instr & Asst libn St Joseph Col (Conn) 58-62, Libn & Asst Prof of hist 62-. 8: Dean of Studs, St Joseph Col, 58-59. 9: CathLA (chm Conn Unit 64-65); ALA; ConnLA. 10: Wadsworth Atheneum, Hartford Conn; AAUP. 14: Ref. 15: St Joseph Col, W Hartford Ct 06117.

ADAMS, ROBERT MONROE. b Aberdeen SD 20 Ja 29. 5: No State Col 50-51 (Eng) BS; Garrett Theol Sem 51-55 (Theol) BD; Peabody Col 65-67 MLS; LSU 67-68 (LS); AuburnU 59-61 (Eng) MA, 68-. 6: Sp. 7: So Union Col: Engl instr 57-59, Libn 64-; AuburnU: Tchg fellow in Eng 59-60, Eng instr 60-62; Asst prof communication skill AirU USAF, Montgomery Ala 62-64. 9: Amer Coun of Trans of Foreign Lang; ALA-ACRL; AA Coun of Tchrs of Eng; Ala Jr Libns; Ala Jr Col Lib Assn; AlaLA Col Eng Tchrs Ala; So Atlantic Mod Lang Assn; SELA. 10: Beta Phi Mu; Ala Coun on Human Rel; ACLU. 14: Ref, bibliog, lib educ. 15: Box 2155, Auburn Al 36830.

ADAMS, RUTH L. b Boston 15 S 12. 5: Wheaton Col (Norton Mass) 30-34 (Psych) AB; Simmons 34-35 (LS) BS. 7: Child libn Rochester Pub Lib, Rochester NY 35-44; Head of child dept Schenectady Co Pub Lib, Schenectady NY 44-. 8: Pub Libns Certif Exam Com, 54-56. 9: ALA (Newbery-Caldecott Com 52-53 & 65-66, Bks Worth Their Keep Com 58-60); -CSD(treas 50-51, chm Let's Read Together Revision Com 66-69); NYLA (Coun 49-51, chmChild Bks & Libs Com 47, pres Child & YP Libns Sect 52-53). 14: Child lib wk. 15: 1075 Park ave, Schenectady NY 12308.

ADAMS, SCOTT. b Agawam Mass 20 N 09. 4: Barbara Winn Adams. 5: Yale 26-30 (Eng) AB; Columbia 39-40 MLS. 6: Fr, Ger, Russian. 7: Supv libn Tchrs Col Lib, NYC 40-43; Order-catlg libn Providence Pub Lib 43-45; Chief acquis div Army Med Lib, Wash DC 45-46, Act libn 46-50; Libn Nat Inst of Health, Bethesda Md 50-59; Program dir for sci info NSF 59-60; Deputy dir NLM 60-. 8: LC Mission to Germany 46; Adv Com on Libns, Fullbright Program 56; Jt Com on Preservation of Sci & Cultural Materials 57 Internal Adv Com on Documentation, Lib & Archives (UNESCO) 67-; Biomed Info Policy Group, OECD 68-; Adv Com UNISIST (UNESCO/ICSU0 68-; Alt repr HEW to COSATI 66-; Hon pres III Internal Cong Med Lib 69. 9: ALA (Coun); SLA; ADI (past pres); MedLA (past pres) CNLA (sec); USBE (sec); DCLA (past pres); ARAS; Amer Soc for Info Sci. 10: Cosmos Club, Wash DC. 11: Spec Serv Award, Public Health Serv 57; Geo & Mary Eliot Award MedLA 64. 12: "OP Market" (44). 13: Yes. 14: Admin, internal communcation. 15: 4621 High st, Chevy Chase Md 20015.

ADAMS, VELMA LEE. b Columbus Miss 20 N 09. 5: Miss State Col for Women 27-30 (Eng) BA; La StateU summers 47, 49, 50, 51 BS in LS; UTex summer 62, grad wk in LS. 6: Fr. 7: High Sch Tchr Van Cleave & Bay Springs Miss 37-40; Tchr-Libn Georgetown & Bentonia Miss 40-50; Asst libn Southern State Col Magnolia Ark 50-53, Head Libn 53-, Assoc Prof of Lib Sci 64-. 8: Certif in Archival Mgt UTex 61. 9: ALA; NEA; ArkLA (chm of Col Sect 55); SWLA (v-chm 56-58, Col & U Lib Sect chm 58-60, mem of Lib Educ Com 60-); Ark EA; Ark Hist Assn. 10: AAUW (sec, pres 56-59); Pilot Club; Columbia Co Tuberculosis Assn Comm; Mortar Bd; Beta Phi Mu. ; Delta Kappa Gamma. 13: Yes. 14: Bk sel, archival materials, child bks. 15: Box 1176 Southern State Col, Magnolia Ark 71753.

ADAMS, ZELLA D(AILEY). b Indianapolis 16 Jl 06. 5: Fla State U 24-28 (Eng Lit) BA; Columbia 32 BSLS. 7: Br libn Queensboro Pub Lib, Jamaica NY 32-46; Adult bk sel ALA Booklist, Chicago 46-47; Chief Libn Pub Lib, W Palm Beach Fla 47-52; Dir of lib ext Fla State Lib 52-56; Chief Libn Pub Lib, W Palm Beach Fla 56-. 8: Taught course in Adult Materials Fla State U Lib Sch summer 54 Bldg consul, N Palm Beach Fla & Lake Park Fla 68. 9: ALA; SELA; FlaLA. 10: Soroptimist Club; AAUW. 13: Yes. 14: Admin, adult bk sel. 15: Pub Lib Flagler Pk, W Palm Beach Fl 33401.

ADAMSON, EUGENIA. b Albertville Ala 12 S 10. 5: Milligan Col 30-32 (Eng) AB; Peabody 36-37 BS in LS, summers 51-55 (Eng) MA. 7: Libn Hiwassee Col 37-42; Libn Milligan Col 42-46; King Col summer 47; Col William & Mary summer 48; Norfolk Pub Lib summer 50; Jacksonville State Col summer 58; Libn Va Intermont Col 46-. 8b Albertville Ala 12 S 10. 09: ALA; VaLA; SELA; Boone Tree Lib Club. 9: ALA; VaLA; SELA; Boone Tree Lib Club. 10: Delta Kappa Gamma. 14: Acquis,catlg. 15: 718 Moore st, Bristol Va 24201.

ADAN, ADRIENNE (HINDS). b New York NY 17 O 42. 5: HebU Jerusalem 60-66 (Pol Sci) BA; UTex 67-68 (LS) MLS. 6: Heb, Fr, Sp. 7: Libn I Tucson Pub Lib, 68-. 9: ALA; ArizLA. 15: 4060 E Fourth st, Tucson Az 85711.

ADCOCK, (ALICE) ELIZABETH. b Riverton Wyo 7 N 17. 4: Harold W Adcock. 5: Colo State Col 33-37 (Eng) AB; UDenver 37-38 BS in LS. 7: Circ libn DePauw U 38-40; Ref asst Colo State Col summers 48-52; Libn Greeley High Sch, Greeley Colo 42-43; Sch libn Colo State Col Lab Sch 52-53; Libn Weld Co Lib, Greeley Colo 54-. 9: ALA; ColoLA (pres 61-62); MPLA (sec & chm Pub Lib Sect); Colo Coun for Libdevel (chm 66-68). 10: Altrusa Interna. 13: Yes. 15: 2418 19th ave, Greeley Co 80631.

ADDESA, FRANK A. b Newark NJ 16 Je 21. 4: Mary Krakowski. 5: Montclair State U 46-50 (Music) AB; Rutgers 54-56 MLS. 6: Ital. 7: Bench lathe operator NJ Gear, Newark NJ 38-42; Tank gunner US Army (Pfc) ETO 42-45; Tchr vocal music Bd of Educ, Union NJ 50-51; Bench lathe operator Gen Electric, Bloomfield NJ 52-53; Lib trainee Pub Lib, Newark NJ 53-55; Sch libn Bd of Educ, Scotch-Plains-Fanwood NJ 55-. 9: NEA; ALA; NJEA; NJSchLA. 14: Wk with yp. 15: 1630 Pershing pl, S Plainfield NJ 07080.

ADDISON, ANNA MARGARET (WININGS). b Amsterdam Ohio 12 Mr 25. 4: Douglas W Addison. 5: Kent State U 43-47 (Hist, Soc Sci, Biol) BS in Ed; Western Reserve U 49-52 MS in LS. 7: High sch tchr Sharon Center Sch, Sharon Center Ohio 47-48; Lib aide (clerical) Cleveland Pub Lib Cleveland 48-Je 52; Y p libn 52-55; Pub Lib of Cincinnati 55-56; Asst Br libn Cleveland Pub Lib 57-58; Br Libn Hartford Pub Lib, Hartford Conn 58-. 9: ConnLA; Greater Hartford Child Libns Group; ALA. 10: Immanuel Cong Church(Hartford) Lib Comm (chm 63-65); Hartford Sem Campus Wives group. 14: Br libs. 15: 92 Girard ave,Hartford Ct 06105.

ADDISON, ELIZABETH RUTH (HEYECK). b Irvington NJ 11 F 29. 4: Lewis Ernest Addison. 5: Trenton State Col 48-52 (Secondary Educ, Hist, Geog) BS; Rutgers 56-59 MLS. 7: Tchr Bd of Educ, Piscataway Twp 52-53; Child libn Union Free Pub Lib, Union NJ53-57; Sch libn Bd of Educ, Newark NJ 58-62; Sch libn Bd of Educ New Providence NJ62-. 9: Union Co SchLA (sec-treas 64-65); NJSchLA (Elections chm 69); NEA; NJEA. 10: Beta Phi Mu; Kappa Delta Pi. 14: Child wk. 15: 25 Woodland rd N, Millington NJ 07946.

ADDISON, LAURA (LOMBARD). b New Orleans La 11 Je 16. 5: LSU 32-35, summer 38 (Fr) AB, summers 48-51 (Eng) MA; UDen 59-60 (Libnship) MA. 7: Tchr-libn E Baton Rouge Parish schs, Baton Rouge La 35-60; Libn I (catlgr) Free Lib of Phila 60-62; Asst prof of LS, Asst libn Milner Lib Ill State U, 62-. 9: ALA; AAUP; IllAHE; IllEA; IllLA; McLeanCoLA; Alpha Beta Alpha. 10: Mem Ed Com, "Ill State U Journal"; Amer Contract Bridge League (life master). 14: Catlg, ref. 15: 602 W Monroe, Bloomington Il 61701.

ADDISON, LOUISE ALCOTT. b Everett Mass 16 F 09. 4: Henry D Addison. 5: BostonU 31 (Sec Sci) BS; Simmons 336 (Lib) 51 Mass Certif of Lib Sci. 6: Fr. 7: Hd Lending Lib Mass Div of Lib Ext, Boston 31-37; Asst ref libn Smith Col 50-59; Chief reader serv UMass 59-61, Educ libn 61-. 8: Organ lib of Prophylactic Brush Co, Florence Mass 44. 9: SLA (Boston Chap: sec 34-35); MassLA; NELA. 10: Commun chest: Woman's Club; PEO. 12: Co-auth "One Hundred Years of Brotherhood; History of florence Congregational Church" (62). 14: Ref, soc scis. 15: 74 Massasoit st, Northampton Ma 01060.

ADDISON, MAEIVES (PARSONS). b Smithfield Va 22 O 24. 4: Lester H Addison. 5: Morgan State Col 41-45 (Educ) BS; Syracuse 56-60 (LS) MS. 7: Tchr Brooks High Sch Calvert Co Bd of Educ 46-47; Libn Turner Station Br Baltimore Co (Md) Lib 51-. 9: ALA; MdLA; Md Adult Educ Assn. 14: Juvenile wk. 15: 317 Pine st, Baltimore Md 21222.

ADELMAN, IRVING. b New London Conn 22 F 26. 4: Florence Less. 5: Northeastern 44-48 (Eng) BA; Columbia 49-51 (Eng) MA, 52-54 (LS) MS. 7: Jr libn Long Beach Pub Lib, Long Beach Cal 54-56; Jr & sr Brooklyn Pub Lib 56-58; Sr II head ref dept E Meadow Pub Lib, E Meadow NY 58-. 8: Mem Nat Adv Bd, McGraw-Hill Encyclopedia & Subscription Book Division; Ref consul & adv wk, pub lib. 9: Nassau Co LA (Intell Freedom Com, Ref Com). 12: Co-auth (with Rita Dworkin) "Modern Drama; A Checklist of Critical Literature on 20th Century Plays" (67). 14: Ref. 15: 73 Autumn lane, Hicksville NY 11801.

ADELMAN, JEAN (SHAW). b Toledo Ohio 23 N 30. 4: Fred Adelman. 5: UPenn 48-54 (Anthrop) BA; UWash 54-55 (Anthrop, Mongolian studies); UPittsburgh (MLS) 63, Advanced Certif 64. 6: Fr. 7: Stud asst UPenn Libs 48-51, Asst to archivist 52-53; Tchg fellow: UWash 54-55, UPittsburgh Grad Sch Lib & Info Sci 63-64; Adjunct instr lib sci Drexel 64-65; Instr lib tech program Commun Col of Allegheney Col of Allegheney Co 67-68; Visiting lecturer UWest Ont Sch Lib & Info Sci 68-69. 9: ALA; SLA; COLT; Tri-State ACRL; PennLA. 10: Beta Phi Mu; Pi Gamma Mu; Phi Beta Kappa. 13: Yes. 14: Clsf, col & univ libs, lib educ. 15: 3915 Beechwood blvd, Pittsburgh Pa 15217.

ADELSPERGER, ROBERT (JAMES). b Hammond Ind 19 Je 25. 5: UIll 52-57 (Eng Lit) BA, 57-58 (LS) MS. 6: Fr, Ital. 7: Asst ref libn Bowling Green StateU 58-59; Asst ser acquis libn UIll(Chicago) 59-60, Asst ref libn 60-64, Spec collectionslibn 64-. 8: Del Conf of US Nat Comm for UNESCO, Chicago 63. 9: ALA (Jr Mem RT Chicago Chap; chm Jr Mem RT 63-64; act treas Intl Rel RT);-RSD (Publs Com 63-; Local Arrangements Com, RareBks/Hist Sect Pre-conf 63; liaison to Jr Mem RT 64-; chm Elections Com 64, 67);-ACRL (Elections Com 65, Rare Bks Sect rep to Memb Com 66-67); IllLA (Intellectual Freedom Com; 64-65, chm 65-67; chm Conf Exhibits Com 64; Publicity & Pub Rel Com 62-64);BSA; Ms Soc; SAA. 10: Caxton Club; Soc Arch Hists; AAUP; Phi Beta Kappa; Phi Kappa Phi. 13: Yes. 14: Rare bks, mss, archives, maps. 15: 1018 N State st, Chicago Il 60610.

ADKINS, BERTHA LAMAR (WACHSMAN). b Shubuta Miss 11 S 31. 4: Robert Edgar Adkins. 5: Miss State Col for Women 49-53 (LS) BS. 6: Fr. 7: Catlg dept Pub Lib, Mobile Ala 53-54, Head circ dept 54-55; Base libn Amer Air Force, Chateauroux France 55-57; Sch libn Amer Air Force, Nouasseur Morocco N Africa 57-60; Sch libn Steuben Jr High Sch, Milwaukee 60-61. 10: Women Overseas Serv League; Welcome Wagon Club; "Reading Mother" to Brown Deer School (kindergarten classes). 14: Catlg, child wk. 15: 8642 N 51st st, Milwaukee Wi 53223.

ADKINS, ELIZABETH FRANCES. b Richmond Va 29 Jl 10. 5: Hollins Col 28-30 (Music, Eng); UVa 30-32 (Eng, Ed) BS in Ed; U of NC 36-37 AB in LS; U of NC 42-46 (Span & Lat Am). 6: Sp, Fr, Ger. 7: Recatlgr UVa Alderman Lib 37-41; Libn in chg of Lat Amer Affairs UNC 42-46; Libn Army Ground Forces Hdqrs Ft Monroe Va 46-47; Libn Med Sch Lib UVa 47-62; Catlgr & Asst Libn in chg Tech Processes Duke U 62; Libn Lib Scott & White Mem Hosp Temple Tex 63-. 9: MedLA,-Wash Reg Group (chm Steering Com)-So Reg Group. 10: AAUW. 13: Yes. 14: Med & nursing. 15: 818 S 27th st, apt 3, Temple Tx 76501.

ADKINS, MARGARET (FIELDER). b Roanoke Va 27 S 09. 4: William Royall Adkins. 5: Nat Bus Col 30; UVa Ext 32-33. 7: Bkmob libn, Pub Lib of Charlotte & Mecklenburg Co, Charlotte NC 53-63, Br libn: E Br lib 63-65, W Br Lib 65-67, S Br Lib 68-. 9: ALA; SELA; NCLA; MecklenburgCoLA. 14: Child, young adult, pub rel, rare bks. 15: 1326 Drexmore ave, Charlotte NC 28209.

ADKINS, THELMA (REXROAD). b Harmony WVa 27 N 11. 4: John M Adkins. 5: U WVa 30-34 (Educ) BS Ed; Tulane 54-55; LSU ext 61, 64, 65; LSUNO (LS) 68-69. 6: Tchr Nitro Jr High Sch, Nitro WVa 34-35; Tchr Wheeling High Sch, Wheeling WVa 35-36; Act registrar & temp dean of women Kanawha Jr Col 36-37; Asst libn Jefferson Parish (La) Pub Lib 60-61; Manager Metairie Br Lib, Metairie La 61-63; Ref libn II, Jefferson Parish La 63-. 9: ALA; LaLA. 10: Kappa Delta Pi; Delta Gamma; Reader's Club of Metairie (La). 14: Ref. 15: N Causeway blvd, Metairie La 70002.

ADKINSON, BURTON W(ILBUR). b Everson Wash 5 Mr 09. 4: Margaret L Klock. 5: UWash 36 (Geog) BA, 39 (Geog) MA; Clark U 42 (Geog) PhD. 7: Research assoc & asst dir Bd of Geographic Names, Wash DC 43-44; Asst chief map intelligence sect OSS, Wash DC 44-45; LC; Asst chief Map Div 45-47, Chief Map Div 47-48, Asst dir Ref Dept 48-49, Dir Ref Dept 49-57; Head Off of Sci Info Serv NSF 57-. 9: ALA (Adv Com to Lib Tech Proj); SLA (pres 59-60); ASIS; Internat Fed for Documentation (pres 62-65). 10: Cosmos Club, Wash DC. 12: "The Role of Scientific Societies Today" (62); "Primary Scientific Publications and the Federal Government" (63); "The Organization of Information - How It Is Done in the USA" (67); "Libraries and Machines - A Review" (67). 13: Yes. 14: Admin. 15: 5907 Welborn dr NW, Wash DC 20016.

ADLER, BETTY. b Havana Cuba 13 My 19. 5: Goucher 33-37 (Internat Rel) AB; Drexel 37-38 MLS. 6: Sp, Ger, Fr, Portu, Ital. 7: Mencken Room Enoch Pratt Free Lib, Baltimore 57-; Compiler cumulative index Md Hist Soc, Baltimore 62-. 8: Consul Off of Coordinator of Inter-Amer Affairs 41. 10: Phi Beta Kappa. 12: Comp "HLM, The Mencken Bibliography" (61); "Census of Ventures into Verse" (65); Comp "Man of Letters" (69); Trans Joseph Basile's "Cultural Development of Managers, Executives & Professionals" (68); Ed "Menckeniana." 14: Catlg, bibliog, indexing. 15: 1701 Eutaw pl, Baltimore Md 21217.

ADMIRE, LESLIE (QUINLAN). b Boston Mass 12 Je 45. 4: Gary D Admire. 5: Barnard 63-64 (Japanese); UHawaii 65-68 (Japanese) BA, 68-69 MLS. 6: Chinese, Japanese, Fr. 7: Stud asst Oriental Lib E-W Ctr, Honolulu Hawaii 66-68. 9: ALA. 10: Phi Beta Kappa; Assn Asian Studies. 14: Ref. 15: 1505 Kewalo st, Honolulu Hi 96822.

ADRIAN, MRS DONNA JEAN (FRAZER). b Mordon Manitoba Can 28 Ag 40. 4: James Ross Adrian. 5: Brandon Col 58-62 (Eng) BA; McGill U 62-63 BLS McGill U 66-68 MLS. 6: Eng, Fr. 7: Clerk Brandon Pub Lib Brandon Man 53-62; Clerk Brandon Col Brandon Man 61-62; Libn Rosemere High Sch Rosemere Que 63-. 14: Sch Libs Org & Admin. 15: 241 Roi du Nord apt 4, Ste Rose de Laval Que Can.

ADZIMA, CHRISTINE ROBERTA (HANLON). b New Haven Conn 7 N 31. 4: Edward S Adzima Jr. 5: New Haven State Tchrs Col 50-54 (Educ & LS) BS, summer 56; BostonU summer 68. 6: Sp. 7: Asst Instr of LS & Supv of Training Sch Libs Tchrs Col of Conn, New Britain 54-57; Clerical asst L-2 Yale Lib summer 54; Asst Summer Sch Lib New Haven State Tchrs Col summer 55; Libn Ellington High Sch, Ellington Conn 62-. 9: ALA-AASchA; NEA; AAUP; ConnLA; ConnSchLA; ConnEA; EllingtonEA. 10: Libn Ellington Hist Soc. 14: Ref, catlg. 15: 356 DRR1 Heather rd, Ellington Ct 06029.

AFFLERBACH, LOIS GRIMES. b Bristol Penn 8 Ag 21. 5: Queens Col 38-42 (Eng) BA; Columbia 43-45 BLS, 48-50 (Lat) MA. 6: Lat, Ger. 7: Clerk ser catlg div NY Pub Lib 42-45; Chief reviser Columbia U Sch of Lib Serv 45-50; Ser libn Paul Klapper Lib Queens Col 51-62; Libn Grad Studies Div City U(NY) 62-64; Libn soc sci div Paul Klapper Lib Queens Col 64-. 9: NYLA; NY Reg Tech Serv Libns; NY Lib Club. 10: Coun on Research in Bibliog. 12: Co-chm, Ed Com "Mental Health Book Review Index" (55-). 14: Catlg, ser, govt docs. 15: 139-75 35th ave, Flushing NY 11354.

AFRICK, LENORE (PETCHAFT). b Oak Park Ill 17 Ag 22. 4: Hyman Africk. 5: Beloit Col 39-43 (Chem) BS. 6: Fr, Sp. 7: Chem libn Armour Auxiliaries, Chicago 43-60; Chem libn Armour Ind Chem Co, McCook Ill 60-. 9: ACS (Chem Lit Div); SLA (pres Ill Chap 53-54); Amer Soc for Info Sci. 10: Phi Beta Kappa; Phi Sigma Iota. 12 Abstr, 'Soap & Detergent Abstracts' in "Journal of the Amer Oil Chemists Soc" (43-60). 14: Ref wk in aliphatic chem. 15: Armour Ind Chem Co Lib, 8401 W 47th st, McCook Il 60525.

AGARD, ROBERT M(ASON). b Williamstown Mass 1 Ap 16. 4: Phyllis Fairweather. 5: WesleyanU 35-39 (Hist) BA; Columbia 39-40 (LS) BS; Brown 40-42 (Hist) MA. 6: Fr. 7: Ref asst BorwnU 40-42; Ref asst LC 42-46; Lecturer CatholicU 44-46; Libn, Asst Prof of Lib Sci Ripon Col 46-50; Lecturer Wis State Col summer 50; Libn Earlham Col 50-61; Asst libn reader serv UMass 61-66; Libn Bennington Col 67-. 13: Yes. 14: Ref, admin, lib arch. 15: Box 49 West st, N Bennington Vt 05257.

AGEE, MARY EVELYN. b Cody Wyo. 5: UDenver 32-36 (Econ) BS Certif in LS; NYU 47-48. 7: Lib asst NY Pub Lib 36-41; Chief libn post libs US Army, Fort Story Va 41-46; Asst libn NY Postgrad Med Sch Lib 46-47; Asst libn Air Reduction Co, NYC 48; Libn Amer Gas Assn, NYC 48-58; Libn main lib us naval Hosp, St Albans LI NY 58-. 8: Consul & adv wk on starting or expanding existing libs in pub utility or natural-gas transmission companies, 48-58. 9: SLA (Sci-Tech Div: Adv Coun 54-56, Exhib Com 52; NY Chap: chm Exhib Com 52, chm Constit & Bylaws Com 55, Directory Com 50-51; sec Sci-Tech Gp 65-66; Pub Utilities Sect: sec 51-52, v-pres 53, pres 54-56, chm Exhib Com 50, 52, 55. 12: Ed "American Gas Association Publications List (49-57); Comp various printed, comprehensive bibliogs on major subjects of interest to the gas industry. 13: Yes. 14: Admin, ref, bibliotherapy. 15: 45 Tudor City pl apt 409, New York NY 10017.

AGENBROAD, JAMES EDWARD III. b Dayton Ohio 9 D 34. 4: Jean Morris Agenbroad. 5: Miami U (Ohio) 52-56 (Hist) BA; Rutgers U 59-60 MLS. 6: Sp. 7: Trainee Dayton Pub Lib, Dayton Ohio 56-57; Clk (Pfc) US Army, Nuremberg Germany 57-59; UNH Lib(Durham); Catlgr 60-61, 62-65, Sr catlgr 65-67, Ser libn 67, Asst libn 67, Asst to libn & Machine Syst libn 68-69; Lib syst analyst Inforonics Inc, Maynard Mass 67-68; Sr info research analyst, info syst off, Wash DC 69-. 9: ALA; NELA; NHLA (Treas 64-65); ASIS. 14: Catlg, lib automation. 15: 9410 Warren st, Silver Springs Md 20910.

AGGARWAL, NARINDAR KUMAR. b Hoshiarpur India 15 F 34. 4: Indra Taneja. 5: DAV Col (Hoshiarpur India) 49-51 (Eng, Econ, Sanskrit) FA; Panjab U Col (Hoshiarpur India) 51-53, 54 (Eng, Econ, Sanskrit) BA; Kan State Tchrs Col (Emporia) 58-59 (LS) MS. 6: Hindi, Urdu, Sanskrit, Panjabi. 7: Catlgr Havard U 59-60; S Asian bibliogr UPenn 60-64; S Asian libn UIll (Urbana) 64-. 8: Trip to India & Ceylon as a repres of Midwest Univ Consortium for Internat Activities to buy bks, 66-67. 9: ALA. 14: Admin, catlg, bibliog (S Asian field). 15: 1914 S Vine st, Urbana Il 61801.

AGGEN, MYRA J. (STECKER). b Chilton Wisconsin 6 Je 18. 4: Chester C. 5: Outagamie Normal 35-37 (Ed) Certif; Milwaukee State Tchrs 37-39 (Ed) Certif. 7: Tchr Twain Sch, Calumet Co Wis 37-38; Tchr Brillion Elem, Brillion Wis 38-41; Tchr Lower Sch, New holstein Wis 43-45; Libn Morton Grove Pub, Morton Grove Ill 54-. 9: CalumetCoTA (v-pres). 10: Toastmistress Interl; Morton Grove Womans Club; Jerusalem Lutheran Womans Club. 15: 8647 Ferris st, Morton Grove Il 60053.

AGNER, MRS SUSIE B(AILEY). b Lexington Miss 1 Ja 08. 5: Miss Delta State Col 26-30 (Soc Studies) BS; LSU summers 49-52 BLS. 6: Sp. 7: High sch soc studies Eudora High Sch, Hernando Miss 30-35; Libn & Study Hall Belzoni High Sch, Belzoni Miss 49-51; Libn & Eng Tchr; Crowville High Sch, Crowville La 51-53; Cheneyville High Sch, Cheneyville La 53-55; Libn Sulphur High Sch, Sulphur La 55-60; Libn Frasch Elem Sch, Su lphur La 60-63; Libn North Crocker Elem Sch, Sulphur La 63-69; Libn E K Key Elem Sch, Sulphur La 69-. 8: Sec of CalcasieU Libn Assn. 9: ALA; NEA; CTA; LaSchL; LaLA; LaTA. 10: Bus & Prof Womens Club. 14: Ref, elem sch libs. 15: 721 McArthur st, Sulphur La 70663.

AGNES, SISTER MARY (O'BRIEN) SC. b NYC. 5: Col of Mt St Vincent 32 (Lat) AB; Columbia 33-36 (Eng) AM, 43-44 BS in LS, 44-49 (Educ Admin) PhD. 6: Lat, Fr. 7: Tchr St Peter High Sch, SI NY 26-32; Tchr- libn Blessed Sacrament High Sch, NYC 32-43; Libn Cathedral High Sch, NYC 43-47; Libn Col of Mt St Vincent 47-51; Libn Elizabeth Seton Sch, Yonkers NY 51-59; Libn, sr adv, Eng tchr St Gabriel High Sch, New Rochelle NY 59-67; Libn, St Barnabas High Sch, Bronx NY 67-. 8: Selections Com Cath Child Bk Club 45-50; High Sch Com Cath Lib Serv 61-. ; Cath Supplnt Com, Wilson HS Catlg, 67-. 9: CathLA (chm High Sch Sect 59-60, chm Greater NY Unit 59-61); ALA, NCTE; NYLA. 12: "History of Catholic Secondary Education in the Archdiocese of New York" (49). 13: Yes. 14: High sch libs, bks for adolescents, bk sel, catlg. 15: 425 E 240 st, Bronx NY 10470.

AGNEW, ELLEN Y (SAVILLE). b Boston 15 Ja 21. 4: Robert Jamieson Agnew. 5: Smith 38-42 (Chem) AB; SUNY (Albany) 63-65 MLS. 7: Chem Texaco, Beacon NY 42-43; Volunteer Blodgett Mem Lib, Fishkill NY 63-65; Asst in ref dept Mid-Hudson Libs System, Poughkeepsie NY 65; Libn central ref coordinator Adriance Mem Lib, Poughkeepsie NY 65-68; Asst catlg libn Richmond Pub Lib, Richmond Va 69-. 9: NYLA; Dutchess Co LA (v-pres 67-68); VaLA. 10: AAUW. 14: Ref. 15: 4613 Shoremeade rd, Richmond Va 23234.

AGNEW, FREDA (CLARK). b Yellow Springs Ohio 29 O 07. 4: Edward Agnew. 6: Fr. 7: Free Library of Phila: Child libn 29-45, Br libn 45-63, Asst chief ext div 64-66; Libn Sch of Nursing Grand View Hosp, Sellersville Penn 66-. 9: ALA. 10: Trustee Pierce Free Lib Bd, Silverdale Pa 68-. 11: Award for Outstanding Commun Serv in Northeast Phila. 12: Short play published (singly) for church organization production (about 45) United christian missionary society. 14: Br admin. 15: Route 2 Box 3, SellersvillePa 18960.

AGNEW, JANET MARGARET. b St Paul 1 N 03. 5: UMan 25 (Eng) BA, 30 (Eng) MA; McGill 33 BLS. 7: Asst catlgr McGill 28-33; Instr McGill Lib Sch 33-38; Asst Prof LSU Lib Sch 39-42; Head Libn Sweet Briar Col 42-47; Head Libn Bryn Mawr Col 47-69. 8: Taught in summer schs at Denver U Lib Sch, 44 & UNC 47. 9: ALA; BSA; PennLA; CLA; Can Biblig Soc. 10: AAUP; AAUW. 12: "Southern Bibliography" (29-42). 14: Rare bks, admin. 15: Bryn Mawr Col Lib, Bryn Mawr Penn.

AGREE, ROSE HYLA. b Poland 25 Ag 13. 4: Morris J Agree. 5: Hunter Col 29-32 (Soc Sci) BA; Queens Col 55-58 (LS) MSE; NYU 64- (Elem Ed). 6: Yiddish. 7: Head Libn Bd Educ UFSD #30, Valley Stream NY 56-. 8: Adv Com, AAAS Child's Sci Bklist; Instr Child Lit; Queens Col summer 64, DrexelInst summer 67. 9: ALA (Elem Sch Lib Com 60-63 (chm Bk Coun Jt Com 67-69); NYLA;Nassau-Suffolk Sch LA (pres 63-65, Liaison Dir, Prof Orgs); NY State Tchrs Assn (chmreg Zone Conf); NYLibClub. 10: LWV; Great Neck Friends of Lib; Great Neck EA. 12: Ed "Added Entries," Nassau-Suffolk Sch LANewsletter (62-64); Comp "How to Eat a Poem and other Morsels" (67). 13: Yes. 14: Childbks, illus, Negro in child bks. 15: 17 Campbell st, New Hyde Park NY 11040.

AGRIESTI, PAUL (ALLAN). b Columbus Ohio. 5: Ohio No 61-64 (Eng) BA; UMich 64-65 AMLS. 7: State Lib of Ohio, Columbus: Bookmobile 65, Inter-lib loan 65, Catlgr 66-68, Asst to state libn 68-. 9: ALA; OhioLA. 10: Sigma Tau Delta. 15: 229 N Terrace ave, Columbus Oh 43204.

AGUAYO, JORGE. b Habana Cuba 4 D 03. 4: Maria Hortensia Lavedan. 5: UHavana Law Sch 21-25 Doctor Civil Law; UHavana Diplomatic 25-27 9consular Serv) Certif; Columbia 41 (LS). 6: Sp. 7: Asst dir Gen Lib UHavana 37-59, Dir Gen Lib 59-60; Prof catlg ; clsf, Lima Peru 44; Prof catlg & clsf UHavana summers 46-52; Prof catlg & clsf, Sch of Libnship UHavana 50-60; Head Br Lib, Pan American Union 62-. 8: Rockefeller Foun Scholarship to study at the Sch of Lib Serv, ColumbiaU, spring sem 41; Invited by the State Dept to spend 4 months in the US 45; Attended, by invitation, the First Assembly of Libns of the Americas 47. 9: ALA; DCLA. 11: Hon degree in libnship, UHavana 55. 12: "Manual practico de clasificacio y catalogacion de bibliotecas (43, 2nd ed 51); Co-comp "Lista de encabezamientos de materia para bibliotecas, 3 v (67). 13: Yes. 14: Clsf, catlg. 15: 2800 Quebec st W 404, Washington DC 20008.

AGUIRRE, GEORGE L. b Akron Ohio 29 My 32. 5: Kent State U 50-58 (Sp) BA; Rutgers U 59-60 MLS. 6: Sp, Fr, Ital, Port, Roum. 7: Head Circ Taylor Mem Lib Cuyahoga Falls Ohio 53-56; Personnel specialist US Army (Specialist 3rd Class) 56-58; Jr asst Akron Pub Lib 58; Head Circ Orange Pub Lib Orange NJ 59-60; Libn Boni,Watkins, Jason & Co Inc NYC 60-61; Libn Esso Standard Eastern Inc NYC 61-, Head Info Center, Esso Standard Eastern Inc NYC 66-68; Mgr lib serv Standard Oil Co (NJ) NYC 68-. 8: Res asst Rutgers U Sch Lib Serv 59; Discussion leader & guest speaker at Am Mgt Assn seminars on Company Libs, Document Reproduction and Info Storage & Retrieval. 9: ALA; SLA-NY Chap (Chm Sci-Tech Group 64-65, treas 65-66); Sociedad de Bibliotecarios de Puerto Rico; ASIS. 10: Instituto de Puerto Rico; Soc Friends of Puerto Rico; Amer Translators Assn. 11: Chamberlain Scholarship, Akron Pub Lib. 13: Yes. 14: Admin, info storage & retrieval, bibliog, ref. 15: 2 Tudor City pl, NYC 10017.

AGUOLU, CHRISTIAN CHUKUNEDU. b Nimo Biafra 22 D 40. 5: UIbadan Nigeria (Classics) Honors BA from ULond; UWash 67-68 (Libnship) ML. 6: Ibo, Fr, Lat, Gr, Ger, Sp, Ital. 7: Lat, Eng & Fr Tchr Secondary Sch, Biafra 65-66; Ref libn UCal (Santa Barbara) 68-. 9: UCalLA. 11: Prize & Bronze Medal in Classics 65. 14: Ref, bibliog. 15: 6668 #F Picasso rd, Goleta Ca 93017.

AHARONIAN, MRS ARSINE (PARAGAMIAN). b Erzeroum Armenia 4 D 13. 4: Vartkes Aharonian. 6: Armenian, Fr. 7: Transit dept Nat Shawmut Bank of Boston 31-47, Credit dept 47-53, Libn 53-. 9: Amer Inst of Banking; Women's Nat Bk Assn. 10: Armenian Women's Educl Club. 15: 40 Water st, Boston Ma 02106.

AHERN, ARLEEN (FLEMING). b Mt Harris Colo 15 O 22. 4: George I Ahern. 5: U Utah 39-43 (Sociol) BA; UDenver 62 (LS) MA UColo 66-67 (Sociol). 7: Lib asst Air Force Base, Salt Lake City 43; Lib asst Colo Woman's Col 52-59; Acquis libn Temple Buell Col 60-. 9: ALA; MPLA; ColoLA (chm Scholarship Com, sec Col & Univ Div, v-pres & pres-elect 69-70); SAA. 10: Adult Educ Coun of Denver; LWV; Altrusa; Mountain Plains Adult Educ Coun. 14: Acquis, rare bks, archives. 15: 746 Monaco pkwy, Denver Co 80220.

AHERN, VIRGINIA (OWEN). b Birmingham Eng 19 Ap 10. 4: Philip Charles Ahern. 5: Simmons 29-33 (LS) BS. 7: Asst & child room Newton Free Lib, Newton Mass 33-35, Br libn 35-37; High sch libn sch dept, Winchester Mass 37-40; Child libn Berkshire Athenaeum, Pittsfield Mass 53-. 9: ALA; MassLA; West Mass Lib Club. 14: Child wk, elem sch libs. 15: 52 Broad st, Pittsfield Ma 01201.

AHL, RUTH ELAINE. b Orange Cal 20 O 36. 5: Valparaiso U 54-58 (Sociol) BA; Drexel 63-65 MS in LS. 6: Sp. 7: Research & Statistics Armed Serv Commsn Lutheran Church, Wash DC 58-60, Supv Refferral Sect 60-61; Probation Off Juvenile Court, Montgomery Co, Rockville Md 61-63; Libn VA Hosp, Wash DC 65-. 9: ALA; MedLA; SLA. 14: Ref. 15: 2409 Homestead dr, Silver Spring Md 20902.

AHLERS, ELEANOR E. b Seattle 16 My 11. 5: UWash 28-32 (Fr) AB; UDenver summers 40-42 BLS; UWash summers 55-57 (Curriculum) MA. 6: Fr, Sp. 7: Tchr-libn High Sch, S Bend Wash 32-36; Tchr-libn High Sch, Mt Vernon Wash 36-42; Libn High Sch, Everett Wash 42-52; Supv of libs Everett Sch Dist, Everett Wash 52-53; Asst Prof of Lib Sci UOre 53-57; Exec Sec of AASL ALA, Chicago 57-61; Supv of lib serv Off of Pub Instr, Olympia Wash 61-66; Assoc Prof UWash Sch of Libnship 66-. 8: Asst dir Sch Libns Wkshop: UOre summer 56; Central Wash State Col, Ellensburg summer 51; Instr Lib Sci: UWyo summers 45-46; San Jose State Col summers 47, 52 Dir KSTC Wkshop summer 64; DirNDEA Inst UWash summer 67. 9: ALA (Coun 62-66); NEA-DAVI; Assn for Supv & CurrDevel; AASchL (pres 65-66, Bd Dir 53-55); PNLA; WashLA; Wash State ASchL (pres50-51). 10: Phi Beta Kappa; Pi Lambda Theta; UWash Faculty Nomin Club 68-69. 11: Hon mem Wash State ASchL 69. 12 "Enriching American History" (57); Guest edALA Bull, Feb 67. 12: "Enriching American History" (57); Guest ed ALA Bull, Feb 67. 13: Yes. 14: Sch libs, lib educ. 15: 2360 43rd st, Seattle Wa 98102.

AHLSTROM, PETER WILLIAM. b Iron River Mich 6 D 35. 4: Sandra Anderson. 5: UMich 54-55 (Engr); Northwest Bible Col 56-59 (Bible) BA; UWash summer 59 (LS); UDenver summers 60-62 (LS) MA. 6: Sp. 7: Libn Northwest Col of the Assemblies of God 59-67; Libn Ida Pub Lib, Idaho Falls 67-. 9: PNLA; IdaLA (v-chm & chm-elect Pub Libs Div 68-69). 12: Ed "Northwest Col Alumni News" (64-67). 13: Yes. 15: 1912 Everest, Idaho Falls Id 83401.

AHMAD, SYED NASEEM. b Delhi Brit India 25 Ag 36. 4: Kausar Musthaq. 5: UKarachi (Pakistan) 55-60 (Math, Chem) BS; Syracuse summer 64 (LS); CatholicU fall 64-65 (LS); UPittsburgh 65 (MLS). 6: Urdu, Arabic, Persian. 7: Jr lib spec UHawaii 65-67; Bibliogr (sci) UMass (Amherst) 67-68; Hd reclsf projects; Asst Prof, AdelphiU 68-. 9: ALA. 14: Ref, sci & tech, documentation & info scis. 15: 8825-148th st apt 4F, Jamaica NY 11435.

AHN, HERBERT K. b Los Angeles 2 D 28. 5: Los Angeles City Col 46-48 (Pre-Med) AA; UCLA 48-50 (Zool) AB, 50-53 (Slavic Langs) AB; UCal 53-54 BLS. 6: Sp, Ger, Russian. 7: Tr catlg dept Lib 52-53; Catlg asst catlg dept lib & Bancroft Lib UCal (Berkeley) 53-54; UCLA; Research asst Inst of Slavic Studies 53-54, Bibliog checker acquis dept Lib 54, Ref libn ref dept Lib 54-55; Clerk typist (Spec 4th Class) Army of the US, Paris France 55-57; Foreign documents libn govt publ room UCLA Lib 57-62; Govt publ libn UNev Lib 62-66; Lib syst analyst & c omp coord UCal (Irvine) 66-. 8: Asst prof org & clsf of lib materials UNev Gen Univ Ext 64-; Lectr; UOre Sch Libnship HEA Wkshops on Lib Automation, summer68; SF Chap ASIS Wkshop on Lib Automation 69; UCal(Irvine) Lib St Assn (pres 68; Chm Comm on Admin Appl, Comp, Fac, Serv 68-;Mem Chancellor's Adv Comm on Comp, Fac & Serv UCal(Irvine) 68-; Mgt Info Sys Coord 68-. 9: CalLA (chm Docs Com 61); NevLA (chm Intel Freedom Com 64-); ALA; ASIS; Coun for Soc Sci Data Archives (mem Info Retr sub com); So Cal Tech Proc Gp (Prog Com chm 67-68, pres-elect 68-69); OrangeCoLA (chm Ser Merchan Com 68-). 13: Yes. 14: Govt pubs, ref, automation, admin. 15: PO Box 4042, Irvine Ca 92664.

AHRENS, MARCELLA. b St Louis 29 Ag 15. 5: St Mary's Col of O'Fallon 34-36; St Louis U 45-52, 58, 63 (Hist) AB; Rosary Col 52-57 MALS. 6: Fr. 7: Libn Bishop DuBourg High Sch, St Louis 54-56; Libn St Elizabeth Acad, St Louis 57-62; Libn St John's High Sch, St Louis 62-63; Libn St Elizabeth Acad, St Louis 63-65; Libn St Mary's Col of O'Fallon 65-68; Community serv libn St Louis Pub Lib 68-. 8: Instr in Lib Sci, St Mary's Col of O'Fallon, Mo 65-68. 9: CathLA; MoLA; ALA. 10: Staff Assn St Louis Pub Lib. 14: Ref, serv to inner city. 15: 1624 Locust st, St Louis Mo 63103.

AHRENS, WILLIAM C. b NYC 2 O 42. 4: Carolyn Flower. 5: UMe 60-65 (Hist & Govt) BA; LIU 65-68 (LS) MS. 7: C W Post Col: Circ libn 65-66, Asst period libn 66-67, Asst to libn 67-68; Supply off (Lieut) USA 66; Asst U libn UMe 68-. 8: Asst Prof of Lib Serv, UMe 69-. 13: Yes. 14: Ad,in, tchg, periodls. 15: UMe, Orono Me 04473.

AIELLO, ALICE PHOEBE (BLACK). b Dane County Wis 17 Jl 28. 4: Albert R Aiello. 5: UWis 45-50 (Journalism) BA, 50-51 MA. 7: High sch libn Racine Pub Lib, Racine Wis 51-52; Child libn Milwaukee Pub Lib 52-56, Young adult libn 56-59, Br libn 59-61; Coordinator Young adult Serv Cuyahoga Co Pub Lib, Cleveland 61-; Asst Prof of Lib Sci West Res U, summer 6465; Lecturer Lib Sci West Res U, summer 64, spring 66, 68; Dep dir Cuyahoga Co Pub Lib, 66-. 8: Weekly TV Program Milwaukee 54-59; Consul Lib Sch West Res U & Kent State U Lib Sch. 9: ALA (v-pres Young Adult Serv Div 64-65, Bd 58-59); OhioLA (chm Child & YP Round Table 64-65, chm com to prepare standards for pub libs); OhioASchL; Exec dir Nat Lib Week State of Ohio 64-65. 12: Chm com to prepare bibliog on Latin Amer for Young Adult Serv Div ALA-YASD. 13: Yes. 14: Young adult serv, sch libs, pub libs, tech serv, admin. 15: 4510 Memphis ave, Cleveland Oh 44144.

AIKIN, JOHN K. b Columbus Ohio 20 Mr 17. 4: Katharina Reuland. 5: SoIll State Tchrs Col 35-38 (Educ) Tchrs Certif; UMd 56-57 (Mil Sci) BS; UIll 62-64 (LS) MS. 6: Ger. 7: Tchr grade sch 39-40; Clerk-typist Civil Serv, Chicago Signal Corps Procurement Depot, Chicago 40-42; US Army: Field Artillery, Ft Bragg NC, Officer Train, Ft Sill Okla, Highest enlisted rank: Master Sgt, highest officer rank: Maj 42-43, Field Artillery in Zone of Interior and in European Theater Post-war Serv Quartermaster Corps in Europe 1st Lt 43-47; USAF Finance & Acctg, Management Analysis, Squadron Comdr, Base Adjutant, Personnel Off, Ala, Austria, Tex, Cal, & Guam Maj 47-62 ret; Head photographic serv UIll Lib (Urbana) 64-. 8: Participated in planning for Austrian State Treaty, Vienna Austria 55. 10: Retired Officers Assn; Chi Gamma Iota; UIll (Urbana) Lib Staff Assn (pres). 14: Reprographics. 15: 304 Sunnycrest ct W, Urbana Il 61801.

AILLET, GENEVIEVE (FUSELIER). b St Martinville La 27 Ag 22. 4: Clarence Johanni Aillet. 5: Southwestern U, La 39-42 (Educ, Eng) BA; LSU 55-57 MS in LS. 6: Fr. 7: Tchr-libn Hahnville High Sch, Hahnville La 42; Lab tech Humble, Baton Rouge La 45-47; Libn Zachary High Sch, Zachary La 51-59; Libn Istrouma Jr High Sch, Baton Rouge La 59-61; Libn Baton Rouge Sr High Sch, Baton Rouge La 61-; Libn LSU Lib summers 57-61; Libn EBR Parish Lib, Baton Rouge La 62-65 Tchr lib sci extension courses LSU Lib Sch 66-68. 9: LaLA; LaASchL. 10: Baton Rouge Lib Club; Kappa Delta Pi; Beta Phi Mu; Phi Kappa Phi. 14: Ref. 15: 9548 Meredith dr, Baton Rouge La 70815.

AIMONE, ALAN CONRAD. b Sycamore Ill 6 D 41. 5: East Ill U 61-66 (Am Hist) BS in Ed; Rosary Col 67-69 (LS) MALS. 6: Fr. 7: Asst libn Wheeling High Sch, Wheeling 66-68; Asst libn Wheaton N High Sch, Wheaton 68-69; Bk shop asst Abraham Lincoln Bk Shop, Chicago 66; Rare bk catlgr West Point Mil Lib 69-. 9: ALA; Amer Assn State & Loc Hist; Ill State Hist Soc. 10: Chicago Civil War Round Table; Confed Hist Soc. 13: Yes. 14: Rare bks, Amer mil hist ref. 15: 30 High Lake ave, W Chicago Il 60185.

AIREL, WALTER F. b Bayonne NJ 23 D 25. 4: Frances Airel. 5: Champlain Col (Plattsburg NY) 53 (Bus Admin) BA; Albany StateU 56 MSLS. 7: (Pfc) US Army, Germany 44-46; Ya libn Rochester Pub Lib, Rochester NY 55-58; Br libn 58-60; Dir Livingston & Wyoming Co Lib System, NY 60-. 9: ALA; NYLA (Memb, Personnel Com); MonroeCoLA (chm 57). 10: Albany Lib Sch Alumni Assn; Kiwanis; Big Tree Ski

Club. 13: Yes. 14: A-v, circ syst, lib syst org. 15: 29 North st, Geneseo NY 14454.

AIRO-FARULLA, JOELYN M. b Chicago Ill 14 Jl 38. 4: Joseph A Airo-Farulla. 5: Northwestern U 56-60 (Psych) BA; UWash 60-62 (Psych) 64-66 (Preventive Med) BS, 66-67 (Libnship) MSLS. 6: Fr. 7: Libn I Free Lib of Phila 68; Libn Wills Eye Hosp and Res Inst, Phila 68-. 9: ALA; MedLA (Phila Reg Gp). 14: Hist of med, automation. 15: 915 Wyndon ave, Bryn Mawr Pa 19010.

AISTARS, AIVARS. b Jaunjelgava, Latvia 13 D 29. 4: Lidija Kalnmals. 5: UIll, Navy Pier 51-52 (Liberal Arts); UChicago 53-55, 57-58 (LS) MA. 6: Latvian, Ger. 7: Ab, mail clk, SP/3 US Army, 55-57; Catlgr UChicago Lib, 58-66; Catlgr UIll, Chicago Circle 66-. 14: Catlg. 15: 6250 N Campbell, Chicago Il 60645.

AIVAZIAN, A GIA. b Kavalla Greece. 5: Amer UBeirut 54-59 (Econ) AA; UCLA 61-66 (Eng Lit) BA, 66-67 MLS. 6: Armenian, Gr, Fr, Ital, Arabic, Turkish. 7: Sec Econ Dept Amer UBeirut 54-59; Sec to asst sales mgr Kaiser Steel Corp Los Angeles 60-64; Sec Near East Ctr UCLA 64-67; Libn catlg Armenian & Gr collections catlg dept Research Lib UCLA 67-. 8: Armenian lang instr 68-. 9: ALA; CalLA. 10: Armenian Youth Cultural Assn; Armenian Allied Arts Assn; Pro-Komitas Choral Soc; Nat Assn for Armenian Studies & Research. 14: Catlg, ref. 15: 8546 Saturn, Los Angeles Ca 90035.

AJAMIAN, HAIG. b Boston 2 S 05. 5: Harvard 25-29 (Hist) AB; Columbia 29-30 (Law), 35-36 (LS) BS, 39-41 (Hist) AM. 7: Gen bkkeeper Bank of Manhattan Trust, NY 31-32; Brooklyn Col Lib: Lib asst 35-38, Chief period & bind div 38-41, Chief period & documents div 41-59; US Army (Pfc) 42-45; Chief soc sci div Brooklyn Col Lib 59-61; Chief soc sci div City Col (NY) 61- Asst Prof 65-. 9: ALA (Com on Wilson Indexes 53-66). 15: 160 W 77th st, NYC 10024.

AKE, ROBERT S. b Ft Wayne Ind 22 Mr 13. 5: Butler U 34-38 (Eng) AB; Columbia 38-39 BLS, 46-48 (Adult Educ) MA. 7: Ref asst bus & econ div, Rochester Pub Lib 40-42; S/Sgt US Army Air Force, US & Europe 42-45; Asst br libn NY Pub Lib 46-48, Br libn 48-52; Pub lib consul Conn State Dept of Educ, Hartford Conn 52-58; Asst dir Enoch Pratt Free Lib, Baltimore 58-64; Dir Finkelstein Mem Lib, Spring Valley NY 64-. 8: Surveys for ALA: Martinsburg WVa (60), Greenwich Conn (62); Survey for Div of Lib Ext, Md: Frederick Md (63) Md Area Lib Serv 69. 9: ALA; AEAUSA; ConnLA; NYLA. 13: Yes. 14: Pub lib admin, lib bldgs, adult educ. 15: Finkelstein Mem Lib, Spring Valley NY 10977.

AKERS, EDWARD JOHN. b Williamson WVa 5 F 29. 4: Mona Jean Coole. 5: Berea Col 46-48; Baker U 52-54 (Psych) AB; John B Stetson 54-55 (Hist, Educ) MA; Fla State U 64 (LS) MS. 6: Fr. 7: Elem tchr Rockledge Elem Sch, Rockledge Fla 54-59; Elem tchr Port Orange ElemSch, Port Orange Fla 59-62; Libn N Ridgewood Elem Sch, Daytona Beach Fla 62-63; LibnMainland Sr High Sch, Daytona Beach Fla 63-65; Guidance supv Navajo Reserv, AnethBoarding Sch 65-69; Lib Chm Aneth Indian Sch, Aneth Utah 65-. 8: Established lib in Port Orange Fla. 9: ALA; FlaEA; Amer Childhood Educ Assn (treas 60-62). 10: Phi Alpha Theta. 13: Yes. 14: Ref. 15: 148 San Juan ave,Daytona Beach Fl 32014.

ALBERT, DOROTHY MAY (MILLER). b Wilmington Del 6 F 33. 4: Rolph Albert. 5: Maryville Col (Tenn) 51-53 (Biol); Auburn U 53-55 (Hirticulture) BS; Catholic U 64-66 MSLS. 6: Fr. 7: Info specialist Frederick Research Corp, Gaithersburg Md; Libn John I Thompson Co, Wash DC 64-; Info specialist Nat Referral Ctr Inst LC 66-67; Info specialist Acquis chief Nat Highway Safety, Wash DC 67-68; Info specialist Nat Educ Assoc, Wash DC 68-. 9: SLA; ASIS; ACS; DCLA. 14: Acquis, ref, info retr. 15: 5241 Nebraska ave NW, Washington DC 20015.

ALBERT, WARREN. b NYC. 5: Brooklyn Col 47-53 (Health Educ) BS; UIll 53-55 (LS) MS. 7: Circ clk Cooper Union, 47-48; Clk Pub Health Dir Mun Ref Lib, NYC 48-50; Serials asst UIll Lib 53-55, Bind libn 55-60; Assoc dir Archive Lib AMA, Chicago 60-. 8: SAA rep to Jt Comm on Hosp Libs 67-68. 9: SAA (Comm on Archives of the Professions, chm 68-69); Oral Hist Assoc; NMA; ASIS (Chicago Area Chap chm 65-67); Assoc of Records Execs & Adminrs. 10: Amer Assoc State & Local Hist. 13: Yes. 14: Records mgt, archives, microfilm systems applications, med bibliog & hist. 15: 1702 N Lawndale ave, Chicago Il 60647.

ALBERTI, DINO A (ANTHONY). b Gary Ind 10 Jl 16. 4: Elizabeth Dunbar Rue. 5: Gary Col (Gary Ind) 35-40; Polytech Inst 63-65 (Hist & Pol Sci) BA, 65-67 (Am Hist) MA; LSU 66-67 (LS) MS. 6: Ital, Sp, Fr, Ger. 7: Laborer-budgetary clk Gary Sheet & Tin Mill, Gary Ind 35-40; Lt, Lt Col, Engrs Hq, 3rd & 6th Army, USA & SWPA 41-46; Locker optr & livestock farmer, Jonesboro La 47-64; Lt Col, Inf Hq, 4th Army & KMAG, USA & Korea 50-52; Hum libn Instr La Polytech Inst, Ruston La 67-. 8: Col Inf, USAR, Mob Designee, P&O Div, O&T, HQ, 4th US Army 47-. 9: ALA; AAUP; AUSA; ROA; SWLA; LaLA (Leg Com 68-70); LaTA. 10: Phi Kappa Phi; Phi Alpha Theta; Beta Phi Mu; Amer Legion; Jackson Parish Farm Bureau. 13: Yes. 14: Humanities, lib ed & admin, automation, military. 15: PO Box 607 (107 Cooper ave), Jonesboro La 71251.

ALBINA-MARIE, SISTER (GAZAILLE). b Holyoke Mass 22 Ja 15. 5: Catholic Tchrs Col (Providence) 37-44 (Educ) Normal Sch Certif; Rivier Col 36-45 (Math) BA; Catholic U 47-48 BS in LS; Simmons Col 53-54. 6: Fr. 7: Elem sch tchr Diocesan Schs, RI & NH 36-46, Jr & high sch tchr 48-51; Head Libn Rivier Col 51-. 9: ALA; CathLA; NELA; NHLA. 14: Admin, ref. 15: Rivier Col, Nashua NH 03060.

ALBRECHT, LOIS (KINDELBERGER). b Wheeling WVa 3 O 30. 4: Charles O Albrecht. 5: Clarion State Col 48-52 (Math, LS) BS in Ed; UPittsburgh 62-63 MLS. 6: Sp. 7: Libn Richland Twp High Sch, Johnstown Penn 52-62; Head tech serv Washington Co Free Lib, Hagerstown Md 63-68; Libn Info storage & retrieval Washington Co Bd of Educ, Hagerstown Md 68-. 8: Ref asst Lib/USA, NY World's Fair 65. 9: ALA; MdLA (Recr Com); Potomac Tech Proc Libns Assn; Cambria Co Sch Libns(Johnstown Penn) (past pres); PennLA; Cumberland Valley LA (pres 68-69); NEA;Washington Co TA; Md State TA. 10: Beta Phi Mu; AAUW. 12: Co-auth "Library Service,southern Style," (66). 14: Acquis, ref, info storage & retrieval. 15: 100 Larch ave, Hagerstown Md 21740.

ALBRECHT, MARION LOUISE. b St Louis 20 Jl 33. 5: U Mo 51-55 (Elem Ed) BS; West Res U 57-58 MSLS. 7: Tchr Ferguson-Florissant Schs Ferguson Mo 55-57; Lib asst Cleveland Pub Lib 57-58; Jr child libn St Louis Pub Lib 58-59; Child libn Daniel Boone Reg Lib Columbia Mo 59-67, Act dir 65-66, Dir of child serv 67-. 8: Exten Course Instr, U Mo 62-63; Instr Lib Inst U Mo summer 64; Libn USA staff NY World's Fair 65 Lect, U Mo 67-69; Exec dir Mo MoNLW 68. 9: ALA (Subs Bks Com 64-70),-LSD Newberry-Caldecott Awards Com 68) MoLA. 10: LWV; Quota Club; Delta Kappa Gamma; Col Bus & Prof Women's Club. 11: Outstanding Woman of the Year in Columbia (Theta Sigma Phi) 68. 14: Child lit lib serv to child, sch libs. 15: Daniel Boone Regional Library Box 935, Columbia Mo 65201.

ALBRIGHT, LOUISE (ROTHROCK). b Grand Rapids Ohio 26 D 15. 4: Don U Albright. 5: West Col for Women 32-36 Biol AB; Ohio U summer 38; Kent State summers 64, 65. 6: Fr. 7: Tchr Bloom Twp Schs, Bloomville Ohio 38-40; Tchr W Lafayette Schs, W Lafayette Ohio 40-42; Scipio-Republic Schs, Republic Ohio: Sub tchr 42-59, Tchr 59-60, Libn 60-64; Libn Defiance City Schs, Defiance Ohio 64-. 9: ALA; NEA; OhioASchL (dir NW region 67-69); OEA. 10: AAUW; LWV. 14: Ya reading guid. 15: 2028 Shawnee dr, Defiance Oh 43512.

ALBRIGHT, ROBERT W. b Seattle Wash 1 S 13. 4: Jay S Buck. 5: UWash 30-38 (Psych) BA; Stanford 41-46, 50-51 (Speech Pathology) MA & PhD; IndU 65-66 (LS) MA. 6: Fr, Sp. 7: Soldier USA, US & Europe 43-46; Tchr UMont 46-48; Tchr UColo 45-51; Tchr Cornell 51-55; Tchr N Dak State 55-57; Ariz State U: Tchr 57-65, Ref libn 66-. 9: ALA; ArizStateLA. 10: Fac Senate, Ariz State U. 12: "The International Phonetic Alphabet: Its Backgrounds and Development 58. 14: Ref, African bibliog. 15: 702 Roosevelt, Tempe Ar 85281.

ALBRIGHT, SUSIE K. b Cooper Tex 1 O 08. 5: Okla U 28-30 (Hist) BA, 39-40 (Hist) MA, 41-42 (LS) BA. 6: Sp. 7: Tchr Cooper High Sch, Cooper Tex 30-39; Bus & soc sci libn U Tex Austin Tex 42-46, Documents libn 46-49; Head of Circ East Tex State Tchrs Col 49-53; Head of circ Tex A&M Lib 53-60; Law Lib So Methodist U 60-. 9: AALL: TexLA. 14: Law. 15: So Methodist U Law Lib, Dallas Tx 72505.

ALBURGER, THOMAS P. b Camden NJ 10 S 37. 4: Marjorie R Polley. 5: Rutgers 56-60 (Humanities) AB; West Res 60-62 MSLS. 6: Fr. 7: Catlg libn Boston Pub Lib 62-63; Med & nursing libn Mt Auburn Hosp, Cambridge Mass 63-. 9: ALA; MedLA (chm Nurs Libs Group 65-66); NELA (Hosp lib sect); Bliss Clsf Assn. 10: Men Libns Club (Boston); ACLU. 14: Catlg. 15: 234 Lakeview ave, Cambridge Ma 02138.

ALBUSH, FIDELIA. b Montrose Colo 31 Jl 25. 5: West State Col (Colo) 43-47 (Pol Sci) BA; UDenver summers 48-51 (LS) MA. 7: Tchr Florence High Sch, Florence Colo 47-59; Libn Montrose Co High Sch, Montrose Colo 49-51; Libn Lakeview Pub Schs, Lakeview Ore 51-54; Libn La Grande High Sch, La Grande Ore 54-57; Libn Eugene (Ore) Pub Schs, Colin Kelly Jr High Sch 57-65; Libn Kennedy Jr High Sch 65-. 8: Instr ULethbridge Lib Sci Dept summers 67-69. 9: ALA; NEA-DAVI; OreEA; OreLA; OreSchLA. 10: EugeneEA. 14: Sch libs. 15: 2030 Van Buren, Eugene Or 97402.

ALDEN, (HOWEL) HENRY. b Topeka Kan 12 Ag 07. 5: Washburn Col 23-26 (Fr) BA; UKan 26-28 (Eng) MA; Columbia 49-50 MS in LS. 6: Fr, Sp. 7: Fellow in Eng UKan 26-27, Instr in Eng 27-28; US Army Transportation Corps (Master Sgt), Persian Gulf Command 42-45; Grinnell Col: Instr in Eng 34-46, Asst Prof, Eng 46-52, Libn, Assoc Prof Eng 52-. 9: ALA; Mod Lang Assn; IowaLA. 10: AAUP; Sigma Delta Chi; Phi Beta Kappa. 13: Yes. 14: Admin. 15: 833 East st, Grinnell Ia 50112.

ALDEN, JOHN (ELIOT). b Brockton Mass 12 F 14. 5: Williams 31-35 (Eng) AB; Brown 35-36 (Romance Lang) AM; UMich 38-41 ABLS. 6: Fr, Ital, Ger, Port, Sp, Lat. 7: Ref asst City Lib Assn, Springfield Mass 36-38; Asst UMich Lib 38-41; Ref asst LC 41-43; Asst & catlgr Houghton Lib, Harvard U 43-46; Curator of rare bks UPenn 46-50; Asst libn Georgetown U 50-52; Asst & keeper of rare bks Boston Pub Lib 54-. 8: Consul on Preservation to Govt of India, 58; Consul on Lib, Gethsemani Abbey, Trappist Kent 58-59. 9: Amer Antiq Soc; BSA; Bibliog Soc (London), etc. 10: Phi Beta Kappa, Club of Odd Vols (Boston); Grolier Club. 11: Fulbright Research Fellow, British Museum, 51. 12: "Rhode Island Imprints" (49); "Bibliographica Hibernica" (56); "The Muses Mourn" (57); rev ed of Lydenberg & Archer "Care & Repair of Books" (60); etc. 13: Yes. 14: Rare bks, bibliog. 15: Boston Pub Lib, Boston Ma 02117.

ALDERFER, ARLETA A (ANDERSON). b Denver 9 Je 11. 4: Elmer J Alderfer. 5: UDenver 28-32 (LS) BA; UColo 55-56 Teaching Certif. 7: Libn Colo Sch of Mines 32-33; Libn Rocky Mountain News, Denver 33-34; Libn Evergreen High Sch, Evergreen Colo 56-. 9: ColoSchLibns; ColoEA. 10: Camp Fire Girls Leaders. 15: Box 6, Evergreen Co 80439.

ALDERMAN, ALICE (RUDRUD). b Westby Wis 6 My 24. 4: Donald Alderman. 5: N Park Col (Chicago) 43-45 (Pre-Med) AA; State U (La Crosse) 63-65 (Eng) BS; UWis 65-66 (LS) MS, 66- (Scandinavian St). 6: Norw, Swed, Ger. 7: Libn I State Hist Soc, Madison Wis 66-68, Libn II, 68-. 9: ALA. 10: Kappa Delta Phi; Beta Phi Mu. 14: Catlg govt publ. 15: 1715 Laurel Crest, Madison Wi 53705.

ALDERMAN, HARRY J. b Yonkers NY 10 Jl 11. 4: Alice M Ross. 5: NYU 27-31 (Eng Lit) BA; Columbia 32-33 (Ger Lit), 34-37 (LS) BLS, 45-46 (LS); American U 49 (Archival Admin) Certif. 6: Ger, Fr, Ital, Sp, Hebrew, Yiddish, Japanese. 7: Lib asst Gen Lib NYU 31-39; US Army Japanese lang spec 42-45; Libn Amer Jewish Com, NYC 39-, Libn-archivist 54-. 9: SLA; ALA; SAA; Jewish Libns Assn; NYLibClub. 10: Ling Soc Amer; Amer Numis Soc; Jewish Bk Coun; Phi Beta Kappa. 12: Contrib "American Jewish Year Book" & "Jewish Book Annual." 14: Spec lib admin, ref, archives. 15: 240 Cabrini blvd, NYC 10033.

ALDERSON, WILLIAM THOMAS Jr. b Schenectady NY 8 My 26. 4: Sylvia Farrell Alderson. 5: Colgate U 43, 46-47 (Hist, Math) AB; Tulane U 45-46 (Hist); Vanderbilt U 48-52 (Hist) MA,PhD. 7: Sr archivist Tenn State Lib & Archives 52-57; Exec sec Tenn Hist Commn 57-61; Asst State Libn & Archivist Tenn State Lib & Archives 59-61, State Libn & archivist 61-64; Chrm Tenn Hist Comm 61-64; Dir Amer Assn for State & Local Hist 64-, Ed "History News" 64-. 8: Visiting Asst Prof of Hist Vanderbilt U 55-56; Instr UTenn (Nashville) 54-61. 9: ALA, SAA (coun); Amer Records Mgt Assn (pres SE chap 63-64); Amer Assn for State & Local Hist (coun 60-64); Org Amer Historians; Nat Trust for Historic Preservation; Tenn Hist Soc; Tenn Assn of Museums (v-pres 64-65, pres 65-66); SoHistA; Assn for the Preservation of Tenn Antiquities (trustee); Amer Assn of Museums. 10: Pres, Colgate U Alumni Assn Tenn chap, Amer & Nashville Rose Societies, Westerners, Rotary Internat, Metropolitan Com on Zoning, Belle Meade Mansion (Bd of Govs), Ft Watauga Assn. 11: Fellow SAA; Amer Assn for State & Local Hist (Award of Merit 59); Advisory Council, Historic Amer Buildings Survey. 12: Asst ed "Tennessee Historical Quarterly" (53), assoc ed (54-55), ed (56-65); "Tennessee Historical Markers" (58), with R M McBride (62); "A Guide to the Study and Reading of Tennessee History" with R H White (59); "Historic Sites in Tennessee" with H G Thomas (63); Ed (with R M McBride) "Landmarks of Tennessee History" (65); "Tennessee, a Students' Guide to Localized History" (66). 13: Yes. 14: Hist archives, mss, preservation & microfilming, admin. 15: 124 Taggart ave, Nashville Tn 37205.

ALDRICH, RACHEL DURHAM. b York Me 5 N 21. 5: Plymouth Tchrs Col 39-43 (Ed) BS in Ed; Simmons Lib Sch 46-47 (LS) BS; HarvardU (Ger). 6: All European. 7: Head catlgr Colby Col Waterville Me 47-51; Intern law catlgr Harvard Law Lib 51-58; Head catlg & processing, William & Mary 58-68; Chief catlg Lib UWis (Parkside) 68-. 8: Consul Richard Abel Co, Portland Ore 68-69; Vol: Racine Co Hosp, Mt Auburn Hosp. 9: VaLA; potomac Reg Catlgrs. 10: Appalachian Mtn Club; College Woman's Club Serv; Red Cross Gray Lady Eastern State Hosp. 13: Yes. 14: Tech processes, catlg, admin, train lib assts. 15: 5704 Wildwood dr, Racine Wi 53403.

ALDRICH, RUTH M. b Dunkirk NY 6 N 42. 5: State U Col (Geneseo NY) 60-64 (LS) BS in Ed; Syracuse 64-65 MSLS. 6: Fr. 7: Circ libn State U Col (Fredonia NY) summers 61-64, Ser libn 65-68; Campus Sch Libn Madison Col (Harrisburg) 68-. 9: VaEA. 10: Kappa DeltaPi. 14: Circ, ref, ser, sch libnship. 15: Apt 10, 953 Mt Clinton Pike, Harrisburg Va 22801.

ALDRICH, MRS WILLIE LEE (BANKS). b Cleveland 9 S 24. 4: Thomas N Aldrich. 5: Livingstone Col 43-45 (Soc Studies, Hist) BA; Atlanta 63 MSLS. 6: Fr. 7: Asst libn Rowan Br Lib, Salisbury NC 54-57; Tchr-libn Cleveland High Sch, Shelby NC 58; Libn Dunbar High Sch, E Spencer NC 59-60; Asst libn Livingstone Col 60-63; Bible tchr Salisbury City Schs Monroe Elem Sch & Price High Sch 52-53, 64; Libn Hood Theo Sem Livingstone Col 63-. 8: Dir of Christian Educ, Salisbury (NC) Dist AME Z, 65 Conf dir of Christian Educ, Western North Carolina Conf 68-. 10: Delta Sigma Theta; Civic League; AAUW. 14: Ref, child libn. 15: 1337 W Horah, Salisbury NC 28144.

ALEMANY, ANA (RAMIREZ). b Santurce PR 28 N 39. 4: Luis G Alemany. 5: UPR 55-61 (Chem) BS; Drexel 64-67 MS in LS. 6: Sp. 7: Asst circ libn UPR Mayaguez 61-62, Doc libn 63-66, Catlgr 66-67; Lib dir Cayey Reg Col, Cayey PR 67-. 9: ALA; Sociedad de Bibliotecarios de Puerto Rico. 10: Asociacion Interamericana de Bibliotecarios y Documentalistas Agricolas. 12: "Las Publicaciones oficiales del gobierno del ELA de Puerto Ric," Bibliog. 14: Lib admin, govt docs. 15: Cayey Regional Col, Cayey PR 00633.

ALEVIZOS, THEODORE. b Milwaukee. 4: Susan Thatcher Bamberger. 5: Marquette U 46-59 (Eng) PhB; Juilliard Sch of Music 50-51 (Voice); Columbia 56-57 (LS) MS; Suffolk U Law Sch 61-66 LLB. 6: Ital, Ger, Gk. 7: Lib asst Milwaukee Pub Lib 51-52; Lib asst NYU Med Sch 56-57; Harvard U: Asst chief of circ Widener Lib 57-61, Asst libn Lamont Lib 61-64, Dir 64- Assoc Univ Lib & Lib of Lamont Lib 66-. 12: Comp (with Susan Alevizos) "Folksongs of Greece" (68). 14: Admin, personnel. 15: Lamont Lib Harvard Univ, Cambridge Ma 02138.

ALEXANDER, DANIEL GREGORY. b NYC 3 Ag 26. 4: Emma Milano. 5: Montclair State 44-48 (Sp, Lat) AB; Columbia 49-50 MSLS; UPenn summer 67 (Educ research). 6: Sp, Ital, Fr. 7: Jr libn Paterson Pub Lib, Paterson NJ 48-50; Ref libn Newark Pub Lib, Newark NJ 50-53; Sch libn Newark Bd of Educ, Newark NJ 53-; Fellow Columbia U Sch Lib erv 68-69. 9: NJLA. 10: Newark Sch Lib Assoc; Newark Tchrs Assoc; Newark YMCA; Friends of NYC Ballet; Mem Found for Amer Dance. 13: Yes. 14: Lib serv to youth. 15: 272 Fourth st, Newark NJ 07017.

ALEXANDER, DOROTHY LAMOUR. b Belzoni Miss 8 My 39. 5: Tougaloo Col 58-62 (Biol) BS; UWash 64-65 M Libr; UOre 65 (Biol); Portlandstate Col summer 68. 6: Ger, Sp. 7: Asst in lib Tougaloo Col 62-64; Sci libn UOre 65-66; Sci libn PacificU 66-68; Libn NW Educ Research Lab,Portland Ore 69-. 8: Mem Faculty Coun PacificU. 9: ALA; SLA; PNLA; OreLA (chmScholarship Com). 10: LWV. 11: Fellow American Acad of Optometry. 14: Ref. 15: Rt 1 Box 126-B, Gaston Or 97119.

ALEXANDER, EDITH (REID). b Manchester NH. 5: UNH 21-25 (Hist) BA; Columbia 26-27 (Hist) MA; Simmons 50-51 MS in LS. 6: Fr. 7: Head of music dept Manchester (NH) City Lib 51-54, Head of fine arts dept 54-57; Asst libn Patients Lib VA Hosp, Providence 57-58; Asst libn Patients Lib VA Hosp, Boston 58-59; Asst ref libn Naval War Col, Newport RI 59-. 9: ALA; RILA. 10: AAUW. 13: Yes. 14: Ref. 15: 40 Toppa blvd, Newport RI 02842.

ALEXANDER, ELENORA CECILIA. b Houston Tex 5 F 06. 5: RiceU 23-27 (Eng) BA; Peabody summers 36-38 BS in LS; Columbia summers 42-46 MLS. 7: Tchr & libn Houston Ind Sch dist (Tex) 27-49, Dir lib serv 49-61, Dir instr materials serv 61-. 8: Director of summer wkshops: N Tex State Col 47 & 48, UKy 49, Fla StateU 57, Immaculate Heart Col (Los Angeles) 58, Brigham YoungU 61; vis lectr: Appalachian State Col summer 52; UTex 56. 9: ALA (chm Ed Com: Advis Subcom on Reviewing & Nonprint Materials in "Booklist"); -AASchL (pres 58-59); mem AASchL-DAVI Standards Revis Com; TexLA (pres 54-55); SWLA (sec 54). 10: Kappa Delta Pi; Delta Kappa Gamma; mem Nat Bk Comm's Exec Adv Coun for Educ Media Sel Centers Proj, NEA, ASCD & DAVI. 11: Tex Libn of the Year 60. 13: Yes. 14: Sch libs, sch media serv. 15: Apt 337 2511 Willowick, Houston Tx 77027.

ALEXANDER, ELINOR M(URIEL). b Salinas Cal. 5: Pomona Col 31-35 (Eng) AB; UCal (Berkeley) 35-36 (LS) Certif; Columbia 40-41 (LS) MS. 7: Libn High Sch, Salinas Cal 36-44; Asst head documents dept Gen Lib UCal(Berkeley) 44-63; Legis indexer Admin-Legis Ref Serv Cal State Lib 63; CoordinatorCont Educ in Libnship UCal Ext (Berkeley) 63-65; Asst libn Pillsbury, Madison &sutro, San Francisco 65-69, Libn 69-. 9: ALA; SLA; CalLA (chm &/or mem var coms);CalASchL (pres No Sect 41-42); No Cal Tech Proc Group. 10: Women's Faculty Club, UCal (Berkeley); Bk Club of Cal. 13: Yes. 14: Govt docs, ref, law. 15: 721 Hilldale ave, Berkeley Ca 94708.

ALEXANDER, HELEN P. b Buffalo NY 24 Jl 11. 4: George H Alexander. 5: Wellesley 29-33 (Bot) BA, 33-36 (Bot) MA; Catholic U 59-63 MS in LS. 6: Fr. 7: Lab asst Wellesley Col 33-37; Asst Sch Nature League, NYC 37-38; Civil serv examiner US Civil Serv Commsn, Wash DC 39-45; Elem sch tchr & sch libn Union Sch, Port au Prince Haiti 56-58; Lib asst Catholic U 59-61; Ref libn US Dept Agric, Beltsville Md 61-64; Libn Patuxent Wildlife Research Center US Dept of Interior, Laurel Md 64-66; Ref libn US Atomic Energy Commsn 66-67; Ref libn Nat Argic Lib 67-. 9: SLA. 13: Yes. 14: Ref, lit searching, biol scis. 15: 6309 Rockhurst rd, Bethesda Md 20034.

ALEXANDER, JOANE L. b Los Angeles Cal 23 Jl 32. 4: Cecil B Alexander. 5: Harding Col 50-54, 56 (Soc Sci) BA; Emory summer 55 (LS); UMich summers 56, 58, 59, 61 (AMLS). 7: Asst libn Harding Col 54-59; Libn Waterford Twp High Sch, Pontiac Mich 59-60; Asst libn Harding Col 60-61; libn Mich Christian Jr Col 6-165; Br libn Davis br Yolo Co Lib, Davis Cal 65-66; Libn Mich Christian Jr Col 66-. 9: ALA; MichLA; CalLA. 10: Friends of the Woodward Mem Lib, Rochester Mich; Friends of the Kresge Lib OaklandU, Rochester Mich. 14: Admin, ref. 15: 800 W Avon rd, Rochester Mi 48063.

ALEXANDER, MOTHER M DE MONTFORT OSU. b Jacksonville Ill 1 O 03. 5: Illinois Col 21-25 (Eng) BA; Catholic U 54-58 MS in LS. 6: Fr, Sp, Ital. 7: Sec tr Dept of State, Washington & abroad 27-42; Asst libn Coll of New Rochelle 57-59, Libn 60-. 9: ALA; CathLA; NYLA. 10: Beta Phi Mu. 12: Tr "Way of Perfection," by St Teresa of Avila (47). 14: Admin. 15: Lib, Col of New Rochelle, New Rochelle NY 10805.

ALEXANDER, MALCOLM DOUGLAS. b Potlatch Ida 17 O 39. 4: Susan Jo Trail. 5: UIda 57-61 (Pol Sci) BA; UWash 64-65 M Libr. 7: Page UIda Lib 57-60, Subprof 60-61; Secondary Sch Tchr-Libn Lake Stevens Sch Dist, Lake Stevens Wash 61-64; Pre-prof in refSeattle Pub Lib 64-65; Ref libn Central Wash State Col 65-67, Asst to dir & data processing coordinator 67-. 9: ALA; NEA; WashEA; PNLA. 10: Phi Delta Kappa. 14: Ref, readers serv, rare bks, data processing. 15: 811 E 4th st, Ellensburg Wa 98926.

ALEXANDER, MARY ANN. b Greenville Tenn 18 Mr 32. 5: E Tenn StateU 50-54 (Elem Educ) BS; Peabody summers 57-60 MA in LS. 7: Libn n point Jr High, Baltimore 54-56; Libn Robinson Jr High Sch, Kingsport Tenn 56-58; Libn Titusville Elem Sch, Titusville Fla 58-59; Libn Tusculum Col 59-61; Libn Perry Hall Elem Sch, Baltimore 61-62; Ref Dept Knoxville Pub Lib, Knoxville Tenn 62-67; Ref libn Kingsport Pub Lib, Kingsport Tenn 67-69; Libn Greene Co Lib, Greeneville Tenn 69-. 9: ALA; TennLA: SELA. 14: Ref. 15: Rte 9, Greeneville Tn 37743.

ALEXANDER, MILDRED RUTH (CHRISTLER). b Hudsonville Mich 22 Ag 19. 4: Henry Clay Alexander. 5: West Mich 38-41, 55 (Soc Sci) BS; UMich 56-61 (LS) MA. 7: Elem tchg pub schs, Hudsonville Mich 40-41; Elem tchg pub schs, Jenison Mich 41-42; Jr high prin & tchg, Burr Oak, Grand Rapids Mich 42-43; Jr high tchg, Bentley, Flint Mich 44-45; Jr high tchg & sr high tchg, Ellsworth Mich 45, 47-48; Jr high tchg sub, Waloon Lake Mich 50-51; Elem & jr high libn pub schs, Holland Mich 51-. 9: NEA; MichEA. 14: Catlg, jr high sch lib .wk, church libs. 15: Lake Shore dr Box 204, Fennville #1 Mich.

ALEXANDER, NORMAN DALE. b Lead SD 8 D 29. 04. Lois Eddy. 5: UNeb 52-56 (Eng, Hist) BA; UDenver 56-57 (LS) MA; UMinn 62-63 (Pub Admin). 6: Sp. 7: (M/Sgt) Army personnel 48-52; Libn Centralia Jr Col 57-58; Head ref libn Mont StateU 58-62; Asst to dir UMinn (Minneapolis) 62-63; Head of pub serv Portland State Col Lib 63-67; Libn & Hd Lib Sci Dept Ore State Col 67-. 8: State lib adv com Bur Bus & Econ Research Study 68-69; faculty Senate Portland StateU 64-67. 9: ALA-ACRL; PNLA (treas 68-); OreLA (chm Const Com 64; chm Lib Development Com 68-69; Parliamentarian 63-68; Exec Bd 63-; v-pres 68-69; pres-); OreASchL; OreEA. 14: Admin, ref. 15: 2922 Anderson Creek rd, Talent Or 97540.

ALEXANDER, PHILIP. b Cracow Poland 17 N 11. 4: Bertha Katz. 5: UTagiellonski (Cracow Poland) 29-34 (Law, Admin) Doctor; USoCal 56-58 (LS) MS. 6: Polish, Ger. 7: Lawyer, Cracow 35-39; Legal adv & camp leader JRO, Kassel Germany 46-49; Manager Zeitlin & Ver Brugge Booksellers, Los Angeles 58-60; Head Libn Cedars-Sinai Med Center, Los Angeles 60-. 8: Lecturer on bibliotherapy, Dept of Psychiatry, Cedars-Sinai Med Center, Los Angeles. 9: Soc Hist Med (exec sec local br). 14: Rare bks. 15: 926 Coronado dr, Glendale Ca 91206.

ALEXANDER, ROBERT (JAMES). b Coatesville Penn 6 Ja 29. 4: Linda Lawson. 5: Grove City Col 46-50 (Hist, Pol Sci) BA; UDubuque 60-64 BD; UChicago 64-65; Drexel 67-69 MSLS. 6: Gr, Hebrew. 7: (S/Sgt) USAF Aircraft Radar Equipment Repairman 50-54; Dist scout exec BSA, West Chester Baltimore Md 55-60; Minister Grace Presbyt Ch Montgomery Penn 65-67; Ser libn LincolnU 68-. 9: ALA. 14: Theol libnship, ser. 15: Ash Park e apt C6 S 4th ave, Coatesville Pa 19320.

ALEXANDER, SAMUEL OLIVER. b Delhi India 10 Ja 37. 4: Farida Fez Hiptoola. 5: St stephen's Col UDelhi 53-56 (Hist) BA, 57-59 (Hist) MA; UPhillipines 56-57 (E Asian hist); Sch of Lib & Info Sci UWest Ontario 67-68 MLS. 6: Hindi, Urdu, Punjabi, gujerati, Ger. 7: Info off Govt of India Tourist Off, Bombay 61-62; Gen sales supv Esso Standard East Inc, Bombay 62-67; Lib asst U W Ontario 67-68; Tutor Sch of Lib & Info Sci U W Ontario 68-. 8: Indian Delegate 1956, 3d Asian Students' Forum, Baguio City, The Phulippines. 9: ALA; CanLA; OntLA. 10: Rotary Club; Jr Chamber Internat, Bhopal (India); U West Ontario Sch Lib & Info Sci Students' Coun. 14: Catlg, lib educ, acquis. 15: Sch of Lib & Info Sci, UWest Ontario, London Ont Can.

ALEXANDER, (HAZEL) SUSANNA. b St James Mo 13 F 17. 5: Stephens Col 36 AA; Northwestern 38 BS; UDenver 52 MALS. 7: Asst libn James Mem Lib, St James Mo 45-49; Stephens Col Lib: Ref & circ libn 49; Asst catlgr & ser libn 49-52, Head lib tech serv dept 52-55; Dir Columbia Pub Lib, Columbia 55-59; Dir Daniel Boone Reg Lib, Columbia Mo 59-65; Dir of field serv Mo State Lib 65-66; Assoc state libn Mo State Lib 66-. 9: ALA (Spec Projs Com); -ASD (J W Lippincott Award Jury); -ALTA (Publs Com); MoLA (pres 63, treas 57-59, chm &/or mem 3 coms 55-56 & 64). 10: LWV; Stephens Col Alumnae Club;Severance Bk Review Club; Fed of Women's Clubs; AAUW. 11: Alumnae Achievementaward (59) from Stephens Col. 13: Yes. 15: 408 Crystal View terr, Jefferson City Mo 65101.

ALEXANDER, WILLIAM D IV. b High Pt NC 4 Jl 40. 4: Martha Linda Thormondson. 5: El Camino Jr Col 58-60 (Psych); Whittier Col 60-62 (Psych) BA; Syracuse 65-66 MS in LS. 6: Fr. 7: Libn asst Santa Maria Pub Lib, Santa Maria Cal 62; MP (E-4) USA, Ger 63-65; Trainee Warner Lib, Tarrytown NY 65; Dir Abington Lib Soc, Jenkintown Penn 66-68; Dir Westerly Pub Lib, Westerly RI 68. 8: Instr URI Ext Div 68-69 (Lib Certif prog). 9: ALA; NELA; RILA; PennLA; NYLA. 10: C of C; Beta Phi Mu. 14: Pub lib admin, reg serv. 15: Broad, Westerly RI 02891.

ALEXANIAN, ANNA. b West New York NJ 30 O 24. 5: Hunter Col 44 (Eng) BA (summa cum laude). 7: Asst libn Price Waterhouse & Co NYC 44-. 9: SLA (archivist Fin Div 52-56, 59-64; chrm Fin Group 56-57; Fin Com NY chap 58-59, 60-61; chrm com to revise by-laws of Bus & Fin Group of NY chap 61-62); Phi Beta Kappa. 14: Rev. 15: Price Waterhouse & Co, 60 Broad st, NYC 10004.

ALFERIEFF, LUBOV (JERNAKOFF). b Tiumen Russia 15 D 11. 4: Nicholas Alferieff. 5: UWash 53-55 (Far East Studies) BA, 56, 57-58 (LS) MA. 6: Russian, Fr, Sp. 7: Sec Reiss, Bradley & Co Ltd, and other, Shanghai China 31-38; Consul UWash Machine Tr Research Proj 58; Ref libn Boeing Sci Research Labs, Seattle 59; Catlg libn IBM Research Center, Yorktown Heights NY 59-. 9: ALA; SLA. 14: Catlg, ref. 15: IBM Research Center PO Box 218, Yorktown Heights NY.

ALFORD, H WENDELL. b Fla 6 N 23. 4: Adileen Gavin. 5: Stetson U 51-54 (Eng, Psych) BA; Southwestern Baptist Theol Sem 54-57 (Theol) BD; N Tex State 58-59 MS in LS. 6: Fr, Sp. 7: US Air Force 42-45; Communications chief US Civil Serv, Eglin Air Force Base Fla 45-51; Chief documents div Stetson 5-154; Chief sers div Southwestern Baptist Theol Sem 54-59; Asst dir lib serv UNo Iowa Lib 59-. 9: ALA; ATheolLA; IowaLA (chm Resources & Tech Serv Sect). 10: AAUP. 13: Yes. 14: Tech serv, admin. 15: 812 E Seerley blvd, Cedar Falls Ia 50613.

ALFORD, RUTH VIRGINIA. b Jackson Co Fla 23 D 07. 5: Chicora 25-29 (Eng) BA; Duke 34 (Eng); Peabody 41-42 BS in LS. 6: Fr. 7: Eng tchr Holmes Co High Sch, Bonifay Fla 29-31; Eng tchr Mt Pleasant High Sch, Mt Pleasant Fla 32-34; Eng tchr Gadsden Co High Sch, Quincy Fla 34-41; Libn Wicomico High Sch, Salisbury Md 42-44; Head ref & circ Minot State Col 44-45; Chief ref libn UDel 45-. 9: ALA; DelLA (sec 48-50, pres 52-54). 12: Ed "Delaware Library Bulletin" (46-48); Ed "Delaware Library Association Manual" (56). 14: Ref. 15: 3 Courtney st, Newark Del 19711.

ALFORD, THOMAS E. b McKeesport Penn 5 Mr 35. 4: Kay Alice Taylor. 5: East MichU 53-58 (Natural Sci) BS; UMich 6-164 MALS. 7: 2nd to 1st Lt us army Artillery 58-61; Flint Pub Lib, Flint Mich: Pre-prof trainee 61-64, Young adult dept 6-163, Br libn Potter br 63-65, Head young adult dept 65-67; Coord y-a serv Mideast Mich Lib Coop, Flint Mich 67-. 8: Lib/USA, World"s Fair 65; Mem West MichU Adv Com Dept of Libnship. 9: ALA (E P Dutton-John MacRae Award Jury 69); -YASD (Activities Com 67-; chm By-Laws Com 67-); MichLA (Planning Com). 10: NAACP; Urban League; Flint Lib Club. 14: Admin, info & computer serv, ya serv. 15: 2050 Barks st, Flint Mi 48503.

ALGUERO, MANUEL SALVADOR. b Republic of Panama 14 N 35. 4: Wendy Lee Freeman de Alguero. 5: UPanama 55-61 (LS) Licenciado; UIll 65 (LS) MS, 68 (Sociol). 6: Sp, Fr, Portu. 7: Asst in Lib UPanama 55-58; Libn in chg Serv InterAmer de Cooperacion Agricola en Panama (SICAP), Panama 58-61; Asst libn Internat Labour Org, Geneva Switzerland 61-64; Asst libn UIll (Urbana) 65, Bibliogr consul on Latin Amer ser 65-66; UNESCO expert in lib org in Colombia, So Amer 69-70. 9: ALA; Amer Sociological Assn. 10: UIll Staff Assn. 11: Scholarship from Govt of Brazil to study documentation in Rio de Janeiro, 61; UN Interneship Programme, Geneva, Switzerland 68. 13: Yes. 14: Educ for libnship, Info stor & retr, Sociology of libnship in Latin Amer. 15: 211 N Coler, Urbana Il 61803.

ALHADEF, REV JOHN JOSEPH SJ. b Los Angeles Cal 13 Ja 25. 5: Loyola ULa 41-42; Santa claraU 44-48 (Humanities) AB, 54-58 (Relig) STMA; GonzagaU 48-51 (Philos) MA; USoCal 59-60 MS in LS. 6: Lat, Sp. 7: Dir Grad Union Bibliog Ctr, Berkeley 66-67; Instr theol Alma Col (Los Gatos Cal) 61-68, Hd libn 60-; Dir Cath Microfilm Ctr, Los Gatos Cal 66-. 8: CathLA rep to Internat Com for Coord Cath Lib Assns, Frankfurt Germany 67; Dir of Microfilming Expeditions: Rome 67, Germany 68. 9: ATLA; CathLA; WTLA; LARC; GTU. 12: "Cumulative Index to 'The California Librarian', vol 1-10, 39-49" (62); "National Bibliography of Theological Titles in Catholic Libraries" (65-). 13: Yes. 14: Research collections. 15: PO Box 1258, Los Gatos Ca 95030.

ALIG, LEONA (TOBEY). b Indianapolis 12 S 12. 5: Butler U 30-34 (Eng) AB; Columbia summers 37-40 (LS) BS. 6: Fr, Ger. 7: Stud asst Butler U Lib 31-35; Ind State Lib; Asst loan div 35, Asst genealogy div 36-41, Ref libn Ind div 41-44, 58-61, Catlgr 45; Mss libn Ind Hist Soc Lib, Indianapolis 62-. 9: ALA; IndLA; SLA. 10: IndHistSoc; Marion Co Hist Soc; AAUW. 14: Ref, ind mss, catlg. 15:5019 E 40th st, Indianapolis In 46226.

ALLAN, ANNA BROOKE. b Charlotte NC 15 Mr 16. 5: Smith Col 35-37 (Eng) AB; American U summer 45. 7: Curator So Hist Collection,UNC Lib (Chapel Hill) Mss Dept 43-. 9: NCLA. 14: So hist mss.

ALLAN, MARGARET (BURRELL). b Hamilton Oh 2 N 15. 4: Harry W Allan. 5: Pomona Col 33-35 (Pre-Lib) AB; UCal 36-37 (Libnship) Certif; UCLA 52 (Tech Bibliog). 7: Asst br libn Kern Co Free Lib, Bakersfield Cal 37-40; Libn Hughes Tool Co Aircraft Div, Culver City Cal 40-59; Libn (admin) USAF Eielson AFB GS-9, Alaska 59-65; Asst libn usaf 21st ABGP (ELDPS-L) GS-9, Seattle 65-69; Libn (Med Scis) USAF Elmendorf (ALHP-LIB) GS-11 Seattle 69-. 9: ALA; AlaskaLA. 14: Ref, bk sel, clsf & catlg in sci. 15: 221 Meyer st, Anchorage Ak 99504.

ALLAN, SUSAN MARY. b NYC 13 Ja 43. 5: Conn Col 60-64 (Am Hist) BA; UMich 66-67 MALS. 6: Sp. 7: Asst libn Henry Ford Hosp Med Lib, Detroit 67-. 10: Phi Beta Kappa. 14: Admin. 15: 450 N Cranbrook rd, Birmingham Mi 48009.

ALLARD, GABRIEL (CLEOMEN) CSC. b Weedon Que Can 18 O 22. 5: UMontreal 46 BA, 50 BTh, 51 BPED; McGill 61 BLS, 65 MLS. 6: Fr, Lat. 7: Tchr Col Ste Croix (Montreal) 51-60, Libn 52-61, Chief libn 61-. 9: Association Canadienne des Bibliothecaires de Langue Francaise (pres 63-64, v-pres Montreal Sect 61-62); QueLA. 10: Commsn des Bibliotheques de la Federation des Colleges Classiques. 12: Project d"un index cooperatif de periodiques de langue franciase pour nos bibliotheques d"enseignement (65). 13: Yes. 14: Ref. 15: College de Maismneuve 3800 Sherbrooke E, Montreal 406 Can.

ALLARD, (META) KAY. b Brooklyn NY 2 Ja 16. 4: Albert Henry Allard. 5: Rice U 33-37 BA; Harris Co Hosp 38 MT; NYSU (Geneseo) 62 MS in LS. 6: Sp. 7: Medical Tech Panama Canal Health Dept 39-42; Interlib loan clerk Monroe Co LS, Rochester Pub Lib 61-62; Ref libn Rochester Inst of Tech Lib 62-68, Chem libn Chem Grad Research Lib 68-. 9: NY State LA; SLA. 14: Ref (sci). 15: 50 Bright Oaks dr, Rochester NY 14624.

ALLARD, SERGE. b Sherbrooke Que Can 3 Je 31. 5: Ottawa U 52 BA, 54 LPh, 60 LTh, 60 BEd, 64 BLS. 6: Fr, Eng. 7: Tchr Col de Rouyn (Rouyn Que) 61-63, Libn 64-. 9: CanLA; QueLA; Association Canadienne des Bibliothe3caires de Langue Franc6aise; Assn des bibl NOQ (pres). 14: Admin. 15: The Lib, College de Rouyn-Noranda, C P 1500, Rouyn Que Can.

ALLARDYCE, LINDA. b Evanston Ill 8 Jl 46. 5: MiamiU (Oxford Ohio) 64-68 (Eng) BA; UIll 68-69 (LS) MA. 6: Fr. 7: Ser libn NorthwesternU 69-. 9: ALA. 14: Ref. 15: 600 Forest ave, Evanston Il 60202.

ALLEMANG, MARY M (JUSTICE). b Logansport Ind 8 Ap 23. 4: Richard D Allemang. 5: Ball State Tchrs Col 41-43 (Eng); IndU 46-48 (Eng) AB; Mich U Ext 48-50; Columbia summer 49 (LS); UIowa 67-69 (LS) MA. 6: Fr. 7: WAVES 43-45 Sp T 2/c (Link trainer instr); Sch libn M H Cent Jr High, Muskegon Hts Mich 48-50; Elem sch libn Cedar Rapids Com Sch Dist, Iowa 69-. 9: ALA. 10: Alpha Xi Delta; Camp Fire Girls; Cub Scouts. 14: Child serv. 15: 3001 Ridgemore dr SE, Cedar Rapids Ia 52403.

ALLEN, ALBERT (HAROLD). b Middletown NY 4 D 29. 4: Frieda Hollstein. 5: Lehigh 49-53 (Hist) AB; NYU 62 (Pub admin) MPA; SUNY (Albany) 68 MLS. 6: Fr. 7: USA 53-56; IBM Corp, Kingston NY: Prod analyst 56-62, Assoc libn 63-67, Sr libn 68-. 9: SLA; SE NY Lib Resources Coun. 10: Phi Alpha Theta. 14: Ref, lit searching. 15: 17 Redwood rd, Saugerties NY 12477.

ALLEN, ANNA M (COVIELLO). b Brooklyn NY 22 My 30. 4: Emil W Allen Jr. 5: U Conn 47-51 (Philos) AB; West Res 51-52 MLS. 7: Libn Grade 2 Brooklyn Pub Lib 52-56; Documents libn St Anselm's Col Manchester NH 65-. 66; Libn N H Tech Inst 68-. 15: Box 204, Warner NH 03278.

ALLEN, BERTHA R(ANKIN). b Ann Arbor Mich 11 Mr 07. 5: UMich 24-25, 26-28 (Fr); Carleton Col 28-29 (Fr) BA; UMich 31-32 BS in LS. 6: Fr, Ger. 7: Libn Air Force Atomic Energy Lib, Albuquerque NM 49-51, Chief 51-57; Air Force Spec Weapons Center: Supv Tech Lib Sandia Corp, Albuquerque NM 57-63; Supv Tech Lib Div Sandia Corp, Albuquerque NM 63-. 9: SLA (Mem Relations Com 59-61; pres Rio Grande Chap 58-59, mem Exec Bd 56-60); ASIS; ALA; NMLA (pres 59-60); SWLA (mem Exec Bd 67-71). 10: Amer Soc for Metals; LWV; NM Ornithol Soc; NMHistSoc; AlbuquerqueHistAssn; Alpha Phi. 14: Admin. 15: Sandia Laboratories, Technical Lib Div, Albuquerque NM 87115.

ALLEN, BETTY (FOWLER). b Portland Ore 16 O 18. 4: Norman P Allen. 5: Whitman Col 36-40 (Eng) BA; UDenver 42-43 BS in LS. 6: Fr. 7: Child Lib Corvallis Pub Lib,

Corvallis Ore 43-44, Libn 45-46; Ref asst Reed Col 45; Cler asst Lib Assoc of portland 40-42, Child libn, bkmob 66-68, Hd child serv 68-. 9: ALA; OreLA; PNLA. 10: Urban League. 14: Child bks. 15: 801 SW 10th ave, Portland Or 97205.

ALLEN, BETTY JANE (ASKEW). b Cincinnati 20 O 27. 4: Carl S Allen Jr. 5: UCincinnati 45-49 (Sociol) BA, 49-50 (Sociol); UMich 52-53 MALS. 6: Fr, Ger, Lat. 7: Acquis asst UCincinnati 50-52; UCincinnati; Acquis asst libn 53-57, Educ & psych libn 57-63, Act ser libn 63-64, Educ & psych libn 64-66; Asst Prof of Educ & Lib Sci 66-. 9: ALA. 14: Ser, acquis. 15: 5871 Belmont ave, Cincinnati Oh 45224.

ALLEN, CAMERON. b Springfield Ohio 7 F 28. 5: Otterbein Col 44-47 (Hist) BA; U Wis 49-51 (Eur Hist) MA; U Ill 54-56 (LS) MS; Duke U 56-59 LLB. 7: Insurance risk surveyor Sanborn Map Co. 47-49; High sch tchr Union Co Sch Dist Ohio 53-54; US Army Corps of Engrs Wash State Korea 51-53; Asst libn Rutgers Law Sch 59-65; Libn 65-. 9: AALL; Law Lib Assn of Greater NY. 10: Amer Soc Genealogists (Fellow). 13: Yes. 14: Ref. 15: Rutgers U Law Sch, 180 University ave, Newark NJ 07102.

ALLEN, CLARA VAN BUREN. b Schenectady NY 3 N 11. 5: NY State Col (Albany) 29-33 MLS; St John's U Summer 39 (LS); Shelton Col 43-46 (Religion) BRE; New Sch for Soc Res 44-47 (Psych); Fuller Theol Sem 49-60 (Psych, Theol). 6: Fr, Sp, Ger. 7: Asst libn Pub Lib Schenectady NY 33-35; Libn-tchr High Sch Ft Plain NY 35-36; Libn Roxbury High Sch Succasunna NY 36-38; Libn supv Pub Schs Williston Park NY 38-43; Libn-tchr Shelton Col NY 43-48; Chief libn Fuller Theol Sem Pasadena Cal 48-64; Supv libn Los Angeles Co Lib San Gabriel Cal 64-67; Head Tch Serv Azusa-Pacific Col, Azusa Ca 67-. 8: Consul Los Angeles Baptist Sem 49-51, San Francisco Theol Sem, San Anselmo 63-64, Azusa Col Lib Azusa Cal 64-65. 9: ALA; ATLA; CalLA-Christian Lib Assn (pres); CURLS; Western Theol LA (pres); San Gabriel Valley LA. 10: San Gabriel Coordinating Coun; Coun of Church Women of San Gabriel Valley. 11: Christian Lib Assn Fellowship. 12: "Expansion of Dewey 200" (50); Asst ed "Fuller Library Bulletin" (48-51), ed (51-59). 13: Yes. 14: Admin, ref, tech serv. 15: 4809 No Armel dr, Covina Ca 91723.

ALLEN, CORNELIUS B. b Bayonne NJ 28 Ja 08. 4: Isabel Christie Allen. 5: NYU 27-31 (Bus Admin) BS, 39-41 (Hist) AB, 48-51 (Amer Hist) AM. 6: Sp. 7: Ref libn NYU Com Lib 40-43; Acquis libn US Navy, Camp Peary, Williamsburg Va 43-45; Asst libn NYU Com Lib 46-49, Libn 49-55; Libn NYU Grad Lib of Bus Admin 55-. 67; Libn Amos Tuck Sch of Bus Admin, Dartmouth Col 67-. 9: ALA; SLA. 10: NY Univ Club. 13: Yes. 14: Ref, acquis. 15: P O Box 964, Hanover NH 03755.

ALLEN, DONALD C. b Toledo Ohio 20 My 13. 4: Alleen Strong. 5: Oberlin Col 31-35 (Pol Sci) AB; West Res 38-39 BS in LS. 6: Fr. 7: Lib asst Wash DC Pub Lib 39-40; Lib asst LC 40-42; Captain Signal Corps US Army 42-46; Admin asst LC 46-47, Head filing sect 47-56; Head lib br Army Signal Intelligence, Wash DC 56-58; Ref libn Housing & Home Finance Agency, Wash DC 58-68; Chief, Ref Sect Lib Dept housing & urban development, Wash 68-. 9: SLA. 13: Yes. 14: Ref. 15: 6111 11th rd N, Arlington Va 22205.

ALLEN, DOROTHY (WOODRUFF). b Chicago Ill 5 Ap 33. 4: John William Allen. 5: Grinnell Coll 50-51; Northwestern U 51-54 (Home Econ) BS; Rosary Col 62-66 (LS) MA. 6: Sp. 7: Classified advert E H Brown Advertising Agcy, Chicago 54-55; Inter decorator: Segno sign of today's living, Winnetka Ill 55, Koeppens Inc, Des Plaines Ill 55-56, Old Colony Home Fashions, Wilmette Ill 57, Pk Ridge Home Fashions, Park Ridge Ill 57-58; Lib asst Travenol Labs Inc, Morton Grove Ill 58-61, Asst libn 66-. 9: ALA; SLA. 14: Sel dissem of info catlg. 15: 92 N Warrington rd, Des Plaines Il 60016.

ALLEN, DOROTHY BURGE. b El Reno Okla 8 My 14. 4: Richard K Allen. 5: UOkla 30-34 (Hist) AB, 35-36 BLS; Columbia 49 (LS) MS; USoCal summer 54 (Sch Lib Problems); UValencia (Spain) summer 56 UVt summer 63; Dartmouth Alum Sch summers 64,65,66 & 68. 6: Sp. 7: Libn Ponca City Jr High Sch, Ponca City Okla 36-39; Sch & ref asst NY Pub Lib 39-41; Asst ind analyst War Prod Bd, Wash DC 42-45; Asst libn Spec Serv of Carribean Command, PR 45-46; Libn at the Amer Inst for Foreign Trade, Phoenix 46-49; Dept Ch for Educ Serv West High Sch, Phoenix 49-56; Eng tchr US Info Serv, Valencia Spain 56-57; Libn Montpelier High Sch, Montpelier Vt 59-65; Consul LegisCoun 68; Coord for Title IV Prog for the Free Pub Lib Serv of Vt 69. 8: Consul in Vt Educ Dept, 65; Consul US Info Lib, Valencoa, Spain, 56-57; Tchr of lib sci summer courses: Wichita U 50, USoIll 51, Wis State Col (Eau Claire) 55 Tchr LSext courses for UVt 66-68. 9: NEA (life mem); ALA (life mem); VtLA; NELA;Vt State LA. 10: AAUW; LWV; Homestay Chm for Experiment in Internat Living; Rep for Vt Coun for World Affairs. 12: "Librarians Be Wise Publicize". 13: Yes. 14: Sch lib serv, servto institns & handicapped; tchg LS. 15: 4 Meadow lane, Montpelier Vt 05602.

ALLEN, EMIL WILLIAM Jr. b Raymond NH 4 Mr 26. 4: Anna M Coviello. 5: Bowdoin 47-50 (Hist) AB; Pratt 51-52 MLS. 7: Sgt US Army Southwest Pacific 44-46; Staff Sgt US Air Force Va 50-51; Libn Grade 2 Sci & Ind Div Brooklyn Pub Lib 52-53, Libn Grade 3 stack curator 53-54; Head Bus & Tech Dept Ferguson Lib Stamford Conn 55-56; Asst State libn NH State Lib 56-64, State libn 64-. 8: Committee to produce New Eng Lib Film (chrm 61). 9: ALA (Fed Rel Com 52-54, Legislative Liaison Com 64-68, Coun 65-); NYLA 52-55;ConnLA 55-56; NHLA 56-; NELA 56- (treas 58-59, dir 63-64, v-pres 64-65, pres65-66); ASC Internat Rel Com (chm 68-). 10: Concord Kiwanis Club (pres 62); NH HistSoc; ACLU; NAACP; Concord Human Rights Coun; Kearsarge Cooperative Sch Bd; NH LibTrustees Assn; Friends of Concord Pub Lib; Warner Town Budget Com; ConcordUnitarian Church (pres 64); Amer Soc for Pub Admin; Concord Hosp Bd; NH MemorialSoc (pres 67-68); Kearsarge Reg Sch Bd; NH Audubon Soc. 13: Yes. 14: Ref, extension work. 15: Box 204, Warner NH 03278.

ALLEN, ESTHER. b Parsons Kan 15 Ag 04. 5: WASH State U 22, 23, 24-26 (Foreign Langs) BA; Willamette U 23-24; UDenver 36 BSLS. 6: Fr, Sp. 7: Tchr Mill Plain High Sch, Vancouver Wash 26-27; Clerk Portland Pub Lib, Portland Ore 27-28; Tchr Springdale High Sch, Springdale Wash 29-32; Tchr Battle Ground High Sch, Battle Ground Wash 32-35; Libn George Fox Col 36-39; Asst in lib Ore State U 39-40; Child libn Vancouver Pub Lib, Vancouver Wash 40-56; Libn Hood River Co Lib, Hood River Ore 56-60; Libn Pacific Co Lib, Raymond Wash 60-62; Libn Camas Pub Lib, Camas Wash 62-. 9: ALA; PNLA; WashLA (Exec Bd 62-65). 10: AAUW; Soroptimist Club; Bus & Prof Women's Club; DAR. 14: Pacific Northwest history. 15: P O Box 651, Camas Wa 98607.

ALLEN, EVIE (ALLISON). b Piedmont Ala 17 S 1897. 4: Gay Wilson Allen. 5: Huntingdon Col 14-17 (Math) AB; Carnegie Lib Sch, Atlanta 18-19 Certif in LS. 6: Fr, Ger, Danish. 7: Libn Valdosta Pub Lib, Valdosta Ga 19-21; Libn Converse Col 21-24; Catlgr Durham Pub Lib, Durham NC 24-27; Temp catlgr LimestoneCol 28; Temp catlgr API (Auburn Ala) 28-29; Catlgr LIU 53-54; Catlgr Fairleigh Dickinson U 54-56; Catlgr Oradell Pub Lib, Oradell NJ56-60. 12: Tr from the Danish "Whitman," by Frederick Schyberg (50). 14: Catlg. 15: 454 Grove st, Oradell NJ.

ALLEN, FRANCIS P(ITCHER). b Rochester NY 12 N 02. 4: Janet MacMaster. 5: Amherst 27 (Hist) BA; Columbia 29 (LS) BS; UMich 32 (LS) MA. 6: Fr. 7: Ref libn Cornell U Lib 29-30; Libn U Museums UMich 30-36; Libn, prof, bibliog, archivist URI 36-69; Instr USFl Col of EducDept of lib & audio-visual educ 69. 8: Adv com to US Dept of Agric Lib 62-65. 9: ALA-ACRL (Bd Dirs);-RSD (chm Wilson Index Com 65-69); RILA (pres 44-46); NELA (v-pres 50-52). 10: Rotary Club; University Club; Grolier Club (NYC); Dunes Club (Narragansett RI);Field Club (Sarasota Fla); Ivy League Club (Sarasota). 12: Comp "University Museums Bibliography," UMich (35). 13: Yes. 14: Rare bks, lib admin. 15: 26 Bayberry rd, Kingston RI 02881.

ALLEN, FRANCIS S. b Rock Falls Ill 17 Ap 10. 4: Marjorie B Caudle. 5: St Charles 28-30 (Humanities); Xavier (Cincinnati) 30-33 (Humanities) LittB; Loyola (Chicago) 33-35 (Eng, Philos); UIll 40-41 BS in LS. 7: Instr, Eng, Lat St Ignatius High Sch, Chicago 35-40; Libn Seattle Col 41-42; US Army Med Adm C Supply Off Field Hosp 42-45; Libn US Army Shrivenham Amer U (England) 45-46; Circ libn Ore State Col 46-49; Col Libn Cal State Polytech Col 49-63; Lib Admin Niles Pub Lib, Niles Ill 63-. 8: Lib Bldg Consul for Batavia Ill Pub Lib 68-69. 9: ALA; IllLA; Lib Admin Conf No Ill. 14: Lib bldg planning & construction. 15: Niles Pub Lib, 7950Waukegan rd, Niles Il 60648.

ALLEN, FRANCIS W(ILBUR). b Waterbury Conn 28 Ap 13. 4: Ruth Gile. 5: Colby Col 30-34 (Hist) BS; U Mich 34-35 ABLS, 35-39 AMLS. 6: Fr, Ger, Sp, Port, Ital, Romanche, Amharic. 7: Asst UMich 35-41; Libn LeMoyne Col Memphis Tenn 41-44; Asst mgr Pilgrim Press Boston 44-46; Catlgr Harvard 46-47; LibnCongregational Lib Boston 47-50; Libn Van Buren Co Lib Paw Paw Mich 51-52; Catlgr West Mich U 53-59, Asst libn 59-67, Sci libn 70-. 8: Assoc libn, Haile Sellassie U 68-69; Ford Found Proj Specialist. 9: ALA; SLA

(Sci-Tech Div-Paper-Textile Sect);MichLA; Ethiopian LA. 10: Tech Assn of Pulp & Paper Industry; Amer Soc of Bookplatecollectors & Designers; Soc of ExLibris Historians; British Bookplate Club; Pi Gammamu; Horticultural Soc of Ethiopia. 12: "Bookplates of Charles R. Capon" (50);"Bookplates of William Fowler Hopson" (61); Ed "American Congregational Assn Bulletin"(47-50). 13: Yes. 14: Catlg, Period. 15: Waldo Lib, Western Mich U, Kalamazoo Mi 49001.

ALLEN, GLADYS WISEMAN. b Benton Wis 17 D 18. 4: Wallace W Allen. 5: UWis 36-40 (Comparative Lit) BA, 40-41 BLS, 46 (Comparative Lit) MA. 6: Lat, Fr. 7: UWis Lib (Madison): Jr & Sr lib asst 41-46, Asst head acquis dept 46-48; Catlg asst Providence Pub Lib 48-49; Catlgr Dorsch Mem pub Lib, Monroe Mich 49-51; Sr lib researcher "Minneapolis Star & Tribune, Minneapolis 51-54; Libn Minn Nat Lab, St Paul 63-67; Free-lance research libn 68-. 9: ALA; MinnLA. 10: Friends of the Minneapolis Pub Lib; UWis Alumnae Club of Minneapolis. 12: Asst ed "Review Index 42-44. 14: Ref. 15: 4-28 Ewing ave S, Minneapolis Mn 55410.

ALLEN, JAMES ALBERT. b Alexandria La 7 N 30. 4: Gloria Ann Bausewein. 5: LSU 48-54 (Bus Admin) BS, 61-62 (LS) MS. 6: Sp. 7: Tchr Lockport High Sch, Lockport La 58-59; Tchr Houma Elem Sch, Houma La 59-61; Trainee LSU Lib 61-62; Asst dir La Col Lib 62-64, Dir 64-65; Libn Little Rock U 65-. 9: ALA-ACRL; -RTSD; ArkLA (chm CRLD); SWLA (sec RTSD). 10: AAUP; Ozark Soc. 14: Lib bldgs, admin, tech serv, ref, lib tech. 15: 22 Alameda dr, Little Rock Ark 72204.

ALLEN, JEAN (SHORT). b High Point NC 30 N 30. 4: Charles A Allen Jr. 5: Mars Hill 49-51 AA; Wake Forest 51-53 (Eng) BA; SEast Bapt Sem 54-56 (Relig Ed); UNC 67-69 MS in LS. 6: Sp, Fr. 7: Tchr Mineval Springs High, Forsyth Co NC 53-54; Missionary tchr Bapt Inst, Guatemala CA 59-67; Prof libn ULouisville 69-. 9: Ohio Valley Tech Serv assn. 10: Phi Beta Kappa; Beta Phi Mu. 14: Catlg. 15: 2825 Lexington rd, Louisville Ky 40206.

ALLEN, JOHN C. b Preble NY 25 S 10. 4: Kathleen Ward Allen. 5: Cortland Normal Sch 28-31 (Educ) Diploma; Syracuse 38-39 (Educ) BS, 39-42 BS (LS); UIll 50-51 MS (LS). 6: Fr. 7: Tchr Preble Sch Dist #2, Preble NY 31-38; Tchr libn Mt Upton Central Sch, Mt Upton NY 39-42; Army Air Corps Radar Technician S/Sgt, S Pacific 42-45; Libn Triple Cities Col 46-47; Syracuse U: Asst to the dir Lib 47-51, Asst to dean & Asst Prof Lib Sch 51-58, Asst Prof Lib Sch 58-. 10: Phi Kappa Phi; Pi Lambda Sigma; Beta Phi Mu. 14: Catlg, clsf, adult reading. 15: 322 Goodrich ave, Syracuse NY 13210.

ALLEN, JOHN CARLIN. b Oswego NY 5 Jl 42. 04. Rita C Allen. 5: Cornell 60-64 (Soc) BS; Syracuse 65-67 (LS) MSLS. 7: Trainee Finger Lakes Lib Syst, Ithaca 65-66; Trainee Onondaga Lib Syst, Syracuse 66-67; Trainee Jr Lib Yonkers Pub Lib, Yonkers 67; Indexer-abstractor Geigy Agric Chem, White Plains 68; Libn & records control mgr blyth & Co Inc NYC 68-. 9: ALA; SLA; ASIS. 13: Yes. 14: Lib org & facility planning, indexing, records control, serv to commun. 15: 45-40 158th st, Flushing NY 11358.

ALLEN, JOHN PRENTICE. b Seattle Wash 26 N 18. 5: Whitman Col 41-42, 46 UColo 42-43 (Japanese Lang); UWash 48-49 (Far East Studies) BA, 51-52 (LS) ML. 6: Japanese, Ger, Fr, Sp. 7: Clerical & bkkeeping Mutal Life of NY, Seattle 37-41; Asst to dir of admissions Whitman Col 41-42, 46-47, 48; Lt USNR, Japanese lang off 42-45, 50-51; Asst libn, ser libn, acquis libn, act dir Cent Wash State Col 52-65; Chief tech serv div Wash StateU Lib 65-. 9: ALA. 10: AAUP. 14: Admin, tech serv. 15: 507 W Main st, Pullman Wa 99163.

ALLEN, JOSEPH SANBORN. b Erie Penn 6 Ja 12. 4: Grace Hildebrand. 5: Col of Wooster 30-34 (Lat) BA; UMich 35-40 AMLS. 6: Fr, Sp, Ital, Ger, Lat. 7: Asst grad reading room UMich Lib 35-36, Asst catlg dept 36-38, Jr catlgr catlg dept 38-41; Catlgr Descr Catlg Div LC 41-44, Sr catlgr & reviser Descr Catlg Div 44-50, Ed of card catlgs Catlg Maintenance Div 50-54, Sr subj catlgr Subj Catlg Div 54-64, Ed of subj headings Subj Catlg Div 64-. 9: ALA; Potomac Tech Proc Libns; DCLA. 10: Nat Fed of Federal Employees; Phi Beta Kappa; Eta Sigma Pi. 12: Asst ed "DC Libraries" (53-55). 14: Catlg. 15: 2904 S 13th rd #301, Arlington Va 22204.

ALLEN, JOYCE M. 4: Benjamin C Allen. 5: West ResU 63 (LS) MSLS. 7: Ref libn Battelle Mem Inst, Columbus 63-. 8: Conducted a survey of Ohio pub sch lib needs and resources. 9: SLA. 14: Ref (sci & tech), sch lib serv. 15: 1521 Waltham rd, Columbus Oh 43221.

ALLEN, KENNETH S. b Holdenville Okla 7 D 20. 4: Faye Gardner. 5: UOkla 46-49 (Econ) BA; UWash 50-51 (Libnship & Bus Sdmin) BLS. 6: Fr, Ger, Sp. 7: US 45th Infantry Div 40, ETO 43-45, Commsn USA, Stolberg Germany 44; Libn bus sect Seattle Pub Lib, Seattle Wash 51; Libn ref div UWash Lib 52, Hd libn sci read rm 53-56, Asst hd acquis div 57-58, Hd acquis div 59-60, Hd acquis & admin asst to dir 60, Assoc dir of libs 61-. 8: Cons: United Control Corp, Seattle 54; Boeing Co, Seattle 55-56; ALA Cons on Col & Univ Lib Buildgs; Involved in planning & construction of several libs at UWash; Mem Planning Comm, Governor's Reg Conf on Libs 68. 9: ALA (mem Build Comm for Col & Univ Libs); -LAD (mem Sect on Builds & Equip 67-69); PNLA; WashLA. 12: "Bookbinding at the University of Washington" (62). 13: Yes. 14: Admin organ, systems devel, budgetary mgt, tech proc, lib buildings. 15: UWash Lib, Seattle Wa 98105.

ALLEN, LOREN H. b Ill 3 O 09. 4: Doris Trout. 5: So Ill U 32-36 (Educ) B·Ed; UMinn 36-37 BS in LS; UIll 48-51 MS in LS. 6: Fr. 7: Libn Johnston City High Sch, Johnston City Ill 45-48; Libn E Richland Community Unit Dist, Olney Ill 48-57; Instr materials Richwoods Community High Sch, Peoria Ill 58-61; Consul instr materials Dept of Pub Instr, Springfield Ill 61-62; Dir instr materials Richwoods Community High Sch, Peoria Ill 62-66; Dir instr materials & lib serv Sauk Valley Col 66-68; Dir learning resourcesIll Central Col 68-. 8: Consul (instructional materials 9: Ill A-V Assn (Bd); IllASchL (Bd); Peoria (Ill) Co Film Lib (chm Bd); ALA;IllLA; NEA-DAVI. 12: "Educational Screen and Audio-Visual Guide" (62). 13: Yes. 14: Org & admin of instr materials programs. 15: Ill Central Col, PO Box 2400, Peoria Il 61611.

ALLEN, MARGERY JEAN (MILNE). b Montreal. 5: McGill 39-42 (Eng, Hist) BA, 45-46 BLS. 7: Lieut (SB) Navy (Canada; WRCNS) 43-45; Catlgr Sir George Williams U Lib(Montreal) 46-48; Catlgr Nat Research Coun Lib, Ottawa, Indexer & catlgr Aero Lib;Subj reviser Defence Research Bd (DSIS), Ottawa 48-54; Acquis libn Sir GeorgeWilliams U (Montreal) 63-64; Clsf Engnr Soc Lib, NY 64-66; Asst libn Clarkson Colof Tech 66-67; Head tech serv Sir George Williams U Lib 68-. 9: Quebec LA; CanLA;ALA. 15: Sir George Williams Univ Lib, 1435 Drummond st, Montreal P Q Can.

ALLEN, MARIAN MEAD. b Ft Wayne Ind 8 Je 04. 5: Smith 21-22; URochester 22-25 (Eng) BA; Columbia 34 BS in LS. 6: Fr, Ger, Sp, Lat, Russian. 7: Child libn Lincoln Br Pub Lib, Rochester NY 25-27; URochester: Asst circ & ref 27-30, Head circ & ref Women's Col 30-50, Libn Women's Col 50-55, Asst libn ref serv 55-. 65, Libn ref serv 65-69; Catlgr Colgate Rochester Divinity Sch, Bexley Hall 69-. 9: ALA (Coun); -RSD (Bd); -Subs Bks Com; -ASD/RSD Com on Orientation; NYLA. 10: AAUW; Assn for the UN; Rochester Mus of Arts & Scis; Rochester Civic Music Assn; Visiting Nurse Assn; Travelers Aid; Mem Art Gallery. 13: Yes. 14: Ref. 15: 80 Highland ave, Rochester NY 14620.

ALLEN, MARY ROSELAND. b Nashville Ark 24 F 46. 5: So Ore Col 64-68 (Educ) BA; UOre 68-69 MLS. 6: Sp. 7: Page Medford Pub Lib, Medfore Ore 64-68; Sub tchr Medford Pub Schs, Medfore Ore 68-69; Grad asst So Ore Col 68; Circ ref libn Medford Pub Lib summer 69. 9: NEA; OreEA. 10. Commun Concert Assn. 14: Child wk. 15: 30 Western ave, Medford Or 97501.

ALLEN, NOLA LEE (RHOADS). b Spokane Wash 28 S 28. 4: James Albert Allen. 5: UWash 46-51 (Eng) BA, 51-53 BA in Ed, 51-54 Standard Gen Certif in Ed, 63-68 Master of Libnship. 7: Pre-prof libn King Co Lib, Seattle 64-68; Libn I San Diego Co Lib La Mesa br 68- br 68-. 14: Ref. 15: 8530 Sandstone dr, Santee Ca 92071.

ALLEN, PAULINE B. b Salix Iowa 11 My 14. 4: Philip A Allen. 5: Morningside Col 32-34 (Eng); USD 36-37 (Eng); OmahaU 62-66 B Gen Ed; UNeb 68-. 6: Fr. 7: Libn Neb Psychiatric Inst, Omaha Neb 62-. 9: ALA. 10: Great Bks Found Coord for Omaha (Neb) area 55-58. 14: Ref, rare bks. 15: 8515 Burt st, Omaha Nb 68114.

ALLEN, ROBERTA (FLETCHER). b Joppa Ill 15 My 07. 5: SoIll U 24-25; Mich State U 26-29 (Pub Sch Music) AB; UMich 62 MLS. 7: Tchr pub schs, Big Rapids Mich 29-33; Asst libn Commun Lib, Big Rapids Mich 40-47; Asst libn Ferris State Col 50-. 9: MichLA. 15: 112 N Stewart, Big Rapids Mi 49307.

ALLEN, RUTH (BROWN) (MRS). b Jersey Ohio 23 O 03. 5: DenisonU 20-24 (Mod Langs) PhB; Chautauqua Sch for Libns 24-26 (LS) Diploma. 7: Asst libn Pub Lib, Grand Forks ND

24-26, Libn 26-37, Ref asst Pub Lib, Albany NY 46; Ref libn UND 47-62; Asst ref libn Pub Lib, Columbus Ohio 62-. 9: ALA; NDLA (past pres); OhioLA. 10: Bus & Prof Women''s Clubs. 14: Ref. 15: 149 E Royal Forest blvd, Columbus Oh 43214.

ALLEN, WALTER COLEMAN. b Troy Oh 23 N 27. 4: (Jean) Diane Heckert. 5: Williams Col 45-49 (Geol) BA; Columbia 50-51 (LS) MS. 6: Sp. 7: Subprof asst Williams Col Lib, 48-50; Ref asst Northwestern U, 51-52; Catlg Dayton Pub Lib, 53-55, Asst hd catlg dept 55-57, Asst hd ref dept 57-59, Hd catlg dept circ 59-61, Hd lit & fine arts div 61-67; Visiting instr Grad Sch of Lib Sci, UIll summer 67, Asst prof 68-. 8: Consul Vandalia (Ill) Pub Lib 68-. 9: ALA-ASD (mem Notable Bks Coun 67-); -RSD (Div Affiliates Com, chm 64-69); -SORT (chm 59-60); AALS; MusLA; Geosci Info Soc; OhioLA (Ref serv RT chm 63-64, district meeting chm 63-65); IllLA. 10: AAUP; Soc of Arch Histns; YMCA. 13: Yes. 14: Ref, lib bldgs, publ, lib sch tchg, bk sel. 15: 1115 W Union st, Champaign Ill 61820.

ALLENDER, ROBERT K. b Louisville Ky 4 Ag 32. 5: U Louisville 50-53, 55-57 (Hist) AB; UKy 57-59 (LS) MS. 7: Company clerk (Cpl) US Army Ft Hood Tex 54-55; Dir Lake Cumberland Reg Lib, Columbia Ky 59-66; Sr Extn Libn Ky Dept of Lib, Frankfort Ky (Hdqrs, Columbia Ky) 66-. 8: Consul on lib furniture & equipment Dept of Libs, Ky 66-. 9: KyLA (chm Pub Lib Sect). 10: Leader Teen 4-H Club. 14: Admin, ref, a-v, lib bldgs. 15: Jeffries st P O Box 33, Columbia Ky 42728.

ALLER, WILMA AUCHMUTY. b Omaha Neb 8 Mr 06. 4: Dwight F Aller. 5: UNeb 29 (Eng, Hist) AB; UDenver 46 BS in LS. 7: Libn West Mil Acad, Alton Ill 42-47; Denver Pub Lib: Libn gen serv dept 47-48, 1st asst 49-55, Hist spec 56-. 9: ALA; ColoLA. 10: Phi Beta Kappa. 14: Hist, biog, travel, ref. 15: 1200 Quebec, Denver Co 80220.

ALLEY, BRIAN L. b Waterville Me 27 F 33. 4: Cornelia Egan. 5: Colby Col 52-56 (Art) AB; Fla State U 62-63 (LS) MS. 6: Sp. 7: Asst Humanities libn Portland State Col 63-65; Ref libn Elmira Col 66, Act dir libs 67-68; Undergrad libn Miami U (Oxford Ohio) 68-. 8: Ref libn Library/USA, NY World''s Fair, 65. 9: SLA; NEA-DAVI. 10: AAUP; Educ Media Coun Ohio. 14: Ref. 15: 126 Plum st, Oxford Oh 45056.

ALLISON, EUGENE S. b Brownsville Penn 14 Je 31. 5: Mt Union Col 49-53 (Eng) BA; Pratt inst 53-54, 57 MLS. 7: US Army Counter-Intelligence Corps 54-56; Clk Carnegie Lib of Pittsburgh Penn 56-57; NYC Pub Lib 57-59; Bucks Co Free Lib, Doylestown Penn 69-. 9: ALA; NYLA (Child & YA Serv Sect: Bd 59-62, pres 65-66); NY Lib Club (Coun 68-69). 14: Admin, adult & ya. 15: Bucks Co Free Lib, 50 N Main st, Doylestown Pa 18901.

ALLMAN, (CORA) MARGARET. b Whistler Ala 26 Je 06. 5: UAla 24-28 (Eng) AB; UNC 39-41 BS in LS, 51-53 MS in LS. 6: Fr. 7: High sch tchr Mobile Co Sch Bd, Mobile Ala 28-39; Libn Elem Sch, Chapel Hill NC 39-41; Libn & reviser Sch of Lib Sci UNC 41-44; Ext libn Durham Pub Lib, Durham NC 44-47; Reg libn State of Tenn, Memphis Tenn 47-49; Libn US Info Serv, Manila Philippines 49-51; Co Libn Wilmington Inst, Wilmington Del 53-56; Lecturer & Libn Sch of Lib Sch UNC 56-61; Br libn Tacoma Pub Lib, Tacoma Wash 61-. 9: ALA; Philippine LA (v-pres 50-51); PNLA; WashLA; Wash State ASchL. 10: Altrusa Internat; Phi Beta Kappa; Kappa Delta Pi; Beta Phi Mu. 14: Lib educ, admin, adult serv, wk with child. 15: 319 N Tacoma ave, apt 806, Tacoma Wash 98403.

ALLMAND, LINDA FAITH. b Port Arthur Tex 31 Ja 37. 5: Lamar State Col of Tech 54-55; N Tex State U 58-60 (LS) BA; UDenver 61-62 (LS) MA. 7: Clerk Gates Mem Lib, Port Arthur Tex 53-55; Sub prof asst Houston Pub Lib 55-58; Libn Denver Pub Lib 60-63; Child coordinator Anaheim Pub Lib, Anaheim Cal 63-64; Br head Dallas Pub Lib 65-. 8: Fac N Tex State U summers 67-; Ill State Lib wkshop on adult serv, Chicago 67. 9: ALA; TexLA (NLW State Com 68, 69); SWLA (Local Arrangements Com 66); DallasCoLA (v-pres 67-68; pres 68-69). 10: Bus & Prof Women''s Club; Beta Phi Mu; Alpha Beta Alpha; Phi Alpha Theta; Alpha Lambda Sigma. 14: Child wk, ref, brs. 15: 2930 Woodmere, Dallas Tx 75233.

ALLSPACH, ELIZABETH ANN. b Charleston WVa 29 My 39. 5: Rice U 56-60 (Psych) BA; UCal (Berkeley) 60-61 MLS. 6: Ger, Fr, Sp. 7: Catlg libn Rice U 61-63; Monograph order div Otto Harrassowitz, Wiesbaden Germany 64-65; Catlg libn Rice U 65-. 10: Houston Chorale. 14: Catlg. 15: 1113 Lyndon #6, Houston Tx 77025.

ALLYN, WILLIAM H. b Lima Ohio 8 My 11. 4: Jane Phillips. 5: Ohio State U 30-32, 42-44 (Marketing) BBA; West Res 59-60 MLS. 7: Self-employed, Chillicothe Ohio 39-60; OhioU: Circ libn 60-62, Admin libn 62-65, Assoc dir of libs 65-67; OhioU (Chillicothe): Libn 67-. 9: ALA (Reg Recruitment Com; Bldgs Com); OhioLA (Recruitment Com; Col & Univ RT Sub-com; Scholarship Com). 13: Yes. 15: 17 Courtland dr, Chillicothe Oh 45601.

ALMAGNO, ROMANO S, Rev. b Providence RI 5 Ag 39. 5: Immaculate Conception Sem (Troy NY) 57-61 (phil) BS; Mt Alvernia Sem 61-65 (theol); UPittsburgh 65-66 MSLS. 6: Fr, Ital, Sp, Lat & Gr. 7: Stud lib asst Immaculate Con Sem, Troy NY 57-61; Stud lib asst Mt Alvernia Sem, Wappingers Falls NY 61-65; Libn Immaculate Con Sem, Troy NY 66-; Prof biblio & methods of philos research, Troy NY. 8: Mem Bd Educ (Franc Prov Immaculate Conception, NY 67-; Advis Bd Amer Teilhard de Chardin Ass 68-. 9: ALA; CathLA (v-pres DFM sect 69-); Va Bibliog Soc; Cambridge Bibliog Soc. 10: Catholic Peace Fellowship; Amer Mus of Nat Hist. 11: "A Basic Teilhard Bibliography 55-68" (68). 14: Bibliog, rare bks. 15: Immaculate Conception Sem Vandenburgh ave, Troy NY 12180.

ALMY, PATTY CARPENTER. b Eatonton Ga 10 Mr 26. 4: Lee A Almy. 5: Brenau 43-44; UGa 44-47 (Journalism) AB; Woman''s Col Ga summers; Peabody 62-64 (LS) MA; Ga Col 67. 6: Sp. 7: Radio continuity WGGS Tifton Ga 48; Feature writer Athens Banner Herald, Athens Ga; Feature writer Atlanta Journal-Constitution; Tchr Butts Co High Sch, Jackson Ga; Publ dir Uncle Remus Reg Lib, Madison Ga; Libn Putnam Co High Sch, eatonton Ga 60-61; Libn Ga Mili Col 61-. 9: ALA; SLA; NEA; GaLA (mem com); GaEA. 10: AAUW; Tri-Delta. 13: Yes. 14: Admin. 15: Sibley Cone Lib Ga Military Col, Milledgeville Ga 31061.

ALPEN, THEODORE R(ICHARD). b Berkeley Cal 9 My 28. 5: San Francisco State Col 46-50 9sox Welf) BA; Los Angeles State Col 52-53 (Soc); UCal (Berkeley) 53-59 (Soc) MA; Sch of Libnship 65-67 MLS. 7: Med aid man Med Co, 12th Inf Regt USA, Germany 50-52; Ref libn Palos Verdes Lib Dist, Palos Verdes Peninsula Cal 67-69. 9: ALA; CalLA. 10: ACLU; Supporter, War Resisters League. 14: Ref, interlib loans. 15: Palos Verdes lib Dist, 650 Deep Valley Drive, Palos Verdes Penin Ca 90274.

ALSMEYER, HENRY (LOUIS) Jr. b San Benito Tex 13 S 26. 4: Marie Bennett Alsmeyer. 5: Tex A&M Col 43-44 (Liberal Arts); UTex 44, 47-48 (Journalism) BJ; Texas A&I 56-58 (Eng) MA; LSU 65-66 (LS) MA; Tex A&M U 68- (Eng). 7: Newspaper writer 48-49; Reporter & staff writer Caller-Times, Corpus Christi Tex 50-58; Faculty Presbyterian Pan Amer Sch, Kingsville Tex 58-60; Managing ed Kingsville Record, Kingsville Tex 60-61; Dir pub rel Maryville Col 61; Texas A&M U; Info specialist 62-66, Asst ref libn 66-67, Humanities & soc sci libn & asst prof 67-70, Asst Dir for Tech Serv 70-. 9: ALA; TexLA. 10: West Lit Assn, Collectors' Inst (Texas); Beta Phi Mu; Sigma Delta Chi. 14: Ref, lib hist. 15: 1207 Joe Orr st, Col Sta Tx 77840.

ALSPAUGH, EMMA (ADELINE). b North Grove Ind 29 N 14. 5: Taylor U 34-38 (Fr, Eng) AB; Ball State Tchrs Col summers 38, 39 (LS); UDenver summers 45-47 BS in LS. 6: Fr. 7: Tchr-libn Jefferson Twp High Sch, Upland Ind 39-41; Libn Frankton High Sch, Frankton Ind 41-. 9: ALA; NEA; IndLA; Ind State Tchrs Assn; IndSchLA (sec 2 terms, Bd Dirs). 14: Ref. 15: 205 S Delaware, Frankton In 46044.

ALSTON, ANNIE MAY. b Henning Tenn 26 N 17. 5: David Lipscomb Col 35-37; Harding Col 37-39 (Eng) BA; Peabody summers 40-43 BS in LS; Chicago summers 48-52 (LS) MA; Harding Grad Sch of Relig MA 67. 6: Fr. 7: Tchr Gibson High Sch Gibson Tenn 39-41; Tchr-libn West Memphis High Sch West Memphis Ark 41-44; Tchr Harding Col 44-47, Libn 47-54; Tchr Byars-Hall High Sch Covington Tenn 54-55; Libn Stranahan Jr High Ft Lauderdale Fla 55-56; Libn Harding Col 56-62; Libn Harding Grad Sch of Religion Memphis Tenn 62-. 8: Exec Dir Nat Lib Week for Ark 59. 9: ALA; ATLA; ArkLA (chm Col Sect 57, pres 58) SELA; TennLA (chm Col Sect 67). 13: Yes. 14: Ref. 15: 1000 Cherry rd, Memphis Tn 38117.

ALTAVESTA, REV SAL. b Woburn Mass 5 O 34. 5: St Michaels Col 54-57 (Eng) BA; Cath U 62-69 (LS) MS in LS. 7: Tchr-libn La Salette Sem, Cheshire Ct 65-69. 9: NCTE; NE Drama Assn. 15: 475 Oak ave, Cheshire Ct 06410.

ALTBERG, ROSE A (BEIM). b Newark NJ 25 Je 28. 4: Dr Reynold G Altberg. 5: NYU 46-49 (Eng Educ) BA; Columbia

51-54 (LS) MS. 6: Fr, Hebrew. 7: Trainee & ref asst Pub Lib, E Orange NJ 51-55; Jr-Sr High Sch libn Sch Dist, Tyrone Penn 55-56; Chief Libn VA Hosp, Altoona Penn 56-. 10: Phi Beta Kappa. 14: Ref, circ, readers adv serv. 15: 130 Wordsworth ave, Altoona Pa 16602.

ALTEPETER, SISTER M PAULINIA OSF. b Dunnington Ind 20 Ag 1898. 5: St Francis Col (Lafayette Ind) 23-27 (Educ) AB; Our Lady of the Lake Col 51-53 MS in LS. 7: Tchr Elem Sch: St John's Ind 25-30, Logansport Ind 30-31, Olpe Kansas 31-44; Tchr: High Sch, Denver Colo 45-47, High Sch, Gallup NM 47-50; Libn UAlbuquerque 54-69. 9: ALA; CathLA; Greater Albuquerque LA. 14: Lib admin. 15: Univ of Albuquerque St Josephs place NW, Albuquerque NM 87120.

ALTER, FORREST HENRICI JR. b Pittsburgh Penn 15 Jl 15. 5: UPittsburgh 32-35 (Math) BA; Columbia summer 38, 46-47 (LS) BS. 7: Clerk Carnegie Ill Steel Corp, Pittsburgh 36-37; Tchr U Sch, Pittsburgh 37-39; Sec to the pres Business Train Col (Pittsburgh) 40-41; Co sec Ice-Capades Inc, Pittsburgh 41-42; (1st Lt) US Army, US & France 42-46; Detroit Pub Lib: Ref asst soc sci dept 47-49, Ref asst music & drama dept 49-50, Home reading asst Parkman Br 51, 1st asst Butzel Br 51, 1st asst a-v dept 51-53; Libn Film Coun of Amer, Evanston Ill 53-55; Liaison rep of Sdult Educ Assn of USA to Nat Inst of Adult Educ (Eng & Wales) & Libn of the Inst, London 55-57; Heart art, music & drama dept Flint Pub Lib, Flint Mich 58-. 9: ALA; MusLA; Adult Educ Assn if USA; Nat Inst of Adult Educ, Eng & Wales (Hon life mem); SLA (Picture Div: v-chm 60-62, chm 62-64; Mich Chap: pres-elect & ed of "Bulletin 65-66; pres 66-67; pres-elect & program chm 68-69; pres 69-70); MichLA (chm Nom Com 49-50, sec Dist 3 49-50, chm Pub Rel Com 53; Adult Educ Sect: v-chm 58-59, chm 59-60, chm Const & By-laws Com 60-61); Adult Educ Assn of Mich (Bd Dirs 62-66, sec 64-66). 10: Flint Lib Club; Internat Inst of Flint; Mich State Coun for Arts Music Com; Greater Flint Arts Coun. 13: Yes. 14: Ref, adult educ, readers adv. 15: Flint Pub Lib 1026 E Kearsley, Flint Mi 48502.

ALTHEIDE, DOROTHY PAULINE. b St Louis 4 My 10. 5: Chicago 26-30 (Hist) PhB; UMinn 45-47 (Educ Psych) MA; UIll 51-52 (Accounting); Catholic U 61-63 MS in LS. 7: Supv of clerical personnel Sears Roebuck & Co, Chicago 32-36; Sec to factory manager Gen Electric X-Ray Corp, Chicago 36-44; High sch tchr, Ill & DC 44-49; Col tchr SD State Col 49-51; Accountant & Accounting off supv US Govt, Fed Amer Socs for Experimental Biol & Nat 4-H Club Found, Wash DC 52-61; Libn-catlgr Brookings Inst, Wash DC 63-65; Libn catlgr US Govt NIH 65-69; Libn catlgr US Post Off Dept 69-. 9: ALA. 10: Beta Phi Mu; Psi Chi. 14: Catlg, documents libnship. 15: 4416 Clearbrook lane, Kensington Md 20795.

ALTMAN, ELLEN (O'BRIEN). b Pittsburgh Pa 1 Ja 36. 4: Carl Altman. 5: Duquesne U 53-57 (Journalism) BA; Rutgers 64 (LS) MLS, 67-. 6: Sp. 7: Ref libn Rutgers 65-67. 8: Consul OhioLA & Ohio Lib Trustees Assn for the Ralph Blasingame study of Ohio Libs 67. 9: ALA. 10: Beta Phi Mu. 12: "The Ohio Library Association and the Ohio Library trustees Association" (67). 14: Interlib coop. 15: 12 Guernsey Hill rd, Lagrangeville NY 12540.

ALTMAN, JO ANN. b Okla City Okla 8 Jn 43. 5: Okla City U 61-65 (Relig) BA; Okla U 65-66 MLS. 7: Pub lib consul Okla Dept of Lib, Okla City 66-. 9: ALA; SWLA; OklaLA. 15: 3405 NW 40, Okla City Ok 73112.

ALTMAN, LILLIAN FRIED. b Oklahoma City Okla 26 N 11. 04 Harold D Altman. ALTMAN, LILLIAN FRIED. 4: Harold Altman. 5: San Diego State Col 29-33 (Hist) AB; George WashingtonU 34-35 (Hist); USoCal 37-38 (LS) BS, 59-60 (LS) MS. 6: Sp. 7: Jr libn Glendale Pub Lib, Glendale Cal 38-41; Libn Hoff Gen Hosp (US Army), Santa Barbara Cal 41-43; Libn Pasadena Area Army Hosp, Pasadena Cal 43-44; OPA San Francisco Standard Oil 45-46; Asst libn USan Francisco 47; Jr libn Oakland Pub Lib, Oakland Cal 48; Libn Tehama Co Lib, Red Bluff Cal 49; Libn III Cal State Lib 50-58; Libn Joaquin Miller Jr High Sch, Sacramento Cal 58-68; libn clk McClatchy Sr High Sch, Sacramento Cal 68-. 9: ALA; CalASchl (pres No Sect 64-65); CalLA. 10: Sacramento Hist Soc. 14: Sch libs. 15: 3099 Freeport blvd #1, Sacramento Ca 95818.

ALTMAN, MIRIAM. b NYC 3 Mr 16. 5: UMich 34-38 (Pol Sci) AB, 38-39 ABLS. 6: Fr. 7: Asst libn Mt Clemens Pub Lib, Mt Clemens Mich 40-56, Dir 56-. 9: ALA; MichLA (Dist sec-treas 62-63, sec Adult Sect 60-61); Adult Educ Assn of Mich. 10: Delta Sigma Rho; Delta Kappa Gamma. 14: Ref, admin, adult educ. 15: 740 Wellington crescent, Mt Clemens Mi 48043.

ALVAREZ PORRATA, IVETTE. b Utuado PR 2 O 35. 5: Seten Hill 52-53; Catholic U of PR 53-56 (Soc Sci) BA. 6: Sp, Eng. 7: Sp prof Utuado High Sch, Utuado PR 56-57; Aux med soc wker City Hosp, San Juan PR 57-62; Dept of State, San Juan PR: Libn I 62-66, Libn II 66-. 10: Eta Gamma Delta. 14: Ref, internat relations. 15: PO Box 3271, San Juan PR 00904.

ALVERSON, (Mrs) MADELINE (GOLDSMITH). b San Anselmo Cal 16 Je 07. 5: UCal (Berkeley) 25-28 (Fr) BA, 40-41 Certif of Libnship; Yale 45-46 (Ed) MA; Universite Laval (Quebec) Summer 46; Stanford summers 49, 50. 6: Fr, Sp, Ital. 7: Music tchr McTyeire Middle Sch Shanghai 35-36; Eng tchr U Shanghai Middle Sch summer 36; Child Libn Hayward Pub Lib Hayward Cal 41-43; US Govt Tr Dept of Censor San Francisco 43-44; Cryptographer US Army Signal Corps 44-45; Tchr of Fr & Sp Madera Union High Sch Madera Cal 46-48; Sch Libn High Jr High Elem Mt View Salinas & Antioch Cal 48-55; Libn Cal Labor Fed AFL-CIO San Francisco 62-. 9: SLA; CalLA. 10: Commun Concerts Assn; Antioch Chamber Music Soc; World Affairs Coun of No Cal; Amer Vet Com (sec San Francisco chap). 14: Serv, ref. 15: 1365 Chestnut st, San Francisco Ca 94123.

ALWARD, DENNIS M(OORE). b Los Angeles Cal 8 N 30. 5: Swarthmore Col 48-52 (Hist) BA; Immaculate Heart Col (Los Angeles) 62-63 (LS) MA. 7: Var ABC, Los Angeles 53-58; Interlib loan libn Honnold Lib, Claremont Cal 60-62; Libn I readers' serv dept Glendale Pub Lib, Glendale Cal 63-68; Libn II Hd Tropico Br 68-. 9: ALA; SLA; CalLA. 10: AHA; Cal Hist Soc. 14: Ref, loc hist (spec collections), docs. 15: 4224 Francis ave, Los Angeles Ca 90005.

ALWARD, EMILY JOAN (MONTGOMERY). b Lafayette Ind 4 Jl 35. 5: UColo 54 (Hist); Purdue 52-55, 56 (Hist) BS; IndU 60-61 (LS) MA. 6: Fr, Russian. 7: Programmer trainee USAF, Dayton Ohio 55-56; Lib asst PurdueU Libs (Lafayette) 57-58, Supv period files 58-60; Grad asst educ reading room IndU (Bloomington) 60-61; Docs & asst ref libn DePauwU 61-69; Asst dir pub serv Frostburg State Col 69-. 10: AAUW. 14: Ref, docs, period, admin. 15: 328 Braddock st apt 213, Frostburg Md 21532.

AMAN, MOHAMMED M. b Alexandria UAR 3 Ja 40. 5: Cairo U 57-61 (LS) BA; Columbia 63-65 (LS) MS; UPittsburgh 65-68 (LS) PhD. 6: Arabic, Fr, Ger. 7: Ref libn Egyptian Nat Lib, Cairo 61-63; Instr lib sci Cairo U summer 63; Libn Arab Info Ctr, NYC 64-65; Searcher Knowledge Availability Syst Ctr UPittsburgh 65-66; Govt docs libn Duquesne U 66-68; Hd lib sci lib & lecturer in lib & info sci Pratt Inst 68-69; Asst Prof of lib sci St John's U (NY) 69-. 9: ALA; -LED; -RTSD; -RSD (chm Lib Sci Libns Com, NEast Reg); NY LA. 10: AAUP. 12: "Analysis of Terminology, Form and Structure of Subject Headings in arabic Literature and Firmulation of Rules for Arabic Subject Headings," PhD diss upittsburgh (68). 13: Yes. 14: Catlg, tech serv, spec libs, lib research, compar libnship, lib educ. 15: 215 Willoughby ave apt 1702, New York NY 11205.

AMATO, ANGELENE HELEN. b Winding Gulf WVa 5 Jl 19. 5: WVaU 41 (LS) BS in Ed, 46 (Ed & LS) MA in Ed, 46-69; Marshall 68 (Sp ed). 7: Libn Clear Fork High Sch, Colcord WVa 41-42; Libn Stoco High Sch, Coal City WVa 42-62; Libn Woodrow Wilson High Sch, Beckley WVa 62-. 8: Consul Cath Christian Doctrine, Beckley Reg Lib 68-69. 9: ALA; NEA; WVaSchLA (chm Regn 68-69); WVaLA; WVaEA; RaleighCoEA; Raleigh CoClTA. 10: Woman's Club of Beckley; Cath Daughters of Amer; Bus & Prof Woman's Club; Beta Sigma Phi. 14: Ref, catlg displays and exhibits, publicity, bk sel. 15: Box 105, Pemberton WVa 25905.

AMATO, MARGARET (DIEFENDERFER). b Tamaqua Penn. 4: Joseph Amato. 5: Kutztown State Col 25-27 (Educ); Penn State 28-29 (Educ); West Chester State Col 39-41 (Educ) BS in Ed; UPenn 43-45 (Educ & Soc Studies); Villanova 62-64 (LS) MSLS. 7: Elem tchr Pub Schs, Tamaqua Pa 27-29; Elem tchr Pub Schs, Haverford Twsp Pa 29-57; Sch libn 57-66; Asst prof (LS) Villanova 66-. 9: ALA; -AASchL; -ACRL; NEA; CathLA; PennLA; PennStateEA. 10: AAUP. 14: Catlg, child lit, bk sel, sch lib devel. 15: 433 Maro lane, Berweyn Pa 19312.

AMBLER, BARBARA HAYES. b Peking China 15 Ja 26. 04 William W Ambler. 5: Oberlin Col 44-48 (Hist) BA; Drexel 53-56 MSLS. 7: Asst libn & interne tchr Oakwood Sch, Poughkeepsie NY 48-49; Copy-ed & proofreader Westminster Press, Phila 49-50; Research report writer Curtis Publishing Co, Phila 51-53; Lib trainee The Free Lib of Phila 53-56; Child libn Upper Darby Free Pub Lib, Upper Darby Penn 56-57; Child libn Mem Lib of Radnor Twp, Wayne Penn 57-64; Asst coordinator of wk with child, The Free Lib of Phila 64-67; Sch libn Radnor Twp Sch Dist, Wayne Penn 67-. 8: Consul in child wk, Penn Lib Adminrs Round Table, 63. 9: ALA; PennLA (Program Chm; chm Child, YP & Sch Libns Sect; treas Southeast chap); DelaCoSchLA. 14: Child wk in pub libs. 15: 736 Upper Gulph rd, Wayne Pa 19087.

AMBLER, MARY ELIZABETH. b Oklahoma City Okla 24 Mr 06. 5: Lindenwood 26-30 (Hist) BA; Columbia; Sch of Lib Serv 30-31 (Catlg) BS; UChicago 38-39 (Adminis) MA. 6: Fr. 7: Catlgr NorthwesternU 31-34; Catlgr Alabama Col 34-38; Libn North Park Col 39-44; Libn Blackburn Col 44-64; Lindenwood Col: Catlgr 64-67, Libn 67-. 9: ALA; IllLA (chm Col & Ref sect 64); MoLA. 11: Lindenwood Col Fellowship. 14: Catlg, admin. 15: Lindenwood Col Lib, St Charles Mo 63301.

AMDOR, JUANITA B. b McLean Co Ill 21 F 15. 4: Linville Cortez Amdor. 5: Ill State U (Normal) 33-35, summers 57-60, 61 (Educ) BA; UIll summers 61-65 (LS) MS. 6: Fr. 7: Elem tchr Rural Sch Dist 57 McLean Co, Bellflower Ill 37-42; Elem tchr Cons Grade Sch Dist 88, Bellflower Ill 55-64, Elem tchr-libn 64-65; Libn Elem Sch Dist 88 & High Sch Dist 311, Bellflower Ill 65-. 9: NEA; ALA; IllEA. 10: Beta Phi Mu. 14: Bibliotherapy, child libn. 15: Bellflower Il 61724.

AMEEL, HENRIETTA R (ZEZULA). b Cedar Rapids Iowa 20 N 08. 4: Donald J Ameel. 5: Coe Col 26-30 (Eng) AB; UMich summers 30, 31, 35 ABLS. 6: Fr, Ger. 7: Lib asst Coe Col 30-36; Head catlgr Utah State U 36-37; Libn UMich Biol Station summers 36, 38-42; Kan State U; Ser catlgr 60-64, Asst head catlg dept 64-65; Asst libn preparations 66-. 8: Kan State U Senate 67-. 9: ALA; KanLA; MPLA. 10: AAUW; Riley Co Assn for Mental Health; Review Club. 14: Catlg. 15: 411 Edgerton ave, Manhattan Ks 66502.

AMEND, JOHN DAVID. b Alva Okla 9 Ag 28. 5: Emporia State Tchrs Col 46-50 (Eng, Fr) BS in Ed; UCal (Berkeley) 52-54 BLS. 6: Fr, Sp. 7: San Diego Pub Lib: Eng tchr-libn 50-52, Child libn 52-57, Sr libn brs 58-59, Sr libn lit & langs 59-62, Supv libn hist & world affairs 63; Dist Libn Eleventh Naval Dist, San Diego 64; Lib consul Cal State Lib 65-. 9: ALA; CalLA. 10: Beta Phi Mu. 12: "Library Service for the County of Madera, Calif" (65). 15: 4040 T st, Sacramento Ca 95819.

AMER, ROSALIE (CUNEO). b Stockton Cal 26 Ag 40. 4: Metwalli B Amer. 5: Mills Col 58-62 (Philos, ; Pol) BA; UIll 63- 58-62 (Philos, Econ, & Pol) BA; UIll 63-64 (LS) MS; U of the Pac 65-66 (Islamic hist) MA. 6: Ital, Arabic, Syriac, Ger. 7: Lib trainee Stockton & Joaquin County Pub Lib Cal summer 62; Grad stud lib asst U of the Pac Lib, Stockton Cal 62- cal summer 62, Grad stud lib asst U of the Pac Lib, Stockton Cal 62-63, Asst catlg libn 64- libn 64- libn 64-65; Hd bibliog serv & lib resources Div of Amer U, Cairo Egypt 67, Hd of tech serv 67-68; Acting Dir of Libs 67- serv 67-68; Acting Dir of Libs 67-; Acting fld dir Lib of Cong PL 480 Project, Am Libs Bk Procurement Cntr Cairo 69. 9: ALA (Internat Rel RT); The Middle East Inst; CalLA. 10: AAUP; YWCA (Cairo Egypt); Diamond Walnut Growers Assn. 11: Fulbright grant, Cairo Egypt 66-67. 14: Middle East collections & bibliog, acad lib admin, tech serv. 15: 20405 E Comstock rd, Linden Ca 95236.

AMES, DOROTHY (RUTH). b Newmarket Ont Can 13 Ag 08. 5: Victoria Col UToronto 26-30 (Household Econ) BA; Toronto 63-64 BLS. 7: Dir Northeastern Reg Lib Co-operative, Kirkland Lake Ont 64-; Chief Libn Twp of Teck Pub Lib, Kirkland Lake Ont Can 65-. 9: OntLA; CanLA; Inst Prof Libns Ont. 10: Beta Phi Mu; Kirkland & Dist Hosp Women's Auxiliary; Kirkland Lake Golf Club; Kirkland Lake Curling Club. 14: Admin. 15: Box 670, Kirkland Lake Ont Can.

AMES, JANICE (FONDY). b Steamboat Springs Col 31 O 28. 4: William E Ames. 5: So Dak State U 45-49 (Journalism) BS; UWash 65-69 MLib. 7: Reporter Belle Fourche Bee, Belle Fourche S Dak summer 45-49; Sec Iowa State U (Ames) 50-51; Bk ed Iowa State U Press (Ames) 51-52; Sec Socony Mobil, St Paul 52-54; Sec Sen Magnusons staff, Wash DC 67, Seattle 68. 15: 4507 Stanford ave NE, Seattle Wa 98105.

AMESTOY, MRS HELEN (MONNETTE). b Los Angeles 26 Ag 20. 4: Michel F Amestoy II. 5: Bryn Mawr 37-41 (Pre-Med); UCLA 61-63 (Hist of Art) BA, 63-64 MLS. 6: Ger, Fr. 7: Lib asst UCLA Engnr Lib 63; Libn Los Angeles Co Pub Lib Carson Br, Torrance Cal 65-67; Lynwood Branch, Lynwood Cal 67-68; Sr libn & Libn-in-chg Angelo M Iacoboni Lib, Lakewood Cal 68-. 9: ALA; CLA. 10: Nat Charity League& bryn Mawr Club of So Cal; UCLA Art Coun; Los Angeles Mus of Art & Mus Alliance; Opera Guild of So Cal; Cal Hist Soc; Beta Phi Mu; So Cal Coun on Lit for Ch & YP, Lakewood Coordinating Coun. 14: Ref, admin - pub libs. 15: 3330 Club dr, Los Angeles 64 Cal.

AMEY, LORNE JAMES. b Montreal Can 2 Ag 40. 4: Elizabeth Bisset. 5: Acadia 59-61 (Bio, Philos) BS, 61-62 (Educ) BEd; UNB 64-65 (Educ) MEd; Columbia 68-69 MLS. 6: Fr. 7: Sci tchr RCAF Sta St Herbert, Montreal 62-64; Bio tchr Protestant Sch Bd of Greater Montreal 65-66; Zoology tchr Can External Aid Off, Nigeria 66-68. 14: Ref, Africana, fine arts. 15: 675 Rue des Sources, Strathmore Que Can.

AMICK, CHARLES W(ILLIAM). b LaCrosse Kan 31 O 29. 5: Friends Jr Col 47-49 (Hist); Friends U 49-51 (Hist) BA; UWichitasummers 55-61 (Hist) MA; UDenver 63-64 (LS) MA. 6: Sp. 7: Farming, Rush Co Kan; Varied duties Ferris Sch, Wilmington Del 53-55;Tchr St Mary of the Plains High Sch, Dodge City Kan 55-56; Tchr Kincaid Rural High Sch, Kincaid Kan 56-57; Auto sales Palm SwedeMotors Inc, Wichita Kan 58-59; Tchr Valley Center High Sch, Valley Center Kan 59-61; Claims authorizer Social Security Adm, Kan CityMo 61-62; Staff Queens Borough Pub Lib, Jamaica NY 64-68; Hd ref dept Broadway Yonkers Pub Lib, Yonkers NY 68-. 8: Queens BoroughPub Lib Ref Bk List Rev Comm 66-67. 9: ALA; NEA; NYLA; WestchesterLA. 10: Yonkers Hist Soc; Bronx Co Hist Soc. 14: Ref, adult serv, local hist. 15: 17 Cross Hill ave, Yonkers NY 10703.

AMIS, JOE DALE. b Sparkman Ark 8 O 37. 4: Felba Mae (Burgess) Amis. 5: Ouachita Baptist Col 55-58 (Secondary Educ) BA; E Tex State U 63-65 MS in LS. 7: Eng-lib Ouachita High Sch, Donaldson Ark 58-60; Libn Roswell Sr High Sch, Roswell NM 60-65; Circ libn Southeast Mo State Col 65-66; Col of Artesia 66-68 (Artesia NM); Head libn South Plains Col 68- (Levelland Tex). 9: NEA-DAVI; ALA; NMLA (treas); ArkLA; SWLA. 14: Ref. 15: 216 Linda lane, Levelland Tx 79336.

AMIS, NANCY RUTH (KEEN). b Elk City Okla 10 D 06. 5: Stephens Col -23 (Eng) HS; Okla Baptist U -26 (Eng) AB; UOkla -59 MLS. 6: Sp. 7: Instr Eng to Allied Offs, I & E, Ft Sill Okla; Tchr Ext Cameron Jr Col; Tchr Lawton High Sch, Lawton Okla 48-59; Head libn Shawnee High Sch, Shawnee Okla 59-61; Asst assoc prof of lib sci Okla State U 61-; Coordinator Lib Ed Dept, Okla State U 68-. 8: Mem N Central Evaluation teams. 9: ALA; OklaLA (pres Sch Libns Div 63-64, sec Second Lib Sect 60-61, chm Lib Educ Div 67-68); OklaEA; SWLA; various com assignments in prof org. 10: AAUW; Theta Alpha Phi; Faculty sponsor Alpha Beta Alpha; Chm Lib Com First Pres Church Stillwater, Okla. 14: Lit yp, ref, sch lib admin. 15: 152 S Melrose dr, Stillwater Ok 74074.

AMNER, MARY (CASE). b Columbus Ohio 12 My 08. 4: F Dewey Amner. 5: Denison U 24-28 (Fr, Classics) BA; Kent State 50-52 (LS) MA. 6: Sp, Fr, Ital, Lat. 7: Lab asst Pharis Tire & Rubber Co, Newark Ohio 42-43; Reserve bk libn Denison U 43-45; Reserve bk libn Kent State U 45-46; Tchr Lat & Eng Kent Roosevelt High Sch, Kent Ohio 46-48; Asst order libn Kent State U 48-52, Order libn 52-57, Asst libn 57-58, Assoc libn tech processes 58-, Assoc Prof lib admin. 9: ALA; -RTSD (Acquis Sect Info Com 57-59); -ACRL (Tri-State Chap: Exec Bd, Program Chm 60-62, pres 64-65); OhioLA (sec Col & Univ Lib Sect 55-56); No Ohio Tech Serv Libns (v-pres & Program chm 63-65). 10: LWV; Coun on World Affairs; Phi Beta Kappa; Faculty Club; AAUW. 13: Yes. 14: Acquis, tech serv. 15: 609 Woodside dr, Kent Oh 44240.

AMOS, AUTUMN. b Burnsville WVa 24 Ag 01. 5: Morris Harvey Col 18-20 (Music) Certif; Cincinnati Conservatory of Music summer 24 (Music); Glenville State Col summers 36-41 (Music, Eng) AB; West Res summers 51-53 MSLS. 6: Fr, Ital. 7: Private tchg Piano & Violin, Burnsville WVa 20-36; Music tchr Glenville State Col Lab Sch, Glenville WVa summer 50; Tchr-libn Burnsville High S, Burnsville WVa 36-. 9: NEA; WVaEA; CTA; CEA; WVMEA. 14: Catlg, ref. 15: P O Box 177, Burnsville WVa.

AMOS, GERALDINE ODESTER. b Lake Providence La 3 O 22. 5: Dillard U 43-47 (Religion, Philos) BA; Atlanta 48-49 BS in LS, summer 54, 55 MS in LS; New Orleans Baptist Theol Sem 56-59 (Religious Educ) MRE. 6: Fr, Sp. 7: Catlg libn Jackson State Col 49-52; Catlg libn Dillard U 52-63; Program spec Ford Found, Lagos Nigeria 63-65; Asst libn Dillard U 65-66; Project spec Ford Found, Addis Ababa Ethiopia 66-. 8: Head of Catlg Sect in establishing a National Library for the Federal Govt of Nigeria. 9: ALA. 10: BTU Assn; AlphaKappa Alpha; Beta Phi Mu. 12: Comp & ed "Directory of Ethiopian

Libraries". 14: Catlg. 15: 5619Urquhart st, New Orleans La 70117.

AMOS, MARY L (RODGERS). b Ft Worth Tex 22 Jl 23. 4: Carroll E Amos. 5: N Tex State U 41-45 (LS) BS; Bowling Green State U 57 (Elem Educ); UToledo 57, 58 Elem tchg certif N Tex State U summer 67; UMich 68-69 AMLS. 7: Asst libn Pub Lib, Ft Worth Tex 45; Period libn U Toledo 46-49; Child libn Hqd Lucas Co Lib, Maumee Ohio 50-57; Elem tchr Maumee Bd of Educ, Maumee Ohio 57-61; Child libn Toledo Bd of Educ, Toledo Ohio 61-69; Instr Bowling Green State ULS Dept 69-. 8: Visiting prof of child lit UToledo summers 59, 61, 63, 65, 68,69; Selection of bks for classroom libs up to 6th grade; Tchg child lit via TV totoledo's 51 elem schs; Tchr child lit, Adrian Col, Mich 66-68; Consul StorytellingFilm, Dayton & Montgomery Co Lib (Ohio). 9: ALA; NEA; OhioLA; OhioASchL; Toledo Tchrs Assn; OhioEA. 10: Delta Kappa Gamma. 14: Child lit, sch libs& educ of libns,storytelling. 15: 4762 Carskaddon ave, Toledo Oh 43615.

AMOS, PAUL STODDARD. b NYC 13 Ap 16. 5: U Chicago 39-40 (Internat Law & Relations) MA; Columbia 52-53 (LS) MS. 6: Fr. 7: Lib intern Brooklyn Pub Lib 53-55; Lib intern Newark Pub Lib Newark NJ 55-57;Libn Bellevue Hosp Sch of Nursing NYC 57-61; Res libn S. B. Penick & Co Jersey Citynj 61-64; Libn St Louis Med Soc 64-65; Libn Worcester Found for Experi BiolShrewsbury Mass 65-66; Libn Meyer Zone Ctr, Decatur Ill 66; Libn Adler Zone Ctr,Champaign Ill 67-. 9: MedLA; SLA-NY chap (chrm, picture Group 61-62). 10: Appalachian Mtn Club. 13: Yes. 14: Ref. 15: The Professional Lib, Adler Zone Center, 2204Griffith dr, Champaign Il 61820.

AMOSS, ALICE M. b Fullerton Md 11 My 1894. 5: Md State Normal Sch 08-12 (Educ) Diploma; Johns Hopkins 12-64 (Sci) BS. 6: Ger, Russian. 7: Tchr Baltimore Co (Md) Bd of Educ 12-18; Libn Chem Corps Dept of Defense, Edgewood Arsenal 18-25; Tchr Baltimore City (Md) Bd of Educ 25-26, Even Sch 25-29; Libn Chem Corps Dept of Defense, Edgewood Arsenal 26-64; Libn even ref Enoch Pratt Free Lib, Baltimore 26-39; Lib consul J I Thompson Co, Wash DC 64-65; Ref libn UBaltimore Langsdale Lib 66-. 9: ACS; SLA; ADI. 10: Amer Guild of Organists. 12: "Where to Find the New Trade Names," brochure. 13: Yes. 14: Ref, admin, org. 15: 7704 Belair rd, Baltimore Md21236.

AMRHEIN, REV THOMAS FRANCIS SCJ. b Pittsburgh Penn 20 Jl 38. 5: Kilroe Sem 57-61 (Philos) BA; Sacred Heart Mon (affiliate of Cath U) 61-65 (Theol) STB; CathU summers 62, 63, 64, 65, 66, 67, 68 (LS) MSLS. 7: Stud libn Sacred Heart Mon, 62-65; Dean of Stud Adult Voc Sem Dehom Sem, Gt Barrington Mass, 65-69, Treas, Libn, Tchr, Principal (Dir of Schs) CADET, Holly Springs Miss 69-. 9: ALA; CathLA; NEA; NCEA; NELA. 10: So berkshire Commun Action Assn. 14: Ref, lib serv. 15: CADET, Holly Springs Ms 38635.

AMSON, ELIZABETH (ROSE). b New York NY 17 Mr 42. 5: Cornell 59-63 (Chem) BA; Columbia 64-66 MS in LS. 7: Research chem Rockefeller U 63-64; Ref asst ColumbiaU Med Lib 65-65; Lit chem Lederle Lab, Pearl River NY 65-67; Asst libn Info & Computer Serv Lib Shell Oil Co 67-. 9: SLA (Docum gp NY chap: treas 67-68, v-pres 68-69, chm 69-70; Pharmac Div Convention Repr 66-67); ASIS. 10: Beta Phi Mu. 14: Ref, data processing. 15: 285 Riverside dr, New York NY 10025.

AN, LINDA (HUANG). b Chungking China 28 S 42. 4: Chung-ming An. 5: Nat Taiwan U 60-64 (Eng lit) BA; Fla State U 64-66 (LS) MS; Drexel 68 (Info Sci). 6: Chinese, Fr. 7: Stud asst Fla State U Physics Dept Lib 65-66; Asst libn Moore Col of Art lib 66; Drexel: Catlgr 66-68, Ser catlgr & asst hd of catlg dept 68-. 15: 4501 Larchwood ave apt 1, Philadelphia Pa 19143.

ANASTASSIADIS, HELEN (GREEN). b Florida NY 25 N 21. 5: Keuka Col 39-43 (Eng, Hist) BA; Geneseo State Tchrs summers 43-47 (LS) BS; Columbia 51, 55 BSLS. 7: Tchr & Libn Prattsburg Central Sch Prattsburgh NY 43-45; Tchr-libn Livingston Manor Central Sch Livingston Manor NY 45-46; Tchr-libn Marlboro Central Sch Marlboro NY 46-48; Campus sch libn West Mich Col Ed Kalamazoo 48-51; Specialist in wk with schs Brooklyn Pub Lib 52-56; Katonah libn & a-v Katonah Elem Sch Katonah NY 56-. 9: NEA; NYLA; NYSTA. 10: Great Bks disc. 13: Yes. 14: Child, sch. 15: 210 Willis ave, Hawthorne NY 10532.

ANCES, MARLAYNE (R). b Innsbruck Austria. 5: Conn Col (Hist, Zool) BA; UMich 65 AMLS. 6: Sp, Fr. 7: Sr libn New Haven Free Pub Lib, New Haven Conn; Soc dir Matson Navigation Co, San Francisco 59-62; Asst ref libn UMd Health Sci Lib 65-67; Libn cylburn Lib Cylburn Wildflower Preserve & Garden Ctr, Baltimore 68-. 8: Adv wk & consul to different profs on various projects Johns HopkinsU Sch Med & Sch Hygiene & Pub Health 68-. 9: ALA; SLA; MedLA; MdLA (Program Chm; Jr Mem RT). 10: Women's Civic League; Cylburn Wildflower Preserve & Garden Ctr Bd Dir; Garden Club Home Garden Com; Federated Garden Club; Beta Phi Mu; Pi Lambda Theta; Phi Kappa Phi. 13: Yes. 14: Ref, hist collections, rare bks, child & ya bks. 15: 627 E 34th st, Baltimore Md 21218.

ANDERL, ROBERT GEORGE. b Jamestown NY 14 Ap 40. 4: Susan Jarvis. 5: Syracuse 58-62 (Geog) BA, 62-65 MLS. 7: Acquis asst Syracuse U Lib 65-67; Hd Tech Serv UNev (Las Vegas) Lib 67-. 14: Tech serv, map collections,automation. 15: 4297 Vegas Valley dr, Las Vegas Nv 89109.

ANDERL, SUSAN JARVIS. b Cooperstown NY 30 Jl 40. 4: Robert G Anderl. 5: Syracuse 58-62 (Zool) BS, 63-66 MLS. 7: Ref & interlib loan UNev (Las Vegas) Lib 67-. 14: Med. 15: 4297 Vegas Valley rd, Las Vegas Nv 89109.

ANDERS, MARY EDNA. b Northport Ala 7 D 21. 5: UAla 40-43 (Hist) AB, Certif in Lib Sci; UNC 46-47 BS in LS, 48-50 (Hist) MA; Columbia 55-58 DLS. 6: Fr. 7: Asst to dir of lib Huntingdon Col 43-45; Libn Huntingdon Col 45-46; Ref asst UNC (Chapel Hill) 47; Libn Tuscaloosa (Ala) Sr High Sch summer 47; Ref libn Birmingham So Col 47-48; Instr-libn Sch of Lib Sci UNC 48-49, Research asst Inst for Research in Soc Sci 50-51; Visiting Instr Lib Sch Fla State U summer 50; Visiting Instr Lib Sch UNC 50-51; Visiting Instr Dept of Lib Sci UAla summer 51; Asst Prof Lib Sch Fla State U 51-53; Soc sci libn UFla 53-56; Visiting Lecturer Div of Libnship Emory U summer 56; Visiting Instr Lib Sch Fla State U summer 58; Spec research sci Ind Development Div Engnr Expt Station Ga Inst of Tech 58-69; Prin Research Sci 69-. 69; Prin Research Sci 69-. 8: Staff of Survey of Lib Functions of the States, 61-62. 9: ALA; SELA; GaLA. 13: Yes. 14: Ref, lib hist. 15: Indl Development Div Ga Inst of Tech, Atlan ta Ga 30332.

ANDERS, RICHARD LEAR. b Cleveland 24 Ja 24. 5: Fenn Col 42-46 (Eng) BA; Columbia 46-47 (Eng) MA; UIll 47-48 BSLS. 7: Catlgr Union Col Lib Schenectady NY 48-49; Head catlgr Mary Washington Col Lib 49-51; Catlgr Wesleyan U Lib Middletown Conn 51-55; Spec catlgr Dartmouth Col Lib 568; Catlgr Amer Antiquarian Soc 68-. 10: AAUP. 14: Catlg. 15: 39 Highland st, Worcester Ma 01608.

ANDERSEN, DORIS FERN ORR. b Red Oak Tex 8 D 16. 4: Richard Edward Andersen. 5: Abilene Christ Col 35-38 BS in LS; Tex WomanU 38-40 BS in LS; E Tex StateU 61-62 MS in LS. 6: Sp. 7: Libn Pecos Pub Schs, Pecos Tex 40-41; Libn High Sch, burkhurnett Tex 41-42; Period libn Amarillo Pub Lib, Amaritto Tex 42-43; Tchr Vernon Pub Sch, Vernon Tex 44-45; Co-owner Henrietta Floral Co, Henrietta Tex 48-58; Co-owner Andersen's Gardens & Nursery, Longview Tex 58-60; Hd libn Margaret Estes Lib lethburneau Col 59-. 9: ALA; NEA; Nat Aerospace Educ Coun; Nat Assn of Elem Kindergarten Educ; TexLA (chm Dist VI 62). 10: Le Tourneau Womens Club; Kappa Delta pi. 12: "An Analysis of the Role of the Library in Accreditation" (62). 14: Acquis, ser (sci & tech). 15: Margaret Estes Lib Le Tourneau Col Box 7001, Longview Tx 75601.

ANDERSEN, LILLIAN (GERTRUDE). b Sharon Wis. 5: Northwestern 41-45 (Span) BA; UIll (Champaign) 59-60 MS in LS. 6: Sp. 7: Copywriter Catalog Engnrs, Chicago 45-46; Assoc ed Sci & Mechanics Pub Co, Chicago 47-59; Tchg asst UIll Lib Sch (Champaign) 59-60; Head ed research Field Enterprises Educ Corp, Chicago 60-68; LibnMiddle W Serv Co, Chicago 68-. 9: SLA (Ill Chapt; chm Memb Directory Com 64-65);IllLA. 10: Gamma Alpha Chi; Alpha Lambda Delta. 14: Research, spec libs. 15: 3835 N Central Park ave, Chicago Il 60618.

ANDERSON, A ISABELLA (RUSS). b Monroe Co Ind 22 O 17. 4: Ray E Anderson. 5: Ind U 36-40 (Chem) AB. 7: Chem libn Victor Chem Wks, Chicago Heights Ill 40-52; Libn Alfred I DuPont Inst, Wilmington Del 55-56; Chem libn Vctor Chem Div Stauffer Chem Co, Chicago Heights Ill 57-65; Tech libn Pullman-Standard, Hammond Ind 65-68; Chem libn Argonne Nat Lab, Argonne Ill 68-. 9: SLA; ACS. 10: Iota Sigma Pi. 13: Yes. 14: Chem lib duties. 15: 698Birch lane, Olympia Fields Il 60461.

ANDERSON, ADA. b Excelsior Minn 30 Jl 33. 5: Hamline U 51-55 (Sociol) AB Carnegie 60-61 MLS. 6: Fr. 7: Lib asst St Paul Pub Lib 51-55; Carnegie Lib of Pittsburgh: Child libn Mt

Washington Br 61-63, Child libn S Side Br 63-64, Child libn Brookline Br 64-65, Child consul Dist Serv Div 65-. 9: ALA; CathLA; PennLA. 14: Child wk. 15: 143 N Craig st, Pittsburgh Pa 15213.

ANDERSON, ALBERT G JR. b Fargo ND 19 Jl 29. 4: Ann Lee O'Connell. 5: ND State U 52 BS; UWyo 53 MA; UIll 56 MSLS. 6: Norwegian, Fr. 7: US Army, Korea 53-55; Libn in chg Masonic Grand Lodge of ND, Fargo ND 56-58; Head circ dept UPittsburgh 58-60; Tech info coordinator Bendix Systems Div, Ann Arbor Mich 60-63; Head libn & asst prof Worcester Polytech Inst 63-67; Head libn & assoc prof Worcester Polytech Inst 67-; Lectr State U NY, Albany summer 67. 8: Consul, US Bur of Mines, Pittsburgh Revision of Geology Glossary, 60; Consul, John Woodman Higgens Armory Mus, Worcester Mass 65-67; Dir Mass Tech Referral Center 69-. 9: ALA; SLA; AID; NEA (sec Col Sect); Intl Assn Tech Univ Libn. 10: Torch Club; Univ Club. 13: Yes. 14: Admin. 15: Worcester Polytech Inst, Worcester Ma 01609.

ANDERSON, ALTHEA WILLIAMS. b Macon Ga 23 Je 25. 4: Hayward S Anderson. 5: Ft Valley State Col 43-47 (Hist, Pol Sci) BA; Atlanta 47-48 BS in LS; Syracuse 52-53 MS in LS. 6: Sp. 7: Circ libn & readers adv Savannah State Col 48-. 9: ALA; GaLA; Ga Tchrs Educ Assn (Libns sec); SELA. 10: LWV; AAUP. 13; yes. 14: Circ, ref, readers adv, child serv. 15: Box 216 Savannah State Col, Savannah Ga 31404.

ANDERSON, ANITA (SUNDBY). b Harmony Minn 10 My 18. 4: Glenn E Anderson. 5: Winona State 36-40 (Soc Stud & Math) BS; UMinn summer 51, 52 (LS); Mankato State summer 62 (LS); Winona State summer 60 (LS). 7: Soc stud instr Pub Sch, Bigfork Minn 40-41; Hist instr Pub Sch, Spring Grove Minn 41-44; Math/hist instr Pub Sch, Rushford Minn 44-46; Math/hist instr Pub Sch, Chatfield Minn 46-48; Math/lib instr High Sch, Canby minn 48-61; Elem lib Elem Sch, Canby Minn 61-. 9: ALA; NEA; MinnASchL (past district chm); CanbyEA (past sec). 10: Canby Womens' Club; Yellow Medicine Co Hist Soc; Pub Lib Trustee. 13: Yes. 14: Elem lib wk. 15: 1101 St Olaf N, Canby Mn 56220.

ANDERSON, ARLENE L. b Pittsburgh Pa 1 F 38. 5: Muskingum Col 56-60 (Elem Educ) BS in Ed; UNC 66-67 MSLS. 7: Tchr Peters Twp Sch Dist, McMurray Penn 60-62; Libn Hampton twp Sch Dist, Allison Pk Penn 62-66; Prof asst Baltimore Co Pub Lib, Towson Md 67-69, child specialist 69-. 9: ALA; MdLA. 14: Child serv. 15: 5915D Radecke ave, Baltimore Md 21206.

ANDERSON, BARBARA ELAINE. b Los Angeles 10 S 34. 5: UCLA 52-56 (Prelibnship) BA; UCal (Berkeley) 56-57 MLS. 6: Ger. 7: Libn I adult & ya Free Lib of Phila 57-59; San Francisco State Col: Libn II curriculum libn 59-60, Libn II asst educ libn 60-61, Libn III educ libn 61-. 8: Fulbright Lectureship 66-67, Pahlavi Univ Shiraz Iran. 9: CalLA (pres Ref Libns Round Table 63); CalASchL (chm Curric Libns Com 60-); ALA. 12: Co-auth "Handbook for Regional Curriculum Depositories" (64); Co-auth "Curriculum Material Depositories" (65); Ed "Curriculum Materials, 1966" (66). 14: Ref, admin, tchg. 15: 2447 Vallejo #3, San Francisco Ca 94123.

ANDERSON, BERYL LAPHAM. b Canso NS Can 15 Ap 25. 5: Dalhousie U 43-46 (Classics) BA, 48-49 (Gk Hist) MA; McGill 55-56 BLS. 7: Tchr, NS & Quebec 46-48, 49-50; Lecturer Dalhousie U (Halifax NS) 50-55; Lecturer & Libn McGill U Grad Sch of Lib Sci 56-62, Asst Prof 62-68; Assoc Prof 68-. 9: CanLA (Catlg Sect; sec-treas, chm); ALA; SLA (MontrealChap; Archivist, chm &/or mem var coms); AALS; Internat Assn Documentalists; QueLA;APLA; ASIS. 10: Classical Assn of Can; McGill Assn of Univ Tchrs. 11: Governor-General's Gold Medal & Avery Prize 46. 12: Ed "Selected Bibliography on Algae," No 5 with Joann Morris (60);Ed "Union List of Serials in Libraries of Montreal & Vicinity" (65); "Basic Cataloguing Tools for Use in Canadian Libraries" (68); Special Libraries in Canada; "A Directory. (1st & 2d eds 68); "Special Libraries in Canada; A Statistical Analysis andCommentary" (69). 13: Yes. 14: Catlg, bibliog, spec libs. 15: Grad Sch of Lib Sci McGill Univ, Montreal 110 Can.

ANDERSON, CAROLYN JOYCE (BIGGS). b Nampa Ida 26 Ap 34. 4: Earl N Anderson. 5: WillametteU 56-60 (Mus Educ) BMEd, 61-66 (Educ) MA; UOre 65-68 MSLS, 68- (Educ, Libnship). 7: Tchr & libn N Marion Sch Dist, Hubbard Ore 60-67; Libn Gresham High Sch Dist, Gresham Ore 67-68; Ref libn UOre Lib (Eugene) 68-. 9: NEA-DAVI; OreLA; PNLA; OreASchL; OreIMA; OreEA. 10: Pi Lambda Theta; Mu Phi Epsilon; University Women's Club. 13: Yes. 14: Ref, pub serv. 15: 379 Conestoga way, Eugene Or 97401.

ANDERSON, CHARLOTTE KENNARD. b Manchester NH 27 O 13. 5: UMich 31-35 (Lang & Lit) AB, 35-36 ABLS, 50-51 AMLS. 6: Fr. 7: Circ asst MvGregor Pub Lib, Highland Park Mich 36-39; Asst in chg of circ Colby Jr Col 39-43; Asst libn UNH 43-. 9: ALA (Coun rep NHLA 48-62); -ACRL (Recr Com 55-57, sec Univ Libs Sect 57-58); NHLA (pres 48-50); NELA (treas 46-47). 10: AAUW; AAUP. 14: Admin, docs. 15: Univ of NH Lib, Durham NH 03824.

ANDERSON, CHARLOTTE L. b Kellerton Iowa 20 Ja 21. 4: Dale G Anderson. 5: Augustana Col 37-38, 38-58 (Bus Admin); URochester 42-43; Marycrest Col 57-58 (LS). 6: Fr. 7: Mgr lib serv Deere & Co, Moline Ill 58-. 8: Mem Adv Council of Libns, Ill Grad Sch of Lib Sci 67-; Mem Ill State Lib Adv Council on Lib Development 67-. 9: SLA (Ill Chap; Spec Com to Study Possibility of Reg Chap 65-66); ALA; Internat Assn of Agric Libns & Documentalists; Asociacion Interamericana de Bibliotecarios y Documentalistas Agricolas. 10: Zonta Internat; Elder, South Park Presbyt Church, Rock Island Ill. 14: Admin. 15: 1402 First st, Moline Il 61265.

ANDERSON, CYNTHIA M. b St Paul Minn 8 N 44. 4: Dennis R Anderson. 5: Col of St Catherine 63-67 (LS, Hist) BA. 6: Sp. 7: Ref libn Ramsey Co Pub Lib, St Paul 66-69. 9: ALA (Jr mems RT); MLA. 14: Ref. 15: 1786 Hillcrest ave, St Paul Mn 55116.

ANDERSON, DELIA C (MAY) (CASH). b Collins Ark 13 O 06. 4: Mack Harvie Anderson. 5: Ark A & M 31, 36-38 (Soc Sci) AB; UArk 49-53 (Ed) MS; LSU 51-55 (LS) MS. 7: Tchr McGehee High Sch, McGehee Ark 38-48; Tchr, libn Desha Central High Sch, Rohwer Ark 48-54; Ark State U: Catlgr 64, Instr summer 64; Instr of lib sci NE La State summers 65-68; High sch libn Delhi High Sch, Delhi La 54-. 8: Committee for Reviewing Evaluation of high schools, Lake Providence La 1959; Monticello La 1963; Pioneer La 1963; Winnsboro La 1961. 9: ALA; NEA; LaLA; LaTA. 10: Kappa Delta Pi; Delta Kappa Gamma; Bus & Prof Women. 14: Tchg, ref, catlg. 15: Rt 1, Box 61. McGehee Ar 71654.

ANDERSON, DONNA LaVERNE (LaMOTTE). b Pasadena Cal 18 S 44. 4: Lowell Terry Anderson. 5: Pasadena City Col 62-64 (Hist) AA; UCal (Santa Barbara) 64-66 (Soc Sci, Hist) BA; USoCal 66-67 MSLS. 7: Lib asst Pasadena Pub Lib, Pasadena 67; Specialist UWis (Milwaukee) 67-. 9: ALA. 14: Ref. 15: 2920 E Park pl, Milwaukee Wi 55211.

ANDERSON, DOROTHY JEAN. b Winnipeg Man Can 19 Je 34. 5: Can Bible Col 52-55 (Christian Educ) 3 yr diploma; Seattle Pacific Col 56-58 (Eng Lit) BA; UWash 60-61 MLS. 6: Ger. 7: Child libn Seattle Pub Lib 58-62; Prof asst child serv div, young adult serv div ALA, Chicago 63-64; Lecturer Child Lib Roosevelt U 64; Lib career consul Ill State Lib, Chicago 65-69; Assoc dir Media Serv Fed City Col, Wash DC 69-. 8: ALA unofficial del to IFLA, Edinburgh Scotland 61; Instr Child Serv Wkshop WestIllU 65; TV Story-telling Series, Seattle 61-62 Recruitment Consul WisLA 69. 9: ALA-CSD (Bd of Dirs); IllLA (Recr Com). 12: "Seattle Images,with Don L Aylard (61); Ed "Ill Libs", May 67. 13: Yes. 14: Child lit, recr of libns, urban lib problems. 15: Federal City Col, 425 2nd st NW, Wash DC 20001.

ANDERSON, EDITH (FEISS). b Denver Colo 27 Je 39. 4: Maj Gerald M Anderson. 5: Hood Col 57-59; Harvard 59-64 (Fine Arts)AB; UMich 64-65 MLS. 7: Gen asst Bedford Pub Lib, Bedford Mass 63-64; Sec Harvrd Grad Sch of Educ60-62; Br libn Ann Arbor PubLib, Ann Arbor Mich 65-66; Sinclair Commun Col Lib, Dayton Ohio 68-. 9: ALA; Miami Valley Consortium. 14: Recruit, manpower & lib training, child lit. 15: 340 Beverly pl, Dayton Oh 45419.

ANDERSON, ELIZABETH (HOREK). b Niagara Falls NY 12 Ja 28. 4: Arthur H Anderson. 5: State U Col (Geneseo NY) 46-50 BS in LS; PMC 65 (Educ); Villanova 66-67 (LS). 7: Catlgr Penn State U 50-53; Elem libn Penn-Delco Union Sch Dist, Chester Penn 62-. 8: Sec, Aston Twp (Penn) Lib Com 65-. 9: ALA; PennLA; DelawareCoSchLA; PennStateEA; NEA; Penn-DelcoEA. 14: Catlg, IMC (elem level). 15: 202 Marianville rd, Chester Pa 19014.

ANDERSON, ELIZABETH C (FARR). b Henagar Ala 20 Ja 23. 4: G Kenneth Anderson. 5: Wayne State 41-45 (Eng) BA, 55 (Eng) MA, 64-66 91s0 msls& seton Hall (NJ) 59 (Educ). 6: Fr, Sp, Ital. 7: Pub Rel Consult & Copywriter Bell Tel Co, Mich 47-52; Libn Bloomfield Hill Sch Dist Wing Lake Sch, 64-67, Lahser High Sch 67-68; Libn, Lib Coordinator K-12 West Bloomfield Sch Dist, 68-. 9: NEA; ALA; MichEA; MichASchL. 10. AAUW. 14: Sch libnship. 15: 5229 Whispering oak, Birmingham Mi 48010.

ANDERSON, EVELYN J(ACOBSON). b Marquette Kan 8 My 13. 5: Bethany Col (Lindsborg Kan) 33-35 (Hist) AB; Chicago 54-57 (LS) MA. 7: Hist tchr North Park Col 35-41; Army libn US Army, CZ 42-45; Sch libn CZ Schs, Panama 45-54; Elem libn Lab Sch UChicago 57-60; Asst Prof of Lib Sci Purdue U 60-64; Asst Prof Lib Sci Educ UMd 64- Summer sch tchg in lib sci; UOkla 57, 58; Drexel Inst, Phila 59,60,64. 8: Review Com "Bulletin of the Center for Children's Books" 57-60; Voting consul for child bks in ALA "Booklist and Subscription Books Bulletin" 58-64. 9: ALA; NEA; DCLA. 10: AAUP; Pi Lamda Theta. 14: Child lit, sch libs. 15: 4313 Knox rd No 606, College Park Md 20740.

ANDERSON, FRANCES LOUISE (WILLIAMS). b Seneca SC 26 My 08. 04. Dr Jerry Cepheus Anderson. 4: Dr Jerry Cepheus. 5: Clark U 27-31 (Eng) BA; Atlanta 36-37 (Educ); SCar State A&M Col 41-42 (LS); Atlanta 47-49 BSLS, 54-55 (Educ), 59-60 (Music), 64-65 (Lib Methods Analysis). 7: Tchr Simpson Jr High Sch, Easley SC 31-37; Tchr Mullins High Sch, Mullins SC 37-38; Tchr Northside Elem Sch, Anderson SC 38-46; Tchr-libn Reed Street High Sch, Anderson SC 46-51; Libn Westside High Sch, Anderson SC 51-. 8: So Assn Cols & Sec Schs for 3 SC high schs 62-65. 9: NEA; Amertchrs Assn; SCLA; Anderson City TA; SCTA; Clrm Tchr Org. 10: Piedmont Med, Dental & Pharmaceutical Auxiliary; Alpha Kappa Alpha; Nat Dental Auxiliary; Wives Civic & Social Club; Organist for sr & youth choirs. 15: PO Box 4004,Anderson SC 29621.

ANDERSON, FRANK J(OHN). b Chicago Ill 29 Ja 19. 4: Jeanette Rioux Anderson. 5: UConn 47-48; UInd 48-50 (Eng, Amer Lit) AB; Syracuse 50-51 MS in LS. 7: Millwright Kingsbury Ordnance Plant, Kingsbury Ind 42-43; Torpedoman US Submarine Serv, Atlantic & Pacific 43-45, Atlantic 51-52; Libn Kan WesleyanU 52-56; Head Baring Ave Br, E Chicago Pub Lib, E Chicago Ind 56-57; Dir The Submarine Lib, Groton Conn 57-60; Libn Kan WesleyanU 60-66; Chief libn Wofford Col (SC) 66-. 8: Consul, USN Submarine Sch Lib 59; Consul, Minn State Col Bd 64; Survey Assoc, Kan Higher Educ Facilities Commsn 65; Visiting Prof UIll Grad Lib Sch summer 65; Consul Morris Col 67, 68; Proprietor Kitemaug Press. 9: ALA; SLA; MPLA (v-pres 63-65, pres 65-67); KanLA (State rep to MPLA 61-); SCLA; SELA. 10: AAUP; Beta Phi Mu; Kan State Hist Soc; US Naval Inst; Naval Records club; League of Lithographed Libns; Salina (Kan) Soc of Art; Almalgamated Printers Assn; PrivLA. 11: ALA-ACRL personal research grant, 65. 12: "Submarines, Submariners and Submarining (63); Article on atomic submarines in "Colliers Encyc (59 & subsequent eds); Ed SLA Conn Valley chap "Bulletin (58-60); Ed SLA Geog & Map Div "Bulletin (65-). 13: Yes. 14: Col lib admin, printing hist. 15: 229 Mohawk dr, Spartanburg SC 29301.

ANDERSON, HAZEL A. b Kanwaka Kan. 5: UKan 26-30 (Sociol) AB, 42-45 LLB. 7: Engnr libn UKan 30-36, Law Libn 36-68, Assoc Prof 68-. 9: AALL (chm Chaps Com, mem several other coms; pres SWChap); ALA-ACRL; KanLA (Council 67-, pres Spec Libs Div, Parliamentarian, & mem varcoms); Mem KanLA Council 67-. 10: AAUP; AAUW; Bus & Prof Women's Club; Bus & ProfWomen's Found. 11: Woman of the Year, Kans Bus & Prof Women, 68. 13: Yes. 14: Admin, legalresearch, lib consultg. 15: Law Lib Univ of Kan, 208 Green Hall, Lawrence Kan66044.

ANDERSON, HERSCHEL VINCENT. b Charlotte NC 14 Mr 32. 5: Duke 50-54 (Pol Sci) AB; Columbia 54-55, 57-59 (LS) MS. 7: Pre-prof Brooklyn Pub Lib 54-55; US Army Signal Corps, Cryptography (Sp-4) 55-57; Pre-prof Brooklyn Pub Lib 57-59; Asst Bkmob libn King Co Pub Lib Seattle 59-62; asst libn Longview Wash Pub Lib 62-63; Libn NC Mus of Art Raleigh 63-64; A1V consul NC State Lib 64-68; Dir Sandhill Reg Lib, Carthage NC 68-. 9: ALA-PLA (chm A-V Com; Memb Com; Recruiting Netwk State Rep); SELA (chm Pub Lib Sect 69-70); NCLA (2nd v-pres 68-69); Educ FilmLA; Film Lib Info Coun. 10: Rotary Intl; Phi Kappa Psi; NC Art Soc; NC Lit & Hist Soc; Bd Assoc Artists of NC. 13: Yes. 14: A-v, art, admin, recruiting. 15: Box 851, Carthage NC 28327.

ANDERSON, HOPE. b Boston Mass 21 D 37. 5: Russell Sage 56-60 (Nutrition) BS; Worcester Jr Col 66-67 (Liberal Arts); Simmons 67-69 (LS) MS. 6: Fr. 7: Child libn: Worcester pub Lib, Worcester Mass 61-2, Tatnuck Br Lib 62-64, Greendale Br Lib 64-67, Child libn Morrill Mem Lib, Norwood Mass 69-. 9: ALA; MassLA. 14: Child lit, storytelling, lib displays. 15: 851 Coventry lane, Norwood Ma 02062.

ANDERSON, ISABELLE T. b Conifer Colo 13 Ag 05. 5: UColo 24-27 (Eng) BA; UIll 29-30 BS in LS; UUtah 54 (Hist). 7: Asst libn UColo Sch of Med 27-29; Libn Ramsey Co Med Soc, St Paul 30-47; Med libn UUtah 47-55; Libn Denver Med Soc 56-60; Dept head NLM 60-61; Asst libn Washington U Sch of Med (St Louis) 61-65; Libn St Joseph's Hosp Med Lib, Phoenix 65-. 8: Tchg: UMinn Lib Sch 37-47; Col of St Catherine Lib Sch 45-47; Denver U Lib Sch 54-60; Cath U Lib Sch 60. 9: MedLA (pres 58-59); ArizLA. 10: Altrusa. 13: Yes. 14: Admin. 15: St Joseph's Hosp, 350 W Thomas rd, Phoenix Az 85001.

ANDERSON, JAMES DOIG. b Caldwell Ida 22 N 40. 5: Harvard 59-63 (Hist) BA; Columbia 63-64 MLS, 68-. 7: Asst libn Sheldon Jackson Jr Col sitka Alaska 64-66; Libn 66-68; Ref libn Lib Assn of Portland, Portland Ore 68; Stud & tchr Columbia Sch of Lib Sci 68-. 9: ALA; AlaskaStateLA. 11: Joseph Towne Wheeler Award, R Krystyna Dietrich Award 64, Columbia. 14: Tchg, bibliog. 15: 148 W 92 st apt 1A, New York NY 10025.

ANDERSON, JAMES F. b Prairie Miss 22 My 41. 5: Miss State U 59-64 Math BS; La State U 65-66 (LS) MS. 7: Circ Asst Miss State U 63-64; Res Asst LSU Lib 65-66; Hd Catlgr Ark State U Lib 66-. 9: ALA; ArkLA (v-chm Col & Univ Div); NEArkLA; Ark Co on Lib Educ. 10: Lions Club. 14: Admin, catlg, acquis. 15: Box 448, State U Ar 72467.

ANDERSON, MRS JEAN R (HOLCOMB RUGEN). b Bronxville NY 24 Jl 28. 4: Eric R Anderson. 5: St Lawrence U 45-49 (Govt, Eng) BA; Columbia 50 (Educ); Newark Col of Engnr 58 Ind-Chem Tech Certif; Columbia MSLS. Drexel Inst of Tech (Info Sci). 6: Fr. 7: Ed asst McGraw-Hill Publ Co, NYC 49-50; Libn Avion Div ACF Ind Inc, Paramus NJ 55-56; Asst libn W L Maxon Corp, NYC 56; Libn W R Grace & Co Polymer Chem Div, Clifton NJ 57-61; Ref libn Bell Telephone Labs, Whippany NJ 62; Libn Mobil Res & Dev Corp, Central Research Div, Princeton NJ 62-. 9: SLA; ASIS; ACS (Div Chem Lit). 10: Beta Phi Mu; Pi Delta Epsilon; Pi Beta Phi. 14: Admin, sci-tech ref, machine-aided lib operations. 15: 337 Glenn ave Lawrence Twp, Trenton NJ 08638.

ANDERSON, JOHN F(IRTH). b Saginaw Mich 5 O 28. 4: Patricia Goble. 5: Mich State U 46-49 (Hist, Pol Sci) BA; UIll 49-50 MS in LS. 7: Yp libn Enoch Pratt Free Lib, Baltimore 50-52; Baltimore Co Pub Lib, Towson Md: Bkmob libn 52-54, Area libn 54, Supv of adult wk 55, Asst Co libn 56-58; Dir Knoxville Pub Lib, Knoxville Tenn 58-62; Dir Tucson Pub Lib 62-68; City Libn San Francisco Pub Lib 68-. 8: Survey of lib bldgs, Flagstaff Ariz 67. 9: ALA (Coun 61-65, chm Coun Apprtmt Com 63 & 65);-PLA (Bd 61-65, chm Pub Lib Activ Com 64-65);-LAD (Bd 64-65, chm Lib Org & Mgt Sect 64-65, chm Lib Devel Com 63 & 65 61-65, chm Pub Lib Activ Com 64-65);-LAD (Bd 64-65, chm Lib Org & Mgt Sect 64-65, chm Lib Devel Com 63 & 65; chm Org Com 65-66); MdLA (rec sec 54); TennLA (Exec Bd 59-, pres Pub Libs Sect 59-60, chm Lib Devel Com 60-61); SELA (chm Lib Devel Com 61); Ariz State LA (Exec Bd 63-, pres Pub Libs Sect 64-65, chm Lib Devel Com 65-); SWLA (chm Policy Com 65-). 12: 'Trauma & Triumph in Tucson' in "The Library Reaches Out," ed by Kate Copeland & Edwin Castagna. 13: Yes. 14: Pub lib admin, lib devel. 15: 280 San Benito way, San Francisco Ca 94127.

ANDERSON, JOSEPH C. b Ga 8 N 15. 5: UDenver 48 (Music Educ) BME, 51 (Music Educ) MME; UGa (Eng) AB Educ; UDenver 60 (LS) MA. 6: Fr. 7: Military Service Clsf & Assignment Off in Personnel (Lt Col) USAF Training Command 42-46; Stud UDenver 46-48; Music tchr Denver Pub Schs 48-60, Libn 60-. 9: ALA; ColoASchL; ColoEA; Denver ClrTA. 10: Reserve Officers Assn. 14: Ref. 15: 1209 Pennsylvania st, Denver Co 80203.

ANDERSON, JOSEPH JAMES. b Dubuque Iowa 28 Je 32. 5: St MarysU (Tex) 49-53 (Hist) BA; UCal (Berkeley) 60-61 MLS. 6: Sp, Fr, Ger, Lat. 7: US Navy LCDR; CIC/Radio/Communications 54-60; Supv br libn Lockheed Missiles & Space Co, Van Nuys Cal 61-64; Manager Tech processes sect Ampex Corp, Redwood City Cal 64-67; Dir Ref Serv Div Nev State Lib, Carson City Nev 67-. 9: SLA; CalLA; NevLA (v-pres Acad & Spec Libs Sect). 10: Carson City Ormsby Co Friends of Lib 68-69. 13: Yes. 14: Acquis, catlg, systems devel, ref, automation. 15: Boot Hill Ranch 5959 Sedge rd, Carson City Nv 89701.

ANDERSON, SISTER JOSEPH MARIA SSND. b New Orleans La 30 S 29. 5: LoyolaU (New Orleans) 49-55 (Educ) BS; Immaculate Heart Col 55-61 (LS) MA. 7: Elem sch tchr Our Lady of Good Counsel Sch, New Orleans 49-55; Elem sch tchr St Aloysius Sch, Tulare Cal 55-61; Asst libn, period libn, a-v libn Notre Dame Col (St Louis) 61-66; Periods libn UDallas 66-67, Hd libn 67-. 9: ALA; CathLA; TexLA; DallasCoLA. 13: Yes. 14: Periods, ref, a-v wk. 15: Rte 2 Box 4, Irving Tx 75060.

ANDERSON, LE MOYNE W. b Wheaton Minn 16 Ag 23. 4: Hollis Pearson. 5: Gustavus Adolphus Col 42-43, 46 (Hist); UMinn 41-42, 46-48 (Hist) BA, 47-48 BSLS; UIll 50-51 (LS) MS, 66-69 (LS). 6: Fr. 7: (Sgt) US Army, US, Africa, Europe 42-45; Ser libn Iowa State U 48-50; UIll (Chicago): Lib adv 51-52, Coun libn 52-55, Ref libn 55-57; Dir of Libs Colo State U 57-. 8: Surveyor, West Wash State Col 62; Consul, Mesa Col65; Casper Col, 66; Adams State Col, 67; Pres Bibliog Center for Research, Denver63-65. 9: ALA (Coun, Purchasing Com, Reg Memb Com);-LAD (chm); -ACRL (Nat Libweek, Internat Relations 67-70);-RSD (Publ Bd 68-70); Chicago Lib Club (treas);IllLA; ColoLA (Exec Com); MPLA; Rocky Mtn Bibliog Ctr for Research (pres 63-65). 10: Amer Scandinavian Found; Alpha Tau Omega; Lions Internat; AAUP; Col Assoc UnivPress (Bd Dirs 61-). 12: Ed "SORT," ALA (55-57); "Report of a Survey of the Western Washington State College Library," with E W Erickson (62); "A Guide to Theses at Colorado State University," with W F Lindgren (63). 13: Yes. 14: Ref, personnel, admin, automation. 15: 2000 Orchard pl, Fort Collins Co 80521.

ANDERSON, MAMIE (LEEPER). b Webster Co Ky 1 D 11. 4: Vernon Anderson. 5: West Ky State Col 30-33 (LS) AB; Peabody summer 63-66 MLS. 7: Libn Freed-Hardeman I Henderson Tenn 35-40; Circ libn Murray State U 53-54, Ser libn 57-. 9: KyLA; FDLA; ALA (chm Col & Ref Sect KLA 69). 10: Murray Col High Sch PTA (pres 50-51). 14: Ser, humanities. 15: College Farm rd, Murray Ky 42071.

ANDERSON, MARGARET ROBERTA. b Los Angeles 15 S 21. 5: UCLA 40-43 (Eng, Hist, Pol Sci) BA; UCal (Berkeley) 44-45 (LS) Certif. 7: Libn I Santa Monica Pub Lib, Santa Monica Cal 45-47; Asst libn Gonzaga U Lib 47-50; Catlgr-abstractor The Rand Corp, Santa Monica Cal 51-52, Libn 52-62; Supv tech info center Nortronics Div of Northrop Corp, Palos Verdes Cal 62-63; Chief Libn No Amer Aviation Sci Center, Thousand Oaks Cal 63-. 9: SLA (chm Sci-Tech Div 61-62, mem Publ Com 57-62, chm Resolutions Com 67-68,pres SoCal chap 56-57). 10: Pilot Club Internat; Santa Monica Club. 13: Yes. 14: Ind lib org & mgt, machine applications to lib ref. 15: 6366 W 84th pl, Los Angeles Ca 90045.

ANDERSON, MARILYN CLAIRE (LYNNE). b St Joseph Mo 8 D 25. 5: UTulsa 44-48 (Speech, Drama) BA; Smith 50-52 (Drama) MA; UWash 60-63 MALS. 6: Fr. 7: Artist-designer Multicolor Silk Screen Co, Tulsa Okla 48-49; Interior decorator-artist Cathey Furniture Co, Tulsa Okla 49-50; Tchr speech & drama Annie Wrights Sem, Tacoma Wash 55-56; Cadet libn-publicity-artist Prince George's Co Lib, Bladensburg Md 56-57; Cadet libn Multnomah Co Lib, Portland Ore 58-59; Libn Everett High Sch, Everett Wash 5967; Media libn Skagut Valley Commun Col, Mt Vernon Wash 67-68; Assoc libn North Country Commun Col, Saranac Lake NY 68-. 9: NEA; WashEA; Wash State SchLA. 11: Fulbright Fellowship to England. 13: Yes. 14: Ref, pub rel. 15: Star Rt Box 980 Arcadia, Marysville Wa 98270.

ANDERSON, MARTHA (PARKER). b Gainesville Fla 16 F 23. 4: William N Anderson Sr. 5: Tenn StateU 43 (Hist, Soc Sci) BS; Temple 51-54 (LS). 6: Fr. 7: Tchr Lincoln high Sch, Gainesville Fla 46-55; Libn Carver Elem Sch, Miami Fla 54-66; Libn Horace Mann Jr High, Miami Fla 66-. 8: Committee on Book Selection Miami Librarians Miami 1968-69 and 1969-70. 9: NEA; FlaEA; DCTA. 10: Alpha Phi Alpha Aux; Jack and Jill. 14: Catlg, child libn. 15: 3249 NW 51 st, Miami Fl 33142.

ANDERSON, MARY (SAMPSON). b Seattle 8 F 21. 4: Glen H Anderson. 5: UCal (Berkeley) 39-43 (Anthropology) AB; Lewis & Clark Col 51-52 (Elem Educ); San Jose State Col summer 57, 63; UCal (Berkeley) 61-62 MLS. 6: Fr. 7: Page Richmond Pub Lib, Richmond Cal 39-43; Soc wker Amer Red Cross, Richmond Cal 45-47; Serv rep Pacific Telephone, Portland Ore 47-51; Elem tchr pub schs, Eugene Ore 52-56; Elem tchr pub schs, San Leandro Cal 56-61; Libn pub schs, Oakland Cal 62-68; Libn pub schs, San Leanbro Cal 68-. 8: Consul for Wkshop on Cultural Diversity: UCal 63; Sch of Libnship, San Francisco 64. 9: Cal Tchrs Assn; CalASchL. 10: Oakland Educ Assn; Town Affiliation Com; Civic Music Assn. 14: Child lit. 15: 1505 Bancroft ct, San Leandro Ca 94578.

ANDERSON, MARY CHRISTINE. b Rockford Ill 23 Ap 40. 5: No IllU 58-62 (Geog) BS in Educ, 64-66 (LS) MA. 7: Tchr E Rockford High Sch 62-64; Catlgr No IllU 66-. 9: ALA; SLA; IllLA. 10: AAUW; Rockford Hist Soc; Swedish Cultural Soc of Amer; Beta Sigma Phi. 14: Catlg (microforms, law, geography), univ libs. 15: 1259 N Main st, Rockford Il 61103.

ANDERSON, MARY JANE (McPHERSON). b Des Moines Iowa 23 Ja 35. 4: Charles Robert Anderson. 5: UFla 53-57 (Ed) BAE; Fla State U 59-63 MS in LS. 7: Elem sch libn Oak Grove Elem Sch Miami Fla 57-61; Reg child libn Santa Fe Reg Lib Gainesville Fla 61-63; Br libn Jacksonville Pub Lib Jacksonville Fla 63-64; Chief child serv Jacksonville Pub Lib Jacksonville Fla 64-67; Pub Lib Consul Fla State Lib 67-. 9: ALA; SELA; FlaLA (chm Recruit Com62-63, chm Sch & Child's Div 63-64). 10: Girl Scouts of Amer; Beta Phi Mu (presGamma Chap 67-68); Fla Comm for Child & Youth 65-, (Exec Bd 67-); Fla State U Libsch Alum Assn (past sec). 12: Ed "Fla State Library Newsletter" (67). 13: Yes. 14: Child & young adult serv. 15: 242 Lafayette Cir, Tallahassee Fl 32303.

ANDERSON, MAY KATHERINE (ARMSTRONG). b Greenville Tex 1 N 17. 5: TSCW 34-38 (LS) BA; TWU 58 MLS. 6: Fr, Lat. 7: Libn Eng High Sch, Honey Grove Tex 38-39; Libn High Sch, Odessa Tex 39-41; Libn Midland High Sch, Midland Tex 52-54; Lib supv pub schs, Midland Tex 54-61; Libn Lee High Sch, Midland Tex 61-. 9: ALA; Tex State Tchrs Assn (chm); TexLA (State assembly mem for Sch Lib Sect 63-65); TexASchL (treas). 10: DAR; OES; KKI; PTA (Life mem). 13: Yes. 14: Admin, sch libs. 15: 4311 W Dengar, Midland Tx 79701.

ANDERSON, MILDRED M(ARIE) (FORNEY). b Pontiac Ill 2 F 17. 4: Carl E Anderson. 5: Eureka Col 33-36; Ill Wesleyan U 36-37 (Eng) AB; UIll 37-38 BS in LS. 7: Asst libn McPherson Col 38-40; Libn Ind Central Col 40-42; Libn Manchester Col 42-45; Chief Libn VA, Dwight Ill 52-59; Libn Flanagan Commun Unit No 4, Flanagan Ill 60-. 9: IllASchL. 10: UIll Lib Assn. 15: Flanagan Il 61740.

ANDERSON, OLGA (SHKLANKA). b Hafford Saskatchewan Can 20 Je 31. 4: Peter George Anderson. 5: USask 47-50 (Biol) BA, 50-51 (Educ); UAlta summers 53-55 (Eng) B Ed; UWash 55-56 MLS. 6: Fr, Ukrainian. 7: High sch tchr Nipawin Sch Dist, Carrot River Sask Can 51-52; High sch tchr Lloydminster Sch Dist, Neilburg Sask Can 52-53; High sch tchr, Thorsby Alta Can 53-55; High sch libn Mercer Island Sch Dist, Mercer Island Wash 56-61; High sch libn Jasper Place Composite High Sch, Edmonton Alta Can 61-64; Sch lib consul Red Deer Pub Sch Dist, Red Deer Alta Can 64-65; Acting hd ref dept Cameron Lib, UAlberta 68-69, Hd ref dept 69-. 8: Instr in Lib Sci UAlta summers 61-62, winter ext 63 & 65 Instr in child lit, summer 67; Instr in LSUAlberta summer 68. 9: ALA; CanSchLA (Prov Rep 62-64, Coun 63-64); Alta Tchrs Assn (Sch Lib Spec Coun: Dir 64-65). 12: Ed "Moccasin Telegraph," CanSchLA (63-64); Ed "Alberta School Library Review," Alta Tchrs Assn (65-67). 14: Yp lit, ref. 15: #1 Selkirkblvd, Red Deer Alberta Can.

ANDERSON, PAULINE H. b Broadalbin NY 27 N 18. 5: Keuka Col 35-39 (Eng) BA; SUNY (Albany) 43 BLS. 7: Chrm-libn Perth Central Sch Perth NY 39-41; Tchr-libn Andover Cen Sch Andover NY 41-44; Head Eng Dept Ilion Sr High Sch Ilion NY 44-46; Libn Abbot Acad Andover Mass 46-50; Co-Dir Andrew Mellon Lib Choate Sch Wallingford Conn 50-. 8: Consul to Eaglebrook Sch Deerfield Mass 63-64; Lib Com of Nat Assn Indep Sch 52-61. 9: ALA; NESchLA; ConnSchLA; Nat Assn Independent Schs (Lib Com 52-61). 12: Ed 1,000 Bks for Indep Sch Libs, publ by Secondary Educ Bd 55; Mem of com to edit 3,000 Bks for Secondary Sch Libs, Bowker 61; comp & ed "Selected Bibliography of Literautre on the Independent School pub by ISEB 59; "The Library in the Independent School (68). 13: Yes. 14: Sec sch libs. 15: The Choate School, Wallingford Ct 06493.

ANDERSON, REBA JEAN. b Chillicothe Mo 9 Mr 28. 5: UMo 52-56 (LS) AB. 7: Sec to libn Livingston Co Mem Lib, Chillicothe Mo 48-52; Stud asst UMo Lib 52-56; Asst libn & head adult serv Moline Pub Lib, Moline Ill 56-63; Asst libn order dept UMo Lib 63-. 9: ALA; MoLA. 10: Phi Beta Kappa. 13: Yes. 14: Bibliog, ref. 15: 1503 Anthony st, Columbia Mo 65201.

ANDERSON, ROBERT G. b Kenosha Wis 17 Ja 43. 5: U Wis Kenosha 61-63 (Eng); Dominican Col Racine 63-65 (Eng) BA; Rosary Col 65-67 MALS. 6: Fr. 7: Dominican Col, Racine Wis: Catlgr 67-68, Asst libn & acquis libn. 10: Explorer Post Advisor. 14: Catlg, tchg. 15: 3624 19th ave, Kenosha Wi 53140.

ANDERSON, ROBERTA (CONKLIN). b Seattle 24 Ag 13. 4: Lyle Anderson. 5: UWash 31-40 (Sociol) BA, BA in LS; Ore Gen Ext 59-65 (Educ); UCal (Berkeley) 64 (LS). 6: Fr, Ger. 7: Jr libn UWash 38-40; Libn Ft Stevens Jr High Sch, Hammond Ore 61-62; Libn Clatsop Commun Col 62-. 8: Ketchikan Alaska, Pub Lib Bd 41-49 (pres 4 yrs). 9: ALA; OreLA. 10:

4-H Leader. 12: "Bibliography of the Community-Junior College" (67). 13: Yes. 14: Ref, org. 15: P O Box 354, Warrenton Or 97146.

ANDERSON, ROSE K (KEMMER). b Rhea County Tenn 23 D 15. 5: UChattanooga 31-34 AB; Columbia summer 35; Rutgers Grad Sch of LS 63-65 MLS. 7: Tchr Pub Schs, Chattanooga tenn 35-37; Gen asst Hi Williams Studio, NYC 37-42; Ref circ libn Queens Col, charlotte NC 65-67, Act libn 67-68, Libn 68-. 9: ALA. 15: 3318 Windsor dr, Charlotte NC 28209.

ANDERSON, ROSEMARY (ERDODY). b Detroit Mich 15 O 42. 4: Raymond E Anderson. 5: Marygrove Col 60-64 (Eng) BA; UMich 64-66 MALS. 7: Pre-Prof Detroit Pub Lib 65-66; Child libn 66-. 14: Child wk (pub lib). 15: 8227 Prest, Detroit Mi 48228.

ANDERSON, RUTH. b Saginaw Mich 20 O 09. 5: UMich 27-31 (Journalism) AB, 31-32 ABLS. 7: Asst loan desk Butman Fish Lib, Saginaw Mich 32-37, Libn in chg 37-43; Libn in chg US Naval Air Station, Grosse Ile Mich 43-45; 1st asst catlg dept Pub Lib, Saginaw Mich 47-63, Chief home reading 63-. 9: ALA; MichLA. 10: AAUW; Chi Omega; Theta Sigma Phi. 14: Catlg, circ. 15: 2317 Adams blvd, Saginaw Mi 48602.

ANDERSON, SARAH (PARK). b Canonsburg Penn 23 D 08. 4: John L Anderson. 5: Col of Wosster 26-30 (Math) BS; UIll 30-31 BS in LS, 34-35 (LS). 7: Catlgr Marshall U 31-34; Br asst Multnomah Co Lib, Portland Ore 49-65; Br libn Multnomah Co Lib, Portland Ore 66-. 9: ALA; PNLA; OreLA. 10: LWV; Beta Phi Mu. 14: Ref. 15: 3540 SW Hume st, Portland Or 97219.

ANDERSON, SHERMAN (AINSLIE). b Maddock ND 18 Ja 19. 5: UMinn 37-42 (Accounting) BBA; Phila Conservatory 46-50 (Theory) B Music; Drexel 50-51 MLS. 7: (1st Lt) US Army Qtrmstr Corps 42-46; Libn I art & music dept Milwaukee Pub Lib 51-55; Phonorecord catlgr Detroit Pub Lib 55-67; Mustic catlgr U Ill Lib Urbana 68-. 13: Yes. 14: Music, catlg. 15: 121 N Race, apt 10, Urbana Il 61801.

ANDERSON, STUART H Jr. b Johnson City NY 3 D 20. 4: Mary Patricia Manning Anderson. 5: St Michael's College Winooski 39-43 (Eng) (Cum Laude); Fordham 46-48 (Soc Casewk) Master of Social Service; Rutgers 65-67 Master of Lib Serv. 6: Fr. 7: CL Teletype Operator Army Air Force, US & India 43-46; Soc Casewkr Youth Counseling Serv, NYC 49; Soc Casewkr Catholic Charities, Syracuse NY 49-52; Engineering Aide NY State Dept of Pub Wks, Binghamton NY 52-54; Claim Examiner Security Mutual Life Ins Co, Binghamton NY 54-64; Sch Tchr Georgetown Central Sch, Georgetown NY 64-65; Libn NJ State Dept of Labor & Industry, Trenton NJ 66-. 9: ALA; SLA. 10: Nat Rehabil Assn; NJ Welfare Coun; NJ State Employees' Assn; MENSA. 15: 35A Hawthorne dr, Somerset NJ 08873.

ANDERSON, MRS TWILA (POSTAL). b Paton Iowa 7 Jl 23. 5: Simpson Col 41-45 (Eng) BA; Northwest Mo State 59-60 (Educ) MS; UMinn 62-63 (LS) MA. 6: Fr. 7: Tchr-libn Pub Sch, Sibley Iowa 50-55; Sch libn Pub Sch, Carroll Iowa 55-62; Asst head ext div State Travel Lib, Des Moines Iowa 63-65; Ref libn Drake U 65-. 8: State lib consul to pub libs 63-65; Fellow, Coe Found Amer Studies, summer 61. 9: Des Moines Lib Club (sec-treas). 10: Iowa Coun for Better Educ; YWCA; Sigma Tau Delta; Alpha Psi Omega. 14: Ref, pub serv. 15: 1016 37th, Des Moines Ia 50311.

ANDERSON, VERLYN DEAN. b Fergus Falls Minn 23 O 33. 4: Evonne Beastrom. 5: Concordia Col (Moorehead Minn) 52-56 (Hist) BA; UMinn summers 58-62 (Curriculum) MA, summers 62-65 MALS; UMinn summers 66, 67, 66-67 (Amer Studs). 6: Norwegian. 7: Music libn Nels Vogel Inc, Moorehead Minn 55-57; Sch libn Hawley Pub Schs, Hawley Minn 57-58; Eng tchr Waconia Minn 58-62; Asst libn Carl B Ylvisaker Lib Concordia Col 62-68, Chief libn 68-. 9: ALA; MinnLA; Amer Studies Assn. 10: AAUP; Norwegian-Amer Hist Assn. 14: Bk selection, acquis, lib admin, bldgs. 15: Carl B Ylvisaker Lib Concordia Col, Moorhead Mn 56560.

ANDERSON, WILMA J. b Canon Ga 12 Ap 19. 5: Paine Col & Seneca Jr Col 39-40; Spelman Col 47-50 (Eng, Psycg) AB; Atlanta 58 MSLS. 7: Tech clerk (Cpl) USAAF (WAC) 43-45; Tchr Toccoa Col Sch, Toccoa Ga 47; Tchrjefferson Co Train Sch, Louisville Ga 50-51; Tchr Hubbard Train Sch, Forsyth Ga 51-53;Res libn Atlanta U 55-56; Libn Fla Normal & Ind Col 56-57; Tchr-libn Bruce St Sch, DeKalb Co Ga 57-58; The Fort Valley State Col; Circ libn 58-60, libn educ div 60-63, Tchr of Lib Sci 63-. 9: ALA; GTEA (Libns sect); SELA. 11: Zeta Phi Beta "Woman of the Year"; Alpha Phi Alpha "Citizenship AchievementAward" (65); Omega Psi Phi Plaque for Service. 15: 1301 Jones st, Fort Valley Ga 31030.

ANDERSSON, LISELOTTE N. b Posen Germany 16 Ag 16. 4: Dr Knud D Andersson. 5: UCologne 36-40 Lib degree; West-German Lib Sch. 6: Ger, Fr, Ital. 7: Libn Volksbucherei Trier, Germany 40, Head Libn in chg 41-44; Libn Elem Sch Lib Newman Sch, New Orleans 56-57; Libn Thomas F Cunningham Ref Lib, international House 59-62; Music libn Maxwell Music Lib Tulane U 62-. 9: Mus LA; New Orleans Lib Club. 14: Music. 15: Maxwell Music Lib, Tulane U, New Orleans La 70118.

ANDERTON, LILLIAN (DICKINSON). b Memphis Tenn 9 Je 16. 5: Hollins Col 32-33; St Mary of the Woods 33-36 (Hist, Eng) BA; Catholic U 33-40 (Educ) Life tchg Credential; Peabody 41 BS in LS; San Jose State 58 (Fine Arts); Sacramento State 64, 65 (Art, Short Story); UUtah 65 (Hist) UCal (Davis) 66-67 (Pol Sci). 6: Lat, Fr. 7: Org Philos Lib Dominican Order, Nashville 42; Ref main br New Orleans Pub Lib 49; Org lib Child Country Sch, Los Gatos Cal 50; Org & trained nuns to run Madeleine Sch Lib, Berkeley Cal 56; Holy Names Col & Prep Sch, evaluated & prepared for state accreditation 57; Raskob Reading Found, org & trained successor, Oakland Cal 60; Ref libn Amer River Jr Col 63-. 8: TV Reading Program sponsored by Jewish Charities, Memphis Tenn 49. Mem survey of 25 USIS libs in Asia,Africa, So Europe 66; various one-man shows 44-60. 9: NEA; CathLA (sec Tenn Unit); Internat Reading Assn (Bay Area Coun: Pub, v-pres 60); CalLA; Cal Tchrs Assn; Cal Jr Col Assn. 10: AAUP; Newman Club Sponsor;Amer River Col Acad Senate; Bd mem Le Petit Theatre du Vieux Carre, New Orleans. 12: Co-ed "Los Rios Dist Faculty Assn Org. 13: Yes. 14: Ref, archives. 15: 3434 Thirteenth st, Sacramento Ca 95818.

ANDO, JEAN ELIZABETH (KUNTZ). b Rochester NY 24 S 40. 4: Hirofumi Ando. 5: Earlham Col 58-60; Internat ChristianU (Tokyo) 60-61; UMich 61-63 BA (Far East Studies), AMLS. 6: Japanese, Fr, Ger. 7: Libn I UMich Lib Ext Serv 64-67; Ext child libn Ann Arbor Pub Lib, Ann Arbor Mich 68-. 9: ALA. 14: Ref, child. 15: 966 Manhattan ave, Dayton Oh 45406.

ANDRE, LESLIE T. b Budapest Hungary 16 Ja 15. 4: Ilona Baan. 5: Gymnazium 34 (Liberal Arts) Baccalaureat; Royal Hungarian Francz Josef U 40 (Law, Pol Sci) Dr rer Pol; West Mich U 62 (LS) MA. 6: Fr, Ger, Lat, Hungarian. 7: Hungarian Govt Employee Ministry of Agric, Budapest 37-38 (1st Lt) R HungarianArmy 39-45; Catlgr Hd Ser & Doc Dept, Asst prof East Ill U 62-. 14: Catlg, rare bks,ser, maps, art. 15: 2 Harrison, Charleston Il 61920.

ANDREASSEN, JOHN C(HRISTIAN) L(UDVIG). b Bloomer Wis 18 Ag 09. 4: Allison Grant. 5: Stout Inst SS 26-27; Tulane 29 (Hist); UWis 27-31 (Hist) PhB; LSU 33-37 (Hist) MA. 6: Scand, Fr, Ger. 7: Tchg Asst LSU 34-37; State & reg dir Hist Rec Surv New Orleans & Ft Worth37-41; Reg field supv serv Proj WPA Ft Worth 41-43; Admin Off FWA WashDC 43-44; DPspecialist UNRRA London 44-45; UNRRA Rep to Sweden Stockholm 45; Dir Relief ServUNRRA Mission to Austria Vienna 45-46; Dir Admin LC 46-52; Chief aeronut div & ChairAeronaut LC 52-53; Assoc dir State Archives Surv Baton Rouge La 55-56; Rec consulto La Attorn Gen, Sec of State & Compt Baton Rouge 56-58; Dir State Archives ofRec Commn Baton Rouge 58-60; Consul Bur Govt Res New Orleans 61; Archivist Can NatRailways 62-67; Univ archivist McGill U 68-. 9: Can Hist Assn (Fellow); SAA; OAH;SHA; Nat Trust Hist Preserva; LaHA; La Landmarks Soc. 10: Hist Assn Montreal; Quebec Heritage. 12: "Internal Improvements in Louisiana 1824-1837" (47); "The Library of Congress and Its Work" ed.; "Paperwprk Records Management in new Orleans" (61); "Louisiana Archives Survey Reports No. 1 and 2" (56); "Newsletter The Louisiana historical Association" Vol 1 (58-59). 13: Yes. 14: Admin, elec data proc, archives & rec mgt. 15: 65 rue St-Louis, St-Eustache, Quebec.

ANDRENE, SISTER CSJB. b Bronx NY 11 S 14. 5: Fordhams 47 (Hist) BS in Ed; St Johns U 51 (LS) BLS, 60-63 (Art). 6: Ital. 7: Tchr, libn Cath Sch, Staten Is NY 47-58; Tchr, libn St John's Villa Acad, NYC 58-60; Tchr, libn Mt St John Acad, Gladstone NJ 60-62; Libn Alphonsus Col, Woodcliff Lk, NJ 62-. 8: Consul: On plans for new library in Woodcliff Lake Township NJ; on lib affairs for Berkeley Bus Sch, East Orange NJ. 9: ALA; CathLA; NJLA; BergenCoLA. 14: Admin, ref, bk sel. 15: Alphonsus Col, Woodcliff LAKE NJ 07675.

ANDREW, DOROTHY S. b Ft Worth Tex 1 Ag 21. 5: Tex Woman's U 38-43 (LS) BA, 63-68 MLS. 6: Fr, Sp. 7: Tex

Woman's U, Asst catlgr 43-45;Bks catlgr Tex A&M U 45-49; Catlgr Peabody Museum of Arch & Ethn Lib Harvard U49-50; Tex A&M U; Bks catlgr 59-60, Ser catlgr 60-63, Ser libn 63-. 8: Catlg of deptl libs Tex A&M U, 54; Consul (unofficial) Veterinary Col Lib, Dacca E Pakistan 54-56. 9: TexLA (sec-treas Col Libs Div 47-48). 14: Catlg, ser acquis. 15: 600 Welsh,College Station Tx 77840.

ANDREWS, BARBARA PARKER. b Nantucket Mass 18 Mr 18. 5: Simmons 40-44 (LS) BS. 7: Catlgr UCincinnati Lib 44-46; LC: Prel catlgr 46-47, Ser catlgr 47-50, Admin asst Descr Catlgr Div 50-62, Research asst Descr Catlg Div 63-65; Libn Nantucket Atheneum, Nantucket Mass 65-. 9: ALA. 15: 1 E York st, Nantucket Ma 02554.

ANDREWS, BERNICE CORNELIA. b Spring Creek Tenn 20 Ag 01. 5: Union U 19-21, 26-27 (Eng, Math) BA (cum laude); Peabody 39-43 BS in LS. 7: Tchr Spring Creek Sch Spring Creek Tenn 21-26; Tchr Mercer High Sch mercer Tenn 26-33; Tchr Pope High Sch Jackson Tenn 33-43; Asst libn Memphis State Memphis Tenn summer 47; Reg lib wk UTenn summer 49; Libn North Side High Sch Jackson Tenn 43-. 8: Helped org libs for Madison Co (Tenn) elem schs, summer 66. 9: NEA; West Tenn Libns Assn (sec 47, v-pres 48, pres 49); TennEdA. 10: OES sec chapter 378; Treas Spring Creek Baptist Church; UDC; Delta Kappa Gamma. 14: Catlg, ref. 15: Spring CreekTn 38378.

ANDREWS, CHARLES R(OLLAND). b Scranton Penn 5 Jl 30. 4: Harriet Williams. 5: Bloomsburg State Col (Penn) 50-54 (Eng) BS in Ed; UOkla 56-59 (Eng) MA; WestRes 63-64 MSLS, 64-67 (Lib Sci, Eng) PhD. 6: Fr, Sp. 7: Army (Penn Nat Guard)Heavy Mortar Co. 109th Inf (Sgt) 47-50; Eng tchr Pennsbury High Sch Yardley Penn54-56; Tchg asst UOkla Dept Eng 56-59; Instr Eng Westminster Col (New WilmingtonPenn) 59-63; Ref libn Cleveland Pub Lib 64-66, Hd Gen Ref Dept 66-68; Chief of refserv Freiberger Lib Case West Res 68-69, Libn 69-. 9: Mod Lang Assn; OhioLA; ALA. 12: Abstracter for "Abstracts of English Studies" (61-). 13: Yes. 14: Ref, bibliog, admin. 15: 2528 Overlook rd, Cleveland Heights Oh 44106.

ANDREWS, CLAIRE (LOUISE). b St Paul Minn 21 Ap 43. 5: Cottey Col 61-62; UWyo 62-66 (Hist) BA; UMich 66-67 AMLS. 6: Fr. 7: Ser catlgr UIpwa (Iowa City) 67-68, Math libn 68-. 9: SLA. 10: United Campus Christ Movement. 14: Ref. 15: Mathematics Lib, Univ of Iowa, Iowa City Ia 52240.

ANDREWS, ELLIOTT E. b Springfield Mass 28 N 21. 4: Constance K Hurley. 5: Brown 41-43, 46-47 BA, 48-49 MA; URI 64 (LS). 7: US Army (Sgt) 42-45; In chg soc studies BrownU 49-51; Libn Providence Journal Co, Providence 51, 53-62; US Army (1st Lt) 51-52; State libn & State Record Commsnr RI State Lib 62-. 8: Lecturer, SyracuseU wkshop on newspaper libs, 60; SLA Consul for newspaper libs 60-. 9: SLA (v-chm Newspaper Div); ALA-AAStateL; AALL; NELA; RILA; SAA. 10: New England Coun; RI Hist Soc; BrownU Alumni Assn; BrownU Club of RI. 13: Yes. 14: Ref, legis & law. 15: RI State Lib State House, Providence RI 02903.

ANDREWS, ELOISE. b Ozark Ala 5 Mr 01. 5: Ala Col 19-22 (Eng); UAla 24-25 (Eng) AB, summers 59-61 (LS) MA. 6: Fr. 7: chr Pinckard Pub Sch, Pinckard Ala 18-19; Gist tchr Jr High Sch, Selma Ala 24-5; Eng & Lat tchr Sr High Sch, Evergreen Ala 27; Eng tchr Sidney Lanier High Sch, Montgomery Ala 27-60, Hd of lib 60-. 9: NEA; AlaEA; MontgomeryTA; ClrTA; AlaLA. 10: Delta Kappa Gamma; Delta Kappa Pi. 14: Catlg, admin. 15: 1524 S Court st, Montgomery Al 36104.

ANDREWS, MRS HELEN (RILLING). b Erie Penn 4 Mr 09. 4: Cecil Bradly Andrews. 5: Lake Erie Col 27-31 9hist) BA; Columbia 31-32 (LS) BS. 7: Erie Pub Lib, Erie Penn: Asst catlg dept 37-40, Head ext dept 40-49, Asst libn 48-49, Libn 49-. 9: ALA; PennLA (Lib Dev Com). 10: Erie Co Hist Soc; AAUW; Jr League; Art Club ofErie Internat Inst; Booker T Washington Ctr. 14: Admin. 15: 630 W 9 st, Erie Pa 16502.

ANDREWS, JAMES C(RANDALL). b Phila 18 Ap 21. 4: Katherine Hamrick. 5: UNC 38-42 (Physics) BS; UIll 46-47 BSLS, 47-48 MSLS. 6: Ger, Sp. 7: Electronics engnr US Naval Research Lab, Wash DC 42-46; Acquis asst UIll Lib (Urbana) 47-48; Libn Union Carbide Nuclear, Oak Ridge Tenn 48-50; Supv of tech info serv E I duPont Savannah River Lab, Aiken SC 51-58; Lib Dir Argonne Nat Lab, Argonne Ill 59-. 8: SLA Prof Consul; UIll Sch of Lib Sci Adv Coun, 65-68 Ford Found Lib Consul in Central Amer; mem Ill State Bd of Higher Educ Lib Com. 9: SLA (Spec Rep to ALA Interlib Loan Com 63-, chm Sci-Tech Div Nuclear Sci Sect 63-64); ADI. 10: Appalachian Mountain Club; Amer Philatelic Soc; Intl Soc of Guatemala Collectors (pres). 13: Yes. 14: Automation in spec libs, lib developt in Central Amer. 15: Argonne Nat Lib 9700 S Cass ave, Argonne Il 60439.

ANDREWS, JEAN (MATILDA). b Kewanee Ill 16 S 19. 5: Knox Col 37-41 (Hist) AB; West Res 42-43 BLS. 6: Fr, Ger. 7: Ref libn Ill State Lib 43-45; Lib Asst Hamtramck Pub Lib Hamtramck Mich 45-46; Lib asst River Forest Pub Lib River Forest Ill 46-47; Bkmob libn Ill State Lib 47-49; Ref libn Pontiac City Lib Pontiac Mich 49-55; Br libn Pontiac Mich 55-66; Head libn Waterford Twp Lib Pontiac Mich 66-. 9: MLA. 10: Zonta Club; Women's City Club (Detroit). 14: Ref. 15: 100 W Hickory Grove rd apt D-4, Bloomfield Hills Mi 48013.

ANDREWS, MRS MARGARET (BUTTERFIELD). b Middletown Ohio 28 F 05. 4: Herbert W Andrews. 5: URochester 22-26 (Hist) AB, 27-28 (Hist) AM; Columbia 37 (LS) BS. 6: Lat, Fr, Ger. 7: URochester Lib: Asst clsf 29-31, Head clsf 31-48, Head ref dept & curator of local hist & univ archives 48-55, Asst libn in chg of spec collections 55-. 9: ALA; NYLA; Five Associated Univ Lib. 10: Rochester Memorial Art Gallery; Rochester Civic Music Assn; Rochester Museum Assn. 11: Phi Beta Kappa; Fellow Rochester Museum of Arts & Sci. 12: Assoc ed "University of Rochester Library Bulletin." 13: Yes. 14: Hist mss, rare bks, archives. 15: 575 Drumm rd, Webster NY 14580.

ANDREWS, MARGARET SUSANNA. b Pine Island Minn 28 Ap 01. 4: Raymond C Andrews. 5: UMinn 21-26 (Law) LLB. 7: Off mgr Lindstrom Coop, Lindstrom Minn 38-52; Legislative Clerk Gov of Minn, 53; State Law Libn State of Minn 53-. 9: AALL (Exec Bd, Publicity Chm); SLA; MinnLA. 10: Minn Cong Parents & Tchrs; Bus & Prof Women; Amer Leg Aux; Lindstrom Study Club; Lindstrom Lib Bd. 15: Lindstrom Mn 55045.

ANDREWS, MELDA (LEATRICE). b Proctor Tex 4 Ap 30. 4: Ernest Charles Andrews. 5: Tarleton Jr Col 47-48 (Chem); UTexas 48-50, 64, 65 (Math) BA; Incarnate Word Col 65-66 (Educ); Our Lady of the Lake Col 66-67 MS in LS. 6: Ger. 7: Research asst UTex Med Br, Galveston 55-58; Math tchr Longfellow Jr High Sch, San Antonio Texas 65-66; Sci libn San Antonio Col 67-. 8: Consul, Carbon Black Proj, UTex, Med Br, Galveston 58. 9: SLA; ALA; TexLA; Bexar Co LA; Tex State Jr Col TA. 10: AAUW; Tex Med Assn Aux. 14: Catlg, bibliog, spec libs. 15: 509 East pk, Weatherford Tx 76086.

ANDREWS, PATRICIA WILSON. b Wash DC 1 My 26. 5: George WashingtonU (Psych) BA. 6: Ger. 7: Lib asst George WashingtonU OQMG Proj, wash DC 46-47; Br libn Off of the Quartermaster Gen Dept Army, Wash DC 47-48; Asst libn Operations Research Off, Wash DC 51-54; Libn CEIR, Wash DC 54-55; Chief ref br Spec Operations Research Off, Wash DC 55-57; Chief libn Inst for Defense Analysis, Arlington Va 57-67; Dir tech info & security Lambda Corp, Arlington Va 67-. 9: SLA (DC Chap Documentation Gp: treas 67-68, chm 68-69); ASIS. 10: Chi Omega. 12: "Psychological warfare in Support of Military Operations, an Annotated Bibliography, with Gwendolyn M Murphy (50). 14: Org & mgt of document collections, lib automation, indexing theory. 15: Barton House apt 721 2525 N 10th st, Arlington Va 22201.

ANDREWS, THELMA. b Lamposas Tex 10 Mr 04. 5: Hardin-SimminsU 21-25 (Sociol) BA; State U Iowa 27-28 (Sociol) MA; Chicago 44-45 (LS) MA. 7: Libn Hardin-SimmonsU 23-56; Libn Abilene Pub Lib, Abilene Tex 56-. 8: Lecturer UTex Grad Sch of Lib Sci, summer 63, 64, 65, 67. 9: ALA; TexLA (pres 57-58). 10: Abilene Womans Club; Abilene C of C. 14: Admin. 15: Abilene Pub Lib 202 Cedar st, Abilene Tx 79601.

ANDREWS, THEODORA ANNE (ULREY). b Carroll Co Ind 14 O 21. 5: Purdue U 39-40, 49-53 (Sci) BS; UIll 54-55 (LS) MS. 6: Fr, Ger. 7: Purdue U Libs; Clerk 45-52, Jr prof asst 53, Asst catlgr 55, Asst ref libn 56, Pharmacy libn 56-. 8: Tchr of Lib Sci summer courses; Syracuse U 5 (58, 59, 61, 63, 65), UIll 2 (60, 62), Ind State U 2 (67, 68). 9: ALA; ADI; MedLA (chm Pharm Group 60-61, rep to Jt Com on Pharm Col Libs 63-); Midwest Reg Group (Bd of Dirs 66-68); SLA (Bd of Dirs 66-69); Sci-Tech Div (chm Pharmaceut Sect Com on Pharmacomedical Nonserial Ind Publs 64-); Ind Chap (pres 62-63, memb chm 64-, chm Automation Conf 64); IndLA. 12: "Thesis Manual," Purdue U (64); Ed "Papers Presented at the Meeting on Automation in the Library-When, Where, and How" (64); Ed "Copnip List," SLA Pharmaceut Sect (64-); "Thesis Manuel for Students in the Pharmaceutical Sci (66). 13:

Yes. 14: Sci lit, pharmaceut lit. 15: 2209 Indian Trails dr, W Lafayette In 47906.

ANDREWS, VIVIAN F (JONES). b Sutton Neb 11 D 09. 4: Roger W Andrews. 5: UNeb 27-31 (Drama-Eng) BS in Ed, (summer) 54 (LS); UWyo summer 55 (LS); Denver U summer 59 (LS). 6: Fr, Ger. 7: Libn High Sch, Alliance Neb 43-54; Yp libn Carnegie Pub Lib Cheyenne Wyo 54-55; Libn Jr High, Alliance Neb 55-67; Lib Coord Pub Schs, Alliance Neb 67-; Libn Chadron State Col summers 56-64; Jr High libn & Lib Supv for schs, Alliance Neb 64-. 8: Tchr Welfare (chm, educ com); Western state div Neb, Lib Improvements (chm) 62 Consul Neb Educl Media Assn. 9: ALA-AASchL (Region V rep State Assembly 60-65); NEA (Local consul on citizenship com); Nat Coun of Women in Admin; NebLA (past sec). 10: AAUW (past local pres); Neb State Hist Soc; Natl Coun of Women in Educ; Alliance Educ Assn (pas pres). 14: Ref. 15: 1231 Laramie, Alliance Nb 69301.

ANDREWS, WILLIAM E(DWARD). b Portland Ore 29 N 21. 5: UOre 39-42, 46-47 (Eng) BA; UDenver 47-48 (LS) MA. 7: US Army Finance Dept, Infantry 43-44, 44-46; City Libn N Platte Pub Lib, N Platte Neb 48-56; Admin asst Pub Lib of Stockton & San Joaquin Co, Stockton Cal 56-59; Dir Washoe Co Lib, Reno Nev 59-. 9: ALA; NebLA (treas 52-54); CalLA; NevLA (treas 64-). 10: No Cal Lib Film Circuit Commsn (pres 65-); Kiwanis Internat. 14: Admin, ref. 15: 5301 Canyon dr, Reno Nv 89502.

ANDRO3CZI, FERENC FRANK. b Semje3nhaza Hungary. 5: Pazmany Peter U Budapest 45-50 (Law and Pol Sci) PhD; Syracuse 62-64 MSLS UIll 68 (Rare bks libnship). 6: Hung, Ger, Croatian-Serb, Russ, Lat, Ital. 7: Admin Naturalized Mill, Sze3csisziget Hungary 50-52; Cartographical draftsman Engnr Hdqrs US Forces in Austria 52-55; Tech Roswell Park M Inst Buffalo NY 56-60; Circ asst Syracuse 63-64; Catlgr & clsfr UDetroit 64-65; Asst libn State U Col (Fredonia NY) 65-NY) 65-67; W Va Wesleyan Col; Head of Catlg & Inst of Lib Sci 67-68; Asst Prof of Lib Sci & Head of Catlg 69-. 9: ALA; WVaLA. 10: AAUP; Commsn Concert Assn. 13: Yes. 14: Catlg, rare bks, admin. 15: 58 S Kanawha, Buckhannon W V 26201.

ANGEL, MICHAEL ROBERT COLIN. b Alberta Can 15 Mr 04. 4: Barbara Ann Jackson. 5: UAlta 58-61 (Hist) BA; UBC 62-63 BLS; UIowa 65- 9hist). 6: Fr. 7: Sub-Lt Royal Can Navy Reserve 58-62; Lib asst Edmonton Pub Lib, Edmonton Alta 61-62, Ref libn catlgr 63-65; Bkstacks libn UIowa 65-66, Res bks libn 66-67; Curriculum libn Ministry of Educ, Guyana (CUSO assignment) 67-. 9: GuyanaLA (Exec 69-). 15: 18 D Drysdale st, Georgetown Guyana, South America.

ANGELA, SISTER MARIE (KREITZ) IHM. b Akron Ohio 10 Ag 04. 5: Marygrove Col 24-35 (Educ) BS; Wayne State U 45-51 (Educ) M ED; Marygrove Col 45-53 (LS) Certif. 6: Fr, Lat, Sp. 7: Tchr-libn St Gregory Sch, Detroit 45-47; Tchr-libn St Philip High Sch, Battle Creek Mich 47-50; Tchr-libn St Mary High Sch, Mt Clemens Mich 50-53; Tchr-libn St Francis de Sales High Sch, Detroit 53-57; Tchr-libn St Matthew Elem Sch, Detroit 57-60; Tchr-libn Girls Catholic Central High Sch, Detroit 60-63; Tchr-libn Holy Redeemer High Sch, Detroit 63-. 9: CathLA (Publ Chm, Mich Unit 60-). 12: "Teens Triumphant" (66). 13: Yes. 14: Wk with high sch studs. 15: 5678 Eldred st, Detroit Mi 48209.

ANGELISSE, SISTER M (BOYCE) IHM. b Pittston Penn 29 My 25. 5: Marywood Col 43-47 (LS) AB. 6: Sp. 7: Libn Archmere Acad, Claymont Del 47-48; Elem tchr Forest Hills, LI NY 51-54; Libn Central Catholic High Sch, Kingston Penn 54-; Asst libn Marywood Col summer 51-64. 9: PennLA. 14: Ref. 15: Central Cath High Sch, Maple ave, Kingston Pa 18704.

ANGELL, LOUISE (BRYAN). b Hico Tex 17 D 02. 5: So Methodist U 19-23 (Eng) BA, 24 (Hist) MA; Tex Woman's U summers 50, 54, 57, 58; Col of Guam 65, 66 (LS). 6: Fr. 7: Head Hist Dept Westminster Jr Col 24-25; Head Eng Dept Meridian Jr Col 25-27; Head Eng Dept & Libn Hico High Sch, Hico Tex 38-62; Soc studies Tumon Jr-Sr High Sch, Guam 62-64; Eng instr Col of Guam 64-65; Asst libn George Washington Jr-Sr High Sch, Guam 64-66; Libn George Washington Jr High Sch, Guam 66-67; Libn Iredell Pub Schs,Iredell Tex 67-. 9: NCTE; Amer Acad Pol & Soc Scis; TexLA; ALA. 10: AAUW; DAR. 14: Ref, child lit. 15: Box 182,Hico Tx 76457.

ANGELL, RICHARD S(LOANE). b Aberdeen SD 3 Ap 05. 4: Dorothy Shugg. 5: Stanford 22-24; Princeton 25-27 (Eng) BS; Harvard 31-34 (Music) AM; Columbia summer 34 (LS), 36-40 (Musicology). 6: Fr, Ger. 7: Music libn Columbia U 34-46, Asst Prof of Lib Serv 42-46; Act chief music div NY Pub Lib 44-45; LC: Chief Copyright Catlg Div 46-51, Chief Descr Catlg Div 51-52, 53-56, Chief Subj Catlg Div 52-, Chief Tech Processes Research Off 66-. 8: Bd of Eds Columbia U Studies inLib Serv; Subcom on Catlg of Educl Motion Pictures, US Nat Commsn for UNESCO; AdvBd Center for Documentation & Communication Research, Sch of Lib Sci West Res U. 9: MusLA (v-pres 37-40, Exec Bd 43-45, Rep on Exec Com of Nat Mus Coun 42-44);Amer Musicological Soc (Exec Bd 45 & 49, Coun 49-51); ALA (Coun 51-55, var specassignments 49-68, chm Catlg & Clsf Sect 59-60); ADI (Coun 62-63, rep on ALA Coun64-69; pres Potomac Valley Chap 58-59; ASA (Z39/SC12 64-68); Internat Fed forDocumentation (Com on Clsf Research 64-; Adv Bd ERIC Clearinghouse for Lib & InfoSci 67-; Subcomm on UDC US Natl Comm for FID 69-70); DCLA; Potomac Reg ProcessingLibns; SLA. 11: Guggenheim Fellow 45-46; Rockefeller Pub Serv Award 56-57. 12: Two papers on thesaurus construction FID/CR Rep ser 8, Copenhagen(68). 13: Yes. 14: Catlg, clsf, bibliog control. 15: 4913 Flint dr, Wash DC 20016.

ANGELO, ELIZABETH JOYCE. b Hartford Conn 11 Ap 10. 5: New Haven State Tchrs Col 40-46, 50-52 Conn State Certif. 6: Fr, Ital. 7: Catlgr Hartford (Conn) Pub Lib. 8: Asst in chg of WPA proj (rehabilitation of card catlg) at Hartford Pub Lib 34-37. 9: ConnLA (past sec-treas Catlg Sect, past chm Jr Mem Round table); Greater Hartford Libns Club (past offr). 10: Amer Assn for UN; Hartford Pub Lib Staff Assn & past ed of Staff Assn Organ "The Sieve"; Commun Folk Dancers of Greater Hartford. 14: Catlg. 15: 137 W Robbins ave, Newington Ct 06111.

ANGIONE, PAULINE V. b Rochester NY 19 S 44. 5: Nazareth Col (Rochester) 62-66 (Biol) BS; UChicago 66-68 (LS) MA. 6: Fr. 7: Research asst UChicago Grad Lib Sch 66-68, Research assoc 68-. 9: MedLA; SLA; ASIS. 11: NLM Traineeship 66-68. 14: Info stor & retr, med libnship, sel dissem of info. 15: Univ of Chicago, Grad Lib School 1116 E 59th st, Chicago Il 60637.

ANGLEMYER, MARY. b Chelan Wash 4 Ag 09. 5: Radcliffe 27-31 (Hist, Govt, Econ) AB; Columbia 34-36 BS in LS. 7: Asst libn Div of Placement & Unemployment Ins, NYC 38-42, Libn 46-48; Libn US Army Air Corps, US, Eng, Germany 42-46; Dir of Libs USIA, Bangkok Thailand 49-53; Asst ed DDC LC 54-56; Lib expert UNESCO, Ubol Thailand 57; Libn The Mil Assistance Inst, Arlington Va 58-66; Publics Selection Offr Dept of the Inter 66-68; Tech Info Spec (Phys Sci), Engnr Agency for Resources Inventories, 68-. 8: Consul Inst of Pub Admin, NY 61-62; Jt auth "Library Manual" for AID 60; Instr on Thailand MAI 59-63; Originator of program & mem of com, Jointly Sponsored Program for For Libns, Wash DC 56-. 9: ALA; SLA; DCLA. 10: Hon mem & hon libn Siam Soc, Bangkok; mem var conservation socs & garden clubs. 13: Yes. 14: Admin, acquis of for area materials, bibliog. 15: 2035 Trumbull Terrace NW, Wash DC 20011.

ANGOFF, ALLAN. b Boston 30 Jl 10. 4: Florence Adelson Angoff. 5: Boston U 27-32 (Journalism-Lit) BS in Jour; Columbia 50-52 MSLS. 6: Fr, Ger. 7: Gen lib asst Boston Pub Lib 27-34; Bk reviewer-feature writer "BostonEvening Transcript" 34-39; Asst ed "North Amer Review" 40-42; Staff Sgt Pub RelWriter US Army-USA/China-Burma-India 42-45; Assoc ed Creative Age Press NY 45-46;Managing ed "Tomorrow Magazine" NY 46-51; Ed-in-chief Emerson Bks NY 51-52; Ed &asst dir NYU Off of Publ 52-53; Ed-in-chief NYU Press 53-57; Sr ref libn & Readers'adv, Montclair Pub Lib, Montclair NJ 57-60; Asst lib dir Fair Lawn Pub Lib, FairLawn NJ 60-65; Dir Glen Rock Pub Lib, Glen Rock NJ 65; Asst libn Ed Ref Lib "NYTimes" 65-68; Dir Pub Rel & Chief of Ref Dept Teaneck NJ Pub Lib 65-. 8: Consul on libs & lit Parapsychology Found 51-; Consul on libs & U presses Ford Found 61-62; Lib consul Clifton (NJ) Jewish Center 64-65; presented papers on libs & the lit of parapsychology at four internat conf held in London & St Paul-de-Vence A-M France 63, 64, 65, 66, 67,68; Chief coord Conf on Creativity, St Paul de Vence 69; elected trustee Parapsychology Found 68 & Admin secy 69-; Consul & lib advis South AfricanInstitute of Parapsychology, Johannesburg 69-. 9: NJLA (chm Program Com 68-69);Bergen & Passaic Lib Club (v-pres 61-62). 10: Chm Evaluation Com Adult Sch ofMontclair NJ 58-59; pres Friends of the Clifton (NJ) Pub Lib 63-64. 12: Co-ed-the World Over" (39-40); Ed "American Writing Today; Its Independence and Vigor"(57); Auth 'Hypnotism in the USA', v 4 in ser "Abnormal Hypnotic Phenomena; A 19thCentury Survey"; Founder & ed of triennial period "Teaneck Points of Reference,"(65-); Bk reviewer, "Lib Journal," (55-). 13: Yes. 14: Ref, pub rel. 15: 159 McCosh rd, Upper Montclair NJ 07043.

ANGOFF, FLORENCE (ADELSON). b Boston 29 O 22. 4: Allan Angoff. 5: Simmons 39-43 BS in LS; Montclair State Col 60-63 (Educ). 6: Fr, Ger. 7: Child libn E Boston Br, Boston Pub Lib 43-45; Yp libn Shute Mem Lib, Everett Mass 45-48; Br libn Bellevue Ave Br, Montclair Pub Lib, Montclair NJ 48-50; Ser libn Montclair State Col 57-62; Libn Clifton (NJ) High Sch 64-. 8: Lib & Reading Consul, Elem Sch Lib, Sch 16, Clifton NJ 63-64; Adv Clifton High Sch Lib Coun, 64-. 9: NJEA; NJSchLA; Passaic SchLA (pres 68-69). 15: 159 McCosh rd, Upper Montclair NJ 07043.

ANGUILANO, MICHEL (ROBERT). b Cleveland 16 My 31. 5: UMiami (Fla) 54 (Eng Lit) BA; Columbia 55 MLS. 6: Sp, Ital, Ger. 7: Catlgr Miami Pub Lib, Miami Fla 55-56, Art & music, a-v libn 56-. 8: World's Fair Library/USA, NY 64. 9: ALA; FlaLA; SELA; Mus Lib Assn; ASIS. 10: Dade Co LA. 14: Ref, a-v. 15: 287 NW 45th ave, Miami Fl 33126.

ANGUS, JACQUELINE A. b Minneapolis 30 S 34. 5: St Cloud State Tchrs Col 52-53; UMinn 53-56 (Humanities) BA, 56-57 (LS) MA. 7: Libn US Army Spec Serv, Germany 57-59; Ref libn Minneapolis Pub Lib 60-62; Libn Brown & Bigelow, St Paul 62-64; Tech processing libn Gen Mills Inc, Minneapolis 64-. 9: SLA - Minn Chap - (Bulletin ed, 66-67, Employment chm 68-69). 14: Catlg, ref. 15: 4425 RhodeIsland ave No, Minneapolis Mn 55428.

ANKER, URSULA H. b Dusseldorf Germany 11 Je 22. 5: King's Col of Household & Soc Sci U London 40-42 Diploma in Inst Mgt; West Res U of Cleveland 49-51; Denver U 52-56; SUNY (Albany) 61-64 (Eng) BA, MLS. 6: Ger. 7: Manager Cafeteria Messrs Rootes Securities (Lord's Court branch) London 42-44; Manager Sch Meals Central Kitchen Surrey County Council, England 44-46; Research asst Dept Biochemistry Albany Med Col 57-61; Asst libn 63-64; Libn 64-. 9: SLA; MedLA-NY Regional & Upstate NY Regional Groups (chm of letter 67-68); Hudson-Mohawk Lib Assn. 14: Med ref. 15: Albany Med Col Lib New Scotland ave, Albany NY 12208.

ANKRUM, EDITH ROHRER. b Lancaster Co Penn 22 S 15. 4: Paul W Ankrum. 5: Millersville State Col 32-36 (LS, Math) BS in Ed; UPenn 38-39; Drexel 63 (LS). 7: Libn Jr-Sr High Sch, Clifton Heights Penn 36-42; Libn Sr High Sch, Quarryville Penn 57-61; Lib supv Solanco Sch Dist, Quarryville Penn 61-. 9: ALA; NEA; PennLA; PennStateEA. 10: Lancaster Co LA. 14: Sch lib supv. 15: RD 1, Quarryville Pa 17566.

ANKRUM, JANET L. b Lancaster Penn 28 My 43. 5: Millersville State Col 61-65 (LS) BS; UIll 65-66 (LS) MS. 7: Ed & alphabetizer Bowker - Books-in-Print, lancaster Penn 62-66; Libn Ridgewood High Sch, Norridge Il 66-68; inst of Millersville State Col, Millersville Oenn 67; Libn Cheltenham High Sch, Wyncote Penn 68-69; Libn Abington High Sch, Abington Penn 69-. 9: HLA; NEA; AASchL; PennStateEA; PennASchL. 10: Alpha Beta Alpha; Beta Phi Mu. 14: Sch libs, ya. 15: RD #1, Quarryville Pa 17566.

ANNA, WILLIAM PETER (JR). b Warren Penn 17 Ap 06. 4: Mary Elizabeth Green. 5: Allegheny Col 24-27 (Hist); Syracuse 27-28 (Hist) AB; Gen Theol Sem 29-32 (Theol); CathU 62-65 (LS) MS in LS. 7: Ref libn DC Pub Lib, Wash DC 67-68; Staff libn DC Tchrs Col, Wash DC 68-. 9: ALA. 10: Proj Hope, People to People, Health Found, SE Asia 60-61. 15: 4938 Powder Mill rd, Beltsville Md 20705.

ANNABLE, DOROTHY. b Salem Mass. 5: Simmons 14-18 BS; Columbia 47-50 MS. 6: Fr, Ger, Sp. 7: Ref libn Pub Lib, Cedar Rapids Iowa 18-19; Head of circ Pub Lib, Mason City Iowa 20-22; 1st Asst ext div Pub Lib, Evansville Ind 22-23; Libn Pub Lib, Walpole Mass 24-29; Exec sec NH Pub Lib Commsn 29-36; Reg libn State of Vt, Rutland Vt 37-39; Organizer of Bethesda Pub Lib Bethesda Md 39-40; High Sch Lib Salem High Sch, Salem Mass 43-65; Head Catlg Dept Winn Lib, Winn Lib, Gordon Col Wenham Mass 66-. 8: Dir Summer Lib Inst NH Pub Lib Commsn 29-35; Instr Bk Sel West Md Col Summer Sch 40; Visitng Instr Grad Sch Educ UNH Summer Session 65. 9: ALA (memb chm for NE); AASchL (Standard & Buildings Com; Dir Region 1); NESchLA (sec 2 yrs, pres 2 yrs); Mass Sch Libns (chm 2 yrs). 10: Zonta, AAUW; Appalachian Mt Club; DKG. 14: Sch lib serv, lib ext. 15: 4 Savoy rd, Salem Ma 01970.

ANNAN, GERTRUDE LOUISE. b Providence RI 19 D 04. 5: Brown 21-25 (Eng) BA. 6: Fr, Lat. 7: Catlgr John Carter Brown Lib, Providence 27-29; Catlgr NY Acad Med 29-33; Head rare bk dept 33-53, Assoc libn 53-56, Libn 56-. 9: ALA; SLA; BSA; MedLA (pres 61-62, chm Publ Com, Finance Com, other coms, Bd 57-60); Med Archivists if NY (pres 62-); NY Lib Club (Coun 59-62). 10: Amer Assn State & Local Hist; NY Hist Soc; Eng Speaking Union. 11: Marcia Noyes award MedLA 68. 12: Ed 3rd ed "Handbook of Medical Library Practice (69). 13: Yes. 14: Rare bks, hist of med. 15: 118 East 91 st, New York NY 10028.

ANNE, SISTER M ELIZABETH RSM. b NYC 8 Jl 37. 5: Mt Aloysius Jr Col 55-57 AA; College Misericordia 57-61 (Eng) AB; Catholic U 61-63 MS in LS. 7: Asst libn Col Misericordia Lib 63-64; Libn Bishop McCort High Sch Lib, Johnstown Penn 64-67; Asst Libn Mt Aloysius Jr Col 67-. 9: ALA; CathLA; PennLA (mem Publs & Publ Relations Com). 10: Beta Phi Mu. 15: Mt Aloysius Jr Col, Cresson Pa 16630.

ANNENBERG, LESTER. b Bronx NY 8 Ap 24. 4: Selma Berlinger. 5: NYU 47-50 (Journalism) BS; Pratt Inst 51-52 (LS) MLS. 7: SSgt High-speed radio operator, USAF 42-45; Ref Libn NY Pub Lib 52-54; Asst Br Libn, Cur Affairs Ldr 54-56; Bus Res Libn Time Inc 56-57; World Affairs Res Libn 57-. 8: Consul libn Amer Bankers Assn 61-. 9: SLA (Newspaper Div). 14: Ref. 15: 1430 Theriot ave, Bronx NY 10460.

ANNETT, ADELE MARIE. b Toronto Can. 5: Toronto 46-50 BA, 62-63 BLS. 7: Catlg libn St Michael's Col (Toronto) 63-66; Sr catlg libn UToronto Lib 66-. 9: CanLA; Inst Prof Libns, Ont; ALA. 14: Catlg, ref. 15: Univ of Toronto Lib, Catalogue Dept, 175 Bedford rd, Toronto5 Ont Can.

ANOUSHIRVANI-TAFRESHI, HOSSEIN. b Arak Iran 25 Ap 16. 4: Malli Marzieh Anoushirvani. 5: Naval Acad of France 36-39 Licentiate; UOre 63-66 (Pol Sci) BS, 66-68 MLS. 6: Fr, arabic, Persian. 7: Capt (Retired) Persian Navy, Iran 36-62; Tech processing Bemidji State Col 67-68; Hd libn Tillamook High Sch, Tillamook Ore 68-. 9: OreASchL. 10: Fulbright Scholarship. 13: Yes. 14: Tech proc, ref. 15: 5103 Mountain View dr, Tillamook Or 97141.

ANSLEY, ANNE C. (COONEY). b Birmingham Ala 6 F 14. 4: Eugene B Ansley. 5: Birmingham-So Col 36 AB; EmoryU & UGa 56-8 Grad study; Peabody Col for Tchrs 65 MLS. 6: Fr. 7: Libn Birmingham Pub Lib 31-37, Libn Child dept 42-45; Libn Atlanta Pub Lib Uncle Remus & Highland Br 56-57; Libn EmoryU Sch of Bus Admin Lib 58-60; Libn Dykes High Sch Lib, Atlanta 60-68; Consul Ga Dept of Educ 68-. 8: Libn Educ Wkshop, Oglethorpe Col summer 67; Assoc Prof Dept of Lib Educ UGa summer 67. 9: ALA; -AASchL; SELA; GaLA; GaEA; Ga Dept Instr Supv. 10: AAUW; Metro Atlanta Lib Club; Delta Kappa Gamma; Alpha Chi Omega. 14: Sch libs. 15: State Dept of Educ 156 Trinity ave SW, Atlanta Ga 30303.

ANSLOW, ELIZABETH (PRATT). b Spokane Wash 28 My 15. 4: Ralph O Anslow. 5: Wash State Col of Educ 33-34; UWash 34-38 (Eng, Lit, Gen Lit) BA, 3-yr Tchg Diploma, Tchr-Lib Certif; Emory 57-60 MLS. 7: Secondary sch libn Entiat Pub Schs, Entiat Wash 38-39; Sec Bur of Govt Research UWash 40; Libn San Antonio Pub Lib, San Antonio Tex 48-49; Elem sch libn Montgomery Co Pub Schs, Kensington Md 50-52; Secondary sch libn Atlanta Pub Schs 60-62; Elem sch libn Madison Pub Schs, Madison Wis 62-63; Monroe St Br libn Madison Pub Lib, Madison Wis 63-. 9: ALA; WisLA. 10: Panhellenic Soc; Girl Scouts; AAUW; PTA. 13: Yes. 14: Pub lib, sec sch. 15: 4810 Marathon dr, Madison Wis 57305.

ANSON, BROOKE B. b Orchard Neb 18 N 34. 4: Julie Williams. 5: Neb Wesleyan (Lincoln) 55-9 (Eng) BA; UFla 59-61 (Eng); UIll 66-68 (LS) MS. 7: Dental tech US Navy 53-55; Lib asst IV UFla 59-60; Grad asst 60-61; Stock clk Gen Dynam, Wahoo Neb 61-62; Tchr & libn O'Neill Pub Sch, O'Neill Neb 62-64; Libn Urbana Jr High, Urbana Ill 64-. 9: IllLA; UrbanaEA. 15: 704 Fairlawn, Urbana Il 61801.

ANTHES, SUSAN HILL. b Manitowoc Wis 3 N 44. 4: Richard Allen. 5: UWis 62-66 (Hist) BA, Lib Sch, 66-67 (LS) MA. 7: Circ libn UWis Law Sch Lib 67-68; Asst ref libn UMiami Lib 68-. 14: Ref, interlib loan. 15: 6271 SW 41st st, S Miami Fl 33155.

ANTHONY, DONALD C. b NYC 29 Mr 26. 4: Mary Miserez. 5: Dartmouth 44; UWis 49-51 (Hist) BA; UGeneva 52-53 "Certificat"; UWis 53-54(LS) MA; Grad Sch of Pub Affairs SUNY (Albany) 64-. 6: Fr. 7: Lib asst Enoch Pratt Free Lib, Baltimore 54-55; Head Libn Eleutherian Mills-Hagley Found, Wilmington Del 55-59; Dir Fargo Pub Lib, Fargo ND 59-61; Assoc libn NY State Lib 61-66; Asst dir Columbia U Libs66-. 14: Admin. 15: 53 Bellewood ave, Dobbs Ferry NY 10522.

ANTIPIN, ROSE (GREEN). b Wilmington Del 18 Jl 17. 6: Fr, Ger. 7: Libn USDA Phila, Upper Darby, Asheville NC

41-44; Catlgr Daniel Baugh Inst Anatomy collection 52-53; Libn Robertshaw-Fulton Controls Co, Phila 58-59; Libn Brown Instruments Div M-H Regulator, Phila 59-62; Libn Inst for Sci Info, Phila 62-64; Consul, Phila; Info spec Science Citation Ind, Inst for Sci Info, Phila 65-68; Libn 3i Co, Phila 69-. 8: Org St Agnes Hosp Lib, Phila 64; Consul Western Electric Engnr Res Ctr Lib, Princeton 64-65; Consul Einstein Med Ctr, Korman Res Ctr, No Div Phila 65 Consul Crowell-Collier-Macmillan 68. 9: ALA;MedLA; SLA; ASIS. 14: Info sci. 15: 7033 N 15th st D-4, Philadelphia Pa 19126.

ANTOINETTE, MARY (ANDALORA) (Sister). b Jamestown NY 24 Ag 23. 5: Fredonia State Teachers Col 40-44 (Ed) B Ed; Canisius 46-48 (Hist); Marywood summers 55-60 MSLS. 6: Ital, Sp. 7: Tchr Lakeview Pub Sch, Lakeview NY 44-45; Tchr S Dayton Pub Sch, So Dayton NY 45-46; Tchr St Thomas Aquinas Sch, Buffalo NY 46-48; Tchr St Agatha Sch, Buffalo NY 49-50; Tchr St Anthony Sch, Batavia NY 50-54; Tchr All Saints Sch, Buffalo NY 54-56; Tchr-libn Bishop Quigley High Sch, Buffalo NY 56-57; Instr Tocaire Col, Buffalo NY 65-67; Libn Mt Mercy Acad, Buffalo NY 57-. 8: Mission Procurator of Sisters of Mercy 60-68. 9: ALA; CathLA; NEA-DAVI; NYStateLA; Wester NY Cath Lib Conf. 14: Child lit, ya bks. 15: 88 Red Jacket pkwy, Buffalo NY 14220.

ANTON, ANASTASIA (PAPPAS). b Fort Dodge Iowa 20 Ap 28. 4: George T Anton. 5: Ft Dodge Jr Col 46-7; DrakeU 47-48; State UIowa 48-50 (Fr, Sp) BA; UMinn 56-57 (LS) MA. 6: Fr, Sp, Gr. 7: Br libn Ft Dodge Pub Lib, Ft Dodge Iowa 51-56; Libn Robbinsdale High Sch, Minneapolis 57-61; Ref Evanston Pub Lib, Evanston Ill 61-63; Ref Winnetk Pub Lib, Winnetka Ill 68-. 10: Winnetka Woman's Club. 14: Ref, reader's adv. 15: 290 Poplar st, Winnetka Il 60093.

ANTON, JEANNETTE (ELISE). b Paide Estonia 3 O 15. 4: Johannes Anton. 5: UTartu (Estonia) 34-42 (Ger) Diploma; UToronto 63-64 BLS. 6: Estonian, Ger. 7: Eng & Ger tchr: Estonia 42-44, Germany 45-48; Bkkeeper, Can 52-62; Staff UToronto Lib 64-. 8b Paide Estonia 3 O 15. 15: 28 Greengate rd, Don Mills Ont Can.

ANTONIEWICZ, MRS ROMEO (ANNA). b Springfield Vt 28 N 10. 4: Romeo Antoniewicz. 5: Middlebury Col 28-32 (Lat) BA; Simmons summers 52-56 (LS) MS. 7: Asst libn Springfield Town Lib, Springfield Vt 33-51, Head Libn 51-62; High sch libn Springfield High Sch, Springfield Vt 62-. 9: ALA; NEA; VtLA (past pres) NELA; NeSchLA; VtSchLA. 10: Springfield Quota Club; Springfield Hosp Corporator; Springfield Collector's Club; Hist Soc of Early Amer Decoration Inc. 15: 2 Orchard lane, Springfield Vt 05156.

ANTWEILER, (MARIE) LEOLA (FREEMAN). b Richmond Va 12 F 24. 4: Ralph J Antweiler. 5: Tex West Col 40-43 (Eng) BA; Penn State U 43 (Aeronautical Engnr); Lake EriCol 57, 58 (Elem Educ); Kent State 59, 61 (Educ); West Res 62-65 MSLS. 6: Sp, Fr. 7: Engnr draftsman Curtiss-Wright Corp, Buffalo NY 44& engr draftsman Matthews & Kenan, San Antonio Tex 45; Elem tchr St Clare Sch, Lyndhurst Ohio 53-54; Elem tchr Madison loc schs, John Adams, Unionville Ohio 55-56; Elem tchr N Madison Elem Sch, Madison Ohio 57-62; Jr high libn Madison (Ohio) loc schs 62-67; Sr High Libn Madson Ohio 67-69. 9: ALA-YASD; NEA; OhioASchL; OhioEA; NE Ohio Tchrs Assn; Madison Educ Assn. 10: AAUW. 14: Young adult serv. 15: 5266 E Chapel rd ext, N Madison Oh 44057.

ANZALONE, ALFRED M. b Kearney NJ 23 Ap 26. 4: Helen M Przybylski. 5: Newark Col of Engnr 43-44, 46-47 (Engnr); Rutgers summer 46 (Engnr); Seton HallU 47-49 (Chem) BS; Rutgers 57-60 MLS. 7: US Army Rifleman 75th Inf Div ETO 44-46, Surgical Tech 46; Lib asst Seton Hall 48-49; Chem F W Berk & Co Wood Ridge NJ 49-51; Organic research chem Picatinny Arsenal, Dover NJ 51-56; Asst chg of planning, Tech Serv Lab Picatinny Arsenal, Dover NJ 56; Lit research chem Picatinny Arsenal, Dover NJ 56-61; Info spec Dept of Defense Plastics Tech Evaluation Center, Dover NJ 61-. 9: ACS; SLA; ASIS; NMA; NJSLA. 10: Alpha Phi Delta; Dover Area Jr Chamber Com. 13: Yes. 14: Info serv, documentation. 15: 32 Hilltop rd, Mendham NJ 07945.

ANZALONE, JOSEPH. b Marion Ill 7 S 23. 4: Louise Arnold. 5: State U Col (Geneseo NY) 40-43, 46-48 (LS) BS; Syracuse summers 55-56 MSLS. 6: Ital, Sp. 7: US Army 43-46; Ref libn Lackawanna Pub Lib, Lackawanna NY 48-49; Asst br dept Buffalo Pub Lib, Buffalo NY 50-51, Asst ref dept 51-53; Libn Alden Central Sch, Alden NY 53-. 15: 1203 Greenfield dr, Alden NY 14004.

AOKI, TOSHIYUKI. b Niigata Japan 16 Je 35. 4: Michiko Yamaguchi. 5: Komazawa U 54-56 (Eng & Amer Lit); Columbia 57-60 (Geog) BS, 60-62 (LS) MS, 62-64 (Chinese & Japanese Thought). 6: Japanese, Chinese. 7: Research asst & bibliog in Chinese & Japanese Columbia U 62-64; Catlgr Yale U Lib 64-66; Bibliog Yale U Lib 67; Asst libn Harvard-Yenching Lib 68-. 9: ALA; AAS. 12: "Denshi Keisanki to Toshokan" (tr of "The Computer and the Librarys," by N S M Cox et al) (68). 14: Catlg, ref, acquis. 15: 63 Dana st, Cambridge Ma 02138.

AOYAMA, SUSIE. 4: Frank Aoyama. 5: UIll 48-51 (OT) BS; UWash 64-66 (LS) MLS. 6: Fr, Japanese. 7: Ref libn Seattle Pacific Col 66-. 9: ALA. 14: Ref. 15: 7637 Place NE, Redmond Wa 98052.

APA, MARY RITA. b NYC 28 D 41. 5: Co of Mt St Vincent 59-63 (Eng) BA; Columbia 63-64 MS in LS. 6: Lat, Fr. 7: Libn Msgr Farrell High Sch, SI NY 64-68; Libn Cardinal Hayes High Sch, Bronx NY 68-. 9: ALA; CathLA (ed NY Chap newsletter); NYStateLA. 10: Lay Fac Assn Archdiocesan High Schs NY. 14: High sch, young adults, ref. 15: 2385 Grand ave, Bronx NY 10468.

APLIN, SUSAN ELVIRA. b San Pedro Cal 28 F 43. 5: UCal 60-64 (Decorative Art) BA, 64-65 mls. 7: Libn (staff) UCal (Santa Barbara) 65-. 14: Catlg. 15: PO Box 11585 UCSB, Santa Barbara Ca 93107.

APOSTLE, FLORENCE (NICHOLLS). b Watertown Mass 28 Ag 08. 4: Basil George Apostle. 5: Cornell U 25-30 (Philos, Psych) AB; Columbia 39-40 (LS) BS, 41-45 (Adult Educ) MA. 6: Fr. 7: Libn I, II Brooklyn Pub Lib, Brooklyn NY 40-43, Chief soc sci div 43-46; Dir Hosp Lib Bur United Hosp Fund, NYC 46-48; Dir bus & prof dept YWCA, Buffalo NY 49-54; Dir adult dept YWCA, Richmond Va 55-56; Br libn Richmond Pub Lib, Richmond Va 56-. 9: SLA (chm Hosp Libs Planning Com 48, NY Chap: chm Hosp & Nurs Group 47-48); ALA (Hosp Div); VaLA. 10: Cornell Club of Va; Va Museum of Fine Arts; Amer Contract Bridge League; var bridge clubs; Kappa Delta Pi; Pi Beta Phi. 14: Ref. 15: 4806 Fitzhugh ave, Richmond Va 23230.

APPEL, RHODA (SARA). b Brooklyn NY 24 O 20. 5: Douglass Col 36-40 (Math, LS) BS; Rutgers 45-49 (Ed) MEd; NJ State Col 49-53; USoCal 69. 7: Asst libn Bd of Educ lib, Newark NJ 41-43; Libn Nat Train Sch for Boys, Wash DC 44-46; Libn Madison Jr High Sch, Newark NJ 46-57; Libn Clinton Place Jr High Sch, Newark NJ 57-65; Asst prof Rutgers Grad Sch of Lib Sci summer 66; Asst prof lib sci Newark State Col Field Serv, Union NJ summers 65, 67, 68; Libn Weequahic High Sch, Newark NJ 65-69; Dir Libs & a-v, Newark NJ 69-. 8: Adv Newark Youth Coun 58-60. 9: ALA; NJEA; NJSchLA (Exec Bd); NewarkSchLA (pres 54 chm Coord Com). 10: AFT; NAACP; LWV; NCJW. 14: Admin, school library, service, human relations, inner city serv, a-v, info sci. 15: 18 Bungalow court, Newark NJ 07112.

APPELL, ALICE JACQUETTE. b Burlington Iowa 12 Ap 14. 5: UIll 35 (Fr) AB, 36 (Fr) AB, 36 (Span) MA, 46 BS in LS. 6: Fr, Sp. 7: Lib asst Peoria Pub Lib, Peoria Ill 39-45; Asst catlg dept UIll Lib (Urbana) 45-46, Asst circ dept 46; Asst Dimond Br Oakland Pub Lib, Oakland Cal 46-47, Act br libn Dimond Br 47; UIll Lib (Urbana): Asst acquis dept 47-48, Bibliog acquis dept 48-51, Act asst acquis libn 51-53, Asst acquis libn 53-60; Asst libn in chg of brs Pub Lib, Long Beach Cal 60-. 9: ALA (Coun 59-63,chm Reg 2 Memb Com); IllLA (treas 52-55); CalLA (chm Pub Rel Com 61-63, chmAccred & Certif Com 69); Pub Lib Execs Assn So Cal. 10: Bouggess-White Scholarship Found; Delta Zeta; Beta Phi Mu; English-Speaking Union. 14: Ref, rare bks. 15: 8-18th pl, Long Beach Ca90803.

APPELT, D(AVID) C(LEMENS). b Upper Moutere New Zeland 3 Ag 15. 4: Natalie Schmidt. 5: UAlta 32-36 (Eng) BA, MA 37 (Eng); UMich 39-41 ABLS Sch of Libnship & Archives U Col, London 61-62. 6: Ger, Fr. 7: Asst catlg dept UMich Lib 40-41; Chief catlgr UAlta Lib 41-45; Libn USask 45-. 9: CanLA; ALA; SaskLA (Coun, pres 49-50); Can Assn Col & Univ Libs (pre66-67). 15: USask, Saskatoon Sask Can.

APPERSON, FRANCES EUGENIA. b Jones Ala 10 Je 09. 5: Alabama Col 25-29 (Eng) AB; UAla 32-33, summers 31, 33 (Eng, LS); Emory 35-36 AB in LS. 6: Sp. 7: Tchr Ala pub schs 29-32, 33-35; Asst catlgr UTenn 36-42, Asst ref libn 42-43; UFla: Asst catlgr & documents 43, Documents libn & asst ref 43-47, Act ref libn, head, documents libn 45-47, Ser libn & head 47-55, Documents libn & head 55-. 9: ALA-RTSD (sec Ser Sect 59-61); FlaLA; SELA. 10: AAUW; UN Assn of the

USA. 12: Ed "Short-Title Checklist of Official Florida Publications (45-). 13: Yes. 14: Docs, ref, catlg. 15: 202B NW 12th terrace, Gainesville Fl 32601.

APPLE, ETHEL B. b Elgin Ill 12 Ja 27. 4: Ralph E Apple. 5: Ill Wesleyan U 46-50 (Mus) BM; No Ill U 64-69 (LS) MA. 6: Fr, Ger. 7: Hd of child dept, Gail Borden Pub Lib, Elgin Ill 51-55; Ref & circ libn Elgin Commun Col 67-. 9: ALA; IllLA. 10: Sigma Alpha Iota. 14: Jr col libs, mus libs. 15: 402 Miller dr, Elgin Il 60120.

APPLEBAUM, EDMOND LEWIS. b Boston 19 D 24. 4: Vasiliki Georgiou. 5: Harvard 46-49 (Eng) AB (magna cum laude); Columbia 50 (LS) MS; Harvard 55 (Pub Admin) MPA. 6: Fr, Ger. 7: 26th Inf Div 43-46, T/5, Reserve Lt Field Artillery 48-53; LC; Spec recruit 50, Head Amer-British Exchange Sect Exchange Gift Div 52, Head European Exchange Sect 53-56, Admin asst processing dept 56-57, Head order sect Card Div 57-59, Asst Chief Order Div 60, Exec Off Processing Dept 60-66, Asst dir Processing Dept 66-68; Asst dir for acquis & Overseas Operations Processing Dept 68-. 8: Chm &/or mem various LC Coms; Federal Council for Sci & Tech Com on Sci & Tech Info Panel on Operational Techniques and Systems 67-68; Panel on Internat Info Actties 68-; Adjunct lecturer UMd Grad Sch of Lib & Info Serv 66-. 9: ALA (State rep; Com on the Award of the Margaret Mann Citation 66-67; Nomin Com, Copying Methods Sect 66-67; ARL (Foreign Acquis Com 68-); ALA-LAD Recruitinh Network 63-66; DCLA (several coms). 10: Phi Beta Kappa; Harvard Club of Washington; Kennedy Sch of Govt. 11: Admin Fellowship, Harvard 54-55; LC Superior Serv Award 67. 13: Yes. 14: Te ch processes, admin, acquis, catlg, automation, lib sci educ. 15: 7322 Edmonston rd, College Park Md 20740.

APPLEBAUM, HANNAH BEATRICE (MULLER). b NYC 21 Jl 16. 4: Edward Applebaum. 5: Hunter Col (Fr) BA; Columbia 37-40 (LS) BS. 6: Fr, Ger. 7: Head catlgr Brooklyn Museum, NYC 38-43; Asst libn Museum of Modern Art, NYC 43-54; Head Libn Grad Sch of Pub Affairs, State U of NY (Albany) 58-67, Bibliog 67-. 9: Hudson-MohawkLA. 10: AAUP; SUNYALibns Org. 12: Bibliog Sections in more than 30 bks publ by Museum of Modern Art & commercial publishers in USA & Europe, 44-54. 13: Yes. 14: Catlg, bibliog, ref, admin. 15: 53 Edgewood ave, Albany NY 12226.

APPLEGATE, HOWARD LEWIS. b Neptune Twp NJ 13 Jl 35. 4: Shelby Coons Applegate. 5: Drew 53-57 (Hist) BA; Syracuse 57-61 (Hist) MA, 61-66 (Hist) PhD. 7: SyracuseU: Asst admin Univ College 60-62, Manuscripts consul Carnegie Lib 61-62, Admin asst to v-pres Acad Affairs 61-66, Instr Hist Dept 64-66, Admin of manuscripts Carnegie Lib 62-67, Asst dir of libs for spec collections & dev Carnegie Lib 67-. 8: Editorial reader, Syracuse University Press 64-; Commissioner, Town of Clay (NY) Planning Board 68-. 9: Mss Soc News ed "Manuscripts" 68-, dir 67-, Memb Com 67-, chm Fin Com 68-; ALA-ACRL (Rare Bks Dect Ad Hoc Com on Mss Collections 68-, chm Subcom on Mss Standards 68-); SAA (Spec Collections Com 67-); Five Assoc Univ Libs (chm Spec Collections Com 68-). 10: Memb, Onondaga Repub Co Com; Compass Society; Syracuse Univ lib Associates Dir 68-, AHA; Organiz Amer Histns; AAUP; Newcomen Soc. 13/ yes. 14: Spec collections, admin, mss, pub rel, devel. 15: 323 Beech st, N Syracuse NY 13212.

ARAI, TOMOE (MURATA). b Kona Hawaii 14 Ag 17. 4: Tim T Arai. 5: Conn Col for Women 43-46 (Social anthropology) BA; Columbia 46-47 (Japanese), 61-63 (LS) MA. 6: Japanese. 7: Sec Columbia U Research in Contemporary Cultures 48-49; Sub tchr Montvale Sch,nj 58-59; Lib asst E Asian Lib Columbia U 60-63; Libn Hunter Col 63-68; Herbert H Lehman Col 68-. 9: NY Lib Club; ALA. 10: NY Buddhist Church Adult Assn. 14: Ref, catlg, hd circ. 15: 245 W 107 st,New York NY 10025.

ARBABI, ELIZABETH MARIE (ROWE). b Longview Wash 1 O 31. 4: Mansur Arbabi. 5: UPuget Sound 49-53 (Eng Lit, Educ) AB; Cal State Polytech Col summer 55 (Educ); CatholicU 60-62 MSLS. 7: Ref Montgomery Co Pub Lib, Bethesda Md 62-63. 10: Beta Phi Mu. 15: 9304 Holland ave, Bethesda Md 20014.

ARBUCKLE, KATHRYN DIANE. b Morocco Ind 15 Jl 34. 5: Ind U 52-56 (Lang Arts) BS; UCal summer 55; Ind U summers 57-59 (LS) MAT. 7: Sec American U summer 63; Libn Dyer Central High Sch, Dyer Ind 56-66; Libn Lake Central High Sch, St John Ind 66-. 66; Libn Lake Central High Sch, St John Ind 66-. 9: NEA; IndSchLA; Ind State Tchrs Assn; Ind Classroom Tchr's Assn. 10: Delta Kappa Gamma; Alpha XI Delta. 14: High sch lib wk. 15: 8821 Schneider, Highland In 46322.

ARBUCKLE, MARYBETH M. b Walla Walla Wash 9 Je 43. 5: UPuget Sound 61-65 (Gen Stud) BA; Walla Walla Col summers 63, 64; UDenver 65-66 (Libnship) MA. 6: Ger. 7: Stud asst UPuget Sound Lib 62-65; Stud asst Whitman Col Lib summers 63, 64; Stud asst UDenver Lib 65-66; Asst humanities ref libn Portland StateU 66-. 9: ALA; PNLA. 14: Ref. 15: 660 Second st apt 16, Lake Oswego Or 97034.

ARCHER, ALICE M (BROWN). b So Natick Mass 7 Ap 05. 4: David M Archer. 5: Simmons 23-27 (LS) BS. 7: Sr asst Clark U, Worcester Mass 27-29; Sr asst (ref dept) Thomas Crane Pub Lib, Quincy Mass 41-46, Art libn 46-47, Ref libn 57-. 14: Ref, art. 15: 48 Whittier rd, Braintree Ma 02184.

ARCHER, H(ORACE) RICHARD. b Albuquerque NM 13 S 11. 4: Margot Hanko. 5: UCal (Berkeley) 37-40 (Eng & Amer Lit) BA, 40-41 Certif Libnship 41, 43 (LS) MA; Chicago 54 (LS) PhD. 6: Ger. 7: Asst Manager College Bk Co Los Angeles 34-36; Asst Argonaut Bk Shop, Los Angeles 36-37; Manager UCal Assoc Stud Store, Used Bk Dept 38-39, Asst 39-40; Libn Jr Grade UCal Lib (Berkeley) 41-42; Fellow UChicago Grad Lib Sch 42-43, research asst 43-44; Supv bibliogr Clark Mem Lib UCLA 44-52; Curator UCLA Lib Spec Collections 52-53; Libn RR Donnelley & Sons Lakeside Press, Chicago 54-57; Libn Chapin Lib Williams Col 57-. 8: Visiting instr UOkla Lib Sch summer 56; Visiting instr USoCal Sch Lib Sci summer 60; Visitinglecturer UMich Lib Sch summer62; Visiting lecturer Simmons Sch Lib Sci spring 65; Visiting lecturer; SUNY(Albany) Lib Sch spring 68, UIll Grad Sch of Lib Scisummer 69. 9: ALA-ACRL (Rare Bk Sect, chm 62-63, ed Rare Bk Manual Proj 57-64, Coun 62-65)-RTSD (Reprint Com 61-63, Lib Tech Proj Adv Com 65-); CalLA 44-53; SLA 54-57; NELA; BSA; Ms Soc. 10: Beta Phi Mu (Publ Com 63-68); Rounce & Coffin Club Los Angeles (sec-treas 44-53); Grolier Club; Caxton Club; Typophiles; Zamorano Club, Los Angeles (libn 46-49); Soc of Printers (Boston) Pittsburgh Bibliophiles; Printing Hist Soc (London); Soc for Italic Handwriting; William Morris Soc; Berkshire Coun Hist Soc (dir 65-); AAUP. 11: UCal Bibliophile Prize (40), Certif of Excellence for Typographic Design (Soc Typographic Arts Chicago 57). 12: "Fine Printing in Clark Memorial Library, Report of the First Decade, 1934-44" (46); "Survey of the History of Printing" MA thesis UCal, Microcard publ (54); "Rare Book Collections" ACRL Monograph 27 (65); "The Private Press: Its Essence & Recrudescence" (in 'Modern Fine Printing') (68). 13: Yes. 14: Bibliog, rare bks, hist of printing & typography, calligraphy, preservation & conservation. 15: Chapin Lib Williams Col, Williamstown Ma 01267.

ARCHER, JOHN H. b Broadview Sask Can 11 Jl 14. 4: Alice Mary Widdup. 5: Scott Collegiate 30-31; Regina Normal Sch 32-33; USask 47 (Hist) BA, 48 (Hist) MA; McGill 49 BLS Queens U 69 PhD. Queens U 69 PhD. 6: Fr, Ger. 7: Tchr rural schs, sask 33-39; Vice-Prin Wawota High Sch, Sask 39-40; Royal Canadian Artillery-1st Cdn Survey Reg't (a/Cpt) 40-45; Admin asst to Legis Libn Sask, Regina Can 49-51; Prov Archivist, Regina Can 57-62; Libn Legis Lib of Sask, Regina Can 51-64; Dir of Libs McGill 64-67; Univ Archivist & Prof of Hist, Queens U Kingston Ont 67-. 67; Univ Archivist & Prof of Hist, Queens U Kingston Ont 67-. 8: Sec Royal Com on Judicial System Sask 56; Spec Proj Off Glassco Commsn (Royal Commsn on Govt Org, Can) 61-62; Spec Commsn on Continuing Educ (chm) Sask; Accreditation team UBC Sch & Libnship 62-63UWest Ontario Sch of Info & Lib Sci 69. UWest Ontario Sch of Info & Lib Sci 69. 9: CanLA (treas 59-62, pres-elect, pres 66-67); Re ginLA (pres 56); SaskLA (pres 61). 10: Bd Dir Can Centennary Coun 63-; Canadian Club Montreal. 11: Coronation Medal 52. 12: "Historic Saskatoon" (48); "The Hudson's Bay Route" with A M Pratt (53); "Saskatchewan: the Story of a Province" with A M Derley (55); "Saskatchewan History" (56-62); "West of Yesterday" (65); "Footprints in Time" with C B Koester (65); "Best of Billy Bock" (68). 13: Yes. 14: Canadiana, govt docs, hist, bk reviews. 15: 119 Earl st apt 3, Kingston Ont Can.

ARCHER, LEONARD BENJAMIN JR. b Petersburg Va 10 Ja 13. 4: Marion Fuller. 5: URichmond 34-38 (Eng) BA; Madison Col(Harrisonburg Va) summer 38 (Educ & Hist); Emory 39 BA in LS. 6: Fr, Sp. 7: Jr asst DC Pub Lib 39; Jr asst Parkman Reg Br Detroit Pub Lib 39-41; Ref dept asst Main Lib 41-42; Sr asst ref Burton Hist Collection 46-48; Libn Goddard Col, Plainfield Vt 48-51; Dir Rutland Free Lib, Rutland Vt 51-58; Dir Oshkosh Pub Lib, Oshkosh Wis 58-. 8: Guest lectr Grad Lib Sch UWis(Madison); Lib Sci Dept, Wis State U(Oshkosh) 59-69; Prof of Pub Lib Admin, UWis(Madison) summer 69. 9: ALA (Comm on Pub Rel Serv toLibs, Comm on Budgeting, Costs and Accounting 65-); CanLA; WisLA (chmIntell Freedom Com 63-65, Personnel and Profess Prob Com). 10: Rotary Club; Men's Debating Soc;

Oshkosh Human Rights Coun; Aurelian Soc; Men's Fac Club of Wis State U(Oshkosh); Wis ArtsFound & Coun; Wis State Hist Soc; PTA. 11: Citizenship Award, Vt DAR 57; Brotherhood Award, Nat Conf Christians & Jews 58. 13: Yes. 14: Admin, intell freedom, loc hist. 15: 520 Mount Vernon st, Oshkosh Wi 54901.

ARCHER, LUCILLE (S). b Nanticoke Penn 24 Ag 27. 4: John C Archer. 5: Marywood 45-49 (BA in LS). 7: NY Public: Mus libn 49-51, Children's libn 62-65; Circ libn Engr's Sch lib, Ft Belvoir Va 52-53; Sci libn Pratt Inst lib, Brooklyn NY 65-. 9: ASIA; SLA. 10: AAUP. 14; Ref. 15: 86 Prospect Park W, Brooklyn NY 11215.

ARCHER, MARION (DANIELS). b Salinas Cal 13 O 23. 4: Ralph Archer. 5: Reedley Jr Col 41-43 (Journalism, Eng) AA; San Jose State 43-45 (Educ) AB; 50-51 (Libnship) Cred. 7: Elem tchr Fresno & Contra Costa Cos 45-50; Child libn Fresno Co Lib 51-54; Elem tchr Tulare & Fresno Cos 54-59; Co schs libn Lake Co, Lakeport Cal 62-. 8: Org of independent sch libs. 9: NEA; CalSchL; Assn Child Libns; CalTA. 10: OES; 4H, Cub Scouts. 14: Child lit. 15: PO Box 961, Lakeport Ca 95453.

ARCHER, MARY ANN ELIZABETH (CULLEY). b b Rochester NY 7 Mr 30. 4: H Brent Archer. 5: SUNY (Genesco) BS in LS (Magna cum laude). 7: Tech libn Rochester Inst Tech 53-55; Sch libn, Spring Tex 60-61; Lib consul St Mary's Hosp, Rochester NY 62-63; Tech libn Wilmot Castle Co, Rochester NY 64; Indexer Tech Assoc of Graphic Arts 65-66; Tech libn Xerox Corp 66-67; Search team coordinator-lit searcher Eastman Kodak Co, Rochester NY 67-. 9: SLA (Bul ed Upstate NY chap); Monroe CoLA. 10: Kappa Delta Pi; Alpha Sigma Alpha; Rochester Mus Soc. 14: Ref, mech lit searching, computer-produced indexes. 15: 270 Mendon rd, Pittsford NY 14534.

ARCHER, MARY LUCILLE. b Jonesboro Tenn 4 Ap 06. 5: Johnson City Bus Col 42-54 (Typing, Bkkeeping); E Tenn StateU 47 (Eng, Hist) BS; Peabody 53 MA in LS. 7: Grade tchr Carter Co, Elizabethton Tenn 30-40; High sch (Eng & Hist) Hawkins Co, Church Hill Tenn; Libn high sch Sullivan Co, Kingsport Tenn 49-61; Libn Milligan Col 61-. 9: ALA; TennLA. 10: Internat Rel Club; AAUW; Altrusa Club; Little Theatre Group. 14: Catlg. 15: 1205 Holston ave, Johnson City Tn 37601.

ARCHIBALD, MRS ELIZABETH (B). b Macomb Ill 17 Ag 09. 4: Gerry Archibald. 5: Carnegie 31 BSLS. 7: Child libn Warren Lib Assn, Warren Penn 32-40, County libn 61-. 9: PennLA. 15: 403 Quaker rd, Warren Penn 16365.

ARCHIBALD, JEAN T (KENWAY). b Newton Mass 31 O 17. 4: John L Archibald. 5: Simmons 35-39 BS in LS. 6: Fr, Sp, Ger. 7: Page Newton Free Lib, Newton Mass 32-42; Asst libn Northfield Sch for Girls,E Northfield Mass 39-42; Libn Mt Hermon Sch, Mt Hermon Mass 42-48; Catlgr St PaulFire & Marine Insurance Co, St Paul 60-61; Asst ref libn & rare bk libnMacalester Col 61-66, Ref libn 66-, Acting libn 69-. 9: NeSchLA (treas 48);MinnLA; ALA. 10: Minn Hist Soc; Pioneer Valley Symphony Orchestra. 13: Yes. 14: Ref, rare bks, col & sch libs. 15: 1425Englewood ave, St Paul Mn 55104.

ARCHIBALD, MARJORIE (DICKSON). b Bovina Center NY 3 O 02. 4: Wilber Thomas Archibald. 5: Cornell 19-23 (Eng) AB; NYS Lib Sch summer 26; Columbia Sch of Lib Serv 27-29 BS. 7: Eng tchr Griffin-Fleischmanns High Sch, Fleischmanns NY 25-27; Libn, Pub Lib & Pub Schs, Hicksville NY 27-28; Libn Poughkeepsie High Sch, Poughkeepsie NY 28-. 8: Adv "World Book Encyclopedia" 64. 9: ALA; NEA; NYLibA (Legisl Com 53); NYStateTA; Sch Libns of Soeast NY; Dutchess CoLA. 10: NY State Hist Assn; Dutchess Co Hist Soc; Nat Wildlife Fed; YWCA; Dutchess Co Soc for Mental Health; Wilderness Soc; Scenic Hudson Preserv Conf; Amer Fprestry Assn. 14: ya, ref. 15: 84 S Randolph ave, Poughkeepsie NY 12601.

ARCHULETA, MRS LENA L(OVATO). b Clapham NM 25 Jl 20. 4: Juan U Archuleta. 5: UDenver 38-42 (Span) AB, 50-51 (LS) MA. 6: Sp. 7: Tchr No NM Normal Sch 42-50; Libn Denver Pub Schs 50-60; Act exec sec Denver ClrTA 60-61; Coordinator Dept of Lib Serv Denver Pub Schs 61-64, Supv 65-66; Supv Off of Sch Commun Relations, Denver Pub Schs 66-. 66; Supv Off of Sch Commun Relations, Denver Pub Schs 66-. 9: ALA; NEA (Adv Com to Com on Educ Implications of Automation 61-64); ColoLA (past pres); ColoASchL; ColoEA. 10: Delta Kappa Gamma; Kappa Kappa Iota; Phi Beta Kappa; Relig Coun on Human Rel; Latin Amer Res & Serv Agency; Latin-Amer Educl Found. 14: Sch lib serv, bks for child. 15: 1840 S Federal blvd, Denver Co 80219.

ARD, HAROLD J. b Herrick Ill 26 Ag 40. 4: Erma J Chapman. 5: Ill State U 58-62 (Educ) BS, 62-64 (Reading); Rosary Col 66-68 (LS) MS. 6: Sp. 7: Ref libn Withers Pub lib, Bloomington Ill; Chief libn Barrington (Ill) Pub Lib 65-68; Exec libn Arlington Hts (Ill) Mem Lib 69-. 8: Lect wkshops in tech proc, Ill State Lib. 9: ALA; IllLA; LACONI (past chm Lib Practices Com). 10: Beta Phi Mu; Rotary. 14: Tech proc, censorship, admin. 15: 500 N Dunton, Arlington Hts Il 60004.

ARD, KATHERINE. b Barnes Miss 13 F 10. 5: Mary Hardin-Baylor 27-29, 34-35 (Eng); Ga U 33 (LS); Sam Houston StateCol 64-65 (Eng) BA; LSU 65-67 (LS) MS. 7: Asst Tom Green Co Lib, San Angelo Tex 29-38; Libn Nueces Co Lib, Corpus ChristiTex 38-48; Libn Montgomery Co Lib, Conroe Tex 48-68; Field consul Tex State Lib, Conroe 68-. 9: ALA; TexLA (pres 47). 10: Women's Com for Houston Symphony; Pi Gamma Mu; Phi appa Phi; Beta PhiMu. 15: Drawer AC, Conroe Tx 77301.

ARENDAS, IRENE. b Passaic NJ 7 N 38. 5: Fairleigh Dickinson U 56-60 (Eng) BA; Rutgers 60-61 MLS. 7: Catlg libn Fairleigh Dickinson U 61-66; Catlg libn Patterson State Col 66-68; Catlg libn US Intl U 68-69; Hd libn RosemeadGrad Sch of Psych 69-. 8: Org of lib at St John The Baptist Russian Orthodox Church, Passaic NJ 64-; Tchr of Lib Sci, FairleighDickinson U & Reading & Study Ins, E Rutherford NJ 62-64. 9: ALA; SLA; CalLA. 12: "Messler Library Handbook," FarleighDickinson U (65). 14: Catlg. 15: 6933 N Rosemead blvd, San Gabriel Ca 91775.

ARENS, IRENE BERNICE (NYGAARD). b Chicago 7 Ap 37. 4: Alvin Armond Arens. 5: St Olaf Col 54-56 (Socio); UOslo (Norway) 56-57 (Lang & Lit); St Olaf Col 57-58 (Soc & Norwegian) BA; UMinn 58-59, 62-63 (LS) MA. 6: Norwegian. 7: Libn US Bur of Sport Fisheries & Wildlife Minneapolis 64-67; Lib asst General Mills Inc, Minneapolis 68; Libn US Reg Poultry Res Lab, East Lansing Mich 68-. 9: SLA. 15: 4364 Oakwood dr, Okemos Mi 48864.

ARETZ, ELIZABETH E. b Sharon Hill Penn 30 N 18. 5: UPenn 36-40 (Eng) BA; Drexel 40-41 (LS) BS. 6: Fr, Ger. 7: Asst in child dept Free Lib of Phila 41; Libn Nurses Sch Phila Gen Hosp 42; Libn Germantown Acad, Phila 43-44; Asst in acquis div Temple U 45-49, Head of acquis div 49-. 9: ALA-ACRL; Phila Area Tech Serv Libns. 10: Women's Univ Club; AAUW; Del Valley Protective Assn. 14: Acquis. 15: 165 E Roosevelt blvd, Phila Pa 19120.

AREY, HELEN P(YLE). b Lancaster Penn 17 Ap 13. 5: Millersville State Col 57-60; Jacksonville U 60-67 (Eng) BA; Catholic U (LS). 6: Sp. 7: Sec to A S Kimmel C P A, Lancaster Penn 49-60; Sec Registrar's Off Jacksonville U 60-63; Sec to Dir Swisher Lib, Jacksonville Fla 63-67; Research lib aide Pr George's Co Mem Lib, Hyattsville Md 67-69. 9: ALA; MdLA. 10: Prince George's Co Mem Lib Staff Assn; Friends of Jacksonville (Fla) PPub Lib. 14: Ref, catlg. 15: 6164 Springhill ter apt 201, Greenbelt Md 20770.

AREY, JANET (BROOKS). b Columbus Ohio 4 Mr 45. 5: UAla 63-67 (Geog) BA; UNC 67-68 (LS) MS in LS. 7: Ref libn Birmingham So Col 68-. 9: SELA. 10: Phi Beta Kappa. 14: Ref. 15: 905 Eighth ave W, Birmingham Al 35204.

ARGO, MRS FRANCES ELOISE (CLARK). b Nevada Mo 3 D 08. 5: UWichita 27-31 (Hist) AB; UIll summer 36 (LS); W Tex State U 57, 58 (Educ); Kan State Tchrs Col (Emporia) 57, 58 (LS) MSUOkla 66 (LS). UOkla 66 (LS). 7: Ref asst Wichita (Kan) City Lib 31-37; Ref asst Amarillo (Tex) Pub Lib 55-58, Head of ref dept 58-76; Spec collections libn W Tex State U Lib 65-66; Chief Libn VA Hosp Lib, Amarillo Tex 66-. 66; Chief Libn VA Hosp Lib, Amarillo Tex 66-. 9: ALA; TexStateLA; MedLA. 10: Girl Scouts; AAUW; YWCA; Alpha Chi Omega; Delta Gamma. 14: Ref, med libnship. 15: 2701 S Patterson apt 4, Amarillo Tx 79109.

ARGUE, DOLORES M. b Arcadia Mich 17 N 29. 5: San Francisco State Col 57-61 (Eng) AB; UCal (Berkeley) 62 MLS; Cal Sec Tchg Credential 67. 7: Asst ref libn Sonoma State Col Lib 62-68; Tchr Rancho Cotate Sr High Sch 68-69, Libn 69-. 9: CalTA: Assn of Petaluna Area Tchrs. 10: AAUP; Assn of Cal State Col Profs. 14: Ref, periods, sch libs. 15: 1106 Duer rd, Sebastopol Ca 95472.

ARIAN, YVETTE (BARDON). b Cleveland Oh 30 Je 22. 4: Edward William Arian. 5: West res 40-43 (Soc); Temple U 55-58 (Educ) BS; Drexel Inst of Tech 63-65 (LS) MLS. 6: Fr. 7: Sec ALA, LC 44-45; Tchr Plymouth-Twsp Sch Syst 58-63; Libn Colonial Sch Dist 65-. 9: ALA; NEA; PennSchLA; PennLA; Colonial Sch Dist TA. 15: 116 Boulder rd, Plymouth Meeting Pa 19462.

ARMBRISTER, ANN (UZZELL). b Goldsboro NC 18 Fe 42. 4: Carl S Armbrister. 5: Duke U 59-63 (Fr) BA; UOkla 65-66 (LS) MLS. 6: Fr. 7: Libn I UTex Lib 66-68, Libn II 68-. 9: ALA. 14: Acquis. 15: 502-B Cater dr, Austin Tx 78704.

ARMBRISTER, ROBERTA F(RANCES). b Max Meadows Va. 5: Berea Col 29-33; Lit BA; Wheaton Col, Wheaton Ill 37-43 Langs, soc sci; UIll summers 38-41 BS in LS; American U 43-54; Pub Admin MA, 1 yr post-grad; George Washington U 58-59; Adult educ. 6: Fr, Sp, Lat, Ger. 7: Trainee Berea Col 30-33; Libn Max Meadows Pub Sch, Max meadows Va 33-34; Libn Wytheville Sch, Pub Lib, Wytheville Va 34-36; Trainee Enoch Pratt Free Pub Lib, baltimore 36-37; Catlgr & ref libn Wheaton Col (Wheaton Ill) 37-43; Catlgr US Dept of Com, Wash DC 43-47; Catlgr br US Navy Dept, Wash DC 47-49; Libn US Agency for Internat Development, Wash DC 55-61; Libn readers serv, for aid & econ spec US Dept State, Wash DC 47-55, 61-. 8: Consult org small libs 33-36, 55-61. 9: ALA (Life mem); SLA; Amer Polit Sci Assn. 10: Dominion Hills Civic Assn, Arlington Va; Prof Writers Club (Wash DC). 11: Meritorious Award us for Operations Admin, 59. 12: Comp of var bibliographies. 13: Yes. 14: Admin. 15: 1001 N Larrimore st, Arlington Va 22205.

ARMES, DORIS L(OUISE). b Harrisburg Penn 11 Mr 22. 5: Albright Col 40-44 (Soc Studies) BS; Pratt 45-46 BLS; American U 64-65 (Internat Serv) MA. 6: Sp. 7: Tchr-libn Allen High Sch, Asheville NC 44-45; Libn Mather Acad, Camden SC 46-50; Tchr-libn Holding Inst, Laredo Tex 50-53;Libn Robinson Sch, San Juan PR 53-64; Libn Allen High Sch, Asheville NC 65-66; Tchr-libn Holding Inst, Laredo Tex 66-. 9: ALA; NEA; TexLA. 10: Pi GammaMu; Methodist Deaconess; AAUW. 14: Sch libs. 15: Holding Institute, Box 269, Laredo Tx 78040.

ARMISTEAD, HENRY T(UCKER). b Phila Pa 16 S 40. 4: Mary E Mallam. 5: UPenn 58-63 (Eng Lit/Zoology) BA; Drexel Institute of Technology 67-68 Library Science MSLS; Drexel Institute of Technology 68- Information Science. 6: French. 7: USA Cler PFC, 63-65; Lib Trainee Free Lib of Phila (NE Reg Lib), 65-67; Acquis libn Jefferson Med Col Lib, Phila 68-. 9: ALA; MedLA; SLA; ASIS; PennLA. 10: Beta Phi Mu; Amer Ornithol Union. 14: Bibliog, ref, ornithol. 15: 39 Benezet st, Phila Pa 19118.

ARMITAGE, ANDREW D. b Charleston W Va 13 F 39. 4: Katherine Young. 5: Morris Harvey Col 57-60 (Hist) BA; Drexel 60-62 MSLS; UDenver 64-65 (Hist); UPittsburgh 67-68 (LS) Adv certif, 68- (LS). 6: Fr, Sp. 7: Lib trainee State of Penn, Harrisburg 61-62; Lib development asst, ref libn Penn State Lib 62-64; Act chief of ref UDenver 64-65; Admin asst YorkU Lib (Toronto) 65-67; Instr Grad Sch Lib Sci UPittsburgh 67-. 8: Instr UDenver Lib Sch. 9: ALA; ColLA; PennLA (chm Pub Lib Div 69); AALL; OntLA. 10: Congress for Change; ADA. 13: Yes. 14: Ref, lib educ, admin, hist bk & lib. 15: GSLIS Univ of Pittsburgh, Pittsburgh Pa 15213.

ARMOUR, (MARY) JEAN. b Dixon Ill 28 Ag 39. 5: No Ill U 57-59 (Home Econ); Lake Forest Col 59-61 (Eng) BA; Rosary Col 62-64 MA in LS. 7: Tchr Nashold Sch, Rockford Ill 61-62; Registrar Elmhurst Pub Lib, Elmhurst Ill 62-64; Catlgr SD State U 64-65; Catlgr UIll (Chicago Circle) 65-68; Ref libn UIll (Urbana) 68-. 9: ALA. 10: Beta Phi Mu; AAUP; ACLU. 14: Ref. 15: 306 S Coles, Urbana Il 61801.

ARMS, AROLINE C. b Gaines Mich 15 N 04. 5: East Mich U 21-23 (Lat) Life Tchg Certif; Wayne State U summer 25; UMich 27(Lat) AB in Educ, 34 (Lat) AM, 55 AMLS; Columbia summer 56 (Certif of Med Libnship). 6: Lat, Fr. 7: Tchr Milan High Sch, Milan Mich 23-24; Tchr Redford High Sch,Detroit 24-55; Libn Evangelical Deaconess Hosp, Detroit 56-. 9: MedLA; SLA. 10: Pi Lambda Theta; Beta Phi Mu; Phi Beta Kappa. 14: Ref. 15: 16594 Westbrookave, Detroit Mi 48219.

ARMSTEAD, HELEN (HOLMES). b Bennettsville SC 27 S 21. 4: Bernard L Armstead. 5: Flora Stone Mather 39-43 (Sociol) BA; West Res 44-45 BS in LS, 62-64 MS in LS. 7: Child libn Cleveland Pub Lib 45-46; Elem sch libn Cleveland Bd of Educ 47-54, Jr high sch libn 54-. 9: ALA; OhioLA; OhioSchL; CTU. 14: Sch libs. 15: 16919 Invermere ave, Cleveland Oh 44128.

ARMSTRONG, CESAR J(OEL). b Havana Cuba 12 Jl 13. 4: Maria Luisa Bustillos. 5: UHavana 34-40 (Law) Dr in Laws, 41 Dr in Pol Sci; La State U 65-66 (LS) MS. 06 Sp, Port, Fr, ital. 7: Priv Law Practice, Havana 40-60; V-pres Industrias Harmigon Cubano, Havana 52-66; Maule Industries, Miami 60-62; Fla State Dept of Pub Welfare, Miami 62-64; Circ dept La State U Lib 65-66; Ref libn Harvard Law Sch Lib 66-. 14: Ref, admin. 15: Harvard Law Sch Lib Langdell Hall, Cambridge Ma 02138.

ARMSTRONG, CHARLES W. b Knoxville Tenn 30 Je 05. 5: UTenn (Knoxville) 23-27 (Lit) AB, 27-29 (Law) LLB; USoCal 48-49 MA in LS. 7: Inspector Civilian Conservation Corps, tenn, Ala, Ga & NC 34-39; Maj US Army US & Europe 40-47; Order libn Los Angeles Co Law lib 49-50, Various positions 50-60, Ref dept 61-. 9: AALL (past pres SoCal Chap). 13: Yes. 14: Ref. 15: 3409 Camino de la Cumbre, Sherman Oaks Ca 91403.

ARMSTRONG, ELIZABETH (PHYLLIS). b Ridgefield Conn 2 My 26. 5: Ithica Col 45-47 (Drama); Tufts 49-51 (Eng) BA; Rutgers 59-60 (LS) MLS (Magna Cum Laude). 6: Fr. 7: Asst commander dir of rec Sp Serv, Europe 52-56; Post Entertainment dir Sp Serv, Ft Knox 56-59; Loan libn UIdaho 60-62; Ref libn Long Beach Pub Lib, Cal 62-63; Hd of pub serv Cal West U Lib 63-65, Hd libn 65-68; Chief libn Cal Inst of the Arts, Los Angeles 68-. 9: ALA; TheatreLA; NEA-DAVI; SLA (San Diego Chap: sec 65-66, v-pres & pres-elect 67-68). 14: Lib admin, automation. 15: 1866 N Rodney dr, Los Angeles Ca 90027.

ARMSTRONG, EVELYN WALKER. b Phila 18 Ap 27. 4: Cornelius W Armstrong. 5: Howard U 45-49 (Pol Sci, Econ) AB; Drexel 53-56 MSLS. 7: Mgr Merck Sharp & Dohme Res Labs, W Point Penn 50-. 8: Visiting Instr lib sci Drexel Inst Tech 63-. 9: SLA; Chm pharmac sect 63-64, Mem Prof Standards Co m 65-67; ADI (Adv Bd 65-66); Drug Info Assn; ACS (Chem Lit Div); Franklin Inst; MedLA; ASIS (Adv Bd 65-66). 14: Info storage & retrieval. 15: Merck Sharp & Dohme Res Labs, West Point Pa 19486.

ARMSTRONG, FRANKLIN F. b Sacramento Cal 25 My 27. 4: Joan Suppes. 5: Sacramento State Col 47-51 (Eng) AB; Columbia 53-54 MSLS. 6: Ger. 7: Pharmacist Mate 3/c US Navy, US 45-47; Bibliog-indexer USDA Lib, Wash DC 54-56; Field libn USAF, Japan 56-57; Ref libn Nat Housing Center Lib, Wash DC 58-59; Ref libn San Diego Pub Lib 59-60; Libn II Cal State Lib 60-64; Libn II Hayward Pub Lib, Hayward Cal 65-. 9: SLA. 14: Ref, admin, bk sel. 15: 335 Bristol blvd, San Leandro Ca 94577.

ARMSTRONG, GENEVIEVE (MARTIN). b Haines Alaska 21 Je 07. 4: Edward Dale Armstrong. 5: UWash 26-31 BS in LS, 32-35 (Pol Sci) BA. 7: Sec-libn UWash Col of Engnr 32-39; Volunteer, circ Arlington Co Pub Lib, Arlington Va 40-41; Libn Geo Mason Jr-Sr High Sch, Falls Church Va 59, 61-62, 63-64; Child libn Thos Jefferson Br Fairfax Co Pub Lib, Fairfax Va 64-68; Asst Supv Childs Serv, Fairfax Co Pub Lib 68-. 9: ALA; VaLA. 10: Zeta Tau Alpha. 14: Child serv, periods. 15: 319 N Underwood st, Falls Church Va 22046.

ARMSTRONG, JOHN B. b Glendale Cal 18 N 24. 4: Roberta Malcolm. 5: UPittsburgh 46-49 (Bus Admin) BS; Carnegie 49-50 MLS. 7: US Army Infantry (Sgt) 43-46; Sr catlgr UNH 50-53; Asst catlgr Purdue U 53-55; UAkron: Head catlgr 55-60, Head tech processes 60-64, Asst libn 64-65; Col Libn Muskingum Col 65-. 9: ALA-ACRL (Tri-State Chap). 10: AAUP. 14: Catlg, admin. 15: 165 Montgomery blvd, New ConcordOh 43762.

ARMSTRONG, JOHN ELDRED. b Indianapolis Ind 30 Jl 08. 4: Elizabeth Goodwin. 5: Princeton 25-29 (Art & Arch); Rollins Col 29-30 (Fr, Ger) AB; Columbia 40-41 BLS, 51 (Med Lit), 61 (Legal Lit). 6: Fr, Ger, Ital, Sp, Lat, Gk. 7: Ref asst Ind State Lib 39-40; Ref asst Ref Dept NY Pub Lib 41-45; Pub health libn Mun ref Lib, NYC 45-49; Prin libn NYC Healrh Dept 49-51; Ref libn NYC Bd of Higher Educ 51-52; Biol sci libn ASTIA (US Defense Dept), NYC 55-56; Spec asst to gen libn NYU 62-65; Lit searcher free-lance 65-. 8: Served as Pres-elect of United Staff Assn of Pub Libs of NYC 48-49. 10: ColumbiaU Sch of Lib Serv Alumni Assn. 13: Yes. 14: Ref. 15: 235 W 102nd st, New York NY 10025.

ARMSTRONG, JUDITH (MIMS). b Jersey City NJ 23 N 33. 5: N Tex U 51-55 (Bus Educ) BBA; Tex Woman's U 61-62 MSLS. 7: Sec Pfizer Labs, Dallas 55-61; Jr libn UMo 62-64; A-v libn Daniel Boone Reg Lib, Columbia Mo 64-65; Govt documents libn Southwest Mo State Col 65-68, Asst Prof LS 69-. 8: Dir, Nat Lib Week, Columbia Mo 65; Exec Dir, NatLib Week in Mo 66. 9: ALA; MoLA (Exhib Chm 65 & 68, treas 68-70). 10: Quotainternat. 12: Bk reviewer "Library Journal" (66-). 14: Ref, govt docs, LS tchg. 15: 2118 S Fairway Apt 3, Springfield Mo 65804.

ARMSTRONG, JULIA RUTH. b Rochester NY 22 F 07. 5: URochester 24-28 (Lat) BA, 28-30 (Lat) MA; Simmons 35-36 (LS) BS. 6: Lat, Fr, Ger. 7: Head bus & econ Rochester Pub Lib, Rochester NY 36-43, Supv of brs 43-48; Asst reg libn Reg Lib Serv Center NY State Lib, Watertown NY 48-51, Reg libn 51-52; NY Pub Lib: Head Bronx Ref Lib 52-55, Head Donnell Ref Lib 55-59, Asst coordinator adult serv 59-62; Ref consul Col of Insurance, NYC 62-63; Lib consul adult bks Thomas Y Crowell Co, NYC 63-68; Lib consul 69-. 8: Consul on Ref Bks for Reg Ref Centers, NY State Lib Ext Div 62-63; chm Com to Study the Lib Needs of Lower Manhattan, NY Pub Lib 56. 9: ALA-RSD (pres 61-62, Com on Wilson Indexes, & var div coms); SLA (NY Chap: chm Publ Group 65-66); NYLA (dir Adult Serv Div 58-59); NY Lib Club. 10: Phi Brta Kappa. 14: Ref, adult serv, bk sel. 15: 433 W 21st st apt 9C, New York NY 10011.

ARMSTRONG, MARGARET JUNE. b Vanceboro Maine 23 Je 11. 5: UMe 28-32 (Hist, Govt) BA; Harvard summer 40; BostonU 50 (Soc studies) MEd; Simmons 59 MSLS; Iowa StateU summer 62. 6: Sp, Fr. 7: Supv Colson-Serv Co, Somerville Mass 44-54; Tchr Parker Sch, Lexington Mass 54-55; Reserve libn Tufts 55-59; Assoc libn Farmington State Col 59-. 9: MeLA; MeSchLA. 10: AAUP; AAUW; Delta Kappa Gamma; Farmington Friends of the Lib; Fac Women's Club. 14: Catlg, ref. 15: 61 Main, Farmington Me 04938.

ARMSTRONG, MARIAN. b Bedford Ind 24 Je 29. 5: IndU 49-52 (Lang Arts) BS Educ, 58 (LS) MA. 7: Libn Edison Sch, Gary Ind 52-56; Libn Paris Amer Sch, Paris 56-57; Libn U Sch, Bloomington Ind 58-68; Asst Prof Div Lib Sci IndU 68-. 8: Instr Div of Lib Sci IndU. 9: ALA-AASchL; AALS; IndLA; IndSchLA. 10: Pi Lambda Theta; Beta Phi Mu. 14: Info sources & serv, sch libs. 15: Grad Lib School Indiana Univ, Bloomington In 47401.

ARMSTRONG, MARY ELIZABETH. b NYC 21 Ja 10. 5: Cornell 27-31 (Eng) AB; Columbia 31-32 (Eng lit). 6: Fr, Russian. 7: Libn (ILL) US Nat Security Resources Bd, Washington DC 48-51; Asst law libn US Off of Price Stabilization, Washington DC 51-53; Libn-catlgr CIA Lib, Washington DC 53-67; Libn-catlgr LC 67-. 14: Catlg (docs, Slavic lang publ). 15: 3811 Newark st NW, Washington DC 20016.

ARMSTRONG, MARY PAULA. b Rocky Ford Colo 5 Ja 32. 5: Miss State Col for Women 59 (LS) AB; UDenver (LS) MA; UUtah 66-67 (Law). 6: Fr, Ger, Sp. 7: Clerk lib USDOD, Anchorage Alaska 51-53, Libn Chateauroux France 54-56; Libn US Govt Panama CZ 61-62; Acquis libn Colo State Col 60-61; Catlgr UUtah 62-65; Libn LDS Bus Col, Salt Lake City 65-67; Tech processes libn Nev State Lib, Carson City Nev 67-. 9: ALA; NevStateLA. 10: AAUW; Alpha Beta Alpha; NICAP; BPW; Procenium Players. 13: Yes. 14: Catlg, child wk, law libnship. 15: PO Box 1256, Carson City Nv 89701.

ARMSTRONG, ROBERT D. b Albert Lea Minn 24 N 31. 4: Margaret Thompson. 5: UCal (Berkeley) 58 AB, 59 MLS. 7: Gifts libn UCLA Lib 59-62; Ser libn UNev Lib 62-63, Spec collections libn 63-. 8: Consul to Spec Collections Dept, UNevada (Las Vegas) 67; Governor's Commsnon Nevada Hist 66-. 9: NevLA; SAA. 10: AAUP; West Hist Assn. 12: "A PreliminaryUnion Catalog of Nevada Manuscripts" (67). 13: Yes. 14: Spec collections, mss,imprints. 15: 490 E Greenbrae dr, Sparks Nv 69220.

ARMSTRONG, ROBERT W. b Detroit 4 Jl 15. 4: Florence Hayes. 5: Wayne U 32-36 (Bus Admin) AB; Columbia 38-39 BLS. 7: Br asst Pub Lib, Brooklyn NY 39-40; Asst journalism libn Columbia U 40-42; (2nd Lt) USAF Armament Off 42-45; Detroit Pub Lib: Lib asst 45-53, Mun ref libn 53-56, Purchasing agent 56-64, Bus dir 64-. 9: ALA (Coun 64-68); SLA (pres Mich Ch ap 55-56); MichLA (pres 6061). 10: Friends of Detroiy Pub Lib (asst treas); Detroit Associated Libs System (bus dir). 13: Yes. 14: Admin, ref, reg lib serv systems. 15: 31699 Southview rd, Birmingham Mi 48008.

ARMSTRONG, ROBERTA MALCOLM. b Buffalo NY 20 D 24. 4: John Buchanan Armstrong. 5: Western Col for Women 42-46 (Hist) BA; Carnegie 49-50 MLS. 7: Asst br libn Hartford Pub Lib, Hartford Conn 50-51; Asst circ libn UNH Lib 51-53; Pub serv asst UAkron 58-65; Asst libn ref Muskingum Col 65-. 14: Ref. 15: 165 Montgomery blvd, New Concord Ohio 43762.

ARMSTRONG, RODNEY. b Atlanta 5 Mr 23. 5: Williams 45-48 (Eng) AB; Columbia 48-50 (LS) MS. 6: Sp. 7: US Naval Reserve, 43-45; Nonprof asst in brs Brooklyn (NY) Pub Lib 48-49, Asstyp dept 49; Libn The Phillips Exeter Acad, Exeter NH 50-. 8: Consul to DeerfieldAcad, Deerfield Mass, on its new lib 64-68; Consul on bldg & lib prog; Foxcroft Sch,Middleburg Va 66-; Middlesex Sch, Concord Mass 67-; St Mark's Sch, Southboro Mass68-; Greenwich C D Sch Conn 69-; Trustee, Kensington Soc Lib, Kensington NH 57-;Trustee, Thomas Bailey Aldrich Mem, Portsmouth NH 55-. 9: ALA; SAA; Mss Soc 9dir 64-); NHLA (Coun 51-52); NESchLA (v-pres 52). 10: NE Hist Geneal Soc; Amer Antiq Soc; Colonial Soc of Mass; Grolier Club, NY; Club of Odd Volumes, Boston; Union Club, Boston. 11: Awarded Trustees Award for Distinguished Serv, The Phillips Exeter Acad, 60. 13: Yes. 14: Yp, rare bks, archives. 15: Davis Lib The Phillips Exeter Acad, Exeter NH 03833.

ARNDAL, ROBERT EDWARD. b Ventura Cal 28 My 30. 5: Fresno State Col 48-53 (Soc Sci) AB; USoCal 55-56 MSLS. 6: Fr. 7: US Army Infantry Pub Info Off (Cpl) 53-55; Libn I Fresno State Col 55; Asst ser libn UCLA 56-59; Acquis libn Hughes Aircraft Co, Culver City Cal 59-61; Catlg libn Gen Dynamics Corp Convair Div, San Diego Cal 61-. 9: SLA; CalLA. 10: Beta Phi Mu. 14: Catlg, lib admin. 15: 18351 Verano pl, San Diego Ca 92128.

ARNDT, ARLEEN I. b Imlay City Mich 6 My 38. 5: Central Mich U 56-60 (Sch Libnship) BA (summa cum laude); UMich summers 61-65 AMLS. 6: Fr. 7: Libn Midland Pub Schs, Midland Mich 6065; Catlgr Shipman Lib Adrian Col 65-. 9: ALA; MichLA. 10: Alpha Gamma Delta. 14: Catlg, child lit. 15: Shipman Lib Adrian Col, Adrian Mi 49221.

ARNETT, HELEN MAE (VALLISH). b Mt Carmel Penn 29 O 14. 4: James E Arnett. 5: UAkron 32-36 (Lat, Fr) AB; West Res 40-41 BSLS; San Jose State Col 46-52 (Supervision) MA; Stanford 58-59 (Tchr Educ); West Res 60-65 (Curriculum & Supervision) PhD. 7: Fr tchr of gifted, Akron Pun Schs, Akron Ohio 36-39, Eng tchr 39-40 Wayne Co libn, Wooster Ohio 41-42; Yp libn Akron Pub Lib, Akron Ohio 44; Eng tchr & head of Eng Dept Salinas Union High Sch, Salinas Cal 44-53; Educ libn & Assoc prof of bibliog UAkron, Akron Ohio 53-. 9: ALA; OhioLA. 10: Delta Kappa Gamma; Pi Lambda Theta. 11: Teacher of Merit (Salinas Cal). 14: Curriculum centers, libs for educators. 15: 691 Payne ave apt 2, Akron Oh 44302.

ARNHEIM, JULIETTE (O'NEIL). b Knoxville Tenn 23 N 39. 4: William M Arnheim III. 5: Sweet Briar 57-61 (Chem) AB; UParis (Sweet Briar jr year program) 59-60. 6: Fr. 7: Asst Libn Interchem Corp, NYC 61-63; Esso Research & Engring Co, Linden NJ: Tech ed 63-66, Ref libn 66-. 9: SLA. 14: Sci-tech ref. 15: 751 St Marks ave, Westfield NJ 07090.

ARNOFF, SELDA (ARGINTEANU). b Schenectady NY. 4: Louis Arnoff. 5: Hunter Col 35-39 (Music, langs) AB (cum laude); Columbia 39-43, 45-51 (Musicology) AM, 43-45, 53-57 BS in LS. 6: Fr, Ital, Sp, Ger. 7: Asst music lib ColumbiaU 43-44; Catlgr NY Pub Lib 44-46; Asst libn Juilliard Sch (NYC) 46-47; Libn & asst to dir of visual educ Lexington Sch (NYC) 47-48; Admin asst & head of catlg dept RutgersU Libs 48-52; Asst libn Pace Col 52-53; Spec appointment in music NY Pub Lib 54; Tch of lib, in chg of catlg, Brooklyn Tech High Sch, Brooklyn NY 55; Tchr of lib NY Sch of Printing 9nyc0, 55-, Libn in chg 60-. 8: Asst examiner, Bd of Examiners, NYC Bd of Educ, 60-; Bk Reviewer, Bur of Libs, NYC Bd of Educ, 57-. 9: ALA (Div of Catlg & Clsf: chm Subcom on Revision of Filing Rules 56-58, mem other coms 55-58); -ACRL; Amer Musicological Soc; Internat Musicological soc; MusLA; Music Tchrs Nat Assn (Com on Lib Resources 47-49); SLA; NJLA (Exec Com 50-51, var offs & assignments in Assn & in Catlg Sect 49-51); NY Reg Catlg Group (sec-treas 50-51); NY Lib Club. 10: OES; Kappa Mu Epsilon. 12: Ed "Reprints of Periodicals in Musicology (53-55). 13: Yes. 14: Catlg, admin, tech serv, info retrieval, bibliog. 15: 3725 Henry Hudson pkwy, Riverdale NY 10463.

ARNOLD, ANN ALICE. b Columbus Ohio 5 Ja 47. 5: UCal (Berkeley) 64-68 (Phy Sci) BA; UCLA 68-69 MLS. 15: 3731 Cedar ave, Long Beach Ca 90807.

ARNOLD, BRENDA (WILSON). b Winnipeg Man Can 28 Ag 10. 7: Asst libn City Lib Las Vegas Nev 40-55; Libn Edgerton, Germeshausen & Grier Inc, Las Vegas Nev 59-. 9: ALA; SLA; NevStateLA (sec-treas). 14: Catlg, ref, lib admin. 15: 213 East Hill ave, North Las Vegas Nv 89031.

ARNOLD, CHARLES HARVEY. b Atlanta 25 My 20. 4: Patricia Streeter. 5: David Lipscomb Col 41-43 AA; UGa 43-44; Transylvania Col 44-45 (Philos); Chicago Divinity Sch 46-49, 56-57 (Theol, Higher Educ) MA, BD. 6: Ger. 7: Minister Congregational Churches, Ill 47-56; Asst libn Chicago Theol Sem 56-57, Libn 57-62; Libn & bibliog Philos & Theol

UChicago 62-. 9: TheolLA. 10: Church historian of the Hyde Park Union Church; Porter Found Bd & Campus Ministry United Church of Christ and UnitedPresbyterian Church. 14: Ref, research, bibliog in philos; Amer theol hist 1876-1939; John Henry Newman and Oxford Movement. 15: 5715 Harper ave, Chicago Il 60637.

ARNOLD, EDMUND (RANDOLPH). b NYC 22 Je 30. 4: Barbara Cook. 5: UConn 52-57 (Hist) BA, 57-63 (Hist) MA; Rutgers 60-62 MLS; SyracuseU 67- (Instr Communications). 6: Fr. 7: USAF Radar operator & tech (S/Sgt) 47-52; Circ libn head dept Wilbur Cross Lib UConn 57-60; Ref asst Orange Pub Lib, Orange NJ 60-61; Research asst Grad Sch Lib Serv Rutgers 61; Bibliog E Stroudsburg State Col 62-64; Ref libn Col Lib State U Col (Potsdam NY) 64-67; Lectr Sch Lib Sci SyracuseU 67-. 8: Assisted in prep of Shaw-Shoemaker "American Bibliography 1811-1817; Fac consul Lib educ Experimental Project SyracuseU Lib Sci Sch 68-. 9: ALA; Amer Educ Research Assn; NYLA. 10: AAUP; Beta Phi Mu. 12: Kemp Lib Bibliogs on Africa (63); "A Bibliography of the Middle East & the Moslem World (65); "A Selected Bibliography of Materials on the Teaching of Social Studies, Co-comp "Historical Materials Relating to Northern New York: a Union Catalog (68). 13: Yes. 14: Ref, ser, documentation, readers serv. 15: School of Lib Sci Syracuse Univ, Syracuse NY 13210.

ARNOLD, FREDERICK LAWRENCE. b Johnstown Penn 26 O 23. 5: UPenn 39-48 (Psych) AB; U de Grenoble 45 Cert d'Etat; Drexel Inst of Tech 49 (LS) BLS. 6: Fr. 7: US Army Inf Sgt, 42-46; Ref asst Lib of Cong, 50-54; Supv Ser Div Princeton U, 54-56; Asst Univ Libn for Ref 56-. 8: Dir Lib, Amer U in Cairo UAR 65-66. 9: ALA; -RSD (pres 64-65); BSA; NJLA. 10: Grolier Club; Princeton Club; SAR. 14: Ref. 15: Sunny Slope Farm, PO Box 3, Lawrenceville NJ 08648.

ARNOLD, MARGARET J. b NYC 15 Ag 20. 5: Syracuse 39-42 (Psych) BA; Simmons 42-43 (LS) BS. 7: Gen asst Detroit Pub Lib 43-45; Gen asst Wellesley Free Lib, Wellesley Mass 45-46; Reviser, assoc dir Simmons Col lib 46-50; Libn Wellesley Free Lib, Wellesley Mass 50-. 9: MassLA; NELA; Reg Adv Coun; Alumni Assn of Simmons Col (Bd). 10: Human Relations Serv of Wellesley; Isabel Babsin Mem Lib; Town Meeting Member; Freedom Agenda; Wellesley Hist Soc; Newton-Wellesley Hosp Aid; LWV. 14: Reg development. 15: 35 Summit rd, Wellesley Ma 02181.

ARNOLD, SISTER MARIA OP (DOROTHY). b Marietta Ohio. 5: St Mary of the Springs 33 (Hist, Eng) BS; Duquesne 56-59 (LS) MEd in LS. 7: Elem Sch Pittsburgh, Detroit-Grosse Pointe, Ohio; Libn High Sch NW Cath, W Hartford Conn 65-. 9: ALA; CathLA. 14: Ref, catlg. 15: 29 Wampanoag dr, W Hartford Ct 06117.

ARNOLD, NANCY IRVIN. b St Marys Penn 23 N 14. 5: Mass State Tchrs Col 33-34; Penn Sch of Horticulture 36-37. 7: Biddle Law Lib UPenn: Circ asst 44-45, Asst in acquis dept 46-58, Head circ & ref libn 58-. 69, Ref libn 69-. 9: AALL. 14: Ref. 15: Biddle Law Lib Univ of Penn, 3400 Chestnut st, Phila Pa19104.

ARNOLD, RUTH GERTRUDE LIBERTY (RABINOFF). b NYC 6 Ap 18. 4: Ladine (Dean) Arnold. 5: Antioch Col 34-39 (Soc Sci) AB; NYU 40-41 (Retailing) MSc in Retailing; Columbia 60-63 (LS) MS; NYU Grad Sch of Educ 63-64. 6: Fr. 7: Copywriter advertising promotion Parents Magazine, NYC 45-49; Lib assoc NYU Dental Lib 63-64; Asst prof of ib sci JerseyCity State Col 64-; Adjunct child lit 69-. 9: NEA; NJEA; Hudson Co EA. 10: Woodstock Guild of Craftsmen, Woodstock NY; Eta Mu Pi. 14: Ref. 15: 565 W 169th st, NYC 10032.

ARNOLD, WILNORA (BARTON). b Burnet Tex 11 N 23. 4: J Barton Arnold Jr. 5: UTex 41-44 (Eng) BA; La State U 45-46 (LS) BS in LS. 6: Spanish. 7: Asst Libn Tex A & M U, 46-48; Libn St Mary's Hall, San Antonio 48-49; Libn John Marshall High, San Antonio 57-61; Asst libn San Antonio College, San Antonio 61-; Instr Grad Sch LS Our Lady of the Lake Col, 66. 9: ALA; SWLA; TexLA; BexarLA (sec). 10: San Antonio Col Fac Senate; AAUP; Delta Kappa Gamma. 14: Ref, lib educ. 15: 7784 Woodridge rd, San Antonio Tx 78209.

ARNOTE, WENDELL K. b Polo Mo 25 D 18. 5: William Jewell Col 36-40 (Sociol) AB; Southern Baptist Sem 40-45 9religious Educ) BD; Peabody 57-59 (LS) MA. 7: Asst ref libn Pub Lib, Nashville 49-59; Dir adult serv pub lib Greensboro NC 59-60; Asst ref libn pub lib, Charlotte NC60-63; Ref libn Frostburg State Col 63-66; Libn admin Worcester Co Lib, Snow Hill Md 66-. 9: ALA-Md Chap (Ref Serv Div); MdLA (Ref Serv Div). 14: Admin. 15: Worcester County Lib, Snow Hill Md 21863.

ARNOTT, LILLIAN (REMICK). b Fitchburg Mass 26 My 22. 5: Atlantic Union Col 40-43 (Eng); Columbia Union Col 43-44 (Eng); Ashland Col 62-64 (Eng) BA; IndU 66-68 (LS) MES. 7: Eng tchr Mt Vernon Acad, 62-64; Libn 64-67; Asst libn Atlantic Union Col, 67-. 9: ALA; MassLA. 15: Box 52, Lancaster Ma 01523.

ARO, BARBARA (HOWARD). b Montrose Colo 19 Ja 33. 4: Richard S Aro. 5: UWyo 51-55 (Sociol) BA; UDenver 64-65 (LS) MA UIowa 67 (Educ, Anthro). 6: Fr, Sp. 7: Clerk-typist Wyo Game & Fish Commsn, Cheyenne Wyo summers 51-55; Asst to ser libn Mont State U Lib 56; Clerk-libn Sch of Home Econ UAriz 59-60; Bind libn Olin Lib Washington U (St Louis) 65-66; Sci libn, UIowa Lib 66-68, Ref libn, UIowaEduc Lib 68; Ref libn Colo State U Libs, Ft Collins 68-. 9: ALA. 10: Pi Beta Phi; Phi Beta Kappa; Phi Kappa Phi; Phi Sigma Iota. 14: Ref, pubserv, Jr col libs, Univ libs. 15: 1801 Orchard pl, Fort Collins Co 80521.

AROESTE, JEAN LISETTE. b Richmond Va 2 O 32. 4: Henry Aroeste. 5: UWis 54 (Comparative Lit) BA; Simmons 62 MS in LS; UCLA 67 (Eng) BA. 6: Fr. 7: Acquis dept Harvard Col Widener Lib 54-62; Ref dept libn III uresearch Lib UCLA 62-. 8: Ref staff Lib/USA, NY Worlds Fair 65. 12: Ed "New Reference Books at UCLA (67-). 13: Yes. 14: Ref, acquis, pub rel. 15: Univ Res Lib UCLA, Los Angeles Ca 90024.

ARONSON, ELEANOR J(AFFRAY). b Garden City NY 30 Jl 15. 4: C(asper) J Aronson. 5: Smith 32-36 Physics BA. 6: Fr, Ger. 7: Stud tchr The Brearley Sch, NYC 36-38; Tchr Kent Place Sch, Summit NJ 38-42; Physicist Bureau of Ordnance Navy Dept, Wash DC 42-46, Libn 46-48; Chief, catlg sect ASTIA Ref Center, Wash DC 48-58; Chief, processing br Off of Tech Serv, Wash DC 58-64; Chief, processing sect Clearinghouse for Federal Sci and Tech Info, Spr9ngfield Mo 64-66, Chief doc standards sect 66-. 9: SLA; ASIS. 14: Catlg. 15: 3401 Oberon st, Kensington Md 20795.

ARSENAULT, HENRI J. b Upper Charlo NB Can 16 N 20. 4: Marie-Antoinette Fournier. 5: St Francis Xavier 47-57 (Chem) BSc; McGill Lib Sch 51-52 BLSc. 7: Libn Fed Dept of Agric, Kentville Nova Scotia 52-58; Fed Dept of Agric, OHawa Ontario: Ref libn 59-61, Hd br libs 61-63; Chief libn Alcan Research & Development Ltd, Arvida PQ 64-. 9: SLA; ASIS. 14: Library management. 15: 274 Morrison, Arvida PQ Can.

ARTANDI, SUSAN. 4: Charles Artandi. 5: Rutgers 63 (Info sci libnship) PhD. 7: Assoc Prof Rutgers Grad Sch of Lib Serv. 8: Principal Investigator "Investigation of Systems for the Intellectual Organization of Information" undr a grant from NSF 63-66; "Automatic Indexing Drug Information" under a grant from PHS NLM in Progres. 9: ALA (mem Adv Bd of Lib Tech Program 69-71); SLA; ASLIB; ASIS (Coun 69-71). 10: Beta Phi Mu; AAUP. 12: "An Introduction to Computers in Information Science," (68); Ed "Rutgers Series on Systems for the Intellectual Organization of Information" 7 vols (64-66). 13: Yes. 14: Info sci & tech systems analysis, computer scis, spec libs. 15: Grad Sch of Lib Serv, Rutgers U New Brunswick NJ.

ARTERBERY, VIVIAN (JUSTICE). b Houston Tex 21 Je 37. 4: Augustus C Arterbery. 5: Howard U 54-58 (Hist) BA; UsoCal 65 MLS, 66-67 (Data Processing). 6: Fr. 7: Catlgr Space Tech Lavs, Redondo Beach Ca& 59-60; Indexer & ref libn Aerospace Corp, Los Angeles 60-61, Ref libn, San Bernardino Cal 62-63, Ref libn, Los Angeles 63-67; Supv circ Charles C Lauritsen Lib, Los Angeles 67-. 9: SLA (corr sec 66-67, Rec sec 67-68, Placement Chm 68-69); ASIS; CalLA; So Cal Tech Proc Gp 9memb Chm 69). 10: Alpha Kappa Alpha. 12: Comp "Directory of Special Libraries of Southern California' (65). 14: Lib automation, ref, admin. 15: 4560 Don Diego dr, Los Angeles Ca 90008.

ARTHUR, ADAH CAROL (WEBBER). b West Liberty Ohio 13 Je 23. 4: Charles Edward Arthur. 5: Wittenburg U 45-48 (Eng) BS in Ed; Ohio State U 49-55; Kent State U 50-55 (LS) MA. 6: Sp, Lat. 7: Libn & high sch Eng tchr Salem Local Schs, Champaign Co Ohio 48-49; Libn Urbana Jr Col 49-51; Lib asst Dayton Pub Lib, Dayton Ohio 51-52; Asst libn Ohio Northern U 52-53; Libn Urbana Jr Col 53-55; Elem tchr Urbana City Schs, Urbana Ohio 55-57; Tchr & libn Graham Local Schs, St Paris Ohio 59-66; Catlg & processing Urbana Col Lib, Urbana Ohio 66-68; Libn Cath Central HS, Springfield Ohio 68-. 9: NEA; OhioEA; Ohio Sch Libn Assn; OhioLA; CathLA. 10: Methodist Church: Women's Soc of

Christian Serv; Beta Kappa Theta; Springfield Art Assn; Champaign Co Mental Health Assn. 13: Yes. 14: Ref, catlg, non-book media. 15: 336 Sweetman st, Urbana Oh 43078.

ARTHUR, HELEN (PYLE). b Didsbury Alta Can 23 Ja 22. 4: Everett L Arthur. 5: Simmons 39-43 (LS) BS; Utica Col of Syracuse 59-63 (Educ) Permanent Certif. 6: Fr. 7: Libn Rome Free Acad, Rome NY 60-. 9: ALA; NYLA; NY Tchrs Assn; Cent NY Libns Assn (pres); Rome Tchrs Assn. 10: Sponsor Rome Free Acad Lib Coun; AAUW; Delta Kappa Gamma. 15: 913 Floyd ave, Rome NY 13440.

ARTHUR, SUSAN (LILLIAN). b Knox County Ky 5 N 16. 5: Cumberland Col 32-34; Berea Col 34-36 (Eng, Soc studies) BA; UKy summers 38-48 (BS in LS); Columbia summer 58. 6: Fr, Sp. 7: Sch libn Pineville City Schs, Pineville Ky 47-51; Catlgr & circ Henderson State Tchrs Col, Arkadelphia Ark 50-51; Asst libnUnion Col Barbourville Ky 52-54; Ser libn Berea Col 56-60; Clsf-catlgr US Army TRECOM Ft Eustis Va 60-61; Sch libn BarbourvilleCity Schs, Barbourville Ky 61-66; Spec Col Libn Berea Col 66-68; Sch libn Barbourville City Schs 68-. 9: ALA; SELA; KyLA; KySchLA; NEA; KEA. 10: AAUW; Garden Club. 14: Catlg, rare bks. 15: 601 N Main st, Barbourville Ky 40906.

ARVIN, CHARLES STANFORD. b Loogootee Ind 17 Ap 31. 5: Wayne U 49-53 (Govt) AB, 56-57 (Hist); UMich 59-60 MALS. 7: US Army (Sgt), Ark, Korea, Mo 53-56; Asst div libn UMich Natural Sci Lib60-62; Ref & bk sel Genesee Co Lib, Flint Mich 62-67, Hd of central serv 67-. 9: ALA; MichLA. 10: Ind Hist Soc; ACLU; Flint Lib Club; Flint Geneal Soc. 14: Ref, bk sel, bibliog. 15: 5157 Winshall dr,Swartz Creek Mi 48473.

ASAWA, EDWARD E. b Norwalk Cal 15 F 30. 4: Hideko Harumi. 5: Meiji U (Tokyo) 48-50 (Lit); Fullerton Jr Col 55-57 (Eng) AA; Long Beach State Col 57-59 (Eng) BA; USoCal 59-61 MSLS. 6: Japanese. 7: Interpreter & Tr US Army (Sgt) 52-55; Tchr Japanese lang Japanese Lang Sch Unified System, Los Angeles 55-61; Stud prof libn Los Angeles Co Pub Lib 60-61, Cat&gr 61-67; Bk evaluator (sr libn) 67-; Libn Los Angeles Co Dept of Mental Health 62-. 8: Org lib for Los Angeles Co Dept of Mental Health, 62; its libn on part-time basis. 9: CalASchL; ITA. 13: Yes. 14: Catlg, bk selection. 15: 14527 Cedar Springs dr, Whittier Ca 90603.

ASCHKENASY, LINDA (SCHULDER). b Brooklyn NY 8 Ap42. 4: Jacob Aschkenasy. 5: Brooklyn Col 59-63 (Eng) BA; Pratt 63-64 MLS. 6: Hebrew, Fr. 7: Libn trainee Brooklyn Pub Lib summer 63; Libn Yeshiva of Flatbush High Sch Lib, Brooklyn NY 64-. 9: ALA. 10: Phi Beta Kappa; Beta Phi Mu. 14: Ref. 15: 451 W End ave, New York NY 10024.

ASH, DONALD E. b Eau Claire Wis 28 Ag 24. 5: Knox Col 47-48; St Thomas Col (St Paul) 48-49; Wis State Col (River Falls) 49-51 (Hist) BS; UWis (Madison) 51-52, summer 55 (Hist, Law); Los Angeles State Col 53-58 (Hist) MA; Immaculate Heart Col 60-62 (LS) MS. 7: US Army Air Corps 43-46; Tchr Thermal Elem Sch Dist, Thermal Cal 53; Tchr Los Angeles City Sch Dist 54-55; Estate admin Los Angeles Co, Los Angeles 56-58; Tchr Victor Valley Union High Sch Dist, Victorville Cal 58-59; Sch libn Mayfair High Sch, Bellflower (Cal) Unified Sch Dist 62-64; Sch libn Morningside High Sch, Inglewood (Cal) Unified Sch Dist 64-. 9: CalASchL; ITA. 14: Sch libnship. 15: Morningside High Sch Lib, 10500 Yukon st, Inglewood Ca 90303.

ASH, LEE (MICHAEL). b NYC 15 S 17. 4: Marian Neal Ash. 5: Pratt 36 (Certif to BLS); Columbia 32-37, Spec stud Sch of Lib Serv 36-38; Chicago (LS) 39-41. 6: Fr, Ger, Ital, Sp, Lat. 7: Asst to libn Explorers Club (NYC) 29-33; Asst to libn Museum of the Amer Indian (NYC) 33-36; Asst libn Burgess lib for Hist (Pol Sci & Econ), Columbia 36-37; Libn News & Research Lib, Associated Press, NYC (org Photolibrary) 37-38; Priv fellowship for research in anthropology & bibliog, State of Okla 38-39; Asst to libn Joint Ref Lib Pub Admin Clearing House, Chicago 39 -40; Research Asst to Prof Pierce Butler UChicago Grad Lib Sch 40-41; State Dir WPA Lib Serv Projs of Ind 40-42; US Army Operating Surgical Tech 42-44; Asst head rare bk dept & head trade order & internat acquis dept, Brentanos Bk Stores (NYC) 44-46; Bibliog in chg med & rare scholarly bks dept, Argosy Bk Stores (NYC) 46-53; Libn Carnegie Endowment for Internat Peace (NYC) 53-57; Ed "Library Journal" 57-59; SEARCH ANALYST ; Ed Selective Bk Retirement Prog, YaleU Lib/Coun on Library Resources Proj, New Haven Conn 59-63; Assoc Prof Grad Sch of Lib Sci, Drexel Inst Tech 63-64; Staff consul Yale Hist Med Lib 67-; Ed & Publ "American Notes & Queries" 62-; Lib & Publ consul (own firm) 62-. 8: Publishers consul Gale Research Corp 65-, G K Hall Inc 64-, etc; Org lib Amer Municipal Assn, Chicago 40; Research Sec Com on Preservation of Cultural Resources in War-Time, Nat Resources Planning Bd, Wash DC 39-41; Dir Postwar Lib & Museum Program, Philippine Found of Amer (NYC) 46-50; Major Lib Consultantships; Nat Com on the Aging Lib (NYC) 57-62; St Francis Monastary Lib (Anglican), Mt Sinai (NY) 61-; Adv for the collections, Harvard Med Lib/Boston Med Lib 62-; Dir Survey of Med Lib Resources of Greater NY 63-; Dir Survey of Bk Resources, Toronto Pub Lib 65-; Dir Survey Conn Rege Med Lib Program 67-68; Univ Rochester Libs consul 66-; consul Med Chir Faculty of Md Lib 67-; consul Hort Soc of NY 67-; Downstate Med Lib (NY), consul 69-; Dir Queens Borough Pub Lib Survey 68-69. 9: ALA (Coun 59-63, NE Reg Recr mem 63-, chm numerous coms, etc); -ACRL; -LAD; -PLD; -RTSD; -RSD; AALS; CanLA; CNLA; LPRC; MedLA (chm var coms, etc); SLA (chm var coms, etc); ConnLA; NELA (Ed "Newsletter"); NYLA; NY Tech Serv Libns; NY Lib Club (past pres, etc); OntLA. 10: AHA; Amer Assn State & Loc Hist; Amer Assn Hist Med; Antiq Bksellers of Amer & Internat League Antiq Bksellers; BSA; Friends NY Acad Med Lib & Yale Univ Lib; Hist Sci Soc; Medieval Acad; Renaissance Soc; SAA; Mss Soc; Mod Lang Assn; Caten Soc of Amer; Soc of Indexers (London); Soc Hist of Discoveries; Scott Inst Polar Research (Cambridge Eng); Clubs; Grolier archons of Colophon Torch; Lay Reader, Prot Episcopal Church. 12: Ed & Publ "Amer Notes & Queries" (62-); Ed NELA "Newsletter" (69-); Books; co-chm "Who's Who in Library Service" (55), Ed (66 & 70); "Guide to Subject Collections in Libraries" (3rd ed 67); "Yale's Selective Book Retirement Program" (63); "Serial Publications Containing Medical Classics" (61); "Conference on Future Programs for Medical Library Cooperation" (65); "Interlibrary Loan Requests of Medical Libraries" (66); "Scope of Toronto's Central Library" (67) WITH Burton Tysinger; "Taste and Design in Library Planning" (70). 13: Yes. 14: Recr, admin, lib resources, acquis, rare bks, lit appraisals, publ, bkselling, lib educ. 15: 31 Alden rd, New Haven Ct 06515.

ASHBROOK, GAIL JUDITH. b Hot Springs Ark 28 F 38. 5: State Col of Ark 56-60 (Educ) BSE; LSU 66-68 (LS) MS. 7: Garland Montgomery Reg Lib; Ark Polytech Col Lib. 9: ALA; ArkLA; 10: AAUW; Beta Phi Mu. 14: Lib sci educ. 15: 136 Magnolia st, Hot Springs Ar 71901.

ASHEIM, LESTER (EUGENE). b Spokane Wash 22 Ja 14. 5: UWash 31-36 (Eng) BA, 36-37 BLAS, 37-41 (Amer Lit) MA, 45-49 (LS) PhD. 6: Fr. 7: Jr ref asst UWash 37-41; Libn US Fed Penitentiary, McNeil Island Wash 41-42; US Army 42-45; Reg libn US Fed Pub Housing Authority, Seattle 46; Asst Prof Grad Lib Sch U Chicago 48-52; Visiting Lecturer Grad Sch of Lib Sci UIll summer 49; Dean of Students Grad Lib Sch UChicago 51-52; Dean & Assoc Prof Grad Lib Sch U Chicago 52-61; Dir Internat Rel Off ALA 61-66; Dir Off Lib Educ 66-. 66; Dir Off Lib Educ 66-. 9: ALA; SLA; IllLA. 10: Phi Beta Kappa; Beta Phi Mu; AAUP. 12: Ed "Core of Education for Librarianship," ALA (54); "Educational Television, The Next Ten Years," with others (62); "Forum on the Public Library Inquiry" (50); 'From Book to Film' in "Reader in Public Opinion and Communication" (50); Ed "The Future of the Book" (55); "The Humanities and The Library," with others, ALA (57); "Library's Public," with Bernard Berelson (49); "New Directions in Public Library Development" (57); "Persistent Issues in American Librarianship" (61); 'Portrait of the Book Reader' in "Mass Communication" (49); "Librarianship in the Developing Countries" (66); Ed "Library Manpower Needs and Utilization" (67). 13: Yes. 14: Lib educ, communication, internat libnship. 15: 50 E Huron st, Chicago Il 60611.

ASHFORD, MRS FREDDYE (GEORGE). b Paducah Ky 21 Mr 14. 4: Jesse Ashford. 5: Ky State Col 37 (Eng) BA; Atlanta 48 BLS; UMo 58 (Elem Educ) MEd. 6: Fr. 7: Prim tchr Lynch Pub Sch, Lynch Ky 34-36; Soc sci tchr Washington High Sch, Caruthersville Mo 37-50; Circ & ref libn Lincoln U 50-, Asst libn 56-. 8: Citizens Com for Pub Sch, Jefferson City Mo 63. 9: ALA; MoLA. 10: AAUW; Mo Assn of Soc Welfare; AKA; Jefferson City Communconcert Assn; Coun of the Arts; WICS. 12: "Student Handbook" (Library); "FacultyHandbook" (65); Selected Bibliogs; "Directory of Missouri Public School Counselorsand Guidance Teachers" (kept up to date). 14: Ref, rare bks, special bibliog on Negroheritage and other Minorities' Heritage. 15: 781 Clark ave, Jefferson City Mo 65101.

ASHLEY, MRS ALICE FREEMAN (JONES). b Salemburg NC 19 Jl 10. 4: George Norman Ashley. 5: Pineland Jr Col 26-28 AA; Meredith Col 28-30 (Hist) BA; UNC 30-31 (Hist), summers 49-51 BS in LS. 7: Hist tchr Pineland Jr Col 31-34,

Libn 49-57; Libn Roseboro-Salemburg High Sch, Roseboro NC 57-. 8: Trustee, Pineland Jr Col 31-57; Trustee Sampson Co (NC) Pub Lib 58-62; Lib Recruiter, Sampson Co 65-. 9: NEA; ALA; NCEA; NCLA. 10: NC Lit & Hist Soc. 14: Ref. 15: P O Box 171, Roseboro NC 28382.

ASHLEY, CARRIE GENE. b Augusta Ga 10 Je 19. 5: Agnes Scott Col 36-40 (Hist) AB; UNC 55156 (LS) MS. 7: Tchr pub schs, SC 40-45; Red Cross Hosp Serv ARC, Augusta Ga, Ft Bragg NC, Ft Jackson SC 45-47; Tchr pub schs, SC 47-48, 50-55; Tchr CZ schs, Panama 49-50; Ext &ibn Greenwood Co Lib, Greenwood SC 56-58; Ref & adult serv libn ABBE Reg Lib, Aiken SC 58-. 9: ALA; SCLA (chm Pub Lib Sect 58-60, chm Recr Com 63-65). 15: Box 909, Aiken SC 29803.

ASHLEY, M CELESTE. b Baltimore 30 Ag 11. 5: Johns Hopkins 43-47 (Eng) BS; UCal(Berkeley) 47-48 (LS) BS; Stanford51-53 (Speech, Drama) MA 67. 7: Asst trea-sec Ashley Chevrolet Sales Inc, Baltimore 32-44; Ser catlgr Johns Hopkins U 46-47;Catlgr (L1) UCal (Santa Barbara) 48-51; Ref & theatre libn (L11) Stanford U 53-. 8: Free-lance theatre critic coveringcommunity theatres for -san Francisco Chronicle" (AP-AG 65). 10: Johns Hopkins Club; Palo Alto Commun Theatre. 14: Theatre ref. 15: 1077 Stanford ave, Palo Alto Ca 94306.

ASHMON, MARTHA ANN. b Columbus Ga 10 F 35. 5: Albany State Col 54-57 (Elem Educ) BS; Atlanta 63-64 MSLS. 6: Sp, Fr. 7: Tchr-libn Calhoun High Sch, Irwinton Ga 57-63; Circ libn Albany State Col (Ga) 64-. , Ref libn 65-67; Ref libn SoU 67-68, Hd libn 68-. 9: ALA; NEA; Ga Tchrs & Educ Assn. 10: Alpha Kappa Alpha; Churchlibn, Galilee Baptist Church, Shreveport La. 11: Outstanding Young Woman of the Year,66. 14: Reader's adv, circ, child wk, ref, admin, acquis. 15: 511 Alabama ave, Shreveport La 71107.

ASHMORE, CONSTANCE MARIE. b Freeport Ill 27 Ag 38. 5: UIll 56-60 (Hist) AB, 60-61 (LS) MS. 7: Catlg asst UIll (Urbana) 60-61, Ser asst 61-63; ser libn (US Peace Corps) ULagos (Lagos Nigeria) 64-65; Asst ref libn UIll (Urbana) 66-. 9: ALA. 10: Stephenson Co (Ill) Hist Soc; Ill State Hist Soc; Sierra Club. 14: Ref. 15: 2319 S First st, Champaign Il 61820.

ASHMORE, MARY R. b Utica NY 15 Ag 31. 5: Col of St Rose 49-50; St Joseph Col 51-53 9elem educ); Le Moyne Col 54-57 (Hist) BA; Syracuse 59-60 (LS) MS in LS. 7: Clk Utica Mut Ins Co, Utica NY 50-51; Housemother House of Providence, Syracuse 53-54; Rec clk St Joseph's Hosp, Syracuse 54; Sec reading instr Le Moyne Col, 54-59; Sch libn St John's Cath Acad, Syracuse 57-59; Br asst Syracuse Pub Lib, 60-63; Br hd, Field wkr Buffalo & Erie County Pub Lib, Buffalo NY 63-68; Hd adult serv Utica Pub Lib 68-. 9: NYLA. 10: Beta Phi Mu. 14: Adult serv. 15: 2614 Sunset ave, Utica NY 13502.

ASHWELL, (SARA) ELIZABETH. b Portland Ore 13 Mr 12. 5: Reed Col 30-34 (Langs & Lit) BA; UCal 38-39 Certif of Libnship Ore State U 68 (Gen Studies) MA. 6: Fr. 7: Lib Assn of Portland, Portland Ore;Clerical asst 34-38, Br libn 39-40, Ref dept 40-41, 1st asst circ dept 41-51, Head lendingdept 51-57, Head educ & psych dept 57-. 8: Consul Judson Baptist Col 67-. 9: ALA; OreLA; PNLA. 10: Northwest Adult EA. 14: Adult educ. 15: Lib Assn of Portland, 801 SW 10th ave, Portland Or 97205.

ASHWORTH, EDITH ELIZABETH. b Danville Va 9 Je 20. 5: Averett Col 37-38 Diploma; Madison Col 39-42 (LS) BS; UVa 52 (Educ) M Ed; UMex 53 (Folklore); Media Inst UVa 68. 7: Sch libn Brosville High Sch 42-53; Libn Va Hills Elem Sch, Fairfax Co (Va) Schs 53- Proj Dir Title II State Demonstration Lib Brookfieldelem 68-69; Media Specialist, Area I, Fairfax Co 69-. 9: ALA; VaLA (Steering Com);VaEA (sec-treas Dist 63-65); Associated SchLibns of Fairfax Co (pres); VaEA (sec SchLibns sect). 14: Child bks, a-v. 15: 7521 McWhorter pl, Annandale Va 22003.

ASKEW, ELIZABETH (ENGLE). b Richmond Va. 5: Westhampton Col 61-64 (Econ) BA; Rutgers 64-65 (LS) MLS. 7: Ref Asst Richmond Pub Lib, Richmond Va 65-68; Assoc Libn Fed Res Bk of Richmond, 68-. 9: ALA; SLA; VaLA. 15: 4809 Rodney rd, Richmond Va 23230.

ASPENGREN, GORDON E(RIC). b Rock Island Ill 30 My 07. 4: Frances Wilson. 5: Augustana Col (Rock Island Ill) 25-28; UMinn Ext 37; AB (Music), BM (Music Educ), MM (Musicology), MS in LS USoCal 38-41, 47-50. 6: Fr, Swedish. 7: Sec wk 29-38; Music supv Nyssa Schs, Nyssa Ore 41-42; US Army (T/Sgt) Anti-aircraft Artillery, US, Europe 42-45; Tchr secondary schs, Los Angeles & Long Beach Cal 46; Organist Angelica Lutheran Church, Los Angeles 46-51; Gifts & exch libn USoCal Lib 50-. 9: ALA; CalLA. 10: Amer Guild of Organists; Phi Kappa Phi; Beta Phi Mu. 14: Acquis, ref. 15: 4871 Dockweiler st, Los Angeles 90019.

ASPNES, GRIEG (GARFIELD). b Montevideo Minn 21 N 12. 4: Frances Gilman. 5: Minn 37-40 (Eng) BA, 40-41 BS in LS. 7: Libn Brown & Bigelow, St Paul 43-50, Advertising Manager 50-56; Research libn Cargill Inc, Minneapolis 56-. 8: Tchr of course in spec libnship, UMinn 62-. 9: SLA (pres 51-52, chm var coms incl Educ & Nomin, chm Advertising Div & Documentation Div; Minn Chap; consult offr); ASIS. 10: ACS; AAAS. 12: Ed "The Organization and Management of Special Libraries," SLA. 13: Yes. 14: Spec libs info centers, ref, indexing, human communication. 15: 4324 S Drew ave, Minneapolis Mn 55410.

ASTBURY, EFFIE CONSTANCE. b Montreal Can 9 D 16. 5: McGill 34-38 (Classics) BA (magna cum laude), 38-39 BLS; Toronto 56 MLS. 6: Fr. 7: Asst order libn McGill Med Lib 39-40, Head circ & ref 40-49; Grad Sch of Lib Sci McGill U: Lecturer 49-53, Asst Prof 53-65, Assoc Prof 65-69, prof 69-. 9: ALA; SLA; AALS; CanLA (coun 58-61); QueLA (coun 57-59);CACUL (coun 67-69). 10: Beta Phi Mu. 13: Yes. 14: Educ for libnship, ref, bibliog, col & univ libs. 15: Grad Sch of Lib Sci McGill Univ, Montreal 110 Can.

ASTLE, DEANA (LEE). b Martinez Cal 18 Jl 45. 5: Pembroke Col in Brown 63-67 (Eng Lit) AB; UCLA 67-68 MLS. 6: Fr, Sp. 7: Asst ser order libn UUtah Libs 68-. 9: ALA; UtahLA; MPLA. 10: Phi Beta Kappa. 14: Ser, automation. 15: Univ of Utah Libs, Salt Lake City Ut 84112.

ATEN, HELEN H(ARPER). b Indianapolis 29 D 1900. 5: Butler U 18-20 (Eng, Foreign Langs); UWis 20-22 AB, 22-23 MA in LS. 6: Fr. 7: Asst br libn, Milwaukee 23-24; Libn City & Co Lib, Ladysmith Wis 24-27; Libn Pub Lib, Manitowoc Wis 27-28; Instr Wis U Lib Sch summer 26; Ref & circ libn Iowa State Travel Lib, Des Moines Iowa 28-. 9: ALA;-ACRL; IowaLA. 10: Des Moines Lib Club. 13: Yes. 14: Ref, rare bks, French 18th Century especially. 15: IowaState Travel Lib, Historical bldg, Des Moines Ia 50319.

ATHERTON, PAULINE ANN (BLAZINA). b Berwyn Ill 2 D 29. 5: Lyons Township Jr Col 47-49; Ill Col 49-51 (Soc Sci) AB; Rosary Col 52-54 MA in LS; Chicago 55- (LS). 6: Sp, Ger. 7: Assoc libn Corn Products Co-Chem Div, Argo Ill 51-53; Tchr 7th ave Sch, LaGrange Ill 53-54; Libn I, adult serv Chicago Pub Lib 54-55; Act ref libn Chicago Tchrs Col 56-58; Cross ref ed World Book Encyclopedia, Chicago 58-59; Asst Prof Dept of LS Chicago Tchrs Col 58-61; Assoc Dir Doc Research Proj Amer Inst of Physics, NYC 61-66; Assoc Prof Sch of Lib Sci Syracuse U 66-. 8: Consul libn Rodfei ZedekCong Lib Chicago 60-61; Consul World Book Encyclopedia Chicago 60-; Proposal reviewer for NSF-OSIS; Consul; System Dev Corp 67, Westat Surveys Inc 69-; Visiting lecturer; Rosary Col Dept of Lib Sci 60-61; SUNY (Albany 65, Atlanta U 66. 9: ADI (treas 64-65); ALA-RTSD (Clsf of Com); SLA (Nucl Sci Div, treas 68-69);USNCFID/UDC; NYLA; NY Tech Serv Libns; FID-CR Commsn; ASIS (chm Sig/Cr 68-). 10: LWV; Phi Beta Kappa. 12: Ed "Classification Research" (Elsinore Conf Proc, 65); Elem Sch Lib Cat Manual (59). 13: Yes. 14: Catlg, clsf, info serv, info stor & retr. 15: 126 jamesville Apt K3, Syracuse NY 13210.

ATHY, DORIS J. b Columbia Mo 3 O 33. 5: UMo 51-55 (LS) BA; UIll 60 (LS) MS. 7: Asst libn Mexico-Audrain Co Lib, Mexico Mo 55-57, Libn 57-62; Libn Jefferson City-Cole Co Lib, Jefferson City Mo 62-67; Libn Thomas Jefferson Lib System 67-. 8: Exec dir, Nat Lib Week, Mo 61-62. 9: ALA; MoLA (treas 62-64, Lib Devel Com 62), chm Legislat Com 68-69. 10: Beta Phi Mu; Phi Beta Kappa. 14: Admin. 15: 1022 Holly dr, Jefferson City Mo 65101.

ATIYEH, GEORGE N. b Amioun Lebanon 21 My 23. 4: Daisy Roper. 5: Amer U of Beirut 46-48 (Hist) BA, 49-50 (Hist) MA; UChicago 51-54 (Orient Lang and Lit) PhD. 6: Sp, Arabic, Fr. 7: Instr and act libn Aleppo Col, Aleppo Syria 45-46; Instr Amer U of Beirut 49-50; Asst prof UPR 54-57, Assoc prof 57-60, Prof 60-67, Chm Dept of Humanities 61-67; Hd Near East Sect LC 67-. 9: Amer Oriental Soc; AHA; Middle East Studies Assn. 12: "Three Historical Essays" (Beirut 56); "al-Kindi the Philosopher of the Arabs" (Karachi 66); Co-auth "Medieval Political Philosophy" (63); Ed "Historia" SanJuan PR. 13: Yes. 14: Ref. 15: 600 N Naylor st, Alexandria Va 22304.

ATKINS, BETH (BRANTZ). b NYC 18 Mr 17. 4: Irving Atkins. 5: Brooklyn Col 34-39 (Hist) AB. 7: Info dept Gen

Motors Overseas Corp, NYC 35-40; Head Libn J M Mathes Inc, NYC 55-62; Head Libn Nat Lead Co, Hightstown NJ 63-. 9: SLA (Adver Div; NY Chap: chm). 10: PTA. 12: Ed "What's New in Advertising & Marketing" (60-62). 14: Ref. 15: 8 Windsor lane, Willingboro NJ 08046.

ATKINS, GENE DALE. b Russellville Ala 8N 38. 5: UAla 56-60 (LS) BS; UIll 61-62 (LS) MS; UOkla summer 68 (Orgm admin, multi-media resources); UIll Ext 62. 6: Fr. 7: Asst ref libn Peoria Pub Lib, Peoria Ill 60-61; Grad asst UIll (Urbana) 62; Chief catlgr Peoria (Ill) Pub Lib 62-63; Asst libn & instr in lib sci Va Mil Inst 63-65; Head tech processes dept Peoria (Ill) Pub Lib 65-66; Miss State U: Asst Prof & Hd (soc sci, humanities, ref) 66-67; assoc Prof & Hd catlg dept 67-. 8: Organist: (& choirmaster) St Andrews Episcopal Ch, Peoria Ill 62-63; Good Lutheran Ch, Lexington Va 64; Methodist Ch, Lexington Va 65; (& choirmaster) Episcopal Ch of the Resurrection, Starkville Miss 67-68; St Lukes Lutheran Ch, Starkville Miss 67-68. 9: ALA; LARC Assn; SELA; MissLA (Awards Com 68; Recruitment Com 69); VaLA (sec Col & Univ Sect 64); MissEA. 10: Amer Guild of Organists; Alpha Beta Alpha; AAUP; Nocturne Mus Club, Starkville Miss. 14: Catlg, ref, rare bks. 15: PO Box 2159, State College Ms 39762.

ATKINS, HANNAH (DIGGS). b Winston-Salem NC 1 N 23. Charles N Atkins. 5: St Augustines Col 39-43 (Sci) BS; Chicago 47-49 BLS; Okla City U Law sch 63-64; UOkla 68. 6: Fr, Sp. 7: Reporter "Winston-Salem Journal & Sentinel, Winston-Salem NC 45-48; Tchr of Fr, Atkins High Sch, winston-Salem NC 45-48; Research asst in biochem Meharry Med Col 48-49; Ref libn FiskU 49-50; Sch libn Kimberley Park Elem Sch, winston-Salem NC 50-51; Br libn Okla City Pub Libs, Okla City Okla 53-56; Ref libn Okla State Lib 62-63; Chief gen ref div & act law libn 63-68; Instr lib sci UOkla 67-68; Instr Sch Law Okla CityU summer 68; State Rep Okla State House of Reps 69-. 8: Ref libn, Library/USA, NY Worlds Fair 64. 9: AALL (past pres SWest Chap); SLA (pres Okla Chap; chm Soc Welfare Sect); ALA; OklaLA (past sec). 10: Governor Commsn on Status of Women; state Adv Com to State Bd Educ on Title III ESEA; Exec Bd Okla Co Mental Health Assn; Exec Bd Okla City Symphony Soc; NAACP; Urban League; visiting Nurse Assn. 11: Outstanding Woman of Okla 65; Distinguished Service Award, Midwest Reg 65; Woman of the Year; Theta Sigma Phi 68. 13: Yes. 14: Ref, law, computer use in libs. 15: Rt 1 Box 447, Okla City Ok 73111.

ATKINS, JANINA. b Warsaw Poland. 4: Thomas V Atkins. 5: UWarsaw Poland 55 Magister MA; Columbia 68 MLS. 6: Fr, Russian, Polish. 7: Catlgr NYU Law Lib 68-69; Catlgr Lehman Col CUNY 69-. 9: SLA; NY Lib Club. 14: Catlg, bibliog. 15: 120 E 34th st, New York NY 10016.

ATKINS, MARJORIE CHRISTINE (STUCKEY). b Florence SC 15F 30. 4: Richard Benton Atkins. 5: Winthrop Col 48-51 (LS) AB; UMd 63-65 (Educ). 6: Fr. 7: Research asst Internat Bk for Res & Devel, Wash DC 51-53; Libn Anchorage Pub Lib, Anchorage Alaska 53-54; Child libn Arlington Pub Libs, Arlington Va 54-56; Elem libn Arlington Pub Schs, Arlington Va 56-57; Elem libn Montgomery Co Pub Sch, Rockville Md 59-. 9: NEA; Md State EA; MdLA. 10: Pi Gamma Mu. 14: Elem sch libs. 15: 13809 Bauer dr, Rockville Md 20853.

ATKINS, THOMAS VICTOR. b Lodz Poland 19 D 23. 4: Janina Atkins. 5: UWarsaw (Poland) 50 Magister MA; Columbia 58 MLS. 6: Fr, Gr, Ger, Russian, Polish, Heb. 7: Searcher 9tech serv) NYC Pub Lib 65, Revisor 65-66, Libn trainee 66-67, Ref libn econ div 68; Sr libn Metro 68; Asst hd of ref Baruch Col cuny 69. 8: Consul libn Royalton Col So royalton Vt 67-. 9: SLA; LACUNY; NY Lib Club. 14: Ref, bibliog, admin. 15: 120 E 34th st, New York NY 10016.

ATKINSON, ANNE ELIZABETH (BEARDSLEY). b Saramac Lake NY 6 S 17. 5: Vassar 36-39 (Fr) AB; Syracuse 39-40 BS in LS. 6: Fr. 7: Ed asst H W Wilson Co, NY 41-43; Asst libn NY Pub Lib, 43; Libn Saranac Lake Free Lib, Saranac Lake NY 46; Com tchr Saranac Lake Study & Craft Guild 44-50; Br libn Buffalo & Erie Co Pub Lib, Buffalo NY 51-. 9: NYLA. 14: Br admin. 15: 275 Mill st, Williamsville NY 14221.

ATKINSON, EDITH (THOMPSON). b Little Rock Ark 21 Mr 07. 4: Thomas Clarence Atkinson. 5: UArk 28-30; La Polytech Inst 33-34; LSU 40-42. 7: Libn Monroe Pub Lib, Monroe La 34-39; Supv br libs Lincoln-Bienville (La) 39-40; La State Lib: Circ dept 40-42, Head circ dept 42-46, Ref dept 46-48, Head Louisiana dept 48-. 9: SLA; LaLA; SWLA. 14: La hist, maps, photographs, rare bks. 15: LA State Lib PO Box 131, Baton Rouge La 70821.

ATKINSON, HUGH CRAIG. b Chicago Ill 17 N 33. 4: Mary Nugent. 5: St Benedicts Col 51-52 (Accounting); Chicago 52-57 (Eng) 57-59 (LS) MA; US Nat Archives 58 Certif. 6: Lat, Fr. 7: Asst in spec collections UChicago Lib 57-58; Readers serv libn Penn Mil Col 59-62; Head ref dept SUNY (Buffalo) 62-64; Asst dir of libs tech serv 64-67; Asst dir of libs pub serv & Asst Prof Lib Admin Ohio StateU 67-. 8: Consul on automated info retrieval to jt Legis Com on Intergovernmental Fiscal Rel NY State Assembly 66-67; USOE grant "Optimum Speed of Library Access vs Related to Optimum Size of Library Collections (69). 9: ALA-RTSD (Lib Materials Price Index Com 66-); -ISAD (Com on Lib Programming Langs 67-69; RT on Soc Responsibilities of Libs; By-laws Com 69-); ASIS; Assn Intl des Documentalists; OhioLA (Com on Lib Automation 64-68). 10: ACLU; AAUP. 12: "The Merrill Checklist of Theodore Dreiser (69); "Twenty-One Letters from Crane to Bryan (68); "The Crane-Munson Correspondence (69). 14: Automation, ref, catlg, admin. 15: Ohio State Univ Libs 1858 Neil ave, Columbus Oh 43210.

ATKINSON, MRS MARJORIE (ANNE) F(AGEN). b Ormond Beach Fla. 5: La State U 34-35, 37-40 (Eng) BA; Fla State U 55-56 (LS) MA. 6: Sp. 7: Asst libn Montgomery Co Lib, Montgomery Ala 56-57; Catlgr Huntingdon Col, Montgomery Ala 57-58; Ref libn Air U Lib MAFB,Montgomery Ala 59-65, Bibliog 65, Chief circ br 65, ndexer 68-. 9: SLA; AlaLA; SELA. 10: AAUW; Beta Phi Mu; 4 other nat hon fraternities. 14: Ref, circ, bibliog, indexing systems. 15: 636 Ponce de Leon ave, Montgomery Al 36106.

ATKINSON, MIRIAM. b Plainfield Ind 4 S 09. 5: Butler U 32 (Eng); Ind U Ext; Ind Summer Sch for Libns 29 Certif. 6: Fr. 7: Indianapolis Pub Lib: Catlg 27-35, Child dept sch serv 35-44, Catlg 44-47, Ext serv 47-60; Libn Herron Museum of Art, Art Assn of Indianapolis 60-. 8: Job Analysis Com, Indianapolis Pub Lib; Bd of Trustees, Plainfield-Guilford Twp Pub Lib, 60-. 9: ALA-CSD (Newberry Award Com, Job Clsf Com); IndLA. 10: PEO; Indianapolis Pub Lib Staff Assn. 14: Catlg, art. 15: Herron Mus of Art Lib, 110 E 16th, Indianapolis In 46202.

ATKINSON, NANCY I. b Detroit Mich 9 D 06. 5: Mills COL (Cal) 26-28; UMich (Ann Arbor) 33-35 Sci AB, 35-36 ABLS. 6: Fr. 7: Asst catlgr East Mich U (Ypsilanti) 36-39; Catlgr Detroit Pub Lib 39-43; Hd catlg dept UIdaho (Moscow) 43. 9: ALA (mem 16th ed DDC Adv Com); PNLA (chm Tech Serv Div 59-61); IdaLA. 10: Phi Beta Kappa; Phi Kappa Phi. 14: Catlg. 15: 606 N Lincoln, Moscow Id 83843.

ATKINSON, NORMA J (SOMERS). b Murphysboro Ill. 4: Dean L Atkinson. 5: USoIll 42-43 (Sociol); USoCal 43-46 (Sociol) AB, 60-61 MLS. 6: Sp. 7: Soc wkr Los Angeles Co 46-48; Catlgr San Marino Pub Lib, San Marino Cal 61-63; Catlgr Syst Development Corp, Santa Monica Cal 63-64; Hd libn Col Stud Personnel Inst, Claremont Cal 64-68; Pub serv libn Chaffey Col 68-. 9: SLA; ASIS; CalLA; CalASchL. 10: Phi Beta Kappa; Beta Phi Mu; Libraria Sodalitas. 12: Mng ed "College Student Personnel Abstracts" (65-68); Jt comp "Definitions of Student Personnel Terms in Higher Education". 15: 1165 N Indian Hill blvd, Claremont Ca 91711.

ATKINSON, WALLACE LIPPINCOTT JR. b Seattle Wash 7 Mr 16. 4: Barbara Storey. 5: UWash 34-38 (Hist) AB; George Washington U 55-56 (Comptrollership) MBA; UOre 62-63 (Secondary Educ) MS, Standard Secondary Tchg Certif 68-69 MLS. 7: Capt Supply Corps USN 38-62; Tchr N Eugene High Sch, Ore 63-68; Libn Junction City High Sch, Oregon 69-. 9: NEA; ALA; OreEA. 10: Phi Gamma Delta; Elks; retired Offrs Assn. 14: Lib admin. 15: 920 Crest dr, Eugene Or 97405.

ATTINELLO, ELEANOR (VARNER). b Rockford Ala 4 D 35. 4: Salvatore Joseph Attinello. 5: UIll (Urbana) 56-60 (Eng Lit) BA, 60-62 (LS) MS; Columbia 63-65 (Eng Lit) MA. 6: Fr. 7: Sec Crane Co, Chicago 53-56; Tech asst Ill Geol Survey, Urbana Ill 56-61; Catlgr UIll Lib (Urbana) 61-62; Gen libn NY Pub Lib 62-63; Bibliog Bowling Green State U 65-. 10: Phi Beta Kappa; Phi Kappa Phi. 14: Rare bks, bk sel. 15: Fuller dr, Bowling Green Oh 43402.

ATTINELLO, SALVATORE J. b Lawrence Mass 4 Je 37. 4: Eleanor Varner. 5: UMass 57-61 (Hist) BA; UIll 61-62 (LS) MS; Bowling Green U 66-69 (Hist) MA. 6: Ger, Ital. 7: Asst libn Col Lib Columbia U Libs 62-65; Instr in Lib Sci Bowling Green State U 65-68, Asst Prof 69-. 9: NEA; ALA-AASchL; OhioLA; OhioEA; OhioASchL. 14: Tchg, admin. 15: Fuller dr, Bowling Green Oh 43402.

ATTINSON, SOLOMON. b NYC 14 Mr 15. 5: News Sch for Soc Research 46-50 (Lit) BS; Columbia 50-51 MS in LS. 7:

Brooklyn Pub Lib 46-53; Prin libn Ed & Publ, Newark (NJ) Pub Lib 53-. 14: Art & music ref, design of lib publs, pub rel. 15: 177 Clifton ave, Newark NJ 07104.

ATTUQUAYEFIO, VERNICE MARIE. b Many La 11 O 32. 5: Southern U 50-54 (Eng) BA; UDenver 62 (LS) MA. 6: Fr. 7: Tchr-libn Irion High Sch, Benton La 54-57; Libn Howard Acad High Sch, Monticello Fla 57-60; Libn Grambling Col 60-. 9: ALA; LaLA; LaEA. 10: Zeta Phi Beta. 14: Ref. 15: PO Box 751, Grambling La 71245.

ATWOOD, FRANCES. b Waltham Mass 20 N 09. 5: Simmons 28-32 (LS) BS. 7: Lib asst Waltham Pub Lib, Waltham Mass 32-40; Chief Libn Vet Hosp, Rutland Heights Mass 40-45; Asst libn Northeastern U 46-53; Head Libn Lasell Jr Col 53-. 9: ALA; MassLA. 14: Admin, ref, catlg. 15: 19 Ipswich rd, Newton Hlds Ma 02161.

ATWOOD, RUTH. b NYC 28 Ag 19. 4: Kenton Atwood. 5: Cornell U 40 (Microbiol) BS; Iowa State U 42 (Physiol) MS; Catherine Spalding Col 57 (LS) MS. 7: Pub serv libn Kornhauser Med Lib, Louisville Ky 62-65, Dir info retrieval 65-68; Dir Louisville Technical Referral Serv Center 68-. 8: Asst Prof ULouisville Speed Sci Sch. 9: ALA; SLA; KyLA. 12: Ed; "Technical Serials in Louisville," "Technical Serials in Kentucky," "Kentuckiana Metroversity Periodicals." 13: Yes. 14: Ref, automation. 15: Kornhauser Med Lib 101 W Chestnut st, Louisville Ky 40202.

AUER, E EVERETT. b E Orange NJ 20 Mr 11. 4: Margaret Ames. 5: Columbia 28-35 (Chem Engring) AB, MS. 6: Fr, Ger. 7: Analytical research chem Amer Cyanamide, Bound Brook 35-39; Research chem US Rubber Co, Wayne NJ 39-63; On Loan Columbia U Div of War Research 43-45; Info specialist Mobil Chem Co, Edison NJ 63-65, Supv tech info 65-. 9: ACS; SLA. 10: AAAS. 13: Yes. 14: Info stor & retr. 15: 36 Riggs pl, S Orange NJ 07079.

AUERBACH, LOIS MINERVA. b Doylestown Penn 9 D 41. 4: Samuel Auerbach. 5: Ursinus Col 59-63 (Hist) BA; UWis 63-64 (LS) MS. 6: Fr. 7: Sch libn E Norristown Sch Dist, Norristown Penn 64-67; Circ libn Van Pelt Lib U Penn 67. 9: NEA; ALA; PennStateEA; PennLA (Hist Documentation Com 65-66). 14: Child bks, sch libs, circ. 15: 1724 Spruce st, Philadelphia Pa 19103.

AUERBACH, ROBERT SHIPLEY. b NYC 14 D 19. 4: Mary Carson Auerbach. 5: NYU 39-50 (Govt) BA; Columbia 45; New Sch for Soc Research 46-47; City Col (NY) 49-50; Peabody 55-56 MA (LS). 7: Asst libn Shepherd Col 56-57; Asst libn Col of Steubenville 57-58; Libn Tecumseh High Sch, New Carlisle Ohio 58-59; Libn Urbana Col 59-61; Catlgr Capital Lib Serv, Greenbelt Md 61-. 9: ALA-SCRL-AASchL; Amer Polit Sci Assn; MdLA; Potomac Tech Proc Libns; Md Assn Jr Col (Learning Resources Div). 10: Amer Philatelic Soc. 13: Yes. 14: Acquis, catlg, ref. 15: 133 Centerway, Greenbelt Md 20770.

AUFDENKAMP, JO ANN. b Springfield Ill 22 Mr 26. 5: MacMurray Col for Women 42-45 (Bus) BA; UIll BLS; Chicago 64-66 (LS). 7: Asst libn Com Lib UIll (Urbana) 46-48; Libn Fed Reserve Bank of Chicago 48-. 8: Lib consul Off of Nat Planning, Monrovia Liberia 62-63. 9: SLA (chm Fin Div 51-52; Ill Chap: pres 54-55, chm Scholarship & Student Loan Com 59-61). 12: Co-author "Special Libraries; A Guide for Management." 13: Yes. 14: Info serv. 15: Box 834, Chicago Il 60690.

AUFSES, HARRIET (WHITMAN). b New York NY 4 O 26. 4: Dr Arthur H Aufses Jr. 5: Hunter Col 44-48 (Eng) BA; Columbia U Tchrs Col 48-49 (Educ) MA; Columbia U Sch of Lib Serv 66-68 (LS) MLS. 6: Fr. 7: Eng tchr NYC Bd of Ed High Sch, 60-66; Libn Yorkville Voc High Sch 66-67; Hd Libn H High Sch 66-67; Hd Libn Hunter Col High Sch 67-. 9: ALA. 10: Phi Beta Kappa; Beta Phi Mu. 14: Sch libnship. 15: 1225 Park ave, New York NY 10028.

AUGUST, SIDNEY. b Phila Penn 21 Ag 18. 4: Rosalie Silber. 5: Temple 35-39 (Eng) BA, 48-52 (Sch Admin) BS Ed, 67-69 (Educ Media); Drexel 39-40 BS in LS, 66-67 (Info Sci). 6: Ger. 7: Asst libn LC 40-41; Catlgr UPenn Law Lib 41-43; US Army Active Duty 43-46; VA Research Off Phila 46-48; Libn Fitzsimons Jr High Sch Phila 48-53; Libn Northeast High Sch Phila 53-66; Hd libn Prof Staff Lib Phila Bd Educ, Phila 66-; Instr lib techn program Commun Col of Phila 69-. 9: SLA (Placement Policy Com 69-); ALA; Spec Libs Coun of Phila (chm Soc Sci Div 69-); Penn Learning Resources Assn; pennLA; PhilaSchLA (pres 55-58). 10: Educ media, lib admin. 15: Professional Staff Lib Phila Board of Education 21st & Parkway, Philadelphia Pa 19103.

AUGUSTINE, ROLF ST CLAIR. b Berkeley Cal 3 My 37. 5: Oakland Jr Col 55-56 (Langs); Ludwig-Maximilians U (Munich Ger) 56 (Ger lang & cult); UMich summer 56; UCal(Berkeley)56-60 (Linguistics) AB; USoCal 61-62 MSLS. 6: Ger, Sp, Fr. 7: Asst catlgr U of the Pacific 63-64; Catlgr (Libn I, Step II) UCal (Santa Cruz) 65-. 9: ALA; CalLA. 10: UCal (Santa Cruz Cal), State Employees Assn. 14: Catlg. 15: 1523 Laurel st, Santa Cruz Ca 95060.

AUGUSTINE, SISTER RAYMOND. b Brooklyn NY 13 My 17. 5: St Joseph Col for Women 38-42 (Math) BA; Pratt 42-43 BLS; Columbia 53-54 (LS) MS. 6: Fr. 7: Tchr St Angela Hall Elem Sch, Brooklyn NY 36-38; Asst libn St Joseph Col (Brooklyn NY) 43-60; Libn St Joseph High Sch, Brooklyn NY 60-68; Catlgr & Ref Libn Brentwood Col, Brentwood NY 68-. 8: Tchr of Lib Sci, St Joseph High Sch, Brooklyn NY 60-. 9: CathLA; NYLA; ALA. 13: Yes. 14: High sch libs, catlg, col libs. 15: 382 Bridge st, Brooklyn NY 11201.

AULD, LAWRENCE W S. b Joplin Mo 19 S 33. 4: Rhoda Landsman. 5: Yankton Col 51-52; Iowa State Tchrs Col 52-55 (Eng) BA; Columbia 56-58 MS in LS. 6: Fr. 7: Tchr Sibley High Sch, Sibley Iowa 55-56 Pre-prof Brooklyn Pub Lib, Brooklyn NY 56-58; Catlgr UTex Lib 58-61; Head catlgr Lib of Hawaii, Honolulu 61-62; Dir of centralized processing State Lib, Honolulu 62-64; Asst libn for tech processes Oakland U (Rochester Mich) 64-67, Asst libn for systems and research 67-68; Hd tech serv Ore State U 68-. 8: Hawaii Governor's Com on State Lib Resources, 63-64. 9: ALA-ACRL;-RTSD;-ISAD; PNLA. 13: Yes. 14: Tech serv, rare bks, lib automation. 15: Lib Ore State Univ, Corvallis Ore 97331.

AULL, SARA (ALBERTA). b China Grove NC 2 Ap 10. 5: Lenoir Rhyne Col 26-30 (Eng) BA; Columbia 31-32 BS in LS; UHouston (Radio, TV) MA. 7: Catlgr ser ref dept NY Pub Lib 34-38; Catlgr Lansing Pub Sch Lib, Lansing Mich 39; High sch libn NY City Bd of Educ 40-42; Catlgr Foreign Econ Admin Lib, Wash DC 43-44; Research asst in pub rel Assn of Amer RRs, Wash DC 45-49; Sci libn UHouston Lib 51-. 9: SLA (Dir 60-63, chm Com on Coms 68-70); -Tex Chap (sec 54-55, v-pres 58-59 &65-66, pres 59-60 & 66-67); TexLA (Lib Devel Com 64-67); SWLA. 10: Soc of Techwriters & Publ; Geoscience Inf Soc; Phi Kappa Phi. 13: Yes. 14: Ref. 15: 2447 Charleston, Houston Tx77021.

AURELIAN, THOMAS FSC BROTHER (JOHN FRANCIS LAVERY). b Providence RI 24 Ja 04. 5: Manhattan Col 23-27 (Arts) AB; Columbia 27-31 (Fine Arts) AM, 31-35 (LS) BLS; UNH 65 Educ Media-Certif. 6: Fr, Ital. 7: Libn Bishop Loughlin High Sch, Brooklyn NY 27-39; Dir libs Manhattan Col 40-58; Dir Biblioteca Lasalliana, Rome Italy 58-60; Hd Eng dept Istituto Universitario, Asmara Ethiopia 60-64; Libn and A-V coord Bishop Bradley High Sch, Manchester NH 64-69; Visiting bibliog MarquetteU Milwaukee Wi 66-; Lib consul Diocese of Manchester, Manchester NH 66-69; Lib supv Dist of LI-New Eng 67-; Libn De La Salle Col, Washington DC 69-. 8: Consul "Compton's Encyclopedia" 50-58; Instr, Church Hist, Lateran Univ, Rome Italy 58-59; Instr, Sci, Itege Menon Sch of Nursing, Asmara Ethiopia 61-62; Lectr USIS Asmara Ethiopia 62-64. 9: ALA (chm Engrg Sch Libs Sect 43-45); CathLA (10 exec, unit & coun appointments 34-). 11: Citation, FordhamU 58; on Promotion of Study of Oriental Rites. 12: Bibliog ed "Catholic Encyclopedia for School and Home" (65); Ed New Hampshire "Circle" 66-69. 13: Yes. 14: Col lib admin. 15: De La Salle Col 4900 La Salle rd NE, Washington DC 20018.

AUST, LORRAINE (LOUCKS). b Hermon NY 19 O 17. 4: James Gerald Aust. 5: Syracuse 34-38 (Eng) BS in Educ, (summers) 59-64 MS in LS. 7: High sch tchr, Potsdam NY 39-41; Asst ed, "Massena Observer," Massena NY 43-44; Reporter, "Morning Sun," Las Vegas Nev 45; Corresp, "The Hornet," Waukomis Okla 49-50; Elem tchr, Meno Okla 50-51; High sch tchr, Garber Okla 54-55; Jr high tchr, Oneida NY

55-56; High sch tchr, Canastota NY 57-59; Secondary sch libn, Chittenango NY 59-. 9: ALA; -AASchL; NYLA; Cent NY LA (Prog & Nom Com 68-69); NY State TA; Chittenango TA (1st v-pres 64-65). 10: Beta Phi Mu; Pi Lambda Sigma Chap. 14: YA, ref. 15: 216 Washington ave, Oneida NY 13421.

AUSTIN, ARLITA KAY (WARRICK). b Peoria Ill 28 Je 44. 4: Julian Morgan Austin. 5: Ill StateU 61-65 (Eng) BS; UIll 65- (LS). 6: Fr, Ger. 7: Lib asst Withers Pub Lib, Bloomington Ill 62-64; Head libn Normal Pub Lib, Normal Ill 65-67; Dir Fon du Lac Twp Lib, East Peoria Ill 67-. 9: ALA; IllLA (Registration Chm 69); IllValleyLA; Pere MarquetteLA (pres 68-69). 10: Alpha Beta Alpha; Amer Bus Womens Assn; E Peoria Chamber Com; Beta Phi Mu; Sigma Tau Delta. 14: Admin, bk selection. 15: 2401 Washington rd, E Peoria Il 61611.

AUSTIN, CAROLINE (DALE). b Montgomery Ala 22 Jl 43. 4: William Benton Austin Jr. 5: Erskine Col 62-65 (Elem Educ) BA; EmoryU 65-67 (LS) Master of Libnship. 7: Libn St Andrews Jr High, Charleston SC 66-67; Catlgr Baptist Col at Charleston, Charleston SC 69-. 9: ALA. 14: Catlg, ref. 15: 2120-A Westrivers rd, Charleston SC 29407.

AUSTIN, DENNIS DALE. b Janesville Wis 18 Ja 42. 5: Wis State U (Oshkosh) 60-64 (LS) BA; UWis 64- (LS). 6: Sp. 7: Stud asst Janesville Pub Lib, Janesville Wis 59-64; Stud asst Wis State U (Oshkosh) 60-64; Catlgr Wis State Law Lib, Madison 64-66; S/Sgt US Air Force 66-; Catlgr Robins AFB, Ga 66-. 9: WisLA. 10: Bd Warner Robbins Little Theatre; Alpha Phi Omega. 13: Yes. 14: Catlg, data processing, info retrieval. 15: 712 S Jackson st, Janesville Wi 53545.

AUSTIN, FRANCIER (FRANKIE CHEEVES). b 10 S 23. 4: Ulysses Jack Austin. 5: Wiley Col 42-46 (Sociol) AB; UChicago summer 48 (Special Reading); UCal summer 49; Prairie View A&M 51-52 (Elem Educ); Syracuse 52-56 MS in LS. 6: Fr, Ger. 7: Pub sch, Kilgore Tex: Tchr 46-50, Speech & drama 50-52, Libn 52-67; Libn Navarro Col, Corsicana Tex 67-. 9: ALA; NEA; TexLA. 10: Top Ladies of Distinction; Nat Fed of Clubs; Commun Action Com; Mayor's Com For Bette Commun Rel; Beautification Com of Amer the Beautiful; Phi Delta Psi; Alpha Kappa Alpha; AAUP; AAUW. 14: Ref, research. 15: 426 Wells st, Kilgore Tx 75662.

AUSTIN, HAZEL BINNS. b Moultrie Ga 20 N 12. 5: Wesleyan Cl (Macon Ga) 29-33 (Biol) AB; Emory 33-34 ABLS; Cplumbia 49 (Med Libnship). 7: Libn High Sch, Moultrie Ga 34-37; Libn Pub Lib, Moultrie Ga 37-40; Lib supv Works Projects Admin, Albany Ga 40-42; US Navy Reserve (Lt) 43-46; Admin libn USVA, Atlanta 46-49; Admin libn USVA, Wash DC 49-67. Asst dir lib serv USVA, Wash DC 68-. 9: ALA. 15: 2800 Quebec st NW, Wash DC 20008.

AUSTIN, JOSEPHINE S. b Havana Cuba 26 Je 05. 5: Oliver College 24-28 (Lat) BA; CaseWest Res 36 BS in LS. 7: Tchr Gaylord High Sch, Gaylord Mich 28-30; Asst S Haven City & Twp Lib S Haven Mich 31-36; Libn Forest Park Pub Lib, Forest Park Ill 36-43; Gen asst Janesville Pub Lib, Janesville Wis 43-48; Bookmobile asst Decatur Pub Lib, Decatur Ill 48-52; Libn Pub Lib, Forest Park Ill 52-. 9: ALA; IllLA; LACONI. 10: Friends of the Lib (Forest Park); Oak Park Coun on Internat Affairs; Great Bks; No Ill Film Coop. 15: 7542 Adams st, Forest Park Il 60130.

AUSTIN, MARTHA L. b Geneva Neb 22 A 28. 4: Loren B Austin. 5: UWash 45-49 (Art) BA, 64-65 (Libnship) Master of Libnship. 6: Sp. 7: Lib asst UWash 52-64; Catlg libn 66-. 9: SLA; PNLA. 14: Spec libs (art, arch, med), catlg. 15: 5316 NE 74th st, Seattle Wa 98115.

AUSTIN, NEAL F(ULLER). b Mangum Okla 9 My 26. 4: Betty Shaw. 5: UOkla 44-48 BALS. 6: Ger, Sp. 7: Libn UOkla Sch of Journalism 48-50; Libn Union Co Lib, Monroe NC 50-52; Libn High Point Pub Lib, High Point NC 52-. 8: Visiting Lecturer High Point Col 62-. 9: ALA (various com assignments); AEAUSA; SELA; NCLA (various offices). 10: Rotary. 11: Thomas Wolfe Memorial Lit Award, 68; AAUW Lit Award, 68. 12: "A Biography of Thomas Wolfe (68). 13: Yes. 14: Admin. 15: PO box 522, High Point NC 27261.

AUSTIN, RICHARD HALL. b Norfolk Va 1 S 34. 5: UVa 53-56 (Engnr); Hofstra Col 58-59 (Physics); UVa 61-62 (Physics) BA; Ga Inst of Tech 64-65 (Info Sci) MS. 6: GER. 7: Parts catlg writer Sperry Gyroscope Co, Great Neck NY 56-57, Asst publ engnr 57-58, Publ engnr 58-59; Head info serv UVa 59-67, Act head sci ref div 62-67; Asst to dir Sch of Info Sci, Ga Inst Tech 67-68; Dir Sci Tech Info Center UVa 68-. 8: Tech lib consul, NASA, Wallops Island 63. 9: ASIS; ACS (Chem Lit Div); VaLA. 12: Auth or co-auth of 4 reports, 62-65; ed "Proc of Symp on Dental Materials (66); ed "Proc of Symp on Accidental Injuries to Child (67). 14: Info sci educ. 15: Sci Tech Info Center, Alderman Lib, Charlottesville Va 22904.

AUSTIN, ROXANNA. b Kenwood Ga 5 Je 19. 5: Ga State Col for Women 35-39 (Hist) AB; UNC summers 43-45 (LS) BS; Fla State U summer 65, 68-69 AM. 6: Fr. 7: Tchr libn Pike Co High Sch, Zebulon Ga 39-41; Elem tchr R L Hope Sch, Fulton Co Schs Atlanta 41-42; Asst libn N Fulton High Sch, atlanta 42-45; Asst to sch lib consul, State Dept of Educ, Atlanta 45-48; Dir Towns-Union Reg Lib, Young Harris Ga 48-52; Lib consul Pub Lib Unit, State Dept of Educ, Atlanta 52-. 8: Visiting lecturer Fla State U Lib Sch 65. 9: ALA (chm Awards Com 63-64; Coun 68-72); NEA; GaEA; GaLA (chm pub Lib Sect 49-50; Constitution Com 64-); SeLA (treas 65-66, chm Sch & Child Sect 48-49); Ga Adult Educ Coun (sec 62-66). 10: Atlanta Lib Club; Delta Kappa Gamma. 13: Yes. 14: State lib agcy, pub libs, bk selection, child & yp wk, bk selection. 15: 156 Trinity ave SW, Atlanta Ga 30303.

AUSTIN, SHIRLEY JEAN (TOWNSLEY). b Florence Ala 23 Ap 36. 4: James William Austin. 5: Florence State Col 55-65 (Soc Sci) BS. 6: Sp. 7: Libn Hyde Park Elem Sch, Jacksonville Fla 57-59; Libn Bozees Sch, Florence Ala 64-68; Tchr Kelso Wash High sch sys 68-. 9: NEA; AlaEA; AlaLA. 10: Kappa Delta Pi. 14: High sch libnship, ref serv. 15: 422 Fifth NW, Kelso Wa 98626.

AUSTINSON, SIGURD M. b Peterson Minn 20 Ja 11. 5: UCal (Berkeley) 41-45 (Eng) AB, 48-49 (Educ), 53-54 BLS. 7: Libn Crowell-Collier Publishing Co, NYC 55-64; Libn Crowell-Collier-MacMillan, Inc, NYC 64-. 67; Catlg libn Fordham U Law Sch 67-. 15: 950 Evergreen ave, New York NY 10472.

AUSUBEL, HILLEL. b NYC 25 N 24. 4: Lucille Whintrop. 5: Yale 42-47 (Music) BA; Columbia 47-48 (Guidance) MA, 48-49 (LS) MS, 50-53 (Music, Music Educ) PhD. 6: Ger, Fr. 7: Libn Brooklyn Pub Lib 49-50; Libn, br & asst br libn The Queens Borough Pub Lib, Jamaica NY 54-63; Libn Mt Vernon High Sch Lib, Mt Vernon NY 63-65; Libn Mt Vernon High Sch Annex Lib, Mt Vernon NY 65-66; Head libn NY Col of Music, NYC 66-68; Ref libn New Rochelle Pub Lib, New Rochelle NY 68-. 9: ALA; NYLA; MusLA. 10: Yale Alumni Assn. 12: "The Effect of Chromaticism on Tonality in the Period between 1890 and 1910," Doctoral dissertation (53). 13: Yes. 14: Ref, admin, research, music lib. 15: 46-10 216 st, Bayside NYC 11361.

AUTEN, VERA. b Rawson Ohio 30 S 10. 5: Ohio Northern U 28-31 (Biol) AB; UMich 32-33 ABLS. 6: Fr, Ger. 7: Libn Jr High Sch, Ashtabula Ohio 36-38; Tchr Pub schs, Ohio 39-45; Libn High Sch, Defiance Ohio 45-50; 1st asst libn Toledo Pub Lib, Toledo Ohio 50-56; Libn VA Hosp, Sunmount NY 56-58; Libn-nursing sch Geisinger Med Center, Danville Penn 58-59; A-v libn Wittenberg U 59-. 9: ALA; OhioLA; A-v Coun of Ohio. 14: A-v material. 15: 477 Woodlawn ave, Springfield Oh 45501.

AUTH, REV CHARLES ROBERT O.P. b Pittsburgh 19 D 11. 5: Holy Cross 29-31; Providence 31-33 BA; Dominican house of Studies (Theol) 38-41; Catholic U 42-43 BSLS. 6: Fr, Lat, Ital, Ger. 7: Chaplain US VA Hosp, Wash DC 50-52; Libn Dominican House of Studies 42-, Sub-prior 59-65. 9: ALA; CathLA; DCLA; CathLA-Washington- Baltimore Unit. 12: "Rosary Bibliography"; "Bibliography of Vincent McNabb (O.P.)." 13: Yes. 14: Theol, ref, bibliog, rare bks. 15: 487 Mich ave NE, Wash DC 20017.

AUTRY, RUTH ANNE. b Tulsa Okla 4 D 42. 5: UOkla 60-64 (Elem Educ) BS in Educ; 64-64 (LS) MLS. 7: Child libn Okla County Lib 65-68; Elem libn Okla City Pub Schs 68-. 9: ALA; NEA; OklaLA; OklaEA; OklaCityEA; OklaCity ClrTA. 14: Child wk. 15: 1105 N Ann Arbor, Oklahoma City Ok 73127.

AUZINS, INESE. b Riga Latvia 15 N 43. 5: Ohio State U 61-65 (Fr) BA; UMich (Ann Arbor) 66 MLS. 6: Latvian, Fr, Sp. 7: Specialist (libn II) UWis Mem Lib (Madison) 67-69. 14: Ser catlg. 15: 315 N Blair st, Madison Wi 53703.

AVAKIAN, ANNE M. b Fresno Cal 6 Ja 06. 5: Fresno State Col 24-27 (Educ, Eng) Tchrs Certif; Pomona Col 28-30 (Eng, Hist) AB; UCal (Berkeley) 31-32 (LS) Certif 06: Armenian. 7: Libn US Forest Serv Inst of Forest Genetics, Placerville Cal34-36; Libn Cal Forest & Range Expt Station, US Forest Serv, Berkeley Cal 36-43; Libn West Reg Research Lab

USDA, Albany Cal 43-. 9: ALA; SLA; CalLA (pres Golden Gate Dist 53; pres Col Univ & Res Lib Sect 65; chm of No Div of Col Univ & Res Lib Div 46; mem Documents Com 51). 14: Spec lib wk. 15: West Reg Res Lab, Albany Ca 94710.

AVANT, JULIA (KING). b Marion La 14 O 34. 5: NWest State Col 53-57 (Soc Studies) BA; LSU 64 (LS) MS; IndU 67- (LS). 7: Bkmob libn Ouachita Parish Pub Lib, Monroe La 57-58, Child libn 59, Catlgr for br lib 60, Asst libn 61-66; Catlgr LSU (Alexandria) 67; USOE Doctoral Fellow IndU (Bloomington) 67-. 9: ALA; LaLA. 10: Delta Kappa Gamma. 15: 2067 Crabapple dr, Shreveport La 71108.

AVDICH, KAMIL Y. b Bileca Yugoslavia 10 Jl 14. 4: Aida Avdich. 5: Col of Orientalistics (Sarajevo Yugoslavia) 35-39 BA; UAl-Azhar (Cairo Egypt) 41-51 PhD; Rosary Col 61-62 MA. 6: Bosnian, Arabic, Fr, Ger, Turkish. 7: Tchr: Col de Jeunnes F Francais, Daher Cairo Egypt 51-52, Amer Syrian Soc, Toledo Ohio 58-59; Bibliogr John Crerar Lib, Chicago 61-62, Order libn 63-65, Asst chief acquis dept 65-67; Hd acquis dept NEast Ill State Col 67-. 10: AAUP; Amer Oriental Soc; Amer Friends of Middle East; Bosnian-Amer Cultural Assn. 13: Yes. 14: Acquis, selection. 15: 4044 Crestwood dr, Northbrook Il 60062.

AVENEY, BRIAN HENRY. b Bronx NY 24 Ja 40. 4: Harriet Walker. 5: Colgate 57-61 (Fine Arts) BA; Columbia 65-67 (LS) MS. 6: Fr. 7: Mus asst Montclair Art Mus, Montclair NJ 61-62; Employment interviewer Prof Placement Serv NYSES, NYC 62-63; Fine Arts Tchr NYC Jr High Schs NYC 63-65; Lib asst Tchrs Col Columbia NYC 65-67; Res asst METRO Science Survey NYC 67-67; Special Recruit Lib of Congress 67-68; Info Systems Res Analyst 68-. 9: Potomac Tech Serv Libns. 10: Beta Phi Mu; Tauber-Beguer Award (Columbia U 67). 14: Automation, programming, bk catlgs, non-bk material, fine & applied arts. 15: 27 3rd st NE, Washington DC 20002.

AVERILL, ELIZABETH A(LDEN) F(ERGUSON). b Schenectady NY 10 Jl 08. 5: UNeb 26-31 (Drawing, Painting) BFA; UIll 36-38 BS in LS; UNeb 62 (A-v materials in tchg). 7: Bethany Br Libn Lincoln City Libs, Lincoln Neb 39-43; Libn Joslyn Art Museum, Omaha 43-52; Catlgr Omaha Pub Libs 52-53; Head art dept Free Lib of Phila 53-56; Libn St Elizabeth Sch of Nursing, Lincoln Neb 57-64; Chief Libn Med & Gen Libs VA Hosp, Lincoln Neb 64-. 9: MedLA; ALA; SLA; NebLA (treas 49-50). 10: Lincoln Lib Assn; Lincoln Artists Guild; Altrusa Club. 12: "Nebraska Art and Artists," microfilmed & in the Archives of Amer Art in Detroit. 13: Yes. 14: Catlg, ref, med, art. 15: 2711 Ryons st, Lincoln Nb 68502.

AVERY, MARIANNA (MOORE). b La Grange Ga 12 S 39. 4: T Eugene Avery. 5: UGa 57-61 (Fr) AB; Emory 61-62, 63-64 MLs; Womans Col Ga summer 63; UGa 66; UIll 67-68. 6: Fr. 7: Asst res libn Theol Lib Emory U 61-62, 63-64; Readers asst Wheaton Pub Lib, Silver Spring Md 62; Lib asst Amer Potash & Chem Corp, Los Angeles 63; Circ & ref libn UGa Law Lib 64-66; Records & acquis libn UIll Law Lib 67-68; Br libn Flagstaff Ariz Pub Lib 68-. 8: Library/USA NY Worlds Fair 65; Consul for moving & reorg Coconino Co Law Lib 69. 10: Girl Scouts Amer; Salvation Army Aux. 14: Acquis, law libs, catlg. 15: 3726 Grandview dr, Flagstaff Az 86001.

AVERY, MAUDE E(DITH). b Wallingford Vt 28 N 1887. 5: Middlebury 06-10 AB; Simmons 21-22 BS. 7: Tchr high schs, NY, NJ, Vt 10-21; Catlgr Penn State Col 22-24; Catlgr, catlgr chg serv Ohio State 24-26, 26-58; Catlgr RI State Lib 58-60; Catlgr Family Serv Inc, Providence 60-66. 9: ALA; RILA; NE Group of Tech Serv Libns. 10: Delta Kappa Gamma; AAUW; United Church Women. 14: Catlg. 15: The Minden Apt 67, 123 Waterman st, Providence RI 02906.

AVRAM, HENRIETTE D. b NYC 7 O 19. 4: Herbert M Avram. 5: Hunter Col (Pre-Med); George Washington U (Math). 7: Programmer systems analyst Dept of Defense, Fort meade Md 53-59; Syst analyst Amer Research Bur, Beltsville Md 59-61; Sr syst analyst datatrol Corp, Silver Spring Md 61-65; Supv Info Syst Analyst LC 65-66, Asst coord of info syst 66-, Dir Proj MARC 66-. 8: Adv NE Bd Higher Educ's Proj NELINET (NE Lib Info Netwk) 68; Participated in MARC Insts (spon by Info Sci and Automation Div, ALA & LC) 68-69; ALA rep to the USA Standards Inst Com X3 66-68; Adv UCal (Berkeley) proj (design of a MARC compatible Tech Proc Ctr); Alternative to chm US Nat Libs Task force on Automation and other Coop Serv; Mem, Adv Com, Guide to Sci Instruments; Chm, wking Task Force on RECON (study on retrospective conversion). 9: ALA; Assn Comp mach; ASIS; USA Standards Inst Com Z39 (Subcom chm, mem Planning Co). 11: LC Superior Serv Award 68, Outstanding Performance Award 66, 67. 14: Lib automation. 15: 1776 elton rd, Silver Spring Md 20903.

AWKARD, MRS JULITA C. b Manila Philippines 18 N 29. 4: Dr Joseph C Awkard Jr. 5: Fla A&M (LS) BS. 6: Tagalog, Sp, Fr. 7: Circ libn Albany State Col (Ga) 61-62; Pharmacy libn Fla A&M 62-. 8: SLA (co-comp of theses project of Com of Pharmaceutical Sect) summer 65. 9: ALA; MedLA; SLA; KDP. 10: St Eugene Circle (Jolly Kids Club) Adv; LWV. 14: Pharmaceutics. 15: 1108 Tanner dr, Tallahassee Fl 32301.

AXAM, JOHN. b Cincinnati 12 F 30. 4: Dolores Ballard. 5: Cheyney State Col 49-53 (Educ) BS; Drexel 55-58 (LS) MS. 6: Fr. 7: Tchr Sch Dist of Phila 53-54; Free Lib of Phila: Lib asst II Wagner Br 54-57, Lib trainee Wagner Br 57-58, Child libn Wagner Br 58-60, Head Queen Mem Br 60-62, Head Paschalville Br 62-64, Head stations dept 64-, Dir Reader Develop Prog 67-. 9: ALA; PennLA. 14: Wk with child & the underprivileged. 15: 1803 Chew ave, Philadelphia Pa 19141.

AXEEN, MARINA E. b St Cloud Minn 29 N 21. 5: St Cloud State Col 41-45 (Educ) BS; UMinn 48-49 BS in LS, 51-53 MS in LS; UIll 66 (Ed) Adv Certif in Ed) PhD in LS. 6: Fr, Ger. 7: St Cloud State Col, St Cloud Minn: Res libn 45-47, Ref libn 58-66; Tchr Duluth Pub Schs, Duluth Minn 47-48; Hd libn Bethel Col & Sem, St Paul 48-58; Assoc prof Ball State 67-69, Prof 69-, Chm Dept Lib Sci 69-. 9: ALA (life mem); NEA; IndSchLA; IndTA. 10: Delta Kappa Gamma; First Baptist Christian Educ Bd. 11: US Off of Educ Bur of Research Grant. 12: "Teaching Library Use to Undergraduates: Comparison of Computer-Based Instruction and the Conventional Lecture" (Final Report, US Dept of HEW, Off of Educ, Bur of Research); "Teaching the Use of the Library to Undergraduates" Report 361, UIll (67). 14: Lib educ, admin, ref. 15: 700 N McKinley ave, apt M-3, Muncie Ind 47303.

AXELROD, HELENE BERNICE (MARGOLIS). b New York NY 8 Ap 25. 4: David Axelrod. 5: Hunter Col 46 (Bus) BA; So Conn state Col 65 (LS) MS. 6: Fr, Sp. 7: Catlgr So Conn State Col, 61-66; Sch Libn Hamden High Sch, Hamden Conn 66-. 9: ALA; ConnSchLA. 10: AFT; ConnFT. 14: Ref, sch libnship. 15: 125 Twin Brook rd, Hamden Ct 06514.

AXFORD, H WILLIAM. b Butte Mont 7 Ap 25. 4: Lavonne Brady Axford. 5: Reed Col 46-50 (Hist) AB; UWash 50-52 (Hist); UDenver 57-58 (LS) MA, 60-68 (Hist, PhD). 6: Ger. 7: US Army T/5 43-46; Asst manager Evergreen Dairy Coop, Seattle 52-55; NM State Rep Nat Found for Infantile Paralysis 55-57; Chief libn The Denver Post 58-60; Asst dir of libs UDenver 60-65; Dir of libs 65-67; Dir libs Fla Atlantic U 67-. 9: ALA (Urban Univs Com; LRTS; Acquis Sect; Policy & Research Com); SLA; chm Conv Prog Com 60-61); FlaLA; SELA. 10: AAUP. 11: Fulbright Lectureship U of Punjab, Lahore W Pakistan 63-64. 13: Yes. 14: Admin, automation. 15: 900 Elderberry way SW, Boca Raton Fl 33432.

AXFORD, LAVONNE (BRADY). b Ft Collins Colo 30 Je 28. 4: H William Axford. 5: UColo 46-52 (Sociol) BA; UDenver 54-56 (LS) MA. 6: Ger, Fr. 7: Asst ref libn Albuquerque Pub Lib, Albuquerque NM 56-57; Act documents libn UColo 58; Asst bus admin lib UDenver 57-58; Libn St Thomas Sem (Denver) 58-65; Head Jefferson Co Lib System, Golden Colo 65-66; Hd libn Arapahoe Jr Col 66-67; Hd libn Dade Ctr, Miami Beach Fla 68-. 8: Have set up & acted as consul for the following major sem libs: Seoul, Korea, Rangoon, Burma; Taught catlg at U of Punjab, Lahore W Pakistan 63-64; Consul: Sterling High Sch, Colo 67, migrant educ in Fla 68-69. 9: ALA. 10: Remainders; Friends of Chamber Music; Botanic Gardens. 14: Admin, ref. 15: 900 Elderberry way SW, Boca Raton Fl 33432.

AXMAN, DONALD HOMER. b Bridgeport Conn 12 My 26. 4: Janet Herb. 5: Yale Sch of Music 47-50 (Comp) Mus B; Simmons 53-57 MSLS. 6: Ger, Fr. 7: T/5 US Army Field Artillery 44-46; Yale U Lib: Res bk asst 51-53, Catlg asst Med Lib 53-54, Ref asst Music Lib 54-56; Catlgr UBridgeport 56-58; Catlgr UMich 58-59; Ser Rec libn Penn State U 59-64; Chief catlg dept UNC (Chapel Hill) 64-67; Asst dir tech serv UConn 67-. 9: ALA; ConnLA. 10: AAUP. 14: Catlg, ser, tech serv,data proc. 15: Box Mtn dr RFD 5, Vernon Ct 06086.

AXMAN, JANET (HERB). b Valley View Penn 28 Jl 27. 4: Donald H Axman. 5: Wilson Col 45-49 (Psych) BA; Rutgers 59-61 MLS. 7: Receptionist ASTM, Phila 49-51; Cryptographic wk US Dept of State, Far East, Europe 51-53, 55-57; Typing supv, catlg dept Penn State U 58-59; Circ Princeton Pub Lib, Princeton NJ 59-61; Asst ref libn Penn State U 61-64; Engnr libn Duke U 64-67; Conn State Lib Hd hist & geneal 67-. 9: SLA; ConnLA; NELA. 15: Box Mtndr RFD 5, Vernon Ct 06086.

AXTHELM, KENNETH W. b St Louis 25 Ag 29. 5: Wash U (St Louis) 47-51 (Music) AB; UIll 51-54 MS in LS. 7: Pre-prof St Louis Pub Lib 52-53; Brooklyn Pub Lib: Staff 54-58, Libn art & music div 58-60, Head a-v dept 60-. 8: Instr in a-v materials, Pratt Inst Lib Sch 64-65. 9: ALA; MusLA; Educ Film LA; NY Film Coun; Film Lib Info Coun (treas). 13: Yes. 14: Films & recordings. 15: 153 Joralemon st, Brooklyn NY 11201.

AYDELOTTE, LOMAN FRANKLIN. b Lubbock Tex 7 D 36. 4: Nola Barrus. 5: Brigham YoungU 59-63 (Hist) BS, 63-65 (Hist) MS; UOkla 67-68 (Hist) PhD, 67-68 (LS) MA. 7: Ref libn UKan 69-. 9: AHA. 10: Phi Alpha Theta. 15: 811 E 12th st, Lawrence Ks 66044.

AYDLETT, DOROTHY (DUNHAM). b Genesco NY 7 Jy 16. 4: Guy D Aydlett. 5: NY State Tchrs Col 37 (Elem Educ) Cert, 42 (LS) BS; State U Col of NY (Genesco) 62 MLS. 7: Libn York Central High Sch, Rets of NY 40-42; Hd Libn (Eastman Kodak Co., Kodak Apparatus Div), Rochester NY 42-. 9: SLA; ALA; MonroeCoLA. 10: Print Club of Rochester; Humane Soc. 15: 901 Elmgrove rd, Rochester NY 14650.

AYERS, ADA LORAINE. b Plainfield NJ 23 My 10. 5: Douglass Col, Rutgers 28-32 (LS) BA; Rutgers 43-50 (Educ) MA. 6: Fr. 7: Child libn Plainfield Pub Lib, Plainfield NJ 32-43; Libn Scotch Plains-Fanwood High Sch, Scotch Plains NJ 43-; Child libn Pub Lib, Newark NJ summers 44-65. 8: Mem Eval Coms, Middle States Assn of Schs & Cols 48-. 9: NEA; NJSchLA (past adv); NJEA; NJSchLA; UnionCoSchLA (sec, v-pres, pres). 10: Douglass Col Alumn Assn; Fanwood Col Women's Club. 13: Yes. 14: Yp reading. 15: Scotch Plains-Fanwood High Sch Westfield rd, Scotch Plains NJ 07076.

AYLWARD, JAMES FRANCIS. b Fall River Mass 6 N 42. 4: Maria Abbatomarco. 5: Calvin coolidge Col 62-66 (Hist) BA; URI 66-68 MLS. 7: Libn Sims Classified Lib Naval War Col Libs, Newport RI 68-. 14: Ref, a-v, automation, info ret. 15: 2C Clock Tower Sandy Pt ave, Portsmouth RI 02871.

AYRAULT, MARGARET W(EBSTER). b Tonawanda NY 8 S 11. 5: Oberlin Col 29-33 (Hist) AB; Drexel 33-34 BS in LS; Columbia 38-40 MS in LS. 7: Gen Asst Drexel Inst of Tech Lib 34; Catlgr & clsf Enoch Pratt Free Lib, baltimore 34-38; Asst ref dept Columbia U Lib 39-40; Head catlgr Carnegie Endowment for Internat Peace Lib, Wash DC 41-43; Chief processing sect USDA Lib, Wash DC 43-50; Chief bibliog control sect Tech Lib US NOTS, Inyokern Cal 50-51; Asst libn US Bur of the Budget, Wash DC 52-54; Head catlg dept U Lib UMich 54-65; Prof Grad Sch of Lib Studies UHawaii 65-. 8: Assisted in org the Lib for the 1st UNRRA Conf, Atlantic City NJ 43. 9: ALA (Coun 3 terms, mem 3 coms, sec Jr Mem Round Table 41-42; Div Catlg & Clsf;pres 56, chm &/or mem 4 coms 59-64); -RTSD (Exec Bd 58-62, mem org com 68-70);DCLA (Asst sec 42-44); MichLA (Tech Serv Sect; v-pres & pres 58-60); Hawaii LA. 10: Delta Kappa Gamma; Beta Phi Mu; Phi Beta Kappa; AAUP. 13: Yes. 14: Catlg, educ for libnship, admin. 15: Grad Sch of LibStudies UHawaii, Honolulu Hi 96822.

AYRE, CAROLYN V (HUNT). b Caro Mich 31 Mr 15. 4: Robert Donald Ayre. 5: West MichU 32-33 (Art); Certif libn (Mich) 67. 7: Libn Caro High Sch, Caro Mich 33-34; Chief clerk Sel Serv, Tuscola Co Mich 40-42; Rural sales mgr Curtis Circulation Co Mich 52-54; Asst catlg div Grace A Dow Mem Lib, Midland Mich 55-61; Catlgr 61-. 9: ALA; MichLA. 10: Midland Art Coun; Midland Hist Soc. 14: Catlg, exhibits. 15: 119 E Carpenter st, Midland Mi 48640.

AYVAZ, ANNE (LAZAREFF). b Tamaris s/m France 23 Ja 09. 4: Simon Ayvaz. 5: BirminghamU (England) 34 (LS); Columbia 32-33 (correspondence) (LS). 6: Fr, Russian. 7: Asst med libn AmericanU (Beirut Lebanon) 26-33, Med libn 32-37, Libn-consul & org chem dept & Fr Sect 37-50; Hd circ desk JafetU Lib 50-59; In charge of Comm Archives Belgian Consul NYC 59-61; Med libn Booth Mem Hosp, Flushing NY 61-. 8: Org lib Sch Ste Anne des Soeurs de Besancon, Beirut Lebanon. 9: MedLA. 14: Ref, rare bks. 15: 32-51 - 83rd st, Jackson Heights NY 11370.

AZZARA, ELIZABETH E. b Irvington NJ 7 S 28. 5: St Elizabeth 46-50 (Eng) AB; Fordham Sch of Soc Serv 50-53 (Soc Wk); Rutgers 55-59 MLS. 6: Ger. 7: Casewker Assoc Catholic Charities, Newark NJ 50-53; Head Ser- Period libn Seton Hall U 54-. 8: Act Exec Asst U Libn Seton Hall U 60-63 Seton Hall University Faculty Senate 61-. 9: ALA; NJLA. 10: AAUP. 14: Period, govt doc. 15: 22 Rector st, Millburn NJ 07041.

B

BAA, ENID M. b St Thomas VI 28 S 11. 5: Sch of Gen Studies Columbia 49 (Eng lit) BS; Grad Lib Sch Hampton Inst 33 (49) BS in LS. 6: Sp, Fr, Portu. 7: Govt of VI, St Thomas VI: Hd dept of pub libs 33-43, Lib consul 50, Dir div pub libs 51-61 & 65-present; Preliminary catlgr Columbia lib 43-48; Fellow libn Queen's Col lib 48-49; Ser catlgr UN lib, NYC 49-50; Ref catlgr NYC Pub lib 50-51; Hd libn Caribbean Org, San Juan PR 61-65. 9: ALA; SLA; Lib Ass (London); Aslib; PuertoRicoLA. 10: Amer Jewish Hist Soc; Caribbean Hist Assn. 11: John Hay Whitney Foundn Fellowship (56). 12: "Preservation of Sephardic records of the island of St Thomas VI" (54); "Libraries of the Caribbean Area" (59); "Inter-l "Libraries of the Caribbean Area" (59); "Inter-Library Cooperation and Its Relation to Problems of Aquisition of Library Materials from the Caribbean Islands (60); "Library and Bibliographic Activities in the Caribbean" (63); "Library and Bibliographic Activities in the Dominican Republix (64); Ed "Current Caribbean Bibliography" (61-65). 14: Bibliography. 15: Estate Hope PO Box 822, Charlotte Amalie St Thomas VI 00801.

BAAK, ODELLA (SOLHEIM). b Valley City ND 26 S 13. 4: Leonard E Baak. 5: St Olaf Col 32-36 (Eng, Lat) BA (cum laude); UMinn summers 39, 41 (LS); Kan State Col (Emporia) 53-54 MS in LS. 6: Lat, Norwegian, Ger. 7: Tchr Eng, Music Westhope High Sch, ND 36-39; Tchr Eng, Lat, Music Faulkton High Sch, SD 39-42; Eng tchr Alexandria (Minn) Sr High Sch 42-45; Res bks libn St Olaf Col 46-53; sst libn Col Emporia 53-60; Visiting Lecturer in Lib Sci Kan State Col (Emporia) 59-60; Asst Prof of Lib Sci & asst libn Morningside Col 60-. 8: Lib consul 5 Tri-Co Insts for pub schs in NW Iowa 66. 9: IowaLA; ALA. 10: Bus & Prof Women's Club; AAUP; Lutheran Acad for Scholarship; Beta Phi Mu. 14: Col lib wk, tchg lib sci, catlg, ref. 15: 4227 Morningside ave, Sioux City Ia 51106.

BAAR, DONNA (LERARIO). b Astoria LI 24 Ag 43. 4: Stephen. 5: Alfred U 61-65 (Eng lit) BA; Syracuse 65-66 (LS) MLS. 6: Fr. 7: Asst ref libn UUtah Lib 66-68, Instr in LS 68-. 9: ALA; UtahLA. 14: Ref, tchg lib sci. 15: 1449 Lincoln st, Salt Lake City Ut 84102.

BAAR, HAZEL FRAZIER. b Jackson Mich 19 D 17. 4: Stuart P Baar Jr. 5: Jackson Commun Col 36-38 AA; Michigan State U 38-40 (Eng) BA; Fresno State Col 58 (Educ Tch's Cert); UMich 63-65 MALS. 7: Hd libn Taipei Amer Sch, Taipei Taiwan 63-64; Ref libn Dearborn (Mich) Pub Lib 64-65; Adult ref lobn Southfield Lib, Southfield Mich 65-66; Hd sociol & educ dept Grand Rapids (Mich) Pub Lib 66-. 8: Instr, McGregor Wkshop, Mich State Lib ssummer 68, 69. 9: ALA; MichLA; Grand Rapids Libn's Club. 10: Women's Nat Bk Assn; Phi Kappa Phi; Beta Phi Mu. 14: Ref. 15: 987 Three Mile rd NE, Grand Rapids Mi 49505.

BAATZ, ROSEMARY. b Crookston Minn 15 F 31. 5: Col of St Scholastica 48-52 (Biol) BA; Amer Conservatory of Music (Chicago) 53-58 (Music Theory) BMus; West Res 6-64 MSLS. 6: Ger. 7: Lit searcher Armour & Co, Chicago 53-53; Med ref Amer Med Assn, Chicago 53-56; Patent & lit searcher Armour & Co, Chicago 56-63; Libn Oak Ridge Inst of Nuclear Studies, Oak Ridge Tenn 64-65; Libn Ill Col of Optometry 65-68; Libn 3M Med Prods Lib, St Paul 68-. 8: Tchg Bibliog of the Natural Scis at UTenn Lib Sch spring 65 Optometric Ext Prog, Decrean Okla, indexing 66-. 9: MedLA. 12: Comp "Optometric Extension Program Postgraduate Courses Inex, 1957-1968". 13: Yes. 14: Admin, indexing. 15: 2040 Hudson rd, St Paul, Mn 55119.

BAATZ, WILMER HENRY. b Ft Wayne Ind 23 O 15. 4: Leia E Cornell. 5: Ind U (Ft Wayne & Bloomington) 35-40 (Eng) AB; Ind U (Bloomington) 40-41 (Eng) MA; Chicago 45-46 BLS. 6: Ger, Fr. 7: Bkmob libn Ft Wayne Ind Pub Lib 35-39; Asst dir Beloit Col Lib 46-47; Chief libn VA Hosp, Tomah Wis 47; Asst chief Br Off 7 VA, Chicago 47-49; Asst dir URochester Libs, Rochester NY 49-50; Chief tech processing dept Pub Lib, Milwaukee 50-55; Supv libn VA, Wash DC 55-60; Chief lib serv div Fed Aviation Agency, Wash DC60-65; Asst dir for Operations & Serv Ind U (Bloomington) 65-. 9: SLA (chm Transportation Div 64-65, advis Coun 64-65)-Milwaukee (now Wis) Chap (chm 52-53); Consult Offr Ind Chap 66-67; Mil Libns (chm DC Chap 64-65); ALA-RTSD (Org Com 67-71 IndLA (treas 68-69). 10: Pres Friends of the Library, Springfield Va 56-60; sec Church Coun, St Mark's

Lutheran Church Springfield Va 58-61; Phi Beta Kappa. 11: Fed Aviation Agency Certif of Achievement 65; Outstanding rating 62-65. 13: Yes. 14: Admin. 15: 3501 Park Lane, Bloomington In 47405.

BABBITT, CHARLES A. b Branford Conn 23 F 35. 4: Heloise Kendris. 5: UMich 52-56 (Bus Admin) BAA; Columbia 57-59 (LS) MS. 6: Lat, Fr. 7: Admin asst Branford Free Lib, branford Conn 59; Lt Col USAF Res Davis-Monthon AFB, Tucson Ariz 59-60, (active duty) Discharged 65; Hd libn N Haven High Sch, N Haven Conn 60-62; Libn Perkin-Elmer Optics Div, Norwalk Conn 62-66; Hd libn Gen Electric Co, Syracuse NY 66-. 9: ALA; NEA; ConnTA. 10: 4-H; Scout Master; Commun Chest. 14: Lib mgt, theoret devel of info & docs proc. 15: Box 445 405 University pl, Syracuse NY 13210.

BABCOCK, GEORGE GIBBS. b Janesville Wis 11 Ap 21. 4: Maralyn M Busjaeger. 5: Carroll Col 45-49 (Sociology) BA; UWis 49-50 BLS. 7: Tech Sgt US Army (Artillery/Infantry) 39-45; Libn Sturgeon Bay Pub Lib, Sturgeon bay Wis 50-52; Libn Portage Free Lib, Portage Wis 52-53; Ref libn Winnetka Pub Lib, Winnetka Ill 53-59, Dir 60-. 9: ALA; Assn of US Army. 15: 902 Lincoln st, Evanston Il 60201.

BABCOCK, NANCY ELIZABETH. b Brockton Mass 8 Ap 16. 5: UNH 33-37 (Eng) BA; Simmons 37-38 BS in LS. 7: Asst Memorial Hall Lib, Andover Mass 38-43; Ref libn City Lib, Manchester NH 43-63; Asst ref libn NH State Lib 64-. 9: ALA; NELA; NHLA. 13: Yes. 14: Ref. 15: 491 Maple st, Manchester NH 03104.

BABICKI, JOSEPH T. b Grodno Poland 27 Jl 19. 4: Gudrun M Pfeifer. 5: UMoscow Russia 36-41 (Hist) BA (Equiv); Wayne State U 46-48 (Hist) MA; UMich 48-49 AMLS. 6: Russ, Polish, Ger, Fr, Sp, Ital, Ukrainian, byelorussian. 7: Jr asst libn Detroit Pub Lib 48-49; Asst libn I Wayne State U 49-69, libn II69-, Instr in Russ 51-66; Libn Adas Shalom Synagogue Lib, Detroit 54-69; Asst Prof& libn East Ill U 69-. 8: Special Instr of Russ for US Army reserve, Detroit55-68. 9: ALA; MichLA; Detroit Philos Soc. 11: Citation by Jewish Bk Coun of Amer59; Carnegie Fellowship in LS, 66; Alexander von Humboldt Found (W Germany) ResearchFellowship 66-67. 12: Contrib to "East Europe in the Sixties" (64). 14: Catlg, admin, bibliog. 15: East Ill U Lib, Charleston Il 61920.

BABIN, ROBERTA (YOUNG). b Waxia La 23 F01. 5: LSNC 21-22 (Eng, Soc Studies); USL 26-27 (Eng, Soc Studies) BA; Tulane 28, 56-57; LSU 40. 7: Eng, Soc Studies Sunset High Sch, Sunset La 23; Sch prin Tech Sch, opelousas La 23-24; Sch prin Notleyville Sch, Opelousas La 23-28; Adult educ tchr WPA, Houma La 38-40; Eng tchr Pecan Island High Sch, Pecan Island La 44-65, Libn Pecan Island High Sch, Pecan Island La 44-. 66. 8: Reporter for "Louisiana Register" 55-65; Columnist & reporter for "Houma Courier" 28-44. 9: ALA; NEA; NCEA; ClrTA; LaLA; LaTchrsAssn. 13: Yes. 14: Ref, readers advisory. 15: 762 N Walnut st, Opelousas La 70570.

BACELLI, MRS HALLIE SYKES. b Hobbsville NC 29 Ag 13. 5: Woman's Col of UNC 30-34 (Eng, Hist) AB; UNC 35-36 ABLS; Appalachian State Tchrs Col 48-50 (Educ, LS) MA. 6: Fr, Ger. 7: Libn Concord High Sch, Concord NC 36-40; Libn Harding High Sch, Charlotte NC 40-43; Post libn US Army, Camp Mackall NC 43-45; Sch lib supv Charlotte City Schs, Charlotte NC 45-46; Sch lib supv Greensboro City Schs, Greensboro NC 46-47; Libn Central Elem & Jr High Sch, Greensboro NC 47-52; Dir lib serv Guilford Co Schs, Greensboro NC 52-. 8: Consul: Concord Pub Lib org 39-40; NC State Dept, on writing the Guidelines & Standards for NDEA III, V. 9: ALA (coms: Magazine Eval 50, Basic Bk Collection for Jr High Schs 50, Basic Bk Collection for High Schs 57); NCLA (sec & com wk; Sch & Child Sect: var offs); SELA (chm Sch & Child Sect); NCEA (chm Greensboo Unit; var other duties). 10: DKG; OES. 12: Ed "North Carolina Libraries" (41-43, 51-53). 13: Yes. 14: Sch libs. 15: 1305 McDowell dr, Greensboro NC 27408.

BACH, HARRY. b Laupheim Germany 23 Mr 22. 4: Grace A Jones. 5: UCal (Berkeley) 40-43 (Fr) AB, 46-47 BLS, 55-56 (LS). 6: Fr, Ger. 7: UOre: Jr ref libn 47-48, Bibliogr 48-49, Ser libn 49-50; Sr asst acquis dept UNeb 50-52; Head acquis & ser depts UIowa 52-55; Head acquis dept San Jose State Col 56-62; Col Libn Riverside Coty Col 62-. 8: Survey of Iowa State Reformatory Lib 53, follow-up 54. 9: ALA (Equip Sect 56-57, Acquis Sect, Policy & Research 57-58, Ser Sect Nom Com 60-61);-ACRL (Adv Com 68-69); CalLA (chm Reg Resources Coord Com 65-66, chm No Cal Tech Proc Group 62-63, Chm Standards Com, Comm Col Div 69); CalTA; Cal Jr Col Assoc. 10: Phi Beta Kappa; ACLU; Urban League; NAACP. 12: "Bibliographical Essay on the History of Scholary Libraries in the United States, 1800 to the Present," UIll Lib Sch Occasional Paper, No 54 (59). 13: Yes. 14: Acquis, admin. 15: 3633 Castle Reagh, Riverside Ca 92506.

BACHENBERG, ELMER V. b Lewiston Neb 17 Ja 23. 4: Mary Katheryn Armstrong. 5: Neb State Tchrs Col 44-49 (Eng) BA; Iowa State Tchrs Col summer 51 (Sch Admin); UIll 54-56 MS in LS; Radcliff-Harvard Inst on Hist & Archival Mgt summer 57 Certif. 6: Ger. 7: Jr high & act prin Mt Auburn Pub Schs, Mt Auburn Iowa 49-52; Jr high instr Nora Springs (Iowa) Consolidated Schs 52-54; Asst agric libn Col of Agric UNeb 55-56; Asst sci libn UNeb 56-57; Asst col libn & act libn Neb Wesleyan U 57-61; Soc & applied sci catlgr Denver Pub Lib 61-64; Head catlg libn Colo State Col 64-. 8: Chm, Bk Fair Exhib in Lincoln Neb, 61; Consul for Rocky Mtn Educ Lab 67-69. 9: ALA; MPLA; NebLA (Constit Com 59-61); ColoLA. 10: AAUP Des; AF&AM; ASA. 14: Catlg, archives, hist records mgt, time-cost motion studies, filing rules, catlg card reprod. 15: 1835 Twelfth ave, Greeley, Co 80631.

BACHMANN, GEORGE THEODORE JR. b Annapolis Md 31 Mr 30. 4: Marjorie Winant. 5: U Md. 48-52 (Hist) BA, 55-60 (Hist) MA; Cath U of Am 56-61 (LS) MSLS. 6: Fr, Ger. 7: Circ asst UMd Lib, 56-58; Br libn Prince Geo Co Mem Lib, 58-60; Catlgr Va Theol Sem, 60-61; Catlgr Lutheran Theol Sem, Gettysburg Pa 61-64; Catlgr Shippensburg State Col, 64-67; Dir of Adult Serv Anne Arvnel Co Pub Lib, Annapolis Md 67-68; Lib Dir Catonsville Commun Col Lib, 68-. 9: ALA; MdLA; Md Assn Jr Cols (Col - Learning Resources Dir). 10: Viola da Gamba Soc of Amer; Active in recitals of Renaissance & Baroque music on instruments of those periods. 12: Asst ed "Journal of the Viola da Gamba Society of America". 14: Adminis. 15: 123 Monticello ave, Annapolis Md 21401.

BACHRACH, ETTA ELIZABETH (CHRISTIANSEN). b S Bellingham Mass 28 My 09. 4: William Bachrach. 5: Hyannis Normal Sch 26-28 (Educ); bostonU 35-37 (Eng) BS in Ed; Columbia 47-48 BS in LS. 6: Russian, Fr, Ger. 7: Tchr, Bellingham & Mendon (Mass) 29-35; Tchr (Boston) 37-38; Lib asst BostonU 38-44; Research analyst US War Dept 44-47; Libn US Census Bur, Wash DC 47; Catlgr DC Pub Lib 48-51; Catlgr, Slavic catlgr & reviser US Armed Forces Med Lib, Wash DC 51-58; Head Slavic Unit NLM 58-62; Catlgr & reviser Smithsonian Inst Lib, Wash DC 62-64; Cyrillic catlgr US Nat Agric Lib, Wash DC 64-. 9: ALA; Potomac Tech Proc Libns. 10: Pi Lambda Theta. 13: Yes. 14: Catlg. 15: 1330 New Hampshire ave NW apt 325, Wash DC 20036.

BACK, ANDREW W. b Weirton WVa 4 F 29. 4: Elizabeth Nadzak. 5: Clarion State Col 50-54 (Soc Studies) BSEd; UPittsburgh 65 MLS; Duquesne U 62-65(LS). 6: Ukrainian, Polish. 7: US Navy Petty Off 3rd Class YN; Geog tchr & asst football coach Hopewell Sch Dist, Aliquippa Penn 54-63, Libn Sr High Sch 63-66; Assoc Prof Lib Sci Slippery Rock State Col 66-. 8: Middle Atlantic States Eval Com, Benjamin Franklin Jr High Sch, New Castle Penn spring 65 Inst mem Inst onNew Media for Library Educ (UPittsburgh) 69. 9: NEA; ALA-ACRL; CathLA; Penn StateEA; PennLA; Pittsburgh Suburban LA; Beaver Co Lib Assn (past pres). 10: AAUP; Lions;Amer Legion. 14: Sch libs, ref, inst mater. 15: 3210 Harding ave, Aliquippa Pa15001.

BACKER, MRS MARY ASKEW. b Cincinnati 26 Ja 1897. 5: UCincinnati 15-18 (Eng) BA; UWis 18-19 Grad in LS; Johns Hopkins 51-54 (Amer Hist) MA. 6: Fr, Ger. 7: Br asst NY Pub Lib 19-20; Br libn Enoch Pratt Free Lib, Baltimore 42-63; Faculty Catonsville Community Col, Catonsville Md 65-66; Lib proj Md Bd of Natural Resources, Annapolis Md 67-69. 8: ALA (sec AFL-CIO Joint Com on Lib Serv to Labor Groups 56-62); Governor's Conf on Role of Educ in Field of Aging 62; State Com for Nat Lib Wk 60, 61, 62. 9: ALA; MdLA; Md Adult Educ Assn. 10: AAUW (pres Baltimore Br 64-65); Women's Civic League of Baltimore; Citizens Planning & Housing Assn of Baltimore. 13: Yes. 14: Br lib admin, bk-talks, commun rel. 15: 216 Rodgersforge rd Apt D, Baltimore Md 21212.

BACON, CONSTANCE MARY (SMITH). b Fall River Mass 28 Ap 25. 5: Temple 51-52 (LS) Certif. 7: Clerk-typist- teletype operator US Maritime Commsn, Phila 42-46; Typist-lib clerk Philco Corp Research Div, Phila 46-53; Sect manager Lit Bros Retail Dept Store, Phila 53-54; Libn, asst off manager Educ Registrar Insurance Soc, Phila 54-61, Libn off manager 61-. 9: SLA (Phila Coun, Mng ed "Bulletin" 56-57). 10: Colonial Phila Hist Soc (Womens) Insur Soc of Phila; Penn Town Hist Soc (charter mem); Society Hill Civic Assn). 14: Research, admin, child bks. 15: 232 S 4th st, Phila Pa 19106.

BACON, ETHEL FRANCES. b Hartford Conn 3 Jl 22. 5: Hartt Col of Music 40-44 (Piano) BMus, 55 (Organ) MusM. 6: Fr, Ger. 7: Catlgr Hartt Col Lib 51-60; Music libn UHartford 60-. 9: MusLA; SLA; ConnLA. 10: Appalachian Mountain Club. 14: Music ref materials. 15: 47 Riverview rd, Rocky Hill Ct 06067.

BACON, OMAR ALBERT. b Ellsworth Wis 30 Mr 11. 4: Margaret Grow Bacon. 5: Wis State Col (River Falls) 32-36 BE; Peabody 38-39 BS in LS; UIll 51-52 MLS. 7: Tchr-libn High Sch, Cornell Wis 37-38; Head Libn So State Tchrs Col (Springfield SD) 39-42, 46-47; Personnel tech Army Air Force 42-46; Head Libn Pub Lib, Waterton SD 47-51; Head Libn Pub Lib, Huntington WVa 52-58; Dir Columbian River Reg Lib, Wenatchee Wash 58-59; Dir Pub Lib of Medford & Jackson Co, Medford Ore 59-. 9: ALA (Coun 55-59); AdultEA; SDLA (pres 59); WVaLA (pres 53-54); OreLA (pres 62-63); PNLA. 10: Rotary Club; C of C; Beta Phi Mu; Phi Gamma Mu; Governor's Com on Aging 67-. 13: Yes. 14: Admin. 15: 2527 Capital ave, Medford Ore 97501.

BADERTSCHER, DAVID GLEN. b Morrow Ohio 31 Ja 35. 4: Betty Jo Downing. 5: Ind StateU 53-57 (Soc Sci) BS, 58-62 (Soc Sci) MS; Rosary Col 64-67 (LS) MA. 6: Sp. 7: Tchr Rockville Pub Schs, Rockville Ind 57-58; Tchr Terre Haute Pub Schs, Ind 58-59; US Army Cts and Bds Clk (Sp/4) 59-61; Tchr Medinah Dist #11, Medinah Ill 61-63; Tchr libn Elgin Acadm Elgin Ill 63-64; Tchr Beachwood Pub Schs, Beachwood Ohio 64-65; Libn trainee chicago Pub Lib 65-66; Circ and asst ref libn UChicago Law Lib 66-. 8: Circ Com UChicago Libs 67-; Circ Systems Task Force UChicago Lib 69-. 9: ALA; AALL; Chicago Assn Law Libs; MedinahTA (pres 62-63). 14: Lib admin, lib automation, ref. 15: PO Box 87, Hazelcrest Il 60429.

BADGER, FRANK W. b Butler Penn 5 S 25. 4: Joan Allison. 5: Clarion State Col 47-50 (Eng) BS; Peabody 51-52 MA (LS); UPenn 58-61 (Amer Civilization) AM. 7: Infantry US Army (Pfc) 43-46; Libn Butler Co Lib, Butler Penn 50-51; Catlgr Baptist Sunday Sch Bd, Nashville 52; Col Libn Morris Harvey Col 52-. 8: Dir of curric studies, Morris Harvey Col 68-. 9: Amer Studies Assn; Amer Soc Arch Hist; WVaLA. 10: Pi Gamma Mu; Phi Alpha Theta. 12: "Developments in the Academic Area of the Liberal Arts College; A Bibliography," with Collins Burnett (68). 13: Yes. 15: 2502 Kanawha ave SE, Charleston WV 25304.

BADGER, SUSAN (DOYLE). b Indianapolis 27 O 41. 4: Dr William Earl Badger III. 5: UIll (Urbana) 59-61; UMich 61-63 (Anthropology) AB, 63-64 (Anthropology) AM, 64-65 AMLS. 7: Engnr asst Gen Electric, Cincinnati 60-61; Lib wk-study scholar Engnr Lib UMich 64-65; Libn II Undergrad Lib UMich 65-67; Res asst Holloman AFB Aeromed Lab 68-69. 14: Ref, bk sel. 15: 200 N Dalmont, Hobbs NM 88240.

BADGETT, DONA (COYTE). b Louisville Ky 16 My 40. 4: T Carl Badgett. 5: Hollins Col 58-62 (Hist) BA; Sorbonne 60 (cours de la civilization) Diplome; UNC 62-63 (LS) MSLS. 6: Fr. 7: Catlgr DukeU Col of Law Lib 63-64; Order libn Wake Forest Col Lib 64; ULouisville Lib 65; Catlgr Fondren Lib So Methodist U 65-. 9: TexLA; Callas CoLA. 14: Gift & exch, ref. 15: 6024 E University apt 116, Dallas Tx 75206.

BADILLO, IRAIDA. b Aguada PR 13 S 32. 5: UPR 49-52 (Eng) BA in Humanities (magna cum laude); Carnegie 53-54 MLS. 6: Sp, Eng, Fr. 7: Lib asst UPR Lib 53, Catlgr 54-55; Post libn Camp Losey PR 55-56; Ref libn US Army War Col Lib, Carlisle Barracks Penn 56-59; Catlgr & ref libn Martin Co Lib, Orlando Fla 59-61; Libn Aerospace Corp ETRO, Patrick AFB Fla 61-68; Sr ref libn Fla Tech U, 68-. 9: SLA; FlaLA. 10: Phi Kappa Phi; Beta Phi Mu. 11: Nina Brotherton Prize, Carnegie Lib Sch. 14: Ref. 15: 8401 N Atlantic ave apt C-6, Cape Canaveral Fl 32920.

BADING, MARY KAY. b Cedar Rapids Iowa 5 Ag 45. 5: Mt Mercy Col 63-67 (Hist) BA; Pratt inst 67-68 MLS. 6: Sp. 7: Staff libn UNotre Dame (Ind) 68-. 14: Ref, catlg. 15: 656 Valley Brook dr SE, Cedar Rapids Ia 52403.

BAE, EUNKYUNG (YOON). b Seoul Korea 30 O 31. 5: Kyung-Hee U (KOREA) 58-62 (Eng Lit) BA; Catherine Spalding Col 62-64 (LS) MS. 6: Korean, Japanese, Chinese, Fr, Russian. 7: 1st stud asst Catherne Spalding Col Lib 62-64; Catlg libn Howard U Lib 64-66, Libn Col of Pharmacy 66-68; Catlg libn Princeton U Lib 68-. 14: Catlg, ref, child lit. 15: PO Box 9, Kingston NJ 08528.

BAECHTOLD, MARGUERITE. b Elmhurst NY 16 Ap 16. 5: Montclair State Col 34-38 (Eng) AB; Columbia 45-49 BLS; Western Michigan U 66-68 Ed S. 6: Fr, Lat. 7: Tchr, libn High sch, Pt Pleasant Beach NJ 39-44; Libn High sch, N Plainfield NJ 44-46; Libn High sch, Ridgewood NJ 46-55; Libn Benjamin Franklin Jr High Sch, Ridgewood NJ 55-60; Libn W Essex High Sch, N Caldwell N J 60-64; Coordinator lib sci minor Newark State Col 64-66; Asst prof dept libship West Mich U, 66. 8: Tchr UVt, summer 64. 9: ALA; AALS; NJLA (Exec Bd 63-66); NJSchLA (past pres); MichASchLA. 11: Beta Phi Mu. 14: Sch lib serv, lib educ. 15: 3226 Tamsin ave, Kalamazoo Mi 49001.

BAEHR, BETTY B(ISCHOFF). b Wash DC 2 D 16. 5: George Washington U 43 (Hist) AB; UKy 47 BS in LS; UMd 62 (Amer Civilization) MA. 7: Asst loan libn UMd 47-48, Loan libn 48-. 9: ALA (Life mem); -RSD: Md Chap; MdLA (Mem Com). 10: Eng Speaking Union; Friends of Surbridge Village. 14: Ref, automation, rare bks. 15: 5302 Baltimore ave, Chevy Chase Md 20015.

BAER, ELEANORA (AGNES). b Springfield Mo 22 D 07. 5: Fontbonne Col 26-27, 28-31 (Eng) AB; St Louis U 39-44 (Educ) MEd; Wash U summer 54; UWis summers 58-61 MS in LS. 6: Sp, Fr. 7: Lib asst St Louis Pub Lib 25-26; Libn Fontbonne Col 29-46, Instr summer 44; U asst libn St Louis U 46-52; Lib asst University City Pub Lib, University City Mo 52-60; Libn Clayton High Sch, Clayton Mo 53-65; Lib Coord Clayton Sch Dist 66-. 9: ALA; CathLA; NEA; Beta Phi Mu; Delta Epsilon Sigma; Mo State Tchrs Assn. 10: AAUW; Mo State Hist Soc. 12: "Titles in Series" (53, 57, 60, 64). 13: Yes. 14: Admin, catlg. 15: 1359 McCutcheon, Brentwood Mo 63144.

BAER, ELIZABETH (HENRIETTA). b Oxford Ohio 10 N 19. 5: Miami U 37-41 (Eng) BA; Simmons 41-42 (LS) BS; Miami U 59 (Hist) MA. 6: Sp. Armenian, Fr. 7: Asst loan libn Miami U 42-43; Child libn Pub Lib of Cincinnati 43-45; Miami U (Oxford Ohio): Clsf 45-51, Head catlgr 51-, Head catlgr Asst Prof 55-62, Head catlgr Assoc Prof 62-. 9: ALA; OhioLA; (Chm Ohio Valley Group Tech Serv Libns chm 63-64). 10: Phi Beta Kappa; Pi Delta Phi; AAUP. 13: Yes. 14: Catlg. 15: 131 E Spring st, Oxford Oh 45056.

BAER, KARL AMADEUS. b Munich Germany 1 D 06. 4: Margaret Stirling. 5: Us of Berlin, Munich, Heidelberg 24-28 Law LLB; UHeidelberg 28-31 Law LLD; Pratt 40-41 BLS; Columbia 43-45 (LS). 6: Ger, Fr, Sp, Port, ital, Dutch, Lat. 7: Catlgr St John's U, Brooklyn NY 41-43; Head catlgr Chemists Club Lib, NYC 43-45; Subj catlgr US Army Med Lib, Wash DC 45-47; Head, rare bk catlgr US Army Med Lib, Cleveland 47-48; Bibliogr & head, bibliog unit Armed Forces Med Lib, Wash DC 48-52; Asst chief Med & Gen Ref Lib Veterans Admin, Wash DC 52-53; Libn Amer Pharmaceutical Assn, Wash DC 53-55; Lecturer Grad Sch of LS, CathU 53-62; Chief libn Nat Housing Center, Wash DC 55-. 8: Chm Prof Consultation Com Wash Chap SLA 59-68; FHA Lib Survey 58; USA Stand Inst (chm Z39 Subcom on Trade Catlgs & Directs 65-). 9: SLA (past chm Biol Sci Div, rep to IFLA 56-, chm PHB Sect 66-67, Wash DC Chap; pres 56-57, Consul Offr 57-68); ADI; AAAS;DCLA; Wash DC Hist of Sci Club; Intl Club; Spec Libs Sect of Internat Fed of Lib Assns (pres 64-70). 12: Ed "Founders of Neurology" with Webb Haymaker (53); Hon mem Adv Bd "International Library Review". 13: Yes. 14: Internat cooperation, bibliog, spec libs. 15: 1625 L st NW, Wash DC 20036.

BAER, MARK H. b Pendleton Pr 24 Je 23. 4: Elizabeth Carter. 5: UWash 46-50 (Pre Law, Pre Med) BA, 50-53 (Hist), 54-55 (Libnship) ML. 6: Fr, Ger. 7: Catlg libn Law Lib UWash, 55-56; Chem libn 56-57; Eng & tech div libn Ore State U, Corvallis 57-59; Dir tech inf serv Ampex Corp, Redwood City Cal 59-66; Libs mgr Hewlett-Packard Co, Palo Alto Cal 66-. 8: Lect UCal (Berkeley) Grad Sch of Libnship 66-; Instr UCal Ext Div Contin Educ in Libnship 64, 65; SLA consul. 9: SLA (chm Placement Policy Com 68-70; past pres San Francisco Bay chap); Inst Electri & Electro Engnrs; CalLA. 12: Ed "Union List of Periodicals: Science-Technology-Economics," San Francisco Bay Reg Chap, SLA (66). 14: Admin, educ, ref. 15: 602 Remington dr, Sunnyvale Ca 94087.

BAERWALD, EVA (LEWY). b Germany 20 Ap 05. 4: Hans George Baerwald. 5: Tech U 24-30 Physics (Engnr Diploma); Friedrich Wilhelm U (Breslau) 24-30 Physics (High Sch Tchr Diploma); West Res 56-58 MSLS. 6: Ger, Fr. 7: Libn West Res Sch Applied Soc Sci 58; Asst libn Albuquerque Pub Lib 59-60; Asst libn Bernalillo Co Med Soc Lib, Albuquerque NM 61-; Asst libn Lib of the Med Scis, Albuquerque NM 63-. 9: MedLA; NMLA; GALA. 10: LWV; Beta Mu. 14: Ref, catlg. 15: 2732 Chama NE, Albuquerque NM 87110.

BAGBY, DOROTHY (LECHLER). b Knoxville Tenn 2 Ag 06. 4: T Wesley Bagby. 5: Randolph- Macon Woman's Col 23-24 (Hist & lang); Converse Col 24-25 (Mus); Queens Col (Charlotte NC) 25-26 (Mus). 6: Fr. 7: Check collect clk Fed Res Bk, Charlotte NC 27-31; Sales Baptist Bk Store, Charlotte NC 57; Ref asst Pub Lib of Charlotte & Mecklenburg Co, 58-. 9: SELA; NCLA; MecklenburgLA. 10: Staff Organization Pub Lib. 14: Ref. 15: 2107 E Seventh st, Charlotte NC 28204.

BAGDASIAN, NAZALY. b Racine Wis 22 Jl 31. 5: UWis 50-54 (Hispanic Studies) BA; UWis 56-57 (LS) MA. 6: Sp, Armenian, Fr. 7: Catlgr-ref lib Racine Pub Lib, Racine Wis 58-63; Catlgr Arizona State U,(Tempe) 63-65. ; Catlg libn Fresno State Col 66-67; Asst catlgr UWis (Kenosha) 68-. 9: WisLA. 14: Catlg, ref. 15: 1932 N Main st, Racine Wis 53402.

BAGERIS, GEORGE NICKOLAS. b Detroit 2 Mr 33. 4: Jeanne Slasor. 5: UMich 51-55 (Hist) BA in Educ; West Mich 58-60 MALS; UMich 62-63 (LS). 6: Ger, Gk. 7: Soc Studies Tchr Schoolcraft Pub Schs, Schoolcraft Mich 55-56; US Army Radio operator (Pvt) Schweinvurt Germany 56-58; Asst libn Pontiac Central High Sch, pontiac Mich 58-59; Head libn Kalamazoo Central High Sch, Kalamazoo Mich 60-62; Coordinator tech processing Livonia Pub Schs, Livonia Mich 63-. 10: Beta Phi Mu. 14: Admin, pub schs. 15: 16661 Prest, Detroit Mi 48235.

BAGGS, ROBERT NATHANIEL JR. b Camden NJ 18 F 37. 4: Audrey Parr Gourley Baggs. 5: Ursinus Col 55-57, 59-61 (Eng) BA; Glassboro State Col 61; Drexel 62-64 MLS. 7: Spec 4th Class US Army, Ft Dix NJ 57-59; Eng tchr Ellwood Swift Jr High Sch, egg Harbor Twp NJ 61-62; Libn-in-chg Bala-Cynwyd Lib Assn, Bala-Cynwyd Penn 64- Actg dir of libs Lower Merion LA, 68-69, Dir 69-. 9: PennLA. 14: Pub Lib Serv, Admin. 15: 111 Kenilworth rd, Merion Station Pa 19066.

BAGINSKI, DORIS ANN. b Middletown Conn 14 Je 38. 5: UConn 56-60 (Hist) BA; Syracuse 61-63 (LS) NS. 6: Fr. 7: Gen asst Hartford Pub Lib, Hartford Conn 60-61; Grad asst Syracuse U Sch of Lib sci 61-63; Enoch Pratt Free Lib, Baltimore: Jr libn gen ref dept 63-64, Sr libn hist travel & biog dept 64-65, Subj Spec soc sci & hist dept 65-. 9: ALA; MdLA. 10: AHA; Beta Phi Mu. 14: Ref, adult serv. 15: 4514 N Charles st, Baltimore Md 21210.

BAGLEY, CATHERINE HOLLAND. b Waterbury Conn 24 Ap 41. 5: Col of New Rochelle 58-62 (Sociol) AB; SUNY (Geneseo) 62-63 MLS. 6: Fr. 7: Head Libn Cardinal Hayes High Sch, Bronx NY 63-68; Asst Libn NE Life Ins Co., Boston 68-69; Libn Hollis Lib, Braintree High Sch, Braintree Mass 69-. 9: ALA. 14: Young adult serv, catlg, ref. 15: 288 Clove rd, New Rochelle NY 10804.

BAGLEY, MARCILE (IVA) LEITER. b Louisville Ohio 8 S 25. 4: Lester Leonard Bagley. 5: Fla State U 43-47 (Home Econ) BS; Presbyterian Sch of Christian Educ 52-54 (Rel Educ) MRE; Fla State U 58-60 (LS) MS. 7: Tchr Millville Elem Sch, Panama City Fla 47-50; Home econ tchr Los Angeles City Col 50-52; Home missionary Presbyterian Church, Ky Mountains 54-56; Tchr Millville Elem Sch, Panama City Fla 56-58; Libn Lynn Haven Elem Sch, Panama City Fla 58-60; Head of journal dept Sci Info Center, Redstone Arsenal Ala 60-63; Chief Missile Intelligence Lib Missile Intelligence Dir, Redstone Arsenal Ala 63-. 8: Mission wk for 3 churches & 2 outposts in the Kentucky Mountains 54-56; Camp wk at Estes Park, Colo 48. 9: Bay Co (Fla) (pres); Bay Co EA (sec). 10: 4-H Club; Girl Reserves; PTA. 13: Yes. 14: Ref, admin. 15: 1219 Blevens Gap rd, Huntsville, Al 35802.

BAGNELL, PRISCA von Dorotka. b Novi-Sad Yugoslavia 16 F 28. 4: Lewis Allen. 5: Syracuse 59-63 (Ger) BA, 63-66 (Soc sci) MA. 6: Serbo-Croatian, Ger, Hungarian, Russian. 7: SyracuseU: Inst AF lang sch 58-63, Sec Slavic catlg dept 64-65, Asst slavic bibliogr acquis dept 65, Asst archivist 66-. 8: Subst instr of German, Skytop; Organ and supv lang course in Hungarian, Skytop; Asst in transl the Venetian Mss in the von Ranske Lib. 9: SAA; AHA. 10: Delta Phi Alpha; Syracuse U Libns Assn. 14: Univ archives. 15: 147 Redfield pl, Syracuse NY 13210.

BAHN, MRS CATHERINE INMAN. b Beaver Dam Wis 23 F 08. 5: Millersville State Col 26-29 (Educ-Sci) BS; Chicago summers 33-34 (Geog); Columbia 37-39 (Geog) MA. 6: Sp, Fr. 7: Tchr of Geog East Jr High Sch, Lancaster Penn 28-37; Instr Geog dept Columbia summers 40-41; Accounting clerk Payroll Div, Panama Canal Balboa Hts CZ 41-50; Act head tchr Pickett Sch, Arlington Va 50-51; Chief of Chart Lib Sect Aeronautical chart & Info Center, Wash DC 51-57; Instr USDA Grad Sch, Wash DC 52-; Head acquis sect Geog & Map Div LC 57-66; Prin recommending offr, Sci/Tech Div 66-. 8: SLA (Geog & Map Div rep to Standards Com 62-64, Spec Classifications & Subj Headings Com 64-65). , chm 56-57. 9: SLA (various com duties);-DC Chap (sec); Amer Assn Geogs (var coms). 10: Arlington hist Soc (sec, dir, ed); Lyon Village Citizens Assn (sec, treas, Federn rep). 12: Bk review ed SLA-Geog & Map Div "Bulletin"; ed "Arlington Hist Society magazine"; ed "Jobs in Geography". 13: Yes. 14: Acquis, maps & atlases, globes, geographical & cartographical pubs & related ref, sci & tech publs. 15: 2613 Key blvd, Arlington Va 22201.

BAHN, GILBERT S(CHUYLER). b Syracuse NY 25 Ap 22. 5: Columbia 39-43 (Chem Engnr) BS; Rensselaer Polytech Inst 49-52, 65 (Mechanical Engnr) MS. 7: Admin off US Army Forces, US & SW Pacific 43-46; Advanced sci program Gen Electric Co, Pittsfield Mass 46-48; Development Engnr Gen Electric Co, Schenectady NY 48-53; Sr thermodynamics engnr, engnr spec, research spec, sr research spec, research scientist, research consul Marquardt Corp, Van Nuys Cal 53-. 8: Gen chm Conferences on Performance of High-Temperature Systems 59, 62, 64; Chm Marquardt Corp Lib Com 61-67; Co-founder & sec Western States Sect, The Combustion Inst 57-; Mem Performance Standardization Wkg Group and Thermochemistry Wkg Group & Interagency Chemical Rocket Propulsion Group. 9: Amer Soc Mech Engnrs; Amer Inst chem Engnrs; Amer Inst Aeron & Astronaut; ACS; Amer Phys Soc; Combust Inst; SLA. 10: Licensed Prof Engnr, Cal, 55, NY, 51; Marquardt Employees Fed Credit Union; San Fernando Valley Chap Cal Credit Union League; Unit Leader & Commsnr Will Rogers Dist, Crescent Bay Area Coun Boy Scouts of America; Vestryman St Aidan's Church, Malibu Cal. 12: Ed "First (60), Second (63), Third (68) Conference on Performance of High temperature Systems"; Ed "Pyrodynamics, The Journal of Applied Thermal Processes" (63-). 13: Yes. 14: Combustion & propulsion, high-temperature chem thermodynamics & thermokinetics, propellant properties, tech data sources. 15: 16902 Bollinger dr, Pacific Palisades Ca 90272.

BAHNSEN, JANE (CUTLER). b Evansville Ind 13 N 10. 5: Vassar 27-28; West Res 28-31 (Philos) AB; UNC53-54 BS in LS. 6: Fr. 7: Sec Grad Sch West Res U 31-34; NC Collection UNC Lib (Chapel Hill): Lib attendant 52-55, Asst libn 55-58, 1st asst libn 58-. 9: NCLA (com on Conserv of Newspapers 56-63). 10: Beta Phi Mu. 13: Yes. 14: Catlg. 15: NC Collection Univ NC Lib, Chapel Hill NC 27514.

BAHRINGER, ELSIE A (SMITH). b Schenectady NY 13 Mr 11. 4: Lee R Bahringer. 5: Syracuse 28-32 (Lat) AB; NYS Col for Tchrs (Albany) summer 35, 36 (LS); Ithaca Col ext 57 (A-V); Syracuse 58-61 (LS) MS. 7: Sub your Home Pub Lib, Johnson City NY 43-48; Br libn Binghamton Pub Lib, Binghamton NY 48-49; Asst to dir Your Home Pub Lib, Johnson City NY 50-53; Consul & sales bk dept Fowler, Dick & Walker, Binghamton NY 53-54; Sub brs & ref) Binghamton Pub Lib, Binghamton NY 55-56; Sch libn Bd of Educ, Johnson City NY 56-63; Child consul Four Co Lib System, Binghamton NY 63-. 9: NEA; ALA; NYLA; NY State Tchrs Assn. 10: US Power Squadron Auxiliary; AAUW; Beta Phi Mu; Women's Nat Bk Assn. 14: Child serv, a-v serv. 15: 115 Thomas st, Johnson City NY 13790.

BAIG, SAMUEL. b Paterson NJ 12 My 10. 4: Lucille Roff. 5: NYU 28-34 (Eng) BA; Columbia 37-39 (Bibliog, Ref) BS. 6: Fr, Ger. 7: Ref asst NY Pub Lib 30-44; Libn Film Lib Ft Belvoir Va 44-45; Chief of ref (sgt) Army War Col Lib, Wash DC 45-46; Head of records & reports M W Kellogg Co, Jersey City NJ 46-52; Chief libn Republic Aviation Corp, Farmingdale LI NY 52-64; Chief libn CBS Labs, Stamford Com 64-66; Chief libn Kollsman Instrument Corp, Elmhurst NY 66-. 9: SLA; Lib Group SW Conn. 10: Contrib to "Bibliographic Index"; free-lance ed Grolier Info Serv Tchr Fundamental Adult Educ. 11: Army Commendation Medal for lit & ref serv to War Dept. 12: Numer bibliogs & indices publ by NY Pub Lib. 14: Bibliog, ref. 15: 65-36 99th st, Forest Hills NY 11374.

BAILEY, AGARD HYDE. b Ft Leavenworth Kan 23 Ag 09. 4: Dr Mabel Driscoll. 5: William Penn Col 47-51 (Eng) AB; State U Iowa 57 (Span) MA; UIll 63 (LS) MS. 6: Sp. 7: Tchr Scattergood Sch, W Branch Iowa 51-56; Tchr Estherville High & Jr Col, Estherville Iowa 56-57; Tchr El Paso High Sch, El Paso Ill 57-60; Asst libn Eureka Col 60-66; Assoc libn Eureka Col 66-. 9: ALA. 10: Amer Assn Tchrs Span & Port. 13: Yes. 14: Catlg, ref. 15: 610 S Dar st, Eureka Il 61530.

BAILEY, ANNE McKENNAN. b Dallas 14 O 32. 5: UMich 50-51; So Methodist U 51-54 (Sociol) BA; UTex 59-60 MLS. 7: Fondren Lib So Methodist U: Periods asst 55-59, Ref asst

60-61, Period libn 61-. 9: ALA; TexLA; SWLA. 10: Phi Beta Kappa. 14: Ref, periods. 15: 6323 Waggoner dr, Dallas Tx 75230.

BAILEY, BERTHA FRANCETA (GREEN). b Clarinda Iowa 9 My 13. 4: Harold Dean Bailey. 5: Clarinda Jr Col 56-58; NW Mo State 58-59 BS in Ed; UIdaho summer 60; USeattle summer 61; DenverU summers 62-65 MALS. 7: Childrens libn Pub Lib, Clarinda Iowa 32-39; Med & Patients' lib Mental Health, Clarinda Iowa 39-43; Life ins agent Prudential, clarinda Iowa 43-46; Store owner, Clarinda Iowa 43-56; High sch & jr col libn Clarinda commun schs 59-66; Hd libn Iowa West Commun Col, Council Bluffs Iowa 66-. 9: ALA; NEA; IowaStateEA; IowaASchL; Iowa Commun & Jr Col LA (pres 69-70); A-V Educ Assn Iowa. 10: Semper Fidelis (Woman's Serv Club); Sunday School Supt. 13: Yes. 14: Catlg, ref. 15: 611 W State st, Clarinda Ia 51632.

BAILEY, BERTHA M. b Pittsburgh Pa 24 Je 13. 5: UPittsburgh 31-34 (Hist) AB, 35 (Hist) MA; Columbia 48 (LS) BS in LS. 7: Tchr Pub schs Pittsburgh 39-42; Libn 42-55; Supv of sch lib serv 55-. 8: Part-time lect, Carnegie Lib Sch 60-62. 9: ALA; NEA; PennLA (chm Child YP & Sch Libns sect 59); Penn StateEA. 10: Pi Lambda Theta; Delta Kappa Gamma; Administrative Women in Education; United World Federalists; Natural Color Camera Club; West Penn Conservancy. 14: Sch libs. 15: 703 Hastings st, Pittsburgh Pa 15206.

BAILEY, DORIS VIVIAN (MOSTELLER). b Seattle Wash 6 Mr 27. 4: George Ernest Bailey. 5: Kan WesleyanU 47-49; UColo 58-59, 65; UDenver 59-62 (Soc Sci, Elem Educ) BA, 66-68 MA in Libnship. 6: Sp. 7: Tchr Elem Pub Schs, Kan 49-54; Tchr pub schs, Thornton Colo 56-66; Sch libn Westminster High Sch, Westminster Colo 67-. 9: ALA; -AASchL; NEA; ColoASchL; ColoLA; ColoEA; AdamsCoTA; WestminsterEA. 10: Rainbow Girls' Mothers' Club; UDenver Grad Sch of Libnship Alum Assn; Parents' Booster Club; PTA. 14: Ref, pub serv. 15: 2561 Barnhard st, Denver Co 80229.

BAILEY, DOROTHY M. b Bisbee Ariz 1 Jl 32. 5: Cottey Jr Col 50-51; Ariz State U 51-54 (Sociol) BS; UDenver 60-62 (LS) MS. 7: Asst teenage dir YWCA, Phoenix 54-56; Dist adv Girl Scouts of Amer, Phoenix 56-59; Lib asst Denver Pub Lib 60; Lib asst Bus Admin Lib UDenver 62; Libn Mercy Hosp, Denver 62-63; Libn Gen Rose Hosp, Denver 64-. 8: Consul, Lutheran Hosp Lib, Denver 65-68; Adv, Beth Israel Hosp, Denver 68-. 9: MedLA; Colo Assn Med Libns. 10: Great Books Discussion Groups; Colo Mountain Club (Denver Group sec 68-69). 14: Ref. 15: 1350 Columbine, Denver Co 80206.

BAILEY, ELEANOR MILNOR. b Knoxville Tenn 4 Ja 14. 4: Don R Bailey Jr. 5: UTenn 31-35 (Eng) BA; Columbia 37-38 (LS) BS. 7: Libn Knoxville Pub Schs, Knoxville Tenn 38-42; Libn Fulton Sylphon Co, Knoxville Tenn 43-46; Asst Ga State Lib 47-49; Ref dept asst Atlanta Pub Lib 49-64, Head Bus & Sci dept 64- Head, Order Dept 65, Libn Tech Processes 66-. 9: ALA; GaLA; SELA. 10: Atlanta Lib Club; DAR; UDC; Phi Mu. 15: 776 N Parkwood rd, Decatur Ga 30030.

BAILEY, ELIZABETH LLOYD DE BROHUN (MRS JOE HARDEN). b Charleston SC 8 Jl 20. 4: Joe H Bailey. 5: Vanderbilt 39-42 (Eng) AB; Peabody 46 BS in LS, 51-53 (LS). 6: Fr, Ger. 7: Lt US WAVES, San Francisco 42-46; Ser libn So Methodist U 46-47; Libn The Selwyn Sch, Denton Tex 58-. 9: Indep Schs Assn Southwest. 10: AAUW; DAR; Delta Kappa Gamma; Nat Audubon Soc. 12: "Checklist of the Birds of the Panhandle of Texas," with husband (56). 13: Yes. 14: Elem lib, ser, sch self-charging systems. 15: 412 Bryan st, Denton Tx 76201.

BAILEY, GEORGE M(URRAY). b Millers Md 13 F 24. 4: Claire Busk Bailey. 5: Franklin & Marshall Col 42-46 (Hist) BA; UPenn 46-47 (Hist) MA; UWis 52-53 MLS. 6: Fr, Sp. 7: Instr in hist Franklin & Marshall Col 47-48, Heidelberg Col summer 48, UWis (Racine & Kenosha) 49-51; Intern in lib admin UCal (Berkeley) 53-54; Ref libn soc sci ref serv UCal (Berkeley) 54-55; Documents libn & sibj spec in soc sci UCal (Davis) 55-59, Head ref dept 58-59; Chief of ref & spec serv Northwestern U 59-63; Exec sec ALA-ACRL 63-68; Chief libn & prof York Col CNNY 68-. 9: ALA (chm SORT); -RSD (chm Hist Sect, chm Coop Ref Serv Com mem Publs Com, Jt Com on Govt Publs); CalLA (chm Docs Com, v-pres Golden Empire Dist); IllLA (chm Mem Com, mem Intel Freedom Com); NYLA (mem Resources Com). 10: Sigma Pi; Beta Phi Mu; Phi Alpha Theta; AAUP. 13: Yes. 14: Ref, col lib admin. 15: 939 Maple ave, Evanston Il 60202.

BAILEY, JACQUELINE (RUTH). b Double Springs Ala 3 My 31. 5: Howard Col 48-51 (Hist) AB; Appalachian State Tchrs Col summer 62 (NDEA Span Inst); UAla 63-65 (Sch Libnship) MA. 6: Sp. 7: Tchr hist & Span, Haleyville Ala 51-57; Span tchr, Decatur Ala 57-64; Libn, Ha leyville Ala 64-67; Ref Libn Col of Educ UAla 67-. 8: Chm Lib Com for Accred by So Assn of Cols & Schs, Austin High Sch, Decatur Ala fall 65. 9: NEA; Amer Assn Tchrs Span & Port (treas Ala Chap 62-63); AlaLA; AlaEA. 10: Delta Kappa Gamma; Sigma Delta Pi; Kappa Delta Pi; Alpha Beta Alpha; Kappa Kappa Iota; PTA. 11: Outstanding Young Women of Amer 65. 14: Ref. 15: P O Box 3161, University, Al 35486.

BAILEY, JANE (MA). b Shanghai China 20 O 14. 4: Paul Bailey. 5: Ginling Col China 31-35 (Eng) AB; Ind U 48-49(Ed, Psych) MA; Denver U 53-54 (LS) MA. 6: Fr, Chinese, Russian. 7: Libn, Eng & Hist Tchr Shanghai High Sch 35-48; Asst catlgrColo State U 54-63; Asst catlgr UUtah 63-. 9: ALA; UtahLA; MtnPlLA; ColLA (Scholarship Com 56-57). 10: AAUW. 14: Catlg. 15: 56 Elizabeth st, Salt Lake City Ut 84102.

BAILEY, JO ANN. b Gatesville Tex 6 My 28. 5: UTex 45-49 (Phys Educ) BS; UDenver 58-59 (LS) MA; URedlands 61-62; UCal (Extension) 61-65. 7: Health & Phys Educ tchr San Angelo Pub Schs, San Angelo Tex 49-52; Child Welfare Wker in Training, State Dept of PubWelfare, Brownsville Tex 52-53; Jr high sch sci tchr Houston Pub Schs, Houston Tex 53-54; Jr high sch Eng tchr San Angelo PubSchs, San Angelo Tex 54-58; Jr High Sch libn Riverside Pub Sch, Riverside Cal 59-60; High sch libn Alvord Unified Sch Dist,Riverside Cal 60-64; Asst Prof of Lib Riverside City Col, Riverside Cal 64-. 9: ALA; NEA; Cal Tchrs Assn; Cal Jr Col Assn; CalLA. 10: Riverside Jr Col Faculty Assn. 11: H W Wilson Scholarship for grad study atUDenver Sch of Libnship. 14: Ref, tchg. 15: 91 Palm circle, Mira Loma Ca 91752.

BAILEY, JOE HARDEN. b Dallas 16 Ja 18. 4: Elizabeth De Brohun. 5: N Tex State U 35-38 (Hist) AB, summers 39-41 (Secondary Educ) AM; Peabody 46 BS in LS, 51-53 (Philos). 6: Sp. 7: Prin Carrollton Elem Sch, carrollton Tex 39-40; Libn Union Grove High Sch, Gladewater Tex 40-42; T/Sgt Med Corps Army of the US, Africa & Europe 42-45; Period libn So Methodist U 46-47; Libn & Head Lib Sch Murray State Col 47-51; Instr Lib Sch Peabody Col 51-53; Libn W Tex State 53-57; Assoc libn N Tex State U 57-. 8: Consul The Selwyn Sch Lib, Denton Tex. 9: KyLA (dir 49-51); SWLA (treas 59-61); TexLA; Tex Clr TA. 10: Tex Panhandle Audubon Soc; Kappa Delta Pi; Phi Delta Kappa; Nat Audubon Soc; Amer Ornithologist Union. 12: "Checklist of the Birds of the Panhandle of Texas," with wife (56). 13: Yes. 14: Admin, bibliog, ref. 15: 412 Bryan, Denton Tx 76201.

BAILEY, LOIS E. b Vestal NY 6 D 19. 5: Houghton Col 38-42 (Eng, Soc Sci) AB; UWis (Madison) 45-46 (Modern european Hist) MA; Syracuse 57-62 MSLS. 7: Soc studies tchr Moravia High Sch, Moravia NY 42-43; Soc studies tchr West Jr High Sch, Binghamton NY 43-44; Grad asst hist dept UWis (Madison) 45-46; Soc studies tchr Homer High Sch, Homer NY 46-55; Soc studies tchr Skaneateles High Sch, Skaneateles NY 55-59, Libn 59-; Summer sch libn Solvay Sr High Sch, Solvay NY 64-65 Lecturer Grad Sch of Lib Sci Syracuse U 67-. 9: NEA; ALA; NYTchrsAssn; NYLA. 10: Beta Phi mu. 15: RD 4, Auburn NY 13021.

BAILEY, MARTHA J. b Beech Grove Ind 24 Jl 29. 5: Drexel 56 (LS) MS; ButlerU (Eng) AB. 6: Fr. 7: Lib asst Eu Lilly & Co, Indianapolis 53-55; Lib asst DuPont, Wilmington Del 56-57; Tech libn Union Carbide Corp, Indianapolis 57-. 9: SLA; ASIS. 10: AAUP; Indianapolis Soc; Indianapolis Art Assn; Indianapolis Jazz Club. 14: Admin, ref. 15: Union Carbide Corp, Indianapolis In 46224.

BAILEY, RICHARD RAYMOND. b Dickinson ND 6 O 40. 4: Elizabeth Lefor. 5: Dickinson state Col 58-64 (Eng, Phys Ed) BS; Minot State Col 65; UOre 66-67 MSLS; Sacramento State Col 68; UCal (Davis) 69. 7: USA personnel specialist specialist 4th class; Eng instr Souris High Sch, Souris ND 64-65; Eng instr Riddle High Sch, Riddle Ore 65-66; Stud asst UOre lib 66-67; Hd ref dept Amer River Col lib 67-. 9: CalTA. 10: BPOE. 14: Ref. 15: 4700 College Oak dr, Sacramento Ca 95841.

BAILEY, ROBERT GANO. b Bound Brook NJ 27 Ap 11. 5: Wesleyan 28-32 (Fr) BA, 32-33 (Fr) MA; Princeton 34-35, 36-39 (Fr) MA; Columbia 52-53 (LS) MS. 6: Fr, Sp, Portuguese, Ital, Ger. 7: Tchr of lang Massanutten Acad, Woodstock Va 33-34; Asst Prof of Fr Davidson Col, 35-36; Instr in rom lang Wesleyan 39-43: Trans-Examiner US Off of

Censorship, San Juan PR 43-45; Consular Off For Serv US Dept of State, 45-52; Asst doc div Lib Columbia, 53-54; Asst libn Wash Col, 54-57; Libn 57-. 8: Evaluation teams of the Middle States Assn of Col & Second Schs 62-. 9: ALA; MLA. 10: AAUP. 14: Catlg, ref, docs. 15: Wash Col Lib, Chestertown Md 21620.

BAILEY, ROBERT H. b Santa Monica Cal 22 Jl 31. 5: UCLA 48-54 (Soc sci) AB; USoCal 64-69 (LS) MS. 7: LA City Sch Dists: Tchr 54-64, Libn 65-67, Lib consul 67-. 9: ALA; NEA; CalASchL; CalTA. 10: Beta Phi Mu; Libraria Sodalitas, USoCal, Bd Dirs. 14: Sch lib. 15: 6237 Woodlake ave, Woodland Hills Ca 91364.

BAILLIE, STUART. b Pittsburgh Penn 28 Ja 14. 4: Sara Aline Johnson. 5: Hiram Col 31-34; WashU 34-35 BA, 35-39 MA; Geo Peabody Sch for Tchrs 40-41 BS in LS; WashU 51-61 EdD. 7: Libn Festus High Sch, Festus Mo 38-40; Asst libn Vanderbilt Med Lib 40-41; Soc sci libn Stevens Col 41-42; Asst ref-circ dept UMo 42-43; Time study eng Emerson Electric Co, St Louis Mo 43-45; Libn Ga Tchrs Col (Atlanta) 45-46; Libn Lutheran High Sch, St Louis Mo 46-47; Libn Engring Sch WashU 47-53; Lib sci tchr WashU 47-53; Dir Grad Sch of Libnship UDenver 53-65, Dir Univ Libs 53-65; Dir of libs San Jose State col 65-. 8: Consul to: 1 col, 1 state & 4 pub libs (Colo, Wyo, Ida), to Aspen Inst, and to Universidad Autonoma de Guadalajara, Guadalajara, Mex. 9: ALA-LAD (chm Statist Coord Com); -ACRL; -LED; SLA; AALS (chm Statist Com 61-63); MPLA; ColoLA (hon life mem); NebLA (hon life mem); CalLA. 10: AAUP. 12: Ed ColoLA Bulletin 54-57; "Library School and Job Success" M Studies in Libnship #3 (64). 13: Yes. 14: Photography. 15: San Jose State Col Lib 250 S 4th st, San Jose Ca 95114.

BAIRD, ALINE SMITH (MRS VERNON). b Kentwood La 11 D 27. 4: Vernon A Baird Jr. 5: LSU 44-48 (Eng Educ) BS, 60-63 (LS) MS. 7: Sch libn Webster Parish, Doyline La 48-49; Libn II La State Lib 65-. 9: LaLA. 15: 383 Ardenwood dr, Baton Rouge La 70806.

BAIRD, DONALD ALEXANDER. b Edmonton Alberta Can 29 Ja 26. 4: Sydney Barlow. 5: UNC 45-49 (Philos, Psych) BA; ColumbiaU 50-51 (Bibliog) MS. 7: Lib asst UBC 49-50; Catlgr pub lib, Vancouver BC 51-54; Hd catlgr pub lib, Victoria BC 54-56; Hd catlgr UAlta 56-60, Asst libn 60-64; Univ libn Simon FraserU 64-. 9: CanLA; ALA; Can Assn Univ Tchrs. 11: Govt of Can Centennial Medal 67. 12: Co-auth "The English Novel" (59). 13: Yes. 14: Bibliog. 15: 3052 Armada rd, Port Coquitlam British Columbia Can.

BAIRD, DOROTHY S. b Elizabethton Tenn 30 Ap 32. 5: E Tenn State U 50-54 (Bus) BS; Peabody 59-61 (LS) MA UMinn 66-67. 6: Fr. 7: Tchr-libn Washington Col Acad, Washington College Tenn 54-57; Libn Lees-McRae Jr Col 57-62; Asst libn King Col 62-66; Asst Prof Appalachian State U 67-68; Asst Prof Lib SciDept E Tenn State U 68-. 9: SELA; TennLA; ALA. 10: Beta Phi Mu; Bus & ProfWomen. 15: 428 W Chestnut st, Johnson City Tn 37601.

BAIRD, HELEN D (ELPHINE). b Bartlesville Okla 19 D 05. 5: Willamette U 23-27 (Eng) BA; UWash summer 30 (Eng); West Res U 30-31 BLS; Columbia 37-39 MS in LS. 6: Lat, Fr. 7: Tchr Newberg High Sch, Newberg Ore 27-30; Child libn Salem Pub Lib, Salem Ore 31-37; Sub libn NY Pub Lib 37-38; Stud asst Columbia Lib 38-39; Instr Villanova summer sch 39; Child libn Akron Pub Lib Akron Ohio 39-43; Head libn Lydia Brunn Woods Lib, Falls City Neb 43-44; Instr of LS Our Lady of the Lake Col 44-46; Asst libn The Abbey Lib, St Benedict's Col (Atchison Kan) 46-. 10: AAUW; Daughters of Isabelle. 13: Yes. 14: Child wk, circ, ref. 15: The Abbey Library St Benedict's Col, Atchison Ks 66002.

BAIRD, MARGARET LUCILLE (ELLIOTT). b Cox City Okla 5 My 30. 4: Lyle Baird. 5: Okla Col for Women 48-52 (Bio) BA, 52-53 (Elem ed) BS; UOkla 66-68 MLS. 6: Lat, Fr. 7: Elem tchr Duncan Pub Schs, Duncan Okla 54-55; Tchr, libn Alex Pub Schs, Alex Okla 64-. 9: ALA; NEA; SWLA; OklaLA; OklaEA. 14: Child, ya. 15: Rural Rt 3, Blanchard Ok 73010.

BAIRD, NANCY (TICE). b Jackson Tenn 21 D 42. 4: Ancil R Baird Jr. 5: UTenn (Martin) 61-63 (Eng), 63-65 (Eng) AB; IndU 66-67 MLS. 7: Bkmob libn Reelfoot Reg Lib, Martin tenn 65; Tchr Parkland Jr Highm Louisville Ky 65-66; Ref libn IndU SE (Jeffersonville) 67-. 14: Ref, multi-media, govt docs. 15: 114 Rice Hall Godfrey ave, Louisville Ky 40206.

BAIRD, POLLYANN (CASTLE). b Danville Ill 19 Ap 23. 4: Billy E Baird. 5: UColo 41-45 BA; UDenver BS in LS. 7: Tchr-libn High Sch, Littleton Colo 45-47; Libn Jr High Sch, Denver 47-49; Libn Elem-Jr High Sch, Georgetown Ill 61-65; Libn High Sch, Catlin Ill 65-67; Edgar Co Comm, Unit #2 67-. 9: NEA; IllEA; IllLA (Prof Relts Com). 10: Delta Kappa Gamma; PEO; Firemen's Auxiliary; Spur, Hesperia Am Legion Aux; Delta gamma. 13: Yes. 14: Org libs, tchg child to use libs, unit libn. 15: Box 486, Ridgefarm Il 61870.

BAIRD, MRS VIOLET (MATTSON). b Crosby Tex 16 F 10. 4: John P Baird. 5: Rice U 27-31 (Eng) BA, 32-34 9ls0 ma& lsu 34-35 BS in LS. 6: Sp, Fr, Ger. 7: Stud asst Rice U 28-34; Ref libn Tex Tech Col 35-42; Ser libn Baylor U 43; Asst libn Southwestern Med Sch 43-47, Libn 47-. 9: MedLA; TexLA. 10: Dallas Hist Soc; Med Center Woman's Club; Phi Beta Kappa; Phi Kappa Phi. 15: 5323 Harry Hines, Dallas Tx 75235.

BAIRNSFATHER, RAGNHILD (MUNSON). b Dayton Ohio 25 S 38. 4: Robert R Bairnsfather. 5: Transylvania Col 56-57 (Eng); Miami U (Ohio) 57-60 (Eng) AB; Simmons 61-63 MSLS. 6: Sp, Swedish. 7: Lib intern Harvard U Grad Sch of Bus Admin Baker Lib 60-63; Asst ref libn Gen & Humanities Ref MIT Hayden Lib 64-. 10: DAR; MIT Lib Staff Assn. 12: "Careers in Science & Engineering, a Selected Bibliography" (64). 14: Ref. 15: 1 Copley st, Winchester Ma 01890.

BAITY, HAZEL. b Mocksville NC 3 F 04. 5: Meredith Col 26 AB; UNC 33 (LS) AB. 7: Tchr Mocksville High Sch, Mocksville NC 26-32; Asst libn Meredith Col 33-34; Libn Gray High Sch, Winston-Salem NC 34-40; Visiting Instr UNC Sch of Lib Sci summers 39-40; Libn Meredith Col 41-. 9: ALA; SELA; NCLA. 10: AAUW; Beta Phi Mu; NC State Lit & Hist Assn; NC State Art Soc. 14: Ref. 15: Meredith Col, Raleigh NC 27602.

BAJEMA, BRUCE D. b Bellingham Wash 31 O 32. 4: Ankie Last. 5: UWash 50-51, 55-56, 57-58 (Pol Sci) BA; Sorbonne 56-57; UWash 58-59 MLS. 6: Fr. 7: (PFC) US Army Sig C, Japan 52-54; Libn II-III Brooklyn Pub Lib 59-61; Br libn Baltimore Co Pub Lib, Arbutus Md 61-64; Co Libn Mendocino Co, Ukiah Cal 64-68; Asst co libn Marin Co, San Rafael Cal 68, Co libn 69-. 8: Chm N Bay Coop Lib System 67. 9: ALA; CalLA. 10: Helibs. 14: Admin, Personnel. 15: Marin Co Civic Center, San Rafael, Ca 94903.

BAKEMAN, CAROL ANN (BERGH). b San Francisco 27 O 34. 4: D Clifton Bakeman. 5: UCLA 55-61 (Eng Lit). 6: Fr, Russian. 7: Hughes Aircraft Co, Culver City Cal: Order libn documents group 54-56, Head lib photo serv 56-59, Ref dept 59-61; Head Econ Lib Planning Research Corp, Los Angeles 61-63; Corp Libn Economic Consultants Inc, Los Angeles 63-68; Hd Econ Lib Daniel Mann Johnson & Mendenhall, Los Angeles 69-. 9: SLA (Adv mgr 60-63); (So Cal Chap Adv Coun 60-65, 68, 68 Conf Com Printing Chm) ASIS; CalLA. 10: Assistance League of So Cal; Amer Guild of Musical Artists; Los Angeles Master Chorale; Nat Assistance League; Opera Assocs of Mus Ctr (Los Angeles); Roger Wagner Chorale. 12: "Bibliography on Thermal Resources" (67). 14: Ref, admin (small spec libs). 15: 15520 Hamner dr, Los Angeles, Ca 90024.

BAKER, ADELLE (MAENARD) WILSON. b Ocala Fla 27 Ap 33. 4: Willie Lee Baker. 5: Atlanta Col of Mortuary Sci Inc 52 (Embalming) Diploma; Fla A&M U 55-59 (LS) BS; Fla Inst of Continuing Studies Ext 63 (A-v Educ). 6: Fr. 7: Asst embalmer Dabney Funeral Home, Leesburg Fla summers 53-55; Stud asst lib serv Coleman Lib Fla A&M 56-59; Itinerant elem sch libn Orange Co, Orlando Fla 59-61; Libn Webster Elem Sch Orange Co, Winter Park Fla 61-68; Ivey Lane Elem Sch Orange Co, Orlando Fla 68-. 9: NEA; ALA; Fla StateTchrs Assn; FlaLA; FlaEA; FlaASchLib; Orange Co Sch L. 10: Alpha Beta Alpha; Bus &Prof Women. 14: Child bks, ref. 15: 771 Lyman ave, Winter Park Fl 32789.

BAKER, ALMYRA (HENRIETTA). b Edmore N Dak 19 Ag 12. 5: St Olaf Col 30-34 (Lat) BA; UMinn 36-39 (LS); UMich 47-49 MALS; UOslo (Norway) summer 57. 6: Norwegian. 7: Tchr, Peterson Minn 34-36, 37-38; Sch libn Foley (Minn) Pub Sch 36-37; Sch libn & tchr Mt Lake (Minn) Pub Sch 39-46; Sch libn Crosby-Ironton Pub Sch, Crosby Minn 47-52; Libn Edison High Sch & South High Sch, Minneapolis 54-57; Asst libn Pacific Lutheran U 57-59; Libn Belle Plaine (Minn) Commun Schs 62-66; Libn Lindstrom-Ctr City-Shafer Pub Sch, Lindstrom Minn 68-. 8: Instr, lib sci Winona State Col, Winona Minn 68-69. 9: ALA; MinnASchL. 14: Sch lib wk, tchg lib sci. 15: 855 W Fourth st, Zumbrota Mn 55992.

BAKER, MRS ANNE M (MULCAHY). b Bay City Mich 6 S 33. 4: Robert E Baker. 5: Bay City Jr Col 51-53 (Liberal Arts) AA; UMich 53-55 (Psych, Sociol) BA, 55-57 MA in LS. 6: Fr. 7: Ref libn Detroit News Lib, Detroit 56-61; Ref asst UDetroit

Lib 61, Acquis libn 61-. 14: Bk sel, ref. 15: Univ of Detroit Lib, 4001 W McNichols rd, Detroit Mi 48221.

BAKER, AUGUSTA (ALEXANDER). b Baltimore 1 Ap 11. 4: Gordon Alexander Baker. 5: NY State Col (Albany) 33 (Eng) AB, 34BS in LS. 7: NY Pub Lib; Child libn 37-53, Asst coordinator of child serv & storytelling spec 53-61, coordinator of child serv61-. 8: Consul, Trinidad Pub Lib, Trinidad BWI, 53; Instr Columbia U Sch of Lib Serv 56-; Lecturer Rutgers U Grad Lib Sch65-67 & others; Founder James Weldon Johnson Memorial Collection Countee Cullen Reg Br NY Pub Lib; Org lib wk with childTrinidad Pub Lib, Trinidad BWI. 9: ALA (Coun 65-68; Exec Bd 68-72);-CSD (Bd Dirs 58-61, 66-69; pres 67-68; chm Newbery-CaldecottAwards Com 66; mem var coms); NYLA (chm 2 coms); NY Lib Club. 10: NAACP; Women's Nat Bk Assn; NY Folklore Soc; Delta SigmaTheta. 11: Dutton-MacRae Award, 53; Parent's Magazine Medal 66; ALA Grolier Award 68. 12: "The Talking Tree" (55); "The GoldenLynx" (60); Ed "Stories; A List of Stories to Tell and to Read Aloud" (58); "Books about Negro Life for Children" (63);Ed-in-chief, "Young Years; Anthology of Children's Literature" (60); Ed "Once Upon a Time" (64); Ed "Recordings for Children"(64). 13: Yes. 14: Storytelling, children's work, library admin, teaching. 15: 115-33 174 st, St Albans NY 11434.

BAKER, BARRY BOYD. b Louisville Ky 3 S 44. 5: LSU 62-66 (Hist) BA, 66-67 (LS) MS. 7: Lib asstship LSU Lib, 66-67; Sr libn 67-68; Asst libn - tech serv & instr LS, Macon Jr Col 68-. 9: ALA; GaLA. 10: Beta Phi Mu. 14: Acquis, art bks, ref. 15: 2020 Vineville ave, Apt 32, Macon Ga 31204.

BAKER, BRUCE S. b Worcester Mass 22 Je 39. 4: Janet (Russell). 5: Clark U 58-62 (Hist) AB; Simmons 62-63 (LS) MS in LS. 7: Asst dir Leominster Pub Lib, Leominster Mass 63-65, Dir 65-. 8: Chm Spec Advis Com re Film Serv in Mass; Chm Exec Com, Central Mass Reg Pub Lib Advis Coun. 9: ALA; MassLA. 10: Rotary Club. 14: Adult serv. 15: Princeton rd, Sterling Ma 01564.

BAKER, (SCHNITZLER) CAROLINE FRANCES. b Muskegon Mich 4 My 22. 5: Aquinas Col 59-62 (Hist, Eng) AB, Tchg Certif; UMich 63-65 MALS. 6: Lat, Fr. 7: Instr in Eng Davenport Col 62-64; Asst libn Aquinas Col 64-67; Docs libn & Instr Lib Sci Central Mich U 67-. 9: NCTE; MichLA. 10: Beta Phi Mu; Phi Alpha Theta; AAUP; AAUW; Nat Geog Soc. 14: Govt docs, maps, child lit. 15: 403 E Grand ave, Mount Pleasant Mi 48858.

BAKER, CHRISTINE (KOJA). b Brooklyn NY 13 Ag 24. 4: Arthur Harold Baker. 5: NYU 42-46 (Biol) BA; Caldwell Col 64-66 (Educ); Montclair State 65-66 (Educ); Rutgers 66-68 MLS. 6: Ger, Sp. 7: Asst libn Heyden Chem Corp, Garfield NJ 46-49; Libn W Essex High Sch, N Caldwell NJ 68-. 9: ALA; NEA; NJEA; EssexCoEA; W EssexEA; EssexCoSchLA. 10: Alpha omicron Pi; Rutgers Alum Assn; Amer Field Serv. 14: Ref, bibliog, ya wk. 15: 28 Maple lane, Essex Fells NJ 07021.

BAKER, CONSTANCE ALICE (COLESTON). b Melrose Mass 8 Je 32. 5: Nev So U 63-67 (Hist) BA; UOre 68 MLS. 6: Fr, Ger. 7: Libn (Instr) East Ore Col 69; Libn (Asst Prof) Ore Tech Inst 69-. 9: ALA. 10: AAUP. 14: Ref. 15: 3933 Kelley dr, Klamath Falls Or 97601.

BAKER, D(ONALD) PHILIP. b Hornell NY 2 F 37. 5: AlfredU 54-58 (Hist) BA, 58-59 (Educ) MSE; Pratt Inst 66-69 MLS. 6: Fr. 7: Research asst US Senate, Wash DC 59-60; Bd of Educ, Darien Conn: Hist tchr 61-67, Dir libs 67-. 9: ALA; ConnSchLA; NEA; (chm Sch Media Programs Standards); NESchLA; ConnEA; DarienEA. 10: Phi Gamma Mu; Beta Phi Mu. 14: Sch lib prog. 15: 30 Glenbrook rd, Stamford Ct 06902.

BAKER, ELIZABETH E(UGENIA). b Pittsburgh 8 S 08. 5: Otterbein Col 26-27; U Pittsburgh 27-30 (LS) AB; Carnegie 29-30 Certif. 7: Continuations catlgr Carnegie Lib of Pittsburgh 30-35; Libn TVA, Wilson Dam Ala 35-44; Headquarters libn ALA, Chicago 44-46; City Libn Ferndale Pub Lib, Ferndale Mich 46-51; Br libn Cleveland Heights (Ohio) Pub Lib 51-53; Libn Greene Co Dist Lib, Xenia Ohio 53-. 9: ALA; OhioLA. 13: Yes. 15: Greene Co Dist Lib, 194 E Church st, Xenia Oh 45385.

BAKER, MRS ELIZABETH MAYER. b Cleveland 1 Ja 10. 5: West Res 32 (Eng) BA, 33 BS in LS; Columbia (courses in Med Lib Serv) 52. 6: Ger. 7: Loan div. Cleveland Pub Lib 33-34; Br asst Cleveland Hts Pub Lib, Cleveland Heights Ohio 34-40; Catlgr Flora Stone Mather Col (Cleveland) 41-42; Head of Patient Lib University Hospitals, Cleveland 49-54; Libn hosp & instit dept Cleveland Pub Lib 54-. 9: SLA (v-pres, chm Hosp Div, Adv Bd Hosp Div, ed Div "Bulletin", chm Interassn Hosp Lib Com); ALA-AHIL (v-pres & pres, var coms); ALA rep to LA (British); MedLA (chm No Ohio Chap); OhioLA. 10: Unitarian Church (var coms); West Res Sch of Lib Serv Alumni assn (pres 55-56); Cleveland Pub Lib Staff Assn (v-pres 66-67, pres 67-68, Exec Bd 67-68). 13: Yes. 14: Hosp & inst lib serv. 15: Cleveland Pub Lib 325 Superior ave, Cleveland Oh 44120.

BAKER, MRS (MARY) EVELYN (SHOEMAKER). b Columbus Ohio 8 My 12. 4: Richard Heinley Baker. 5: Ohio State U 29-34 (Fr) BA; West Res 34-35 BSC in LS. 7: Ohio State U; Catlgr 35-37, 38-44, Bibliog 55-56, Asst libn & instr U Sch 56-57, Act Dept libn 57, Act admin asst 58, Ser catlgr 58-67, ser catlgr & instr in lib admin 63-67, Sr catlgr & asst reviser & instr 67-68, Hd ser div, catlg dept & Asst Prof 68-. 9: ALA; OhioLA; Ohio Valley Group Tech Serv Libns; Franklin CoLA (cor sec). 10: Ohioana Lib Assn (regis chm); Faculty Womens Club; Univ Womens Club (past pres); Pi Lambda Theta; First Congrat Church (past chm of lib staff). 14: Ser catlg. 15: 2444 Arlington ave, Columbus Oh 43221.

BAKER, MRS FLORA (JOHNSTONE). b El Campo Tex 3 N 07. 5: Southwest Tex State Tchrs Col 27-30 (Eng) BA; Southwest Tex State Col 57-60 (Elem Educ) MEd; Tex Woman's U 61-64 MLS. 7: Tchr Wharton Co Schs, Bonus Tex 27-28; Asst libn Southwest Tex State Tchrs Col 30-34; Catlgr Southwest Tex State Col 57-. 66; Hd of catlg dept 66-. 8: Trustee Pub Lib Bd 43-47. 9: TexLA; Tex State TA; Tex Assn Col Tchrs; SWLA; AAUP. 10: San Marcos Pub Lib Bd; Jr Sorosis Study Club (pres 60-62); Friends of the Library; San Marcos Pub Lib Bd (pres 68-69). 14: Catlg. 15: 620 W San Antonio st, San Marcos Tx 78600.

BAKER, FLORENCE (SELLERS). b Meriden Conn 21 D 06. 4: G(eorge) Houston Baker. 5: Swarthmore 24-28 (Eng) BA; Drexel 28-29 BS in LS. 6: Fr, Sp. 7: Circ & ref asst Bryn Mawr Col Lib 29-30; Libn in Chg Day Missions Lib, New Haven Conn 30-32; Catlgr Yale Divinity Sch Lib 32-39, 55-62, Sr catlgr & research asst 62-65, Sr catlgr 65-. 9: ATheolLA. 10: Kappa Kappa Gamma. 14: Catlg. 15: Yale Divinity Sch Lib, 409 Prospect st, New Haven Ct06511.

BAKER, HAZEL (COPELAND). b Jewett Ohio 26 Ag 07. 4: Jack F Baker. 5: Wooster Col 26-27; Cleveland col of West Res 28-32 (Eng); Kent State summers 32-36 (Elem) BS in Educ, summers 56-62 (LS) MA. 6: Fr. 7: Tchr grade sch Hammondsville Ohio 30-37; Tchr grade sch & high schs Kirtland Ohio 37-39; Tchr grade sch Salineville Ohio 46-62; Libn high sch Salineville Ohio 65-. 8: Art supv Kirtland Ohio 37-39 Art tchr Southern Local 58-67. 9: NEA; OhioEA. 10: Several commun & church orgs; Delta Kappa Gamma. 14: Catlg, ref, rare bks. 15: 66 E Main st, Salineville Oh 43945.

BAKER, HELEN M (MALMBERG). b Lee Ill 28 Mr 18. 4: Roger M Baker. 5: UIll 38-41 (Com, Eng) BS, 49-52 (LS) MS in LS. 7: Tchr Ottawa Township High Sch, Ill 41-42; Sec Alcoa Corp Chicago 43-44; Indexing World Bk Encyc, Chicago 45-55; Libn Kansas City Pub Lib 59-67; Hd libn Plaza Br, 67-69. 9: ALA; MoLA. 10: Mortar Bd; Beta Phi Mu; Woman's C of C. 14: Ref, lib ext. 15: 416 E 66 Terr, Kansas City Mo 64131.

BAKER, HOWARD M(ICHAEL). b Chicago Ill 6 Mr 22. 4: Baker, Joanne T (Kaye). 5: De Paul 54-60 (Pol sci) Bachelor's; Rosary Col 63-65 (LS); Purdue 64-65 (Hist). 7: Clerk US War Dept, Ill 42-46; Clerk US RR Retirement Bd, Chicago 46-55; Clerk US Dept of Justice, Chicago 55-62; Supv libn US VA Hosp, Downey Ill 62-64; Asst libn St joseph's Col, E Chicago Ind 64-65; Ref libn Upper Iowa Col 65-68; Asst libn Lea Col on Lake Chapeau 68-. 9: MinnLA; IllLA. 10: US Capitol Hist Soc; Freeborn Co (Minn) Hist Soc; Ill State Hist Soc. 14: Ref, US hist, govt docs. 15: 2011 W Trail, Alberta Lea Mn 56007.

BAKER, JOSEPH DAMIEN. b Baton Rouge La 7 N 41. 4: Joan Hanson Geiser. 5: LSU 59-63 (Eng) BA, 63-64 (LS) MS. 6: Ger. 7: Grad asst Lib LSU 63-64; Munitions staff off usaf 1st Lt, RAF Sta Bentwaters Eng S 65-67, Storage & handling off (Capt) 67-68; Weapons off USAF Capt, Takhli Royal Thai AFB Thailand 69-70; Hd govt docs dept Lib StetsonU 70-. 9: ALA. 14: Univ lib admin. 15: Rte #2 Box 84A, Baton Rouge La 70815.

BAKER, JULIA E (CHAPMAN). b Crawfordsville Ind 21 F 13. 4: E G Stanley Baker. 5: Oberlin Col 30-31; DePauw U 31-34 (Ger) AB Grad Sch Lib Serv, Rutgers U 68-69. 6: Fr. 7: Wabash Col Lib: Gen asst 34-36, 37, Asst libn 43-44, Act head libn 44-45; Catlg libn Drew U Lib 54-, Asst head of catlg dept 65-. 9: ALA; ASIS. 10: Human Rel Coun; Phi Beta Kappa; Phi

Sigma Iota; Alpha Psi Omega. 14: Catlg, rare bks, systems analysis, lib automation. 15: Drew Univ Lib, Madison NJ 07940.

BAKER, (GLOSSIE) LAVONNE. b Ind 31 Jl 19. 4: Orlen Ervin Baker. 5: Ball State U 36-40 (Eng, Bus ed) BA; UAriz 65-68 Lib Certif. 7: Asst med libn Ball State Hosp 40-41; Libn San Bernardino Co, San Bernardino Cal 49-50; Libn Flowing Wells Schls, Tucson Ariz 66-. 8: Learning Resource Ctr Consul, Action Lab with Assn of Clr Tchrs 68-69. 9: NEA; ALA; ArizEA; ArizSchLA. 15: 70 N Lazy pl, Tucson Az 85705.

BAKER, MARGARET K. b Worcester Mass 23 Mr 11. 4: Stephen Baker. 5: Simmons 28-32 (LS) BS; Boston U 60 (LS); UVt Ext 61, 63, 65, 64 (Econ). 7: Asst libn Rutland City Lib, Rutland Vt 33-37; Reg libn Free Pub Lib Serv, St Johnsbury Vt 37-39; Reg libn Free Pub Lib Serv, Rutland Vt 39-45; Sch libn Middlebury ID4, Middlebury Vt 57-60; Libn Middlebury Union High Sch, Middlebury Vt 57-. 8: Vt state com for implementation of sch lib standards 60-69 (chm 63-68). 9: ALA; NEA; NESchLA (cor sec 63-65); VtASchL (pres 60-62); VtEA. 11: Delta Kappa Gamma. 14: Sch libs. 15: 10 Morningside, Middlebury Vt 05753.

BAKER, MARGARET VIRGINIA. b Savannah Ga 27 Ag 12. 5: Randolph-Macon Woman's Col 29-31; Ga State Woman's Col 31-33 (Eng) AB; UNC summers AB in LS. 7: Libn Valdosta High Sch, Valdosta Ga 34-40; Catlgr UGa Lib 40-41, Ref asst 41-43; Libn Washington Sem 43-45; Ref asst UFla Lib 46; Libn Emory Jr Col 46-48; Dir S Ga Reg Lib, Valdosta Ga 48-. 9: GaLA; SELA. 10: DAR; AAUW; Delta Kappa Gamma; Phi Mu; Valdosta Arts Center Inc; Lowndes Co Hist Soc. 14: Ref, admin. 15: 1017 Slater st, Valdosta Ga 31601.

BAKER, MARTHA H. b San Antonio Tex 23 Je 08. 5: UTex 26-29 (Chem) BA; U Denver 54-55 (LS) MA. 7: Ref dept, Head period dept San Antonio Pub Lib, S an Antonio Pub Lib, San Antonio Tex 30-54; Staff various depts Colo Springs Pub Lib 42-54; Asst libn Fitsimons Gen Hosp Med Lib, Colo 56-57; Libn Webb Mem Lib Penrose Hosp, Colo Springs Colo 60-. 9: MedLA; ColoLA. 10: AAUW. 15: Webb Mem Lib, Penrose Hosp, Colorado Springs Co 80907.

BAKER, MARY CAROLYN SND de N (SISTER). b Dayton Ohio 14 F 24. 5: Athenaeum of Ohio 44-52 (Educ) BS in Ed; Rosary Col 59-64 MA in LS. 7: Elem tchr St Augustine Sch, Cincinnati 49-51; Elem tchr Cardinal Pacelli Sch, Cincinnati 51-52; Elem tchr St Patrick Sch, Columbus Ohio 52-55; Elem tchr St Peter Canisius, Chicago 55-61; Elem tchr St Alexander, Villa Park Ill 61-63; Tchr-libn Notre Dame High Sch, H amilton Ohio 63-66; Libn Stephen Badin High Sch, Hamilton Ohio 66-. 9: CathLA; ALA; OhioASchL. 10: Beta Phi Mu. 14: Young adult serv. 15: 926 S Second st, Hamilton Ohio 45011.

BAKER, MARY CATHERINE. b Spokane Wash 1 S 10. 5: UIda 27-28; UCal(Berkeley) 28-31 (Eng) AB, 31-32 (LS) Certif; UWash 34-35 (Eng) MA; UMich summer 36 (LS); UCal(Berkeley)summers 37, 40 (LS, Educ); Gonzaga U summer 38 (Educ); UWash 66 (Educ). 7: Libn Whitworth Col 32-34; Libn Sr High Sch, Wenatchee Wash 35-36; Libn Spokane High Schs, Spokane Wash 36-40; Libn US Pub Health Serv Rocky Mountain Lab, Hamilton Mont 40-42; Libn US Naval Hosp, Oakland Cal 42-47, 52-55; Libn US Naval Hosp, San Diego 47-48; Libn US Naval Air Station, Alameda Cal 48-52; Libn US Navy, Pearl Harbor, Hawaii 55-60; Command Libn US Army, Schofield Barracks Hawaii 60-61; Libn US Army Post Lib, Ft Lewis Wash 61; Dist libn Thirteenth Naval Dist, Bremerton Wash 61-66; Libn US A F 66-. 9: ALA (Life mem, pres Hosp Libs Div 53-54); SLA (sec-treas Pacific NW Chap 65-66); CalLA. 10: AAUW. 13: Yes. 14: Admin. 15: 7500 Air Base Group, APO NY 09125.

BAKER, MARY E (McCARTHY). b Chisholm Minn 16 N 19. 4: Ralph M Baker. 5: Hibbing Jr Col 37-39; Col St Catherine 39-41 (LS) BS. 6: Fr, Ger. 7: Asst libn St Mary-of-the-Woods Col 41-42; Sch libn Mt Iron High Sch, Mt Ironminn 42-43; Jr libn, libn UMinn (St Paul) 47-59; Libn 3M Co, St Paul 59-. 8: AdvCoun on Title III of the Lib Servs & Construction Act, State Dept of Educ, St PaulMinn 67-. 9: SLA (pres Minn Chap 59-60); CathLA; MinnLA; NMA; Tech Assn of thePulp & Paper Industry. 15: 1864 Ryan ave W, St Paul Mn 55113.

BAKER, MARY ELIZABETH. b Waterbury Conn. 5: Mt Holyoke 29 (Eng) BA; Columbia 38 (LS) MS. 7: Libn Jr & Sr high schs, New Haven Conn 29-40; Libn pub schs NYC 40-41; Prof asst Free Pub Lib, New Haven Conn 41-44; Libn Lyman Hall High Sch, Wallingford Conn 44-55; Libn Amity Reg High Sch, Woodbridge Conn 55-. 8: Wilson Com on Indexes 62-63. 9: ALA; NELA (Exec Coun); NESchLA (v-pres, pres); ConnSchLA (v-pres). 13: Yes. 14: Sch libs. 15: 1931 Chapel st, New Haven Ct 06515.

BAKER, NANCY ANN. b Charleston WVa 6 O 21. 5: UPenn 39-43 (Kdg-Prim) BS in Ed; UPittsburgh 62-65 M in LS. 6: Fr. 7: Tchr Penhurst State Sch, Spring City Penn 43-44; Tchr Upper Darby Twp Schs, Upper Darby Penn 44-48; Tchr Mt Lebanon Twp Schs, Mt Lebanon, Pittsburgh Penn 48-65, Libn 65-. 8: Sec-treas, West Penn Educ Conf Lib Div fall 68. 9: NEA; ALA; PennStateEA; PennLA; Suburban Independent Lib Gp. 10: Zeta Tau Alpha; College Club of South Hills, Pittsburgh. 15: 19 Ralston pl, Pittsburgh, Pa 15216.

BAKER, RICHARD ALLAN. b Stoneham Mass 18 Mr 40. 4: Patricia Stec. 5: UMass 57-62 (Hist) BA; Mich State 64-65 (Hist) MA; Columbia 67-68 (LS) MSLS. 6: Fr. 7: Commd off US Army First Lt 62-64; Hist instr Holy Apostles Sem, Cromwell Conn 65-67; Ref libn LC 68-. 8: Participated in LC six-month "Special Recruit" training program 68-69. 9: ALA. 10: AHA. 11: Columbia Univ Joseph Towne Wheeler Award 68. 14: Ref, lib educ, lib hist. 15: 4134 Suitland rd apt C, Suitland Md 20023.

BAKER, ROY DENVER. b Fayetteville Ark 2 Ja 17. 5: Ball State U 46-47; Colo State Col 48-49 (Bus Ed, soc Sci) AB; UDenver 49-51 (LS) MA. 7: US Air Force 1033rd Signal Platoon, US, Eng, Africa, Italy 41-45; Bkmob libnReg-Pub Lib, Olympia Wash 51-52; Libn II Travel Br Denver Pub Lib 52-54; Supvr ofLibs Tahoe-Truckee Unified Sch Dist, Truckee Cal 54-. 8: Leader, Great Bks Discussion Group for Tahoe-Truckee (Cal) communities, 56-. 9: CalSchLA; Tahoe-TruckeeEA. 10: Truckee-Donner Hist Soc (chm). 13: Yes. 14: Admin. 15: Truckee Ca 95734.

BAKER, SAMUEL MONROE JR. b Knoxville Tenn 28 D 29. 5: Randolph-Macon Col 48-49 (Eng); Guilford Col 49-52 (Eng, Hist) BA; UNC (Chapel Hill) 52-53 (LS) BS; UNC (Greensboro) 55-56 (Creative Writing); UNC (Chapel Hill) 57-60 (Eng) MA. 6: Fr, Ital. 7: Asst head ref USCar Lib 53; Admin asst to spec serv & asst to post lib US Army 53-55; Libn Hagerstown Jr Col 60-62; Asst head acquis Tulane U Lib 62-64; Head acquis LSU (New Orleans) 64; Catlgr Wake Forest U 65; Head Periods Miami-Dade Jr Col 65-66; Dir New Haven Col Lib 66-. 9: ALA; NELA; NYLA; com LA (chm Pub Rel Com 67-68, asst chm & chm Prog Com 68-70; Exec Com Col & Univ Sect). 10: AAUP; Bk Com New Haven Festival of Arts 67-69. 13: Yes. 14: Acquis, admin, rare bks. 15: 4 Wall st, New Haven, Ct 06511.

BAKER, VERNA (TOMLINSON). b Somerton Phila 14 Ap 15. 5: UNC summers 56-58 (LS) Tchr-Libn Certif; Bryan Col 62-63 (Elem Educ) BS; Peabody 63-64 (LS) MA. 6: Fr. 7: Asst to expeditor British Admiralty Delegation, Naval Aviation Supply Depot, Phila 44-45; Sec to fiction ed The Westminster Press, Phila 47-53; The Ben Lippen Sch, Asheville NC: Sec to Headmaster 53-54, Libn-sec 54-57, Libn 57-58; Sec to pres Faith Theol Sem 58-62; Asst libn King's Col 64-68, Reader's serv libn 68-. 9: ALA; Christian Libns Fellowship; WestchesterLA. 12: "Here in the Spring, and Other Poems," (68). 14: Ref. 15: 149 Central dr, Briarcliff Manor NY 10510.

BAKER, VIOLET (MAY). b St Joe Ind 4 O 09. 4: Roy L Baker. 5: Ball State Tchrs Col 38 BS, 47 MS. 7: Elem sch tchr DeKalb Co, Auburn Ind 29-38; Elem sch tchr Riverdale, St Joe Ind 46-63; Elem libn East DeKalb, Butler Ind 64-; Elem libn Riverdale Sch, St Joe Ind 64. 9: NEA; ALA; IndSchLA; Ind State Tchrs Assn; Ind ClrTA. 10: Ladies Literary Club, St Joe Ind. 15: RR #1, Hicksville Ohio 43526.

BAKERAITIS, DOLORES ELAINE. b Bay City Mich 9 D 22. 5: Bay City Jr Col 41-43 (Eng) AA; Central MichU 44-46 (Eng) BA; UIll 47-48 BS in LS, Fifth Year. 6: Fr. 7: Tchr Brown City Jr & Sr High Sch, Brown City Mich 46-47; Asst libn in high sch E Cleveland Pub Lib, E Cleveland Ohio 48-50; Lib asst UOmaha Lib 50; Lib asst Wilmette Pub Lib, Wilmette Ill 51; 1st asst in br lib Cleveland Heights Pub Lib, Cleveland Heights Ohio 52-54; Br ref libn Cuyahoga Co Lib System, Cleveland 54-55; Asst in adult serv Lansing Pub Lib, Lansing Mich 55-68. 9: ALA (var assignments 48-); MichLA (com duties 55-). 14: Adult serv, ref, vertical file wk. 15: 1608 Third st, Bay City Mi 48706.

BAKEWELL, IRENE FLORENCE. b Detroit 27 Ap 29. 5: Wayne State U 47-57 (Span) BA; UMich 55-58 MALS. 6: Sp, Fr. 7: Wayne State U: Stenographer 46-52, Lib asst 53-58, Jr asst libn 58-63, Asst libn 63-. 9: ALA; ASIS. 14: Catlg, microprint, electronic data proc. 15: 338 Channing, Ferndale Mich 48220.

BAKRIS, EUGENIA. b Detroit Mich 16 Jl 42. 5: UMich 59-63 (Bot) BA, 64-65 (LS) MS; UHawaii 67- (Bot). 6: Gr, Fr. 7: Libn I Los Angeles Co Pub Lib 65-66; Libn I UCal Los Angeles 66-67; Jr lib spec UHawaii 67-. 14: Ref (sci & tech). 15: CM1B40 Univ of Hawaii, Honolulu Hi 96822.

BALAY, ROBERT ELMORE. b Wichita Kansas 6 P 30. 4: Harriette Anderson. 5: Friends U 48-49; Macalester Col 49-52 (Eng) BA; UMinn 52-54 (Eng) MA; Columbia 58-59 (LS) MS. 6: Ger. 7: Asst libn Grumman Aircraft Corp Bethpage NY 59-62; Sr libn Gen Precision Inc, Little Falls NJ 62-64; Ref libn (Kresge Sci Lib, Wayne State Univ), Detroit 64-68; Hd Ref Dept Yale Lib, 68-. 9: SLA (v-pres & pres-elect Com Valley Chap 69-70). 14: Ref, lib automation. 15: 97 Livingston st, New Haven Ct 06511.

BALDAROTTA, ANTHONY. b Paceca Sicily 21 S 19. 4: Betty Ann Krahn. 5: UWis 46-50 (Rom Lang) BA, Lib Sch 50-51 (LS) MALS. 6: Ital, Fr, Sp. 7: Genl asst Milwaukee Pub Lib, Wis 51-52, Br asst, 52-53, Child libn 53-54, Br hd 54-55; Chief Extension Libn Rockford Pub Lib, Rockford Ill 55-56; Asst Dir, No Ill Lib Sys, Rockford Ill 66-. 9: ALA; IllLA. 10: Ill Municipal Retirement Fund; Rockford Municipal Employees Coun; Rockford Municipal Credit Union. 14: Public libs, Pub serv, child serv. 15: 3715 Thornwood dr, Rockford Il 61107.

BALDERSON, SALLY (HITCHENS) (ELLEN). b McKeesport Pa 28 Ap 29. 5: Bucknell 47-51 (Eng, Pol Sci) AB; UPittsburgh 64-69 (LS) MLS. 6: Sp. 7: Sales Dora S Kerr Antiques and Imports, Chautauqua NY summers 45, 46, 47; Copy writer (jr) G C Murphy Co, McKeesport summers 49, 50; Sales - photo Varden Studios, McKeesport 51, 53; Sales - mus instr, Woodbury NJ 52; Priv nursery sch tchr, Audubon NJ 52; Substi tchr Philadelphia Pub Sch 56; Clk Immel's McKeesport 63; Tour leader for House of Travel Europe 56; Lib asst Carnegie Free Lib, McKeesport 65-66; Acting child libn 66-67; Child libn 68-69. 8: Counselor for freshman girls, Bucknell University, junior year, 49-50. 9: ALA; PennLA. 10: Mortar Bd; College Club; Twentieth Cent Club; Phi Delta Gamma; Phi Mu; Women's Society for Christian Serv. 14: Child wk, catlg, ref. 15: 1702 Manor ave, McKeesport Pa 15132.

BALDWIN, RUTH M. b Due West SC 29 S 18. 5: Muskingum Col 36-39 BA; UIll 39-40 BS in LS, 44-45 (LS) MS, 53-55 (LS) PhD. 10: Sierra Club; AAUP. 13: Yes. 14: Research, admin, adult bk selection (tchg), hist child bks (collecting & personal research). 15: 423 LSU ave, Baton Rouge La 70808.

BALDYS, MARY MARCIA (SISTER). b Calumet City Ill 23 Mr 15. 5: Loyola U (ed) PhB; Roasary Col 61 MA in LS; UMinn 58 Lib certif. 6: Polish, Brazilian. 7: Prin & libn St Hedwig Ind High Sch 55-60; Tchr St Turibius Sch, Chicago 60-61; Libn & Eng tchr Our Lady of Mercy Amer Sch, Rio de Janeiro 61-63; Libn: Holy Innocents Sch, Chicago 63-65, St Helen Sch, Chicago 65-66, St Peter and Paul Sch, Chicago 66-68, Good Shepherd Sch, Chicago 68-69. 8: Affiliated Our Lady of Mercy Sch with the Cath U of Amer (In Rio de janeiro) 61; Set up a lib & was mem of Erie Neighborhood House adv bd 64-65, Lib consul for the Felician Lib Serv 65-69; Pres Chicago Archdiocesan Jr High Organ 65-66; Conducted several lib wkshops for the Wis Unit. 9: ALA; CathLA; IllLA. 10: Ill Jr Acad if Sci; Ill Hist Soc; Moderator of Young Christian Students. 13: Yes. 14: Ref, catlg. 15: 2733 S Kolin ave, Chicago Il 60623.

BALIMA, MILDRED GRIMES. b Wash DC 7 Mr 40. 5: Sarah Lawrence 57-61 (Soc sci) BA; Columbia 64-67 (LS) MS. 6: Fr. 7: Page Mt Vernon Pub Lib, Mt Vernon NY 56-57; Stud asst Sarah Lawrence Col Lib 57-61; Asst Westchester Co LA, Union Cat NY summer; Libn trainee Yonkers Pub Lib, Yonkers NY 61-62; Radio Upper Volta Eng news announcer, Upper volta W Africa 62-63; Stringer Reuters Ouagadougou Upper Volta W Africa 63-64; Libn population Coun NYC 64-65; Libn & bibliogr African sect LC 68-. 8: LC Spec Recruit 67-68. 9: African Studies Assn. 10: Urban League. 14: Ref, bibliog. 15: 600 3rd st SW, Wash DC 20024.

BALKE, MARY NOEL (SCHOALES). b Londonderry N Ireland 25 D 18. 4: Nicholas Balke. 5: Sheffield U (Britain) 36-39 (Math, Mod Lang) BA. 6: Fr, Ger. 7: Lib asst Sheffield Pub Libs, Yorkshire Britain 39-42; Asst libn Brown-Firth Research Estab, Sheffield Britain 40-42; Libn & info off Ministry of Supply, SRDE Britain 42-45; Catlgr UN Info Off, London Britain 45; Ref libn Ottawa Pub Lib, Canada 59-62; A/Hd bus & tech 62-64; Chief libn Nat Gallery of Canada, Ottawa 64-. 8: Free-lance writer and broadcaster, Yorkshire Post, Manchester Guardian, Toronto Globe & Mail, Can Broadcasting Corp. 9: CanLA (chm Art Libs Com 67-68); Assoc of Lib Assn (Gt Brit); SLA; Inst Profess Libns Ont; Profess Inst Pub Serv Libns Gp; Lib Assn Ottawa. 10: Ottawa Ski Club; Ottawa Little Theatre. 11: Canadian Womens Press Club Memorial Award 53. 14: Ref, admin. 15: 2694 Dupont st, Ottawa 8 Ont Can.

BALKEMA, JOHN B. b Orange City Iowa 10 Ag 27. 5: Morningside Col 44-48 (Eng) BA; Drexel Inst 54-58 (LS) MS. 6: Ger, Fr. 7: Ref libn NYU Medical Center NY 57-59; Libn NY Psychiatric Inst NY 59-62; Ref libn Downstate Med Center Brooklyn 62-64; Dir pub serv Welch Med Lib Johns Hopkins U 64-. 8: Instr Med Bibliog SUNY (Albany) summer 63. 9: MedLA (chm Com on Internat Coop); SLA (dir Baltimore Chap); ASIS; Baltimore HospLA. 14: Ref. 15: 1900 E Monument st, Baltimore Md 21205.

BALKEMA, K(ATHLEEN) LAUREL (CASE). b Grand Rapids Mich 29 N 42. 4: Philip A Balkema. 5: Wheaton Col (Wheaton Ill) 60-68 (Lit) BA; Mich Dept of Educ 68 Tching Certif; UMich 66-69 AMLS. 6: Ger. 7: Bkmob & child libn Kent Co Lib, Grand Rapids Mich 65-67; Sch lib admin Godfrey Lee Pub Sch, Wyoming Mich 67-69; Elem libn East Grand Rapids Pub Sch, Grand Rapids Mich 69-. 9: MichLA (sec-treas Sch Lib Sect). 15: 2454 Normandy dr SE apt 113, Grand Rapids Mi 49506.

BALL, ALICE DULANY. b Washington DC. 5: UCLA 30-34 (Eng) BA, 34-36 MA, 37-41 (Eng). 6: Fr. 7: Tchg asst UCLA 34-36, 39, Sec Eng Dept 36-38, 39-41, Accessioner Clark Lib 41; Gp hd Lockheed Aircraft, Burbank Cal 42-44; Expediter Hughes Aircraft Corp, Culver City Cal 45; Asst & act dir Amer Bk Ctr for War-devasted Libs, Wash DC 46-48; Exec dir US Bk Exchange Inc, Wash DC 48-. 9: SLA (chm Governmental Rel Com 61-66; pres Wash Chap 60-61); ALA (chm Acquis Sect); MedLA; CNLA (Trustee 68); SALALM (Bd 68-); DCLA (pres 68-69). 10: Chi Delta Phi; Phi Beta Kappa. 13: Yes. 14: Acquis, ser, exchange, lib educ. 15: 2931 Kanawha st NW, Washington DC 20015.

BALL, BERNARD EDWARD. b Buffalo NY 6 Ja 35. 4: Juanita Stout. 5: Buffalo State Tech Inst 52-54 (Mech Tech) AAS; SUNY (Buffalo) 60-62 (Educ) BS; UDenver 62-63 (LS) MA. 7: Clerk-page Buffalo & Erie Co Pub Lib, Buffalo NY 54-56; Electronics Tech US Navy 56-57; Instrumentman Olin Mathieson ChemCorp, Model City NY 57-60; Tech reports catlgr Bell Telephone Lab, Whippany NJ 63-65, Lib systs analyst, Murray Hill NJ 65,Ref libn Holmdel NJ 65-. 9: SLA. 14: Ref. 15: 189 Chapel Hill rd, Atlantic Highlands NJ 07716.

BALL, DUDLEY B. b Randolph Vt 17 O 19. 4: Helena Huse. 5: UVt 35-39 (Pol Sci) PhB; AmerU 39-40 (Pub Admin). 7: Lib asst AmerU 39-40; US Army 42-46; Exec Dir Conn Merit Syst Assn, Hartford Conn 55-64; LC 40-42, Legis ref serv, 46-55, Asst chief stack and reader div 64-65, Chief 65-. 15: 9604 Jacqueline dr, Oxon Hill Md 20022.

BALL, (ALICE) ELIZABETH. b Montclair NJ 28 F 13. 5: Douglass Col 30-34 (LS) AB. 6: Fr. 7: Lib asst E Orange Pub Lib, E Orange NJ 34-39; Br libn Newton Pub Lib, Newton Mass 40-41; Reg libn Mass Div of Lib Ext, Pittsfield Mass 42-46; Reg libn Vt Free Pub Lib Serv, St Albans Vt 46-49, Rutland Vt 50-59; Dir B H M Reg Lib, Washington NC 59-61; Dir Suwannee River Reg Lib, Live Oak Fla 61-67; Co libn Rutherford Co Lib, Rutherfordton NC 67-. 9: ALA; SELA; NCLA. 10: Nat Audubon Soc, Fla Audubon Soc, Carolina Bird Club. 14: Admin, story-telling programs, film programs. 15: PO Box 245, Rutherfordton NC 28139.

BALL, MRS HAZEL (DALE). b San Antonio Tex 7 S 18. 5: Tex Women's U 35-39 (Home Econ) BS, 59-60 (Educ) MA, summers 62-64 MLS; Odessa Col even 60-61 (Art); Drexel summer 65 (LS). 6: Sp, Fr. 7: Priv sec Paymaster Feeds, Abilene Tex 55-59; Instr developmental reading Odessa Col 63-65, Instr child lit 61-65; Libn Ector Co Ind Sch Dist, Odessa Tex 60-61; Head Libn Arabian Amer Oil Co Schs, Dhahran Saudi Arabia 65-. 8: ALA del to IFLA conf, Helsinki 65, The Hague 66. 9: ALA; TexLA; Tex State Tchrs Assn; Knife & Fork Club. 11: Outstanding Libn award, Tex Parents & Tchrs Assn, 64. 14: Chilt lit, rare bks, Middle East hist & archaeol. 15: 2417 Jarratt, Austin Tx78703.

BALL, HELEN (COULTER). b Oxford Ohio 25 O 19. 5: Miami U (Ohio) 37-41 (Fr, Eng) AB, 41-42 (Eng & Amer Lit) MA. 7: Loan desk asst libn Miami U (Oxford Ohio) 41-42, Res libn 42-50, Spec serv libn & audio ref 50-64, Loan libn,

King Undergrad Lib 65-. 8: Instr of Eng UMiami (Ohio). 10: Ed assistance on preparation of textbooks; Music Club; Woman's Club; Univ Club; Phi Beta Kappa. 14: Circ. 15: King Undergraduate Lib, Miami Univ, Oxford Oh 45056.

BALL, JOYCE (CSAPOSS). b E Paterson NJ 31 O 32. 4: Robert S Ball. 5: Douglass Col for Women 50-54 (Econ, Sociol) AB; Ind U 54-59 (LS) MA. 6: Sp. 7: Sec lib asst Celotex Corp, Chicago 54; Lib asst ICA Ind U Thailand Project Ind U 56-59; Asst chief govt document div Stanford U Libs 59-66; Chief govt publns dept UNev 66-. 8: Adv, For Statl Documents Proj (Internat Studies Grant, Stanford U) Ed bd mem, Congressl Info Serv 69-. 9: ALA (Interdiv Com on Pub Docs 67-, Memb Com 68-); Nev Lib Week (Pub chm 68). 10: Sigma Delta Pi; Alpha kappa Delta; PTA. 12: Ed "Foreign Documents; Census of Population Publications" (62); Ed "ForeignStatistical Documents" Hoover Inst Bibliog ser 28 (67). 13: Yes. 14: Ref, govt docs, for doc specialist. 15: 1785 Carlinst, Reno Nv 89503.

BALL, KATHARINE LUCY. b Toronto 26 Jl 04. 5: Toronto 22-26 (Eng) BA; Oxford U 26-28 (Eng) BA, MA; Toronto 46-47 BLS. 6: Fr. 7: Circ asst UToronto Lib 28-42; Squadron Off Royal Can Air Force 42-45; Catlgr UToronto Lib 45-46, Head catlgr 47-51; Asst Prof UToronto Lib Sch 51-59, Assoc Prof 59-64, prof 64-. 9: CanLA (pres, chm Catlg & Clsf Sect); ALA (Coun, chm Com on Catlg Policy & Research);OntLA (chm Reg Group of Catlgrs); Inst of Prof Libns of Ont. 10: Can Assn Univ Tchrs; Univ Women's Club, Toronto; Pi Beta Phi. 11: Can Centennial Medal. 13: Yes. 14: Catlg, documentation. 15: Sch of Lib Sci UToronto, 167 College st, Toronto 2B Can.

BALL, (GENEVRA) LOUISE. b Mayville NY 22 Jl 34. 5: Stetson U 52-56 (Soc Sci) BA; Syracuse summers 62-67 MS in LS. 7: Tchr Sanford Grammar Sch, Sanford Fla 56-57; Elem tchr Longwood Sch, Longwood Fla 57-58; Elem tchr Enterprise Sch, Enterprise Fla 58-62, Elem tchr & libn 62-63; Libn Boston Ave Sch, DeLand Fla 63-. 9: Assn of Childhood Educ (lst v-pres, hist, cor sec); ALA; NEA; FlaLA; FlaASchL (Life mem); Fla A-V Assn; FlaEA. 10: AAUW; DAR; W Volusia (Fla) Mem Hosp Auxiliary; Bus & Prof Women; Garden Club. 14: Child serv. 15: PO Box 241, DeLand Fl 32720.

BALL, MICHAEL JAMES. b Kalamazoo Mi. 4: Mary Lou Alling. 5: West MichiganU 58-63 (Sociol) BS, 67-68 MLS. 7: Photographer (Sgt) Michigan Air Nat Guard, Battle Creek Mich 63-69; Libn I Grand Rapids Pub Lib, Grand Rapids Mich 68-. 14: Ref. 15: Library Plaza, Grand Rapids Mi 49509.

BALL, PHYLLIS. b Phila 31 Jl 20. 5: UAriz 38-43 (Eng) BA. 7: UAriz Lib: Asst in acquis 45-53, Acquis libn 53-59, Spec collections libn 58-65, U hist, mss & archives libn 65-. 9: ArizLA; SWLA; SAA. 10: Ariz Hist Soc; Phi Beta Kappa. 13: Yes. 14: Mss, rare bks. 15: 2306 E Waverly, Tucson Az 85719.

BALL, ROBERT J. b Tacoma Cal 11 Mr 16. 4: Jane Koffard. 5: UCal (Berkeley) 33-38 (Forestry) BS; Immaculate Heart Col 64-66 (LS) MLS. 7: Lt cmdr US Navy SW Pacific 43-46; Assoc prof of life sci Pasadena City Col 38-66, Libn & assoc prof of lib serv 67-. 8: Ranger, Nat Park Serv summers 38-65. 9: CalLA; CalSchLA; CalTA. 10: Xi Sigma Pi; Alpha Zeta; Sierra Club; Nat Wildlife Fed. 14: Catlg, ref. 15: 235 Iris ave, Corona Del Mar Ca 92625.

BALLANCE, PAUL S. b Maple NC 7 S 06. 4: Susan Covington. 5: NCStateU 25-29 (Voc ed) BS; Columbia 29-31 BLS. 7: Ref asst NY Public Lib 29-36; Hd Sci & Tech Rochester Pub Lib, Rochester NY 36-42; Libn Tex Engineers lib, Col Sta Tex 43-49; Libn Tex A & M Col lib 44-49; Libn Greensboro Pub Lib, Greensboro NC 49-51; Dir Pub Lib, Winston- Salem NC 51-65; Dir libs Forsyth Co Pub Lib, Winston-Salem NC 65-. 8: Consul: Lubbock, Tex Pub Lib; Le Tourneau Tech Inst Longview Tex; Danville Pub Lib Danville Va; Mem NC State Lib Commsn and NC State Lib Bd 53- (chm of latter 67-). 9: ALA (chm Bus & Tech Sect 38-40, mem Bldgs Commsn 52-54); SELA; TexLA (past treas); NCLA (Pub Lib Sect: chm, v-pres 63-65, pres 65-67, Exec Bd 63-69). 10: Kiwanis Club; Rotary Club; Lion's Club; C of C; 12: Comp "First 50 Years of Public Library Service in Winston-Salem" (56); "List of Books in Texas Engineers Library" (45); Comp "Union List of Periodicals in Selected NC Libraries" (59); Co-editor, North Carolina Index (55-). 14: Pub lib admin. 15: Rte 8, Winston-Salem NC 27106.

BALLANTYNE, BERNICE (FAUGHNAN). b Montreal. 4: Ian A Ballantyne. 5: McGill 45 (Arts) BA, 46 BLS. 7: Libn RCA Victor, Montreal 46-47; Libn Omutt Hosp, Montreal 47-51; Libn Priory Sch, Montreal 63-. 15: 237 Kindersley ave, Montreal 305 Can.

BALLANTYNE, MADELINE (ROGERS). b Eagleville Mo 20 N 11. 4: J Dean Ballantyne. 5: Graceland Col 30-32 (Home Econ) AA; NE Mo State summers 33-35 (Hist); Simpson Col 36-37 (Hist) BA; UWisc 65-66 (LS) MA. 7: Tchr Walnut Grove Rural Sch, Eagleville Mo 32-36; Tchr Milo Indepenent Sch, Milo Iowa 37-44; Tchr Van Vert Independent Sch, Van Wert Iowa 51-52; Tchr Grand Valley Commun Sch, Kellerton Iowa 52-56, 57-61; Tchr Lamoni High Sch, Lamoni Iowa 56-57; Graceland Col Lib: Lib clk 61-66, Asst libn 66-. 9: ALA; Iowa Library Association. 10: Pi Gamma Mu; Iowa Hist Soc; RLDS Profess Tchrs. 14: Ref. 15: Rte 2 Box 84, Lamoni Ia 50140.

BALLARD, NANCY LEE. b Bedford Va 25 Ag 27. 5: Madison Col 44-48 (Math, LS) BA in Ed; AmericanU 66-. 7: Libn & tchr Henry Co Pub Schs, Bassett Va 48-56; Libn (ref) Off Chief of Engrs, Wash DC 56-60; Chief pub serv sect Industrial Col of Armed Forces 60-64, Asst libn 64-66, Lib dir 66-. 9: SLA; ALA; DCLA. 14: Admin, ref. 15: 1200 S Court House rd, Arlington Va 22204.

BALLARENE, CATHERINE R. b Jersey City NJ 22 S 23. 5: Notre Dame Col 41-45 (Chem) BA; Rutgers 61-62 MLS. 7: Asst research chem Nopco Chem Co, Harrison NJ 45-51; Export correspondent Fisher Sci Co, NYC 51-54; Sec Sinclair Oil Corp, NYC 54-57; Asst libn Union Carbide Plastics Co, Bound Brook NJ 57-59; Chem Lever Brothers Co, Edgewater NJ 59-61; Libn Isotopes Inc, Westwood NJ 62-67; Libn NY Pub Lib, Res Libs, Sci & Tech Div, NYC 68-. 9: SLA; ACS. 14: Ref (Sci & Tech, periodicals). 15: NY Pub Lib Research Libs, Science & Tech Div, 5th ave & 42nd st, New York, NY 10018.

BALLENTINE, VERNA BLANCHE (MAXSON). b Grand Rapids Mich 10 S 08. 4: Mattis W Ballentine. 5: Rollins Col 26-30 (Modern Lang) AB; Columbia 30-31 (LS) BS; UCal (Berkeley) 46 (Child Lit). 7: Head ref dept Rollins Col Lib 31-37; Br libn Order ref libn Tampa Pub Lib, Tampa Fla 37-45; Child libn Oakland Pub Lib,Oakland Cal 45-52; Pub rel libn Tampa Pub Lib, Tampa Fla 52-58, head circ dept 58-61; Supv libn Oakland Pub Lib, OaklandCal 61-66, Prin child libn Oakland Pub Lib 66-. 9: FlaLA (treas 2 yrs, ed of "Bulletin" 2 yrs, treas Pub Libs Sect 2 yrs, chm Int Freedom Com 1 yr); CalLA; Assn Child Libns NoCal. 12: Ed "Fla Lib Assn Bulletin" (32-34). 14: Child wk, ref. 15: 3348 Betty lane, Lafayette Ca 94549.

BALLEW, NELL B(ARRON). b Plano Tex. 5: Arlington State Col 25-26; Southwestern Jr Col 31-32; Tex Woman's U 60-61 (LS) BS; N Tex State U 64-68. 6: Sp. 7: Asst libn Navarro Jr Col 61-65, Documents libn 65-66, Period-documents libn 66-. 9: TexLA; Tex Jr Col Assn; AAUP, B & PW Club. 14: Ref, govt docs. 15: Box 249, Corsicana Tx 75110.

BALLIOT, ROBERT LAINE. b Douglas Ariz 19 F 31. 4: Marilyn Sue Smith. 5: Wash State U 53-57 (Eng) BA; UMich 57-59 AMLS. 7: US Army Signal Corps (Sgt) 51-53; Asst circ libn Ore State U 59-60, Engnr tech libn 60-62; Head Educ-Psych Lib State UIowa 62-63; Col Libn State U Col (Fredonia NY) 63-65; Undergrad libn UIll (Urbana) 65-67; Sci libn Wesleyan U 67-. 8: Visiting Instr Peabody Col summer 65-67, 69. 14: Admin. 15: 36 Knowles ave, Middletown Ct 06457.

BALLOU, HUBBARD (WALTER). b Peking China 26 Ja 17. 4: Patricia Kennedy. 5: Yenching U (Peking China) 34-36 (Liberal Arts); Yale 36-39 (Pre-Med) AB; Columbia 46-47 (LS) BS; UIll 47-48 (LS). 7: Master of the Scis The Darrow Sch, New Lebanon NY 39-42; Army of the US Mil Intelligence Mil Govt (lst Lt) 42-46; Photoduplication libn UIll Lib (Urbana) 47-48; Head photographic serv Columbia U Lib, NYC 48-. 8: Lecturer on Photoreproduction Columbia U Sch of Lib Serv, 50-; USASI PH5, 57-; Adv on Microrecording, "Industrial Photography," 58-65, "Systems" 60-64; Consul, Coun on Lib Resources project on "New Shaw List" 60, ALA Lib Standards for Microfilm Com 60-65. 9: Nat Microfilm Assn (Fellow, Assoc ed "National Micro-News" 59-, Dir 65-68); ALA (chm Photodup Order Form Com, Copying Methods Sect 60-63; Rep to ASA PH5 56-); Soc photographic Scis & Engnrs (Sect ed on "Copying" and "Copying Equipment" for "Abstracts of Photographic Sci & Engnrg" 63-64); ASIS (Assoc ed "American Documentation" 58-60; US Corresp on Document Reproduction to Internat Fed for Documentation); Royal Photogr Soc of GtBrit; SLA. 12: Ed "Guide to Microreproduction Equipment," annually 59-); 'Microcopying' in "Information Processing Equipment" (55); 'Microphotography' in "Encyclopedia International" (64); 'Copying Methods Notes,' series in "Library resources and Technical Services" (64). 13: Yes. 14: Reprography, espec microreproduction. 15: 90 Morningside dr, NYC 10027.

BALLOU, MARY ELLEN (LEE). b Mineola NY 21 Mr 28. 4: Dr Robert A Ballou. 5: Trinity Col 46-50 (Eng) AB; Columbia 50-57 MLS; Newark State Col 65-67. 7: Lib asst BBDO, NY 51-53, Advertising copywriter 53-55; Tchr libn Pt Pleasant Beach (NJ) Elem Sch 66-. 9: ALA; NJLA. 14: Ya, child. 15: 404 Boston blvd, Sea Girt NJ 08750.

BALLOU, PATRICIA (KENNEDY). b Detroit 2 Jl 24. 4: Hubbard W Ballou. 5: Oberlin Col 42-46 (Hist) BA; Columbia 46-47 BS. 7: Ref asst Brown U Lib 47-48; Ser asst City Col Lib (NY) 48-50; Asst ref libn Barnard Col Lib 61-. 10: Phi Beta Kappa. 15: 90 Morningside dr, NYC 10027.

BALLOU, YOLANDA ROBERTO. b Wakefield Mass 29 O 21. 4: LANCE C Ballou. 5: UMass 55 (Eng, Journalism) BA; Simmons 56 MSLS; UConn 58. 6: Ital, Fr, Sp. 7: Br libn Lucius Beebe Mem Lib, Wakefield Mass 44-51; Lib asst Kemp Pub Lib, Wichita Falls Tex 51-52; Lib asst Newton FreePub Lib, Newton Mass 55-57; Libn Foxboro High Sch, Foxboro Mass 56-57; Windsor High Sch, Windsor Conn 57-59, Conard High Sch,W Hartford Conn 59-65, Endicott Jr Col 65-. 9: ALA; Conn SchLA; NESchLA; NE Jr Col Coun of Libns. 10: Phi Theta Kappa. 14: Ref, catlg. 15: 30-C Shore dr, Northshore Gardens, Peabody Ma 01960.

BALOGH, CORNELIA O. b Budapest Hungary. 5: State Tchrs Col (Szeged Hungary) 53-56 (Biol, Geog) Tchg Certif; USoCal 57-59 (Geog) BA, 59-60 MSLS. 6: Ger, Hungarian. 7: Tchr Pomaz Jr High Sch, Pomar Hungary 55-56; Clerk admissions off USoCal 57-59; Ref stud asst USoCal Lib 59-60; Catlgr UCLA 60-62; Sci & tech libn Cal State Col (Los Angeles) 62-. 9: CalLA; SchLA. 10: Sierra Club. 14: Ref. 15: 6603 W 6th st, Los Angeles Ca 90048.

BALOGH, MARY RUTH. b Omaha 12 Jl 23. 4: Dr Charles Joseph Balogh. 5: Duchesne Col 41-45 (Eng) BA; Col of St Catherine 45-46 (LS) MA. 6: Fr. 7: Asst libn Omaha U 46-47; Law libn Creighton U Law Sch, Omaha 47-49; Ref libn Omaha Pub Lib 49-50; Libn Minneapolis Gas Co 59-61; Libn Christ the King lib, Minneapolis 64-68; Libn Bur of Sport Fisheries & Wildlife (Int Dept) 68-. 9: SLA. 10: LWV; Friends of Edina Pub Lib; Col Alumnae Chap (pres); Christ the King Women's Club (sec); Med auxiliaries; LWV. 14: Ref. 15: 5204 Halifax ave S, Edina Mn 55424.

BALZ, CHARLES F(RANCIS). b Wilkes-Barre Penn 3 F 23. 4: Marjorie Dourand. 5: King's Col 46-50 (Biol) BS; Syracuse 50-51 (LS) MS. 6: Fr. 7: (Sgt) US Air Force 43-46; Libn St Regis Paper Co, Watertown NY 51-52; Libn IBM Corp, Vestal NY 52-53, Mgr document control 53-56; Project mgr security serv IBM Corp, Owego NY 56-60, Project mgr info retrieval lib serv 60-64, Project mgr info retrieval & off serv 64-. 9: SLA; ADI. 10: Company of Mil Histns. 12: 'MERGE: A Current Awareness and Retrospective Searching System for Technical Documents,' with R H Stanwood, Chap 9 of "Technical Preconditions for Retrieval Center Operations" (65); 6 IBM Corp reports, mainly on data processing & info retrieval (61-63); Comp & Ed, with Stan wood "Literature in Information Retrieval & Machine Translation" (61 , 66). 13: Yes. 14: Lib mgt. 15: IBM Corp, Owego NY 13827.

BALZ, ELIZABETH LOUISE. b Delaware Ohio 6 Mr 12. 5: Capital U 29-33 (Chem) BS, 34-35 (Educ) BS in Ed; Columbia 38-39 BS in LS. 7: Typist Ohio State U Lib 35-38; Catlgr Yale Divinity Sch Lib 39-42; Ser catlgr NY Pub Lib 42-44; Ref & circ libn Capital U 44-47, Asst libn & catlgr 47-51; Libn Evangelical Lutheran Theol Sem 51-. 9: ALA; ATheolLA; OhioLA. 10: Bd of Mgrs, Pauline Home for the Aged; Bus & Prof Unit of Columbus SymphonyOrchestra; Luth Hist Conf. 14: Admin, catlg. 15: 865 S Remington rd, Columbus Oh43209.

BALZ, ELOISE EDNA. b Covington Ky 9 Mr 17. 5: East Ky State Col 35-38 (Educ) BS; UKy 48-56 (LS) MS. 6: Fr. 7: Tchr Covington Bd of Educ, Covington Ky 38-48, Libn 48-58; Libn Indian Hill Exempted village, Cincinnati 58-. 9: NEA; ALA; KyLA; KyASchL (pres 56-57); KyEA; OhioASchL (sec 64); OhioEA. 10: Phi Beta Mu. 14: Sch lib wk. 15: 34 Requardt lane, S Ft Mitchell Ky 41017.

BAMBER, DOROTHY. b Staten Island NY 10 Ag 10. 5: Douglass Col 27-31 (Soc Sci) BA; Columbia 37-41 (LS) MA. 7: Adult & child libn NY Pub Lib 36-41, Ya libn 41-43; DC Pub Lib: Child libn 45-48, Sub-br libn 48-49, Bkmob libn 49-50; Asst coordinator of wk with ya Enoch Pratt Free Lib, Baltimore 54-56; Readers adv White Plains Pub Lib 56-62, Order libn 62-. 9: NYLA; WestchesterLA (sec 2 yrs, var positions in YA & Child Libns Sect). 10: Soroptimist. 13: Yes. 14: Bk sel, ya, readers adv. 15: White Plains Pub Lib, White Plains NY 10602.

BANFILL, ARNOLD (DREW). b E Agnus Que Can 16 F 14. 5: Bishop's U 32-35 (Hist) BA; McGill 35-40 (Law) BCL, 46-47 BLS. 6: Fr. 7: Asst to dir Harvard Law Lib 47-51; Libn Bishop's U (Lennoxville Que) 51-67; Catlgr McGill U Law Lib 69. 8b E Angus Que Can 16 F 14. 07: 67; Catlgr McGill U Law Lib 69. 9: CanLA. 11: Awarded degree ofDoctor of Civil Law, honoris causa, by Bishop's U 67. 12: Comp "Catalogue of theeastern Townships Historical Collection in the Bishop's University Library" (65). 14: Catlg. 15: 2330 Madison ave Apt V204, Montreal 261 Que Can.

BANGOURA, LORRAINE (SCHILDBERGER). b Grafton N Dak 24 My 37. 4: Ibrahima Sory. 5: Valley City State Col 65-69 (Eng) BS; UDenver 62-63 (LS) MA. 6: Fr, Czech. 7: Asst catlgr UWis (Milwaukee) 63-65; Tchr & elem libn Amer Commun Sch, Conakry Guinea 66-68; Asst catlgr Milner Lib Ill StateU (Normal) 68-69; Asst catlgr Memorial Lib MarquetteU 69-. 9: WisLA; McLeanCoLA. 10: AAUP. 12: "A Bio-bibliography of Dr Malcolm Wyer (66). 14: Catlg. 15: 531 N 17th st, Milwaukee ND 53233.

BANHEGYI, TIBOR E. b Budapest Hungary 9 Jl 14. 5: U of Law (Budapest) 33-37 Doctor of Law; Columbia 60-61 MLS. 6: Hungarian, Fr, Ger. 7: Legal adv to US legation, Budapest NYC 45-51; Ref asst Coun on For Rel Lib, NYC 61-. 15: Council on Foreign Relations Inc 58 E 68 st, New York NY 10021.

BANICK, ALBERT (NICHOLAS). b NYC 6 D 10. 5: NYU 28-31 (Hist) BS; Columbia 31-32 (Soc Studies) MA; St John's U (NY) 39-42 BLS. 6: Fr. 7: Asst ref libn & act law libn St John's U Law Sch 42-44; Libn Park Ridge (NJ) High Sch 44-46; Tech libn Specialties Inc, Syosset NY 46-49; Asst libn circ dept Queens Borough Pub Lib, Jamaica NY 52-54; Libn East st Elem Sch, Hicksville NY 54-. 9: NEA; Assn Supvn & Curr Devel; ALA; NYLA; Nassau-Suffolk SchLA; Hicksville SchLA (pres 69-). 10: Newman Alumni Assn of LI; St John's U Lib Sci Alumni Assn. 12: "Bibliography of Science Books for the 3-Track Elem Curriculum" (58). 13: Yes. 14: Wk with child. 15: 45 Harvard st, Garden City NY 11530.

BANISTER, JOHN ROBERT. b Saginaw Mich 3 F 12. 4: Nancy Simpson. 5: Bay City Jr Col 32-34 (Engnr) AA; UMich 34-36 (Soc Sci) AB; UIll 37 BS in LS. 6: Fr, Ger. 7: Gen asst Pub Lib, Saginaw Mich 29-34; Stud asst UMich 34-36; Asst ref libn Mich State Lib 37-42; Order libn TVA Tech Lib, Knoxville Tenn 42-44; Chief ext dept Pub Lib, Lansing Mich 44-46; Reg libn Ill State Lib 46-48; Pub lib consul UFla gfd 48-51; Dir of Libs Bradley Mem Lib, Columbus Ga 51-. 8: Consul Albany, -Manchester, Madison & Valdosta Ga, Bradenton Fla Pub lib bldg 65-. 9: ALA (Coun 40-44, chm Jr Mem Round Table 46); SELA (chm Pub Lib Div 48-49); GaLA (1st v-pres 60-61). 10: Rotary Club; Commun Serv Assn; Columbus Symphony Orchestra; Appeals Review Bd United Givers. 12: Ed "Junior Librarian," Mich (38-41); Ed "Florida Public Library Newsletter" (48-49). 13: Yes. 14: Admin, bldg design, automation. 15: 2952 Roswell lane, Columbus Ga 31906.

BANKER, SANFORD JOHN JR. b St Paul 5 Ag 30. 4: Karen Thul. 5: St Cloud State Col 53-57 (Hist) BS; UMinn 58-60 (LS). 7: Communication Oper US Army (Cpl), Ala 50-51; Order filler Red Owl Stores Inc, Hopkins Minn 51-53, summers 54-57; Catlgr & child libn Anoka Co Lib & Anoka Pub Lib 59-60; Libn & Chief Libn VA Hosp, St Cloud Minn 60-. 10: Sch Lib consul Knights of Columbus. 14: Catlg, admin. 15: VA Hosp, St Cloud Mn 56301.

BANKS, DORIS (HARPER). b Auburn NY 1 My 25. 5: State Teachers Col SUNY Genesco 42-46 (LS) BS; Syracuse 48-52 MSLS; USoCal 62-67 (Pub Admin) MPA. 7: Libn Mohawk Central Sch, Mohawk NY 47-50; YP libn Pub Lib, Brookline Mass 50-53; YP libn City Lib, Phoenix 53-54; Chief libn Robertshaw-Fulton Controls Co Anaheim Cal 55-57; Chief libn Hughes Aircraft Co, Fullerton Cal 57-67; Assoc col libn adminis serv Cal State Col, Fullerton 67-. 9: ALA; SLA; CLA (Conf chm 66 Coun 68); So Cal Tech Processes Gp (pres 68-69). 11: Beta Phi Mu; John Cotton Dana lecturer, U So Cal 60. 14: Admin, systems analysis. 15: 2025 Victoria dr, Fullerton Ca 92631.

BANKS, FLORENCE EVELYN (STOVEL WISELOGLE). b Sault Ste Marie Ont Can 5 Mr 14. 4: Graham F Banks. 5: Flint Jr Col 52-57 (Eng); UMich 57-59 (Eng) AB in Educ, 60-64 AMLS; West Mich U 65- (LS). 6: Fr. 7: Off manager Genesee Co Lib, Flint Mich 52-57, A-v libn 57-62; Tchr Bentley Jr High Sch, Flint Mich 58-61, Libn 58-62; Libn Bentley Elem Schs, Flint Mich 58-62; Supv of sch libs Fenton Pub Schs, Fenton Mich 62-; Tchr Adult High Sch, Flint Mich

63-; Coord sch libs W Bloomfield Schs, Orchard Lake Mich 67-68; Dir lib serv, Ferndale Schs, Ferndale Mich 68-. 8: Consul Reading & Lib Serv Com Mich Cong P&T 60-. ; Summer staff West Mich U 66. 9: ALA-AASchL; NEA; MichLA (chm Recruiting Com 56-57; Memb Com 59-60; chm Sch & Child Sect 67-68; chm Fall Inst Sch & Child Sect 65); MichASchL (chm Recruiting Com 63-64; 1st v-pres 68-69; Conf Chm 68-69; pres 69-70). 11: UMich Hopwood Award for a novel, 58. 14: Sch libnship, a-v, catlg. 15: 5881 Dixie hwy, apt H159, Waterford Mi 48095.

BANKS, GEORGE S JR. b NYC 16 F 30. 5: Georgetown U 47-51 (Pol Sci) BS; UPenn 53-56 (Bus Admin) MBA; Columbia 68-69 (LS) MS. 6: Sp. 7: Logistics off (1st Lt) USMC 51-53; Sales admin Gen Motors Overseas Operations, NYC 56-61; Export mgr Ballthrall Trading Co, Phila 63-68. 9: ALA. 14: Ref, admin. 15: 49 Western ave, Morristown NJ 07960.

BANKS, PAUL N(OBLE). b Montebello Cal 15 Ap 34. 5: Compton Col 52-53; Carnegie 53-56 (Printing management); Columbia 56-58 (Graphic arts). 6: Fr, Ital. 7: Typographer prod coordinator Viking Press, NYC 56-60; Asst Carolyn Horton, Rare Bk Restorer, NYC 60-62; Proprietor Paul N Banks, Rare Bk Restorer, NYC 62-64; Conservator Newberry Lib, Chicago 64-. 8: Consul on conserv, LC 68-; Chm Study Com on Bk Conserv, Com to Rescue Italian Art, 66-; Mem Advis Com on Conserv of Lib Materials Publ Proj, Lib Tech Program, ALA 65-; Consul, NLM (sponsored rare bk restor proj, Northwest U Dental Sch Lib 68-70). 9: ALA (Spec sub-com on Florence 67-69; Bkbinding Com 67-); Guild of Bk Wkers (chm, Pub Com 56-64); Internat Inst for Conserv of Hist and Artistic Wks and its Amer Group (Assoc 62-69, Fellow 69-; mem-at-large of Amer Gp 67-69; mem Paper Study Com 68-). 14: Conserv of lib materials. 15: 60 West Walton st, Chicago Il 60610.

BANNER, GERALD T(HEODORE). b Brooklyn NY 8 S 35. 5: Goddard Col 54-56 (Hist); New Sch for Soc Res 61-65 (Hist) BA; Pratt Inst 65-67 (LS) MLS. 7: Trainee Brooklyn Pub Lib, Bklyn NY 65-67; Pub serv libn Plymouth State Col 67-68; Ref libn UMaine (Portland) 68-. 8: Instr UMe (Portland) Grad School, Dept of Lib Serv 69-. 9: MeLA. 10: Beta Phi Mu. 14: Ref, coop among small coll, federal aid. 15: 7 Forest Park, Portland Me 04101.

BANNETT, ROCHELLE (OVED). b Brooklyn NY 19 S 44. 4: Paul Martin Bannett. 5: Queens Col 61-65 (Sociol) BA; Pratt Inst Grad Lib Sch) 67-68 (LS) MLS. 7: Dept Libn NYC Dept of Soc Serv, 68-. 9: SLA. 10: Phi Beta Kappa; Beta Phi Mu. 15: 142-10 Roosevelt ave, Flushing NY 11354.

BANNIGAN, BERNICE (GATES). b Utica NY 19 N 15. 4: George E Bannigan. 5: NY State Col for Tchrs (Albany) 37-41 (Lat) BA, summers 42-44 BS in LS. 7: Asst circ dept Utica Pub Lib, Utica NY 41, Br asst 42, Info asst 43-48, Head music, art, religion, philos & foreign depts 48-. 9: ALA; CathLA; NYLA. 10: AAUW; Boys' Club of Utica Inc Women's Auxiliary; Munson Williams Proctor Inst. 14: Adult serv. 15: 14 Watson, Utica NY 13502.

BANTA, JOHN J. b Astoria NY 24 My 32. 4: Joan Walker. 5: Pace Col 56-58 (Bus Admin). 7: Harbor craft crewman (cpl) US Army, 110 Harbor Craft Batt. 52-54; Deputy-libn Assn of the Bar, NYC 58-65; Libn Strasser, Spiegelberg, Fried & Frank, NYC 65-67; Chief Law Libn Hughes Hubbard & Reed, NYC 1967-. 9: AALL; Law Lib Assn of Greater NY; Assn of Law Lib Upstate NY. 14: Reference. 15: Hughes Hubbard & Reed, One Wall St, NYC 10005.

BARACCA, PHILIP E. b Pittsburgh 20 Ap 28. 5: Duquesne U 46-49 (Eng, Soc Studies) B Ed; UPittsburgh 63-64 MLS. 7: Spec Serv US Army, US, Italy; Self-employed Insurance, Pittsburgh; Spec agent NYLife Ins Co, Pittsburgh 54-59; Tchr Penn Inst (Glenmore Acad), Pittsburgh 59-60; SoHills Catholic High Sch, Pittsburgh; Eng tchr 60-61, Tchr head reading dept 61-62,Libn 62-; Instr of Lib Sci Duquesne U Sch of Educ 69. 9: ALA; Internat Reading Assn(v-pres); CathLA (sec High Sch Sect; West Penn Unit; chm Publicity, ed); PennLA(Planning Com); Pittsburgh Lib Club (pres). 10: Cath Lay-Tchrs Guild; Acad of Arts &sci; Pittsburgh Landmarks Assn; West Penn Hist Assn. 12: Ed West Penn CathLA "Newsletter"; Ed Diocesan Lay-Tchrs Guild "Journal." 13: Yes. 14: Ref, bk sel, rare bks. 15: 209 S Braddock ave,Pittsburgh Pa 15221.

BARAN, WOLODYMYR. b Demianiw Ukraine 2 F 13. 4: Oksana Nakoneczna. 5: UCracow Poland 33-37 (Law) Master; West Res 56-57 (LS) MS. 6: Ukrainian, Fr, Ger, Polish, Russ. 7: Asst libn Wayne Co Lib System, Ecorse Mich 57-59, Libn River Rouge Mich 60-. 9: ALA. 14: Ref. 15: 12274 Moran, Detroit Mi 48212.

BARASCH, DONNA C(YNTHIA) (STONEWALL). b Boston Mass 9 My 46. 4: Kenneth L Barasch. 5: UCal at Riverside 64-68 (Hist) BA; UCLA 68-69 MLS. 6: Ger. 7: Lib research analyst N Amer Rockwell Autonetics Div, Anaheim Cal 69-. 9: ALA. 14: Info sci. 15: 343 Bedford rd apt 22, Orange Ca 92668.

BARBARA, SISTER MARY PBVM. b Hudson Mass 31 O 34. 5: Worcester State Tchrs Col 52-54; Regina Coeli Col 54-58 (Eng) BA; Villanova 61-65 MSLS; Certified Elem Tchr 63, Certified Libn 65 Vassar NSF Inst 68 (Geol); West Mich NSF Inst 69 (Phys Sci). 6: Sp. 7: Tchr StLeo's Sch, Leominster Mass 56-58; Tchr Sacred Heart Sch, Fitchburg Mass 59-60; TchrSt Leo's Sch, Leominster Mass 61-63; Tchr St Bernard's Sch, Fitchburg Mass 64-66;Tchr Regina Coeli Col 65-66, Libn part & full time 54-67; Tchr St John's, Clintonmass 67-68; Tchr & libn St Mary's Sch, Stamford Conn 68-69. 9: ALA; CathLA;Central MassLA; ConnLA. 14: Catlg, ref, aiding col studs in use of lib, child lit. 15: St Mary's Convent, 540 Elm st, Stamford Ct 06902.

BARBARE, LOIS (ANNIE). b Taylors SC 27 F 13. 5: Greenville Woman's Col 29-31; USCar 31-33 AB; Emory 38 AB in LS. 7: Tchr Darlington (SC) Schs 34-37; Supv WPA Lib Prog 38-41; Army libn Stark Gen Hosp, Charleston SC 42-44; Asst exec sec SC State Lib Bd, Columbia SC 44-57, Tech serv libn 57-. 9: ALA; SELA; SCLA (pres 54). 10: LWV. 14: Acquis, tech serv. 15: 1614 Senate st, Columbia SC 29201.

BARBE, WAVERLY WILSON. b Surry Co Va 26 O 13. 5: URichmond 33-35 (Eng) BA; Chicago 36-37 (Eng); Peabody 38-39 BS in LS, 39-40 (Eng) MA. 6: Fr, Ger, Sp. 7: Reviser & libn George Peabody Col 39-40; Catlgr UAla 41-42, Head catlg dept43-51, Libn Educ Lib 51-67, Assoc Prof of Lib Sci 67-. 9: AlaEA; AlaLA. 10: Sigma Phi Epsilon; VaHist Soc; SAR; Phi Delta Kappa; Kappa Delta Pi; Pi Gamma Mu. 14: Catlg, ref. 15: 13 Audubon pl, Tuscaloosa Al 35401.

BARBEE, KENT (HODNETT). b Milton Va 13 Ag 1891. 4: C C Barbee. 5: Wake Forest Col 43-45 (Eng) BA; Emory 47-48, 50 (LS) BA. 6: Fr, Sp. 7: Circ libn Wake Forest Col Lib 48-61; Libn Wake Forest Pub Lib, Wake Forest NC 62-. 9: NCLA. 10: Garden Club; Woman's Club. 14: Circ. 15: 222 N Main, Wake Forest NC 27587.

BARBER, GARY DeFOREST. b N Tonawanda NY 26 F 41. 4: Nancy (Feltham). 5: SUNY (Fredonia) 59-64 (Lib Arts, Mus) BA, (Geneseo) 64-67 (LS) MLS. 6: Fr. 7: Lib trainee Buffalo & Erie Co Pub Lib, Buffalo 64-67, Jr libn 67-69; Asst libn SUNY (Fredonia) 69-. 9: NYStateLA. 14: Ref. 15: Main rd, Sheridan NY 14135.

BARBER, HELEN M(ARGARET). b New York NY 19 Je 36. 5: Elmira 53-57 (Biol & Eng) BA; (Case) West Res U Sch of LS, MS in LS; UIll 65-67 (Bot) MS; Summer sessions: Columbia Tchrs Col 58; UMich 56, 62. 6: Ger. 7: Eng tchr Sanderson Acad, Ashfield Mass 57-58; Gen Sci 7-8, Biol tchr Odessa Cent Sch, Odessa NY 58-59; Nature Counselor Camp Francis (GSA) S Kent Conn summer 59; Courier, Frontier Nursing Serv, Wendover Ky 59; Stud-in-Train State Lib, Columbus Ohio 60-61; Asst Ref Libn (zool spec) Cornell U Libs 62-65; Libn II (biol sci catlgr) USoCal Lib 67-. 9: Amer Inst of Biol Scis; Bot Soc of Amer; Internat Assn for Plant Taxonomy; ALA; SLA (Biol Scies & Nat Resources Div); CalLA; OhioLA. 10: Beta Phi Mu; Nat Audubon Soc; AAAS. 14: Catlg & ref (biol scis & Oceanog). 15: 3789 Menlo ave #302, Los Angeles Ca 90007.

BARBER, KATHERINE (KELEHER). b Norfolk Va 26 Ag 40. 4: John Farwell Barber. 5: Knox Col 58-62 (Fr) BA; UChicago 63-66 (LS) MA. 6: Fr. 7: Lib asst Knox Cal Lib 59-62; Lib asst (ser) UChicago Lib 62-64; Lib asst Aerojet Gen Corp, Sacramento Cal 64; Libn Ctr for Health Admin Studies, Chicago 64-67; Indexer ALA, Chicago 67; Research assoc AMA, Chicago 67-. 9: MedLA. 14: Ref (clinical med). 15: 2409 N Geneva ter, Chicago Il 60614.

BARBER, L A (HASSELL). b Hamilton Ont Can 25 Je 45. 4: Lynn Barber. 5: McMaster 63-66 (Fr) BA; UBC 67-68 BLS. 6: Fr, Ger. 7: Lib asst McMasterU 66-67; Soc sci libn UAlgary 68-69, Humanities libn & rare bks 69-. 9: ALA; CanLA; AltaLA. 14: Ref, rare bks. 15: Apt 114 1340 Univ dr NW, Calgary 42 Alta Can.

BARBER, N LYNN. b Mont Belvieu Tex 16 O 23. 5: UTex 41-45 (Hist) BA; U Houston 46-48 (Hist) MS; UDenver 57-59 (LS) MA. 6: Sp. 7: Soc Sci tchr Jr-Sr High Schs, Tex 46-52; High sch libn, Prince George's Co Md 52-53; Head libn Ark State Col 58-59; 1stState Bkmob libn Tex State Lib 57-58; Circ libn Trinity U (San Antonio Tex) 59-60; Head libn Atlantic Christian Col 60-61; LibnSt Mary's Co Bd of Educ, Leonardtown Md 61-62; Pub serv libn Washington & Lee U 62-63; Dir St Lucie-Okeechobee Reg Lib, Fla 63;Acquis libn Southeast Mo State Col 63-65; Ref libn N Tex State U 65-66; Hd libn Paul Quinn Col 66-67; Ref-doc libn NevSoU 67;Dir Bristol Va-Tenn Pub Lib 67; Doc libn UVa Sch of Law 67; Doc libn Tarlton Law Lib UTex 68-. 8: Mem of seven-man Lib Planning Com, Southeast Mo State Col Consul James Connally Tech Inst. 9: ALA; ConservativeLA; SELA;TexLA; AALL; VaLA. 10: AAUP; Miss Valley Hist Assn; Delta Upsilon; Alpha Beta Alpha; Sertoma Internat; Forty Acres Club; Longhorn Club. 14: Admin, ref. 15: PO Box 205, Mont Belvieu Tx 77580.

BARBER, RAYMOND R. b Duluth Minn 22 Mr 25. 4: Lois A Strom. 5: Duluth Jr Col 46-47 (Electrical Engnr); Mich Tech 47-49 (Chem Engnr) BS; West Res 49-50 (LS) MS. 6: Fr, Ger. 7: USN Fire Control Operator 2C 43-46; Tech asst Carnegie Lib of Pittsburgh 50-52; Ref libn General Electric, Richland Wash 52-55; Libn Boeing Airplane Co, Seattle 55-59; Lib unit chief The Boeing Co, Seattle 59-64; Libn Corning Glass Works, Corning NY 64-. 9: SLA; ADI. 14: Ref, admin, info retrieval systems. 15: 117 Goff rd, Corning NY 14830.

BARBER, RAYMOND WILLIAM. b Akron Ohio 25 F 38. 5: UAkron 56-60 (Hist) BA; UKy 61-65 (LS) MS. 7: Libn West Jr High Sch, Akron Ohio 61-68; Coord media serv Kent State U 68-. 9: ALA; OhioLA; OhioSchLA; ASCD; NEA-DAVI; NASSP. 10: Summit Co LA; Akron Adult Educ Coun. 13: Yes. 14: Sch lib admin, a-v serv. 15: 819 Saxon ave, Akron Oh 44314.

BARBERENA, ELVIA. b Mex City Mex 30 Ap 30. 5: Universidad Nacional Autonoma de Mex 47-50 (Eng Lit) MA; UCal (Berkeley) 57-59 MLS. 6: Sp. 7: Ref asst Benjamin Franklin Lib, Mex City 50-55, Head ref dept 56-66, Asst Libn 67-. 8: Tchr of Ref & Bibliog, Escuela Nacional de Bibliotecarios y Archivistas, Mexico DF. 9: Associacio3n Mexicana de Bibliotecarios (Consejo Te3cnico 65-66, v-pres 67-69); ALA. 10: Beta Phi Mu. 12: Comp "Directory of Mexico City Libraries" (67). 13: Yes. 14: Ref. 15: Ave Azcapotzalco 218, Mexico 16, DF.

BARBERENA-BLASQUEZ, ELSA. b Mexico DF 28 O 34. 5: Mex City Col 58-60 (Art Hist) BA; UCal (Berkeley) 63-64 MLS. 6: Sp, Ital, Fr, Ger. 7: Lib asst Nacional Financiera SA, Mex DF 56-58; Lib asst Societa Dante Alighieri, Mexico DF 61; Lib asst UN Lib, Mexico DF 62-63; U of the Americas(Mex DF): Ref libn 64, Act libn 65, Ref libn 65-; Libn Societa Dante Alighieri, Mexico DF 64-. 9: Asociacion Mexicana de Bibliotecarios; Societa Dante Alighieri. ; ALA. 11: Italian govt scholarship. 12: Comp "Directory of Mexico City Libraries" (67). 13: Yes. 14: Ref, art libs . 15: Ave Atzapotzalco 218, Mexico 16 DF.

BARBOUR, SISTER JANE MARIE CDP. b Owensboro Ky 13 F 05. 5: Our Lady of the Lake Col 34 (Math) BA; Catholic U 41 (Educ) MA; Our Lady of the Lake Col 44 BS in LS; Columbia 57 MS in LS, 64-65 (LS). 6: Ger, Fr, Sp. 7: Tchr high schs, Tex Okla & La 25-44; High sch libn Our Lady of the Lake High Sch, San Antonio Tex 44-55; Faculty Dept of Lib Sci Our Lady of the Lake Col 44-55, Head Dept of Lib Sci 55-66, Prof lib sci & dir grad program lib sci 66-. 8: Rep Coun Nat Lib Assns 69-; Appointed by Pres Adv Coun for Col Lib Resources Higher Educ Act Title II 66-68; Governor's Conf on Tex Libs. 9: ALA (Coun 62-66, Nat Commsn on Plan for Lib Educ)-AASchL (Prof Rel Com 57-65; Jury for Distinguished Sch Admin Award 68-69); CathLA (Regina Award Medal chm 66; Nat Unit Coord 65-69; Adv Coun, Prof Rel); SWLA; TexLA (pres 63-64); Tex State TA (Lib Devel Com); BexarLA; Tex Coun Lib Educ. 10: Alpha Beta Alpha; Theta Sigma Phi. 11: ALA Letter Libn 56; TALA Founder's Plaque 68. 13: Yes. 14: Lib educ. 15: Our Lady of the Lake Col, 411 SW 24th st, San Antonio Tx 78207.

BARCKLAY, SUSAN (JANET SPERBER). b Portland Ore 10 Jl 22. 5: WHITMN Col 40-44 9hist) BA; Simmons 46-47 BS in LS. 7: Asst libn Linfield Col 47-50; Ref libn Mid-Columbia Lib, Kennewick Wash 51-52; Asst libn Kaiser Aluminum & Chem Corp, Spokane Wash 54-58; Libn Geiger Field USAF Lib, Spokane Wash 59-63; Ref libn Spokane Co Rural Lib, Spokane Wash 64, Dir 65-. 9: WashLA; PNLA; ALA. 14: Admin. 15: E 24426 Third ave, Liberty Lake Wa 99019.

BARCLAY, DOT (HICKMAN). b Bicknell Utah 4 Mr 23. 4: William Lloyd Barclay. 5: Utah State U 41-44 (Eng); UUtah 49-51 (Educ) BS. 6: Fr. 7: (Spec Q 1st Class) Tech Res Lib US Navy US Naval Commun Washington DC 44-46; Hd of child serv Palos Verdes Dist Lib, Palos Verdes Cal 55-. 9: ALA; CalLA. 14: Child wk. 15: 202 Via Anita, Redondo Beach Ca 90277.

BARCLAY, LUELLA KNOX. b Monroe Neb 4 N 06. 4: Charles P P Barclay. 5: Whitman Col 24-25; Lamar Col 26-27; UWash 37-39 (Pol Sci) BA, 39-40 BLS. 7: Ser libn Hartford Sem Found, Hartford Conn 40-42; Bkmob libn Harris Co Lib,Houston 42-43; Libn US Army, San Antonio Tex 43-44; Libn US Army, Bastrop Tex43-45; Ser libn UHouston 51, Head circ 51-67, Humanities libn 67-. 9: ALA; TexLA;Houston Lib Club. 10: Outdoor Nature Club; Univ Oaks Civic Club. 15: 4382 Varsity lane, Houston Tx 77004.

BARCUS, THOMAS R. b Plainview Tex 4 O 08. 5: So Methodist U 24-2 (Comparative Lit) BA; Columbia 28-29 bls& umich 31-33 AMLS. 6: Fr, Ger. 7: Ref asst lib ext serv UMich 29-34, Head econ-math reading room 34-36, Head grad reading room for soc sci 36-38; Asst to chmAdv Group on Academic Libs, Carnegie Corp 38-43; Libn USask 43-45; Chief Exchange & Gift Div LC 45-48, Tech off processingdept 48-. 8: Surveyed col libs for Carnegie Corp & N Central Assn 38-43; Instr in ref wk UMich Sch of Lib Sci 43-44. 9: ALA; SaskLA (pres 44); Can Lib Coun (44-45); ALA (Com on Memb); ACRL; DCLA. 12: Alumni Reading Lists (UMich) (31,34); "Carnegie Corporation & College Libraries, 1938-1943" (43).00778 13: Yes. 14: Acquis. 15: Apt 305, 215 C st SE, Wash DC 20003.

BARD, HARRIET (ELY). b Springfield Mass. 5: Oberlin Col 24-26; Boston U 26-28 (F) AB; UMich 41 ABLS. 7: Libn pub lib, Hagerstown Ind 37-45; Libn pub lib, Richmond Ind 45-. 8: Pres, Ind Li Certif Bd 45-52. 9: ALA (Coun 50-52); IndLA (pres 50). 10: American Red Cross; Musical Arts Soc; Wayne Co Tubercul Assn (mem Exec Bd). 11: Designated as Indiana Librarian of the Year (1966) by Ind Lib Trustees Assn. 13: Yes. 14: Admin. 15: Morrisson-Reeves Lib, Richmond In 47374.

BARD, THERESE (BISSEN). b Caledonia Minn 8 Ag 26. 4: Imre Bard. 5: St Theresa 43-46, 47-48 (Hist) AB; USoCal 49-50(Educ); UCal(Berkeley) 56-57 (Libnship) MLS. 7: US Army WAC Mil Instr (1st Lt) 51-56; Ref libn Newberry Lib, Chicago 57-59;Sch libn Bd of Educ (Chicago) 59-63; Sch libn Oak Park Sch Dist 97, Oak Park Ill 63-64; Sch lib consul Centennial Sch DistR-100, San Luis Colo 65-66; Instr LS Wis State U, Stevens Point 67-. 9: ALA. 14: Sch libnship. 15: 309 Fairview Vill, R4,Stevens Pt Wi 54481.

BARDEEN, JANICE E. b Penn Yan NY 3 Je 26. 5: Denison U 44-48 (Hist) BA; Columbia 49-50 (Hist, Bibliog & Tchg) MA; U Chicago Lib Sch Ext 60-64 Lib Sch Diploma. 6: Sp, Lat. 7: Catlgr NY Hist Soc NYC 50-52; Catlg & ref libn Keuka Col 53-62; Hd cat ref libn Orlando Pub Lib Orlando Fla 63-. 8: Established 3 church libs; NY State Hist Assn; Nat Button Soc. 9: ALA. 14: Catlg, ref. 15: 1012 Lake Highland dr, Orlando Fl 32803.

BARDEN, BERTHA R. b Columbus Ohio 9 S 1883. 5: Vassar Col 01-06 (Lat, Gk) AB, 06 AM; West Res 07 Lib Sci Grad. 7: Prof Emeritus West Res (Sch of Lib Sci) 54-; Church libn Hyde Pk Union Church, Chicago 60-68. 9: ALA. 12: Book numbers (pamphlet) (37); Comp with Barbara Denison "Guide to the SLA Loan Collection of Classification Schemes and Subject Heading Lists" (5th ed 61). 14: Catlg, clsf. 15: 1481 Rydal Mount rd, Cleveland Heights Oh 44118.

BARDENHEIER, SISTER PHYLLIS CSJ. b St Louis Mo 23 O 37. 5: Fontbonne Col 58-61 (Hist) BA; Rosary Col 64-69 (LS) MS. 7: Tchr Amer Martyrs, Kingsford Mich 61-2; Tchr St Matthew's, Mobile Ala 62-65; Tchr-libn St Mary's, Bridgeton Mo 65-69. 8: Lib consul, Archdiocesan Lib Coun. 14: Elem sch libn, child serv. 15: 4601 Long rd, bridgeton Mo 63042.

BARDER, BARBARA (HILYER). b Minneapolis. 4: Joseph R Barder. 5: Beaver Col 46-47 (Educ); UPenn 47-50 (Hist, Eng) BS in Ed; Drexel 50-51 MS inLS; Temple 52-53 Tchrs Certif. 6: Fr. 7: Ref libn Free Lib of hila 51-53; High Sch libn US Army Dependent's Sch, mannheim/Rhei 56-62; High sch libn Lansdowne- Aldan High Sch, Lansdowne Penn 62-. 8: Taught Eng to adults in Finland at theFinnish-Amer Soc 53-54; A-v Coord at Mannheim Amer High Sch 56-62, Mannheim, Germany. 9: NEA; PennEA; Del Co SchLA; Del Co Bk Reviewers Assn. 10: Kappa Delta; AAUW. 14: Ref. 15: 4117 Fountain Green, Lafayette Hill Pa 19444.

BARDIN, HENRY JAMES III. b Richmond Va 7 My 34. 5: URichmond 53-56 (Eng) BA; UVa 56-58 (Eng) MA; Pratt 62-64 MLS. 7: Instr UAla 58-60; Brooklyn Pub Lib 62-64; Hd tech proc Pratt Inst Lib 65-. 8: Lect Pratt Inst Grad Sch of Lib

& Info Sci 67-. 10: Beta Phi Mu. 15: 175 Willoughby st, Brooklyn NY 11205.

BAREFOOT, GARY FENTON. b Johnston Co NC 13 My 39. 5: Mt Olive Jr Col 57-59 (Liberal Arts) AA; UNC 59-61 (Eng) AB, summers 61-64 MSLS. 6: Fr. 7: Lib asst UNC(Chapl Hill) 59-61; Libn High Point City schs, High Point NC 61-63; Lib Mt Olive pub Schs, Mt Olive NC 63-65; Catlgr Mt Olive jr Col 64-65, Head Libn 65-. 9: ALA; NCEA (pres Sch Libns West Dist 63-64); NCLA (chm Mem Com Sch Libs Sect 63-65, chm for mem RT 67-69. 10: Phi Delta Kappa; Beta Phi Mu; Phi Theta Kappa. 12: Assoc ed "North Carolina Libraries". 14: Ref, Admin, spec collections. 15: 302 N Church st, Mt Olive NC 28365.

BARETSKI, CHARLES ALLAN. b Mt Carmel Penn 21 N 18. 4: Gladys Yartin. 5: Newark U Rutgers U 39-45 (Humanities) BA;Columbia 45-51 BS in LS, MS in LS; American U 51, 55 Archival Diploma, Advanced Archiv Adm Diploma; U Notre Dame 56-58 (Pol Sci)MA, (Pol Sci) PhD; NYU 59-65 (Govt & Intl Rel) MA, 65-69 (Pol) PhD. 6: Fr, Ger, Ital, Polish, Russian. 7: Newark NJ Pub Lib; Lib asst receiving & pamphlet depts 38-42, Chief of period div 42-43, Sr lib asst art & music dept 43-45,Jr libn 45-46, Sr libn art & music depts & lending ref 47-48, Sr libn art & music dept 48-54, Prin libn br Branch Brook Lib 54, Prin libn br Van Buren Br 54-56, 57-; Research assoc U Notre Dame Grad Sch 56-57. 8: Internship in US National Archives to preparpreliminary inventory in US Dept of State Archives 51; Res consul Charter Reform Movement for Newark City Govt 53-54; Founder &dir Inst of Polish Culture Seton Hall U 53-54; Faculty Pol Sci Dept Rutgers U Col Newark 65-66; Archivist-Histn Amer Coun of PolishCultural Clubs Inc 54-; Participant, Nat Archives Conf on Archives of US For Rel 69. 9: ALA (Jr mem Round Table; Exec Bd 50-53,Pub Rel Chm 50-51, Reg chm, Staff org's RT Steering Com 60-63);-LED (Com mem 50-51); NJLA (chm Educ for Libnship Com 50-51, chmInternat Com to Honor Founding of Newark NJ 65-66). 10: Writers Soc of NJ; Middle States Coun for the Soc Studies; Acad FreedomCom; Polish Amer Unity League; Neighborhood Improvements & Serv Task Force, Model Cities Prog, Commun Devel Admin, Newark; EducNeeds & Sch Requirements Com, Assoc Commun Couns of Newark; Newark Pub Lib Staff Assn. 11: Second Annual Brotherhood Award,Newark City Govt 62; Plaque & Listing, Commun Leaders of Amer 69; Distinguished Achievement Award, The Two Thousand Men ofAchievement, London 69; Clean Govt Award, Clean Govt, Essex Co NJ 62. 12: Asst ed & ed "Polish American Historical Assn Bulletin"(59-65); "The Polish Pantheon; A Roster of Men and Women of Polish Birth or Ancestry who have Contributed to American Culture andWorld Civilization" (58); "Commemorative History of the Polish University Club of New Jersey, 1928-1963" (63); Assoc ed "AmericanCouncil Polish Cultural Clubs Bulletin" (64-65); Ed "The Higher Horizons Educational Program in New York City" (61). 13: Yes. 14: Ref, admin, archival sci. 15: 229 Montclair ave, Newark NJ 07104.

BARGERSTOCK, MARIE D (LONG). b Trenton NJ 24 My 10. 4: Gerald George Bargerstock. 5: RUTGERS 31-38 (Educ) BS Ed; Douglass Col Rutgers U 38-39 BSLS. 6: Fr, Ger. 7: Lib asst Free Pub Lib, Trenton NJ 35-41; Catlgr US Securities & Exch Commsn, Wash DC 41; Chief libn US Naval Hosp, Phila 41-51; Chief libn US Naval Engnr Res Center, Phila 51-60; Chief Lib Serv VA Hosp, Lyons NJ 60-64; Chief Lib Serv VA Hosp, Coatesville Penn 64-66; Hd libn Naval Air Eng Ctr, Phila 66-. 9: SLA; Spec Libs Coun of Philadelphia & Vicinity; Coun of Libns,East Coast Navy Labs. 10: Kappa Delta Pi; Alumni Assn Grad Sch of Lib Serv ofRutgers U. 14: Admin, bibliotherapy. 15: 725C Park View Apts, Collingswood NJ08107.

BARHAM, MARY LEA. b BRENT Okla 17 Ag 33. 5: Okla State U 51-56 (Elem Educ) BS; UOkla summers 58, 62 MLS. 6: Sp. 7: Lib asst Okla State U 51-62; Vetrinary med libn Okla State U 62-63; Readers serve libn Midwestern U 63-65; Asst libn San JacintoCol 65-. 8: Or & estalishd a Govt Doct Depository Dept & a Curr Materials Lb at MIDWESTERN U. 9: Amer Assn Jr Cols; TexLA; SWLA. / Col & univ admin, govt docs, ref, curr materials. 114: Col & univ admin, govt docs, ref, curr materials. 15: 701 Princeton lane,Deer Park Tx 77536.

BARIANI, GERALDINE D(ONNA). b Denver 14 My 15. 5: UDenver 33-36 (Bus) BS in Com, 36-37 BSLS; Ind U 39-41 (Bus) MS. 7: Asst ref & circ dept Northwestern U 37-38; Libn Sch of Bus Ind U 38-62, supv of dept libs 41-43; Ref libn Colo Sch of mines Lib 62-. 9: ALA; SLA; ColoLA; MPLA. 10: Phi Chi Theta. 13: Yes. 14: Ref. 15: #8 Mines Park, Golden Co 80401.

BARIL, (J GEORGES) HUBERT. b Montreal Que 23 Ap 24. 4: Huguette Prescott. 5: Universite de Montreal 59 BA, 62 BLS. 6: Fr. 7: Libn Commsn des Ecoles de Montreal, 49-59; Dir of Libs Serv Commsn des Ecoles de Quebec, 59-61; Libn Ecole secondaire Jean-de-Breeuf, Quebec 61-63; Chief Libn Ecole Cure Antoine-Labelle CSR des Milles-Isles, Sve-Rose (Laval) 63-64; Dir of Sch Libs Serv Commsn Seolaire Reg Duvernay, Laval 64-66; Dir of Sch Libs Serv Commsn Secolaire Reg Lanaudiere, Joliette 66-67; Asst Dir Serv de b'ibliographie Centrale des Bibliotheques, Montreal 67-. 8: Reader on sch libs, the Arts School, Laval (Quebec) 61-63; Sec Comit de direction de la Commission des Directeurs de bibliotheques seolaires de la Federation des Commissions Seolaires Catholiques du Quebec 64-67. 9: Association Canadienne des Bibliothecaires de Langue Francaise (Dep chm Quebec Sect 62-63; chm Sch Libns Dir 66-67); CLA; ALA; QuebecLA. 14: Bk sel, bibliog. 15: Serv de bibliographie Centrale des Biblibtheques, 1940 est, boul Henri-Bourassa, Montreal Que 360.

BARKER, AILEEN MARGARET. b Ft McMurray Alta Can 3 N 43. 5: Mount Allison U 61-64 (Hist) BA; McGill 64-65 BLS. 7: Asst catlgr Prov Lib, Halifax NS 65-66; Bkmob & Br Cape Breton Reg Lib, Baddeck NS 66-67; Catlgr East Counties Reg Lib, Halifax NS 67-. 9: CanLA; Atlantic Provinces LA; HalifxLA. 14: Catlg. 15: 1623 Cambridge st, Halifax NS Can.

BARKER, CATHERINE JANE (WHERRY). b Regina Saskatchewan Can 16 Ja 44. 4: Ian K Barker. 5: Ont Veterinary Col 62-67 (Veterinary Med); UGuelph 67-68 (Gen Sci) BS; UToronto 68-69 BLS. 7: Catlgr UWaterloo 69-. 9: ASIS. 14: Catlg. 15: 62 Cedar st apt 1, guelph Ont Can.

BARKER, DALE L(OCKARD). b Pensacola Fla 18 O 19. 4: Caroline Jones. 5: Ga Inst of Tech 46-49 (Electrical Engnr) BEE; UIll 49-50 (LS) MS, 59-60 (LS) PhD. 7: Tech Sgt US Marine Corps Communications 42-45; Ga Inst of Tech: Acquis libn 50-51, Asst libn in chg of tech processing 51-52, Assoc dir of libs 52-60; UGa Lib Sys analyst 66-69; UMiami Assoc dir of libs 69-. 8: Act dir Southeastern Interlib Research Facility, 56. 9: ALA; SELA; ASIS; FlLA. 10: AAUP; AAAS. 13: Yes. 14: Sci lit, ser, bibliog control, resources, admin. 15: 43- Aragon ave, Coral Gables Fl 33134.

BARKER, LILLIAN (HABER). b NYC 18 Mr 24. 5: Washington Sq Col, NYU 40-44 (Eng) BA; Sch of Lib Serv Columbia 46-47 (LS)BS in LS, Sch of Gen Studies 48. 6: Fr, Ger. 7: Stud asst Washington Sq Col, NYU 44; Educ Serv Off USNR - WR (WAVES) 45-46;Asst Pop Lib Enoch Pratt Free Lib, Baltimore 46-48; Ref libn United Hosp Fund of NY, NYC 48-50; Field libn US Army, Germany50-51; Asst libn West Md Col 61-66; Dir stud ref ctr proj Enoch Pratt Free Lib 66, Br libn 67, Hd County Serv Dept 67-. 9: MdLA; ALA-RSD. 14: Interlib coop systems, ref. 15: 3507 Foxcliffe ct, Randallstown Md 21133.

BARKER, MARJORIE W(HEELER). b Goffstown NH 14 S 14. 5: Goucher Col 32-36 (Fr, Ger) BA; Enoch Pratt Free Lib Train Class 36-37 UMd Sch of Lib and Info Serv (66) MLS. 7: Enoch Pratt Free Lib, Baltimore 36-39; Br libn Laurel Md 63-69; Supt of Adult Serv Nashua (NH) Pub Lib 69-. 9: ALA; MedLA; MdLA. 10: Goucher alumnae Assn; AAUW; Alpha Gamma Delta; Soroptimist; AFS; Md Alum Assn. 15: Nashua Pub Lib, Nashua NH 03060.

BARKER, RICHARD THOMAS. b Mooresville NC 3 O 32 04: Dorothy Barber. 4: Dorothy Barber. 5: Appalachian State Tchrs col 51-55 (Eng) BS, 55-56 (LS) MA; Rutgers 65-66 (LS). 6: Fr. 7: Circ libn Appalachian State Tchrs Col 56; US Army 56-58;Circ libn Appalachian State U 58-63, Asst libn 63-. 9: ALA; SELA; NCLA. 10: AAUP; Phi Delta Kappa; Jr C of C. 14: Admin, ref. 15: Keystone dr, Boone NC 28607.

BARKER, VICTORIA (SIEGFRIED). b Seattle 13 D 09. 4: Gordon Hitchcock Barker. 5: Stanford 27-31 (Eng) AB; UCal 31-32 Certif of Libnship; UColo 48-50 (Anthropology). 6: Fr, Ger. 7: Catlgr Stanford U Lib 32; Head catlg dept Mont State Col Lib 32-36; Head catlg dept UIda Lib 36-37; Head clsf & catlg dept UColo Libs 37-46; Head catlgr Navy Dept Bur of Ordnance Tech Lib, Wash DC 46-48; Libn west hist collection UColo 48-50; Head Libn Boulder Labs Nat Bur of Standards Dept of Com, Boulder Colo 51-64; Lib consul Pierce Col, Athens Greece 64-65; Free Lance Spec Projects 67-68. 9: ALA; SLA; Bibliogl Center for Research (Rocky Mount Reg: pres 61-63, chm Exec Com 60-61); MPLA; ColoLA. 10: Delta Kappa Gamma. 13: Yes. 13: Yes. 14: Admin, catlg, spec libs. 15: 835 8th st, Boulder Co 80302.

BARKEY, PATRICK TERRENCE. b Flint Mich 11 F 22. 4: Mary Ann Schutte. 5: Pomona Col 48 (Eng) BA; UMich 48-49 AMLS. 6: Ger. 7: AOM 3/c US Navy 42-44; A-v libn Flint Pub Lb, Flint Mich 49-57; Head circ dept UNotre Dame(S Bend Ind) 57-60; Head circ dept East Ill U 60-64; Head Libn Tex Col of arts & Ind 64-67; Dir U libs UToledo 67-. 9: ALA; OhioLA. 13: Yes. 14: Admin. 15: 3263 Milstead dr, Toledo Oh 43606.

BARKLEY, KATHERINE (TRAVER). b Troy NY 25 S 14. 4: Robert Barkley. 5: Hood Col 31-35 (Zool) BA; West Res U 58, 63, 64 (LS). 7: Asst to libn John Hay High Sch, Cleveland 56-58; Asst to libn Northtown-Shiloh Br Lib (Dayton, Montgomery Co Pub Lib), Dayton Ohio 58-60; Br libn Vandalia Br 60-64; Med libn Jewish Hosp, Cincinnati 65-. 9: SLA (Cincinnati Br: Program Chm & pres-elect); MedLA (Midwest Reg Br (Program Com & host to Cincinnati Conv 68). 10: AAUW. 14: Ref, hist of med. 15: Jewish Hosp Med Lib, Burnet ave, Cincinnati Oh 45229.

BARKSDALE, MARY M(ORTON). b Randolph Va 12 Ag 11. 5: Randolph-Macon Woman's Col 28-32 (Eng Lit) AB; UVa summers 31, 33;Columbia summers 36-39 BLS; Longwood Col summers 52-53 State Certif for Sch Lib; Temple summer 57 (Comparative educ abroad); UNCsummer 62 (LS). 6: Fr, Ger. 7: Prin Charlotte Co Elem Schs, Charlotte Co Va 32-37; Libn Charlotte Co Pub Lib, Charlotte C H Va37-40; Dist lib supv WPA, Albany Ga, Richmond Va 40-42; Circ, ref Va Polytech 42-43; Analyst US Air Force Intelligence, Wash DC44-45; Ref libn Enoch Pratt Free Lib, Baltimore 45-49; Libn Randolph-Henry High Sch, Charlotte C H Va 51-68; Coord Lib ServDanville (Va) Commun Col 68-. 8: State Bd of Educ Eval Com 54, 65, 67; State Sch Lib Devel Program 61; Org Dist E, VaEA, Schlib assts 62; Instr, lib sci Madison Col 61-62, UVa Ext 62-67. 9: ALA (Loc Recr Rep); NEA; VaLA (pres 54-55); VaEA (Sch LibSect). 10: Va Museum of Fine Arts; Chase City Woman's Club; Nat Travel Club; Assn Preserv Va Antiquities; Delta Kappa Gamma;Amer Red Cross; Internat Rel Com. 13: Yes. 14: Ref, lib educ, recr of libns, tchg. 15: Windemere, Randolph Va 23962.

BARKSDALE, MILTON KENDALL JR. b Richmond Ky 15 S 45. 5: East KyU 63-67 (Math) BS; UKy 67-68 MSLS. 6: Fr, Russian. 7: Chief acquis div Crabbe Lib East Ky U 69-. 9: ALA; KyLA. 10: Beta Phi Mu. 14: Lib automation, info sci, acquis. 15: 103 Bristol dr, Richmond Ky 40475.

BARKSDALE, MRS ROBBIE A(NDREWS). b Ozark Ala 8 Ag 05. 4: Jelks Barksdale. 5: Alabama Col 22-26 (Fr) BA; Columbia 30-31 (LS) BS, 36-40, 58 (LS) MS. 6: Fr, Sp, Ger. 7: Tchr-libn Thomasville High Sch, Thomasville Ala 26-38; Tchr-libn Franklin Co High Sch, Russellville Ala 28-30; Reviser Columbia U Sch Lib Serv 30-31, Head reviser 31-35, 36-38; Catlgr Brown U 35-36; Assoc Columbia U Sch Lib Serv 36-40; Ed asst19th Cent Readers Guide H W Wilson Co, NYC 40-42; Order libn Auburn U 48-51, Ser libn 51-52; Libn Lee-Tallapoosa Reg Lib,Dadeville Ala 52-54; Ser catlgr Auburn U 54-, Instr 61-65, Asst prof 65-. 9: ALA; AlaLA (mem var coms; Col, Univ & Spec Libs Div: chm 63-64, pres 65-66); SELA; NY Reg Catlg Group. 10: Kappa Delta Pi; Delta Kappa Gamma; AAUW; DAR; Friends of Hollifield Mem Lib; City Cemeteries Bd; Auburn Univ Faculty Coun; Woman's Club; PTA. 14: Catlg. 15: 610 Meadowbrook dr, Auburn Al 36830.

BARLOW, BARBARA JEAN (PAIGE). b Concord NH 21 Mr 28. 4: Edward James Barlow. 5: UBridgeport 46-50 (Math) BA; Drexel 52-53, 56-57 MS in LS; San Jose State Col 67, 68, 69 Cal State Standard Secondary Credential. 6: Sp. 7: Lib asst spec serv, Fort Monmouth NJ 51-52; Lib asst spec serv, Fort Dix NJ 52-53; Hosp libn spec serv, Okinawa 53-56; Libn spec serv, Poitiers France 57-59; Tech libn, Ft Huachuca Ariz 59-61; Ref libn, Ampex Corp Redwood City Cal 61-69; Sch libn Ravenswood High Sch, E Palo Alto Cal 69-. 9: SLA; NEA. 10: Amer Math Soc. 14: Ref. 15: 1533 Orillia ct, Sunnyvale Ca 94087.

BARLUP, JANET E (CASSEL). b Lancaster Penn 6 F 35. 4: James Barlup. 5: Sacramento state Col 63-65 (Math) BA; UWash 66-67 (Libnship) MLib; WashU (St Louis) 67-68 certificate in Compter/Libnship. 7: Statistical methods analyst State of Cal, Sacramento 65-66; Communications specialist Health Sci Lib UWash 68-. 9: MedLA. 14: Lib automation. 15: 411 N 44th st, Seattle Wa 98103.

BARNARD, A(LFRED) J(AMES) R. b Can 5 Ja 20. 4: Frances Longacre. 5: Tufts Col 39-42 BS in Chem (magna cum laude); Harvard 42-44 (Chem) MA; Lehigh U 48-50 (Chem) PhD. 6: Ger, Fr. 7: Austin Tchg Fellow in Chem Harvard U 42-44; Jr chem Godfrey L Cabot Co, Boston 42-43; Med dept US Army 44-46; Research Div J T Baker Chem Co, Phillipsbrg NJ 46-48; Lit consul 48-50; Assoc W F Greenwald & M G Mulinos MD Consuls, NYC 50-51; Dir tech info J T Baker chem Co, Phillipsburg NJ 51-67, Mgr tech info serv 67-68, Mgr research analytical & info serv 68-. 8: Adv bd "Microchemical Journal" 62-; gen sec, Internat Symposia on Microchemical Techniques, 61 & 65; Lecturer, summer Insts for Col Tchg, 62-64. 9: Amer Microchem Soc (Bd Dirs 64-65); ACS (sec Lehigh Valley Sect 58, co-chm for anal chem, Middle Atlantic Reg Mtg 66; Chem Notation Assn; Soc Applied Spectroscopy; SLA. 10: Phi Beta Kappa. 12: Ed "Chemist-Analyst" (51-67) Co-ed "Chelates in Analytical Chemistry" 3v (67-70) Co-author "Quantitative Analytical Chemistry" 2v (69). 13: Yes. 14: Lit of analyt chem, mgt of chem info, chem structure notation. 15: J T Baker Chem Co., N Broad st, Phillipsburg, NJ 08865.

BARNARD, MRS JEAN LYNN. b Tiffin Ohio 24 O 18. 5: UMich 36-40 AB, 49-51 AMLS. 6: Ger. 7: Auditor's asst Sylvestre Oil Co, Mt Vernon NY 40; IBM operator, Mich 40-41; File clerk USES, Pensacola Fla 41; Clerk ship serv dept 41-42; bkkeeper West Side Distrib Co, Ann Arbor Mich 43; Payroll clerk King- seeley Corp 44-45; Stack asst Mich 49-50; Print catlgr Clements Lib, Mich 51; Asst catlgr Miami U (Oxford Ohio) 51-54; Catlg libn I, II, III UMich 54-60, Head spec proj unit 60-66, Tech serv libn IIIB 66-. 9: ALA; MichLA. 12: Ed "Library Notes," UMich Lib Staff Assn (64-65). 14: Catlg. 15: 522 W Stadium blvd, Ann Arbor Mi 48103.

BARNEBURG, FREDDY LOUISE (BUCHANAN). b Tyler Tex 3 S 38. 4: Kenneth Frederick Barneburg. 5: Marylhurst Col 56-60 (Elem Educ) BS in Ed; UDenver summer 62, 62-63 MA in LS. 7: Tchr Portland Pub Schs, Portland Ore 60-62; Child libn Lib Assn of Portland, Portland Ore 63-64; Polk Co Lib Spec (Ore) 66-68; Asst prof libnship UOre summer 68; Dist lib supv Douglas Co Sch Dist #116, Dillard Ore 68. 8: Instr div continuing educ Ore State Syst Higher Educ 65-; Consul Random House 67-; Regular story hours tv & radio. 9: OreEA; OreASchL (chm Nomin Com 68); PNLA; IRA; ALA (Subscription Bks Bulletin Com 68-69); NEA-DAVI; NAEB; OIMA. 10: AAUW; Nat Storytelling League; Alpha Delta Kappa. 12: Guest ed "The byron Bugle (Ja 67, Ja 69). 14: Wk with prim child, train tchrs for libnship. 15: 515 W Ballf, Roseburg Or 97470.

BARNES, CHRISTOPHER R. b NYC 10 D 36. 4: Katharine Kephart. 5: Miami U 55-56 (Bus); Colo Col 56-60 (Eng) AB; UMich 60-62 AMLS. 7: Asst libn Engring Lib Cornell U 61-62, Asst libn Undergrad Lib 62-66; Hd libn Keene State Col 66-. 9: NELA; NHLA; NHColLibns. 10: MENSA. 13: Yes. 15: Upper Troy rd, Fitzwilliam NH 03447.

BARNES, CLARENCE. b Waycross Ga. 5: Savannah State Col 66 (Eng) BS; Atlanta U 67 (LS) MSLS. 6: Fr. 7: US Army Med Corp, 59-61; Asst ref libn Morgan State Col 67-69. 9: ALA. 14: Ref. 15: Morgan State Col, Baltimore Md 21212.

BARNES, CONSTANCE INGALLS. b Atchison Kan 30 Jl 03. 4: Russell Barnes. 5: UKan 22-25 (Fr) BA; UMich 50 (Fr) MA, 55 MLS. 6: Fr, Russian. 7: Libn Cranbrook Acad of Art, Bloomfield Hills Mich 55-. 9: OklaLA. 10: LWV; Planned Parenthood. 15: Lib, Cranbrook Acad of Art, Bloomfield Hills Mi 48013.

BARNES, ELIZABETH (RAUGHLEY). b New Florence Penn 22 Jy 15. 4: Russell Bates Barnes. 5: Penn State 33-37 (Eng lit) BA, (Cert in Sec ed); Pratt 37-38 (LS Cert). 6: Fr. 7: Asst libn Pop Lib Enoch Pratt Free Lib, Baltimore 38-40; 1st Asst NEA Hdqs Lib, Washington DC 40-42; Asst in Eng, salvage & reclamation div DuPont Co, Wilmington Del 42-43; Asst Libn Garden City Lib, Garden City NY 52-53; Catlg libn Hofstra U L, 54-59. Hd catlg libn, 59-. 9: ALA; NYLA (sec-treas Resources & Tech Serv Sect 68-); Nassau Co LA; NY Tech Serv Libns. 10: Hofstra Univ Fac Women's Club. 14: Catlg, personnel training & mgt. 15: 44 Martin ave, Hempstead NY 11550.

BARNES, EUGENE BURDETTE. b Minneapolis 27 N 17 04: Katherine Jett. 5: UMinn 37-41 (Hist) BA, 41-43 (Hist) MA, 41-43 (LS) Certif; Chicago 45-47 (LS) PhD. 6: Fr, Ger, Russ, Sp. 7: Catlg libn UCLA 43-45; Head acquis libn UOre 47-. 9: SAA; Far West Slavic Confer. 10: AAUP. 12: Jr ed "La Geste de Monglanne" (66). 13: Yes. 14: Acquis. 15: Univ of Oregon Library, Eugene Or 97403.

BARNES, FRANCES (KERR). b Lexington Ky. 4: A Edward Barnes. 5: UKy 32-36 (Eng) BA; UTex summers 59-66 MLS. 7:

Asst child libn Abilene Pub Lib, Abilene Tex 57-60, Ya libn 60-61; Asst libn Cooper High Sch, Abilene Tex 61-66, Libn 66-. 9: ALA; TexLA. 15: 1233 Washington blvd, Abilene Tx 79601.

BARNES, KATHARINE (DAY). b Beirut Lebanon 15 Ja 05. 4: Gerald Barnes. 5: Vassar 27 (Eng) AB; Simmons 62 (LS) MS. 6: Fr. 7: Eng tchr Medfield High Sch, Medfield Mass 54-55; Lib asst Wayland Pub Lib, Wayland Mass 55-56; Lib asst Morse InstLib, Natick Mass 56-60; Ref libn Mary Reed Lib UDenver 62-64; Spec collections libn Denver Pub Lib 64-. 9: ALA; ColoLA; MPLA;SLA. 10: Phi Beta Kappa. 14: Ref, rare bks, aeronautics. 15: 2010 S Fillmore st, Denver Co 80210.

BARNES, MARJORIE. b Chattahoochee Fla 25 S 18 05: Col of William & Mary 36-40 Hist) BA; Fla State U 63 (LS) BS. 7: Communications off WAVES (Lt) 43-46; Sec Keen, O'Kelley & Spitz Attorneys at Law, Tallahassee Fla 46-53; Ref libn Air U Lib Maxwell AF Base, Montgomery Ala 65-. 10: Beta Phi Mu. 14: Ref. 15: Route 2 Box 416A, Millbrook Al 56054.

BARNES, MARY W(INIFRED). b Richland Center Wis 2 Mr 08. 5: Lawrence Col 26-30 (Lat) BA; UIll 31-32 BS in LS, summers 57, 58, 61, 62 MS. 7: Catlgr Pub Lib, Columbia Mo 36-38; Catlgr Pub Lib, Eau Claire Wis 38; Catlgr Karrmann Lib State U Wis (Platteville) 39-, Hd tech serv 67-. 9: ALA; NEA; WisEA; WisLA. 10: Monday Evening Club; Alpha Delta Kappa; AAUW (sec 67-). 14: Catlg. 15: 480 W Pine st, Platteville Wi 53818.

BARNES, MILDRED E(MILY). b Far Rockaway NY 25 Mr 13. 5: Vassar 29-33 (Comparative Religion) AB; Chicago 33-36 (Comparative Religion) MA; Columbia 36-38 BS in LS. 6: Fr. 7: Libn Biblical Sem in NY, NYC 36-38; Catlgr Rutgers U Lib 38-40; Ref asst catlgr Soc Security Bd Lib, Wash DC 41-42; Asst libn & head catlgr Fed Pub Housing Authority Lib, Wash DC 42-47; Head catlgr USAEC Lib, Wash DC 47-57; Act chief catlg sect NIH Lib, Bethesda Md 58-63; Chief catlg serv br Dept Lib US Dept of the Interior, Wash DC 63-. 9: SLA; Potomac Tech Proc Libns. 12: "Housing and Planning Classification" (45); "QCD, a Preliminary Classification for Nuclear Science and Technology" (58). 14: Catlg, clsf, subject headings & clsf devel. 15: 2807 Connecticut ave NW, Wash DC 20008.

BARNES, NANCY (STEFFEN). b Hubbard Ore 2 O 42. 4: Richard B Barnes. 5: Mt Angel Col 60-64 (Eng) BA; UWashington Lib Sch 64-65 (Libnship) M in Libnship. 6: Fr, Sp. 7: Asst readers serv libn UAlaska Lib, College Alaska 65-7; Ext libn Nez Perce Co Free Lib, Lewiston Idaho 67-68; Libn Lewiston Carnegie Lib, Lewiston Idaho 68-. 9: ALA; PNLA; IdahoLA (sec Pub Lib Div). 10: Beta Phi Mu. 14: Geneal, readers serv. 15: Lewiston Carnegie Lib Pioneer Park, Lewiston Id 83501.

BARNES, NORMA A (BOLLHOEFER). b 23 Ap 20. 5: U N Iowa 37-41 (Eng, Speech) BA; UTulsa 54-57 (Eng, Educ) MTA; UOkla 64-67 (LS) MLS; Okla State U summer 68 (LS). 6: Ger. 7: Tchr Iowa Falls Pub Sch, Iowa Falls Iowa 41-44; Tchr-libn Tippecanoe Twp Sch, Tippecanoe Ind 45-46; Tchr Plymouth Pub Schs, Plymouth Ind 46-52; Tchr dept chm Tulsa Pub Sch, Tulsa Okla 53-64, Libn E Central High Sch 64-. 8: Spec Instr in Lib Sci UOkla 69; Mem eval teams No Central Assn of Sec Schs & Cols. 9: ALA; -LAD-LOMS (Statistics Com for Sch Libs); NEA; OklaLA (Com on Recr, Intel Freedom Com); OklaEA. 10: Beta Phi Mu; Delta Kappa Gamma; Kappa Delta Pi. 13: Yes. 14: Ya reading guidance. 15: PO Box 3701, Tulsa Ok 74152.

BARNES, ROBERT W. b Rochester NY 21 Ap 27. 4: Ethel M O'Connor. 5: U Rochester 47-51 (Eng) BS; Syracuse 52-53 (LS) MS. 7: Rochester Pub Lib, Rochester NY: Ref asst 53, Sci ref asst 54-56, A-v asst Reynolds AV Dept 58-60, Dir Reynolds AV Dept 61-. 15: Reynolds AV Dept Rochester Pub Lib, 115 South ave, Rochester NY 14604.

BARNES, RUSSELL FRANKLIN. b Dayton Ohio 28 My 12. 4: Dorothy Henderson. 5: Miami U (Oxford Ohio) 35 (Econ) BA; Columbia 38 BLS, 43 MLS. 7: Clerical asst Dayton Pub Lib, Dayton Ohio 35-36; Jr asst NYU 38-43; Armed Forces staff sgt AGD US Army 43-46; Libn Minn Hist Soc, St Paul 46-49; Libn James Jerome Hill Ref Lib, St Paul 49-. 9: SLA-Minn Chap (pres). 14: Ref, info sci. 15: Hill Ref Lib 4th st & Market st, St Paul Mn 55102.

BARNES, MRS SHIRLEY (HARDIN). b Tupelo Miss 19 N 23. 5: UKy 42,45-47 (LS) BA. 6: Fr. 7: Libn High sch, Irvine Ky 47-48; Pub Lib, Winchester Ky: Child libn 50-51, Catlgr 52-53, Sub 54-55, Bkmob driver 57-58; Libn Southeastern Christian Col 59-. 9: ALA; KyLA (Jr Col Libns Group). 10: PTA. 15: 51 Meadowbrook, Winchester Ky 40391.

BARNETT, GOLDIE ELLEN. b Enterprise Okla 22 Ja 05. 5: UTulsa 25-29 (Eng) BA; UOkla (LS) BA. 6: Fr. 7: Libn Norman Pub Lib, Norman Okla 30-60; Libn Seminole Pub Lib, Seminole Okla 60-. 9: OklaLA. 10: AAUW. 12: Article on Norman, Okla in "Collier's Encyclopedia" (58); Article on Seminole, Okla in "Encyclopedia Americana" (63). 14: Catlg, ref, readrs adv, bk sel. 15: 410-1/2 Highland, Seminole Ok 74868.

BARNETT, HELEN (KLAYMAN). b Middletown Ohio 28 Ja 27. 4: Nathan Barnett. 5: UCincinnati 44-48 (Sociol) BA; Rutgers 59-61 MLS. 7: Sr libn Linden Pub Lib, Linden NJ 62-63; Sch libn Piscataway Twp Bd Educ, Piscataway Twp NJ 64-65; Asst libn Town of Mt Royal Lib, Town Mt Royal Que 65-67; Libn Del Tech & Comm Col 68-. 8: DelLA. 10: Phi Beta Kappa. 15: 11 Clermont rd, Wilmington De 19803.

BARNETT, JACQUELINE (GERTRUDE). b Houston 10 Ja 43. 5: Sam Houston State 61-64 (Hist, Ed, LS) BS; Tex A & M U 64-65,67-68; LSU 65-67 (LS) MS. 6: Russian, Czech. 7: Stud asst Sam Houston State Lib 61-64; Carnegie Pub Lib, Bryan Tex; Lib asstsummers 62 & 63, Bkmob libn summer 64; Tex A & M U Lib; Asst ref dept 64-65, Asst libn basic div 67-; Trainee LSU Lib 65-67. 9: ALA; TexLA. 14: Ref. 15: 403-D Cross, Col Sta Tx 77840.

BARNETT, JEAN (DRABBE). b Monroe Mich 10 Je 45. 4: Baron Gale Barnett. 5: UPittsburgh 62-65 (Eng) BA, 65-66 (LS) MLS; UCal 67- (Eng). 6: Fr. 7: Stud asst UPittsburgh Lib 63-66; Asst ref libn UCal (Riverside) 66-68; Humanities Catlgr 68-69. 9: ALA; CalLA. 10: Beta Phi Mu; AAUP. 12: Ed "Hue and Cry" UCal (Riverside Lib) 68-69. 14: Catlg, ref (humanities). 15: U of Cal Lib, Riverside Ca 92507.

BARNETT, MRS JUANITA (McMILLAN). b Hope Ark 3 My 15. 4: Dr. James Russell Barnett. 5: Ouachita Baptist Col 32-36 (Eng) AB; Peabody 36-37 BS in LS. 7: Libn Ouachita Baptist Col 36-40; Sec First Presbyterian Church, Arkadelphia Ark 55-56; Libn Ouachita Baptist U 56-. 9: ALA; ArkLA (var offs in Col Sect 58-69). 10: Woman's Lib Assn Arkadelphia Ark. 12: Ed "Periodical holdings in the Arkansas Foundation of Associated Colleges" (rev ed 63). 14: Catlg, ref. 15: 610 Pine st, Arkadelphia Ar 71923.

BARNETT, JUDITH (BRODKIN). b NYC. 4: Stanley M Barnett. 5: Barnard 55-59 Hist) AB; Drexel 61-62 MS in LS. 6: Fr, Sp, Swedish. 7: Lib asst Marine Hist Assn, Mystic Conn 59-60; Libn I ref Free Lib of Phila 62-63; Sr libn ref Newark Pub Lib, Newark NJ 63-64; sr Catlgr Temple U Lib 65-. 9: ALA. 10: Phi Beta Kappa; Beta Phi Mu. 14: Catlg. 15: 3900 Ford rd, apt 17B, Phila Pa 19131.

BARNETT, MARY G (HARRISON). b Toronto. 5: Toronto 35-39 (Eng, Hist) BA, 40-41 BLS. 6: Fr. 7: Staff UToronto Lib 41-43; Lt Women's Royal Can Naval Serv (WRCNS) in Naval Intelligence 43-45; Asst libn Berkeley Divinity Sch(New Haven Conn) 45-48; Asst libn Wycliffe Col (Toronto) 52-55; Libn UToronto 56-60; Asst libn Anglican Theol Col(Vancouver BC) 60-64; Libn (Class 2) circ dept UToronto Lib 64-. 9: CanLA; (Inst of Prof Libns Ontario). 14: Bk sel, pub serv dept. 15: Apt 402 36 Castle Frank rd, Toronto 5 Canada.

BARNETT, MRS MARY (NORWOOD). b Goldsboro NC 30 Ja 26. 4: Douglas Allen Barnett. 5: Salem Col (Winston- Salem NC) 44-46 (Span Lit); George Washington U 46-48 (Span Lit) BA; UNC 55-57 MS in LS. 6: Sp, Fr. 7: Sec Off of the Pres George Washington U 48-52; Sec Sen Richard B Russell Campaign Hdqrs Wash DC 52; Off Manager & sec to Dir Albert Coates Inst of Gov Chapel Hill NC 52-54; Sec to Asst Dean UNC Med Sch, Chapel Hill NC 54-55; Asst libn Greensboro Pub Lib, Greensboro NC 57-59, Head ext dept 59-60; Catlgr Mt Olive NC 63-64; Asst catlg libn UNC (Greensboro) 65; Head libn Morganton-Burke Pub Lib, Morganton NC 65-. 8: NCLA (Personnel Manual Com 58-59). 10: NCLA; Greensboro (NC) Lib Club; Burke Libns Club (program chm); AAUW; mem xhm of Morganton NC Chap. 14: Catlg, personnel admin. 15: Morganton-Burke Pub Lib, Morganton NC 28655.

BARNHART, JANET HOOVEN. b Norristown Penn 21 D 38. 5: UIda 57-58 (Educ); Kan State Tchrs Col(Emporia) 58-62 (Pol Sci, LS) BA; UIda 64- (Pol Sci). 7: Stud lib asst Col Lib Kan State Tchrs Col 58-62; Catlg Enoch Pratt Free Lib,Baltimore 62-63; Head Libn Co Lib, Moscow Ida 63-64; Libn VA Hosp, Ft Lyon Colo64-65; Libn VA Hosp, Lyons NJ 65-67; Libn VA Hosp, Coatesville Penn 67-68; Adminlibn

USAF, Iraklion Crete 68-. 9: ALA; PennLA; USAEE (Lib div). 14: Catlg. 15: Box 84469 31st Security Group, APO NY 09291.

BARNUM, JOYCE LILLIAN (RADER). b Seattle 28 F 27. 4: Walter Keith Barnum. 5: UWash 43-47 (Eng0 ba& colgate Rochester Divinity Sch 47-48; Eastman Sch of Music 47-48; UWash 61-64 (LS) ML. 6: Fr. 7: Ref libn UWash Lib 64-. 9: ALA; PNLA. 10: Beta Phi Mu; Mu Phi Epsilon; Cellist, Cascade Symphony. 14: Ref. 15: 16920 26th ave NE, Seattle Wa 98155.

BAROCO, JOHN VINCENT. b Pensacola Fla 10 Ap 28. 5; UMiami(Fla) 49-51 (Hist) BA; Mex CityXXX05: UMiami (Fla) 49-51 (Hist) BA; Mex City Col (Mex) 51, 54-55; Fla State U 52-53 (LS) MA; Chicago 55-60 (Anthropology). 6: Sp, Fr. 7: US Navy 45-46; Lib Dir Mex City Col(Mex) 54-55; Asst acquis libn UMiami(Fla) 56; Admin asst UChicago Libs 56-57; Research grants UChicago Anthropology Dept 57-58; Research grant Pan American Union Fellowship, Guatemala-Mexico 59; Research asst UChicago Anthropology Dept 60; Lib Dir UNESCO-CREFAL, Patzcuaro Mex 61-62; Museum Libn Ariz State Museum, Tucson 64-. 8: Consul Lib Use Study, UChicago Lib 60. 9: ALA; ArizStateLA. 14: Admin, lib serv to bi-cultural commun, lib devel in Latin Amer. 15: 4005 N Stone ave, Tucson AZ 85705.

BARON, CLAIRE (LIBRESCOT). b Phila 3 O 12. 4: Murray Baron. 5: Hunter Col 28-32 (Eng) BA; Columbia 32-34 (Eng) MA, 37 MSL, (Afri Hist); UColo 58 (LS). 6: Fr. 7: Personal libn to Gov Herbert H Lehman 34-36; Libn Walton High Sch, NYC 38-42; Eng tchr, NYC various 38-42; Libn Milton Sch, Rye NY 58-. 8: Lib/ USA, NY World's Fair 65. 9: ALA; NY State LA; Westchester LA; NEA; NY State TA. 10: World Federalists; For Policy Assn; Freedom House; Metro Museum of Art, etc. 13: Yes. 14: Tchg lib skills to yp, reading & soc studies curr. 15: Milton Harbor House, Rye NY 10580.

BARON, HERMAN. b Phila Pa 23 D 41. 5: Drexel 59-64 (Finance) BS in Bus Admin, 65-66 MS in LS; UIowa 66-67 (Bus). 7: Contract auditor US Defense Contract Audit Agcy, Phila 65-66; Docs Libn UIowa Libs (Iowa City) 66-67; Mgr Journal Serv Inst for Sci Info (Phila) 67-. 9: ALA; SLA; ASIS; PennLA. 14: Ser, automation, internat, rel. 15: ISI 325 Chestnut st, Phila Pa 19106.

BARON, MICHAEL S. b Springfield Mass 15 Je 43. 5: AIC 61-65 (Hist) BA; Cath U of Am 65-66 (LS) MSLS. 7: Ref asst Washington DC Pub Lib, 65-66; Ref asst City Lib, Springfield Mass 66-67; Ref circ libn AIC. 67-68; Coord ref serv West Mass Reg Lib Sys, Springfield Mass 68-. 9: ALA; West Mass Lib Club. 14: Reference, interlib loan, in-serv training. 15: 263 School st, Chicopee Ma 01013.

BARR, MARGARETTA JEAN. b New Wilmington Penn 13 d 09. 5: UNM 32 (Eng) AB; Emory 34 ABLS. 7: Asst libn Pub Lib, Santa Fe NM 35-40; Asst libn Westminster Col (New Wilmington Penn) 40-42; Libn Eavenson Alfred & Auchmuty, Pittsburgh 42-43; Libn Army Post Lib, Ft Eustis Va 43; Libn Army Post Lib, Camp ReynoldsPenn 43-44; Chief Libn Army Gen Hosp, Martinsburg WVa 4 Asst chief lib div VA Br Off, Phila 47-49; Post Libn Post Lib, Ft Monmouth NJ 49-53; Dir Pub Lib, Princeton NJ 53-64; Dir Pub Lib, Nutley NJ 64-65 Admin asst, Lucas Co Pub Lib, Maumee Ohio 68; Admin asst Toledo Pub Lib, Toledo Ohio 69-. 9: ALA OhioLA. 14: Pub lib admin, personnel. 15: 3217 Glanzman rd, apt 73-H, Toledo Oh 43614.

BARRETT, ANN (DOBSON). b Lincoln Neb 13 F 42. 4: Olin Barrett. 5: Stanford 59-63 (Hist) BA; UTex 64-66 MLA. 6: Ital, Fr. 7: Lib internship Yale U Lib 66; Period & gov docs libn Humanities & Soc Sci Lib Cal Tech Lib 67-. 13: Yes. 14: Ref with periods, gov docs. 15: 815 S Euclid, Pasadena Ca 91106.

BARRETT, ARLINE (RIEDESEL). b Rochester NY 19 Ja 24. 4: Robert W Barrett. 5: SUNY (Geneseo) 41-45 (LS) BS; URochester 47-50. 6: Ger, Fr. 7: Libn East Aurora Elem Sch, East Aurora NY 45-47; Asst libn Kodak Park Research Lib, Rochester NY 47-50; Libn Kodak Park Photographic Tech Lib, Rochester NY 50-. 9: SLA-Upstate NY Chap (pres 64-65). 10: Kappa Delta Pi. 15: 200 Coolidge rd, Rochester NY 14622.

BARRETT, DONALD J. b St Paul Minn 30 S 27. 4: June Clay. 5: Col of St Thomas-St Paul 45-46, 47-50 (Chem) BS; UMinn 50-53 (LS) MA. 7: Lib clk St Paul Pub Lib 43-45; Col St Thomas, St Paul: Lib clk 45-46 & 47-50, Ref libn 50-54; Clk typist US Army 46-47; Libn Electronic Supply Off, Great Lakes Ill 54-55; USAF Acad Lib: Chief ref br 55-59, Chief pub serv div 59-. 9: ColoLA. 10: Air Force Assn. 14: Ref, pub serv, admin. 15: 2110 Afton way, Colorado Springs Co 80909.

BARRETT, LENNA MAE (McMILLEN). b Okemah Okla 7 D 33. 4: Joe C Barrett. 5: Ok State U 52-55; Northeast State Col 65-67 (Elem educ & LS) BS in Educ. 7: Libn Pryor High Sch, Pryor Okla 67-. 9: ALA; NEA; OklaLA; OklaEA. 10: Assn of Clrm Tchrs; Kappa Kappa Iota Sor. 14: Sch libn. 15: 12 Payne, Pryor Ok 74361.

BARRETT, MARGUERITE E. b Denver 9 Ap 10. 5: UDenver 40-44 (Educ) BA; UDenver 44-45 BLS. 7: Asst ref libn Pub Lib, W Hartford Conn 54-59; Ref libn Hollins Col 59; Chief Libn Pub Lib, Chanute Kan 59-62; Asst ref libn Pub Lib, Lorain Ohio 62-69; Col libn East Iowa Commun Col 69-. 8: Great Books Leader, 52-65. 9: CathLA; KanLA (Coun 59-62). 10: Ladies Auxiliary, Brotherhood ofRailroad Trainmen; AAUW; Bus & Prof Women. 14: Admin, ref, rare bks. 15: 713 S Seventh ave, Clinton Ia.

BARRETT, MARY I. b Wilkes-Barre Penn 30 Jl 10. 5: Marywood Col 27-31 (LS, Eng) AB; Penn State U 32-33 (Eng). 6: Fr. 7: Libn Harter High Sch, W Nanticoke Penn 31-34; Prin lib asst State Lib, Harrisburg Penn 35-40; Genealogical research, Wilkes-Barre Penn 40-42; Post libn & chief catlgr Post Lib, Ft Monmouth NJ 42-47; Libn Col of St Elizabeth 47-49; Libn King's Col(Wilkes-Barre Penn) 49-. 8: Com which prepared "Report on Personnel Administration in New Jersey Libraries," publ 49; Subcom on Lib serv in Penn Survey 58; Dir Northeast Penn Union Catlg. 9: ALA-ACRL; PennLA (Coun Rep to ALA 64-68, chm Awards Com 61,62, chm Friends of Lib Com 55, chm Mem Com 56); Northeast PennLA (pres 2 terms). 11: Pope Pius XII Award for Libnship, Marywood Col 46. 13: Yes. 14: Admin, coop. 15: 56 W North st, Wilkes-Barre Pa 18702.

BARRETT, MILDRED (ECKERT). b Cleveland Ohio 12 Mr 12. 4: Richard L Barrett. 5: West Res 42 AB, 42 BSLS, 58 MSLS. 7: Jr asst Cleveland Pub Lib 42-43; Asst libn Case Inst of Tech 43-45; Ref & circ libn NM StateU 45-60; Pub serv libn 60-65; Asst libn 65-. 9: ALA; SLA (pres Rio Grande Chap 61-62); NMLA (pres 67-68); NM Lib Devel Coun. 10: AAUP; AAUW. 14: Ref. 15: 455 El Prado, Las Cruces NM 8801.

BARRETT, MONTGOMERY BRINTON. b Phila 16 Ag 13. 5: UPenn 31-35 (Hist) AB; Institut universitaire de Hautes Etudes Internationales(Geneva) 35-37 (Internat Rel) Diplome; UPenn 38-40 (Educ) MS in Ed; Drexel 39-40 BS in LS. 6: Fr, Lat, Ital, Sp. 7: Asst libn The Cooper Union for the Advancement of Sci & Art, NYC 40-43; Asst libn The Lawrenceville Sch, Lawrenceville NJ 43-47; Libn Bloomfield Col & Sem 47-51; Chief ref libn USIS Paris Info Center 51-54; Co-owner, manager The New Yorker Bkshop, NYC 55-59; Chief tech processes The Smithtown Lib, Smithtown NY 57-. 9: ALA; Suffolk Co LA (chm Direc com 64). 10: Civil Serv Employees Assn (NY State). 11: Fellowship, 36-37 granted by the Institut universitaire de Hautes Etudes Internationales, Geneva. 12: Ed "The School Library Journal," NJLA (46-50). 14: Tech serv, labor rel. 15: 7 Fordham dr, Smithtown LI NY 11787.

BARRETTE, ELISE (DRAPER). b Gainesboro Tenn 21 Jl 12. 4: Paul Barrette. 5: Tenn Polytech Inst 27-31 (Eng) BS; Peabody summers 33-37 BS in LS, 39-44 (LS) MA; Chicago summers 44 (LS). 6: Fr, Sp. 7: Libn & tchr Central High Sch, Gainesboro Tenn 31-37; Libn David Lipscomb Col 37-42; Libn Shorter Col 42-46; Dir Lib Educ E Tenn State U 46-. 9: ALA; SELA; TennLA. 10: Kappa Delta Pi; Phi Gamm Mu. 13: Yes. 14: Lib educ. 15: East Tenn State Univ, Johnson City Tn 37601.

BARRON, ASSUNTA (MANTI). b Dolgeville NY 11 Je 30. 5: Geneseo State Tchrs Col 48-52 (LS) BS; Syracuse 59-62 (LS) MS. 6: Ital. 7: Child libn Caniteo Central Sch, Canisteo NY 52-53; Child Libn J Prendergast Lib, Jamestown NY 53-54; Child Libn Annapolis Pub Lib, Annapolis MD 54-57; Head libn Herkimer Free Lib, Herkimer NY 61-67; High Sch Libn Frankfort Schuyler Central Sch, Frankfort NY 67-. 9: NY State TA. 10: AAUW; Beta Phi Mu. 14: Admin. 15: 39 Dolge ave, Dolgeville NY 13329.

BARRON, LYNN (TAYLOR SMITH). b Greenwood SC 16 My 44. 4: Porter Gable Barron. 5: Mary Baldwin Col 62-63; USoCar 63-66 (Eng) AB; UNC 66-67 (LS) MS in LS. 6: Fr. 7: Child dept asst Richland Co Pub Lib, Columbia SC 66; Asst ref libn USoCar 67-. 9: SELA; SCLA. 10: Jr League; Beta Phi Mu. 13: Yes. 14: Ref. 15: 1831 Green st, Columbia SC 29201.

BARRON, ROBERT EDWARD. b Woodhaven NY 25 Mr 30. 4: Joan Helen Roeder. 5: State of NY (Albany) 48-52 (Hist) BA, 52-53 (LS) MSLS, 69; Columbia Tchrs Col summer 61; State U of NY (New Paltz) 61-62, 63-64; NYU 65. 6: Sp, Lat. 7: Pub rel spe US Army, 53-56; Asst Dir Armed forces Info Sch Lib, Ft Slocum 53-55; Pub rel dir USFA Area Com, Salzburg Austria 55; Hd of adj Gen files sect, Ft Dix NJ 55-56; Ref dept Trenton Free Lib, Trenton NJ 55-56; Dir N Castle Free Lib, Armonk NY 56-59; Libn White Plains High Sch Libs, White Plains NY 59-66; Ref dept New Rochelle Pub Lib, New Rochelle NY 60-66; Sch pub lib liaison Div of Lib Dev, NY State Lib, State Educ Dept 66-. 8: Nat Lib Week Com, NY 67-. 9: ALA-AASchL; NEA-DAVI; NYLA; NY State Tchrs Assn; NY State Educ Communic Assn; Eastern Sch Libns; Hudson-Mohawk LA; NY Lib Club; Sch Libns of So-east NY (pres 64-66) 64-66. 10: Kappa Phi Kappa; Pi Gamma Mu. 12: "Bibliographic Guide for Advanced Placement-Latin" (65); "Towards a Common Goal" (68); "Proceedings of the Conference on School-Public Library Relations" (68). 14: Serv to students, catlg, ref, admin. 15: 17 Rural pl, Delmar NY 12054.

BARRON, TILTON MARSHALL. b Phillipsburg Kan 19 Ja 16. 4: Sue Clark. 5: Colo Col 33-37 (Pol Sci) AB; Columbia 38-40 BLS, 47-48 (LS). 6: Fr. 7: Page NYU Wash Sq Lib 37-38, stack supv 38; Asst NYU Col of Dentistry Lib 38-40; Evening supv Brooklyn Col Lib 40-41; Ref asst UAla 42; Act head circ Queens Col Lib, Queens NY summer 42; Circ libn Penn State Col 45-46; Libn Ursinus Col 48-54; Libn Clark U 54-. 9: ALA; BSA; MassLA; NELA. 10: Bohemians; Dickens Fellowship; Citizens Plan E Assn; Friends of the Worcester Pub Lib; Beta Theta Pi. 12: Bk reviews "Worcester Telegram and Gazette"; misc ed wk. 14: Admin, ref. 15: Clark U Lib 1 Downing st, Worcester Ma 01610.

BARROWS, RICHARD S. b Brookline Mass 1 Jl 20. 5: Harvard 39-43 (Philos) SB, 45-48 LLB; Simmons 59 (LS). 7: Deck off US Naval Reserve, World War II Ensign 42-45; Examining attorney Abstract & Title Guaranty Co, Detroit 48-51; Closing attorney US Army Engnrs, Detroit Dist 51-52; Assoc Law Firm Kneeland & Splane, Boston 52-56; Asst libn in chg Treas Room Harvard Law Sch 56-57; Law Libn & Asst Prof of Law Mont State U 57-60; Law Libn US Post Office Dept, Wash DC 60-61; Libn Off of the Judge Advocate Gen US Navy Dept, Pentagon 61-. 9: AALL (Com on Chaps, Com on Nomin; chm Federal Agency Activities Com 66-67); Law Libns Soc Wash DC (pres 64-66); DCLA. 13: Yes. 14: Law lib admin. 15: Office of Navy Judge Advocate Gen, Washington DC 20370.

BARRY, JAMES WM (JR). b Altoona Penn 27 Je 19. 5: UPittsburgh 37-39, 45-47 (Hist) AB; Carnegie 47-48 bsls& upittsburgh 51-52 (Gen Educ & Hist of Amer Sci & Tech) MEd. 6: Ger, Sp. 7: Schedule chief Ra-aacs US Air Force T/Sgt 42-45; Stud asst lib UPittsburgh 46-47; Stud asst brs Carnegie Lib of Pittsburgh 47-48, Sr asst schs dept 48-49; Asst order libn Purdue U 49-51; Br asst Carnegie Lib of Pittsburgh 51-52; Liaison with DLC & ref USDA US Dept of Agric, Wash DC 52-54; Admin asst UPittsburgh 54-55; Head acquis sect NLM 55-63; Libn Lib of Sci & Med Rutgers 63-. 8: Reorg Com, NLM 60; Civil Serv Commsn Middle Mgt Inst 60; American Univ Inst on Info Storage & Retrieval 60; Seminars onacquis of Latin Amer Lib Materials, Acquis Com 61-63; Consul Visiting Libn Univ Med Sci, Faculty Med Sci, Bangkok Thailand68-69. 9: ALA-RTSD (Exec Bd 63-64, Nom Com 60-61 & 64-65, Interlib Coop Com 61-65; Acquis sect; chm 63-64, mem 3 coms 57-63;Ser sect; sec 57-59, chm &/or mem 2 coms 57-65);-ACRL (mem adv com coop educ & prof orgs 67-69); MedLA (Rep to US Commsn forUNESCO 61-64, chm Med Sch Libs Group 64-65, mem Com on Curr 65-68; Panel mem Exchange Annual Meetg 66; NY Reg Group Com onContin Educ; mem 65 & 67-, chm 66-67); DCLA (treas 56-58, Exec Bd 60-61 & 63-, Com 55-56, 59-60); NJ Lib Res Comm (mem SubcomMed Lib Res 67-). 10: Phi Alpha Theta. 11: Suprior service award NLM, 60. 13: Yes. 14: Admin, tech serv, ref. 15: Lib of Science & Medicine, Rutgers, The State Univ, New Brunswick NJ 08903.

BARRY, ROZANNE (MARIE). b Chicago 1 O 37. 5: UKan 55-59 (Internat Rel) BA; UCal(Berkeley) 61-62 (LS) MLS. 7: Lib asst Kan City(Mo) Pub Lib 60-61; Ref libn LC 62-64; Libn admin Spec Serv, Korea 64-. 66, Vietnam 69-. 12: Ed "African Newspapers in Selected American Liraries" (3d ed GPO 65). 14: Ref, govt publs. 15: 4509 Summit, Kansas City Mo 64111.

BARTEKY, TIBOR VICTOR. b Budapest Hungary 15 D 24. 5: P Pazmany U of Sci 44-48 (Law, pol Sci) Grad, 48-51 (Law, Pol Sci) Dr in each; USoCal 60-61 (LS) MS; UMinn summer 67 (Lang Educ). 6: Fr, Ital, Ger, Sp, Lat, Portu, Hungarian, Slavic lang. 7: Asst Prof theol Sem, Budapest 48-51; Concentration camp, Hungary 51-53; Corp lawyer, Budapesy 53-56; Asst Prof Col Cevenol, France 57-59; Libn II Cal State Lib 61-63; Soc sci libn pacific Lutheran U 63-65; Prof dept chm, Oral Roberts U 65-69; Asst city libn New Orleans Pub Lib 69-. 9: LaLA. 10: AAUP; Amer Coun on the Tchg of For Langs; Amer Assn Tchrs of Fr, of Germ, of Ital, of Ital, Sp & Portu. 12: "Mysticism in Modern Islam" (in hungarian) (50). 13: Yes. 14: Admin, collection bldg, tech serv, catlg (acad or res libs). 15: 6109 Rosalie ct, Metairie La 70003.

BARTER, MARY CUNNINGHAM. b Philadelphia 9 D 12. 4: Leland L Barter. 5: UPenn 30-34 (Eng) BS in Ed; Pratt 55-57 MLS. 7: Legal sec, Phila 36-46; Amer Friends Serv Com, Phila & NYC 46-49; Queens Borough Pub Lib, Jamaica NY; Various 54-61, HeadEduc Div 61-65, Asst libn Central Lib 65-67; Springfield Town Lib, Springfield Vt 67-. 8: Tchr Lib Sci courses UVermont Ext,Springfield Vt 68. 9: ALA (chm Basic Refer Bks Com 65-68, Coun-Rep Vt Chap 69-); NELA (Rep Vt on Adv Coun 69-); VaLA(Exec Bd 68-). 10: Beta Phi Mu; Grads Assn Pratt Inst Grad Lib Sch; Quota Club. 12: Ed "Recommended Reference Books for Smalland Medium Sized Public Libraries" (ALA 69). 13: Yes. 14: Admin, ref. 15: 4 Bluebird ct, Springfield Vt 05156.

BARTH, BARBARA (MYERS). b Geneva NY 19 My 22. 4: Joseph A Barth. 5: Syracuse 40-44 (Hist) AB, 45 BLS. 7: Child libn Newton Pub Lib, Newton Mass 45-48; Child lbn Winchester Pub Lib, Winchester Mass 48-50; Base libn USAF Lib Serv, Kadena AFB, Okinawa 50-51; Base libn USAF Lib Serv, Great Falls AFB Mont 51-53; Youth libn Phoenix Pub Lib 58-62, Asst br libn 62-66, Acting br libn 66-67; Libn San Diego Pub Lib 67-. 9: ALA; Ariz State LA;CalLA. 10: Emblem Club of the US. 14: Ya, br wk. 15: 6025 Kantor st, San Diego Ca 92122.

BARTH, BARBARA ANNE. b Whittier Cal 9 N 32. 5: Fullerton Jr Col 50-51 (Eng); Biola Col 51-54 (Bible, Chr Ed) BA; UCLA 60-64 (Anthro) BA, 64-66 MLS, 67 (Anthro). 7: Libn (staff) LA Public Library 66-68; Children's libn Whittier Pub Lib Whittwood Br 68-. 9: ALA; SLA; CalLA. 10: American Museum of Natural History. 14: Bibliog, ref, collecting. 15: 12313 E Orange dr, Whittier Ca 90601.

BARTH, EDWARD W. b Chicago 7 Mr 30. 4: Ruth Richmond. 5: Luther Col 49-51 (Hist) AB; State UIowa summer 54 (Ind Mgt); UDenver 54-55 (LS) MA; San Diego State Col evens 56-60 (Educ); UMd evens 61-62; UMinn summer 65 (LS); George Washington U 67-.´7: Asst bk tore manager Luther Col 49-51; Co Libn Waukon Pub Schs, Waukon Iowa summer 51; Jr/Sr High Sch Libn Huron Pub Sch, Huron SD 51-52& us army, Japan, Korea 52-54; Jr high sch libn La Mesa-Spring Valley Sch, La Mesa Cal 55-61; Col Libn San Diego State Col summer 56; Pub libn San Diego Pub Lib, San Diego summers 58-61; Montgomery Co Schs, Montgomery Co Md: Jr high sch libn 61-63, Manager processing center 63-65, Sr high sch libn 65-. 9: ALA (life mem, chm Peace Corps Subcom 62-64);-YASD; AASchL; Md State LA (chm Study Needs 63, mem Recr Com 64); MdLA (mem&/or chm Scholarship Com 68-69); NEA; Md State TA; Montgomery Co LA (chm Legisl Com 63); Montgomery Co EA (Sch delegate 61-62). 10: Cub Scouting. 11: NDEA Summer Inst for Libns UMinn, summer 65. 12: 'Are We in Touch' in "Top of the News" (spring 63). 13: Yes. 14: High Sch lib, media fields. 15: 13802 Loree lane, Rockville Md 20853.

BARTH, JOSEPH MICHAEL. b Jamaica NY 10 Mr 45. 5: Iona Col 63-66 (Eng) BA; St John'sU (Jamaica NY) 67-69 (LS) MLS. 6: Sp. 7: Caseworker NYC Dept of Welfare 66-67; Libn a-v US Mil Acad Lib, West Pt 68-. 9: ALA; MusLA. 10: Mensa. 13: Yes. 14: A-v libnship, ref. 15: 102-19 216 st, Queens Vil NY 11429.

BARTHOLD, (EMMA) ELOISE. b Wood Co Ohio 20 N 14. 5: Bowling Green State U 32-36 (Fr) BA, BS in Ed; West Res summers 37-46 (Fr) MA, BSLS. 6: Fr, Sp. 7: Tchr Rossford Bd of Educ, Rossford Ohio 36-; Libn Toledo Pub Lib, Toledo Ohio 48-. 9: NEA; OhioEA. 10: Vergilian Soc; Delta Kappa Gamma; Sigma Delta Pi; Kappa Mu Epsilon. 14: Ref. 15: 416 Oregon rd, Toledo Oh 43605.

BARTHOLOMAE, ANNETTE M (CROGSTER). b Milwaukee 21 F 08. 4: George Thomson Bartholomae. 5: Reed Col 25-29 (Hist) BA; Columbia 29-30 BSLS Portland State U 67-68 (Hist) MA. 6: Fr, Sp. 7: Child libn Lib Assn, Portland Ore 30-38; Libn pub Lib, Pocatello Ida 38-42; Libn Serv Club No. 2, Camp White Ore 42-45; Ref libn Lib Assn, Portland Ore 48-60; Soc sci libn Portland State Col 60-. 9: OreLA. 10:

LWV; Lib Staff Assn, Portland State Col. 12: Ed "Oregon Library News" (63-65). 14: Hist. 15: 4246 SW McDonnell ter, Portland OR 97201.

BARTHOLOME, SISTER MARITA CHM. b Great Falls Mont 10 O 23. 5: Col of Great Falls 41-44; Marycrest Col 44-45, 46-47 (Bus Educ) BS; Col of St Catherine 50-54 Summers BS in LS; UWis 64-65 (LS) MA. 6: Fr. 7: Bus Educ tchr & libn St Leo's High Sch, Lewistown Mont 47-53; Libn Central Catholic High Sch, Great Falls Mont 53-57; Head libn & Chm of Lib Sci Dept Marycrest Col 57-. 9: ALA; CathLA; IowaLA (local rep Recruiting Network 65-, mem &/or chm Scholarsh Com 66-68, sec Col Lib Sect 69; Quad-City Libns; Midwest Academic Libns Conf. 12: "Articulation in Library Education in the Midwest Area: a Survey" (65). 14: Admin, lib educ. 15: The Cone Library M arycrest Col 1607 W 12th st, Davenport Ia 52804.

BARTLETT, DOROTHY (LUCILLE) (WOOD). b Richmond Va. 4: Kenneth F Bartlett. 5: Randolph-Macon Woman's Col 28-32 (Hist) BA; Emory 33 BA in LS. 7: Lib asst head child dept Richmond Pub Lib, Ricmond Va 33-40; Map asst archives div Va State Lib 40-42; Chief circ dept City Lib Assn, Springfield Mass 42-43; Map curator, National Archives, Wash DC 43-44; Map analyst, chief map research sect Foreign Econ Admin, Wash DC 44-45; Map analyst Dept of Agric, Beltsville Md 46; Chief ref sect Map Lib Dept of State, Wash DC 46-47; Map libn Cent Intel Agency, Wash DC 48-61; Head ref & bibliog sect Geog & Map Div LC 62-. 9: ALA; SLA (DC Chap; v-chm Geog & Map Group 64-66, chm 67); Assn Amer Geogrs. 10: AAUW; Assn PRESERV Va antiqs. 13: Yes. 14: Maps, ref. 15: 1713 Wainwright dr, Reston Va 22070.

BARTLETT, JUDITH GILBERT. b Kent Conn 23 F 39. 5: Wheaton Col 57-60 (Hist); Centenary 60-61 (Hist) BA; LSU 62-63 MLS. 7: Libn Shreve Mem Lib, Shreveport La 61-62; Sr libn NYC Pub Lib 63-66; Acquis libn Wagner Col Lib 66-67; Acquis libn York Col Lib, Queens NY 67-. 14: Acquis. 15: 42 Commerce st, New York NY 10014.

BARTLETT, MABEL. b Brooklyn NY. 5: Conn Col 26-30 (Hist) BA; Columbia 38 BS in LS. 6: Fr, Sp. 7: Lib asst Conn Col 39-40; Catlgr ref asst LI Hist Soc, Brooklyn NY 40-43; Lib asst Pub Lib of New London, Conn 43-44; Catlgr State U Iowa 44-46; Head catlg dept Osterhout Free Lib, Wilkes-Barre Penn 46-48; Head tech processes dept LIU 48-. 9: ALA; NY Tech Serv Libns. 10: AAUP; Amer Bible Soc. 14: Catlg. 15: 143 Linden blvd, Brooklyn NY 11226.

BARTLEY, ANNA JANET (COX). b St John NB Can 3 My 16. 4: Melville W Bartley. 5: Acadia U 34-37 (Eng) BA; Toronto 38 (Eng) MA, 39 BALS. 7: Order dept UToronto Lib 39-40; Catlg Pub Lib, Port Arthur Ont 60-. 10: Univ Women's Club. 14: Catlg, ref. 15: 209 Winnipeg ave, Port Arthur Ont Can.

BARTLEY, BARBARA (GRACE). b Columbus Wis 18 Ja 19. 5: UWis 41 (Educ,Eng) BS, 50 (Educ, Guidance, Personnel) MS, 60 (LS) MS. 6: Fr. 7: Libn, tchr High Sch, Brillion Wis 41-42; Libn, tchr High Sch, Oconomowoc Wis 42-44; Libn, tchr High Sch, Janesville Wis 44-49; Asst dean of women WVa U 50-52; Eng tchr High Sch, Waukesha Wis 53-56; Sch libn Sch System, Columbus Wis 56-59; Asst Prof Lib Sci, ref libn Wis State U(Oshkosh) 60-62; Asst Prof Lib Sci UWis(Milwaukee) 62-, Asst to the dir 67-. 9: ALA (Subs Bks Bul Com 65-); -ACRL; -AASchL; -YASD; -LED; -RSD; WisEA (Lib Sect); WisLA. 10: Delta Kappa Gamma; Beta Phi Mu; Pi Lambda Theta; Wis Lib Sch Alumni Assn. 13: Yes. 14: Ref, ya, sch libs, instr materials centers. 15: 5015 N Diversey blvd, Milwaukee Wi 53217.

BARTLEY, LEWIS A. b Wausaukee Wis 21 N 09. 5: Ill Wesleyan U 33-34 (music); Bradley U 34-35; Ill Wesleyan U 35-36 (bus admin) AB; State U of Iowa summers 40-42 (commerce) MA; UIll summers 54-55 (LS); UWis summers 56-59 MSLS. 6: Fr, Ger. 7: Tchr of Com & Music Rutland (Ill) Twp High Sch 36-39; Prin Rutland (Ill) Elem Sch 39-40; Tchr Com & Music Sa Jose (Ill) Commun High Sch 40-42; Tchr of Com & Music Arispie-Indiantown Twp High Sch, Tiskilwa Ill 42-43; Master, Head of Dept of Bus Educ, Shattuck Schl, Faribault Minn 43-45; Prin Harvel (Ill) Commun High Sch 45-47; Visiting Instr in Bus, Lincoln Col (Lincoln Ill) summer 47; Assoc Prof & Head of Dept of Bus Admin, W Va Wesleyan Col 47-48; Instr Com & Bus Admin, Galesburg Undergrad Div UIll 48-49; Instr in Bus Admin So Ill U 49-50; Tchr Music & Soc Studies, Lorimor Independent Schs, Lorimor Iowa 50-51; Prin New Boston (Ill) Commun High Sch 51-54; Tchr Bus Educ Commun High Sch, Blue Island Ill 54-56, Libn 56-59; Libn Naperville (Ill) Commun High Sch 59-. 8: Pres C M S Conf 46-47; Pres Naperville High Sch Tchrs Assn 63-65; IllEA deleg 57-68; NEA deleg 63-68. 9: NEA; IllEA. 10: Am Philatelic Soc; Nat Philatelic Soc; Beta Phi Mu. 14: Catlg, ref. 15: 1032 Front st, Aurora Ill 60505.

BARTLEY, MARGUERITE (VESTAL). b Nashville Tenn 16 Ap 05. 4: Loran Gale Bartley. 5: UMich 26 (Eng) AB; Rutgers 62 MLS. 6: Fr 07: Sch libn Detroit Pub Schs 26-27; Ref staff Montclair Pub Lib, Montclair NJ 62-. 10: Bus & Prof Women's Club; Phi Beta Kappa; Pi Lambda Theta; Sorelle Club Verona NJ. 14: Ref. 15: 15 Howard st, Verona NJ 07044.

BARTLING, JULIA. b Austinville Iowa 9 F 19. 5: UIowa 46-50 (Eng) BA; UMich 50-52 AMLS. 6: Fr, Ger. 7: Lib asst Enoch Pratt Free Lib, Baltimore 52-54; UIowa Lib: Ref libn 54-56, Act head ref dept 56-58, Head ref dept 58-. 9: ALA-RSD (chm "Library Journal" List Com 64-65; IowaLA (sec 58-60, rep to ALA Coun 65-69). 13: Yes. 14: Ref. 15: Univ of Iowa Lib, Iowa City Ia 52240.

BARTOLINI, R PAUL. b Ladd Ill 21 Jl 20. 4: Myrtle J File. 5: Ill State Normal U 42 (Soc Sci) B Ed; Utah 43-44 (Ger Culture) ASTP Dip; UIll46 (LS) BS, 46-47 (LS) MS, summer 49, 50, 51 (LS). 6: Ger. 7: Admin NCO Army of the US,Okinawa 42-45; Asst ref libn UIll Lib(Urbana) 46-47; Asst head libn Wichita U 47-48;Lib Dir Kan State Col (Pittsburg) 48-53; Coord Adult serv Free Lib of Phila 53-56;Supv neighborhood & ext serv Milwaukee Pub Lib 56-65; Lib Dir Lake Co Pub Lib,griffith Ind 65-. 8: Lib bldg consul 60-. 9: ALA (Life mem, Coun 49-54 Jt Com Serv to Labor 53-57, Wiscoord Fed Rel Off 58-59); -LAD (Com on Econ Status 66-69); -ALTA (Intel Freedom Com65-69); -PLA (Bd dirs 68-72, mem 2 coms 65-72); IndLA (Life mem, mem &/or chm 2 coms);KanLA (pres 51-52); WisLA (pres 62-63). 10: Adult Educ Coun of Metro Phila;Research Clearinghouse of Metro Milwaukee; Wis Governor's Com on the UN 62-65; PTA;Pi Gamma Mu; Kappa Phi Kappa; Beta Phi Mu; Rotary. 12: 'The American Library Association Retirement Plan' in "Retirement for Librarians" ed by Herbert Goldhor (ALA 51). 13: Yes. 14: Pub lib bldgs, rare bks, Coloradoiana. 15: 624 N Oakwood ave, GriffithIn 46319.

BARTON, BEVERLY A. b Providence 6 S 30. 5: RI Col of Pharmacy 48-52 (Pharmacy) BS; Simmons 58-60 (LS) MS; Northeastern, Boston Col, RI Col, Providence Col (Educ). 7: Act chief pharmacist Kent Co Mem Hosp, Warwick RI 52-56; Act Libn RI Col of Pharmacy 53-54, Instr 52-57; Instr NE Col of Pharmacy 57-59; Libn Warwick Veterans Mem High Sch, Warwick RI 60-62; Hd libn Pilgrim High Sch, Warwick RI 62-. 8: Asst in pre-clinical instr Pawtucket em Hosp Sch of Nursing, Pawtucket RI 52-53, 56-57; Consul, Eastern States Mining Corp, Boston Mass 60. 9: ALA; RILA; NESchLA. 10: AAAS; Amer Pharmaceut Assn, RI Pharmaceut Assn Lambda Kappa Sigma; RI Civil Defense Admin. 13: Yes. 14: Data proc, ref. 15: 121 Oakhurst ave, Warwick RI 02886.

BARTON, ELIZABETH MARGARET. b Phila. 5: UPenn 46 (Eng) AB; Drexel 46-49 BS in LS; UPenn 47-54 (Eng) AM. 6: Fr, Ger. 7: UPenn; Card preparation 42-44, Ser asst 44-49, 1st asst ser dept 49-58, Catlgeditor 58-. 9: Phila Area Tech Serv Libns. 14: Catlg. 15: 4101 Pine st, Phila 19104.

BARTON, MARY ANN (AHRENDT). b LeMars Iowa 27 Jl 42. 4: Richard Barton. 5: Wartburg Col 60-64 (Eng) BA; Rosary Col 66-67 MALS. 7: Eng tchr Lincoln High Sch, Manitowoc Wis 64-65; Eng tchr Mt Horeb High School, Mt Horeb Wis 65-66; Ref & circ libn Mundelein Col 67-. 9: ALA. 14: Ref, acquis. 15: 816 Michigan, Evanston Il 60202.

BARTON, MARY NEILL. b Winchester Va 20 Mr 1899. 5: Agnes Scott 18-22 (Math,Fr) BA; Columbia 27 (LS) BS, summers 38, 39, 41, 42, 45 MS. 6: Fr. 7: Lib asst U of the South 25; Ref asst Enoch Pratt Free Lib, Baltimore 27-29, 1st asst Ref Dept 29-39; Instr Ref & Bibliog Drexel 37; Instr Ref & Bibliog Columbia summers 43, 46; Head gen ref dept Enoch Pratt Free Lib, Baltimore 38-59, ret; Consul & part- time libn 59-. 8: Organized lib Carnegie Institution of Washington, Dept of Embryology. 9: ALA-ACRL (chm Ref Libns Sec 42-43, Coun 51-53, 57-58, pres Ref Serv Div 57-58); MdLA (chm var coms); Baltimore Bibliophiles. 10: Md Hist Soc; LWV; Walters Art Gallery; Baltimore Museum of Art; Phi Beta Kappa. 11: William G Baker Award (58); Isadore Gilbert Mudge Award (59). 12: Co-author (with Virginia W Kennedy) "Samuel Taylor Coleridge; A Selected Bibliography"; "General Reference Department Staff Manual" (with E F Watson) (50) (Japanese tr 61); "Reference Books: A Brief Guide for Students" (5th ed 62, 6th ed 65); Comp & ed "A Topical Guide to Materials for Reference and Research in Libraries of the Baltimore Metropolitan Area." 13: Yes. 14: Ref serv, ref bks. 15: 500 W University pkwy, Baltimore Md 21210.

BARTON, RICHARD LEE. b Chicago Ill 12 Ag 41. 4: Mary Ann (Ahrendt). 5: Mason City Jr Col 59-61 AA; Wartburg 61-63 (Hist) BA; UWis 64-66 (Educ, Hist) MA; Rosary Col 67-68 MALS. 7: Tchr Freeport Sr High Sch, Freeport Ill 63-64; Tchr N Pk Acad, Chicago 66-67; Lib asst NorthwesternU summer 66; Lib asst NEast Ill State Col 67-68; Act circ libn UIll (Chicago Circle) 68-69, Asst circ libn 69-. 10: Beta Phi Mu; AAUP. 14: Lib automation, ref. 15: 816 Michigan, Evanston Il 60202.

BARTON, VIRGINIA LEE (JENNINGS). b Redlands Cal 8 Je 22. 4: Wesley Barton. 5: UCal (Santa Barbara) 39-43 (Educ) BA; UWash summers 58-61 MA in LS, 65 (NDEA Inst). 6: Sp. 7: Tchr Port Hueneme Elem Sch, Port Hueneme Cal 43-45; Tchr Rochester Elem Sch, Rochester Wash 48-49; Asst to libn Centralia Sch Dist, Centralia Wash 54-56; Libn, Tchr Green Hill Sch, Chehalis Wash 60-68; Area supv, Timberland Reg Lib 68-, Asst dir 69-. 8: Instr NDEA Inst for Sch Libns, U Ariz, summer 66; Supv bibliotherapy, Green Hill Sch. 9: NEA; Internat Reading Assn; WashStateASchL (past chm reg 3); WashEA; CalEA; WashLA; ALA; PNLA. 10: Lewis Co Mental Health Assn; Lewis Co Hist Soc; Beta Phi Mu; Delta Kappa Gamma; AAUW. 13: Yes. 14: Ref, bibliotherapy, superv. 15: 751 Pennsylvania ave, Chehalis Wa 98532.

BARTOO, GILBERTA ELLEN. b Stoneboro Penn 18 Ag 16. 5: Edinboro State Col 34-36 (Elem educ), 36-37 (Sec educ), 38-39 summer 44, 45 (Elem Educ) BS; Clarion State Col 58-59 (LS) Master's Equivalent. 7: Tchr Brown Sch, Greene Twp Erie Co 44-45; Tchr Conneaut Lake Elem Sch, Conneaut Lake Pa 45-46; Nurses' Aide Edinboro Nursing Home, Edinboro Pa 52-54; Kitchen Helper YWCA, Warren Pa 57-58; Lib aide Warren Area Joint Sch Bd 58; Libn Warren Lib Assoc, 59; Libn Warren State Hospital, Commonwealth of Pa 60-. 9: ALA; -AHIL (Jt Com on Rev Standards); -YASD; -ASD; PennLA. 14: Serv for psychiatric nursing educ, psychiatric patients. 15: 333 Prospect st, Warren Pa 16365.

BARTOW, BARBARA. b Paterson NJ 16 S 25. 5: UDel 43-47 (Hist) BA; UPenn 49-50 (Hist) MA; Drexel 54-55 MSLS. 7: Lib asst UPenn 50-54; Catlgr UDel 55-65, Hd catlgr 65-. 9: ALA-ACRL; Phila Area Tech Proc Gp; DelaLA. 14: Catlg. 15: 502 N Bancroft pkwy, Wilmington De 19805.

BARTZ, ALICE PUGH. b Vineland Va 19 Je 15. 4: Warren F Bartz. 5: Westhampton Col URichmond 32-36 (Eng) BA; UNC summer 36-38 (LS) BLS; Temple 62, 64 (Hist, reading); Drexel 62, 64 (LS). 6: Ger, Fr. 7: Asst child libn Richmond Pub Lib, Richmond Va 36-38; Asst child libn NY Pub Lib 38-40; Child libn Free Lib of Phila 40-43;Libn Frankford High Sch, Phila 54-55; Libn Germantown Acad, Phila 56-60; Libn Abington (Penn) Sch Dist 61-68; Sch lib dev advEast area br, Div of Sch Libs Dept of pub instr, Upper Darby Penn 68-. 8: Libn for Patient & Med Libs, Friend's Hosp, Phila 53-61. 9: ALA; AASchL (mem Stud Assist Com); NEA-DAVI; PennLA (a-v chm 68-69); PennStateEA; PennSchLA (pres 66-68). 10: AAUW; Dau ghter of American Colonists; Frankford Hosp Aux. 13: Yes. 14: Multo-medic sch lib devel. 15: 646 Pine Tree rd, Jenkintown Pa 19046.

BASIUK, EMIL. b Ukraine 11 Mr 15. 4: Lena Mikula. 5: Pontifical Col for Expan of Faith(Rome) 36-42 (Theol) BA; University for Foreigners 43-44 (Ital Lit); West Res 61-62 (LS) MS. 6: Ukrainian, Polish, Russian, Fr, Ital, Sp, Lat. 7: Interpreter Ital Mil Hdqrs, Rome 42-43; Sec-interpreter Allied Mil Govt, Perugia 44-45; Receptionist Off Transit Hotel, Perugia 45-46; Sec Brufani-Palace Hotel, Perugia 46-47; Receptionist Anchorena Hosp, Buenos Aires 47-58; X-ray file clerk UHosps, Cleveland 58-59; Bkkeeper Delta Import Co, Phila 59-60; Asst ref libn Loyola U(Chicago) 62-67, Libn Dent Sch Lib 67-. 9: CathLA. 10: Ukrainian nat Mus, Chicago. 13: Yes. 14: Ref, a-v, documentation. 15: 3814 W Thomas st, Chicago Il 60651.

BASKIN, CLARIBEL GEE. b Soochow China. 5: Duke 36-40 (Germ) AB; UNC (Charlotte) 66 (Libnship) MSLS. 6: Fr, Ger. 7: Readers' serv libn Miami-Dade Jr Col N Campus, Miami Fl 66-69. 9: ALA. 14: Comp lit, archives. 15: 1107 Columbus blvd, Coral Gables Fl 33134.

BASKIN, MATTIE V. b Stamford Tex 4 D 10. 5: Tex Woman's U 28-29; W Tex State U 33-34 (Prim Educ) BS; Hardin Simmons U 31-32; E Tex State U summer 62, 63 MS in LS. 7: Tchr New Hope Common Sch Dist, Jones Co Tex 32-33; Elem tchr Stamford Ind Schdist, Stamford Tex 34-42; Tchr Elem Schs Ector Co Ind Sch Dist, Odessa Tex 42-64,Libn Gonzales Elem Sch 64-. 9: Tex State Tchrs Assn; Tex Clrm Tchrs; TexLA. 14: Elem libn. 15: 1300Parker dr, Odessa Tx 79762.

BASLER, BEATRICE (KOVACS). b Austria 2 Je 45. 4: Thomas Gordon Basler. 5: Syracuse 62-66 (Eng) AB; Rutgers 66-67 MLS. 6: Sp, Ger, Hungarian. 7: Libn Nassau Acad of med, Garden City NY 67-. 9: MedLA (chm Subcom on New Mems, 1971 MedLA Conv); NY Reg Med Lib Assn; Med & Sci Libns (chm). 14: Lib automation, recr, rare bks, ref. 15: Nassau Academy of Medicine, Garden City NY.

BASLER, ROY P(RENTICE). b St Louis Mo 19 N 06. 4: Virginia Anderson. 5: Central Col (Mo) 23-26 (Eng, Hist) AB; Duke 28-31 (Eng, Phil) AM, PhD. 6: Fr. 7: Eng tchr Caruthersville High Sch, Caruthersville Mo 26-28; Grad asst & fellow in Eng DukeU 28-31; Hd Dept of Eng Ringling Col 31-34; Hd Dept of Eng State Tchrs Col, Florence ala 34-43; Prof of Eng UArk 43-46; Hd Dept of Eng Peabody Col, Nashville 46-50; Exec sec & ed in chief Abraham Lincoln Assoc, Springfield Ill 47-52; LC: Chief gen ref & bibliog div 52-54, Assoc dir ref dept 54-58, Dir ref dept 58-68, chief mss div with chair of Amer Hist 68-. 8: Soc Amer Histns; AHA; The Mss Soc. 10: Mod Lang Assn; Phi Beta Kappa; Sigma Tau Delta; Pi Gamma Mu; Authors Guild; Cosmos Club. 11: Diploma of Honor, Lincoln Mem Univ 39; Distinguished Alumni Award, Central Col 49; Hon D Litt, blackburn Col 52. 12: "The Lincoln Legend" (35); "Abraham Lincoln: His Speeches and Writings" (46); "Sex, Symbolism, and Psychology in Literature" (48); "The Collected Works of Abraham Lincoln", 8 vols (53); "A Guide to the Study of the United States of America" (60); "Lincoln" (62); "Walt Whitman's Memorandum during the War & Death of Abraham Lincoln" (62); "A Short History of the American Civil War" (67). 13: Yes. 14: Mss. 15: Lib of Cong 10 1st st SE, Wash DC 20540.

BASLER, THOMAS G. b Cleveland 8 Mr 40. 4: Beatrice Kovacs. 5: UMiami Fla 58-62 (Biol) B Ed, 62-63 (LS); Fla State U 63-64 (LS) MS; Emory 64-65. 6: Fr. 7: Med lib intern A W Calhoun Med Lib Emory U 64-65; Ref libn Miami-Dade Jr Col 65-66; Libn Inst of Marine Scis, Miami Fla 66-68; Lib Amer Mus of Natural Hist 68-. 8: Consul, Archival Restoration Assocs, Schomburg Collection 68-. 9: MedLA; ALA; SLA; FlaLA; ASIS; Geosci Info S 10: Amer Assn State & Loc Hist; Amer Mgt Assn; NY Lib Club. 13: Yes. 14: Admin, preserv & restoration, lib educ, recr. 15: Am Museum Natural Hist, 79th st & Central Park W, New York NY 10024.

BASORE, ERNA KATHERINE (FAJEN). b Rich Hill Mo 11 F 12. 5: Pittsburg State Tchrs Col summer 32; Ext & correspondence UKan, Emporia State Col, & Warrensburg State Tchrs Col 31-63. 6: Ger. 7: Tchr Pub Schs, Mo 31-32; Clerk Dept of Treasury Internal Revenue, Kan City Mo 50; Lib asst US Army War Col 50-51; Lib asst circ US Army Command & Gen Staff Col 51-57, Ref libn 57-. 11: Dept of the Army, 2 Superior Performance Awards 57, 68. 12: "Queen of Battle" (64). 13: Yes. 14: Ref (mil art & sci), mil hist. 15: 1112 Osage,Leavenworth Ks 66048.

BASS, ELIZABETH (ELVING). b Philadelphia Penn 27 N 43. 4: Abraham Bass. 5: UWis 61-65 9eng) BA; UMich summer 63; UWis 65-66 (LS) MS. 6: Fr. 7: UWis: Libn Sch of Bus 66, project asst Lib Sch summer 66; Wilson Lib UMinn: Ref libn 66-, Hd bibliog collection 67-. 9: ALA. 10: ACLU; UNAUSA; Phi Beta Kappa; Phi Kappa Phi. 14: Ref, bibliog, bk sel. 15: 2120 Como ave, St Paul Mn 55108.

BASS, HELEN (JONES). b Turon Kan 2 Ja 16. 4: Russell B Bass. 5: Christian Col 34-36 (Eng) AA; UDenver 36-38 (Eng,LS) BA & certif in LS; Rosary Col 63-65 MA in LS. 7: Asst Indianapolis Pub Lib, Indianapolis 38-43; Asst Oak Park Pub Lib, Oak Park ill 58-68, Hd of readers' serv dept 68-. 9: ALA; IndLA. 10: AAUW; Boy Scouts of Amer (Bd); Beta Phi Mu; PTA. 14: Adult serv. 15: 311 N Elmwood, Oak Park Il 60302.

BASS, LINDA LOUISE. b Okla City Okla 9 Jl 42. 5: Sophie Newcomb 60-62; UOkla 62-64 (Finance) BBA; UDenver 66-67 (LS) MA. 6: Fr. 7: Libn (staff) Seattle Pub Lib 67-. 9: PNLA. 10: Jr League; Eng Speaking Union. 14: Ref, acquis. 15: 701 NW 38th, Okla City Ok 73118.

BASSETT, BETTY ANNE. b Beaver Falls Penn 26 My 43. 5: Grove City Col 61-65 (Hist) BA; West Res 65-66 MSLS. 6: Fr. 7: Libn Highland Suburban Elem, Beaver Falls Penn summer 66-67; Libn Berkshire High Sch, Burton Ohio 66-. 8: Steering Com for "Library Careers" Project of Noeast Ohio 68. 9: ALA; AASchL; NEA; OhioLA; OhioASchL (Recr Com); OEA. 14: Ref. 15: 14418 N Cheshire st, Burton Oh 44021.

BASSETT, CLANCY BECKSTEAD. b Santa onica Cal 23 O 27. 4: Grace Satoda. 5: UCLA 49-50, 51-54 (Pol Sci) BA;

USoCal 54-55 (LS) MS, 59 (Pub Admin, Educ) Jr Col Tchg Certif. 7: USAF: Japan 46-49, Marshall Islands, S Pacific, Hawaii 50-51; Ref libn Los Angeles Pub Lib Hist Dept 55-60, Supv Central Magazine Pool 57; Circ libn Santa monica City Col Lib 60-66; Period libn 66-. 8: Ref adv, Los Angeles Pub Lib Hist Dept 63; Lib adv St Augustine Epis Church Lib, Santa Monica 68-. 9: Amer Soc Pub admin; NEA; CalTA; CalLA. 10: Ida Hist Soc; USoCal Lib Sch Alum Assn; Jap Amer citizens League. 14: Ref, period, geneal. 15: 1316 Cedar st, Santa Monica Ca 90405.

BASSETT, MRS FRANCES (GEARHART). b Lexington Miss 16 F 05. 5: Miss State Col for Women 23-27 (Eng) AB; Emory 28-29 AB in LS; Columbia 36-37. 7: Eng tchr Raymond Pub Sch, Raymond Miss 27-28; Sr asst Pub Lib, Springfield Mo 29-31, Catlgr 31-51; Head catlgr & 1st asst Fed Power commsn Lib, Wash DC 51-52; Catlgr & documents libn Drury Col Lib 52-67, Head cataloger libn 68-. 9: ALA; MoLA. 14: Catlg. 15: Drury Col Lib, Springfield Mo. 65802.

BASSETT, FRED J. b Green Bay Wis 31 Ja 18. 4: Louise A Cormier. 5: St Norbert Col 46-49 (Chem) BS; UWis 50-51 BSLS. 7: Chem libn UWis(Madison) 51; Chem libn Purdue 52-56; Lit chem Upjohn Co, Kalamazoo 56-60, Head libn 61. 9: ACS (Dir of Chem Lit; treas 59-60, 61-62; Kalamazoo Sect; sec 67-68, chm-elect 69); MedLA; ASIS; NY Sci Acad. 14: Info processing, lib systems analysis, use studies. 15: The Upjohn Co Tech Lib, Kalamazoo Mi 49001.

BASSETT, MARY (HENRIAN). b Holcomb Rock Va 12 Mr 02. 5: Longwood Col 20-22; Lynchburg Col 24-25; UVa 28-29 (Educ) BS; Peabody summers 34-36 BS in LS; Columbia summers 45-48 MS in LS; UIll 53-54 (LS). 7: Tchr elem schs, Pittsylvania Co Va 22-24; Tchr elem schs, Henry Co Va 25-26, 30-35; Libn So Christian Inst(Edwards Miss) 36-53; Staff NY Pub Lib summer 45; Asst libn Lynchburg Col 47, 54-56, Libn 56-67; Ref libn Lynchburg Pub Lib 67-. 9: ACS (Dir of chem lit; treas 59-60, comm 61-62; Kalamazoo Sect; sec 67-68, chm-elect 69); MedLA; ASIS; NY Acad Sci. 10: AAUW. 14: Ref. 15: 108 Yeardley ave, Lynchburg Va 24501.

BASSETT, MILDRED AVIS (COATS). b New Berlin NY 23 N 12. 4: Allen B Bassett. 5: Cornell U 29-33 (Eng) BA; Columbia 33-34 (LS) BS. 6: Fr, Sp. 7: Reviser Sch of Lib Serv Columbia U 34-35; Catlgr Scarsdale Pub Lib, Scarsdale NY 35-38; Child libn Brooklyn Pub Lib 38-49; Sch libn New Berlin Central Sch, New Berlin NY 62-64; Ref libn Hartwick Col 64-. 9: ALA; NYLA. 10: DAR; Hartwick Women's Club; AAUP; LWP. 14: Catlg, ref. 15: 33 Cedar st, Oneonta NY 13820.

BASSETT, ROBERT J. b Coshocton Ohio 22 Jl 29. 5: Murray State Col 47-51 (Hist) AB; UMich 55-56 AMLS. 6: Ger. 7: US Navy 51-55; Asst ref libn bus ref br Brooklyn Pub Lib 56-59; Order libn Polytech Inst(Brooklyn) 59-63; Order libn Tenn Tech U 64-66; Asst acquis libn UTenn 66-. 9: ALA; TennLA; SELA. 10: Beta Phi Mu; Kappa Delta Pi. 14: Acquis. 15: 7905 Livingston dr, Knoxville Tn 37919.

BASSETT, (MARY) RUTH. b Wilkinsburg Penn 14 Ag 17. 5: UPenn 35-38 (Lat) BS in Ed, 39 (Lat) MS in Ed; Drexel 43-48 BS in LS. 6: Sp, Lat. 7: Tchr Cherryhill Twp High Sch, Penn Run Penn 40-41; Tchr, libn Mansfield Sr High Sch, Mansfield Penn 42; Libn Smyrna High Sch, Smyrna Del 43-45; Libn Upper Merion High Sch, Bridgeport Penn 46-48; Asst libn Upper Darby Sr High, Upper Darby Penn 48-53, Libn 53-. 9: NEA; ALA; PennStateEA. 15: 3637 Rosemont ave, Drexel Hill Pa 19026.

BASSETTI, LOUIS CHARLES. b Chicago Ill 6 Ap 35. 5: St Joseph's Col 53-57 (Eng) BA; UDenver 67-68 (Libnship) MA. 6: Ger. 7: Cryptographer USA Security Agcy, US & Germany 57-60; Claims adjuster Soc Security Admin, Chicago 60-67; Special asst to chief libn Hammond Pub Lib, Hammond Ind 67; Ref libn USAF Acad Lib 68-. 9: ColoLA. 10: Beta Phi Mu; Colo Mountain Club. 14: Pub serv, ref. 15: 4334 N Chestnut apt B5, Colorado Springs Co 80907.

BASTILLE, JACQUELINE DELIA. b Nashua NH 5 Je 29. 5: UNH 48-52 (Fr) BA; UMich 56-57 MALS. 6: Fr. 7: Libn Free Lib of Phila 57-59; Libn of R & D Lib Smith Kline & French Labs, Phila 60-66, Chief libn 67-. 9: SLA (Pharmac sect; sec 64-65, chm 68-69); MedLA (chm Phila Reg Group 63-64); Spec Libs Coun of Phila (sec 62-63). 14: Admin, automation of Document stor & retr. 15: R & D Information Center, Smith Kline & French Lab, 1500 Spring Garden st, Phila pa 19101.

BATCHELDER, JOYCE (BODEN). b Decatur Ill 24 Ja 29. 4: John Batchelder. 5: Millikin U 46-49 (Eng) AB; Columbia 61-63 (LS) MS. 7: Sch libn Katonah-Lewisboro Sch System, Cross River NY 63-. 9: ALA; NYLA; NY State Tchrs Assn. 10: Beta Phi Mu. 14: Sch libs. 15: Allison rd, Rt 1, Katonah NY 10536.

BATCHELDER, MURIEL G(RACE). b Bridgewater Mass 21 D 09. 5: Mt Holyoke 27-31 (Eng) BA; Columbia 38-40 BLS. 6: Fr. 7: Circ asst NY Pub Lib 31-40; Ref libn Pub Lib, Ridgewood NJ 40-43; Res & circ libn Conn Col Lib 43-49; Pub Lib, Mt Vernon NY: Chief circ dept 49-54, Chief ref dept 54-56, Asst dir 56-60, Dir 60-66; Libn Hyannis Pub Lib 66-. 9: ALA; MassLA (Program Com 68-69); Cape Cod LibClub (v-pres 67-69). 10: Quota; Columbia Lib Sch Alum Assn (pres 58-60); AAUW. 13: Yes. 14: Admin, adult serv. 15: PO Box 63, Wellfleet Ma 02667.

BATCHELOR, LILLIAN L. b Camden NJ 17 N 07. 5: UPenn (Langs) 26-30 BS; Drexel 29-30 BS in LS; Columbia 42-46 (LS, Educ) MA, 48-52 (Curriculum, Supervision) EdD. 6: Fr. 7: Libns asst Camden Pub Lib, Camden NJ 26-32; Libn Ogontz Jr Col 30-32; Libn & tchr Jr-Sr High Sch, Prospect Park Penn 32-37; Libn & tchr Vaux Jr High Sch, Phila 37-38; Libn & Eng Head Bok Tech High Sch, Phila 38-48; Supv high sch libs Bd of Educ, Phila 48-. 66; Asst dir in charge of libs 66-; Adjunct prof LS Drexel 57-. 8: Consul or dir of 4 wkshops in Tex, Kans, Los Angeles, and phila, 58-66; Consul NDEA-AASchL Purchase Guide; Consul Title III; mem natl chap Sch Lib Quarters & Equipment; chm Urban Sch Libs; mem Natl steering com, Natl Lib Week; Sch Lib Stand Com, 60. 9: NEA; ALA(Coun); -AASchL (past pres); PennSchLA (Exec Bd); SCD (Exec Bd). 10: YWCA; Metro Lib Coun; Colonial Phila Hist Soc; AAUW; ASCD. 12: "School Library and the Gifted" (60). 13: Yes. 14: Sch libs, sch library quarters, lib education. 15: 2559 Baird blvd, Camden NJ 08105.

BATEMAN, BETTY (BELLINGER). b Elkhart Ind 10 Ap 14. 4: Bedford Byron. 5: UAkron 36 (Eng) AB; West Res 37 BS in LS. 6: Fr, Sp. 7: Asst libn Kent State U 37-41; Asst libn Bethany Col (BethanyWVa) 41-42; Asst libn USMC, Camp Lejeune NC 42-44; Libn USMC, Miramar Cal 44-46; Libnbus ref Dallas Pub Lib 46-47; Owner-manager Mountain Meadows Inn, Paradox Lake NY47-53; Libn Tex Engnrs Lib, College Station Tex 54-59; Chief lit research StanfordResearch Inst, Menlo Park Cal 59-63; Lib manager IBM Systems Dev Div, PoughkeepsieNY 63-. 8: Lecture-Engnrg Ref Materials UCal, San Francisco 62. 9: ALA; ASLIB; SLA (numerous assignments & duties); ASIS. 10: PTA; Sierra Club. 12: Comp Index to 3 AF Manuals in civil engnrg; Numerous bibliographies in engnrg fields; IBM Tech Rpt. 14: Ref, bibliog wk, admin. 15: 8 Horizon Hill dr, Poughkeepsie NY 12602.

BATEMAN, MARY RUTH. b Troy NY 13 N 21. 5: Russell Sage 46-47; Syracuse 47-49 (Eng) AB, 49-50 MS in LS. 7: Clk typist USN, Wash DC 41-42; Clk typist USA, Watervliet NY 42-44; Cpl USMC 44-46; Catlgr Cleveland Pub Lib 50-51; Libn Boyce Thompson Inst, Yonkers NY 51-59; Tech libn Union Carbide Corp, Tuxedo NY 59-. 9: SLA (NY chap: chm Biol Sci sect, sec Sci/Tech sect). 1: Phi Beta Tau. 14: Catlg, bibliog. 15: PO Box 324, Tuxedo NY 10987.

BATEMAN, NELLIE HARD. b Columbia Miss 18 N 07. 4: Robert Leighton Bateman. 5: UAla 25-27 (Eng) AB; Emory 30 ABLS; UAla 46 (Eng) MA Emory 63-65 MLn. 6: Fr, Sp. 7: Sec-libn State Dept of Educ, Atlanta 39-41; Asst state supv WPA Lib Proj of Ga, Atlanta 41-42; Br libn Carnegie Lib of Atlanta 42-44; Catlgr UAla Lib 44-46; Catlgr UGa Lib 46-48; Libn Morgan Co High Sch, Madison Ga 49-52, 53-54; Asst dir Augusta Lib, Augusta Ga 56-58; Dir Uncle Remus Reg Lib, Madison Ga 52-53, 54-56, 58-66; Asst libn & instr in Lib Sci Georgia Col(Milledgeville) 66-. 9: ALA; SELA; GaLA (sec-treas 56-58, chm Libnship as a CareerCoun 67-69); NEA. 10: AAUW; DAR; Morgan County Civil War Centennial Assn (sec); Delta Kappa Gamma; AAUP. 14: Ref, catlg, tchg undergrad lib sci. 15: 312 Poplar st, Madison Ga 30650.

BATES, CAROL. b Kilgore Tex 27 Mr 42. 5: Kilgore Col 60-62 AS; E Tex State U 64-65 (Eng & LS) BA; UIll 66-67 (LS) MS. 6: Ger. 7: Catlgr E Tex State U 65-66; Grad asst UIll Lib Sch 68; Catlgr UIllLib 68-. 10: UIll Lib Staff Assn. 11: Beta UIll Lib Sch 68; Catlgr UIllLib 68-. 14: Catlg. 15: Apt 1-W 301 W Green st, Champaign Il 61820.

BATES, ELIZABETH R(YAN). b Salt Lake City 13 Ag 14. 5: UUtah 31-34 (Anthropology); UAriz 34-36 (Archaeol) BA; Columbia 37 (Anthropology) USoCal 58-59 (LS) MA. 7: Research wkr Fed Theater Project, NY 36-38; Legal sec Atty Roland S Bates, Los Angeles 50-58; Catlgr UCal(Riverside) 59-62; Engnrg libn USoCal 62-65; Head Engnrg Lib Stanford 65-. 8: Ref libn Lib/USA NY Worlds Fair 64. 9: ALA; SLA; CalLA. 10: USoCal Lib Sch Alumni Assn; AAUP; Amer Soc for Engrg Educ. 14: Ref, lib org & mechanization. 15: 154 Oak ct,Menlo Park Ca 94025.

BATES, HENRY ELMER Jr. b Quincy Mass 2 D 32. 4: Mary T McKenna. 5: Bentley Col of Accounting & Finance 50-52 (Accounting); BostonU 56-60 (Hist) AB; Simmons 60-62 MLS. 7: Accountant Bethlehem Steel Co, Quincy Mass 52; Finance-Sgt US Army, Toul France 53-56; Desk asst Thomas Crane Pub Lib, Quincy Mass 56, Tech libn 57-62, Ref libn 62, Asst libn 62-64, Head Libn 64-67; Hd libn Newton Free Lib, Newton Mass 67-. 9: Adult Educ Assn; MassLA (Treas). 10: Rotary Club; Quincy Toastmasters Club; Jackson Homestead. 14: Admin. 15: 40 Prospect ave, Wollaston Ma 02170.

BATES, MARY (BENNETT). b Ordway Colo 28 O 26. 4: Melvin L Bates. 5: Linfield Col 44-46 (Mus); Cascade Col 46-47 (Mus); Linfield Col 47-48 (Mus) BA; UWashington summers 55-58 (Libnship) M in Libnship. 7: Tchr Yamhill High Sch, Yamhill Ore 48-49; Tchr Lafayette Elem Sch, Lafayette Ore 49-50; Tchr Lexington High Sch, Lexington Ore 53-54; Libn Arlington pub schs, Arlington Ore 61-63; Libn Blue Mountain Commun Col 63-. 9: NEA; ALA; PNLA; OreEA; OreLA; (chm Intel Freedom Com); OreASchL; Ore Instr Media Assn. 10: Woman's Club; Civic Music Assn; Col Commun Theater; AAUW. 14: Admin of libs, ref. 15: Box 1091, Pendleton Or 97801.

BATES, MARY NELSON. b Nashville 20 Jl 05. 5: Vanderbilt 23-27 (Math) BA; Emory 30-31 BA in LS. 7: Asst libn Knoxville High Sch, Knoxville Tenn 31-33, Head libn 33-36; Head of ref & circ Greensboro Pub Lib, Greensboro NC 36-38; Head libn Knoxville High Sch, Knoxville Tenn 38-43; Head libn Naval Air Tech Training Center, Jacksonville Fla 43-44; Dist libn First Naval Dist, Boston 44-45; Dist libn Eighth Naval Dist, New Orleans 45; Reg libn Middle Tenn State Col 45-52; Field libn Pub Lib Div Tenn State Lib & Archives 52-60, Asst dir 60-63, Dir 63-67; Br libn Pub Lib of Nashville & Davidson County, 67-. 9: ALA; SELA; TennLA; Nashville Lib Club. 10: Women's Nat Bk Assn; Zonta Internat. 13: Yes. 14: Pub lib admin. 15: 1006 Woodmont blvd, Nashville Tn 37204.

BATES, SUSIE MABELL (THOMBS). b Westbrook Me 2 Ja 13. 4: Ralph S Bates. 5: Simmons 32-34, 35-37 (LS) SB; State Col (Bridgewater Mass) 61-64 (Educ) MEd. 6: Fr, Ger, Sp, Lat. 7: Child libn Waterville Pub Lib, Waterville Me 37-38; Ser libn Marine Biol Lab Lib, Woods Hole Mass 38-43; Documents libn John Hay Lib BrownU 43-47; Catlgr head of tech serv Cushing-Martin Lib Stonehill Col 59-66; Hd of Catlg Dept Clement C Maxwell Lib Bridgewater State Col (Mass) 67-. 9: NEColLA; NE Col Tech Libns; MassLA. 10: Mass Archaeol Soc; Old Bridgewater Hist Soc; Soc of Mayflower Descendants; Ousamequin Club (Bridgewater); Faculty Wives Club State Col (Bridgewater); Bond Astronom Club. 14: Catlg. 15: 42 Leonard, Bridgewater Ma 02324.

BATESON, RUTH (H). b Chicago Ill. 5: UMich 58-61 (Eng) AB, 62-65 (Eng) MA, 67-68 AMLS. 6: Ger. 7: Tchr: Dexter High Sch, Dexter Mich 61-66, Kamehameha Schs, Honolulu 66-67; Ref libn Huron High Sch, Ann Arbor Mich 68-. 9: NEA; MichASchL; MichEA; Mich A-V Assn. 10: Phi Beta Kappa; Phi Kappa Phi; Beta Phi Mu; Mensa. 14: Ref. 15: 643 Manor dr, Ann Arbor Mi 48105.

BATLINER, DORIS JANE. b Louisville Ky 24 Mr 29. 5: Nazareth Col 47-51 (Chem) AB, 57-59 (LS) MS. 6: Fr, Sp, Ital, Ger, Port, Russ. 7: 58-69; Group Libn Chemetron Chemicals, Louisville Ky 69-. 8: Mem Exec Com Greater Louisville Tech Referral Center Com 68-69; mem governor's Com on Libs 67-. 9: SLA; KyLA. 10: Amateur Theatrical Assn; Wandering Minstrels; Holy Name Choral Club. 13: Yes. 14: Ref, indexing. 15: 1752 Shady lane, Louisville Ky 40205.

BATMAN, MAXINE. b Roachdale Ind. IndU 33-34; UIll 46-51 (Eng, Ger, LS) MS. 7: Libn Roachdale Pub Lib, Roachdale Ind 41-43; Child libn Goshen Pub Lib, Goshen Ind 43-45; Jr Lib Asst US Naval Train Sta, Sampson NY 45-46; Clk UIll Lib catlg dept 46-50; Hd libn Vincennes & Knox County Pl, Vincennes Ind 51-. 9: IndLA (chm Scholarship & Loan Fund Com, past pres). 10: Vincennes Hist & Antiquarian Soc; AAUW; Delta Kappa Gamma. 11: Librarian for the Year, Ind. 15: 502 N 7th st, Vincennes In 47591.

BATSCHE, CAROL (RIPPERE). b Annapolis Md 14 Jl 06. 4: George. 5: Union Col (Ky) 24-27; UAla 27-28 (Eng) BS Educ; Cinc Pub Train Class 29-30 (LS) Certif. 6: Fr. 7: Lib asst acquis Cincinnati Pub Lib 29-32, Lib asst br libs 39-50; Asst libn (Acting libn) UCincinnati Col Med Lib 55-63; Ref libn Clendening Med Lib, Kansas U Med Ctr 63-66, Asst dir Pub Serv 66-68; Hdqrs Serv Charloote Co Lib Syst, Port Charlotte Fla 69-. 9: MedLA; FlaLA. 10: LWV; DAR; Kappa Delta Pi. 13: Yes. 14: Ref. 15: 460 NE Laramore ave, Port Charloote Fl 33950.

BATSON, ANN KERKSIECK. b Memphis Tenn 29 S 20. 5: LSU 37-41 (Educ) AB, 41-42 BS in LS. 6: Fr, Ger. 7: Adult & children's circ asst Cossitt Lib, Memphis Tenn 42-43; Children's libn Shreve Memorial Lib, Shreveport La 43-44;Hd of ext dept, hd of children's room, supv of juvenile wk in br Mobile Pub Lib, Mobile Ala 45-53; Demonstration libn forstate lib St Mary Parish Lib, Franklin La 53-54; Sr libn circ dept LSU Lib 54-55;Bkkeeper & mgr Broussard Investment & Ins Agcy Inc & Abbeville Bldg & Loan Assn,Abbeville La 57-60; Asst prof Dept of Lib Dupre Lib USoLa 60-. 9: ALA (Memb Comfor La); LaLA (Standing Com on Const By-Laws & Manual). 10: U Southwestern La (Fac Sen Com on Fac Research & Fellowships);Madam et Mademoiselle; PTA; La State U Alumni Assn (treas of Vermillion Parish Gp). 14: Catlg. 15: 106 S st Valerie,Abbeville La 70510.

BATTELL, FREDERIC C(HAPMAN). b Mediapolis Iowa 26 S 10. 4: Gertrude Smith. 5: Iowa StateU 34 (Forestry) BS; UIowa 40 (Eng) BA; Columbia 41 (LS) BS; UIowa 47 (Journalism) MA. 7: Forest surveyor US Forest Serv, Ida, Mont, Iowa 34-35; CCC camp forester US Soil Conservation Serv, Ohio 35-38; Supv Amer Imprints Survey Hist Records Survey WPA, Iowa 38-39; Col of the City of NY: Lib asst circ dept 40-42, Head catlgr Sch of Bus & Civic Admin 42-43; Supv of dept libs UIowa 43-47; Libn Minn & Ont Paper Co, Minneapolis 47-65; Libn Mando Div of Boise Cascade Corp, Minneapolis 65-66; Libn N Central Forest Exp Station US Forest Serv, St Paul 66-. 8: Instr course in spec libs Col of St Catherine 50-54. 9: SLA (sec 51-52, chm 51 Nat Conv, mem chm Sci-Tech Div 54-57, pres Minn Chap 50-51, v-chm Paper & Textiles Sect 68-69, chm69-70); Iowa City Lib Club (pres 44-). 10: St Anthony Park Assn. 12: Assoc ed "The Mandonian" house organ (49-65). 13: Yes. 14: Admin, ref. 15: 2269 Carter ave, St Paul Mn 55108.

BATTELL, GERTRUDE (SMITH). b Mecklenberg County Va 12 N 10. 4: Frederic Battell. 5: Lynchberg Col 28-29; Averett Jr Col 29-30; Washington Co Lib Train Class 30-31 Certif; UIowa 46-47; UMinn 47-48 (Ger) BA. 6: Fr, Ger. 7: Child libn NY Pub Lib 31-34, 35-36, 40-43; Child libn Washington Co Lib, Hagerstown md 34-35; UIowa: Circ asst 38-40, Bot chem pharm libn 45, Math phys libn 46; Inst of Agric UMinn (St Paul): Biochem libn 48-51, Ser libn 51-53, Pub serv libn 53-56, Asst libn 56-65; In chg interlibrary loans, UMinn (Minneapolis) 65-. 9: ALA; SLA; MinnLA. 14: Ref, ser, interlib loans. 15: 2269 Carter ave, St Paul Mn 55108.

BATTEN, SARA (MAGDALENE STOREY). b Murfreesboro NC 6 N 15. 4: James William Batten. 5: Chowan Col 32-36 (Eng, Lat, Math) AB (summa cum laude); UNC 58-60 MS in LS. 7: High sch tchr, Enfield NC 37; High sch tchr & tchr libn, Glendale Sch, Kenly NC37-45; High sch tchr & tchr libn, Micro NC 45-46; High sch tchr, Wilmington NC 46-47;High sch tchr & tchr libn, Micro NC 47-48; Catlgr Joyner Lib EC U (Greenville NC)60-. 9: NCLA; NCEA; ALA; SELA. 10: Beta Phi Mu; EC Univ Faculty Wives Club; AlphaBeta Alpha. 14: Catlg. 15: 1014 E Wright rd, Greenville NC 27834.

BATTIN, PATRICIA (MEYER). b Gettysburg Penn 2 Je 29. 4: William T Battin. 5: Swarthmore 47-51 (Eng) BA; UMinn 53-54 (Amer stud); Syracuse 66-67 (LS) MLS. 7: Sec Indust Rel Center, Minneapolis 51-53; Lib Trainee State U of NY (Binghamton) 64-66, Asst libn 67, Assoc libn Catlg 68-. 10: Phi Beta Kappa; Beta Phi Mu. 14: Catlg. 15: 3128 Briarcliff ave, Vestal NY 13850.

BATTISTELLI, LOLA BRATTY. b Toronto Can 28 Je 41. 4: Vincent. 5: UToronto 59-63 (Hist) BA, 64-65 (Lib) BLS. 6: Fr. 7: Libn Canada Assoc for Adult Educ, Toronto 65-68; Libn Edmonton Journal Lib 68-. 14: Ref. 15: 10320 122nd st, Edmonton 40 Alberta Can.

BATTON, DELMA (JANE) HECK. b Tampa Fla 10 D 15. 4: James Harold Batton. 5: State Tchrs Col (Trenton NJ summer 35-37 (LS); Col of William & Mary 37-38 (Eng); UPenn summer 46 (Eng); UIll 48-51 BS in LS UFla summer 68 Inst on Institutional Libs NDEA Certif. 6: Fr, Ger, Sp. 7: Sch libn State Home for Girls, Trenton NJ 34-35; Circ asst PrincetonU Lib 36-37; Asst child & adult-Free Lib of Phila 38-43; Asst libn US Naval Hosp, Phila 43-46; Order libn Principia Col 46-48; Asst catlg dept UIll Lib 48-51; Del State Lib: Field consul 61-, Act state libn 64-65, 67-68, Act asststate libn 66, Title IVa consul 68; Dir Dover Pub Lib, Del 69-. 8: Coord for Del Jaycee/CSD pilot proj "Good Reading for Youth," 63-

Consul LSCA IVA & IV B Studies, 67-68. 9: ALA (Advis Coun to Jaycee Good Reading 66-70);-AAStateL; DeLA (Publ Com, sec 66-67, v-pres 68, pres 69-70). 10: Century Club & Chorus; AAUW; Del Assn for Retarded Child; Dover Day Care Center, PFA. 12: Ed DelLA Bulletin (65-66). 13: Yes. 14: Consul serv, child's & yp areas, pub & sch libs. 15: 1081 S Bradford st, Dover Del 19901.

BATTS, NATHALIE C(HLAN). b Baltimore 3 N 18. 5: Notre Dame of Md 36-40 (Hist, Soc Studies, Educ) AB; Columbia summers 42, 45, 46 BLS; Mt Holyoke 46-51 (Econ) MA; Columbia 62-66 (LS) MLS. 7: Jr asst Enoch Pratt Free Lib, Baltimore 41-45; Mt Holyoke Col Lib: 1st asst circ 45-49, Order libn 49-51; Grad Sch of Bus Lib ColumbiaU: Asst ref libn 51-55, Ref libn 55-62; Ser catlgr ColumbiaU Libs 62-. 9: Amer Econ Assn (Life mem); ALA; ASIS; NyTech Serv Libns (sec-treas); USA Standards Inst (mem 2 coms). 10: Amer Numismatic Assn. 12: "Small business" 51; "Orginization Charts" 53. 13: Yes. 14: Catlg, bibliog, info sci. 15: 21 Claremont ave, New York NY 10027.

BATY, ELIZABETH G. b Centralia 5 Ap 11. 4: Arthur N Baty. 5: Centralia Jr Col 27-29; UWash 29-31 BS in LS, 31-35 (Lit) BA. 6: Fr, Ger, Sp. 7: UWash Lib circ div: Jr libn 31-36, Sr libn 39-40; Catlgr Lib of Hawaii, Hilo 37-38; Libn lit l hist dept Multnomah co Lib, Portland Ore 60-61; Gen libn lit & hist dept Long Beach (Cal) Pub Lib 69-. 9: ALA. 14: Ref. 15: 6215 Beaumont ave, La Jolla Ca 92037.

BATZDORFF, SUSANNE M (BIBERSTEIN). b Breslau Germany 25 S 21. 4: Alfred Batzdorff. 5: Brooklyn Col 39-43 (Eng Lit) AB (summa cum laude); Pratt 43-44 BLS; Columbia 46-47 (Eng Lit) AM. 6: Ger, Sp. 7: Catlg libn Cooper Union Lib 44-46; NY Post-Grad Med Sch & Hosp, NY: Asst libn 47-48, Head Libn 48-50; Free Lib of Phila: Asst head lit dept 61-63, Head humanities dept Northeast Reg Lib 63-. 9: ALA; PennLA. 10: AAUW. 14: Ref. 15: 2519 Tulip lane, Neshaminy Woods, Langhorne Pa 19047.

BAU, DAVID H. b Shanghai China 3 O 12. 4: Fanny Chen. 5: UNanking 30-34 (Agric) BS; UMd 41-42 (Bus Admin); UMich 63 (LS) AMLS. 6: Chinese. 7: Var pos in the Chinese govt 34-41; Agric econ Bd of Econ Warfare, Washington DC 42-45; Agric adv Supr Com for Allied Powers, Tokyo 45-47; Agric econ Food and Agric Org, Washington DC 47-51; Res assoc Ctr for Chinese Stud UMich 62-64; Libn Ctr for Res on Econ Dev, Ann Arbor Mich 64-65; Subj catlgr LC 65-. 8: Consul to the Food Mission to China 46. 14: Catlg. 15: 121 6th st SE, Washington DC 20003.

BAUBLITS, RUTH O (BAUGHMAN). b Lima Ohio 24 Ja 20. 4: John E Baublits. 5: OhioNoU summers & ext 39-42; Bowling Green StateU 43-46 (Eng) BA; West Res summers 49-53 MS in LS; Ariz StateU 54-55 (Tchg); UDenver 62 & 64 (LS). 7: Asst libn Lima (Ohio) Pub Lib 46-54; Eng tchr Coolidge (Ariz) & PUHS system ariz 55-57; Asst libn PUHS system PUHS High Sch, Ariz 57-64; Head Libn PUHS system Carl Hayden High Sch 64-. 8: Promoting the idea of functional Instr Materials Centers in Phoenix, 64-66. 9: NEA; ALA; ArizEA; ArizSchLA. 14: Sch lib, methods of serving non-readers. 15: 2143 W Coolidge, Phoenix Az 85915.

BAUCOM, CHARLES VAN. b Lefors Tex 7 Ja 30. 5: Abilene Christian Col 48-52 (Hist) BA; East Tex State Col 56 (Hist) MA,65 MS in LS. 7: Eng tchr pub schs, Ackerly & Stamford Tex 52-55; Eng tchr-libn Wall Tex High Sch 55-59; Acquis libn East TexState Col, Commerce Tex 59-64, Acquis libn & instr in lib sci 63-64; Dir of lib York Col 64-65. 9: ALA; MPLA; NebLA; TexLA(sec-treas dist 6, 62-63, chm 63). 10: Co-leader York Great Bks Gp 67-69; York Co HistLA; Disciples of Christ Hist Soc. 14: Acquis, catlg. 15: 905 Delaware, York Nb 68467.

BAUER, ALICE LEE (GOOGE). b Winston-Salem NC 9 D 17. 5: Salem Col (Winston-Salem NC) 33-37 (Hist) AB; UNC 37-38 BSLS; UMich summer 41 (LS). 6: Fr, Ger. 7: Catlg asst UGa 38-41; Ser asst UIll(Urbana) 41-42; Ser asst UChicago 42-45; Lib asst Salem Col (Winston-Salem NC) 49-51; Sci ser catlgr Duke U 51-54; Head tech processes libn WVaU 54-65; Head catlgr UCincinnati 65-. 9: ALA-ACRL (Tri-State chap); WVaLA (treas 6 yrs); OhioLA. 14: Catlg, ser. 15: UCincinnati MainLib, Cincinnati Oh 45221.

BAUER, HARRY C(HARLES). b St Louis 22 Jl 02. 5: UMo 21-23 (Engnr); WashingtonU 24-27 (Math) BA, 27-29 (Physics) MS; St Louis Lib Sch 29-31 Certif. 6: Ger. 7: Chief of circ dept UMo Lib 31-34; Chief tech lib Tenn Valley Authority, Knoxville Tenn 34-42; US Air Corps CombatIntelligence Major 42-45; UWash: Asst libn 45-47, Dir of libs 47-59, Prof of libnship 59-67, Prof Emeritus 67-, sec of thefaculty 62-66. 8: Founder & Pres, Bibliographic Dowsers of Amer. 9: ALA; PNLA; WashLA. 10: Sigma XI, Pac NW Internat Writers Conf; Allied Arts of Seattle; Seattle Creative Activities Center; ACLU; Oval Club;Scabbard & Blade& pi Mu Epsilon; Seattle Art Museum; Rainier Club; Kiwanis Internat; Retired Off Assn. 11: Bronze Star; Air Medal; Purple Heart. 12: "Seasoned to Taste" (61). 13: Yes. 14: Ref. 15: 4203 Brooklyn ave NE, Seattle Wa 98105.

BAUER, SARAH (MacDONALD). b Fitzgerald Ga 9 D 1900. 4: Frederick H Bauer. 5: Randolph-Macon Woman's Col 18-22 (Eng Lit) AB; Carnegie Lib Sch of Atlanta 24 Diploma. 6: Fr. 7: Libn Langwood Col 14-27; Catlg dept Emory U Lib 27-28; Asst libn Mansfield State Tchrs Col 28-35; Asst libn Slippery Rock 50-57; Kent State: Hd & sci & tech 57-65, Red div 67-. 9: ALA; TriStateCRL. 10: Kappa Alpha Gamma. 14: Ref. 15: 182 N Prospect, Kent Oh 44240.

BAUER, SISTER MARY CELIA, SSND. b Mascoutah Ill 3 S 10. 05 State Col 40 (Eng) BS; Rosary Col 50 AB in LS; St LouisU 60 (Educ) MEd. 6: Fr, Ger. 7: Tchr -45; Libn & tchr St Joseph High Sch, Conway Ark 45-46; Libn & tchr Aviston Commun High Sch, Aviston Ill 46-50; Prin & libn Our Lady of Good Counsel Sch, New Orleans 50-53; Prin & libn St Martin's Sch, St Louis Ill 53-59; Libn Sacred Heart High Sch, New Orleans 59-60; Libn Cardinal Ritter Lib Notre Dame Col Lib (St Louis) 60-. 9: CathLA (Greater St Louis Unit: chm Col Sect 64-66; New Orleans Unit: sec 59-60); Nat Adv Bd for Second Schs 58-60; ALA; MoLA. 13: Yes. 14: Catlg, admin. 15: Notre Dame Col, 320 E Ripa ave, St Louis Mo 63125.

BAUGH, JOANNE DAVIS. b Greensboro Penn 31 Ag 29. 4: Lloyd Baugh. 5: Waynesburg Col 48-52 (Bus Admin) BS; George Washington U summer 54 (Bus Admin); WVaU 54-55; UPittsburgh 64-66 MLS. 6: Sp. 7: Tchr: West Greene Sch Dist, Rogersville Pa 51-55, Uniontown City Sch Syst, Uniontown Pa 55-66; Libn Uniontown Area Sch Dist, uniontownPa 66-67; Libn Penn State U (Uniontown) 67-. 8: Staff, Wkshop for Lib Assts, W Va U summers 66, 67; Memb, Vis Com, Middle States Assn Commsn of Second schs. 9: ALA; PennLA. 10: AAUP; Xi Si Epsilon; Uniontown Col Club. 11: Beta Phi Mu. 14: Ref, acquis, admin. 15: 26 Martha st, Uniontown Pa 15401.

BAUGH, RUTH (MERRICK). b Penn 24 Jl 17. 4: Edward R Baugh. 5: SUNY (Albany) 34-38 (Eng) AB; UWash 69 Libnship) MA. 6: Fr. 7: Engring asst GE, Schenectady NY 41-44; Adult asst King Co Lib Syst Bellevue Br 62-65, Admin Issaquah Br 65-69, Admin Lake Hills Br 69-. 9: WashLA. 14: Adult sel, ref, serv. 15: R3 Box 3671, Issaquah Wa 98027.

BAUGHMAN, ELIZABETH RUTH. b Effingham Ill 17 My 25. 5: East Ill State U 44-48 (Soc Sci, Educ) BS in Educ; UIll 48-49 (Hist) MA; UCal 59-60 MLS. 7: Ed Newberry Lib, Chicago 49; Head ref libn Chicago Hist Soc 49-59; Asst in catlg instr Sch of Lib Serv UCLA 60-67,Lecturer 67-. 9: ALA; CalLA (chm Pub Com, 65-). 10: UCal Lib Schs Alumni Assn (pres 67). 14: Catlg, ref. 15: 1132A - 19th st, Santa Monica Cal 90403.

BAUGHMAN, JAMES CARROLL. b Oil City Penn 13 N 41. 04; Carolyn (England) Baughman. 5: Clarion State 59-63 (LS & Eng) BS in Ed; Drexel 64-67 MS in LS. 6: Fr. 7: Libn Phillipsburg High Sch Phillipsburg NJ 63-65; Libn Weymouth East Jr High Weymouth Mass 65; Supv of sch libs Mass Dept of Ed Boston 66-68; Grad fellow Case West Res 68-. 9: ALA. 10: Beta Phi Mu. 11: Fellowship Award; HEA; Title II-B. 14: Sch libs, lib educ. 15: 1438 Golden Gate blvd, Mayfield Hts Oh 44124.

BAUM (MARTHA) PATRICIA. b Valdosta Ga 17 Mr 29. 5: Mary Washington Col 46-50 (Dramatic Arts, Speech) BA; Emory 54 (LS) MLn. 7: Tchr DM Brown Sch, Petersburg Va 50; Asst libn Northside High Sch, Fulton Co Atlanta 50-51; Stud asst EmoryU Lib 51-52; Eng tchr Chamblee High Sch, DeKalb Co Chamblee Ga 52-54; Asst catlgr Ga Tech Lib 54-59; Ga State Lib Dept, Atlanta: Ref libn 59, Asst state libn 59-66, Doc libn-catlgr 66-. 9: GaLA. 14: Catlg, ref. 15: 2101 Powell lane apt 2, Decatur Ga 30033.

BAUM, JUDITH. b Czechoslovakia 12 O 38. 4: Stuart Baum. 5: CCNY 55-60 (Psych) BA; Rutgers 66-67 MLS. 6: Hungarian. 7: Bibliogr ERIC Clearinghouse CUNY 67-68; Ref libn NYU 68; Psych libn City College of CUNY 68-. 14: Ref (soc scis). 15: 226 W 72 st, New York NY 10023.

BAUM, WILLIAM W(ARICK). b Akron Ohio 28 S 22. 4: Mary Shera. 5: Kent StateU 46-50 (Journalism) AB; West Res 54-55 (LS) MS. 7: AUS Ordinance Ammunition Clerk Sgt

USA ; ETO 42-45; AUS Infantry Second Lt Motor Off ETO 45-46; Freelance , pub rel, Akron & Cleveland Ohio 50-54; Clerk & off mgr, Textor Labs Inc Cleveland 55-59; Asst mgr Textor Div of Commercial Testing & Engnrg Co, Cleveland 59-62; Adult serv asst Cuyahoga Co Pub Lib Berea Br, Berea Ohio 62-68; Ref libn IF Freiberger Lib West Res 68-. 9: OhioLA; Tri-State ACRL. 10: Nat & Cleveland Audubon Socs; Amer Ornithologists Union; Wilson Ornithological Soc; Kirtland Bird Club. 14: Ref, natural scis humanities. 15: 1257 Cranford ave, Lakewood Oh 44107.

BAUMANN, AGNES M(CGRATH). b NYC. 4: Alfred W Baumann Jr. 5: Brooklyn Col 42 (Soc Sci) BA; Columbia 44 (LS) BS. 6: Fr. 7: Ref libn Queens Borough Pub Lib, Jamaica NY 44-. 14: Ref. 15: 5101F 39 ave, LI, NY 11104.

BAUMANN, CHARLES HENRY. b Brooklyn NY 24 O 26. 4: Nancy Nicholas. 5: WashU (St Louis) 47-51 (Educ) BS; Pratt 51-52 MLS; UWyo 56-60 (Hist); UIll 62-63 (LS). 6: Fr. 7: Asst circ ref libn Champlain Col SUNY (Plattsburgh) 52-53; Br libn Pub Lib, Niagara Falls NY 53-54; UWyo: Documents libn 54-56, Acquis libn 56-, Asst dir 61-69; Libn East Wash State Col 69-. 9: ALA; MPLA (Exec Bd); WyoLA (Exec Bd). 10: AAUP. 13: Yes. 14: Acquis, bldgs, admin. 15: 803 Hancock, Laramie Wy 82070.

BAUMANN, MILDRED ELIZABETH. b Springfield Ill 10 My 06. 5: UIll: 25-29 (Eng) AB, 29-30 BS of LS. 7: Lincoln Lib, Springfield Ill: Lib asst 30-32, Libn of high sch dept 32-57, Ref libn 57-. 9: ALA; IllLA. 10: Sangamon Co Hist Soc. 14: Ref. 15: 539 Washington, Springfield Il 62702.

BAUMGARTEN, Dr WALTER, Jr. b St Louis 3 Mr 12. 5: Harvard 30-33; WashU (St Louis) 33-35 (Hist, Lit) AB, 35-39 (Med) MD. 7: St Louis Med Soc Lib: Chm Lib Com 61-63, Curator 64-. 8: Practice of Internal Med 45-; Mo Heart Assn (pres 56-58); St Louis Heart Assn (pres 60-62). 9: MedLA; Mo State Med Assn; St Louis Heart Assn (Bd 52-69, pres 60-62); St Louis Health & Welfare Coun (chm Health & Hosp Div53-58). 14: Med hist, rare bks. 15: 5505 Delmar blvd, St Louis Mo 63112.

BAUMGARTNER, BARBARA (ELAINE) W(ALKER). b Alexander M Baumgartner. 5: Oberlin Col 57-61 (Eng lit) AB; Drexel Inst 64-68 MSLS. 7: Eng tchr John Dickinson High Sch, Wilmington Del 61-63; Lib asst Bryn Mawr Col Lib 64-66; Libn Sudlersville Middle Sch Sudersville Md 66-68; Child libn Free Lib of Philadelphia, 68-. 9: ALA. 14: Wk with child. 15: 6200 Germantown ave, Philadelphia Pa 19144.

BAUMGARTNER, HARRIET M(AY). b Brooklyn NY 18 Jl 07. 5: Hunter Col 27-30 (Lat) BA; Columbia 34-40 MLS. 7: Queens Borough Pub Lib: Ref sch catlgr 31-36, Readers adv 37-44; Info spec Off of War Info, NYC 44-45; Documentation spec Dept of State, Wash DC 45-48; Asst chief field serv sect Dept of State & USIA Overseas Lib Prog, Wash DC 48-55; Chief bk appraisals br US Info Agency, Wash DC 55-. 8: Instr in bk sel, EmoryU Lib Sch summers 46 & 48. 9: ALA (Life mem); DCLA. 14: Bk sel & review, readers adv wk. 15: 3620 16th st NW, Wash DC 20010.

BAUMGARTNER, ROBERT W. b Neenah Wis 30 D 30. 5: UWis 54-59 BA (Internat Rel), MA (LS). 7: Army (Cpl) 51-54; NorthwesternU Lib: Asst documents dept 59-61, Bus libn 61-63, Documents libn 63-. 9: ALA; IllLA. 14: Govt publ. 15: 903 Austin st, Evanston Ill 60202.

BAUMLER, JUNE LEE (HANSON). b Oak Park Ill 19 Je 42. 4: John V Baumler. 5: Northwestern U 60-64 (Eng Educ) BS; Simmons 66-68 (LS) MS. 6: Fr. 7: Eng tchr Dist 100, Carpentersville Ill 64; Child rm asst Weston Pub Lib, Weston Mass 65-67; Ref libn Belmont Mem Lib, Belmont Mass 68-. 9: ALA; MassLA; NE Screen Educ Assn (charter mem). 14: Ref, ya. 15: 16 Hill rd, Belmont Ma 02178.

BAUMRUK, ROBERT. b Chicago 23 F 30. 5: Morton Jr Col 48-50 (liberal arts) B of Gen Educ; Chicago 50-56 (LS) MA. 7: Order libn Ind Rel Center UChicago 55-56; Chicago Pub Lib: Ref asst libn I Soc Sci Dept 56-58, Asst tech dept 58-59, Head newspaper div 59-64, Act head publ dept 64-65, Hd publ dept 65-67, Act chief Soc Sci and Bus 67, Chief Soc Sci and Bus 68-. 9: ALA; SLA (Ill Chap; Mem Chm 65-66); IllLA; Chicago Lib Club (sec 61-62 & 65-66,v-pres 67-68, pres 68-69). 12: Ed "SORT Bulletin" (63-64); Ed "Book Bulletin,"Chicago Pub Lib (64-67). 15: 78 E Washington st, Chicago Il 60602.

BAUNER, RUTH (ELIZABETH). b Quincy Ill 21 S 28. 5: West IllU 46-50 (Eng) BS in Ed; Biblical Sem (NY) summer 51; West MichU summer 54; UIll 54-56 (LS) MS; SoIllU summer 56- (Educ Admin & Supv). 7: Asst Res Lib West IllU summer 50; Tchr-libn Sandwich Twp High Sch, Sandwich Ill 50-54; Circ dept asst UIll (Urbana) 55; SoIllU: Asst educ libn & head of instructional materials center 56-63, Act educ libn 63-64, Educ libn 65-, Asst prof Dept of instructional materials 69-. 8: Consul Nat Conv, NEA-DAVI 62; Jt Com AASchL/Nat Commsn on Tchr Educ & Prof Standards to prepare publ on prof lib for tchrs 64-68. 9: ALA; AASchL; IllLA; IllASchL (2nd v-pres 62-63, program chm for state meetings). 10: AAUP; Beta Phi Mu; Alpha Delta; Sigma Tau Delta; Amer Sci Affiliation. 13: Yes. 14: Ref, instr materials centers, tchg. 15: 704 W Mill, Carbondale Il 62901.

BAURER, JOAN (ADAMS). b Holyoke Mass 28 Ap 36. 4: Herbert T Baurer. 5: State Col (Westfield Mass) 54-58 (Educ) BS Educ; Simmons 68 MSLS. 6: Sp. 7: Tchr Senior high sch, Longmeadow Mass 58-59; Ensign US Navy Guided Missiles Sch, Dam Neck Va 59-60; Hd libn Hermes Electronics Co, Cambridge Mass 60-61; Ed coord Computer Control Co, Framingham Mass 61-62; Hd libn Allied Research Assoc, Concord Mass 62-63; Tech libn Sylvania Electronics Syst, Waltham Mass 63-67. 8: Cons on spec libs 68-. 9: SLA (Memb Com for Proposed Fla Chap); SELA. 10: Museum of the Arts, Fort Lauderdale; Jr Symphony Soc, Fort Lauderdale. 14: Admin of spec libs. 15: 2453 NE 51 st apt D312, Ft Lauderdale Fl 33308.

BAUS, CAROLA G. b Phila Pa 3 O 23. 5: Temple 44-48 (Mod lang) BA; Drezel 47-48 BLS. 7: Moore Col of Art, Phila 48-51; Scarsdale Pub Lib, Scarsdale NY 51-52; Temple Dental Pharmacy Lib, Phila 52-59; W Orange Pub Lib, W Orange NJ 59-64; Free Library of Phila, Phila 64-. 9: ALA; PennLA. 14: Catlg. 15: 7415 Dungan rd, Phila Pa 19111.

BAUXAR, J JOSEPH. b Oklahoma City Okla 9 S 10. 4: Alice McIntyre. 5: UOkla 28-32 (Anthrop) BA, 32-33 (Educ); UChicago 37-38, 49-50 (Anthrop) AM; UWis 57-58 (LS) MA. 6: Fr. 7: Archaeologist UOkla 34-37; Ethnohistorian anthrop lab UTenn (Knoxville) 38-42; Flight radio operator (S/Sgt) Air Transport Command 42-45; Archaeologist River Basin Survey, Wash DC 46-49; Research asst Ill State Mus 50-53; Instr Rockford Evening Col Rockford Ill 53-57; Asst libn Rockford Col 58-63, Act hd 63-64; Univ archivist No Ill U DeKalb Ill 64-. 9: SAA; Amer Soc Ethnohistns; IllLA. 13: Yes. 14: Historical records. 15: 1101 Suburban apts, DeKalb Il 60115.

BAXTER, CAMILLE LOUISE. b Terminal Island Cal 19 Ap 15. 5: UCLA 32-36 (Fr) BA, 36-37 (Educ) Secondary credential; UCal (Berkeley) 44-45 (LS) BS; USoCal 58 (LS) MA. 6: Fr, Ital, Sp. 7: Lib asst pub lib, S Pasadena Cal 39-40; Libn Redondo Union High Sch, Redondo Cal 40-44; Libn San Pedro High Sch, San Pedro Cal 45-55; Libn & a-v coordinator Los Angeles Harbor Col 55-, Lib cording 68-. 9: CalLA; CalASchL; Cal Tchrs Assn; Cal Jr Col Assn. 10: AAUP; Eng-Speaking Union; Pi Delta Phi; Los Angeles Mus Assts. 13: Yes. 14: Catlg, period a-v areas. 15: Los Angeles Harbor Col 1111 Figueroa pl, Wilmington Ca 90744.

BAXTER, JEANETTE (HARRELSON). b Tabor City NC 12 J 37. 4: Everett Wayne Baxter. 5: Winthrop Col 54-58 (Elem ed) BS; SEast Baptist Theo Sem 59-61 (Bible & theo) UNC at Chapel Hill summers 62-66 MS in LS. 7: Tchr Royall Elem Sch, Florence SC 58-59; Tchr Little Creek Elem Sch, Norfolk Va 61-62; Elem libn Norview Elem Sch, Norfolk Va 62-65; Elem libn Wrightsboro Elem Sch, Wilmington NC 65-67; Asst libn SEast Commun Col, Whiteville NC 67-. 9: ALA; SWLA; NCLA. 10: Beta Phi Mu. 14: Ref, child wk. 15: PO Box 11, Tabor City NC 28463.

BAXTER, RUTH (WALLACE). b Summitt Miss 12 F 08. 5: Judson Col 25-29 (Hist, music) BA; UMiss summer (LS); LSU summer 30 (Fr). 7: Tchr & libn High Sch, Johns Miss 29-30; Tchr & libn High Sch Olive Branch Miss 30; Tchr & libn High Sch, Stringer Miss 32-34; Tchr & libn High Sch, Blue Mountain Miss 35-36; Personnel clerk US War Dept, Clinton Miss 44-45; Personnel clerk USVA, Jackson Miss 45-53, Asst libn 53-. 14: Ref. 15: Va Center Med Lib, Jackson Ms 39216.

BAXTER, VIRGINIA (MACDONALD). b Portsmouth Va 28 Je 18. 4: Joe Warren Baxter. 5: Col of William and mary 36-40 (LS) BA. 6: Fr. 7: Libn Ruffner Jr High Sch Norfolk City Sch Bd 40-44; Sub ref libn sub br libn Norfolk Pub Lib summers 42-44; Lib asst US Navy, Naval Train Station, Norfolk Va 44-46; Libn Hinds Co Lib, Jackson Miss & Raymond Miss 46; Libn Dept of Archives & Hist, Jackson Miss 46-47; Libn USAF, Gunter Base Lib, Gunter AFB Ala 56-. 9: VaLA; MissLA; AlaLA; SELA. 10: DAR; PTA; Pilot Club. 14: Ref, readers serv. 15: 3561 N Georgetown dr, Montgomery Al 36109.

BAYARD, MARY IVY (STECKER). b Hazleton Penn 14 D 40. 4: Peter A Bayard. 5: Wilson Col 58-62 (Eng) AB; Drexel 62-63 MS in LS. 7: Ref libn Norristown Pub Lib, Norristown Penn 63-66, Hd adult serv 66-67; Asst dir Montgomery Co - Norristown Pub Lib, Norristown Penn 68-. 8: Teaching ref materials in the Soc Scis, Drexel, fall 65; Taught ref wkshop sponsored by Penn State Lib, spring 65. 9: ALA; Memb Chm, Penn 68-70; PennLA; (chm Com on State Docs 65-66; Chm Memb Com 66-68, chm Awards Com 68-69; v-chm SE chap 68-69). 10: Lib Pub Rel Assn of Greater Phila; Bds sellers' Assn (Phila); Phila Museum of Art. 14: Admin. 15: 542 Dekalb st, Norristown Pa 19401.

BAYLESS, JUNE ELIZABETH. b Chicago. 5: UTenn 33-37 (Eng) BA; Peabody 38-39 BS in LS. 7: Assoc libn Knoxville High Sch, Knoxville Tenn 39-45; Pub Lib, Pasadena Cal: Libn 45-48, Br libn 48-51, Chief circ dept 51-52; City Libn Pub Lib, San Marino Cal 52-69; City Libn Pub Lib, Beverly Hills Cal 69-. 8: UCal Statewide Avd Coun on Educ for Libnship 61-66; Lib Serv Adv Com East Los Angeles Jr Col 57-58; USoCal Lib Sch Adv Coun 60; Scarecrow Press Awards Jury 64-65. 9: ALA (Coun 61-65, Fed RelCoord, Cal 53-57; SoCal Mem Chm 54-56); -ASD (treas 54-56, Lib Devel & StandardsCom 58-61; Publ Liaison Com, Friends of the Lib 64-66); -PLA (pres 70, chm Stand RevCom); CalLA (v-pres 59, pres 60; SoDist v-pres 55, pres 56, Coun 67-69); Mem Cal AdvCoun on Educ for Libnship 63-67; Pub Lib Exec Assn SoCal. 10: San Marino C of C; Pasadena Symphony Assn; Friends of the Huntington Lib; Friends of San Marino Pub Lib; Pasadena Lib Club; Cal Hist Soc; Altrusa Internat; Alpha Omicron Pi. 13: Yes. 14: Admin adult serv,child serv, Californiana. 15: 1066 San Pasqual st, apt 23, Pasadena Ca 91106.

BEABES, MARY KATHERINE. b Somerset Penn 19 Mr 22. 5: Clarion State Col 39-43 (LS, Eng) BS in Ed Syracuse summer 54; UPittsburg 66-67 MLS. 7: Libn Bellwood-Antis Joint Sch Dist, Bellwood Penn 43-45; Libn Southmont Borough Pub Schs, Johnstown Penn 45-56; Libn Hempfield Area Sch Dist, Greensburg Penn 56-68; Lib coord Owen J Roberts Sch Dist, Pottstown Penn 68-. 9: NEA; ALA; Penn State EA; PennLA. 14: Sch libs, ya. 15: 782 Worth blvd, Pottstown Pa 19464.

BEACH, CECIL (PRENTICE). b Knoxville Tenn 12 Jl 27. 4: Marcia Gibson. 5: UChattanooga 46-50 (Eng) BA; Fla State U 51-52 (LS) MA. 6: Sp. 7: (Yeoman) US Navy 44-46; Bkmob libn Chattanooga Pub Lib, Tenn 48-50; Ext libn Decatur-DeKalb Lib, Decatur Ga 52-54; Dir Piedmont Reg Lib, Winder Ga 54-60; Dir Gadsden Pub Lib, Gadsden Ala 61-65; Dir Tampa Pub Lib, Tampa Fla 65-. 9: ALA (var coms); FlaLA (pres); AlaLA (pres Pub Lib Div); GaLA(treas & var coms); SELA (program chm). 10: Gadsden Comm Coun (pres 64); Kiwanis,C of C. 13: Yes. 14: Admin. 15: 900 Ashley st, Tampa Fl 33602.

BEACH, SISTER DOROTHY. b Boston Mass 25 Jl 21. 5: Trinity Col 39-43 (Eng) BA; Catholic U 50-52 MS in LS, 60-62 (Medieval Hist) MA. 6: Fr. 7: Sec ABC, NYC 43-44; Communications Ensign US Naval Res (Womans Res), Wash DC 44-46; High sch tchr Sisters of Notre Dame, Ilchester Md & Phila 48-50; Asst libn Trinity Col Lib, Wash DC 50-. 14: Ref, catlg. 15: Trinity College, Washington DC 20017.

BEACH, ROBERT FULLERTON. b Brooklyn NY 14 Jl 11. 4: Eva Ripley. 5: WesleyanU 28-32 (Eng) BA; Columbia 32-33 (LS) BS, summers 37-40 (LS) MS. 7: Ref & circ asst YaleU Lib 33-36; Supv of res Berea Col Lib 36-43; Libn Garrett Biblical Inst 46-51; Libn Union Theol Sem (NYC) 51-. 8: Staff summer session Columbia Sch of Lib Serv 60, 62, 64, 66, 68. 9: ALA (Coun 52-54); ATheol LA (sec 47-50, v-pres 53-54, pres 54-56; chm, Alumni Asso, Columbia U Sch of Lib Serv 66-67. 13: Yes. 14: Theol Sem Libs. 15: 99 Claremont ave NYC 10027.

BEACH, RUTH (MILDRED). b Glen Ridge NJ 30 Jl 20. 5: Hood Col 39-40; Cedar Crest Col 40-43 (Hist) BA; McGill 50-51 BLS. 7: Archivist Nat Archives, Wash DC 44-46; Clerk Naval Records Mgt Center, Los Angeles & San Francisco 46-48; File org Shaw-Walker Co NYC 48-49; Clerk pictures collection NY Pub Lib 49-50; Post libn US Army Spec Serv, Japan & Korea 51-53; Libn pictures collection NY Pub Lib 54-64; Acquis Montclair State Col 64-. 9: SLA (sec Picture Div; NY chap: chm Picture group). 10: AAUW; Cosmopolitan Club of Montclair. 14: Acquis, pictures. 15: 12 Victoria terrace, Upper Montclair NJ 07043.

BEACH, VERL E (GOODWIN). b Genoa Neb 5 Ag 06. 4: Louis M Beach. 5: Neb State Tchrs Col 29-30 (Art) 2 yr certif; Ore StateU 56-57 (Educ) BS; UOre summers 58-65 (US) MS. 7: Elem tchr, Neb 24-28, 30-32; Elem tchr, Ill 32-34; Elem tchr Ore 57-60; Elem libn, Philomath Ore 60-. 9: NEA; OreEA; OreLA; OreSchLA. 14: Child lit, rare bks, ref, a-v. 15: 1940 N 23 st, Corvallis Or 97330.

BEACOCK, E STANLEY. b Elmvale Ont 21 Ja 21. 4: Nadine M Beacock. 5: QueensU (Kingston Ont) 39-42 BA; Toronto 46-47 BLS, 69 MLS; Columbia summer 65 (Bus Admin); U West Ont summer 68 (Mgt) Certif. 7: Artillery Can Army 42-46; Libn Lambton Co Lib, Wyoming Ont 47-49; Libn Hardin Co Lib, Kenton Ohio 49-53; Libn Troy-Miami Pub Lib, Troy Ohio 53-61; Asst dir London Pub Lib & Art Museum, London Ont 61-66; Dir Midwest Reg Lib Syst, Kitchener Ont 66-. 9: CanLA; ALA; OntLA; Inst Prof Libns Ont (Bd Dirs). 10: London C of C; Torch Club; London Coun for Adult Educ. 14: Admin, reg libs. 15: 637 Victoria st N, Kitchener Ontario Can.

BEACOM, MARJORIE (ALEXANDER). b Penn 12 F 23. 5: Sullins Col 40-42 (Art & Sec); Cal State (Los Angeles) 60-63 (Eng) BA; USoCal 63-66 MSLS. 6: Fr. 7: Ref libn Alta Pub Lib, Altadena Cal 66, Phono record catlgr 67; Libn Cal Inst of Tech, Pasadena Cal 68-. 9: ALA. 14: Catlg, ref. 15: 1400 S Los Robles ave, Pasadena Ca 91106.

BEAD, CHARLES C(ONRAD). b Berlin Germany 1 S 05. 4: Hildegard Minz. 5: UBerlin 32 (Law); UErlangen (Germany) 35 Dr Jur; UIll 46 BS in LS. 6: Fr, Ger, Sp, Lat, Gk. 7: US Army intelligence & censorship Prisoner of War Camp Tech Sgt 43-45; LC; Sr descr catlgr 46-50, Sr subj catlgr 50-62, Prin catlgr Subj Catlg Div 62-67, Asst chief subj catlg div 67-. 9: ALA; AALL; DCLA. 10: Beta Phi Mu. 13: Yes. 14: Catlg & clsf, (law & soc scis). 15: 4201 Mass ave NW, Wash DC 20016.

BEAL, CATHERINE (NORA). b Omaha 22 F 04. 5: OmahaU 21-23; Grinnell Col 24-26 (Hist) BA; Columbia 32-33 (LS) BA. 7: Omaha Pub Lib: Asst catlg dept 26-30, Head South Br Lib 30-52, Supv adult serv 52-67, Supv exten serv 67-. 9: ALA; NebLA (pres 37-38); Oma Adult Educ Coun (pres 60-61). 10: AAUW. 15: Omaha Pub Lib, 1823 Harney st, Omaha Nb 68102.

BEAL, GEORGE. b Newton Mass 16 Ap 12. 4: Amey Owen. 5: Dartmouth 30-32 (Eng); BostonU 33-35 (Eng) AB, 35-36 (Eng) AM; Bentley Col Accounting & Finance 37-39 (Accounting) Diploma; Simmons Col Sch of Lib Sci 65-67 (LS) MS. 6: Fr, Lat. 7: Eng instr High Sch, Plainville Conn 36-37; Accountant H P Hood & Sons, Boston 39-46; Eng instr BostonU 46-50; Credit mgr Hub Distributors Boston 50-51; Asst v-pres NY Termimal Warehouse Co, Atlanta & Boston 51-65; Hd circ dept Baker Lib Harvard 65-68; Hd circ dept Wessell Lib Tufts 68-. 8: Eng lectr BostonU 58-68. 9: Mod Lang Assn; ALA. 14: Readers serv. 15: 152 Curtis st, Somerville Ma 02144.

BEALL, BARBARA ANN. b Wash DC 6 Ag 40. 5: UDel 58-60; George Washington U 60-62 (Eng lit) AB; Sch Lib Serv Columbia 62-63 (Lib Serv) MS. 6: Fr, Sp. 7: Catlgr Engineering Soc Lib, NYC 63-65; Research assoc Chase Manhattan Bank, NYC 65-67; McKeldin Lib UMd: Assoc libn I 67, Assoc libn II 67, Assoc libn II Rare Bk Room 67-. 9: ALA; ACRL; SLA (Wash DC chap Mus & Document divs); DCLA. 10: AAUP; Univ of Md Chapter AAUP. 11: Phi Beta Kappa; Beta Phi Mu. 14: Ref, archives, loc hist, document. 15: 11616 Lockwood dr, Silver Spring Md 20904.

BEALL, ELIZABETH A. b Pittsburgh Pa 4 Ap 21. 5: Carnegie-Mellon U 39-44 (Bus Studies) BS; UPittsburgh 63-64 MLS. 7: Sec & Receptionist T Mellon & Sons, Pittsburgh 52-55; Sec J H Overpeck Co, Pittsburgh 51-57; Exec Sec Chemstrand Corp, Decatur Ala NYC 57-63; Children's Libn NY Pub Lib, 64-66; Libn St Mary's Sch, Peekskill NY 66-67; Catlgr Carnegie Lib of Pittsburgh, 67-69; Catlgr Rollins Col, 69-. 9: ALA; FlaLA. 14: Catlg. 15: 104C Jamestown dr, Winter Park Fl 32789.

BEAM, EVELYN (ROPER). b Calhoun Ala 7 Je 09. 4: Arnett R Beam. 5: Hampton Inst 28-32 (Fr, Soc Studies) BS in LS. 6: Fr. 7: Libn Dart Hall Br Lib, Charleston SC 32; Libn Huntington High Sch, Newport News Va 32-34; Instr lib sci AtlantaU 34; Lib asst Hampton Inst, Hampton Va 39-40; Libn Robert Robinson Br, Alexandria Va 40-42; Clk US War Prod Bd, Wash DC 42-43; Lib asst LC 43-. 10: Delta Sigma Theta; NAACP; Dir Child Choir, Calvary Episcopal Church, Wash 54-. 14: Catlg. 15: 524 Okla ave NE, Wash DC 20002.

BEAMGUARD, ELIZABETH PARKS. b Fayetteville Tenn. 5: UTenn 31 (Eng, Span) AB; Emory 44 (LS) BS. 7: Sch libn

Tenn Educ Assn, Chattanooga 40-44; Dir Huntsville-Madison Co Lib, Huntsville Ala 44-55; Libn UAla Ext Center, Huntsville Ala 53-54; Ala Pub Lib Serv: Field rep, Montgomery Ala 56-60, Dir 60-. 8: Instr, spec lib course UAla summer 62 & 66; Dir of TVA Demonstration: Southeastern Coun of Adult Educ, SoStates Wk Conf on Adult Educ, White House Conf on Youth, & White House Conf on Aging; Mem of original Mayor's Huntsville-Redstone Arsenal Liaison Com; one of two libns from So selected to attend Allerton Park Conf on Lib Educ. 9: SELA; SEAdult Educ Assn; Amer Soc Pub Admin; ALA; AlaLA. 10: Ala Com on Child & Youth; Governor's Com White House Conf on Aging; Ala Writer's Conclave, Ala Federated Women's Clubs; Delta Kappa Gamma; AAUW; Altrusa Internat. 11: Resolution from Ala Legis. 12: "Poetry in American Voices" (32); Ed "Library Notes," AlaLA. 13: Yes. 14: Consul serv to child & youth; early Amer hist. 15: 3373 Dartmouth circle, Montgomery Ala 36111.

BEAN, REV GORDON A. b Toronto 13 Mr 30. 5: St Michael's Col of UToronto 48-51 (Philos) BA; St Augustine's Sem (Toronto) 51-55 (Theol); UMich 64-65 AMLS. 7: Asst pastor St Brigid's RC Church, Toronto 55-60; Asst pastor St Margaret's Church, Midland Ont Can 60-64; Chaplain Can Army (Militia) Grey & Simcoe Regt 60-64; Libn St Augustine's Sem & Col (Scarborough Ont) 65-. 8: Pastor, Cath Deaf Congregation Toronto. 9: ALA; CathLA; Can Lib Assn; OntLA. 10: Beta Phi Mu. 15: St Augustine's Sem Kingston rd, Scarborough Ont Canada.

BEAN, ROBERT GORDON. b London Ont Can 16 Mr 33. 4: Ann Burchell. 5: UWest Ont 51-54 (Geog) BA; Toronto 60-61 BLS. 6: Fr. 7: Catlgr UWaterloo (Waterloo Ont) 61-64, Head of Catlg Dept 64-68, Sys libn 68-. 9: CanLA; ALA; OntLA; Institute Prof Libns Ont. 14: Catlg, systems, automation. 15: 44 Austin dr, Waterloo Ont Canada.

BEAR, JEAN (TRIMBLE). b Richmond Va 29 S 40. 5: King Col 59-63 (Eng) BA; Pittsburgh 63-64 MLS. 7: Ref libn Richmond Pub Lib, Richmond Va 63-66, Hd ref dept 66-. 9: ALA; VaLA (gr Mem RT). 10: Beta Phi Mu. 14: Ref. 15: 904 W Ladies Mile rd, Richmond Va 23227.

BEARD, ANNETTE (HUDDLESTON). b Montgomery Ala 20 S 33. 4: Timothy Field Beard. 5: UAla 52-56 (LS) BS. 6: Sp. 7: Libn Jr High Sch, Anniston Ala 56-58; Libn Life Off Mgt Assn, NYC 58-. 9: SLA (chm Insurance Div 67-68). 10: DAR. 14: Ref. 15: 38 Barrow st, New York NY 10014.

BEARD, CHARLES EDWARD. b New Orleans 21 Jl 40. 5: UAla 58-62 (Hist) BA; Fla State U 62-64 (LS) MS. 6: Ger. 7: Grad asst Fla State U Lib 62-63; Tchr Caldwell Elem Sch, Scottsboro Ala 63-64; Asst br libn Jacksonville Pub Lib, Jacksonville Fla 64; Admin off, act head of ref dept US Army Command & Gen Staff Col Lib, Ft Leavenworth Kan (1st Lt) QM Corps 64-66; Hd ref dept U Ala, 66-69, Hd Acquis dept U Ala 69-. 10: ALA; SeLA; Ft Leavenworth Hist Soc; Assn of the US Army; Beta Phi Mu; Phi Alpha Theta. 12: Bk rev "Military Review" (65-). 14: Ref, admin, acquis. 15: P O Box 506, Scottsboro Al 35768.

BEARD, DORA M. b Vidalia La 31 Ja 15. 5: LSU 31-35 (Eng) BA, 55-60 (LS) MS. 7: Serv rep Southern Bell Telephone Co 36-40; Sec E I duPont de Nemours, Baton Rouge La 41-44; Sec Ethyl Corp, Baton Rouge La 46-51; Research libn Pub Affairs Research Coun, Baton Rouge La 51-63; Asst libn & Asst Prof of Lib sci, Northeast La State Col 63-. 9: SLA (chm Chap Program 59-60, Publicity chm 61-62); LaLa (sec 62-63, chm Subject Specialists Sect 69-70; La Tchrs Assn. 10: SWLA; AAUW; Delta Kappa Gamma; Beta Phi Mu. 11: SLA-La Chap award as outstanding grad of LSU Lib Sch (60). 12: Co-author "La State Agencies Handbook" (60); "A Selective Subject Index: PAR Research 1951-1960". 13: Yes. 14: Ref admin. 15: 1007 Park ave, Monroe La 71201.

BEARD, DOROTHY (WALTER). b Milton Ore. 4: Erwin J Beard. 5: UOre 26-27 (Math); Whitman Col 28-31 (Math) AB; UWash summers 63-67 M Lib. 6: Sp. 7: Libn Sr High Sch, Walla Walla Wash 60-. 9: NEA; WashStateASchL (treas). 10: AAUW; YWCA; Delta Kappa Gamma. 14: Catlg, documentation, sch libs. 15: 116 E Maple, Walla Walla Wa 99362.

BEARD, JOHN ROBERT. b Milk River Alta Can 29 D 18. 4: Patricia D Hehir. 5: Calgary (Alta) Normal Sch 38-39 (Educ) Tchrs certif; UBC 49-52 (Fr,Span) BA; Toronto 53-54 BLS; Columbia 56-59, 65 (LS) DLS. 6: Fr, Sp. 7: Tchr elem schs, Alta Can 39-42; Tech Consolidated Mining & Smelting Co, Trail BC 42-50, 52-53; Ref asst Windsor Pub Lib, Windsor Ont 54-56; Circ libn Bus Lib ColumbiaU 56-58; Tchg asst Sch Lib Serv ColumbiaU 58-59; Head acquis div Vancouver Pub Lib, Vancouver BC 59-61; Chief libs devel sect UNESCO, Paris 62-64; Assoc libn Montclair State Col 65-66, Head libn 66-. 9: ALA; CanLA; NEA; NJLA; NJEA; AAHE. 10: AAUP; Montclair State Col Faculty Assn; Coun of NJ State Col & Univ Libns. 11: Fellowships from Can Coun 60 & 61. 12: "Canadian Provincial Libraries," (CanLA 67). 13: Yes. 14: Admin. 15: 310 W 79th st Apt 10WF, NYC 10024.

BEARD, PATRICIA DAWN (HEHIR). b Toowoomba Queensland Australia 1 Mr 22. 4: John Robert Beard. 5: Queensland State Tchrs' Col 39-40 (Ed) Tchr's Certif; UBC 51-53 (Eng, Pol sci); UWest Ont 55-56 (Eng, Pol sci) BA; Columbia 56-58 Lib Sci MLS, 67- (LS). 6: Fr. 7: State sch tchr Queensland, Australia 40-48; Vancouver Pub Lib: Lib clerical 48-54, children's libn 59-62; Lib asst Windsor Pub Lib, Windsor Ont 54-55; NYC Pub Lib: Lib trainee 56-58, children's libn 58-59, Sr children's libn 67-68; Libn Amer Studs' & Artists' Ctr, Paris 64; Hd children's dept Spainbrook Br Yonkers Pub Lib, Yonkers NY 66-67. 9: ALA; CanLA; NYLA. 10: Beta Phi Mu. 11: Higher Educ Act of 65 Fellowship 68, 69. 14: Child serv. 15: 310 W 79th st, apt 10wf, New York NY 10024.

BEARDEN, JOAN (LADEN). b Jersey City NJ 29 Jl 34. 4: Michael M Bearden. 5: Allegheny Col 51-53; Ohio StateU (summer) 54; TulaneU 53-55 (Econ) BA; LSU 68-69 9ls0 ms. 6: Fr, Sp. 7: Trainee LSU (Baton Rouge) 68-69, Sr libn 69; Asst libn Fla Jr Col 69-. 9: ALA-ACRL; LaLA. 10: Beta Phi Mu. 14: Educ for libnship, hist of books & libs, devel of jr col libs. 15: Fla Jr Col at Jacksonville, Jacksonville Fl 32207.

BEARDSLEY, FRANCES M. b Auburn NY 20 Ag 41. 5: Barnard 59-60; SUNY at Albany 61-64 (His) BA, 64-68 MLS. 7: Stud asst Lib Sch Lib SUNY at Albany 62-63; Children's libn Wingate Br Schenectady Co Pub Lib, Schenectady NY 65-. 9: ALA-PLA; AASchL; -CSD; NYLA; Hudson-MohawkLA. 14: Child serv. 15: 210 2 Westside ave, Schenectady NY 12306.

BEARRY, ANNIE LAURIE. b Bessemer Ala 2 Ag 38. 5: UUtah 56-61 (Fr) BA; UCal (Berkeley) 62-63 MLS UKan 66 (Eng). 6: Fr. 7: Stud asst UUtah Lib 57-61; Clerk & apprentice libn Richmond Pub Lib, Richmond Cal 62-63; Asst order libn & instr in lib sci UUtah Lib 63-67, Lit libn and instr in Lib Sci 68-. 9: UtahLA; ALA. 10: Beta Phi Mu. 14: Acquis, tchg lib sci, ref wk in humanities. 15: 860 E 5th SApt 12, Salt Lake City 84102.

BEARY, EUGENE GEORGE. b Whitman Mass 2 Mr 26. 5: Boston U 47-51 (Geol) AB; Simmons 64-66 (LS) MS. 7: Ref libn US Army Quartermaster R & E Center, Natick Mass 58-62; Libn Armed Forces Food & Container Inst, Chicago 62-63; Ref libn US Army Natick Labs, Natick Mass 63-66, Chief ref serv 66-68, Chief lib serv group 69-. 9: SLA; MassLA. 14: Ref, admin, translations, lib automation. 15: 12 Alfred ter, Randolf Ma 02368.

BEASLEY, CLARENCE JR. b Gainesville Fla. 5: Brigham Young 58-60 (Hist) LS; Syracuse 63-67 (LS). 7: (SSGT) USAF active duty 53-57; Page Washoe Co Lib, Reno Nev 57; Stud asst UFla 57; Staff memb Brigham Young, 57-58; Libn I Jefferson Parish Lib, Gretha La 61-63; Asst libn St Johns River Jr Col, Palatka Fla 64-66; Libn Oceanway Elem-Jr High Sch, Jacksonville Fla 66-68; Adminis libn St John The Baptist Parish Lib, La Place La 69-. 9: ALA; FLA; LaLA; SWLA; DuvalCoLA. 14: Admin. 15: PO Box 672, La Place La 70068.

BEASLEY, DAVID RICHARD. b Hamilton Can 4 My 31. 4: Viola Nicholas. 5: McMaster U 50-53 (Eng Lit, Hist) BA; Sorbonne 54-55 (Modern Fr Lit); Pratt 64 MLS. 6: Fr, Ger. 7: Salesman Weston's, London 53-54; Tchr London Co Coun, London 56; Tchr Hochschulle fur Wien, Vienna 57-58; Tchr Grace Church Sch N YC 59-61; Soc researcher Columbia U & JBG, NYC 62-63; Catlgr NY Pub Ref Lib 65-, Econ ref 65-, Labor econ spec 68-. 10: NY Lib Guild AFSCME Local 1930 (pres 68-); Coordin, City & Co pubs bibl. 14: Catlg., Ref. 15: 141 East 26th st, NYC 10010.

BEASLEY, ROGER EVAN. b Hammond Ind 19 Je 40. 5: IndU 58-62 (Russian) AB, 62-64 (Slavic lang & lit) MA, 64-67 (LS) MA. 6: Russian, Other Slavic langs, Ger, Sp, Fr. 7: IndU: Rare bk catlgr Lilly Lib, 64-65 Slavic sect catlgr 66-67; Slavic bibliogr SyracuseU Carnegie Lib 67-. 14: Bibliog. 15: 601 Allen st, Syracuse NY 13210.

BEATON, MAXINE (BAILEY). b Mass 13 Ap 15. 4: William B Beaton. 5: Simmons 32-36 (LS) BS. 07. Guest Lecturer

UDenver Sch of Libnship; Med Libn Mass Gen Hosp Sch of Nursing, Boston 37-39; Med Libn Bellevue Hosp Sch of Nursing, NYC 39-41; Med libn Burbank Hosp, Futchburg Mass 43-44; Coun AAF Convalescent Hosp, Ft Logan Colo 44-45; Med Libn Presbyterian Med Ctr, Denver 51-. 8: Consultant: Denver Clinic, Denver Colo 66-; Colo Assocd Nursing Homes, Denver Colo 68-; General Rose Mem Hosp, Denver Colo 66; Luth General Hosp, Denver Colo 67; Mental Health Inst, Mt Pleasant Iowa 66. 9: SLA (pres Colo Chap 53-54 & 63-64; sec Hosp Div 54-55, v-chm 55-56; chm 56-57); MedLA; ColoLA (2d v-pres 68-69); Colo Coun for Lib Develop 66-; Colo Coun of Med Libns 53-. 14: Hosp Libs. 15: 1725 Albion st, Denver Co 80220.

BEATTIE, PEGGY (FAIRCLOTH). b Toronto Can 12 Ap 16. 4: William Beattie. 5: UToronto 34-35, 37-38 BA, 39-40 BLS. 6: Fr, Ger. 7: Reviser UToronto Lib Sch 40-44; Lib asst Toronto Pub Lib 44-45; Sec-treas Ont Lib Assoc, Toronto 51-61; Catlgr Can Inst for Intl Affairs, Toronto 65-. 14: Catlg. 15: 135 Alexandra blvd, Toronto 12 Ont Can.

BEATTY, WILLIAM KAYE. b Toronto 5 F 26. 4: Virginia L(ewis). 5: Harvard 46-49 (Lat,Gk); Columbia 50-51 (Classics) BA, 51-52 (LS) MS. 6: Lat. 7: Lib interne HarvardU, Cambridge Mass 49; Circ asst Col of Physicians of Phila 52-53; Asst libn Readers' Serv, Phila 54-56; UMo: Assoc libn & Asst Prof Med Bibliog 56-57, Assoc libn & Assoc Prof Med Bibliog 57-62; Libn & Prof Med Bibliog NorthwesternU Med Sch 62-. 8: Consul; Yale Nursing Index Project 60; "Biol Abstracts," 61; UVt Col of Med Lib61; Presbyt-St Lukes Hosp Lib, Chicago 64; NLM Com on Sel Lit "MEDLARS," 65-; Pub Health Serv Adv Com on Sci Publs 65; NLM Com on Manpower Training 66-; Consul on Lib Bldgs& progs. 9: Amer Assn Hist Med (Coun 65-68); ALA-AHIL (chm Spec Com Respons forMaterials 61, Bd Dirs 62-64, chm Conf Prog Com 62-63; pres 65-66); MedLA (Bd dirs66-69, chm Com Period Ser Publ 55-61, chm Med Soc group 56, chm Med Sch group 60, chm "Vital Notes on Med Period" Com 61; SLA (Bd Dirs 64-; Biol Sci Div; Exec Bd 60-65,sec-treas 61-62, chm 63-64; Hosp Div; chm 60-61, chm Inter assn Hosp Lib Com63-64, pres Ill chap 69-70); Lib Assn (Gt Brit); Soc Med Hist, Chicago (Coun 63-). 10: Amer Med Writers Assn; Boston Athenaeum; Chicago Literary Club; Franklin Inn Club; Phi Beta Pi. 12: Ed "Transactions & Studies of the College of Physicians of Philadelphia," (55-56);Ed "Vital Notes on Medical Periodicals," (55-); Ed "The Reminder" (Biol Sci Div SLA60-61); Ed Bd, "Familiar Medical Quotations" 63-68. 13: Yes. 14: Med bibliog, med hist. 15: 1509 Forest ave, EvanstonIl 60201.

BEATY, M PAUL JR. b Philipsburg Penn 27 D 38. 4: L Gay Herbst. 5: Ind UPenn 59-63 9geog) BS in Ed; UPittsburgh 65-66 MLS. 7: Personnelman, 2nd Class, USN 56-59; High sch tchr Huntingdon High Sch, Huntingdon Penn 63-64; Jr High Tchr Albuquerque Schs 64-65; Asst catlg libn UDel 66-68; Asst catlg libn E Stroudsburg State Col 66-. 14: Admin, personnel, acquis, catlg. 15: RD #1 Box 240A, E Stroudsburg Pa 18301.

BEAVER, DORIS J (JUNE). b Hegins Penn 28 Jl 17. 4: Somer C Beaver. 5: Indiana UPenn 34-38 BS Ed; UPittsburgh 63-65 LS MLS. 7: Elem teacher pub schls, Gratz Penn 38-42; Elem tchr pub schls, Bethel Park Penn 42-46; Elem tchr pub schls, Snowden Twp, Penn 60-66; Elem libn South Park Sch Dist, Penn 66-. 9: ALA; PennLA; PennStateEA. 14: Sch libs. 15: 6454 Library rd, Library Pa 15129.

BEAVER, LUCILE E(LIZABETH). b Gainesville Ga 1 F 26. 5: Agnes Scott Col 42-46 (Math) BA with high honor; UGa 46-48 (Math) MA; Columbia 48-49 (LS) MS. 6: Ger, Fr. 7: Libn-hostess Riverside Mil Acad, Gainesville Ga & Hollywood Fla 49-54; Army libn Spec Serv Libs, Giessen & Ulm Germany 54-56; Asst command libn NACom US Army Spec Serv, Frankfurt Germany 56-59; Libn-recruiter Dept of the Army Spec Serv, Wash DC 59-63; Ref libn act chm info retrieval Fed Aviation Agency Lib Serv Div, Wash DC 63-65, Chief ref & research br 65-. 9: ALA; SLA (DC chap: Sci-Tech, Mil Libns & Transportation groups). 10: Phi Beta Kappa; Sigma Xi; Pi Mu Epsilon; Smithsonian Assocs. 14: Ref, pub rel, recrment, lib educ, info retr. 15: 1400 S Joyce st B-709, Arlington Va 22202.

BEAVIN, HELEN IRENE (SHINN). b Rugby ND 5 Ap 37. 4: Bartlett C Beavin. 5: UWis 55-59 (Eng educ) BS; 59-60 (LS) MS. 7: Libn East High Sch, Madison Wis 60-63; BostonU Sch of Educ: Ref libn 63-64, Asst libn 64-66; Res libn UMich 66-68, Libn circ serv and res 68-. 9: ALA-ACRL. 10: Pi Lambda Theta; Phi Kappa Phi; Beta Phi Mu. 14: Univlibs, sch libs. 15: 1814 Arbordale dr, Ann Arbor Mi 48103.

BEAVIN, MARY (WHEELER). b Youngstown Ohio 19 N 18. 4: Alfred D Beavin. 5: Coucher Col 37-42 (Eng) AB; UDenver 42-43 BS in LS. 6: Fr. 7: Page Enoch Pratt Free Lib, Baltimore 34-41; Chamber of Com Lib, YMCA 42; Asst libn Midland Co (Tex) Lib, Midland Tex 43-44, Libn 44-46; Trustee & org of small libs in Vt 58-63; Ref & adult serv libn TB Scott Lib, Wisconsin Rapids Wis 63-66; Dir Stevens Pt Pub Lib, Stevens Pt Wis 66-68; Libn Kellogg-Hubbard Lib, Montpelier Vt 68-. 9: ALA; WisLA (Recr Com 64-); VtLA; NELA. 14: Ref, adult serv. 15: TB Scott Lib, Wisconsin Rapids Wi 54494.

BEBBINGTON, MARGUERITE. b Providence 16 My 22. 5: Upsala Col 40-44 (Chem) BA; Pratt 59-62 MLS. 7: Asst chem Bakelite Corp, Boomfield NJ 44-46; Internat Nickel Co Inc, NYC; Lib asst 46-47, Tech asst 47-56, Lit chem 56-62, Lit spec 62-63; Libn Tetanium Pigment Div Nat Lead Co, Sayreville NJ 63-. 8: Consul in chem lit, Monclair State Col, summer 68-69. 9: ACS (Chem Lit Div, Abstract for chem documentation); Natl Assn of Correcion Engnrs (chm Abstract Subcom 49-55); SLA (ed Metals Div "News", NY Chap, Directory Com 58-59, NJ Chap, 2nd v-pres 64-65, mem &/or chm var coms). 10: Woman's Club of Upper Montclair NJ; Beta Phi Mu. 14: Ref. 15: P O Box 58, South Amboy NJ 08879.

BEBEAU, GORDON H. b Manistique Mich 25 Jl 20. 4: Jean Trantanella. 5: No Mich Col 46-49 (Hist) BS; UWis 49-50 BSLS. 7: Libn UWis Lib (Madison) 50-52; Libn Sturgeon Bay Pub Lib, Sturgeon Bay Wis 52-55; Ref libn Mich State Lib 55-56; Dir Valparaiso Pub Lib, Valparaiso Ind 57-61; Dir Appleton Pub Lib, Appleton Wis 61-. 9: ALA; WisLA. 15: 907 E Frances st, Appleton Wi 54911.

BECERRA, BERTA A. b Sagua la Grande Las Villas Cuba 13 Jl 08. 5: Havana U 25-29, 46 doctor in Pedagogy), 47-49 (LS); Lib of Congress spec fellowship to study lib schs org in var lib schs in US 49-50 Diploma in Lib Educ. 6: Sp, Portu, Ital. 7: Asst dir Biblioteca Sociedad Economica Amigos del Pais Havana 45-48, Dir 48-60; Dir Escuela Cubana de Bibliotecarios, Havana 50-60, Prof 50-54; Libn Lat Amer Studies UNC Lib (Chapel Hill) 62-64, Lat Amer bibliogr 64-. 9: Asociacion Cubana de Bibliotecarios (v-pres 49, pres 50-51 & 56-57); ALA; Lat Amer Studies Assn; Sem Acquis Lat Amer Lib Materials; IFLA (pres Hispanic-Amer Sect 58-60). 12: "La Ciencia del Bibliotecario," (49); "Bibliografia del Padre Bartolome de las Casas" (49); "La Imprenta en Cuba en el siglo XVIII" (51); "Indice de la Revista de la Facultad de Letras y Ciencias de la Universidad de la Habana" (44). 13: Yes. 14: Bibliog. 15: 106 Hamilton rd, Chapel Hill NC 27514.

BECHAM, GERALD (CHARLES). b Thomaston Ga 20 Jl 38. 5: La Grange Col 56-60 (Piano) BA; Emory 61-63 (LS) MLn. 6: Ger. 7: Tech libn Thiokol Chemical Corp, Huntsville Ala 63-64; Tech libn AEDC Lib ARO Inc, Arnold Air Force Station Tenn 64-. 9: SLA. 11: Tommie Dora Barker Fellowship Emory U. 14: Catlg, ref. 15: AECD Library ARO Inc, Arnold Air Force Station Tn 37389.

BECK, BEATRICE MAE (ANDE). b Pasadena Cal 1 S 34. 4: Myron Beck. 5: John Muir Col 52-54 (Hist) AA; Whittier Col 54-55 (Psych) BA; USoCal 55-56 MS in LS Claremont Grad Sch 67-. 7: Page Pasadena Pub Lib, Pasadena Cal 52-53; Br libn Altadena Pub Lib, Altadena Cal 57-59; Child libn Los Angeles Co Lib, El Monte Cal 59-60; Educ libn Cal State Col (Los Angeles) 60-68, Acquis libn 68-69; Hd Catlg dept Cal StatePolytech Col 69-. 9: CalStateEA; CalLA; SoCal Coun on Child & YP's Lit. 10: Pilambda Theta; Delta Phi Upsilon. 13: Yes. 14: Child lit. 15: 1428 Oxford ave, Claremont Ca 91711.

BECK, MARGARET V. b Elk River Minn 19 Jl 13. 5: St Cloud State Col 31-33, 41-42 (Elem Educ) BS; UDenver summers 59-62 (LS) MA. 7: Elem tchr, Anoka Co Minn 33-40; Elem tchr, Groveland Minn 42-44; Elem tchr, Austin Minn 44-59, Elem libn 59-. 8: Instr; UDenver Inst summer 67, UDenver summer session 68. 9: NEA; ALA; -AASchL; MinnEA; MinnASchL (sec 66-68). 12: Co-auth of a series of Lib Skill Bks & Guide Bks (65-68). 14: Elem sch media ctrs. 15: 305 First ave NW, Austin Mn 55912.

BECK, RICHARD JOSEPH. b St Paul 1 Jl 28. 4: Shirley Lewis. 5: St Thomas Col 46-49 (Econ) BA; UMinn 49-50 BS in LS, 54-55 (LS) MA. 7: Exch libn Iowa State 50; US Army (Engrs-cpl) 51-52; Ref libn Iowa State 53, Clsfr 53-54; Bibliographic searcher UMinn(Minneapolis) 54-55; Loan libn UDetroit 55-57; Sci libn UIdaho 57-60, Assoc libn Head Pub Serv 60-67, Act libn 67-68, Assoc dir 68-. 8: Chm Nat Lib Week for Idaho 64. 9: ALA; (mem &/or chm several coms); IdahoLA; (pres 68-69 mem various coms); PNLA (mem several coms). 10: Moscow Toastmasters Club (pres); Idaho State

Employees Assoc, Univ chap (past pres). 12: Ed "The Bookmark" quarterly publ UIdaho. 13: Yes. 14: Ref, admin. 15: 418 C st, Moscow Id 83843.

BECK, VIRGINIA E. b Dorchester Mass 28 Ag 18. 5: Simmons 36-40 (LS) BS. 6: Fr, Ger, Sp. 7: Temp catlgr Thomas Crane Pub Lib, Quincy Mass 41; Asst libn NEasternU 41-42; Store mgr Campbell & Hall Inc, Boston 42-50; Bk buyer & libn Charles E Lauriat Co, Boston 50-56; Libn Mass Dept of Com, Boston 57-62; Catlgr Mus of Fine Arts, Boston 65-. 12: "Love on the Run" (54); "Stormy Voyage" (55); "The Pastoral Heart" (60). 13: Yes. 14: Catlg. 15: 82 Otis st, Milton Ma 02186.

BECKER, ALAN IRA. b NYC 25 Ag 36. 4: Ruth (Friedman). 5: Manhattan Sch of Mus 54-58 9composition & Applied mus) Bachelor of Mus; UMiami 59-60 (Mus educ); Syracuse 61-63 MSLS. 6: Fr. 7: Musician various symphony orchestras -58; Lib asst Mus lib UMiami 58-59; Libn Miami Pub Lib 61-66; Dir Hallandale Pub Lib, Hallandale Fla 66-. 8: Adv & consul Hallandale (Fla) Pub Lib construction 68. 9: FlaLA (Resolutions com 69); Brow and Co LA. 14: Music libnship, Fla collections, conserv, lib admin. 15: 11517 NE 12th ave, Miami Fl 33161.

BECKER, BARBARA (LOUISE) KELLER. b Findlay Ohio 21 N 23. 5: Oberlin Col 41-45 (Modern langs) AB; UMich 47-48 ABLS. 6: Fr, Ger. 7: Stud asst Findlay Pub Lib, Findlay Ohio 38-41; Stud asst Oberlin Col Lib 41-45; Libn Jones, Day, Cockley & Reavis Attys, Cleveland 45-47; Asst in acquis UMich Law Lib (Ann Arbor) 47-48; Asst libn-catlgr Findlay Pub Lib, Findlay Ohio 51-52; Libn Mich Mun League, Ann Arbor Mich 59-63; Asst libn-catlgr Parke Davis & Co, Ann Arbor Mich 63-. 8: Ann Arbor Pub Lib Adv Coun 58-62 & chm of Ext Serv. 9: SLA; (Pharmaceut Div rep., Microfilm Com) MichLA; Washtenaw Co LA (v-pres). 10: Muscular Dystrophy Assn (pres Washtenaw Co Chap); Friends of the Ann Arbor Pub Lib (pres). 13: Yes. 14: Catlg. 15: 2761 Aurora, Ann Arbor Mi 48105.

BECKER, HELEN ELIZABETH. b St Ignatius Mont 8 Mr 24. 5: Laval U 40-42 (Fr); Swarthmore 42-44 (Fr) BA; West Res 46-47 BS in LS; Lehigh 56-57 (Hist)MA. 6: Fr, Sp. 7: Lib trainee Govt Prtg Off, Wash DC 45-46; Jr libn Indianapolis Pub Lib, Indianapolis 47-48; Spec serv libn US Army Europe 48-56; Asst libn (catlgr) Atlas Chem Ind Inc, Wilmington Del 57-67; Consul Conn State Lib 67-. 9: ALA; SLA; ConnLA; NELA. 14: Catlg, ref, admin. 15: 21 Sharon lane, Wethersfield Ct 06109.

BECKER, HELEN. b Barberton Ohio 2 S 22. 5: UPittsburgh 39-43 (Eng lit) AB; Carnegie 50 MLS. 6: Ger, Fr, Srbo/Croat, Russian, Yiddish, Polish. 7: Carnegie Lib, Pittsburgh; Art catlgr 50-54, Bibliog 54-60, Head catlg dept 60-61; Catlgr Hunt Botanical Lib, Carnegie 61-62; Sr mss catlgr LC 63; ger Lang catlgr Hillman Lib UPittsburgh 64-67, SLavic bibliog 68, Staff asst planning & admin 68-. 8: Instr Carnegie Lib Sch 55-56 & 59-60; Survey, "Union List of Serials of the Pittsburgh Area"; Survey Com, Adult Serv Program Carnegie Lib, Pittsburgh. 9: ALA; BSA; SLA; Ms Soc; PennLA; Tri-State ACRL. 10: Amer Soc Advanced Slavic studies. 13: Yes. 14: Catlg, rare bks, bibliog. 15: 5548 Darlington rd, Pittsburgh, Pa 15217.

BECKER, JAMES LOUIS. b San Francisco 9 Ja 27. 5: City Col of San Francisco 53-55 AA; UCal 57-58, 60 (Pol Sci) BA; UWash Law Sch 59-60; Seattle U 60-61 (Educ); West Mich U 62-64 (LS) MA. 6: Sp, Port, Lat. 7: Sales asst Hallmark Greeting Cards, San Francisco 55; Warehouseman Liberty Industrial Sales Co, San Francisco 56; File clerk Bank of America, San Francisco 56; Clerk-salesperson Campus Textbook Exchange, Berkeley Cal 61-62; Stud asst West Mich U Lib, Kalamazoo 62-63; Asst Kalamazoo Pub Lib 63-64; Asst libn St Louis Pub Lib, Mun Ref Lib 64-67, 1st asst libn applied sci dept 67-. 9: ALA; SLA; CathLA; MoLA; Greater St Louis Lib Club (pres-elect 67-68). 10: Amer Polit Sci Assn; St Louis Pub Lib Staff Assn, Alpha Gamma Sigma. 14: Catlg, clsf, ref, docs, documentation & research. 15: 3733 Lindell blvd, St Louis Mo 63108.

BECKER, JOAN (ELBERT). b Toledo Ohio 16 O 25. 4: Lester F Becker. 5: Wilson Col 43-47 (Hist) BA; Carnegie 58-60 MS in LS. 7: Tchr soc studies Dundalk Jr-Sr High Sch, Baltimore 47-48; Asst libn Chatham Col 60-. 9: ALA-ACRL (Tri-State Chap); PennLA. 14: Catlg. 15: Chatham Col Woodland rd, Pittsburgh Pa 15232.

BECKER, JOHN (HENRY). b Miamisburg Ohio 28 Ap 25. 4: Marian Havens. 5: Otterbein Col 46-50 (Hist) BA; UIll 50-51, 52 (LS) MS; Ohio State U summers60-66 (Hist) MA. 7: Asst libn Heidelberg Col 51-53; Ser Libn Bowling Green StateU 53-54; Libn Otterbein Col 54-. 8: Ref asst Ohio StateU summers 58 & 59. 9: ALA; OhioLA. 15: 94 E Broadway, Westerville Oh 43081.

BECKER, JOSEPH. b NYC 15 Ap 23. 4: Arlene Berlin. 5: Polytech Inst (Brooklyn NY) 41-44 (Aero Engnr) BAeE; CatholicU 47-55 MSLS; UCLA 58-60 Research Fellow in Computer Sci. 7: Clerk NY Pub Lib 39-43; 1st Lt US Army Tokyo & Wash 44-46; Data processing & lib consul, Bethesda Md 46-66; Interuniv Communications Coun (EDUCOM), Bethesda Md vice-pres 66-. 8: Proj Consul to ALA for Lib-21 Seattle World's Fair 60-62; Proj Consul to ALA for Lib/USA NY World's Fair, 63-65; Lecturer Sch of Lib Sci CatholicU, 63-. 9: ALA; Assn Comput Mach; ASIS. 12: "Information Storage and retrieval; Tools, Elements, Theories," with RM Hayes (63); "Data Processing Equipment in Libraries," ALA Bull Ser (64-65). 13: Yes. 14: Electronic data processing, lib automation, lib educ. 15: 5805 Marbury rd, Bethesda Md 20034.

BECKER, KATHERINE JANE (MORRIS). b Chicago Il 2 Jl 18. 4: Robert M Becker MD. 5: UChicago 36-40 (Related Arts) BS; UWis 61-66 LS MS. 7: Asst dir admissions UChicago 40-48; Asst placement dir MIT 48-49; Lib consul IMC Abraham Lincoln Jr High Sch, Madison Wis 66-. 8: Jr High Bk Sel Com 66-, chm 67-68. 9: ALA; WisLA; WisEA; WisSoutheastEA; Madison Tchrs, Inc. 10: Phi Beta Kappa; LWV. 14: Child & ya lit, instr material cts. 15: 4015 Hammersley ave, Madison Wi 53705.

BECKER, PATRICIA (WARREN). b Winston-Salem NC. 4: Stanley E Becker. 5: Woman's Col UNC 48-52 (Physics) BA; UNC 55-59 MSLS. 7: Catlgr & order libn Union Carbide Nuclear Div ORGDP Plant, Oak Ridge Tenn 57-62; Catlgr Oak Ridge Inst of Nuclear Studies, Oak Ridge Tenn 63-64; Catlgr NC State Lib 64-65; Libn IBM Corp, Raleigh NC 65-. 9: SLA-Oak Ridge Chap; sec 58-59, treas 63-64, chm recr 62-63, chm placement64-65;-NC chap; chm Nom Com 67, Rec Com sec 68-, Engrg div; chm Bylaws Com 66-67. 12: Comp "Bibliography on Masers, 1954-1961" (62) & Sup 1 (63); Comp "Bibliography on Lasers" (62). 14: Tech libs. 15: 2604 Dover rd, Raleigh NC 27608.

BECKERMAN, EDWIN PAUL. b NYC 27 N 27. 4: Jean Friedburg. 5: UMo 46-49 (Eng) AB; Columbia 51-52 MSLS. 7: Libn NY Pub Lib 52-59; Pub lib consul NY State Lib 59-61; Asst dir Yonkers Pub Lib, NY 62-63; Dir Woodbridge Pub Lib, Woodbridge NJ 64-. 8: Consul 5 NJ & Ohio pub l co libs; Associated with Nelson Assoc in study of Dade Co (Fla) lib system; NJ State Dept of Educ Bd of Examiners. 9: ALA; NJLA (chm Legis Com, mem Lib Devel Com). 10: Rotary Club. 12: Former ed "New Jersey Libraries". 14: Lib admin. 15: 27 Longview dr, Princeton NJ 08540.

BECKERT DORIS LORRAINE (FRACCHIA). b Healdsburg. 4: Orion Robert Beckert. 5: San Jose State Col 56-58 (Eng); San Francisco State Col 59-61 (Eng) BA; UCal (Berkeley) 61-62 MLS. 7: Libn Pioneer Sr High Sch, San Jose Cal 62-64; Hd libn Napa High Sch, Napa Cal 64-67; Sp serv libn Amer River Col, Sacramento Cal 67-. 9: CalLA; CalASchL. 10: Boy Scouts of Amer. 14: Ref. 15: 5034 Oleander dr, Carmichael Ca 95608.

BECKETT, MABEL (ROANE). b Banner Miss 28 Jl 16. 4: Charlie M Beckett. 5: Northeastern State Col (Okla) 35-38 (Eng) BS; NoTex StateU; summers 53-55 BS in LS, Summers 65, 67, 68, MLS. 7: Elem sch tchr elem sch, Shady Point Okla 38-40; Elem sch tchr elem sch, Muse Okla 40-41; High sch Eng high sch, Slate Spring Miss 41-42; High sch Eng high sch, Hitchita Okla 42-43; Elem sch tchr, Henryetta Okla 44-46; High sch Eng, Ellard Sch Bruce Miss 46-47; Jr high sch Eng high sch, Mulberry Ark 50-51; High sch Eng Cooper Sch, Lubbock Tex 51-52; High sch Eng Springlake Sch, Earth Tex 52-53; High sch Eng Klondike Sch, Lamesa Tex 53-55; Libn high sch, Denver City Tex 55-59; Libn high sch, Anahuac Tex 59-. 9: NEA; ALA; TexLA; Tex State TchrsA. 10: Delta Kappa Gamma; Fed Women's Club. 15: Box 721, Anahuac Tx 77514.

BECKHAM, ANN (L). b Wilmington 10 Jl 09. 4: William T Beckham. 5: Peabody Col 29-33 (Eng) BS, 33-34 BS in LS; Winthrop 54 LS; USoCar 55 Eng, 57 LS. 7: Libn Richland Co & Dentsville High Sch, Columbia SC 53-66; Catlgr USoCar 66-. 14: Catlg. 15: 111 Marietta st, Columbia SC 29204.

BECKHAM, REXFORD STUART. b Chandler Tex 5 O 31. 4: Marie Page. 5: UCal (Berkeley) 48-52 (Eng) AB, 54-55 MLS; Chicago 63-64 (LS). 6: . 7: Stud asst UCal Lib (Berkeley)

49-52; (Sgt) US Army 52-54; UCal Lib (Berkeley): Stud asst 54-55, Intern in admin 55-56, Art-Anthropology libn 56-60; Asst dir sci & tech UNeb Lib 60-63; Fellow Grad Lib Sch UChicago 63-64; Asst dir tech servs Ohio State U Libs 64-67; Hd tech processes UCal Lib (Santa Cruz) 67-. 8: Bibliog consul; Educ Resources in Anthropology proj, UCal under a grant from the Course Content Improvement Sect, NSF 59-61. 9: ALA (Stat Com Col & Univ Libs); -ACRL (Tech Proc Com of Large Res Libs 64-67, chm 66-67); -RTSD (Tech Serv Cost Com);OhioLA; Ohio Valley Tech Serv Group (chm 66-67). 12: Comp Anthropology; a Basic List of Books and Periodicals for College Libraries in "Resources for the Teaching of Anthropology," ed DG Mandelbaum (63). 13: Yes. 14: Admin, resources. 15: 3640 Vienna dr, Aptos Ca 95003.

BECKMAN, MARGARET (LILAS ARMSTRONG). b Hartford Conn 22 Ja 25. 4: Arthur K Beckman. 5: UWest Ont 42-46 (Eng, Hist) BA; Toronto 48-49 BLS. , 69 MLS. 7: Child lib Pub Lib, Galt Ont 49-50; Catlgr UWest Ont 50-51; Head catlgr Waterloo Col (Ont) 58-60; Head catlg dept UWaterloo (Ont) 60-64; Dir of tech servs 64-66; Syst libn UGuelph (Ont) 66-. 8: Lib bldg Consul, AlgonquinCol Ottawa. 9: ALA; CanLA; OntLA; ASIS. 10: Waterloo (Ont) Pub Lib Bd; MidwesternReg Lib Coop Bd; Ont Coun of Health. 12: "Preparation of Machine-Readable Records."(68). 13: Yes. 14: Lib org, bldgs, systems design, lib automation. 15: Univ of Guelph,Guelph Ont Can.

BECKMAN, MIRIAM RUTH. b Spokane Wash 19 O 06. 5: UPuget Sound 24-28 (Hist) BA; UWash summer 29; BostonU 30-33 (Sociol) MA; UWash 63-64 MLib. 6: Fr. 7: Tchr Eng & hist Adna High Sch, Adna Wash 28-30; Parish wkr Congregational Ome Missions, Boston 30-33; Tchr nursery sch, Seattle 44-46; Pacific LutheranU Lib: Circ supv 57-64, Soc & natural sci libn 64-68, Chief of ref & bibliog serv 68-. 14: Ref. 15: 1101 E 56, Tacoma Wa 98467.

BECKWITH, ANGELINE M. b Gresham Wis 4 Mr 10. 4: Chauncey Beckwith. 5: Rosary Col 28-32 (Lat, Eng) BA; UWis 55 BLS, 66 (Lib Curriculum). 6: Ger, Lat. 7: Tchr: Gresham Wis 33-40, Chilton Wis 40-45; Univ libn, Madison Wis 45-48; Spec libn Forest products Lab, Madison Wis 48-55; Sch libn, Madison Wis 55-66; Coord lib serv, Madison Wis 66-. 8: Coord of wkshop on instr materials, (UWis) Whitewater 68. 9: ALA; NEA-DAVI; WisEA; WisLA. 10: Kappa Gamma Pi. 13: Yes. 14: Sch libs. 15: 401 N Eau Claire ave, Madison Wi 53705.

BECKWITH, AVIS (MARIETTA BROWN). b Alma Mich 28 Je 09. 4: Ford D M Beckwith. 5: UMich 26-30 AB, 30-31 AB in LS; 33-36; East Mich 56-63 Elem Provisional Tchr's Certif. 6: Fr, Sp, Ger. 7: Asst Period Reading Room UMich (Ann Arbor) 31-35, Asst Grad Reading Room Mod Langs 35-36, Asst in reclsf 36-37; Asst libn (ref) Bradley Col 37-39; Consul Mich State Lib Div 58-59; Ref asst Lansing Pub Lib 59; Bus Admin Lib UMich 60-61; Sec & lib asst Howell Pub Schs, Howell Mich 61-62, Tchr 67-. 9: ,ichLA. 10: United Presbyterian Women; DAR; UMich Alum Assn; Howell Delphian; Family Living Gp Mich Child Study Assn. 14: Ref. 15: 610 W Crane st, Howell Mi 48843.

BECKWITH, FRANCES L. b Joliet Ill 10 O 05. 5: Joliet Jr Col 22-24 Certif; UChicago 24-26 (Lat, Math) AB; UMich 27-28 (Lat) AM; Drexel 29-30 BS in LS. 6: Fr, Lat. 7: Tchr St Johns High Sch, St Johns Mich 28-29; Lib asst Colo State Col Lib 30-32; Survey wker UChicago Grad Lib Sch 33-34; Libn US Forest Serv N Central Reg Milwaukee 35-42; Communications off (Lt) USN, Wash DC & Joliet Ill 42-46; Libn N Central Br USDA Lib, Madison Wis 46-53; Libn Marquette Sch Med 53-. 8: Alumni consuk for N Central area Drexel Inst 55-61; Exec Com Coun Midwest Reg Med Lib 68-70. 9: MedLA; SLA (Wis Chap: program chm 54-55, v-pres 55-57, pres 57-59, Hospitality-Pub Rel 59-). 14: Admin, ref. 15: 1732 N Prospect ave, Milwaukee Wi 53202.

BECKWITH, HELEN IRENE (KONSTANTY). b Cooperstown NY 18 O 44. 4: David R Beckwith. 5: Denison 62-66 (Hist) BA; Syracuse 66-67 (LS) MS; WashU (St Louis) 67-68 (Computerized libnship). 6: Sp. 7: Act ser libn Hartwick Col Lib summer 67; Trainee in computer libnship WashU Sch of Med Lib (St Louis) 67-68; Asst lib syst analyst Upstate Med Ctr Lib, Syracuse NY 68-. 9: MeLA; Upstate NY Med Lib Assn. 10: Beta Phi Mu. 14: Lib automation, systems analysis, med libraries. 15: 109 Croyden lane, Dewitt NY 13224.

BECKWITH, HERBERT (HENRY). b Pittsburgh 16 Mr 30. 5: Carroll Col (Wis) 48-50 (pre-engnr); Lake Forest Col 54-56 (Fr) BA; UNC 56-58 MSLS. 6: Fr. 7: Circ desk libn Ohio State U 57-58; Ref libn & asst catlgr Lake Forest Col 58-60; Circ-ref libn Cal Inst of Tech 60-61; Ref libn (Sci & Soc Sci) Ariz State U (Tempe) 62-67; Soc sci libn Kansas State U 67-68; Ref libn Vt Free Pub Lib Serv 68-. 9: ALA; VtLA. 10: Friends of the Tempe Pub Lib (charter mem). 12: Co-auth (with E Williams) "Author and Subject Indices to Kansas State University Dissertations, Master's Theses & Master'sReports 1886-1968" (69). 14: Ref, circ, application of punched cards & computers in libs., interlib coop. 15: Box 361, Montpelier Vt 05602.

BEDA, MARGARET CLARISSA (CAPPS). b St John New Brunswick Can. 4: Lt Col (Ret) Stephen W Beda. 5: McGill 45-48 (Eng lit) BA, 48-50 (Eng lang & lit) MA, 59-60 BLS. 6: Fr, Ger. 7: Asst Registrar's Off Mc Gill 48-51; Tchr Miss Edgar's Sch, Montreal 51-52; Va Beach Pub Lib, Va Beach Va: Hd libn 60-63, Lib dir 63-. 9: ALA; VaLA. 10: Pembroke Meadows Civic League; AAUW. 14: Bk sel, ref, catlg. 15: 629 Cardiff rd, Va Beach Va 23455.

BEDELL, KATHRYNNE (N). b Patchogue NY 8 S 30. 5: Geneseo State Tchrs Col 48-52 BS in LS; Hofstra Col 54-57 (Elementary Educ) MS. 7: Libn Bay Shore Pub Schs, Bay Shore NY 52-55; Libn West Islip Pub Schs, West Islip NY 55-. 8: Lib coordinator, West Islip Pub Schs 57-62. 9: NEA; NY State Tchrs Assn; NYLA; NY State Sch LA. 10: Sagtikos Manor Hist Soc. 14: Child lib wk. 15: 26 Mowbray ave, Bay Shore NY 11707.

BEDFORD, LOUISE (CHILDERS). b Des Moines Iowa 6 My 17. 5: Drake U 34-38 (Hist) AB; UKy summers 51-55 MSLS. 6: Lat, Fr. 7: Tchr Montgomery Co Schs, Mt Sterling Ky 38-42; Expediter General Electric Co, Cincinnati 42-50; Tchr & libn Montgomery Co Schs, Mt Sterling Ky 50-55; Libn Mt Sterling City Schs, Mt Sterling Ky 55-. 8: Consul in setting up research lib system at General Electric Jet Propulsion Plant at Lockland Ohio summer 52; Instr in Lib Sci-UKy summers 61-63, 67 Mem Governor's Planning Com for Ky Libs 67-; Mem Sch Lib Educ Adv Com, Sch of Lib Sci UKy. 9: ALA; NEA; KyLA; Ky Assn Sch Libns (sec 63-64, State Bd 64-65); KyEA; Central KyEA (pres Libns Sect 64-65). 10: Mt Sterling Woman's Club; Central Ky Woman's Club; DAR. 14: Sch libnship, superv & admin, tech sch libship. 15: Jeffersonville Ky 40337.

BEDIKIAN, ELIZABETH (OBERHELMAN). b New Orleans 9 O 34. 4: Victor Bedikian. 5: Tulane 52-56 (Gen Bus) BBA; Columbia 56-57 MS in LS. 7: New Orleans Pub Lib; Howard-Tilton Mem Lib, Tulane U; Columbia Grad Sch of Bus Lib; Bus Lib Newark (NJ) Pub Lib, Asst bus libn, Kan City (Mo) Pub Lib 57-59; Libn The California Co, New Orleans 59-60; Research asst in econ Moodies Serv Ltd, London 61; Libn Delasalle High Sch, New Orleans 61-62; Libn I bus & sci dept New Orleans Pub Lib 63-67, Libn III 67-. 9: ALA, .LaLA. 10: Beta Gamma Sigma. 14: Ref. 15: 4929 Dryades st, New Orleans La 70115.

BEDNARSKI, HANNA (JADWIGA). b Poland. 4: Jan Adam. 5: Warsaw U (Phil) Master of Phil; McGill 61-62 BLS (62). 6: Polish, Fr. 7: Sec Com sec of the Polish Legation, Stockholm 46-49; Clk (staff) Univ Lib, Edmonton Alberta 59-61; Libn UAlberta, Edmonton Alberta 62-. 8: Library displays, from 1963 till present. 9: CanLA; ALA; AltaLA; EdmontonLA; Assn Prof Libns U Alta (Assn of Acad Staff U of Alta). 10: AASUA; Can-Polish Assn; Lib Assn of Alta. 14: Ref (soc sci). 15: Rutherford Lib UAlberta, Edmonton Alta.

BEDSOLE, DANNY T. b Louann Ark 30 My 30. 4: Leola Amena. 5: Anderson Col 48-51 (Math) AB; UMich: 54-56 (Math) AM, 56-57 AMLS, 57-61 (LS) PhD. 7: (Cpl) US Army 52-54; Spec projs libn United Aircraft Corp, E Hartford Conn 57-61; Manager tech lib Aerojet-Gen Corp, Sacramento Cal 61-65; Dir of Lib & Tchg resources Austin Col 65-, Acad dean 67-. 9: SLA (chm Stats Com 64-66, chm Com on Govt Info Serv 64-65,treas Tex chap 68-69). 13: Yes. 14: Info storage & retrieval, lib admin. 15: 1109 Grand ave, Sherman Tx 75090.

BEDWELL, ROSE L (BIETZ). b Delmont SD 18 Mr 23. 4: Thomas H Bedwell. 5: So State tchrs (Springfield S D) 41-56 (Elem Educ) BS; UNeb 57-58 (Sec Educ) MA Lib Certif 64. 6: Ger. 7: Tchr Pub Schs, S Dak & Neb 42-64; Acquis libn No Ariz U 64-66; Libn flagstaff Pub Schs, Marshall, Flagstaff Ariz 66-. 9: NEA; ALA; NCTE; AEAUSA; ArizStateLA. 14: Child bks. 15: 2903 N Patterson, Flagstaff Az 86001.

BEEBE, (ANNIE) JEANETTE. b Lakewood Ohio 21 S 01. 5: Oberlin 19-23 (Eng) AB; West res U 29-30 BS in LS, 35-41 (Hist) MA. 6: Lat, Fr, Ger. 7: Sub tchr, Cleveland 23-24; Lib asst high sch & br libs, Cleveland Pub Lib 24-29; Lib asst Flora Stone mather Col, West Res U 30-42; Catlgr USA Med Lib, Cleveland div 42-48; Ref libn Ritter Lib, Baldwin-Wallace

Col 48-61; Hd catlgr & hd of tech proc 61-67; Assoc libn 67-68; Assoc catlgr 68-. 9: ALA; No Ohio Tech Serv Libns. 10: AAUP; Cleveland-Oberlin Women's Club. 12: Ed "Flora Stone Mather College Library Staff Manual" (35). 14: Catlg, ref. 15: 98 E Center st, Berea Oh 44017.

BEEBE, ANN (IDA). b Yakima Wash 18 O 19. 5: UWash 36-41 (Scandinavian Langs) BA, 41-42 (LS) BA; Berkeley Baptist Divinity Sch 45-47 (Religious Educ) MA; Columbia 58-(Anthropology). 6: Danish. 7: Child libn Walla Walla Pub Lib, Walla Walla Wash 42-43; Jr libn Catlg Div UWash Lib 44-45; Tchr & libn Cal Sch for the Blind, Berkeley Cal 47-50; Libn Oakland Pub Schs, Oakland Cal 50-51; Child libn Yakima Valley Reg Lib, Yakima Wash 51-54; Lecturer Ext Div San Francisco State Col, Hayward Cal 56; Sr libn Alameda Co Lib, Hayward Cal 54-56; Asst Prof Lib Sci NoIllU 56-58; Prin Child libn Monmouth Co Lib, Freehold NJ 58-59; Le cturer Seton Hall U 61-63; Visiting lecturer USask summers 61- 64; Elem lib servs consul Bloomfield Pub Schs, Bloomfield NJ 60-. 8: Bk Review Advis Com "School Library Journal" 61-63; Educ Consul T Y Crowell Co NY; Educ Consul J B Lippincott Co NY 65-; Tchr child lit Prince of Wales Col (P E I Can) summer 68; Educ consul Henry Z Walck 69-. 9: ALA (var coms); Assn of Child Libns Northern Cal (sec 49), Bk Review Chm 55; NEA; NSEA; NJSchLA. 10: Altrusa Internat; Internat Platform Assn. 12: "How to Use the Library" (65). 13: Yes. 14: Child Libnship, Child lit, lit educ. 15: 186 Franklin st, Bloomfield NJ 07003.

BEEBE, RICHARD WILLIAMS. b Batavia NY 24 My 39. 5: URochester 57-61 (Geog) BA; UBritish Columbia 61-63 (Geog); SUNY at Buffalo summer 66 (Ed); SUC at Genesco 67-68 MLS. 6: Fr, Ger, Chinese (Mandarin), Malay. 7: Lab asst geog dept UBritish Columbia 61-63; Secondary sch tchr US Peace Corps, Kanowit, Sarawak, Malaysia 64-65; Lab asst geog dept Simon Fraser U 66; Acquis libn Milne Lib SUC, Geneseo NY 68-. 9: ALA; -ACRL. 14: Acquis, ser. 15: 131 Main st, Geneseo NY 14454.

BEEBEE, MARY ELIZABETH (BELL). b Van Buren Ark 10 Ja 16. 4: C Scripps Beebee. 5: Lindenwood Col 34-36 (Fr); UIll 36-38 (Educ,Fr) BS of Ed; UIll Grad Lib Sch summer 39; Rutgers 55-57 MLS. 6: Fr, Sp. 7: Eng tchr & asst libn Centralia Twp High Sch, Centralia Ill 38-39; Trainee Columbia U Lib summer 41; Libn E Orange High Sch,E Orange NJ 56-66; Libn C J Scott High Sch, E Orange NJ 66-. 9: NEA; NJEA; NJSchLA. 10: Kappa Alpha Theta. 14: Sch lib serv. 15: 384 N Walnut st, East Orange NJ 07017.

BEELER, ETHEL L. b Cabool Mo 3 S 12. 5: StateU Iowa 33-37 (Journalism) BS; Chicago 43-44 BLS. 6: Fr. 7: Free lance advertising & feature writer, Cedar Rapids Iowa 37-40; Pub Lib of Des Moines Iowa: Br lib asst 41-42, 1st asst circ dept 44-47, Head circ dept 47-53, Coordinator home reading servs 53-. 68, Act div 68-69. 8: Mem Adv Com Local TV station (KDIN). 9: ALA; IowaStateLA; IowaAdult Educ Assn. 10: Iowa Pub Employees Assn; Quota Internat; Des Moines C of C; Des Moines Lib Club. 15: Pub Lib, Des Moines Ia 50309.

BEELER, LINDA DIANN. b Peru Iowa 11 Ap 39. 5: Cotty Col 57-59 (Liberal Arts) AA; U of No Ia 59-61 (LS) BA; Chicago 61-67 (LS) MA. 6: Fr. 7: Asst libn Thornridge High Sch, Dolton Ill 61-64, Head Libn 64-, Instr in Lib Sci; Miss State U, summer 67; State U of Ia, summer 68; Portland State Col, Oregon summer 69. 8: Mem several NCA Eval coms. 9: ALA-AASchL; IllLA; NEA. 10: Kappa Delta Pi; PEO; OES. 14: High sch libs. 15: 11121 S Vernon Apt 1C, Chicago Il 60628.

BEEMAN, VIRGINIA MAE. b Muskegon Mich 19 O 31. 5: UMich 53-54 (Eng) AB, 55 MA in LS. 7: Sr ref libn Hacklsy Pub Lib 55-. 9: ALA (Dist Memb chm 62-; chm Local NLW 61); MichLA. 10: Port City Palyhouse; Muskegon Urban League; Interfaith Coun on Human Rights; NAACP. 11: Jonathan Walker Award Muskegon Urban League 67. 14: Ref. 15: 972 E Isabella ave, Muskegon Mi 49442.

BEEN, PHYLLIS H. b Detroit Mich 6 Ap 47. 5: Wayne StateU 64-68 (LS) BS. 6: Sp, hebrew. 7: Sch libn Birmingham Pub Schs Quarton Sch 68-69; Pub libn Oak Park Pub Lib 67-; Sch libn Southfield Pub Schs Lathrup Elem 69-. 8: Mem gp introducing high sch srs to field & prof of lib sci, Detroit area 68. 9: NEA; MichEA; MichASchL. 14: Child libn, catlg, storytelling. 15: 22111 Parklawn, Oak Park Mi 48237.

BEER, FLORENCE (GREENBERG). 4: Sylvan. 5: Brooklyn 47-54 (Ed, Art) BA; UPittsburgh 65-69 MLS. 6: Hebrew, Yiddish. 7: Libn Hillel Acad, Pittsburgh 64-68; Libn Syracuse Hebrew Day Sch 68-. 9: ALA; Assn of Jewish Libns. 14: Child wk. 15: 315 Scott ave, Syracuse NY 13224.

BEFU, KEI T. b Sacramento Cal 29 Ap 30. 4: Harumi Befu. 5: UCal (Berkeley) 54-56 (Sociol) AB, Sch of Libnship 62-64 MLS; UMo 62; San Jose State Col 68. 6: Ger, Chinese, Japanese. 7: Catlgr UMich Asia Lib 64; Catlgr UMo catlg dept 64. 9: ALA. 10: Beta Phi Mu; AAUW; Amer Anitrop Assn. 14: Catlg, col libs, Japanese. 15: 3078 Stelling dr, Palo Alto Ca 94303.

BEGIN, JOSEPH-OCTAVE. b St Joseph de Levis Can 16 S 10. 5: ULaval 28-32 (Classics) BA; UMontreal 35-36 (Lit Franc) MA; L'Immaculee-Conception (Montreal) 36-38 (Philos) Licence, 41-45;Licence (Theol) UMontreal 51-52 (Hist) MA; Rosary Col 60-61 MALS. 6: Fr, Eng. 7: Libn Chabanel Hall Chinese lang Sch (Peking) 40-41; Prof hist Tafari Makonnen Sch (Addis-Ababa) 48-50; Libn Col Saint-Ignace (Montreal) 50-55; Libn Col Jean-de-Brebeuf (Montreal) 56-60; Libn LaurentianU (Sudbury Ont) 60-69; Libn ULaval 69-. 9: ALA; CanLA; Inst Prof Libns Ont. 10: Can Hist Assn. 14: Ref bibliog, rare bks. 15: Coll des Jesuites 1150 St Cyrille, Quebec Province de Quebec Can.

BEGUM, MARCIA JANE. b Providence 8 My 33. 5: Colby Col 50-54 (Eng) AB; Simmons 55-56 MSLS. 6: Sp. 7: Eng tchr Reading Sch Dept, Reading Mass 54-55; YA libn Providence Pub Lib 56-68, Lib infor coord 68-. 9: ALA; RILA (record sec 59-61). 10: Providence Pub Lib Staff Assn. 14: Ya wk, readers adv wk, pub relations. 15: 60 Forest ave, Cranston RI 02910.

BEHAR, SOLOMON. b Brooklyn NY 3 F 27. 4: Patricia McGraw. 5: Brooklyn Col 47-51 (Philos) BA; ColumbiaU 51-53 (LS) MS; UNM 54-56 (Eng). 6: Fr, Sp, Lat, Hebrew, Yiddish, Gk. 7: Able-seaman US Merchant Marine 45-46; Lib asst Brooklyn Col Lib 50-51; Lib sch intern NY Pub Lib 51-53; Ref libn Mechanics Inst Lib (San Francisco) 56-58; Circ libn & catlgr San Francisco Pub Lib 59-60; Bibliog UCal Lib (Berkeley) 61-. 66, Hd gift div 66-. 14: Bibliog, ref (humanities). 15: 6450 Regent st, Oakland Ca 94618.

BEHR, ALICE SHAVER. b Charleston WVa 3 N 32. 5: WVU 50-54 (Chem) BS; West Res 62-64 MSLS. 7: Union Carbide Corp,Oak Ridge Tenn, Asst libn 54-59, Assoc chem 59-60; Libn Union Carbide Corp, Tarrytown NY 67-. 9: SLA; ALA; ACS. 14: Catlg, docs (company & Govt). 15: 90 F Shaver, Heaters WV 26627.

BEHRENDS, MARILYN JO (SMITH). b Auburn, Neb 19 My 30. 4: Dean Behrends. 5: William Woods Col 49-50 (Music); Neb WesleyanU 50-52, 54-55 BS in Music; UDenver 62-63 (LS) MA. 7: Med sec Bryan Mem Hosp, Lincoln Neb 52-54; Med sec Lincoln Clinic, Lincoln Neb 56-57; Med sec St Elizabeth Hosp, Lincoln Neb 57-59; Libn Auburn Pub Lib, Auburn Neb 60-62; Ref libn Wausau Pub Lib, Wausau Wis 63-64; Ref libn Salina Pub Lib, Salina Kan 64-67; Libn Holmesville High Sch, Holmesville Neb 67-68; Libn Creston High School,Creston Ia 68-. 9: ALA. 14: Ref. 15: 1710 Highland ave, Salina Ks 67401.

BEHYMER, E(DGAR) HUGH. b Liberty Ind 3 Ag 07. 5: Ind U 28-34 (Eng) AB; UMich 34-36 ABLS; Chicago 38-40 (LS) MA; University Col (London) 49-50 (LS). 7: Asst law libn Ind U Law Lib (Bloomington) 28-34; Sec UMich Law Lib 34-36; Libn LSU Law Lib 36-38; Research bibliog UAla Lib 40-41; Libn Bethany Col (Bethany WVa) 41-55; Dir of Libs C W Post Col 55-; Dir Grad Lib Sch LIU (Brookville NY) 59-66, Dean 67-. 8: Fulbright Lecturer LA of Australia 52. 9: ALA-ACRL (past pres Tri-State Chap); NyLA; Nassau County LA; WVaLA (past pres). 13: Yes. 14: Tchg catlg. 15: C W Post College Apt AE10, Greenvale NY 11548.

BEHYMER, MARIE (GENEVIEVE). b Atlanta Mo 9 F 10. 5: Northeast Mo State 39 (Elem Educ) BS in ED; UMo 46 (Educ) MS in ED; UMich summers 53, 54, 56; Wash U summer 52. 7: Libn Alton Pub Schs, Alton, Ill 52-. 8: Grad Asst & Instr in Dept of Instr Materials at So Ill U summers 62-64, 67-68. 9: ALA; NEA; IllLA; IllASchlL; IllEA. 10: Bus & Prof Women; Zonta Internat; Trustee of College avePresbyterian Church. 13: Yes. 14: Young adults. 15: 2500 Donald apt B, Alton Il 62002.

BEIERS, KATHERINE (HUGHES). b Langdon ND 12 Jl 32. 5: Col of St Catherine 50-55 (LS) BS; USoCal 62-64 (LS) MS. 6: Fr, Russ. 7: Child libn Brooklyn Pub Lib 55-56; Ref libn UPenn 56-57; Bkmob & catlgr King County Seattle 57-58; Ref libn Alhambra Pub Lib, Cal 62-69; Ser libn U of Cal (Santa Cruz) 69-. 14: Bus & fin. 15: 135 Gharkey st, Santa Cruz Ca 95060.

BEIK, DORIS (HUMPHREY). b Union NY. 4: Paul H Beik. 5: SUNY (Albany) 32-36 (Eng) AB, 37-40 BS in LS. 6: Fr,

Russian. 7: Libn Ethelbert B Crawford Memorial Lib, Monticello NY 37-39; Asst libn circ dept Swarthmore Col Lib 49-63, Asst libn catlg dept 63-67, Hd catlg dept 67-68, 69-. 9: ALA. 10: SUNY (Albany) Alumni Assn. 14: Catlg. 15: 4 Whittier pl, Swarthmore Pa 19081.

BEILBY, MARY (HEYING). b Alma Mich 10 Ja 40. 4: Albert Beilby. 5: Alma Col 58-62 (Eng) BA; UCLA 64-65 MLS. 7: Eng tchr Fraser Pub Schs, Fraser Mich 62-64; Catlg, ref libn CornellU 65-67; Ser acquis libn PrincetonU 67-68; Acquis libn SUNY (Cortland) 68-. 14: Acquis, ref. 15: SUNY Cortland Memorial Lib, Cortland NY 13045.

BEILKE, PATRICIA FAY (HEMPHILL). b Austin Tex 10 O 33. 4: Wallace George Beilke. 5: West MichU 51-55 (Fr) BA; UMich summer 53; West Mich U 57-58; MA; UCal Ext 59-60, 62-63; UWis summer 65 (NDEA Lib Sci); West MichU 67-68 MSL, 68-70. 7: Childlibn Allen Park Br, Plymouth Br, Lincoln Park Br Wayne Co Lib, Wayne Co Mich 55-57;Libn LaMesa-Spring Valley (Cal) Sch Dist, Spring Valley Jr High Sch 58-61, LibnLaMesa Jr High Sch 61-67. 9: ALA; CalLA (sec Palomar dist 67); ASCD; NEA-DAVI;MichASCD; CalASchL (sec So sect 65-67). 10: Kappa Delta Pi; Beta Phi Mu. 14: Wk with yp & tchrs, sch lib suprv, sch lib research. 15: 317 Sage ave, KalamazooMi 49007.

BEIRIGER, ELIZABETH A. b Monte Vista Colo 22 N 25. 5: Loretto Heights Col 46-50 (Span) BA; UDenver summers 59-62 (LS) MA. 6: Sp. 7: Sch libn-tchr Sargent Consolidated Sch, Monte Vista Colo 50-55; Sch libn-tchr Misawa Dependents Sch, Misawa Japan 55-56; Sch libn-tchr Morton High Sch, Morton Wash 56-57; Sch libn-tchr Izmir Dependents Sch, Izmir Turkey 57-58; Sch libn-tchr Zaragoza Dependents Sch, Zaragoza Spain 58-60; Sch libn Royal Oaks Elem Sch, Madrid Spain 60-. 9: ALA (Life mem); NEA (Life mem); Overseas EA. 14: Sch libs & child serv. 15: Paseo de la Habana 9-4-dcha, Madrid Spain.

BEITER, ELIZABETH (PERRY). b Gansevoort NY 3 O 12. 4: David Beiter. 5: Simmons 30-34 (LS) SB. 7: Lib asst Troy Pub Lib, Troy NY 34-38, Catlgr 38-46; Libn Stillwater Free Lib 49-. 10: Fortnightly Club. 15: 13 Park ave, Stillwater NY 12170.

BELCHER, FAYE. b Belcher Ky 29 F 32. 5: UKy 52-56 (Educ) BA, 58-61 (Educ & LS) MA; Peabody Col 68-69 (Educ). 7: Tchr Pike Co Bd of Educ, Elkhorn City Ky 51-60, Libn 60-62; Libn Lexington Bd of Educ, Lexington Ky 62-64; Libn Pike Co Bd of Educ, Elkhorn City Ky 64-65; Tchr of Lib Sci Morehead State U 64-65, Ref libn 65-68. 8: Consul, Pikeville City Schs Inserv Wkshop, Sept 65. 9: ALA; SELA; KyLA. 10: AAUW; Morehead Bk Club. 14: Ref. 15: Morehead Ky 40351.

BELCHER, OPAL E. b Belcher Ky. 5: UKy 57 (Educ) AB, 61 (LS, Educ) MA, summers 62, 63, 65 (LS, Educ). 7: Elem libn Pide Co Schs, Elkhorn City Ky 61-64, High sch libn 64-67; Dir instr materials ctr Buchanan Co, Grundy Va 67-69; Instr children's lit Pikeville Col (Proj Bootstrap) 67-68; Instr children's lit Murray State Univ summer 69. 9: NEA-DAVI; VaEA. 14: Lib educ, instr materials ctrs. 15: Box 482, Elkhorn City Ky 40522.

BELCHER, THELMA (BRADLEY). b Bristol Tenn Va 26 Ag 18. 4: Ollie Brown Belcher. 5: Tuskegee Inst 32-36 (Hist) BS; Wayne State 55-57 (Sch LS) MEd; UMich 59-62 AMLS. 6: Fr, Sp. 7: Asst libn Tuskegee Inst 36-37; Libn Inkster High Sch, Inkster Mich 55-. 9: MichASchL. 10: Delta Sigma Theta. 14: Sch serv. 15: 5621 Oakman blvd, Detroit Mi 48204.

BELENY, ELIZABETH S. b New Castle Penn 16 Mr 37. 5: Kent StateU 55 (Eng-Drama); Fashion Acad 56 (Theatre Design, Costumes); NY Sch of Interior Design 58; London Co Coun Sch of Arts 61 (Costume Design). 6: Fr. 7: Numerous positions in theatres 55-60; Asst libn Erwin Wasey Ruthrauff & Ryan Inc, NY 57-61; Libn Erwin Wasey Ruthrauff & Ryan Ltd, London 61-62; Research libn Bus Internat Corp, NYC 62-65; Assoc ed Marketing Research 66-. 9: SLA (Bus/Fin, Museum/Pict & Advert/divs); Internat Executives Assn; Internat Advert Assn. 12: "How to FindInformation About Foreign Firms" (66); "Choosing Brandnames and Trademarks inInternational Markets" (67). 14: Ref, rare bks. 15: 81 Irving pl, New York, NY 10003.

BELFOR, SHARON ANN. b Rochester NY 15 N 44. 5: SUNY at Buffalo 62-66 (Sociol) BA; UDenver 66 (LS); SUNY at Albany 66-67 (LS) MS. 7: Ref libn RIT Wallace Memorial Lib, Rochester NY 67-. 9: ALA. 14: Sci ref. 15: 253 Barry rd, Rochester NY 14617.

BELHOBEK, JEANIE (BROWN). b Cleveland Ohio 10 D 44. 4: George Hubbard Belhobek. 5: De Pauw 62-66 (Hist) BA; IndianaU 66-68 MLS. 6: Fr. 7: Ref libn IndU SE (Jeffersonville) 68-. 9: ALA; Louisville Lib Club. 10: Jr League. 14: Ref. 15: 2025 Brownsboro rd apt 407, Louisville Ky 40206.

BELINA, LENORE M. b Alpha Minn 10 D 05. 4: Frank J Belina. 5: Mankato State Col 23-25 (Math) Certif; UKy 28-30 (Educ) BA in Educ; DenverU summers 55-58 MA in libnship; West State Col summer 64-. 7: Tchr: Okabena Consolidated Sch, Okabena Minn 25-26, Jackson Jr High Sch, Jackson Minn 26-28, Pikeville High Sch, Pikeville Ky 30-31; Tchr & libn Grand Junction High Sch, Grand Junction Colo 44-47; Libn Central High Sch, Grand Junction Colo 54-67; Docs libn NM StateU 67-. 9: ColoASchL (charter mem); ColoLA (Com mem); NMLA (Com mem). 14: Govt docs. 15: 1835A Rentfrow dr, Las Cruces NM 88001.

BELISLE, GERMAIN. b St Guillaume Que Can 23 O 25. 4: Cecile Brunet. 5: Seminaire Chambly (Que) 39-45 9arts); UOttawa 45-53 (Arts, Philos) BA, BPh, BLS. 6: Fr, Eng, Lat. 7: Libn UOttawa 49-53; Libn & Ed Queen's Printer, Ottawa 53-60; USherbrooke (Que): Sci libn 60-63, Chief Libn 63-65, Chief Med Libn 65-. 8: Prof, UOttawa Lib Sch Official Publ 57-59 & 64 Mem of the provisional consul com on the UQuebec Lib 69. 9: AssociationCanadienne de Bibliothecaires de Langue Francaise (pres 61-62, dir 66-69); BibliogSoc of Canada (Coun 69-). 12: Ed "Canadian Government Publications du Governement canadien Catalogue," catalogue general (53) annual (54-59); other catalogues during the same period. 13: Yes. 14: Sci & med, admin. 15: 2350 Rue Bachand, Sherbrooke Que Can.

BELK, MRS ROSE K. b Seneca SC. 5: Winthrop Col 19-23 AB; UNC 41-42 BSLS. 7: Catlgr Historical foundation, Montreat NC 42-44; Ref & circ libn Col of William & Mary 44-53; Libn Colonial Williamsburg (Va) 53-. 9: VaLA. 10: AAUW; LWV; Presbyterian Church. 14: Ref, catlg. 15: Box 1173, Williamsburg Va 23185.

BELKNAP, GERDA (MOORE). b Columbia SC 2 D 41. 5: USC 60-63 (Ed) AB; UNC 63-64 MS in LS. 7: Libn Evans Jr High Sch, Spartanburg SC 64-65; Libn Exec Coun of the Episcopal Church NY 65-67; Libn Crayton Elem & Jr High Sch, Columbia SC 67-. 9: ALA; NEA; SCEA; SCLA; RichlandCoEA. 10: Jr League. 15: 4429 Woodside Haven dr, Columbia SC 29206.

BELKNAP, HELEN R. b Painesville Ohio 22 Ap 15. 5: Oberlin Col 38 (Art Hist) BA; West Res 39 BLS. 7: Art libn StateU Iowa 40-42; Head art dept Kalamazoo Pub Lib 42-46; Catlgr Fogg Art Museum HarvardU 46-52; Libn printed bks & period, Winterthur Museum Lib 52-. 9: ALA; SLA; DelLA. 14: Catlg, ref (art). 15: Winterthur Museum, Winterthur De 19735.

BELKNAP, SARA YANCEY. b Ocala Fla 2 Mr 1895. 5: Rollins Col 16-19 BA; Columbia 19 (Educ) BS, (Eng) MA, 31 (LS) BS. 6: Fr, Sp, Ital. 7: Tchr Gorton Sch, Yonkers NY 21-, Libn 30-53; Founder-Dir UFla Archives of Dance-Music-Theatre 53- Hd of ref Flagler Col 68-. 9: NyLA. 10: Theatre groups; Fla Arts Coun; AAUW. 12: "Guide to Dance Periodicals"; "Guide to the Musical Arts"; "Guide to the Performing Arts"; "Latin Amer Performing Arts. 13: Yes. 14: Indexing, edg. 15: 601 N Newnan st, Jacksonville Fl 32202.

BELL, ADELAIDE R(USSELL). b Hartford Conn 31 O 15. 4: Paul Hadley Bell. 5: Oberlin Col 32-36 (Econ & Soc) BA; Rutgers 60-62 MLS. 6: Fr. 7: Statistical clerk Milbank Mem Fund, NYC 36-41; Bkkeeping & payroll clerk Pitney-Bowes, Stamford Conn 43-44; Ridgewood Lib, Ridgewood NJ: Jr lib asst 61-62, Yp Libn 62-. 10: Village Com on Youth, Ridgewood NJ. 14: Ref, ya. 15: Ridgewood Lib 125 N Maple ave, Ridgewood NJ 07450.

BELL, BARBARA (LATTIMER). b Hobart NY 30 Je 41. 4: Richard Henry Bell. 5: Fla StateU 59-63 (Eng Educ) BS, 64-65 (LS) MS. 7: High sch tchr Pinellas Co Sch Syst, Fla 63-64; Grad asst Fla State U Lib 64-65; Ref libn Yale U Lib 66-. 10: Beta Phi Mu; YaleU Lib Staff Assn. 14: Ref. 15: 606 Yale sta, New Haven Ct 06520.

BELL, BARBARA L (HALL). b Brainerd Minn 10 Ag 32. 5: HamlineU 50-54 (Eng) BA; Peabody 57-58 (LS) MA Lib Mgt Inst Emory 67. 7: Libn Glasgow High Sch, Glasgow Ky 55-56; Libn Kinmundy-Alma Comm Sch, Kinmundy Ill 56-57; Asst Vanderbilt Med Lib 57-58; Libn Grand View Col 58-. 9: ALA; Iowa Jr Col Assn (chm Lib Sect 62-65, chm Const Com 68); IllLA (sec Acad Sect 60-61, 67 chm Recr Com 64-65. 14: Ref. 15: 605 Grandview, Des Moines Ia 50313.

BELL, CHARLES ETTA. b Elgin Tex 23 Ap 31. 4: Ulysses Simpson Bell. 5: Prairie View A&M Col 49-53 (LS, Educ) BS; UDenver summers 56-58 (LS) MA; UTex summer 66; E Tex StateU 65. 7: Libn Pickard Sch, Brenham Tex 53-55; Tchr J J Rhoads Sch, Dallas 55-56; Libn N W Harllee Sch, Dallas 56-59; US Army Spec Serv Lib: Head libn, Whittier Alaska 59-60; Child libn, Fairbanks Alaska 60-61; Lib supv, Ansbach Germany 62-64; libn L G Pinkston High Sch, Dallas 64-. 9: ALA; No Tex Tchrs Assn; TexLA; NEA. 10: Court of Calanthe; YWCA; Clr Tchrs Dallas; Dallas Libns Club. 14: Catlg, ref. 15: 6523 Prosper st, Dallas Tx 75209.

BELL, CLARA LU. b Wash DC 23 D 29. 5: Goucher Col 47-51 (Pol Sci) AB; Johns Hopkins 51-53 (Pol Sci); UMich 54-55 MSLS. 6: Fr, Russian. 7: Lib asst hist, pol econ, pol sci Johns Hopkins U Lib 51-54; Ref libn St Agnes & Bronx Ref Center NY Pub Lib 55-56; Ref & ed asst McGraw-Hill Publ Co Lib, NY 56-59; Ref libn US Central Intelligence Agency, Wash DC 59-. 9: ALA; SLA. 10: Beta Phi Mu. 14: Ref. 15: 5480 Wisconsin ave, Chevy Chase Md 20015.

BELL, EDITH HELEN (BURGESS). b Waldoboro Me 7 My 26. 5: Gorham State Tchrs Col 43-47 (Eng-Lit) BS; UMe 59-65 (Hist) MEd. 7: Tchr Windham Sch Dept, Windham Me 47-49; Jr High Tchr Westbrook Sch Dept, Westbrook Me 56-60, Jr High Libn 60-. 10: Girl Scouts of Amer (var offs); First Congregational Church of Windham (organist, treas, church sch tchr). 14: Jr High lib. 15: RD 2, South Windham Me 04082.

BELL, ELSIE LILIAS (COOK). b Clydebank Scotland 12 Je 22. 4: Digby Bell. 5: UMich 46-50 (Mus) BM; UOkla 64-68 MLS. 7: Sec Gray & Smith Detroit 40-43; Secretary (chief yeoman) USN Res (WAVES), NY 43-46; Sec Okla Health & Welfare Assn 54-57; Mus dir WNAD UOkla 62; Br hd & area supv Okla Co Libs, Okla City 68-. 9: ALA; OklaLA. 10: LWV. 14: Admin, ref, ya. 15: 515 Chautauqua, Norman Ok 73069.

BELL, FRANCES. b Howe Tex 26 S 36. 5: N Tex State U 54-55, 63-66 (Eng) MA; UTex 55-58 (Eng) BA. 7: Y-a libn Dallas Pub Lib, Dallas 61-64, Adult libn 64-68, Asst to coord adult serv 68-69; Dept Hd Popular Lib 70-. 9: Dallas Co LA (sec-treas 69-70). 15: 4103 Rawlins apt B, Dallas Tx 75219.

BELL, FREDRICK. b St Joseph Mo 2 D 11. 4: Fern (Wilson). 5: USMA 32-36 (Sci) BS; Harvard Grad Sch Bus Adm 54 (Mgt) Diploma; St Mary'sU (San Antonio) 66 (Ed); Our Lady of the Lake Col (LS) MS. 7: Mgt & Engineering (Brig Gen) USAF Dayton Ohio 61; Hd circ dept TrinityU 67-68; Field consul Tex State Lib, San Antonio 68-. 8: Chief, Lien-Fen Peace Team Nationalist/Communist China, Lin-Fen China 46; Tex State Lib consul for pub libs in So Tex 68-69. 9: ALA; TexasLA; BexarLA. 10: Daedalian Soc; Air Force Assn; Retired Officers Assn; Harvard Alum Assn. 11: A variety of US military and foreign honors. 14: Pub lib serv, lib admin. 15: 11002 Dreamland, San Antonio Tx 78230.

BELL, GERALDINE OVETA (WATTS). b Camden Ala 29 Ag 36. 4: Milton Ray Bell. 5: Ala State Col 53-57 (Eng) BS; IndU 61-65 (LS) MA UPenn summer 66. 6: Fr. 7: Libn Wilcox Co Train Sch, Millers Ferry Ala 57-59; Libn Monroe Co Train Sch, Beatrice Ala 59-66, libn Alden High Sch, Alden Ala 66-67; Libn Hayes HighSch, Birmingham Ala 67-. 8: Consul for Mary Gardner Pub Lib, Monroeville Ala 65-66; Acting Hd Tech Serv Ala A & M Col, Normal Alasummer 67, Lab libn summer 69. 9: NEA; Amer Tchrs Assn; AlaState Tchrs Assn;AlaSchL (sec 66-67, v-pres & pres-elect 68-). 10: Alpha Kappa Alpha; Monroe Co (Ala) Educator's Fed Credit Union. 14: Ref. 15: Box 1683, Wenonah Park rd,Birmingham Al 35228.

BELL, INGLIS FREEMAN. b Medicine Hat Alberta 27 Mr 17. 4: Grace Wilkins. 58: A Checklist of Twentieth-Century Criticism" (59); "On Canadian Literature, 1806-1960" (65); Ed "British Columbia Library Quarterly," (56-59); Ed "Canadian Literature; A Checklist" (59-62); "Canadian Literature, Literature Canadienne 1959-1963" (66). 7: (Lt) Can Army 41-45; UBC: Libn I ref 52-54, Libn II circ 54-56, Libn III circ 56-61, libn IV circ 61-62; Asst libn 62-64, Assoc libn 64-. 8: Consul Bldgs British Columbia Inst of Tech 66; Consul Personnel McGill U libs 69. 9: CanLA (Mem Com); BSCan (v-pres, pres 68-70); ALA (sec Lib Period Round Table); BCLA (Coun Lib Devel Com); Can Assn Col & Univ Libs (v-pres & pres-elect 69-71). 12: "The English Novel, 15 78-1958: A Checklist of Twentieth-Century Criticism" (59); "On Canadian Literature, 1806-1960" (65); Ed "British Columbia Library Quarterly," (56-59); Ed "Canadian Literature: A Checklist" (59-62); "Canadian Literature, Literature Canadienne 1959-1963" (66). 13: Yes. 14: Bibliog. 15: 4334 W 8 ave, Vancouver 8 BC Can.

BELL, JANET E. b Honolulu 1 N 10. 5: UHawaii 28-32 BA; UWash 32-33 BSLS. 7: UHawaii Lib: Lib asst 33-35, Hawaiian & Pacific libn 36-62; Censor of registered mail US Censor's Off, Honolulu 41-42; UHawaii: Curator Hawaii War Records Depository 46-, Curator Hawaiian & Pacific Collection 62-. 9: ALA; Amer Assn State & Loc Hist; HawaiiLA; Hawaiian Hist Soc (Lib Com chm 53-63, trustee 65-68). 10: AAUP; Mortar Board; Friends of the East West Center; Lahaina Restoration Found; Honolulu Commun Theatre; Anthropol Soc of Hawaii; Univ of Hawaii Found (Life mem); Bishop Mus Assn; Honolulu Acad of Arts; Honolulu Symphony Soc; Chamber Music Soc. 12: "Official Publications of the Territory of Hawaii 1900-1959" with others (62); Ed "Current Hawaiiana" (44-). 13: Yes. 14: Spec collections, rare bks, ref. 15: P O Box 3373, Honolulu Hi 96801.

BELL, JO ANN (GIBSON). b Golden Tex 12 Ag 33. 4: Wilmer W Bell. 5: N Tex State U 56-59 (Elem Educ) BSE, 65- (LS). 7: Elem tchr Spring Br Ind Sch Dist, Houston 59-61; Elem tchr Richardson Ind Sch Dist, richardson Tex 61-62, Materials & elem libs coordinator 62-. 9: Tex State Tchrs Assn; TexLA NEA-DAVI; Tex Assn of Ed Tech. 10: Alpha Lambda Sigma; Alpha Delta Kappa; Delta Kappa Gamma. 14: Child bks, elem sch libs. 15: 801 Carney, Garland Tx 75040.

BELL, JO PORCHER. b Hibbing Minn 21 Je 43. 5: UMinn; 61-64 (Hist) BA, 64-66 (LS) MA; Stanislaus State Col 68; UHawaii 68. 6: Sp, Chinese. 7: Tchg asst Lib Sch, UMinn 65; Libn Kenny Rehabilitation Inst, Minneapolis 65; Acquis libn Col of St Thomas (St Paul) 65-67; Acquis libn Stanislaus State Col 68-. 9: ALA; CCUFA; ACSCP (sec localdist); CalLA (sec Yosemite dist). 14: Asian studies. 15: Stanislaus State Col,Turlock, Cal 95380.

BELL, JoANN. b Wilmington NC 25 Mr 41. 4: Michael P Bell. 5: Duke 59-63 (Hist) BA; UNC 65-66 (LS) MS. 7: Asst libn E Carolina U 66-67; Lib dir Pitt Tech Inst 67-. 8: State Advis Com on Commun Cols. 9: ALA; MedLA; SLA; NCLA; SELA; NC Commun ColLA. 10: Beta Phi Mu; Duke Alum Assn; Pitt Co Loyalty Fund; Greenville Jaycettes. 14: Ref. 15: 203 Nichols dr, Greenville NC 27834.

BELL, MARION V(IRGINIA). b Plainfield NJ 2 Je 23. 5: Dickinson Col 46 (Hist) AB; Toronto 48 BLS. 6: Fr. 7: Ref asst Enoch Pratt Free Lib, Baltimore 48-50; Ref asst Kent StateU 50-51, Enoch Pratt Free Lib, Baltimore; Sr ref asst 51-59, Admin asst Ref Dept 59-60, Head gen ref dept 61-. 9: SLA; ALA (Md Chap: chm 58-59, Ref Serv Div); MdLA. 12: "Pooles Index: Date & Volume Key, with Jean C Bacon, ACRL Monog #19 (57). 14: Ref, bibliog. 15: 913 Southerly rd, Towson Md 21204.

BELL, MATTHEW JOSEPH. b Boston Mass 11 Je 41. 4: Mary L McGivern. 5: Assumption Col 59-64 (Natural Sci) AB; CatholicU 64-66 (LS) MSLS. 7: Asst libn Mgt Sci Div Arthur D Little Inc, Cambridge Mass 65-. 9: SLA. 14: Admin. 15: 19 Sycamore lane, Hingham Ma 02043.

BELL, MERTYS (WARD). b Arlington Ga 13 Jl 17. 4: Thomas Edward Bell. 5: Ga State Col for Women 33-37 (Hist) AB; UNC summers 38-42 BS in LS; UNC (Greensboro) 63-64 (Lib Educ). 7: Tchr hist Lat libn Ringgold High Sch, Ringgold Ga 37-38; Libn Douglas Pub Schs, Douglas Ga 38-40; Dist lib supv WPA of Ga, Savannah & Macon Ga 40-42; Dir of Reg Lib Athens Reg Lib, Athens Ga 42-43; Circ asst br supv Seattle Pub Lib, King Co Lib, Seattle 43-45; Co Libn Moultrie Carnegie Lib, Moultrie Ga 45-46; Catlgr lib dept Greensboro Pub Schs, Greensboro NC 55-60; Libn Guilford Tech Inst, Jamestown NC 63-66; Libn Rockingham Commun Col 66-68; Acquis libn UNC (Greensboro) 68-. 9: ALA; SELA; NCLA (Lib Resources Com); Commun Cols LA (pres 68-69); Greensboro Lib Club (treas 69-70). 10: Mem NC Lit & Hist Assn; Amer Assn State & Loc Hist; Weatherspoon Art Gallery; Friends of the Lib U NC (Greensboro); Pi Gamma Mu. 14: Jr col lib admin, catlgr, acquis. 15: 5608 Cambridge rd, Greensboro NC 27407.

BELL, ROBERT (EUGENE). b Tarrant City Ala 13 O 26. 5: Birmingham-SoCol 44-50 (Eng) BA; Harvard 50-51 (Eng) AM; Columbia summer 52 (LS);LSU summer 53, 66-67 MS in LS; UCal (Berkeley) 67-. 6: Fr, Ger. 7: Asst circ dept Birmingham Pub Lib, Birmingham Ala 49-50; Mobile Pub Lib, Mobile Ala; Head of ref dept 51-54, Asst dir 54-55; Asst dir Ft Worth Pub Lib, Ft Worth Tex 55-60; Exec dir Book Club of Cal, San Francisco 60-62; Asst bus & sci New Orleans Pub Lib 62-63; Head adultservs Mobile Pub Lib, Mobile Ala 63-65; Act head art & music dept New Orleans Pub Lib 65-66; Head adult serv N Orleans Pub Lib 66-. 9: AlaLA (var coms); ALA. 10: Antiqn Bksellers Assn of Amer; Amer Assn of Museums; Phi Beta Kappa; Omicron Delta Kappa; Eta Sigma Phi; Phi Kappa Phi; Cal Arts Soc; Sierra Club. 12: "A Bibliography of Mobile, Alabama" (56); "The Butterfly Tree, a Novel" (59); ed "Quarterly News-letter" (Bk Club of Cal)(60-62). 13: Yes. 14: Rare bks, spec collections, bibliog. 15: 545 Sutter st, Rm 302, San Francisco Ca 94102.

BELL, SARAH JANE (HODGES). b Muskogee Okla 2 Ag 18. 4: Clarence E Bell. 5: Shorter Col 34-35; LangstonU 35-38 (Eng) BS; AtlantaU 44-45 BSLS; UOkla 52-56 MSLS; Okla StateU 65 (LS). 6: Fr. 7: Tchr-libn Washington High Sch, Red Bird Okla 40-41; Tchr-libn Manual Train High Sch, Muskogee Okla 45-47; Br libn Dunbar Br Lib, Okla City Okla 48-52; Libn Dunbar Elem Sch, Okla City Okla 52-54; Libn Douglass High Sch, Okla City Okla 54-66; Sch lib supv State Dept of Educ 66-68; Field libn Okla city schs 68-. 9: ALA (Mem Com Okla); NEA; OklaLA (sec, Recr Com, Nomin Com); OklaEA (sec, v-pres, chm Lib Sect). 10: YWCA; Urban League; Entre Nous Study Club; Delta Sigma Theta; Queen of Hearts Bridge Club. 11: Grace E Herrick Award, OklaU. 14: Sch libnship, instr materials centers. 15: 1112 Euclid, Oklahoma City Ok 73117.

BELL, SYLVIA IRENE. b Timaru New Zealand 19 Ja 30. 5: UOtago New Zealand 49-54 (Hist, Pol Sci) BA; New Zealand Lib Sch 55 Diploma. 7: Libn-in-Charge Pub Lib, Blenheim NZ 55-57; Catlgr, Readers' Adv Pub Lib, Palmerston N NZ 57-59; Hendon Pub Lib & J M Whitaker 59-61; Act ref libn Pub Lib Palmerston N NZ 62; Libn-in-Charge Knox Col 63-65; Libn-Bibliogr YorkU 66-. 9: NZLA (Offr Otago Br & Profess Sect); OntLA; Inst Profess Libns Ont. 15: Box 606, Woodbridge Ont Can.

BELL, WINNIE ELIZABETH. b Waxahachie Tex 7 Jl 25. 5: Harding Col 46-49 (Bus Educ) BA; Peabody 60-61 (LS) MA; Drexel 64 Spec stud. 7: Sec Security State Bank, Wewoka Okla 49-59; Asst libn Harding Col Lib 59-. 9: ALA; ArkLA. 10: AAUW; Harding Bus Women. 12: Ed "Periodical Holdings in the AFAC (3rd ed 68). 14: Ref, catlg. 15: 100 S Turner, Searcy Ark72144.

BELLAMY, MRS LAURETTA (MOLONEY). b San Luis Colo 6 N 18. 5: UColo 36-40 (Span) BA, summers 40,41 (Span), 47-48 (Span), 50 (Span); UDenver summer 57 (LS); UColo summer 58 (Span),63-68 (Span). 6: Sp, port, Fr, Lat, Ital, Catalan, Old Provencal. 7: Tchr of Span, Lat & Eng & libn Limon High Sch, Limon Colo 40-41; Tchr of Span, Eng & Journalism & libn Aurora High Sch, Aurora Colo 41-44; Tchr of Span, Lat & Eng Sargent High Sch, Monte Vista Colo 45-47; Instr & conversation dir Language House U Colo 47-48; Asst Prof Span & Lat NM West 48-49; Catlg libn UColo 49-. 9: ALA; Amer Assn Tchrs Span & Port (past sec Colo Chap); MPLA (past sec-treas Catlg Sect); ColoLA (past pres, mem Exec Com No Dist Chap). 10: AAUP; University Club; Colo HeartAssn; Territ Daughters of Colo; Mortar Board; Phi Beta Kappa. 12: Comp "A List of the Plays in Garcia Rico y Cia's Coleccion de comedias espanolas de los siglos XIX y XX" with A C Klemme (56). 13: Yes. 14: Ser catlg (Romance langs). 15: 1510 13th st,Boulder Co 80302.

BELLEFLEUR, MARTHE LEMIEUX. b Roberval Can 29 Je 18. 4: Joseph Bellefleur. 5: UMontreal 62 Bachelor of LS. 6: Fr. 7: Asst libn & hd catlgr Bibliotheque St-Sulpice, Montreal 49-60; Bibliothecaire en chef du Catalogue et clsf des Ec Hautes Etudes Coms, Montreal 61. 8: Libn to Societe Historique de Montreal 64-66. 9: CanLA; Assn Canadienne des bibliothecaires de langue francaise. 10: Can Fed of Univ Women; Assn des Femmes diplomees des Universities (Montreal); Societe Paul Claudel. 14: Ref. 15: 535 ave Viger, Montreal PQ Can.

BELLEY, DAVID (O). b La Malbaie Co Charlevoix PQ Can 3 D 42. 4: Claudette Boivin Belley. 5: MonctonU 64-65 BA; OttawaU 65-66 BLS. 6: Fr. 7: Libn catlgr USherbrooke PQ 66-. 14: Catlg. 15: 1560 Cabana sr apt 6, Sherbrooke Que (Prov) Can.

BELLINGER, ROBERT CHARLES. b Bay City Mich 12 N 35. 5: Bay City Jr Col 53-55 (AA); Kalamazoo Col 55-57 (Span) BA; West Mich U 57-58; UWis 64-65 MA in LS. 6: Sp, Fr. 7: Tchr Rockford Ill Pub Schs 58-59; Asst Dept Manager Hills Dept Store, Milwaukee 59-60; Libn I Milwaukee Pub Lib 60-67, Reglibn Lib for the Blind & Physically Handicapped 69-; Libn Santa Clara Co Lib, San Jose Cal 67-69. 9: ALA (RT for the Blind & Physically Handicapped);-AHIL; CalLA; WisLA. 10: Bay Area Young Adult Assn; Nat Braille Assn; Coord Coun for the Visually Handicapped (Milwaukee); Volunteer Serv Ctr; Nat Multiple Sclerosis Soc; Beta Phi Mu. 13: Yes. 14: Serv to the blind & physically handicapped. 15: 814 W Wisconsin ave, Milwaukee Wi 53233.

BELLINGHAM, HAROLD. b NYC 16 Ja 09. 4: Ellen Forsyth Bellingham. 5: Hope Col 28-32 (Hist) AB; Columbia 37-40 BS in LS. 6: Fr, Sp. 7: Interlib loan lib US Dept of Defense, Wash DC 45-56; Catlgr US Dept of State, Wash DC 46-47; Catlgr UDenver 47-50; Head catlgr UIowa 50-53; Catlgr Los Angeles Co Med Soc, Los Angeles 53-59; Catlgr UNM Lib 59-63; Assoc libn for pub serv UNM Med Lib 63-68; Catlgr UNM Lib (& in charge of bind) 68-. 9: MedLA; NMLA. 14: Catlg. 15: Zimmerman Library, Univ of N Mex, Albuquerque NM 87106.

BELLIS, GENEVIEVE H(OEHN). b Lilbourn Mo 10 Jl 10. 4: Tom Bellis. 5: Southeast Mo State Col 28-31 (Eng) BS in Ed; Catholic U 57-59 MS in LS. 6: Sp. 7: Sec US Govt, Wash DC, Chicago, Kansas City Mo, bogota Columbia SAmer 35-44; Libn Arlington Co Libs, Arlington Va 57-62; Base libn Bolling AFB Lib, Wash DC 63; Br libn Columbus Mem Lib of Pan Amer Union, Wash DC 64-66; Ref libn Fairfax Co Pub Lib, Fairfax Va 66-. 9: . 10: AAUW. 12: "Ten Rooms and Two Patios" (48). 13: Yes. 14: Ref. 15: 2606 S Troy st, Arlington Va 22206.

BELLO, RAYMOND P(AUL). b Lakeland La 8 F 34. 5: LSU 52-56 (Educ) BS, 63 (Educ) MEd, 66-67 MSLS, 67-68 Post Master's Fellowship Program in LS. 6: Fr. 7: Specialist 4 US Army, Ark, Colo, La 57-59; Staff Sgt US Army, La 61-62; Tchr W Baton Rouge Parish Sch Bd, Port Allen La 56-57, 59-61, 62-66; Asst docs libn LSU Lib (Baton Rouge) 68-69, Head acquis div 69-. 9: ALA; SWLA; LaLA. 12: Ed "Bulletin of the Louisiana Chapter of the Special Libraries Association". 13: Yes. 14: Acquis, govt docs. 15: 980 Government, Baton Rouge La 70802.

BELLOLI, JOSEPH A(THONY). b San Jose Cal 14 Ja 09. 4: Florence C Amaral. 5: San Jose State Col 30-34 (Eng) BA; UCal 34-35 (LS). 6: Fr, Ger, Sp. 7: Jr asst UCal Col of Agric (Davis) 36; Asst ref libn San Jose Pub Lib 36-38; City Libn Pub Lib, Pacific Grove Cal 38-43; Cost inventory Hendy Iron Co, Sunnyvale Cal 43-44; Lib supv Vallejo Housing Authority 44-45; Bkkeeper & salesman Automobile Bus, San Jose 45-46; Chief humanities & soc sci libn StanfordU 46-. 9: CalLA. 10: Exchange Club, Stanford Faculty Club. 13: Yes. 14: Ref, bibliog, research materials. 15: Stanford U Lib, Stanford Ca 94305.

BELMONTE, HELEN (MARION). b Jacksonville Fla 30 S 41. 4: Stan Belmonte. 5: UWash 59-63 (Pol Sci) BA; Universidad de San Marcos 61 (Peruvian Culture); Universidad Nacional Autonoma de Mexico 63 (Span); UWash 63-64 MLS. 6: Sp, Fr, Ger. 7: Med sec Seattle 56-63; UN hostess Seattle World's Fair UN Pavillion summer 63; Tchr Universidad de San Marcos, Lima Peru 61; Lib asst UWash Bus Lib 62-63; Libn hist div Brooklyn Pub Lib 64-. 9: NY Lib Club. 10: Pan American Union; UWash Sch of Libnship Alumni Assn. 14: Ref. 15: 6633 Ovington ct, Brooklyn NY 11204.

BELSER, THOMAS ARVIN Jr. b Montgomery Ala 29 Mr 27. 4: Mary Littlejohn. 5: VanderbiltU 48-54, 58 (Hist) BA, MA, PhD. 6: Fr. 7: USAAF Control Tower Operator (Cpl) 44-46; Asst Prof of hist Jacksonville State col 54-57; AuburnU: Asst Prof of hist 57-63, Assoc Prof of hist 63-64, Assoc Prof of hist & archivist 64-68, Prof of Hist & Archivist 68-. 9: So Hist Assn; SAA; Ala Hist Assn; Ala Acad Sci. 10: Phi Alpha Theta. 13: Yes. 14: Mss. 15: Dept of Archives Auburn Univ, Auburn Al 36830.

BELT, (SARAH) JANE (WORTH). b Cumberland Md 5 Ag 28. 4: Paul F Belt. 5: Millersville State Tchrs Col 46-50 (LS) BS in Ed; Syracuse 54-56 MS in LS; Wenatchee Valley Jr Col 61-. 7: Bkmob libn Montgomery Co Lib, Dayton Ohio 50-53; Child libn Dayton Pub Lib, Dayton Ohio 53-54; Cadet libn in educ Home Econ & Arch Lib SyracuseU 54-55; Educ libn (Cadet) SyracuseU 55-56; Child libn No Central Reg Lib, Wenatchee Wash 56-58; Bkmob libn Col River Reg Demo Lib, Wenatchee Wash 58-59; Libn Sch of Nursing Central Wash Deaconess Hosp, Wenatchee Wash 67-. 8: Governor's Lib Conf (Prog Com), Moses Lake Wash 68; Set up all bkmob routes & serv for the Chelan, Douglas Cos in the Columbia River Lib Demonst 58-59. 9: ALA; MedLA; WashLA. 10: Venture Club; Beta Phi Mu. 14: Nursing materials, child serv. 15: Rte 3 Box 3193, Wenatchee Wa 98801.

BELT, STEPHEN G. b Toledo Ohio 24 Ag 31. 5: Williams 49-51; Mich State Col 51-54 (Eng Lit) BA; Mich State U 57-59

(Eng Lit)MA; UMich 60 MA in LS. 6: Fr. 7: US Army Message Centre Mo (Pfc) 54-56; Libn ref dept Enoch Pratt Free Lib, Baltimore 60-. 10: ACLU; Baltimore Urban League. 14: Ref. 15: 2303 Montebello ter,Baltimore Md 21214.

BELZER, JOAN (WEISMAN). b Minneapolis 2 Mr 43. 4: Dr Irvin Belzer. 5: UMinn 61-64 (Sociol) BA; UCLA 64-65 MLS. 6: Sp, Hebrew. 7: Ref libn UCLA 65; Ref libn USoCal 65-66; Lib Consul, S D State Lib Comms 66-68. 10: Phi Beta Kappa. 14: Ref, Bibliog. 15: 21 River Terrace court, Minneapolis, Minn 55414.

BEMIS, NANCY M. b Spokane Wash 2 Ap 31. 5: East Wash Col 49-53 (Educ) BA in Educ; UWash 54-55 MLS. 6: Fr, Sp. 7: Libn Wenatchee High Sch, Wenatchee Wash 55-57; Libn Orleans Amer High Sch, Orleans France 57-59; Libn US Army Seoul AreaCommand, Korea 60; Libn US Army 1st Cavalry Div, Korea 60-64; Libn USAF Kanto Mura & Grant Hts Housing Areas, Japan 64-66;Post libn, Ft Devens Mass 66-67; Dist libn 23rd Direct Support Group 8th US Army, Korea 68-. 9: ALA. 10: Royal Asiatic Soc. 14: Ref, ext serv. 15: Spec Ser Lib 15-23rd Dir Support Group, APO San Francisco 96271.

BEN-ZVI, HAVA (BROMBERG). b Warsaw Poland 30 D 29. 4: Ephraim Ben-Zvi. 5: Teachers Col (Haifa Israel) 49-50 (Educ) Teaching Cred; Cal State Col (Los Angeles) 60-62 (Sociol) BA; Immaculate Heart Col Cal 62-63 MALS. 6: Hebrew, Russian, Polish. 7: Tchr Pub Schs, Haifa Israel 50-57; Libn Loma Linda 63-67; Los Angeles Co PubLib 67-. 9: CalLA. 14: Admin. 15: 1684 Huntington dr, S Pasadena Ca 91030.

BENCSIK, GABOR. b Budapest Hungary 29 Je 10. 4: Julia Magassy. 5: U of Science (Budapest) 33-39 (Law, pol Sci) PhD (Pol Sci); Columbia 57-60 MLS. 6: Fr, Ger, Hungarian. 7: Queens Borough Pub Lib: Gen asst 60-61, Ref libn 61-63, Br libn 63-. 9: NYLA. 15: 222 E 87, NYC 10028.

BENDER, ALICE (COVELL). b Chicago 2 N 27. 4: Joseph C Bender. 5: Colby Col 45-49 (Eng) BA; Simmons 50-51 MS in LS; UHawaii summer 61, 68; UIll summer 65. 7: Child libn Lib of Hawaii, Honolulu 51-60; Child libn NY Pub Lib 60-61; Sch libn Paramus Pub Schs, Paramus NJ 61-63; Sch libn Kamehameha Schs, Honolulu 63-. 9: Hawaii Assn Sch Libns. ; Hawaii LA (dir 69-70); ALA. 14: Child lit. 14: Child lit. 15: 1937 Kakela dr, Honolulu 96822.

BENDER, BETTY (WION). b Mt Ayr Iowa 26 F 25. 4: Robert F Bender. 5: Drake U 42-44; No Tex State Teachers Col 44-46 (LS) BS; UDenver summer 50,56-57 (LS) MS. 6: Sp, Ger. 7: Asst catlgr No Tex State Col 46-49; Catlgr So Meth U 49-51; Ref libn Ind State Lib 51-52; SoMethU: Period libn 52-53, Head order dept 53-56; Ark State Col: Act libn 58, Ref libn 58-59; Libn East Wash State Hist Soc, Spokane Wash 60-67; Catlgr St Louis Pub Lib 66-67; Ref libnSpokane Pub Lib 68, Hd circ libn 68-. 8: Visiting Instr UDenver Grad Sch of Libnship summers 57-60, 63; fall 59; Instr Whitworth Col, spokane Wash summers 62, 64; springs 63, 64. 9: ALA; PNLA; TexLA (pres Col Lib Sect 52-53); WashLA (ALA Mem Chm 63-). 10: AAUW; Zonta Internat; East Wash State Col Faculty Wives. 14: Catlg, acquis, ref, circ. 15: 119 NSixth st, Cheney Wa 99004.

BENDER, DAVID R. b Canton Ohio 12 Je 42. 4: Harriet Posgay. 5: Kent State 60-64 9soc studies) BS in Ed; UHawaii Inst on Asian Studies summer 66; Case WestU 65-69 MSLS. 7: Libn Willoughby-Eastlake S High Sch, Willoughby Ohio 64-69; Instr Lakeland Commun Col, Mentor Ohio 68; Consul Sch Lib Serv State Dept of Educ Title II ESEA Columbus Ohio 69-. 8: Adv Coun, Lakeland Commun Col, Lib Tech Aides' Prog 68-69. 9: ALA; OhioASchL; Educl Media Coun of Ohio; OhioLA; OhioEA. 10: Kappa Sigma. 13: Yes. 14: Admin, supv. 15: 22 E Gay st, Columbus Oh 43215.

BENDER, HENRY EDWIN JR. b Evanston Ill 6 Mr 37. 4: Barbara E Caven. 5: Purdue 54-58 (Engnr Sci) BS; UNM 58-64 (Nuclear Engnr); UDenver 64-65 (LS) MA. 6: Sp. 7: Stud aide Argonne Nat Lab, Argonne Ill summer 57; Designengnr ACF Ind, Albuquerque Div, Albuquerque NM 58-64; Lib consul Kaman Nuclear, ColoSprings Colo 65; Libn IBM Systems Development Div, San Jose Cal 65-. 9: Amer SocMech Engnrs; SLA. 10: Railroad Club of NM; Railway & Locomotive Hist Soc; NatRailway Hist Soc; Rocky Mtn RR Club; Citizens Against Air Pollution. 12: Ed "New Mexico Railroader" (59-64). 14: Catlg, computerization of tech serv. 15: 6257 solano dr, San Jose Ca 95119.

BENDER, J TERRY. b Wash DC 8 Ag 25. 5: Williams 46-49 (Hist) AB ; Princeton 49-50 (Hist); Columbia Sch Lib Sci 52-53 (Rare Bks) MS. 6: Fr, Ger, Lat. 7: Statistician USA Ordnance Div Eur Thea Oper 43-46; Clerical asst Williams Lib 50-51; Antiquarian bk seller Brick Row Bk Shop, NYC 51-52; Bibliog asst dept spec col Columbia 52-53; Spec col Libn StanfordU Lib 53-55; Chief of Spec Col StanfordU 55-61; Libn & dir The Grolier Club, NYC 61-64; Curator of Rare Bks SyracuseU Lib 64-69; Spec Collections Libn Hofstra U Hempstead NY 70-. 8: Libn to Bk Club of Cal 53-55; Chm of Exhib Com, Bk Club of Cal 56-59; Bd Dirs Bk Club of Cal 56-61; Sec treas Roxburghe Club of San Francisco 56-57; Spec Col Com, Five Assoc Univ Libs, 09: ALA; -ACRL (chm Rare Bk & Mss Sect 58-59); Les Bibliophiles Internationales& (London) Bibliog Soc; BSA. 10: Book Club of Cal; Roxburghe Club of San Francisco; Grolier Club. 12: Numerous separate catalogues of exhibits, etc. 14: Rare bks, mss, spec col, bibliog. 15: Hofstra U Lib, Hempstead NY 11550.

BENDER, ROSE S(UBERMAN). b NY 18 Ag 10. 4: Alfred Bender. 5: Hunter Col 34 (Fr) BA; Queens Col (NYC) 63 (LS) MA. 6: Fr, Sp. 7: Attendance clerk Bayside High Sch, Queens NY 50-59; Libn W Hempstead Sr High Sch, W Hempstead NY 59-62; Libn Great Neck Jr High Sch, Great Neck NY 62-. 8: Instr Lib Sci Queens Col (NY) 64-. 9: ALA; NYLA; NY State Tchrs Assn. 13: Yes. 15: 4 Spruce pl, Great Neck LI NY 11021.

BENDIX, DOROTHY. b Berlin Germany 31 O 13. 5: Columbia: 41 BLS, 46 (Sociol) MA, 65 DLS. 6: Ger. 7: Columbia U Libs NYC 39-43; Brooklyn Pub Lib 43-45; Prin labor & soc sci libnnewark Pub Lib, Newark NJ 45-51; Coordinator adult group servs Detroit Pub Lib 51-56;Instr NY State Teachers Col, (Geneseo) summer 57; Instr Pratt Inst Lib Sch 58-59;Assoc Prof Grad Sch of Lib Sci Drexel Inst of Tech 59-. 8: Consul (Public libraryspecialist), Penn State Lib 59-68. 9: ALA (Coun 65-69, memb com on 2 jt coms 65-)-ASD (Spec Proj Com 65-66, Nom Com 55-56); PennLA (chm Conf Eval Com 62, mem IntelFreedom Com 62-64, Adult Serv Com 64-65). 10: AAUP; LWV; AEAUSA; Penn Assn AdultEduc. 11: Fund for Adult Educ Leadership Train Award 56-57. 12: "Some Problems in Book Selection Policies and Practices in Medium-SizedPublic Libraries" (59); Ed "Library Service to Labor Newsletter" (49-52); Guest edIntell Freedom Issue "PennLA Bulletin" May 63; "Labor Unions and Public LibraryService," Doctoral Dissertation Columbia 65; Ed "Problems of Library Service inMetropolitan Areas" 65; Ed "Problems of Library Work with the Undereducated" (66). 13: Yes. 14: Pub libs, adult serv, lib educ, pub lib serv to the disadvantaged. 15: 3408Powelton ave, Phila Pa 19104.

BENEDICT, BETTY JEAN (ZAHN). b Morristown NJ 17 Ap 32. 4: Joseph T Benedict. 5: Wellesley 50-54 (Chem) AB; Grad Sch of Lib Serv Rutgers 66-68 MLS. 6: Fr, Ger. 7: Lab asst chem Nick el Processing Corp, Montclair NJ 55-57; Lab asst chem Merck & Co, Danville Penn 57-58; Lib asst White Labs, Kenilworth NJ 60-61. Fairleigh Dickinson U; Asst period libn 63-68, period libn 68-. 9: SLA. 14: Period. 15: 667 Beechwood dr Wash twp, Westwood NJ 07675.

BENEDICT, ESTELLE. b New York NY 27 S 31. 5: UCal at Berkeley 49-53 Eng BA; USoCal 57-58 MLS. 6: Fr, Sp. 7: Libn LA Co Pub Lib Malibu Bkmob 59-61; Ref & catlg libn US Dept of Com Ref Lib NY 63-65; Med libn Hosp for Joint Diseases NY 66-. 8: Consul Med Lib, Inst for the Crippled and Disabled, NY 65. 9: SLA; MedLA (NY Reg Gp). 14: Admin, ref, acquis. 15: 136 W 13th st, New York NY 10011.

BENEDICT, RICHARD F(OSTER). b Water Mill NY 10 Je 22. 4: June Teeling. 5: Ernest Williams Sch of Mus 40-42; UCal (Berkeley) 48-49; Catholic U 49-52 (Music) BM, 52-53 MS in LS. 6: Fr. 7: Catlgr UNH 53-54; AFPTRC, San Antonio Tex: Chief of tech processing 54-58, Head Libn 58-59; Chief Libn Ryan Aero Electronics Div, San Diego 59-60; Head of ref Gen Dynamics Astronautics, San Diego 60-62; Chief of Info Serv Lab for Electronics, Boston 62-63; Asst libn UFla 63-66; Tech info specialist Lawrence Radiation Lab Lib, Livermore Cal 66-67; Chief systs div Air U Lib 67-. 9: ALA; SLA; ASIS. 10: AAUP; EAA; NRA; AOPA; Phi Beta Kappa. 14: Admin, info sci. 15: 1243 Adell st, Prattville Al 36067.

BENEDICT, RUSSELL H(OWARD). b Muskegon Mich 20 Ap 24. 5: Emmanuel Missionary Col 9andrewsU) 42-43, 45-49 (Hist, Bio); IndU 51-56, 67 (Ch Mus); Fla StateU 62-63 (LS); Mich State summer 65 (A-V, Educ). 7: Surgical tech & supv US Army Med Dept, SW Pacific Theatre 43-45; Tchr Richmond Jr Acad, Richmond Va 49-50; Mus dept hd Oak Park Acad, Nev Iowa 56-57; Priv mus studio tchg, Indialantic Fla 57-61; Grad asst Fla StateU Lib 62-63; Asst catlgr FurmanU 63-64; Learning resources tchr Ind Acad, Cicero Ind 66-67; Travelling elem libn Bloomington Schs, Bloomington

Ind 67-68; Catlgr Central StateU (Ohio) 68-. 8: Chm Lib Com for the elem and intermed schs, Educ Dept Mich Conf of seventh-day Adventists; Adv In-serv wkshop for elem & intermed tchrs, Educ Dept Ind conf of Seventh-day Adventists; Memb Tech Com, Lib Div, Dayton-Miami Valley Consortium. 14: Catlg, ref, admin, a-v. 15: 5370 Manchester rd, W Carrollton Oh 45449.

BENENFELD, ALAN R. b Brooklyn NY 3 O 39. 5: NYU 57-61 (Metallurgical Engnrg) BMetE, Cornell U 61-64 9materials Sci); Rutgers 64-65 MLS. 6: Fr, Ger. 7: Research asst in metallurgy CornellU 61-64; Lib asst ref RutgersU 64-65; Materials sci libn MIT, Cambridge Mass 65-66; Research staff (Proj Intrex) Elec Syst Lab MIT 66-. 9: ALA; ASIS (NewEngland Chap; chm 69, Program chm 68). 10: Tau Beta Pi; Alpha Sigma Mu. 13: Yes. 14: Lib automation, info stor &retr, admin, tech serv. 15: MIT Elec Syst Lab, Bldg 35-407, Cambridge Ma 02139.

BENEPE, CLAIRE BLODAU. b Nashville Tenn. 4: Garth W Benepe. 5: Vanderbilt 26-30 (Eng) BA; Peabody Col 26-34 BS in LS; UChicago 38. 6: Ger, Fr, Sp, Lat. 7: Ref libn Nashville Pub Lib 19-30; Ref libn VanderbiltU 30-31; Dir sch libs Nashville City Schs 31-38; Lib tech US Govt Union Catlgs, Chicago 39-40; Inter-Amer libn Lib Intl Rel, Chicago 41; Advertising/paint mfr Brocado Inc, Chicago 41-62; Catlgr Glenview Pub Lib, Glenview Ill 62-65, Asst libn 65-68; Tech proc hd Northbrook Pub Lib, Northbrook Ill 68-. 8: Lib instr Peabody Col summers 34-38; Org 1st sch libs in Nashville Pub Schs. 9: ALA; IllLA. 10: Altrusa Club; AAUW; Chicago Art Inst. 14: Adult ref, catlg, admin. 15: 1505 Plymouth pl, Glenview Il 60025.

BENGLE, SISTER STELLA MIRIAM SNJM. b Detroit 23 F 09. 5: Outremont Scholasticate 49 Superior Diploma; St Rose Col 57 (Eng) BA; Villanova 61 MLS. 6: Fr. 7: Jr & Sr high sch tchr, Montreal; Jr high sch tchr, Hochelaga Convent 32-57; Tchr, St Thomas High Sch 57-64; Libn St Thomas High Sch, Pointe Claire Que 64-. 9: Prov Assn Rel Tchrs. 14: Ref. 15: 24 Sources rd, Valois Que Canada.

BENGTSON, BETTY (JEAN) GRIMES. b Milledgeville Ga 22 Je 40. 4: Peter Yeager Bengtson. 5: Duke 58-62 (Hist) BA; CatholicU of Amer 66-67 MS in LS. 6: Fr. 7: Catlgr LC Copyright Off 62-63; Asst cat libn Macalester Col 67-68; Cat libn Col of Notre Dame, Belmont Cal 68-. 9: ALA. 10: Beta Phi Mu. 14: Catlg, acquis. 15: 275 Puffin st, Foster City Ca 94404.

BENGTSON, MARJORIE CAROLYN. b Wheaton Ill 21 Ja 34. 5: Chicago Teachers Col 52-56 (Educ) BEd; Chicago 58; UIll 58-59 (LS) MS. 7: Tchr Chicago Pub Schs 56-57; Asst ref libn UIll (Chicago) 59-68, Asst docs libn 68-. 9: ALA-ACRL; IllLA; Chicago Reg Group Libns Tech Serv (sec-treas 62-63); Chicago Lib Club. 14: Ref, US docs. 15: 5134 W Strong st, Chicago Il 60630.

BENICE, SISTER M. b Windber Penn. 5: Canisius Col 38-42 (Eng, Lat) AB; SUNY (Buffalo) 42-44 (LS) BLA; Niagara U 47-51 (Eng) MA. 6: Pol, Fr, Lat, Ger, Sp. 7: Tchr-libn Immaculate Heart of Mary Acad, Buffalo NY 39-55; Prin & libn Transfiguration Sch, Buffalo NY 55-61; Villa Maria Col; Acad dean 66-68, Libn 61-66, 68-. 9: ALA; CathLA; NCTE; NYLA; NYEC; West NY Cath Lib Conf (sec 4 terms 45-62, offr 3 sects 48-64); Nat CathEA; NY State Assn Jr Cols. 10: NY State Eng Coun; Col Eng Assn; Polish Arts Club. 12: Ed "Library Bulletin" West NY Cath Libns Conf (56-58). 13: Yes. 14: Catlg, admin, a-v educ media. 15: 600 Doat st, Buffalo NY 14211.

BENJAMIN, JANE (ANDERSON). b Lansing Mich 23 Ap 41. 4: Richard C Benjamin. 5: Mich State 59-63 (Soc sci) BA; UMich 64-66 AMLS. 7: Eng tchr Potterville Pub Schs, Potterville Mich 63-64; Washtenaw Co Lib, Ann Arbor Mich: Pre-prof 65-66, Libn 66-67, Asst dir 67, Act dir 67-68, Asst dir 68-69, Ref libn-catlgr 69-. 9: ALA; MichLA; Ann Arb or Lib Club (sec 68-). 14: Interlib loan, personnel. 15: 3302 Alton ct, Ann Arbor Mi 48105.

BENN, ALICE E(DNA). b Detroit 8 Jl 13. 5: Wayne U 31-35 (Educ, LS) BA, 46-50 (Bus Admin) MA. 6: Fr. 7: Tchr & libn Detroit Pub Schs 35-42; Libn in chg Ford Aircraft Sch Lib Ford Motor Co, Dearborn Mich 42-46, Sr libn train dept lib 46-52, Libn pub rel research lib 52-55, Archives asst Ford Motor Co Archives 55-56, Archives asst Research & Info Dept 56-65, Archivist admin serv serv dept, Ford Motor Co Archives 65-. 9: ALA; SLA; SAA; Hist Soc of Mich; Dearborn Hist Soc. 10: Soroptimist. 11: Hon Life Memb Internat Mark Twain Soc. 12: "Management Dictionary" (52). 13: Yes. 14: Admin, ref, hist records, archives. 15: 22726 Nona ave, Dearborn Mich 48124.

BENNE, MAE (MAXINE). b Morrowville Kan 22 F 24. 5: UNeb 46-50 (Educ) BS; NW State Teachers Col (Mo) summer 50; UIll summers 53-55 MSLS. 7: Tchr-libn Decatur Commun High Sch, Oberlin Kan 50-53; Asst libn Shawnee MissionHigh Sch, Merrian Kan 53-54; Child libn Yakima Valley Reg Lib, Yakima Wash 55-59;Commun libn Wayne Co Lib, Detroit 59-61; Child & yp libn N Central Reg Lib,Wenatchee Wash 61-65; Asst Prof Sch of Libnship UNeb 65-. 9: ALA (mem Newbery-caldecott Com 68); PNLA (sec Young Reader's Choice Award); WashLA. 13: Yes. 14: Child pub sch. 15: 5025 22nd ave NE, Seattle Wa 98105.

BENNER, EVANGELINE ANNA. b Allentown Penn 16 D 46. 5: Shippensburg State Col 64-68 (Eng) BS in Ed; Rutgers (New Brunswick) 68-69 MLS. 6: Fr. 7: Adult ref libn Baltimore Co Pub Lib 69-. 9: ALA. 10: Kappa Delta Pi. 13: Yes. 14: YA, a-v serv. 15: 28 Spruce st, Emmaus Pa 18049.

BENNETT, ADELLE (MOORE). b Gary Tex 11 N 10. 4: James Hartwell Bennett. 5: Berea Col 30-34 Fr BA; Emory 34-35 AB in LS. 6: Fr. 7: Tchr libn Rocky Mount High Sch, Rocky Mount Va 35-37; Libn Andrew Lewis High Sch, Salem Va 37-51; State Dept Lib & personnel, Wash DC summer 44-45; Catlgr Roanoke Co Pub Lib, Salem Va 66-. 10: AAUW; Garden Club; Salem Woman's Club; WSCS. 14: Catlg. 15: 3533 Garst Mill rd SW, Roanoke Va 24018.

BENNETT, AGNES L (HANSON). b Livingston Mont 20 N 28. 4: Robert David Bennett. 5: Luther Col 47-51 (Eng) BA; UMich 51-52 MALS. 7: Catlgr Fresno Co Free Lib, Fresno Cal 52-53; Catlgr UIdaho Lib (Moscow) 53-57, Asst ser libn 59-60; Catlgr stanislaus State Col Lib 61-. 9: ALA; CalLA. 10: Assn of Cal State Col Profs; Cal State Employees Assn. 14: Catlg. 15: Stanislaus St Col Lib, 800 Monte Vista ave, Turlock Ca 95380.

BENNETT, ALMA A(GNES). b Gainesville Tex 13 Ag 10. 5: Kan State Tchrs Col (Emporia) summers 33-39, 40-41 (LS) BS, Lib Certif, 42-47 (Psych, Eng) MS. 6: Fr. 7: Libn High Sch, Caney Kan 32-40; Libn OttawaU (Kan) 41-43; Ext libn Kan State Tchrs Col (Emporia) 43-47; UMo: Soc sci libn 47-, Asst libn & Asst Prof Lib Sci 50-59, Sr asst libn head soc sci dept 59-. 9: ALA-ACRL (chm Mo Chap 59-60); SLA; MoLA. 10: Kappa Delta Pi; PEO. 14: Ref. 15: Frederick apt #408 1001 University, Columbia Mo 65201.

BENNETT, BETTY (BESSE). b Omaha 18 F 21. 5: MunicipalU Omaha 38-42 (Hist) BA; UIll 42-43 BSLS; UIowa 46-48 (Pol Sci, Geog) MA; Tex Woman'sU 59-60 MLS. 6: Fr. 7: 1st asst Govt Documents Lib UIowa 43-50; Kan State Col (Pittsburg): Ref & documents libn 50-57, Ref libn & archivist 57-67; Ref & research libn Stephen F Austin State Col 67-. 9: ALA-ACRL; TexLA. 10: AAUW; AAUP. 14: Ref, govt docs, archives, maps. 15: 1525 Walnut st, Nacogdoches Tx 75961.

BENNETT, CARSON WESLEY. b Scottsburg Ind 1 F 11. 4: D Ethlynn Pauline Kerns. 5: Butler U 29-33 (Econ, Hist) BA; George Peabody Col 40 BS in LS; UChicago summer 50; Indiana State U 50-53 (Soc sci) MA. 6: Sp. 7: Libn Ind Boys Sch, Plainfield 40-41; Supv WPA Defense Area, Charlestown Ind 41-42; US Coast Guard 42-45; Sr libn Indianapolis Pub Lib 45-48; Circ libn Auburn U 48-50; Dir lib Rose Polytechnic Inst 50-63; Dir lib Heidelberg Col 63-. 8: Consul Ind Tech Inst Fort Wayne 58. 9: SLA (Ind Chap, Del-at-Large); ALA (two terms as chm of the Subject Specialists, two terms on the Nom Com); IndLA (chm Col & Univ RT); OhioLA. 10: AAUP; Admin Bd St Paul's United Meth Church. 14: Admin, ref. 15: 50 Achre ct, Tiffin Oh 44883.

BENNETT, COLLEEN GRACE. b Decherd Tenn 14 F 12. 5: Middle Tenn State Teacher's Col 31-35 (Eng) BS; Peabody 35-36 BS in LS, 62 MA in LS. 7: Libn Boyd Jr High Sch, Knoxville Tenn 37; Libn S Knoxville Jr High Sch, Knoxville Tenn 37-43; Clerk TVA, Knoxville Tennsummer 43; Libn Knoxville High Sch, Knoxville Tenn 43-51; Libn summer sch, Knoxville Tenn summers 45-51; Libn evening high sch,Knoxville Tenn 42-44; Libn East High Sch, Knoxville Tenn 51-68; Libn Fulton High Sch, Knoxville Tenn 68-; Ref Br libs KnoxvillePub Lib 57-. 8: Tchr UTenn Lib Dept, Knoxville summer 57. 9: NEA; ALA; SLA; TennEA. 10: Delta Kappa Gamma; Sec of Commission on Educ; Knoxville Teachers' League (corr sec 54-56). 14: Ref pub lib wk, sch lib wk. 15: Sevierville Pi ke Route 9, Knoxville Tn 37920.

BENNETT, FLEMING. b Everson WVa 20 Ag 10. 4: Violet Mackey. 5: Fairmont (WVa) State Col 27-31 (Eng, Soc Sci)

AB; West Res 39-41 BSLS; Chicago 47-50 (LS). 6: Fr, Ger. 7: Libn Fairmont Jr High Sch, Fairmont WVa 34-41; Libn Findlay Sr High Sch, Findlay Ohio 41-42; Asst ref libn West Va U 42-46, Chief A-V aids libn 46-47; Head acquis dept Columbia 50-52; U libn UAriz 52-64; Libn Inst of Food & Agric Sci UFla 64-. 9: ALA (Coun 54-58); -ACRL (chm A-V Com 52-55, chm Agric & Biol Sci Subsect 65-66); ArizLA (pres 56-58). 10: AAUP. 12: Ed "Arizona Librarian" (62-64). 13: Yes. 14: Admin, acquis. 15: 318 SW 40th terrace, Gainesville Fl 32601.

BENNETT, GORDON LATTA. b Lincoln Neb 20 My 08. 4: Emma Louise Schwalb. 5: UNeb 26-31 (Span, Eng) AB; UMich 35; UDenver 36-37 BS in LS. 6: Sp. 7: Lib asst Neb Legis Ref Bur, Lincoln Neb 27-32; Lib asst Neb Pub Lib Commsn, Lincoln Neb 33-35; Lib asst UNeb 36; Lib asst Lincoln City Lib, Lincoln Neb 36; Ref asst Denver Pub Lib 37-40; Libn Pulaski Co Lib, Little Rock Ark 40-42; Exec sec WVa Lib Commsn, Morgantown WVa 42; Dir Colo State Lib 43-. 8: Exec dir Colo Nat Lib Week 59; Dir Bibliog Center Rocky Mount Reg 59; Coun Educ TV Channel 6 Inc KRMA; Nat Educ Adv Com; Voice of Youth Governor's Manpower Coord Com. 9: ALA-PLD (dir 55-58); ColoLA (pres 45-46,Exec Bd 58-61, Lib Devel Com 64-); MPLA; ColoASchL; ColoEA; NEA. 10: Denver Kiwanis Club; PTA; Latin Amer Educ Found. 12: Colo ed Crowell-Collier Educ Corp encyclopedias; "Library Lens" & "Capitol Hill Library Crier" Colo State Lib quarterlies. 13: Yes. 14: Admin. 15: 32 StateServices bldg, Denver Co 80203.

BENNETT, HELEN LOUISE (BURKHART). b Clinton Iowa 30 Jl 17. 5: Phillips U 35-37; Southwestern State Col 37-39 (Eng & Span) BA; UDenver 52-53 (LS) MA. 6: Sp. 7: High Sch Eng tchr pub sch, Stafford Okla 39-40; High sch Eng tchr pub sch, Indiahoma Okla 40-41; Circ asst pub lib, KansasCity Mo 47-50, Readers Adv 51-52; Ref libn Denver Pub Lib 53-54; Head of Ref Dept pub lib Kansas City Kan 54-60; Curator SnyderCollection UMo (Kansas City) 61-67, Ref libn 67-. 9: ALA-Subs Bks Com 61-63; MoLA. 10: AAUP. 14: Ref, catlg, rare bks. 15: 1710 Brush Creek blvd, Kansas City Mo 64110.

BENNETT, MRS JESSIE (LORENA) WINTZ. b Morgan Tex 10 Ja 08. 4: Alvin L Bennett. 5: Meridian Jr Col 25-26 AA; UTex summer 28, 46-49 (Eng) BA, 50-52 MLS. 6: Sp. 7: Tchr Blackwell Ind Sch Dist, Blackwell Tex 27-30; Tchr USAF, Amarillo Tex 42-44; Libn Austin Ind Sch Dist, Austin Tex 49-. 9: ALA: TexLA (sec Ref Round Table 65-66); Austin Lib Club. 14: Ref, catlg, recr young libns. 15: 5814 Trailridge dr, Austin Tex 78731.

BENNETT, JULIA (MADALEINE GATES). b Great Bend NY 29 N 14. 4: Edwin A Bennett. 5: Mt Holyoke 32-35 (Hist) BA;St LawrenceU 35-36 (Educ) MA; Simmons 60-63 (LS) MS. 7: Br libn pub lib of Youngstown & Mahoning Co, Youngstown Ohio 51-54;Readers asst Reuben McMillan Lib, Youngstown Ohio 55-59; Lib asst Research Div Raytheon Co, Waltham Mass 60-61, Libn 62-. 9: SLA. 14: Ref, bibliog. 15: 52 Grove st, Lexington Ma 02173.

BENNETT, MARGARET (WEIR). b Cuthbert Ga 7 Ag 18. 4: Carl D Bennett. 5: Campbellsville (Ky) Jr Col 35-37; Valdosta State Col 37-39 (Eng) AB; Emory 39-40 BALS, summer 55 (Med Libnship) Grade I Certif. 7: Asst in lib Agnes Scott Col, Decatur Ga 40-42; Catlgr Pack Mem Pub Lib, Asheville NC 43-44; Catlgr A W Calhoun Med Lib,Emory U 54-56, summer 57; Catlgr Mercer U 57-59; Catlgr Detamble Lib St Andrews Presbyterian Col 60-63, Act libn 63-66, Assoclibn, catlgr 66-. 9: ALA; NCLA; SELA. 10: AAUP. 14: Catlg. 15: St Andrews Presbytn Col, Laurinburg NC 28352.

BENNETT, MATTIE (ELLIS). b Baker La 12 Ag 08. 5: Leland Col 40 (Elem Educ) BA; Atlanta 61 MLS. 6: Fr. 7: Tchr Livingston Parish Sch Bd, Maurepas La 34-39; Tchr E Feliciana Parish Sch Bd, St Francisville La 42-43; Lib asst E Baton Rouge Parish Lib, Baton Rouge La 43-60, Libn 61-. 14: Ref, bk sel. 15: 1160 N 36th st, Baton Rouge La 70802.

BENNETT, MELVIN. b Mangum Okla 23 N 19. 5: Okla State U 37-41 (Bus Admin); UOkla 46-47 BALS, BA (Econ); Emory 49-50 ML. 6: Fr. 7: Clerk catlg dept Okla State U 38-41; Tech/Sgt Co clerk Quartermaster Detachment, Alaska Highway Can 42-45; Asst libn SEMo State Col 47-49; Ref libn Tex A & M 50-51; Head Tech Lib AF Missile Test Center, Patrick AFB Fla 51-56; Research asst Radiation Inc, Melbourne Fla 56-57; Asst head sci & tech dept Carnegie Lib, Pittsburgh 58-65; Head Engnrg Lib Penn State U (Univ Park) 65-. 9: SLA; PennLA (Ser Com, US govt docs com). 10: Philatelic soc. 12: "Science and Technology; A Purchase Guide for Branch and Small Public Libraries" (63, sups for 63 & 64); "Index to US Patents Prior to 1871" (65); "The Pennsylvania State University Libraries Union List of Current Periodicals" (69). 14: Ref, admin. 15: 2006 Highland dr, State College Pa 16801.

BENNETT, WILANNA (FONTAINE). b Clarksdale Miss 1 S 38. 5: Delta State 58-60; Mississippi State Col for Women 60-62 (Soc sci) BS; Mississippi State U summer 61; LSU 63-65 (LS) MS; Millsaps 65-67. 6: Sp. 7: Miss Lib Commsn, Jackson Miss: Gen ref 62-63, Miss Lib Commsn, Jackson Miss: Catlgr 65-66, Miss Lib Commsn, Jackson Miss: Hd dept inst 66-. 9: ALA; -AHIL; -AED; MLA; LLA. 10: Jackson Music Assn; Jackson Symphony Orchestra. 11: Merit Award, City of Clarksdale 58; Outstanding Young Women of Amer, 65. 14: Instit lib serv & catlg. 15: 1315 N Jefferson st apt 205, Jackson Ms 39202.

BENSINGER, CLAIRE. b Vincennes Ind 31 Jl 35. VincennesU 53-55 (Mod Langs) AA; Evansville Col 55-57 (Journalism) BA; IndU 58-59 (LS) MA. 7: Gen assignment reporter "Henderson Gleaner & Journal," Henderson Ky 57-58; Catlgr U Louisville Lib 59-61; Catlgr UNM Lib 61-66; Ctlgr Sandia corp Lib 67-. 9: ALA; NMLA; SLA. 14: Catlg. 15: 2315 General Arnold NE, Albuquerque NM 87112.

BENSON, HAZEL A SARTWELL. b Mooers NY 17 Ja 07. 4: Alfred Benson. 5: Houghton Col 23-27 (Fr, Rel Educ) AB; Columbia -38 (Tchg of Fr) AM; StateU Col (Geneseo NY) -62 MLS. 6: Fr. 7: Tchr Fr & hist Bliss High Sch, Bliss NY 27-30;Tchr Fr & hist Tomkins Cove High Sch, Tomkins Cove NY 30-34; Tchr Fr guidance NY MillsHigh Sch, NY Mills NY 34-39; Libn Tomkins Cove Pub Lib, Tomkins Cove NY 46; TchrMontville Dist, Bear Mountain NY 55-60; Dist libn N Rockland Cent Dist, Stony Pt NY60-. 9: NEA; ALA; NYState Tchrs Assn; NYLA; Rockland Co SchLA; LARC. 10: AAUW; PTA. 14: Acquis,catlg, processing, superv. 15: PO Box 121, New City NY 10956.

BENSON, HELEN C. b Tipton Ind 11 Je 20. 4: Stanley E Benson. 5: Monroe Commun Col 64-66 (Liberal Arts) AA; SUNY (Brockport) 66-68 (Lit) BA; SUNY (Geneseo) 68-69 MLS. 6: Fr. 7: Asst to ed Inst for Defense Analyses, Wash DC 59-62. 9: ALA. 14: Rare bks, ref. 15: 153 Allwood dr, Rochester NY 14617.

BENSON, JAMES ALLEN. b Hutchinson Kan 13 Jl 43. 5: UKan 61-65 Hist BA; Rutgers 65-66 MLS, 68- (Lib Serv); Tex SouthU 66-67 Hist. 6: Ger, Sp. 7: Tex SouthU: Circ libn 66, Ref & circ libn 66-67; Ref & interlib loan libn SW Tex State Col 67-68; Research fellow Rutgers Grad Sch of Lib Serv 68-. 8: Rutgers Grad Sch of Lib Serv: Stud-Fac Com 68-, Curr Com 69-. 9: ALA; ADLIB (Exec Bd); TexLA. 10: Tex Assn of Col Tchrs. 12: Co-comp "The Student Editorials of Lyndon Baines Johnson" (68). 13: Yes. 14: Ref, research in libnship, planning lib serv. 15: 189 College ave rm 343 Grad Sch of Lib Serv RutgersU, New Brunswick NJ 08903.

BENSON, JEAN (LAMB). b New Haven Conn 11 O 25. 4: Raymond Benson. 5: Wellesley 43-47 (Fr) BA; UCal (Berkeley) 49-51 (Compar Lit) MA; Columbia 52-53 MLS. 6: Fr. 7: Ref & ed asst rare bk dept Boston Pub Lib 47-49; City Col Lib (NY); Catlgr & asst to libn 53-62, Head catlgr, Asst Prof63-. 9: ALA; NY Tech Servs Libs; LACUNY. 10: Sierra Club. 13: Yes. 14: Catlg. 15: 390 Riverside dr, NYC 10025.

BENSON, JOSEPH. b Chicago. 4: Martha J Benson. 5: Wright Jr Col 45-47; Chicago 48-51 (LS) AM. 7: Catlgr Nat Soc for Crippled Child & Adults, Chicago 51; Asst libn Wright Jr Col 51-56; Mun ref libn Mun Ref Lib, Chicago 56-67, Libn Jt Ref Lib 67-. 8: Adv Coun of Proj URBANDOC 64-; Mayor's Commsn on Chicago Architectural Landmarks 57-. 9: ALA; SLA (chm Soc Sci Div); AALL (treas 67-). 10: Arts Club. 14: Admin, catlg. 15: Joint Reference Lib, 1313 E 60th st, Chicago Ill 60637.

BENSON, LINDA R (FRIED). b Philadelphia Penn 16 F 43. 4: William E Benson. 5: Mt Holyoke 61-65 (Fr) AB (Magna Cum Laude); Columbia 65-66 MS. 6: Fr, Sp. 7: Ref libn ColumbiaU Libs 66-. 10: Phi Beta Kappa; Beta Phi Mu. 13: Yes. 14: Ref. 15: 400 W 119 th, New York NY 10027.

BENSON, MARIANA (STEELE). b Algona Iowa 23N41. 4: Jeffrey L Benson. 5: State Col Iowa 59-63 (LS, Foreign Langs) BA Chicago 63-66 (LS). 6: Fr, Sp. 7: Elem sch libn UChicago Lab Schs 63-. 9: ALA. 14: Child lit, wk with child, storytelling. 15: 541 Circle dr, Park Forest S Il 60466.

BENSON, NETTIE LEE. b Arcadia Tex 15 Ja 05. 5: Tex Presbyterian Col 22-24; UTex 24-25, 28-29 (Hist) BA, 29-30, summer 36 (Hist) MA, 41-42, 48-49 (Latin Amer Studies) PhD. 6: Sp, Port. 7: Tchr Instituto Ingles-Espanol, Monterey Mex 24-25, 26-27; Tchr Sinton Pub Schs, Sinton Tex 27-28; Tchr Hartley Pub Sch, Hartley Tex 29-30; Span & Eng tchr Ingleside High Sch, Ingleside Tex 31-32, 40-41; Libn Latin Amer Collection UTex 42-. 8: Consul, Stechert-Hafner Inc to initiate Latin Amer Coop Acquis Proj, traveling in So Amer 60, 61 & 62. 9: ALA; Seminar on Acquis of Latin Amer Lib Materials; Col & Univ Libs; TexLA. 12: "La Diputacio3n provincial y el federalismo mexicano" (55); Transl "Report of Ramos Arizpe to the Spanish Cortes in 1811" Studies XI (50); and Transl "The United States versus Porfirio Di3az" by Daniel Cosi3o Villegas (63). Ed "Mexico and the Spanish Corte3s; Eight Essays" (66); Latin American Books and Periodicals "Library Trends" (Jan. 67). 13: Yes. 14: Bibliog, ref, acquis (Latin Amer Lib materials). 15: Latin Amer Collection Univ of Texas, Austin Tx 78712.

BENSON, STANLEY H. b Sparta Ill 1 O 29. 4: Sara E Collins. 5: Southern Ill U 47-51 (Soc Studies) BS in ED; Southwestern Baptist Theol Sem 51-54, 56-59 (Religion) BD, ThD; UTex 63-64 MLS. 6: Gk, Ger. 7: Tchr High Sch, Steeleville Ill 54-55; Lib asst Tex Christian U 59-61; Minister First Baptist Church, Vienna Ill 61-63; Head libn Ky So Col 64-68; Hd libn Gardner-Webb Col 68-69; Hd libn Berry Col, 69-. 9: ATheolLA; KyLA;Louisville Lib Club (v-pres, pres elect 65-66, pres 66-67); SELA. 14: Admin, tech processes, tchg lib sci. 15: Berry Col,Mt Berry Ga 30149.

BENTLEY, ELIZABETH (LELAND). b Lincoln Neb 15 Ja 12. 4: Frederick Wallace Bentley. 5: UNeb 29-31 (Eng); Wells Col 31-33 (Eng) BA; West Res 33-34 BLS. 6: Fr, Ger, Lat. 7: Child libn Pub Lib, Cedar Rapids Iowa 34-35; Child libn Col Lib, Oberlin Ohio 37-45; Child libn Cuyahoga Co Lib, Chagrin Falls Ohio 54-59; Sch libn Chagrin Falls Pub Schs, Chagrin Falls Ohio 59-62; Child libn Bennett Martin Pub Lib, Lincoln Neb 63-. 65, Coord of YP serv 65-. 9: NebLA. 10: PEO; Kappa Alpha Theta; Lotos Club; Neb Art Assn. 14: Child lit. 15: 2828 Jackson dr, Lincoln Nb 68502.

BENTLEY, HOWARD BEEBE. b Norfolk Mass. 5: Principia 43-47 (Eng, Econ) AB; Simmons 53-54 (LS). 6: Fr, Ger, Romance langs. 7: Libn II Brooklyn Pub Lib, Brooklyn NY 54-55; Free lance lib organizer & consul55-56; Libn II Econ Div NY Pub Lib 56-57; Admin libn Alanar Corp, Newark NJ 57-59;Research libn Time Inc, NYC 59-. 8: Consul to URBANDOC, 64. 9: SLA (var coms,incl chm "Special Libraries" Com, chm Planning, Bldg, & Housing sect; chm NY ChapNewspaper & News Div); CNLA; ALA. 12: "Building Construction Information Sources" (64). 13: Yes. 14: Admin, ref. 15: 8 East 48 st, New York NY10017.

BENTLEY, JANE (FRAME). b Huntsville Ala 6 Ag 28. 4: Jack H B entley. 5: Howard Col 46-50 (Eng) BA. 7: Libn Defense Documentation Ctr Huntsville Off, Huntsville Ala 64-66; Libn Info Programs Br Redstone Sci Info Ctr, Huntsville Ala 66-68; Chief operations sect Lib Br Redstone Sci Info Ctr, Huntsville Ala 68-. 9: Nat Microfilm Assn; ASIS; SLA (sec-treas Ala Chap 55-56); AlaLA (treas 58-59 & 63-64; v-pres 60-61; pres 61-62). 10: AAUW; Bus & Prof Women's Club; Bd Trustees Huntsville Symphony Assn. 14: Lib automation. 15: 3922 Crestview dr NW, Huntsville Al 35805.

BENTLEY, JANICE (BABB). b Philadelphia Penn 13 Ja 33. 4: Charles A Bentley. 5: UIll 50-54 (Econ) AB, 54-56 (LS) MS. 7: Dir Dept of Info Nat Assn of Real Estate Bds, Chicago 56-63; Libn Continental Nat Amer Group, Chicago 63-. 9: SLA (chm Housing, Bldg & Planning Sect 62-63, chm Soc Sci Div 65-66, 2nd v-chm Bus & Fin Div 60-61, Ill Chap: v-pres 66-67, pres 67-68); ASIS (sec-treas Chicago Chap 63). 12: "Real Estate Information Sources, with Beverly F Dordick (63); "Real Estate Appraisal Bibliography, with Beverly F Dordick (64). 14: Spec libs in finance. 15: CNA Group 310 S Michigan, Chicago Il 60604.

BENTLEY, MARTHA C. b Rochester NY 4 D 18. 5: CornellU 36-40 (Hist) BA; Simmons 40-41 BSLS. 7: Child libn Detroit Pub Lib 41-43, 46-58; Ensign US Coast Guard (WR) 43-46; Queens Borough Pub Lib, NYC: Asst consul child serv 58-63, Consul child serv 64; Consul child & ya serv N Bay Cooperative Lib System, Santa Rosa Cal 64-. 9: ALA (Newbery Caldecott Com 65-66); CalLA; NYLA. 10: AAUW; LWV; Audubon Soc; Sierra Club. 13: Yes. 14: Child wk. 15: 3695 Sonoma ave, Santa Rosa Cal 95405.

BENTLEY, PHYLLIS (DYSON). b La Crosse Wis 8 S 06. 5: La Crosse (Wis) Normal Sch 24-26; UWis 26-28 (LS & Eng) BA & Diploma from Lib Sch; Columbia 36-37 (LS) MS. 7: Asst libn Free Pub Lib, Burlington Iowa 28-30; Asst libn Minn State Teachers Col 30-53; Asst libn circ Beloit Col 53-54; Guest libn Minn State Teachers Col summer 54; Asst libn Stout Inst 54-55; Head libn Stout StateU 55-. 9: ALA; NEA; WisLA; WisEA. 10: AAUP; AAUW. 14: Col libs. 15: 221 Second st, W Menomonie Wi 54751.

BENTLEY, RUTH (SHEARER). b Wayne Co Ky 29 Jl 11. 4: C Frank Bentley. 5: David Lipscomb Col 29-30; Eastern Ky State Col 30-32 (Eng); UKy 48-54, 60, 61 AB, MS in LS. 6: Fr. 7: Elem tchr Wayne Co Schs, Monticello Ky 30-32; Sch libn Laurel Co Schs, London Ky 47-. 8: Mem Natl Lib Weeks Com 65, 66; Wk on "Rural Vista Kit" for Natl Lib Com 67. 9: ALA-AASchL; SELA; KyLA (pres); KyASchL (treas, pres); Upper Cumberland Dist Libns (chm). 11: Outstanding Sch Libn of Ky, 68. 13: Yes. 14: Ref, sch libs. 15: Rt 4 Box 251, London Ky 40741.

BENTON, EVELYN (FLEMING). b Ponchatoula La 10 Ag 21. 04; Douglas C Benton. 5: Ok la State U 39-43 (Mus) BFA; UTex 59-60 (LS). 6: Sp. 7: Tulsa Pub Lib: Circ asst 44, Tech dept 1st asst 45; Okla State U: Ref asst 46-48, Jr ref libn 48-50; Piano tchr, Baytown Tex 58-60; Asst libn, Lee Col Lib, Baytown Tex 60-66; Dir Deer Park Pub Lib, Deer Park Tex 67-. 9: ALA; SWLA; TexLA (Memb Com, sec Dist 5); Tex Munic Libns Assn (chm Nom Com). 10: Sigma Alpha Iota; Phi Kappa Phi; Baytown Unit Fellowship; Baytown Little Theater. 14: Admin, ref, catlg. 15: 3401 Woodcrest, Baytown Tx 77520.

BENTON, FLORA (VIRGINIA HUFF). b Roanoke Va 8 O 21. 4: Stanley T Benton. 5: Radford Col 39-41 (Eng); OhioU 55-56 (Hist); OhioNoU59-61 (Educ) BS; UToledo 63-64 MA in LS; 65-66. 7: Page Pub Lib, Roanoke Va 35-41, Ref asst 41-42; Catlg asst EmoryU Lib 43; Sec Nat Red Cross, Atlanta 44; Catlg asst Pub Lib, Pickerington Ohio 47-49; Elem sch tchr pub schs, Celina Ohio 59-62; Libn High Sch Toledo Bd of Educ, Toledo Ohio 62-64; Lib coordinator Oregon Bd of Educ, Oregon Ohio 64-. 9: ALA; OhioASchL; OhioEA; IRA(v-pres); OCIRA. 10: Kappa Delta Pi; Phi Kappa Phi. 12: Ed OhioASchL "Bulletin". 14: Sch libs, child wk. 15: Box 237, Route 2, Curtice Oh43412.

BENTON, MARJORIE (GLASS). b Mo 15 Ag 15. 4: Byrl E Benton. 5: Doane Col 33-37 (Eng) AB; UIll 37-38 BS in LS. 7: Ser catlgr SD State Col 38-39; Sub catlgr Pub Lib, Des Moines Iowa 57-61, Catlgr 61-65, Br libn 65-67, Hd mus dept 67-. 9: ALA; IowaLA. 10: Des Moines Symphony Assn. 14: Music. 15: 7510 College dr, Des Moines Ia 50322.

BENTON, RITA. b NYC. 4: Arthur L Benton. 5: Juilliard Sch of Music 33-38 (Piano) Diploma; Hunter Col 34-39 (Music) BA; UIowa 49-51 (Musicology) MA, 57-61 (Musicology) PhD. 6: Fr. 7: Tchr of music theory, High Sch of Music & Art NYC 39-40; Asst in piano UIowa 51-52, Catlg asst 52-53, Music libn 53-. 8: Consul on music lib reorgan to Grinnell Col 60. 9: ALA; Amer Musicological Soc (Coun 65-67, 69-71); Internat Assn of Music Libs (pres Research Libs Commsn & mem of Coun 64-); Internat Musicological Soc; MusLA (pres 62-65; Exec Bd several terms); Socie3te3 Francaise de Musicologie; Soc for French Hist Studies. 10: Iowa City Friends of Music (v-pres 65-). 11: 2 travel & 2 research grants 62-65. 12: Comp "Directory of Music Research Libraries, Pt I" (67). 13: Yes. 14: Materials of research, bibliog, hist materials. 15: Music Library Eastlawn, Iowa City Ia 52240.

BENTRUP, MAUD MERRITT (COOK). b Baton Rouge La 25 Mr 08. 4: Walter Carl Bentrup. 5: LSU 25, 27-29 (Educ, Soc Studies) AB; Northwest La State Col 26; UIll 30-31 BS in LS; Columbia 39; LSU summer 61. 7: Catlgr LSU 29-43; Instr LSU Lib Sch summer 39; Head catlgr USouthwestern La 43-49; Libn McMaster and Hamrick Schs, Columbia SC 50-54; Libn Northeast La State Col 54-. 9: ALA; SWLA; LaLA (pres 61-62, chm col & Ref Sect 59-60); La Col Conf (chm Lib Sect 57); La Tchrs Assn. 10: AAUW; Amer Camellia Soc; Delta Kappa Gamma; Sigma Tau Delta; Kappa Delta. 14: Admin, tech processes. 15: 305 K st, Monroe La 71204.

BENTZ, DALE M(ONROE). b York County Penn 3 Ja 19. 4: Mary Gail Menius. 5: Gettysburg Col 35-39 (Fr, math) AB; UNC 39-40 BSLS; UIll 48-51 MS. 6: Fr, Sp, Ger. 7: Stud asst Gettysburg Col Lib 35-39; Asst period dept UNC Lib 40-41; Ser catlgr DukeU Lib 41-42; Chief clerk statistical control sect Air Force, Denver 42-46; Asst libn E Carolina Col 46-48; Head processing dept UTenn Lib 48-53; Assoc dir of libs UIowa 53-. 8: Consul on Reclsf: UMiss 52, Lake Forest Col 54. 9: ALA-Div Catlg & Clsf (Exec Com 60-63, chm 2 coms 54-58 & 59-60); -ACRL (chm 3 coms 54-58 & 61-64); -RTSD (Bd Dirs 65-69, chm Nomin Com 58-59); SELA (chm Jr Mem Round Table 47-48); TennLA (chm Intel Freedom Com 49-50); IowaLA (pres 59-60, chm 3 coms 54-59). 10: Beta Phi Mu (pres

66-67); AAUP; Boy Scouts; Kappa Phi Kappa; Phi Sigma Iota ; Bd of Educ, Iowa City Commun Sch Dist; Triangle Club UIowa. 12: Ed "UTenn Lib Lectures" nos 1-3 (52). 13: Yes. 14: Catlg, lib admin. 15: 1615 East Collece, Iowa City Ia 55240.

BENTZ, DONALD NICHOLAS. b Sheboygan Wis 6 My 21. 5: UWis 39-41, 46-48 (Amer Hist) BS, 48-49 (Amer hist) MS, 49-50 (Amer Hist); UNev summer 52; Fresno State Col summer 52; UWis 54-55 (LS) MS; UMich 57-58 (LS) MA (6th yr). 7: US Army Tank Destroyers (2d Lt US Army Reserves) 42-45; Tchr & libn Mineral Co High Sch, Hawthorne Nev 50-52; Tchr & libn Visalia Jr High Sch, Visalia Cal 52-53; Tchr & libn Highland Jr High Sch, San Bernardino Cal 53-54; Tchg asst Col of Ed UWis 54-55; Asst Prof Lib Sci & period serv libn, Ball State Tchrs Col 55-57; Lecturer in Lib Sci UMich Ext Serv 57-58; Asst Prof of Lib Sci UAriz 58-66; Asst prof of LS Wis State U 66-67; Assoc prof of LS Head Dept of LS West Carolina U 67-. 9: ALA-AASchL (Bd of Dir); SWLA; Ariz State LA (Intel Freedom Com & other coms); Wis Lib Sch Alumni Assn; Mich Lib Sch Alumni Assn. 10: AAUP; Phi Delta Kappa; Alpha Beta Alpha; ALA; NCLA; NEA; NCEA. 12: Comp "Directory of Public School Librarian in Tucson and Vicinity" (64). 13: Yes. 14: Tchg lib sci, admin. 15: Col of Educ UAriz, Tuscon Az 85721.

BENTZLER, GEORGIANE C. b Malone Wis 26 Mr 27. 4: Donald James Bentzler. 5: Wis State U 44-48 (Eng) BS; Peabody 53-57 (LS) MA. 6: Ger. 7: Libn Bear Creek High Sch, Bear Creek Wis 48-50; Libn Berlin High Sch, Berlin Wis 50-51; Libn Beaver Dam High Sch, Beaver Dam Wis 51-53; Libn East High Sch, Green Bay Wis 53-54; Libn Franklin Jr High Sch Racine Wis 54-57; Libn Cedarburg High Sch, Cedarburg Wis 57-63; Instr & Guest lecturer UWis (Milwaukee) 61-63; Libn Marshfield Sr High Sch, Marshfield Wis 63-65; H libn UWis (Marshfield-Wood County Center) 65-. 8: Implementation Com Wis, Standards for Sch Libs. 9: ALA-AASchL; WisLA; WisEA (pres Sch Lib Sect 60-62). 10: Delta Kappa Gamma; AAUW. 14: Catlg, reading interests of young adults, sch lib, admin. 15: 614 N Plum ave, Marshfield Wi 54449.

BENYON, ELIZABETH VIOLA. b Chicago 1 S 1900. 5: Chicago 18-22 (Hist) PHB; 06: Fr, Ger. 7: Catlgr UChicago Law Lib; Catlgr 43-50, Act law libn 50-51, Asst law libn 52-65, Adv in preparations 65-67; Consul libn CookCo Law Lib, Chicago 67-. 9: ALA; AALL; Chicago ALL. 10: Consul to various law libs. 12: "Class K" LC (48); Ed "Conference on Classification Proceedings" (61). 13: Yes. 14: Catlg, clsf. 15: Cook County Law Lib, Civic Ctr 29th floor, Chicago Il 60602.

BEQUETTE, MRS NEVA (LEBOND). b Seattle 14 Ap 10. 4: William C Bequette. 5: UWash 32 (Eng) BA, 33 BS in LS; Columbia 61 MS in LS. 6: Ger, Fr. 7: Clerk prof circ & brs, Seattle Pub Lib 33-34; Head Libn Ellensburg Pub Lib, Ellensburg Wash 36-39; Stud asst Columbia U Lib 39-40; Head art & music div San Jose State Col Lib 40-42; Head Libn Salem Pub Lib, Salem Ore 42-44; Co Libn Umatilla Co Lib, Pendleton Ore 44-49; Reg Libn Mid-Columbia Reg Lib, Kennewick Wash 49-. 8: Instr Lib Sci UWash summer 65 Wash Title III Com mem 67-69. 9: ALA (var coms); WashLA (pres 57-59, mem lib devel com 60-65, mem State-Wide Serv Com 66, chm Legisl Com 67-69); PNLA (Lib Devel Com 60-64). 10: AAUW; Tri-Cities Womens Club. 11: Dorothy Canfield Fisher Award, 64; Woman of Achievement, Kennewick 63. 13: Yes. 14: Admin, bk sel, a-v. 15: 3019 S Auburn pl, Kennewick Wa 99336.

BERAHA, EMMY. b Yugoslavia. 4: Max Beraha. 5: UBelgrade 38 (Hist of Art) BA; Rutgers 55 MLS; NY StateU 65 Certif Exam. 6: Ger, Serbo-Croatian, Ital, Fr. 7: Queens Borough Pub Lib, NYC: Lib trainee 62, Staff 65, Sr libn 65-, Asst br libn 67. 9: ADI; ALA; NYLib Club. 14: Ref. 15: 23-50 143rd st, New York NY 11357.

BERBERIAN, KEVORK ROUPEN. b Beirut Lebanon 1 S 27. 4: Marcia Ann Fick. 5: Haigazian Col Beirut Lebanon 60-65 (Eng lit, Armenology) BA; SUNY (Geneseo) 65-67 MLS. 6: Armenian, Turkish, Fr, Arabic. 7: Nazarene 1st Sch Damascus Syria: Tchr 50-53, Prin 53-55; Prin Armenian Evang Sch (Christian Soc Ctr), Beirut Lebanon 55-62; Catlgr umass, Amherst Mass 67-. 14: Catlg. 15: 524 Lincoln apts Lincoln ave, Amherst Ma 01002.

BERENSON, HOWARD. b NYC 26 My 21. 5: UCal (Berkeley) 48 (Eng) BA; UIll 50 MSLS; Stanford 48-51 (Educ) MA. 6: Fr. 7: US Army Air Corps 42-46 (Cpl); Libn Menlo-Atherton High Sch, Atherton Cal 50-52; Ref libn City Col (NY) 52-54; LibnUniondale High Sch, LI NY 54-57; Libn Hicksville Pub Schs, LI NY 57-. 9: Nassau-Suffolk SchLA; NY State TA; NEA. 10: Amer Personnel & Guidance Assn; Amer Sch Couns Assn; Natl Vocat Guidance Assn. 14: Ref. 15: 134-29 218th st, Springfield Gardens NY 11413.

BERENSON, IRWIN ROBERT. b NYC 24 Ag 26. 4: Marion (Bodker) Berenson. 5: City Col (NY) 46-51 (Soc Sci) BSS; Syracuse 53-55 MS in LS; Pratt 63 (LS) Certif. 7: Prof intern ColumbiaU Libs 51-52; Br libn Syracuse U Libs 53-55; Young adult libn Rochester Pub Lib, Rochester NY 55-56; Spec libn Jewish Young Mens Assn, Rochester NY 55-56; Ref libn Hewlett-Woodmere Pub Lib, Hewlett LI NY 56-59, Asst dir & adult serv libn 59-61; Asst dir Penisula Pub Lib, Lawrence LI NY 61-66, Dir 66-. 8: Consul for Blue Ribbon Award Films, sponsored by Encyclopedia Film Lib Assn. 9: Nassau Co LA (Bus Mgr). 12: Ed "Odds & Bookends" Nassau Co LA (65). 13: Yes. 14: Ref, a-v. 15: 220-18 75th ave, Bayside NYC 11364.

BERG, EDNA (BARROWCLOUGH). b Paterson NJ 17 Mr 15. 4: Lloyd Berg. 5: Montclair State Col 32-36 (Eng) BA; Columbia Sch of Lib Serv 36, 40; Mont State U 60-61 (Eng) MS. 6: Fr, Ger. 7: Tchr Hampton Pub Sch, Hampton NJ 36-37; Lib asst Free Pub Lib, Paterson NJ 37-39; Lib asst Purdue U 39-42; Libn Bozeman Sr High Sch, Bozeman Mont 61-. 8: Instr Lib Sci Mont StateU, Bozeman Mont 64-65; Instr NDEA Inst for Sch Libns, Indiana U, 66; Instr Grad Lib Sch, Indiana U, 67. 9: ALA; NEA; MontLA; MontEA. 10: AAUW; Girl Scout Coun; Mont Cong Parents & Tchrs. 14: High sch libs. 15: 1314 S Third ave, Bozeman Mt 59715.

BERG, FRANCES (BROWN). b Phila Penn 26 Ag 20. 5: Temple 38-47 (Chem) BA; CornellU summer 47 (Microscopy); Phila Textile Inst 47-58 9fiber Indentif & Microscopy). 6: Fr. 7: Analyst & research chem H Kohnstamm & Co, Camden NJ 42-46; Patent searcher Hercules Powder Co, wilmington Del 47-52; Lit searcher & libn Catalytic Construction Co, Phila 52-59; Tech info spec Gen Electric Co, Phila 59-. 8: Fellowship sullivan Mem Lib, TempleU 46-47. 9: SLA (Sci-Tech Sect); ACS. 12: "Bibliography of Russian Literature on Magneto Hydrodynamics (62) with Rosa Bernstein. 15: 2746 Belmont ave, Phila Pa 19131.

BERG, FRANCES RUSSELL. b Schenectady NY 22 F 17. 5: Middlebury Col 34-38 (Eng) BA; NYS Col for Teachers (Albany) 37-42 BS in LS; SUNY (New Paltz at Farmingdale) 5967; Columbia NDEA Inst for supvs 67-. 6: Fr. 7: Eng tchr Draper High Sch, Schenectady NY 38-40; Eng tchr Red Hook Central Sch, Dutchess Co NY 40-42; Head Eng Dept, Woodmere High Sch, Woodmere NY 42-45; Head genealogy & heraldry sect NY Pub Lib 45-53; Libn Lawrence Pub Schs, LI NY 55-60; Head Libn Lawrence Jr High Sch, Lawrence NY 60-; Supv of sch libs, Lawrence NY 65-. 8: Consul in Heraldry for NY Pub Lib 53-. 9: NYState Tchrs Assn (Moder Censorship Panel 61). 10: DAR. 11: UN citation for Heraldic Research Oslo Norway 52. 13: Yes. 14: Genealogy, heraldry, central proc system. 15: 195 Broadway, Lawrence LI NY 11559.

BERG, FRANCES T. b Rockyford Colo 29 F 24. 5: UIll 43-47 (Soc Studies) BA; CW Post Col 61-63 (LS) MA. 7: Clerical GM Otis Elevator, Wash DC 42-43; Stud asst UIll (Urbana) 43-47; Elem sch libn Malverne Sch Dist #12, Malverne NY 63-66; Sr High Sch Libn Oceanside Sch Dist, Oceanside NY 66-68; Elem Sch LibnFreeport Sch Dist #9, Freeport NY 68-. 9: NEA; NYState Tchrs Assn; ALA; NYLA; NStateSchLA. 10: PTA; CW Post Col Lib Sch Alumni Assn 65-66. 14: Elem libs, sr high schs. 15: 35Hempstead ave, Malverne NY 11565.

BERG, HELEN (JACK). b Minersville Penn 22 D 31. 4: Donald R Berg. 5: Kutztown State Col 49-53 (LS, Eng) BS in Ed. 7: Libn Pottstown Jr High Sch, Pottstown Penn 53-54; Libn Boyertown Jr High Sch, Boyertown Penn 54; Asst libn State Col (Kutztown Penn) 59-. 14: Sch libs, periods. 15: 534 College Gardens dr, Kutztown Penn 19530.

BERG, MARGARET (MARY EATON). b Phillips Neb 28 Mr 17. 4: Glen V Berg. 5: UNeb 35-41, 43 (Eng) AB, 49-51 (Journalism), 51-56 (Eng) Init Second Tchg certif; UMich 59-60 MALS. 6: Fr, Ger, Sp. 7: Stud asst UNeb Lib 35-41; Stenographer Jos E Seagram & Sons Inc, Louisville Ky 41; Sec Spec Engnrg Div, Panama Canal Diablo Heights CZ 41-42; Sec off manager ind rel dept Carnegie-Illinois Steel Corp, Pittsburgh 42-43; Communications off WAVES USNR Serv Force Atlantic Fleet 43-45; Chief clerk Oak Ridge Rec & Welfare Assn, Oak Ridge Tenn 45-46; UMich libn (Ann Arbor): Searcher catlg dept 57-59, Catlg libn 60-67, Tech serv libn 67-. 8: Tech serv adv, Kanpur Indo-Amer Program, IndianInst of Tech/Kanpur, Kanpur, U.P., India (associated with USAID) 67-69. 9: ALA; MichLA; Ann Arbor Lib Club. 10: UMich Faculty Womens Club; LWV; Sigma Kappa. 14: Catlg, rare bks. 15: 1033Baldwin ave, Ann Arbor Mi 48104.

BERG, ROBERT MONT. b Oakland Cal 5 Jl 21. 5: UCal 39-42 (Art hist) BA, 55-56 MLS. 7: Mgr bk dept Campus Textbook Exchange, Berkeley Cal 48-55; Order libn San francisco State Col 56-. 15: San Francisco State College Lib 1630 Holloway st, San Francisco Ca 94132.

BERGE, LAURA E(LIZABETH WHELPLEY). b Fremont Neb 28 S 03. 5: UNeb 23-26 (Eng); UMich 26-27 (Eng) AB, 65-66 MA in LS; Chadron State 60 (Educ, LS) Certif. 6: Fr. 7: Circ mgr Sci News Letter Sci Serv Wash DC 31-33; Sec Amer Assoc Univ Profs, Wash DC 56-58; Eng & Fr tchr Libn High Sch, Oshkosh Neb 60-65; 67-68; Hd libn Hiram Scott Col, Scottsbluff Neb 66-67, 68-. 9: ALA; NEA; NebLA (v-pres 67-68, pres 68-69); NebStateEA. 10: AAUW; Woman's Nat Demo Club, Wash DC. 14: Ref, for libs. 15: 121 W 20th st, Scottsbluff Nb 69361.

BERGE, MIRIAM (HASS). b Bismarck ND 18 Jl 16. 5: Yankton Col 34-38 (Eng) AB; Cal State (Los Angeles) 52-56; USoCal 60-65 (LS) MS. 7: Tchr Covina Valley Schs, Covina Cal 52-61; Sch libn Las Palmas Jr High sch, Covina Cal 61-64; Sch libn Covina High Sch, Covina Cal 64-. 9: CalASchL. 14: Sch lib wk. 15: 19336 E Casad, Covina Cal 91722.

BERGEN, ANN R(ATCLIFF). b Wash DC 23 Ja 36. 4: John V Bergen. 5: UWisc Madison 53-57 (Chem) BS, 57-58 (LS) MMA. 7: UWis: Stud asst lib cir dept 53-55, Stud asst McCardle Mem Lab 55-57, Tchg asst chem dept 57-58, Tchg asst lib sch 58, chem libn 58-60; Current journal abstractor Intelligence Div DuPont Co, Wilmington Del summer 56; Sci libn Ida StateU lib 62-66, 67-68; Sci catlgr UKan libs 68-. 9: ALA; SLA. 14: Ref, catlg. 15: 532 Lawrence ave apt C, Lawrence Ks 66044.

BERGEN, DAN. b Albert Lea Minn 25 My 35. 4: Carol Lee Janson. 5: UNotre Dame 53-57 (Hist) AB, 57-58 & 61-62 (Pol sci) MA; UChicago 60-61 Libnship MA, summer 62, 63 Libnship; UMinn 67- (Amer studies) MA. 6: Fr, Sp. 7: Supply off (1st Lt) USAF 58-60; Assoc libn & instr pol sci St Benedict's Col, Atchison Kan 62-63; Asst dean Sch of Lib Sci SyracuseU 64-65; Asst prof Sch of Lib & Info Serv UMd 65-66; Assoc prof Dept of Lib Sci UMiss 66-. 8: Consul NLM 65-66; Research fellow, Inst of Marketing, communications, NYC. 9: ALA; Amer Studies Assn; MissLA; Soc for Gen Systems Res. 10: AAAS; AAUP. 13: Yes. 14: Libnship, systems theory, philosophy, cultural anthropol, linguistics, communication, soc scis. 15: Route 1, Oxford Ms 38655.

BERGER, ALVIN CARL. b Lebanon Penn 13 Mr 26. 5: Clare Schaeffer. 6: Ger. 7: Radioman US Navy 44-45; Tchr Lebanon Sr High Sch, Lebanon Penn 49-54; Libn E Stroudsburg State Col 55-. 9: . 10: AAUP; Beta Phi Mu. 14: Circ, catlg music, phonorecords. 15: 10 Club ct, Stroudsburg Penn 18360.

BERGER, CAROL ANN (KUZNOFF). b Stamford Conn 16 O 42. 4: William J Berger. 5: CatholicU 60-64 (Eng) AB, 64-69 MSLS. 7: Reader's adv DC Pub Lib, Wash DC 64-65; Catlgr & abstractor Vitro Labs Lib, Silver Springs Md 65; Asst libn Prince George's Co Bd of Educ, Bowie Md 66; Libn ARINC Research Corp Lib, Annapolis Md 67-68; Libn Herner & Co Lib, Wash DC 68-. 9: DCLA. 14: Ref, catlg, admin. 15: PO Box 1432, Landover Md 20785.

BERGER, DORIS L (GOLDSTEIN). b NYC 18 N 09. 4: Henry Berger. 5: Hunter Col 26-30 (Span) BA; Queens Col 62-56 (LS) BS; 65 Lib Certif, Albany NY. 6: Sp. 7: Tchr in train New Utrecht High Sch, Brooklyn NY 30-31; Tchr clerk Brooklyn Tech High Sch, Brooklyn NY 31-33, Sub tchr 36-37; Libn Cornwell Ave Elem Sch, W Hempstead NY 62-68; Libn Sr High Sch W Hempstead NY 68-. 9: NY State Tchrs Assn; Nassau-Suffolk SchLA; NYLA. 10: PTA; Sigma Delta Pi. 12: Co-auth "Fin ancing Public Library Ex pansion" (68). 14: Reading guidance, tchg lib skills. 15: 39 Milburn ct, Freeport NY 11520.

BERGER, HELEN VIOLA (SAMUELSON). b St Paul Minn. 5: Macalester Col 24-28 (Fr, Eng) BA; UMinn 44 (LS) BS. 6: Fr. 7: St Paul Pub Lib: Asst period & for dept 28-38, Ref libn 38-40, In chg period & for dept 40-43, In chg St Anthony Park Br 44, 1st asst soc sci tech dept 45-47; Los Angeles Pub Lib: Catlgr 47-60, Catlg reviser 60-61, Sr libn in catlg dept 61-67, Sr libn in chg Felipe de Neve Br 68-. 9: ALA, CalLA. 10: AAUW; Amer Scand Found. 11: Trip to Queen Elizabeth's Coronation 53, awarded by Brit Bk Centre. 13: Yes. 14: Catlg ref, sr br libn. 15: 2820 W 6th st, Los Angeles 90057.

BERGER, LOUISA. b Asheville NC 5 D 44. 4: Martin E Berger. 5: Barnard 62-66 (Hist) BA; UPittsburgh 66-67 MLS. 7: Adult serv libn Brooklyn Pub Lib, Brooklyn NY 67-69; Libn Youngstown State U 69-. 10: Beta Phi Mu. 14: Ref. 15: Youngstown State Lib, Youngstown Oh 44503.

BERGER, MICHAEL GEORGE. b NYC 16 Ag 40. 5: UCLA 60-63 (Geog) BA, 63-65 (Geog), 65-66 MLS. 6: Ger. 7: Ref libn I UCLA Col Lib 66-67; Ref libn II UCLA Biomed Lib 67-. 14: Ref, systems analysis. 15: Biomedical Lib Univ of Cal, Los Angeles Ca 90024.

BERGER, OSCAR ROBERT. b Tuebingen Germany 7 Mr 27. 5: San Francisco State Col 57-61 (Second Educ) AB; Immaculate Heart Col 62 MALS. 6: Ger, Sp. 7: US Army Interpreter, Germany 52-54; Asst law libn, San Francisco Sch of Law 62-66; Ref & Circ Libn U Cal Hastings Sch of Law, San Fran 66-. 9: AALL. 14: Catlg. 15: 519 32nd ave, San Francisco Ca 94121.

BERGER, ROSE SUE. b Brooklyn NY 3 My 16. 4: Abraham L Berger. 5: Brooklyn Col 33-38 (Biol) BA; Col of the City of NY 38-39 (Educ); Queens Col (NY) 57-62 (Lib Educ) MS in Ed, 65 (LS) Certif in Lib Sci. 6: Fr, Jewish. 7: Jr prof asst Signal Corps, Ft Monmouth NJ 42; Biol tchr NYC Schs 43-45; Tchr-libn Jericho (NY) High Sch 59-60; Tchr-libn Central High Sch Dist #3 Sanford High Sch Calhoun Sr High Sch 60-63; Tchr-libn Wantagh (NY) Sr High Sch 63-64; Tchr-libn John P McKenna Jr High Sch, Massapequa NY 64-. 9: ALA; AASchL; NYState Tchrs Assn; Nassau-Suffolk SchLA. 10: Massapequa Tchrs Assn; Nat Cong of Parents & Tchrs; E Meadow Commun Concert Assn; 4-H groups. 14: Reading guidance, performing arts materials. 15: 1421 Sylvia lane, East Meadow NY 11554.

BERGERON, CLAIRE A. b Ottawa Ont Can 16 Jl 44. 4: Gilles Bergeron. 5: Col Bruyere (Ottawa) 62-66 BA, UOttawa 66-67 BLS. 6: Fr, Sp. 7: Catlgr Nat Lib of Can, Ottawa 67-. 14: Catlg, ref. 15: 558 Coronation ave apt 3, Ottawa Ont Can.

BERGERON, GILLES-I. b Jonquiere Que Can 28 Je 41. 4: Claire Lecours. 5: Col de jonquiere 56-62 BA; UOttawa 63-64 BPh, 66-67 BLS. 6: Fr. 7: Tchr high sch: Que Can 64-65, Phicoutimi Que Can 65-66; Catlgr UOttawa, Central Lib 67-69, Hd libn Faculty of Soc Sci 69-. 9: Association canadienne de bibliothecaires de langue francoise. 14: Catlg, ref, admin. 15: 558 Coronation ave apt 3, Ottawa 8 Ont Can.

BERGEY, DOROTHY (MABEL). b Guernsey Sask Can 7 Ap 13. 5: USask 46-49 (Accounting) BCom; Toronto 61-62 BLS. 7: Elem sch tchr rural schs, Sask 32-42; Clerk QMS (WO 11) Can Army CWAC, Can 42-46; Lib clerk Defence Research Bd, Suffield Experimental Sta, Ralston Alta 49-52; Clerk Defence Research Bd, Naval Research Establishment, Halifax NS 52-54; Clerk Defence Research Bd, Defence Research Member, CJS, Wash DC 54-60; Lib clerk Defence Research Bd, Defence Research Med Labs, Toronto 60-61; Libn Defence Research Bd Naval Research Establishment, Halifax NS 62-69; Defence Research Bd Hdqs DSIS/B&P Lib, Ottawa Ont 69-. 9: CanLA; SLA;Prof Inst Pub Serv (Libns div); OttawaLA. 10: Univ Women's Club. 14: Catlg, ref. 15: 330 Metcalfe st, apt 310, Ottawa 4 Ont Can.

BERGGRUEN, HERBERT. b Hannover Germany 19 Je 06. 4: Joanne Frisch. 6: Fr, Ger. 7: Research libn Automobile Manufacturers Assn, NYC 29-40; Manager central ref dept Automobile Manufacturers Assn, Detroit 41-56, Head econ & hist Sect of pat lib 57-63, Libn & Res supv 64-. 9: SLA. 10: Unitarian Serv Com; (reg chm). 12: Automobile Manufacturers Assn's monthly chronology of important events (40-64) and its Current News Digest (45-56). 14: Automative tech lit. 15: 320 New Center Bldg, Detroit Mi 48202.

BERGHAUS, MARY J. b West Palm Beach Fla 1 Je 40. 5: Divine Providence Tchr Training Sch 57-61 (Educ); UPortland 62-65 (Eng, Hist) BA; UWash 65-66 MLS. 6: Sp. 7: Tchr sacred Heart Sch, Kingston Mass 58-61; Tchr St Joseph's Sch, Vancouver Wash 61-64; LC: Spec recruit 66-67, Staff research asst for acquis & overseas operations 67-. 8: Mem, Program for Outstanding Lib Sci Grads LC 66-67. 9: FlaLA; DCLA. 10: UWash Sch of Libnship Alum; Delta Epsilon Sigma. 14: Acquis, tech serv, child & sch libs. 15: 510 N st SW No N421, Washington DC 20024.

BERGHOLZ, DONNA ANN (CHAPIN). b Midland Mich 14 Mr 34. 4: Harry Bergholz. 5: UMich 51-55 (Ger) BA, 56-57 MALS. 6: Ger. 7: Descr catlgr DukeU 58-60, 62-. 10: Phi Beta Kappa. 14: Catlg. 15: 211 Vance st, Chapel Hill NC 27514.

BERGHOLZ, HARRY. b Berlin Ger 16 Ja 08. 4: Donna Ann Chapin. 5: UBerlin 26-33 (Humanities) MA; PhD; Sorbonne summer 38 License; Istituto di Cultura Italiana, (Lausanne) 43-44 Diploma; UMich 56-57 MALS. 6: Ger, Fr, Swedish, Dano-Norwegian, Dutch, Ital, Sp, Lat. 7: Tchr Germany, Eng, Switzerland; Lecturer Lawrence Col 47-48; Asst Prof Germanic Langs & Lit Dept UMich 48-57; Visiting Assoc Prof Dept of Germanics UNC (Chapel Hill) 58-59; Chief bibliog UNC 5766, Head bibliog serv dept 66-, Lecturer comp lit dept 66-. 9: NCLA; NYLib Club. 10: Mod Lang Assn; AAUP. 12: 4 books; also transl volumes edited Ed "The Bookmark" (58); Co-ed "Modern Language Journal" (50-55). 13: Yes. 14: Admin, bk sel. 15: 211 Vance st, Chapel Hill NC 27514.

BERGIN, MARION (M). b Birmingham Ala. 4: David Paul Bergin. 5: Northwestern (Eng) AB; UOkla MLS. 6: Fr, Sp, Lat, Ger. 7: Ed asst Okla Law Review UOkla 57-58; Asst catlg dept UArk 59-60; Asst acquis libn UOkla 60-61; Humanities & Rare Bk Coll Libn, UOkla 61-65; Asst law libn 65-67; Asst law libn 65-67; Asst to dir UFla Libs 67-68; Libn Law Firm Fulbright Crooker Freeman Bates & Jaworski Houston 69-. 9: ALA; AAL. 11: Graceherrick Award UOkla Sch Lib Sci. 12: Ed "Oklahoma Librarian" (60-67); Ed asst-okla Law Review" (57-58). 13: Yes. 14: Catlg, ref, rare bks (law & humanities). 15: 3623 Durness way, Houston Tx 77025.

BERGLAND, ELSIE. b Berwyn Ill. 5: J Sterling Morton Jr Col 25-27 (Biol Sci) Certif; UWis 27-30 (Biol Sci) BS, 35 (Biol Sci, Phys Ed) MS; UMich summer 38 (Public Health, Prev Med); Chicago summer 45 (LS); UIll 45-47 (LS) BS in LS. 6: Fr. 7: Instr of hlth & phys educ Louisville Collegiate Sch, Louisville Ky 30-32; Asst prof hlth & phys educ Ill StateU 32-45; Staff asst UIll (Urbana) 45-47; Circ, ref libn UIll Lib of Med Sci (Chicago) 47-55; Assoc libn & catlgr UColo Med Cntr Lib 55-57; ssoc prof of LS Colo StateU Libs 57-. 9: ALA; MedLA; ColoLA; MPLA. 10: Colorado Mountain Club; Beta Phi Mu; Delta Kappa Gamma. 12: Comp "Serial Publications in the Life Sciences" 67. 13: Yes. 14: Ref. 15: 1014 Castlerock dr, Fort Collins Co 80521.

BERGMAN, BRUCE J. b McGregor Iowa 30 My 32. 5: Macalester Col 50-54 (Internat Rel) BA; Stanford 56-57 (Internat Rel); UWis 58-59 MALS. 7: US Army 54-56; Ref libn NY Pub Lib 59-61; Readers serv libn Pace Col 62-68, Asst dir 68-. 14: Ref.

BERGMAN, HUGH RICHARD. b St Louis 14 Je 31. 4: Ann Bane. 5: St LouisU 49-53 (Hist) BA; UIll 56-57 MSLS; St LouisU 59-60, 64-65 (Hist, Educ). 7: (Pfc) US Army 53-55; Libn St LouisU 55-64; Libn Christian Brothers Col (St Louis) 64-. 14: Circ. 15: 5826 Pershing ave, St Louis Mo 63112.

BERGMAN, LOIS ALLENE (SUMMERS). b Callao Mo 3 Ap 09. 5: William Woods 25-27 (Music) AE; State Col Iowa summers 49-51 (Jr High Sch Educ) BA, summers 53-55 (Hist) MA; UColo summers 57-59 (LS); State Col Iowa summers 61-62 (LS); West MichU summers 64-65 (LS). 7: Soc studies tchr Jr High Sch, Belle Plaine Iowa 49-51; Soc studies tchr Anson Jr High Sch, Marshalltown Iowa 51-58, Libn 58-65; Head Libn Sr High Sch, Marshalltown Iowa 65-. 8: Mem &/or chm, Adv Sch Com, Title II area VI, Iowa 65-. 9: ALA-AASchL (State Assembly Planning Com; rep for Reg IV); NEA Iowa State ES (chm Court & By-Laws Com 62-65) IowaASchL (pres 67-68); Marshall-Town EA. 10: Kappa Delta Pi; Delta Kappa Gamma; Alpha Beta Alpha. 12: "Teachers' guide to Historical Information." (60). 14: Ref. 15: 10 N 10th st, Marshalltown Ia 50158.

BERGMANN, ROSEMARIE (LOUISE ELIZABETH). b Hambach Germany 10 Jl 25. 4: Alexander Bergmann. 5: UVienna 44-45; UMunich 47-48 (Fine Arts) BA equivalent; UMarburg 46-47, 48-51 (Art Hist) PhD; McGill 62-63 BLS. 6: Fr, Ger, Ital. 7: Asst in arts dept Marburg U 49-51; Asst, Chief Libn NDG Child Lib, Montreal 53-56; Asst music libn CBC, Montreal 57-58; Photo & slide libn McGill Arts Dept 61-63, Lecturer 63-67, Asst prof 67-. 8: Libr Consult, Montreal Mus, Fine Arts. 9: Can Youth Hostel Assn; Col Art Assn of Amer. 10: Can Amateur Musicians; Amer, Recorder Soc. 12: Comp Catalog of Canadian Amateur Music Library, No. 1 (63). 13: Yes. 14: Art & music bks, sheet music, slide catalg, Illuminated Bks. 15: Dept of Fine Arts McGill Univ, Montreal 2 Can.

BERGMANN, WINOGENE L. b Milwaukee 7 D 10. 5: Milwaukee Downer Col 27-31 BA; University Col (Exeter Eng) 31 Certif; Columbia summers 48-52 (LS) MS. 6: Fr. 7: Sch libn Juneau High Sch, Milwaukee 33-56; Sgt in WAC-Air Force, Aircraft Dispatcher 44-46; Curriculum libn & supv of lib serv Milwaukee Pub Schs 56-. 8: Consul for Book Trails program, The Wis Sch of the Air WHA Madison; Adv Com for Lib Insts sponsored annually by WEA, WLA, UW, UW-M in Madison Wis mem Planning Com for Ann Lib Inst; Wis State Com on Certification of Libns. 9: ALA-AASchL (sec Supv Sect 64, Ad hoc Jt Com); NEA-DAVI (Com wk); ASCD; WisEA (pres Sch Lib sect 65-66); WisLA (memResolutions Com, Asst dir & dir Natl Lib Week 68-70); WISASCD. 10: AAUW; Inter-Group Coun of Milwaukee (pres 65-66); Mayor's Commsn on Beautification 65- (v-chm 69); Delta Kappa Gamma. 13: Yes. 14: Superv of sch libs, curr developt, profess materials center, bk evaluation. 15: 709 E Juneau ave, Milwaukee Wi 53202.

BERGNES, GEORGIA B. b New York NY 8 F 22. 4: Paul Alvin Bernes. 6: Greek. 7: Asst map curator Map Dept Amer Geog Soc NY 54-65; Tech libn WDC A: Glaciology Amer Geog Soc NY 65-. 9: SLA (Geog & Map Div; past sec & v-chm NY chap). 14: Maps, catlg, ref, bibliog, glaciology. 15: World Data Center A Glaciology, American Geographical Society, Broadway & 156th st, New York NY 10032.

BERGSTROM, CHARLOTTE STUART. b NYC 29 My 24. 4: William H Bergstrom. 5: Mt Holyoke 42-44 (Zool); URochester 44-45 (Eng) BA; Syracuse 59-63 MS in LS. 7: Libn Pebble Hill Sch, Dewitt NY 64-. 9: ALA; NY State LA; OOSchLA. 10: . 15: Whetstone rd, Manlius NY 13104.

BERKEY, ADA E. b Somerset Penn 23 Jl 17. 5: Mt Holyoke 35-38 (Hist) AB; State UIowa 38-39 (Hist) AM; UMich 46-47 ABLS. 7: Circ libn Penn State Lib 40-45; Res libn Mt Holyoke Col 45-46; Ref libn West MichU 47-58, Music libn 58-. 9: ALA (life mem); MusLA (sec-treas Midwest Chap 67-69). 10: Chamber Music Soc of Kalamazoo. 14: Music. 15: 809 Weaver ave, Kalamazoo 49007.

BERKOWITZ, ALBERT M. b New Rochelle NY 27 Je 21. 4: Mary Coe. 5: NYU 38-42 (Marketing) BS; CatholicU 59-61 MS in LS. 7: Chief Yeoman US Maritime Serv 42-46; Member of managers staff National Symphony orchestra, Wash DC 46-49; Asst manager Hayes Concert Bur, Wash DC 49-59; Br libn DC Pub Lib 61-66; Hd loan & stack sect NLM 66-. 69; Dep chief, Ref serv div 69-. 9: DCLA; MedLA. 10: Washington Drama Soc; Beta Phi Mu. 13: Yes. 14: Ref, admin, interlib loan, lib netks. 15: 3722 Chesapeake st NW, Wash DC 20016.

BERLAD, BELLE (DIANE). b Brooklyn NY. 5: Brooklyn Col 45-50 (Lit) BA; USoCal 59-60 MSLS. 6: Ger, Fr, Sp. 7: Lib staff World-Telegram & Sun, NYC 40-54; Libn-file supv Andrews Clark & Buckley, NYC 55; Asst libn Bureau of Advertising ANPA, NYC 55-58; Libn Stromberg Carlson Co, San Diego 59; Libn A C Spark Plug, Los Angeles 60-61; Head libn Lockheed Propulsion Co, Redlands Cal 61-. 8: Mem Lib Tech Advis Com, San Bernadino Valley Cal. 9: SLA. 11: EE Award, Lockheed Propulsion Co. 14: Admin, ref research. 15: 325 E Cypress ave, Redlands Ca 92373.

BERLIN, CHARLES. b Boston 17 Mr 36. 4: Judith Armet. 5: Harvard 54-63 AB, AM, PhD; Hebrew Tchrs Col 52-56 BJEd, 56-59 MHL; Simmons 63-64 (LS) MS. 6: Hebrew, Yiddish, Fr, Ger, Arabic, Lat. 7: Instr in hist, Hebrew Tchrs Col 58-62; Lecturer on Modern Hebrew, Harvard 62-65; Lee M Friedman Bibliog in Judaica, Harvard Col Lib 62-. 8: Lecturer Harvard Summer Sch 64, 65; Consul on Lib Serv Col of Jewish Studies, Chicago 64-65. 9: ALA; Assn of Jewish Libs (pres 68-69, pres Research & Spec Libs Div 67-68). 10: Trustee Hebrew Tchrs Col. 14: Hebraic, Judaic bibliog. 15: Widener 188 Harvard Col Lib, Cambridge Ma 02138.

BERLIN, EDITH (ELINOR). b Cleveland 4 S 19. 4: Seymour S Berlin. 5: West Res 36-40 (Eng) BA, 40-41 BS in LS. 6: Fr. 7: Asst libn Dayton Pub Lib, Dayton Ohio 41-43; Chief mail & records BCPOE War Dept, Baltimore 43-45; Libn Eastern Jr High Sch, Silver Spring Md 59-62; Libn White Oak Jr High, Silver Spring Md 62-. 8: Adv Com to Coun Bd of Educ. 9: NEA; ALA; Md State Tchrs Assn; MdLA; Montgomery Co SchLA (past pres). 10: LWV. 11: Phi Beta Kappa. 14: Curriculum materials. 15: 6410 Bannockburn dr, Bethesda Md 20034.

BERLINER, ELEANOR F(FRIEDMAN). b NYC . 4: Joachim F Berliner. 5: Hunter Col (Eng) BA; Columbia (LS) MA. 6: Ger. 7: Tchr of Lib NYC Bd of Educ, NYC. 9: NYLA; NYLib Club; NYCSchLA (corr sec 59-60, prog chm 62-63, pres 64-65). 10: Sierra Club; Audubon Soc. 14: Wk with high sch studs. 15: 89 Metropolitan Oval, NYC 10462.

BERMAN, ALLAN BERTRAND. b Bayonne NJ 13 My 31. 4: Harriet Werner. 5: Bayonne Jr Col 49-51 (Liberal Art) Diploma; Montclair State Col 51-54 (Soc Studies) AB, 62-66 (Hist); Columbia 57-61 (Secondary Admin) MA; Newark State

Col 67-69 (Lib Studies) State Certif. 7: Camp dir summers 49-55, 57; Journalist 3d Class news ed-reporter "The Sweeper" USN Mine Force, Charleston SC 55-56; Tchr (spec educ) Bd of Educ, bayonee NJ 57-57; Tchr Bd of Educ, Orange NJ 58-59; So Orange Jr High Sch, So Orange NJ: Tchr 59-67, Asst libn & a-v coord 67-68, Libn & a-v coord 68-. 9: NEA; NJEA; EssexCoEA; South-Orange-MaplewoodEA; EssexCoSchLA. 10: Phi Delta Kappa. 14: Bldg a competent lib and tchg child its proper function and use. 15: 18 Highland pl, Maplewood NJ 07040.

BERMAN, EVELYN (ALINTUCK). b Boston Mass 30 Ag 24. 4: Herbert Berman. 5: Smith 42-46 Govt AB; Simmons Sch Lib Sci 64-67 LS MS. 6: Fr, Sp. 7: Federal Reserve Bank Econ Res Lib, Boston 68; Catlgr Northeastern U Sch of Law 68-. 14: Catlg. 15: 30 Ellis rd, W Newton Ma 02165.

BERMAN, MARSHA F. b Los Angeles 23 F 35. 5: UCLA 52-57 (Music) BA; UCal (Berkeley) 57-59 MLS. 6: Fr. 7: Libn Brooklyn Pub Lib 59-62; Libn San Francisco Pub Lib 62-63; Libn Brooklyn Pub Lib 63-64; Sr libn UCLA Educ & Psych Lib65-67; Asst mus libn UCLA Mus Lib 67-. 9: MusLA (mem Placement Com, sec-treas So Cal Chap 68-69; Amer Musicological Soc. 10: UCLA Lib Staff Assoc (pres 68-69). 14: Music, ref, adult serv. 15: 153 W Channel rd, Santa Monica Ca 90402.

BERMAN, MURRAY A. b NYC 18 Ag 30. 4: Natalie C Margulies. 5: Fla So Col 53-54 (Liberal Arts); Fla StateU 54-56 BS, 56-57 MSLS; Cal State Col (LA) 63-67 (Theater Arts). 7: United States Air Force, Airman First Class, Classification Specialist 48-52; Lib trainee Brooklyn Pub Lib, Brooklyn NY 56-; Br lib asst Denver Pub Lib 57-59; Asst ref libn soc sci & bus admin Sacramento State Col 59-62; Readers asst Pomona Pub Lib, Pomona Cal 62-64; Libn Cal High Sch, Whittier Cal 64-68; Asst spec collections libn Honnold Lib, Claremont Cal 68-69; Hd ref dept Honnold Lib Claremont Col 69-. 8: Drama Asst Cal High Sch, Whittier Cal 65-68; Afro-Amer Bibliogr, Honnold Lib, Claremont Cal 68-. 9: Amer Educl Theatre Assn; CalLA (past mem Intel Freedom Com); Amer Educl Theatre Assn So Cal. 10: ACLU; Whittier Area Fair Housing Com. 12: Principal investigator "Influenza: an Amotated Bibliography"; Ed "Birth Defects"; Ed "Cystic Fibrosis". 14: Ref. 15: 10140 Regetta ave apt 7, Whittier Ca 90604.

BERMAN, SANFORD. b Chicago Il 6 O 33. 4: Lorraine Oliver. 5: UCLA 51-55 (Pol sci) BA; CatholicU of Amer 58-61 MSLS. 6: Sp, Ger. 7: Messengerlclk LA Pub Lib 50-52; Reader in Eng Eng Dept UCLA 54-55; Info specialist (SP/4) USA Heidelberg WGer 55-57; Asst chief acquis dept DC Pub Lib, Wash DC 57-62; Field libn USA Spec Serv Libs W Ger 62-66; Libn Schiller Col, Kleiningersheim W Ger 66-67; Period libn UCLA Research Lib 67-68; Asst libn UZambia Lusaka Zambia 68-. 8: Del Internat Social Tchrs Conf Rome 67; Defense witness "Open City", obscenity trial Los Angeles Cal Oct 68. 9: ALA; ZambiaLA. 10: Phi Beta Kappa; Phi Beta Mu; Amnesty Internat; ACLU; Cal State Seal of Merit 50. 12: "Spanish Guinea: an annotated bibliography" (61); co-ed Yin-Yang (Worms/Mannheim, West Germany 66). 14: Bk sel, period, intel freedom, serv to minorities, Africana, avant-garde & radical lit. 15: Lib University of Zambia PO Box 2379, Lusaka Zambia.

BERMAN, SEYMOUR. b Atlantic City NJ 2 My 24. 5: Harvard 46-50 (Eng) BA; UMich 50-51 MLS. 6: Fr, Ger. 7: Tech Sgt US Army AF 42-45; Detroit Pub Lib: Ref libn 51-55, Home reading libn 55-58, Head foreign lang 58-61; Dir Brentwood Pub Lib, Brentwood NY 61-. 9: ALA; NYLA; Suffolk-CoLA. 10: Rotary Club. 15: 21 Penataquit ave, Bay Shore NY 11706.

BERMAN, SUSAN NANCY. b Detroit Mich 6 D 44. 5: UMich 62-66 (Fr) BA, 67-68 AMLS; UDetroit 63; Wayne State 66. 6: Fr, Sp, Ital. 7: Contingent sales & clerical wk Winkelman's, Detroit summers 65-67; Libn I (child) Detroit Pub Lib, Chaney Br 68-. 14: Child wk, ref serv. 15: 18317 Ohio ave, Detroit Mi 48221.

BERNARD, HUGH Y(ANCY). b Athens Ga 17 Jl 19. 5: Piedmont Col 37-38; UGa 38-41 (Hist & Pol Sci) AB; Columbia 46-47 BS in LS; George WashingtonU 57-61 (Law) JD. 6: Fr, Ger. 7: Tchr gen sci high sch, Moultrie Ga 41; Army of the US, Air Corps USA & Philippine Islands 42-46; Clerk-Supv VA Reg Off, Atlanta 46; LC: Catlgr Copyright Off, Wash DC 47-52, Reviser Copyright Off 52-59, Sr catlgr Ms Sect Desc Catlg Div 59-60; Law Libn George WashingtonU 60-, Asst Prof of Law 66-68, Assoc Prof of Law 68-. 9: Amer Bar Assn; Amer Judicature Soc; SLA; DCLA; AALL (Com on "Law Library Journal" 64-; Catlg & Clsf Com 60-63; Com on Directories & Statis 63-64); Law Libns Soc, Wash DC (past pres). 10: Bar of the Dist of Columbia (US District Court, US Court of Appeals); Nat Lawyers Club; Phi Beta Kappa; Phi Alpha Delta; Order of the Coif; Kappa Delta Pi; Assn Amer Law Schs; Amer Acad Polit & Soc Sci. 12: "The Law of Death and the Disposal of the Dead" (65); Contrib "Subject Headings for the Literature of Law and International Law" AALL Pub ser no 6 (63); "Public Officials, Elected and Appointed" (68). 13: Yes. 14: Lib admin, Catlg, acquis, budget or fin mgt. 15: 1911 Paul Spring Parkway, Alexandria Va 22308.

BERNARD, SISTER M JOSEPH. 5: St John's U (Eng) BA (magna cum laude), MLS. 7: Lib asst Barnard Col Lib; Tchrs Col Lib Columbia U; Libn Mt St Mary Acad, Newburgh NY; Libn Mt St Mary Col (NY) 55-. 9: ALA-ACRL; CathLA; NYLA. 15: Mt St Mary Col Lib, Newburgh NY 12550.

BERNARD, RICHARD F. b Los Angeles 5 Ag 25. 4: Priscilla Julia (Chavez) Bernard. 5: US Merchant Marine Acad 43-45 (Marine Transportation) BS; UCLA 47-50 (Anthropology) BA; UCal (Berkeley) 52-53 BLS, 54-57 (Anthropology) MA. 6: Sp, Port, Fr, Ger. 7: Ref libn Bancroft Lib, UCal(Berkeley) 53-61; Bibliog UWis Lib(Madison) 61-65; Chief Dept of Special Collections UMinn Lib(Minneapolis) 65-66; Hd Pub Serv Huntington Lib 66-67; Asst Prof Sch of Libnship UBC 67-. 9: ALA; CanLA. 14: Spec collections, area studies, educ for libnship. 15: 5487 Green Leaf rd, Vancouver BC Can.

BERNARD, VIRGINIA (BILMAZES). b Haverhill Mass 19 Jl 23. 4: Kenneth R Bernard. 5: Simmons 41-45 (LS) BS; NY State Tchrs' Col for Women summer 48; BostonU 48-54 9educ). 6: Gr, Fr. 7: Ref asst pub lib, Fitchburg Mass 45-47; Boys & girls libn pub lib, Haverhill Mass 47-48; Libn Newburyport High Sch, Newburyport Mass 48-54; Ref libn Bradford Jr Col 54-55; Asst command libn USAF, TAF England 55-57; Libn Haverhill High Sch, Haverhill Mass 58-62; Ref libn pub lib, Haverhill Mass 69-. 9: ALA; MassLA; NELA; Merrimack Valley LA. 10: Women's City Club; Haverhill Col Club; John Greenleaf Whittier Club; Haverhill Girls Club; Haverhill Hist Assn. 14: Ref, hist collections. 15: 3 North ave, Plaistou NH.

BERNARDI, HELEN FRANCES. b Joplin Mo 25 N 42. 5: Northeastern Okla A & M Jr Col 60-62 AA; Okla StateU 62-65 (LS) BS in Ed. 6: Fr. 7: Soc studies tchr Tulsa Pub Schs, Tulsa Okla 65, Libn 65-. 9: NEA; ALA; OklaEA; OklaLA (sec); Tulsa Sch LA. 10: Alpha Beta Alpha; AAUW. 14: Ref, child & yp. 15: PO Box 2, Miami Ok 74354.

BERNATH, KATHLEEN (LOEB). b Los Angeles 11 N 10. 4: Edward J Bernath. 5: UCal (Berkeley) 28-30; UCLA 30-32 (Philos) AB; Columbia 59-61 (LS) MS. 6: Sp, Port. 7: Catlgr Henry E Huntington Lib, San Marino Cal 61-67; Catlgr Pub Lib Upland Cal 67-68, Tech Serv Libn 68-. 9: ALA; CalLA. 10: Assistance League of Upland; Honnold Lib Soc; Chaffey Commun Cultural Center (bd dirs). 14: Rare bks, org & use of lib materials. 15: 325 E Yale st, Ontario Ca 91762.

BERND, LELA M(ARY). b Manson Iowa 24 O 04. 5: Grinnell Col 24-25; Morningside Col 30-33 (Eng Lang & Lit) BA; UMinn 45-46 BS in LS. 7: Tchr Calhoun Co Rural Schs, Iowa 23-24, 26-27; Libn Pub Lib, S Bend Ind 46-60, Head land & lit dept & Interlib Loan libn 61-. 9: ALA; IndLA. 10: AAUW; LWV; Chamber Music Soc; Wesleyan Serv Guild. 14: Ref, adv wk. 15: 613 Park a ve, South Bend In 46616.

BERNDT, AUDREY JOANNE. b Otter Creek Twp Wis. 5: TaylorU 57-61 (Eng) AB; UMinn 61-62 (LS) MA. 6: Fr. 7: Asst libn in charge catlg TaylorU 62-68; Catlg & ref Wis StateU (Eau Claire) 68-. 9: ALA. 14: Ref, catlg. 15: 276 W Belleview, Winona Mn 55987.

BERNDT, MARION (ANN MAUER). b Cleveland 23 Je 27. 4: Donald W Berndt. 5: Notre Dame Col (South Euclid Ohio) 45-49 (Eng) BA; West Res 49-50 MSLS. 6: Sp. 7: 1st asst Main Boys & Girls Room Lakewood Pub Lib, Lakewood Ohio 50-55; Libn Hq 1st Cav Div, Tokyo Japan 55-56; Supv libn Camp Fuji Japan 56-57; Supv libn Reg Camp, Tokyo Japan 57; Area supv Seoul Area Command Hq 8th US Army, Korea 57-58; Staff libn Hq USARYIS/IX Corps, Sukiran Okinawa 58-61; Staff libn Hq USARSO Ft Amador CZ 61-65; Libn recreation & educ div PSSD, TAGO, Dept of Army Wash DC 65; Chief tech serv lib div post spec serv, Ft Hood Tex 65-66; Chief libn Ft Bragg NC 67-. 8: Adv OkinawaLA 58-61; Guest lecturer Lib Sci U of the Ryukyus 61; Guest lecturer Lib Sci CZ Jr Col 62. 9: ALA; SLA; OkinawaLA (58-61); Assn of Gradlibs of the Isthmus of Panama (61-65); NCLA; Cape Fear

LA. 10: Altrusa; AAUW. 11: Sus Sup Perf Award 60; Out Perf Awards 61 & 64; USCONTIC Cert Achiev 67. 14: Admin. 15: 6228 Cool Shade dr, Fayetteville NC 28303.

BERNEIS, REGINA F. b Budapest Hungary 22 S 19. 4: Hans L Berneis. 5: Wayne State U 36-40 (LS) BA; West Mich U 61-64 (LS) MA. 6: Fr. 7: Libn Detroit Pub Schs 40-48, 50; Libn NM Western Col summer 49; Libn Portage Pub Schs, Portage Mich 60-65; Asst Dir NDEA Inst West Mich U summer 65, Asst prof & Libn 65-. 8: Instr Materials Com Mich State Curriculum Planning Commsn; Chm MEA Lib Meeting Reg V 64. 9: ALA; Mich Assn Sch Libns; MichLA; (mem Scholarsh Com 67). 10: Beta Phi Mu, AAUW; Art League (Kalamazoo), Faculty Woman's Club (pres 68-69). 12: Assoc ed "School Libraries" (65-). 13: Yes. 14: Child & yp wk, catalg, ref., Rare bks, Acad Libs. 15: 2537 Applelane ave, Kalamazoo Mi 49001.

BERNEKING, CAROLYN (BAILEY). b Kan City Mo 21 Je 15. 4: Christian Berneking. 5: UKan City Musical Conservatory 33-34 (Piano); UKan 34-37 (Piano) BM; AuburnU 52 (Ger); UKan 62 (Music Hist). 6: Ger. 7: Catlgr AuburnU 50-53; Catlgr Elizabeth Pub Lib, Elizabeth NJ 53-58; Ser libn UKan Lib 58-64, Admin asst 64-68; Lib Cent Jr High Sch, Lawrence Ks 68-. 9: KanLA; NJLA. 10: DAR; Lawrence Music Club; Womens Literary Club; Mu Phi Epsilon Alumna; Pi Beta Phi. 13: Yes. 14: Catlg, data proc. 15: 706 W 12th st, Lawrence Ks 66044.

BERNER, RICHARD C. b Seattle 31 D 20. 4: Thelma Kass. 5: UWash 40-46 (Econ) BA; UCal (Berkeley) 47-52 (Hist) MA, 54-55 MLS. 6: Fr. 7: Col 10th Mountain Div US Army 43-46; Mss clerk Bancroft Lib UCal (Berkeley) 53-55; Libn Hist & Pol Sci Grad & Map Lib, Ohio State U 55-56; Gen libn UIda 56-57; Bk orders libn UWash 57-58; Curator of Mss UWash Lib 58-67, U archivist 67-. 8: Archival consul, The Boeing Co 64-66. 9: SAA (Com on Mss & Spec Collections 60-67, Educ Com 64-65, Prog Com 66, Com on Col & Univ Archives 67-); ALA (Adhoc Com to Establish Unit for Mss libns 68-); Org Amer Histns; AHA; West Hist Assn (Memb Com 64-65, Prog Com 67); Forest Hist Soc; Wash State Hist Soc; Amer Records Mgt Assn. 10: ACLU; NAACP; UWash Staff Assn; Pacific NW Labor Hist Com; Urban League. 13: Yes. 14: Mss, archives acquis, hist research & writing. 15: Univ of Washington Lib, Seattle Wa 98105.

BERNER, WILLIAM (SHERMAN). b St Paul 1 Jl 39. 4: Gisela Starck. 5: UMinn 57-61 (Hist) BA, 61-62 (LS) MA; UIll 66-(LS). 6: Fr, Ger. 7: Asst libn Soc Studies Div UNeb Libs 62-64, pre-catlg libn pub serv div 64-66; Research assoc Lib Research CtrUIll (Urbana) 66-. 9: ALA (mem com 64-); IllLA. 10: UMinn Lib Sch Alumni Assn; AAUP; Theta Delta Chi; Beta Phi Mu. 12: Co-auth "Financing Public Library Expansion (68). 13: Yes. 14: Tech serv, lib referendums, bk sel, educ for libnship. 15: 2031 D Orchard st, Urbana Il 61801.

BERNIER, CHARLES L(EWELLYN). b Winona Minn 23 S 07. 4: Marie Ropeter Bernier. 5: Mont State Col 25-30 (Ind Chem) BS; Ohio StateU 30-32 (Organic Chem) MS, 32-35 (Organic Chem) PhD. 7: Assoc ed Chem Abstr Amer Chem Soc, Columbus Ohio 53-57, Ed "Chemical Abstracts" 57-61; Dir ASTIA AF Defense Doc Center DSA, Alexandria Va 61-64; Head communications br NICHDNIH, Bethesda Md 64; Sci commun spec NLM, Bethesda Md 64-65; Research spec Instr in Lib Sch Rutgers 65-68; Prof SUNY (Buffalo) 68-. 8: Internat Union of Pure & Applied Chemistry; Commsn on Ciphering Codification & Punched-Card Techniques 57-61; Consul on info systems to 2 groups, 67-68. 9: ACS; ASIS; Amer Inst Chemists. 10: . 13: Yes. 14: Info sci, tech serv, systems, indexing, abstracting. , tchg. 15: Delaware Towers 9-I 1088 Delaware ave, Buffalo NY 14209.

BERNIER, ELISE E. b St-Cyrille de Lessard Cte L'Islet 30 Mr 17. 4: Gertrude Bernier. 5: Col Ste- Anne de la Pocatiere (Kamouraska) 32-41 BA; ULaval 42-43; (Philos). 6: Fr, Eng. 7: Libn Ecole Superieure d'Agriculture, La Pocatiere 45-62; Libn Institut de Tech agric 62-. 9: Assn canadienne des bibliothe3caires de langue francaise; ALA. 10: Bd of Trade, La Pocatiere Kamouraska. 14: Catlg, ref. 15: E Bernier CP 36, La Pocatiere Kamouraska Que Can.

BERNIER, ROGER (BERTRAND). b Drummondville Que Can 28 S 42. 4: Denis Marquis. 5: Seminaire de Sherbrooke 60-64 (Lit, Philos) BA; UMontreal 64-65 (LS) B Bibl. 6: Eng. 7: Libn Seminaire de Sherbrooke 65-67; Libn USherbrooke 67-. 8: Tchr, LC clsfn, College Sainte-Anne-de-la Pocatiere, Que summers 68, 69. 9: Association canadienne des bibliothecaires de langue francaise. 10: Young C of C, Sherbrooke. 14: Catlg. 15: 1500 Rue Chagnon #1, Sherbrooke Que Can.

BERNINGHAUSEN, DAVID KNIPE. b Beaman Iowa 5 F 16. 4: Elizabeth Smith. 5: Iowa State Tchrs Col 33-36 (Speech) BA; Columbia 38-41 BLS; Drake U 39-43 (Eng) MA; UNC 44 (Eng); Harvard U 50-51 (Educ Fellow). 7: Tchr Edgewood (Iowa) High Sch 36-37; Tchr Valley Jr High Sch, W Des Moines Iowa 37-41; Asst libn Iowa State Tchrs Col 41-44; Dir of libs Birmingham-So Col 44-47; Dir of libs Cooper Union 47-53; Dir Lib Sch UMinn (Minneapolis) 53- Visiting prof UHawaii 69. 8: Consul Nat Taiwan U, Taipei Taiwan 62-63Consul UTunis, Tunis Tunisia 68; Dir NDak State Lib survey 67. 9: AALS (pres 59-60); ALA (Com on Intel Freedom, Com on Accred); MinnLA (pres 57-58). 10: AAUP (pres 61-62). 11: Drake U Alumni Distinguished Serv Award 64. 12: Ed "Undergraduate Library Education" (59); ed "Libs of Seven South Dakota Institutions of Higher Education" (65). 13: Yes. 14: Admin, lib educ, intell freedom. 15: 1912 Dupont ave S, Minneapolis Mn 55403.

BERNS, HAZEL (SILVERSTEIN). b NYC 29 Ap 20. 4: Milton Berns. 5: St John's U 36-38 (Pre Law); St John'sU Sch of Law 38-41 LLB; Pratt 56-59 MLS. 7: Lib trainee Hewlett-Woodmere Pub Lib, Hewlett NY 56-59, Jr libn 59-61, Sr libn 61-63, Asst dir 63-. 10: Phi Beta Mu. 14: Wk with child & ya, ref, catlg, ref, admin. 15: 1182 Frocan ct, Hewlett NY 11557.

BERNSTEIN, ERIC. b Schwerin-Warthe Germany 10 N 05. 5: Friedrich WilhelmU (Berlin) 24-28; HalleU (Halle/Saale) 28-29 Doctor of Law; CatholicU (LS). 6: Fr, Ger. 7: Lawyer, Berlin 32-33; Real estate broker, Berlin 34-38; Bus man, Indianapolis 39-41; Dist rep Amer Automobile Assoc, Wash DC 41-44; Sales rep mgr, Wash DC 44-55; Stastical clk US Census Bur, Suitland Md 55-56; Sr catlgr LC 56-. 12: "Irrtum und Geschaftsgrundlage" (Berlin 33). 14: Catlg (law bks, rare bks, tech bks). 15: 1615 Rosemont ct, McLean Va 22101.

BERNSTEIN, NORBERT. b Francfort Am/Main Germany 10 F 26. 4: Estelle Novak. 5: BostonU 47-50 (Langs) AB; Columbia 52 MSLS. 6: Fr, Ger. 7: Buck Sgt US Army Air Corps 44-46; Document searcher NY Pub Lib 51-54; Asst head catlgr Providence Pub Lib 54-56; Dir tech proc dept Youngstown Pub Lib, Youngstown Ohio 57-60; Head Libn Seymour Lib, Auburn NY 61-66; Asst dir for readers' serv BrandeisU Lib 66-. 9: NYLA. 10: Friends of Swampscott Pub Lib; B'Nai Brith. 13: Yes. 14: Admin, catlg, rare bks. 15: 20 Evans st, Auburn NY 13021.

BERNSTEIN, SANDRA B. b Wash DC 19 D 41. 5: Brooklyn Col 58-63 (Biol) BA; Columbia 64-66 (Lib Serv) MS. 6: Hebrew, Fr. 7: Brooklyn Pub Lib, Brooklyn NY: YA libn trainee 63, Children's serv libn trainee 64-66, Children's serv libn 66-67; Asst ref libn Med Lib Columbia U 67-68; Ref libn Amer Mus Natural Hist, NYC 68. 9: SLA; MedLA (NY reg Gp); NY Lib Club. 10: Brooklyn Col Alum Assn; CLU; SLS Alum Assn, Columbia. 14: Ref. 15: Amer Mus of Natural History, Central Park W at 79th st, New York NY 10024.

BERNSTEIN, ZITA (WALDMAN). b Melville Sask Can 27 Je 27. 4: Mark A Bernstein. 5: UMan 47 (Music) AMM, 43-48 BA; Toronto 53-54 BLS. 6: Fr. 7: Catlgr Pub Lib, Winnipeg Man 59-63; Catlgr UMan Lib 63-67, Asst libn 67-. 9: ManLA. 14: Catlg. 15: 218 Oxford st, Winnipeg 9 Man Canada.

BEROLZHEIMER, HOBART F(RANCIS). b Chicago 25 O 21. 5: UIll 38-42 (Eng) AB, 42-43 (Eng) AM (Chicago) 44-45 BLS, summers50-52. 6: Fr. 7: Research asst Fr Dept UIll (Urbana) 40-43; Ref asst Chicago Pub Lib 44-45, 1st asst bk sel div 45-48; Acquislibn UCal(Santa Barbara) 48-53; Head Lit Dept Free Lib of Phila 53-. 8: Part-time instr ref wk Drexel Inst 64-. 9: ALA (Steering Com 47-48, memb chm Penn 62-63, chm Reg 8 63-68);-RSD (chm New Ref Tools Com 68-69); TheatreLA (Exec Bd 66-);LPRA; PennLA (mem Chm 61-64, chm SE Chap 63-65, chm Awards Com 64-65, chm Adult Serv Com 65-66, chm Scholarship Com 66-67; chmOrg & Bylaws Com 68-69; mem Exec Com 68-69). 10: Phila Reg Writers' Conf; Phi Beta Kappa; Pi Delta Phi. 13: Yes. 14: Ref, adultserv, pub rel. 15: Free Lib of Phila Logan Sq, Phila Pa 19103.

BERRING, ELSA J. b Orange NJ 9 S 42. 5: Wilson Col 60-64 (Sociol) BA; Ohio StateU 64-65 (Sociol); Rutgers 65-66 MLS. 6: Fr. 7: Ref libn Plainfield Pub Lib, Plainfield NJ 66-68; Ref libn Fairfax Co Pub Lib, Fairfax Va 68-. 9: VaLA. 14: Ref. 15: 6129 Leesburg pike, Falls Church Va 22041.

BERRISFORD, PAUL DEE. b St Paul 3 N 25. 4: Margaret Cullen. 5: UMinn 50 (Hist) BA, 50-52 (Educ) BS, 50-52 BSLS. 7: Pharmist Mate USN 41-44; Libn Crystal Falls Mich schs 52-53; Libn St Paul pub schs 53-57; Instr UMinn Lib Sch

(Minneapolis) 54-55; Asst Prof & chief catlg libn UMinn (Minneapolis) 56-67, Asst dir for processing 68-. 8: Lib consul UMinn Ford Foundation at UConcepcion, Concepcion Chile. 9: ALA; "RTSD (CCS Descrip Catlg Com 68-690& minnLA; Twin City Catlgrs Round table (chm 57-58, 65-66). 10: Phi Delta Kappa; AAUP. 13: Yes. 14: Catlg. 15: 2245 Princeton ave, St Paul Mn 55105.

BERRY, ALMEDIUS BLANCHE. b Chesterfield Co Va 25 Je 20. 5: Va State Col 37-41 (Teacher-Librarian) BS; Syracuse 44-45 BSLS. 7: Sec Robert F Jones Chesterfield Co Farm Agent, Chesterfield Co Va 41-42; Tchr Evans Elem Sch, Dinwiddie Co Va 42-44; Asst libn Keney Br Hartford Pub Lib, Hartford Conn 45-47; Asst libn Detroit Pub Lib 48-49; Libn Southside High Sch, Dinwiddie Co Va 49-. 9: NEA; ALA; VaEA; VaTA (past off libns dept); VaLA. 10: Alpha Kappa Alpha; Beta Phi Mu. 14: Ref, high sch lib wk. 15: Rt 1 box 180, Colonial Heights Va 23834.

BERRY, ELLENE. b NYC 28 Ja 11. 4: Robert C Berry. 5: Hunter Col 32 (Eng) BA; Columbia 50 (LS) MS. 6: Fr, Sp, Ger. 7: Hd libn Evander Childs High Sch, Bronx NY 50-. 8: Reading Com, Bur of Libs, NYC Bd of Educ. 9: NYCSchLA; NYLib Club. 13: Yes. 14: Sch libs. 15: 1079 Pelhamdale ave, Pelham NY 10803.

BERRY, JOHN NICHOLS III. b Montclair NJ 12 Je 33. 5: Boston U 54-55, 57-58 (Hist) AB; Simmons 59-60 (LS) MS. 7: (Sp3) US Army Ft Bragg NC 55-57; Youth-Ref Reading Pub Lib, Reading Mass 59-60; Ref libn Simmons Col Lib 60-62; LecturerSch of LS Simmons 61-64; Asst dir Simmons Col Lib 62-64; Asst ed "Library Journal" 64-66; Mng ed New Bk Proj R R Bowker Co66-69; Ed in chief "Library Journal" 69-. 9: ALA; MassLA (Publ Comm, ed of Publs); NY Lib Club; Nat Lib Week Comm for Mass 64; SLA (chm Publ Div 69); ASIS. 10: Melvil Dewey Chowder & Marching Soc; Lib Pub Rels Coun. 11: H W Wilson Lib Period Award (62). 12: Ed "Bay State Librarian" (62-64), ed "Directory of Library Consultants," (69). 13: Yes. 14: Pub lib admin, censorship, bk sel, lib educ. 15: Library Journal 1180 Ave of the Americas, NYC 10036.

BERRY, JUNE. b Torrington Conn 1 Je 25. 5: Brigham YoungU 43-47 (Educ) BA; UUtah 50-52 (LS) MS Brigham Young U 66- (Curriculum). 6: Ger, Lat. 7: Bind supv Brigham YoungU Lib 47-48; Libn Brigham YoungU Lab Sch 48-68; Guest instr Col of Ida summers 68, 69. 8: Consul, Utah Wkshop on Econ Educ Curr, Provo Utah 52-66; Consul; Beaver Sch Dist, Milford Utah50, Kane Co Sch Dist, Kanab Utah 64-66, Bassett Sch Dist, Bassett Cal 63-64; Curric consul, Utah Wkshop on Econ, Educ 52-66;Consul Educ Serv Unit 18, Scottsbluff Neb 68; Curric writer, Rocky Mtn Educ Lab, Provo Utah 66-67. 9: ALA (Ya Bk Sel Com); UtahLA (Sch Sect; chm Memb Com); UtahEA (var off in past). 10: Utah Coun on Reading; IRA, AAUW, PTA; Utah Acad Sci Arts & Letters. 12: "Services of School Libraries in Utah" (56); "Library Service in Utah; A Graphic View" (59); ed "Utah Council Reading Review" (67-69). 13: Yes. 14: Sch libs, geneal, communications. 15: RFD 1 Box 129, Payson Ut 84651.

BERRY, KATHRYNE (CAMPBELL). b Stanford Ky 4 O 15. 4: John D Berry. 5: East KyU 33-37 (Soc Sci) AB; Peabody Col summer 38 (LS). 7: Tchr jr high sch, Irvine Ky 37-43; Supv Seagram's Distillers, Louisville Ky 43-45; Clk US Govt, Honolulu 45-50; Bkkeeper creamery, Oakland Cal 50-51; Clk Credit Bur, Bellflower Cal 51-54; Saleswoman real estate, Hawaiian Gardens Cal 548; Clk Fullerton Pub Lib, Fullerton Cal 58-59, Bkmob libn 59-61, Order libn 61-. 9: CalLA; OrangeCoLA. 14: Bk sel. 15: 325 N Basque ave, Fullerton Ca 92633.

BERRY, LEONA P. b Redwing Kan 9 My 16. 5: York Col 36-40 (Hist) AB; Ft Hays Kan State Col 41-42 (Eng) MS; UDenver 48-49 MALS; UMich summer 58 UDenver summer 68. 7: Elem sch tchr Russell Co Schs, Russell Co Kan 34-36, 40-41; Eng tchr Atwood Community High Sch, Atwood Kan 42-44; Eng tchr Hoisington High Sch, Hoisington Kan 44-47; Eng Instr William Penn Col 47-48; Ref libn Central Wash State Col 49-54; Libn Southwestern Col (Kan) 54-56; Circ libn Kan State Col (Pittsburg) 56-57; Ref libn East MichU 57-66, Asst soc sci libn 66-. 9: ALA; SAA. 10: AAUP; AAUW; Delta Kappa Gamma. 14: Ref, archives. 15: 905 Hillside ct, Ypsilanti Mi 48197.

BERRY, LOIS THARRINGTON. b Charlotte County Va 19 Jl 14. 5: Far,ville State Tchrs Col 31-33 (Elem educ) Diploma; Longwood Col 48-51 (LS) BS; Grad Sch of Lib Sci UNC at Chapel Hill 60-66 MSLS. 6: Ger. 7: (M/Sgt) US Army Corps Engrs (Atomic Bomb Proj) 41-46; Act libn Simpson Col summer 47; UMich; tchgfellow 49-52, Instr 52-56, Asst Prof 56-60, Assoc Prof 60-65, Prof 65-, Dean Sch Lib Sci 69-. 8: President's Adv Com, E Carolina U 67-. 9: ALA; -AASchL; -YASD; -CSD; NCLA; NCASchL. 10: AAUP; Longwood Alum Assn; Kappa Delta Pi. 12: "Evaluation of the High School Books in the Fields of the Social Sciences on the Virginia State-Aid Lists, 65" (Thesis 66). 14: Ref, pub serv, educ media ctrs. 15: 4000 S Elm st, Greenville NC 27834.

BERRY, MRS MARIE BRAUN. b San Antonio Tex 15 Ag 15. 4: Clarence Matthew Berry. 5: San Antonio Jr Col 34-35 (Hist, Eng); Tex Lutheran Col 36 (Hist, Eng); St Marys U even 37-40 (Hist, Eng); Our Lady of Lake Col 55-57 (LS) BA. 6: Ger. 7: San Antonio Pub Lib, San Antonio Tex: Lib asst 34-45, Ref libn 54-58, Head of hist, gen ref & soc sci dept 58-68, Ref Libn 68-. 9: ALA; CathLA (Memb Chm San Antonio Unit 60-62); SWLA; TexLA; Libns Coun of San Antonio (pres 58-59). 10: Alpha Beta Alpha; AAUW; Tex State Hist Soc; San Antonio Hist Assn; San Antonio Conserv Soc; State Assn of Tex Pioneers. 11: Outstanding Staff Award, San Antonio Pub Lib Staff Asso 68. 14: Ref, Texana, hist. 15: 213 Overhill dr, San Antonio Tx 78228.

BERRY, PATRICIA ANNE (WALSH). b Toronto Ont Can 23 Jl 17. 4: John Desmond Berry. 5: St Michael's Col; UToronto 35-39(Fr) BA; Sch of Lib Sci UToronto 45-46 BLS. 6: Fr. 7: Lib asst Toronto Pub Lib, Toronto Ont Can 41-43; Spec duty libn (Pettyofficer) WRCNS, Can & overseas 43-45; Child libn Enoch Pratt Free Lib, Baltimore 46-48; Child libn Sudbury Pub Lib, Sudbury OntCan 48-50; Commun libn St Joseph Col, N Bay Ont Can 50-55; Libn Toronto Pub Lib, Toronto Ont Can 55-66; Chief libn prof libMetropolitan Separate Sch Bd, Toronto Ont Can 66-. 9: OntLA. 14: Ref, readers adv, wk with child. 15: 162 Princess ave,Toronto 441 Ont Can.

BERRY, PAUL L(UCIEN). b San Jose Cal 4 S 21. 4: Doris Patterson. 5: AmericanU 39-43 (Rel Philos) BA; Yale 43-44 (Theol); CatholicU 46-49 (LS); AmericanU 57-63 (Pub Admin). 7: LC: Asst in order div 45-49, Head ser record sect 49-52, Asst chief order div 52-53, Chief ser div 53-61, Coordinator for org & development of collections 61-64, Assoc dir of admin 64-66, Dir of admin 67-68, Assoc dir ref dept 68-69, Dir ref dept 69-. 8: ChmFed Lib Com Task Force on Automation 65-. 9: ALA; Nat Microfilm Assn; DCLA (Bus Mgr "DC Libraries" 60-). 13: Yes. 14: Admin, ref. 15: 2104 Cascade rd, Silver Spring Md 20902.

BERRY, R EDWIN. b North Bangor NY 27 D 27. 4: Ellen Cochrane Berry. 5: St LawrenceU 51 (Chem) BS; Syracuse 55 MSLS. 7: Jr libn Niagara Falls Pub Lib, Niagara Falls NY 55-56; Sr libn Reg Lib Serv Center, Watertown NY 56-58; Sr lib supv Lib Ext Div, Albany NY 58-61; Supv Allegheny Co Lib Serv Carnegie Lib, Pittsburgh 61-62; Dir Clinton-Essex-Franklin Lib System, Plattsburgh NY 62-65; Assoc lib supv Lib Ext Div, Albany NY 65-. 8: Adv, Pub Rel Projs, LSCA Title I, NY State, 66-. 9: ALA (chm State Libs Stat Com); NYLA. 10: Beta Phi Mu. 12: Ed "The Bookmark". 13: Yes. 14: Ref, stat, pub rel, publ. 15: Box 42 Cow Alley, Spencertown NY 12165.

BERRY, SARA NEAL (COUSE). b Binghamton NY 4 Jl 08. 4: Emmitt Berry. 5: Pasadena Jr Col 27-29; Occidental Col 29-31 (Eng) AB; San Jose State Col 31-32 (LS) Credential. 7: Br libn Glendale Pub Lib, Glendale Cal 32-36; Lab sch libn Fresno State Col, Fresno Cal 57-. 8: The Laboratory School Lib was given an ESEA Title II, Phase II grant in 67; Read projects for State of Cal for 68 ESEA Title II, Phases I & II. 9: ALA; CalLA (Rep for Yosemite Dist to Child Serv Div) 68. 12: Co-auth "Building Library Skills". 14: Lib wk with child. 15: 4406 E Iowa, Fresno Ca 93702.

BERRYMAN, CAROLYN (WINIFRED). b St Albans Vt 8 Ap 08. 5: St LawrenceU 26-28; Wayne StateU 28-32; Simmons 32-33 BS, 36-37 Library certif. 6: Fr, Sp. 7: Sec Chevrolet Motor, Detroit 28-32, 34-36; Jr & Sr asst Detroit Pub Lib 37-46, Head bus & com div 47-48; Asst ref libn Hackley Pub Lib, Muskegon Mich 49-. 9: NEA; ALA; MichLA; MichEA. 14: Ref. 15: 1433 Clinton st, Muskegon Mich 49442.

BERSAGEL, VIRGINIA MERLE. b Wakonda SD 24 Je 22. 5: No State Col (Aberdeen SD) 40-41; St Olaf Col 41-44 (Econ) BA; Columbia 60-64 (LS) MS. 7: Sec Dow Chem Co, NYC 44-48; Sec to research dir Conservation Found, NYC 48-56; Head of ref files Inst of Life Insurance, NYC 56-59, Asst libn 59-66, Assoc libn 66-69, libn 69-. 9: SLA (Chm Insur Div 65-66; mem & chm Tellers Com 63-66; NY Chap; chm Insur Group 58-60, 2nd v-pres & ed NY Chap "News" 66-67, Mem Non-Serials Publ Com 67-68, Chm NY Chap Recruitment & Training Com 67-68). 14: Subj ref. 15: Inst of Life Insur 277 Park ave, NYC 10017.

BERTALAN, FRANK JOSEPH. b Edwardsville Ill 18 S 14. 4: Helen Scheck. 5: Ill StateU 36-38 (Math) BEd; UIll 38-42 (LS) BS, MS; CatholicU 58-62 (Higher Educ) PhD. 6: Hungarian. 7: Asst circ libn UIll (Urbana) 40-42; Communications off (Rank-Commander) US Navy, Atlantic Fleet & Eng 42-46; Head ref & bibliog serv Dept of Health, Educ & Welfare, Wash DC 46-50; Chief lib serv div Legis Ref Serv LC 50-55; Head engnr info br US Navy Bur of Aeronautics, Wash DC 55-58; Dep exec asst sci info Off of Naval Research, Wash DC 58-62; Asst Prof Lib Sci CatholicU 62-63; Chief Emergency Measures Proj Div Exec Off of the Pres, Wash DC 63-65; Dir Sch of Lib Sci, U Okla 65-. 8: Adv to US Senate Fin Com for Lib reorg, Wash DC 54; Consul to Commandant US Coast Guard for planning a formal library system, Wash DC 60; Consul to NASA Goddard Space Flight Center, Greenbelt Md 62, for developing Lib acquis policies & procedures. 9: ALA; SLA; AALS; OklaLA SWLA. 10: Kappa Delta Pi; Kappa Mu Epsilon. 12: "Books for Junior Colleges" (54); "Provision of Federal Benefits for Veterans" (55); "Proposed Scope and Coverage of theGoddard Space Flight Center Library" (63); "The Junior College Library Collection" (68). 13: Yes. 14: Documentation, lib sch admin, ref & bibliog in sci & tech. 15: Sch of Lib Sci Univ of Okla, Norman Ok 73069.

BERTHEL, JOHN H(ALLOCK). b Washington Penn 27 Mr 14. 4: Elizabeth Bagby Edwards. 5: Columbia 34-38 (Hist) BA, 38-39 (Hist, Pol Sci) MA, 39-41 (Hist, Pol Sci), 41-42 (LS) BS. 6: Fr. 7: Libn Columbia Col (NY) 42-44; Dept libn Columbia U 44-48, Nicholas Murray Butler Libn 48-54; Hist Instr Columbia Col (NY) 45-48; Instr Sch Lib Serv Columbia U 49-50; Libn Johns Hopkins U 54-. 8: Served on 20 Middle States Accred groups 48-53; Bldg & prog consul to several cols 48- Chm Lib Adv Bd, US Naval Acad, early 60's; George Wash U Lib Adv Coun 67-68. Chm Lib Adv Bd, US Naval Acad, early 60's; George Wash U Lib Adv Coun 67-68. 9: ARL (Chm Univ Micro films Com 67-68); ALA; MdLA. 10: AAUP; Baltimore Bibliophiles. -5 13: Yes. 14: Lib admin, ref, hist of res libs, lib arch, lib automation. 15: 3701 Patterson ave, Baltimore 21207.

BERTHOLD, ARTHUR (BENEDICT). b Dundaga Latvia 8 Ja 05. 4: Katherine Buvinger Hornketh. 5: Colgate 27-31 (Comparative Lit) BA; Columbia 31-32 (LS) BS; Chicago 33-34 (LS) MA. 6: Ger, Latvian, Russian, Sp, Dutch, Fr. 7: Bibliogr trainee NY Pub Lib 35-36; Bibliogr Union Lib Catlg, Phila 36-37, Bibliogr & assoc dir 37-42; Bibliogr & Research analyst OSS, Wash DC 42-45; Chief preparations div UChicago Lib 45-48; US Dept of State Lib, Wash DC: Chief Bibliog Br 48-50; Chief tech serv br 50-51, Chief readers serv br 51-53, Act libn 53-54, Asst libn 54-. 8: Del, FID Conf, Zurich 39; ALA Union Catlg Survey team 39-40. 9: ALA (Catlg Code Rev Com); DCLA. 10: Internat Club of Washington; Beta Phi Mu Amer Name Soc. 11: US Dept of State Commend Service Award 51. 12: Ed "Journal of Cataloging & Classification"; Auth "On the Systematization of Documents in Ancient Times" (38); "Union Catalogs" (36); "Russian Corporate Headings" (39); "Union Catalogs in the United States" (42); "Library of the Department of State" (58). 13: Yes. 14: Personnel train, catlg & clsf, bk sel. 15: 2601 Woodley pl NW, Washington DC 20008.

BERTHOLD, KATHERINE (HORNKETH). b Trenton NJ 8 Ja 07. 4: Arthur B(enedict) Berthold. 5: Wilson Col 25-29 (Fr) BA;Columbia 31-32 (LS) MS, 35-36 (Adult Educ); Temple 36-40 (Span); Northwestern 40 (Art). 6: Fr, Sp. 7: Asst libn Sch Lib ServLib ColumbiaU 32-34; Gen serv asst Teachers College ColumbiaU 35-36; Head circ dept TempleU Lib 36-42; Lib asst US Army AFWeather Div, Wash DC 43; Libn Off of Strategic Serv, Wash DC 43-45; Spec asst ALA, Chicago 46-48; Libn Trans Assn of Amer,Chicago 48; Chief sub Bib Br USIA, Wash DC 51-. 9: SLA; DCLA. 10: AAUW; Corcoran Art Gallery. 13: Yes. 14: Internat rel, bibliog. 15: 2601 Woodley pl NW, Wash DC 20008.

BERTHRONG, MERRILL GRAY. b Cambridge Mass 18 Jl 19. 4: Geraldine Merritt Brock. 5: Tufts 37-41 (Hist) BA; Fletcher Sch Law & Diplomacy 46-47 (Hist) MA; UPenn 50-58 (Hist) PhD. 6: Fr. 7: Pilot (Captain) USAF 42-45; Instr UConn (New London) 47-50; Instr Drexel Inst, RutgersU 52-58; Hd res bk dept UPenn 56-57, Hd circ dept UPenn 57-58, Libn admin 58-64; Dir libs & assoc prof hist, Wake ForestU 64-. 8: Fulbright Research Scholar, France 55-56. 9: ALA; NCLA; SELA. 10: AHA. 14: Col & univ lib admin. 15: Box 7777 Reynolds sta Wake Forest Univ, Winston-Salem NC 27109.

BERTON, ALBERTA D. b Phila 9 S 16. 5: UPenn 34-35 (Pre Med), 35-36 (Med Record Libn). 7: Med Research-Med Histn-Lit Search-Med Textbk Ed & Med Ref 25 yrs; Research libn William H Rorer Inc, Fort Washington Penn60-64; Research libn The Nat Drug Co Div of Richardson-Merrell Inc, Phila 64-67; Dir Med Documentation Serv Col of Physicians,Phila 67-. 8: Campaign res, United Fund-Health & Welfare Coun 56-60; Exec sec, Com on New Growth, Nat Res Coun. 9: SLA (treas Pharmaceut Div 67-69, Bus mgr, Copnip List 68; Phila Chap 1965 Conv Loc ARR Com, chm Memb Com 65, 66, Com to study Chap Bull 66, sec 66-67, Sci-Tech Sect 68-69); MedLA (Phila Chap; Liaison Com for Cont Educ 64-65, Prog Com 65, 66, Ed Jim List 66, Ed & bus mgr Jim List 68-); ASIS; NMA; Drug Info Assn (Charter member); Franklin Inst (Educ Memb); Nat Info Ret Colloq (Planning Com, chm-elect 69-70); PennLA. 12: Principal investigator "Influenza; an Amotated Bibliography"; Ed "Birth Defects"; Ed "Cystic Fibrosis". -4 14: Lit searching, abstracting, editing, transl, tech writing, publ. 15: Med Documentation Serv Col of Physicians 19 S 22nd st, Philadelphia Pa 19103.

BERTRAM, LEE ANN(ETTE) (WHITTLE). b Harlingen Tex 10 O 38. 4: Riley R Bertram. 5: Southwestern U 56-60 (Chem) BS; Carnegie 60-61 MLS; Emory 61-62 Med LA Grade II Certif. 7: Catlgr Sci Lib Eli Lilly & Co, Indianapolis 62-64, Info Systems asst 65-67, Catlgr sci lib 67-. 9: MedLA; SLA (sec Ind Chap 65-66). 10: Delta Delta Delta. 13: Yes. 14: Catlg, sel dissemination info, lib data proc. 15: 90 Herriott st, Franklin In 46131.

BERTRAM, SHEILA JOAN (KELLEY). b Smooth Rock Falls Ont 1 Mr 40. 4: Edward Frank Bertram. 5: McMasterU 58-62 (Chem) BS; Toronto 62-63 BLS; U Ill 65-66 MS, 66-. 7: Staff UAlta 63-65; Fac Sch of Lib Sci UAlta 69-. 9: CanLA;OntLA; ALA. 14: Sci libs, educ for libnship. 15: 807 W Illinois #10, Urbana Il 61801.

BERTRAN, ROSEMARIE M. b Baltimore 6 My 34. 5: DrewU 52-56 (Psych) BA; Columbia 57-58 MSLS. 7: Child libn Queens Borough Pub Lib, Jamaica NY 57-63; Consul Chautauqua-Cattaraugus Lib Syst, Jamestown NY 63-66; Adult consul Ramapo Catskill Lib Syst, Middletown NY 66-. 9: ALA (Aurienne Award Com 62-65); FLIC; NYLA (Adult Serv Standards Com 67-; Awards Com 66, 68, 69; chm Child & YA Serv Sect; Bd 66-67; 2nd v-pres 65-66). 11: Recipient, medal for commun lib serv, VFW 63. 12: Ed Chautauqua-Cattaraugus Lib System "Newsletter" (64-66). 13: Yes. 14: Pub libs (standards & larger units of serv, patterns of statewide lib devel. 15: 241 Commonwealth ave, Middletown NY 10940.

BESANT, LARRY X. b Centralia Ill 13 Mr 35. 4: Jean Hofstetter. 5: Centralia Jr Col 58-59 AA; UIll 59-61 (Chem) BS,MSLS. 7: Staff Sgt USAF Air Intelligence Operations 54-57; Grad asst Bkstacks UIll (Urbana) 61-62; Tech processes libnChemical Abstracts Serv, Columbus Ohio 62-64, Asst libn 64-68; Asst libn UHouston Tech Serv 69-. 9: SLA (chm Chem Div 68-69,chm Scholarship Com 68; mem Tex Chap Publs Com); TexLA; ACS-Houston Sect (chm Textbks & Per Com, Expos Com). 14: Lib automation, tech serv. 15: 4059 Aberdeen, Houston Tx 77025.

BESS, ELVIN DALE. b East St Louis Ill 20 O 16. 4: Anita Allen. 5: WashU (St Louis) 45-49 (Phil) AB; UKy 66-67 MSLS. 6: Fr, Sp. 7: Tank unit commander (1st Lt) USA, US & Philippines 40-45; Sr lib asst UCLA 50-52; Tech publ checker Douglas Aircraft Co, Santa Monica Cal 52-54; Spares analyst Glenn L Martin Co, Baltimore 55-56; Logistics rep Convair-Astronautics, San Diego Cal 56-61; Seminarian Benedictine Order, S Union Ky 62-66; Intern in biomed lib admin Welch Med Lib Johns HopkinsU 67-68; Asst libn Lib of Med Sci Sch of Med UNM 68-. 8: Acting Librarian, Library of the Medical Sciences, School of Medicine, University of New Mexico 1968-. 9: MedLA; NMLA; Greater albuquerqueLA. 14: Admin. 15: Lib of Med Sci School of Med Univ of New Mexico, Albuquerque NM 87106.

BEST, EMILY (DOZIER). b Athens Ga 14 F 10. 4: George H Best. 5: Shorter Col 27-28; UGa 28-31 (Eng, Fr, Educ) AB; Emory 31-32 AB in LS. 6: Fr. 7: Tchr & libn Maysville High Sch, Maysville Ga 32-33; Tchr Greensboro High Sch, Greensboro Ga 33-34; Tchr Athens City Schs, Athens Ga 34-43; Hd libn Daniel Field Air Base, Augusta Ga 43-44; Catlgr UGa Lib 44-50; Asst libn post lib, Ft Monmouth NJ 51-55; Tchr Barnesville Grammar sch, Barnesville Ga 58-66; Asst libn Gordon Military Col 66-. 9: GaEA; GaLA; Ga Assn Jr Cols (Lib Sect). 10: AAUP; Amer Legion Aux; Delta Kappa Gamma; Phi Beta Kappa; Phi Kappa Phi. 14: Catlg, ref. 15: Augusta Lambdin Lib Gordon Military College, Barnesville Ga 30204.

BEST, RUTH (ANDREW). b Newton NC 15 O 15. 5: Catawba Col 32-36 (Hist) AB; Peabody summer 38 (Elem

Educ); UNC 39-40 BA in LS; Appalachian State Teachers Col summer 63 (LS); UNC (Greensboro) 65 (REduc). 6: Fr, Ger. 7: Tchr pub schs, NC 36-39; Asst libn Longwood Col summer 40; Elem libn city schs, Burlington NC 58-. 8: Child Libn Lib/USA, NY World's Fair, 64. 9: ALA; AASchL; NEA; Assn Childhood Educ; SELA; NCLA; NCASchL (dir). 10: Bus & Prof Women's Club; NC Lit & Hist Assn; Alpha Delta Kappa; NC Art Assn. 14: Wkg with child, child bks. 15: 201 Tarpley st, Burlington NC 27215.

BESTEHORN, UTE WILTRUD. b Cologne Germany 6 N 30. 5: UCincinnati 51-54 (Ger) BA, 54-55 (Educ) BE, 57-58 (Educ) MEd; West Res 60-61 MSLS. 6: Ger. 7: Practice tchg Bd of Educ Withrow Jr High Sch, Cincinnati 54; Soc studies tchr Bd of Educ Cutter Jr High Sch, Cincinnati 55-57; Asst Med Record Lib Bethesda Hosp, Cincinnati 58-59; Tchr-libn Felicity-Franklin Sr High Sch, Clermont Co Ohio 59-60; Cleveland Med Lib 61; Libn Sci & Ind dept Pub Lib of Cincinnati & Hamilton Co, Cincinnati 61-. 9: SLA (Cincinnati Chap: Archivist 63-64, ed "Queen City Gazette" 64-66); OhioLA. 10: Delta Phi Alpha. 14: Ref. 15: 3330 Morrison ave, Cincinnati Oh 45220.

BESWICK, BARBARA LOUISE (LANTZ). b Albany NY 25 Ag 38. 4: C Dane Beswick. 5: State U at Albany 60 (Sch Libnship) AB, 64 MLS. 7: Elem sch libn Scotia-Glenville Central Schs, Scotia NY 60-63; Elem sch libn Colonie Central Schs, Albany NY 63-. 9: East NY SchLA (sec 66-68).01225 14: Child lit, catlg. 15: 1 Barker st, Albany NY 12205.

BESWICK, JAY W. b Berea Ohio 25 Mr 13. 5: Baldwin-Wallace Col 30-35 (Eng) AB; West Res 34-40 BS in LS, (Eng) AM; Columbia 40-41 MS in LS. 6: Fr. 7: Subj heading wk-WPA Newspaper Abstracting Proj, Cleveland 36-37; Lib asst Ohio State Archaep& & Hist Soc, Columbus O hio 38; Asst lit dept Pub Lib, Cleveland 38-, Asst hd lit dept 57-68, Hd Lit Dept 68-. 9: ALA; OhioLA. 10: Cleveland Hiking Club. 12: "The Work of Frederick Leypoldt" (42). 14: Ref, bk sel: Lit & Lang. 15: 194 S eminary st, Berea Oh 44017.

BETCHER, WILLIAM MARTIN. b Pittsburgh 6 My 28. 4: Janet Pickenpaugh. 5: Carnegie Inst of Tech 46-48 (Painting & Design); UPittsburgh 48-52 (Eng & Hist) BA; Carnegie Inst of Tech 52-53 MLS. 6: Sp. 7: Ref asst Carnegie Lib, Pittsburgh 53-56; Ref asst Legis Ref Serv LC 56-58; Libn Penn Economy League Inc, Pittsburgh 58-63; Ref asst UPittsburgh 63-65; Ref asst Ohio U 65-66, Ref libn 66-67, Asst libn serv div 67-. 9: ALA; SLA (Adv Coun 64)-Pittsburgh Chap (treas 59-62, v-pres 63-64, pres 64-65); OhioLA. 10: Carnegie Lib Sch Assn (Nat treas 59-62); Kappa Phi Kappa; AAUP. 14: Ref. 15: 70 Maplewood dr, Athens Oh 45701.

BETHKE, BETTY JO (PACE). b Bethany Okla 7 O 24. 4: Dale L Bethke. 5: UTulsa 46-51 (Drama) BA; Immaculate Heart Col 66-69 (LS) MA. 7: Children's libn Azusa Pub Lib, Azusa Cal 65-67; Lib intern Pomona Pub Lib, Pomona Cal 67-68; Sch libn S Hills High Sch, Covina Cal 68-. 9: ALA; CalLA; CalASchL. 15: 2924 Mesa dr, West Covina Ca 91790.

BETHMAN, JANE (DAVID). b Arnold Penn 23 Je 21. 4: Lynn H Bethman. 5: UWash 47-49; UPittsburgh 50-51 (Educ) BS; UWash 64-65 MLS. 7: Sec dept store, Pittsburgh 41-43; Personnel supv US Navy (Womens Reserve), NY & San Francisco 43-46; Tchr Pittsburgh pub schs 51-52; Tchr Highline pub schs, Seattle 52-55; Libn Federal Way pub schs, Federal Way Wash 65-. 9: NEA; WashEA; WashLA; Wash State ASchL. 14: Sch libnship (elem level). 15: 805 S 208th st, Seattle Wa 98148.

BETTERLY, MILDRED V (PALMER). b Reading Kan 24 D 1895. 4: Walter A Betterly. 5: Col of Emporia 15-19 (Eng) BA; Kan State Tchrs Col (Lib) Certif. 7: Kan State Tchrs Col Lib 21-32; State Traveling Lib Commsn & State Lib Topeka Kan 45-49; State Traveling Lib Commsn summer 53; Topeka Pub Lib, Topeka Kan 53-. 9: KanLA. 10: PEO; Daughters of Amer Colonists. 14: Catlg, ref. 15: 307 Roosevelt, Topeka Ks 66606.

BETTS, SALOME. b Montezuma Ga 3 Mr 13. 5: Randolph-Macon Women's Col 31-35 (Math) AB; Emory 35-36 AB in LS. 7: Child libn NY Pub Lib 36-42; Research analyst US Govt, Wash DC 42-46; Asst todir of wk with child Enoch Pratt Free Lib, Baltimore 46-48; Child libn Hawaii Co Lib,Hilo Hawaii 48-50; Research analyst US Govt, Wash DC 50-61; Br libn Atlanta Pub Lib61-. 10: Phi Beta Kappa. 14: Child wk, pub lib wk. 15: 1086 St Charles pl NE, Atlanta Ga 30306.

BETZ, CAROLYN (ANDERSON). b Pueblo Colo 4 S 40. 5: Pueblo Col 58-60 (Liberal Arts) AA; UDenver 60-62 (Eng) BA. 7: Lib page McClelland Pub Lib, Pueblo Colo 55-60; Clk-typist library UDenver 60-62; Intermed clk-typist lib San Francisco State Col 63-64; Lib asst Sacramento State Col 64; Lib asst Foothill Col 65-66; Acting libn Syntex Corp, Palo Alto Cal 66-. 9: SLA. 14: Acquis, catlg. 15: 3865 LaDonna ave, Palo Alto Ca 94306.

BEUTHEL, ELLENGAIL (MAPES). b Jefferson County Colo 24 Ap 29. 4: Donald G Beuthel. 5: UDenver 47-51 (Span) BA, 59-62 (LS) MA. 7: Elem sch libn Denver pub schs 51-52, Tchr 52; Catlgr UDenver Law Lib 53-54; Elem sch libn Denver pub schs 54-55; Catlgr Law Lib Dawson, Nagle, Sherman & Dorsey, Denver 59; Catlgr Law Lib Hughes & Dorsey 60; High sch libn Denver pub schs 62-. 9: ALA; NEA; ColoASchL; ColoLA; ColoEA; Denver CTA. 10: Beta Phi Mu, Phi Beta Kappa, Sigma Kappa. 14: High sch libs, catlg. 15: 3450 S Cherry, Denver Co80222.

BEVINGTON, ELIZABETH (HODSON). b Sheridan Ind 17 Jl 08. 5: Edward W Bevington. 7: Gen asst Pub Lib, Cedar Rapids Iowa 36-43; Acquis head Ind State Lib 47-48; Lib asst Union Hosp Sch of Nursing, Terre Haute Ind 54; Unit libn Community Unit C-2 Schs, Marshall Ill 54-. 9: ALA; AASchL; NEA; IllLA, IllASchL; IllEA. 10: AAUW; Beta Phi Mu. 14: Rare bks, ref. 15: 1625 N 8th st, Terre Haute Ind 47804.

BEVIS, (LEURA) DOROTHY. b Duluth Minn 19 Ap 04. 5: Pomona Col 27 (Lit, Hist) BA; PurdueU 45 (Personnel Admin); USoCal 47 BS in LS; Uwash 51 (Compar Lit) MA; Columbia 59-60 (LS). 6: Fr, Sp. 7: Social wker YWCA, Los Angeles 27-28; Research spec Dawson's Rare Bk Shop, Los Angeles 29-39; Ed & manager San Pasqual Press, Pasadena Cal 39; Asst ed promotion dir UCal Press (Berkeley) 40-43; USCG (WR) Lt Commander Personnel, Seattle 43-46; Ref libn Long Beach Pub Lib, Long Beach Cal 47; Adult serv coordinator Glendale Pub Lib, Glendale Cal 48; Br libn Seattle Pub Lib 52, Spec assignment adult educ 53; Visiting prof Sch of Lib Sci USoCal summer 51; Visiting Lecturer Sch of Lib Serv ColumbiaU summer 60; Faculty UWash 47-, Assoc dir Sch of Libnship 59, Prof 60-. 8: Spec assignment adult educ Seattle Pub Lib 52; Consul Decision is Destiny Wkshop UWash 65; Consul USOE Conf of Lib Educrs 65; Adv No Central Reg Lib Conf 64; Co-Sponsor Fed Records Center Inst 64; Ref consul, Tri-State Lib Conf 63; Consul, Rocky Mountain Conf on Lib Educ 62; Wash State Chm Nat Lib Week 58; Consul, Idaho LA Conf 57; Spec eval Sutro Lib of Cal State Lib 57 Wash State Lib, 66-68; ALA Surveyor for Lib Educ, Korea, Philippines, Lebanon, 68; -Consul on sch libnship, Medeli3n Columbia 61; Accreditation visits for NW Higher Educ Assn 65. 9: ALA (Coun-at-large 65-68 Z 39 Rep ASA 55-60); -LED (rec sec 61-62, Publ Com 61-); -RTSD (asst ed "LRTS" 60-64); AALS (v-pres & pres-elect 64-66, Rep to ALA Coun 58-&65); PNLA (Exec Bd 65; chm Lib Ed Div 58-59 & 65-66, mem Publ Com 55, chm Pub Rel Com 48-49); WashLA (Exec Bd 58-59 & 61-62, chm Publ Com 56-57). 10: Phi Beta Kappa; Beta Phi Mu; AAUP; Wash Hist Soc; UWash: Inst of Govt: Women's Faculty Club, Faculty Senate Publ Com, Adult Educ Com, Faculty Senate Fin Aids Com, Faculty Senate For Students Com. 11: Theta Sigma Phi Award Seattle'w Six Women of Achievement 65. 12: "Silver Farthing" (33); Ed "Institute of Government Proceedings" (50); "Changing Patterns of Reference(52); 'Virginia Wolf, Symbol and Thought' in "Twentieth Century Literature" (59) "Inventory of Washington State Libraries and Library Resources", (69). 13: Yes. 14: Ref, bibliog, rare bks, interna libnship & lib educ. 15: Sch of Libnship Univ of Wash, Seattle 98105.

BEWLEY, GLADYS (PALMER). b NJ 19 Mr 23. 4: Philip B Bewley. 5: Douglass Col 40-44 (Span) BA; Rutgers 59-63 MLS. 6: Sp, Fr. 7: Ref libn catlgr PUB Lib, Haddonfield NJ 63-66; Asst Dir 67-; Asst Pub Lib Consul Drexel-Penn State Lib, 66-67. 9: ALA; NJLA. 10: Beta Phi Mu. 14: Admin, catlg, ref. 15: 208 Mt Vernon ave, Haddonfield NJ 08033.

BEWLEY, MRS LOIS M (CROOK). b Regina Sask Can 3 Ap 26. 5: UBC 43-47 (Hist, Eng) BA; Toronto 48-49 BLS; UIll 65- (LS)66 MS in LS. 7: Libn I Vancouver Pub Lib, Vancouver BC 49-54; Archives libn MacMillan-Bloedell Co, Vancouver BC 55; Researcher Encyclopedia Canadiana, Vancouver BC 55-56; Libn I Vancouver Pub Lib, Vancouver BC 57-61; Act libn on loan Ext Lib UBC 61; Libn II Vancouver Pub Lib, Vancouver BC 62-65; Research assoc Lib Research Ctr UIll (Urbana) 66-67; Project coord N Sacramento Valley Lib Coop, Chico Cal 67-68; Lect & Coord of continuing educ, Libnship UCal Sch of Libnship (Berkeley) 68-. 9: ALA; CanLA; BCLA (past pres); AALS; CalLA. 10: Vancouver Pub Lib Staff Assn; Assn BC Libns; Beta Phi Mu. 13: Yes. 14: Tchg. 15: School of Librarianship, Univ of Cal, Berkeley Ca 94720.

BEWSEY, JULIA J. b Frankfort Ind 25 Je 28. 5: ButlerU 46-50 (Span) BA; IndU 57-60 (LS) MA, 65- (LS). 7: Jr libn Indianapolis Pub Lib 46-50; Assoc libn Eli Lilly & Co, Indianapolis 51-60; Asst prof & Asst Libn Ill StateU 60-. 9: ALA; ASIS; IllLA; McLean CoLA. 10: Zeta Tau Alpha; Alpha Beta Alpha. 12: Comp of index for "Diabetes" (56-57); Comp, KWIC Index of Ill StateU Theses and Dissertations" (68-). 14: Catlg, automation. 15: 301 Oakdale ave, Normal Ill 61761.

BEYERLY, HAROLD. b Rotterdam Holland 31 Ja 26. 5: CZ Jr Col 43-44; London U 47 (Russ); Columbia 47-51 (Russ) Ba, MA, 51-52 (LS) MS. 6: Eng, Fr, Russ, Serbo-Croatian, Sp, Ger, Dutch. 7: Pvt US Army 45-47; Libn trainee LC 52-53, Catlgr 53-55, Ref libn 55-57; Catlgr United Nations Lib, Geneva Switzerland 57- 60, Ref libn 60-64; Acquis libn Dag Hammarskjold Lib, United Nations NY 64-68, Libn UNIDO Lib (UN), Vienna Austria 68-. 15: UNIDO, Vienna Austria.

BEYMER, CHARLES RICHARD. b Tacoma Wash 10 S 27. 4: Kathleen Jannucci. 5: Washington State Col 46-49 (Math, Econ); UWAash summers 49 & 50; UWis 49-50 (Econ) BS; UCal at Berkeley 52-53 (Astron); UWis Lib Sch 54-55 MSLS. 6: Fr, Sp. 7: S 1/C USN Reserve 45-46; Stud asst Circ dept UWis Lib 54-55; Marquette Lib: Acquis libn 55-57, Asst catlg libn 57-59; Asst catlgr Cornell Lib 59-61; UNotre Dame Lib: Asst acquis libn 61-63, Hd gen sci dept 63-66; Hd tech serv Cal State Polytech Cal 66-. 9: ALA; -ACRL; -RTSD. 10: Cal State Employees Assn; Boy Scouts. 14: Admin, acquis, bibliog. 15: 217 Westmont, San Luis Obispo Ca 93401.

BIAGINI, MARY KATHRYN. b Charleroi Penn 30 N 42. 5: Cal State Col 60-63 (Eng) BS; Kent State 64-65 MLS. 6: Ital. 7: Eng tchr Innes Jr High Sch, Akron Ohio 63-64; Libn Hyre Jr High Sch, Akron Ohio 65-68; Instr & coordinator of Fed programs Sch of Lib Sci Kent State 68-. 8: Consulting Materials Specialist, Sch of Lib Sci, Kent State U Kent Ohio 67.68. 9: AAL; AALS; OhioLA; OhioASchL. 10: Beta Phi Mu. 14: Sch lib, ya serv, bk sel. 15: 1350 N Howard st apt 612, Akron Oh 44310.

BIALAC, VERDA (JOAN HOSTETLER). b Flandreau SD 29 Ja 37. 4: George D Bialac. 5: Goshen Col 54-59 (Eng) BA; Ind U 60-62 (LS) MA. 6: Sp, Fr. 7: Eng & Span tchr Millersburg High Sch, Millersburg Ind 59-60; Head libn Shawnee Mission West High Sch, Shawnee Mission Kan62-65; Libn 1 asst catlgr Omaha Pub Lib 65-68; Inst libn 111 Rainier State Sch, Olympia Wash 69-. 9: ALA; WashStateLA. 10: Pi Lambda Theta; YWCA. 14: Catlg, admin. 15: 1443 Raini er ct #4, Tacoma Wa 98466.

BIANCARDO, LENA L. b NYC 21 My 18. 4: Joseph M Biancardo. 5: Brooklyn Col 39 (Eng) AB; Columbia 41 BLS, 50 MLS. 6: Ital. 7: Lib asst circ NY Pub Lib 41-42; Chief of tech serv Queens Col Lib (NY) 43-. 9: NYLib Club; NY Resources & Tech Serv Libns. 10: AAUP. 15: Queens Col Lib, Flushing NY 11367.

BIANCHI, RUTH (ZINGELBACH). b Israel 9 Mr 45. 4: James Bianchi. 5: UCLA 62-66 (Ger) BA, 66-67 MLS. 6: Ger. 7: Child libn LA Co Pub Lib 67-. 9: CalLA. 10: Phi Beta Kappa. 14: Child, ya serv. 15: 3326 Keystone ave 10, Los Angeles Ca 90034.

BIBBY, MILTON STUART. b Elba NY 9 D 20. 4: Irene E Sexton. 5: Brockport State Tchrs Col 39-40; UBuffalo 47-49 (Eng) BA; Syracuse 49-50 MSLS. 7: Gunnery sgt USMC 40-46; Clk Buffalo Pub Lib, Buffalo NY 47-49, Jr libn 50-52, Sr libn I 53-54; Hd bk care Buffalo & Erie Co Pub Lib, Buffalo NY 54-64, Hd order dept 64-. 8: Mem, Adv Com on Acquis Procedures for ANYLTS (Association of New York Libraries for Technical Services) 1969. 9: Assn NY Libs Tech Serv (Adv Com on Acquis Procedures 69); NYLA (Legisl Com 55-57, Exhibit Com 65). 14: Tech serv. 15: 239 Warren ave, Kenmore NY 14217.

BICHTELER, JULIE (HALLMARK, NOTT). b Houston 27 My 8. 4: Klaus Bichteler. 5: UTex 56-60; Chem; BS, 63-65 MLS; So Methodist U 65-68 (Geol). 7: Research asst Biochem Dept UTex summer 59 & 63; Chem Dow Chem Co, Midland Mich 60-62; Intern NASA Manned Spacecraft Center Tech Lib Houston 64 SCAS libn Sci Lib So Methodist U 64-; Lecturer Grad Sch LibSci U Tex (Austin) 69-. 9: SLA; Employ (chm Tex Chap 65-66, Sec 68-69); TexLA; Geosci Info Soc; SLA sec Tex Chap 68-69. 10: Iota Sigma Pi; Phi Beta Kappa. 12: Ed "Texas Looks at Science Information, Proceedings of a Symposium" SLA (66). 13: Yes. 14: Sci ref, interlib loan. 15: Grad School of Lib Sci Univ of Texas, Austin Tex 78712.

BICKFORD, ISABEL H. b Waynesburg Penn 2 Mr 14. 4: Richard H Bickford. 5: UCal (Berkeley) 33-37 (Econ) BA; Claremont Col 40-41 (Sociol, Educ) Genl Sec; SUNY (Geneseo) 64-66 MLS. 7: Tchr Home Econ & Sci: Chaffey Union High Sch, NY 41-43, Coachell Valley Union High Sch, 44-45, Fullerton Union High Sch 45-46; Sci libn Willaimsville Sr High Sch, Williamsville NY 65-. 15: 162 Highland dr, Williamsville NY 14221.

BICKFORD, SHIRLEY (SHACTER). b Rochester NY 13 Ag 23. 5: Brockport State Teachers Col 41-45 (Educ) BEd; URochester even 45-48 (Art); Geneseo State Teachers Col summers 52-56 MSLS. 6: Fr. 7: Elem tchr Indian Landing Sch, Rochester NY 45-48; Elem tchr George M Diven Sch, Elmira NY 50-51; Elem tchr Hendy Ave Sch, Elmira NY 51-53, Libn K-8 53-64, Libn K-6 64-. 9: NYLA; NYState Tchrs Assn; Sch Libns So Tier (NY). 10: Beta Phi Mu. 14: Child lit, rare bks. 15: 69 Ohio ave, Elmira NY 14905.

BICKSTON, DEVERTT DRAKE. b Rockford Ill 2 Jl 33. 4: Diane Davis. 5: UColo 58-61 (Eng) BA; UTex 66-68 MLS. 6: Fr. 7: Radio Announcer KGFL, Roswell NM 56-57; USAF-S/Sgt Radio Maint Var bases, Korea, Japan, US 53-57; Insurance investigator Retail Credit Co, Denver 57-61; Tchr Grant High Sch, Fox Lake Ill 61-63; Tchr Arlington High Sch, arlington Tex 63-66; Lib ref asst UTex (Austin) 67-68; Info spec So Methodist U (Dallas) 68-; Field rep Industrial Info Serv 68-. 10: Dallas C of C; Lasso Club. 12: Ed "Industrial Information Services Newsletter" (68). 14: Consulting with bus firms about info prob, lit searching, bibliog, holding educ seminars for indus. 15: 3057 Fondren, Dallas Tx 75205.

BIDA, OLGA (JUDD) S(TOTZ). b Easton Penn 22 Je 09. 5: Mt Holyoke 27-31 (Archaeol) AB; LehighU summer 30 (Educ); Muhlenberg Col summer 31 (Educ); Penn State Col Fr Inst summer 32-33 (Fr); Columbia 45-46 BS in ls. 6: Fr. 7: Tchr of Lat & libn Wolf Jr High Sch, Easton Penn 35-45; Catlgr Great Neck Lib, Great Neck NY 46-47; Catlgr Hempstead Pub Lib, Hempstead NY 48-54; Instr even Lib Sch Pratt Inst 49-51; Asst lib dir Hempstead Pub Lib, Hempstead NY 54-. 9: Nassau Co LA. 10: Mt Holyoke Club of LI; South Shore Club. 14: Admin, ref. 15: 210 Cedar st, Hempstead NY 11550.

BIDDISON, DONALD GERALD. b Milwaukee Wi. 5: UWis 53-57 (Eng Lit) BA, 59-60 (LS) MA. 6: Sp. 7: Stud asst Wis State Hist Soc Lib, Madison Wis 55-57; Milwaukee Pub Lib Jr Libn 57-59; Milwaukee Pub Lib Libn Sci Div 60-62; Milwaukee Pub Lib Hd Natural Sci & Ag Dept 62-64; Milwaukee Pub Lib Br Hd E Br 64-66; Milwaukee Pub Lib Br Hd N Br 66; UWis Asst ref libn 66-. 9: ALA. 14: Admin, ref. 15: 2525 S Shore dr, Milwaukee Wi 53207.

BIDLACK, RUSSELL EUGENE. b Manilla Iowa 25 My 20. 4: Melva Helen Sparks. 5: Simpson Col 38-41, 46-47 (Eng) AB; UMich 47-48 ABLS, 48-49 AMLS, 49-50 (Hist) AM, 50-54 (LS) PhD. 7: (M/Sgt) US Army Corps Engrs (Atomic Bomb Proj) 41-46; Act libn Simpson Col summer 47; UMich: Tchg fellow 49-52, Instr 52-56, Asst Prof 56-60, Assoc Prof 60-65, Prof 65-, Dean Sch Lib Sci 69-. 9: ALA; MichLA. 10: Mich Hist Soc. 12: "Letters Home (60); "The Nucleus of a Library (62); "John Allen and the Founding of Ann Arbor (62). 13: Yes. 14: Catlg, hist of libs, hist of child lit. 15: 1709 Cherokee rd, Ann Arbor Mi 48104.

BIEBEL, SUSAN C. b New Brunswick NJ 18 S 42. 5: Col of Wooster 60-64 (Math) BA; Columbia 67-68 MLS. 6: Fr, Ger. 7: Media estimator Doyle Dane Bernbach Inc, NYC 65-67; Research asst LC 68-. 9: ALA. 14: Ref, lib automation. 15: 7301 Keystone lane apt 301, Forestville Md 20028.

BIEBUSH, BARBARA ANN. b Vallejo Cal 10 Ap 32. 5: Oceanside-Carlsbad Col 50-52 AA; Stanford 52-54 AB; UCal (Berkeley) 55-56 MLS. 7: Libn Santa Rosa Center, San Francisco State Col 56-59; Army libn, Augsburg & Lenggris Germany 59-61; Base libn March AF Base, Cal 62; Ref libn Sonoma State Col 62-. 8: Lib/USA NY World's Fair, 65. 9: CalLA. 10: AAUP; Assn Cal State Col Professors; Phi Beta Kappa; Beta Phi Mu; AFT. 14: Ref. 15: Sonoma State Col Lib, 1801 E Cotati ave, Rohnert Park Ca 94928.

BIEL, JOSEPH L. b NYC 31 Mr 30. 4: Rachel Melrose Biel. 5: Rutgers 62-66 MLS; Trenton State Col 56-59 (Elem Educ) Teaching Cert; Ohio State 50-53 (Hist) BA; CCNY 49-50 Liberal Arts. 7: Clk NY Pub Lib 48-50; Specialist 2 USA Ft Meade Md 54-56; Tchr Bordentown Twp Pub Schs Bordentown NJ 56-58; Tchr Hamilton Twp Pub Schs Trenton NJ 58-63; Elem Sch Libn S Brunswick Twp Pub Sch Monmouth Jct NJ 63-67; Act Coord of Lib Serv Englewood Pub Schs Englewood NJ 67-68; Dean of Lib Instruction Pennsbury Sch Dist

Fallsington Penn 68-. 9: ALA; NEA; NJLA; PennStateEA; BCSchLA; NJSchLA. 10: ACD. 14: Sch lib, child lit. 15: 9 Harbor rd, Levittown Pa 19056.

BIELENBERG, (WALDO) LARRY. b Los Angeles 18 Mr 39. 4: Jill McGrew. 5: Wartburg 57-60 (Hist); Pepperdine 62 (Hist); Cal Lutheran 63-65 (Hist) BA (Magna Cum Laude); USoCal 65-68 MS in LS. 6: Ger. 7: Asst mgr Standard Stations Inc Inglewood Cal 61-64; Lib trainee USoCal 65-66; Libn Lutheran High Sch 66-69; Dir of tech serv Concordia Sem 69-. 9: ALA; CalASchL. 10: Beta Phi Mu. 14: Catlg, ser, ref. 15: Concordia Sem 801 De Mun, St Louis Mo 63105.

BIEN, BETTINA (HERBERT). b Wash DC 21 Jl 17. 5: Wheaton Col Norton Mass 34-38 (Botany) BA; American U 48-49 (Econ); NYU 51-52 (Econ); Columbia U Sch of Lib Sci 64-67 MLS. 6: Sp, Ger. 7: Sec 39-42; Admin asst Foreign Econ Admin Wash DC Bolivia & Austria 39-43; Sec in export dept Smith Kline & French Philadelphia 46-47; Asst to exec dir Fed for Freedom Wash DC 47-48; Off mgr Thos L Phillips realtor Wash DC 48-51; Sr staff mem economist libn & dir of debate materials Fed for Econ Educ Irvington NY 51-. 9: AEA; AHA; ALA. 12: "The Works of Ludwig von Mises" Bibliog (62). 14: Ref, econ research. 15: 19 Pine lane, Irvington on Hudson NY 10533.

BIERMAN, KENNETH JOHN. b Aberdeen SD 27 My 44. 5: Hanover Col 62-66 (Eng, Math) BA; UOkla 66-68 (LS, Math) MLS. 6: Ger. 7: Asst ed "Mathematical Log" Mu Alpha Theta, Norman Okla 66-68; Supv automated ser holding list, UOkla 67-68; Data processing coord Okla Dept of Libs, Okla City 68-. 9: ALA; SWLA; OklaLA. 11: H W Wilson Scholarship Recipient. 13: Yes. 14: Lib automation, tech serv, ref. 15: Oklahoma Dept of Libraries 109 State Capitol, Oklahoma City Ok 73105.

BIERWAGEN, EMMA T. b Dresden ND 19 D 04. 5: UCal 31 (Ger) AB, 32 Gen Secondary Certif, 34 Library Certif, 34 Spec Secondary Cred of Libnship; Interstate Col of Personology 65 Analyst, Instr. 6: Ger. 7: Asst & child libn Oroville Pub Lib, Oroville Cal 35-37; Libn Porterville Pub Lib, Porterville Cal 38-42, Br libn McKinley Br Lib 42-68; Personnel libn Sacramento City Lib 68-. 9: CalLA (pres Golden Empire Dist); Amer Assn Personologists. 10: Sacramento City Employees Assn (pres); AAUW; Sierra Club; Nat Health Fed; Interstate Col of Personology; Amer BusWomens Assn. 15: 3141 McKinley blvd Apt C, Sacramento Ca 95816.

BIETH, RUBY MYRA (HUDSON). b Ottawa Ont Can. 5: UToronto 35-37 BA, 37-38 BLS. 6: Fr, Ger. 7: Libn Lambton Co Lib Assn Sarnia Can 38-40; Lib asst "Toronto Star", Toronto Can 40-41; Hd Naval Serv Lib, Ottawa Can 41-47; Asst Hartford Pub Lib, Hartford Conn 47-67, Act hd art, mus & recreation dept 67-. 9: ALA; ConnLA. 10: Wadsworth Atheneum; Humane Soc; Wilderness Soc; Audubon Soc. 14: Art, mus, films, ref. 15: Hartford Pub Lib 500 Main st, Hartford Ct 06103.

BIGBEE, ELLEN ORA. b Simpson County Ky 12 O 25. 5: Ky State Col 51-55 (Home Econ) BS; West Ky State Col summers 56, 57 (LS) State Certif; Peabody summers 61-63 (LS) MA. 7: Biol & hist tchr High Street High Sch, Bowling Green Ky 55-56; Sci tchr & libn Lincoln High Sch, Franklin Ky 56-65; Biol & asst libn franklin-Simpson Sr High Sch, Franklin Ky 65-68; Libn Franklin Elem Schs & Asst Libn Franklin-Simpson Sr High Sch 68-. 9: NEA; KyEA; KyASchL; Third Dist (Ky) EA; Simpson Co EA. 10: Commun Theatre Gp. 14: Catlg. 15: Palm st, Franklin Ky 42134.

BIGGANE, ARLENE FRANCES. b Saskatoon Sask 14 S 45. 5: UBrit Columbia 63-67 (Eng & Sp) BA, 67-68 BLS. 6: Fr, Sp. 7: Libn Grade I UAlberta 68-. 9: CanLA; ALA; Assn Prof Libns Alta. 14: Catlg. 15: Apt 907 11145-87 ave, Edmonton 61 Alberta Can.

BIGGERT, ELIZABETH COLETTE. b Columbus Ohio 23 S 15. 5: St Mary of the Springs Col 33-37 (Eng) BA; West Res 37-38 BS in LS. 6: Fr. 7: Asst catlgr Toledo Pub Lib, Toledo Ohio 39-40; Catlg & ref asst Ohio Hist Soc, Columbus Ohio 40-43; Lt (jr grade) US Navy libn WAVE Midshipman Sch, Northampton Mass 43-46; Mss libn Ohio Hist Soc, Columbus Ohio 46-53; Ref libn Columbus Pub Lib, Columbus Ohio 53-56; Libn Econ Lib Battelle Mem Inst, Columbus Ohio 56-. 9: SLA (chm Nomin Com-Metals/Materials Div 65-66); CathLA (pres Columbus Unit 56-57). 10: Franklin CoLA; Reserve Off Assn; Columbus Symphony Orchestra; Kappa Gamma Pi; Columbus Gall of Fine Arts; Franklin CoHist Soc. 12: "Guide to the Manuscript Collections in the Library of the Ohio State Archaeological and Historical Society" (53). 13: Yes. 14: Bus & econ. 15: 2409 E Broad st, Columbus Oh 43209.

BIGGLESTONE, W E. b Chicgo Ill 20 Jl 24. 4: Mary Grady. 5: UAriz 46-50 (Hist) AB; Stanford 50-51 (Hist) MA. 7: Archivist (staff) Nat Archives, Wash DC 59-60; Archivist Firestone Tire & Rubber Co, Akron Ohio 60-66; Archivist Oberlin Col 66-. 9: SAA; AHA; Ohio Hist Soc. 15: Oberlin Col Archives, Oberlin Oh 44074.

BIGGS, KATARINA (BRACKER). b Providence RI 12 Jl 46. 5: Central Wesleyan 62-64; Furman 64-66 (Educ) BA; Peabody Lib Sch 67-68 MLS. 7: Singer in traveling show Splendor Productions for Chrysler Corp, Detroit 66-67; Lib asst Peabody Mus Lib Nashville Tenn 68; Period libn Tenn A&I State U 68-. 9: TennLA (Memb Chm 69). 14: Ref, music, nat sci. 15: Rte 4 Grandview circle, Travelers Rest SC 29690.

BIGGS, MARTHA LYDIA. b Dubuque Iowa 24 D 07. 5: Lake Forest Col 25-29 (Eng) BA; UWis 29-30 (LS) Certif; UIll 48-50 (LS) MS. 6: Fr, Ger. 7: Asst libn Bradley Polytech Inst, Peoria Ill 30-37; Assoc libn Lake Forest Col 37-43, Head libn 37-. 9: ALA-ACRL (chm Col Libs Sect 57-58, 65-66); IllLA (chm Col & Ref Libs Sect 54). 10: AAUP; Delta Kappa Gamma. 13: Yes. 14: Admin. 15: Donnelley Lib Lake Forest College, Lake Forest College, Lake Forest Il 60045.

BIGNELL, DOUGLAS (CHARLES). b England 20 Ag 33. 4: Barbara Brown. 5: UBC 65-68 (Hist) BA, 68-69 BLS. 6: Fr. 7: Stud nurse (RN) Royal Lancaster Infirmary, UK 51-54; Sgt royal Army Med Corps British Army, UK & Cyprus 54-57; Psychiatric stud nurse Lancaster Moor Hosp, UK 57-60; Psychiatric nurse BC Govt Health Serv, Essondale BC 60-68; Med libn USask 69-. 9: CanLA; ALA; MedLA. 14: Med libnship. 15: Medical Librarian Univ of Saskatchewan, Saskatoon Sask Can.

BIL, DRAHA. b Czechoslovakia. 4: Milos Bil. 5: Gymnasium (Czechoslovakia) Matura; CharlesU (Prague) (Law) Dr iur utr; Columbia 60-61 (LS) MS. 6: Czech, Slovak, Ger, Fr. 7: Attorney and Surrogate Judge, Czechoslovakia; Catlgr Columbia Med Lib 62-64;Internat Law Libn ColumbiaU Law Lib, Hd 64-67; Hd HUD Fed Lib 67-. 8: Bibliogresearch for the Hague Ac Intern Law Recrueil de cours, 66. 9: AALL; Amer Soc ofintern at Law; Hague Academy Internat Law; AAA, The Netherlands. 10: Columbia UnivAlum Assn. 14: Internat law, law, ref, libn mgt & admin. 15: 110-50 71st rd,Forest Hills NY 11375.

BILANCIO, LEWIS. b Trenton NJ 16 F 15. 4: Gloria Lewis. 5: Trenton State Teachers Col 35-39; Rutgers 39-40 SB; Columbia 40-42 BLS; UIll (Champaign-Urbana) ASTP 43; U Train Center (US Army) (Florence Italy) 45; Chicago 46-49 (LS) AM; Ecole Berlitz (Paris) summer 50 (Fr conversation); UPerugia (Italy) 50; URome (Italy) (Istituto di Palegrafia e Biblioteconomia) 49-52. 6: Fr, Ital. 7: Fellow in the Lib Ref Col of the City of NY 40-41; Stack chief NY Pub Ref Lib41-42; Tech Sgt US Army, US, Africa, Italy 42-46; Grad lib asst UChicago 46-48; GradFulbright Grantee, Rome Italy 49-51; Libn II Free Lib of Phila 53-54; Tchr-libnSolebury Sch, New Hope Penn 54-55; Glassboro State Col; Instr in Lib Sci 55-56, Reflibn 56-. 8: Great Books Group organizer and leader 53-65; Tour Director andgroup org (Europe) 57-; Drexel Institute, Phila summer 65. 9: Libs Unlimited (v-pres). 10: C of C; Glassboro Tercentenary Com; Kappa Delta Pi; Ruling Elder,presbyterian Church. 11: Fulbright Fellow, Italy 49-51; Men of the Year, GlassboroC of C, 67. 12: Ed "Bibliomancer" (62-68); Ed "Libraries Unlimited Newsletter" (67-). 13: Yes. 14: Ref. 15: Lib Glassboro State Col, Glassboro NJ 08028.

BILINSKI, REV DONALD (STANLEY) OFM. b Waite Park Minn 14 D 16. 5: St Francis Col (Burlington Wis) 34-39 (Philos) BA; St Mary of the Angels Major Sem 39-42 (Theol); Chicago 43-44 BLS; Amer U 51 Catholic U (LS) 52; Harvard 53. 6: Polish, Lat. 7: Admin of Libs Franciscan Fathers, Assumption Prov 43-, Dean of Studies 51-54, Councilman 54-60, Educ bd mem 54-. 9: ALA; CathLA; (chm Seminary sect); WisLA; Wis CathLA (past chm); Franciscan Educ Con (chm & sec Lib sect); Amer Correctional Chaplains Assn. 12: Ed "Franciscan Librarian Contact" (47-); Jt auth "Franciscan Subject Headings". 14: Catalog archives, Museology. 15: Provincial Lib 774 Lake Shore dr, Lake Geneva Wi 53147.

BILLER, FLORENCE ELIZABETH. b Grafton ND 8 Ja 15. 5: MiamiU (Ohio) 33-37 (Eng) AB; UMinn 49-50 BSLS. 7: Asst ed Oral Hygiene, Evanston Ill 45-49; Asst co libn Whitman Co Lib, Colfax Wash 50, Co Libn 50-54; Reg libn Ft Loudoun Reg Lib, Athens Tenn 54-58; Co Libn Lassen-Plumas

Cos, Susanville Cal 58-60; Lib consul Cal State Lib 60-66; Dir lib constr dept Fla State Lib 67-68; Dir Palm Beach Co Lib Syst, WestPalm Beach Fla 69. 9: ALA (chm Dorothy Canfield Fisher Award Com 62-63); CalLA;FlaLA; SELA. 13: Yes. 14: Lib consul serv, adult serv, pub lib admin. 15: 241 Mercury cir apt 5, N Palm Beach Fl 33403.

BILLERT, JULIA A. b Hoosick Falls NY 13 Jl 38. 5: SUNY (Plattsburgh) 62-66 (Liberal Arts) BA, SUNY (Albany) 66-69 MLS. 6: Ger. 7: Asst libn SUNY (Plattsburgh) 65-69; Hd catlgr Bemidji State Col 69-. 9: ALA; NYLA; SUNYLA. 10: AAUP. 13: Yes. 14: Catlg. 15: A C Clark Lib Bemidji State Col, Bemidji Mn 56601.

BILLINGS, HAROLD WAYNE. b Cain City Tex 12 N 31. 4: Bernice Schneider. 5: Pan Amer Col 49-53 (Physics) BA; UTex 54-57 MLS. 6: Fr, Sp. 7: Tchr Pharr-San Juan-Alamo High Sch, Pharr Tex 53-54; UTex; Catlgr 54-57, Asst chief catlg libn 57-64, Acquis libn 64-67, Asst Libn 67-. 9: TexLA, ALA. 12: Ed The Leafless American, by Edward Dahlberg (67); Edward Dahlberg; American Ishmael of Letters (68). 13: Yes. 14: Acquis, Catlg, rare bks. 15: 2201 Delcrest dr, Austin Tx 78704.

BILLINGS, JANE (ELIZABETH KELLY). b Watertown Wis 10 Je 16. 4: Robert E Billings. 5: Northwestern Col 34-36; UWis 36-38 (US Hist) BA, 38-39 BLS, 62 MA in LS. 6: Ger. 7: Asst Watertown (Wis) Pub Lib 34-36; Libn Finney Pub Lib, Clintonville Wis 39-49; Supv sch libs Pub Schs, Clintonville Wis 49- Visiting lecturer UWis Lib Sch summers 63-69. 8: Wis Governor's Adv Coun on Lib Devel (chm 69). 9: ALA (Grolier-Americana Scholarship Com, NCTE-AASchL Jt Com on Censorship); NEA; WisLA (past sec, past pres); WisEA (past pres Sch Lib Sect). 10: Wis Hist Soc (Life mem); Wis CTE; AAUW; Amer Field Serv; Delta Kap pa Gamma; UWis Lib Sch Alumni Assn; Wis Coun of Tchrs of Eng, Wis Dept A-V Instr. 11: Wisconsin Librarian of the Year, 63, WisLA. 12: Ed "Library Curriculum Guide" Wis Dept of Pub Instr (67-69). 13: Yes. 14: Reading guidance of superior studs in sch lib wk. 15: 158 N Clinton ave, Clintonville Wi 54929.

BILLINGS, KATHRYN ANN (HEISMAN). b Oshkosh Wis 18 Ja 29. 4: Robert Keeler Billings. 5: UWis 46-50 (Eng) BA, 50-51 MA in LS. 6: Sp. 7: Stud asst UWis Lib (Madison) 47-51; Asst ref & circ libn Kellogg Pub Lib, Green Bay Wis 51-55; Asst libn hist & lit dept Pub Lib of Cincinnati & Hamilton Co Ohio 55-58; Asst hd home reading div Madison pub Lib, Madison Wis 58-60; Asst libn art & music dept Kan City (Mo) Pub Lib 60-62, Asst br libn SE Br 63; Ropkins br libn Hartford Pub Lib, Hartford Conn 63-65, Bkmob libn 66-. 9: ConnLA. 14: Wk with adults in art, mus, lit, a-v materials. 15: 350 Connecticut ave, Newington Ct 06111.

BILLINGS, ROBERT KEELER. b Lewiston Me 10 S 20. 4: Kathryn Heisman. 5: UMich 38-53 (Econ, Eng) AB, MA; UKy 58 (LS); UWis 58-60 (LS) MS. 6: Fr. 7: Army Finance Dept, US, India 43-46; Asst libn Times-Star Newspaper, Cincinnati 55-57; Instr Eng Dept UKy 57; Lib asst Madison Pub Lib, Madison Wis 58-60; Libn Kan City Art Inst, Kan City Mo 60-63; Libn Hartford Conn Pub Lib 63-65; Libn E Hartford Conn Pub Lib summer 65; Libn Central Conn State Col 65-69, Catlg Dept 69-. 9: ALA. 14: Catlg. 15: 350 Connecticut ave, Newington Ct 06111.

BILLINGSLEY, ALICE (SCHNELL). b Buffalo NY 1 D 21. 5: Buffalo State Tchrs Col 38-39 (Home Econ); UBuffalo 46-53 (Gen Sci) BA; Catholic U 57 (Med Libnship); American U 62-64, 69 (Mgt of Sci & Tech). 6: Ger. 7: Head libn Durez Plastics & Chem, N Tonawanda NY 49-55; Chemist NAS, Wash DC 55-57; Research analyst NSF, Wash DC 57-62; Sci tr off NLM, Bethesda Md 62-67; Admin asst Vitro Labs, Silver Spring Md 67-. 8: Consul, UDC Clsf in meteorol & occanog, and systems design 68-. 9: SLA (ed "DC Chapter Notes") ASIS (ed "PUP Newsletter; past chm Potomac Valley Chap). 10: DC Com for Equal Status of Woman. 14: Automated systems & procedures analysis. 15: 10406 Hutting pl, Silver Spring Md 20902.

BILLINGSLEY, MARGARET (KYLE). b Covington Ky 10 My 14. 4: William Billingsley. 5: DePauwU 32-36 (Fr) AB; Pratt 36-37 BLS. 7: Libn Pratt Free Lib, Brooklyn NY 37-38; Child libn Pub Lib, Cincinnati 38-41; Co supv Cuyahoga Co Lib, Cleveland 42-43; Child libn Boys & Girls Lib, Newton Mass 43-45; Child libn Pub Lib, Indianapolis 45-46; Child libn Pub Lib, Cincinnati 62-. 9: ALA; OhioLA. 14: Child wk. 15: 2381 Dixie hwy, Fort Mitchell Ky 41017.

BILLINGTON, DONNA JEAN. b Eugene Ore 11 Ap 02. 5: BostonU 22-23 (Eng, Art); Tex ChristianU 26-28, 50-51 (Eng, Fr) BA; Tex WomansU 31-32 bs in LS, 53 MLS. 6: Fr. 7: Stud asst libn Tex ChristianU 25-28; Asst libn 30-31; Prof asst Ft Worth Pub Lib, Ft Worth Tex 34-37; Asst libn & head libn Paschal High Sch, Ft Worth Tex 37-43; Libn W C Stripling & Rosemont Jr High Sch, Ft Worth Tex 43-44; Libn Harris Col of Nursing, Ft Worth Tex 44-48; Libn US Pub Health Serv Hosp, Ft Worth Tex 48-; Med libn 48-57; Patients libn 57-. 9: ALA-AHIL (Awards Com 65-67); SWLA; TexLA. 10: AAUW; Ft Worth Fed Bus Assn; Tarrant Co Assn for Mental Health. 14: Ref, bk sel, catlg. 15: 4907 South dr, Ft Worth Tx 76132.

BINA, PRISCILLA K (MORROW). b Springbrook N Dak 28 D 11. 4: Gordon J Bina. 5: UNDak 29-33 (Hist, Soc) BA; UIll 33-34 BS in LS; Lake Forest Col 57-58; Rosary Col 68. 7: Sch libn Wilmette Pub Sch, Wilmette Ill 35-37; Child libn Irving Pk Figueroa br lib LA Pub Lib 38-38; Child libn Kern Co Pub Lib Taft Cal 39-42; Staff schs div Wash DC Pub Lib 43-45; Lake Forest Pub Lib, Lake Forest Ill 68-. 15: 766 E Highview ter, Lake Forest Il 60045.

BINDER, RICHARD ALAN. b Oak Park Ill 30 Ap 45. 5: Knox Col 53-67 (Hist) BA; UIll 67-68 MS in LS. 6: Farsi, Fr. 7: Stud asst Ryerson Lib Art Inst of Chicago summers 64, 65, 66; Stud asst Knox Col Lib 64-67; Peace Corps Volunteer, Iran 68-: Libn UTehran Ctr for Grad Studies Research & Train in Intl Affairs 69-, Instr Grad Sch of Lib Sci UTehran 69-. 9: ALA; IranLA. 10: Beta Phi Mu. 14: Ref, research in cinema. 15: 5016 W 19th st, Cicero Il 60650.

BINDMAN, FRED M. b NYC 24 Ag 29. 4: Roberta Ganz. 5: Boston U 47-51 (Musicology) Mus B, 51-52 (Composi- tion); Simmons 52-53 MLS. 6: Ger, Fr. 7: Ref asst music div, Boston Pub Lib 52; Music catlgr & reviser copyright Office LC 53-57; Sr music catlgr LC 57-, Asst hd mus sect desc cat div LC 68-. 9: MusLA; Amer Musicological Soc;ALA; DCLA; Assn of Recorded Sound Collections. 10: Phi Mu Alpha. 14: Catlg & clsf of music mss &holographs & of phonorecords, record reviewing. 15: 832 Loxford Terrace, Silver Spring Md 20901.

BINGHAM, ELIZABETH (CLAUGHTON). b Auburn Ala 11 Ap 18. 4: Harold Jaynes Bingham. 5: Hollins Col 36 (Hist) AB; Vanderbilt 37 (European Hist) MA; Columbia 64 (LS) MS; USoCal 50-51, 54-55, 64 (European Hist) 06: Fr, Ger. 7: Asst hist Army Serv Forces War Dept, Wash DC 42-45; Lecturer Central Conn State Col 47, 52-53, 56-58; Libn ref dept USoCal 64-66; Hum bibliog SML Yale 66-. 10: Conn Valley Mental Health Assn; Conn Assn of Mental Health; Cromwell (Conn) Home Club; Cromwell (Conn) Hist Soc. 14: Ref, bibliog. 15: 93 Shunpike rd, CromwellCt 06416.

BINGHAM, GERTRUDE S. b Cadiz Ky. 5: ULouisville 51 (Econ) BA; UIll 52 (LS) MS. 7: Asst catlg libn Ind U (Bloomington) 52-. 9: ALA, Ohio Valley gp Tech Serv Libns. 10: Beta Phi Mu. 14: Catlg. 15: Indiana Univ Lib, Bloomington In 47401.

BINGHAM. REBECCA (JOSEPHINE TAYLOR). b Indianapolis Ind 14 Jl 28. 4: Walter D Bingham. 5: Indiana U 46-50 (Soc studies) BS in Ed, 65- LS; UTulsa 58-62 (Educ) MA. 6: Sp. 7: Asst libn Alcorn A&M 50-51; Ser libn Tuskegee Inst 52-53; Act libn Jarvis Christian Col 55-57; Sch serv libn Indianapolis Pub Lib summer 57; Jr high sch libn Tulsa Pub Sch Tulsa Okla 60-62; Louisville Pub Sch, Louisville Ky Jr high sch libn 62-66; Louisville Pub Sch, Louisville Ky Supv of lib serv 66-. 8: Sch Lib Educ Adv Com UKy 68-; Staff Higher Educ Inst for Sch Libns East Ky U summer 68. 9: ALA; -AASchL (National Lib Week Com 68-70); NEA; SELA; KyASchL; KyLA; KyEA (Del Assembly 69; pres Fifth Educ Dist Sch Libns 68); Ky Assn Supvr & Curr Devel. 10: Pi Lambda Theta; Kappa Delta Pi; Child Theatre Bd; Louisville Lib Club. 12: Ed "Bulletin" KyASchL (67-68). 14: Sch libs. 15: 3608 Dumesnil st, Louisville Ky 40211.

BINKELE, MRS STELLA (KAUFFMAN). b Pigeon Mich 30 Je 11. 5: Goshen Col 30-34 (Eng) BA; UIll 35-36 BLS. 6: Fr, Ger. 7: Libn Goshen Col 36-42; Army libn US Army Lib, Camp Chaffee Ark 43-44; Libn Ligonier Pub Lib, Ligonier Ind 54-55; Head Libn Plymouth Pub Lib, Plymouth Ind 55-66; Hd libn Goshen Pub Lib, Goshen Ind 66-. 9: ALA; IndLA. 10: AAUW. 14: Ext, rare bks. 15: 622 S Fifth st, Goshen In46526.

BINNINGTON, JOHN P. b London Eng 26 N 14. 4: Blanche Caddo. 5: U of the South 33-37 (Eng) BA; Wesleyan U 38-40 (Eng) MA; Columbia 40-41 BLS. 7: Circ Libn URhode Island 41-42; USN Communications Lt (jg) 42-46; Assoc Libn US Merchant Marine AlaV 46-47; Brookhaven Nat Labor Assoc libn Upton LI NY 47-52; Brookhaven Nat Labor Hd Research Lib Upton LI NY 47-. 8: Gp leader SLA deleg to the Soviet Union 66. 9: SLA; LI Libs Research Coun. 2: Mutual Exchange in the Scientific Library and Technical Information

Center Fields. 10: Trustee Bellport Memorial Lib. 14: Admin. 15: 21 Browns lane, Bellport NY 11713.

BINNS, FREDERIC WOLFE. b Sewickley Heights Penn 19 S 17. 4: Grace L Worthington. 5: Princeton 36-40 (Modern Langs) AB; Catholic U 58-62 (LS) MS. 6: Fr, Sp, Ger, Lat. 7: (Sgt) USAF, US, ETO 42-45; Ed & publ The Wagging Tail, Hanson Mass 46-53; Ed The Hanson Courier, Hanson Mass 53-54; Compositor & pressman Hanson Press, Hanson Mass 51-56; Freelance writer 56; Tech writer The Martin Co, Baltimore 56-57; Asst br libn, br libn, asst coordinator o f adult serv Baltimore Co Pub Lib, Towson Md 57-. 9: ALA-RSD; MdLA; Potomac Tech Proc Lib (Coun 66-68). 10: Boy Scouts; Junior Ward, Trinity Church, Long Green Treas, Trinity Day Sch. 13: Yes. 14: Adult serv, bk sel, ref. 15: Sweetair rd, Baldwin Md 21013.

BINO, MARIAL DESOLYN. b Hurley Wis 11 My 16. 5: UWis (Superior) 39 (Eng) ME; UMinn (Duluth) summer 53; UWis 53-54; Columbia 59 MS in LS; UVienna (Austria) summer 60; Columbia 66 (Developmental Psych) MA. 7: Tchr Iron Belt High Sch, Iron Belt Wis 41-42; Instr UWis(Menomenie) 42-43; Instr UWis(Eau Claire) 43-45; Tchr Arbor-Vita-WoodruffHigh Sch, Woodruff Wis 45-46; Soc wker Iron Co Welfare Dept, Hurley Wis 46-50; Visiting lecturer UWis(Platteville)summer 63; Sch Dist libn Joint Sch Dist 1, Hurley Wis 50-; Instr Gogebic Commun Col, Ironwood Mich 67. 9: ALA; NEA; WisLA; WisEA; WisCTE. 13: Yes. 14: Sch libs, adol lit, childlit, lib admin. 15: 221-1/2 Silver st, Hurley Wi 54534.

BINTNER, MARY (WILLET). b Mineola NY 26 Ja 32. 5: Ursinus 50-54 (Fr) BA; Drexel 54-55 MS in LS. 6: Fr. 7: Libn Brooklyn Pub, Brooklyn NY 55-56; Libn St Joseph's Hosp Sch of Nursing, Phila Penn 57-58; Bkmob libn LA Pub 59-60; Dir Hillsdale Pub, Hillsdale NJ 60-63; Asst dir Bergenfield Pub, Bergenfield NJ 63-. 9: ALA; NJLA (Memb Chm). 10: Beta Phi Mu. 14: Adult serv. 15: 3040 Edwin ave, Fort Lee NJ 07024.

BIONDI, PRISCILLA A. b Springfield Mass 23 S 37. 5: UMass 55-59 (Eng) BA; Trinity Col Conn 59-62 (Eng); Yale 60 (Eng); Simmons 65-66 (LS) MS. 7: Underwriter Conn Gen Life Ins Co, Hartford Conn 59-65; Hd libn Ins Lib Assoc of Boston 66-. 9: SLA. 14: Ref. 15: 107 Jersey st, Boston Ma 02215.

BIRCH, GRACE (MORGAN). b NYC 3 Je 25. 4: Kenneth F Birch. 5: Hunter Col 42-46 (Sociol); UBridgeport 61-63 (Psych) BA; Pratt Inst 65-67 MLS. 6: Fr, Ger. 7: Jr asst E br Bridgeport Pub Lib 49-53, Jr asst H A Bishop Hist Room 54-58, Sr asst E br 58-60, Act hd H A Bishop Hist Room 60-62, Act br libn Black Rock br 62-64, Br libn Black Rock br 64-66; Asst town libn Fairfield Pub Lib 66-. 8: Instr lib sci So Conn state Col 68-. 9: ALA; NELA; ConnLA (chm Adult Serv Sect 69-70). 10: Alpha Sigma Lamda. 11: CLA Scholarship 65. 14: Admin, ref, automation. 15: 175 Brooklawn ave, Bridgeport Ct 06604.

BIRCH, ROBERT L(OUIS). b Mobile Ala 9 Ag 25. 4: Grace Kay. 5: Mary Knoll Col Syst 44-47 (Relig), UMiami (Fla) 48-51; (Philos, Eng) BA; Catholic U 53-58 MS in LS. 6: Sp, Fr, Ger. 7: Grad asst UMiami (Fla) 49-51; US Army (Cpl) Finance, Ft Jackson SC 51-53; Grad lib asst Catholic U 53-55; Lib spec Georgetown U Lib 55-57; Foreign lang catlgr Patent Off Sci Lib, Wash DC 57-59; Info spec Pan Amer Union, Wash DC 59-60; Ref libn US Patent Off Sci Lib, Wash DC 60-68; Faculty Grad Sch US Dept of Agric, Wash DC 58-, Ref libn Nat Agric Lib 68-. 8: Lecturer Grad Sch USDA, 58-; Info-processing sems spons by Amer U, 63-65; Amer Transl Assn, 64-65; Radio Talks for Voice ofAmerica; Bibliog consul, President's Commsn on the Patent System 65-66; Presents Annual Lincoln Day Prog at Ford's Theater,Wash DC. 9: Sci Index Group (Coord); Lincoln Group DC, (nat memb org; Patent Off Soc; Soc Fed Linguists. 10: Mensa (Libns Gp). 12: Ed Med radiation symposia in English & Spanish; indexer, var med & bacteriological symposia, etc. 13: Yes. 14: Stylistics, info stor & retr, communication, rel of phraseology Co indexability, catlg, ref. 15: 3108 Dashiell rd, Falls Church Va 22042.

BIRD, JUDITH (FALLER). b New Suffolk NY 25 S 45. 4: Russell Bird. 5: SUNY Col (Oneonta) 62-67 (Liberal Arts, Lit) BA; LIU 67-68 MLS. 6: Fr. 7: Acquis libn SUNY (Farmingdale) 68-. 9: SUNYLA. 14: Acquis. 15: 52 Engelke ave, Huntington NY 11746.

BIRD, NANCY K(ARNES). b Radford Va 19 D 06. 5: Lynchburg Col 22-24, 25-26 (Eng) AB; Radford Col 24-25, summer 28 (Eng, LS); UTenn summers 31, 32 (LS); Peabody summers 34-37 BS in LS; Columbia 45-46 (LS) MS. 6: Lat, Fr, Ger. 7: Tchr Eng, algebra Radford High Sch, Radford Va 26-28; Tchr, tchr-libn Livingston Acad, Livingston Tenn 28-35; Tchr-libn Blacksburg High Sch, Blacksburg Va 35-37; Libn Groveland High Sch, Groveland Fla 37-39; Period & binding libn UFla 39-45; Fla State U: Period & binding libn 46-56, Interlib loan libn 56-60, Head spec collections 60-. 9: ALA; SELA; FlaLA (chm Col & Spec Libs Div 64-65). 10: AAUP; Tallahassee Hist Soc; Fla Heritage Assn. 13: Yes. 14: Ref, bibliog, rare bks. 15: 522 W College ave, Tallahassee Fl 32301.

BIRD, SARA (GREY) PROCTOR. b Salisbury NC 18 O 15. 4: Speight Leonard Bird. 5: Winthrop Col 32-36 (Pub Sch Music) BS, summer 37 (LS); UMich 54-56 AMLS; Winthrop Col 55-56 (Eng). 6: Fr. 7: Tchr Pub Sch Music Pub Schs, Bethune SC 36-38; Libn 37-38; Asst libn, asst in circ, documents, head ser & govt Documents Deptm Hd Acquis Dept Winthrop Col 47-. 9: ALA; SELA; SCLA. 10: AAUW. 14: Acquis. 15: 801 Milton ave, rock Hill SC 29732.

BIRD, VIOLA AVIS (FOSTER). b Fall River Wis 7 Je 05. 4: Win W Bird. 5: Lawrence Col 27 (Pol Sci) BA; USoCal Law Sch 27-28; UWash Law Sch 50 LLB; UWash 53 Master of Law Libnship. 7: Asst law libn UWash Sch of Law 53-. 8: Tchr, Legal Bibliog UWash 54-. 9: AALL (Schlarsh chm 64-67; mem Exec Bd 68-71). 12: Co-Auth "Order Procedures," AALL Publ Ser No 2 (60); Ed 'Current Comments Column' in "Law Library Journal" (60-66). 14: Legal ref, reader serv. 15: 5233 Pullman ave NE, Seattle Wa 98105.

BIRD, WARREN PHILLIP. b Rochester NY 27 D 33. 5: Georgetown U 53-56 (Physics) BS; Columbia 63-64 (LS) MS. 6: Fr, Ger, Sp, Ital. 7: Biophysicist Columbia U 58-64, Lib systems analyst 64-65; Chief lib mechanization Duke U Med Center 65-68, Assoc Dir and Asst Prof of Med Lit 68-. 8: Visit Lecturer Sch of LS, UNC (Chapel Hill) 67-. 9: MedLA; (com on Cont Educ) SLA; NCLA; ASIS; BSA Inst Electric & Electron Engnrs. 10: AAAS. 12: Ed "Library Telecommunications Directory" (68-69). 13: Yes. 14: Lib systems, Automation, Lib Communic. 15: Duke U Med Center Lib, Durham NC 27706.

BIRDSALL, SHIRLEY ANNE. b Wichita Falls Tex 16 N 32. 5: Harding Col 50-54 (Soc Sci) BA; LSU 57-59 MS in LS. 7: Ref libn LSU Law Lib 59-62; Libn Harding Col 62-. 9: ALA; ArkLA (past chm Col sect); SWLA. 10: AAUW; Beta Phi Mu; Beta Sigma Phi. 13: Yes. 14: Ref, admin, catlg. 15: Beaumont Mem Lib Harding Col, Searcy Ar 72144.

BIRDSALL, WILLIAM FOREST. b Farmington Minn 30 O 37. 4: Ann Page. 5: UMinnesota 55-59 (Hist) BA, 59-61 (LS) MA. 7: Ref libn Iowa State U of Sci & Tech Ames Iowa 61-63; Hd pub serv Wis State U at LaCrosse 65-. 10: AAUP; ACLU. 14: Ref, archives. 15: 1410 State, La Crosse Wi 54601.

BIRDSEY, BETTY (JEAN). b Winfield Kan 30 My 28. 5: Eastman Sch of Music 46-50 (Applied Music) MM; Ind U 50-52 (Cello); UDenver54-55 MA in LS. 7: Asst UIll (Urbana) 55-57; Music catlgr, asst fine arts dept Dallas Pub Lib 58-64; Asst Conserv of Music Oberlin Col 65-. 9: ALA; MusLA. 14: Music. 15: 688 E College, Oberlin Oh 44074.

BIRDSEYE, LUCILE E. b Centralia Wash 19 Ap 09. 4: Story Birdseye. 5: UWash 30 (liberal arts) BA, 30 (libnship) Certif. 7: Asst children's libn Seattle Pub Lib 30-32; Bk mob libn King Co Lib, Seattle 63-65; Ref libn King Co Lib, Bellevue Wash 65-. 9: ALA; PNLA; WashLA. 14: Ref. 15: 10602 SE 29th, Bellevue Wa 98004.

BIRDSEYE, STORY. b Spokane Wash 28 N 06. 4: Lucile E Wonderly. 5: UWash 30 (Pol Sci) BA, 30 LLB. 7: Practice of Law, Seattle 30-55; Judge of Superior Court State of Wash, Seattle 55-. 8: Trustee King Co (Wash) Lib System 53-. 9: ALA-ALTA (past pres); WashLA; PNLA. 10: Amer Bar Assn; Amer Judicature Soc; Order of Coif; Silver Beaver. 13: Yes. 14: Lib trustee educ. 15: King Co Courthouse, Seattle Wa 98104

BIRDSONG, GAIL E. b Kansas City Mo 28 F 44. 5: Grinnell Col 62-66 (Sp) BA; Rutgers 67-68 MLS. 6: Sp. 7: Prof asst Baltimore Co Pub Lib, Randallstown Md 68-. 9: MdLA. 15: 2814 St Paul st, Baltimore Md 21218.

BIRDWELL, EFFIE (NEOMA). b Mineral Wells Tex 28 Ja 26. 5: Hardin Jr Col 43-44 (Chem); UTex 45-48 9chem) BS. 6: Ger, Fr. 7: Clerk-typist US Civil Serv, Shepherd Field Tex 44-45; Libn Monsanto Co, Texas City Tex 48-. 9: SLA (pres Tex Chap 57-58); ASIS. 13: Yes. 14: Spec libs. 15: 318 Sixth ave N, Texas City Tx 77590.

BIRKEL, PAUL EDWARD. b Louisville Ky 13 Jl 31. 5: Bellarmine Col 50-54 (Eng) AB (summa cum laude); Catholic U 54-55 MS in LS. 6: Fr. 7: Catlg libn Bellarmine Col 55-60; Ref asst Pub Lib of Cincinnati & Hamilton Co Ohio 60-61; Assoc ed Catholic Periodical Index, Wash DC 61-63; Tech serv libn Bellarmine Col 63-66; Asst catlg libn ULouisville 66-68; Hd acquis dept USan Francisco 68, Hd techproc USan Francisco 69-. 9: ALA. 10: Beta Phi Mu. 12: Assoc ed "Catholic Periodical Index," v 11 (61-62). 14: Tech serv. 15: 480 Vallejo, San Francisco Ca 94133.

BIRKY, GWENDOLINE EVELYN. b Milford Neb 29 Mr 10. 5: Neb Wesleyan U 28-32 BS in Ed; UDenver 50-55 (LS) MA. 7: Elem tchr Bd of Educ, Hastings Neb 34-53; Elem tchr Bd of Educ, Lincoln Neb 53-55, High Sch libn 55-64, Elem libn 64-65, Catlgr 65-. 8: Exch tchr Bournemouth Eng 47-48; Sec to Supt of schs & Bd of Educ Hastings Neb 43-44; Head Libn YMCA Conf Camp Estes Park Colo summers 63-65; Church Libn First Methodist Church Lincoln Neb 56-67. 9: ALA; NEA; ACE; Neb State LA (sec 68-70); Lincoln Lib Assn (pres-elect 66-67); MPLA; Neb State Tchrs Assn; Lincoln EA (sec 64-66 & 68-69). 10: Nat Fed of Bus & Prof Women's Clubs (Nat Bd 54-55); State Fed of Bus & Prof Women's Clubs (past state pres); AAUW (various offs); Wesleyan Serv Guild; Delta Kappa Gamma (var offs). 11: ALA tour of Europe (59). 14: Ref, sch libs, catlg. 15: 2503 N 48th, Lincoln Nb 68504.

BIRLEM, LYNNE MARIE. b SE Harbor Me 28 Mr 40. 5: Jackson Col Tufts U 58-62 (Eng) AB; Simmons 68-69 (LS) MS. 7: Tchr: Weymouth High Sch, Weymouth Mass 62-64, Ponaganset High Sch, N Scituate RI 64-66, Biddleford Jr High Sch, Biddleford Me 66-67, Houlton High Sch, Houlton Me 67-68; Media specialist Quincy High Sch, Quincy Mass 69-. 10: AAUW. 14: Sch media ctr. 15: SW Harbor Me 04679.

BIRMINGHAM, MARY ALICE (TREACY). b St Paul Minn 30 My 41. 4: Francis R Birmingham Jr. 5: Col of St Catherine 59-63 (Eng, Hist) BA; Catholic U 65-66 MSLS. 7: Exec sec Nat Fed of Catholic Col Studs, Wash DC 63-64; Sec US House of Rep 64-65; Libn DC Tchrs Col 66-. 9: ALA; NEA; DCLA. 14: A-v materials & serv. 15: 7603 Riverdale rd, New Carrollton Md 20784.

BIRNBAUM, HENRY. b Switzerland 7 Mr 17. 5: UColo 50-52 (Internat Rel) BA (magna cum laude); Columbia 52-54 MS in LS. 6: Ger. 7: Personal serv manager Hoover Mfg & Sales Co, NYC 36-41; US Army (AUS) 41-45;Admin asst & rep LC Mission in Europe 45-46; Lib asst LC Acquis Div 46-47; Researchanalyst Office Chief Coun War Crimes, Nurnberg 47-48, Asst case ed 48-49; BrooklynCol Lib; Asst acquis div 52-54, Catlg libn 54-57, Chief circ libn 57-61; Dir oflibs Pace Col Lib 61-. 8: Consul Survey of Circ Procedures at the NY Acad of Med,67. 9: ALA (Internat Rel Round Table 54-, chm Ad Hoc Com on Circ Libns 59-60);-ACRL (Col Libs Sect); -RTSD (Catlg & Clsf Sect 54-, Spec Com 57); -LAD Circ Servsect, chmn Program & Action Com 68-70; Info Sci & Automation Div; SLA; NY Tech ServLibns; Lib Assn City Cols NY (Brooklyn Col del to Exec Coun 56-59); NY Lib Club(treas 64-66); Archons of Colophon, Convener 66-67. 10: NY Hist Soc; Phi Beta Kappa; Pi Gamma Mu; Delta Phi Alpha. 12: "IBM Circulation Control at Brooklyn College Library" (60). 13: Yes. 14: Admin. 15: 40 East 10th st, New YorkNY 10003.

BIRO, JULIANE S (BING). b Mainz Germany 7 My 30. 4: Ivan Biro. 5: Manhattanville 49-53 (Russian, Fr) BA; Fordham 54-58 (Russian Area Studies) MA; Columbia U 58-61 (LS) MLS, 66-67. 6: Ger, Fr, Sp, Ital, Russian. 7: Translator Nat City Bank, NYC 53-54; Catlgr of Rare Bks & Prints William H Schab, NYC 54-61; Art libn NY Pub Lib 662-68; Senior asst in charge of childrens wk Mt Kisco Pub Lib Mt Kisco NY 68-. 9: SLA; WestchesterLA. 12: Trans Franz Born, "Jules Verne: The Man Who Invented The Future" (64. 14: Art, rare bks. 15: RR 1 Box 410 Kitchawan rd, S Salem NY 10590.

BIRO, RUTH (LIND) GHERING. b Butler Penn 7 Ag 40. 4: William Louis Biro. 5: Agnes Scott Col 35-38, 39-40 (Eng) AB; UAla summer 58; Emory 61-62 (LS) MLn, 69. 6: Lat, Sp, Fr. 7: Ref asst Duquesne U Lib 62-65; Lib asst UPittsburgh Grad Sch Lib Sci Lib 65; Asst ref libn in chg of the African collection Duquesne U Lib 65-68; Instr in Lib Sci, DuquesneU Sch of Educ 68-. 8: Reg Coun Faculty Inst on Internat Educ, 65-68; Faculty DeveloptInst in Educl Media (Ohio State U) 69. 9: Pittsburgh Suburban LA; Hungarian LA. 10: Participant in Univ of Pittsburgh 1st Inst on Comparative Libnship; AAUW. 12: "Books On Africa; 'CORE College' Acquisitions 1965-1966" (66). 13: Yes. 14: Catlg (African Materials), ref, East-Central European Materials, lib sci educ. 15: 631 Maryland ave, Pittsburgh Pa 15232.

BIRRELL, ALEXANDER THOMAS. b Okla City Okla 16 Mr 30. 4: Ann Finch. 5: UOkla 48-50 (Music), 53-56 (Fr) BA, 56-57 MLS. 6: Fr. 7: Act ref libn Okla State Lib 56-57; Cal State Lib: Libn ref sect 57-58, Libn catlg sect 58-59, Asst ref libn 59, Asst catlg libn 59-60, Supv catlg libn 60-64, Head tech serv 64-. 66; UCal (Davis) Hd catlg dept 66-. 9: CalLA (sec Tech Proc Round Table, mem Ed Com, pres Golden Empire Dist 68); No Cal Tech Proc Group (sec-treas); Lib Assnof UCal (chm Davis DIV). 14: Tech proc. 15: 1209 Bucknell dr, Davis Ca 95616.

BIRTHA, JESSIE M. b Norfolk Va 5 F 20. 4: Herbert M Birtha. 5: Hampton Inst 36-40 (Secondary Ed; English, History) BS; Drexel 59-62 (Children's libnship) MLS. 7: Tchr Penn Normal Sch, St He&ena's Is SC 41-42; Tchr Bd of Educ, Norfolk Va 42-46; Free Lib of Phila: Lib trainee 59-62, Libn I 62-67, Libn III 67-. 9: ALA; PennLA. 14: Child libnship. 15: 433 Glen Echo rd, Philadelphia Pa 19119.

BISE, MARGARET (GILMOR). b Pittsburgh 13 My 09. 5: West Ky Tchrs Col 36-40 (Elem Educ) BS; UDenver 55-58 (LS) MA. 7:Elem sch tchr Jenkins Sch , Jenkins Ky 30-42; Elem tchr Sacajawea Sch, Richland Wash 46-49; Libn Jefferson Elem Sch, Richland Wash 50; Libn Naramasu Amer Sch, Tokyo 51-52; Jr High Sch tchr Amer Sch, Ramstein Germany 53; Elem tchr Amer Sch, Munich Germany 54; Sch libn Elm Grove Sch, Oak Ridge Tenn 56-. 8: Visiting Lecturer; Dept of Lib Serv UTenn summers 62, 63, 66; VisitingLecturer; Appalachian State U, Boone NC summer 68; Instr NDEA Inst Middle TennState U summer 67; Visiting Prof, Educ Media, Purdue U 68-69. 9: ALA; NEA; TennLA; SELA; TennEA. 10: Delta Kappa Gamma. 11: John Cotton Dana Award, 61. 13: Yes. 14: Elem sch libs. 15: 240 N Purdue ave,Oak Ridge Tn 37830.

BISHOP, CHILSON (MARY E LEAGUE). b Edinburg Ind 24 N 15. 4: Chilson M Bishop. 5: ButlerU 33-37 (Lat, Eng) AB, 38-39 (LS); IndU 56; West Mich U 65. 6: Fr. 7: Tchr Libn Jonesboro High Sch, Jonesboro Ind 38-40; Hd libn Jonesboro Pub Lib, Jonesboro Ind 41-45; Hd Libn Marion Pub Lib Marion Ind 47-62; Dir Crawfordsville Pub Lib & Processing Ctr, Crawfordsville Ind 63-. 9: IndLA (sec 56-70). 10: AAUW; Bus & Prof Women; Zonta Internat; LWV. 14: Mgt, build. 15: 409 Hughes, Crawfordsville In 47933.

BISHOP, DAVID FULTON. b NYC 23 N 37. 4: Nancy Driscoll. 5: URochester 55-60 (Music Educ) B of Music; Catholic U 61-65 MS in LS. 7: Musician (S/Sgt) US Air Force Band, Wash DC 60-64; Asst head Reclsf Proj UMd 64-65, Head ser sect of catlg dept 65-66; Asst head catlg dept 66-67, Hd ser dept 67-. 9: ALA. 14: Catlg, ser, libautomation. 15: 6412 Telegraph rd, Lanham Md 20801.

BISHOP, DAVID. b Newfoundland Can 23 S 28. 5: Memorial U (St John's Newfoundland) 45-47 (Pre-Med); Dalhousie U (Halifax NS) 49-52 (Econ) BA; Columbia 57-58 (LS) MS. 6: Fr, Lat. 7: Navigator trainee Royal Air Force Eng 48-49; Stud asst NS Research Edtn Lib, Halifax NS 50-52; Concrete inspector BC Internat Engng, Kemano BC 52-53; Chief steel inspector G S Eldridge & Co, Vancouver BC 53-57; Ref libn L A County Med Assn Lib, Los Angeles 58-61; Dental libn UCLA Biomedical Lib 61-63, Ser libn 63-65; Libn UAriz Col of Med 65-. 9: ALA; MedLA (ed com, recr com); Ariz State LA (pres spec libs dir 68-69). 10: Ariz Acad of Sci; AAUP; Assn Amer Med Cols; Libraries Ltd (v-pres 69-70). 13: Yes. 14: Med bibliog, admin. 15: 139 W Suffolk dr, Tucson Az 85704.

BISHOP, MRS DIANE (DE ROLLIN). b Santa Monica Cal 6 Ap 37. 4: Howard Earl Bishop. 5: UCLA 54-59 (Latin amer Studies) BA; Amer Inst for Foreign Trade 59-60 (Span, Fr) BFT; Columbia 63-64 MLS. 6: Sp, Portu, Fr, Ital. 7: Clerk typist Grad Div UCLA 60-61; Linguist Defense Dept, Wash DC 61-63; Child libn 1st asst, act head Prince George's Co (Md) Mem Lib 64-66, Child libn 66-. 9: ALA; MdLA (sec child & ya div, 65-66 & 69). 10: Phi Beta Kappa. 14: Child wk. 15: 5909 89th ave, Hyattsville Md 20784.

BISHOP, DELBERT ALVIN. b Springfield Mo 1 D 27. 4: Wanda Lee Whitlock. 5: Southwest Mo State 46-47 (Hist); Drury Col 48-50 (Hist) AB; UMo(Kansas City) 57-61 (Hist) MA. 7: Cook US Navy 45-46, Commissaryman 2nd class 51-55; Archives asst & Archivist Fed Records Center GSA, Kansas City Mo 56-60; Archivist Harry S Truman Lib, Independence Mo 60-61; Archivist Dwight D Eisenhower Lib, Abilene Kan 61-63; Supv archivist Fed Records Center GSA, Kansas City Mo 63-67; Ctr mgr Fed Records Ctr GSA, Denver 67-. 9: SAA; Org Amer Histns; AmerAssn for State & Local Hist; Mo State Hist Soc; Kan State Hist Soc; Neb State HistSoc; West Hist Assn; State Hist Soc of Colo, Hist Soc of

Montana; Utah State HistSoc; Amer Records Mgt Assn. 10: The Kansas City Posse, The Westerners; The DenverPosse, The Westerners. 13: Yes. 14: Archives & records mgt, fed Govt records. 15: Gen Serv Admin, Fed Records Ctr, Bldg 48 Denver Fed Ctr, Denver Co 80225.

BISHOP, MRS EDITH P. b Seattle 23 Je 07. 5: UWah 25-29 BS in LS. 7: Asst child libn Seattle Pub Lib Ballard Br 29-30; Child libn Missoula Pub Lib, Missoula Mont 30-32; Br libn King Co Pub Lib, Seattle 46, asst child libn 46-49; Los Angeles Pub Lib: Child libn 50-51, Asst coordinator child 51-54, Br libn 54-57, Coordinator ya serv 51-61, Dir of Brs 61-. 9: ALA; CathLA; CalLA (pres YA Round Table). 10: Phi Beta Kappa, Soroptomist Club. 13: Yes. 14: Child, ya, admin. 15: 10318 Richlee ave, Southgate Ca 90281.

BISHOP, ELEANOR (BOIT) C(RAFTS). b Reading Mass 23 Je 10. 4: C Nelson Bishop. 5: Wellesley 28-32 (Amer Hist) BA; Radcliffe summer 54 (Inst for Archives & Hist Mgt) Inst on Publ of Hist Agencies & Mus VanderbiltU & Am Assoc for State & LocalHist 67 Certif. 7: Asst Ms Div & Archives Baker Lib Harvard Grad Sch of Bus Admin 59-. 9: SAA (Preserv Methods Com 63-64); Amer Assn State & Loc Hist. 10: Nat Soc Women Descendants of Ancient & Honorable Artillery Co(Nat registrar 56-59); Reading (Mass) Antiq Soc; DAR; NE Hist & Geneal Soc. 12: "One Hundred Years of Papermaking" (38); "Reading's Colonial Rooftrees" (44); Ed"Bulletin," Bay State Hist League (63-). 13: Yes. 14: Mss, archives. 15: Lowell st, Reading Ma 01867.

BISHOP, EMMA B. b Port Royal SC 14 D 22. 4: James Cox Bishop. 5: Winthrop Col 39-43 (LS) BA. 7: Libn Hand Jr High Sch, Columbia SC 43-45; Head catlg dept Clemson Col Lib 46-49; Asst libn Beaufort Co Lib, Beaufort SC 58-. 9: ALA; SCLA. 10: Bus & Prof Women's Club. 14: Catlg. 15: PO Box 294, Beaufort SC 29903.

BISHOP, GWYNNETH HEATON. b Toronto Can 5 Mr 37. 4: Richard Thornton Bishop. 5: UToronto 55-59 (Hist) BA, 59-60 BLS; UCal ext (LS). 6: Fr. 7: Libn Canadian Inst of Intl Affairs, Toronto Ont Can 60-61; Acquis libn Jackson Lib of Bus StanfordU 61-66; Admin asst to dir SUNY (Binghamton) Lib 66-67, Hd acquis dept 67-. 9: NYLA. 10: Jr League of Binghamton; AAUW; Susquehanna Conservation Coun; Sierra Clubs. 14: Acquis, admin. 15: 8 Goethe st, Binghamton NY 13901.

BISHOP, J(ESSIE) CATHERINE. b Baltimore 1 Mr 27. 5: West Md Col 45-48 (Hist) AB; Catholic U 58-59 MSLS. 6: Fr, Sp. 7: Agency sec Continental Amer Life Insurance Co, Baltimore 48-53; Sec Prudential Insurance Co of Amer, Baltimore 53-58; Catlgr Johns Hopkins U 58-66, Catlgr-Reviser 66-67, Sr asst catlg libn 68-. 9: ALA; MdLA. 14: Catlg, rare bks. 15: 6111 Bellona ave, Baltimore 21212.

BISHOP, MINNIE (SLADE). b E Spencer NC. 4: Sanford D Bishop. 5: ShawU 32-35 (Eng) AB; Columbia summer 37; Hampton Inst 39 BSLS. 6: Fr, Ger. 7: Ellerbe High Sch, Ellerbe NC 36-38; Br libn Evansville Pub Lib, Evansville Ind 39-40; Libn A M & N Col 9pine Bluff Ark) 40-43; Libn Ala State Col (Grad Div) summer 43; Libn Mobile Cen Ala State Col 43-65; Libn Mobile State Jr Col 65-. 9: NEA; ALA; Amer Assn Jr Cols; Assn for Higher Educ; SELA; AlaStateTA; AlaLA; AlaJrColLA. 10: YWCA; Friends of Mobile Pub Lib; Mobile Allied Arts Assn; Delta Sigma Theta. 14: Admin, ref. 15: 2413 Ridge rd, Mobile Al 36617.

BISHOP, OLGA BERNICE. b Dover NB Can 24 Je 11. 5: Mt Allison U 32-38 (Hist) BA; Carleton U 44-46 (Admin) B Pub Admin; Mt Allison U 49-51 (Hist) MA; UMich 51-52 AMLS, 62 (LS) PhD. 7: Sec Mt Allison Mem Lib, Sackville NB 32-40; Sr admin off RCAF Record of Serv, Can Civil Serv, Ottawa 40-46; Act libn Mt Allison Mem Lib, Sackville NB 46-53; Gen libn U West Ont 53-54, Med libn 54-65; Assoc Prof Sch of Lib Sci UToronto 65-. 8: Consul, Toronto Can: Acad Med Lib 65-66, Ont Dept Mines Lib 67-68, Ont MedLA Lib 65-68. 9: ALA; CanLA (coun, chm Research & Spec Lib Sect); Can Assn Colo & Univ Lib (sec); MedLA; SLA; Bibliog Soc Can; OntLA (chm Col & Univ Sect); Inst Prof Libns Ont (pres & dir). 10: University Women's Club; Faculty Club; Beta Phi Mu. 12: "Publications of the Governments of Nova Scotia, Prince Edward Island, New Brunswick 1758-1952" (57); "Publications of the Government of the Province of Canada" (63). 13: Yes. 14: Admin, ref, spec libs, med libs, govt publs. 15: 1 Kilbarry rd, Toronto 7 Ont Can.

BISMUTI, GENE. b Everett Mass 19 My 21. 4: Susan Swink. 5: Seattle U 46-49 (Bus Admin) BCS; UWash 49-50 BA in Lib. 6: Ital. 7: USAAF (Sgt) 42-46; Bus ref asst Seattle Pub Lib 50-52, Gen ref asst 51-52; Asst ref libn & legis ref libn Wash State Lib 52-58; Research consul 58-63; Asst chief Undergrad Lib UWash 63-65; Dir reader serv Wash State Lib 65-. 8: Spec assignments, Indexer of Legis Bills 61, 63, 65, 67, 69. 9: ALA; Coun of State Govts (Nat Legis Conf Div); PNLA; WashLA. 12: Co-comp "Legislative Record, Washington State Legislature" (61, 63, 65, 67). 14: Ref, legis lib serv, admin. 15: 1825 McCormick way, Olympia Wa 98502.

BITNER, HARRY. b Kansas City Mo 22 Jl 16. 4: Anne Goldstein. 5: UMo(Kan City) Sch of Law 36-39 LLB; UMo(Kan City) 39-41 (Pol Sci, Hist) AB; UIll summers 39-42 AB in LS; Columbia 48-52 (Admin & Pub Law). 6: Fr, Ger. 7: Law Libn UMo(Kan City) 39-42, Law Libn & Instr in Law 42-43; US Army Signal Corps, Europe 43-46; Ref libn Biddle Law Lib UPenn 46; Assoc law libn Columbia U Law Sch 46-54; Libn US Dept of Justice, Wash DC 54-57; Law Libn Yale Law Sch 57-65; Law Libn & Prof of Law Cornell Law Sch 65-. 9: ALA; SLA; AALL (pres 63-64); Amer Soc Legal Hist; CNLA (v-chm 64-66) Legal Research, with co-auth 53, third ed 69. 12: Co-auth "Effective Legal Research" (53, 3rd ed 69). 13: Yes. 14: Admin, ref. 15: 406 Winthrop dr, Ithaca NY 14850.

BITZER, MARY ELIZABETH. b Harrisburg Penn 26 Jl 22. 5: Col of William & Mary 40-44 BA in LS; UMadrid summer 60. 7: Stud asst Col of William & Mary 43-44; Libn Radnor High Sch, Wayne Penn 44-45; Circ libn US Merchant Marine Acad, Kings Point LI NY 45-47; Prin catlgr Ext Div Penn State Lib 48-49; Asst libn Mitchel Air Force Base, Hempstead LI NY 49-50; Libn US Steel Corp, NYC 51-56; Asst to exec off NY Pub lib 58-60; Sub libn & tchr Harrisburg secondary schs, Harrisburg Penn 63-. 9: SLA. 10: Phi Mu; Eng-Speaking Union; Art Assn of Harrisburg. 14: Ref, admin. 15: 115 S 24th st, CampHill Pa 17011.

BIXBY, MARGARET HELEN. b Tacoma Wash 18 D 09. 5: U of Puget Sound 28-30 (Hist); UWash 30-32 (Gen Lit) BA, 32-33 BS in LS. 7: Asst child libn Tacoma Pub Lib, Tacoma Wash 35-44; Child libn Olympia & Thurston Co Lib, Olympia Wash 44-45; Child libn Pierce Co Pub Lib, Tacoma Wash 46-. 9: ALA; PNLA; WashLA (Exec Com 54-55, Legis Com 64-65). 10: Altrusa Internat; Zeta Tau Alpha. 14: Child & yp serv. 15: 501 No D st, Tacoma Wa 98403.

BIXLER, DOROTHA JEAN (ADAMS). b Wilcox Mo 23 Ja 27. 4: Gordon George Bixler. 5: NW Mo State Col 46-49 (Eng, Speech) BS, Sec Ed; UMinn 62-64 (LS) Certif; UWis 68- (LS). 6: Sp. 7: Tchr Wilcox Mo 45-46; High sch Eng & speech ychr, Malvern Iowa 49-50; Libn Pub Lib, St Joseph Mo 50-51; Tchr Pre-sch nursery, Des Moines Iowa 61-62; Libn Elem schs, Robbinsdale Minn 65-66; Libn LaFollette Middle Sch, Madison Wis 66-. 8: Consul LaFollette Middle School. 9: ALA; -AASchL; WisLA; WisEA-DAVI; SoWisEA; MTI. 10: Beta Sigma Phi; WSCS. 14: Sch lib consul. 15: 1148 Beech st, Sun Prairie Wi 53590.

BIXLER, PAUL (HOWARD). B Union City Mich 27 O 1899. 4: Norma Hendricks. 5: Hamilton Col 19-22 (Eng) AB; Wharton Sch UPenn 22-23 (Econ); Harvard 23-24 (Eng) MA; West Res 32-33 BSLS. 6: Sp. 7: Instr in Eng Ohio Wesleyan U 24-26; Reporter "Cleveland Plain Dealer" 26; Reporter "Cleveland Press" 27; Instr in Eng West Res U 28-35; Libn Antioch Col 35-65. 8: Staff mem Ford Found Study on Policy & Program, 49; Adv Soc Sci Lib URangoon 58-60 (Ford Found grant to ALA); Ford Found grantee for Bibliog Research in Southeast Asia 62-63; Lib consul for Ford Found in Argentina 64-69; Visiting scholar Univ Center, Atlanta 63; Survey (with Carl White), Mexican Libs 66-67; Sem on Non-West materials Columbia Sch Lib Serv summer 67; Inst on Asian materials Hawaii Grad Sch Lib Studies summer 68. 9: ALA (Coun 48-51 & 56-59; exec sec Intel Freedom Com 52-56); OhioLA (pres 48-49). 10: ACLU; Assn for Asian Studies; AAAS; Amer Acad Polit & Soc Sci; Lat Amer Studies Assn; Burma Research Soc. 11: Judge Nonfiction Nat Bk Award, 55. 12: Auth of chaps in "Administration of the College Library" (44); Ed "Antioch Review Anthology" (53); Ed "Freedom of Communication" (54); Ed "Newsletter," for Int Freedom Com of ALA (52-56); Chm ed bd "Antioch Review" (43-58); Auth The Mexican Library (69); "Intellectual Freedom Newsletter" (ALA) (52-56); "Antioch Review," (43-58); "Freedom of Comm munication," (53); "Freedom of Book Selection," (54); "Antioch Review Anthology," (54); Guest ed, "Librs of the Far East," sect of 6 articles in "Librs of the Far East," sect of 6 articles in Lib Journ, Nov. 15, 1962. 13: Yes. 14: Col lib admin, train of overseas libns. 15: 1345 Rice rd, Yellow Springs Oh 45387.

BJORGO, MAYNARD. b Bemidji Minn 8 Jl 22. 4: Nancy Lee. 5: UMinn 40-42 (Physics); Chicago 46-47 (Meteorology) BS, 47-48 (Philos); Minn State Tchrs Col (Moorhead) 53 (Educ) BS; UMinn 55-56 (LS) MA. 6: Fr. 7: Weather off (Capt) USAF 42-46, 48-49, 50-52; Eng tchr Sauk Centre & Fergus Falls Minn 54-55; Instr ref & acquis Central Mich State Col 56-57; Libn II ref Fresno State Col 57-58; Instr ref & period libn St Cloud State col 58-66; Ref Wis State U (Eau Claire) 66-67; Asst Prof Lib SciLakehead U 67-. 9: ALA; OLA. 13: Yes. 14: Ref, lib educ. 15: RR #2, Port ArthurOnt Can.

BJORKE, WALLACE SKEEM. b Rugby ND 30 Jl 26. 5: Willamette U 44-48 (Music) BM; UMich 48-51 (Music) MM, 54-57 AMLS. 7: UMich: Tchg asst 48-49, Tchg fellow 49-51, Order clerk 51-57, Serv libn 57-60, Music libn 61-. 9: ALA; MusLA; Internat Assn of Music Libs. 14: Pub serv, catlg (music). 15: 200 Brookside dr, Ann Arbor Mi 48105.

BJORKLUND, EDITH MARIE. b Minneapolis Minn 19 Jl 41. 5: UChicago 59-63 (Eng) BA, 67-68 (LS) MA. 6: Fr, Ital. 7: Acquis supv Law Sch Lib UChicago 64-67; Original catlgr 67-68; Hd pre-catlg dept UWis (Milwaukee) Lib 68-. 10. Mensa. 13: Yes. 14: Acquis, bibliog, ref. 15: 3264 N Summit ave, Milwaukee Wi 53211.

BJORNCRANTZ, LESLIE (BENTON). b Jersey City NJ 1 Mr 45. 4: Carl Edward Bjorncrantz. 5: Wellesley 63-67 (Eng) BA; Columbia 67-68 MLS. 6: Fr, Lat. 7: Ref asst Alderman Lib UVa (Charlottesville) 68-. 9: ALA (ACRL; RSD). 10: Phi Sigma; Beta Phi Mu. 11: Wellesley Col Scholar. 14: Ref, pub serv. 15: 1800 Jefferson Park ave apt 60, Charlottesville Va 22903.

BLACK, DOROTHY M(ILLER). b Little Rock Ark 6 Je 1900. 5: UArk 18-22 (Eng) AB; UIll 23-28 (LS) MA. 6: Fr. 7: Asst pub lib, Little Rock Ark 22-23, Ref libn 23-25, Act libn 25-26,Ref asst UIll 26-40, Asst ref libn 40-46, Assoc ref libn & Asst Prof 46-62, Assoc reflibn & Assoc Prof 62-68, Assoc ref libn & Assoc Prof Emerita 68-. 9: ALA (chm Subscr Bks Com 37-39); -ACRL (chm Ref Sect 49-50); IllLA. 10: Beta Phi Mu; AAUP; ACLU; Nat Audubon Soc. 12: "Guide to Lists of Master's Theses" (66); Ed Ill Lib Sch Assn "Newsletter" (41-53). 13: Yes. 14: Ref, govt publs. 15: 1501 Delmontct apt 3, Urbana Il 61801.

BLACK, FERNE M. b Cleveland 16 My 20. 5: Ohio U 38-40 (Eng); Los Angeles State Col 58-59 (Eng) BA; USoCal 60-61 MS in LS. 7: Research libn Aeronutronic Div of Philco, Newport Beach Cal 61-65; Info spec Battelle Mem Inst, Columbus Ohio 65-66; Supv acquis group Aerospace Corp, El Segundo Cal 66-67; Libn Seven Cotransp-land use study, Cleveland 67-68; Asst libn Parma Heights Pub Lib, ParmaHeights Ohio 69-. 9: Amer Inst Aeron & Astron; SLA (mem &/or chm 5 chap coms);OhioLA. 10: Beta Phi Mu. 14: Acquis, admin. 15: 1387A Bluff ave, Columbus Oh 43212.

BLACK, JANE (LABINO). b Pittsburgh 26 Mr 36. 4: John Clark Black. 5: Seton Hill Col 54-58 (Modern European Hist) BA; UToledo 59-60 (Art); McGill 61-62 BLS. 6: Fr. 7: Lib asst Toledo (Ohio) Museum of Art Ref Lib 59-61, Asst libn 62-64; Catlgr State U Iowa Lib 64-66; Asst art libn Hillyer Art Lib Smith Col 66-67; Dir Lynchburg Pub Lib, Lynchburg Va 67-. 9: ALA; CanLA; Internat Assn of Documentalists; SELA; VaLA. 10: Pi Gamma Mu. 14: Catlg. 15: 26 A Princeton cir W, Lynchburg Va 24503.

BLACK, JEAN PHYLLIS. b Duluth Minn 22 My 03. 5: Mt Holyoke 20-24 (Hist, Pol Sci) AB; UMich 24-25 (Hist) MA, 25-26 (Hist) PhD; UWash 31-32 BS in LS. 6: Ital, Fr. 7: Instr Col of St Catherine 28-29; Libn Seattle Art Museum 33-36; Research Assoc Hoover Lib, Stanford U 37-39; Asst Prof Hist, pol sci Our Lady of the Lake Col 39-41; Asst Prof Lib Sci Rosary Col 41-43; Libn Iowa State Hist Soc, Iowa City Iowa 43-46; Libn Portland State U 46-. 69. 9: ALA; -ACRL; PNLA; OreLA (pres 63). 10: AAUP; AAUW; Phi Beta Kappa. 11: Eleanora Duse fellowship of Italy-Amer Soc of NY 25-26; Post doctoral Soc Sci Res Coun fellowship 29-30. 13: Yes. 14: Admin, catlg, ref. 15: 1881 SW 11th ave, Portland Or 97201.

BLACK, JOHN HOUSTON. b Camden NJ 11 F 46. 5: Columbia 64-68 (Eng) BA, 68-69 MS. 6: Fr. 9: ALA. 14: Non-print media, film, inst libs. 15: 45 Country Club rd, Willingboro NJ 08046.

BLACK, LAWRENCE. b Bronx NY 28 My 40. 4: Linda Black. 5: Brooklyn Col 58-60; LIU 60-63 (Hist) BA; Pratt 64-65 MLS. NYU 67-; NY State Prof Certif; Med Lib Assoc Certif Grade#1. 7: Tchr Bd of Educ of NYC, Brooklyn NY 63-64; Hosp libn VA Hosp, Northport NY 65-66; Ref libn NYU Gen U Lib 67-68; Sr libn NY State Inst for Basic Research,Staten Island NY 68-. 9: NY Lib Club; ALA; MedLA; -NY Reg Grp. 14: Ref, admin. 15: 29 Arlo rd, Staten Island NY 10301.

BLACK, PATRICIA (HEBERT). b Patterson La 21 S 30. 4: Ralph E Black. 5: Huntingdon Col 47-50 (Eng Lit, Art) AB; Fla State U 50-51 (LS) MA. 7: Art libn & 1st asst fine arts dept Atlanta Pub Lib 51-62, Head Fine Arts Dept 62-64; Head Art Div Rochester Pub Lib, Rochester NY 64-68; Asst Hd Reynolds A-v Dept, Rochester Pub Lib 68-69, A-v consul Monroe Council Lib Sys 69-; Instr (part time) Lib Sch SUNY(Geneseo) 66-. 9: NYLA; Metro Area Communications Coun; Film Lib Info Coun, NEA-DAVI, NY State AV Assn, & FLA, Roch. A-V Assn. 10: Mem Art Gallery, Rochester NY. 14: Art ref, a-v (recordings, films, pictures), pub rel. 15: 870 Arnett blvd, Rochester NY 14619.

BLACK, RALPH EUGENE. b Cartersville Ga 5 Ap 24. 4: Patricia Hebert. 5: UGa 46-49 (Psych) AB; Fla State U 58-60 (LS) MA; Glasgow U (Philos) PhB. 6: Fr. 7: US Army Chaplain's asst 43-46; Atlanta Pub Lib; Lib asst Fine Arts, A-v 55-58, Libn I Ref 58-60, Head pub serv 60-62, Act asst dir 62, Coordinator of brs 62-64; Assoc Prof Lib State U Col(Geneseo) NY 64-68; Assoc Prof Lib Sch Peabody 68-69; Assoc Prof Lib Sci SUNY(Geneseo) 69-. 8: Lib/USA 64. 9: ALA (Coun 65-69; Notable Bks Coun); Adult Educ Assn; GaLA; SELA (chm Lib Educ sect 67-68); NYLA; Retrospective Notable Bks Coun. 10: AAUP; Beta Phi Mu. 12: "Phonograph Records for Public Libraries," Ky microcards (60). 13: Yes. 14: Bk sel, adult serv info sci. 15: Arnett blvd, Rochester NY 14619.

BLACK, SALLY W. b Northampton Mass 2 Je 42. 4: William W Black. 5: Earlham Col 60-65 (Eng) AB; Rutgers 66-68 MLS. 7: Trainee Monmouth Co Lib, Freehold NJ 66-67; Research asst RutgersU 67-68; Libn (staff) RutgersU Lib (New Brunswick) 68-. 14: Ref, lib research. 15: 65 Huntington st, New Brunswick NJ 08901.

BLACKBURN, ALICE KISER. b LaJunta Colo 2 F 17. 4: Charles E Blackburn. 5: UWash 37-41 (Eng) BA, 41-42 BS in LS. 6: Fr, Ger. 7: Libn UWash Bur of Bus Research 42-47; Libn I, II Ref Div UWash Lib 59-64; City Libn Neill Pub Lib, Pullman Wash 64-. 9: ALA; PNLA; Wash State LA. 10: AAUW; Phi Beta Kappa. 13: Yes. 14: Ref, pub lib, admin. 15: 1401 Charlotte st, Pullman Wa 99163.

BLACKBURN, F(RANCIS) M(ARION). b Akron Ohio 31 My 17. 4: Carolyn G Blackburn. 5: Kent State U 36-41 (Eng) AB, 41-46 (Eng) MA, 50-51 MALS. 7: Chief clerk US Army Air Corps, US 42-46; Proprietor Blackburn's Bk Store, Akron Ohio 48-51; Acquis libn Ariz State U 51-53; Base libn Sheppard AFB, Wichita Falls Tex 53-56; Asst to libn UMo 56-58; Libn W Tex State U 58-. 9: ALA; SWLA; TexLA; Tex Assn Col Tchrs. 10: AAUP. 13: Yes. 14: Admin, acquis. 15: Box 265 W T Sta, Canyon Tx 79015.

BLACKBURN, HALLIE DAY (BACH). b Cannel City Ky 2 N 06. 4: William O Blackburn. 5: UKy 24-28 AB in ED; Pratt 28-29 BS in LS. 7: Asst libn E Ky State Col 29-30; Libn Henry Clay High Sch, Lexington Ky 30-31; Asst catlgr UKy Lib 31-34; Libn Grant Co Lib, Williamstown Ky 53-54; Sr ext libn Dept of Libs, Frankford Ky 54-. 9: SELA; KyLA. 14: Ext, catlg. 15: RR 1, Dry Ridge Ky 41035.

BLACKBURN, JOY (MARTIN). b Marietta Ohio 28 O 25. 4: Paul Edward Blackburn. 5: Ohio Wesleyan 43-47 (Psych) BA; UMinn 47-48 (Psych) MA; UPittsburgh 58-60 (Soc psych, Math). 7: Clin fellow Stud counseling Bur UMinn at Minneapolis 47-48; Asst to dean Col Arts & Sci Ohio State 48-54; Research libn Graham Lab Jones & Laughlin Steel, Pittsburgh 55-57; Research asst Off Educ Planning Health Professions 60-61; Research libn Tech Marketing Assoc, Concord Mass 64-66; Libn Wash Nat Ins Co, Evanston Ill 66-. 9: SLA. 10: Phi Beta Kappa. 12: Jones and Laughlin "Research Bulletin," quarterly (55-57). 14: Communic, ref. 15: 515 Meadow rd, Winnetka Il 60093.

BLACKBURN, ROBERT HAROLD. b Vegreville Alta Can 3 F 19. 4: F Patricia Gibson. 5: UAlta 36-40 (Eng) BA, 40-41 (Eng) MA; Toronto 41-42 BLS; Columbia 46-47 (LS) MS. 7: Air Navigator & Instr RCAF (Flight Lt) 42-45; Gen asst pub lib, Calgary Alta 45-46; Asst libn UToronto 47-54, Chief libn 54-. 8: Carnegie Travel Fellowship US & Europe 49 Co-chm Can Lib Week; tour of Ger libs as guest of W Ger Govt 64; Can Adv Colliers Encyclopedia; Adv Com 'Who's Who in Lib Serv' 4th ed; IFLA (chm Toronto Com 67), Can repres to Warsaw & Frankfurt. 9: CanLA (pres 58-59); Can Assn of Col

& U Libs (pres 63-64); Assn of Research Libs (Bd mem 65-67); Center for Research Libs (Bd chm 67); ALA (Coun 67-71);-ACRL (mem Bd of Dirs). 10: Streetsville Pub Lib Bd (chm 57-65); Nat Research Coun of Canada (Com on Sci Info 60-). 11: LLD UWaterloo 65 Carnegie Travel Fellowsh; Guest visit to W German Libs 64. 12: Ed Newfoundland Suppl Encyclopedia of Can (49); ed Joint List of Ser in Toronto Libs (53). 13: Yes. 14: Admin. 15: Streetsville, Ontario Can.

BLACKBURN, TERENCE (GENE). b Warren Ohio 8 Ja 46. 5: Flint Jr Col 63-65 (Mus Lit); Mich StateU 65-67 (Mus Lit) BA; UMich 67-68 AMLS. 6: Ger, Ital. 7: Libn (staff) mus dept Boston Pub Lib 68-. 14: Ref, mus. 15: 199B Longwood ave, Brookline Ma 02146.

BLACKFORD, IRENE. b Brodhead Wis 18 Jl 18. 5: UWis 36-38, 39-41 (Eng) BA; UWis 41-42 BLS. 7: Ref asst Lima Pub Lib, Lima Ohio 42-49; Ref libn Janesville Pub Lib, Janesville Wis 49-66, Dir 66-. 8: Co-admin of Rock Co Lib Serv 69. 9: WisLA. 14: Admin. 15: Janesville Pub Lib 316 S Main st, Janesville Wi 53545.

BLACKLEDGE, THERESA (POWELL). b Jones Co Ms 29 D 17. 4: Clifford M Blackledge. 5: University of Southern Mississippi 38-50 (English) BS, 50-56 (Elmenetary Educ) MA, 62-68 (LS) MS. 7: Jones Co Schs, Jones Co Miss, Tchr 38-58, Libn 59-68; Libn Jones Co Jr Col, Ellisville Miss 68-. 9: ALA; NEA; MissLA(chm Recr Com); MissEA; MissASchL (past pres); DCT (past dir Dist VI). 10: Alpha Delta Kappa. 15: Route 2, Ellisville Ms 39437.

BLACKMAN, LaVONNE. b Fort Smith Ark 4 O 29. 5: Fort Smith Jr Col 47-48; Freed Hardeman Col 48-49; Harding Col 49-51 (Soc studies) BA; George Peabody Col for Tchrs 55-58 (LS) MA. 7: Tchr South Christian Home, Morrilton Ark 51-52; Tchr Spec Sch Dist, Ft Smith Ark 52-56; Bkmob lib Tenn Reg Lib Serv, Murfreesboro Tenn 56-58; Libn Van Buren Jr High, Van Buren Ark 58-59; Libn Northside High Sch, Ft Smith, Ark 60-63; Libn Southside High Sch, Ft Smith Ark 63-66; Asst libn & Instr in lib sci State Col of Ark 66-. 9: ALA; ArkLA; ArkEA. 10: Bus & Prof Women. 14: Period. 15: 567 Locust, Conway Ar 72032.

BLACKMON, WILBUR DEE. b Lancaster SC 18 S 21. 4: Jane Puryear lackmon. 5: UArk 46-50 (Bus Admin) BS BA, 62 (LS); Peabody 62-63 MA LS. 7: T/5 US Army, USA & Hawaii 41-45; Owner-manager Priv Bus, Hobbs NM 53-61; Head bus & sci dept Abilene Pub Lib, Abilene Tex 63-64; Ref libn Hardin-Simmons U Lib 64-65; Dir of libs Sul Ross State Col 65-67; Assoc lib dir Stephen F Austin State Col 67-. 9: ALA-ACRL;-LAD;TexLA;SWLA. 14: Admin. 15: 310 Warren dr, Nacogdoches Tx 75961.

BLACKSHEAR, MARTHA JULE. b Headland Ala. 5: Samford U Howard Col 33-37 (Eng) AB; Florida State U 49-50 (Lib serv) MA. 7: Tchr Chilton Co High Sch, Clanton Ala 37-41; Girl Scouts Houston Girl Scout Coun Houston 41-43; Girl Scouts Columbus Girl Scout Coun Columbus Ga 43; Amer Red Cross Station Hosp, Ft Rucker Ala 43-45; School libn Leon High Sch Tallahassee Fla 50-52; Pub libn Decatur-Seminole Reg Lib, Bainbridge Ga 52-53; State sch libs consul State Dept of Educ Montgomery Ala 53-67; Lib med & specialist SE Ala Educ Media Project, Troy Ala 67-. 8: Evaluation Committee of the American Film Festival New York City Summer 68; Professor Library Science, University of Alabama Tuscaloosa Ala Summer 69. 9: NEA; ALA; DAVI; SELA (treas 61); AlaLA (v-pres 59, pres 60, Exec Coun 61-65); AlaSchLA (Exec Coun & cor s4c 53-67). 10: Bus & Prof Womens. 12: "Building and Renovating School Libraries" (63); "Questions School Administrators Ask About School Libraries (64). 14: Lib media, sch material ctr. 15: 103 E Church, Headland Al 36345.

BLACKSHEAR, ORRILLA (THOMPSON). b Otsego Columbia Co Wis 14 My 04. 5: Central State Col (Steven's Point Wis) 33-37 (Eng) BS; UIll summers 38, 39, 43 (LS) BS. 7: Rural schs tchr Columbia Co, Wis 24-26; High sch libn Ripon High Sch, Ripon Wis 37-40; Head libn Ripon Pub Lib, Ripon Wis 40-45; Head libn William's Free Lib, Beaver Dam Wis 45-47; Consul Wis Free Lib Com, Madison Wis 47-51, Dir Trav Lib 51-57; Asst dir Madison Pub Lib, Madison Wis 57-68; UWis Lib Sch 68-. 8: Dir Summer Session for Bkmob Libns UKy 54; Consul Wkshop for Libns of Small Libs conducted by State Lib Mich 50 Tchr LS extenscourse, UWis 4 yrs; monthly radio program "Invitation to Reading" 47-69. 9: ALA;-ASD; AHIL (chm & memb of var coms); WisLA (var com assignments); AEAUSA. 10: AAUW; V-chm Com on Aging (Madison); Welfare Coun; Madison Art Assn; Wis Artsfoundation Coun; Zeta Phi Eta; Madison Civics Club; Altrusa. 11: Libn of the Year Award WisLA 62. 12: Ed "Wis LibBulletin" (47-57); ed "Buying List of Bks for Small Libs" (8th ed 54); Auth "BkSelection" Pam 5 in ALA Small Lib Proj (63); bk ed "Capitol Times" (Madison Wis60-61); Co-auth UWis Extens Course A-50 "Introduction to Library Service" (58). 13: Yes. 14: Pub lib materials & readers servs. 15: 1662 Monroe st, Madison Wi 53711.

BLACKWELDER, FANNY GREGORY (BRADLEY). b Mocksville NC 14 N 10. 5: Queens Col (NC) 29-30, 32-33 (Eng, Hist) AB; UNC 33-34 AB in LS. 7: Tchr Cooleemee High Sch, Cooleemee NC 34-35; Libn Amelia Co High Sch, Amelia Va 35-36, 36-37; Libn Rock Hill High Sch, Rock Hill NC 37-38, 38-39; Libn Davie Co Pub Lib, Mocksville NC 59-66; Libn Pub Lib ofCharlotte & Mecklenburg Co, Charlotte NC 67, Coordinator of child serv 68-. 15: 1300 Reece rd, Charlotte NC 28209.

BLACKWELDER, MARY (FONNER). b Waynesburg Penn. 4: John J Blackwe&der. 5: Carnegie 28-32 BS in LS. 6: Fr. 7: Asst to archivist Penn State Lib, Harrisburg Penn 33-38; Ref libn NY Pub Lib, NYC 39-43; Catlg supv Cooper Union Mus, NYC 56-68; Registrar Cooper-Hewitt Mus of Design Smithsonian Inst, NYC 68-. 9: SLA (Mus Div: sec-treas, Nom Com chm, Memb Com) 67-. 15: 131 Riverside dr, New York NY 10024.

BLACKWELL, KATHRYN D. (MRS). b St Joseph Mo. 5: UMinn 45 BSLS, 56 (Eng Lit) BA, 57 (LS, Amer Studies) MA. 7: Circ, ref Macalester Col 45-60, Act libn 58-60; Libn Minneapolis Sch of Art 60-. 9: ALA (Nomin Com for Melvil Dewey Award 64, chm Art Subsect 66-67);-LAD (State Rep Minn); SLA (Nat Dir 65-68, Dir Picture Div 65-68); MinnLA (chm Col Sect 59-61, chm Recr Com 59-61, chm Const Rev Com 58, mem Ref Sect 45-, Exec Com 60-61); Sch Libns of Twin Cities. 10: AAUW; Minn Lib Sch Alumni; Nat Toastmistresses Club; Zonta Club; AAUP. 14: Art, child lit, ref, music, theater. 15: 7350 Winnetka Heights dr, Golden Valley, Minneapolis Mn 55427.

BLAINE, EARLE C (HUGHES) b Niagara Falls NY 11 Mr 15. 4: Earle C Blaine. 5: SUNY Col (Buffalo) 65 (Educ) BS in Ed; SUNY Col (Geneseo) 69 MS in LS. 6: Fr. 7: Libn Cayuga Drive Elem Sch, Niagara Falls NY 65-68; Libn Trott Voc High Sch, Niagara Falls NY 68-. 14: Rare bks. 15: 8914 Rivershore dr, Niagara Falls NY 14304.

BLAINE, MARTHA M. b Williamstown Ky 28 F 06. 5: East Tchrs Col 33-41 (Elem Educ) BS; UKy 48-56 (LS) MA. 7: Elem tchr, Dry Ridge Ky 33-53; High sch libn, Grant Co (Ky) High Sch 53-56; Grant Co (Ky) elem libn 56-. 9: NEA; KyEA; KySchLA; KyLA. 10: DAR; Carlsbad Garden Club, Pub Lib Bd; Tchrs clubs. 14: Catlg. 15: Dry Ridge Ky 41035.

BLAIR, EDITH (DANIEL). b Wash DC 27 Je 23. 4: Albert U Blair. 5: Miner Tchrs Col 41-45 (Eng) BS; Catholic U 46-47 BS in LL; UMich 51-52 AMLS. 7: Prelim catlgr LC 47; Lib asst Associated Col of Upper NY (Utica) 47-48; Asst libn Utica Col of Syracuse U 48-49; Ref libn Howard U 49-53, Med libn 53-60; Ref libn NLM, Bethesda Md 60-. 10: Phi Kappa Phi. 12: "Directory of Medical Libraries Outside the US and Canada" (63); Assoc ed "MedLA Bulletin" 55-56. 13: Yes. 14: Ref. 15: 1813 Randolph st NE, Wash DC 20018.

BLAIR, KEITH G. b Sioux City Iowa 3 Mr 13. 4: Eleanor Morsch Blair. 5: State U of Iowa (Iowa City) 37-41 (Gen Sci) BA; Columbia 41-42 BLS. 7: Ref asst NY Pub Lib Sci Tech Div 42-43; US Navy Electronics Tech 2nd Class Petty Off 43-45; Assoc libn Gen Chem Co, NYC 46; Libn US Maritime Commsn, Sheepshead Bay NY 46-47; Head ref & bibliog serv Navy Electronics Lab, San Diego 47-57; Head ref serv Gen Dynamics/ Astronautics, San Diego 57-58; Chief libn Gen Dynamics/Convair, San Diego 57-62; Lib supv Gen Dynamics/ Astronautics, San Diego 62-66; Chief Lib Gen Dynamics/Convair 66-. 8: SLA Consul, San Diego 62-; Assoc Prof LS San Diego State Col 65-66. 9: SLA (Consul 58-, Bd of Dirs, Advis Coun chm-elect 69-70; treas Aerospace Div 61-62);-San Diego Chap (var offs); CalLA (Coun-at-large 69-71); ASIS; Nat Mgt Assn. 10: Toastmasters Internat; Convair Club 457 (paspres); Amer Legion; Past Commander La Mesa Cal Post 282; Convair Mgt Club (chm Scholarship Awards Program 61-63). 13: Yes. 14: Documentation retrieval, lib career promotion, microtech, mgt. 15: 3770 Nassau dr, San Diego 92115.

BLAIS, GASTON. b East Broughton Quebec Can 11 My 35. 5: Sem de Quebec 48-56 BA; Le Bret Sem 57-61 (Phil, Theol); UMontreal 63-64 BLS. 6: Fr, Ger. 7: Jr catlg ULaval 61-62, Dept hd Educ Sci Lib 62-63, Acquis libn 64-65, Film libn 66;

Reading adv & bibliogr Ministry of Cultural Affairs, Que Can 67-. 9: Assn canadienne des bibliothecaires de langue francaise (pres Sect de Que 65-66). 14: Bibliog, ref, a-v, rare bks. 15: Quebec Pub Lib Serv Ministry of Cultural Affairs Govt bldgs, Quebec 4 P Que Can.

BLAISDELL, ROBERT M(ANLEY). b Boston Mass 4 Ja 20. 4: Jean C Mahler. 5: TuftsU 39-43 (Hist) AB; Simmons 48-49 (LS) BS; Boston 56, 57 (Educ); uhartford 61, 62 (Educ); Danbury State Col 65 (Educ). 6: Fr. 7: Instr Friends Acad, S Dartmouth Mass 47-48; Ref asst Sci & Tech Dept Boston Pub Lib 48; Ref asst Md dept & civics & sociol dept Enoch Pratt Free Lib, Baltimore 49-51; Head catlg dept TuftsU 51-52; Head ser div Baker Lib Harvard Grad sch of Bus 52-55; Libn Conn State Dept of Educ, Waterbury Conn 55-59; Supv of sch libs, W Hartford (Conn) Pub Schs 59-65; Dir of Lib Serv Danbury State Col 65-. 8: Consul on planning of lib complex, William H Hall High Sch Lib, W Hartford Conn 64-65; Participant in radio & TV prog on sch libs in Conn. 9: ConnEA; ConnLA; ConnSchLA (Legis Com, Standards Com). 10: W Hartford Educ Fund Com; AAUP. 12: "The Principals Role in the Organization and Administration of Elementary School Libraries (61); "The Integration of the Library Program With the Elementary School Curriculum (61); "Supervision of Parent Volunteers in Elementary School Library Programs (62). 15: 7 Old Washington rd, Ridgefield Ct 06877.

BLAISE, SUE ANN. b Tulsa Okla 17 My 34. 4: Thomas Mitchell Blaise. 5: OklaU 52-55 9nursing) Certif, 65-67 (Eng, Anthrop, LS) BA, 67-68 MLS; Okla CityU 61-63 (Math). 7: Psychiatric staff nurse UOkla, LA Co Hosp, Charity Hosp New Orleans 55-58; Pub health nurse City of New Orleans 58-59; Supv OklaU Med Ctr 59-64; Lib asst Norman Pub lib, Norman Okla summer 66; Staff nurse UOkla health serv 65-66; Lib asst UOkla 66-67; Staff nurse Central State Hosp, Norman Okla 67-68; Lib consul Okla Dept of Libs, Okla City 68-. 8: Staff & adv Inst for Train in Libship "Inst Libnship, Analysis & Challenge", Edmond Okla 69. 9: ALA; AHIL (mem Spec Projects Com 69-71); OklaLA; SWestLA. 11: H W Wilson Scholarship. 14: Lib research, development spec lib programs, adult serv. 15: 918 W Brooks, Norman Ok 73069.

BLAKE, DOROTHY (WAGER). b Heflin Ala 16 S 28. 4: Bruce Blake. 5: Jacksonville State Col 46-49 (Educ, Eng) BS; Peabody 50-53 (LS) MA; Emory 61-63 (LS) 6th yr certif. 7: Tchr E Clinton St Grammar Sch, Huntsville Ala 49-51; Asst libn Decatur High Sch, Decatur Ga 51-54; Libn sch prob lab Emory summers 53-63; Tchr Decatur High Sch 55-57; Elem sch libn Atlanta Pub Schs 58-61, Resource libn Area V 61-64, Coordinator of libs 64-; Instr Lib Sci Ga State Col 63-. 8: Visiting Instr Methods & Materials Oglethorpe U 55; Consul NDEA Inst for Sch Lib Personnel UGa summer 65; Visiting Lecturer Sch Libs Emory 65 Consul; UGa Dept of Libr Educ 65-67, 69; AtlantaU Sch of Lib Serv 66; UTenn Dept of Lib Sci 69. 9: NEA; ALA; SELA; GALA; GAEA; Ga Educ Media Assn. 10: AAUW; Kappa Delta Pi; Delta Kappa Gamma. 14: Sch libs, as total learning resources ctrs. 15: Industrial Ser Center, 2930 Forrest Hill dr SW, Atlanta Ga 30315.

BLAKE, ELIZABETH DIANA. b Kingston Ont Can 2 Je 23. 5: Queen's U 41-46 (Hist) BA; McGill 54-55 BLS. 6: Fr. 7: Ref libn Aluminium Labs Ltd, Kingston Ont 46-51; Circ libn Queen's U (Kingston Ont) 52-54, 55-56; Asst libn Nat Defence Col 56-67; Libn admin serv Queen's U, Kingston Ont 67-. 9: Inst of Prof Libns Ont; Queen's U Alumnae Assn (pres 64-66). 14: Ref. 15: 83 Beverley st Kingston Ont Can.

BLAKE, FAY M. b NY 15 S 20. 5: Hunter Col 36-40 (Eng) BA; USoCal 45 (Educ) Jr HS Certif, 59-61 MS in LS; UCLA 61-63 (Eng) MA; UVienna 63 (Ger) Certif; ULeningrad 65 (Russian) Certif. 6: Ger, Fr, Yiddish. 7: Hydraulic press diesetter Challenger Lock Co, Los Angeles 56-57; Bkkeeper Reliable Mattress Co, Los Angeles 57-58; Bkkeeper Sanitary Mattress Co, Huntington Park 58-61; Gifts & exch libn UCLA 61-. 69; Assoc in acad & research libs Div of Lib Development, NY State Educ Dept 69-. 9: ALA (Ad hoc Com on Manpower); -ASD/By laws Com); CalLA (Legis Com 64, Intel Freedom Com 65, Chm, com on (Acad Status 68-69, sec Col, Univ on Research Lib Div, So Sect). 10: Phi Beta Kappa; Beta Phi Mu; SANE; ACLU, AAUP, Phi Kappa Phi, Libns Assn, UCal (sec). 13: Yes. 14: Lib exch, academic status, lib netwks. 15: 39 Dove st, Albany NY 12210.

BLAKE, JOHN B(ALLARD). b New Haven Conn 29 O 22. 4: Jean Place Adams. 5: Yale 39-42 (Hist) BA; Harvard 46-51 (Hist) MA, PhD. 6: Fr, Ger. 7: (1st LT) USAAF meteorology 43-46; Fellow hist med Johns Hopkins 51-52; Fellow hist med Yale 52-55; Asst histn Rockefeller Inst, NYC 55-57; Assoc curator div of med sci Smithsonian Inst, Wash DC 57-59, Curator 59-61; Chief hist of med div NLM, Bethesda Md 61-. 8: Lecturer in Pub Health & Hist of Med, Yale Sch of Med 55-57; Consul to Historian, Rockefeller Inst 57-60; Mem Hist of Life Scis Study Sect Nat Inst Health 59-63. 9: AHA; Hist Sci Soc; Amer Assn Hist Med (sec-treas 56-67 Coun 67-); MedLA. 11: Fielding H Harrison lecturer, Amer Assn Hist Med 64, Hon MD, Conn State Med Soc 66, Ida & George Eliot Award, Med Lib Assn 68. 12: "Benjamin Waterhouse and the Introduction of Vaccination Reappraisal" (57); "Public Health Lib in the Town of Boston 1630-1822" (59); Ed with Charles Roos "Medical Reference Works 1679-1966," a selected bibliography (67); Ed "Education in the History of Medicine" (68). 13: Yes. 14: Hist of med. 15: Nat Lib of Med 8600 Rockville Pike, Bethesda Md 20014.

BLAKE, KENNETH POND JR. b Boston 21 Mr 26. 4: Harriet Stowell. 5: Brown 44-48 (Pol Sci) AB; Boston U 48-49 (Educ, Hist) AM; Simmons 55-56 (LS) SM. 7: Tchg-prin Wells Mem Sch, Harrisville NH 50-52; Chm hist dept St Stephen's Episcopal Sch, Austin Tex 52-55; Ref asst Yale U Lib 56-57, Libn of the res bk room 57-59; Colby Col Lib: Readers serv libn 59-64, Act libn 64-65, Libn 65-. 9: ALA; NELA; MeLA (chm Col & Univ sec 66-67, treas 67-). 10: AAUW; Soc for the Preservation of New England Antiquities; New England Historic Genealog Soc; Maine Hist Soc. 13: Yes. 14: Admin, ref. 15: 3 Brescia ct, Waterville Me 04901.

BLAKE, MARGERY S. b Windsor Conn 14 Ap 28. 5: Wellesley 45-49 (Hist) BA; Columbia Lib Sch 65-67 (Soc sci) MS. 6: Fr. 7: Sec Conn State libn 50-57; Trainee NY Pub Lib 65-67; Ref asst Firestone Lib Princeton NJ 67-68; Libn Woodrow Wilson Sch Princeton 68-. 9: ALA. 10: Firestone Staff Assn. 14: Ref, soc scis. 15: 33 Maple st, Princeton NJ 08540.

BLAKE, MARY K. b Chestnut Hill Penn 23 Ap 33. 4: Robert Vincent Blake. 5: William & Mary 50-54 (Philos) BA; Drexel 63 MLS. 6: Ger. 7: Hosp libn Spec Serv, Ft Hood Tex 64-65; Asst libn Auerbach Corp, Philadelphia 66-67; Chief libn spec serv HSA,Taipei 67-69. 9: SLA. 10: Phi Kappa Phi. 11: Outstanding Scholarship Award,Drexel 63. 14: Mil libnship, catlg. 15: 225 W Jefferson, Media Pa 19063.

BLAKE, MILDRED (EVERIL). b Cleveland 14 S 1898. 5: Lake Erie Col 17-21 (Math) AB; West Res 31-46 BS in LS. 6: Fr. 7: Tchr Columbus Sch for Girls, Columbus Ohio 22-23; Libn Dept of Surgery West Res U Sch of Med & U Hosps 24-44; Asst Army Med Lib Hist of Med Br, Cleveland 45-46; Subj catlgr Army Med Lib, Wash DC 47, Libn Pentagon Br 48; Med ed hist unit Surg Gen's Off (Army), Wash DC 49-52; Asst libn R Matas Med Lib Tulane Med Sch 52-55; Libn Lovelace Found for Med Educ & Research, Albuquerque NM 55-66, Research lib consul 66-. 9: SLA; MedLA (chm Publ Com 53-58, chm Nomin Com 62, chm Bibliog Com 60-61, mem Ida & George Eliot Prize Essay Com 63-); NMLA. 10: AAUW. 12: Assoc ed "MedLA Bulletin" (50-52). 15: Apt O 515Girard blvd SE, Albuquerque NM 87106.

BLAKE, THERESA. b Millis Mass 28 S 12. 5: Vassar 30-34 (Hist) AB; Simmons 34-35 (LS) BS. 6: Fr, Ger. 7: NYC Pub Lib: Libn 2nd grade 37-, Sr libn -59; Dartmouth Lib: Ref asst 59-67, Ref libn 67-. 9: ALA; NELA. 10: Planning Bd; Enfield NH 64-66. 14: Ref. 15: Norwich Vt 05055.

BLAKELY, FLORENCE (ELLA). b Clinton SC 3 S 23. 5: Presbyterian Col 40-43 (Hist) BA (Magna Cum Laude); George Peabody Col 44-45 BS in LS, summers 59 & 60 MA in LS; Duke 49-53 (Hist). 7: Asst libn Presbyterian Col 44; Ref libn Greenville Pub Lib, Greenville SC 45-47; Br libn Greenville Co Lib, Greenville SC 47-48; Duke Lib: Ref libn 48-56, Hd ref dept 56-. 8: Visiting lecturer, School of Library Science, Univ of North Carolina, Chapel Hill, Summer 62; member Winchester (Eng) Excavation Party, summer 64. 9: ALA (life mem); SELA (chm Ref Sect 56-58); NCLA (chm Jr Memb RT 51-53, chm Resources Com 65-67, chm Dev Com 67-69). 10: Beta Phi Mu; AAUW; MC Lit & Hist Assn; Soc of Mayflower Descendants. 11: Council on Lib Resources Fellow 70. 14: Ref, bibliog. 15: Perkins Lib, Duke Univ, Durham NC 27706.

BLAKESLEE, ESTHERE (OGDEN). b Atlanta Ga 1 D 17. 5: Agnes Scott Col 35-38, 39-40 (Eng) AB; UAla summer 58; Emory 61-62 MLibnship, 69 diploma Advanced Libnship. 7: Home serv sec Amer Red Cross, Anniston Ala 40-41; Piano tchr priv studio, Covington La 44-46; Clr & music tchr Sch Organic Educ, Fairhope Ala 46-48; Casewker Cal State Dept Welfare, Pasadena Cal 48-49; Dir extra-prof & programs Mobile Infirmary Sch Nursing, Mobile Ala 53-56; High sch libn Mobile Co Bd of Educ, Mobile Ala 56-61, 63; Elem libn DeKalb Co Bd of Educ, Atlanta 63-69; Sch media coord,

Gwinett Co Ga 69-. 9: NEA; GaEA; GaLA; SELA; Atlanta Lib Club. 10: Delta Kappa Gamma. 15: 570 Ridgecrest rd NE, Atlanta Ga 30307.

BLAKESLEE, NINE JANE. b Spartansburg Penn 5 D 12. 5: Penn State U 44-51 (Soc Studies) BA in Ed; Case West Res summers 58-61 MS in LS. 7: Asst circ dept Erie Pub Lib, Erie Penn 31-46, Asst ext dept in chg of sub-br libs 46-48; Asst circ dept Pattee Lib Penn State U 48-51; Libn Wilson Jr High Sch, Erie Penn 51-. 9: PennLA (chm NW Dist 59-60, div v-pres 61-62); Erie Tchrs Assn (pres 53-54). 10: DAR (var offs); DAC; Phi Kappa Phi; Delta Kappa Gamma; Erie Co Hist S (past pres & dir). 14: Secondary sch libs, wk with young adults. 15: 167 E 34 st, Erie Pa 16504.

BLAKNEY, HELEN (NEAL). b McAllen Tex 8 S 20. 4: Paul S Blakney. 5: Rice 38-41; UTex at Austin 41-42 (Eng) BA; Tex Woman's U 64-67 MLS. 7: Sec West Reserve Life Ins Co, Austin Tex 42-47; Sec Gambill Ins Co, Denton Tex 50-54; SoMethodistU: Catlgr 67-69, Act hd catlg dept 69-. 9: ALA; TexLA (sec-treas Reg Gp of Catlgrs & Clsfrs 69-70); Dist VII LA. 14: Catlg. 15: 520 Waggoner, Arlington Tx 76010.

BLALOCK, MARTHA (HELEN) CHASE. b Berkeley Cal 21 S 06. 4: Edward Franklin Blalock. 5: UCal (Berkeley) 23-27 (Eng) AB, 27-28 (Eng) Gen Secondary Credential; San Jose State Col 54-62 (LS) Libnship Credential MA. 6: Sp. 7: Tchr-libn Mountain View High Sch, Mountain View Cal 46-54; Head Libn Los Altos High Sch, Los Altos Cal 55-. 8: Supv, lib field wkers from San Jose State Col 59-. 9: NEA; ALA; AASchL; CalTchrs Assn; CalASchL (publ chm 57-58, co-chm no sect Sr High Sch div 69-70); CalLA. 10: Quadalco Club; Mountain View Parks & Recreation Commsn; Mountain View Woman's Club (hon life mem). 11: Named Woman of the Year by Mountain View Bus & Prof Women's Club, 60. 13: Yes. 14: Ref, catlg, yp. 15: 1332 Miramonte, Mountain View Ca 94040.

BLANCHARD, J RICHARD. b Delphos Kan 3 Mr 12. 4: Christine Johnson. 5: UOkla 29-33 (LS) AB; Geo Washington U 34-35 (Eng) AB; UIll 49-53 (LS) MS. 6: Sp, Fr. 7: Ref asst LC 33-46; US Navy 44-46; Libn Tech Intelligence Center ONI, US Navy, Wash DC 46; Head ref dept USDA Lib, Wash DC 47-49; Libn of Col of Agric and div libn in sci & tech UNeb 49-51; U libn UCal(Davis) 51-. 8: Consul for Rockefeller Found, Santiago Chile 59; Consul for AID, State Dept, Buenos Aires Argentina 62; Visiting Prof, Japan Lib Sch Keio Univ, Tokyo 64; Mem Accred Survey, San Jose State Col 53. 9: SLA; ALA (Coun 54-56 & 60-63, chm Oberly Mem Fund Com 54-56, Nomin Com 56, Del to Internat Cong of Libs & Documentation Centers - Brussels 55); -ACRL (chm Pure & Applied Scis Sect 56); CalLA (pres Golden Empire Dist 54, pres Col Univ & Res Libs Sect 56). 10: Beta Phi Mu. 11: Oberly Mem Award. 12: "Literature of Agricultural Research," with H Ostvold. 13: Yes. 14: Ref, admin. 15: Univ of Cal Lib, Davis Ca 95616.

BLANCHARD, WARD STEVENS. b Brooklyn NY 25 S 12. 5: San Jose State Col 49-52 (Educ) AB; USoCal summer 53; LSU 53-55 (LS) MS. 6: Fr. 7: US Navy Seabees (60th Bn) MM1/c 42-45; Lib asst LSU Lib 54-55; Jr libn order dept Mich State U Lib 55-56; Catlgr Monterey Co Lib, Salinas Cal 56-57; Ref libn Long Beach Pub Lib, Long Beach Cal 57-59, Head processing div 59-61; Col Libn Southwestern Col 61-63; Col Libn Oakland City Col 63-64; Col Libn Col of Marin 64-67; Dir of Lib Serv Ohlone Col 67-. 9: ALA; CalLA (chm Tech Proc Round Table64, sec Jr Col Libns Round Table 64, pres 67, Adv Mgr "California Librarian" 59-60,chm So Cal Reg Tech Proc Group 61). 14: Admin, proc, a-v. 15: Ohlone Col, PO Box909, Fremont Ca 94537.

BLANCK, SARABETH (KING). b Kansas 24 N 20. 4: Harold E Blanck. 5: Ottawa U Kan 38-42 (Sociol) BA; UUtah 55-64 (LS); TWU 65- (LS). 7: Libn High Sch, Monticello Utah 59-64; Libn Skylone High Sch, Salt Lake City 64-65; Libn Richardson N Jr High Richardson Tex 65-. 8: Welfare Dir, Millard Co Utah 50-51. 9: ALA; NEA; TexLA. 10: PEO. 12: Free-lance writing (travel articles). 14: Sch libs. 15: 13906 Ramblewood Trail, Dallas Tx 75240.

BLAND, CATHERINE (VAUGHAN). b Petersburg Va. 4: Philip M Bland. 5: Va State Col 37-41 (Eng) AB; West Res 41-42 BS in LS, summer 65. 7: Libn Ky State Col 43-49; Acquis libn Howard U 49-51; Catlg libn Va State Col 51-68, Acting Lib Dir 68-. 9: ALA; VaLA; Va Tchrs Assn; AAUW. 14: Catlg. 15: Va State Col, Petersburg Va 23803.

BLAND, EVELYN JANE. b Loga WVa 7 N 07. 5: UKy 26-30 (Educ, Biol) AB in Ed; Columbia summers 32-36 Prof Certif in Lib Serv; UKy summers 39, 40, 42 (Educ, LS) MA in Ed. 7: Tchr & libn Holden Jr High Sch, Holden WVa 30-32; Libn Logan Sr High Sch, Logan WVa 33-. 8: Mem Logan Co Pub Lib Bd 68-69. 9: ALA; NEA; WVaLA; WVaEA; WVa ASchL. 10: Delta Kappa Gamma; Logan Woman's Club. 15: 601 Stratton, Logan WVa 25601.

BLAND, THEODORE S. b Hobart Okla 16 Ag 04. 4: Susan M McFarling. 5: UOkla 23-27 (Govt) AB, 31-32 (LS) AB, 36-44 (Eng) MA. 7: Ser libn UOkla Lib 29-30; Libn Dept of Geol UOkla 31-38; Supt ser & exch State U Iowa Lib 38-39; Libn Off Ch of Engnrs US Army, Wash DC 40-55; USAF, Eglin AFB Fla; Libn Air Force Armament Center 55-58, Tech libn Armament Dev & Test Cntr Ground Center 58-64, Dir of Libs 64-; Instr Fla StateU (part time) 60-68; Assoc prof U West Fla (part time) 69. 10: Phi Beta Kappa; Lib Bd, Ft Walton Beach Fla; Lib Bd, Okaloosa Co Fla. 14: Ref, admin. 15: PO Box 1016, Ft Walton Beach Fl 32548.

BLANDING, SYLVIA J. b Enterprise Kan 7 N 21. 4: Louis W Blanding. 5: Kan Wesleyan U 39-43 (Hist); U Mo at Kansas City 65-69 (Hist); Kansas State Tchrs Col 64-66 (LS). 7: Lib asst Johnson Co Pub Lib Shawnee Mission Kan 61-64; Libn Trinity Lutheran Hosp Sch of Nursing, Kansas City 64-. 9: ALA; SLA. 14: Med, nurs & loc hist. 15: 5126 Outlook, Shawnee Mission Ks 66202.

BLANDY, CONSTANCE A. b Woodbury NJ 7 Mr 35. 5: Douglass Col 52-53; UPenn 53-56 (Sociol) BA; UDenver 56-57 (LS) MA. 7: Ya libn Schenectady Co Pub Lib, Schenectady NY 57-59; Army libn USAREUR Spec Serv, Germany 59-61; Adult asst Enoch Pratt Free Lib, Baltimore 62-63, Admin asst 63-64; Ya consul Onondaga Lib System, Syracuse NY 64-65, Adult consul 65-66; Asst dir Mt Vernon Pub Lib, Mt Vernon NY 66-. 9: ALA; NYLA; WestchesterLA (chm Admin sect 68-70); LPRC; NY Lib Club. 10: Alpha Chi Omega; YWCA. 14: Adult serv, admin, pub relations. 15: 290 Collins ave, Apt 7-E, Mt Vernon NY 10552.

BLANK, ANNETTE (CHOTIN). b Bronx NY 1 Je 25. 4: Franklin Blank. 5: Wilson Tchrs Col 43-48 (Educ) BS in Ed; Catholic U summer 47; USoCal 50-51 MS in LS. 7: Sales clerk The Hecht Co, Wash DC 43-45; Clerk Off of Price Admin, Wash DC 45-46; Lib asst Wilson Tchrs Col 46-48; Lib asst Los Angeles Co Gen Hosp, Los Angeles 48-50; USoCal Lib 50-51; Sch libn Towson Jr High Sch, Towson Md 51-52; Child libn GS-5 DC Pub lib 53; Child libn 1,2,3 Enoch Pratt Free Lib, Baltimore 60-64, Bkmob libn III (Juv) 64-. 9: ALA; MdLA. 10: Camp Fire Girls. 13: Yes. 14: Child & ya. 15: 5477 Cedonia ave, Baltimore Md 21206.

BLANK, CHARLES S. b Chicago Ill 16 Ap 38. 5: UChicago 55-57 (Liberal Arts); Birmingham So Col 57-59 (Mus) BA; Indiana U 59-61 (Musicology) MM; Fla State U 62-63 9lib Sci) MS. 7: Asst libn Alleghany Co Lib, Cumberland Md 64, Libn 65-68; Asst Dir Wash Co Free Lib, Hagerstown 68-. 9: ALA; MdLA. 14: Admin. 15: 100 S Potomac st, Hagerstown Md 21740.

BLANKEN, EVA (WINTER). b Budapest Hungary 9 Ja 31. 4: Robert R Blanken. 5: Lib Sch UBudapest 48-51 BSLS; UBudapest Russian Tr Sch 51-54 Engring & Russian Trs diploma. 6: Russian, Ger, Fr, Hungarian. 7: Asst hd period dept Nat Lib Ctr, budapest 49-52; Hd libn Tech Research Inst, Budapest 52-56; Ref & circ libn Pennsalt chem Corp research & development, Phila 57-58; Hd research libn Scott Paper Co research & development, Phila 58-65; Admin asst to dir 3I Info Intersci Inc, Phila 66-67; Info specialist Info Ctr for Hearing Johns Hopkins Med Sch 67-68; Hd lib & files Aircraft Owners & Pilots Assn, Bethesda Md 69-. 9: SLA; ASIS. 13: Yes. 15: 2424 Penna ave NW, Washington DC 20037.

BLANKENBURG, JUDITH B. b Herndon Kan 10 Ja 33. 5: Ft Hays Kan State Col 51-55 (Hist) BA; Kan State Tchrs Col 68-69 (LS) ML. 7: Tchr & libn Natoma High Sch, Natoma Kan 55-56; Tchr & libn Delphos High Sch, Delphos Kan 56-59; Tchr & libn Plainville High Sch, Plainville Kan 59-61; Sch libn Dept of Defense Schs, Europe 61-65; Sch libn Foreign Dependents Children, Japan 65-67; Sch libn Topeka Pub Schs, Topeka Kan 67-68; Asst libn Colby Commun Jr Col, Colby Kan 68-. 9: ALA; KanLA. 10: AAUW. 14: Catlg, pers serv. 15: 109 W Sixth, Oakley Ks 67748.

BLANKENSHIP, WINSON CALKIN. b Camden Co Mo 4 Ag 25. 4: Elizabeth Booth. 5: Mo Valley Col 50-53 (Eng, Educ) BS; Syracuse summers 52-53; UMo (Kansas City) 55-56; Kan State Tchrs (Emporia) 55-56 (LS) MS; Bradley U evenings 57-58; UsoCal summer 59 (Admin); Okla State U 58-61 (higher educ) EDD; UColo summer 68; UWis evenings 68-69. 7: Libn high sch, Raytown Mo 53-56; Period libn Bradley U 56-58;

Instr Lib Sci Okla State U 58-61; Lib Dir Midwestern U 61-64; Assoc Prof Lib Sci Wis State U (Whitewater) 64-65, Prof Lib Sci 65-, chm Lib Sci Dept 67-. 8:Adv wk with Episcopal Day Sch Lib Wichita Falls Tex; Supv of Lib Practice wk for sch libns at Wis State U (Whitewater) Adv Wk with various Wis sch Libs. 9: ALA; WisLA; SoWisEA; NEA-DAVI; Wis Davi; Wis EA. 10: Alpha Sigma Phi; Sigma Tau Delta; Alpha Phi Omega. 13: Yes. 14: Ref, admin. 15: 466 S Pleasant St, Whitewater Wi 53190.

BLANSHINE, DONNA (LOUISE DAVIES). b Wash DC 12 Jl 45. 4: James Allison Blanshine. 5: W Va Wesleyan Col 63-67 (LS) BS. 6: Fr. 7: Asst Libn St Mary's Col of Md 67-. 9: ALA. 10: AAUP; Church Libn Unit Meth Church, Lexington Park Md. 14: Acquis. 15: 110 Old Rolling rd, California Md 20619.

BLASINGAME, RALPH (UPSHAW). b State College Penn 9 O 20. 4: Mariann Carpino. 5: Penn State U 38-42 (Eng Lit) BA; Columbia 46-52 BS, MS. 7: USAF (Maj) 42-46; Lib asst City Col (NYC) 47-49; Research asst Sch of Lib Serv Columbia U 49-50, Asst to the dean 50-52; Asst state libn Cal State Lib 52-57; State Libn Penn State Lib 57-64; Assoc Prof Grad Sch of Lib Serv Rutgers 64-66, Prof 66-. 8: Chm Penn Bd of Reg Lib Resource Centers, 61-64; Spec ed Crowell-Collier Educ Corp, 63-; Consul: Fla State Lib Bd, 63; Kent-Caroline (Md) Pub Libs Assn 65; New Castle (Penn) Free Pub Lib Bd 65; Pottsville (Penn) Free Pub Lib Bd 65; WVa Lib Commsn 64-65. State Lib of Ohio 66-67. 9: ALA (Coun, treas 64-68; chmadv Com on Off for Recr 62-65, chm ALA-NEA Jt Com, mem Commsn on a Nat Plan forlib Educ); -LAD (pres 61-62); NJLA. 10: AAUP. 11: Doctor of Letters, St Francis Col, 63; Dis- tinguished Service Award PennLA, 64. 12: Contrib M F Tauber's "Technical Servicesin Libraries" (54); Auth "Library Service in West Virginia; Present and Proposed,"(65); "Survey of Ohio Libraries and State Library Services," (67). 13: Yes. 14: Pub lib devel, lib educ. 15: 24 Pineridge dr, E Brunswick NJ 08816.

BLATT, ANNE. b Vienna Austria 18 Ja 28. 5: Hunter Col 57-62 (Eng Lit) AB; Columbia 62-64 (LS) MS. 6: Ger, Fr. 7: Legal sec & researcher Schwartz & Frohlich, NYC 56-64; Res & ref libn City Col (NYC) 64-. 9: ALA; NY Lib Club. 10: AAUP; Beta Phi Mu. 14: Ref, catlg, automation. 15: 170 E 94 st, New York NY 10028.

BLATZ, SISTER IMOGENE OSB. b Bloomington Minn 20 F 11. 5: Col of St Benedict 30-31, summers 35-41; St Cloud State Col summer 34; Seattle U 35-39; Holy Names Col 41-42 (Educ) BA; UPortland summer 49; Col of St Catherine summers 50-54 BS in LS; Marquette U summer 55. 6: Ger. 7: Tchr Holy Rosary Sch, Tacoma Wash 32-41; Tchr Visitation Sch, Tacoma Wash 42-45; Tchr Holy Rosary Sch, Tacoma Wash 45-52; Tchr & prin st Joseph Minn 52-55; Libn St Benedict's High Sch, St Joseph Minn 55-59; Asst libn Col of St Benedict 55-60, Libn 60-. 9: ALA; CathLA; MinnLA. 10: Amer Benedictine Acad. 14: Catlg. 15: Col of St Benedict, St Joseph Minn 56374.

BLAU, EDMUND J. b New York NY 2 Je 15. 5: CornellU 31-35 (Chem) BChem; UChicago 35-36 (Chem) SM; Ohio StateU 48-53 (Phys Chem) PhD. 6: Ger, Fr. 7: Jr chem Indiana Ordnance Wks, Charlestown Ind 41-42; USA electronics tech (T/Sgt) 42-46; Chem Nat Bur of Standards, Wash DC 46-48, Sr chem 53-56; Sr chem Johns HopkinsU Applied Physics Lab, Silver Spring Md 56-63, Bibliogr 63-, Lib syst analyst 68-. 9: ASIS; ACS; Amer Phys Soc; Pgilos Soc of Wash DC. 10: Phi Lambda Upsilon; Sigma Phi Sigma. 13: Yes. 14: Lib automation, bibliogr, info retrieval. 15: 3010 Homewood pky, Kensington Md 20795.

BLAUSTEIN, ALBERT PAUL. b NYC 12 O 21. 4: Phyllis Migden. 5: UMich 38-41 (Hist) AB; Columbia 46-48 LLB, 53 (LS); Rutgers 58 (LS). 7: Newspaper rep & rewrite man City Bur of Chicago & Chicago Tribune 41-42; US Army (Pvt to 1st Lt) 42-46; Priv law practice, NYC 48-50, 52-55; Korean War, 50-52 JAGC 1st Lt - Maj; Asst Prof & Law Libn NY Law Sch 53-55; Prof of Law & Law Libn Rutgers U S Jersey (Camden NJ) 55-. 8: Spec studies consul, Survey of Legal Prof, Amer Bar Assn, 48-54; Spec law lib consul, Haile Sellassie I Univ, Addis Ababa Ethiopia, 62; Spec consul on law libs in Africa for Inst of Internat Educ & Intl Leg Center 63-; Law Lib Consul, USIA to Select Bks for drafting 1967 Vietnam Const 66; Law lib consul, 1967, US Aid to Vietnam. 9: Numerous. 10: Numerous. 12: Assoc ed "Public Relations for Bar Associations" (52 & 53); Co-auth "The American Lawyer" (54); "Fiction Goes to Court" (54 & 62); Co-auth "Desegregation and the Law" (57, 59 & 62); "Civil Law, Civil Affairs Legislation; Selected Cases and Materials" (61); "Manual on Foreign Legal Periodicals and Their NDEX" (62); "Civil Rights USA" (62 & 63); "Fundamental Legal Documents of Communist China" (62); "Human and Other Beings" (63); Co-auth "Civil Rights and the American Negro" (68); "Black Man, White Man" (70). 13: Yes. 14: Law lib admin, legal bibliog, teaching legal research & writing. 15: Rutgers-Camden Law School Lib, Camden NJ 08102.

BLAUVELT, THOMAS JOSEPH. b Queens NY 10 Mr 44. 4: Marion Donohue. 5: Cathedral Col 62-66 (Philos) BA; Queens Col 67-69 MLS. 7: Trainee Bus Lib ColumbiaU 67-68; Ref libn Freeport Mem Lib, Freeport NY 68-. 9: ALA; NassauCoLA. 14: Ref. 15: Freeport Mem Lib W Merrick rd, Freeport NY 11520.

BLAZEK, RONALD DAVID. b Chicago 13 Je 36. 4: Genevieve Kanape. 5: UIll (Chicago) 54-56 (LAS); Chicago Tchrs Col 56-58 (Educ) BEd, 58-61 (Sch Libnship) M Ed; UIll 63-65 (LS) MS, 65- (LS). 6: Sp, Fr. 7: Tchr Cooper Elem Sch, Chicago 58-60; Libn Montefiore Soc Adj Sch, Chicago 60-62; Libn Marshall High Sch, Chicago 62-64; Hd circ dept Chicago State Col 65, Asst prof lib sci 67-. 8: Tchr, Citizenship & Americanization for Adults, Chicago Bd of Educ 61-64; Consul, Sch Libs and Instr Materials Ctrs, State of Ill Off of Pub Instr 65-66. 9: ALA; -AASchL; -ACRL; IllLA (Intel Freedom Com 66-68). 10: AAUP; Beta Phi Mu. 11: HEA Fellowship, UIll 68-69. 14: Col & univ libs, sch libs, adult educ, lib educ. 15: 8029 S Massasoit, Oak Lawn Ill 60459.

BLAZZARD, MARY BETH (JECKER). b San Rafael Cal 27 Ap 38. 4: Norse N Blazzard. 5: Stanford 56-59 (Hist) AB; UCal at Berkeley 66-67 MLS. 6: Fr, Ger. 7: Auditor IRS San Francisco 62; Tchr US Army, Germany 62-65; Catlgr UCal at Davis Law Lib 68-. 9: ALA. 10: LWV. 12: CompUnion List of Scientific & Technical Serials in the University of Michigan Library(58); Ed "Library Cooperation in New York City" (62-64); Ed "Directory ofcooperating Libraries in Metropolitan New York City" (63, 64); 'Technical Informationin the Library' in "Students Engineering Handbook" (68). 14: Catlg, tech serv. 15: 1214 Bucknell dr, Davis Ca 95616.

BLEAN, KEITH C JR. b Los Angeles Cal 27 D 30. 5: UCal at Santa Barbara 56-58 (Hist) BA; UCal at Berkeley 63-64 (LS) MLS. 6: Ger, Fr. 7: Tech instr USAF Air Weather Serv (staff sgt) 49-53; Catlgr Stanford Libs 65-66; Admin asst catlg division Stanford 66-69; Hd catlg dept UCal at Santa Barbara 69-. 8: Lib Systems Consul, Automation Div (Project BALLOTS), StanfordU Libs 68-69. 9: ALA (Coun of Reg Gps 68); No Cal Tech Processing Gp (chm 68). 14: Tech processing, automation. 15: 2147 Mountain ave, Santa Barbara Ca 94101.

BLEDSOE, ROBERT (VALENZUELA). b New Orleans 26 Ja 34. 5: Tulane 52-55 (Span) BA; LSU 58-60 (LS) MS. 6: Sp. 7: Clerical Nat Bank of Com in New Orleans 56-58; Staff Tulane U 60-. 9: ALA; SLA; LaLA; New Orleans Lib Club. 10: Phi Beta Kappa; Phi Sigma Iota; Phi Kappa Sigma. 14: Acquis. 15: 7004 St Charles ave, New Orleans La 70118.

BLEECKER, CHESTER VINCENT. b Scott City Kan 20 Mr 19. 4: Elaine (Majchrzak) Bleecker. 5: Kan U 38-42, 45-46 (Violin) BM, 47-49 (Composition) MM; Columbia 50-51 (Langs); Simmons 59-62 (LS) MS. 6: Fr, Ger, Ital, Lat. 7: S/sgt Crypto US Army Africa 42-45; Instr Baker U 47-48; Instr Kan U summer 48-49; Tchr city schs, Haddam Kan 49-50; Asst Prof UNH 51-58; Head Art & Music dept Brookline Pub Lib, Brookline Mass 58-62; Head libn Peabody Inst Lib, Danvers Mass 62-64; Head libn Warwick Pub Lib, Warwick RI 64-. Lecturer U RI Grad, Sch of LS (part-time). 9: ALA; NELA; RILA. 13: Yes. 14: Ref, catlg. 15: 21 Delwood Rd, Warwick RI 02889.

BLEECKER, MRS RUTH (MERCER). b Phila 18 Mr 21. 5: Colo State U 39-43 (Music) BM; UKan 47-48 (Music Educ) MME; Rutgers U 59-63 MLS. 6: Fr, Ger, Ital. 7: Sec & music libn Rutgers U 58-63; Curator of music Boston Pub Lib 63-. 9: MusLA; NEMusLA. 10: Beta Phi Mu. 14: Ref. 15: 222 Babcock, Brookline Ma 02146.

BLEICHER, EDWIN CHARLES. b Brooklyn NY 16 Ag 06. 4: Henrietta Kaastra. 5: St John's Col (NY) 27-30 (Eng) BS; NYU even 31-33; Columbia 36-37 (LS) BS. 7: Sales correspondent Chase Securities Corp, NYC 30-33; Lib asst Morristown (Pub) Lib, Morristown NJ 35-36; Asst libn The Lawrenceville Sch, Lawrenceville NJ 37-42; Army Airways Communication System, US Army Air Corp (Pvt-T/Sgt) Communications, US & Alaska 42-45; Asst libn The Lawrenceville Sch, Lawrenceville NJ 46-48, Assoc libn 48-. 9: ALA; NJAIST (chm Lib/a-v div). 10: Pres Bd Trustees, The Lawrenceville CommunLib. 13: Yes. 14: Circ, ref. 15: John Dixon Lib, The Lawrenceville Sch, Lawrenceville NJ 08648.

BLEVINS, MARY LOUISE (ALDRICH). b Hornell NY 21 Ja 24. 5: Fredonia State Tchrs Col 41-43 (Educ); AlfredU 43-45 (Eng) BA; Syracuse 49-50 MS in LS. 6: Fr. 7: US Army 45-47; Admin asst Dunkirk Free Lib, Dunkirk NY 47-49; Sch libn Cuyahoga Co Pub Lib, Garfield Hts Ohio 54-58; Libn Kenton Local Schs, Kenton Ohio 58-62; Libn Arcanum Local Schs, Arcanum Ohio 62-67; Ref libn A F Inst of Tech, Wright-Patterson AFB 67-. 8: Lib consul Hobart Welding Co Tech Ctr, Troy Ohio 63-. 10: Pi Lamda Sigma; ArcanumClrTA. 14: Ref serv. 15: 620C Dodge ct, Dayton Oh 45431.

BLEVINS, ROBERT McDOWELL. b Volant Penn 7 S 17. 4: Marguerite Jane Blevins. 5: Geneva Col 35-39 AB; Syracuse 49-50 MSLS. 7: USN 44-46; Bkmob libn Athens Co Lib, Nelsonville Ohio 50-52; Child bkmob libn Cuyahoga Co Lib, Cleveland Ohio 52-56; Dir Hardin Co Lib, Kenton Ohio 57-61; Dir Carnegie Pub Lib, Greenville Ohio 62-68; Asst dir Grove City Pub Lib, Grove City Ohio 69-. 10: Lions Club. 15: 1666 Eastfield dr, Columbus Oh.

BLEW, MRS KATIE ARNEST. b Oakland Cal 3 N 31. 4: Robert W Blew. 5: UCLA 50-54 (Hist) BS, 62-63 MLS. 7: Libn Los Angeles Pub Lib 63-65; Libn II San Fernando Valley State Col 65-67, Libn III 67-. 9: CalLA. 14: Ref. 15: 19754 Schoolcraft st, Canoga Park Ca 91304.

BLEY, MRS RUTH (CHASE). b Schenevus NY 9 S 13. 4: Philip H Bley. 5: Hartwick Col 30-34 (Eng, Hist) BA; State U Col (Albany NY) 35-36 BS in LS; Ohio U 47-48 (Spec). 7: Tchr Dist Sch in Town of Roseboom NY 34-35; Tchr-libn Schenevus High Sch, SchenevusNY 36-38; Tchr-libn Cherry Valley C S, Cherry Valley NY 38-40; Libn Schenectady CoLib, Schenectady NY 49-50; Libn V State U Col (Buffalo NY) 62-. 9: ALA; NYLA; SUNYLA. 10: Faculty Assn of SUNY; Consul for church lib. 14: Ref. 15: 239 Hamilton blvd, Kenmore NY 14217.

BLEYHL, NORRIS A(RTHUR). b Snyder Neb 7 My 15. 4: Zella E Smith. 5: Midland Col 32-34; UNeb 34-36 (Hist) BA; UDenver 37-38 BS in LS; UMinn 46-47, 49-51 (Hist) MA, PhD. 7: Circ asst Lincoln City Lib, Lincoln Neb 36-37; Catlgr UOmaha 38-39; Asst period dept & bus lib Temple U 39-43; Tech Sge Med Dept US Army 43-46; Libn Mesa Col 47-49; Col libn Chico State Col 51-66; Dir of Libs 66-. 9: CalLA. 10: Phi Alpha Theta; Butte Co Hist Soc. 14: Lib admin, lib sci instr. 15: 237 W Lincoln ave, Chico Ca 95926.

BLIGHT, RALPH (ERNEST). b Mitchell Ont Can 18 D 22. 4: Gladys Heath. 5: UWest Ont 44-47 (Gen Arts) BA; Huron Col 47-49 (Theol) Leth; UToronto 59-60 BLS. 7: Clergyman anglican Ch of Can Diocese of Huron Can 49-59; Libn pub lib, Milton Ont Can 60-61; Libn Penetanguishene High Sch Penetanguishene Ont Can 65-67; Catlgr Waterloo LutheranU 67-. 9: OntLA. 14: Catlg, ref. 15: 1579 Applewood rd, Port Credit Ont Can.

BLISS, DOROTHY HELEN. b Greeley Colo 4 Ag 08. 5: Colo State Col 25-29 (Educ) BA; UDenver summers 37-39 BS in LS; UOre 53-54 (Educ) MEd USC 66-67 MS in LS. 7: Child libn Greeley Pub Lib, Greeley Colo 36-41; Circ libn Moline Pub Lib, Moline Ill 41-43; Spec serv libn Casper Air Base, Casper Wyo 43-44; Spec serv libn Camp Carson, Colo Springs Colo 44-45; Catlg libn Coun Bluffs (Iowa) Pub Lib 45-47; Ref libn East Ore Col 47-68, Assoc prof, LS 69-. 9: ALA (sec Col Sect 62-63); -ACRL (Memb Com 63-64); OreLA (pres 58-59, v-pres 57-58; chm Nom Com 59-60, Const Com 57-58; chm Memb Com 56-57; chm Constit Revision Com 61-62). 10: AAUP; AAUW; Delta Kappa Gamma. 14: Ref, loc & reg hist, Indian hist. 15: E Ore Col, La Grande Or 97850.

BLOCK, JEAN P. b Lockport NY. 4: Richard L Block. 5: Geneseo State Tchrs Col 41-45 BS in LS; NY State U Col (Geneseo) 60-65 MS in LS. 7: E I duPont de Nemours & Co, Buffalo NY: Staff 45-47, Asst libn 47-50, Libn 50-. 9: SLA. 10: Red Cross. 14: Ref, espec in scis. 15: E I duPont de Nemours & Co, Sta B, Buffalo NY 14207.

BLODGETT, PHILIP R. b Chicago Ill 19 Ap 08. 4: Adah Smith. 5: Bowdoin 26-30 (Hist) AB; UMich 31-32 ABLS. 6: Fr, Ger. 7: Ref asst Chicago Pub Lib 30-36; Libn Fed Reformatory, El Reno Okla 36-39; State supv WPA Lib Proj, Ky 39-41; Asst libn Klamath Co Lib, Klamath Falls Ore 41-43; Libn Clasop Co Lib, Astoria Ore 43-49; Dir Everett Pub Lib, Everett Wash 49-. 9: ALA; PNLA (chm Constit Rev Com); WashLA; OreLA (pres & mem var coms). 10: Delta Upsilon; Bowdoin & Mich Alum Assns; Wash State Golf Assn; Kwanis Club; Elks Lodge; Golf & Country Club; Citizens Adv Com. 11: John Cotton Dana Award (twice). 14: Bk sel, acquis. 15: Everett Pub Lib, Everett Wa 98201.

BLOEMENDAAL, LAWRENCE. b Alton Iowa 10 Ag 21. 4: Frances Brink. 5: Northwestern College 62-66 (Soc Sci) BA; U S Fla 66-67 (Lib, A-v) MA. 7: Bloemendaal Hatchery, Alton Iowa: Laborer 39-44, owner operator 46-66; Soldier USA, US & Asia 44-46; Elem libn & asst to supt Floyd Valley Commun Schs, Alton Iowa 67-. 8: Current appointments include; Title I, ESEA Coord dir; Title III, NDEA Coord. 9: NEA; IowaASchL; Iowa State EA. 15: Box 199, Alton Ia 51003.

BLOOD, BETTINA (BIAS). b Huntington WVa 24 Ag 45. 4: Allen Holt Blood. 5: W Va Wesleyan Col 63-67 (LS) BS; Marshall summers 64, 66; Peabody Col 67-68 MLS. 7: Stud asst WVa Wesleyan Col 66-67; Asst in ch lib serv Methodist Publ House, Nashville summer 67; File clk Disciples of Christ Hist Soc, Nashville 68; Acquis libn Morrill Memorial Lib, Norwood Mass 68-. 9: ALA; Old Colony Lib Club. 14: Bk selection, ref, wk with youth. 15: 36 Walpole st, Norwood Ma 02062.

BLOOD, HELEN (LOUISE). b Gustavus Ohio 7 Ja 16. 5: Hiram 35-39 (Gen lit) AB; Case-West Res 41-42 BS in LS. 7: Adult bkmob Lucas Co Lib, Maumee Ohio 42; Warren Pub Lib, Warren Ohio 43; Hd city circ & ext 43-47; Reader's adv Kent State Lib 47-50; Asst libn John McIntire Pub Lib Zanesville Ohio 50-52; Hd libn Tiffin-Seneca Pub Lib Tiffin Ohio 52-. 9: ALA; OhioLA. 10: AAUW; Lay Adv Bd: Mercy Hosp; St Francis Home for Aged. 14: Bk sel, admin. 15: 470 Sycamore st, Tiffin Oh 44883.

BLOOM, CHARLES WALTER. b Passaic NJ 21 O 22. 5: Yuba Jr Col 39-41 (Eng) AA; UCal (Berkeley) 41-43 (Eng) AB, 46-48 (Eng) MA, 51-52 BLS. 6: Fr, Ger. 7: Cryptographer USAAF (AACS) (Sgt), S Pacific 43-46; Instr Eng UCal (Santa Barbara) 48-51; Libn III Humboldt State Col Lib 52-. 9: ALA; CalLA. 10: Phi Delta Kappa; Sierra Club; Amer Forestry Assn; Phi Beta Kappa; Wilderners Soc. 14: Ref, water resources libnship. 15: 12 E 15th st, Apt 4, Arcata Ca 95521.

BLOOMBERG, MARJORIE (BRAWER). b Paterson NJ 27 Mr 20. 4: Irving Bloomberg. 5: NYU (Educ) BS; Pratt 65 MLS. 7: Libn Midland Sch, Rye NY 63-66; Hd libn New Rochelle High Sch 66-. 9: ALA; NEA; NY State Tchrs Assn. 10: Beta Phi Mu. 14: Sch lib serv. 15: 6 Ridgeway rd, Larchmont NY.

BLOOMER, GERTRUDE (EVELYN). b Mishawaka Ind 17 S 08. 5: Ind U 37-41 (Fr) AB; UIll 42-43 BSLS. 6: Fr, Ger, Ital. 7: Libn The Wm S Merrell Co, Cincinnati 43-. 9: SLA; (chm Pharmaceutical div 66-67); ALA; OhioLA. 11: Science-Technology Div, SLA Publ Award 61. 12: Ed "Union List of Periodicals in Pharmaceutical Libraries" (52); Ed "Union List of Scientific and Technical Periodicals in Libraries of Greater Cincinnati and Vicinity" (58); Ed "Scientific Meetings" (57-62). 13: Yes. 14: Admin. 15: 1060 Springfield Pike, Wyoming, Cincinnati 45215.

BLOOMFIELD, MASSE. b Franklin NH 20 Ag 23. 4: Fay Koenigsberg. 5: UNH 40-42, 46-48 (Bacteriology) BS; Carnegie 50-51 MLS; USoCal 63- (LS). 7: Navigator US Army Air Force (Capt) 42-45; Catlgr USDA Lib, Wash DC 51-52; Catlgr US Naval Ordnance Test Sta Lib, China Lake Cal 52-55; Asst libn Atomics Internat (Div of North Amer Aviation), Canoga Park Cal 55-62; Superv Culver City Lib, Culver City Cal 62-. 9: ASIS; SLA. 13: Yes. 14: Admin, indexing. 15: 20733 Stephanie dr, Canoga Park Cal 91306.

BLOOMFIELD, ROSEMARY JUNE ELSPETH. b Edinburgh Scotland 17 Je 29. 5: Loughborough Col 9england) 53-54; Wash State Lib Certif 66. 7: Br supv Worcestershire Co Lib, Worcester England 51-56; Br libn Norfolk Co Coun, Norfolk England 57-66; Circ libn Yakima Valley Reg Lib, Yakima Wash 63-65; Ref libn Pierce Co Lib, Tacoma Wash 66-67; Supv commun libs Sno-Isle Reg Lib, Marysville Wash 67-. 9: Lib Assn (England); WashLA (mem Recruitment Sub-com). 10: Fellow Royal Soc of Arts & Com, London. 15: Apt A Madison Manor 8th and Fir, Mt Vernon Wa 98273.

BLOOMQUIST, HAROLD (JOHN). b Muskegon Mich 27 O 28. 5: Muskegon Jr Col 46-48; Albion Col 48-50 (Eng) AB; Columbia 51-54 (LS) MS, 54- (Sci & Med Libnship). 6: Fr, Sp, Ger. 7: Page Hackley Pub Lib, Muskegon Mich 44-46, Catlg asst 46-48; Catlg asst Albion Col Lib 48-50; Asst to supt of transportation Inter-State Motor Frt Co, Grand Rapids Mich 50-51; Desk asst Columbia Zoology-Botany Lib 51-53, Libn 53-54; Sr ref asst Columbia Med Lib 54-57, Med ref libn 57-58; Asst libn for resources & acquis Harvard Med Lib 58-61, Asst libn 61-65; Asst libn Harvard U Francis A Countway Lib of Med 65-67, Act libn 67-68, libn 69-. 8: Consul to Ed dental sect "Stedman's Medical Dictionary" 61-; Sci Adv Com on

PAHO Reg Med Lib, Brazil 68-; Lib consul Med Col of Ohio 67-; Com on selection of lit for MEDLARS 68-. 9: MedLA (chm Com on Continuing Educ 64-65); SLA; Amer Assn of Dental Editors; Coun on Research in Bibliog Inc (Bd dir); MedLa-NY Reg Group (by-laws Com, chm 57-58); MedLA-NE Reg Group. 10: Harvard Lib Club; Harvard Club of Boston. 12: Ed "Science Reference Notes" (55-58); "The Status and Needs of Med Sch Libs in the US" (62); Ed bulletin of MedLA. 13: Yes. 14: Admin, ref, bk sel. 15: 10 Shattuck st, Boston Ma 02115.

BLOOMSBURGH, ESTHER (GEORGE). b Haverhill Mass 22 D 17. 4: Ralph Bloomsburgh. 5: Smith 36-40 (Econ) BA; Drexel 62-65 MS in LS. 7: Asst libn Ambler Campus Temple U 66-. 9: ALA; MusLA; Assn for Recorded Sound Collections; PennLA. 10: Beta Phi Mu. 14: Ref, music. 15: 3008 Edmonds rd, Lafayette Hill Pa 19444.

BLOSS, MEREDITH. b Cressey Mich 17 D 08. 4: Maureen Williams. 5: Oberlin 29-32 (Eng) AB; Columbia 39-40 (LS) BS. 6: Fr. 7: Dir of pub rel & asst libn Hartford Pub Lib, Hartford Conn 40-43; US Army 43-46; Libn Adriance Mem Lib, Poughkeepsie NY 47-48; Asst libn Pub Lib of Youngstown & Mahoning Co, Youngstown Ohio 48-52; Asst city libn Milwaukee Pub Lib 52-58; City Libn New Haven Free Pub Lib, New Haven Conn 59-. 9: ALA; ConnLA (v-pres 65-66; pres 66-67). 10: Kiwanis Club of New Haven; Grad Club, New Haven. 13: Yes. 14: Admin, bk sel. 15: 65 Beckett ave, Short Beach Ct 06405.

BLOSTEIN, PAUL J. b Chicago 5 Ap 26. 5: UCal(Berkeley) 48-50 (Behav Scis) AB; UDenver 55-58 (LS) AM; USoCal 60-62, 66 (Telecommunic) AM UCLA 67 (Info Mgt Tech) Standard Cal Jr Col Credential in Soc, Info Sci & Libnship, 68. 6: Fr, Sp. 7: Br libn Oakland (Cal) Pub Lib 50-51; Ref libn Main Oakland Pub Lib (Cal) 51-58; Ref libn Lewis & Clark Col Lib 58-59; Asst catlg libn San Diego State Col 59-60; Asst sci libn USoCal 61; Chief pub serv Inglewood (Cal) Pub Lib 62; Bus-sci-tech spec Alhambra (Cal) Pub Lib 64; Systems analyst Los Angeles Co Pub Lib 64; Info research analyst, space & info systems div No Amer Aviation Inc, Downey Cal 63-66; Asst libn Instr Media Resource Ctr Antelope Valley Col 67-69. 8: Publ for Oakland (Cal) Centennial Com & Gerontol Com, Oakland Pub Lib 51-58; Co-producer of a series of radio programs on commun devel, Oakland Pub lib 54; Design of an analytical index to bks on Amer Indian Ethnol, Oakland Pub Lib 58 Aerospace tech reports and bibliogs 63-66; Comprehensive Plan for an Integrated Mt Info Retr System for Los Angeles Co Pub Lib 64. 9: ALA; SLA; ASIS; CalLA; Assn of Cal State Col Profs. 12: "Natural Language Display Within Command and Control Systems" (64); "Preliminary Analysis & Design of Automated Circulation & Registration Systems" (64); "Bibliography on Ground Requirements for Advanced Space Exploration" (66); "Guide to the Literature of Aerospace Management" (66). 14: Ref, catlg & index, bibliog, lib publ & promotion, info retrieval systems analysis & design, instr media ctr. 15: 44224 N Cedar ave, Lancaster Ca 93534.

BLOUNT, EDWARD F. b Holyoke Mass 26 D 16. 5: Yale 35-39 (Hist) BA; Harvard 39-40 (Hist) MA; Yale 40-42, 46-49 (Hist); Columbia 53-55 MSLS. 6: Fr. 7: US Army Adjutant Gen Corps Personnel Clsf Off (Capt) 42-46; Instr of Hist Capital U 49-50; Hist Tchr Nichols Sch, Buffalo NY 52-53; Catlgr Amherst Col Lib 55-57; Sr ser catlgr Yale U Lib 57-59, Sr subj catlgr 59-67; Asst libn Bates Col 67-. 8: Capt 51-59, Major 59-66, Lt Col 66-69;Adjutant Gen Corps US Army Reserve. 9: ALA; NY Tech Serv Libns (Com Wk 60-63);MeLA. 10: Yale Lib Staff Assn (pres 64-65); Twin Cities Lib Coun (Lewiston-Auburn). 14: Ref, admin. 15: 166 Wood st, Lewiston Me 04240.

BLOUNT, VIOLA (MOORE). b Boston 30 D 20. 4: Richard Blount. 5: Bryn Mawr 38-42 (Fr) AB; West Res 56-61 (LS) MS. 6: Fr. 7: Cryptographer US Navy, Wash DC 42-44; Libn Hawken Sch, Lyndhurst Ohio 58-63; Libn Cuyahoga Co Lib, So Euclid Ohio 63-64, Mayfield Heights Ohio 64-65, S Euclid Ohio, 66-. 9: ALA; OhioLA. 14: Young adult, adult serv. 15: 1971 Laurelhill dr, S Euclid Oh 44121.

BLOWERS, G ELAINE. b Mankato Minn 23 Jl 32. 5: NE Mo State Col 59 (Elem, Educ) BS in educ; No Ill U 66-67 MA in LS; UMd 61-62. 7: Tchr public schs Knox Co Mo 49-57, Aurora Ill 57-60; Tchr Dept Def Schs, Chize France 60-61); Libn Dept Def Schs, Wiesbaden Germany 61-63; Tchr Dept Def Schs Karamursel Turkey 63-64, Ramstein Germany 64-66; Libn No Ill U 67-69, Docs libn 69-. 9: ALA; IllLA. 15: 510 S Main st, Sandwich Il 60548.

BLUE, ELEANORE CECILIA. b Spokane Wash. 5: Wash U 47-51 (LS) BS; St Louis U 53-57 LLB. 7: Staff Washington U (St Louis) 51-59; Law libn Washburn U 59-60; Law libn UMo (Kan City) 60-. 9: AALL; MoLA. 10: Greater Kansas City Club; Mo Bar; Kansas City Bar. 12: Ed "University of Kansas City Law Review" (56); Humanitarian Doctrine Evidence. 14: Legal bibliog. 15: Univ of Mo (Kansas City) Law Lib, 5100 Rockhill rd, Kansas City Mo 64110.

BLUE, GARTH (ALVIN). b Regina Sask Can 10 Ap 41. 4: Sharon Hosegood. 5: USask 58-59, 61-62 (Psych, Eng) BA; UBC 63-64 BLS. 7: Lib asst Regina Pub Lib, Regina Sask 62-63; Temp libn Sask Wheat Pool Lib, Regina Sask 63; Ref libn Sask Legis Lib, Regina Sask 64-66; Libn Lib Regina (Can) Dept of Agric 66-69; Libn Lib Regina (Can) Dept ofReg Econ Expan 69-. 9: CanLA; SaskLA; ReginaLA (pres 65-66). 14: Govt docs. 15: 2850 Angus st, Regina Sask Can.

BLUE, KATHRYN JOAN. b Quincy Ill 23 Fe 46. 5: Cornell Col (Iowa) 63-67 (Ger) BA; UWis (Madison) 67-68 MALS. 6: Ger, Fr, Russian. 7: Asst catlgr Swem Lib William & Mary Col 68-. 9: ALA; VaLA. 14: Catlg. 15: 725R Lafayette st, Williamsburg Va 23185.

BLUE, MARGARET (LINN). b Seattle 15 Je 34. 5: Marylhurst Col 52-56 (Eng Lit) BA; UWash 58-59 M of Libnship; Columbia 65- (LS). 6: Fr. 7: High Sch libn Othello High Sch, Othello Wash 56-57; Libn Marylhurst Col 57-58; Asst libn ref & circ U Portland 59-61; Elem libn & lib sci instr Central Wash State Col 61-65; Asst Prof Lib Sci San Diego State; Coord dept of lib educ Okla State U; Asst ref libn Cal West U. 14: Sch lib wk, lib educ, catlg. 15: 4711 Coronado ave, San Diego Ca 92107.

BLUE, MARGARET R. b Le Mars Iowa. 5: Cornell 52-56 (Math) BA; UPittsburgh 66-67 MLS. 7: Grad asst tchr Ohio State 56-63; Tchr volunteer US Peace Corps Ijebu-Ode, Nigeria 63-65; Asst libn UNebr 67-. 9: ALA; SLA; NebLA; LincolnLA. 10: Bus & Prof Women. 14: Tech serv, automation. 15: 2910 S 42nd st, Lincoln Nb 68506.

BLUM, FRED. b NYC 27 N 32. 4: Beula Eisenstadt. 5: Oberlin 50-54 (Piano) BM; Ohio U 54-55 (Piano) MFA; State U Iowa 55-59 (Musicology) PhD; UKoln (Germany) 59-60 (Musicology); Freie U Berlin (Germany) 60-61 (Musicology). Catholic U 67-68 MSLS. 6: Ger, Fr. 7: Tchg asst Ohio U 54-55; Research & tchg asst State U Iowa 55-59; Staff music div NY Pub Lib summer 59; Exch tchr German Academic Exchange (Bonn), Berlin 60-61; Ref libn LC 61-66, Ed Nat Register of Microform Masters 66-67; Hd spec serv dept Catholic U Libs 67-. 8: Lib/USA, NY World's Fair 65; Inst on Computer-Based Lib Info Systems, UMo 68. 9: ALA; MusLA (chm Wash-Baltimore Chap 64-66; chm Com on Microforms & Photoduplication, chm Preservat Standards Subcom); DCLA. 11: Deutscher Akademischer Austauschdienst grant, 59-60; Deutscher Paedagogischer austauschdienst grant, 60-61. 12: "Susanne Langer's Music Aesthetics," dissert (59); "Music Monographs in Series; A Bibliography of Numbered Monograph Series in the Field of Music Current Since 1945" (64); "Jean Sibelius; An International Bibliography" (65); "Guide to Selected Research Material on Microforms" (68); Asst ed "DC Libraries" (67-). 14: Lib admin, automation, info stor & retr, microforms, research and pub. 15: 2400 Queens Chapel rd, Hyattsville Md 20782.

BLUM, JANET H. b Greensboro NC 11 F 41. 4: William R Blum. 5: Peace Col 59-61 AA; UNC 61-63 (Eng) AB, 63-64 MS in LS. 7: Catlg ref libn May Mem Lib, Burlington NC 64-67; Elem sch libn Newport Schs, Newport R I 67-. 9: ALA; SELA; RIASchL. 14: Catlg, ref, child. 14: Catlg, ref, child. 15: 12 Shore dr, Middletown Ri 02840.

BLUM, JOHN PHILLIP. b Warren Ohio 2 Ap 30. 4: Judith Arnold. 5: UNMex 54-57 BA; UCal (Berkeley) 60-61 MLS. 6: Sp. 7: Circ asst UNMex Lib 56-58; Adult serv div Berkeley Pub Lib, Berkeley Cal 60-61; Curator Museu pub Lib, Berkeley Cal 60-61; Curator Museum of NM, Santa Fe 62-67; Law libn NM Supreme Court Law Lib 67-. 9: ALA; NMLA; AALL. 14: Ref, admin. 15: 115 Camino Escondido, santa Fe NM 87501.

BLUM, NORBERT. b Vienna Austria 25 Ag 21. 5: Washington & Lee U 40-41 (Liberal Arts); Sampson Col 47-48 (Liberal Arts); Cornell U 49-51 (Pol Sci) BA; State U Col (Geneseo NY) 60-61 (LS) MS Ed. 6: Ger. 7: T/5 in Intelligence Unit US Army, N Africa, Europe 43-45; Catlgr N Co Lib System, Watertown NY 62-. 67; Acting supv of tech serv 68, Supv of tech serv 69-. 9: ALA; NYLA. 10: Phi Beta Kappa; ACLU; Diabled Amer Veterans. 14: Catlg, tech serv. 15: Hotel Woodruff, Watertown NY 13601.

BLUM, SARAH (MALES). b NYC 3 O 11. 4: Solomon Blum. 5: Hunter Col 27-31 (Ger) AB; Tchrs Inst of the Jewish Theol Sem 27-31 (Hebrew) BJP; No Tex State Col 55-58 BS in LS. 6: Ger, Fr, Hebrew, Yiddish. 7: Asst to dir Educ Radio Script Exch of the US Off of Educ, Wash DC 36-40; 1st asst gen ref dept Pub Lib, Ft Worth Tex 54-61, Head gen ref dept 61-. 9: ALA; TexLA. 10: Nat Coun of Jewish Women; Phi Beta Kappa. 14: Ref. 15: 2504 Dean lane, Ft Worth Tx 76107.

BLUMENFELD, CATHERINE (ECK). b St Paul 9 S 37. 4: Michael Blumenfeld. 5: Radcliffe 55-59 (Govt) AB; Columbia 63-64 (LS) MS. 6: Fr. 7: Pre-prof asst Boston Pub Lib 59-60; Lib spec Ford Found Lib, NYC 60-63, Lib asst 64-67; Consul Fed City Col 67, Asst libn 68, Assoc dir of media serv 68-. 8: Consul on devel & planning, Fed City Col Wash DC 67. 10: Beta Phi Mu; Am Contract Bridge League. 12: Cont to "Media Power," ed by T Trevor (68). 13: Yes. 14: Admin, planning. 15: 1940 Biltmore st NW, Washington DC 20009.

BLUMSTEIN, TIMMIE SUSAN. b NYC 1 My 40. 5: Goucher 58-62 (Fr) BA; Columbia 64-65 MLS. 6: Fr, Ital. 7: Asst to libn French Inst Lib, NYC 62-65; Bk libn Amer Heritage Publishing Co Lib, NYC 65-. 14: Ref. 15: 308 E 79, NYC 10021.

BLYTHE, ESTHER ALFRIEND. b Macon Ga 30 O 37. 4: Gerald G Blythe. 5: Duke 56-60 (Pol Sci) BA; Simmons 62-64 MLS; Harvard summer 63 (Pol Sci); UVa 66-67 (Govt). 6: Fr. 7: Prof asst Harvard Bus Sch 60-62, Lib asst 62-64, Ref libn 64; Libn docs div Harvard U Lib 64; Circ libn URichmond, Richmond Va 65-66; Ref libn Fairfax Co Pub Lib McLean br, McLean Va 67-. 14: Ref. 15: Arlington Va.

BOAG, LINDA (LEE) (CANTON). b Mount Olive Ill 9 D 43. 4: Robert Boag. 5: El Camino col 62-65 (Liberal Arts) AA; UCLA 65-67 (Eng) BA, 68-69 MLS. 6: Sp, Ger. 7: Catlgr long Beach Pub Lib 69-. 9: ALA; CalLA. 14: Catlg, rare bks. 15: 2617 Manhattan ave, Hermosa Beach Ca 90254.

BOARD, PERMELIA E. b near Owensboro Ky 30 O 1900. 5: West Ky State Tchrs Col 27 (Educ) AB; Bowling Green Bus U summer 28; Peabody summer 35; Fla State U 50 (LS) MA. 6: Lat. 7: Tchr Daviess Co (Ky) Elem Schs 21-24, Prin 24-26; Asst prin Catlettsburg City Schs, Catlettsburg Ky 27-29; Libn Catlettsburg High Sch, Catlettsburg Ky 29-32; Tchr-libn Waynesburg Ind Sch, Waynesburg Ky 33-34; Tchr-libn Warren Co Schs, Rockfield & Oakland Ky 34-36, 39-42; Libn Tarpon Springs Sr High Sch, Tarpon Springs Fla 42-. 8: State Adv to Fla High Sch Lib Council's pres, 56-57. 9: NEA; FlaEA; FlaASchL; FlaLA; Pinellas Co Clr Tchrs. 10: Tarpon Springs Hosp Found; Rebekah Assembly of Fla. 14: Catlg. 15: 464 E Orange st, Tarpon Springs Fla 33589.

BOARDMAN, CHARLOTTE KATHARINE. b Cedar Grove NJ 9 N 17. 5: Rutgers (Newark) 57-63 (Math) AB, Grad Sch of Lib Serv, New Brunswick NJ (LS) 64-67. 7: Thomas A Edison Inc, W Orange NJ; Libn 49-57; Asst libn Radio Corp of Amer, Camden NJ summer 58; Libn Lockheed Electronics Co, Plainfield NJ 63; Search libn Gen Precision Aerospace, Little Falls NJ 63-64, Catlgr 64-68; Libn Amer Smelting & Refining Co Cent Research Lab, S Plainfield NJ 68-. 9: SLA (sec NJ Chap 53-55). 14: Ref, catlg, admin. 15: 9 High st apt W-1, Montclair NJ 07042.

BOARDMAN, ELIZABETH G. b Cedar Grove NJ 26 Je 16. 5: Rutgers U 50-54 (Bot) AB, 54-56 (Horticulture) MS; UNC 62-63 (Botany), 63-67 MS in LS. 7: Night supv Montclair Commun Hosp, Montclair NJ 48-50; Night nurse Douglass Col Infirmary 50-54; Grad res asst horticulture Col of Agric, Rutgers 54-56; Res asst & Instr Field Crops Dept NC State Col (Raleigh) 56-62; Bot lect NC Col at Durham 62-63; Ref libn NY Col of Agric & Tech (Farmingdale) 64; Agric & biol sci bibliogr & ref libn UCal (Davis) 65-. 9: ALA; Internat Assn for Hort Sci; SELA. 10: AAAS; ALBS. 14: Subj spec (agric & biol). 15: 908 Snyder dr, Davis Ca 95616.

BOARDMAN, NEIL S(ERVIS). b Stillwater Minn 16 Ja 07. 4: Una Watts. 5: UMinn (LS) BS. 7: Ind U: Circ libn 48-61, Undergrad Libn 61-65, Admin asst 65-68; Libn, Advanced Tchrs Col, Kano Nigeria 68-70. 8: Lib consul, Inst of Educ & Research, Univ of the Punjab, Lahore Pakistan, 63-65. 12: "The Long Home," novel(48); "The Wine of Violence," novel (64, End ed 65, Span ed 66). 13: Yes. 15: Ind Univ Libs, Bloomington In 47405.

BOATMAN, MAURICE WILSON. b Montezuma Iowa 11 F 13. 4: Doris Nay. 5: Iowa State Tchrs Col 31-35 (Eng) BA; Columbia 36 (LS) BS; UMich 64 MALS. 7: Ref asst NY Pub Lib 36-41; Self-employed 41-55; Ref libn Grinnell Col 55-61, Assoc libn 61-64; Libn Millikin U 64-. 9: ALA; IllLA (chm Col & Research Libs sect 69); Midwest Acadc Libns Conf (chm 68, 69). 10: Kiwanis Club; Phi Kappa Phi. 14: Admin. 15: 417 Timber dr, Decatur Il 62521.

BOAZ, MARTHA. b Stuart Va. 5: Madison Col 31-35 (Eng) BS; Peabody 37 BS in LS; UMich 49-50 MA in LS, 51-52 (LS) PhD. 6: Fr, Ger. 7: Critic tchr of Eng & sch libn, Bridgewater Va 35-37; Tchr of Latin & Eng & sch libn, Jeffersontown Ky 37-40; Asst libn Madison Col (Harrisonburg Va) 40-49; Assoc Prof of Lib Serv UTenn 50-51; Instr of Lib Sci UMich 51-52; Libn in Pub Serv Dept Pasadena Pub Lib, Pasadena Cal 52; Dean & Prof, Sch of Lib Sci USoCal 53-. 8: Lib Consul, Pakistan, US State Dept AID, 62; Lib Consul "Britannica Book of the Year"; Adv Bd: Pacific Oaks Friends Sch, Los Angeles Trade-Tech Col. Lib Repre for US State Dept in Vietnam 66-. 9: AALS (pres 61-62, Res Com 59-); ALA (chm Lippincott Award Com 63-, chm Com to Study Content of Ref Courses 63-65, mem Lib Admin Devel Com 63, mem Commsn on a Nat Plan on Lib Educ; chm Intel Freedom Com 64-); -LAD (Com on Ethics); -LED (pres 68-69); CalLA (pres 62, mem Lib Educ Div, mem Intel Freedom Com, mem; Lib Devel & Stand Com, Prof Educ Com, Reg Resources Com 61, Nat Lib Week Com); Cal SchLA (Hon mem); Pub Lib Execs Assn So Cal. 10: Kappa Delta Pi; Delta Kappa Gamma; AAUW; Beta Phi Mu; Charles Fletcher Mem Assn. 11: Sesquicentennial Award, UMich 67. 12: "Fervant and Full of Gits" (61); Ed "A Living Library" (58); Ed "Modern Trends in Documentation" (59); "The Quest for Truth v 1 (61) v2 (67); Co-auth "Reviews in Library Book Selection" (58); Ed Bd "Highlights for Children"; "Qualitative Analysis of the Criticism of Best Sellers" (55); "A Study of Professional Training for Librarians in Pakistan," mimeo (Karachi 62); Strength Through Cooperation (a survey of 60 public libraries); Reviser "A Guide to General Book Publishers" (50); Ed Bd "Highlights for Children". 13: Yes. 14: Bk sel, bibliog, rare bks, contin educ, research methods, lib educ, admin. 15: 1849 Campus rd, Los Angeles Ca 90041.

BOAZ, RUTH (LAVONNE). b Water Valley Ky 27 Mr 26. 5: Memphis State U 48 (Eng) BS; George Peabody Col for Tchrs 53 (LS) MA. 7: Circ asst Memphis Pub Lib, Memphis Tenn 48-50, 60-64; Libn Wynne High Sch, Wynne Ark 51-52; Asst libn Ill Wesleyan U, Bloomington Ill 53-54; Librarian I San Francisco State Col summer 53, 54-55; Catlgr Methodist Publ House, Nashville Tenn 56-59; Asst libn & sr lib supv NY State Educ Dept, Albany NY 64-68; Educ program specialist US Off of Educ, Wash DC 68-. 9: ALA. 10: AAUW; DAR. 14: Lib statistics, research, evaluation. 15: Federal Office Bldg 6 400 Maryland ave SW, Washington DC 20202.

BOBB, JOHN MORROW. b Hollidaysburg Penn 20 Ag 18. 5: Allegheny Col 35-37; Penn State U 40-42 (Liberal Arts) BA; Carnegie 50-51 (LS) MLA. 7: Armed Serv Adjutant Gen Dept, USA & Pacific 43-46; Prescription Prod Div, The Borden Co, Pittsburgh 49-50; Engnr libn Penn Sate U 51-56; Asst chief libn Oak Ridge Nat Lab, Oak Ridge Tenn 56-. 9: SLA (treas Sci-Tech Div 65-66, By-laws Com 69-71; Pres Oak Ridge Chap 60-61; TennLA (chm spec libs sect 65-66). 10: Toastmasters Internat; Oak Ridge Club; TennArchaeol Soc; Golf & Country Club Playhouse; Commun Art Center, Commun Music Assn; Phi Kappa Psi; Pi Gamma Mu. 13: Yes. 14: Admin. 15: PO Box X, Oak Ridge Tn 37831.

Bobbitt, Margaret S Eidel (Mrs James C). b Reed City Mich 29 Jl 08. 4: James Chilton Bobbitt. 5: Wittenberg U 26-30 (Eng) AB; Drexel 31 BS in LS. 7: Marshall Col: Asst libn 32-47, Ref libn in chg of period room & documents 47-56, ref libn in chg of pub serv 56-60; Ref libn & documents Marshall U 60-. 9: ALA-ACRL (Tri-State Chap); WVaLA (sec 36-37 & 54-55, pres 56-57, chm Col Sect 46, chm Legis Com 63-64, Fed Coord 64-65, mem Recr Team 64-). 10: AAUP; AAUW; Huntington Panhellenic Assn; Chi Omega. 12: Ed (with others) "West Virginia Libraries" (55-56). 14: Ref, govt docs, Interlib loan serv. 15: 1662 Glenway lane, Huntington WVa 25701.

BOBEN, MARIAN (STEVENS). b Kingston Pa 27 Je 41. 5: Mount Holyoke 59-60; UPenn 60-63 (Amer studies) BA; Drexel 65-67 MSLS. 6: Fr. 7: Library asst Haverford Col Lib 64-66; Children's libn Wolfson Memorial Lib, King of Prussia, Penn 67-. 9: ALA; PennLA (Planning Com, New Libns sect). 10: Phi Beta Kappa; Montgomery Lib Dist. 14: Serv to child & ya. 15: 254 Old Eagle School rd, Wayne Pa 19087.

BOBINSKI, GEORGE S. b Cleveland 24 O 29. 4: Mary Lillian Form. 5: West Res 47-51 (Hist) BA, 51-52 MSLS; UMich 61 (Hist) MA, 66 (LS) PhD. 6: Polish. 7: US Army Mil Intelligence 52-54; Ref asst Bus Info Bur Cleveland Pub Lib 54-55; Asst dir Royal Oak (Mich) Pub Lib 55-59; Dir of

Libs State U Col (Cortland NY) 60-67; Assoc Prof Sch of Lib Sci UKy 67-68, Asst Dean 68-. 8: Consul, Clawson (Mich) Pub Lib Reorg, 56-57. 9: ALA; MichLA (Dist treas 59-60); Chm Conf SUNY Head Libns 63-64; East Col Libns (treas 63-64); SUNY 4-yr Col Libns (chm 63-65); NYLA (dir Col & Univ Sec 64-66) KyLA; AALS. 10: AAUP; Polish-Amer Hist Assn; ACLU; Beta Phi Mu. 12: "A Brief History of theLibraries of Western Reserve University, 1826-1952," ACRL Microcard Series (55);Ed bd of "CHOICE" 66-; "Andrew Carnegie's Role in American Public Librarydevelopment," doctoral dissertation (66); "Carnegie Libraries; Their History andImpact on American Public Library Development," ALA (69). 13: Yes. 14: Admin, lib educ, libhist. 15: Sch of Lib Sci, Univ of Ky, Lexington Ky 40506.

BOBINSKI, MARY (FORM). b Rochester NY 29 Ag 28. 4: George S Bobinski. 5: URochester 47-51 (Eng) BA; West Res 51-52 MSLS. 7: Dir of children's wk Royal Oak (Mich) Pub Lib 52-53, 55-59; Supvr of sch librs Ft Bragg NC 53-54; Children's libn Miles Park Br Cleveland Pub Lib 54-55; Lecturer Sch of Lib Sci UKy 68-. 8: Consul Cortland (NY) Sch Dist Liba 66-67. 9: ALA; KyLA. 10: LWV. 14: Wk with child, lib educ. 15: 2200 Richmond rd, Lexington Ky 40502.

BOCCACCIO, MARY ANDREA. b San Antonio Tex 15 N 43. 5: Albion 61-65 (Hist) BA; UPenn 65-67 (Hist) MA; Wayne State 67-68 MSLS. 6: Ger, Fr. 7: Archival asst Wayne State 68-69; Archivist Rockefeller Foundation, NYC 69-. 9: SAA; SLA; Amer Records Mgt Assn (NY Chap). 10: Phi Alpha Theta. 11: Mich Scholar in Col Tchg. 14: Archives, preserv. 15: 250 E 73rd, New York NY 10021.

BOCHE, MARJORIE (STERN). b Eureka Cal 10 F 16. 7: Libn Chicago Midway Labs 51-55; Lib asst Lockheed Missile Systems Div, Van Nuys Cal 55-56; Libn Amer Machine & Foundry, Pacoima Cal 56-58; Libn Sundstrand Aviation, Pacoima Cal 58-60; Libn System Development Corp, Santa Monica Cal 60-. 9: SLA-SoCal Chap 9sec 63-64, memb chm 64-65, publ chm 65-66). 14: Ref. 15: 16526-1/2 Sunset blvd, Pacific Palisades Cal 90272.

BOCK, ARLINE ECKARD. b Dalton Ohio 18 My 11. 4: Irving M Bock. 5: UAkron 29-33 (Lat) BA; USoCal 39-40 bsls, 59-60 MSLS. 6: Fr. 7: High sch tchr Copley High Sch, Copley Ohio 33-39; Dist libn Montebello Unified Sch Dist, Montebello Cal 40-59; Circ libn Occidental Col Lib 60-61; Educ-curriculum libn Cal state Col (Los Angeles) 61-66, Sci-Tech libn 66-. 9: ALA; NEA (life mem); CalLA (hospitality chm annual conf 64); CalLASchL. 10: Libraria Sodalitas; USoCal Lib Sch Alumni Assn; AAUW; Cal State Employees Assn; Fac Women's Assn. 14: Ref. 15: 6257 S Washington ave, Whittier Cal 90601.

BOCK, ELIZABETH (ZIMMERMAN). b St Louis 6 Jl 16. 5: Jefferson Col 34-39 (Bus Admin) BS in Bus Ad; LSU 40-41 BS in LS; San Francisco State Col 58-62 (Humanities) MA. 6: Fr. 7: Lit asst St Louis Pub Lib 36-40; Grad fellowship LSU 41; Prof libn St Louis Pub Lib 41-42; Prof libn Metropolitan Life Insurance Co, San Francisco 42-43; Depot libn Ninth Serv Command Lib Depot, Presidio of San Francisco 44-46; Asst command libn Ninth Serv Command, later Sixth US Army, Presidio of San Francisco 46-56; Supv libn Sixth US Army Lib & Lib Depot & Presidio Post Lib System, Presidio of San Francisco 56-. 8: Lib/USA NY World's Fair, 64 Hist Activs Offr, Presidio of San Francisco 66-68. 9: ALA (Life mem);-PLA;-LAD; CalLA (sec Golden Gate Dist 67); Pub Lib Execs Cent Cal. 10: Beta Phi Mu;Amer Studies Assn; AAUW; Phi Kappa Phi; San Francisco Chamber Mus Soc; SanFrancisco Mus of Art; Bay Area Educ TV; San Francisco Symph Found. 14: Admin, ref. 15: 3917-ACalifornia st, San Francisco Ca 94118.

BOCK, FAYE (NORTON). b Denison Tex 31 Ja 17. 4: Granville H Bock. 5: Austin Col 34-35; UOkla 35-38 BA in LS. 7: Libn Lubbock Jr High Sch, Lubbock Tex 38-43; Libn Lockhart Elem Sch, Lockhart Tex 51-52; Head films & recordings dept Austin Pub Lib, Austin Tex 53-63, Catlgr 64-67, Dir tech serv 67-. 9: TexLA. 13: Yes. 14: Catlg, a-v materials. 15: Austin Pub Lib Box 2287, Austin Tx 78767.

BOCK, JOLEEN (DOROTHY) (WESSEL). b Bennington Kan 30 S 25. 5: UDenver 43-48 (Theatre Arts) BA, MA; USoCal 61-63 MSLS; UCLA 57-59 (Jr Col Admin). 7: Asst coord tchr in-serv ed UNeb Ext Div (Lincoln) 52-54; Catlgr Whittier Union High Sch Dist, Whittier Cal 58-60, Libn 60-63; Head libn Rio Hondo Jr Col 63-69; Dir lib serv Col of the Canyons 69-. 9: ALA-ACRL (chm-elect Jr Col Lib Sect 69); -LED (Interdiv Com on Train Programs for Supportive Lib Staff; Curriculum Com; Coun on Lib Tech); Tri-Co Area Cal Commun Col Lib Coop (chm). 13: Yes. 14: Lib admin (planning jr col libs); lib tech asst program & curriculum planning. 15: 1306 Armacost #9, Los Angeles Ca 90025.

BOCK, NANCY JEAN. b Quincy Mass 11 D 44. 5: UNH 62-66 (Art ed) BS; UIll 66-67 (LS) MS. 7: LC: Spec recruit program 67-68, Descr catlgr 68-. 9: ALA. 10: Phi Kappa Phi; Beta Phi Mu; AAUW. 15: 429 N st SW apt S-701, Washington DC 20024.

BOCKMAN, EUGENE J. b NYC 23 Jl 23. 4: Pauline Berg. 5: City Col NY 41-42, 46-49 (Soc Sci) BSS; Pratt 49-50 BLS; City Col NY 50-51 (Soc Sci) MA; Columbia 53-58 (LS). 6: Ger. 7: Staff/Sgt USAAF USA & Asia 42-45; Tchr of Soc Studies NYC Bd of Educ 50-52; Asst br libn NY Pub Lib, Woodstock Br 52-53, Br libn 53-58; Mun ref libn NY Pub Lib, NYC 58- Instr Pol Sci Hunter Col 66-68; Sec to Congressman James Scheuer (Bx-NY) 66. 8: Consul in pub admin NYU Med Sch 67, ABC-TV 68. 9: AALL; ALA; SLA; NYLA. 10: City Club of NY; Local Sch Bd 3 NYC. 11: USAAF Distinguished Flying Cross, Air Medal w/2 OLC. 12: Ed "Municipal Reference Library Notes"; Contrib -book of Knowledge." 13: Yes. 14: Govtl ref & research, pol sci, pub admin. 15: 61 Jane st, New York NY 10014.

BOCKMAN, MARILYN (MODERN). b New Orleans La. 4: Sigurd S Bockman. 5: LSU 47-51 (Educ) BS; Columbia 54-55 (LS) MS. 7: Tchr & libn Belle Chasse High Sch, Belle Chasse La 51-54; Asst libn American Petroleum Inst, NYC 55; Catlgr & ref libn Arabian Amer Oil Co, NYC 55-59; Hd libn Amer Assn of Advertising Agencies, NYC 60-65, Staff exec mem info serv 65-. 8: Consul Amer Assn of Advertising Agencies, NYC. 9: SLA (pres NY Chap 63-64, chm & mem nat & local coms); ALA; Amer Assn Info Specialists; NY Lib Club. 10: Alpha Xi Delta; Advertising Women of NY. 12: SLA NY "Chapter News" 58-59. 13: Yes. 14: Lib admin & org, ref serv. 15: American Assoc of Advertising Agencies 200 Park ave, New York NY 10017.

BOCKNEK, JOYCE LEAH. b Toronto Ont Can 28 Ag 27. 5: Toronto 47-49 BA, 50 BLS. 7: Lib asst Globe & Mail, Toronto 50-64; Libn Bell Canada, Toronto 64-. 9: SLA;OntLA. 10: Univ Alumnae Dramatic club. 14: Ref. 15: 525 Chaplin Crescent, apt 715, Toronto 12 Can.

BODAK, TRUDY B. b Geraldton Ont Can 5 Ag 45. 5: Queen'sU 64-67 (Hist, Geog, Sp) BA; UToronto 67-68 BLS. 6: Fr, Sp. 7: Catlgr UAlberta 68-. 14: Catlg. 15: 8323-82 ave, Edmonton 82 Alberta Can.

BODIFORD, DOROTHY (LOUISE HINES). b Selmer Tenn 5 Ja 21. 4: Edward Paul Bodiford. 5: Ark State Tchrs (Educ) BSE UMiss (LS) MLS. 7: Tchr Marvell Pub Schs, Marvell Ark 59-60, Tchr-libn 60-. 9: ALA; NEA; ArkLA; ArkEA. 10: PTA. 14: Ref. 15: Marvell, Ark 72366.

BODLEY, ROSEMARY T. b Milan Mich 23 My 25. 4: Dean G Bodley. 5: UMich 43-44 (LS & A); Mich State Col 44-45 (Home Econ); East MichU 62-65 (LS) AB; UMich 65-67 MALS. 7: Elem libn Dearborn Pub Schs, Dearborn Mich 65; Admin ref libn UMich Law Lib (Ann Arbor) 65-67; Libn Pinckney High Sch, Pinckney Mich 67-68; Libn Lincoln Concolidated Nigh sch, Ypsilanti Mich 68-69; Libn Pioneer High Sch, Ann Arbor Mich 69-. 9: ALA; MichASchL; Mich A-V Assn. 10: Kappa Delta Pi. 14: Secondary sch libs. 15: 2051 Chaucer dr, Ann Arbor Mi 48103.

BODURTHA, EDWARD F. b Portland Ore 13 F 11. 4: Jean Krema Bodurtha. 5: Springfield Jr Col 29-30; Brown 30-33 (Lat) AB; Columbia 40-41 (LS) BS. 6: Fr, Ger. 7: Infantry & Air Corps 42-46; Libn Shattuck Sch, Faribault Minn 41-42, 46-51; Libn Brattleboro Union Dist High Sch, Brattleboro Vt 51-59; Libn Plainview Commun Sch, Plainview Minn 59-. 9: ALA; NEA; MinnEA. 14: High sch lib, element lib. 15: 140 6th st nw, Plainview Mn 55964.

BOEHME, LOUISE (MENEELY). b Troy NY 7 Je 13. 4: G Ernest Boehme. 5: Bryn Mawr 30-34 (Math) AB; State U NY (Albany) 58-64 (LS) MA. 6: Ger, Fr. 7: High sch libn Berlin Central Sch, Berlin NY 58-. 9: NYLA; Hudson-Mohawk LA; East NY Sch Libns Assn; NY State Tchrs Assn, ENYSchLA. 15: RD 1, Cropseyville NY 12052.

BOEHME, RICHARD WILLIAM. b Buffalo NY 13 Jl 36. 4: Elaine Hannah. 5: UBuffalo 57-63 (Geol) BA, MA; UPittsburgh 63-65 MLS. 6: Ger. 7: Lib asst Lockwood Mem Lib U Buffalo 62-63; Lib trainee U Libs UPittsburgh 63-65; Asst col libn Mem Lib State U Col (Cortland NY) 65-. 8: Grad Asst Geol Dept UBuffalo 60-62. 9: Paleontol Soc; Soc of

Vert Paleont. 10: Beta Phi Mu; Sigma Xi. 14: Tech serv, info retrieval, sci collections. 15: 49 North Main st, Cortland NY 13045.

BOELKE, JOANNE HELEN. b Springfield Minn 11 O 38. 5: Gustavus Adolphus 56-57; UMinn 57-60 (Eng) BA, 62-64 (LS) MA. 7: Ref & catlg libn Owatonna Pub Lib, Owatonna Minn 60-62; Ref libn Madison Pub Lib, Madison Wisc 64-67; Doc analyst ERIC Clearinghouse for Lib & Info Sci UMinn Minneapolis Minn 68-. 9: ALA; MinnLA. 10: Phi Beta Kappa; Beta "hi Mu/ 12: "Library Technicians: A Survey of Current Developments" (68); co-auth "Library Service to the Disadvantaged: A Bibliography" (68). 14: Ref. 15: 400 6th ave SE, Minneapolis Mn 55414.

BOEPPLE, ROLLAND E(MERSON). b Baltimore 25 D 27. 4: Saeko Nakano. 5: Elizabethtown Col 46-49 (Eng Lit) AB; USoCal 59-62 MS in LS UCLA & UCI (Computer Sci & Mgt Systs). 7: Libn Orange (City) Pub Lib, Orange Cal; Libn trainee, Libn Los Angeles Pub Lib 59-62, Intermittent sub libn 62-; Head catlgr Douglas Aircraft Co, Long Beach Cal 62-64; Ref libn Anaheim Pub Lib, Anaheim Cal 64-65; Ref libn Philco Aeronutronic Div, Newport Beach Cal 65-. 67; Hd Libn Santa Ana Col 67-. 9: SLA; CalLA; CalTA; Orange Co (Cal) LA; Cal Jr Col Assn. 14: Info sci, automation, mgt systems, lib bldgs. 15: 6071 Cerulean ave, Garden Grove Cal 92641.

BOERUM, (MRS) MARIE (GREGERSON). B Pemberton Minn, 21 N 16. 5: No State Tchrs Col 34-38 (Soc Sci) BS in Ed; Peabody 41-42 BS in LS. 7: High sch libn Gallatin Co, Bozeman Mont 42-43; Lib US Army Pocatello Ida 43-44; Libn (Educ & Hosp) Newark Free Pub Lib, Newark NJ 44-52; Ref libn Fresno Co Free Lib, Fresno Cal 53-55; Br libn Newark Free Pub Lib, Newark NJ 55-57; Br libn Fresno Co Free Lib, Clovis Cal 57-59; Head ref dept Fresno Co Free Lib, Fresno Cal 59-. 8: Consul Essay & General Lit Index. 9: ALA; CalLA (pres Ref Libns div 68). 14: Ref. 15: 4455 N 1st, Fresno Ca 93726.

BOES, WARREN NORMAN. b Grand Rapids Mich 3 S 29. 4: Margaret Camp. 5: UMich 47-51 (Hist) AB, 53 (Hist) MA, 54 AMLS. 6: Ger. 7: Jr circ libn UMich 54-55, Sr circ libn 55-56, Assoc div libn 56-58; Dir of Libs Polytech Inst (Brooklyn NY) 58-64; Asst dir of libs Syracuse U 64-65, Act dir of libs 65-66, Dir of libs 66-. 8: Lib consul Coun of Higher Educ Inst of NYC 62-64; Lib consul Case-Western Reserve U 67-68. 9: ALA; Amer Soc Engnr Educ (chm Engnr Sch Lib Com 63-65); SLA; NYLA; NY Lib Club; Metro Col Inter-lib Assn (pres 63); Central NY Ref Research Coun (v-pres). 10: AAUP; Appalachian Mountain Club; Chm of Bd United Campus Christ Fellowsh, Syracuse 67-. 12: Comp "Union List of Scientific & Technical Serials in the University of Michigan Library" (58); Ed "Library Cooperation in New York City" (62-64); Ed "Directory of Cooperating Libraries in Metropolitan New York City" (63, 64); "Technical Information & The Library" in "Students Engineering Handbook" (68). 13: Yes. 14: Sci & engnr, pub serv, admin. 15: 124 Circle rd, Syracuse NY 13210.

BOESHORE, ELINOR S (FRANCES STRAUSS). b Lebanon Co 2 Sg 25. 4: Robert Leon Boeshore. 5: Lebanon Valley 43-47 (Mus ed) BS; Millersville State 58-60 (Elem ed) Certif; Millersville State 64-67 (LS) Certif & Masters Equiv. 7: Sub tchr Jonestown Schs, Jonestown Penn 48-50; Private Tutor Adj Gen A J Biddle Children, Indiantown Gap Penn 55-58; Elem tchr North Lebanon Schs, Jonestown Penn 58-64; Elem libn North Lebanon Sch Dist, Fredericksburg Penn 64-. 9: ALA; NEA; IRA; PennLA; Penn StateEA; Keystone State Reading Assn. 10: AAUW; Co Lib Bd (Lebanon Co); Jonestown Borough Planning Commsn. 14: Guidance through reading. 15: 131 N King st, Jonestown Pa 17038.

BOGAN, MARY ELIZABETH. b Pottsville Penn 6 Ap 40. 5: Col of Mt St Vincent 58-62 (Hist) AB (cum laude); UMich 62-63 AMLS. 6: Fr. 7: Page, Saratoga Springs Pub Lib, Saratoga Springs NY 55-58; Page & gen asstsummers 58-62; Child libn Point Loma Br San Diego Pub Lib 63-. 8: Re-org Library atthe Cabrillo Nat Monument. 9: ALA (Memb chm Palomar dist 67-69 & 69-71); CalLA. 10: Assn for the Educ of Young Child; Phi Kappa Phi; Col of Mount Saint Vincentalum Assn; U Mich Alum Assn. 14: Child wk. 15: 4731 Santa Cruz ave, San Diego Ca92107.

BOGIE, THOMAS MARTIN. b Dallas 1 My 29. 4: Alice Miller. 5: So Methodist U 46-49 (Philos, Hist) BA, 49-50 (Philos) MA; Chicago summers 55-57 (LS). 7: Bkmob asst Dallas Pub Lib 50-52, Period asst Ref Dept 52, Ref asst 52-55, 1st Asst gen ref dept 55-56, Head gen ref dept 56-57, Head community living dept 57-58, Chief tech serv 58-. 8: Instr in tech serv Sch of Lib Sci Tex Woman's U 61-67. 9: ALA; (mem Exec Com, Aquis sect 68-); SWLA; TexLA (chm Catlogers Roundtable 65-66, Lib Development Com 64-66. 10: Bk reviewer for "Library Journal. 13: Yes. 14: Tech serv. 15: Dallas Pub Lib 1954 Commerce st, Dallas 75201.

BOGORFF, ROBERT AARON. b Stamford Conn 22 Ag 39. 4: Toby Brokstein. 5: NYU 57-61 (Phil) BA; LIU (C W Post Col) 64-66 (LS) MS. 6: Fr. 7: Catlgr SUNY Maritime Col (Ft Schuyler) 64-66, Tech serv libn 66-68; Unit hd tech processing Conn State Lib, Hartford 68-. 9: ConnLA; NY Lib Club. 10: Sierra Club; NY Zoological Soc. 14: Automated tech processing. 15: Buff Cap rd, Tolland Ct 06084.

BOGUE, JAMES WALTER. b Cleveland Ohio 1 Ag 17. 5: Canisius Col 34-35 (Classics); Col of the Holy Cross (Worcester Mass) 35-38 (Philos, Chem, Biol) AB; Columbia 49-50 (Eng) MA, 51-53 (LS) MS. 6: Lat, Sp, Fr. 7: Salesman Bogue-Buffalo Co, Buffalo NY 39-41; Capt MAC US Army 41-45; Asst sales mgr Bogue-Buffalo Co, Buffalo NY 46-48; Pre-prof main reading rm NY Pub Lib 48; Instr Eng UPuerto Rico 50-52; Ref libn soc sci div Brooklyn Pub Lib, Brooklyn NY 53-56; Asst libn & head ref dept Ariz StateU Lib 56-58, Instr Eng 58-60; Libn hd ref dept Phoenix Col 60-. 9: ALA; ArizStateLA; Ariz Col Assn. 10: AAUP. 13: Yes. 14: Ref, lib educ, a-v. 15: 1202 W Thomas rd, Phoenix Az 85013.

BOHANAN, MARY JO (MORGAN). b Albany Ky 16 S 44. 4: Charles S Bohanan. 5: Transylvania Col 62-66 (Hist) BA; UPittsburgh 68 MLS. 7: Adult serv libn Mt Lebanon Pub Lib, Pittsburgh Penn 69-. 9: PennLA. 14: Ref. 15: 30 Clove dr apt 1, Pittsburgh Pa 15236.

BOHANAN, WM J JR. b Palm Beach Co Fla 6 Ap 28. 5: Palm Beach Jr Col 50-52; Ga So Col 53-55 (Eng) BS Ed; Peabody 59-60 (Eng) MA, 62-63 MA(LS). 6: Sp. 7: Tchr Houston Co Schs, Perry Ga 52-53; Tchr Chatham Co Schs, Savannah Ga 55-59; Tchr Pasco High Sch, Dade City Fla 60-62; Libn Mehlville Sch Dist, St Louis 63-65; Libn UKy, Hopkinsville Commun Col 65-66; Libn Mehlville Sch Dist, St Louis 66-69; Adj faculty WashU (St Louis), 67-69. 8: Lib Consul, Franklin Inst, Merida Yucatan Mexico, summer 64; NSF Grant, Colo State Col of Educ, summer 58. 9: ALA; -AASchl; NEA; KyLA; Fla Tchrs Assn. 10: Phi Delta Kappa. 14: Catlg, ref. 15: 325 Edmor, W Palm Beach Fl 36831.

BOHEM, HILDA (MARKS). b NYC 9 Ag 23. 4: Endre Bohem. 5: ULouisville (Pre-med) BA; UCLA 64-65 MLS. 7: Free lance writer for motion pictures & TV, Los Angeles 45-64; Asst libn USoCal Undergrad Lib 65-. 66; Bibliog Harry A Levinson Rare Books, Beverly Hills Cal 66-. 15: 1629 No Crescent Heights, Los Angeles 69.

BOHLEY, RONALD G. b Indianapolis Ind 17 F 42. 4: Barbara Helm. 5: Purdue 60-64 (Soc Studies) BA; IndU 65-67 (LS) MA. 6: Fr. 7: Lib intern PurdueU 64-67; Libn St Elizabeth Sch of Nursing, Lafayette Ind 66-67; Hd libn PurdueU N Central Campus, Westville Ind 67-. 8: Lib dir (on consul basis) Ind Pub Lib, Mich City 68-69. 9: ALA. 10: Beta Phi Mu; AAUP. 15: 510 E Tenth st, Michigan City In 46360.

BOHLING, (JAMES) CURT. b Hammond Ind 13 Jl 38. 4: Diane Daniels. 5: Drury Col 56-59 (Eng); Southwest Mo State Col 59-60 (Eng) BA; UIll 61-62 (LS) MS. 6: Sp. 7: Lib Dir Mexico-Audrain Co Lib, Mexico Mo 62-64; Libn Ind U 64-65; Lib Dir Webster Mem Lib, Decatur Mich 65-. 9: SLA; MichLA; Mich Lib Film Circuit (pres 67-69). 13: Yes. 14: Admin. 15: Rt 1, Decatur Mi 49045.

BOHLING, RAYMOND A. b Auburn Neb 12 Ja 28. 4: Doris M James. 5: Wartburg Col 45-46 (Elec Engnr); Omaha U 48-51 (Psych) BA; UDenver 51-52 (LS) MA. 6: Ger. 7: Electrician's Mate US Navy Sub Serv 46-48; Asst libn Col of Med UNeb(Omaha) 52-55, Sci libn UNeb(Lincoln) 55-58, Asst dir for sci tech 58-60; Supv of dept libs UMinn(Minneapolis) 60-63, Asst Dir of Libs 63-. 9: ALA; SLA-Minn Chap (dir 62-63, 65166, v-pres 63-64, pres 64-65, annual convention treas Mpls 66); MinnLA; ASIS. 10: AAUP; (YMCA); (Bd Dirs, Northwest Br St Paul); City Planning Commsn, New Brighton Minn. 14: Industrial psych with grad courses at UMinn. 15: 2142 Inca lane, New Brighton Mn 55112.

BOHNSDAHL, NAOMI CRUMLEY. b Jackson Co NC 15 Ag 08. 4: Gunnar William Bohnsdahl. 5: George Washington U 26-30 (Eng) AB; UNC summers 39-41 BS in LS. 6: Fr. 7: Tchr high sch, Clyde NC 30-33; Tchr of Math Jr High Sch, Canton NC 34-37; Libn High Sch, Canton NC 38-46; Libn summer Sci Serv Wash DC 42; Libn summer Enoch Pratt Free Lib, Baltimore 43; Libn summer Curtis Bay Coast Guard Yard, Baltimore 44; Tchr Jr High Sch, Canton NC 52-57; Libn High Sch, Canton NC 58-67; Libn, Haywood Co, Lib, Waynesville NC summer 67-68; Libn Pisgah Sr High, Canton NC 67-. 8: YMCA Camp Coun Canton NC 55-58. 9: ALA-AASchL; NCLA; NCEA; NC High Sch Libns Assn. 10: Kappa Kappa Gamma; Delta Kappa Gamma; Home Demonstration Club; Women's Aux Program & Mission Wk in Diocese. 14: Ref, Tchg Lib Sci to col-bound seniors. 15: 103 Skyland Terr, Canton NC 28716.

BOISSE, JOSEPH (ADONIAS). b Marlboro Mass 20 Je 37. 4: Josette A Smongeski. 5: Stonehill 61-63 (Fr) AB; Brown 63-65 (Fr) MA; Simmons 66-67 (LS) MS. 6: Fr, Sp, Lat. 7: Lang tchr Canterbury Sch, New Milford Conn 65-66; Lib intern (acquis) MIT 66-67; Lib Consul (title IV) Free Pub Lib Serv, Montpelier Vt 67-68; Asst dir lib LawrenceU 68-. 8: TV script adv NLW Com, Montpelier Vt 68; Org consul Trinity Lutheran Ch Lib, Appleton Wis 69. 9: ALA; WisLA; NE Wis Intertype Libs (sec). 10: Delta Epsilon Sigma. 13: Yes. 14: Admin. 15: Lawrence Univ Lib, Appleton Wi 54911.

BOISSE, JOSETTE ANNE (SMONGESKI). b Elmhurst Long Island NY 29 Je 42. 4: Joseph A Boisse. 5: Stonehill 60-64 (Fr) AB; Simmons 64-67 (LS) MS. 6: Fr. 7: Child serv consul Free Pub Lib Serv, Montpelier Vt 67-68; Hd ext serv Oshkosh Pub Lib, Oshkosh wis 68-. 8: Consul Wis Intellectual Freedom Com, Oshkosh 69-; Coord Wis Educ Tele Network, Oshkosh 68-69; Asst tchr Introduction to Lib Sci UWis ext div course (Oshkosh) 68-69. 9: ALA; WisLA. 13: Yes. 14: Child serv, consul, tchg of lib sci. 15: PO Box 1093, Oshkosh Wi 54901.

BOISSONNAS, CHRISTIAN (MARC). b Paris France 21 Mr 42. 5: Cornell 60-64 (Animal Breeding) BS; Syracuse 64-65 MSLS. 6: Fr. 7: Industrial & Labor Relations 46 Cornell: Asst catlg libn 65-67, Assoc catlg libn 67-68, Catlg libn 68-. 14: Personnel wk, industrial relations, catlg. 15: 1089 Taughannock blvd, Ithaca NY 14850.

BOISSONNAS, SUSAN (LUDLUM). b Mineola NY 20 Ja 41. 4: Christian M Boissonnas. 5: Cornell U 59-63 (Span Linguistics) BA; Syracuse 63-64 MSLS. 6: Fr, Sp. 7: Asst libn catlg dept Cornell U Libs 64-66; Catlgr of coll DeWitt Hist Soc, Ithaca NY 67-68; Asst libn catlgdept (Reclass Proj) Cornell U Libs 68-. 9: ALA. 10: Beta Phi Mu. 14: Catlg, tech serv, automation in libs,conting educ, personnel. 15: 1089 Toughannock blvd, Ithaca NY 14850.

BOLAND, GARY L. b Enid Okla 21 Jl 40. 4: Diane Lingle. 5: OklaU 62 (Hist, Pol Sci) BA, 65 (Law) Juris Doctor, 67 MLS. 6: Fr, Ger. 7: Lawyer Charles R Ogden Law Off, Guymon Okla 65-66; Central libn Okla Co Libs, Okla City 66-67; Ref libn Harvard Law sch 67-. 8: Moderator "Money & You" Channel 4 TV, Okla City summer 67. 9: AALL; ASIS; NELA. 10: Com 408 "Info Retrieval" of Patent, Copyright & Trademark Bar; Amer Bar Assn; Fed Bar Assn; Okla Bar Assn. 14: Admin. 15: 345 Brookline st, Cambridge Ma 02139.

BOLAND, MARY BLANCHE. b Cairo Ill 8 Ap 16. 5: Col of St Francis 33-37 (Eng) BA; UIll 38-42 (Eng, Educ) MA, 41-49 BS in LS. 6: Fr. 7: Libn Lawrenceville Twp High Sch, Lawrenceville Ill 43-46; Libn hughes High Sch, Woodward High Sch, Heinold Jr High Sch, Cincinnati 46-57; US Army Dependents' Educ Group, Paris, Munich & Wuerzburg Germany 57-60; Libn Cincinnati Bd of Educ, Walnut Hills High Sch 61-. Tchr of bibliog UCincinnati summer 66. 8: John Hay Fellow, UOre summer 62. 9: ALA; CathLA (chm-elect Greater Cincinnati Unit); OhioASchL; OhioEA. 14: Sch lib admin, bk sel for yp, ref. 15: 358 Shiloh st, Cincinnati Oh45220.

BOLAND, STUART MORTON. b NYC. 5: UCal 27-31 (Pol Sci) AB, 32-33 (LS) BS, 33-34 (Govt Admin). 6: Sp, Portu, Lat, Fr. 7: San Francisco Pub Lib: Libn 33-35, Temp sub 36-37, Jr libn 37-38, Libn 39-41; US Army War Col Lib, Wash DC 42-44; Sr libn San Francisco Pub Lib 45-54, Prin libn 54-65. 8: Originator of National Library Week; Org San Quentin Prison Lib (Cal); Helped org Okla A&M Univ Lib; Made daily Broadcasts from San Francisco Lib for 5 yrs;Org; SF Commun Center Library; SF Col for Women Lib; Sonoma Pub Lib; San Quentinprison Lib; Oklahoma A&M Lib, etc 40-60; Deleg ALA conferences 53-63; Deleg CalLAconv & conf 54-64; Four travel scholarships; A-V-Cinema-Radio & TV to Europe & Asia58-62; Chm SF A-V Comm 58-; Orig SF Chinatown Lib Annl Family-Night, Open House FilmFestival 61-; Chm Radio-TV Com 54-62; SF Pub Lib Info & Educl Broadcaster; Found &dir Chinatown Lib Cult Center & Research-Ref Clearing House; SF PUB Lib PubRelations Com; etc. 9: ALA (chm Memb Com & Radio TV Com); CalLA (Parliament, mem A-V Com, dir Nat Lib Week 66-67). 10: Athens Athletic Club; NY Athletic Club; Nat Travel Assn; Breakfast Club. 11: Citizen-of-the-Month, San Francisco. 12: "Immortalia" (book of verse); "The Blue Rose" (children's play); "Eternalia" (drama); "Doomsrood" (passion play); "Legends of the Golden City"; "Legends of San Francisco" (fantasy). 13: Yes. 14: Pub libs (child, teen-agers, ya). 15: San Francisco Pub Lib, Civic Center, San Francisco Ca 94102.

BOLAND, WINNIFRED JOAN. b Watrous Sask Can 5 S 31. 4: William Guy. 5: USask 49-52 BA; McGill 54-55 BLS; UWash 63-65 MLS. 7: Circ desk & period USask 52-54; Ref libn Sask Prov Lib, Regina Sask 55-57; Ref dept USask 57-61; Bus dept Seattle Pub Lib 61-65; A/S/Lt RCN R(Ret) 53-57; Libn UWash Lib Undergrad Lib Ref sect 65-. 10: Beta Phi Mu. 14: Ref. 15: 2020 NW 63 rd, Seattle Wa 98107.

BOLD, FRANCES ANN. b Evansville Ind 30 My 30. 5: Mary Washington Col of UVa 48-52 (Art) BA; UNC 54-56 MS in LS. 6: Fr. 7: Lib asst Falls Church Pub Lib, Falls Church Va 52-53; Lib asst Hollins Col Lib 53-54; Asst br libn Arlington Co (Va) Pub Lib 57-58, Br libn 57-64; Lib Dir Pottstown Pub Lib, Pottstown Penn 64-67; Dir Free Pub Lib, New Bedford Mass 67-. 9: ALA; Lib Assn (Gt Brit); VaLA;MassLA; NELA. 10: Beta Phi Mu; Phi Sigma Iota; YWCA; Bibliog Soc UVa. 11: Fulbright Scholarship in Lib Sci to Gt Brit, 56-57. 14: Preserv & repair of bks. 15: 415County st apt 307, New Bedford Ma 02740.

BOLD, RUDOLPH. b Brooklyn NY 10 D 38. 4: Virginia Sottile. 5: St John's U (Brooklyn NY) 56-60 (Psych, Philos) BA; Pratt 63-65 MLS. 7: Admin asst Mus of Modern Art NYC 61; Libn Queens Pub Lib, Jamaica NY 63-69, Ridgewood NY 69-. 8: Young Adult Spec, Queens Pub Lib 64-; Speakers' Bureau. 9: ALA. 10: Beta Phi Mu; Co Com-man, NY State Conserv Party. 14: Lib admin, ya wk. 15: 49 Campbell ave, Williston Park NY 11225.

BOLDING, MRS SAMUEL M (HELEN BYRD). b Vimville Miss 8 S 13. 4: Samuel M Bolding. 5: Millsaps Col 31-35 (Eng) BA (cum laude); UAla summers 38-40 Certif in Lib Sci; Auburn U summer 58. 7: Tchr of high sch Eng & Lat, Mendenhall Miss 35-36; High sch libn Pascagoula High Sch, Pascagoula Miss 36-39; High sch libn Ala Pub Schs 39-43; Asst libn Col of Educ Lib UAla 45-46; Head popular lit dept Birmingham Pub Lib, Birmingham Ala 48-50; Libn Montgomery Pub Lib, Montgomery Ala 59-68, Adult adv 68-. 8: Mem STATE OF Ala Advis Com for High Sch Libs 68-. 9: AlaLA. 10: Kappa Delta Pi; Ala Fed of Music lubs; Montgomery Music Study Club; OpelikaMusic Club; Bus & Prof Women's Club; AAUW; Member Kappa Kappa Iota. 14: Ref, readersadv, bk reviewing. 15: 620 Ponce de Leon ave, Montgomery Al 36106.

BOLDRA, ALICE (AMICK). b Clarinda Iowa 18 Ja 15. 5: Tarkio Col 33-36 (Eng); Cal State Col at LA 52-53 (Eng) AB; USoCal 53-55 MSLS. 7: Children's libn LA Co Pub Lib, Inglewood Cal 55-56; Libn-in-charge Non-med collection LA Co Gen Hosp 56-60; Libn-in-vharge LA Co Pub Lib, Lenox Cal 60-64; Children's lib Haw Reg Hdqrs Lib LA Co, Hawthorne Cal 64-68; Libn-in-charge LA Co Pub Lib Lawndale Cal 68-. 8: Innovated a pre-sch story-time & film prog in Los Angeles Co. 9: ALA; CalLA. 10: LWV; Lennox Women's Club; Lennox Co-ordinating Coun; So Cal Coun on Lit for Child & YP. 14: Child & parents. 15: 4851 W 96th st, Inglewood Ca 90301.

BOLEF, DORIS. b Phila 26 Mr 22. 4: Dan I Bolef. 5: Temple 39-43 (Secondary Educ) BS; Drexel 44-45 (LS) BS; Columbia 47-51 (LS) MS. 6: Ger. 7: Jr contractor RCA Victor Div, Camden NJ 43; Sub tchr Phila Bd of Educ 44; Libn Bellevue Sch of Nursing Lib, NYC 45-49; Lib consul Mary Immaculate Sch of Nursing, Jamaica NY 50-51; Lib consul Mercy Hosp Sch of Nursing, Pittsburgh 54-55; Lib consul Sewickley Valley Hosp Sch of Nursing, Sewickley Penn 56-57; Catlg reorg Koppers Res Lab Lib, Verona Penn 57-59; Consu Westinghouse Astronuclear Lab Lib, Mt Lebanon Penn 60-61; Catlgr UPittsburgh Sch of Health Prof Lib 63; Catlgr Washington U Med Sch Lib (St Louis) 63-67, Deputy libn 67-. 9: SLA (chm Hosp Div); MedLA; ALA. 10: LWV; Women's Internat League for Peace & Freedom. 13: Yes. 14: Catlg. 15: 6612 Waterman, St Louis 63130.

BOLES, JANET (KAY). b Burkburnett Tex 26 Jl 44. 5: UOkla 62-66 (Govt) BA; UMich 66-67 mals& utex (Austin) 69- (Govt). 6: Ger. 7: Asst libn NY Legis Ref Lib, Albany 67-68; Libn Lyndon Baines Johnson Lib, Austin Tex 69-. 9: SLA; Amer Pol Sci Assn. 14: Ref, bibliog. 15: 2812 Rio Grande #103, Auston Tx 78705.

BOLICK, MARJORY AYLEENE (CRABB). b Medicine Hat Alta Can 13 Ap 19. 4: Watcil Byron Bolick. 5: UOttawa 37-41 (Eng) BA; UWash 55-57 (LS) ML. 6: Fr. 7: Tchr Alta Can 41-50; Tchr Pub Sch Bd, Medicine Hat Alta 52-56, Libn 55-56; Sch libn Ridcau High Sch Ottawa Collegiate Inst Bd 57-66, Supv of Libs 66-. 8: Chm of Steering Com for lib sect of Ottawa Schs Centennial Exhibition Com, 67. 9: ALA; CanSchLA (v-chm, chm 66-67); Can Col of Tchrs; OntLA; Ont Secon Sch Tchrs Assn; OttawaLA. 10: U Women's Club. 13: Yes. 14: Sch libnship, ref, educ. 15: 43 Sunset blvd, Ottawa 1 Can.

BOLING, MARTHA. b Terre Haute Ind 31 Ag 15. 5: Ind State Tchrs 34-38 (Eng, Soc Sci) BS, 39-40 (LS); Ind StateU 63 (LS) MS. 7: Libn: Robinson Twp High Sch, Robinson Ill 40-50, Barrington Consolidated High Sch, Barrington Ill 50-61, Elgin Commun Col 61-. 9: NEA; ALA; IEA; IllLA; IllASchL (bd mem). 10: Zonta Intl; FISH. 14: Admin, bk sel. 15: 307 S Cook, Barrington Il 60010.

BOLL, JOHN JORG. b Berlin Germany 12 Ag 21. 4: Ruth Senn. 5: Union Col (Schenectady NY) 38-42 (Langs, Lit) AB; Columbia 42-43, 48-49 MS in LS; UIll 61 (LS) PhD. 6: Ger, Fr. 7: Research analyst Psych Warfare Br US Army (T/Sgt) 43-46; Research analyst Off of Chief of Coun for War Crimes 46-48; Catlgr Copyright Off LC 49-52; Asst UIll Lib (Urbana) 52-54; Instr Simmons Col Sch of Lib Sci summer 54; Asst libn for tech processes UTex 54-56; Asst Prof U Wis Lib Sch (Madison) 56-61, Assoc Prof 61-68, Prof 68-. 9: ALA-ACRL; WisLA; AALS. 10: AAUP; Beta Phi Mu. 12: "American College Library Buildings 1800-1875" (PhD dis); Introduction to Cataloging" (prelim ed 66-68). 13: Yes. 14: Catlg, nat bibliog structure, arch, indexing. 15: 2710 Sommers ave, Madison Wi 53704.

BOLLING, THOMAS E. b San Diego Cal 14 Je 41. 4: Rosemary Warden. 5: PacificU 59-63 (Phil) BA; UCal (Berkeley) 63-64 (Oriental Lang); UOre 67-68 MLS. 6: Mandarin. 7: Reader PacificU 63; Stud prof asst Porterville State Hosp, Cal 62, 63; Step one clk Educ & Psych Lib UCal (Berkeley) 64-65; Med corpsman & clk/typist (Sp/4) US Army 65-67; Libn Rogers' City Lib Forest Grove Ore 68-. 9: ALA-RSD hist sect; -PLA; PNLA; OreLA. 10: Ore Hist Soc; Tualatin Plains Hist Soc; Valley Art Assn. 13: Yes. 14: Ref 9hist), pub lib. 15: PO Box 121, Forest Grove Or 97116.

BOLOTEN, SHIRLEY (ASPLER). b London England 8 Ag 34. 4: Herbert Boloten. 5: McGill 51-55 (Philos) BA, 66-69 MLS. 6: Fr. 14: Child serv. 15: 7496 Briar rd, Cote St Luc, Montreal Que Can.

BOLSTAD, MARGARET (THOMES). b Minneapolis Mn 14 Je 14. 4: Milo M Bolstad. 5: UMinn 32-36 (Geol) BA, 36-37 (Geol) MA; UMo 58-60, 64 (LS). 7: Instr Macalester Col 37-38; Ref libn Stephens Col, Columbia Mo 59-. 9: ALA; MoLA (Conv treas 68). 10: Phi Beta Kappa; AAUP. 14: Ref. 15: 835 Greenwood ct, Columbia Mo 65201.

BOLTON, ELIZABETH GRIER. b Charlotte NC 9 Jl 12. 5: Agnes Scott Col 29-31; UNC 31-33 (Eng) AB in Educ; Columbia 41-43 (Guidance, Personnel) MA; UNC 52-53 (LS) BA. 6: Fr, Ital. 7: Asst dean & housecoun Duke U & NJ Col for Women 43-48; Tchr of Eng & libn US Navy Dependents' Schs, Naples Italy & Izmir Turkey 53-56; Libn Roanoke Rapids High Sch, Roanoke Rapids NC 56-58; Catlgr UNC Lib (Chapel Hill) 59-. 9: NCLA. 10: AAUW. 14: Catlg. 15: 224 McCauley st, Chapel Hill NC 27701.

BOLTON, LUCILE I. b Northfield Mass 23 Ag 20. 5: Green Mountain Col 41 (Hist) AA; Boston U 46 (Hist) BS of Educ; Syracuse summer 50 (Sci), summer 65, 66, 67, & 69 (LS). 7: Hosp br lib ext Thomas Crane Pub Lib, Quincy Mass 47-53; Chief of bk serv div of lib ext, Boston 53-57; Catlg libn Forbes Lib, Northampton Mass 58-62; Lib Dir Greenfield Pub Lib, Greenfield Mass 62-. 9: MassLA (Intel Freedom Com); West Reg (Mass) Adv Coun (Exec Com 62-); West Mass Lib Club (pres 66-68). 10: Quota Internat; AAUW. 14: Catlg. 15: Greenfield Pub Lib 402 Main st, Greenfield Ma 01301.

BOMAR, MISS CORA PAUL. b Memphis Tenn 8 S 13. 5: UTenn 39 (Hist) BS in Educ; Peabody 46 BS in LS; UNC 50 (Elem Educ & Supv) MA. 7: Tchr Elem Sch, Trezevant Tenn 32-39; Tchr-libn Central High Sch, Bruceton Tenn 39-41; Libn Milan High Sch, Milan Tenn 41-42; Prod supv Milan Arsenal Plant, Milan Tenn 42-45; Libn & a-v dir Hoke Smith Jr High Sch, Atlanta 45-46; Ref libn UTenn Jr Col 46-47; Libn Elem Sch, chapel Hill NC 47-49; Instr supv Grades 1-12, Orange Co NC 49-51; Visiting Lecturer UNC(Chapel Hill) 50, 53, 54, 60, 61, 64; Visiting Lecturer USCar(Columbia) 55; Head supv lib & instr materials serv sect, NC Dept of Pub Instr 51-67, Dir div educ media 67-. 8: Governor's Commsn on Lib Resources, NC 64-65; Com to plan curr for the Advancement Sch, NC 63; Testified before House & Senate Educ Com 61, 62, 63, 65, 67, 69 as ALA witness; Adv Com of UNC Sch of Lib Sci; Ed Adv Com to "School Library Journal"; Ed Tech Coun of Nat'l Cath Ed Assn, 69-72. 9: ALA (Coun 62-67, Legis Com 62-66, Adv Com to Off of Recr 62-63); -AASchL (Exec Bd 58-60, pres 62-63, chm Legis Com 64-66); State Sch Lib Supvs (chm); ALA-LED v-pres, pres-elect 69-70; NEA; Assn Supv & Curr; Nat Coun TE; NCLA (Exec Bd 58-62, 64-67, ALA Coun Rep 64-67, chm Recr Com 57); NCASchL (Exec Com); SELA (Exec Bd 58-62, Lib Devel Com 62-64, pres 68-69); NCEA. 10: Raleigh Altrusa Club; AAUW; Amer Assn for UN; Pi Gamma Mu; Delta Kappa Gamma; Internat Platform Assn; Beta Phi Mu. 12: "Reference Materials for School Libraries" (60, 2nd ed 65, 3rd ed 68); "Learning Resources Library; A Planning Guide" (65); "School Libraries in Action," a film; Auth or co-auth several NC curr bulletins; guest ed "ALA Bulletin," (Feb 64); "Guide for Developing Curriculum Materials Centers for Teacher Education," (69). 13: Yes. 14: Sch libs, devel of system-wide serv. 15: 2105 St James rd, Raleigh NC 27607.

BOND, JANET I (BAILEY). b Kempton Penn 24 Je 41. 4: Richard C Bond. 5: Kutztown State Col 62-66 (LS) BS. 7: Catlgr Kutztown State Col 66-. 14: Catlg. 15: Rte 2, Kempton Pa 19529.

BOND, MIRIAM (PICKETT). b Waseca Minn 31 Ag 12. 5: UMinn 30-34 BA; UDenver 63-64 (Libnship) MA. 7: Ya libn Denver Pub Lib 64-67; Asst circ libn Iowa StateU (Ames) 67-68, Asst Prof & hd undergrad serv dept 69-. 9: ALA; IowaStateLA. 10: Iowa State U Fac Women's Club; ACLU; Audubon Soc; Amer Friend's Serv Com; SCLC; LWV; Kappa Kappa Gamma; Mortar Bd. 14: Undergrad studs. 15: 111 Sheldon, Ames Ia 50010.

BOND, RUTH HILL (EVELYN). b Atlanta 9 Je 08. 4: Roy Jackson Bond. 5: Lagrange Col 25-29 (Fr) AB; Emory summers 32, 34-37 (Fr) MA; Mercer U 53-54 (Educ); Woman's Col of Ga 59 (LS); Fla State U summers 61, 63, 65 (LS) MS; Ga So Col 64-65 (Educ). 6: Fr, Sp, Lat. 7: Libn Tignall High Sch, Tignll Ga 24-25; Stud catlgr LaGrange Col 25-29; Tchr-libn Madison Co High Sch, Danielsville Ga 29-31; Tchr-libn Buena Vista High Sch, Buena Vista Ga 31-33; Tchr-libn Winterville High Sch, Winterville Ga 33-36; Tchr-libn Paulding Co High Sch, Dallas Ga 36; Tchr-libn Schley Co High Sch, Ellaville Ga 43-45; Libn Millen High Sch, Millen Ga 46, 47-48; Tchr-libn Eastman High Sch, Eastman Ga 48-51; Elem libn Bibb Co Elem Schs 57-60; Libn Groves High Sch, Savannah 62-. 9: ALA; NEA; GaLA; GaEA; SELA; Chatham CoEA. 10: Beta Phi Mu; Nurses' Aid (ARC); PTA. 14: Sch libs. 15: 106 Keystone dr, Savannah Ga 31406.

BOND, W H. b York Penn 14 Ag 15. 4: Helen Lynch. 5: Haverford Col 37 AB; HarvardU 38 MA, 41 PhD. 7: Sheldon Traveling Fellow Harvard U 40-41; Research Fellow Folger Shakespeare Lib 41-42; Civil Servant US Navy Dept 42-43; Commissioned off US Naval Res 43-46; Asst to libn Houghton Lib Harvard 46-48, Curator of Manuscripts 48-64; Fulbright Fellow Asst keeper (temporary) Manuscript Dept British Museum (London) 52-53; Libn Houghton Lib 65-; Lecturer in Bibliogr HarvardU 64-67, Prof of Bibliogr 67-. 8: Trustee; Ralph Waldo Emerson Mem Assn, Concord (Mass) Free Pub Lib, Heritage Foundation, Deerfield Mass. 12: Ed "Jubilate Agno" (5 4); "Supplement to the Census of Medieval and Renaissance Manuscripts in the United States and Canada" (62); Co-ed Alexander Pope's tr of Homer's "Iliad" (65); "The Houghton Library, 1942-1967" (67); Ed "The Records of a Bibliographer" (67). 13: Yes. 15: Houghton Library Harvard Univ, Cambridge Ma 02139.

BONDOW, LOUISE. b Neenah Wis 22 O 44. 5: Wis State U (Oshkosh) 62-65 (LS, Eng) BA. 6: Ger, Sp. 7: NDEA bibliog UAriz Lib 65-. 14: Acquis, catlg. 15: PO Box 2, Arizona City Az 85223.

BONE, ESTHER (J). b Cleveland 3 Ap 04. 5: Kent State 25-27, 54-58 (Hist) BA, 60-65 MLS. 7: Gen ref The Ferguson Lib, Stamford Conn 36-44; Admin asst Amer Red Cross-Mil Liaison Sect, Newport News Va 44-46; Asst libn Shaker Heights Jr High Sch, Shaker Heights Ohio 46-50; Asst libn soc sci div Kent State U 51-68, Asst hd ref dept 68-. 9: ALA-ACRL (Tri-State Chap). 10: Alpha Phi; LWV. 12: Co-ed "The Serif". 14: Ref. 15: 1227 E Main st #1, KentOh 44240.

BONE, LARRY EARL. b Memphis Tenn 31 O 32. 5: Southwestern-at-Memphis 50-54 (Fr) BA; West Res 54-55 (LS) MS. 6: Fr, Sp. 7: Asst educ libn San Francisco State Col summer 55; Asst libn Highland br Memphis Pub Lib, Memphis Tenn 55-56, Libn Randolph br 56-57; Asst head Gifts Sect LC 58; Libn George Mason Col of UVa 58-59; Head libn Avon Lake Pub Lib, Avon Lake Ohio 59-62; Dir Mentor Pub Lib, Mentor Ohio 62-63; Co libn Shelby Co Libs, Memphis Tenn 63-66; Asst to dir & Instr Grad Sch of Lib Sci UIll(Urbana) 66-67, Asst dir & Asst Prof 67-. 8: Staff, Lib/USA NY World's Fair 65 Vis Asst Prof, UWash Sch of Libnship 68; Deputy libn, Amer Lib in Paris 68-69. 9: ALA; -RSD (Lib Journal List Com 67-68); OhioLA (chm Ref Sect 61-62); Tenn LA (chm Intel Freedom Com 63-66); Lake Co(Ohio) LA (pres 62-63). 10: Phi Beta Kappa; Memphis Libns Com; Beta Phi Mu. 12: Ed "Library Education: An International Survey" (68); Ed "Teaching the Adult Selection Courses" (69).13: Yes. 14: Admin, bk sel, lib educ. 15: 3506 Barron rd, Memphis Tn 38111.

BONER, MRS MARIAN (OLDFATHER). b Cleburne Tex 25 Je 09. 4: Charles Paul Boner. 5: UTex 26-31 (Physics) BA, MA, 50-55 LLB. 6: Fr, Sp. 7: Research asst UTex Law Sch Found 56-59; Ref libn UTex Sch of Law 60-65, Assoc law libn & Asst Prof of Law 65-. 9: AALL. 10: State Bar of Tex; Order of the Coif; Kappa Beta Pi. 13: Yes. 14: Ref, admin. 15: UTex Law Lib 2500 Red River, Austin Tx 78705.

BONETT, SUSAN (PATE HARTMETZ). b Wichita Kan 17 Ja 37. 4: Herman R Bonett. 5: UWichita 54-58 (Hist) BA; UDenver 58-59 (LS) MA; UKan 64- (Law). 7: Asst libn Bradford Mem Lib, El Dorado Kan 59-60; Acquis bibliog Watson Lib UKan 61-63; Asst law libn Law Lib UKan 63-67; Ref Coord Trails Reg Lib, Warrensburg Mo 69-. 14: Catlg; Ref. 15: 603 N College, Warrensburg Mo 64093.

BONFILI, BARBARA JUNE (DAVIS). b Morgantown W Va 20 D 23. 4: Dominick L Bonfili. 5: W Va U 58-61 (Elem ed, Eng, Soc studies, LS) BS Elem Ed; UPittsburgh 62-65 MLS. 6: (Read) French, Italian. 7: Catlgr W Va U, 61-65; Hd libn Morgantown High Sch, Morgantown W Va 65-; Visiting instructor Lib Sci W Va U 69-. 9: ALA; WVaLA. 14: Ref, catlg, admin. 15: 746 Amherst rd, Morgantown WVa 26505.

BONIFACE, EDWARD IRVIN. b Wash DC 21 Jl 34. 4: Anne Bierstein. 5: WesleyanU (Conn) 52-56 (Eng Lit) BA; UNC 62-63 MSLS; American U 64-65 (Automatic Computers). 7: File clerk Copyright Catlg Div LC summers 52-56, Searcher Serv Div Copyright Off 56-57; Postal clerk US Army (Pfc), Ft Meade Md 57; Searcher Compliance Sect Copyright Off LC 57-59, Searcher Loan Div 59-60; Tech period libn Nat Aero & Space Admin, Wash DC 60-64; Asst chief Reports Lib US AEC, Wash DC 64-66; Programming Libn Rensselaer 66-67, Hd, Lib Data Processing Off, 67-. 08: Asst program dir "Systems Study as Related to Library Operations"; USOE Title IIB HEA Grant1Supported, Rensselaer Poly Inst 6 Je 68. 8: SLA. 9: SLA. 10: Beta Phi Mu. 14: Computer applications to libs. 15: 1180 Van Curler ave, Schenectady NY 12308.

BONK, WALLACE JOHN. b Two Rivers Wis 13 Mr 23. 4: Joyce Johnson. 5: UWis 41-43; UMinn 46-49 (Eng) BA, MA; UMich 52-56 AMLS, PhD. 7: US Army (Pfc) 43-46; Asst Prof of Eng E Tex U 49-52; UMich Lib fellow catlg dept 52-54, Instr Dept of Lib Sci 54-56, Asst Prof 56-61, Assoc Prof 61-65, chm Dept of Lib Sci 65-67, Prof 66-. 9: ALA; AALS; SLA; MichLA. 10: Signature Club, Ann Arbor; Phi Beta Kappa. 12: "Building Library Collections," with M D Carter (3rd ed 69); "Use of Basic Reference Sources in Libraries" (64). 13: Yes. 14: Lib educ, ref, bk sel, admin. 15: 2002 Shadford rd, Ann Arbor Mi 48104.

BONN, GEORGE S(CHLEGEL). b Cincinnati 19 S 13. 5: Ohio State U 31-35 (Chem Engnr) BChE, 35-36 (Chem Engnr) MS; Chicago 47-48, 51 AM(LS). 6: Fr, Japanese. 7: Research engnr Engnr Exp Station Ohio State U 36-37; Research engnr City Water & Power Dept, Springfield Ill 37-41; US Army Med Admin Corps (Capt) 41-46; Assoc Ed Better Roads Magazine, Chicago 46-47; Libn Tech Inst Northwestern U 49-51; Assoc Libn Rice Inst 51-53; Visiting Prof Japan Lib Sch Keio U (Tokyo) 54-55; Asst/Adjunct Prof Grad Sch of Lib Studies Rutgers U 56-64; Chief sci & tech div NY Pub Lib 58-64; Prof, Assoc Dean Grad Sch of Lib Studies UHawaii 65- Adv Dept of Lib Sci UDelhi 67-69; Lib adv Indian Co of Agric Research, Delhi India 69. 8: Fulbright Research Scholar, Japan 53-54; Lib consul Turkey, 55-56; Engnr sch lib surveys & lib sch adv wk var times; Survey of Can lib resources in sci & tech, 65 Consul, Cal State Lib, Sacramento Oct-Dec 66. 9: ALA-ACRL/SSS; -RSD; -LED; -COA; AALS; ASIS; AsLib; SLA; ACS "Engnr Index" Trustee mem 59-64; ASA Z39; HawaiiLA. 10: AAAS; AAUP; Japan Soc (NY); Vachel Lindsay Assn, Springfield Ill; Sigma Xi. 11: Fulbright Research Grant, 53-54. 12: "Japanese Journals in Science and Technology" (60); "Training Laymen in Use of the Library" (60); "Science-Technology Literature Resources in Canada" (66); ed "Library Education and Training in Developing Countries" (66); "Technical Information for California Business and Industry" (67). 13: Yes. 14: Ref, lit of sci-tech, lib educ.

BONNAFFON, ANNA CLARKE. b Phila 14 O 25. 5: UPenn 44-48 (Eng) BA; Drexel 48-49 BS in LS. 6: Fr. 7: Asst libn Woman's Med Col (Phila) 49-50; Asst libn Phila Naval Hosp 50-57; Med libn Valley Forge Gen Hosp, Phoenixville Penn 57-59; Med libn Walson Army Hosp, Ft Dix NJ 59-. 9: MedLA. 14: Ref. 15: Med Lib Walson Army Hosp, Ft Dix NJ 08640.

BONNELL, ALICE HARRISON. b Mt Vernon NY 16 My 07. 5: NY State Col for Tchrs (Albany) 25-29 (Hist) BA; Columbia summers 29, 38-40 (LS) BS, 51-52, 53-54 (Hist). 6: Lat, Fr. 7: Yp libn Mt Vernon Pub Lib, Mt Vernon NY 29-41; Asst libn Horace Mann High Sch, Tchr's Col 41-42; Columbia U Libs: Lib asst spec collections 42-48, Asst libn spec collections 48-, Curator Columbiana 64-. 9: MusLA. 10: Bd of Dirs Internat Bach Soc. 13: Yes. 14: Rare bks, mss. 15: 410 Riverside dr, NYC 10025.

BONNER, ARLENA LYNN (CAMPBELL). b Richmond Va 6 Ag 40. 4: David Hill Bonner. 5: Madison Col 58-62 (LS) BS; William & Mary 63. 7: Sales clerk Thalhimers, Richmond Va 57; Coder Va Highway Dept, Richmond Va 58; Billing clerk Reynolds Medals, Richmond Va 60, Switch bd operator 61; Summer recreation libn Henrico Co, Richmond Va 62-63; Libn Henrico Co, Richmond Va 62-65; Libn Nansemond Co, Suffolk Va 65-. 66; Libn Portsmouth Va 66-. 9: NEA; ALA; VaEA. 10: AAUW. 14: Child bks. 15: 1177 Normandy dr, Suffolk Va 23434.

BONNER, FLOY S (SMILEY). 4: Lawrence W Bonner. 5: Alabama State Col 30-38 (Eng) BS, 47-48 (Eng, LS) Master's. 7: Sch libn Autauga Co Train Sch 49-66, 67; Sch libn Billingsley High Sch 67-. 8: Adv for the Parent-Tchrs Organ of Autauga Co Training Sch (12 yrs). 9: NEA; AlaSchLA (treas 6 yrs, pres 2 yrs); Ala State TA. 10: State chm Lib Student Assts Organ of Ala. 11: Tchr of the Year, Ala State TA 61-62. 14: Circ, story hour, ref. 15: PO Box 6, Autaugaville Al 36003.

BONNER, HARRIET (C). b DeWitt Ark 3 F 29. 4: Lloyd A Bonner. 5: Ark State Tchrs Col 47-51 (Eng) BSE; Tex Woman's U 57-63 MLS. 6: Sp. 7: Tchr-libn DeWitt High Sch, DeWitt Ark 51-52; Tchr-libn Velma-Alma High Sch, Velma Okla 52-56; Tchr Duncan Sr High Sch, Duncan Okla 57-59, Libn 60-. 9: ALA; NEA; OklaLA; OklaEA. 10: Delta Kappa Gamma; AAUW. 14: Ya. 15: 812 Beech, Duncan Ok 73533.

BONNER, LUCY (GOODRICH). b Medina Tenn 23 O 18. 4: Melvin C Bonner Jr. 5: Union U 32-35 (Biol) BS; Peabody 39-41 BLS; Okla State U 51; USoCal 59-61 (LS) MS. 6: Sp. 7: Libn Danville Pub Schs, Danville Va 39-42; Libn US Navy Naval Intelligence Lib,Wash DC 43-45; Instr Trinidad State Jr Co 46-47; Circ libn Tex Tech Col 47-48; LibnOkla State U Agric Lib 48-52; Libn Lynwood High Sch, Lynwood Cal 52-. 9: NEA; CalLA; CalASchL; Cal Tchrs Assn. 10: DeltaKappa Gamma. 14: Org of libs for new secon schs; ref, readers adv serv, col libs. 15: 3635 Cedar ave, Lynwood Ca 90262.

BONNER, ROBERT J. b Hazelton Penn 3 Jl 41. 4: Sharyn (Evans). 5: King's Col Wilkes Barre Penn 59-65 (Econ) BA; Rutgers 65-66 MLS. 6: Latin, French. 7: Ref libn Pottsville Free Pub Lib, Pottsville Penn 66-68; Dist ext libn Penn State U Libs 68-. 8: Wkshop Instr Penn State Lib (Ref & basic lib procedures). 9: ALA; PennLA. 14: Ext wk, ref, admin. 15: 1132 South Atherton st, State College Pa 16801.

BONNET, PAUL ANDREW. b Rochester NY 7 Je 35. 4: Anne Black. 5: URochester 53-54 (Chem); UCLA 54-60 (Pol Sci) BA; UCal (Berkeley) 63-64 MLS. 7: Foreign banking off trainee Bank of America, San Francisco 61; Salesman Air Reduction Pacific Co, Emeryville Cal 61-62; Ref libn UCLA 64-65; Asst head loan dept UCal (Davis) 66-67; A-v dir W Valley Col 67-. 14: Personnel, admin, bldgs & equipment. 15: 20900 Big Basin Way, Saratoga Ca 95070.

BONNETTE, PAUL EARL. b Burlington Vt 16 Ja 20. 4: Blanche St Cyr. 5: St Michael's Col (Vt) 59-63 (Eng) BA; Rutgers 63-64 MLS. 6: Fr. 7: Asst libn St Michael's Col (Vt) 64-67, Hd catlgr 67-. 9: ALA-ACRL; CathLA; Champlain Valley LA (pres 68-69). 14: Catlg, ref. 15: 26 Colonial sq, Burlington Vt 05401.

BONNEY, SISTER MARY BRENDAN OP. b Vancouver Wash 19 Je 15. 5: Marylhurst Col Elem Credentials; Queen of Holy Rosary (Eng) BA; Portland U MA in LS; USF Secondary Credentials; St Marys (Cal) Theol School 69. 6: Lat. 7: Libn San Gabriel High Sch, San Gabriel Cal 52-57; Libn St Elizabeth's High Sch, Oakland Cal 57-60; Libn Marycrest High Sch, Portland Ore 60-64; Libn Sacred Heart High Sch, Los Angeles 64-68; St Elizabeth's High Sch, Oakland Cal 68-. 8: . 9: ALA; CathLA (chm No Cal Unit); CalASchL. 14: Wk with ya, ref. 15: 1530 34th ave, Oakland Ca 94601.

BONWITT, KENNETH LEONARD. b Berlin Germany 4 Ag 25. 4: Miriam Lota Langer. 5: San francisco State Col 63-66 (Ger) BA; UWash 66-67 (Libnship) MA. 6: Ger, Fr. 7: Sgt british Army of the Rhine Royal Army Serv Unit War Crimes Investigation Unit 44-47; IBM operator: Kidder Peabody, NYC 48-51, ARAMCO, NYC 51-60; Libn Miami Dade Jr Col 67-. 9: FlaLA. 14: Circ, ref, computerization. 15: 732 82nd st, Miami Beach Fl 33141.

BOOK, ORPHA. b North Manchester Ind 2 O 09. 5: Manchester Col 27-31 (Eng) BA; UIll summers 37-40 BS in LS; UMich summers 33, 58 (Lat, LS); UColo summer 49 (LS); Ind State Col summer 58 (LS). 7: Tchr Chester twp High Sch, N Manchester Ind 31-41; High sch libn Sch City of Elkhart, Elkhart Ind 41-64; Ref libn Manchester Col, N Manchester Ind 64-. 9: ALA; IndLA; IndSchLA (pres 51-52, Historian 50, 59). 14: Ref. 15: 306 Wayne st, N Manchester In 46962.

BOOKE, DOROTHEA CATHERINE. b Dickinson NDak 29 Ag 16. 5: State Col (Dickinson ND) 42-44 (Home Econ); StateU (Fargo ND) 44-45 (Home Econ); UWis 45-47 (Home Econ) BS; UMich 65-66 (LS) Masters. 7: Tchr High Sch, Carsonville Mich 62-63; Libn High Sch, durand Mich 63-65; Libn State Col, Glenville W Va 66-67; Libn Pub Lib, Dickinson ND 68-. 9: NEA; ALA; MichLA; NDakLA. 13: Yes. 14: Educ. 15: Box 975, Dickinson ND 58601.

BOOKER, MRS ALICE (RELYEA). b Waterbury Conn 17 Ap 27. 4: Ralph W Booker. 5: Simmons 46-50 (LS) BS. 7: Lib asst Rutgers U (Camden) 50 & 51; Catlgr Quartermaster Research & Dev Lib,Phila 51-52; Ref asst Washington U (St Louis) 52-53, Libn Biol Lib 53-54; Lib asstBeaver Col 61-63; Libn F Jackson Daniel Mem Lib, St Peter's Episcopal Church,Glenside Penn 61-; Dir Church Libns Exchange Grad Sch of Lib Sci, Drexel Inst ofTech 67-68. 8: Church & Synag LA. 10: Episc Soc for Cult & Rac Unity. 14: Spec libs, inter-lib coop. 15: 654 NEaston rd, Glenside Pa 19038.

BOOKMYER, JANE (OWINGS). b Pittsburgh 22 Ja 23. 4: Paul O Bookmyer. 5: Carnegie 40-42, 45-47 BS; UPittsburgh 64-65 (LS) MS. 6: Fr, Sp. 7: Sec Carnegie-Illinois Steel Corp, Homestead Penn 42-45; Sec US Steel Corp, Pittsburgh 47-51; Asst libn Pittsburgh Plate Glass Co Glass Research Center, Pittsburgh 65- Ref libn 69. 9: SLA-ACRL; ASIS. 14: Ref, bibliog, preparation. 15: 109Woodland ave, Glenshaw Pa 15116.

BOONE, LOU ANN (SCHEPERS). b McBain Mich 10 Mr 33. 4: Wendell G Boone. 5: West Mich U 51-55 (LS) BS, 64. 6: Fr. 7: Bkmob libn Grand Traverse Area Lib, Traverse City Mich 55-57; Child libn & catlgr Traverse City Pub Lib, Traverse City Mich 60-61; Asst dir Grand Traverse Area Lib Fed, Traverse City Mich 61-62; Head Lib for the Blind Mich State Lib 62-66; Ottawa Ill; Dir Reddick's Lib 67-, Dir Starved Rock Lib Syst 67-. 9: ALA (Round Table on Lib Serv to the Blind);-ASD (Com on Lib Serv to Aging Popul 66-68). 10: Zonta Internat. 13: Yes. 14: Adult serv, automation, systems devel. 15: 207 N Dibble blvd, Lansing Mi 48917.

BOONE, MAURICE PERRY. b Houlton Me 25 Jl 07. 5: UNB 25-29 (Classics) BA; Toronto 29-31, 38-39 (Classics) MA, 40-41 BLS. 7: Lecturer in Lib Sci UToronto 41-42; Asst libn & Lecturer in Lib Sci Ontario Col of Educ 42-43; Chief catlgr USask 43-44; Chief libn & Asst Prof of Lib Sci Acadia U 44-50; Legis libn Legis Lib, Fredericton NB 50-. 8: Summer sch tchr: UNB, 50's; Bowling Green State U, 63. 9: CanLA; Bibliog Soc Can; APLA. 12: Ed "Union List of Scientific and Technical Periodicals in Libraries of the Maritime Provinces and Newfoundland" (51). 13: Yes. 14: Catlg, rare bks. 15: 338 Saunders, Fredericton NB Can.

BOONE, NANCY (BATES). b Asheville NC 22 Ja 29. 4: Samuel Moyle Boone. 5: St Genevieve-of-the-Pines 47-49 AA; UNC 49-51 (Eng) AB, 51-54 MSLS. 6: Fr, Lat. 7: Catlgr UNC 53-67, Hd Catlg maintenance 67-. 14: Catlg. 15: 57 Oakwood dr, Chapel Hill NC 27701.

BOONE, PATRICIA ELLEN. b Los Angeles Cal 22 Ag 30. 5: UCLA 48-52 (Soc studies & Educ) BA; ULondon Eng 57; USoCal 64-66 (LS & Sch admin) MSLS & MS Ed. 7: Elem tchr USA Ger 52-53, 56-57; Jr high sch tchr Hawthorne Sch Dist Hawthorne Cal 53-55; Jr high sch tchr USAF, Japan 58-59; High sch tchr LA City Schs 60-61, 62-64; Elem sch tchr USAF, Morocco 61-62; High sch libn Grossmont Union High Sch Dist, San Diego Cal 66-67; High sch libn LA City Schs 68-. 9: ALA; CalTA (Mem So Coun 55). 10: Letter of Commendation, US Army, Goeppingen, Germany 53. 14: Research. 15: 21453 Pac Cst Hwy, Malibu Ca 90265.

BOONE, SAMUEL MOYLE. b Gates NC 9 Ap 19. 4: Nancy Pritchette Bates. 5: UNC 46-49 (Journalism) AB, 59-64 MSLS. 6: Fr. 7: Radio Operator US Army Air Force T/4th Italy Africa 42-45; Chief photographic serv UNC Lib (Chapel Hill) 52-. 9: ALA;-RTSD (Copying Methods Sect, chm Bylaws Com 60-64, chm Simplified Payments Com 64-; Reprod of lib materials sect, v-chm & chm-elect 69); NCLA; NMA. 10: . 12: Ed Bd "North Carolina Libraries". 13: Yes. 14: Lib photocopying, interlib communications. 15: UNC Lib, Photographic Ser, Chapel Hill NC 27514.

BOONE, WILLIE G. b Morganton NC 26 Ag 13. 5: Wake Forest Col 32-35 (Eng) AB; UNC summers 55-58 (Educ, LS) M Ed. 7: Tchr High Sch, Murphy NC 35-38; Tchr High Sch, Warsaw NC 38-41; Tchr-libn Jr High Sch, Shelby NC 42-46; Tchr High Sch, Concord NC 47-51; Tchr High Sch, Clinton NC 51-55; Libn High Sch, Durham Co 56-59; Head Libn Durham High Sch, Durham Co 59-. 8: Instr Materials Consul, NC State Dept of Pub Instr, 59-60; Executive Secretary North Carolina High School Library Assoc 67-. 9: NEA; ALA NC High SchLA (Exec dir 67-); NCEA (past pres Lib Div); CarTA. 10: Bus & Prof Women's Club; OES. 14: Sch libs. 15: 2918 University dr, Durham NC 27701.

BOORD, MILLER. b Danville Ill 16 F 10. 4: Patricia A Romig. 5: UIll 28-33 (Econ) AB; Peabody 50-51 (Soc Studies) MA, 51-52 MALS. 7: Ind engnr CarnegieIll Steel Corp, Chicago 39-41; Adjutant US Army US & SPacific (Capt) 41-46; Standards analyst F L Jacobs Co, Danville Ill 46-50; Student asst Lib Sch Peabody Col 50-52; Dist libn Ill State Lib, Anna Ill 52-54; Libn Pub Lib, Mason City Iowa 54-57; Reg libn head pub serv & lib development, Ill State Lib 57-65; Head libn Randolph-Macon Woman's Col 65-. 8: Adjunct Prof So Ill U 57-60; Commun Development Dept Dir of Lib Serv & Construction Act proj for state of Ill 60-65. 9: ALA; VaLA. 10: Beta Phi Mu; Phi Delta Kappa; Pi Gamma Mu. 13: Yes. 14: Lib admin & buildings, ref. 15: 26D Princeton Circle W Apt 60, Lynchburg Va 24503.

BOORKMAN, CHARLES JOHN. b Aurora Ill 31 Mr 09. 4: Ruth Ellen Reuss. 5: UIll 33 AB, 38 BS in LS; USoCal 54 MA. 7: Libn reg Project Nat Youth Admin, Quoddy Village Me 38-42; USNR 5th Serv Command War Dept Columbus Ohio 43-43; Sci libn Cal State Col at San Jose 45-48; Libn Cal State Col at LA 48-49; Libn Cal State Col at Long Beach 49-. 10: Kappa Delta Rho; Phi Kappa Phi; Rotary Club; Torch Club; AAUP. 11: MedLA scholarship 57; GSA certificate59. 12: Bks & pamphlets on mech & allied trades (41); bks & pamphlets on econ citizenship (41). 14: Bldg. 15: 6441 DeLeon st, Long Beach Ca 90815.

BOOSER, RONALD JAMES. b Erie Penn 9 O 34. 4: Joan Murray. 5: Westminster Col 52-56 (Chem) BS; Syracuse 61 (LS); American U 65 (Tech mgt). 7: Engnr-lit searcher Gen Electric, Erie Penn 56-60; Spec tech info Gen Electric, Syracuse NY 60-62; Manager-Apollo Tech Info System Gen Electric, Daytona Beach Fla 62-64; System analyst Gen Electric, Huntsville Ala 64-65; System analyst, Head EDIS Proj Howard Research Corp, Arlington Va 65-67; Info sys specialist IMI Gen Syst Sciences 67-68; Account rep, IBM CorpWashington DC 69-. 8: Organized Aerospace Sect of SLA Consul to IMI, 68. 9: SLA (chm Transportation Div 60, chm Aerospace Sect 63). 10: Scoutmaster, CYO sports coach. 13: Yes. 14: Info systems & analysis, computer application to info systems. 15: 7310Wilburn dr, Capitol Heights Md 20027.

BOOTH, ADA (MARGARET) PFOHL. b Winston-Salem NC 10 Je 15. 4: Robert Edmond Booth. 5: Salem Col 32-36 (Eng) AB; Simmons 36-37 BSLS; UMich 42-44 AMLS. 7: Asst libn Meredith Col 37-42; Asst order dept Gen Lib UMich 42-43; Catlgr rare bks William L Clements Lib, Ann Arbor

Mich 43-46; Sub Grosse Pointe Pub Lib, Grosse Pointe Mich 61-63, Ref asst 63-. 9: ALA; MichLA; MichEA. 10: Founders' Soc, Detroit Inst of Art; Friends of thedetroit Pub Lib. 13: Yes. 14: Ref. 15: 872 Balfour rd, Grosse Pointe Mi 48236.

BOOTH, BARRY E(UGENE). b LeMars Iowa 3 N 41. 5: UDenver 60-64 (Fr) BA, 64-65 (LS) MA; So Ill U 68. 6: Fr. 7: Asst humanities & fine arts libn So Ill U 65-67, Humanities libn 67-68, Interlib loan lib 68-69, Interlib cooper libn 69-. 8: Lib consul for Sioux Empire Col, Hawarden Iowa 65. 9: IllLA. 14: Interlib coop. 15: 4734 Lake dr #25, Granite City, Il 62040.

BOOTH, (MRS) DEE MORRISON. b Ridgefield Park NJ 28 D 06. 5: Cornell 24-28 (Eng) AB; Rutgers 54-57 MLS. 7: Lib trainee Pub Lib, Elizabeth NJ 54-57; Adult serv State Lib, Trenton NJ 57-59; Generalist Pub Lib, NYC 59-60; Child libn Pub Lib, Chatham NJ 60-. 9: ALA; CathLA; NJLA. 14: Child bks, story telling. 15: 47C Lafayette ave, Chatham NJ 07928.

BOOTH, ELIZABETH (HAWKINS). b Schenectady NY 28 Ap 07. 4: Raymond E Booth. 5: Wellesley Col 24-28 (Fr) BA; Simmons 28-29 BLS. 6: Fr, Ger. 7: Lib asst NY Pub Lib 29-37, Asst libn 38-39; Asst libn, catlgr Upper Darby Lib, Upper Darby Penn 48-66; Area ref libn Ocean C Lib, Tom River N J 66-. 14: Catlg, ref. 15: 16 E California ave, Beach Haven Park NJ 08008.

BOOTH, MRS MARTHA OWENS. b Amory Miss 3 Ag 23. 5: Miss State Col for Women 41-45 (LS) BS; UIll summer 61 (LS); LSU summer 64 (LS); Miss State U 65 (LS) LSU 66-67 (LS) MS. 6: Fr, Lat, Sp. 7: Circ asst Jackson (Miss) Pub Lib 45-47; Libn VA Hosp, Jackson Miss 47-50; Libn VA Center, Houston 50-51; Libn VA Center, Jackson Miss 51-53; Libn Milam Jr High Sch, Tupelo Miss 60-61; Dir Capitol Area Reg Lib, Raymond Miss 61-62; Act chief circ Miss State U 62-64, Res libn 64-66, Catlgr 67-68, Sr catlgr 68-. 9: MissLA. 10: YWCA; Beta Phi Mu; Phi Kappa Phi. 14: Catlg, ser. 15: PO Box 1006, StateCollege Ms 39762.

BOOTH, PHEBE B. b Superior Wis 10 Ag 05. 5: Wis State Tchrs Col 28 (Eng) BE; UMinn 36 (LS) BS. 7: Asst Superior Pub Lib, Superior Wis 27-28; Br libn Racine Pub Lib, Racine Wis 29-30; Admin in lib serv Superior Pub Lib, Superior Wis 36-39, Gen asst 39-45; Catlgr Waukegan Pub Lib, Waukegan Ill 45-64, Head tech processes 65-. 9: ALA; IllLA (chm Catlgr Sect 52-53). 10: Altrusa Club. 12: "Subject Matter of Pilately" (44). 13: Yes. 14: Catlg. 15: Waukegan Pub Lib, Waukegan Il 60085.

BOOTH, ROBERT EDMOND. b Bridgeport Conn 21 My 17. 4: Ada Pfohl Booth. 5: Wayne State U 41 (Hist) AB; Columbia 42 ABLS; UMich 43 AMLS; West Res 60 (LS) PhD. 7: Lib Fellow Queens Col Lib (NY) 41-42; Grad asst UMich Lib 42-43; Jr asst DetroitPub Lib 43-44; Ed & bibliog University Microfilms, Ann Arbor Mich 44-46; Ref libnpeabody Inst Lib, Baltimore 46-47; Assoc libn MIT 47-56; Research Assoc & Instrwest Res U Sch of Lib Serv 56-60; Chm & Prof Dept of Lib Sci Wayne State U 60-. 8: Consul; Ponce PR Pub Lib, 59-60; Hudson (Ohio) Lib & Hist Assn, 59-60; Head,info Serv Div, Center for Application of Scis & Tech, Wayne State U 64-66; Researchassoc Ctr for Urban Studies 67-68; Dir Off for Urban Lib Research 68-. 9: ALA (chm&/or mem var coms); SLA; MichLA (pres 69-70); AALS; ASIS. 10: AAUP; Beta Phi Mu;Phi Delta Kappa; Founders' Soc Detroit Inst of Art; Friends of the Detroit Pub Lib &Grosse Pte Pub Lib; Mich Heart Assn A-V Com; EDUCOM summer study conf, 66. 12: "Bibliography of Aerospace Bibliographies" (65); Co-comp of several KWICindexes; "Culturally Disadvantaged," (67). 13: Yes. 14: Lib educ, diffusion of innovation,info storage & retrieval, urban libnship. 15: 872 Balfour rd, Grosse Pointe Mi 48236.

BOOZE, EDNA LOIS. b Beardstown Ill 19 Ag 42. 5: Ill State U 60-63 (Eng) BS; UIll 66-67 (LS) MS. 7: Libn Durand High Sch, Durand Ill 63-64; Libn Argenta High Sch, Argenta Ill 64-67; Asst dir Free Pub Lib, New Bedford Mass 67-68; Adult bk reviewer "Booklist & Subscription Books Bulletin" ALA Chicago 68-. 9: ALA; IllLA. 10: AAUW; Beta Phi Mu. 14: Bk sel, ref. 15: 3550 Lake Shore dr, Chicago Il 60657.

BORCHELT, (STELLA) LOUISE. b Coles Co Ill 24 Mr 09. 5: Western Col 26-28 (Classics); Radcliffe 28-29 (Classics); Chicago 29-30 (Classics) PhB; UIll 31-32 BLS. 7: Jr prof asst Evanston Pub Lib, Evanston Ill 23-34; Prof asst Morton High Sch & Jr Col, Cicero Ill 35; Sr prof asst Evanston Pub Lib, Evanston Ill 35, Act br libn 35-37, Acquis libn 37-. 9: ALA (var com duties); IllLA (var com duties); Chicago Lib Club (several coms). 10: AAUW; YWCA (Bd & coms); LWV; Evanston City Employees Safety Commsn 57-61. 14: Bk sel, acquis. 15: 1321 Washington st, Evanston Il 60202.

BORCHERS, MARGARET E (BORG-BREEN). b Kioshan Honan China 25 D 14. 4: Raymond L Borchers. 5: Luther Col 33-35, 36-38 (Eng, Mus) BA; UMinn 39-40 BLS. 6: Norwegian. 7: Ref UIowa Lib (Iowa City) 40-41; Ref Luther Col Lib 41-42; Org pub sch lib, Omaha neb 43; Org ch lib, Lincoln Neb 62-65; Ref Nebraska State Lib Commsn, Lincoln 60-. 10: Boy Scouts; Campfire Girls; 4H Club; PTA; Univ Wives Org. 14: Ref. 15: 6200 Walker ave, Lincoln Nb 68507.

BORCHIN, ANNA (PANSOCK). b Czechoslovakia 31 My 09. 4: Andrew Borchin. 5: UKy 28-38 (Eng, Hist) BA, 50-54 (LS, Educ) MA. 6: Slovak. 7: Tchr Lynch Pub Schs, Lynch Ky 28-43; Statistical clerk Wright Aeronautical Corp, Cincinnati; Tchr Erlanger Schs, Erlanger Ky, Libn 46-53; Libn Cincinnati Pub Schs 53-. 8: Eval Com, So Assn of Secon Schs; Exec dir Nat Lib Week, Ohio, 65. 9: ALA; OhioASchL (past pres); CathLA (chm Cincinnati Unit 67-69). 10: Delta Kappa Gamma. 12: Ed OhioASchL "Bulletin." 13: Yes. 14: Wk with yp. 15: 3175 Hulbert ave, Erlanger Ky 41018.

BORCHUCK, FRED PAUL. b Newark NJ 6 F 34. 4: Gelia Hammer. 5: Rutgers 59-62 (Eng) BA, 63-65 MLS. 6: Ger. 7: Catlg, ref libn, loan libn, Albert R Mann Lib Cornell U 65-. 14: Catlg, ref, circ, admin. 15: 317 Hook pl, Ithaca NY 14850.

BORDELON, DIANNE C. b Warner Robins Ga 8 S 43. 4: Raynald Louis Bordelon. 5: LSU (New Orleans) 61-65 (LS, Educ) BA, 65-66 (LS) MS; La Certif Admin Libn. 7: Lib asst Jefferson Parish Lib, Metairie La 65; Admin libn St John the Baptist Parish Lib, Laplace La 66-68; Libn St James Parish Lib, Litcher La 68; Br libn Prince William Co Pub Lib, Manassas Va 69. 8: Sec Coord Com La Stage Lib Proc Ctr 67-68. 9: ALA; CalLA. 14: Ref, circ, admin, pub relations. 15: 4522 S Park dr, Metairie La 70001.

BORDEN, JOSEPH C(ARLETON). b S Orange NJ 22 My 09. 5: Harvard 27-31 AB; Union Theol Sem 32-33; Columbia 35-40 (LS) BS. 7: NY Pub Lib: Asst prep div ref dept 35-38, Head searching sect prep div ref dept 38-42, Head bk order sect acquis div ref dept 42-47; Assoc libn in chg of acquis dept UArk 47-65; Head Ser Unit processing div Purdue U Libs 65-. 9: ALA (Bk Acquis Com 51-53);-ACRL (Com on Const & Bylaws 54-57);-RTSD (chm &/or mem 3 coms 60-65);-SRT (sec-treas Southwestern Reg 49); SWLA (Exec Bd, Ark rep 52; Consul to Com on Col & Univ Lib Standards 52-55, treas 61-64); ArkLA (chm Col & Ref Sect 52-53, pres 64). 12: Contrib to Hawkins' "Scientific, Medical and Technical Books Published in the USA 1930-1944," & to its supls & the 2nd ed; Ed bd "Serial Slants" (52-54). 13: Yes. 15: 2410 Happy Hollow rd Apt B-9, W Lafayette In 47906.

BORDEN, LOIS MARIE. b Pittsburgh 20 S 14. 5: Adelphi Col 32-36 (Eng) AB (cum laude); Pratt 36-37 BLS. 7: Asst child dept NY Pub Lib 37-38; Queens Borough Pub Lib, Jamaica NY: Asst ext dept 38-44, Libn, 1st asst 44-45, Br libn 45-58; Sr libn NY Pub Lib 58, Supv libn 59-. 9: NY Lib Club. 13: Yes. 14: Tech serv, br admin. 15: 311 E 37th st, NYC 10016.

BORDEN, MARY FRANCES. b Tacoma Wash 23 N 19. 5: UWash 39-43 (Hist) BA, 43-44 BA in Libnship. 6: Fr,Sp. 7: Tacoma Pub Lib, Tacoma Wash: Br asst, child libn 44-45, Br libn Mottet Br 45-49, Br libn Moore Br 50-55, Asst dir 55-. 8: Tacoma-Pierce Co Lib Coun. 9: ALA (Memb Com 57-61);-PLA;-YASD;-RTSD;-ASD;-LAD;-IRRT;-ERT; Wash State Memb Chm 57-60; CathLA; PNLA (various coms); WashLA (Exec Bd57-59, Exec Dir Nat Lib Week 65). 10: Quota Club; Allied Arts; UPS-Tacoma SymphonyGuild; Brotherhood of RR Trainmen Auxiliary; AAUW; Educ Task Force, Urban Coalition;Tacoma Arts for Youth Coun. 14: Serv to the disadvant, computer tech, pub rel,personnel, circ systems, lib organ & admin. 15: Tacoma Pub Lib, 1102 S Tacoma ave,Tacoma Wa 98402.

BORDERS, FLORENCE (EDWARDS). b New Iberia La 24 F 24. 4: James B Borders. 5: Southern U 41-45 (Eng) BA; Rosary Col 46-47 BA in LS, 64 MA in LS Post Master's fellow LSU 66-67. 6: Fr, Sp. 7: Lib asst UChicago 46; Asst libn catlg Bethune- Cookman Col 47-58; Catlgr Tenn A & I U 58-59; Head of tech serv Grambling Col 59-. 8: Consul; Palm Beach Co Wkshop 49; Tenn Tchrs Assn 59; Mem So Assn Eval Com Consul LaEA Lib Dir 66. 9: ALA; CathLA; LaLA; LaEA. 10: St Benedict Cath Circle; Zeta Phi Beta. 14: Catlg. 15: P O Box 466, Grambling La 71245.

BORDERS, GLENN HOUGHTON. b Pontiac Mich 22 Je 27. 4: Grace (Sutton). 5: George Washington U even 49-62 (Hist) BA; McGill 63-64 BLS. 6: Fr. 7: Asst order libn Naval Acad Lib (Annapolis) 54-55; Asst to chief art sect NLM 55-56;

Circ libn Smithsonian Inst Lib, Wash DC 56-57, Asst ref libn 57-58; Libn Off of Weights & Measures Lib Nat Bur Standards, Wash DC 59-63; Assoc libn State U Col Lib (Fredonia NY) 64-65; Chief standards Communication Center Nat Bur Standards, Wash DC 65-66; Cons libn Unemployment Insurance Serv US Dept Labor, Wash DC 66-67; Supvrrare bk rdg rm LC 67-. 9: ALA-ACRL; CanLA; SLA. 10: AAUP; Nat Conf on Weights & Measures. 14: Admin, tech serv. 15: 8005 Eastern ave apt 209, Silver Spring Md 20910.

BORDNER, GEORGE WILSON. b Kutztown Penn 1 Ap 18. 4: Reba J Basom. 5: State Tchrs Col (Kutztown Penn) 36-39 (LS) BS in Educ; Columbia 48-49 MS in LS. 7: Supv Lib Proj WPA, Reading Penn 40-41; US Army (M/Sgt) Admin NCO Hdq Hawaiian Dept 41-45; Libn Monongahela Pub Lib, Monongahela Penn 45-46; Tchr-libn admiral Farragut Acad, St Petersburg Fla 46-48; Asst libn State Tchrs Col (Mansfield Penn) 49-53; Libn Mechanicsburg High Sch, Mechanicsburg Penn 53-55; Assoc libn Franklin & Marshall Col 55-61; Dir tech serv State Lib, Harrisburg Penn 61-. 9: ALA; PennLA. 14: Tech proc. 15: 3814 Lamp Post lane, Camp Hill Pa 17011.

BORENSTEIN, GERTRUDE (PERLMAN). b Cambridge Mass. 4: Emanuel Borenstein. 5: Mass Col of Art 24-28 (Art) BS Ed; Adelphi U 57 (Art); C W Post Col LIU 60-65 MLS. 6: Fr, Ger, Portu. 7: Assoc Dir Child Art Centre, Boston; Art tchr Pub Schs, Second Supervisory Dist, Patchogue NY 56-58; Sch libn Pub Schs, Glen Cove NY 60-62; Sch libn Pub Schs, W Hempstead NY 62-64; Child libn Bethpage Pub Lib, Bethpage NY 65; Sch libn Terryville Sch, Pt Jefferson Station NY 65-68; Broward Co Pub Sch, Fla 68-. 9: NEA; NY State Tchrs Assn; Nassau-SuffolkSchLA; NY State Art Tchrs Assn; FlaTA. 15: 1701 S Ocean dr, Hollywood Fl 33020.

BORGESON, EARL C. b Boyd Minn 2 D 22. 4: Barbara Jones. 5: UMinn 40-43, 45-49 (Law) BS in Law, LLB; So Br UIda 43-44; UWash 49-50 BS in Law Libnship. 7: US Navy 43-45; Asst law libn UWash 50; Asst ref libn los Angeles Co Law Lib 50-52; Asst libn Harvard U Law Sch 52-53, Act libn 53-54, Law libn 54-. 8: Exhibit consul World Peace Through Law Center 65; Survey of Asian law lib & research facilities for Amer Bar found 63 Dir Seminar on law librarianship & legal research techniques, U Philippines summer 66. 9: ALA; ABA (com on law lib coop) (Exec Bd) 66-67, pres 68); Law Libs of NE (past pres). 10: Sch Com Sudbury Mass 60-63; Sudburg Little League. 13: Yes. 14: Admin. 15: 16 Wilson rd, Sudbury Ma 01776.

BORING, MICHAEL RAY. b Everett Wash 15 Je 42. 4: Sharon Winkle. 5: UWash 60-61, 65-67 (Libnship) MA; West Wash State Col 61-64 (Educ) BA. 6: Ger. 7: Elem libn Elma Pub Schs, Elma Wash 64-65; Jr high libn No Thurston Schs, Lacey Wash 65-67; Ref libn S Puget Sound Reg Lib, Olympia Wash 66-67; High sch libn William W Miller High Sch, Olympia Wash 67-69; Supv sch libs Olympia Pub Schs, Olympia Wash 69-. 8: Lib consul Off of Pub Instr Wash 66-68; Mem State Reading Com Off of Pub Instr wash 67-. 9: ALA; NEA; Wash State Assn Sch Libns (pres-elect 69-71); WashLA; WashEA. 10: Olympia YMCA. 11: Laura Hahn Mem Scholarship UWash. 13: Yes. 14: Coord of var media. 15: Olympia Public Schools, Olympia Wa 98501.

BORLAND, MARY ELIZABETH (O'CONNOR). b Oelwein Iowa 27 Je 11. 5: Col of St Catherine 29-33 (Fr) BA; UDenver 60-64 (LS) MA. 6: Fr, Sp. 7: Tchr-libn Santa Fe City Schs, Santa Fe NM 51-53; Asst catlgr NM State Lib 54-64, Chief tech serv div 64-. 9: NMLA; SWLA. 13: Yes. 14: Catlg. 15: 1929 Kiva rd, Santa Fe NM 87501.

BORMANN, SISTER MARY CLARA BVM. b Cedar Rapids Iowa 17 S 14. 5: Clarke Col 40 (Hist) BA; Col of St Catherine 45 BSLS; UMich 56 MALS. 6: Fr. 7: Tchr Gesu Sch, Milwaukee 37-38; Mundelein Col Lib: Clerical asst 38-44, Asst libn 45-51, Libn 52-. 9: CathLA (sec Col Sect; off in Ill Unit 59-; chm Jt Com CathLA- ala 65-); IllLA. 12: Ed "Periodical Holdings in Eleven College Libraries in Chicago Area" (62). 13: Yes. 14: Admin, catlg. 15: Mundelein Col, Learning Resource Ctr, 6339 Sheridan rd, Chicago Il 60626.

BORN, GERALD M. b Hammond Ind 16 My 36. 5: Purdue U 54-55 (Entymology); Butler U 55-59 (Hist, Pol Sci, religion) BA; Christian Theol Sem 59-60; Ind U 60-62 (LS) MA. 6: Ger. 7: Catlg asst Christian Theol Sem (Indianapolis) 55-60; Ref asst Ind U Lib 60-61; Catlgr Bartholomew Co Lib, Columbus Ind 61-64, Dir 64-66;Bldg consul Ill State Lib 66-68; Resources coordinator N Suburban Lib Syst, Morton Grove Ill 68-. 8: Consul Forest Park Pub Lib. 9: ALA (life mem); IndLA(treas 64-65, chm com on reorg 65); IllLA. 10: Rotary; SAR. 12: Co-ed Bldg issue of "IllinoisLibraries" (68). 13: Yes. 14: Admin, lib bldgs, lib resources. 15: 630 Green Bay rd,Kenilworth Il 60043.

BORN, JEAN S. b Tucson Az 29. 4: John W Born. 5: UAriz 46-51 (Physics, Math) BS; Ariz State 65-; UDenver 65-67 (LS) MA. 6: Ger. 7: Grad asst UAriz; Engr asst GE Co 51-56; Libn asst Ariz State Lib Ext Serv 64-67; Libn Maricopa Co Jr Col Dist 67-. 9: ALA; ArizStateLA. 14: Catlg, automation, ext. 15: 1644 W 6th ave, Mesa Az 85201.

BORNSTEIN, REVA (RICE). b Detroit Mi 7 O 36. 4: Morris Bornstein. 5: Mich State 54-56 (Elem ed); Wayne State 56-58 (Bus admin) BS, 58-59 (LS) Tchg certif; UMich 59-62 (LS) MS. 6: Fr, Hebrew. 7: Libn Elem schs, Oak Park Mich 59-62; Libn Elem schs, Brookline Mass 62-63; Libn High schs, Ann Arbor Mich 63-. 9: ALA; MichASchL. 10: LWV. 14: Child lit. 15: 1503 Warwick ct, Ann Arbor Mi 48103.

BORNT, PHYLLIS. b Schenectady NY 14 S 29. 5: Central Col 47-51 (Eng lit) BA; Columbia 51-52 MS in LS. 6: Fr. 7: Lib catlgr Bridgeport Pub Lib, Bridgeport Conn 52-55; Sr libn Brooklyn Pub Lib, Brooklyn NY 55-60; Br libn Schenectady Co Pub Lib, Schenectady NY 60-. 9: ALA; NYLA. 14: Adult serv. 15: 61 Sacandaga rd, Scotia NY 12302.

BOROVANSKY, VLADIMIR T(HEODORE). b Prague Czechoslovakia 25 My 31. 4: Dagmar Borovansky Korbel. 5: CharlesU (Prague) 60-65 MLS. 6: Czech, Russian, Ger. 7: Tech info specialist Research Inst Ferric Metallurgy, Prague 59-64, head doc dept 64-67; Sci ref libn Ariz State U Lib 68-. 9: ArizLA. 10: Czechoslovak Soc for Art & Sci in Amer Inc. 13: Yes. 14: Ref. 15: Arizona State Univ Lib, Tempe Az 85281.

BOROWSKI, JOSEPH F JR. b Calumet City Ill 16 N 27. 4: Inga Hallstrom. 5: Chicago Musical Col 49-52 (Music) BMus Ed; Roosevelt U 52-57 (Music) M Mus Ed; UIll(Chicago) 49-51; UIll(Urbana) 60-64 (LS) MS. 6: Sp. 7: Mus dir Forman High Sch, Manito Ill 52-53; Mus supv Sesser High Sch, Sesser Ill 53-54; Mus supv Roberts-Thawville Schs, Roberts Ill 54-57; Mus supv & libn Cissna Park High Sch, Cissna Park Ill 57-62; Head Libn Kankakee High Sch, Kankakee Ill 62-64; Head Libn Glenbrook South High Sch, Glenview Ill 64-. 8: Kankakee (Ill) Pub Lib consul, 64. 9: ALA; IllLA; IllSchLA; IllEA. 13: Yes. 14: Instr materials centers, info storage & retrieval. 15: 1089 Valley Stream dr, Wheeling Il 60090.

BOROWYK, MICHAEL. b Ukraine 6 Ap 22. 4: Dora Holian. 5: Sch of Economics (Munich) 45-48 (Econ) BA; UOttawa 55-60 (Slavic) MA, 58-59 BLS Ukranian Free U (Munich) 66-69 (Hist) PhD. 6: Ukrainian, Russian, Polish, Ger. 7: Catlgr, libn 3 Nat Museum of Can Lib, Ottawa 59-. 9: CanLA; Bibliog Soc Can; OttawaLA. 10: Shevchenko Scientific Soc in Can. 13: Yes. 14: Catlg. 15: 1290 Snowdon st, Ottawa 8 Can.

BORST, MARLENE ALITA. b Paterson NJ 31 Ag 42. 5: State U Col (Geneseo NY) 60-64 (LS) BS. 7: Libn-bkmob Mohawk Valley Lib Assn, Schenectady NY summers 64, 65; Libn Fonda-Fultonville Central Sch, Fonda NY 64-65; Libn Spencerport Central Sch, Spencerport NY 65-68; Jr High libn in Amer Dependent Sch, RAF Wethersfield, Essex Eng. 9: ALA; NYLA. 15: Box25, Seward NY 12199.

BORTHWICK, HOWARD HALL. b Woodland Cal 30 Mr 26. 5: George Washington U 43-47 (Hist) AB, 47-48 (Hist) MA; Carnegie 51-52 MLS. 7: Circ desk supv DC Pub Lib 49-51; Montgomery Co (Md) Pub Lib: Bkmob libn (Gaithersburg) 52-54, Br libn (Wheaton) 54-57, Ext libn (Bethesda) 57-63, Chief div of pur serv (Bethesda) 63-. 9: ALA; MdLA (2nd v-pres 62-63). 14: Public serv. 15: 13700 Creekside dr, Silver Spring Md 20904.

BORTNER, ALBA P. b Wilmington Del. 4: Doyle McClean Bortner. 5: Wilson Col (Fr, Eng) AB; Temple (Reading); UMe (Child Lit); Rutgers 65 MLS. 6: Ital, Fr. 7: Tchr of Eng & journalism Vineland High sch, Vineland NJ; Tchr of Eng Lewiston High Sch, Lewiston Me; Ref child dept Freeport Mem Lib, Freeport LI NY; Child libn Montclair Pub Lib, Montclair NJ 65-. 9: ALA; NJLA. 10: AAUW; LWV; College Club, Montclair Women's Club; Montclair Art Mus; Mus ofMod Art (NYC). 14: Child wk, ref, pub relations. 15: 66 Clinton ave, Montclair NJ 07042.

BORTNER, MARIAN V. b Bradford Penn 2 Ja 06. 5: Grove City Col 24-26, 28-29 (Eng, Fr) Litt B; Columbia summers 35, 36, 38, 41 BS in LS. 6: Fr. 7: Eng tchr High Sch, Wilcox Penn 29-30; Eng tchr High Sch, Brookville Penn 30-37, Libn 37-39; Libn High Sch, Meadville Penn 39-43; Libn Roosevelt Jr High Sch,Erie Penn 45-47 ; Libn Academy High Sch, Erie Penn 45-57; Mem High High Sch, Erie Penn 60-. 8: Act libn Clarion

State Col summers 46 & 56. 9: NEA; Penn StateEA; ErieEA; PennLA. 10: AAUW; Delta Kappa Gamma. 14: Yp, circ. 15: 518 Holland st, Erie Pa 16507.

BORTON, DONALD CHARLES. b St Joseph Mich 2 My 32. 4: Barbara Johnson. 5: George WashingtonU 58-61 AA, 61-66 (Bio) BS; UMd 66-68 MLS. 7: HSSA to midshipman USN, Great Lakes, Memphis, Newport, Annapolis 50-52; Lab tech Auto Specialties Mfg Co, St Joseph Mich 52-55; Lab tech-test engnr Whirlpool Corp, St Joseph Mich 55-58; Lab tech-physicist-tech libn Gillette Research Inst, Wash DC 58-68; Libn supv Nat Lib of Med, Bethesda Md 68-. 8: MedLA Certif Grade I. 9: AAAS; AIBS; ASIS (pres Natl Capitol Area Stud Chap 68); MedLA; SLA; DCLA. 10: Phi Epsilon Phi (Delta Chap); Beta Phi Mu. 13: Yes. 14: Ref, MEDLARS demand search, biomed communications networks, reg lib syst. 15: 9918 Thornwood rd, Kensington Md 20795.

BOSCO , SISTER JOHN (SANDERS) CPPS. b St Louis 4 Ap 23. 5: St Louis U 59 (Hist) AB; St Catherine 62 (LS); Rosary Col 63 (LS); Utah State (LS). 7: Tchr-libn Sacred Heart Elem Sch, Florissant Mo 62-63; Tchr libn Holy Family Elem Sch, St Louis 58-59; Tchr To establish a school, LaPaz Bolivia 59-60; Libn St John High Sch, St. Louis 63-. 8: Adv wk for elem sch libs. 9: ALA; CathLA (Greater St Louis Unit; chm Cath Studs Lib Guild); MoSchLA; Greater St Louis Lib Club (treas). 14: Yp lit. 15: 5021 Adkins ave, St Louis 63116.

BOSEN, SHIRLEY ELIZABETH. b Santa Barbara Cal 28 D 27. 4: Evan Lee Bosen. 5: UCLA 45-48 (Pol Sci) AB, 60-61 MLS. 7: Libn Lowell High Sch, La Habra Cal 61-64; Libn pub serv Fullerton Jr Col 64-66, Hd libn 66-. 9: Cal Tchrs Assn; CalLA; ALA. 10: Beta Phi Mu; Delta KappaGamma; Cal Jr Col Fac Assn. 14: Catlg, ref, admin. 15: 3501 Sunnywood, FullertonCa 92632.

BOSHEARS, ONVA K JR. b Bloomington Ind 31 Ag 39. 5: Greenville Col 57-61 (Soc Sci) AB (cum laude); UIll 61-62 (LS) MS; Asbury Theol Sem 62-65 (Theol, Rel Educ) MRE; UMich 65-. 6: Fr, Ger. 7: Asst libn Asbury Theol Sem (Wilmore Ky) 62-65; Co-0rdg Libn for Residence Halls Libs, UMich 65-67; Dir of lib serv, Assoc prof of Theol Bibliog, Asbury Theol Sem Wilmore Ky 67-. 8: Ordained Minister, Free Method Church of N Amer. 9: ATheolLA; Amer Acad of Relig; Kyla. 10: Theta Phi; Phi Alpha Theta; Pi Kappa Delta; Alpha Kappa Sigma. 13: Yes. 14: Admin, ref, bibliog. 15: Asbury Theol Sem, Wilmore Ky 40390.

BOSS, (WOODRUFF) RICHARD. b Arnheim Netherlands 31 O 37. 4: Christine Buckner. 5: UUtah 53-56 (Pol Sci) BA; UWash 56-70 (LS) MA; UUtah & UWash 60- (Pol Sci) PhD cand. 6: Dutch, Ger. 7: Order libn UUtah 62-63, Asst dir libs 63-66, Assoc dir 66-; Tchg Dept LS UUtah 62-, Sch Libnship Wes Mich U summer 68. 8: UUtah Faculty Coun 65, mem Exec Com 68; Mem Bd Trustees; Bibliog Center for Research, Denver 68-; v-pres & pres- elect, Reg Info Netwk Group 68-. 9: American Library Association (Utah JMRT Liaison 67); -TRSD (Tech Serv Cost Com 67-); -ACRL (Com on Lib Surveys 67-, Coun nominee 69); UtahLA (v-pres 67, pres 68); MPLA (chm Nom Com 68). 10: AAUP; Jr C of C; Newcomers; Phi Kappa Phi; Phi Beta Kappa; Beta Phi Mu. 13: Yes. 14: Admin, acquis, automation, a-v. 15: 2320 Garfield ave, Salt Lake City Ut 84108.

BOSSEAU, DON L. b Pittsburgh Kan 28 N 36. 4: Kay Seavey. 5: Kansas State Col 54-56 (Math, Sci); Kan StateU 56-58 (Engring) BS; UKan 60-61 (Engring) MS; UHawaii 65-66 mls. 6: Fr. 7: Asst engr GE Aircraft Nuclear Project, Cincinnati 57; Engr Allis-Chalmers Nuclear Div, Milwaukee 58-60; Staff assoc Gen Atomic Corp, La Jolla Cal 61-65, Asst libn 65; Dir lib syst development UCal (San Diego) 66-. 8: Visiting faculty suny 9geneseo) Grad Sch of Lib Sci 69, Consul Educ Data Syst Corp, Newport Beach Cal 69; Faculty UOre Inst on Lib Automation (Eugene) summer 68. 9: Com on Lib Automation; ALA; ASIS. 10: AAUP; Amer Acad of Sci. 11: US AEC Grad Fellowship 60-61; SLA Scholarship 65. 13: Yes. 14: Lib admin & mgt, lib syst development. 15: 1227 Umatilla, Del Mar Ca 92014.

BOSSHARDT, MARGARET E(TTA). b Winona Minn 15 N 32. 5: Hanline U 50-54 (Hist) BA; Carnegie Lib Sch 55-56 MSLS. 7: Detroit Pub Lib: Children's libn 56-66; Detroit Pub Lib: Asst personnel dir 66-68; Dir Marshall-Lyon Co Lib, Marshall Minn 68-. 9: ALA; MinnLA. 14: Adult serv, child & ya. 15: 1302 Birch st apt 27, Marshall Mn 56258.

BOSSUYT, KATHRYN MAY (KNOBLOCH). b Davenport Iowa 25 D 19. 4: Maurice J Bossuyt. 5: Col of St Teresa Winona Minn 37-41 (Eng, Fr) BA; Catholic U of Amer 42-47. 6: Fr. 7: Auditor USA Finance Off Wash DC 42-45; Libn Dept of Lib Sci Catholic U 46-47; Hd adult circulation dept Moline Pub Lib Ill 47-51; Tchr St Anthony's Sch Casa Grande Ariz 56-57; Libn Casa Grande Union High Sch Casa Grande Ariz 59-68; Dir elem lib Amphitheater Pub Sch Tucson 68-. 8: Chm Casa Grande Pub Lib Com 52; Pub Lib Bd: mem 54-60, pres 55-57. 9: NEA; ALA (State Recruitment Com 62); CathLA; ArizEA; Amphitheater ClrTA; ArizStateLA (Exec Bd 67-69; Sch Lib Div: v-pres 64-65, pres-elect & Prog chm 67-68, pres 68-69). 10: Delta Kappa Gamma. 14: Wk with child & ya. 15: 965 W Las Lomitas rd, Tucson Az 85704.

BOSTIAN, MRS IRMA R (CARSTEDT). b DeKalb Ill. 4: J Calvin Bostian. 5: No Ill U 46-50 (Speech); UIll 64-65 (LS). 7: USA (CIC) Lt 60-61; 1st Asst ext dept Flint River Reg Lib, Griffin Ga 63-65;1st Asst order dept Atlanta Pub Lib 65-66; V-pres Amer Lib Line Inc, Atlanta Ga 66-. 9: ALA; IllLA (chm Memb Com 69). 10: Lawyers' Wives Assn; Springfield Art Assn; Kappa Delta P; Delta Zeta. 12: Ed "Illinois Libraries. 14: A-v serv, lib publs. 15: 15 Timber Hill dr, Springfield Il 62707.

BOSTON, HELEN S(CHAYER). b Denver 4 Jl 09. 5: UDenver 26-28; Northwestern 28-30 (Sociol) BS; Columbia 53-54 MSLS. 7: Br libn Denver Pub Lib 30-38, Ref libn 41-43; US Army libn Camp Luna NM, Camp Crowder Mo, Ft Monmouth NJ 43-49; Br libn Newark Pub Lib, Newark NJ 54-60, Ref libn 60-63; Ref libn Dept of Health Educ & Welfare, Wash DC 63-65; Hd ref & pub serv Fed Housing Admin Lib, Wash DC 65-68; Hd Bibliog SecHousing & Urban Dev Lib 68-. 9: ALA; DCLA. 14: Ref. 15: 2731 Ordway st NW, Wash DC 20008.

BOSWELL, PEGGY (BISHOP). b Megargel Tex 30 S 30. 5: Tex Woman's U 48-51 (LS) BA; UDenver 67-68 Libnship MA. 7: TSCW Lib, Page, Denton Tex 49-51; Waco Pub Lib, Library asst, Waco Tex 51-52, Catlgr 52-56; Denver Pub Lib Bkmob libn 56-58, Libn I 68-. 9: ALA; ColoLA. 14: Ref, bk sel. 15: 4617 South Lincoln st, Englewood Co 80110.

BOSWORTH, MRS RUTH (FAWCETT). b Youngstown O 3 D 17. 4: Robbins R Bosworth. 5: Lake Erie Col 36-40 (Music) BA; West Res 61-65 (LS) MS. 6: Fr, Ital. 7: Violinist Youngstown Symphony, Youngstown Ohio 33-40; Music tchr Bettsville High Sch, Bettsville Ohio 41-42; Lib consul Kenston Sch, Chagrin Falls Ohio 64; Catlgr Case West Res U 65-. 8: ALA; NoOhio Tech Serv Org. 10: Amer Field Serv. 14: Catlg. 15: 8799 Bainbridge-Auburn rd, Chagrin Falls Oh 44022.

BOTH, GABOR. b Eperjes Hungary 29 Je 14. 4: Stephanie Meszner. 5: Charles U (Prague) 32-38 Dr Jur; McGill 60-61 BLS. 6: Hungarian, Ger, Russian, Czech, Fr. 7: Municipal judge, Hungary 39-42; Reviser Bank of Hungary, Budapest 43-51; Catlgr Pub Lib, Edmonton Alta 61-64; Head of tech serv Law Lib McGill U 64-. 9: CanLA; QueLA. 12: Indexer "Index of Canadian Legal Periodical Literature" (65-). 14: Catlg. 15: 3644 Peel st, Montreal 2 Can.

BOTHAM, JANE. b Madison Wis 2 Ja 34. 5: UWis 51-55 (Speech) BS; Carnegie 56-57 MLS. 6: Sp. 7: Child libn Milwaukee Pub Lib 55-56; Child libn Carnegie Lib of Pittsburgh 56-57; Ya spec & child libn NY Pub Lib 57-60; Br libn Madison Pub Lib, Madison Wis 60-63; Libn in Chg main child room San Francisco Pub Lib 63-. 8: Child Libn Seattle World's Fair, 62. 9: ALA (Assoc ed "Top of the News" 61-64, mem Aurianne Award Com 60-61); -CSD,Publ Planning Com 69-; CalLA; Assn Child Libns, No Cal. 14: Child lib wk. 15: San Francisco Pub Lib,Civic Center, San Francisco Ca 94102.

BOTHELL, LARRY L. b Greeley Col 22 O 32. 4: Janet Bowers Bothell. 5: Harvard 50-54 (Phil) AB; Union Theol Sem 56-59 (Theol) BD; Princeton 60-64 (Ch Hist) PhD. 7: Specialist 3rd class (personnel) USA 54-56; Episcopal Theol Sch, Cambridge Mass: Relig & hist master 59-60, Assoc libn & instr in ch hist 64-66, Assoc libn & asst prof of ch hist 66-69, Dir of lib & assoc prof of Amer relig studies 69-. 8: V-pres bd of dir Gen Theol Lib, Boston. 10: ATheolLA. 14: Acquis, rare bks, inter-lib coop. 15: 8 St Johns rd, Cambridge Ma 02138.

BOTTEN, MARY (AGATHA). b Windthorst Can 5 Ag 07. 5: Concordia Col 25-29 (Eng) BA; UWis 33-34 Certif. 6: Norse, Danish. 7: Libn Newark High Sch, Newark Ohio 35-37; Asst libn & catlgr Pub Lib, Coshocton Ohio 37-39; Libn Sheridan Co Lib, Plentywood Mont 39; Asst libn Pacific Lutheran Col 40-43; Circ asst UWash Lib 43-45; Asst libn Grays Harbor Co Lib, Montesano Wash 45-47, Libn 47-54; Head catlg dept Duluth Pub Lib, Duluth Minn 54-56; Head child dept Pub Lib, San Bernardino Cal 56-. 9: ALA; PNLA; CalLA; So Cal Coun on Child Lit. 10: World Affairs Coun. 14: Lit for child & yp, bk publ, catlg. 15: 1415 Genevieve, San Bernardino Ca 92405.

BOUCHER, JEAN TAYLOR. b Carroll Iowa 29 D 26. 4: Tom Boucher. 5: Wartburg Col 43-47 (Eng) AB; UWash 48-49 (LS) AB. 7: Asst ref libn Lib of Hawaii, Honolulu 49-51; Libn Japan Lib Sch Keio U (Tokyo) 51-52; Catlgr Seattle Pub Lib 52-53; Catlgr UWash 54; Asst libn & med libn VA Hosp Lib, Walla Walla Wash 55-56; Ref libn Westchester Br Los Angeles Pub Lib 57-58; Libn Shannon & Wilson Inc, Seattle 65-. 9: SLA. 14: Spec libs, spec collections. 15: 2203 N 143rd , Seattle 98133.

BOUCHER, LORNA MARJORIE (MARVIN). b Bear River NS Can 6 Ja 25. 4: Richard Ronald Boucher. 5: St Francis XavierU 42-45; Sir George Williams 60-61 BA; McGill 61-62 BLS. 7: Asst libn Montreal Child Lib 62-63; Order libn Georges P Vanier Lib Loyola Col Montreal 63-. 8: Lecturer (lib wk) Loyola Col summer 68 & 68-69. 15: Apt 231 7400 Sherbrooke st W, Montreal 262 Que Can.

BOUCHER, MARY (SCHINDLER). b San Francisco 19 Ag 13. 4: John T Boucher. 5: UCal 35 (Pol Sci) BA, 39 (LS) Certif. 7: Sch libn Burlingame Elem Sch Dist, Burlingame Cal 39-41; Ref libn San Carlos Br San Mateo Co Lib, San Carlos Cal 53-. 9: CalLA. 10: AAUW. 15: 51 Cambridge, San Carlos Ca 96346.

BOUCHER, REV RAYMOND. B St-Pascal Kamouraska 24 F 29. 5: College de Sainte-Anne-de-la -Pocatiere 42-50 BA; ULaval 50-54 (Theol) LTh; Cath U 60-61 MS in LS. 6: Fr, Eng. 7: Tchr College de Sainte- Anne-de-la-Pocatiere 54-58, Libn 56-. 8: Pres de la Commsn des Dir de Bibliotheque de la Fed des Col Classiques 63-68; Visiteur des Bibliotheques de Col Classiques Affilies al'ULaval 64-6:; Co-dir de la Centrale de Catalogage de la Fed des Col Classiques 64-66; Dir du Stage en Bibliotheconomie de la Bibliotheque duCol de Sainte-Anne 64-. 9: Assn Can des Bibliotheques de Langue Francaise; CanLA; CathLA; ALA. 10: La Societe Historique de la Cote-du-Sud (sec 63-67, treas 67-). 12: "Les Etapes de la redaction d'un travail de recherche en bibliotheque" (64); "Guide du personnel de la Bibliotheque du College de Sainte-Anne-de-la-Pocatiere" (65). 13: Yes. 14: Ref, admin, bldgs, lib educ. 15: College de Sainte-Anne-de-la-Pocatiere, La Pocatiere Que Can.

BOUCHER, ROMUALD. b Danville Prov Que 6 F 21. 5: UOrrawa 38-43 BA, 43-47 (Theol); Columbia 66-67 MSLS. 6: Fr. 7: Prof UOttawa (High Sch) 47-58; Asst libn UOttawa Central Lib 59-. 9: ALA; CanLA; Association canadienne des bibliothecaires de langue francaise; OttawaLA. 14: Admin. 15: 305 Nelson st, Ottawa 2 Can.

BOUCHER, MRS VIRGINIA (PARKER). b Bloomington Ill 26 My 29. 4: Stanley W Boucher. 5: Colo Col 47-51 (Eng Lit) BA; UMich 51-52 AMLS. 7: Libn I UColo Libs 53-55, 57-58; Libn I UCal Radiation Lab (Berkeley) 55-56; Libn Cutter Labs, Berkeley Cal 56-57; Libn Western Interstate Commsn for Higher Educ, Boulder Colo 60-63; Mun ref libn Mun Ref Lib, Boulder Pub Lib, Boulder Colo 65-67; Hd interlib loan serv,UColo Libs 67-. 9: ALA; MPLA; ColLA; SLA (sec Col chap 67-68, chm Planning, Bldg& Housing sect of Soc Sci Div 67-68). 10: LWV. 13: Yes. 14: Spec lib wk in human & soc sci. 15: 845 Lincoln pl, Boulder Co80302.

BOUCHER, VIVIAN E. b Lemberg Sask Can 17 Ag 15. 4: Leonard H Boucher. 5: Dakota Wesleyan U 33-37 (Eng) BA. 6: Ger. 7: Libn VA Hosp, Sheridan Wyo 62-65; Libn OAR, Holloman AFB NM 65-66; Ref libn USA, White Sands Missile Range 66-. 9: SLA; ASCAP; Border Reg LA. 10: Phi Kappa Phi. 14: Ref. 15: 2021 Lester, Las Cruces NM 88001.

BOUCHER, WILLIAM DENNIS. b Yorktown Heights NY 15 Mr 31. 4: Lorraine Caprara. 5: W Tex State Col 51-52 (Bus); Marist Col 59-60 (Bus) BBA. 7: USAF Spec Serv 50-54; Staff asst Engnr Lib IBM Corp, Poughkeepsie NY 55-62; Ref libn Avco Corp, Wilmington Mass 63-65, gp ldr data Support 66-. 9: SLA. 14: Ref, info retrieval, indexing. 15: 86 Haverhill st, N Reading Ma 01864.

BOUDREAU, ALLAN. b Albany NY 1 Ag 36. 4: Ingeborg Goetze. 5: Russell Sage Col 55-58 (Acctg) BS; NYU 62-64 (Pub Admin) MPA, 65- (Higher Educ). 6: Sp, Fr. 7: (Pvt to Sgt) US Army Info Spec 53-55; Jr admin asst NY State Lib 58-59, Admin asst 59-62; Asst dir NYU Libs 62- Pub accountant NY State 69-. 8: Consul, NY State Emancip Proclam Shrine Com,Albany NY 62; NYU Com on Current Tchg Loads, NYC 64-67; NYU Data Proc Com, NYC64-67; Consul various equipment mfrs & architects, NYC 62-; NY Metro Ref & Res LibAgency Spec Proj Com 66-. 9: ALA (life mem);-LAD;-ACRL; Nat Soc Pub Accts; Internatfed for Documentation; Lib Assn (Eng). 10: IRA Foundation (pres 68-); Phi Delta kappa. 12: "The Role of the Library in Scientific and Scholarly Research" (64). 13: Yes. 14: Admin, research. 15: One Washington Sq Vil, New York NY 10012.

BOUDREAU, INGEBORG. b Weehawken NJ 18 My 43. 4: Allan Boudreau. 5: SUNY (Albany) 59-63 (Eng) AB; NYU 63-64 (Comm Arts) MA; Columbia 65-66 (LS) MS; NYU 68 (Hiher Educ); Permanent certif NY State Secondary Sch Eng tchr. 6: Ger, Fr. 7: Period asst NY State Lib, Albany 61-63; Lib dir Child bk Coun, NYC 64-. 8: Lib/USA NY World's Fair 64-65; Publ consul Grosset & Dunlap St Martin's Press, NYC 65-; Consul; sch lib planning & bk selection, NY 66-, Ch & Synagogue Lib Assn 69-. 9: ALA-ACRL; -CSD; -AAStateL; NYLA. 12: "Aids to Choosing Books for Children" (67, 68, 69). 13: Yes. 14: Admin, bk selection, research. 15: One Washington Sq Village, New York NY 10012.

BOUDREAU, JAMES A. b Medford Mass 26 Ag 22. 4: Muriel Page Boudreau. 5: Boston Col 40-42, 46-48 (Hist) AM; Simmons 51-53 (LS) MS. 6: Fr. 7: US Army 42-46; Asst in hist Boston Col 48-49; Instr econ Newton col 49-50; Libn Stonehill Col 50-52; Asst dir of lib Simmons Col 52-59; Dir of Lib, Prof of hist Bentley col 59-69; Dir of libs Babson Col 69-. 8: Consul: Lybrand Ross Bros & Montgomery 58-; Baker Guidance Center for Child 59; Stenotype Inst of Boston 64-65; Camp Dresser & McKee, Engnrs, 62; Lecturer, Lib Sci, Simmons 53- Champlain Jr Col Vt 66-. 9: ALA-ACRL;NELA (chm Col sect 68); MassLA. 10: AAUP; Simmons Col Sch of Lib Sci Alum Assn(pres 68). 14: Lib admin. 15: Baker-Vanguard Lib Bentley Col, Beaver & Forest sts, Waltham Ma 02154.

BOUGAS, STANLEY J. b Norfolk Va 7 D 21. 4: Athena Douvarges. 5: Washington Sq Col NYU 46-50 (Hist) AB; Columbia 50-52 MSLS; Emory 55-62 LLB. 6: Sp, Fr, Gk. 7: USAF 42-45; Clerical NY Pub Lib 46; sst night libn & manager Assn of Bar of City of NY 46-53; Asst ref libn NYU Law Lib 53-54; Law Libn & admin asst, Dean, Emory U Sch of Law 54-62; Law Libn & Assoc Prof Law Catholic U of PR 62-65; Lecturer Inter Amer U Ponce Ext (PR) 64-65; Law Libn Dept of Health Educ & Welfare, Wash DC 65-66; Asst Prof of Law & Assoc Law Libn, Washington Col of Law, American U 66-67, Assoc Prof of Law & Law Libn 67-; Dir Alumni & Placement 69-. ; Dir Dept of Commerce Lib Wash DC 69-. 8: Visiting lecturer in legal lit, Sch of Lib & Info Serv UMd summer 66 Consullaw firm & Govt law lib 67-. 9: AALL (pres SE Chap 59-60); SLA (treas Ga Chap 59);PRLA; Law Libns Soc Wash DC (Bd mem 68-); AALL (Co-chm Com Statistics 68-); AALS. 10: Phi Alpha Delta. 12: "Outline of Federal Jurisdiction," mimeo (64). 13: Yes. 14: Admin, tchg. 15. Dept of Commerce Lib, Wash DC 20235.

BOULA, JAMES A. b Chicago Il 11 S 13. 4: Lillian Younger. 5: Crane Junior College Diploma 1933 Architecture; University of Illinois BS 1937 Education; Graduate: University of Chicago MA 1949 Library Science; University of Chicago PhD Candidate Curriculum. 7: Math tchr Kan, USA 5th Div Inf Aviation Engrs, Iceland & S Pacific World War II; Dir instr materials Joliet Township, High Sch & Jr Col 49-59; Dir of Instr materials & Title II Ill State Dept of Educ 59-. 8: Consul N Central Evaluator. 9: NEA-DAVI; ALA (life mem); IllEA; IllASchL; IllA-VA; ACSSAVO; AASA; IllASA (Bd com mem in several). 12: "Instructional Materials Bulletin," A-3, Off Supt of Pub Instr; "Standards for School Library Programs in Illinois"; "Illinois State Plan for Title II"; "Guidelines for Title II". 15: 711 S Second ave, Maywood Il.

BOULA, MRS LILLIAN Y(UNGER). b Chicago 30 Ag 15. 4: James Albert Boula. 5: UIll 36 BA, UIll 37 BS in LS; Chicago State 68 MS in Ed. 7: Asst libn River Forest Pub Lib, River Forest Ill 37-39; Libn Proviso Twp High Sch, Maywood Ill 39-43; Hdqrs libn 6th Serv Command & 5th Army, Chicago 43, 44-46; Libn Northwestern CATS, Chicago 43-44; Libn Proviso Twp High Sch, Maywood Ill 50-63; Instrl materials spec in Soc Studies 65-. 8: AASchL Nat Lib Week Com (chm). 9: ALA-AASchL; NEA-DAVI; AFT; AASA. 10: AAUW. 12: Ed Bd "School Librarian"; Ed Bd "Illinois Education." 14: Instr materials. 15: 711 So Second, Maywood Il 60153.

BOULDIN, MRS MABEL (STOKES). b Altheimer Ark 9 Je 09. 5: Loyal U 35-40 (Educ) BSED; UIll 50 MS LS. 6: Fr. 7: Tchr Ross Elem Sch, Chicago 36-43, Libn 43-46; Libn Gillespie Elem Sch, Chicago 46-51; Libn Phillips High Sch, Chicago 51-. 9: ALA; Internat Reading Assn; Ill Assn of SchL; High Sch Libns Chicagoland (treas). 10: Mildred B Haessler Ballet Group; Nat Coun of Negro Women; Chicago UrbanLeague; Phi Delta Kappa; Bd dirs Chicago Area Reading Assn 64. 12: Ed "Krinon," OffJl of Phi Delta Kappa; Ed staff, Chicago Area Reading Assn "Newsletter";

"PromotingMaximal Reading Growth Among Able Readers" (54). 13: Yes. 14: Reading guidance. 15: 8333 S Langley ave, Chicago Il 60619.

BOULDIN, MYRTLE M(AE). b McKenzie Tenn 12 S 01. 5: Bethel Col (McKenzie Tenn) 22-26 (Eng) AB; Peabody Col summers 27-29, 48-49 (LS) MA; Columbia summer 32. 7: High sch tchr & libn, Fla: Moore Haven 26-32, 44-48, 49-50 (asst prin 28-29), Auburndale 32-33, St Cloud 34-36, Pinetta 36-37, Jay 37-38, Niceville 38-39, Everglades 42-44; Tchr Trezevant Grade Sch, Trezevant Tenn 39-40; Tchr & libn Huntingdon High Sch, Huntingdon tenn 40-41; Libn Bethel Col (McKenzie Tenn) 50-. 9: NEA; TennLA; SEL. 10: Bethel Col alumni Assn; PTA. 14: Admin, ref. 15: 210 W Cherry ave, McKenzie Tn 38201.

BOURKE, MARY ANN. b NYC 2 My 47. 5: Col of Mt St Vincent 64-68 (Eng) BA; Columbia 68-69 (LS) MS. 6: Fr, Lat. 9: ALA. 14: Ref. 15: 34-35 - 82 st, Jackson Heights NY 11372.

BOURNE, CHARLES P. b San Francisco Cal 2 S 31. 4: Elizabeth Scheidtmann. 5: UCal 9berkeley) 53-57 (Electrical Engring) BSEE; Stanford 62 (Ind Engring) MSIE. 7: USMC Res active duty 50-51; Sr research engr Stanford Research Inst, Menlo Park Cal 57-66; V-pres Info Gen Corp, Palo Alto Cal 66-. 8: Lecturer UCal Sch of Libnship; Exec dir Nat Acad Sci SATCOM & COSUP panel on copyright; Mem adv bds: Chem Abstracts Serv, Annual Review of Info Sci, Documentation Abstracts, Encyclopedia of Lib & Info Sci, Wiley Bk Serv on Info Sci. 9: ASIS (pres-elect); ALA-ISAD (dir); US Rep FID Study Com on Theory of Machine Techniques & Syst. 10: IEE; ACM; NMA. 11: ADI annual award of merit 65. 12: "Methods of Information Handling" (63). 13: Yes. 14: Lib analysis, automation & evaluation, study nat syst & issues. 15: 1619 Santa Cruz ave, Menlo Park Ca 94025.

BOUSFIELD, HUMPHREY G. b Newark NJ 29 D 03. 4: Mary G Bousfield. 5: NYU 27 (Eng Lit) AB, 31 (Educ) MA; Columbia 35 BS in LS. 7: Supv even serv NYU 27-29; Instr high sch div Columbia Grammar Sch, NYC 28-29; Chief of readers dept Wash Sq Lib NYU 29-39, Asst libn 39-43; Assoc Dir UIll (Urbana) 43-44; Chief Libn & Chm of Lib Dept Brooklyn Col 44-. 8: Surveys & evaluations, Middle States Assn; Several private surveys & consultantships; Past chm Jt Com ala & LBI; Spec Adv Com, Higher Educ Facilities Act, NY State Educ Dept 64-. 9: ALA-ACRL (Grants Com); NY Lib Club. 10: Coun of Higher Educ Inst; Kingsbridge Hist Soc; Del Co Hist Soc; Inst for Early NYC Hist. 12: "Circulation Work in College & University Libraries," with C H Brown (33). 13: Yes. 14: Admin. 15: Brooklyn Col Lib, Brooklyn NY 11210.

BOUTINON, MRS ELIZABETH RUTH (ASSET). b Yonkers NY 22 Ja 07. 4: Jacques Charles Boutinon. 5: UMich 30 (Journalism) AB; Columbia 34 (Bus Libnship). 6: Fr. 7: Asst libn McCann-Erickson Inc, NY 30-35; Libn Campbell-Ewald Inc, NY 35-37; Libn Warwick & Legler Inc, NY 37-39; Asst libn Nat Ind Conference Bd Inc, ny 39-43; Libn McKinsey & Co Inc, NY 43-61; Libn Lee Higginson Corp, NY 61-65; Libn Faulkner Dawkins & Sullivan, NY 65-. 9: SLA (many com assignments; Adv Div; sec-treas 52-53, chm 54-55; sec NY Chap41-42). 10: Adirondack Mountain Club; Appalachian Mountain Club; Volunteers of the Shelters. 13: Yes. 14: Ref (finan). 15: Faulkner Dawkins & Sullivan, One New York Plaza, New York NY 10004.

BOVA, PATRICK. b Erie Penn 1 Je 38. 5: Georgetown U 56-60 (Eng lit) AB; UChicago 62-65 (LS). 7: Libn Nat Opinion Research Ctr Chicago 61-. 8: Coun of Soc Sci Data Archives Standards Com. 9: SLA; ASIS. 14: Data Archives in the Soc Sci. 15: National Opinion Research Center, 6030 S Ellis, Chicago Il 60637.

BOVEE, MARTHA (LOIS). b Butte Mont 29 S 34. 5: UDenver 52-55 (Chem) BS; UHawaii 59-60 (Chem); UDenver 60-61 (LS) MA; UCLA 61-62 (Internship Med Lib). 6: Fr. 7: Chem Colo Sch of Mines Research Found, Golden Colo 56; Chem US Naval OrdnanceTest Station, China Lake Cal 56-59; Tchg asst Dept of Chem UHawaii 59-60; Stud asstUDenver Lib 60-61, Research asst 61; Research libn Dept Microbiology UColo MedCenter 61; Med lib intern Biomedical Lib UCLA 61-62; Asst libn US Naval Ordnance Lab,Corona Cal 62-63; Head Catlg Biomed Lib UCal (San Diego) 63-65, Hd Tech Processing65-68; Hd Ser Dept UCal (San Diego) 68-. 14: Tech proc. 15: Serials Dept Lib Univ of Cal (San Diego),La Jolla Ca 92037.

BOWDEN, ANN (HADDON). b E Orange NJ 7 F 24. 4: . 5: Radcliffe 42-44, 46-48 (Scandinavian langs & lits) AB; Columbia 50-51 (LS) MS. 6: Ger, Lat, Swedish. 7: (Cpl) USMC Womens Reserve 44-46; Descr catlgr Yale U 48-49; Ref asst in chg Henry L Stimson Collection, Yale U 51-53; Mss catlgr Humanities Research Center, UTex 58-60; Humanities Research Center libn, UTex 60-63; Academic Center Libn UTex 63; Dir of films & recordings Austin Pub Lib, Austin Tex 63-65; Lecturer Grad Sch of Lib Sci UTex 64-65, Asst Prof 65-; Coordinator of adult serv Austin Pub Lib, Austin Tex 65-67, Asst Dir of Lib 67-. 9: ALA (Memb Com for Texas 65-, chm 68-); BSA; SWLA(Audit Com 68); TexLA (chm Publ Com 65-69, sec-treas Pub Lib Div 65-66, chm DistVIII Nat Lib Week in Texas State Com 66-67). 10: AAUW. 12: "An Exhibition of Manuscripts andfirst Editions of T S Eliot" (61); "T E Lawrence/Fifty Letters; 1920-35" (62); "TheFirst Editions of T S Eliot" (61); "T E Lawrence/Fifty Letters; 1920-35" (62); Assted & assoc ed "The Papers of the Bibliographical Society of America" (67-). 13: Yes. 14: Rarebks, admin. 15: PO Box 2287, Austin Tx 78767.

BOWDEN, DOROTHY (PRESTWOOD). b Coffee Co Ala 2 Mr 25. 4: Earl Max Bowden. 5: UAla 42-45 (Eng, LS) BS, 47-48 (Secondary Educ) MA. 7: Libn UAla 46, & summers; Libn Tuscaloosa High Sch, Tuscaloosa Ala 46-47; LibnBrookwood High Sch, Brookwood Ala 48-53; Tchr High Sch, Seale Ala 53-56; Elem tchr,56-58; Eng tchr Ft Payne High Sch, Ft Payne Ala 58-59; Elem tchr Vidalia Elem Sch,Vidalia Ga 59-60; Eng tchr Treutlen Co High Sch, Soperton Ga 60-61; Tchr Elba ElemSch 61-63; Libn Northport (Ala) Jr High 63-. 9: NEA; AlaEA. 10: PTA; Community Improvement Club;Delta Kappa Gamma; Kappa Delta Pi; Alpha Lamda Delta; Triangle. 14: Supv reading program of individual pupils, ref. 15: 74 Vestavia Hills,Northport Al 35476.

BOWDEN, ELEANOR M. b Sextonville Wis 13 N 14. 5: MacMurray Col 32-34; UWis 34-35; No Ill U 36-38 (Eng) BS; UWis 56-57 (LS) MS. 7: Eng tchr Bd of Educ, Crandon Wis 40-43; Lib asst Bd of Educ, Park Ridge Ill 43-44; Eng tchr Bd of Educ, Blue Island Ill 44-45; Eng tchr Bd of Educ, Reedsburg Wis 45-52; Eng tchr Bd of Educ, Crandon Wis 52-56; Sr high libn Bd of Educ, Janesville Wis 57-59; Libn Bd of Educ Central U High Sch, Madison Wis 59-69; E Sr High Sch, Madison Wis 69-. 9: ALA; WisLA (treas Sch Lib Div 64); WisEA;NEA. 10: Beta Phi Mu. 14: Secon sch instr materials. 15: 921 High st, Madison Wi 53715.

BOWDEN, EVA. b Timberland NC 9 Ag 06. 5: UNC (Greensboro) 24-28 (Eng) AB; UNC (Chapel Hill) summers 46-48; Emory summers 43-45 AB in LS, 57 (Med Libnship). 6: Fr, Sp. 7: Tchr of Eng & Fr &/or Hist & Sci NC State High Sch System 27-43; Asst libn Greensboro Col 43-45; Libn Lander Col 45-47; Asst libn Flora McDonald Col 47-49; Asst supv of the indexing & card distrib sect Atomic Energy Lib, Oak Ridge Tenn (summer 49); Libn UTex Dental Br (Houston) 49-. 9: ALA; MedLA; TexLA; SWLA. 10: AAUW; AAUP; Amer Bus Women's Assn; United Church Women of Houston. 11: MedLA scholarship 57; GSA certificate 59. 12: "Library Handbook for Dental Students" (50); "Library Handbook for Dental Hygiene Students (67 & 68). 13: Yes. 14: Admin, ref, catlg, biblio, spec coll. 15: 4707 Fannin ct, Apt 6, Houston Tx 77004.

BOWEN, ADA M (SELTZER). b Kempton Penn 7 Je 42. 4: John W Bowen. 5: Kutztown State Col 60-64 (Lib Educ) BS; Fla State U 64-65 (LS) MS. 7: Asst ref libn USoFla 65-68, Assoc ref libn 69-. 9: ALA; FlaLA (Ref RT; sec 67-68, chm 69-70). 10: Beta Phi Mu; Kappa Delta Pi. 14: Ref. 15: 8014 Hiawatha st, Tampa Fl 33615.

BOWEN, HELEN (JOHNSON LEGETTE). b Statesboro Ga 3 N 28. 5: Ga So Col 45-47; Woman's Col of Ga 47-49 (Eng) BS; Emory 56-58 (LS) MLn, 65-67 Diploma for advanced study of libnship. 7: Asst libn Statesboro Reg Lib, Statesboro Ga 49-50; Tchr-libn McEachern High Sch, Powder Springs Ga 50-54; Tchr-libn Hahira High Sch, Hahira Ga 54-55; Ser libn Ga So Col 56-58; Head Libn No Fla Jr Col 58-60; Libn Moultrie Jr High Sch, Moultrie Ga 61-64; Libn Statesboro Jr High Sch, Statesboro Ga 64-. 9: NEA; GaEA; SELA; GaLA. 15: 14 E Parrish st, Statesboro Ga 30458.

BOWEN, MRS EVELYN (TABAKA). b Lakeville Minn 19 Ag 06. 5: UMinn BSLS. 7: Hackley Pub Lib Muskegon Mich 29-39; Wayne Co Lib Detroit 39-41; Detroit Pub Lib Detroit 41-43; Waseca Co Lib Waseca Minn 43-46; Chisholm Pub Lib Chisholm Minn 46-48; Clallam Co Lib Port Angeles Wash 48-49; Bremerton Pub Lib Bremerton Wash 49-55; Kitsap Reg Lib Bremerton Wash 55-. 9: ALA; Wash State LA (treas 63-64); PNLA. 10: Delta Kappa Gamma (pres local chap); AAUW. 14: Admin. 15: 2456 Marine dr, Bremerton Wa 98313.

BOWER, CORA LOUISE. b Galesburg Ill 13 Ag 13. 5: Knox Col 30-34 (Fr) AB; UMich 36-37 ABLS; Chicago summer 64 (LS). 6: Fr. 7: Circ asst DePauw U Lib 37-40; Head of circ Pub Lib, Galesburg Ill 40-43; Br libn Pub Lib, Flint Mich 43-44; Head of circ Joseph Schaffner Lib, Northwestern U 64-. 9: ALA; SLA. 10: Phi Beta Kappa; Art Inst of Chicago; Delta Delta Delta;Friends of Lit. 14: Ref. 15: 415 Fullerton pkwy, Chicago Il 60614.

BOWER, DAVID ALLAN. b Weymouth Mass 21 D 45. 5: East Nazarene Col 63-67 (Hist) AB (cum laude); Rutgers 67-68 MLS. 6: Fr. 7: Asst libn Curry Col 68-. 10: Mus of Fine Arts (Boston); Alumni Assn Rutgers Grad Sch of Lib Serv; The Trustees of Reservations; SAR Mass Soc. 13: Yes. 14: Period, acquis. 15: 1627 Main st, Marshfield Hills Ma 02051.

BOWER, MRS TRUE V (GEHMAN). b Canton Ohio 17 O 16. 4: Aaron R Bower. 5: Otterbein Col 35, 36, 38 9sociol, Hist, Pol Sci) AB; Kent State 37; West Res summers 50-53 MSLS. 7: Tchr-libn Green Twp Bd of Educ, Greensburg Ohio 47-53; Catlgr Canal Fulton Pub Lib, Canal Fulton Ohio 57-58; Sch libn Akron Bd of Educ, Akron Ohio 58-. 8: Consul to Monitor Craft Inc, subsidiary of Crawford Lib Bindery, Akron Ohio. 9: OhioEA (life mem); AkronEA; ALA; NEA; OhioASchL (memb &/or chm Legis Com 58-62); AASchL (State Assembly Planning Com 68-). 10: Col Club; Marquis Biog Lib Soc (adv mem). 12: "Career Novel and Biography as a Source of Occupational Information in Junior High Schools" (with Frank L O'Dell) (68). 14: Sch libnship, legis. 15: 8205 Wales Ave NW, North Canton Oh 44720.

BOWER, VERNA CLAIRE HARRIET. b St Louis 23 Je 37. 4: Leland Miller Bower. 5: SE Mo State Col 54-58 (Eng) BS; Peabody 59-62 (LS) MA. 7: Libn & Eng tchr N Kirkwood Jr High Sch, Kirkwood Mo 58-59; Libn Lindbergh N Jr High Sch, St Louis 59-. 9: Md State Tchrs Assn; MoLA; MoASchL; SuburbLA St Louis (pres 69-71); LindberghTA (sec 69-70). 10: Jr C of C Wives. 14: Sch libs. 15: 13512 Clayton rd, Creve Coeur Mo 63141.

BOWERMASTER, MRS IZORA W. b Phillipsburg NJ 10 S 17. 4: Paul M Bowermaster. 5: Millersville State Col 38 (Eng, LS) BS in Ed; Drexel 46 BS in LS. 7: Elem tchr Lancaster Co Penn 39-40; Elem tchr, Delaware Co Penn 40-43; Libn High Sch, Audubon NJ 43; Libn High Sch, Media-Del Co Penn 43-47; Child libn Lancaster (Penn) Free Pub Lib 47-52; Libn McCaskey High Sch, Lancaster Penn 61-. 9: NEA; Penn State EA; Lancaster Co; PennLA. 14: Clsf, catlg, child lit. 15: 1720 Windy Hill rd, Lancaster Penn 17602.

BOWERS, CHARLOTTE S(HELNUTT). b Walnutgrove Ga 31 O 09. 4: James Edwin Bowers. 5: Ga Col at Milledgeville 25-29 (Eng) AB; Appalachian State U summers 57-60 (LS) M Ed; George Peabody Col for Tchrs summers 61-64 MALS. 7: Tchr Danburg High Sch, Danburg Ga 30-31; Tchr Canon High Sch, Canon Ga 34-36; Tchr Danville High Sch, Danville Ga 36-41, 43-; Prin-tchr Montrose Elem Sch, Montrose Ga 47-49, 47; Tchr-libn Chester High Sch, Chester Ga 51-53; Tchr-libn Dexter High Sch, Dexter Ga 53-55; Libn Wilkinson Co High Sch, Irwinton Ga 55-58; Assoc dir-catlgr Oconee Reg Lib Ref libn Middle Ga Reg Lib Macon Ga 66-. 14: Ref, catlg, acquis. 15: Allentown Ga 31003.

BOWERS, DOROTHY W. b Chambersburg Penn 17 O 16. 4: William S Bowers. 5: Wilson 33-63 (Hist) BA; Drexel 66 MSLS. 6: Fr. 7: Asst libn Franklin Co Lib, Chambersburg Penn 57-60; Asst libn Coyle Lib, Chambersburg Penn 60-63, 65; Asst libn UPenn Lib Phila 66; Ref libn Free Lib of Springfield Township Phila 66-67; Hd ref dept Dickinson Col Lib Carlisle Penn 67-. 9: ALA; PennLA. 14: Ref. 15: Irwinton RD 2, Mercersburg Pa 17236.

BOWERS, HERBERT EDWIN. b Washington NJ 29 Mr 17. 4: Patricia Clark. 5: Columbia Col 35-39 (Math, Music) AB; Columbia 46-48 BS in LS, 50-55 (A-v Educ)MA; UPenn NDEA Inst for Adv Study in Educ Media featuring programmed instr summer66. 6: Fr, Ger. 7: Aviation Cadet USAAF AAFSETC 56th aafftd 41-42; Civilian Flight Instr USAAF, Americus Ga 42-44; Pilot F/O US Air Transport Command, CBI Theater 44-46; Asst libn The Hill Sch, Pottstown Penn 48-58; Ref libn Lafayette Col 58-59; A-v libn & Instr, lib sch libn, exhibits chm Drexel Inst 59-62; Libn & a-v dir Neshaminy Sch Dist, Langhorne Penn 62-66; Libn Sr High Sch Dist of Bensalem twsp, Cornwells Hts Penn 66; Visitingdir lib-learning ctr, Iolani Sch, Honolulu 66-67; Libn readers serv period doc deptMiami-Dade Jr Col, Miami 67-. 9: ALA (life mem); NEA; Penn Learning ResourcesAssn; Penn State Educ Assn; Nat Soc for Progr Instr 68; FlaLA; Dade Co LA; Fla Assnof Pub Jr Cols. 10: Faculty mem Cum Laude Soc. 13: Yes. 14: Ref, govt docs, programmedinstr. 15: PO Box 1542, Hollywood Fl 33022.

BOWERS, MIRIAM A(LMA). b Hope Kan 18 Je 12. 5: Southwestern State Col 30-34 (Eng, Math); LaVerne Col 37-38 (Eng, Math) AB; Claremont Grad Sch 38-39 (Eng); Immaculate Heart Col (LS) MA. 6: Ger, Fr. 7: Elem tchr Union Ridge Rural Sch, Thomas Okla 33-35; Prof of Eng Upland Col 39-47; Relief work Mennonite Central Com, Germany 47-51; Lib asst Chaffey High Sch & Col, Ontario Cal 53-54; Prof of Eng, Upland Col 54-56, libn 56-65; Asst libn LaVerne Col 65-. 9: ALA; CalLA. 10: Zonta Internat. 14: Ref, catlg. 15: 565 N Laurel ave, Upland Ca 91786.

BOWERS, MIRIAM (HARDER). b Versailles Mo. 4: Melvin Bowers. 5: Upland Col 36-40 (Eng) BA; Claremont Grad Sch 40-46 (Educ) Secondary Credential; Immaculate Heart Col 54-56 Libnship Credential. 7: Lib clerk Chaffey High Sch & Jr Col, Ontario Cal 46-48, 52-56; Asst libn Chaffey Jr Col 56-. 9: ALA; CalLA; Cal Tchrs Assn. 10: Altrusa Intl. 14: Catlg. 15: 636 E 7th st, Upland Ca 91786.

BOWERS, RHODA E. b Hagerstown Md 19 N 06. 5: Hood Col 24-28 (Lat) AB; Drexel Inst summer 29-30; Muhlenberg Col 30-31, 31-32;Columbia summers 36-40 BS in LS. 7: Libn Quakertown Jr-Sr High Sch, Quakertown Penn 30-38; Libn A D Eisenhower High Sch, Norristown Penn 38-. 9: ALA-AASchL; NEA; PennLA; PennStateEA; PennSchLA. 10: Soroptimist Club; AAUW; Hist Soc of Montgomery Co; Beta Phi Mu. 13: Yes. 14: Sch libs, ref. 15: 1806 Chain st, Norristown Pa 19401.

BOWLER, VIRGINIA. b Salt Lake City Utah 9 Jl 15. 5: UCLA 40 (Educ) EdB; UOre 65-68 MLS. 6: Sp, Ital. 7: Elem sch tchr Los Angeles City & Co 40-46; Asst libn Tongue Point job Corps Ctr, Astoria Ore 65-68; Catlg libn UCal (Irvine) 69-. 9: ALA; -AASchL; -ACRL; OreLA; OreSchLA. 14: Catlg, acquis. 15: 524 N 10th st, Corvallis Or 97330.

BOWLES, GARRETT HENRY. b San Francisco 3 F 38. 4: Margaret Jepsen. 5: UCal(Davis) 55-60 (Music) AB; San Jose State Col 61-62 (Music) MA; UCal (Berkeley) 63-65 MLS. 6: Ger. 7: Lib asst Gen Lib UCal (Berkeley) 63-65; Libn III Stanford U Libs 65-. 9: ALA; MusLA; chm, No Cal Chap (68-69); Amer Musicol Soc, CalLA. 11: Beta Phi Mu. 14: Music catlg, acquis. 15: 54 Roosevelt cir, Palo Alto Ca 94603.

BOWLEY, DOROTHY E. b Jefferson Iow 23 My 09. 4: B A Bowley. 5: State U Iowa 28-31 (Biol) BA, 57-58 9educ); UIowa summers 62-65 (Lib Educ) MA. 7: Soc studies, Eng tchr Madrid Pub Sch, Madrid Iowa 58-60; Lit tchr Jefferson Commun Schs, Jefferson Iowa 60-63, High sch libn 63-. 9: ALA; NEA; IowaLA; Iowa State EA; IowaASchL (treas 67-69). 10: PEO (pres 50-53); OES. 14: Ref, ya. 15: 617 S Wilson, Jefferson Ia 50129.

BOWMAN, MRS A(NNIE) LOUISE. b Troutville Va 4 O 06. 4: Raymond P G Bowman. 5: UVa 37 BS; UNC 52 BS in LS. 6: Fr, Ger. 7: Lib asst Dickinson Col 44-52; Ref libn Va Polytech Inst 53, Catlgr 53-. 9: ALA; VaLA; SELA; Potomac Tech Proc Libns. 10: AAUW. 14: Catlg. 15: 103 Dunton dr, Blacksburg Va 24060.

BOWMAN, BEN COOK. b Los Angeles Cal 22 D 12. 4: Marion Hatch. 5: UOregon 32-34, 36-38 (Eng) BA, 38-40 (Eng) MA; UChicago 40-41, 46-48 BLS. 6: Sp. 7: Grad asst in Eng UOregon 38-40; Sgt USA Sig Corps, Asiatic-Pac Th 41-45; Grad asst in Eng UIll at Urbana 46; Trainee hd pub serv asst libn Newberry Lib, Chicago 46-61; Dir of libs UVermont 61-65; Chief libn Hinter Col 66-69; Dir libs & prof Bibliog URochester 69-. 8: Materials Consultant Specialist Japan Lib School Proj 51-52, Ankara Lib School Project 55; Library Consultant National Endowment for the Humanities 69. 9: ALA (Nat Lib Week Com 65-66); -ACRL (Pub Com 64-68; chm Com Appts & Noms 67-68; H W Wilson Indexes Com 66-); VLA (pres 65); NYLA. 10: Caxton Club, Chicago; Grolier Club, New York. 14: Admin, col devel, interlib coop systems. 15: Rush Rhees Lib, University of Rochester, Rochester NY 14627.

BOWMAN, JAMES R. b Ill 4 N 24. 5: Knox Col 42-43, 45-48 (Hist) AB; UMinn 48-49 (Amer Studies) MA, 49-50 BS in LS. 7: LC; Spec Recr 50-51, Catlgr Copyright Off 51-52, Sr catlgr Descr Catlg Div 52-60, Head Monthly Checklist Sect & Ed "Monthly Checklist of State Publications" 60-62, Head Pre-1953 Imprints Sect & Ed "National Union Catalog" 62-63; Dir LC Public Law 480 Project, Djakarta Indonesia 63-66, Dir LC Public Law 480 Project of Shared Catlg Off, Belgrade Yugoslavia 67-. 9: ALA-ACRL; -RTSD; DCLA. 10: Phi Beta

Kappa. 12: Ed "Monthly Checklist of State Publications"; Ed "Weekly List of Unlocated Research Books"; Ed "Accessions List: Indonesia." 14: Catlg, acquis, bibliog. 14: Catlg, acquis, bibliog. 15: Belgrade Dept of State, Washington DC 20521.

BOWMAN, JANE (BELKNAP). b Atlanta Ind 14 Jl 23. 4: Ezra A Bowman. 5: State Tchrs Col (Lock Haven Penn) 40-42 (Soc Studies); State Tchrs Col (Millersville Penn) 42-43, 46-47 (LS) BS n Ed; Syracuse summers 55-57 MS(LS); UCal (Santa Barbara) summer 58; UPacific summer 60; Pacific Oaks Col summer 63; UCal (Berkeley) summer 65, 66, 67. 7: MaM 2/c US Navy (WR) 43-45; Libn Captain Jack Jr High Sch, Mt Union Penn 54-57; Libn Avalon Schs Long Beach Unified Sch Dist, Santa Catalina Island Cal 57-. 9: ALA (Life mem); NEA (Life mem); Cal Tchrs Assn; CalLA; TALB. 10: Beta Phi Mu; Alpha Beta Alpha. 13: Yes. 14: Child, yp. 15: Box 1335, Avalon Ca 90704.

BOWMAN, MARY ANN (WELLS). b Crawfordsville Ind 15 Ag 40. 4: Joel Pitkin Bowman. 5: Col of Wooster 57-61 (Ger) AB; UCLA 62-63 MLS. 6: Ger, Fr. 7: Sr lib asst UCal Lib (Berkeley) 61-62; Engnr lib asst UIll(Urbana) 63-66; Asst catlgr, Austin Peay State U, Clarksville, Tenn, 67-68; Asst acquis libn TrinityU, San Antonio, 68; Bibliogr, Acquis dept, UIll Urbana 68-. 10: ACLU. 14: Ref. 15: 2210 Perkins Rd RR4, Urbana Il 61801.

BOWMAN, MIRIAM ALLEN. b Mt Jackson Va 19 Ja 33. 5: Madison Col 51-55 (LS) BS; UNC 57-58 (LS) MS. 6: Fr. 7: Libn Williamsburg Jr High Sch, Arlington Va 55-56; Tchr New Market High Sch, New Market Va 56-57; Libn Wakefield Sr High Sch, ArlingtonVa 58-61; Libn Chateauroux Air Force Base Sch, Chateaurdux France 61-62; Supv libn ref Naval Research Lab, Wash DC 62-63; Libn Off of NavalResearch, Wash DC 63-. 9: ALA; SLA. 14: Ref. 15: Off of Naval Res Lib, 4215 Main Navy Bldg, Wash DC 20360.

BOWMAN, OLMA (BIRD) "JUNE". b Chicago 9 N 06. 4: Selwyn Taylor. 5: UIll 24-26, 26-28 (Eng) BA; Ohio Wesleyan U 26; UWis 29-30 Diploma in Lib Sci; USoCal summers 55-57 (LS) MS. 7: 1st asst loan desk Oak Park Pub Lib, Oak Park Ill 28-29; Asst libn VA Hosp,Hines Ill 31-32; Libn Stevens Hotel, Chicago 35-36; Act libn Sr High Sch, Royal OakMich 36-37; Libn St Charles Pub Lib, St Charles Ill 37-44; Army Libn, Oahu, Guam,Philippines, Japan 44-49; Asst libn Evanston Twsp High Sch, Evanston Ill 50-53; LibnSanta Barbara High Sch, Santa Barbara Cal 53-. 8: Consul for "Standard Catalog forhigh School Libraries," 65-68. 9: ALA;-YAS (Com Richer by Asia proj 59-66); NEA;AASchL; CalLA; Cal Tchrs Assn; CalASchL (Soc Chm So Sect 61-62). 10: Altrusa Club; AAUW; UN Assn of USA. 14: Sr high sch wk. 15: 618B WPedregosa st, Santa Barbara Ca 93101.

BOWMAN, ROBERT JAMES. b Teulon Man Can 29 Mr 35. 5: UMan 56-61 (Hist, Pol Sci) BA; McGill 63-64 BLS. , 67-69 MLS. 6: Fr. 7: Lab asst Civil Serv of Can, Winnipeg Man, Ft William Ont 53-56; Tchr Fort Qu'Appelle High Sch, Sask 61-62; Libn subprof Regina Pub Lib, Regina Sask 62-63; Libn catlgr Fraser-Hickson Inst, Montreal 64-65; Libn ref Loyola Col (Montreal) 65-. 9: CanLA; QueLA. 14: Ref. 15: 76 Fourth blvd, Terrace Vaudrauil Quebec Can.

BOWRON, ALBERT (WILSON). b Hamilton Ont Can 13 O 19. 5: ; summ66. 0 6: Ger. 7: Lib asst fine arts Vancouver Pub Lib, Vancouver BC 49-50; Lib asst gen Hertfordshire Co Lib, Hertfordshire Eng 50-51; Co Libn Lambton Co Lib, Wyoming Ont 51-54; Chief Libn Galt Pub Lib, Galt Ont 54-59; Head tech serv div Toronto Pub Lib, Galt Ont 54-59; Head tech serv div Toronto Pub Lib 59-64; Dir Scarborough Pub Lib, Scarborough Ont 64-. 8: Consul "Library Journal," 62-63; Lib Consul, West Berlin Germany, 64; Study tour of Swedish pub lib 68-. 9: CanLA (Coun adv group); OntLA (past pres); META, Toronto (dir); Inst Prof Libns Ont; Ont, Prov Lib Coun. 11: Study tour Fellowship Awarded by Can Coun, 61. 12: "Librarian's Guide to Metropolitan Toronto" (65); "Librarian's Directory to Metro Toronto" (67). 13: Yes. 14: Admin, tech serv, arch, info systems, surveys. 15: 164 MacPherson ave, Toronto 5 Ont Can.

BOYCE, EMILY STEWART. b Raleigh NC 18 Ag 33. 5: East Carolina U 51-55 (LS & Hist) BS, 59-60 (Psych) MA; UNC (Chapel Hill) 63-64 (LS). 7: Libn Tileston Jr High Sch, Wilmington NC 55-57; Child libn Wilmington Pub Lib, Wilmington NC 57-58; Asst catlgr & Instr in Lib Sci E Carolina Col 59-61; Assoc supv lib & instrl materials serv State Dept of Pub Instr, Raleigh NC 61-62; Head, Dept Spec Collections E Carolina Col 62, Assoc Prof Dept of Lib Sci 64-. 9: ALA1AASchL (chm Stud Assts Com 62-65); NEA; SELA (chm Sch & child sect 66-68); NCLA; NCEA; (chm Pub Com 66-69). 10: AAUP; NCASchL; Beta Phi Mu; Alpha Beta Alpha. 14: Lib quarters & equipment, automation in libs, catlg, adminis. 15: 1005 E Third st, Greenville NC 27834.

BOYCE, GEORGE KENNETH. b Clifton NY 12 My 06. 4: Aline L Abaecherli. 5: Cornell 23-27 (Lat) AB, 27-28 (Ancient Hist) MA; Yale 29-33 (Ancient Hist) PhD; UMich 36-38 ABLS. 6: Ital, Fr, Ger, Lat. 7: Var positions, circ & order depts UMich Lib 36-39; LibnAmer Acad (Rome) 40; Intel Off (Maj) USAAF, NC & Rome 42-46; Curator of autograph mss& chief ref dept Pierpont Morgan Lib, NYC 46-54; Catlgr hist of med div NLM,Cleveland 55-56; Hd catlg dept Law Lib UMich 57-64, Hd rare bks sect catlg dept64-66, Hd catlg dept law lib 67-. 9: BSA; Renaissanc Soc of Amer. 11: Fellow Amer Acad in Rome (Italy) 33-35. 12: "Corpus of the Lararia of pompeii," Memoirs of Amer Acad in Rome, v 14 (37); "Italian Mss in the Pierpont Morgan Lib," with M P Harrsen (53); "Modern Literary Mss in the Morgan Library" (52). 13: Yes. 14: Rare bks & mss, catlg. 15: 841 Oakland ave, Ann Arbor Mi 48104.

BOYCE, HAROLD W(ALTER). b Mishawaka Ind 13 My 27. 4: Nedra Murdock Boyce. 5: 4102 S Washington, Marion In 46952. 7: Minister Wesleyan Churches, Ind 47-62; Tchr Clinton-Hanna Sch, Wanata Ind 57-61; Tchr Marion Commun Schs, Marion Ind 61-66; Marion Col, Libn 66-67, Dir of lib serv 67-. 9: ALA; Christian Libns Fellowship; IndLA. 14: Admin. 15: 4102 S Washington, Marion In 46952.

BOYCE, JOSEPH A. b Trinidad WI 12 Ap 38. 4: Katherine Bryant. 5: Shrter Jr Col 51-59 AA; Morris Brown Col 59-61 (Philos, Rel) BA; Atlanta 61-64 MSLS. 6: Fr, Sp. 7: Asst libn Interdenominational Theol center, Atlanta 64-65; Asst libn Md State Col 65-. 8: Assisted with planning of new lib bldg; Instr for lib orient; In charge ofdisplays. 10: Grove Park-Center Hill Civic Assn; Alpha Kappa Mu. 14: Catlg, ref, acquis. 15: Md State Col, Princess Anne Md 21853.

BOYCE, MRS MARIE SUMMERS. b Grove Springs Mo 4 Ag 03. 4: Edward G Boyce. 5: Drury Col 21-25 (Hist) BA; Peabody 50-63 MALS. 7: Tchr Marshfield High Sch, Marshfield Mo 25-26; Tchr Taylorsville High Sch, Taylorsville NC 26-28; Sec Bd of Christian Educ, Richmond Va33-37; Libn-tchr French Camp Acad, French Camp Miss 45-48; Libn-tchr Chamberlain-Hunt Acad, Port Gibson Miss 49-60; Hostess Erskine Col 60-61,Libn 61-. 9: ALA; SCLA; SELA. 10: AAUW; Due West Bk Club. 14: Ref, rare bks. 15: Box 204, Due West SC 29639.

BOYD, BARBARA GRAY. b Boston 17 Jl 17. 5: Fresno State Col 35-39 (Eng) AB; UCal 39-40 Certif; UCLA 59-60 (Pub Admin) MPA. 7: Various Orange Co Free Lib Santa Ana Cal 41-44; Various Kern Co Free Lib, Bakersfield Cal 41-48; Co Libn Modoc Co Free Lib, Alturas Cal 48-51; Co Libn Kitsap Co Lib, Bremerton Wash 51-55; Consul Cal State Lib 55-59; Lecturer UCLA Sch of Lib Serv 60-64; Libn, br libn Los Angeles Pub Lib 64-. 66; Asst Co Libn Alameda Coy Lib 67-. 8: Consul to Los Angeles Co Lib, Whittier Pub Lib & Santa Fe Springs City Lib in formation of Los Cerritos-Whittier Lib System; Consul to Orange Co Lib & Placentia & Yorba Linda Dist Libs in formation of a lib system; Part-time lecturer, UCLA 64-. 9: ALA; PNLA (chm Pub Lib Div 54); CalLA (pres So Dist 63, chm Prof Educ Com 64-65). 14: Pub lib admin. 15: 5800 Balboa dr, Oakland Ca 94611.

BOYD, DORIS (JARVIS). b Burlington Iowa 13 Ja 12. 4: Herbert Boyd. 5: Burlington Jr Col 29-30; UIowa 30-33; Drake U 50-51 (Phys Educ) BS in Educ; West Res 51-52 MS in LS. 7: Jr welfare wkr Co Bd Soc Welfare, Des Moines & Ottumwa Iowa 41-42; Outside rep Household Finance Co, Des Moines Iowa 42-43; Grain size tester Des Moines Ordnance Plant, Des Moines Iowa 43; Girls' wker Roadside Settlement, Des Moines Iowa 44; Clerical to prof asst Pub Lib (var depts), Des Moines Iowa 44-51; Circ asst & yp libn Pub Lib, Des Moines Iowa 52-55; Libn Bedford Co Lib (Cuyahoga Co), Bedford Ohio 55-56; Libn Meredith Publishing Co, Des Moines Iowa 56-. 9: SLA (chm Publ Div 63-64); ALA (Coun 56). 10: Zeta Tau Alpha. 13: Yes. 14: Ref. 15: Meredith Publishing Co 1716 Locust st, Des Moines Iowa 50303.

BOYD, ELSIE M. b Memphis Tenn 27 Ap 08. 4960 Ridge ave, Cincinnati Oa 45209. 5: Siena Col 28-31 (Eng) AB; Col of St Catherine 36-37 (Art) BS in Art; Catholic U 40-46 (Eng) MA, 55-56 MS in LS. 6: Fr, Ger, Lat. 7: Tchr Nazareth Col (Nazareth Ky) 37-43; Tchr OLN Acad, Roanoke Va 43-48; Tchr-libn Acad of O L Nazareth, Wakefield Mass 48-55; Prof Lib Sci Catherine Spalding Col 56-59; Libn Cincinnati Pub Lib 59-. 8: Act head Lib Sci Dept, Catherine Spalding Col, 57-59.

9: ALA; OhioLA. 13: Yes. 14: Ref. 15: 4960 Ridge ave, Cincinnati Oh 45209.

BOYD, GRACE E (MRS). b Bolton Mass 10 Je 23. 5: UMass 41-45 (Home Econ, Engnr) BS. 6: Ger. 7: Libn for Lit Ctr Lincoln Lab MIT 59-. 8: Instr, Boston Chap SLA, Spec course for Lib Assts, 67, 68; Chm, SLA-SFIPS SJCC Com (SJCC5Spring Jt Computer Conf 69). 9: SLA (Transl Activities Com 65-69, Govt Info Serv Com 69-71; Boston Chap; Chm Spec Prog's Com 66-69, Mailing for Bull 65-68; v-chm & chm Sci-Tech Gp 67-69); Soc Federal Linguists. 10: Nat Grange. 12: Ed "Lincoln Log," MIT Lincoln Lab (62-63); co-comp "A Guide to Scientific and Technical Journals in Translation" (68). 14: Translations, ref, for lit, govt publ. 15: RFD Box 455, Bolton Ma 01740.

BOYD, HARMON ARTHUR. b Carterville Ill 21 D 14. 4: Lucy Hickson Boyd. 5: Ind State U 47-50 (Bus ed) BS, 50-52 (Soc sci & LS) MS, 52-53 Lifetime Tchg License (Ind) Pub Lib Certif. 7: Shoe Inspector International Shoe Co Anna Ill 34-42; A US Inf Lt Col 42-46; Libn US Penitentiary, Terre Haute Ind 49-66; Ref libn Vigo Co Pub Lib, Terre Haute Ind 66-. 9: ALA; Correct EA; IndLA. 10: Assn of the US Army. 14: Ref. 15: 1101 Wood Lane dr, Terre Haute In 47802.

BOYD, HERBERT R. b Des Moines Iowa 18 O 13. 4: Doris Jarvis. 5: Iowa State U 36-40 (Agric & Sci) BS; State U of Iowa 41-42 (Med & Sci); West Res 55-57 MSLS; Drake U 62-65 (Econ & Bus Admin) MA. 7: Dir of libs Grand View Jr Col 56-57; Asst chief research & reports Govt Agency, Des Moines Iowa 45-. 8: Masonic Lib Com Des Moines Iowa 57-; Gout Agency lib com 67-. 11: US Bur Employment Security Certif of Award. 13: Yes. 14: Documentation. 15: 1314 63rd, Des Moines Ia 50311.

BOYD, JESSIE EDNA. b Anaheim Cal 13 Ag 1899. 5: UCal (Berkeley) 20-21 (Hist) AB, 22 (Hist) MA, 28-29 Certif in Libnship; Columbia summer 46. 7: Libn Fremont High Sch, Oakland Cal 32-35; Libn U High Sch, oakland Cal 36-46; UCal: Lecturer in child lit Sch of Libnship 31-33, Lecturer in Sch Lib Admin 36-58, Supv of Sch Lib Practice Sch of Educ 36-47; Dir of Sch Libs Oakland Pub Schs, Oakland Cal 48-63; Supv of Directed Lib Practice USan Francisco 64-. 8: Consul, Sch Lib Wkshop, Orange Co, Santa Ana Cal, 64; Lecturer, Sch Lib Admin & Child Lit UOre, summers 36-37. 9: NEA (Life mem); ALA (Coun 45-49 & 60-64, Subs Bks Bul Com 65-67, chm Jt ALA-NEACom 55-56)-AASchL (Bd Dirs 56-58 & 60-64); CalASchL (pres 41-42, Hist & Rec Chm 65-70;pres No Sect 39-40); CalLA. 10: Friends of the Oakland Pub Lib; Bd dirs, Adv CounFriends of Cal Libs; Beta Phi Mu; Delta Kappa Gamma; AAUW; Col Women's Club, Berkeley;Book Club of Cal; Cal Hist Soc; Alameda Co Hist Soc; Friends of the Bancroft Lib;Women's Fac Club UCal. 11: Hon life mem; Cal Congress PTA, CalASchL, Assn of ChildLibns. 12: Co-auth "Books, Libraries and You" (3rd ed 65); Ed (wih others) "Basic Book Collection for High Schools," ALA (42). 13: Yes. 14: Educ for libnship, supv, child lit, priv presses, fine printing. 15: 100 Bay place, apt 805, Oakland Ca 94610.

BOYD, KENNETH WADE. b Jacksonville Fla 2 O 38. 4: Linda Adams. 5: The Citadel 56-60 (Hist) AB; Drexel 62-63 (LS) MS; Ga State Col 65- (Philos). 7: US Army (CIC) Lt 60-61; 1st asst Ext Dept Flint River Reg Lib, Griffin Ga 63-65; 1st asst Order Dept Atlanta Pub Lib 65-66; V-pres Amer Lib Line, Inc, Atlanta Ga 66-. 9: ALA; GaLA; SELA. 14: Tech processing. 15: 216 Adair ct apt 1, Decatur Ga 30030.

BOYD, MARY ANN (McCOMB). b Chicago Il 18 Mr 26. 4: Clarence W Boyd Jr. 5: Stanford 44-47 (Psych) AB; Florida State 62-63 (LS) MS. 7: Libn Amer Personnel & Guidance Assoc Wash DC 60-62; Readers serv libn Marine Corps Educ Ctr Va 64-64; Libn SEast Materials Ctr U of S Fla 66-68; Asst prof div of libnship Emory U 69-. 8: Instr Inst on the Operation of Educ Info Serv Ctrs EmoryU 68 & 69. 9: ALA; SLA; FlaLA; FlaA-VA. 10: Phi Beta Kappa; Beta Phi Mu. 11: Fellow, Fla StateU. 14: Ref, spec libnship. 15: Div of Librarianship, Emory Univ, Atlanta Ga 30322.

BOYD, MAURICE R. b Ashland Ohio 13 O 33. 5: Baldwin-Wallace Col 51-53; Ohio State 53-55 (Pol sci) BA; Kent State 58-59 MSLS. 6: Sp. 7: Bk mob libn PGCML, Bladensburg Md 60-62; UMd: Assoc soc sci libn 62-65, off-campus libn 66; Reader's adv Prince Georges Co Men Lib, Hyattsville Md 67-. 8: Ref libn, Lib/USA NY World's Fair 65. 9: ALA; MdLA. 14: Adult readers serv. 15: 3900 Hamilton st a304, Hyattsville Md 20781.

BOYD, SANDRA (HUGHES). b Council Bluffs Iowa. 4: J Hayden Boyd. 5: Colo Col 57-61 (Econ) BA; UMinn 62-64 (LS) MA. 7: Price economist Bur Labor Statistics, Chicago 61-62; Libn Lutheran Brotherhood Ins Co, Minneapolis 64-66; Catlgr Ohio StateU (Columbus) 66-67, Libn Journalism Library 67-68. 8: Mem Ohio StateU Faculty Lib Sch Com (appointed to coordinate establishment of a lib sch) 68. 9: SLA; ALA; OhioLA. 14: Ref, spec libs. 15: 1746 Northwest blvd, Columbus Oh 43212.

BOYD, TRENTON. b Baton Rouge La 17 Jl 44. 5: UMo at Columbia 62-67 (Wildlife Conservation) BS in Agric, 67-68 MA in LS. 6: Fr. 7: Genealogist Columbia Mo 66-68; Lib liaison & bibliog food sci & nutrition dept UMo 67-68; Sci ref libn Wichita State U 68-. 9: ALA; MoLA. 14: Sci ref. 15: PO Box 8216 Munger Station, Wichita Ks 67208.

BOYD, VIRGINIA (DEAN). b Anderson Co SC 29 Ja 29. 4: Glover Boyd Jr. 5: SC State A&M Col 46-50 (LS) BS; Atlanta summer 52, 57-58, summer 59 (LS) MS. 6: Fr. 7: Libn Bond-Wilson High Sch, Charleston SC 50-54; Tchr libn Wright High Sch, Abbeville SC 54-55; Libn, sec & dir of music New Deal Sch, Starr SC 54-57; Eng tchr Westside High Sch, Anderson SC 63-65, Tchr libn 65-68; Libn Southwood Middle Sch, Anderson SC 68-.9: NEA; Anderson Co (SC) Tchrs Assn. 10: PTA; Young Matron's Circle; School Dist #5 (Anderson SC) Profess Libns; Sponsor Campfire Girls. 15: 396 Stewart Circle, Anderson SC 29621.

BOYD, (RUTH) VIRGINIA. b Pelham Ga 1 O 38. 5: Young Harris Col 56-58 AA; Ga Col at Milledgeville 62-65 (Hist) AB; George Peabody Col for Tchrs 65-66 MLS. 7: Bkkeeper Pelham Fed Savings & Loan Assn, Pelham Ga 58-62; Asst libn Ga SWest Col 66-. 9: ALA; GaLA; SELA. 11: Beta Phi Mu. 14: Catlg, govt docs. 15: 224 Frieda lane, Americus Ga 31709.

BOYD, WILLIAM BAGGETT. b Tarpon Springs Fla 5 Mr 18. 4: Betty Nollman. 5: Fla So Col 36-40 (Journalism) BS; Fla StateU 55-57 (Educ) MS; UFla 62 (LS) Certif. 7: Eng tchr Jackson High Sch, Jacksonville Fla 40-42; Lt USN 7th Fleet 42-46; Voc tchr St Petersburg Sr High, St Petersburg Fla 46-50; Eng tchr & libn Disston Jr High, St Petersburg Fla 50-64; Libn St Petersburg Jr Col 64-. 9: NEA; Fla Educ Assn; Fla Libs. 10: United States Power Squadron. 12: "Audio Visual Techniques" (68). 14: A-v, lib orientation instr. 15: St Petersburg Jr College PO Box 13489, St Petersburg Fl 33733.

BOYER, MRS ALTA E. b Lodi NY 18 O 14. 4: Charles H Boyer. 5: William Smith Col 36 (Eng, Span) BA; Gen Motors Inst of Tech 42 (Retailing, Compt); Syracuse summer 59 (LS); State U Col (Geneseo NY) 64 MLS. 7: Willard State Hosp, Willard NY: Lib trainee 57-62, Asst libn 62-63, Hosp libn 63-. 9: NYLA (Inst Libs Com); MedLA. 10: PTA; Lodi Yacht Club; Alumnae Coun, William Smith Col 68-. 12: "A Survey of Nursing," NY Dept of Mental Hygiene (63); "Nursing Car and Rehabilitation of the Geriatric Patient," NY Dept of Mental Hygiene (65). 14: Ref, visiting libs. 15: Watkins Glen rd, Lodi NY 14860.

BOYER, CALVIN JAMES. b Charleston Ill 4 Mr 39. 4: Roberta Davis. 5: East Ill U 58-62 (Foreign Langs) BS in Ed; Bradley U summer 62; UTex 63-64 MLS. 6: Fr, Sp. 7: Libn Beardstown Commun High Sch, Beardstown Ill 62-63; Lib asst UTex 63-64; Head acquis dept Tex A&M U 64-67, Dir Midwest U Lib. 9: TexLA; SWLA. 10: TACT; AAUP. 13: Yes. 14: Admin, acquis, automation. 15: 507 Kyle, College Station Tx 77840.

BOYER, JEAN WARREN (ARCHER). b Portobello Scotland 6 My 32. 4: Alan Gordon Boyer. 5: Toronto 61 (Fr) BA, 62 BLS. 6: Fr. 7: Lib asst Joint Intelligence Bur, Melbourne Australia 51; Child libn Prahran Mun Lib, Melbourne Australia 52-54; Lib asst YP dept Calgary Pub Lib, Calgary Can 55-56; Lib Asst boys & girls div Toronto Pub Lib 56-59; Catlgr-in-chg Secondary Sch Lib Processing Centre, Educ Centre Lib Toronto Bd of Educ 62-64; Tech dir prof div Can Lib Supply Co, Toronto 64; Asst libn Ont Inst for Studies in Educ (Toronto) 65-66; Asst hd catlg div Temple U Lib 66-67, Bibliog 68-. 8: Lecturer in catlg Sch of Libnship, Ont Col of Educ, Toronto summer 65. 9: Inst Prof LibnsOnt; ALA; PennLA. 10: AAUP. 14: Catlg, ref, bibliog. 15: Apt F5 27 E Central ave,Paoli Pa 79301.

BOYER, LAURA MERCEDES. b Madison Ind 3 Ag 34. 5: UMiss 52-54; George Washingon U 54-56 (Religion) AB; UDenver 58-59 (Secondary Educ) AM; Peabody 60-61 (LS) AM. 7: Pub sch Eng tchr 57-58, 60; Asst circ libn UKan Lib 61-63; Asst ref libn U of the Pacific 63-65, Ref libn 65- 09: ALA; CalLA. 9: ALA; CalLA. 10: Phi Beta Kappa; Beta Phi Mu; Kappa Delta Pi. 14: Ref, circ. 15: 1020 W Bianchi apt 109, Stockton Ca 95207.

BOYER, RUTHANNE (GOLDTRAP). b Aurora Ill 25 N 37. 4: James Fredrick Boyer. 5: Purdue 55-56, 63-65 (LS & Sociol) BA; Rosary Col 66-67 MALS. 7: Child libn Skokie Pub Lib, Skokie Ill 65-66; Hd child dept Deerfield Pub Lib, Deerfield Ill 67-68, Act hd libn 68, Ref libn 68-. 9: ALA; -YASD; -LED; ISAD; Lib Research RT; RT on Social Responsib in Libs (charter mem); IllLA (Pub Lib sect). 10: AAUW. 13: Yes. 14: Recr, prof educ, automation. 15: 1640 Hertel lane, Deerfield Il 60015.

BOYKIN, AGNES G. b Amelia County Va 2 Je 11. 4: Charles P Boykin. 5: Longwood 28-32 (Hist) BS Ed; William & Mary summer 47 & 48 (LS) ABLS; Columbia summer 49 (LS). 7: Tchr Blackstone Elem Sch, Blackstone Va 32-41; Tchr James Madison, Arlington Va 41-43; Tchr Amelia Elem, Amelia Va 43-45; Amelia High, Amelia Va: Eng & hist tchr 45-47, libn 47-50; Libn Jackson E&em, Arlington Va 50-51; Libn McKinley Elem, Arlington Va 57-58; Libn Kenmore Jr High, Arlington Va 58-. 8: Eval Com State of Va Highland Springs High Sch Henrico Co Va; Chm Materials Ctr & Student Activities Com 65; Eval Com Binford Jr High Richmond Va; Chm Instr Serv & A-V Com 67. 9: ALA; VaEA (Dept of Libns); VaLA; ArlingtonEA; Arlington Pub Sch Libns. 10: Delta Kappa Gamma; Springfield Civic Assn. 14: Ref ya. 15: 7027 Leesville blvd, Springfield Va 22151.

BOYKIN, EDNA LESTER (LaVERNE). b Valdosta Ga 4 N 27. 4: Dr Leander L Boykin. 5: Paine Col 44-48 (Sociol) AB; Atlanta 54-55, summers 54-55 MS in LS, 57. 6: Fr. 7: Tchr Mt Moriah Voc High Sch, Climax Ga 48-49; Tchr Hutto High Sch, Bainbridge Ga 49-51; Tchr Brooks High Sch, Quitman Ga 51-54; Asst Prof of Educ & dir of Lib Sci Program So U 55-61; Asst Prof of Lib Serv Atlanta U 61-63; Asst Prof of Lib Serv Fla A&M U 64-66, Dir Curr Lab Fla A & M U 66-. 9: ALA; FlaLA; NEA. 10: Pi Gamma Mu; Psi Chi; Alpha Beta Alpha; AAUP; Le Moyne Art Found. 13: Yes. 14: Tech serv, ref, lib serv internship. 15: PO Box628, Tallahassee Fl 32304.

BOYKIN, JOSEPH FLOYD JR. b Pensacola Fla 7 N 40. 4: Evelyn Larson. 5: Pensacola Jr Col 58-60; Fla State U 60-62 (Hist) BS, 64-65 (LS) MS. 7: Tchr Escambia Co Bd of Pub Instr, Pensacola Fla 63-64; Asst to libn UNC(Charlotte) 65-68, Act hd libn 68-. 9: ALA; NCLA; SELA. 10: AAUP; LARC. 14: Admin, automation. 15: 2237 Milton rd, Charlotte NC 28205.

BOYKIN, LUCILLE (ANDERSON) (MRS). b Osborne Kan 20 Ag 21. 5: State Tchrs Col (Emporia Kan) 41-46 LS Certif & BS in Educ; UDenver summers 49-53 (Sociol); American U Inst of Genealogical Research summer 63 Certif; Tex Christian U 55-56 (Spec Educ). 7: Libn High Sch, Ottawa Kan 46-49; asst libn & catlgr High Sch & Jr Col, Santa Maria Cal 49-51; High sch libn High Sch, Latmar Colo 51-53; Head libn Pub Lib, Lamar Colo 53-54; Bkmob libn Jackson Co Lib, Jackson Mich 54-55; Catlgr Dallas Pub Lib 56-58; Ser libn 58-61; Gr 9 libn Spec Serv 4th US Army Missile 8th Army Korea 61-62; dept head Tex Hist & Genealogy Dallas Pub Lib 63-. 8: Lecturer for annual wkshop Genealogical Research Local History and Genealogical Soc 64, 65; Lecturer for wkshop Okla Genealogical Wkshop Col of Continuing Educ UOkla (65). 9: ALA-Tex Div (Memb Com 64-, Ref Com, Hist Sub-Com 64-). 10: Local Hist & Genealogy Soc Dallas (Bd 64-); AAUW. 12: Ed "Perhaps Ill Be With M Gaspar (51). 14: Rare bks, ref, catlg, geneal research. 15: 4927 Bryan st Apt S, Dallas Tx 75206.

BOYLAN, DOUGLAS BRUCE. b Sarnia Ont Can 25 Ag 36. 4: Kathryn Anne (Sault) Boylan. 5: Carleton U 61 9hist, Pol Sci) BA; McGill 64 BLS; Carleton U 64 Certif in Archival Prin & Admin. 6: Fr. 7: Lecturer Prince of Wales Col (Charlottetown PEI) 61-63; Legis Libn & Prov Archivist, Prov of Prince Edward Island, Charlottetown 64-. 8: Sessional Lecturer, St Dunstans U (Charlottetown PEI) 64-; PEI del contin com of officials, constit conf 68-. 9: ASA; APLA (pres 64-65); ALA. 10: Can Hist Assn; Internat Inst of Conserv. 12: Ed for PEI, "Atlantic Provinces Checklist." 14: Admin, govt docs, archives. 14: Admin, govt docs, archives. 15: Legislative Lib, Box 1000 Charlottetown Pei Can.

BOYLAN, MERLE NELSON. b Youngstown Ohio 24 F 25. 5: Youngstown U 46-50 (Biol Sci) BA; UAriz 50-51 (Biol Sci); Ind U 51 (Biol Sci); Carnegie 55-56 MLS. 6: Fr, Ger. 7: Libn UCal Pub Health Lib (Berkeley) 56-58; Sci libn UAriz 58-59; Engnr libn Gen Dynamics/Convair, San Diego Cal 59-61; Engnr libn Gen Dynamics/Astronautics, San Diego Cal 61-62; Head of tech processes Lawrence Radiation Lab, Livermore Cal 62-64, Lib mgr 64-68; Chief lib NASA-Ames Research Ctr, Moffett Field Cal 68-. 9: ALA; ASIS. 12: "IBM 1401 Computer Produced and Maintained Printed Book Catalogs at the Lawrence Radiation Laboratory, 1964 UCRL-7555" (64); "Automated Acquisition, Cataloging, and Circulation in a Large Research Library, UCRL-50406" (68). 14: Machine systems, catlg, ref. 15: 841 Division st, Pleasanton Ca 94566.

BOYLAN, NANCY (TOLL) GERMAN. b Kansas City Mo 16 Je 29. 4: Richard P Boylan. 5: Kansas U 46-49 (Eng); UMo (Kansas City) 49-51 (Eng) BA, 50-51 (Law); UIllsummer 60 (LS); Kan State Tchrs Col summer 64, 66 (LS) MS. 7: Training asst buyer Macy's Kansas City, Kansas City Mo 52; Lib asst Washington U Engnr Lib 57-59, Engnrg libn 60; Documents libn Linda Hall Lib, Kansas City Mo 60-66; Acquis libnClendenning Med Lib Kan U Med Ctr 66; Hd libn Midwest Research Inst, Kansas City67-68; Hd Gov Docs Dept U Iowa 68-. 12: "Checklist of PeriodicalTitles Currently Received in Medical Libraries in the Southern Region" (60); Ed"Bulletin of the Medical Library Association" (61-69). 13: Yes. 14: Ref, catlg, govt publs, lib ed. 15: Apt 916, Westhampton Vil, Coralville Ia 52240.

BOYLE, JEANNE (BAUMULLER). b Englewood NJ 30 Ja 45. 4: Peter Boyle. 5: Douglass Col 63-67 (Eng) AB; Rutgers 67-68 MLS. 6: Fr. 7: Clk circ dept RutgersU (New Brunswick) 67, Grad asst ref dept 67-68; Ref referral libn NJ State Lib, Trenton NJ 68-. 14: Ref. 15: 34 Model ave, Hopewell NJ 08525.

BOYLE, JOHN RAYMOND. b Summit Hill Penn 2 F 41. 5: King's Col 59-63 (Hist, Govt) BA; Drexel 63-64 MSLS. 7: Ref libn W Orange Pub Lib, W Orange NJ 65- Acquis Lib, Tech Serv Lib, DIA, Wash DC 66-68, Chief 69-. 9: ALA; SLA. 14: Tech serv, acquis, ref. 15: 5055 Seminary rd, apt 935, Alexandria Va 22311.

BOYLE, RUTH (ROGERS). b Hamilton Square NJ 7 Ja 10. 4: Joseph E Boyle. 5: NJ Lib Sch 29-31 Certif; UPenn 30-32; Rutgers 58-59 (LS), 59 (Eng) AB. 7: Lib asst Trenton Pub Lib, Trenton NJ 29-34; Asst libn E Trenton Br Lib, Trenton NJ 42-49; Libn Watson AF Labs, Eatontown NJ 49-51; Ref libn Signal Corps R & D Labs, Ft Monmouth NJ 51-56; Libn Automatic Switch Co, Florham Park NJ 56-. 9: SLA; Amer Soc for Testing Materials. 10: Friends of the Livingston Pub Lib. 13: Yes. 14: Ref. 15: 80 Elmwood dr, Livingston NJ 07039.

BOYNO, MARY ANN (WHITE). b Mineral Wells Tex 28 Ag 45. 4: Edward Alexander Boyno. 5: St Norbert Col 63-66 (Eng) BA; Rutgers 67-68 MLS. 6: Fr. 7: Ref Fordham U Lib 68-69; Ref Free Pub Lib of Woodbridge, Woodbridge NJ 69-. 14: Ref, govt publ. 15: 132 Myrtle ave apt 16, Fort Lee NJ 07024.

BOYNTON, JANET H(ELEN). b Bradford Penn 20 My 17. 5: St Bonaventure U 35-40 (Soc Sci) BA, 40-41 (Eng) MA; Catholic U 45-46, 48-49 BS in LS. 7: Clerk-steno US Navy Dept, Wash DC 41-42; Lib asst US Navy Dept Libs, Wash DC 42-45; Circ libn Catholic U 45-46, Catlgr 48-49; Jr catlgr UMiami 49-50; Catlg libn St Bonaventure U 50-62; Tech serv libn URochester Med Center, Rochester NY 62-. 9: MedLA; Monroe Co Lib Club. 14: Catlg. 15: 701 University Park, Rochester NY 14620.

BOYSWORTH, WILLA MATHESON. b Andrews NC. 5: Fla State U 24-26 (Eng) LI; UNC 26-28 (Eng, Hist) AB, 37-40 BSLS. 7: Prof of Lib Sci Longwood Col, Farmville Va; Dir of Lib Serv Hampden-Sydney Col; Dir of Lib Serv Huntingdon Col; Fulbright Prof Lib Sci to Dacca, East Pakistan; Dir of Lib Sci Central Fla Jr Col; Dir of Lib Serv Miami-Dade Jr Col; Prof of Lib Sci College of Guam; Dir Lib Serv Santa Fe Jr Col. 8: Fulbright Prof to Pakistan; Aid in org of Asia Fed of Lib Assns, Tokyo Japan; Consul to H W Wilson on "Standard Catalog for Public Libraries. 9: ALA; SELA; FlaLA; Pakistan LA; GuamLA. 10: AAUW; AAUP; Guam Woman's Club; Guam Rehabilitation Center; Col of Guam Faculty Wives Club. 11: Medal of achievement from Asia Fed of Lib Assns; Certif of commend from Pakistania govt. 13: Yes. 14: Admin, tchg of lib sci. 15: Santa Fe Jr Col Gainesville Fl 32601.

BOYVEY, MARY R (O'NEILL). b Ft Worth Tex 10 S 20. 5: TWU 38-40 (LS, Eng) BA; UTex 45 (Eng) MA 69-; UChicago 56 MALS. 6: Sp. 7: Libn H S Lockhart ISD, Lockhart Tex 43-45; Libn H S Big Spring ISD, Big Spring Tex 45-47; Libn HS Orange ISD, Orange Tex 47-48; Libn Jr H S Beaumont ISD, Beaumont Tex 48-51; Libn Jr H S Corpus Christi ISD, Corpus Christi Tex 51-63; State Dept of Educ, Lib consul, Austin Tex 63-65, Program dir 65-. 9: ALA; NEA-DAVI; ASCD; NCTM; TexLS; Tex Assn of Educ Tech; TexStateA; TexASCD. 11: Delta Kappa Gamma. 14: Sch libs. 15: 505 W 7th apt 212, Austin Tx 78711.

BOZONE, BILLIE R(AE). b Norphlet Ark 7 O 35. 5: Miss State Col for Women 53-57 (LS) BS; Peabody 57-58 (LS) MA. 7: Asst ref libn Miss State U 58-61, Ser libn 61-63; Asst ref libn UIll(Urbana) 63-65; Asst libn New England Mutua Life Insurance Co, Boston 65-67; Sr ref libn UMass (Amherst) 67-68; Hd circ dept Smith 68-69, Asst libn 69-. 9: SELA; MissLA (chm Col Sect). 10: Alpha Beta Alpha; Alpha Psi Omega; Theatre Guild; Girl Scouts leader. 13: Yes. 14: Ref, admin. 15: 108 Lessey st, Amherst Ma 01002.

BRACE, PHYLLIS (ARLENE) MAYER. b Jersey City NJ 18 D 31. 4: William Brace. 5: Simmons 49-53 (Pre-prof Studies) BS; Chicago 53-55 (LS) MA. 7: Asst order dept Northwestern U 55-56; Libn Nat Congress of Parents & Tchrs,chicago 56-58; Libn Southeast Jr Col 58-60; Asst libn Amundsen Jr Col 60; Sec extdiv Fla State Lib 61; Br libn Oak Park Pub Lib, Oak Park Ill 61-68, Br libn Mazeand Dole Brs 69-. 8: Lib Consul Research & Devel Div Continental Can Co, 58-59. 9: ALA; Chicago Reg Group of Libns in Tech Serv (sec-reas 58-59);Chicago Lib Club; IllLA. 10: Chicago Grad Lib Sch Alumni Assn; AAUW. 14: Readers serv, pb libs. 15: 215 Marengo ave, Forest Park Il 60130.

BRACE, VERNA S(CHILLING). b Proctor WVa 8 Mr 04. 4: Clarence E Brace. 5: Kent State 32-33 Certif; UDenver 44 (Educ) BA; UColo 54; UDenver 62 (LS) MA. 6: Fr. 7: Tchr Elem Sch, Ohio 24-26, 33-34; Tchr Jr High Sch, Colo 35-43; Tchr Lakewood Jr High Sch, Colo 43-65, Libn 57-. 8: Chm Lang Arts, Lakewood Jr High Sch 50-57. 10: Kappa Delta Pi. 14: Ref, rare bks. 15: 1151 Fillmore, Denver Co 80206.

BRACE, WILLIAM. b Cortez Colo 20 Ag 29. 4: Phyllis Mayer Brace. 5: Brigham Young U 47-50 (Hist) BA; Chicago 53-54 (LS) MA. 7: Instr ref dept Brigham Young U 54-56, Instr circ libn 56-57; Asst Prof Chicago tchrs Col 57-60; Asst Prof Lib Sch Fla State U 60-61; Asst Prof Dept of Lib Sci Rosary Col 61-65, Assoc Prof 65-. 9: SLA; ALA; -LED (chm Publ Com 63-66); AALS; IllLA(chm Recrt Com 66-); Chicago Lib Club (pres 68-). 10: AAUP. 13: Yes. 14: Educ for libnship, ref. 15: 7900 W Divisionst, River Forest Il 60305.

BRACKETT, CHARLES H. b Chicago Ill 18 Ja 32. 4: Stephanie Lea Snow. 5: Azusa Pacific Col 51-55 (Biblical Lit & Theol) AB (magna cum laude); Pasadena Col 55 (Hist); USoCal 54-56 MS in LS, 62-67 (Amer Studies) MA. 7: Catlg libn Azusa Pacific Col 56-57; Decimal clsf specialist LC 67-. 9: ALA. 10: Nat Assn of Evangelicals. 14: Catlg. 15: 1602 Carey lane apt 37, Silver Spring Md 20910.

BRACKWINKLE, HILDA L. b Elberfield Ind 20 N 15. 5: Evansville Col 33-37 (Lat) AB; UIll 39-40 Voc Home Econ; Ind U 42 (Eng); Ind State Col 56-61 (LS) MS. 7: Tchr-Lat, home econ New Point High Sch, New Point Ind 37-38; Tchr-Lat, home econ Vienna High Sch, Vienna Ill 38-39; Tchr Folsomville High Sch, Folsomville Ind 40-45; Tchrllibn Eng Lat lib Lynnville High Sch, Lynnville Ind 45-52; Tchr home econ, bio, lib Fayetteville High Sch, R R Bedford Ind 52-53; Tchrllibn Eng, Lat, lib Plainville High Sch, Plainville Ind 54-56; Tchr-libn Lat, biol, lib Orleans High Sch, Orleans Ind 56-56; Libn Worthington High Sch, Worthington Ind 57-58; Tchr-libn Eng, lib Brook High Sch, MSD SoNewton, Brook Ind 58-67; S Newton Jr-Sr High Sch, R R Kentland Ind 67-. 8: Sch sec Lynnvile Hih Sch 53-54. 9: NEA; ALA-AASchL; IndSchLA (sec 59-61, bd Dirs 65-66; Area 4: chm Lib Devel Com 65-66); Ind State Tchrs Assn; Ind ClrTA. 14: Bk sel, stud guidance. 15: Box 216, Brook In 47922.

BRADAC, MARY F. b Chisholm Minn. 4: Joseph G Bradac. 5: Col of St Catherine BS in LS; Columbia summers (Educ); UMich MALS. 6: Fr, Ital. 7: Head ref dept High Sch, Hibbing Minn, Head circ dept; Army libn US Army, Cheyenne Wyo summers; Head loan dept UND; Head Communications Lib Stephens Col; Pub serv & tchg Educ Div Lib, Central Mich U 57-. 9: ALA-AASchL; MichLA; MichASchL. 10: Youth Study Club; Alpha Beta Alpha; AAUW; Central Mich U Faculty Dames; PTA; Faculty Women's Club. 14: Sch libs, child & yp, circ. 15: 628 W Preston, Mt Pleasant Mi 48858.

BRADBURY, JOHN FRANCIS. b Boston 1 Je 22. 4: Louise Shubert. 5: URochester 51-54 BS; Simmons 54-55 (LS) MS; Chicago 62- (LS). 7: (Pfc) US Army Infantry, US, Europe 43-46; Ref asst educ div Rochester Pub Lib, rochester NY 55-57; Libn Pittsford High Sch, Pittsford NY 57-60; Ser libn East Ill U 60-61; Lib supv Cicero Elem Schs, Cicero Ill 61-64; Instr Dept Lib Sci No Ill U 64-67; Asst Prof Lib Sci Ill State U 67-. 8: Dir NDEA Summer Inst for Sch Libns, 65. 9: ALA-AASchL (Instr Materials Com64-); IllLA (Recr Com); IllASchL (chm Recr Com 64-66, treas 66-67, chm ProfRelat Com 68-). 10: NEA-DAVI. 13: Yes. 14: Sch libs, materials for youth. 15: 1217 Searledr, Normal Il 61761.

BRADDON, (ISABEL) BERNICE. b Chatham Ont Can 4 My 11. 5: UCal(Berkeley) 30-34 (Eng) BA; UCal 35 Gen Secondary Cred; USoCal 45 (LS); San Jose State Col summers 54-56 (LS) Lib Cred, summers 60-61 (LS) MA in Lib. 7: Kern Jt Union High Sch Dist, Bakersfield Cal; Eng tchr 35-42, Asst libn Bakersfield High 42-49, Libn act dist supv 49-52, Supv Libn 53-. 8: Consul to Adv Com, Sch Lib Research Proj, State Dept of Educ (Cal) 63-. 9: NEA; ALA; Cal Tchrs Assn; CalASchL. 10: Delta kappa Gamma; Sierra Club; Kern Co (Cal) Hist Soc; Friends of the Kern Co Lib. 14: Catlg. 15: 2000 24th st, Bakersfield Cal 93301.

BRADEN, IRENE ANDREA. b Hondo Tex 26 S 38. 5: UTex 56-60 (Eng) BA; UMich 60-61 AMLS; Kan State U 62-64 (Hist) MA; UMich64-67 (LS) PhD. 7: Catlg libn Sam Houston State Tchrs Col, Huntsville Tex 61-62; Head circ dept Kan State U (Manhattan) 62-64; Grad asst UMich Dept of Lib Sci 64-66; Libn for gen admin & research Ohio State U 66-. 8: Dir HEA Inst 69. 9: ALA;-ACRL (Publ Com 67-); OhioLA (chm Constit Com 67-68;mem Lib Devel Com 68-69). 10: Phi Kappa Phi; Phi Alpha Theta; Pi Lambda Theta. 12: Jt auth "Physiological Factors Relating to Terrestrial Altitudes; A Bibliography"(68). 13: Yes. 14: Undergrad libs, admin. 15: 684 Riverview dr #65, Columbus Oh43202.

BRADFIELD, MARJORIE A (BLACKISTONE). b Wash DC 10 My 11. 4: Horce F Bradfield. 5: UMich 30-34 (Romance lang) BA, 39-40 (Fr, lib serv) MSLS; Columbia 34-35 (Lib serv) BSLS. 6: Fr, Sp. 7: Libn Roosevelt High Sch, Gary Ind 35-38; Library asst Detroit Pub Lib 38-52, 64-66; Libn Harris Sch, Detroit 68-. 8: First Prof Negro Libn hired by Detroit Pub Lib; Chm Lib Com; Neighborhood Serv Prog Detroit 68-. 9: ALA; MichLA. 10: Delta Sigma Theta; Bd memb St Peter Claver Commun House; past chm Speaker's Bur Detroit NAACP; past chm Detroit Archdiocesan Coun of Cath Women (Legislation Com). 14: Ref, lib serv. 15: 3230 Oakman blvd, Detroit Mi 48238.

BRADFORD, (JOSEPH) EDWARD JR. b Houston 16 D 37. 5: UMd(Munich Germany) 55-56; Cameron State A&M Col 56; UOkla 56-59 (Eng Lit) BA, 59-61 (Eng Lit) MA, 62-63 MLS. 7: Queens Borough Pub Lib, Jamaica NY: Staff 63, Research asst ext serv 63-64, Dept asst ext serv 64-66, Asst chief tech proc 66-68, Chief tech proc 68; Hd tech serv York Col LibCUNY. 9: ALA; NYLA. 14: Tech proc, admin. 15: 87-05 89th ave, Woodhaven NY 11421.

BRADFORD, EMMA L. b Hodge La 25 D 43. 5: Grambling Col 61-65 (Speech, Drama) BS; LSU (Baton Rouge) summers 65, 66 (LS); AtlantaU 66-67 MSLS; UPittsburgh summer 68 (Lib Educ Media Inst). 6: Fr. 7: Hd libn Sevier Elem Sch Lib, Ferriday La 65-66; Off asst At&antaU 66-67; Co-ord lib educ program Grambling Col Lib 67-. 8: Consul High Sch Career Day Conf, Winnfield La 67; Col supv Student Tchg Team; Mem Col Lib com. 9: LaEA. 10: Alpha Kappa Alpha. 11: Rockefeller Scholarship AtlantaU 66-67. 13: Yes. 14: Lib educ, col lib serv. 15: PO Box 384, Grambling La 71245.

BRADLEY, ALBERT PEARCE. b Bridgewater England 19 S 18. 4: Katie (Garrity) Bradley. 5: UHouston 46-46 (Physics); UTrx 46-49 (Physics) BS, 49-51 MLS. 7: Wirephoto Operator AP, Wash DC 38-41; Weather Forecaster USAAF Warrant Off JG 41-46; Physics Librarian UTex 49-51; Libn US Naval Ordnance Test Sta Annex Pasadena Cal 51-53; Libn Atomics International Canoga Park Cal 53-60; Clsf Coordinator Atomics International Canoga Park Cal 60-64; Hd Libn NASA Manned Spacecraft Ctr, Houston 64-. 9: SLA (pres So Cal Chap 59; held various off in So Cal Chapter & Tex Chap 53-); TexLA (v-chm, Spec Libs Div 68-69). 10: Sigma Pi Sigma. 14: Lib admin, ref. 15: NASA Manned Spacecraft Center, Houston Tx 77058.

BRADLEY, ALCYONE B (MALLINSON). b Dawson NM 14 O 19. 4: Sam N Bradley. 5: Ark State Tchrs Col (Eng) BSE; Fla State U 53-54 (LS) MS. 7: Catlgr A-V Center Dade Co (Fla) summers; Catlgr Nat Everglades Park (Fla) 65-; Libn High Sch Lib, Homestead Fla 54- Libn S Dade Center Miami-Dade Jr Col. 9: ALA; Dade Co Sch Libs; FlaEA; CTA. 14: Catlg, acquis. 15: 25600 SW 182nd ave, Homestead Fl33030.

BRADLEY, BEN W(ILLIAM). b Fife Tex 21 Ka 19. 4: Mary E(lizabeth Sharpe). 5: St Mary's U San Antonio Tex 36-38; UTex at Austin 38-41, 46-47, 65-68 MLS; UMd at College Park 51-53 (Military sci) BS. 7: USA (Lt col), US, SW Pacific & Europe 41-46, 47-62; Jr libn San Antonio Col 68-. 9: ALA; SWLA; TexLA; Tex Jr Col TA. 10: AAUP. 11: Bronze star medal with oak leaf cluster; Army commendation medal with two oak leaf clusters. 14: Ref. 15: 301 Blanco rd, San Antonio Tx 78212.

BRADLEY, DORIS ANNE. b Phila 21 F 30. 5: Wilson Col 47-51 (Fine Arts) AB; UNC 51-52 BS in LS. 6: Ger, Sp, Fr. 7: Catlgr UGa Lib 52-53; Catlgr Pub Lib of Charlotte & Mecklenburg Co, Charlotte NC 53-58; Army libn US Army Spec Serv, Germany 58-60; Sr ser catlgr Yale U Lib 61-63; Asst chief catlg dept Washington U Lib (St Louis) 63-66; Hd ser catlg U of Rochester Lib 66-68, Hd tech serv libn UNC (Charlotte)Lib 68-. 9: ALA; SELA; NCLA. 14: Catlg, ser. 15: 1933 Milton rd apt 1, Charlotte NC 28205.

BRADLEY, FLORENE JORDAN. b Magnolia Ark 18 Ag 17. 4: Steve Bradley. 5: Southern State Col 35-37; Henderson State Tchrs Col 37-39 (Eng, Hist) BA; Peabody summers 45-47 BS in LS. 7: Tchr-libn Burdette High Sch, Burdette Ark 39-42; Tchr-libn Calhoun High Sch, Calhoun Ark 42-43; Tchr-libn Magnolia High Sch, Magnolia Ark 43-51; Reg Libn Columbia-Lafayette Reg Lib, Magnolia Ark 51-62; Reg Libn Columbia-Lafayette-Ouachita-Magnolia Reg Lib, Ark 62-; Reg libn Columbia-Lafayette-Ouachita Calhoun Reg Lib, Ark 65-. 9: ALA (Notable Bks Coun, Dorothy Canfield Fisher A ward Com);-PLA (Nom Com); SWLA (chm Pub Lib Sect); ArkLA (pres 54, Pub Lib Activities com 67-70). 10: Quota Club; Bus & Prof Women's Club; AAUW; Delta Kappa Gamma; LWV; C of C; Columbia Co Fair Bd; Wesleyan Serv Guild. 11: Magnolia Woman of the Year 63; Magnolia Citizen of the Year 68. 15: 405 W Calhoun, Magnolia Ark 71753.

BRADLEY, JOHN. b Ridley Park Penn 18 My 43. 5: Ursinus 61-65 (Eng) BA; Drexel 65-66 MSLS. 6: Sp. 7: Asst Libn Ocean Co Col 66-67; Asst Libn Bucks Co Commun Col 67-. 9: ALA; PennLA. 2: "Your Library" (69). 14: Admin, a-v, acquis. 15: 1503 Orthodox st, Philadelphia Pa 19124.

BRADLEY, MELISSA. b Boston Mass 29 Ag 43. 5: UKy 61-65 (Hist) BA; Ecole Francaise de Middlebury 65; UIll 65-67 (LS) MS. 6: Fr. 7: Asst educ & soc sci libn UIll (Urbana) 66-67; Ser acquis libn UMass 67-68, Ser catlgr 68-. 15: 38 Kellogg ave, Amherst Ma 01002.

BRADLEY, ELIZABETH. b Ely Nev 24 S 18. 4: Robert L Bradley. 5: UNeb 36-39 (Journalism); UMo 39-41 (Journalism) (Bachelor of Journ); Marshall 59-61 (LS) MA; Emory 63 (LS). 6: Sp. 7: Med libn Veterans Adminis, Huntington W Va 62-. 9: MedLA; SLA. 14: Research. 15: 1540 Spring Valley dr, Huntington W Va 25701.

BRADLEY, (JENNIE) RUTH. b Santa Ana Cal 14 Ag 09. 5: Santa Ana Col 27-29 (Math) AA; UCLA 29-31 (Phil) AB; Riverside (Cal) Lib Sch 31-32 (LS) Certif; Columbia Lib Sch summers MSLS. 7: Asst libn, libn Santa Ana High Sch, Santa Ana Cal 36-48; Libn Santa Ana Col 48-62; Libn American Col for Girls, Istanbul Turkey 62-65; Science Libn UCal at Irvine 65-66; Acting Libn Sweet Briar Col 66-67; Branch Libn Wahiawa Hawaii State Lib Wahiawa Oahu 68-69; Act libn Robert Col Istanbul Turkey 69-. 9: ALA. 10: Women's Overseas Serv League. 14: Admin, rare bks. 15: 230 E Almond ave, Orange Ca 92666.

BRADLEY, SHEILA (HARVEY). b Vancouver BC Can 1 My 43. 4: J Murray Bradley. 5: UBC 61-64 (Eng, Pol Sci) BA, 65-66 BLS. 6: Fr. 7: Jr catlg CarletonU 66, Jr ref libn 67, Ref libn 67, Sr ref libn 68-. 9: CanLA; ALA. 14: Ref. 15: Ref Dept Lib CarletonU, Ottawa 1 Ont Can.

BRADLEY, VERDELLE (VANDERHORST). b Jacksonville Fla. 4: Dr Walter O Bradley. 5: Fla A&M U 37-41 (Hist) AB; Atlanta 41-42 (Ref) MSLS; Columbia 60 (LS) MS. 6: Fr, Ger. 7: Libn Barber-Scotia Jr Col 42-44; Ref libn Fla A&M U summer 44; Newark Pub Lib educ dept, Newark NJ 44-46; Libn Va Union U 46-. 8: Adv Com Southeastern States Coop Lib Survey, 46-47 Lib eval; Knoxville Col 68, Spelman Col 69; Lib consul Spelman Col 69. 9: VaLA. 10: Alpha Kappa Alpha; Jack & Jill Inc; Links of Amer Inc. 14: Ref, admin. 15: Va Union Univ, Richmond Va 23220.

BRADOW, MARGARET ELAINE (AMEND). b Olin Iowa 26 Ap 32. 4: George W Bradow. 5: Coe Col 50-52; UIowa 52-54 (Gen Bus) BSC; UIll 62-63 (LS) MS. 7: Mus tchr Boddicker Sch of mus, Cedar Rapids Iowa 49-57; Readers asst pub lib, Cedar Rapids Iowa 57-62, Libn II 63-. 9: IowaLA. 14: Ref. 15: 1636 34 st NE, Cedar Rapids Ia 52402.

BRADSHAW, CAROL D'ANN. b Glenwood Springs Col 9 O 38. 5: Colo State Col 56-60 (Eng) BA; UDenver 65-66 (LS) MA. 7: Tchr Limon Pub Schs, Limon Colo 60-61; Clk 1st Nat Bank of Denver 61-65; Libn Ft Lewis Col 66-. 14: Catlg.

BRADSHAW, LILLIAN MOORE. b Hagerstown Md 10 Ja 15. 4: William T Bradshaw. 5: West Md Col 33-37 (Hist) AB; Drexel 37-38 BS in LS. 7: Asst circ dept Utica Pub Lib, Utica NY 38-41, Asst hd circ dept 41-43; Adult libn Enoch Pratt Free Lib, Baltimore 43-44, Asst coord wk with ya 44-46; Br hd Dallas Pub Lib, Dallas Tex 46-47, Readers adv 47-52, Hd circ dept 52-55, Coord adult serv 55-58, Asst dir 58-61, Act dir 61-62, Dir 62-. 8: Bd of consuls, "Library Journal 62-63; Lib consul for vars bldgs and serv. 9: ALA (Coun 68-72; chm 4 coms 66-69); -ASD (sec 58-59, dir 62-65, v-pres 66-67, pres 67-68; chm 3 coms 60-69); -LAD (Friends of Libs Com 62-68; Pub Rel Sect: dir Exec Com 64-66); -PLA (mem 3 coms 63-69); TexLA (pres 64-65, chm &/or mem 5 coms 55-60); SWLA (Ed Bd 58-62); Friends of Tex Libs (corr sec 60-62, Adv Bd 63-65). 10: Assn for Grad Educ and Res in N Tex; Tex Munic League; Nat Lib Week; Dallas Co Commun Action Com; OEO; Beta Phi Mu; LWV; Zonta Club; Goals for Dallas Task Force. 11: Tex Libn of the Year Award 61. 13: Yes. 14: Adult serv, lib admin. 15: Dallas Pub Lib 1954 Commerce st, Dallas Tx 75201.

BRADSHAW, LUCY (LANEY) HYMAN. b Clinton NC 20 Jl 22. 4: Joseph Elton Bradshaw. 5: Winston-Salem State Col 39-43 (Elem Educ) BS; Atlanta 45-46 (LS) BS, 52, 53, 55 MSLS. 6: Fr. 7: Winston-Salem Tchrs Col: Lib sst 43-45, Asst libn 46-62, Act libn 62-63, Libn 63-. 9: ALA; NCLA. 10: Beta Phi Mu; Piedmont Univ Center of NC Inc. 14: Catlg, admin. 15: 442 26th st NW, Winston-Salem NC 27105.

BRADSHAW, RICHARD HENRY III. b Berkeley Cal 24 N 39. 4: Patricia Forster. 5: UCal at Berkeley 57-63 (Pol sci) AB, 64-65 (Educ) Secondary credential; USan Francisco & San Jose State Col 66-67 (LS) Credential; San Jose State Col 68-69 MLS. 6: Ital. 7: USA 445 Civil Affairs Co Ssg E-6 61-67 Field First Sgt; Sales, Reynolds Metals Co, San Francisco 63-64; Tchr DelValle High Sch, Walnut Creek Cal 65-67; Lib coordinator Reed Elem Sch Dist, Tiburon Cal 67-69. 8: Dir Title II Phase II Elem & Sec Educ Act, Exemplary Lib 67-68 Del Mar Middle School, Tiburon Cal Evaluator Title II Phase II Projects. 9: ALA; -AASchL; -YASD; CalTA; CalASL; Sch Libns Assn of Marin Co Cal (pres). 10: Marinwood Volunteer Fire Dept; East Bay Child Theater; Planned Parenthood League; Amer Red Cross Standard & Advanced First Aid Ski Patrol. 12: "The Underground Press in the United States". 14: Underground publ, censorship, a-v in sch libs. 15: 786 Idylberry rd, San Rafael Ca 94903.

BRADT, ELIZABETH JANE (PEASE). b Mineola NY 18 S 39. 4: Richard Carl Bradt. 5: Simmons 57-60 (LS); Chicago 60-61 BA, 62-63 (LS) MA. 7: Ed asst U Chicago Press "Library Quarterly" 61-62; Ref libn Skokie (Ill) Pub Lib 62-63; Child libn Delmar (NY) Pub Lib 63-64; Asst catlgr Russell Sage Col Lib 64-65; Libn NY State Off for Reg Development, Albany NY 65-67; Catlgr Penn State U Libs (U Pk) 68, Personnel libn 68-. 9: ALA; SLA; Coun of Planning Libns; PennLA. 10: Beta Phi Mu; AAUP. 13: Yes. 14: Personnel. 15: RD 1 Box 178A, Belleforte Pa 16823.

BRADY, BETTY ANN. b Salem Mass 9 My 36. 5: Fla State U 57-60 (LS) BA, 60-61 Lib Certif. 7: Lib stud asst Orlando Jr Col 55-56; Asst child libn Orlando Pub Lib, Orlando Fla 60-66, Lib aide III Child Dept 67-. 9: ALA; FlaLA. 10: Fla State U Alumni Assn; Fla State U Lib Sch Alumni Assn. 14: Wk with child & yp. 15: 1122 West Yates st, Orlando Fl 32804.

BRADY, SISTER ELIZABETH (MARIE). b El Paso Tex 1 S 14. 5: Immaculate Heart Col 42 (Hist) BA, 6 (LS) MA. 7: Immaculate Heart Col: Gifts & exch 57, Period Libn 58-60, Ref libn 60-65; Ref libn Xavier U (New Orleans) 65-66, Libn art dept 66-67; Asst libn commun action program Enoch Pratt Pub Lib, Baltimore 67, Admin asst 67; Asst libn-sel coord Federal City Col Media Ctr 68-. 8: Exhibit dir; immaculate Heart Col 60-65, Xavier U. 9: Cath LA; ALA; CalLA (Display consul 65-68). 10: Bk Discussion Leader. 12: "Eric Gill: Twentieth Century Book Designer (62). 13 Yes. 14: Fine printing, lib exhibits, ref. 15: 2401 H st NW, Washington DC 20037.

BRADY, GARY (EUELL). b Waxhaw NC 14 Ja 35. 5: Queens Col 53-57 (Eng, Hist) BA; Winthrop Col 60-61 (LS). 6: Fr. 7: Tchr & libn Waxhaw High Sch, Waxhaw NC 57-60; Libn Hartsell High Sch, Concord NC 60-66; Libn Pub Lib of Charlotte & Mecklenburg Co summers 64-68; Libn Central Cabarrus High Sch, Concord NC 66-. 9: NEA; NCEA; NCLA; SELA. 10: Carolinas Genealogical Soc; West Hist Soc; Waxhaws Hist Festival & Drama Assn; Union co Republican Exec Com. 14: Y-p bks, ref, catlg. 15: Rt 5 Box 488, Concord NC 28025.

BRADY, JAMES J. b Cincinnati 1 S 23. 4: Marilyn Huedepohl. 5: Xavier U 46-50 (Physics) BS. 7: USMC 43-45 Ord Sgt; Gen Electric, Cincinnati; Engnr asst 50-51, Tech writer 52-53, Supv acquis & processing 53-60, Supv tech documents 61-64, Manager FPD Tech Info Center 64-. 9: ASIS, Amer Soc for Metals; AIAA. 13: Yes. 14: Info mgt. 15: General Electric Co Bldg 700 N-32, Cincinnati 45215.

BRADY, LILA. b Indianapolis 21 Mr 26. 5: Ind U 45-48 (Hist) BA; UWis 48-49 (Hist) MA; UIll 53-54 (LS) MS; Ind U 61-66 (Journalism) MA. 7: Ref asst Ind State Lib 49-54, Ref libn 54-58; Pub rels libn Indianapolis Pub Lib 58-68; Asst dir Lake Co (Ind) Pub Lib 68-. 9: ALA; LPRC; IndLA;Adult Educ Coun Ind; AEAUSA; Pub Rels Soc of Amer. 10: Beta Phi Mu; Theta Sigma Phi;Nat Fed of Press Women; Pi Sigma Alpha; Woman's Press Club Ind; Lake Co Adult EducCoord Coun. 12: Ed "Library Occurrent," Ind State Lib (55-58 & 60-63). 13: Yes. 14: Pub rel, admin, adult educ. 15: Lake Co Pub Lib, 221 W Ridge rd, Griffith In 46319.

BRADY, LYNN ANN (STRASSBURGER). b NYC 26 Jl 42. 4: Arthur Daniel. 5: Col of New Rochelle 60-64 (Sociol) BA; St John'sU 64-67 MLS. 6: Fr. 7: Libn Nanuet Middle Sch, Nanuet NY 67-. 9: ALA. 14: Sch lib wk. 15: Bldg 8L Jeanne Marie apts, nanuet NY 10954.

BRADY, SISTER MARION CSJ MA. b Denver Colo 5 Ap 19. 5: Fontbonne Col 39-53 (Sociol) BA; Col of St Teresa summers 46-48; UIll summer 54; Col of St Catherine summers 55-59 (Libnship) MA. 7: Tchr of deaf St Joseph Inst for Deaf, St Louis Mo 42-47; Elem tchr: Immaculate Conception Sch, St Joseph Mo 47-50, Nativity Sch, St Louis Mo 50-52, St Cecilia Sch, Peoria Ill 52-54, St Marys Sch, Peoria Ill 54-58; Tchr-libn Reicher High Sch, Waco Tex 58-67; Libn St Josephs Acad, St Louis Mo 67-. 8: Org elem sch libs, Waco Tex 66-67; Org Central Lib for St Josephs Inst for Deaf; Sect for trainees in deaf educ, adult bks, child bks summers 68 & 69. 9: ALA; CathLA; Greater St Louis Lib Club. 14: High sch. 15: 2307 So Lindbergh blvd, St Louis Mo 63131.

BRADY, MARLENE ROSE (NORQUIST). b Klamath Falls Ore 18 Ap 32. 4: Remus LeMoyne Brady. 5: UOre 50-54 (Secondary Educ) BS; UPortland 60-64 MLS, summer 66. 7: Tchr-libn Molalla Union High Sch, Molalla Ore 54-57, Tchr 59-60, Libn 60-. 8: Lib consul for State Dept of Accreditation. 9: NEA-DAVI; OreEA; OreLA; OreSchLA. 10: Willamette Valley Knife and Fork Club. 14: Ref, bk sel, accessions. 15: 1029 Johnson st, Oregon City Or 97045.

BRADY, MARY FRANCES. b NYC. 5: Hunter Col 19 BA; Columbia 22 MA, 58 (LS) MS. 7: Libn David A Boody Jr High Sch, Brooklyn NY 30-53; Tchr of lib James Madison High Sch, Brooklyn NY 53-67; Asst examiner NYC Bd of Educ 67-. 67; Asst examiner NYC Bd of Educ 67-. 9: ALA; NYLA; NYC Sch Libns Assn (pres 60-62); NY Lib Club. 12: "New York City, Yesterday, Today and Tomorrow", Bibliog (39). 14: Ya bks. 15: 3900 Kings highway, Brooklyn NY 11234.

BRADY, MARY T. b New York NY 8 Ag 20. 5: Hunter Col 38-42 (Eng) BA; Pratt Inst 43-44 BLS. 7: Clk stenographer NYC Pub Lib 42; Libn Mott Haven, Bronx Ref Ctr & Highbridge Brs, NYC 44-48; Sr libn Tremont, Ft Wash & Br ref specialist with off of Adult Serv, Francis Martin Br 49-62; Supv libn Francis Martin Reg Br 62-67; Telephone ref serv Mid-Manhattan Lib 67-. 9: ALA; SLA; CathLA. NYLA; NY Lib Club. 14: Ref. 15: 8 E 40 st, New York NY 10016.

BRADY, SHIRLEY M. b St Paul 24 My 26. 5: Col of St Catherine 44-48 (Eng) BA; UMinn 50-51 BS in LS. 7: St Paul Pub Lib; Asst Riverview br 51-54, Asst child room 54-62, Head of child room 62-63, Libn 64-. 14: Child & ya. 15: 957 Goodrich ave, St Paul Mn 55105.

BRAGER, BEVERLY J. b Mt Horeb Wis 17 D 28. 5: UWis 46-50 (Eng) BA, 50-51 (LS) MA. 7: Catlgr Gilbert M Simmons Lib, Kenosha Wis 51-53, Ref libn 53-59; Br libn Madison Pub Lib, Madison Wis 59-60, Asst supv of home reading div 61-63, Young adult libn 63-64, Supv art & music div 65-. 9: ALA; WisLA (chm Adult Serv Div). 10: AAUW; Madison Art Assn; Wis Arts Found & Coun. 14: Adult serv. 15: 556 Glen dr, Madison Wis 53711.

BRAHM, WALTER THOMAS. b Massillon Ohio 9 O 10. 4: Estelle Hudson. 5: West Res 28-32 (Ger) AB, 33 BLS. 7: Stud asst Pub Lib, Massillon Ohio 24-25; Stud asst West Res U 28-33, Ref staff 33-37; Head Sci & Tech Dept Pub Lib, Toledo Ohio 37Asst dir 38-42; State libn State Lib, Columbus Ohio 42-64; State libn State Lib, Hartford Conn 64-. 8: Tchr, ref & admin courses West Res ULib Sch 36; Conceived & initiated survey of Ohio Libs by Lib Survey Commsn appointed by Ohio Legis, 45; Suggested plan for statewide libsurvey in Conn 66; Surveyed var pub & co libs in Penn, Ohio, NJ 49-61; Lib bldg surveys of 7 Ohio pub libs 45-60. 9: ALA-AAStateL (past pres);OhioLA; ConnLA; NELA. 10: Alpha Tau Omega. 11: Named Outstanding Libn of Year by OhioLA, 59; Lib Bdg Inst Award for lib devel, 60; OhioanaLAAward for meritorious serv, 61. 12: Auth or co-auth of 7 reg or pub libs surveys (49-64) and of 7 bldg surveys (45-61); Comp "Index ofPublications of Western Reserve University" (37); Ed "News from the Ohio State Library" (56-63). 14: Lib legis, org & mgt, lib bldgs,innovative lib devel progs. 15: 96 Wildwood rd, W Simsbury Ct 06092.

BRAIG, CHRISTIAN C. b NYC 2 Ap 41. 4: . 5: Moravian Col 58-62 BA; Moravian Theol Sem 62-63; Drexel 63-64 MLS. 6: Ger. 7: Catlg libn Drew U Lib 64-66; Catlgr Cedar Crest Col 66-. 9: ALA; ATheolLA. 14: Catlg. 15: 207 W Lexington st, Allentown Pa 18103.

BRAIN, E PATRICIA. b Detroit 2 Ap 25. 5: Flint Jr Col 43-44; Mich State U 44-47 (Psych) BA, 47-48 (Educ) State Secondary Certif; UMich 50-51 (Educ) MA, 59-60 MALS. 7: Eng tchr Flint Bd of Educ, Flint Mich 48-50, 51-59, Libn 60-. 9: ALA; MichEA; MichLA; MichASchL. 10: Del to State Republican Convention 52,56,65; Pi Lambda Theta; Beta Phi Mu; Flint Lib Club; Flint Republicans Club; Del to Nat Confof Repub Women in Wash DC 68-69. 14: High sch libs. 15: 720 W Hamilton ave, Flint Mi 48504.

BRAINARD, EDITH MAE. b Grant Twp, Guthrie Co Iowa. 5: State U Iowa 23-27 (Span) BA, 27-28 (Span, Eng Lit) MA; UMinn 31-32 (LS) BS; Chicago 44-45 (LS). 6: Sp. 7: Libn Pub Lib, Eldora Iowa 33-36; Libn Southestern Col 36-42; Libn Itasca Jr Col 42-43; Libn Gustavus Adolphus Col 43-44; Libn Ill Wesleyan U 45-47; Libn Millikin U 47-51; Ref libn John McIntire Lib, Zanesville Ill 52-53; Libn McKinley Mem Lib, Niles Ohio 53-. 8: Lecturer Catlg UMinn Lib Sch, summers 37-42; Served on var coms of state lib assns in Kansas Ill. 9: KanLA (pres 40-41, var coms); IllLA (chm sev coms of Col Sect). 10: Bus & Prof Women's Club; Mayor's Com on Comic Bks; Girl Scout Coun; Trustee, Trumbull Art Guild, Gilmer Howse, Warren Ohio. 13: Yes. 14: Admin, personnel. 15: 412 Brown st, Niles Oh 44446.

BRAINARD, ELSIE KATHERINE. b Boston 30 D 35. 5: Bridgewater State Col 53-57 (Soc Studies) BS in Ed; Rutgers 59-61 MLS. 6: Sp, Russian. 7: Elem tchr Bd of Educ, Calexico Cal 57-58; Preprof asst Pub Lib, boston 58-59; Traine Pub Lib, Newark NJ 59-61; Libn Bd of Educ, Bridgewater-Raritan NJ 61-. 9: NJ Sch LA; NJLA. 10: LWV; IRA. 14: Child wk. 15: 180A Cedar lane, Highland Park NJ 08904.

BRAITHWAITE, MARY ANNE (KNUTH) (DOLAN). b Pittsburgh Penn 7 Jl 36. 4: Dale Edward Braithwaite. 5: Chatham Col 54-58 (Chem) BS; UPittsburgh 63-66 MLS. 6: Ger. 7: Jr engr Westinghouse Researchm Pittsburgh Penn 58-59; Research asst Penn StateU 59-61; Act libn PPG Ind, Pittsburgh Penn 62-64, Tech serv libn 67-. 9: SLA. 10: Berkeley hills Parents Assn Lib (chm); Beta Phi Mu. 14: Tech vocabulary & Thesaurus 441 Woodland rd Berkeley Hills, Pittsburgh Pa 15237.

BRAMBLE, ANNABELLE FURMAN. b Charleston SC 23 D 12. 4: Geoffrey Stephens Bramble. 5: Col of Charleston 31-35 (Hist) AB; UIll 35-36 BS in LS. 7: Libn Med Col of SC 36-49; Asst libn Wright-Patterson Air Force Field, Dayton Ohio 50; Med libn Atomic Bomb Casualty Commsn, Hiroshima 50-52; Head br lib Sutherland Co, Sydney Australia 53-56; Lib consul schs, Charleston SC 57-58; Lib consul schs State Lib NJ 59-61; Head tech serv pub lib, Princeton NJ 61-64, Asst dir 65-. 9: ALA; NJLA. 14: Catlg. 15: Pub Lib 65 Witherspoon st, Princeton NJ 08540.

BRAMEYER, CHRISTINE (MATHIS). b Fountain City Wis 7 F 16. 4: Henry A Brameyer. 5: St Olaf Col 33-37 9eng) AB; State U Iowa 37-38 (Eng) AM; UMinn 47-49 BS in LS; Bread Loaf Sch of Eng summer 45; Columbia U Tchrs Col summer 54; Loyola U (Chicago) 55; Chicago Tchrs Col 61-62; Fla Inst for Continuing U Studies 62-64 Rosary Col summer 68. 6: Ger. 7: Instr, Asst Prof Dept of Eng Augustana Col (Sioux Falls SD) 39-47; Jr libn acquis dept UMinn Libs (Minneapolis) 47-49; Libn VA Hosp, Northport LI NY 49-50; Biol libn UChicago 50-54; Libn prof Lib Bd of Educ, Chicago 54-62; Libn Pasadena Elem Sch, St Petersburg 62-65; Libn Senn High Sch, Chicago 65-66; Libn Waller High Sch, Chicago 66-6; Catlglibn Div of Libs, Bd of Educ 68-. 9: ALA; NEA; ChicagoEA. 10: Alpha Delta Kappa; Bus & Prof Women's

Club. 14: Sch lib wk, catlg. 15: 5630 N Sheridan rd,Chicago Il 60626.

BRAMLEY, MARY (BAILEY). b Dorchester Mass 26 My 21. 4: David Lewis Bramley. 5: Simmons 39-43 (LS) BS. 6: Fr, Ger. 7: Reviser Simmons Sch of Lib Sci 43-44; Libn US Naval Training Center, Bainbridge Md 45; Catlgr Enoch Pratt Free Lib, Baltimore 45-46; Libn Eunice Thompson Lib, No Woburn Mass 60-; Catlgr woburn Pub Lib, Woburn Mass 62-. 14: Catlg. 15: 13 Kendal dr, N Woburn Ma 01801.

BRANBURY, J ARTHUR III. b Banbury England 24 D 30. 5: Leeds 55-58 (LS) Certif; Sorbonne 50-54 (Fr Lot) Bachelors. 6: Fr, Hebrew, Gaeolic. 7: Circ libn co lib, Shropshire England 59-61; Bkmob libn co lib, Surrey England 61-63; Hd libn St Charles Sem, Liege Belgian 63-65; Libn Inst for Advancement of Diabetic Research, Hershey Penn 65-66; Lib consul, Paradise Penn 67-. 8: Consul to Formosa govt on project for intercontinental lib loan 67; Research & lib recruitment for Slippery Rock State Col 68; Consul on establishing boat-mobile libs in outer islands of Bahamas 68. 9: BLA; PSLA. 10: Intl Clasf Org; CARE Pkg Inst. 13: Yes. 14: Interlib loan, bkmob serv. 15: RFD 1, Paradise Pa 17562.

BRANCH, BENJAMIN HARRISON JR. b Leesburg Va 27 Ag 19. 4: Marjorie Lee Browne. 5: Guilford Col 39-43 (Hist) BS; Drexel 47-48 BS in LS; UIll Lib Sch 51-52 (LS) MS. 7: Farm wker; Overlea Farm, Hamilton Va 43; Overlook Orchards, Leesburg Va 43-47;Stud asst Presbyterian Hist Soc, Phila 47-48; Reserve room libn UMiami(Fla) 48-49,Asst acquis libn 49-51; Jr sci & tech asst Ill Water Survey, Urbana Ill 52; Asstlibn Friends Hist Lib, Swarthmore Penn 52-53; Asst libn UMd 53; US Geol Survey,Wash DC; Libn binding 54-55, Libn asst acquis 55-58, Libn order wk 58-61, Libnacquis phys sci & engnr 61-63; George Washington U Circ asst 63-66, Ref asst 63-. 8: Chm Com on Periodical Problems US Dept of the Interior, First Biennial Dept-WideLib Conf, 64; Chm ser panel US Dept of the Interiod, 3rd Biennial Depart Lib Wkshop68. 9: ALA-ACRL. 10: Mem Permanent Bd, Baltimore Yearly Meeting (orthodox) 46-65. 12: "The Branch, Harris, Jarvis, and Chinn Book: A Family Outline" (64). 14: Acquis, admin, ref. 15: Apt 68, 5800 N Sixteenth st, Arlington Va 22205.

BRANCH, OLIVE HARLLEE. b Clinton SC 5 F 13. 5: Converse Col 29-33 (Eng) AB; Emory 33-34 BS in LS. 7: Libn High Sch, LaFollette Tenn 34-35; Libn High Sch, Spartanburg SC 35-41; Catlgr Duke U 41-42; Libn Post Lib, Ft Moultrie SC 42-45; Libn Army of Occupation, Germany 45-46; UTenn: Asst circ libn 47, Head order dept 48-63, Acquis libn 63-. 9: ALA; SELA; TennLA. 14: Acquis. 15: Lib Univ of Tenn, Knoxville Tenn 37916.

BRANCH, MRS RUTILLIA (EUBANK). b Seminole Tex 12 My 09. 4: DeWitt Branch. 5: Tex Tech Col 25-29 (Eng) BA; UIll 29-30 BS in LS. 7: Stud asst Tex Tech Lib 26-29; Libn Lubbock Co Lib Tex 30-32, Runnells Co Lib, Ballinger Tex 33-34, Midland Co Lib, Midland Tex summer 34; Catlgr Kemp Pub Lib, Wichita Falls Tex 34-. 14: Catlg, ref, state & loc hist. 15: 1805 Polk st, Wichita Falls Tx 76309.

BRANCH, REBECCA (ROGERS). b Mullins SC 7 My 1900. 4: Chester Wilder Branch. 5: Coker Col 18-20; UTex 37-38 (Span) AB; Peabody summers 53, 57, 58 (LS) MA. 6: Sp. 7: Missionary So Baptist Foreign Missions, Mexico 22-36; Tchr Demmit Co Sch Bd, Carrizo Springs Tex 38-41; Tchr Hillsborough Co Bd of Pub Inst, Tampa Fla 41-67. 8: Military Intelligence World War II. 9: NEA; FlaEA; FlaLA; Fla Hist Soc. 15: Rt 2 Box 762, Plant City Fl 33566.

BRAND, BARBARA (BERGER). b San Antonio Tex. 4: Douglas L Brand. 5: Swarthmore 60-64 (Hist) BA; UWis 64-65 (LS) MA. 6: Fr. 7: Lib intern circ Columbia U 65-66, Asst libn Sch of Lib Serv Lib 66-68; Ref libn Undergrad Lib UNC (Chapel Hill) 68-69. 8: Organized and first president of Nu Chapter, Beta Phi Mu at Columbia 67. 9: ALA. 10: Beta Phi Mu. 14: Ref, bibliogr. 15: Colony Apts A-1, Chapel Hill NC 27514.

BRAND, MRS MARVINE (McNEIL). b Philadelphia Miss 16 Ja 26. 4: Johnnie L Brand. 5: UMiss 43-46 (Chem) BA. 6: Ger. 7: Asst libn res & development div Amer Oil Co, TEXAS City Tex 46-52, Libn 52-63; Sci libn Rice U Lib 63-68; Admin asst to asst dir pub serv UHouston Lib 69-. 9: ACS; SLA (Tex Chap: Employment Com, 3rd v-pres). 10: Delta Gamma; Houston Lib Club; Beta Beta Beta. 14: Sci ref. 15: University of Houston Lib, Cullen Boulevard, Houston Tx 77004.

BRANDELL, GERTRUDE AVEY. b Cincinnati 21 F 1900. 5: UCincinnati 21-28; Miami U 26; Chicago even 52-58. 7: Br libn College Hill Lib, Cincinnati Pub Lib 21-23, Br libn Price Hill Lib 23-28; Br libn Howen Sch, Evanston Ill; Pub Lib 28-37, Br libn South Br 37-65; Lib asst Educ Dept Cincinnati Pub Lib 65-66, Br libn Price Hill & Overlook Brs 66-. 9: ALA; IllLA (past offr & mem personnel com); OhioLA. 10: Ill League of Municipal Employees. 13: Yes. 14: Circ. 15: 1640 Rockford pl, Cincinnati Oh 45223.

BRANDES, JUDITH. b NYC. 4: Mack Brandes. 5: NYU 48-52 (Educ) BS; Pratt 55-56 MLS; Columbia 64-66 (Supv & Curriculum Improvement) Prof Diploma. 6: Fr, Jewish. 7: Sales R H Macy, NYC 30-33; Tchr Brooklyn Kindergarten Soc, Brooklyn NY 48-52; Tchr Neighborhood Playhouse, Brooklyn NY 52-53; Tchr Long Beach Schs, Long Beach NY 53-55; Libn Long Beach Pub Lib, Long Beach NY 55-56; Sch libn Island Park Schs, Island Park NY 56-. 8: Lib consul on curriculum revis coms for Island Park schs. 9: ALA; NEA; NYLA; NY State Tchrs Assn; Nassau-Suffolk SchLA. 10: Island Park Facult Assn. 14: Org libs, supervisor. 15: 186 Washington ave, Island Park NY 11558.

BRANDES, JULIAN. b Cincinnati 19 Je 16. 5: UCincinnati 34-38 (Ger) BA; UMih 47-48 ABLS. 6: Ger, Fr. 7: Asst ref libn & readers adv Pub Lib of Cincinnati 39-55; Ref libn UHouston Lib 55-62, Educ & bus admin libn 63-66, Asst humanities libn 67-. 9: ALA; TexLA; SWLA; Tex Assn Col Tchrs. 10: Houston Lib Club; AAUP; Sunday Evening Club. 13: Yes. 14: Ref. 15: Univ of Houston Lib, Cullen blvd, Houston Tx77004.

BRANDHORST, WESLEY THEODORE. b Portland Ore 9 My 33. 4: Jane Smythe. 5: UCal(Berkeley) 51-55 (Eng) BA, 56-57 MLS; American U 58- (Anthropology). 6: Fr. 7: Spec intern & ref libn LC 57-59; Info systems analyst Documentation Inc, Bethesda Md 59-62; Manager ref dept & chief catlg div NASA Sci & Tech Info Facility, College Park d 62-64, Asst dir for user serv 65-68; Principal info scientist Leasco Sys & Res Corp 69-. 8: SLA Repres on AFIPS Pub Info Com 69-. 9: SLA; ASIS; ALA. 10: AAAS; Amer Anthropol Assn. 11: Spec Intern, LC, 57. 13: Yes. 14: Ref, info retr, lib automation, standards, coop networks. 15: 10902 Jolly way, Kensington Md 20795.

BRANDON, ALFRED N(ORTHRUP). b Ogden Utah 10 S 22. 4: Mabel L Pomeroy. 5: Atlantic Union Col 40-45 (Theol) THB; Syracuse 47-48 (LS) BS; UIll 50-51 (LS) MS; UMich 54-56 (Hist) MA. 06: Fr, Ger. 7: Asst libn Atlantic Union Col 46-48, Head libn 48-52; Libn Transportation Lib UMich 52-53; Head libn Loma Linda U 53-57; Visiting lecturer Syracuse U Lib Sch summers 50, 52-55; Head libn UKy Med Center 57-63; Dir & libn Welch Med Lib Johns Hopkins U 63-69; Chm & Prof Dept Lib Sci Mt Sinai Sch Med 69-. 8: Med lib consul to Temple Sch of Med, URochester Med Center, Pan Amer Health Org, Nat Insts of Health, Mich State U, NLM. 9: MedLA (pres 65-66); SLA; ALA. 10: Pi Lambda Sigma; Beta Phi Mu. 12: "Checklist of Periodical Titles Currently Received in Medical Libraries in the Southern Region" (60); Ed "Bulletin of the Medical Library Association" (61-69). 13: Yes. 14: Med libnship, admin & org, hist of med. 15: Dept Lib Sciences, Mt Sinai Sch of Med, 5th ave & 100th st, New York NY 10029.

BRANDON, WANDA (JANEL). b Anson Tex 26 Jl 41. 5: Tex Woman's U 59-63 (LS) BS summer 66 & 67; East NM U Ext 65 & 68. 7: YA libn Abilene Pub Lib, Abilene Tex 63-64; Elem & jr high libn Eunice Municipal Schs, Eunice NM 64-. 9: ALA; NEA; NMLA; NMEA; Lea Co LA; EuniceEA. 10: Beta Sigma Phi. 14: Ref, y-a lit, child lit. 15: Box 1369, Eunice NM 88231.

BRANDT, ELEANOR (MARY). b Lakewood Ohio 13 N 10. 5: Oberlin 28-32 (Eng) AB; West Res 32-33 BS in LS. 7: Circ asst Akron Pub Lib, Akron Ohio 33-35; Libn Franklin Sylvester Lib, Medina Ohio 35-43; USNR (WAVES) Lt(jg) Comm Intell, Wash DC 43-45; Contact & admin div VA Dist Off, Dallas 46-47; Chief libn VA Hosp, Dallas 47-. 9: ALA (var coms). 10: Pilot Club of Dallas (offs). 14: Hosp lib serv. 15: 7806 Greenway blvd Apt 61, Dallas 75209.

BRANDT, JUDITH ANN. b Steubenville Ohio 12 Je 34. 5: Ohio U 52-56 (Govt & Pol Sci) AB; Ohio No U Col of Law 56-59 LLB; West Res 58 (LS). 7: Law libn William Mitchell Col of Law 5-60; Law Ed Bobbs-Merrill Co law div, Indianapolis 60-64; Law libn Ohio No U 64-. 9: AALL; OhioRALL. 10: AAUW; AAUP; Delta Zeta Kappa Beta Pi. 14: Legal research legal writing, law lib admin. 15: 709 -/2 S Gilbert st, Ada Oh 45810.

BRANDT, WILLIAM REED. b NYC 25 Ap 18. 4: Mary Atlee Brandt. 5: Hamilton Col 35-39 (Lit) AB; Columbia 41 BLS. 6: Fr. 7: Ref asst NY Pub Lib 41-43; US Army 43-46; Photographic serv div NY Pub Lib 46-49; Asst libn University Club Lib, NY 49-52; Head Libn Lane Lib Ripon Col 52-. 9: ALA (Life mem); -ACRL; WisLA (mem &/or chm various coms). 10: Friends of Wis Libs. 14: Admin, tech serv. 15: Lane Lib Ripon Col, Ripon Wi 54971.

BRANNER, SHIRLEY (PRAGER). b Providence 13 Jl 28. 4: Robert Branner. 5: Pembroke 45-49 (Music) BA; Yale 49-54 (Music Hist) MA; Columbia 57-58 (LS) MS. 6: Fr, Ger. 7: Circ attendant Yale U Music Lib 50-53, Ref libn 53-54; Catlgr UKan Lib 54-57; Catlgr & asst libn Juilliard Sch of Music (NYC) 58-61; Catlgr Columbia U 62; Indexer Soc of Arch Histns, NY 64-. 9: Internat Assn of Mus Libs; ALA; Amer Musicological Soc; MusLA (Publs Com, Bibliog Chm NY Chap); NY Tech Serv Libns. 10: Dir Columbia Com for Commun Serv. 14: Catlg. 15: 440 Riverside dr, apt 62, NYC 10027.

BRANSCOMB, LEWIS C APERS JR. b Birmingham Ala 5 Ag 11. 4: Marjorie Stafford. 5: Birmingham-So Col 29-30 (Pre-Med); Duke U 30-33 (Eng) AB; UMich 38-39 ABLS, 39-41 AMLS; Chicago 45-47 PhD. 6: Fr, Ger. 7: Clerk Young & Vonn Supply Co, Birmingham Ala 33-38; Head order dept UGa 39-41; Libn Mercer U 41-42; Libn & Prof of Lib Sci USCar 42-44; Asst dir of pub serv & Assoc Prof of Lib Sci UIll(Urbana) 44-48; Assoc Dir of Libs & Prof of Lib Admin Ohio State U 45&r of Libs Admin 52-. 8: Lib consul to Punjab Agric Univ, Ludhiana Punjab India 67; Ohio Lib/ brmingham-So Col 29-30 (Pre-Med); Duke U 30-33 (Eng) AB; UMich 38-39 ABLS, 39-41 AMLS; Chicago 45-47 PhD. 9: ALA (chm Nomin Com 54-55); -ACRL (Dir 53-55, pres 58-59); chm Academic Status Com, ULS); MILC, now CRL (Bd Dirs 53-, chm 61-62); OhioLA (chm Col & Univ Sect 52-53, chm Adminrs RT); Inter-Univ Lib Coun. 10: ACLU; AAUP; Torch Club; Crichton Club; Faculty Club; Ohio Hist Soc; UN Assn of US; Ohio Com to Abolish Capital Punishment; Sigma Alpha Epsilon; Beta Phi Mu; Bd Trustees Ohio Col Lib Ctr. 12: 'Ernest Cushing Richardson' in "Pioneering Leaders in Librarianship" (53); 'Library specialization through Institutional Specialzation' in "Problems and Prospects of the Research Library. 13: Yes. 14: Admin, personnel, lib resources, faculty status. 15: 1858 Neil ave, Columbus Oh 43210.

BRANSON, BARBARA. b Raleigh NC 14 Ap 38. 5: Wake Forest Col 56-60 (Sociol) BA; UNC 60-62 MS in LS. 6: Fr. 7: Descr catlgr Duke U 62-. 10: Beta Phi Mu; AAUW; Phi Beta Kappa. 14: Catlg. 15: 708 Louise circle, Durham NC 27705.

BRANSTETTER, EVELYN (HUESTIS). b Lincoln Neb 11 S 11. 4: Neil V Branstetter. 5: Neb Wesleyan U 28-30; UNeb 30-32 (Hist) BS in Educ, 33-34 (Hist) MA; UDenver 57 (LS) MA. 6: Fr, Sp. 7: Instr Balboa Jr High Sch, Balboa CZ 37-42; Instr Beatrice & Syracuse Neb High Schs 34, 35, 42; Instr UNeb Tchrs Col 43; Instr Balboa High Sch, Balboa CZ 43-44; Libn & insr CZ Jr Col 44-47; Libn US Army Caribbean, Ft Clayton CZ 50-51; Command libn USAF Southern Command, Albrook AFB CZ 51-64; Hdqrs libn Air Force Systems Command, Andrews AFB 64-, Command libn 68-. 9: ALA; SLA (sec-treas Mil Lib Div 65-66); DCLA; Internat Platform Assn. 10: Assn of Grad Libns of the Isthmus of Panama (charter mem); Ky Hist Soc. 14: Lib admin, mil libs. 15: 7447 Gwyndale dr, Clinton Md 20735.

BRANYAN, BRENDA MAY (BERTELSEN). b Coloma Mich 16 Jl 32. 4: Rollin U Branyan Jr. 5: Benton Harbor Commun Col 50-52 AA; West Mich U 52-54 (LS) BA, 66-67 MLS. 6: Fr. 7: Sch libn Highland Jr High Sch Lakeview Sch Dist, Battle Creek Mich 54-69; Instr Lib Sci West Ill U 69-. 8: Admin asst Higher EducInst for Sch Lib Personnel, West Mich U summer 68; Consul Jr High Sch Lib CatlgH W Wilson co NYC; Instr Dept of Lib, West Mich U summer 69. 9: NEA; MichASchL;MichEA; Mich A-V Assn; ALA. 10: Beta Phi Mu. 14: Instr materials, lib orientation for yp. 15: Mem Lib, West Ill Univ, MacombIl 61455.

BRASHER, ROBERT E JR. b Henderson Tex 28 S 20. 4: Marilyn Belle (De Lonjay) Brasher. 5: Mangum Jr Col 38-40; Okla City U 46-48 (Eng) BA; UDenver 49-50, 54 (LS) MA. 6: Fr, Russian, Ital, Ger. 7: Clarinetist-clerk (Sgt) US Army (45th Inf Div Band), US, Sicily, Italy, France, Germany 40-45; Postman us post Off, Okla City Okla 46-49; Catlg libn Sonoma Co Free Lib, Santa Rosa Cal 50-55; Catlg libn Whittier Pub Lib, Whittier Cal 55-56; Ser catlg libn Cal State Col (Long Beach) 56-. 9: CalLA (chm Tech Proc Round Table 59-60); SoCal Reg Tech Proc Group; Mem & offr var Cal State Col (Long Beach) Lib coms & staff orgs. 14: Catlg, ref. 15: 6855 Driscoll st, Long Beach Ca 90815.

BRATTON, JOHN THOMAS. b Camden Ark 17 O 33. 4: Grace E Kojima. 5: Hendrix Col 51-55 (Li & Philos) AB; LSU 55-58 60-62 (LS) MS; UColo 63-65 (Hist). 6: Fr. 7: Lib trainee LSU Lib 55-57, Catlgr 57-58; US Army Adjutant Gen's Corps Personnel spec Sp4 58-60; Catlgr LSU Lib 60-63; Catlgr UColo 63-65, Head order dept 65-66; Catlgr URochester (NY) 66-67; Acquis Libn Ida State U 67-68; Ser libn UDenver 68-69, Hd acquis-ser dept 69-. 9: ALA; NEA (life mem); ColoLA. 10: AHA; AAUP. 14: Acquis, catlg. 15: UColo Libs Denver Co 80210.

BRATTON, ROSE (JOHNSON). b Richmond Ind 18 Mr 20. 4: Meredith Bratton. 5: IndU 38-42 (Pol sci) AB; Pratt Inst 67-68 MLS. 6: Fr. 7: Assoc Ed "Modern Packaging Magazine", NYC 48-51; Assoc Ed "American Exporter Magazine", NYC 52-53; Ed "McCall's Home Service Bulletin", NYC 53-59; Doc analyst Project URBANDOC, NYC 68-. 8: Consul Women's Activities Prog NYC 59-66. 9: SLA; ASIS; Coun of Planning Libns; Soc Arch Histns. 10: LWV; Elect Women's RT; Amer Women in Radio & TV. 14: Computerized bibliog tech, urban planning documentation, pictorial documentation. 15: 3 Peter Cooper rd, New York NY 10010.

BRAUCHER, JANE ELLIOTT. b NY 20 F 30. 5: UPenn 47-50 (Sci); Duke U 56-57 BS; Catholic U 59-61 MS in LS; American U Law Sch 63-64 (Law). 6: Fr, Sp, Swedish. 7: Pub health & welfare wk -59; Asst libn Mil AssistanceInst, Arlington Towers Va 59-61; Asst libn Securities & Exchange Commsn, Wash DC61-65; Libn All Souls Church (Unitarian), Wash DC 62-64; Chief legal & legis refPentagon 65-69; Chief Fed Highway Admin Lib 69-; Instr in Lib Sci Grad Sch, Dept ofagric 66-. 9: ALA; SLA (v-chm Soc Sci DC chap 63-); AALL. 10: Sidwell Tennis Club;Corcoran Gallery; Racquet Club. 12: Ed "Law Library Lights," Wash DC 65-66; Auth"Introduction to Cataloging Workbook, 1967". 14: Ref, admin. 15: 2512 Q st NW, Wash DC 20007.

BRAUDE, ROBERT MICHAEL. b Los Angeles 27 S 39. 4: Sharon Katz. 5: UCLA 57-62 (Psych) BA, 62-64 MA, 63-64 MLS. 6: Lat, Sp, Fr. 7: UCLA: Lib clerk Biomed Lib 57-61, Research asst Dept of Psych 61-63, Lib clerk William A Clark Lib 63-64, Libn I ref dept Biomed Lib 64-65, Libn II MEDLARS Biomed Lib 65-. 68; Assoc libn UColo Med Ctr Lib (Denver) 68-. 8: Lib consul, Allergan Pharmaceuticals, Santa Ana Cal 67. 9: MedLA; ColoLA. 14: Pub serv, systems analysis. 15: 4200 E 9th ave, Denver Co 80220.

BRAUDY, JUDITH (SIEGEL). b Brooklyn NY 4 Ja 45. 4: Robert S Braudy. 5: Harpur Col suny 9binghamton) 62-66 (Russian Lang & Lit) BA; Drexel 66-67 MSLS. 6: Russian, Fr. 7: Ref libn Free Lib of Phila NE Reg Lib 67-68; Adult serv libn Cherry Hill Free Pub Lib, Cherry Hill NJ 68-. 9: ALA; NJLA; Libs Unlimited, CamdenCoLA. 10: ACLU. 14: Adult serv, ref. 15: 277 White Horse pike, Audubon NJ 08106.

BRAULT, JEAN-REMI. b Verdun Que Can 16 S 26. 5: Col de Montreal 39-47 BA; Grand Seminaire de Montreal 47-51; UOttawa 59-61 (Hist) MA. 6: Fr, Eng. 7: Prof et dir de la bibliotheque, Seminaire Ste Theresa-de-Blainville 51-. 8: Dir-adjoint du Service des Bibliotheques de la Federation des Colleges classiques. 9: CanLA; Association canadienne des bibliothecaires de langue francaise (pres Sect des Colleges); QueLA. 13: Yes. 14: Ref. 15: College Lionel-Groulx, Sainte-Therese-De-Blainville, Cte TerrebonneQue Can.

BRAUN, CONSTANCE (TODD). b Flushing LI NY 12 Jl 31. 4: Louis Carl Braun. 5: Ind state Col (Ind Penn) 49-50 (Elem Educ); Geneva Col 63-65 (Elem Educ) BSEd; UPittsburgh 66-68 MLS. 6: Sp. 7: Libn Highland Sch Dist, Beaver Falls Penn 66-67; Juvenile & curriculum libn Geneva Col 68-. Child lit tchr 69-. 8: Establishing church lib for Col Hill Presbyterian Ch, Beaver Falls Penn 68-. 9: ALA; PennLA. 10: Beta Phi Mu. 15: 128 McLanahan dr, Beaver Falls Pa 15010.

BRAUN, LOIS BAKER. b Ravenna Neb 31 Jl 15. 4: Wendell Ayers Braun. 5: Neb Wesleyan U 31-32; Baker U 32-35 (Eng) BA; Kan State Col (Emporia) 35-36 (LS) 5th yr. 7: Child libn Kan City (Mo) Pub Lib 36-38; Prof sub Des Moines Pub Lib, Des Moines Iowa 56-58, Supv wk with child 58-. 9: ALA; IowaLA (pres Child Serv Div 59-60). 10: Alpha Chi Omega; PEO. 14: Wk with child. 15: 4005 Forest ave, Des Moines Ia 50311.

BRAVARD, ROBERT STATON. b Dayton Ohio 2 N 35. 4: Cynthia Ann Buttolph. 5: Wilmington Col 53-57 (Hist, Eng) BA; Syracuse57-59 MS in LS. 6: Fr. 7: Asst libn Findlay Col

59-60, Head libn 60-63; Asst libn, tech serv, Lock Haven State Col 63-. 9: PennLA. 10: Beta Phi Mu; Phi Alpha Theta; Sigma Tau Delta; Alpha Phi Gamma. 12: Consul for "Choice." 13: Yes. 14: Tech serv. 15: 205 N Fairview st, Lock Haven Pa 17745.

BRAWLEY, SISTER MARY ANNE. b Elizabeth NJ 19 My 34. 5: St Joseph Col 52-56 (Eng) AB; St John's U 61-66 MLS. 7: Tchr Queen of Peace Sch, Wash DC 56-61; Tchr E Seton High Sch, Bladensburt Md 61-63; Tchr St Joseph Col, Emmitsburg Md 67-69; Libn Seton High Sch, Endicott NY 63-. 9: ALA; CathLA; NYLA; So Tier Sch Libns. 10: WNBA. 14: Reading guidance. 15: 210 Madison ave, Endicott NY 13760.

BRAWLEY, PAUL LEROY. b Granite City Ill 27 S 42. 5: So Ill U 60-65 (Music, Eng) BA; Simmons 65-68 (LS); MS; UOkla 69 (LS). 6: . 7: Acquis asst So Ill U Lib 64-65; Rare bks asst Countway Med Lib, Boston 65; Boston Pub Lib; Recordings libn 65-66, A-v libn 66-69; Ed Nonprint Reviews The Bklist & Subs Bks Bull ALA, Chicago 69-. 9: ALA; EFLA; NEA-DAVI; Film Lib Info Coun; NELA. 10: Sigma Pi; Lambda Iota Tau; Phi Eta Sigma; Nat Geogr Soc. 14: A-v materials & bibliog control thereof, instr materials ctrs. 15: 166 E Superior st, Chicago Il 60611.

BRAWNER, LEE B. b Seguin Tex 1 My 35. 4: Nancy J Wallis. 5: Tex A&M U 53-55 (Personnel admin); No Tex State U 55-57 BALS; Peabody 61 MALS. 7: Prof asst lit & hist dept Dallas Pub Lib 57; 1 st asst Jefferson Br Lib, Dallas 57-58; Active duty with US Army Res, Ft Chaffee Ark 57-58; Head popular lib & circ dept Dallas Pub Lib 58-60; Libn Tenn State Lib & Archives 60-61; Head Lakewood Br Lib, Dallas 61-62; Dir Waco Pub Lib, Waco Tex 62-64; Chief of br serv Dallas Pub Lib 64-67; Asst state libn Tex State Lib 67-. 9: ALA (Sm Lib Proj Pub Com 68-69); SWLA (v-pres & pres-elect 68-70, loc arr chm 66); TexLA (Dist Planning Chm 68-70, chm Pub Lib Div 64, mem Legis Task Force Com 69; Memb Com 64-65, chm Standards for Tex Pub Libs Suppl 65). 10: Phi Epsilon; Alpha Lambda Sigma (pres 57); Friends of Tex Libs; Tex State Hist Assn; Amer Assn State & Loc Hist; Austin Soc Pub Admin. 14: Admin, bldg planning. 15: 2405 Loyola, Austin Tx 78723.

BRAY, MARGARET (MARY). b Saginaw, Mich 10 Ag 10. 5: UMich 28-32 (Lang) AB; Columbia 43 (LS) BS. 6: Ger, Fr. 7: Saginaw Pub Lib: Loan desk asst 33-38, Registration libn 38-40, Ref asst 40-46, Hd processing 46-. 9: ALA; MichLA. 10: Hosp Aux. 14: Catlg, ref. 15: 1155 So Warren ave, Saginaw Mi 48601.

BRAY, ROBERT STUART. b Cincinnati Oh 9 S 15. 4: Virginia Elizabeth Ballard. 5: George Washington University 33-41 Zoology BS; Catholic University of America 47-50 Library Science. 7: Page DC Pub Lib 35-40; messenger, deck attendant, Jr libn ref asst LC 40-44; Lt (jg) USN 44-46; Hd exchange section asst chief card div asst chief Navy research chief tech info div LC Wash DC 46-57; Chief div for Blind & Physically Handicapped LC 57-. 8: Adv Bd of Recording for the Blind Inc Bd of Trustees Amer Found for the Blind; Serv Adv Com to Amer Found for the Blind; Bd mem Nat Accreditation Coun on Agencies Serving the Blind & Visually Handicapped; Adv Bd Christian Record Braille Found; chm Lib Com, President's Com on Employment of the Handicapped. 9: ALA-AHIL (pres); Adult Educ Assn; Amer Assn of Homes for the Aging; Amer Assn of Instr of the Blind; Am Assn of Workers for the Blind; Amer Correctional Assn; Amer Pub Health Assn; Coun for Exceptional Child; National Assn of Physically Handicapped; National Braille Assn; National Multiple Sclerosis Soc; National Rehabilitation Assn; National Society for Prevention of Blindness. 10: Goose Creek Country Club. 11: Migel Medal for outstanding service to the blind, American Found for the Blind 63; Apollo Award for outstanding contribution to visual welfare of Amer people from Amer Optometric Assn 68; Francis Joseph Campbell Citation from ALA's Round Table on Library Service to the Blind for outstanding contribution to library service to blind persons 68. 14: Bks for handicapped persons. 15: Division for the Blind and Physically Handicapped, Lib of Congress, Washington DC 20542.

BRAZEE, EDWARD BROOKS. b Klamath Falls Ore 2 O 37. 4: Judy Frank. 5: UOregon 60-62 (Hist) BA; UWash 62-63 Master of Libnship. 7: USAF 56-59; Ref libn Oregon State U Lib 64-. 9: PNLA. 10: Sierra Club. 14: Ref. 15: 2131 NW 11th st, Corvallis Or 97330.

BRAZER, SHIRLEY. b Winnipeg Man Can 9 Ap 40. 5: UMan 57-62 BA; UOttawa 63-64 BLS. 7: Circ clerk United Col (Winnipeg) 62-63; Subprof Forest Hill Pub Lib, Toronto 63; Circ & ref libn Brandon Col (Man) 64-65; Boys & girls gen libn Etobicoke Pub Lib, Toronto 65-. 9: CanLA; OntLA. 14: Child wk in pub Lib. 15: Etobicoke Pub Lib 36 Brentwood rd N, Toronto 18 Can.

BREARLEY, ANNE (CLAYTON). b Blackburn England 13 O 26. 4: Neil Brearley. 5: UManchester 45-48 (Eng) BA (Hons); ALA (British Lib Assn) 56. 6: Fr. 7: Libn Research dept Tootal Broadhurst Lee Co Ltd, Manchester UK 51-56; Ref libn UBC 56-61; Head sci div UBC Lib 61-62; Info off Canadian Uranium Res Foundation 62-65; Hd soc sci div UBC Lib 65-66; Asst prof UBC Sch of Libnship 66-. 8: U of Victoria Lib summer 68; Nat Sci Lib Ottawa summer proj 67. 9: CanLA (chm Research & Spec Libs sect 68-69); ALA; BCLA; ABCL; SLA (PNM Chap Bd mem 66-67); AALS; CanALS. 10: UBC Fac Assn. 12: "Scientific Policy Research & Development in Canada: A Bibliography," Nat Sci Lib 68. 14: Sci/tech lit, ref, info serv, spec libs. 15: 1858 Quilchena Crescent Vancouver 13 BC Can.

BREAZEALE, MARY RUTLEDGE. b Verona Tenn 9 S 14. 4: William M Breazeale. 5: Vanderbilt (Hist) BA; Peabody BS in LS. 6: Fr. 7: Loan libn Vanderbilt U; Catlgr Widener Lib, Harvard U 41-45; Catlgr Penn State U 53-56; Readers consul Randolph-Macon Woman's Col 56-. 10: LWV; Lynchburg Pub Lib Bd; Head Start. 14: Ref. 15: Randolph-Macon Woman's Col, Lynchburg Va 24504.

BREAZNELL, MILDRED K. b Virginia Minn 17 F 08. 5: UMinn 26-28; Barnard Col 28-30 (Eng) BA; Columbia 32-33 BLS. 7: Libn Duluth Jr Col 34-35; Catlgr Eveleth Pub Lib, Eveleth Minn 40-41; 1st asst NY Pub Lib 41-42; Tech libn Army Air Force Train Aids Div 42-45; Head Libn First National City Bank, NYC 45-51; Pub rel libn Gen Motors Corp, NYC 52-58; Manager Standard & Poor's Corp Lib, NYC 60-. 9: SLA; Amer Stat Assn. 14: Admin. 15: 176 E 77th st, NYC 10021.

BRECKENRIDGE, KIT (SANDERSON). b Freeport Ill 18 N 39. 4: Lee Breckenridge. 5: BradleyU 57-61 (Eng, Math) BA; UIll 61-62 (LS) MA. 7: Child libn Free Lib of Phila 62-66, Hd central child dept 66-68, Hd bk selection off of wk with child 69-. 9: ALA; PennLA. 14: Child lit. 15: 1833 Lombard st, Philadelphia Pa 19146.

BREDEL, SISTER MARY ELVIRA OSF. 5: DePaul U (Chicago) -29 (Lat) AB; UIll(Urbana) -34 (LS) ABLS, -37 (LS, Eng) AM. 6: Ger, Fr. 7: Tchr St Francis Acad, Joliet Ill 24-26; Tchr St Mary's High Sch, Columbus Ohio 26-32; College of St Francis, Joliet Ill: Asst libn 32-39, Libn & Instr in Lib Sci 37-42, Libn & Asst Prof 42-48, Libn & Prof Lib Sci 48-53, Pres 53-62, Prof Lib Sci 62-. 9: ALA; CathLA (Ill Unit; pres 48-4 10: Beta Phi Mu. 13: Yes. 14: Bk sel. 15: Col of St Francis, Wilcox & Taylor sts, Joliet Il 60435.

BREED, CLARA E. b Fort Dodge Iowa 19 Mr 06. 5: Pomona Col 27 BA; West Res 28 (LS) BS. 7: San Diego Pub Lib: Child libn E San Diego Br 28-29, Supv libn 29-45, Act city libn 45-46, City Libn 46-. 8: Mem San Diego City & Co Centennials Commsn 50-51; Appointed by Governor to Pub Lib Devel Bd, State of Cal, 63-66; Adv Coun UCal Sch of Libnship, 56-60. 9: ALA (Coun 44-48 & 52-56; chm Sect for Lib Wk with Child 42); -LAD (Bd Dirs Sect on Lib Org & Mgt 60-62; mem Adv Com for Studies in Pub Lib Serv to Child 58-65); -PLA (pres 62-63 & many com duties); Pub Lib Execs Assn So Cal (pres 59); CalLA (2nd v-pres 52; pres 2 dists & 1 sect & mem var coms, coun 68-69). 10: Altrusa Club; Delta Kappa Gamma; San Diego Woman's Club; Geneal Soc; San Diego City & Co Centennials Commsn; off &/or mem var loc orgs; Pres Pub Lib Executives Assn of So Cal 59. 11: "Woman of the Year," Women's Serv Clubs, 55; Lay Citizen's Award for outstanding contrib to educ in 58, Phi Delta Kappa. 13: Yes. 15: 820 E st, San Diego 92101.

BREED, PAUL F. b Norwich NY 20 O 16. 5: Chicago 46-50 (Hist) PhB, 51-55 (LS) MA. 6: Fr. 7: (T/Sgt) Army Ordn, Pacific Area 41-45; Asst ref libn U Chicago Lib 53-55; Head ref dept UDetroit Lib 55-59; Wayne State U Lib: Asst libn hum div 59-65, Univ bibliog 65-. 9: ALA. 12: Jt auth "Songs in Collections; an Index" (65). 13: Yes. 14: Ref, documents. 15: 1960 E Pearl st, Warren Mi 48091.

BREEN, RUTH (ALICE). b Schroon Lake NY 10 N 29. 5: SUNY(Albany) 47-51 (Eng) BA; Syracuse 52-53 (LS) MS. 6: Fr, Lat. 7: Circ & ref libn Rider Col 53-59; Zool libn Cornell U 60-61, Entom libn 61-. 9: ALA-ACRL; SLA. 10: AAUW; Beta Phi Mu. 14: Ref, bibliog. 15: Entomology Lib Comstock Hall, Cornell Univ, Ithaca NY 14850.

BREEN, VIRGINIA (WISE). b Somerset Md 2 Ag 07. 4: Glenn H Breen. 5: George Washington U 27-29 (LS) AB, 29-32 (LS) AM; UIll 31-32 (LS). 6: Fr, Sp. 7: Clsf Pan Amer Union, Wash DC 28-29; Asst DC Pub Lib 29-31; Asst libn Fed Emergency Relief Admin, Wash DC 33-35; Libn WPA 36-39; Libn Fed Works Agency, Wash DC 39-42; Assoc libn Bur of Pub Roads, Wash DC 42-50; Libn St Marks-Incarnation Lutheran Church, Wash DC 52-66; Catlgr St Marks Lutheran Church, Evansville Ind 68. 9: SLA. 10: DAR; Daughters of the Amer Colonists; Colonial Dames of the 17th Cent; Magna Carta Dames. 14: Ref, cat. 15: 525 Audubon dr, Evansville In 47715.

BREGZIS, ILZE (BIRKHANS). b Riga Latvia 17 D 34. 4: Ritvars Bregzis. 5: Carleton U 54-58 (Eng Lit) BA; Toronto 59-60 BLS. 6: Latvian. 7: Clerk typist Credit Bur of Ottawa & Hull, Ottawa 53-57; Clerk Can Dept of Revenue, Taxation Br, Toronto 58-59; Catlgr Imperial Oil Ltd, Toronto 60-63; Catlgr Coop Bk Centre of Can, Toronto 65-66; Hd tech serv Ont Inst for Stud in Educ, Toronto 66-. 9: SLA; Inst Prof Libns Ont. 15: 2573 St Clair ave E, Toronto 16 Can.

BREGZIS, RITVARS. b Latvia 15 Ap 20. 4: Ilze Birkhans. 5: ULatvia 39-44 (Hist); Bonn U 46-48 (Hist); Toronto 50-51 (Hist) MA, 53-54 BLS. 6: Latvian, Ger, Lat, Fr, Sp. 7: UToronto Lib: Catlgr 54-56, Asst head catlg dept 56-61, Head catlg dept 61-63, Asst libn tech serv 63-. 9: ADI; Assn Computing Machinery; ALA; Inst Prof Libns Ont (Bd); OntLA; MusLA. 13: Yes. 14: Info tech, lib tech serv, automation. 15: 2573 St Clair ave E, Toronto 16 Can.

BREILAND, MILDRED (SCHUBERT). b Rock Port Mo 6 Jl 15. 4: John G Breiland. 5: Neb State Tchrs Col 33-37 9educ, Hist, Eng) BA; UMich 39-40 BALS; UNM 53-. 7: Catlgr UMich 40-41; Head of ser UNM 41-44; Catlgr UCLA 47-48; Ref libn Albuquerque Pub Lib, Albuquerque NM 51-53; Libn Albuquerque High Sch, Albuquerque NM 53-63; Head catlgr Lib Proc Center Albuquerque (NM) Pub Schs 63-. 9: ALA; SWLA; NMLA (past pres); NMEA (past pres, mem Sch Libns Sect). 14: Catlg. 15: 908 Georgia SE, Albuquerque NM 87108.

BREINICH, JOHN A. b Davenport Iowa 20 O 43. 5: St Ambrose Col 61-63 (Psych); UIowa 63-65 (Psych) BA; UIll 65-66 (LS) MS. 7: Catlgr St Ambrose Col 65-65; Asst to libn UConn Health Ctr Lib 66-. 9: MedLA; SLA (Conn Valley Chap, Dir at large). 14: Admin. 15: Univ of Conn Health Center Lib, 1000 Asylum ave, Hartford Ct 06105.

BREITENSTEIN, (JULIAN) BRADLEY. b NYC 13 O 17. 5: St Bonaventure U 36-40 (Bus) BBA; Syracuse summers 46-50 (Educ) MA, 50-51 MS (LS). 7: US Army (1st Lt) Adj Gen Corps 42-46; Soc studies tchr De Veaux Sch, Niagara Falls NY 46-47; Soc studies tchr Camden Central Sch, Camden NY 47-49; Soc studies tchr Wappingers Falls Central Sch, Wappingers Falls NY 49-50; Prof asst Bridgeport Pub Lib, Bridgeport Conn 51-55; Lib Dir Olean Pub Lib, Olean NY 55-66; Lib dir Massapequa Pub Lib Massapequa NY 66-. 9: ALA; NYLA; Nassau CoLA. 13: Yes. 14: Pub lib admin. 15: Olean Pub Lib, Olean NY 14760.

BREKKE, ALICE BELINDA. b Elmore Minn 9 D 11. 5: West Col of Educ & UMont 31 (Eng) BS; Colo State Col 55 (Elem Educ) MA; UDenver 60 (LS) MA. 7: Tchr pub schs, Meagher Co Mont 32-42; Prin & tchr pub schs, Jerome Ida 42-43; Tchr high sch, Roundup Mont 43-44; Tchr pub schs, Big Timber Mont 44-49; Tchr pub schs, Bozeman Mont 49-58; Asst libn & Asst Prof in Lib Instr Black Hills State Col 60-64; Ref libn Gustavus Adolphus Col 64-. 8: Exam Bd, Meagher Co (Mont) Schs, 38-41. 9: NEA; ALA-ACRL; MinnLA. 10: Bus & Prof Women; Delta Kappa Gamma; Kappa Delta Pi; AAUW. 14: Ref. 15: 1005 S Washington, St Peter Mn 56082.

BRENAN, ANNE V (SCHIEWE). b Titusville Penn 13 F 22. 5: Allegheny Col 40-44 (French, german) AB; NYU 50-51; UMich 60-62 MSLS. 6: Ger, Fr. 7: Advertising, NYC: Prentice Hall Inc 44-47, Hanes Hosiery Inc 52, (Mgr) The Coward Shoe 53-56; Promotion, NYC: Young Amer 47-48, Marguerite Tuttle Inc 48-52; Advertising Hahne & Co, Newark NJ 52-53; Act hd Ionia Pub Lib, Ionia Mich 58-62; Child libn Lakewood Pub Lib, Lakewood Ohio 62-. 9: OhioLA (Pub Com 1968 Conf). 10: Lakewood Pub Lib Staff Assn. 14: Child bks, rev, eval, child wk, advertising, bk talks, story-hours. 15: 15120 Esther ave, Lakewood Oh 44107.

BRENDEL, SHIRLEY JEAN (LONCARICH). b Miami Okla 6 O 36. 5: Ft Hays Kan State Col 59-63 (Hist) AB; UDenver 64 (LS) MA. 6: Fr, Ger. 7: Sec to libn Ft Hays Kan State Col 56-61, Lib asst circ summers 61-63; Asst catlgr UArk 64-. 9: ALA; ArkLA. 10: Phi Alpha Theta; Phi Kappa Phi. 14: Catlg. 15: 314 Sutton, Fayetteville Ar 72701.

BRENDER, MAURITA (PETERSON). b Sault Ste Marie Mich 5 Mr 44. 4: Ronald F Brender. 5: UMich 62-65 (Mus Lit) BMus, 65-66 MALS. 7: Humanities ref East Mich U 66-67, Mus catlgr 67-68; Ref libn Ann Arbor Pub Lib, Ann Arbor Mich 68-. 9: MusLA. 13: Yes. 14: Art & music ref. 15: 1109 Elder blvd, Ann Arbor Mi 48103.

BRENEAU, DONALD L. b Detroit Mich 19 N 34. 4: Elizabeth Kelly. 5: Sacred Heart Sem Detroit 55; Wayne State 59-62 (Eng lit) BA; UMich 63-65 MALS. 7: USN radio announcer & public relations Journalist 2d Class 55-59; Wayne State Lib: Lib asst 62-65, Jr asst libn (catlgr) 65-68, Libn II (ser libn) 68-. 8: Part-time instr, Wayne State U Dept of Lib Sci, fall 67 & summer 68. 9: ALA. 14: Tech serv. 15: 232 Academy, Ferndale Mi 48220.

BRENNAN, SISTER IRENE M. b Iowa Falls Iowa 5 My 04. 5: Clarke Col 25-28 (Eng) AB; UIll (Champaign) 29, 33 BS in LS, MA; LoyolaU (Los Angeles) summers 53-56 (Educ). 6: Fr. 7: Tchg Mt St Joseph Acad, Dubuque Iowa 25-27; Tchg Clarke Col 27-30, Libn 30-33; Libn Mundelein Col 33-52; Tchg Holy Family High Sch,Glendale Cal 52-57; Tchg St Mary High Sch, Chicago 57-59; Libn Immaculata High Sch, Chicago 59-; Ref & tech serv UNotre Dame (Ind) summer 68. 8: Consul for org, reorg, or expansion, 7 cath, elem & high sch libs in middle west 40-65; Com mem World Bk Evaluation 67. 9: ALA; CathLA; Ill Unit: chm 50, chm Secon Sect 65, Memb Chm 60-61); A-V Arch (com mem 67-); Chicagoland Libns. 10: NCTE; Beta Phi Mu. 13: Yes. 14: Wk with tchrs, bibliogs, ref, catlg. 15: 640 Irving Park rd, Chicago Il 60613.

BRENNAN, JOAN (DONAHEY). b Ashland Ohio. 4: Benson E Brennan. 5: Ashland Col 35-36; Ohio State 56-57; Col of Steubenville 57-59 (Educ) BS; Kent State 61-67 MLS; Ohio Dominican Col 69. 7: Bkmob libn Jefferson Co Lib, Steubenville Ohio 59-60; Libn Brilliant Bd of Educ, Brilliant Ohio 60-64; Libn Columbus Bd of Educ, Columbus Ohio 65-. 9: NEA; ALA; OhioEA; OhioASchL; ColumbusOTA; ColumbusEA. 10: Columbus Gallery of Fine Arts. 14: Child lit. 15: 4796 Ridgerun dr, Columbus Oh 43229.

BRENNAN, ROBERT GILBERT. b Mt Vernon NY 26 Mr 27. 4: Dawn Tolson. 5: Mt Union Col 46-51 (Sociol) AB; Pratt 51-52 MLS. 7: Stock clerk Ward Leonard Electric Co Regulator Div, Mt Vernon NY 45-46; Clerk- purchasing & transportation off Bd of Missions & Church Ext Methodist Church NYC 47-49; Lib asst Mt Union Col Lib 49-51; Helper boiler crew Babcock & Wilcox Co, Alliance Ohio 51; Ref libn Dayton Pub Lib, dayton Ohio 52-54; Lib Dir Howard Whittemore Mem Lib, Naugatuck Conn 54-62; Head soc scis & bus lib Chico State Col Lib 62-66, Pub serv libn 66-. 8: Stud Affairs Com of Faculty Coun Chico State Col 64-67, Fac Elections Com 65-, Orientation Com 65-66, Fac Senate 67-, Long Range PlanningCom 69-. 9: CalLA. 10: Assn Cal State Colprofs 62-. 14: Ref. 15: 11 Woodside lane, Chico Ca 95926.

BRENNER, EVERETT H. b Lynn Mass 3 F 26. 4: Joan Greenberg. 5: Bates Col 43-48 (Chem) BS; UMich 48-50 (Ger) MA; UZurich 50 (Ger). 6: Ger. 7: US Army Inf & Signal Corps (T/4 Sgt), ETO 44-46; Chem Interchemical Corp, NYC51; Lit chem Texaco Co, Beacon NY 52-58; Lit chem Dow Chem Co, Williamsburg Va 58;Manager central abstracting & indexing serv Amer Petroleum Inst, NYC 59-. 8: LecturerPratt Inst Lib Sch, Brooklyn NY 64-; Consul 64, Bd of Trustees "Engineering Index"69-. 9: ACS (Lit Div); ADI (NY Metro chap: chm, mem Adv Bd 63-65). 13: Yes. 14: Thesaurus bldg (faceted vocabularies), abstracting. 15: Amer Petro Inst 555 Madison ave, New York, NY 10022.

BRENNER, LAWRENCE. b Lynn Mass 19. S 39. 5: Northeastern U 57-62 (Soc Studies) BS in Ed; U of Mass Ext Courses 62-63 LS Certif Salem State Col 68-. 6: Fr, Jewish. 7: Wire room asst "Boston Herald Traveler" 58-60; Reading room asst Boston Med Lib 60-62; Asst med libn Boston City Hosp 62-63, Sr med libn 63-. 8: Exec Bd Upper Swampscott Improvement Assn Swampscott Mass 65; Planning Com Boston City Hosp Centennial Program 64. 9: MedLA; (NE/BostonMedLA Coun); ALA-AHIL; NELA (Hoop sect); Mens' Libn Club. 10: Upper Swampscott Improvement Assn Swampscott Mass; Jr Achievements Lynn Mass 56-57; Swampscott Jr C of C. 11: Scholastic Art Award NE Reg 57. 12: 'History of the Medical Library' in "History of the Boston City Hospital 1905-1964". 14: Catlg, ref , hist of med. 15: Boston City Hosp Med Lib 818 Harrison ave, Boston 02118.

BRENNER, MRS HELEN ANN (DRIVER). b Winchester Ind 29 D 10. 4: Andrew M Brenner. 5: DePauw U 28-32 (Eng Lit) AB; Ind U 58-59 (LS) MA. 7: Act libn Winchester Pub Lib, Winchester Ind; Child libn Morrisson- Reeves Pub Lib,

Richmond Ind 59-. 9: ALA; IndLA (Child & YP Round Table: Bd 61-, chm 64). 10: AAUW. 14: Child lit, wking with underpriv child. 15: Morrisson-Reeves Pub Lib, N Sixth & A sts, Richmond In 47374.

BRENNER, WILLIS FRANKLIN JR. b Culver Kan 4 N 35. 5: Kan State U 53-57 (Speech) BS; Kan State Tchrs Col 63-65 (LS) MS. 7: Personnelman 2nd Class US Navy 59-63; Asst order libn UNeb(Lincoln) 65-68; Hd publ serv Mikkelsen Lib & Learn Resource Ctr Augustana Col 68-. 9: ALA; SDLA. 14: Tech serv, ref. 15: 633 S Dakota ave, Sioux Falls SD 57104.

BRENNI, VITO JOSEPH. b Highland NY 15 Mr 23. 5: NY State Col for Tchrs (Albany) 40-43, 46-47 (Eng) AB; Columbia 47-49 (Tchg of Eng) MA, 50-51 (LS) MS, 57-58 (LS). 6: Fr. 7: Cannoneer Field Artillery US Army (Cpl) 43-46; Tchr of Eng & for langs, Fonda NY 49-50; Chief ref libn WVaU 51-57; Tchg fellow Sch of Lib Serv Columbia U 57-58; Ref libn econ div NY Pub Lib 59-60; Chief ref libn Villanova U 60-62; Asst Prof of Lib Sci & Hd Lib Educ Duquesne U 62-65 66-68; Visiting lect Col of Libnship (Aberystwyth Wales) 68-. 9: ALA; CathLA; BSA. 10: AAUP. 12: Comp "Water Resources of West Virginia; a Bibliography" (54); "West Virginia Authors; "American English; a Bibliography" (64); "Edith Wharton; a Bibliography" (67). 13: Yes. 14: Ref, bibliog, govt publ, lib educ, bk sel, acquis. 15: 66 S Prospect st, Plattsburgh NY 12901.

BRENTLINGER, HOWARD R. b Cambridge Mass 23 Mr 27. 4: Jane Walker. 5: Harvard 44-45, 47-49 (Hist) AB; Syracuse 49-50 MS in LS. 7: Jr libn Rochester Pub Lib, Rochester NY 50-52, Sr libn 52-56; Dir Cornell Pub Lib, Ithaca NY 56-67; Dir Tompkins Co Pub Lib 67-. 9: ALA; NYLA. 10: Kiwanis; PTA. 13: Yes. 14: Pub lib admin, adult serv. 15: 301 Columbia, Ithaca NY 14850.

BRESIE, MAYELLEN. b Lafayette La 25 Ag 28. 5: UTex 45-49 (Span) BA; Stephen F Austin summer 49; Sam Houston Col (Puebla Mex ext) summer 50; UTex 62-64 MLS. 6: Sp, Portu. 7: Tchr Lufkin Ind Schs, Lufkin Tex 49-51; Tchr Tyler Pub Schs, Tyler Tex 51-52; Sec UTex Dental Br, Houston 52-62; Sr lib asst UTex Lib 63-64, Libn I catlgr 64-67; Libn Lilly Lib IndU 67-. 9: Assn Mex Bibliotecarios. 10: Beta Phi Mu. 14: Catlg, Latin Amer bibliog & period, rare bks. 15: 461 Jefferson ave, LufkinTx 75901.

BRESLIN, CICELY (AIKMAN). b El Paso Tex 4 Je 23. 4: Paul Breslin. 5: UChicago 40-42 art; Art Stud League 42-46 Art; New Sch for Soc Research 66 (Eng). 7: Lib asst NYU 51-54; Bk buyer Mus Shop American Mus of Natural Hist, NYC 54-56; Libn Colegio Franklin D Roosevelt, Lima Peru 56-58; Asst libn Walden Sch, NYC 60-64; Circ libn Mills Col, NYC 66-67; Circ libn Hunter Col 67-; Libn Amer Mus Hayden Planetarium, NYC 58-. 9: IFLA (Astronomical Libraries Subsection); NY Lib Club. 10: Art Students League. 14: Ref, research. 15: 226 E 83rd st, New York NY 10028.

BRESNAHAN, REV JOHN F. b Medford Mass 29 S 18. 5: Villanova 38-42 (Philos) AB; Ctholic U 43 (Eng); Villanova U 49-53 (LS) MS, 61 (Religion) MA. 6: Lat, Fr, Sp. 7: Libn Villanova Prep Sch, Ojai Cal 44-57; Asst libn Augustinian Col 58-60; Asst libn Mgr Bonner High Sch, Drexel Hill Penn 61-62; Libn Biscayne Col 62-. 9: ALA; CathLA; SELA; FlaLA. 15: Biscayne Col Lib, Miami Fl 33054.

BRETT, WILLIAM HOWARD III. b NYC 2 Mr 14. 4: Alice Robison Brett. 5: Stanford 31-38 (Soc Sci-Journalism) BA; UCal(Berkeley) 40-41 (LS) Certif, 46-49 MSLS. 6: Fr. 7: Clerk Farm Security Admin USDA, San francisco 38-40; Mil Serv Jr libn Army War Col (Wash DC) 41-42, Dir Sch for Army Libns Europe 45; Libn II UCal(Berkeley) 46-48; Jr Libn Adult Educ Oakland Pub Lib 49-50; Mil Serv Lib Offr Hq 6th Army Presidio of San Francisco 50-51, Chief of Lib Serv, Command and Gen Staff Col 51-53 (Capt); Adult Educ libn Oakland Pub Lib 53-56, Chief ref libn 56-59, Asst libn 59-. 8: Act dir Oakland Museums 62-63. 9: ALA (var coms); CalLA (past pres). 10: Pub Lib Execs of Central Cal (pastpres); East Bay Adult Educ Coun (var offs); Oakland Chamber of Com; CulturalAdvancement Com; Coun of commun serv Oakland area; Adult Educ Study Commsn (Alumni);Assn Sch of Libnship UCal; Oakland Museums Assn; US Army Res (Lt Col). 13: Yes. 14: Adult educ. 15: 5666LaSalle ave, Oakland Ca 94611.

BRETZ, ROBERT LAWRENCE. b Rochester NY 9 Jl 28. 4: Linda Mazza Bretz. 5: Cooper Union Art Sch 47-49 (Arch); State U Col (Geneseo NY) 58-61 (Lib Educ) BS Ed; URochester 61-62 (Art Hist). 7: Libn The George Eastman House Inc, Rochester NY 61-65, Asst curator 65-68; Ref libn & rare bk libn Rochester Inst of Tech 68-. 9: SLA; Priv Libs Assn. 10: William Morris Soc; Printing Hist Soc; Internat Small Printers Assn. 14: Bibliog. 15: Wallace Mem Lib, Rochester Inst of Tech, Rochester NY 14623.

BREUER, ERNEST HENRY. b Hungary 2 My 02. 4: Minna Hirschfeld Breuer. 5: NYU 22-25 (Govt, Econ) BCS; Harvard Law 26-29 LLB; Pratt 47-48 BLS. 6: Ger. 7: Spec investigator Nat Assn of Credit Men, NYC 25-26; Attorney private practice NYC 30-38; Attorney Cohen & Wolf Esqs, Cincinnati 38-43; Field Dir Amer Red cross, Tinian Pacific 43-45; Attorney private practice NYC 45-48; Asst law libn NY State Lib 48-51, State Law Libn 51-. 8: Law Lib consul to NYS Judicial Conf Bar Assns. Pub NY State Law Libs. 9: AALL (Exec Bd, chm var coms); Law Lib Assn of Greater NY (pres); Assn of Law Libs of Upstate NY (pres); Amer Soc for Legal Hist (Exec sec Eastern States Br). 12: "Constitutional Developments in New York 1777-1958"; "The New York State Court of Claims, Its History and Jurisdiction" (59); "History of Moreland Act Investigations in New York" (65). 13: Yes. 14: Law lib admin, ref, bibliog. 15: 143 Melrose ave, Albany NY 12203.

BREWER, MRS DORALOUISE (BRITT). b St Louis 15 S 08. 4: Melvin C Brewer. 5: Washington U 25-29 (Fr, Eng, Hist) AB; St Louis Lib Sch 30-31 (LS) Certif. 6: Fr. 7: Reviser St Louis Lib Sch 31-32; Lib asst St Louis Pub Lib 32-34; Libn Emerson Elec Mfg Co, St Louis 34-36; Lib asst tchrs room St Louis Pub Lib 36-43; Procedure writer Emerson Elec Mfg Co, St Louis 43-45; St Louis Pub Lib: Lib asst ser 45-46, Ser libn 52-58, Acquis libn 58-. 10: Alpha Zeta Pi; Nat Wildlife Fed. 12: "Study of Order Routines and Procedures in the St Louis Public Library" (58); "Effect of the Depression on the St Louis Public Library, May 1930-April 1937," with others (37). 14: Ser, acquis. 15: 7831 Lafon pl, University City Mo 63103.

BREWER, ERNESTINE T. b Durham NC 7 Ag 36. 5: NC Col (Durham) 53-57 (Span) AB; Rutgers 65 MLS. 6: Sp. 7: Sch libn, Newark NJ 57-62; Sch libn Rutherford Jr High Sch, Rutherford NJ 62-. 9: NEA; NJEA; NJSchLA; Bergen Co (NJ) EA. 10: Wk with youth groups & citizen participation in educ groups. 13: Yes. 14: Wk with ya, ref. 15: 15 Rhode Island ave, E Orange NJ 07018.

BREWER, GLORIA (JEANINE). b Greeneville Tenn 15 My 38. 5: Ind Central Col 56-60 (Eng) AB; Ind U 61-62 (LS) MA. 6: Fr. 7: Asst catlg libn Dayton & Montgomery Co Pub Lib, Dayton Ohio 62-63, Asst ref libn 63-66; Asst catlg libn; Ohio U Lib (Athens) 66-68, Marshall U Lib 68-. 9: ALA. 10: AAUW; Church libn. 14: Ref, catlg. 15: 1521-1/2 Sixth ave, Huntington WV 25701.

BREWER, IMOGENE (BAKER). b Chattanooga Tenn 29 Ag 30. 4: Paul D Brewer. 5: Carson Newman Col 48-52 (Eng) AB; Southwestern Baptist Theol Sem 52-53; Peabody summer 64; UTenn 64-65 (LS) MS. 7: Catlgr Carson-Newman Col 65-. 9: ALA (Tenn recruit netwk 66-) TennLA (sec 66-67). 10: Pi Lambda Theta. 14: Catlg. 15: 804 Russell, Jefferson City Tn 37760.

BREWER, JEANEICE (ORLANDO). b Marmaduke Ark 24 Jl 22. 5: Ark State Col 41-50 (Bus Admin) BS; UMiss 55-57 MLS. 7: Tchr Pub SchsGreene Co Ark 41-52; Indexer Dept of Defense Wash DC 52-53; Libn High Sch Paragould Ark 53-55; Libn High Sch Wilson Ark 55-56; Jr libn UMo56-61, Asst libn 61-. 9: ALA; MoLA. 10: Bus & Prof Women's Club; Delta Kappa Gamma. 14: Ref, interlib loan. 15: 211 Hitt apt 205, ColumbiaMo 65201.

BREWER, JOSEPH (HILLYER). b Grand Rapids Mich 9 O 1898. 5: Dartmouth 20 (Eng) AB; Oxford 22 (Eng) BA, 33 MA; Columbia 46 BS in LS. 6: Fr, Ger. 7: (2nd Lt) Inf US Army 18; Priv sec to ed "The Spectator," London 22-24; Ed Staff D Appleton & Co, NYC 25-26; Asst ed Payson & Clarke, NYC 26-28; Pres Brewer, Warren & Putnam, NYC 28-33; Pres Olivet Col 34-44; Pres Hotel Morton Corp, Grand Rapids Mich 43-; Assoc in lib serv Columbia U 46-48; Assoc libn Queens Col (NY) 45-, Deputy libn 60-, Prof 66-. 8: Survey Com Univ of Montreal, 46; Lib Consul: Acad of the New Church, 61; Briarcliff Col, 65; Evaluation teams, Middle States Assn, 47-. 9: ALA-ACRL; BSA; NYLA; NY Lib Club (pres 51-52). 10: AAUP; Beta Phi Mu; Archons of Colophon; Grolier Club; Fellow, 01780 11: LLD, Olivet Col 9mich). 13: Yes. 14: Acquis. 15: 151 East 83 st Apt 9F, New York NY 10028.

BREWER, MARGARET LOFA (DOSSETT). b Winthrop Ark 6 O 29. 4: Durward Brewer. 5: So State Col 47-49 (Educ); Okla StateU 51-53 (Hist) BA; UMo 55-56 (LS) MEd. 6: Sp, Fr. 7: Tchr Arkinda Sch Dist, Arkinda Ark 47-49; Tchr & libn

Gillham Sch Dist, Gillham Ark 49-51; Purchasing asst Okla StateU 52-55; Asst libn UMo (Columbia) 56-. 8: Lib consul Riverview Gardens Sch Dist 64; Lib consul Project Communicate 66; Lib consul Mo Dept of Educ 68-69; Lib evaliatpr 69. 9: National Library Week (exec dir for Mo); Mo Assn of Sch Libns (ed of newsletter); Mo Congress of Parents & Tchrs (lib chm); MoLA (chm Intellectual Freedom Com) Mo State Tchrs Assn (commun pres). 10: AAUW; Pi Gamma Mu; Delta Kappa Gamma. 12: "Elementyary School Library; Theory and Practice" (69). 13: Yes. 14: Elem sch libnship, ref, admin. 15: 2274 Concordia dr, Columbia Mo 65201.

BREWSTER, BEVERLY J (KLINE). b Chicago 19 O 38. 5: Ind U 56-60 (Span) AB, 61 (LS); UMich summers 62-64 AMLS; UPittsburgh 66- (LS). 6: Sp, Fr. 7: Soc wker Children's Aid Soc, Ottawa 60; Ref libn Port Huron Pub Lib, Port Huron Mich 61-63; Chief tech serv Port Huron Pub Lib, Port Huron Mich 63-65; Catlgr Bur of the Budget Lib, Wash DC 65-66; Asst instr Grad Sch of Lib & Info Scis UPittsburgh 69-. 8: Consul & res assoc, Sch of Libn & Info Serv, UMd summer 67; Free-lance indexer 65-66. 9: ALA. 10: Soc of Indexers (Eng); Volunteers of the Shelters. 12: Asst ed "Who's Who in Consulting (68). 14: Index, review, internat & compar libnship, tech serv, Latin America. 15: Grad Sch of Lib & Inf Sci, Univ of Pittsburgh, Pittsburgh Pa 15213.

BREWSTER, EVELYN SYLVIA (VOGNILD). b Volin SD 1 F 16. 4: George R Brewster. 5: Yankton 32-34 Diploma in Ed; UDenver 42-43 Diploma in LS, 47-48 (LS) BA, 48-49 (Ed) MA. 7: Field libn S Dak State Lib Commsn Pierre S Dak 43-47; Libn Grad Sch of Libnship UDenver 47-49; Libn Deadwood Pub Lib Deadwood S Dak 49-57; Colo State Lib Denver: Area lib supv 57-66, Lib serv coordinator 66-. 9: ALA; MPLA (pres 69); ColoLA (pres 64); S Dak LA (pres 54 & 55); ColoASL. 10: PEO Sisterhood. 11: Delta Kappa Gamma. 14: Lib organ & mgt. 15: 1125 Jersey st, Denver Co 80220.

BREWSTER, OLIVE NESBITT. b San Antonio Tex 19 Jl 24. 5: Our Lady of the Lake Col 41-45 (Eng) BA, 45-46 BS in LS. 6: Sp, Fr. 7: Asst libn & catlgr Aeromedical Lib USAF Sch of Aerospace Med Randolph AFB & Brooks AFB Tex 46-. 9: ALA. 14: Catlg. 15: 1906 Schley ave, San Antonio Tx 78210.

BREYFOGLE, SUSAN (COLTHARP). b Fort Wayne Ind 11 Ag 41. 4: Russel P Breyfogle Jr. 5: UMich 63 (European Hist) BA, 67 MLS. 6: Fr, Swahili. 7: Tchr US Peace Corps, tanzania 63-65; Ref libn Genesee Co Lib, Flint Mich 66; Libn I bus & ind dept Flint Pub Lib, Flint Mich 67-68, Br libn II 68-. 14: Br lib wk. 15: 1309 1/2 N Stevenson, Flint Mi 48504.

BRIAN, RAY. b Stockton Cal. 5: UCal(Berkeley) 42-43, 46-49 (Psych) BA, 49-52 (Psych) MA, 52-53 BLS; UCLA, San Francisco State Col, UCal(Berkeley) 60-. 6: Ger, Fr, Sp. 7: Libn I Ref UCLA 53-55; Libn Lear Inc, Santa Monica Cal 54-55; Personnel analyst State Personnel Bd, Sacramento Cal 56-57; Adult probation off Contra Costa Co, Richmond Cal 57-61; Libn Hyman Labs Inc, Berkeley Cal 61-63; Libn Cal Acad of Sci, San Francisco 63-. 8: Lecturer UCal(Berkeley) Sch of Libnship 69. 9: SLA (Employment chm San Francisco Bay Reg Chap 62-63, Recr chm 66-67, Educ Com 66-, CCSF Lib Tech Adv Com 67-, dir 67-69); ASIS; ALA; AALS; CalLA. 10: Amer Psychol Assn; UCal Lib Sch Alum Assn (pres 70); ACLU. 13: Yes. 14: Ref, rare bks, admin, research. 15: 616 Belvedere st, San Francisco Ca 94117.

BRIANS, JANET (LEONARD). b Effingham Co Ill 2 Jl 35. 4: Robert John Brians. 5: USoCal 52-56 (Internat Rel) BA; UCal(Berkeley) E Asian Studies MA; UCLA 61-62 MLS. 6: Ger, Dutch, Indonesian. 7: World Affairs Catlgr USoCal 64-66. 9: CalLA. 10: Phi Beta Kappa; Phi Kappa Phi. 14: Catlg. 15: 23801 Topar ave, Los Altos Ca 94022.

BRICE, CAROL A. b Lewistown Mont 24 D 08. 5: UCLA 26-30 (Eng) BA; Grad Sch of Libnship UWash 31-32 BLS. 6: Fr. 7: Ref lib asst Lib UWash 32-37; Bibliogr Lib Stanford U 37-43; Libn Aero-Med Lab Wright Field Air Materiel Comm Dayton Ohio 43-47; Ext libn Hawaii Co Lib Hilo Hawaii 48-65; Dir Hawaii Pub Lib Hilo Hawaii 66-. 9: ALA; HiloLA. 10: AAUW; ZONTA. 14: Admin, ref, reg hist & ref. 15: 5 Hina st, Hilo Hi 96720.

BRICH, GEORGE MICHAEL. b Palmerton Penn 31 Mr 35. 4: Audrey L Kemmerer. 5: E Stroudsburg State 59-61 (Eng) BS in Ed; Drexel 63-67 MALS. 7: Airman 1st class USAF 54-57; Lenape RHS, Medford NJ: Eng tchr 61-64, Libn 64-67; Asst libn & hd tech serv NorwichU 67-. 9: ALA; -ACRL; ISA. 10: Association desprofesseurs d'universites de langue francaise du Que; Association des facultes demusique des universites canadiennes; Can AAUP; Music Educrs Nat Conf. 14: Tech serv & automation. 15: PO Box 163, Northfield Vt 05663.

BRICHFORD, MAYNARD J. b Madison Ohio 6 Ag 26. 4: Jane A Hamilton. 7: Hiram Col 44-50 (Soc Studies) BA; UWis 50-53 (Hist) MS. 9: SAA (Coun). 12: "Descriptive Inventory of Resources for the Ecology of Mental Health and Work With the Disadvantaged" (67). 14: Archival theory (train & practice), mgt & systemsanalysis, sci & tech documentation. 15: 409 Eliot dr, Urbana Il 61801.

BRICKER, GEORGE HARRY. b Mechanicsburg Penn 29 S 10. 4: Florence Miller. 5: Franklin & Marshall Col 29-33 (Philos) AB; Lancaster Theol Sem 33-36 (Systematic Theol) BD; UPittsburgh 41-43 (Adult Educ) MEd; Gettysburg Theol Sem 47-48 (Church Hist); TempleU 50-53 (Hist Theol); Drexel 57-60 MS in LS. 6: Grk, Hebrew, Fr, Ger. 7: Pastor St Johns Evangelical & Reformed Ch, Johnstown Penn 36-44; Pastor Trinity-Salem Parish Evangelical & Reformed Ch, Waynesboro Penn 45-52; Pastor St Peters Evangelical & Reformed Ch, Lancaster Penn 53-56; Libn & Professor of Theol (Liturgics) Lancaster Theol Sem 57-; Dir Crozer-Lancaster Theol Libs, Chester & Lancaster Penn 69-. 8: Circ mgr of "Theology and Life 58-64; Instr, Theol Libnship Drexel Grad Sch of Libnship 65-; St Charles Sem, Phila; Adv Com, Bd of Trustees 68-. 9: ATheolLA (pres 65-66, Com on Appraisal 68-); Evang & Reformed Hist Soc (treas); United Church of Christ (Hist Commsn); PennLA; LancasterCoLA. 10: Amer Soc Church Hist; Lancaster Co Histns; Torch Club; Lancaster Clisoph Soc; Phi Beta Kappa; Beta Phi Mu. 12: Co-ed "Lancaster Series on the Mercersburg Theology v 1 "Philip Schaff: The Principle of Protestantism (64); v 4 "John W Nevin: The Mystical Presence and other Writings on the Eucharist (66). 14: Theol libnship, lib admin. 15: Philip Schaff Lib Lancaster Theol Sem 555 W James st, Lancaster Pa 17603.

BRICKEY, MARY LOU (HUDSON). b Guthrie Ill 7 Ag 32. 5: Ill State Normal U 50-52 (Math); UIll 60-62 (Eng) BA, 63 MSLS. 6: Fr. 7: Acquis clerk Decatur Pub Lib, Decatur Ill 57-60; Catlgr UIll(Urbana) 62-63; Catlgr Cal State Col (Fullerton) 64; Head of processing dept of lib & archives State of Ariz 65-. 9: SLA; ArizLA; SWLA. 10: Univ of Ill Lib Sch Assn; Beta Phi Mu. 14: Catlg. 15: 4506 W Rose lane, Glendale Ariz 85301.

BRICKEY, OLIVIA ANN (COLLINS). b Clayton NM 7 O 30. 4: Ray N Brickey. 5: Colo Woman's Col 48-49 (Eng) AA; N Tex State U 60-64 (Eng); UMd 64-66 (Eng) BA, 66-67 MLS; George WashingtonU 68- (Amer Studies). 6: Sp. 7: Admin sec Phillips Petroleum Co, amarillo Tex 50-55; Catlgr LC 68-. 10: Phi Beta Kappa; Beta Phi Mu. 14: Catlg, rare bks. 15: 523 Sixth st SE, Washington DC 20003.

BRIDEGAM, WILLIS E JR. b Pottstown Penn 15 O 35. 4: Mary Hospador. 5: Eastman Sch of Mus 53-57 (Organ) BM; Syracuse 58-63 (LS) MS. 7: US Army Reserves Sp 4 57-63; Continuations Catlgr Rush Rhees Lib URoch 58-62, Asst hd order dept 62-64, Hd order dept 64-65, Hd acquis dept 65-66; Med libn & Asst Prof of Med Bibliog edward G Miner Lib URochester Sch of Med 66-. 9: ALA; SLA; Upstate NY Reg Med Assn (Sec-treas 67-68); Monroe Co LA; Rochester Acad Med (Lib Com). 10: SUNY Biomed Communication Netwk; URochester Admin Anonymous. 14: Admin. 15: 39 Collingsworth dr, Rochester NY 14625.

BRIDGE, PETER H. b Chicago Ill 23 D 33. 5: Harvard 52-56 (Classics) BA (cum laude); Columbia 59-60 MSLS. 6: Ger, Fr, Sp. 7: Capt artillery USA Res, Cincinnati 57-68; Acquis libn UCincinnati 58-59; Spec recruit LC 60-61; Hd gift sect exchange & gift dept LC 63-68, Asst chief 68-. 9: DCLA. 11: Grolier Fellowship Columbia Lib Sch 59. 14: Acquis. 15: 431 New Jersey ave SE, Washington DC 20003.

BRIDGES, BARBARA (SUE). b New Orleans La 7 O 42. 5: H Sophie Newcomb Col 60-64 (Mus Hist) BA; Inst Technologico de Monterrey (Mexico) summer 62 (Sp); Tulane 64-66 (Musicology); UTex at Austin 66-69 MLS. 6: Fr. 7: Stud asst ms div Tulane Lib 61-66; UTex at Austin undergrad lib: Sr lib asst summer 67, Libn I (ref) 68-. 9: ALA; SLA; TexLA; SWLA. 10: AAUW. 14: Ref, hist mss, educ for libnship. 15: 2216 San Gabriel 4, Austin Tx 78705.

BRIDGEWATER, MARION (JOYCE). b Carnegie Penn 20 D 18. 4: Herbert L Bridgewater. 5: Trniity Col for Women 35-39 (Eng) AB; Carnegie Lib Sch 39-40 BS in LS; Penn StateU 40-41 Secondary Certif; UDayton 66- (Eng). 6: Fr. 7: Grad asst ref dept Penn State Lib State Col Penn summers 41, 42; Libn Millcreek Twp High Sch, Erie Penn 42-44; Asst ref libn DuquesneU Lib 58-60; Catlgr & asst libn West Psychiatric Inst & Clinic Lib upittsburgh Sch of Med 60-63; Asst ref libn Hunt Lib Carnegie-MellonU 60-66; Hd ref UDayton AEL Lib 66-. 8: Instr Duquesne Lib Sci Sch 62-63; Spec lectures for

Freshman classes in lib orientation West Psychiatric Inst & Clinic & Duquesne. 9: ALA-ACRL; AAUP (Dayton Chap); OhioLA. 10: AAUW; Alumni Assn of Trinity Col. 14: Ref, reader's serv. 15: 206 Telford ave, Dayton Oh 45419.

BRIDGMAN, WILLIAM GERALD. b Thomaston Ga 13 O 34. 4: Carolyn Rainey. 5: Columbia Bible Col 52-53; MercerU 54-56, 59-61 (Soc Studies) BA; Ga State Col 579; Peabody Col 66-67 MLS. 7: Specialist 4 US Army 56-58; Lib employee Robins AFB Lib, Ga 60-63; Staff assoc Random House Sch & Lib Serv Inc, S Ga 63-65; Lib asst Ga Col (Milledgeville) 66; Libn Wash Memorial Lib, Macon Ga 67-68; Dir Pine Mt Reg Lib, Manchester Ga 69-. 8: Taught catlg UGa Ext (Macon) 68. 9: ALA; GaLA; SELA. 10: Kiwanis Club of Manchester Ga; Beta Phi Mu. 14: Admin, catlg. 15: 505 Webster dr, Manchester Ga 31816.

BRIDGWATER, DOROTHY WILDES. b Meriden Conn 21 Mr 01. 5: Simmons 18-22 (LS) BS; Yale 24-31 (Hist) MA. 6: Fr. 7: Libn Lindenwood Col 22-24; Yale U Lib: Catlgr 24-27, Catlgr & ref asst 27-39, Research asst, sr catlgr & asst ref libn 39-43, Research asst, reviser, catlg dept & asst ref libn 39-45, Research asst, asst ref libn 45-59, Research asst, asst head ref dept 59-. 9: ALA; ConnLA. 10: New Haven Colony Hist Soc; Hamden Hist Soc. 13: Yes. 14: Ref. 15: 31 Moulton st, Hamden Ct 06517.

BRIEL, PHYLLIS M. b Williamsport Penn. 5: Millersville State Tchrs Col 31 (LS) BS in Educ. 7: Libn Montoursville Area Joint High Sch, Montoursville Penn 57-. 10: Bus & Prof Women's Club; Penn Guild of Craftsmen. 15: 625 Fifth ave, Williamsport Pa 17702.

BRIERLEY, NANCY LEA (CLEMENTS). b Wash DC 16 S 32. 5: UMd 50-54 (Home Econ) BS; UWis 60-61 (LS) MS. 6: Sp. 7: Lib asst ref UMd Lib 56-59; Child libn Prince George's Co Mem Lib, Hyattsville Md 60; Tchg asst UWis Lib Sch 61; Libn I Madison Pub Lib, Madison Wis 61-62; Ref asst Worthington Pub Lib, Worthington Ohio 65; Ref libn Arlington-Grandview Libs 66; Med libn Ohio State U Sch Med 67-68; Ref libn Gen Motors Inst Lib, Flint Mich 69-. 9: SLA; WisLA (Intel Freedom Com); ALA. 10: Beta Phimu; Omicron Mu; Q & S; Colonial Hills (Ohio) Civic Assn; LWV; Northwest Area Humanrelations Coun; Parents Without Partners. 13: Bk reviewer "School Library Journal.". 14: Ref, bk sel, reader's adv, child & ya. 15: GMI Library, 1700 West 3rd ave,Flint Mi 48502.

BRIESEMEISTER, LAURA (B). b Barberton Ohio 7 Jl 04. 5: Lake Erie Col 22-26 BA; West Res 36-37 BS in LS. 7: Tchr, Hinckley Ohio 26-27; Tchr, Painesville Ohio 27-31; Lib asst Morley Lib, Painesville Ohio 31-35; Canton Pub Lib, Canton Ohio: Catlgr 36-37, Act libn 37-38, Dir 38-54; Br libn Toledo Pub Lib, Toledo Ohio 54-58; Dir Port Huron Lib, Port Huron Mich 58-. 9: ALA (Fin Com); OhioLA (Exec Bd, pres); MichLA (Memb Com). 10: Toledo Staff Assn; Quota Club; Canton Col Club; AAUW; LWV; Port Huron Citizens League; Lake Huron Lore Marine Hist Soc; St Clair Co Hist Soc. 13: Yes. 14: Admin, ref, tech proc. 15: 1115 Sixth st, Port Huron Mi 48060.

BRIGGS, DAVID WALTER. b Peoria Ill 24 Mr 42. 5: UIll 60-64 (Hist) AB; UCal (Berkeley) 64-65 MLS. 6: Ger, Fr. 7: Ref dept UCal (Santa Barbara) 65-66, Bibliographer 68-; Train NCO US Army (Germany) 66-68. 9: ALA; CalLA; SoCal Tech Processing Group. 10: Beta Phi Mu. 14: Bibliog, hist libs. 15: 5959 Mandarun dr, Goleta Ca 93107.

BRIGGS, J(OHN) EDWARD. b Binghamton NY 21 D 27. 4: Mary Constance Carberry. 5: Syracuse 49-52 (Eng, LS) BA, 53-54 MLS. 7: Proof reader Vaill-Ballou Press Inc, Binghamton NY 52-53; Jr libn Your Home Pub Lib, Johnson City NY 54-55; Libn NY State Electric & Gas, Binghamton NY 55-56; Eng tchr E Jr High Sch, Binghamton NY 56-57; Jr libn Binghamton Pub Lib, Binghamton NY 57-61; Order libn Four Co Lib System, binghamton NY 61-63, Gen consul 63-67; Assoc Libn SUNY (Binghamton) Library, Catlgr 67, Ser Libn 67-68; Ref Lib 68-. 9: NYLA. 10: Harper Film Soc SUNY (Binghamton) (sec-treas 67-). 14: Adult serv, ya serv, ref, serials, films. 15: Box 116 Rt 1, Shadeyside Farm, Chenango Forks NY 13746.

BRIGGS, NATHALIE E. b Woonsocket RI 22 Ja 12. 5: RI State Col 29-33 (Biol) BS; Syracuse 33-34 (LS) BS. 7: Gen asst to Head catlg dept RI State Col, Kingston 34-. 9: ALA; RILA. 10: Pettaquamscult Hist Soc; Chi Omega. 14: Catlg. 15: Univ of Rhode Island Lib, Kingston RI 02881.

BRIGGS, REBECCA. b Maryville Mo 3 Mr 05. 5: Northwest Mo State Col 24-28 (Eng) BS; UIll 28-29 BS in LS; UMich 41-42 (LS) MA. 7: Catlg libn Lawrence Col 29-41; Catlg libn Stephens Col 41-42; UIll(Urbana): Catlgr 43-50, Asst catlg libn 50-55, Asst ser libn 55-. 9: ALA (Catlg Code Rev Com, Subcom on Ser 56-66). 10: Beta Phi Mu. 14: Catlg, serv. 15: 1505 S Broadway, Urbana Ill 61801.

BRIGGS, RUTH M(ARIAN). b Toronto Can 25 F 06. 5: UToronto 27 (Fr, Span) BA. 6: Fr. 7: Sec UToronto 28-33; Sec Connaught Med Research Labs UToronto 33-40, Personnel asst 40-45, Libn 45-. 9: CanLA; MedLA (chm Nom Com 65-66, chm Recruit Com 68-69); SLA-Toronto Chap (pres 62-63, chm var coms). 14: Ref, admin. 15: Lib Connaught Med Research Lab UToronto, 1755 Steeles ave W, Willowdale Ont Can.

BRIGHT, DOROTHY H (VAN FLEET). b Toledo Ohio 12 Ja 07. 4: Lewis M Bright. 5: Various pos in ref & br wk Toledo Pub Lib, Toledo Ohio 25-41; Lib asst US Bur of Pub Rds Lib Wash DC 44-45; Libn Highway Research Bd of the NAS Wash DC 46-. 9: SLA; Coun of Planning Libns; DCLA. 14: Admin. 15: 4501 Connecticut ave NW apt 213, Washington DC 20008.

BRIGHT, EVELYN LAURADELL. b Columbia SC 11 D 11. 5: Benedict Col 30-32 (Sci); WVa State Col 32-34 (Educ) AB in ED; Pratt 48-49 BLS. 6: Fr. 7: Tchr elem schs Bd of Educ, Columbia SC 35-40; Tchr elem schs Bd of Educ, Greensboro NC 40-44; Libn NY Pub Lib 44-51; Asst libn Bd of EducNYC 51-53, Tchr of lib, Libn in charge 53-. 8: Summer Sch Instr SC State Col Educ & Eng 35-37. 9: ALA; NYCSchLA. 10: Alpha Kappa. 14: Catlg. 15: 48 St Nichols pl, New York, NY10031.

BRIGHT, FRANKLYN FURMAN. b Rochester NY 24 Mr 19. 4: Frances Loomis. 5: Oberlin Col 37-41 (Pre-Lib) AB; UMich 41-42 BALS. 6: Fr, Ger. 7: US Army Infantry (S/Sgt) 42-45; Head acquis dept Brown U Lib 46-48; Head acquis dept UWis Lib (Madison) 48-65, Chief tech serv div 65-. 9: ALA; SELA; GaLA (v-pres 68-69). 10: Phi Beta Kappa. 14: Tech serv. 15: 3737 Ross st, Madison Wi 53705.

BRIGHT, LEWIS M. b Toledo Ohio 6 O 13. 4: Dorothy H VanFleet Bright. 5: U of the City of Toledo 31-35 (Hist) PhB; UIll 35-36 BS in LS; Columbia 45-46 MS in LS. 6: Fr, Ital. 7: Ref asst & catlgr Ft Wayne Pub Lib, Ft Wayne Ind 38-41; Ref asst & catlgr US Fed Trade Commsn Lib, Wash DC 41-42, Asst libn 43-45; US Dept of State Lib, Wash DC: Ref libn 46-47, Chief ref sect 47-53, Chief reader serv 53-. 9: ALA; SLA (chm Internat Rel Sect 57-59; Exec Bd Washington Chap 63-65); CNLA (Com on Visiting For Libns 61-64); DCLA (Exec Bd). 10: . 14: Admin, ref, bibliog. 15: 3850 Tunlaw rd NW, Wash DC 20007.

BRIGHT, MIRIAM ELEANOR. b Trempealeau Wis. 5: UWis 44-47 Sp BA, 47-48 BLS. 7: Catlgr Wash State 48-49; Ser catlgr Mich State U 49-. 14: Catlg, rare bks. 15: 1421 Gilcrest st, East Lansing Mi 48823.

BRIGHTWELL, JUANITA (SUMNER). b Sylvester Ga 4 Ja 18. 4: Louie Brightwell. 5: Ga Southwestern Col 34-36; Woman's Col of Ga 36-38 (Eng) BS Ed; Emory U summer 62-65 (LS) ML. 7: Elem tchr Weston High Sch, Weston Ga 37-38; Libn, Eng tchr Smithville High Sch, Smithville Ga 41-42; Libn Americus High Sch, Americus Ga 42-43; Asst libn Carnegie Lib, Americus Ga 52-55; Elem tchr New Era Elem Sch, Americus Ga 55-56; Eng tchr Americus High Sch, Americus Ga 56-62; Libn Lake Blackshear Reg Lib, Americus Ga 62-. 9: ALA; SELA; GaLA; GaEA. 10: AAUW; BPW; UDC; DAR. 11: Recipient Teacher Merit Scholarship 1962-65. 15: 1307 Hancock dr, Americus Ga 31709.

BRILL, GLORIA P. b Newark NY. 5: Colby Jr Col 44-45; Syracuse 45-49 (Eng, Ed, LS) BA, 55-56 MLS. 7: Libn High Sch Alleghany NY 49-50; Asst libn Norton AF Base 50-56; Coordinator adult serv San Berbardino Co Lib 57-. 9: ALA; CLA. 10: Bus & Prof Women. 15: 104 W 4th st, San Bernardino Ca 92401.

BRIMM, HENRY MULLER. b Columbia SC 3 F 1898. 4: Josephine Craven. 5: Presbyterian Col (Clinton SC) 13-17 (Bible, Philos) BA; Columbia 27-28 (LS) BS, 35-36 (LS). 7: US Navy Quartermaster 2/c 17-19; Libn Presbyterian Col (Clinton SC) 23-25; Asst libn USCar 28-30; Libn Union Theol Sem (Richmond Va) 30-. 9: ATLA; VaLA. 11: Lit D, Davis & Elkins Col, 44; ThD (Honoris Causa), Faculte Libre de l'Eglise Reforme de France, Montpellier France, 50; LLD, Presbyt Col, Clinton SC, 65. 12: Ed "Scholars' Choice". 15: Lib Union Theol Sem, 3401 Brook rd, Richmond Va 23227.

BRINER, JEANNE MARIE (LYONS). b Chicago Ill 22 Ja 26. 4: William Briner. 5: NYU 44-52 (Amer Civilization) BA; Columbia 52-55 (Tech Serv) MLS; NYU 58-60 (Geol); UAriz 62 (Geol). 6: Sp. 7: Lib clk NYU 45-56; Lib asst Amer Mus of Natural Hist, nyc 56-62; Bibliog UAriz 63-66, 67-; Sr catlgr WittenbergU 66-67. 9: ArizLA. 14: Acquis. 15: PO Box 4701, Tucson Az 85717.

BRINKLER, BARTOL. b Portland Me 2 O 15. 5: Princeton 33-37 (Eng) BA, 37-40 (Eng) MA; Columbia 46-47 Libnship BS. 6: Fr, Ger. 7: Instr in Eng LSU 40-41; T/3-Med Specialist USA 41-45; Harvard Col Lib, Cataloger & clsfr: 47-50, Asst in charge of subj catlg 50-57, Chief subj catlgr 57-67, Clsf specialist 67-. 8: Consultant on classification (in both cases this included the construction of a special classification system & supervision of reclassification) for Dumbarton Oaks Research Library, Washington DC 56-69, and J F Kennedy-Institut fur Amerikastudien, Freie Universitat, Berlin Ger 67-. 9: ALA-RTSD (mem &/or chm Com on Subj Hdings 54-60); NE Tech Serv Libns 9sec-treas 49-50, v-chm 54-55, chm 55-56). 14: Clsf & subj catlg. 15: 26 Concord ave, Cambridge Ma 02138.

BRINTON, (EDGAR) HARRY. b Kansas City Mo 5 Jl 16. 4: Jane O Dallimore. 5: UDenver 38 AB; Columbia 57 MS. 6: Fr. 7: Govt documents libn Okla A&M Col Stillwater Okla 38-39; Libn Topeka High Sch Topeka Kan 39-40; Head govt documents U of Kan City, Kan City Mo summers 39-40; Catlgr & manager travel libs Mo Lib Commsns Jefferson City Mo 40-41; Chief order dept chief ext serv & act libn Pub Lib, Kan City Mo 41-59; Dir of Libs Pub Lib Jacksonville Fla 59-. 8: Pub Lib consul (recognized by State of Fla); New Smyrna Beach; Ormond Beach; Holly Hill; Suwannee River Reg (Live Oak; Edgewater; Gainesville. 9: ALA; SELA (legisl chm); FlaLA (past pres); MoLA (past pres). 10: Jacksonville Area Chamber of Commerce; Civitan Club of Jacksonville; Bd of Trust Jacksonville Episcopal High Sch. 12: Former ed "MoLA Quarterly". 13: Yes. 14: Admin. 15: 122 N Ocean st, Jacksonville Fl 32202.

BRISBIN, CHARLES E(LGIN). b Holden Alta Can 1 F 18. 5: UAlta 40-41 (Elec Engnr), 46-47 (Arts) BA; Toronto 59 BLS. 7: Surveyor Bear Oil Co, Edmonton Alta 48-50; Off manager Industrial Power Installations, Edmonton Alta 50-56; Asst manager Commercial Electric Co, Edmonton Alta 56-58; Manager No Engine & Equip, Edmonton Alta 58-59; Libn N York Pub Lib, Willowdale Ont 59-60; Chief Libn Waterloo Pub Lib, Waterloo Ont 60-63; Chief Libn Hamilton Pub Lib, Hamilton Ont 63-. 9: CanLA; OntLA. 10: Royal Hamilton Yacht Club; Hamilton Press Club. 15: Hamilton Pub Lib, 55 Main st W, Hamilton 10 Ont Can.

BRISKA, BONIFACE. b Latvia 30 O 02. 4: Vera Kuga. 5: Agricultural Acad in Latvia 36-41 (Agronomy) Agronomist (MS); SUNY(Albany) 62-65 MLS. 6: Russian, Ger, Latvian, Latgalian. 7: Asst libn SUNY(Albany) 65-. 8: ALA; SUNY Faculty Assn. 10: Latgalian Research Inst; Latvian Press Soc in Amer. 12: "Latgali Politiskajos Patmalos" (57); "Humoreskas" (65). 13: Yes. 14: Slavic Bibliog & catlg. 15: 298 Washington ave, Albany NY 12203.

BRISKEY, ALDEN R. b Gering Neb 24 S 17. 4: Jean Frances Schuyler. 5: UIda 50-51 (Spec stud); Mesa Col 61-63 (Assoc Arts); West State Col at Gunnison 63-64 (Eng) BA; DenverU 64-65 Libnship. 6: Fr. 7: Marine (Plt Sgt) USMC 38-47; Soldier (Msgt) USA 47-59; Off mgr Colo State Lib 60-61; Priv investigator W J Burns Intnl Det Ag, Denver 65-67; Lib dir Douglas Co Public Lib, Castle Rock Colo 67-. 9: ALA; MPLA; ColoLA. 10: OES; Vol Fire Dept. 14: Lib mgt, contracting. 15: PO Box 737 131 Hillside dr, Castle Rock Co 80104.

BRISKEY, JEAN F (FRANCES SHUYLER). b Ringling Mon 8 Mr 17. 4: Alden R Briskey. 5: San Diego State Col 34-38 Eng AB; USoCal 38-39 BS in LS. 6: Fr, Ger, Sp. 7: Jr libn San Diego State Col 39-41; Children's libn Ocean Beach Br San Diego Pub Lib 41-43; Muscogee Co Sch Dist, Columbus Ga: Bkmob asst 57, Asst catlgr 57-58; Libn (admin) GS8 Spec Serv NACOM, Aschoffenburg Ger 58-59; Area lib consul Colo State Lib 60-. 9: ALA; MPLA; ColoLA. 14: Catlg. 15: Box 737, Castle Rock Co 80104.

BRISLEY, MELISSA (ANN). b Santa Monica Cal 10 Ap 44. 5: Reed 62-66 (Amer Studies) BA; UChicago 66-67 (LS) MA. 7: Asst ref libn IndU 67-. 9: ALA; IndLA. 10: AAUW. 14: Ref, pub serv. 15: Reference Dept Main Lib Indiana Univ, Bloomington In 47401.

BRISLIN, JANE F. b Pittsburgh Penn 23 F 20. 5: Mt Mercy Col 38-42 (Biol) BA; UPittsburgh 44-51 (Biol); Carnegie 54-58 MLS. 6: Sci-Fr, Sp. 7: Lab tech St Francis Hosp, Pittsburgh 42-43; Research asst Mellon Inst Pittsburgh 43-51, Research bibliog 51-58, Jr Fellow 58-59; Free lance bibliog Pittsburgh 59-60; Research assoc UPittsburgh Sch of Dentistry 60-64; Jr Fellow Mellon Inst Pittsburgh 65-66; Asst libn Graphic Arts Tech Foundation, Pittsburgh 66-68, Abstractor/Ed 66-, Libn 68-. 8: Wk on Grants from Nat Inst of Dental Research, US Pub Health Serv 59-64, and Highway Res Bd, NRC 65-66. 9: SLA. 10: Beta Phi Mu; Bd Trustees, Pittsburgh Reg Lib Ctr. 12: "Survey of the Literature of Dental Caries, 1948-1960," with Gerald J Cox (64); "Graphic Arts Abstracts" (66-). 14: Sci-tech bibliog. 15: 340 S Highland ave, Pittsburgh Pa 15206.

BRISTER, DONALD ROBERT. b Endicott NY 2 Ap 43. 5: Ithaca Col 61-65 (Eng) BA; Syracuse 65-66 (LS) MS. 6: Lat, Sp, Ger. 7: Catlgr asst libn SUNY at Binghamton 66-. 9: ALA. 10: Beta Phi Mu. 14: Catlg. 15: 527 Central st, Endicott NY 13760.

BRISTER, MABEL. b Bogue Chitto Miss. 5: Miss Woman's Col (Eng, Music) BA; Tulane (Eng); Miss State U (Eng, Educ); Appalachian State Tchrs Col summers 44-52 (LS) MA. 6: Fr, Sp. 7: Eng Tchr high schs Miss; Libn Hazelhurst & Natchez Miss high schs 44-49; Lib staff Appalachian State U 49-53; Catlg libn & Asst Prof of Lib Sci Delta State Col 53-68; Libn Profess Lib, App State U 68-. 8: Supv of stud tchrs in Lib Sci Appalachian State U 50-53. 9: SELA; MissLA (sec Col & U Sect); MissEA. 10: AAUW; Kappa Delta Pi; Delta Kappa Gamma. 12: "Manual of Suggestions for Supervising Teachers in Library Science" (55). 13: Yes. 14: Catlg, tchg lib sci. 15: 105 Faculty Apts ASU, Boone NC 28607.

BRISTER, MARJORIE F(ERRIER). b Aberdeen Wash 11 D 10. 5: UWash 30-34 (Eng) BA, 34-35 (LS) BA. 6: Ger, Fr. 7: Ref libn Lib Assn of Portland, Portland Ore 35-40; City & Co Libn Pub Lib, Raymond Wash 40-42; Ref libn UWash 42-43; US Army Spec Serv Libn, Ft Lewis Wash 43-44; Hosp libn Madigan Gen Hosp, Ft Lewis Wash 44-46; Ch Camp Libn, Fort Lewis Wash 46-51; Asst circ dept Seattle Pub Lib 63-65; Ser libn Mont State U 65-, Hd acquis dept 67-. 9: ALA; PNLA; MontLA. 10: Mont Inst of Arts (Hist group); AAUP; AAUW; DAR. 14: Catlg, ref, ser, Acquis. 15: 1014 S Third, Bozeman Mt 59715.

BRISTOL, RUTH (AITKEN). b Cambridge Mass 27 Ja 01. 4: Roger Pattrell Bristol. 5: Boston U 19-23 (Eng) AB; Simmons summers 552-55 (LS) MS. 6: Fr. 7: Libn Thayer Sch of Engnr Dartmouth Col 38-41; Asst libn Vail Lib Elec Engnr Mass Inst of Tech 48-49; Head libn Kenwood High Sch, Baltimore Co Md 50-55; Libn Va Div of Mineral Resources, Charlottesville Va 58-63; Various consul in Lib Serv 63-. 9: ALA; SLA; VaLA. 10: LWV; AAUW; Geoscience Info Soc (Org & Founding Mem); AAAS. 14: Info exch among scis & techs. 15: 1808 Barracks rd, Charlottesville Va 22903.

BRITCHER, ELIZABETH COTTON. b Wash DC 26 Mr 14. 5: George Washington U 32-36 (Biol) BS; Simmons 42 (LS) BS. 7: Field sec Girl Scouts, Charleston WVa 36-38; Temp asst Pub Lib, Wash DC 39; Asst in child care dept NY Orthopaedic Hosp, White Plains NY 39-41; Ya libn in br Enoch Pratt Free Lib, Baltimore 42-43; Base libn Army Air Corps, Dale Mabry Field Fla 43-45; Lib asst White Plains Pub Lib, White Plains NY 50-63, Ya & ref asst 63-. 9: ALA; NYLA; WestchesterLA. 10: Simmons Col Lib Sch Alumni Assn; Girl Scouts; Col Club of White Plains. 14: Ref, ya. 15: 192 N Kensico ave, White Plains NY 10604.

BRITE, AGNES. b Bridgeton NC 18 Ap 20. 5: Atlantic Christian Col 37-39 (Soc Sci); Appalachian State Tchrs Col 39-41 (Soc Sci) BS; Peabody 46-47 BS in LS. 7: Ref libn Newark Bus Lib Newark NJ 47-48; Ref libn Wilmington (Del) Pub Lib 48-50; Br libn E I duPont de Nemours & Co, Wilmington Del 50-55; Libn New Eng Mutual Life Insurance Co, Boston 55-. 9: SLA (chm Ins Div, chm Prof Standards Com);-Boston Chap (pres). 10: phi beta kappa; phi mu alpha; aaup; pueblo metro mus assn (bd of dirs 67-); amer guild of organists (dean hartford chap 50-51). 12: Ed & Indexer "Ins Period Index." 14: Ref. 15: 501 Boylston st, Boston 02117.

BRITT, MARGARET ELIZABETH (TROGLOUR). b Brooklyn NY 3 Je 06. 4: Joseph J Britt. 5: Seton Hall U Col 59 (Eng) BA; Rutgers 60-63 MLS. 7: Free Pub Lib, Bayonne NJ: Probation asst 24, Asst 25, Jr asst 26, Sr asst 27-39, Head of catlg dept 39-59, Prin libn 59, Asst lib dir 59-. 8: Catlgr, Alanar bk processing center. 9: ALA; NJLA; NY Tech Serv Libns Assn; Hudson Co LA. 10: UN Assn of USA. 14: Catlg, ref, admin. 15: 129 W 53 st, Bayonne NJ 07002.

BRITTON, GWENDOLYN AUDREY. b Muskogee Okla. 5: Muskogee Jr Col 34-36 AA; Okla Baptist U 36-38 (Hist, eng) BS in Ed; Peabody summers 42-44 BS in LS. 6: Fr. 7: Libn West Jr High Sch, Muskogee Okla 42-. 9: NEA; OklaEA. 10: DAR. 13: Yes. 14: Ref, catlg. 15: 1218 Boston ave, Muskogee Okla 74401.

BRITTON, HELEN (HENDERSON). b Tuskegee Ala 20 N 22. 4: Albert Jefferson Britton. 5: Leland Col 39-43 (Eng) BA in Ed; State U Iowa44-45 (Eng) MA; UMich 52-53 MALS; Bradley U 51. 7: Instr Leland Col 43-44; Instr Bishop Col 45-46; Instr Tuskegee Inst 46-47; Instr Southern U47-50; Tchr Boston High Sch, Lake Charles La 50-51; Libn I Free Lib of Phila 53-55; Asst prof Grambling Col 55-56; Libn III La State Lib 56-62;Catlg libn Ohio State U (Columbus) 62-63, 66-68, Circ desk & bk stack libn 63-66, Sr catlg libn & asst catlg reviser 68-. 8: Commun Survey ofSt Martinville La in interest of lib serv in St Martinville Parish, 59. 9: ALA;-ACRL; OhioLA; Ohio Valley Gp Tech Serv Libns. 10: Pi Lambda Theta; Alpha Kappa Alpha; AAUP; Marquis Biog Lib Soc; Columbus Urban League; Pilots Internat; Ohio State U Fac Club Women. 14: Catlg. 15: 200 Melyers ct, Worthington Oh 43085.

BRITTON, INA (CAVENER). b Hammon Okla 17 Ap 06. 4: Leo F Britton. 5: Central State (Edmond Okla) summer 23-24 life elem certif;UOkla 27, summer 27, 31, 64, 65 (Hist) BA, MA; UWis 34-35 (LS) Diploma. 6: Fr, Sp. 7: Libn Kiefer & Clinton Okla High Schs 27-31; Libn, tchr ofhist Jacksonville Col 31-34; Instr of lib sci Our Lady of the Lake Col summer 37; Libn Intermountain Union Col 35-36; Libn Whitworth Col 36-37;Libn Child High Sch, Edgerton Wis 37-42; Libn Milwaukee U Sch 42-46; Libn Tulsa Pub Schs, Daniel Webster, Tulsa Okla 46-52; Libn Connor StateAgric Col 64-66; Asst libn McMurry Col 66-68; Libn pub schs, Dibble Okla 68-. 9: ALA (Life mem); NEA; OklaLA; OklaEA. 10: Delta Kappa Gamma;Daughters of the Confederacy. 13: Yes. 14: Admin, except child. 15: 123 N Jones, Drumright Ok 74030.

BRITTON, ISABELL (NOONE). b Lawrence Mass 11 Ap 20. 4: Dick S Britton. 5: Simmons 39-43 (LS) BS. 6: Fr. 7: Lib asst Mem Hall Lib, Andover Mass 43-45; Asst libn Ft Devens Army Base, Ayer Mass 45-46; Base libn Wright-Patterson AFB, Dayton Ohio 46-47; Chief Libn Guided Missiles Lib MIT 47-54; Chief Libn Raytheon Co Missile Systems Div, Bedford Mass 54-. 9: SLA; MassLA. 10: Mass Hortic Soc. 13: Yes. 14: Admin, computerized info retr. 15: 137Olive ave, Lawrence Ma 01841.

BROACH, JEANNE (D). b Meridian Miss 27 Ap 13. 5: Miss State Col for Women 30-34 (Eng, Soc Sci) AB; UAla 34-35 (Eng) MA; LSU 48, 50 BS in LS. 7: Tchr high sch, Aliceville Ala 35-36; Tchr high sch, Newton Miss 36-37; Tchr Kate Griffin Jr High Sch, Meridian Miss 37-42; (Lt) Communications US Naval Reserve 42-45; Libn Meridian Pub Lib, Meridian Miss 47-. 9: ALA; SELA; MissLA (pres 57-59, Exec Bd 55-60). 10: Fortnightly; LWV; C of C. 14: Admin. 15: Meridian Pub Lib, 2517 7th st, Meridian Ms 39301.

BROADBENT, MARV(IN) (RAY). b Broken Bow Neb 11 Mr 30. 4: Ruth Scheerer. 5: UNeb 47-61 (Eng, Sp) BSEd; NorthwesternU 62-68 (Sp); Rosary Col 65-68 MALS. 6: Sp. 7: Lt Naval Intelligence 52-59; Marine traffic controller, Panama Canal Co Canal Zone 59-60; Tchr Neb Pub Schs, Aurora Neb 60-61; Tchr & libn Ill Pub Schs 61-68; Proprietor Marv Broadbent Bksellers, New Carrollton Md 62-; Acquis libn OAS Pan Am Union, Wash DC 68-. 9: Ill Stud Libns Assn (sponsor 67-68). 10: Amer GI Forum of Ill. 14: Lat Amer acquis. 15: 5710 - 85th ave, New Carrollton Md 20784.

BROADHEAD, EDWARD HALL. b Jamestown NY 5 Ap 10. 5: Denison U 28-31 (Music) AB; Duke U 32-33 (Hist) MA; UMich summer 39 (Organ) M Mus; Columbia 47-48 BSLS. 6: Fr. 7: U organist Duke U 33-44; Organist First Congregational Church, Meriden Conn 45-47; Libn, tchr Hartt Col of Music 46-60; Organist Second Church of Christ Sci, Hartford Conn 47-48; Minister of Music Asylum Hill Congregational Church, Hartford Conn 48-56; Organist Temple Beth Israel, W Hartford Conn 51-53; U libn UHartford 57-60; Dir of Lib Fairleigh Dickinson U 60-65; Head Libn So Colo State Col 65-. 9: ALA; ColoLA; MPLA. 10: Phi Beta Kappa; Phi Mu Alpha; AAUP; Pueblo Metro Mus Assn (Bd of dirs 67-); Amer Guild of Organists (dean Hartford chap 50-51). 14: Admin. 15: So Colo State Col, Pueblo Co 81001.

BROADNAX, WILLIAM THOMAS JR. b Columbus Ga 18 F 35. 5: Knoxville Col 54-58 (Eng) BS in Ed; Drexel 61-65 (LS); Villanova U 63-65 MSLS. 6: Sp. 7: Eng tchr Phila Bd of Educ 61-65; Libn Deptford Twp High Sch, Deptford NJ 65-Hd libn BOCES #1 Spec Educ Dept, Yorktown Hts NY 10598. 8: Citizen Adv Comfor new Ossining High Sch; Citizen Reading Com, Ossining Bd of Educ. 9: NEA;ALA;-Westchester Sch Lib System; NYLA;-BOCES Soc. 10: Omega Psi Phi; NAACP;Interfaith Coun for Action; Ossining Choral Soc. 14: Ref, ya serv, child serv. 15: 71 Charter cir, Ossining NY 10562.

BROADUS, ROBERT NEWTON. b Stanford Ky 3 D 22. 4: Eleanor Hammond. 5: David Lipscomb Col 41-43; Pepperdine Col 43-45 (Relig) BA; Chicago 46-47 BLS; USoCal 48-52 (Speech) PhD. 7: Libn Pepperdine Col 47-53; Libn David Lipscomb Col 53-55; Lecturer Peabody Lib Sch 54, 55; Assoc Prof No Ill U 55-56; Lib spec Sperry Rand Corp, Chicago 56-61; Assoc Prof No Ill U 61-65, Prof 65-. 8: Consul to Dir of Libs, No Ill U, on lib equipment planning, 62-64. 9: ALA; SLA; IllLA. 10: AAUP; Phi Kappa Phi. 13: Yes. 14: Catlg, bk sel, bibliog humanities, col & univ libs, tech processes, inforetr. 15: 8 Pheasant Run, DeKalb Il 60115.

BROADWELL, JUDITH (INGRAM LOWY). b NYC 29 O 32. 4: George Peake Broadwell. 5: Hunter Col 50-54 (Creative Writing) AB; Columbia 55-58 (Scenic Design) 62-65 (LS) MS. 6: Fr, Ger. 7: Eng tchr, sch libn JHS 60-133, NYC 54-64; Sch libn JHS 22, NYC 64-. 9: ALA; NYLA. 10: Delta Pi. 14: Child & ya. 15: 162 E 92nd st, NYC 10028.

BROCHU, LUCIEN. b Drummondville Que Can 2 O 20. 4: Georgette Davy. 5: UMontreal Seminaire St-Hyacinthe 42 BA; ULaval (Que) 47 BMus,55 Licence en Musique. 6: Eng, Fr. 7: Prof a l'Ecole de Musique de l ULaval 47-; Maitre-de-Chapelle Notre-Dame-du-Chemin, Que 48-65; Prof AuConservatoire de Musique de la Prof de Que 48-60; Bibliothecaire a l'Ecole de Musique de l U'Laval 47-, Dir 62-. 9: Internat Assn of Mus Libs;CanLA. 10: Association des Professeurs de Universites de Langue Francaise du (Que); Association des Facultes de Musique des Universites Canadiennes; Can AAUP; Music Educrs Nat Conf. 14: Ref, catlg. 15: Ecole de Musique, Universite Laval, Que Can.

BROCK, (DEWEY) CLIFTON JR. b Anderson SC 13 S 30. 4: Eunice Miller Brock. 5: Clemson U 47-51 (Eng) BS; UMich 55-57 MALS; Fla State U 58-60 (Pol Sci) MA; UNC 61- (Pol Sci). 7: Navy journalist US Navy 51-55; Jr ref libn UMich Sch of Bus Admin Lib 56-57; Asst Soc Sci libn Fla State U Lib 57-59; Lecturer Sch of Lib SciUNC 61-63; Chief bus admin & soc sci div UNC Lib 59-66, Assoc Univ libn UNC 66-. 9: ALA; NCLA. 10: AAUP; So Polit Sci Assn. 12: "Americans for Democratic Action; Its Role in National Politics" (62); "A Guide to Library Resources for Political Science Students at theUniversity of North Carolina" (65); "The Literature of Political Science; A Guide for Students, Teachers and Librarians" (69). 13: Yes. 14: Ref, govt docs, admin. 15: 316 Burlage dr, Chapel Hill NC 27514.

BROCK, LOIS WELLINGTON. b Boston 6 Jl 16. 5: Wells Col 33-37 (Classics) BA; West Res 37-38 (Classics) MA; Kent State 52-54 (LS) MA. 6: Fr, Ger. 7: Sci tchr Buffalo Sem Buffalo NY 38-43; Chem Nat Aniline Div Buffalo NY 43-46; Tech libn Gen Tire & Rubber Co Akron Ohio 46-. 9: SLA; ACS. 10: Akron Coun Engnrg & Sci Socs; Col Club of Akron (Program chm 67-69). 11: Phi Beta Kappa. 12: Ed 'Society News' in "Akron Tech Journal." 13: Yes. 15: The General Tire & Rubber Co, Akron Oh 44309.

BROCKMAN, MARTHA D. b Clifton Hill RR Mo 20 O 13. 05 NE Mo State Tchrs 31-41 Eng BS, 57 UMo 47-53 Certif Lib Sci Peabody 58-62 MS in LS. 5: MNE Mo State Col, Kirksville Mo 31-41 (Eng) BS; UMo 47-53 Certif LS; Peabody 58-62 MS in LS. 7: Rural & elem, Randolph Co Mo 31-41; Eng tchr Brashear High sch, Brashear Mo 41-42; Eng tchr Renick High Sch, Renick Mo 42-47; Eng tchr W Plains High Sch, W Plains Mo 47-49; Tchr-libn Paris Mo 49-55; Tchr-libn Moberly Jr Col 55-62; Dir of Lib Central Methodist Col 62-66; Ref libn Northeast Mo State Col Kirksville Mo 66-. 9: ALA; MoLA; MoSchLA; Mo State Tchrs Assn. 10: Alpha Delta Kappa; AAUW; Bus & Prof Women. 14: Ref. 15: 721 Cleveland, Moberly Mo 65270.

BROCKMAN, WANDA (ZERILDA). b Portland Ore 4 My 17. 5: Reed Col 35-40 (Lit) BA; UCal 41-42 Certif in Libnship. 6: Fr. 7: Circ asst Ore State Col 42-44; Union catlgr Ore State System of Higher Educ, corvallis Ore 44-45; Seattle Pub Lib: Asst ref dept 45-57, 1st asst ref dept 57-60, 1st asst hist & govt dept 60-62, Head lit, lang, phil, relig dept 62-. 9: ALA; PNLA. 10: Women's Univ Club, Seattle. 14: Ref, pub libs. 15: Seattle Pub Lib 4th & Madison, Seattle 98104.

BROCKMEYER, MARGOT (GOWDY). b Belmond Iowa 14 N 36. 4: Roger L Brockmeyer. 5: Cottey Col 54-56 AA;

Cornell Col (Iowa) 56-58 (Hist) BA; UIll 62-63 MSLS. 7: Tchr Anamosa Hogh Sch, Anamosa Iowa 58-60; Libn (staff) Vassar Col 64-66, 67-. 8: Consul Col of Bus & Pub Admin, Fla Atlantic U69; Consul ICAITI, Guatemala, for Bi-National Develop Corp, Boulder Colo 69. 9: SLA (pres-elect Colo chap); ColoLA. 10: Phi Beta Kappa; Beta Phi Mu. 14: Catlg. 15: Vail rd, Poughkeepsie NY 12603.

BROCKWAY, DUNCAN. b Manchester NH 23 Jl 32. 4: Lois Simpson. 5: St John's Col (Annapolis Md) 49-53 (Liberal Arts) BA; Harvard Divinity Sch 53-55; Princeton Theol Sem 55-56 BD; Rutgers 58-60 MLS. 6: Fr. 7: Stated Supply Windham Presbyterian Church, Windham NH 56-58; Tchr Sanborn Sem 56-57; Lib asst UNH 57-58; Order libn Princeton Theol Sem 58-62; Pastor Frenchtown Presbyterian Church, Frenchtown NJ 62-65; Acquis libn & catlg of 16th & 17th cent imprints, Hartford Seminary Found, Hartford Conn 65-66, Libn 66-. 9: ALA; AtLA. 13: Yes. 14: Acquis, catlg, rare bks, admin. 15: Case Mem Lib Hartford Sem Found, 55 Elizabeth st, Hartford Ct 06105.

BRODE, MILDRED (HOOKER). b Greensboro Vt 14 Ap 1900. 5: UVt 17-21 (Math, Physics) PhB; George Washington U Even 21-25 (Physics); OhioState U 30-31 (Physics) MS, 32-33 (Educ) BS in Educ; Columbia 37-38 BS in LS. 6: Fr, Ger, Sp, Russian. 7: Asst Physicist Nat Bur of Standards,Wash DC 21-26; Supv Spectroscopy Proj MIT 38-39; Baker Lib Dartmouth Col; Catlgr 39-41, Ref dept 41-42, Chief ref dept 42-44, Instr Physics42-44; Chief libn Nav Ship Rsearch & Devel Ctr, Wash DC 44-. 9: SLA (pres 63-64; pres Wash DC Chap 55-57); ALA; ASIS; DCLA. 10: AAAS; AAUW;Bus & Prof Women's Club. 13: Yes. 14: Admin, ref. 15: 4607 Connecticut ave NW, Wash DC 20008.

BRODERICK, DOROTHY M. b Bridgeport Conn 23 Je 29. 5: New Haven State Tchrs Col 47-53 (LS) BS; Columbia 54-56 (LS) MS. 6: Sp. 7: Pub lib child consul NY State Lib 60-62; Assoc Prof West Res 63-. 9: ALA (Coun 64-68); WNBA; OhioLA. 11: United Educators Fellowship 65. 12: "Leete's Island Adventure" (62); "Training a Companion Dog" (65); "Introduction to Child Wk in Pub Libs" (65); Ed "Top of the News" 63-64;"Hank" (66); Co-comp "Time for Stories Past and Present" (68); "Time for Biography" (69). 13: Yes. 14: Child lit, ya lit. 15: 3637 Cross st, Madison Wi 53711.

BRODERICK, JOHN C (CARUTHERS). b Memphis Tenn 6 S 26. 4: Kathryn Lynch Broderick. 5: SW (Memphis) 43-45, 46-48 (Eng) AB; Yale 45-46 (Japanese) Army Lang Certif; UNC 48-52 (Eng) MA, PhD. 6: Fr. 7: Reporter "Memphis Press Scimitar", Memphis Tenn 43-44, 46-49; Pfc USA 45-46; Instr in Eng UTex (Austin) 52-57; Prof of Eng Wake ForestU 57-65; Visiting Prof of Eng UVa 59; Adjunct Prof George WashingtonU 64-; Specialist Amer Cultural Hist LC 64-65, Asst chief mss div 65-, Act chief mss div 67-68; Visiting Prof of Eng UNC (Chapel Hill) 68. 8: Consul in bibliog George WashingtonU 64; Adv bd Calendars of American Lit Mss 66-; Assoc ed The Writing of Henry David Thoureau 66-. 9: Mod Lang Assn; Amer Studies Assn; Bibliog Soc of Amer; Mss Soc; Soc of Amer Archivists; Thoureau Soc. 11: ACLS Grant 62-63; Danforth Award 60. 12: "Whitman the poet" (61); "Dreisler Sister Carrie: a Study Guide" (64). 13: Yes. 14: Mss, spec collections. 15: 8005 Inspection House rd, Rockville Md 20854.

BRODERICK, PATRICIA (MULGREW). b Carlisle Penn 22 Ja 27. 5: Col Misericordia 44-48 (Soc Sci) BA; Case-West Res 61-62 MSLS. 7: Soc wkr Penn Dept of Health Bur of TB Control, S Mt Penn 49-50; Health educ sec Cumberland Co TB & Health Assoc, Carlisle Penn 50-51; Eng tchr Rockwood Joint Schs, Rockwood Penn 57-59; Eng tchr N Syracuse Sch Syst, Matly Dale NY 59-60; Eng tchr Westmont Sch Syst, Johnstown Penn 60-61; Baltimore Co Pub Lib, Towson Md: Prof asst libn 62, Br libn 63, 65-67; Coordinator of co serv C Burriatz Lib, Frederick Md 63-65; Penn State Lib Bur Lib Development, Harrisburg Penn: Lib development adv 67-69, Lib development supv 69-. 9: ALA; PennLA. 10: Beta Phi Mu. 14: Pub lib devel. 15: 4201-A King George dr, Harrisburg Pa 17109.

BRODMAN, ESTELLE. b NYC 1 Je 14. 5: Cornell U (Histology) 31-35 AB; Columbia 35-53 (LS & Med Hist) BS, MS, PhD. 6: Ger, Fr, Lat. 7: Var poss Columbia U Med Lib 37-49; Assoc for Extramural Planning NLM 60-61, Asst libn for ref serv 49-61; Visiting Prof Keio U Japan Lib S. Tokyo 62; Libn & Assoc Prof Med Hist Wash U Sch of Med 61-64 Prof 64-. 8: Numerous surveys & consultantships; Survey of Nat Inst of Health Lib 49150; Consul Mich U Biomedical Info Center 65; Consul Nat Inst for Mental Health Info Clearinghouse 64-69; AAMC-MLA Com on Guidelines for Med Libs 63-64; Mem Nat Adv Commssn on Libs 66-68. Expert, Tech Asst Program, UN (India) 67-68; Taught libnship Columbia 46-50, at Catholic U 57 Keia Univ, Tokyo, 62; Tchr med hist, Washington U Sch of Med 63-. 9: ALA (many offs); MedLA (pres 64-65, many other offs); SLA (nat dir 49-52, many other offs). 10: Taught libnship Columbia 46-50, at Catholic U 57; Tchr med hist Washington U Sch of Med 63-. 11: Woman of the Year St Louis Chap of AAUW 64. 12: "Development of Med Bibliog" (54); Ed "Bull of the Med Lib Assn" (47-57). 13: Yes. 14: Ref, transmission of sci info, computer tech, admin, educ of libns, hist of med. 15: Wash U Sch of Med 4580 Scott ave, St Louis Mo 63110.

BRODOWSKI, JOYCE HELENE. b Trenton NJ 16 S 32. 5: Douglass Col 49-53 (Eng) AB; Columbia 53-55 (LS) MS; Rutgers 57-62 (Eng) AM; Columbia 64- (LS). 6: Fr. 7: Jr libn Trenton Free Pub Lib Trenton NJ 53-55; Acquis libn Trenton State Col Trenton NJ 55-60, Readers' adv Humanities 60-66, 68-, Assoc Prof & asst libn readers serv 66-68. 9: ALA; BSA; Priv LibAssn; NJLA (sec 60-61, Archivist 61-64, Publ Expediter 55-65, var coms, v-pres67-68; Col & Univ Sect; sec-treas 66-67, v-pres 69-70); NJEA. 10: William MorrisSoc; AAUP; NJ State Faculties Assn. 12: Assoc ed "New Jersey Libraries" 61-64. 14: Rare bks, hist of bks & printing, hist of libs, ref. 15: 59 Gedney rd, Trenton NJ 08638.

BRODY, CATHERINE ALBERTA VERONICA (TYLER). b Chicago Ill 7 S 27. 4: Stanley J Brody. 5: Rosary Col 45-49 (Eng) AB; St Louis U 49-51 (Eng); Pratt Inst 62-65 MLS; Hunter 67- Eng. 6: Fr. 7: Tchy fellow St Louis U 49-51; Contributing ed "Popular Horsemen Magazine," Harrisburg Penn 48-53; Lib consul ESEA Title II, NYC 66; Catlgr Hunter Col 66; Br libn graphic art & com art NYC Commun Col 66-67; Ref libn NYC Commun Col (Brooklyn) 67-. 9: ALA; (JMRT); SLA; BSA; Lib Assn CUNY (Del 67-, Conf Com 68 & 69, Prog Com 68-69, etc); NY Lib Club. 10: Beta Phi Mu; New Yorl Shavians; William Morris Soc; Victorian Soc in Amer; Soc Hist Discoveries. 14: Rare bks, fine printing, hist of bks & printing. 15: 649 E 14th st, New York NY 10009.

BROEDE, CAROL EVE (KARMATZ). b New Brunswick NJ 2 O 38. 4: Bruce A Broede. 5: Syracuse 56-58 (Bacteriology); UWis 58-60 (Amer Inst) BS; Drexel 64-65 (LS) MS. 6: Ger. 7: Stud asst UWis Memorial Lib 58-60; Libn C D Smith Pharmaceutical Co, New Brunswick NJ 64; Lib asst UPenn Math-Physics Lib 64-65; Readers serv libn Franklin Inst Lib, Phila 65-66; Lib analyst Boeing Co Vertol Engring Lib Ridley Pk Penn 66-67; Libn Sun Shipbuilding & Dry Dock Co, Chester Penn 67-68. 8: Spec asst, Honnold Lib, claremont Cols, Claremont Cal 68-. 9: SLA. 14: Sci & tech, bus & indus, ref & admin. 15: 1037 Lake Forest dr, Claremont Ca 91711.

BROESTL, JOHN ANTHONY. b Cleveland 13 Je 26. 5: John Carroll U 44, 47-49 (Eng) BA, 49-53 (Eng) MA; West Res 50-51 MS in LS; Ind U 52 (Linguistics). 6: Fr. 7: Infantryman (Sgt) US Army 44-46; Tchr Eng, Lat Lucas (Ohio) High Sch 49-50; Sr libn, catlg dept Indianapolis Pub Lib 51-53; Catlg asst Fla State U Lib 53-54; 1st asst catlg dept Lib of Hawaii, Honolulu 54-55; Station libn Barbers Pt Naval Air Station, Oahu Hawaii 55-56; Base libn Hickam AFB, Oahu Hawaii 56-58; Catlgr Minn Hist Soc Lib, St Paul 58-63, Head of tech serv 63-68; Catlg Librn 69-. 15: Minn Hist Soc Lib, St Paul Mn 55101.

BROGAN, DOROTHY B(ULLARD). b Ft Lupton Colo 23 Je 23. 5: Colo State Col of Educ 41-45 (Biol, Phys Sci) AB, 46-51 (Biol Sci) MA; UDenver 53-58 (LS) MA. 7: Critic tchr Colo State Col of Educ 46-49; Tchr High Sch, Mont Air Colo 49-52; Tchr Jr High Sch, Englewood Colo 53-55; Tchr High Sch, Long Beach Cal 55-57; Libn Denver Pub Lib 59-. 8: Tchr of Biol Sci, Colo State Col of Educ, 50. 9: ALA; ACS (Chem Lit Sect). 10: Botany Club. 115: 7820 E 17th st, Denver Co 80220. 14: Ref. 15: 7820 E 17th ave, Denver 80220.

BROGAN, GERALD E(DWARD). b Bentonville Ark 15 Ag 24. 4: Coweta Adkins. 5: Colo State Col 46-50 (Eng) AB; UDenver 50-51 (LS) MA. 7: (Sgt) US Army Air Corps 43-46; Libn I Denver Pub Lib 51-54; Long Beach City Col: Circ libn 54-59, Head Libn bus & tech div 59-65, Chm lib & a-v div 65-66; Coord Lib Serv Hawaii Commun Col 66-67; Soc sci libn Chico State Col 67-68;Col libn Col of the Redwoods 68-. 8: Mem, Adv Bd, Grad Sch of Lib Studies, UHawaii. 9: ALA; NEA; CalLA; Cal Tchrs Assn. 12: Co-auth "Effective Use of Libraries" (69). 14: Jr Col admin. 15: College of Redwoods, Eureka Ca 95501.

BROMBERG, ERIK. b Centerville Iowa 24 Ag 14. 4: Ailene Jane McMahon. 5: Ohio State U 31-36 (Hist) Ba, bsc, MA; UNeb 36-38; UWash 48-49 BLS. 6: Fr, Ger. 7: Soc Sci tchr Wymore (Neb) High Sch 38-41; US Army Med Corps Sgt

Major 41-45; Train Off US VA Seattle 45-50; Asst ref libn Wash State Lib 50-52; Libn Puget Sound Naval Shipyard Bremerton Wash 52-55; Libn US Dept of Interior Bonneville Power Admin, Portland Ore 55-66; Dir of Libs US Dept of Int Wash DC 67-. 8: Consul & lecturer Yugoslav Govt 65. 9: SLA (Govt Rel Com 61-66, chm educ Com 65-67); chm Pugent Sound chap 55. 10: Phi Beta Kappa. 13: Yes. 14: Admin. 15: US Dept of Interior, Washington DC 20240.

BROMLEY, M JANE. b Hamilton Ont Can 24 Mr 34. 5: New Haven State Tchrs Col 52-56 (Educ) BS; So Conn State Col 60-61 (LS) MS; Harvard summer 63. 7: Tchr Bd of Educ Branford Conn 56-57; Serv Club rec asst Spec Serv Kitzingen Germany 57-59; Libn Village Improvement Assn West Haven Conn 60-61; Libn Beloit Col 61-65; Intern libn City of Westminster London 65-66; Dir Roselle Pub Lib, Roselle NJ 67-. 9: ALA; NJLA. 10: LWV. 14: Ref, circ, admin. 15: 138 Division ave, Shelton Ct 06484.

BRONDUM, NANCY (HUGHES). b San Bernardino Cal 17 N 29. 5: UCLA 47-51 (Soc) BA; UCopenhagen 63-64 (Psych); USoCal 64-65 MSLS; Boston U fall 67 (Adult Educ). 6: Danish. 7: Catlgr Harvard Col 65-66; Libn Camp, Boston 66-68; Hd commun servSanta Ana Pub Lib, Santa Ana Cal 68; Child libn Orange Co Pub Lib, Garden Grove Cal68-. 15: 455 Dartmoor ave, Laguna Beach Ca 80120.

BRONSON, BARBARA. b Spencer Iowa. 5: Pomona Col 31-33 (Hist) BA; USoCal 41-42 BS in LS; UIll 50-51 (LS). 7: Ref libn Pasadena Pub Lib, Pasadena Cal 42-43; Post libn Camp Roberts Army, Camp Roberts Cal 43-46; Asst staff libn Eighth US Army, Yokohama Japan 46-49; Bibliog UIll(Urbana) 49-51; Chief libn US Army, Ft Benning Ga 51-57; Staff libn Third US Army, Ft McPherson Ga 57-59; Lib consul Ga State Dept of Educ, Atlanta 59-. 9: ALA; SELA; GaLA (v-pres 68-69). 10: Atlanta Lib Club; AAUW; Soroptimist Fed; Phi Kappa Phi; Beta Phi Mu. 11: John Cotton Dana Award, 55. 14: Ref, tech serv, admin. 15: Apt 1705, 710 Peachtree st NE, Atlanta Ga 30308.

BRONSON, JOHN O JR. b Memphis Tenn 6 Ap 37. 4: Patricia P Packer. 5: UMiss 64-65 MLS; Miss State U 59-61 (Eng, Hist) BS; NortheastMiss Jr Col 57-59 (Eng, Hist); Memphis State U 56, summer 59 (Eng, Hist). 7: Page Memphis Pub Lib, Memphis Tenn 53-57; USAF Res A/3c WelfareSpec 55-63; Field rep Miss Lib Commsn, Jackson Miss 61-62; Field sec Acacia Nat Fraternity, Evanston Ill 62-64; Instr Lib Sci UMiss 64-65; LibnJohn C Calhoun Jr Col 65-67; Hd libn Chesapeake Col, Wye Mills Md 67-. 9: ALA; AlaLA; Ala Jr Col LA (v-pres); MdLA; Md Assn Jr Col (sec-treasLearning Resources Div). 10: Geneal Soc; Northeast Miss Hist Soc; Hist Soc Talbot Co Md. 14: Catlg, admin (Jr Col), ref. 15: Box 23, Wye Mills Md 21679.

BRONSTON, MRS ESTHER (MARY) C(RENSHAW). b Richmond Ky 6 Je 11. 4: Irvin W Bronston. 5: Wilberforce U 29-33 (Math) BS in Ed; Hampton Inst 33-35 BS in LS; UIll summers 40-43 MS in LS. 7: Libn & math tchr Voorhees Normal & Ind Sch, Denmark SC 35-37; Libn W Ky Ind Col 37-38; Libn W Ky Vocational Train Sch, Paducah Ky 38-39; Reserve bk dept libn Wilberforce U 39-47; Reserve bk dept libn Central State U (Wilberforce Ohio) 47-68; Libn Wilbur Wright High Sch, Dayton Ohio 68-. 9: ALA-AASchL;-YASD;OhioLA. 10: AAUW. 13: Yes. 14: Ref, circ, reserve bks, lib admin. 15: Rt 5, Xenia Oh45385.

BROOK, MICHAEL. b Bristol Eng 1 O 26. 5: Pembroke Col (Oxford) 44-47 (Mod Hist) BA (converted to MA); Leeds Sch of Libnship 51-52 ALA. 6: Fr, Swedish. 7: Jr asst UBristol Lib (Bristol Eng) 48-50; Asst libn USheffield Lib (Sheffield Eng) 53-55; Sub-libn dept of local hist & archives Sheffield Pub Lib, Sheffield Eng 55-57; Reading room supt USouthampton Lib (Southampton Eng) 57-61; Asst ref libn Minn Hist Soc, St Paul 62-63, Ref libn 63-. 9: Lib Assn (Gt Brit); MinnLA. 10: Hist Societies in Sweden, UK, US. 14: Ref, bibliog. 15: Minn Hist Soc, St Paul Mn 55101.

BROOKE, WILFRED LEE JR. b Rochester NY 5 Jl 30. 4: Mary Domermuth. 5: Knox Col 48-50 (Music); Elmhurst Col 54-56 (Eng) AB; Roosevelt U (Psych) 60;Rosary Col 61-65 MLS. 7: USN Musician 3rd class 50-54; Chem sales Fred L BrookeCo, Chicago 56-60; Proviso East High Sch, Maywood Ill; Eng Instr 60-63, Libn 63-64,Catlgr 64-65; Libn Proviso West High Sch, Hillside Ill 65-66; Dir of info PlannedParenthood Assn, Chicago 66-. 9: IllLA; IllASchL. 10: Unitarian Social Action Com (chm); Oak Park-Riverforest Citizens Com for Human Rights; Housing chm West Suburban Org for FairHousing. 11: Short Story Award, Elmhurst Col 56. 12: Ed "Suburban Human Relations Handbook"; Auth of Programmed Instr in Lib Sci (5 brochures). 15: 208 N Scoville, Oak Park Il60302.

BROOKS, BENEDICT III. b Pearl Creek NY 18 Ap 35. 5: URochester 52-56 (Fr) AB; Columbia 56-57 (LS) MS; Penn State U 58-61 (Chem); Yale U Sch of Med 61-65 (Med) Nat Bds, part 1. 6: Fr, Sp, Ger, Ital, Russian. 7: (Pvt E-2) US Army basic train, Ft Dix NJ summer 57, Mil Intelligence, Ft Holabird Md fall 57; Gen catlgr Penn State U Lib 58, Sr catlgr 59-61; Catlgr Yale U Sch of Med, Med Lib 61-65; Lecturer in Dept of Lib Borough of Manhattan Commun Col Lib 65-66; (SSG E-6) US Army Res, New Haven Conn61-63; Indexer Biol & Agric Index H W Wilson Co, Bronx NY 66-68; Instr catlg div Brooklyn Col Lib 68-. 9: MedLA; SLA; ALA; LACUNY; NY Lib Club. 10: Metro OperaGuild; Phi Beta Kappa; Phi Sigma Iota; Beta Phi Mu; Metro Museum of Art. 12: Indexer"Library Literature," H W Wilson (66-69). 13: Yes. 14: Ref, catlg (med & other sci libs). 15: Box 56 - 155 W 68th st, New York NY 10023.

BROOKS, EULAN (VON). b Clarksville Tex 29 Mr 36. 4: Dwan (Lemmond). 5: No Tex State U 55-58 (Mus) Bachelor of Music, 58-66 (Musicology) Master of Arts; UTex at Austin 61-66 (LS). 6: Ger. 7: Tchr Malakoff Pub Schs, Malakoff Tex 53-55; Tchr Dallas Pub Schs, 55-58; Tchr Garland Pub Schs, Garland Tex 58-62 UTex at Austin: Verifier (order dept) 62-64, Mus libn 64-, Asst prof of mus 67-. 9: MusicLA (prog chm, Mid-Winter 69); ALA; Amer Musicol Soc; TexLA (chm, Arts R T 68-69); Tex Assn of Col Tchrs. 10: Soc of UTex Libns; Lib Staff Assn UTex. 14: Mus libnship, mus bibliog. 15: 1715 E 38 1/2 st, Austin Tex 78722.

BROOKS, GREGG McKINNEY. b Woodland Cal 15 Ja 40. 5: Gallaudet Col 60-65 (LS) BS. 6: Fr, sign lang. 7: Catlg libn Walt Disney Studios, Burbank Cal 65-. 10: Cal Assn of the Deaf; Nat Assn of the Deaf. 14: Catlg & research wk on motion pictures. 15: 14210 Dickens st #6, Sherman Oaks Ca 91403.

BROOKS, HALLIE (BEACHEM). b West Baden Ind 9 O 07. 4: Frederic Victor Brooks. 5: B utler U 34 (Eng) AB; Columbia 40 BLS; Chicago 46 (LS) MA, 49-50. 6: Fr, Sp. 7: Asst libn Indianapolis Pub Lib Indianapolis 23-30; Libn Atlanta U Lab Sch 30-42; Mem of faculty Atlanta U Sch of Lib Serv 42-. 8: Lib consul secondary sch study of the Assn of Col and Secondary Schs 40-42; Dir of field serv Atlanta U Sch of Lib Serv 42-45; Consul in reading at wkshops in Ala, La & Ga. 9: ALA (chm Asia Found Grant Com, Lib Educ Div); AALS (chm Com on Instr & Materials); SELA (Com on Lib Educ); Atlanta Lib Club (Intellectual Freedom Com). 10: AAUP; Atlanta U Women's Club; NAACP (chm Freedom Fund); Gate City Day Nursery Assn (Bd); Grady Homes; Girls Club (Bd); United Appeal (co-chm Negro Div & mem of Budget Panel); Beta Phi Mu; Pi Lambda Theta. 12: Ed "The Role of the Lib in Improving Educ in the South" (Conf Proceedings) 65. 13: Yes. 14: Rare bks, communications, bibliog of the humanities, modern bk pub. 15: Box 264 Atlanta U 223 Chestnut st SW, Atlanta Ga 30314.

BROOKS, HARLEY CALVIN JR. b Harrogate Tenn 6 Ap 33. 4: Barbara Collier Brooks. 5: Lincoln Mem U 47-51 (Eng) BA; Peabody 56-57 (LS) MA; UNM 59-61; Chicago 61-62. 6: Sp. 7: Meter record clerk Dayton Power & Light, Dayton Ohio 51-53; US Army 53-55; Tchr Pruden High Sch, Pruden Tenn 55-56; Libn Hiwassee Col 57-59; Catlgr UNM 59-61; Asst libn Southeast Jr Col 62; Circ libn U Chicago 62-64; Head circ dept Ohio State U 64-68; Libn Peabody Col 68-. 9: ALA; TennLA. 12: Ed Adv Bd, "Peabody Journal ofEducation". 13: Yes. 14: Circ, admin. 15: 4405 Farriswood dr, Nashville Tn 37204.

BROOKS, HAZELLE A. b Mehoopany Penn 21 My 12. 4: Foster R Brooks. 5: Dickinson Col 30-34 (Soc Studies) AB; Marywood Col 57-62 MS in LS. 7: Tchr & asst prin Mehoopany High Sch 36-41; Libn Tunkhannock High Sch, Tunkhannock Penn 56-. 8: Eval Team for Middle Atlantic States at Jr-Sr High Sch in Wellsboro Penn 67. 9: PennLA; A-V Coords Assn for Northeast Instrl Materials Center (sec). 15: Mehoopany Pa 18629.

BROOKS, JANET (STRATTAN) (PETERS). b Detroit 27 D 18. 5: Butler U 36-38 (Fr); Ohio State U 40-41 (Fr, Eng) BS in Ed; UMd 67-69 MLS. 6: Fr. 7: Research asst Ohio State C of C 41-43; Research asst Machinery & Allied Products Inst 43-46; Partner & manager Brooks-Stratton Insur Agency 50-55; Tchr, Montgomery Co Md 56-58; Libn John I Thompson & Co, Wash DC 59-60; Libn circ period & interlib loan US Naval Observatory, Wash DC 60-63; Asst libn ref libn & chief catlgr US Naval Observatory, Wash DC 63-65; Libn catlg & info spec in astronom Naval Automated Research & Devel

Info System, Physical sci indexer & abstracter, Carderock Md 65-66; Act chief Sci & Tech Info Off USA Engrs Geodesy Intelligence & Mapping Agency, Ft Belvoir Va 66-67; Dir lib serv US Nat Commsn on Prod Safety, Wash DC 68-. 8: Ed consul: R Blum & Assocts, Wash DC 69-; Surveys and Research Corp 67; Archival consul Nat Coun for the Prevention of War 68-. 9: SLA (chm Mil Libns Group, DC chap 68-69); ALA; Soc Tech Writers & Publrs; DCLA; ASIS; AALL. 10: Washington Ethica Soc; Toastmistresses; Amer Humanist Assn; Kappa Alpha Theta; ACLU. 14: Lib adm in & planning. 15: 4620 Windom pl NW, Wash DC 20016.

BROOKS, JOYCE H. b Sweet Grass Mont 15 D 16. 5: UWash 34-38 (Anthropology) BA, 56-60 M of Libr. 6: Fr, Ger. 7: Br libn Col of Eng Lib UWash 39-41; Exec sec & admin asst, bus firms, Seattle 47-56; Libn Skagit Valley Jr Col 56-57; Libn Sch of Libnship UWash 57-58, Br libn Geog & Map Libs 58-63; Ref libn soc sci & bus div San Jose State Col 63-. 9: SLA; Cal Tchrs Assn. 10: Alpha Xi Delta. 14: Ref, spec collections. 15: San Jose State Col Lib, San Jose Cal 95114.

BROOKS, KAREN COX. b Decatur Ill 12 D 44. 4: Carl J Brooks. 5: East IllU 63-67 (Soc Sci) BS in Ed; UIll 67-68 (LS) MS. 7: Libn Jr High Sch, Rochelle Ill 68-. 10: Beta Phi mu. 14: Sch libs, child lit. 15: May Mart apts E-6, Rochelle Il 61068.

BROOKS, LOUISE (McDONALD). b Monroe La 14 F 19. 5: La Polytech Inst 36-40 Soc sci BA; George Peabody Col summers 40, 41, 44 BS in LS. 6: Fr, Lat. 7: Tchr libn Gilbert High Sch Gilbert La 40-43; Libn Winnsboro High Sch, Winnsboro La 43-45; Libn USA, Camp Shelby Miss 45-46; Asst libn Hattiesburg Pub Lib, Hattiesburg Miss 46-47, Hd libn 47-52; Tchr libn Weston High Sch, Weston La 52-53; Libn Jonesboro Elem Sch, Jonesboro La 53-54; Libn Jonesboro-Hodge High Sch, Jonesboro La 54-. 9: ALA; LaLA; LaTA. 10: DAR. 14: Ref. 15: 404 No Polk st, Jonesboro La 71251.

BROOKS, PHILIP C. b Wash DC 14 Ja 06. 4: Dorothy Holland. 5: UMich 24-28 (Hist) BA; UCal 29-33 (Hist) MA, PhD. 6: Sp. 7: Tchg asst George Washington U 33-34; Examiner, Staff Off, Nat Archives 35-48; Records Off Nat Security Resources Bd 48-50; Chief Archivistof Records Br; Chief Fed Records Center San Francisco 53-57; Dir Harry S Truman Lib Independence Mo 57-. 8: Records Management, Adv Republic of Panama (Point IV Tech Asst program) 54-55. 9: AHA; SAA (sec 36-42, pres 49-51); Jackson Co (Mo) Hist Assn (v-pres 60-); Org of Amer Histns. 12: "Diplomacy and the Borderlands" (49); "Public Records Management" (49); Archivos y Documentos (Panama) 55; "Research in Archives" (69). 13: Yes. 14: Archival mgt, hist & nature of the presidency, US diplomatic hist. 15: 1332 W Truman rd, Independence Mo 64050.

BROOKS, ROBERT EDWARD. b Detroit 7 F 34. 5: Morgan State Col 54-58 (Sociol) AB; So Conn State Col 61-65 (LS) MA. 6: Fr. 7: Circ asst Yale Law Lib 58-61, Ref libn 61-. 9: AALL; Law Libns of NE. 10: So Conn State Col LA. 14: Ref. 15: Yale U Law Lib 127 Wall st, New Haven Ct 06520.

BROOME, HEATHER CLAIRE (PLATT). b England 20 S 24. 4: Kenneth R Broome. 5: Cambridge U 43-46 Chem MA; Immaculate Heart Col LA 59-60 LS. 6: Fr, Ger. 7: Research chem Distillers Corp, Epsom Eng 46-49; Research libn US Borax Research Corp, Anaheim Cal 60-64; Libn Foremost Dairies, San Francisco 65-66; Info chem (temp) Chevron Research Corp, Richmond Cal 66-67; Libn Lester Gorsline Assocs Belvedere-Tiburon Cal 67-. 9: SLA. 14: Reference, cataloging. 15: 335 Fawn dr, San Anselmo Ca 94960.

BROOME, LORICE (ANDERSON). b Columbia Miss 21 Je 37. 4: Wilford A Broome. 5: Mississippi State Col for Women 59-59 LS BA; Sacramento State Col 64-65. 7: Libn St Martin High Sch Bilox Miss 60-61; Libn Bayon View Jr High Sch Gulfport Miss 61-62; Libn Aerojet General Corp Sacramento Cal 62-65; Libn Dependents Sch, APO NY 09291 Crele 66-68; Libn Columbia City Schs Materials Ctr Columbia Miss 69-. 9: NEA; ALA; MissEA; MissLA. 14: Ref, readers adv to ya. 15: RT 1 Box 22, Columbia Ms 39429.

BROPHY, CHARLES A JR. b Columbus Ohio 9 Jl 13. 4: Mary Jane Belt Brophy. 5: Ohio State U 32, 38-40 (Psych) BS; UIll 41-42 BSLS. 7: Libn Army, Ft Harrison Ind 42-46; Asst chief libn VA, Columbus Ohio 46-49; Circ libn UNM 49-50; Med libn White Cross Hosp, Columbus Ohio 50-51; Battelle Mem Inst: Ref & bibliog 51-53, Libn Slavic br 53-62, Head Libn 62-. 8: Consul, "Chemical Abstracts," 55-56; Adv Counl, Title III, LSCA, Columbus. 9: SLA; ALA; Aslib; ASIS. 10: Amer Ord Assn; Highway Research Bd. 12: Chief comp "Titanium Bibliography 1900-1951." 13: Yes. 14: Russian sci & tech lit. 15: 303 S Ardmore rd, Columbus Oh 43209.

BROSE, FRIEDRICH (KARL-HEINZ). b Potsdam (Germany) 29 F 36. 4: Sharon L Hoffman. 5: Deutsche Hochscgule fuer Politik/Freie Universitaet Berlin 56-59 (Pol sci); Australian Nat U 60-63 (Japanese/E Asian Civilization) BA; U New S Wales 64 (LS) Diploma in Libnship; Columbia 65 (Eng for Foreign Students); McGill 66 LS MLS; San Diego State Col present (Ger lit). 6: Ger, Fr, Japanese. 7: Libn I Australian Nat Lib, Canberra 63-64; Bibliog asst ColumbiaU Lib, NYC 65-66; Librarian II UCal Lib, Santa Barbara 67-68; Acquis libn US Internat U Lib, San Diego 68-. 9: ALA; So Cal Tech Processes Gp (Prog Com). 14: Tech processing. 15: 2245 Ulric st apt 8, San Diego Ca 92111.

BROSE, KATHERINE A(GNES). b Dubuque Iowa 21 Ag 04. 5: State U Iowa 22-26 (Eng) BA; UIll 28-29 BS in LS. 7: Circ asst State U Iowa 26-28, Reviser summer sch for lib train summer 29; Catlg reviser Lib Sch UIll(Urbana) 29-30; Head of circ dept Mills Col 30-. 9: ALA; CalLA. 10: Beta Phi Mu; Phi Beta Kappa. 14: Circ, catlg, ref. 15: Box 9106 Mills Col, Oakland Cal 94613.

BROSKY, CATHERINE M. b Pittsburgh. 5: Carnegie 42-46 (Chem) BS, 46-47 BSLS; UPittsburgh 63-64 (LS). 7: Libn Carnegie Lib of Pittsburgh46-52; Asst libn Region V US Bur of Mines 52-55; Libn Grad Sch Pub Health, UPittsburgh 55-. 8: Proj dir lib serv W Penn Reg Med Program 68-. 9: ALA; MedLA (treas Pittsburgh Group); ASLib; ACS; SLA (pres Pittsburgh Chap); ADI (sec-treas Pittsburgh Chap). 10: NY Acad Scis; Sigma XI. 14: Med info, admin. 15: 252-1/2 McKee pl, Pittsburgh Pa 15213.

BROSS, DOROTHY (RODGERS). b Albany NY 11 O 17. 5: Russell Sage 57-66 (Social sci) BA; SUNY at Albany 66-68 MLS. 7: VA Hosp, Sec Albany NY 51-66, Lib stud trainee 66-67; Lib stud trainee NYS Dept of Educ, Albany NY 66-68; Asst libn NY State Dept of Health, Albany NY 68-. 9: ALA; MedLA. 14: Ref, catlg. 15: 12 Bohl ave, Albany NY 12209.

BROTHER, SHIRLEY. b Owingsville Ky 25 F 15. 5: Birmingham-So Col 31-33, 36, 37 (Hist) AB; UAla 33-36 (LS) BS; Emory 40-41 (LS) AB. 7: High sch libn, Ala 36-40; Field rep Ala Pub Lib Serv, Montgomery Ala 45-52; Capt WAC Tng Bn Women's Army Corps 52-55; Field rep Ala Pub Lib Serv, Montgomery Ala 55; Libn Johnson Co Lib, Merriam Kan 55-59; Parish demonstration libn Jackson Parish Demonstration Lib, Jonesboro La 59-61; Consul Cal State Lib 61-63; Admin asst La State Lib 63-67; US Off of Educ Reg IV Lib serv prog off, Atlanta 67-. 8: Surveyor, Waco Pub Lib, Waco Tex, 65. 9: ALA; SWLA; LaLA (chm Fed Rel Com 65-, chm Recr Com); AlaLA (sec 47-50). 10: AAUW; LWV; Altrusa. 13: Yes. 14: Admin, org, co & reg serv. 15: 3060 Pharr court,nw 3207, Atlanta G 30305.

BROTHERS, MRS CASSIE MARIE (CAMPBELL). b Wabash Ark 20 O 28. 4: William John (Bill) Brothers Jr. 5: UArk 46-50 (Educ) BSE; UMiss 60-62 MLS. 7: Tchr Helena-W Helena Sch System, Helena Ark 51-56, Libn 56-. 9: ALA; NEA; ClrTA; Ark ClrTA (Memb Com, Constit Com); ArkLA; SWLA; ArkEA. 10: Sigma Alpha Iota; Delta Kappa Gamma; Phillips Co (Ark) Hist Assn; PTA. 12: Comp "Bibliography of Arkansas & Arkansas Author's materials" (62). 14: State & loc hist. 15: 123 Summit dr, Helena Ar 72342.

BROTHERTON, MRS DOROTHY M (PATTON). b Johnson City NY 5 F 11. 4: Arthur R Brotherton. 5: Wheaton Col 31-34 (Eng) BA; Albany State Col summer 34 (Eng); Syracuse 45-49 (Educ) MA. 7: Tchr Bd of Educ, Binghamton NY 34-36; Tchr Bd of Educ, Sinclairville NY 40-44; Tchr Bd of Educ, Frewsburg NY 44-48; Tchr & libn Phoenix Christian High Sch, Phoenix 50-57; Asst libn VA, Whipple Ariz 57-. 10: AAUW. 15: PO Box 1775, 311 E Union, Prescott Az 86301.

BROUGH, KENNETH JAMES. b Scotch Grove Iowa 22 Ag 06. 4: Ruth Bloomer Brough. 5: Grinnell Col 23-27 (Hist) BA; UColo 30-31 (Educ) MA; Columbia 35-42 BSLS; Stanford 46-49 (Higher Educ) PhD; UCal(Berkeley) 47-48 (LS). 6: Sp. 7: Tchr Portales High Sch, Portales NM 27-34; Libn & Dean of Instr East NM Col 34-43; (1st Lt) 54th AAA Tng Bn US Army 43-46; Asst ref libn Stanford U 46-47; Col Libn San Francisco State Col 49-. 8: NM Lib Commsn, 46; West Col Assn Accred Coms, 50-61. 9: ALA; CalLA. 10: Phi Beta Kappa; Phi Delta Kappa; Assoc Cal State Col Profs; Cal State Employees Assn; Cal Hist Soc. 12: "Scholar's Workshop: Evolving Conceptions of Library Service" (53). 13: Yes. 14: Admin. 15: 2364 S Court, Palo Alto Ca 94301.

BROUSSARD, HARRY (CLAUDE). b New Orleans 7 Mr 41. 4: Leslie Broussard. 5: Tulane 58-63 (Fr) BA; LSU 63-65 (LS) MS; UTex 66-67. 6: Fr. 7: Acquis libn Tex State Lib 65-66; Ser libn Tulane U Lib 67-. 9: ALA; LaLA. 10: Beta Phi Mu; AAUP. 14: Acquis, catlg, mechanization, ser. 15: 5601 Chamberlain dr, New Orleans La70122.

BROW, ELLEN (HODGES). b Williams Cal 23 D 36. 4: William Hooker Brow. 5: UCal at Davis 54-59 (Pol sci) BA; San Jose State Col 63-66 Libnship MA; UWisconsin at Madison 66-. 6: Portu, Sp, Fr. 7: Statistical clk Dept of Ag Econ UCal at Davis 56-58; Tchr primary grades, Colegio Americano de Quito, Ecuador 60-61; Teacher Eng as for lang Centro Ecuatoriano-norteamerican, Quito Ecuador 60-61; Catlgr Memorial Lib UWis at Madison 65-66; Research asst for acquis Land Tenure Ctr Lib Madison Wis 66-67; Asst to Hispanic bibliog UWis at Madison 68-. 9: ALA; SALALM; LASA. 14: Hisoanic bibliog. 15: 2102 Kendall ave, Madison Wi 53705.

BROWAND, KENNETH S. b Tyrone Penn 28 D 22. 4: Luella Brady. 5: Penn StateU 48-52 9sociol) BA; Mich StateU 60-62 (Educ); West MichU 62-63 (Educ) Secondary tchg Certif; UMich 60-65 MLS. 7: Petty off 1st Class USN, Pacific Area 42-45; Toolmaker Douglas aircraft, Long Beach 46-48; Tool designer Leedy Engring, Grand Rapids Mich 53-58; Bkmob libn Kent Co Lib, Grand Rapids Mich 58-60; Hd libn Kentwood Pub Schs, Grand Rapids Mich 60-62; Hd libn Kalamazoo Central High Sch 62-65; Admin asst Kalamazoo Pub Lib 65-68; Reg lib dir Central Fla Reg Lib, Ocala 68-. 8: Adv com to Fla State Libn on State processing Ctr 68-; Adv com to Review Fla State Plan for LSCA 69-. 9: ALA; FlaLA; SELA. 10: Exchange Club of Ocala. 14: Pub lib admin. 15: 738 NE 17th ct, Ocala Fl 32670.

BROWARD, MARJORIE ANN (GRIMES). b Austin Minn 28 Jl 24. 5: Luther Col 42-45 (Eng, Hist) BA; UMich 47-48 BALS. 7: Ref libn Luther Col 48-50; Circ libn UIowa 50-51; Arch libn Ga Inst of Tech 51-53; Asst libn State Bd of Health Lib, Jacksonville Fla 53-54; Part-time positions org libs for Baptist Mem Hosp, Riverside Hosp, St Vincent's Sch of Nursing, Brewster Sch of Nursing, Jacksonville Fla 54-58; Bkmob libn Jacksonville Pub Lib, Jacksonville Fla 58-60; Libn Bartram Sch for Girls, Jacksonville Fla 62-63; Bus libn UColo 63-; Dir Colo Tech Ref Ctr 67-. 8: Consul Col of Bus & Pub Admin, Fla Atlantic U 69; Consul ICAITI, Guatemala, for Bi-National Develop Corp, Boulder Colo 69. 9: SLA (pres-elect Colo Chap); ColoLA. 10: AAUW. 14: Pub serv. 15: Bus Lib Univ of Colo Libs, Boulder Co 80302.

BROWDER, MARTHA (HOLSINGER). b Rockingham Co Va 31 D 13. 4: Edward R Browder. 5: Madison Col 30-33 (Hist) BS, summer 46 (LS); William & Mary summer 47 (LS); Chicago summer 48 (LS); UVa 59-63 (Educ) MEd. 6: Fr, Sp. 7: Tchr McGaheysville High Sch, McGaheysville Va 33-43; Tchr & asst libn McIntire High Sch, Charlottesville Va 43-50; Libn Scottesville High Sch, Scottesville Va 50-51; Tchr & asst libn Highland Springs High Sch, Richmond Va 51-53; Libn Waynesboro Elem Schs, Waynesboro Va 53-55; Libn Waynesboro High sch, Waynesboro Va 55-. 9: ALA; NEA; VaEA (Lib Sect); VaLA; SELA. 10: AAUW. 14: Sch libs, child libn. 15: 1915 Park rd, Waynesboro Va 22980.

BROWINSKY, OLENA (BARANYCZ). b Muszyna Poland 10 F 05. 4: Ivan Browinsky. 5: Uchytel's'kyi Seminar (Stryl Ukraine) 24-29 (Polish,Ukrainian) Tchrs degree; Universitat zu Innsbruck (Austria) Philosophisch Fakultat 45-47 (Ger); UCincinnati 59-60 (LS). 6: Ger, Lat, Polish,Russian, Ukrainian. 7: Tchr Ukrainian-Polish Schs, Poland (now Ukraine) 30-39; UCincinnati Lib; Typist & chief typist 52-54, Chief catlgclerk 55-60, Catlg libn 60-. 9: ALA; Ohio Group Tech Serv Libns. 10: Internat Club (Cincinnati). 14: Catlg. 15: Univ of Cincinnati Lib, Cincinnati Oh 45221.

BROWN, ADELE H(EEREN). b Pittsburgh 9 Jl 13. 5: Oberlin Col 30-34 (Sociol) AB; Carnegie 34-35 BS in LS; Oberlin Col 38-41 (Hist of Art)MA. 7: Catlgr Carnegie Lib of Pittsburgh 35-38, Asst ref dept, brs 42-45; Schenectady Co (NY); Pub Lib; Br libn 45-51, 58-65, Head ext div51-56, Head ref div 56-58, Coordinator brs & ext 65-. 9: ALA; NYLA; Hudson-Mohawk Lib Assn (sec, v-pres). 15: 1578 Regal ave, Schenectady NY12309.

BROWN, ALBERTA L. b Chicago 9 Ja 1894. 5: Tabor Col (Eng) AB; UWis 24-25 (LS) Certif. 6: Ger. 7: Catlgr Pub Lib, Council Bluffs Iowa 20-24; Head Libn Creighton U 25-29; Head Catlgr UND 29-33; Head Libn St Mary's Col (Notre Dame Ind) 33-38; Libn H A Brassert Co, Chicago 38-41; Head Libn The Upjohn Co, Kalamazoo 41-59; Lib consul, Kalamazoo 59-. 8: Assoc Prof Dept of Libnship West Mich Univ, 62-64; Visiting Prof in Spec Lib65-69; Spec Legis Rep for MichLA, 65-69; Lib consul Borgess Hosp, Kalamazoo 68-. 9: SLA (pres 57-58; chm Sci-Tech Div 53-54; chm Pharmaceut Sect 48-49); MichLA(chm Spec Lib Div 68-69). 10: Friends of the Kalamazoo Pub Lib; Kalamazoo Co Lib Bd; Altrusa Club. 11: Upjohn Award, 54; SLA Hall of Fame, 61. 12: "Scientific and Technical Libraries," with 2 co-auth (64). 13: Yes. 14: Admin. 15: 3234 Butternut lane, Kalamazoo Mi 49007.

BROWN, MRS ALICE EMMERT. b Sunnyside Wash 7 Mr 11. 4: Donald F Brown. 5: Mt Morris Col 28-32 (Eng) AB; UIll 32-33 (Fr) MA; Drexel 61-62 (LS) MS. 6: Fr, Sp. 7: Child libn Free Lib of Phila, Wyoming Br 62-63; Child libn Wolfsohn Mem Lib, King of Prussia Penn 63-66; Hd & child libn W Phila Br Free Lib 66-68; Asst Hd stations dept Free Lib Phila 68-. 9: ALA; PennLA. 14: Child lit. 15: 108 Wooded lane, Villanova Pa 19085.

BROWN, ALICE L (COWLES). b Cleveland 10 Mr 19. 4: Jordan F Brown. 5: Allegheny Col 36-40 (Eng) BA; Carnegie 40-41 BS in LS. 7: Child libn Kirkwood Pub Lib Kirkwood Mo 41-42; Corporal WAAC & WAC 42-45; Asst libn Cleveland Heights (Ohio) Pub Lib 46-47; Asst in child dept Tacoma Pub Lib Tacoma Wash 47- 50; Asst br libn 52-54; UNev (Las Vegas): Ref & docs libn 61-67; Docs libn 67-. 9: NevLA (chm So Dist). 14: Child wk, ref, docs. 15: 104 Beech st, Henderson Nv 89015.

BROWN, ATLANTA (THOMAS). b Bennettsville SC 30 O 31. 4: Samuel E Brown. 5: SC State Col 49-53 (LS) BS; UWis 63 (LS) MS. 6: Fr. 7: Libn Carver Elem Sch Columbia SC 53-58; Libn George Mason Sch Richmond Va 58-63; Libn George Gray Sch Wilmington Del 63-. 8: Consul for Spring Wkshop for Wilmington Elem tchrs 65. 9: ALA; NEA; DelLA; Del Tchrs Assn; Wilmington EA. 10: Delta Sigma Theta; YWCA; Coun on Human Rel. 13: Yes. 14: Child bk sel, ref. 15: 4502 Pickwick dr Limestone Gardens, Wilmington De 19808.

BROWN, BARBARA ELIZABETH. b Montreal Can 27 My 33. 5: McGill 53 BA, 58 BLS Toronto 68 MLS. 6: Fr, Ger. 7: Catlgr Lib of Parliament, Ottawa 58-. 9: CanLA; ALA; OntLA; Lib Assn Ottawa; Inst of Prof LibnsOnt. 10: U Women's Club of Ottawa. 14: Catlg, govt docs. 15: 102 Broadway ave, Ottawa 1 Can.

BROWN, BARBARA JEANNE. b Charles City Iowa 9 O 41. 5: Iowa State U 59-63 (Eng) BS; Columbia 63-64 (LS) MS. 6: Fr, Ger. 7: Asst circ libn Cornell U 64-66, As libn Undergrad Lib 66-68, Assoc Libn ref 68-. 9: SLA (chm Directory Com 67-68). 10: Cornell Univ Lib Staff Assn. 14: Pub serv, ref. 15: A3-2 Lansing apts W, 20 Triphammer rd, Ithaca NY 14850.

BROWN, BETSY C. b Shelbyville Ky 25 Ag 24. 5: Eastern State Tchs Col 42-44 (Elem ed); UKy 44-46 LS. 7: Children's libn Pub Lib, Youngstown Ohio 46-48; Army libn Armed Forces, Ger 48-51; Army libn Armed Forces, Ft Knox Ky 51-54; Hosp libn Army Hosp, Downey Ill 54; Bkmob libn Pub Lib. Kenosha Wis 54-67; Hd ext dept G M Simmons Pub Lib, Kenosha Wis 67-. 9: ALA; WisLA. 10: AAUW; Delta Kappa Gamma. 15: 2418 73rd st, Kenosha Wi 53140.

BROWN, BETTY (MARTIN). b Cincinnati 11 My 30. 5: UVt 47-50 (Hist) BA; UIll 55-56 MS in LS; Bryn Mawr 65- (Hist). 6: Ger, Fr, Lat. 7: Asst to head a-v dept Louisville Free Pub Lib 56-58; CatlgrFree Lib of Phila 58-60; Volunteer worker Amer Friends Serv Com, Germany 60-62;Catlgr Drexel Inst of Tech Lib 63-65, Instr in catlg 64-. 9: ALA. 10: AAUP; MedAcad of Amer. 14: Catlg, rare bks. 15: 1510 Sheraton-Chase apts, Baltimore Md21202.

BROWN, BETTY JEAN (MATHIS). b McAlester Okla 11 D 37. 4: John Gray Brown. 5: Okla Baptist U 56-61 (Phys ed) BS; UOkla 64-66 MLS. 7: Okla Dept of Libs, Okla City: Catlg libn 66-69; Act div libn tech serv div 69-. 9: ALA; SLA; SWLA; OklaLA. 10: Beta Phi Mu. 14: Catlg. 15: 2020 No Shartel apt 4, Oklahoma City Ok 73103.

BROWN, BRUCE McCLAVE. b NYC 11 Je 17. 4: Helen Brown. 5: Middlebury Col 34-38 (Hist) AB; NYU 45-46 (Soc Studies) MA; Columbia 46-47 BS in LS. 7: Various positions in commercial art, advertising & printing 40-45; Ref libn Englewood Free Pub Lib, Englewood NJ 47-48; Colgate U Lib: Asst ref libn 48-52, ref libn 52-59, Act libn 59-60, U Libn 60-. 8: Lib mem of Middle States Assn eval teams (- sch & 5 col libs 62-69). 9: ALA; NYLA (pres Col & Univ Sect 62-63); chm Scholarship Com 66-68); Central NY Ref & Resources Coun (sec-treas 67-). 10: AAUP; Hamilton Club; Electric Railroaders

Assn. 13: Yes. 14: Admin, ref, rare bks. 15: Rt 2 Earlville rd, Hamilton NY 13346.

BROWN, CARLENE (PERRY). b Milo Me 28 Ag 38. 4: Charles E Brown. 5: Colby Col 56-60 (Eng Lit) AB; Simmons 62-64 MSLS. 6: Fr, Sp. 7: Order clerk Little Brown & Co, Boston 60-61; Asst to libn First Nat Bank of Boston 61-64; Ser libn USan Francisco 64-65; Bibliog Gen Lib UCal(Berkeley) 65-. 14: Bibliog, catlg. 15: 1656 Oak View ave, Kensington Ca 94707.

BROWN, CAROLYN (BLISS). b Stafford Springs Conn 20 My 24. 4: Robert R Brown. 5: UConn 42-44; Simmons 44-46 (LS) BS. 7: Catlgr Temple U 46-50, Supv tech processing 50-52; LC: Catlgr 52-58, Sr catlgr 58-65, Supv libn catlg 65-. 9: ALA; DCLA. 14: Catlg. 15: 7420 Nancemond st, Springfield Va 22150.

BROWN, CATHERINE MARY (MAHER). b Jersey City NJ 4 Jl 26. 4: Stewart J Brown. 5: Carnegie 44-48 (Psych, Eng) BS, 50-53 MS in LS. 6: Sp. 7: Psychometrist Kaufmann's Dept Stores, Pittsburgh 48-49; Lib asst UPittsburgh Lib 49-53; Post Libn US Army Caribbean, Ft Clayton CZ 53-56; Br coordinator CZ Lib-Museum, Balboa Heights CZ 60-64, Asst ref libn 64-. 9: SLA; ALA. 10: Pacific Civil Coun repres 67-68; Cz Col Club; Army-Navy Club. 14: Ref. 15: Box 989, Balboa CZ.

BROWN, CHARLOTTE (STOVER). b Phila 21 S 19. 5: Waynesburg Col 36-40 (Eng, Lat, Fr) AB; UPittsburgh 42-43; UWash summer 63-65 (LS) M Libn. 6: Fr, Lat. 7: Tchr-libn Findlay Twp, Imperial Penn 40-43; Libn Sonoma Valley High Sch, Sonoma Cal 54-66; Dist libn Sonoma Unified 66; Pub serv libn Chabot Col 66-. 8: Consul, Sonoma Valley Unified Sch Dist 62-66. 9: ALA; Cal Tchrs Assn;CalASchL. 14: Bks for ya & child. 15: 2020 Santa Clara, Richmond Annex Ca 94804.

BROWN, (DOUGLAS) CLARA. b Portland Ore 13 Ap 05. 4: Clair Allan Brown. 5: UWash 35 (Fine Arts) BA, 36 (LS) BA; Wash State Col 37 (Fine Arts) MA. 6: Sp, Ger, Fr. 7: Washington State Col: Circ asst 37-44, Head of acquis 44-47, Ref libn 47-48; Ser libn LSU 48-. 9: ALA; LaLA. 10: Baton Rouge Gem & Mineral Soc (past v-pres, sec & treas). 14: Ser. 15: 1180 Stanford, Baton Rouge La 70808.

BROWN, CURTIS L(ESLIE). b Vienna 31 My 21. 4: Gertrude Popper. 5: Bolyai U (Cluj) 44-45 (Chem); UVienna 45-46 (Philos, Psych); George Washington U 47-53 (Phys Chem) MS. 6: Ger, Fr, Hungarian, Rumanian, Ital, Sp, Dutch, Swedish, Portu, Norwegian, Russian. 7: Tech abstracor-indexer Nat Research Coun Nat Acad of Sci, Wash DC 47-53, Head abstracting dept, Prevention of Deterioration Center 53-55; Inst of Paper Chem (Lawrence U), Appleton Wis: Bibliog & Instr of Sci Ger 55-56, Tech ed & Instr of Sci Ger 56-60, Tech ed & act (admin) libn 60-. 9: ACS (Div Chem Lit); ADI; SLA. 10: Attic Theatre Inc; Amer contract Bridge League; Archery Club; YMCA; PTA. 12: Ed "Prevention of Deterioration Abstracts," NRC-NAS (53-55); Ed "Abstract Bulletin of The Institute of Paper Chemistry" (56-). 13: Yes. 14: Tech ed, documentation, mechanized info retrieval. 15: P O Box 1048, Appleton Wi 54911.

BROWN, CYNTHIA ROBLIN. b Winnipeg Can 2 Ap 19. 4: Stanley Wiswell Brown. 5: UMan 35-39 (Hist) BA; McGill 39-40 BLS; Toronto 56-57 MLS. 6: Fr, Sp. 7: Pub rel off Dept of Pub Info, Ottawa 40-42; Intelligence agent British Security Coordination, NYC & Lima Peru 42-45; Asst dir Ind Rel Centre, McGill U 48-50; Head Libn Faculty of Med UMan 57-63; Head Libn Sch of Med UMass 66-. 8: Orig mem, Com on Med Sci Libs in Can; Consul, org Rehabil Sch Lib, Winnipeg 64; Spec assignment, Faculty of Med Lib UMan 65. 9: CanLA (Com on Prof Libnship, Com on Stat); MedLA (NE Reg Group); ManLA (chm of Publicity Com, chm Exhib at Annual Conf); SLA; ALA; Spec Libs - Boston. 10: Gamma Phi Beta; Jr League; St Agnes Hosp Guild; Civil Defense radio operator; Red Cross Blood Clinic; Royal Winnipeg Ballet /com; Winnipeg Symphony Orchestra Com; Bd, Middlechurch Home for the Aged; Winnipeg Winter Club; Tuxedo Horsemans Club. 11: Commend from Sir William Stephenson (serv performed for Brit Security Coord). 13: Yes. 14: Admin, rare bks (hist of med). 15: 26 Spaulding st, Amherst Ma 01002.

BROWN, DALE WALLIS. b Benton Ky 21 Jl 32. 4: Molly Kunning. 5: David Lipscomb Col 49-53 (Speech) BA; Peabody 54-55 (Educ) MA; UMich 60-65 AMLS; Wayne State 57-(Educ). 7: Instr David Lipscomb Col 54-56; Eng & Soc Stud tchr Livonia Pub Schs, LivoniaMich 56-57, Libn 57-58; Instr Dept of Lib Educ Wayne State U 58-61; Asst Prof LibSci Educ UMd 61-. 69; Dir of Lib & Media Serv for Pub Schs, Alexandria Va 69-. 8: Mem of visitation & evaluation teams Nat Coun for Accreditation of Tchr Educ 62, and Middle States Assn of Col and Secondary Schs 65. 9: ALA; AASL; NEA (Div of a-v instr); MdLA; Md State Tchrs Assn; ASL of Md (past sec). 10: AAUP; Disciples of Christ Hist Soc; NCTE. 12: Contrib "Curriculum Guide for Elementary Sch Libs" Detroit Pub Schs. 13: Yes. 14: Sch libs,child lit, educ media. 15: 456 McKeldin Lib UMd, College Park Md 20740.

BROWN, DAVID C(ARL). b Milwaukee Wis 30 S 29. 4: Rita K Rasmussen. 5: UWis 47-56 (Hist) BS; Rutgers 57-58, 63-64 (Libnship) MLS. 7: Milwaukee Pub Lib: Jr libn 56-57, Libn I 58-60; Imstr in lib sci Wis State U at Whitewater 61-63; Asst libn Breckinridge Lib Marine Corps Base, Quantico Va 65-. 8: Consultant on government documents, New Brunswick (NJ) Public Library, 64. 9: ALA. 10: Toastmasters Internat; Sierra Club; Nat Wildlife Fed; Alum Assn Grad Sch of Lib Serv, RutgersU. 14: Catlg, acquis. 15: PO Box 252, Quantico Va 22134.

BROWN, DEE ALEXANDER. b Alberta La 28 F 08. 4: Sally B Stroud. 5: Ark State Tchrs Col 29-31 (Hist) AB; George Washington U 37 BLS; UIll 49-50 (LS) MS. 6: Fr. 7: Lib asst USDA, Wash DC 34-39; Libn Beltsville Research Center, Beltsville Md 39-42; US Army (Sgt) 42-45; Libn US Army Ordnance, Aberdeen Proving Ground Md 45-48; Agric libn UIll(Urbana) 48-. 9: ALA (chm Oberly Award Com). 10: Beta Phi Mu; Agric hist Soc; Org Amer Histns; Authors Guild. 12: Ed "Agricultural History" (56-58); Auth "The Galvanized Yankees" (63); Fort Phil Kearny" (62); "Griersons Raid" (62); "The Bold Cavaliers" (59); "The Gentle Tamers" (58); "Trail Driving Days" (52); "The Year of the Century" (66). 13: Yes. 14: Agric & Amer hist subj areas. 15: 226 Mumford Hall Univ Ill, Urbana Il 61801.

BROWN, DONALD RAYMOND. b Lebanon Penn 19 N 30. 5: Ursinus Col 48-52 (Hist) AB; UIll 52-54 (Hist) MA; UWis 56-57 (LS) MS. 6: Ger. 7: Spec agent US Army Counter-Intell Corps, Chicago & Minn 54-56; Ref libn I & II Hist & Travel Dept Detroit Pub Lib 57-61; Chief ref libn west MichU 61-68. 8: Bibliog for Hist Soc of Mich 58-59. 9: ALA-RSD (mem-at-large Hist Sect 68-71); MichLA (chm Ref Sect 65); Amer Assn Arch bibliogrs. 10: Beta Phi Mu; Assn for State & Local Hist; Soc Arch Histns; Chicago Sch Arch. 13: Yes. 14: Ref, archives, libs in hist agencies, art inst, rare bks. 15: 1932 S Westnedge ave, Kalamazoo Mi 49001.

BROWN, DOROTHEA (THOMPSON). b Rock City Falls NY 3 Ja 15. 4: Stanley H Brown. 5: Green Mt Jr Col 31-32; Barnard 32-35 (Hist) AB; Columbia 35-36 BS in LS. 7: Jr libn, Sr libn Mt Vernon Pub Lib, Mt Vernon NY 36-41; Br libn Schenectady Co Pub Lib, Schenectady NY 43-. 10: YWCA. 15: 1450 Grenoside ave, Schenectady NY 12308.

BROWN, EDWARD (GERARD). b Vancouver BC Can 4 Mr 20. 4: Grace Katherine Thompson. 5: UBC 45 (Eng, Philos) BA; Toronto 57-58 BLS. 6: Fr. 7: Soc wker CNIB, Toronto 46-57, Chief Libn 58-. 9: Amer Assn of Workers for the Blind. 12: Ed "Braille Courier" (58-). 15: 1929 Bayview ave, Toronto 17 Can.

BROWN, EILEEN J. b Medford Mass 19 Jl 11. 5: Montclair State Col 29-34 (Soc Studies) AB; Simmons 46-47 (LS) BS. 7: Sub tchr Bd of Educ, Verona NJ 34-36; Head of bk dept Kresge Dept Store, Newark NJ 36-43; Child libn Verona Pub Lib, Verona NJ 43-46; Prin child libn Passaic Pub Lib, Passaic NJ 4-57; Supv libn child & yp Bloomfield Pub Lib, Bloomfield NJ 58-. 9: ALA; NJLA (Sect for Serv to Child & YP); LPRC. 10: AAUW; Bloomfield Better Human Rel Coun. 14: Child wk. 15: Bloomfield Pub Lib 90 Broad st, Bloomfield NJ 07003.

BROWN, ELAINE SUZANNE. b Phila Penn 22 Ap 39. 4: Vaikai K Brown. 5: Drexel 57-63 (Biol Sci) BS; West Res 63-65 MSLS. 7: Research asst center for Doc & Communication Research, West ResU 65-. 14: Info sci. 15: 6149 Trask rd, Thompson Oh 44086.

BROWN, ELIA LILLIAN (DELL'ORCO). b Providence 14 F 28. 4: Johnny D Brown. 5: Pembroke 46-50 (Span) AB; Simmons 56-58 (LS) MS; Worcester State Col 62-65(Elem Educ) M Ed. 6: Sp, Ital. 7: Tchr Town of Northbridge, Whitinsville Mass 50-51; Span-Eng steno Whitin Machine Wks, Whitinsville Mass 52-54; Tchr Town of Uxbridge, Uxbridge Mass 54-55, Eng-Sp tchr 55-58, Libn & tchr 58-60, Libn 60-. 8: Catlgd lib at Milford High Sch Milford Mass summer 62; Libn US Army Dependents Sch Stuttgart Germany 58-59 Libn Balmer Elem Sch, Whitinsville Mass summer 68. 9: NEA; Mass State LA; Mass Tchrs Assn; Uxbridge Tchrs Assn. 14: Young adult & child lit. 15: 20 Moody st, Uxbridge Ma 01569.

BROWN, ELIZABETH ANNE. b Minneapolis. 5: UMinn 44 (Hist) BA (cum laude), 44 BSLS (cum laude); UCal 48 (US Hist) MA. 6: Lat, Fr. 7: Lab asst Shell Development Co, Emeryville Cal 44-46; Tchg asst UCal(Berkeley) 47; Br asst Oakland Pub Lib, Oakland Cal 46-51; Libn Resources Dept UMinn Lib (Minneapolis) 53-65, Instr-libn 65-. 9: ALA (Memb Com Minn 68-69); SLA; MinnLA (Memb Com 65-66, 68-69, Nom Com 66-67). 10: AAUP; Minn Hist Soc. 14: Acquis, bibliog, bk sel. 15: Univ of Minn, Wilson Lib, Minneapolis Mn 55455.

BROWN, ELISE (VUILLEUMIER). b New Rochelle NY 19 S 15. 5: Adelphi U 28-32 (Eng) BA; Queens Col 55-58 (LS). 7: Eng tchr NY Bd of Educ, Elmhurst NY 32-38; Sch libn E Meadow Bd of Educ, E Meadow NY 55-. 9: NEA; NY State Tchrs Assn; Nassau-Suffolk SchLA. 14: Wk with child of jr high sch age. 15: 7 Roydon drive W, North Merrick NY 11556.

BROWN, ELIZABETH E. b Charlotte Mich 29 Ag 21. 5: Albion Col 39-43 (Chem) BA; Pratt 52-53 MLS. 6: Fr, Ger, Sp. 7: Info spec Enjay Co, NYC 43-50; Reports indexer Bakelite Co, Bound Brook NJ50-52; ref libn IBM Research Lib, Yorktown Heights NY 53-69; Libn IBM CommercialAnalysis Library, White Plains NY 69-. 9: ALA; SLA (sec-treas Engrg Div 69-);ACS; ASIS; NYLA; WestchesterLA. 10: AAAS; Phi Beta Kappa. 14: Ref, lib automation. 15: 221 S Broadway, Tarrytown NY 10591.

BROWN, ELIZABETH LOUISE. b Toledo Ohio 18 My 18. 5: UToledo 36-41 (Eng lit) BA, (Ed) MA in Ed; West Res 41-42 BLS. 7: Libn Toledo Pub Lib, Toledo Ohio 42-48; Br libn Whitmer High Sch Lucas Co Lib, Toledo Ohio 48-60; Libn Johnson High Sch DO Do/s Schs Japan 60-62; Libn Scott High Sch Toledo Bd of Ed, Toledo Ohio 62-63; Adult educ tchr Speed Reading/Reading Improve 1st Educ Ctrs, Johnson & Fuchu 60-; Libn Chofu High Sch DO Do/s Schs, Japan 63-; Visiting lecturer Bowling Green U (Ohio) summers 60, 61. 8: Lib coord; Chofu Schools 63-64; Consul & chm Sch libns (DOD) in Japan 66-68. 9: ALA; NEA; OverseasTA; FarEastTA. 10: Delta Kappa Gamma; Internat House of Japan; Col Women of Japan; Pan Pacific SE Women's Assn. 11: USOE Inst; UHawaii Lib Sch 68; AAUW; Intergp Rel, Scholarship 54. 14: Sch libs, media resources, adult educ. 15: 6114th AB Sq CMR Box 3119, APO San Francisco 96525.

BROWN, ELOISE (FRANCES). b NYC 24 Ag 27. 5: Miner Tchrs Col 45-49 (Elem Educ) BS; Syracuse summers 50-55 MSLS; USoCal summer 60. 7: Tchr pub schs, Wash DC 50-60, Libn 60-67, DCTC col instr, Wash DC 67-68; Asst dir Dept of Lib Sci Pub Schs, Wash DC 67-. 8: Founder & consul of vol lib Payne Elem Sch, Wash DC 58-60; Consul River Terrace Elem sch, Wash DC 61-63; Libn in pilot project Goding Demonstration Sch, Wash DC 61-63; Chm of lib com NW Settlement House for Nat Sorority Phi Delta Kappa, Wash DC 67; Consul Central Educ Reg Lab 67; Consul & writer Greater Cities Educ Radio Project AmericanU 67. 9: DC Assn of Sch Libns. 10: Phi Delta Kappa. 13: Yes. 14: Ref, sch lib serv for child. 15: 4210 E Capitol st NE apt 203, Wash DC 20019.

BROWN, EMMA ISOBEL. b St John's Newfoundland 29 S 31. 5: Mem U of Newfoundland 62-66 9modern lang) BA; UToronto 66-67 BLS. 6: Fr. 7: Stenographer Grace Gen Hosp Sch of Nursing, (St John's) 50-62; Catlgr Memorial U Lib (St John's) 67-. 9: CanLA. 10: Can Assn Univ Tchrs. 14: Catlg. 15: 2a O'Dea pl, St John's Newfoundland Can.

BROWN, ERNEST GROGAN. b Houston 21 S 36. 4: Patricia Mahoney. 5: Baylor U 54-57 (Hist) BA; Simmons 62-65 (LS) MS. 6: Ger. 7: Off manager Grogan Butane Co, Atlanta Tex 57-62; Head of circ dept Robbins Lib, Arlington Mass 62-65; Asst to dir SUNY (Buffalo) 65-67, Order libn 67-. 9: ALA; NYLA. 15: 2669 Eggert rd,Tonawanda NY 14150.

BROWN, EVELYN (DAY). b NJ 20 Jl 19. 4: J Kenneth Brown. 5: Bucknell U 37-41 (Soc Studies) BS Educ; UPenn 48 (Educ) MS Educ; Drexel 64 (LS) MS. 7: Tchr Jr High Sch, Burlington NJ 41-49; Libn Pub Lib, Huntingdon Valley Penn 65-. 9: ALA; PLA. 10: Phi Beta Kappa. 14: Catlg, ref. 15: 3897 Byron rd, Huntingdon Valley Pa 19006.

BROWN, FRANCES ELIZABETH. b Cullowhee NC 22 Mr 13. 5: West Car Col 31-35 (Eng) BS; Peabody Col 41-42 BS in LS, 59 (LS) MA. 7: Eng Princeton High Sch, Princeton NC 35-36; Eng Western Carolina Col 36-37, Asst libn 37-43; Libn Cadiz High Sch, Cadiz Ohio 43-47; Prof libn Cleveland Pub Lib 47-59; Hd libn Harford Jr Col Bel Air Md 59-. 9: ALA; MdLA; Md Assn Jr Cols. 14: Admin. 15: 502 S Kenmore ave, Bel Air Md 21014.

BROWN, FRANCES GREER. b Beckley W Va 29 F 12. 5: Mary Baldwin Col 29-33 (Eng) AB; UVa summers 33-36 LS, 36-37 (Eng) MA; Columbia summers 38-41 BLS. 6: Fr, Ger, Lat, middle Eng, Sp, Portug. 7: Libn Stratford Col 37-38; Libn Thomasville High Sch, Thomasville Ga 38-39, 41-42; Checker & catlgr ser rec LC 41-51, Continuations specialist order 51-52, Ref libn govt publ 52-65; Ref libn Fairfax Co Pub Lib, springfield Va 65-. 14: Ref, govt ser, lit. 15: Fairfax Co Pub Lib, Springfield Va 23880.

BROWN, FRANCES J. b NYC. 5: Col of Mt St Vincent BA; Syracuse BS in LS. 7: NY Pub Lib; Fordham Prep Sch Lib; Chief libn Financial Lib First National City Bank, NYC 54-. 9: SLA (mem Finance Com 68-70) -NY chap; sec-treas Bus & Fin Group 65-66); chm Local Arrangements Com SLA Conf 67. 10: Volunteers of the Shelter. 11: National City Found Domestic Travel Award, 62. 14: Admin. 15: First Nat City Bank Fin Lib 399 Park ave, NYC 10022.

BROWN, FREDDIEMAE EUGENIA (BOWMAN). b Racine Wis 16 O 28. 4: Ellis Brown Jr. 5: Fisk 47-51 (Sociol) BA; UMich 56-59 MALS; Wayne State 59-60. 6: Fr. 7: Adminis asst Racine Pub Lib, Racine Wis 51-53; Clerical asst order dept Madison Free Lib, Madison Wis 53-55; Detroit Pub Library; Clk 55-56, Pre-prof asst 56-59, Libn I, II, III 59-66, Chief of div 66-. 8: Pres Staff Assn Detroit Pub Lib 67-68; Chm Program for Reading for Adult Illiterates Detroit Pub Lib 68-. 9: ALA (subscr Bks Bull Com 66-68); MichLA (sec-treas Dist III 67-68). 10: NAACP; Assn for the Study of Negro Life & Culture; Alpha Kappa Alpha; AAUW; Fisk Alum Club. 14: Commun gp planning activities. 15: 2204 So Ethel, Detroit Mi 48217.

BROWN, HARLAN C(RAIG). b Cleveland 26 Ja 06. 4: Helen Abel Brown. 5: UMinn (Fr, Ger) BA, 31 BS in LS; UMich 35 AMLS. 6: Ger, Fr. 7: Asst libn SD State Col 31-34; Gen serv asst UMich Lib 35-36; Circ libn NC State Col 36-39; Capt Inf, AUS 42-46; Dir NC State Col Lib 39-64, Assoc dir 64-. 8: Mem Com on USDA lib 50; Assisted in reorgn of NC State Prison lib. 9: ALA; SELA; SDLA (v-pres 34); NCLA (pres 49-50). 10: Torch Internat. 11: Phi Kappa Phi. 14: Admin. 15: 3217 Merriman ave, Raleigh NC 27607.

BROWN, HELEN (MAUL). b Denver Colo 22 My 27. 4: Ira V Brown. 5: Colorado Womans Col 44-46 (Eng) AA; UDenver 46-48 (Eng) BA, 48-51 (LS) MA. 7: Asst catlgr URedlands 48-50; Ser catlgr UDenver 50-53; Penn State U: Ser records libn 53-57, Microform catlg libn 66-68, Supv ser & microform catlg & reclsf project 68-. 9: ALA; PennLA. 11: Phi Beta Kappa. 14: Catlg ser, microforms. 15: 1923 Park Forest ave, State College Pa 16801.

BROWN, HELEN MARGARET. b Troy NY 17 Jl 12. 5: Vassar 29-33 (Eng) AB; Columbia 33-34 (LS) BS, 38-42 (LS) MS. 6: Fr, Ger. 7: Staff mem Vassar Col Lib 34-44, Order libn 40-43, Ref libn 43-44; Libn MacMurray Col Jacksonville Ill 44-47; Li'n Skidmore Col 47-53; Libn Wellesley Col 53-. 9: ALA (Coun 44-48, 59-63);-ACRL (chm Col Sect 46-47; Com on Standards 53-55, 57-60; Com on Grants 62-68; pres 65-66); MassLA (chm Col Sect 54-55; Recruiting Com 61-62); Hudson-Mohawk LA (pres 52-53). 10: AAUP; AAUW. 13: Yes. 14: Admin. 15: Wellesley Col Lib, Wellesley Ma 02181.

BROWN, MRS HILDA W (MITCHELL). b Bradford Eng 29 Je 11. 4: Donald Macy Brown. 5: E Stroudsburg State Col 28-32 (Eng) BS; Duke U 35; Marywood Col summers61-66 MLS. 6: Fr. 7: High sch tchr, Pocono High Sch, Tannersville Penn 32-42; Sch libn Pocono Mountain High Sch, Swiftwater Penn 61-. 9: Penn State EA (sec Pocono Mountain Chap). 10: PTA; Amer Red Cross; Church Sch Supt; Girl Scouts. 14: Serv to ya. 15: Mt PoconoPa 18344.

BROWN, HUGH A. b Pontotoc County Mis 14 Jl 13. 5: Clarke Col 34-36; Mississippi Col 37-39 (Lang) BA; UMiss 50 (Ed) MA, 57 MLS. 6: Fr. 7: High sch tchr Pontotoc Co Miss pub sch 39-57; Libn SWest Baptist Col 57-63; Libn Bethel Col, Hopkinsville Ky 63-64; Carson-Newman Col Ref libn 64-67; Hardin-Simmons U Dir lib 67-. 8: Mem visiting com So Assn of Schs & Cols. 9: ALA; NEA; SWLA; SELA; TexLA; MissEA (bd mem & sec Dept of Clr Tchrs. 14: Admin, ref. 15: 1241 Ambler, Abilene Tx 79601.

BROWN, JANET E(LDER). b Buffalo NY 29 Jl 20. 5: UBuffalo 38-42 (Eng Lit) BA, 43-45 (Amer Lit) MA; McGill 48-49 BLS; Cornell U summer 52 (Pol Sci). 6: Fr, Ger. 7: Circ asst UBuffalo 42-43, Period libn 43-47, Act ref libn 47-48; Catlgr Sarah Lawrence Col 49-52; Order libn SUNY Harpur Col (Endicott NY) 52-53, Head readers serv (Endicott & Binghamton) 53-65, Hd ref ILL 65-. 9: BSA; NYLA. 10: Phi

Beta Kappa; ACLU; AAUP. 12: "Saga of Elsie Dinsmore" (45). 14: Admin. 15: 26 Roosevelt ave, Endicott NY 13760.

BROWN, JEAN ISOBEL (TAYLOR CUFFLING). b Montreal Can. 4: Scott A Brown. 5: Sir George Williams U 55 BA; McGill 57 BLS; Columbia summer 62 (LS); UVt summer 65-67. 6: Fr. 7: Steno Can Inds Ltd, Montreal 45-51; Sec Dunany Investments Ltd, Montreal 51-52; Sec Aluminum Co of Can, Montreal 52-56; Ref libn Toronto Pub Libs 57-58; Asst libn Shawinigan Water & Power Co Ltd, Montreal 58-60; Libn Protestant Sch Bd of Greater montreal 60-. 9: ALA; CanLA; Que Assn of School Libns; QueLA (chm Young Peoples Sec68-69, v-pres 69-70). 10: Montreal Mus of Fine Arts; Can Amateur Music MakersAssn; Provincial Assn of Protestant Tchrs; MontrealTA. 14: Ya & child serv. 15: #33, 4865 Queen Maryrd, Montreal 248 Can.

BROWN, JEANNE (REANEY). b Toledo Ohio 28 S 26. 4: Dean Brown. 5: Pasadena City Col 43-45 (Drama) AA; Cal State Col (Los Angeles) 56-60 (Speech, Drama) BA, MA; UCLA 61-62 MLS. 7: Advertising traffic handler "The Register," Santa Ana Cal 53-54; Tchr speech &drama Glendale High Sch, Glendale Cal 60-61; Libn Pasadena Pub Lib, Pasadena Cal 63,libn Pasadena City Col 63-68, libn-tchr 68-. 9: CalLA; CalASchL. 10: AAUW; PasadenaCity Col Fac Senate offr 67, rep 68-. 14: Ref (fine arts). 15: 1616 Hyland ave, Arcadia Ca 91006.

BROWN, JOHN (ANTLIFF). b Lethbridge Alta Can 13 Mr 18. 4: Mary Ethel Anderson. 5: UAlta 44-49 (Hist, educ) BA, B Ed; UBC 64-65 BLS. 6: Fr. 7: Tchr rural & small town schs, Alta 37-47; Tchr City of Calgary Pub Schs, Calgary Can 47-48; Mount Royal Col (Calgary): Tchg & admin 49-65, Libn 66-. 9: CanLA; ALA; Alta Tchrs Assn; Library Council. 10: Canadian Club (dir 68). 14: Ref, admin. 15: 3635-6th st SW, Calgary Alta Can.

BROWN, JULANNE H. b Winthrop Minn 6 N 29. 5: Gustavus Adolphus Col 47-51 (Sec Train) BA; UMinn 55-56 MLS. 7: Libn I Omaha Pub Lib 56-. 9: ALA; NebLA. 14: Child wk. 15: 115 N 33rd st apt 6, Omaha Nb 68131.

BROWN, KATHERINE (MOHLER). b Deedsville Ind 28 O 16. 4: Chester C Brown. 5: IndU 35-39 (Eng) AB; West ResU 48-49 (LS) MS. 7: Lib asst scottsburg High Sch, Scottsburg Ind 39-40; Bkkeeper & clk General Ins Agcy, Scottsburg Ind 41-48; Ref libn Muncie Pub Lib, Muncie Ind 49-54; Asst libn ALA Hdqrs Lib 54-56; Asst dir Muncie Pub Lib, Muncie Ind 56-. 9: ALA; IndLA. 10: Altrusa Intl; Psi Iota Xi. 12: Ed "Focus on Indiana Libraries (57-58). 14: Ref, bk selection, personnel. 15: RFD #4 Box 362, Muncie In 47302.

BROWN, KATHRYN S. b Schenectady NY 21 Ja 16. 4: Arthur B Brown Jr. 5: SUNY(Albany) 34-39 (Eng & LS) BS, 59-61 (Eng & Educ) MS, 62 (LS) NDEA AV Inst 66-67. 6: Ger, Fr. 7: Asst libn catlgr Mercer U 40-42; Post libn US Army Air Corps Roblins Field Ga 42-45; Ref libn Harmanus Bleecker Pub Lib, Albany NY 48-50; Consul libn NY State Educ Dept Archives & Hist Div, Albany 50-55; Asst Med libn NY State Dept Health Div Labs & Res, Albany 55-59; Libn Colonie Central Sch Dist 1, Albany NY 59-. 8: Bibliog for Biol High Sch Curriculum for NY State Dept of Educ 65. 9: ALA; NEA; NYLA; NY State Tchrs Assn; East NY Sch Libns Assn; Hudson-Mohawk LA; NEA-DAVI; NYSECA; ASCD; Capital Area ASCD; NYS ASCD; Colonie Tchrs Assoc. 14: Yp, catlg, doc. 15: 1645 Central ave, Albany NY 12205.

BROWN, KEITH GRAHAM. b England 26 D 17. 4: Mildred Pavlis. 5: NY City Col 35-39 (Lang) BA; Columbia 46-50 BS in LS; Tex Christian U 51-55 (Educ) MEd. 6: Fr. 7: Clerk Municipal Ref Lib NYC 39-40; S/Sgt US Army Pacific 42-45; Catlgr "NY Herald Tribune" 40-45; Catlgr Inst of the Aeronautical Sciences NYC 46-50; Tech info spec Gen Dynamics, Ft Worth Tex 50-. 14: Admin, catlg. 15: 5032 Gilbert dr, Ft Worth Tx 76116.

BROWN, KENNETH. b Curtin WVa 7 Ag 25. 4: Nan Elmslie. 5: WVa Wesleyan Col 46-48 (Econ); Ohio U 48-49 9bus Admin, Econ) BS; Columbia 51-52 MS in LS. 7: Reg consul WVa Lib Commsn, Charleston WVa 52-56; Supv of co serv Carnegie Lib of Pittsburgh 56-61; Dir Chautauqua-Cattaraugus Lib System, Jamestown NY 61-63; Dir Cabell-Huntington Pub Lib, Huntington WVa 63-65; Dir of Libs Asheville & Buncombe Co, Asheville NC 65-. 9: ALA; NCLA. 13: Yes. 15: Pub Lib, Pack Square, Asheville NC 28801.

BROWN, KENNETH RICHARD. b Hallstead Penn 9 S 34. 5: Boston U 53-57 (Amer Hist) AB; Simmons 58-60 (LS) MS. 7: Lib asst MIT 55-57; Adults libn Boston Pub Lib 58; Ref libn Boston U Bus Sch Lib 58-60; Head ref dept Occidental Col Los Angeles 60-62; Chief libn Garrett Corp Los Angeles 62-68; Lib dir Sch of Eng Pahlavi U (Shiraz Iran) 68-. 8: Lectr, Col of Educ, Dept of Lib Sci, UTehran, Tehran Iran Feb 69. 9: SLA (chm Directory Com 67-68). 12: Ed "Directory of Special Libraries of Southern California" (3rd ed 68). 13: Yes. 14: Admin, devel of libs. 15: Univ of Penn Team PO Box 232, Shiraz, Iran.

BROWN, LAURA MAY (TOLMAN). b Schenectady NY 25 Ja 14. 4: Carlton Harold Brown. 5: Colby Col 31-36 (Hist) BA; SUNY(Albany) 57-61 MS of LS. 7: Sch libn Van Corlaer Sch, Schenectady NY 58-. 8: Ch Social Studies Curric Study Com Schenectady NY Pub Schs 67-69; Schenectady Curric Coun 68-. 9: NYLA; NY State Tchrs Assn; East NY Sch LA. 10: Schenectady Photo Soc. 14: Sch libs. 15: 213 Third st, Scotia NY 12302.

BROWN, MRS LAURIE JANE (PLIMPTON). b Medina NY 4 S 08. 5: Elmira Col 26-27; Geneseo State Tchrs Col 27-30, 46-47 (Tchr-Libn) BS; Rochester Bus Inst 39-40 Certif; UBuffalo summers 53-57; Sorbonne-American Sch summer 55 (Libs, Museums & Archives) Certif; URochester summer 58. 7: Tchr Pub Sch, Ithaca NY 30-31; Tchr Rochester Bus Inst 41-43; Tchr-libn Pub Central, Wellsville NY 43-46; Libn Northfield & Mt Hermon Schs, Mass 47-52; Libn Maryvale High Sch, Cheektowaga NY 52-56, 57-58; Tchr-libn Dependents' Sch US Govt, Orleans France 56-57; Libn Greece Central Sch Dist 1, Rochester NY 59-66, Dist catlgr instr materials 66-. 8: Com on Lib Study, 65; Greece Central Sch Dist 1, 65-66. 9: NEA; NYLA; NYStateTA. 10: Rochester Assn for the UN; Rochester Internat Friendship Coun; Rochester Cosmopolitan Club; Internat Friendship Hospitality Family. 13: Yes. 14: Rare bks,mss, archives, ref. 15: 143 Willis ave, Rochester NY 14616.

BROWN, LETA (LUYSTER). b Linneus Mo 21 N 11. 4: Max James Brown. 5: TCU 29-33 (Eng) AB; UMo (Columbia) summer 29; NW Mo State Col67-68. 6: Fr, Ger. 7: Tchr Bucklin Pub Schs, Bucklin Mo 34-37; Asst libn Maryville Pub Lib, Maryville Mo 56-62; Circ libn NW Mo State Col62-. 9: MoStateTA; MoLA. 10: Friends of the Library, Maryville Mo; AAUW; Alpha Beta Alpha. 14: Circ, ref. 15: 404 S Walnut, Maryville Mo64468.

BROWN, LOUISE (BARBARA RAZIN). b Medford Mass 13 My 37. 4: Daniel Leonard Brown. 5: Simmons 54-58 (LS) SB; State Col (Framingham Mass) 65-67; Sch lib certif (Mass) 67. 6: Fr, Hebrew. 7: Catlgr Tufts U Med & Dental Lib 56-60; Asst libn & catlgr Wayland Free Pub Lib, Wayland Mass 66-. 9: MassLA. 10: B'nai Brith; the Academy (Simmons); Women's Amer ORT; Alumnae Assn of Simmons Col. 14: Catlg, med-dental libs, public libs, book review. 15: 74 School st, Wayland MA 01778.

BROWN, LUTHER. b NC 9 Mr 12. 4: Marie (Haber) Brown. 5: Connors State Col 32-33 (Gen) AA; Northeastern (Okla) State Col 33-35 (Sci, Soc Sci) BS; Okla State U 37-38 (Admin, Hist) MS; Colo State Col 41 (Psych, guidance); Peabody (Curriculum, Soc Sci) PhD. 6: Fr, Sp. 7: Elem & sec tchr, prin pun schs, Dewey Okla 35-42; Summer camps NE Okla, Bartlesville Okla 35-42; US Navy (WW II) Enlisted & Off, US, Pacific 42-46; Prof, tchrs educ & placement Northeastern (Okla) State Col 46-55; Pres NW State Col (Okla) 55-56; Curriculum & instruction State Col (St Cloud Minn) 56-58, Dir Learning Resources Center, Chm Dept of Info Media (lib & a-v educ) 58-. 8: Curr & tchr Educ, TEPS Commsn Okla, 46-56; Adv Learning Resources Center; SW State Col, Marshall Minn 64-66, UMinn, Crookston 65; Adv Com (Info Media) Minn State Dept of Educ 65-66; Minn Citizens Commsn on Pub Educ 64; Minn Higher Educ Facilities Commsn (Col Rep) 64-65; Adv Commsn to Coord Higher Educ (Minn) re Learning Resources & ETV. 9: ALA (Life mem); NEA -DAVI; Nat Soc Study Educ; Midwest Acad Libns; OklaEA (Life mem); MinnLA (Certif Com); Acad Libns Minn (past pres); MinnASchL; MinnEA; A V Coordinators Assn Minn (Exec & Ed Bd); DAVI Tchr Educ Com. 10: Kiwanis Club; C of C; Alpha Phi Omega. 14: Org, admin supv info media (lib & av educ). 15: State Col, St Cloud Mn 56301.

BROWN, MABEL CLAIRE. b Ottawa Can 13 N 32. 5: Toronto 60 (Nursing) BS Nursing, 65-66 (LS). 7: Gen staff nurse Ottawa Civic Hosp, Ottawa 53-54; Instr Nursing Sch Toronto E Gen Hosp, Toronto 57-59; Libn Nurses' Lib Toronto West Hosp, Toronto 60-. 9: Can Nurses Assn; MedLA; Regd Nurses Assn Ont; Tor Nursing Libns (chm 63-65). 13: Yes. 15: 31 Christie st, apt 1, Toronto 4 Ont Can.

BROWN, MARGARET CORNELIA. b Williamsport Penn 7 N 15. 5: Mt Holyoke 33-37 BA; Columbia 37-38 BA; UChicago 45-46 (LS) MA. 7: Catlgr Columbia U Lib 38-40; Catlgr Col of the City of NY 40-47; Head of tech serv Pub Lib of Brookline Mass 47-53; Chief processing div Free Lib of Phila 53-. 9: ALA; PennLA. 13: Yes. 14: Tech serv, admin, personnel. 15: Free Lib of Phila 19th & Vine sts, Phila Pa 19103.

BROWN, MARIJKE (MICHAELS). b Amsterdam Holland 2 Je 43. 4: David R Brown. 5: Grinnell Col 61-64 (Speech); RI Col 64-65 (Eng) BA; Rutgers 67-68 MLS. 6: Sp, Ger. 7: Child development specialist Bradley Hosp, Riverside RI 65-67; Ref libn E Brunswick Pub Lib, E Brunswick NJ 68-. 14: Reader's serv. 15: 365 Prentiss lane, piscataway NJ 08854.

BROWN, MARION ELIZABETH. b Tarentum Penn 3 Ja 04. 5: Beaver Col 22-23; Smith 23-26 (Eng Lit) BA; Carnegie 26-27 BS in LS. 7: Jr lib asst Cleveland Pub Lib 27-31; Lib asst DC Pub Lib 31-36; Readers asst Carnegie Lib, Pittsburgh 36-43; Dist libn Hqs 11th Naval Dist, San Diego 43-46; Area libn Com Nav Forces West Pacific, Guam 46-49; US Info Serv: Dir Libs, Athens Greece 50-52, Dir Libs, Baghdad Iraq 52-54, Dir Libs, The Hague 55-57, Saigon 60-62, Manila 62-67; Sr bibliog & libn, ics/bb; USIA, Wash DC 67-. 9: PhilippineLA. 10: Smith Col Alumnae Assn. 14: Adv wk with adults. 15: 3014 Dent pl NW, Washington DC 20007.

BROWN, MARION ELIZABETH. b Woodstock Ont Can. 5: McMasterU 29-33 (Modern Langs) BA; UToronto 33-34 BLS; Brown -54 (Amer Civilization) AM. 6: Fr, Ger, Sp, Ital. 7: Catlgr, hd ref dept QueensU (Kingston) 35-38; Catlgr hd rare books dept Smith Col 38-43, 46; Serv with the WRNS (3rd Officer) 43-45; Hd dept special collections BrownU 46-55; Hd dept rare bks & spec collections UToronto 55-. 9: ALA-ACRL (sec Rare Bks Sect 65); CanLA; Bibliog Soc Can (1st v-pres 62-64; pres 64-66); SAA; OntLA; Inst Prof Libns Ont; Mss Soc. 13: Yes. 14: Rare bks. 15: apt 1912 50 Cambridge ave, Toronto 355 Ont Can.

BROWN, MARION GRACE. b Cleveland 2 My 16. 5: West Res 34-38 BA, 39-40 BS in LS; American U 52-55 (Pol Sci). 7: Act asst libn Northwestern U Sch of Law 42-46; Libn US Army, Philippines 47; Histn US Army; Graves Registration Serv, Philippines 47-48; Asst libn Nat Educ Assn, Wash DC 52-56; Base libn USAF, Italy 57-58; Acquis libn Naval Applied Sci Lab, Brooklyn NY 59-. 9: SLA; NY Tech Libns Assn. 15: Naval Applied Sci Lab, Tech Lib Bldg 1 Code 222, Flushing & Wash aves, Brooklyn NY 11251.

BROWN, MARJORIE H. b Gardena Cal 28 Ap 06. 5: Whittier Col 24-28 (Zool) BA; UCal(Berkeley) 28-29 (Educ) Certif; Riverside Lib Serv Sch 42-43 (Libnship) Certif. 7: Asst libn Ventura Co Lib, Ventura Cal 43-44, Br libn 44-49, Libn II 49-64, Supv libn 64-. 9: ALA; CalLA. 10: Bus & Prof Women's Club. 14 Bk sel, acquis. 15: 254 Eugena dr, Ventura Ca 93002.

BROWN, MARY (GRACE HAWKINS). b Petersburg Va 22 O 15. 4: Ernest Mason Brown. 5: Mary Washington Col 34-38 (Eng) BS; UVa summers 39, 40, 48 (LS) Certif; William & Mary Col summer 47 (LS); Fla So summer 57 (LS); Columbia summer 58 (Med Lit & LS). 7: Tchr-libn Floyd Co Sch Bd, Floyd Va 39-41; Tchr-libn Surry High Sch, Surry Va 41-43; Libn Bolling Jr High, Petersburg Va 43-63; Tchr of Eng & hist Petersburg High Sch, Petersburg Va 63-; Med libn Petersburg Gen Hosp, Petersburg Va 56-. 9: NEA (chm Libns Sect Dist D 53-55); ALA; MedLA; VaEA; VaLA. 10: Country Club of Petersburg; Amer Cancer Soc (local sec 66-67); AAUW; Kiwanis. 13: Yes. 14: Ref, research. 15: Petersburg Gen Hosp, Petersburg, Va 23803.

BROWN, MARY ANN. b Wrigley Tenn 10 Ag 36. 5: Peabody Col 54-58 (Bio) BS, 58-59 MALS; EmoryU A W Calhoun Med Lib Internship 61-62. 7: Asst in acquis A W Calhoun Med Lib emoryU 59-60, Asst pub serv 62-65; Ref libn Med Ctr Lib DukeU 65-68, Ext libn 68-. 8: MedLA Certif Grade II. 9: MedLA (sec-treas So Reg Gp 63-64; Com recruit 68-). 10: AAUW. 14: Ref. 15: Med Center Lib Duke University, Durham NC 27706.

BROWN, MARY ELIZABETH (DOLFIN). b Englewood NJ 14 Ag 16. 4: Halcott Anderson Brown. 5: Fla State Col for Women 33-37 (Eng) BA; UVa 37-38 (LS) Certif; Fla State U 60 (LS) MA. 7: Tchr Bay Co High Sch, Panama City Fla 38-41, Libn 41-42; Libn Bay Co Pub Lib, Panama City Fla 43-45; Libn Lynn Haven Elem Sch, Lynn Haven Fla 48-55; Libn Gulf Coast Jr Col 57-. 9: ALA; FlaLA; FlaASchL; Bay County Sch LA; Bay County EA. 10: AAUW; Beta Phi Mu. 13: Yes. 14: Admin. 15: 706 Ill ave,Lynn Haven Fl 32444.

BROWN, MARY JO. b Hartshorne Okla 24 D 29. 5: UOkla 47-54 (Mus) BMus, MM; Eastman Sch of Mus summer 58 (Mus); IndU 60-63 (Musicology, LS) MA; UIowa 65-66. 6: Fr, Ger, Ital, Sp. 7: Instr (piano) Radford Sch for Girls, El Paso Tex 55-56; Asst Prof of mus w va Wesleyan Col 56-59; Instr (piano) Birmingham-So Conservatory, Birmingham Ala 59-60; Stud personnel serv IndU (Bloomington) 60-63; Catlg libn UIowa Libs (Iowa City) 63-67; Asst Prof of lib sci & asst libn Ill StateU (Normal) 67-. 9: MusLA; Amer musicological Soc; IllLA. 10: AAUP. 14: Mus libnship. 15: Milner Lib Illinois State Univ, Normal Il 61761.

BROWN, MARY LINUS SISTER. b Pittsburgh Pa 4 S 13. 5: Mt Mercy Col 45 (Sociol) BA; Catholic U 60 MS in LS. 6: Fr, Sp. 7: Libn & tchr Diocese of Pittsburgh and Greensburg Penn

Canevin High Sch, Pittsburgh Penn 63-. 8: Coord, ESEA Title II, Diocese of Pittsburgh 65; A-V Com, Cath Sch Journal 43-44; Adv Com, ESEA Title II Lib Bks, Penn Sch Lib Resources sel 66-67; Conduct prog for In-Serv Train for Adult Volunteer Lib Aides; Coord Lib aide Prog under Title I, Pittsburgh Pub Schs. 9: CathLA (BkList Com Cath Suppl to wilson Sr High Sch Catlg; Wes Penn Unit: chm 65-67, chm Elem Sect 45-47, chm Secon Sect 51-56); PennLA. 14: Lib admin, wkshops for insts for furthering lib educ. 15: Canevin High Sch Lib, 2700 Morange rd, Pittsburgh Pa 15205.

BROWN, MARY RUTH. b Lexington Ky 3 My 25. 4: George W Brown. 5: UKy 42-44, 46-48 (Educ) AB, 59-60 MSLS. 6: Sp. 7: Tech US Civil Serv, Honolulu 44-46; Tchr Fairhope High Sch, Fairhope Ala 47-48; Tchr libn Joseph High Sch, Joseph Ore 51-56; Asst libn Reno High Sch, Reno Nev 56-59; UKy; Catlgr Margaret I King Lib 60-62, Catlgr Agric Lib 62-64, Asst libn Agric Lib 65-66, Hd Libn Agric Lib 66-. 8: Lib adv, NE Thailand Agri Ctr 67-. 9: ALA; Internat Assn Agric Libns & Documentalists; KyLA; Ky Assn Contin Educ; Ky Hist Soc. 10: Beta Phi Mu; AAUP. 13: Yes. 14: Admin. 15: Rte 1 Box 144B, Winchester Ky 40391.

BROWN, MATTIE ARNELL (HAWKS). b Gary Ind 29 Ja 43. 4: Clarence Edward Brown Jr. 5: Clarion State Col 61-64 (LS) BS; UPittsburgh 64-68 MS. 6: Fr. 7: Stud asst Clarion State Col 61-64; Asst libn Mt Alto VA Hosp, Wash DC summer 63; Sch libn Butler Area Schs, Butler Penn 64-68; Hd tech serv New Castle Pub Lib, New Castle Penn 68-. 9: PennLA; PennStateEA. 14: Catlg, ref, info retr. 15: 719 Etna st, New Castle Pa 16101.

BROWN, MORTON R. b Atlanta 26 Ag 22. 5: Columbia 49 (Eng) BA, 50 MSLS. 7: M/Sgt US Army 42-45; Libn NY Pub Lib 50-59; Libn Smith Barney & Co Inc NYC 59-. 9: SLA. 13: Yes. 15: Smith Barney & Co Inc, 20 Broad st, NYC 10005.

BROWN, MILDRED (PRIDE). b Horatio Ark 14 Ja 04. 4: Louis Gray Brown. 5: Hendrix Col 21-25 (Eng) AB; LSU 43-44 BS in LS. 6: Fr. 7: Tchr High Sch, Fordyce Ark 25-27; Tchr High Sch, Hoxie Ark 27-30; Tchr High Sch, Ohio Co Ky 38-42; Tchr High Sch, Horatio Ark 42-43; Libn Jr High Sch, Bastrop La 44-. 14: Ref, child reading. 15: 365 W Hickory, Bastrop La 71220.

BROWN, NANCY TROWELL. b Anderson SC 30 My 40. 4: Edward Sol Brown. 5: Winthrop Col 58-62 (LS) BS. 7: Libn Beaufort Elem Sch, Beaufort SC 62-63; Libn Goose Creek Elem Sch, Goose Creek SC 63-66; Librarian Goose Creek High Sch 66-. 9: NEA; ALA; SCEA; SCLA. 4: Yp libs. 15: 7661 Pinehurst st, Charleston Heights SC 29405.

BROWN, NORMAN A. b Antwerp NY 28 Ap 12. 4: Marion Fuller. 5: Hobart Col 30-34 (Eng) BA; Syracuse U 50-51 MS in LS, 51-53 (Econ). 6: Fr. 7: Tchr High Sch, Russell NY 36-37; Tech 2 US Army - 5th Armored Div 40-45; Clk NY Air Brake Co, Watertown NY 46-50; Libn Main Lib, Rochester NY 53-54; Libn NY State Reg Lib Serv Ctr, Watertown 54-57; Libn IBM Corp, Owego NY 57-. 9: SLA. 10: Endicott Toastmasters Club. 14: Catlg, ref, admin. 15: 2726 Crescent dr, Endwell NY 13760.

BROWN, NORMAN B. b Rochester NY 25 F 26. 4: Mary Ann Randall. 5: URochester 45-48 (Eng, Hist) AB; West Res 48-49 MS in LS; UIll 52-54 (LS). 6: Ger, Fr. 7: Ref libn Union Col Lib (Schenectady NY) 49-52; UIll Lib (Urbana): Asst ref libn 53-57, Documents bibliog 57-58, Ser acquis libn 58-. 9: ALA. 10: Phi Beta Kappa; Beta phi Mu. 13: Yes. 14: Ser acquis, ref. 15: 1612 Sangamon dr, Champaign Il 61822.

BROWN, PATRICIA (MAHONEY). b Somerville Mass 10 S 39. 4: Ernest Grogan Brown. 5: Emmanuel Col 57-61 (Eng) BA; Simmons 61-62 (LS) MS. 6: Sp. 7: A-v libn Boston Pub

Lib 6 2; Music libn Robbins Lib, Arlington Mass 62-65; Libn Fish, Richardson & Neave, (Attys Boston) 65-66; Head acquis SUNY (Buffalo) Law Lib 66-67; Circ & readers' adv serv Kenmore Pub Lib, Kenmore NY 67-. 15: 2669 Eggert rd, Tonawanda NY 14150.

BROWN, PATRICIA ANN (CHARLTON). b Ft Sumner NM 21 O 30. 4: John Franklin Brown. 5: No Tex State U 47-51 (LS) BA; Tex West fall 51 (Educ); O ur Lady of the Lake Col summer 65 (NDEA Inst). 6: Sp. 7: Libn Goldsmith Elem Sch, Ector Co Independent Sch Dist, Goldsmith Tex 51-55; Child libn Midland Pub Lib, Midland Tex 58-59; Libn Hays Elem Sch, Odessa Tex 59-66; Libn Ector Jr-Sr High Sch, Odessa Tx 66-. 9: TexLA; Tex State Tchrs Assn; TexASchL; Tex Clrm TA. 10: Kappa Delta Pi; Kappa Kappa Iota; Beta Sigma Phi. 14: Bk sel, reading adv to child, ref. 15: 1702 Palomar lane, Odessa Tx 79761.

BROWN, PATRICIA IRENE. b Boston 23 Ap 31. 5: Suffolk U 51-55 (Eng, Hist) AB; Suffolk Law Sch 61-65 (LLB); Suffolk U 65- (Bus Admin). 6: Fr, Sp. 7: Typist Rustcraft Publ Co, Boston 48-50; Pitcher All Amer Girls Baseball League, Chicago 50-51; Suffolk U; Stud lib asst 51-55, lib asst 55-64, asst libn 64-. 9: AALL; Mass Bar Assn; Boston Bar Assn; Amer Judicature Soc. 10: Phi Alpha Theta. 14: Legal research. 15: 20 Derne st, Boston Ma 02114.

BROWN, PATRICIA LYNN. b Lafayette La 1 O 28. 5: U Southwestern La 44-47 (Chem Engnr) BS; UTex 47-49 (Organic Chem) MA. 7: Instr Smith Col 49-50; Research assoc Albany Med Col 50-51; Lit searcher EthylCorp, Detroit 51-55; Sr tech writer-ed Westinghouse Atomic Power Div, Pittsburgh55-57; Texas Instruments, Dallas; Manager of info serv 57-64, Tech info consul &manager of central lib serv 64-67; Sr info scientist Battelle Mem Inst, Columbus67-. 9: ACS; Soc Women Engnrs (pres 61-63); SLA; Engnr Socs Lib Bd 61-63, 68; NatSecurity Ind Assn (Sci & Tech Oriented Info Subcom 65-). 10: Inst Electric & Electro Engnrs; Soc Tech Writers & Publ; AAAS; Iota Sigma Pi. 12: Contrib auth &indexer "The Technical Report" (54); Contrib auth "Ann Rev of Info Science, Vol 3"(68); Ed "Women in Engineering". 13: Yes. 14: Lib mechanization, info storage & retrieval, tech lit searching. 15: 2590 Wellesley dr, Columbus Oh43221.

BROWN, PEARLIE (MURRAY). b Kings Mtn NC 24 Mr 40. 4: Marvin W Brown. 5: N Car Col 57-61 (Health ed, LS) BS. 6: Fr. 7: Libn Carver High Sch, Spindale NC 61-64; Tchr Pleasant Ridge Sch, Gastonia NC 64-65; Asst libn Gaston Col 66-. 9: ALA; NCLA; NCEA; Commun Col LA. 10: Gaston Col Fac Assn. 11: Zeta Phi Beta. 14: Ref librarian. 15: Rte 1 Box 218, Kings Mountain NC 28086.

BROWN, PHYLLIS (BROWN). b Medford Mass 12 N 20. 4: Calvin Clinton Brown Jr. 5: Syracuse 38-40; UNH 41-43 (Econ) BS; SUNY (Geneseo) 54-56 (Elem Educ) MS, 56-59 (LS) MS. 7: Economist Nat War Labor Bd, Boston 43-45;Staff asst Amer Red Cross, Honolulu & Guam 45-46; Libn Lima High Sch, Lima NY 56-57; Libn Churchville-Chili Central, Churchville NY 59-,Dept hd 68-; Libn ALA Exhibit US Pavilion, World's Fair NY 64. 8: World's Fair Child Lib. 9: NYLA; NY State Tchrs Assn; Monroe Co Tchrs Assn. 14: Child bks. 15: 320 N ave, Avon NY 14414.

BROWN, PHYLLIS L. b Detroit 4 Mr 14. 5: Our Lady of the Lake 34-36 (Math) BA, 44-46 BS in LS, 52-54 (Educ) M Ed. 7: Tchr San Antonio Ind Schs, San Antonio Tex 36-41; Tchr Somerset Ind Schs, Somerset Tex 41-42; Tchr San Antonio Ind Schs, San Antonio Tex 42-46; Child libn San Antonio Pub Lib, San Antonio Tex 46-48; Girl scout prof Bexar Co Girl Scout Coun, San Antonio Tex 48-54; Libn Laredo Jr Col 51-63; Sci-tech libn Tex A&M U 63-65; Order libn Northwestern State Col 65-68; Ser Libn 68-. 9: ALA-ACRL (sec Jr Col Sect 62-63); SLA; TexLA; Tex Assn Col Tchrs; La Tchrs Assn; LaLA. 10: AAUP; AAUW; Delta Kappa Gamma; Delta Zeta. 14: Acquis, sci ref, ser. 15: P O Box 4312 NSC, Natchitoches La 71457.

BROWN, PRISCILLA (MAGOUN). b Cambridge Mass 10 N 19. 5: Wellesley 37-41 (Psych) BA; DrexrXXX BROWN, PRISCILLA (MAGOUN). 7: Circ asst Swarthmore Col Lib 42-45; Libn I brs Child & Sch Dept Denver Pub Lib 45-52; Child libn Littleton Pub Lib, Littleton Colo 62-66; Asst child dept Penrose Pub Lib, colo Springs Colo 67-69. 9: ALA; ColoLA. 10: Littleton Coun for Human Rels. 14: Child wk. 15: Penrose Pub Lib, Colorado Springs Co.

BROWN, ROBERT (WILFRED). b Lucknow Ontario 3 N 24. 4: Antonie Meckes. 5: UBritish Columbia 50 (Eng, Fr) BA, 51; Victoria Summer Sch 53-55 LS. 6: Fr. 7: Purchasing Agent Railway & Power Engineering Corp, Vancouver 46-47; Sch Dist 28, Quesnel BC Can Tchr 51-54; Sch Dist 44: N Vancouver: Tchr libn 54-68, Chief libn 68-. 8: Served on a joint committee of the British Columbia Teachers' Federation and the British Columbia School Librarians' Association convened to report on needs in British Columbia School Library Development 67. 9: CanLA; ALA; CanSchLA; BCSchLA (past pres). 10: Liturgical Committee St Stephen's Catholic Church, North Vancouver. 12: Ed BCSchLA "Newsletter" & Journal "The Tikinagan" (68-69). 14: Sch lib devel. 15: 2327 Kilmarnock Crescent, North Vancouver BC Can.

BROWN, REV ROBERT E SM. b Dayton Ohio 31 Mr 06. 5: UDayton 24-28 (Eng) BA; UFribourg (Switzerland) 31-37 (Theol, Philos, Ordination); Columbia 40-42 MS in LS; West Res summer 40 (LS). 6: Lat, Fr. 7: Tchr St Mary Parish Sch, Pittsburgh 25-27; Tchr Cathedral Latin High Sch, Cleveland 27-30; Tchr Holy Redeemer High Sch, Detroit 30-31; Stud UFribourg Switzerland 31-37; Tchr-Chaplain Trinity Col (Sioux City Iowa) 37-38; Tchr-Chaplain Mt St John (Dayton Ohio) 38-39; Tchr-Chaplain Chaminade High Sch, Santa Cruz Cal 39-40; Chaplain St John Home, Brooklyn NY 40-42; Libn-Chaplain N Catholic High Sch, Pittsburgh 42-47; Libn-Chaplain Chaminade High Sch, Dayton Ohio 47-59; Libn-Chaplain Cathedral Latin, Cleveland 59-62; Libn-Chaplain N Catholic H igh Sch, Pittsburgh 62-65; Libn-Chaplain Moeller High Sch, Cincinnati 65-69; Archivist chaplain Marianist Prov, Marianist Col 69-. 8: Instr in bk sel, Duquesne U, summers 44-47. 9: ALA; CathLA; West Penn LA; OhioSchLA. 15: Univ of Dayton, East Campus, Marianist Col, 4100 Patterson rd, Dayton Oh 45430.

BROWN, MRS RUTH W(ELCH). b Bear Lake Mich 13 Mr 19. 5: Muskegon Jr Col 36-38 AA; Mich State U 38-40 (Eng, Hist) AB; West Res 40-41 BS in LS; Mich State U 57-62 (Educ); UMich 68-69 (LS). 7: Yp libn Cleveland Pub Lib 41-43; Sub tchr Whitehall Dist Schs, Whitehall Mich 57-58; Ref libn Hackley Pub Lib, Muskegon Mich 58-60; Sch libn Whitehall Dist Schs, Whitehall Mich 60-. 9: ALA; MichASchL; NEA; MichEA. 14: Ref. 15: 6324 Michillinda rd,Whitehall Mi 49461.

BROWN, SARAH (COLE). b Conway Ark 3 D 11. 4: Sterling Felan Brown. 5: Hendrix Col 29-33 (Eng) BA; Chicago summer 34; UIll 39 BS in LS. 6: Ger, Fr. 7: Asst libn Alabama Col 39-41; Post Libn USAF, Maxwell Field Ala 41; Asst libn Air Corps Tactical Sch, Maxwell Field Ala 42-43; Libn Combat Intelligence 4-engine Sch, Maxwell Field Ala 44-45; UAla Med Center Lib: Head catlgr 48-51, Asst libn 51-55, Dir 55-. , Asst Prof 67-. 8: Cons Comprehensive Health Planning Off, Ala Dept Pub Health 68-69. 9: MedLA (Bd Dirs 67-, mem &/or chm MedLA-NLM Liaison Com 66-69; Amer Assoc Dent Schs (v-chm Sect on Dent Libs & Info Servs 68-69); SLA; AlaLA (v-pres & pres-elect 68-69); Birmingham Lib Club. -0 10: Amer Assn Hist Med; Assn Amer Med Cols; Assn Amer Dent Schs; Amer Assn Hist Dentistry. 12: Mem ed com "Rare Books and Collections in the Reynolds Historical Library; A Bibliography (68). 13: Yes. 14: Catlg, rare bks, lib admin. 15: 1919 7th Ave S, Birmingham Al 35322.

BROWN, SHIRLEY LOUISE (SCOTT). b Cedar Rapids Iowa 27 J141. 4: Jeffrey Warner Brown. 5: Iowa State U 59-63 (Eng) BS; UIowa 64-65 (Lib Educ) MA; UColo summer 62. 7: Tchr-libn Haley Sch Dist 103, Lyons Ill 63-64; Libn Pensacola Jr Col 65-67; Libn Mayfair High Sch Bellflower Unified Sch Dist, Lakewood Cal 67-. 9: CalASchL. 10: Pi Lambda Theta. 14: Acquis. 15: 117 Ninth st NW, Cedar Rapids Iowa 52405.

BROWN, SIBYL (COKER). b Muleshoe Tex 18 Ja 18. 4: Olie Theoran Brown. 5: Hardin-Simmons U 35-36; W Tex State U 36-39 (Eng) BA; East NMU summer 40, 42 (Educ); So West Baptist T Sem 43-44 (Rel Educ); USoCal 52-56 MSLS. 7: Eng tchr high sch Pettit Tex 39-41; Tchr Central Grade Sch, Portales NM 41-43; Mechanic Consolidated Aircraft Ft Worth Tex 43; Tchr grade sch Rotan Tex 47-48; Tchr San Gabriel Valley Acad, Temple City Cal 51-52; Libn Cal Baptist Col Riverside Cal 52-. 8: Consul to area church libs. 9: ALA; CalLA; Christ Libns Assn. 10: AAUW;Riverside Music Assn. 13: Yes. 14: Rare bks. 15: 8432 Magnolia ave, Riverside Ca 92504.

BROWN, STANLEY DOWDELL. b Chicago Ill 4 N 06. 4: Dorothy Jane Russell. 5: Columbia Union Col 26 (Hist) AB; UMd 34 (Eng) AB, 35 AM; UNC 37 AB in LS; UChicago 42; Ohio State 54 (Hist) AM. 7: Licensed minister WPenn Conf of Seventh-day Adventists 26-32; South Jr Col, Collegedale Tenn: Libn & hd Eng 35-40, Libn 40-44; South Missionary Col, Collegedale Tenn: Libn 44-68, Assoc libn 68-. 9: ALA. 14: Acquis. 15: Box 293, Collegedale Tn 37315.

BROWN, THOMAS M(ARKWELL). b Los Angeles 19 My 30. 4: Leila Marie Jackson. 5: UCal(Berkeley) 48-52 (Eng) BA; Los Angeles State Col 53-54 (Educ) Secondary Credential; Chicago 59-60 (LS) MA. 7: Tchr Hollenbeck Jr High Sch, Los Angeles 53-54; Libn Anglo-Chinese Sch, Ipoh Malaya 54-59; Libn UChicago Lab High Sch 60-61; Lib consul Methodist Schs, Malaya Bd of Missions Methodist Church, Malaya 61-65; Libn sci & ref New Trier Twp High Sch, Northfield Ill 65-66 dept chm lib 66-. 8: Lib Consul Methodist Schs, Malaya 61-65; Chm Basic Book List for English School Libraries, Malayan Dept of Educ, 64-65. 9: ALA;-AASchL; MalayanLA (Coun 62-63; chm Sch Libs Com63); IllLA (chm adhoc com on manpower train & utilization); IllASchL (treas 69-);NEA; IllEA. 10: Beta Phi Mu; mem Bd of Educ Sch dist #34, Glenview Ill 68-; ACLU. 12: Ed "Malayan Library Journal," v 3. 13: Yes. 14: Sch libs. 15: 7 Happ rd, Northfield Il 60094.

BROWN, VIRGINIA (TAYLOR). b Indianapolis 30 S 16. 4: Louis J Brown. 5: Miami U 34-38 (Eng) AB; Carnegie 39-40 BS in LS. 7: Res libn Miami U 38-39; Co libn Clinton Co, Wilmington Ohio 40-41; Circ desk Lane Pub Lib, Hamilton Ohio 41-42; High sch libnBellefontaine High Sch, Bellefontaine Ohio 43-46; Circ libn Miami U (Middletown) 65-68, Hd libn 68-. 9: ALA; OhioLA; COLT. 10: Middletown Hist Soc; Coun ofWorld Affairs; Univ Women's Club; Delta Zeta; Elder, Presbyterian Church. 14: Readersserv, admin. 15: 2403 Superior ave, Middletown Oh 45042.

BROWN, VIVIAN SARITA. b Charlotte NC 1 Ag 44. 5: UNC (Greensboro) 62-64 (Eng); UNC (Chapel Hill) 64-66 (Eng Educ) BA, 66-67 MSLS. 7: Lib clk Pub Lib of Charlotte & Mecklenburg Co, Charlotte NC summers 64-66; Y-a libn Charlootte Pub Lib, Charlotte NC 67-. 9: ALA; MecklenburgLA. 14: Y-a serv. 15: 2119 Canterwood dr apt 1, Charlotte NC 28213.

BROWN, REV WILLIAM J CSB. b Buffalo NY 9 N 30. 5: Assumption U 55 (Hist) BA; U St Michael's Col 60 (Theol) STB; West Res 65 MS in LS. 7: Tchr St Thomas High Sch, Houston 55-57; Tchr Aquinas Inst of Rochester 61-64; Libn St Michael's Col Sch (Toronto) 64-68; Consul sec sch libs Met Separate Sch Bd, Toronto 68-. 9: ALA; CanLA;SchLA; CathLA; NEA-DAVI; Educ Media Assn of Can; Internat Reading Assn; NCTE; Instof Profess Libns of Ont; OntEA; Ont Eng Cath TA; OntLA. 10: Beta Phi Mu. 14: Sch libs. 15: 1515 Bathurst st, Toronto 10 Can.

BROWNE, ALMA ESTES. b Boston 27 Ag 02. 5: Simmons 19-23 (LS) SB. 6: Fr, Sp. 7: Asst Lib Simmons Col Sch of Soc Wk 23-28; Asst in chg 28-46; Simmons Col Lib: Asst in chg summers 28, 29, 31, Asst in lib 46-59, Lib asst 59-62,Circ libn 62-. 9: ALA. 10: Bellevue Hill Improvement Assn. 14: Circ, catlg of col archives. 15: 170 Stratford st, W Roxbury Ma 02132.

BROWNE, CYNTHIA E. b Plainfield NJ 3 Mr 26. 5: Conn Col 43-47 (European Hist) BA; Simmons 51-52 (LS) MS; Trinity Col (Hartford Conn) 65- (Amer Hist). 7: Off clerk Keats Bk Co, Stamford Conn 47-51; Catlgr in chg of deptl catlg Harvard U Lib 52-64; Chief tech processes div Conn State Lib 64-68; Catlgr Trinity Col 68-. 9: ALA; NE Tech Serv Libns; ConnLA. 10: Conn Hist Soc. 14: Tech serv. 15: 37 Huntington st, Hartford Ct 06105.

BROWNE, FRANCES S VAN VALKENBURGH. b Schenectady NY 9 O 15. 4: J Elmore Browne. 5: Hunter Col 32-36 (Eng) BA; Columbia 48-49 (LS) MS; UNM 61-62 (Educ). 6: Sp. 7: Libn NY State U (New Paltz); Tchr Los Lunas Train Sch, Los Lunas NM 57-59; Instr of Lib Sci St Josephs Col (Albuquerque NM) 59-61; Libn Espanola High Sch, Espanola NM 61-. 9: MedLA; SLA. 10: Finlandia Found; Sierra Club; YMCA. 14: Sch lib serv, lib educ. 15: PO Box 43, Corrales NM 87048.

BROWNE, JOSEPH PETER CSC. b Detroit 12 Je 29. 5: UNotre Dame 46-51 (Philos) AB; Holy Cross Col (Wash DC) 51-55 (Theol); Georgetown U 54 (Ger); Angelicum (Rome) 56-58 (Theol) STL, STD; UVienna 57 (Ger); Catholic U 59-64 MS in LS. 6: Ger, Fr, Lat, Ital. 7: Asst Pastor Holy Cross Church, S Bend Ind 55-56; Prof of moral theol Holy Cross Col (Wash DC) 59-64, Libn 59-64; Head Dept of Lib Sci UPortland 64-, Dir of Summer Session 65-67, Libn 66-. 8: UPortland, chm, Acad Senate 68-; State Exec Dir Natl Lib Week 65-66. 9: CatLA (chm Lib Educ Sect 68-69; v-pres & pres-elect 69-); ALA-ACRL; OreLA (v-pres 66-67, pres 67-68); OreASchL; PNLA. 10: (Beta Phi Mu) Cath Theol Soc of Amer. 12: "Some Moral Implications of the Privilege Against Self-Incrimination in the Fifth Amendment to the Constitution of the United States" (60). 13: Yes. 14: Ref, lib educ. 15: 5000 N Willamette blvd, Portland Or 97203.

BROWNE, L HAYGOOD. b Ala 10 F 10. 5: UCincinnati 32 BA; George Washington U 48-49 (Legal Bibliog). 6: Fr. 7: Law clerk Off Gen Coun US Dept of Navy, Wash DC 49-53, Head Libn 53-. 9: AALL; Law Libns Soc, Wash DC. 13: Yes. 14: Law periods, research assistance to attorneys. 15: 3133 Connecticut ave NW, Wash DC 20008.

BROWNE, RUSSELL ALEXANDER. b Cairo Ga 6 S 20. 4: Margaret Woodall Browne. 5: Emory 37-40, 45-47 (Journalism) AB, 67-68 (Libnship) M Ln. 7: Program dir Radio Station WRNY, Rochester NY 47-54; Mgr Radio Station WCLB, Camilla Ga 54-67; Libn Dalton Jr Col 68-. 10: Rotary Club. 15: Lib Dalton Jr College, Dalton Ga 30720.

BROWNE, RUTH B. b N Adams Mass 17 Jl 13. 5: Simmons 33-37 BS in LS. 7: Child libn N Adams Pub Lib, N Adams Mass 37-41; Br child libn Providence Pub Lib 41-44; Br libn Schenectady Co Pub Lib, Schenectady NY 44-50; Child libn N Adams Pub Lib, N Adams Mass 54-55, Libn 55-. 9: ALA; NELA; MassLA; West Mass Lib Club (past pres). 15: N Adams Pub Lib, N Adams Ma 01247.

BROWNELL, GLADYS M. b Schenectady NY 10 Mr 04. 5: Mt Holyoke 24-28 (Eng) AB; Columbia 29-30 (LS) BS. 6: Fr. 7: Gen asst Wells Col Lib 30-38; Catlgr Swarthmore Col Lib 38-44; Sr catlgr Worcester Free Pub Lib, Worcester Mass 44-46; Head Catlgr Colby Col Lib 46-47; Asst libn Bard Col Lib 47-53; Act libn 49, 50-51; Libn Skidmore Col Lib 53-. 8: Mem of & sec to the Bd of Trustees of Capital Dist Lib Coun 66-68. 9: ALA-ACRL (Sec Col Sect 56-57); NYLA. 10: AAUP. 14: Bldg bk collection. 15: Skidmore Col, Saratoga Springs NY 12866.

BROWNING, MRS OLIVE (NICKLE). b Harrison Ont Can 12 Ag 23. 4: G Russell Browning. 5: U West Ont 43-46 BA; Toronto 46-47 BLS. 7: Asst libn Oshawa Pub Lib, Oshawa Ont 47-50; Chief Libn Weston Pub Lib, Weston Ont 50-60; Child libn Mimico Pub Lib, Mimico Ont 60-66; Chief libn Port Credit Pub Lib, Port Credit Ont 66-. 14: Pub lib wk. 15: 8 Tecumseh ave, Port Credit Ont Can.

BROWNLEE, JERRY W. b Mobile Ala 30 M 38. 4: Lorian Leslie Brownlee. 5: Spring Hill Col 60-64 (Pol sci) BS; LSU 65-67 MSLS. 7: Mobile Pub Lib, Mobile Ala: Ref asst 64-66, Hd ref & circ 67-68; Hd libn Livingston U, Livingston Ala 68-. 9: ALA; -ACRL; AlaLA. 14: Admin, acquis, interlib systems. 15: Box 729, Livingston Al 35470.

BROWNSON, HELEN L (MYERS). b Kan City Kan 1 My 17. 4: Eugene C Brownson. 5: Kan City Jr Col 34-36; UKan 36-38 (Span) AB. 6: Sp, Fr. 7: Sec, tech aide Com on Med Research Off Sci Res & Dev, Wash DC 42-47; Com sec Spec Com on Tech Info Res & Dev Bd Dept of Defense, Wash DC 47-51; NSF: Research analyst Off of Sci Info 51-54; Program dir Sci Documentation 54-58; Program dir Documentation Research 58-64; Program dir Research & Studies 64-66; Employed US Govt 66-. 9: ADI (Coun 53-55); Ling Soc Amer. 10: Club de Las Americas; Phi Beta Kappa. 12: Ed "Literature Notes, abstracts sect in "American Documentation (51-57). 13: Yes. 14: Documentation, info research. 15: 3850 Tunlaw rd, Wash DC 20007.

BROWNSTEIN, RUTH LYNN (KRUGMAN). b Brooklyn NY 10 Ag 14. 4: Sidney Brownstein. 5: Brooklyn Col 31-39 (Music) BA; Pratt 44-45 BLS. 7: Libn Post Lib, Ft Hamilton NY 41-43; Libn W Hempstead (NY) Pub Lib 56-58; Libn Hebrew Acad of W Hempstead, NY 61-62; Libn Plainedge High Sch, N Massapequa NY 62-65; Libn Turtle Hook Jr High Sch, Uniondale NY 65-. 9: NY State Tchrs Assn; Nassau-Suffolk SchLA. 14: Reading guidance for yp. 15: 707 Knollwood dr, W Hempstead NY 11552.

BRUBAKER, ROBERT LOUIS. b Centralia Ill 30 N 29. 4: Linda Lou Switzer. 5: So Ill U 47-50 (Music Educ); UIll 54-56 (Hist) BA; UWis 56-59, 61-62 (Amer Hist) MS; Chicago 65-69 (LS) MA. 6: Ger, Fr. 7: Bassoonist (S/Sgt) USAF Band, Scott Field Ill 50-53; Host tchr Elgin High Sch, Elgin Ill 59-61; Dept of Spec Collections UChicago Lib 65-66; Curator of mss Ill State Hist Lib 62-65; Asst Prof Grad Sch of Lib Serv UCLA 69-. 8: Consul Chicago Area Hist Records Com 66. 9: ALA, BSA; Bibliog Soc; Gutenberg Gesellschaft; Printing Hist Soc; Bibliog Soc UVa; SAA. 10: Phi Beta Kappa; AAUW. 12: Three brochures in series of guides to mss in the Ill State Hist Lib. 13: Yes. 14: Bibliog, hist of bks & libs, communic theory, adminis of research libs, rare bks & mss, lib educ. 15: Grad Sch of Library Service, Univ of California, Los Angeles Ca 90024.

BRUBECK, KATHERINE (McCALLIE). b Trenton NJ 4 N 10. 4: Harold E Brubeck. 5: Goucher Col 29-33 (Romance langs) AB; Columbia 33-34 BLS; Fla State U 53-54 (LS) MA. 6: Fr, Sp. 7: Asst libn NJ State Col (Glassboro) 34-37; Libn High Sch, Millburn NJ 37-43;Libn Fla Naval Acad, St Augustine Fla 43-47; Head Libn Jacksonville U 49-57; Libnfor new schs Baltimore Pub Schs 57-58; Head Libn Commun Col of Baltimore 58-. 9: ALA-ACRL (chm Md Jr Col Libns, Jr Col sect 67-);-RSD; MdLA (past sec col sect);FlaLA; Md Tchrs Assn (past chm col sect); Md Assn of Jr Cols. 10: Beta Phi Mu; AAUW. 13: Yes. 14: Admin, standards for jr col libs. 15: 3705 Sylvan dr,Baltimore Md 21207.

BRUCE, HELEN G HARDIE. b Scotland 21 Je 23. 4: John Bruce. 5: U Aberdeen 45-52 MA. 7: Lib asst City of Aberdeen, Scotland 40-45; Lib asst City of Nelson, BC 61; Lib asst UVictoria (BC) 63-65; Libn Bur of Econ & Statistics, Victoria BC 65-. 9: SLA. 15: 1008 Deal st, Victoria BC Can.

BRUCE, MARGUERITE (CARRARA). b Fort Lee NJ 29 Ja 15. 4: J Clark Bruce. 5: West Md Col 32-36 (Eng) BA; Columbia 37-39 (Tchg of Eng) MA, 47-54 MS in LS. 7: Tchr: WPA, Ft Lee NJ 36-39, Ft Lee High Sch 39-42, Englewood Jr High Sch, Englewood NJ 42-43; 1st Lt WAC 43-46; Libn Coronado High Sch, Coronado Cal 46-. 9: NEA; Cal Assn Sch libns (sec So Sect 68-69); CalTA. 10: Delta Kappa Gamma; Soroptimist Club. 14: High sch lib serv. 15: 1847 Lyndon rd, San Diego Ca 92103.

BRUCH, VIRGINIA IRENE (SULLIVAN). b Hickman Ky 26 My 21. 4: Truman Elwood Bruch. 5: Murray State Col 40-43 (LS, Eng) BS. 6: Fr. 7: Libn Union City High Sch, Union City Tenn 43-44; Catlgr Lawson McGee Pub Lib, Knoxville Tenn 46; Catlgr Fed Trade Commsn, Wash DC 49-55; Catlgr Army Lib, Pentagon 55-64; Act head catlg sect tech serv br Army Lib, Pentagon 65-66, Chief 66-. 8: Wkshop leader 5th annual Church Lib Wkshop, Wash DC 65. 9: SLA; DCLA. 14: Catlg. 15: 15 W Howell ave, Alexandria Va 22301.

BRUCK, EDITH. b Prague. 4: Otto E Bruck. 5: UBerlin (Hist of Fine Arts); UPrague (Hist of Fine Arts) Lic Phil; UOttawa 59-60 BLS, 60-61 (LS). 6: Fr, Ger, Czech. 7: Catlgr Nat Research Coun Can Nat Sci Lib, Ottawa 60-67, Asst libn div building res NRC 67-. 9: CanLA; ALA; Prof Inst Pub Serv Can (Libn Group); Lib Assn Ottawa (sec-treas 60, Coun 65). 10: Alumni Assn Univ of Ottawa, Lib Sci Chap; UDC. 14: Catlg, ref, automation inforetr. 15: 111 Wurtemburg apt 805, Ottawa 2 Can.

BRUDVIG, GLENN L. b Kenosha Wis 14 O 31. 4: Myrna Michael. 5: UND 48-50, 52-56 (Hist) BS, MA; UMinn 58-62 (LS) MA. 7: Tchr Pub High Sch, Mahnomen Minn 54-55; Tchr Pub High Sch Herman Minn 56-58; Order libn & archivist UND Lib 58-62, Asst libn 62-63; Supt of dept libs UMinn Lib(Minneapolis) 64, Bio-Med Libn 64-, Asst dir for research & dev 69-. 9: ALA; SLA; MedLA; NDLA (pres 63-64); ASIS. 14: Med libnship, automation. 15: 203 Patton rd, New Brighton Mn 55112.

BRUER, JOHN MICHAEL. b Knoxville Tenn 23 Jl 40. 4: Susan Crumpton Bruer. 5: Vanderbilt 58-62 (Gk) BA, 62-65 (Lat) MA; Peabody 63-65 MLS. 6: Gk, Lat, Russ, Fr, Ger. 7: Sub-prof ref asst Tenn State Lib 58-62; Sub-prof circ asst Joint U Libs, Nashville 63-65; Head circ dept Mem Lib UNotre Dame (Notre Dame Ind) 65-66; Admin Asst to dir of Libs, UKy 66-68, Admin Asst to dr of Libs & to asst dr for tech serv 68-. 8: UKy Lib Press. 9: ALA; SELA. 11: Selected to LC Internship Program for 65 (declined). 13: Yes. 14: Admin, tech serv, printing, calligraphy. 15: Univ of Kentucky Libraries, Lexington Ky 40506.

BRUETTE, VERNON R. b Green Bay Wis 18 Je 32. 5: UWis 51-55 (Linguistics, Pre-med) BA; Columbia 62-64 (LS) MS. 6: Ger, Fr. 7: Head card prep sect NY Pub Lib 56-62; Ref asst NY Acad of Med (NY) 62-64; Asst project dir Survey of Med Lib Resources of Greater NY (NY) 64-65; Research systems libn SUNY (Downstate Med Center) 65-. 9: MedLA; SLA; NY Lib Club; NY Tech Libns. 12: Co-auth "Report of the Survey of Medical Library Resources of Greater New York, with Lee Ash (66). 13: Yes. 14: Systems analysis. 15: 228 W 17th st apt 5C, New York NY 10011.

BRUGGEMAN, LON (FRANKLIN). b Carroll Iowa 30 Mr 38. 5: Northwest Mo State Col 56-60 (Eng) BS; UDenver summers 60-64 (LS) MA; Coe Col summer 65 (French Foreign Lang Inst). 6: Fr. 7: High sch libn Comm Sch, Spirit Lake Iowa 60-62; High sch libn Comm Sch, Laurens Iowa 62-65. 9: NEA; Iowa State EA; IowaLA; IowaASchL (mem; constit & By-Laws Com, Area 5 Lib Select Com); Iowa Dept Clr Tchrs. 10: Laurens Golf & Country Club; Laurens Booster Club. 14: Ref. 15: 114 W Garfield, Laurens Ia 50554.

BRUGGER, E JANE. b Canonsburg Penn 1 S 17. 5: Muskingum Col 35-39 (Eng) AB; Drexel 39-40 BS in LS. 7: Lib asst Pub Lib,Wilkinsburg Penn 40-42; Lib asst Pub Lib, Sewickley Penn 42-46; Catlg libn Kanawhaco Pub Lib, Charleston WVa 46-62; Catlg libn Marshall U Lib 62-. 9: ALA; Ohio Valley Reg Tech Serv Libns; WVaLA (pres 61-62). 10: Soroptimist Fed of Amer; AAUW. 14: Catlg. 15: 619 Elm st,rear, Huntinton WVa 25703.

BRUGUERA, EVA ANITA (OLIVIA MAKELA). b Viipuri Finland 23 D 27. 4: Jorge Bruguera. 5: UHelsinki (Finland) 46-48, fall 49 (Fr); Sorbonne 48-49, 51-52 (Fr) Certif & Dipl; UPittsburgh 52-56 (Fr) MA; Carnegie 60-61 MLS. 6: Fr, Finnish, Sp. 7: Lib clerk UPittsburgh Lib 52-53; Libn VA Hosp, Menlo Park Cal 61-62; Order libn Stanford Research Inst, Menlo Park Cal 62-63; Med libn VA Hosp, Palo Alto Cal 63-. 9: MedLA; SLA. 10: Finlandia Found; Sierra Club; YMCA. 14: Med libnship. 15: 2427 Benjamin dr, Mountain View Ca 94041.

BRUGUERA, JORGE. b Barcelona Spain 10 N 23. 4: Eva A Bruguera. 5: UParis 48-51 (Fr Lit) Diploma; UPittsburgh 53-56 (Fr, Span Lit) BA; Carnegie 57-60 MLS; San Jose State Col 60-61 (Educ) Credential. 6: Catalan, Fr, Sp. 7: Span conversationalist UPittsburgh 53-60; Libn trainee UPittsburgh 57-60; Ref libn San Jose State Col 60-61; Asst to head libn Engineer & Physics Libs, Stanford U 61-64, Head Libn Math-Statistics Lib 64-66, Hd order dept 66-67, Hd Computer Sci Lib 67-. 9: SLA; CalLA; ASIS; ACM. 10: Sierra Club. 14: Ref. 15: Computer Sci Lib Stanford Univ, Stanford Ca 94041.

BRUHNS, ULLA (VEDGAARD). b Copenhagen Denmark. 4: Finn B Bruhns. 5: Cal State Col at Los Angeles (Amer studies) BA; Immaculate Heart Col 66-68 (LS) MA. 6: Danish, Fr. 7: Ref libn Citrus Col 67-. 9: ALA; CalLA. 14: Ref. 15: 226 Mauna Loa dr, Monrovia Ca 91016.

BRUHWILER, ANNETTE B. b Rutherford NJ 28 Jl 15. 4: William Bruhwiler. 5: Wellesley 34-38 (Ger) AB; Middlebury 38-41 (Ger) MA; Columbia MLS. 6: Ger, Fr. 7: NYC Pub Lib Ref libn 45-50; Fairleigh Dickinson Hd period 58-67, Dir 67-. 15: 222 Ridge rd, Rutherford NJ 07070.

BRUINGTON, HARRY S. b Lark N Dak 24 N 25. 4: Dorothy Dickman. 5: Walla Walla Col 48-52 (Educ) BA, 63 (Educ) MA; Portland State Col 60-67; UOre 68-69 MLS. 7: Med tech (Pfc) USA, US & Pacific Theatre 45-46; Elem tchr & prin Ore Conf of SDA 52-60; Secondary tchr & libn Portland Union Acad, Portland Ore 60-68. 9: AmericanLA. 14: Sch libs, acquis, ref. 15: 6370 River rd, Junction City Or 97448.

BRUMBY, SEWELL MARION. b Cedartown Ga 20 My 11. 4: Mary Hart. 5: US Mil Acad (W Point) 28-32 BS; Columbia 59-61 (LS) MS; UGa 61-64 LLB. 7: Regular off Cadet through Col US Army 28-60; Fellow Lib Col of the City of NY 60-61; Law Libn UGa 61-. 9: ALA; ConnLA (past sec). 10: LWV; UMe Alumni Assn; Fairfield Hist Soc; PhiBeta Kappa; Phi Kappa Phi; AAUW. 14: Bk sel, tech serv, admin, bldgs. 15: Law Lib Univ of Ga, Athens Ga 30601.

BRUN, CHRISTIAN (MAGNUS FROM). b Trondheim Norway 3 O 20. 4: Jane Fristoe Brun. 5: UWash 39-41, 46-48 (Econ, Bus) BA; UNC 49-50 BS inLS; UMich 51-52 AM in LS. 6: Norwegian. 7: Infantry US Army 42-45; Asst curator of rare bks UPenn 50-51; Asst curator of maps & curator ofmaps W L Clements Lib UMich 52-63; Head Dept of Spec Collections UCal(Santa Barbara) 63-, Univ archivist, UCAL (Santa Barbara) 63-. 9: Assn State & Loc Hist; Soc for the Hist of Discoveries; Soc for the Adv of Scand Study; Amer Scand Found; West Hist Assn. 12: "Guide to the Manuscript Maps in the William L Clements Library" (59); Co-auth "Maps and Charts Printed in America Before 1800, ABibliography," (67). 13: Yes. 14: Rare bks, early cartography, West hist, Scand lit, hist of printing. 15: 5663 Via Trento, Goleta Ca 93017.

BRUNDIN, ROBERT E(LLIOTT). b Los Angeles 10 D 29. 4: Gretchen Pauli. 5: UCal(Berkeley) 48-53 (Journalism) AB, MJ; Nat U of Mex 57-58 (Span); UCal (Berkeley) 58-59 (Educ, LS) MLS; Stanford 60- (Educ). 6: Sp. 7: Reporter "Calexico Chronicle," Calexico Cal 53-54; Photographer US Army (Cpl), USA, Germany 54-56; Carrier US Post Off, Whittier Cal 56-57; Libn San Jose City Col 59-63, Dir of Lib Serv 63-. 9: CalASchL (Jr Col chm, No sect 68-69); CalLA; Cal Jr Col Faculty Assn. 10: Amer Fed Tchrs. 11: Kellogg Fellow, Stanford, 66-67. 12: "The Library in the Junior College:

Planning Guidelines" (65). 14: Admin, acquis. 15: 1120 Fairlands ct, Campbell Cal 95008.

BRUNER, BERNICE ISABELLE. b Evnsville Ind 2 Ap 13. 5: Evansville Col 30-34 (Lat) AB; UIll summers 40-42 BS in LS. 7: Tchr-libn Gas City High Sch, Gas City Ind 35-40; Tchr-libn Noblesville High Sch, Noblesville Ind 40-42; Libn Bellaire Pub Lib, Bellaire Ohio 42-46; Libn Vanderburgh Co Pub Lib, Evansville Ind 46-52; Chief div of wk with schs & child Evansville Pub Lib, Evansville Ind 52-. 8: Instr lib materials; Evansville Col 61-62, Ind State U 66-68. 9: ALA;Newbery-Caldecott Award Com, Subscr Bks Com; IndLA (past pres child & yp roundtable). 10: AAUW. 13: Yes. 14: Child wk. 15: 8312 Petersburg rd, Evansville In 47711.

BRUNNEMER, FRED A. b Brooklyn NY 20 Je 14. 4: Mabel B Bethel. 5: Brooklyn Col 32-36 (Econ) BA; Pratt 37 BLS. 7: Sch libn Brooklyn High Sch for Specialty Trades, Brooklyn NY 37-40; Lib asst Queensborough Pub Lib, NYC 40-41; Post libn Ft Slocum NY 41-44; Agent Metropolitan Life Ins Co, Hempstead NY 44-58; Sch libn Herricks Jr High, New Hyde Park NY 58-60; Sch libn Island Trees High Sch, Levittown NY 60-. 9: NY State Tchrs Assn; NYLA; Nassau-Suffolk Sch Libn Assn (treas 68-). 10: Pratt Inst Alumni Assn (life mem & past pres 48-49). 15: 11 No dr, New Hyde Park NY 11040.

BRUNNSCHWEILER, TAMARA (PETERSON). b Riga 23 Je 23. 4: Dieter Brunnschweiler. 5: URiga 41-43 (Nat Sci); UVienna 43-47 (Philos) MA; UZurich 47-49 (Geog) PhD; UMich 59-60 (LS) ML. 6: Latvian, Ger, Sp, Russian. 7: Asst meteorologist Swiss Meteorol Off, Zurich 51-52; Asst to Libn Clark U 53-55; Asst stat Zurich Switz 56-57; Mich State U; Ser bibliog 58-60, Head map libn 60-62, Head acquis dept 62-64, Latin Amer Bibliog 65-. 8: Ref consul, UCali Colombia summer 68. 9: Assn of Amer Geographers; ALA; SLA. 12: "Die Erdoel Production Europas" (Vienna 49); "Current Periodicals; a Select Amstated Bibliography in the Area of Latin American Studies" (68); Amazonia Brasileira; a Brief Area Study (69). 13: Yes. 14: Bibliog, ref, Latin America. 15: Mich State Univ Lib, East Lansing MI 48823.

BRUNS, LINDA M. b Herrin Ill 22 Ap 46. 5: So Ill U 64-67 (Eng) BA; UIll 67-68 (LS) MS. 6: Fr. 7: Libn Amer Oil Co, WhitingInd 68-. 9: SLA. 10: Beta Phi Mu. 14: Lib automation. 15: King Arthur Courts 32 - 12, Northlake Il 60164.

BRUNS, VALBORG (RENANDO). b Seattle. 4: Raymond E Bruns. 5: UWash 37 (Gen Lit) BA, 38 BALS (Chicago) 4 2 (LS); UPuget Sound 68-69 (Lit). 6: Swedish, Fr, Sp. 7: Asst catlgr RR Retirement Bd, Chicago 41-43; Chief catlgr War Prod Bd, Wash DC 43-45; Chief libn 118th Sta Hosp, Fukuoka Japan 46-47; Area libn US Army, Vienna Austria 48-49; Post libn US Army, Wurzburg Post Germany 49-50; Chief libn Madigan Gen Hosp (Army), Tacoma Wash 51-. 8: Tacoma-Pierce Country Lib Coun; Governor's Conf on Libs 68. 9: Wash State LA; ALA. 10: Altrusa Club; The Mountaineers. 13: Yes. 14: Ref, readers adv, admin. 15: Spec Serv Lib Madigan Gen Hosp, Tacoma Wa 98422.

BRUNTON, DAVID W. b Oak Park Ill 9 N 29. 4: Marilyn Halbe. 5: Ripon Col 50-54 (Hist) AB; UIll 55-56 (LS) MS. 7: 1st Lt Corps of Engnrs Active 46-49, Reserve 50-61; Catlgr Earlham Col Lib 56-57, Asst libn 57-60; Head libn Elmhurst Col 60-61; NevState Lib; Dir Cooperative Proc Center 61-62, Law libn 62-64, Dir Tech Proc Div 63-64; Exec dir Cal Lib Assn, Berkeley Cal 64-69. 9: ALA-ACRL (Col Sect, chm Nomin Com 68); Amer Soc of Assoc Execs; Cal Soc of Assoc Execs (Memb Com 65); NevLA (treas 63-64; Exec dir NatLib Week Nev 62); CalLA. 10: AAUP; ACLU (sec West Contra Costa Coun 69). 13: Yes. 14: Catlg, lib legis, assn activities. 15: 626 Ocean ave, Point Richmond Ca 94801.

BRUNTON, MARILYN (HALBE). b Elmhurst Ill 29 Ap 28. 4: David W Brunton. 5: Ripon Col 46-50 (Bio) AB; UCal (Berkeley) 67-68 MSLS. 7: Asst libn Ripon Col 50-54; Lib asst UIll (Urbana) 55-56; Researcher Our Wonderful World, Champaign Ill 56; Bkmob libn richmond Pub Lib, Richmond Cal 68-. 8: Jr Great Bks leader Richmond (Cal) Unified Sch Dist 66-67; PTA lib chm Stage Sch, Richmond Cal 65-66. 9: CalLA. 10: League of Women Voters; ACLU; PTA; Point Richmond Civic Gp; Save the San Francisco Bay Assn; Richmond Art Ctr; Citizens for Excellent Educ; Bay Area Educ Television Assn. 14: Child serv, spec serv to urban minorities. 15: 626 Ocean ave, Point Richmond Ca 94701.

BRUSEAU, LAURENCE LYNN. b Port Angeles Wash 17 Je 39. 4: Joan Eileen Hassing. 5: Everett (Wash) Jr Col 57-59 (Hist, Psych); Northwestern 59-61 (Psych) AB; UMich 61-62 AMLS. 7: Acquis libn UMich 62-. 68; Acquis libn Portland State U 68-. 10: Phi Beta Kappa; Beta Phi Mu; Phi Kappa Phi. 14: Acquis, ref. 15: 3206 N E 42nd ave, Portland Or97213.

BRUST, ELEANOR ADELAIDE (ROTTACH). b NYC 23 Jl 18. 4: John Jackson Brust. 5: Fairleigh Dickinson 61-65 (Ed) BS; Rutgers 66-67 MLS. 6: Ger. 7: Report writer Dun & Bradstreet N YC 36-39; Libn adult dept Bergenfield F P Lib Berg NJ 55-61; Ref libn Fairleigh Dickinson 61-65; Libn tchr Ft Lee Intermed Sch Ft Lee NJ 67-. 8: Tenafly Commun activity in schs & town relationship 51-; Leader of Great Bks Gp, Bergenfield Free Pub Lib 56-61. 9: ALA (-ACRL, RSD); Nat Congress of Parents & Tchrs; NEA; ALA; -ACRL; -RSD; NJLA; NJEA; NJSchLA; Bergen Co SchLA; Fort Lee Tchrs Assn; Fed Tchrs Assn. 14: Ref, lib sci tchg. 15: 38 North Lyle ave, Tenafly NJ 07670.

BRUTON, BERNICE NADINE (HAND). b Spokane Wash 13 Ap 14. 4: Rodney Clinton Bruton. 5: Mills Col 31-35 (Fr) BA; UWash 37-38 (LS) BA; Mills Col 40-41 Cal Secondary Tchg Credential, Spec Tchg Credential in Libnship; UCal(Berkeley) summer 41; UWash summer 59 (LS); East Wash State Col summers & even 60-63, 65 (Materials of Instruction) MEd. 6: Fr. 7: Fr Instr Spokane Col 38-39; Asst supv NYA proj, catlg Spokane elem sch libs Spokane (Wash) Pub Lib 38-39; Staff UIda 39-40; Libn Joint Union High Sch, Delano Cal 41-42; Libn Oceanside-Carlsbad Joint Union High Sch & Jr Col, Oceanside Cal 42; Ensign to Lt WAVES Off Train Sch Smith Col, Dist Intel Off 13th Naval Dist San Francisco, Libn West Sea Frontier Intel Off Fed Off Bldg San Francisco, Sr off in chge of WAVES on CINCPAC staff, Libn in chg of CINCPAC Intel Lib 42-46; Head Libn Lewis & Clark High Sch, Spokane Wash 49-. 9: NEA; WashEA; WashLA; Wash State ASchL; PNLA. 14: Ref, geneal research. 15: West 919-19th ave, Spokane Wash 99203.

BRUTON, HARRY W. b Colo Springs Colo 29 Je 29. 5: Colorado Col 47-51, 55-56 (Eng) BA; UDenver 58-59 MALS. 6: Fr. 7: Personnel spec (Cpl) US Army 51-53; Documents catlgr USAF Acad Lib 59-60, Ser & documents libn 60-62; Chief tech serv USAF Inst of Tech, Wright-Patterson AFB Ohio 62-64; Head catlg libn So Colo State Col 65-. 9: ColoLA; MPLA. 10: AAUP. 14: Catlg, tech serv. 15: APT 202-A, 900 W Abriendo ave, Pueblo Co 81005.

BRY, ILSE. b Berlin Germany 14 S 05. 5: Univs of Berlin, Munich, Vienna 24-29 (Philos) PhD; Columbia 39-42 BS in LS, 43-46 (Psych) MA (47). 6: Ger. 7: Lib asst Pub Lib, Berlin-Charlottenburg 29-33; Reviser Columbia Sch of Lib Serv 42; Lib asst catlgr Columbia U Libs 42-46; Asst ed "Psychological Abstracts" (Amer Psychol Assn) 46-47; Research asst in psych Sampson Col 46-47; Libn NY Psychoanalytic Inst, NYC 47-53; Lib assoc in chg of Neuropsychiatric Lib NYU, Bellevue Med Center, NYC 53-57; Res scientist Res Center for Mental Health, NYU 63-. 8: ALA rep on Nat Adv Com on Loc Health Depts, Nat Health Coun, 53-57; Chm Ed Com Mental Health Bk Review Index, NYC 57-; Dir of Res & 2nd v-pres, Coun on Res in Bibliog, NYC 65- Coun of Bio Eds, Com on Ed Policy, 68-69. 9: ALA; MedLA; SLA; ASIS; Adult Educ Bd (Subcom on Bk Appraisal) (Research) 49-57; NY Lib Club. 10: Internat Coun of Psychologists (Fellow); Amer Psychol Assn; Coun of Biol Editors; AAAS (Fellow); AAUP; Fed of Amer Scientists; NY Acad Scis; Hist Sci Soc; Soc for Gen Systems Res; World Fed for Mental Health; Columbia U Sch of Lib Serv Alumni Assn. 12: Ed "Mental Health Book Review Index," v 1 (56-). 13: Yes. 14: Research in bibliog & lib problems. 15: Res Center for Mental Health NYU, 4 Washington pl, NY NY 10003.

BRYAN, ALICE I. b Arlington NJ 11 S 02. 5: Columbia 29 (Psych) BS, 30 (Psych) MA, 34 (Psych) PhD; Chicago 51 (LS) MA. 6: Ger, Fr. 7: Instr Child Educ Found, NYC 29-39; Instr Sarah Lawrence Col 29-30; Head Dept of Psych Pratt Inst Sch of Fine & Applied Arts 30-34; Columbia U Sch of Lib Serv: Assoc & consul psychologist 36-39, Asst Prof 39-53, Assoc Prof 53-59, Prof 59-. 8: Dir of Personnel & Personnel Admin Study for The Pub Lib Inquiry, NY 49-51; Univ Coun Columbia U, 50-56; Licensed Psychologist, NY State 59-. 9: ALA; AALS; NYLA. 10: Amer Psychol Assn; East Psychol Assn; NY Psychol Assn; Sigma Xi. 12: "The Public Librarian" (52). 13: Yes. 14: Research methods, human rel in admin, pub communication. 15: Sch of Lib Serv Columbia Univ, NYC 10027.

BRYAN, BARBARA (HUNT). b Aberdeen Miss 26 Jl 31. 5: Bennett Col (Greensboro NC) 48-52 (Eng) BA; Syracuse 52-54 MSLS; Chicago Tchrs Col summer 61 (Educ); UMd summer 68 (Lib admin) Certif. 7: Hd libn Rust Col 54-55; Asst libn Morgan State Col 55-57; Instr Bennett Col (Greensboro NC) 57-60; Libn Commun Consolidated Schs, Evanston Ill 61-62,

63-66; Asst libn Dillard U 62-63; Asst libn Jackson State Col 66-67; Libn Bennett Col (Greensboro NC) 67-. 8: Consul So Assn Cols & Schs at Dillard and Xavier Univs, New Orlenas 69. 9: NCLA; Greensboro Lib Club. 10: NAACP; YMCA. 14: Admin, catlg, spec collections. 15: 703 Reid st #2, Greensboro NC 27406.

BRYAN, BARBARA (LEE) DAY. b Livermore Falls Me 20 My 27. 4: Robert S Bryan. 5: UMe 44-48 (Psych) BA; So Conn State Col 60-64 MSLS. 6: Fr, Sp. 7: Catlg dept asst Yale U Lib 48-49; Departmental lib catlgr Harvard Col Lib 49-51; Subj catlgr Yale U Lib 51-52; Catlgr Fairfield Pub Lib, Fairfield Conn 52-54, ref libn 54-57, asst libn & order libn 57-65; Asst dir of libs Fairfield U 65-. 8: Governor's Com on Libs (Conn) 62-63; Conn Nat Lib Week Com 63. 9: ALA; ConnLA (past sec). 10: LWV; UMe Alumni Assn; Fairfield Hist Soc; Phi Beta Kappa; Phi Kappa Phi; AAUW. 14: Bk sel, tech serv, admin, bldgs. 15: 2255 Mill Plain rd, Fairfield Ct 06431.

BRYAN, ELIZABETH (OVERTON). b Patchogue NY 22 Ja 13. 4: William W Bryan. 5: Conn Col 29-33 (Hist) AB; Columbia 36-37 BS in LS. 7: Br asst Brooklyn Pub Lib 37-40; Asst Easton Pub Lib, Easton Penn 41-42; Order libn Bradley U 56-. 9: ALA; IllLA. 14: Acquis. 1523 E Marietta, Peoria Il 61614.

BRYAN, HELEN (LAMB). b Clinton Mass 14 Ag 15. 4: James E Bryan. 5: Wheaton 38 (Sociol) AB; Rutgers 63 MLS. 6: Fr. 7: Child libn Pub Lib, Glen Ridge NJ 63-64, Adult serv libn 64-67; Asst ref libn Pub Lib, Bloomfield NJ 67-. 9: ALA; NJLA. 14: Ref, readers' adv wk. 15: 666 Highland ave, Newark NJ 07104.

BRYAN, JAMES EDMUND. b Easton Penn 11 Jl 09. 4: Helen Lamb. 5: Lafayette Col 29-31 (Econ) BS; Drexel 32 BLS; American U 37 (Pol Sci) MA. 7: Asst Pub Lib Wash DC 32-36; Libn Easton (Penn) Pub Lib 36-38; Head adult & lending dept Carnegie Lib, Pittsburgh 38-43; Asst Dir Pub Lib Newark NJ 43-58, Dir 58-. 8: Consul on pub lib bldgs, sites, programs. 9: ALA (pres 62-63, chm var coms)-PLA (pres 59-60); NJLA (pres 52-54, chm var coms). 10: Middle Atlantic States Reg Conf (chm 49, prog chm 47); Boy Scouts of Amer (Scouting commsnr 56-59); Visiting Nurses Assn (Bd Dir); Kiwanis Club; Rutgers U Grad Sch Lib Serv (Advis Bd chm). 11: Litt D Rutgers 64; Alumni Citation Drexel 61; Dist Achieve Award Drexel Grad Sch of Lib Sci 63. 13: Yes. 14: Pub lib admin, bldgs, programs, legis. 15: 5 Washington st, Newark NJ 07101.

BRYAN, MINA R. b Sidney Ohio 23 Ja 08. 5: The Col of Wooster 26-30 (Hist) BA. 6: Fr. 7: Libn-conf sec John H Scheide, Titusville Penn 30-44; Assoc ed Papers of Thos Jefferson Princeton U 44-57; Libn The Scheide Lib, Princeton NJ 59-; Managing Ed "Princeton Univ Lib Chronicle" 62-. 8: Bd of Trustees Princeton Lib (NYC). 9: BSA. 10: Phi Beta Kappa. 12: Assoc ed "The Papers of Thomas Jefferson" vols 1-13 (50-56); "The Princeton U Lib Chronicle" vols XXIV-. 13: Yes. 14: Rare bks, mss. 15: Scheide Lib Princeton U, Princeton NJ 08540.

BRYAN, RUTH MILDRED (TOLIN). b Metzger Ore 17 D 09. 4: John J Bryan. 5: UCLA 31-33 (Lat) AB, 34-36 9eng) MA; USoCal 60-62 MS in LS. 6: Fr, Sp, Ital. 7: Faculty Colo Woman's Col 43-45; Catlgr Azusa Pub lib, Azusa Cal 60-62; Asst humanities libn Cal State Col (Long Beach) 62-. 9: CalLA. 10: Phi Kappa Phi; Beta Phi Mu; Phi Delta Gamma; Alpha Mu Gamma; PTA; CommunityConcert Assn; Cal State Employees Assn. 14: Catlg (art), ref in humanities. 15: 341 Eliot lane, Long Beach Ca 90814.

BRYAN, WILLIAM W. b Easton Penn 31 D 11. 4: Elizabeth Overton. 5: Lafayette 31-35 (Econ) BS; Drexel 35-36 (LS) BS. 7: Br asst Brooklyn Pub Lib, Brooklyn NY 36-40; Asst libn Lafayette Col 40-44; Sgt USA 45-46; Asst to dir Carnegie Lib, Pittsburgh Penn 46-48; Libn Scranton Pub Lib, Scranton Penn 48-55; Dir Peoria Pub Lib, Peoria Ill 55-; Dir Ill Valley Lib Syst, Peoria 66-. 8: Lib bldg consul. 9: ALA (Coun 65-); PennLA (pres 52-53); IllLA (pres 62-63); Ill State Lib Adv Com 65-). 10: Rotary. 11: Lib Citation Award 64. 13: Yes. 14: Admin, bldgs. 15: 107 NE Monroe, Peoria Il 61602.

BRYANT, BONITA I (WEGNER). b Madison Wis 10 O 38. 5: MacMurray Col 56-60 (Eng) AB; UWis at Madison 66-67 (LS) MA. 6: Fr, Ger. 7: Lib asst Sandia Corp Lib, Albuquerque NM 62-66; Bibliog U North Iowa Lib 67-. 8: Library Consultant Chamberlain Mfg Co Waterloo Iowa 68-. 9: ALA; -ACRL. 10: Beta Phi Mu; AAUP; AAUW; United Campus Chris Ministry UNIowa. 15: 610 E Seerley blvd apt 5, Cedar Falls Ia 20613.

BRYANT, DAVID R. b Chicago 21 Mr 39. 5: John Carroll U 57-58 (Sci); Loyola U (Chicago) 58-61 (Hist) BS; Northwestern 61-64 (Law) JD; Rosary Col 64- (LS). 6: Lat. 7: (Pvt) US Army active 57, inactive 57-65; Asst in ref & for Law Northwestern U Sch of Law 64-67; Acquis libn Cook Co Law Lib, Chicago 67-. 9: Amer Bar Assn; AALL; Ill State Bar schicago ALL. 13: Yes. 14: Acquis, ref, admin, govt docs. 15: 2900 Chicago Civic Center, Chicago Il 60602.

BRYANT, DOUGLAS WALLACE. b Visalia Cal 20 Je 13. 4: Rene Kuhn. 5: UMunich 32-33; Stanford 35 AB; UMich 38 AMLS. 7: Tr Hoover Inst & Lib StanfordU 34-35; Asst curator of printed bks W L Clements Lib UMich 36-38; Sr ref asst Tech Dept Detroit Pub Lib 38-41; Asst chief Burton Hist Collection 41-42; US Naval Res 42-46; Lt Commander Head of Tech Info Br Engnr Div of Aeronautics Navy Dept, Wash DC 42-46; Asst libn U Lib ucal (Berkeley) 46-49; Dir of Libs attache Amer Embassy US Info Serv, London 49-52; Admin asst libn Harvard Col Lib 52-56; Assoc dir Harvard u lib & assoc libn of Harvard Col 56-64; Univ libn HarvardU 64-. 8: US Nat Commsn for UNESCO 53-55; Rapporteur Internat Cong of Libs & Documentation Ctr, Brussels 55; Consul to Ford Found for estab of Inst of Libnship, Univ of Ankara, Turkey 54; Consul to Rockefeller Found on publ of Brit Mus Gen Catalogur, London 56; General Rapporteur Nat Bk Com Conf on Amer Bks Abroad, Princeton 55; Coord Com for Slavic & East Europ Lib Resources (chm 59-61); Guest lectr in Japanese Nat Univs 63; Consul to John F Kennedy Inst for Amer Studies, Free Univ Berlin 64-68. 9: Internat Fed of Lib Assns (v-pres 52-58); Internat Fed for Documentation (v-pres 56-58); ALA (chm Internat Rel Com 52-55); ARL (chm Com on Slavic & East European Studies 56-59, chm Com on Preserv of Research Lib Materials 60-67, pres 69-70); Ctr for Research Libs Chm Bd Dirs 69-70). 10: Mass Hist Soc; Amer Antiq Soc; Club of Odd Volumes, Boston. 13: Yes. 14: Univ lib admin. 15: Harvard Univ Lib, Cambridge Ma 02138.

BRYANT, FREDERICK DAVID. b El Paso Tex 18 Jl 24. 5: UFla 42-46 (Pol Sci-Law) AB; Emory 46-47 ABLS, 55 (Med Libnship). 7: Catlgr UFla 47-48; Ref documents NLM 49; A-v UFla 50; Catlgr NLM 50-52; Catlgr UFla 52-54; Dir The J Hillis Miller Health Center Lib, Gainesville Fla 56-64; Dir The Milton S Hershey Med Center Lib, Hershey Penn 65-. 8: Exec sec Fla Lib Assn 54-64; Bus manager "Bulletin MedLA 58-62; Consul to 11 Fla hosps in setting up med libs; UFla Senate 64; Instr in med libnship and bibliog EmoryU 64. 9: MedLA; ASIS; FlaLA (sec 54-64); PennLA (3 coms 65-); Phila Reg LA. 12: Ed "Florida Libraries 54-60. 14: Admin, catlg, machine meth. 15: 2303 Market st, Harrisburg Pa 17103.

BRYANT, GENEVA (CARRIER). b Waynesburg Ky 7 S 13. 4: James T Bryant. 5: Tex TechU 55 (Elem Educ) BS; Tex WomansU 63 MLS. 6: Sp. 7: Elem tchr Pleasant Point Elem, Waynesburg Ky 32-33; Machinist & inspector Chrysler Corp, New Castle Ind 33-34; Elem tchr, Tex: Horn Sch, anson 43-45; Hermleigh Pub Schs, Hermleigh 45-48; Wellman Pub Schs, Wellman 48-57; Central Elem Sch, Plainview 57-58; Libn Estacado Jr High Sch, Plainview Tex 58-. 9: TexLA; TexStateTA (treeas Reg Lib Div 60-61). 10: Delta Lamda. 14: Catlg, ascessions, a-v materials & proc. 15: 3002 W 16th st, Plainview Tx 79072.

BRYANT, JACK W. b Los Angeles 8 Ja 26. 4: Jean Bacon. 5: UCLA 51 (Fr) BA; USoCal 52 MSLS; UParis 53-54. 6: Fr, Sp, Ital. 7: Asst to libn Hoover Lib Stanford Cal 54-57; Admin asst circ & popular lib Enoch Pratt Free Lib, Baltimore 57-60; Dir Crandall Lib, GlensFalls NY 60-62; Dir Greenwich Lib, Greenwich Conn 62-66; Dir Worcester (Mass) Pub Lib & Central Mass Reg Lib Syst 66-. 8: Exec dir Nat Lib Week, Conn 62-63; Consul Fairfield (Conn) Pub Lib 65, Lancaster (Mass) Pub Lib 67, Torrington (Conn) Pub Lib 68; Lectr,Simmons Col, Lib Sci 69. 9: ALA (chm Memb Com Reg X 64-; Pub Rel Sect; Film Proj Com 65-);-LAD (Pub Rel Sect; sec 64-66, Goals & PoliciesCom 65-67); NYLA (Memb Com 62); NELA (chm Memb Com 65-67); MassLA (Planning Co 66-); WestchesterLA (chm Nomin Com 64); ConnLA (chm Prog Com65); LPRC (Exec Bd 65-). 10: Rotary; Bohemian (Worcester). 12: "Suburban Service in the Library Reaches Out" (65). 13: Yes. 14: Admin, pub rel,bldg surveying & planning. 15: Worcester Pub Lib, Salem sq, Worcester Ma 01608.

BRYANT, JOHN L. b Lamesa Tex 30 Ag 39. 5: Baylor 57-60 (Music) B Mus; UMich 60-61, 63 (Music) M Mus; UCal (Berkeley) 64-66 MLS. 6: Fr, Ger. 7: E/4 Band US Army Res, Dallas Tex 61-64; Tchr Dallas Pub Schs, Dallas Tex 63-64; Phono record libn San Francisco State Col 66-69; Asst mus libn NorthwesternU 69-. 8: Organist-choirmaster: St Paul's United Ch, Dallas Texas 62-64, St Francis Lutheran Ch, San

Francisco 67-68; Organist Temple Methodist Ch, San Francisco 68-69. 9: MusicLA; Amer Musicological Soc. 10: Amer Guild Organists; Alpha Chi. 14: Catlg. 15: Music Lib Northwestern Univ, Evanston Il 60201.

BRYANT, LILLIAN (DABNEY). b Penn 21 O 29. 4: Dr Winston M Bryant Jr. 5: Va Union 48-52 (Sociol) BA; Pratt 53-54 MLS. 7: Asst libn Nat Farmers Union, Denver 54; Libn grade II NY Pub Lib 55-56; Libn meharry Med Col 56-60; Asst libn Hahnemann Med Col 60-62; Libn US Housing & Home Finance Agency, Phila 62-64; Asst libn Hahnemann Med Col 64-67; Libn Child Hosp, Phila 67-. 9: MedLA. 14: Catlg, ref, admin. 15: 4636 Sansom st, Phila 19139.

BRYANT, MELROSE (McGURK). b Lexington Ky 12 Je 25. 5: UKy 43-47 (Langs, LS) BA; Ind U 48-49 (Langs); William & Mary Col 54 (Amer Lit). 6: Fr, Ger. 7: Catlgr Ind U 47-50; Asst libn Army Trans Corp Lib, Ft Eustis Va 50-55; Bibliog asst Air U Lib, Maxwell AFB Ala 56-62; Ref libn USAFE Hq ref lib, Wiesbaden Germany 62-64; Bibliog asst Air U Lib, Maxwell AFB Ala 64-. 9: SLA. 14: Ref. 15: 1747 S Court st, Montgomery Al 36104.

BRYANT, NORAH (PAGE). b Winnipeg Can 28 Ja 18. 4: W Hayden Bryant. 5: McGill 35-39 BA, 59 BLS. 6: Fr. 7: Libn Westmount Pub Lib, Montreal 59-62, Chief libn 62-. 9: CanLA; Quebec LA (Coun, co-chm Pub Lib Sect, co-chm Pub Lib Mtl Reg 68-69). 14: Admin, bk sel. 15: 4574 Sherbrooke W, Westmount 6 Que Can.

BRYANT, SOLENA (VIANNA). b Rio de Janeiro Brazil 23 Je 25. 4: William Cullen Bryant. 5: Sch of Law Rio de Janeiro 44-46; Columbia 49-53 (Latin Amer Studies) BA, 54-56 (LS) MS; UIowa 64-65 (Hist) MA. CUNY 66- (Luso-Brazilian Lit). 6: Fr, Portu, Ital, Sp. 7: Trainee Itamaraty, Rio de Janeiro 45-47; Fellow Barnard Col Lib 49-53; Trainee NY Pub Lib 53-56; Asst libn Amer Metal Co, NYC 56; Catlgr & ref City Col (NYC) 57-66; Lat Amer bibliog Queens Col (Flushing NYC) 66-. 8: Tr, Inter-Amer Juridical Com (Rio de Janeiro) 44-45. 9: ALA; SLA; NY Lib Club. 10: Latin Amer Studies Assn; SALEM. 11: Gulbenkian Fellowship 67-68; NDEA 68-69. 13: Yes. 14: Bibliog & ref (Latin Amer). 15: 204 Burns st, Forest Hills NY 11375.

BRYK, DONALD C. b Brooklyn NY 25 S 27. 4: Joyce (Kuhasz). 5: Tufts 48-51 (Eng) AB; Cornell 53-55 (Mgt) MBA; Pratt Inst 65-67 MLS. 7: Lt(jg) USN, USS Albany 51-53; Sales mgr Geo F Stuhmer & Co, Brooklyn NY 56-67; Reserve & A-v libn Queensborough Commun Col Bayside NY 67-. 9: ALA; QCC. 10: Phi Kappa Phi; Nassau Co Demo Co Man 66-. 14: Ref. 15: 30 Pinetree lane, Roslyn Heights NY 11577.

BRYNTESON, SUSAN S. b Huntington WVa 18 F 36. 5: UWis(Madison) 58 (Philos) BA, MA in LS 63. 7: Ser lib asst & ser libn UWis(Madison)58-63; Acquis libn San Diego State Col 63-64; Catlg libn Skidmore Col 64-65; Ser libn UWis(Madison) 65-66; Catlg libn Skidmore Col 66-69; Hdorder dept UMass(Amherst) 69-. 9: ALA; NELA. 14: Acquis, ser. 15: 222 N East st, Amherst Ma 01002.

BRYSON, EVELYN LOUISE. b Hilham Tenn 25 F 29. 4: William Bryson. 5: David Lipscomb Col 47-57; Tusculum Col 57-60 (Sociol) BA; Peabody 61-62 MA(LS). 7: Proofreader Typecraft Inc, Richmond Va 61; Libn J R Tucker High Sch, Henrico Co Va 62-64; Catlg libn Med Col of Va 64-65; Asst ref libnRollins Col 65-66; Hd catlgr Med Col of Va 66-. 9: ALA; MedLA; SELA; VaLA; Richmond Area Spec Libs Assn. 10: Beta Phi Mu; Richmond Area Assn for Retarded Child. 14: Catlg. 15: Box 286 Medical College of Va, Richmond Va 23219.

BRYSON, JULIETTE. b Ashland Ky 5 Ja 22. 5: UKy 39-43 (LS) AB; UIll 51-52 MS in LS. 6: Fr. 7: Br asst Youngstown Pub Lib, Youngstown Ohio 43-45; Child libn Dearborn Pub Lib, Dearborn Mich 45-49; Bkmob libn 49-51; Head ext dept Topeka Pub Lib, Topeka Kan 52-53; Head circ dept Kanawha Co Pub Lib, Charleston WVa 53-61; Adult serv consul Mid-Hudson Libs, Poughkeepsie NY 61-65; Deputy dir Mohawk Valley Lib Assn, Schenectady NY 65-69; Lib Ashland (Ky) Pub Lib 69-. 9: ALA; NYLA. 10: Soroptimist Club. 14: Adult serv. 15: 1316 State st apt 4, Schenectady NY 12304.

BRYSON, VERENA LAMAR (LEWIS). b Brevard NC 22 F 27. 4: William J Bryson. 5: UNC(Greensboro) 44-46; USC 46-48 (Hist, Pol Sci) BA,48-49 BS in LS. 7: Circ & ref libn Furman U 49-50; Ref libn Greenville Co Lib 52-53; Asst lib Furman U 53-55; Libn Donaldson AFB, GreenvilleSC 60-62; Ref libn Greenville Co Lib 63-. 9: ALA; SCLA. 10: Alpha Delta Pi. 11: Outstanding Librarian Award from Mil Air Transport Serv 61;John Cotton Dana Scrapbk Recognition Award 61; Sustained Superior Performance Award from Civil Service Admin 61. 14: Admin, ref. 15: 127 Howell circle, Greenville SC 29607.

BUCHAN, BARBARA (LYNN). b Calgary Alberta Can 25 F 44. 5: UWest Ontario 62-66 (Eng) BA; UToronto 67-68 BLS. 6: Fr. 7: Lond Pub Lib, Lond Can; Art Libn 66-67, Mobile Libn 68-. 14: Catlg, ref, adv serv. 15: 455 Moore st, London Ont Can.

BUCHAN, RONALD LEE. b Charlotte NC 13N 40. 4: Carol B Dahlgren. 5: Concordia Jr Col (Bronxville NY) 58-60 AA; Concordia Sr Col (Ft Wayne Ind) 60-62 (Phil) BA; Pratt Inst 63-66 MLS; Columbia 65; UVa (Charloote) (Arch Hist). 6: Ger. 7: Asst libn Concordia Jr Col (Bronxville NY) 62-66; Period libn UVa (Charlottesville) 66-67, Asst acquis libn 67-. 8: Dir Va Place Name Soc. 9: BSA; ATheolLA; Bibliog Soc of UVa; VaLA. 10: Colonnade Club; Friends of McIntire Pub Lib; Va Place Name Soc; Va Folklore Guild; Medieaeval Circle of UVa; UVa Chap of Soc of Arch Histns. 14: Bibliog, lib hist, lib arch, hist of the bk, hist of bkselling, publ. 15: PO Box 5484, Charlottesville Va 22903.

BUCHANAN, GERALD. b Forrest Co Miss 26 Jl 37. 4: Dottie Renick. 5: William Carey Col 54-57 (Eng) BA; LSU summer 62 (LS); USoMiss 62-65 (LS) MS. 7: Eng tchr Okolona High Sch, Okolona Miss 57-59; Eng tchr Perkinston Col 59-62, Asst libn 62-65; Miss Nat Guard (Sp5) 60-64; Libn Perkinston Col 65-. 9: ALA; MissEA; MissLA; SELA. 10: Deacon Perkinston Baptist Church. 14: Jr Col libs. 15: PO Box 71, Perkinston Ms 39573.

BUCHANAN, JOHN. b Glens Falls NY 13 S 31. 4: Susi Erhardt. 5: St Lawrence U 54-58 (Hist) BA (magna cum laude); Inst on Hist & Archival Mgt Radcliffe Col summer 60 Certif. 6: Ger. 7: Radio operator US Army (Pvt), USA, Germany 51-54; High sch tchr Newark Valley Central Sch, Newark Valley NY 58-60; Asst archivist Cornell U 60-64; Co Archivist & histn West Electric Co Inc, NYC 64-66; Archivist Met Mus of Art 66-. 9: SAA. 10: Mystery Writers of Amer; Phi Beta Kappa; Pi Sigma Alpha. 13: Yes. 14: Archives, hist mss. 15: 401 E 86th st, apt 9-H, NYC 10028.

BUCHANAN, MRS MATYLDE M(ILDRED BENJAMIN). b Lexington Miss 27 Je 10. 5: Jackson State Col 40 (Eng) AB; Atlanta 55 MSLS; Chicago summer 62 (Reading Wkshop) NDEA Multi-Media Inst Queens Col City U of NY summer 66. 6: Fr, Ger. 7: Lat tchr Corinth Jr High Sch, Corinth Miss 27; Eng tchr Pike Co Train Sch, Magnolia Miss 29; Eng tchr Alexander High Sch, Brookhaven Miss 35, Tchr-libn 37; Eng tchr, tchr-libn Central High Sch, Bogalusa La 43; Eng tchr, tchr-libn Holmes co Train Sch, Durant Miss 44; Eng tchr, tchr-libn Grenada High Sch, Grenada Miss 45; Libn Alexander High Sch, Brookhaven Miss 48- Visiting ProfLib Sci Alcorn Col summers 58, 59, 60, 64, 65, 67, 68. 9: ALA; MissLA; Miss Tchrs Assn (past off annual State Conf Group in Lib Area). 10: Zeta Phi Beta; Bertha LJohnson Lit & Garden Club; Miss State Fed of Corored Women's Clubs; Jackson StateCol Alum Club. 13: Yes. 14: Ref, tchg, lib sci. 15: 530 E Washington st, Brookhaven Ms 39601.

BUCHANAN, PEGGY (GIBSON). b Pittsylvania County 12 Ja 40. 4: Walter Allen Buchanan. 5: Averett Col 58-60; Radford Col 60-62 (LS) BS in Ed. 7: Libn George Washington High Sch, Danville Va 62-67; Libn York High Sch, Yorktown Va 67-. 8: Sponsor, Dist E Stud Lib Assts 63-64. 9: VaEA; VaLA. 10: Danville Concert Assn. 14: Catlg, a-v aids. 15: 14 Church st, Yorktown Va 23490.

BUCHER, MARTHA A. b Dayton Ohio 21 Mr 21. 5: UDayton 39-43 (Sociol) AB; Columbia 60-61 MSLS. 6: Fr. 7: Ref asst Wright Patterson AFB Lib, Dayton Ohio 43-45; Libn Engnrs Club of Dayton, Ohio 45-53; Sec to command libn Hdqrs USAF in Europe, Wiesbaden Germany 53-54; Libn Geo A Pflaum Publ, Dayton Ohio 55-56; Libn Good Samaritan Hosp Lib, Dayton Ohio 56-60; Ref asst Dayton & Montgomery Co (Ohio) Pub Lib 61-63, Head ind & sci div 64-. 9: ALA; SLA; OhioLA. 10: Dayton Chamber Music Soc. 14: Ref. 15: Dayton & Montgomery Co Pub Lib, 215 E Third st, Dayton Oh 45402.

BUCHER, MRS RUTH (PAYNE). b NYC 21 Ag 16. 5: UWis 34-36, 37-38 (Fr) BA; Geneva Col for Women (Switzerland) 36-37; Columbia 38-39 (LS) BS. 6: Fr. 7: Sr asst libn Rochester Pub Lib, Rochester NY (39-42); Asst in ref dept CossittLib, Memphis Tenn 43; Sr libn Mt Pleasant Pub Lib, Pleasantville NY 62-. 9: WestchesterLA. 10: Girl Scouts; Adv Com Adult Educ. 15: 3 Hays Hill rd, Pleasantville NY 10570.

BUCHHEIM, GUNTHER (ARNO FRITZ). b Dobeln Germany 26 O 24. 4: Rosemarie Matz. 5: Humboldt Universitat (Berlin) 46-49 (Botany); Freie Universitat (Berlin) 49-53 (Botany) Doctor of Natural Sci. 6: Ger. 7: Scientific asst Technische Hochschule, Aachen Germany 54; Tsxonomic Botanist Botanischer Garten und Museum, Berlin 55-63; Bibliogr Hunt Botanical Lib, Pittsburgh Penn 63-. 10: Internatl Assn of Plant Txonomots; Internatl Sic for Horticul Sci. 12: Co-comp "Handworterbuch der Pfanzennamen" (64); Co-ed "Botanico-Periodicum-Huntianum" (68). 13: Yes. 14: Bot bibliog (esp period). 15: Hunt Botanical Lib, Pittsburgh Pa 15213.

BUCHHOLZ, LUCY (LEE DOUGLASS). b Ivy Va 21 Ap 26. 5: UVa 43-46 (Ed) BS in Ed; San Antonio Col 63-64 (Govt); SWest Tex State Col 64 (Ed); UVa 65-69 (A-V ed) M Ed. 7: Circ asst Alderman Lib UVa 46-48; Circ asst Fondren Lib Rice U 49-53; Owner Capri Italian Restaurant, San Antonio Tex 56-60; Tchr Royalgate Elem Sch S San Antonio Tex 63-64; Tchr S San Antonio Jr High Sch 64-65; Tchr McIntire Sch, Albemarle Co Va 65-66; Libn Meriwether Lewis Sch Albemarle Co Va 66-. 9: ALA; -AASchL; NEA-DAVI; VaLA; VaEA. 10: Lychnos Soc U Va. 14: Child lit, a-v educ. 15: 1613 Meadowbrook Hts rd, Charlottesville Va 22901.

BUCHTA, TOM (TOMMY LEE). b Martin County Ind 4 D 39. 4: Lila Sue Jarchow. 5: Ind State U 58-62 Art ed BS; Rosary Col 62-65 MALS; Nat Col of Ed 63; UMd 67. 6: Ger. 7: Sch dist 68, Skokie Ill: Libn 62-64, Media libn 65-66, Act coordinator 66-67, Coordinator instr material 67-; Libn Evanston Pub Lib, Evanston Ill 62-63; Children's libn Skokie Pub Lib, Skokie Ill 64; High sch lib Dependent Schs, Ger 64-65. 9: NEA; ALA (By-Laws Com); AASchL; NEA-DAVI; IllEA; IllLA; IllASchL (chm of reservs 70); Ill A-V Assn. 14: School lib learn ctrs. 15: 9300 N Kenton ave, Skokie Il 60076.

BUCK, JAMES E. b Pittsburgh Penn 16 N 44. 4: Joyce A Milcarek. 5: Alliance Col 62-66 (Eng) BA; UPittsburgh 66-67 MLS. 6: Fr. 7: Asst ref libn IndU 67-69; Asst libn WashburnU 69-. 8: Participation in NY Pub Lib Radio Programs; Tchr course in popular lit RutgersSch of Lib Serv. 9: ALA. 14: Ref, acquis, admin. 15: Washburn Univ Lib, Topeka Ks 66621.

BUCK, MARJORIE G(RIMES) BOUQUET. b Dover NH 17 Ja 13. 4: John Webster Buck. 5: Universities of Grenoble, Perugia, Paris (Sorbonne) 29-31; Mass Col of Art 31-34 (Art); Boston U 46-48; Simmons 49-51 (LS) Certif. 6: Fr, Ital, Sp. 7: Boston Pub Lib; Asst dir off 37-44, Admin asst 44-46, Asst to chief libn ref & research serv 46-57, Deputy supv ref & research serv57-59, Coordinator of the Arts 60-61; Asst libn Aetna Life Insurance Co, Hartford Conn 61-63; Admin asst & circ libn Wethersfield Pub Lib,Wethersfield Conn 63-67, Lib dir 67-. 9: ALA; NELA; ConnLA. 10: Lib-Sch Coun; Greater Hartford Libns Club (pres 66-67). 14: Admin, ref. 15: 411 Hartford ave, Wethersfield Ct 06109.

BUCK, RICHARD M(acDONALD). b Albion NY 16 Je 30. 5: SUNY Albany 48-53 (Soc Sci) BA, MA; Columbia 58-60 (Hist), LS MS in LS. 7: US Army Infantry Adm Clerk (Sgt), Ft Carson Colo 53-55; Tchr Albany Bd of Educ, Albany NY 55-58; Receptionist Art Gallery Komor Galleries, NYC 58-59; Clerk NY Pub Lib 59, Trainee (A-D) 59-60, Libn to sr libn 60-, Sr adult libn Bk Order Off 65-67; Libn III Asst to chief Research Lib of Performing Arts Lincoln Ctr 67-. 8: Participation in NY Pub Lib Radio Programs; Tchr course in popular lit Rutgers Sch of Lib Serv. 9: ALA; TLA. 10: ANTA. 14: Adult serv, group discussion leadership, lit collection bldg. 15: 601 W 115, Apt 75, New York NY 10025.

BUCKINGHAM, BARBARA L (SIEVERS). b Highland Park Mich 18 D 38. 4: James E Buckingham. 5: Wayne State 57-61 (Secondary Educ, Speech) BS, 65-69 MSLS. 7: Br libn Warren Pub Lib, Warren Mich 65-68; A-v dept hd Macomb Co Lib, Mt Clemens Mich 68-. 8: Lib adv Detroit Waldorf Sch 68-. 9: EFLA; MichLA. 10: Warren-Ctr Line Human Rel Coun. 14: Film, spokem rec & tape, child lit. 15: Macomb County Lib County Service Center, Mt Clemens Mi 48043.

BUCKINGHAM, BETTY JO. b Prairie City Iowa 6 Ag 27. 5: Iowa State Tchrs Col 45-48 (Eng) BA; State U Iowa summer 49 (LS); UIll summers 50-53 (LS) MS W MichU summer 67 (LS). 7: Eng tchr Earlham Commun Schs, Earlham Iowa 48-50; Tchrs-libn Harlan Sch Dist, Harlan Iowa 50-54; High Sch Libn Ft Madison Independent Sch, Ft Madison Iowa Iowa 54-60; Jr High Libn Kurtz Jr High Sch, Des Moines Iowa 60-64; Lib consul State Dept of Pub Instr, Des Moines Iowa 64-. 9: ALA; NEA-DAVI; IowaLA; Iowa State EA; IASchL (var past offs); AVEAI. 10: Kappa Delta Pi; Beta Phi Mu. 13: Yes. 14: Sch lib admin. 15: Box 83 RR 2, Prarie City Ia 50228.

BUCKLEY, ALICE MARIE. b Boston 5 Ap 14. 5: Simmons 32-36 (LS) BS; Boston Col 50-54 (Educ) Ed M. 6: Ger, fr. 7: Child libn NY Pub Lib 36-37; Child libn Brookline Pub Lib, Brookline Mass 37-38; Child libn Boston Pub Lib 38-50; Libn E Boston High Sch, E Boston 50-52; Libn Jamaica Plain High Sch, Jamaica Plain Mass 52-. 8: Bk Reviewer Kliatt Paperback Book Guide 67-. 9: ALA; CathLA; NESchLA (Ed "Newsletter" 55-61); Mass SchLA (pres 60-64). 10: Soroptimist Internat; DeltaKappa Gamma; Girl Scouts; Nat Wildlife Assn; Spellman Philatelic Mus; Women's NatBk Assn. 14: High sch libs. 15: 157 Aldrich st, Roslindale Ma 02131.

BUCKLEY, AMELIA KING. b Carlisle Ky 18 My 08. 5: UKy 25-27; Goucher Col 27-29 (Pol Sci) AB; UKy 48-58 (LS) AM. 7: UKy Lib 48-53; Libn Keeneland Assn Lib, Lexington Ky 53-. 9: ALA; KyLA. 10: LWV. 12: "Keeneland Association Library; A Guide to the Collection" (58); "The Racing Commissioners' Manual" (66). 14: Sporting bks, rare bks. 15: 119 Forest ave, Lexington Ky 40508.

BUCKLEY, CLAIRE (KAHKOLA). b Bellows Falls Vt 13 S 45. 4: John J Buckley. 5: UVt 63-67 (Lat) BA; Columbia 67-68 (LS) MS. 6: Lat, Gr, Fr. 7: Asst ref libn UVt Bailey Lib 68-. 10: Phi Beta Kappa. 14: Ref. 15: 239 So Union st, Burlington Vt 05401.

BUCKLEY, FRANCIS JAMES JR. b Lynn Mass. 4: Victoria D McKenzie. 5: NC State Col 60-62; UMich 62-65 (Hist) BA, 65 (LS) MA. 7: Detroit Pub Lib: Ref asst gen info dept 66, Ref asst sociol & econ dept 69-; Clk (Sp 4) USA Train Ctr, Ft Bragg NC 67; NCOIC (Sp 4) USA Lib Serv Ctr, Saigon 68. 9: ALA; MichLA (Jr Mem RT). 10: Univ City Commun Assn; Univ City "B" Dist Area Coun. 14: Ref. 15: 5137 Commonwealth, Detroit Mi 48208.

BUCKLEY, JAMES WHITNEY. b Los Angeles 16 Ag 33. 4: Margaret Ann Wall. 5: Los Angeles Harbor Coll 51-53; Long Beach State Col 58-60 (Eng) BA; USoCal 60-61 MSLS. 7: US Army Med Corps, Germany 55-57; Los Angeles Co Pub Lib: Br libn W Gardena Br 61-62, Br libn Carson Br 62-63, Br libn Montebello Br 63-68; Reg libn Orange Co Pub Lib 68, Dir pub serv 69-. 8: Lib/USA Ref Center, NY World's Fair 65. 9: ALA; CalLA (Com on Coms 64, Recrt Com 67-); Pub Lib Execs of So Cal. 10: Orange Coworld Affairs Coun; USoCal Sch of Lib Sci Alumni Assn; Rotary; Amer Soc for PubAdmin. 14: Admin, pers, pub rel. 15: 25191 Sea Vista dr, Dana Pt Ca 92629.

BUCKLEY, JOHN JOSEPH. b Boston 23 D 20. 4: Dorothea Harty Buckley. 5: Tufts U 40-43, 46 (Liberal Arts) AB; Columbia 46-47 BLS; Mass State Col (Boston) 63-68 M Ed. 7: Asst libn Amer Numismatic Soc, NYC 48-49; Copy ed The Letters of Theodore Roosevelt MIT 49-51; Period libn USAF Cambridge Res Center, Boston 51-55; Ref libn US Army QM Research Center, Natick Mass 55-58; Libn Stonehill Col 58-59; Bibliog Yale U Sch of Nursing 60; Libn Highland Central Sch, Highland NY 60-61; Libn Hyde Park High Sch, Boston 62-. 8: Consultant; Keene State Col, Keene NH (Planning movement of lib to new bldg) summer 64; New England Mobile Bk Fair, Newton Highlands, Mass (set up & operated catlg serv for ESEA Title II processed bks) 66, 68; Information Dynamics Corp, Reading Mass (set up & operated indexing & abstracting serv for journals of interest to Army Quartermaster Sci) 66, 67. 10: Great Books Group Leader. 12: Copy ed "The Letters of Theodore Roosevelt, v 1-4" 51-55; Indexer, "Chicago History," Journal, Chicago Hist Soc 60, 63, 66, 69. 15: 157 Aldrich st, Boston Ma 02131.

BUCKMAN, THOMAS R(ICHARD). b Reno Nev 3 My 23. 4: Gunhild Margareta Malmkjell. 5: U of the Pacific 43-44, 46-47 (Liberal Arts) BA; UStockholm (Sweden) 48-51 (Hist of Lit) Certif; UMinn 51-52 (Scandinavian Studies) MA, 52-53 BSLS. 6: Swedish, Danish, Norwegian, Ger, Fr. 7: US Navy deck off (Lt jg) 43-46; Asst ref libn Ore StateU 53-54; Asst libn Modesto Jr Col 55-56; UKan: Head acquis dept 56-60;Assoc dir 60-61; Dir of libs 61-68; Dir internat rel off ALA (Chicago) 66-67; Univ libn & prof bibliog NorthwesternU 68-. 9: ALA (Internat Rel Com 67-); ARL (Bd dirs 67-); BSA. 10: Linnean Soc of London (fellow); Caxton Club (Chicago). 11: Amer Scand Found Fellowship to Sweden 54-55; Guggenheim Fellowship 64-65. 12: Transl Par Lagerkvist, "Modern Theatre: Seven Plays and an Essay (66); Ed "Bibliography and Natural History, Essays (66). 13: Yes. 14: Acquis, rare bks, ref, documentation, internat aspects of libnship. 15: 624 Noyes st, Evanston Il 60201.

BUCKNALL, CAROLYN (FOREMAN). b Port Arthur Tex 14 D 31. 4: Malcolm R Bucknall. 5: UTex 50-53 (Eng) BA, 58-60 MLS; Columbia 54. 6: Fr. 7: Ser catlgr UTex Lib

(Austin) 59-61, Hd acquis dept 67-; Ser catlgr UWash Lib 61-63; Hd ser catlg & acquis UMass Lib 63-65; Hd acquis dept SUNY (Binghamton) 65-67. 9: ALA. 10: Phi Beta Kappa. 12: "Analysis of Publications issued by the American Library Association, 1907-57," ACRL Microcard Series No 118 (59). 14: Tech serv. 15: 808 W ave, Austin Tx 78701.

BUCKNER, ANNA (EVERETT). b Brunswick Ga 19 S 13. 4: Ben F Buckner. 5: Ga State Col for Women 30-34 (Chem) BS; Peabody Lib Sch 34-35 BS in LS; Columbia summer 39; Ohio State summers 56, 57. 7: Libn All Saints Episcopal Col 35-40; Circulation asst DC Pub Lib 41-42; Ref asst US Weather Bur Lib Wash DC 42-43; Ref asst Columbus Pub Lib Columbus Ohio 59-62; Bexley Pub Lib, Columbus Ohio: Ref asst 62-64, YA libn 68-; Libn Bexley High Sch, Columbus Ohio 64-68. 8: Tchr of Library Materials for the Business Man, Franklin U, Columbus Ohio 63-68. 9: ALA; OhioLA; Franklin Co LA. 14: Young adults. 15: PO Box 6733, Columbus Oh 43209.

BUCKWALTER, MABEL (HERR). b Lancaster Co Penn 25 My 12. 5: Millersville State Tchrs Col 30-34 BS, summers 34-35 Elem Certif in Penn; Penn State Col summers 38-40 MEd; West Res summers 42-45 BS in LS; Columbia summer 49 (LS). 7: Tchr Coleraine Twp Lancaster Co Penn 34-37; Tchr libn Hatfield Joint Consolidated Sch, Hatfield Penn 37-39; Libn Shaler High Sch, Glenshaw Pgh Penn 39-45; Asst libn Upper Darby Sr High Sch, Upper Darby Penn 45-48; Tech coun Lib Ext Div State Dept of Educ, Baltimore summer 47; Libn Tolleston Sch, Gary Ind 48-49; Libn Albert Leonard Jr High Sch, New Rochelle NY 49-52; Libn New Rochelle Pub Lib, New Rochelle NY summer 50; Libn New Rochelle High Sch, New Rochelle NY summers 51, 52; Libn Farmingdale Sch, Farmingdale NY 52-53; Libn Freeport Jr & Sr High 53-55; Libn Farmingdale Pub Lib, Farmingdale NY summers 53-54; Libn Atlantic Ave Sch, Lynbrook NY 55-. 9: NEA; Nassau Co LA; NY State Tchrs Assn; NYLA; LTA. 15: 148 Pine st, Freeport NY 11520.

BUDELL, ELIZABETH E(RB). b Westminster Md 25 N 17. 4: William Budell. 5: West Md Col 34-38 (Hist) BA, 39 (Art) Post grad; Rutgers 58-60 MLS. 6: Fr. 7: Tchr Hampstead (Md) High Sch 39-41; Libn Passaic Twp Pub Lib, Stirling NJ 57-60; Asst Dir Berkeley Heights (NJ) Pub Lib 60-62; Dir Madison Pub Lib, Madison NJ 62-. 8: Adv bd, Lib Services & Construction Act of NJ 68; Exec dis NJ Natl Lib Week 65-66. 9: ALA (Recruitment, Materials Com, Confer Com); NJLA (Exec bd 66-69, chm 3 coms); Morris Co LA; LPRC. 10: Alumni Assn Rutgers Lib Sch (pres); Bus & Prof Woman's Club; Past Dir NJ Nat Lib Week; Marquis Biog Lib Soc (Adv Mem). 12: "How to Build achurch Library" (55); Ed "New Mexico Libraries" (68). 13: Yes. 14: Admin, ref. 15: 110 Cross Hill rd, Millington NJ 07946.

BUDER, CHRISTINE LUCILLE. b St Louis 12 S 24. 5: Culver-Stockton Col 44-48 (Bus Admin, Econ) BS; UIll 48-49 MSLS. 6: Fr. 7: Sec personnel serv American Red Cross Midwest Area, St Louis 43-44; Asst libn Culver-Stockton Col 49-52; Asst curator Disciples of Christ Hist Soc, Nashville 52-55; Libn Christian Bd of Publ, St Louis 55-62; Circ libn NM State U 62-65, Ref libn 65-66, Soc sci & bus admin div libn 66-. 9: ALA; NMLA. 10: Beta Phi Mu; AAUW. 12: "How to Build a Church Library" (55); Ed, "New Mexico Libraries" 68-. 14: Ref, Southwest lit. 15: PO Box 4141, University Park NM 85001.

BUDGE, EDWIN STRATFORD III. b Los Angeles 25 Ag 37. 4: Ronnie Lee Budge. 5: UHawaii 57-58; U Utah 58-64 (Hist) BA; Magna cum laude; UCal(Berkeley) 64-65 MLS; UMd 66-68 (Hist) MA; UCal(Berkeley) 68-. 6: Fr, Ger. 7: US Marine Corps (Cpl) 56-58; Lib asst ref dept UUtah Lib 63-64; Lib asst Interlib Loan UCal(Berkeley) Lib 64-65; Libn OutstandingGrad Train Program LC 65-66, Asst hd Reg Lib for Blind 66, Admin off Shared Catlg Div 66-67; Ref libn UCal(Berkeley) 68-69. 8: Assoc tchr bibliog UCal (Berkeley) 69. 9: ALA; CalLA. 10: Phi Alpha Theta; Phi Kappa Phi. 14: Admin, ref. 15: 2525 LeConte ave, apt 16, Berkeley CA 94709.

BUDGE, RONNIE LEE (BRAUNSTEIN). b NYC 10 F 42. 4: Edwin S Budge. 5: Barnard Col 59-63 (Anthropology) AB; UMich 63-64 AMLS. 6: Fr. 7: Stud asst Wollman Lib, Barnard Col 62-63; Stud & col asst Cohen Lib, Col of the City of NY summers 62, 63; LC: Libn trainee 64-65, Info systems research asst 65, ref libn 65-68; Hd ref div San Leandro Commun Lib Ctr 68-. 14: Ref. 15: 2525 Le Conte ave apt 16, Berkeley Ca 94709.

BUDINGTON, WILLIAM S. b Oberlin Ohio 3 Jl 19. 5: Williams Col 36-40 (Eng) BA; Columbia 40-41 (LS) BS; Va Polytech Inst 46 (Elec Engnr) BS; Columbia 47-51 (LS) MS. 7: Ref libn Norwich U 41-42; US Army Master Sgt, Manhattan Dist 42-46; Engnr libn Columbia U 47-50, Supv Engnr & Phys Sci Libs 50-52; Assoc libn John Crerar Lib, Chicago 52-65, Libn 65-69, Exec Dir & Libn 69-. 8: Accredit teams, Middle States Assn of Cols & Sec Schs US/USSR Exchange Team Spec Libns 66. 9: ALA (Coun 60-64, 67-71; chm Pure & Applied Sci Sect; dir Photocopy Methods Sect); -RTSD (chm Reprod Lib Materials Sect 67-68); SLA (pres Ill Chap 57-59; 2nd v-pres 59-60; pres 64-65); ASIS; ACS (Chem Lit Sect). 10: Amer Soc Engr Educ; Phi Beta Kappa; Tau Beta Pi; AAAS; Coxton Club. 13: Yes. 14: Ref, admin, photoduplication. 15: John Crerar Lib, 35 W 33rd st, Chicago IL 60616.

BUDINSKY, CORNELIA. b Komarom Hungary 18 Ja 19. 4: Geza Budinsky. 5: Tchrs Train Col(Budapest) 33-38 (Teaching) Diploma; Col of Com(Budapest) 38-40 (Bus & Econ) Diploma; Ind U 58-59 (LS) MA; UNotre Dame 65 (Govt, Internat Rel) MA. 6: Hungarian, Ger. 7: Libn UNotre Dame (Notre Dame Ind) 59-. 9: RILA (pres 58-60, exec bd 53-64); NELA (sec 60-61); Ext Libns NE States (sec65-66). 10: Ladies of Notre Dame, Notre Dame Ind. 14: Ref, catlg. 15: 1032 Stanfield st, S Bend In 46617.

BUDLONG, DOROTHY WOOLLEY. b Providence 23 Ag 10. 5: Pembroke 28-32 (Fr) AB; Simmons 32-33 BS. 6: Fr. 7: Asst Providence Athenaeum 28-35; Libn RI State Planning Bd, Providence 35-37; Sec Providence USO Com, Provid ence 41-46; Asst YWCA, Providence 47-49; Circ & ref libn Elmwood Pub Lib, Providence 49-55, Libn 55-64; Supv of adult serv RI Dept of State Lib Serv, Providence 64-. 8: Adv Com on Sch Libs; Sec, Legis Commsn on Libs 62-64. 9: RILA (pres 58-60, Exec Bd 53-64); NELA (sec 60-61); Ext libns NE States (sec 65-66). 10: RI Simmons Col Club; Pembroke Col Club of Providence; The Players; Adult Educ Assn in RI; RI Histl Soc; ALA. 14: Adult serv, admin. 15: 455 Morris ave, Providence RI 02906.

BUDUROWYCZ (BOHDAN) BASIL JOSEPH. b Zukow Ukraine 8 S 21. 5: Philos-Theol Hochschule, Regensburg Germany 46-48 (Hist); Toronto50-53 (Hist, Slavic Studies) BA, MA, 54-55 BLS; Columbia 55-59 (Hist) PhD. 6: Ger, Polish, Russian, Ukrainian. 7: Bibliogr UToronto Lib 59-65; Bibliogr Center for Russian and East European Studies UToronto 65-68; Assoc Prof Dept of Slavic Lang &Lit UToronto 65-. 8: Research asst UToronto Lib, 65-. 10: Beta Phi Mu; AHA; Can Assn of Slavists; Nat Geog Soc; Shevchenko Sci Soc. 12: "Polish-Soviet Relations, 1932-1939" (63). 13: Yes. 14: Bk sel, ref. 15: 184 Rusholme rd, Toronto 4 Can.

BUECHLER, JOHN L. b Milwaukee 26 Mr 26. 4: Berniece Nelson. 5: Marquette U 46-51 (Eng) BA, MA; UWis 54-55 MA in LS; Ohio State U 57-58 (Eng); UFla 61-62 (Hist). 7: Aerial gunner (Sgt) US Army Air Force 44-46; Instr of Eng Marquette U 51-54; Asst humanities libn UNotre Dame(Notre Dame Ind) 55-56; Libn Eng & Speech Grad Lib Ohio State U 56-59; Head spec collections UFla 59-62; Head spec collections UVt 62-. 8: Served as liaison person for the SELA Col & Univ Sect, and the ALA-ACRL Rare Bks Sect 61. 9: BSA; Company of Mil Histns; Vt Hist Soc; Chittenden Co (Vt) Hist Soc; Vt Arch & Col Soc; Champlain Soc. 13: Yes. 14: Rare bks, mss. 15: 20 Victoria dr, South Burlington Vt 05401.

BUEHL, ELEONORE R(OSINA). b Montague Mich D 06. 5: Baldwin-Wallace Col 25-29 (Fr, Educ) AB; West Res 30-32 BS in LS; UIll summers 37-40 MS in LS. 6: Ger, Fr. 7: Asst libn & catlgr Baldwin-Wallace Col Lib 29-33; Catlgr & ref asst Boston U Col of Bus Adm 33-42; Catlgr Tufts Col Lib 43-46; Head catlgr Bucknell U Lib 46-47; Head catlgr Tex State Col for Women Lib 47-48; Assoc catlg libn Cornell U Lib 48-54; Libn Gen Electric Advanced Electronics Center, Ithaca NY 54-57; Classifier Iowa State Col 57; Head catlgr Schs of Health Professions UPittsburgh 57-64; Catlgr UMass 64-65; Libn Baltimore City Hosps, Baltimore 65-. 9: ALA-ACRL; MedLA; SLA. 10: Bus & Prof Womens' Club; AAUW; Soroptimist. 14: Catlg. 15: Baltimore City Hosps, 4940 Eastern ave, Baltimore Md 21224.

BUEHLER, DALE ALLAN. b Hazleton Penn 28 F 32. 5: Franklin & Marshall Col 50-54 (Sociol) AB; Drexel 57-60 MS in LS. 7: Admin off (2d Lt) USAF 54-55; Acquis & asst libn Wilkes Col Lib 62-. 9: PennLA-ACRL. 10: Delta Sigma Phi. 14: Acquis, catlg, col lib serv. 15: Eugene Shedden Farley Library, Wilkes College, Wilkes-Barre Pa 18703.

BUEHLER, NANCY D. 4: Eberhard Buehler. 5: William Smith Col 54 (Govt) BA; Rutgers 68 MLS. 7: Asst libn Milbank Lib Columbia Presbyterian Med Ctr 60-66, Libn Milbank Lib 68-. 14: Lib serv for patients. 15: 69 Fifth ave, New York NY 10003.

BUENING, REV ROBERT BERNARD. b Cincinnati 26 Je 31. 5: Aethenaeum of Ohio 50-54 (Philos) AB; Xavier U summers 52-55 (Eng); Mt St Joseph Col summers 55-60 Lib Certif. 6: Ger. 7: Libn Elder High Sch, Cincinnati 58-. 9: CathLA (chm High Sch Sect 62-63); OhioLA; OhioASchL. 14: Ya interests. 15: Elder High Sch, Vincent & Regina aves, Cincinnati Oh 45205.

BUFF, DOROTHY (DORCHESTER). b Brooklyn NY 4 O 14. 4: Ernest Buff. 5: Syracuse 31-35 (Hist, Educ) AB, Certif to teach, Certif as libn; Columbia 37-40 BS in LS. 6: Fr. 7: Hist tchr Teaneck High Sch, Teaneck NJ 35-36; Lib asst Pace Col 37-40; Morris Co Free Lib, Whippany NJ; Sr libn child & educ 56-58,Sr libn ya & adult serv 59-61, Asst lib dir 62-. 9: ALA; NJLA. 10: AAUW; LWV; Delta Zeta. 14: Ref. 15: 79 Mine Mount rd, Bernardsville NJ 07924.

BUFFA, FRED (FERDINAND). b Brooklyn NY 26 Ja 43. 5: Brooklyn Col 60-64 (Eng) BA, 66- (Eng, Educ); Pratt Inst 64-66 MLS. 6: Fr. 7: Tchr health educ after sch ctr PS 105, Brooklyn NY 63-68; Tchr health educ vacation day camp PS 102, Brooklyn NY summers 64-66; Sub tchr of lib sci East Dist High Sch, Brooklyn NY 66, Tchr of lib sci 66-. 9: CathLA (chm high sch sect 62-63); OhioLA; OhioASchL. 11: Carpenter Mem Award. 14: Tchg, y-a serv. 15: 1048 72nd st, Brooklyn NY 11228.

BUFFUM, CHARLES WALBRIDGE. b Dobbs Ferry NY 14 D 1900. 4: Katherine D Swartwout. 5: Amherst Col 18-22 (Eng, Hist) AB; NY State Col Tchrs 27 (Educ); Syracuse 30-32 (LS) BS, 31-33 (US Hist); USDA Grad Sch 46-47 (Cartography). 6: Fr, Ger. 7: Tchr math Falconer High Sch, Falconer NY 26-28; Instr math Rensselaer Polytech Inst 29; Instr math Syracuse U 29-30, Instr Lib Sci 31-33; LC: Catlgr 35-41, Map catlgr 41-, Sr map catlgr currently. 9: ALA; SLA; Assn of Amer Geog (Handbk-Direc Com 56); DCLA. 12: US collab, "Bibliographie Cartographique Internationale" (50-); Contrib to LC Clsf Class G (3d ed 54); Assoc ed "Geography & Map Bulletin," SLA (56-); Ed "Catalog of National Exhibits, 17th International Geography Congress," Wash DC (52). 14: Maps, catlg & clsf, geog names. 15: 4201 52nd st, Bladensburg Md 20710.

BUGERA, JULIA ADAMS (SAPALA). b Detroit Mich 1 Fe 38. 4: William Bugera Jr. 5: Hillsdale Col 55-57; UMich 57-58, 64 (LS); West MichU 58-59 (Eng) BA, 59-60, 64-65 (Libnship) MA. 6: Fr. 7: Asst libn Kalamazoo Pub Lib 59-60; Ref libn Upjohn Co, Kalamazoo Mich 60; Libn Baldwin Pub Lib, Birmingham Mich 61-63, Adult serv libn 65-66; Ref libn Hamtramck Pub Lib, Hamtramck, Mich 63-64; Tech libn Space/Defense Corp, Birmingham Mich 66-67; Libn Whirlpool Corp, Benton Harbor Mich 67-68; Instr Dept Libnship West MichU 68; Libn Bendix Corp Research Labs, Southfield Mich 69-. 9: SLA. 14: Ref. 15: 3185 Ayrshire dr, Bloomfield Hills Mi 48013.

BUGG, MAYME (PINKARD). b Nashville. 4: George W Bugg. 5: Tenn A&I State U 23-25 (Bus Educ) Certif; Howard U 25-27 (Educ) AB; Gregg Col 26 (Bus Educ) Certif; UIll summers 38-41 BS in LS Wash U, 66, 68; So Ill U summer 66, 68, (Instructional Materials) summer 69. 6: Fr. 7: Bus educ tchr Booker Washington High Sch, Atlanta 27-29; Bus educ tchr Vashon High Sch, St Louis 29-31; Sec Tenn A&I U 32-34; Lib asst Fisk U 34-37; Libn Pearl High Sch, Nashville 37-40; Libn Meharry Med 45-50; Libn Vashon High Sch, St Louis 50-68; Libn O'Fallon Tech Center, St Louis 68-. 9: Mo State Tchrs Assn; MoLA; Greater St Louis LA; St Louis TA. 10: YWCA; Annie Malone Orphans Home; Alpha Kappa Alpha; Jack & Jill of Amer, Inc; Howard U Alum Assn. 11: SAIS Hon Scholarship Soc, Tenn State Col; Scholarship to Howard U. 13: Yes. 14: Ref, Negro bibliog. 15: 5042 Northland ave, St Louis Mo 63113.

BUGINAS, SCOTT J. b Oak Park Ill 26 D 33. 4: Mavis Gleason. 5: Ripon Col 51-52; Miami U(Ohio) 52-55 (Bot, Zool) BA. 6: Ger. 7: Head of ref & circ Battelle Mem Inst, Columbus Ohio 55-62; Ref libn Lockheed Missiles & Space Co, Palo Alto Cal 62-64; Head of info serv Lawrence Radiation Lab, Livermore Cal 64-. 67, Lib mgr 68-. 9: SLA (News ed Metals Div 62-63). 13: Yes. 14: Ref. 15: 1207 Gonzaga ct, Livermore Ca 94550.

BUHLER, CURT F(ERDINAND). b NYC 11 Jl 05. 5: Yale 23-27 (Greek, Ital) BA; Trinity Col UDublin 28-30 (Mediaeval Lit) PhD, 47 (Mediaeval Lit) Litt D; UMunich 31-33 (Germanic Phil). 6: Ger, Fr, Ital. 7: Morgan Lib, NYC; Staff mem 34-39, Curator, early printed bks 39-48, Keeper of printed bks 48-65, Research fellow 66-, Act dir 69. 8: Rosenbach Fellow (UPenn) 47, 58-59; Guggenheim Fellow 65; Visiting Fellow, All Souls, Oxford 69; Spec lecturer UNotre Dame 58; Gutenberg Soc (Mainz) 62; So Methodist U 62; Member bd Intl Union of Academies 67-. 9: BSA (pres 52-54); Renaissance Soc of Amer (pres 61-62); Mediaeval Acad of Amer; Mod Lang Assn (exec coun 57-60); ACLS (sec 60-). 10: Amer Philosophical Soc; Amer Acad Arts & Sci; Gutenberg Gesell, Mainz. 12: "The History of Tom Thumbe (65); "Neue Kunst und Neue Welt (63); "The Fifteenth-Century Book (60); "William Caxton and His Critics (60); "Univ & Press in XVc Bologna (58); "Fifteenth Century Books and The Twentieth Century (52); "The Dicts and Sayings of The Philosophers (41). 13: Yes. 14: Mediaeval mss & rare bks. 15: 33 E 36th st, New York NY 10016.

BUIKA, GINA (GAERTLER). b Austria. 4: James J Buika. 5: UHeidelberg 34-38 (Lit) Dr phil; Simmons 40-41 (LS) BS; Radcliffe 38-39 (Eng, Educ). 6: Fr, Ger. 7: Asst libn LI Col of Med 41-42; Libn Amer Soc of Anesthetists, NYC 42-43; Libn Horticultural Soc of NY, NYC 43-45; Advertising manager Med dept The Macmillan Co, NYC 45-47, Advertising manager internat dept 47-60; Info spec Amer Nurses' Assn, NYC 62-63; Med libn & info spec NY Med Col Center for Chronic Disease 64-. 8: Internat adv consul, R R Bowker Co, 61; Adv consul UN Publ Div Spanish Sect, 65; Med Com Midtown Internat Center, 64; Publ Com Internat Adv Assn; US Com Observer World Med Assn. 9: SLA; MedLA; Amer Med Writers Assn. 10: Radcliffe Club, Mus of Mod Art. 15: 50 Park ave, NY NY 10016.

BUIST, ELEANOR. b Brooklyn NY 9 Jl 16. 5: Vassar 33-37 (Ger) AB; Cornell U 43-45 (Russian); Middlebury Col summers 46-49 (Russian) MA; Columbia U 48-50 (Russian area studies); Columbia 52-54 (LS) MS. 6: Russian, Ger, Lat, Gk, Fr. 7: Sec to chief metallurgist Remington Rand Propeller Div, Binghamton NY 41-43; Asst to the treas Cornell U 43-45; Research sec RussianInst Columbia U 46-51, Research asst in Russian studies 51-54; Columbia U Libs; Sr ref asst 54-63, Sr ref libn 63-64, Slavic bibliogr 64-66. 8: Exec sec coord com for Slavic & East Europ Lib Resources, 62-66; Adv on publ of Cyrillic Union Catalog, Microprint ed 63; Consul ongen bibliog to P H Horecky, ed "Russia and the Soviet Union; A Bibliographic Guide to Western Language Publications" U of Chicago Press 64. 9: Amer Assn for the Advancement of Slavic Studies; ASIS; ALA; -ACRL (Exec Com & Chm Slavic & East European Subsect 65-66); NY Tech Serv Libns; NY Lib Club. 11: Senior Fellow, Russian Inst of Columbia U 61-62, 68-; Title II Fellow Columbia U Sch of Lib Serv 67. 12: Co-auth "Guide to Reference Books," 7th ed, 3rd & 4th sup (60, 63). 13: Yes. 14: Ref, bibliog, info sci. 15: 90 LaSalle st, New York NY 10027.

BUJA, REV ARNOLD F(RANCIS) SDB. b San Francisco Cal 1 D 14. 5: Don Bosco Col 36-40 (Philos) BA; Immaculate Heart Col 65 MA in LS. 7: Libn Don Bosco Tech Inst, South San Gabriel Cal 55-. 8: Archdiocesan (LA) Lib Com chm 64-. 9: ALA; SLA; CathLA (Exec Com, Southwest Unit). 10: Chaplain, Boy Scouts. 12: Co-ed High Sch sect of Catholic Booklist (67-). 14: Catlg. 15: PO Box 1218, Rosemead Ca 91770.

BUKSBAZEN, JACQUELINE A (JONES). b Quincy Mass 7 Mr 32. 5: UAriz 51-56 (Anthropology) BA; UDenver 56-57 (LS) MA. 7: Chief base libn USAF Lib Serv, Japan 57-58; Base libn USAF Lib Serv, Korea 58-59; Catlgr UNH 62-63, Asst loan libn 63-64; Child libn Los Angeles Pub Lib 65-67; Catlgr Tucson Pub Lib 67-68; Base libn USAF Lib Serv Loring AFB, Me 68-. 14: Ref, child wk, catlgr. 15: 29 West Gate Trailer Park, Limestone Me 04750.

BULAONG, GRACE (FABELLA). b Manila Philippines 22 N 39. 4: Renato A Bulaong. 5: UPhilippines 55-59 BSLS, 63-67 (Asian Studies) MA; UMich 62-63 AMLS. 6: Sp, Fr. 7: Libn I UPhilippines 59-60, 63-67; Instr II Inst of Lib Sci, Asst Prof No IllU 67-68; Libn III Queen'sU, Kingston Ont Can 68-. 9: PhilippineLA (sec 65-67); Philippine Hist Assn. 10: Filipino Assn of Kingston. 12: "Satire and Society" (69). 13: Yes. 14: Catlg. 15: 190 University st, Kingston Ont Can.

BULL, CAROLINE (ARDEN). b Thomasville Ga 16 O 28. 4: Richard Claggett Bull. 5: UNC 47-49 (Eng), 55 (LS); Fla State U 56-58 (LS) BA, 60-61 (LS) MS UMd 67-68 (LS). 6: Fr. 7: Staff asst Cumberland Co Pub Lib, Fayetteville NC 55-56; Asst libn Wilson Co Pub Lib, Wilson NC 58-59; Child libn Braswell Mem Lib, Rocky Mount NC 59-60; Actress Asolo Theatre Festival, Sarasota Fla 60; Res Room asst Fla State U 60-61; Young Adult Serv Supv Arlington Co Pub Lib, Arlington Va 61-65; Instr UVa Ext (Arlington) 63-65; Lib Consul Woodbury Forest Sch, Orange Va 65-66; Ya serv coordinator Prince George's Co (Md) Mem Lib66-67; Asst Prof Fla State U 68;

Communications Analyst Smithsonian Inst 68-. 9: ALA; DCLA. 10: Smithsonian Associates; Friends of the Nat Zoo; Beta Phi Mu. 11: Philip Wylie Award Fla State U; H W Wilson Co Scholarship, Fellowship UMd67-68. 14: Lib educ, ref, bibliog, info systems. 15: Box 235, Alexandria Va 22314.

BULL, JACQUELINE. b Greenville Miss 24 Ap 11. 5: UKy 29-34 (LS) AB, 39-48 (Hist) PhD. 6: Sp, Ger. 7: UKy Lib: Sec to libn 34-37, Asst ref libn 37-42, Archivist 44-60, Head spec collections 60-. 9: ALA; SAA; Amer Studies Assn; KYLA (pres 52-53); Ky Hist Soc. 10: AAUP. 11: Rockefeller Fellowship in Soc Scis, 42-43. 12: Ed (with Frances Dugan) "Bluegrass Craftsman" (59). 13: Yes. 14: Rare bks, mss. 15: Univ of Ky Lib, Lexington Ky 40506.

BULL, MARGARET G. b Kunsan Korea 25 F 05. 5: Agnes Scott Col 22-26 (Eng) AB; URichmond 33-34 (Eng) MA; UNC 54-55 MSLS. 7: Instr Fassifern Sch, Hendersonville NC 34-41; Instr Greenbrier Col 41-54; Montclair Pub Lib, Montclair NJ: Ref asst 55-56, Head of ref 56-61, Asst dir 61-. 9: ALA; NJLA. 10: Beta Phi Mu; Bus & Prof Womens Club. 14: Ref, bk sel. 15: 7 Trinity pl, Montclair NJ 07042.

BULL, MRS RUTH P. b Perryman Md 3 F 11. 5: Johns Hopkins U summers 28, 32, 49, 50, 51, 60, 63; Goucher Col 51-53 (Eng) BA; West Res summers 53, 55, 57, 58, 60 MSLS. 7: Asst br libn Enoch Pratt Free Lib, Baltimore 29-41, Br libn 41-42; Upper sch libn The Park Sch, Baltimore 48-51; Elem sch libn Mars Estates Sch Bd of Educ of Baltimore Co, Towson Md 53-62; Elem sch libn Ft Garrison Sch, Towson Md 62-65; Reviewer of child bks for Booklist ALA, Chicago 65-. 9: ALA; IllLA (Dir Chicago chapt); Chicago Lib Club; Child Reading RT; Coun For Relations (Chicago chap). 13: Yes. 14: Lib wk with child. 15: 777 N Michigan ave, apt 2402, Chicago Il 60611.

BULLARD, BARBARA (BORGER). b Penn. 4: A V Bullard Jr. 5: UNC at Chapel Hill 64-66 LS MS. 7: Asst libn Mt Olive Col 66-. 9: ALA; NCLA; SELA. 10: Beta Phi Mu; Swimming Club; Mt Olive Exten Homemakers Club. 14: Catlg, ref. 15: 103 Smith Chapel rd, Mount Olive NC 28365.

BULLARD, ROSETTA (DAUGHERTY). b W Plains Mo 28 Ja 42. 5: Central Col 59-60; SE Mo State Col 60-63 (Hist) AB; UIll (Urbana) 63-64 (LS) MS. 7: Lib aide y-a dept St Louis pub Lib 63; Child libn Saguaro Br of Phoenix Pub Lib 64-67; Asst ref libn Mo State Lib, jefferson City Mo 68-. 9: ALA; MoLA. 13: Yes. 14: Child lit & serv, ref serv. 15: 8th & Jefferson sts, Hermann Mo 65041.

BULLEN, ROBERT WHITEFIELD. b Vicksburg Miss 12 Ag 27. 4: Ida Andrus. 5: Millsaps Col 44-47 (Eng) BA; Emory 50-51 (LS) MA. 7: Lib asst Waterways Expt Sta, Vicksburg Miss 47-50; Libn UGa(Atlanta) 51-53; Head ser dept Miss State Col 53-57; Consul WVa Lib Commsn, Charleston WVa 57-60; Dir Piedmont Reg Lib, Winder Ga 61-62; Visiting Prof Emory U 64-65; Dir Cobb Co-Marietta Pub Lib, Marietta Ga 62-68; Visiting Prof UGa 65-67; Admin serv libn N Suburban Lib Syst, Morton Grove Ill 68-. 8: State Supt of Educ Prof Adv Com 64-68, chm 67-68. 9: ALA; -LED (chm Bylaws Com 67-69); SELA (Lib Development Com 64-66); GaLA (chm Memb Com 63-65, chm Pub Lib Sect 65-67, Exec Bd 65-67); IllLA. 10: Kiwanis Club; SAR; Pi Kappa Alpha; PTA. 12: "McDowell County WVa Library Survey" (57); "Conf for Lib Trustees Proceedings" (61); "Marshall Co WVa Library Survey" (57); "Survey for Library Development in Raleigh and Fayette Counties" (59); Ed "Nor'easter" (68-). 13: Yes. 14: Pub lib admin. 15: 5814 Dempster st, Morton Grove IL 60053.

BULLOCK, FRANCES E. b Moline Ill 25 O 13. 5: Wellesley 31-35 (Eng composition) BA; Union Theol Sem 64-65; Columbia 65-68 (LS) MS. 6: Fr, New Testament Gr. 7: Sec to ed "The Annalist" NY Times 35-37; Sec to assoc dir metallurgy Crucible Steel Co NYC 40-45; Sec registrar's off Union Theol Sem 61-66, Circ libn 66-. 9: ATheolLA. 14: Circ, bibliog. 15: 80 La Salle st, New York NY 10027.

BULMAN, LEARNED T(HOMAS). b Norwich Conn 23 F 23. 5: UMo 43-44; Washington & Jefferson Col 46-48 (Hist) AB; Columbia 48-49 (LS) MS; Montclair State Col 54-55 (Guidance & Educ). 7: US Army 43-45; Jr-Sr libn Detroit Pub Lib 49-51; Co-ordinator of youth serv E Orange Pub Lib, E Orange NJ 51-66; Asst dir 67-. 8: Reviewer & adv to "Sch Lib Journal" 50-67; Ed 'Adult Books for Young Adults' "Sch Lib Journal" 63-67 ALA rep to NCTE for "Books for You" 53-57; Lecturer on travel & books; Publishers' Consul. 9: ALA (life mem) -YASD (var coms & chm of some); NJLA (var com duties, pres of Sect for Serv to Child & YP 65-67; NYLib Club; Melvil Dui Chowder and Marching Assn. 10: East Orange Youth Guidance Coun; past pres-High 12 Club of E Orange; past pres E Orange Little Theatre; Church Elder. 13: Yes. 14: Young adult wk, pub lib admin. 15: 17 Summit st, East Orange NJ 07017.

BULTHUIS, G. THOMAS. b Grand Haven Mich 21 Je 35. 4: Nancy Gale Bulthuis. 5: Calvin Col 53-55, 60-63 (Hist) AB; UMich 63-64 (LS) MA. 6: Ger. 7: Asst libn Grand Valley State Col 64-. 9: CalASchL (Jr Col chm No sect 68-69); CalLA; Cal Jr Col Faculty Assn. 10: Amer Fed Tchrs. 11: Kellogg Fellow, Stanford 66-67. 14: Ref; Admin. 15: Grand Valley State Col, Allendale Mi 49401.

BUMBAUGH, THELMA (RUTH). b New Castle Penn 9 D 13. 5: Hiram Col 44-49 (Religion) AB; Kent State U 50-53 (LS) AM. 6: Sp, Ger. 7: Asst libn New Castle Sr High Sch, New Castle Penn 31-33; Sec New Castle Brick Co, New Castle Penn 34-35; Bank employee Lawrence Savings& Trust Co, New Castle Penn 37-44; Asst libn Hiram Col 46-48, Head libn 58-, Assoc prof LS 58-. 9: ALA-ACRL (Tri-State Chap); OhioLA; NoOhioTechProcLibns (chm Col & Univ Round Table 62-63). 10: LWV; AAUP. 14: Catlg. 15: 6857 Cheryl dr, Hiram Oh 44234.

BUMBERG, AMY ELIZABETH (EVANS). b Aalt Lake City Utah 1 Ag 43. 4: Harold Bumberg. 5: UWis 61-65 (Natural Sci) BS; UPittsburgh 69 MLS. 6: Sp. 7: Asst tech libn J&L Steel Corp, Pittsburgh Penn 66-68; Libn trainee VA Hosp, Pittsburgh Penn 68-69; Libn (geol) UMinn (Minneapolis) 69-. 9: SLA; ALA; MeLA. 10. YWCA. 15: 3710 Minnehaha ave, Minneapolis Mn 55406.

BUMGARDNER, HELEN AYERS. b Athens Sangamon Co Ill 6 My 29. 4: Melvin Lonas Bumgardner. 5: Northwestern U 47-51 (Speech); UWash summers 55-58 MLS. 6: Fr. 7: Tchr Feitshan's High Sch, Springfield Ill 51-53; Cadet libn Lib Assn of Portland, Portland Ore 54-57; Libn Tacoma Sch Dist 10, Tacoma Wash 57-59; Head libn Wash State Hist Soc, Tacoma Wash 61-63; Libn Clover Park Sch Dist 400, Lakewood Center Wash 63-. 9: ALA; NEA; WashEA; Wash State ASchL, Rec sec, (Reg chm); WashLA; CPEA. 10: Phi Beta; PTA. 12: Ed "Library Leads". 13: Yes. 14: Washington State hist. 15: 3217 North 29, Tacoma Wa 98407.

BUMP, DONALD. b Ashland NH 28 Mr 29. 5: Plymouth State Col 47-51 (Sci, Educ) BEd, 62 (Eng) MEd; Rutgers 62-65 MLS; UWash summer 65 (NDEA Inst). 6: Fr. 7: Elem tchr Dublin Consolidated Sch, Dublin NH 51-53; Sci tchr Hood Mem Sch, Derry NH 53-56; Asst to pres Laconia Shoe Co, Laconia NH 56-57; Eng tchr & libn Plymouth High Sch, Plymouth NH 57-61; Eng tchr No Valley Reg High Sch, Demarest NJ 61-63; Libn E Orange High Sch, E Orange NJ 63-65; Libn Scarsdale High Sch, Scarsdale NY 65-. 9: ALA-AASchL;-ACRL (rare bk sect);-RTSD; NEA-DAVI; NYStateLA; NY Tech Serv Libns; NY State EA. 10: SAAB Club of Amer; Westchester Co Sports Car Club; PTA. 14: Sch libs, col & univ libs, rare bks, bldg collections, acquis. 15: 90 Woodruff ave, Scarsdale NY 10583.

BUMP, RUTH ELIZABETH. b Amenia NY 6 F 07. 5: NJ Col for Women (28) (Math) BA; Columbia (39) BS in LS (51) MS in LS. 6: Fr. 7: Math tchr Jr High Sch Wood Ridge NJ 28-30; Sch libn Moorestown Public Schs, Moorestown NJ 30-61; Lib coordinator Moorestpwn Schs 61-67; Instr LS Trenton State Col 67. 8: Participated in TV program on elem sch libs for NJEA; Instr LS Glassboro State Col summer 68; Assoc prof of LS 68-. 9: NEA; AASchL; ALA; NJEA; NJ Sch Libns Assn (past v-pres & archivist). 10: AAUW; Moorestown Women's Club; Phi Beta Kappa; Beta Phi Mu. 14: Sch lib wk. 15: Pine Tree Apts 294 W Second st, Moorestown NJ 08057.

BUNCO, MERLE ANN. b Derby Conn 31 Jl 36. 5: So Conn State Col 54-58 (Ed) BS, 66- (LS). 7: Howard Whittemore Memorial Lib Naugatuck Comm Children's libn 58-65, Hd libn 65-. 8: Consul Southbury Pub Lib, Southbury Conn 67-68. 9: ALA; ConnLA; NELA. 14: Sch libs, col & univ libs, rare bks, bldg collections,acquis. 15: 196 Prospect st, Ansonia Ct 06401.

BUNDSEN, PATRICIA (LANDRUM). b Wash DC 17 Mr 41. 4: Bruce Bindsen. 5: UMd 58-62 (Eng) BA. 6: Fr. 7: Lib asst Hyattsville Pub Lib, Hyattsville Md 56-57; Med Records Clk CIA, Langley Va 58-62; Searcher LC 62-63; Asst Readers Serv Libn Applied Physics Lab, Silver Spring Md 64-67; Hd Libn Leasco Sys & Research Corp, Bethesda Md 67-. 9: SLA; (Documen Gp); ASIS (Info Analysis Ctrs Gp). 10: Archeol Soc of Md; Wilderness Soc. 12: Asst ed "List of Scientific-Technical Journal titles and holdings in the Washington-Baltimore Area" (66). 14: Ref, clsf systems. 15: 5921 Cherrywood ter, Greenbelt Md 20770.

BUNDY, ANNALEE M(ARSHALL). b Chicago Ill 11 F 38. 4: John W Bundy. 5: UNH 56-60 (Pol sci) BA; Simmons 60-61 MSLS. 7: Lib asst UNH Lib 56-60; Asst libn Pine Manor Jr Col 60-61; Hd & assoc hd College of Guam Lib, Agana Guam 61-63; Tech libn E I DuPont de Nemours Maydown, Londonderry N Ireland 63-65; Hd children's room Schenectady Co Pub Lib Schenectady NY 65-66; Documents & period libn Grad Sch of Pub Affairs SUNY at Albany 66-67; Co-ordinator of serv Medford Pub Lib, Medford Mass 67-. 9: ALA; MassLA. 14: Admin, tech serv, child wk. 15: 22 Stowell rd, Winchester Ma 01890.

BUNGE, CHARLES ALBERT. b Kimball Nb 18 Mr 36. 4: Joanne Vonstoeser. 5: UMo 54-57, 58-59 (Philos) AB; UIll 59-60 (LS) MS, 64-67 (LS) PhD. 6: Fr, Ger. 7: Ref libn Daniel Boone Reg Lib, Columbia Mo 60-62; Ref libn Ball State Tchrs Col Lib 62-64; Research asst Lib Research Center, Urbana Ill 64-65; Instr UIll Grad Sch (Lib Sci Urbana) summer 65; Research asst Lib Research Center, Urbana Ill 64-66, Research assoc 66-67; Asst Prof UWis Lib Sch 67-. 9: ALA; AALS; WisLA. 10: Phi Beta Kappa; Beta Phi Mu. 12: "Professional Education and Reference Effi ciency" (67). 13: Yes. 14: Ref, bk sel. 15: 840 Woodrow st, Madison Wi 53711.

BUNKER, CHARLOTTE JANE. b Inuvil Ceylon 21 O 39. 5: Oberlin Col 57-61 (Eng Lit) BA; Columbia 64-65 (LS) MS. 7: Eng tchr United Church Bd for World Ministries, Izmir Turkey 61-64; Catlgr Yale Divinity Sch Lib 65-. 9: ALA; AALS; WisLA. 14: Catlg. 15: 611 Whitney ave, New Haven Ct 06511.

BUNKER, NORMAN J. b Lansing Mich 2 O 18. 4: Evelyn Langenderf. 5: Mich State U 38-41 (Journalism) AB; UMich 47-49 AMLS. 7: Br asst Pub Lib, Dearborn Mich 49-50; Head Libn Carnegie Lib, Ironwood Mich 50-54; Lib Dir Ingham Co Lib, Mason Mich 54-60; Head Libn No Mich Col 60-64; Libn Mich State Highways Dept, Lansing Mich 64-. 8: Tchr, lib sci, No Mich U 60-64. 9: SLA; PLRC; MichLA (2nd v-pres 50; chm Co Lib Sect 56). 10: Rotary; Mich Week Com; Com on Aging. 13: Yes. 14: Spec libnship, documentary retr systems. 15: 815 N Capitol, Lansing Mi 48906.

BUNN, DUMONT CYRIL. b Vero Beach Fla 15 Ja 36. 4: Christine Cooper. 5: UGa 55-59 (Eng) BA; Emory 59-61 MLS. 7: Asst libn Emory U Dental Sch 62; Asst to head acquis dept Ga State Col Lib 62-64; Head catlgr Mercer U 64-65, Head of Pub Serv 65-. 9: SELA; GaLA. 14: Ref, admin, pub serv. 15: 2456 Kingsley dr, Macon Ga 31204.

BUNNELL, CONSTANCE (OSMOND). b Provo Utah 13 Ja 06. 4: Merrill J Bunnell. 5: Utah State 22-24; Brigham Young U 24-26 (Eng) AB; Columbia 60-63 (LS) MS. 6: Fr. 7: Hig h Sch Eng Dept Head, Ogden Utah (5 yrs); Bk reviewer Salt Lake City (8 yrs); Ext libn Carnegie Free Lib, Ogden Utah 35-42; Libn Central Sch, Ogden Utah 42-44; Libn Mamaroneck NY High Sch 61-63, Hd libn 63-. 9: ALA; NEA; NYLA; NY State TA; WestchesterLA; Westchester A-V Assn. 14: Admin, ya lit, child lit. 15: 749 Forest ave, Larchmont NY 10538.

BUNTING, ANNE CARROLL. b Memphis Tenn 8 D 36. 5: Miss State Col for Women 54-58 (LS) BA; UNC 64-66 (LS) MS; Medical Libn Certif Class I. 6: Fr, Sp. 7: Lib asst Carnegie Pub Lib, Clarksdale Miss 58-59; Libn e e bass Jr High Sch, Greenville Miss 59-64; Lib asstship UNC(Chapel Hill) 64-66 Asst libn Hd of tech processes and pub serv UTenn Med Units Lib 66-. 8: Tchr of Bibliog of med lit UTenn Med Units 67-. 9: ALA; MissLA; SELA; MedLA. 10: Alpha Beta Alpha; Sigma Tau Delta. 14: Catlg, ref. 15: Univ of Tenn Med Units Lib, 62 S Dunlap, Memphis Tn 38103.

BUNTON, MRS AVIS (FISHER). b Sterling City Tex 23 Mr 1900. 5: Mary Hardin Baylor 19-20, 21-22 (Educ) Certif; Trinity U 53-55 (Educ) BS; Our Lady of the Lake Col 55-56 (LS) Certif. 7: Asst catlgr, head acquis dept, head circ dept Trinity U 55-. 9: TexLA; SWLA. 14: Acquis, catlg, ref, circ. 15: 491 Olmos dr E, San Antonio Tex 71282.

BUNTY, NANCY LEE (RITZ). b Pittsburgh 15 Je 36. 4: Thomas F Bunty. 5: UPittsburgh 54-58 (Educ) BA, even 63-65 MLS. 6: Fr. 7: Eng tchr Bd of Educ, Pittsburgh 58-61, 62-63; Eng tchr Baldwin-Whitehall, Pittsburgh 61-62; Libn Bd of Educ, Pittsburgh 63-. 9: Penn State EA. 10: Phoebe Brashear Assn; Pi Lambda Theta. 11: Frick Found summer study UParis 60. 14: Ref, admin, pub serv. 15: 660 Garden pkwy, Circleville Oh 43113.

BUPP, RENO W. b Wooster Ohio 6 Ja 10. 4: Ruth Paxton Bupp. 5: Col of Wooster 27-31 (Hist) BA; Ohio State U 39 (Hist) MA; Fla State U 50 (LS) MA. 6: Fr. 7: High sch tchr Big Prairie High Sch, Big Prairie Ohio 31-37; High sch tchr Fairport Harbor High Sch, Fairport Harbor Ohio 37-43; Pharmacist Mate US Navy 44-45; High sch tchr Fairport Harbor High Sch, Fairport Harbor Ohio 46-48; Asst libn Fla State U Lib 50-56, Head soc sci div 56-. 9: SELA; FlaLA. 10: Phi Beta Kappa. 15: 1401 Pichard dr, Tallahassee Fla 32303.

BURCH, MARION J. b Anadarko Okla 14 F 18. 4: Juanita Burch. 5: NoTexU 48-60 (Educ, LS) MA. 7: AMMIc US Navy 44-46; County Supt of Pub Schs, Marietta Okla 48-59; Admin Pub Lib, Lisbon Ohio 59-60; Admin Pub Lib Newton Iowa 61-. 9: ALA; IowaLA. 15: Pub Lib 400 1st ave W, Newton Iowa 50208.

BURCHER, HILDA (BEAZLEY). b Caroline Co Va 5 Je 38. 4: Eugene Stearns Burcher. 5: Mary Washington 56-60 (Eng) BA; UMd 65-67 (LS) MS. 7: Eng tchr, Fairfax Co Va 60-65; Ref libn, Fairfax Co Va 69-. 10: Beta Phi Mu. 14: Ref, bibliog, y-a serv. 15: 603 Beverley dr, Alexandria Va 22305.

BURCHETT, KENNETH WALTON. b Alpha Wash 1 Ag 26. 5: UPortland 47-51 (Soc Sci) AB (cum laude); Ore Gen Ext Div summers 51, 52, 54, 58, 59; East Wash State Col summer 53; UPortland summers 58-61 (Educ) MEd, 62-64 MLS; UNev summers 62-63 UOre summer 66; IndU summers 67 & 68. 6: Sp, Fr. 7: Libn Centennial High Sch, Gresham Ore 63-68; Libn Puyallup High Sch, Puyallup Wash 68-. 9: NEA; ALA; WashEA; Wash State ASchL. 14: Readers guidance, bk sel, ref. 15: 7104 N Syracuse st, Portland Or 97203.

BURDEN, GERALDINE RICE. b Ashland Ohio 9 N 26. 4: Jay Burden. 5: Col of Wooster 48 9econ) BA; Kent U 68 MLS. 6: Fr. 7: Asst ref dept Andrews Lib, Wooster Ohio 67-. 9: ALA. 15: 1352 E Wayne ave, Wooster Oh 44691.

BURDEN, MRS ROSINE (KELLEY). b Fullbright Tex 15 Je 04. 5: E Tex State Tchrs Col 23-26 (Eng) BA; Tex Tech summers 39, 40; UTex summer 41; Tex Women's U summers 47-49 BS in LS. 6: Eng & Sp tchr High Sch, Gladewater Tex 26-27; Tchr Elem sch, Seminole Tex 37-46; Tchr Houston Elem Sch, El Paso Tex 47-49; Libn Austin High Sch, El Paso Tex 49-55; Libn Burges High Sch, El Paso Tex 55-. 9: NEA; ALA; Tex State Tchrs Assn; TexLA; El Paso Tchrs Assn; Trans-Pecos Tchrs Assn. 14: Catlg, ref. 15: 1112 Duke circle, El Paso Tx 79903.

BURDETTE, ELEANOR MARY. b Chicago. 5: George Washington U 36-40 (Eng Lit) AB; Catholic U 47-48 BS in LS. 6: Fr. 7: Asst order dept Catholic U 47-48, Asst head order dept 48-52, Asst ref libn 52-53; Chief acquis br research info Div of Nat Advisory Com for Aeronautics, Wash DC 53-56, Asst libn Hdqrs Lib 56-58; Head tech processes & asst to libn Hdqrs Lib NASA, Wash DC 58-62, Ref libn 62-. 8: Chm, Spec Libs Task Force for Nat Lib Week 67. 9: DCLA; SLA (Wash DC chap;sec Sci-Tech Gp 66-67, chm Elect Com 65-67, corr sec 67-68). 14: Ref, acquis. 15: 1722 19th st NW, Apt 702, Wash DC 20009.

BURDICK, LOIS (BREYER). b Chicago Ill 13 F 41. 4: Morton L Burdick. 5: UMich 58-60; Loyola U 60-61; Nat Col of Ed 60-62 (Elem ed) B Ed; Drexel 66-67 MSLS. 7: Tchr Mary Mapes Dodge Sch Chicago Pub Schs 62-62; Tchr Sch #92 Baltimore Pub Schs 62-63; Hd typist Milton S Eisenhower Lib Johns Hopkins U 63-66; Hd ser catlgr Robert Manning Strozier Lib Florida State U 67-. 9: ALA (-ACRL; -RTSD); FlaLA; SELA. 10: Beta Phi Mu. 14: Catlg, ser. 15: 504 W Call st, Tallahassee Fl 32301.

BURDICK, OSCAR (CHARLES). b Milton Wis 2 Ja 29. 4: Mary Elizabeth Pederson. 5: Milton Col 46-50 (Music) BA with Certif in Pipe Organ; Alfred U Sch of Theol 50-52, 53 Bd; Pacific Sch of Religion 52-54; UCal (Berkeley) 56-58 MLS. 6: Ger, Fr. 7: Pastor Seventh Day Baptist Church, Daytona Beach Fla 54-56; Asst libn Pacific Sch of Religion 56-62, Assoc libn 62-; Organist, Arlington Commun Church, Berkeley Cal 58-; Assoc libn Grad Theol Union 66-. 9: ATheolLA (chm Period Exchg Com 61-64). 10: Amer Guild of Organists. 14: Admin, ref, acquis, catlg. 15: Pacific Sch of Religion, 1798 Scenic ave, Berkeley Ca 94709.

BUREL, MARY (GREGORY MAYSE). b Sapulpa Okla 19 D 20. 4: Walter D Burel. 5: UOkla 39-42 (Drama, Ed) BA; Florida State U 64-65 MSLS. 6: Fr. 7: High Sch Tchr Jenks Okla & Dayton Ohio 42-57; Asst Libn Wright Pub Lib, Dayton Ohio 57-59; Hd libn Riverside Elem Sch, Titusville Fla 60-62; Hd libn Tropical Elem Sch, Merritt Island Fla 62-64; Hd libn Madison Township Sch Libs, Old Bridge NJ 65-66; Hd libn Coyle Free Lib, Chambersburg Penn 66-68; Dir Conococheague Dist Lib, Chambersburg Penn 68-. 8: Coord planning & exec merger of co & pub (city) libs, Chambersburg

Penn; libn in charge of planning new brs & new sch libs. 9: ALA; PennLA. 10: Little Theatre; Bk Discussion Gp. 14: Admin. 15: RD #1 Box 312, Gettysburg Pa 17325.

BURESH, VITUS. b Dickinson ND 23 S 23. 5: St Procopius Col 41-45 (Philos) BA; St Procopius Sem 45-49 (Theol); Catholic U 46, 48, 49-50 MS in LS. 6: Czech, Lat. 7: Asst libn St Procopius Col 45-56, Libn 56-60; Chaplain St Anthony Hosp, Chicago 60-64; Spec collections libn St Procopius Col 64-67; Archivist St Procopius Abbey 64-. 8: Ministerial wk 49-; Tchg in Nurs Sch 60-64. 10: Amer Benedictine Acad. 12: Tr; "Legend of Blessed Agnes ofbohemia" (63); "Saint Procopius" (64); "Historical Documents of Ancient Bohemia"2v (64). 14: Rare bks, archives. 15: St Procopius Abbey, Lisle Il 60532.

BURG, LEON. b Newark NJ 10 S 16. 4: Gertrude Gunz. 5: Col of the City of NY 31-36 (Eng, Physics, Math) BS; UMich 63-67 MLS. 7: Inspr Engr Equipt US Navy Bur Ordnance, Centerline Mich 42-47; Engnr info spec Dev & Engnr Dept Eng Data & Records Br, Detroit Arsenal 48-62; Tech Reports libn Research & Eng Dir STINFO & Tech Data Co-Ord Br, Army Tank-Automotive Center 63-67; Tech info specialist Research Lib Vehicular & Components Labs Dir 67-. 8: Engnr Change Coord, Final Dr Task Force 53-55; Detroit Arsenal Rep, Enr Forms Com, Ordn Engnr & Drafting Manual 54-58; Instr of Contractor Personnel, Engnr Data & Records Systems 52-62; ASTIA & DDC Liaison Rep, Res & Engnr Directorate ATAC 63-. 9: SLA (Host repr Mil Libns Div 1970 Detroit Conf); ASIS. 10: Boy Scouts. 14: Sci & tech info retrieval, res & devel documentation. 15: 204 Worcester pl,Detroit Mi 48203.

BURGAN, JOHN SYDNEY. b Baltimore 25 S 30. 5: Johns Hopkins U 48-51; 54-56 (Hist) AB; Rutgers 58-59 MLS. 6: Fr, Ger, Chinese. 7: Sr libn Linden Pub Lib, Linden NJ 59-61, Prin libn 62; Adult spec Catonsville Area Lib Baltimore Co Pub Lib, Towson Md 62; Enoch Pratt Free Lib, Baltimore: Admin asst Herring Run Br 63, Admin asst to asst dir 63-65, Head co serv dept 65-67, Chief ext div 67-. 9: ALA-RSD (Md affil chm 67-68); MDLA (treas 65-69,1st v-pres-elect 69-70). 14: Ref, ext serv, admin. 15: 5106 Underwood rd, Baltimore Md 21212.

BURGARELLA, MARY M. b Gloucester Mass 27 Je 23. 5: Salem State Col 41-45 BS in Ed; Simmons 45-46 BS in LS. 7: Asst catlg libn Penn StateU 46-51; Hd catlgr Greenwich (Conn) Lib 51-53; Spec serv libn US Army, Japan 53-55; Base libn USAF, Philippines 56; Chief libn USAF, Hawaii 56-59; Hd tech serv Robbins Lib, Arlington Mass 59-60; Pub lib consul Conn State Dept Educ, Hartford Conn 60-65; Sr supv lib devl Mass Bur of Lib Ext, Boston 65-. 9: ALA; MassLA; NELA. 15: 54 Beach rd, Gloucester Ma 01930.

BURGESON, CLAIR D JR. b Jamestown NY 28 Jl 29. 4: Joyce Carlberg. 5: SUNY (Albany) 58-61 (Eng) AB; Columbia 62-65 (LS) MS. 6: Ger. 7: Personnel clerk, lib clerk US Army, US, Korea 55-58; Libn 6-9 Bd of Cooperative Educ Serv, Vahalla NY 61-62; Libn K-9 Union Sch Dist #7, Harrison, E White Plains NY 62-63; Libn White Plains High Sch, White Plains NY 63-66; Dir of libs Ramapo Sch Dist #1, Suffern NY. 9: NEA; NY State Tchrsassn; NYLA; WestchesterLA; Sch Libns So NY (sec-treas); Rockland Co SchLA (pres 69). 10: Cub Scouts. 14: Sch libs, child lit. 15: 35 Laurel rd, Sloatsburg NY 10974.

BURGESS, CAROLINE M. b Marblehead Mass 17 Ag 11. 7: Lib Staff Bd of Governors of the Federal Reserve System, Wash DC 35-57, Chief libn 56-57; Cosmos Club, Wash DC Libn 58-. 9: SLA. 14: Ref. 15: 2301 Connecticut ave, Wash DC 20008.

BURGESS, DEAN. b Buffalo NY 27 Mr 37. 4: Marguerite Barco Burgess. 5: Kenyon Col 54-58 (Eng) AB; UNC 64-65 MS in LS. 6: Sp. 7: Pilgrim Prod (co mgr), NYC 58-60; Lib asst (acquis) Hughes Lib (Old Dominion Col) 60-63; Ref asst Portsmouth Pub Lib, Portsmouth Va 63-65, Ref libn 65-66, Asst city libn 67-. 9: ALA; SELA; VaLA (mem Activities Com 67-). 10: Torch (bd of dir); Norfolk Little Theatre (bd of dir). 11: Paul Newman Award. 13: Yes. 14: Admin. 15: 601 Court st, Portsmouth Va 23704.

BURGESS, ELEANOR S(AUNDERS). b Clinton Mass 27 N 09. 5: Wheaton Col (Norton Mass) 27-31 (Eng Lit) AB; UWis 35-36 Certif in LS; UMich 59 MA in LS. 7: Asst in child dept Providence Pub Lib 31-35; Child libn glen Ellyn Pub Lib, Glen Ellyn Ill 36-38; Child libn & asst libn Lyndhurst Pub Lib, Lyndhurst NJ 38-40; Prof wrker Girl Scouts of Amer, Kalamazoo, Portland Me 40-45; Br child libn Providence Pub Lib 45-46; Coordinator child wk Scranton Pub Lib, Scranton Penn 46-48; Chief child dept Grand Rapids Pub Lib, Grand Rapids Mich 48-. 9: ALA (Child Serv Div); Womens Nat Bk Assn; Delta Kappa Gamma; MichLA (Pub Lib Div Child R T) (off & var coms). 10: Grand Rapids Libns Club; Beta Phi Mu; Phi Kappa Phi; Grand Rapids Assn for Childhood Educ; Central Volunteer Serv Bd. 13: Yes. 14: Child bks, hist, rare bks. 15: Grand Rapids Pub Lib, 111 Lib st NE, Grand Rapids Mi 49502.

BURGESS, EMILY EATON. b Rock Island Ill 9 F 11. 5: Augustana Col Rock Island Ill 29-33, 46 (Chem) BA; UIowa 34-35; UVt summer 47; Pratt 50-51 MLS. 6: Fr. 7: Advertising "Daily Times," Davenport Iowa 37-43; Yeoman 2/c WAVES 43-45; Soc ed "Daily Times," Davenport Iowa 46-47; Tchr Rock Island Sch Bd, Rock Island Ill 47-50; Head Sci & Engnr Lib Pratt Inst 51-53; Ref libn Augustana Col(Rock Island Ill) 53-. 9: IllLA. 10: AAUP; Beta Phi Mu. 14: Ref. 15: 2414 20th ave, Rock Island Il 61202.

BURGESS, RHODA MILDRED. b San Antonio Tex 8 O 5: UTex 44-48 (Span) BA; UNC 48-49 BSLS. 6: Sp, Fr. 7: Lib asst UArk 49-52; Br asst Tacoma Pub Lib, Tacoma Wash 52-53; Period libn So Methodist U 53-54; Sr lib asst UArk(Little Rock) 54-62; Sr lib asst UArk (Fayetteville) 62-. 9: ALA; ArkLA; SWLA. 10: LWV. 14: Ref. 15: 609 Storer, Fayetteville Ar 72701.

BURGESS, ROBERT S(TONE). b Pulaski Tenn 22 N 17. 4: Jean Hamilton. 5: Vanderbilt 34-38 (Math) AB; Peabody 38-39 BS in LS; Chicago 41-42, 46-47 (LS) MA; Grad Sch of Pub Affairs SUNY (Albany) 64-65. 6: Sp. 7: Sci libn Stephens Col 39-41; Asst libn UCol Northwestern U 41-42; Libn Shimer Col 42-43; Libn Talladega Col 43-48; Chm Dept of Libnship NY State Col for Tchrs (Alba ny) 48-59; Spec in lib development & Visiting Prof Dept of Lib Sci, Yonsei U, Seoul Korea 59-61; Prof Sch of Lib Sci SUNY (Albany) 61-. 8: Lib consul to University City Mo sch system Mr 66; Consul on Lib Educ, UPuerto Rico 66; Consul & surveyor SUNY Indonesian Project in Tchr Educ (founded by F ord Foundn) summer 67. 9: ALA; NYLA; Hudson-MohawkLA; KoreanLA (Hon mem); Assoc de Bibliotecarios de Puerto Rico. 10: AAUP; Phi Beta Kappa; Torch Club; Sigma Delta Pi; Kappa Delta Pi. 12: Ed "The Classified Catalog" (Seoul, Korea 60). 13: Yes. 14: Lib sch tchg, polit & soc aspects of libnship, info retrieval. 15: Sch of Lib Sci SUNY, Albany NY 12203.

BURGESS, RUTH C. b Syracuse NY 20 Ag 12. 4: Robert S Burgess. 5: Wellesley Col 30-34 (Hist) AB; Drexel summer 35 (LS); Simmons summer 36 (LS) RI Col summer 68. 6: Fr, Ger. 7: Libn Ellis Sch, Newton Square Penn 35-36, Libn & tchr 36-37; Sec Temple U 37-39; Eng tchr to refugees Amer Friends Serv Com, West Branch Iowa 39-40; Libn Health & Welfare Assn Lib, Pittsburgh 57-64; Asst in art & music dept Providence Pub Lib 65-67; Libn M V Quirk Jr High Sch, Warren RI 67-. 8: Adv Coun for Island Int Lib System; Consul on lib serv to Pittsburgh Reg Planning Assn. 9: SLA-Pittsburgh Chap (Program Com). 10: Women's Internat Leaguefor Peace & Freedom; Bd mem Providence Shelter & Bannister House. 14: Ref, organ,sch libs. 15: 117 Maple rd, Warren RI 02885.

BURGESS, WILLIAM E. b Ashland Ky 20 N 29. 5: UPittsburgh 48-53 (Geog) BA; Columbia 64-66 (Lib serv) MS. 6: Fr. 7: USAF 1/Lt PhotoIntelligence Off 53-56; Eng Sperry Rand Corp, NY 56-61; Sr scientist Raytheon Corp, NY 61-64; Sr engr Sperry Rand Corp, NY 64-66; Syst analyst Autonetics N Amer Rockwell, Anaheim Cal 66-68; Project mgr CCM Info Sci Inc, NY 69-. 8: Chm ERIC Adv Task Gp on Descrip Catlg; Mem ERIC Adv Task Gp on Indexing & Abstracting. 9: ALA; SLA; ASIS; LARC (Cal). 11: Beta Phi Mu. 12: Chief ed "Current Index to Journals in Education". 14: Lib automation, catlg, publ. 15: 7910 34th ave, Jackson Heights NY 11372.

BURGHARDT, JAMES H. b Pittsfield Mass 8 D 23. 4: Helen I Hill. 5: Williams Col 46-48 (Pol Econ) BA; Columbia 49-50 MSLS. 7: Lib asst ref dept NY Pub Lib 50-55; Head soc sci & sci Lib Assn of Portland 55-62; Asst libn Bonneville Power Admin, Portland Ore 62-64; Asst libn Lib Assn of Portland, Portland ore 64-. 9: ALA; PNLA; OreLA. 15: 801 SW 10th ave, Portland Or 97205.

BURGHARDT, RUSSELL G. b Great Barrington Mass 27 Jl 15. 4: B Great Barrington Mass 27 15. 5: Johns Hopkins 34-38 (Lat) BA, 38-41 (Lat); Columbia 46-47 (LS) BS, 48-50 (LS). 6: Fr, Ger, Greek, Ital, Lat. 7: Stud asst Johns Hopkins U Lib 34-37; City col Lib (NYC): Catlgr 47-51, Asst chief catlgr 51-62, Head ser div 62-. 9: ALA. 10: Phi Beta Kappa. 14: Ser, acquis, catlg. 15: 125 Sheldon st, Wyckoff NJ 07481.

BURGOYNE, LILA (PETERS). b Perry Utah 17 O 10. 4: Irvin C Burgoyne. 5: Weber Col 28-30 (Elem ed) AA; Utah State U 31-33 (Speech) BS; UIda summer 33; UUtah 51 (LS) Utah certif. 7: Tchr Perry Elem Sch, Perry Utah 30-31; Tchr Madison High Sch, Rexburg Ida 33-35; Libn Onequa & Longfellow Schs, Salt Lake City 51-59; Libn Roosevelt Jr High Sch, Salt Lake City 59-. 8: Mem of the UEA Spec Com on Dues and Services, Salt Lake City Utah 60-61; Mem of the Supert of Salt Lake City Schs Adv Coun 58-61. 9: ALA; NEA; Salt Lake LA; UtahLA (pres); MPLA; Salt Lake TA (pres). 10: Delta Kappa Gamma; Theta Alpha Phi; Women's Legis Coun of Utah (six yrs). 12: "THE Family of Jeppa Hanson Jeppson (68). 14: Child & ya. 15: 1371 Browning ave, Salt Lake City Ut 84105.

BURGUNDER, BERNARD F JR. b Wilkes-Barre Penn 3 My 29. 5: Cornell U 47-50 (Econ) AB, 50-52 (Finance) MBA; Columbia 63-64 MLS. 6: Fr. 7: US Air Force Procurement (1st Lt) 52-53; Manufacturers-Hanover Trust Co, NYC 54-56; Salesman Manzo Realty Co, NYC 46-63; Ref libn Pratt Inst 64; Asst libn NYU Dental Col 64-. Libn S High Sch, Valley Stream NY 66-. 14: Ref; Cat. 15: One Grove ct, New York NY 10014.

BURHANS, BARBARA CARROLL. b Morristown Tenn 9 N 27. 5: George Washington U 45-48 (Eng Lit) BA; Catholic U 49-51 MS in LS UMd (Col Pk) 48-49 (Lit); Columbia 63 (LS). 6: Fr, Ger. 7: Circ asst Alexandria Lib, Alexandria Va 49-51; Jr ref libn UWVa Lib 51-54; Ref libn Gen Ref Div Cleveland Pub Lib 54-55; Catlg libnNLM, Bethesda Md 55-. 9: ALA; MedLA; SLA. 14: Catlg, ref, med libnship, info sci. 15: Apt 910-5480 Wisconsin ave, Chevy Chase MD 20015.

BURHANS, CYNTHIA CONSTANCE. b Morristown Tenn 12 O 30. 5: George Washington U 48-51; UWis 51-52 (Eng) BS; UMich 56-57 (LS) MA. 67; Ref Div of Chronic Diseases Programs PHS 67-. 09: ALA; SELA; DCLA; VaLA; MedLA. 7: Elem tchr Fairfax Co Va, Ft Belvoir Va 52-54; Typist-indexer Nat Geographic, Wash DC 54-56; Ser checker UMich 56-57; Assthumanities libn UGa 57-61; Catlgr Smithsonian Inst, Wash DC 61-62; Ref & catlg LC 62-65; Ref Pentagon, Wash DC 65-67; Ref Divof Chronic Diseases Programs PHS 67-. 9: ALA; SELA; DCLA; MedLA. 10: AAUP. 14: Ref. 15: 1806 Orchard st, Alexandria Va 22302.

BURINSKI, (BURNS) WALTER WARREN. b Grand Rapids Mich 3 Mr 39. 5: St Joseph's Sem Grand Rapids Mich 56-58; Athenaeum of Ohio 58-60 (Philos) AB; St John's Sem (Plymouth Mich) 60-63 (Theol); UMich 65 AMLS. 6: Lat, Fr, Sp, Hebrew, Gk. 7: Lib asst Grand Valley State Col 62, 64; Head stud libn St John's Prov Sem (Plymouth Mich) 61, 63; Ref libn Mich State U Lib 65-, Interlib loan libn 66-. 9: ALA; MichLA. 10: MichStateU Lib Staff Assn. 14: Ref, acquis, admin, interlib coop. 15: Mich State Univ Lib, E Lansing Mi 48823.

BURK, SALLY (McKEEN). b Rutherford NJ 23 Jl 12. 4: Joseph Caden Burk. 5: Doug lass 31-35 (LS) BA; Rutgers 58 MLS. 7: Child libn Princeton Pub Lib, Princeton NJ 36-40; Asst libn Rutherford Pub Lib, Rutherford NJ 48-50; Ref libn Paterson State Col 50-. 9: NJLA (Col & Ref sect, Hist & Bibliog sect); SLA. 10: Paterson State Fac Assn. 14: Archives. 15: Paterson State Col Lib, 300 Pompton rd, Wayne NJ 07473.

BURKE, ANNA FRANCES. b West Burke Vt. 5: Conn Col for Women 30-34 AB; Drexel 45 BS in LS. 7: Lib coordinator St Johnbury Athenaeum St J Acad St Johnsbury Vt 39-42; Libn Overbrook Sch fpr the Blind, Phila 42-45; Libn Dwight Morrow High Sch, Englewood NJ 45-51; Libn Cornell Med Col, NYC 52-63; Acquis libn Clendening Med Lib U Kan 64-66; Assoc libn Lib of Med Sci UNM 66-68; Assoc libn Med Research Lib SUNY downstate Brooklyn 68-. 9: MedLA. 10: LWV; Amer Assoc for UN. 15: Medical Research Lib, 450 Clarkson ave, Brooklyn NY 11203.

BURKE, ELEANOR. b Chicago 12 O 12. 5: Smith 30-34 (Fr) BA; Sorbonne 32-33 (Fr) Certif; Columbia 34-35 (LS) BS. 6: Fr. 7: Apprentice Joint Ref Lib, Chicago 35-36; President's Commsn on Govt Reorgan, Wash DC 36; Asst Pub Lib, Evanston Ill 36-40; ALA 40-44; US Navy Women's Auxiliary Lt(jg) 44-46; UCal Head of loan dept (Berkeley) 46-50; Sch Lib Supv Dist 108, Highland Park Ill 51-68. 8: Bd of Dirs Glencoe Pub Lib Glencoe Ill 61-67 (pres 65-67). 9: ALA; IllLA; IllEA. 15: 207Beach rd, Glencoe Il 60022.

BURKE, JOHN EMMETT. b Chicago 22 Ag 08. 4: Lois Evelyn Perkins. 5: DePaul U 26-30 (Eng) AB, 30-31 (Biol) BS, 35-36 (Eng) AM; Chicago 45-47 BS in LS; U Denver 56-57 (Lib Admin) EdD. 6: Fr. 7: Asst prin tchr of Eng High Sch, Evanston Ill 30-36; Dean of Men, asst libn St Mary's Col(Winona Minn) 36-40; Head Libn Christian Bros Col 43-49; Head Libn & Asst Prof of Lib Sci Peabody Col 49-53; Dir Lib Serv & Prof of Lib Sci E Tex State U 53-. 9: ALA-ACRL; Amer Assn Col Tchrs Educ; NEA; SWLA; TexLA; Tex State Tchrs Assn; Tex Assn Col Tchrs. 12: "School Librarian at Work" (54); "Guideposts to Improved Library Service" (58); "Planning the Modern Functional College Library" (61); "Specifications Covering Furniture and Equipment for the Library" (63); "The Rising Tide: Research Libraries" (65). 13: Yes. 14: Univ lib admin, tchg lib sci. 15: 1201 Earl st, Commerce Tx 75428.

BURKE, REDMOND A(MBROSE). b Missouri Valley Iowa 4 Ag 14. 5: UIll 32-36 (Eng) AB, 36-38 (Eng) AM; Catholic U 42-44 BSLS; Chicago 44-48 (LS) PhD. 6: Ger, Fr, Lat. 7: Assoc Prof Eng & asst libn Dowling Col 39-44; Assoc Prof Lib Sci & philos Rosary Col 44-51; Dir of Libs DePaul U 48-67; Assoc dir Catholic U Press 67-. 8: Ordained priest Roman Cath Church 39; Educ consul on univ libs Educ Br US Mil Govt in Germany 49 & 51; Auxiliary chaplain US Army, Austria & Germany 51. 9: ALA; Chicago Assn of Law Libs (pres 54-55); CathLA (Exec Coun 61-); IllLA. 10: Grolier Club; Century Club; CaxtonClub; Arts Club of Chicago; Univ Club (Chicago) (Lib Com 64-). 11: Fellow, Royal Soc of Lit. 12: "What is theIndex" (52); "Culture and Communication Through the Ages" (52); Assoc ed "Catholicbooklist" (53-); Ed "Workshop on Law Library Problems" (53); "Buecher und Zeitung(53); Ed bd "Fathers of Church" (67-). 13: Yes. 14: Rare bks, mss, bibliog hist, lit. 15: Catholic Univ of Am Press, 620 Mich ave NE, Wash DC 20017.

BURKE, RITA M (FARRELL). b Carbondale Penn 13 Ja 17. 4: Thomas J Burke. 5: Marywood Col 59-63 (Eng) BS in Ed, 63-64 MS in LS. 7: Tchr Eldred Central Sch, Eldred NY 63; Consul St Joseph's Hosp Sch of Nursing, Carbondale Penn 63-64, Libn 64-. 9: ALA; CathLA; MedLA; NoEPennLA. 10: Natl dir Nat Coun of Cath Women; Lackawanna United Fund; Muscular Dystrophy Assn; Diocesan Cath Women; Consul-advis Pa Church Women United Exec Bd. 14: Med libnship, ref. 15: St Joseph S Hosp Sch of Nurs, Carbondale Pa 18407.

BURKETT, CHERRELL (CREEL). b Morris Ala 8 O 28. 4: William E Burkett. 5: Samford U 59-62 (Sci) BS; UAla 64-66 (Sch Libnship) MA. 7: Clk typist City of Memphis, Memphis Tenn 49-51; Jefferson Co, Birmingham Ala Sci tchr 62-65, Libn 65-. 9: ALA; NEA; SELA; AlaLA; AlaSchLA; AlaEA. 10: Kappa Delta Phi. 14: Catlg. 15: Rte 1 Box 112 B, Morris Al 35116.

BURKETT, RICHARD SOUTHERN. b Sunderland England 21 Ap 16. 4: Kathleen Mary (Shaw). 5: St John's Col UCambridge 35-39 Hist Tripos Part I, Law Tripos Part II, 38 BA, 49 MA; Univ Vol ULondon 49 Diploma of Libnship. 6: Fr, Ger. 7: British Army; Intelligence Corps (field security) 40-41, Royal Army Pay Corps (Capt & Paymaster) 41-47, serv in England, Algeria, Italy, Yugoslavia MacClean's mission to Tito 44-45; Asst libn Univ Col, London 48-52; Asst libn UGhana 52-56; Libn Fourah Bay Col (Univ Col of Sierra Leone) 56-61; Libn UIfe, West Nigeria 61-65; Libn Charterhouse 65-67; Hd readers serv div ULethbridge Lib 67-. 8: Sierra Leome Lib Bd 59-61; Nigerian Educ Lib Adv Com 61-65; Univ of Ife Lib Adv Panel 61; Nigerian Univ Law Seminar; Iniv of Ife 65. 9: Can Assn Univ Tchr Univ of Ife Lib Adv Panel 61; Nigerian Univ Law Seminar; Univ of Ife 65. 10: ULethbridge Fac Assn. 13: Yes. 14: Rare bks, govt docs, period. 15: 1269 - 4th ave S, Lethbridge Alberta Can.

BURKEY, BARBARA ANN. b Pittsburgh 9 D 42. 5: Wilson Col 60-64 (Lat) AB; Columbia 64-65 MS in LS. 6: Fr, Lat. 7: Lib aide Paoli Area High Sch System, Berwyn Penn summer 62, 63; Ref libn LC (GR&B) summer 65, Recruit 65-66, Ref libn local hist& geneal rm 66-67; Sr ref libn Thomas Jefferson rm 67-. 9: ALA. 10: Phi Beta Kappa. 14: Ref. 15: 301 G st SW, Wash DC20024.

BURKHARDT, DOLORES ANN. b Meriden Conn 28 Jl 32. 5: UConn 50-55 (Secondary Educ, Fr, Span, Eng) BA; So Conn State Col 55-60(LS) MS; Central Wash State Col summer 62; Columbia summer 64-66; UConn 67- (Media). 6: Fr, Sp. 7: Secondary sch lib tchr FarminHigh Sch, Farmington Conn 55-66; Lib tchr, Conn; N Haven High Sch, N Haven 66-67, E Farms Sch, Farmington 67-. 8: Spec consul,Conn State Dept of Educ 66-68. 9: ALA-AASchL; NEA; NESchLA (Planning Com 61-69, pres-elect & Prog chm 68-69); ConnSchLA (sec 58-60,Pub Rel dir 62-64, chm Sch Lib Devel Com 66-); ConnEA; Farmington TA. 10: AAUW; Farmington Conn Tchrs Assn. 14: The Sch Lib as aLearning Resources Media Ctr. 15: 812 Savage st, Rockwood Hills, Southington Ct 06489.

BURKHART, MARIE (WELLSTEAD). b Perrysburg Ohio 27 N 09. 5: UMich 27-31 (Eng) BA; Bowling Green State U 50-58 (Educ, LS) MA in Ed. 6: Fr. 7: Elem tchr Perrysburg Schs, Perrysburg Ohio 32-35, 45-46; Eng tchr, Journalism Holland High Sch, Holland Ohio 46-51; Tchr-libn OttawaHills High Sch, Ottawa Hills Ohio 51-62; Libn Perrysburg High Sch, Perrysburg Ohio 62-, Coord of elem libns 68-. 9: OhioASchL (sec, program chm, pres, chm spec surveycom, Scholarship Com). 10: Delta Kappa Gamma; Alpha Delta Pi; Bus & Prof Womens Club. 11: Phi Kappa Phi. 15: 707 Louisiana ave, Perrysburg Oh43551.

BURKHART, VELDA (BETTS). b Grantsville WVa 15 Jl 18. 4: Grover Wayne Burkhart. 5: Glenville State Col 35-37, 41-43 (Eng) AB; UMich summers 45-48 ABLS. 6: Ger, Fr. 7: Tchr elem schs, Calhoun Co WVa 37-42; Tchr-libn High Sch, Cairo WVa 43-46; Catlgr Ohio State U Lib 46-49; Catlgr Ohio Wesleyan U Lib 49-52; Catlgr Kenyon Col Lib 62-65; Catlgr Ohio State U Libs 65-68; Catlgr Va Polytech Inst 69-. 10: Citizens Com for Educ, Mt Vernon; Pi Lambda Theta. 14: Catlg. 15: 601 Dickerson lane, Blacksburg Va 24060.

BURKHEART, (HILDA) SUE. b Murfreesboro Tenn 29 Je 44. 5: Middle Tenn State U 62-65 (Bus ed) BS; George Peabody Col 65-66 MLS. 7: Catlgr Columbia State Commun Col, Columbia Tenn 66-. 14: Catlg. 15: 289 Browning rd, Nashville Tn 37211.

BURKHOLDER, SISTER MARY DOROTHEA SSND. b El Paso Tex. 5: Loyola U of the South 33 (Hist) AB; Our Lady of the Lake Col 38 BSLS; St Louis U 41 (Hist) MA; UIll 61 (LS) MS. 6: Fr. 7: Libn Prof of hist Notre Dame Jr Col 36-54; Libn Notre Dame Col 54-60; Libn UDallas 61-67; Sch lib supv Archdioces of San Antonio 67-. 9: ALA; CathLA; TexLA. 10: Beta Phi Mu. 12: Ed "The Kingdom of Books." 13: Yes. 14: Ref, admin, child lit, supv. 15: Archdiocese of San Antonio School Office, 9123 Lorene lane PO Box 13190,San Antonio Tx 78213.

BURKMAN, CHARLES HOMER. b Elizabeth NJ 20 My 26. 4: Sarah-Alicia Wilt. 5: Princeton 47-52 (Eng) AB; Rutgers 58-62 MLS. 6: Lat, Fr, Ital, Ger. 7: Hospitalman US Navy 44-46; Reviewer Educ Testing Serv, Princeton NJ 54-59; Sr asst searcher Princeton U Lib 59-60, Asst ref libn 60-. 9: ALA; NJLA. 10: Friends of the Princeton Univ Lib; ACLU; NJ Hist Soc; Hunterdon Co Hist Soc; Hist Soc Princeton; Friends of the Pingry Lib. 14: Ref, bibliog. 15: 18 EProspect st, Hopewell NJ 08525.

BURKS, ALICE ANNE. b Waco Tex 4 Mr 45. 5: William Jewell Col 63-67 (Eng) BA; IndU 67-68 MLS. 7: Ext libn Thomas Jefferson Lib Syst, Jefferson City Mo 68-. 9: ALA; MoLA. 14: Ext wk. 15: 905B St Mary's blvd, Jefferson City Mo 65101.

BURMEISTER, ERWIN C. b Davenport Iowa. 4: Marie-Anne Burmeister. 5: Monmouth Col 49-52; UIll 52-53 (Hist) BS, 53-54 (LS) MS. 6: Fr. 7: Hd tech processes U of the Pacific 62-. 12: Comp "Place Names of the World" (69). 14: Catlg, ref, rare bks. 15: Univ of the Pacific, Stockton Ca 95204.

BURMEISTER, FLORENCE ESTELLE. b Cleveland 17 Ap 29. 5: Flora Stone Mather Col 53-56 (Psych) AB; West Res 57-58 MSLS. 7: Cleveland Pub Lib, Lib aide 48-55, Asst child libn E 131 st br 56-57, Child libn Miles Park br 58-60, Child libn Fleet br 60-61;Child Bks Reviewer "Booklist and Subscription Books" Bulletin, Chicago 62-63; Head yp & child dept Skokie Pub Lib, Skokie Ill 63-, LectrDept of LS Rosary Col 67-. 8: Chm Child Lib Activities Wkshop, Ill Bur Oak Lib System 68 & 69; Chm Child & Pub Relations in Libs Wkshop; Ill North Suburban LibSystem 69, Ill DuPage Lib System 69-. 9: ALA-CSD (Chm Elections Com 65); mem Newbery-Caldecott Awards Com 69-70); ALA-RTSD (Mem Child Catlg Com 68-69); AALS; IllLA (Chm Child Libns Div 66-67, Mem Dues Structure Com 67, del to Ill Commsn on Child 67-68); Lib Admin Coun NoIll (pres Child Serv Sect 64-66, chm Child Ref Materials Wkshop 69); Chicago Lib Club; Child Reading R T of Chicago (Mem Child Reading R T Award Com 68, chm Pub Com 68-69). 10: Case West Res Sch of Lib Sci Alumni Assn; Beta Phi Mu. 13: Yes. 14: Lib serv for child & ya, sch libs, ref, lib educ. 15: 201 E Walton st, Chicago Il 60611.

BURNDORFER, HANS. b Austria. 4: Sheila (Gow) Burndorfer. 5: UBC 59-63 (Hist) BA, 63-64 BLS. 6: Ger. 7: Libn America House, Vienna 50-57; Lib asst Pub Lib, Vancouver BC 57-63; Libn UBC 64-. 9: ALA; CanLA; BCLA. 13: Yes. 14: Bibliog, mus lbnship. 15: Univ of British Columbia, Vancouver BC Can.

BURNESS, JEAN F. b Toronto 17 Ap 27. 5: Toronto 44-47 BA, 47-48 BLS. 6: Fr. 7: Ref libn Toronto Pub Lib 48-54; Bkmob libn Cape Breton Reg Lib, Sydney NS 54-55; Ref libn McLaughlin Pub Lib, Oshawa Ont 55-56; Spec libn Prudential Insurance Co Can Head Off, Toronto 56-57; Chief libn, spec libn Ontario Dept of Health, Toronto 57-. 9: CanLA (chm 65 conf pub com); MedLA; SLA; Bibl Soc Can; Inst Prof Libns Ont(sec-treas 60-62, pres 62-63). 10: Amer Assn of Museums; Canadian Museums Assn;Stephen Leacock Assocs. 12: Ed Inst Prof Libns Ont "Newsletter" (59-60). 13: Yes. 14: Spec libs, ref. 15: 87Riverdale ave, Toronto 279 Ont Can.

BURNETT, ANNE. b Richmond Cal 21 Jl 11. 5: Stanford 28-32 (Soc Sci, Journalism) AB. 7: Asst libn Pacific Gas & Electric Co, San Francisco 33-43; Libn San Francisco Bay Region Div Inst of Pacific Rel, San Francisco 44-47; Libn World Affairs Coun of No Cal, San Francisco 47-52; Asst libn Pacific Gas & Electric Co, San Francisco 53-57, Libn 58-. 9: SLA. 15: 245 Market st, San Francisco Ca 94106.

BURNETT, DONALD EWING. b Anna Ill 2 F 38. 5: So Ill 57-59 (Soc Sci); Murray State Col 59-63 (Soc Sci) BS, 63-65 (LS), 68 (Educ & LS) MA. 7: Recreation dir Peoria Park Bd, Peoria Ill 63-65; US Army Infantry 685th Trans Co, Peoria Ill; Reserve's Sgt, Ft Leonard Wood Mo 60-65; Libn Peoria Pub Schs, Peoria Ill 63-66; Libn Anna dist 37, Anna Ill 66-69. 9: ALA;IllASchL (loc arr chm 1965 conv); Ill Valley LA (sec-treas 65-66); IllEA (Del 66-69);Union Co Assoc Ed (Leg chm 68-72). 10: Tau Kappa Epsilon; Kappa Delta Pi. 14: Ref. 15: 702 N Main st, Anna Il 62906.

BURNETT, PHILIP M(ASON). b Peterborough NH 4 Je 08. 4: Esther Pelton. 5: Yale 26-30 (Hist) BA; Harvard 31 (Hist); Columbia 31-33 (Hist) MA, 40 PhD; UCLA 63-64 MLS. 6: Fr, Sp, Ger. 7: Research asst Carnegie Endowment for Internat Peace NY 33-39; Hist instr City Col(NY) 41; Hist instr Bennett Jr Col 41-42; Various positions in research, in internat orgs coordination US Dept of State, Wash DC 42-56; Personnel work Wash DC then chief of econ sects in Asuncion Paraguay & San Salvador El Salvador as member of US Foreign Serv 56-63; Libn for econ & govt Ind U Lib 64-66; Dir libs UWis (Parkside) 67-. 8: KenoshaLA (pres 68-69). 10: Beta Phi Mu. 12: "Reparation at the Paris Peace Conference" 2v (40). 13: Yes. 14: Ref, acquis, soc sci,lib admin. 15: Lib Univ of Wis-Parkside, Kenosha Wi 53140.

BURNETT, RUTH (PITKIN). b Coventry Conn 23 My 19. 4: Richard W Burnett. 5: Simmons 37-41 (LS) BS. 6: Fr, Ger. 7: Asst Boston Pub Lib W Roxbury Br 34-41; Asst Simmons Col Lib 37-41; Asst to Prof of Catlg Simmons Col Sch of Lib Sci 41-42; Libn Sch of Lib Sci 42-43; Libn Maria Mitchell Assn Lib, Nantucket Mass summers 41, 42; Asst in bus sci & ind depts Providence Pub Lib 43-45 & summer 49; Libn New England Electric System Lib, Boston 46; Asst libn State U Col Oneonta NY 62-. 9: NYLA; ALA. 14: Ref, acquis. 15: RD 2, Oneonta NY 13820.

BURNHAM, JEAN (WILLARD). b Waltham Mass 21 Ag 05. 4: William Burnham. 5: Simmons 23-27 (Lib) BS. 7: Catlgr Hispanic Soc of Amer, NYC 27-34; Descr catlgr Yale Divinity Sch, 57-62; Hd catlgr NY Soc Lib, NYC 63-. 9: ALA; SLA. 10: Guild of Bkworkers. 14: Rare bk catlg; bk restor & preserv. 15: New York Society Lib 53 E 79th st, New York NY 10021.

BURNHAM, JOHN P. b Framingham Mass 18 Je 35. 4: Rebecca Dow. 5: UMe 53-57 (Hist, Govt) BA; Clark U 57-58 (Hist) AM; Simmons 62-63 (LS) MS. 7: US Army Reserve (Signal Corps) PFC 58-59; Bkmob libn Me StateLib 59-62; Ref libn & archivist UMe (Orono) 63-67; Hd libn Farmington State Col (Me)67-. 8: Tchg lib sci courses Univ of Me 66-. 9: ALA; MeLA; NeLA. 10: AAUP; Phi Beta Kappa; Phi Kappa Phi; Me Hist Soc. 12: Ed, MeLA "Bulletin" 66-; Indexer, "Down East Magazine" v1-11 (65). 14: Ref,Me imprints & mss, Mosher imprints, admin. 15: 115 Main st, Farmington Me 14938.

BURNIE, VALERIE (ANITRA EMILY). b Charlotte NC 10 Ap 41. 5: Queens Col (Charlotte NC) 59-63 (Mus) B Mus; UNC (Chapel Hill) 63-64 (Music); Memphis StateU 64-65 (Music) MA; Fla StateU 66-67 MSLS. 6: Fr. 7: Mus libn Converse Col 67-. 9: MusLA; SCLA; SELA. 14: Catlg, ref. 15: Converse College, Spartanburg SC 29301.

BURNS, ALICE H. b Luray Va 25 Ja 33. 4: James Pat Burns. 5: Wittenberg U (Educ) BS 64-65 (Guidance, Counseling); UDenver68 MA Libnship. 6: Sp. 7: Psychometrist UNM 1954; Ref asst, Asst dept head of Ref Dept Warder Pub Lib, Springfield Ohio 59-; Libn WestHigh Sch, Denver Colorado 68-. 9: OhioLA; ColoLA; ColoSchLA; Colo A-V Assn; ALA (chm Denver High Sch Libns 69). 10: Alpha Delta Pi;YWCA Swim Club; Book Club; Friends of the Mountain Libs (v-pres); Beta Phi Mu; US Ski Assn. 14: Ref. 15: PO Box 987, Evergreen Co80439.

BURNS, MRS ANNA (CANNADAY).)(: NYLA; ALA. b Memphis Tenn 13 D 24. 4: Edmond B Burns. 5: Sophie Newcomb 42-43; LSU 43-45 (Hist) BA, 45-46 BS in LS Northwest State Col (History) 66-67 MA. 7: Parish libn Madison Parish Lib, Tallulah La 46-47; Catlgr La State Lib 47-48; Libn Oberlin High Sch, Oberlin La 55; Asst libn & Asst Prof LSU(Alexandria) 60-. 9: ALA; LaLA; SWLA; La Hist Assn; Central La Hist Soc (sec). 10: Lutheran Womens Missionary League (pres La Dist); AAUW; Delta Kappa Gamma; Phi Alpha Theta. 11: Delta Kappa Gamma Scholarship Award 66, 67. 12: "A History of the Louisiana Forestry Commission" (68); Index to Forests and People Magazine. 13: Yes. 14: Catlg tchg bks & libs, free-lance indexing. 15: 5014 Chestnut dr, Alexandria La 71301.

BURNS, CAROL JOYCE. b Seattle Wash 12 F 34. 5: Chouinard Art Inst 54-57 (Costume design) BFA; (UWash) 53-54, 58 (Gen studies) BA, 59 M of Libnship. 7: Libn circ div UWash Lib 59-64; Lib Assoc of Portland, Portland Ore: Libn lit & hist dept 64-65, Hd art dept 66-. 9: ALA; PNLA; OreLA. 10: Portland Art Assn. 14: Ref, art bks. 15: 901 SW King st, Portland Or 97205.

BURNS, DOROTHY ELIZABETH (HAMM). b Herkimer NY 24 S 12. 4: Robert Louis Burns. 5: SUNY(Albany) 28-30, 31-32 (Eng); West Ill U summers 53-56 (Eng) BS in Ed; UIll summers 58, 60-62 (LS) MS. 7: Elem tchr Van Hornesville Central Sch, Van Hornesville NY 32-35; Elem tchr Raleigh Co Schs, Beckley WVa 43-44; Elem tchr Lewistown Grade Schs, Lewistown Ill 53-56; Elem tchr Central, Kelvin Grove Schs, Lockport Ill 56-57; Libn Wilmington High Sch, Wilmington Ill 57-62; Libn Joliet Twp High Sch, Joliet Ill 62-64; Asst libn Joliet Jr Col 64-66; Dir Central catlg Joliet Twp High Sch 66-. 9: ALA; IllLA; IllASchL. 10: AAUP; Amer Fed Tchrs; Beta Phi Mu; LWV. 14: Ref, catlg. 15: 113 Union st, Joliet Il 60433.

BURNS, HELEN MARIE. b Baltimore 15 Ag 22. 5: Col of Notre Dame of Md 44 (Eng) BA; Drexel 48 BS in LS; NYU 59 (Hist) MA, 65 (Hist) PhD. 6: Fr, Sp. 7: Price & Specification Clerk US Govt Printing Off, Wash DC 45-46; Lib asst Documents Lib Govt Printing Off, Wash DC 46-47; Jr libn Midwood br Brooklyn Pub Lib 48-49; Libn Md State Planning Commsn, Baltimore 49-53; Asst law libn Legal Lib Fed Res Bank, NYC 53-57, Law libn 57-66, Chief Law Lib Div 66-. 9: ALA; SLA; AALL; AHA; Org of Amer Histns; Econ Hist Assn; NY Hist Soc; LLA Greater NY (Bd 62-63 sec 67-). 10: Eng Speaking Union (NY Chap). 12: Contrib "Manual of Procedure for Private Law Libraries" (62). 13: Yes. 14: Lib admin, ref, info retrieval. 15: Law Lib Div Fed Reserve Bank of NY, New York NY 10045.

BURNS, JERRY K. b Long Island NY 5 D 22. 5: UMiss 43 (ASTP); Ga Sch of Tech 43-44 (ASTP); UWis 46-49 (Ed, Hist) BS, 59-64 (LS) MS, (Fr, Hist). 6: Fr, Ital. 7: USA (Inf, ASTP, & CWS) 43-46; Gisholt Mach Co 41-43, 46; Oscar Mayer, Madison Wis 51; City of Madison, Madison Wis 51-54; Sinaiko Bros Coal & Oil Co, Madison Wis 54-57; State Highway Commsn, Madison Wis 57; Gift libn UWis, 57-65; Hist libn CUNA Internat, Madison Wis 65-. 9: SLA. 14: Archivist, museum wk. 15: 811 E Gorham st, Madison Wi 53703.

BURNS, JOAN (GLORIA) (EASTMENT). b New Jersey 6 Mr 18. 4: Robert Burns. 5: Newark State Col 35-39 (Fine Arts Educ) BS; Columbia 42-45 (Arch); Rutgers MLS. 7: Art tchr Whippany Schs, Whippany NJ 39-41; Draftswoman: Bell Tele West Electirc, NYC 42-44, Time Inc (Arch Forum), NYC 44-48; Arch illustrator ColumbiaU 46-52; Newark Pub Lib, Newark NJ: Lib trainee 60-63, Sr art libn 64-69, Prin art libn 69-. 9: ALA; NJLA. 14: Ref, spec collextions, indexing. 15: 99 Vreeland ave, Nutley NJ 07110.

BURNS, JOHN A. b Baltimore 25 S 28. 4: Joan Carroll. 5: Johns Hopkins U 46-50 (Eng) BA; Columbia 54 (LS) MS. 7: Pre-prof NY Pub Lib 51-54; Admin asst Enoch Pratt Free Lib, Baltimore 54-59; Dir Ossining Pub Lib, Ossining NY 59-62; Asst dir Onondaga Lib System, Syracuse NY 62-65; Reg libn Prince George's Co Mem Lib, Hyattsville Md 65-67; Assoc dir Anne Arundel Co Pub Lib, Annapolis Md 67-. 9: ALA (Jt Com on Lib Serv to Labor Gps);-ASD; MdLA (pres 69). 13: Yes. 14: Admin. 15: 49 Bay dr, Annapolis Md 21403.

BURNS, MARIE JOSEPHINE (TINTO). b Glasgow Scotland 26 Mr 37. 4: Donald Francis Burns. 5: D'Youville Col 54-59 (Hist) BA; Genesco State Col 61-65 MLS. 6: Fr. 7: D'Youville Col: Lib tech 56-61, Libn 69-; High sch libn Buffalo Bd of Educ, Buffalo NY 62-67. 9: SLS. 10: AAUW; D'Youville Col Alum Assn. 11: Outstanding Young Women of Amer, 67. 14: High sch lib wk. 15: 188 Northwood dr, Kenmore NY 14223.

BURNS, MARJORIE (BEERS). b Verona Penn 17 N 26. 4: Frank E Burns. 5: William & Mary 44-46; Pomona 47-48 (Sociol, Psych, Eng); UMinn 48-49 (LS) BA. 7: Libn hosp & shut-in serv Cleveland Pub Lib, Ohio 49-51 Libn (child) Bkmob & sta Seattle Pub Lib 56-58, 68-. 10: Past sec Lake Hills Commun Club; Past pres Cascade Lib Bd; Past pres Maynard Hosp Aux. 14: Child wk, hosp & shut-in serv with emphasis on possibilities in retirement homes. 15: 1232 143rd ave SE, Bellevue Wa 98004.

BURNS, MARY (MEHLMAN). b Gloucester Mass 5 S 27. 4: Richard J Burns. 5: Mt St Mary Col 45-49 (Eng) AB; Boston Col 49-50 (Eng) AM; Simmons 54-66 MS. 7: Tchr Mt St Mary Sem, Nashua NH 50-52; Child libn Boston Pub Lib 52-59; Instr Hist Dept framingham State Col 62-69, Lecturer Child Lit Dept of Grad & Continuing Studies 67-, Col libn 69-. 8: Participant & research asst in Educ Through Vision Project Phillips Acad, Andover Mass summers 67 & 68; Participant Invitational Conf on Tchg of Child Lit in Col & Univ, Milwaukee 68. 9: ALA; NCTE; NE RT Child Libns; Mass State Col Assn; East Mass Child Review Bd. 10: Intl Reading Assn; Framingham Hist Soc; Mt St Mary Col Alum Assn; Museum of Fine Arts (Boston); Friends of the Symphony (Boston). 13: Yes. 14: Child lit & its significance in tchr-train curriculum. 15: 11 Joanne dr, Framingham Centre Ma 01701.

BURNS, MILDRED E(LAINE). b Grand Forks ND 9 D 05. 5: Ohio Wesleyan U 23-27 (Hist, Pol Sci) BA; UMich summers 27, 28, 30, 34; UArk summers 51-53, 37-38 (Hist) MA; E Tex State U summers 59, 61-65 MSLS. 6: Sp, Fr. 7: Elem tchr Norphlet Sch Dist, Norphlet Ark 27-31; Eng tchr Sulphur Springs High Sch, Sulphur Springs Ark 33-34; Elem tchr Pulaski Co Sch Dist, Jacksonville Ark 34-36, Fuller Sch, Sweet Home Ark 36-37; Instr hist pol sci Bible Central Wesleyan Col 38-41; Tchr hist and govt High Sch Pangborn Sch Dist, Pangborn Ark 41-42; Tchr hist and govt High Sch Hulbert-W Memphis Sch Dist, Hulbert Ark 42-47; Tchr hist & govt, Keiser High Sch, Keiser Ark 47-58, Libn 49-58; Hist & libn Burdette High Sch, Burdette Ark 58-60; Libn Greenwood High Sch, Greenwood Ark 60-. 9: NEA; ALA; AASchL; ArkEA; ArkLA. 10: Delta Kappa Gamma; Kappa Kappa Iota; Ark Coun for Soc Studies. 14: Sch lib. 15: Box 305, Greenwood Ar 72936.

BURNS, NORMA E. b Toronto Ont 15 O 24. 4: Neil Burns. 5: UToronto 43-46 (Lang) BA; UOttawa 62-65 BLS. 7: Lib clk UToronto 66-69; Libn North Electric Co R&D Labs, Ottawa Ont 65-. 9: SLA; CanLA; OttawaLA. 14: Ref, lib admin. 15: 48 Crystal Beach dr, Ottawa 14 Ont Can.

BURNS, OLLIE (HAMILTON). b Monroe La 13 Je 11. 4: Alex Andrew Burns Jr. 5: Southern U 29-31, 35, 36, 37 (Liberal Arts); Grambling Col 34, 35, 45, 46, 47 (Elem Educ) BS; Ark A&M Col 51; LSU summer 53-57 (LS) MS; UMich summer 65 (NDEA Inst). 6: Fr. 7: Elem tchr Jackson Parish Sch Bd, Jonesboro La 34-36; Ouachita Parish Sch Bd: Elem tchr, Monroe La 36-38, High sch tchr-libn, Sterlington La 47-60, Elem sch libn, Monroe La 60-. 9: NEA; ALA; LaEA (chm & pres Lib Dept 64-66). 10: Sepacivso Club. 13: Yes. 14: Wk with child, ref. 15: 2025 Adams st, Monroe La 71204.

BURNS, RICHARD KEITH. b Black Mountain Ky 9 Ja 35. 4: Frances Forgeone. 5: Morehead State Col 53-57 (Eng) BS; UIll 58-60 MSLS. 6: Fr. 7: Lib asst Morehead State Col 54-57; Ref libn Louisville(Ky) Free Pub Lib 57-58; Circ asst UIll 58-60; Asst ref libn Arlington(Va) Pub Lib 60; Dir Falls Church(Va) Pub Lib 60-. 8: Pub Lib Devel Com for Va Research Assoc, Natl Adv Commsn on Libs 68; Washington Metro Coun of Goverts, Libns Tech Com 67-. 9: ALA-FSD (chm Potomac Valley Chap 63); VaLA (chm Pub Lib Sect 64; State Exec Dir Nat Lib Week 66; Activities Com 64; Nat Lib Week Com 64); DCLA (Memb Com 64-65; Nat Lib Week Exec Dir 69; Comm on Objectives 67-); VaLA (Intell Freedom Com). 10: Rotary Club. 11: Certificate, Intl City Managers Assn, Seminar on Lib Admin. 12: Ed "Virginia Librarian" (69-); Ed "Falls Church by Fence and Fireside." 13: Yes. 14: Bk sel, admin, pub serv (adult), ref. 15: Falls Church Pub Lib 120 N Virginia ave, Falls Church Va 22046.

BURNS, ROBERT WHITEHALL JR. b St Louis 5 Jl 28. 4: Georgine Bush. 5: Emory 46-49 (Hist); UColo 49-51 (Hist) BA; UDenver 54-55 (LS) MA. 7: US Army Artillery (2nd Lt) 51-54; Head of ref Omaha Pub Lib 56-57, Br asst 55-56; Loan libn

UIda 57-59, Sci & tech libn 60-68; Libnfor research & development Colo State U 68-. 8: Ref libn, Library 21 Seattle World's Fair, 62; Lecturer UDenver Grad Lib Sch, Je-Ag 64. 9: SLA; ALA; ASIS; Soc for Bibliography of Natural Hist. 10: Beta Phi Mu. 13: Yes. 14: Ref, automation. 15: 1504 Emigh, Ft Collins Co.

BURNS, RUTH (BLAKE). b Duncan Okla 5 O 25. 4: Louis F Burns. 5: Kan State Tchrs Col 47-59 (Educ) BS Ed; Kan City U 50-55; USoCal 61-64 (LS) Sch libn Certif, 66 MSLS. 7: Radioman WAVES (Seaman 1c) 44; Libn Antioch Sch, Overland Park Kan 55-60; Asst libn Santa Ana Col 63-66; Dist elem libn Orange Unified Sch Dist, Orange Cal 66-. 8: Tchr, child lit, Santa Ana Col, 65. 9: Orange Co LA (corr sec 66); Orange Co SchLA (treas 67-68). 14: Child lit. 15: 19121 Biddle dr, Irvine Ca 92664.

BURNS, SUSAN. b Chicago Ill 30 N 42. 5: Purdue 60-64 (Soc studies) BA; UIll 65-67 MSLS. 6: Fr. 7: Catlgr US Dept of Health, Educ, & Wel, Wash DC 67-68; Libn Kanto Mura Lib, Tokyo 68-. 9: ALA. 10: Pi Delta Phi. 14: Ref. 15: 6114th Air Base sq CMR Box 3076, APO San Francisco Ca 96525.

BURNS, WILLIAM J JR. b Dubuque Iowa 13 Ap 40. 4: Patricia Anne Knight. 5: Loras Col 58-62 (Fr) BA; UMich 62-63, 65 MSLS; NoIll U summer 63, 64; Rosary Col 64 UMich 66. 6: Fr, Lat, Sp. 7: Clothing salesman Fuhrman's Clothing Store, Dubuque Iowa 57-62; Lib clerk Loras Col 58-62; Bus off & med lib St Joseph's Mercy Hosp, Dubuque Iowa summer 62; St Joseph's Mercy Hosp Med Lib, Ann Arbor Mich 62; High sch libn W Dubuque Commun High Sch, Epworth Iowa 63; Elem sch libn, Arlington Heights Ill 63-64; High sch libn Palatine High Sch, Palatine Ill 64-65; Grad asst UMich 65-66; Dir Area VIII IMC; Coordinator ESEA Title II, Dubuque Ia 66-. 9: ALA; NEA-DAVI; ISEA; AVEA Iowa (regl rep); ILA; State Hist Soc of Iowa. 10: Iowa State Title II Coms; Local Family Life Educ Com. 14: Admin, pub rel, instrl media admin. 15: 2318 Martin dr, Dubuque Ia 52001.

BURR, ELIZABETH. b Waco Tex 27 My 08. 5: Oxford Col for Women 25-27 (Eng); Cleveland Col West Res 30-31 Lib Certif; UIll 42-43 (Eng) BA. 6: Fr. 7: Child libn Lincoln Lib, Springfield Ill 31-42; Child libn Pub Lib, Champaign Ill 42-43; Head child dept Lincoln Lib, Springfield Ill 43-46; Consul child yp serv Div for Lib Serv Dept of Pub Instr, Madison Wis 46-. 8: Program chm 5th Govt Conf on Child & Youth, 57; Wis Governor's Com on Child & Youth. 9: ALA-CSD (pres 60-61, chm Newbery & Caldecott Com 60); IllLA (chm Child Sect); WisLA (Exec Bd; Child Sect). 10: Wis Hist Soc; Wis Arts Foun & Coun; Wis Coun Better Radio & TV; Wis Assn of the Amer Coun for Better Radio Broadcasts. 11: Wis Librarian of the Year, WisLA 56. 13: Yes. 14: Child libnship, state lib agency ext serv. 15: 302 S Owen dr, Madison Wi 53705.

BURR, MARY (BAUGHMAN). b Anderson Ind 11 F 11. 4: Roberts D Burr. 5: DePauw U 29-33 (Hist, Eng) BA; UWis 34-35 (LS). 6: Ger, Sp. 7: Ref libn, Sr libn dept of soc sci Pub Lib, Detroit 35-42; Asst libn High Sch-Tarrytowns, Tarrytown NY 56-64; Sr ref libn Pub Lib, White Plains NY 64-67; Hd ref dept 67-. 9: ALA; Westchester LA; NY State LA. 10: Friends of the Lib; Hist Soc of the Tarrytowns; PTA. 14: Ref. 15: 50 Sunnyside ave, Tarrytown NY 10591.

BURRELL, EUGENE HENRY. b S Bend Ind 9 My 17. 4: Bette J Krainik. 5: Ind U 35-39 (Eng) AB; Bryant & Stratton Col 39-40 Certif; UMinn 48-49 BSLS. 7: Steno-typist Nat Engnr Co, Chicago 40-41; Master Sgt US Army DEML, ETO 42-45; Gage clerk Bendix Products, S Bend Ind 47-48; Ref asst Detroit Pub Lib 49-65; Head ref dept Elkhart Pub Lib, Elkhart Ind 65-. 9: ALA; IndLA. 10: Libn Elkhart Co Hist Soc; Amer Assn State & Local Hist. 14: Ref. 15: 3406 Benham ave, Elkhart In 46514.

BURRELL, BARBARA LOIS. b Penticton BC 10 Jl 21. 4: Ray A Burrell. 5: McGill 40-43 BA; Toronto 62-63 BLS. 7: Sub prof on bkmob N York Pub Lib, Toronto 60-62; Ref libn Nat Lib, Ottawa 63-. 9: CanLA; OntLA; Inst Prof Libns Ont; Lib Assn Ottawa. 10: Prof Pub Serv Inst. 14: Ref. 15: 1210 Meadowlands dr E, Apt 2, Ottawa 5 Can.

BURRIESCI, NEVA N (HUDSON). b Ft Worth Tex 23 D 27. 4: Frank Burriesci. 5: UIll 45-49 (Tchg of Soc Studies) BS, 50-52 MS in LS. 6: Sp. 7: Tchr-libn High Sch, Crossville Ill 49-50; Libn I Detroit Pub Lib 52-54; Army libn Army Libs, Kitzingen Germany 54-55; 1st asst sci & ind dept Dallas Pub Lib 55-58, head commun living dept 59-62; Asst libn Gen Electric Co Atomic Power Div, San Jose Cal 62-64; Libn II central research Santa Clara Co(Cal) Pub Lib, San Jose Cal 64-66; Regl Libn I, Hd Cupertino Br 66-. 8: Active in pub rels when with Dallas Pub Lib (as Head of Commun Living Dept) 59-62; Speech making to various church & sch groups; Also promoted Ferguson Mem Lib on Aging and Municipal Ref making speeches and meetings. 9: ALA; CalLA; PeninsulaLA (67-68). 10: Sierra Club; Soroptimist Club; Friends of Cupertino Lib. 14: Pub libs, pub serv, ref. 15: 540 Westlake dr,San Jose Ca 95117.

BURRIS, MIRIAM BUZZELL. b Chicago 25 Jl 24. 4: Robert H Burris. 5: Bebit Col 42-43; UIll 46 (Eng) AB; Nat Col of Educ 48 (Educ) BE; UDenver 63(LS) MA. 7: Instr Eng Dept UIll(Urbana) 46-47; Elem tchr Arlington Co Schs, Arlington Va 48-50; Stewardess United Airlines 51-52; Elem libn Cherry Creek Sch Dist, Arapahoe Co Colo 63- Sub tchr Amer Dependent Schs, Yokota Japan 59-62; Honorarium instrUDenver 67-. 9: ALA; ColoASchL. 13: Yes. 14: Sch lib, child bks. 15: 536 Quentin st, Aurora Co 80011.

BURRIS, RAY EDZELL. b Aiken SC 4 S 28. 4: Leota Branch. 5: Miner Tchrs Col 46-50 (Hist) BS; Catholic U (LS). 7: Statist clerk Census Bur, Suitland Md 50-52; Clerk GAO, Wash DC 52-58; Lib asst Armed Serv Tech Info Agency, Arlington Va 58-59; Libclerk NASA Hdqrs Lib, Wash DC 59-62, Catlgr 62-65; Catlgr Food & Drug Admin Hdqrs Lib, Wash DC 65-. 9: SLA; DCLA (Hospit Com 65-66);Potomac Tech Proc Libns. 14: Catlg. 15: 104 Walnut st NW, Wash DC 20012.

BURRISS, BERTRAM MURPHY JR. b Camden NJ 20 F 33. 4: Greta (Hill) Burris. 5: E Carolina Col 54-58 (Sci) BS; Fla State U 63-64 (LS) MS. 7: US Coast Guard Radio Operator (Petty Off 2nd Class) 51-54; Tchr sci & math Morson Jr High Sch Raleigh NC 58-59; Tchr chem & biol Cocoa High Sch Rockledge Fla 59-60; Engng aid space Tech Labs Inc Cocoa Beach Fla 60, Tch libn 61-63; Tech libn Corning Glass Wks Electronics Research lab Raleigh NC 64-66, Tech info specialist Corning Glass Wks, Corning NY 66-67; Mgr tech infoserv Ampex Corp, Redwood City Cal 68-. 9: SLA; ASIS. 10: Beta Phi Mu. 14: Spec lib admin. 15: 453 N Rengstorff ave, apt 20, Mt View Ca 94040.

BURROW, MINIFRED ELIZABETH (WAUGH). b Batesville Ark 22 D 10. 5: Philander Smith 34 (Eng) AB; Langston U summer 36, 42, 44; Northwestern 53 (Educ) MA; UOkla 60 MLS. 6: Fr, Lat. 7: Tchr Eng & music Jr High Sch, Newport Ark 32-34; Tchr Eng & music High Sch, Arkadelphia Ark 34-36; Tchr Eng & music High Sch, Duncan Okla 36-37; Tchr Eng & music High Sch, Waurika Okla 37-45; Tchr Eng & music High Sch, Crescent Okla 45-47; Tchr Eng, lib & music High Sch, Tatums Okla 47-54; Asst libn Langston U 54-56; Libn Dunjee High Sch, Okla City Okla 64-. 8: Tchr of Communic Skills, Guthrie Job Corps for Women, Guthrie Okla. 9: NEA;Nat Assn Colored Women's Clubs; ALA; NCTE; OklaEA; OklaLA; Okla Educl T-V Authority. 10: YWCA; NAACP; WCTU Ministers Wives Coun; AAUW; OES; ISIS; Phi Delta Kappa;Heroines of Jericho; Golden Circle. 11: Federated Club "Woman of the Year" 65. 14: Catlg, ref. 15: 317 S Second, Guthrie Ok 73044.

BURROWS, ELIZABETH BAIRD. b Waukegon Ill 2 O 21. 4: William C Burrows. 5: N Ill State Tchrs Col 39-41; UIll 41-43 (Eng) BA; UMich 46-47 ABLS. 6: Fr. 7: Tchr Ottawa Twp High Sch, Ottata Ill 43; Commun Off US Navy 43-46; Asst libn Fed Res Bank of Cleveland 47-65; Libn Alcan Aluminum Corp Cleveland 65-. 9: SLA. 10: Kappa Delta Pi; Alpha Lambda Theta. 14: Admin. 15: Alcan Aluminum Corp, PO Box 6977, Cleveland Oh 44101.

BURROWS, MURIEL E (BROWN). b Denver Col 29 Ap 41. 4: John M Burrows. 5: Tyler Jr Col 58-60 (Eng); UOkla 60-62 (Eng, Hist, LS) BA; UDenver 62-63 MA in LS. 7: Tulsa City-Co lib sys, Tulsa Okla: Asst br libn 63-64, Br libn 64-65; Hd children's dept Tulsa Central Lib 65; Ark Lib Commsn, Little Rock: Catlg & ref 65-68, Consul children's bk sel 68-. 9: ALA (PLD, CD, YAD); ALA; -PLD; -CD; -YAD; SWLA; ArkLA. 14: Child wk. 15: 1717 Louisiana st apt 24, Little Rock Ar 72206.

BURROWS, SUZANNE. b Santa Cruz Cal 23 Ja 40. 5: San Jose State Col 57-62 (Libnship) BA, 63-68 (Libnship) MA. 7: Libn I San Jose State Col Lib 62; Libn Campolindo High Sch, Lafayette Cal 62-65; Libn John F Kennedy High Sch, Fremont Cal 65-. 9: ALA; CalASchL (Treas Nor Sect); A-V EA Cal; CalLA; CalTA. 15: 4848 Golden rd, Pleasanton Ca 94566.

BURSINGER, BESS C(ALDWELL). b Newberry SC 29 My 19. 4: George P Bursinger. 5: Winthrop Col 36-40 (Hist) AB; Peabody 44 BS in LS. 7: Libn High Sch, Nichols SC 40-41; Libn High Sch, Whitmire SC 41-44; Libn US Naval Hosp,

Portsmouth Va 44-46; Libn VA Hosp, Oteen NC 46-48; Chief Libn VA Hosp, Tomah Wis 48-. 9: ALA; MedLA. 13: Yes. 14: Hosp libs. 15: VA Hosp, Tomah Wi 54660.

BURSON, MRS PHYLLIS (SHEIDLER). b Seattle 31 Mr 14. 5: UWash 32-38 (Pol Sci) BA, 38-39 (LS) BA; UIda Col of Law 39-45 (Law). 7: Acquis clerk UWash Lib 34-39; Lib asst UIda Lib 39-40, Libn Law Lib 40-45; Asst libn Del Mar Col 51-53; Supv of adult serv La Retama Pub Lib, Corpus Christi Tex 53-56; Libn 56-. , Dir of Libs 66-. 8: Catlg instru UIda 40-41; Legal Bibliog instr UIda Col of Law 43-54; Bldg consul 3 Tex libs 66-69; conducted Pub Lib Mgt Wkshop, Tex State Lib 68; participated in study by Natl Bk Com for OEO 67. 9: ALA (Pub Libs Activities Com 67-69); TexLA (v-pres & pres-elect 69-71, mem &/or chm 7 coms 54-69, Exec Bd repres at-large 62-65); Coastal Bend Regl Planning Commsn Lib Serv & Facilities Com 68-. 10: Nueces Co Hist Survey Com; Girl Scouts; AAUW; UF sect chm. 11: Corpus Christi Woman of the Year, 63; Tex Libn of the Year 66. 13: Yes. 14: Admin. 15: La Retama Pub Lib, 505 N Mesquite st, Corpus Christi Tx 78401.

BURSTEIN, ROSE ANNE. b NYC 3 My 22. 4: Lucien Burstein. 5: Olivet Col 43 (Soc Sci) AB; Yale 48 (Soc Sci) MA; Columbia 65 MLS. 7: Econ analyst State Dept, Wash DC 44-45; Ref asst New Haven Pub Lib, New haven Conn 47-48; Lib asst Benton & Bowles Agency, NYC 49-50; Research libn William Weintraub Agency, NYC 50-52; Sci libn Sarah Lawrence Col 56-. 9: SLA; WestchesterLA. 15: 40 Flint ave, Larchmont NY 10538.

BURSTINER, ELAINE. b NYC 5 Ag 37. 5: CCNY 55-59 (Sociol) BA. 7: Libn Arthur Young & Co, NYC 59-62; Libn Sales Management "The Marketing Magazine", NYC 62-. 9: SLA. 10: Amer Jewish Com. 14: Ref. 15: 50 E End ave, New York NY 10028.

BURT, CLINTON ROBIN. b Salt Lake City 9 My 31. 4: Nancy (Nee) Becraft. 5: U Utah 48-52, 55 (Pol Sci) BS; USoCal 55-56 MS in LS. 6: Fr. 7: (Cpl) US Army AAA, Korea 52-54; Ser asst USoCal 56, Engnr libn 56-57; Tech libn Raytheon Co, Goleta Cal 57-59; Ext libn Utah StateLib 59, Asst libn legis ref 60-61; Libn AC Electronics Def Research Lab Gen Motors Corp, Goleta Cal 61-. 8: Exec dir for Utah, Nat Lib Week, 60; Consul to Kears Commun Lib Devel Com, 60. 9: BSA. 12: Ed "Utah State Libraries" (59-60). 13: Yes. 14: Admin. 15: 3210 CalleRoselas, Santa Barbara Ca 93105.

BURTCH, SOLGLAD. b Chicago 1 N 12. 5: Tufts Col 28-32 (Eng, Math) BS; Simmons 39-40 (LS) BS. 6: Fr. 7: Libn Pub Lib, Scottsville NY 42; Libn Pub Lib, Sidney NY 43-44; Child libn br libs, Providence 45; Recataloged two lib systems for Mass Div Pub Lib 46-47; Catlgr & asst to libn, Weston Mass 48-52; Catlgr, Stoneham Mass 52-. 14: Catlg. 15: 684 Lowell st, Lexington Ma 02173.

BURTIS, MRS ALYCE (RODGERS). b Charleston SC 10 My 21. 5: Syracuse 39-43 (Zool, Hist) AB; Drexel 45-46 (LS); Trenton State Col summer 46 (LS); Columbia summers 47-52 MLS; Rutgers 62-63 (LS). 7: Libn Upper Freehold High Sch Lib, Allentown NJ 45-50; Libn Flemington High SchLib, Flemington NJ 51-56; Act libn Flemington Free Pub Lib, Flemington NJ summer55; Instr Lib Sch Trenton State Col 67-; Libn Hunterdon Central High Sch Lib,Flemington NJ 56-69; Libn Zuegner Mem Lib Hunterdon Central High Sch, Flemington NJ69-. 9: NEA; ALA; NJEA; NJSchLA; NJLA; Hunterdon Co EA; Hunterdon Central TA. 10: AAUW; NJ Schoolwoman's Club. 14: Wk with youth. 15: 5 Hickory Trail, Flemington NJ 08822.

BURTNIAK, JOHN. b Ethelbert Man Can 12 F 41. 5: UOttawa 61-64 BA; Toronto 64-65 BLS, 65-69 MLS. 6: Ukrainian, Fr. 7: Catlgr Brock U Lib (St Catherines Ont Can) 65-, Hd catlg 66, Acquis libn 66-67, Admin asst to chief libn67-68, Acquis & ser libn 68-69. 9: CanLA; OntLA; Inst of Prof Libns of Ont. 10: Ont Hist Soc; Arch Conservancy of Ont; BibliogSoc of Can; Great Lakes Hist Soc; Welland Co Hist Coun; Lincoln Co Hist Coun; OntGenealogical Soc. 14: Admin, loc hist, rare bks. 15: RR 2 Barron rd, Niagara Falls Ont Can.

BURTON, ROBERT EDWARD. b Detroit Mich 16 F 27. 4: Mary Kathryn Rutten. 5: UMich 45-48 (Math) BS, 54-56 AMLS; Wayne State 48-50 (Phil). 7: Hd libn Speedway Labs union Carbide Corp, Speedway Ind 56-59; Hd libn Union Carbide Metals Co, Niagara Falls NY 59-62; Hd sci & tech libs UMich (Ann Arbor) 62-. 9: BSA; Bibliog Soc UVa. 10: Hist Soc of Mich: Great Lakes Foundation; Nat Wildlife Federation; Wilderness Soc. 13: Yes. 14: Admin, sci & tech libs. 15: Univ Lib Univ of Mich, Ann Arbor Mi 48104.

BURWASH, RUTH VIRGINIA (SOFTLEY). b Chicago 7 Ag 15. 4: Henry Edward Burwash. 5: Los Angeles Jr Col 34-35; UCLA 35-37 (Eng), summer 41 (Educ); Riverside Lib Sch 37-38. 7: Br libn A K Smiley Pub Lib, Redlands Cal 38-42; City schs libn Anaheim City Schs, Anaheim Cal 42-44; Asst libn US Naval Hosp, Seattle 44; Hosp libn US Naval Hosp, San Leandro Cal 44-46; Libn Birmingham VA Hosp, Van Nuys Cal 46-47; Head circ dept A K Smiley Pub Lib, Redlands Cal 47-50; Libn VA Hosp, Long Beach Cal 51-54; Chief libn VA Hosp, San Fernando Cal 54-61; Admin libn US Naval Air Station, Alameda Cal 61-66; Supv Libn Williams AFB, Az 66-. 9: ALA (Armed Forces Lib Sect); CalLA (presarmed Forces LIBNS Round Table 65); ArizLA. 11: Superior Quality Performance Awardas Base Libn 68. 14: Ref, org & planning. 15: 2081 E Alameda dr, Tempe Az 85281.

BURY, PETER P. b Hartford Conn 29 N 27. 4: Gertrude Thompson. 5: Boston U 44-48 (Hist) AB, 48-49 (Hist) MA; Simmons 54-55 (LS) MS. 7: 1st Lt USA (Artillery), US & Korea 50-53; Libn (staff) Detroit Pub Lib 55-58; Lib consul State of Conn, Hartford Conn 60-62, Hd libn Glenview Pub Lib, Glenview Ill 58-60, 62-. 8: Bldg Prog, Site Study & Eval of Lib Serv: Oak Lawn Ill 66; Blue Island Ill 68; Wheeling Ill 69; Site study & bldg prog for Worth Ill 67; Tinley Park Ill 68; Eval of lib serv for Council Bluffs Iowa 68. 9: ALA (chm Ill Mem Com); IllLA (treas 67, chm of NLW Ill 65); LACONI (pres 60-61). 10: No Suburban Lib System Advis Com: Rotary Club; Glenview Art League. 14: Adminis, bldg, ref. 15: 1930 Glenview rd, Glenview Il 60025.

BUSBIN, O MELL JR. b Winterville Ga 19 My 37. 5: High Point Col 55-59 (Eng) AB; Appalachian State Col 61 (LS) MA; Ohio State U 62; UNC summer 64 (LS). 7: Tchr Surry Co Pub Schs, Surry Co NC 59-61; Asst libn U Sch Ohio State U 61-64, Libn 64-66, Instr Lib Educ Col of Educ 64-65; Asst Prof Lib Sci Clarion State Col 66-67;Visiting lecturer Dept Lib Serv UTenn summer 67; Asst Prof Lib Sci Appalachian StateU 67-. 9: ALA; SELA; NCLA; NCTE. 12: Ed "North Carolina Libraries" (68-). 13: Yes. 14: Sch lib serv, lib educ. 15: PO Box 411, Boone NC 28607.

BUSBOSO, JEAN PHYLLIS (DURHAM). b Charlottesville Va 25 O 34. 4: Ernest B Busboso. 5: Mary Washington Col 53-57 (Sp) BA; UMd 66-68 MLS. 6: Sp. 7: Tchr pub sch: Orange va 57-58, Hawthorne Nev 58-60, Alexandria Va 60-66; A-v libn Fairfax Pub Lib, Fairfax Va 68-. 9: ALA; DCLA. 14: A-v materials. 15: 5000 Andrea ave, Annandale Va 22003.

BUSBY, ESSIE NAOMI. b Gilmer Tex 25 Ja 06. 5: E Tex State 38 (Span) BA, 56 BS in LS. 6: Sp. 7: Tchr Pub Schs of Tex 25-36, Tchr & prin 36-43; Libn-Eng Gwinnett Co Ga 51-53; Libn-Eng Forney High Sch, Forney Tex 53-56; Libn S Oak Cliff High Sch, Dallas 56-. 9: TexLA; Tex State Tchers Assn; Dallas Co Libns. 10: Dallas Libns; Dallas ClrTchrs; PTA; Womens Soc of Christian Serv. 15: 2138 Gus Thomasson rd, Mesquitte Tx 75149.

BUSCH, BETTY JEAN (MOSHER). b Ypsilanti Mich 12 N 43. 4: Robert L Busch. 5: UMich 62-65 (Russian) BA, 66-67 AMLS. 6: Russian, Fr, Ger. 7: UMich: Sec 61-66, Lib wk-study scholar 66-67, Subj catlgr 67-68; Sch libn St Joseph Acad, Adrian Mich 68-. 9: A,A; CathLA; MichLA. 14: Catlg, Slavic area, sch libs. 15: 5046 Treat Highway, Adrian Mi 49221.

BUSH, ALFRED L. b Denver 5 Ja 33. 5: Brigham Young U 51-53, 55-57 (Archaeol) BS; Harvard 58; Inst for Archival and Hist Mgt Diploma. 7: (Cpl) US Army, CZ 53-55; Asst ed Papers of Thomas Jefferson, Princeton U 58-62; Curator Philip Ashton Rollins Collection of West Americana and assoc curator of mss, Princeton U Lib 62-; Curator American Alpine Museum 65-. 9: AHA; Assn of Amer Indian Affairs; BSA; Manuscript Soc; Royal Geog Soc (Fellow); Soc for Early Hist Archaeol; West Hist Assn; Utah State Hist Soc. 10: Cal Bk Club; Grolier Club; Hudson's Bay Record Soc; Amer Alpine Club; Princeton Club of NY. 12: Ed "The Papers of Thomas Jefferson," v 16 with Boyd & Wilmerding (61); "The Life Portraits of Thomas Jefferson" (62); "Wilde and the Nineties," with Ellman and Johnson (66); Ed BDS, "Manuscripts," and "The Princeton University Library Chronicle". 13: Yes. 14: Rare bks, mss. 15: 40 Bayard lane, Princeton NJ 08540.

BUSH, BERNARD. b NYC 14 Jl 29. 4: Elaine Stark. 5: NYU 46-50 (Hist) AB; Columbia 54-56 MLS, 56-61 9hist) MA. 6: Fr. 7: Ya libn NY Pub Lib 56; Ref libn Zionist Archives & Lib, NY 57-58; Asst libnCarnegie Endowment for Internat Peace, NY 58-61; Libn NJ Hist Soc, Newark NJ 61-62;Hist ed NJ State Lib 62-69, Exec dir NJ Hist Commsn 69-. 9: Amer Assn State & LocHist; NJLA; NJ Hist Soc; AHA; Organ of

Amer Histns Amer Jewish Hist Soc; TrentonHist Soc. 12: Proj dir "New Jersey and the Negro; A Bibliography, 1715-1966" (67). 13: Yes. 14: Hist programs. 15: 41 Fran ave, Trenton NJ 08628.

BUSH, BERNICE (CARPENTER). b Guilderland NY 30 Ja 05. 5: Syracuse 22-26 (Eng) AB, summer 26 (LS) Certif; Bread Loaf Sch of Eng summer 38 (Eng); SUNY(Albany) 46 BSLS; SUNY(Plattsburg) summer 58 (Soc Studies). 7: Libn High Sch, Whitehall NY 26-28; Libn & Eng Central Sch, Otego NY 31-46; Libn High Sch, Canajoharie NY 46-48; Asst libn Milne Sch NY State Col for Tchrs(Albany) 48-53; Libn Sr High Sch, Glens Falls NY 53-. 8: Mem Middle States Accredit Team for secondary schs. 9: NEA; ALA; NYLA; NY State Tchrs Assn; Hudson-Mohawk LA. 10: Delta Kappa Gamma; AAUW; Zonta Internat (local pres 69-70). 12: Jt auth "Fare for the Reluctant Reader," 2 eds. 14: Reading guidance. 15: 17 1/2 Sherman ave, Glens Falls NY 12801.

BUSH, EILEEN (RAFFERTY). b White Plains NY 24 Ap 09. 4: Kimberly Bush. 5: Smith 27-31 (Eng lit) BA; Pratt Inst 64-65(LS); South Conn State Col 65-67 MLS. 6: Fr, Ger, Ital. 7: Train supv & employment interviewer R H Macy & Co, NYC 31-40; Nursery sch tchr, Riverside & Old Greenwich Conn 52-56; Sec Cleveland,Duble & Arnold Real Estate, Greenwich Conn 56-62; Circ & ref libn Perrot Memorial Lib, Old Greenwich Conn 62-65; Acquis libn YaleDivinity Sch 66-68; Ref-period libn Deerfield Acad, Deerfield Mass 68-69.02234 9: ALA. 14: Ref, bk sel & admin. 15: Box 171, Old Deerfield Ma 01342.

BUSH, JOHN DEXTER. b Lock Haven Penn. 5: UPenn 42-48 (Chem) AB; Columbia 48-49 (Eng Lit) MA; Sorbonne 49-50 Degre Annuel; Columbia 57-60 (Music libnship) MS. 6: Ital, Fr, Ger, Sp. 7: Chem Crown Can Co, Phila 53-54; Sr desk asst Columbia U Music Lib 57-60, Asst libn 60-. 14: Catlg . 15: Columbia Univ Music Lib, New York NY 10027.

BUSH, JOYCE (FRIEDLAND). b NYC 24 Mr 31. 4: Alan R Bush. 5: Radcliffe 48-52 (Govt) BA; Columbia 66-68 MS in LS. 7: Claims adjuster Conn Genl Life Ins Co, NYC 52-53; Lib clk White Plains Pub Lib, White Plains NY 66-, Jr libn 69-. 9: ALA; WLA. 10: League of Women Voters; Beta Phi Mu. 14: Ref. 15: 2 Willows lane, White Plains NY 10605.

BUSH, L DORCAS. b Douglas Co Kan. 5: UMo(Kan City) 51 (Chem) BA; Columbia 53-54 (LS) MS. 7: Med libn Geigy Chem Corp; Libn Bendix Corp, Kan City Mo 61-62; Catlgr UKan (Lawrence & Kan City) 62-64; Act supv readers serv Eli Lilly & Co, Indianapolis 65-. 9: SLA; MedLA; ACS. 10: AAUW; Nature Study Club of Ind; Ind Geol & Gem Soc. 13: Yes. 14: Ref, catlg, transl. 15: Eli Lilly & Co Sci Lib, 740 S Alabama, Indianapolis In 46106.

BUSH, LILA DEWELL. b Salina Kan 11 Jl 25. 5: Washburn U 43-45; UMo 63-66 (Soc studies) BS, 67-69 (LS) MA. 7: Ms libn State Hist Soc, Columbia Mo 66-67; Research asst UMo 69-. 9: ALA; MoLA. 11: Pi Lambda Theta. 14: Readers serv, ref, circ. 15: 2704 Braemore rd, Columbia Mo 65201.

BUSH, MARGARET. b Webster SDak 14 Ag 37. 5: UCal at Berkeley 55-59 (Eng) BA, 59-60 MLS; Pacific Sch of Theol (Theol); Union Theol Sem (Theol). 7: Sr clk docs sec Lawrence Radiation Lab, Berkeley Cal 59; Children's libn 60-61; Sr children's libn NYC Pub Lib 61-67; Hd children's dept Oak Park Pub Lib, Oak Park Ill 67-. 9: ALA; IllLA (child serv Sect: v-pres & pres-elect 68-70). 10: Beta Phi Mu; Child Reading RT of Chicago; Lib Admin Coun No Ill. 14: Child serv. 15: 321 S Maple, Oak Park Il 60302.

BUSH, NAOMI (SALVESON). b Hesper Iowa 25 N 16. 5: Luther Col 34-38 (Eng) BA; UMinn 39-40 BLS; Luther Col summer 56; Winona State Col summer 65. 7: Tchr-libn Sch Dist #90, Burtrum Minn 38-39; Tchr-libn Clover High Sch, Clover Va 40-42; Libn Viroqua High Sch, Viroqua Wis 42-43; Gen helper US Naval Amm Depot, Hastings Neb 44; Gen helper US Naval Air Station, Corpus Christi Tex 44; Saleslady Silver's Dept Store, Macon Ga 45; Libn SP-4 US Marine Base, Camp Lejeune NC 45-46; Off sec Harris & Ballenger Ins Agency, Cordele Ga 46-47; Asst libn Austin Pub Lib, Austin Minn 48-51; Asst libn (GS-5) Post Lib Camp J H Pendleton, Oceanside Cal 51; Libn, head of lib dept Winona Sr High Sch, Winona Minn 56-58; Libn Kasson-Mantorville Schs, Kasson Minn 58-. 9: ALA-AASchL; NEA; MinnASchL; MinnEA. 10: Kasson-Mantorville EA; PTA; Pub Lib Bd. 14: Ref, catlg, sch lib mgt. 15: 108 NW 1st ave, Kasson Mn 55944.

BUSH, PATRICIA AGNES. b Chicago 17 Je 29. 5: Rosary Col 47-51 (LS) BA; Loyola U(Chicago) 54-56. 7: Ref documents libn & asst catlgr Northwestern U Joseph Schaffner Lib 51-55, Asst libn & head catlg dept 55-. 9: ALA; SLA. 14: Catlg, ref, docs. 15: 9329 S Winchester ave, Chicago Il 60620.

BUSH, VIRGINIA MAE (RATAI). b Virginia Minn 27 O 43. 4: James A Bush. 5: Va Jr Col 61-63 AA; UMinn (Minneapolis) 63-65 (Eng) BA, 65- (LS). 6: Fr. 7: Grad lib asst UMinn Lib acquis dept (Minneapolis) 65-66; Libn St Paul Pub Lib Commun Rel Off, St Paul 67-. 10: YMCA. 14: Commun rel, child wk. 15: 4112 28th ave, S Minneapolis Mn 55406.

BUSHA, CHARLES H(ENRY). b Liberty SC 14 D 31. 5: Furman U 54-58 (Pol Sci) BA; Rutgers 60-61 MLS. 6: Fr. 7: (2nd Lt) Forward observer US Army 1st Cav Div, Korea & Far East 53-54; Libintern Greenville Pub Lib, Greenville SC 58-60; Head of tech processes GreenvilleCo Lib, Greenville SC 61-62, Ref libn 62-63; Ref consul SC State Lib Bd, ColumbiaSC 63-67; Capt SC Nat Guard, SC 54-67; Fellow Grad Lib Sch IndU. 8: Conducted feasibility study for estab of Greenville Textile Tech Info Center, Greenville SC, 65. 9: SCLA; SELA;ASIS; BSA. 12: Comp "Bibliography of Business, Scientific & Technical Books" (63); "Prospectus of a Proposed Information Research Center Specializing in Textiles and Textile Technology" (65). 13: Yes. 14: Ref, lib serv to bus & ind, communication & libs. 15: 128 N Roosevelt ave, Bloomington In 47401.

BUSHEE, RALPH WALDO JR. b Monticello Ill 22 O 20. 5: Coe Col 38-42 (Eng) BA; McCormick Theol Sem 42-45 BD; UIll 42-46 (Eng) MA, BS in LS; Chicago 46-47; Art Inst of Chicago 50-51. 6: Fr, Ger, Hebrew, Sp, Gk. 7: Asst Minister First Presbyterian Church, Lake Forest Ill 42-45; Minister First Presbyterian church, Kansas Ill 45-46; Asst in Eng UIll(Urbana) 45-46; Libn Transportation Assn of Amer, Chicago 47; Asst in order dept Newberry Lib, Chicago 47-48; Trainee Nedwick's Bk Store, Chicago 48-52; Owner & manager Ralph Bushee Bkseller, Chicago 52-55; Libn Allerton Pub Lib, Monticello Ill 55-56; Asst libn Decatur Pub Lib, Decatur Ill 56-59; Order libn So Ill U 59-61, Rare bk libn 61-. 8: Consul, Lib of The Inst for Sex Res, 65-66. 9: IllLA (chm RTSD 59-60). 10: Beta Phi Mu; So Ill Open Hunt; The Decatur Ill Club; Carbondale UnivClub; Ms Soc; Amer Com on Irish Studies. 13: Yes. 14: Rare bks. 15: Rt 4, Carbondale Il 62901.

BUSHING, VERA R(OSE). b Chicago 6 Je 12. 5: Valparaiso U 42-46 (Geog) BA; Chicago 46-47 BLS. 6: Ger, Fr, Sp. 7: Valparaiso U Lib 47-. 9: ALA; IndLA. 10: Pi Gamma Mu. 14: Catlg. 15: 203 McKinley st, Valparaiso In 46383.

BUSSELLE, VERA G (ANDERSON). Jasonville Ind 20 D 12. 4: Arthur E Busselle. 5: DePauw U 31-35 (Hist) AB; Ind U summers 36-38 Tchg license in Lib Sci; USoCal BS in LS. 7: High sch libn Linton Stockton High Sch, linton Ind 35-43; High sch libn Peru High Sch, Peru Ind 43-46; Catlgr Ind State Lib 46-50; Field Enterprises Educ Corp, Chicago: Asst libn 50-60, Sr libn 60-64, Asst head libn 64-. 9: SLA. 10: Beta Phi Mu; Phi Kappa Phi; Pi Lambda Theta. 14: Catlg, ref. 15: 3803 W Timothy lane, McHenry Il 60050.

BUSTER, FRANCES (F). b Southampton NY 30 Ag 16. 4: Thwodore J Buster. 5: Skidmore 33-37 (Mus) BS; Pratt Inst 38-39 (Catlg) BLS. 6: Fr. 7: Br asst & catlgr Brooklyn Pub Lib, Brooklyn NY 39-42; Asst chief & catlgr ser dept Wash Square Lib NYU 42-46, Chief ser dept 47-60; Ed ser rec & new ser tilles LC 50-52, Asst ed Dewey decimal clsf 52; Sr sub catlgr E European acc ind 52-55; Prin acquis off ref dept 55-67; Assoc libn & chief tech serv DHEW Lib, Wash DC 67-. 15: 5530 Bouffant blvd, Alexandria Va 22311.

BUSWELL, ROSALIND F. b Barton Vt 23 D 09. 5: Clark U even 54- (Eng, Hist) Diploma in Gen Studies. 7: Gen asst ref & circ Forest Park Br City Lib, Springfield Mass 28-47; VA; Libn P-1, Togus Me 47, Libn P-1, Rutland Heights Mass 47-48, Chief libn, Rutland Heights Mass 48-65, Chief libn, Providence 65-. 9: ALA; MedLA; RILA. 10: Nat Audubon Soc. 14: Med & hosp libs, lib serv to patients. 15: 201 Angell st, Providence RI 02906.

BUTCHER, PATRICIA (SMITH). b Waterbury Conn 26 D 45. 4: John E Butcher. 5: Albertus Magnus 63-67 (Hist) BA; Rutgers 67-68 MLS. 6: Fr. 7: Anglo-Amer catlgr YaleU Law Lib 68; Reader's adv in educ & psych Trenton State Col 68-. 9: ALA; AALL; SLA. 12: Ed "Thepapers of Thomas Jefferson," v l6 (with Boyd & Wilmerding) (61); "The Life Portraitsof Thomas Jefferson" (62); "Wilde and the Nineties," with Ellman and Johnson (66);Ed Bds, "Manuscripts," and "The Princeton University Library Chronicle". 13: Yes. 14: Ref. 15: 4 Pierson pl, Hopewell NJ 08525.

BUTLER, BARBARA A (HUNT). b Niagara Falls NY 24 Ja 37. 4: Joseph A Butler. 5: SUNY(Buffalo) 55-59 (Art educ) BS; West Res 60-61 MS in LS. 6: Fr. 7: Elem art tchr Bd of Educ Niagara Falls NY 59-60; Jr libn Nioga Lib System Niagara Falls NY 61-64; Supv of bkmobs Tampa Pub Lib, Tampa Fla 64; Elem sch libn Fuguitt Elementary Sch, Largo Fla 65-. 8: Ref libn at Library/USA, NY World's Fair 64. 9: ALA; Fla Assn Sch Libns; Pinellas Co LA. 10: Fla Westcoast ETV, Inc; Nat Geographic Soc. 14: Child serv, pub rels, ref. 15: 125 Midway Island, Clearwater Fl 33515.

BUTLER, CATHERINE J. b Homestead Penn 9 S 1898. 5: Penn State Col 17 (LS) Certif; Chautauqua Sch for Libns 28-30 (LS) Certif; Voluntary plan of Certification in Penn Grade A Certif. 6: Fr. 7: Adult lending & ref Carnegie Free Lib, Duquesne Penn 16-23; Catlgr & child wkCarnegie Lib, Homestead Penn 23-43; Dir Carnegie Lib, Homestead Penn 43-64; Catlg libnLa Roche Col 64-. 8: Weekly radio program WHOD, 49-57; Appointed to the Ecumenicalcommsn of the Diocese of Pittsburgh, 63-. 9: ALA (Friends of the Lib Com 47-54);CathLA (sec & chm Elem Sect 50,51; Regina Medal Award Com 69; pres W Penn Unit 61-63);SLA; PennLA (Friends of Lib Com 49-56; Local Arrangements 69; NLW State Com 69; pres SW Dist 51 & 58); Pittsburgh Lib Club (pres 47-48; trustee 61-62). 10: SteelValley C of C Bus & Prof Women; Steel Valley Artists Series; Acad of Sci & Arts ofPittsburgh; Citizens for Decent Lit; Altrusa Internat; Pittsburgh Symphony Soc;Greater Pittsburgh Coun on Adult Educ; Pius X Bk Club. 11: John Cotton Dana Pubaward, 47; Americanism Citation by B'nai B'rith, 51. 12: Comp; "Friends of theLibrary Handbook, Public Library ed," ALA (51), "History of Friends of Carnegielibrary of Homestead" (63), "Handbook for Western Pennsylvania Unit, CatholicLibrary Association" (66). 13: Yes. 14: Catlg, wk with child, Friends of the lib. 15: 221 Kennedy ave, Munhall Pa 15120.

BUTLER, E CARMEN (JONES). b Ill 1 Mr 12. 4: Fred A Butler. 5: Occidental 32-34 Eng AB; UCal at Berkeley 36-37 Certif of Libnship. 6: Ital, Fr, Ger, Sp. 7: Libn Glendale Unified Sch Dist (Hoover High Sch) 37-43; Libn Kern Co Free Lib, Bakersfield Cal 62-64; Br libn Ventura Co & City Lib (Camarillo Br) 64-. 9: ALA; CalLA. 14: Readers serv, ya. 15: 298 N Dos Caminos ave, Ventura Ca 93003.

BUTLER, CHARLES EDWARD. b Denver Colo 9 Jl 09. 4: Eleanor Walters. 5: UDenver 27-31 (Eng) BA, 31-32 BS in LS; Chicago 37-38 (LS); UMich summers 48-50 AMLS. 7: Asst order dept Denver Pub Lib 32-33; Asst to sec ALA, Chicago 33-37; Ref libn West Wash Col of Educ 38-39; Libn Kanawha Co Pub Lib, Charleston WVa 39-49; US Army Air Force T/Sgt 42-45; Libn WVa U 49-56; Libn Canisius Col 56-59; Libn Longwood Col 59-. 9: VaLA. 11: Yale Univ Younger Poets Series Award, 45; Hopwood Award in Poetry UMich summers 49, 50; Guggenheim Fellowship in Creative Writing 51. 12: "Cut Is the Branch," poems (45); "Follow Me Ever," novel (50). 14: Bk sel. 15: 602 First ave, Farmville Va 23901.

BUTLER, EVELYN. b Saginaw Mich 23 Ag 15. 5: UMich 37 (Span) AB, 38 ABLS, 46 AMLS. 6: Sp. 7: Libn UMich Inst of Pub & Soc Admin(Detroit) 38-42; Tech libn New Britain Inst Lib, New Britain Conn 42-46; Libn UPenn Sch of Soc Wk 46-. 8: SLA consul to Schs of Soc Wk; Howard U & Hunter Col, Syracuse U; Temple U. 9: ALA; Amer Pub Welfare Assn; Nat Assn Soc Wkers; SLA (Soc Sci Div: chm 52-53; chm Soc Welfare Sect 51 & 60-63; pres Conn Chap 45-46); Spec Libns Coun of Phila (sec 47, dir 58-60); PennLA. 10: AAUW; Phila Fellowship Commsn. 11: UMich Alum Scholar 33-37. 12: Jt comp "Building a Social Work Library" (62). 13: Yes. 14: Soc wk, admin. 15: 124 W Queen lane, Phila Pa 19144.

BUTLER, FLORENCE WINIFRED. b Newry Minn 27 Ap 04. 5: Winona State Col 34 (Eng) BS in Ed; ColumbiaU 42 BLS. 6: Fr. 7: Tchr Rural Schs, minn 21-24; Child libn Winona Free Pub Lib, Winona Minn 25-37; Instr child lit Morningside Col 45-; Visiting lecturer Sch of Lib Sci Case Western Res 65; Dir of wk with child Sioux City Pub Lib, Sioux City Iowa 37-. 8: Mem of ALA gp touring Swedish libs 60; Miriam Wessel Memorial lecture, Detroit 66; Wkshop dir Mo State Lib, Jefferson 68. 9: ALA (Coun 54-57; Subscription Bks Bulletin Com; Lib Serv Act Com); -CSD (chm Lists & Serv; chm Liaison with Bkstores; Org Com); IowaLA (past sec; past pres); IowaStateEA (Bd Mem Lib Serv 40-). 10: Soroptimist Intl; Sioux City Commun theatre; AAUW; Womans Club. 11: Woman of Year Award Agora Club Morningside Col 57; Woman of Year Award Bus & Prof Club 53. 13: Yes. 14: Child serv. 15: Bellevue apts D-3, Sioux City Ia51104.

BUTLER, FRANCES C (FOOTE). b Chicago Ill 29 Je 09. 4: John Lee Butler. 5: Ward belmont Col 26-27; IndU 27-30 (Fr) AB, 60-62 MALS, 65-66 (Letters). 6: Fr, Ital, Sp. 7: Asst bus libn, Indianapolis 31-45; YWCA 48-49; Sears Roebuck & Co, Indianapolis 49-50; Schmid & Smith (real estate off), Indianapolis 50-51; Libn Caldwell Larkin (Advertising agy), Indianapolis 51-55; Asst bus lib Indianapolis Pub Lib 61-65; Asst ref div Ind State Lib, Indianapolis 66-. 9: ALA; IndLA. 10: Intl Travel Study Clubs; IndU Women's Club; AAUW; Alpha Chi Omega; Beta Phi Mu. 14: Ref. 15: 5151 N New Jersey st, Indianapolis In 46205.

BUTLER, HARLEY RANDALL. b Le Mars Iowa 28 S 27. 5: UCal (Berkeley) 45, 47-51 (Hist) BA, 51-52 (Hist) MA, 52-53 (Hist), 53-54 BLS. 6: Fr, Sp. 7: Cal State Col (Los Angeles): Asst order libn 54-56, Order libn 56-57, Supv acquis libn 57-59, Chief of circ serv 59-60, Chief of tech serv 60-65, Asst col libn 65-68, Assoc col libn 68-. 8: Adv Com, Lib Sci Program, Los Angeles Trade-Tech Col 63-. 9: ALA; CalLA. 10: AAUP; Assn Cal State Col Profs. 14: Admin. 15: 4003 Berendo apt 319, Los Angeles Ca 90005.

BUTLER, HARRY A. b Dallas 25 Ap 31. 4: Mary Jane Reagan. 5: Abilene Christian Col 48-51 (Gk) BA; Pepperdine Col 51-52 (Religion) MA; Vanderbilt 54-59 (Religion) PhD; USoCal 61-62 (LS) MS. 6: Fr, Ger, sp, Hebrew, Gk. 7: Instr in religion David Lipscomb Col 55-57; Chaplain Whittier Col 60; Pepperdine Col: Ref libn 61-62, Asst libn 62-63, Act libn 63-64, Libn 64-66; Assoc prof lib sci Fla State U 66-67; Libn Iliff Sch of Theol 67-. 9: ALA; AALS; ATheolLA; Soc of Bibl Lit & Exegesis; Amer Acad of Relig. 15: 9634 W Kentucky ave, Denver Co 80226.

BUTLER, HELEN E. b Polk Co Ore 28 Ja 08. 5: Ore Normal Sch 24-26 (Prim Educ) Diploma; UOre summers until 39 (Educ) BS; UWash 57 MLS; Mont State U summers (LS). 6: Sp. 7: Tchr inter grades & lib Dallas Pub sch, Dallas Ore 26-44, libn High Sch 39-44; Merchandising, Dallas Ore 44-47; Clerk State Dept Tax Commsn, Salem Ore 49-52; Libn Bend Sch Dist, Bend Ore 52-59; Head Libn Lower Columbia Col (Wash) 59-68; Hd Libn Oregon City Pub Lib, 68-. 9: NEA; SW WashLA (chm 61); PNLA; WashEA; WashLA; WashASchL (pres 61). 10: AAUP; AAUW; Delta Kappa Gamma; Neighbors of Woodcraft; Mayflower Descendants; DAR. 14: Ref, admin, adult educ. 15: 713 Monroe, Oregon City Or 97045.

BUTLER, JOSEPH THOMAS JR. b White Castle La 24 Ja 38. 4: June Barrosse. 5: LSU 56-59 (Educ) BS, 59-61 (LS) MS. 7: US Army, Ft Jackson SC 61; Asst ref libn Mobile Pub Lib, Mobile Ala 61-62; Asst libn Spring Hill Col 62-64; Acquis libn Southeastern La Col 64-. 9: ALA; LaLA. 10: Kappa Phi Kappa. 13: Yes. 14: Catlg, acquis, oral hist, Govt docs. 15: 107 Florencedr, Hammond La 70401.

BUTLER, NAOMI (WITMER). b Boonsboro Md 25 Ag 34. 4: Philip A Butler. 5: Shepherd Col 57 (Eng) AB; UNC 65-66 MSLS. 7: Libn Middletown Elem Sch, Middletown Md 57-67; Yellow Springs Elem Sch Lib, Frederick Md 67-68; Shippensburg State Col Dept of LS 68-69; Valley Sch Lib, Jefferson Md West Md Col Dept LS 68-. 9: NEA; Md State Tchrs Assn; Cumberland Valley LA; Educal Media, Assn of Md (pres 69-). 13: Yes. 14: Child wk, tchg lib sci media, yp wk. 15: Rt 2, Boonsboro Md 21713.

BUTLER, PAMELA DOROTHY. b Seattle 8 My 43. 5: UWash 61-64 (Russian) BA, 64-65 MLS, 65- (Russian Lit). 6: Russian, Fr, Ger, Polish. 9: ALA. 10: Amer Assoc Advancement of Slavic Studies; Amer Assoc of Tchrs of Slavic & E Europ Langs. 14: Slavic & East European. 15: 4714 22nd ave NE, APT 6, Seattle Wa 98105.

BUTLER, SHERMAN L. b Homestead Fla 18 D 26. 4: Fusako Matsushita. 5: Trenton State Col 64-65; Park Col 66 (Econ) BA; Rockhurst Col summer 66; UOkla 67-68 MLS. 6: Fr. 7: Seaman USN, Pacific area 44-46; Clk typist T/5 USA, Germany 46-48; Electronics tech T/Sgt USAF, France, Japan, Labrador Alaska 48-65; Interlib loan lib UFla 67-. 9: AAUP; ALA; FlaLA. 10: Pi Sigma Alpha; Beta Phi Mu. 14: Ref. 15: 3530 SW 24th ave, Gainesville Fl 32601.

BUTLER, W ROYCE. b Lethbridge Alta Can 23 Ja 14. 5: UBC 35-39 (Eng) BA; Toronto 40-41 (Eng); UCal(Berkeley) 58-59 MLS. 6: Fr, Ger. 7: Res & gen manager Marine Lumber Co Ltd, Vancouver BC 59; Head order dept Honnold Lib Associated Cols (Claremont Cal) 59-61;Head acquis div Boston U 61-62; Head Div of Tech Serv & Asst Prof Grad Sch of Libns UDenver 62-65; Asst dir York U Libs (Toronto) 65-66, Assocdir of libs 66; U libn & Prof of bibliog Oakland U (Mich) 67-. 8: Mem, Adv Bd Lib Tech Proj, Oakland Commun Col 68-. 9: ALA; MichLA. 10: AAUP. 12: Ed "Colorado

Academic Lib" (63-65). 13: Yes. 14: Acquis, admin, lib sch tchg. 15: 141 Wimberly dr,Rochester Mi 48063.

BUTORAC, FRANK GEORGE. b Crosby Minn 12 F 27. 5: UMich 48-50 (Pol Sci) AB; Cornell Law Sch 50-51 (Law); UMich 51-52 (Educ) Tchg Certif; Harvard summer 53 (Educ); UMich 53-56 (Educ Admin) AM; UMich 56-58 AMLS; UNotre Dame 59, 60-62 (Phil, Lat); Holy Cross Col(DC) 62-66 (Theol); Catholic U summer 63 (LS); Georgetown U summer 65 (Span) NYU 68-. 6: Sp, Fr. 7: Radar operator 2/c US Navy, Atlantic & Pacific WW II 44-47; Sales corr & train program US Rubber Co, Mishawaka Ind 52-53; Elem tchr Jefferson Sch, Wayne Mich 53-54; Tchr of soc studies Slauson Jr High Sch, Ann Arbor Mich 54-55; Supv tchr of soc studies (rank of Asst Prof) Lincoln Consol High Sch of East Mich U 55-57; Circ libn Gen Lib & Asst Engnr Lib UMich 58-59; Order libn Holy Cross Col 62-66; Registrar (Assoc Prof) Trenton Jr Col (NJ) 66-67; RegistrarMercer Co Commun Col (Trenton NJ) 67-68, Asst dir commun & ext serv 68-. 9: ALA-ACRL (Ref serv div); LA Div (Resources & Tech Serv Div-ALA); NJ Sch Col Assn;Amer Assn for Higher Educ; Assn of Univ Evening Cols); ATheolLA; CathLA; NEA; Natstudy of Educ; MichEA; AERUSA; NJEA. 10: Theta Delta Chi; Phi Delta Kappa; Phi Delta Phi alpha Phi Omega; Toastmasters Internat; Cornell Law Assn; Washtenaw Co (Mich)Hist Soc; Torch Club; Lions Club; Navy League of the US Elks; Moose; Cath Tchrs Guild;Cath Alum Club; Amer Legion; Amer Assn of Col Registrant & Admission Offrs; NJ Assn forAdult Education; Knights of Columbus; Parkview Tennis Club (Trenton NJ); PenningtonPlayers (NJ); Middle States Assn of Col Registrars & Admissions Offrs; Delaware ValleyRegistrars Assn. 14: Admin, ref, acquis. 15: 640 W State st, Trenton NJ 08618.

BUTT, BONNIE SUE (BERRY). b Covina Cal 31 D 42. 4: David C Butt. 5: Pasadena Col 60-61 (Soc sci); Citrus Col 61-62 (Soc sci) AA; Cal State Col 62-66 (Soc sci) BA; Immaculate Heart Col 66-67 (LS) MA. 6: Fr. 7: Hd libn Baldwin Park Lib, Baldwin Park Cal 67-. 9: ALA; CalLA. 10: Woman's Club; Friends of the Baldwin Park Lib. 14: Pub lib admin, ref. 15: 3707 Gibson, Elmonte Ca.

BUTTARS, GERALD ANDERSON. b Logan Utah 12 O 39. 4: Jeannie Webb. 5: Utah StateU 57-59, 62-66 (Bio Sci) BS; Brigham YoungU 67-69 (LS) MS. 7: Lab tech Thiokol Chem Corp, Brigham City Utah 59, Process inspector 62-64; Missionary Mormon Ch, Toronto Can 59-61; Bkmob libn Utah State Lib Commsn 65-67, Reg libn for the blind 67-. 9: UtahLA. 14: Pub lib admin. 15: 4749 W 3280 S, Granger Ut.

BUTTARS, HONOR GENEVIEVE (BAILIE). b Milestone Sask Can 3 Jl 13. 4: Rev Melville Buttars. 5: Queen's U(Kingston Ont) 31-35 (Eng) BA; Toronto 35-36 BLS. 6: Fr. 7: Circ asst Queen's U & UToronto Libs 36-39; Ref libn McLaughlin Pub Lib, Oshawa Ont 59-, Ref libn & youth room 61-65. 14: Ref. 15: 29 Olive ave, Oshawa Ontario Can.

BUTTERFIELD, ELIZABETH. b Buffalo 17 Je 01. 5: Oberlin Conservatory 19-20; Oberlin col 21-23; UBuffalo 24, 30 BA BSLS. 6: Fr. 7: Libn Buffalo & Erie Co Lib, Buffalo NY 24-55; Soc wkr Family Serv, Buffalo NY 56-57; Libn Maryvale Sr High Sch, Cheektowaga NY 59-. 9: NYLA; NYTA; ErieCoTA; Suburban Libns Assn (pres). 10: Human Rel Project Maryvale High Sch (chm). 13: Yes. 14: Y-a. 15: 37 Linwood ave, Williamsville NY 14221.

BUTTERFIELD, MARY JANE BOLNER. b Green Bay Wis 8 Jl 42. 4: William Henry Butterfield. 5: Ariz State U 60-64 (Liberal Arts) BA, 64-66; UMich 67-68 AMLS. 6: Sp, Ger. 7: Apt mgr: Univ Houses Ariz, Tempe Ariz 64-66, Miller-Maple Townhouses, Ann Arbor Mich 67-68; Stud asst Music Lib, UMich (Ann Arbor) 67, Wk-study scholar Lib Sci Lib 67-68, Off clk dept of Lib Sci 68; Asst soc sci libn East Mich U 68-. 9: ALA; MichLA. 10: AAUP; Beta Phi Mu; Assn for the Study of Negro Life & Hist. 14: Ref serv. 15: 1215 Washtenaw, Ypsilanti Mi 48197.

BUTTERFIELD, VELMA (ENLOW). b LaJunta Col 28 Ag 14. 5: Colo Woman's Col 31-33 (Journalism) AA; USoCal 33-34 (Journalism); Black Hills State Col 55 (Communications, Soc sci) BS in Ed; UDenver 62 MA in LS. 7: Ed Sundance Times, Sundance Wyo 40-45; Libn & grade 6 Belle Fourche Schs, Belle Fourche S Dak 53-54; Libn & Eng Deadwood High Sch, Deadwood S Dak 56-59; Libn Los Alamos High Sch, Los Alamos NM 59-69; Asst ser libn Texas A&M U 69-. 9: ALA; NEA; NMLA. 14: Soc sci, humanities, ref, jr col. 15: 301 Stasney st apt 1002, College Station Tx 77840.

BUTTERWORTH, JOANNE. b Atlanta Ga 10 N 41. 5: Randolph-Macon Woman's Col 58-62 (Chem) AB; USCar summer 61; Emory 62 (LS); Ga Inst of Tech 63-64 (Info sci) MS; UCal at Berkeley 66, 67. 6: Ger, Russian, Sp, Fr. 7: Asst libn Ga Inst of Tech 63; Asst libn Shell Development Co, Emeryville Cal 65-67; Tech libn Memorex Corp, Santa Clara Cal 67-. 9: ASIS; SLA. 10: Cal Young Republicans; YMCA. 14: Ref, info storage & retrieval. 15: Memorex Corp, 1181 Shulman ave, Santa Clara Ca 95052.

BUTTOLPH, JANET (HOWE). b Burlington Vt 9 S 28. 4: David Lyman Buttolph. 5: Mt Holyoke 45-49 (Fr) BA; Columbia 65-66 MS in LS. 6: Fr. 7: Exec sec to area mgr R H Donnelley Corp, Wash DC 49-51; Order libn SUNY (Binghamton) 66-67, Docs libn 67-. 14: Govt docs, computer applications to libs. 15: RD 1 Andrews rd, Vestal NY 13850.

BUTTON, EDITH MAUD DICKSON. b Stellarton NS. 4: Hubert Edward Richardson Button. 5: Acadia U 31 BA; McGill 63 BLS. 6: Fr. 7: Asst reg libn Albert-Westmorland-Kent Reg Lib, Moncton NB Can 64- Spec asst to Reg Libn 68-. 9: CanLA; APLA. 10: Univ Women's Club. 15: 53 Kensington dr, Moncton NB Can.

BUTTS, CAROL JAYNE. b Wild Rose Wis 9 Ja 28. 5: Lawrence Col 45-49 (Hist) BA; UMich 50-51 MA in LS. 6: Ger. 7: Child lib pre-prof Milwaukee Pub Lib 49-50; Circ lib Penn State Col 51-52; Libn I UWis Lib 52-57; Libn II catlgr ext div UWis 57-59; Catlgr Lawrence U 59-69; Hd libn Lakeland Col 69-. 8: Instr in lib course for pub libns UWis Ext 58, 60, 62. 9: WisLA. 10: AAUW; Wis Acad Scis, Arts & Letters; Wis Geneal Soc. 14: Catlg, ref, admin. 15: 1413 Fla ave, Sheboygan Wi 53081.

BUURSTRA, ANNETTE KATHRYN. b S Holland Ill. 5: Calvin Col 45-47, 49-51 (Hist) AB; UMich 53-56 AMLS Mich State U 64- (Hist). 7: Tchr Grosse Pointe Chr Sch, Grosse Pointe Mich 47-49; Tchr Calvin Christian Sch, S Holland Ill 51-52; Calvin Col & Sem: Lib asst 53-56, Circ libn 56-62, Knollcrest libn 62-65, Ref libn 65-68; Ref libn Mich State U (E Lansing) 68-. 9: ALA; MichLA (sec-treas Col Sect 62-63, sec-treas Ref Sect 66-67). 14: Ref. 15: 705-104Cherry lane, E Lansing Mi 48823.

BUXBAUM, LILLIAN (T). b New Haven Conn 2 Je 03. 7: Lib asst Milwaukee Pub Lib 21-26; Libn Boys Tech High Sch, Milwaukee 26-30; Libn Simpson & Curtin, Phila 58; Asst libn Penn RR Co, Phila 58-63 (Grade III); Libn Free Lib of Phila 63-64; Act head bus lib Drexel Inst of Tech 64-65; Libn Blue Cross of Greater Phila, Phila 65-. 9: SLA; MedLA; Spec Libs Coun, Greater Phila. 14: Ref. 15: Kennedy House apt 1419, 1901 J F Kennedy blvd, Philadelphia Pa 19103.

BUXTON, FRANCES (HURD). b Honolulu Hawaii 21 S 11. 4: Robert A Buxton. 5: UHawaii 28-32 (Lit) BA; Emort 32-33 BA in LS. 7: Ref libn Lib of Hawaii, Honolulu 34-47; Jr libn ref dept Oakland Pub Lib, Oakland Cal 47-53; Sr libn in charge of Cal Room Oakland Pub Lib 53-. 8: Consul Jr League of Oakland Historic Preserv Survey, Oakland Cal 67-. 9: ALA; CalLA. 10: Conf of Cal Historical Soc; Alameda Co Hist Soc; Friends of the Okaland Pub Lib; Oakland Municipal Civil Serv Employees Assn. 14: Californiana. 15: 2808 Clay st, Alameda Ca 94501.

BYAM, MILTON S(YLVESTER). b NYC 15 Mr 22. 4: Yolanda Shervington. 5: City Col of NY 40-47 (Eng) BSS; Howard U 43-44 (ASTP); Columbia 48-49 (LS) MS; NYU 50-51 (Eng). 6: Sp, Fr, Ital. 7: T/5 92nd Infantry Div Fifth Army AUS 43-45; Brooklyn Pub Lib Trainee 47-49, Br libn 50-56, Supt of Brs 56-60, Chief Pub Serv 60-65, Deputy Dir 65-68; Chm Dept of Lib Sci St Johns U 68-. 8: Lecturer in Lib Sci Pratt Inst Lib Sch 56-66, St John's U Lib Sch 57-68; Adv Com St John's U Congress for Libns 59-67; Ad Hoc Com on Certif, NY State Educ Dept 64; Co-chm Brooklyn Citizens Com for Nat Lib Week 59-60; "High John" Adv Com 69-; NY State Pub Libns Certif Exam Com 61-66; NY State Civil Serv Examiner 66-; Panel of Fellows Program 67-. 9: ALA;-PLA (Study Com);-LAD (Fringe Benefits Com); NYLA (Co-chm Memb Com 63-, sec-treas Adult Serv Sect 60, chm Intell Freedom Com 67); CathLA (Adv Bd); NY Lib Club (Bd Dirs 56-57). 10: Flushing Suburban Civic Assn; Brooklyn Pub Lib Staff Assn; AAUP; Grace Episc Church (Jamaica) Urban Commsn; LI Diocese Queens Commun Planning Bd. 11: Bronze Star Medal for Heroic Achievement in Action; Brooklyn Pub Lib Friends of Lib Award; Savannah State Col Lib Award. 13: Yes. 14: Admin, group serv, lib ed pub libs. 15: 162-04 75th rd, Flushing LI NY 11366.

BYARS, (ETHEL) GAYE. b Birmingham Ala 12 D 27. 5: Samford U 44-48 (Eng) BA; Emory 48-49 MLS. 6: Fr. 7: Circ asst Fla State U 50; Ref libn Samford U 50-54; Adult serv supv LANE Pub Lib, Hamilton Ohio 54-58; Ref Libn Air ULib Maxwell AFB ALA 58-62, Bibliogr 62-. 9: SLA (dir Ala Chap 62-63); AlaLA. 14: Ref, bibliog. 15: 619 E Patton ave, Montgomery Al 36111.

BYARS, MARY KATHRYN (PATRICK). b Pacolet Mills SC 16 Ag 21. 4: Hugh Heyward Byars. 5: Furman U 38-42 (Eng) BA (Lib Sci); USCar (LS). 6: Fr. 7: Tchr Kershaw High Sch, Kershaw SC 42-43; Asst to registrar Woman's Col Furman U 43-47; Continuity writer, Radio Sta WFBC, Greenville SC 47-49; Sec & educ asst Trinity Meth Church, Greenville SC 51-60; Asst to children's libn Greenville Co Lib 61-63; Asst libn Greenville Sr High Sch 63-65; Libn Augusta Circle Sch Greenville SC 65-69. 9: ALA; SoCalLA; SoCalEA; Greenville Co EA. 10: Friends of the Greenville Co Lib; Delta Kappa Gamma; Greenville Co Elem Libns Assn. 14: Child wk. 15: 5 Edisto st, Greenville SC 29605.

BYBEE, MARY JANE. b Mexico Mo 1 N 35. 5: Christian Col 54-56 AA; UMo 56-58 (LS) BS. 7: Jr libn UMo 58-. 9: ALA; MoLA. 10: AAUW; Pi Lambda Theta; PEO. 14: Acquis. 15: 108 Belvedere apts 206 Hitt st, Columbia Mo 65201.

BYBLOW, SISTER MECHTILDE SMI. b Springside Sask Can 29 Je 15. 5: UAlta 37-40 (Eng) BA, summers 43-4 BEd; St Johns U 58 MLS; UToronto summer 65. 6: Ukrainian, Fr. 7: Prin & tchr Sacred Heart Acad, yorkton Sask 43-50; Prin & libn St Mary's Villa Acad, Sloatsburg NY 50-53; Tchr Ituna High Sch, Ituna Sask 53-57; Tchr & libn Sacred Heart Acad, Yorkton Sask 57-59; Prin & libn Byzantine Catholic High Sch, Cleveland 59-65; Libn St Joseph's Col U Div (Yorkton Sask) 65- Libn Sacred Heart Acad YorktonSask 65-. 9: CanLA; CathLA; SasASchL. 10: Sask Tchrs Fedn, Sask, Eng Tchrs'Assn. 14: Catlg, ref, admin. 15: St Joseph's Col, Univ Div, Yorkton Sask Can.

BYCZKOWSKI, (DASHKIEWICZ) MARIE. b Belorussia 5 Ja 43. 4: Alêx Byczkowski. 5: Douglass Col 62-66 (Russian Studies) AB; Rutgers 66-68 MLS. 6: Russian, Belorussian. 7: Ser & ref libn Wilkes Col Lib 68-. 9: AAUW; ALA. 10: Amer-Belorussian Youth Assn; Nat Slavic Honor Soc. 14: Ref, ser. 15: 580 N Franklin st, Wilkes-Barre Pa 18703.

BYERGO, FREDERICK H. b Chicago Ill 4 S 40. 5: LawrenceU 58-62 (Phil) BA; Rosary Col 67-68 MLS. 6: Fr. 7: Hd libn Cook Memorial Lib, Libertyville Ill 68-. 9: ALA; Laconi; IllLA. 10: Phi Mu Alpha. 14: Ref, admin. 15: 800 N Milwaukee, Libertyville Il 60048.

BYERLEY, MARY VIRGINIA (HENINGER). b Chilhowie Va 18 O 14. 4: James Lacy. 5: Fla StateU 60 (Educ) BS, 61 (LS) MS. 7: Libn: Brevard School Syst, Eau Gallie Fla 61-63, Brevard Jr Col, Cocoa Fla 63-64, Golden Hill Acad, Ocala Fla 64-68, Marion Co Schs, Dunnellon Fla 68-. 9: NatLA; FlaLA; MarionCoLA. 14: Sch libn. 15: 1427 NE First, Ocala Fl 32670.

BYERLY, IMOGENE (JONES) (McCARTHY). b Russellville Ark 29 Jl 11. 4: Theodore Carroll Byerly. 5: Barnard 29-33 (Eng Lit) AB; Columbia 33-38 (Col Libs) BLS; UMd 50-53 (Amer Civilization) MA. 6: Fr, Sp. 7: Asst to dir Three Arts Club (stud residence), NYC 33-38; Staff libn Barnard Col 38-40; Libn US Tariff Commsn, Wash DC 41; Staff libn DC Tchrs Col 44-66, Chief libn 66-. 9: ALA; NEA; DCLA; DCEA. 11: Agnes and Eugene Meyer Fellowship 67. 13: Yes. 14: Admin col & univ lib. 15: Six J Ridge rd, Greenbelt Md 20770.

BYERS, MRS EDNA (HANLEY). b Trenton Ohio 30 Mr 1900. 4: Noah Ebersole Byers. 5: Bluffton Col 18-23 (Fr) AB; UMich 26-27 AB in LS, summers 30, 31, 34 MA in LS. 6: Ger. 7: Sec to pres Bluffton Col 21-26, Libn 27-32; Ref asst NY Pub Lib summers 43-45; Lecturer UMich summers 52-55, 57; Libn Agnes Scott Col 32-. 8: Consul on lib bldg plans: Bennett Col 37-38, Rockford Col 39-40, Conn Col 40-41, Columbia Theol Sem 51-52, King Col 59-60; Consul on bk collections: Bennett Col 37-38, Tex Wesleyan 46-47. 9: ALA (Bldg Com 37-45);-ACRL (Bldg Com 55-59); SELA; GaLA; Atlanta Lib Club (pres 41-42). 10: Phi Beta Mu. 12: "College and University Buildings" (39); "Robert Frost at Agnes Scott College: a Bibliography" (63). 14: Admin. 15: 226 E Hancock st, Decatur Ga 30030.

BYMAN, JUDITH A. b Meriden Conn 11 N 35. 5: Simmons 53-57 (Biol) BS, 61-62 (LS) MS. 7: Research asst Harvard Sch of Pub Health 57-60; Circ asst Harvard Med Sch Lib 61-62; Reader's serv libn Edward G Miner Lib URochester Sch of Med & Dentistry 62-68; Instr & asst libn Monroe Commun Col Lib 68-. 9: MedLA-Upstate NY Reg Group. 14: Ref. 15: 1000 E Henrietta rd,Rochester NY 14623.

BYRD, CECIL KASH. b Winchester Ky 23 O 13. 4: Esther Sample. 5: Anderson Col 37 (Hist, Eng) AB; Ind U 38 (Hist, Govt) AM, 42 (Hist) PhD. 6: Ger, Fr, Indonesian. 7: Communications & exec off USS LST 338 43-45; Ind U: Tutor in Amer & European hist 39-41, Curator of rare bks & spec collections 42-46, Asst dir of libs 46-48, Assoc dir of libs 48-, Staff Grad Div of Lib Sch 49-64; Univ Libn 64-. 9: ALA-ACRL (Lib Bldgs Com 54-57, Bd on Bibliog 55-61); BSA; IndLA. 10: Caxton Club; Grolier Club. 11: Fellow, Carnegie Project in Advanced Lib Admin, Grad Sch of Lib Serv Rutgers U 58; Lib Adv to Natl Inst Adm, Djakarta Indonesia 61-62; Bldg consul to U of Islamabad Pakistan 68; Mem bk survey team to Indonesia 67. 12: "A Bibliography of Indiana Imprints, 1804-1854," with Howard H Peckman (55); Ed "Indiana University Bookman," "A Bibliography of Illinois Imprints 1814-1858," "Library Development in Eight Asian Countries," with David Kaser, C Walter Stone. 14: Admin, rare bks, lib bldgs. 15: Main Lib Ind Univ, Bloomington In 47405.

BYRD, IDA FAY (CAUDLE). b Iredell Co NC 28 My 38. 4: Kenneth Edwin Byrd. 5: Pfeiffer 56-57; Appalachian State Tchrs Col 57-59 (Eng) BS, 59-61 (LS) MA, summer 62 Certif Supv. 7: Tchr-libn Jonesville (NC) High Sch, 59-62, Libn & a-v coordinator 62-64; Instr in Lib Sci Marshall U 64-66; Dir Learning Resource Ctr Wilkes Commun Col (Wilkesboro)66-. 9: NEA-DAVI; ALA; NCLA; NCEA; NC Commun Col LA (dir West Gp 68-69). 10: AAUW;Fac Wives; Ladies Circle. 14: Ref. 15: RT 1, Roaring River NC 28669.

BYRD, MARION (ELAINE). b Johson City Tenn 26 D 34. 5: E Tenn StateU 53-57 (Eng) BS; Peabody Lib Sch 58-59 MALS. 7: Period libn Middle Tenn StateU 59-62; Period libn & asst ref libn DukeU Woman's Col Lib 62-. 10: Christian Bus & Prof Women's Coun; Book Club (chm). 14: Period, ref. 15: Woman's College Lib Duke Univ, Durham NC 27708.

BYRD, PATRICIA. b Salem Ore 17 Mr 23. 5: Willamette U 40-45 BA; UWash 58-59 (LS) ML. 6: Ger, Fr. 7: Casewker Ore State Pub Welfare, Portland Ore 45-55, Casewk supv 55-58; Gen reading room libn UWash 59-61; Soc wk libn Portland State Col 61-. 9: ALA; OreLA. 10: AAUP. 14: Ref. 15: 2235 SW VistaPortland Or 97201.

BYRD, RUBIA MAI. b Monticello Fla 22 O 42. 5: Fla A&M U 60-64 (LS) BS; Atlanta 65,67,68,69 (LS) MA. 6: Fr. 7: Head Libn Douglas Anderson High Sch, Jacksonville Fla 64-68; Libn Carter GWoodson High Sch, Jacksonville Fla 68-69. 9: ALA; NEA; FlaLA; Fla Tchrs Assn;FlaEA. 13: Yes. 14: Ref. 15: 1241 Hart st, Jacksonville Fl 32209.

BYRER, BEVERLY ELAINE. b Bourbon Ind 24 N 35. 5: Bob Jones U 55-56 (Home Econ); Purdue U 53-54, 56-58 (Home Econ) BS; Ind U 60-62 MSLS Bowling Green State U 66-67 (Biol). 6: Ger. 7: Asst buyer Robertson's Dept Store, SBend Ind 58-59; Asst libn Bendix Products Div, S Bend Ind 59-60; Tech libn Dow ChemLib, Midland Mich 62-64; Sci libn Bowling Green State U 64-67; Research libn Youngstown Sheet & Tube Co, Youngstown Ohio 67-. 9: SLA; ASIS (Libns Gp). 14: Ref,sci info. 15: Box 336 RT 1, Berlin Center Oh 44401.

BYRN, JAMES HARRY. b Frederick Okla 10 Ja 35. 4: Mary Jane Steele. 5: Cameron State Agric Col 53-55 (Engring) AA; UOkla 55-58 (Hist) BA, 68-69 MLS; UTex (El Paso) 65 (Hist). 7: (Capt) USA 58-68; Asst syst analyst Bizzell Lib UOkla 68-69; Dir Cameron Col Lib 68-. 9: ALA; OklaLA. 10: Reserve Offr Assn. 13: Yes. 14: Admin. 15: 3309 Atlanta ave, Lawton Ok 73501.

BYRNE, JERALDINE W(OZNAK). b Plainfield NJ 29 Ag 41. 4: Michael Byrne. 5: Elmira Col 59-60; UWis 60-63 (Greek) BA; UMinn 63-64 (LS) MA. 6: Fr, Grk. 7: Asst ref libn NorthwesternU 64-66; Asst acquis libn UIll (Chicago) 66-67; Asst acquis libn UCal (Riverside) 68-. 9: CalLA. 14: Acquis, gifts & exchange, nat bibliogr. 15: 910 W 21st, Upland Ca 91786.

BYRNE, SISTER ANNE LUCILLE. b Orange NJ 2 My 13. 5: Col of St Elizabeth 33-37 (Educ); Fordham 38 (Educ); State Tchrs Col 39 (Educ); Col of St Elizabeth 42 (Educ) BS; Catholic U 53-58 MLS. 6: Fr. 7: Elem tchr OLV Elem Sch, Jersey City NJ 35-49; High sch tchr Bayley-Ellard High Sch, Madison NJ 49-58, Libn 58-. 8: Prepared first catlg for Cath Lib Serv (Alesco) now serv 3000 schs; Adv Coun,title II Nat

Educ Act; Bk Sel Com, Cath Sup, H W Wilson Co; Supv of Province Libs,Sisters of Charity of St Elizabeth, Convent Station NJ 64-; chm Paterson DiocesanLib Coun 60,62,66,68. 9: ALA; CathLA (v-chm NJ Unit 63); NEA; NJLA; NJSchLA; Morris Co LA. 11: National Citation 1968, Encyclopedia Brittanica Awards Program. 12: "Handbook of Policies and Procedures for Volunteer Librarians (67). 14: Adult educcourses in lib sci. 15: Bayley-Ellard High Sch Lib, Madison ave, Madison NJ 07940.

BYRNS, JAMES FITZGERALD. b NYC 7 Ag 24. 5: St Joseph's Col & Sem(Dunwoodie NY) 44-48 (Philos) BA, 48-49 (Theol); Fordham 49-50 (Hist) MA; Columbia 51-53 MLS. 6: Lat, Fr. 7: Radio operator (PFC) US Army Air Force 43-44; Lat instr Castle Heights Mil Acad, Lebanon Tenn 51; Libn aide catlg div NY Pub Lib 51-53; Libn Brooklyn Pub Lib 53-56, Br libn 56-59; Libn Newspaper Agency Corp, Charleston WVa 59-60; Head of tech serv dept WVa Lib Commsn, Charleston WVa 60-61; Br libn Brooklyn Pub Lib 61-. 9: ALA; NYLA; NY Lib Club. 14: Ref, admin. 15: 220 Berkeley pl, Brooklyn NY 11217.

BYRUM, JOHN DONALD. b Wenatchee Wash 10 Je 40. 5: Harvard 58-62 (Hist) AB (magna cum laude); Rutgers 65-66 MLS. 6: Fr, Ger, Ital. 7: Asst to period libn UWash 64-65; Catlgr PrincetonU Lib 66-68, Hd catlgr 68-. 8: Inst on Middle Management in Libnship, umd's Sch of Lib & Info Serv 69. 9: ALA; NY Tech Serv Libns. 10: Beta Phi Mu. 12: Abstractor "Historical Abstracts and America: History and Life" (66-68). 13: Yes. 14: Catlg. 15: 253 Mount Lucas rd, Princeton NJ 08540.

BYSIEWICZ, SHIRLEY RAISSI. b Thompsonville Conn 16 Je 30. 4: Stanley J Bysiewicz. 5: UConn 49-51 (Pol Sci) BA, 51-53 LLB So Conn State Col 67 MSLS. 6: Fr, Lat, Gk. 7: Research assoc Conn Pub Expenditure Coun, Hartford Conn 52; Attorney at Law Raissi & Raissi Attys, Thompsonville Conn 54-; ProsecutingAtty, Town of Enfield, Thompsonville Conn 55-56; Prof of Law & Law libn UConn Law Sch 56-. 8: Lib consul to Middlesex Bar Lib, Middletown Conn, 59; Examiner for State of Conn Lib Examinees. 9: Amer Bar Assn; AALL (chm Microfacs Com 62-65; Law Lib Journal Com; Bus Mgr 68-); pres NE chap AALS (pres NE chap 65-67); Conn Bar Assn (Civil Rights Com 67-); Hartford Co Bar Assn (chm Com on Legal Status of Women). 12: Co-auth "Forms of Town Government in Connecticut" (51); Auth Survey of County Law Libraries in Connecticut (67); Co-auth Selected Annotated Bibliography on Education for Professional Responsibility." 13: Yes. 14: Legal catlg & bibliog; co law libs. 15: Univ of Conn Law Sch, W Hartford Ct 06105.

C

CABALLERO, ISABEL SEIJO. b Havana Cuba 7 My 26. 4: Alfredo A Caballero. 5: Havana U 46-50 (Arts) Dr in Philos & Arts, 50-51 (LS,52-60 (Educ) PhD. 6: Sp, Fr, Ital, Portu. 7: Head Libn Inst Nacional de Examen y Diagnostica INED, Havana Cua Cuba 52-54; Dir of Lib Palace of Fine Arts, Havana Cuba 54-60; Libn Pro-Arte Musical Assn, Havana Cuba 55-61; Head Libn Cuban Engnrs Assn, Havana Cuba 55-61; Dir Hosp, Havana Cuba 60-61; Catlgr Cornell U Med Lib 64; Asst libn NY Pub Lib 61-65; 1st asst per dept NY Acad of Med, NYC 65-66; Interlib loan libn UMiami Sch of Med Lib 67-. 8: Consul catlgr for "Libros in Vent, R R Boker Co, 64. 9: MedLA; SLA; NY Lib Club; Fla Med Libns. 13: Yes. 14: Catlg, interlib loan. 15: 21 NW 170th st, N Miami Beach Fl 33169.

CABEEN, SAMUEL KIRKLAND. b Easton Penn 22 Ja 31. 5: Lafayette Col 48-52 (Chem) BA; Syracuse U 52-54 (LS) MS. 6: Fr. 7: US Army Chem Corps (Sp-3) 54-56; Asst libn Amer Metal Climax Inc, NYC 56-58; Tech libn Ford Instrument Co LI NY 58-64; Asst to dir Engineering Societies Lib NYC 64-68, Dir 68-. 9: SLA;-NY Chap (Group chm 61-62, treas 62-65, pres-elect 65-66, pres 66-67); ASIS; ACS; NY Lib Club; Archons of Colophon; ALA. 10: Phi Gamma Delta; Amer Contract Bridge League. 14: Admin. 15: Engineering Societies Lib, 345 E 47th st, New York NY 10017.

CABLE, CAROLE (LAW-GAGNON). b New Orleans La 21 Ja 44. 4: Thomas Monroe Cable. 5: Tulane 62-65 (Hist, Art Hist) BA; UItal per Stranieri (Perugia Italy) 65; UTex 65-68 MLS. 6: Fr. 7: Lib asst, rare bks catlgr UTex (Austin) 66-68. 14: Rare bks. 15: 406 East 30th, Austin Tx 78705.

CACCESE, LOUIS WILLIAM. b Franklinville NJ 11 Ap 36. 4: Lesley Gross. 5: PMC Col 54-58 (Eng) BA; Drexel 64-66 (LS) MS. 6: Fr. 7: USA Inf (Capt) Fort Dix NJ 58-59; Libn Delsea Reg High Sch, Franklinville NJ 59-67; Lib dir Camden Co Col, Blackwood NJ 67-. 9: ALA; NJLA (Col & Univ Div sec-treas 68-69); NJEA; Two-Year Col Assn of NJ; Reserve Officers Assn of the US. 14: Admin. 15: Jamestown square apt C-1, Blackwood NJ 08012.

CACCESE, VINCENT. b SI NY 2 Jl 36. 5: UCLA 57 (Zool) BA; USoCal 60 (LS) MS. 6: Fr, Ger, Ital. 7: Asst order & catlg libn USoCal Sch of Med Lib 59-60; Asst sci & tech ref libn Cal State Col(Long Beach) Lib 60-63, Head sci & tech 63-65; Head ser & govt publs UCal(Irvine) Lib 65-67, Coord Br Libs 67-. 9: SLA (SoCal Chap; Com on Union Listof Ser in SoCal Libs); CalLA. 10: So Cal Acad of Scis; Beta Phi Mu. 13: Yes. 14: Research libs. 15: 859 Catalina st, Laguna Beach Ca 92651.

CADDY, REV JAMES L. b Cleveland 11 D 37. 5: Borromeo Col of Ohio 56-60 (Hist) AB; West Res 60-66 MS in LS. 6: Lat, Fr. 7: Libn Borrom eo Col (Wickliffe Ohio) 57-60; Libn St Mary Sem (Cleveland) 61-64, Head libn 64-. 9: ALA; CathLA (chm Adult sect, No Ohio unit). 10: NAACP, Citizens for Educl Freedom; Cath Interracial Coun, Liturgical Conf; Fd mem Cleveland Conf of Priests. 14: Theol ref wk, rare bks, catlg, visual aids. 15: 1227 Ansel rd, Cleveland Oh 44108.

CADE, BARBARA JANE (COX). b Miami Fla 10 Jl 28. 4: Kyle Richard Cade. 5: Womans Col of Ga 45-49 (Soc Studies, Educ) BS in ED; Emort U summers 50-53 MLS; UGa summer 65-67, 68 Cert in Lib Educ. 7: Semi-prof libn Woman's Col of Ga 49-50; High sch libn Atlanta Pub Schs 50-66; Res libn (supv) 66-; Temp instr W Ga Col 68, 69. 8: NDEA Inst, UGa summer 65. 9: ALA; NEA; GaLA (treas 68-69); GaEA; SELA; ASCD. 10: Delta Kappa Gamma. 14: Sch libs, ref. 15: 1820 Hurt rd SW, Marietta Ga 30060.

CADE, ROBERTA GERTRUDE. b Osborne Kan 28 D 36. 5: UDenver 54-58 (Eng) BA, 66 (LS) MA. 7: Eng tchr Pub Schs, Englewood Colo 58-60; Eng tchr Pub Schs, Lamar Colo 61-63; Sch libn, Kenosha Wis 63-68; Sch pub lib coordinator Mid-York lib syst 68-. 8: Bd of Dirs Swancott Home. 9: AAUW; NEA; NYLA; Central NYLA; NYStateA-v Assn; KenoshaEA (sec & v-pres); KenoshaLA (sec & v-pres). 14: Sch libnship. 15: 141 Genesee st, New Hartford NY 13413.

CADLE, DEAN. b Middlesboro Ky 16 Ja 20. 4: Jo Dannel. 5: Berea Col(Ky) 38-40, 46-47 (Eng) BA; Stanford 47-48 (On Wallace Stegner Creative Writing Fellowship); State U Iowa 49-50 (Eng) MA;UKy 56-57 (LS) MS. 7: Sgt US Air Force photographer & photo lab tech 42-46; Instr Union Col Barbourville Ky 50-53; Instr Detroit Inst of Tech 54-55; Asst ed "Wilson Library Bulletin, H W Wilson Co, (NY) summer 58; Ext libn Ky State dept of Libs (Frankfort Ky) 57-59; Asst in catlg dept UKy Lib 59-60; Libn UKy Southeast Commun Col (Cumberland Ky) 60-66; Asst lib UNC (Asheville) 66-. 9: SELA; Buncombe Co Lib Assn (pres). 10: AAUP. 11: Winner of nat short story contest sponsored by "Tomorrow Magazine (46). 12: Ed Bd "Western Review 49-50; Asst Ed "Wilson Library Bulletin summer (58). 13: Yes. 14: Acquis. 15: Univ of NC, Asheville NC 28801.

CADY, FAITH LUCILLE. b Gilbertsville NY 31 D 15. 5: Col of St Rose 34-38 (Lat) BA; Simmons 39-40 BS in LS; Catholic U 49-50 (LS). 7: Child libn Curtiss Mem Lib, Meriden Conn 41; ClerkSelective Serv System, Albany NY 41-43; Law-legis asst Social Security Admin, Washdc 43-47; Libn catlgr Civil Serv Commsn, Wash DC 47-48; Libn catlgr Dept of State,Wash DC 48-51; Libn catlgr Bur of Naval Weapons, Wash DC 51-61; Hd tech lib Bur ofNaval Personnel, Wash DC 61-. 9: SLA. 10: Amer Red Cross. 12: Ed "Monthly List of CurrentAccessions, BuPers Technical Library". 14: Catlg, ref. 15: 5112 Connecticut ave NW, Wash DC 20008.

CADY, FLORENCE (DAVIS). b Salem Ohio. 4: Robert F Cady. 5: Ohio Wesleyan 29-33 (Eng, Fr)BA; Ohio Wesleyan 33-35 (Eng) MA; West Res 37-40 (LS) BS. 7: Sec Elyr Home for the Aged, Ely ria Ohio 35-36; Sec Sch Nursing West Res 36-40; Lib asst Cleveland Pub Lib 40-42; Lib asst San Antonio Pub Lib, San Antonio Tex 43; Post libn Liberal Army Air Field, Liberal Kan 43-44; Lib asst Cuyahoga Co Pub Lib, Cleveland 61-67; Act supv ya Wor Cuyahoga Co Pub Lib 67; Hd readers' asst div Pub Lib Youngstown & Mahoning Co, Youngstown Ohio 67-. 9: ALA; OhioLA. 10: Zeta Tau Alpha; Ohio Hist Assn; West Res Hist Assn. 14: Programming for ya. 15: 227 N Cadillac dr, Youngstown Oh 44512.

CAFFEY, HELEN PAULINE. b Philippine Islands 4 D 06. 5: Incarnate Word Col 25-27; UColo 27-28 (Educ) AB, BE; Emory 29-30 AB in LS; UCal 46-47, 48-49 (LS). 7: Ref asst Carnegie Lib of Atlanta 30-38, Br libn 38-46; Asst Richmond Pub Lib, Richmond Cal 48-49; Asst Ventura Cal 49; Head Libn Thomas Branigan Mem lib, Las Cruces NM 50-. 9: ALA; SWLA; NMLA. 10: Altrusa Club; AAUW; Story League of Las Cruces; Dona Ana Co (NM) Hist Soc; Delta Kappa Gamma. 14: Ref, bk sel. 15: PO Box 547, Mesilla Park NM 88047.

CAGE, ALVIN C. b Flushing NY 26 Ap 43. 4: Lee Huber. 5: CUNY (Hunter Col) 60-64 (Econ) BA; Rutgers 64-66 MLS. 6: Fr. 7: Libn trainee Queens Borough Pub Lib, NYC 64-66; Acquis libn Tex So U 66-67, Coord tech serv 67-. 8: Lectr on acquis mechanization AALL inst on acquis 69. 9: TexLA (conf treas 69). 13: Yes. 14: Acquis & mechanization. 15: 4110 McKean, Houston Tx 77055.

CAGE, WALETHA (HUBER). b Okla City 30 D 40. 4: Alvin Cage. 5: Bethany Nazarene Col 60-61; Temple Jr Col 61-62; Tex Woman'sU 62-64 (LS) BS. 6: Sp. 7: Child libn Queens pub Lib, Queens NY 64-66; Libn Houston Independent Sch, Houston Tex 67-68; Child libn Houston Pub Lib, Houston Tex 68-. 9: SLA;-NY Chap (Group chm 61-62, treas 62-65, pres elect65-66, pres 66-67); ASIS; ACS; NY Lib Club; Archons of Colophon; ALA. 10: Phi GammaDelta; Amer Contract Bridge League. 15: 4110 McKean, Houston Tx 77055.

CAGEN, ESTHER (HIRSCH). b Cleveland 6 D 07. 4: Samuel Cagen. 5: Cleveland Sch of Educ 24-26 Certif; West Res 57-61 (Educ) BS Ed, 62-63 MLS; Kent U summer 65 NDEA Lib Inst. 6: Fr, Ger. 7: Sch lib asst Cleveland Pub Lib 26-36; Head child's room Cleveland Heights Pub Lib, Cleveland Heights Ohio 53-57; Elem sch libn Cleveland Heights Sch Sys, Cleveland Heights Ohio 57-. 8: Instr Children's Lit West Res U 65-68; Instr Child Lit, Cleveland State U 69-. 9: NEA; OhioLA; OhioSchLA. 10: Beta Phi Mu. 13: Yes. 14: Wk with child. 15: 1911 Forestview dr, ClevelandHeights Oh 41118.

CAHALAN, GERTRUDE. b Weir Kan 4 N 03. 5: State U Iowa 23-27 (Hist) BA, 27-28 (Hist) MA; Columbia summers 37-41 BS in LS. 7: Statistical clerk Central Pub Serv Corp, Chicago 30; Newark Pub Lib, Newark NJ: Jr lib asst 36-37, Child libn 38-43, Br libn 43-53, Sr lending & ref libn 53-. 9: ALA; SLA; Adult Educ Assn; NJLA; NJ Adult Educ Assn. 10: NJ Hist Soc. 12: Ed "Newark Public Library New," (52). 14: Ref, loc hist. 15: 376 Mt Prospect ave, Newark NJ 07104.

CAHALAN, THOMAS H. b Harpers Ferry Iowa 4 My 15. 4: Alice Patterson. 5: UIowa 35-37, 39-40 (Math) BA; UIll 40-41 BS in LS, 41-45 (LS)MS; American U 64-66. 7: Circ asst UIll Lib(Urbana) 41-42, Newspaper libn 42-46; Libn UOre Dental Sch 46-64; Head acquis libn Nat Inst ofHealth Lib 66-69; Asst acquis libn Northeastern U 69-. 9: ASIS; ALA-ACRL;-RTSD;-LAD;-LED; SLA (Biol Sci Div, Documentation Div, Sci-Tech Div);MedLA (chm Gifts & Grants Com 50-51, mem & chm Nomin Com 52-55, mem Microcard Com 57-58, mem Fed Rel Com 64-65, sec & chm Dental Group50-51, 58-59, 61, sec Pacific NW Group 57-59); PNLA (Bd dirs 53-55, chm Exhib Com 53); OreLA (treas 55-56, chm Exhib Com 49, Bd Dirs 53-55). 13: Yes. 14: Admin, automation. 15: 32 Allen rd, Tewksbury Ma 02173.

CAHALANE, EDMOND P(ATRICK). b Chicago 17 Mr 17. 4: Mary Murayama. 5: Train Class Chicago Pub Lib 39-40 Certif; Loyola U(Chicago) 38-41 (Philos) AB;St Louis U 43-44 (ASTP Ger Lang, & Area) Certif; Chicago 46 BLS; UMich 49-50 AMLS;USoCal summer 53 (LS); Grad Sch US Dept of Agric 56-57 (LS); Catholic U spring 57(LS). 6: Ger, Fr, Lat. 7: Acquis asst Chicago Pub Lib 40-41; Sgt US Army Air Forces 41-45; Ref libn US Air Force Tech Lib, Chanute Field Ill 41-42; Intel clerk US Army Mil Intel, Bayreuth Germany 48-49; Chief catlgr SCAP, CIE Info Centers Br, Tokyo Japan 50-51; Dir Hakodate SCAP, CIE Info Ctr, Hakodate Japan 51-52; Acquis asst USoCal Lib summer 53; NLM: Acquis asst 54; Head ser sect 54-58; Catlgr Spec Projs Off tech Lib US Bur Naval Weapons, Wash DC 58-59; Chief ref libn San Francisco Reg Off US Defense Documentation Center, Oakland Cal 59-61; Catlg-acquis libn Ames Res Center Tech Lib NASA, Moffett Field Cal 61-65; Sr tech libn Tech Info Ctr Xerox Corp, RochesterNY 66-67; Sr catlgr Eng Lang Sect, Descr Catlg Div LC, Wash DC 67-68, Supv specproblems unit, Eng Lang Sect, Descr Catlg Div 68-. 9: MedLA; Potomac Tech Proclibns. 14: Bibliog, catlg, ref, acquis, info retrieval. 15: 7421 Keystone lane apt 302, Forestville Md 20028.

CAHALANE, MARGARET (ELIZABETH). b Wash DC 22 Ap 42. 5: UColo 60-65 (Hist) BA; Case-West Res 65-66 (LS) MS. 6: Fr. 7: Stud asst UColo, 63-65; Asst ref libn Purdue 66-. 9: ALA (Jr Mem RT). 14: Soc sci, ref, doc. 15: 2410 Happy Hollow rd A-17, W Lafayette In 47906.

CAHILL, CAROL ANNE. b Brockton Mass 14 Mr 39. 5: Smith 57-61 (Eng) AB; Simmons 63-64 (LS) MS. 6: Fr. 7: Ref libn Arthur Young & Co, NYC 61-63; Ref libn Harvard Bus Sch Baker Lib 64-. 9: SLA (Pub Rel Com 66-67, Spec projs 68-69). 10: Harvard Lib Club (Treas 64-65). 14: Ref. 15: Reference Dept, Baker Lib Harvard Business School, Cambridge Ma 02138.

CAHILL, ELLEN F. b St Edward Neb. 5: St Ambrose-Marycrest Col 43 (Eng) BA; UDenver 53 (LS) MA UWis (Milwaukee) 68 (Inst-Non-Bk Materials) Certif. 7: Libn McQuaid JesuitHigh Sch Rochester NY 54-57; Asst libn Peru State Col 57-58; Child libn Los AngelesPub Lib 58-60; Libn Columbus Sr High Sch, Columbus Neb 60-; Asst Prof Ed Admin UNeb(Lincoln) summers 62-; Dir Centralized Lib Processing, Columbus City Schs, ColumbusNeb 68-. 9: ALA; -AASchL; Neb State LA; Neb Educ Media Assn. 14: Sch libnship,catlg. 15: 2708 27th st, Columbus Nb 68601.

CAHOON, HERBERT (THOMAS FULLER). b West Chatham Mass 29 D 18. 5: Harvard 36-40 (Hist) AB; Columbia 42-43 SBLS. 6: Fr. 7: Stud asst Harvard Col Lib 37-40, Asst catlg dept 40-41; Ref asst NY Pub Lib 41-48, First asst rare bk div 48-54; Dir lib serv & Curator of Autograph MSS Pierpont Morgan Lib, NYC 54-. 9: ALA; Bibliog Soc (London); BSA; NY Lib Club. 10: Bibliographical Soc UVa; James Joyce Soc; Manuscript Soc; Melville Soc; Poetry Soc of Amer; Assn Internationale de Bibliophilie (Paris). 12: "Thanatopsis" (poems 49); "Herman Melville: a check List" (51); Co-comp "Bibliography of James Joyce"; Contrib "Oxford Companion to the Theatre" (51); "The Clifton Waller Barrett Library" (60); "The Overbrook Press Bibliography" (63). 13: Yes. 14: Autograph mss, rare bks. 15: 29 E 36th st, New York NY 10016.

CAIL, NADA (HENDERSON). b Jacksonville Fla 2 N 40. 4: John Wilson Cail. 5: Warren wilson Jr Col 58-60 (Eng) AA; Bennett Col 60-62 (LS) BA; Villanovia 65-68 (LS) MS. 6: Fr, Ger. 7: Tchr-libn Phila Bd of Educ, 62-63; Circ ref libn Benjamin Franklin inst, Phila 63-65; Dir nursing lib Hahnemann Med Col Sch of Nursing, Phila 65-68; Dir tech serv Villanovia Sch Law 68-. 8: Consul in establishing lib for Commun Health Ctr, Phila 67-68. 9: AALL; SLA. 10: Delaware Valley Bennett Col Alumnae Assn; NAACP. 11: SLA Scholarship award. 13: Yes. 14: Ref & research, lib admin. 15: Box 124 3 Penambler rd, Pennllyn Pa 19458.

CAIN, ALEXANDER MATHIESON. b Aberdeen Scot 2 Ja 30. 5: AberdeenU 46-50 (Eng) MA; UParis 50-52; AberdeenU 52-54 PhD. 6: Fr, Ger, Ital, Swedish, Dutch. 7: Asst keeper British Mus dept of printed bks, London England 54-66; Lib systems analyst & Asst Prof med bibliography SUNY (Syracuse) biomed communication network 66-. 8: Sec Anglo-Amer Conf on Mechanization of libs, Oxford England 66. 9: MedLA; ASIS; MedLA Upstate NY. 10: AAUP. 12: Associate Ed "Bulletin of the Medical Library Association" (69-). 13: Yes. 14: Lib automation, catlg, subj indexing. 15: 875 Ostrom ave, Syracuse NY 13210.

CAIN, JACK. b Newmarket Ontario Can 16 D 40. 5: UToronto 58-62 (Eng) BA; UBritish Columbia 65-66 (LS) BLS. 6: Fr. 7: Asst hd Catlg Dept UToronto Lib 66-69. 9: ALA. 14: Catlg. 15: UToronto Lib, Ontario Can.

CAIN, ROBERT EVANS. b Marble City Okla 21 Jl 38. 5: Lawrence Col 57-61 (Eng) AB (cum laude); Simmons 62-64 (LS) MS. 6: Fr. 7: Asst mgr Libns Club Swimming Pool, Antioch Ill 59; Lifeguard Sherwood Park Inc, Lake Villa Ill summer 60; Circ asst Lawrence Col Lib 59-61; Eng tchr Cherry Creek high Sch, Englewood Colo spring 61; Ser asst Tufts U Lib 61; Circ asst Belmont PubLib, Belmont Mass 62-63; Ref libn Reading Pub Lib, Reading Mass 63-64; Ref libncary Mem Lib, Lexington Mass 64-66, Ref supv 66-. 9: ALA; MassLA (Pub Rel Com 68);NELA (chm Pub Rel Com 66-68); LPRC; NE Screen Educ Assn. 10: ACLU; Urban League of Greater Boston. 13: Yes. 14: Ref, pub rel, admin. 15: 14 Washburnst, Watertown Ma 02172.

CAIN, ROBERT LOUIS. b Alba Tex 17 D 24. 4: Kathleen Cypert. 5: Baylor 46-50 (Hist) BA; LSU 52-55 (LS) MS; Columbia 60 (LS); UChicago 62-63 (LS). 6: Fr, Ger, Ital. 7: Docs & sci ref libn NWest State Col (La) 55-63; Hd readers serv 63-65; Asst to dir PurdueU Libs (Lafayette) 65-67; Libn II Wash StateU Lib 68-. 8: Visiting libn Indian Inst of Tech, Kanpur India 66-67. 9: ALA. 10: AAUP; Alpha Beta Alpha. 14: Ref, admin. 15: 210 Harrison, Pullman Wa 99163.

CAIN, RUTH (RODEN). b Florence Ala 26 O 31. 4: Arthur R Cain. 5: Florence State Col 49-50, 63-65 (Eng); UAla 50-52 (Eng) AB; UNC 65-68 MSLS. 6: Fr. 7: Lib asst Baptist sem Lib, Louisville Ky 52-54; Lib asst Louisville Pub Lib, Louisville Ky 54-55; Tchr fants Jr High Sch, Anderson SC 57-58; Tchr Tchr Train Col, Two Nigeria 61-62; Libn city & Reg Planning Dept UNC (Chapel Hill) 65-68; Asst docs expediter LC 68-. 15: 2205 Georgian way, Wheaton Md 20902.

CAIN, STITH MALONE. b Nashville 25 S 11. 4: Mary Elizabeth Woodcock Cain. 5: Vanderbilt 30-34 (Hist) BA; UVa 34-36 (Econ) MA; Peabody 37-38 BS in LS, 44-45 (Educ) M of Ed. 6: Fr. 7: Dir of Libs Haines City (Fla) Pub Schs 38-40; Asst libn Morehead State Col 40-42; Army libn Camp Wallace Tex, Camp Fannin Tex 42-44; Head libn NM State Tchrs Col 45-46; Head libn Union Col (Barbourville Ky) 46-47; Head libn Central Col (Fayette Mo) 47-53; Head libn Ill Wesleyan U 53-57; Head libn Wis State U (Whitewater) 57-. 8: Consul to Iowa Wesleyan Col Lib & to Dakota Wesleyan U Lib 56, 59, 60; Adv Coun to Bloomington (Ill) Pub Schs. 9: ALA (Memb Com); -ACRL (var coms); NMLA (v-pres 45-46); WisLA (chm Col & Univ Libs Sect 67-68); KyLA (chm Col Lib Sect 46-47); WisEA; TennHA. 10: Assn of Wis State U Faculties (chm Col Sect); Assn of Wis State U Head Libns (Coun chm); Kiwanis (pres 65); Pi Gamma Mu; Phi Delta Kappa; Madison (Wis) Civil War Round Table; Bus Manager "MoLA Quarterly". 11: Du Pont Fellowship in Econ UVa; Scholarship George Peabody Col for Tchrs Grad Lib Sch. 13: Yes. 14: U lib admin. 15: 775 W Main st, Whitewater Wi 53190.

CAINE, BEATRICE (ROTHSCHILD). b Chicago Ill 15 Ap 17. 4: Edmund Arthur Caine. 5: UAla 34-38 (Eng) BA; Emory 38-39 (LS) BA. 6: Fr & Ger. 7: Ref libn NY Pub Lib 39-43; Libn Coca-Cola Co, Atlanta Ga 43-44; Hd period dept USC 44-45; Catlgr Ga State Dept of Educ, Atlanta 48-49; Catlgr OglethorpeU 50; Acquis libn Ga Inst of Tech 51-. 9: GaLA; SELA; Metropolitan Atlanta Lib Club. 10: Beta Phi Mu; League of Women Voters; Sigma Delta Tau; Chi Delta Phi; Alpha Lambda Delta& mortar Bd; AAUP. 14: Acquis. 15: 1956 Lebanon dr NE, Atlanta Ga 30324.

CAIRNS, ELEANOR C(HISHOLM). b Boston 23 Jl 09. 5: Columbia 39-41. 7: Lib asst Baker Lib Harvard Bus Sch 28-35; Asst catlgr Harvard Col Lib 35-39; High sch libn Dalton Schs, NYC 39-42; Catlgr Harvard Col Lib 43-45; Libn Burbank Hosp Sch of Nursing, Fitchburg Mass 45-63; Libn Child Hosp Sch of Nursing, Boston 63-66; Libn Med Lib Me Med Ctr, Portland Me 66-. 8: Consul to 3 nursing sch libs & 1 hosp med lib, 57-65. 9: ALA; MedLA (Mass Chap; presHosp Lib Group 65); Nat League Nurs; Nat Tuberc Assn (voting mem); Mass League Nurs(Bd Dirs 65-); Mass Tuberc & Health League (Clerk of Corp, Exec Com, Med Educ Com55-); Boston Tuberc Assn (Exec Com, Nurs Educ Com 63-); MeLA. 10: Amer Cancer Soc;Nat Tuberculosis & Respiratory Disease Assn; Me Tuberculosis & Health Assn; AltrusaClub. 11: Del to Internat Congress of Union Against Tuberc, Rome, 63. 13: Yes. 14: Bk sel (med), med ref. 15: 131 Chadwick st, Portland Me 04102.

CALARCO, PASCAL JEROME. b Kitchener Ont 28 F 26. 4: Marcella Louise Wittig. 5: UWindsor 54 (Philos) BA; Ontario Col of Educ UToronto 55 High Sch Asst's Certif; Toronto 59 BLS. 6: Fr, Ital. 7: (Pvt) Can Army Overseas, Europe 44-46; Tchr StJerome Sch, Kirkland Lake Ont 54-55; Tchr-libn St Lawrence High Sch, Cornwall Ont58-59; Tchr-libn Lawrence Heights Jr High Sch, N York Ont 60-62; Tchr-libn SouthwoodSecondary Sch, Galt Ont 62-64; Tchr-libn Forest Heights Collegiate, Kitchener Ont64-65; Dir of sch libs Kitchener-Waterloo (Ont) High Sch Bd 65-66; Sch lib consul ont Dept Educ, Waterloo Ont 66-. 9: CanLA (YP's Sect); OntLA (Com for Sch LibStands 63, chm Sch & Interm Sect 62); OntEA (v-chm Sch Lib Div). 10: Can Operaguild. 14: Sch lib serv, profess educ for sch libns. 15: 279 Weber st N, WaterlooOntario Can.

CALDER, CAROL ANN. b Sydney Nova Scotia Can 9 Jl 38. 5: Marianapolis Col 57-58 BA; McGill 58-60 (Eng Lit); UToronto 66-67 BLS. 7: Asst to advertising mgr Can Cement Co Ltd, Montreal 60-61; Hd circ Sir George WilliamsU Lib 61-66; Circ libn UToronto 67-68; A-v libn Ontario Inst for Studies in Ed, Toronto 68-. 9: CanLA; SLA. 14: Pub serv. 15: #1605 50 Prince Arthur ave, Toronto 5 Ontario Can.

CALDWELL, FRANCES (THORNBURG). b Detroit Mich 29 Ag 16. 5: Wayne State U 34-38 (Hist) BA; Wayne State U 62-64 (LS) M Ed. 7: IBM operator Mich Blue Cross, Detroit 39-44; v-pres Alfred B Caldwell Inc, Detroit 44-69; Libn Detroit Bd of Educ, 64-. 8: Recreation Center for the Handicapped for the City of Detroit, Book Selection Committee-Detroit Public Schools 67. 9: ALA; -AASchL; MichEA; DetroitEA. 1: Internat Platform Assn. 10: Sigma Kappa; Bushnell Child Study Club; Bushnell Child study Club Nursery School; (memb 3 alum assns) Wayne State U. 14: Child lit. 15: 16700 Shaftsbury rd, Detroit Mi 48219.

CALDWELL, GEORGE HOWARD. b Holton Kan 29 S 26. 4: Marcia Sweetman. 5: UKan 44-48 (Pol Sci) BA; Harvard 48-50 (Govt) MA; Wichita U 51-53 (Educ); Columbia 54-55 MSLS. 7: Tech writer Boeing Aircraft Co, Wichita Kan 51-54; LC: Intern trainee 55-56, Bibliogr legis ref serv 56, Asst head European exch sec 56-57; Head govt documents sect UKan Lib 57-61, Head ref dept 61-66; Hd Pub Ref Sect LC 66-. 9: ALA. 10: Phi Beta Kappa; Omicron Delta Kappa. 13: Yes. 14: Ref, docs. 15: 10010 Frederick ave, Kensington Md 20795.

CALDWELL, JOHN (CHARLES). b Latrobe Penn 28 Ag 26. 4: Clara Jane Tovo. 5: St Vincent Col 46-50 (Hist) BS; UPenn 50-51 (Amer Civilization) MA; Drexel 53-54 MSLS. 7: Yeoman 3rd class US Navy 45-46; Prod expediter ACF-Brill Motors, Phila 51-53; Catlgr Drew U 54-56, Asst libn tech serv 56-61; Libn Cal Lutheran Col 61-. 9: Amer Studies Assn; CalLA. 10: Luth Soc for Worship, Music, & the Arts; Beta Phi Mu. 13: Yes. 15: Cal Luth Col Lib, Mountclef Village, Thousand Oaks Cal 91360.

CALDWELL, ROSEMARY (SCHILLY). b St Louis Mo. 5: Maryville Col 30-34 (Philosophy) AB; LSU 40-41 (LS) BS; UIll 44-45 MS. 6: Fr. 7: Libn Barat Catholic Action Ctr, St Louis 34-37; Sub-prof asst Divoll Br St Louis Pub Lib 39-40; Asst Stat ions Dept St Louis Pub Lib 41-43; Libn Champaign Jr High Sch Champaign Ill 43-46; Libn Amer Lib Assoc Hdqrs Chicago 46-47; Libn Haven Sch Evanston Ill 47-48; Dental Ln med l n Loyola U Chicago 48-54; 1st asst ya dept Educ Dept St Louis 54-59; Chief app sci dept St Louis Pub Lib 59-67; Ref libn St Louis U Med Ctr 68-. 9: MedLA; SLA; (various officer & coms in Greater St Louis Chap); CathLA (various offices & coms in Greater St Louis Unit). 10: Beta Phi Mu. 15: 4321 S Compton ave, St Louis Mo 63111.

CALDWELL, ROSSIE JUANITA (BROWER). b Columbia SC 4 N 17. 4: Dr Harlowe Evans Caldwell. 5: Claflin Col 33-37 (Eng) BA (magna cum laude); SCar State Col 49-52 (Educ) MS; UIll 54-59 MSLS; Columbia summer 61; Duquesne U summer 65. 6: Fr. 7: Tchr-libn Reed st High Sch, Anderson SC 37-39; Tchr-libn Emmett Scott High Sch, Rock Hill SC 39-42; Tchr-libn, libn Wilkinson High Sch, Orangeburg SC 42-43, 45-57; War Dept clerk-stenogr, Tuskegee Army Air Field 43-45; Asst Prof SCar State Col Lib Serv Dept 57-. 8: Instr, NDEA Inst on Elem Sch Libnship, Scar State Col, summer 66. 9: NEA;ALA; SCLA; SCEA; SELA. 10: Alpha Kappa Alpha; Links Inc; Methodist Wesleyan ServGuild; AAUP; Beta Phi Mu; NAACP; Nat Assn of Col Women. 12: Comp "Profile oflibrarians (A Directory)," PalmettoEA (64, Sup 65-67). 13: Yes. 14: Sch libnship, new lib media. 15: PO Box 686, Orangeburg SC 29115.

CALDWELL, SUSAN ELLEN. b Roanoke Va 15 O 42. 5: Radford Col 61-64 (LS) BS 64-67 (Eng) MS. 7: Asst libn & a-v Pulaski High Sch, Pulaski Va 64-68; Lib Radford High Sch, Radford Va 68-. 9: NEA (Libns Sect); VaEA (Libns Sect); VaLA. 10: Kappa Delta Pi; Pi Gamma Mu. 14: Second sch libs. 15: Rt 3, Box 650, Riner Va 24149.

CALE, PATRICIA SUE. b Wytheville Va 10 O 42. 4: Robert Fieldon Cale. 5: Radford Col 61-64 (LS) BS. 7: Tchr Wythe Co Schs, Wytheville Va 65, Libn George Wythe High Sch, Wytheville Va 65-; Libn Wytheville Elem Sch 67, 68. 9: VaEA (sec-treas Dist I Lib); VaLA. 14: Ref serv. 15: 645 W North st, Wytheville Va 24382.

CALFEE, LENORA ANN (McMULLEN). b Clearwater Fla 20 My 35. 4: Howard F Calfee. 5: St Louis Inst of Mus Summer 55; Asbury 56-58 (Mus Ed); UFla 58-60 (Music Ed) BA; Fla State U 63-64 MLS. 7: Billing clk City Fuel Po& Co Clearwater Fla 53-54; Billing clk Howard Scoggins Golf Co, Dunedin Fla 54-55; Semi-sr clk Minute Maid Corp, Dunedin Fla 55-56; Mus tchr Horace Mann Jr High Sch, Brandon Fla 60-61; Lib asst Gen Nuclear Eng Co, Dunedin Fla 62-63; Oak Ridge Nat Lib, Tenn: Lib spec, 64-68, Tech Libn (cat) 68-. 9: SLA (sec Sou Appalachian Chap). 14: Catlg. 15: 214 Virginia rd, Oak Ridge Tn 37830.

CALHOUN, CARROLL R. b Roan Mountain Tenn 12 Jl 29. 4: Bonnie McBride. 5: E Tenn State U 47-51 (Eng, Soc Studies) BS; Appalachian State Tchrs Col summers 53-56 (LS) MA. 6: Sp. 7: Pub info clerk USAF, Tyndall AFB Fla 51-52; Libn Valdese High Sch, Valdese NC 52-56, Libn Grandview Jr High Sch, Hickory NC 56-62; Lib supv NC Ind Educ Center Program, Raleigh NC 62-63; Lib supv Dept of Commun

Cols(Raleigh NC) 63-66; State supv Fed Programs for Instrl Materials & ESEA Title II Dept of PublInstr, Raleigh NC 66-. 8: Consul on Libs for Technician Educ Dept of Health, Educ & Welfare, 65. 9: NEA; NCEA; NCLA; ALA; SELA. 10: Jr C of C; Lions Club. 14: Supv, ref, acquis, catlg. 15: 403 Lakeside dr, Garner NC 27705.

CALHOUN, KIMIKO HAZEL (KUSACHI). b Hood River Ore 16 D 29. 4: Harold G Calhoun. 5: Ore State Col 48-51 (Phys Educ) BS; UWash 59-69 MLib. 7: Tchr: Glendale High Sch, Glendale Ore 51-54, Wy East High Sch, Hood River Ore 54-55, Seattle Pub Schs 57-; Health educ dir YWCA, Portland Ore 55-57. 9: NEA; WashEA; SeattleTA. 14: Sch lib serv. 15: 5231 16th ave SW, Seattle Wa 98106.

CALHOUN, WANDA JUNE. b Mayfield Ky 23 Ja 32. 5: Murray(Ky) State Col 50-53 (Math, LS) BS; UMich 53-55 AMLS. 7: Div libn UMich 53-58; Head Libn Heidelberg Col 58-63; Head Libn Fla Presbyterian Col 63-. 8: Visiting specialist in lib serv for United Bd for Christ Higher Educ in Asia (Philippines, Hong Kong, Taiwan, & Korea) 65-66 (On leave from Fla Presbyterian Col). 9: ALA; FlaLA. 10: AAUP. 14: Col lib admin, catlg. 15: Fla Presby Col Lib, St Petersburg Fl 33733.

CALI, JOSEPH JOHN. b Amsterdam NY 17 O 28. 5: Union Col(Schenectady NY) 47-51 AB; West Res 51-52 MS in LS; UMich 57- (LS). 6: Fr, Ger. 7: Sci & music libn Antioch Col 52; Sgt artillery US Army, Germany 52-54; AntiochCol; Sci & music libn 54-55, Period & music libn 55-65, Assoc libn 62-, Libn forpub serv 65-. 15: Olive Kettering Lib, Antioch Col, Yellow Springs Oh 45387.

CALKIN, HOMER L. b Clearfield Iowa 5 My 12. 4: Corrine Reynolds. 5: Simpson Col 30-32 (Music); State U Iowa 33-39 (Hist) BA, MA, PhD. 6: Fr. 7: Tchr Lyons Twp High Sch, LaGrange Ill 41-42; Org & propaganda analyst Dept of Justice, Wash DC 42-43; Army Mil Intelligence (1st Lt) 43-46; Lecturer American U 46, 47; Archivist Nat Archives, Wash DC 46-50; Chief records mgt staff Dept of State, Wash DC 50-58, Mgt analyst 58-68, Hist 68-. 8: Com to formulate an archival policy for The Methodist Church Chm Archives Com, The United Methodist Church. 9: AHA;SAA; SoHistSoc; OrgAmerHistns; State Hist Soc Iowa; Cosmos Club. 12: "Castings Fromthe Foundry Mold" (68). 13: Yes. 14: Church archives. 15: 1117 S Quincy st, Arlington Va 22204.

CALLAHAM, BETTY (ELGIN). b Honea Path SC 8 O 29. 5: Duke 46-50 (Hist, Educ) BA; Emory 53-54 (Hist) MA, 60-61 (LS) ML. 6: Fr. 7: Tchr Newton Elem Sch, Newton NC 50-51; Tchr NC Sch for the Blind, Raleigh NC 51-53; Tchr Columbus High Sch, Columbus Ga 54-55; Tchr Hanna High Sch, Anderson SC 55-60; SC State Lib Bd, Columbia SC: Field serv libn 61-64, Field consul 64-65, Dir field serv 65-. 8: Lib/USA NY World's fair, 64; Conf Coord, SC Governor's Conf on Pub Libs, 65. 9: ALA; SELA; SCLA (chm Com on Lib Respons & Relnships 64, chm Pub Libs Sect 65). AAUW; SCarolinianaSoc; Beta Phi Mu. 11: Scholarship Emory U Div of Libnship 60; Beta Phi Mu Award 62. 12: "The Carnegie Library School of Atlanta (1905-1925)." 14: Ref, adult serv. 14: Ref, adult serv, admin. 15: 1830 St Michaels rd, Columbia SC 29210.

CALLAHAN, GERALDINE. b Saratoga Springs NY 17 S 25. 5: SUNY(Albany) 47 (Fr) AB, 52 MLS. 6: Fr, Ger. 7: Asst libn Metal & Thermit, Woodbridge NJ 48-49; Res libn Amer Smelting & Refining, Barber NJ 49-52; High sch libn Port Jervis High Sch, Port Jervis NY 52-65; Sr ref libn Newark Pub Lib, Newark NJ 65-. 9: SLA (Bus & Fin Div, NY chap). 10: Volunteers of the Shelters. 14: Ref. 15: 34 Commerce st, Newark NJ.

CALLAHAN, JOSEPH FRANCIS. b Detroit Mich 6 Jl 38. 5: Detroit Engring Inst 57-58 (Drafting) Diploma; UDetroit 60-65 (Geog) AB; UMich 65-66 AMLS; Wayne State 67- (Geog) MA. 6: Fr. 7: Draftsman Mercier Brick Co, Dearborn Mich 58-62; Plant employee Brickley Dairy Farms, Detroit 62-66; Ref libn Detroit Pub Lib 67-. 9: ALA (Jr Mems RT). 14: Ref. 15: 8080 Sprague, Detroit Mi 48214.

CALLAHAN, LINDA A (DURGIN). b Somerville Mass 8 F 44. 4: Kevin W Callahan. 5: Emmanuel Col (Boston) 61-65 (Chem) AB; Simmons 65-66 (LS) MS. 7: Asst res libn Cabot Corp Billerica Res Ctr 66-68; Res libn Cabot Corp Tech Info Serv 68-. 9: ACS; SLA (Boston Chap: sec-treas Sci-Tech Group 68-69). 14: Catlg, ref. 15: 161 Highland ave, Arlington Ma 02174.

CALLAHAN, ROSE (ELIZABETH). b South Hill Va 28 O 35. 5: UNC(Greensboro) 53-57 (Eng) AB; UNC(Chapel Hill) 63-64 MSLS. 6: Sp. 7: Eng tchr Princess Anne High Sch, Lynnhaven Va 57-60; Asst ed Med Economics, Oradell NJ 61-62; Research asst Richardson Found, NYC 62-63; Ref libn McGraw-Hill Inc, NYC 64-67; Asst libn Port of NY Authority 67-. 9: SLA. 10: Beta Phi Mu. 14: Ref. 15: 80 E End ave, New York NY 10028.

CALLAN, REV HENRY THOMAS. b Pittsfield Mass 10 Mr 32. 5: Assumption Col (Mass) 49-54 (Eng) BA; Chateau de Lormoy Sem Paris 54-58 (Theol); Catholic U 61-62 MS in LS. 6: Fr, Sp. 7: Head libn & hist tchr Assumption Prep Sch, Worcester Mass 62-69; Hd libn & hist tchr Milton Acad, Milton Mass 69-. 9: ALA; CathLA; NELA. 10: Archaeol Assn Amer; Friend of the Worcester Pub Lib; Worcester Art Museum. 14: Ref, rare bks. 15: Assumption Prep Lib, 670 W Boylston st, Worcester Ma 01606.

CALLARD, CAROLE SUE (CRAWFORD). b Charleston W Va 8 Ag 41. 4: Donald P Callard. 5: Morris Harvey Col 59-63 (Hist) BA; MarshallU 63-64 Sic Educ Vertif; W VaU 64; UPittsburgh 65-66 MLS. 7: Tchr Blessed Sacrament Elem Sch, S Charleston W Va 62-64; Libn trainee W Va Lib Commsn, Charleston 64-65; Adult serv libn Tompkins Co Lib, Ithaca NY 66-. 9: ALA. 10: Beta Phi Mu. 14: Ref, adult serv. 15: 805 N Tioga st, Ithaca NY 14850.

CALLARD, DONALD POPE. b Charleston W Va 29 D 37. 4: Carole Crawford. 5: Marietta 55-58 (Eng); Morris Harvey Col 58-60 (Eng) BA; UPittsburgh 64-65 MLS. 7: Asst libn Inst of Ophthalmology Columbia-Presbyterian Med Ctr, NYC 61; Bds clk (Spec/4) USA Adj Gen Corps 61-63; Asst catlgr Kanawha Co Pub Lib, Charleston W Va 64-65; Sr asst libn catlg cornellU 66-69; Hd tech serv Haile Sellassie I U Libs, Addis Ababa Ethiopia 69-. 9: MusLA. 14: Catlg, tech serv. 15: 805 N Tioga st, Ithaca NY 14850.

CALLAWAY, INEZ NMN. b Louisville Miss 9 S 09. 5: Sunflower Jr Col 30-32 Certif; Delta State Col 33-35 9elem Educ) BS; UDenver 45-46 BSLS. 7: Elem tchr pub sch, Miss 35-40; Elem tchr Indian serv, Window Rock Ariz 40-45; Libn Fitzsimons Army Hosp, Denver 46-47; Libn VA Hosp, Albuquerque NM 47-52; Chief Libn VA Hosp, Grand Junction Colo 52-55; Chief Libn Glenn Dale Hosp, Glenn Dale Md 55-58; Chief Libn VA Hosp, Wash DC 58-. 15: VA Hosp, 50 Irving st NW, Wash DC 20422.

CALLETTO, MARY JOYCE ANN. b Lyons NY 26 N 32. 5: State U Col (Geneseo NY) 50-54 (LS) BS. 6: Fr, Ital. 7: Child libn Maplewood Mem Lib, Maplewood NJ 54-63; Child libn Monmouth Co Lib, Freehold NJ 63-. 8: Child World Lib, Library/USA World's Fair 65 local a-v lib wk. 9: ALA-CSD (Newbery-Caldecott Com 67); Educ Film LA; NJLA (var offs); NY Film Coun; Women CathLA. 10: BPW. 11: Am Film Festival Juror. 14: Child wk, a-v materials. 15: 100 Broad st, Freehold NJ 07728.

CALLIS, LUCILE. b Providence Ky 14 Ag 14. 4: Henry Callis. 5: West Tchrs Col (Ky) 31-34 (Eng) AB; Peabody 58-60 (LS) MA. 7: Sec Peabody Col 37-42; Tchr-libn S Hopkins High Sch, Nortonville Ky 57-59; Reg libn Ky State Dept of Libs, Owensboro Ky 60-. 8: Mem Governors Planning Com on Libs 67-68. 9: KyLA; SELA. 10: AAUW; Bus & Prof Women; Beta Phi Mu; Kappa Delta Pi. 14: Regl lib devel. 15: Rt 2, Utica Ky 42376.

CALLISON, HELEN (LEPPARD). b Chicago Ill 20 Jl 27. 4: Preston Harvey Callison. 5: USCar 43-47 (Eng, Psych) AB, 67-69 (LS); Columbia Col 59-60 (LS). 7: Tchr Walterboro Schs, Walterboro SC 47-48; Tchr Greenville City Schls, Greenville SC 48-49; Libn Sp Serv USA, Ft Jackson SC 54-57; Tchr Brookland-Cayce Schs, W Columbia SC 57-58, 49-50; Libn Airport High Sch, W Columbia SC 62-69. 9: SCLA (chm Sch Libns Sect 68-69). 10: High sch lib club, sponsor; Girl Scout leader. 14: Wk with yp; educ libnship. 15: 1520 Alpine dr, West Columbia SC 29169.

CALLOW, MARJORIE SHERMAN. b Dexter Iowa 3 My 12. 4: William Warren Callow. 5: UCLA 30-34 (Economics) AB; USan Francisco 58-60, 62 Libnship Credential; San Francisco State Col 60-61 (Educ); San Jose State Col 62, 65-67 MA Libnship. 7: Libn Woodside Priory Sch, Portola Valley Cal 60-61; A-v media specialist Hillside High Sch, San Mateo Cal 61-62;Libn Arroyo High Sch, San Lorenzo Cal 62-63; Asst libn-chief catlgr for Amer Studies, Burlingame Cal 63-64; Libn Bellarmine Col Prep, SanJose Cal 64-66; Libn-media specialist M D Silva Intermed Sch, Newark Cal 66-. 9: ALA; -AASchL; NTA; CalLA; CalASchL; CalTA. 10: Friends of the San

Mateo Pub Lib; AAUW; San Mateo Br: (Scholarship, Fellowship, Member, Prog, Choral, Cal Fact & Legend Comms); Girl Scout & Campfire Gorls consul & leader. 12: "A Directory of Special Libraries in the San Francisco Bay Region Available to the Public (67). 14: Catlg, ref, sch lib admin. 15: 605 Comet dr, Foster City Ca 94404.

CALLOWAY, JOSEPHINE ANN. b Tacoma Wash 26 Mr 21. 5: Dominican Col of San Rafael (Cal) 38-39, 40-42 (Hist) BA; UWash 39-40 (Hist); Catholic U summers 44-49 (Hist), 49-50 MSLS. 6: Fr. 7: Libn Metro Life Ins Co, San Francisco 60-. 9: SLA. 14: Ref, bk sel. 15: Metro Life Ins Co, 600 Stockton st, San Francisco, Ca 94120.

CALVANO, MARY FLORENCE. b Erie Penn 28 D 17. 5: Villa Maria Col 36-40 (Biol) BS; UPitt 40-42 (Biol); Allegheny Col summer 42 (Chem); West Res 55-56 (Documentation) MSLS. 6: Ital, Fr, Sp, Ger. 7: Sub tchr Erie Sch Syst, Erie Penn; Lib asst Erie Pub Lib, Erie Penn 40-42; Chem Keystone Ordnance Wks, Geneva Penn 42-43; Spectrographer Aluminum Forgings, Erie Penn 43-45; Hd bus & tchr div Erie Pub Lib, Erie Penn 45-48; Hd chem lib, Hd health physics & Met Lib Oak Ridge Nat Lab, Oak Ridge Tenn 48-54; Ref libn Battelle Memorial Inst, Columbus Ohio 54-55; Tech lit spec Amer Sterilizer Co, Erie Penn 56-64; Libn Lord Corp, Erie Penn 64-. 9: ALA; SLA; ASIS. 10: Villa Maria Col Alum Assn; Bus & Prof Womens Club; AAUW. 11: Beta Phi Mu; Hosp Aux. 14: Lib admin, info sci. 15: 1635 W 12th st, Erie Pa 16512.

CALVERT, LOIS (MARGARET). b Rockford Ill 19 My 40. 5: Beloit Col 58-60 (Eng); UWis 60-62 (Eng) BS; UDenver 62-63 (LS) MA. 7: Asst ser libn UColo Lib 63-66; Assoc law libn & catlgr UColo Law Lib 66-. 9: ColoLA; AALL. 15: 601 Cascade, Apt B-West, Boulder Co 80301.

CAMENIETZKI, KERSTIN E M (HULTBERG). b Malmo Sweden 2 Je 38. 4: Schalom Camenietzki. 5: UppsalaU (Sweden) 57-63 (Scand lang, lit) fil kand; Lib Sch Bd of Educ, Stockholm 64-65 diploma (DBS). 6: Scand, Ger, Fr, Hebrew. 7: Libn I Ref dept UKansas Lib 65-69, Libn II 69-. 14: Ref. Libn II 69-. 15: 1716 Louisiana, Lawrence Ks 66044.

CAMERON, ALBERTA. b Cookeville Tenn 12 Ag 19. 5: Tenn Polytech Inst 36-40 (Bus Admin) BS; Peabody 45-46 BS in LS. 7: Upper Cumberland Reg Libn, Cookeville Tenn 46-47; High sch libn Fla Dept Educ, Fernandina Fla 47-49; High sch libn Fla Dept Educ, Sarasota Fla 49-50; Accountant & records libn Cooke- ville Hosp, Cookeville Tenn 50-51; Period libn Tenn Tech U 51-66; Acquis libn 66-. 9: ALA; SWLA; TennLA. 10: Cookeville Study Club; Tech Faculty Women's Club. 14: Acquis. 15: 313 N Dixie ave, Cookeville Tn 38501.

CAMERON, CONSTANCE MAY (BROADHURST). b Somerset Mass 23 My 37. 4: J Kent Cameron. 5: Bates Col 55-59 (Eng) AB; Simmons 59-64 MSLS. 6: Fr, Russian. 7: Asst Bates Col 57-59; Gen asst Parlin Mem, Everett Mass summer 58; Pre-prof B oston Pub Lib 59-61; Reader asst Providence Pub Lib 62-68, Pub Lib Coordinator 68-. 9: ALA; RILA; MassLA; NELA. 10: ACLU; Providence Pub Lib Staff Assn. 14: Adv wk, interlib coop (systems). 15: 274 Buttonwoods ave, Warwick RI 02886.

CAMERON, ELOISE (AUSTIN). b Benton Ill 28 Ja 13. 5: Fla State Col for Women 30-34 (Educ) AB; UKy 52-56 MS in LS. 7: Tchr DeSoto High Sch, Arcadia Fla 34-36; Tchr Miami Edison Sr High Sch, Miami Fla 36-37; Tchr Plant City Pub Schs, Plant City Fla 48-57; Libn St Petersburg Jr Col 57-. 9: FlaLA. 10: Alpha Gamma Delta. 14: Catlg. 15: 6721 8th ave N, St Petersburg Fl 33710.

CAMERON, HILDA ROBINA. b Poughkeepsie NY 22 My 16. 5: New Paltz Normal Sch 34-37 (Educ) Certif; New Paltz State Col 50-51 (Sci) BS in Ed; Columbia summers 44-46 (LS); Syracuse summers 48-49 (LS). 7: Adriance Mem Lib, Poughkeepsie NY: Ref asst 49-54, Circ libn 55-58, Ref libn 59-63; Ref coordinator So Adirondack Lib Systems, Saratoga Springs 63-65; Lib Dir Crandall Lib, Glens Falls NY 66-. 8: Ref libn Lib/USA, NY World's Fair 64. 9: ALA; NYLA. 10: AAUW; Zonta; Glens Falls Hist Assn. 14: Ref, catlg. 15: 175 Lake ave, Saratoga Springs NY 12866.

CAMERON, JOHN KENNETH. b Bay City Mich 5 S 04. 5: Bay City Jr Col 22-25; UMich 25-28 AB, 28-31 AMLS; Chicago (41-42). 7: Lib asst Bay City Mich Pub Lib 22-25; Lib asst UMich(Ann Arbor) 25-34; Libn Mercer U 34-40; Libn Bowling Green State U 40-41; Lib asst UChicago 41-42, 45-46; Clerk USAAF (Sgt) European Theater 42-45; Chief ref Air U Lib (Maxwell AFB Ala) 46-63, Chief reader serv 64-67; HdReader's Serv Marquette U Lib 67-. 9: ALA; SLA (Ala Chap; pres 64-65); BSA; AlaLA (life mem, pres 53-54); SELA (Coun 57-60; chm & memb of var other lib coms). 13: Yes. 14: Ref, lib hist. 15: 3456 N 84th, Milwaukee Wi 53222.

CAMERON, MARION DICK. b Toronto 21 D 18. 5: UToronto Trinity Col 37-41 (Modern Lang) BA; Toronto 46-47 BLS, 55-56 MLS. 6: Fr, Ger. 7: Asst catlgr Pub Lib, Windsor Ont 47-55; Head catlg dept UGuelph Guelph Ont 56-. 8: Tchr of catlg under sponsorship of Ont Dept of Educ 54-59. 9: CanLA; ALA; OntLA; Can Assn Univ Tchrs; Inst Prof Libns Ont; Bibliog Soc of Can. 10: Univ Women's Club of Guelph. 14: Catlg. 15: 671 Woolwich st apt 407, Guelph Ont Can.

CAMERON, SISTER MARY DAVID SSND. b Yonkers NY 27 N 06. 5: Col of Notre Dame Md 23-27 (Eng) AB; Catholic U summers & 37-38 (Fr) AM; Johns Hopkins 31-33 (Eng, Fr); Catholic U summers 39-43 BS in LS. 6: Fr, Lat. 7: Tchr of Fr, Hist St John's High Sch, Westminster Md 27-28; Tchr of Eng, Fr Catholic Girls Central High Sch, Cumberland Md 29-31; Col of Notre Dame(Md); Instr of Eng, Fr, Lat 31-41, Asst libn 39-62, Libn 62-. 8: Lib consul on eval coms, Commsn on Higher Educ, Middle States Assn. 9: ALA-ACRL; CathLA (chm Wash DC-Md Unit 46-48); MdLA. 10: Delta Epsilon Sigma; Beta Phi Mu. 12: "The College of Notre Dame of Maryland, 1895-1945" (47); Tr Paul Claudel "Coronal" (43); Tr Brother Lawrence "Practice of the Presence of God" (45). 13: Yes. 14: Ref, admin. 15: Col of Notre Dame of Md, 4701 N Charles st, Baltimore Md 21210.

CAMERON, MARY E(VELYN). b Moose Jaw Sask Can. 5: USask 33 (Eng) BA; Toronto 40 BLS. 7: Asst catlgr USask 34-35; Chief Libn Regina Col(Regina Sask) 35-40; 1st asst catlgr Smith Col 40-44; Chief Libn Galt Pub Lib, Galt Ont 44-50; Chief Libn Halifax Mem Lib, Halifax NS 50-. 9: CanLA (Coun 52-55, 66-69); APLA (Pres59-60); HalifaxLA (past pres). 10: Zonta Club. 14: Pub lib admin. 15: Halifax Mem Lib, 5381 Spring Garden rd, Halifax NS Can.

CAMERON, MARY TRIMBLE. b Durham NC 31 Jl 38. 5: Wellesley Col 56-58; UMich 58-60 (Hist) BA; UNC 60-63 MS in LS. 6: Fr. 7: Asst child room Pub Lib of Brookline, Brookline Mass 62-66; Child libn Chapel Hill Pub Lib, Chapel Hill NC 67-. 9: ALA. 10: Beta Phi Mu. 14: Child wk. 15: 404 Laurel Hill rd, Chapel Hill NC 27514.

CAMERON, ULYSSES. b Sanford Hts NC 2 D 30. 4: Ida R Womack. 5: HowardU 48-52 (Mus educ) BMEd, 52-53 (Educ); AtlantaU 64-65 MLSL. 6: Fr. 7: Pilot USAF, US & Gt Brit 53-62; Libn Enoch Pratt Free Lib, Baltimore 63-68; Assoc dir of media servs Fed City Col 68-. 9: ALA. 10: Pi Kappa Lambda. 13: Yes. 14: Acquis, ref. 15: 3243 Belmont ave, Baltimore Md 21216.

CAMERON, WILLIAM JAMES. b New Zealand 29 O 26. 4: Pamela Margaret Brand. 5: Victoria UWellington 45-53 (Eng) BA, MA; UReading (Berks Eng) 53-57 (Eng) PhD. 6: Fr, Sp. 7: Jr lectr Victoria UWellington (New Zealand) 50-53; Asst lectr UReading (England) 53-56; UAukland (New Zealand): Lectr 58-60, Sr lectr 60-64; Prof of English McMasterU 64-68; Assoc Dean & Prof Sch of Lib & Info Sci U Western Ont 68-. 8: Research asst YaleU 57, 61-62, 62-; Commonwealth fellow (attached to Nat Lib, Canberra Australia) 66. 9: CanLA; ALA; OntLA. 12: "A Bibliography of English Poetical Miscellanies, 1660-1720, in the Alexander Turnbull Library" (54); "John Dryden in New Zealabd" (60); "A Short- title Catalogue of Books Printed in Britain and British Books Printed Abroad 1641-1700 Held in Australian Libraries" (62); "New Light on Aphra Behn" (61); Co-auth -experiments in New Zealand Bibliography" (64); "The Company of White-Paper-Makers of england 1686-1696" (64); "New Zealand" (65); Co-auth "Short Title Catalogue of books printed in the British Isles, the British Colonies and the United States of America and of English books printed elsewhere 1701-1800 held in the libraries of the Australian Capital Territory" (66); Co-auth "Robert Addison's Library" (67); Co-auth -the HPB Project: Phase I" (68); "Poems on Affairs of State, Augustan Satirical Verse, 1660-1714, Volume 5: 1688-1697" (69). 13: Yes. 14: Rare bks, bibliog, computer control of knowledge. 15: 1510 Western rd, Lond Ont Can.

CAMM, MARGARET A CRAWFORD. b Mexico Mo 10 Ap 16. 5: North Mont Col 36-39 (Lib) Certif; UMont 39-41 (Lib) BA in Lib Econ. 7: Spec serv libn Ida State Lib, Helena Mont 58-59, 64-67; Co libn; High sch libn, Mont; Libn USN; Libn USAFB, Malmstrom AFB Mont 48-51, 59-64; Libn USAFB, Mt Home Ida 52-53, 67-68; Chief libn VA Ctr, Boise Ida 68-. 9: MedLA; IdaLA; MontLA (pres 66-67); PNLA. 10: Altrusa; Zonta. 14: Readers adv serv. 15: 123 Village lane, Boise Id 83702.

CAMMACK, ELEANORE A. b Greencastle Ind 18 Ap 06. 5: DePauw U 24-28 (Eng Lit, Hist) AB; UIll 28-29 BS in ls& american U summer 55 Archives Inst Certif. 6: Fr. 7: Order asst Purdue U 29-44, Order libn 44-55; Archivist DePauw U 55-. 8: Com on Archival Policy, Methodist Church Consul on Meth, archival wk, Commsn on Archives & Hist, Lake Junaluska NC68. 9: SAA (Church Arch Com); Ind Hist Soc. 10: Bus & Prof Women; Ind Museum Soc; Putnam Co Hist Soc. 12: Comp "Indiana Methodism" (64). 13: Yes. 14: Mss, Methodism. 15: Arch of DePauwUniv & Ind Methodism, Greencastle In 46135.

CAMP, BERT ELLEN (WEIR). b Oklahoma City Okla 27 Je 12. 5: NM State U 29-32 (Eng); USoCal 37-38 (Eng) BA; Sul Ross State Col 56-58 (Eng) MA; UDenver 58-61 (LS) MA. 7: Tchr Lea Co Schs, Monument NM 32-33; Tchr Hobbs Mun Schs, Hobbs NM 33-37, Tchr-libn 38-41; Asst libn NM Mil Inst, Roswell NM 62-67; Hd libn NM Mil Inst, Roswell NM 67-. 9: ALA; NMLA. 10: Delta Kappa Gamma. 14: Ref, catlg. 15: PO Box 584, Roswell NM 88201.

CAMP, LOIS SUE (NIX). b Rockmart Ga 29 D 05. 4: James Casper Camp. 5: Young Harris Col 24-26 Diploma; UGa 26-28 (Hist) AB (cum laude); Emory 32-33 ABLS, 56-58 (T-6 program) M Ls, T-6. 6: Fr, Lat. 7: Asst in music & dramatics Young Harris Col 26-27; High sch tchr-libn Clay Co Schs, Hayesville NC 29-31; High sch tchr-libn Towns Co Schs, Hiawassee Ga 38-42; Pub welfare wker & Dir Ga Pub Welfare, Douglas Ga 42-43; Malaria educator US Pub Health Serv, Douglas Ga 43-44; Catlgr Ga State Lib 47-48; High sch libn Atlanta Pub Schs 48-56; Lib supv Atlanta Pub Sch System 56-. 8: Tchr Educ Coun of Ga 61-; Part-time instr in lib sci Ga State Col 61-. 9: ALA; NEA; SELA; GaLA; GaEA. 10: Delta Kappa Gamma; Atlanta Lib Club; Wesleyan Service Guild; Coun of So Mountains. 13: Yes. 14: Catlg, supv of sch libs, lib educ. 15: 731 Luckie LANE NE, Atlanta Ga 30329.

CAMP, THOMAS EDWARD. b Haynesville La 12 Jl 29. 4: Elizabeth Anne Sowar. 5: Centenary Col(La) 46-50 (Eng) BA; Vanderbilt U Divinity Sch 50-51; LSU 51-53 MS in LS. 6: Sp. 7: Asst in bind dept LSU Lib 51-53; US Army SP-4 Communications Sect, Ft Hood Tex 53-55; Circ libn Bridwell Lib Perkins Sch of Theol So Methodist U 55-57; Libn Sch of Theol U of the South 57-. 9: ALA; ATheolLA (exec sec 65-67); SELA. 10: Amer Guild of Organists; Ecce Quam Bonum Club; Sewanee Civic Assn. 12: "Using Theological Books and Libraries," with Ella V Aldrich (63). 13: Yes. 14: Ref. 15: Lib Sch of Theol Univ of the South, Sewanee Tn 37375.

CAMPAIGNE, LAURA E (FLETCHER). b Albany NY 6 Je 11. 4: William M Campaigne. 5: NY State Col for Tchrs 29-33 BS in LS, 34-39 (Guidance) MS in Ed. 6: Fr. 7: Asst libn Albany High Sch, Albany NY 34-39; Libn Albany High Sch Annex, Albany NY 46-47; Catlgr NY State Col for Tchrs(Albany) 47-48, Ref libn 55-56; Catlgr NY State Lib 56-59; Asst libn Russell Sage even div(Albany) 59-60; Libn Mem Hosp, Albany NY 59-62; Libn St Peter's Hosp Med Staff Lib, Albany 63-. 9: MedLA; Hudson-MohawkLA. 13: Yes. 14: Med ref. 15: 181 Milner ave, Albany NY 12208.

CAMPBELL, MRS ALMIRA (TAYLOR). b Hyde Park Mass 26 My 20. 4: Vincent A Campbell. 5: Colby Jr Col 38-40 (Liberal Arts) AA; Mt Holyoke 40-42 (Fr) AB; Simmons 42-43 (LS) BS. 6: Fr. 7: Asst accessions dept Yale Law Sch Lib 43-45; Asst order dept Mt Holyoke Col Lib 48; Act libn Mt Hermon Sch, Mt Hermon Mass 48-49, Head libn 49-54; Head libn Stoneleigh-Prospect Hill Sch, Greenfield Mass 60-68; Catlgr Deerfield Acad, Deerfield Mass 68-. 9: ALA; MassSchLA; NESchLA. 10: AAUW; Gill Mass PTA (pres 57-59); Trustee Greenfield Pub Lib; Franklin Co Mt Holyoke Club (pres 63-65); Greenfield Txpayers Assn. 14: Sch lib wk, ctlg. 15: 103 Burnham rd, Greenfield Ma 01301.

CAMPBELL, B(ILLY) WILMON. b Los Angeles 14 S 27. 4: Patricia Jean Cowan. 5: USoCal 47-48 (Internat Rel); UCLA 48-52 (Latin Amer Studies) AA, BA; UCal (Berkeley) 53-54 BLS; UCLA 65 (Bus Data Processing & Computer Programming). 7: Med lab tech USAAF (Pvt) 45-46; Stud asst res bk room UCal (Berkeley) 53-54; Period & film libn of Hawaii, Honolulu 54-56; Asst acquis libn Los Angeles State Col 56-57; Ser libn San Fernando Valley State Col 57-63; Hughes Aircraft Co Tech Doc Ctr, Culver City Cal; Catlgr 63, Asst supv for tech processes 63-65, Supv 65-. 8: Consul on KWOC indexing of spec collections, Hughes Aircraft Co Aerospace Group, 65-. 9: SLA. 10: UCal Schs of Lib Sci Alumni Assn; Alpha Mu Gamma. 14: Tech proc, automated info retrieval, tech docs. 15: 17336 Elkwood st, Northridge Ca 91324.

CAMPBELL, BETTYE (WASHINGTON). b Chicago 15 Jl 31. 5: Bennett Col 49-53 (Eng) BA; Syracuse 53-54 (LS) MS. 6: Ger. 7: Ya libn Detroit Pub Lib 54-55; Ref libn Syracuse U Lib 55-56; Research libnFed Reserve Bank of Chicago 57-59; Libn Dwight D Eisenhower High Sch, Blue Islandill 59-69, Chm Lib 64-65. 9: ALA; IllLA. 10: Phi Beta Mu. 14: Ref, reader guid, col admin. 15: 9428 S Michigan ave, Chicago Il 60619.

CAMPBELL, BEULAH (MARY) BURTON. b Dallas WVa 8 Ag 17. 4: Ralph Everett Campbell. 5: UMd 35-38 (Home Econ, Educ) BS; West Liberty State Col summer 38; WVa U summer 42; Kent State 58-64 MLS. 7: Tchr Kitzmiller High Sch, Kitzmiller Md 38-42; Tchr-libn Mogadore local schs, Magodore Ohio 48-63, Elem libn O H Somers Sch 63-. 9: NEA; ALA; OhioEA; OhioSchL; SCEA;NEOTA; SCLA. 14: Sch libs. 15: 3476 Gary dr, Mogadore Oh 44260.

CAMPBELL, CORDELIA (ANNE) GULLEDGE. b Verbena Ala 3 N 11. 4: James Larue Campbell. 5: Judson Col 28-32 (Hist, Eng, Speech) AB; West Res 32-33 BS in LS. 7: Tchr-libn Verbena Elem Sch, Verbena Ala 33-35; Asst libn Air Corps Tactical Sch, Maxwell Field Ala 35-41; Libn Air Corps Proving Ground Command, Eglin Field Fla 41-46; Libn Lake View High Sch, Lake View SC 63-. 9: SCLA; SCEA; Dillon Co EA. 10: DAR. 14: Ref. 15: Rt 3, Dillon SC 29536.

CAMPBELL, CORINNE ADELE. b Tacoma Wash 10 My 40. 5: Wash State U 58-62 (Eng) BA; UWash 64-66 (Libnship) M of Libr. 7: Eng tchr Prosser High Sch, Prosser Wash 62-64; Eng tchr S Kitsap High Sch, Port Orchard Wash 64-65; Boeing Co, Renton Wash: Sr tech lib asst 66-67, Sr res libn 67-. 8: Participant in Washington State Governor's Conference on Libraries, 67. 9: SLA. 10: Phi Kappa Phi; Pi Lambda Theta; Beta Phi Mu. 12: Ed "Interface" Bull Pac Nwest Chap SLA (67-). 14: Spec libs, ref, retrieval systems. 15: 2480 Dexter ave N apt 4, Seattle Wa 98109.

CAMPBELL, DOROTHY (WILSON). b Rocky Mount NC 11 Ja 26. 4: Joseph E Campbell. 5: NC Col(Durham) 42-46 (Eng) AB, 46-47 BS in LS; Catholic U 52-53, 54 MS in LS. 7: Asst libn Winston-Salem State Col 47-51; Br libn Prince George's Co Mem Lib(Md) 51-52; Catlgr Md State Col(Princess Anne) 53-54, Act libn 54-55; Asst ref libn Howard U summer 55; Circ libn NC Col(Durham) 56-60, Instr Sch of Lib Sci 63-. 9: ALA; NCLA. 10: Durham Acad Med Auxiliary. 14: Col lib, bibliog. 15: 605 Linwood ave, Durham NC 27701.

CAMPBELL, DOUGLAS A. b NYC 12 N 44. 4: Kay Darsey. 5: ClemsonU 62-67 (Hist) BA; UKy 67-68 MSLS. 7: Laborer Concord Water Works, Concord NH summers 64 & 65; Patrolman Concord Police Dept, Concord NH summer 66; Patrolman Traffic Div State Highway Dept, Concord NH summer 67; Ser specialist M T King Lib UKy 68; Lib syst off Air Force Acad lib 69-. 9: ALA. 14: Lib automation, lib admin. 15: 1928 N Prospect, Colorado Springs Co 80907.

CAMPBELL, ERIC RANDALL. b Proton Ontario Can 12 Jl 29. 5: Graceland 59-62 (Relig, Soc Stud) BA; Kan State Col 65-66 (Hist) MS; UMich 66-67 AMLS. 6: Fr. 7: Various Can Imperial Bank of Com Toronto 50-59; Casewker Ontario Dept of Soc & Fam Servs, Toronto Can 63-65; Ref libn No York Pub Lib, Downsview Ont Can 67-68; Ref asst & ctlgr Detroit Pub Lib 68; Lib dir Blue Ridge Commun Col, Weyers Cave Va 68-. 9: ALA; -SLA; VaLA. 10: AHA; Amer Histns. 14: Ref, acquis, catlg. 15: Box 993, Harrisonburg Va 22801.

CAMPBELL, EVELYN (MATILDA). b Arichat NS Can 29 O 08. 5: Mt St Vincent 29 (Eng Langs) BA; McGill 31 BLS; Columbia 44 (Ref Bk Sel) CTF;Dalhousie U 62-63 (Fr, Russian Hist). 6: Fr. 7: Sch prin L'Ardoise, River Bourgeois, Barton-Brighton 29, 32-34, 35-36; Libn Prov Sci Lib 36-48; Chief Libn NS Res Found 48-. 9: CanLA; ALA; APLA (sec-treas 44-56); NS Inst Sci (Libn, corr sec). 10: AAAS; Univ Women's Club. 12: "Selected Bibliography on Algae, 1-6." 13: Yes. 14: Ref, bibliog. 15: 1101 Wellington st, Halifax NS Can.

CAMPBELL, FRANK (CARTER). b Winston-Salem NC 26 S 16. 5: Salem Col 33-38 (Piano) B Mus; Eastman Sch urochester(NY) 40-42 (Musicology) M Mus, 42-43 (Musicology). 6: Ger. 7: Catlgr Sibley Lib Eastman Sch, Rochester NY 43; Libn Music Div LC 43-59; Asst Chief NY Pub Lib mus div 59-66; Chief 66-. 8: Prof of Music Hist Amer Univ 50-53; Music Critic "Washington Evening Star" 53-59. 9: Mus LA (sec 48-50, pres 67-69); Amer Musicological Soc; Internat Assn of Mus Libs. 10: The Bohemians; Opera Soc of Washington; Cantata Singers; Festival Orchestra Soc. 12: Assoc ed "Music Library Associaition NOTES" (50-67). 13: Yes. 14:

Ref, admin, tech serv (music). 15: Lincoln Center Lib & Mus of the Performing Arts, 111 Amsterdam ave, New York, NY 10023.

CAMPBELL, GRACE. b Old Kilpatrick Scotland 8 Jl 08. 5: Acadia U (Wolfville NS) 29-31 (Eng) BA; McGill 49-50 BLS. 6: Fr. 7: Clerical asst Prince Edward Island Libs, Charlottetown 32-49, 53-55; Prof asst No Central Sask Prince Albert Reg Lib 51-52, Reg libn 55-. 9: SaskLA (pres 59); CLA; APLA. 10: University Womens Club; Toastmistress Club. 14: Admin. 15: 145-12th st East, Prince Albert Sask Can.

CAMPBELL, HELEN (LOUISE) WOERNER. b Indianapolis 17 O 18. 4: Thomas Boyd Campbe ll. 5: Ind U 36-41 (Bus Admin); B utler U 64-67 BS. 6: Fr. 7: Asst or der libn Ind U 37-42; Sch of Dentistry Ind U libn 42-46, Catlgr 60-65, Asst libn 65-66, Libn 66-. 9: SLA (treas Ind Chap 63-64). 14: Tech proc. 15: 1865 N Norfolk st, Indianapolis In 46224.

CAMPBELL, HENRY CUMMINGS. b Vancouver BC Can 22 Ap 19. 4: Sylvia Frances Woodsworth. 5: UBC 37-40 BA; Toronto 40-41 BLS; Columbia 45-46 MA. 6: Fr. 7: Libn & film producer Nat Film Bd, Ottawa 41-46; Archives sect UN, NY 46-49; Head sect for bibliog & documentation UNESCO, Paris 49-50; Head Clearinghouse for Libs, UNESCO, Paris 50-56; Chief Libn Toronto Pub Lib 56-. 8: Canadian Privy Coun Survey of Sci Info 67-68; Canadian Urban Research Coun Info Survey 69-. 9: CanLA; CanAAdultEduc. 12: "Unesco Bulletin for Libraries" (50-56); "Handbook on the International Exchange of Publications" (56); "How To Find Out About Canada" (67); "Metropolitan Public Library Planning Throughout The World" (67); "Canadian Libraries" (69). 13: Lib trends. 14: Adult educ. 15: 373 Glengrove ave, Toronto Can.

CAMPBELL, IVAH F. b Chippewa Falls Wis. 5: UWis 40-45 (Eng) BA, 45-46 BLS; UIll 51-52 (LS) MS. 6: Fr, Russ. 7: Libn I Milwaukee Pub Lib 46-51; Asst libn Argonne Nat Lab, Argonne Ill 52-. 9: SLA. 14: Catlg. 15: 110 S Monroe st, Hinsdale Ill 60521.

CAMPBELL, (MARTHA) LOUISE SIMMONS. b Freeport Fla 3 D 08. 5: Fla State Col 25-29 (Ed, Hist, Eng) AB in Ed; Fla StateU 55-57 (LS) MLS. 7: Hist tchr Jackson Co Bd, Graceville Fla 29-30; Hist & Eng tchr Okaloosa Co Bd, Laurel Hill Fla 30-33; Welfare wker FERA, De Funiak Springs Fla 33-35; Dist welfare supv State Welfare Bd, Crestview Fla 35-37, 41-45, Gainesville Fla 47-50; High sch libn Okaloosa Co Bd, Crestview Fla 57-60; Catlgr lib Fla StateU, Tallahassee Fla 60-67; Ref & period libn Okaloosa-Walton Jr Col, Niceville Fla 67-. 9: ALA; NEA; SELA; FlaLA; FlaEA; Fla Assn Pub Jr Cols. 10: AAUP. 11: Delta Kappa Gamma; Phi Kappa Phi; Beta Phi Mu; Kappa Delta Pi; Phi Alpha Theta. 14: Ref, period. 15: PO Box 363, Niceville Fl 32578.

CAMPBELL, LUCY (BARNES). b Windsor NC. 4: Alfonso L Campbell Sr. 5: NC Col at Durham 3741 (Eng) AB, 41-42 BS in LS, summers 58-60 MS in LS. 6: Fr, Ger. 7: Libn Darden High Sch, Wilson NC 42-45; Circ libn Ala State Col, Trenholm Memorial Lib 45-52, Libn grad reading room 52-63; Circ libn Hampton Inst, Huntington Memorial Lib 63, Sct dir & coord stud activities 64, Asst ref libn in charge oeruid 64-65, Asst Prof & period libn 66-. 8: Coord residence hall reading rms (pilot program of 10 stud operated reading rooms, jt effort Ford Foundation & Hampton Inst). 9: ALA; NEA; SELA; VaLA. 10: Alpha Kappa Alpha; YWCA; NAACP. 14: Period, ref, Peabody (Negro) collection. 15: Box 6302 Hampton Inst, Hampton Va 23368.

CAMPBELL, LYALL (GARTH). b Halifax Nova Scotia 15 Ap 34. 4: Sheila Ellman. 5: D Alhousie U 55-58 (Hist, phil) BA, 60-62 (Hix 05: D Alhousie U 55-58 (Hist, phil) BA, 60-62 (Hist) MA; UToronto 63-64 BLS. 7: Elevator operator St Regis Hotel, Vancouver BC 54; Dispatcher BC Forest Serv, Hope & Lake Cowichan BC 55; Eng tchr Dalhousie High Sch, Dalhousie New Brunswick 59-60; Lecturer hist dept Prince of Wales Col 63-64; Ref libn UToronto Lib 64-65; Libn in charge of reading rm ULondon Inst of Educ, London Eng 65-66; Hist libn Humanities dept London Pub Lib, London Ont 67-. 9: CanLA. 11: Cana Coun Humanities & Soc Sci Research Grant 69. 14: Ref. 15: 2356 Hunter st, Halifax Nova Scotia Can.

CAMPBELL, MARC T JR. b Putneyville Penn 4 Mr 25. 4: Dorothy Smith. 5: Clarion (Penn) State Tchrs Col 46-50 (Soc Studies) BS in Educ; Peabody 50-51 MA in LS; Ft Hays Kan State Col 58-62 (Hist) MA. 7: US Navy 43-46; Circ libn Rollins Col 51-53; Ext libn Ft Hays Kan State Col53-55, Ref libn 55-64, Head libn 64-. 9: ALA; KanLA; MPLA; KanASchL; NEA; KanState Tchrs Assn. 10: Amer Legion; VFW; Toastmasters; Amer Radio Relay League; US Naval Inst. 14: Ref, lib admin. 15: 516 W 27th st, Hays Ks 67601.

CAMPBELL, MARGARET (W). b Greenfield Ind 16 N 05. 5: Earlham Col 21-23 (Chem, Eng) Certif; LaSalle Ext U(Chicago) 24-26 (Bus Admin); Catholic Hosps Seminar, St Louis 62. 7: Continental Ill Bank & Trust Co Financial Lib, Chicago 24-28; Libn Field Mus,chicago 28-29; Rental lib & bk sale Cape Cod Gift Cottage, Chicago 46-51; SalesHenry C Lytton's, Evergreen Park Ill 52-55; Med staff libn Little Co of Mary Hosp,Evergreen Park Ill 61-64; Period libn Chicago Med Sch 64-. 9: MedLA; IllLA. 10: Morgan Park Woman's Club; Internat Chrysanthemum Soc. 12: Co-comp, "Chicago Medical School, Current List of Serials" (66). 14: Rare bks. 15: 8945 Utica ave, Evergreen Park Ill 60642.

CAMPBELL, MARGARET G. b Dayton Ohio 22 Ap 13. 5: Ohio Wesleyan U 31-35 (Chem) BA; West Res 51-52 MS in LS. 6: Ger, Fr. 7: Lab tech; Mt Sinai Hosp, Cleveland Ohio 36-39, SC State Bd of Health, Columbiasc 39-45; US Army Lib Serv, France, Germany 52-54; Ref asst Shaker Heights Pub Lib,Shaker Heights Ohio 55-60, Br libn 60-69, Dir 69-. 8: Command libn (US Army), Berlin Germany 53-54; Service Club dir: Amer Red Cross, Munich Germany 45-46, Amer Red Cross & US Army, Korea 47-49, Ft Sill Okla 50-51. 9: ALA; OhioLA. 10: Womens Overseas Serv League;Eng Speaking Union; Amer Overseas Assn (Amer Red Cross); Shaker Hist Soc. 14: Ref. 15: 2540N Moreland blvd, Shaker Heights Oh 44120.

CAMPBELL, MARILYN (MORRIS). b Seattle Wash 18 O 32. 4: Richard W Campbell. 5: Mills Col 50-54 (Hist, Govt) BA; UWash 66-69 MLib. 15: 4818 E Mercer way, Mercer Island Wa 98040.

CAMPBELL, MARILYN ELEANOR SMITH. b Berkeley Cal 25 O 22. 5: UCal 40-44 (Hist, Pol Sci, Econ) BA; UWash 57-59 (Educ) Elem Certif, 60-64 MLS. 6: Fr. 7: Elem tchr Lake Washington Sch Dist, Kirkland Wash 58-61, Elem sch libn 61-62; Elem sch libn Bellevue Sch Dist, Bellevue Wash 62-63; lib consul King Co Schs Off, Seattle 63-66; Supv libs Seattle Sch Dist 66-. 9: NEA; ALA; Assn Sch Curr Devel; WashStateASchL: WashStateLA; WashEA-DAVI. 10: Treas of the Coun of town of Clyde Hill, Wash; Pi Beta Phi; Seattle Schs Mgt Assn; A & S League. 13: Yes. 14: Sch lib wk. 15: 3012 92nd pl NE, Bellevue Wa 98004.

CAMPBELL, MARILYN I. b Columbus Ohio. 5: Ohio Wesleyan (Pol Sci) BA; Columbia (LS) BS. 7: Ref asst Columbus Pub Lib,Columbus Ohio, Head Gen Ref Div 61-. 9: ALA; OhioLA. 10: Westside & Ohio Ave Day Nurseries Assoc Bd. 14: Ref. 15: 2618 Bryden rd, Columbus Oh 43209.

CAMPBELL, MARY (ELIZABETH). b London Ontario 23 Jl 39. 5: Victoria Col UToronto 57-61 (Household Sci) BA; Sch of LS UToronto 65-66 BLS. 6: Fr, Sp. 7: Underwriter Mfr Life Ins Co, Toronto 61-65; Catlgr Ontario Inst for Studies in Ed Lib, Toronto 66-. 9: CanLA; ALA; SLA; Internat Assn of Documentalists& Inst Prof Libns Ont. 10: Eng-Speaking Union, Commonwealth in Can. 14: Catlg. 15: Balmoral ave, Toronto Ontario.

CAMPBELL, MARY JOAN. b Winnipeg Can 18 Ag 20. 5: UMan 37-41 (Eng) BA; McGill 45-46 BLS; Chicago 59-62 (LS) MA. 6: Fr. 7: Catlgr UMan 46-48; Libn St Luke's Hosp Sch of Nursing, Chicago 48-50; Asst catlgr UIll Med Sci Lib (Chicago), Acquis libn 56-. 9: ALA; MedLA (Memb Com); IllLA (Recr Com); Chicago Lib Club. 10: AAUP; Soc of Typographic Arts; Sierra Club; Chicago Coun on For Rel. 14: Acquis. 15: 411 W Fullerton ave, Chicago Il 60614.

CAMPBELL, NINA (LOUISE) S(ITTLER). b Anselmo Neb 15 Ag 16. 4: Robert D Campbell. 5: UNeb 33-37 (Elem Educ) BS; UDenver 40-41 BS in LS; Colo State Col of Educ 43-46 (Educ) MA. 6: Sp. 7: Elem tchr pub schs, Overton Neb 37-38; Elem tchr pub schs, Council Bluffs Iowa 38-40; Bks arts reviser UDenver Sch of libnship summer 41; Asst libn NM State Tchrs Col 41-42; Catlg reviser UDenver Sch Libnship summer 42; Catlgr Tex Col Arts & Ind 42-43; Catlg instr UDenver Sch Libnship 46; Catlgr Colo State Col Educ 43-46; Child libn Shreve Mem Pub Lib, Shreveport La 48-49; Catlgr Ind U Sch of Med Lib 51-57, Asst & ref libn 57-. 9: MedLA. 10: Phi Beta Kappa; Pi Lambda Theta; Alpha Lambda Delta; Sigma Tau Delta. 14: Ref, catlg. 15: 304 Woodland lane, Carmel In 46032.

CAMPBELL, PAULINE (BROWN). b Troy Mo 14 S 17. 4: William Kenneth Campbell. 5: Wash U 51 (Educ) BS, 58 (Educ) MA. 7: Tchr rural & elem schs, Lincoln Co Mo 35-50; Libn Sch Dist R-III of Lincoln Co, Troy Mo 50-. 9: NEA;

ALA; Mo State Tchrs Assn; MoLA; MoASchL (pres 55-56, chm Publ Rel Com 57-61); Lib Curriculum Comm Dept of Educ Mo 62-63; Lincoln Co Tchrs Assn (pres 63-64); Lincoln Co Lib Bd of Trustees 65-. 10: Mark Twain Literary Clu b; Lincoln Co Library Bd 59-62; Kappa Delta Pi. 14: Sch libn. 15: 1055 S Main, Troy Mo 63379.

CAMPBELL, RITA R (RICARDO). b Boston 16 Mr 20. 4: W Glenn Campbell. 5: Simmons 37-41 BS; Harvard (Radcliffe Col) 42-45 MA, 45-46 PhD. 6: Fr, Ger. 7: Res asst Harvard U 42-44, Tchg Fellow & tutor 46-47, Instr 47-48; Asst Prof Tufts Col 48-51; Labor economist Wage Stabilization Bd US Govt 51-53; Economist Ways & Means Com US House of Rep 53; Visiting Prof San Jose State Col 60-61; Archivist & research assoc Herbert Hoover Archives, Stanford U 61-68; Sr staff mem Hoover Inst 69-. 8: Consultantships. 9: SAA; Amer Econ Assn. 10: Phi Beta Kappa; Mont Pelerin Soc. 12: "Voluntary Health Insurance in the US(60). 13: Yes. 14: Med Economics, info retr. 15: Herbert Hoover Archives Hoover Institution, Stanford Ca 94305.

CAMPBELL, TEDDY THAXTON. b Memphis Tenn 19 D 36. 4: Audrey Jean Wilson. 5: Memphis State U 54-62 (Educ) BS, summer 64 (LS) State Certif as Libn; E Tenn State U summer 65 (LS) Ind U 66-68 MS in Admin Educ 68- (LS and educ). 6: Sp. 7: Off clerk City of Memphis, Memphis Tenn 57-60; Tchr W Memphis(Ark) Jr High Sch 60-64; Libn asst Memphis State U Lib summers 60-64; Libn Memphis U Sch for Boys, Memphis Tenn 64-; Libn UTenn Downtown Center Lib 65-67; Assoc lbn Mooney Mem Lib UTenn Memphis Med Units, Memphis Tenn 67-. 9: ALA (-Tem chap; sec-treas Ref Serv Div 66-67, co-chm 67-68); NEA; SELA; TennLA (life mem); WestTennEA; MedLA (life mem); Mid-South Assn Indep Schs; Memphis Libs Assn. 10: Kiwanis Club; Memphis Men's Garden Club; Jr C of C; Better Films Coun of Memphis Tenn; Germantown Civic Club; Poplar Estates Homeowner Assn. 14: Catlg. 15: 6988 Neshoba rd, Germantown Tn 38038.

CAMPBELL, WINIFRED J (CULIK). b Cleveland Ohio 15 Jl 18. 4: Robert Van Duyne Campbell. 5: Radcliffe 35-39 (Govt) AB; Columbia 39-41 BSLS. 6: Fr, Ger. 7: Asst (stud) Columbia libs ed 39-41; Ed asst "Who's Who in Library Service" Columbia 41-42; Catlgr Harvard Col Lib 42-45; Catlgr Swarthmore Col Lib 63-64; Catlgr Haverford Col Lib 64-66; Subj catlgr Harvard Col Lib 66-. 9: ALA. 10: LWV; Radcliffe Club of Phila. 14: Catlg, ref. 15: 23 Old Village rd, Acton Ma 01720.

CAMPEAS, ROSELYN (HALPERIN). b Brooklyn NY 11 Ag 28. 4: Hyman Campeas. 5: Pratt Inst 66-67 MLS; Brooklyn Col 60-65 (Eng) BA; Herzliah Hebrew Tchr Inst NYC 46-50 (Hebrew) Tchrs Certif. 6: Hebrew. 7: Tchr Brooklyn Jewish Ctr, Brooklyn NY 52-67; Tchr of lib Bd of Educ Brooklyn NY 67-. 9: ALA. 10: Phi Beta Kappa; Alpha Sigma Lambda; Beta Phi Mu. 15: 72-65 Yellowstone blvd, Forest Hills NY 11375.

CAMPION, ELEANOR ESTE. b Media Penn 18 Ag 12. 5: UPenn 30-34 (Eng) AB; Drexel 35 BS in LS. 6: Fr, Ger. 7: Staff Union Lib Catlg of Phila 36-38; State dir Neb Union Catlg WPA, Lincoln Neb 38-39; Asst state dir Statewide Lib Serv III WPA, Chicago 40; State Dir Statewide Lib Serv Penn WPA, Harrisburg Penn 40-42; Personnel asst Amer Chicle Co, Long Island City NY 42-44; Personnel asst Gen Foods Corp, NYC 45; Dir Union Lib Catlg of Phila 49-. 8: Consul Catlg-in-Source Proj, Neb Union Catlg. 9: ALA; ADI; PennLA. 12: Ed "Union List of Microfilms Cumulated Edition" (50,51). 13: Yes. 14: Coop acquis, bibliog, ref wk. 15: 101 Mill Creek rd, Ardmore Pa 19003.

CAMPION, VIOLA (LANG). b Holdingford Minn 3 My 12. 4: Daniel Francis Campion. 5: Col of St Catherine 30-34 BS in LS; St Thomas Col summer 56; Col of St Catherine summers 54-57 (LS) MA. 6: Ger, Sp. 7: St Paul Pub Schs: Ref libn for Bd of Educ 37-57, Libn Central High Sch 57-59, Libn Hazel Park Jr High Sch 59-60, Libn Como Park Jr High Sch 60-65, Libn Wilson Jr High Sch 65-. 9: MinnEA; St Paul Sch Libns (chm & chm Spec Com). 10: Volkfest Assn Minn. 14: Catlg. 15: 1120 Portland ave, St Paul Mn 55104.

CANADA, MARY WHITFIELD. b Richmond Va 13 Je 19. 5: Emory & Henry Col 36-40 (Eng, Lat) BA; Duke 40-42 (Eng Lit) MA; UNC 55-56 BSLS. 7: Duke U Lib: Asst circ 42-46, Libn undergrad reading room 46-55, Ref libn 56-. 9: ALA (Life mem); NCLA; SELA. 10: Beta Phi Mu; Va Hist Soc (Life mem); Duke UFac Club; Trinity Col Hist Soc; Grad Eng Club. 13: Yes. 14: Ref. 15: 1312 Lancaster st, Durham NC 27701.

CANAVAN, ROBERTA (NOLAN). b Elizabeth NJ 11 N 42. 4: Richard Canavan. 5: Caldwell Col for Women 60-64 (Eng) AB; Seton Hall 64 (Eng); Rutgers 66-68 MLS. 7: High sch Eng tchr Bd of Educ, Linden NJ 64-65; Co-libn Linden NJ High Sch 65-66; Libn Joseph E Soehl Jr high Sch, Linden NJ 66-. 9: NJEA; Union Co Sch Libns. 10: League of Women Voters; Local Democratic Club; Sigma Tau Delta; Delta Epsilon Sigma; Pi Delta Epsilon. 13: Yes. 14: Secondary sch libs. 15: 1217 Stiles st N, Linden NJ 07036.

CANELAS, DALE BRUNELLE. b Chicago Ill 13 J 38. 4: Marcelo Canelas. 5: Loyola U 56-58, 59-60 (Sp) BS; UNacional De Mexico 58-59 (Sp, Hist); Rosary Col 65-66 MALS. 6: Sp. 7: Ref Libn Park Ridge Pub Lib, Ill 66-67; Palatine Pub Lib, Ill: Asst dir 66-67, Act dir 68-69; Budget & Planning Off NorthwesternU Lib Ill 69-. 9: ALA; IllLA; LACONI (Nom Com Ref Div 68). 14: Admin, col devel, ref. 15: 15 N Elm st, Mt Prospect Il 60056.

CANFIELD, HELEN SARA. b Hartford Conn 17 Mr 18. 5: St Joseph Col 34-38 (Eng, Hist) BS; Carnegie 40-41 BSLS; Columbia 47, 58(LS) MS. 6: Fr. 7: Asst Hartford(Conn) Pub Lib 38-40; Child libn Akron(Ohio) Pub Lib 41-44; (Sgt) Women's Army Corps (Air Force), NewGuinea & Philippines 44-46; Child libn NY Pub Lib 46-47; Head child dept Enoch Pratt Free Lib, Baltimore 47-50; Supv child wk Hartford(Conn)Pub Lib 50-. 8: Instr child lit Evening Col Central Conn State Col 58-; Gave Caroline H Hewins Lecture at NELA Sept 1969 meeting. 9: ALA (advertising mgr "Top of the News" 53-57; Newbery-Caldecott Com 65; Nomin Com 66; Mildred L Batchelder Award Com 67); ConnLA(chm Child Sect 54; chm Scholarship Com 58-60, 64; Personnel chm 66-67; rep to NELA 56); NELA. 10: Pen Women; Pilot Internat; AAUW. 13: Yes. 14: Child wk, early child bks. 15: 111 Wadhams rd, Bloomfield Conn 06002.

CANNON, ANNE (FLORA) (CHAFFE). b Toronto Ontario Can 6 Ap 29. 4: Donald B Cannon. 5: UToronto 48-52 (Eng) BA; ColumbiaU 52-53 MSLS. 6: Fr. 7: Jr libn Toronto Pub Lib 54; Libn I YorkU Lib, Toronto 68-. 14: Govt docs, ref. 15: 26 Thornhill ave, Thornhill Ontario Can.

CANNON, PERRY. b Birmingham Ala 1 S 30. 5: Birmingham-So Col 48-52 (Eng) AB; UNC 52-53 BS in LS; UAla 56-59 (Eng) MA. 7: Circ asst Birmingham Pub Lib, Birmingham Ala 52; Ref asst UNC(Chapel Hill) 52-53; Ref libn Enoch Pratt Free Lib, Baltimore 53-56; Catlgr UAla 56-64, Head Catlg Dept 64-67; Asst libn Col of Gen Studies, Birmingham Ala 67-68, Act libn 68-. 9: ALA; SELA; AlaLA (chm Col, Univ, & Spec Libs Div 58-59). 10: AAUP. 14: Catlg, adv serv, ref. 15: Box 553, Fultondale Al 35068.

CANRIGHT, MARGERY (MITCHELL). b Longmont Colo 23 O 17. 4: Norman P Canright. 5: Pomona Col 40 BA; UCal (Berkeley) 62-64 MLS. 7: Asst libn Intnat Longshoremen's & Warehousemen's Union, San Francisco 60-65, libn 65-. 9: SLA; UCal Lib Sch Alumna Org. 14: Spec libs. 15: 150 Golden Gate ave, San Francisco Ca 94102.

CANTER, LOUIS. b New Haven Conn 28 Ag 15. 4: Margaret Susan Schutt. 5: Trinity Col 33-37 (Eng Lit) BS; Syracuse 39-40 BLS; UMd 48-52 (Eng Lit). 7: Libn Park Br Hartford Pub Lib, Hartford Conn 40-41; Warrant off US Army, US, N Africa, Europe 41-46; Asst libn Engnr Socs Lib, NYC 46-47; Libn Nat Bur of Standards Ordnance & Electronics Div, Wash DC 47-51; Libn Johns Hopkins U Applied Physics Lab 51-56; Manager Lib Gen Dynamics Convair, San Diego Cal 56-66; Mgr Lib Jet Propulsion Lab, Cal Inst of Tech 66-68; Mgr Tech Info Ctr TRW Sys Group, Redondo Beach Cal 68-. 9: SLA (past chm Engnr Sect, chm Aerospace Div 68-69; pres San Diego Chap; chm SoCal Chap; chm Wash DC Chap); Nat Mgt Assn; CalLA; ASIS; Los Angeles Chap (pres 69). 10: Phi Kappa Phi; Pi Lambda Sigma. 13: Yes. 14: Tech lib admin, documentation tech & mechanization. 15: 514 Pacific ave, Solana Beach Ca 92075.

CANTERBURY, NANCY JO. b Montgomery WVa 8 S 30. 5: Va Intermont Col 48-50 (Liberal Arts) AA; Concord Col 50-53 (Secondary Educ) BS in Ed; UKy summers 59-62, 64 MS in LS. 7: Asst libn Concord Col 53, summers 54-55; Tchr & libn Kingston High Sch, Kingston WVa 53-55; Libn Doddridge Co High Sch, West Union WVa 55-56; Asst libn and instr in Lib Sci Concord Col 66-67; Program specialist of lib serv State Dept of Educ, Charleston WVa 67-. 8: Advisory WVa Recruitment for Libns, ALA 63-65; Proj on Study of WVa Sch Libs under ALA Grant 59 (treas); Coord WVa Stud Lib Assts Assn Ann Conf 68-; State/Nat Lib Week Com (69). 9: ALA; AASchLibns; NEA; WVaLA (var offs). 10: Nat Fed of Women's Clubs; Alpha Sigma Tau; Alpha Beta Alpha. 13: Yes. 14: Ref, catlg. 15: Kimberly, WV 25118.

CANTRALL, REBECCA JANE. b Clarksburg W Va 16 Ja 25. 5: Bethany Col 42-44 (Econ); OhioU 44-46 (Bus Admin) (BS in Commerce); Carnegie Inst of Tech 54-55 MLS. 7: Lib Asst Mellow Nat Bank & Trust Co, Pittsburgh 47-54; Libn Carnegie Lib of Pgh Bus Br Pittsburgh 55-63; Asst Libn US Steel Corp, Pittsburgh 63-. 9: ALA; SLA (Pittsburgh Chap: chm Pub Rel Com, chm Archives Com, mem various other coms); pennLA (treas 55-6060. 10: Zeta Tau Alpha; Ciloets; Andrew Carnegie Athletic Assn. 14: Ref, catlg. 15: 1420 Centre ave, Pittsburgh Pa 15219.

CANTRELL, CLYDE HULL. b Caroleen NC 23 S 06. 4: Ethel Marie Williams. 5: UNC 29-33 (Romance Langs) AB, 34-36 (Romance Langs) MA, 36-37 ABLS; WVaU 37-38(Span); UIll 50-51 (LS) PhD. 6: Sp, Fr, Ital, Portu. 7: Supv circ dept UNC Lib (Chapel Hill) 33-37; Circlibn NC State U (Raleigh); Head circ div WVa U Lib 41-42, Asst libn 42-43; Assocprof Span & Dir of Lib Birmingham-So Col 43-44; Dir of Libs Auburn U 44-, Dir of Libs& Prof 59-. 8: Archivist Ala Acad Sci 55-. 9: ALA-ACRL; Coun for Basic Educ; SAA; Instituto Internat de laLiteratura Iberoamericana; Mod Lang Assn; SELA; AlaLA (pres 46-47); Ala Hist Assn. 10: AAUP; Southern Hist Assn; Ala Writers' Conclave; Auburn Faculty Club; Phi Betakappa; Mu Beta Psi; Phi Sigma Iota; Beta Phi Mu. 12: "Graduate Degrees Awarded and Titles of Theses (UWVa) 1894-1940" (41); "Southern Literary Culture: A Bibliography of Masters' and Doctors' Theses," with W R Patrick (55); Ed "A History of the Alabama Academy of Science" (63). 13: Yes. 14: Admin. 15: Box 290, Auburn Al 36830.

CANTU, JANE (QUALE). b Rochester Minn 24 N 38. 4: Robert Clark Cantu. 5: UMinn 56-60 (Psych) BA; UCal (Berkeley) 63-64 MLS. 6: Sp, Fr. 7: Research asst UMinn (Minneapolis) 58-59, Tchg asst 59-60; Lib asst Mayo Clinic Lib, Rochester Minn 62; Lib asst UCal Med Sch Lib (San Francisco) 63; Research asst UCal Lib Sch (Berkeley) 63-64; Ref libn Francis A Countway Med Lib, Boston 64-68; Consul 68-. 9: MedLA: Am Assn for the Hist of Med. 10: Distaff Club Mass Gen Hosp; Mortar Board; Phi Beta Kappa. 13: Yes. 14: Ref, hist of med, exhibits. 15: 211Newton st, Weston Ma 02193.

CANTWELL, JACQUELYN. b Montreal Can 23 Mr 26. 4: Edward Marc Cantwell. 5: Marianopolis Col 43-47 (Gen) BA; McGill 65-67 MLS. 6: Fr. 7: Lab Tech, Montreal 47-48; Catlgr MacDonald Col McGill 67-69. 9: CanLA; ALA; QuebecLA. 14: Ref, catlg. 15: 63-29 Haring st, Rego Park NY 11374.

CAO, HILDA (JOFTIS). b Havana Cuba 8 Je 22. 5: UNev 57-63 (Romance Kang) BA; UCal (Berkeley) 65-67 MLS. 6: Sp, Fr, Catalan, Portu. 7: Asst ref libn UNev 67-68, Asst catlgr 68-. 8: Lib sci tchr UNev. 9: NevLA. 10: Alliance Francaise, Sierra Club, AAUP. 14: Catlg, ref. 15: 3200 Lodestar lane, Reno Nv 89503.

CAO, JERRY FINLEY. b Madisonville Ky 21 Jl 31. 4: Myra Evelyn Webster. 5: La Sierra Col 60-64 (Hist) BA; USoCal 64-65 MSinLS, 68 (LS). 6: Fr, Ger. 7: US Army Sgt (Stenographer) 52-54; Serv station manager Standard Oil(Cal), Los Angeles 55-60; Catlgr USoCal 65; Catlgr State U Iowa 65-66, Hd Govt Docs Dept 66-68. 9: ALA. 14: Catlg, govt docs. 15: 1621-FAmberwood dr, So Pasadena Ca 91030.

CAO, MYRA EVELYN (WEBSTER). b Lockport NY. 4: Jerry Finley Cao. 5: La Sierra Col 46-51 9eng) BA, summers 61 & 62 (Elem Educ) Certif; UIowa 66-68 (LS) MA. 6: Sp. 7: Sec flintkote Co, Lockport NY 52-53; Sec entom dept Loma LindaU 54-55; Tchr elem sch Little Lake City Sch Dist, Santa Fe Springs Cal 55-57; Tchr sub Culver City Jr High Sch, Culver city Cal 58; Tchr elem sch La Sierra Elem Sch, Riverside Cal 60-63; Researcher entomol dept Loma LindaU 63-64; Lib clk USoCal 64-65; Grad asst Sch of Lib Sci UIowa 68; Catlgr USoCal 68-. 9: CalLA. 10: Friends of UIowa Libs. 13: Yes. 14: Catlg. 15: 1621F Amberwood dr, S Pasadena Ca 91030.

CAPEHART, ELIZABETH (RUTH) BARR. b Georgetown SC 14 S 22. 4: Wm C Capehart. 5: Converse Col 39-40; USC 40-42 (Fine Arts) BA; UNC 42-43 BS in LS UIll 67. 6: Fr, Ger. 7: Asst libn UMiami (Coral GablesFla) 43-44; Asst ref libn Charlotte Pub Lib, Charlotte NC 44-45; Hosp recreation wkrAmer Red Cross, Camp Shelby Miss 45-46; Asst to civilian personnel offs US NavyGuantanamo Bay Cuba 46-47; Libn Quantico Post Schs USMC Schs, Quantico Va 50-51; LibnCamp LeJeune Schs USMC Camp LeJeune NC 57-60; Chief tech serv sect Armed Forces Staffcol (Norfolk Va) 60-. 9: SLA; SELA; VaLA. 10: Onslow Co Hist Soc; Garden Club. 14: Ref, catlg. 15: Armed Forces Staff Col Lib,hampton blvd, Norfolk Va 23511.

CAPEL, ELNA MAE. b Molena Pike Co Ga 25 S 17. 5: Woman's Col of Ga 34-38 (Eng) AB; Mercer U summer 48; Appalachian State Tchrs Col summer 50; UNC summers 53-56 MLS. 6: Fr. 7: Tchr-libn N Camden High Sch, white Oak Ga 38; Tchr-libn Summertown High Sch, Summertown Ga 38-40; Tchr-libn Enigma Consolidated High Sch, Enigma Ga 40-41; Tchr-libn Meriwether High Sch, Woodbury Ga 41-42; Tchr-libn Luthersville High Sch, Luthersville Ga 42-45; Tchr-libn Bonaire High Sch, Bonaire Ga 45-46; Tchr-libn Warner Robins High Sch, Warner Robins Ga 46-49, Libn Warner Robins High Sch, Warner Robins Ga 49-65, Libn Warner Robins Sr High & Warner Robins Jr High 55-56; Tchr of Vets Warner Robins High Sch even 51-52; Asst libn Roberts Mem Lib Middle Ga Col 65-. 9: NEA; ALA; GaEA (sec dist sect of Child & YP Div 62-65); SELA; GaLA. 10: AAUW; Alpha Delta Kappa. 14: Catlg. 15: 708 Third st, Cochran Ga 31014.

CAPIZZI, CAROL (KAY). b NYC 18 Mr 32. 5: Brooklyn Col 49-53 (Painting, Philo, Eng) BA; Columbia 55-58 MSLS. 7: BrooklynPub Lib; Libn trainee 55-57, Child libn 58-60, Reg child libn 60-62; Head child deptYonkers Pub Lib, Yonkers NY 62-63; Child bk ed Doubleday & Co Inc, NYC 63-64; Asstlib dir Free Pub Lib of Woodbridge, Woodbridge NJ 64-67; Consul Plenum Publ Corp 67;Libn Baldwin Sch NYC 67-68; Consul NYC Bd of Educ 68; Planner Anti-Poverty Programcommun Dev Agency NYC 68-. 8: Child bk consul, Plenum Publ Corp NYC & Bro-Dart Ind,NJ 67. 12: Assoc ed "New Jersey Libraries". 14: Admin, child serv, commun action. 15: 41 W 74 st, New York NY 10023.

CAPLAN, (NAOMI) CAROL. b Nashville Tenn 26 N 38. 5: Memphis State U 60-62 (Hist) BS; George Peabody Col for Tchrs 62 (LS) MA. 7: Catlgr Ga State Col 63-65; Enoch Pratt Free Lib, Baltimore Md: Catlgr 65-67, Sr children's libn 67-. 9: ALA. 14: Child lit, catlg. 15: 2502 Ken Oak Rd, Baltimore Md 21212.

CAPOZZI, MARIAN RITA. b Baltimore Md 11 My 27. 5: UMd 45-49 (Home Econ) BS; Towson State, Johns Hopkins, West Maryland, summers 50-64 (E duc); NYU, CatholicU 65-67 (LS) MS. 6: Fr, Ger. 7: Tchr, libn Baltimore Co Sch, Edgemere Md 50-55; Tchr adv USA Dependent Sch, Rochefort France 55-56; Libn USA Dependent Schools, Stuttgart Germany 56-57; Libn Baltimore Co Sch, Inverness Md 57-61; Tchr, libn Westchester Co Sch, Valhalla Rye New Rochelle NY 62-65; Supv lib serv Bd of Educ Balto Co Towson Md 66-. 8: Advis 1969 Young Reader's Advis Com (Doubleday). 9: ALA (consul Manpower Research Proj 69); -CSD; Mildred L Batchelder Award Sel Com 71); -AASchL; NEA-DAVI; MdLA; Educ Media Assn of Md; Tchrs Assn of Baltimore Co. 10: Beta Phi Mu; Delta Delta Delta. 14: Admin of sch libs/media ctrs. 15: 6802 Dunhill rd, Baltimore Md 21222.

CAPPS, ELEANOR S (GEORGE). b Chicago 27 F 15. 5: George Washington U 32-35 (LS) AA. 7: Lib asst UMd 49-53, 54-56; Documents libn Air Force Off of Sci Research, Wash DC 58-66; Hd tech processes and ass libn, Tech Ref Lib Naval Med Res Inst, Bethesda Md 66-. 9: SLA (Memb chm Mil Libns Div); DCLA. 14: Documentation, indexing, tech processes. 15: Point of Rocks Estates, Point of Rocks Md 21777.

CAPPS, MARIE (THEODORA PAPPAS). b Aberdeen SD 1 Je 21. 4: Jack Lee Capps. 5: Central Wash State Col 39-43 (Educ, Hist) BA; UWash 48-49 (Far East); SUNY (Albany) 65-68 MLS. 7: Tchr Sunnyside Sch, Sunnyside Wash 47-48; Tchr Seattle Sch, Seattle 48-49; Tchr usa dependent Sch, Kumomoto Japan 49-50; Tchr USA Dependent Sch, Kokura Japan 50-51; Tchr USA Dependent Sch, Frankfurt Germany 51-53; Libn US Mil Acad Lib 69-. 14: Mss, maps. 15: Quarters 35 USMA, West Point NY 10996.

CAPRIO, DORIS (WELD). b Rockland Mass 3 Ja 02. 5: Simmons 21-25 (Educ) BS. 7: Tchr-libn City of Newark NJ 27-44; Hosp libn Va, Ariz, Mo, NY, Conn 50-. 9: MedLA. 14: Catlg, ref. 15: 555 Willard ave, Newington Ct 06111.

CAPRITTA, DIANNE (MARY). b Schenectady NY 24 Ag 42. 5: Smith 60-63 (Geol); UIll 63-65 (Geol) BS; Union Col 65-66; Syracuse 66-67 MSLS. 7: SUNY Col of Forestry (Syracuse): Catlgr 67-68, Acquis libn 68-. 9: ALA; SLA; Geosci Info Soc; NYLA; SUNYLA (staff rep Col of Forestry). 14: Tech serv. 15: 303 Miles ave, Syracuse NY 13210.

CARAWAY, EDNA (BUSBY). b Hunt Co, Greenville Tex 18 Ja 13. 4: Glenn (Franklin) Caraway. 5: E Tex State U 61 (LS) BS, 62 (LS) MA. 7: Libn Greenville Pub Lib, Greenville Tex 61; Libn Wilkinson Jr High Sch, Mesquite Tex 62-. 9: Tex State Tchrs Assn; TexLA; SWLA; Mesquite TA; Teen-Age LA;

Dallas Co LA. 14: Catlg, ref. 15: 3605 Briscoe st, Greenville Tx 37743.

CARBONARO, DOROTHY ROSE MARIE. b Chicago Il 9 Ag 29. 5: DePaul 46-51 (Eng, Chem) BA; Chicago State Col 63-65 (LS) MS. 6: Ital. 7: Eng & chem tchr Austin High Sch, Chicago 58-64; Libn Whittier Sch, Oak Park Ill 64-65; Libn USA Dep Sch, Fulda Germany 65-67; Libn Amer Dental Assoc Chicago 67-. 9: ALA; SLA; MedLA; IllLA. 14: Admin. 15: 528 N Cuyler ave, Oak Park Il 60302.

CARBONE, SUZANNE (WIRTH). b Reedsburg Wis 23 Ap 42. 4: Robert F Carbone. 5: St Olaf Col 60-61; UWis 61-65 (Art Hist) BS 61-65(LS) MS. 6: Ger. 7: Lib aide lib sch UWis 64, Faculty asstship 64-65; Child libn Coop Child Bk Ctr, Madison Wis 66-68; Instr UWis summersessions 69-. 9: SLA. 14: Art ref, child libn. 15: 2051 Allen blvd apt 2D, Middletown Wi 53562.

CARBONELL, AMPARO GOMEZ. b Camaguey Cuba 15 O 30. 4: Ney. 5: UHavana 48-52 (Phil & letters), (Lib) 53-54; UMiami 64-65 (LS) Certif. 6: Sp. 7: Libn Instituit of Camaguey, Camaguey Cuba 54-59; Catlgr Jose Maile Pub Lib, Havanna 59-61; Dade Co Pub Schs, Miami Fla: Libn aide 61-67, Libn 67-. 9: ALA; DadeCoSchL; Dade Co Clr TA. 10: Woman's Club. 14: Catlg, clsf. 15: 7615 SW 21 st, Miami Fl 33155.

CARBRAY, MARY (Di FABIO). b Cranford NJ 29 Ja 16. 4: Richard John Carbray. 5: Mt Holyoke 33-37 (Fr) BS; UCol Dublin 49-50 Diploma in LS 50; Wash State Lib Certif 65. 6: Fr, Ital. 7: Asst personnel dir Ask Mr Forest Travel Serv, NYC 38-44 & 46; Lt (jg) USNR asst to dist dir of 13th ND, Seattle 44-46; Asst train supv Bliimingdale's Dept Store, NYC 46-47; Ref libn USIS lib, Dublin Ireland 50-52; Ref & circ libn Lake Forest Pub Lib, Lake Forest Ill 52-53; Libn Lake Forest Acad, Lake Forest Ill 54-58; Catlg & ref libn Barat Col, Lake Forest Ill 61-63; Ref libn SeattleU Lib summers 62-64; Catlgr Oak Park Pub Lib, Oak Park Ill 64-65; Art dept libn Seattle Pub Lib 66-. 9: PNLA. 14: Ref. 15: 1500 Grand ave, Seattle Wa 98122.

CARDENAS-ABREU, RENE. b Cruces Las Villas Cuba 17 Ja 21. 4: Herminia Artau Amado. 5: Inst of Havana 37-42 BA&S; UHavana 42-48 (Law) LLD; Kan State Tchrs Col 64-65 (LS) MA. 6: Sp, Portug. 7: Lawyer, Havana 48-56; Judge Judiciary Power, Mantua & Guines (Cuba) 56-60; Catlgr YaleU Lib 65-67; Asst libn Fla AtlanticU 68-. 9: ALA; FlaLA; SELA. 10: Havana Bar Assn (in exile), Miami Fla; Judicatura Cubana Democratica, Mimiam Fla; Elsie PineLA. 14: Catlg. 15: 145 NW 9th st, Boca Raton Fl 33432.

CARDONA, MARIAELENA (ARGULLO). b Managua Nicaragua. 4: Francisco J Cardona. 5: Barnard 44-45; UConn 47-48; UPR 52-58 (Span Lit) BA; Pratt 59-62 MLS. 6: Sp, Fr, Portu. 7: Libn Ind Res Labs Economics Development Adm, Hato Rey PR 55-57; NY Pub Lib: Lib tech asst 58-62, Libn head of Latin Amer Bibliog Projects 62-64, Libn II catlgr Latin Amer Area 64-65; Indexer Hispanic Found LC UFla Lib 65-67, Catlgr Latin Amer Area 66-67; LatAmer Bibliogr, Libns Research asst Caribbean Studs Inst UPR Rio Pedras 68-. 8: Bibliog consul for "Libros En Venta" (63-64) Chief Catlgr "Fichero Bibliografico Latinoamericano" 62-64. 9: ALA; Sociedadde Bibliotecarios de Puerto Rico. 10: SALALM. 12: Chief catlgr "Fichero Bibliografico Latinoamericano" (62-64). 14: Catlg, bibliog, indexing. 15: 2208 Park blvd st, Park blvd, Santurce PR 00913.

CARDWELL, MARIAM (ANN). b Shelbyville Ky 4 Jl 15. 5: Ohio Wesleyan 32-36, 37 (Fr) BA, 37-39 (Educ) MA; UKy summers 51-53 (LS). 6: Fr, Sp. 7: Eng tchr Shelby Co Bd of Educ, Ky 39-44, Eng & sci tchr 44-47, Eng tchr 47-49, Eng tchr & libn 49-60, Libn 60-. 9: ALA; KyLA; KyEA; KyASchL (Exec Bd 66-67); Shelby Co EA; Shelby Co Clr T (pres48-49). 13: Yes. 14: Ref. 15: Shelby County High School, Box 30, Shelbyville Ky 40065.

CAREY, ALBERTA (MUNDY). b Atlantic City NJ. 4: David Lee Carey. 5: Hampton Inst 43-47 (Secondary Educ) BS; NYU 52, 55 (Eng Educ) MA; Columbia 61-62 (LS) MA. 6: Fr. 7: Tchr of soc studies & Eng Worcester Co High Sch, Snow Hill Md 49-61; Tchr of lib Wm Grady Voc-Tech High Sch, Brooklyn NY 62-63; Tchr of lib James Monroe High Sch, Bronx NY 63-. 9: NYCSchLA. 10: Amer Fed Tchrs; United Fed of Tchrs; NAACP. 14: Tchrs lib usage to high sch studs. 15: 752 Macon st, Brooklyn NY 11233.

CAREY, ARTHUR EDWARD. b Topeka Kan 8 S 43. 4: Kjestine Rindom. 5: So Ill U 63-67 (Phil) BA; Kan State Tchrs Col 67-68 ML. 6: Sp. 7: Readers adv Topeka Pub Lib, Topeka Kan 67-68; Ref asst Kan State Tchrs Col 67-68; Ref libn Mont StateU 69-. 9: ALA; MontLA. 10: Colo Mt Club; Mont Conservation Coun; Amer Contract Bridge League. 14: Ref, rare bks, maps. 15: PO Box 1162, Bozeman Mt 59715.

CAREY, EILEEN F (Schumann). b Burlington Wis 5 D 24. 4: John T Carey. 5: UWis 45-48 (Eng) BS Ed; N Ill U 63 (LS) MALS. 6: Fr. 7: Lib analyst Battelle Mem Lib, Columbus Ohio 52-54; Sch Dist Lib N Baltimore Ohio 54-56; Libn-tchr Waterman High Sch, Waterman Ill 57-58; Unit libn Burlington Central Sch Dist Ill 58-61; Libn DeKalk High Sch, DeKalb Ill 61-66; Libn Boone High Sch, Orlando Fla 66-67; Acquis libn Pensacola Jr Col 67-. 9: ALA; NEA; FlaLA; WFlaLA; FlaEA. 10: Advis Bd Commun Action Prog, Pensacola Fla. 14: Acquis, ref. 15: 412 Sunnydale lane, Cantonment Fl 32533.

CAREY, MRS ELEANOR (MUNSON). b New Haven Conn 22 F 06. 5: Wheaton Col (Mass) 24-28 (Eng) AB; Columbia 29-30 (LS) BS. 6: Fr. 7: Lib asst Metropolitan Museum of Art, NY 30-36; Libn Hamden High Sch, Hamden Conn 36-39; Asst libn Transylvania Col 46-47; Libn Mary Todd Sch, Lexington Ky 58-. 9: NEA; KyEA; KyLA; KyASchL. 10: DAR; UKy Women's Assn; Nat Cong Parents & Tchrs. 13: Yes. 14: Sch lib wk. 15: 787 Robin rd, Lexington Ky 40502.

CAREY, FAYE (KINGSBURY). b Belknap Ill 15 Ja 17. 4: Dr Raymond G Carey. 5: UEvansville 33-37 (Soc Sci, Eng, Fr) AB; Northwestern 38-40 (Theatre) MA; UDenver 61-62 (LS) MA. 6: Fr. 7: Tchr Bosse High Sch, Evansville Ind 37-41; Instr Shimer Col 41-42; Tchr The Kent Sch, Denver 53-60; Ref libn Colo Woman's Col 62-. 8: Ref libn Lib/USA, NY World's Fair, 65; Exec Dir, Nat Lib Week, Colo 66. 9: ALA (Memb chm Region IV); MPLA; ColoLA. 10: Treasurer,alum Assn Grad Sch of Libnship, UDenver; Allied Arts, Inc; Eng-Speaking Union. 14: Ref. 15: 1590 S Monroe st, Denver Co 80210.

CAREY, FRANCES L(OUISE). b E Newark NJ 4 O 17. 5: St Joseph Col(Md) 35-39 (Eng) BS; Catholic U 40-41 BS in LS; Trinity Col(Conn) 47-50 (Hist) MA. 6: Fr. 7: Libn Nat Highway Users Conf, Wash DC 41-43; Libn Baker & Co, Newark NJ 43-45; Loan libn Col of New Rochelle 45-46; Asst libn St Joseph Col(W Hartford Conn) 46-51; Head catlgr US Naval War Col, Newport RI 51-57, Asst dir of libs 57-68; Assoc Dir of Libs 68-. 9: SLA; RILA; ASIS; Oral Hist Assn. 10: AAUW; Art Assn of Newport. 14: Catlg, admin. 15: Asst Dir of Libs, Naval War Col, Newport RI 02844.

CAREY, GERTRUDE MARIE. b Lowell Mas 5 Ag 46. 5: Lowell State Col 64-68 (Hist) BA; LSU 68-69 MSLS. 6: Sp. 7: Stud asst Lowell State Col 65-68; Stud asst LSU (Baton Rouge) 68-69. 14: Ref, a-v. 15: 35 Nashua rd, Billerica Ma 01862.

CAREY, JOHN T. b Oswego NY 4 Je 39. 4: Jeanne Noyes. 5: St BonaventureU 60-62 (Lat) BA; Simmons 66-68 (LS) SM. 7: Tchr Scio Central Sch, Scio NY 62-63; Lance Corp US Marine Corps (Field Radio Oprt) 63-65; Sub-prof libn Pub Lib, Cambridge Mass 65-67; Asst reg admin West Reg Pub Lib Syst, Springfield Mass 68-69; Dir Groton (Conn) Pub Lib 69-. 8: Mass Bd of Lib Commsners Spec Adv Com 68-69; Exec com Mass Lib Film Coop 69-. 9: ALA; West Mass Lib Club; NELA; MassLA (prog com 68-69; nominating com 68-69). 13: Yes. 14: Catlg, a-v. 15: 220 State st, Springfield Ma 01103.

CAREY, M PATRICIA. b Newport NH 15 Mr 22. 5: UNH 40-42 (Sociol); Fla State Col for Women 45-47 (Pol Sci) BA; UVa 47-48 (Pol Sci) MA; Johns Hopkins 54-55 (Middle East); Catholic U 59-60 MSLS. 7: Cryptographer War Dept, Miami Fla 43-45; Documentalist Defense Dept, Wash DC 48-59; Hdqrs libn Fairfax co Pub Lib, Fairfax Va 59-. 8: Adv Fairfax Co Historic Landmarks Preserv Commsn; mem Citizens Com Fairfax CoPub Sch Centennial Celebration. 9: ALA; VaLA; SELA. 12: Ed 'Virginiana' column "Virginia Librarian" (60-63). 13: Yes. 14: Ref. 15: 5421 Back Lick rd, Springfield Va 22151.

CAREY, THERESA (ZIPP). b Seattle Wash 17 N 44. 4: Paul W Carey. 5: SeattleU 62-66 (Hist) BA; UWash 65-67 MLS. 7: Clerical Seattle Pub Lib 64-66, Pre-prof 66-67, Ref libn Multnomah Co Lib, Portland Ore 67-68; Asst acquis libn Portland State U Lib 68-. 9: PNLA. 14: Acquis. 15: 5415 N Strong, Portland Or 97203.

CARFAGNO, HELEN (RILEY). b Los Angeles Calif 28 F 13. 4: Simon A Carfagno. 5: UCLA 3136 (Eng) BA, 48-53 (Eng) MA; UCal at Berkeley 36-37 (Libnship) Certif. 6: Eng, Fr. 7: Branch libn Fresno Co Lib, Fresno Cal 37-42; UCLA: Catlgr 42-47, Ref libn 47-55, Hd grad reading rm 55-63; Sub libn Chico State Col Lib 64-66; Ref & readers serv libn Butte

Co Lib, Oroville Cal 68-. 10: UCLA Lib Staff Assn. 14: Ref, catlg. 15: 666 Elliott rd, Paradise Ca 95969.

CARGILL, JENNIFER SUE. b Ruston La 15 Jl 44. 5: La Polytech Inst 62-65 (Hist) BA; LSU 65-67 (LS) MS. 6: Fr. 7: Trainee LSU Lib 65-67; Asst acquis libn UHouston Lib 67-68; Asst sci libn 68-69; Optometry libn 69-. 9: SLA (Tex Chap Memb Com 68-69, treas 69-70); TACT; TexLA; SWLA. 10: AAUP; Faculty Club; UHouston; Phi Kappa Phi; Beta Phi Mu. 14: Acquis, reviewing, ref. 15: 6441 Gulf Freeway apt 264, Houston Tx 77023.

CARHART, FORREST F(REER) JR. b Sheffield Iowa 11 Jl 17. 4: Mary Elizabeth (Peregrine). 5: Drake U 35-39 (Pol Sci) AB; UMich 39-41 ABLS, 41-43 AMLS. 7: Page Jr asst & sub br libn Des Moines Pub Lib, Des Moines Iowa 32-39; U Mich Gen Lib (Prof asst circ dept 40-41, in chg 1st floor Study Hall 41-42, in chg Angell Hall Study Hall 42, Libn Math-Econ Lib 42-43, 1st asst circ dept 43; Asst libn WVa U Lib 43-48; Loan l ibn Iowa State Col Lib 48-49; Asst dir of libs UDenver 49-52; Staff libn Hq Air Force Personnel & Train Research Center, Lackland AFB Tex 52-55; Deputy dir USAF Acad Lib 55-59; Asst dir ALA Lib Tech Proj, Chicago 59-63, dir 63-; Dir ALA Off for Research & Development, Chicago 65-. 8: Consul WVa State Dept of Forestry Lib 47. 9: ALA (Coun 55-57, chm &/or mem 3 coms 49-57);-LAD (Org Com 56-57);-RTSD (Bd dirs Acquis Sect 57-59);-ACRL (Res Planning Com 50-54; SLA (chm Hospitality Com Ill Chap 64-65); IllLA. 10: Jr C of C; AAUP; Bibliog Center for Res (Rocky Mountain Reg); UMich Lib Sch Alumni Assn; ChicagoLibClub; Inst Res Coun Inc; Tau Kappa Epsilon; ASA Z39, Z85, & PH5; USAF Acad Command; Incentive Awards Com. 12: Contrib to Encyclopedias. 13: Yes. 14: Admin, research. 15: 50 E H uron st, Chicago Il 60611.

CARHART, MARY ELIZABETH (PEREGRINE). b Denver 16 Jl 21. 4: Forrest F Carhart Jr. 5: UDenver 39-43 (Eng) AB, 51-52 (LS) MA. 7: Libn Greenlee Elem Sch, Denver Pub Schs 52-54, Libn South High Sch 54-59; Head Libn Thornridge High Sch, Dolton Ill 59-64; Sr catlgr Roosevelt U 64-65; Head catlgr Center for Research Libs, Chicago 65-. 9: NEA; ALA-AASchL (rep to ALA Memb Com 61-63, rec sec 63-64); -LAD (Recr Com 61-64, Retirement Homes 63-65); ColoLA; MPLA; IllLA; IllSchLA; ChicagoLibClub. 10: Kappa Delta Pi; Alpha Gamma Delta; South Holland Pub Lib Bd. 14: Catlg, admin. 15: 1460 N Sandburg Ter, Apt 1712, Chicago Il 60610.

CARIANI, VANDA PAULA (BERTAZZONI). b Boston 21 Ap 23. 4: Anthony Robert Cariani. 5: Boston U 40-44 (Chem) AB; Simmons 48-51 (LS) MS. 6: Ital, Fr, Lat, Ger. 7: Research chem Atlantic Research Assn, Cambridge Mass 44-48; Ref libn sci-tech dept Boston Pub Lib 48-56; Instr in Lib Sci UMiss 57-64; Engnr libn & Asst Prof Lib Sci Memphis State U 64-. 9: SLA; TennEA. 12: Co-auth "Manual for Cataloging with Sample Cards" (68). 14: Sci-tech, ref, catlg. 15: 722 Eaton st,Memphis Tn 38117.

CARL, HERBERT A. b Hempstead NY 3 S 15. 4: Virginia Hulbert. 5: Duke U 34-38 (Econ) AB; Columbia 46-47 (LS) BS. 7: Casualty & fire insurance agent Liberty Mutual Insurance Co, NYC 38-42; Signalcorps (Cpl) US Army, USA & India 42-46; Ref asst Yale U Lib 47-48; Br libn DC PubLib 48-56; Lib research spec Div of Lib Programs US Off of Educ, Wash 56-59, ResearchLibn 59-67, Spec asst to dir 67-. 9: ALA (Life mem). 10: Brooke Manor Country Club; Chevy Chase(Md) Lib Adv Com. 12: Co-ed US Office ofEducation's "State Plans Under the Library Services Act," with Sups 1-3 (58-63). 13: Yes. 14: Lib research, admin. 15: 9908 Old Spring rd, Kensington Md 20795.

CARLEY, CLARA E (GETMAN). b Ilion NY 19 O 18. 4: Harold E Carley. 5: Mt Holyoke 36-38; St LawrenceU 38-40 (Eng) BA; SUNY (Geneseo) summers 39, 40 (LS) Certif; UWis summers 63, 64, 66 MLS. 6: Fr, Ger. 7: Libn Onondaga Central Sch, Nedrow NY 40-41; Asst libn Cann asst libn Onondaga Central Sch, Nedrow NY 40-41; Asst libn Cannon Free Lib, Delhi NY 52-54, Hd libn 54-59; Catlgr Olin Lib CornellU 59-60; Libn Groton Elem Sch, Groton NY 62; Libn trainee Finger Lakes Lib Syst, Ithaca NY 62-66, Bkmob libn 66-67, Ref serv specialist 67-. 8: Permanent interlib loan com mem S Central Research Lib Coun 68-; Com mem S Central Research Lib Coun for compilation local hist bibliog 69-; Research & recommendation for uniform syst card in prep for formation Dade Co Lib Syst; Madison (Wis) Pub Lib 66. 9: ALA; NYLA. 0: Alpha Delta Pi; Beta Phi Mu; Alumni Assn UWis Lib Sch. 12: Comp "A List of Periodicals and Newspapers in the Finger Lakes Library system". 14: Ref, catlg consul for the syst. 15: 569 Ellis Hollow Creek rd, Ithaca RD #2 NY 14850.

CARLEY, MARCIA MARIE (REID). b Alliance Neb 20 Je 23. 5: Neb State Tchrs Col 40-43 (Educ) BA; UDenver 57 9ls0 ma. 6: Fr. 7: Tchr Dalton High Sch, Dalton Neb 46-48; Tchr Gurley High Sch, Gurley Neb 50-56; Libn Sidney High Sch, Sidney Neb 56-64; Libn J L Parrish Jr High Sch, Salem Ore 64-. 9: NEA; ALA (Memb rep Reg 4 62-64); OreEA; NebLA (sec 62-64); OreSchLA (Dist 2chm 68-69). 10: AAUW; Delta Kappa Gamma. 14: Sch wk. 15: 1193 24th st NE, Salem Or 97301.

CARLIN, IRENE DOROTHY. b Holyoke Mass. 5: Pembroke 24 (Eng) PhB; Brown 30 (Educ) MA; Columbia summer 28 (LS); Simmons 50 (LS) BS. 6: Fr. 7: Eng tchr & libn high sch, Cranston RI; Eng tchr high sch, Pawtucket RI; Libn Amer High Sch, Heidelberg Germany; Libn Tolman High Sch, Pawtucket RI, Hd of Lib. 8: Mem of Com to suggest rev of RI Sch Lib Standards 68-69. 9: ALA; NESchLA; RISchLA; RILA. 15: 199 West ave, Pawtucket RI 02860.

CARLSEN, DOROTHY (SONN). b Newark NJ 11 Ja 22. 4: Stuart E Carlsen. 5: Bucknell 40-43 (Eng) BA; Rutgers 65-68 MLS. 7: Asst Libn Montclair Acad, Montclair NJ 67-68; Child libn Guernsey Mem Lib, Norwich NY 68-. 10: AAUW; LWV; Hosp Auxiliary; Newcomers Club. 14: Child wk, story hours, bk sel. 15: M-12 Midland Park apts, Norwich NY 13815.

CARLSON, ELIZABETH ANNE. b Sheridan Wyo 6 My 39. 5: Sheridan Col 57-59 (Math) AS; UWyo 59-61 (Math) BS; UIll 61-63 (LS) MS. 7: Stud lib asst Sheridan Col 57-59; Stud lib asst UWyo 59-61; Stud lib asst UIll(Urbana) 61-62; Libn Big Bend Commun Col, Moses Lake Wash 62-65; Tech serv libn State Law Lib, Olympia Wash 66-. 9: ALA; AALL; WashLA. 10: Admin Women in Educ; Wyo Archaeol Soc; Phi Theta Kappa. 13: Yes. 14: Tech serv, serv, docs. 15: 1510 SE 46th st, apt J-25, Lacey Wa 98501.

CARLSON, IRVING G(EORGE). b Philadelphia 16 S 18. 4: Josephine S Carlson. 5: Hofstra Col 35-39 (Humanities) BA; Columbia 39-41 (LS) MS; NYU 44-45 (Educ) MA. 6: Fr. 7: Libn gen asst Brooklyn Pub Lib 41-43; Unit supv US Off of Strategic Serv, Wash DC 43-44; Acess libn Columbia Med Lib 44-46; Asst libn Amer Merchant Marine LA, NY 46-47;Head doc analysis sect USNavy Electronics Lab, San Diego 47-57, Assoc libn 57-. 8: Lib Consul Systems Labs Corp, Los Angeles 57. 14: Ref. 15: 1335 Trieste dr, San DiegoCa 92107.

CARLSON, JOAN A. b Brownsville Tex 4 N 36. 5: MacMurray Col 54-58 (Chem) BA; West Res 59-60 MS in LS. 6: Ger. 7: Assoc libn Union carbide Corp (Parma Ohio) 60-67; Asst mgr 68-. 9: SLA (Cleveland Chap: v-pres 65-66, pres 66-67). 14: Ref, processing, acquis. 15: PO Box 6116, Cleveland Oh 44101.

CARLSON, JOHN B. b Brooklyn NY 7 D 25. 4: Patricia Blake. 5: Sampson Col 48-49 (Lang arts) AA; UMich (Marketing) BBA, 64-65 AMLS. 7: USN aviator (Ens) 43-47; Serv rep Goodyear Tire Co, Detroit 51-54; Order rep Amer Seating Co, Grand Rapids Mich 54-55; Sales rep Mich Bell Tel Co, Grand Rapids Mich 55-64; Self-employed food processing, Grand Rapids Mich; Libn Creston High Sch, Grand Rapids Mich 65; Libn Grand Rapids Jr Col 66; Dir LRC Montclair Commun Col 66-. 8: Media Consul for the Amer Assn of Jr Cols 68. 9: ALA; MichLA; Mich Coun of Commun & Jr Col Lib Adminors (sec). 15: 290 Cummings NW, Grand Rapids Mi 49504.

CARLSON, LIVIJA (PELECIS). b Latvia 30 Mr 40. 4: Douglas Carlson. 5: UMinn 58-62 (Eng Lit) BA, 62-63 (LS) MA. 6: Latvian, Russ, Ger. 7: Lib asst St Barnabas Hosp Minneapolis 61-63; Catlgr UMinn (St Paul) Lib 63-67,Acquis libn 67-. 9: MinnLA; Twin Cities Catlgrs RT. 10: Twin Cities Catlgrs Round Table. 14: Catlg, acquis. 15: Rte 1,Jordan Mn 55352.

CARLSON, LYNN CHERYL. b Chicago Ill 3 Ja 46. 5: No IllU 63-67 (Soc Sci) BA; UWis 67-68 (LS) MA. 7: Period libn LoyolaU (Chicago) 68-. 14: Period, ref. 15: 8547 W St Joseph ave, Chicago Il 60656.

CARLSON, MELVIN ALFRED JR. b Minot NDak 28 O 42. 5: Olivet Nazarene Col 60-64 (Eng Lit) AB; UIll 64-66 (LS) MS. 7: Grad asst UIll(Urbana) 64-66; Specialist fifth class US Army 66-69; Catlgr UVt 69-. 9: ALA. 14· Catlg, acquis. 15: University of Vermont, Burlington Vt.

CARLSON, RALPH ALBERT. b Cleveland 17 F 32. 5: John Carroll U 50-55; Mexico City Col 55-57 (Span, Educ) BA; West Res 58-59 MS in LS. 6: Sp. 7: Catlg asst Detroit Pub Lib 59-63; Head of processing Norfolk Pub Lib System, Norfolk

Va 63-. 9: ALA; VaLA; SELA. 10: Nat Exchange Club; Beta Phi Mu. 13: Yes. 14: Catlg. 15: 1202 Pembroke Towers 601 Pembroke ave, Norfolk Va 23507.

CARLSON, WILLIAM HUGH. b Waverly Neb 5 S 1898. 4: Claire Over. 5: UNeb 20-24 (Journalism) AB; NY State lib Sch (Albany) 26 Certif; UCal 36-37 MA in LS. 6: Swedish, Norwegian, Danish. 7: Reporter "Aurora Republican" Aurora Neb 23-24; Asst Neb Legis Ref Bur Lib Lincoln Neb 24-25; Supv dept libs UIowa 26-29; Libn UND 29-34; Visiting libn Vanderbilt U 35-36; Libn UAriz 37-42; Assoc libn UWash 42-45; Dir of Libs Ore State System of Higher Educ & Libn Ore State U 45-65; Lib Planning & Research Assoc Ore State System of Higher Educ 65-68; Dir of Libs Emeritus Ore State Sys of Higher Educ, 68-. 8: Surveyor Tex A & M Col Lib 49 (with R Orr); Adv Dillard U Lib 51; Surveyor(with C Hintz) Portland Ore high sch libs 59; Consul on var acad libs bldgs Visg Libn Willamette U 68-69. 9: ALA (BSA: chm Postwar Planning Coun for Col & Univ Lib 42-45); -ACRL (pres 47-48); -LED (pres 52-53); ArizLA (pres 39-40); PNLA (pres 52-53). 10: Kiwanis Club; Phi Kappa Phi; Soc Adv Scand Studies. 12: "College and University Libraries and Librarianship" with others, ALA (46); "Development and Financial Support of Seven Western and Northwestern University Libraries" (38); "Nebraska Voters Handbook" with others (24); "A Report of a Survey of the Library of Texas A and M College, October 1949 to February 1950" (with R Orr) (50); "Libraries and Library Service in the Portland High Schools," with C Hintz (59); assocd with Ore State U Press 67-. 13: Yes. 14: Univ lib admin, personnel, lib educ, acad lib bldgs. 15: Ore State Univ Lab, Corvallis Or 97331.

CARLSSON, VERA MURIEL (ROBINSON). b Minneapolis 9 S 21. 5: UMinn 39-43 (Educ) BS, 45-46 BS in LS. 6: Fr. 7: Tchr & libn New London High Sch, New London Minn 43-45; Asst manager Folwell Hall Bkstore UMinn summer 45; Sr clerk Walter Lib UMinn 45-46, Jr libn 46-48, Libn 48-49; Tchg asst lib sch UMinn 49-50; Libn law lib UMinn 50-64, Instr & libn 64-. 9: AALL (Com chm 56-57);- Minn Chap. 14: Acquis, documents. 15: Law Library U Minn, Minneapolis Mn 55455.

CARLTON, LUCILLE VIRGINIA (BURBANK). b Hampton Va 6 Jl 25. 4: Peter Anthony Carlton. 5: Col of William & Mary 42-46 BA in LS; Catholic U 54-56 MS in LS. 6: Sp, Fr, Lat. 7: Asst libn Charles Taylor Mem Pub Lib, Hampton Va summers 45, 46; Child libn Pub Lib, Newport News Va 46-49; Child libn Berkshire Athenaeum, Pittsfield Mass 49-52; Asst br libn Louisville Free Pub Lib, Louisville Ky 52-53; Asst jr high libn So Jr High Sch, Louisville Ky 53-54; High sch libn Anacostia High Sch, Wash DC 54-55; High sch libn Herndon High Sch, Herndon Va 55-58; High sch libn Lee High Sch, Springfield Va 58-62; High sch libn Thomas Edison High Sch, Alexandria Va 62-. 8: Instr in lib sci, Catholic U & UVa Extension Center 61- Instr in child lit Amer U, Wash DC (62-64). 9: ALA; NEA; Internat Reading Assn; VaLA; VaEA (Sch libs Dept); Assoc School Libns of Fairfax Co Va (ASLFC); N Va Libns Assoc (chm 63-64); Greater Wash Reading Coun; Fairfax CoEA. 10: YWCA; Civil Air Patrol (2nd Lt); Woman's Internat Bowling Congress Inc; Phi Beta Kappa; Kappa Delta Pi. 11: Asst dir Reading Improvement Lab 63-64. 12: "Basic Library Techniques" (66). ' 13: Yes. 14: Child & yp lib wk, tchg lib sci courses. 15: 2805 Fort dr, Box 4066, Alexandria Va 22303.

CARMACK, BOB D. b Quail Tex 15 Mr 37. 4: Virginia Shattuck. 5: Colo State U 59-61, 62-65 (Hist) BA; UDenver 65-66 (LS) MA. 7: Asst libn humanities div UNebraska 66-67; Undergrad libn 67-. 8: Served on a team of consuls for Neb Wesleyan Lib, Lincoln Neb 67-68. 9: ALA; NebLA. 14: Ref, admin. 15: 420 So 38th, Lincoln Nb 68510.

CARMACK, LUCILE. b Bristol Va 9 Ja 09. 5: UVa 36 (Eng) BA; Col William & Mary summer 41; Peabody summers 42-44 (LS) MA; AmericanU (Eng); UWash summer 65 (NDEA Inst). 6: Fr. 7: Elem tchr Washington Co Va 28-38; Secondary tchr Russell Co Va 38-40, Secondary libn Lebanon 40-43; Secondary libn Fairfax Co Va Falls Church 43-47; Secondary libn Roosevelt High Sch, Wash DC 47-60; Secondary libn Woodrow Wilson High Sch, Wash DC 60-67; Dir Bristol Pub Lib, Bristol Va 67-. 9: NEA; ALA; AASchL; DCLA; DCASchL;VaLA; TennLA. 10: Delta Kappa Gamma; Connecticut ave Citizens Assn; Action Com for DC Sch Libs. 13: Yes. 15: Rte 1, Bristol Va 24201.

CARMAN, FRANCES (ELLEN). b Cambridge Ohio 4 Ag 06. 5: Ohio State U 24-28 (Hist) BS in Ed; West Res 29-30 BS in LS; Columbia summer 40 (LS). 7: Sch lib asst Cleveland Pub Lib 28-29; Jr High Sch libn Flint Pub Schs, Flint Mich 30-42; Sec summer lib sch Penn State U 41; Libn Morley Lib, Painesville Ohio 42-46; Br libn Berkshire Athenaeum, Pittsfield Mass 46-47; Br libn Cuyahoga Co Pub Lib, Cleveland 47-54; Libn Stockbridge Lib, Stockbridge Mass 54-56; Libn Bennington Free Lib, Bennington Vt 56-61; Ref asst State U Col (Cortland NY) 61-64; Lib dir II Liverpool Pub Lib, Liverpool NY 64-. 9: ALA; VtLA (pres 60-61); NYLA; MichEA (chm Reg 2 Lib Sect); MichLA; Mich Schmaster 's Club; OhioLA; MassLA. 10: AAUW. 13: Yes. 14: Small indep libs, br libs, wk with child & yp. 15: 600 James st, Syracuse NY 13203.

CARMICHAEL, BETTY L. b Greene County Ind 27 Ja 22. 5: IndU 40-44 (Ed) BS, 52-55 (Ed) MS; UDenver 64; UOkla 65. 7: High sch tchr Hancock & Polson Mont 44-51; High sch tchr-libn: Crete Ill 51-52, Batesville Ind 52-55; Libn Sr high sch Columbus Ind 55-56; Libn Jr high sch Columbus Ind 56-67; Lib coord Bartholomew Consolidated Sch Corp, Columbus Ind 67-. 8: Particip Lib 21; Seattle World's Fair 62. 9: ALA; NEA; IndSchLA (Rec sec, Mem chm); IndStateTA. 11: Delta Kappa Gamma. 14: Sch libnship. 15: Library Proc Center 722 6th st, Columbus In 47201.

CARMICHAEL, MARY (DARGAN). b Port Washington NY 20 S 19. 4: Robert Stewart Carmichael. 5: Adelphi U 38-42 (Hist) BA; Columbia 46-47 BSLS LIU (Documentation); Rutgers (Documentation). 7: Clerk Amer Tel & Tel, NYC 42-43; Lt (jg) admin USCoast Guard (WR) 43-46; Asst Libn research lib Brookhaven Natlab, Upton NY 47-48; Chief Libn Tech Lib USNaval Train Device Center; Port WashingtonNY 48-50, 57-66, Orlando Fla 66-. 9: SLA (Fla Chap; Org Com 69; So Atlantic Chap;Treas Fla Gp 69); East Coast Navy Labs Coun of Libns (Chm 65-66, sec 64-65, Progplanning & Long-Range Planning coms). 10: Girl Scouts; PTA; Flower Hill Hose Coladies Auxiliary; STINFO; Kappa Kappa Gamma; Cath Daughters Amer. 14: Admin, documentation. 15: 611 Powell dr Oakland Estates, Altamonte Springs Fl 32701.

CARMICHAEL, MRS ELEANOR (JOHNSON). b Mooresville Ind 31 Ag 16. 4: Charles W Carmichael. 5: Earlham Col 34-38 (Eng) AB; Columbia 40-41 (LS) BS Ind U 66- (LS). 7: Asst catlgr Iowa State Tchrs Col 41-42; Libn Dept of Arch & Fine Arts Cornell U 42-46; Physics libn Purdue U 46-49; Libn John Herron Art Inst Indianapolis 56-60; Period serv libn DePauw U 60-66, Catlg libn 66-. 9: Ohio Valley Group of Tech Servlibns (sec 62-63, chm adv bd 64-65); ALA; IndLA. 10: AAUW. 12: "A Chronology of Scientific Development, 1848-1948" with Karl Lark-Horovitz (49). 15: 702 Highwood ave,Greencastle In 46135.

CARMODY, TERENCE FRANCIS. b NYC 6 Ag 38. 5: UNC 56-61 (Eng) AB; UDublin(Trinity Col) 61-63 (Eng) MLitt; Pratt 63-64 MLS NYU (Eng). 6: Fr, Ger, Latin. 7: Lib assoc NYU University Heights Lib 64-66, Grad asst Eng 67-68. 10: NY Shavians;The Soc for the Libs NYU; NYU Eng Grad Assn; Amer Com for Irish Studies; Mod LangAssn. 13: Yes. 15: Brookville rd, Glen Head NY 11545.

CARNES, FRANCES (LAURET) COX. b Mexico City Mexico 19 S 04. 4: Otis G Carnes. 5: UTex 21-25 BA; Columbia 28-29 (LS) BS, 35-36 (LS) MS. 6: Sp, Fr, Ger. 7: Lib asst Stephen F Austin State Tchrs Col 28; Lib asst North Tex State Tchrs Col 28-29; Libn New Haven State Normal, New Haven Conn 29-35; Act libn UTex Educ Lib summer 47; Libn Westminster Jr Col 47-49; Catlgr Harvard Divinity Sch (Boston) 49-52; Catlgr McMurry Col 52-54; Libn Pub Lib, Mt Pleasant Iowa 54-56; Ser libn Central Col (Fayette Mo) 56-59, Act libn 59; Asst libn Pembroke State Col 59-68; Libn 68-. 9: ALA; SELA; NCLA. 10: Mortar Board; Women's Soc of Christian Serv (pres 62-). 14: Catlg, acquis. 15: Box 745, Pembroke NC 28372.

CARNEY, MARY J. b Kankakee Ill. 5: Col of St Francis (Joliet Ill) 42-46 (Eng) AB; UIll 54-55 MS in LS. 7: Libn Unit Dist No 4 Clifton Ill 50-54, 56-60; Libn St Anne High Sch St Anne Ill 55-56; Libn Kankakee E Jr High Sch, Kankakee Ill 60-64; Libn Kankakee Sr High Sch, Kankakee Ill 64-66; Libn Kankakee Eastridge Sr High Sch, Kankakee Ill 66-. 9: ALA-AASchL; IllLA; IllASchL. 10: Delta Kappa Gamma; Beta Phi Mu. 14: Sch libs. 15: 430 So Myrtle, Kankakee Il 60901.

CARNEY, THOMAS (L). b Cedar Rapids Iowa 28 S 43. 4: Dawn Kofron. 5: UIowa 61-67 (Psych) BS, 67-68 (LS) MA. 7: Commun serv Cedar Rapids Pub Lib 68-. 9: ALA; IowaLA. 14: Adult serv. 15: 428 Third ave SE, Cedar Rapids Ia 52401.

CARNINE, MRS HELEN (WILSON). b Strong City Kan 23 O 15. 4: Harry J Carnine. 5: Kan State Tchrs Col 9emporia) 34-38 (LS) BS in Ed & Lib Certif; Rutgers 59-61 MLS. 6: Fr.

7: Asst libn Wyandotte High Sch, Kansas City Kan 38-39; Instr UWyo 47-52; Catlgr Pub Lib Cedar Falls Iowa 55-56; Asst ref libn Paterson State Col Wayne NJ 61-. 9: SLA. 14: Ref. 15: 654 High Mountain rd, Paterson NJ 07508.

CARNOVSKY, LEON. b St Louis 28 N 03. 4: Ruth French. 5: UMo 23-27 (Philos) AB; Chicago 29-32 (LS) PhD. 6: Fr, Sp, Ger. 7: Asst to libn Washington U (St Louis) 28-29; Instr to Assoc Prof UChicago 32-44, Prof 44-. 8: Visiting Lecturer UCal(Berkeley) 37, 39; Visiting Prof Syracuse U 55; Visiting Prof Columbia U 60, 64; Surveys: NY State Lib, Battle Creek Mich, DePaul U Lib, Vancouver Pub Lib, Racine Pub Lib, Chicago, Cleveland, Mansfield Ohio, Greensboro NC, Mich State Lib; Lib educ in the Pacific Northwest; Survey of lib functions of the States; Chicago Schs Survey; US Educ Mission to Japan, 46; Consul US Army of Occupation in Germany; Faculty Unesco seminar for libns, Eng 48. 9: ALA; AALS (pres 42-43). 10: AAUP; Quadrangle Club, Chicago. 11: Fulbright Fellow to France, 51-52; Melvil Dewey Medal, 62; Festschrift "Library Quarterly," (O 68). 12: "Appraisal of the Cleveland Public Library" (39); "Survey of the Greensboro Public Library" (52); "Library Service in a Suburban Area," with E A Wight (36); "Library," with D Waples (36); "Survey of the Michigan State Library," with others (39); "Librarians and Readers in the State of New York," with D Waples (39); "Metropolitan Library in Action," with C B Joeckel (40); Contrib of papers or chapters to; "Some University Student Problems" (33); "Library Trends" (37); "Current Issues in Library Administration" (39); "Practice of Book Selection" (40); "Reading in General Education" (43); "Books and Libraries in Warime" (45); "Education for Rural America" (45); "Education for Librarianship" (49); "Survey of the Los Angeles Public Library" (50); "Encyclopedia of Educational Research"; "Comptons Encyclopedoa;" Ed; "Library in the Community," with L Martin (44); "International Aspects of Librarianship" (54); Managing Ed "Library Quarterly" (42-60); Jt Ed "The Medium-Sized Public Library" (63); Ed "Public Library in Urban Setting" (68); Ed "Library Networks - Promise and Performance" (69). 13: Yes. 14: Pub lib, comparative libnship, educ for libnship. 15: Grad Lib Sch Univ of Chicago, Chicago Ill 60637.

CARNOVSKY, RUTH (FRENCH). b Chippewa Falls Wis. 4: Leon Carnovsky. 5: Carroll Col 24-28 (Lat) BA; Yale 28-31 (Lat, Gk); UIll 32-34 (Gk) PhD; UMinn 44-45 (LS) BS. 6: Gk, Lat, Fr, Ger. 7: Prof Lat & Gk Iberia Col 38-42; Research staff in ancient hist Ind U 43-44; Art libn Minneapolis Pub Lib 45-48; Assoc Prof UDenver Sch of Libnship 49-53; Visting Prof Japan Lib Sch, Keio U (Tokyo) 53-54; Asst Prof Grad Lib Sch UChicago 54-60, Assoc Prof Grad Lib Sch 60- . 8: Dean of Studs, Grad Lib Sch UChicago 56-. 9: ALA (chm Catlg Policy & Research Com 64; Exec Com Catlg & Clsf Sect 66-68, chm 1st Esther J Piercy Award Jury 69);-LED (Liaison with MusLA 68-). 12: Co-auth "Studies in the Texts of St Jeromes "Vitae Patrum (43); "Toward "Tward A Better Cataloging Code (56); Ed "Library Catalogs: Changing Dimensions (63). 13: Yes. 14: Catlg, art & music libs. 15: Grad Lib Sch Univ of Chicago, Chicago 60637.

CAROL, MARCEL C. b NYC 15 D 25. 4: Shirley June. 5: UOkla 48-52 (LS) BA; UIll 54-55, 57 (LS) MS. 7: Ref asst Kan City (Mo) Pub Lib 52-54; Ref asst Dallas Pub Lib 55-57, Br head 57-65; Libn Baylor in Dallas Lib 65-. 9: MedLA. 14: Ref, admin, rare bks. 15: 1547 Kings highway, Dallas Tx 75208.

CARP, HELEN (TOPOL). b Brooklyn NY 15 My 23. 4: Albert A Carp. 5: Brooklyn Col 40-42 (Liberal arts); NYU 42-44 (Retailing) BA; Drexel Grad Sch of Lib Sci 60-66 (LS) MS. 7: Asst buyer Ohrbach's, NYC 44-45, Buyer, Newark NJ 45-46; Asst buyer Factor-Greenstein NYC 47-48, Buyer 48-49; Asst Circ libn Villanova U 66-67; Libn Columbia Sch, Phila 67-. 9: ALA; PennLA; PennSchLA; IndepSchLA, Philadelphia. 10: Beta Phi Mu. 14: Sch libs. 15: 1513 James rd, Wynnewood Pa 19096.

CARPENTER, BARBARA E (ODGERS). b Detroit 24 Ja 30. 4: Nicholas E Carpenter. 5: Albion Col 48-51 (Eng, Music) BA; Columbia 52-54 MSLS. 6: Fr. 7: Tchr Berk ley Pub Schs, Berkley Mich 51-52; Libn adult circ br NY Pub Lib 54-55; Asst libn Henry Ford Hosp Med Lib, Detroit 55-56; Jr libn catlg dept UMich Lib (Ann Arbor) 56-57; Jr libn catlg d ept Ind State U Lib 65-67; Ref libn W Shore Pub Lib, Camp Hill Penn 67-. 9: ALA-ACRL. 14: Catlg, med libs. 15: 8 Oakwood cir, Camp Hill Pa 17011.

CARPENTER, CECILE LORETTA. b Seattle 23 N 38. 5: Wash State Col 57-58; UWash 58-61 (Eng) BA, 63-64 (LS) M of L. 6: Fr. 7: Jr libn Lib Assn of Portland, Portland Ore 64-66, Sr libn 66-. 9: ALA; OreLA; PNLA (Ore Chm Com Biog Data on Pac NW Authors). 10: LWV. 14: Ref, state docs, indexing. 15: 801 SW 10th, Portland Or 97205.

CARPENTER, ELIZABETH. B New Hope Ala 7 D 06. 5: Huntingdon Col 24-28 (Piano) BMus; NYU 35-36 (Arts & Sci), summers 48-49 (Psych) MA; George Peabody Col summers 29-31 (Mod lang) BS; UAla; UGa. 6: Fr, Sp, Ger. 7: Piano & Fr tchr Duncan High Sch, Duncan Miss 28-30; New Hope High Sch, New Hope Ala: Libn & piano, Fr, & Eng tchr 30-50, Libn 50-. 9: NEA (life mem); ALA; ClrTA; SELA; AlaSchLA. 10: Delta Kappa Gamma; AAUW; Organist New Hope Meth Church for 40 years; Mem Ala Sesquicent Com 69. 14: Ref, catlg. 15: New Hope Al 35760.

CARPENTER, GERALD LAWRENCE. b Appleton Wis 20 My 42. 5: St Norbert Col 60-62; Wis State U 62-65 (LS) BS; UWis at Madison 65-66 (LS) MS. 7: Hd ext serv Oshkosh Pub Lib, Oshkosh Wis 66-68; Asst ref libn Wis State U 68-. 14: Ref. 15: 429-A Algoma blvd, Oshkosh Wi 54901.

CARPENTER, JANELLA ANN. b Knoxville Tenn 20 S 36. 5: UTenn 54-58 (Educ) BS; Peabody 60-63 (LS) MA; Appalachian State U 65, 67. 7: Libn Elizabeth Sch, Charlotte NC 58-63; Libn Merry Oaks Sch, Charlotte NC 63-64; Libn Rama Road Elem Sch, Charlotte NC 64-. 9: ALA; NEA; ClrTA; NCEA; NCLA; MecklenburgLibrary Assoc. 10: Delta Kappa Gamma, Beta Phi Mu; Beta Sigma Phi. 14: Sch libs, & child wk. 15: 2401 Randolph rd, Charlotte NC 28207.

CARPENTER, KENNETH EDWARD. b Altoona Penn 13 N 36. 4: Mary Wilson. 5: Bowdoin 54-58 (Hist) AB; Russian Inst of Columbia U 58-59 (Russ Hist); Simmons 61-64 MS in LS. 6: Fr, Ger. 7: Asst in reading room, Houghton Lib Harvard U 59-61, Asst to libn 61-62; Ref libn Bowdoin Col 62-63; Asst to ed of "Bibliography of American Literature" Houghton Lib 63-67; Assoc in Kress Lib 67-68, Curator 68-. 9: ALA; BSA. 10: Phi Beta Kappa. 13: Yes. 14: Rare bks, bibliog. 15: Kress Lib of Bus and Econ, Harvard Bus Sch, Soldiers Field rd, Boston Ma 02163.

CARPENTER, KENNETH JOHN. b Glendive Mont 16 Ap 16. 4: Patricia Healy Carpenter. 5: UCal (Santa Barbara) 50 (Eng) BA; UCal (Berkeley) 52 (Eng) MA, 52 BLS. 7: Admin Asst UCal Lib (Berkeley) 52-55, Head rare bks dept 55-62; Asst dir of libs UNev 62-. 9: ALA; Printing Hist Soc; NevLA. 10: AAUP; ACLU; Nev Art Gallery (ed dirs). 13: Yes. 14: Tech serv, rare bks, tchg. 15: Univ of Nev Lib, Reno Nv 89507.

CARPENTER, LUCY. b Memphis Tenn 12 D 28. 4: Frank Thomas Carpenter. 5: LeMoyne Col 45-49 (Eng) BA; Columbia 49-50 (Secondary Educ); Talladega Col 54 (Span); Atlanta 55-57 MSLS; Chicago 60 (LS); Chicago State Col 67 (Educ). 6: Sp 07: Asst libn Talladega Col 56; Jr High Sch libn Bd of Educ, Memphis Tenn 57-59; Catlgr Chicago Pub Lib 59-66; High sch libn Chicago Bd of Educ 66-. 9: Chicago Lib Club; ALA; Church & Synagogue LA. 10: Beta Phi Mu; NAACP. 11: Evangelistic Tour & Crusade, Ghana, W Africa 68 with Bishop H W Goldsberry. 12: Ed "Church Library Outreach Quarterly"; "Poems; Power to Live By" (62). 14: Catlg. 15: 5358 S Prairie ave, Chicago Il 60615.

CARPENTER, LOLA. b Norwich ND 7 Ap 09. 5: State Tchrs Col (Minot ND) 25-29 (Educ, Com) BA; Gregg Col 37 (Com) Tchrs Diploma; UMinn 33-34, 39-40 (LS) BS; IndU 65 MA in LS. 6: Ger, Sp. 7: Catlgr-asst libn State Tchrs Col (Dickinson ND) 29-44; Cryptographer Women's Army Corps (Cp l) 44-45; Accountant Monte Vista Inn, Dutch Flat Cal 46-47; Owner-Operator Phonograph Record Store, Indianapolis 47-53; Sr libn Catlg Div Indianapolis Pub Lib, Indianapolis 53-62; Libn Perry Central Jr High Sch, Indianapolis 62-66; Sr libn br & stations div Indianapolis Pub Lib, Indianapolis 66-67; Asst Sup Tech Serv Indianapolis-Marion Co Pub Lib, Indianapolis 67-. 9: ALA; IndLA. 10: Bus & Prof Wom Club. 14: Catlg, lib admin. 15: RR2 Box 119, Greenwood In 46142.

CARPENTER, MARY ELIZABETH (MORGAN). b Atlanta. 4: Lawrence Reid Carpenter. 5: Samford U summers 53-59 (Soc Sci, Educ, Eng) BS; UAla 64 Certif Sch libnship MA (LS) 65; UTenn summer 67 (LS). 6: Sp. 7: Sec & bkkeeper Commonwealth Life Insurance, Birmingham Ala; Tchr Jeffer son Co Bd of Educ, Birmingham Ala 50-58; Libn spec collections Samford U Birmingham Ala 58-59; Asst libn Shades Valley High Sch, Jefferson Co Bd of Educ, Birmingham Ala 59-62; Head libn Berry High Sch Jefferson Co Bd of Educ, Birmingham Ala 62-. 8: Consul John Carroll High Sch Accred 66, Faculty Jacksonville State U summer 67. 9: NEA; ClrTchrsAssn; AlaLA (mem 3 coms, sec Sch Div 65-66, v-pres

66-67, pres 67-68); SELA; AlaEA; ALA. 10: PTA; Alpha Lambda Delta; Kappa Delta Epsilon; Alpha Beta Alpha; Mountain Laurel Garden Club; Shades Crest Civic Club; Cleophas Lit Club; Armantine Lit Club. 11: Honors Day Recipient Samford U 57, 58, 59; Runner-up "Favorite Tchr Ala" 68; UAla Alum Lib Sc (pres 68-69). 14: Rare bks, Ala materials, ref, yp serv. 15: 537 Park ave, Birmingham Al 35226.

CARPENTER, MICHAEL (ANTHONY). b Los Angeles Cal 30 Jl 40. 4: Rosemarie Hlad. 5: Occidental 58-63 (Phil) AB; UCLA 66-67 MLS. 6: Fr, Ger. 7: Clk UCal at Santa Barbara Lib acquis dept 66; LC: Searcher Preservation Off Pilot Preservat Proj 67, Spec recruit 67-68, Ser catlgr 68-. 9: ALA; ASIS. 10: AAUW. 11: Beta Phi Mu. 14: Catlg, automation, ser, bibliog control. 15: 1019 E Capitol st apt 2, Wash DC 20003.

CARPENTER, MYRA SCHWEININGER. b Pittsburgh 20 Ap 15. 4: Lawrence S Carpenter. 5: Col of Wooster 33-37 (Biol & Eng) BA; Carnegie 37-38 BLS. 6: Lat, Fr, Ger. 7: Sch libn Ambridge High Sch, ambridge Penn 38-39; Sch libn Avonworth High Sch, Ben Avon Penn 39-40; Child libn Norwalk Pub Lib, Norwalk Ohio 52-61; Sch libn Norwalk Jr High, Norwalk Ohio 61-. 9: ALA; OhioEA; OhioASchLibns; NWOhioEA; N Central Libns Assn (pres). 10: Roundabout Reading Club; Child Conservation League; Advisory Bd of Rainbow Girls; Delta Kappa Gamma. 14: Ref, lib instr. 15: 205 W Main, Norwalk Oh 44857.

CARPENTER, MYRTLE (LUCILE) (COX). b Lancaster Wis 22 S 14. 4: Glenn J Carpenter. 5: UMinn 31-35 (LS) BS; UWis 61-65 MSLS. 6: Fr. 7: Circ asst State UIowa 35-40; Ref libn Pub Lib, Wausau Wis 40-42; Sch libn Pub Lib Sys, Madison Wis 42-44; Navy libn US Dept of Navy, Olathe Kansas, Great Lakes Ill 45-46; YP libn Pub Lib, San Diego Cal 47-48; High sch libn Lancaster Commun Schs, Lancaster Wis 56-64; Supv libn SW Wis Pub Lib Serv Ctr Fennimore Wis 64-65; Reader serv libn Wis State 65-. 9: ALA; WisLA; SoWisEA; SoWisLA; AWSUF; WLTA. 10: AAUW. 12: "Masters Theses and Seminar Papers, Wisconsin State Universities 35-68"; v 1 - Myrtle L Carpenter, editor. 14: Reader serv, ref. 15: 128 So Taylor, Lancaster Wi 53813.

CARPENTER, RAYMOND LEONARD. b Watertown NY 1 D 26. 4: Patricia Anderson Carpenter. 5: St Lawrence U 46-49 (Sociol) AB; UNC (Chapel Hill) 49-51 (Sociol) MA, 59 (LS) MS, 59-68 (Sociol) PhD. 6: Fr. 7: Private US Army Inf & Japanese Lang Studies Yale, Minn, Rutgers 44-45; Asst manager Bull's Head Bookshop UNC Lib 9chapel Hill) 52-55; Lib asst ext dept UNC Lib (Chapel Hill) 52-55; Lib asst ext dept UNC Lib (Chapel Hill) 56, Chief order & searching Sect 57; Instr Sch of Lib Sci UNC 58; Grad Fellow So Friendship Fund UNC 59; Bibliog Searcher Duke U Lib summer 59; Lecturer Sch of Lib Sci UNC (Chapel Hill) 60-68; Assoc prof 68-. 8: Instr in Libnship Venezuela Peace Corps Proj UNC 62; Instr US VA Bk Selection Institute UNC 63; Consul Governor's Commsn on Lib Resources in NC 64 Proj dir US Off Educ research contract 66-67; Chief investigator "The Man of Knowledge & the Admin of Soc Change," pt of NASA proj "Sciences in Interaction" 69- Research Contract 1966-67, Principal 02485 9: ALA; A Sociol A; AALS; SELA; NCLA. 10: AAUP; Beta Phi Mu; Alpha Kappa Delta. 11: Library Bind Inst Award; Grad Fellowship from Southern Fellowships Fund. 12: Asst Managing Ed "Library Resources and Technical Services 1959-1960"; Transl & Ed "Mission of the Librarian" Ortega y Gasset, with James Lewis (61); "The Public Library Executive" (68). 13: Yes. 14: Research, educ, admin, soc sci lit. 15: Sch of Lib Sci, Univ of NC, Chapel Hill NC 27514.

CARPENTER, ZOE IRENE. b Fort Dodge Iowa 29 Mr 31. 5: No U of Iowa 49-53 (Eng) BA; Catholic U 57-60 MSLS. 7: Assoc libn (ref) UMd (College Park) 60-69; Info scientist Johns Hopkins U (Silver Spring Md), Applied Phys Lab 69-. 14: Computers in libs. 15: 6802 Highview ter, Hyattsville Md 20782.

CARPER, ANNA M. b Palmyra Penn 13 Ag 19. 5: Elizabethtown Col 37-41 (Eng) AB; Columbia 50-51 (LS) MS. 6: Fr, Ger, Lat. 7: Tchr-libn Fredericksburg High Sch, Fredericksburg Penn 41-47; High sch tchr S Lebanon Schs, Lebanon Penn 47-50; Head catlgr UMd 51-60; Head Libn Elizabethtown Col 60-. 8: Mem, Eval Team, Middle States Assn of Colo & Secon Schs 62, 64. 9: ALA-ACRL;PennLA (sec Col & Res Libs Sect 63). 10: Delta Kappa Gamma. 14: Catlg. 15: 306-1/2E High st, Elizabethtown Pa 17022.

CARPER, MYRTA (THOMAS) MRS. b Madison Heights Va. 5: Oglethorpe U 37 (Lit, Journalism) AB; Atlanta Lib Sch 24 (LS) Certif; Oglethorpe U 38 (Lit & Journalism) MA; Emory 65 (LS) MA, 63-65 (LS) 6th yr Certif. 6: Fr. 7: Catlgrmitchell Col summer 24; Libn Oglethorpe U 25-44; Libn Ga State Col 45-49; Libn GaState Col 45-49; Libn Prof Lib Atlanta Pub Schs 50-; Tchr lib sci and Fr & Russianlit Oglethorpe U, var times. 9: ALA; NEA; GaEA (lib dept); GaLA; SELA; AtlantaEA;Metro Atlanta Lib Club. 10: AAUW; Alpha Delta Kappa; Oglethorpe U Alum Assn. 15: 37 B Inwood Circle NE, Atlanta Ga 30309.

CARPINO, EILEEN R. b Yorkville Ohio 13 Ag 21. 5: Catherine Spalding Col 40-44 (Art) BS; Catholic U 44-46 (LS) BS. 6: Fr, Ital. 7: Libn Mt St Mary's Col (Los Angeles) 46-48; Asst libn Col of Steubenville 48-50; Bkmob libn Martins Ferry Pub Lib, Martins Ferry Ohio 51-54; Asst libn Wheeling Col 55-63, Libn 63-. 9: ALA; -ACRL; CalLA; WVaLA;WPenn ColLA; Tri-State ACRL (pres 65-66). 10: LWV; Cath daughters of Amer; Cath Womans Club; Cath Soc Serv Dept for Diocese of Steubenville (Bd); Sch Bd for St John's Central High Sch, Bellaire Ohio. 14: Ref. 15: 15 North Third st, Martins Ferry Ohio 43935.

CARR, BEULAH (MOTT). b Viola Iowa 30 N 1900. 4: Roland (Provoost) Carr. 5: Iowa State Tchrs Col 19; Grinnell Col 20-23 (Philos); Columbia summer 25; UDenver 35-36 (LS) BA; Colo State Tchrs Col 36-37 (Educ) MA. 7: Asst cashier Farmers Savings Bank, Gaza Iowa 23-35; Sr High Sch Libn Greeley High Sch, Greeley Colo 37-38; Libn Fairhope Pub Lib, Fairhope Ala 57-. 9: ALA; AlaLA. 10: Kappa Delta Pi; Sigma Pi Lambda. 15: Box 252, Fairhope Al 36532.

CARR, CATHERINE DAISE. b St Helena Island SC 28 My 37. 4: Robert Edward Carr. 5: SC State Col 53-57 (LS) BS; Atlanta summer 63 (LS). 6: Fr. 7: Libn St Helena High Sch, Frogmore SC 57-59; Libn Robert Smalls Elem Sch, Beaufort SC 62-65; Libn St Helena Elem Sch, Frogmore SC 63-65; Tchr Burroughs Elem Sch, brunswick Ga 65; Libn Burroughs Elem Sch, Brunswick Ga 65-66; Libn Risley High Sch, Brunswick Ga 67-68. 9: NEA; ALA; Amer Tchrs Assn; GaTchrsEA. 10: First African Baptist Church; Delta Sigma Theta. 14: Catlg & child lit. 15: Rte 1 Box 177, Frogmore SC 29920.

CARR, CHARLES EDWARD. b Wildwood NJ 13 Mr 39. 5: Wagner Col 57-61 (Hist, Pol Sci) BA; Drexel 61-62 MSLS. 06: Sp. 7: Sr libn Burlington Co Lib, Mt Holly NJ 62-65; Prin Libn Burlington Co Lib Br Cinnaminson NJ 65-. 9: NJLA; NJCoLib Staff Members Assn (chm 63-65). 10: Phi Mu Alpha Sinfonia. 14: Ref. 15: 2000 Atlantic ave, Wildwood NJ 08260.

CARR, DOROTHY MAY. b Uxbridge Mass 17 Ag 07. 5: Pembroke 26-30 (Eng) AB; Boston U 30-31; Simmons 31-32 BS. 6: Fr, Lat. 7: Asst Waltham (Mass) Pub Lib 32-34; Asst libn Graves Lib Kennebunkport Me 49-62, Libn 62-64; Head libn St Francis Col (Biddeford Me) 64-. 9: ALA; MeLA; NELA. 10: Trustee Graves Mem Lib 49-; Kennebunkport Hist Soc (sec 56-62, Bd). 14: Catlg. 15: Lane to the Lock, Lock st, Kennebunkport Me 04046.

CARR, GOLDIE (Z). b Zagreb Yugoslavia 17 D 42. 5: UBritish Columbia 61-65 (Slavic Studies, Russian) BA, 65-66 BLS. 6: Serbo-Croatian. 7: Librarian I Bus & Econ Seattle Pub Lib 66-. 14: Ref in bus, econ and fin. 15: #107-433 Belmont East, Seattle Wa 98102.

CARR, KATHRYN (PENN). b La Granoe Ga. 5: South U 36-39 (Eng, Soc sci) AB; Atlanta U 42-43 (Pub lib) BS in LS. 7: Tchr libn Onachite Parish Sch Bd, Monroe La 39-42; Sr libn War Dept Sp Serv 43-47; LA Pub Lib: Libn 47-48, 49-50, Sr libn 51-60, Prin libn 60-63, 67-; Lib specialist UCLA/USAID, Nigeria 64-67. 8: Instr Exten Sch, SoU 41-42 (Negro hist); Adv to libs in Lagos, Nigeria. 9: ALA; IFLA; CalLA. 10: Nat Assn of Col Women; Nat Urban League; League of Allied Arts. 11: Alpha Kappa Alpha; Phi Delta Gamma. 14: Catlg, automation, organ, admin, personnel. 15: 2000 N Ivar ave apt 12, Hollywood Ca 90028.

CARR, MARJORIE (FOLZ). b Colon Repub of Panama 1 Jl 21. 4: Rear Admiral Bruce L Carr USN (ret). 5: UNH 37-41 (Fr) BA; Rosary Col 63-67 MA. 6: Fr. 7: Dist libn Sch Dist 58, Downers Grove Ill 63-. 9: ALA; IllEA; NEA; ETA. 10: AAUW; DAR. 14: Wk with child. 15: Downers Grove Pub Schs, 935 Maple ave, Downers Grove Il 60515.

CARR, MARY JANE. b Tipton Ind 28 F 13. 5: Butler U 31-33; DePauw U 33-35 (Eng) BA; UIll 41-42 BSLS; UMich 51-52 MALS. 6: Fr, Ger. 7: Recept Registrar's Off, Purdue U 36-41; Catlg libn Purdue U Lib 42-53, Head card prep unit 53-57; Libn Rockford Col 57-63; Acquis libn DePauw U 63-. 9: ALA; IndLA. 14: Tech serv. 15: 215 Wood st apt 1, Green Castle In 46135.

CARR, MARY LYNNE (HOPKINS). b Okmulgee Okla 5 N 34. 4: Albert L Carr. 5: UTulsa 53-56 (Eng) BA; UWis 66-67 (LS) MA. 6: Sp. 7: Tchr pub schs: Sapulpa Okla 56-57, Okla City 57, DeWitt Neb 58-59, Reedsburg Wis 63-64; Bkmob libn Dane Co Lib Serv, Madison Wis 67-68; Libn Co-op Child Bk Ctr, Madison Wis 68-. 9: Wisla 9child & y-p Sect Film Bibliog Com). 14: Storytelling, bibliog compilation & research. 15: 1313 Tompkins dr, Madison Wi 53716.

CARR, MILDRED LEE. b Norfolk Va 10 F 15. 4: E William Carr. 5: William & Mary 31-34 (Eng) BA; Columbia 38-39 (LS) BS; UNC at Chapel Hill summer 67 (Data processing, Libs). 6: Fr. 7: Enoch Pratt Lib, Baltimore: Asst circ 35-38, First asst lit dept (readers adv) 39-42; Ref libn Md State Teachers Col, Towson Md 51-52; Asst circ libn UNC at Greensboro 58-. 9: ALA; SELA; NCLA. 12: Ed, "The St John's College List of Great Books," Enoch Pratt Free Lib 43; Ed & Comp "Catching up with the Twentieth Century," Womans ColU NC 61. 14: Pub serv, exhibits. 15: 202 Meadowbrook ter, Greensboro NC 27408.

CARR, OPAL GLADYS. b Augusta Kan 28 Ja 08. 5: UOkla 29 (Home Econ) BS, 33 BALS, 58 MLS. 7: UOkla: Asst ref libn 31-45, Ref libn 45-58, Libn hist govt geog area 58-. 9: ALA; SWLA; OklaLA. 10: American Rose Soc; Coun of Norman Garden Clubs. 14: Ref, docs. 15: 1025 McNamee, Norman Ok 73069.

CARR, RICHARD JOSEPH (THOMAS). b Washington DC 24 My 35. 4: Ana Lucia Villamar Carr. 5: CatholicU 52-58 (Eng) BA; UMd 59- (LS). 6: Sp, Thai, Ger, Fr, Lao, Portu, Ital, Lat, Dutch. 7: Ger tchr Abbey High Sch, Wash DC 56-58; Soldier US Army, SC & Germany 58-60; Tchr of Eng as for lang Chulachomklao Acad, Bangkok 61-64; Sp catlgr LC 64-. 12: Translated Cuban poet Nicolas Guillen (69); Thai grammar bk (Bangkok). 14: Catlg, ref (Hispanic materials). 15: 4700 Bennett ave, Bradbury Hts Md 20023.

CARR, WEAMENA (MARGUERITE). b Oklahoma City Okla 24 Ap 12. 5: LA Pub Lib Sch summer 29; UCLA 31, 39, 41, 42; UCal at Riverside 57; Riverside City Col 58-60, 62, 64. 7: Jr libn LA Pub Lib 29-45; Riverside Pub Lib, Riverside Cal: Libn Rubidoux Br 48-60, Sr libn Arlington Br 60-68, Area supv 69-. 9: ALA; CalLA. 10: PTA; Girl Scouts of America; Soroptimist Club. 15: 5786 De La Vista, Riverside Ca 92509.

CARR, WILLIAM CECIL. b Kaitangata Otago New Zealand 25 Mr 05. 4: Naomi Cottam. 5: Brigham Young U 27-34 summer 35-39 (Eng Hist) BA; UCal (Berkeley) 39-46 (Pol Sci) PhD; UDenver 63-64 (LS) MA. 6: Fr, Ger. 7: Prin tchr LDS Sems Utah 34-39; Soc studies tchr McClymonds High Sch, Oakland Cal 44-45; Grad tchg fellow pol sci UCal (Berkeley) 42-44, 45-46; Asst Prof hist-pol sci Brigham Young U 46-56; Chm Soc Studies Dept Church Col of New Zealand, (Tempel View) 58-62; Soc sci documents ref libn Brigham Young U 64-65; Col Libn West Wyo Commun Col 65-. 9: ALA; UtahLA; MPLA. 10: Utah Hist Soc; Amer Assn State & Local Hist. 14: Ref, govt docs, hist of libs, bibliog, lib educ. 15: 270 N 700 West, Green River Wy 82935.

CARR, ZELMA KATHRYN (BURNETT). b Arkadelphia Ark 6 My 05. 4: Love C Carr. 5: Fla State Col for Women 38-45 (Elem Educ, Soc Studies) BA; UHouston summer 49 (Psych); Fla State U summers 54-57 (LS) MA. 6: Sp. 7: Tchr Pace Elem Sch, Pace Fla 29-33; Tchr Holt Elem Sch, Holt Fla 33-42; Tchr Blount Jr High Sch, Pensacola Fla 42-45; Tchr Holt Elem Sch, Holt Fla 45-53; Tchr Southside Elem Sch, Crestview Fla 53-54; Admin Okaloosa Co Pub Lib, Crestview Fla 64-65; Libn Southside Elem Sch, Crestview Fla 54-65 Supv educ media Okaloosa Co Schs, Crestview Fla 66-69. 8: Curriculum Guide Com State Dept of Educ Fla. 9: NEA; ALA; FlaEA; FlaASchL; FlaA-V Assn. 10: Pilot Club; PTA; Kappa Delta Pi. 11: Tchr of the Year for Crestview 56. 14: Child libn, ref. 15: PO Box 276, HoltFl 32564.

CARRAWAY, EDWARD (EARL). b Morehead NC. 5: E CarU 57-61 (Mus) AB; Wichita StateU 63-66 (Mus); UOkla 67-68 MLS. 6: Fr. 7: Tchr High Sch, Newport NC 62-63; Lib asst wichita StateU 64-66, Ref libn 67-68, Circ libn 68-. 9: ALA; KanLA. 10: Beta Phi Mu; NAACP. 11: Evangelistic Tour & Crusade, Ghana W Africa 68 with Bishop H W Goldsberry. 12: Ed "Church Library Outreach" quarterly; "Poems; Power to Live By" (62). 14: Lub automation, ref, circ, pub serv. 15: 1547 N Yale blvd, Wichita Ks 67208.

CARRICK, (ROBERT) BRUCE. b Winnipeg Man Can 10 F 07. 4: Barbara Brockley. 5: UBC 25-29 (Econ) BA; McGill 35-36 BLS. 6: Fr. 7: Audit clerk Riddell, Stead, Hodges, & Winter, Chartered Accountants, vancouver BC 29-35; Gen asst Fraser Valley Union Lib, Abbotsford BC 36-40; Reg Libn Fraser Valley Union Lib, Abbotsford BC 40-45; City Libn Brandon War Mem Pub Lib, Brandon Man 46-48; Co Libn Whitman Co Lib, Colfax Wash 49-50; Co Libn Spokane Co Lib, Spokane Wash 50-60; City Libn Spokane Pub Lib, Spokane Wash 61-. 9: WashLA (pres 58-59); PNLA. 10: Photographic Soc of Amer; Delta Upsilon. 13: Yes. 14: Admin, bk sel. 15: W 1309 19th ave, Spokane Wa 99203.

CARRIER, ESTHER JANE. b Punxutawney Penn 22 Je 25. 5: Bob Jones Col 42-44; Geneva Col 44-46 (Eng) AB; Carnegie 46-47 BS in LS: Penn State U 47-50 (Eng) MA; UMich 57-60 AMLS, PhD. 7: Circ ref asst Penn State u lib 47-50; Libn Houghton Col 50-. 9: ALA. 12: "Fiction in Public Libraries, 1876-1900" (65). 14: Ref. 15: Houghton Col, Houghton NY 14744.

CARRIER, LOIS (JACQUELINE). b Saskatoon Sask Can 24 F 30. 5: USask 47-50 (Eng) BA; Toronto 51-52 (LS) BLS, 65-66 (LS), 68 MLS. 7: UAlta; Asst ref dept 53-60, libn Boreal Inst 60-62; UCalgary; Head ref & circ 62-65; UBC; Hd Soc Sci Div 66-. 9: CanLA; ALA; Assn of BC Libns (pres 68-69); BCLA. 13: Yes. 14: Ref. 15: 804-1644 W 12th ave, Vancouver 9 BC.

CARRINGTON, DAVID KENT. b Wash DC 10 Ap 38. 4: Mary Elinor Meacham. 5: UMd 56-61 (Geog) BS; Fla State U 65-66 (LS) MS. 6: Fr. 7: US Off Geog Interior, Wash DC: Geog analyst 61-65, Chief source materials sect 66-68; Coordinator single map automation proj LC 68-. 8: Consul John Carroll High Sch Accred 66, Faculty Jacksonville State U summer 67. 9: SLA (chm Geog & Map Gp, Wash DC Chap 67-69); Geosci Info Soc. 11: Honors DayRecipient Samford U 57,58,59; Runner-up "Favorite Tchr Ala" 68; UAla Alum Lib Sci(pres 68-69). 14: Tech processing, automation, acquis. 15: 5470 Sanger ave, Alexandria Va 22311.

CARRINGTON, MRS WILLIE R. b Louisville Ky. 5: Ind U 30 (Fr) AB, 36 (Fr) MA; Columbia 60 (LS) MS. 6: Fr. 7: Tchr Livingstone Col 34-37; Tchr Louisville (Ky) High Sch 32-34; Tchr Jr High Sch, Wash DC 42-46; Libn head of fine arts dept New Rochelle (NY) Pub Lib 60-. 9: ALA; NYLA; WestchesterLA. 10: Phi Beta Kappa; Womans Club; Alpha Kappa Alpha; Natl Assn for Study of Negro Life and Hist. 14: Fine arts, music. 15: New Rochelle Pub Lib, New Rochelle NY 10805.

CARRISON, DALE K. b Macomb Ill 29 Ap 36. 4: Marion J Gillett. 5: West Ill U 54-58 (Bus Educ) BS, MS; UIll 60 (Educ); NoIll U 60 (LS); UDenver61-62 (LS) MA, 64-69 (Higher Educ) PhD. 6: Fr. 7: Period libn West Ill U 57-58; Libn United Twp High Sch, E Moline 58-61; Lib Sci Instr West Ill U 62-64; Lib Sci Instr UDenver 64-68; Exec Dir Lib Mankato State Col 68-. 8: Consul; Devel of Lib Sci, Instr Prog, Ill State Lib 64; Job Corps Lib Breckenridge Job Corps Ctr Ky 65; Planning Grant ESEA Title III Project BoulderColo 67; Central Colo Coop Pub Lib Sys Staff Devel Proj, Denver 68. 9: ALA-AASchL;NEA-DAVI; MPLA; MinnLA; MinnASchL. 10: Pi Omega Pi; Phi Delta Kappa; Beta Phi mu; AAUP. 13: Yes. 14: Admin, lib educ, tech serv. 15: 104 Lilliandr, Mankato Mn 56001.

CARROL, ARTHUR L. b Roxbury Mass 19 O 24. 4: Sarah V Tyrrell. 5: Syracuse 46-50 (Speech) BS, 50-51 MS (LS). 6: Gk. 7: US Army Off Strategic Serv (OSS) 43-46; Libn DC Pub Lib 51-52; US Army Engnr Sch Lib, Ft Belvoir Va: Catlg libn 52-53, Ref libn 53-55, Chief archives br 55-60, Chief lib div 60-66; Chief Libn, Navy Mine Defense Lab 66-68; Tech Info Off Naval Ship R & D Lab(formerly Mine Defense Lab) 68-. 9: SLA; Coun of Libns, E Coast Navy Labs (sec69-70). 10: Sigma Tau Rho. 14: Admin. 15: 443 Bunkers Cove rd, Panama City Fl 32401.

CARROLL, C(ARMAL) EDWARD. b Grahn Ky 8 O 23. 4: Greta Sjostrom. 5: UToledo 47 PhB, MA 50, BEd 51; UCal(Los Angeles) MLS 61; UCal(Berkeley) 65-69 PhD. 6: Fr, Ger. 7: Pub sch tchr Ohio & Ill 47-56; Dir CurriculumLib UCLA 56-60; Asst educ libn USoCal 61-62; Ref libn educ & psych UCal (Berkeley)62-65; Head libn So Ore Col 65-67; Dir Libs Wichita State U 67-. 69; Dir Libs UMo Columbia 70-. 8: Ref libn & consul to the Cal Coordinating Com on Higher Educ 63-65. 9: ALA; KanLA. 10: Layreader Episcopal Church 58-; Phi Delta Kappa; Wichita Bibliophiles. 13: Yes. 14: Admin,educ for libnship. 15: UMo Lib, Columbia Mo 65201.

CARROLL, CELIA (GREEN). b Electra Tex 18 Fe 45. 4: James Larry Carroll. 5: Our Lady of the Lake Col 63-64; Wagner Col 65-66; UTex (Austin) 67-68 (Eng) BA, 68-69 MLS. 6: Fr. 7: Asst dir ext Austin Pub Lib, Austin Tex 68-69, Coord child serv 69-. 9: TexLA. 14: Child serv. 15: 203A Laguna Vista, Austin Tx 78746.

CARROLL, REV CLIFFORD ANDREW, S J. b Duluth Minn 23 Ap 06. 5: Gonzaga U 29-33 (Econ) AB, 33-34 (Econ) MA; Alma Col 38-41 (Theol) STL; St Louis U 44-47 (Econ) PhD. 6: Fr, Ital. 7: Libn & tchr of econ Seattle U 35-38; Asst libn Alma Col 38-41; Guest Lecturer in Econ Seattle U 42; Libn Gonzaga U 45-63, Dir of libs & Prof of Econ 64-. 8: Sometime dean & regent of Sch of Econ & Bus Gonzaga U; Founder of the Industrial Rel Sem at Gonzaga U; Labor arbitration both independently & for the Amer Arbit Assn. 9: ALA; Bibliog Soc (London); CathLA; NEA; Amer Arbit Assn (mem Nat Panel); PNLA; PacNW Bibliog Center; WashLA. 10: West Assn of Art Museums. 14: Rare bks, bks in hist of labor rel. 15: Crosby Lib, Gonzaga Univ, Spokane Wa 99202.

CARROLL, DEWEY (EUGENE). b Monterey Tenn 30 Ag 26. 4: Elizabeth Ann (Cade). 5: UChattanooga 46-49 (Psych, Hist) BA; Emory 53-54 (Libnship) MS; UIll 58-60 (LS) Ph D. 6: Ger, Fr. 7: USN Operations Off (Lt) 51-53; Atlanta Pub Lib: Asst ref libn 54-55, Hd sci & indus div 55-56; EmoryU: Sci libn 56-58, Faculty mem div of libnship 60-63; Faculty mem Ga Inst of Tech 63-65; Faculty mem UIll Lib Sch 65-69; Dir of libs UTenn at Chattanooga 69-. 9: ALA; ASIS; SELA; TENNLA. 10: AAUP. 12: "Newspaper and Periodical Production in countries of Europe 1600-1950" (65); Ed "Proceedings of Clinic on Library Applications of Data Processing" (66-69). 14: Lib admin, lib automation, info retrieval systems. 15: 205 Arrow dr, Signal Mountain Tn 37377.

CARROLL, DOROTHY (LEIGH) EDWARDS. b New Madrid Mo 6 Je 41. 4: James A Carroll. 5: UMiss 59-63 (Home Econ) BS, 65-69 MLS. 7: Clk typist period dept UMiss Lib 63-66; Act sr libn period 66-. 9: Miss Civil Air Patrol; MissLA. 14: Period, ser publ. 15: Box 38, Lexington Ms 38677.

CARROLL, ELIZABETH. b Gloucester Mass 27 Ag 13. 5: Regis Col 36 (Eng) AB; Simmons 41 BS. 7: Staff aide Amer Red Cross, Manila PI 45-46; Lib supv AFWESPAC, Manila PI 46-48; Staff lib USAFIK, Seoul Korea 48-49; Staff libn Yokohama Command, Yokohama Japan 49-50; Command libn Alaskan Air Command, Elmendorf AFB Alaska 51-56; Command libn Tech Train AF, Gulfport Miss 56-57; Post libn US Army Ft Richardson Alaska 57-60; Asst libn Alaska Methodist U 60-63; Hd 63-. 9: ALA; Alaska State LA (v-pres 63, pres 65). 14: Admin, bk sel. 15: PO Box 325, Eagle River Ak 99577.

CARROLL, ELOISE THERESE. b Lackawanna NY 16 S 42. 5: Marywood Col 60-64 (Span) AB, 64-65 MS in LS. 6: Sp. 7: Page Scranton Pub Lib, Scranton Penn 58-60; Clerk-typist Scranton Sch Dist, Scranton Penn 62-65; Libn Lackawanna Jr Col 65-. 8: Chm Lib Com Mercedian Sch of Nursing, Scranton Pa 69-. 9: ALA; PennLA; NEPennLA. 14: Ref, circ. 15: 1426 W Gibson st, Scranton Pa 18504.

CARROLL, FRANCES LAVERNE. b Scammon Kan 6 D 25. 5: Kan State Tchrs Col (Pittsburg) 44-49 (Eng) BS; UDenver 54-56 (LS) MS; West Res 61 (LS) UOkla 67-68 (Educ). 6: Ger. 7: Tchr High Sch, Caney Kan 47-49; Libn Field Kindley High Sch, Coffeyville Kan 49-53; Elem lib supv pub schs, Coffeyville Kan 53-62; Libn Jr Col, Coffeyville Kan 53-62; Asst Prof UOkla 62- Asst Prof Lib Sci Drexel Inst of Techsummer 65. 8: State Sponsor, Oklahoma Student Lib Assn Inst dir OklaU 66,67,69; Research grant, USOE, 68. 9: ALA;OklaLA (chm Lib Educ div); OklaEA. 10: AAUW; Beta Sigma Phi; Beta Phi Mu; DeltaKappa Gamma. 13: Yes. 14: Lib educ, sch libnship. 15: Box 464 Faculty Exchange, NormanOk 73069.

CARROLL, HARDY. b Kernersville NC 24 F 30. 4: Mary Gotwals. 5: Guilford Col 47-51 (Philos) BA; Hartford Theol 51-54 (Philos of Religion) BD; UEdinburgh 54-56 (Hist); Temple 61-63 (Math, Educ); Drexel 63-65 MS in LS Case West Res Univ 67-69 (Info Sci). 7: Tchr Sch Dist of Phila 61-63; Catlgr UPenn 57-59, 63-65; Asst catlg libn Penn State U 65-. 66; Personnel libn Penn State U 66-67;Lib Educ Fellow Case West U 67-69. 9: ALA; ASIS. 14: Catlg, info sci, lib educ. 15: 2656 Hampshire rd, Cleveland Heights Oh 44106.

CARROLL, HAZEL (JARVIS). b Wilkesboro NC 31 Ja 36. 4: John J Carroll. 5: Appalachian State Tchrs Col 54-58 (LS) BS; UNC (Greensboro) 65-68 MEd. 7: Libn Bessemer Elem Sch, Greensboro NC 58-6 2; Libn Sumner Elem Sch, Greensboro NC 62-63; Asst dir of libs Guilford Co Sch, Greensboro NC 63-. 9: ALA; NCEA; NCLA; SELA; NCASchL (Awards & Scholarship Com); Greensboro Lib Club. 10: Lit & Lib Com of Centre Friends Meeting. 14: Catlg, wk with child. 15: Rte #1 Box 381, Greensboro NC 27406.

CARROLL, ISABEL R. b Bangor Me 25 Mr 18. 5: Regis Col 35-39 (Eng) AB; Simmons 42-43 (LS) BS Columbia 52. 7: Eng tchr John Baptist High Sch, Bangor Me 39-40; Child libn Pub Lib Rochester NY 43-45; Asst Pub Lib Bangor Me 40-43, 45-47,; Child libn Pub Lib Milton Mass 47-50; Child spec West Mass Lib Fed, Conway Mass 50-52; High Sch libn Mt Vernon NY 52-. 9: ALA; Intern Reading Assn; NYLA; NY State Tchrs Assn. 10: BPW; Regis Col Alumnae Club; Simmons Col Alumnae Club. 14: Sch & child libs. 15: 25 E Cedar st, Mt Vernon NY 10052.

CARROLL, KENNETH D. b Centralia Ill 21 N 21. 5: Ind State Tchrs Col 43 (Hist, Fr, Math) AB; So Ill U 40-44 (Psych, Romance Langs, Educ) BS; UMich 47-48 (Romance Langs & Lit) MA, 48-49 (Linguistic Sci). 6: Fr, Sp, Ital. 7: Chm Fr Dept Kemper Mil Jr Col 45-46; Chm Romance Langs Dept Cumberland Col 46-47; Fellow Romance Langs & Lit UMich 47-49; Asst Prof Romance Langs Colo Col 49-50; Tech libn Chicago Rawhide Mfg Co 50-59; Supv, Lit Searcher, tech info center Lockheed Missiles & Space Co 59-64; Sci info spec Xerox Corp 64-65, Manager tech info serv dept 65-67; Dir Clearinghouse on Educ Differences & Asst Libn Grad Sch of Educ Harvard67-68; Sr Info Scientist Amer Inst of Physics 68-. 9: SLA (var coms & group off59-67); Wk on exhibits for SLA & Amer Soc for Metals; ASIS; NMA; Soc Info Display;Soc Photogr Engnrs & Scientists. 11: Citation for work on Polaris Missile System, Admiral Rickover USN. 12: Numerous reports available through CFSTI,DDC etc. 13: Yes. 14: Admin, info systems, lit search. 15: 301 E 22 st, New York NY 10010.

CARROLL, MRS LUCILE C. b Beaumont Tex. 5: UTex 34 (Hist) BA; LSU 51 BS in LS. 6: Sp, Fr. 7: High sch libn South Park Ind Sch Dist, Beaumont Tex 34-43; Libn Midland Co Lib, Midland Tex 45-53; Asst libn Pub Lib, Decatur Ill 53; Head Libn Midland High Sch, Midland Tex 54-. 8b Beaumont Tex. 09: ALA; TexLA; Tex State Tchrs Assn; Tex Assn of Educ Tech. 9: ALA; TexLA; Tex State Tchrs Assn; Tex Assn of Educl Tech. 10: Beta Phi Mu; Delta Kappa Gamma; PTA; Friends of the Midland Pub Lib; MidlandSymphony Orchestra; Commun Theatre; Midland Civic Concerts. 14: Ya serv, ref. 15: 613 W Storey,Midland Tx 79704.

CARROLL, MARGARET LORRAINE (KELLY). b Indianapolis 5 Mr 19. 5: Butler U 36-40 (Hist) AB; UIll 40-41 BS in LS. 7: Libn Madison Ave Br Indianapolis Pub Lib 41-42; Libn Indianapolis Pub Lib 52-55; Tchr Orchard Country Day Sch, Indianapolis 55-60; Cook Gnaw Bone Camp, Nashville Ind 55-65; Libn Park Sch, Indianapolis 60-. 15: 7200 N College, Indianapolis In 46240.

CARROLL, MARIAN McAMBLEY. b Bradford Penn 30 My 16. 4: John J Carroll. 5: Randolph-Macon Woman's Col 32-36 AB; UMich 37-39 ABLS, 56-57; St Lawrence U 57-58; NY State High Sch Libnship Certif. 6: Fr. 7: Asst catlg dept UMich Lib 38-39; Asst libn Tusculum Col 39-40; Supv WPA Lib Proj, Flint Mich 41; Catlgr Wm F Clements Lib UMich 50-51; Ref libn St Lawrence U 51-54; Libn Canton Jr-Sr High Sch, Canton NY 54-56, 57-61; Lib adv to Calcutta Metropolitan Planning Org, Calcutta India 62-66; Docent Nat Gallery of Art 66-. 9: SLA; DCLA. 10: Delta Kappa Gamma;AAUW. 14: Wk with yp, ref. 15: 4807 Falstone ave, Chevy Chase Md 20015.

CARROLL, RUTH (NATALIE) CARTER. b Burton Tex 22 Ja 18. 4: Dr Carl Mark Carroll Jr. 5: Tillotson Col 37-41 (Eng) AB (magna cum laude); UDenver 44-45 BS in LS; UTex 52 (LS). 6: Fr. 7: Eng tchr Texas Deaf & Blind Sch, Austin Tex 41-44; Asst libn Kan City Mo Pub Lib 45-46; Asst libn Meharry Med Col 46-51; Head catlgr Tex So U 51-54; Asst & head libn Wheatley Sr High Sch, Houston 54-60; Head libn Worthing Sr High Sch, Houston 61-. 9: ALA; TexLA. 10: YWCA; Houston Med Forum Woman's Auxiliary; Jack & Jill of America Inc; Alpha Kappa Alpha; Alpha Nu. 14: Sch libnship, catlg & circ in col libs. 15: 3306 Binz ave, Houston Tx 77004.

CARRUTHERS, JOAN AUDREY. b Toronto Ont Can 17 D 30. 5: UWest Ont 49-53 BA; UToronto 53-54 BLS. 6: Fr. 7: Hd ref dept YorkU 66-. 15: 131 Bloor st W apt 917, Toronto Ont Can.

CARSON, DORIS (LUELLA MILLER). b Tescott Kan 2 Je 11. 4: Andrew B Carson. 5: Kan Wesleyan U 29-33 (Eng, Fr) BA (magna cum laude); UKan summers 36, 39, 39-40, 41 (Eng) MA; UIll summers 50-54 (LS) MS. 7: Instr Kan Wesleyan U 33-34; Tchr Eng & Lat Healy (Kan) High Sch 34-36 & Nortonville (Kan) High Sch 36-37; Tchr language arts, vocal music Norcatur (Kan) Grade Sch 37-39; Tchr Eng & Lat Lucas (Kan) 42-43; Operator Goodyear Engnr Corp

Charlestown Ind 43-44; Tchr libn Cheyenne Co High Sch St Francis Kan 45-46; Asst libn McPherson (Kan) Pub Lib 47-48; Asst libn Kan Wesleyan U 48-50; Libn McPherson (Kan) High Sch 50-57; Asst Prof & catlgr Wichita State U 57-. 8: Visiting lecturer & catlgr Fort Hays Kan State Col summers 56, 57; Visiting lecturer in catlg UIll Grad Sch of Lib Sci summer 58 tchr of catlg Wichita State U summer 69. 9: NEA; ALA (com on Retirement Homes); KanLA (Dist chm 54-55, treas 62-63, budget off 64; chm Intel Freedom Com 59-60; chm Res & Tech Serv Sect 66-67); KanASchL (Dist Chm 55-56, Pub Chm 56-57, chm High Sch Standards Com 55); MPLA. 10: Beta Phi Mu; AAUP; Wichita Lib Club; Wichita Oratorio Soc. 13: Yes. 14: Catlg. 15: 1855 N Lorraine, Wichita Ks 67214.

CARSON, EURETTA RANK. b Phila 5 Ag 08. 5: Drexel 32. 7: Child libn Phila City Inst 27-37, Adult libn 37-44; Br libn Free Lib of Phila 44-46; Sch of Nursing libn Chestnut Hill (Penn) Hosp 62-. 9: SLA. 10: Nat League for Nursing; Germantown Horticultural Soc. 15: Chestnut Hill Hosp Sch of Nursing, 8835 Germantown ave, Phila Pa 19118.

CARSON, JOSEPHINE R. b Middletown Conn 24 Ap 16. 4: Leslie F Carson. 5: Brown 34-38 (Hist) AB, 52-56 (Hist of Sci) MA; URI 64-65 MLS. 6: Fr, Ger, Ital, Russian. 7: Brown U Lib; Asst circ dept 38-40, Asst Biol Sci 40-43, Asst Biol Sci & Phys Sci 43-44, Libn Biol Sci Lib 44-45; Tchr Middletown RI 45-47 ; Brown U; Asst Phys Sci Lib 47-48, Catlgr for the Biol & Phys Sci 48-52, Libn Biol Sci Lib 52-. 14: Ref. 15: 230 Ives st, Providence RI 02906.

CARSON, SHEILA M. b Liverpool England 7 Ap 33. 5: Randolph-Macon Woman's Col 51-55 (Hist) AB; Emory 55-56 summer 58 (European hist) MA; Simmons 60-62 (LS) SM. 7: High sch hist tchr St Agnes Sch, Albany NY 56-59; High sch Soc st & Eng tchr High Sch, Duxbury Mass 59-60; Child lib Milton Pub Lib, Milton Mass 60-62; Asst catlgr Bryn Mawr Col Lib 62-64; Child libn Greater Olney Br Free Lib of Philo 64-69; Br supv Chestnut Hill Br Free Lib of Phila 69-. 9: ALA. 10: Phi Beta Kappa. 14: Catlg, wk with child. 15: 601 W Cliveden st, Philadelphia Pa 19119.

CARSTATER, SISTER MARY ESTHER. b Jamestown NY 30 Jl 31. 5: Nazareth Col (Rochester) 49-55 (Eng) BA; Geneseo State U Col of Educ 57-60 MS in Pub Libnship. 6: Fr, Lat. 7: Tchr St Andrew's Sch, Rochester NY 52-54; Tchr St Charles' Sch, Rochester NY 54-57; Tchr Our Lady of Mercy High Sch, Rochester NY 57-59; Tchr & asst libn Notre Dame High Sch, Elmira NY 59-62; Libn Our Lady of Mercy High Sch, Rochester NY 62-; Libn & tchr Catherine McAuley Col, Rochester NY summers 60-. 9: ALA; CathLA; NYLA; West NY Cath Lib Conf; Monroe Co Lib Club; NY State AV Assn. 10: Lib consul Rochester Diocese; Cons Genesco Valley Sch Dev Lib Assn. 11: Genesco Valley Lib Com; First Place National Poetry Contest, Cath Daughters of Amer 60. 13: Yes. 14: Ref, bibliotherapy. 15: 1437 Blossom rd, Rochester NY 14610.

CART, MICHAEL. b Logansport Ind 6 Mr 41. 5: NorthwesternU 59-63 (Radio-TV News) BSJ; Columbia 63-64 (LS) MS. 7: Admin specialist (Sp/5) US Army, Ft Knox Ky Bangkok 64-67; Ref libn & catlgr US Army Armor Sch Lib, Ft Knox Ky 65-66; Asst dir Logansport-Cass Co pub Lib, Logansport Ind 67-68, Dir 68-. 9: IndLA (sec; Fed Rel coord); Ind Lib Film Serv Authority. 10: Logansport Kiwanis Club. 13: Yes. 14: Lib admin, child & y-p serv. 15: 606 E Broadway, Logansport In 46947.

CARTER, BOBBY R(USSELL). b Baytown Tex 26 N 41. 5: Lee Col 60-62; UHouston 62-65 (Communications) BS; LSU 65-67 MS. 7: Stud clk UHouston Libs 64-65; Lib trainee LSU Lib (Baton Rouge) 66-67; Pharmacy libn UHouston 67-69; Hd catlg dept UTex Med Br Lib 9galveston) 69-. 9: SLA; MedLA; TexLA. 10: Sigma Delta Chi; Alpha Epsilon Rho; AAUP; Tex Assn Col Tchrs. 14: Ref, pub serv, catlg. 15: 7316 Linden, Houston Tx 77012.

CARTER, CATHERINE. b Council Bluffs Iowa 26 My 25. 5: Grinnell Col 43-44; UKan 44-47 (Sp) AB; UMich 47-49 MALS; Columbia 53-55 (Ling) MA. 6: Sp, Fr. Ger. 7: Catlgr UIowa 49-51; Asst catlgr libn Penn StateU (Univ Park) 51-53, Assoc catlg libn 55-. 8: Wk on agric vocabulary proj, Nat Agric Lib, Wash DC 66. 9: ALA; PennLA. 14: Catlg. 15: 447 Hillcrest ave, State College Pa 16801.

CARTER, CIEL MICHELE. b Los Angeles Cal 20 S 23. 5: Pomona Col 44-48 (Eng) BA; Simmons 65-66 (LS) MS. 6: Fr. 7: Reporter & ed Various newspapers, Cal 48-55; Real estate sales, security analysis, Cal 55-62, 63-64; Security analysis, Switz 62-63; Night supv MIT Libs 65-66; Head research lib F I duPont & Co, NYC 66-67; Assoc for Computing Machinery, NYC: Mgr info ctr 67-69, Asst to exec dir 69-. 9: ASIS; SLA; Assn for Computing Machinery. 10: Mensa. 12: "Guide to Information Sources in the Computer Sciences" (69). 14: Ref, bibliog. 15: Apt 15H 14 Horatio st, New York NY 10014.

CARTER, CLAUDIA J. b Littleton NH. 5: UNH 50 (Eng) BA; Columbia 58 (LS) MA. 6: Fr. 7: Asst acquis libn (UNM 58-60); Asst acquis libn Rice U 60-64; Ser libn USoFla64-. 9: ALA; FlaLA; SELA. 10: Fla Hist Soc. 14: Ser, acquis. 15: 13813 21st st, Tampa Fl 33612.

CARTER, CONSTANCE. b Whitefield NH 19 Ap 37. 5: Smith 55-59 (Zool) BA; UNC 64-65 MS in LS. 7: Research asst NY Zool Soc dept tropical research 59-60; Special asst in geol Museum of Comparative Zool Lib Harvard U 60-61, Catlgr 62-64; Intern LC 65-66, Ser catlgr 66-67, Sci ref libn 67-68, Sci ref specialist 68-. 9: ALA;DCLA. 10: British Field Studies Coun; Beta Phi Mu; Archivist, Appalachian TrailConf 66-. 14: Tech serv, ref serv. 15: 110 D st SE, Wash DC 20003.

CARTER, DOROTHY (WOOD). b Minneapolis 26 S 09. 4: Bryce L Carter. 5: UKan 34 (Eng, Educ) BS in Ed; UWash 62 (LS) MS. 7: Child libn Main Lib, Seattle 60-61; Head Libn Issaquah (Wash) Lib King Co Br 62-65; Libn King Co Jail, Seattle 65-68; Libn Cedar Hills Alcoholism Treatment Ctr, Seattle 68-. 9: ALA; PNLA; WashStateLA. 10: AAUW; Seattle Symphony League; Wash Correctional Assn; Correctional Educ Assn; Beta Phi Mu. 14: Pub rel, inst lib wk. 15: 4417 137th SE, Bellevue Wa 98004.

CARTER, ESTHER MAY. b Russiaville Ind 3 O 23. 5: Kokomo Jr Col 41-43; Earlham Col 41-45 (Soc Sci) BA; UIll summers 53-57 (LS) MS;IndU 66-69 (LS). 7: High sch tchr Lynn Pub Schs, Lynn Ind 45-48; High sch tchr Tyner Pub Schs, Tyner Ind 48-49; High sch tchr Albion Pub Schs, Albion Ind 49-50; Tchr-libn Fowler Pub Schs, Fowler Ind 50-54; Tchr-libn N Vernon high Sch, N Vernon Ind 54-55; Libn Crown Point High Sch, Crown Point Ind 55-57; Campus sch libn West Mich U 57-63, Dept of Libnship 63-, Asst Prof 57-. 8: Bus & Production mgr "School Libraries" 59-61 Dir NDEA Title XI Inst for Sch LibPersonnel, West Mich U summers 65,66. 9: ALA; NCEA; NCLA; SELA; NCASchL (Awards & Scholarships Com); Greensboro LibClub. 10: Beta Phi Mu; Pi Lambda Theta. 14: Sch libnship, lib educ. 15: 1007short rd, Kalamazoo Mi 49001.

CARTER, HARRIET IRENE. b Columbus Ohio 6 Ag 05. 5: Ohio State U 26 (Educ) BS; Chicago 44 (LS) BS. 7: Lib asst Chicago Pub Lib 26-27; Asst in adult educ dept Chicago 28-45; Libnpub & High Sch Lib, Iron Mountain Mich 45-47; Libn Carnegie Pub Lib, Elkhart Ind47-50; Head ext div Ind State Lib 50-60; Chief ext serv Flint Pub Lib, Flint Mich60-. 8: -65. 9: ALA (chm awards com); MichLA (chm 2 coms). 10: Flint Lib Club (pres 63-64). 11: Libn of theYear 68, Flint Lib Club. 12: Ed "Public Libraries" (53-55); Ed "Extension Division Bulletin" Ind State Lib (51-60). 14: Adult educ, ext. 15: 1026 E Kearsley st, Flint Mi 48502.

CARTER, HELEN. b Sheldon Mo 20 Jl 08. 5: UMo 25-33 (Math) BS in Ed, 36-37 (Educ) MS in Ed, 60-61 (LS). 6: Ger, Sp. 7: Tchr var pub elem schs, Mo 26-32; Tchr Richards Pub Sch, Richards Mo 33-35; Supv MU Statewide Testing, Columbia Mo 35-37; Tchr Trenton High Sch, Trenton Mo 37-38; Supv MU Statewide Testing Program, Columbia mo 39; Catlg UMo Lib 61-. 8: Stat wk on GE Lighting expt, Joplin Pub Sch, Joplin Mo 38-39. 9: ALA; MoLA. 10: Pi Lambda Theta; Pi Mu Epsilon. 14: Catlg, clsf. 15: 603 Morningside dr, Columbia Mo 65201.

CARTER, JOHN M. b Jackson Miss 17 D 36. 4: Carolyn Robertson Carter. 5: Millsaps Col 55-59 (Eng) BA; Emory 60-61 (LS) ML UIll 68 seminar in computer-based lib sys Cert. 7: Tchr-libn Tonopah High Sch, Tonopah Nev 59-60; Libn & Instr East Ill U 61-64; Assoc Prof & Head of Circ Miss State U 64-65; Dir Jackson Mun Lib, Jackson Miss 65-66; Asst Dir & Assoc Prof, Miss State U Lib 66-. 8: Expert witness in censorship trial, Jackson Miss 69. 9: ALA; MissLA; SELA. 10: AAUP. 13: Yes. 14: Circ systems, admin. 15: Miss State Univ Lib, State College Ms 39762.

CARTER, JOHN W. b Montalba Tex 18 My 12. 5: U Puget Sound 38-42 (Music) BA; NYU 46-47 (Musicology) MA; UWash 51-55 (LS) MS. 7: Music Instr Col of Puget Sound 47-51; Music Instr Bothell Pub Schs 51-57; Bkmob libn Mid-Columbia Reg Lib, Kennewick Wash 58-60; Fine arts libn Everett Pub Lib, Everett Wash 60-63; Head libn Pasco Pub Lib, Pasco Wash 63-65; Head libn Walla Walla Pub Lib, Walla Walla Wash 65-. 9: ALA; WashLA; PNLA. 10: Rotary;

C of C; Comm Serv Coun. 14: Admin, fine arts. 15: Walla Walla Pub Lib, 111 Palouse, Walla Walla Wa 99362.

CARTER, LILLY (ISABELLE). b Mayo Fla 9 S 11. 5: Fla State U 31-34 (Educ) AB; Columbia summers 47, 49, 50, 51 MSLS. 7: Tchr High Sch Mayo Fla 34-35; Tchr High Sch Trenton Fla 35-37; Tchr Cathedral Sch for Girls Orlando Fla 37-41; Clerk UFla Libs (Gainesville) 41-43; Order libn UFla Lib 43-55, Acquis libn 55-63; Libn Gainesville Pub Lib, Gainesville Fla 64, Asst dir 64-. 9: ALA (Jt Com to compile a list of subscription agents 60-63); SELA; FlaLA (sev offs). 10: Kappa Delta Pi. 14: Acquis, admin. 15: PO Box 183, Gainesville Fl 32601.

CARTER, MARY ANN (PELCH). b Santa Barbara Cal 24 S 20. 5: UCal (Santa Barbara) 42-46 (Group-Music, Sci hist, Eng) BA; Kan State Tchrs Col (Emporia) 46-47 (LS) Certif. 7: Ref & circ asst libn Palo Alto Pub lib, Palo Alto Cal 47-49; Ref asst libn McHenry Pub Lib, Modesto Cal 50-51; Ref libn Modesto Jr Col 58-60; Educ psych curriculum libn Chico State Col 60-. 10: Assn Cal State Col Prof; AAUW; Kiwani-anns; CalLA (pres, deleg to State ColLibs div); Chico Area Coun of Churches. 14: Ref. 15: Educ Lib Chico State Col, First st,chico Ca 95927.

CARTER, MARY DUNCAN. b St Paul 3 My 1896. 5: Chicago 14-17 (Soc Sci) PhB; NY State Lib Sch (Albany) 22-23 BLS; Chicago 31-32, 41-42 (LS) PhD. 6: Fr, Ger. 7: Asst & head Short Loan Desk Chicago Pub Lib 18-21; Libn Bemis Co Consulting Engnrs, Chicago 21-22; Asst libn & Assoc Prof Skidmore Col 23-24; Asst dir & Asst Prof McGill U Lib Sch 27-37; Dir & Prof Lib Sch USoCal 37-46; Dir USIS Lib owi, cairo Egypt 45-46; Middle east reg libn & attache American Embassy, US State Dept, Cairo Egypt 47-50; Visiting Prof Lib Sci Dept UMich 56-57, Prof Lib Sci Dept 57-66, Prof em 66-. 8: Libn Consul Aircraft War Production coun Los Angeles 42-43; Lib Consul Grolier Soc NY 51-56; Lecturer, Simmons Col Lib Sch, summers 53-54. 9: ALA (Coun 34-39); SLA (Bd Dirs 42-46); CanLA; CalLA (pres 44); QueLA; MichLA. 10: AAUW; Pi Lambda Theta. 12: "The Story ofMoney, Farrar & Rinehart" (32); "Building Library Collections" with W J Bonk (59,2nd ed 64, 3rd ed 69). 13: Yes. 14: Admin (pub & spec), bk sel, reading interests of adults. 15: Apt 205 1750 S Ocean blvd, Pompano Beach Fl 33062.

CARTER, MARY JOSEPHINE. b Barstow Tex 2 Mr 07. 5: UCLA 26-30 (Eng) BA; USoCal 31-32 (Child Libs) Certif. 7: Child libn Los Angeles Pub Lib 32-43; US Civil Serv; Base Libn US Army Corps Taft Cal 43-45, Chief Libn US Army Ground Fcs Marysville Cal 45-47, Asst & Command Libn XXIV Corps, Seoul Korea 47-48; Staff libn 4th US Army, San Antonio Tex 49-52; Command Libn Far East Air Forces, Tokyo Japan 52-57; Command Libn Pacific Air Forces, HONOLULU 5". 9: ALA (dir Armed Forces Libns Sect); -PLA; HawaiiLA. 10: Honolulu: Friends of the Lib; Bishop Mus; Friends East-West Center; ULU Mau Village Exposition; Symphony Soc. 13: Yes. 14: Admin, mil lib serv. 15: Apt 1402, 1309 Wilder ave, Honolulu Hi 96822.

CARTER, NANCY CAROL (SCHWEBEL). b Tacoma Wash 12 N 42. 4: Lee Carter. 5: Texas A & I 60-65 (Hist) BS, MS; OklaU 65-67 MLS. 7: Tchr: Premont Pub Schs, Premont Tex 63-64, Kingsville Pub Schs, Kingsville Tx 64-65; Asst acquis libn OklaU Libs 67-. 9: ALA; OklaLA. 10: Beta Phi Mu. 14: Acquis, bibliog. 15: 719 Asp, Norman Ok 73069.

CARTER, OMA BELLE (BIXLER). b Burlingame Kan 1 F 13. 4: William Taylor Carter. 5: Abilene Christian Col 31-34 (Eng), 52 (Secondary Educ) BS; Kan State Tchrs Col (Emporia) 55 MS in LS. 7: Act libn Abilene Christian Col 33-34; Libn Okla Christian Col 53-64; Libn Edmond High Sch, Edmond Okla 64-67; Lib cousul 67-. 8: Consul in org & bldg planning of lib Christian Col of Southwest 63-64. 9: ALA; OklaLA; OklaEA. 10: AAUW; Alpha Chi; 12: "How to Organize the Small Library in the Home or Church" (58, 61). 14: Catlg, org. 15: 1912 South blvd, Edmond Ok 73034.

CARTER, ROBERT G. b Hillsboro Iowa 8 S 28. 5: UNM 47-49 (Eng); UIowa 49-51 (Eng) BA; UMich 55-56 AMLS. 7: Army Med Serv, Germany 51-53; Acquis libn UMich Lib (Ann Arbor) 56-. 14: Exch prog. 15: 1400 Broadway, Ann Arbor Mi 48105.

CARTER, ROBERT L. b Indianapolis 3 Mr 28. 4: Beverly Stone. 5: Earlham Col 45-49 (Philos) BA; Butler U 50 (Eng); UIll 51-52 (LS) MS. 7: Lib asst Indianapolis Pub Lib 50-51; Jr libn Enoch Pratt Free Lib, Baltimore 52-54; Sel & acquis libn Prince Georges Co Md 54-56, Reader & info serv libn 56-57; Sr lib supv NY State Lib 57-59; Dir N Country Lib System, Watertown NY 59-66; Dir Lincoln Trail Libs, Campaign Ill 66-. 8: Vistg lect Grad Sch of LS, UIll spring sem 67, 68. 9: ALA; IllLA. 10: Beta Phi Mu; YMCA. 13: Yes. 14: Pub lib admin, adult serv, a-v. 15: 103 1/2 East Daniel st, Champaign Il 61820.

CARTER, ROBERT LYMAN. b Phila 26 Ja 31. 5: Temple 48-52 (Journalism) BS; George Washington U 54-56 (Educ) AM; West Res 58-59 MS/LS. 6: Fr, Sp, Ital. 7: Research clerk The Patent, Trademark & Copyright Found of The George Washington U, Wash DC 56-58;Libn bus & econ dept Enoch Pratt Free Lib, Baltimore 59-63; Ref libn Millikin U 63-65; Bibliog Ind State U 65-. 14: Ref, rare bks, bibliog, interlib loan, spec collections. 15: Indiana State U Lib, Terre Haute In 47809.

CARTER, ROBERT RAY. b Riverside Cal 29 F 32. 5: Orange Coast Col 56-57 AA; Cal State Col (LA) 57-60 (Eng) BA; Immaculate Heart Col 63-66 MALS. 7: Tchr Woodrow Wilson Jr high Sch, Pasadena Cal 60-64, Hd libn 64-67; Visiting prof UOre summer 67; Instr libn pasadena City Col 67-. 9: NEA; CalTA; CalLA; CalASchLibns (Publicity Chm 66-68). 10: Pasadena Sch Libns (chm 66-67). 12: Assoc ed "California School Libraries"; "Library Skills" (68); "English Languages & Literaure" (68). 13: Yes. 14: Instr, ref. 15: 4501 Richard dr, Los Angeles Ca 90032.

CARTER, (CHARLES) ROSS. b Vancouver BC Can 18 Mr 29. 4: Sue Hughes. 5: UBC 49-51 (Hist) BA, 51-52 (Educ) Dipl; UWash 56-57 (Libnship) ML. 7: Libn III Brooklyn Pub Lib, Brooklyn NY 57-59; Asst dir Plainfield Pub Lib, Plainfield NJ 59-63; Asst av libn Portland State U, Portland Ore 63-65; Asst libn Yakima Valley Reg Lib, Yakima Wash 65-69; Libn Vancouver City Col, Vancouver BC 69-. 9: ALA; WLA; NLW (chm 68-69); PNLA. 14: Admin, bk sel. 15: Eagle Cliff, Bowen Island, BC Can.

CARTER, SELINA JEWELL (ALEXANDER). b Birmingham Ala 3 Ja 28. 4: Buford William Carter Jr. 5: Judson Col 45-46 (Religious Ed); Howard Col 55-62 (Human Rel) BS; UDenver 62-63 (LS) MA. 7: Serv rep So Bell Tel & Tel Birmingham Ala 46-51; Ordnance Property Clerk US Govt Ft Hood Tex 51; Records mgt clerk US Govt Birmingham Ordnance District Ala 51-53; Records mgt clerk US Govt Ft Richardson Alaska 53; Records mgt officer US Govt Birmingham Ordnance District Ala 54-59, Procurement asst 59-62; Catlg libn Howard Col Birmingham Ala 63-65; Reader serv libn & asst libn Samford U 65-68; Circ libn Col of General Studies, UAlabama, Birmingham 68-. 8: Church Lib Week; So Baptist Assemblies; Glorieta NM & Ridgecrest NC 65; Tech Serv for Church Libs; Sunday Sch Bd of So Baptist Convention 65-; Birmingham Baptist Church Lib, Org 67-. 9: SAA; Kappa Delta Pi; AlaLA (Recruitment Com); SELA. 10: Ala Hist Soc; Birmingham Women's Jr C of C (Bd of Dir 69-). 14: Catlg, archives. 15: 937 Shadybrook cir, Birmingham Al 35226.

CARTER, MRS SHIRLEY ANN (LAWRENCE). b Chillicothe Mo 15 F 29. 4: George W Carter. 5: NTAC 46-48; NTSC 48-50 (LS) BA; Tex Tech U 51-56 (Educ) ME. 7: Libn Levelland Sr High Sch, Levelland Tex 50-54; Libn Hobbs Sr High Sch, Hobbs NM 54-55; Libn Wink Ind Schs, Wink Tex 55-56; Libn Austin Elem Sch, Odessa Tex 56-59; Libn Hood Jr High Sch, Odessa Tex 60-. 9: TexStateTchrsAssn; TexLA. 14: Child bks. 15: 1412 E 42nd, Odessa Tx 79760.

CARTER, YVONNE (BREAUX). b Crowley La 3 Ag 22. 5: USL 39-43 (Math Educ) BS (Ed); Peabody 50 (LS) BS in LS, 60 (LS) MA, 66 (LS) Ed S. 7: Tchr Calcasiew Parish, Sulphur La 42-43; Prin Sardis High Sch, Sardis Tenn 44-45; Tchr Gueydan High Sch, gueydan La 45-49, Libn 45-64; Asst Prof of LS Northwestern State Col 64-65; Libn Gueydan High Sch, Gueydan La 65-66; Asst Prof of LSUSL 66-67; Prog Off Title II ESEA OE Dallas Tex 67-. 9: ALA; AASchL; LaASchL; NEA; LaTA; LaLA; Laa-vA. 10: Nowest La Hist; Attakapas Hist; Delta Kappa Gamma; Beta Phi Mu; Kappa Delta Pi; Kappa Kappa Iola; Alpha Beta Alpha. 11: Delta Kappa Gamma State Scholarship 59; Kappa Kappa Iota Natl Scholarship 60. 13: Yes. 14: Sch lib wk. 15: 301 G st SW Apt 213, Washington DC 20024.

CARTLEDGE, LOUISA (BURNS). b Brevard NC 18 Jl 23. 5: Randolph-Macon Woman's Col 41-45 (Hist) BA; UNC at Chapel Hill 50-52 (Dramatic art) MA, 64-66 MS in LS. 6: Fr, Ger. 7: Field asst Amer Red Cross, Wash DC 45-46; Hist tchr St Margaret's Sch, Tappahannock Va 57-60; Hist tchr-libn University Lake Sch, Hartland Wis 60-64; Ref libn Emory 66-. 9: ALA. 10: Phi Beta Kappa; Beta Phi Mu. 14: Ref. 15: 5403 Villa rd, Knoxville Tn 37918.

CARTWRIGHT, JANET (BARTLETT). b Poughkeepsie NY 3 Ap 1899. 4: Walter A Cartwright. 5: Vassar 17-21 AB; Columbia 30 (LS) BS, 33 (LS) MS. 6: Fr. 7: Asst Vassar Col Lib 24-28; Asst Columbia U Lib Sch Bus Sch Arch Central Ref 29-33; Catlgr Boston Pub Lib 33-34; Asst Ossining Pub Lib, Ossining NY 39-41; Head catlgr Adriance Mem Lib, Poughkeepsie NY 41-59; Libn Hyde Park Free Lib, Hyde Park NY 59-. 9: ALA; NYLA; Dutchess Co LA. 10: Jr League of Poughkeepsie NY. 14: Catlg, org loc hist collections. 15: 5 Crumwold place, Hyde Park NY 12538.

CARTWRIGHT, MOIRA CATHERINE (JONES). b MacLeod Alta Can 16 Je 21. 4: Henry L Cartwright. 5: UAlta 39-42 BA; UToronto 66-67 BLS. 6: Fr, Ger. 7: Supv Dept of Nat War Serv, Ottawa 42-45; Abstractor & tr Aluminum Labs Ltd, Kingston Ont 47-48; Libn Aluminium Labs Ltd, Kingston Ont 48-66; Consul Spec Libs Assoc 68-; Freelance translator Can Dept of Sec of State 68-. 8: Consul on company libs 54-55; John Cotton Dana Lecturer. 9: CanLA; Assn of Spec Libs & Info Bureaux; SLA (chm Metals Div 59-60 chm Resolutions Com 66-67); AID. 10: Kingston Bd of Educ; Can Fed of Univ Women; Kingston Symphony Assn; Can Inst of Internat Affairs; Assn of Women Electors. 13: Yes. 14: Admin, subject indexing. 15: P O Box 758, Kingston Ont Can.

CARTWRIGHT, PHYLLIS BERGEN. b Middletown Ohio 29 My 25. 5: MiamiU (Oxford Ohio) 43-45 (Music, Fine Arts); UMiami (Coral Gables Fla) 51-55; 02552 cartwright, phyllis bergen. 7: Music tchr Dade Co Bd of Pub Instr (Miami Fla) 55-56; Lib sec Broward Co Bd of Pub Instr (Ft Lauderdale Fla) 58-59; Tchr-libn 59-61; Catlg libn Armstrong Col 61-64; Asst libn Converse Col 64-65; Act libn 65; Libn 65-67; Hd catlg dept Fla AtlanticU 67; Hf tech serv 67; Asst dir tech serv 68-. 8: Instr if lib sci, UGa Ext at Armstrong Col (64); org Jewish Educ Alliance Lib (Savannah Ga) 64; Consul, First Methodist Church Lib (Savannah Ga) 64; Instr lib sci: Winthrop Col summer 66; FurmanU 66-67. 9: ALA; SELA; FlaLA. 10: AAUP; Sigma Alpha Iota; AAUW. 14: Lib educ, catlg, acquis, ser. 15: Lib Fla Atlantic Univ, Boca Raton Fl 33432.

CARUFEL, GERTRUDE SICARD de (SISTER) (OSU). b Shawinigan Que 18 S 20. Coll Marie de l'Incarnation (Lettres) BA (Laval); UOttawa 56-57 (Eng Lit); Catholic U 63-65 MSLS. 6: Fr, Eng. 7: Prof of Eng secondary sch, Grand Mere Can; Prof of Eng Col Marie de l'Incarnation 55-63, Hd libn 65-68; Prof of catlg STAGE de la Pocatiere; Hd libn CEGEP de Trois-Rivieres 68-. 8: Exec des dirs de bibliotheque de la FCC, sec 67-68; Exec des dir de bibliotheque de CADRE 68-, Conseil nat de l'ACBLF 68-69. 9: Assn canadienne des bibliothecaires de langue francaise (Sect des colleges; v-pres 67-68, pres 68-69). 14: Catlg, admin. 15: 725 Hart, Trois-Rivieres Que Can.

CARY, BETTY J (MASTERS). b Hornell NY 31 D 26. 4: Paul R Cary. 5: Elmira Col 44-48 (Hist) BA; Syracuse 64-66 (Latin) MSLS. 7: Bkkeeper, clerk, tchr (Lat, Hist), factory wkr, dry cleaner, food processor; Lib trainee Syracuse Pub Lib, Syracuse NY 64-65; Asst libn SUNY at Morrisville 65-68; Libn Georgetown Central Sch, Georgetown NY 68-. 9: ALA; NYLA; NYStateTA. 10: Beta Phi Mu. 14: Ref. 15: 13 Sims lane, Cazenovia NY 13035.

CARY, DONALD EDWIN. b Colrain Mass 11 F 05. 4: Edith McKane. 5: Williams Col 23-27 (Econ) BA; Columbia 37-38 (LS) BS. 6: Fr. 7: Lib asst Williams Col Lib 27-28; Radio prod Westinghouse Elec Co, Chicopee Falls Mass 28-29; Lib asst Williams Col Lib 29-37; Lib asst Columbia U Lib 38; Lib asst NY Pub Lib 39; Lib asst Williams Col Lib 39-58; Asst libn Williams Col Lib 58-. 10: West Mass Auxiliary Police Assn Inc; Williamstown (Mass) Auxiliary Police Assn; Williams Col Faculty Club. 14: Circ, reserved bk div. 15: Benlise dr, Williamstown Mass 01267.

CARY, PHYLLIS (ELAINE). b Worcester Mass 25 F 46. 5: Clark U 64-68 (Eng) BA; Simmons 68-69 MS in LS. 6: Fr. 7: Libn Art Inst of Boston 69-. 9: ALA. 14: Ref, rare bks, bk sel. 15: 22 Woodland rd, Shrewsbury Ma 01545.

CARY, VERONICA F. b NYC 9 F 11. 5: Douglass Col 29-33 (Eng) BA; Columbia 43-45 BS in LS. 7: Gen asst Trenton Pub Lib, Trenton NJ 35, Sr asst 38, Chief of circ 46; Field libn NJ State Lib 58; Dir Trenton Pub Lib, Trenton NJ 61-. 9: ALA; NJLA (pres 65-66). 10: AAUW; Zonta. 15: 230 Garfield ave, Trenton NJ 08609.

CARYL, DELMAR H. b Boyceville Wis 26 My 13. 4: Mary Margaret Van Marter. 5: East Wash Col 34-37 (Educ) 3 yr diploma, 38-40 (Educ) BA; UWash 41-43 BA in LS. 7: Lib catlgr East Wash Col 40-41; Readers adv UWash Lib 41-42; Libn Mukilteo Pub Schs, Mukilteo Wash 45-47; Sci desk libn UWash Lib 47-50; Asst libn Everett Jr Col 50-66; Dir lib 66-. 10: Assn fpr Higher Educ; Natl Fac Assn of Comm & Jr Colls; ACLU Snohomish Co Tchrs Credit Union (pres); Nie-eight Kilo Corp (pres); Bd Trustees Meadowdale Comm Club; Aircraft Owners & Pilots Assn. 12: "With Angels to the Rear" (c 60). 14: Catlg, admin. 15: 15631 75th place W, Edmonds Wa 98020.

CASE, LEWIS B. b St Louis Mo 16 My 27. 5: Purdue 44-45 (Engineering); UChicago 46-48 (Liberal Arts) BA; Harris Tchrs Col 67-69 LS. 7: Lib clk Jr Col Dist, St Louis 65-66; Catlg aide St Louis Bd of Educ 67-. 9: ALA; MoLA. 14: Catlg. 15: 3643 Castleman, St Louis Mo 63110.

CASE, ROBERT N. b Lorain Ohio 22 Mr 31. 4: Charlotte Lewis. 5: Miami U 49-53 (Educ) BS; West Res 57-60 MSLS. 7: Pfc US Army (QM), Kokura Japan 53-55; Eng tchr Napoleon High Sch, Napoleon Ohio 55-58; Libn Rocky River High Sch, Rocky River Ohio 58-65; State Supv Sch Libs Ohio Dept of Educ, Columbus 65-68; Dir Sch Lib Manpower Project ALA, Chicago 68-. 8: Ref Libn Library/USA-NY Worlds Fair 64; Instr summer session Kent State U Lib Sch 65. 9: ALA-YASD (chm Nat LibWk 65-66); OhioASchL (pres 67-68); NEA; OhioEA. 10: Beta Phi Mu. 12: Comp "Top of News Index" (63-65). 13: Yes. 14: Sch libs. 15: 2603 Sheridan rd apt A,Evanston Il 60201.

CASE, THERESA M. b Schenectady NY 29 Mr 26. 5: Col of St Rose 58-61 (Educ) MS; SUNY at Albany 45-48 (Soc sci) BA, 61-64 MLS. 6: Sp, Fr. 7: Libn & Eng tchr Mayfield Central Sch, Mayfield NY 48; Bkkeeping Dept Supv Citizens Trust Co, NY 49-52; Accounting clk GE Co, Schenectady NY 52-68; Libn & tchr Draper Schs, Rotterdam NY 58-62; Libn Schenectady Pub Schs, NY 62-68; Dir of lib serv Schenectady Commun Col, Schenectady NY 68-. 8: Adv wk on various sch curr coms. 9: ALA; NYStateTA; NYStateLA; Hudson-MohawkLA; EastNYSchLA (past v-pres); SUNYLA. 10: Phi Gamma Mu; Delta Kappa Gamma. 15: 2212 Green point ave, Schenectady NY 12303.

CASELLAS, ELIZABETH REED (BRANNON). b New Orleans La 7 Ja 25. 4: Joaquin Casellas. 5: Chicago Musical Col 42-48 (Music) BM; Columbia 49-52 (Educ) MA & Prof Diploma;UParis 53-54 (Fr lang); Columbia 59-64 MS in LS. 6: Fr. 7: Instr Valparaiso U 46-47; Asst libn J M Mathes Inc NYC 55-57; Libn Communications Counselors Inc NYC 57-59; Head libn Cresap McCormick & Paget NYC 59-60; Head libn Stewart Dougall & Associates NYC 60-65; Research asst Columbia U Sch of Gen Studies 64-65; Asst Prof UHawaii Grad Sch of Lib Studies 65-66; Hd bus sci & tech deptOrlando (Fla) Pub Lib 66-69; Hd Grad Sch of Bus Admin Lib Tulane U 69-. 8: Lecturer SLA NY Chap Adv Group "Media Sources" (58); SLA NY Chap Consul Serv (Bus Libs) 64; Bibliog in bus & econ UHawaii 65-66. 9: SLA (chm & founder of Fla Gp 68-69, chm Soc Sci Gp, NY chap 59-60, sec Adv GpNY chap 64-65; ALA; SELA; FlaLA. 10: AAUW; Amer Mgt Assn. 11: Phi Mu Gamma Award in Musical Composition 48. 13: Yes. 14: Bus & sci ref, tchrlib sci. 15: C/o Grad Sch of Bus Admin Library, Tulane Univ, New Orleans La 70118.

CASEY, ALICE (GURD). b Brooklyn NY 7 S 07. 5: Art Studs League 25-28; Rutgers (LS). 7: Asst dir & child libn New Milford (NJ) Pub Lib 47-. 9: ALA; Nat Trust for Hist Preservation; NJLA; Bergen-Passaic Lib Club. 10: Bergen Co Hist Soc. 14: NJ hist, child bks. 15: 618 River rd, New Milford NJ 07646.

CASEY, GENEVIEVE M. b Minneapolis 13 Jl 16. 5: Col of St Catherine 33-37 (LS) BA; UMinn 40 (Journalism); UMich 56 (LS) MA. 6: Ger, Lat. 7: Gen asst Detroit Pub Lib 37-46; US Army libn European Theatre 46-47; Ext dept Asst Detroit Pub Lib 48-61; State libn Mich State Lib 61-68; Assoc Prof Lib Sci Wayne State U 68-. 8: Chm State Lib Law Com; Chm Jt Com on Educ for Library Serv to Disadvantaged; Consul NY, Ind, Hawaii State libs 68-. 9: ALA-AHIL (pres 60-61); MichLA; CathLA; SLA. 10: Phi Beta Mu. 12: Bk Rev. 14: Lib educ, research. 15: 574 Goldengate W, Detroit Mi 48203.

CASEY, HELEN. b Nottingham Ohio. 4: William Way Casey. 5: Flora Stone Mather West Res 24 (Eng, Lat) AB; West Res 26 BLS. 6: Fr, Ital. 7: Desk asst E Cleveland Pub Lib, E Cleveland Ohio 24-26; Child libn Cleveland Pub Lib 26-40; Libn Fairport Pub Lib, Fairport Ohio 49-57; Libn Bay Village Br Cuyahoga Co Lib, Bay Village Ohio 57-. 9: ALA; OhioLA; Lake Co Libns (pres 55-56). 10: LWV; Theta Phi Omega; Bay Village Women's Club; AAUW; French Club; Bridge Club. 14: Adult serv. 15: 24724 E Oakland, Bay Village Oh 44140.

CASEY, NORA M. b Darwin Minn. 5: UMinn 28-32 (Hist) BS, 47 BS in LS. 7: Eng & hist tchr Minneapolis Pub Schs 32-41; Eng & hist tchr Pub High Sch, Claremont Minn 42-43; Hist & lib Pub High Sch, New Prague Minn 44; Tchr Women's Army Corps, Ft Des Moines Iowa 44-45; Clk WAC Walter Reed GH, Wash DC 46; Libn Pub High Sch, Mound Minn 47-49; Libn VA Minneapolis 49; Libn VAH Minot N Dak 50-54; Chief libn VAH Cincinnati 54-. 9: ALA; SLA. 15: Library VA Hosp 3200 Vine st, Cincinnati Oh 45220.

CASEY, WANDA M (SWENSON). b Minneapolis 1 S 22. 4: E L Casey. 5: Bismarck Jr Col 39-41 AS; UMinn 41-42 (Elem Educ); Valley City State Col 56-60 (Soc Sci) BS; ND State, UND 56-60 (Admin); UOre 60-63 (LS) MS. 7: Libn Valley City High Sch, Valley City ND 56-59; Elem libn So Lane schs, Cottage GROVE Ore 59-65; Head Libn Stagg High Sch, Stockton Cal 65-. 9: NEA; ALA; OreLA; No Cal LA. 14: Ref. 15: PO Box 14, Wilseyville Ca 95257.

CASGRAIN, MILDRED (CHALONER) DAVIS. b Winthrop Mass 20 Mr 08. 4: Ardoin Edmond Casgrain. 5: Boston Art Sch 30; Corcoran Gallery of Art 37; UNH summers 63-65. 6: Fr. 7: Lib asst Covington, Burling law off, Wash DC 48-49; Lib asst Falls Church Pub Lib, Falls Church Va 49-51; Lib asst US Geological Survey Lib, Wash DC 52-54; Lib asst Walter Reed Med Lib, Wash DC 57-62; Patients' Lib Nat Inst Health, Bethesda Md: Asst libn 62-63, Supv libn 64-. 9: ALA. 10: Arts Club of Washington. 14: Admin, adult serv. 15: 4000 Cathedral ave, Washington DC 20016.

CASON, CLEO S. b Dahlonega Ga 24 Je 10. 4: Charles M Cason. 5: N Ga Col 26-28; Amer Ext Sch of Law (Chicago) 49 LLB; UAla 51-53. 7: Admin asst to Commander Redstone Arsenal, Redstone Arsenal Ala 44-47; Chief Tech Lib, Redstone Arsenal Ala 49-62; Chief Libn Redstone Sci Info Center, Huntsville Ala 62-. 9: SLA (pres Ala Chap 55-56); SELA; AlaLA (chm Col Univ & Spec Libs Div 59-60). 10: Aladdin Club. 11: Woman of the Year Award 61. 14: Admin. 15: Redstone Sci Info Center, Redstone Arsenal Al.

CASON, DAVID H. b Thomaston Ga 30 S 37. 5: Emory 56-60 (Hist) AB; Mercer U 60-61 M Ed; Emory 63-65 M LS. 7: Tchr Spalding Jr High Sch 61-62; Tchr No Clayton High Sch, College Park Ga 62-63, Libn 63-67; Libn N Clayton Sr High 67-. 9: ALA; GaEA; NEA. 10: Ga Hist Soc. 15: POBox 806, Thomaston Ga 30286.

CASON, JUNE. b Atlanta Ga 19 Jl 33. 5: Gordon Col Barnesville Ga 50-51; Wesleyan Col Macon Ga 51-54 (Chem) AB. 6: Fr, Ger. 7: E I duPont de Nemours & Co, Augusta Ga: Tech asst 54-57, Lib specialist 57-60; Sr chemist E I duPont de Nemours & Co, Gibbstown NJ 60-61; Tech libn FMC Corp, Baltimore 62-. 9: ACS; SLA (Baltimore Chap: v-pres 68-69, pres 69-70). 14: Chem lit. 15: FMC Corp PO Box 1616, Baltimore Md 21203.

CASPER, RODERICK J. b Los Angeles Cal 28 O 20. 5: Loyola U 39-40 (Eng); LA City Col 41-42 (Eng) AA; UCLA 46-48 (Eng) BA; USC 62-67 MSLS. 6: Fr. 7: Personnel clk USA (rank: Sgt) 42-45; Organist-choirmaster St Therese RC Church, Alhambra Cal 45-59; Lib asst LA City Sch Syst 60-64; Readers serv libn Millikan Memorial Lib Cal Tech 64-. 9: SLA; CalLA. 12: Ed Caltech Publications of the Staff (64); Ed SLA Cal Chap Bull (68-). 14: Automation, ref. 15: 6305 Lomitas dr, Los Angeles Ca 90042.

CASS, HARRIET LOUISE (BERGER). b Toronto Can 25 Mr 43. 4: William Cass. 5: UToronto 62-64 (Pol Sci) BA, 64-65 BLS. 6: Fr. 7: Research libn Bank of Nova Scotia, Toronto 65-68; Soc sci libn Simon FraserU, Vancouver BC 68-69; Ref libn Ont Inst for Studies in Educ, Toronto 69-. 9: SLA. 14: Ref. 15: 60 Glengrove ave W, Toronto 12 Ont Can.

CASSADY, THEODORE J. b Oakdale Tenn 6 N 07. 4: Juanita McDowell. 5: UKy 28-34 (Law) BA in Hist, LLB Law; American U 47 (Archives Admin). 6: Sp. 7: Dist Dir WPA Prof Projs, E St Louis 35-40; Club supv Amer Red Cross, London 42-45; Asst state archivist Ill State Lib 46-57; Chief Archives-Records Mgt, Springfield 57-. 8: Consul on archival admin, States of Mo, Cal, & Ga. 9: Nat Soc Pub Admin; SAA; State & loc hist socs. 10: Ill Civic Exch; Amer Assn State & Loc Hist. 11: Fellow SAA. 13: Yes. 14: Archives documentation. 15: State Archives Bldb, Springfield Il 62706.

CASSEL, JEAN RICHARDS. b Palmyra Neb 15 O 13. 5: Doane Col 31-35 (Biol) BA; UDenver 36-37 BS in LS; Columbia 46-47. 6: Ger. 7: Catlgr U Iowa Lib 37-42; Catlgr U Tex Lib 43-44, Music libn 45-46, 47-57; Sr catlgr Columbia U 46-47; U Tex Lib: Rare bks libn 57-59, Undergrad libn 59-63, head Bk sel & acquis Undergrad Lib 63-. 9: ALA; TexLA (sec 53-54, Bus Mgr 'Texas Library Journal' 65-66). 10: Nat Audubon Soc; Austin Lib Club; Staff Assn of the UTex Lib; Delta Kappa Gamma. 13: Yes. 14: Bk sel, catlg. 15: 608 Jessie st, Austin Tx 78704.

CASSELL, KAY ANN. b Van Wert Ohio 24 S 41. 5: Carnegie 59-63 (Modern Langs) BA; Rutgers 63-65 MLS Brooklyn Col 66-69 (Comparative Lit) MA. 6: Fr, Sp. 7: Lib trainee Linden Pub Lib, Linden NJ 63-65; Ref libn Brooklyn Col Lib 65-68; Adult serv libn NJ State Lib,Trenton NJ 68. 9: ALA; NJLA; NJ Assn Adult Educ; Profess Assn, NJ Dept of Educ. 10: Beta Phi Mu; Sigma Kappa; YWCA; AAUW. 14: Ref, adult serv, serv to thedisadvantaged. 15: 1 Highgate dr, Trenton NJ 08625.

CASSIDY, FRANCES (CLEAR). b NYC 5 Ag 12. 5: NYU 32-36 (Eng) BA; Pratt Inst 36-37 BLS. 7: Jr libn Brooklyn Pub Lib, Brooklyn NY 37-38; Asst libn Fresno Co Lib, Fresno Cal 38-40; Story analyst Metro-Goldwyn-Mayer Studios, Culver City Cal 41-48; Child libn Los Angeles Pub Lib 49-50; Story analyst Universal-Intl Studios, Universal City Cal 52-57; Circ libn University of California (Riverside) 60-. 8: Research asst to various motion picture writers. 9: ALA; CalLA; Libns Assn UCal (Riverside) (V-pres 68-69). 14: Circ, lib & personnel admin, pub rel. 15: 3249 Redwood dr, Riverside Ca 92501.

CASSIDY, MELINE (SHAMLIAN). b Sivas Armenia 7 Ag 16. 4: Charles Willia, Cassidy. 5: Wayne State 36-37, 53, 67- (Liberal arts); Miami U, Oxford Ohio 62-63 (Liberal arts); Fairleigh Dickinson 63-65 (Liberal arts). 6: Armenia. 7: Library asst Detroit Pub Lib 34-41; Lab tech AC Spark Plug Gen Motors, Flint Mich 42-44; Children's asst Lane Pub Lib, Hamilton Ohio 62-63; Ser libn Fairleigh Dickinson 63-65; Asst libn Nat Bank of Detroit 66; Ref asst & period libn Baldwin Pub Lib, Birmingham Mich 66-. 9: SLA. 14: Ref, ser. 15: 24561 Mulberry dr, Southfield Mi 48075.

CASSIDY, PHOEBE ANN (ANDERSON). b Washington Penn 31 Ja 37. 4: Terence W Cassidy. 5: Col of Wooster 54-58 (Chem) BS; West Res 58-59 MS in LS; Med Lib Assn Certif 67. 7: Research asst West Res U Ctr for Documentation & Communication Research 59-61; Libn West State Sch & Hosp, Canonsburg Penn 65-66; Acquis libn WashU (St Louis) 66-67; Asst libn St Louis Col of Pharmacy 68; Libn UTMB Opthalmology Lib, Galveston Tex 68-. 9: MedLA. 12: "Index to the William Beaumont MD (1785-1853) Manuscript Collection" (68). 14: Ref, catlg. 15: UTMB Lib, Galveston Tx 77550.

CASSIDY, TERENCE WILLIAM. b Erie Penn 14 Ja 34. 4: Phoebe Ann Anderson. 5: UIll 59-60 MSLS; Park Col 53-55, 58-59 (Pol Sci) BA. 7: Army personnel spec Sp/3 (E-4) (Ft Bragg NC) 56-58; Libn Mo Valley Room Kanasas City Mo Pub Lib 60-63; Libn Kan City Mo Art Inst Lib 63-64; Asst order libn Ind U Libs 64-67; Asst libn tech serv Washington U Sch of Med Lib (St Louis) 67-68; Asst libn UTex (Galveston) Med Br Lib 68-. 9: ALA; SLA; MoLA. 10: Amer Econ Assn; The Westerners; The Lexington Group. 14: Acquis, rare bks, catlg. 15: UTMB Lib 912 Mechanic st, Galveston Tx 77550.

CASSIDY, THOMAS R. b Bay City Mich 11 O 17. 5: George WashingtonU 36-41, 45-47 (Eng) AB; UMich 47-50 (LS, Eng) ABLS, MA. 6: Fr. 7: US Army 41-45; Bkfinder Govt Printing Off, Wash DC 35-41, 45-47; Ref libn UOre (Eugene) 50-52; Br libn Suitland Md 52-54; Reader & ref libn, Hyattsville Md 54-55; Base libn USAF: Lodd AFB Alaska 55-60, bolling AFB Wash DC 60-62, Nha Trang RVN 67-68; Hd preservation sect Nat Lib of Med, Bethesda Md 62-67; Serv ctr libn USAF, Ran Son Nhut RVN 68-. 9: ALA. 13: Yes. 15: 7AF (DPSRLD) APO 96307.

CASSLER, PHYLLIS SUSAN. b Pittsburgh Penn 3 My 42. 5: UPittsburgh 63-64 (Elem Educ) BS; Syracuse 65-67 MSLS. 6: Fr, Ital, Sp, Ger. 7: Ref libn Oberlin Col 67-68; Acquis libn Boston Col 68-. 9: ALA. 14: Ref, acquis, readers' serv. 15: 1160 Commonwealth ave apt 26, Allston Ma 02134.

CASTAGNA, CAROLYN JEAN. b Seattle 30 Ja 33. 4: Frank Castagna. 5: West Wash Col of Educ 50-51; UWash 51-53 (Sociol) BA, 58-61 MLS. 6: Ger. 7: Info clerk "Seattle Times" 54; Tchr armenian United Sch, Baghdad Iraq 54-56; Tchr Peter Burnett Jr High Sch, San Jose Cal 57-58; Lib asst UWash 58-61, Catlg libn 61-67; Asst catlg libn NM State U (Las Cruces) 67-68;Hd catlg libn UMich (Dearborn) 68-. 9: ALA. 14: Catlg. 15: Univ of Mich, Dearborn CampusLib, Dearborn Mi 48128.

CASTAGNA, EDWIN. b Petaluma Cal 1 My 09. 4: Rachel Dent. 5: Santa Rosa Jr Col 28-30 (Eng) Jr Certif; UCal

(Berkeley) 33-35 (Eng) AB, 35-36 Certif in Libnship; UNev 48-49 (Pub Admin); Glendale Col 50 (Pub Personnel Admin); Cal State Dept of Educ Glendale Cal 50, (Basic Prin of Org & Mgt); Long Beach City Col 51 (Motion & Time Study & Wk Simplification). 7: Prof asst Alameda Co Lib, Oakland Cal 37; City Libn Ukiah Pub Lib, Ukiah Cal 37-40; Pvt to Capt 4th Armored Div & 771st Tank Battalion US & Europe 42-46; Dir Washoe Co Lib, Reno Nev 40-49; Chief Libn Glendale Pub Lib, Glendale Cal 49-50; City Libn Long Beach Pub Lib, Long Beach Cal 50-60; Dir Enoch Pratt Free Lib, Baltimore 60-. 8: Consul on lib bldgs, org, & serv of 10 Cal pub libs (one with M Boaz & one with E C Perry) 56-65 Mem Md Governor's Commsn to Revise Pub Lib Laws 68-; Tchr of Lib Sci USoCalucla. 9: ALA (pres 64-65, chm Com on Legisl 66-68, chm Intel Freedom Com 68-);MdLA; CalLA (pres 54); NevLA (one of founders & 1st pres 46-47). 10: Rotary Club;UN Assn of Md; Md Hist Soc; Baltimore Mus of Art; Walters Art Gallery; CitizensPlanning & Housing Assn; Baltimore Bibliophiles, Zamorano Club (Los Angeles; Unionde Bibliofilos Taurinos (Spain). 11: Bronze Star Medal for Heroic Achievement,Purple Heart Medal; Yelland Award for article in "California Librarian". 12: "History of the 771st Tank Battalion" (46); "The Library Reaches Out" Co-edwith Kate Coplan & auth of chap 65; "Long Warm Friendship; H.L. Mencken and the e.p.f.l. (66). 13: Yes. 14: Bk sel, adult educ, admin. 15: Enoch Pratt Free Lib, 400 Cathedral st, Baltimore Md 21201.

CASTAGNOZZI, CAROL A. b Yonkers NY 4 D 43. 5: Syracuse 62-66 (Eng) BA; Rutgers 67-68 MLS. 7: Ref libn Cal State Col (Hayward) 68-. 15: 24035 2nd st, Hayward Ca 94541.

CASTELL, WILLIAM (RENTOUL). b Toronto 6 N 08. 4: Mildred Ruth Joyce. 5: UToronto 28-32 (Eng, Hist) BA; UMinn 34-35 BLS; UMich 35-36 MLS. 6: Fr. 7: Chief libn Pub Lib, Ft William Can 37-45; Dir Pub Lib System, Calgary Can 45-. 9: CanLA (pres); AltaLA (past pres). 10: Fort Williams (Ont) Bd of Educ. 14: Rare bks, ref. 15: Calgary Pub Lib, 616 2nd st SE, Calgary Alta Canada.

CASTELLUCCI, ARTHUR. b Roseto Penn 5 N 32. 4: Norma Ellis. 5: Kutztown State Tchrs Col 54-58 (LS, Geog) BS; Syracuse 61-63 MLS. 6: Sp, Ital. 7: Libn Towanda Valley High Sch, Towanda Penn 58-61; Libn Raub Jr High Sch, Allentown Penn 61-62; Libn Haverford Twp Sr High, Havertown Penn 62-64; Libn Darmstadt Elem Sch, Darmstadt Germany 64-66 Ref Lib & Inst West MD Col 66-68; Asst Prof Villanova U 68-69. 9: ALA; PennLA. 10: AAUP; OEA; Beta Phi Mu; German-Amer Club. 13: Yes. 14: Storytelling, ref, bk sel, sch lib admin, interlib loan. 15: Garibaldi ave, Roseto Pa 18013.

CASTLE, LAVELLE (CONEY). b Tex 14 D 07. 5: E Tex State Col 28 (Home Econ) BS; Pratt 51 MLS. 7: Home econ tchr high sch, Tex 28-38; Asst co home supv Farm Security Admin, Tex 38-42; Ref asst Pratt Inst Lib 49-50; Tex A&M Lib: Sr circ asst 51-52, Ref asst 52, Head ref dept 52-68, Hd basic div 68-. 9: TexLA; TexAssn Col Tchrs. 11: Faculty Distinguished Achievement Award in Individual Student Relations, presented by the Assn of Former Students of Tex A&M U 65. 15: Tex A&M Univ Lib, College Station Tx 77843.

CASWELL, ELEANOR (WALLACE). b New Castle Penn 30 Ja 1900. 5: Thiel Col 18-22 (Eng) AB; Columbia 25; UPittsburgh 26-27; Marywood Col summers 49-53 BS in LS. 7: Tchr High Sch, Stockton NY 22-23; Tchr Jr High Sch, Beaver Falls Penn 23-24; Tchr High Sch, Ambridge Penn 24-29; Lib asst State Tchrs Col, Millersville Penn 49; Libn Wyoming Sem, Kingston Penn 49-; Act libn Cooper Mem Lib, Clermont Fla summer 65 Libn Cooper Mem Lib Clermont Fl 66-. 9: ALA; PennLA (chm NE Dist 61). 10: AAUW; Wilkes Barre-UN Assn. 14: Ref, catlg. 15: 1447 - 4th st, Clermont Fl 32711.

CASWELL, VIRGINIA (DEWHURST). b Milford Conn 10 Je 29. 4: Paul Meldon Caswell. 5: URochester 47-51 (Art Hist) BA; Columbia 52-53 (LS) MS. 7: Technical Libn Jack & Heintz Inc, Cleveland 57-59; Tech libn Brush Berylium Co, Cleveland 60-62; Supv Ref Serv McDonnell Aircraft Corp St Louis 62-66; Research Info Analyst Lockheed Missiles Space Co, Sunnyvale Cal 66-68; Tech Info Specialist UCal Livermore 68-. 9: SLA. 14: Ref, lit search. 15: 41777 Grimmer blvd apt F-3, Fremont Ca 94538.

CATALDO, JOAN D. b Jamaica LI NY. 5: Queens Col 52-56 (Anthropology-Sociol) BA; Pratt 57-59 MLS. 7: Libn James C Buckley Inc, NYC 59-61; Asst libn Amer Gas Assn Inc, NYC 61-. 9: SLA. 10: Beta Phi Mu; Pratt Inst Grad Lib & Info Sci Sch Alumni Assn. 14: Ref. 15: 119-11 Linden blvd, Ozone Park LI NY 11420.

CATE, CHARLOTTE WESTER. b Henderson NC 27 Jl 17. 4: Walter Refford Cate. 5: Meredith Col 34-38 (Eng) AB; UNC 38-39 ABLS; UNC Greensboro 58-60 M Ed. 6: Fr. 7: Child libn Rock Hill Pub Lib, Rock hill SC 41-42; Libn Marine Corps Schs, Quantico Va 42-46; Libn Reidsville Sr High Sch, Reidsville NC 39-41, 57-68; Libn Rockingham Commun Col 68-. 9: NCLA; ALA; SELA. 10: Delta KappaGamma; Twentieth Cent Study Club. 15: 608 Parkway blvd, Reidsville NC 27320.

CATHERINE, SISTER ROSE (MC LAUGHLIN) CSJ. b St Paul 5 S 1891. 5: Col of St Catherine 10-14 (Fr, Eng) BA; UMinn 15-16 (Fr) MA, 20 (Pharmacy) Certif, summer 22 (Hist) Certif, summer 26 (Fr) Certif; Chicago summer 31 (Tchg of Fr) Certif; UMinn 43-44 (Span), summers 44-49 (Span) Certif; Col of St Catherine summers 51-54 BS in LS, summers 55, 64 (LS) Certif. 6: Fr, Sp, Lat, Ital. 7: Tchr Frenh, Lat, Eng Derham Hall, St Paul 16-17; Tchr Lat Eng St Mary's Acad, Graceville Minn 17-18; Tchr Fr, Lat Derham Hall, St Paul 18-20; Tchr Hist Lat, Eng St Joseph's Acad, St Paul 21-24; Tchr hist, Lat, Eng I C High Sch, Watertown S D 24-28; Tchr Fr, Lat, hist St Joseph's Acad, St Paul 28-33; Tchr Fr, Lat Acad of the Holy Angels, Minneapolis 33-40; Tchr Fr, Span, Lat St Joseph's Acad, St Paul 40-49; Tchr Eng, Lat & Libn St Mary's High Sch, Waverly Minn 49-52; Tchr-Libn St Mary's High Sch, Bird Island Minn 52-53; Libn Derham Hall, St Paul 53-55; Libn St Joseph's Acad, St Paul 55-65; Libn St Mary's High Sch, Waverly Minn 65-. 8: Reading consul, mem of curriculum committee St Joseph's Acad, St Paul Minn 36-60. 9: ALA; CathLA; MinnLA. 10: Lambda Alpha Psi; Booster Club. 14: Bk sel, ref. 15: St Mary's Convent, Waverly Mn 55390.

CATHEY, VELMA LEE (COLE). b Crawford Co Ark 4 Ja 09. 4: Finis G Cathey. 5: UArk 27-31 (Hist, Ger) BA, summers 35, 36, 38 (Hist, Educ); N Tex State U 48-49 (Hist, Govt) MA, 49-51 BS in LS. 7: Soc studies sci lib High Sch, Eudora Ark 31-41; Supv La Ordnance Plant, Shreveport La 42-43; Ammunition Issuing Off USNR (W) Lt jg Bur of Ordnance, Wash DC 43-46; Ed Hdq Air Train Command Info Sect, Barksdale Field La 46-47; N Tex State U: Instr Hist 48-50, Asst catlgr 50-55, Documents libn 55-. 9: ALA (chm of subcom); SWLA; TexLA (chm Docs Group 68,69, sec Docs Div). 10: Phi Alpha Theta; Kappa Delta Pi; Alpha Lambda Sigma; Delta Kappa Gamma; AAUW; Shakespeare Club. 14: Docs, archives, law. 15: 910 Stanley, Denton Tx 76201.

CATHON, LAURA E(LIZABETH). b Pittsburgh 17 O 08. 5: Bethany Col 29 BA; Carnegie 32 BS in LS. 7: Tchr Eng & Lat High Sch New Martinsville WVa 29-30; 1st asst Central Boys & Girls Div Carnegie Lib of Pittsburgh 34-48; Instr ref wk Carnegie Lib Sch of Carnegie Inst of Tech 44-46; Head Central Boys & Girls Div Carnegie Lib of Pittsburgh 48-. 8: ALA-CSD Rep as consul for the rev ed of "A Parent's Guide to Children's Reading" by Nancy Larrick. 9: ALA (sec-treas & chm staff org round table 49-51, subs bks com 58-60, coun 61-65); -CSDC (chm Publs Planning Com 57-59, Newbery-Caldecott Com 7 yrs, chm Nomin Com 55 & 57, sec 54-55, treas 61-64, chm Develop Com 64-); PennLA (chm Nomin Com 54, mem Pub Rel Com 55, sec 59-60); Sect of Wk with Chi ld Schs & YP; v-chm 8-49, 68-69, chm 49-50. 10: YWCA; Kappa Delta. 12: Comp with T Schmidt "Treasured Tales; Stories of Courage and Faith" (60); "Perhaps and Perchance Tales of Nature" (62); Ed com "Subject and Title Index to Short Stories for Children" ALA (55); Chm Ed Com "Stories to Tell to Children" (7th ed 60). 13: Yes. 14: Serv to child. 15: Carnegie Lib of Pittsburgh, 4400 Forbes ave, Pittsburgh Pa 15213.

CATLETT, PATRICIA (GLENWOOD). b Morrow La 28 Ag 15. 5: LSU 31-34 (Math) AB, summers 35-38 BS in LS; Columbia summer 46 (LS); UMich summer 51, 53, 56 AMLS. 7: Math tchr & libn Elton High Sch, Elton La 34-38; Libn Lake Charles High Sch, Lake Charles La 38-41; Reviser-libn LSU Lib Sch summers 39-42; Catlgr Southeastern La Col 41-43; Libn US Army Ft Taylor, Key West Fla 43-44; Libn US Army Camp Rucker, Ala 44-45; Asst ref libn LSU summer 48; Ref libn & tchr of Lib Sci Southeastern La Col 46-. 9: ALA (State Mem Chm 2 yrs); -ACRL (State Rep 2 yrs); La Tchrs Assn; LaLA (treas1 yr, sec 1 yr, chm Jr Mem Round Table 1 yr, sec Col & Ref Sect 1 yr); LaCol Conf(sec Lib Sect 1 yr). 10: Phi Kappa Phi; Kappa Delta Pi; Beta Phi Mu; Treas; LSU LibSch Alumni Assn; Bd Dir, 1st United Meth Church, Hammond La; Bd dir, Hammond UnitedGivers Fund; Phi Mu. 12: "Student Library Handbook," (64 ref ed 67). 14: Ref. 15: Box 676,College sta, Hammond La 70401.

CATLIN, ANNE (COOGAN). b Bryn Mawr Penn 7 Jl 12. 5: Womans Col UNC 30-34 (Hist) BA; UNC 42-43 BS in LS. 6:

Fr. 7: Asst circ lib Bryn Mawr Col 36-42; Catlgr Hampden Sydney Col 43-44; 1st asst gen ref Grosvenor Lib, Buffalo NY 45-47; Head ref & circ Carnegie Inst of Tech 47-51; Libn Lynchburg Col 51-56; Catlgr Chatham Col 59-60; 1st asst ref UPittsburgh 60-62; Dir of Libs Juniata Col 62-. 9: ALA-ACRL; PennLA (chm Loc chap 65-66). 10: AAUW; LWV. 14: Admin, ref. 15: 1703 Washington st, Huntingdon Pa 16652.

CATRON, ADA RUTH (OSBORNE). b Grayson Co Va 11 Mr 38. 4: Bobby Vance Catron. 5: Radford Col 56-59 (LS) BS. 7: Libn Fries High Sch, Va 59-64, 65-69. 9: VaEA; Grayson Co EA. 10: Grange; WSCS. 14: Catlg, a-v. 15: PO Box 476, Galax Va 24333.

CATTIE, MARY M. b Phila 8 S 27. 5: Chestnut Hill Coll 45-49 (Fr) AB; West Res 61-62 MS in LS; St Josephs Col 65-66 (Bus Admin). 6: Fr. 7: Sec La Salle Col 50-61; Asst libn NY Life Insurance Co, NYC 62, Libn 62-64; Libn I bus sci ind dept Free Lib of Phila 64-66; Libn-in-Chg Auto Ref Col 66-. 9: SLA; ALA. 14: Ref (bus), auto, ind. 15: 2991 W School House lane, Sycamore 33W, Phila Pa 19144.

CATTIE, MAUREEN M. b Philadelphia Penn 20 My 42. 5: Rosemont Col 60-64 (Eng Lit) AB; Drexel 64-65 MSLS. 7: Libn I Free Lib of Phila 65-67, Libn II Educ, phil, & relig dept 67-. 9: ALA. 14: Ref. 15: Free Library of Philadelphia, Philadelphia Pa 19103.

CAUDLE, VIOLET K. b Iredell Co NC 30 Je 25. 5: Lenoir Rhyne Col 49-52; Appalachian State Tchrs Col 52-53 (LS) BS; Emory summers 57-58. 7: Clerk Army Libs WAC (Cpl) 45-49; Circ libn Gaston Co Pub Lib NC 53-55; Chief libn Greene Co Pub Lib, Snow Hill NC 55-59; Chief libn Iredell Co Lib, Statesville NC 59-67; Asst dir Iredell Pub Lib, Statesville NC 67-. 9: ALA; NCLA; SELA; Nat Trust Hist Preservation; Soc Preservation of Antiquities; NC Lit & Hist Assn. 10: Bus & Prof Women's Club; WAC Vet Assn. 14: Pub libs, bkmob serv. 15: 224-1/2 N Center, Statesville NC 28677.

CAULKER, OLIVE SELBY. b Normal Ala. 5: Fisk U 40-44 (Religion) BA; UChicago 45-46 (Religious Educ) MA; Peabody 58-59 MA(LS). 6: Fr, Ger. 7: Tchr of relig & head catlgr University Col of Sierra Leone (Freetown Sierra Leone W Africa) 46-63; Head of Tech Processes Marquette U Mem Lib 64-. 8: Over the years in Africa, taught in church ministerial training programs,helped org civic groups, helped found child care homes, served on the Lib Bd of Sierra Leone, a govt body. 9: ALA; WisLA. 10: AAUP; Marquette Faculty Assn forInterrac Justice; ACLU. 14: Catlg. 15: 4561 N 45th st, Milwaukee Wi 53218.

CAUMARTIN, CHRISTINE. b Penetang Can 19 Ap 26. 5: Wayne State U 45-50 (LS) BS in Ed; UMich 50-51 MALS. 6: Fr. 7: Libn Mownier Elem Sch, Detroit 52-63; Libn Cass Tech High Sch, Detroit 63-64; Libn Mackenzie High Sch, Detroit 64-66; Libn Denby High Sch Detroit 66-. 9: ALA-AASchL; MichASchL; 10: Det Fed Tchrs; USO; Wayne State U Lib Sci Alumni. 14: Ref, bk reviewing. 15: 15081 Tracey ave, Detroit Mi 48227.

CAUSLEY, MONROE SWEENEY JR. b Bay City Mich 28 D 29. 5: Bay City Jr Col 48-50 (Hist); Central MichU 60-62 (Hist) BA; UMich 62-63 AMLS; fla AtlanticU 69- (Geog). 6: Ger. 7: US Navy YNT3 (YC3), Key West Fla & Keflavik Iceland 51-53; Clk Bay City Pub Lib, Bay City Mich 54; Circ dept NY Pub Lib, NYC 55; Hd bkmob Saginaw Pub Lib, Saginaw Mich 55-60, Hd bus & tech dept 63-65, Hd ref dept 65-67; Hd tech serv Ft Lauderdale Pub lib, Ft Lauderdale Fla 67-68; Hd ref dept & asst dir, hd pub serv Fla AtlanticU Lib 68-. 8: MLA Legis Com 66. 9: ALA; SLA; SELA; FlaLA. 14: Ref, govt docs. 15: 3699 NW 4th ave, Boca Raton Fl 33432.

CAVALLARI, ELFRIEDA (LASMANE). b Talso Latvia 9 S 29. 4: Ford D Cavallari. 5: UNRRA U Munich Ger 45 (Chem); Ukrainian Politech Munich Ger 45-49 (Pharmaceutical chem); Clark U 51-53 (Ger) AB; Simmons 61-63 (LS) MS; Centenary Col La 55-57 (Sp). 6: Latvian, Ger, Russian, Polish, Okrainian, Sp. 7: Library asst Clark U 52-53; Libn Free Pub Lib, Worcester Mass 54-55; Libn Tex East Transmission Corp, Shreveport La 57-58; Documentation engr Itek Corp, Lexington Mass 62-64; Libn AFCRL Research Lib, Bedford Mass 64-. 9: SLA (Boston Chap: chm of Recr Com 67-69). 10: AAUW. 14: Catlg. 15: 18 Lantern lane, Chelmsford Ma 01824.

CAVANAGH, G S TERENCE. b Winnipeg Can 16 S 23. 4: Dorothy E Brown. 5: UMan 46-50 BA; McGill 50-51 BLS. 6: Fr. 7: Med Lib McGill U 51; Brooklyn Pub Lib 52-53; Chief Libn U Kan Med Center 53-62; Dir, curator of Trent Collection Prof of Med Lit, Med Center Lib Duke U 62-. 8: Research fellowship Hist of Med Div UCLA 61; NLM Facilities & Resources Com 68-. 9: MedLA; Amer Assn Hist Med; BSA. 10: AAAS. 13: Yes. 15: Med Center Lib, Duke Univ Durham NC 27706.

CAVANAUGH, ELIZABETH (JENNETT). b Owasso Mich 4 Je 12. 4: Woodrow W Cavanaugh. 5: Our Lady of the Lake Col 29-32 (Lat) BA, 32-33 BLS. 6: Sp. 7: San Antonio (Tex) Indep Sch Dist: Asst libn San Antonio Voc & Tech Sch Lib 34-44, Libn Burbank High Sch 44-49, Libn L W Fox Voc & Tech Sch 49-. 9: NEA; Tex State Tchrs Assn; Bexar Co (Tex) LA. 10: Alpha Delta Kappa. 14: Ref, lit for ya with emphasis on poor readers. 15: 637 N Main ave, SanAntonio Tx 78205.

CAVE, CLIFFORD ROY. b Berkeley Cal 29 Je 15. 5: Pomona Col 34-36 (Soc Studies) BA; Union Theol Sem 36-39 BD; Columbia 47-51 (European Hist); USoCal 61-63 (Libnship) MS. 6: Fr. 7: US Army, SW Pacific, Philippines, Japan 43-46; Tchr Pasadena City Col 46-47; Instr hist Adelphi Col 52-59; Ref libn Orange Co Pub Lib, Orange Cal 64-66, Br libn Lazuna Beach 66-. 9: AAUPL AHA; CalLA; OrangeCoLA. 14: Ref, admin. 15: Box 564, Laguna Beach Ca 92652.

CAVELL, CHARLOTTE ANTHONY. b Chicago 12 Jl 06. 5: UCal(Los Angeles) 23-27 (Fr) AB; UCal Sch of Libnship 27-28 Certif; USoCal 56-59 (Educ) MS in Ed. 6: Fr. 7: Catlgr & circ libn UCLA 28-36; Catlgr Beverly Hills (Cal) Pub Lib 36-49; Jr Col catlgr Los Angeles City Schs 49-60, Elem order libn 60-65, Lib coord Professional Lib 65-. 9: NEA; ALA (chm Reg Catlgrs Gp); CalLA "So Dist (Sec-treas); Cal Tchrs Assn; CalASchL (Publ chm). 10: Kappa Phi Zeta; Delta Kappa Gamma; Women's U Club of Los Angeles; Bus & Prof Women's Club; Prytanean. 13: Yes. 15: 450 N Grand ave, Los Angeles Ca 90012.

CAVENDER, EUGENIA (PARKER). b Dalton Ga 27 Je 31. 4: William J Cavender. 5: Ga State Col for Women 48-52 (Soc Studies) AB; Peabody 53, 56, 57 (LS) MA. 7: Asst libn Dalton Reg Lib, Dalton Ga 52-55; Libn North Whitfield High Sch, Dalton Ga 55-58; Bkmob libn Dalton Reg Lib, Dalton Ga 58-60; Libn North Whitfield High Sch, Dalton Ga 60-65; Dir lib serv Whitfield Co Bd of Educ, Dalton Ga 65-. 8: Elem sch lib consul, Dalton Ga 60-. 9: GaLA (sec). 14: Admin. 15: 109 Todd ave, Dalton Ga 30720.

CAVIN, LOUTRELL E. b Chesterfield Ala 4 D 19. 5: Bob Jones U 36-39; GSCW 39-40 (soc sci) BS; App State Tchr's Col summer 44 (LS). 6: Fr. 7: Tchr & libn Powder Springs Cons Sch, Powder Springs Ga 40-41; Libn Cave Springs Cons Sch, Cave Springs Ga 41-42; Libn Reidsville High Sch & Tatnall Co, Reidsville Ga 42-44; Tech libn USAF, Eglin Field Fla 44-46; Staff libn USAF, Philippines & Okinawa 47-51; Staff libn USAF, 2AF Barksdale AFB La 51-52; Command libn USAF, SAC Offutt AFB NB 52-. 9: ALA; NebLA. 10: Joselyn Museum. 14: Admin. 15: SAC (DPSR) Offutt AFB NB 68113.

CAWLEY, INEZ (CARLTON). b Hughton Sask 21 S 18. 5: USask 36-40 (Fr) BA, UToronto 64-65 BLS. 6: Fr. 7: Ottawa Pub Sch Bd: Sub tchr (Fr) 51-56, Violin tchr 56-61; Lib asst Cauleton U 61-64; Govt docs libn Waterloo Lutheran U 65-. 9: CanLA; OntLA. 14: Govt docs, acquis, catlg, ref. 15: 166 Elgin Crescent, Waterloo Ont Can.

CAWLEY, REV ROBERT P. b Cedarhurst LI NY 18 Jl 33. 5: Mary Immaculate Sem 56-62 (Philos) BA; SUNY(Albany) 62-63 MLS, 63-64 (Educ) MA; Wharton Sch UPenn 64-65; Notre Dame U (Ind) 65 (Bus Admin). 6: Fr, Ger. 7: Libn Sem of Our Lady of Angels, Albany NY 62-64; Asst treas Congregation of the Mission, Phila 64-66; Asst dir of libs St John's U (Jamaica NY) 66-. 9: ALA; CathLA; NYLA; Hudson-MohawkLA. 10: SUNY(Albany) Lib Sch Alumni; Phi Delta Kappa; Melvil Dui Marching and Chowder Soc. 14: Catlg, ref, tech processes. 15: St John's Univ, Jamaica NY 11432.

CAWTHON, JUNE (BRICE). b Knoxfork Ky 10 Ap 23. 4: Jesse Marvin Cawthon. 5: Berea Col 41-45 (Eng, LS) AB; Emory 50-51 MLS. 7: Libn Black Star High Sch, Alva Ky 45-47; Libn Pineville City Sch, Pineville Ky47-48; Libn Jefferson Jr High Sch, Oak Ridge Tenn 48-50; Libn Elberton city schs,Elberton Ga 51-53; Lib Consul Athens Reg Lib, Athens Ga 53-65; Asst Prof Lib EducUGa Col of Educ 65-. 9: GALA (v-pres pub lib sect, sec Educ for Libnship sect,Libnship as a career com, Special Committee to Make Recommendations on the StateCatlg Serv); SELA. 10: Entre Nous Club. 14: Bk sel, ref, catlg. 15: 240 Pine Needle rd, Athens Ga 30601.

CAWTHORNE, EDYTHE O (MAYBERRY). b Des Moines Iowa. 5: Howard U 31-33 (Eng); Lincoln U 34-36 (Eng) BA; UMinn 55-56 MA in LS. 7: Sub-prof asst Pub Lib, Omaha 54-55; Child libn Multnomah Co Lib, Portland Ore 56-59; Libn Ore Educ Assn, Portland Ore 60-61; Field consul & child & yp spec Iowa State Travel Lib 61-. 8: Lib/USA 64; Iowa Governor's Commsn on Child & Youth 63- Vis Prof Drake U 68-; Dir Title II Inst Drake U 69. 9: ALA; IowaLA (chmchild sect 63, Exec Com 66). 10: Iowa Town & Country YWCA (Exec Com). 14: Pub lib, child & yp, ext. 15: 3110 E 7th st, Des Moines Ia 50316.

CAYLOR, HENRIETTA (GRIBBLE). b Dalton Ga 17 O 25. 5: WGa Col 41-43; UGa 45-47 (Home Econ) BSHE; Emory 59-61 MLN. 7: Clerk Bell Aircraft Corp, Marietta Ga 43-45; Home econ tchr Spalding Co Sch,Griffin Ga 47-48; Elem tchr Dalton Pub Schs, Dalton Ga 48-50; Sch libn Atlanta Ga;Bolton Beecher Hills & Venetial Hills 61-63; Beecher Hills & Venetial Hills 63-64;Beecher Hills & Continental Colony 64-66; Continental Colony 66-69. 9: ALA;-AASchL; GaLA; GaEA; AtlantaEA. 14: Sch libs, acquis, tech processing. 15: 1454 Willow Trail SW, Atlanta Ga 30311.

CAYTON, ROBERT FRANK. b Covington Ky 6 Jl 29. 4: Vivian Pelley. 5: East Ky State Col 47-50 (Eng) AB; Columbia U 50-51 (LS) MS; UCincinnati 53-62 (Eng); Ohio U 63-68 (Am lit) PhD. 6: Fr, Sp, Ital, Ger, Lat. 7: Catlgr Va Polytech Inst 51-52; Univ Cincinnati: Period & res bk room libn 52-54; Lecturer on libnship 59-63, Head ser div 54-63; Head Libn Marietta Col 63-. 8: Mem Bd of Trustees & Sec Ohio Col Lib Center 67-; Bldg consul, Washington Co Pub Lib, Marietta O 68-. 9: ALA (Internat Orgs Com 61-64); -RTSD (mem-at-Large Ser Sect Exec Com 63-66); -ACRL (Tri-State Chap 64-); Ohio Valley Group Tech Serv Libns (sec 61-62); Ohioana LA; OhioLA (Col & Univ Round Table; v-pres & pres-elect 68-); Ohio Col Assn (Com of Libns 65-66. 10: AAUP; Washington Co (Ohio) Hist Soc; Sigma Tau Delta; Mod Lang Assn. 11: Certif of Merit, Ky State Poetry Soc (67); 12: Bk reviewer for "Library Journal" (63-). 13: Yes. 14: Rare bks, ser, admin. 15: 427 Fifth st, Marietta Oh 45750.

CAZAYOUX, VIVIAN BLANCHE. b Greenville Miss 15 O 22. 5: LSU 39-42 (Educ) BS, 42-43 BS in LS UWis 66-67 MS in LS, 66-67 (LS). 6: Fr. 7: Asst East Baton Rouge Parish Lib, Baton Rouge La 43; Ref asst Texas A&M Col Lib 44; Catlgr La State Lib 45-46, Head La dept 47-48, Head films & recordings 49-60; Libn Ascension Parish Lib, Donaldsonville la 60-64; Libn St Landry Parish Lib, Opelousas La 64-66; Lib consul La State Lib 67-69, Assoc State Libn for Lib Dev 69-. 8: Ref libn-Library/USA NY World's Fair 64 Chm State Bd of Lib Examrs 67-. 9: ALA (A-V Bd 53-57, chm 56-57; Nom Com65; Memb Com 62-, ASL Stand Com 68-, Com on Instr in Use of Lib 68-); Adult EducAssn (Delegate Assembly 55-56; Memb Com 56); LaLA (var offs 48-59, pres 53-54); Adult Educassn of La (pres 56-57). 10: Jr League of Baton Rouge. 12: "Public Library Services and Their Use by the ProfessionalStaffs of Family Welfare Agencies". 13: Yes. 14: Adult serv, lib devel. 15: 2109 Perkins rd,Baton Rouge La 70808.

CAZDEN, ROBERT EDGAR. b NYC 29 Ag 30. 4: Joann Cohn Cazden. 5: UCLA 51-52 (Eng) AB; USoCal 53-54 (Musicology) MA; UCal at Berkeley 54-55 MLS; UChicago 65 (LS) PhD. 6: Ger, Fr. 7: Gifts libn UCal at Berkeley 55-57; Bibliog coordinator Oregon State U 59-65; Assoc prof UKy Sch of Lib Sci 66-. 9: ALA; BSA; Bibliog Soc UVa; Printing Hist Soc (London). 10: Soc for the Study of Labour Hist (London); Leo Baeck Soc. 12: "German Exile Literature in America 33-50: a History of the Free German Press and Book Trade" (69). 14: Hist of printing, publ & the bktrade; acad libs, nat and subj bibliog, acquis. 15: 1245 Eldermere rd, Lexington Ky 40502.

CEBALLOS, LILLIAN (PEREZ). b Havana Cuba 28 F 26. 4: Eloy Hipolito Ceballos. 5: HavanaU 45-49 Dr in Phil & Letter; Escuela de Bibliotecarios 51-52 Bachiller en Ciencias Bibliotecaria. 6: Portug, Ital, Fr, Sp. 7: Catlg II: Sociedad Economica amigos del Pais, Havana 51, Ministerio de Hacienda, Havana 52-56, 62-63; Asst ref hispanic Foundation LC 51-52; Dir Lib of Ministerio de Relaciones, Havana 58-60; Asst chief Bk Div USBE, Wash DC 66-. 8: Lectr clsf & catlg in archives Escuela de Archiveros 60-61. 9: ALA; NCLA; SELA; Nattrust Hist Preservation; Soc Preservation of Antiquities; NC Lit & Hist Assn. 14: Catlg. 15: 1824 Metzerott rd, Adelphi Md 20783.

CECILIANNE, SISTER MARY, SSJ. b E Chicago Ind 26 D 18. 5: DePaul U 40-50 (Eng) AB; Rosary Col 51-54 9ls0 ma& deLourdes 55-57 Certif in Theol; Loyola 58-62 (Hist). 6: Polish. 7: Tchr-libn St Barbara High Sch, Chicago 53-59; Tchr-libn Immaculata Col (Chicago) 60-62; Libn Immaculata Col (Bartlett Ill) 62-. 69; Asst libn St Joseph Col (Calumet) 69-. 9: CathLA; ALA. 14: Catlg. 15: Immaculata Col, 801 W Bartlettrd, Bartlett Il 60103.

CEDRINS, JOHN (JANIS). b District Valmiera Latvia 8 N 22. 4: Irene Cedrins. 5: UBonn (Germany) 46-49 (Philos) PhD; UChicago 55-56 (LS) MA. 6: Latvian, Ger, Dutch. 7: Tchr Gymnasium, Flensburg Germany 45-46; Asst acquis dept UChicago Libs 55-56; Asst libn Amer Dental Assn, chicago 56-61; Asst dir Bur of Lib & Indexing Serv, Amer Dental Assn, Chicago 61-. 9: SLA (Ill Chap: chm Memb Com 64-65, treas 65-67, auditor 67-69); MedLA. 10: Caxton Club; Art Inst of Chicago. 12: Ed "J Rainis, Joseph and His Brothers" (2nd ed). 13: Yes. 14: Tech serv, rare bks, hist bibliog. 15: 1439 W Hutchinson st, Chicago Il 60613.

CEKAS, ALDONA (NOAKAS). b Lithuania 22 Je 38. 4: George G Cekas Md. 5: Hunter Col 56-60 (Ger) BA; Simmons 60-62 (LS) MS Rutgers 65-69 (Ger). 6: Lithuanian, Ger, Fr. 7: Jr lib asst Hunter Col 60; Libn & tchr Franklin Jr Sch, Metuchen NJ 63-65 Ref libn N Plainfield Lib NJ 67-. 8: Bibliog Com of the NJ Sch LA for compiling bibliog of bks about NJ ("New Jersey in the Classroom") for children. 9: ALA. 10: American-Lithuanian Girl Scout Leader (Guide) in NY 53-61, Providence 61-62. 11: The Herman Ridder Memorial Honorary Prize for Recitation of Poetry (Hunter Col). 14: Ref, young adults lit. 15: 50 Aylin st, Metuchen NJ 08841.

CELESTINE, SISTER MARY (NAES). b St Louis 10 Ja 07. 5: Mary Rogers Col 31-35 (Educ) B of Ed; St Louis U 47-48 (Hist); Rosary Col 59-60 MA in LS UHawaii summer 66; Chaminade Col (Honolulu) summer 69. 6: Fr, Ger, Sp. 7: Libn Maryknoll Col High Sch Dept 60-61; Libn Maryknoll Novitiate (Jr Col) (Valley Park Mo) 61-62; Libn Maryknoll Novitiate (Jr Col) (Topsfield Mass) 62-64; Libn Maryknoll High Sch, Honolulu 64-65; Libn Maryknoll Convent, Honolulu 65-66; Libn St Ann'shigh Sch, Kaneohe Hawaii 66-69. 9: ALA; CathLA; HawaiiASchL. 13: Yes. 14: Catlg, ref. 15: 46-131 Haiku rd, Kaneohe Hi 96744.

CELINE, SISTER MARY (O'BRIEN). b Troy NY 2 Je 22. 5: St Rose Col 47-51 BE; SUNY (Albany) 57-61 MSLS; Col of St Rose 63-70. 6: Fr, Lat. 7: Prim tchr Sisters of Mercy Vincentian Inst, Albany 44-47; Prim tchr Annunciation Sch, Ilion NY 47-50; Prim tchr Blessed Sacrament Sch, Albany NY 50-53; Prim tchr Vincentian Inst, Albany NY 53-54; Prim tchr Sacred Heart of Mary Sch, Watervliet NY 54-57; Tchr-Libn St Bernard's Acad, Cohoes NY 57-68; Libn Maria Col 68-. 9: CathLA; NYLA. 10: AAUW. 12: "I Charge Each of You" (66). 14: Sch libnship. 15: 634 New Scotland ave, Albany NY 12208.

CELINETTE, SISTER MARY CSSF (BARUSH). b Buffalo NY 23 N 14. 5: Mt St Joseph Tchrs Col 37-43 (Ed) BS; Notre Dame U 48 (Eng); Nazareth Col 52-54 (LS) Certif; Syracuse 60 (LS); SUNY at Genesco 63-65 MLS. 6: Eng, Fr, Polish. 7: Tchr jr high sch, Buffalo Lackawanna NY 36-55; Tchr & libn Villa Maria Acad, Buffalo NY 55-65; Asst libn & instr lib sci Villa Maria College, Buffalo NY 65-. 9: ALA; CathLA; NatSciTA; NYStateLA; WestNY Cath Libns Conf. 14: Ref. 15: 240 Pine Ridge rd, Buffalo NY 14225.

CELMS, AINA (KALNINS). b Riga Latvia 1 Ag 36. 4: Roalds Celms. 5: West Mich U 56-60 (Eng, Lit) BA, 60-61 (LS) MA. 6: Latvian. 7: San Diego Pub Lib ; Ref libn Hist & World Affairs Sect 61-62, Interlib Loans libn 62-63, Ref libn Hist & World Affairs Sect 63-64, Br libn Point Loma Br Lib 64-. 9: CalLA. 14: Ref. 15: 831-1/2 26th st, San Diego Ca 92102.

CELNIK, MAX. b Berlin Germany 15 Je 33. 4: Faith Caplan. 5: Brooklyn Col 51-55 (Eng) BA; Rutgers 56 MLS; Col of Jewish Studies Jewish Theol Sem 57 BHL. 6: Ger, Hebrew. 7: Libn NY Pub Lib ref dept 56-57; Libn Cong Shearith Israel, USA 56; Col libn Yeshiva U Stern Col for Women 57-58; Instr lib admin GradSch of Ed YeshivaU 58-60, Asst prof lib admin 67-. 8: Lib Consul United Synagogue of Amer 59-60; Lib Consul Fed of JewishPhilanthropies of NY 65 and various others 66-; Dir of High Sch Libs, YeshivaU; Orgof Yeshiva Elem high sch, synagogue & commun center libs. 9: Jewish LA (sec 58-64);Assn of Jewish libs (exec sec 67-68). 10: AAUP; Fed Jewish Philanthropies. 11: Citation of Merit for distinguished serv infostering Judacca libs in soc welfare agencies, Fed of Jewish Philanthropies, 65. 12: "The Synagogue Library Organization and Administration" (60 2nd ed 68); "A BasicBooklist for Synagogue and School Libraries" (60); "A

Bibliography on Judaism and Jewish-Christian Relations" (65); Ed in chief "Physicians Book Compendium" (69-)Ed dir PCMI Lib Info Systems, Nat Cash Register 69-. 13: Yes. 14: Col lib admin,micropublishing, medical lit. 15: National Cash Register, Dayton Oh.

CENTING, RICHARD RONALD. b Detroit 16 S 36. 5: Wayne State U 54-61 (Eng) BA; UMich 61-64 MLS. 7: (Pfc) US Army 58-60; Pre-prof Detroit Pub Lib 61-63; Ref libn "Detroit News" 64; Ref supv Campbell-Ewald Co, Detroit 64-67; Ref libn Oakland U (Rochester Mich) 67-68; Admin asst to dir Ohio State ULibs, Columbus 69-. 9: SLA. 10: AAUP. 13: Yes. 14: Ref, admin. 15: Ohio State Univ Libs, 1858 Neil ave, Columbus Oh 43210.

CEPULKAUSKAS, NIJOLE LIGIJA SAULE. b Rokiskis Lithuania 22 Ap 20. 5: UVilnius Law Sch (Vilnius Lithuania) 38-42 (Law) Diploma Juris; McGill 56-57 BLS. 6: Ger, Russ, Po l. 7: Law clk & act magistrate Circuit Court of Vilnius, Vilnius Lithuania 43-44; Title searcher Jeffery Jeffery & Frost, Toronto 52-56; Ref libn Toronto Pub Lib Bus & Tech Sect 57-59; Bibliog-catlgr Cromwell Lib Amer Bar Found, Chicago 59-63; Asst libn Rush Med Col Lib Presbyterian-St Luke's Hosp, Chicago 63-64; Asst libn Lib of the US Courts, Chicago 64-. 9: AALL; SLA; Internat Assn Law Libs; Chicago Assn of Law Libs (chm Publ Com 63-64). 10: Kappa B eta Pi. 12: Comp "Selective Bibliography on Land Tenure" (62). 14: Catlg, ref, admin. 15: Lib of the US Courts, Chicago Il 60604.

CERJANEC, MRS RUTH (WADE). b Central Falls RI 22 Ap 13. 4: Earl Franklin Cerjanec. 5: Pembroke 29-33 (Langs & lits) AB (magna cum laude); Brown 34-35 (Educ); RI Col 32-55 (Educ); Simmons 59-60, MS 63 (LS); UWash summer 65 (LS); UColo summer 68 (Ed media). 6: Fr, Ger, Ital, Lat, Sp. 7: Tchr-libn Central Falls High Sch, Central Falls RI 33-43; Head libn US Naval Air Facilities, Quonset RI 43-47; Sub tchr various schs 47-57; Tchr Barrington High Sch, Barrington RI 57-59; Libn Dighton-Rehoboth Reg High Sch, Rehoboth Mass 60-66; Consul, curr serv (sch libs) R I Dept of Ed, 66-. 9: ALA; NESCHLA; NEA; AASchL; NELA; Mass Sch Libns Assn; Mass Tchrs Assn; RI Ed; RILA (Exec Bd 67-68); RISCHLA (chm Nom Com 68-69); RI a-v Assn; RI ASCD. 10: Pembroke Col Alumnae Assn (chm of class secs 62-63); Officer of local PTA groups; Phi Beta Kappa; Quota. 12: "Rhode Island Title II Handbook" (67); Ed "Rhode Island Media News" (66-). 14: Sch libs. 15: 22 Binford st, Central Falls RI 02863.

CERRATO, ANTHONY J. b Yonkers NY 13 Je 13. 4: Louise Damiano. 5: Fordham U 35 (Chem) BS; Fordham Law Sch 38 LLB. 6: Ital, Sp. 7: Family Court Judge, Westchester Co NY. 9: Amer Bar Assn; NY State Bar Assn. 10: Rotary Club; Pres, NY State Lib Trustees Found; Racquet Club; Westchester Country Club. 11: ALA Outstanding Lib Trustee Award, 50; Hon life mem NYLA, 52; Kiwanis Citizen of Year Award, 64; Velma K Moore Mem Award, 64. 15: 20 S Broadway, Yonkers NY 10701.

CERUTI, THERESA (REYNOLDS). b Cambridge Mass 21 My 15. 4: William Tracy Ceruti. 5: Vassar 32-36 (Hist) BA; Tobias Matthay Pianoforte Sch 36-38, 39 (Piano) Certif as Tchr; Pratt 60-62 MLS. 6: Fr, Ital. 7: Lib asst rare bk dept Boston Pub Lib 44-48; Ed asst Pantheon Books Inc, NYC summer 48; Ed asst Metropolitan Museum of Art, NYC 48-49; Free lance research, writing, ed wk, NYC 49-55; Membership co-ordinator Ethical Soc, NYC 55-60; Records analyst Tenneco Chemicals Inc, NYC 64-65; Coord member serv Amer Inst of Aeronautics & Astronautics 66; Records Analyst Breed, Abbott & Morgan 67-. 8: Grand juror NY County 54-64; House Com Bd of Trustees Paul Revere House, Boston 40-. 13: Yes. 14: Info retrieval, catlg, rare bks, fine bindings. 15: 52 East 72d st, NYC 10021.

CESARE, BURTON LEO. b Rochester NY 9 N 43. 4: Beth Ann Zabrosky. 5: Hobart Col 61-65 (Amer hist) BA; SUNY at Albany 65-66 (Hist) MA, 66-68 MLS. 6: Sp. 7: Stud lib asst Hist dept SUNY at Albany 66-67; Asst circ libn & circ libn E G Swem Lib William and Mary 68-. 9: ALA; VaLA. 10: Pi Gamma Mu. 14: Admin, pub serv. 15: 700 Conway dr apt 103, Williamsburg Va 23185.

CESARIO, MRS VIRGINIA NAILLE. b Baltimore 9 D 23. 5: Col of William & Mary 40-42; George Washington U 43-44; Col of William & Mary 44-45 (Philos) AB; Columbia 46-47 BLS. 6: Fr. 7: Clerk Seaboard Nat Bank, Norfolk Va 43-43; Sci Sp 4 Nat Bur of Standards, Wash DC 45-46; Circ asst City Col Lib (NYC) 47-64, Admin asst 64-68, Asst chief libn pub serv 68-. 9: ALA (various coms); -LAD; -ACRL; Ny LibClub; Lib Assn of CUNY; Ny Lib Club. 10: AAUP; Phi Beta Kappa; City Col Fac Com. 14: Circ, personnel, admin. 15: City Col Lib, Convent ave at 135 st, New York NY10031.

CETTA, MARJORIE (MONAGAN). b Waterbury Conn 20 Ap 22. 5: Trinity Col (Wash DC) 39-43 (Fr) BA; Columbia summer 45-48 BS in LS; UConn 48-59 (Educ) MA in Ed; UMinn summer 65 (NDEA). 6: Fr. 7: Lib asst Bronson Lib, Waterbury Conn 43-47; Libn UConn Waterbury Br 47; Lib tchr City of Waterbury 47- Instr So Conn State Col Dept of Lib Sci 67-68. 9: NEA; ConnSchLA; ConnEA. 10: Waterbury Tchrs Assn; Beta Phi Mu. 13: Yes. 14: Sch, ref. 15: 84 Euclid ave, Waterbury Ct 06710.

CHABOT, JULIETTE. b Montreal 24 Ja 02. 5: College Marguerite Bourgeoys (Montreal) BA; U Montreal Lic (Phil); McGill MLS; Inst Catholique (Paris) Diploma. 6: Fr, Eng, Ital, Lat. 7: Staff Montreal Pub Lib 30-44, Asst chief libn 44-65. 8: Del of the CanLA to attend a pub lib conf at UManchester (Eng) under the auspices of Unesco 48; Invited to participate in a conf held at the Lib Sch of the Inst Catholique of Paris, 65; Prof U Montreal Lib Sch 40-60. 9: CanLA; Assn canadienne des Bibliothecaires de langue francaise (pres 55-56, hon life mem). 12: "Vocabulaire technique des bibliothecaires"; "Vedettes matiere utilisees dans la redaction de Biblio", prelim ed; "Classification Fauteux" prelim ed; Comp "Bio-bibliographic des ecrivains canadiens"; "La Ville de Montreal et le probleme des bibliotheques publiques" (66). 14: Catlg, admin, bk sel. 15: 4245 rue de Lanaudiere, Montreal Can 34E.

CHACE, BEATRICE (MARGUERITE). b Hudson NY 21 Ag 11. 5: Simmons 31-34 (LS) BS; Columbia summers 41-44 (LS) MS. 7: Dir Sch Libs Hudson High Sch, Hudson NY 34-. 8: Consul to var libs in Columbia Co NY 34-. 9: ALA; NEA; NYLA (pres East Zone Sch Libns 49); NYState Tchrs Assn; Hudson-MohawkLA (charter mem); Hudson TA (pres 52, Exec Com 66-). 10: Bus & Prof Women's Club; Delta Kappa Gamma; YWCA; Columbia Co Humane Soc; Columbia Mem Hosp Women's Auxiliary; Hudson Fortnightly. 14: Sch libnship. 15: 6 Becraft ave, Hudson NY 12534.

CHADBOURN, ERIKA (SAMMETH). B Nuremberg Germany 21 Ja 15. 4: James H Chadbourn. 5: Cecilien-Gymnasium Ger 24-34 (Eng, Fr) Abitur; UDela 34-36 (Fr) BA; Drexel 36-37 BS in LS; Simmons 65-66 (Ref, Catlg); UDenver summer 68 (Archives adminis) Certif. 6: Ger, Fr. 7: Asst circ libn Middlebury Col 37-38; Asst to libn Hunterdon Co Lib, Flemington NJ 38-39; Asst catlgr Temple U Lib, Phila 39-40; Curator of ms Harvard Law Sch Lib 66-. 9: SAA; SLA. 10: Sierra Club; Appalachian Mt Club; Wilderness Soc; Mass Audubon Soc. 14: Modern ms collections. 15: 12 Blakeslee st, Cambridge Ma 02138.

CHADWELL, PATRICIA ANN. b Tulsa Okla 4 Ag 41. 5: Tex Womans U 58-62 (LS) BS, BA, 63-64 MLS; UTex (Arlington) 67. 6: Ger, Fr. 7: Page Pryor Pub Lib 54-58; Stud asst Brally Lib Tex Woman's U 59-62; Ref asst Ft Worth Pub Lib, Ft Worth Tex 62-63, Head, Southwest & Gen Dept 63-. 9: TexLA (sec-treas, Archives RT 68-69); SWLA. 10: Fort Worth Geneal Soc; Tex State Geneal Soc; Tarrant Co (Tex) Hist Soc. 14: Ref, readers adv, hist collections. 15: 2966 A McCart, Ft Worth Tx 76110.

CHADWICK, CATHERINE S(TRAHORN). b Spokane Wash 4 Ag 07. 4: Paul Chadwick. 5: U of Puget Sound 25-28 (Fr) BA; Wash State U (31); UCal(Berkeley) (33) (LS)BA, 34 Grad Certif. 6: Fr, Sp, Lat. 7: Tchr Hanford High Sch, Hanford Wash 28-30; Tchr Rockford High Sch, Rockford Wash 30-31; Tchr E Wenatchee Jr High Sch, Wenatchee Wash 31-33; Libn Taft Br Kern Co Lib, Taft Cal 49-55; Dir Lib Ser Mont State Lib 55-57; Ext libn Ariz Dept Lib Archives, Phoenix 57-61; Dir Ventura Co & City Lib, Ventura Cal 61-. 8: Consul & adv wk in Nev 57-58; Admin Libn Black Gold Coop Lib System 64-. 9: ALA; SLA; CalLA (pres 68); ArizLA; MontLA;PNLA; SWLA; Chm &/or mem State & Reg Coms. 10: PTA; AAUW; Soroptimist Club; MentalHealth Assn; Bus & Profess Women. 13: Yes. 14: Coop lib programs, lib devel, ext of serv. 15: PO Box 771, Ventura Ca 93001.

CHADWICK, KATHERINE BIDDLE. b Honolulu 1 Ap 26. 5: Bryn Mawr 45-47; Cornell U 48-50 (Fine Arts) BA; Columbia 62 (LS) MS. 7: Photo libn Associated Press, NYC 50-61; Ref libn Greenwich Pub Lib, GreenwichConn 62-69, Asst dir 69-. 9: ALA; ConnLA; Westchester LA. 14: Ref. 15: Old Redding rd,Weston Ct 06880.

CHADWICK, THORA (LIBBY). b Greenfield Mass 31 O 37. 4: Peter G Chadwick. 5: Wilson Col 55-59 (Pol sci) AB; Rutgers 64-67 (Lib serv) MLS. 6: Fr. 7: Research asst US

Govt, Wash DC & Frankfurt Germany 59-63; Ser clk Johns Hopkins U Lib 63-64; Libn trainee Newark Pub Lib, Newark NJ 64-66; Children's libn Metuchen Pub Lib, Metuchen NJ 67-. 9: ALA; AASchLA; NJLA. 10: Metuchen-Edison Racial Relations Coun. 14: Wk with child. 15: 17 Mayfield pl, Metuchen NJ 08840.

CHAFFIN, ANNE (MORTON). b Midway Ala 4 D 14. 4: Samuel M Chaffin. 5: St Petersburg Jr Col 32-33; Alabama Col 33-34; UAla 34-36 (LS, Eng) BS. 7: Sch libn Chilton Co High Sch, Clanton Ala 36-39; Sch libn Okeechobee High Sch, Okeechobee Fla 41-42; Expediter Cameron & Barkley Co, Tampa Fla 42-44; Dir Jr Red Cross, Tampa Fla 44-45; Libn Hq Third Air Force, Tampa Fla 45-46; Base libn MacDill AFB, Tampa Fla 46-52; Base libn Rhein-Main AFB, Frankfurt Germany 52-54; Area libn 7100 Air Base Gp, Wiesbaden Germany 54-55; Staff libn Hq 7100 Support Wg, Wiesbaden Germany 54-56; Bibliog Air U Lib, Maxwell AFB, Montgomery Ala 57-. 9: SLA; AlaLA; SELA. 14: Ref. 15: 578 Farmington rd, Montgomery Al 36109.

CHAFFIN, EMMA LeGRAND. b Mocksville NC 20 Ag 1898. 5: Trinity Col Durham NC 17-21 (Educ) AB; Columbia 42 (Nursing, LS) AM. 7: Tchr Elem & High Sch, NC 21-26; Stud & grad nurse Guilford Gen (NC) & Bellevue(NYC) 26-38; Libn Bellevue Sch of Nursing, NYC 38-45; Libn Watts Hosp Sch of Nursing,Durham NC 49-. 9: Charter member MedLA. 10: Amer Nurses Assn; Nat League for Nursing. 15: 1019 Iredell st, Durham NC 27705.

CHAIKIND, HANNAH (KREISWIRTH). b NYC 24 N 12. 4: Samuel Chaikind. 5: Hunter Col 30-34 (Eng) BA; Columbia 37-38 (Eng); So Conn State Col 61-63 (LS) MS. 7: Tchr Grover Cleveland High Sch, NYC 36-37; Tchr Flushing High Sch, NYC 37-38; Libn Hamden High Sch, Hamden Conn 63-. 9: ALA; ConnSchLA; Hamden EA. 15: 125 Dessa dr, Hamden Ct 06517.

CHAIT, WILLIAM. b NYC 5 D 15. 4: Beatrice Faigelman. 5: Brooklyn Col 31-34 (Hist) BA; Pratt 34-35 BSLS; Columbia 37-38 MSLS. 7: Page Brooklyn Pub Lib 31-34, Libn I and II 35-41; Br libn 41-45; Serv Command Libn 2nd Service Command, US Army Governors Island NY 45-46; Chief in-serv train & personnel control, milwaukee Pub Lib 46-48; Dir Kalamazoo Pub Lib 48-56; Dir Dayton & Montgomery Co Pub Lib, Dayton Ohio 56-. 8: Tchrs lib admin West Mich U spring 55, summer 56; Visiting lecturer UIll Grad Sch of Lib Sci, summer 64, 69; Bldg consul on many pub libs; vis lect, Kent State U Grad Sch LS, summer 67; chm Steering Com Ohio Lib Devel Plan 67-. 9: ALA (Coun 68-72); LAA; (chm Personnel Admin Sect 58-60); -PLA (pres 64-65); MichLA (pres 55-56); OhioLA (pres 64-65). 10: Beta Phi Mu; Dayton Discussion Club; Dayton City Beautiful Coun; Montgomery Co Hist Soc. 12: 'State-Wide Retirement Plans for Employees of Local Government Units' in "Retirement for Librarians" (51); "Survey of the Public Libraries of Asheville and Buncombe County, North Carolina" with Ruth Warncke (Ala 65); "Survey of the Public Libraries of Norwalk, Connecticut," with Robert S Are (Ala 66). 13: Yes. 14: Pub lib admin & bldgs. 15: Pub Lib, 215 E Third st, Dayton Oh 45402.

CHAKLOSH, CYNTHIA LEE (EATON). b Detroit 6 N 31. 4: Peter Chaklosh. 5: Mich State U 49-51; UMich 52-54 (Fine Arts) AB, 55-56 AMLS UMich 66-67 (Educ) AM. 7: Libn I Redford Twp, Wayne Co Mich 56-58; Head libn II Inkster Pub Lib, Wayne Co Mich 58-59; Head libn III River Rouge Pub Lib, Wayne Co Mich 59-61; Head libn III Wayne-Nankin Pub Lib, Wayne Co Mich 61-62; Head child serv Wayne Co Hdqts, Wayne Co Mich 62-66; Jr High Sch Libn Livonia Pub Schs (LivoniaMich) 68-. 9: ALA; MichASchL. 10: Pi Lambda Theta; Phi Kappa Phi. 13: Yes. 14: Child, pub serv. 15: 36028 Joy rd, Livonia Mi 48150.

CHALFANT, BARBARA L. b Vicksburg Miss 3 Mr 18. 5: All Saints' Col 36-37; Stephens Col 37-38 Assoc BA; LSU 38-40 BA; Peabody 40-41 BS in LS. 6: Fr. 7: Libn Rhea Co High Sch, Dayton Tenn 41-42; Libn High Sch, Yazoo City Miss 42-43; Libn High Sch, Biloxi M Bibliogr 50-. 9: SLA (Mem chm Ala Chap 63-65); AlaLA (sec-treas Col Univ & Spec Libs Sect 61). 13: Yes. 14: Ref, research. 15: 1923 Norman Bridge court, Montgomery Ala 36104.

CHALKER, MARY (FRANCIS). b Twillingate Nfld 15 Je 39. 5: Memorial UNewfoundland 56-57; Queen's U Kingston 57-58, 60-61 (Hist) BA; UToronto 61-62 BLS. 7: Circ & catlg MemorialU 62-64; Catlgr BalnelU, Lond Eng 64-66; Libn Canadian Dept of Fisheries, St John's Nfld 66-67; Hd of ser div Ontario Inst for Studies in Educ, Toronto 67-. 8: Set up a small fisheries lib 66-67. 9: CanLA; SLA. 14: Catlg, ser. 15: 55 Oakmount rd apt 1411, Toronto 9 Ont Can.

CHALKER, WILLIAM JENNINGS. b Jacksonville Fla 6 F 15. 5: UFla 34-37 (Educ) BAE; Peabody summers 47-50 BS in LS, 50-51 MS in LS. 6: Sp, Fr. 7: Tchr Span & Eng Taylor High Sch (Taylor Fla) 37-39; Private tutoring Span, Fr 39-41; Tech Sgt Armed Forces US Army Communications-Intelligence 41-45; Tchr Span, Eng Christ Sch (Arden NC) 46-50; Dir of lib NY State U Col (Fredonia) 51-60; Acquis libn jacksonvilleU 60-61; Dir of lib 61-. 9: ALA; SELA; FlaLA. 10: Torch Club. 11: Louis Shores Award. 14: Lib admin, acquis. 15: 2527-A Forbes st, Jacksonville Fl 32204.

CHALLMAN, JEAN (CARSON). b Oakland Cal 5 Ja 12. 4: Robert C Challman. 5: Stanford 29-33 (Psych) BA; Ohio State 35-36 (Social wk) MA; Vassar 45 (Family Living); UMinn 60-62 (LS) MA. 7: Social wker 35-44; Bkmob Anoka Co Lib, Spring Lake Park Minn 62-65; Libn Metropolitan State Jr Col (Minneapolis) 65-. 9: ALA; MinnLA. 10: AAUW; LWV; Pi Beta Phi; ACLU; Minn State Jr Col Fac Assn (pres libns Sect 69-70). 13: Yes. 15: 3915 Beard ave So, Minneapolis Mn 55410.

CHAMBERLAIN, CARROLL GAY. b Ovid Mich 21 F 45. 5: UMich 62-66 (Hist) BA, 66-67 AMLS. 6: Fr. 7: Libn Ovid-Elsie Schs, Ovid Mich summers 64, 66, 67; Libn Amer Internatl sch, The Hague Holland 67-69; Acquis libn Rutgers Law Lib 69-. 8: Represented Amer Intl Schs of The Hague at Intl Bk Fair, Frankfurt 67, 68. 9: ALA. 10: Delta Gamma. 14: Ref, ya wk. 15: 2346 N Hollister rd, Ovid Mi 48866.

CHAMBERLAIN, DOROTHY E(LIZABETH). b Chicago 10 Jl 06. 5: Agnes Scott 23-27 (Eng) AB; Columbia 27-28 (LS) BS. 6: Fr. 7: In chg vertical files Irving Trust Co, NYC 28-30; Catlgr Columbia U Libs 30-44; Head tech processes Grosvenor Lib, Buffalo NY 44-45; Head law catlg sect Columbia U Lib 45-. 9: ALA; AALL; NY Tech Servs Libns; Law Lib Assn of Greater NY; NY Lib Club. 10: Women's Faculty Clubof Columbia U (sec 65-68). 12: Ed "Foreign Law Classification in the ColumbiaUniversity Law Library" by A Arthur Schiller. 14: Catlg. 15: Law Lib 304 Law Sch Bldg,Columbia U, New York NY 10027.

CHAMBERLAIN, LAWRENCE CARLETON. b St Louis 17 Ap 21. 5: St Louis U 38-43 (Lat) AB, 43-45, 47-49 (L AT) AM; Catholic U 57-62 MSLS. 7: Instr Rockhurst High Sch, Kansas City Mo 46-47; Br asst St Louis Pub Lib 47-48; Documents libn St Louis U 48-56; Catlg dept asst Georgetown U 56-62, catlgr 62-64, spec collections catlgr 64-. 9: CathLA (Washington-Maryland Unit). 14: Rare bks, catlg. 15: Georgetown U Lib, 37th & O sts NW, Wash DC 20007.

CHAMBERLAIN, MIRIAM (JONES). b Anderson SC 28 Ja 30. 5: Wesleyan Col (Macon Ga) 47-49; UNC(Chapel Hill) 49-51 (Amer Hist) AB; Emory 51-52 M Libnship. 7: Ref asst Duke U Lib 53-56; Ref asst UFla Lib 56-58; Documents libn Emory U 58-66; Dir bank info ctr C & S Nat Bank, Atlanta 66-68; Chief bibliog(r) Ga State Col Lib (Atlanta) 68-. 9: ALA; SLA (sec Ga Chap 62-64); SELA; GaLA. 14: Ref, documents. 15: 1549 Farnell ct apt 1, Decatur Ga 30033.

CHAMBERLIN, EDGAR WILBUR. b Mishawaka Ind. 4: Edith Martens Chamberlin. 5: IndU 42-43, 46-49 (Hist) BS in Ed; UIll 50-52 MS in LS. 7: Sgt US Army Air Corps, Eng 43-45; Asst ref dept Pub Lib, Indianapolis 49-50; Asst bus, tech dept Pub Lib, Kan City Mo 52-54; Head bus & tech dept Pub Lib, S Bend Ind 55-59; Asst dir Ind State Lib 60-67; Exec dir Kaskaskia Lib Sys Belleville Ill 67-. 8: Exec dir, Nat Lib Week, Ind 62. 9: ALA; IllLA. 12: Ed Focus on indiana Libraries" (59 & 60); Ed "Library Occurrent" (63-). 13: Yes. 14: Admin (personnel), ref (bus & tech). 15: 1230 N 17th st, Belleville Il 62221.

CHAMBERLIN, RICHARD RALPH. b Great Barrington Mass 8 S 35. 5: Northeastern U 53-58 (Hist) BA; Mich State U 61-62 (Hist) MA; UDenver 62-63 (LS) MA. 7: Circ-ref libn Springfield Col 63; Documents libn Wellesley Col 63-67; Ref Libn Ind U of Penn, 67-. 10: YMCA; Nat Grange. 13: Yes. 14: Docs, maps & atlases. 15: RD #1, Indiana Pa 15701.

CHAMBERLIN, VIRGINIA GRACE (SWIFT). b Minneapolis Minn 20 S 09. 4: David Holmes Chamberlin. 5: Valley City State Tchrs 26 (Ed); UMinn 31 (Eng, LS) BS. 7: Station Libn Minneapolis Pub Lib 37-41; Pub Lib, Burbank Cal: Libn I 49-52, Libn II 52-53, Supv Libn 53-. 9: ALA; CalLA. 10: Altrusa Club; Alpha Omicron Pi; Burbank Coordinating Coun; Valley Univers Women; Boy Scouts of America, Merit Badge Counselor. 14: Adult serv, br admin, a-v. 15: 3315 W Verdugo ave, Burbank Ca 91505.

CHAMBERS, BEATRICE. b NYC 28 D 25. 5: Taylor U 45-49 (Eng Lit) AB; Pratt 51-52 MSLS. 7: Clerical asst NYPL

49-50; Child libn NY Pub Lib 52-57; Child libn Mineola Mem Lib, Mineola NY 57-63; Libn ref & catlg San Diego Co Lib, San Diego 63-. 9: CalLA. 14: Catlg, ref. 15: 4186 Madison ave, San Diego Ca 92116.

CHAMBERS, ELIZABETH. b New Cumberland WVa 24 Jl 16. 5: UCincinnati 35-39 (Eng) BA; UIll (Urbana) 40-41, 59-60 BS in LS, MS; Berkeley (Cal) Baptist Divinity Sch 53-54 (Rel Educ) MA. 6: Fr, Hiligaynon. 7: Gen catlgr UCincinnati 41-43; Catlgr Mich State Col (East Lansing) 43-44; Headcatlgr ULouisville 45-51; Jr libn Wash State Col 51-52; Dir of libs CentralPhilippine U 54-. 9: ALA (chm Jr Mem RT); PhilippineLA; ATheolLA; Ohio Valley RegGroup of Catlgrs (chm); West Visayas LA (chm). 10: YWCA. 11: Phi Beta Kappa. 13: Yes. 14: Catlg, reading guidance. 15: Central Philippine Univ, Iloilo Philippines K-421.

CHAMBERS, FRANCES (BANKO). b Wilkes-Barre Penn 23 My 41. 5: Col Misericordia 58-62 (Eng) AB; Rutgers 63-65 MLS; Hunter Col 66-69 (Eng) MA. 6: Fr. 7: Asst to libn City Col (NY) 65-. 10: Mod Lang Assn; William Morris Soc. 14: Acquis, bibliog, rare bks. 15: 99 Chrystie st, New York NY 10002.

CHAMBERS, FREDA C(ONRAD). b Wayland Iowa 15 F 08. 5: Coe Col 25-29 (Com, Finance) BA; UDenver 35-36 BS in LS; Drexel 52 (LS). 6: Fr, Ger. 7: Gen asst Cedar Rapids Pub Lib, Cedar Rapids Iowa 31-35; 1st asst Albuquerque Pub Lib, Albuquerque NM 36-37, Libn 37-44; Libn St Mary's Hosp Sch of Nursing & Hosp Med Lib, Phila 50-55; Catlg libn Coe Col Stewart Mem Lib 55-63; Libn Roswell Pub Lib, Roswell NM 63-65; Head catlgr Riverside Pub Lib, Riverside Cal 65-. 8: Asst Liaison Libn, Eighth Serv Command for NM 42-44. 9: ALA; NMLA(treas 36-37, pres 40-41); SWLA (sec 38-40); CalLA. 10: AAUW. 15: 10351-North Lynn cir apt L, Mira Loma Ca 91752.

CHAMBERS, MARCY. b Pittsburgh Penn 30 Ja 41. 5: George Washington U 59-63 (Art Hist) BA; UPittsburgh 65-66 MLS. 6: Fr. 7: Asst Reference Libn Toronto Pub Lib 66-67; Asst Reference Libn U Rochester Lib 67-. 9: ALA. 10: Beta Phi Mu. 14: Ref, art libs. 15: 64H Clintwood ct, Rochester NY 14620.

CHAMBERS, MOREAU B(ROWNE) C(ONGLETON). b Winchester Ky 24 My 09. 4: Ruth Hanners. 5: Miss Col 28-32 (Hist) BA; Duke summers 39, 40, 42 (Hist) MA; CatholicU 66-68 MSLS; AmerU 68 (Mod Archives Admin) Certif. 6: Fr, Ger, Sp. 7: Archaelogical hist & archival staff Miss Dept Archives & Hist, Jackson 34-42; Staff NYC Pub Lib 42-43; Recognition off & naval aviation histn (Lt Comdr) USN Res 43-46; Diplomatic histn US Dept of State, Wash DC 46-53; Supv Colonial Williamsburg's (Va) Archaelogical Lab 54-57; Histn Army Transportation & Engring Command, Ft Eustis Va 57-62; Hist lecturer William & Mary ext Hampton Va 60-61; Histn Defense Gen Supply Ctr, Richmond Va 62-66; Archivist CatholicU 67-. 8: Mem Smithsonian Inst expedition to Bering Sea reg of Alaska excavating Eskimos Sites on St Lawrence Is 31; Asst archaeologist CWA program in Shiloh Nat Military Pk, Tenn 33-34; Maintained archival liaison (Dept of State Nat Archives) 47-49. 10: Archaelogical Soc of Va (V-pres & pres 55-59); Amer Mil Inst; Layreader Episcopal Ch. 12: Bibliog study of Miss imprints during Reconstruction Era. 13: Yes. 14: Archival serv, bibliog research. 15: 5206 Devonshire rd, Richmond Va 23225.

CHAMBERS, NORMA M. b Atlanta 30 Jl 30. 5: Ga State Col of Bus Admin 47-50, 55 (Psy); Emory summer 55 (Med Libnship). 6: Sp. 7: USPHS, Communicable Disease Center Atlanta: Lib asst 50-56, Libn 56-58, Acquis libn 58-. 9: MedLA; SLA; GaLA. 14: Ref, acquis. 15: Natl Commun Disease Center Lib, Atlanta Ga 30333.

CHAMBERS, ORVILLE THOMAS. b Middleport Ohio 16 Ja 16. 4: Marion Knapp. 5: Ohio U 40 (Eng) BS in Ed, 47 (Eng) MA; Peabody 50 BSLS; Emory 55 (Med Libnship) MedLA Grade I Certif. 7: Instr of instrumental music, Meigs Co Ohio 40-42; US Army 42-45; Instr in Eng Ohio U 47-49; US Army 50-52; Libn Air U Lib Med Br 52-65; Asst to the chief for ref activities, utilization & distrib sect PHS A-V facility Communicable Disease Center 65-; Indexer Air U Lib 67- . 9: MedLA; SLA (sec-treas 64-65 Ala Chapt); SELA; AlaLA (sec 59-60, pres-elect 65). 10: Amer Fedn of Musicians; Toastmasters Internat. 12: "Union List of Health Science Periodicals Available in Selected Libraries in the State of Alabama" (60). 13: Yes. 14: Ref (med). 15: 5701 Carriage Hills dr, Montgomery Al 36111.

CHAMBLEE, OLIVIA. b Weir Miss 25 Ag 31. 5: Miss State Col for Women 55-57 (LS) BS; UAla summers 57, 59, 63; Emory summers 60, 61. 6: Fr. 7: Mail Off Ridgecrest Baptist Assembly, Ridgecrest NC summer 54; Libn Truett-McConnell Col 58-64; Libn Lilburn High Sch, Lilburn Ga 64-65; Libn Lilburn Elem Sch, Lilburn ga 65-68; Libn Epworth Elem Sch, Epworth Ga 68-. 9: NEA; GaEA; GaLA. 10: PTA. 14: Ref, child lit. 15: 122 N Jefferson circle, Oak Ridge Tn 37825.

CHAMPE, (ELIZABETH). b Toledo Ohio. 5: UMich. 7: Research libn Fuller & Smith & Ross Inc 53-. 9: Amer Marketing Assn; ASIS; SLA. 10: Bus Economists Club; Jr League of Amer. 15: 13800 Fairhill rd, Shaker Heights Oh 44120.

CHAMPION, JERRYE (YVONNE) GRAY. b Prentiss Miss 23 Ag 40. 4: Freddie M Champion. 5: Tougaloo Col 57-61 (Eng) BA; UOkla 63-65 MLS. 6: Ger. 7: Tchr-libn Webster High Sch, Eupora Miss 61-62; Tchr Columbus Pub Schs, Columbus Miss 62-63; Ref libn Tougaloo Col 64-65; Ref libn Phoenix Pub Lib, 65-66; Pub Lib Consul Ariz State Lib Dept, Phoenix 66-67; Hd pub serv ScottsdalePub Lib, Scottsdale Ariz 67-. 8: Reader's adv wk for disadvantaged child, Columbus Miss 62; Conducted a weekly story hour for child, Tougaloo Col 64-65 Lib consul, State of Ariz. 9: ALA; Ariz Statela& swla. 10: Delta Sigma Theta; YWCA. 14: Ref, ya serv. 15: 10601 N 39th st,Phoenix Az 85028.

CHAMPLAIN, CONSTANCE JOYCE (KELLY). b Perth Amboy NJ 2 Mr 42. 4: John L Champlin. 5: OhioU 59-61 (Educ); Syracuse 61-63 (Educ) BS; Peabody Col 67-69 MLS, EdS. 7: Tchr; Wetzel Road Sch, Liverpoo l NY 63-64, US Peace Corps, Philippines 64-66, Lake St Sch, Spencer Mass 66-67; Libn (circ) pub lib, Nashville 67-68; Libn Country Music Hall of Fame, Nashville summer 68; Libn (ref) UT enn (Nashville) 68-69, Instr bks for child 69; Libn Nashville Pub Schs 69-. 9: ALA; Assn for Childhood Educ Intl; T ennEA; TennLA; Metropolitan NashvilleEA; Middle TennLA; Middle TennEA. 10: Beta Phi Mu. 13: Yes. 14: Tchg, child bks & serv, libs & lib educ in developing countries. 15: 2144 Capers ave, Nashville Tn 37212.

CHAN, ALMA (YU CHING LEE). b Hong Kong China 23 N 39. 4: Ping Kuen Chan. 5: Chung Chi col 58-62 (Geog) Diploma; ChineseU of Hong Kong 65-66 (Geog) BS; UMich 68 AMLS. 6: Chinese. 7: Thcr, Hong Kong: St Gabriel Col 62-63, Bernard Col 63-66; Lib asst Simon Fraser U 66; Lib asst UToronto 66-67; Libn (Staff) Detroit Pub Lib. 9: ALA. 10: UMich Lib Sci Alumni. 14: Catlg. 15: 5201 Woodward ave, Cat Dept Detroit Pub Lib, detroit Mi 48202.

CHANCEY, GENEVA CLARICE. b Ducktown Tenn 11 0 17. 5: Carson Newman Col 35-37; Peabody 37-39 (Eng) BS, summers 40-42 BS in LS. 7: US Army Major WAAC, WAC 42-46; USVA; Chief tech processes Richmond Va 46-47, Asst chief libn, Richmond Va 48-49, Chief Libn Kecoughtan Va 49-55 Chief Lib US Naval Train Ctr Bainbridge Md 56; US Post Office Dept, Wash DC; Head processing sect 56-57, Head ref sect 57-64, Libn 64-. 9: SLA. 14: Admin, ref. 15: 4000 Tunlaw rd, Wash DC 20007.

CHANDLER, ANN ROEBUCK. b Nacogdoches Tex 29 Ag 41. 4: Freddy Wayne Chandler. 5: Stephen F Austin State Col 59-62 (Elem Educ) BS; E Tex StateU 67-68 MS in LS. 7: Circ asst Stephen F Austin State Col 62-67, Curriculum & a-v libn 68-. 9: TexLA; SELA. 10: AAUW. 14: Curriculum, a-v. 15: 213 Crestwood, Nacogdoches Tx 75961.

CHANDLER, BERTHA (KRONE). b Pittsfield Mass 13 Ap 13. 5: Simmons 30-34 (LS) SB; Gorham State Col summer 62; UMe summer 65; U of State NY (Oswego) 66-. 6: Fr, Lat, Ger, Sp. 7: Libn Pub Lib, Monson Mass 36-37; Acquis Dept Harvard U Baker Lib 37-3 gen asst to libn pub lib, St amford Conn 38-40; Asst libn Patchogue Pub Lib, Patchogue NY 40-41; Med libn Pownal State Hosp, Pownal Me 59-61; Circ libn Bates Col 61-62; Libn & A-V Supv Gray-New Gloucester High S ch & Sch Admin Dist #15, Gray Me 62-. 8: Trustee, New Gloucester Pub Lib. 9: ALA (mem com);-AASchL; MeSchLA (treas); NESchLA (Standards Com). 10: Me Ext Serv; Amer Forestry Assn. 14: Sch, pub & col libs, media centers. 15: Gray-New Gloucester High Sch, Gray Me 04039.

CHANDLER, JAMES G(REENOUGH). b Dedham Mass 8 My 17. 4: Barbara Dunlap. 5: UHawaii 38-40 (Eng); Pomona Col 40-42 (Eng) AB; Catholic U 47-50 BSLS. 7: Asst in Music Lib & circ dept UHawaii 39; Ref asst Coordinator of Info & Offof Strategic Serv, Wash DC 42-45; Various lib & liaison positions Dept of State,Wash DC 46-52; Ref libn & chief Ref lib CIA, Wash DC 52-67; Asst dir for reader servumd 67-. 9:

ALA. 10: Beta Phi Mu; AAUP; Phi Beta Kappa; Appalachian Mountain Club. 12: Comp "Checklist of Periodicals Published in the Republic of Ireland" (52); Ed "Behind the Bamboo Curtain" by A.M. Dunlap (55). 14: Ref, lib admin, interlib serv, undergrad libs. 15: 4835 Stillwell ave, Alexandria Va 22309.

CHANDLER, PORTIA (SPENCER). b LaFayette Ala 19 Je 24. 5: Spelman Col 42-46 (Eng) BA; Atlanta U Sch of Lib Serv (Pub LS) 54-56. 7: WAC Disbursing specialist, US & Ger 49-53; Libn Ohen Shalom Synagogue, Chester Penn 58-59; Cat libn East Penn Psych Inst-Prof Lib, Phila Penn 60-65; Br libn J Oewis Crozer, Chester Penn 65; Ref libn Cheyney State Col 65-66; Libn Jr High Sch Sch Dist of City of Chester Penn 66-. 9: ALA; NEA; PennStateEA; ChesterEA. 14: Catlg, reader's adv. 15: 2001 W 9th st, Chester Pa 19013.

CHANDLER, SAMUEL C. b Idaho Falls Ida 4 My 19. 4: Ruth Darlene Stowell. 5: Ricks Col 38-40 (Ed) AA, Brigham Young 46-47 (Eng) BA, 49-50 (Eng lit) MA; George Peabody Col 50-51 MALS. 7: Circ libn Idaho State Col 51-52; Sci libn Brigham Young 52-58; City libn Daly City Pub Lib, Daly City Cal 58-. 9: ALA; CalLA. 10: Pub Lib Exec of Central Cal; Toastmasters Internat. 14: Lib admin. 15: Daly City Pub lib, 275 Southgate ave, Daly City Ca 94015.

CHANDLER, THOMAS W JR. b Carrollton Ga 12 N 24. 5: W Ga Col 42-43, 46-47 (Liberal Arts) Jr Col Certif; Emory 47-49 (Fine Arts) BA; Emory 49-51 M of Libnship. 7: US Army Med Det, US-Europe 43-45; Order libn, Head of acquis dept of lib Ga State Col 51-61; Head Libn Oglethorpe Col 61-. 8: Consul for Org Lib Materials, So Assn, Atlanta summer 63; Consul for Lib Bldg etc Gordon Mil Col 65. 9: GaLA. 10: Bonsai Soc. 14: Admin, spec collections, ref, acquis. 15: 2873 Hermance dr ne, Atlanta Ga 30319.

CHANDONNET, LUCILLE M. b Manchester NH 24 My 02. 5: Simmons 20-24 (LS) BS; UPoitiers (France) summer 25. 6: Fr. 7: Child libn People's Lib, Newport RI 25-29; City Lib, Manchester NH; Gen asst 29-30, Bk sel & order libn 30-, Asst city libn 59-; Act libn 66; Asst lib dir 68-. 8: Consul Library Guild, Notre Dame Col. 9: ALA; NELA (past sec); NHLA (2nd v-pres 67-68); NELA. 10: Simmons Club of NH; Manchester Col Women's Club; Manchester Hist Assn; Inst of Arts & Scis; Friend of the Currier Art Gallery. 14: Adult bk sel. 15: City Lib, 405 Pine st, Manchester NH 03104.

CHANEY, SUZANNE FLORENCE. b Spokane Wash 3 D 19. 5: UOre 37-42 (Hist) BA; UWis 47-48 BLS; Wash State U 54-58 (Pol Sci) MAPS. 6: Fr. 7: Aircraft communicator CAA, Dillon Mont & Redmond Ore 42-46; Documents libn UIda 48-51; Libn I Wash State U Lib 51-56, Libn II 56-61, Libn III 61-67; Collections Libn UNB 67-. 9: ALA; CanLA; ASPA; PPA; PNLA; WashLA. 10: CFUW. 12: 'Grants in Aid and Public Library Service' in "Public Libraries of the Pacific Northwest." 14: Documents, ref, col dev. 15: 24-15C Waggoners Lane, Fredericton NB Canada.

CHANG, BYRON P. b Fukien Rep of China 17 O 26. 4: Pi-hua Chi. 5: Nat TaiwanU 53 (Hist) BA; Villanova 65 MS in LS. 6: Chinese. 7: Tchr Provincial Chien-kuo Sch, taipei Taiwan 53-64; Acquis asst ColumbiaU 66-67; Asst libn SUNY (Oneonta) 67-68; Libn III MichU (Ann Arbor) 68-. 9: ALA. 12: "Oversea Chinese in India" (58). 13: Yes. 14: Catlg, ref. 15: 314 E Washington, Ann Arbor Mi 48108.

CHANG, FREDERICK (YIU TUNG). b Hong Kong 27 F 37. 5: Chu Hai Col 58-62 (Educ) BA; UOttawa 63-64 BLS. 64-65, summer 66 (Educ) Med; Kan State Tchrs Col 67-68 MSLS. 6: Chinese, Japanese. 7: Tchr Loyal Sec Sch, Hong Kong 62; Ref libn Mt Allison U (Can) 65-67; Curriculum & ref libn East Wash State Col, 68-. 9: CanLA; Wash Sate LA. 14: Ref. 15: East Washington State Col Lib, Cheney Wa 99004.

CHANG, HENRY CHUNG-LIEN. b Canton China 24 Jl 41. 4: Marjorie Li. 5: Nat Chengchi U 58-62 (Sociol) LLB; Summer Inst in Amer Studies 63 Amer Studies Certif; UMo (Columbia) 64-65 (Sociol) MA; UMinn (Minneapolis) 67-68 MALS. 6: Chinese, Japanese, Tibetan lang, fr. 7: 2nd Lt Chinese Army. Taipei 62-63; Stud asst UMo Lib (Columbia) 65; Lib asst braille Inst Lib, Los Angeles 65-67; Ref libn govt docs Wilson Lib UMinn (Minneapolis) 68-. 8: Chm Nat Youth Congress, Taipei China 61-62. 9: ALA; Amer Soc Assn. 10: YMCA; Minn Alumni. 13: Yes. 14: Documentation, lib research. 15: 1003 19th ave NE, Minneapolis Mn 55455.

CHANG, ISABELLE (CHIN). b Boston 20 F 24. 4: Dr Min Chuch Chang. 5: Simmons 42-46 BSLS; Yale 46-47 (Oriental Studies); Worcester State Tchrs 64 (Schl Lib Admin); Clark U 65-67 (Educ) AM; State Col at Bridgewater 68. 6: Chinese, Fr, Lat, Sp, Ital. 7: Page Boston Pub Lib summer 43; Gen asst Yale Med Lib 45; Catlgr Yale U Lib 46-48; Lib dir Shrewsbury Free Pub Lib, Shrewsbury Mass 59-64; Sch Libn Shrewsbury Jr-Sr High Sch, Shrewsbury Mass 64-. 9: ALA; NELA; MassLA (sec-treas Young Adult Div 63-64). 10: Library Trustee of Shrewsbury Pub Lib 65; Bay Path Club (Central Mass); Womens Club; PTA. 11: Chandler Award for distinctive literary writing 65. 12: Whats Cooking at Changs (59); Chinese Cooking Made Easy (69); Chinese Fairy Takes (65); Tales From Old China (69). 13: Yes. 14: Bk sel, admin. 15: 15 Fiske, Shrewsbury Ma 01541.

CHANG, L EO. b Nanking China 7 O 27. 4: Margarita Cheng. 5: U of Nanking 46-49 (Pol Sci); Duquesne U 50-51 (Pol Sci) BA; UPittsburgh 51-53 (Hist) M Litt; Carnegie 53-54 MLS. 6: Chinese. 7: Ref asst Pub Lib of Youngstown & Mahoning Co Ohio 54-61, Head Ref Dept 61-66; Doc ref libn Earlham Col, Richmond Ind 66-. 14: Ref. 15: 648 Northwood dr, Richmond In 47374.

CHANG, LUCY (GI) (DING). b China 2 Ap 13. 4: Chang Kuei-yung. 5: UShanghai 28-32 (Ed, Eng) BA; UWash 59-60 MSLS. 6: French, German, Japanese, Chinese. 7: Instr in Eng, Nat Taiwan U, Taipei Taiwan 54-57; Asst catlg libn VPI 60-61; Catlg libn Wm & Mary Lib 61-62; Catlg libn Loyola U Chicago 62-63; Assoc libn Nat Central Lib, Taipei Taiwan 63-64; Prof of Eng Nat Cheng-Chi U & Col of Chinese Culture, Taipei Taiwan 63-65; Asst law libn Loyola U Sch of Law Chicago 66-67; Ser libn Ida State U Lib 67-68; Catlg libn U Richmond 68-. 9: ALA; VaLA. 14: Catlg, bibliog. 15: 104 W Franklin st, Richmond Va 23220.

CHANIN, MRS LEAH F. b Galveston Tex 29 N 29. 4: Louis Chanin. 5: Stephens Col 46-48 (Econ) AA; So Methodist U 48-50 (Econ, Sp)BA; Mercer U 50-54 LLB. 6: Sp. 7: Attorney at Law Private Practice, Macon Ga 58-63; Law libn & instr of law, Mercer U Law Sch 64-. 9: ABA; AALL (pres-elect SE chap); State Bar of Ga; Macon Legal Aid Soc (pres-elect); Editorial Bd Law Library Jour. 10: Hadassah; Macon Bar Assn (sec 59-62, publ rel chm 64-66). 11: Woman of Year, Hadassah. 12: Ed Bd "Law Library Journal". 13: Yes. 14: Legal bibliog. 15: Walter F George Sch of Law Mercer U, Macon Ga 31207.

CHANKALIAN, CYNTHIA. b Jersey City NJ 16 O 46. 5: Moravian Col 64-68 (Hist) BA; Columbia 68-69 MS. 10: Phi Alpha Theta. 15: 161 Moore ave, Leonia NJ 07605.

CHANOVE, BARBARA L (FAGAN). b Lexington Ky 13 Ap 29. 4: Wilson E Chanove. 5: UKy 47-51 (LS) AB. 6: Fr. 7: Catlgr UKy 51-53; Catlgr Lexington Pub Lib, Lexington Ky 58-63; Libn in Art & Music Dept Cincinnati Pub Lib 63-. 9: ALA; KyLA; OhioLA; Lexington Libns Assn. 14: Catlg. 15: 10941 Tangleberry ct, Cincinnati Oh 44240.

CHAO, THERESA MEI-FONG. b Shanghai 27 Ag 42. 4: Chao Henry Hua. 5: Nat Chengchi 60-64 (West Lit) BH; UOkla 65-67 MLS. 6: Chinese. 7: Libn Research & Devel Lib Consolidated Papers Inc 67-. 9: ALA. 14: Ref, lib automation. 15: PO Box 544, Wisconsin Rapids Wi 54494.

CHAPEL, DOROTHY JEAN (GOYNES). b Hope Ark 24 Ag 19. 4: Dewey E Chapel. 5: Henderson State Tchrs Col 46 (Elem Educ) BA; E Tex State Tchrs Col 52 (Educ) MS; Tex Woman's U 65 MLS; UPittsburgh 68 (New media lib inst). 6: Sp. 7: Tchr Bismarck High Sch, Bismarck Ark 46-50, Libn 50-61; Libn Hot Springs High Sch, Hot Springs Ark 61-63; Libn Arkadelphia High Sch, Arkadelphia Ark 63-64; Dept chm and assoc prof of lib sci Ouachita Baptist U 64-. 9: ALA; NEA; ARKEA; SWLA; AAHE. 10: Alpha Delta Kappa. 14: Tchg lib sci, lib educ. 15: 221 N 12th , Arkadelphia Ark 71924.

CHAPIN, RICHARD E. b Danville Ill 29 Ap 25. 4: Eleanor Lang. 5: Wabash Col 43-48 (Econ) AB; UIll 48-49 MLS, 50-55 (Mass Communications) PhD. 7: Lt (jg) US Navy 43-46; Ref asst Fla State U 49-50; Circ asst UIll (Urbana) 50-53; Asst dir-Sch of Lib Sci UOkla 53-55; Assoc Libn Mich State U 55-59, Dir of Libs 59-. 8: Visiting Prof, UIll, 57; Consul Mich State U-Vietnam 58; Field reader US Off of Educ 59-60 Consul US Dept of Ag 62, US Dept of Comm 63, Kellogg Fdn 66-67, Educom 68. 9: ALA (chm Copyright Com 60-63, chm Nom Com 68-69); -ACRL (chm Univ Libs Sec [illegible]); MichLA (treas 62-63, pres 66-67). 10: Lansing Rotary Club; E Lansing Human Rel Com. 12: "Mass Communications: A Statistical Analysis" (57). 13: Yes. 14: Admin, mgt, bldg. 15: Mich State Univ Lib, E Lansing Mi 48823.

CHAPIN, RUTH T(RIMBLE). b Greensburg Penn 10 Jl 02. 5: UPittsburgh 21-25 (Eng) AB, 28-32 (Zool) MS. 6: Fr. 7: Tchr & libn Confluence (Penn) High Sch 25-27; Sec & asst curator Carnegie Mus Bird Dept, Pittsburgh Penn 27-40; Controller's off ColumbiaU 41-53; Research assoc in ornithology IRSAC, Belgian Congo 53-58; Lib asst & catlgr Amer Mus Nat Hist, NY 58-. 8: Bibliog research & ed "Birds of Western Pennsylvania," by W E Clyde Todd; Bibliog research for "Birds of Labrador" by Todd. 10: Pi Beta Phi; Amer Ornithologists Union; Soc of Woman Geographers; Linnaean Soc of NY. 13: Yes. 14: Catlg, ref. 15: 419 W 119 st 9E, New York NY 10027.

CHAPMAN, DOROTHY (HILTON). b Victoria Tex 4 S 34. 4: Warren Adlee Chapman. 5: Tuskegee Inst 53-58 9eng, Soc Studies) BS; Carnegie 58-60 MLS. 6: Fr. 7: Asst libn Richard B Harrison Pub Lib, Raleigh NC 60-61; Asst libn St Augustine's Col 61-. 9: ALA; NCLA. 14: Catlg. 15: 833 Coleman, Raleigh NC 27610.

CHAPMAN, DWIGHT L(ESLIE). b Casper Wyo 8 S 30. 4: Opal (Miller) Chapman. 5: No Ida Col of Educ 48-51; Wash State U 51-52 (Psych) BS; UMich 53-60 AMLS, MA (Educ). 7: Lib asst Wash State U Lib 52-53; Lib serv Fellow Museums Lib UMich 53-55, divlibn Museums Lib 55-60; Asst libn Amundsen-Mayfair br 60-62, Libn Amundsen-Mayfairbr 63-. 8: Libn (part-time basis) Liberal Arts Col, of the Jewish Univ of Amer Skokie Ill 62- Mem, Lib Commsn, Village of Glendale Heights Ill. 9: ALA-ACRL (JrCol Sect; Standards & Criteria Com 60-66). 10: Village Bd of Trustees, Glendale Heights Ill 63-65. 13: Yes. 14: A-V materials, admin, recordings,bldg planning. 15: 4626 N Knox ave, Chicago Il 60630.

CHAPMAN, EDWARD ARNOLD. b Shelbyville Ind 24 Mr 06. 4: Mary Alice Moore. 5: UMich 24-30 (Engnr) BSE(ME), 33-35 MLS. 7: Asst libn Ind State Lib 36-38; Dir lib asst program-WPA, Wash DC 38-42; Asst dir div program & review-War Pub Serv, Wash DC 42; Exec asst to asst commissioner Fed Wks Agency, Wash DC 42-43; Chief copyright admin sect US Office Alien Property Custodian, Wash DC 43-45; Asst mgr & sec bd of dir, J W Edwards Co, Ann Arbor Mich 45-46; Dir of libs Rensselaer Polytech Inst 46-. 8: Consultantships; Howard U Engnr & arch lib 53; Franklin Inst Lib 57; Mohawk Valley Commun Col Lib 59; Watervliet Arsenal Tech Info Serv 63; Middle States Assn, Lib Surveyor on call var insts 57-. 9: ALA; SLA; ASIS; Amer Soc for Engng E duc; NYLA; Hudson-Mohawk LA. 10: Troy Boys Club; Kiwanis; AAUP; Troy Pub Lib Bd dirs. 13: Yes. 14: Admin. 15: Rensselae r Polytechnic Inst, Troy NY 12181.

CHAPMAN, ELLEN L(AWRENCE). b Long Beach Cal 7 S 42. 4: Ronald Fettes. 5: UNM 60-64 (Sp, Portu) BA; UHawaii 67-68 MLS. 6: Sp, Portu, Fr. 7: Vol US Peace Corps, Brazil 64-66; Lib intern US Dept of Housing & Urban Development, Wash DC 68-. 10: Delta Gamma; Beta Phi Mu. 14: Ref, bibliog. 15: 1778 Halekoa dr, Honolulu Hi 96821.

CHAPMAN, GEOFFREY LEIGH. b Sydney NSW Australia 6 S 37. 4: Margaret Kennedy. 5: USydney Australia 54-58 (Lat) BA; UBritish-Columbia 65-66 BLS. 6: Fr, Lat. 7: Tchr Narrabri High Sch, NSW Australia 58-62; Tchr Nakusp Secondary Sch, BC Can 63-65; Chief Libn Loyalist Collegiate & Vocational Inst, Kingston Ont 66-68; Visiting Lecturer UBritish Columbia, Vancouver Can 67; Asst Prof UMantoba, Columbia Winnipeg 68-. 9: ALA; -AASchL; CanLA; CanSchLA; Lib Assn of Australia; Inst Prof Libns Ont; ManitobaLA; ManitobaASchL. 11: Ruth Cameron Medal UBC Sch of Libnship 66. 14: Sch libnship, ref. 15: Faculty of Ed Univ of Manitoba, Manitoba Winnipeg 19 Can.

CHAPMAN, LORNA (ZUBRIS). b Glen Lyon Penn 26 Ap 33. 4: Charles E Chapman. 5: Wayne State U 50-51 (LS); West Mich U 52-54, 61 (LS) BA, 67. 7: Asst libn Chrysler Guided Missile Tech Lib, Warren Mich 51; ComstockTwp Lib, Comstock Mich 58; Kalamazoo Pub Lib, Bkmobile dept 62-64, Hd East Br Lib64-. 9: MichLA. 10: Eastside Improvement Assn. 14: Circ & br wk (pub & spec libs). 15: 8210 W OP ave R #8, Kalamazoo Mi 49001.

CHAPMAN, LUCY (FERGUSON) WARE. b Woodford Co Ky 16 N 09. 4: Morris Whitfield Chapman. 5: UKy 28-33 9eng, LS) AB, summers 59-63, 65 (LS) MS. 7: Libn Jr High Lib, Louisville Ky 34-35; Libn ref & circ Centre Col 58-64; Libn ref dept Dept of Libs, Frankfort Ky 64-. 9: ALA; SELA; KyLA (Pub Lib Sect). 10: DAR; Audubon Soc; Ky Hist Soc. 14: Ref, bk sel. 15: 1129 Ojibwa trail, Frankfort Ky 40601.

CHAPMAN, MARGARET LOUISE. b New Bern NC 6 Ap 16. 5: Greensboro Col 33-34, 35-38 (Hist) AB; UNC 42, 44-45 BSLS, 47-51, 54-56 (Hist) MA. 6: Fr. 7: Libn New Bern Pub Lib, New Bern NC 40-43; Stock control asst Barbour Boat Wks, New Bern NC 43-44; UNC at Chapel Hill: Asst catlgr 45, Alumni recorder 45-47, Catlgr 47-51; Fla State U Catlgr 51-54; Catlgr & asst law libn UNC at Chapel Hill 54-56; Hd of bibliog room UFla 56-58; Libn Yonge Lib of Florida Hist UFla 58-62; Spec collections libn U So Fla 62-. 9: ALA; FlaLA (chm Ref RT 57-58; chm Col & Spec Div 62-63, pres 65-66). 10: Hillsborough Co Hist Comsn; Fla Hist Soc. 12: Ed "Florida Breezes," by Ellen Call Long (62). 14: Rare bks, Floridiana. 15: Univ of So Florida Lib, Tampa Fl 33620.

CHAPMAN, MARY JANE (POLACK NILSEN). b Seattle Wash 18 Ag 45. 4: David Duane Chapman. 5: UWash 63-66 (Anthrop, Sociol) BA, 66-67 MLS. 6: Ger. 7: Reader's serv libn Highline Commun Col 67-. 8: Tchg lib circ procedures & lib use (ref course for technicians); Adv to Black Student Union on Campus. 10: AAUP; Soc for the Prevention of Old Fishes. 14: Ref, tchg, rare bks, sci ref, wk with disadvantaged groups. 15: 16612 19th SW, Seattle Wa 98166.

CHAPMAN, RONALD F(ETTES). b Bristol England 12 F 32. 4: Ellen Lawrence. 5: Glendale Col 58-60 AA; LA State Col 60-63 (Speech) BA; UHawaii 67-68 MLS. 6: Fr, Ilocano. 7: Br mgr West Union Telegraph Co, LA 52-54; Personnel specialist (Sp/4) US Army, Honolulu 54-56; Asst operations mgr Western Union Telegraph Co, LA 56-64; Volunteer US Peace Corps, Philippines 64-66; Ref libn UHawaii 68; Spec recruit LC 68-69, Info syst research asst 69-. 10: Beta Phi Mu; Phi Kappa Phi. 13: Yes. 14: Lib automation, ref, admin. 15: 1778 Halekoa dr, Honolulu Hi 96821.

CHAPPELL, GUY DeWITT II. b Phila 16 Ja 31. 4: Yvonne Worrell Chappell. 5: Earlham Col 49-51 (Eng); Fla So Col 55-58 (Amer Culture) BS, 58 (Eng, Econ) AB; Drexel 61-62 MSLS. 6: Sp. 7: Retail clerk Doubleday & Co Book Shops, Phila 51-52; Sgt US Army ASA SignalCorps; Specialties Courier-Mail Clerk; Ed, Newspaper Mgr Motion Picture Theater52-55; Asst to dir of men & head resident counselor for men; Fla So Col 56-58; Industrial catlgr Nice Ball Bearing Co, Phila 60; Mobile Pub Lib, Mobile Ala; Adminasst to dir 62-63, Parkway Br libn 63-64, Head of commun serv 64-65; Asst libn Commun Col of Phila 65-67; Hd libn Darien Lib Inc, Darien Conn 67-68; Libn Amer LawInst, Phila 68-. 8: TV bk reviewer Mobile Ala 64-65; Ala co-chm for Nat Poetry Day 64-65; Co-ord Nat Lib Week TV hour show, Mobile Ala 63, 64 Phila Lib Surv Resources & Student Use Planning Com 67. 9: ALA (sec-treas) Jr Mems Round Table 64-65; AlaLA; PennLA; ConnLA Lib Admin Gp,Fairfield Co Conn; AALL. 10: Jr C of C; Mobile Chamber Music Soc; Allied Arts Counof Metro; Mobile Allied Arts Festival Com; Amer Fed of Adv Clubs, Mobile; MobileAmer Landmarks Celebration; Gulf Coast Folk Festival, Mobile; Plays & Players ofPhila; Omicron Delta Kappa; Joe Jefferson Players, Mobile; Pi Kappa Phi; Delta SigmaPi; Pi Delta Epsilon. 11: Hy Jordan Sobillof Poetry Award 56; First Prize, Fla Acadsci (Undergrad Div) 58. 13: Yes. 14: Pub rel, ref, lib publs, lib admin, adult serv, techserv. 15: 406-F Croskey Mews, Phila Pa 19146.

CHAPUT, GILLES (LEOPOLD DENIS). b Ste-Scholastique 1 S 42. 4: Francine Quevillon. 5: Simmons 30-34 (LS) SB; Gorham State Col summer 62; UMe summer 65; U of StateNY (Oswego) 66-. 6: Fr, Eng. 7: Asst catlgr-in-chief USherbrooke (Can) 64-66; Chief Catlgr 66-. 9: ALA (mem com); -AASchL; MeSchLA (treas); NeSchLA (Standards Com). 10: Meext serv; Amer Forestry Assn. 12: Histoire du canada; Table de classification F(q)5000 (69) 14: Sch, pub & col libs, media centers. 15: 2810 Rue Maricourt, Sherbrooke Que Canada.

CHAR, LAN HIANG. b Pekalongan Indonesia 27 Ap 29. 4: Benjamin P S Char. 5: U Indonesia 48-51 (Chinese) BA, 51-56 (Chinese) MA; Columbia 58-59 (LS) MS. 6: Indonesian, Dutch, Japanese, Eng, Chinese, Fr, Ger. 7: U Indonesia: Lecturer Chinese lang 56-58, Lecturer Chinese bibliog 60-62; Lecturer Lib Sci 60-62, Curator of Chinese Lib 60-62; Lang & area spec Chinese/Korea East-West Center Lib, Honolulu 62-63, Land & area spec Southeast Asia 63-. 9: HawaiiLA (sec Spec & Ref Sect 64-). 12: Tr into Indonesian, "Twelve Citizens of the World by L S Kenworthy (Djakarta 62). 14: Ref. 15: 2228 Hoonanea st, Honolulu Hi 96822.

CHARITON, HELEN (DUNN). b Oneida NY 5 D 21. 4: William Chariton. 5: Geneseo State Tchrs Col 39-43 (LS) BS; Syracuse (LS) MS. 7: Jr high sch libn & pub libn, Oswego Pub NY 43-44; High sch libn , Canastota NY 44-47; Pub Libn, Canastota NY 50-58; Jr high sch libn, Oneida NY 58-60; Dir of pub lib, Canastota NY 60-. 10: Canastota Garden Club. 11: Dorothy Canfield Fisher Award 62. 14: Child & adult reading serv. 15: Rte 46, Durhamville NY 13054.

CHARITON, MAY (KANTER). b NYC 18 Ja 26. 4: Ted Chariton. 5: Hunter Col 43-47 (Psych) AB; LIU 62-67 MLS. 7: Bus off rep NY Tele Co, NYC 46-48; Ed asst Coronet Magazine, NYC 48-51; Ref libn Henry Waldinger Mem Lib, Valley Stream NY 67-. 14: Ref. 15: 6 Meadowbrook lane, Valley Stream NY 11580.

CHARLES, E RENNIE. b Toronto 20 O 17. 4: Flora June Farley. 5: Toronto 36-41 (Eng) BA; Ontario Col of Educ (U of T) 41-42 Ont High Sch Tchg Certif; West Res 51-58 MS in LS; Ont Col of Ed 58-65 MEd. 6: Fr, Ger. 7: Signals off Royal Can Corps of Sigs (Cdn Army) Can & GB 41-45, Cipher off (Lt)Eng 43-45; Personnel off (Capt & Maj) Can Army Militia, Can 52-65; Tchr Train &Re-Establishment Inst, Toronto 45-48; Master tchr End Dept Ryerson Inst of Tech,Toronto 48-63; Asst chm End Dept Ryerson Polytech Inst 67-69, Asst chm JournalismDept 69, Pres com on lib dev 67-. 8: Lecturer Ext Div, UToronto 49-; Lecturer & consul in bus & tech communication for 30 bus, industrial, & prof orgs. 9: Amer Bus Writing Assn (Can rep); Soc Tech writers & Publrs; Ont Second Sch Tchrs Fed (past pres Ryerson Br). 11: C D (Canadian Mil decor). 13: Yes. 14: Admin. 15: 43 Halford ave, Toronto 9 Canada.

CHARLES, KAREN (BENTS). b Cumberland Wis 4 My 40. 4: Lewis W Charles. 5: Northland Col 58-62 (Music) BA; UWis 62-63 MSLS. 7: Ref libn div for lib serv Dept of Pub Instr, Madison Wis 63-66; Libn Portage Pub Lib, Portage Wis 68-. 9: WisLA. 14: Ref. 15: 106 Summit st, Portage Wi 53901.

CHARLES, PAMELA JEAN (POINTER). b Portland Ore 11 Ja 47. 4: Glen Charles. 5: URedlands 64-65; Cal State (Fullerton) 65-66; UCal (Berkeley) 66-67 (Eng Lit) AB, 68 MLS. 6: Fr, Ger. 7: Hd libn Pasadena City Sch Dist Wash Elem 69-. 8: Consul Library Guild, Notre Dame Col. 9: CalASchL; CalTA. 10: Simmons Club of NH;Manchester Col Women's Club; Manchester Hist Assn; Inst of Arts & Scis; Friend of theCurrier Art Gallery; Simmons Club of NH; Col Women's Club. 14: Sch libnship, serv to the disadvantaged. 15: 7648 Lantana dr, Buena Park Ca 90620.

CHARLTON, BARBARA ANN (KOS). b Rochester Minn 7 Ja 26. 4: Charles L Charlton. 5: Col of St Catherine 43-47 (LS, Journalism) BS. 7: Libn Dept Chem Lib Wash U (St Louis) 47-51; Libn sci & tech ref Sacramento State Col 61-. 9: CalLA. 14: Sci. 15: 6150 Park Oaks dr, Circus Heights Cal 95610.

CHARPENEL, MAURICIO E. b Mexico D F 15 S 30. 4: Blanche Loving. 5: U of the Americas 4850 (Art Hist); Central Mo State Col 5657 (Art) BA; Universidad Nacional Autonoma de Mexico 5759 (Sp) MA; Drexel 65 (LS); UTex 6568 MLS. 6: Sp, Fr, Portu. 7: Instr sp Guilford Col (Greensboro) 6264; Instr sp Dept of Romance Langs UNC (Greensboro) 5964; Senior lib asst Latin Amer collections UTex (Austin) 6566; Academic asst to dean Grad Sch Lib Sci 6667; Publ coord & libn Latin Amer Studies UTex 67. 9: Asociacion Mexicana de Bibliotecarios. 11: Blanche W Knopf Award Bk Collecting Contest Sponsored by Humanities Research Ctr UTex. 12: Luis G Inclan; periodicos e impresos; Mexico, D F, Ediciones de la Linterna, 1959, 50p ilus; Imprentas de la ciudad de Mexico en el siglo XIX; Mexico, D F, Editorial Bolivar, 1960, 51 p ilus. 13: Yes. 14: Lat Amer child lit, Lat Amer bibliog & bk publ, materials for bilingual educ. 15: Inst of Lat Amer Studies UTex 214 Archway, Austin Tx 78705.

CHARPENTIER, ARTHUR A. b Waterbury Conn 13 Ag 19. 4: Phyllis Smith. 5: Springfield Col 37-41 (Gp wk) BS; BostonU 46-48 (Law) LLB; Admitted Mass Bar 48. 7: (Capt) FA Armored US Army 41-46; Libn Boston U Sch of Law 48-50; Asst libn Assn of the Bar of nyc 50-57, Libn 57-67; Libn Yale Law Sch 67-. 8: Adv com to LC on Clsf 58-67; Lib consul Judicial Conf of State of NY 61-67. 9: AALL (pres 65-66); Int Assn Law Libs (v-pres 68-); Amer Bar Assn (Lib Serv Com 69-; Adv Com to Law Lib of LC 68-); Amer arbitration Assn (Lib Com 66-); Law Lib Assn of Greater NY (pres 57-58); Law Libns of new England; Assn of Bar of NYC. 12: Ed "Opinions on Professional Ethics" (54); Ed "Counsel on Appeal" (68); "Court Libraries in the State of New York" (61). 13: Yes. 14: Law lib admin. 15: Yale Law School, New Haven Ct 06520.

CHARVET, PIERRE EDOUARD. b Grandview Wash 23 D 18. 4: Geraldine Sargent. 5: Mt Angel Col 38; Gonzaga U 38-41 (Philos, Arts & Sci), 59-60 (Educ) BEd; UWash 60-61 MSLS. 6: Fr, Ger, Lat. 7: S/Sgt US Army Sig Corps Finance 41-45; Statistician Macy's, San Francisco 46-47; Engnr clerk Amer Pres Lines, San Francisco 47-50; Farmer Wash 50-58; Bkmob libn NC-Moses Lake Wash 61-62; Br libn Spokane Pub Lib, Spokane Wash 62-65. 14: Reader guidance, br admin, child wk; Great Bks Disc Group. 15: 5017 Jefferson, Spokane Wa 99208.

CHASE, ANGELA GUILD. b Exeter NH 23 Jl 20. 5: UNH 38-41 (Langs); UDenver 41-42 (LS) BA. 6: Fr. 7: Asst Keene Pub Lib, Keene NH 42-43; Bkmob libn NH State Lib 43-45; Ref asst Kanawha Co Pub Lib, Charleston WVa 45-47; Sr asst circ dept Mt Vernon Pub Lib, Mt Vernon NY 47-49; Asst bus sci & tech dept Hartford Pub Lib, Hartford Conn 49-. 9: ALA; ConnLA; SLA (Conn Valley Chap; ed Union List of Periods 53, mem chm 54); Hosp chm 67; Hartford Libns Club. 14: Tech & bus ref. 15: Hartford Pub Lib, 500 Main st, Hartford Ct 06103.

CHASE, EDWARD HUTCHINSON. b NYC 24 Je 1897. 4: Maude A Banks. 5: NYU 16-17, 19-23 (Bus admin) BSC; South Conn State Col 58-61 (LS). 7: Ensign USN 17-19; Off mgr Hooper-Holmes Bur, New Haven Conn 32-62; Libn N Haven Conn Memorial Lib 62-. 9: ALA; ConnLA (Exec Bd sec 63-64); NELA. 10: West Haven Conn Pub Lib Exec Bd; Town Bd of Fin. 14: Pub lib admin. 15: 534 Second ave, West Haven Ct 06516.

CHASE, ELEANOR (JACKSON). b Bremerton Wash 13 O 41. 5: Lewis & Clark Col 59-63 (Hist, Political sci) BS; UCal 63-64 Libnship MLS. 7: Ref libn Corvallis Pub Lib, Corvallis Ore 64-65; Asst libn Pol Sci Br UWash Libs 67-. 9: ALA; PNLA. 14: Ref. 15: 2032 Franklin ave E, Seattle Wa 98102.

CHASE, MRS ELIZABETH (HOWARD). b Cleveland 1 N 20. 4: William M Chase. 5: UMich 38-42 (Liberal Arts) AB; State U Col (Geneseo NY) 58-62 MLS. 6: Fr. 7: Interlib loan libn Monroe Co Lib System, rochester NY 58-. 14: Interlib loan. 15: 678 Lake rd, Webster NY 14581.

CHASE, ELIZABETH (WAGNER) JOHNSON. 4: Harold F Chase. 5: Phila Col of Pharmacy & Sci 39 (Bacteriology) BS; Drexel 50 (LS) MS. 6: Fr, Ger. 7: Research chem asst USDA, Phila 41-46; Libn Phila Col of Pharm & Sci 46-63; Acquis libn Drexel Inst of Tech 63-64; Libn Phila Col of Pharm & Sci 64-. 9: SLA; MedLA; PennLA. 10: AAUW; Lambda Kappa Sigma. 14: Catlg, ref. 15: Lib Phila Col of Pharm & Sci 43rd & Woodland ave, Phila 19104.

CHASE, ESTHER (STEVENS). b New Orleans La 19 O 20. 5: Simmons Col 38-42 (LS) BS. 7: Bkmob libn Framingham Town Lib, Framingham Mass 58-60; Libn Sharon Pub Lib, Sharon Mass 60-67; Asst libn Belmont Mem Lib, Belmont Mass 67-. 9: NELA; MassLA. 14: Admin, ref, adult serv. 15: 147 S Main st, Sharon Ma 02067.

CHASE, FRANK R. b Chicago 9 Je 15. 4: Anne Cameron. 5: UIll 38-42 (Amer Hist) BA; Columbia 46-47 BSLS. 6: Fr. 7: Ref & ser libn Bradley U 47-52; Asst ref libn Peoria Pub Lib, Peoria Ill 52-59; Asst sci libn So Ill U 59-65; Hd ref libn & coordinator of pub serv East Ky State 65-. 9: ALA-ACRL; KyLA. 14: Ref. 15: Rte 2 Box 30-A, Richmond Ky 40475.

CHASE, JAMES W. b Silverdale Wash 17 Mr 25. 5: UWash 45-49 (Chem) BS, 49-50 Secondary Tchg Certif; 52-54 M of Lib. 7: Dist Libn Twisp Pub Schs, Twisp Wash 51-52; Dist Libn Elma Pub Schs, Elma Wash 52-53; Ref libn Pub Lib, Bremerton Wash 53-54; Asst libn Clover Park High Sch, Tacoma Wash 54-56; Tech center libn Weyerhaeuser Co, Longview Wash 56-59; Sr ref libn Aero-Space Group Boeing Co, Seattle 59-64, Tech lib serv supv 64-68, Procedures Analyst 68-69; Libn Skagit Valley Col 69-. 9: SLA (Pac NW Chap;pres 59-60, chm var coms); WashLA. 10: UWash Sch of Libnship Alumni Assn; Beta Phimu; Phi Delta Kappa. 13: Yes. 14: Ref. 15: Skagit Valley Coll, 2405 College way, Mt Vernon Wa98273.

CHASE, JEANNE M. b Buffalo NY. 4: Charles R Chase. 5: Col of New Rochelle 44-48 (Psych) BA; SUNY Col at Genesco 65-67 MLS. 7: Case wkr Erie Co Dept of Soc Welfare, Buffalo NY 48-50; Psychiatric soc wkr NYS Dept of Mental Hygiene & Child Guidance, Buffalo NY 50-55; Sch libn Maryvale Central Schs, Cheektowaga NY 67-68; Sch libn Spry Jr High Sch, Webster NY 68-. 9: ALA; NYStateTA. 14: Sch lib. 15: 55 Timber Brook lane, Penfield NY 14526.

CHASE, JOY DORIS. b India 28 N 40. 5: UWis at Madison 64-66 (LS) MA; Queen Mary's Col U Madras India 59-63 (Eng lit) BA; Bethel Col St Paul Minn 63-64; London Sch of Journalism Eng (by corr) diploma in Journalism. 7: Dormitory counselor UWis at Madison 64-66; Pre-prof libn Etobicoke Pub Lib, Toronto summer 65; Libn I Div for Lib Serv, Madison Wis summer 66; Libn catlg dept State U Wis 66-67; Libn II (pub rel) Gilbert M Simmons Pub Lib, Kenosha Wis 67-. 9: ALA; KenoshaLA. 10: International Club, Wisconsin Union (Newsletter chm 65-66); Kenosha Co Literacy Council; Greater Kenosha Arts Coun. 14: Adult serv, pub rel. 15: 605 - 60th st apt 4, Kenosha Wi 53140.

CHASE, VERA O. b Glens Falls NY 11 Ap 16. 5: Simmons 33-37 (LS) BS. 7: Circ asst URochester Women's Col 37-42; Libn in chg of Publs Camp Evans Signal Lab, Belmar NJ 42-45; Ref asst Tufts Col 45-46; Lib asst Sperry Gyroscope Co, Great Neck NY 46-48; Head bus & tech div Schenectady Co Pub Lib, Schenectady NY 48-66; Ref catlg Gen Electric R&DC Schenectady NY 66-. 9: SLA (Upstate NY Chap; Dir-at-Large, pres 63-64); NYLA; Hudson -Mohawk LA. 10: YWCA; Schenectady Simmons Club; Girl Scouts. 14: Ref. 15: 906 Bedford rd apt 6, Schenectady NY 12308.

CHASE, VIRGINIA. b Kibbie Mich 23 Ap 06. 5: Mich State U 24-28 (Eng, Hist) AB; Carnegie 28-29 (LS) BS; Columbia 31-32 (LS) MS. 7: Sr asst child dept Duluth Pub Lib, Duluth Minn 29-31; Asst supt wk with child & libn central child rm, Queens Borough Pub Lib, NYC 32-44; Assoc & libn central child rm, Queens Borough Pub Lib, NYC 32-44; Assoc Prof Drexel Lib Sch 44-45; Supv wk with child Free Lib, Worcester Mass 45-46; Instr Lib Sci UMich Ann Arbor Mich summers 49-51, 54-58; Head boys & girls dept Carnegie Lib of Pittsburgh 46-. 9: ALA (exec Bd 59-63, Grolier Award Com 65-66, Coun 58-61, 68-71); -CSD (Bd Dirs 57-60, 68-71, CLA Chm 48-49; Pres Div Libs for Child & Yp 50-51); NYLA (chm Child Lib Sect 37-38); PennLA (chm Spec Com on Org for Child & Yp Sect, chm Eval Com 64); CathLA-West Penn Unit. 10: Zonta Internat. 13: Yes. 14: Wk with child. 15: Carnegie Lib of Pittsburgh, 4400 Forbes ave, Pittsburgh Pa 15213.

CHASE, WILLIAM D(eROY). b Lakeview Mich 8 Ap 22. 4: Helen E Marquardt. 5: UMich 43 BA, 53 MA Columbia-Amer Press Inst 67 (Lib Seminars). 6: Ger, Fr. 7: Geogr Off ofStrategic Serv, Wash DC 44-45; Tchg Fellow UMich (Ann Arbor) 47-48; Asst curator ofbks Clements Lib UMich (Ann Arbor) 47-48; Chief lib sect Aeronautical Chart Serv ofUSAF, Wash DC 48-49; Chief libn "The Flint Journal," Flint Mich 49-. 8: Publ & owner of Apple Tree Press, Flint Mich 54- Specialistgrant US Dept of State with assignment to Saigon Vietnam to help establish news libsat Vietnam Press My-Ag 66. 9: SLA (chm Newspaper Div 57); NMA; ASIS; Flint Lib Club. 10: Shaw Soc of Amer; Flint Adult Mental Health Clinic; Flint Community PlannedParenthood Assn; Flint Inst of Arts. 12: Ed "Last Will & Testament of George Bernard Shaw" (54); Ed "Chase's Calendar of Annual Events" (58-); Ed "Newspaper Libraries" (55). 13: Yes. 14: Newspaper libs, lib automation, rare bks. 15: 1113 Kensington ave, Flint Mich 48502.

CHASEN, LAWRENCE I. b Phila 20 S 24. 4: Frankie Vivian Frank. 5: Std Even Sch (Phila) 42 (Sociol); Gratz Hebrew (Col) 44 (Lang) Certif. 6: Hebrew, Ger, Russian, Sp. 7: Tech libn Phila Signal Depot, Phila 44-47; Libn Naval Rec Station, Phila 47-49; Chief Libn Boeing Vertol Div, Morton Penn 49-56; Mgr ge missile & Space Div, King of Prussia Penn 56-. 8: Indexing Consul Amer Inst of Aeronautics & astronautics, 64- Indexing Consul IRON AGE, Chilton Publ Co 68-. 9: SLA; ADI. 11: Awarded GE Co The Man in A Thousand Award for pioneering achievement in the GE Random Access Retrieval System. 13: Yes. 14: Info retrieval, admin. 15: 238 Sherbrook blvd, Upper Darby Pa 19080.

CHATTON, MILDRED (VICK). b Portsmouth Va 2 Ag 16. 4: Dr Milton John Chatton. 5: Westhampton Col URichmond 33-37 (Eng) BA; UNC 40 (LS) BS; San Jose State Col 60- (Curriculum materials). 7: Asst child room Richmond Pub Lib, Richmond Va 37-40; Asst child room & 1st asst NYPub Lib Port Washington Br Tremont Br, Hunt's Pt, 40-42; Libn Serv Club Lib, Camp Lee Va 42-43; Asst libn Lib Ed Div, Spec Serv, Pentagon 43; Libn Mason General Hosp, Brentwood NY 43; Asst libn San Jose Pub Lib, San Jose Cal 59; Libn San Jose High Sch, San Jose Cal 59-68; Asst Prof Dept of Libnship, San Jose StateCol 68-. 9: NEA; Cal Tchrs Assn; CalASchL (pres 67-68); CalLA; AVEAC. 10: Delta Kappa Gamma; PTA (Life mem). 12: Manag ed "California School Libraries" (65). 14: Readerserv, ref, lib educ. 15: 1189 Crescent dr, San Jose Ca 95125.

CHATWIN, DOROTHY BAXTER (KELLY). b Edmonton Alta 15 F 11. 5: UBC 32 (Fr) BA, 33 (Fr) MA; UWash 37 BA in LS. 6: Fr. 7: Ref dept UBC 37-47; Ed Canadian Index Can LA, Ottawa 47-56; Libn Can Inst of Internat Affairs, Toronto 56-57; Libn Toronto Ref Lib 57-59; Asst head adult serv & in chg of ref No York Pub Lib, willowdale Ont 59-66, Hd Bathurst Br 66-67, Coordinator ref & research 67-. 9: CanLA; OntLA;Inst Prof Libns Ont; ALA. 14: Ref, Canadiana. 15: Apt 414 3 Du Maurier blvd, Toronto 12 Can.

CHAUSSE, DELBERT NORMAN. b Medford Ore 12 Jl 36. 4: Mary Ann Fuerst. 5: So Ore Col 55-59 (Soc Studies) BS; UDenver 61-62 (LS) MA; Humboldt State Col 63-65. 7: US Army & US Army Reserve 59-65; Tchr Tonapah Sch System, Tonapah Nev 59-61; Libn Eureka City Schs, Eureka Cal 62-66; Asst libn Reedley Jr Col 66-67; Lib supv Mt Pleasant Sch Dist, San JoseCal 67-. 9: NEA; ALA; Cal Tchrs Assn; CalSchLA. 10: Gamma Theta Upsilon. 14: Sch libs. 15: 3130 Woodmont dr, San Jose Ca 95118.

CHAUSSE, MARY ANN (FUERST). b Omaha 21 O 35. 4: Delbert Norman Chausse. 5: Peru State Col 53-57 Soc Sci, Biol) BS; UDenver 61-62 (LS) MA. 7: Tchr Superior City Schs, Superior Neb 57-61; Libn South High Sch, Omaha 62-63; Sci libn Humboldt State Col 63-66. 9: ALA; CalLA; CalSchLA. 10: Beta Beta Beta; Kappa Delta Pi; Beta Phi Mu. 14: Sch libs. 15: 3130Woodmont dr, San Jose Ca 95118.

CHAVES, FRANCISCO MARIANO. b Santiago de Cuba Cuba 20 S 16. 4: Mari Isabel Roque. 5: U Miami 35-36 (Econ), 63-64 (Sp lit); U Havana 37-40 (Law) Doctor of Laws; Kan State Tchrs Col 67-68 (LS) Master of Libnship. 6: Sp, Portu, Fr. 7: Law practice sr partner Chaves, Hernandez & Revilla, Havanna 40-60; Owner mgr Paperback Bk Shop, Hollywood Fla 61-66; Sp instr Casals Lang Ctr, Coral Gables Fla 66; Grad asst to prof of catlg Kan State Tchrs Col & grad asst dept of acquis 67-68; UGa: Asst catlg libn 69, Supv rush catlg sect 69-. 14: Catlg, acquis, admin. 15: 2360 W Broad st apt N7, Athens Ga 30604.

CHAVEZ, MARIAN A (AUSHERMAN). b Abilene Kan 15 N 27. 5: Sterling 44-46; Muskingum 46-48 (Speech & Drama) BA; Ohio State 48-50 (Speech & Hearing therapy) MA; Western Res 56-59 (Nursing) BS in Nursing, 59-62 MSLS. 7: Hearing & vision consul Ohio Dept of Health 50-56; Gen duty nurse Univ Hosps, Cleveland 59-60; Ref asst West Res U 60-62; Ref libn Columbia U Med Lib 62-65; Asst med libn UNM 65-67; Med ref libn Case West Res U 67-68; Asst med libn UUtah 68-. 9: SLA; MedLA. 14: Ref. 15: 130 S 13th E #507, Salt Lake City Ut 84102.

CHAZANOW, LILLIAN (TURNER). b Tulsa Okla. 4: Syd S Chazanow. 5: UOkla 34-38 (Eng) BA; Columbia 56-61 (LS) MA. 6: Fr. 7: Ed asst UOkla Press 35-39; Verbatim reporter UN, NY 46; Libn Queens Borough Pub Lib, Queens NY 61-. 9: ALA. 10: Phi Beta Kappa. 14: Child libnship. 15: 255-02 75th ave, Floral Park NY 11004.

CHEADLE, HELEN N. b Sanborn Iowa 4 D 20. 5: Marquette 44-47 (Philo, Eng) Ph B; UWis 47-48 BLS; UMich 54-56 (Hist) MA. 7: UNotre Dame: Asst catlgr 48-50, Libn medieval inst 50-54; Ref libn hist & travel dept Detroit Pub Lib 56-58; No Ill U: Asst catlg libn 58-65, Asst hd catlg dept 65-68; Hd tech serv Kenyon Col 68-. 9: ALA; OhioLA. 10: AAUP. 14: Catlg. 15: 6 Highland dr, Mount Vernon Oh 43050.

CHEAVENS, DORCAS (H). b Wilmington Del 6 Ag 08. 5: UDel 27-31 (Eng) BA; Columbia 34-35 BS in LS. 7: Act Co libn New Castle Co Free Lib, Wilmington Del 48-50; Head bus & tech dept Wilmington Inst Free Lib, Wilmington Del 51-52; Research libn duPont Tech Lib, Wilmington Del 52-58; Br libn Chestnut Run Br duPont Tech Lib, Wilmington Del 58-59, Act asst libn (admin) 59-62, Asst libn serv 62-63, Asst libn 63-65, Head libn 65-. 8: Local Convention Rep Sci-Tech Div for SLA Nat Convention 65. 9: ALA; SLA; ASIS; ACS; Tech Assn of Pulp & Paper Ind; Soc of the Plastics Ind; DelLA (pres 55-56, com chm); Del Chap ACS (Chem Lit Group). 14: Tech lib wk. 15: Du Pont Tech Lib, Room 3154, Wilmington De 19898.

CHEE, CHENG-KHEE. b Fukien China 14 Ja 35. 4: Sing-Bee Ong. 5: Nanyang U (Singapore) 57-60 (Chinese Lang & Lit) BA; UMinn 62-64 (LS) MA. 6: Chinese, Malaya. 7: Asst libn Nanyang U Lib (Singapore) 61-62; UMinn: Stud asst Main Campus Lib 63-64, Tchg asst Col of Educ U Minn 64, Ref libn (Duluth Campus) 65-68; Instr & sr libn 68-. 9: ALA; SingaporeLA; MinnLA. 14: Ref. 15: 704 E 2nd st apt 18, Duluth Mn 55805.

CHEESEMAN, (ELIZABETH) MARGARET. b Muncie Ind 3 Mr 31. 5: Northwestern U 49-53 (Eng, Fr, Math) BS; Chicago 55-57 (LS) MA. 7: Tchr & libn Mt Morris High Sch, Morris Mich 53-55; Asst libn Lab Sch UChicago57-58; Bkmob libn Grace A Dow Mem Lib, Midland Mich 58-60; Head libn Lakeview HighSch, Battle Creek Mich 60-66; Supv inst lib serv coordinator lib serv to blind andphysically handicapped, Penn State Lib 68-. 8: Exec dir Nat Lib Week in Mich 63 (Certif of Recognition) Sch lib consul Mich State Lib66-68. 9: ALA;-PennLA; MichASchL. 10: Amer Correct Assn; Internat Platform Assn. 11: Schuman Award, Certif of Merit, NLW 63. 13: Yes. 14: Admin, yp, institutions. 15: 135Williams Grove Mobile Homes RD 2, Mechanicsburg Pa 17055.

CHEN, CHING FAN. b Foochow China 16 N 17. 4: Helen C Chen. 5: North-Eastern U 40 (Econ) BA; Nankai Inst of Econ 41 (Econ) MA. 6: Chinese. 7: Research assoc Nanking U (China) 41-44; Instr West China Union (China) 44-45; Asst Prof Cheng-hua U (China) 45-46; Research assoc UWash 46-47; Instr Goddard Col 51-52; Asst curator & lib assoc NYU 47-. 9: SLA. 10: NYU Faculty Club. 14: Documentation, automation systems. 15: 139-21 - 85th dr, Apt 1A, Jamaica NY 11435.

CHEN, CHING-CHIH (LIU). b Fukien China 3 S 37. 4: Dr S H Chen. 5: Nat Taiwan U 55-59 (Foreign Langs) BA; UMich 59-61 AMLS. 6: Chinese, Fr. 7: Serv libn UMich (Ann Arbor) Mich 61-62; Ref libn Windsor Pub Lib, Windsor Ont 62; Ref & circ libn McMaster U (Ont) 62-63, Sci libn 63-64; Ref libn UWaterloo (Ont) 64-65; Supv libn Engnrg & Sci Lib 65-66; Hd libn 66-68; Asst Libn Sci Lib MIT 68-. 9: ALA; CanLA; OntLA; Inst Prof Libns Ont. 13: Yes. 14: Ref (sci & engnr). 15: 11 Nassau dr, Winchester Ma 01890.

CHEN, DOLORES. b Taiwan 8 D 38. 5: Providence Eng Col 58-61 (Eng) AA; Providence Col 63-64 (Eng) BA; Wayne State 65-66 MSLS; Columbia summer 68 (LS). 6: Chinese, Fr. 7: Teacher Huatan High Sch, Changhua Taiwan 61-63; Tchr Lunchien High Sch, Taichung Taiwan 65; Catlgr Weber Co Lib 67-67; Catlgr West Col Lib 67-. 9: ALA. 10: Chinese Assn of Tchrs; Sino-Amer Cult & Econ Assn. 14: Catlg, ref, acquis & admin. 15: Corson Hall apt 3, Western College, Oxford Oh 45056.

CHEN, EFFIE YUEH-HUA (CHUANG). b Taiwan China 22 Mr 35. 4: James Chewen Chen. 5: Taiwan Normal U 53-57 (Home Econ) BEd; Drexel 59-61 (Food & Nutrition) MS, 61-62 MLS. 6: Chinese, Japanese. 7: Catlgr Princeton U Lib 63-65; Catlgr Citizens Lib, Washington Penn 65-68; Catlgr Princeton U Lib 68-. 14: Catlg. 15: Princeton Univ Lib, Princeton NJ 08504.

CHEN, FLORA FU-HWA (SHEN). b Hu-Nan China 8 N 34. 4: William Yu-Fang Chen. 5: Nat Taiwan U 52-56 (Eng Lit) BA; Taiwan Normal U 57-59 (Eng Lit) MA; UDenver 59-60 MLS; Cornell U 6 1 (Eng Lit); Toronto 6 2 (19th Century Thought). 6: Chinese, Fr. 7: Lib asst, Nat Central Lib, Taiwan 56-57; Ser libn Cornell U Lib 60-61; Catlgr UMan Lib 62-64; Catlgr USask Lib 64-67; Catlgr Can Agric Research Station, Sask 67-. 9: SaskLA. 12: Yang Tzu (pen name), Lan lu Chi Title (poems) (68). 14: Catlg. 15: 2234 Munroe ave, Saskatoon Sask Can.

CHEN, JOHN H M. b Shanghai China 24 Je 31. 4: Susan. 5: Va PolytechU 56-57 (Educ) MS; Columbia 62-63 (LS) MS; NYU 61-64 (A-V Media) MA; Penn StateU 67-69 (Higher Educ & Educ Admin) EdD. 6: Fr, Sp, Chinese. 7: Head libn SUNY (S Fallsburg) 63-65; dir of lib W Va Inst of Tech 65-66; Dir of lib, Lynchburg Col 66-69; Dir of libs, Wis StateU (Stevens Point) 69-. 8: Various consul lib serv, NY, W Va, Va, Mass. 9: ALA; NEA; Amer Assn for Higher Educ; NYStateLA; WVaLA; VaLA; WisLA. 10: Rotary Internat; AAUP; Alpha Phi Omega. 11: Meritorious Serv Award if W Va. 12: "Originia of Asian People (55); "Audio-Visual Materials & Instruction (60); "A Study on Aborigines in Formosa (56); "Formosa-As I See It (54); "A Survey of the Libraries of Selected Land-Grant Colleges & Universities (69). 13: Yes. 14: Lib admin, tech serv, lib automation, tchg lib & info sci, special collections. 15: PO Box 503, Stevens Point Wi 54481.

CHEN, LYNN CHIA-LING (WANG). b Peking China 3 D 32. 4: Dick Chen. 5: Nat Taiwan U 51-55 (Lit) BA; UMinn 55-57 (LS) MA. 6: Chinese, Eng, Sp. 7: Student asst UMinn Lib (Minneapolis) 56-57; Lib asst Stanford U Lib 57-58; Refer libn ENLO Park Lib, Menlo Park Cal 58-59; Prof Asst II Minneapolis Pub Lib (Minneapolis) 59-60; Catlgr Hopkins Pub Lib, Hopkins Minn 63-. 9: ALA; MinnLA. 14: Ref, catlg. 15: 5731 Woodland rd, Minnetonka Mn 55345.

CHEN, NANCY VERONICA (KOO). b Shanghai China 25 F 40. 4: Shium Andrew Chen. 5: Maryknoll Com Col (Hong Kong) 59-60 (Bus) Diploma; Marymount Col (Tarrytown NY) 61-64 (Hist); Kan State Tchrs Col 64-65 (Hist) BA, 65-66 (LS) MS. 6: Chinese. 7: Exec sec Pfizer Corp, Hong Kong 60-61; Libn Flint Hills Area Voc Tech Sch, emporia Kan 66; Hd libn Butler Co Commun Col 66-. 9: ALA; PennLA. 10: Phi Gamma Mu. 14: Ref, acquis, planning & org new libs. 15: 438 Vista dr, Butler Pa 16001.

CHEN, RUBY (SWEN). b China 26 Jl 06. 5: Ginling Col 23-25, 26-28 (Mus) BA; Eden Sem 47-48 (Relig Educ); Peabody Col 48-50 (LS) MA; UNC summer 60, spring 62 (LS). 6: Chinese. 7: Tchr, China: Ming Deh High Sch, Nanking 25-26, Baldwin High Sch, Nanchang 28-30, McTyeire High Sch, Shanghai 30-32, Secondary Sch for Girls 33-47; Libn (circ) Webster Groves Pub Lib, Webster Groves Mo 50-52; Libn (catlg dept) SoMethodistU Fondren Lib 52-60; Libn (ref dept) Mars Hill Col 60-62; Libn (catlg dept) DukeU Med Ctr 63-64; Libn (catlg dept Oriental sect) UNC (Chapel Hill) 64-. 12: Yang Tzu (pen name), Lanlu chi Tutle (poems) 68. 14: Oriental studies, esp Chinese culture. 15: 504 North st, Chapel Hill NC 27514.

CHEN, SHERRY S R. b Szechwan China. 5: Nat TaiwanU (Lang & Lit) BA; SUNY (Geneseo) 69 MLS. 6: Chinese. 7: Tchr High Sch, Taipei Taiwan 66-67; Exec sec German Co, Taipei Taiwan 65-67; Lib stud asst Lib Sch Lib SUNY (Geneseo) 68-. 9: ALA. 14: Catlg, acquis, ref. 15: 10 Court st, Geneseo NY 14454.

CHEN, SIMON PING-JEN. b Peking China 25 S 31. 4: Maureen Teh-Yung (Ku). 5: Nat Taiwan U 50-54 (Hist) BA; St Vincent Col 55-56 (Soc Sci); Catholic U 56-59 MSLS. 6: Chinese, Japanese, Ger, Fr. 7: Asst St Vincent Col Lib (Latrobe Penn) 55-56; Grad lib asst Catholic U 56-59; Catlgr UChicago Lib 59-61; Asst catlg libn UNev Lib 61-63; Asst catlg libn No Ill U Lib 63-67; Hd of catlg dept West Ky U Lib 67-. 9: KyLA. 10: Amer Contract BridgeLeague. 12: Comp "A Checklist of Non-Official Imprints Published in District of columbia in 1847" (59). 13: Yes. 14: Catlg, col & research libs. 15: 54 Highland dr, Bowling Green Ky 42101.

CHEN, SUE YING (ENG). b NYC 1 F 36. 4: Dr Peter K Chen. 5: Rutgers Newark Col 54-58 (Hist of Art) BA; UChicago 58-59; Catholic U 63-65 MSLS. 6: Fr, Ger, Chinese. 7: Lib trainee Newark Pub Lib, Newark NJ 59-60; Lib asst Art Inst of Chicago 60-61; Lib asst Pittsburgh Plate Glass Co, Pittsburgh 62-63; Ref libn Smithsonian Inst, Wash DC 64-. 10: Phi Beta Kappa. 14: Ref, circ. 15: 4010 Wexford dr, Kensington Md 20795.

CHEN, SUMI (ARIMA). b Oakland Cal 13 D 24. 4: William Pin. 5: Tsuda Col (Japan) 42-45 (Eng Lit) BA; UIll 55-57 MSLS. 6: Japanese. 7: Asst child libn Detroit Pub Lib 57-60; Catlgr Chapman Col 66-67; Catlgr Orange Co Pub Lib, Orange Cal 67-. 0: World Affair Coun of Orange Co; Faculty Women's Club; CSCF; PTA; AAUW. 14: Catlg, child lit. 15: 515 Wilson cir, Placentia Ca 92670.

CHEN, WANDA WANCHUN (HAN). b Kweichow China 1 D 39. 4: Chi-hau Chen. 5: Nat TaiwanU 56-60 (For Lang) BA; UIll (Urbana) 60-62 (LS) MS. 6: Chinese, Japanese, Fr. 7: Stud asst UIll (Urbana) 61-62; Catlgr UWash Lib 62-64; Oriental specialist Francis A Countway Lib of Med HarvardU 64-. 9: ALA; MedLA. 14: Catlg, ref. 15: 141 Elm st, Somerville Ma 02144.

CHEN, WEN CHAO. b China 14 O 19. 4: Lilia (Chao) Chen. 5: Grinnell Col 47 (Pol sci) BA; St Louis U 49 (Pub admin) MA, 51 (Pol sci) PhD; UChicago 57 (LS) MA. 6: Chinese, Fr. 7: Kalamazoo Col: Asst Prof of pol sci 53-56, Libn 54-, Assoc Prof of pol sci 56-58, Prof of pol sci 58-, Dean of spec serv 67-. 9: ALA; Amer Soc Pub Admin; Amer Pol Sci Assn; MichLA; Midwest Conf of Pol Sci. 10: AAUP. 14: Admin, tchg. 15: Kalamazoo College, Kalazoo Mi 49001.

CHEN, WILLIAM PIN. b Chien-Tien Chekiang China 17 D 4. 4: Sumi Arima. 5: Nat Wu-Han U 37-41 (Pol Sci) BA in Law; UIll 48-49 (Pol Sci) MA, 49-55 (Pub Admin) PhD, 55-57 (LS) MS. 6: Fr, Ger, Eng, Chinese. 7: Asst sec Hupeh Prov Govt, China 41-4; Act chief dept of pol train Administrators Train Corps of Hupeh Prov, China 42-45; Assoc Prof Col of Engnr Nat Wu-Han U (China) 44-45; Sec Mil Supplies Bureau Dept of Defense, China 45-48; Assoc Prof Shanghai Col of Law (Shanghai China) 47-48; Asst libn Detroit Pub Lib 57-60; Head tech serv Cal State Col 60-68, Assoc Col Libn 68-. 9: ALA; CLA; SoCal Reg Tech Serv Group (chm-elect 65-67). 10: World Affairs Coun Orange Co Cal. 12: State Control over Local Law Enforcement in the United States, (Microfilm rd 1955); Library Automation or Else (67). 13: Yes. 14: Catlg, clsf, acquis, ser. 15: 515 Wilson circle, Placentia Ca 92670.

CHEN, WILLIAM YU-FANG. b Liu-Ho Kiang-Su China 11 My 27. 4: Flora Fu-Hwa (Shen). 5: Nat Ch engchi U (China) 49-50 (Journalism) BA, 57-59 (Journalism) MA; UToronto 62-63 BLS. 6: Japanese, Ger. 7: Copy reader The New Life Daily News, Taipei 51-53; Eng interpreter The Chainese Army, Tainan Taiwan 54-56; Div head Taipei Post Off, Taipei Taiwan 59-62; Catlgr Saskatoon Pub Lib, Saskatoon Sask 63-67; Catlgr USaskatchewan Lib. 9: SaskLA; CanLA. 12: "Press Freedom and Self-Control" in Chinese (Formosa 64). 13: Yes. 14: C atlg. 15: 2234 Munroe ave, Saskatoon Sask Can.

CHEN, WOEI REN. b Taiwan 9 Jl 39. 4: Marian Mei Y. 5: Taiwan Theol Col 65 (Rel) B Th; YaleU Divinity Sch 68 (Ethics) BD; UPittsburgh 69 MLS. 6: Chinese, Ger, Grk, Hebrew. 7: Catlgr Hartford Sem Found, Hartford Conn 69-. 12: Tr "Nestorian Church in China" (65). 13: Yes. 14: Catlg, bibliog, ref. 15: 55 Elizabeth st, Hartford Ct 06105.

CHENEY, FRANCES NEEL. b Wash DC 19 Ag 06. 4: Brainard Cheney. 5: Vanderbilt U 24-28 (Sociol) BA; Peabody 30-34 BS in LS; Columbia 38-40 MS in LS. 7: Vanderbilt U: Libn chem dept 28-29, Circ libn 29-30, Ref libn 30-37; Ref libn Joint U Libs, Nashville 37-43; Asst to Chm of Poetry LC 43-44, Bibliogr gen ref & bibliog div 44-45; Head ref dept Joint U Libs, Nashville 45-46; Peabody Lib Sch: Asst prof 46-49, Assoc prof 49-60, Assoc dir 60-, Prof 67-. 8: Visiting Prof Japan Lib Sch Keio U, Tokyo Japan 51-52; Consul US Field Seminar on Lib Ref Serv 59. 9: ALA (Exec Bd 56-61, Coun 54-68, chm Subsc Bks Com 62-63, chm Pub Libs Ref Survey Com); -RSD (past pres); -LED (past pres); AALS (past pres); BSA; SELA (past pres) TennLA (past pres). 10: Centennial Club; Colonna Club; Query Club; Tenn Hist Soc; Tenn Folklore Soc; Beta Phi Mu. 11: Mudge Award 62; Beta Phi Mu Good Tchg Award 59; D Littmarquette U 66. 12: Ed "Tennessee Librarian" (49-51, 53-55); Comp "Sixty American Poets, an Annotated Bibliography" (44); "An Annotated List of Selected Japanese Reference Materials" (52). 13: Yes. 14: Ref, bibliog. 15: 112 Oak st, Smyrna Tn 37167.

CHENEY, JOHN T. b Berkeley Cal 7 Ja 11. 4: Violet Braidfoot. 5: UCal 29-33 (Eng) AB, 33-34 (LS) Certif; UVa 38 (Eng); UCal 38-39 (LS) MA. 6: Fr, Ger, Ital, Sp. 7: Lib asst Tennessee Valley Authority 35-38; Jr libn UCal Lib (Berkeley) 38-41; Libn spec projects UVa 41-43; DC Pub Lib: Jr libn, libn 43-52, Chief lit div 52-56, Consul in adult educ 56-57, Act Personnel off 57-64, Asst dir in chg of personnel 64-68, Asst dir adm 68-. 8: Planning Com Nat Conf on Citizenship Wash DC. 9: ALA; SLA; ASIS; Amer Soc for Engrg Educ; NYLA; Hudson-Mohawk LA. 10: Troy BoysClub; Kiwanis; AAUP; Troy Pub Lib Bd dirs. 12: Contrib "Collier's Encyclopedia" & "Yearbook". 14: Admin. 15: 1728 Que st NW, Wash DC 20009.

CHENG, CHAO-SHENG. b Taiwan Rep of China 10 Ag 39. 5: Taiwan Normal U 49-53 (Educ) BSEd; UPittsburgh 68 MLS. 6: Chinese, Taiwanese. 7: Asst catlgr Lib Inst of Mod Hist Academia Sinica, China 61; Catlgr Lib Academia Historica, China 63-64; Asst libn Lib inst of Nuclear Sci Tsing Hua U, China 65-66; Asst instr Dept of Adult Educ Taiwan Normal U 66-67. 9: ASIS; ChineseLA; ChineseEA. 13: Yes. 14: Educ for libnship, info sci. 15: 272 N Bellefield ave, Pittsburgh Pa 15213.

CHENG, JAMES KUO-CHIANG. b Nanking China 20 Ag 36. 4: Lo-Lan Lo. 5: George Fox Col 60 (Hist) BA; Seton HallU 62 (Asian Studies) MA; Peabody 65 MLS. 6: Japanese, Sp, Chinese. 7: Ed Free China Monthly (NY) 63-64; Assoc prof (Hist) Warner Pacific Col 65-67; Dir lib 65-67; Asst libn Educ Lib UAlta (Edmonton) 67-68; Corresp Newsdom Weekly & Travelling Mag, Hong Kong 68-; Dir libs Okanagan Reg Col, Kelowna BC 68-. 9: ALA; PNLA; BCLA. 10: AHS; Far East Assn; Chinese Writers Club; Chinese Culture Assn; Rotary Club; Canadian Club. 11: Outstanding Young Man of Amer 67; Commun Leaders of Amer Award 69. 12: "The Stranger (Hong Kong) 63; "Man Without A Country (Taiwan) 65; Tr "The Night in Lisbon (64); "Song of a Wanderer (66); Tr "Middle Night (69); "The Dirty Group (in progress). 13: Yes. 14: Ref, rare bks, admin, pub rel. 15: Okanagan Regional College Box 550 Kelowna, British Columbia Can.

CHENIER, ANDRE. b Maniwaki 20 Jl 30. 4: Nicole Desjardins. 5: U d'Ottawa 49-53 BA, B Ph, 55 BLS. 6: Fr, Eng. 7: Libn Central Mortgage & Housing Corp, Ottawa 55-57; Hd libn Col des Jesuites 57-64; Chief central lib U Sherbrooke 64-. 14: Ref. 15: Bibliotheque generale, Universite de Sherbrooke, Sherbrooke Quebec Can.

CHERNACK, LUCILLE (RADLO). b Boston 5 Je 16. 4: David Chernack. 5: State Tchrs Col (Bridgewater Mass) 35-38 (Eng) BS in Ed; URI 63-65 MLS. 7: Stud asst Boston Pub Lib 31-38; Stud asst State Tchrs Col (Bridgewater Mass) 36-38; Saleslady Old Corner Book Store Inc, Boston 38-40; Tchr Cranston (RI) schs 51-54; Sch libn Park View Jr High Sch, Cranston RI 54-. 9: ALA; RISchLA (pres 59-63); RIEA. 14: Sch lib wk. 15: 9 University ave, Providence RI 02906.

CHERNIK, BARBARA EILEEN (EISENLOHR). b Wash DC 18 F 38. 4: Glenn Edwin Chernik. 5: Dickinson Col Carlisle Penn 55-59 (Hist) BA; UIll 59-60 (LS) MS. 6: Ger. 7: Children's libn Arlington Co Pub Libs, Arlington Va 60-62; Army libn USA, Metz Fr 62-64; Asst hd boys & girls lib G M Simmons Library, Kenosha Wis 65-66; Tech proc libn Kenosha Tech Inst, Kenosha Wis 67-. 9: ALA; WisLA (sec Col & Univ Sect 68-69). 10: AAUW; Commun Concerts Assn. 14: Child wk, catlg, lib educ. 15: 5113 33rd ave, Kenosha Wi 53140.

CHERON, THEODORE (YA). b Gomel Russia 15 Ag 20. 4: Mary N Sherbinina. 5: UCLA 52-54 (Slavic lang) BA; USC 64-68 MSLS. 6: Russian, Ukrainian, Belorussian, Polish, Ger. 7: Slavic lang chem lit Chem Abstract Serv, Ohio State U 57-59; Translator McGraw-Hill, NYC 59-60; Lit searcher Aerospace Corp, El Segundo Cal 60-61; Translation & research info specialist Philco-Ford, Aeronutronic Div, Newport Beach Cal 61-. 8: Free-lance transl of Russian tech bks into Eng. 9: SLA. 14: Trans, catlg, ref. 15: 2232 Jeanette pl, Costa Mesa Ca 92627.

CHERRY, LOUIS A. b Scotland Neck NC 26 N 19. 4: . 5: Wake Forest Col 36-40 (Hist-Govt) AB; Drexel 40-41 BS in LS. 6: Fr. 7: 1st asst read room Yale Law Sch Lib 42-43; Asst libn UNC Law Sch 9chapel Hill) 43-44; Libn & asst dir Inst of Govt UNC (Chapel Hill) 44-47; Chief Records Sect Armed Forces Staff Col, Norfolk Va 47-49; Prin ref lib & chief ref sect Lib US Dept of State, Wash DC 49-. 12: Ed "Popular Government" (44-46). 13: Yes. 14: Ref, area studies, bibliog. 15: 4600 Tarpon lane, Alexandria Va 22309.

CHERRY, RONALD L. b Cedar Rapids Iowa 5 Jl 34. 4: Belva J Wieben. 5: State UIowa 52-53, 56-59 (Pol Sci) BA, 59-61 (Law) LLB; UWash 66-67 Master of Law Libnship. 6: Fr. 7: Pfc US Army, Germany 54-56; Asst govt doc libn UIowa Libs 57-61; Assoc Law Off of Clarence R Off, N English Iowa 61-62; Partner Cherry & Griffin Attorneys at Law, Dysart Iowa 62-66; City attorney, Dysart Iowa 62-66; Asst libn Harvard Law Sch Lib 67-. 8: Consul UNew Delhi Law Sch & Indian Law Inst, New Delhi India 68. 9: AALL (chm spec com on recs & briefs). 10: Beta Phi Mu; Amer Bar Assn; iowa State Bar Assn. 14: Law libs, admin, ref. 15: 18 Winter st, Sudbury Ma 01776.

CHESHIER, ROBERT GRANT. b Goldendale Wash 28 S 30. 4: Sylvia Joy (Addicoat) Cheshier. 5: UWash 54-60 (General Studies) BA, 60-63 (LS) MA; Chicago 64 (LS). 6: Russ. 7: Aircraft mech UWash 55-57; Engring aide Boeing Co, Seattle 57-60, Procedures analyst 60-61, Info specialist 61, Br libn 61-64; Ed UChicago Industrial Research Ctr 64; Hd libn Chicago Med Sch 65-66; Dir Cleveland Health Scis Lib, Cleveland Ohio 66-. 9: Internat Assn of Documentalists & Info Officers; ADI; MedLA; SLA. 10: Toastmasters. 13: Yes. 14: Advanced info wk with sci personnel, admin. 15: 1100 Euclid ave, Cleveland Oh 44106.

CHESKI, RICHARD MICHAEL. b Canton Ohio 29 S 35. 4: Mary Ella Sica. 5: Alliance Col 53-55; Kent State 55-57 (Speech, Drama) BA, 58 (Educ) BS in Ed, 63 (LS) MA. 6: Polish. 7: Tchr-libn Columbia Local Sch, Columbia Station Ohio 58-59; Asst advertising Manager E W Bliss Co, Canton Ohio 59-61; Dir of pub rel & head of adult serv Canton Pub Lib, Canton Ohio 61-63; Dir Ella Everhard Pub Lib, Wadsworth Ohio 63-64; Dir Rodman Pub Lib, Alliance Ohio 64-. 69; Asst dir Columbus Pub Lib, Columbus Ohio 69-. 9: ALA (Reg Memb Chm 69);OhioLA (chm State Adv Com, Title IV B). 10: Kent State Lib Sch Alumni Assn; AdvBd Kent State Lib Sch; Rotary; Alliance Hist Soc; Stark Co (Ohio) Hist Soc; Beta PhiMu; Polish Amer Hist Assn. 14: Admin, data proc, circ. 15: 4795 Wynwood ct,Columbus Oh 43220.

CHESLEY, WINONA LOETTA (HALLOCK). b Springfield Ill 23 S 14. 4: Leonard R Chesley. 5: MacMurray Col for Women 32-36 (Eng, Latin) BA; UMich (summer) 40, 41 (winter) 43 ABLS. 6: Latin, Fr, Ger, Sp. 7: Tchr, Ill: Scales Mound High Sch 36-38, Dana Township High Sch 38-39, Golden Community High Sch 39-41; Lib asst Field Mus of Nat Hist, Chicago 41-43; Hispanic Soc of Amer NYC 43-45; US Army WAC Surgical Tech T-4 45-47; US Army Special Serv libn, Camp Stoneman Cal 51-52; Child libn asst, Jacksonville Ill 53-54; US Army Special Serv libn, H Belnoir Va 57-62; Ref libn Seattle Pub Lib 62-63; Catlgr UWash 63-66, Bk Orders libn 66-. 9: SLA; ALA; PNLA (Bibliog Com). 10: Audubon Soc; Pt Reyes Bird Observ; Wash Kayak Club. 12: Comp Wash sec of "PNLA Bibliography" (66-69). 14: Tech serv. 15: 9508 30th ave NE, Seattle Wa 98115.

CHESNEAU, PHYLLIS ELIZABETH. b American Falls Ida 4 S 11. 4: David J Chesneau. 5: UOmaha 28-30, 34-35 (Eng, Pol Sci) AB. 7: Tchr Omaha Pub Sch System 35-41; Engnrs asst Teletype Corp, Chicago 40; Berkshire Athenaeum, Pittsfield Mass: Asst circ dept 47-52, Exec asst 52-60, Asst libn 60-. 9: ALA; MassLA; West Mass Lib Club (pres 61-62). 15: 44 Bank row, Berkeshire Athenaeum, Pittsfield Ma 01202.

CHESNUT, DOROTHY S. b Harrell Ark 10 O 25. 4: Robert W Chestnut. 5: Limestone Col 42-44; Montclair State Col 64-67 (Eng) BA; Rutgers 67-68 MLS. 7: Circ y-a ref Verona Pub Lib, Verona NJ 57-66; Ref W Orange Pub Lib, W Orange NJ 68-. 9: NJLA. 10: Beta Phi Mu. 11: NJLA Fellowship, Emdin Award 67. 14: Ref. 15: 60 South Prospect st, Verona NJ 07044.

CHESTER, MARJORIE. b Astoria Ore 13 N 07. 5: UOre 26-30 (Eng) BA; Wash State U summer 32; UWash 35, 39; UDenver 42 BS in LS; USoCal 50; San Jose 60. 7: Tchr & tchr-libn Roseburg pub schs, Roseburg Ore 30-41; Libn Eugene High Sch,Eugene Ore 41-46; Instr of Lib Sci UOre 42-45 & summers 45-47; Asst in summerwkshops UOre 52, 53; Instr in Lib Sci Portland State U 57; Supv of instr materialsSalem pub schs, Salem Ore 46-. 9: ALA; NEA; Assn for Supv & Curr Devel; PNLA;OreLA; OreASchL; Ore Instr Materials Assn; Ore Assn of Sch Supvs. 10: AAUW; SalemCity Club; Salem Art Assn; Marion Co Hist Assn. 14: Sch libs. 15: 1390 Ferry st, Salem Or 97308.

CHEVERIE, ELIZABETH (JEAN WARD). b Buffalo NY 3 O 25. 4: Edward A Cheverie. 5: State U Col (Geneseo NY) 43-47 (Lib Educ) BS, summers 49-53 (Lib Educ) MS. 7: Asst libn Woodward Mem Lib, LeRoy NY 47-48; Elem tchr Royalton-Hartland C S, Gasport NY 49; Libn Attica Central Sch, Attica NY 49-51; Asst libn Book Trailer, Youngstown O 51-52; Libn Avoca Central Sch, Avoca NY 53-55; Libn Franklin Jr High Sch, Kenmore NY 55-58; Libn Barker Elem Sch, Barker NY 62-. 8: NDEA Sch Lib Inst Geneseo NY 65. 9: NEA (life mem); NY State Tchrs Assn (chm Lib Sect, NW Zone 68); Niagara-Orleans Area Assn of Sch Libns. 10: PTA; Trustee Barker Free Lib 64-69, Pres 65-68. 14: Elem sch libs. 15: 1719 Pallister ave, Barker NY 14012.

CHEW, KATHERINE LIANG (PEIHUA). b China. 4: Frank Chew. 5: U So Miss 60-61 (LS) BA; LSU 61-62 (LS) MS. 6: Chinese. 7: Staff Los Angeles Pub Lib 62-66; Admin asst to Coord Br Admin Prince George Co Mem Lib, Hyettsville Md 66-67;Act hd ref dept & Interlib loan libn UMiami Richter Lib (Coral Gables) 67-68; Libndade Co Bd of Pub Instr, Miami Fla 68-. 8: Citizen Adv Com 12th Councilmanic Dist Los Angeles. 9: ALA; NEA; FlaLA; Dade Co SchLA. 10: BetaPhi Mu; AAUW; Phi Lambda Pi; AAUP; PTA. 12: "Prince George's Co Mem Lib Manual ofProcedures" (rev ed 67). 14: Ref, admin, tchg. 15: 901 Sistina ave, Coral GablesFl 33146.

CHIANG, HAVEN. b Kiangsu China 9 O 25. 4: Pih-Yun Chen. 5: Nat ChenchiU 45-49 (Intl Rel) BA; UOrrawa 56-58 (Intl Rel) MA; McGill 60-61 BLS. 6: Chinese. 7: Catlgr N York Pub Lib, Toronto Can 62-63, Bkmob supv 63-66, Libn supv 67-. 9: Inst of Prof libns of Ont. 14: Catlg, ref, govt docs. 15: 869 Bathurst st, Toronto 4 Ont Can.

CHIAPPETTA, JOHN DONALD. b Kenosha Wis 24 D 22. 4: Viola Marie Forgianni. 5: UWis 46-48 (Liberal Arts); Northwestern U 48-50 (Eng) BS; USoCal 60-63 MSLS. 7: Draftsman Bell Aircraft Co, Buffalo NY 42, Cpl US Army, South Pacific 43-45; Libn Antioch Twp High Sch, Antioch Ill 50-58; Libn Morongo Unif Sch Dist, 29 Palms Cal 59-. 8: Asst dean of lib sci, UWyo summer 65. 9: ALA; NEA; CalASchL; Cal Tchrs Assn. 10: Lions Club (treas). 14: Reader's advis, educ for libnship, high sch libnship. 15: 73355 Sun Valley dr, 29 Palms Ca 92277.

CHICOREL, MARIETTA (EVA) (SELBY). b Vienna. 5: Wayne State U 47-52 (Humanities) BA; UMich 57-60 MALS; UWash 65 IBM Field Courses 69. 6: Ger. 7: Instr Ger Wayne State U 50-51; Bibliog UDetroit Lib 54-56; Interlib loans Gen Motors Res Lib, Warren Mich 56-58; Adult serv libn Oak Park Pub Lib, Oak Park Mich 58-61; Consul col & univ lib statistics ALA Nat Lib Statistics Proj 64; Asst chief acquis div UWash Lib 62-66; Chief ed -ulrich's International Periodicals Directory" R R Bowker Co, NYC 66-68; Projectmgr Crowell Collier MacMillan Info Scis, Inc, NYC 68-69; Lib's Publishing consulChicorel Pub Co, NYC 69-. 8: Consul; Col & Univ Lib Stat, Ala Nat Lib Stat Proj64; Wash Governor's Commsn on Status of Women, Educ Com 63-65; NLM 64. 9: ALA(Coun); -RTSD (Bd Dirs 68-72, sec Acquis Sect 65-68, chm Lib Materials Price Index Com65-67; ABPC/RTSD Jt Com 67-68; chm Nomin Com RTSD/SS 68); SLA (NY Chap 1 v-pres &pres-elect Publ Gp); ASIS (Publ Com 67-69). 10: Bk Sellers League; Women's Nat Bkassn; UMich Lib Sci Alumni. 12: 'College and University Library Statistics' in-guide to Library Statistics; Handbook of Concepts, Definitions, and Terminology" ALA(66); Ed Amer Jew Com Seattle Chap "Newsletter" (62-64); Ed "Ulrich's InternationalPeriodicals Directory" 12th ed, 2v (67-68), plus 3 suppl of new titles (66,67,68). 13: Yes. 14: Ref, tech serv, admin, planning, coord, systems analysis. 15: 330 W 58th st, apt 12 N, NYC 10019.

CHIDDELL, PHILIP REX. b Edmonton Alta 31 Jl 28. 4: Modena Anne Brown. 5: UBC 50-53 (Hist) BA; Fuller Theol Sem 53-56 (Religion) BD; UWash 57-58 (LS) ML. 7: Ref libn UOre Lib 58-60, Soc sci libn 60-61; Ref libn Vancouver Pub Lib, Vancouver BC 62-64, Branch libn 64-65; Libn Vancouver City Col (BC) 65-. 9: Assn Br Columbia Libns. 10: Staff Assn UOre Lib. 13: Yes. 14: Ref, catlg. 15: 372 E 47th ave, Vancouver BC Can.

CHIEN, MARGARET CHIH-YU. b Chuking China 23 N 44. 5: Nat TaiwanU 61-65 (Hist) BA; Yale 65-66 (E Asian Hist); Rutgers 66-68 MLS. 6: Chinese, Japanese. 7: Research asst Academia Sinica, Taiwan summer 63; Asst to ed World Bank's Co, Taiwan summer 64; Sr asst catlgr RutgersU (New Brunswick) 67-68, Catlgr 68-69; Catlgr SUNY (Buffalo) 69-. 11: Chinese Culture & Nat Sci Scholarship, Central Chinese Govt; Nat TaiwanU Bk prize. 14: Catlg, acquis. 15: 99 W Winspear ave, Buffalo NY 14214.

CHILDERS, LEONA ELIZABETH (HAWKINS). b Oklahoma City Okla 23 N 11. 4: William Walter Childers. 5: UOkla 30-34 BA in LS; Southwestern Tchrs Col ext 36; UTex summers 38, 39; Wittenberg Col summer 58 Utah State U 68. 6: Fr, Ger. 7: Pub Lib Carnegie Lib, Cordell Okla 34-38; Jr & sr high sch libn tchr, Mercedes Tex 38-41; Civil Serv US Govt, Midland & Randolph Field Eagle Pass Tex 41-45; Tchr I & E Program, Guam MI 48-49; Libn/tchr Dependent Sch, Clark AFB PI 49-50; Libn Sr High Sch, Sumter SC 50-53; Libn Jr High Sch, Springfield Ohio 57-58; Tchr Elem Sch, Sumter SC 58-60; Libn High Sch, New Braunfels Tex 60-66; Libn High Sch, San Antonio Tex 66-67; Tchr High Sch,New Braunfels Tex. 9: Tex State Tchrs Assn; ClrmTA. 10: AAUW; Wesleyan ServiceGuild. 14: Admin, ref, catlg, circ. 15: 550 W Merriweather st, New Braunfels Tx 78130.

CHILDERS, THOMAS ALLEN. b Chillicothe Ohio 2 Jl 40. 5: UMd 58-62 (Eng) BA; Rutgers 62-63 (Lib serv) MLS, 67- (Lib serv). 7: Spec serv libs USA, Ft Lewis Wash 63-65; Sr adult asst (spec ya wk) Baltimore Co Pub Lib, Towson Md 65-67; Research fellow Rutgers U 67-. 9: ALA. 10: ADLIB. 12: "Book Catalog & Card Catalog: a Cost & Service Study" (mimeo, CLR 67). 14: Ref systems. admin, eval of serv. 15: 35 Drift st, New Brunswick NJ 08901.

CHILDRESS, JULIA (EDDINS). b Stanly Co Palmerville NC 25 Ja 06. 4: Thomas R Childress. 5: Meredith Col 23-27 (Lat, Soc Studies) AB; UNC summers 37-40 (LS) BS. 6: Fr. 7: Elem & high sch tchr Stanley Co (NC) System 34-37; Cleveland Elem Sch, Rowan Co (NC) 37-40; Spencer High Sch, Rowan Co (NC) 40-51; Granite Quarry Elem Sch, Granite Quarry (NC) 51-53; Libn Spencer High Sch, Spencer (NC) 53-58; Libn N Rowan High Sch, Spencer (NC) 58-. 9: NEA; NCEA; NCLA; RowanCoLA. 10: Alpha Delta Kappa. 14: Ref, bk sel for yp. 15: 207 S Rowan ave, Spencer NC 28159.

CHILDS, JAMES B(ENNETT). b VanBuren Mo 2 Je 1896. 4: Eleanor A Pirkner. 5: UIll (Urbana) 14-21 BA, BLS. 6: Ger, Fr, Sp. 7: Catlgr John Crerar Lib Chicago 21-25; LC: Chief docs div, Chief catlg div, Chief docs off, Spec in govt doc bibliog 25-. 8: Del to World Lib & Bibliog Congress Rome 29. 9: ALA; Lib Assn (Gt Brit); BSA. 10: Amer Pol Sci Assn; Amer Econ Assn; Cliff Dwellers Chicago; Cosmos Club Wash DC. 12: "Memorias of the Republics of Central America and the Antilles" (32); "Government Documents Bibliography in the U.S. and Elsewhere"(3d ed 42); "Guide to Official Publications of Other American Republics" (5v 45-49); "Author Entries for Government Publications" (39);"German Federal Republic Official Publications 1949-57" (58); German Democratic Republic Official Publications" (60-61); "SpanishGovernment Publications after July 17, 1936" (6v 65-69) & Ed "Papers of the Bibliographical Society of America" (26-36). 13: Yes. 14: "Govt publs, bibliog, catlg. 15: 1221 Newton st NE, Washington DC 20017.

CHILDS, JANE LEE (McCORMACK). b Milton Mass 31 Mr 43. 4: Edwin Sherman Childs. 5: Simmons 61-65 (Bus admin) BS, 65-66 MSLS. 7: Libn Channing Lab of Infectious Diseases Harvard Med Sch 65-67; John Hancock Mutual Life Ins Co, Boston Mass: Asst Librarian 67-68, Libn 68-. 9: SLA; ALA. 10: DAR; Simmons Col Fund Drive, 68-70. 14: Ref. 15: 52 Cypress st, Newton Centre Ma 02159.

CHILDS, MARGARETTA (PRINGLE). b Charleston SC 29 S 12. 4: St Julien Ravenel Childs. 5: Wellesley Col 28-32 (Hist) BA; Johns Hopkins U 33-36 (Hist) Ph D; Emory 67-68 (Libnship) M Ln. 6: Fr. 7: Archival asst SC Hist Soc, Charleston SC 62; Libn St Stephen High Sch, St Stephen SC 60-61; Stock clk Naval Supply Ctr, Charleston SC 63-65; Libn Boulder Bluff Elem Sch, Mt Holly SC 66-67; Libn Curtis Bay

Elem Sch, Baltimore 67; Asst catlgr Welch Med Lib, Baltimore 68-. 9: ALA; AHA. 10: SC Hist Soc; Md Hist Soc; LWV. 14: Rare bks, child lit. 15: 218 E Preston st, Baltimore Md 21202.

CHILDS, MARIAN LAYBOURNE (JONES). b Port Arthur Ont Can 12 My 43. 4: Bruce Allan Childs. 5: Queen'sU 62-65 (Math) BA; UToronto 65-66 BLS. 6: Japanese, Ger. 7: Ref libn Ft William Pub Lib, Ft William Ont Can 66-. 9: CanLA; OntLA. 14: Ref. 15: 209 Balmoral st, Ft William Ont Can.

CHIN, ELISE (YING-SHU LIU). b Soochow Kiangsu China 20 F 31. 4: George Chao Chin. 5: Nat Taiwan U 50-54 (Eng Lit) BA; Seattle Pacific Col 58-60 (Christian Educ); UWash 61-63 MLibnship. 6: Chinese. 7: Tchr 1st Provincial High Sch, Taichung Taiwan 55-57; Libn UWash Lib 63-. 9: ALA. 10: Faculty Women's Club, UWash. 14: Catlg. 15: 3546 NE 125th, Seattle Wa 98125.

CHIN, FRANCES (WANG). b Peking China 24 S 12. 4: Rockwood Q P Chin. 5: UColo 30-33 (Bot) BA; UMich 33-34 (Pub Health) MSPH; ULondon Sch of Hygiene & Tropical Med 34-35 (Bacteriology) Post-Grad Diploma;UMich 37-41 (Microbiology) PhD; UKy 61-62 MSLS. 6: Chinese, Fr. 7: Lab asst Div of Labs NY State Dept Health, Albany NY 36-37; Head Dept of Bacteriology Nat Inst of Health, Chungking China 41-44; Catlgr Med Center Lib UKy (Lexington) 62-63; Head catlgr Welch Med Lib Johns Hopkins U 63-64; Catlgr Brown U Lib 64-65; Assoc Prof Grad Lib Sch URI 65-. 9: MedLA (mem com 65-66); ALA; NEMedLA; NELA; NETSL; RILA ISAD; OVTSL (sec 63). 10: Treas Norton Pub Lib 67-68; Beta Phi Mu; Sigma Xi; Phi Sigma; Iota Sigma Pi; AAUP. 14: Catlg, med libnship. 15: 2 Lynwood rd, Storrs Ct 06268.

CHING, ELLEN (KUI YIN). b Honolulu Hawaii 24 Jl 29. 5: UHawaii 49-53 (Home Econ) BS; Peabody 56-57 (LS) MA. 7: Sch libn Dept of Pub Instr, Kahuku Hawaii 53-56; Libn E Cleveland Bd of Educ, E Cleveland Ohio 57-61; Libn Hawaii Dept of Educ, Honolulu 61-64; Libn Eugene Sch Dist #4, Eugene Ore 64-. 9: NEA; ALA; EugeneEA; OreSchLA; OreEA; OreIMA. 10: Beta Phi Mu. 11: Participant 1965 NDEA Inst for Sch Libns & Sch Lib Supvrs UWash; Participant NSF Tcher-Computer Course, UOre 69. 14: Ya & child reading programs. 15: 2760 Willamette st, #-6, Eugene Or 97405.

CHING, WINNIE H (CHEN). b Shanghai China 29 Jl 37. 4: Charles Y Ching. 5: Taiwan Normal U 54-59 (Educ) BS; So Ill U 59-61 (Educ) MS; Rutgers 61-63 MSLS. 6: Chinese, Fr. 7: Tchr Taipei High Sch, Taipei Taiwan 58-59; Lib-trainee Queens Borough Pub Lib, Jamaica NY 61-62; Asst libn Nazareth Col (Nazareth mich) 63-64; Ref libn Mills Col of Educ 64-67; Ref libn Brentwood Pub Lib, Brentwood NY 67-68; Smithtown Elem Sch Distlib, Smithtown NY 69-. 9: NYLA; NYLib Club. 14: Ref. 15: 21 Grissom way, Hauppauge NY 1187.

CHINIK, MILDRED (KATELLA). b Pittsburgh 20 My 10. 5: UPittsburgh 29-32 (Fr) AB; Carnegie 35-36, 36-37 BS in LS. 6: Fr, Lithuanian. 7: Carnegie Lib, Pittsburgh; Page & clerical positions 25-36, Asst juv South Side br 37-38, Asst juv Wylie ave br39-40, Asst juv Carrick Brookline 41-43, Child libn Knoxville-Carrick 44-51, Libn of br Carrick br 52-62, Libn of br Knoxville br 62-. 9: ALA; CathLA; PennLA. 10: Knights of Lithuania. 14: Pub libs. 15: 4649 Cook ave, Pittsburgh Pa 15236.

CHITTENDEN, CAROL CHRISTINE (BORG). b Atlanta Ga 25 Mr 45. 4: W LeRoy Chittenden. 5: UKan 62-67 (Eng, Pol Sci) BA; IndU 67-68 MLS. 6: Fr. 7: Stud asst Dept Spec Collections UKan 62-67, Libn I Dept Spec Collections Spencer Research Lib 68-; Stud asst Lilly Lib IndU 67-68. 14: Rare bks, catlg, natural hist, early 18th century Eng hist. 15: Spencer Research Lib Univ of Kansas, Lawrence Ks 66044.

CHITWOOD, (JULIUS RICHARD) JACK. b Magazine Ark 1 Je 21. 4: Aileen Newsom. 5: Quachite Col 38-42 (Music) BA; Ind U 47-48 (Music) MMus; Chicago 48-51 (LS) MA. 7: Staff Off (Maj) 422d Infantry, US & Europe 42-46; Music tchr Edinburg Pub Schs, Edinburg Ind 46-47; Music & a-v libn Roosevelt Col 48-51; Humanities libn Drake U 51-53; Catlgr Chicago Tchrs Col 53; Coordinator adult serv Indianapolis Pub Lib, Indianapolis 54-51; Dir Rockford Pub Lib, Rockford Ill 61- Dir No Ill Lib Syst 66-; Sec bd of mgrs Ill Lib Materials Processing Ctr 68-. 8: Mem Advis Com, Ill State Lib 66-; Chm Sub-Com for System Devel 66-; Mem AdvisCom, Grad Sch of Lib Sci, UIll 65-68. 9: ALA-ASD (Bd chm Standards Com;-LAD (chm in-servtrain com, chm Bldg & Equip asst 67-68, pres-elect 68-69); Exec dir Ind NatLib Week 59, Ill Nat Lib Week 64; -PLA (chm sub-com on materials, standards revcom 66-67); IllLA (pres 65-66). 10: Rotary; Interprofes Men's Clubs; RockfordSymphony (Exec Bd); Unitarian Church (pres); C of C. 13: Yes. 14: Admin, adult servs. 15: 215 North Wyman st,Rockford Il 61101.

CHITWOOD, LERA CATHERINE. b Columbiana Ala 14 S 42. 5: Carson-Newman Col 60-64 (Eng) BA; Emory 62-68 M Libn. 7: Atlanta Pub Lib: Lib asst 64-65, YA libn 66-67; Tchr DeKalb Co, Doraville Ga; Libn I, II & act hd Bus & Sci Lib, Atlanta 68-. 14: Bus ref. 15: 1363 Benning pl NE #2, Atlanta Ga 30307.

CHIU, HELEN HANG-YUEN (NG). b Hong Kong China 18 N 40. 4: Norman Chiu. 5: St Mary's Sch (Hong Kong) 479; UHong Kong 59-63 (Hist) BA; UToronto 64-66 (Hist), 66-67 BLS. 6: Chinese, Fr. 7: Tchr: Hong Kong Govt Inst 59-64, Confucion Tai Shing Secondary Sch, Hong Kong 63-64; Lib asst UToronto 64-66; Tech libn Placer Development Ltd, Can 67-68; Act hd sci div UCalgary 68-. 8: Red Cross link leader 63-64; Career mistress 63-64. 9: ALA; SLA; Geosci Info Soc. 14: Ref, indexing, documentation. 15: 304-1239 17th ave NW, Calgary 43 Alberta Can.

CHIU, KAI-YUN. b Republic of China 5 Mr 38. 5: Tunghai U 57-59 (Pol Sci); Col of the Holy Names 59-61 (Pol Sci) BA; UCal (Berkeley) 61-62 MLS Columbia U 67 (LS). 6: Chinese. 7: Sr adult asst Enoch Pratt Free Lib, Baltimore 62-64, Docs libn 66-68; Docs libn John Hopkins U Lib 68-. 9: SLA;-RSD (Md Affiliate). 14: Ref in soc scis, govt docs. 15: 3024 Essex rd, Baltimore Md 21207.

CHIZEVER, MADELINE P. b Boston Mass 5 Ap 36. 4: Calvin K Chizever. 5: Simmons 53-57 (LS) BS; Rutgers summer 57 (LS). 6: Fr, Sp. 7: Prof asst Acquis Dept Harvard Law Lib 57-60; Prof asst Catlg Dept Waltham Pub Lib, Waltham Mass 63; Asst libn Lib Co of the Baltimore Bar 65-67; Ref libn US Soc Security Admin, Baltimore 67-68; Chief libn US Pub Health Serv Hosp, Baltimore 68-. 9: ALA; SLA; MedLA; Baltimore Hosp libn Assn (pres 68-70). 12: Eds comp "Medicare, a Bibliography of Selected References (68). 14: Ref, admin. 15: 803 Judy lane, Baltimore Md 21208.

CHO, KEIKO (NAKAI). b Winnipeg Can 12 Ap 43. 4: Hyunjin Cho. 5: UMan 61-64 (Fr, Lat) BA; UToronto 64-65 BLS; Royal Conservatory of Toronto 66 (Piano) ARCT. 6: Fr, Japanese. 7: atlgr UMan 65, Hd libn Educ Lib 65-67; Catlgr Kee Lib UWis (Milwaukee) 67-68; Catlgr Fondren Lib RiceU 68-. 14: Catlg, music. 15: 3916 Swarthmore, Houston Tx 77005.

CHO, SUNG YOON. b Korea 10 S 28. 4: Wanda Cho. 5: Seoul Nat U Law Sch 53 LLB; Tulane 57 (Internat Law) MA, 63 (Internat Law) PhD George Washington U 66 (Comp Law) MCL (Amer Practice). 6: Korean, Japanese, Chinese. 7: Research asst LC 59, Legal spec 63-, Sr legal spec68-. 9: Amer Soc Internat Law; AALL; Assn Asian Studies. 13: Yes. 14: Legal ref. 15: 7310 Taft rd, Camp Spring Md 20031.

CHOATE, C RAY. b Torrington Wyo 16 Jl 41. 4: Rosia Pasteur. 5: UWyo 59-63 (Eng) BA; FreieU (Berlin) 63-65 (Lit); Columbia 65-66 (LS) MS; UMass 67. 6: Ger. 7: Asst Eng tchr "Deutsche Akademis Die Austauschadencst", W Berlin (Paul-Natorp-Schule, OW2 & Robert-Blum-Schule, OW2) 64-65; Asst ref libn NYU 66; Ref libn UMass 66-. 9: Mod Lang assn. 11: Fulbright Fellowship to FreieU (Berlin) (63-65). 14: Ref, readers serv. 15: Box 161, Hawk Springs Wy 82217.

CHOO, SOO-UN. b Pusan Korea 11 My 24. 4: Virginia B Choo. 5: Paul Smiths Jr Col 55-57 (Liberal Arts) AA; Wilkes Col 57-59 (Econ) BA; Trenton state Col 60-62 (Educ); Rutgers 59-62 MLS; Seton HallU 68- (Asian Studs). 6: Chinese, Fr, Japanese, Korean. 7: Stud asst Paul Smiths Col Lib 55; stud asst Wilkes Col Lib 57; Libn Toms River Schs (Toms River NJ) 59; Libn Ocean Co Lib (Toms River NJ) summer 63; Libn Henry Hudson Reg Schl (Highlands NJ) 62; Head libn Brick Twp High Sch (Brick Town NJ) 63-; Tech libn Naval Air Test Facility (Lakehurst NJ) 64-67. 8: Lang instr, Japanese & Korean USAFI, APO 902 52. 9: ALA; NJ Media Assn; NEA; NJEA; OceanCoLA; BTEA. 14: Admin, catlg, ref. 15: 451 River terr, Toms River NJ 08753.

CHOSKE, LORANNE (JOYCE). b Frederic Wis 17 N 41. 5: Walla Walla Col 60-64 (Hist) BA; UWash 65-68 MLS. 6: Sp. 7: Libn Blue Mountain Acad, Hamburg Penn 64-67; Asst libn Walla Walla Col 68-. 9: ALA; WashLA. 10: ABWA. 14: Ref, ya. 15: #12 119 E Whitman, College Place Wa 99324.

CHOU, HAROLD. b Peking China 27 Ja 09. 4: Daisy Kuo. 5: Yenching U 30 (Educ) BA; UPittsburgh 65 MLS. 68. 6:

Chinese. 7: Sec-clerk Chinese Maritime Customs, China 31-48; Tchr St Stephen's Col (Hong Kong) 49; Photographer Jt Commsn on Rural Reconstruction, Taiwan 50; Tr Australian Ext Affairs Dept, Hong Kong 50-54; Instr UHong Kong, Hong Kong 50-63; Tr "Upper Room" Chinese Ed, Hong Kong 60-62; Instr UPittsburgh summer 63; Catlgr Duquesne U Lib 63-67; Catlgr Edinboro State Col, Asst Prof 67-68 (also teaching LS); Assoc Prof (also teach Chinese) 68. 10: Pittsburgh Lib Club; PSEA. 12: Tr into Chinese: "Upper Room" 17 issues (61-63); "Short Stories by Saki," H H Munro (62); "Major Methodist Beliefs" by Mack B Stokes (64); "Short Stories from Eng & Amer authors" (64). 14: Catlg, ref; South-East Asian collections, microform collection. 15: 65 Valley View, Edinboro Pa 16412.

CHOU, PEI HUA (KAO). b Liao-pei China 14 Ja 38. 4: Chun-Chao Chou. 5: Tunghai U 55-59 (Hist) BA; Colorado Col 59-60 (Hist); UDenver 60-61 (LS) MA. 6: Chinese, Fr. 7: Asst documents libn UKan Lib 61-64, Ref libn 64-65; Catlgr Prof Lib Serv, Santa Ana Cal 65-67; Hd Govt Pub Dept UCa, Irvine Cal 67-. 9: ALA; CalLA. 14: Ref, govt docs, ctlg. 15: 20110 Acacia st, Santa Ana Ca 92707.

CHOUDHURI, NIGAMANANDA (DIPU). b Suri Birbhum W Bengal India 12 Je 36. 5: Suri Vidyasagar Col 52-54 BS; UCalcutta 54-58 (Physics) BS; Berliner Bibliothekar Schule (W Berlin) 62-65 Diplom Bibliothekar; Simmons 66-68 MS. 6: Ger, Bengali, Hindi, Sanskrit. 7: Demonstrator in Physics KC Col (W Bengal Indai) 58-60; Stud-trainee in mech engr Firma E K Spieth, Altbach, NW Germany 60-61; Stud libn Amerika Gedenkbibliothek, W Berlin 62-65; Intern Harvard U Libs 65-67; Catlg shared catlg div ger sect LC 67-68; Catlg York U Libs (Toronto) 68-. 14: Catlg. 15: 87 Harlandale ave, Willowdale Ont Can.

CHOW, DOROTHY (WEI). b China. 4: Chien Chow. 5: George Washington U 51 (Govt) BA; Catholic U 65 MSLS. 6: Chinese, Fr. 7: Acquis libn Welch Med Lib, Johns Hopkins U 64-66; Hd acquis dep Albert S Cook Lib Towson State Col, Baltimore Md 66-. 9: MedLA. 14: Tech proc. 15: 1022 Woodson rd, Baltimore Md 21212.

CHOW, ROSE (JONG). b NYC 4 F 23. 4: Jack Chow. 5: UDubuque 45-48 (Eng) BA; Pratt 50-51 MLS. 6: Chinese. 7: Asst br libn Chatham Square Br NY Pub Lib 48-58; Tchr-libn E Meadow Pub Schs, E Meadow LI NY 58-. 9: NassauLA. 10: Chinese Center on LI; LIChinese Circle. 14: Readers adv, bk sel. 15: 763 Goodrich st, Uniondale LI NY 11553.

CHOW, SHANG-MEI (TANG). b China 5 F 41. 5: Nat Taiwan U 59-63 (For Lang & Lit) BA; SUNY (Albany) 64-67 MLS. 6: Chinese, Fr. 7: Tchr Taipei Second Girls' High Sch, Taipei Taiwan 63-64; Libn (Staff) Schenectady Co Pub Lib, Schenectady NY 67; Libn 9staff) UNC (Chapel Hill) 68-. 10: UNC Women's Club. 14: Catlg, ref. 15: C-8 Camelot apts Estes dr, Chapel Hill NC 27514.

CHOW, TSO-HUAI. b Hunan China 19 F 34. 4: Wei-Moa Tsad. 5: Chung-Hsin U (Taiwan) 51-55 (Econ) BS; New Asia Research Inst (HongKong) 57-59 (Chinese Hist) MA; Peabody 64-65 MLS; Kansas State U 60-64 (Bus admin) MS. 6: Chinese, Japanese. 7: Asst ed Farms' FriendMagazine, Taiwan 56-57; Dean of Stud Fu-Ten High Sch, Hong Kong 59-60; Sr libn Queens Borough Pub Lib, NY 65-69; Dep dir New Asia ColLib Chinese U of Hong Kong 69-. 13: Yes. 14: Asian studies, research. 15: 6 Farm rd, Kowloon Hong Kong.

CHOWDHURY, MAN D. b Calcutta India 26 Ag 26. 5: Calcutta U 42-48 (Bus Admin) BC, 49-51 (Law, Econ); Grad Faculty New Sch 61, 64 (Econ); Pratt Inst 60-63 MLS Columbia U 67 (LS). Columbia U 67 (LS). 6: Sanskrit, Bengali, Hindi, Fr. 7: Trainee adult serv Brooklyn Pub Lib 60-63; Prof asst readers serv Fordham U Lib 63-64; Asst libn period NY State Lib 64-68; Libn Harlem Hosp Ctr Med Sci Div Columbia U Libd 68-. 68; Libn Harlem Hosp Ctr Med Sci Div Columbia U Libd 68-. 9: ALA; -ACRL; SLA; ASIS; AAMC; Amer Econ Assn; Lib Assn (Gt Brit); Royal Econ Soc (Fellow); NYLA. 13: Yes. 14: Acad libs, bibliog, admin. 15: Med Sci Div Columbia Univ Libs 630 W 168th st, New York NY 10032.

CHRANE, OLEENE (ROCHESTER). b Bangs Tex 4 Ap 17. 4: George Chrane. 5: Daniel Baker Col 34-36; Sul Ross State 46-49 (Elem Educ) BA; NTex State 56-62 (Secondary Educ) MEd; N Tex State Lib Certif. 7: Tchr Crane Ind Sch Dist, Crane Tex 49-51; Tchr Tolar Ind Sch Dist, Tolar Tex 51-56; Tchr Stephenville Ind Sch Dist, Stephenville Tex 56-57; Tchr Tolar Ind Sch Dist, Tolar Tex 57-61; Libn Rocksprings Ind Sch Dist, Rocksprings Tex 61-65; Libn Marble Falls Ind Sch Dist; Marble Falls Tex 65-. 9: Tex State Tchrs Assn (Dist Sec; TEPS chm). 10: Tolar Garden Club; Delta Kappa Gamma; Kappa Delta Phi. 14: Bks for yp. 15: Box 283, Marble Falls Tx 78654.

CHRISMAN, DIANE (SCHUTTA). 03: b Lackawanna NY. 4: David F Chrisman. 5: UVM 55-59 (Eng) BA; Simmons 59-60 MS in LS. 7: Libn jr & sr Buffalo & Erie Co Pub Lib, Buffalo NY 60-. 9: NYLA; ALA. 15: 38 Briarwood dr, Lancaster NY 14086.

CHRISMAN, LARRY GEORGE. b Glendale Cal 27 N 40. 4: Shirley Ann (Anderson). 5: Allan Hancock Col 58-60 (Soc sci) AA; Wash State U 60-62 (Prelaw) BA; USoCal 64-66 (LS) MS. 6: Fr, Ger, Sp. 7: Librarian I, II USoCal 66-. 9: ALA. 14: Catlg. 15: 724 E Alvin ave, Santa Maria Ca 93454.

CHRIST, JOHN MICHAEL. b Kan City Kan 4 F 34. 4: Peggy Ann Phalen Christ. 5: Creighton U 52-54, 58-60 (Journalism) AB; Rutgers 60-61 MLS. 7: US Army Ft Stewart Ga Pfc Artillery (Radar) 55-57; Ref libn Creighton U 61-63; Head Libn Rockhurst Col 63-. 8: Kan City Reg Coun for Higher Educ, chm Lib Sub-Com for Central Purch & Proc. 9: MoLA (Recr Com). 13: Yes. 14: Admin. 15: 5225 Troost ave, Kan City Mo 64110.

CHRIST-JANER, VIRGINIA. b Dewey Okla 6 Ag 13. 4: Albert Christ-Janer. 5: Stephens Col 31-33 (Eng) AA; UMo 33-36 (Eng) BS in Educ; Columbia 37 (Comparative Lit); UMo 37-38 (Eng) AM; Cranbrook Acad of Art 45-47; Pratt 62-63 MLS. 6: Fr. 7: Libn for humanities div Dormitory Libs, Stephens Col 34-38, Instr in lit 38-41; Midwest Col Wkshop UChicago summer 39; Instr of Eng Christian Col 42; Instr of Eng Mich State Col 44-45; Instr of Eng asst libn George Williams Col 48-49; Libn NY Pub Lib NY 64-69; Asst curator dance coll, Lib Perf Arts, Lincoln Ctr 69-. 8: Five yearsresearch on "American Hymnbook"; Spec assignment, NY Pub Lib, indexing "New York PubClipper, 1853-1924". 9: ALA; SLA; NYLib Club. 10: Beta Phi Mu; Pi Lambda Theta. 12: Ed wk on two of husbands books "Boardman Robinson" (46) & "Eliel Saarinen" (48). 14: Ref, rare bks, automation in libs. 15: Apt 8E 160 E 48 st, NYC 10017.

CHRISTENSEN, CAROL (MAE). b St Paul Minn 1 Jl 38. 5: Bethel Col St Paul 56-60 (Bio) BA; UMinn 61-67 (Lib) MA. 7: Sci tchr St Paul Pub Schs, St Paul Minn 60-61; Asst libn Bethel Col (St Paul) 61-. 9: ALA; MinnLA. 14: Admin, ref, period. 15: 3122 Shorewood dr, St Paul Mn 55112.

CHRISTENSEN, DAVID W. b Pottsville Penn 16 Ja 19. 5: UDel 49-52 (Eng) AB; Columbia 52-53 MSLS. 7: Readers adv DC Pub Lib 53-58, Br libn 58-. 9: ALA; DCLA. 14: Ref. 15: 4300 Old Dominion dr, Arlington Va 2207.

CHRISTENSEN, EVAN J. b Brigham City Utah 20 N 30. 4: Geraldine Ogden. 5: Utah State U 55-59 (Pol Sci) BS; UIll 59-61 MSLS. 6: Swedish, Norwegian. 7: Missionary Church of Jesus Christ Latter Day Saints, Sweden 50-53; Cpl US Army, Italy & Austria 53-55; Clerk Food King Inc, Brigham City Utah 56-59; Lib clerk UIll (Urbana) 60-61; Libn Tidewater Oil Co, Los Angeles 61-68; Sci libn Weber State Col 68-. 9: SLA; CalLA. 14: Admin. 15: 1359 36th st, Ogden Ut 84403.

CHRISTENSEN, MARGUERITE A(LICE). b Trout Lake Wis. 5: UWis 34-38 BA, 38-39 BLS. 6: Fr. 7: Libn pub & high sch libs, Bloomer Wis 39-41; Asst Wis State Col (Superior) 41-43; Asst libn Carroll Col 43-45; Asst ref libn UWis (Madison) 45-66; Hd gen ref dept 67-. 9: ALA. 10: Nat Audubon Soc; Madison Audubon Soc. 14: Ref. 15: 4469 Hillcrest dr, Madison Wi 53705.

CHRISTENSEN, RODNEY EDWARD. b Chicago Ill 11 Mr 29. 4: Barbara Saillor. 5: UIll 48-51 (Soc sci); NoIllU 56 (Social sci) BS, 57 (Soc sci) MS; USoCal 66 MSLS. 6: Sp. 7: USA 52-54; Tchr High Sch, Globe Ariz 57-66; Libn LA Pub Lib 67-68; Soc sci ref libn UOregon 68-. 9: ALA; OreLA. 14: Ref, bus, Latin Amer hist. 15: 2087 Alder, Eugene Or 97405.

CHRISTENSEN, RUTH MARTHA. b Glendale Cal 15 Jl 23. 4: Rex Blythe Christensen. 5: UCLA 41-44 (Hist) BA, 45-46 (Hist) MA; Immaculate Heart Col 62 MA in LS; 3 California Cred entials-Sch Lib, Gen Secondary, Lifetime Jr Col; USoCal Sch of Ed 67-. 6: Sp, Fr. 7: Grad research histn dept of hist, UCLA 45-62; Educ libn Cal State Col (Los Angeles) 62-68; SW Mus libn, Highland Pk, Los Angeles 68-. 8: Activities associated with Jr Col Libs Sect of ACRL; Read paper on "The Junior College Library as an Audio-Visual Center" at 63rd ALA Conf; planned & chaired wkshop on spec materials including a-v at 65th ALA Conf. 9: ALA (Life mem, Mem Recr Netwk);-ACRL (A-V Com 64-68, chm 66-67, Jr Col Lib

Sec; Stand Com 64-66, chm ad hoc com to revise JCLS Bylaws 67-69; Recorder 68 Preconf); CalLA (various duties); CalASchL; SoCal Coun Lit Child & YP; NEA-DAVI; A-V Educ Assn Cal, So Sect. 10: AAUP; LWV; Friends of So Pasadena Lib; Friends of The Huntington Lib; UCLA Alum Assn (life mem); Art Coun Cal State Col, Los Angeles. 13: Yes. 14: Ref, spec materials, bibliog, research. 15: 1506 Stratford ave, South Pasadena Ca 91030.

CHRISTENSEN, SIBYL (MAXINE). b Cedar Rapids Iowa 23 N 26. 5: State U Iowa 55-58 (Eng) BA, 67-68 (LS) MA. 6: Fr. 7: PO Clk PO Dept, Lost Nation Iowa 44-55; Clerical Wk Protein Blenders, Iowa City Iowa 55-58; Eng Tchr Iowa City Commun Schs, 58-65; Self-Employed Sales Amway Corp, Iowa City 65-68; Sch Libn Mid-Prairie Jr High, Kalona Iowa 68-. 9: NEA; Iowa State EA; Mid-Prairie EA; IowaASchL; Iowa City EA (sec 62-63, pres 63-64). 10: Phi Beta Kappa. 14: Sch libnship, acquis, ya. 15: RR 5 Linder r, Iowa City Ia 52240.

CHRISTENSON, HELEN (SMITH). b Lee Mass 26 Ap 01. 4: H Lloyd Christenson. 5: Simmons 20-24 (Eng) BS. 7: Catlgr NY Pub Lib 24, 27, 29; Catlgr Lenox Lib Assn, Lenox Mass 54-. 9: West MassLA. 14: Catlg, ref. 15: 19 Debra ave, Lee Mass 01238.

CHRISTIAN, MRS CLYDE (HILLYER). b Waco Tex 3 My 09. 4: Alfred B Christian. 5: American U 43- (Pub Admin). 7: Clerk to Archivist Dept of Army, Wash DC 42-54; Record Manager Archivist Deptof Defense, Ft Geo G Meade Md 54-. 9: Soc Amer Arch; mem of state & local hist socs. 10: Garden Club. 14: Catlg, ref in govt records. 15: 6500 Truman rd, Hyattsville Md 20783.

CHRISTIAN, MABLE (IRENE) DIVERS. b Jellico Tenn 27 Ap 15. 4: Henry Thomas Christian. 5: Knoxville Col 41-45 (Sociol, Eng) AB; Bethune-Cookman Col 60-61 (LS) Fla Certif; UWis summers 60, 63, 65, 67-68 MSLS. 6: Fr. 7: Tchr Beardsley Jr High Sch, Knoxville Tenn 45-46; Soc sci tchr Kinterbish High Sch, Cuba Ala 46-48; Clerk Daytona Beach Housing Authority, Daytona Beach Fla 50-59; Tchr-libn R J E High Sch, Starke Fla 59-61; Asst libn Daytona Beach Jr Col Volusia Center 61- 66, Daytona Beach Jr Col 66-. 8: Part-time adult educ tchr Campbell St Sch Center Daytona Beach Fla, 56-59; S Co-sponsor Phi Theta Kappa 61-66 & 68 09: ALA; FlaLA; FlaEA; Fla Adult EA; Fla State Tchrs Assn; NEA. 10: Alpha K appa Mu; Zeta Phi Beta; Nat Coun of Negro Women; YWCA; Hon mem Phi Theta Kappa; Silver Leaf Charity Club. 14: Acquis, tech serv, readers serv. 15: 940 School st, Daytona Beach Fl 32014.

CHRISTIAN, PORTIA. b Noblesville Ind 12 Ja 08. 5: Oxford Col for Women 26-28 (Eng Lit); Butler U Even (50-58) Eng Lit BA; Columbiaeve 59-61 MLS. 7: Libn & archivist Caldwell, Larkin & Sidner-Van Riper, Indianapolis 34-55; Asst libn US Brewers Assn, NYC 56; Own bus 207 E 34th st Inc, NYC 56-58; Bibliogr & bkseller The Book Mailer Inc, NYC 58-60; Lib asst McKinsey & Co Inc, NYC 60-61; Instr in Lib Sci Ind U 61-63, Asst bus libn 63-68; Libn Acad of Food Marketing St Joseph's Col 68-. 8: Consul to US Grinding Wheel Co NYC, records mgt 55. 9: ALA-LAD(Ind Rep 62-63); SLA (Ind Chap treas 50, pres 54, chm Admis Com 64-65); IndLA (chmscholarship & Loan Com 65, mem Recr Com 62-68). 10: Women's Nat Bk Assn 59-. 11: US Legion of Merit, with citation 45. 12: Ed "Beth El Temple Sisterhood Cookbook" (50). 14: Ref serv, instr in use of lib resources, admin, catlg. 15: 101 Conshocken st,Llanberris Apt B-2, Bala Cynwyd Pa 19004.

CHRISTIANO, KATHERINE (LEACH). b Wash DC 24 Ap 43. 4: Lawrence A Christiano. 5: UBridgeport 60-64 (Eng Lit) BA; Drexel 64-65 MS in LS. 7: Catlgr UBridgeport 657; Ref libn Greenwich Lib, Greenwich Conn 67-68, Hd catlg dept 68-. 9: ConnLA. 15: 45 Valley rd, Cos Cpb Ct 06807.

CHRISTIANSEN, BERNIECE M. b Von Ormy Tex 20 Mr 14. 4: Royce P Christiansen. 5: St Mary's U 46 (Sociol) BA; Out Lady of the Lake Col 48 BS in LS. 7: Asst br libn San Antonio Pub Lib, San Antonio Tex 47-48; Hosp libn Brook Gen Hosp, Ft Sam Houston Tex 48-49; Co libn New Madrid Co, New Madrid Mo 49-53; Ref libn Gen Electric Co Hanford Atomic Energy Works, Richland Wash 54-57; UN Documents libn UCLA 57-58; Asst acquis libn UHouston 58-59; Research libn Tex Research Inst of Mental Sci, Houston 59-. 9: SLA-Tex Chap (chm Employment Com 62-64); MedLA; Wash State Lib Assn (sec 55-57). 14: Ref. 15: 1300 Mour Sund, Houston TX 77025.

CHRISTIANSEN, DOROTHY EILEEN. b New Rochelle NY 27 O 42. 5: SUNY at New Paltz 60-64 (Elem ed) BS; Pratt Inst 65-66 MLS. 7: Tchr Yonkers Bd of Educ, Yonkers NY 64-65; Ctr for Urban Educ, NYC: Lib clk 65-66, Asst libn 66-. 9: ALA; SLA. 10: Beta Phi Mu. 14: Ref, bibliog. 15: 47 Adams st, New Rochelle NY 10801.

CHRISTIANSEN, EDWARD W JR. b Savannah Ga 10 N 23. 4: Helen Patricia Priest. 5: LoyolaU 40-43 (Accounting); Okla State 43 (Math); Washburn 51-53 (Econ) BA; LSU (New Orleans) 67-68 (LS); Tule 67-68 (Hist). 7: Pilot & personnel staff (Lt Col) USAF 42-64; Pres Choctaw Development Co, Ft Walton Beach Fla 65-66; Chief circ H T Memorial Lib TulaneU 66-. 14: Circ, automation. 15: 4745 Charlene dr, New Orleans La 70127.

CHRISTIANSON, ELIN (BALLANTYNE). b Gary Ind 11 N 36. 4: Stanley D Christianson. 5: Chicago 54-58 (Liberal Arts, LS) BA; Chicago 58-59 (LS) MA, 69-. 7: Ed asst "Journal of Business," UChicago 57-59; Asst libn J Walter Thompson Co, Chicago 59-63, Libn 64-68, Consul 68-. 9: ALA (chm Study of Regl ed of Periodicals,consul to Coun Com on Access to Libs); ASIS; SLA (Adver & Marketing Div, chm 67-68,dir 68-69); Co-chm Spec Proj Com 61-64, Rep to Spec Clsf Com 64;-Ill Chap; AsstBulletin Ed 60-61, Ed 61-63 (Memb chm 63-64, treas 65-66). 12: "Subject Headings inadver, Marketing & Communications Media," with E G Strable (64); Ed "The InformantAdver, Marketing & Communications Media," with E G Strable (64); Ed "The Informant";SLA-Ill Chap Bulletin 60-63; Ed "What's New in Adver & Marketing" 64-66, 67-68; Edasst "Journal of Business" (57-59). 13: Yes. 14: Info retr, spec libs. 15: 1478 E 56th st,Chicago Il 60637.

CHRISTIE, SYLVIA MERRILL. b Minneapolis 28 F 11. 4: George Norman Christie. 5: UMinn 29-33 (Fr) BS, 54-55 (LS) MA. 6: Fr, Sp. 7: Libn Pub Schs, Minneapolis 55-. 9: NEA; MinnASchL; MinnEA. 10: Minn Alumni Assn. 14: Child wk. 15: 4920 Morgan ave So, Minneapolis Mn 55409.

CHRISTMAN, EMILY ELIZABETH (SCHROEDER). b Reading Penn 21 Ap 08. 5: Kutztown State Tchrs Col 25-28 (Educ) BS, summers 29-32; Penn & Temple 25-26, 40. 7: Tchr & libn Bensalem Sr High Sch, Cornwells Heights Penn 28-60, libn & supv 60-. 8: Consul & adv to several elem & high sch libs; Adv to Bucks Co Tech Lib; Prepared annotated list of bks for Imperial Bk Co of P hila. 9: NEA; Penn State EA; Phila Sub LA; Bucks Co (Penn) LA. 10: Alpha Delta Kappa. 14: Ref, proc. 15: Bensalem Sr High Sch, 2201 Street rd, Cornwells Heights Pa 19020.

CHRISTMANN, MARJORIE (HELD). b Evanston Ill 12 N 29. 4: Henry A Christmann. 5: Grinnell 47-48; WashU 48-51 (Psych) BA; Rosary Col 63-65 MLS. 6: Fr, Sp. 7: Order libn Northwestern U Lib 52-54; Ref libn Glenview Pub Lib, Glenview Ill 63-64; Asst libn Northbrook Pub Lib, Northbrook Ill 64-. 9: ALA; IllLA; LACONI (chm nominating Com, Ref Div). 10: Kappa Kappa Gamma; Lyons Sch Parent Club; AAUW; Ill Child Home & Aid Soc; Evanston Woman's Club; WashU Alumnae Assn. 14: Pub rel. 15: 1335 Pine st, Glenview Il 60061.

CHRISTOPHER, IRENE. b Greece 17 N 22. 5: Boston U 40-44 (Eng) AB; Simmons 44-45 BS in LS. 6: Fr, Ger, gk. 7: Gen asst Røbbins Lib, Arlington Mass 45-46; Boston U: Circ libn 46-48, Head of ref serv 48-62, Libn Nursing Social Wk Lib 62; Dir Emerson Col Lib 62-68; G K Hall & Co 68; Lib Harvard Gordon McKay Lib 68-. 68; G K Hall & Co 68; Lib Harvard Gordon McKay Lib 68-. 8: Asst libn Interchemical Corp NYC summer 56. 9: ALA (Memb Com 63-64, New Ref Tools Com 68-); -ACRL (Com on Nat Lib Week 62-63); -RSD (Catlg Use Com 63-68, chm 68-); NELA; MassLA; SLA (Boston Chap: Sec 50-53, dir 68-70, chm Mem Com 53- 55, chm Nomin Com 55-56, Mem Com on Loc Affairs for Nat Conf 55-57, mem Program Com 57-58); NE Tech Serv Libns (Recr sec 64-66, mem Nomin Com 62-63 chm 66-67, NE col libns (chm Nom Com 66-67, sec-treas 68-69); Libns of Small Cols of Boston (chm Nom Com 67-68); Boston U Lib Club (pres 55-56, mem Exec Bd 56-58). 10: AAUP; Mass Soc for Univ Educ of Women. 13: Yes. 14: Ref. 15: 107 Poplar st, Watertown Ma 02172.

CHRISTOPHER, LAURA ALICE. b Santa Monica Cal 24 O 41. 5: UMd Munich Br 59-61; UCal at Berkeley 61-63 (Soc sci) AB; UIll 63-64 MSLS. 7: Libn Freeport Commun Col 64-66; Ref libn Educ & Psych Lib UCLA 66-67; Research libn Amer Inst for Research, Palo Alto Cal 67-. 9: SLA; CalLA. 14: Ref. 15: 945 High School Way apt 5, Mountain View Ca 94040.

CHRISTOPHERSON, ERMA (WENTWORTH). b Princeton Minn 5 Ag 22. 4: Walter Christopherson. 5: Gustavus adolphus Col 40-44 (Eng) BA; UMinn 51-55 BS in LS. 6: Ger. 7: Eng

Instr High Sch, Cloquet Minn 44-45; Eng Instr High Sch, Hastings Minn 45-47; Libn High Sch, Hackensack Minn 47-50; Libn High Sch, Remer Minn 50-61; Lib Sci Instr State Col (Bemidji Minn) 61-65, Child lit instr 65-. 9: ALA; MinnEA. 10: AAUP. 14: Child lit. 15: 803 Donald ave, Bemidji MN 56601.

CHRISTY, ANNA BELLE (PEERS). b Deer Lodge Mont 3 D 17. 4: Leon Eugene Christy. 5: Spokane Jr Col 36-38 (Eng) AA; Whitworth Col 38-40 (Eng) BA, 40-41 (Educ) Tchg certif; UWash 45-46 BS in LS. 7: Tchr High Sch, Pine City Wash 41-42; Tchr-libn High Sch, Anatone Wash 42-43; Tchr-libn High Sch, Ridgefield Wash 43-45; Asst libnGraceland Jr Col 46-47; Catlg libn Jackson Co Lib, Independence Mo 47-49; Libn Cass Co Lib, Harrisonville Mo 47-59; Libn Cass Co Lib,Harrisonville Mo 59-64; Admin SW Mo Lib Serv, Bolivar Mo 64-67; Extens libn Kinderhook Reg Lib, Lebanon Mo 67-. 8b Deer Lodge Mont 3 O 17. 07: 67; Extens libn Kinderhook Reg Lib, Lebanon Mo 67-. 9: ALA; MoLA (Certif Bd 63-70). 14: Ext wk, catlg, Bk talks. 15: 201 Jessie,Lebanon Mo 65636.

CHU, ELAINE (I-NAN-LIU). b Chang-Sar China 2 Ag 35. 4: Shi-Pei Chu. 5: Nat TaiwanU 55-59 (Psych) BS; Pratt Inst 61-63 MLS. 6: Chinese, Ger. 7: Lib asst Pratt Inst Lib 62-63; Catlgr NC State U Lib 63-64; Circ & ref libn Shaw U Lib 64-65; Art ref libn NC Mus of Art Ref Lib, Raleigh 65-68; Med libn St Elizabeth Hosp Med Lib, Covington Ky 69-. 10: Chm ch lib com 1st Baptist Ch of Springdale, Cincinnati. 14: Ref, catlg. 15: 821 Rosemont ave, Cincinnati Oh 45205.

CHUBAK, BENJAMIN. b USA 3 Ap 13. 4: Sydell N Berns. 5: City Col (NYC) 29-37 (Biol, Psych) BS; Columbia 37-42 BS in LS, 45-46 (Adult Educ, Personnel) MA. 6: Fr, Ger, Lat. 7: Chief acquis div City Col (NYC) 45-. 9: ALA; NYLib Club. 10: Kappa Delta Pi. 13: Yes. 14: Acquis, ref. 15: 8615 4th ave, North Bergen NJ 07047.

CHUN, MAY (C HONG). b Honolulu Hawaii 2 My 23. 4: David U S Chun. 5: IndU 46 (Eng) BS; UHawaii 53 Tchr's Certif, 67 MLS, (Ed admin) M Ed. 7: Libn, Waipahu Hawaii: Waipahu Elem Sch 47-49, Vice-prin 49-50; Libn Pearl City Sch, Pearl City Hawaii 53-54; Libn Lunalilo Sch, Honolulu 54-56; Libn Jefferson Sch, Honolulu 58-62; Hawaii State Dept of Educ: Program asst sch lib serv 62-65, Program specialist sch lib serv, Act dir sch libs & instr materials br 68-. 8: Adv Com Grad Sch of Lib Studies, UHawaii 65-66, 68. 9: HLA; -AASchL (State Assembly Del 65); HawaiiLA chm Child Sect 63-64. 12: Ed of State newsletter, "ALOHA IKE AKEA," 64-69. 14: Sch libs. 15: 295 Ulua st, Honolulu Hi 96821.

CHUNG, SUNOK (WUN). b Seoul Korea 26 O 39. 4: Woo Hong Chung. 5: EWHA WomansU (Seoul Korea) 58-62 (Eng Lit) BA; USoCal 67-68 (LS) MS. 6: Korean. 7: Sec to pres Christian Ctr, Seoul Korea 623; Asst libn Ewha Woman'sU, Seoul Korea 63-65; Inventory controller A-I Kotzin Co, LA 66-67; Asst libn Orange Co Lib La Habra 69-. 14: Adult ref. 15: 1741 E La Habra blvd, La Habra Ca 90631.

CHUNN, JEAN (JOHNSON). b Richmond Va 7 Ap 45. 4: Anson Bob Chunn. 5: UMiss 63-66 (Eng) BA, 67-68 MLS; Fla StateU 66 (LS). 7: Jr libn ref dept UMiss Lib 67-68, Sr libn ref dept 68-. 9: MissLA. 14: Ref. 15: 209 Avent st, Oxford Ms 38655.

CHURCH, CORNELIA B(ASSETT). b New Paltz NY 21 Jl 06. 5: UMass 28 (Home Econ) BS; UWis 41 BLS. 7: Asst ref dept Worcester Pub Lib, Worcester Mass 31-42, Head bus sci & tech dept 43-48, Head adult dept 49-56; Reg libn Reg Lib Center, Greenfield Mass 56-64; Asst Dir West Reg Pub Lib System, Springfield Mass 64-. 68, Reg Admin 68-. 9: ALA; NELA; MassLA. 15: 220 State st, Springfield Ma 01103.

CHURCH, EARLYN (DEAN). b Canada 13 Ag 39. 4: Theodore H Church. 5: UAlberta 57-60 9pol Sci) BA; UToronto 60-61 BLS. 7: Asst libn Imperial Oil, Toronto Can 61-62; Indexer Nat Ind Conf Bd, NY 62-69; Libn McCall Corp, NY 64-65; Libn Sullivan Stauffer Calwell Boyles, NY 67-68; Asst libn Port of NY Authority 68-. 8: Vol serv Universidad del Pacifico, Lima Peru 66. 12: "NICB Cumulative Index" (62-69). 14: Indexing, thesaurus prep. 15: 2330 Linwood ave, Fort Lee NJ 07024.

CHURCH, HELEN L. b Indianapolis Ind 17 Ag 16. 5: Iowa State Tchrs Col 35-36, 37-40 (Eng) BA; DenverU 48-49 (S) MA. 7: 1st Lt WAAC, Ft Des Moines Iowa 42-43; Order catlg libn pub lib, Richland Wash 54-56, 58-59; USAF: Admin libn, Japan 56-58, Chief libn, Libya 59-61, chief libn, Korea 63-66; Past libn USA, Ft Lewis Wash 61-63; Dist libn 13th Naval Dist, Bremerton Wash 66-. 9: ALA; WashLA. 10: Bus & Prof Women. 14: Admin 15: Box 4156 Wycoff Station, Bremerton Wa 98310.

CHURCH, WILLA (M). b North Little Rock Ark 19 My 08. 5: Mary Hardin-Baylor Col 25-28 (Eng) BA; West Res 36-41 BS in LS; UMinn 51-55 (Curriculum). 6: Fr. 7: Eng tchr Austin High Sch, Austin Minn 29-42, Libn 42-46; Libn Gen Lib Stephens Col, Columbia Mo 46-47; Libn Austin Sr High Sch, Austin Minn 47-64, Coordinator of sch lib serv 64-. 8: Instr in Lib Sci UMinn(Duluth) 50. 9: MinnSchLA (pres); ALA; AASchL; NEA; MinnEA. 10: AAUW; Delta Kappa Gamma; PEO. 14: Admin. 15: Admin Bldg, 202 Fourth ave, NE Austin Mn 55912.

CHURCHILL, KATHRYN (MARGARET HUGHES). b Hood River Ore 2 Je 09. 4: Irving Lester Churchill. 5: Muskegon Jr Col 27-29; UMich 29-32 BA, BA in LS. 6: Fr. 7: Catlg & circ asst Ousterhout FreeLib, Wilkes-Barre Penn 32-34; Libn Bucknell U Jr Col (Wilkes U) 34-37; Act catlgr Coe Col 49; Libn Mercy Hosp Sch of Nursing, Cedar Rapids Iowa 50-55; Asst in tech serv Pub Lib, Cedar Rapids Iowa 58-61, Head kenwood Br Lib 61-66; Catlg libn Coe Coll 66-69; Order libn Warren Wilson Col 69-. 8: Re-catlgd collection Silliman U Sch of Nurs Lib Dumaguete Philippines 55-56; Visiting Consul in lib serv Tunghai U Lib Taichung Taiwan 64-65. 10: Cedar Rapids Col Club; Cedar Rapids Ladies' Lit Club; Wednesday Shakespeare Club; PEO; LWV; Phi Kappa Phi; Phi Beta Kappa; Phi Tau Phi. 13: Yes. 14: Catlg, ref, admin. 15: Warren Wilson Col, Swannanoa NC 28778.

CHURCHILL, REV ARTHUR R. b LI NY 22 Je 33. 5: St Francis Col (Loretto Penn) 52-56 (Philos) BA; Villanova U 61-64 MS in LS;St Francis Sem 56-60 (Theol). 6: Fr, Lat. 7: Libn St Francis Sem 58-60; Instr Bishop Egan High Sch, Levittown Penn 61-63; Asst libn Col of Steubenville 63-64; Asst libn St Francis Col (Loretto Penn) 64-65; Libn Bishop Egan High Sch, Levittown Penn 65-. 9: ALA; CathLA-East Penn Unit; PennLA; Bucks Co LA. 10: Cath Hist Soc of Phila. 13: Yes. 14: Admin, catlg. 15: Bishop Egan High Sch (611) Wistar rd, Fairless HillsPa.

CHURCHWELL, CHARLES DARRETT. b Dunnellon Fla 7 N 26. 4: Yvonne Ransom. 5: Morehouse 48-52 (Math) BS; Atlanta U 52-53 (Col & Univ Lib Admin) MLS; UIll 58, 63-66 (Col & Univ Lib Admin) PhD. 7: Sgt 4th Grade Army Air Force US & Philippine Is 45-47; Ref asst Alabama State Col summer 52; Instr lib sci Prairie View A&M Col 53-58;Ref libn circ dept New Pub Lib, NYC 59-61; Bkstacks libn UIll (Urbana) 64-65; Asst circ libn 65-67; Asst dir pub serv UHouston 67-. 8: Adv Com Atlanta U Lib Sch; Visit Com, So Assn of Col & Schs; Adv to Amer Gen Ins Co of a Prog for the Unemployed. 9: ALA; TexLA; SWLA. 10: AAUP; NAACP; Nat Urban League. 14: Col & univ lib admin, ref. 15: 3801 Cullen blvd, Houston Tx 77004.

CHURGIN, SYLVIA JOSEPHINE. b Bronx NY 17 Ja 25. 4: Charles Judge Churgin. 5: Syracuse 50-54 (Plant Sci) BS, 63-64 (Plant Physiology), 65-67 MSLS. 7: Jr scientist (biochem) SUNY Col of Med (Syracuse) 54-67, Asst ref libn 67-. 9: MedLA; SUNYLA. 10: Nat Audubon Soc; Phi Beta Kappa; Beta Phi Mu; Botany Club of Syracuse. 13: Yes. 14: Ref. 15: 414 Hibbell ave, Syracuse NY 13207.

CHVATAL, DONALD (PAUL). b Waverly Iowa 14 My 40. 4: Nancy (Mackey) Chvatal. 5: St John's U (Collegeville Minn) 58-60, 61-63 (Philos) BA; UIll(Urbana) Ill summer 62, 63-64 MSLS. 6: Lat, Fr. 7: Exch libn St John's U (Collegeville Minn) 59-60, 61-63; Instr-libn St Augustine's Col (Nassau Bahamas) 60-61; Asst in circ UIll(Urbana) 63-64; Humanities ref libn Fla Atlantic U 64-65; Asst ref libn UMont 65-67, Dir of pub serv 67-68; Br mgr, Richard Abel & Co., Dallas Tex. 9: MontLA (Exhi b Co-chm 65-66); PNLA (chm Printing & Publ Com 66-68). 14: Ref, admin, collections devel. 15: 812 Gaye lane, Arlington Tx 76010.

CHWALEK, SISTER ADELE MARIE. b Ludlow Mass 3 Je 39. 5: Our Lady of the Angels Jr Col 57-59; Col of St Catherine 65-67 (LS) BA. 6: Polish. 7: Libn Longview Lib Learning Ctr, Enfield Conn 67-. 9: ALA; CathLA; ConnLA. 15: 1333 Enfield st, Enfield Ct 06030.

CIAMAGA, LILLIAN (MARIE). b London Ont Can 9 N 29. 4: Gustav S J Ciamaga. 5: UWest Ont 50-53 BA (Toronto) 54-55 BLS. 6: Fr. 7: Child libn Hamilton Pub Lib, Hamilton Ont Can 55-56; Elem sch libn Runkle Pub Sch, Brookline Mass 56; Supv high sch lib, Brookline Mass 57; Head child & yp & sch lib serv pub lib, Brookline Mass 57-63; Head sch libs sect Educ Centre Lib, Toronto Ont Can 63-65, head secondary sch libs sect 65-68, hd ref & circ sect 68-. 8: New Eng Sch Development Coun Lib Com 58-62; Ont Dept of Educ, Curr Consultative Com 66-67. 9: ALA; CanLA; OntLA; ASIS. 10: Art Gallery of Toronto. 14: Ref & spec libs, info serv. 15: Education Centre Lib, Toronto Bd of Educ, Toronto 28 Ont Can.

CIARAMELLA, MARY A. b Union City NJ 1 Ap 31. 5: Columbia 51-57 (Chem) BS, 61-63 (LS) MS. 6: Ger, Russian. 7: Asst lab supv Container Labs Inc, NYC 60-62; Tech reports libn Columbia U Engnrg Lib 63-65; Tech libn The Lummus Co Newark NJ 65-67;Chief libn The Lummus Co, Bloomfield NJ 67-. 9: SLA. 13: Yes. 14: Ref, indexing, catlg, transl. 15: 689 Columbus ave, New York NY 10025.

CIBOCH, LORRAINE (ANN). b Cicero Ill 22 S 22. 5: UIll 44 (Chem) BS, 47 BSLS. 7: Chem Libby, McNeill & Libby, Blue Island Ill 45-46; Ref libn Ed "Gas Abstracts" instr gas lit, Inst of Gas Tech (Chicago) 47-51; Libn Amer Can Co, Canco Res Center, Barrington Ill 51-60; Libn Charles Bruning Co Res & Dev Dept, Mt Prospect Ill 60-61; Chief libn Fansteel Metallurgical Corp, NChicago Ill 62-63; Res libn Teletype Corp, Skokie Ill 64-65; Libn Bell & Howell Bus Equipment Group, Lincolnwood Ill 65-68; Automation libn UIll Med Ctr, Chicago 69-. 8: Adv Coun of Libns, Grad Sch of Lib Sci UIll 64. 9: SLA (Dir 59-62, pres Ill Chap 62-63, dir 63-64); ACS; ASIS (sec-treas Chicago Area Chap 62-63). 13: Yes. 14: Org, info systems for tech & engnrg libs, automation. 15: 5060 N Marine dr, Chicago Il 60640.

CIERESZKO, ESTHER M. b Chester County Penn. 4: Leon S Ciereszko. 5: W Chester State Col 35-39 (Secondary ed) BS; UOkla 52-53 BALS, 67 (Hist of sci). 7: Insurance clk Indemnity Ins Co of N Amer, Phila 39-42; Lab tech Sharp & Dohme, Glenolden Penn 42-45; Blood bank tech Salt Lake Co Hosp Salt Lake City 45-46; Research asst UOkla 54-57; Bkmob libn Cleveland-Garvin-McClain Co, Norman Okla 57-59; Med libn Presbyterian Hosp, Okla City Okla 59-. 8: Visit lecturer (on use of lib), High Sch Research Program in Chem, UOkla summer 64. 9: MedLA; ALA; OklaLA. 10: Coterie. 11: Phi Sigma. 14: Lib orgam. ref, bibliog. 15: 639 S Lahoma, Norman Pk 73069.

CIERLEY, EVALYN (REICH). b Ada Okla 12 Mr 15. 4: Morris B Cierley. 5: E Central State Col (Okla) 32-36 9span, Ger) AB; UOkla summer 36; UIll 36-41 BS in LS, MA in LS. 6: Sp. 7: Asst Educ Lib UIll (Urbana) 37-44, Libn Educ Lib 44-50; Libn Sch of Nursing Lib St Elizabeth Hosp, Covington Ky 50-54; Libn Sch of Nursing Lib Good Samaritan Hosp, Lexington Ky 54-. 9: ALA; MedLA; Nat League Nursing; KyLA; Ky League Nursing. 10: Delta Kappa Gamma; Beta Phi Mu: 13: Yes. 14: Spec libs, ref. 15: 282 Malabu ct, Lexington Ky 40502.

CIERZNIEWSKI, ROBERT JOHN. b Bay City Mich 12 Je 24. 5: Bay City Jr Col 42-43 (Sci); UMich 46-48 (Sci) BS, 50-52 AMLS. 7: Naval Reserve (Lt) Active Duty, Pacific 43-46; Circ libn Bay City (Mich) Pub Lib 49-53; Dow Chem Co Patent Dept, Midland Mich 53-. 9: ACS; CathLA (Mich Unit: chm Nat Bk Week 61); MichLA (Const & By-Laws Com 65). 10: Amer Philatelic Soc; Bay Co (Mich) Hist Soc; Comm Concert Assn, Bay City (pres& mem of Bd). 14: Ref, philatelic lit. 15: 225 N Sheridan, Bay City Mi 48706.

CIESIELSKI, JOSEPH STANLEY. b Chester Penn 26 Mr 40. 5: Villanova U 57-61 (Pol Sci) AB, 61-62 MS in LS. , 63-69 JD. 7: Lib asst Villanova U Lib 58-61; Tchg asst Villanova U Dept of Lib Sci 61-62; Asst libn Villanova Law Sch 62-69; Law Libn U of San Diego Law 69-. 8: Lecturer Dept of Lib Sci Villanova U 62-69. 9: AALL; CathLA; -East Penn Unit (treas 64-65, v-chm Col & Univ sect 66-67, chm 68); PennLA; Law Lib Assn of Greater NY. 14: Ref, catlg, admin. 15: Law Lib Garey Hall Villanova U, Villanova PA 19085.

CIKO, ANTHONY. b Studenci Yugoslavia 6 Je 19. 4: Agnes M Ribarich. 5: UZagreb (Yugoslavia) 41-43, 45-47 (Law) candidate; IndU 58-59 (LS) MA. 6: Ger, Croatian, Fr, Lat, Ital, Slavic lang. 7: Jr libn Buffalo Pub Lib, Buffalo NY 59; Asst libn Roswell Park Mem Inst, Buffalo NY 60-69; Med libn E J Meyer Mem Hosp, Buffalo NY 69-. 9: SLA. 14: Ref, med libr, cat Slavic. 15: 71 Relich ave, Lackawanna NY 14218.

CIMA, KATHERINE ANN (SNOW). b Rochester NH 5 D 26. 4: Louis Cima. 5: Skidmore Col 44-48 (Eng) BS; ULondon summer 48; Simmons & Columbia summers 49-50 MLS; UMd 62-65 (Educ), 67 (Eng); Frostburg State Col 68 (Educ). 7: Lib asst & sub libn Brooklyn Pub Lib 48-49; Head of Dept of Child Wk Great Neck Lib, Great Neck NY 50-52; Ref libn LC 53-58; Tchr-libnTakoma Park Jr High Sch, Montgomery Co Pub Schs, Md 58-60; Asst head of loan dept & bk room head UMd 61-62; Elem sch libn Montgomery Co PubSchs, Md 62-67; Elem sch libn Pr Geo's Co Pub Schs, Md 67-. 9: MdLA; MdStateTA; NEA. 10: Oakview Citizens Assn; PTA. 14: Child libs, a-v media. 15: 1419 Dilston rd, Silver Spring Md 20903.

CIMA, LOUIS. b NYC 23 Jl 19. 4: Katherin Ann Snow. 5: UTurin (Italy) 39-47 (For Lang & Lit) PhD; Columbia 49-51 (European Hist); CatholicU 54-55 (LS); George WashingtonU 60-64 (Geol). 6: Ital, Fr, Sp. 7: Research analyst Bur of Soc Sci Research, Wash DC 54-54; Ser catlgr LC Ser Div 54, Bibliog searcher Order Div 54-55, Order libn 55-57; Hd order sect 57-58, Sci acquis specialist Sci Div 58-63; Prof asst NSF OSIS, Wash DC 63-66, Asst program dir 66-. 8: Mem Adv Com White Oak Pub Lib, Silver Spring Md 64-. 9: Geol Soc of Amer; Amer Geophysic Union. 10: PTA; Oakview Citizens Assn. 12: Surveys & reports on sci info activities in earth scis & phys scis. 13: Yes. 14: Sci info, admin. 15: 1419 Dilston rd, Silver Spring Md 20903.

CINELLI, CARYL JEAN. b Chicago Ill 2 D 45. 5: Mundelein Col 63-67 (Home Econ) BA; Rosary Col 68-69 MLS. 6: Fr. 7: Sales Wieboldts Randhurst Plaza, Mt Prospect Ill 62-63; Sales Marhsall Fields State & Washington, Chicago 63-65; Light assembly Motorola Augusta Plant, Chicago summer 65; Lib asst Kemper Insurance Co, Chicago 66-69; Asst libn Lutheran Gen Hosp, Park Ridge Ill 69-. 9: SLA; MELA. 14: Ref. 15: 1217 N Tyrell, Park Ridge Il 60068.

CINQUEMANI, FRANK L(EONARD). b Jamaica NY 16 N 22. 4: Dorothy Kyte. 5: Queens Col (NY) 46-49 (Econ) BA; Columbia 50-51 MS in LS; NYU 58-64 (Higher Educ) MA in Ed. 6: Sp. 7: Sgt tech Grade 3 Signal Corps US Army 42-46; Clerk Equitable Life Assurance Soc of the US, NYC 41-42, 46; Summer sub econ div NY Pub Lib 50; Asst bus ref libn Sch of Bus Lib Columbia U 50-51; Bernard M Baruch Sch of Bus & Pub admin City Col (NYC): Asst bus ref libn 51-63, Bus ref libn 63-65, Ref libn 65- Bernard M Baruch Col Ref Libn 68-. 9: ALA; SLA; NY Lib Club. 13: Yes. 14: Ref. 15: 136 W 16th st, New York NY 10011.

CIOLLI, ANTOINETTE. b NYC 20 Ag 15. 5: Brooklyn Col 33-37 (Hist) AB, 37-40 (Hist) AM; Columbia 40-43 BS in LS. 6: Fr. 7: Tchr of hist & civics, Brooklyn (NY) high schs 43-44; Brooklyn Col: Circ libn 44-46, Instr in hist Sch of Gen Studies 44-50, Ref libn 47-59, Chief sci libn 59-. 9: ALA; SLA (NY Chap sec Mus Group 50-51 & 52-53); NY Lib Club. 10: AHA; AAUP; Beta Phi Mu. 12: "Basic Reference Books in the Sciences" with Daniel J Yett. 13: Yes. 14: Ref. 15: 1129 Bay Ridge parkway, Brooklyn NY 11228.

CIRCIELLO, JEAN (MILES). b Fresno Cal 8 D 45. 4: Francesco Circiello. 5: Raymond Col 63-65; UBarcelona (Spain) 65-66 (Sp); UCal (Berkeley) 67 (Comparative Lit) BA, 68 MLS. 6: Sp, Ital. 7: Libn Federal Water Pollution Control Admin Pacific SW Reg, San Francisco 69-. 9: ASIS; SLA. 14: Info sci, spec libs. 15: 2149 1/2 Russell, Berkeley Ca94705.

CITRON, HELEN (ROOME). b Eden NY 21 O 41. 4: Stanley Citron. 5: Fla StateU 59-63 9hist) BA; Emory 64-66 (LS) MA. 6: Fr, Sp. 7: Circ asst Fla State U Lib 61-62; Gift & exchange asst Ga Inst of Tech Lib 63-65, Gift & exchange libn 65-. 9: SELA. 14: Acquis. 15: 3483 Glenwood rd apt #6, Decatur Ga 30032.

CIUCKI, MARCELLA A. b Hammond Ind 30 Ja 31. 5: Ind U 48-52 (Math) AB, 59-62 (Edc) MS, 62-63 (LS) MA. 6: Polish. 7: Correspondent-analyst Lever Bros Co, Hammond Ind 52-59; Tchr E Chicago Pub Schs, E Chicago Ind 60-61; Asst libn UChicago 61-62; Libn US Naval Ordnance Lab, Silver Spring Md 63-66; Chief of ref serv Lake Co Pub Lib, Griffith Ind 66-. 9: SLA; ALA; IndLA. 10: Beta Phi Mu. 14: Info retrieval, info systems. 15: 4336 Ash ave, Hammond IN 46327.

CLAPP, MARILYN M (SHELTON). b Los Angeles Cal 1 D 39. 4: Michael H Clapp. 5: Palomar Jr Col 57-59 AA; San Diego State Col 60-62 (Lit) BA; UWash 66-67 MLS. 7: King Co Lib Syst, Seattle: Libn 64-66, Libn hd bkmob dept 67-68, Asst undergrad libn UMiami 68-. 69; Sr libn in chg Ref Serv, Fullerton Pub Lib, Cal 69-. 9: ALA. 14: Pub serv. 15: Fullerton Pub Lib, Fullerton Ca.

CLAPP, MAXINE B(EARD). b Owatonna Minn 10 Je 21. 4: Robert F Clapp Jr. 5: UMinn 39-43 (LS) BS. 7: UMinn: Jr lib asst ref dept 43-44, Lib asst ref dept 44-46; Jr Libn Sch of Arch 46, Libn Sch of Arch 47-52, Sr libn ref dept 52-53, Prin libn in chg of archives 53-63; Instr & archivist 63-66, Asst prof & archivist 66-. 9: SAA. 10: AAUP. 14: Archives, hist mss, ref. 15: 3620 35th ave S, Minneapolis Mn 55406.

CLAPP, ROBERT GEORGE. b Glen Dean Ky 8 Ja 10. 5: Vanderbilt 27-31 BA, 31-33 (Eng) MA; Peabody summers 34-35 (Educ) BS in LS, 37-39 BS in LS. 6: Lat, Fr. 7: Clerk Gen Shoe Corp, Nashville 33-34; Instr E Miss Jr Col 34-35; Instr Jt University libs, Nashville 38-47; US Army 42-45; Prof Fla State U 47-; Asst Dean 51-67. 9: ALA; SELA; FlaLA. 10: Phi Beta Kappa. 14: Acquis, admin. 15: 1239 Camellia dr, Tallahassee Fl 32301.

CLAPP, VERNER W(ARREN). b Johannesburg South Africa 3 Je 01. 4: Dorothy Ladd. 5: Trinity Col (Hartford Conn) 18-22 AB; Harvard 22-23 (Philos). 7: Asst Mss Div LC 22, Asst Reading Rooms 23-40, Dir Admin Dept 40-43, Dir Acquis Dept 43-47, Chief Asst Libn 47-56; Pres Coun on Lib Resources Inc, Wash DC 56-67, Consul 67-. 8: Libn UN Conf on Internat Org San Francisco 45; Chm US Lib Mission to Advise on the Establishment of a Nat Diet Lib 47-48; Consul on the libs of the UN 46-53 Mem, Nat Adv Commsn on Libs 66-67. 9: ALA; SLA; BSA; BSCan; ADI; Amer Antiq Soc; DCLA. 10: Cosmos Club (Wash DC); Columbia Hist Soc (Wash DC); Grolier Club (NYC). 11: ALA LippincottAward 60; Order of the Sacred Treasure (Japan) 68. 12: "The Future of the Researchlibrary" (63); "Copyright - a Librarian's View" (68). 13: Yes. 14: Acquis, exch, catlg, bibliog, bibliog control, ref, mss, rare bks, serials, govt documents, bks for the blind, legis ref, preservation & restoration, binding, photoduplication, sound-recording, standards, testing, copyright. 15: 4 West Irving st, Chevy Chase Md 20015.

CLARE, SISTER MARGARET OP. b Jersey City NJ 10 Mr 14. 5: Seton Hall U 41 (Educ) BS; Catholic U 47 BS in LS. 6: Fr. 7: Libn St Dominic Acad, Jersey City NJ 42-56; Registrar Caldwell Col 56-57; Prin St Dominic Acad, Jersey City NJ 57-63; Libn St Mary's High Sch, Rutherford NJ 63-; Supv of Dominican High Schs 65-. 9: CathLA (chm No NJ Sect 64-). 15: 64 Chestnut st, Rutherford NJ 07070.

CLARK, A ZANE. b Freedom Wyo 8 My 36. 4: Renee Von Niederhauser. 5: Ricks 53-56; Utah State U 56-57 (Speech0 bs& udenver 58-60 (LS) MS. 7: Asst Libn Ricks Col 59-64; Asst Libn Church Col of Hawaii 64-68; Hd circ dept Fresno State Col 68-. 9: ALA; CalLA. 14: Ref. 15: 2547 Harvard ave, Clovis Ca 93612.

CLARK, ALFRIEDA (SORRELS). b Gloster Miss 5 D 35. 4: M C Clark. 5: Southwest Miss Jr Col 53-55 AA; USoMiss 55-57 BS. 7: Asst circ libn USoMiss 57-58; Libn Jefferson Mil Col 58-59; Asst libn Hinds Jr Col 61; Catlgr Waterways Expt Station, Vicksburg Miss 61; Libn Jefferson High Sch, Fayette Miss 61-62; Catlgr Waterways Expt Station, Vicksburg Miss 62-64, Head catlgr 64-. 9: MissLA. 15: 206 Enchanted dr, Vicksburg Ms 39180.

CLARK, ALICE S (SANDELL). b Oneonta NY 24 N 22. 5: SUNY at Albany 40-41 (Lat), 67-68 MLS; SUNY Col at Oneonta 42, 63-67 (Soc sci, ed) BA; Ohio State 68 (Math). 6: Ger. 7: Lecturer in lib sci SUNY at Albany Sch of Lib Sci 68; Asst hd of personnel Ohio State U Libs 68-. 8: Asst dir HEA Inst in Libnship summer 69, on Quantitative Methods in Libnship: Standards, Mgt, Research. 9: ALA; ASIS. 10: Beta Phi Mu; Kappa Delta Pi; NY State Hist Assn. 14: Personnel, catlg. 15: 74 Georgetown dr, Columbus Oh 43214.

CLARK, BILLIE C. b Jefferson City Mo 14 Mr 45. 5: WVa State Col 63-67 (Elem Educ) BS in Ed; UIll 67-68 MS in LS. 6: Fr. 7: Libn US Dept of Health, Educ & Welfare, Wash DC 68-. 10: Pi Delta Pi; Kappa Delta Pi. 14: Catlg. 15: Box 11, Institute WVa 25112.

CLARK, CARMEN E(RCELL). b Lexington Va 1 O 14. 5: Longwood Col 31-35 (Lat) BS; UNC 41-42 BS in LS. 6: Fr, Lat. 7: Longwood Col; Asst libn 35-37, Asst libn catlgr 37-39, Asst libn in charge ref & circ 39-41, 42-44, Act libn 44-46;Ref libn AirU Maxwell AFB, Ala 46-51; Chief ref sect Army War Col, Carlisle Barracks Penn 51-69, Chief serv br 69-. 12: "Key References" (annual 58-). 14: Ref (mil hist). 15: US Army War Col Lib, Carlisle Barracks Pa 17013.

CLARK, CATHERINE. b Smyrna Tenn. 5: Tenn Col 18-22 (Eng) AB; Duke summer 33; Peabody 41-42 BS in LS. 6: Fr. 7: Tchr in secondary schs, Tenn 22-42; Libn Central High Sch, Murfreesboro Tenn 42-45; Libn Middle Tenn State Col 46-49; Dir of Lib Middle Tenn State U 49-67, Assoc libn 67-. 9: ALA (Nat Lib Week Com 63, mem Com 64-66); SELA; TennEA; TennLA (pres 61-63, chm Col Sect 57-58, chm Educ Com 67-69). 10: AAUW; Delta Kappa Gamma. 14: Admin. 15: 105 Second ave, Murfreesboro TN 37130.

CLARK, CATHERINE (CONNOR). b Chicago 19 Je 16. 4: Richard Clark. 5: Chicago 34-37 (Pol Sci) AB; Pratt 62-64 MLS. 7: Catlgr Suffolk Cooperative Lib System, Patchogue NY 64, Head catlgr 64-66; Asst hd acquis SUNY (Stony Brook) 66-67, Hd catlgr 67-. 9: ALA; NYLA; Suffolk Co LA. 10: Beta Phi Mu. 14: Catlg. 15: 231 Middle rd, Blue Point NY 11715.

CLARK, COLLIN. b San Jose Cal 11 S 31. 5: UCal(Berkeley) 49-53 (Eng) BA, 58-60 MLS. 7: Cpl Regimental S3 clerk 11th Armored Cavalry US Army, Ft Knox Ky 54-55; Instr in Eng Ryukoko U (Kyoto J apan) (Asia Found) 56-58; Head of tech serv Solano Co Free Lib, Fairfield Cal 60-62; Head of adult serv Vallejo Pub Lib, Vallejo Cal 62-. 9: ALA; CalLA (Coun 69, chm Adult Servs Com 68); -Golden Gate Dist (sec 64). 13: Yes. 14: Bk sel, ref, ya, a-v. 15: Vallejo Pub Lib, PO Box 272, Vallejo Ca 94590.

CLARK, CONSTANCE JANE. b Salinas Cal 15 Ag 34. 4: Glen H Clark. 5: Wayne State U 57 (Eng) AB; UCal (Berkeley) 63 MLS. 6: Fr, Sp. 7: Engr libn UNevada 63-65, Eng ineering/Mines libn UNev 67-. 9: ALA; NevLA. 10: AAUP; Sierra Club. 14: Ref, spec libs. 15: 10 Fransden circle, Reno Nv 89502.

CLARK, DENE LOWELL. b Ames Iowa 1 Ja 31. 5: UIowa 49-53 (Marketing) BS; UMinn 58-60 (LS) MA. 7: Personnel clerk US Army (Pfc) 53-55; Underwriter Anchor Casualty Insurance Co, St Paul 55-58; Ref asst Minneapolis Pub Lib60-61; Catlgr Carnegie Lib of Pittsburgh 61-63; Ser libn St Louis Pub Lib 63-65; Hd catlg dept NE Mo State Col 66-68; Hd catlgdept Chico State Col, Chico Cal 68-. 15: 1227 Esplanade apt 12, Chico Ca 95926.

CLARK, DONALD T. b Seattle 13 Mr 11. 4: Emily Espenshade. 5: Willamette U 29-30, 31-32 (Eng); UCal (Berkeley) 32-34 (Eng Lit, Zool) AB; Columbia 35-36 (LS) BS, 37-39 (Econ Hist); Harvard 40-42 (Bus Admin) MBA. 6: Sp. 7: Page circ asst Berkeley Pub Lib, Berkeley Cal 30-31, Asst br libn 32-35; Asst doc div Ore State Lib 31-32; Ref asst NY Pub Lib 35-40; Asst libn Harvard U Grad Sch of Bus Admin 40-48, Assoc libn 48-57, Libn 57-62; University libn UCal (Santa Cruz) 62-. 8: Instr USAAF Statistical Off Candidate sch 42-44; Instr USAAF Contract Termination Course Off Train Sch 44; Lecturer Simmons Col Sch of Lib Sci Summer 49, summer 53; Lecturer Harvard U Grad Sch of Bus Admin 53-56; Lecturer Mgt Train Program UWest ont Summers 54-55; Lecturer Advanced Mgt Program UHawaii summer 56-57; Tchr & consul to In-Company Mgt Development Programs: Bell System Exec Conf, NE Tel & Tel Co, NY Tel Co, Bell Telephone Co of Can, Grad Sch of Insurance Admin; Consul on Lib Org: Price Waterhouse & Co, Bolt Beranek & Newman Inc, Ohio U, UVa Grad Sch of Bus Admin; Adv Com Cal Statewide Survey of Pub Lib Serv, 64-65; Citizens Adv Bd Santa Cruz Pub Lib 64-65; Examining Com Boston Pub Lib 50; Assoc in Spec Lib Admin Simmons Col 48-56. 9: SLA (num coms & var offs); ALA (Coun);-ACRL; Harvard Lib Club (past pres); MassLA; CalLA. 10: Pub Affairs Info Serv (Bd of Trustees 48-); Town of Lexington Mass: Long-Range Planning Com (past chm), Approp Com (past chm), Sch Com (past chm); Bd of Trustees, Cary Mem Lib; Lexington Commun Assn (past v-pres); Amer Red Cross (Home Serv Com Boston, Metropol Chap 46-62); Family Serv Assn of Greater Boston (past memb Bd of Trustees); Santa Cruz & Mus Com 63-; Commonwealth Club of Cal; Bk Club of Cal; Roxburghe Club; Grolier Club; chm Acad Senate 69-. 12: Co-ed "Dictionary of Business and Finance" by Clark & Gottfried (57); Co-ed "World of Business" by Bursk Clark & Hidy (62) 4 vols; Ed 57-60, Publ 60-62 "The Executives"; Ed Bd "Harvard Business Review" 50-55; Ed Bd "Business History Review" 55-58. 13: Yes. 14: Admin, rare bks, Californiana, Robinson Jeffers. 15: 500 Sand Hill rd, Santa Cruz Ca 95062.

CLARK, DOROTHEA (IRENE SHOEMAKER). b Syracuse NY 3 Mr 21. 4: Richard W Clark. 5: Syracuse 38-42 (Home Econ Educ) BS, 62 (LS) MS. 6: Fr. 7: Homemaking tchr Elbridge Central Sch, Elbridge NY 42-44; Casewker home serv dept Amer Red Cross, Syracuse NY 45-46; High sch libn Jordan-Elbridge Central Sch, Jordan NY 59-. 9: ALA; NEA; NYLA; NY State Tchrs Assn. 10: Trustee, Elbridge (NY) Free Lib. 14: Reading guidance, admin, ref. 15: Jordan-Elbridge High Sch, Jordan NY 13080.

CLARK, ELSIE MAY (SNYDER). b Portsmouth Va 16 Jl 26. 4: Elijah Garland Clark. 5: Carson Newman 45-49 (Hist) BA; Tex Wesleyan 63-65(Ed research) M Ed. 6: Sp. 7: Eng tchr & libn Keller Independent Schs, Keller Tex 56-57; Accountant Chance Vought Corp, Dallas 57-60; Ser libn Vought Aeronautics, Dallas 60-65; Acquis libn LTV Aerospace Corp,

Dallas 65-67; Asst libn Tex Instruments, Dallas 67-. 9: SLA. 14: Ref. 15: 2714 Roberts Cir, Arlington Tx 76010.

CLARK, FRANCES (DYE). b Spartanburg SC 23 Jl 22. 4: Edward S Clark. 5: Converse Col 39-45 (Eng) AB; SUNY (Albany) 56-60 MSLS. 7: Chief clerk Ordnance Service Command, Camp Polk La 42-44; Eng tchr Cornwall High Sch, Cornwall NY 45-47; Libn Cornwall Central High Sch, Cornwall NY 56-. 9: NY State TA; NYLA; SELA; Class Room TA. 10: Trustee for Cornwall (NY) Pub Lib; Cornwall Garden Club; Cornwall Book Club. 14: Ref. 15: 58 Laurel ave, Cornwall NY 12518.

CLARK, GEORGIA ANN (BERGLUND). b Duluth Minn 19 S 42. 4: George S Clark. 5: Col of St Scholastica 60-64 (Hist) BS; UMich 64-65 AMLS. 6: Ger. 7: Lib asst Duluth Pub Lib, Dulith Minn 58-64; Lib asst Col of St Scholastica 60-61; Circ libn UMich Law Lib (Ann arbor) 64-65, Circ libn (hd) III 65-67, Ser libn IV 67-. 10: Pi Gamma Mu; Women of the Fac. 14: Ref. 15: 2934 Washtenaw 2A, Ypsilanti Mi 48197.

CLARK, GEORGIA H(ALLER). b Nashville Ark 25 Jl 06. 5: So Methodist U 24-28 (Eng) BA; Columbia 31 BS in ls, summer 41. 7: Libn Pub Lib Texarkana Ark-Tex 31-38; Ref asst UArk Lib 38-40, Head ref dept 40-. 9: ALA; ArkLA. 12: "Arkansas Books and Writers; a Bibliography" with V L Jones (52); Ed "Arkansas Checklist of State Publications" (43-). 14: Ref, Arkansiana, govt pub. 15: 521 Adams st, Fayetteville Ar 72701.

CLARK, GERTRUDE M(UNK). b Vienna Austria 14 Mr 15. 4: Albert M Clark. 5: Occidental Col 39-40 (Mod Lang) AB; USoCal 40-41 (LS) BS. 6: Ger, Fr, Ital. 7: Libn USoCal 40-42; Libn & tech tr J Hendy Iron Wks, Sunnyvale Cal 43-44; Chief libn Harrower Lab, Glendale Cal 46-49; Libn Los Angeles City Pub Lib 49-51; Chief libn Los Angeles Co Med Assn 51-57; Libn Health Dept Los Angeles City Pub Lib 57-59; Libn Stuart Co Div Atlas Chem Ind, Pasadena Cal 59-68; Asst Med Sci Libn UUtah 68-. 8: Lib consul Pharmacol Res Inst Mario Negri, Milan Italy 63-64; Lecturer USoCal Lib Sch 56-58. 9: SLA; MedLA (Group chm 55); Med Lib Group So Cal (pres 55-56, v-pres 54-55). 12: Chm Publ Com "Union List of Periodicals, Libs So Cal" (63). 13: Yes. 15: 1963 S 12 East apt 502, Salt Lake City Ut 84105.

CLARK, HAZEL (WILKINSON). b Los Angeles 28 My 01. 4: Walter E Clark. 5: Park Col 19-22 (Eng); UDenver 45-46 (Eng) BA, 46-48 BS in LS, 46-48 (Educ) MA. 6: Lat, Fr. 7: Tchr Horace Mann Jr High Sch, Denver 40-41; Tchr Baker Jr High Sch, Denver 41-48; Libn Whittier Sch, Denver 48-55; Libn East High Sch, Denver 55-66; Libn & tchr Hillel Acad, Denver 66-69. 8: Libn East High Summer Sch 48-64. 15: 2081 Ivanhoe st, Denver 80207.

CLARK, HELEN (THOMPSON). b Orange NJ 19 Ag 07. 4: Littarvey Clark. 5: Geneseo Normal Sch 30 Life Tchg K-8; State U Col (Geneseo NY) 50 (Lib Educ) BS, 54 (LS) MS. 7: Libn Estel Jr High Sch, Gloversville NY 30-38; Tchr Central High Sch, Auburn NY 45-49; Libn West High Sch, Auburn NY 49-. 8: Asst Prof Lib Sci State U Col (Geneseo NY) summer 61-67; Title II ESEA fundsconsul for Auburn Sch Dist. 9: ALA; NEA; NYLA; CathLA; NYState Tchrs Assn. 10: Auburn Col Club; Sch Improvement Com; AuburnInnovation Com; Cayuga Co Communications Council (pres); Parochial Sch Bd of Educ. 11: Award for outstanding prof serv in Auburn NY 60. 13: Yes. 14: Admin, reading guidance, lib org. 15: 25 Linn ave, Auburn NY 13021.

CLARK, HELEN M(ARIE). b Martinsville Ind 30 My 1900. 5: Ind U 17-21 (Lat) AB; UIll 25-27 BS in LS. 7: Tchr Dakota Wesleyan Acad Mitchell SD 21-23; Tchr-libn Sr High Sch, Mitchell SD 23-25; Libn Classics Seminar UIll 25-26; U High Sch, Urbana Ill 26-27; Sch lib adv Ind State Lib 27-36; Dir wk with schs Enoch Pratt Free Lib, Baltimore 36-39; 40-41; Instr Syracuse U Lib Sch, summers 36-41; Sch Lib adv Ore State Lib 39-40; Asst state libn Mich State Lib 42-45; Dir div lib ext Md Dept Educ, Baltimore 46-60; Dir Central Fla Reg Lib, Ocala Fla 61-67; Extension Libn Santa Fe Reg Lib, Gainesville Fl 32601 (67-). 9: ALA(Coun 45-50); FlaLA (Chm Legis & Planning Com 64-67); MdLA; (life mem). 10: LWV; Soroptimist; AAUW; Md Cong P&T; Phi Beta Kappa; Mortar Board. 13: Yes. 14: Publib ext, interlib coop, child wk, ya. 15: 2613 NW 4th pl, Gainesville Fl 32601.

CLARK, JAMES POLLARD. b Sheffield Ala 10 S 25. 4: Cruse Patton. 5: U of the South 46-49 (Philos) BA; Yale 49-50 (Philos); UMich summer 51-54 AMLS. 6: Ger, Lat, Gk. 7: US Navy 43-46; Asst libn U of the South 50-58; Head Libn UTenn 58-60; Chief of reader's serv Redstone Sci Info Center, Redstone Arsenal, Huntsville Ala 60-68; Dir of libs USA Spec Serv Agcy Europe, Munich, Germany 68-. 9: ALA; SELA; AlaLA. 14: Admin. 15: 515 Franklin st SE, Huntsville Al 35801.

CLARK, JAY B. b Ft Worth Tex 27 Je 38. 4: Marjorie (Trulan) Clark. 5: Rice 57-61 (Hist) BA; Trinity U 62-64 (Hist) MA; Denver U 65-67 (Libnship) MA. 7: Trinity U: Ref & ser libn 64-65, Ref & archivist 66-67, Asst to dir tech serv & archivist 67-68; Chief tech serv Houston Pub Lib 68-. 8: Instr in Amer hist, Trinity U 66-67. 9: ALA; SLA; TexLA (pres-elet Acquis RT). 10: Bexar Co Hist Assn; Toastmasters Internat. 14: Tech serv. 15: 2635 Albans, Houston Tx 77005.

CLARK, JEAN E (MERRISS). b NYC 21 My 23. 5: P utney School, Putney Vt 38-40 Theatre; Bennington 45 (Pol sci & Arts) BA; St Johns Col Annapolis Md 47-49 Great Bks Program; Simmons 58-60 MSLS; UCincinnati 60-64 Transportation & Traffic Mgt Assoc in Commerce. 6: Ger. 7: Ref asst Govt & bus dept Cincinnati Pub Lib 60-62; Hd bus admin lib UCincinnati 62-63; Films & recordings libn Cincinnati Pub Lib 63-65; A-v consul Div of Lib Development NY State, Albany 65-. 8: Film Editor, Willard Pictures Inc, NYC, 42-47; Asst to Charles Walker, Head, Yale School of Industrial Relations 55-56; Asst to Francis B Biddle, former US Attorney General 56-57; Research Asst, Union Tank Car Co, Chicago 57-59. 9: ALA; -PLA (chm A-v Standards); SLA; MusicLA; FLIC (Bd of Trustees); NEA-DAVI; EFLA; CINE (Judge); NYLA; NY Film Coun; NYState A-v Assn. 10: PTA; Nat Coun on Alcoholism. 14: A-v, govt, bus, transport. 15: 244 Delaware ave, Delmar NY 12054.

CLARK, MRS JENNIE BETH (SWAYZE). b Benton Miss 20 Je 08. 5: Millsaps Col 26-29 (Eng) BA; Amer Acad (Rome) 30 (Topography); LSU 50 BS in LS. 7: Eng tchr Benton High Sch, Benton Miss 30-40, Libn 40-47; Libn Columbia High Sch, Columbia Miss 47-56; Lib sch libn LSU 56-. 9: ALA; LaLA; Miss Sch LA (pres 52-53). 10: Phi Mu; YWCA; AAUW. 13: Yes. 14: Ref, child bks. 15: 1785 Country Club dr, Baton Rouge La 70808.

CLARK, JUDITH (MEIS). b Sioux City Iowa 25 S 37. 5: UAriz 55-56, 57-59 (Educ) BA; San Diego State 56-57 (Educ); Immaculate Heart Col 65-67 (LS) MA. 6: Sp. 7: Child libn Orange Co Pub Lib, Fountain Valley 67-68, Ref libn, La Habra 68, Ext serv libn, Orange 68-. 9: CalLA; OrangeCoLA. 14: Child, ya, pub inst. 15: 5419 W Ballast, Santa Ana Ca 92704.

CLARK, JULIET B. b San Francisco 11 S 05. 5: Dominican Col 23-27 (Music) BM; UCal (Berkeley) 38-39 (Grad Lib Sci Certif, (Educ, Fr) MA; Sorbonne 29-30 (Fr Lit). 6: Fr. 7: Head Libn Dominican Col (San Rafael) 40-43; Ref libn Sacramento Pub Lib, Sacramento Cal 43-47; Head supv libn San Francisco State Col 47-53; USan Francisco: Head acquis 53-60, Head gifts & exch 60-64, Act head libn 64-, Consul spec proj 68-. 9: ALA; CalLA; SLA. 10: Cal Bk Club; World Affairs Coun; Cal Hist Assn; Symphony Assn of San Francisco; Wilderness Soc Sierra Club. 13: Yes. 14: Ref, rare bks, admin. 15: 205 Golden Gate ave, Belvedere Ca 94920.

CLARK, L LOUISE. b Stuart Va 6 Je 06. 5: Madison Col 32 (Fr, Eng) BS; William & Mary Col 46 (LS) AB. 7: Tchr Patrick Co (Va) 26-40; Libn Patrick Co Lib (Stuart Va) 41-54; Libn Franklin-Patrick Reg, Stuart Va 54-. 9: ALA; SELA; VaLA. 10: JEB Stuart Womans Club. 14: Admin. 15: Stuart Va 24171.

CLARK, LOIS S(NEED). b Nampa Ida 4 N 17. 4: John Edward Clark. 5: Los Angeles City Col 36-39 (Fr) AA; UCal(Los Angeles) 39-42 (Fr) BA; USoCal 42-43 BS in LS. 6: Fr. 7: Child libn Los Angeles Pub Lib 43-52; Child libn Redondo Beach Pub Lib, Redondo Beach Cal 58-62; Sr child libn Inglewood Lib, Inglewood Cal 62-. 9: ALA; CalLA (Nom Com 63-64; child Serv Dir, v-pres & pres-elect 69-70); Sch &Child Libns Assn of So Cal (treas 64-65, pres 65-66). 10: Palos Verdes Woman's Club (pres 58-59); LWV. 14: Pub rel, child serv. 15: 416 E Regent st,Inglewood Ca 90301.

CLARK, LOLA (WILLIAMSON). b Sloan Iowa 22 S 1895. 4: Harry Miller Clark. 5: Morningside Col 13-15; Iowa StateU (Ames) 15-17 (Econ) BS; columbia summers 24-28 (Eng) MA. 6: Fr. 7: High sch tchr: Milford Iowa 17-18, Odebolt Iowa 18-20, El Paso Ill 20-31; High sch libn: Grinnell Iowa 56-61, Waverly Iowa 61-67, New Hampton Iowa 67-. 9: NEA; ALA; IowaStateEA; IowaASchL. 10: AAUW; Charles City Womans Club. 11: Spec award from Pres Roosevelt for Red Cross wk World War II. 14: Ref. 15: 405 Ferguson st, Charles City Ia 50616.

CLARK, LOVE FORREST. b Drift Ky 2 F 21. 5: Caney Jr Col 39-41; East Ky State Col 45-47 (Eng, Hist) AB; Ohio State U summer 49; UKy summer 50, 52-54 MS in LS; UMinn summer 65 (NDEA) Rutgers summer 66; HEA Inst La State U summer 68. 7: Tchr Floyd Co Schs, Prestonsburg Ky 41-44; Libn Martin High Sch, Martin Ky 47-52; Libn U Sch Miami U (Oxford Ohio) 52-62; Libn Alfred I Du Pont Schs, Wilmington Del 62-. 8: Served on Advis Com for Del Educ TV for Del (Hist) 65-66. 9: NEA; ALA; -AASchL (com to prepare bk list of paperbacks for elem schs 66-69); DelStateEA. 10: Delta Kappa Gamma; Sigma Sigma Sigma; Del Storytellers; Group Emphasizes Social Service; Alfred I DuPont Fac Assn. 14: Sch lib instr materials centers, ya lit & activities, bk reviewing, educ media, the film as an art form. 15: 13 Clifton Park dr, Wilmington DE 19802.

CLARK, MARGARET D (FLICK). b Bedford Iowa 5 D 08. 4: Robert S Clark. 5: Westhampton Col 26-30 (Eng, hist) BA; UIll summer 35, 36, & 37 BS in LS. 7: Sub prof asst Des Moines Pub Lib, Des Moines Iowa 30-37; Asst lending-ref dept Newark Pub Lib, Newark NJ 37-40; Gen asst Central Lib Queens Borough Pub Lib, Jamaica NY 41-46, Ref asst 49-56, Asst br libn 56, Head of div 57-. 9: ALA-PLA (Hist Sect); -RSD. 14: Ref (hist, travel, biog). 15: 141-45 Union Turnpike, Flushing NY 11367.

CLARK, MARGARET MARY. b Cleveland 7 D 05. 5: West Res 23-27 BSLS. 7: Child libn Cleveland Pub Lib 27-40, Head Lewis Carroll Room 40-. 8: Radio storytelling broadcaster, station WBOE 40-; Lecturer in child lit, Grad Sch West Res U 49-55. 9: ALA-CSD (chm 50, Bd 52-58); CathLA; OhioLA. 10: Cath Collegiate Assn; Women's Nat Bk Assn; Friends of the Lib (Cleveland). 12: Co-author "Children's Books Too Good To Miss" (59, 63, 66); Auth "Keeping up with Children and Books" (59, 61, 66); Ed "Adventuring with Books" 50. 13: Yes. 14: Child wk. 15: Clev eland Pub Lib, 325 Superiod ave, Cleveland Oh 44114.

CLARK, MARGARET MITCHELL (MILAM). b New Orleans La 15 S 39. 4: Richard Lee Clark. 5: Tulane 57-59 (Liberal Arts); UMd (Germany) 61-64 (Liberal Arts); UMd (College Park) 64-66 (Govt & Pol) BA (cum laude), 66-68 MLS. 6: Ger. 7: Admin asst in charge Army Educ Ctr, Oberammergau Germany 63-64; Research asst UMd Sch Lib & Info Serv (College Park) 66-68; Catlgr Law Lib UVa 68-. 9: AALL; Amer Pol Sci Assn. 10: Pi sigma Alpha. 12: Assoc ed "Who's Who in Consulting" (68). 14: Admin, catlg, law libnship. 15: Law Lib Univ of Va, Charlottesville Va 22901.

CLARK, MARGERY MARSTON. b Manhattan Kan 30 O 26. 5: UDel 44-48 (Hist) BA; Catholic U 58-62 MS in LS. 7: Interlib loan libn Johns Hopkins U Applied Physics Lab (Silver Spring Md) 58-62; Assoc libn Nat Housing Center, Wash DC 62-. 9: SLA (Soc Sci Dir); -Wash DC Chap (sec). 10: Montgomery Co Hist Soc; Md Acad of Sci; Phi Kappa Phi; Beta Phi Mu. 14: Ref. 15: 4523 Everett st, Kensington Md20795.

CLARK, MARGUERITE (MOSELEY). b Redlands Cal 8 F 13. 4: Walter J Clark. 5: Pacific U 31-34 (Philos); Whitworth Col 34-36 (Modern Langs) BA; UWash 47-48 BSLS. 6: Fr. 7: Tchr High Sch, Hanford Wash 36-37; Tchr-libn High Sch, Davenport Wash 37-40; Catlgr Biblical Sem ny 40-41; Libn High Sch, Walla-Walla Wash 42-45; Libn Lewis & Clark High Sch, Spokane Wash 45-46; Libn High Sch, Forest Grove Ore 51-. 9: ALA-AASchL; NEA; OreEA; OreASchL (scholarship com, chm Reg 60-61). 10: AAUW; Pacific Univ Guild. 14: Bk sel. 15: 2040 15th ave, Forest Grove Ore 97116.

CLARK, MARJORIE (JUSTUS). b Tallulah Falls Ga 19 Ja 29. 4: Royce Jack Clark. 5: Piedmont Col 48 (Eng) AB; Emory 66 (Libnship) M Libn. 6: Fr, Sp. 7: Tchr Gwinnett Vo Pub Schs 48-50; Tchr Hall Co Schs 50-54; Tchr Atlanta Pub Schs 54-63; Tchr Hall Co Schs 65-66; Librarian Gainesville Jr Col, Gainesville Ga 66-. 9: ALA; NEA; GaLA; GaEA; SELA. 10: Torch Club. 14: Admin, ref. 15: Route 1, Flowery Branch Ga.

CLARK, MARY VIRGINIA (WAHL). b NYC 27 Jl 40. 4: Arthur Thomas Clark. 5: DePauw U 58-62 (Bacteriology) BA; UHawaii summer 61; IndU 62-63 (LS) MA; Catholic U summer 65. 6: Ger. 7: Lib intern NLM, Bethesda Md63-64, Asst head catlg maintenance sect 64-65, Ref libn 65-. 9: MedLA. 10: Beta Phi Mu; Alpha Omicron Pi; PEO. 12: "Medical Reference Works," Suppl. I (67-68). 14: Catlg maintenance, NLM printed catlg, biomed ref, info storage & retrieval. 15: 4714 Cherokee st apt 102, College Park Md 20740.

CLARK, NANCY JEWEL. b Greensboro NC 13 Je 44. 5: UNC (Greensboro) 62-66 (Eng) BA; UNC (Chapel Hill) 68-69 MSLS. 6: Fr. 7: Tchr Greensboro Pub Schs, Greensboro NC 66-68; Lib asst UNC Lib (Chapel Hill) 68-69, Ref asst 69-. 9: ALA; NCLA. 14: Ref. 15: Humanities Div Louis Round Wilson Lib, Univ of NC, Chapel Hill NC 27514.

CLARK, PALMER (PRICE). b Philadelphia 3 S 18. 4: William Carl Clark. 5: George Washington U 36-42 (Fr) AB; Catholic U 52-57MS in LS. 7: Clerk-typist Bd of Governors Fed Reserve Wash DC 38-39; Lib asst DC Pub Lib 37-44; Lib asst George Washington U 39-41; Clerk-stenographerUS War Dept, Wash DC 41-43; Airline hostess Pennsylvania-Central Airlines, Wash DC 43; Clerk-stenographer US War Dept CampDavis NC 44; Sec Va, Wash DC 45-47; Thesis typist, Wash DC 49-57; Newspaper correspondent Herndon Chantilly Times Herndon Va 58-62; CatlgrWarrenton Subscription Lib, Warrenton Va 60; Sch libn Dunn Loring Elem Sch, Fairfax Co Va 58-62; Catlgr of personal lib of Dr A H Kiessling,Falls Church Va 65; Libn II Falls Church pub lib, Falls Church Va 65-66; Catlgr Arlington Co Pub Lib, Arlington Va 66-67; Ref libn spec servlib, Ft Belvoir Va 67-. 9: ALA. 12: Comp 3 cookbks, "Out of the Frying Pan" (64); "Christmas Kitchen" (65); "For Goodness, Bake" (67). 13: Yes. 14: Bibliog, publ rel, ref. 15: 3516 W Ox rd, Fairfax Va 22030.

CLARK, PATRICIA ANN. b Ossining NY 20 Je 37. 5: Chatham Col 55-59 (Eng Lit) AB; Carnegie 59-61 MLS. 7: Lib trainee UPittsburgh 59-61; Ref libn NY Pub Lib, 61-64; Ref libn US Info Agency, Wash DC 64-. 9: DCLA. 14: Ref. 15: 1914 Connecticut ave NW, Wash DC 20009.

CLARK, PHILIP MAIZE. b Lewisburg Penn 13 Mr 40. 5: Susquehanna U 58-62 (Pol Sci) AB; Penn State U 63-64 (P penn State U 63-64 (Pub Admin) MPA. 7: Production controller Middletown Air Material Area, Olmsted AFB Pa 62-63; Grad asst Inst of Pub Admin Penn State 63-64, Research asst 64-67; Assistant research specialist Urban Studies Ctr RutgersU 67-69; Instr Grad Sch of Lib Serv Rutgers 69-, Exec asst Bur Info Sci Research 69-. 8: Dir, Seminar for Lib Bldg Consuls Rutgers 68; Res assoc MDA-consul "A Study of Rockland County (NY) Libraries" by Ralph Blasingame & Assocs 68; Mem Co-adjunct fac, Grad Sch of Lib Serv, rutgers 68. 9: ALA; Amer Soc Pub Admin; Amer Pol Sci Assn. 14: Admin, res, methodology. 15: 86 Livingston ave, New Brunswick NJ 08903.

CLARK, PHYLLIS. b Binghamton NY 31 Ja 27. 5: Hartwick Col 45-49 (Eng Lit) AB; Syracuse 53-54 MS (LS). 6: Fr, Ger. 7: Libn I Free Lib of Phila 54-57; Spec serv libn US Govt Spec Serv, Ulm Germany & Stuttgart Germany 57-62; Head Fine Arts Dept Yonkers Pub Lib, Yonkers NY 62-. 8b Binghamton NY 27 Ja 31. 07: Libn I Free Lib of Phila 54-57; Spec serv libnUS Govt Spec Serv, Ulm Germany & Stuttgart Germany 57-62; Head Fine Arts A-V Depts,Yonkers Pub Lib, Yonkers NY 62-67; D'. Hastings-on-Hudson (NY) Pub Lib 67-68; A-VConsul Westchester Co Lib Sys, 68-. 9: ALA (chm Com oncoop Interlib Loan Systems 60); NYLA; Westchester LA; NY Lib Club. 10: Gamma PhiDelta; Westchester Audio Visual Assn; Film Lib Info Coun; Chaminade Club of Yonkers. 12: Command Performance" (musical comedy) USARPEB-Bremerhaven Germany 60. 13: Yes. 14: Admin, fine arts, a-v serv. 15: 64 Locust Hill ave, Yonkers NY 10701.

CLARK, PRUDENCE FULLAM. b Brattleboro Vt 22 Ja 26. 5: Oberlin Col 43-47 (Physics) BA; UCal (Berkeley) 62-63 MLS. 7: Lens computer Eastman Kodak Co, Rochester NY 47-48; Jr physicist URochester Synchrocyclo tron Lab 48-49; Ref libn UCal (Davis) 63-, Asst hd ref dept 67-68, Hd phys sci br libs 68-. 9: ALA; SLA; CalLA. 10: Phi Beta Kappa; AAAS-. 14: Ref, subj spec in phys scis. 15: 632 Rutgers dr, Davis CA 95616.

CLARK, RAE (ANN). b NYC 19 My 43. 5: UPittsburgh 61-65 (Bacteriology) BS, 66 MLS. 7: Libn NY State Dept of Health 67-. 14: Ref, catlg. 15: 363 State st, Albany NY 12210.

CLARK, RAYMOND B JR. b Easton Md 10 Jl 27. 5: Washington Col (Chestertown Md) 44-48 (Hist) AB; UPenn 48-49 (Hist) MA; UDel 53-55 (Amer Dec Arts) MA; Catholic U 58-63 MSLS. 6: Fr, Sp, Ger. 7: Catlgr Yale U Lib 49-50; Asst curator of mss UVa Lib 50-51; Sr ed Penn Mag Hist & Biog Index Vol 1-75 Hist Soc Penn Phila 51-52; Supv local hist & genealogy room LC 56-59; Libn World Confed Orgs Teaching Prof, Wash DC 59-62; Ref libn & head Md room P G Co Reg Lib, Hyattsville Md 63-64; Histn Joint Chiefs of Staff, Pentagon Wash DC 65-66; Prof lecturer Geo Washington U 66-68; Hd catlg dept Lib Sci Div John I Thompson Co, Wash DC 69-. 8: Consul Admin of Lib Amer Coun on Educ

Wash DC 63; Instr No Va Center UVa Arlington Va 62-64; Instr Seminars on Amer Culture NY State Hist Assn, Cooperstown NY 58, Nat Adv Com, World Conf on Records & Geneal, Geneal Soc (Mormon) 68-69. , Nat Adv Com, World Conf on Records & Geneal, Geneal Soc (Mormon) 68-69. 9: ALA; SLA (treas Soc Sci Group DC Chap 64-66); Nat Geneal Soc (Coun 58-6 0, Act pres 60-61, herald 66-67, pres 67-68, Coun 68-70); Md Hist Soc; Hist Soc Del; Md Geneal Soc v-pres (69-70). 10: Sons of the AR; Soc of Ark & Dove; Colonnade Club; UVa English-speaking Union; Beta Phi Mu. 12: Ed & publ Maryland and Delaware Genealogist (59); Queen Ann County Maryland Marriage Licenses (63); Baltimore County Tax List 1699-1706 (64); Washington County, Maryland 1800 Census; Talbot County Maryland Marriage Licenses (65); Genealogical Research in Maryland (63). Comp "Talbot Co Md Marriage Licenses" (vol 2) (67); Caroline Co Md Marriage Licenses, 1774-1825 (69). 13: Yes. 14: Spec collectional (local area), rare bks, mss, maps, ref, admin catlg. 15: 4201 S 31st st apt 545, Arlington Va 22206.

CLARK, RHETA ADELE. b S Glastonbury Conn 18 F 02. 5: Conn Col 23 (Eng) AB; Columbia Tchrs Col 31 (Sch Admin) MA, Sch Lib Sci 41 (Sch Libs) BS. 7: Tchr Newington High Sch (Newington Conn) 23-26; Lyman Hall High Schm Wallingford Conn: Tchr 26-30, Libn 26-44, Dean of Girls 30-44; sch lib consul Conn State Dept of Educ (Hartford Conn) 44-. 8: Established Rheta A Clark Award for excellence in scholarship at Soconn State Col. 9: ALA-AASchL; NEA-DAVI; -Assn Supv Curr Devel; NCTE; Acei; ConnSchLA; ConnEA; ConnLA; NESchLA; NELA. 10: AAUW; YWCA; Delta Kappa Gamma. 13: Yes. 14: Sch libs. 15: PO Box 2219, Hartford Ct 06115.

CLARK, RUDOLPH B. b Delton Va 31 O 23. 5: Lincoln Mem U 44-48 (Hist, Sociol) AB; Peabody 49 (LS) BS. 7: Sub tchr Draper High Sch, Draper Va 43-44; Asst libn Lincoln Mem U (Harrogate Tenn) 47-48, Act libn 48; Libn & Assoc Prof of Lib Sci Union Col (Barbourville Ky) 49-52; Instr in Lib Sci Lincoln Mem U (Harrogate Tenn) 53-54, Libn 52-. 8: Commissioner, sec-treas Powell-Clinch Utility Dist; Adv Bd, Trust Com Commercial Bank, Middlesboro Ky; Pres Clark Insurance & Real Estate Agency, Harrogate Tenn; Lincoln Mem Alumni Assn (chm publ rel com, mem of Exec Com); County treas of Easter Seal Soc, mem of reg bd. 9: ALA;-Ky sect (pres Col & Ref Libns 51-52); TennLA; KyLA (sec 51-52); SELA. 10: Kiwanis; Phi Gamma Mu; Zeta Sigma Pi; Phi Delta Kappa; Sigma Delta Pi;Optimist. 14: Admin, ref. 15: Box 96, Harrogate Tn 37752.

CLARK, RUTH HANNA. b Kemp Tex 10 Ja 12. 4: L Harvey Clark. 5: West Tex State U 28-30, 32-33 (Sp) BA; Tex Woman's U summers 34, 50, 51 BLS, 64 MLS. 6: Sp. 7: Elem tchr West Way Sch, Hereford Tex 30-32; Tchr-libn Friona High Sch, Friona Tex 33-37; Elem tchr Lancaster Pub Sch, Lancaster Tex 44-47; High sch libn Lancaster High Sch, Lancaster Tex 47- Ref libn Dallas Baptist Col 68-. 9: ALA; SWLA; TexLA; TexASchL (pres 61-62); Tex State Tchrs Assn; Teen-Age Lib Assn of Tex (Scholarship Com 62-). 10: PTA; Delta Kappa Gamma. 14: Ref, ya serv. 15: 1019 East Ledbetter dr, Lancaster Tx 75216.

CLARK, THOMAS A. b Iuka Miss 12 Mr 36. 5: USoMiss 54-58 (Hist) BS; UMiss 66-68 MLS. 7: Libn Belmont High Sch, Belmont Miss 58-66; Circ libn Valdosta State Col Lib 66-. 9: ALA; SELA; GaLA. 10: AAUP. 14: Circ. 15: Greenbriar apt 15, Ashley st, Valdosta Ga 31601.

CLARK, TURNER. b McKenzie Tenn 9 Mr 13. 5: Bethel Col 32, 35, 37-39 (Sci) BA; Peabody 39-40 BS in LS. 7: Tchr Weakley Co Tenn 35-36; Stud lib asst Bethel Col 39-40; Lib asst Newark Pub Lib, Newark NJ 40-42; Med Aid US Army 94th Inf Div, ETO-US 42-45; Dir Shelby Co Libs, Memphis Pub Lib, Memphis Tenn 46-60; Asst dir Memphis Pub Lib 60-. 9: ALA (Exec Bd); SELA; TennLA (v-pres 62-63, pres 64). 10: Memphis Pub Affairs Forum. 14: Admin. 15: Memphis Pub Lib 258 S McLean, Memphis Tn 38104.

CLARK, WENONA (CHURCHILL). b El Dorado Springs Mo 5 Ja 06. 4: Walter R Clark. 5: Central Methodist Col 23-27 (Eng, Fr, Educ) AB. 6: Fr. 7: Chief Libn VA Center, Prescott Ariz 49-. 9: ArizStateLA. 10: AAUW; Prescott Camera Club. 14: Hosp libnship, med ref. 15: 804 Country Club dr, Prescott AZ 86301.

CLARKE, AVIS GERTRUDE. b Webster Mass 12 Jl 02. 5: Simmons 19-23 (LS) BS. 6: Fr, Ger. 7: Asst catlgr Brown U 23-27; Asst catlgr Amer Antiquarian Soc, Worcester Mass 27-30, Chief catlgr 30-. 12: "An Alphabetical Index to the Titles in American Newspapers" 1821-1936,a union list, ed by Winifred Gregory 5v (58) (Typed copy available fromUniversity Microfilms, Inc., Ann Arbor Mich. 14: Catlg, rare bks. 15: 3 Wheelock st, Oxford Ma 01540.

CLARKE, CATHERINE V (CONDON). b Adair Iowa 20 O 06. 4: William Edward Clarke. 5: Clarke Col 23-26 (Eng) BA; Columbia 27-28 (LS) BS. 6: Lat, Fr. 7: Pub lib, Des Moines Iowa; Jr asst 26-27, Libn I 28-29, Br libn 29-32, 1st asst circ 32-38, 51-52, Head circ dept 53-. 9: ALA; IowaLA. 10: Des Moines Lib Club; Bishop Drumm Guild; Mercy Hosp Guild; Cath Mothers Club; AAUW; Des Moines Status of Women Coun. 14: Bk sel, reader guidance, admin. 15: 526 40th st, Des Moines Ia 50312.

CLARKE, HAYDEE G(ARCIA). b Cuzco Peru 18 Ja 35. 4: Robert F(landers) Clarke. 5: Colegio San Jorge (Lima Peru) 48-52 (Liberal Arts) Diploma; Biblioteca Nacional Lib Sch (Lima Peru) 53-54 (LS) Diploma. 6: Sp, Portu. 7: Libn in acquis Biblioteca Nacional, Lima Peru 55-57; Tech libn Ministryof Pub Educ, Lima Peru 57-62; Chief med libn Hospital del Nino, Lima Peru62-64; Med libn Chestnut Lodge, Rockville Md 65-66; Med libn Cedar Lodge;Rockville Md 65-; Libn (catlg) Inter Amer Devel Bank, Wash DC 66-67; Libn MdNat Cap Pk & Planning Commsn, Silver Spring Md 67; Asst libn readers servGeorgetown U Med Lib 67-. 9: Assn of Peruvian Libns. 13: Yes. 14: Latin Amer Libnship, admin, catlg, med libnship. 15: 2710 Elsmore st, Fairfax Va 22030.

CLARKE, JACK ALDEN. b Bay City Mich 20 F 24. 4: Anna Holler. 5: Mich State 49 (Hist) BA; UWis 50 (Hist) MA, 51 (LS) MA, 54 (Hist) PhD. 6: Fr, Ger, Sp. 7: Sgt US Army 43-45; Interne LC 52-53; Dir Wash Cathedral Lib 53-55; Dir Doane Col Lib 55-56; Asst libn UWis(Madison) 56-62; Dir Wis State U (Eau Claire) 60-65; Asst dir UWis Lib Sch 65-68; Act dir 68-69, Assoc Prof 65-67, Prof 67-. 9: ALA; WisLA (chm Col & U sect 64-65). 10: Wis Acad of Sciences, Arts, and Letters; AAUP. 12: "Research Materials in the Social Sciences" (67); "Huguenot Warrior, The Life and Times of Henri de Rohan" (67). 13: Yes. 14: Ref, admin. 15: UWis Lib Sch, 425 Henry Mall, Madison Wi 53706.

CLARKE, JAMES P(ETER). b Wilkes-Barre Penn 9 O 26. 4: Mary C Kerins. 5: King's Col 46-50 (Eng) AB; Drexel 50-51 MS in LS. 6: Sp. 7: Ref asst Brooklyn Pub Lib 51-53; Sr libn Monmouth Co Lib, Freehold NJ 53-56; Act dir Mercer Co Lib, Trenton NJ 57; Ext libn Scranton Pub, Scranton Penn 57-58; Head adult serv Monmouth Co Lib, Freehold NJ 59-60; Asst Prof Dept of Libnship Marywood Col 61-67, Dir of Lib 67-. 9: ALA; CathLA; PennLA (v-pres & pres-elect 68-69). 10: Marywood Col Lay Faculty Assn. 13: Yes. 14: Lib educ, admin. 15: 1704 Wyoming ave, Scranton Pa 18509.

CLARKE, JOAN DORN. b NYC 4 F 25. 5: Emmanuel Col (Boston) 41-45 (Eng) AB (cum laude); Simmons 54-57 (LS) MS. 6: Fr, Sp, Anglo-Saxon, Ger. 7: Advertising copywriter & advertising manager Sears Roebuck & Co, T W Rogers Co, Gilchrist Co 45-48; Lib asst & interne in lib train program Harvard Col Lib 48-55; Libn King Philip High Sch, Wrentham Mass 57-60; Libn Girls' Latin Sch, Boston 60-. 8: Consul on spec libs 60-; Evaluation of Secondary Sch libs 61-62; Recruiting mem ALA Recruiting Network 62-65; Intellectual Freedom Com MassLA 62-64. 9: ALA; Authors League of Amer; MassLA; MassSchLA (chm Boston Area Group 60-64). 10: Kappa Gamma Pi; Pan Amer Union; Intercol Club of Boston; Eng Speaking Union. 12: "Your future As A Librarian" (63); "St Margaret, Queen of Scotland" (66). 13: Yes. 14: Ref, hist research. 15: 37 Concord ave, Cambridge MA 02138.

CLARKE, MARIAN G M. b Urbana Ohio 10 Mr 11. 5: Ohio Wesleyan U 28-29; UMich 29-32 (Lit , Langs) AB, 32-33 ABLS; Trinity Col 56-59 (Govt). 6: Fr, Ger, Sp. 7: Stud asst UMich Lib (Ann Arbor) 29-32, Lib asst 33-34; Lib asst Ohio Wesleyan U 34-35; Ref & circ libn Allegheny Col, Meadville Penn 35-38; Libn ORDWES Wesleyan U (Middletown Conn) 48-54; Ser libn Trinit y Col (Hartford Conn) 55-59, Chief of readers serv & curator Watkinson Lib 59-. 9: ALA; ConnLA (chm Col & U Sect 65-66). 10: LWV; Urban League of Hartford; Wethersfield Equal Opportunities Coun. 12: "David Watkinson's Library" (66). 14: Rare bks, ref, admin. 15: Trinity College Lib, Hartford Ct 06106.

CLARKE, NORMAN FORD. b St Paul 7 My 28. 4: Mary Porter. 5: Ind U 46-50 (Journalism) AB; UMinn 50, 53-55 (Pol Sci) MA, MSLS; UMich 59- (LS). 6: Fr, Ger. 7: Pub Info Off US Army, Ft Benning Ga & Korea 51-53; Spec asst to Assoc Dir UMinn Libs (Minneapolis) 53-55; Documents libn Eppley Lib UOmaha 55-56; Head libn Thaw Mem Lib Jamestown Col 56-62; Asst Prof Dept of Lib Sci UKy (Lexington) 63-65; Prof

& Chm Dept of Lib Sci Ind State U 65-. 8: Development Com NDLA (chm 59-60). 9: ALA (mem com 58-60); MPLA (exec bd 58-60); NDLA (pres 61-62); KyLA(exec bd 64-65); Ohio Valley Group Tech Serv Libns (chm 66-69); IndLA (chmLib Educ Com 67-68); SLA; ASIS; IndSchLA. 10: Nat Coun of United PresbyterianMen (ND Synod pres 57-59); Rotary; AAUP; ACLU. 12: Ed UKy Microcards Lib Ser (65-). 13: Yes. 14: Lib educ, catlg, govt documents. 15: 4 Marion way, Terre HauteIn 47802.

CLARKE, POLLY ELIZABETH (STOTTS). b Southland Tex 21 Mr 29. 4: George R Clarke. 5: N Tex State U 48-52 (Elem Ed, LS) BS, summers 55-57 (Secondary Educ, Supv) MEd, 60-64 (Col Tchg, LS). 7: Libn Dallas Indp Sch Dist 52-60; Instr N Tex State U 61-63; Asst Prof Northeastern State Col(Tahlequah Okla) 63-. 8: Dir & instr, NDEA Lib Inst, Northeastern State Col, summer 65. 9: ALA; OklaEA; OklaLA; SWLA. 10: . 14: Sch libnship. 15: Northeastern State Col, Tahlequah OK 74464.

CLARKE, ROBERT F(LANDERS). b Newport News Va 20 Je 32. 4: Haydee Garcia Caceres. 5: US Coast Guard Acad 49-50 (Gen Engnr); US Naval Acad 50-54 (Gen Engnr) BS; Rutgers 60-61 MLS, 61-63 (LS) PhD. 6: Fr, Ger. 7: Capt USAF Personnel Off & aerial navigator-bombardier 54-60; Libn Health serv off (Lt Cdr) US Pub Health Serv 63-; NLM, Bethesda Md: Lib systems analyst 63-64, Asst to the chief tech serv div 64, Deputy chief tech serv div 64-; Lib techniques instr Temple Sch, Wash DC 65-; Chief lib serv Nat Clearinghouse for Smoking & Health, Arlington Va 66-68; Spec asst to chief NIH Lib, Bethesda Md 68-. 8: Adv to Montgomery Co (Md) Pub Lib Bd 64-; Consul in lib serv to Info Br Div of Water Supply & Polution Control, Bur of State Serv Pub Health Serv. 9: ALA); SLA; MedLA (Ed Com "Vital Notes"); DCLA (Mem Com). 10: Beta Phi Mu; Commsn Offs Assn of the Pub Health Serv; Sports Car Club of Amer; US Naval Acad Alumni Assn; Rutgers Grad Sch of Lib Serv Alumni Assn; No Va Bd of Realtors. 12: "Sports Car Events-1959"; Ed "Smoking & Health Bibliographical Bulletin," "Smoking & Health Bibliography," "Directory of Ongoing Research in Smoking & Health". 13: Yes. 14: Admin, research in info handling, applications of stats. 15: 2710 Elsmore st, Fairfax Va 22030.

CLARKE, VIRGINIA. b Albany Tex 8 N 07. 5: McMurry Col 25-26 (Span) 4-yr tchg certif; Sul Ross State Col summers 30-31 (Span) 6-yr tchg certif; No Tex State Col summers 32-39 (Span, LS) BA, Lib Certif, summers 40-44 (Educ, LS) MA Degree, Supv Certif. 6: Sp. 7: Tchr of Span & middle grades Post Sch, haskel Co Tex 26-27; Elem tchr Albany Pub Schs, Albany Tex 28-35, All-level libn 36-42; Instr in Lib Serv No Tex State Col summers 42, 58-59, All-level libn & supv of Sch Lib Practice 43-55, 58-. 8: Consul in lib serv, Tex Educ Agency 56; Elem Lib Experiments, Andrews Tex 57; NDEA Institute consul in Tex & Okla summers 65-69. 9: NEA; ALA; TexASchL; Tex State Tchrs Assn; Tex Coun on Lib Educ. 12: "Non-Book Library Materials" (53, suppl 65). 13: Yes. 14: Elem sch libs, org of non-bk materials, servs. 15: Box 5465, N T station, Denton TX 76203.

CLARKEN, MARY LOUISE. b Newark NJ 18 Mr 28. 5: Col of St Elizabeth 45-49 (Sociol) AB; Rutgers 60-63 mls. 7: Order libn Assoc Prof Seton Hall U 51-. 9: . 10: AAUP; Kappa Gamma Pi. 14: Acquis, ref. 15: 294 Vose ave, South Orange NJ 07079.

CLARKSON, JOAN SCHREIBER. b Toronto 29 Je 29. 5: Trinity Col UToronto 48-52 BA; UToronto 53-54 BLS. 6: Fr. 7: Libn (grade 1) circ dept UToronto Lib 54-62, Libn (grade 2) 62-. 9: CanLA; OntLA; Inst Prof Libn Ont. 10: Canadian Mental Health Assn; Crest Canadian Players Found; Natl BalletGuild of Can; Ont Hist Soc. 14: Interlib loans, bk sel, circ, ref. 15: 153 LaScelles blvd, Toronto 7 Ont Can.

CLARY, ANN ROANE. b Wash DC 5 Ap 31. 5: Wilson Tchrs Col, Wash DC 49-50; Mary Washington Col of UVa 50-52 (Eng) BA; Catholic U 54-55 MS in LS. 6: Fr. 7: Elem tchr Montgomery Co Md 52-54; Chief libn Amer Nat Red Cross Nat Hdqrs Lib, Wash DC 55-60; Ref libn Bd of Governors of the Fed Reserve System, Wash DC 60-65, Asst chief libn 66-67, Chief libn 67-. 9: SLA-DC Chap; DCLA. 14: Ref. 15: 3225 McKinley st NW, Wash DC 20015.

CLARY, JOHNNIE MARY (HURT). b Nashville Tenn 12 Mr 06. 5: Peabody Col 26-37 (Educ) BS, 37-40 BS in LS; Okla StateU 68-69. 7: Tchr Nashville City Schs 26-37, Libn 37-59; Libn Dept of Defense Schs: Germany 59-61, Eritrea (Africa) 61-62, France 62-63, Japan 63-. 9: NEA; OverseasEA; Far EastEA. 14: Elem sch libs. 15: 616 Shelby ave, Nashville Tn 37206.

CLASEN, MILTON G. b Riverside Cal 13 Ja 41. 5: Cal Concordia Col 59-61; Concordia Sr Col (Ft Wayne) 61-63 BA; Concordia Sem 63-67 BD; LSU 67-69 MS. 7: Lib trainee LSU (Baton Rouge) 69; Asst catlg libn Tex A & I U 69-. 14: Catlg. 15: Lib Tex A & I Univ, Kingsville Tx 78363.

CLASON, BARBARA E. b Midland Mich 25 Je 16. 5: Wichita State U 33-37 AB in Educ; UOkla summers 41-46 (Eng Lit) MA, 55-56 MALS. 6: Fr, Lat, Sp. 7: Tchr high schs & jr cols, Kan & Okla 37-55; Catlgr UKan Libs 56-63, Admin asst to hd of prepar dept 64-66, asst hd catlgr 67-. 9: ALA; MPLA; KanLA. 10: AAUP; Bus & Prof Women's Club; AAUW; DAR; Douglas Co (Kan) Hist Soc. 14: Catlg. 15: 1205oread ave apt 17, Lawrence Ks 66044.

CLASSEN, JOANNE (E). b Hastings Neb 23 S 29. 5: Hastings Col 47-51 (Eng) AB; UDenver 52-53 (LS) MA. 7: Child libn P Billings Mem Lib, Billings Mont 53-54; Asst libn Pub Lib, Grand Island Neb 54-59; Reg demonstration bkmob libn Mo State Lib 59-62; Asst br libn (Libn III) Denver Pub Lib 62-68, Libn IV Denver Pub Lib 68-. 68, Libn IV Denver Pub Lib 68-. 9: ALA; ColoLA. 10: YWCA; NWest Denver Commun Rel Coun. 14: Ya wk, ext . 15: 1540 So Albion, Denver Co 80222.

CLAUDIA, SISTER M (CARLEN) IHM. b Detroit 24 Jl 06. 5: Marygrove Col 24-26 (Lang); UMich 26-28 (LS, Lang) ABLS, 36-38 AMLS; Chicago summer 53 (Lib Educ). 6: Lat, Ger, Ital, Sp, Fr. 7: Asst libn St Mary Acad, Monroe Mich 28-29; Asst libn Marygrove Col 29-44, Libn 44-; Index ed "New Catholic Encyclopedia" Catholic U 63-66. 8: Dir of volunteers servicing commun center libs 48-57; Moderator Nat Lit Commsn Nat Fed Cath Col Studs 51-55; Dir Research Annual (Marygrove Col) 50-63; Consul Collier-Macmillan Cath Sch Lib Catlg; Mich Week Cultural Activities Com 52-55 Consul; McGraw-Hill Encyclopedia of World Biography 68-, World Book Encyclopedia 69-. Consul: McGraw-Hill Encyclopedia of World Biography 68-, World Book Encyclopedia 69-. 9: ALA (Coun 58-62, 68-71, chm var coms); CathLA (pres 65-67, chm var coms; Mich Unit: Hon life mem , chm 52-54); BSA; MichLA (chm Col Sect 56-57); DCLA (Memb Com). 10: Phi Beta Kappa; Phi Kappa Phi; Beta Phi Mu. 11: Marygrove Lib Guild (citation) Award. 12: "Guide to the Encyclicals" (39); "Guide to the Documents of Pius XII" (51); "Dictionary of Papal Pronouncements" (58); Adv Bd "The Pope Speaks," quarterly (54-). 13: Yes. 14: Ref, bibliog. 15: Marygrove Col Lib, Detroit Mi 48221.

CLAUSMAN, GILBERT (JOSEPH). b Los Angeles 8 N 21. 5: Willamette U 39-42, 46-47 (Eng Lit) AB; Columbia 47-48 (LS) BS, 52 (LS) MS. 7: Pharmacist Mate 1st Class US Navy 42-45; Ref asst NY Acad of Med, NYC 48-51, 1st asst in chg of circ 52-55; Libn NYU Med Center 55-. 9: MedLA (Bd Dirs 59-62, Exch Mgr 60-62, ny reg Group: treas 51-54, chm 56-57, Exec Com 57-58). 10: AAUP; Melvil Dui Marching & Chowder Soc; Archons of Colophon; NY Lib Club. 11: Hon mem NYU Sch Med Alum Assn 69. 13: Yes. 15: 550 First ave, NYC 10016.

CLAUSON, PENELOPE PARRISH. b Brooklyn NY 20 D 17. 4: James W Clauson. 5: Smith 34-38 (Hist) AB; Rutgers 66 MLS. 6: Fr, Sp. 7: Trainee Montclair Pub Lib, Montclair NJ 64-66; Libn Kimberly Sch, Montclair NJ 66. 9: ALA; NJLA; NJSchA; EssexCoLA. 10: LWY; Jr League; United Commun Serv of North Essex. 14: Sch libnship. 15: 8 Erwin Pk, Montclair NJ 07042.

CLAUSSEN, NORMA AVELINE. b Stuart Iowa 20 Jl 33. 5: UCLA 51-55 (Pol Sci) BA; UWash 64-65 MLS. 6: Ger, Sp. 7: Sr lib asst UCLA circ dept 55; Admin asst The RAND Corp, Santa Monica 55-57; Statistical analyst System Development Corp, Santa Monica Cal 57-63; Asst libn RCA W Coast Div, Van Nuys Cal 65-66; Ref libn UCal (Santa Barbara) 66-. 9: ALA; CalLA. 10: Sierra Club. 14: Ref, catlg. 15: 3449 Richland dr, apt 8, Santa Barbara CA 93105.

CLAVER, SISTER M PETER (DUCAT) OP. b Milwaukee. 5: Ursinus Col 38-42 (Eng) AB; UIll (Urbana) summer 43 (LS); Rosary Col 45-47 BS in LS; Catholic U summer 50 (Hist); Rosary Col summer 51-53 MA in LS; Columbia U 55-57, 59-60 DLS. 6: Fr, Ger. 7: Asst ser libn Jackson Lab Lib DuPont Co, Deepwater NY summers 39-42; Libn Woodstown (NJ) Pub High Sch 42-44; Asst ref libn Rosary Col 45-47; Tchr Visitation High Sch, Chicago 47-49; Libn Heelan High Sch, Sioux City Iowa 49-54; Ref libn Rosary Col 54-55, Dir Dept of Lib Sci 58-. 67; Dir Dom Ed Ctr 68-. 8: Consul in planning new sch libs; Dir of a series of cultural symposiums co-sponsored with the Thomas More Assn 58-65. 9: ALA-LED (past pres); CathLA (Adv Coun, Mem Com, past chm Ill

Unit); SLA; Adult Educ Assn; WisLA (chm LED). 12: Co-ed "Catholic Booklist" (45-49). 13: Yes. 14: Admin, ref, lib planning. 15: Rosary Col, River Forest IL 60305.

CLAVER, SISTER PETER (FAHY). b Rome Ga 17 Jl 1899. 5: Trinity Col 19-23 BA; Catholic U 59 (Educ) MA; Catherine Spaulding 61 MSLS; Emory 60 (Med Bibliog & Ref). 7: Med libn Holy Name of Jesus Hosp, Gadsden Ala. 8: Pres Etowah Co Coun of Comm Serv 68-69. 9: CathLA (chm Pub Rel, HealthSci Sect 68-69; Adv Coun rep to the ALA-AHIL Com on Hosp Lib Stands 69-71). 14: Ref. 15: Holy Name of Jesus Hosp, Gadsden Al 35902.

CLAY, THYRA MAGRETA (HENRIKSEN). b Askov Minn 3 O 16. 5: Colo State Col 35-37 (Ed); UMont 64-65 (Lib serv) BA; Case-West Res 65-66 MSLS. 6: Danish, Norwegian, Ger. 7: Libn Mineral Co, Superior Mont 57-58; Lib asst City of Anchorage, Anchorage Alka 58-64; Readers' serv libn Mont State Lib, Helena Mont 66-. 9: AlaskaLA (sec-treas 63-64) MontLA (sec 69-). 14: Ref, readers serv. 15: 1924 Winne ave, Helena Mt 59601.

CLAYMAN, BEVERLY JOAN. b Pampa Tex 7 Ag 32. 5: UCLA 51-55 (Ed) BA; UsoCal 65-66 MSLS. 6: Sp. 7: Syst simulation designer Syst Development Corp, Santa Monica Cal 55-63; Ref libn Santa Monica Pub Lib 66-67; Info spec sr TRW Syst Group, Redondo Beach Cal 67-68; Acquis libn Cal State Col at Dominquez Hills 69-. 9: ALA; SLA; CalLA. 14: Lit research, ref, acquis. 15: 2226 Linnington ave, Los Angeles Ca 90064.

CLAYTON, HOWARD. b Leonardville Kan 8 Mr 29. 4: Wilma Jean (Pennington) Clayton. 5: Kan State Tchrs Col 47-49, 53-54 (Music, Educ) BSEd , 57 (LS) MS; Amer Conservatory of Music (Chicago) 49-53 (Music) BM, MM; UOkla 61-65 (Educ, LS) PhD; UIll 56, 61. 06: Fr, Ger. 7: Music tchr Paxton Commun Schs, Paxton Ill 54-56; Libn Libertyville High Sch, Libertyville Ill 56-57; Asst libn West Ill U 57-59; Pub serv libn Kan State Col (Pittsburg) 59-62; Head of Lib Dept Southwestern Col 62-64; Spec instr UOkla 65; Head of Lib Dept State U Col (Brockport NY) 65-68; Grad fac UOkla 68-. 9: ALA; KanLA; KanSchLA; OklaLA; SWLA. 10: Kiwanis Internat. 12: "An Investigation of Personality Characteristics Among Library Students at One Midwestern University" (68); Ed "Library-College Journal" (68-). 13: Yes. 14: Educ. 15: 1514 Rowena lane, Norman Ok 73069.

CLAYTON, JOHN MIDDLETON JR. b West Grove Penn 4 My 41. 4: Norma Louise Towne Clayton. 5: W Chester State Col 59-63 (Mus) BS; Drexel 63-66 (LS) MS. 6: Fr. 7: Libn Penns Grove Reg High Sch, Penns Grove NJ 63-66; Tchr Avon-Grove High Sch, West Grove Penn 66-67; UDela: Reader serv libn 67-69, Archivist 69-. 9: ALA; DelLA. 14: Univ pub serv, archives. 15: 81 Madison dr College Park, Newark Del 19711.

CLAYTON, MARGUERITE V. b Tillar Ark 27 Jl 10. 5: Henderson State Tchrs Col 31-34 (Hist, Govt) BA; UColo 36 (Hist); Peabody 42, 45 & 46 BS in LS, 59 MA(LS). 7: Tchr-High Sch Hist & Govt pub schs, Ark 34-39; High sch libn pub schs, Ark, Ala, Tex 39-48; Lib supv city schs, Aberdeen Wash 48-50; Head acquis Mo State Lib 50-52; Chief bibliog serv for Japan USIA, Tokyo 52-53; Head ref dept White Plains Pub Lib, White Plains NY 54-59; Asst Prof Tex Woman's U Sch of Lib Sci 59-. 9: ALA; AALS; TexLA (chm Ref RT 67-68); ArkLA; Tex Assn Col Tchrs (sec-treas TWU chap 68-69); SWLA; Tex Coun on Lib Educ (sec 65-67). 10: AAUP; AAUW; Eng-Speak Union. 14: Ref, sel, pub libs, Am lib resources. 15: 2211 N Locust st, Denton Tx 76201.

CLAYTON, SHERYL (HOWARD). b Kan City Mo 17 My 29. 4: George Clayton. 5: Prairie View A & M Col 45-48 (Sociol) BA; UIll 51-58 (LS) MS Simmons Col summer 66 (LS). 7: Libn-tchr Sch Dist 188, Lovejoy PO Ill 49-53; Tchr Sch Dist 189 E St Louis Ill 54-64, Libn 64-. 10: Bridge Club; PTA; Mem Bd of Educ Sch Dist184, E St Louis, Ill. 14: Sch lib serv. 15: 519 Jefferson, East St Louis Il 62205.

CLEE, RICHARD M. b Jersey City NJ 22 Ag 30. 4: Frances Eleanor (Maclean) Clee. 5: UToronto 49-53 (Arts) BA, 59-60 BLS; Ontario Col of Educ summers 64-65 High Sch Asst "B" Certif, High Sch Specialist Certif. 6: Fr. 7: Acquis libn York U (Toronto) 60-63; Libn Banting Inst, Toronto 63-64; Libn Thistletown Collegiate Inst, Etobicoke Ont 64- Free lance writer in motor sports field 57-. 9: OntTchrs Fed; Inst Prof Libns Ont; OntLA (chm Pub Com 63-64). 12: Ed "Doorway" mag of Coop Bk Centre of Can Ltd (63-64). 13: Yes. 14: Acquis, sch libnship. 15: 21 Rondale blvd, Toronto 19 Canada.

CLELAND, MARY ELIZABETH. b New Brighton Penn 1 My 32. 5: Geneva Col 50-54 (Hist, Eng) BA; Columbia 54-55 (Hist); West Res 58-59 MSLS. 7: Tchr Ontario Pub Schs, Ontario Ohio 55-58; Ref libn West Res U Lib 59-62; Asst libn Geneva Col 62-. 9: ALA; PennLA. 10: AAUW. 14: Ser, ref, govt docs. 15: 3021 6th ave, Beaver Falls Pa 15010.

CLELLAND, MARJORIE (BOLTON). b Cleveland 13 Ap 12. 4: James L Clelland. 5: Flora Stone Mather Col West Res 31-35 (Biol) BA; West Res 36-38 BSLS. 6: Ger. 7: Libn & botanist Garden Center, Cleveland 34-40; Libn Hudson Lib & Hist Soc, Hudson Ohio 40-47; Libn Portage Co Dist Lib, Hiram Ohio 48-52; Br libn Akron Pub Lib, Akron Ohio 52-61. 8: Private Press Printer & publ of "Truffles and Tripe"; mem of NAPA and APA,proprietor of the Partridge Press. 9: ALA; OhioLA. 10: Woman's Club; LWV. 13: Yes. 14: Admin. 15: 2712 Hudson-Aurora rd, Hudson Oh44236.

CLEMENT, EVELYN (GEER). b Springfield Mass 1 S 26. 4: J Randall Clement. 5: Okla Col for Women 44-46 (Voice, Music); UTulsa 61-65 (Hist) BA; UOkla summer 65 (LS); IndU 68- (LS). 6: Fr, Sp, Ger. 7: Serv rep Mich Bell Telephone, Detroit 46; Stenographer UOkla Dept of Short Courses 51-52; Bkmob libn Tulsa City-Co Lib, Tulsa Okla 60-64, Ref libn 64-66;Learning resources libn Oral Roberts U 66-68; Instr Sch of Lib Sci UOkla (Tulsa)66-. 8: Dir, USDE Inst on multi-media resources, Okla U 68; Asst dir USDE Inston bibliog control of media, Okla U 69; Mem Steering Com, Nat Lib Week, Okla68. 9: ALA (chm LAD/LOMS Statist Com for Ref Serv 68-); SLA (chm Recr Com,Okla Chap 67-68); NEA-DAVI; AALS; OklaLA (chm Com on Recr 67-68); SWLA. 10: LWVTulsa Co (Okla) Hist Soc; UN Assn; Tulsa Civic Music Assn; Phi Alpha Theta;Pi Gamma Mu; Beta Phi Mu. 14: Ref, educ media, lib hist. 15: 2917 S Cincinnati,Tulsa Ok 74114.

CLEMENT, HOPE E A. b NS Can 29 D 30. 5: King's Col 48-51 (Fr) BA; Dalhousie U 51-53 (Eng) MA; UToronto 54-55 BLS. 6: Fr. 7: Libn Dalhousie U Law Lib (Halifax NS) 53-54; Catlgr Nat Lib of Can 55-59, Head, Canadiana Sect 60-66; Chief Nat Bibliog Div 67-. 9: CanLA. 10: . 12: Ed "Canadiana". 14: Catlg, bibliog, automation. 15: 252 Daniel ave, Ottawa 3 Canada.

CLEMENT, KEITH GORDON. b Munising Mich 11 Ag 17. 4: Dorothea Shaffstall. 5: Mich State U 35-39 (Hotel Admin) BA; UMich 63-65 MALS. 7: Catering Manager Hotel Noble Jonesboro Ark 39; Naval Aviator US Navy (Lt Cmdr) 39-45; Owner-manager Shingleton Oil Co, Shingleton Mich 46-; Act dir Mich State Lib UPBr, Escanaba Mich 65-67; Asst prof Mich Tech U 67-68; Instl Liaison Libn Wash State Lib, OlympiaWash 68-. 9: MLA; WLA; PNLA. 14: Admin. 15: 2503 Fir st, Olympia Wa 98501.

CLEMENTS, HELEN LEE (PEELER). b San Bernadino Cal 1 Ag 44. 4: (Luther) Davis Clements. 5: Okla State U 62-66 (Eng) BA; UIll 66-68 (LS) MS. 7: Grad asst catlg dept Lib UIll at Urbana 66-68; Info desk libn UOkla Lib 68-69. 9: ALA; OklaLA. 10: Beta Phi Mu; Phi Kappa Phi. 14: Ref, ya. 15: 1205 W 2nd, Elk City Ok 73644.

CLEMONS, JOHN ELTON. b Chiefland Fla 1 Ag 28. 4: Jean Pryor. 5: UFla 44-47 (Soc Sci); Fla State U 47-48 (LS) BA, 48-49 (LS) MA. 6: Sp. 7: Stud asst Agric Lib UFla 45-47; Grad asst Fla State U Lib Sch 48-49; Asst in period Fla State U Lib 49-51; Educ NCO (Sgt) USMC Parris Island SC 52-54; Gen asst Fla State U Lib 54-55, Instr & bibliog 55-59, Asst Prof & bibliog 60-66; Assoc Prof Div Libnship Emory U 66-68, Assoc Prof's Asst Dir Div Libnship68-. 9: ALA; -LED (SEast Reg Rep 68-69); SELA (Exec Bd 64-68, chm Com on Libnshipas a Career 66-68, Exch Chm 68-70); FlaLA (chm col & spec libs sect 60-61); GaLA(chm Educ for Libnship Sect 67-69). 10: Theta Chi; Lions Club; Beta Phi Mu. 12: Co-comp "Graduate Thesis and Dissertation Handbook" (65). 13: Yes. 14: Admin, automation, research methods, educ for libnship. 15: Div of Librarianships, Emory Univ, Atlanta Ga 30322.

CLEMONS, LECLARE F. b Brooklyn NY 17 Je 1899. 5: Hunter Col 24-28 (Eng) BA; Columbia 39-41 BSLS, 41-55 (Curr & Materials) MA. 6: Fr, Sp, Lat. 7: Tchr Hamilton Inst for Girls, 19-25; Tchr Columbia Grammar Sch, NYC 25-31; High Sch & Elem libn 38-54; High sch libn Dalton Schs, NYC54-56; Head libn Bank St Col of Educ (NY) 56-67; Libn spec ed Hunter Col 67-68; Mus libn City Col 69; Libn Juilliard Sch 69-. 8: Consul Goddard Col new lib. 9: ALA; NEA; Assn of Priv Schs, NYC & Vicin (chm Lib Com); NYLA; NY State Assn Nursing Educ; Early Childhood Educ Coun of NYC; Metro Col Inter-lib Assn. 10: AAAS; Amer Coun of Parent Corps; Violoncello Soc, NYC; Amateur Chamber Music

Players. 13: Yes. 14: Admin, bibliog, ref, music. 15: 400 Central park W, New York NY 10025.

CLEVELAND, EDITH (FRANCES). b Canton Mass 15 O 30. 5: Simmons 48-52 (LS) SB. 7: Asst libn Carnegie pub Lib, Greenville Ohio 52-61; Libn J R Clarke Pub Lib, Covington Ohio 61; Head circ dept Lima Pub Lib, round Table 63-64) Spec asst adult serv div Akron Pub Lib 63-69, Sec asst lang, lit, histdiv 69-. 8: Consul & catlg Covington High Sch Lib 61-62. 9: ALA; OhioLA (secJr membs RT 63-69, ed of "Newsletter" for Ref Serv RT 68-). 10: Bus & ProfWomen's Club; AAUW; Akron Pub Lib Staff Assn; Comm Chest Com (various offs); StanHywet Hall Found. 14: Ref in humanities. 15: 627 W Market st, apt 6, Akron Oh44303.

CLEVENGER, GENE W. b Raytown Mo 10 Ap 37. 4: Sue Hamilton. 5: UMo (Kan City) 60-64 (Biol) BS; UDenver 65-66 MSLS. 6: Ger. 7: Pfc USA 56-58; Clerical Raytown Water Co, Raytown Mo 55-64; Ref asst Kan City Pub Lib, Mo 63-64; Grad research asst UDenver 65-67; Spec consul Colo State Lib, Denver 67; Syst libn YorkU 67-69; Libn (hd) NM Inst of Mining & Tech 69-. 9: SLA. 12: Ed "Business Book Review Index" (69). 14: Syst, automation. 15: New Mexico Institute of Mining & Tech, Socorro NM.

CLEVER, ELAINE (COX). b NYC. 4: Fred E Clever. 5: Penn State U 41-43 BA; Drexel 61 MS in LS; Drexel (Info sci) 66-68. 6: Fr. 7: "ElPaso Times & Herald Post" El Paso Tex 44; Avon Sch, Barrington NJ 54-59; Libn Woodland Sch, Barrington NJ 59-63; Libn Haddon High Sch NJ 63-64; Asst head circdiv Temple U Lib 64-66, Hd libn 66-. 8: Library/USA 64 SLA-ADI Panel on lib info, NY 66; Consulfor Anak-Tech Info Syst 68-; Grant in Lib Research U.S. Off of Educ 69-. 9: ALA;ASIS; AAUP. 10: Theta Sigma Phi; ACLU; WIL; Beta Phi Mu. 11: First prize Penn Newspaper Adv Mgrs Award 43; SLA-ADI Panel on libautomation, NY 66. 14: Info systems, lib automation. 15: Sherry Way (Hunt Tract), Haddonfield NJ 08034.

CLIFFORD, JAMES ROLAND. b Los Angeles Cal 21 Jl 41. 4: Susan Gene Heasly. 5: UAriz 59-60 (Chem); Cal State Col (Long Beach) 60-64 (Phil) BA; USoCal 66-68 MLS. 7: Intelligence analyst (Sp/4) USA 64-66; Ref libn Palos Verdes Lib Dist, Palos Verdes Pen Cal 66-. 8: Staff US Army Intelligence Sch, Ft Holabird Md 65-66. 9: ALA; CalLA. 14: Ref. 15: 355 Freeman ave apt 3, Long Beach Ca 90814.

CLIFFORD, KATHLEEN EMMONS. b Las Animas Colo 27 S 08. 5: Alliance Francaise (Paris) 25-26 (Fr) Diploma; UGrenoble (France) 26-27 (Fr) Certif; UMich (Ann Arbor) 27-31 (Langs Lit) AB; UWash 31-32 BS in LS; UWyo summer 41 (Portu). 6: Fr, Portu, Sp, Ital, Ger, Lat. 7: Sr ref asst UWash Lib 32-33; Dir & tchr Amer Sch, Agana Guam 33-35; Libn US Naval Station Lib, Agana Guam 35; Sub libn child dept DC Pub Lib 36; Libn & tchr of Fr Arlington Hall Jr Col 36-38; Descr catlgr LC 38-45, 47-48, 50-52; Consul Biblioteca Nacional Rio de Janeiro Brazil 45-46; Org Dir USIS Lib, Lisbon Portugal 48-49; Sub catlgr & clsfr LC 52-. 8: LC rep at Internat Lib Conf Montevideo Uruguay 46; Unofficial State Dept rep at internat Cong on the Hist of Art, Portugal 49. 9: ALA; DCLA. 10: Alpha Omicron Pi. 114: Catlg. 13: Yes. 14: Catlg, clsf. 15: 2204 S Knoll rd, Arlington Va 22202.

CLIFFORD, NEALE (FORD). b Williamsport Penn 20 Mr 43. 4: Stanley E Clifford. 5: SUNY (Geneseo) 61-65 (Lib Educ) BS, 65-69 MLS. 7: Libn Frankfort High Sch, Frankfort NY 65-66; Libn Haverling Jr-Sr High Sch, Bath NY 66-68; Ref libn Lemon Grove Co Lib, Lemon Grove Cal 68-. 8: Lib consul Christ United Methodist Ch, San Diego 69. 9: NYLA; CalLA. 14: Ref, ya. 15: 4164 37th st apt 7, San Diego Ca 92105.

CLIFFORD, SUSAN GENE (HEASLY). b Long Beach Cal 20 F 46. 4: James Roland Clifford. 5: Cal State Col (Long Beach) 63-67 (Eng) BA; USoCal 67-69 MLS. 6: Lat. 7: Med libn Long Beach Memorial Hosp, Long Beach Cal 66-67; Gen libn Long Beach Pub Lib, Long Beach cal 67-. 9: ALA; CalLA. 14: Ref, y-a serv. 15: 355 Freeman ave apt 3, Long Beach Ca 90814.

CLIFT, DAVID H. b Mason Co Ky 16 Je 07. 4: Eleanore Flynn Clift. 5: UKy 24-30 BS in Com; Columbia 30-31 BS in LS. 7: Stud asst UKy Lib 27-30; Desk asst Pub Lib, Lexington Ky summer 30; Stud asst Columbia U Libs 30-31; Ref asst NY Pub Lib 31-37; Asst to Dir of Libs Columbia U 37-42; (1st Lt) US Army Off of Strategic Serv 42-45; Deputy, then Act Chief LC Mission to Germany 45-46; Assoc Libn Yale U 45-51; Instr New Haven State Tchrs Col summer 48; Exec Sec ALA Chicago 51-58, Exec Dir 58-. 8: Consul & lecturer Reunion Technica Bibliotecarios Agricolas de America Latina,Turrialba, Costa Rica 53; Chm Yrbk Com Nat Soc Study of Educ (for 'Adult Reading'Part II of the NSSE "Yearbook" (56); Head Deleg of US Libns to the Soviet Union61, under the US-Soviet Cultural Exch Agreement; Guest Program of the Fed Republicof Germany ("Librarians from the U.S.A.") 63; Adv Com on the Lib Serv Program inthe US Off of Educ 61-64; Libn of Congress' Liaison Com 62-; Consul Ford Found &Univ of Brasilia on lib program at Univ 63-68; Del IFLA Rome 64, & continuing; Bdof Visitors, Duke U lib 64-. 9: ALA; ConnLA (pres 50-51); NY Lib Club (pres 41-42). 10: UKy Lib Assocs; Delta Sigma Pi; Tavern Club (Chicago); Hon Order of KyColonels; Alpha Beta Alpha (Hon Mem). 11: UKy Founders' Day Award forDistinguished Achievement in Libnship, 57; Joseph W Lippincott Award for Notableachievement in Libnship 62; UKy Distinguished Alumni Centennial Award, 65; Hontrustee, Amer Lib in Paris 69-. 12: "Report of a Survey of the University of Minnesota Library" with Keyes D Metcalf (49); Issue ed "Library Trends" (Ja 55); ("Library Associations in the United States & British Commonwealth"). 13: Yes. 14: Org & wk of lib assns, admin, lib educ. 15: ALA 50 E Huron st, Chicago 60611.

CLIFTON, JOE ANN. b Alton Ill 14 Ap 29. 4: Robert F Clifton. 5: Santa Monica Col 51-54 (Psych) UCLA 69-. 6: Lat. 7: Systems & Procedures Hughes Aircraft, Culver City Cal 53-54; Chief libn Guidance & Control systems Div Litton Industries Inc, Woodland Hills Cal 54-. 8: Adv comm Pierce Col lib 62-65. 9: SLA (var offs 68-69);-Documentation div (3 chmship); -SoCal chap (various duties); ASIS (program chm69); Amer Mgt Assn; Amer Inst of Mgt; Amer Soc for Info Display (chm Arch/LibCom 67-); CalLA; Ame Computing Machinery. 10: Parents for Basic Educ (Exec v-pres60-64). 14: Admin, research, info retrieval, data processing. 15: 5500 Canoga ave,Woodland Hills Ca 91366.

CLIMIE, (MARGARET) KATHERYN. b Sault Ste Marie Ont 14 Ja 13. 5: UToronto Lib Sch 37-38. 7: Libn Sault Ste Marie (Ont) Pub Lib 32-, Chief Libn 51-. 9: CanLA; OntLA; Inst Prof Libns Ont. 10: Bus & Prof womens Club. 15: Pub Lib, Sault Ste Marie Ont Canada.

CLINE, GLORIA JANE (STARK). b Acadia Parish La 22 S 36. 4: Robert William Cline. 5: USoWest La 56-60 (Elem ed) BA; UTex 66-67 MLS; UMiami 69-. 7: Libn I (ref) UTex Undergrad Lib 67-68; Instr children's lit UMiami 69; Libn F M Hamilton Lab Sch, Lafayette La 69-. 9: ALA; -ACRL; -AASchL. 10: Phi Kappa Phi; Kappa Delta Pi; Beta Phi Mu. 14: Ref, child wk. 15: 401 S 4th st, Eunice La 70535.

CLINE, HENRIETTE (FECHENBACH). b Dallas Tex 5 Je 11. 4: Clarence Lee Cline. 5: UChicago 27-28; UTex 28-31 (Eng) BA; Columbia 31-32 (Col & Univ Libs) BLS. 6: Fr, Sp. 7: Catlgr UTex main catlg dept 35-37, Catlgr Undergrad Lib 61-63, Catlgr Rare Bks Lib 63-67, Hd catlgr 67-. 9: ALA; TexLA; Tex Assn Col Tchrs. 10: UTex Ladies Club; UTex Eng Wives. 14: Catlg (espec rare bks). 15: 1401 Hardouin ave, Austin Tx 78703.

CLINE, HERMAN H. b Olympia Wash 27 S 40. 5: St Martin's Col 59-61 (Class Langs); UWash 61-64 (Mod For Langs) BA, (LS) ML Columbia U 67-68; NYU 68-. 6: Fr, Ger, Ital, Lat, Sp, Port. 7: Catlg libn UWash Lib 64-66; Instr City Col CUNY 66-. 9: ALA (Int Rel RT) -ACRL (Com of Commun Use of Acad Libs); Semin on Acquis of Lat Amer Material (chm Com on Reporting Bibliog Activities 67-69). 10: AAUP; JMRT; RT of Soc Responsibilities. 12: "Report of Bibliographic Activities, 1966-1968" (69). 14: Catlg, acquis, bibliog. 15: City Col of CUNY, Cohen Lib 201 A, Covent ave at W 135th, New York NY 10031.

CLINE, MARY ANNA (LENTZ). b Gold Hill NC 2 Je 11. 4: Mack Cline. 5: UNC 29-33 (LS) AB. 7: Libn Concord Pub Lib, Concord NC 58-. 15: Rt 2, Gold Hill NC.

CLINE, MILDRED A(NNE). b Portland Ore 13 Ja 10. 5: Reed Col 28-32 (Pol Sci) AB; UWis 34-35 (LS) Certif; NYU 41-42, 46 (Govt) AM; UWash 67-68 (LS). 7: Asst circ dept Lib Assn of Portland (Portland Ore) 35-41; Br asst NY Pub Lib 41-42; Lib Assn of Portland, Portland Ore: Mun ref libn ref dept 42-51; Head gen reading dept 51-56; Head lit & hist dept 56-59; Head ref libn San Fernando Valley State Col Lib 59-61; Head humanities-sci libn 61-64; Head readers serv div Ore State Lib 64-67; Catlgr Lib Assn of Portland, Portland Ore 68-. 8: Alumni Regent Reed Col 45-47; Bd Mgrs Pac; Northwest Bibliog Ceter 53-55. 9: ALA (Coun mem-at-large) 58-62; OreLA; CalLA; PNLA (2nd v-pres, program chm 49-50). 10: LWV. 14: Ref, tech serv. 15: 1480 24th st NE, Salem Or 97301.

CLINE, WILLIAM VERN. b Port Huron Mich 27 Ag 28. 5: Wayne State U 54-57 (Eng, Sociol) AB; UMich 57-59 AMLS. 6: Ital, Fr, Swedish, Ger. 7: Detroit Pub Lib: Pre-prof Knapp Br 57-59, Libn I Franklin Br 59-62, Libn II Downtown Lib 62-63, Libn III Lincoln Br 63- Br libn Campbell Br 68-. 9: ALA. 10: Phi Beta Kappa; Alpha Kappa Delta;Il Circolo Italiano; Metro Opera Guild. 14: Adult educ. 15: 14239 Faircrest ave, Detroit 48205.

CLINEFELTER, MRS RUTH (ELIZABETH WRIGHT). b Akron Ohio 2 N 30. 5: UAkron 52 (Pol Sci) BA, 53 (Hist) MA; Kent State U 56 (LS) MA. 7: Res room libn UAkron 52-53, Gen ser libn, Instr in Bibliog, & Asst Prof of Bibliog 53-61, Lecturer in gen studies program 60-61, Soc sci libn & Asst Prof of Bibliog 61-. 9: ALA-ACRL (Tri State Chap); AHA; Archael Assn of Amer. 10: Phi Sigma Alpha; Friends of the University Lib; AkronArt Inst; Stan Hywet Hall Found; AAUP; Pi Sigma Alpha; Phi Alpha Theta. 14: Hist. 15: U of Akron Lib, Akron Oh 44304.

CLINGMAN, PHYLLIS H (SMITH). b Riparius NY 16 Ap 27. 4: Charles A Clingman. 5: State Tchrs Col (Geneseo NY) 45-49 (LS) BEd; St Lawrence U (Canton NY) summers 50-54 (Educ) MS. 7: Libn High Sch, Hoosick Falls NY 49-51; Libn Bd of Coop Ed Serv, Katonah NY 51-54; Libn Central Sch, Warrensburg NY 54-57; Libn Elem Sch, Hudson Falls NY 57-. 9: NYLA; NY State Tchrs Assn; East NY Libns Assn. 10: NY State Volunteer Ambulance & First Aid Assn. 14: Elem, child serv. 15: 10 McHugh st, South Glens Falls NY 12804.

CLINKSCALES, CORRIE ELIZABETH (BETH). b Starr SC 9 My 17. 5: Erskine Col 39 (Eng) AB; Emory 49 BA in LS. 6: Fr. 7: Tchr, SC: Ellen Woodside High Sch, Pelzer 39-42, Ware Shools High Sch, Ware Shoals 42-49; Libn York High Sch, York SC 49-50, Greer Sr High Sch, Greer SC 50-53, Elberton High Sch, Elberton Ga 53-55, Boys High Sch, Anderson SC 55-62, Lakeside Jr High Sch, Anderson SC 62-. 8: Dir stud tour of Europe summer 69. 9: NEA; SCEA; SCLA; AndersonCoEA; Anderson Dist 5 Libns. 10: DAR; Shamrock garden Club; Delta Kappa Gamma. 14: Ref. 15: Box 7, Iva SC 29655.

CLINTON, JOYCE (OVERTON). b New Rochelle NY 11 Ap 42. 4: LeRoy Clinton. 5: State U Col(Geneseo NY) 60-64 (Elem Educ, LS) BS. 7: Libn Oregon ave Jr High Sch, Medford LI NY 64-66; Libn NYS Dept of Law, NYC 67-. 9: ALA; Nassau-Suffolk SchLA; AALL. 14: Child & ya serv, ref, legal research. 15: 512 W 122nd st, NYC 10027.

CLINTON, SHIRLEY (WILSON). b Columbia SC 29 Ap 35. 4: Taylor Clinton. 5: SC State Col 53-58 (LS) BS; Allen-Benedict summers 57, 58, 61, 65 Certif in Elem Educ. 7: Tchr Elem Sch, Great Falls SC 60-62; Elem Sch, Lancaster SC: Libn 62-64, Tchr 64-65, Libn & reading tchr 65-. 9: NEA; Clr Tchrs Assn. 10: Veleda Bridge Club; BY Soc; Quette; ISIS. 14: Catlg, ref. 15: 410 N French st, Lancaster SC 29720.

CLISH, JEAN FRANCES. b Portland Me 3 N 27. 5: UChicago 53-58 (Humanities, Gk, Hist, Lit) AM; Simmons 64-65 (LS) MS. 6: Fr, Ger, Lat, Gk. 7: Recreation wker Amer Nat Red Cross, Korea 58-59 ; Admin asst Cambridge YWCA, Cambridge Mass 60-64; Documents libn & admin asst Tufts U 65-. 9: ALA. 14: Docs. 15: 50 Orchard st, Cambridge Ma 02140.

CLOAK, FERN IRENE. b Kelletville Penn 7 Jl 11. 5: Ohio Wesleyan U 30-34 (Eng) AB; Drexel 48 BS in LS; UPenn 48 (Ger). 6: Fr, Ger, Sp. 7: Fr & Sp tchr Union High Sch, New Castle Penn 35-42; Aeronautical Publications Off US Naval Air Station WAVES (Lt jg), Norfolk Va 42-46; Lib asst US Naval Aircraft Factory, Phila 46-47; Head libn RCA Labs, Princeton NJ 48-. 9: SLA. 10: Phi Mu; Bus & Prof Women's Club; Princeton Musical Amateurs. 14: Ref, admin. 15: RCA Labs, Princeton NJ 08540.

CLOGG, MARGARET J(EAN). b Moncton NB Can 14 Je 42. 5: UNB 59-63 (Psych) BA; Simmons 66-67 (LS) MS. 6: Fr, Sp. 7: Gen libn Douglas Lib Queen'sU 67-69, Sr libn 69-. 9: CanLA. 10: Elizabeth Fry Soc. 14: Ref. 15: Queen's Univ Lib, Kingston Ont Can.

CLOPINE, JOHN J. b Bloomington Neb 8 Mr 16. 4: Marjorie S Showers 5: UCLA 34-35 (Hist); Bethany Col (Bethany WVa) 46-48 (Hist) AB; Catholic U 48-51 MSLS. 7: Head libn Sch of Foreign Serv, Wash DC 49-51; Head libn Naval Intelligence Sch, Wash DC 51-57; Assoc libn Dept Health Educ & Welfare, Wash DC 57-59; Head libn NIH, Bethesda Md 59-61; Asst dir VA Lib Serv, Wash DC 61-63; Head libn Bethany Col (Bethany WVa) 63-. 8: Consul WVa Lib Commsn 63-66; Bldg consul Brooke Co Pub Lib, WVa 68-. 9: ALA (life mem); MedLA; SLA (life mem; chm Milit Libns Div 57-58; Wash DC Chap;var offs); DCLA; Tri-State ACRL. 10: Brooke Co WVa Lib Bd; Unitarian Laymen's League; Beta Phi Mu. 12: "History of Library Unions" (51); "Handbook, SLA Washington Chapter" (55). 13: Yes. 14: Ref, bk sel, weeding. 15: Box 245, BethanyWV 26032.

CLOPINE, MARJORIE (SHOWERS). b NYC 25 Je 14. 4: John J Clopine. 5: Penn State 31-35 (Eng) BA; Drexel 35-36 (LS) BS; Columbia 42-43 (LS) MS; uchicago 49 (Med Libnship). 6: Fr. 7: Gen asst Drexel Inst 37-42; Asst libn Gen Chem Div Allied Chem Corp, Long Island City 43-46; Bibliogr us dept of Com Off of Tech Serv, Wash DC 46; Med libn USVA Hosp, Wash DC 46-49; Assoc libn US Naval Observatory, Wash DC 49-52, Libn 52-63; Assoc libn Bethany Col (Bethany W Va) 67-69. 8: Consul in astronomy, Dewey Decimal Clsf, Ed Off LC (56). 9: SLA (Mil Libns Div: sec-treas 60-61; Wash DC Chap: co-chm Memb Com 50-51, Nominating Com 50-52, Sci-Tech Gp treas 51-52, chm 53-54, Mil Libns Gp Memb Chm 56-57). 10: Bethany bk Club; Wheeling Garden Ctr Lib; LWV. 12: "Determination of Criteria for Dictionaries and Condensed Handbooks of Science (49). 13: Yes. 14: Catlg, rare bks, ref. 15: 2296 Coffeepot blvd NE, St Petersburg Fl 33704.

CLOTFELTER, CECIL F. b Anthony Kan 3 Ap 29. 4: Mary (Long) Clotfelter. 5: Okla Baptist U 47-51 (Span) BA; UHabana summer 50 (Span); Okla State U 53-54, 58 (Span) MA; UOkla 58-59 MLS. 6: Sp, Fr. 7: Asst libn Rodgers Lib, NM Highlands U 59-67; Asst dir of lib for tech prep Tex A&M U 67-69; Tech serv libn EastnMU 69-. 9: NMLA (treas 65-66). 10: Las Vegas Rifle & Revolver Club. 13: Yes. 14: Tech serv. 15: 2301 Bristol, Bryan TX 77801.

CLOTFELTER, ELIZABETH RITTER. b Bardstown Ky 22 O 17. 5: Centre Col 35-37, 38-39 (Hist, Eng) BA; Wellesley 37-38; UKy 53 (Hist) MA, 57 MS in LS. 6: Fr, Ger, Lat. 7: Sub tchr Paris City Schs, Paris Ky 40-41; Eng tchr Clintonville High Sch, Clintonville Ky 41-42; Soc sci tchr Cynthiana High Sch, Cynthiana Ky 42-45; Soc sci tchr Paris High Sch, Paris Ky 45-49; UKy Lib: Asst acquis dept 50-51, Asst catlg dept 51-54, State documents libn 54-57, Monographs catlgr 57-. 9: ALA; Ohio Valley Group Tech Serv Libns; KyLA. 10: UKy Lib Staff Assn; Friends of Lexington Pub Lib. 14: Catlg. 15: Univ of Ky Lib, Lexington Ky 40506.

CLOTFELTER, MARY (LONG). b Noble Okla. 4: Cecil F Clotfelter. 5: UOkla 42-46 (Eng) BA, 46-47 BA in LS. 6: Lat. 7: Catlgr Okla Baptist U 47-59; Head Libn Carnegie Pub Lib, Las Vegas NMex 62-67; Bryan Pub Sch Lib Processing Ctr, Bryan Tex 68-69. 9: OklaLA (sec Col & Univ Sect); NMLA. 10: AAUW; LWV. 14: Catlg. 15: 2301 Bristol, Bryan TX 77801.

CLOUDSLEY, DONALD H. b Buffalo NY 11 Ja 25. 5: Bethany Col (Bethany WVa) 42-44, 46-48 (Hist) BA; Carnegie 48-49 MLS. 7: Var positions Buffalo & Erie Co Pub Lib, Buffalo NY 49-61; Head Brighton Lib Kenmore & Town of Tonawanda Lib, Tonawanda NY 61-65; Dir Kenmore & Town of Tonawanda Lib, Kenmore NY 65-. 9: NYLA. 10: Beta Theta Pi; Rotary. 13: Bk reviewer for "Library Journal." 14: Admin, bk sel. 15: 711 Crescent ave, Buffalo NY 14216.

CLOUGH, MARY EVALYN. b Kan City Mo 10 Jl 30. 5: UCLA 50-52 (Music) BA; Columbia 54-56 (LS) MS; UPittsb urgh 68 Adv Certif. 6: Fr. 7: Catlgr Columbia U Med Lib 55-56; Catlgr NY Acad of Med, NYC 56-58; Tech libn Republic Aviation Corp, Farmingdale LI NY 58-60, Sr tech libn 60-64; Libn Glass Research Center Lib PPG Industries Inc (Pittsburgh) 64-. 9: ALA; SLA; NY Tech Serv Libns; ASIS. 14: Admin, tech serv, automation. 15: 6813 Penn ave, Pittsburgh Pa 15208.

CLOW, RICHARD H. b Geneva NY 26 Ap 17. 4: Shirley Gilbert. 5: Trinity Col, Conn 35-39 (Hist, Chem) BS; UPenn 41-42 (Bus admin) MBA Prog; Immaculate Heart Col LA 64-65 MALS. 6: Ger. 7: Prod cont mgr Taylor Inst Co, Rochetser NY 42-46; Prod mgr Grant Oil Tool Co LA 47-65; E G & C Inc, Santa Barbara Cal: Libn 65-69, Sr libn 69-. 9: SLA; ASIS; CalLA. 10: Alpha Delta Phi. 14: Ref, automatic info retrieval. 15: 2416 Selrose lane, Santa Barbara Ca 93105.

CLUGSTON, KATHARINE (WOODS). b Evanston Ill 6 Ap 06. 5: Carleton Col 22-26 (Eng) AB; UColo 27-28 (Eng Lit) MA; American U 44-45 (Archival Methods). 7: Instr Dept of Eng Arkansas State Tchrs Col 33-40; Asst card preparation sect Acquis Dept LC 40-43, Head Searching Sect Acquis Dept 44-46, Head motion picture unit Copyright Off 46-58, A-v spec

Descr Catlg Div 58-64, Head A-V Sect Descr Catlg Div 65-. 8: Rep of Theatre LA on Joint Com on the Union Hist of Serials & on Bd of Dir of USBC 50-. 9: Theatre LA; Educ Film LA; Wash DC Film Coun; NEA-DAVI (Comm on Catlg a-vmaterials). 10: Phi Beta Kappa. 11: Participant in Civil Serv Admin intern Program 45. 12: Co ed "US Govt Films for Public Educational Use" (60-63). 13: Yes. 14: Catlg, bibliog controls of a-v materials. 15: 4816 Brandywine st NW, Wash DC 20016.

CLULEY, LEONARD E. b Rosebush Mich 19 Je 34. 4: Barbara Booth. 5: Central Mich Col 56 (Fr) AB; UMich 64 MALS. 6: Fr. 7: Tchr Montrose Twp Schs, Montrose Mich 56-57; Spec 4 US Army, Wash DC 57-59; Clk-typist Int Coop Admin, Wash DC 59; Tchr Bad Axe High Sch, Bade Axe Mich 59-63; Catlgr Mich State U (E Lansing) 64-. 14: Catlg. 15: Lib Mich State U, E Lansing Mi 48823.

CLUM, AUDNA T. b Troy NY 14 F 13. 5: NY State Col for Tchrs (Albany) 30-34 (LS, Hist) BS, 41 (Hist, Educ) MS. 7: Asst libn Milne Sch, Albany NY 35-37; Libn Knickerbocker Jr High Sch, Troy NY37-38; Curr consul NY State Educ Dept, Albany NY summers 44-; Ref asst NY State Colfor Tchrs (Albany) summers 64-65; Libn Jr-Sr High Sch, Averill Park NY 38-; Chm oflibs Averill Park Central Sch Dist. 8: Curric consul in bibliog, NY State Educdept. 9: ALA; NY State Tchrs Assn; NYLA; East NY SchLA. 10: Delta Kappa Gamma;Rensselaer Co (NY) Hist Assn; PTA (Life mem); Hudson-Mohawk LA. 12: Bibliog in NY state syllabi. 14: Wk with yp, bibliog. 15: 554 Third ave,Troy NY 12182.

CLUNE, JOHN R. b Bronxvlle NY 22 N 33. 5: Cathedral Col 52-54 (Eng, Classics); St Joseph's Sem Dunwoodie 54-58 (Phil, Theol) AB; Pratt Grad Lib Sch 64-66 MLS; LIU 67- (Eng). 7: Gen supply specialist USA Inf, US & Korea 59-61; Soc investigator NYC Dept of Welfare 61-63; Eng tchr Walton High Sch, NYC 63; Adult serv trainee & libn Brooklyn Pub Lib 64-66; Ref libn Kingsborough Commun Col 66-. 8: 1969 Program Com for RT on Social Responsibilities for Atlantic City ALA Conf. 9: ALA; -ACRL (Jr Col Sect); Lib Assn CUNY; NY Lib Club. 10: Beta Phi Mu. 12: Ed "Library Information (Newsletter). 14: Ref, lib orientation. 15: 624 E 20th st, New York NY 10009.

CLUXTON, HARRIETTE M. b Minneapolis 14 Ag 14. 4: Everett W Cluxton. 5: Macalester Col 32-36 (Lat) BA; UMinn 44 (LS) BS. 6: Lat. 7: Tchr-lib or libn high schs jr cols, Minn & Iowa 36-47; Libn Mid-Western Area Amer Red Cross, St Louis 47-49; Libn High Sch, Welston Mo 49-53; Sub tchr High schs, Ind & Iowa 53-55; Libn Ill Col of Optometry 55-61; Libn Cleveland Health Museum 61-62; Libn med staff Huron Road Hosp Cleveland 62-63; Med libn Ill Masonic Hosp, Chicago 63-. 8: Consul Ill Col of Optometry 68-. 9: MedLA; SLA (chm Jt Com on lib serv in hospitals, CNLA 67-);-Ill Chap (Employment chm 67-); Amer Acad Optometry; Nursing Sch Libns, MetroChicago; Assn of Visual Sci Libns. 10: Audio-Jazz Club of Chicgo. 12: Ed Ralph Barstow's "How to Succeed in Optometry" (2nd ed 59). 13: Yes. 14: Ref, admin, editing. 15: 1030 Superior st, Oak Park Il 60302.

CLYDE, WALTER ERIC. Dutton cr, Ottawa 9 Ont Can. b Penicuik Scotland. 4: Margaret J (Wilson). 5: Edinburgh 48-52 (Math) BS; Toronto 57-58 BLS. 6: Fr. 7: Nat Research Coun, Ottawa: Interlib loan libn 58-60, Asst ref libn 60-61, Libn applied physics div 61-64, Head catlgr Nat Sci Lib 64-. 9: SLA. 10: Prof Inst Pub Serv Can. 14: Catlg, tech serv, documentation. 15: 2138 Dutton cr, Ottawa 9 Ont Can.

CLYMER, BENJAMIN FRANKLIN JR. b Wilmington Del 3 O 15. 5: UDel 33-37 (Eng) BA; UPenn 48-49 MBA; UNC 57-59 MS in LS. 6: Fr. 7: US Army EM (pvt, sgt) US & overseas 37-42; Battery Off AAA Bn SWPacific Platoon CMdr & Battery CO 42-45; Staff Off Pentagon Bldg US Army G-2 Gen Staff, Wash DC 46-48; Staff Off NY Port of Embarkation, Brooklyn NY 49-50; Transportation Sch Ft Eustis, Ft Eustis & Ft Monroe Va 50-53; Staff G-4 Trieste Salzburg US Army HQ 53-55; Exec Off Army Trans Bn, LeVerdon France 55-57; Ref libn Old Dominion Col 60-. 9: ALA; Res Off Assn; VaLA. 10: AAUP; Norfolk Museum of Arts & Sciences; Norfolk Little Theater; Phi Kappa Phi. 14: Ref, info retrieval systems, interlib loans serv. 15: Box 97 Old Dominion Col, Norfolk Va 23508.

COACHMAN, DOROTHEA (LOVE). b Brooklyn NY 7 Ap 15. 4: Joseph E Coachman. 5: Mt Holyoke 32-36 (Econ, Sociol) BA; Newark State Tchrs Col 60-62 Tchr Certif; Rutg ers 60-61 MLS. 6: Fr. 7: Statistician Underwriter Personnel Dir Pr udential Insurance Co, Newark NJ 36-43; Asst field dir Amer Red Cross, European Theater 44-46; Maplewood Pub Lib, Maplewood NJ 52-56; S Orange Pub Lib, S Orange NJ 58-61; Sr libn North Jr High Sch, Bloomfield NJ 61-66; Hd libn Hanover Pk High Sch, Hanover NJ 66-. 8: Tchr in lib sci, Newark State Col 64-65. 9: ALA (Com on Significant Bks for YA); NEA; NJSchLA (Record sec v-pres, pres); NJEA (Curr Wkshop Com); Essex Co Sch LA (pres). 10: Beta Phi Mu; NJ AV Coun. 13: Yes. 15: 8 Roosevelt rd, Maplewood NJ 07040.

COALE, ROBERT PEERLING. b Chicago. 5: UChicago 54-58 (Pol Sci) BA, 60-62 (LS) MA. 6: Sp, Port, Fr. 7: Asst catlgr Center for Research Libs, Chicago 61-62; Catlgr The Ayer Collection Newberry Lib, Chicago 62-65; Deputy chief catlgr Newberry Lib, Chicago 65-66; Asst libn, Southeast Col (Chicago) 66-67, Chm Lib Dept & Chief libn 68-. 9: ALA; CalLA. 10: Caxton Club, Chicago; Pan Amer Coun of Chicago. 13: Yes. 14: Rare bks,hispanic & Hispanic-American Hist, catlg, admin, jr col libs. 15: 1150 N LaSallest, Chicago 60610.

COBAUGH, HELEN SHULTZ. b Scotdase Penn 26 My 06. 4: George Daniel Cobaugh. 5: Carnegie Sch Fine Arts 23, 27-30 (Mus) Tchrs Certif; Oberlin 23-27 (Mus, Fr) AB; Eden Sem 39 (Relig); UPittsburgh 64-67 MALS. 6: Fr. 7: Priv elem sch tutor, chautauqua NY 23-24; Waitress Chautauqua Inst, Chautauqua NY 23-24; Volume lib sales, Pittsburgh & Chautauqua NY 25-26; Tchr: Braddock Elem Schs, Braddock Pa 27-29, Wilkinsburg Pub Schs, Wilkinsburg Pa 29-32; Mus tchr Kirkwoon Schs, St Louis Mo 56-57; Child libn Pub Lib of St Louis (Mo) 57-58; Tchr Greentree Schs, Greentree Pa 62-64; Child libn Carnegie Lib of Pittsburgh 64-. 8: Dir woman's choir Wilkinsburg Jr Women's Club; Dir child choir Mifflin Ave Methodist Ch. 9: ALA; NEA; PennMusEA. 10: AAUP; Oberlin Col Alumni Assn; League of Women Voters; Conf of Midwest Sect of Congregational Chs; Pittsburgh Symphony Soc; Chautauqua Soc of Pittsburgh; PTA; GSA. 14: Child wk. 15: 990 Summer pl, Pittsburgh Pa 15243.

COBB, CORA ELEANOR. b NYC 6 F 32. 5: NortheasternU 49-53 (Eng) BA; Simmons 53-54 (LS) MS; BostonU 56-57 (Math); UCLA 59 (Math). 6: Ger. 7: Asst libn Soc Lib, whitinsville Mass 55; Catlgr Boston Col Law School Lib 55-56; Programmer: Melpar Inc, boston 56-57, Intl Computer Corp, Boston 57-58, 3M Co, Culver City Cal 62, Land-Aire corp, Point Mugu Cal 62-63; Statistician Liberty Mutual Ins Co, Boston 58; Assoc engr Douglas Aircraft Co, Santa Monica Cal 58-59; Asst catlg lib Beverly Hills Pub Lib, Beverly Hills Cal 61-62; Syst analyst Empire Data Processing Corp, Denver 63-65; Fiscal consul Colo State Lib, Denver 65-. 9: ColoLA. 12: Ed "Capitol Hill Library Crier" (67-68). 14: Info retrieval, lib automation, lib statistics, catlg, lib finance. 15: 1362 Lincoln st, Denver Co 80203.

COBB, EDITH GENEVA. b Cherokee Falls SC 12 N 09. 5: Limestone Col 26-27; UWis Certif in Lib Methods. 6: Fr. 7: Libn S C Sanatarium, State Park SC 34-. 9: ALA. 12: Ed SoCar San Piper 48-. 14: Libn to hosp patients. 15: Box 115, State Park SC 29147.

COBB, JOSEPHINE. b Portland Me. 5: Simmons 31 BS; Boston U 35 MA. 7: Rare Bk Room Boston Pub Lib 31-34; Mass State Archives, Mss of the Colonial period 35-36; Spec in iconography Nat Archives 36-. 8: Consul on illustrations: US Capitol Hist Soc, the Lincoln Group of the District of Columbia, the Columbia Hist Soc, the Civil War Centennial Commsn, the Lincoln Sesquicentennial Commsn; Consul for selection of candidates for Photography's Hall of Fame etc. 9: SLA (chm Picture Div 56-57); Amer Assn State & Soc Hist; Amer Assn Museum; Photographers' Internat Hall of Fame. 10: Quota International; Lincoln gps; Civil War RTS. 11: Four Lincoln Awards. 12: Exhibition Record of the Washington Art Assn 1857-1861 (65). 13: Yes. 14: Appraisal & hist of art items. 15: 2393 North Kenmore st, Arlington Va 22207.

COBB, JUDITH. b Boston Mass 31 Ja 38. 5: UMass 54-55, 58-59 (Mus) BA; Syracuse summer 63, 64-65 MSLS. 7: Circ asst Mt Holyoke Col 59-61, Ser asst 61-62, Asst in charge of res 62-64; Adult ref Baltimore Co Pub Lib 65-66; Ser libn Towson State Col 66-68; Hd Pub Serv Catonsville Commun Col 68-. 9: ALA; -RSD (Md affiliate); MdLA; Md Assn Jr Cols (Learning Resources Div); Potomac Tech Proc Libns. 10: AAUP; Smithsonian Assocs; Beta Phi Mu. 14: Ref, ser. 15: 639 Plymouth rd, Baltimore Md 21229.

COBB, LUCILLE MARIE. b Ford Kan 2 Jl 10. 5: Wichita U 27-28, 29-32 (Eng, Music, Educ) AB in Ed; Southwest Mo summers 40, 46 (Eng, Com); UMo summer 42 (Eng); Kan State (Pittsburg) ext 51-52 (LS); UDenver 52-53 (LS) MA. 6: Fr. 7: Tchr Charity High Sch, Charity Mo 37-40, 41-43, 45-47; Tchr Philipsburg High Sch, Philipsburg Mo 40-41; Inspector

US Midwest Procurement, Wichita Kan 43-45; Tchr lafontaine High Sch, Lafontaine Kan 47-52; Asst libn NM Inst of Mining & Tech, Socorro NM 53-56; Sr asst libn head spec materials dept UMo 56-. 9: MoLA. 14: Non-bk materials, rare bks. 15: 704 Hunt rd, Columbia Mo 65201.

COBB, MARY LOUISE (BROWN). b Rose Hill NC 16 Mr 37. 4: William Small Cobb Jr. 5: Wake Forest Col 55-59 (Lat, Eng) BA; Columbia Tchrs Col 60-61; Peabody 64-65 MLS. 6: Lat, Fr. 7: Lib asst Union Theol Sem, NY 59-60; Asst tchr Riverside Church Nursery Sch, NY 60-61; Lat tchr Lexington Sr High Sch, Lexington NC61-62; Lat tchr Northwest High Sch, Winston-Salem NC 62-63; Lib asst Joint U Libs, Nashville 63-64, catlgr 64-65; Ref doc libn GrinnellCol 65-67; Asst catlg William & Mary 67-. 9: ALA; VaLA. 10: Beta Phi Mu; Eta Sigma Phi; Mortar Bd, Williamsburg Pub Lib Bd, Bd Dirs Twentieth Century Gallery, Williamsburg. 14: Catlg, Govt documents, ref. 15: 112 Oak rd, Williamsburg VA 23185.

COBB, NANCY (LOU LANCASTER). b Wagoner Okla 24 O 36. 4: Doyle Cobb. 5: Okla Col for Women 54-58 (Bus Educ) BS; UOkla 58-59 MLS; East NM U 60. 6: Sp, Ger. 7: Sec Lancaster Agency, Wagoner Okla summers 51-58; Stud asst Nash Lib Okla Col for Women 54-58; Stud asst UOkla Lib 59; Ser pub serv libn East NM U 59-61; Asst libn E Central State Col (Ada Okla) 61-63; Libn First Baptist Church, Ada Okla 61-. 9: ALA; OklaLA; SWLA. 14: Ref, circ, pub serv. 15: 2100 E 18th st, Ada Ok 74820.

COBB, NELL. b Statesboro Ga 4 D 04. 5: Tift Col 22-25 (Soc sci, Eng) BA; Emory 42-42 (LS) BA; UNC summers 36, 40. 6: Fr. 7: Libn USN Cape Kennedy Fla & Charleston SC 43-46; VA Hosps, Ga Penn Wash & Ore 42-62; VA Hosp, Brecksville Ohio 62-65; Army lib serv: Taegu dist Korea 65-67, 4th US Missile Command Korea 67-69, Spec serv lib Letterman Gen Hosp San Francisco 69-. 9: ALA; State teachers assn & lib assns. 14: Lib serv to mil personnel & veterans. 15: Special Services Lib, Letterman General Hospital, San Francisco Ca 94129.

COBERLY, JEAN ANN. b Elkins W Va 25 Je 42. 5: Fla StateU 60-61 (Eng); UFla 61-63 (Eng) AA; StetsonU 64 (Eng) BA; Emory 66 MLS. 6: Sp, Fr. 7: Tchr: Ocala High Sch, Ocala Fla 65, Dan McCarty High Sch, Ft Pierce Fla 66-67; Libn J C Mitchell Sch, Boca Raton Fla 68; Libn Fla AtlanticU 68-. 14: Ref. 15: 201 SW 7th st apt 9, Boca Raton Fl 33432.

COBLE, GERALD M. b Prior Mo 11 S 26. 4: Donna Hennigh. 5: UColo 47-52 (Eng) BA; UDenver 51-52 MALS; Chicago 57-58 (LS). 6: Fr, Ger. 7: Lib asst Colo State Hist Soc, Denver 51-52; Asst libn West State Col of Colo52-53, Libn 53-55; Lib adv UPeshawar (W Pakistan) 55-57; Asst libn Pub Serv UOkla58-59, Dir Sch of Lib Sci 59-63; Admin libn Machine Applics VA, Wash DC 63-66; HdLib Serv Br Bur Naval Personnel, Wash DC 66-. 9: ALA (var coms); ASIS; DCLA; SWLA(chm var coms 61-63); OklaLA (var offs). 13: Yes. 14: Automation, lib educ, hosp & med libnship, catlg. 15: 7420 Baltimore ave, Takoma Park Md 20012.

COBLE, MARGARET (ELIZABETH) WATSON. b Wadesboro NC 26 S 14. 4: Mack A Coble. 5: Woman's Col of UNC 32-35 (Fr, Eng) AB; UNC 65- (LS). 6: Fr. 7: Tchr Fr, Eng High Sch, Oakboro NC 35-39; Tchr Endy Sch, albemarle NC 45-54; Jr high sch tchr Oakboro Sch, Oakboro NC 54-61; Libn West Stanly High Sch, Oakboro NC 61-66; Lib Coordinator Title I, ESEA of Stanly Co Schs 66-. 9: NCEA (sec 3 times). 10: Alpha Delta Kappa; Woman's Club. 11: Tchr of Year Award,Oakboro Sch. 14: Ref, catlg. 15: Box 245 Oakboro NC 28129.

COBLENTZ, RUTH (IRENE). b Bunker Hill Ind 23 D 03. 5: Manchester Col 21-22, 25-27 (Eng, Fr) BA; UIll 30-31 BS in LS; IndU summer 30 (LS). 6: Fr. 7: Elem sch Bunker Hill Schs, Bunker Hill Inc 22-25, High sch (Eng) 27-30; High sch libn Gary Pub Schs (Gary Ind) 31-45; Libn Manchester col 45-. 8: Ind sch lib coun (Indianapolis) 45-55; chm Ind Col & Univs RT 67-68. 9: ALA; IndLA. 10: AAUW. 14: Admin, catlg. 15: 1008 Wayne st, N Manchester In 46962.

COBURN, LEONARD. b Chicago Il 28 D 21. 4: Barbara Bitting. 5: UIll 46-50 (Econ) BS, 50-51 (LS) MS. 7: Inspector Kankakee Ordnance Wks (Joliet Ill) 41-42; Aviation Radio Tech US Navy (Petty Off 2d Class) 42-46; Circ asst UIll (Urbana) 51; Circ asst 51-52; Physics libn 53-54; Engnr libn 54-65; Coordinator of engnr lib serv 65-. 9: ALA; IllLA. 10: ACLU; AAUP; Urban League; YMCA; UN Assn of the US. 14: Sci & tech, info storage & retrieval. 15: 1409 S Grove, Urbana Il 61801.

COBURN, LOUIS. b NYC 13 Ag 15. 4: Selma Spielman. 5: City Col (NY) 32-36 (Eng) BA; Columbia 36-37 BLS; City Col 37-41 (Educ) MS in Ed; NYU 51-61 (Admin) DED. 6: Ger, Fr. 7: Lib fellow City Col (NY) 37-38; Lib asst Samuel Gompers Voc & Tech High Sch (Bronx NY) 38-46; US Army AF (1st Lt) Communications 42-45; Tchr of lib Samuel Gompers Voc & Tech High Sch (Bronx NY) 46-56; Tchr of lib, Jamaica High Sch (Queens NY) 56-63; Asst prof Queens Col Lib Sci Dept (NY) 63-. 8: Chm Standing Com on Vacat High Sch Libs, Bd of Educ (NYC) 46-52. 9: ALA; NYCSchLA; nyla; NYLC (chm Nominating Com); NYTSL. 10: AAUP; Friends of Queens Col Lib; NYU Alumni Assn. 12: "A Plan for Centralized Cataloging in the elementary School Libraries of New York City, Unpubl Doctoral Diss (61); "Case Studies in School Library Administration (68). 13: Yes. 14: Catlg, ref, sch lib admin. 15: 137-01 63rd ave, Flushing NY 11367.

COBURN, MORTON. b Chicago 28 D 21. 5: UIll 46-49 (Educ) BS, 50 (LS) MS. 7: (Pvt) US Armed Serv, South-west Pacific 42-45; Stack supv & ref libn UKan 50-52; Head gift & exch div & bk purchase div Ohio State U 52-56; Dir of lib Edmonton Pub Lib, Edmonton Alta 56-. 9: CanLA; ALA; AltaLA. 10: Edmonton Welfare Coun; Rotary Club; Can Inst of Internat Affairs. 13: Yes. 14: Admin, lib bldgs, arch. 15: #7 Sir Winston Churchill sq, Edmonton 15 Alta Can.

COCHICO, ERLINDA (JOVEN). b Manila Philippines. 23 Ja 37. 5: U of the East 57-61 (LS) BSE; UPhilippines 66-67 (LS); De Paul 67-68 (Supv, Admin). 6: Sp, Tagalog. 7: Lib asst Col Lib, Manila Philippines 59-60, Libn 61-67; Period libn De Paul U 67-. 8: Reader's adv, Manila Philippines 61-67. 9: ALA. 10: Batangas Club (Manila Philippines); UEast Lib Sci Club. 14: Catlg, ref, period, research. 15: 4751 N Paulina, Chicago Il 60640.

COCHIOS, CHARLES A. b Easton Penn 6 Mr 28. 4: Ruth Coleman Cochios. 5: Kutztown State Col 56-60 (LS) BS in Educ; Rutgers 61 (LS); Temple 65 MS in Ed. 6: Lat, Grk. 7: Libn Elem Sch, Flemington-Raritan (Flemington NJ) 60-61; Lib dir Pub Lib (Philipsburg NJ) 61-62; Libn Jr High Sch, raub (Allentown Penn) 62-67; Elem sch libn Easton Area Jt Schs, Easton Penn 67-. 9: ALA; NEA; PennStateEA. 14: Ref wk. 15: 4611 Bayard st, Easton Pa 18042.

COCHRAN, ALICE HOLMES. b Newton Miss 20 Mr 23. 4: Dr William Norman Cochran. 5: Augusta Ga Jr Col 41-42; LSU 42 (Dramatics); Converse Col 61-63 (Eng) BA; Emory 64 (LS) Libnship. 6: Fr. 7: Bkmob asst Spartanburg Pub Lib (Spartanburg SC) 46-48; Clerical asst 61-62; Asst libn Converse Col Lib 62-65; Order & acting ref libn Wofford Col Lib 65-66; Order libn 66-. 9: SCLA. 10: Jr League of Spartanburg (SC); Garden Club; Bk Club; Assembly. 13: Yes. 14: Ref, bibliog, bk sel, op bks. 15: 18 Woodburn rd, Spartanburg SC 29302.

COCHRAN, JEAN D(OROTHY). b Irwin Penn 12 Jl 10/ 05: Guilford Col 28-32 (Eng) AB; UNC 39-41 BS in LS. 6: Fr. 7: Tchr pub sch, Kernrsville NC 33-41; Asst libn Davidson Co Pub Lib, Lexington NC 41-43; Catlgr UGa Libs 43-44; Hd libn Carnegie Pub Lib, Sumter SC 45-48; DirAugusta-Richmond Co Pub Lib, Augusta Ga 49. 8: Pub Lib consul with emphasis on lib bldgs: Elbert Co Lib, Elberton Ga 63-67; Toombs Co Lib, Vidalia Ga 65-66; DeSoto Trail Reg Lib, Camilla Ga 64-65; Sequoyah Reg Lib, Canton Ga 65; Athens Reg Lib, Athens Ga 67-68; Merritt Island Pub Lib, Merritt Island Fla 67-68; Northeast Ga Reg Lib, Clarkesville Ga 65-66; etc. 9: ALA (various coms); SELA (chm Pub Lib Sect); GaLA (2nd v-pres, pres 67-69; Pub Lib Sect: sec, chm). 10: AAUW; Augusta Art Club; Augusta Bird Club; Augusta Music Club; LWV. 14: Admin, personnel, adult serv, tech serv. 15: 2515 Parkway dr, Augusta Ga 30904.

COCHRAN, JULIENNE. b Cal 19 Je 07. 4: Stefan A Wado-Cochran. 5: UCLA 26-28 (Econ) Jr certif; Mills Col 28-30 (Econ) AB; Stanford 45-46 (Econ) MA; West Res 58-60 MSLS. 6: Fr, Sp. 7: Libn S Dak Col 55-57; Law libn UIda 57-58; Libn Akron Pub Schs, Akron ohio 60-64; Libn Chicago Pub Schs, 64-65; Asst ref libn Cook Co Law Lib, Chicago 65-68; Asst Prof NoIllU 68-. 9: ALA; ALA-ACRL; NEA; AALL; Chicago Law Libns; Chicago Hist Soc; Ill Hist Assn; BSA. 10: DAR; Nat League Pen Women; Nat Federation of Press Women. 12: "Guaranteed Annual Wage" (46); "First Aid to Teachers of Ohio History" (62); "Readers' Guide to Thomas Beer" (63); "Published Writings of Paul Monroe" (66); "Lex Scripta" (68); "Riots" (69). 13: Yes. 14: Bibliog (Lincoln), bus, pol sci, law. 15: Univ Center Northern Ill, University DeKalb Il 60115.

COCHRAN, PEGGY (DELANEY). b Amsterdam NY 29 Je 15. 4: Robert P Cochran. 5: St LawrenceU 33-37 (Eng) BA; NY State Col 40-41 BS in LS; UState NY Pub Libn Prof Certif 51; PennLA Certif 61. 7: Tchr-libn Champlain High Sch (Champlain NY) 37-40; Jr libn ref & catlg asst, Woodlawn br libn Schenectady Co Lib (Schenectady NY) 40-45; Libn "Schenectady Gazette (Schenectady NY) 51-54; Asst libn Paoli Lib (Paoli Penn) 61-65; libn 65-67; Lib asst Easttown Lib (Berwyn Pa) 67-. 9: PennLA. 14: Ref. 15: 149 Waterloo rd, Berwyn Pa 19312.

COCKS, ANNA R. b Moscow Mich 18 Jl 18. 4: Richard E Cocks. 5: West Mich U 35-40 (Chem) AB; Peabody 40-41 BS in LS. 6: Fr, Ger, Sp. 7: Asst libn Agric Lib Penn State U 41-42; Libn br lib Pub Lib, Kalamazoo 42-43; Acquis & tech processing libn Lib Miles Labs, Inc, Elkhart Ind 57-. 9: ACS (Chem Lit & Med Chem Sects); MedLA; ALA-ACRL;-RTS; SLA (Ill Chap; Sci-Tech Div Pharmaceut Sect); ASIS. 10: AAAS; AAUW. 12: Ed-in-chief "CORNIP List" SLA (63-64). 13: Yes. 14: Catlg, clsf, acquis. 15: 1772 Rainbow Bend blvd, Elkhart In 46514.

COCKSHUTT, MARGARET EVELYN. b Brantford Ont Can 27 F 27. 5: Toronto 44-48 (Eng) BA, 48-49 BLS; Columbia summer 64 (LS); Toronto 64 MLS. 6: Fr. 7: Lecturer & libn UToronto Lib Sch 49-61; Lecturer & asst to the dir 61-64; Asst prof 64-66; Assoc prof 66-. 9: ALA; Assn Canadienne des Bibliothecaires de Langue Francaise; AALS; CanALS (chm Nomin Com 66-67); CanLA (chm Com for Liaison with the Jt Planning Commsn 55-56, chm Libns Com 58-61, sec-treas Catlg Sect 54-55); Can Assn Col & Univ Libs (dir 66-68, v-pres 68-69); SLA (sec Toronto Chap 58-60); Inst Profess Libns Ont (Coun 59-60, Registrar & mem Bd Dirs 63-66); OntLA (chm Nomin Com 53-54); Ont Assn Col & Univ Libs (chm Com on Profess Devel 66-68). 10: Beta Phi Mu; Can Assn Univ Tchrs; Mem Corp Trinity Col, UToronto. 12: "Basic Filing Rules(61); Co-comp "Sample Catalogue Cards (68). 13: Yes. 14: Lib educ, research methods. 15: Sch of Lib Sci Univ of Toronto, Toronto 5 Can.

CODY, MAY ELOISE (WESTVEER). b Holland Mich 20 Jl 08. 4: Nelson A Cody. 5: Hope Col 25-26; UMich 26-29 ABLS. 6: Fr, Ger, Sp, Lat. 7: Reclsf asst UMich (Ann Arbor) 29-31; Jr catalog & sr catlgr 31-46; Reviser & libn III 46-62; Libn IV 62-66, Libn V 66-. 9: ALA; MichLA. 10: Women of the Faculty; AAUW; Mich Alumnae; Faculty Womens Club. 14: Catlg. 15: 2136 Georgetown blvd, Ann Arbor Mi 48105.

CODY, PATRICIA ESTHER (TRUOG). b Oskaloosa Iowa 17 D 44. 4: Howard High Cody. 5: UIowa 63-67 (Eng) BA; 67-68 MALS. 6: Fr. 7: Reader's adv Davenport Pub Lib, Davenport Iowa 68-. 15: 636 Main, Davenport Ia.

CODY, SARAH ISABELLE. b Tampa Fla. 5: Fla State Col for Women 37-41 (Hist) AB; Emory 41-42 (LS) AB; West Res 56-58 MS in LS. 7: Children's libn Cleveland Pub Lib 42-61; Tchr Polk Co Bd of Educ, Frostproof Fla 61-62; Supv of children's wk Cleveland Heights Pub Lib, Cleveland Heights Ohio 62-63; Dir Cleveland Heights-Univ Heights Pub Lib 63-. 8: Consul Central Fla Reg Lib 62. 9: ALA; OhioLA (Exec Bd 67-70). 10: Women's Nat Bk Assn; LWV. 11: Beta Phi Mu. 14: Child wk, admin of libs. 15: Cleveland Heights Univ Heights Pub Lib, 2345 Lee rd, Cleveland Heights Oh 44118.

COE, D WHITNEY. b Oswego NY 23 Mr 37. 5: Syracuse U 55-59 (Internat rel) BA, 66-67 MLS; UCal at Berkeley 59-61 (Russian hist) MA. 6: Russian, Fr, Ger. 7: Hist tchr Carthage Jr-Sr High, Carthage NY 62-66; Princeton U: Slavic catlgr 67-68, Hd descr catlg sect 68-. 10: Phi Beta Kappa; Pi Sigma Alpha; Phi Kappa Phi; Beta Phi Mu; AHA. 14: Catlg, subj spec, Slavic. 15: Alexander rd, Princeton NJ 08540.

COE, DORIS TIGHE (MRS ROBERT). b Cleveland Ohio 21 Jl 07. 5: West Res 25-29 (Lat) AB, 31-32 BS in LS. 6: Fr. 7: Desk asst Cleveland Pub Lib, Cleveland Ohio 25-29; Correspondent clk Ohio Bell Tele Co, Cleveland 29-31, 32-39; Tchr (high sch) Cleveland Bd of Educ Cleveland Ohio 39-42; Hosp recreation wker Amer Nat Red Cross, Camp Lee Va, England, France, Germany 42-46; Tchr, readers adv, supv acad dept Saranac Lake Rehabilitation Guild, Saranac Lake NY 49-54; Asst br libn Cleveland Pub lib, Cleveland Ohio 57; Br libn Willoughby Pub Lib, Willoughby Ohio 64-66; Bk selection coord San Diego Co Lib 68-. 9: CalLA. 10: League of Women Voters. 14: Bk selection, ref. 15: 4647 Alabama st, San Diego Ca 92116.

COEFIELD, OTIS (WHITE). b Bertie Co NC 30 Ap 27. 4: Marilyn Hines. 5: Richmond Col 49-52; E Carolina Col 54-55 (Sociol) BS; Emory 56-57 (LS) ML. 7: US Army Signal Corps Cryptographer 45-48; Grad asst Microfilm Lab Emory U Lib 56-57; Ref libn VA Polytech Inst Lib 57-58; Period libn E Carolina Col Lib 58-64; Tchr-libn sci summers 60-62; Head libn Atlantic Christian Col 64-. 9: ALA; SELA; NCLA. 14: Admin, ref. 15: Hermitage rd, Wilson NC 27893.

COEN, JAMES A(RLEY). b Bridgeville Penn 25 O 40. 4: Diann Denning. 5: Washingotn & Jefferson Col 58-63 (Physics) BA 62; Rutgers 63-65 MLS; upittsburgh 66-. 6: Fr, Ger. 7: Stud asst Lib Washington & Jefferson Col 59-63; Trainee E Orange Pub Lib (E Orange NJ) 63-65; Ser & documents libn Hamilton Lib Edinboro State Col 65-67; Asst libn Tech Serv Washington & Jefferson Col 67-. 9: ACRL (Tri-State Chap); ASIS; Amer Soc for Information Science. 13: Yes. 14: Ser, docs, documentation catlg, ref. 15: 375 Duncan ave, Washington Pa 15301.

COENENBERG, RICHARD. b Medford Ore 12 O 30. 5: UOregon 48-52 (Bus Admin) BS, 58 (Pre-LS); UCal 59-60 MLS. 7: Merchant Seaman Amer Pres Lines, San Francisco 60; San Francisco Pub Lib: Ref Docs 60-62, Admin Asst 62-67; Dit Bay Area Ref Ctr, San Francisco 67-. 8: Supv Neighborhood Youth Corps Lib Proj 65-67; Supv Fillmore Street Ref Proj 68-69. 9: ALA; SLA; CalLA; PLECC. 14: Ref. 15: Bay Area Reference Center, SF Pub Lib Civic Center, San Francisco Ca 94102.

COFFEY, CHRISTINE (LeROY). b Marshall Co Tenn 10 Ja 10. 5: UNC 30 AB; UMich 34 ABLS; Chicago Grad Lib Sch 40-41. 6: Fr, Sp. 7: Jr asst Catlg Dept UNC 30-34; Head catlg dept NC State Col 34-45; Instr UNC Lib Sch summer 48; Asst dir Ext Div Va State Lib 45-56; Asst dir & head of ext Iowa State Travel Lib 56-. 8: Adv Coun on the Va Economy Research Com on Recreation 48-52; Iowa Governors Commsn on Child & Youth; Iowa Del to White House Conf on Child & Youth (60). 9: ALA (legis coun) 50-52; AEA; IowaLA; Iowa Adult Educ Assn (treas) 65. 10: ACLU; Iowa Clu. 11: Iowa Adult Educ Assn Achievement Award (65). 13: Yes. 14: Lib ext, admin. 15: Iowa State Travel Lib Hist Bldg, Des Moines Ia 50319.

COFFEY, DOROTHY. b Ann Arbor Mich 7 F 22. 5: Manhattanville Col 39-41; UMich 41-43 9eng Lit) AB, 67-69 AMLS. 14: Ref, child lit. 15: 2004 Medford C121, Ann Arbor Mi 48104.

COFFEY, JUDITH ANN. b West .Point NY 31 D 44. 5: Dunbarton Col 62-66 (Eng) BA; Catholic U of Amer 66-67 MS in LS. 6: Fr. 7: Asst libn Amer Psychiatric Assn, Wash DC 65-67; Libn tech lib Comsat Corp, Wash DC 67-. 9: ALA; SLA; NMA; ASIS; DCLA. 10: Beta Phi Mu; AAAS. 15: Apt #209 2545 MacArthur blvd NW, Wash DC 20007.

COFFEY, MEGAN CAROL (PAGE). b Brantford Ont 18 S 40. 4: Grant Coffey. 5: Victoria Col UToronto 58-62 (Modern Hist) BA; Toronto 63-64 BLS. 7: Tchr Paris Dist High Sch, Paris Ont 62-63; Libn UToronto Lib 64-. 9: CanLA; Inst Prof Libns Ont. 10: Beta Phi Mu. 14: Circ. 15: 35 Claxton blvd, Toronto 10 Ont Can.

COFFIN, GEORGIA R. b Longmont Colo 20 Mr 15. 5: UColo 33-37 (Sociol) BA; UDenver 38-39 BS in LS; UIll 46-48 (LS) MS. 6: Fr, Ger. 7: Libn Henderson State Tchrs Col 39-42; Acquis catlg rare bks asst UIll (Urbana) 42-52; Rare bks libn Cornell U 52-57; Tchr UDenver Lib Schsummer 57; Dir Jefferson Co Pub Lib, Golden Colo 57-63; Head of catlg dept UWyo 63-68; Hd catlg ctr, State Lib of Ohio 68-. 8: Consul to Sublette Co Wyo for bldg program 65. 9: ALA; OhioLA. 15: 5006 Dierker rd, Columbus OH 43221.

COFFIN, JANE MARILYN (LEWIS). b Grasmere NH 14 D 31. 4: Stewart T Coffin. 5: UNH 50-52 (Liberal Arts) 53-55; Keene State 53-65 B Ed; Summers 55-59 MLS. 6: Ger. 7: Secondary Eng tchr Sanborn SemKingston NH 55; Lib asst Robbins Lib, Arlington Mass 55-59; Document asst MIT Lincoln Lab, Lexington Mass 59-60; Lib asst Wayland Pub Lib,Wayland Mass 64-. 9: ALA (Life mem). 10: Mass Hortic Soc; Appalachian mountain Club; Mass Audubon Soc; Wilderness Soc. 14: Pub & sch libs. 15: RFD 1 Old Sudbury rd, Lincoln Ma 01773.

COFFIN, LEWIS C(HARLES). b Ashland Me 15 F 09. 4: Elizabeth Van Brakle. 5: Bowdoin Col 26-30 (Govt) AB; Geo WashingtonU Law Sch 30-34 JD. 6: Sp, Ger, Fr. 7: Asst card div LC 31-37; Asst chief union catlg div 37-48; US Naval Reserve (Lt Commander) Deck Off, Pacific Ocean Areas 42-46; lc; chief exch & gift div 48-51; Chief order div 51-52; Assoc dir processing dept 52-64; Law libn & gen coun 64-. 8: Com of Experts, UNESCO (Paris) 48 & 56 on Internat Exch of Publs; US Delegation to Internat Com of Experts to Draft New Conventions for Internat Exch of Publs (Brussels) 58; Headed LC Teams to Cairo and to Israel to Establish PL480 Offs for Acquis of Publs (61 & 63). 9: Internat Assn of Law Libs pres 68-; AALL; PL480 Rep 65-; USBE Rep 65-; ALA; DCLA; Dag Hammarskjold Col (Bd Trustees(. 10: Amer Bar Assn; Fed Bar Assn. 12: Co-auth "Science Information Personnel (61); Ed "Directory of Computerized Information in Science & Technology (68); Adv ed "Automatic Documentation and Mathematical Linguistics (Journal). 13: Yes. 14: Acquis, ref, law libnship. 15: 6432 Barnaby st NW, Wash DC 20015.

COFFMAN, ELIZABETH (MORRIS). b Livingston County 30 Je 16. 4: Richard L Coffman. 5: NW Mo State Col 58-63 (Elem Educ) BS; UIll 63-64 (LS) MS. 6: Fr. 7: Tchg rural sch (Green Grove) N of Chillicothe Mo 35-39; Tchg Chillicothe Bus Col 39-41; Sec va, st Louis & Chillicothe Mo 42-48; Sec Livingston Co Mem Lib, Chillicothe Mo 53-58, Act libn 58-64, Libn 64-69; Tech Serv Coordinator Wyo State Lib 70-. 9: MoLA (chm Pub Lib Div 65; area chm Recruitment Network 67-). 10: Women's Federated Club; AAUW; C of C. 14: Ref, child serv, pub rel. 15: Wyo State Lib, Cheyenne Wyo.

COFFMAN, PATRICIA J. b Birmingham Ala 11 Mr 27. 5: Bethel Jr Col & U (ky) 45-48 (Soc Studies); Cumberland U Law Sch 49-51 (Law) LLB; Peabody Col 55-56 (Soc Studies) BA, 62-63 MA in LS; NYU summers 62-64 (Law) LLM. 7: Law clk to Fed judge, Fairbanks Alaska 52-54; Asst law libn Vanderbilt U 54-55; Law libn & asst prof of law Mercer U 55-56; Law libn & asstprof of law USanta Clara 56-60; Law libn & assoc prof of law Samford Col 60-62; Law libn & assoc prof of law DrakeU 64-65; Law libn & assocprof of law UAlta 65-69; Law libn & prof of law Tulane Sch of Law 69-. 8: Law lib bldg consul: Samford College 62, USanta Clara 59, Drake 55, UAlta 66-69. 9: AALL. 10: Tenn Bar Assn. 11: NYU Summer Law Tchr Scholarship. 12: Co-auth annual supplement to ", A Bibliography of Materials on Legal Education, NYU" (64). 14: Law lib development projects, legal research, admin. 15: Tulane School of Law, New Orleans La 70118.

COFTA, MARY ANN T (TORMA). b Cleveland Ohio 30 S 30. 4: Paul Lewis Cofta. 5: John Carroll U 55-62 (Hist) B of Soc Sci; West Res 62-64 MLS. 6: Ger, Fr. 7: Govt docs libn Cleveland Pub Lib 64-. 9: SLA (chm Recr Com 66-67, Hosp Com chm 67-68); OhioLA. 12: "Serials Manual for Documents" (68). 14: Govt docs. 15: 6917 Brecksville rd, Independence Oh 44131.

COGEN, JILL R. b Cleveland Ohio 13 Ja 43. 5: San Fernando Valley State Col 61-62 (Hist); Valley Col 62-63 (Hist); UCLA 63-65 (Hist) BA, 65-66 MLS. 7: Arch & fine arts libn USoCal 66-67; Audio libn Music Lib UCLA 67-. 9: MusLA; UCal Lib Sch Alumni Assn. 10: Pi Gamma Mi. 15: 360 So Reeves dr apt 2, Beverly Hills Ca 90212.

COGGESHALL, LUCINDA (ERRINGTON). b Ithaca NY 23 Ja 33. 4: James Coggeshall. 5: Occidental Col 505-2 (Psych); Pomona 53 (Ed); USoCal 55-57 (Ed) BS, 66-68 (LS) MS. 7: Eng Coordinator Creole Sch, Laguinillas Ven 61-63; Lib Asst Anaheim Pub Lib, Anaheim Cal 64-65; Hd Ref Dept Fullerton Pub Lib, Fullerton Cal 68-69; Asst Libn Orange Coast Col 69-. 9: ALA; CalA; OrangeCoLA; OrangeCoSchLA. 11: Beta Phi Mu. 14: Ref, docs. 15: 1792 Ridgewood st, Orange Ca 92667.

COGGIN, EDITH ANDREWS. b Nashville Tenn 6 My 10. 4: Charles U Coggin Jr. 5: Randolph Macon Woman's Col 28-32 (Math) AB; George Washington U 42-43 (Psych); Peabody 62-65 MLS. 6: Fr. 7: Elem tchr Davidson Co Schs, Nashville 32-34; Case wker Tenn Emergency Relief Admin, Nashville 34-36; Elem tchr nashville Pub Schs 36-42; Elem tchr Davidson Co Schs, Nashville 49-50; Libn Nashville Pub Lib 65-. 9: ALA; TennLA. 10: AAUW; Gamma Phi Beta; Pi Gamma Mu; Girl Scout Leader. 14: Pub serv, circ, readers adv. 15: 4326 Signal Hill dr, Nashville TN 37205.

COGSWELL, GEORGE R(ALSTON). b Big Spring Tex 22 O 39. 5: Arlington State Col 57-62 (Hist) BA; UTex 62-65 MLS. 7: UTex Lib: Clerical asst loan dept 62-63, Clerical asst ref dept 63, Sr lib asst Arch Lib 63-65, Libn I lib order dept 65-66, Libn II 66-68, Libn II Collections deposit lib 68-. 9: ALA-ACRL. 14: Tech serv. 15: Box 7465 Univ Sta, Austin Tx 78712.

COHAN, LEONARD. b NYC 20 Jl 30. 4: Ida Newirth. 5: City Col (NY) BS in SS; Columbia MS in LS. 7: Lib asst Columbia U 51-52; Headlibn Parsons Sch of Design, NYC 52; Asst post libn US Army Engnr Center, Ft Belvoir Va 52-54; Lib asst City Col (NY) 54-55; Sr libn BrooklynPub Lib Bus Ref 55-56; Head libn NYC Commun Col 56-64; Dir libs Polytech Inst (Brooklyn NY) 64-. 8: Dir Tech Info Proj, Mod Lang Assn 59-61;Consul on lib bldgs & col lib org 56-; Adv ed; Faraday Press, Inc 67-, Science Associates International Inc 67-. 9: Metro Col InterlibAssn (pres); Acad Libs of Brooklyn (pres). 12: Co-auth "Science Information Personnel" (61); Ed "Directory of Computerized Information inScience & Technology" (68); Adv ed "Automatic Documentation and Mathematical Linguistics" (Journal). 13: Yes. 14: Sci documentation, educ ofinfo specialists, lib bldgs, admin. 15: 63 Ave A Apt 18-H, New York NY 10009.

COHEE, ROBERT NATHAN. b Greenwood Del 10 My 27. 4: Marilyn Goodis. 5: UDel 46-50 (Eng) BA; Drexrl 52-54 MS in LS. 6: Sp. 7: F 1/C US Navy 45-46; (2d Lt) Artillery US Army 52-53; Circ libn Mem Lib UDel 54-58; Libn Elkins Park Free Lib (Elkins Park Penn) 58-59; Head libn hazleton Pub Lib (Hazleton Penn) 59-62; Readers serv libn Elizabethtown Col Lib 62-63; Head libn Scranton Pub Lib (Scranton Penn) 63-. 9: PennLA (chm Tech Development Com) 64-65; NEPennLA (pres) 60-61. 10: Scabbard & Blade; Kiwanis; Scranton UN Com. 14: Ref, admin, intellectual freedom. 15: 700 Harrison ave, Scranton Pa 18510.

COHEN, ALLEN. b NYC 7 N 35. 5: City Col of NY 53-57 (Eng) BA; Pratt 61-62 MLS; New Sch Soc Res 67 MALS. 6: Fr, Modern Grk. 7: Social investigator NY Welfare Dept (NYC) 60-61; Lib fellow Music Lib City Col of NY 61-62; Ser catlgr NY Pub Lib 62-66; Acquis & catlg libn NYC Community Col 66-67; Hd catlgr John Jay Col Crim Justice, CUNY 67-. 9: ALA; Amer Soc Indexers; NY Lib Club; NY RT Soc; Pratt Lib Alum Assoc. 10: ACLU; Beta Phi Mu. 13: Yes. 14: Catlg, acquis, ref. 15: 33 Monroe pl, Brooklyn NY 11201.

COHEN, DAVID. b NYC 24 My 09. 4: Evelyn Zuckerman. 5: City Col (NY) 26-30 (Soc Sci) BBS, 30-34 (Hist, Educ) MSE; Columbia 37-39 MSLS; New Sch for Soc Research 48-54 (Sociol); Columbia 67-68. 6: Fr. 7: Ref libn City Col (NYC) 30-42; Recr train instr US Navy, Sampson NY 43-46; Elem tchr NYC Bd of Educ, Brooklyn NY 47-54; Reg manager World Book Encyclopedia, Queens NY 54-59; Libn Jonas Salk High Sch, Levittown NY 59-60; Libn plainview High Sch, Plainview NY 60- Tchr Lib Sci summer courses; Hofstra U 65, Miami U 66, Queens C 67. 8: Title II B Fellow, Columbia U 67-68; Lib consul Greenvale Sch LI 66-67. 9: Nassau-Suffolk SchLA (past pres, chm Freedom to Read Com); NYLA (mem Intell Freedom Com); ALA;-AASchL (chm Treatment of Minorities inLib Bks Com). 10: Amer Fed Tchrs; LI Intel Freedom Com; ACLU; Amer Jewish Cong; Coun for Interracial Bks. 12: Ed "Recommended Paperback Books for Elem Sch" (3d ed 69). 13: Yes. 14: Ref, paperbacks, bk sel policy. 15: 68-71 Bell blvd, Bayside NY 11364.

COHEN, EDNA L(IEBERMAN). b Boston Mass 21 My 21. 4: Harold Cohen. 5: Simmons 38-42 (LS) BS. 6: Fr, Ger. 7: Asst child libn Boston pub Lib, Mattapan Br 42-43; Asst libn serv lib US Army (Ft Ord Cal) 43-44; Ordnance libn Benica Arsenal (Benica Cal) 44-45; Ref libn Newton Free Lib (Newton Mass) 59-. 15: 19 Chestnut ter, Newton Centre Ma 02159.

COHEN, ELINOR M. b NYC 1 F 36. 5: Queens Col 52-54 (Chem); NYU 54-56 (Chem) BA; Columbia 66-68 (LS) MS. 7: Chem Evans Research & Devp Corp, NYC 56-61; Gen Foods Corp, Tarrytown NY Chem 61-65, Libn 66-. 9: SLA; ACS. 14: Spec lib admin. 15: 316 Woodland Hills rd, White Plains NY 10603.

COHEN, GILBERT. b NYC 2 Ja 29. 4: Shirley Ann. 5: Queens Col 47-51 (Eng) BA; Rutgers 57-59 MLS. 7: Sr clerk RutgersU Newark Colleges Lib (Newark NJ) 57-50; Sr libn Newark Pub Lib (Newark NJ) 59-61; Head of circ RutgersU Newark Colleges Lib (Newark NJ) 61-67; Hd of Ref RutgersU (Newark) Dana Lib 67-. 8: Research asst NJLA Lib Development Com 62-63. 9: ALA; NJLA. 10: Beta Phi Mu. 12: "Library Service to Labor (63). 13: Yes. 14: Ref. 15: 30 Maple ave, Springfield NJ 07081.

COHEN, JACKSON BERNARD. b Detroit Mich 13 Jl 29. 5: UPittsburgh 48-52 (Eng) AB 53-56 (Eng) MLitt; Carnegie 56-57 MLS; UCincinnati 64-68 (Sci, Hist). 6: Fr. 7: Sales clerk Kaufman S Dept Store (Pittsburgh) summer 52; Salesman Mandel Lighting & Equipment Co (Pittsburgh) 52; Carnegie Lib of Pittsburgh Page Tech Dept (53); Clerk Tech Dept 53-55; Sub-prof asst Tech Dept 55-57; Libn Tech Dept 57; Libn sci & ind dept Pub Lib of Cincinnati & Hamilton Co 57-. 9: ALA; SLA (chm Scholarship & Stud Loan Fund Com 65-66; Cincinnati Chap: pres 63-64, Mem Chm 60-61); ohioLA (Ref

Serv Round Table Panelist 60). 10: Beta Phi Mu; Phi Kappa Phi; Staff Assn, Pub Lib of Cincinnati & Hamilton Co; Phi Epsilon Pi. 12: "Machine Tool Referral Guide (66). 13: Yes. 14: Ref wk, pub lib serv to ind. 15: Pub Lib 800 Vine st, Cincinnati Oh 45220.

COHEN, LORRAINE (STERLING). b Warsaw Poland 17 D 17. 4: Sol E Cohen. 5: Chicago Tchrs Col 36-40 (Educ) BE; Queens Col (NY) 58-63 (Lib Educ) MA. 6: Yiddish. 7: Sub tchr Chicago Sch System 40-41; Sec Childres Aid Soc (NYC) 42-43; Libn Main Street Sch (Port Washington NY) 59-. 9: ALA; NEA; NYLA; Nassau-SuffolkLA; NYStateTA. 13: Yes. 14: Ref, read guidance. 15: 184-15 69th ave, Flushing NY 11365.

COHEN, MARTIN. b Boston Mass 11 D 15. 4: Pearl Young Cohen. 5: Harvard 33-37 (Eng) AB; Boston Tchrs Col 37-38 (Educ) MA; Simmons 45-46 91s0 bs. 6: Fr, Ger. 7: (1st Lt) US Army Transportation Corps 40-45; Ref libn Decatur Ill Pub Lib 47-49; Ref libn Newark NJ Pub Lib 46-47; community Group Coun Kalamazoo Mich Pub Lib 49-60; Asst prof Dept of Libnship West MichU 60-. 9: ALA; MichLA. 13: Yes. 14: Pub lib serv, a-v, materials selection, communications media. 15: Dept of Librarianship Western Michigan U, Kalamazoo Mi 49001.

COHEN, MORRIS L. b NYC 2 N 27. 4: Gloria Weitzner. 5: Chicago 45-48 BA; Columbia 48-51 LLB; Pratt 58-59 MLS. 7: Attorney (NYC) 51-58; Asst libn RutgersU Law Sch 58-59; Asst libn ColumbiaU Law Sch 59-61; Law libn & assoc prof of law SUNY (Buffalo) 61-63; Part-time instr at Drexel Inst & ColumbiaU Lib Schs in Law Libnship 64-. 8: Biddle law lib Prof of Law UPenn 63-; Dir Nat Educ Insts AALL 64-65; Lib accredit inspector Assn Amer Law Schs; Consul on lib bldg & planning. 9: ASIS (Com on Ethics); AALL (past chm Educ Com & Of Com on Applic of Sci Devices to Legal Research, Jt Com of AALL-AALS; Adv Com to AALS Lib Study Proj, pres-elect 69-70); Internat Assn of Law Libs; ALA (Com on Constit & By-Laws, chm subsec on law & pol sci 67-69); BSA. 10: Amer Bar Assn; ACLU; AAUP. 12: "Legal Bibliography Briefed (65); "Legal Research in a Nutshell (68). 13: Yes. 14: Admin, lib bldgs, arch. 15: Biddle Law Lib Univ of Penn, 3400 Chestnut st, Phila Pa 19104.

COHEN, NATHAN MARSHALL. b Bradford Penn 1 D 21. 4: Constance Coen. 5: Penn StateU 40-43 BA; Syracuse 48-49 BSLS. 7: Circ manager Fairfield Publs Inc (Fairfield Conn) 46-47; Asst to dir Jewish Commun Coun (Bridgeport Conn) 47-48; Asst chief & act chief bus econ div D C Pub Lib 49-52; Br libn 52-56; Asst libn Transportation Intelligence Agency (Wash DC) 56-57; Research libn Lib Serv Br USOE (Wash DC) 57-64; Head LSCA Reports Unit, Lib Serv Br USOE (Wash DC) 64-67; Prog spec HEA II-A Div Lib Prog 68-. 9: ALA; DCLA. 12: "Vocational Training Directory of the United States (53, 55, 58); Co-auth "State Library Extension Services (61); "Statistics of Libraries (61); "Library Science Dissertations (63); Auth "State Library Extension Service (66). 13: Yes. 14: Lib stats, ext. 15: 4822 N 16th st, Arlington Va 22205.

COHEN, NINA (TAORMINA). b Rochester NY 6 Ag 28. 4: Ira S Cohen. 5: Queens Col (NY) 45-49 (Music) BA; IndU 51-52 (LS) MA. 6: Sp. 7: Jr libn Grosvenor Lib, Buffalo NY 52-55; Ref libn Lockwood Mem Lib, Buffalo NY 55-57; Asst libn Town of Tonawanda Libs, Tonawanda NY 58-60; Acquis libn SUNY (Buffalo) 60-64, Hd readers serv SUNY (Buffalo) 64-67; Dir West NY Lib Resources Coun, Buffalo NY 67-. 8: Consul NY State Jt Legis Com on Intergovtal Fiscal Affairs 66-67. 9: ALA (mem RSD/RTSD Interdiv Com on Pub Docs; Sem Acquis Latin Amer Lib Materials; NYLA (Bd Dirs; RTSS). 12: Comp "Undergraduate Collections: Retrospective and Current Titles, XIII SALALM, wking pap no 6 (68). 14: Tech serv, admin, automation. 15: 159 Morris ave, Buffalo NY 14214.

COHEN, PEARL YOUNG. b Exeter NH 14 Ja 18. 4: Martin Cohen. 5: Simmons 37-41 (Eng) BS; West MichU 56-58 (LS) MA. 6: Fr, Ger. 7: Sec to dir Sch of Eng Simmons Col 41-44; Dir of pub rel Simmons Col 44-47; Ref asst Kalamazoo Pub Lib 58-60; Sch libn South Jr High Sch (Kalamazoo) 60; readers adv Kalamazoo Pub Lib 62-64; Ref libn Humanities Div Mich StateU Lib (East Lansing) 64-65; Hd Bkmob Dept Kalamazoo Lib Syst 66-. 9: MichLA. 10: Audubon Soc; Symphony Soc. 14: Adult serv. 15: 3923 Devonshire ave, Kalamazoo Mi 49007.

COHEN, PHYLLIS M. b 9 O 35. 5: Fashion Inst of Tech 53-54 (Fashion design); CCNY 54-58 (Art) BA; UMich 60-62 (LS, Lithography) AMLS. 6: Fr. 7: Ware libn Avery Lib Columbia U 59-60; Slide libn's asst Arch Lib UMich 61; Art & mus libn Brooklyn Pub Lib, NYC 62-65; Indexer Art Index H W Wilson Co, NYC 66; Asst libn Art & Arch Sch Lib Cooper Union 67-. 9: ALA (Art Subsect: Nom Com 68-69); SLA (Museum Div). 10: Col Art Assn. 11: Columbia U One Woman Show 60; Detroit Inst of Art 62; Jersey City Mus 66 etc. 14: Catlg art lib, art ref, illus bks, lithog, painting. 15: 205 Third ave, New York NY 10003.

COHEN, RICHARD. b Miami Fla 11 F 28. 5: Morehouse Col 45-46 (Biol); Fla A&M U 46-49 (Biol) BS, 49-50, 57-59 (Educ) MEd; Rutgers 60-62 MLS. 7: Tchr Dade Co Fla Bd of Pub Instr (Miami) 50-54, 56; (Cpl) US Army (Camp Pickett Va & Ft Sam Houston Tex) 54-56; Brooklyn Pub Lib Libn trainee 58-61; Libn sci & ind 61-63; Sr libn bus lib 63-66; Tchr-libn NYC Bd Educ 66-. 8: Consul Volusia Co (Fla) Bd of Pub Instr (58). 9: ALA; SLA (NY Chap; Bus & Fin Sect); NY Lib Club. 10: Bksellers League of NY; Alpha Beta Alpha. 14: Ref, sch libs. 15: 78 Manhattan ave, New York NY 10025.

COHEN, SAMUEL. b Safad Israel 2 Mr 19. 5: Govt Law Sch Jerusalem 43-48 (Law) Diploma; Columbia 52-55 (Pol Sci) MA; NYU Sch of Law 55-56 (Comparative Law) LLM; Columbia Law Sch 58-61 (Law) LLB; Columbia Sch of Lib Serv 67-69 (LS) MS610 W 110 st, New York NY 10025. 6: Fr, Hebrew, Arabic. 7: Attorney, Haifa Israel 49-52; Libn NY Law Sch 62-65; Practicing attorney, Tel Aviv Israel 65-67; Ref libn Columbia U Law Sch 67-. 9: AALL; Law Lib Assn of Greater ny. 10: Bar of Israel; NY Bar. 12: Co-auth "Legal Aspects of Foreign Investment in the United States" (59). 13: Yes. 14: Legal research, ref wk. 15: 610 W 110 st, New York NY 10025.

COHEN, SIDNEY. b Cleveland 17 N 23. 4: Betsy Edith Cohen. 5: Ohio U 47-50 (Speech, Drama) BSED; Kent State summers 58-61 (LS) MA. 7: T/4 rank US Army, Pacific Theatre 44-46; Sub tchr Cleveland Pub Schs 51-52; Asst credit manager Midland Electric Co, Cleveland 53-56; Tchr EngSpeech & Drama Millersburg High Sch, Millersburg Ohio 56-59; Libn & a-v aid dir Madison Local Sch, Groveport Ohio 59-60; Libn & visual aidecoordinator Rossford High Sch, Rossford Ohio 60-63; Head libn Marvin Mem Lib, Shelby Ohio 63-66; Hd libn Ohio State U (Mansfield) 66-. 8: Directed speech programs & plays at the above schs: Millersburg & Rossford; Awarded dist VFW certif for directing champion speaker 62; Wrote & directed programs for Amer Red Cross Club in Camp Schimmelfennig Japan 45; Dir United Jewish Appeal, Athens Ohio 49. 9: NEA; ALA; OhioLA; OhioEA; OhioAS chL. 10: Toastmasters Internat; Kiwanis. 13: Yes. 15: Rd 2, Shelby OH 44875.

COHN, ALAN M. b St Louis Mo 21 Ag 26. 4: Sally Ray. 5: Washington U (St Louis) 46-49 (Eng) BA, 49-50 (Eng) MA, 50-54 (Eng); UIll 54-55 MSLS. 6: Fr. 7: Radioman 3d Class US Navy 44-46; Grad asst in Eng WashingtonU (St Louis) 51-53; Humanities libn SoIllU 55-; Assoc prof Eng 67-. 9: BSA; MUSLA. 10: Mod Humanities Res Assn; Mod Lang Assn; Caxton Club of Chicago; Phi Beta Kappa; Beta Phi Mu. 13: Yes. 14: Ref. 15: 700 W Cherry st, Carbondale Il 62901.

COHN, ELIZABETH ANN (RIECKENBERG). b Steelville Ill 10 O 40. 4: Dickford Cohn. 5: Carthage Col 58-62 (Eng) AB; UIll 62-64 MSLS. 6: Fr, Ger. 7: Libn I Free Lib of Phila 64-66; Catlg libn St Olaf Col (Northfield Minn) 68-. 9: ALA. 14: Catlg. 15: 320 N Linden st, Northfield Mn 55057.

COHN, ELIZABETH RIERA. b Chestnut Hill Phila Penn 31 Ag 17. 4: J Bradley Cohn. 5: UPenn 33-37 (Hist) BA, 37-41 (Hist) MA; Drexel 49-52 MLS. 6: Fr. 7: Bibliog asst Union Lib Catalogue (Phila) 49-51; Asst libn Amer Machine & Foundry Co (NYC) 51-52; Asst libn NY Botanical Garden (NYC) 52-54; Libn Coverdale & Colpitts (NYC) 55-. 9: SLA; NY Lib Club. 10: Hist Soc of Windham Co (Vt); Farm Bur (Windham Co Vt); US Equestriam Team; mem 5 horse assns. 14: Admin, catlg. 15: Coverdale & Colpitts 140 Broadway, New York NY 10005.

COHN, EMMA. b NYC 23 Mr 22. 5: Wash Sq Col 40-43 (Eng, Philos) BA; Columbia 52-54 MLS. 6: Fr. 7: Sec C W Berthiez (Paris) 48-50; Asst corner Bk Shop (NYC) 50-52; Asst NY Hist Soc (NYC) 52-54; Young Adult Libn Tremont Br NY Pub Lib 54-56; Asst libn Nathan Straus Young Adult Lib 56-59; Asst libn Mosholu Reg Br 59-63; Young Adult Spec Bronx Borough Off 63-68; Asst Coordinator Off of ya serv NY Pub Lib 68-. 8: Mem of ed coms of ALA-YASD for "Richer by Asia, "African Encounter; Rep of YASD-IFLA 65- (chm A-v Com). 9: ALA; NYLA; Film Library Information Council. 10: Museum of Modern Art. 12: Ed "Top of the News (57); Co-ed (with Brita Olsson) "Library Service for Young Adults (68); Ed "Films for Young Adults, (66) Assoc ed "Film Library

Quarterly. 13: Yes. 14: Young adult serv, art, films. 15: 2827 Valentine ave, Bronx NS 10458.

COHN, WILLIAM LOEWY. b Joliet Ill 9 D 34. 4: Anne Levine. 5: Vanderbilt 57-59 (Eng) BA, 59-60, 65 (Eng) MA; Peabody 61-62 (LS) MA. 6: Ger. 7: Clerk-typist US Army Ft Bragg NC 55-57; Instr NC Col (Durham) 60-61; Ref asst Joint U Lib, Nashville 61-62; Libn I Chicago Pub Lib 62-63; Asst ref UNH 63-64; Humanities & fine arts libn SoIllU 64-66; Dir Drury Col Lib 66-68; Dir of pub serv E Carolina U Lib 68-. 9: ALA; NHLA (treas); IllLA; MoLA; NCLA; SELA. 10: AAUP. 13: Yes. 14: Ref (humanities & fine arts), admin. 15: 2504A E 3rd st, Greenville NC 27834.

COIL, NEAL (ASA). b Buckland Ohio 11 F 22. 4: Marie Ann (Presar). 5: Ohio No U 49-52 (Hist, Pol Sci) BA; Ohio State U 52-53 (Hist) MA; IndU 55-56 MALS. 7: US Army Armored Force (Staff Sgt) 42-46; Instr Hist Ohio No U 54-55; Ref libn & asst prof lib sci Ball State U 56-59; Head of ref dept IndState U 59-63; Ref libn & asst prof of lib sci Ball State U 63-65, Head ref libn & asst prof of lib sci 65-66; Libn Undergrad Lib Bowling GreenState U 66-68; Asst Prof Dept of Lib Sci Ball State U 68-. 10: Phi Alpha Theta; Beta Phi Mu; Phi Delta Kappa. 14: Ref, bibliog, historiography, US hist, educ for libnship. 15: Ball State Univ Lib, Muncie In 47306.

COIRA, MARGARET CHRISTINE. b Bloomsburg Penn. 5: Lock Haven State Tchrs Col 26-30 (Eng, Soc Studies) BS; Columbia summers 33-36 (Eng) MA; Cambridge U (Eng) summer 36 (Eng); Clarion State Col summer 53 (LS); syracuse summers 54-60 (LS) MS. 7: Eng tchr LockHaven Bd of Educ, Lock Haven Penn 32-53; Libn Jr High Sch, Lock Haven Penn 53-60; Asst libn Baltimore Co Pub Lib, Catonsville Md 60-61; Patients' libn VA, Baltimore 61; Asst libn Mansfield State Col 61-62; Libn Red Land High Sch, Etters Penn 64-. 9: NEA; Penn StateEA; PennLA; Penn Sch LA. 10: Beta Phi Mu; Highland Women's Club. 14: Ref. 15: 316 Limekiln rd, New Cumberland PA 17070.

COKER, CHARLES FREDERICK WILLIAMS. b Columbia SC 3 Jl 32. 5: UNC 49-53 (Hist) AB, 53-54 (Hist) 62-63 MSLS; OxfordU 54 (Hist). 6: Lat, Fr. 7: Capt ISMC Inf 57-62; Asst archives admin NC Dept of Archives & Hist, Raleigh 63-. 8: Miss consul USMC, Quantico Va 67. 9: SAA; NC Lit & Hist Assn. 10: Phi Beta Kappa; Amer Mil Inst; US Naval Inst; Co of Mil Histns; Marine Corps Assn. 12: "Henry Clay Cochrane Papers" (68); Ed "Journal of John Graham" in "Military Collector and Historian XIX" (67). 13: Yes. 14: Archives, mss. 15: PO Box 1563, Raleigh NC 27602.

COKER, ELIZABETH. b Salem Mass 1 Jl 09. 5: Keuka Col 26-30 (Eng) BA (cum laude); Pratt 31-32 Lib Certif. 6: Fr. 7: Asst child libn Pratt Inst 32-40; Greenwich Lib, Greenwich Conn: Sch & hsop libn 40-42, Head ext dept 42-63, Bk order coordinator 63-65; Hd adult serv 65-. 65 ; Hd adult serv 65-. 9: ConnLA. 10: AAUW. 14: Circ, ref. 15: 25 Mortimer dr, Old Greenwich Ct 06870.

COLAIANNI, LOIS ANN (HAWKS). b Utica NY 18 Ag32. 4: Edmond R Colaianni. 5: URochester 49-53 (Biol) BA; UCincinnati 58-59 (Psych); UCLA 63-64 MLS. 7: Med lib internship Biomed Lib UCLA 64-65, MEDLARS searcher 65-68; Head med info & communications serv 68-. 9: MedLA; Med Libns Group So Cal (pres). 14: Ref. 15: Biomed Lib, Univ of Cal, Los Angeles Ca 90024.

COLBURN, EDWIN B. b Stafford Conn 10 O 15. 4: Dorothy D Doe. 5: Amherst 33-37 (Eng) BA; Columbia 39-41 BLS; Northwestern 49-50 MA. 7: Tchg asst Amherst Col 37-38; Gen asst NY Pub Lib 39-47; Chief of tech serv NorthwesternU Lib 48-50; Supv of processing dept Cleveland Pub Lib 50-54; Chief of indexing serv The H W Wilson Co (Bronx NY) 54-63; v-pres & chief of indexing serv 63-67, Sr v-pres & dir of indexing ser 67-. 8: Consul on lib equipment US Off of Educ (51); Index Adv Bd "Encyclopedia-International 63-64; Decimal Clsf Ed Policy Com 58-. 9: ALA-RTSD (pres 57-58); -Div Catlg & Clsf (exec sec 50-54); CNLA (sec-treas 55-58). 13: Yes. 14: Ref, tech serv. 15: 140 Ellison ave, Bronxville NY 10708.

COLBURN, FRANCES L (MRS). b Searcy Ark 24 S 26. 5: Ouachita Baptist Col 44-45 (Speech); Tex Womans U 45-47 (Speech) BS, 60-61 MLS. 6: Fr. 7: Speech tchr Magnolia Ark Sch Dist, Magnolia Ark 47-48; Tchr Shelby Co Sch Dist, Memphis Tenn 48-51; Jr high Eng tchr Ft Worth Ind Sch Dist, Ft Worth Tex 55-60; Libn Corpus Christi Ind Sch Dist, Corpus Christi Tex 61-65; Tech libn Celanese Chem Co, Corpus Christi Tex 65-. 9: NEA; Clr Tchrs Assn; Tex State Tchrs Assn; Tex StateLA. 10: PTA; Alpha Beta Alpha; Faculty Club. 14: Ref. 15: 4518 Marie, Corpus Christi TX 78411.

COLBURN, VIRGINIA. b Oberlin Ohio 26 Ja 40. 4: S Z Haidri. 5: Douglass Col 57-61 (Latin Amer Studies) BA; Rutgers 65-68 MLS; UOkla summer 61 (Ling). 6: Sp. 7: Circ libn Mobil Chem Co, Metuchen NJ 65-66; Libn & dir tech info Smith, Miller & Patch Inc, New Brunswick NJ 66-67; Adult serv libn Mamaroneck Free Lib, Mamaroneck NY 68-. 8: Mgt study on needs & processing of photocopies in tech research lib Smith, Miller & Patch Inc, New Brunswick NJ 67. 9: ALA; NYLA; WestchesterLA. 10: AAUW; DAR. 12: "Literature Resources for the Pharmaceutical Industry" (69); Ed "SMP Researcher" (66-67). 14: Sci mgt, bibliog, pub rel, lit criticism. 15: 21 N Chatsworth ave, Larchmont NY 10538.

COLBY, BETTY (KELSEY). b Northfield Minn 20 D 16. 4: Carroll Durgin Colby. 5: St Olaf Col 35-39 (Sociol) BA; West Res 39-41 7: Libn Huntington Jr High; Abington Penn 58; Head tech processes Osterhout Pub Lib (Wilkes-Barre Penn) 59-64; Libn VA Hosp (Wilkes-Barre Penn) 64-66; Dir lib serv Luzerne Co Commun Col (Wilkes-Barre Penn) 67-. 9: ALA; -ACRL; -RTSD; PennLA; NEPennLA. 10: LWV; UN Assn; PTA; United Fund; NASW; AAUW; Beta Phi Mu. 14: Admin, ref. 15: 87 Park pl, Kingston Pa 18704.

COLBY, CHARLES C(LIFTON) 3d. b Newark NJ 2 N 23. 4: Jacqueline Zeldin. 5: Harvard 41-45 (Bio) AB (Awarded in absentia based on course work taken at Harvard, UNH & Yale); Harvard Med Sch 45-46 (Med); Simmons 46-47 (LS) BS. 6: Fr, Ger. 7: Pfc USA 43-46; Messenger Boston Pub Lib 46; Subject catlgr Army Med Lib, Wash DC 47-48; Ref libn boston Med Lib 49-54; Med libn UMO (Columbia) 54-56; Libn 56-65; Assoc libn for med lib serv Countway Lib Harvard Med Sch 65-. 8: Lectr Lit of Sci & Tech Simmons Col 58, 65, 66-67; Specialist in med libs US State Dept Off of the High Commsner for Germany summer 50. 9: MedLA. 13: Yes. 14: Admin. 15: Countway Library 10 Shattuck st, Boston Ma 02115.

COLBY, HELEN C. b Ambridge Penn 15 Ja 17. 5: UNH 41 (Sociol) BS; UWash 66 Libnship ML. 7: Exec sec Girl Scouts, Md, NJ, NH, Me 41-52; Laconia Union #30 Laconia NH: Tchr 55-63, Libn 63-. 9: ALA; NEA; NESchLA; NHEA; NH A-v Assn. 14: Sch lib Assts assns & confs. 15: RD 3 Eastman Shore, Laconia NH 03246.

COLBY, ROBERT A(LAN). b Chicago 15 Ap 20. 4: Vineta Blumoff. 5: Chicago 37-41 (Eng) BA, 41-42 (Eng) MA; NYU 42-43 (Eng); Chicago 47-49 (Eng) PhD; Columbia 51-53 (LS) MS. 6: Sp, Fr, Ger, Ital. 7: US Army (Cpl) Med Corps personnel, info educ 43-46; Instr of Eng DePaul U 46-47; Instr of Eng Ill Inst of Tech 47-49; Asst Prof of Eng Lake Forest Col 49-51; Head div of the arts Queens Col Lib (NY) 53-64; Assoc Prof of Lib Sci So Conn State Col 64-66; Assoc Prof of Lib Sci Queens Col (NY) 66-69, Prof 69-. 9: BSA; Mod Lang Assn (Victorian Bibliog Com); ConnLA; NY Lib Club. 10: AAUP; Columbia Sch of Lib Serv Alumni Assn. 12: "The Equivocal Virtue: Mrs Oliphant and the Victorian Literary Market Place," with Vineta Colby (66). ; "Fiction with a Purpose; Major and Minor Nineteenth Century Novels" (67). 13: Yes. 14: Ref, bibliog, lib educ, hist of the bk, hist of culture. 15: 33-24 86th st, Jackson Hts NY 11372.

COLE, (MARY) ELIZABETH. b Huntland Tenn 4 Ag 21. 5: Tenn PolytechU 40-45 (Eng) BS; UTenn summer 48-49 (LS); Peabody summers 50-53 (LS) MA. 7: Tchr Elem Sch (Winchester Tenn) 42-43; High sch libn Cumberland Co (Crossville Tenn) 45-46; Eng tchr York Inst (Jamestown Tenn) 46-48; high sch libn Maury Co (Mt Pleasant Tenn) 48-52; Bkmob libn Tenn Tech 52-54; Reg libn Blue Grass Reg (Columbia Tenn) 54-60; Consul Fla State Lib 60-67; Dir Pub Lib Serv State Lib & Archives, Nashville Tenn 67-. 9: ALA (Good Reading for Youth Com 63, State Lib Planning Com 68-71); FlaLA (sec 63-64); SELA (sec Publ Lib Sect 61-63, Nat Lib Week Wkshop 64). 10: Exec dir Nat Lib Week in Tenn (60); Exec dir Nat Lib Week in Fla (62-63); nat Soc Colonial Dames. 12: "A Survey of Library Service in Pinellas County Fla (64); "A Survey of Library Service in Volusia County Fla (64); a survey of Library Service in Pinellas County Fla (64) "A Survey of Library Service in Volusia County Fla (64); "A Survey of Library Service in Polk County Fla (65). 13: Yes. 14: Publ rel, ref. 15: 812 Capitol Towers Apts, Nashville Tn 37219.

COLE, CLARE STEWART. b Trenton NJ 9 Je 16. 4: Herbert H Cole. 5: Douglass 40 (Eng) AB; Rutgers 65 MLS. 7: Sussex Co Lib, NJ: Jr libn 60-64, Ref libn 65, Asst dir 66-. 9: ALA; -ACRL (Info Sci & Automation Div); NJLA (Hist & Bibliog Sect). 10: Beta Phi Mu. 14: Ref, lib devel, lib educ. 15: Box 366 226 [illegible]n st, Newton NJ 07860.

COLE, DORIS MARIE. b New Berlin NY 12 Ap 05. 5: Syracuse 21-25 (Eng) AB, summers -39 BS in LS; Chicago 38-39 (LS); Syracuse summer 41 (Ed Psych) MS. 6: Fr. 7: Eng tchr Earlville High Sch, Earlville NY 25-27; Speech tchr libn Delaware Acad, Delhi NY 27-29; Eng tchr Sea Cliff High Sch, Sea Cliff NY 29-31; Libn Massena High Sch, Massena NY 31-38; Ref libn World Book Encyclopedia Chicago 38-39; Supv of Libs Massena Pub Schs, Massena NY 39-61; Prof Lib Educ State U Col (Geneseo NY) 61-62; Assoc Prof Sch of Lib Sci Syracuse U 62-69. 8: Consul to var sch libs 56, 63, 68. 9: ALA (Coun 67-70); NYLA (pres 68, pres sch lib sect 57-58, coun 59-61 & 65-69); NEA; AALS; NYState Tchrs Assn. 10: AAUP; Delta Kappa Gamma; Internat Reading Assn. 11: Citizen of the Year, Massena C of C 61. 12: Ed "Top of the News" (60-62). 13: Yes. 14: Ref, wk with child & ya, sch lib. 15: 212 Lockwood rd, Syracuse NY 13214.

COLE, DOROTHY ETHLYN. b Chicago Il 17 S 07. 5: Chicago 34 (Eng) PhB, 43 AM, 62-63. 7: Libn Riverside-Brookfield High Sch (Riverside Ill) 26-30; Asst child libn Oak Park Pub Lib (Oak Park Ill) 30-32; Ref libn Central YMCA Col 34-43; Libn Grad Lib Sch UChicago 43-46; Ed "Library Literature 46-56; Lib consul "Grolier-Americana (NYC) 56-58; Asst prof Drexel Lib Sch 59-; Visiting lecturer SyracuseU summers 62, 63; Assoc prof Sch of Lib Sci SUNY (Albany) 59-; Visiting lectr UPR 68-69. 9: ALA (Nom Com 53, Coun 55-59); Lib Period Round Table (chm 54); NYLA; NY Lib Club (pres 55-57); East NY Sch Libns Assn (pres 61); AALS. 10: AAUP; Amer Guild of Organists; Capitol Hill Choral Soc; (Exec Com) Friends of Albany Pub Lib. 12: Ed "Whos Who in Library Service (3rd ed 55). 13: Yes. 14: Ref, bibliog of humanities & soc sci, publishing, research in libnship. 15: Sch of Lib Sci State U of NY Albany NY 12203.

COLE, ELIZABETH M(AYHEW). b Newton Mass 29 D 13. 5: Hood Col 30-34 (Eng) AB; Drexel 34-35 BS in LS. 7: Lib asst DC Pub Lib 35-40; Readers adv tech & sci div 40-54; Supv libn US Naval Ordnance Lab Lib (White Oak SS Md) 54-57; Asst chief tech lib, USAEC (Germantown Md) 57-61; Chief tech & sci div DC Pub Lib 61-. 8: Consul John Shellman Baer Natural Hist Collection; C Burr Artz Lib (Frederick Md) 58-61. 9: ALA; SLA; DCLA. 13: Yes. 15: 5009 40th pl #401, Hyattsville Md 20781.

COLE, GENEVIEVE BADLEY. b Portland Ore 6 D 09. 4: Frank Linden Cole. 5: Pacific Col 25-30 (Educ) BA; UWash 62-63 (LS) ML. 7: Sub tchr Sch dist #1, Portland Ore 42-60; Asst libn Shambaugh Lib George Fox Col 63-. 9: ALA; OreLA. 10: Williamette Christian Col Libns Assn; Portland Area Spec Libns Assn; AAUW. 14: Circ, ref. 15: 300 N Meridian st, Newberg Or 97132.

COLE, GENEVIEVE. b Harriman NY 8 Mr 08. 5: NY State Col for Tchrs (Albany) 25-29 (Chem) AB; UWis 50-52 MS (Bot) MA (LS). 6: Fr. 7: Tchr high Sch (Renssalaerville NY) 29-30; Sci tchr High Sch (Monroe NY) 30-44; Sci sec Woods Hole Oceanographic Inst (Woods Hole Mass) 45-47; Asst in biol Rockford Col 47-50; Stud asst Biol & Med Libs UWsi (Madison) 51-52; Libn Biol Div Oak Ridge Nat Lab (Oak Ridge Tenn) 52-56; Libn Treadwell lib Mass Gen Hosp (Boston) 57-. 8: Lib consul Boston Chap of Spec Libs Assn (Boston) 60-61. 9: MedLA (sec 66-68, chm Subcom on Recr 64-65); sla; Repr on Jt SLA-AHIL Com on Lib Serv in Hosps 68-70 & Jt ALA-AHIL Com on Standards for Libs in Health Care Fac 68-70; Biol Scis Div (sec-treas 60-61, chm 62-63); Boston Chap (sec 63-64, chm Recr Com 59-60). 10: Phi Sigma; Beta Phi Mu; College Club of Boston; English-Speaking union; Beacon Hill Civic Assn; AAAS; Service League; Museum of Science. 13: Yes. 14: Ref, hist of med, rare bks. 15: 77A Revere st apt 3, Boston Ma 02114.

COLE, GEORGIA (RANKIN). b Stanford Ky 27 My 26. 4: Herman Cole Jr. 5: East Ky State Col 42-45 (Eng, Hist) AB; UKy 47-53 MS in LS; IndU 65- (LS). 7: High Sch (Somerset Ky) 45-46; Libn High Sch (Evarts Ky) 46-50; Libn Lafayette High Sch (Lexington Ky) 50-53; Libn Dependents Sch (Heidelberg Germany) 53-55; Libn Dependents Sch (Paris) 55-56; Coordinator Lib Serv Dependents Sch, USAF (Europe) 56-58; Dir Div of sch libs & tchg materials (Ind) Dept of Pub Instr 58-62; Asst prof Dept of Lib Sci UKy 62-65; Coord instr materials Vigo Co Schs, Terre Haute Ind 66-. 8: Dir NDEA; Inst for Sch Libns, UKy summer 64. 9: NEA; AASchL (chm Exhib Com 58-59, co-chm AASchL-NCTE Jt Com on the Role of Tchrs & Libns in Bk Sel 64-; sec 61-62, 2nd v-pres 63-64); KyLA (2nd v-pres 64-65); IndASchL; IndLA. 12: "Status of School Libraries at the Elementary Level in Indiana 1959-60 (61). 13: Yes. 14: Sch libs, child & yp lit. 15: 216 Woodridge dr, Terre Haute In 47803.

COLE, (HELEN) ROSAMON. b Hillsboro NH 27 Mr 14. 5: UNH 31-34 & summers (Eng) BA; Simmons 35-36 (LS) BS, summers 53-57 (LS) MS. 7: Asst libn Plymouth Tchrs Col 36-40; Asst examining clerk US Civil Serv Commsn, Wash DC 40-41; Bkmob libn State Lib, Concord NH 41-46;Libn Lincoln Jr High Sch, Meriden Conn 46-51; Libn Meriden High Sch, Meriden Conn 51-52; Libn Spaulding High Sch, Rochester NH 52-62; LibnMonadnock Regional High Sch, Swanzy Center NH 62-. 9: ALA; NEA; NHSchLA; NESchLA. 14: Sch lib wk. 15: PO Box 74, Hillsboro NH 03244.

COLE, HERMAN JR. b Clark Co Ind 23 O 25. 4: Georgia Rankin Cole. 5: Canterbury Col 46-50 (Soc Sci) AB; IndU 50-56 (Educ) MS; UKy 64-65 (LS) MS. 7: (Signalman 2/C) US Navy 43-46; Secondary tchr New Washington High Sch (New Washington Ind) 50-52; Personnel wk Goodyear Eng Co (Charleston Ind) 52-56; Dist sales rep Coronet Films (Chicago) 56-64; Dir of lib Rose Polytech Inst 65-. 9: ALA; IndLA. 14: Admin, acquis. 15: 216 Woodridge dr, Terre Haute In 47803.

COLE, HOWSON WHITE. b Pensacola Fla 7 S 25. 4: Elizabeth Hill. 5: Col of William & Mary (Norfolk) 43-44; Col of William & Mary 46-49 (Econ) BA; UVa 49-52 (Hist) MA. 6: Sp. 7: (Signalman 2/C) US Navy Pacific 44-46; Archivist VA State Lib 52-53; Curator of Mss Va Hist Soc (Richmond Va) 53-. 13: Yes. 14: Mss catlg & ref. 15: PO Box 7311, Richmond Va 23221.

COLE, JOHN Y JR. b Ellensburg Wash 30 Jl 40. 5: UWash 58-62 (Hist) BA, 62-63 (LS) ML; John Hopkins 64-66 (Pol Sci) MLA; George Washington U 67-69 (Amer Civ). 6: Fr. 7: US Army Intelligence Corps (1st Lt) 63-66; Libn US Army Intelligence Sch Lib, Ft Holabird Md 64-66; LC; Legis rep serv asst serv libn 67-68; Ref dept off tech asst 69-. 9: ALA-ACRL. 10: . 14: Ref, acquis, admin. 15: 122 6th NE, Wash DC 20002.

COLE, MARGARET PAYNE. b Astoria NY. 5: Mt Holyoke 27-28; Barnard 28-31 (Eng Lit) AB; Columbia 31-32 (LS) BS, 50-53 (LS) MS New Sch for Soc Research 46-48. 7: Child libn ref asst, br 1st asst Queens Borough Pub Lib, Jamaica NY 32-35, Catlgr 35-48, Supt bk sel 49-66; Acquis libn Hofstra U 66-. 9: ALA; Women's Nat Bk Assn; NYLA; NYLib Club; LPRC; NY Reg Tech Proc Libns; Nassau Co LA. 10: Queensborough Council of Social Agencies; Booksellers' League of NY; Beta Phi Mu. 13: Yes. 14: Bk sel, acquis. 15: 36-36 31st st, LI NY 11106.

COLE,MARTHA F. b Boston Mass 15 Mr 21. 5: Manhattanville 39-43 Hist BA; Simmons 46-47 (LS) BS. 6: Fr. 7: Catlgr Harvard Col Lib 48-58; Spec collections lib Boston Col Lib 58-59; Catlgr Brandeis Lib 59-62; Libn Med lib Beth Israel Hosp, Boston 63-. 9: SLA; (past treas Boston Chap); MedLA. 15: 195 School st, Belmont Ma 02178.

COLE, MAUD D. b Fremont Ohio. 5: UToledo 29-33 (Hist) AB; UMich 33-34 ABLS; US Dept of Agric Grad Sch. 7: Asst transportation libn UMich (Ann Arbor) 34-37; 1st asst Rochester Pub Lib, Rochester NY 37-38; Ref libn Ft Hays Kan State Col 38-40; Asst in chg of Exch LC Exch & Gift Div 43-45; Ref libn & atlas catlgr Map Div 45-52; Asst Amer hist div NY Pub Lib 52-54, 1st asst rare bk div 54-. 9: SLA (past chm Geog & Map Div); ALA; BSA; NY Lib Club. 10: Soc Hist of Discoveries. 13: Yes. 14: Rare bks. 15: 21-45 28th st, Astoria NY 11105.

COLEBROOK, PETER KENLIE. b Vancouver Can 6 My 44. 4: Catherine (Kennedy). 5: Notre Dame U of Nelson 62-66 (Eng) BA; UIll 66-67 (LS) MS. 7: Gen Asst Calgary Pub Sch Bd, Calgary Alta 67-68; Reg Consul Niagara Reg Lib Syst, St Catharines Ont 68-. 8: Adv to Welland Co Coop Lib 68-. 9: CanLA; OntLA; BCLA. 14: Admin, ref, adult serv. 15: apt 1005 16 Tremont dr, St Catharines, Ont Can.

COLEGROVE, CATHERINE ANNE. b Cedar Falls Iowa 26 Ap 09. 5: Stanford 30 (Hist) AB; USoCal 50 MS in LS. 7: Asst Pasadena (Cal) Pub Lib 32-43; US Army EURDATC Clerk-typist (Cpl) 44-46; Asst ref & rare bks Huntington Lib 47-49; Ref asst Lib of Hawaii 50-53, Head philos, religion & educ sect 53-61; Head ref sect Hawaii State Lib 61-65, Head reader serv bib & res 65-. 9: ALA-RSD; HawaiiLA. 12: Ed "Hawaii Library Assn Journal" (51, 54-62). 13: Yes. 14: Ref. 15: 320 Poopoo pl, Kailua HI 96734.

COLEHOUR, S(AMUEL) PHILIP. b Mt Carroll Ill 6 Jl 07. 4: Gretchen Howell Colehour. 5: UWis 26-30 & summers (Humanities, LS) BA; Harvard 30-32 (Humanities) AM, Ph D; N Tex State U 56-57 (LS, Ed) Tchg Certif; George Peabody Col 58-59 MALS. 6: Fr. 7: Asst libn Knox Co Pub Sch Libs, Knox County Tex 57-58; Hd Humanities Lib Chico State Col

59-63; Libn Winters Sr High Sch, Winters Tex 63-. 9: ALA; CalLA; TexLA. 14: Acquis. 15: PO Box 218 507 E Seventh st, Knox City Tx 79529.

COLEMAN, BARBARA (NASH). b Lincolnton Ga 13 D 32. 5: Spelman Col 52-55 (Biol) BA; Atlanta 61-62 MSLS. 6: Fr. 7: Head Libn Donaldson AFB, Greenville SC 62-63; Base Libn Paine Field, Everett Wash 63-66; Hd libn Hamilton AFB, Ignacio Cal 66-. 9: ALA; Pub Lib Devel Bd. 10: Bus & Prof Women's Club; Cath Daughters of Amer. 14: Lib admin. 15: 711-47th st, Everett WA 98200.

COLEMAN, CRENOLA SNEED. b Lafayette Springs Miss 16 D 16. 5: UMiss 34-37 (Hist) BA; Peabody Col 46 BSLS. 7: Tchr Hurricane High Sch, Thazton Miss 37-40; Libn Camp Ground high Sch, Water Valley Miss 40-41; Libn Sallis High Sch, Sallis Miss 41-46; Tchr New Albany High Sch, New Albany Miss 43-45; Libn Magnolia High Sch, Magnolia Miss 45-49; Hd child dept Jackson Pub Lib, Jackson Miss 49-51; Libn Kosciusko Jr High Sch, Kosciusko Miss 60-66; Lib supv Kosciusko Sch Libs, Kosciusko Miss 66-68; Asst prof lib sci UMiss, University 68-. 9: NEA; MissEA; MissLA; MissASchL. 10: Federated Clubs; Ladies' Faculty Club; UMiss; Delta Zeta; Delta Kappa Gamma. 14: Educ in libnship, child lit. 15: 1152 S 14 st, Oxford Ms 38655.

COLEMAN, ELLEN SNELL. b Murfreesboro Tenn 5 Je 03. 4: Woodrow Coleman. 5: George Peabody Col 38 (Mus, Home econ) BS, 44 BS in LS, 59 MALS. 6: Fr. 7: Tchr & libn St Bernard Acad, Nashville Tenn 38-41; David Lipscomb Col: Prin & tchr 41-43, Libn 43-44; Watkins Inst, Nashville: Asst libn 44-47, Libn 47-56; Eng tchr Franklin High Sch, Franklin Tenn 56-58; Libn & tchr Fairview Elem Sch, Fairview Tenn 62-68; Libn Fairview High Sch 68; Ref libn Pub Lib of Nashville & Davidson Co, Nashville 67-. 9: NEA; ALA; TennEA; TennLA. 10: Tenn Bot Gardens & Fine Arts Center; Assn for the Preserv of Tenn Antiquities. 14: Ref. 15: 1206 Belle Meade blvd, Nashville Tn 37205.

COLEMAN, EARLE E. b Greensboro NC 19 F 25. 5: URochester 41-43; George Washington U 46 -48 (Foreign Affairs) AB; Simmons 49-50 MS in LS. 6: Fr. 7: Lt (Jg) US Naval Reserve, US & Pacific 43-46; Research asst "Bibliography of Amer Lit" Harvard U 50-55; Head c atlgr Eleutherian Mills Hist Lib, Wilmington Del 55-61; Libn Corni ng Museum of Glass, Corning NY 61-62; Curator of rare bks & spec collections Princeton U 62-67, Bibliog of hist 67-. 9: BSA. 10: Grolier Club. 13: Yes. 14: Catlg, rare bks. 15: 2 E Stanworth dr, Princeton NJ 08541.

COLEMAN, HENRY EDMUNDS JR. b Halifax Va 5 D 09. 5: Centre Col (Ky) 27-31 (Hist) AB; UNC 31-33 (Eng) AM; UIll 33-34 BS in LS; UMich 38-39 AMLS. 6: Fr. 7: Gen asst Northwestern U Lib 34-36; Supt ser & exch UIowa Lib 36-37, Supv dept libs 37-38; Ref libn West Wash Col 39-41; Libn Washington Col 41-42, 46-47; Libn Washington & Lee U 48-68, (Lib Emeritus 68-). 68, (Lib Emeritus 68-). 8: US ArmyAF 42-46. 9: ALA; VaLA. 10: Beta Phi Mu. 12: Comp (with T R Palfrey) "Guide to Bibliographies of Theses: US and Canada" ALA (2nd ed 37). 13: Yes. 14: Admin, acquis. 15: 2606-A Monument ave, Richmond Va 23220.

COLEMAN, JANET GREER. b Lincoln Neb 8 Ap 14. 4: Samuel D Coleman. 7: Libn Agric Experiment Station Oklahoma State (Stillwater) 35-39; Libn Geol-Geog Dept NorthwesternU (Evanston) 46-48; Catlgr Highland Park Pub Lib (Highland Park Ill) 49-58; Asst libn Field Enterprises Educ Corp (Chicago) 58-. 9: SLA. 14: Catlg, ref. 15: 2017 Fremont, Chicago Il 60614.

COLEMAN, JEAN ELLEN. b Brooklyn NY. 5: Hunter Col 51-56 (Hist) AB, 57-61 (Educ) MS; Pratt Institute 63-64 MLS. 6: Sp. 7: Lib clerk Brooklyn Pub Lib 50-55; Tchr San Carlos Indian Sch (Ariz) 56-57; Libn trainee Brooklyn Pub Lib 57-58; Tchr Jewish Guild for the Blind (NY) 58-63; Asst libn Lexington Sch for the Deaf (NY) 64-65; Libn Brooklyn Pub Lib (NYC) 66-68; Libn-Admin Bkmobile Serv Trust (Brooklyn NY) 68-. 8: Instr, Kan State Tchrs Col Sch of Libnship summer 69. 9: ALA. 10: Beta Phi Mu; Com for Commun Involvement; Pub Educ Assn. 14: Child & ya serv. 15: 577 Grand st, New York NY 10002.

COLEMAN, LAURA M. b Spring Glen Penn 3 Mr 23. 5: Millersville State Col 41-45 (LS, Educ) BS; UPittsburgh 65-66 MLS. 6: Ger. 7: Libn Hegins Twp Sch Dist, Hegins Penn 45-46; Lib asst NJ Col for Women 47-48; Docs asst & hd Penn State Lib, Harrisburg 46-47, 49-53; Docs libn Ida StateU (Pocatello) 54-58; Ser libn Penn StateU (Univ Park) 58-59; Ref libn Lycoming Col 59-65; Readers serv libn Williamsport Area Commun Col 66-. 9: PennLA. 14: Ref, ser, docs. 15: 344 E 4th st, Williamsport Pa 17701.

COLEMAN, MacDONALD. b Vanguard Sask Can 4 Mr 19. 4: Janet Orr Wilson. 5: USask 40-44 (Hist) BA, 45 BEd; UToronto 47 BLS. 6: Fr. 7: Br libn Regina Pub Lib, Regina Sask 47-49; Chief libn Brandon Pub Lib, Brandon Man 49-60; Asst chief libn Calgary Pub Lib, Calgary Alta60-64; Chief libn Red Deer Pub Lib, Red Deer Alta 64-. 9: AltaLA (pres 64); ManLA (v-pres 59). 10: Great Bks Groups. 12: "The Face of Yesterday; "A History of Brandon, Manitoba. 13: Yes. 14: Pub libs. 15: Pub Lib, Red Deer Alta Can.

COLESAR, REBECCA (CORDELIA) (BISBEE). b Riverside NJ 5 D 37. 4: Louis J Colesar Jr. 5: Oberlin Col 55-59 (Hist) AB; Rutgers 59-61 MLS. 7: Stud trainee RutgersU Lib 59-61; Ref libn III NJ State Lib 61-66; Bur of law and legis ref 61-64; Bur of Archives & Hist: 65-; Libn III 65-66; archival examiner 66-67; Archivist 67-. 9: ALA; NJLA (chm Geneal Com, Hist & Biog Sect); SAA. 10: NJ Hist Soc; AAUW; Rutgers Grad Sch of Lib Serv; Alumni Assn; US Coast Guard Auxiliary; Geneal Soc of NJ. 14: Archival & Geneal ref, NJ hist, geneal. 15: 15 W Union st, Burlington NJ 08016.

COLGROVE, KATHERINE L. b Willimantic Conn 12 Mr 04. 5: Conn Col 22-26 (Lat) BA; Drexel 31-32 BS in LS. 7: Catlgr Silas Bronson Lib (Waterbury Conn) 33-43; Trinity Col Lib (Conn) 43-49; Libn Watertown Lib (Watertown Conn) 50-53; Catlgr Silas Bronson Lib (Waterbury Conn) 54-. 9: ConnLA. 10: Conn Col Club. 14: Catlg. 15: 38 Crescent, Waterbury Ct 06710.

COLISH, JOHN LOUIS. b Greene Twp Penn 20 Jl 25. 4: Catherine M O Reilly. 5: Pace Col 46-49 (Accounting) BBA; Rutgers 63-65 MLS. 7: (Aviation Radioman) US Navy 43-46; Intelligence asst Central Intelligence Agency (Wash DC) 50-54; Airline reservations agent Trans World Airlines (Wash DC) 55; Admin asst The Rust Engnrg Co (Wash DC) 55-57; Self-employed with newspaper franchise (Plainfield NJ) 57-59; Sub clerk US Post Off (Elizabeth NJ) 59-61; Fed Credit Union Examiner, Bur of FCUs (NYC) 61-63; Sr libn Linden Pub Lib (Linden NJ) 63-67; Ser and acquis libn, Clarkson Col of Tech Lib 67-. 14: Acquis. 15: RFD #3 Hatch rd, Potsdam NY 13676.

COLL, JOHN DANIEL. b San Francisco 17 F 34. 4: Charlotte Gaffney. 5: USan Francisco 51-52; UCal (Berkeley) 52-55 (Hist) AB, 55-56 MLS. 6: Fr, Lat. 7: Libn San Francisco Pub Lib 56-58, Sr libn tech serv div 58-66, Spec acquis 66-. 9: SLA; CalLA. 10: San Francisco Coun for Civic Unity; Friends Com on Legis; Electric Railroaders Assn; Nat Assn of RR Passengers; Ry & Locomotive Hist Soc. 14: Ref serv (soc scis & hist). 15: 1530 5th ave, San Francisco CA 94122.

COLLESTANEH, REZVANIEH (EGHRARI). b Tehran Iran 22 Ag 24. 4: A H Collestaneh. 5: Col Arts & Lit UTehran 48 (Eng) BA, 67 (LS); Rosary Col 69 MALS. 6: Persian, Arabic, Fr, Ger. 7: Clk tr Fowler Insurance Co, Tehran Iran 49; Tchr lectr, Eng Scotland 50; Broadcaster-scriptwriter, New Delhi India 50-51; Receptionist US Embassy, Tehran Iran 51-53; Lecutrer-tchr Zeitouna U (Tunis) 59-61; Tchr Nat Inst for Eng Lang, Tehran 66. 9: ALA; IranLA. 10: Bhar Commun of the US; World Citizen; Internat Fellowship of India. 13: Yes. 14: Catlg (Persian & Arabic bks), rare bks. 15: 4 Erie, Oak Park Il 60302.

COLLETT, MARY JOAN. b St Louis 13 S 26. 5: Maryville Col (St Louis) 43-47 (Eng) BA (magna cum laude); WashingtonU (St Louis) 47-50 (Eng) MA; UIll (Urbana) 53-54 MS in LS. 6: Fr, Sp. 7: Info Dept Southwestern Bell Tel Co (St Louis) 48; Dir pub rel Maryville Col (St Louis) 49; Asst libn clayton Pub Lib (Clayton Mo) 50-53; Browsing room libn UIll (Urbana) 53-54; Reg consul W Va Lib Commsn (Spencer W Va) 54-56; Instr lib sci Rosary Col 56-57; Head ext dept Gary Pub Lib (Gary Ind) 57-64; Libn Grailville (Loveland Ohio) 64-66; Reg libn USIS Panama 66-69; Reg libn USIA (Wash DC) 69-. 9: ALA. 13: Yes. 14: Pub lib wk, recr, lib educ. 15: US Info Agency, Wash DC 20547.

COLLIER, BARBARA L. b Coxsackie NY 1 Ap 37. 5: SUNY (Fredonia) 54-56 (Music); SUNY (Geneseo) 56-59 BS in LS; University Col (Dublin) summer 59 (Irish hist & lit); Syracuse summer 62 (LS); UFla 68 (Anthropology). 7: Young adult libn Rochester Pub Lib (Rochester NY) 59-60; Elem libn horseheads Central Sch (Horseheads NY) 60-61; Jr high libn Greece Central Sch, Greece (Rochester NY) 61-62; Army libn US Army (Germany) 62-67; Ext libn US Army (Ft Benning

Ga) 67-68; Act chm circ dept UFla Libs (Gainesville) 68-. 9: ALA; FlaLA. 11: Outstanding Performance Rating, Army 66; certif of Achievement, Army 67. 14: Ya, ref, readers adv, admin, ext. 15: 3816 NW 45 st, Gainesville Fl 32601.

COLLIER, CARMEN P. b NYC 31 Jl 13. 4: Charles Vines Collier. 5: Katharine Gibbs Sch 31-33 (Bus admin); UTampa 33-36 (Eng); UFla 34-35 (Sp); Our Lady of the Lake 52-54 (Mod lang) BA, MSLS; U Nat Autonoma de Mexico 56 (Sp lit); Lib admin & mgt at USan Francisco 61. UCal at Berkeley 63 & 65, UCLA 65 & 67, UChicago 66. 6: Sp, Ger. 7: Ed Gen Foods Corp, NY 31-33; Med sec Fla 33-39; Sch consul Sloan's Bk & Toy Shop, Fla 51-52; Libn Ballast Point Sch, Fla 49-51; Consul Castroville High Sch, Tex 53; Libn Alamo Heights Schs, Tex 54-56; Libn St Francis High Sch, Cal 56-57; Libn Alemany High Sch, Cal 57-59; LA Co Pub Lib: Reg children's libn 57-64, Coordinator children's serv 64-. 8: Sch lib consul, CathLA 66-. 9: CathLA (Steering Com, Conv; sec SW Unit); ALA (A-V Com); CalLA; -CSD (pres Exec Bd, chm Lib Devel & Standards Com, Child Wk Consul; Standards Revision, etc); Sou Cal Coun on Lit (Exec Bd); Cal Ctr of Films (Exec Com) YA Reviews (sec Exec Bd). 10: PTA; LWV; Amer Red Cross. 12: Staff reviewer, "Best Sellers," Scranton Penn (58). 14: Child serv. 15: 8156 Deerfield dr, Huntington Beach Ca 92646.

COLLIER, DOROTHY BLACKWOOD. b Portsmouth Va 14 Mr 18. 5: UNH 37-41 (Langs) BA; West Res 48-49 (LS) BS. 6: Sp, Fr, Ger, Port. 7: Jr clerk typist Civil Service Commsn (Wash DC) 42-43; Clerk typist Bur of Supplies & Accounts Navy Dept (Wash DC) 43-44; Clerk Off of strategic Serv (Wash DC) 44-45; Libn State Dept (Wash DC) 45-55; Asst libn Internat Cooperation Admin (Wash DC) 55-61; Libn tr Govt Print Off (Wash DC) 62-. 9: SLA. 10: DAR; Encore Club (DC). 14: Catlg, ref, hist, geneal. 15: 9408 Worth ave, Silver Spring Md 20901.

COLLIER, (MARY) JEAN PIERCE. b Milford Ill 2 Ag 14. 4: John G Collier. 5: UIll 39-43 (Sociol) BA. 6: Fr. 7: Asst libn Milford Township Pub Lib, Milford Ill 34-37; Br libn Wayne Co Lib, Detroit 38-39; Tech UIll Lib at Urbana 39-42; Research asst Yale U 43-44; Tex Med Ctr Lib, Houston: Catlgr 55-64, Tech serv libn 65-66, Act libn 67-68, Libn 69-. 8: Established & maintained Oak Forest Elementary School Library, Houston, Texas 51-53; Consultant Garden Oaks Elementary School Library, Houston Texas 53; Faculty "Workshop for Hospital Librarians" Houston Texas 67; Dallas 68. 9: ALA; MedLA; SLA (Tex Chap Archivist 67-68); TexLA; Houston Lib Club; Tex Coun for Health Sci Libs. 11: Alpha Kappa Delta. 14: Catlg, ref, admin, rare bks. 15: 2431 Nottingham, Houston Tx 77005.

COLLIER, SUSAN E. b Doty Wash 9 F 14. 5: Centralia Jr Col 31-33; Linfield Col 36-38, 40 (Chem, Math) BA; WashingtonU (St Louis) 50. 7: US Naval Res (Lt) 42-46; US Geological Survey (Rolla Mo) 46-49; Geodetic computer Bonneville Power Admin (Portland Ore) 50; US Navy Extended Active Duty (Lt & Lt Commander) (Billets) 50-58; Communications Watch Off CNO (Wash DC) 50-53; OIC Classified Message Center CNO (Wash DC) 53-54; RPIO Pearl Harbor Com14 (Hawaii) 54-56; Head Intelligence Sect Operations Evaluation Group CNO (Wash DC) 58-60; Info spec & research libn The Martin co (Orlando Fla) 61-64; Tech libn R&D Lab, Ingersoll-Rand Co (Bedminster NJ) 64-. 9: Amer Soc of Photogrammetry; Amer Congress of Surveying & Mapping; SLA; US Naval Inst. 10: Soc Women Engrs. 14: Info research, automated storage & retrieval, bibliog, ref. 15: Ingersoll-Rand Res Inc Box 301, Princeton NJ 08540.

COLLIER, THELMA JOHNS. b Bulcher Tex 5 D 02. 4: Walter J Collier. 5: N Tex State U 37 (Elem Educ) BS, 39 (Elem Educ) MA, 49 Lib Certif. 7: Tchr Montague Co Schs 21-36; Tchr-libn St Jo High Sch 42-49; Tchr Denison Pub Schs 50; Libn Graham Sr High Sch 51-52; Libn Denison Sr High Sch 53-62; Asst ref libn N Tex State U 63-. 9: TexLA (sec-treas Dist 7). 10: Bluebonnet Study Club; Delta Kappa Gamma; Tex StateTA; NEA; TexLA; Woman's Shakespeare Club. 14: Ref. 15: 1213 Hillcrest, Denton Tx 76201.

COLLIER, VIRGINIA SPORE. b Dallas 14 F 19. 5: UTex 36-40 (Eng) BA; Emory 41 BS in LS. 6: Fr, Sp. 7: Co libn Austin Pub Lib, Austin Tex 40-43; Asst libn McCloskey ArmyHosp Lib, Temple Tex 43-44; Asst br libn Oakland Pub Lib, Oakland Cal 45; Libn Okmulgee Pub Lib, Okmulgee Okla 53-60; Dir of bkmobs TulsaCity-Co Lib, Tulsa Okla 60-66, Br libn Nathan Hale Br 67, Dist libn West Br area 68; Lib consul Okla Dept of Libs 68-. 9: ALA (memb chm Okla 64-, Com on Interlib Coop 64-67); SWLA (chm Pub Lib Sect 60-62); OklaLA (sec 58-59, chm Pub Lib Div 56-58, chm ResolCom 63, mem Bylaws & Const Com 64-65). 10: AAUW; LWV; Tulsa Club. 11: Okmulgee Co, Mother of the Year, 59. 12: Ed "Texas News Notes," TexLA (42-43). 14: Lib construction. 15: 4316 NW 56 t, Oklahoma City OK 73112.

COLLINGS, LOIS W. b Des Plaines Ill 22 Ap 16. 4: Wayne R Collings. 5: Rockford Col 34-38 (Hist) BA; Chicago 45-46 BLS. 6: Fr, Lat. 7: Elem tchr Pub Schs (Des Plaines Ill) 38-42; Sch libn Des Plaines (Ill) Jr High 42-46; Sch libn Lakeview Sch (Battle Creek Mich) 46-47; Libn Christian Col 47-50; child coordinator Lincoln City Libs (Lincoln Neb) 61-64; Assoc dir 64-67; Hd libn WesleyanU (Lincoln) 67-. 8: Bibliog research for agric Econ Dept uneb 58-59. 9: ALA; MPLA; NebLA (pres 64-65, Exec Bd 63-66); Neb Educ Media Assn. 10: Altrusa International; Beta Phi Mu; LincolnLA. 13: Yes. 14: Child lit, admin. 15: 2700 Van Dorn, Lincoln Nb 68502.

COLLINGS, WAYNE R. b Paris Ida 27 Mr 19. 4: Lois Wiffin Collings. 5: Utah StateU 37-42 (Hist) BS; Chicago 46-47 BLS. 7: US Army (Tech Sgt) AACS, European Theatre 42-45; Agric libn UMo (Columbia) 47-54; Agric libn UNeb 54-. 8: Consul in establishing lib at AtaturkU (Erzerum Turkey) 59; consul Kan States MASUA program in engring educ UAssiut (Egypt) 67. 9: ALA-ACRL (sect chm 64-65; pres Sgric & Bio Subsect Sub, Specialists Sect 65-66); NebLA (chm Col & U Lib Sect 62-63); IAALD. 10: AAUP; Gamma Sigma Delta. 13: "Land-Grant College Libraries in the Moslem World 968). 14: Agric & biol scis, admin, ref. 15: 2700 Van Dorn, Lincoln Nb 68502.

COLLINS, ANN (GRIFFIN). b Birmingham Ala 3 My 05. 4: Robert H Collins Jr. 5: Huntingdon Col 22-23 (Liberal Arts & LS); AuburnU summer 23; Emory summer 24; UGa 23-24, 24-25 (Soc Sci) AB; UAla summers 62-65 MA in Libnship. 6: Fr. 7: Temp asst Carnegie Lib, Atlanta summer 26; Tchr-Fr Sidney Lanier High, Montgomery Ala 25-29; Tchr-Fr & Eng Mildred Dean Sch, Montgomery Ala 38-39, 39-40; Tchr-Fr & Eng Cuthbert High Sch, Cuthbert Ga 48-49, 49-50; Libn City-Co Lib, Cuthbert Ga 58-61; Hd libn Andrew Col 61-. 9: ALA; GaLA; SELA. 10: Cuthbert Garden Club; Cuthbert Music Club; Great Bks Gp; Delta Kappa Gamma; Kappa Delta Pi. 14: Catlg, ref. 15: 143 North st, Cuthbert Ga 31740.

COLLINS, ANNE CRATHORNE (COUGHLIN). b Chicago Ill 25 Jl 39. 4: James Wagner Collins Jr. 5: Pembroke 57-61 (Amer Lit) AB; Harvard 62-63 (Educ) EdM; Columbia 67-69 MLS. 6: Fr. 7: Tchr: Walden Pub Schs, NY 63-64, Boston Pub Lib, Roxbury 64-65, Mt Vernon Pub Schs, NY 65-66; Lib asst ColumbiaU 66-67; Libn trainee NY Pub Lib 67-. 8: Elected mem of Columbia Sch of Lib Serv stud coun 68-69. 9: ALA. 14: Child wk in pub libs. 15: 79 West 12th st, New York NY 10011.

COLLINS, AUDREY W. b Albany Ga 26 D 17. 5: Ga State Col for Women 35-39 (Eng) AB; George Peabody Col 55-57 (LS) MA; Ball StateU 60-64. 6: Fr, Sp. 7: Tchr Gordon High Sch, Gordon Ga 39-40; Tchr Albany Voc Sch, Albany Ga 40-42; Tchr Albany High Sch, Albany Ga 47-57; Ser libn East IllU 57-60; Period libn Ball StateU 60-. 9: ALA. 14: Ser. 15: 708 N McKinley, Muncie In 47303.

COLLINS, BARBARA L. b Plainfield NJ 18 D 45. 5: Albright Col 63-67 (Eng) BA; Rutgers 67-68 MLS. 6: Fr. 7: Asst ref catlgr Scotch Plains Pub Lib, Scotch Plains NJ 68-. 9: NJLA. 14: Ref, catlg. 15: 218 E Ninth st, Plainfield NJ 07060.

COLLINS, BLANCHE WALLACE. b Visalia Cal 8 F 03. 5: Mills Col 21-24 AB; Carnegie 25 Libnship Certif. 7: Child libn Pub Lib (Long Beach Cal) 25-28; Br libn 28-43; Head sci & tech dept 43-51; Asst libn 51-60; City libn 60-. 9: ALA; CalLA (pres Pub Libs Sect 64); Pub Lib Exec Assn of So Cal (v-pres 58, pres 63). 10: LWV; Libraria Sodalitas; AAUW; Bd of Long Beach Chap; Nat Conf of Christs & Jews; Advis Bd Long Beach Chap; Advis Bd long Beach Fiar Housing Found Assn; Beta Pi Mu; Altrusa Club; Los Angeles Philharmonic Symphony Assn; Adv Com, Los Angeles Co Dept of Mental Health; Cal Cong Parents & Tchrs. 11: Citizens Award, Long BeachTA; Commendation for Dedicated Pub Serv, C of C; Proclamation of Merit, Long Beach City Coun. 13: Yes. 14: Admin. 15: 4008 E 5th st, Long Beach Ca 90814.

COLLINS, ELEANOR STUART. b Rochester NY 5 Mr 08. 5: Hiram Col 27-29 (Liberal Arts); Simmons 29-31 (LS) BS; Smith 39-41 (Hist of Art) BA. 6: Fr, Ital, Ger. 7: Ref asst Rochester (NY) Pub Lib 31-37; Curator of bks Smith Col Art Dept 37-41; Head slide & photo collection Art Inst, Chicago 41-44; Ref libn Pease Mem Lib, Ridgewood NJ 44-46; Curator slide & photograph collection Dept of Hist of Art UMich (Ann Arbor) 46-. 8: Consul, Org of Slide Collection Honolulu Acad of Arts 62. 9: College Art Asso. 10: Friends of the Ann

Arbor Pub Lib, Ann Arbor Mich. 14: Catlg visual aids. 15: 703 S Forest ave, Ann Arbor MI 48104.

COLLINS, ELIZABETH (HARPER). b Centreville Md 23 D 15. 4: Jackson Rosse Collins. 5: Goucher 37 (Econ & Sociol) AB; Rutgers 57 MLS. 6: Fr. 7: Desk asst Enoch Pratt Free Lib, Baltimore 37, 40, 44-45, 53-54; Co lib admin Queen Annes Co Free Lib, Centreville Md 54-59; Co lib admin talbot Co Free Lib, Easton Md 59-68; Ref libn Chesapeake Col, Wye Mill Md 69-. 8: State Lib Commsn to revise pub lib laws 68-69. 9: ALA; MDLA (v-pres 61-62); Assn of Md Pub Lib Admin (pres 64). 10: AAUW; Delta Kappa Gamma; Queen Annes Co Hist Soc. 15: Chesapeake College Lib, Wye Mills Md 21679.

COLLINS, EUGENIA AVERY. b Gallion Ala 26 My 11. 5: Ala Col 28-32 (Hist) AB Sec; UAla summer 38; UFla summer 39; Peabody summers 43-45 BS in LS. 7: Tchr Greensboro High Sch (Greensboro Ala) 34-35; Tchr & libn in Fla High Schls 38-45; Libn Judson Col 45-53; Asst libn Third US Army post Lib (Camp Gordon Ga) 53-54; US Army Libs in Korea HQ 8th US Army 54-59; Libn I Prof Atlanta Pub Lib 60; Libn US Artillery & MSL Center 9ft Sill Okla) 60-61; Asst libn White Sands Missile Range (NM) 61-. 9: ALA (life mem); AlaLA (life mem). 14: Catlg, ref. 15: Post Lib Bldg 464, White Sands Missile Range NM.

COLLINS, EVELYN ALDWYTH. b Albion NY 17 F 08. 5: URochester 26-30 (Lat) AB; State Tchrs (Albany NY) 34-35 (LS) BS. 7: Soc studies tchr Albion (NY) High Sch 36-38, Libn 38-. 9: NEA; ALA-AASchL; NY State tchrs Assn; NYLA. 10: PTA; Cobblestone Soc. 15: 124 W Academy st, Albion NY 14411.

COLLINS, EVRON SHARLENE. b Bowling Green Ohio 23 Ap 37. 5: Bowling Green StateU 55-59 (Eng) BA; UIll 59-60 MS in LS. 6: Fr. 7: Biol libn northwesternU 60-63; Head circ dept Bowling Green StateU Lib 63-. 9: ALA; OhioLA. 14: Circ. 15: Bowling Green State Univ Lib, Bowling Green Oh 43402.

COLLINS, FORREST WARREN JR. b Charlotte NC 4 S 39. 5: Davidson Col 57-61 (Eng, Hist) AB; UMich 64-65 AMLS; UCal (La) 69, (African Studies) MA. 6: Fr, Swahili. 7: Clerk Pub Lib of Charlotte & Mecklenberg Co (Charlotte NC) 64; Clerk Undergrad Lib UMich 65; Libn NY Pub Lib Amer Hist Div 65-; Libn inf div 68. 8: Peace Corps 65-68; NY Pub Lib Survey of Africana 68. 9: ALA. 10: Beta Phi Mu. 14: Ref, rare bks, Africana. 15: 702 Norwood st, Shelby NC 28150.

COLLINS, GERALD A. b Lebanon Penn 3 Ag 42. 5: Millersville State Col 60-64 (Ed) BS; Drexel 66- (LS). 7: Lib aide Lebanon Commun Col, Lebanon Penn 58-64; Cocalico Sch Dist, Denver Penn: Elem libn 64-68, Dir lib serv 68-. 9: NEA; ALA; Nat Trust for Hist Preserv; PennStateEA; CocalicoEA; Found of Penn. 10: Lebanon Co Hist Soc; Commun Concert Assn; Lebanon Coun of Churches (Bd of dirs); Evangelical & Reformed Hist Soc. 14: Child libnship. 15: 905 S Third ave, Lebanon Pa 17042.

COLLINS, HILDA (LAWRENCE). b Los Angeles 18 Ap 05. 5: UCal(Los Angeles) 28 (Eng) AB; USoCal 29 Certif of Libnship. 7: Br child lib Los Angeles City Lib 29-37; Supv child lib Los Angeles Co Lib, Los Angeles 37-42; Child libn Tulare Co Lib, Visalia Cal 50-54, County libn 54-68; Reg libn SEast Sask Reg Lib, Weyburn Sask 68-. 9: ALA; CanLA; CalLA (Dist Pres); SaskLA. 10: AAUW; Bus & Prof Women's Club; Internat Platform Assn; Can Fed Unit Woman. 14: Admin, wk with child. 15: 938 W Iris st, Visalia CA 9327.

COLLINS, JEAN L. b Pittsburgh Pa 22 Je 25. 5: UPittsburgh 58 (Eng Lit) BA. 7: Sec Providence Mutual Insurance Co (Pittsburgh) 43-44; Sec Allegheny Co Memorial Park (Pittsburgh) 45; Sec to res dir Sch of Retailing UPittsburgh 46-50; Research asst 51-53; Libn 54-55; Marketing libn ketchum Macleod & Grove Inc (Pittsburgh) 56-58; Supv Info Serv Ketchum Macleod & Grove Inc (Pittsburgh) 68-. 9: SLA. 10: Phi Beta Kappa. 15: 30 Ansonia pl, Pittsburgh Pa 15210.

COLLINS, JOHN F. b St Louis 13 D 22. 4: Jean Forbus Collins. 5: So Methodist U 46-48 (Econ) BA; UWash 63-65 (LS) M of L. 6: Fr. 7: (1st Sgt) US Army 43-46; Tchr, Seattle 48-63; Libn Edison Tech Sch, Seattle 63- Libn Seattle Commun Col 66-. 9: ALA; Wash State ASchL. 10: Seattle Commun Col Fed of Tchrs. 15: 2820 34th ave S, Seattle WA 98122.

COLLINS, MARGARET M. b Wilkes-Barre Penn 24 Je 40. 5: Dunbarton Col of Holy Cross 58-62 (Sociol) BA; Marywood Col 62-64 (LS) MS. 7: Libn Ref Dept Osterhout Free Lib (Wilkes-Barre Penn) 63-. 9: CathLA; PennLA. 14: Ref. 15: 258 S River st, Wilkes-Barre Pa 18702.

COLLINS, ORAL EDMOND. b Alton NY 9 My 28. 4: Joyce Towle. 5: Berkshire Christian Col 46-50 (Theol) AB in Th; Gordon Divinity Sch 50-53 (Theol) BD; Simmons 53-56 (LS); NYU summer (Hebrew);Brandeis U 64- (Judaic Studies). 6: Grk, Hebrew, Ger. 7: Instr Berkshire Christian Col 51-54; Libn & assoc prof of Bible 54-66; Libn & prof of Bible 66-. 9: Christ Libns Fellowship (var offs 60-65); BerkshireLA. 13: Yes. 14: Admin, bk sel. 15: Berkshire Christian Col Stockbridge rd, Lenox Ma 01240.

COLLINS, RAYMOND BERNARD. b Cleveland Ohio 1 Je 21. 4: Doris M Collins. 5: Adelbert Col West ResU 46-49 (Lit) BA; West Res 49-50 MS in LS. 7: (Pharmacists Mate 1/C) US Navy 42-46; Cleveland Pub Lib: Page & head page Main Lib 46-49; Stud aid various brs 49-50; Bkmob libn 50-56; Br libn Sterling Br 56-57; Cuyahoga Co Lib Br libn Suburban Brs 57-59; Reg supv Parma Reg 59-61; Tech serv dir Hdqrs (Cleveland) 61-66; Cleveland Pub Lib: Hd Catlg Dept 66-67; Cuyahoga Commun Col: Dir Metro Campus Lib 67-68; Cleveland State U Lib: Asst Dir for Syst & Tech Serv 68-. 9: ALA; OhioLA. 14: Tech serv, admin. 15: 363 West River rd, Valley City Oh 44280.

COLLINS, RUBY L. b Mass 7 Jl 14. 5: Radcliffe 32-36 (Eng Lit) AB; Simmons 38-39 BLS; Columbia 53-58 (Philos Found) MA. 7: Catlgr Antioch Col 39-42; Asst NY Pub Lib several brs 42-43; Acquis asst State U of Mich 43-44; Child libn Hasbrouck Heights Pub Lib (Hasbrouck Heights NJ) 44-45; Head libn McGraw-Hill Publ Co (NYC) 45-47; Libn & researcher Vilhjalmur Stefansson Lib (NYC) 47-51; Catlgr & chief of circ Hunter Col 51-53; Coordinator of ref & readers servs Tchrs Col ColumbiaU 54-58; Coord lib tech progr Cambrian Col (Ont) 68-. 9: ALA; SLA; NY Catlgrs Assn; canLA; OntLA; Inst Prof Libns Ont. 14: Catlg, ref, lib educ. 15: Cambrian College 261 Notre Dame ave, Sudbury Ontario Can.

COLLINS, WANETA I (GRAVES). b Milford Ill 19 S 10. 5: ButlerU 28-32 (Educ) BS, 57-59 (Educ) MS. 6: Fr. 7: Typist Tipton Co Commissioners (Tipton Ind) 56-58; Tchr Tipton Sch System (Tipton Ind) 59; Head libn Tipton Co Lib (Tipton Ind) 59-. 9: ALA; IndLA (Child & yp RT; sec-treas 64-65, chm 65-66). 10: Kappa Kappa Kappa; Ind Button Soc. 14: Admin. 15: Tipton County Pub Lib 127 E Madison, Tipton In 46072.

COLLINSWORTH, BARBARA LEE (HOWLE). b Detroit Mich 16 Jl 34. 4: Edward L Collinsworth. 5: Central Mich U 51-55 (Hist, Sch Libnship) BA; UMich 66-67, summers 59, 65, 66 AMLS. 6: Sp, Fr. 7: Sr high libn Clawson Pub Schs, Clawson Mich 55-56; Elem libn Pontiac Pub Schs, Pontiac Mich 57; Sr High libn Lake Orion Commun Schs, Lake Orion Mich 57-59; Jr high libn Walled Lake Consolidated Schs, Walled Lake Mich 59-68; Coord lib serv Co commun Col 68-. 9: ALA; COLT; MichASchL; MacombCoLA. 10: Beta Phi Mu. 14: Lib educ, wk with yp. 15: 33654 Colfax dr, Sterling Heights Mi 48077.

COLLISON, ROBERT (LEWIS WRIGHT). b London England 2 My 14. 4: Mary Marshall. 5: ULondon 36-39; Chartered libn & fellow of The Lib Assn 34. 6: Fr, Ger, Lat, swahili. 7: Asst Hendon Pub Lib, London England 30-33; Lending libn Exeter City Lib, Devon England 33-35; Chief catlgr Essex Co Lib, Chelmsford England 35-36; Deputy borough libn Colchester Pub Lib, Essex England 36-39; Deputy borough libn Ealing Pub lib, London England 39-46; British Army, Africa & SE Asia 40-46; Ref libn USIS, London England 47-48; Ref libn City of Westminster, London England 48-58; Libn BBC, London England 58-68; Hd ref dept Univ Research Lib, LA 68-; Prof Grad Sch of Lib serv UCLA 69-. 8: Chm Documentation Com British Standards Inst 67-. 9: Soc of Indexers (v-pres 67-); The Hispanic & luso-Brazilian Couns, London (chm Lib Com 61-68); AsLib (past v-chm & mem Exec Com); The (Brit) Lib Assn Sr Examiner 50-68. 11: Fulbright Scholar UCLA 51-52. 12: "Bibliographical Services Throughout the World" (52); "Bibliographies, Subject & National" (3rd ed 68); "Indexes and Indexing" (3rd ed 69); "Encyclopaedias & Their Bibliographical History" (2nd ed 67); "Library assistance to Readers" (5th ed 67); "Commercial & Industrial Record Storage" (69); "Indexing Books" (69). 14: Ref wk. 15: 933 Hilgard ave, Los Angeles Ca 90024.

COLLURA, MAUREEN (FENNIE). b Buffalo NY 15 Je 38. 4: Frank Charles Collura. 5: Rosary Hill Col 56-60 (Hist) BA; Pratt Inst 62-63; SUNY (Geneseo) 64-66 MLS. 6: Sp. 7: Libn trainee NY Pub Lib 63; Libn trainee Buffalo& Erie Co Pub Lib 64; Libn Buffalo Pub Sch 66-67; Asst ref libn Butler Lib

SUNY (Buffalo) 68-. 14: Ref (child). 15: 701 Auburn ave, Buffalo NY 14222.

COLMER, MARY CLEO (WHITE). b McComb Miss 10 Ja 20. 4: Dr Arthur R(ussell) Colmer. 5: Miss Womans Col 37-40 (Chem); Miss Col 40-41 (Chem) BA; LSU 49-51 BS in LS, 57-58 (Educ) MA. 6: Sp. 7: Math tchr Taylorsville High Sch (Taylorsville Miss) 41-42; LSU: Jr catlgr 51-52; Sr catlgr 52-54, 58-62; Chem libn 54-58; Asst libn 62-63; Asst prof Lib Sch 63-67; Assoc libn 67-. 9: ALA; LaLA. 10: Phi Kappa Phi. 13: Yes. 14: Catlg. 15: 6039 Chandler dr, Baton Rouge La 70808.

COLOMBO, ELDA. b Chicago Ill 1 A 09. 5: Chicago 4 (Humanities) BA, 46 BLS. 6: Ital, Fr. 7: Chicago Pub Lib: Jr ib asst 26-36; Ref libn 36-54; Br libn 54-59; Chief of Educ Dept 59-65; Asst libn Cent Lib 65-. 9: ALA; NEA; IllLA (v-chm Lib Sect); Chicago Lib Club; AEA USA; Adult Ed Coun 9ed Comm); AEA Ill. 13: Yes. 14: Pub lib admin. 15: Chicago Pub Lib 78 E Washington st, Chicago Il 60602.

COLQUETTE, RICHARD LEE. b Wynnewood Okla 3 Jl 26. 5: UArk 43-44; Army Spec Train Program Tex A&M, UVa 44-45; LSU 46-48 BA U Nac de San Marcos (Lima Peru); Columbia 51-53; LSU 63-65 MS (LS). 6: Sp. 7: US Army 44-46, 50-51; Comptroller trainee Standard Oil Co (NJ, US, Venezuela, Can) 53-56; Accountant Humble Oil & Refg Co (Baton Rouge La) 56-63; LSU: Lib trainee 63-64; Sr libn 64-65; Chief acquis libn 65-68; Asst dir tech serv 68-. 9: ALA; LaLA; SWLA (chm Tech Svcs Sec 68-). 10: Baton Rouge Lib Club; Beta Phi Mu; Sigma Alpha Epsilon; Phi Kappa Phi; Phi Eta Sigma; Beta Gamma Sigma; Alpha Kappa Psi; Mu Sigma Rho. 13: Yes. 14: Tech serv, Latin Amer studies. 15: 439 N 5th st apt 30, Baton Rouge La 70801.

COLQUITT, KAY C. b Dallas Ga 4 Mr 41. 5: Emory-at-Oxford 59-61; Emory 61-63 (Eng) BA, 66-69 MLS. 7: High sch tchr DeKalb Co Bd of Educ, Decatur Ga 63-65; Asst research scientist Ga Tech Ind Development Div, Atlanta 65-. 9: GaLA; SELA. 12: "Directory of Scientific Resources in Georgia" (67); "Directory of Statewide and Regional Associations and Organizations in Georgia" (68). 14: Catlg, ref. 15: Industrial Dev Ga Inst of Tech 1132 West Peachtree st, Atlanta Ga 30309.

COLSON, JOHN. b Kingman Ind 9 D 26. 4: Marjo rie Brian. 5: Ohio U 44-50 (Amer Hist) AB; West Res 50-51 MS in LS; Chicago 60-61, 68-69. 6: Fr. 7: T/5 US Army Philippines Japan 44-46; Libn I Milwaukee Pub Lib 51-53; Suc libn State Hist S of Wis, Madison Wis 53-60, Acquis libn 61-65; Asst Prof UMd Sch of Lib & Info Serv 66-. 9: SLA (chm Soc Sci Div 58-59); WisLA (chm Col Libs Sect 64-65, chm Int Freedom Com 65-66; MdLA. 11: Beta Phi Mu Award 61. 12: Ed "Soc Sciences Div Bulletin" SLA (58-60). 13: Yes. 14: Lib hist, lib educ. 15: Sch of Lib & Info Serv, College Pk Md 20742.

COLSON, JUDITH (KELLY). b Syracuse NY 1 S 36. 4: Theodore Colson. 5: Roberts Wesleyan Col 54-58 (Eng) BA; Syracuse 59-60 MSLS. 6: Fr. 7: Jr libn Syracuse Pub Lib, Syracuse NY 60-61; Documents acquis libn UMich (Ann Arbor) 61-63, Ser acquis libn 63-67; Doc libn UNB 67-. 9: ALA; CanLA, APLA. 10: Beta Phi Mu. 14: Acquis docs, maps, ser. 15: 230 Winslow st, Fredericton NB Can.

COLTHARP, JENNIE SUE. b Hickory Flat Miss 18 O 06. 5: Miss State Col for Women 24-28 (Hist, Eng) AB; Tulane summers 33, 34, 36 (Hist); UAla summer 35 (LS); LSU summers 38-41 BS in LS, summer 68. 6: Fr. 7: Libn High Sch, Indianola Miss 36-40; Libn Sr High Sch, Vicksburg Miss 40-45; Libn Metairie Park Country Day Sch, New Orleans 45-48; Libn High Sch, Potts Camp Miss 48-68; Libn Sr High Sch, Holly Springs Miss 58-68; Librarian Middle Sch, Amory Miss 69-. 8: Organized elementary library in Holly Springs; consultant for a clinic for school librarians at Abilene Christian College, Texas. 9: ALA; LaLA (treas); MissLA (chm, Awards Com 69- treas); SELA; MissEA. 14: Instr materials for grades 5-8. 15: Hickory Flat Ms 38633.

COLTMAN, NATALIE (WALSH). b Reading Mass 26 O 09. 5: Vassar 27-31 (Eng) AB; Drexel 59-60 MS in LS. 6: Fr, Sp. 7: Sec Riis & Bonner Publicity Agency (NY) 33-35; Account exec R W Riis Assoc Publicity Agency (NY) 35-39; Sec to pres John Day Publ Co (NY) 40-43; Asst libn Delaware Valley Col 57-60; Head libn 60-63; Head catlgr Bucks Co Free Lib (Doylestown Penn) 64-67; Tech serv libn 67-. 9: ALA; PennLA. 10: Beta Phi Mu; Doylestown Country Club; Forest Lake Fishing Club. 14: Ref, catlg, bk sel. 15: Rt 1 Box 165, Perkasie Pa 18944.

COLTON, FLORA (LOUISE DEIBERT). b Birdsboro Penn 1 Mr 17. 4: George A Colton. 5: Wilson Col 35-39 (Eng) BA; Drexel 44 BS in LS; UPenn 55 (Anthropology) MA. 7: Tchr Fairview Borough & Twp Joint High Sch (Fairview, Erie Co Penn) 40-41; Tchr Upper Chichester Twp Joint High Sch (B00thwyn Penn) 41-43; Ref asst UPenn Main Lib 43-52; Head ref dept UPenn Van Pelt Lib 52-68; Instr advanced ref Drexel 64, summer 60; Libn Hdqrs Lib ALA (Chicago) 68-. 8: Instr adv ref Drexel Sch of Lib Sci summer 60m fall 64. 9: ALA-ACRL (pres Phila Chap 59-61); SLA; PennLA (chm Interim Com on Penn State Docs 60-61). 14: Ref. 15: 8545 S Avalon ave, Chicago Il 60619.

COLVERD, MARTIN (HENRY). b London England 22 S 28. 5: Balliol Col Oxford U 49-52 (Mod hist); Johns Hopkins 55 (Hist); Sch of Lib Serv Columbia 65-67 MS. 6: Fr. 7: British Army Pay Corps 47-49; Far east trainee Harrisons & Crosfield Ltd, Lond Eng 52-54; PX store mgr USA Aberdeen Md 54-56; Amer Electric Power Co NY: Asst records mgr 56-63, Libn 63-66; Proj analyst Pandex Inc, NY 67; Research Asst Rothines Assocs, NY 67; ColumbiaU: Asst libn engineering lib 67-68, Asst libn Burgess-Carpenter Lib 68-. 8: Survey of the tech serv operations of the Memphis Pub Lib system 67. Currently wking on a computer-rpduced indexing system as a research asst to Theodore C Hines Columbia U. 9: ALA; ASIS. 10: Beta Phi Mu; Oxford Union Soc. 12: "Technical Services for the Memphis and Shelby County Public Libraries," (67). 14: Lib admin (emphasis on computer applications). 15: 410 Park pl, Fort Lee NJ 07024.

COLVILLE-STEWART, SANDRA BRONWEN. b Devynock United Kingdom 11 F 44. 5: UEdinburgh 63-66 (Biochem) BS; NWest Polytech 67 British ALA. 6: Fr. 7: Lib asst Brixton Sch of Building, London UK 66; MEDLARS search analyst UCLA Biomed Lib 68-. 9: The Lib Assn (UK); Med Lib Group of So Cal; UCLA Libns' Assn. 14: Ref, SDI. 15: 427 Montana ave, Santa Monica Ca 90403.

COLVIN, DOROTHY (TOMPKINS). b Syracuse NY 8 Ag 18. 5: SyracuseU 55-57 (LS); SUNY(Geneseo) 57-61 MLS. 6: Fr. 7: Libn Carthage Free Lib, Carthage NY 45-55; Libn South Jr High, Watertown NY 55-57; Libn Copenhagen Central Sch, Copenhagen NY 57-59;Libn Ballston Spa Central Schs, Ballston Spa NY 59-62; Hd child serv Albany Pub Lib, Albany NY 62-64; Child libn Harrison Memorial Lib,Carmel Cal 64-67; Consul child serv Ramapo Catskill Lib Syst, Middletown NY 67-. 9: ALA; NYLA (sec-treas CYSS 62-64). 14: Children's serv. 15: RD #1 Ski Run rd, Bloomingburg NY 12721.

COLVIN, LAURA CATHERINE. b Richmond Va 26 N 05. 5: Col of William & Mary 30 (Eng) AB; UMich 34 ABLS, 38 AMLS. 6: Fr, Ger. 7: Sec to libn & gen asst Col of William & Mary 30-33; Catlgr Swarthmore Col Lib 34-35; Asst libn & head catlgr Agnes Scott Col Lib 35-42; Ed "Union Library Catalog of Atlanta-Athens Area" Emory U Lib 40-42; Act chief catlg dept Swarthmore Col Lib 42-43; Simmons Col Sch of Lib Sci: Asst Prof 43-48, Assoc Prof 48-52, Prof 52-67; Prof Sch of Lib & Info Sci, UWest Ont 67-. 8: Guest faculty mem for summer sessions: UIll Lib Sch 39; Columbia Sch of Lib Serv 45, 46; UCal(Berkeley) Sch of Libnship 55, 61; Consul Acquis Unit UNLib, NYC summer 51 Ext Exam, Tech Serv, Inst of Libnship, Fac of Educ, U of Ibadan, Nigeria, J 69, Consul Tech Serv, 65- 9: Coun of Nat Lib Assns (v-chm 49-50); AALS; ALA (Coun 43-47, Nomin Com 54-55, Dewey Award Jury 58-59); -ACRL; -Catlg & Clsf Sect (v-pres 48-49, pres 49-50, chm 3 reg groups, chm &/or mem 3 coms); -LED; -RTSD (Conf Program Com 60-61; Com mem of Catlg & Clsf Sect 54-; Com mem of Ser Sect 60-61); AALS; CNLA (v-chm 49-50); Lib Assn (Gt Brit); MassLA (Educ Com 61-63); NELA; NE Tech Serv Libns; CanLA; OntLA; Can Assn Lib Schs. 10: AAUP; Phi Beta Kappa; Phi Kappa Phi; Alpha Chi Omega; Can Asso of Univ Tchrs. 11: Margaret Mann Citation, 65. 12: "Cataloging Sampler: A Comparative and Interpretive Guide" (63). 13: Yes. 14: Catlg, clsf, tech serv, univ libnship, catlg code revision; lib educ. 15: Sch of Lib & Info Sci, Univ of West Ont, London Ont Can.

COLVIN, MARY (MINTER). b Woolsey Ga 26 D 06. 4: James Joseph Colvin. 5: Ga State Woman's Col 22-24 (Eng) 2-yr diploma, 24-26 (Educ) BS; Emory 30-31 (LS) BS. 7: Lib asst Ga Inst of Tech 31-44; Tech ref libn AEDC Lib ARO Inc, Arnold AF Station Tenn 53-56, lib sect supv 56-. 9: SLA. 14: Bk sel, ref. 15: AEDC Lib ARO Inc, Arnold Air Force Station, Tn 37389.

COMAN, EDWIN TRUMAN JR. b Colfax Wash 18 My 03. 4: Evelyn Buckingham Brownell. 5: Yale 22-26 (Econ) BA; UCal 32-33 (Libnship Certif); claremontU 33-34 (Econ) MA. 6:

Fr, Sp. 7: New bus solicitor Amer Trust Co (San Francisco) 26-28; Bond salesman Dean Witter & Co (San Francisco) 29-32; Lib research asst Claremont Col 33-36; Exec sec Soc for Oriental Studies (Claremont Cal) 34-36; Dir & asst prof (Bus Hist) StanfordU Grad Sch of Bus Lib 36-42, 45-50; (Capt) USAF 42-45; University libn UCal (Riverside) 51-66 (ret). 8: Consul UMiami Bus Lib 59-61; Bldg consul USanta Clara 61; Bldg consul Cal Acad of Sci (San Francisco) 62-63; Consul on building lib collection Cal Baptist Col 63-66; Consul on org spec lib Bank of America (San Francisco) 64; Consul study org Honnold Lib ClaremontU 65; Consul planning org & staffing a spec financial lib bank of Cal (San Francisco) 65; Survey resources & serv to bus & industry in state of Ore 66; Accreditation teams of the West Col Assn, consul ALA. 9: ALA (Coun 50-51); -ACRL (chm Bldg Com 59-61); SLA (Com on Recruitment 57-58); CalLA (pres 49). 10: Kiwanis Club Bd 58; Bishops Warden, St Michaels Episcopal Mission 63-65; Citizens Com to Plan New Riverside Pub Lib Bldg 62; Chm Advis Com on State Correctional Insts Libs 61-64; Trustee Lib Assn of La Jolla; Trustee San Miguel Sch for Boys; Exhibit Com; San Diego Zool Soc. 11: Sla Award for Most Outstanding contribution to Special Librarianship in 1949. 12: "Sources of Business Information (49, Rev Ed 64); "Time, Tide and Timber with H M Gibbs (49). 13: Yes. 14: Admin, bldgs, hist of bus. 15: 5784 Bellevue ave, La Jolla Ca 92037.

COMAROMI, JOHN PHILLIP. b Flint Mich 4 Ap 37. 4: Myung Ock Park. 5: Northwestern U 55-56 (Chem Engnr); Flint Jr Col 58-59 (Eng); Flint Col UMich 59-61 (Eng) AB; UMich 61-64 AMLS, 64-65 (Eng) MA. 6: Ger, Fr, Sp. 7: US Army Security Agency 56-58; High sch libn Flushing High Sch (Flushing Mich) 63-64; Asst ref libn C S Mott Lib (Flint Mich) 64-65; Circ libn 65-66; Instr LS UMich 66-68; Asst prof Sch of Libnship UOre 69-. 9: ALA. 10: Mich Eng Tchrs Assn; Phi Beta Kappa. 14: Admin, educ for libnship. 15: 1505 Em Rey dr, Eugene Or 97405.

COMBS, ADELE (WESTGATE). b Mendota Ill 10 Ja 33. 4: Richard E Combs. 5: Ind U 51-56 (Sociol) AB, 56-57 (LS) MA. 6: Fr. 7: Asst documents libn Ind U 57-64; Ref libn Columbia U 64-65, Ref libn E Asian Lib 65-66; Hd libn Vernon Court Jr Col 66-68; Ref libn NorthwesternU 68-. 10: Beta Phi Mu. 14: Ref, govt docs. 15: 1927 Sherman ave, Evanston IL 60201.

COMBS, RICHARD EARL. b Clinton Ind 10 Ja 34. 4: Adele Wesgate Combs. 5: IndU 56-61 (Sociol) AB, 61-62 (Eng); Columbia 64-65 (LS) MS. 6: Fr. 7: PH-3 US Navy 52-56; Copy ed IndU Press (Bloomington Ind) 62-63; Brooklyn Pub Lib 64-66; Libn Peoples Lib (Newport RI) 66-68; Instr URI 67-68; Hd libn Northbrook Pub Lib (Northbrook Ill) 68-. 8: Bldg consul: Newport Pub Lib (Newport RI) 66-68, Northbrook Pub Lib (Northbrook Ill) 68-69; Dir Newport Commun Ctr 67-68. 9: ALA; RILA (pres 68-69); NELA (dor 68-69; chm Publ Com 67-68). 11: Ed "Rhode Island Library Association Bulletin (66-68). 14: Ref, admin, bldg consul. 15: 1927 Sherman ave, Evanston Il 60201.

COMEAU, REGINALD ALFRED. b St Leonard NB Can 22 N 34. 5: UHartford 57-61 (Behavioral sci) BA; So Conn State Col 62-67 MSLS. 6: Fr. 7: Off personnel clk Army Ordanance adminis specialist Sp 3rd class 55-57; Coder & auditor Norwich- Scottish Ins Co, Hartford Conn 61; Acquis libn UConn Sch of Law 62-65; Sch libn Housatonic Valley Reg High, Falls Village Conn 65-67; Gen lib asst lib serv ctr, Calgary Alberta Can 67; Reg coordinator, S Co Interrelated Lib Syst, Westerly RI 68-. 9: ALA; RILA. 14: Admin. 15: 1487 Farmington ave, Farmington Ct 06032.

COMFORT, FRANCES MECK. b Harrisburg Penn 21 Je 18. 4: Robert M Comfort. 5: Syracuse 36-40 (Eng) AB; Drexel 40-41 BS in LS. 6: Fr. 7: Catlgr Bethlehem Pub Lib (Bethlehem Penn) 41-42; Dist Lib Off US Navy Lt (jg), Phila Navy Yard 42-45; Libn Harrisburg Area Community Col 64-67, Prof & chm Instr Serv Div 68-. 9: ALA; PennLA. 10: AAUW; Phi Beta Kappa. 14: Ref, admin. 15: 3300 N Cameron st, Harrisburg Pa 17110.

COMFORT, MRS HILDA (ELIZABETH) KOONTS. b Lexington NC 6 O 16. 4: Clifford W Comfort. 5: Gulf Park Col 58-60 AA; USoMiss 62-64 (LS) BS. 6: Fr. 7: Child libn Gulfport Carnegie Harrison Co Lib (Gulfport Miss) 64; Libn West Jr High Sch (Gulfport Miss) 64-68; Libn First Meth Church 9gulfport Miss) 68-. 9: NEA; ALA; MissEA; MissLA. 10: Phi Theta Kappa. 14: Catlg. 15: 281 Pinewood circle, Mississippi City Ms 39562.

COMINS, DOROTHY J(ULIA). b Detroit 27 Je 08. 5: UMich 26-28 BA in LS; State U of Iowa 31-35 (Fr) MA. 6: Fr, Sp. 7: Circ asst, catlgr Flint Pub Lib, Flint Mich 28-30; Catlgr State U of Iowa Lib 30-35; 1st asst catlg dept Enoch Pratt Free Lib, Baltimore 35-42; Exec asst ALA Internat Relations Off, Wash DC 42-47; Ref libn Biblioteca Artigas-Washington, Montevideo Uruguay 47-49; Ser reviser catlg dept NLM 49-54; Head of catlg dept Wayne State U Lib 54-. 8: Sent by LC to teach in new Lib Sch at Biblioteca Economica de los Amigos del Pais, Havana 50-51. 9: ALA-RTSD (chm Ser Sect 58-59, pres 62-63, var coms); MdLA (treas 2 yrs); DCLA (sec 52-54); MichLA. 10: AAUW; Detroit Women's City Club. 11: King Christian X Medal of the Liberation (47). 13: Yes. 14: Catlg. 15: Wayne State U Lib, Detroit MI 48202.

COMPAIN, RITA (ROMER). b NYC 4 D 26. 4: Ernest A Compain. 5: Brooklyn Col 43-47 9sp, Pol Sci) BA; Queens Col 59-60 (LS); Hofstra 56-59 (Educ); LIU 60-65 MLS. 6: Sp. 7: Child libn Brooklyn Pub Lib Kings Hwy Br 47-49; Tchr lib & coord Oceanside Jr High sch, Oceanside NY 59-60; Youth gp leader Temple B'nai Israel, Elmont NY 61-65; Libn Dist #17, Franklin Square NY 61-; Libn Lib USA World's Fair, NY 65-. 8: In-serv lecturer Wantagh Sch Lib 67; Story telling Inst C W Post of LIU 66. 9: NEA; ALA; NYLA (chm Serv Standards Com 60); Nassau-SuffolkLA; NYStateTA. 10: AAUW. 13: Yes. 14: Storytelling, ref, tchg lib sci. 15: 12 Grace ct W, Great Neck NY 11021.

COMPTON, HERBERT. b Gosford Australia 8 Jl 36. 5: UNew England Australia 53-56 (Hist) BA; UNew S Wales 64-65 (LS Diploma); UToronto 67-68 BLS. 6: Fr, Ger, Sp. 7: Catlgr UNew S Wales 64-67; Catlgr UToronto 68-. 8: Reorganized Tusbab High Sch Lib, New Guinea 67. 9: ALA; CanLA; Lib Assn of Australia; Nat Trust (Australia); Amnesty Internat. 11: TE Rofe Essay Prize 52. 14: Catlg. 15: 267 St George st apt 405, Toront 5 Ontario Can.

COMPTON, LUVENIA. b Wayne Co WVa 18 F 14. 4: H V Compton. 5: UKy 58-62 AB, 64-65 MSLS. 7: Off manager US Employment Serv, Ashland Ky 41-47; Claims examiner Dept of Soc Security, Ashland Ky 47-55; Tchr Boyd Co Sch Dist, Catlettsburg Ky 59-61, 64; Libn Norwalk High Sch, Norwalk Cal 65-66; Libn Lompoc Unified Sch Dis, Lompoc Cal 66-68; Dis. Libn Rim-of-the World Unified Sch Dis, Lake Arrowhead Cal 68-. 9: Cal Tchrs Assn; ALA; Cal Sch Libns. 10: Beta Phi Mu; AAUW. 14: Sch libnship. 15: Box 475, Cedar Glen CA 92321.

COMPTON, MARJORIE (POWERS). b Osceola Mills Penn 19 D 27. 4: Robert A Compton. 5: Penn State U 44-47 (Comm, Finance) BA; Drexel 51-52 MS in LS. 6: Ger, Fr. 7: Asst to curator Penn State U Lib 47-51, Sr catlgr 52-60; Asst libn Kutztown State Col Lib 60-65; Libn SE Br Reading Pub Lib (Penn) 66-. 9: PennLA. 14: Catlg of a-v aids, child. 15: Rt 2, Kempton PA 19529.

COMPTON, SUSAN LaNELL. b Batesville Ark 20 Ag 17. 5: Little Rock Jr Col 35-36; Ark State Tchrs Col 36-39 (Eng) BSE; Peabody 47-48 BS in LS. 6: Fr, Lat. 7: Jr & sr clerk Hygienic Lab Ark State Bd of Health, Little Rock Ark 42-47; Asst catlgr UArk Gen Lib 48-49; Head catlgr Ark Lib Commsn, Little Rock Ark 49-. 9: ALA (Life mem); ArkLA; Ark Resources & Tech Serv Group (chm). 10: Nat League of Amer Pen Women; Pub Welfare Forum; Amer Fed Women's Clubs; YWCA; AAUW; Ark Choral Soc. 12: Free-lance writer, 38-; Ed "Arkansas Libraries" 49-; Spec ed for Ark "Collier's Encyclopedia" 62-68; Bk of Poems "BeautyTransient & Other Poems" (69). 14: Ref, catlg, rare bks. 15: 506-1/2 Ctr st, Little Rock AR 72201.

COMRAS, REMA. b NYC 26 O 36. 5: UFla 54-58 (Pol Sci) BA; Syracuse 59-60 MS in LS. 6: Fr. 7: Lib asst Grey Advertising Agency, NYC 58-59; Libn Queens Borough Pub Lib, Queens NY 60-61; Libn US Army Spec Serv, France & Germany 62-64; Asst head libn Hialeah Kennedy Lib, Hialeah Fla 64-. 8b NYC 26 0 37. 09: ALA; FlaLA; DCLA. 9: ALA; FlaLA. 10: Beta Phi Mu. 14: Ref, readers adv serv. 15: 1735 Lenox ave, Miami Beach FL 33019.

CONARD, MILDRED (IOLA). b Shepherdstown WVa 8 D 03. 5: Shepherd Col 37 (Eng) AB; Drexel summers 30-31 (LS); Simmons 48 (LS) BS. 6: Sp. 7: Elem tchr, Jeff erson Co WVa 22-28; Jr high tchr, Harpers Ferry WVa 28-31; Tchr-libn High Sch, Harpers Ferry WVa 31-44; Libn Sr High Sch, Martinsburg WVa 44-66; Instr of Lib Sci Shepherd Col 67-. 8: WVa Reading & Lib Com 52-62; WVa Lib Standards Com 60-64; Instr in Lib Sci WVa U summer 53; West Md Co l summers 55, 57, 59, 61; UMd summer 56. 9: ALA; WVa Recr Com 63-;

NEA; WVaLA (chm Sch Lib Sect 62-64); WVaEA; WVaClrTA. 10: Kappa Delta Pi; Delta Kappa Gamma; AAUW. 14: Sch libs, tchg libnship. 15: Shenandoah Junction, WV 25442.

CONAWAY, CHARLES WILLIAM. b Anniston Ala 11 Jl 43. 5: Jacksonville State Col 61-64 (Eng) AB; Fla StateU 64-65 (LS) MS; Emory summer 68 (Archives Inst); Rutgers 68- (LS). 6: Ger. 7: Asst ref libn Fla AtlanticU 66; Hd ref libn 66; Fellow in lib serv RutgersU 68-. 9: ALA; SLA; SELA; ASIS; FlaLA; ADLIB. 10: Beta Phi Mu; AAUP. 14: Ref, acad lib admin, info sci, lib educ. 15: Grad School of Lib Ser Rutgers Univ, New Brunswick NJ 08903.

CONBEER, GERALDINE C. b Shamokin Penn 22 Ja 09. 5: State Tchrs (Millersville Penn) 28-31 (LS) BS in Ed; UPittsburgh 36-40 (Educ Admin) MS in Ed; Drexel 46-50 BLS. 6: Fr. 7: Libn Ramsay High Sch, Mt Pleasant Penn 32-43; Libn Butler Jr High Sch, Butler Penn 43-44; Libn Jr High Sch, Erie Penn 44-45; Libn State Col (W Chester Penn) 45, Act head libn 65-66, Hd tech processing 67-. 9: PennLA. 10: AAUW. 14: Tech process, admin. 15: 417 W Barnard st, West Chester PA 19380.

CONDIT-SMITH, THOMAS (OSBORN). b Ottumwa Iowa 13 F 15. 5: Seton HallU 36-40 (Eng) BS; Syracuse 40-41 BLS; Seton HallU 41-42 (Educ) MA; NYU 45-47 (Educ). 6: Fr, Ital. 7: Catlgr Seton HallU 41-42; Gen clerk US Army 42-45; Libn Newark Bd of Educ 47-48; Catlgr, Sr libn Morris Co Free Lib (Morristown NJ) 48-. 9: ALA; NJLA. 10: Kappa Delta Pi; Beta Pi Chap. 14: Catlg. 15: 2 Wetmore ave, Morristown NJ 07960.

CONDIT, ANNA R. b NYC 22 Mr 24. 5: Swarthmore 41-43 (Pol Sci); Phila Sch of Occupational Therapy 43-46 (Occupational Therapy) OTR; UDenver 58-60 (Soc Sci) AB; Rutgers 60-61 MLS. 7: Occupational therapist NJ State Hosp (Trenton NJ) 46-48; Sec various firms (Colorado Springs Colo) 48-50, 52-53; Asst to office & personnel managers Nestle Co (Colorado Springs Colo) 50-52; Sec off manager Pike Realty Co (Colorado Springs & Denver) 53-55; Sec to Gen Counsel Great Western Sugar Co (Denver) 55-59; Ser catlgr UColorado 61-63; Ser catlgr KanU 63-68; Lib syst spec 68-. 9: ALA; SLA; MPLA; KanLA. 10: AAUP; AAUW; LWV; KanU Fed Credit Union; Nat Audubon Assn; Kan Ornithological Soc; Denver Field Ornithologists. 12: Ed "Kansas Union List of Serials (65). 14: Catlg, sers. 15: 505 Learnard ct, Lawrence Ks 66044.

CONDIT, MARTHA OLSON. b E Orange NJ 8 S 13. 4: Milton Armstrong Condit. 5: Pratt 33-34 (Certif); Rutgers 53 (Hist, Psych) BA, 55-58 (LS) MS. 07: Page Free Pub Lib (E Orange NJ) 27-31; Jr asst 31-34; Lib asst Hunterdon Co Lib (Flemington NJ) 34-36; Child libn Nutley Pub Lib (NJ) 36-43; child libn Passaic Pub Lib (NJ) 43-45; Child libn Franklin Br Lib (E Orange NJ) 45-56; Sch libn Pub Sch (Montclair NJ) 56-65; Coordinator of elem libs 65-. 8: Co-adj staff Grad Sch of Educ & Grad Sch of Lib Serv, Rutgers; Consul: Second Ann Comm Libns Wk Conf, Ala Pub Lib Serv, & UAla 61. 9: ALA; NJEA; NJSchLA (pres); EssexCoSchLA; MontclairEA. 10: Montclair Operetta Club. 13: Yes. 14: Sch libnship, child lit. 15: 65 Hathaway lane, Essex Falls NJ 07021.

CONDITT, PAUL CLOUGH. b Ft Worth Tex 6 N 34. 5: Trinity U (Tex) 52-56 (Humanities) BA; Columbia 56-58 (LS) MS. 7: Libn II Brooklyn Pub Lib 58; US Army clerk-typist Spec 59-60; Gen libn UIda 61-62, Loan libn 62-68, Acquis libn 68-. 13: Yes. 15: 204 N Garfield st, Moscow ID 83843.

CONDRAY, MRS KATHRYN (McNEILL). b Carthage Ark 26 O 12. 5: Ark A&M Col 35-40 (Eng) BA; Peabody 59-61 (LS) MA. 7: Elem tchr (Thornton Ark) 41-42; Sr high tchr (Artesian Ark) 42-43; Elem tchr (Fairview Ark) 43-44; Jr high tchr (Fairview Ark) 44-45; Libn Sr High Sch (Camden Ark) 45-48; Elem tchr (Camden Ark) 55-56; Libn Fred Whiteside Sch (Camden Ark) 56-66; Asst libn & asst prof of LS So State Col 66-. 9: NEA; ALA; ArkLA (treas); NEA; AEA USA; ArkEA. 10: AAUW; Delta Kappa Gamma; Pro Women Garden Club; DKG; Ark Coun on Lib Educ. 14: Ref. 15: 702 Oakwood rd, Camden Ar 71701.

CONDRON, JONEL (WILLIAMS). b Munday Tex 3 Jl 18. 4: C B Condron. 5: N Tex State U 35-39 (Eng) BA, 56-58 (LS) BS, 66-68 (LS) MLS. 7: Libn Throckmorton High Sch, Throckmorton Tex 39-45, 47-65; County sch libn Throckmorton Co 65-66; Lib serv libn N Tex State U 66-. 9: ALA; SWLA; TexLA; Tex Assn of Col Tchrs; Tex State TA. 14: Ref. 15: 1508 Kendolph, Denton Tx 76201.

CONDUITTE, CATHERINE JESSICA. b San Juan PR 30 O 41. 4: John Van Wezel. 5: Fla StateU 59-63 (Inter-Amer Studies) BA; Columbia 63-64 MSLS. 7: Spec serv libn us army, Giessen Germany 64-66; Libn I Miami Pub Lib, Miami Fla 67-68; Libn II Allapattah Br 68-. 9: ALA; FlaLA; SELA. 10: LWV. 14: Child & pub lib wk. 15: 157 SE 12th st apt 12, Miami Fl 33131.

CONDUITTE, GRETCHEN (GARRISON). b Sewickley Penn 10 F 09. 4: Arthur Owen Conduitte. 5: UCLA 27-31 (Philos) AB, 31-32 BSLS. 7: Asst libn Bennington Col Lib 32-35; NY Pub Lib circ dept 35-41; Dir First Reg Lib, Hernando Miss 60-62; Libn Jackson Free Lib,Jackson Tenn 62-64; Southside Br Libn Pub Lib, Jacksonville Fla 64; Community rel libn Pub Lib, Jacksonville Fla 56-64; Libn Monroe CoPub Lib, Key West Fla 64-67; Orlando Pub Lib 67-, Coordinator Commun Rel 68-. 8: Judge, John Cotton Dana Publ Awards, 59. 9: ALA (chm Fol Com 55, chm Pub Rel Sect 57-59, mem Recr Adv Com 62-66); LPRC; SELA (Scholarship Com 62-66); FlaLA (Exec Sec 64-66). 10: LWV; AAUW; Human Rel Coun. 11: Dana Publ Award, Jackson Tenn, 53. 13: Yes. 14: Pub rel. 15: 3508 N Westmoreland dr, Orlando Fl 32804.

CONE, GERTRUDE ELLEN MARY. b Syracuse NY. 5: URochester 27-31 (Hist, Eng & Amer Lit) AB; SUC (Geneseo) summers 31-33, 35 (LS) NY State Sch Libns Certif; UVt 44-45 (Hist, Pol Sci). 6: Fr, Lat, Ger. 7: Tchr-libn; Moira High Sch, Moira NY 31-34, Ft Edward High Sch, Ft Edward NY 34-35, Sr High Sch, Bristol Conn 39-42; Libn Sr-Jr High Sch, Plattsburgh NY 42-44; Asst col libn SUC (Plattsburgh) 45-61; Nardin Acad, Buffalo NY; Tchr-libn 61-65, Libn 65-. 8: Assoc ed "York State Tradition; Consul & lecturer Champlain Valley hist SUC (Plattsburgh) summers 59-60. 9: ALA; CathLA; NEA; NYLA; West NY Catholic Libns Conf (sec 63-64); NYStateTA. 10: AAUW; Theta Alpha Epsilon; N Co Mineral Club; Marquis Biographical Lib Soc. 13: Yes. 14: Eng & Amer hist especially of Champlain Valley, hist research & bibliog. 15: 135 Cleveland ave, Buffalo NY 14222.

CONE, MICHELE (NASH). b Tucson Ariz 10 Ap 44. 4: Robert Edward Cone. 5: Brooklyn Col 61-65 (Eng) BA; Pratt 65-67 MLS. 6: Sp. 7: Libn trainee Brooklyn Pub Lib, Brooklyn ny 65-66; Ref libn Fla A&M U 67; Patients libn UMich Hosp 67-68; Acquis libn Undergrad Lib UMich 68-. 9: ALA. 10: Beta Phi Mu. 14: Acquis, ref. 15: 2151 Medford rd, Ann Arbor Mi 48104.

CONEY, DONALD. b Jackson Mich 21 F 01. 4: Dorothy Bell Pettit. 5: UMich 25 (Philos) AB, 27 (LS) AM. 6: Fr. 7: Various positions UMich 20-27; libn UDel 27-28; Asst libn UNC (Chapel Hill) 28-31; Prof of lib sci & asst dir Lib Sch UNC 31-32; Supv tech processes Newberry Lib (Chicago) 32-34; lecturer Lib Admin (Chicago) 33-34; Libn UTex 34-45; U Libn & Prof of Libnship UCal (Berkeley) 45-, 68; Consul 68-. 8: (Vice Chancellor) Admin UCal (Berkeley) 55-56; Staff UChicago Grad Lib Sch summers 35 & 41 Instr in lib sci Grad Courses UIll summer 37. 9: ALA-ACRL; CalLA. 13: Yes. 14: Lib admin. 15: 1007 Overlook, Berkeley Ca 94708.

CONFORTI, (LORETTA) GAY. b Los Angeles Cal 18 Jl 39. 5: Fullerton Jr Col 57-59 (Elem Educ), 62-64 (Bio); Cal State Col (Fullerton) 59-61 (Elem Educ) BA; San Jose State Col 64-65 (Dietetics); UCLA 66-67 MLS. 7: Tchr Fullerton Elem Schs, Fullerton Cal 61-62; Lib asst Orange City Pub Lib child room, Orange Cal 65-66; Child libn Orange Co Pub Lib Costa Mesa Br 67-. 9: CalLA; OrangeCoLA; OrangeCoEmployeesAssn; So Cal Coun on Lit for YP. 14: Child wk. 15: 8181 Garfield apt 4, Huntington Beach Ca 92646.

CONGDON, GERTRUDE (POPE). b Phillipsburg Kan 25 Ap 10. 5: UOttawa (Kan) 27-28; UWis 28-31 (Eng) BA, 30-31 (LS) Certif; UMo (Kan City) 54-58 9educ) MA. 7: Br child libn (Kan City Mo) Pub Lib 31-48; Sch libn The Barstow Sch (Kan City Mo) 51-. 9: ALA; AASchL: Nat Assn Indep Schs; Jr Bklist Com 57-67; MoLA; MoASchL. 14: Child bks, wk with elem & high sch studs. 15: 4939 Adams st, Shawnee Mission Ks 66205.

CONGDON, RODNEY H(AXSTUN). b South Glens Falls NY 11 Je 33. 5: Union Col 52-57 (Eng) BA; Columbia 59-61 (LS) MS. 6: Fr, Ger. 7: Asst law libn Fed Reserve Bank of NY (NYC) 61-66; Sr law libn 66-. 9: AALL; Law Lib Assn Greater NY. 14: Ref. 15: 33 Liberty st, New York NY 10045.

CONGER, EVELYN MARCELLE. b Fargo NDak 30 D 16. 5: MacPhail Col of Mus 33-35 (Violin) Tchr's Certif; UMinn 35-39 (LS) BS. 7: Catlgr & ref circ libn Pub Lib, Sioux City Iowa 39-4 2; Hosp libn & br libn Pub Lib, Minneapolis 42-44;

Pharm mate USN Hosp, San Diego 44-45; Libn Pub Lib, Minneapolis 46; Chief libn VA Ctr, Hot Springs SD 46-48, 55-. 9: ALA; -AHIL (By-Laws Com 60-62); MPLA; SD State LA (Certif & Loan Fund Com, 62-66). 10: AAUW. 14: Catlg, med ref. 15: 406 Jennings ave, Hot Springs SD 57747.

CONGER, LUCINDA (DICKINSON). b Fort Bragg NC 11 Je 41. 4: Bruce C Conger. 5: Radcliffe 59-63 (Anthrop) AB; Rutgers 63-64 MLS. 6: Fr. 7: Ref libn UCal at Davis 64-65; LC; Descr catlgr 65-66, Ref libn 66; Annex libn Princeton U 66-. 9: ALA. 14: Ref, tech services, circ. 15: 443 Herrontown rd, Princeton NJ 08540.

CONIBEAR, PAULINE. b Bristol England 2 D 35. 5: Bristol U 54-56 (Lar) BA; Birmingham U 57-58 (Ed) Certif; UBritish Columbia 66-67 BLS. 6: Fr, Ital, Greek. 7: Asst mistress Weston-Super-More Grammar Sch for Girls, Eng 58-60; Asst mistress hd of dept Rose Green High Sch, Bristol Eng 60-65; Carleton U: Lib tech 65-66, Gen libn & asst chief catlgr 67-. 9: CanLA; ALA; AAM; OttawaLA. 14: Catlg, ref, ser. 15: 554 Driveway, Ottawa 1 Ont Can.

CONKLIN, ELIZABETH L. b Phila Penn 16 O 20. 4: George N Conklin. 5: Rosary Col 39-43 (LS) AB. 06: Fr, Sp. 7: Asst ref libn OEM Lib (Wash DC) 45; Br libn USNTC (Great Lakes Ill) 43-45; Asst ref libn WPB Lib (Wash DC) 45-46; Asst catlgr WesleyanU (Middletown Conn) 55-61; Asst libn acton Lib (Old Saybrook Conn) 61-63; Libn Essex Lib Assn (Essex Conn) 63-. 9: ALA; ConnLA. 15: 10 Bayberry rd, Old Saybrook Ct 06475.

CONKLIN, GLADYS. b Harpster Ida 30 My 03. 4: Irving Conklin. 5: UWash 21-25 BS in LS. 7: Child libn Pub Lib, Ventura Cal 26-28; Child libn NY Pub Lib 28-31; Child libn Los Angeles Pub Lib 33-42; Child libn Pub Lib, Hayward Cal 50-65 (ret). 8: Bk reviewer for "School Library Journal" 56-65. 9: ALA; CalLA (pres Child Sect 63); Assn Child Libns of N Cal (pres 52). 10: Audubon Soc. 12: Bks pub by Holiday House; "I Like Caterpillars" (58); "I Like Butterflies" (60); "We Like Bugs" (62); "If I Were a Bird" (65); "I Caught a Lizard" (66); "Bug Club Book" (67); "Lucky Ladybugs" (68); "When Insects are Babies" (69); "How Insects Grow" (69). 13: Yes. 14: Child wk. 15: 16582 Kent ave, San Lorenzo Ca 94580.

CONLEY, BETTY RUTTER. b Washington Co Va 4 Je 31. 4: Walter Wayne Conley. 5: Radford Col 47-51 (Eng) BA; E Tenn State U 63-66 (LS) MA. 6: Sp. 7: Libn Valley Inst Elem Sch, Bristol Va 59- Ext Inst Lib Sci UVa. 9: NEA; ALA; VaEA; VaLA. 10: Boone Tree Trail; Delta Kappa Gamma. 14: Child libn. 15: 56 Cherry lane, Bristol Va 24201.

CONLEY, BINFORD HARRISON. b Madison Co Ala 13 F 33. 4: Thelma Bond. 5: Morehouse Col 50-53 (Eng) AB; Atlanta 58-60 MSLS. 7: Asst libn Readers Services Trevor Arnett Lib, AtlantaU 57-60; Libn Scar State Col 60-62; Libn Ala A&M Col 62-. 9: ALA; SELA; AlaLA. 12: Ed "Proceedings of the Conference of Black Writers (65, 66). 14: Ref. 15: PO Box 101, Normal Al 35762.

CONLEY, PATRICIA (ANN BRINKMAN). b Owensville Mo 2 Je 37. 4: William Joseph Conlry II. 5: William William Woods Col 55-56; NorthwesternU 56-57 (Liberal Arts); Rosary Col 57-59 (Eng) AB, 59-60 MALS. 7: Stud asst Rosary Col 58-60; Ser libn St Marys Col (Notre Dame Ind) summer 59; Ref & ser libn Dominican Col (San Rafael Cal) 60-61; Lib asst Kecoughtan Va (Hampton Va) 61; Ref & circ libn Huntington Mem Lib Hampton Inst 63-65; Emmanuel Luth Parish Lib 66-. 9: ALA; Col & Res Libs (Ref Div). 10: Lutheran Womens Missionary League; AAUW. 14: Ref, circ. 15: 133 Peachtree lane, Hampton Va 23369.

CONMY, PETER THOMAS. b San Francisco Cal 8 Jl 01. 4: Emiliette Constance Storti. 5: UCal 20-24 (Educ) AB, 24-27 (Educ) MA, 30-37 (Educ) EDD, 45-47 BLS; Stanford 39-41 (Hist) MA; USan Francisco 50-52 (Law) LLB. 6: Lat. 7: Tchr, coun, evening prin San Francisco Pub Schs 22-43; City libn Oakland Pub Lib (Oakland Cal) 43-69. 9: ALA (mem com); CathLA; NEA; CalLA (var offs 50-61); CalTA. 10: Rotary Club; Sierra Club of Oakland; Native Sons of the Golden West; Cal Hist Soc; Young Mens Inst. 11: Knight of St Gregory, by appointment of Pope Paul VI (64). 12: "Public Library and the State (63); "Public School-Public Library Relations (44). 13: Yes. 14: Admin, Cal hist, church hist. 15: 125 14th, Oakland Ca 94612.

CONNELL, JoANN. b Cincinnati Ohio 30 Ap 22. 5: Smith 40-42; New Sch for Soc Research 63-66 (Sociol) BA; Pratt Inst 66-67 MLS. 6: Fr. 7: Ref libn NY State Psychiatric Inst, NYC 67-. 9: MedLA; SLA; NY Lib Club. 14: Ref. 15: 305 W 86th st, New York NY 10024.

CONNELL, SISTER JOAN. b Pittsburgh Penn 14 F 31. 5: Seton Hill Col 47-54 (Eng) BA; Duquesne U 54-61 (LS) MEd; UAriz 61-64 (Hist) MA; Chicago 63-69 (LS) MA (Hist) PhD. 6: Fr, Ital. 7: Secondary sch libn & tchr Pittsburgh Catholic Sch System 53-57; Eng tchr & dir of spec act Salpointe High Sch (Tucson Ariz) 57-59; Libn & dir of speech act 59-64; PhD Candidate (Chicago) 64-69; Dir Seton Hill Col Lib 69-. 8: State Speech Org, Ariz 9pres) 60-64; Ariz Speech & Drama Assn (sec) 60-62. 9: ALA; CathLA; AHA; West Hist Assn. 10: AAUW; Phi Alpha Theta. 13: Yes. 14: Lib hist, acad libs. 15: Seton Hill Col, Greensburg Pa 16232.

CONNELL, SUZANNE (SPARKS) McLAURIN. b Bennettsville SC 12 S 17. 4: Allen Arthur Connell. 5: UNC 34-38 (Eng) AB, 39-40 (Ref) AB in LS. 7: Lib asst Wash DC Pub Lib Mt Pleasant Br 40-41; Post libn War Dept, Camp Sutton NC 43-44; Post libn McGuire Gen Hosp, Richmond Va 45-46, Chief libn 46-52, 59-62; Chief libn VA Hosp, Lake City Fla 52-56; Various Air U Lib, Maxwell AFB Ala 56-59; Chief of circ & extension greensboro Pub Lib, Greensboro Pub Lib, Greensboro NC 62-63; Asst libn Base Lib MCB Camp Lejeune NC 63-66; Asst Wilmington Pub Lib, Wilmington NC 67-. 9: ALA; -AHIL (pres 55-56). 10: Phi Beta Kappa. 14: Ref hosp lib wk. 15: 502 Brunswick st, Southport NC 28461.

CONNELL, WESSIE. b Cairo Ga 21 N 15. 6: Fr, Lat. 7: Libn Cairo Pub Lib (Cairo Ga) 39-64; Lib dir Roddenberry Mem Lib (Cairo Ga) 64-. 8: Ga Adv Com for Fed Lib Consul Projects. 9: ALA; LPRC; AEA; SELA; GaLA. 10: Delta Kappa Gamma; Camellia Garden Club; Cairo Womans club; Cairo Bk Club. 11: John Cotton Dana Award (48, 49, 58, 59); Kiwanis Award (Citizen of the Year) 48; Man of the Year Award (Only Time presented To A Woman) 60. 12: "So Youre Going to Have a Drive in "The Wonderful World of Books. 13: Yes. 14: Admin, pub rel. 15: Roddenberry Mem Lib, Cairo Ga 31728.

CONNER, ANNA M. b Prospect Park Penn 19 My 11. 5: Ursinus Col 29-30; UPenn 30-33 (Lat) BS in Ed; UNC summers 40-42 BS in LS. 6: Fr, Sp. 7: Lib asst Prospect Park (Penn) Pub Lib 37; Tchr-libn Federalsburg High Sch, Federalsburg M d 37-39; Admin tchr- libn A I DuPont Spec Sch Dist, Wilmington Del 39-43; Naval libn USNTC Bainbridge Md 43-46; Chief libn VA Hosp, Memphis Tenn -51; Chief libn VA Hosp Ft Howard Md 51-67; Chief libn VA Ctr, Martinsburg WV 67-. 9: SLA; MedLA; ALA; MdLA; Baltimore Hosp LA. 14: Readers adv serv. 15: Kent ter 114 #5, Martinsburg WV 15401.

CONNER, CAROL N (MRS). b Sidney Neb 12 F 21. 5: UNeb 39-43, 58 (Eng) AB; UDenver summers 61-64 (LS) MA. 6: Fr. 7: Ref libn Soc Sec Bd, Wash DC 43-45; Asst chief libn VI Hosp, St Cloud Minn 63-68; Chief libn VA Hosp, Sheridan Wy 68-. 10: AAUW. 14: Med libnship, admin. 15: Quarters 27-D VA Hosp, Sheridan Wy 82801.

CONNER, LABAN CALVIN. b Ocala Fla 18 F 36. 5: UOmaha 59 (Educ) B Gen Ed; Kan State Tchrs Col 64 (Lib Educ) MS. 6: Sp. 7: Tchr Liberty City Elem Sch, Miami Fla 59-63; Libn Orchard Villa Elem Sch, Miami Fla 63-65; Libn Community & Migrant Program, Fla City Elem Sch 65-66; Libn Springview Elem Sch, Miami Springs Fla 66-68; Coordinator lib serv Dade Co Pub Schs, Miami 68-. 66; Libn Springview Elem Sch, Miami Springs Fla 66-68; Coordinator lib serv Dade Co Pub Schs, Miami 68-. 9: FlaASchL; FlaLA; ALA. 10: YMCA; Boy scouts. 14: Reading guidance, ref. 15: 3043 NW 61st st, Miami Fl 33142.

CONNER, PEARL C(OLE) (MRS). b Albany Ky 15 D 01. 5: UKy 38 (Bus Educ) AB, 41 (Bus Educ) MA, 48 BSLS. 7: Com tchr Clinton Co High Sch, Albany Ky 37-42, Libn 42-51; Chief libn Sec Dept of Com CAA Tech Dev & Evaluation Center, Indianapolis 51-59; Libn Wright-Patterson AFB Tech Lib, Dayton Ohio 59-. 9: ALA; SLA. 10: Kappa Delta Pi. 14: Acquis. 15: 874 Edinboro ct, Dayton OH 45431.

CONNETTE, EARLE. b Greencastle Ind 30 Jl 10. 4: Ann Muehler Connette. 5: Ind StateU 30-33 (Music) BS, 35 (Music) MS; IndU 44 (Aesthetics) PhD; UDenver 63 (LS) MA. 6: Fr, Ger. 7: Asst prof Murray State Col 35-37; Asst prof N Tex StateU 38-42; US Army Infantry (Capt) 42-44; Assoc prof umo 44-46; Assoc prof SyracuseU 47-48; Assoc prof Wash StateU 49-50; Libn Colfax High Sch (Colfax Wash) 58-63; Libn Soc (Sci Div) Wash StateU 63-65; Libn & chief mss (Archives Div) 66-. 9: SAA; PNLA. 12: Comp "Pacific Northwest Quarterly Index, Vols 1-53 (63). 13: Yes. 15: 903 East C st, Moscow Id 83843.

CONNOLLY, BRENDAN S J. b Boston 10 F 13. 5: Boston Col 37 (Eng) AB, 38 (Philos) AM; Weston Col 44 (Theol) STL; Catholic U 46 BSLS; Chicago 55 (LS) PhD. 6: Lat, Fr, Sp. 7: Eng Instr Boston Col 38-40; Lib Sch Instr Catholic U 50-51; Libn Weston Col 51-59, Assoc Ed "New Testament Abstracts," Weston Mass 56-60; Dir of Libs Boston Col 59-. 8: Consul & adv wk in Mass, Conn, Me, Ind, Ottowa, Rochester, Iraq, and PI 55-. 9: ALA; CathLA; MassLA. 10: AAUP. 12: "The New Humanism" (38); "The Roots of Jesuit Librarianship, 1540-1599" (55); "A Life in Four Weeks" (42); Assoc ed "New Testament Abstracts" (56-60). 13: Yes. 14: Acquis. 15: Bapst Lib Boston Col, Chestnut Hill 67 MA 02167.

CONNOLLY, CHARLES S(TEPHEN). b Winoosky Vt 9 Ja 18. 4: Dorothy Connolly. 5: BostonU 46-48 (Liberal Arts) AA; BustonU Law Sch 48-51 LLB. 7: Libn BostonU Law Lib 52-. 9: AALL; NELL. 10: Mass Bar Assn. 13: Yes. 15: Boston U Law Lib, Boston Ma 02108.

CONNOLLY, ELIZABETH J. b NYC 21 Mr 19. 5: St Joseph's Col for Women (Brooklyn NY) 36-40 (Soc Sci, Psych) BA; Columbia 44-45 (LS). 6: Fr. 7: Sr clerk USAF (Wash DC & Winston-Salem NC) 42-46; Payroll clerk Advertising Agency (NYC) 46-48; Tech libn USAF Air Material Command (NYC) 48-53; Post libn US Army Ft Slocum (New Rochelle NY) 53-55; Libn US Army Ft Totten (Flushing NY) 55-67; Ref libn US Mil Acad Lib (West Point) 68-. 9: ALA (var com & sect offs); NY StateLA; CathLA (mem &/or chm var com 67-69). 10: AAUW. 14: Ref, admin. 15: 2940 Grand Concourse apt 6K, Bronx NY 10458.

CONNOR, BILLIE MARIE (BATTEN STRUBLE). b Brighton Mo 4 O 34. 4: John M Connor. 5: SW Mo State Col 51-55 (Sp) BS in Ed; U de Guanajuato (Guanajuato Mexico) 56 (Sp); Rutgers 58-59 MLS; Wichita State U 63, 64. 7: Tchr & libn Auburn High Sch, Auburn Ill 55-58; Ext libn SW Reg Lib, Bolivar Mo 59-62; Ref libn bus & tech serv Wichita Pub Lib, wichita Kan 62-68; Bibliog (free-lance), Los Angeles 69-. 9: SLA (Heart of Amer Chap: treasurer 65-66, pres-elect 66-67, pres 67-68); ALA. 10: AAUW. 14: Ref, bibliog. 15: 3707 San Rafael ave, Los Angeles Ca 90065.

CONNOR, CAROLE LYNN. b Omaha Neb 15 Mr 41. 5: Cottey Jr Col 59-61; State UIowa (Iowa City) 61-63 (Elem Educ) BA; UMich (Ann Arbor) 67-68 (LS) MA. 6: Fr. 7: Tchr: Libertyville Elem Pub Sch, Libertyville Ill 63-65, Des Moines Pub Sch, Des Moines Iowa 66; Lib asst Des Moines Pub Lib, Des Moines Iowa 66, Ref libn & bibliog asst 68-69, Br libn 69-. 9: ALA; IowaLA; Des Moines Metropolitan LA. 14: Child wk. 15: 3407 Grand ave apt 113, Des Moines Ia 50312.

CONNOR, ERMA (MARY). b Du Bois Penn 10 Mr 07. 5: Clarion State Col 25-27 (Eng, Soc), summers 45-55 (LS) BS. 7: Elem tchr, Brooks (Du Bois penn) 27-31; Tchr, Wilson (Du Bois Penn) 31-40; Tchr-libn 40-46; Libn Pub Lib (Du Bois Penn) 46-52; Libn Jr High Sch (Du Bois Penn) 52-. 9: NEA; PennStateEA. 10: Bus & Prof Women. 14: Ref. 15: 17 S Highland st, Du Bois Pa 15801.

CONNOR, JEAN LOUISE. b Newton Iowa 21 Jl 19. 5: Middlebury Col 37-41 (Eng Lit) AB; Columbia 41-42 BLS; SUNY (Pub Admin). 7: Rochester pub Lib (Rochester NY): Ref asst, jr libn 42-44; Ya libn, Sr libn 44-46; Br libn, Sr libn 46-48; Readers Adv White Plains Pub Lib (White Plains NY) 48-54; Lib Ext Div NY State Lib: Sr lib supv 54-57; Assoc lib supv 58-63; Dir 63-. 9: ALA-AAStateL (Exec Bd); NYLA; Amer Assn Pub Admin. 10: Phi Beta Kappa. 11: Amer Assn Pub Admins (Capital Dist Chap); Governor Charles E Hughes Award for Pub Admin (68). 13: Yes. 14: State lib ext wk, pub lib serv, admin. 15: 64 1/2 Willett st, Albany NY 12210.

CONNOR, JOHN MICHAEL. b NYC 22 My 08. 4: Billie Marie Connor. 5: Manhattan Col 27-31 (Bus Admin) BS in Bus Admin; Columbia 33-34 (LS) MA, 39-50 (Adult Educ) MA. 6: Fr, Sp. 7: Stud asst, lib asst Columbia U 29-35; Ref libn, asst libn Col of Physicians-Surgeons, NYC 35-46; Nat Dir Victory Book Campaign, NYC 42-43; Instr US Army Med Corps 43; Spec Serv Supply 44-46; Chief reader serv div US Dept of State, Off of Intelligence Research, Wash DC 46-50; Asst city libn City of San Bernardino (Cal) Pub Lib 50-53; Tech libn US Naval Air Missile Test Center, Pt Mugu Cal 53-56; Chief Libn Los Angeles Co Med Assn, Los Angeles 56-. 8: Group discussion leader, Commun Educ Proj, San Bernardino Valley Col 52-53; Leader Adult Group Discussion Programs, Ventura Jr Col 54-56. 9: ALA (Jr mem RT; chm 40-41, Nomin Com 41-42); SLA (Chap Liaison Off 65-67; Chm Chap Rel Com 65-67; So Cal Chap,Pub Rel Off 60-61 & 65, pres 62-65; Nat Conf chm 65-68; Conf Adv Com 65-68, chm 68-69; chm H W Wilson Chap Award Com 69-70); MedLA(pres So Cal Group 64-65; NYLA (chm Entertain Com 38-40, chm Memb Com 39-41). 10: Sierra Club; Environm Health Com. 11: Study Grant Fund for Adult Educ, 53; Superior Accomplishment Award, US Naval Air Missile Test Center, 57. 12: "Latin America: Literature of Adult Education" (52); "Discussion Guide: Ways of Mankind" (53). 13: Yes. 14: Admin, ref (med). 15: 634 S Westlake ave, Los Angeles CA 90057

CONNOR, LURENE (LOIS) MICHELS. b McLeansboro Ill 19 Jl 38. 4: Benjamin Duane Connor. 5: So Ill U 56-60 (Eng) BS in Ed; SoIllU 67 (IM) MS in Ed. 7: Libn McLeansboro Twp High Sch, McLeansboro Ill 59-62; Unit libn Community Unit Sch Dist 186, Murphysboro Ill 62-67; Libn Alto Pass Comm High Sch, Alto Pass Ill 67-. 8: Adult sponsor Little Egypt Stud Libns Assn 60-61; Adult sponsor Ill Stud Libns Assn 60-61. 9: ALA; NEA; IllLA; IllEA; IllASchLS (com duties); Union Co EA. 14: Child lit, elem sch libs. 15: P O Box 543, Murphysboro IL 62966.

CONNOR, MARTHA ANGELINE. b Phila Penn 29 Ag 08. 5: UPenn 26-30 (Eng) BS in Educ, 30-32 (Eng) MA; Drexel 33-34 BS in LS. 6: Fr, Ger. 7: Catlgr Franklin Inst Lib (Phila) 34-35; TempleU Lib: Catlgr 36-37; Head Catlg Dept 38-44; Head Ref Dept 44-45; Swarthmore Col Lib: Tech serv libn 45-63; Act libn 48, 62-65; Assoc libn 65-. 9: ALA-ACRL (sec Col Sect 68-69; pres Phila Chap 57-59); Phila Area Tech Serv Libns. 14: Catlg, acquis. 15: 325 Dartmouth ave Apt D 1, Swarthmore Pa 19081.

CONNOR, MARY ANN. b Rochester NY 22 Ap 19. 5: Nazareth Col 37-41 (Eng) AB; West Res 43 BLS; URochester 51-52; West Res 57 MLS. 6: Fr. 7: Libn Rochester Pub Lib (Rochester NY) 43-51; Libn Rush-Henrietta Central High Sch (Henrietta NY) 53-60; Libn Bd of Cooperative Educ Serv 9penfield NY) 60-. 9: NYLA; NY State Tchrs Assn. 14: Sch lib catlg, admin. 15: 334 Eaglehead rd, East Rochester NY 14445.

CONNORS, JEAN M. b Staten Island NY 8 My 25. 4: Myles Francis Connors. 5: Elmira Col 43-47 (Eng) BA; C W Post 64-66 MSLS. 6: Fr, Sp. 7: Libn Mattituck Grad High Sch, Mattituck NY 64-68; Lower Sch Lib French Acad, Locust Valley NY 68. 9: SuffolkSchLA (pres 68-69). 15: 5 Crane rd, Lloyd Harbor, Huntington NY 11743.

CONNERS, MILDRED SAWYER. b Searsport Me 30 Mr 14. 4: John J Connors. 5: UMe 32-36 (Ger) BA; UMich 36-37 ABLS. 6: Ger, Fr, Sp. 7: Lib asst Brookline Pub Lib (Brookline Mass) 37-39; Lib asst Fogg Art Museum (Cambridge Mass) 39-46; Harvard Col Lib: Lib asst ser 49-52; Asst chief ser receipts 54-61; Chief ser receipts 61-66; Catlgr 66-. 10: Phi Beta Kappa. 14: Ser, catlg. 15: 32 Thorndike st, Arlington Ma 02174.

CONNORS, WILLIAM EDWARD. b St Joseph Mich 20 S 35. 4: Jeanette Anna (Frost). 5: Kalamazoo Col 53-57 (Eng lit) BA; Ohio Wesleyan 57-59 (Eng lit) MA; UMich 59-60 MALS. 6: Fr, Ger. 7: Securities salesman B C Morton Co, Kalamazoo 57; Instr in Eng Garrett Graduate Sch of Theol summer 58; Instr in Eng Ohio Wesleyan 57-59 summer 59; Catlg libn NYS Sch of Ind & Labor Rel at Cornell 60-63; Chief of reclsf UMd Libs 63-66; Visiting lecturer SUNY at Albany Sch of Lib Sci 67-69, Assoc libn tech serv SUNY at New Paltz 66-. 14: Bibliog in the humanities, tech serv, automation. 15: 149 Plains rd, New Paltz NY 12561.

CONOVER, ROBERT WARREN JR. b Manhattan Kan 6 O 37. 5: Kan StateU 55-59 (Eng) BA; UDenver 60-61 (LS) MA. 6: Fr. 7: Asst instr Kan StateU 59-60; Fresno Co (Cal) Free Lib: Libn I Ref & readers adv 61; Libn II Bkmob 62; Libn II Br libn 62; Libn III Readers adv & adult serv 65-67; Co libn Yolo Co Free Lib (Woodland Cal) 68-69; City libn Fullerton Pub Lib (Fullerton Cal) 69. 8: A-V consul to San Joaquin Valley Lib System. 9: CalLA (pres Yosemite Dist); ALA. 10: Fresno Jr C of C; Fresno Co (Cal) Hist Soc; Pi Kappa Alpha. 11: Jr C of C Presidents Award. 14: Pub rel, readers adv serv, a-v materials, admin, bldg planning. 15: 301 N Pomona, Fullerton Ca 92632.

CONRAD, AGNES C. b Pasadena Cal 7 S 17. 5: Col of Holy Names 35-39 (Hist) BA; UCal (Berkley) 39-40 (LS) Certif. 7: Catlgr Huntington Lib (San Marino Cal) 41-42; Post libn USAAF (Victorville Cal) 42-45; Catlgr UCLA 45-50; UHawaii Catlgr 50-51; Govt documents libn 51-53; Head circ dept 53-55; Territorial & State Archivist, State of Hawaii (Honolulu) 55-. 9: ALA; SAA (Fellow); (Mem Exec Bd); HawaiiLA (pres) 62; Internat Coun of Archives. 10: Soroptimist Club of Honolulu; Hawaiian Hist Soc; Conservation Comm for Hawaii. 12: Jt ed "Proceedings of the Constitutional convention, State of Hawaii

(60); Jt comp "Official Publications of the Territory of Hawaii, 1900-1959 (62). 14: Archives, mss. 15: 185 Ohana st, Kailua Hi 96734.

CONRAD, ETHEL (EYMAN). b Massillon Ohio 27 D 22. 5: Oberlin Col 40-44 (Eng) AB; West Res 44-45 BS in LS, 51-52 (Educ) MA. 6: Fr, Ger. 7: Ref asst Lakewood Pub Lib, Lakewood Ohio 45-51; Ref asst Canton Pub Lib, Canton Ohio 52-57; Libn Washington High Sch, Massillon Ohio 57-59; Massillon Pub Lib, Massillon Ohio: Head of adult serv 59-61, Asst libn 61-65, Head Libn 65-. 9: ALA; OhioLA (chm Adult Serv RT 67-68). 10: Stark Co (Ohio) Libns; LWV; YWCA; AAUW. 14: Ref, archival materials. 15: 1118 Fourth st NE, Massillon Oh 44646.

CONRAD, VIRGINIA L. b Carmel Ind 3 My 25. 5: UMd 65 (Bus Admin) BA; Ind U 66 (LS) MA. 7: Admin asst Amer Red Cross, Europe,Japan, US 55-65; Asst acquis libn Ind State U 66-68; Asst acquis libn Wis U 68-69, Syst & automation libn 69-. 9: ALA; Ohio Valleygp of Tech Serv Libns. 10: AAUW. 14: Acquis, automation, systems coop. 15: 1121 Carriage dr apt 7, Whitewater Wi 53190.

CONROY, BARBARA JEAN (BULLER). b Sioux Falls SD 1 6 My 34. 5: SD State Col 52-56 (Eng) BS; UDenver 56-57 MA. 7: Libn I Documents Div UCal(Berkeley) 57-61; Head Bus Div Denver Pub Lib 61-64, Head Sociol & Bus Dept 64-68; Proj dir Staff Development Proj Central Colo Pub Lib Syst 68-, Coordinator, Cooperative Educ Development for Lib Personnel; West Interstate Com for Higher Educ, Boulder Colo 68-. 9: SLA (Colo chap; sec 63-65, pres-elect 65-66, pres 66-67); MPLA; ColoLA (chm Intel Freedom Com 66-68); Adult Educ Coun Metro Denver; Amer Soc Training & Devel; AEAUSA. 10: Colo Mountain Club; Nat Ski Patrol System; Bus & Prof Women. 13: Yes. 14: Adult educ, admin, mgt. 15: 1427 Otis apt 3, Lakewood Co 80214.

CONSUELO, SISTER MARY RSM. b 6 Je 06. 5: Villanova 37 (Philos) AB, 42 (Lat) MA, 46 BS in LS. 06: Fr, Lat. 7: Tchr in Elem & Sec Schs in Archdiocese of Phila -42; Libn John W Hallahan CGHS (Phila) 42-53; Libn Gwynedd-Mercy Col 53-. 8: Nat chm, Cath Bk Week (60 & 61). 9: ALA; CathLA (chm-elect East Penn Unit); PennLA. 15: Gwynedd-Mercy Col, Gwynedd Valley Pa 19437.

CONVERSE, KATHRYN ANN (GEMLICH). b Cleveland Ohio 8 My 39. 4: John Emerson Converse. 5: Hiram Col 57-61 (Eng) AB; West Res 61-67 MS in LS. 6: Sp. 7: Libn Independence High Sch, Independence Ohio 62-64; Asst order libn Kent State U 64-67; Catlgr Flint Pub Lib, Flint Mich 68-. 15: 629 E Eldridge ave, Flint Mi 48505.

CONWAY, BERNARD CHRISTOPHER. b Pittsburgh Penn 1 Je 40. 5: Duquesne 59-61; Conception Sem 64-66 (Phil) BA; Boston Col summer 65; UPittsburgh 67-68 MLS. 7: Asst supv rec Swindell-Dressler Co, Pittsburgh Penn 66-67; Asst ref libn & govt docs libn UDayton 69-. 10: Audubon Soc. 12: Bks pub. by Holiday House; "I Like Caterpillars" (58); "I Like Butterflies" (60); "We Like Bugs" (62); "If I Were a Bird" (65); "I Caught a Lizard" (66); "Bug Club Book" (67); "Lucky Ladybugs" (68); "When Insects are Babies" (69); "How Insects Grow" (69). 14: Ref, tech serv. 15: 300 College Park ave, Dayton Oh 45409.

CONWAY, WILLIAM E(GBERT). b Red Bluff Cal 5 Ap 18. 4: Leona Lee Conway. 5: UCal(Berkeley) 34-38 (Pol Sci) AB, 38-39 (LS) Certif. 6: Fr. 7: Catlgr William A Clark Mem Lib UCLA 39-42; Tech sgt chief clerk US Army Infantry 42-46; Catlg libn William A Clark Mem Lib UCLA 46- 58, Supv Bibliog 58-66, Libn 66-. 9: ALA-ACRL; CalLA (chm Publ Com 63-64). 10: Phi Beta Kappa. 14: Catlg, rare bks. 15: 2520 Cimarron st, Los Angeles Ca 90018.

COOCH, AMELIA. b Pottsville Penn 15 N 07. 5: Kutztown State Col 26-30 (LS) BS in Ed; UPittsburgh 39 (Educ, Guidance) M in Ed; West Res 50 BS in LS. 7: Libn Ebensburg-Cambria High Sch, Ebensburg Penn 30-37; Libn Pottsville Jr High Sch, Pottsville Penn 37-49; Libn Pottsville High Sch, Pottsville Penn 37-49; Libn New Kensington High Sch, New Kensington Penn 49-. 9: NEA; Penn State EA; PennLA. 10: Delta Kappa Gamma; Bus & Prof Womens Club; New Kensington Womens Club; Soroptimist. 14: Catlg, ref. 15: 404 7th st, New Kensington Pa 15068.

COOGAN, HELEN MARGARET. b Sioux Falls SD 12 Mr 20. 5: Mt St Marys Col 37-41 (Chem) BS; Immaculate Heart Col 61 (LS) MA. 7: Lab tech Childrens Hosp, Los Angeles 42-45; US Navy lab tech Pharmacists Mate3/c 45-46; Lab tech Med Arts Lab, N Hollywood Cal 46-57; Acquis & catlgr N Amer (Aviation) Rockwell Corp Atomics Internat,canoga Park Cal 59-60; Ref & acquis libn N Amer (Aviation) Rockwell Corp Sci Center, Thousand Oaks Cal 62-. 9: SLA (sec So Cal Chap);cathLA (sec SW Unit); CalLA (sec Black Gold Dist). 12: Co-auth "The Mossbauer Effect Data Index (67). 13: Yes. 14: Ref, acquis. 15: 4256 Riverton ave, N Hollwood Ca 91602.

COOK, C(HARLES) DONALD. b Scottsbluff Neb 6 J123. 5: UAriz 45 (Eng Lit) BA; Columbia 46 (LS) BS, 56 (LS) MS; UGeneva(Switzerland) 50. 6: Fr, Ital, Ger, Sp. 7: Catlg asst UAriz 43-45; Catlgr Columbia U Libs 46-47; Documents libn UN Lib, Geneva 47-52; Assoc in lib serv Columbia U Sch Lib Serv 52-57; Asst to the Dir personnel Columbia U Libs 57-60, Coordinator of catlg 60-69; Res Planning Off, Ont Universities Bibliographic Centre Proj 69-. 8: Middle States Assn Lib rep on eval teams: 4 cols & univs 59-6468. 9: ALA (Council, 67-68)-ALA-RTSD (Nomin Com 58-59, Bd Dirs 65-66, 67-68, Conf Prog Com 65-66, chm Standard Lib Keyboard Com 65-66; -Catlg & clsf sect execcom 61-62, chm 65-66, conf prog com 64-66); RTSD-ISAD Interdiv Com on a Universal Numb System for Lib Materials, 66-, chm 66-68; ISAD Machine-Readable Catlg FormatCom 67-68; Inst on the Use of the LC Clsf 66, (co-chm); -LAD (mem 2 sect coms 59-62)-Internat Rel Round Table (Nomin com 56-57, sec 64-67); -ACRL (Univ libs sect); ASIS;NY Tech Serv Libns (sec-treas 55-56, pres 58-59, Conf of East Col libns org com 63);NY Lib Club (Coun 66-, Scholarship Com 66-); NY Metropolitan Ref & Research Lib agency, Inc. (Tech serv com 67-, chm 67-); NY State Adv Com on Centralized Processing66. 10: Columbia Sch of Lib Serv Alumni Assn; AAUP; Archons of Colophon Melvil DuiChowder & Marching Assn; Phi Beta Kappa; Beta Phi Mu. 12: Contrib "Technicalservices in Libraries" (54); Jt auth "Library Guide" (57); Jt auth "The ColumbiaUniversity Libraries" (58); Jt auth "Sample Catalog Cards" (58); Asst to ed "Collegeand Research Libraries" (54-59); Asst ed "Catlg & Clsf," Library Resources & Tech Services" (67-); Jt ed, "The Use of the Library of Congress Classification" (68). 13: Yes. 14: Catlg, tech serv, acad lib admin. 15: 4 Devonshire pl, Toronto 181 Ont Can.

COOK, DANIEL C. b NYC 29 Jl 37. 5: NYU 56-59 (Eng) BA; Columbia 68-69 MLS. 6: Italian. 7: Trainee NY Pub Lib Br 59-60; Researcher "NY Daily News", NYC 61-68; Libn (staff) ColumbiaU E Asian Studies Lib 69-. 9: SLA; ASIS. 14: Ref, syst. 15: 229 E 79 st, New York NY 10021.

COOK, DONALD (CARTER). b Chateaugay NY 8 Je 32. 4: Jeannine Salvo. 5: NY State Col for Tchrs (Albany) 49-53 (Eng) BA; Chicago 55-56 (LS) MA; Columbia 60-65 (LS). 7: US Army Personnel Admin Clerk (Cpl) 53-55; Acquis libn SUNY (Stony Brook) 57-63, Supv of Pub serv 63-65, Asst dir for pub serv 9: ALA; Suffolk Co LA;LI Lib Resources Coun. 12: Ed Suffolk Co LA "Data (64). 14: Readers serv, acquis, admin. 15: 40 Seabrook lane, Stony Brook NY 11790.

COOK, DONALD W. b Ord Neb 27 F 28. 4: Hideko (Sato) Cook. 5: UCal 50-51; Col of Puget Sound 51-52; Seattle U 52; UWash 52-59, 65-66 (Far east, LS) BA, MLS. 6: Japanese. 7: SFC USA, Japan 46-52; Remodeling self-employed, Seattle 59-60; Off mgr Puget Sound Builders Inc, Seattle 60-61; Methods analyst Boeing Aircraft Co, Seattle 61-65; Lib asst Boeing Aircraft Co, Renton Wash 65-66; Tech libn USN, Seattle 66-67; Hd mun libn city admin, Auburn Wash 67-68; Admin libn USN Housing, Yokohama Japan 68-. 9: ALA; Amer Mgt Assn; Japan-Amer Soc of Yokohama. 11: Merit award, Boeing Aircraft Co, 65. 14: Tech libnship, computer applications. 15: 142 Yamate-cho Naka-ku, Yokohama Japan.

COOK, DORIS E. b Jay Me 19 Ap 12. 5: Smith 29-33 (Lat) BA; UVt 33-35 (Lat) MA; Columbia 39-43 BS in LS. 6: Lat, Fr. 7: Asst to libns sec Conn State Lib 35-38, Catlgr 38-46, Head newspaper dept 46-58, Archivist 58-61, Act head tech processes 62; Mss catlgr Conn Hist Soc, Hartford Conn 62-. 9: SAA; ConnLA. 10: Hartford Libns Club; Appalachian Mt Club. 14: Catlg of mss & archives, indexing. 15: 181 Sigourney st, Hartford Ct 06105.

COOK, EARLEEN (HOLLEMAN), b San Antonio Tex 11 D 25. 4: Joseph Lee Cook. 5: St Mary's U 48-50 (Hist); Our Lady of the Lake Col 50-52 (Hist) BA; UTex 52-54(Hist) MA; Tex Women's U 60 MLS. 6: Fr. 7: Asst to archivist UTex 55-60; Ref libn Emory U 61-64; Ser & bind libn Tex Christian U 64-65; Period ref libn Arlington State Col 65-67; Spec serv libn UTex (Arlington) 67-. 14: Ref, spec collections. 15: 916 W Inwood, Arlington Tx 76010.

COOK, EDGAR T. b NYC 6 Ja 24. 5: Occidental Col 41-43, 46-48 (Philos) AB; USoCal 49-52 (Music, LS) MS in LS. 7: 2nd lt, Bombadier USAAF 43-46; Acquis libn Cal State Col (Long Beach) 52-58, Asst libn Tech Serv 58-68; Lib servconsul Bro-Dart Industries Inc, El Segundo Cal 68-. 8: Libn, ALA Century 21 Exhibit, Seattle Worlds Fair 62. 9: ALA; MusLA; CalLA; SLA; SoCal Tech Proc Group; SoCal Med Lib Group. 10: Phi Mu Alpha. 14: Tech serv, music libnship, lib automation. 15: Bro-Dart Industries Inc 645 Hawaii st, El Segundo Ca 90245.

COOK, ESTHER CLARE. b St Johnsbury Vt 22 je25. 5: UVt 43-47 (Music Educ) BS in Music Ed, 49-50 (Music) MA; West Res 61-62, 63-65 MS in LS. 7: Music & art tchr pub schs, Vt & NY State 47-49, 51-53; Commercial artist Amer Greeting Corp, Cleveland 55-60; Catlg libn ULouisville 62-63; Music catlgr Chicago Pub Lib 65-. 68; Catlgr Staunton (Va) Pub Lib 68-. 9: ALA; VaLA. 10: Phi Beta Kappa; Betaphi Mu. 14: Catlg, ref. 15: 4 Church st, apt 101, Staunton Va 24401.

COOK, FLORENCE (SOLT). b Findlay Ohio 18 S 12. 5: Findlay Col 30-32; Bowling FGreen State U 57-60 (Eng) AB; West Res 61-65 MS in LS. 6: Fr. 7: Lib asst Findlay Pub Lib, Findlay Ohio 56-59; High sch libn Defiance High Sch,Defiance Ohio 60-61; Head catlgr Thomas Lib Wittenberg U 61-66; Sr bibliog BowlingGreen State U 66-68, Hd bibliog dept 68-. 9: ALA; OhioLA; No Ohio Tech Serv Libns. 10: Sigma Tau Delta; Beta Phi Mu. 14: Catlg, bibliog. 15: 215 Wolfly ave, BowlingGreen Oh 43402.

COOK, HARRY FREDERIC. b St Paul 24 Jl 04. 4: Frances Schuler. 5: UMinn 30 (Bus) BBA; Columbia 32 BSLS, 40 MSLS. 7: Page, clerk, ref asst Pub Lib, St Paul 21-29; Lib asst USDA, Wash DC 29-30; Ref libn Pub Lib, Reading Penn 30-31; Br libn, catlgr, chief of bus sci & tech div Queensborough Pub Lib, Jamaica NY 33-40; Serv command libn Hdq 2nd Ser Com US Army, Govs Island NYC 41-45; Chief of USAF Lib Serv, Wash DC 45- 63; Chief of USAF Lib Serv USAF Mil Pers Center, Randolph AFB Tex 63-66; Asst Prof Grad Dept Lib Sci, Our Lady of the Lake Col 9san Antonio Tex) 68-. 8: Chm, Adv Com of Fed Libns on Personnel & Org for Rept on Fed Deptl Libs, Brookings Inst, 63;Lib educ Equivalency Test Com, US Civil Serv Commsn, Wash DC 62-63; Consul, Sci & Tech Info Div, Off Chief Engr Dept/Army 69. 9: ALA (pres Armed Forces Sect 50-51); sla (pres Mil Libns Div 55-56). 10: United Staff Assn of the Pub Libs of the City of NY; Lib Com Arlington Co (Va) Planning commsn; AAUP. 11: Achievement Citation, ALA Armed Forces Libns Sect 66; Citation USAF Acad 66. 13: Yes. 14: Admin, personnel, ref. 15: Grad Dept LS Our Lady of Lake Col, San Antonio Tx 78229.

COOK, IRENE (SMITH). b Silver Creek Miss 15 S 29. 4: John B. Cook. 5: Miss State Col for Women 47-51 (LS) BS. 7: Libn Lincoln Co. Lib, Brookhaven Miss 51; Child libn Fish Pub Lib, Natchez Miss 51-55; Libn Braden Jr High Sch, Natchez Miss 56-57; Catlgr Research Center Lib Waterways Expt Station, US Army Corps of Engnrs, vicksburg Miss 61-67; Libn Carr Jr High Sch, Vicksburg Miss 67-. 9: MissLA. 15: 156 Beverly dr, Vicksburg Ms 39180.

COOK, JEANNINE (SALVO). b NYC 11 Ap 29. 4: Donald Carter Cook. 5: Hunter Col 47-51 (Chem) BA; Columbia 56-58 (LS) MS, 60- (LS). 7: Chem Chas Pfizer, Brooklyn NY 51-55, Lit chem 56-58; Med libn Amer Cyanamid, NYC 58-60; Engnr libn Columbia U 60-62; Assoc libn SUNY (Stony Brook) 62-63; Ref libn Smithtown Lib, Smithtown NY 65-67; Ref libn Emma S Clark Lib 67-68, Act Dir 68-. 9: ACS; SLA; MedLA; SuffolkCo LA. 12: Ed "Science Reference Notes (61-62). 14: Sci lit, pub libs, admin. 15: 40 Seabrook lane, Stony Brook NY 11790.

COOK, JOHN LOGAN JR. b Charlotte NC 30 Je 17. 4: Sara Stoddard. 5: Wilson Tchrs Col (Wash DC) 36-40 BS in Ed; Catholic U 47-52 MS in LS. 6: Ger. 7: Lib asst Catlg Div LC 40-42; Libn Can Div War Prod Bd, Ottawa Can 42; US Army Battalion libn 17th Base Post Off 42-46; Legal libn US Civilian Prod Admin, Wash DC 46-47; Chief Law Lib US Atomic Energy Commsn, Wash DC 47-51, Chief Tech Lib 51-61; Dir of Libs USAF Inst of tech, Wright-Patterson AFB 61-67; Dir AF Lib Serv Hdqr USAF Personnel Cntr, Randolf AFB Tx 67-. 8: Libn-consul for AFIT-SAC Minuteman Educ Program 62-; Lib instr for DOD-STINFO Course, School of Systems & Logistics (AFIT) 64-; Instr LSWittenberg U, Springfield Ohio 67. 9: SLA (chm Dayton Ohio Chap 63; chm Military Libns Div 66); ASIS; ALA; SWLA; BexarLA. 14: Admin, mechanization. 15: Richfield dr, San Antonio Tx 78239.

COOK, JOHN S(IDNEY). b Milwaukee Wis 21 S 15. 4: Edith Utz. 5: Milwaukee State Tchrs Col 33-37 (Educ) BE; uwis 39-40 BLS. 6: Fr. 7: Jr lib asst US Coast & Geodetic Survey, Wash DC 41, Lib asst 42; Asst libn AAF Tech & Tech Intelligence Lib (Cpl), Seymour Johnson AAF, NC 43-44; US Coast & Geodetic Survey, Wash DC: Chief map info sect of lib 46, Asst libn 47, Chief lib br 47-, 66; US Environmental Sci Serv Admin, Rockville Md: Chief Geophysical Sci Lib 66-. 9: SLA; DCLA. 11: Dept of Com Meritor Service Award, 53. 15: Chief, Geophysical Sciences Lib ESSA US Dept of Commerce, Rockville Md 20852.

COOK, JOSEPH LEE. b Paris Tex 25 S 28. 4: Earleen Holleman. 5: UTex 56-60 (Zool) BA; Emory 61-63 MLS. 6: Ger. 7: Flight Instr Uvalde Flying Serv, Uvalde Tex 48-52; Draftsman Cities Service Oil Co, Midland Tex 52-54; Draftsman Kerr-McGee Oil Co, Midland Tex 54-56; Draftsman UTex 60-61; Pub serv libn Emory U 63-64; Chief loan libn Tex Christian U 64-66; Asst Univ libn 66-. 14: Lib admin, lib automation. 15: 916 W Inwood, Arlington Tx 76010.

COOK, JOSEPHINE ELEANOR. b Red Oak Iowa 19 Jl 09. 5: Pomona Col 26-30 BA; UCal (Berkeley) 31-32 Certif in Libnship MLS. 7: Stud asst Pomona Col Lib 27-30; 1st asst libn Visalia Pub Lib, Visalia Cal 34-42; Libn ref dept Santa Ana Pub Lib, Santa Ana Cal 42-. 9: CalLA. 14: Ref. 15: 1303 N Olive, Santa Ca 92706.

COOK, KATHLEEN (WISELEY). b Robinson Ill 19 O 13. 5: Tex Christian U 30-33 (Eng); Hardin-Simmons U 63-64 (Eng); N Tex State U 64-65 (LS) BA. 7: Catlgr LaRetama Pub Lib, Corpus Christi Tex 50-57, Head tech processing 57-62/ Catlgr Abilene Pub Lib, Abilene Tex 62-64; Head Libn Orange Pub Lib, Orange Tex 65-. 9: ala; TexLA (chm Memb Com 68-69); Tex Municipal LA (sec 68-69). 10: AAUW. 14: Catlg. 15: 509 W Cypress, Orange Tx 77630.

COOK, MARGARET GERRY. b Trenton NJ 28 N 03. 5: Smith 21-25 (Math, Fr) AB (cum laude); Drexel 25-26 BS in LS; Columbia 41-469educ) AM, 45-48 (Tchg of Eng); UPenn 48-49 (Amer Studies). 6: Fr, Ital, Ger, Sp. 7: Libn Jr High Sch,Trenton NJ 26-27; Asst catlgr Ind U (Bloomington) 27-28; head catlgr Warder Pub Lib,Springfield Ohio 28-31; Asst libn NJ State Tchrs Col (Montclair) 31-41, Libn 41-48;Lecturer NYU 47; Assoc Prof Lib Sci Drexel Inst 48-52; Br libn Enoch Pratt Free Lib,Baltimore 52-68. 8: Lecturer in Lib Sci Sch of Educ UBC Can summers 60, 63; Examiner with Middle States Assn of Col & Secondary Sch. 9: ALA-RSD (sec-treas Md Affiliate of ALA-RSD 65-68); MDLA. 10: ACLU; ADA; AAUW. 12: "New Library Key" (57, 2d ed 63, rev ed 65). 13: Yes. 14: Ref, reader serv, lib educ. 15: 2214 Erdman ave, Baltimore Md 21213.

COOK, MARY (MANNING). b Ottawa Ill 14 Mr 08. 5: Wellesley 26-30 (Art Hist) BA; Mills Col 37-39 (Art Hist) MA; UCal(Berkeley) 44-45 Certif in Libnship, 56 (Art Hist, Hist of Printing). 6: Fr, Ger, Sp. 7: Sub-prof asst in catlg div LC 31-33, 36-37; Art libn & lecturer in art hist Mills Col 41-42; Gen asst Mills Col Lib 42-44; Ref libn & lecturer in art hist Mills Col 45-. 9: ALA-ACRL (Dir-at-Large 56-59); Cal LA (Col, Univ & Res Lib Sect; sec 63; mem Reg Resources Coord Com 58-61); Bay Area Ref Libns Coun (chm 60). 10: Bk Club of Cal; Wellesley Club of No Cal. 14: Rare bks. 15: 5933 Camden st, Oakland Ca 94605.

COOK, MILLER FREDERICK. b Boston 15 Je 21. 5: Harvard 40-47 (Romance Langs) BA (cum laude); Simmons 48-49 BS in LS. 6: Fr, Sp, Ital. 7: S/Sgt Military Intelligence Dept, US Army Aerial Photo Interpreter 43-45; Asst libn Museum of Comparative Zoology Lib Harvard U 49-51; Libn Emerson Col Lib 51-52; Ref libn Winchester Pub Lib, Winchester Mass 52-60; Head libn Perkins Sch for the Blind, Watertown Mass 60-61; Head of ref Medford Pub Lib, Medford Mass 61-63; Asst libn Waltham Pub Lib, Waltham Mass 63-. 9: MassLA; Charles River Lib Club; Mens Librarians Group; Alumni Assn of Lib Sci Simmons Col; Harvard Mut Soc. 14: Admin, ref. 15: 46 Kenwood st, Brookline Ma 02146.

COOK, RICHARD LOWELL. b Northfield Minn 4 S 32. 4: Guinevere Sherwood COOK. 5: Luther Col 50-52; St Olaf Col 52-53; Andrews U 55-57 (Eng, Hist) BA; Chicago Lithographic Inst 60-61 (Lithography) Diploma; UMich 68-69 (LS) MA. 6: Sp, Urdu. 7: Cashier, co clk, personnel specialist (Pfc) USA Med Corps, Canal Zone Panama 53-55; Tchr 7th Day Adventist Pontiac Jr Acad, Pontiac Mich 57-59; V-prin, press mgr & Eng dept chm 7th Day adventist Pakistan Union Sch & Col, Chuhankana W Pakistan 61-67; Prin Lariat Boys Ranch, Stapleton Neb 68-69; Asst libn 7th Day Adventist Atlantic

Union Col 69-. 14: Tchg, catlg. 15: Atlantic Union Col, South Lancaster Ma 01561.

COOK, SAMUEL CHARLES. b Brooklyn NY 28 Ap 40. 4: Blanche Wiesen. 5: Hunter Col 57-61 (Pol Sci) AB; UNC 63-64 MS in LS; Polytech Inst of Brooklyn 67-70 (Hist of Sci) MS. 6: Ger. 7: Catlgr Hunter Col 64-65; Catlgr NYU 66; Hd acquis dept Polytech Inst of Brooklyn 66-69; Ser libn Grad Ctr CUNY 69-. 9: LACUNY; Hist of Sci Soc. 14: Acquis. 15: 200 Riverside dr, New York NY 10025.

COOK, SARAH ANN. b Redlands Cal 16 My 35. 5: Mary Washington Col 53-57 (Hist) BA; UKy 59-61 MSLS. 7: Ser catlgr UKy 61-63; Asst order libn Purdue U 63-66; Hd acquis dept Portland State U 66-68; Biblio-libn Approval Dept R Abel & Co 68-. 9: BSA; Printing Hist Soc; Private LA; ALA. 13: Yes. 14: Acquis, rare bks, catlg. 15: 610 SW Maplecrest dr,Portland Or 97219.

COOK, SYBILLA (AVERY). b Buffalo NY 20 Ag 30. 4: John D Cook. 5: Smith 48-50; Northwestern U 50-51 (Ed) BS; Rosary Col 66-68 (LS) MA. 6: Fr. 7: Tchr Lyons Sch Glenview Ill 51; Lib aide Kildeer Countryside Sch, Long Grove Ill 61-66; Libn Laura B Sprague Sch, Deerfield Ill 68-69; Libn Cumberland Sch, Des Plaines Ill 69-. 9: ALA; -AASchL; IllLA; IllASL. 10: Beta Phi Mu. 14: Sch & child libs. 15: Route 2 Box 246, Long Grove Il 60047.

COOK, VERLA R. b Chicago 27 Ap 22. 5: East Mich U 40-44 (Music Educ) BS; Catholic U 49-52 MSLS. 7: Elem vocal music tchr Detroit Pub Schs 44-45; Clerk-typist US Army Ground Forces, Wash DC 45-46; Sec USDA Wool Div, Wash DC 46-51; Libncatlgr US Dept of Com, Bur of Pub Roads Lib, Wash DC 51-67, Chief tech processes sect 67-. 9: SLA; DCLA; Potomac Tech Proc Libns. 10: Wash & Cathedral Choral Socs. 14: Catlg, ref. 15: 4312 Brandywine st NW, Wash DC 20016.

COOKE, ANNA DORSEY. b Baltimore Md 22 F 37. 5: William & Mary 55-59 (Educ) AB; UWyo summer 60 (Amer Studies); UAla 64-65, 66, 67 (Libnship) MA. 6: Fr. 7: Tchr: Hot Springs Co High Sch, Thermopolis Wyo 59-62; George Dewey High Sch, Subic Bay Philippines 62-64; Libn Palisades High Sch, Bucks Co Penn 65-67; Asst ref libn ubaltimore 67-68; Libn Lane High Sch, Charlottesville Va 68-. 9: VaLA; VaEA. 10: Eng Speaking Union of the US; Kappa Delta Pi; United Daughters of the Confederacy. 14: Sch libnship. 15: 502 Yarmouth rd, Towson Md 21204.

COOKE, ANNA LOUISE (LEE). b Jackson Tenn 14 F 23. 4: James A Cooke. 5: Lane Col 40-44 (Soc Sci) BA; Tenn A&I State U summers 44, 45, 48, 49; Atlanta U summers 51-55 MSLS ULouisville 67 (Certif in Admin). 7: Prin Douglas Jr High Sch, Stanton Tenn 44-46; Tchr Jackson City Sch, Jackson Tenn 47-51; High sch libn Jackson City Sch, Jackson Tenn 51-62; Catlg libn Lane Col 62-, Act libn Lane Col 67-. 8: Evaluative Com So Assn of Secondary Schs & Col Memphis Pub Schs 57, and Chattanooga Pub Schs 64-65; Critical Analysis Study, World Book Encyclopedia 64 EvalCom of So Assn of Second Schs & Col, Jackson City Schs 68; Educ Survey Adv ComJackson City Sch 67-68; Mem Salute to Higher Educ Com 68. 9: ALA; TennLA; TennEduc Congress (chm lib sect 64); WTenn Educ Congress (chm lib sect 59); TEA. 10: Jackson Mental Health Assn; Delta Sigma Theta; Links Inc; Amer Cancer Soc;Commun Concert Assn. 12: Ed "The Reporter," Lane Col Alum Quarterly. 13: Yes. 14: Catlg, ref. 15: 120 Halest, Jackson Tn 38301.

COOKE, CONSTANCE B. b Chicopee Mass 14 S 40. 4: John C Cooke. 5: UMass 58-62 (Elem ed) BA; West Res 62-63 MSLS. 6: Fr, Ital. 7: Asst lib bus ind & sci Providence Pub Lib, Providence RI 63-64; Asst catlgr UGa 64-67; Readers' serv libn Elizabethtown Col 67-. 9: ALA; PennLA. 14: Ref, catlg, child serv. 15: 680 N Mt Joy st, Elizabethtown Pa 17022.

COOKE, EILEEN D. b Minneapolis 7 D 28. 5: Col of St Catherine 48-52 (LS) BS. 7: Adult asst libn bkmob Minnespolis Pub Lib 52-57; Br asst Queens Borough Pub Lib, Queens NY 57-58; Br asst & hosp libn Minneapolis Pub Lib 58-62, Pub rel spec 62-64; Asst dir Wash off ALA 64-68, Assoc dir 68-. 8: Mem Visit Com, Case West Res U Lib Sch. 9: ALA; MinnLA; DCLA. 13: Yes. 15: 2430 Pennsylvania ave NW, Wash DC 20037.

COOKE, ELEANOUR RUTH. b Chicago Ill 26 N 11. 5: St Mary of the Woods 30-33 (Journalism) BA; Rosary Col 59-61 MALS. 6: Sp. 7: Asst ref & readers serv libn Oak Park Pub Lib, Oak Park Ill 61-62; Hd catlgr Bk Proc Ctr, Oak Park Ill 62-68; Period libn De PaulU 68-. 8: Helped set up catlg clsf code for bk processing ctr. 9: ALA; IllLA. 10: Friends of the Oak Park Pub Lib. 14: Catlg, ref. 15: 177 N Linden ave, Oak Park Il 60302.

COOKE, ETHEL (MILLER). b Reading Penn 16 N 12. 5: Kutztown State Col 30-34 (LS) BS in ED; Syracuse 37-40 BS in LS. 7: Libn Northeast Jr High Sch, Reading Penn 36-. 9: NEA; PennEA. 10: YWCA. 14: Catlg, child wk. 15: 1026 N 10th st, Reading Pa 19604.

COOKE, GORDON DAVID. b Detroit 2 Mr 27. 4: Yayoi Kobayashi. 5: Hamilton Col 45-47 (Hist); Georgetown U 47-50 (Diplomatic & Consular Practice) BS, 54-57 (Hist) MS. 6: Ger. 7: (Pfc) Battery A 192nd FA Bn, 43rd Inf Div, US, Germany 50-52; USBC, Wash DC: Period clerk 57-59, Ser libn 59-62, Chief ser div 62-63, Chief of ser div & asst dir 63-. 10: Phi Alpha Theta; Lambda Chi Alpha. 15: 6906 24th ave, Hyattsville Md 20783.

COOKE, IRENE (SMITH). b Daingerfield Tex 3 O 14. 4: John G Cooke Jr. 5: U SoWest La 30-34 (Eng) BA; LSU summers 34-37 BS in LS. 6: Fr, Sp. 7: Elem libn & asst catlgr USL, USL, Lafayette La 34-38; Sch lib supv La State Lib, Winnfield La 38-39; Catlgr Centenary Col, Shreveport La 62-. 9: ALA; LaLA; Caddo-Bossier Lib Club. 10: Colo Mountain Club; Nat Ski Patrol System; Bus & Prof Women. 13: Yes. 14: Catlg, archives. 15: 119 Taliaferro pl, Shreveport La 71101.

COOKE, MADELEINE (DAVIES). b Brooklyn NY 11 D 12. 4: Wendell W Cooke. 5: Barnard 30-36 (Fine Arts) BA; Columbia 63-66 MS. 7: Child libn Summit Pub Lib, Summit NJ 66, Ref libn 66, Catlgr & dir tech serv 66-. 14: Catlg, exhibits. 15: 38 Valley View ave, Summit NJ 07901.

COOKE, MARGARET D. b Hamilton Can 25 Jr 21. 5: UToronto 39-42 BA, 45-49 BLS. 7: Asst libn Hamilton Pub Lib, Can 47-50; Asst, hd circ dept McMaster U Lib 52-56; Ref libn CBC, Toronto 56-. 8: LAW; Meteorological Observer, RCAF (W) 42-45. 15: 354 Jarvis st, Toronto Ont Can.

COOKLOCK, RICHARD A. b Milwaukee 18 Jl 24. 4: Barbara Zielke Cooklock. 5: UWis 46-49 (Eng) BA, 49-51 (Eng) MA, 51-52 MALS; Chicago summer 55 (LS). 6: Fr. 7: US Army (Pfc) Inf, US, N Africa, Italy 42-45; Lib Sci Instr Wis State U (River Falls) 52-55, Head Libn 55-. 9: ALA; WisLA (treas; chm & sec Col & Univ Sect). 10: AAUP; Pierce Co (Wis) Hist Soc; Beta Phi Mu. 13: Yes. 14: Col lib admin. 15: 653 S Main st, River Falls Wi 54022.

COOKSTON, JAMES SANDERS. b Winnfield La 7 Je 27. 5: La Polytech Inst 43-44, 47-49 (Eng) BA; LSU 50-51 (Educ) M Ed, 53-55 (LS) MS. 6: Fr. 7: US Army (Sgt) 44-46; Tchr Istrouma Jr High Sch, Baton Rouge La 50-55, Libn 55-56, 57-58; LSU; Supv U Lab Sch 56-57, Staff Lib summers 56-58, Instr Lib Sch58-59; Lecturer LSU Lib Sch 62-63; Admin asst & dir recr proj LA State Lib 59-63;Head Soc Sci Div LSU Lib 63-65; State supv of sch libs State Dept of Educ, Batonrouge La 65-. 8: Fac mem NDEA and HEA Lib Insts, LSU 67,68. 9: NEA; ALA; LaLA(pres 67-68); SWLA; LA Tchrs Assn; CathLA. 10: Beta Phi Mu; Phi Delta Kappa; KappaDelta Pi; Phi Kappa Phi; Pi Kappa Alpha; LA Hist Assn; Baton Rouge Lib Club (pres 58). 12: Asst ed LaLA "Bulletin (59-62); Ed "Lousiana Genealogical Register (53). 13: Yes. 14: Sch libs, child lit, recr. 15: 1956 Tamarix, Baton Rouge La 70808.

COOLEY, MARGUERITE (BOWERS). b Wellington Kan 6 S 09. 5: UKan(Lawrence) 31 (Foreign Lang, Psych) AB; Peabody 52 MALS. 6: Sp. 7: Asst libn Medford Pub Lib, Medford Okla 33-38; Bkkeeping 1st Nat Bank, Snyder Okla 41-42; Civilian bkkeeper Telephone Serv Ft Winfield Scott, San Francisco 43-44; Lib asst VA Hosp, McKinney Tex 48-50; Ref asst George Peabody Col Lib 51; Libn Ariz State Dept of Lib & Archives, Phoenix 52-61, Dir 61-. 9: ALA-ACRL; CalLA (chm Publ Com 63-64). 10: Altrusa Club (offs). 14: Ref in law & Southwest hist. 15: Dept of Lib and Archives Capitol, Phoenix Az 85007.

COOLIDGE, COIT. b Fall River Mills Cal 27 Ap 06. 4: Nancy Palmer. 5: Stanford 24-28 (Eng) AB; Columbia 28-29 BLS; UCal 33-34 (LS) MA. 7: Clerical NY Pub Lib 28-29; Asst libn University Club, NYC 29-31; Asst libn Chaffey Jr Col 31-33; Newspaper room, Ref dept Pub Lib,Oakland Cal 34-37; City libn Pub Lib, Hayward Cal 37-39; City libn Pub Lib, Richmond Cal 40-66. 8: Consul on Pub Lib Bldgs;Richmond Cal 49; San Leandro Cal 60; Sunnyvale Cal 60; Coos Bay Ore 65; So San Francisco67; Livermore Cal 66; Great Falls Mont 67; Turlock Cal 69; Adv coun, UCal Berkeley Schof Libnship 56-57; Cal State Adv Com on Correctional Libs 60-62. 9: ALA; CalLA (pres 45, chm 2 coms

49, 64). 10: Rotary Internat; Citizens Adv Com for KQED (Educ TV station, San Fracisco). 13: Yes. 14: Pub lib bldgs, pub lib procedures, up-dating of pub lib methods. 15: 965 35th st, Richmond Cal 94805.

COOMBS, DONALD JAMES. b Fla 27 S25. 5: UCLA 47-51 (Eng) BA, MA; UCal (Berkeley) 64-65 MLS. 6: Sp, Fr, Ger. 7: T/4 US Army Spec Serv 44-46; Methods analyst Lockheed Aircraft, Marietta Ga 51-53; Acct exec PR, O S Tyson & Co, NY 55-58, 60-61; Chief ed Polaris Publs Lockheed Missiles, Sunnyrale 62-64; Acquis libn usan Francisco 65-; Ser hd UCLA 67-. 8: Free-lance ed, textbks, Harcourt-Brace, 60. 9: CalLA; SLA; ALA (Descr Catlg Com). 10: Phi Beta Kappa. 14: Acquis, rare bks, bibliog, ser. 15: Univ of Calif, Los Angeles Ca 90024.

COON, WENDELL B(ACON). b Waverly Iowa 6 Ja 06. 4: Dorothy Delavan. 5: Neb State Tchrs Col (Kearney) 24-27 (Eng, Educ) AB; Chicago 27-28 (Eng); USoCal 40-41 BS in LS. 7: Bkseller, asst buyer Bullocks Bk Store, Los Angeles 29-40; Jr libn asst Los Angeles Co Law Lib, Los Angeles 41; Jr libn, ref Los Angeles Co Pub Lib, Los Angeles 41-42; US Army (T/Sgt) 42-45; Asst to command libn US Army, Ft Douglas Utah & Presidio San Francisco 42-45, asst command libn US Army 45-46, Sixth Army Command libn & Dir Ref Lib & Lib Depot 46-54, Sixth US Army (Area) Libn, Hqrs Sixth US Army 54-, Dep Sixth Army Command Spec Serv Off 66-. 8: Var personnel sel bds for San Francisco Bay Area cities, 55-; Pioneered for var services & duties of Army gen libs. 9: ALA (Life mem; Judge, JohnCotton Dana Awards 53; chm Equipt Com 58 Conf, ALA Notable Bks Com 58-61); LPRC;CalLA (chm Elect Com 46-); Pub Lib Execs of Cent Cal; Fed Lib Com Reg Rec Rep 66-). 10: Beta Phi Mu; Roxburgh Club; West Hist Assn; HELIBS of No Cal; Gleeson LibAssocs (USan Francisco); Mental Health Assn; etc; Assn US Army; Friends San FranciscoPub Lib. 11: Army Commendation Ribbon (45) for contrib to Army Lib Serv, 43-45;Outstanding Performance Award 59, 64, 67. 13: Yes. 14: Personnel mgt, admin, audio materials, lib publ, bkmob serv, bk sel & acquis. 15: 1886-15th ave, San Francisco Ca94122.

COONEY, ELEANOR (TROWT). b Wenham Mass 3 S 12. 4: Wilfred O Cooney. 5: Simmons 29-33 (LS) BS. 6: Fr, Ger. 7: Circ asst Jones lib, Amherst Mass 34-38; Libn pub lib, Littleton NH 38-40; Tufts Lib: Asst libn 51-57, Dir 57-. 9: ALA; MassLA (vice-pres & pres-elect, past chm Educ Com & Legis Com); Greater Boston Pub Lib Admin (past pres); Simmons Col Alum Assn; Cohasset AFS Com; NELA; Old Colony Lib Club (past pres). 14: Admin, ref. 15: 62 Cedar st, Cohasset Ma 02025.

COONEY, JANE (HANSON). b Montreal Can 18 Mr 43. 4: Patrick E Cooney. 5: Marianopolis Col 59-63 BA; UToronto 63-64 BLS. 7: Ref libn Calgary Pub Lib, Calgary Alta 64-65; Circ libn McGill U 65-66; Ref libn Metro Toronto Pub Lib 66-. 9: CanLA (memb com). 14: Ref. 15: 2 Sultan st 205, Toronto 5 Ont Can.

COONEY, JOAN DORIS. b Hempstead NY 18 Je 27 05: Bethany Col (Bethany W Va) 45-50 (Sociol) BA; Carnegie 50-51 MLS. 7: Ref asst & ya libn Hempstead Pub Lib, Hempstead NY 51-59; Asst ref libn Hofstra U 59-. 9: NYLA; Nassau Co LA. 10: Friends of Hempstead Pub Lib. 14: Ref. 15: 9 Liberty ct, Hempstead LI NY 11550.

COONEY, LEO JOSEPH. b Jacksonville Ill 30 Mr 35. 4: Virginia McCaskill Cooney. 5: UFla 56-57 (Ind Mgt) BSBA; Ga Inst Tech 65-66 (Info Sci); Peabody Col 67-69 MLS. 7: Process engr RCA, W Palm Beach Fla 60, Cost estimator 61, Computer programmer 62; Syst analyst Gen Electric, Redstone Arsenal Ala 63; Syst analyst Re dstone Sci Info Ctr, Redstone Arsenal Ala 63-67, Computer specialist 67-. 9: AlaLA. 14: Lib a utomation. 15: 712 Owens dr, Huntsville Al 35801.

COONROD, FLORENCE E. b Cohoes NY 7 Je 18. 5: William Smith Col 35-39 (Fr) BA; NY State Col for Tchrs (Albany) 39-40 BS in LS; Russell Sage Col 41-43 (Span); NY State Col for Tchrs 49, 56-58 (LS); UIll Med Center (Chicago) 64 (Med Lit). 6: Fr. 7: Bkkeeper Cohoes Savings Bank, Cohoes NY 40-44; Bkkeeper North River Savings Bank, NYC 44-45; Statistical clerk Mutual Chem Co, NYC 45-47; Bkkeeper Intercity Sales Co, Boston 48-49; Asst Instr NY State Col for Tchrs (Albany) 49-50; Asst libn NY State Dept Agric & Markets, Albany NY 51-58; Asst libn NY State Med Lib, Albany NY 58-. 9: MedLA. 10: Amer Guild of Organists; Saturday club of Cohoes. 14: Circ, ref. 15: 16 Imperial ave, Cohoes NY 12047.

COOPER, ALICE MILDRED. b Potomac Ill 26 O 22. 5: East Ill U 39-43 (Com) B Ed; UIll 44-47 BS in LS, 48-51 (LS) MS. 7: Period asst UIll Lib (Urbana) 45-47, Ser catlgr 47-53; Br libn Peoria Pub Lib, Peoria Ill 53-57; Asst libn Metcalf Sch Ill State Normal U 57-58; Head of child serv Aurora Pub Lib, Aurora Ill 58-65; Dir of child serv Lincoln Lib, Springfield Ill 65-67; Asst ref libn Booth Lib, East Ill U 68-. 9: ALA; IllLA (chm Child Libns Sect 63). 10: Beta Phi Mu. 14: Child wk, ref. 15: Rt 1, Gilman Il 60938.

COOPER, ANNA JARMAN. b Wilmington NC 29 Ja 06. 5: NYU 38 (Hist) BS, 42 (Amer Hist) MA; Peabody 58 MA in LS. 7: Circ libn Brooklyn Col 29-42, Ref libn 42-46; Ref libn Dickinson Col 46-50; Libn Caldwell Co Pub Lib, Lenoir NC 50-54; Asst libn Salem Col (Winston-Salem NC) 54-60, Libn 60-. 9: ALA; SELA; NCLA. 10: Altrusa. 14: Catlg, ref. 15: Salem Col, Winston-Salem NC 27108.

COOPER, ANNA MARY. b Evansville Ind 6 Je 11. 4: Louis Baxter. 5: IndU 29-32; UEvansville 56-57 (Eng, Educ) AB; UNC 60-61 (LS). 6: Fr, Sp. 7: Asst libn Inst of Govt UNC (Chapel Hill) 61; Libn I & II VA, LA 61-65; Libn II Orange City Pub Lib, Orange Cal 65-. 9: CalLA; OrangeCoLA; So Cal Tech Processes Gp. 10: AAUW; League of Women Voters; Friends of the Lib. 14: Bk selection, rare bks, y-a serv, ref serv, pub rel. 15: 164 W Alessandro, San Clemente Ca 926721.

COOPER, ARTHUR GERALD. b Far Rockaway NY 2 Ja 39. 4: Karen Berlin. 5: Queens Col 56-60 (Lib Educ) BA, 60-61 (Lib Educ) MS in ED & Diploma in Lib Ed. 6: Sp. 7: Libn J P McKenna Jr High, Massapequa Park NY 60-64; Libn Willis Ave Sch, Mineola NY 64-. 9: NYState SchLA; NY State Tchrs Assn. 15: 18 Peter Lane, Plainview NY 11803.

COOPER, BEULAH E. b Tuskegee Inst Ala 21 Ja 04. 5: Hampton Inst 26-28 (LS) Diploma; Bradley Polytech Inst 31-33 (Langs & Lit) AB; NYU 39-40 (Personnel Admin) MA; Chicago 48 (Med Ref & Bibliog). 6: Sp, Fr. 7: Libn Ft Valley Normal Sch (Ft Valley Ga) 28-31; Libn Miles Col 34-35; Libn Bennett Col (Greensboro NC) 35-39; Libn NYU Com Lib 39-41; Camp libn US Army Fort Dix NJ 41-45; Camp libn US Army Camp Kilmer NJ 45; Chief libn VA Hosp, Tuskegee Ala 46-. 8: Sec Macon Co (Ala) Lib Bd of Trustees, 66-. 9: MedLA. 10: Tuskegee Civic Assn; Links Inc. 14: Med lib ref & bibliog. 15: PO Box 684, Tuskegee Inst Al36058.

COOPER, ELIZABETH C. b Nashville 29 Ja 11. 5: Okla City U 30-35 (Hist, Eng) AB; UOkla 35-36 (LS) BA. 7: Lib asst Carnegie Lib, Okla City Okla 36-39; Libn Taft Jr High Sch, Okla City Okla 39-41; Hosp libn VA, Wadsworth Kan 41-42; Post libn US Army, Camp Gruber Okla 42-44; Act libn Okla State Lib 44-45; Libn overseas US Army, European Theatre 45-48; Ref libn Okla State Lib 48-51; Sec Okla Lib Commsn, Okla City Okla 51-52; Station libn US Navy, Norman Okla 52-58; Station libn USAF, Clinton-Sherman AFB 58-60; Adult serv libn Okla City Libs, Okla City Okla 61-65; Coordinator adult serv Okla Co Libs, Okla City Okla 65-66; Consul & act dir of lib development Ill State Lib 67-68; Dir Los Alamos CoLib 68-. 8: Bldg consul to Okla State Lib. 9: ALA (coun 65-66); SWLA (exec bd 60-62); OklaLA (pres 60-61, state repto Ala 65-, mem Exec Bd 60-62); Okla Adult Educ Assn (exec bd 61, sec 62, pres65-66). 10: Soroptimist Internat; Womens Civic Clubs Coun; Commun Coun; Civic Com of C of C. 14: Pub serv, adult serv, field wk, admin. 15: 929 Northwest 21, Okla CityOk 73106.

COOPER, ESTELLE M (BANNEN). b Greenville Mich 12 N 08. 4: Lloyd A Cooper. 5: West Mich U 30 (Lat) AB; UMich 69 (LS) MA. 6: Sp, Fr, Ger. 7: Libn area schs, Greenville Mich 67-68; Libn high sch, Greenville Mich 68-. 15: 791 Baldwin Lake rd, Greenville Mi 48838.

COOPER, FREDA (GAINES) (ATKINSON). b Shawsville Va 4 N 14. 4: Wise Edward Cooper. 5: Radford Col 33-35 (Educ), summers 43, 45, 45-46 (Elem Educ) BS, summers 50, 59 (LS). 7: Tchr Friendship Sch 35-36; Tchr Mt Pleasant Sch 37-39; Tchr Tex Sch 39-40; Tchr Shawsville (Va) High Sch 46-50, Libn 50-54; Libn Alleghany Dist High Sch, Shawsville Va 60- Materials coord Montgomery Co Sch Bd, Christiansburg Va (summer 68). 9: NEA;VaEA (Dept of Sch Libns). 10: YMCA. 14: Catlg, lib serv to studs, rare bks. 15: Alleghany Dist High Sch, Shawsville Va 24162.

COOPER, HELEN MARGARET. b Lansdowne Penn 3 Ag 13. 5: Ohio Wesleyan U 31-35 (Eng) BA; UIll 35-36 BS in LS, 36-39 MS. 6: Fr, Ger. 7: Catlgr UIll(Urbana) 36-39; Catlgr of music The Newberry Library, Chicago 39-41; Catlgr Yale U Lib 41-42; Asst catlg libn, catlg libn Penn State U 42-50; Bkmob libn Washington Co Free Lib, Hagerstown Md 50-59;

Libn Coyle Free Lib, Chambersburg Penn 59-64; Libn Wilson Col 64-. 9: ALA; PennLA. 10: AAUW. 14: Admin, ref, inter-lib coop. 15: 1314 Wilson ave, Chambersburg Pa 17201.

COOPER, JANET (ROSEMARY). b NYC 18 D 42. 5: West Res 60-64 (Eng) BA; Simmons 64-65 (LS) MS; SUNY(Buffalo) 65-68 (Eng). 7: Asst catlgr SUNY(Buffalo) 65-68; Libn Bancroft Sch, Andover Mass 68-. 9: ALA; NYLA. 14: Catlg, rare bks, ref, ya. 15: 2 Anderson pl, Boston Ma 02114.

COOPER, JOANNE (SIMON). b NYC 7 N 26. 4: David Cooper. 5: Cornell 44-45 (Eng); NYU 45-48 (Eng, Phil) BA; LIU 62-69 MSLS. 6: Sp. 7: Asst ref libn Merrick Lib, Merrick NY 68-. 9: ALA; Nassau Co LA. 10: LWV. 14: Ref, docs. 15: 1035 Schuman pl, Bladwin NY 11510.

COOPER, LENOX G JR. b Wilmington NC 15 Jl 36. 4: Bonnie Brown. 5: UNC (Chapel Hill) 54-56, 59-61 (Eng) AB, 65-67 MS in LS. 6: Sp. 7: USN 57-58; Admin asst & investment analyst First Nat Bank, Atlanta 61-63; Ins & real estate agt Lenox G Cooper Ins, Wilmington NC 63-65; Libn Sandhills Commun Col 67-68; Asst acquis libn UGa Lib 68-69, Asst to dir 69-. 9: ALA; SELA; GaLA. 10: Beta Phi Mu; PIKA. 14: Admin, acquis. 15: 2012 S Milledge ave, Athens Ga 30601.

COOPER, LEONE ANDERSON. b Va. 5: Westhampton Col URichmond 27-31 (Lat, Hist) AB; Peabody Col summers 47-50 (LS) MA; UVa summers 35-36, 38-39 (LS); William & Mary summers 40, 44 (LS). 7: Tchr Franklin Co (Va) Schs 31-39; Tchr Randolph-Henry, Charlotte 39-40; High sch libn, Court House Va 40-42; Libn Charlotte Co Pub Lib, Court House Va 42-45; Lobn Va High Sch, Bristol Va 45-. 9: ALA; NEA-DAVI (reg legisl chm 69); VaLA (pres Sch Lib Dept 54-55); VaEA (sec Tchg Materials Sect). 10: Delta Kappa Gamma; Charlotte Woman's Club; LWV. 14: Sch lib wk. 15: 712 Lawrence ave, Bristol Va 24201.

COOPER, LUCY. b NYC. 4: Jack Cooper. 5: Hunter Col 37-40 (Fr) BA; Pratt 62-64 MLS. 6: Fr. 7: Tchr High Sch of Art & Design RBd of Educ, NYC 42-45; Interior designer, NYC 47-; Libn Maxwell High Sch Bd of Educ, NYC 64-. 9: NYC Libns Assn; NY Lib Club. 10: Beta Phi Mu; Phi Beta Kappa; Brooklyn Lib Coun; Bur of Commun Educ Coun; 71st Precinct Youth Coun. 14: Wk with ya, adult functional illiterates. 15: 25 Eastern parkway, Brooklyn NY 11238.

COOPER, MARGARET K. b Hugo Okla 23 Je 29. 4: Reginald D Cooper. 5: Langston U 47-51 (Biol) BA; UOkla 56-57 MLS; UNeb 58-; UWis(Madison) summer 65. 6: Fr. 7: Tchr-libn Douglass Sch, Vian Okla 51-54; Tchr-libn Douglass Sch, Bartlesville Okla 54-56; Asst circ libn UNeb 57-60, Sr asst sci libn 60-62; Jr high sch libn Fremont Jr High Sch, Stockton Cal 62-. 9: ALA; NEA; Cal Tchrs Assn; CalASchL; Delta Kappa Gamma. 10: LWV; Links. 12: Jt auth "A Study of the Negro in the Historical Development of the United States"(68). 14: Instr materials centers. 15: 44 E Pine st, Stockton Ca 95204.

COOPER, MARIANNE V (ABONYI). b Budapest Hungary 14 Ap 38. 4: Herbert W Cooper. 5: Syracuse 57-60 (Liberal Arts) BA; Columbia 60-61 (LS) MS. 6: Hungarian, Fr, Russ. 7: Grad asst Hunter Col 60-61; Chem libn Columbia 61-66; Info Scientist Amer Inst of Physics 67-. 9: SLA; ALA; ASIS. 10: Phi Beta Kappa. 14: Documentation,research, library automotion. 15: 17 St Lawrence pl, Jericho NY 11753.

COOPER, MATTIE SUE. b Overton Co Tenn 15 Je 14. 5: Tenn Polytech Inst 38 (Hist) BS; Peabody 41 (LS). 7: Co Libn Overton Co, Livingston Tenn 39-42; Libn Livingston Acad, Livingston Tenn 42-43, 44-45; Libn US Army, Camp Gorda Ga 43-44; Asst libn Tenn Tech U 45-. 9: TennLA (Chm Col & Univ Sect 61-63); SELA; TennEA. 10: Delta Kappa Gamma;Kappa Delta Pi; Pi Delta Kappa; Coterie Club; Algood Bk Club; Tenn Tech CommunConcert Assn. 14: Admin, ref. 15: Box 6A Tenn Tech, Cookeville Tn 38501.

COOPER, MURIEL (KIPLE). b Independence Iowa 22 F 43. 4: Clyde Daniel Cooper Jr. 5: UWis (Madison) 61-65 (Pol Sci) BA; No IllU 65-67 (LS) MA, Tchg Certif. 7: Libn valley High Sch, Elgin Iowa 67; Asst libn Upper Iowa Col 67-68, Hd libn 68-. 9: ALA. 14: Sch libnship, lib admin. 15: 327 Parkside dr, Sycamore Il 60178.

COOPER, MYRTLE ELIZABETH (BURDICK). b Blaine Wash 2 My 08. 4: Theron Warren Cooper. 5: Whitman Col 26-27 (Eng lit); UWash 27-28 (Eng lit), summer 63-67 (LS) MA; Pacific U 30-32 (Eng lit) BA. 7: Bon Marche, Seattle: Personnel dept 28-30, Sales 32-35; Sales Coles Dept Store, Billings Mont 36-38; Billings Pub Lib: Clk 53-59, Reader's asst 59-63, Br admin 63-66, Ref dept hd 66-. 8: Member adv com for "The Library Image: a Manual of Library Interpretation," Montana 60. 9: ALA; Nat Fed of Press Women: MontStateLA; Mont Press Women; Mont Assn for Mental Health. 10: DAR; Colonial Dames XVII Cent. 11: Kappa Kappa Gamma. 14: Ref, Montana hist col. 15: 632 Burlington ave, Billings Mt 59102.

COOPER, ROBERT GILBERT. b St Louis Mo 24 F 30. 4: Vivian Bernice Rabun. 5: Union Col Lincoln Neb 48-52 (Ed, Rel) BS in Ed; USoCal 62-66 MS in LS. 7: Elem sch tchr Texas Conf of SDA, Fort Worth Tex 52-62; Loma Linda U: Ref circ libn 62-64, Period libn 64-67; Hd libn SWest Union Col 67-. 9: ALA. 14: Admin. 15: Route 4 Box 289, Cleburne Tx 76031.

COOPER, SUSAN ELIZABETH. b London Ont Can 9 Mr 11. 5: UAlberta 28-31 (Fr) BA; Columbia 40-41 BS in LS. 7: Edmonton Pub Lib, Can: Gen asst 41-42, Asst catlgr 42-48, Hd circ 48-54, Hd catlg 54-62, Br libn 62-. 9: CanLA; AltaLA. 15: 11146-83 ave, Edmonton Alberta Can.

COOPRIDER, DAVID OLEN. b Zion Ill 17 Jl 36. 4: Nancy Tarter. 5: Millikin U 55-58 (Hist) BA; UIll 63 (LS) MS. 7: Tchr Blue Mound High Sch, Blue Mound Ill 58-62; Asst libn Millikin U 62-63; Libn Blue Mound High Sch, Blue Mound Ill 63-66; State Reg Sch Supv Title II ESEA, III of the Superintendent of Pub Instr 66-; part-time exten instr in LS UIll 68-69. 9: NEA; IllEA; IllLA. 15: 51 LaSalle dr, Decatur Il 62521.

COOVER, JAMES B. b Jacksonville Ill 3 Je 25. 4: Georgena Walker Coover. 5: Colo State Col 45-49 (Music) AB, 49-50 (Music) MA; UDenver 51-53 MALS. 6: Ger, Fr, Ital. 7: US Army T/5, Eng, France, Germany 43-45; Asst dir Bibliog Center for Research, Denver 50-53; Music libn George Sherman Dickinson Music Lib, Vassar Col 63-67; Prof of mus, Curator Mus Lib SUNY (Buffalo) 66-. 8: Middle States Assoc Eval Teams 61, 62 & 65; Consul, Music Lib Union Theol Sem 59, Swarthmore Col 62, Oberlin Col 57; Consul to NY StateCoun on the Arts 64-; Mayor's Commsn on The Arts, Poughkeepsie NY 66-67. 9: MusLA (pres 59-60, mem many coms; chm bibliog Com); Association internationale des Bibliotheques musicales; Col Mus Soc. 10: AAUP; Player & mgr: Hudson Valley Philharmonic Orch. 12: "Photoduplication Services: A Survey, 1951 (51); "A Bibliography of Music Dictionaries (52); "Music Lexicography, Including a Study of Lacunae, 1500-1700 (58); Co-auth "Medieval and Renaissance Music on Long-Playing Records, with R Colvig (64); Ed "The Rainbeau Catalog, facsimile ed (62). 13: Yes. 14: Bibliog, data processing. 15: Vassar Col, Poughkeepsie NY 12601.

COOVER, ROBERT WINGERT. b Waynesboro Penn 15 D 22. 4: Dorothy Black Coover. 5: UMd 46-49 (Hist) BA; UMd 49-51 (Educ); Catholic U 51-56 MS in LS; UWash summer 63 (Search Strategy); Cal West U 63-64 (Data proc, Sys, Proceds; Drexel 66-67 (Info Sci). 6: Fr. 7: Tchr soc studies, Eng Anne Arundel Co Sch Bd, Millersville Md 49-51; Circ libn, ref asst US Naval Acad Lib (Annapolis) 51-55, Asst catlgr 55; Head catlgr US Navy Postgrad Sch, Monterey Cal 55-56; Tech info spec G E Small Aircraft Engnr Dept, Lynn Mass 56-58; Engnr libn Gen Dynamics-Convair, San Diego 58-62, Lib supv, tech info spec 62-65; Supv tech info center Chrysler Corp Space Div, New Orleans 65-66; Adjunct instr LS. 9: SLA (SD Chap: chm Recr Com 62-63, chm Employment Com 64-65; ASIS. 10: Phi Alpha Theta. 12: "History of the Maryland State Library, 1827-1939 (59). 14: Tech processes. 15: Apt F-8 1000 W Aaron dr, State College Pa 16801.

COPE, GABRIELE E (MEYER). b Kassel Germany 7 N 19. 4: Ray Cope. 5: Fr W Univ (Berlin Germany) 43-44 (World Hist); Karl'sU (Prague) 44-45 (World Hist) BA; Syracuse 64-65 (LS) MS. 6: Ger. 7: Asst libn II (catlgr) SUNY Col of Forestry (Syracuse 65-66, Asst libn III (hd catlg) 66-67, Assoc libn (hd tech serv) 67-68; Asst Prof lib sci & tech serv libn Neb WesleyanU 68-. 9: ALA; SLA; AAUP; NYLA; NebLA; LincolnLA. 10: Beta Phi Mu; Pi Lambda Sigma. 14: Tech serv, catlg, acquis. 15: 1831 Broadmore dr, Lincoln Nb 67506.

COPE, JOHNNYE LOUISE. b Eden Tex 15 D 23. 5: N Tex State U 42-45 (Eng)BA; Ohio State U 48-49 (Eng) MA; UMich 52-54 MA in LS; Certif in archival mgt 60. 6: Sp. 7: Instr Eng N Tex State Lab Sch, Denton Tex 45-48, 49-52; Fellow UMich Lib Ext Dept 52-54; Asst in ref dept El Paso Pub Lib, El Paso Tex54-55; Head ref dept Trinity U Lib (San Antonio Tex) 56-66; Hd ref dept N Tex State U 66-. 9: TexLA; SWLA. 14: Ref, archives. 15: 1315 Greenbrier st, Denton Tx 76201.

COPELAND, DELBERT HENRY. b Philadelphia Miss 3 D 28. 4: Julia Ann Bivins. 5: E Central Jr Col 47-48 AA; Miss So Col 48-50 (Eng) BS, summers 52-54 (Educ) MA; UMiss (LS). 7: Tchr: Goodhope High Sch, Carthage Miss 50-51, Bratt Jr High Sch, Atomore ala 52-55, Leesburg High Sch, Leesburg Fla 55-64; US Army, Korea 51-52; Dir lib serv Lake Sumter Jr Col 64-. 8: State Textbook Adoption Com in Lit for Lake Co; Sec Adv Bd of Leesburg Pub Lib 58-60; Chm Lib Com Leesburg High Sch 57-59; Dir of Radio Youth progral; So Assn Evaluation Com. 9: FlaLA; Fla Assn Pub Jr Cols. 14: Ref, admin. 15: 907 North Shore dr, Leesburg Fl 32748.

COPELAND, ELIZABETH H(ARRELL). b Tarboro NC 12 Mr 17. 5: E Carolina Col 34-38 (Eng, Hist) AB, 38-39 (Eng) MA; Peabody 40-42 (LS) BSLS. 6: Fr. 7: Asst libn Reynolds High Sch, Winston-Salem NC 42-43; Libn Shepard-Pruden Lib, Edenton NC 43-45; Ref asst Research Dept Curtis Publ Co,Phila 45-46; Research libn Bur of Mun Research, Phila 46-49; Dir BHM Reg Lib, Washington NC 49-54; Dir Sheppard Mem Lib, Greenville NC 54-. 8: ALA staff for Lib USA NY Worlds Fair 64; LC vol reader Bks for Blind; Guest lecturer Dept Lib Sci E Car U 68 & 69. 9: ALA; SLA; SELA (var offs); NCLA (var offs); Certif Bd (chm Pub Lib Sect 67-69). 10: NC Lit & Hist Soc; Pitt Co Hist Soc; East Carolina Art Soc; Pitt Co Interracial Com; NC Travel Coun: Pitt Co Interracial Coun: Amer Cancer Soc; East Area TB Assn Bd. 14: Admin, ref, rare bks, educ. 15: 703 E Fifth st, Greenville NC 27834.

COPELAND, EMILY A(MERICA). b Tifton Ga 17 Ap 18. 5: Spelman Col 33-37 (Biol) AB; Atlanta 41-42 BSLS; Columbia 43-46 MSLS; NYU49-50 (Higher Educ, Admin); Columbia U 59-60; USoCal 69. 6: Fr, Ger. 7: Tchr of Eng & biol Tift Co Schs, Tifton Ga 37-38; Libn Finley High Sch, Chester Pub Sch, Chester SC; Lib asst Atlanta U & Spelman Col summers 38-42; Head Libn Gammon Theol Sem 42-44; Acquis libn Atlanta U 44-45; Sch wk & ref, child serv NY Pub Lib 45-46, 59-60; Head Dept of Lib Sci SC State Col 46-51; Head Dept of Lib Serv Fla A&M U 51- Guest Prof No MichU summer 67. 8: Org in-serv program for libns of SC held annually 46-51; Spec consul Southeastern Coop Study, which publ "Southeastern Libraries; SC Lib Devel Com; SC Lib Educ Planning Com; Adv to SC Lib Bd on sel of bks & materials for Negro libs Adv mem Marquis Biog Lib Soc, 69. 9: ALA (Memb Com rep SC 47-51, sec Jt Com on Libnship as a Career 55-56, Exec Planning Com 62);-AASchL (Dele Assembly rep SC 47-51 & Fla 53-59);-LAD (Fa rep 57-); FlaLA (pres 53-56; Recr Com 56-59, Film Com 57-59); SELA (Lib Educ Com). 11: Carnegie Grant in Aid, 38;Gen Educ Bd Fellowship 49-50; Certif of Merit Award, Spelman Col 68; Fac DevelGrant, Fla A & M U 69. 12: "Handbook for the Guidance of School Library Internship"(63); Ed "School Library Workshop Bulletin" (54-56). 13: Yes. 14: Lib educ, sch libs, infosci. 15: 614 Howard ave, Tallahassee Fl 32304.

COPELAND, J(AMES) ISAAC. b Clinton SC. 5: Presbyterian Col 27-31 (Hist) BA; Peabody 31-32 BS in LS, 32-34 (Hist) MA; Chicago summers 36, 38, 39, 40 (LS, Educ); UNC 45-48 (Hist) PhD. 7: Asst ref & period Peabody Col 32-35; Libn Furman U 36-42; Libn Presbyterian Col 42-45; Documents libn UNC (Chapel Hill) 47-50; Libn & Prof of Hist Peabody Col 52-67; Dir So Hist Collection & Prof hist UNC (Chapel Hill) 67-. 9: ALA (Coun 62-65); Bibliog Soc of Amer; Org of Amer Histns; sc hist Assn; So Hist Assn; SELA (var offs; treas 60-62; chm Intellectual Freedom Com); SCLA (pres 42-43); TennLA; SAA; AHA; NCLA; NC Hist Soc (chm Memb Com 67). 10: Kiwanis Club; Nashville Council on Human Relations (Bd 61-63); Nashville Lib Club. 12: Ed "Democracy in the Old South and Other Writings of Fletcher M Green (69). 13: Yes. 14: Ref, admin, lib hist, mss. 15: P O Box 576, Chapel Hill NC 27514.

COPELAND, JOHNNIE (HUNTER). b Montgomery Ala 19 Mr 24. 5: Ala A&M Col 40-43 (Elem Educ) BS; Fisk U summers 44, 45, 48 (Secondary Educ); Syracuse summers 51, 52, 53 & 54 MSLS; Columbia 55 (LS). 6: Fr. 7: Libn Sumter Co Train Sch, Livingston Ala 43-45; Libn Ind High Sch, Tuscaloosa Ala 45-46; Libn Academy St High Sch, Troy Ala 50-51; Libn Hooper City High Sch, Sayreton Ala 51-54; Ya libn NY Pub Lib 54-55; Asst libn Ala A&M Col 55-57; Libn Carver High Sch, Birmingham Ala 59-65; Head Libn Wenonah Jr Col 65-. 8: Libn Tenn A&I State U Lib summers 60-65. 9: ALA-ACRL; NEA; Amer Tchrs Assn; Ala State Tchrs Assn; AlaASchL; Ala Jr Col Libns Assn. 10: YWCA; Alpha Kappa Alpha. 13: Yes. 14: Catlg. 15: Wenonah Jr Col Lib, Rt 10 Box 486, Birmingham Al 35211.

COPELAND, L(OWELL) GRIFFIN. b Valdosta Ga 7 D 19. 4: Gretchen Hill Copeland. 5: David Lipscomb col 37-39 (Liberal Arts) Diploma; Harding Col 39-41 (Fr) AB; Peabody 43-44 (Sp) MA, 52-53 MA in (LS). 6: Fr, Sp. 7: Jr High Tchr Statenville Pub Schs, Statenville Ga 41-42; Span & Eng Tchr Bell High Sch, Bell Fla 42-44; Span tchr Falfurrias High Sch, Falfurrias Tex 44-46; Instr of Span & Eng Fla Col 46-52, Instr of Span, Head libn 52-. 8: Minister of the gospel, preaching in churches of Christ 41-. 9: Amer Assn of Tchrs of Span & Portu (Fla Chap v-pres 57, treas 64-66); ALA (Served on 3 com of U & Col Sect); Phi Delta Kappa. 10: Friends of the Library,temple Terrace Pub Lib (v-pres 65-66, pres 66-68). 14: Admin. 15: Florida Col, Temple TerraceFl 33617.

COPELAND, PATRICIA SUE. b Blountsville Ala 11 Ja 37. 5: AuburnU 54-58 (Home Econ) BS. 7: Lib asst LSU Med Lib (New Orleans) 58-61; Hd circ Tulane U Med Lib 61-64, Hd ref & circ 64-. 9: MedLA; (So Reg Assn memb chm). 10: Kappa Delta Alumni Assn. 14: Ref, interlib loans. 15: 2833 St Charles ave, New Orleans La 70115.

COPELAND, SANDRA (KAY). b Okla City Okla 26 Mr 44. 5: Grinnell Col 62-66 (Anthrop) BA; Tulane 66-67 (Anthrop); LSU 67-69 (LS) MS. 6: Lat, Ger. 10: Phi Kappa Phi. 14: Ref & pub serv (soc scis). 15: 2808 Calhoun st, New Orleans La 70118.

COPENHAVER, CHRISTINA (VESTLING). b Urbana Ill 7 O 43. 4: John W Copenhaver Jr. 5: Carleton Col 60-64 (Fr) BA (cum laude); UMinn 64-65 (LS) MA. 6: Fr, Russian, Lat. 7: Anesthesia aide Carle Hosp, urbana Ill summer 62; Tchg asst Lib Sch UMinn 64-65; Ref libn Hamline U 66-68; Instr UMinn Lib Sch 68-. 9: ALA; MinnLA (co-chm & chm Ref Sect 66-68). 10: Beta Phi Mu. 12: Co-auth "Library Service to the Disadvantaged, a bibliography (68); ERIC Clearinghouse for Library and Information Sciences (68). 14: Ref, col libs, lib educ. 15: Univ of Minn Lib School Walter Library, Minneapolis Mn 55455.

COPPE, THOMAS M. b St Paul 4 Ag 32. 5: Carleton Col 50-51; UMinn 51-54 (Romance Lang) BA; Columbia 54-55 (Fr) MA, 56-58 MSLS. 6: Fr, Sp, Ital, Hebrew, 07: Catlgr NY Hist Soc, NYC 58-62; Catlgr Oakland U 63-64; Catlgr Toledo Pub Lib, Toledo Ohio 64-67; Hammond (Ind) Pub Lib 67; Catlgr Dayton & Montgomery Co Pub Lib 68-. 8: Reorg & recatlg lib at Davis Bus Col, Toledo Ohio 64-65. 9: ALA-RTSD; OhioLA. 14: Catlg. 15: 1333 W Fairview ave apt 26, Dayton Oh 45406.

COPPOLA, DOMINICK A. b NYC 23 F 14. 4: Esmeralda Cravanzola. 5: Brooklyn Col 31-35 (Eng) AB; Columbia 52-55 MS. 6: Fr, Ital, Sp. 7: Exec V-Pres, Sec Stechert-Hafner Inc, NYC 35-, pres 35-. 8: Exec bd Seminars on Acquis Lat Amer materials. 9: ALA; CathLA; MedLA; SLA. 13: Yes. 14: Acquis of books in print throughout the world. 15: c/o Stechert-Hafner Inc 31 East 10th st, New York NY 10003.

CORAL, LENORE (FRANCES). b Detroit 30 Ja 39. 5: Chicago 57-61 (Music) BA, 62-65 (LS) MA; Kings Col ulondon 65-67(Music). 06: Fr. 6: Fr. 7: Clerk UChicago Lib 59-61, Asst Music libn 62-65, Fine Arts libn UCal (Irvine) 67-. 8: Res asst Music Dept UChicago 64-65. 9: MusLA (Com on the Applications of Technology to Music Bibliog); Amer Musicological Soc; Internat MusLA; Royal Mus Assn. 11: Fulbright grant, London 65-67. 12: Comp "A Concordance of the Thematic Indexes to the Instrumental Works of Antonio Vivaldi (65). 14: Music libnship. 15: 787 Diamond, Laguna Beach Ca 92651.

CORBIN, JOHN BOYD. b Moody Tex 7 Ap 35. 5: Temple Jr. Col 53-55 AA; N Tex State Col 55-57 (LS) BA; UTex 59-60 MLS. 7: Catlgr Dallas Pub Lib 57; Sp/4 US Army Spec Serv Libs, Ft Belvoir Va 57-59; Lib asst UTex 59-60; Acquis libn Arlington State Col 60-63; Dir of tech serv Tex State Lib 63-67; Asst libn for systs analysis Tarrant Co Jr Col (Ft Worth Tex) 67-. 8: Consul Okla Dept Libs 68; Part-time instr N Tex State U Dept Lib Serv 68-69; Guest lecturer DEW Inst on State Lib UOkla summer 69. 9: ALA-RTSD (Bk Catlgs Com 67-71; Standards Com 67-69); -ACRL (coord So Reg Spec Projs Com Jr Col Libs 69-70; chm Pro-tem Discussion Gp Tech Serv Dirs Proc Ctr 66); TexLA (sec-treas Col & Univ Div 69-70); SWLA. 10: Austin Lib Club; Friends of Tex Libs; UTex (Austin) Grad Sch Lib Sci Alumni Assn. 12: "Technical Processing Manual for Small Public Libraries: Cataloging (62); "Catalog of Genealogical Materials in Texas Libraries (65); "Technical Services Manual for Small Libraries (65); "Index of State Geological Survey Publications Issued in Series (65); Ed "Texas libraries (65-66). 13: Yes. 14: Tech serv, centralized processing, lib automation, syst analysis. 15: 1912A W Sanford st, Arlington Tx 76010.

CORBIN, RICHARD T. b Phila 12 D 38. 5: Subiaco Col 57-61 (Philos) BA; Baylor 63-64 BLS; Peabody 67-68 MLS. 7: Lib asst Baylor U Lib (Waco) 63-64; Young adult libn Cleveland Pub Lib 64-65; Ref asst Nashville Pub Lib 67-68; Ref asst AtlantaPub Lib 68-. 9: ALA; SELA; GaLA. 14: Ref. 15: PO Box 1021, Atlanta Ga 30301.

CORDELL, HOWARD WILLIAM. b Industry Ill 13 Je 21. 4: Margaret Wilson. 5: West Ill U 39-43 (Bus Educ) BS, 47-49 (Bus Educ) MS; UIll 56-57 MSLS. 6: Fr. 7: (Cpt) USAFR USAF, US & So Pacific 43-46, 50-51; tchr Comm High Sch, Little York Ill 46-49; Tchr Jr Col (Burlington Iowa) 49-50; Acquis libn West Ill U 51-62; Instr Grad Sch Lib Sci UIll(Urbana) 62-63; Assoc Dir Fla Atlantic U Lib 63-66; Hd ref dept UIll (Chicago Circle) 66-67; Dirs Libs Cornell Col (Mt Vernon Iowa) 67-. 9: ALA; FlaLA (chm Intel freedom Com; IowaLA (chm-elect Col Sect). 13: Yes. 14: Ref. 15: 508 Third ave S, Mt Vernon Ia 52314.

CORDERO, JOSE A. b NYC 11 N 22. 4: Ruth Reiman. 5: Queens Col 41-42, 46-48 (Hist) BA; Columbia 48-50 (LS) MS; IBM 63 (1401 Computer Prog) Certif. 6: Sp. 7: Infantry unit cmdr US Army (Capt) 42-46; Lib fellow City U(NY) 49-50; Asst dir Free Lib, Summit NJ 50-52; Ref Army War Col, Carlisle Penn 52-56; Chief Documents Lib Rome Air Develop Cntr, Rome NY 56-57; Head research info retrieval Lederle Labs, Pearl River NY 57-63, Head lib & tech records dept 63-. 13: Yes. 14: Lib mgt, info retrieval. 15: Lederle Labs, Pearl River NY 10965.

CORDTS, GERTRUDE M. b Boone Iowa 26 My 13. 5: UIowa 36-38 (Eng) BA; UIll 38-39 (LS) BS. 6: Ger. 7: Jr asst Ericson Pub Lib, Boone Iowa 33-36; Bkmob libn Athens Co Lib, Nelsonville Ohio 39-41; Libn Bryan Pub Lib, Bryon Ohio 41-44; Child libn Seattle Pub Lib 44-46; Sr child libn Oakland Pub Lib, Oakland Cal 46-59, Supv ref libn 59-. 8: Chm Com on Standards for Cal Child Libs 59-60. 9: ALA; CalLA (chm Child & YP Sect 57); Assn of Child Libns of No Cal (pres; Com on Standards 59-60). 10: Conf of Cal Hist Socs; LWV. 13: Yes. 14: Child libnship, ref. 15: 4026 Aspen pl, Oakland Ca 94602.

COREN, ELAINE H (LIBRESCOT). b Phila Penn. 4: Harry V Coren. 5: Hunter Col (Pol Sci) BA; Columbia (Pol Sci) MA, 60 (LS) MS. 7: Publicity & promotion Helena Rubinstein inc, NYC 47-57; Libn F D Whalen Jr High Sch, NYC 63-67; Libn Mt Vernon High Sch, NY 67-. 9: SLA; NYLA; WestchesterCoLA. 15: 15 Manor pl, Larchmont NY 10538.

COREY, LELAND A(UBREY). b Nowata Okla 23 Mr 22. 5: Okla Baptist U 39-43 (Hist) AB; Central Baptist Theol Sem 44-47 (Theol) ThM; UKan 49-51 (Hist)MA; Kan State Tchrs Col (Emporia) 53-54 (LS) M; Washington U (St Louis) 65-66. 6: Ger. 7: Libn & research asst Central Baptist Theol Sem 51-53; Grad stud asst Kan State Tchrs Col Lib (Emporia) 53-54; Bind libn Kan State Col (Manhattan) 54-55; Libn E Tex Baptist Col 55-57; Catlg libn Mary E Bivins Pub Lib, Amarillo Tex 57-58; Libn Hannibal-LaGrange Col Ext Center, St Louis 58-. 66; Catlg libn William Jewell Col 66-68; Tech serv libn Danville Jr Col68-. 8: Pastoral & interim pastoral wk in Baptist Churches, 43-50 & 54. 9: ALA; IllLA. 10: Boy Scouts. 14: Admin, catlg, ref, ser, circ. 15: 611 Jewell st, Danville Il 61832.

CORGAN, CATHERINE M. b Wilkes-Barre Penn 13 F 35. 5: Col of New Rochelle 53-57 (Hist) BA; Columbia 59-60 MS in LS (cum laude). 6: Fr. 7: Osterhout Free Lib, Wilkes-Barre Penn: Ref asst 57-59, Act head adult circ 60-62, Head adult circ 62-64, Head adult serv 64-65, Asst libn &head adult serv 65-67, Asst libn & coord dist serv 67-. 9: ALA; PennLA (pres NE Penn Chap). 10: Beta Phi Mu. 15: 363 Glen Summit, Mountaintop Pa 18707.

CORKILL, NILA JEAN. b Imperial Neb 17 F 35. 5: Kearney State Col 53-57 (Eng) BA; UDenver 62-63 (LS) MA. 7: Asst libn McCook Pub Lib, McCook Neb 57-61; Clerk Adams Drug, Imperial Neb 61-62; Stud asst UDenver Lib 62-63; Catlg libn UOmaha 63-. 9: NebLA (sec-treas Col & Univ Sect 65-66, chm Personnel Com 69). 14: Catlg. 15: 4822 Chicago st, apt 1, Omaha Nb 68132.

CORKLE, VIOLET (SCHWARTZ). b Chester Penn 5 F 31. 4: William Irvin Corkle. 5: State Tchrs Col 49-55 (Acct, Eng) BS Ed; Drexel 63-69 (LS). 7: Tchr Shippensburg Area Sch Dist, Shippensburg Penn 55-63; Elem libn Caesar Rodney Spec Sch Dist, Camden Del 63-67, Jr High libn 67-. 8: Lib Bd Trustees, Shippensburg Pub Lib 60-63. 9: NEA; ALA; DESA; DelLA; Caesar Rodney TA. 14: Sch libs (especially second level). 15: 2017 Highland ave Buchanan Acres, Dover De 19901.

CORLEY, NORA T(ERESA). b Montreal. 5: McGill 51 (Geog) BA, 52 BLS, 61 (Geog) MA. 6: Fr, Russian. 7: Asst libn Law Lib McGill U 52-54; Libn in chg Arctic Inst of North Amer, Montreal 54-. 9: SLA (pres Montreal chap 64-65; chm Geog & Map Div 69-70): QuebecLA (Eng sec 58-59); Assn of Canadian Map Libs. 10: Canadian Assn of Geographers. 13: Yes. 14: Ref, catlg, hist geog. 15: 703 Roslyn ave, Westmount 217 Que Can.

CORMIER, EVELYN (STUART). b New Orleans 6 My 10. 4: Carroll Winn Cormier. 5: L State Normal Col 30-32 (Eng, LS) AB; LSU 32-36 BS in LS. 7: Stud asst La State Normal Col 30-32, Assisted in org of train sch lib 31; LSU Lib Sch Lib summers 33-36; Instr Lib Sci Loyola U (New Orleans)summer 38; Asst New Orleans PubLib summer 44-46, Libn Algiers Br summer 48, Libn Royal Br summer 50; Catlgr LSU (New Orleans) summer 62; Libn Martin Behrman Jr-Sr High Sch, New Orleans 32-64; Libn Edna Karr Jr High Sch, New Orleans 64- Libn I New Orleans Pub Lib summer 66-68. 9: LaLA (treas 57, chm Audit Com 60-61, mem Pub Rel Com 55-57; Sch Lib Sect: chm, sec, treas); SWLA (chm Jr. Memb Round Table, Memb Chm); La Tchrs Assn; New Orleans Lib Club (var offs); Jr Memb Round Table (chm 3 units 35-38). 10: Delta Kappa Gamma; Delta Sigma; Beta Sigma Phi. 11: "Order of the Rose Beta Sigma Phi; Certif of Merit and key to city (New Orleans). 12: Co-auth "Reading and LibrarySkills, Grades 7-8, Div of Instr New Orleans Pub Schs Curr Bulletin No. 20" Ed"Conference on Louisiana Materials," State Dept of Educ Bul 782. 13: Yes. 14: Sch lib (Jr & Sr high). 15: 6307 GeneralMeyer ave, New Orleans La 70114.

CORNEIRO, NINA A(NGELA) (CARRUTH). b Boston 8 Ap 16. 4: Phillip L(eo) Corneiro. 5: Pratt 51-52 Lib Sci Certif. 7: Libn St Thomas Pub Lib, St Thomas VI 37-45; Supv libn Dept of Interior, VI 45-48; Supv libn St Thomas Pub Lib, St Thomas VI 48-55; City libn St Thomas Pub Lib, Charlotte Amalie VI 55-61; Hd libn Charlotte Amalie High Sch, St Thomas VI 61-. 8: Mem of Accreditation Com of Middle States Assn of Col & Secondary schs: Christiansted High Sch VI 63, St Dunstans Episcopal High Sch, Christiansted St Croix VI 69. 9: ALA. 10: Com Music Assn Charlotte Amalie St Thomas VI (off); Caribbean Chorale. 14: Admin, catlg, sch libs. 15: Box 225 Charlotte Amalie, St Thomas VI 00801.

CORNELISSE, LOIS (SHIVELY). b Harvey Ill 15 Mr 07. 4: Carel M Cornelisse. 5: Grand Rapids Jr Col 26-28; UMich 28-30 AB in LS. 6: Fr. 7: Asst in catlg dept UMich Lib (Ann Arbor) 30-33; Circ asst Grand Rapids Pub Lib, Grand Rapids Mich 37-41; Libn Aeroproducts Div Gen Motors Corp, Vandalia Ohio 43-46; Ref libn UDayton Lib 62-. 14: Ref. 15: 1514 Peters rd, Troy Oh 45373.

CORNELL, GEORGE WADE. b Ashtabula Ohio 7 Ja 20. 4: Barbara Greene. 5: Kent State 39-41, 46-47 (Eng, biol) BS in Ed; West Res 48-49 MS in LS; Ohio State U 61-62, 68 PhD. 6: Sp, Fr. 7: US Army, US, France, Germany 42-46; Eng tchr Warren Twp Sch, Leavittsburg Ohio 47-48; Head catlg libn Kent State U 50-53; Libn for tech serv Antioch Col Lib 49-50, 53-69; Dir of Lib Serv SUNY Col (Brockport) 69-. 9: SAA; OhioLA; Ohio Valley Reg Group Tech Serv Libns; ALA. 12: "The College Archive: A Study in Administration (68 diss). 14: Tech serv, hist of Amer educ, acad archives, admin. 15: Library SUNY College, Brockport NY 14420.

CORNING, DALE I. b Caldwell Ida 25 Ja 41. 5: Col of Ida 59-64 (Soc studies) BA; LSU 65-66 (LS) MS. 7: Ida State Lib, Boise Ida: Ref libn 67, Lib consul 67-68; Dir Coeur d'Alene Pub Lib, Coeur d'Alene Ida 68-. 9: ALA; Amer Mgt Assn; PNLA; IdaLA. 11: Beta Phi Mu. 14: Acquis, admin. 15: Box 1041. Coeur d'Alene Id 83814.

CORNISH, LENA B. b Lansing Mich 13 Ja 09. 4: Elwyn H Cornish. 5: Mary Hardin Baylor 26-28 (Journalism); Kalamazoo Col 28-29 (Eng) AB; West Mich U 58 (LS) MA; UMex(Mexico City) summer 59. 6: Sp. 7: Bkkeeper Community Chest, Kalamazoo Mich 31-38; Tchr Lawton Pub Schs, Lawton Mich 45-46; Tchr libn Decatur Pub Schs, Decatur Mich 51-61; Libn Portage Pub Schs, Portage Mich 61-. 8: Production mgr for school libraries 62-65. 9: NEA; ALA; MichEA; MichASchL; MichLA. 14: High sch libs. 15: Rt 1, Lawton Mi 49065.

CORNWALL, (MARY) FAITH (KINGSCOTE). b Victoria BC Can 17 N 15. 5: UBC 31-34 (Lat, Math) BA; Toronto 53-54 BLS. 7: Tchr various high schs, BC 35-41; Can Army (CWAC) (Capt), Can, UK 41-46; Asst to tech examiner Civil Serv Commsn, Ottawa 46; Nat Research Coun, Ottawa: Research asst 47-49, Head reports sect Div Mech Eng 49-53, Libn Flight Research Lib 54-56; Ref libn Sudbury Pub Lib,

Sudbury Ont 56-57; Catlgr Can Dept of Agric, Ottawa 57-59; Head tech serv Dept of Nat Defence, Ottawa 59-63; Head tech processes Cal West U 64-65; Catlgr Henry E Huntington Lib, San Marino Cal 65-. 14: Catlg. 15: 1715 E Oakwood st, Pasadena Ca 91104.

CORNWELL, BERTHA TERRY. b Marshall Tex 9 O 1898. 4: B L Cornwell. 5: Baylor U 33-39 (Eng); N Tex State Col 40-46 (LS) BS, MS; UHouston 50, 54 (Educ). 6: Ger. 7: Sch libn Sour Lke Ind Sch Dist, Sour Lake Tex 20-60; Exec sec pres Sour Lake State Bank, Sour Lake Tex 27-33; Curator Broning Lib Baylor U 33-39; Coordinator sch libs French Ind Sch Dist, Sour Lake Tex 44-45; Assoc ed weekly newspaper "The Oil City Visitor, Sour Lake Tex 60-. 9: ALA-ATLA (Tex Memb Chm 63-68, var other assignments); TexLA (sec 44-45; Tex Libtrustee Round Table 63-64). 10: Womans Fed Club of Sour Lake; E Tex Nature Club of Beaumont. 11: Trustee of the Year for Tex, 63. 13: Yes. 14: Sch libs, typography. 15: PO Box 546, Sour LakeTx 77659.

CORNYN, SISTER M ANGELA SSND. b Chicago . 5: Chicago Tchrs Col 28-29; Mt Mary Col 29-34 (Hist) BA; Marquette U 35-41 Hist) MA; Rosary Col 42-47 (LS). 6: Fr. 7: Tchr Notre Dame High Sch, Milwaukee 32-41, 44-50; Tchr-libn Huntington Catholic High Sch, Huntington Ind 41-44; Tchr & Prin St George Sch, Kenosha Wis 50-52; Col Libn Mt Mary Col (Milwaukee) 52-. 8: Ed staff for quarterly; "Books for Catholic Colleges. 9: ALA-ACRL; CathLA; Asst sec-treas, chm Col & Univ Sect 2 yrs); WisLA; WisCathLA; IllCathLA; var offs in both state assns. 12: Ed CathLA Col & Univ Lib Sect Newsletter. 13: Yes. 14: Admin, acquis. 15: Mt Mary Col Lib, Milwaukee Wi 53222.

CORONTZES, ARTHUR N(ICHOLAS). b Charleston SC 17 N 23. 4: Helen Carabatsos Corontzes. 5: USoCar 46-50 9eng, Fr) AB; Emory 51-52 (LS) ML. 6: Gk. 7: Gen studies libn Price Gilbert Lib Ga Tech 52-58; Asst libn Citadel Lib The Citadel 58-. 9: SCLA. 14: Admin, pub serv. 15: The Citadel, Charleston SC 29409.

CORRIGAN, ADELINE. b Cleveland. 5: Notre Dame Col 26-30 (Eng) AB; West Res 30 BSLS. 6: Fr, Sp. 7: Cleveland Pub Lib: Child libn 31-46, Asst supv wk with child 47-53, Supv wk with child 53-65, Asst to dir 65-. 8: Consul to faculty, Sch of Lib Sci West Res. 9: ALA; OhioLA. 10: Delta Kappa Gamma; Welfare Fed of Cleveland. 13: Yes. 14: Pub lib serv. 15: 3716 Lytle rd, Shaker Heights Oh 44120.

CORRIGAN, BROTHER EDMUND CFX. b Brooklyn NY 28 F 36. 5: Catholic U 56-60 (Hist) AB; St Johns U 62 (LS); Adelphi Col 68. 6: Fr, Sp, Lat. 7: Libn Leonard Hall Sch, Leonardtown Md 60-62; Libn Nazareth High Sch, Brooklyn NY 63-. 8: Eval team, Middle States Eval Com; Coordinator of New Projs, Brooklyn Diocese Schs 68. 9: ALA; CathLA (v-pres Supv Sect); NYLA; Xaverian Bros Educ Assn (chm Lib D)LA; NEA-DAVI; LIEEC; NYSECA. 13: Yes. 14: High sch libs. 15: Nazareth High Sch, E 57th st & ave D, Brooklyn NY 11203.

CORRIGAN, DOROTHY D. b Rockford Ill. 4: Richard Corrigan. 5: UAla 39-40; Brown Bus Col 40-41; Rockford Col 60-. 7: Bk Review Ed Armed Forces Management Magazine, Rockford 55-56; Lectr Adult Educ Coun, Chicago 60-; Producer performer Semi-EducEntertainment Prod, Rockford 62-; Producer performer WREX-TV Series "Let's Look at Books" Rockford 61-62; Lib consul Keith Country DaySch, Rockford 64-65; Lib consul Bradley & Bradley Architects, Rockford 64-66; Writer Sci Research Assoc, Chicago 65-66; LecturerNat Lecture Bur, Chicago 65-; Trustee consul Ill State Lib, Springfield 66-. 8: Rockford Pub Lib Bd dirs 56-68. 9: ALA-ALTA (pres65-66); Ill Lib Trustee Assn (pres 67-69). 10: Nat Bd, Nat Bk Com 66-; Nat Soc for the Study of Communic 69-. 11: DistinguishedService Citation for Trustees, Ill 65. 12: "The Drama of Prayer" 63; "Sci Res Assocs, Materials and Methods Extension Service" 65;Seven juvenile & juvenile-sci bks (63-68). 13: Yes. 14: Trusteeship. 15: 1931 Old Orchard ct, Rockford Il 61107.

CORRIGAN, JEROME K. b Minnespolis 7 My 25. 5: UCincinnati 43-44 (Army Star Train Program in Engnr); UMinn 46-48 (Hist) BA (cum laude), 48-50 (Hist), 50-52 BS in LS. 7: Minneapolis Pub Lib; Shelver 47-48, Lib aide clerical 49-52, Child libn 52-55, Adult asst 55-56, Br libn Jordan br 56-62, Br libn Franklin br 62-67, Br libn Oxon Hill Br Prince George's Co Mem Lib 67-. 9: ALA (Life mem)-ASD (chm Jt Com on Serv to Labor Gps, Steering Com for Stafforg Round Table); MdLA; DCLA. 10: Chi Phi; UMin Lib Sch Alumni Assn. 14: Wk with ya (culturally deprived), admin, personnel. 15: Oxon Hill Br Lib, 5450 Oxon Hill rd, Oxon Hill Md20021.

CORRY, ANN MARIE. b Minneapolis Minn 31 D 43. 5: Washburn U 61-65 (Eng, Hist) BA; UDenver 65-66 (LS) MA. 6: Fr. 7: Clk Kan State Hist Soc Lib, Topeka Kan 62-65; Catlgr UIowa Libs 66-68; Ref libn Educ & Psych Lib UIowa 68-. 9: ALA; IowaLA. 14: Catlg, acquis. 15: 2034 9th st 29, Coralville Ia 52240.

CORRY, BROTHER EMMETT OSF. b NYC 28 D 34. 5: St Francis Col 53-60 (Eng) AB; Columbia 60-62 (LS) MS; UWash summer 65 (NDEA Inst). 6: Ger, Fr. 7: Stud libn St Francis Col (Brooklyn NY) summers 58-60; Libn Bishop Ford High Sch, Brooklyn NY 62-69; Asst libn St Francis Col 69-. 8: SchLib Consul to Supt of Schs, Diocese of Brooklyn (NY)65-; ESEA Title II Adv Comms for NY State& City. 9: ALA-AASchL; CathLA (chm sec sch sect of Brooklyn-LI unit 67-69); NEA-DAVI; NYLA (Sch Lib Superv sec); NY City Sch Libns Assn. 10: Parents Assn; Metropolitan Opera Guild; Metropolitan Museum of Art; ABS; James Joyce Soc. 13: Yes. 14: Schlibnship, superv. 15: St Francis Col, 180 Remsen st, Brooklyn NY 11201.

CORS, PAUL B(EAUMONT). b Janesville Wis 13 Ag 30. 5: UWis 48-50; Ripon Col 51-53 (Classics) BA; Rutgers 58-59 MLS. 6: Lat, Ger, Fr, Ital, Gk, Sp. 7: Lib asst Wis Free Lib Commsn, Madison Wis 56-58; Catlg asst Rutgers U Lib 58-59; Catlg libn NM State U Lib 59-64; Head of tech processes Wyo State Lib 64-. 9: ALA; MPLA; WyoLA (chm Intel Freedom Com 68-). 10: Beta Phi Mu; Phi Beta Kappa. 13: Yes. 14: Catlg, clsf, intel freedom. 15: 514 E 23rd st, Cheyenne Wyo 82001.

CORTALE, JOSEPH A. b Yonkers NY 5 Ap 46. 5: C W Post Col 63-67 (Hist) BA; LIU 67-69 (LS) MS. 7: Catlgr Maritime Col SUNY (Ft Schuyler) 67-. 9: NYLA. 14: Catlg. 15: 1960 Nereid ave, New York NY 10025.

CORTES, MARGARET LOIS (FERGUSON). b Portland Ore 6 F 18. 5: Chico State Col 35 (Eng); UCal(Berkeley) 35-39 (Eng) BA; San Francisco State Col 39-40 (Educ) Kind/Prim Cred; UCal (Berkeley) summer 40 (Eng), 63-65 MLS & Tchg Cred. 6: Fr, Sp. 7: Dir Childrens Community, Mill Valley Cal 40-42; Asst dir Jack & Jill Parents Coop Nursery Sch, Walnut Creek Cal 53-54; Tchr Danville Elem Sch Dist, Danville Cal; Reader Allens Press Clipping Bur, San Francisco 62; Sr lib asst UCal Lib (Berkeley) 63-65; Libn I Contra Costa Co Lib, Danville Cal 65-. 9: ALA; CalLA. 14: Ref. 15: 2540 Stone Valley rd, Danville Ca 94526.

CORTH, ANNETTE (SIEGEL). b Newark NJ 14 O 27. 4: Richard Corth. 5: Douglass Col 45-49 (Ger) BA; Columbia 61-62 MLS. 6: Ger. 7: Exec secy Various NYC & Newark NJ 50-61; Libn I (Info Div) NY Pub Lib 62; Ref libn Eng Soc Lib NYC 62-63; Ref libn Bell Telephone Labs, Whippany NJ 63-67; Supv Central Info Serv CIBA Chemical & Dye Co, Fairlawn NJ 67-. 9: SLA (treas NJ Chap); ASIS. 14: Ref. 15: 10 Plymouth rd, Nutley NJ 07110.

CORUM, FREDERICK MAXWELL. b Newark NJ 3 N 15. 5: Gretchen Waldrep Corum. 6: Fr, Lat. 7: Eng tchr Col of the Ozarks 40-41; Chaplain US Navy (Lt) 42-46; Eng tchr Pikeville Col 48-51; Catlgr Buffalo & Erie Co Pub Lib, Buffalo NY 53-64; Head catlgr SUNY(Binghamton) 64-. 9: ALA; NYLA. 10: Phi Beta Kappa. 15: 927 Byford blvd, Endwell NY 13763.

CORUM, GLORIA. b Ida 9 Je 23. 5: U of Puget Sound 47 (Eng Lit) BA; UWash 48. 6: Fr, Sp. 7: Ext dept ref dept Child libn Moore Br, Br libn Mottet Br, Br libn S Tacoma Br, Tacoma Pub Lib 48-. 9: ALA; WashLA; PNLA. 14: Yp, br libs. 15: 3411 S 56th, Tacoma Wa 98409.

CORY, JOHN MACKENZIE. b Asheville NC 13 Ja 14. 4: Patricia O'Connell. 5: UCal (Berkeley) 30-32, 34-36 (Hist) BA, 36-37 Libnship Certif; Hastings Col of Law UCal 32-34 (Law); UChicago 38-40 (Libnship). 7: Libn jr grade UCal (Berkeley) 37-38, Assoc libn 45-48; Research asst UChicago Grad Lib Sch 40; Dir libs UAla (Tuscaloosa) 40-42; Sr pub lib specialist US Off of Educ, Wash DC 42-43; Chief lib program div US Off of War Info, Wash DC 42-43; Chief warrant off USAAF Transport Command 43-45; Exec sec ALA 48-51; Chief circ dept NYC Pub Lib 51-63, Deputy dir 63-; Lecturer ColumbiaU Sch Lib Serv 52-; Exec dir METRO NY Metropolitan Ref & Research Lig Agy 66-. 8: Consul: sev publ libs 52-69, US Civil Aeronautics Bd 45-47, US OFff of Educ 52. 9: ALA (exec sec 48-51); AlaLA (pres 41); NYLA (pres 56). 10: Grolier Club; Univ Club (NYC). 13: Yes. 14: Admin, automation, interlib coop. 15: NY Pub Lib 42nd st & 5th ave, New York NY 10018.

COSGRAVE, PEARL-JOAN. b Lincoln Neb 2 My 06. 5: UNeb 23-26 (Fr) BS(Ed), 27-28 (Eng) AM; UDenver 31-32 (Eng); Chicago 37-38, summer 39 (LS); UWis summer 62 (Grad Inst for Em Coun) UChicago Grad Sch of Ed summer 65; Colo State U (Fort Collins) Inst in Tech &Ind Communications summer 66. 6: Fr, Sp. 7: Asst libn & Instr in Lib Sci St Marys Col (Notre Dame Ind) 38-39; Head Libn Joliet Twp High Sch, Joliet Ill 39-40; Sec to Senators Neb Unicameral, Lincoln Neb 61; Counselor II Neb State Emp Serv, Lincoln Neb 61-63; Speech tchr Scotts Bluff Col summers 64, 65, Head Libn & Instr 63-65; Head Libn Hiram Scott Col 6-66; Prof Dept of Eng Chadron State Col 66-. 9: ALA-ACRL-YASD; Speech Assn of Amer; Amer Personnel & Guidance Assn; Nat VocatGuidance Assn; NEA; NebLA; NebCTE. 10: Chi Delta Phi; Gamma Alpha Chi; Neb WritersGuild; Oma Writers Conf; Neb State Hist Soc; U Chicago Grad Lib Sch Alumni Assn;Nat Writers Club; NCTE; Mod Lang Assn. 13: Yes. 14: Tchg, train stud personnel, ref, circ, readers adv. 15: 841 East Sixth st, Chadron Nb 69337.

COSGROVE, LISBETH. b Pittsburgh Penn 7 Mr 12. 5: IndU 49-52 (LS) MA. 7: US NAVY (WAVE) Wash DC Communications 43-45; Asst libn Hammond Pub Lib, Hammond Ind 31-43; Hd adult serv Aurora Pub Lib, Aurora Ill 52-. 9: ALA; IllLA. 10: AAUW. 14: Adult serv. 15: 545 W Downer, Aurora Il 60506.

COSGROVE, MRS EDITH (EDRINGTON). b Cairo Ill 7 S 19. 4: James J Cosgrove. 5: So Ill U 37-41 (Home econ) B Ed; UTex summers 50-52, 58 (LS); UDenver summer 65 (LS), MLS 68. 7: Ref libn La Retama Pub Lib, Corpus Christi Tex 48-52; Libn Miller High Sch, Corpus Christi Tex 52-61; Libn Arapahoe & Paddock Elem Schs, Boulder Colo 61-63; Libn Cullen Jr High Sch, Corpus Christi Tex 63-65; Libn Richard King High Sch, Corpus Christi Tex 65-. 9: NEA; ALA; Tex State Tchrs Assn; TexLA. 14: Ref, ya. 15: 9871 Daisy dr, Corpus Christi Tx 78410.

COSGROVE, PETROVNA D (LAZENBY). b Biddeford Me 7 Jl 14. 4: Robert E Cosgrove. 5: Flint Jr Col 59-61 (Eng) Assoc in Arts; (Flint Col) UMich 61-63 (Eng) BA; UMich 63-68 MLS. 6: Fr. 7: Clk Bloomingdale Br NYC Pub Lib 52-59; Act asst libn Zimmerman Br Flint Pub Lib, Flint Mich 59-67; Act asst libn Jefferson Br Cleveland Pub Lib 65-67; Clk law lib Cornell U 67-68; Adult serv libn Tompkins Co Pub Lib, Ithaca NY 68-. 10: LWV. 14: Adult serv, ref. 15: 117 Grandview ct, Ithaca NY 14850.

COSGROVE, (ZOE) LEIGHTON WILKERSON WHITE. b St Paul 19 F 32. 4: Donald W Cosgrove. 5: Radcliffe 49-50; UMinn 50-52 (Fr) BA (summa cum laude), 52-53 (LS) MA, 53-56 (Eng). 6: Fr. 7: Tchg asst Dept of Eng UMinn (Minneapolis) 54-56; Jr libn readers aid St Paul Pub Lib 56-57; Libn ref Donnell Lib NY Pub Lib 58; Ref asst J J Hill Ref Lib, St Paul 58-63; Ref libn 3 M Tech Lib 3M Co, St Paul 63-68; Libn 3 M Tape Lib 68-. 9: ALA; SLA (Memb Com 69-71); Minn Chap (treas 65-66, v-pres, pres 67-69); MinnLA; ASIS. 10: AAUW; Phi Beta Kappa; UMinn Alumnae Club (pres 66-67). 12: "Guide to the Search Facilities of Central Research Library & Suppl, 3M Distrib MinnLA" (64); "3M Library Services" (67); "3M LibrariesList of Journals" (68). 14: Ref. 15: 1243 Brighton sq, New Brighton Mn 55112.

COSKEY, EVELYN GRAY. b Jersey City NJ 16 N 32. 5: Warren Wilson Col 56-58 (Eng) AA; Berea Col 58-60 (Eng) BA; UKy 62-63 (LS) MS. 6: Sp. 7: Asst libn Enoch Pratt Free Lib, Baltimore 64; Ext libn Kanawha Co Pub Lib, Charleston WVa 64-. 9: WVaLA. 10: Mountain State Cat Club. 14: Ext wk, juv libnship. 15: 1524 Lee st, Charleston WVa 25311.

COSSETTE, REV JOSEPH SJ. b St-Narcisse (Cte Champlain, Que). 25 Ap 13. 5: ULaval 35 BA (Classique). 6: Fr, Eng, Lat, Sp, Gk. 7: Prof of hist & Regent Col du Sacre-Coeur(Sudbury Ont) 41-43, 47-49; Prof titulaire St Boniface Col(UMan) 50-53; Prof titulaire Col du Sacre-Coeur (Sudbury Ont) 53-55; Libn & Prof of hist Col St-Ignace(Montreal) 56-. 9: Inst dhistoire de lAmerique francaise; CanHistAssn; Soc Hist de Montreal. 12: Ed "Revue dhistoire de lAmerique francaise (57-). 14: Catlg, admin. 15: 1700 E boul Henri-Bourassa, Montreal 12 Can.

COSTA, JOSEPH (JAMES). b Frackville Penn 31 Jl 32. 4: Marie Pribish. 5: Bloomsburg State 50-52, 57-59 (Soc Studies) BS Ed; Kutztown State 61-63 (LS) Lib Certif; Villanova 63-66 MSLS; Lehigh 67- (EducAdmin). 7: Weapons instr (SSgt) USAF, Sampson AFB NY & Sheppard AFB Tex 52-57; Tchr & coach: Nativity BVM High Sch, Pottsville Penn 59-60, Kulpmont High Sch, Kulpmont Penn 60-61; Libn & tchr Frackville High Sch, Frackville Penn 61-65; IMC specialist & dir N Schuylkill High Sch (jointure), Frackville Penn 65-67; Libn Penn State U (Schuylkill Haven) 67-. 8: Dir, Libs, N Schuylkill Sch Dist 66-67. 9: NEA; PennStateEA; PennLA. 10: PIAA Official (Football, Basketball, Track & Field Baseball); IAABO (col Basketball); EAIFO (col Football); Lib Bd, Frackville Fub lib; Webelos Den header; Little League Coach; Frackville Softball League; (Schuylkill Campus Fac Assn; Veterans Club Adv, Young Republican's, Adv; Liberal Art Students Adv). 14: Lib admin, IMC dir, ref. 15: 494 W Pine st, Frackville Pa 17931.

COSTABILE, SALVATORE LOUIS. b Hazleton Penn 24 D 34. 4: Mary Rae Lynch. 5: Georgetown U 52-56 (Hist) BSS, 56-59 (Govt); Catholic U 61-63 MSLS. 6: Ital. 7: Riggs U Lib, Georgetown U: Card ordering asst 56, Catlgr 56-57, Circ libn 58-62, Acquis libn 63-66; Spec asst to chief tech serv div Nat Lib of Med 66-67, Hd sel acquis sect67-68, Deputy chief tech serv div 68-69; Fac UMd Sch of Lib & Inf Serv 70-. 12: "Bibliography in "Nations, Peoples and Countries in the USSR, Study of Population and Migration" (64); Bk rev ed "Military Affairs" (64-). 8: Survey & cost estimate for Southeastern U for improvements to be made on lib facilities (62). 9: CathLA (v-pres Univ & Col Sect 65); Amer Mil Inst (Off-Libn 64-). 12: "Bibliography in "Nations, Peoples and Countries in the USSR, STUDY OF Population and mmigration (64); Bk rev ed "Military Affairs (64-). 13: Yes. 14: Acquis, admin. 15: 3515 Turner lane, Chevy Chase Md 20015.

COSTANZO, ANTHONY JOSEPH. b Phila 19 Je 27. 4: Rosemary Catherine Di Nelli. 5: Gettysburg Col 47-51 (Chem) AB; Drexel 53-56 (Chem) MS; Temple 57-62 (Chem); Drexel 62-66 (Info Sci) MS. 6: Fr, Ger. 07: Chem E I duPont de Nemours Co, Phila 52; Chem Allied Chem Corp, Glenolden Penn 52-60; Head of chem records sect Wyeth Labs Inc, Radnor Penn 60-65; Tech info supv Atlantic Richfield Co, glenolden Penn 65-. 9: ACS (Chem Lit Div); ASIS; SLA. 10: 69th st Athletic Assn. 14: Infor retrieval (chem). 15: Arco Chemical Co Div of Atlantic Richfield Co 500 S Ridgeway ave, Glenolden Pa 19036.

COSTELLO, DONALD JOSEPH. b Jersey City NJ 29 Ap 27. 5: St Peters Col (Jersey City NJ) 45-48 (Eng) AB; Rutgers 58-60 MLS. 6: Fr, Lat. 7: Libn asst Lib St Peters Col (Jersey City NJ) 58-60, An asst libn 60-. 10: Confraternity of Christian Doctrine. 14: Catlg, tech serv. 15: 32 Irving st, Jersey City NJ 07307.

COSTELLO, JOAN MARY. b Wilkes-Barre Penn 14 S 30. 5: Col Misericordia 50-54 (Eng) BA; Drexel 63-64 MS in LS. 7: Tchr Belvidere High Sch, Belvidere NJ 54-56; Sub tchr Wilkes-Barre City Schs, Wilkes-Barre Penn 56-57; Records clerk E I Du Pont, Newark Del 57; Adultdir Catholic Youth Center, Wilkes-Barre Penn 57-59; CASEWKER Dept of Pub Assistance, Wilkes-Barre Penn 59; Copy ed Internat Correspondence Schs, Scranton Penn 59-60; Program dir Catholic Youth Center, Wilkes-Barre Penn 60-62; Libn Osterhout Free Lib, Wilkes-Barre Penn 62-68; Asst libn Scranton Pub Lib, Scranton Penn 68-. 9: PennLA; ALA. 10: Quota Club, AAUW; LWV; Drexel Lib Sch Alum. 14: Circ,adult serv, pub rel, admin. 15: 143Hanover st, Wilkes-Barre Pa 18702.

COSTELLO, MICHAEL A. b Newark NJ 7 O 10. 4: Louise Fulcoli. 5: Rutgers 28-32 (Hist) AB; NJ State Col 37-39 (LS) Certif; Rutgers 46-49 (Educ, LS) MA. 7: Instr Newark State Col 35-37, Asst libn 37-40; Instr libn Jersey City State Col 40-43; US Army 43-45; Asst Prof libn Fairleigh Dickinson U 45-49; Libn admin Picatinny Arsenal, Dover NJ 49-. 9: SLA (chm Mil Libs Div); ASIS; NJLA; ALA. 13: Yes. 14: Admin. 15: 224 Forest Ave, Glen Ridge NJ 07028.

COSTELLO, PHILLIP ANTHONY. b N Andover Mass 7 D 12. 4: Dorcas Curley. 5: Villanova 32-35 (Philos); Boston Col 35-36 (Eng) AB; Simmons 64-65 MSLS. 7: Spec investigator US Govt 37-47; Self-employed bk bus, Boston 47-57; Bk salesman various publs, New England 57-64; Libn Merrimack Col 65-. 9: ALA; CathLA; MassLA; NELA. 10: AAUP. 14: Admin. 15: 298 Salem st, Andover Ma 01810.

COSTELLO, ROBERT CHARLES. b Croton-on-Hudson NY 28 F 36. 5: SUNY (Albany) 57-61 (Bus) BS, 61-62 (Bus) MS, 64-65 MLS. 7: Pfc US Army 54-56; Tchr of com subj Westhampton Beach High Sch, Westhampto Beach ny 62-64; Asst libn Hudson Valley Community Col 65-68; Hd libn, Sch of Bus Admin USoCal 68. 15: 920 S Hobart blvd, Los AngelesCa 90006.

COSTELLO, VIRGINIA SMITH. b Santa Fe NM 12 My 16. 5: St Marys Hall 33-35; Washburn Col 35-36; UNeb 36-38 (Fr)

AB; McGill summer 38; Columbia 39-40 BS in LS; Colo State Col 46-48 (Foreign Langs) MA. 6: Fr, Sp, Lat. 7: Ref & yp libn NY Pub Lib 40-42; Head ref libn & Assoc Prof of Lib Sci Colo State Col 42-. 8: Lib consul of the Col Educ Planning Serv for the Greeley Sr High Sch, 61-62; Tchr Ref Materials for Sch Libs, summers 63, 64; Instr ofPracticum, summer 68. 9: ALA-ACRL; MPLA; ColoLA; ColoEA. 10: Ski Club;Kappa Delta Pi; Pi Lambda Theta; Phi Sigma Iota; Delta Kappa Gamma; Pi Beta Phi;Colo State Hist Soc; Colo Civil Serv Eval Com. 14: Ref, govt docs. 15: 2646 15th ave court, GreeleyCo 80631.

COSTIN, MICHAEL J. b Buffalo NY 29 S 37. 4: Barbara Wei-Hao Shen. 5: Syracuse 55-57 (Eng); UAriz 57-60 (Eng) BA; UDenver 63-64 (LS) MA. 6: Fr, Sp, Lat. 7: Tchr of Eng, Fr & Lat Coachella Valley Jt Union High Sch Dist, Indio Cal 60-61; Tchr of Eng & Fr Amphitheater High Sch, Tucson 61-63; Acquis searcher UDenver Libs 63-64; Trainee LC 64-65, Subj catlgr 65-67; Hd catlg dept UCal (Santa Barbara) 67-69; Asst Univ Libn (Tech Serv) NorthwesternU 69-. 9: ALA; So Cal Tech Processer Group. 11: LC Annual Recr Program for Outstanding Lib Sch Grads. 14: Catlg, admin, automation. 15: Asst Univ Librarian Northwestern Univ, Evanston Il 60201.

COTTAM, KEITH (M). b St George Utah 13 F 41. 4: Laurel Springer. 5: Utah StateU 59-63 (Sociol) BS; Pratt Inst 63-65 MSLS. 6: Fr. 7: Libn trainee & libn Brooklyn Pub Lib, Brooklyn NY 63-65; Asst soc sci libn So IllU 65-67; Soc sci libn Brigham YoungU 67-. 9: ALA-ACRL; UtahLA (v-chm/chm-elect Univ Sect 69-71). 10: Rocky Mt States Dir; League of Amer Wheelmen; Beta Phi Mu. 13: Yes. 14: Educ for libnship, pub rel, ref, bibliog. 15: Lib Brigham Young Univ, Provo Ut 84601.

COTTER, SISTER MARY ADRIENNE. b Austin Minn 14 D 12. 5: Col of St Teresa 51 (Lat) BA; Rosary Col 51-52 MA in LS. 6: Lat, Fr. 7: Ref libn Col of St Teresa 52-65, Instr in Lib Sci 65-. 9: CathLA (chm Elem Sect 64-68). 14: Ref, child libs. 15: Col of St Teresa, Winona Mn 55987.

COTTER, MICHAEL GEORGE. b Prescott Wis 12 O 37. 4: Mary Suennen Cotter. 5: Wis StateU (River Falls) 55-60 (Hist) BA; UWis 63-65 (Comp Tropical Hist) MA, 65-66 MALS. 6: Fr, Vietnamese. 7: Sp/5 US Army 60-63; Bk selection (So Asia) Harvard Col Lib 66-67, Bk selection (Africa & SE Asia) 67-. 8: US Army Lang Sch Vietnamese lang course, Monterey Cal 61. 10: Assn for Asian Studies. 13: Yes. 14: Bibliog. 15: 328 Huron ave, Cambridge Ma 02138.

COTTEW, MAURINE (GREENE). b Tabor Iowa 21 My 12. 5: Graceland Col 30-32 (Educ) AA; UColo 39; Northwest Mo State Tchrs Col 59-60(Elem Educ) BS; UDenver 60-61 (LS) MA; UIll 66-67 Certif of Advanced Libnship. 7: Rural sch tchr, Thurman Iowa 33-35; Elem & jr high tchr Tabor Cons Sch, Tabor Iowa 35-40, 42-44; Elem tchr Thurman Cons, Thurman Iowa 44-45; Jr high tchr Essex Ind Sch, Essex Iowa 52-57; Jr high tchr Shenandoah Pub Sch, Shenandoah Iowa 57-59; Undergrad Lib Sci Colo State U summer 63; Lib orientation No Ill U 61-65, Educ libn 65-. 9: ALA; NEA; IllLA; IllEA; Amer Assn Higher Educ. 10: Kappa Delta Pi; PEO. 14: Ref. 15: 808 Ridge dr N113, DeKalbIl 60115.

COTTMAN, JESSIE MARIE. b Pocomoke Md 15 N 28. 5: Md State Col 45-50 (Hist, Govt) AB; Catholic U 53; Columbia 54-58 MSLS Drexel Inst of Tech 63; UMd 64. 6: Fr. 7: Libn Worcester High Sch Lib, Newark Md 51- Ref libn Md State Col 66-. 9: NEA; Md State Tchrs Assn; MdASchL (Worcester Co Memb Chm). 14: Ref. 15: Rt 1Box 232, Pocomoke Md 21851.

COTTON, BETTY ANNE. b Wash DC 7 My 47. 5: Vanderbilt 65-68 (Art Hist) AB; Peabody Col 68-69 MLS. 6: Fr, Lat, Ger. 7: B us info libn Nashville & Davidson Co Pub Lib 69-. 9: ALA. 14: Bus ref. 15: Lampkin Bridge rd Rte 1, College Grove Tn 37046.

COTTON, DOROTHY ANNETTE (PALMER). b Newport News Va. 4: James Alton Cotton. 5: Va State Col 27-31 (Hist) AB; Columbia 48-52 (LS) MS; Col of William & Mary summer 65. 6: Fr, Sp. 7: Elem tchr John marshall 31-35; Elem tchr P L Dunbar 36-39; B T Washington: Elem tchr 40-51, Dept tchr soc studies 38-49, Tchr-libn 50-51, Libn 52-. 8: Instr Lib Sci Hampton Inst, summers 58-64. 9: NEA; Amer Tchrs Assn; Nat Tchrs Assn; Va Tchrs Assn; VaEA; VaLA; ALA. 10: AAUW; YWCA; Links Inc; Girl Friends Inc. 13: Yes. 14: Child libs, ref. 15: 114 E Pembroke ave, Hampton Va 23369.

COTTON, ELIZABETH N(ELSON). b Brooklyn NY 3 Jl 15. 4: Charles R Cotton Jr. 5: Douglass Col 33-37 (Soc studies, LS) BA; Drexel 64-67 MS in LS. 6: Fr, Ger. 7: Libn Freehold High Sch, Freehold NJ 37-41; Libn Lib Merchantville Pub Schs, Merchantville NJ 41-46; Libn Nether Providence Jr-Sr High Sch, Wallingford Penn 46-48; Libn Swarthmore High Sch, Swarthmore Penn 48-49; Hd libn & instr materials coordinator Pennsauken High Sch, Pennsauken NJ 59-. 8: Sec; Consul Lib Technicians Camden Co Vocat & Tech Schls 67-69. 9: ALA; NJLA (mem various com); NJSchLA (chm nom com 68, 50 reg chm wkshop 68); NJEA; NJ A-V Anu; Pennsauken EA (sec 63-64); Libs Unlimited (Exec Bd, mem various com). 10: Beta Phi Mu; The Merchantville Playcrafters; The Pennsauken Hist Soc; DAR. 14: Instr media, catlg. 15: 6710 Grant ave, Pennsauken NJ 08109.

COTTON, KENNETH WAYNE. b Groveton NH 27 Ag 26. 4: Donna M Smith. 5: UNH 44-48 (Eng) AB; Ohio U 56, 57 (Hist) MA; Simmons 60-62 MSLS. 7: Statistical analyst US Army, Ryukyus Command 54-56; Circ asst Boston U 59-62; Acquis asst State U Col (Cortland NY) 62-65, Head of acquis 65-66; Hd libn Westfield State Col (Westfield Mass) 66-. 9: ALA. 14: Acquis, tech serv. 15: Pomeroy Meadow rd, Southampton Ma 01073.

COTTONY, LILLIAN V(ILAND). b Slater Iowa 19 Mr 09. 4: Herman V Cottony. 5: UDenver 28-32 (LS) BA, 32-33 (LS); George Washington U 35-36, 39-40 (Math, Russian). 6: Fr, Sp, Ger, Russian. 7: Asst libn Nat Bur Standards Lib 37-42; Libn Central Radio Propagation Lab Lib, Wash DC & Boulder Colo 51-55; Environmental Sci Serv Admin lab, Boulder Colo: Period libn 57-63, Ref libn & asst libn 63-68, Deputy chief libn 68-. 9: SLA; Biblig Ctr for Research, Denver (Interlib Loan Com 63-). 11: Sustained Superior Performance Award 60; Superior Accomplishment Award 67. 14: Ref. 15: 1051 10th st, Boulder Co 80302.

COUCH, CECIL REDDING JR. b Dallas Tex 7 Jl 30. 5: So Methodist U 47-51 (Sec ed, Biol) BS; UTex at Austin 67 MLS. 6: Sp, Ger, Lat. 7: Hist tech USAF, Ft Worth & Mass 52-56; Catlgr Temco Aircraft Corp, Garland Tex 58-59; Hd catlgr UTex at Arlington 59-67; Libn Col of the Mainland 67; Catlgr Ft Worth Pub Lib 67-68; Research libn Lone Star Gas Co, 68-. 9: ALA; SLA; TexLA (chm Reg Gp of Catlgr 66-67); SWLA; Dallas Co LA. 10: Kappa Phi Kappa; AAUP; Jr C of C. 14: Catlg, ref, rare bks, lib educ, recr. 15: 807 So Edgefield, Dallas Tx 75209.

COUCH, WILSON LeROY. b Painesville Ohio 10 Jl 29. 4: Dorothy Beck. 5: Hiram Col 48-53 (Soc Studies) BA; UWyo 59 (Amer Studies); Kent State 60-65 MLS. 7: Tchr-libn Newberry Loc Sch, Newberry Ohio 53; Tchr-libn Pierpont Loc Sch, Pierpont Ohio 54-55; Tchr-libn Crestwood Loc Sch, Mantua Ohio 55-58; Tchr-libn Boston-Northampton Sch, Peninsula Ohio 58-60; Libn Kenston Loc Sch, Chagrin Falls Ohio 60-62; Libn Marion Harding High Sch, Marion Ohio 62-66; Libn Sandusky Area Supplementary Educ Ctr, Sandusky Ohio 66-. 9: OhioASchL (Dist Memb Chm 58-60, State Memb Chm 60-66, treas 64-66; No Central Ohio Sch L (pres 65-67). 10: Kiwanis Club. 14: Sch libs, youth wk. 15: 512 Hancock st, Sandusky Oh 44870.

COUGHLAN, MARGARET NOURSE. b Baltimore 21 Je 25. 5: Pembroke 44-48 (Eng) BA; Carnegie 50-51 MLS. 6: Fr. 7: Child libn Enoch Pratt Free Lib, Baltimore 51-66; Child Specialist, Towson Area Br Baltimore Co Pub Lib 66-68; Sr Ref Libn and Bibliog Child Bk Sect Lib of Congress 66-. 9: ALA; MdLA. 15: Apt 5 108, 800 4th st SW, Washington DC 20024.

COUGHLIN, BETTY M. b Davenport Iowa. 5: Marycrest Col 41-44 (Soc Sci, LS) BS; West Res 52 MS in LS. 7: Davenport Pub Lib, Davenport Iowa: Asst br dept 44-47, Head ext dept 47-53, Asst ref dept 53-57, Head ref dept 57-. 8: ALA Exhibit, Lib/USA, NY Worlds Fair 64. 9: ALA (Coun 69-); IowaLA (sec 60-62). 10: Beta Phi Mu; Mercy Hosp Auxiliary Assn. 14: Ref. 15: 321 Main st, Davenport Ia 52801.

COUGHLIN, CAROLINE M. b NYC 6 D 44. 5: Mercy Col Dobbs Ferry NY 62-66 (Eng, Theatre) AB; EmoryU 66-67 (Libnship) MLS. 7: Div of libn Emory U: Grad asst 66-67, Instr 68-; Ref libn 1st Nat City Bank, NYC 67-68. 8: Guide & Supv of Guide Staff NY State Exhibit 64-65 World's Fair NYC 64-65. 9: ALA; AALS; SELA; GaLA. 11: Beta Phi Mu. 14: Bk sel, child serv. 15: Div of Librarianship Emory U, Atlanta Ga 30322.

COUGHLIN, MARY (CRATHORNE). b Gottingen Germany 28 N 06. 4: Laurence Coughlin. 5: UIll 24-28 (Journalism) AB; Rutgers 62-65 MLS. 7: Eng tchr Fisher Community High Sch, Fisher Ill 28-30; Ed scout "American Home, "Better Homes &

Gardens 51-61; Lib trainee Newark Pub Lib, Newark NJ 62-65, Jr libn 65-66; Sr libn 66-. 10: Theta Sigma Phi. 13: Yes. 14: Ref. 15: 25 Clifton ave, Newark NJ 07104.

COUGHLIN, VIOLET L MRS. b Montreal Can. 5: McGill (Chem) BSc & Tchg Diploma, 37-38 BLS;Columbia summers 55-57 (Adult Educ) MA, 58-59 (LS); Columbia 66 DLS. 6: Fr, Ger. 7: Med lab tech Royal Victoria Hosp, Montreal High Sch tchr chem Montreal HighSch; McGill U; Catlgr Redpath Lib 41, Libn Royal Victoria Col 41-51, Lecturer Lib Sch51-56, Asst Prof Lib Sch 56-65, Assoc Prof Lib Sch 65-69; Visiting Prof Grad Sch ofLib & Info Sci PittsburghU 66-67; Tchr Grad Lib Sch UHawaii summer 68; Prof Grad LibSch McGill 69-. 9: CanLA; ALA-LED (Rec sec 61); AALS (chm Instr Com 62-); QueLA (pres 54-55, Archivist 55-, chm Lib Legis Com 56-58). 10: Beta Phi Mu. 12: "Larger Units of Public Library Service in Canada" (68). 14: Communications media, bk sel, pub lib org & ext, serv to child & yp in sch & pub libs. 15: 3800 Wilson ave, Montreal 28 Que Can.

COUGHLIN, VIRGINIA LEE. b Cumberland Iowa 16 F 41. 5: NW Mo State Col 58-62 (Math) BS; UDenver 66-67 Libnship MS. 7: Math tchr Manilla Commun Sch, Manilla Iowa 62-65; Creighton U; Period libn 65-66, Docs libn & part-time tchr in LS 67-. 9: ALA; -Jr Mem RT; NCathLA; NebLA. 14: Govt docs, ref, tchg. 15: 2340 Bel Court, Omaha Nb 68144.

COUGLE, MARY (SANDS). b Atlanta 13 Je 03. 5: Fla State U 57 (LS); USO Miss 59-61 (Hist, LS) BA; LSU summer 62 & 63 MS in LS; AmU summer 67 (Archives) certif. 6: Sp. 7: Libn Beaufort High Sch, Beaufort Victoria Australia 51-55; Br libn for Reg Lib, Ballarat Victoria Australia 51-55; Child dept & ext supv Mobile Pub Lib, Mobile Ala 57-59; Circ libn USoMiss 61-62, Ref educ & sci 62-63; Documents & archives libn Nicholls State Col 63-. 9: ALA; LaLA; AAUW. 10: Pi Gamma Mu; Phi Alpha Theta; Phi Lambda Pi; Phi Kappa Phi; Alpha Beta Alpha; Phi Beta Mu; Bus & Prof Women; Alpha Lambda Delta. 14: Fed & state docs, archives, hist. 15: 158 St Joseph st, Thibadoux La 70301.

COULSON, BARBARA (A)NN. b Cookeville Tenn 25 D 42. 5: Tenn TechU 60-64 (Eng) BA; Peabody Col 66-67 MLS. 7: Tchr Citrus High Sch, Inverness Fla 64-66; Reg child libn Central Fla Reg Lib, Ocala Fla 67-. 9: FlaLA. 10: Sigma Tau Delta; AAUW. 14: Reg libnship, ref. 15: 728 SE Second st, Ocala Fl 32670.

COULTER, M(ARGARET) CELIA. b Bovina Center NY 12 Ja 16. 5: Cornell U 34-38 (Hist) AB; NY State Col for Tchrs (Albany) 54-55 MS in LS. 7: State U Col (New Paltz NY): Ref libn 55-60, Asst libn in chg of reader serv 60-63, Ref libn 63-. 9: ALA; NYLA. 10: Delta Kappa Gamma. 14: Ref, periods, inter-lib loan. 15: 3 Lookout ave, New Paltz NY 12561.

COULTER, PANOLA. b Akron Ohio 26 Jl 08. 5: UAkron 25-29 (Eng) AB; West Res 30-31 BS in LS. 7: Asst Pierce Lib UAkron 29-30; Revisor & Asst Instr West Res U Lib Sch 31-32; Subasst Catlgr Mich State Col (E Lansing) 33; First Asst Tech processes Akron Pub Lib,akron Ohio 34-. 9: ALA; OhioLA; No Ohio Tech Serv Libns. 10: Phi Sigma Alpha; Pilt Club of Akron; College Club of Akron. 14: Catlg. 15: 119 Merriman rd, Akron Oh 44303.

COULTER, SHIRLEY (YVONNE). b Oshawa Ont 17 Mr 26. 5: Toronto Victoria Col 46-49 BA; Toronto 49-50 BLS. 7: Child libn Glace Bay Br, Cape Breton Reg Lib, NS 50-54; Asst child libn in chg of brs Halifax Mem Lib, NS 54-60; Supv of sch libs & Libn Tchrs Lib Dept of Educ, Prov of NS 60-. 09: CanLA; CanSchLA (chm 63-64); APLA. 10: NS Civil Serv Assn. 12: Ed APLA "Bulletin (59-62). 13: Yes. 14: Sch lib devel & materials, educ. 15: Provincial Lib Sch Libraries Sect 2nd Floor Trade Mart, Brunswick st, Halifax NS Can.

COUNCILL, MILDRED SOUTHERLAND. b Mt Olive NC 3 Ag 07. 4: Charles Bower Councill. 5: Appalachian State Tchrs Col 56 (LS) BS (magna cum laude), 62 (LS) MA. 6: Fr. 7: Supv Wayne Co (NC) Sch Libs 40-45; Libn Eastover Elem Sch, Charlotte NC 52-55; Libn Mt Olive Jr Col 55-65; Libn Lib Sci Lib Appalachian State Tchrs Col 65-67; Hd libn Wayne Commun Col 67-. 8: Visiting Com of So Assn 64-; Exec dir, at Lib Week, NC, 62. 9: NEA; ALA (Pres; NCLA 67-69, past chm Comof Recr for High Sch & Col Studs, Chm-Elect Col & Univ Sect 63-65); NCEA; SELA; NCLA(past chm libnship as a career com). 10: NC Col Conf; Delta Kappa Gamma; AAUW;AAUP; 20th Cent Club; DAR Daughters of Amer Colonists; Phi Theta Kappa. 13: Yes. 15: PO Box133, Mt Olive NC 28365.

COURAIN, MARGARET C. b Bayonne NJ 23 N 27. 5: Douglas Col 44-48 (Chem) BS; Columbia 52-55 (LS) MS. 6: Ger, Sp. 7: Mgr Res info Merck Sharp & Dohme Res Labs Merck & Co Inc, Rahway 66-. 8: Setting up Med Info Center at West Point, Penn, for MSDRL 63-65; AMA Wkshops on Biomed Vocabulary Control, 65. 9: ASIS; (NY Chap: sec; Exec Bd); Drug Info Assn (Found mem 65). 10: Maplewood Garden Club; Chamois Ski Club; NJ Landscape Design Appraisers Coun; Beta Phi Mu. 13: Yes. 14: Design & eval of info systems. 15: Merck Sharp & Dohme Res Labs, Rahway NJ 07065.

COURTIS, SHIRLEY. b Manchester Eng 10 Ja 29. 5: McGill 47-51 (Hist) BA, 51-52 BLS. 6: Fr. 7: Catlgr Queens U (Kingston Ont) 52-53; Asst libn Engnr Inst of Can, Montreal 53-54, Libn 54-62; Libn Noranda Research Centre, PointeClaire Que 63-. 9: SLA (pres Montreal Chap 59-60); CanLA; QueLA. 13: Yes. 14: Spec libs. 15: Lib Noranda Res Centre, 240 Hymus blvd, Pointe Claire Que Can.

COURTRIGHT, HARRY RICHARD. b Midland Mich 12 N 37. 5: Central Mich U 57-61 (LS) AB; UMich 61-62 MALS. 7: A-v div Macomb Co Lib, Mt Clemens Mich 62-63; Dir Pub Lib, Escanaba Mich 63-64; Ext dir Kellogg Pub Lib, Green Bay Wis 64-65, Head of adult & ext serv 66-67; Lib development adv Penn State Lib 67-. 67; Lib development adv Penn State Lib 67-. 8: Dir at Lib Week, Mich 64-65. 9: ALA; MichLA (Pub Rel Com 62-64, Intel Freedom Com 63-64, chm Dist 7 64); WisLA (Pub Rel Com 65-, Personnel & Prof Problems Com 65, chm-clect Tech Serv Sect). 10: Kiwanis Club; C of C. 13: Yes. 14: Admin, ext, a-v. 15: 110 Locust st, Harrisburg Pa 17101.

COUSTON, GEORGE T(HOMAS). b Lidorikion Greece 27 Jl 23. 4: Georgia Mastrogiannis. 5: UIll 49-52 (LS) BS, 52-53 (LS) MS. 6: Gk. 7: Catlgr Chicago Pub Lib 53-58; Cross-ref ed Field Enterprises Educ Corp,Chicago 58-. 9: ALA; ASIS; Chicago Reg Group of Libns in Tech Serv (pres 58-59). 14: Catlg, clsf, indxing. 15: 13425 Burley ave, Chicago Il 60633.

COUTIN, JOSE DeJESUS. b Baracoa Oriente Cuba 30 S 17. 4: Rita Hilda Macari. 5: UHavana 39-44 Doctor of Law; Kan State Tchrs Col 65-67 MS in Libnship; UCal (Berkeley) 68. 6: Sp, Ital, Portu. 7: Lawyer, Baracoa Ote Cuba 45-62; Tchr Cuban Pub Syst, Baracoa Ote Cuba 46-62; Tech sec Patronato de Baracoa, Baracoa Ote Cuba 55-60; Soc wkr Fla State Dept of Pub Welfare, Miami 62-65; Lib asst CornellU Olin Lib 67-68; Catlg Cornell U Law Lib 68-. 8: Lawyer and tech sec C of C, Agric & Navigation Baracoa Cuba 52-62; Pub notary 50-62. 9: ALA; AALL. 14: Tech processing, catlg, acquis. 15: 107 Salem dr, Ithaca NY 14850.

COUTS, DORIS VIRGINIA. b Salesville Ohio 27 D 15. 5: Muskingum Col 37-39; Edinburgh U 45. 7: Lib asst Pub Lib, New Philadlphia Ohio 39-44; Womens Army Corps (Cpl), Iowa, Ohio, Germany & Scotland 44-46; Lib asst Pub Lib, New Philadelphia Ohio 46-47; Lib asst US Dept of the Army Lib 47-51; Lib asst Off of the General Coun, Ofc of the Quartermaster Gen (Army), Wash DC 51-55; Ref libn law US Dept of the Army Lib, Wash DC 55-57; Asst law libn US Post Off Dept Lib, Wash DC 57-61, Law Libn 61-. 9: AALL; Law Libns Soc Wash DC; DCLA. 14: Legal & legis ref. 15: 5649 Shadyside ave SE apt 201, Suitland Md 20023.

COUVILLON, EVA V. b Los Angeles Cal 12 S 44. 4: Arthur R Couvillon. 5: Immaculate Heart Col 61-65 (Psych) BA, 67-68 MALS. 6: Sp. 7: Catlg libn RAND Corp, Santa Monica Cal 68-. 9: SLA. 14: Catlg. 15: 21 Spinnaker, Marina Del Rey Ca 90291.

COUZINS, ELINOR R. b Boston 29 O 15. 5: NJ Col for Women 44-48, 53 (Sociol) BA; Rutgers 62-65 MLS; Columbia 65 (Med Lit). 7: Sec to claims chief Colo State Employment Off, Denver 59; Asst libn Mass General Hosp Nursing Sch Lib Treadwell Med Lib, Boston 62; Catlgr circ dept NY Pub Lib 63-65; NASA Electronics Research Ctr, Cambridge Mass 66; Countway Lib of MedHarvard 67-. 9: ASIS; MedLA. 14: Catlg, med ref. 15: 2 Worthington st, Roxbury Ma 02120.

COVENTRY, ROSE M(ARGARET). b Coeur dAlene Ida 6 Ja 14. 5: Reed Col 32-34 (Eng); UIda 37-0 (Eng) BA; Col of St Catherine 40-41 BS in LS. 7: Catlgr Ida State Lib 41-. 8: Head of Coop Catlg Experl Proj (in Idaho) 60-63. 9: ALA; PNLA; IdaLA. 14: Catlg. 15: 1809 N 1th st, Boise Ida 83702.

COVEY, ALAN DALE. b Alameda Cal 3 F 17. 4: Alma Ann Munsell. 5: UCal (Berkeley) 35-40 AB, 41 Gen Secondary Tchg Cred, 46 Certif in Libnship; Stanford 55 Ed D. 7: (1st Lt) US Army Field Artillery 41-45; Libn UCal(Berkeley) 46-49; Asst libn for pub serv San Francisco State Col 49-51; Libn Stanford U 51-52; Col Libn Sacramento State Col 52-62; U Libn Ariz State U 62-. 8: Sec Cal State Com on Adult Educ; Cal State Com on Criteria for Accred Lib Sci Programs, 59-60; Adv Com to UCal Lib Schs, 60-61. 9: CalLA (pres 59-60); Ariz State LA (pres Col & Univ Sect 64-65). 12: "Evaluation of College Libraries for Accreditation Purposes, Ed Diss (55); Co-ed "A Fine Contagion, CalLA (58); Comp "Books for schools, monthly 60-61); Ed "Arizona Librarian (67-69). 13: Yes. 14: Fine printing. 15: Ariz State Univ Lib, Tempe Az 85281.

COVEY, DOROTHY ELLEN (RUMSEY). b Woodland Cal 9 Jl 20. 4: Elwin Harmon Covey. 5: Sacramento Jr Col 38-40 (Hist) AA; UCal 40-42 (Hist) AB, 42-43 Certif of Libnship. 7: Jr ref libn A&M Col of Tex 43; Clerk in chg of Chem Div Lib Clinton Labs, Oak Ridge Tenn 44; Lib asst Golden Gate Br Oakland Pub Lib, Oakland Cal 47-48; Lib asst San Carlos Br San Mateo Co Lib, San Carlos Cal 54-62; Documents libn, libn I San Mateo Co Lib, Belmont Cal 62-. 9: CalLA (Docs Com). 10: Sierra Club; AAUW. 13: Yes. 14: Ref, docs. 15: 411 Hill way, San Carlos Ca 94070.

COVEY, ELWIN H. b Napa Cal 29 Je 22. 4: Dorothy Ellen (Rumsey) Covey. 5: UCal at Berkeley 39-42 (Chem), 47-49 (Bus admin) BS, 63-67 (Libnship) MLS. 6: Fr, Ger. 7: Research asst UChicago Metallurgical Lab (Manhattan Atomic Proj), Chicago 42-43; Chem Clinton Labs UChicago Monsanto Chem Co (Manhattan Atomic Proj), Oak Ridge Tenn 43-46; Jr exec UCal Radiation Lab chem div, Berkeley 46-49; Sci staff asst Program Off Naval Radiological Defense Lab, San Francisco 49-; Ref libn San Mateo Co Lib Syst, Belmont Br, Belmont Cal 67-. 8: Manhattan Proj participant under Drs Seaborg & Perlman 42-46. 9: ALA; SLA; ASIS. 10: Akpha Zeta; Phi Beta Mu; Boy Scout Councils; Sierra Club. 14: Lib automation, Nat data banks & info systems. 15: 411 Hill Way, San Carlos Ca 94070.

COVEY, MARTHA H(UNT). b Beckley WVa 22 F 26. 5: UWash 43-44; Lynchburg Col 44-47 (Eng) AB; Peabody 52-53 MA(LS). 7: Tchr Altavista High Sch, Altavista Va 4748; Asst libn Lynchburg Col 49-51; Film libn & gen asst Lawson-McGhee Lib, Knoxville Tenn 53-54; Asst in Lib UFla 54-58; Ref libn Emory U 58-60; Asst ref libn USFla 60-6, Act head ref & pub serv 62-63; Br libn Mobile Pub Lib, Mobile Ala 63-68; Ref supv Ga State Dept of Educ, Atlanta 68-. 9: SELA; GaLA. 14: Bk sel, ref, readers adv. 15: 310 Poncede Leon ave NE, Atlanta Ga 30383.

COVINGTON, FRANCES WHEAT. b Austin Tex 7 Ap 18. 5: UUtah 36-40 (Eng) BA; Enoch Pratt Free Lib Train Class 40-41 Training Class Certif; UNC 45-46 BS in LS. 7: Enoch Pratt Free Lib, Baltimore: Libn popular lib dept 41-45, Br libn Hamilton Br 46-49, Br libn Covans Br 49-60, Br libn Northwoo Br 60-. 9: ALA; MdLA. 10: Md Ornithol Soc; Cylburn Wild Flower Refuge; Child Study Center. 14: Adult serv. 15: 934 Belgian ave, Baltimore Md 21218.

COVINGTON, LENA. b Wadesboro NC 1 D 06. 5: Meredith Col 23-27 (Hist) AB; Emory 38-39 AB in LS. 7: Duke U Lib: Asst order dept 30-38, Clsfr 39-43, Head clsf & reviser subj catlg dept 43-49, Head subj catlg dept 49-62, Coordinator of catlg 62-. 9: ALA; SELA; NCLA. 10: NC Lit & Hist Assn. 14: Catlg. 15: 2739 Sevier st, Durham NC 27705.

COVINGTON, MARY W. b Danville Va 8 Ap 27. 5: UNC 45-49 (Hist) BA; Columbia 52-54 MSLS. 7: Bkmob libn Danville Pub Lib, Danville Va 50-52; Libn Neurological InstColumbia-Presbyterian Med Center, NYC 52-54; Sr ref asst Med Lib Columbia U 54-56;Head libn & off manager Union Carbide Ore Div, NYC 56-65; Info analyst Copper Development Assn, Copper Data Center, NYC 65-. 8: Prof consul, SLA; H W Wilson Co Com on Indexing "Applied Science and echnology Index, 64-66. 9: ADI; SLA (Metals/Materials Div: Elect Chm 61-62; NY Chap: pres 64-65; v-pres & ed "Chapter News, 59-60, chm Bylaws Com 58-59; Sci-tech Group: chm 60-61, treas 59-60, Arrangements Chm 58-59). 10: Columbia U Lib Sch Alumnae Assn. 14: Info systems & centers, consul, market research. 15: 60 E 9th st, New York NY10003.

COVINGTON, VIRGINIA (MAE). b Georgetown Ky 1 Mr 16. 5: Georgetown Col 33-37. 6: Fr. 7: Eng tchr & libn Mayslick High Sch, Mayslick Ky 39-43; Jr & sr high sch libn Lloyd Mem High Sch, Erlanger Ky 43-44; Head Libn Georgetown Col (Ky) 44-. 9: KyLA (past sec-treas Col & Ref Sect). 10: Beta Phi Mu; Pi Kappa Delta; DAR; Amer Guild of Organists; Georgetown Bk Club; Womans Assn Georgetown Col. 14: Admin, catlg, ref. 15: Georgetown Col Lib, Georgetown Ky 40324.

COWAN, CLAUDE ALEXANDER. b Birmingham Ala 21 Ag 30. 5: Maryville Col 48-52 (Philos) BA; McCormick Theol Sem 52-55 (Theol) BD; Peabody 59-60 MA (LS. 6: Lat, Ger, Gk. 7: Minister Seventh Presbyt Church, Indianapolis 55-57; Minister Old KingsportPresbyt Church, Kingsport Tenn 57-59; Circ ref libn McCormic Theol Sem 60-64; AsstDivinity libn Joint U Libs, Nashville 64-67; Catlgr Ga State Col (Atlanta) 68-69; Hd Tech Serv & Asst Prof Birmingham-So Coll Lib 69-. 9: ATheolLA; ALA. 10: Beta Phi Mu. 14: Catlg, ref, admin. 15: Birmingham-So Coll Lib, Birmingham Al 35104.

COWAN, GEORGIA C(OLEMAN). b Greenwood SC 17 N 10. 5: UNC(Greensboro) 27-29; Meredith Col 29-31 (Hist) AB; UNC 40-41 BS in LS. 7: Lib asst for State Aid Program, NC Lib Commsn 41-43; Jr libn US Naval Train Center, Bainbridge Md 43-44; Asst catlg dept Armed Forces Med Lib, Wash DC 44-47; DC Pub Lib: Lib asst 48-49, Readers adv hist div 49-57, Chief biog div 57-. 9: ALA; DCLA. 14: Ref. 15: 2720 Wisconsin ave NW, Wash DC 20007.

COWAN, LENORE (JOHNSON). b Bozeman Mont 28 Ja 28. 4: William Wheatley Cowan. 5: American U 46-49 (Eng Lit); UWis 50-51 (Eng Lit) BA; Columbia 59-62 MLS. 7: NY Pub Lib: Clerk 56-57, Sr clerk 57-59, Lib trainee 59-62, Sr libn 62-66; Supv libn 66-68; Curator of Picture Collection 68-. 9: SLA-Picture Div (sec-treas 68-70, chm NY Chap 67-68). 14: Picture libn. 15: Picture Collection Room 73 NY Pub Lib 42nd st & Fifth ave, New York NY 10018.

COWARD, ROBERT YEOMAN. b Pt Huon Mich 29 Jl 20. 4: Hester Hartman. 5: Pt Huron Jr Col 38-40 AA; UMich 40-42, 46-50 (Ger, LS) AB, ABLS, AMLS; UIll 53-55; Ind U 63. 6: Ger, Fr. 7: Asst circ UMich Gen Lib 41-42; (S/Sgt) US Army 42-46; Sr libn UMich Gen Lib 47-52; Head Libn Franklin Col 52-. 8: Consul on lib construction, Ind State Lib, 65-66. 9: ALA; IndLA (chm Lib Action Com). 10: AAUP. 12: "Catalog of the David Demaree Banta Collection (60, 2nd ed 65). 13: Yes. 14: Admin, bk sel. 15: Rt 5 Box 33A, Franklin In 46131.

COWELL, RUTH FRANCES. b Olean NY 11 S 09. 5: Mt Holyoke 27-32 (Hist of Art) AB; St Bonaventure Col 32-33 (Eng Lit) MA; NYS Col for Tchrs (Albany) 38-39 BS in LS. 7: Instr Dunkirk Collegiate Center of Alfred U 37-38; Instr Olean High Sch, Olean NY 38; Ref asst Carnegie Lib of Pittsburgh 39-42; Ref & lend libn Newark Pub Lib, Newark NJ 42-45; Lib Dir Manhasset Pub Lib, Manhasset NY 45-. 8: Lib consul, Mineola Pub Lib, 56; Part-time lib sch tchg in 3 NY State Cols 55-. 9: ALA; NYLA (com duties); Nassau Co (NY) LA (off & com chm). 10: AAUW. 14: Admin, ref. 15: 30 Onderdonk ave, Manhasset NY 11030.

COWEN, JULIETTE (ANTHONY). b Hartford Conn 7 N 39. 4: W Walker Cowen. 5: Sweet Briar Col 60-62 (Lat) AB; Brown 62-64 (Lat, Gk) MA; Simmons 63-64 (LS) MS. 6: Lat, Fr, Ger, Gk. 7: Stud asst in acquis Harvard Col Lib 63-64; Asst rare bk catlgr NY Pub Lib 64-65; Sr asst in rare bk div UVa Lib 65-66; Rare bk catlgr 66-68; Ref libn McIntire Pub Lib 68-. 9: ALA; Bibliog Soc Va. 14: Rare bks. 15: McIntire Public Library, Charlottesville Va 22901.

COWERN, AGNES G. b Indianapolis 24 Je 09. 5: UMinn 27-31 (LS) BS; Rosary Col 69 (LS). 7: Staff libn VA Hosp, Wood Wis & Hines Ill 36-38; Chief Libn VA Hosp, Cheyenne Wyo, Knoxville Iowa, St Cloud Minn 38-46; Chief lib div VA Br 8, Ft Snelling Minn 46-49; Chief Libn VA Hosp, Sioux Falls SD, Omaha Neb; VA Research, Chicago, Hines Ill 49-. 9: ALA; MedLA. 14: Hosp & med libs. 15: 219 N 2nd ave, apt 20, Maywood Il 60153.

COWGILL, LOGAN O. b Wabash Ind 24 F 19. 4: Martha Anne OBrien. 5: Ind U35-40. 6: Fr, Sp. 7: Ordnance engnr OChOrdnance, Wash DC 41-46; Bibliogr Hispanic Found LC 46-48; Libn OChEngnrs, Wash DC 49-63, C Sc & Tech Info Div 63-67; Asst mgr Water Resources Sci Info Ctr 67-. 8: Chm Adv Com on Acquis, Brookings Institution Survey of Fed Libs, 60-61; Army Ad Hoc Com on Sci & Tech Info, 62; Sub-Com on Info Retrieval, Com on Water Resource Research, 65-67; Fed Lib Com TaskForce on Acquis 66-, Task Force on Relation of Libs and Info Systems 67-. 9: BSA;SLA (chm Mil Libns Div 63-64, pres DC Chap 65-66, chm Statistics Com 68, chm NatRes Div 68-); ASTS; Geo-Sci Info Soc. 10: Soc Hist of Tech; Soc Arch Histns; Nat Trust for Hist Preserv; Grolier Club(NY); etc. 12: Brookings Institution, Fed Dept Libs, "Paper on Acquisitions (63). 14: Sci & tech info systems, tech lib operaions. 15: 26 Sixth st SE, Wash DC 20003.

COWLES, (MARGUERITE) ROSE. b Port Sulphur La 21 Je 41. 5: LSU (New Orleans) 58-63 9hist) BA; LSU (Baton

Rouge) 64-66 (LS) MS; USoMiss 67- (Hist). 6: Fr. 7: Typist LSU (New Orleans) Lib 63-64; Libn II USoMiss Lib 66-. 9: ALA. 10: Phi Alpha Theta. 14: Ref, soc sci. 15: PO Box 205 So Sta, Hattiesburg Ms 39401.

COWLES, LOIS HART. b Kensington Conn 8 Ag 06. 5: Wheaton Col (Mass) 29 (Philos) AB; West Res 51 MSLS. 7: Organist Stanley Mem Church, New Britain Conn 30-40; Organist First Baptist Church, New Britain Conn 40-46; Gen lib asst New Britain Pub Lib, New Britain Conn 32-48, Head catlg dept 48-53; Ref libn Mary Cheney Lib, Manchester Conn 53-57; Sr ref asst Hartford (Conn) Pub Lib 57-. 9: ConnLA (chm Proced Com 60-62); NELA. 10: AAUW; Nat Audubon Soc. 14: Ref, catlg, loc hist. 15: 38 Winthrop st, New Britain Ct 06052.

COWLES, MARY E(STHER). b Jefferson Ohio 2 N 10. 5: Hiram Col 28-32 (Eng, Hist) AB; West Res 32-33 BS in LS. 6: Fr. 7: Apprentice Hiram Col 29-32; Asst catlg dept Ohio State U 34-42, Catlgr 42; Oberlin Col: Catlgr 42-58, Head catlg det 58-61, 1st asst catlg dept 61-65, Sr catlgr 66-. 9: ALA; OhioLA; No Ohio Tech Proc Libns. 14: Catlg. 15: 410 Caskey dr, Oberlin Oh 44074.

COWLEY, JOYCE (MARTIN). b Ark 26 Ja 08. 5: Tex Womens U 26-29 (Art) Ark State Tchrs Col summer 55 (LS); W Tex State U summer 59 (Art) BS; No Tex State U summer 61 (LS). 7: Libn high sch, Marshall Ark 55-56; Amarillo Pub Lib, Amarillo Tex: Ref asst 56-60, Asst to catlgr 61-62, Bkmob dept head 62-65, Ref dept head 65-66, Asst libn 66-. 9: Tex State LA. 10: AAUW. 14: Ref. 15: PO Box 2171, Amarillo Tx 79105.

COWPERTHWAIT, MARTHA COLES. b Mt Holly NJ 8 S 21. 5: Wilson Col 40-44 (Eng) AB; Drexel 44-45 (LS) BS. 7: Asst libn Moorestown Free Lib, Moorestown NJ 45-53; Libn St Marys Hall, Burlington NJ 53-59; Libn Moorestown Friends Sch, Moorestown NJ 59-. 9: ALA (Recr Com); NJSchLA; Burlington Col Sch Libns (past chm); phila Area Independent Sch Libs. 10: AAUW. 15: 318 E Main st, Moorestown NJ 08057.

COX, ANNE (DuBOSE). b Columbia SC 11 N 18. 4: Albert F Cox. 5: Flora Macdonald 35-39 (Eng) AB; Emory 42-43 AB in LS, 56-59 (LS) ML. 7: Tchr Boone Trail High Sch Harnett Co Schs, Mamers NC 39-41; Res libn Emory U Lib 43-48; Libn Slaton & Anne E West Schs, Atlanta 59-63; Libn Sch Problems Lab Emory U summers 63-65; Catlg libn spec collections Emory U Lib 64-. 9: GaLA; SELA. 10: Beta Phi Mu. 15: 1721 Hummingbird lane NE, Atlanta Ga 30307.

COX, CARL RAYMOND. b Norris City Ill 16 S 20. 5: Wright Jr Col 37-39 (Pre-Med); Central YMCA Col (Chiago) 39-41 (Eng) BA; Columbia 48-49 (LS) MS. 6: Fr, Ger. 7: Lib asst "The Chicago Sun" 42, 45-47; Cryptographer US Army Air Corps (S/Sgt)42-45; News & picture ed Acme Newspictures Inc, Chicago 47-48; Subj catlgr LC 49-51;Subj catlgr NY Pub Lib 51-53; Prin libn tech serv Cal State Lib 53-58; Asst dir oflibs tech serv UMd 58-65; Dir Lib Systems Development SUNY Hdqrs (Albany) 65-68; Prof& chief libn Herbert H Lehman Col CUNY 68-. 9: ALA-RTSD (spec com on reg proc57-59, com mem in 3 sects); -ACRL; -LAD; -ISAD; SLA (treas Wash DC Chap); NYLA. 10: Amer Philatelic Soc; AAUP. 13: Yes. 14: Tech serv, applic of data proc to libs, admin. 15: 499 N Broadway apt 4D, White Plains NY 10603.

COX, CARL T(HOMAS). b Knoxville Tenn 21 Je 29. 4: Josephine Rives. 5: Carson-Newman Col 47-51 (Hist) BA; Peabody 56-57 (LS) MA,59-61 (LS) ED, 64-68 Ed D. 7: Tchr DeKalb Co Bd of Educ, Decatur Ga 51-56; US Army(Sgt) Instr, Ft Jackson SC 52-54; Dir Tchg Materials Centre, State U Col, Cortland NY 57-65; Visiting Prof Peabody Lib Sch summers 58-60, 64, 67-68; Asst Prof DeptLib Serv UTenn 65-. 8: Staff, Lib 21, Seattle Worlds Fair, 62. 10: YMCA. 13: Yes. 14: Non-bk materials, ref. 15: Dept of Lib Serv Univ of Tenn, Knoxville Tn 37914.

COX, DORIS (WALKER). b Montbrook Fla 11 D 19. 4: Alfred Rankin Cox Jr. 5: Fla State Col for Women 36-39 (Eng) AB; Fla State U 53-56 (LS) MA, 58-(Educ)., 58-68 (Educl admin) PhD. 7: Tchr-libn Summerfield Pub Schs, Summerfield Fla 39-40; Libn Reddick Cons Sch, Reddick Fla 40-42, 47-49; Libn Elizabeth Cobb Jr High Sch, Tallahassee Fla 53-62; Libn Leon High Sch, Tallahassee Fla 62-63; Instr Lib Sch Fla State U 63-64; Instr Lib Sci Dept West Carolina Col summers 61-64; Asst Prof Lib Educ UGa 65-68; Assoc prof & chm Dept LS Appalachian State U 68-. 09: FlaASchL (Exec Bd). 10: Delta Kappa Gamma; Beta Phi Mu; Phi Kappa Phi; Kappa Delta Pi. 12: "Instructional Materials Centers, Capci Bibliog No 8, NEA Res Inst, ASCD. 14: Sch libs, curr devel, learning processes. 15: Hound Ears Lodge and Club Route 3, Boone NC 28607.

COX, DOROTHY JANE. b Marion Ill 2 My 23. 5: So Ill U 40-44 (Hist, Eng) BS, 47-51 (Hist) MA; UIll 58-61 (LS) MS; UWis summer 65. 6: Fr. 7: Tchr high sch, Pinckneyville Ill 44-52; Tchr high sch, Coquille Ore 52-54; Tchr-libn high sch, Zeigler Ill 54-56; Libn Coolidge Jr High Sch, Granite City Ill 56-65; Instr instr materials So Ill U 66-. 9: NEA-DAVI; ALA-AASchL; IllEA; IllLA; IllASchL (pres 66-67). 10: Delta Kappa Gamma; Beta Phi Mu. 14: Sch libs, catlg non-bk materials. 15: 1103 S Court st, Marion Il 62959.

COX, HELEN (SOHN). b Niles Mich 7 Jl 29. 4: Richard W Cox. 5: Flint Jr Col 46-47; Valparaiso 47-50 (Eng) BA; UMinn 65-68 (LS) MA. 6: Fr, Ger. 7: Lib asst Flint Pub Lib, Flint Mich 42-47; Lib asst ValparaisoU 47-50; Lib asst Concordia Sem summer 48-50; Lib asst City Lib, New Richmond Wis 63; Info ctr coord ADVOTECH 18 (pub 4-co voc-tech col for adults), New Richmond Wis 68-. 9: WisLA; Wis Assn for Voc & Adult Educ. 14: Ref, bibliog. 15: 254 W Third st, New Richmond Wi 54017.

COX, LOIS ANNE (WILLIAMS). b Carbondale Penn 29 My 28. 4: Robert Watts Cox. 5: Paterson State Col 58-63 (Gen Elem) BA; Rutgers 65-69 MLS; Drexel 67; Fairleigh Dickinson 69. 6: Sp. 7: Sub tchr, Haskell NJ, Franklin Lakes NJ, Oakland NJ 59-63; Tchr Franklin Lakes Bd of Educ, Franklin Lakes NJ 63-65; Tchr & libn Wyckoff Bd of Educ, Wycoff NJ 65-68; Libn hd of acquis Bergen Commun Col 68-. 8: President's Ad-Hoc Com for Establishing a Faculty Senate Bergen Commun Col 68-69. 9: NEA; NJSchLA (memb chm Bergen Co 68-69); NJLA; NJEA; BergenCoSchLA. 10: Crystal Lake Homeowners Assn; Kappa Delta Pi. 14: Acquis, sch libnship, ref, pub serv. 15: 125 Lakeshore dr, Oakland NJ 07436.

COX, (ANNIE) LOUISE (HART). b Merryville La 29 O 07. 4: Leonard Alford Cox. 5: Stephen F Austin State Col 25-28 (Eng) BA; UTex summers 32-33, 36, 49 (Eng) MA, summers 58-59 (LS) Temp Certif; Tex Womans U summer 60 (LS); N Tex U summers 61-62 (LS) Prof Certif. 6: Sp. 7: Tchr Buna High Sch, Buna Tex 28-9; Tchr Three Rivers High Sch, Three Rivers Tex 29-32; Tchr Oak Hill High Sch, Henderson Tex 34-35; Tch Pine Tree High Sch, Pine Tree Tex 35-37; Tchr Rochester High Sch, Rochester Tex 38-39; Tchr French High Sch, Beaumont Tex 40-41; Libn & tchr Houston Pub Schs, 46-. 8: Asst lib & a-v coord, Westbury Sr High Sch, Houston. 9: NEA; ALA; Tex State Tchrs Assn; TexLA. 13: . 14: High sch libs. 15: 7503 Thurow, Houston Tx 77017.

COX, MARTHA (BALDWIN. b Mt Union Penn 4 D 28. 4: John A Cox. 5: Bucknell U 4-50 (Eng, Hist) AB; Carnegie 52-53 MS in LS. 6: Sp. 7: Elem tchr Mt Union Schs, Mt Union Penn 50-52; Ref asst in chg of period Penn State U 53-56; Ref asst Penn State U Lib 56-65; Jr high sch libn Westerly Parkway Jr High Sch, State College Penn 65-. 14: Ref. 15: 735 N Allen, State College Penn.

COX, MARTHA (JANE McCORMICK). b Lisbon Ohio 2 Jl 28. 4: J Morgan Cox. 5: Col of wooster 46-48; Carnegie Inst of Tech 48-51 (Eng) BS; Kent State U 63-64 (LS) MA. 6: Ger. 7: Lisbon Pub Lib summers 44-48 Lepper Lib, Lisbon 44-48; Libn Malone Col 64-. 9: ALA; OhioLA; Ohio Col Assn (sec-treas Lib Sect). 10: AAUW; Stark Co (Ohio) LA (pres 68). 14: Admin. 15: 515 25th st NW, Canton Oh 44709.

COX, MARY LILLIAN. b Lyons Kan 10 Je 37. 5: Austin Col 55-57; N Tex State U 57-59 (LS) BA; UTex 61-62 MLS UColo summer 67. 7: Asst libn Southwestern U 59-61; Asst libn catlgr UColo 62-65, Assoc libn ser catlgr 65-. 9: ALA-ACRL;-RTSD; ColoLA. 14: Catlg, ser, ref. 15: 1647 Seventh st,Boulder Co 80302.

COX, MARY SUE. b Brevard NC 2 Jl 11. 5: Furman U 30-33 (Hist) AB; Columbia 37-38 (LS) BS. 7: Bkmob asst Greenville Co Lib, Greenville SC 38-40; Co libn Greenwood City & Co Pub Lib, Greenwood SC 40-41; libn Greenwood City and Co Pub Lib 41-42; Libn Cherokee City & Co Lib, Gaffney SC 42-43; Br libn Greenville Co Lib, Greenville SC 42-45, Co Libn 45-61, Ext & asst libn 61-. 9: ALA; SELA; SCLA (pres 46, mem Stand Com). 14: Ext serv. 15: 316 W Stone ave, Greenville SC 29609.

COX, MERNA J. b Chattanooga Tenn 9 O 17. 5: UChattanooga 35-39 (Fr) BA; UNC 43 BS in LS. 6: Fr, Sp. 7: Tchr Chattanooga Pub Schs, Chattanooga Tenn 40-41, Sch libn 41-43; Child libn Rock Hill (SC) Pub Lib 43-45; Child libn

Durham (NC) Pub Lib 45-46; Child libn Worthington Pub Lib, Worthington Ohio 46-5; Head child div Phoenix Pub Lib 53-56; City Libn Coronado Pub Lib, Coronado Cal 56-. 9: ALA; CalLA (pres Palomar Dist 68). 10: Soroptimist Internat. 14: Admin, ref, child wk. 15: 345 D ave,apt 4, Coronado Ca 92118.

COX, NAOMI (BAKER). b Vernon Ala 23 N 10. 4: Dewey L Cox. 5: Athens Col 28-31 (Eng) AB; Birmingham So Col summers 29-30; UAla summers 47-50 (LS) Certif, summers 52-55 (Secondary Educ) MA. 7: Thcr, Ala: Kate Duncan Smith DAR Sch, Grant 31-33, Vincent Sch, Vincent 33-35, Liberty Sch, Ethelsville 35-37, Chilton Co High Sch, Clanton 42-45, holt High Sch, Holt 45-48; Libr, Ala: Gorgas High Sch, Samanta 48-51, Holt High Sch, Holt 51-55, Alexandria Schs, Alexandria 55-65; Lib supv Calhoun Co Schs, Anniston Ala 65-. 9: ALA (state sch rep 68-69); NEA; AlaSchLA (pres 68-69); AlaLA (treas 68-69); SELA; AlaEA. 10: Bus & Prof Women's Club; Variosa Club of Alexandria; Delta Kappa Gamma; AAUW. 14: Sch lib. 15: 1415 Christine ave apt 4, Anniston Al 36201.

COX, REBA (WEST). b Muskogee Okla 12 S 08. 4: James Burl Cox. 5: Northeastern State Col 41-45 (Educ, Soc Sci) BS; Okla State U 53-55 (Educ) MA; UOkla 60-62 MLS; Okla State U 67. 6: Sp. 7: Tchr of soc studies in pub schs, Tahlequah Okla 47-60; Asst prof LS Northeastern State Col (Okla) 60-. 9: NEA; OklaLA; OklaEA. 10: AAUW; Delta Kappa Gamma; DAR; Phi Kappa Phi; Alpha 13: Yes. 14: Periods, ref. 15: Grand ave, Tahlequah Ok 74464.

COX, WILLIAM H JR. b Cleveland 29 N 23. 5: UMich 44-48 (Eng Lit) AB, 49-51 MLS. 6: Fr. 7: Pub Lib, Rochester NY: Ref asst 51-57, Personnel off 57-64, Adult serv consul 64-. 8: NY State Ad Hoc Com on Certif, 64. 9: ALA (Notable bks coun 65-67); NYLA (Coun 61-65, chm recr com 59-61, memPersonnel Admin Co 56-58, pres Adult Serv sect 67-68). 10: Phi Beta appa; Phi Kappa Phi. 13: Yes. 14: Adult serv. 15: Rochester Pub Lib 115 South ave, Rochester NY 14604.

COXE, ELIZABETH G. b Phila 21 F 33. 5: Colo Col 51-55 (Hist) BA; UDenver 62-63 (LS) MA. 7: Ref libn USAF Acad 64-. 14: Ref. 15: 900 Saturn dr, Colorado Springs Colo 80906.

COYLE (MARY) IRENE. b Ackley Iowa 4 Mr 13. 5: Clarke Col 30-34 (LS, Eng) BA; Wash U (St Louis) 58, 59 (LS); UDenver summer 59 (LS); USoCal summers 60-65 MS in LS. 6: Fr. 7: Asst libn St Josephs Acad, Des Moines Iowa 35-36; Libn Pub Lib, Ackley Iowa 36-55; Rec dir Blanchard Lodge, Boulder Colo 55-57; Libn St Louis U High Sch, St Louis 57-. 9: CathLA (Exec Bd 58-, Greater St Louis Unit); MoLA; MoASchL. 10: St Louis Lib Assocs; NCTE; AAUW; Libraria Sodalitas; Great Books Discussion Group; Girl Scouts Adv; Alum Assn USoCal; clarke Col Alum Assn. 14: Ref, readers adv, acquis, catlg. 15: 5047 Waterman, apt 102, St Louis Mo 63108.

COYLE, EDITH McINTOSH. b Knoxville Tenn 1 O 14. 4: Wilbur Franklin Coyle Jr. 5: Mars Hill Jr Col 33-35; UNC 35-37 (Eng Lit) AB, 38-39 ABLS; Johns Hopkins 43-45 (Classical Archaeol) MA. 6: Lat, Fr. 7: Act libn Black Mountain Col 39-40; Catlgr Millsaps Col 40-41, Asst libn 41-42; Catlgr UMd Sch Med Lib 42-49; Libn Naval Med Field Research Lab Lib, Camp Lejeune NC 49-55; Ser libn UMd Health Sci Lib 56-64, Asst libn for tech serv 65-. 8: Instr in Lib Sci Millsaps Col, summers 40-42. 9: MeLA. 10: Archaeol Inst Amer. 14: Acquis, catlg. 15: 5 Maryland ave, Towson Md 21204.

COYLE, GEORGIA (SPINNEY). b N Conway NH 19 Ag 24. 4: Philip W Coyle. 5: Pratt 46-47 (LS). 7: Asst child libn Brooklyn Child Museum, Brooklyn NY 47-48; Child ibn James Prendergast Free Lib, Jamestown NY 48-53; Child libn Warren Lib Assn, Warren Penn 53-54, Dir 54-. 8: Adv Com, Penn Lib Survey, 57; Penn Adv Coun on Lib Devel, 65. 9: PennLA (sec 58, chm Lib Devel Com 59; chm Pub Lib Sect 57). 10: Warren Co (Penn) Hist Soc. 13: Yes. 14: Admin. 15: P O Box 489, Warren Pa 16365.

COYNE, FUMIKO H. b Tokyo 24 Je 39. 4: Brian J Coyne. 5: Waseda U 61 (Sociol) BA; UChicago 67 (LS) MA. 6: Japanese. 7: Asst Far East Lib UChicago 65-67; Catlgr Ctr for Research Libs, Chicago 67-. 9: ALA. 14: Catlg, ref, docs libnship. 15: Center for Research Lib, 5721 S Cottage Grove ave, Chicago Il 60637.

COZENS, MRS CONSTANCE (BOWAN). b Salt Lake City 6 Ja 31. 4: Wilmer R Cozens. 5: Los Angeles City Col 49-51 (Eng) AA; UCLA 51-55 (Eng, Speech) BA & Gen Secondary Credential; USoCal 60-65 MSLS. 7: Tchr Los Angeles Bd of Educ 55-60; Libn I State of Cal Dept of Mental Hygiene, Metropolitan State Hosp 60-65, Libn II 65-. 9: Soc Mental Health Libns. 10: Salvation Army Family Serv Agency (Los Angeles). 14: Spec libs (psychiatry & psychology). 15: Metro State Hosp Lib 11400 Norwalk blvd, Norwalk Ca 90650.

CRABB, GEORGE WADE. b Nashville Tenn 23 Mr 38. 4: Elizabeth Anne (P'Pool) Crabb. 5: SWest at Memphis 56-60 (Hist) BA; Vanderbilt 60-61 (Hist) MAT; Peabody Col 63-64 MALS. 6: Fr. 7: High sch tchr Union Co Schs, Morganfield Ky 61-63; East Ky U: Catlgr 64-67, Hd catlgr 67-69. 15: Rte 2 Lakewood Estates, Richmond Ky 40475.

CRABTREE, CLARA J. b Durham NC 24 Ap 28. 4: Bruce Wilson Crabtree. 5: E Carolina Col 49-51 (Educ) BS; UNC 64 (Educ) M Ed, 66 Certif in LS. 7: Tchr High Point Pub Schs, High Point NC 51-52; Tchr Durham Co Schs, Durham NC 52-54; Tchr Tarboro Pub Schs, Tarboro NC 54-56; Durham Co Schs, Durham NC: Tchr 57-59, Libn 59-64, Dir of libs 64-. 9: NEA; ALA; ACEI; NCEA (pres East Cent Dist Sch Libns); NCLA; SELA; IRA. 10: Delta Kappa Gamma. 14: Sch libnship, instr in use bks & libs. 15: Rte 1 Box 347A, Bahama NC 27503.

CRABTREE, JEAN ELIZABETH. b Ellendale ND 15 My 15. 5: ND State Tchrs Col 33-35; UND 35-37 (Eng) BA; Columbia summers 40-43 BS in LS. 7: Eng tchr Walsh Co Agric Sch, Park River ND 37-42; Eng tchr Lincoln High Sch, Manitowoc Wis 42-43; Libn Mt Vernon Sem, Wash DC 43-45; Ass libn Garden City High Sch, Garden City NY 45-54; Head Libn Garden City Sr High Sch, Garden City NY 54-. 8: Instr St Johns U 51-52; Visiting lecturer USoCal summer 58; Expert-Consul Lib Serv Br Off of Educ, Wash DC summer 60; Ed Adv Bd "Science Quarterly 64; ALA Observer, Conf of Non-Govtal Orgs, US Mission to UN 54-57 Mem NDEA Inst, Simmons Col 66. 9: ALA (Coun 60-64, Adv Com to Access Study62-63, Com on Org 67-71); -AASchL (Rec sec 60-61; Chm Instr Materials Com 58-64);-YASD (Asia Proj Com 57-59, Dir of Subject Specialists Com 60-61, Nomin Com 64-65,YASD-TV Liaison Com 64-; chm 66-69); NEA; NYLA; Nassau-Suffolk SchLA; NY State TchrsAssn. 10: PTA; Phi Beta Kappa. 13: Yes. 14: Sch libs, serv to ya. 15: Garden City Sr High Sch, Merillon ave & Rockaway rd, Garden City NY 11530.

CRACHI, ROCCO. b Brooklyn NY 13 F 14. 4: Rosary Protheroe. 5: NYU 31-35 (Eng Lit) BA; Georgetown U 35-37 (Pol Sci); UCal 46-47 BLS. 7: USAF (Lt Col) 40-51; Chief archives Air U Lib, Ala 47; Chief Air Tactical Sch Lib, Tyndall AFB Fla 47-50; Mil personnel staff off 46, Admin Staff Off 47-51; Asst chief serv div CADO (sub ASTIA), Dayton Ohio 50-51; Head loan dept Gen Lib UCal (Berkeley) 51-59; Supv bks tech info center Lockheed Missiles & Space Div, Palo Alto Cal 59-61; Head tech processes Los Alamos Sci Lab Lib, Los Alamos NM 61-62; Chief Central Lib Lockheed-California Co, Burbank Cal 62-. 9: ALA (Com on Annuities, Pensions & Life Insur 47-51): SLA; (So Cal Chap: Ed "Bulletin 64-66, treas 66-67, v-pres 67-68, pres 68-69; sci-Tech Div: Ed "Sci-Tech News 67-); CalLA; ASIS. 10: Polynesian Soc; Book Club of California; Soc Hist of Tech; Amer Astronaut soc; Libraria Sodalitas. 12: "Retirement Policies of Life Insurance Companies in "Retirement for Librarians (51). 14: Admin, tech proc. 15: 2748 Hollister terrace, Glendale Ca 91206.

CRADY, STEPHEN LEE. b Peoria Ill 16 Ap 41. 4: Arletta E King. 5: West Ill U 60-63 BS Ed; So Ill U 64-65 (Instr Materials) MS Ed. 7: Tchr Westmer High Sch, Joy Ill 63-64; Grad asst So Ill U 64-65; A-v Dir West Sr High Sch, Aurora Ill 65-68; A-v Dir Ill Cent Col 68-. 9: NEA-DAVI; IllEA; Ill A-V Assn. 15: 1110 E Maywood, Peoria Il 61603.

CRAFT, GUY CALVIN. b Atlanta 19 D 29. 4: Eddie Barnes. 5: Morehouse Col 47-51 (Eng) AB; Atlanta 56-57 MSLS. 6: Fr. 7: Head Libn Fla Mem Col 57-62; Head Libn Edward Waters Col 62-63; Circ libn Va State Col 63-64; Chief catlgr Elizabeth City State Col 64-65; Head Libn Albany State Col 65-. 9: ALA. 10: Omega Psi Phi; YMCA. 13: Yes. 14: Catlg, rare bks. 15: Albany State Col, Albany Ga 31705.

CRAFT, IRENE LOUISE. b Wayne Kan 6 N 04. 5: Ft Hays State Col 22-30 (Hist) BS in Ed; UNeb 30-31, 38-39 (Hist) MA; UIll 39-41 BS in LS, 41-43 MS in LS. 7: Tchr pub schs: Belleville Kan 22-24, 25-29, 33-35, Alta Vista & Goodland Kan 35-38; Asst in hist UNeb 38-39; Asst UIll Natural Hist Lib (Urbana) 40-43; Asst UIll Law Lib (Urbana) 43; Asst ser libn Ore State U 44-51, Ser libn 51-. 9: ALA (Coun 54-57, Memb Com); -ACRL; SLA; PNLA; OreLA. 10: AAUW;

AAUP; Bus & Prof Womens Club; Beta Phi Mu; Phi Kappa Phi. 12: With others "Reporton Policies and Programs of the US Department of Agriculture Library". 14: Ser. 15: 636 N 27th, apt 11, Corvallis Or 97330.

CRAFT, PATRICIA (SKOG). b Detroit Mich 8 D 39. 4: Willard L Craft. 5: UMich 57-61 Chem BS in Chem; UWash 62-63 M of Libnship. 7: Child Libn Seattle Pub Lib 63-66; Elem Sch Libn Wooster City Schs, Wooster Ohio 66-67; Period libn Adrian Col 68-. 9: ALA. 14: Wk with child. 15: 6327 Palmyra rd, Palmyra Mi 49268.

CRAGGS, ANNE OLGA (KOLODY). b Saskatoon Sask Can 23 Ag 42. 4: Brian Craggo. 5: USask 60-63 (Hist) BA; UBC 64-65 BLS. 6: Fr, Ukrainian. 7: Lib asst Provincial Lib, Regina Sask Can 63-64; Child libn NYC Pub Lib 65; Br supv in charge child serv SEast Sask Reg lib, Weyburn Sask Can 66-68; Child libn NWT Pub Lib Serv, Hay River NWT 68-. 10: Can Univ Women. 14: Child serv. 15: Box 1101, Hay River Northwest Territories.

CRAGIN, SHELAH-BELL. b Selma Ala 23 Ag 43. 4: Charles C Cragin Jr. 5: Miss State Col for Women 64 (LS) BS; Fla State U summer 62; UAla (Tuscaloosa) summer 63; Tex Christian U 65; Tex Woman's U 66 MLS. 6: Sp. 7: Stud asst Miss State Col for Women Lib 62; Ref asst Ft Worth Pub Lib; Hd gen ref & personnel dept El Paso Pub Lib, El Paso Tex 66-67, coord extension serv 67-68, Asst dir 68-. 8: El Paso Major Resource Ctr consul to commun libs in Trans-Pecos. 9: ALA-RSD (liaison to JMRT); SWLA; Border Reg LA (chm nominating Com 66; Ed Com 67-68; Nominating Com 67; rep-at-large 67; ed Newsletter 68; Exec Bd 69); TexLA (ALA Memb Com 68-; Nat Lib Week in Tex Core Com 68-; sec-treas Pub Lib Div 69-70; v-chm Jr Mem RT 69-70). 10: El Paso Hist Assn; El Paso Mus of Art Assn. 13: Yes. 14: Lib admin, ref. 15: 501 N Oregon, El Paso Tx 79901.

CRAHAN, ELIZABETH (SCHMIDT). b Cleveland Ohio 6 O 13. 4: Marcus E Crahan. 5: Wellesley 31-32; USoCal 32-37 (Arch) B Arch, 59-60 MS in LS. 6: Ger, Fr. 7: Gen lib asst Lib Los Angeles Co Med Assn 60-61, Hd ref serv 61-67, Asst libn 67-. 9: SLA (So Cal Chap: chm Bio Sci Div 63-64; Corresponding sec 64-65; Pub Rel Dir 65-66; Publicity Chm SLA Conf 68); MedLA; CalLA; Med Lib Gp So Cal (chm Scholarship Com 66-67; sec Med Lib Scholarship Found 67-). 10: Libraria Sodalitas Bd Dir. 14: Ref, hist med. 15: 341 South Westmoreland ave, Los Angeles Ca 90005.

CRAIG, MRS ALGERENE M (AKINS). b Austin Tex 28 Ap 11. 4: Isaac Arnold Craig Jr. 5: Samuel Huston Col 27-30; Prairie View A&M Col 30-31 (Eng) BS; USoCal 45; UTex 58 (LS); Prairie View A&M Col 60 (Elem Educ) M Ed. 6: Sp. 7: Soc Sci Tchr St Paul Jr Col 31; Blackshear Elem Sch, Austin Tex; Prim tchr 32,Intermediate tchr 33, Libn 34, Asst Prin & libn 45, Asst prin 46-47, Libn 48-. 9: NEA (Life mem); ALA; TexLA; Tex State Tchrs Assn. 10: Austin Lib Club; YWCA; Zeta Phi Beta. 11: Austin Tex Pub Schs Tchr of the Year, 63; Commun Serv Award, 65. 13: Yes. 14: Wk with child & ya, storytelling. 15: 1809 Pennsylvania ave, Austin Tx 78702.

CRAIG, SISTER AGNES GREGORY SC. b Irvington NJ 5 O 26. 5: Caldwell Col 44-48 (Eng) BA; Seton Hall U 54-56 (Educ); St Johns U (NY) 56-60 MLS. 6: Fr. 7: Tchr-libn St Johns High Sch, Paterson NJ 54-56; Tchr-libn St Marys High Sch, Jersey City NJ 56-60; Libn Marylawn of the Oranges, S Orange NJ 60-. 8: Chm Elizabeth Seton Lib Coun; Area Coun mem, NJ Lib Devel Program; Archdiocese of Newark, Lib coord. 9: ALA-AASchL; CathLA (High Sch Sect: chm Nomin Com 65); NJLA; NJSchL. 10: Elizabeth Seton Lib Coun. 13: Yes. 14: Ya serv, tchr-libn-student coop. 15: Marylawn of the Oranges, 445 Scotland rd, S Orange NJ 07079.

CRAIG, DALE WARREN. b Bellaire Ohio 13 S 40. 4: Sharon Ann Trutt Craig. 5: Ohio U at Martins Ferry 59-60; Ohio State 60-63 (Internat rel) BA; Kent State 63-66 MSLS. 6: Sp. 7: Miscellaneous laborer Rodefer-Gleason Glass Co, Bellaire Ohio 59-60; Cuyahoga Co Pub Lib, Cleveland: Lib intern 63-66, YA libn 66-67, Adult services & YA libn (Hd) 67; Hd libn Northland Pub Lib, Pittsburgh 67. 8: Particg staff member, Ohio State Lib YA Wkshop, 67. 9: ALA; OLA; PennLA (New Libns Sect: chm of the By-laws Com 68-69). 10: Beta Phi Mu. 14: Admin, adult serv, YA serv. 15: 3603 Oakcrest dr, Gibsonia Pa 15044.

CRAIG, FLORENCE (STEVENS). b Norfolk Conn. 4: W Parker Craig. 5: Simmons 23 BS; West Res 40-46. 6: Fr, Sp. 7: Catlgr Adelbert Col West Res U 23-26; Cuyahoga Co Pub Lib, Cleveland: Head catlg dept 26-40, Head catlg & order dept 30-40, Br libn 40-43, Dir of adult educ 43-, Coord adult serv; Commun rel libn Cleveland Hts, Univ Hts Pub Lib 67-. 8: Visiting lecturer in lib sci: Fla State U summer 64 & 67, Kan State Tchrs Col summer 65. 9: AEAUSA (pres 56, mem Del Assembly 58-65); ALA (chm Adult Educ Bd 51-53; Com on Org 57-62; Goals Award Jury 67-69); -PLD (chm Adult Educ Sect 46-48);-ASD (chm Notable Bks Coun 55, pres 61-62; Bd 63-66); Ohio Assn of Adult Educ (pres 60-62); OhioLA (Bd, chm Intel Freedom Com 57-62; chm Adult Educ Sect). 10: Motion Picture Coun of Greater Cleveland. 11: Award for distinguished service in adult educ, Ohio Assn for Adult Educ, 59. 13: Yes. 14: Adult serv. 15: 3638 Mt Laurel, Cleveland Hgts Oh 44121.

CRAIG, JAMES L(IVINGSTON). b Springfield Mass 18 Ja 41. 4: Susan Helms. 5: Cornell U 58-61, 62-63 (Vertebrate Zool) BS; Harvard 61-62; Rutgers 63-64 MLS. 6: Ger. 7: Stud asst City Lib, Springfield Mass 57-58; Asst Mann Lib Cornell U 59-61; Farmhand Kern Farm, Goshen NY 59; Asst Lib Museum of Comparative Zool, Harvard U summer 61; Searcher acquis dept Harvard Col Lib 61-62, summer 63; Asst catlg ref libn Mann Lib Cornell U 64-66; Asst libn admin libns off, Yale U Lib 66-67, Asst hd catlg dept; Biol Scis libn UMass (Amherst) 68-. 9: ALA; SLA. 10: Beta Phi Mu. 14: Tech serv, personnel, biol sci. 15: 452 River dr, Sunderland Ma 01375.

CRAIG, JEAN E. b Springfield Mass 3 My 44. 5: Colby Col 62-66 (Classics, Eng) AB; UMich 66-67 AMLS. 6: Lat. 7: Ref asst Paley Lib Temple U 67-69; Catlgr UPenn Van Pelt Lib 69-. 10: Phi Beta Kappa. 15: 2125 Locust st, Philadelphia Pa 19103.

CRAIG, JOHN JR. b Jersey City NJ 21 Ag 21. 4: Betty Richards. 5: Maryville Col (Tenn) 44-47 (Eng) BA; Columbia summer 45-57; Princeton Theol Sem 47-50 (Theol) BD; State U Col (Geneseo NY) 64-65 MLS. 7: pastor Presbyterian Churches, Vernon & Vernon Ctr NY 50-53; Pastor First Presbyterian Church, Greenport NY 53-59; Pastor First Presbyterian Church, Carthage NY 59-62; Asst pastor First Presbyterian Church, Batavia NY 62-64; Interim pastor First Presbyterian Church, LeRoy NY 64-65; Asst libn Fairleigh Dickinson U 65-68; Asst libn Sullivan Co Comm Col 68-. 14: Admin, ref, bk sel, ser. 15: R D 2 Box 120, Monticello NY 12701.

CRAIG, (JOSEPH) EDDY (GILLINGHAM) JR. b Brooklyn NY 9 O 31. 4: Julianne Carlstrom. 5: Colorado Col 49-54 (Econ) BA; So Conn State Col 63-68 MSLS. 7: Partner Texorado Oil Co, Gladewater Tex 54-62; Libn Avon Ol Farms, Avon Conn 62- Instr SoConn State Col 67-68. 14: Acquis, catlg, ref. 15: Avon Old Farms, Avon Ct 06001.

CRAIG, MRS RAYMOND B (LOIS LEITER). b Richland Co Ohio 14 Je 09. 4: Rymond B Craig. 5: Miami U 27- 31 (Lat, Eng) BS in Educ; Ohio State U summer 36-38 (Eng); Kent State U summer 55-60 (LS) MA. 7: Tchr Lostcreek High Sch, Casstown Ohio 31-40; Tchr Pickerington High Sch, Pickerington Ohio 51-52; Tchr Liberty Union High Sch, Baltimore Ohio 53-54, Libn 55-65; Libn Belpre City High Sch, Belpre Ohio 65-. 9: ALA-AASchL; NEA; OhioASchL (rec sec, pres 65, chm Research Com); OhioEA; OhioLA. 10: AAUW; Kappa Delta Pi; Delta Kappa Gamma; Mortar Board; Eta Sigma Phi;Alethenai Lit Soc. 13: Yes. 14: Ya serv, ref, catlg. 15: 1802 Rockland ave, Belpre Oh 45714.

CRAIN, OSMON A. b Morris Ill 21 My 20. 5: St Olaf Col 37-48 (Eng, Hist) BA; UHouston 52; Ill Tchrs Col 64-66 (LS) M Ed. 7: Tchr libn Chicago pub schs 64-67; Tchr libn Hammond Pub Schs 67-68; Hd branch Div Hammond Pub Lib 68-. 9: ALA-CSD; -YASD; IndLA; IndSchLA; ChicagoLA. 10: Amer Fed Tchrs. 14: Catlg,new media of libs, admin, pub rel. 15: 5945 Hyslop pl, Hammond In 46320.

CRAM, KENDALL J. b Warsaw Poland 3 S 32. 5: Vanderbilt 50-54 Eng BA; Peabody Col 58-59 MALS. 7: Tennessee State Lib: Libn (Staff) 59-65, Hd ref dept 65-. 9: ALA; TennLA (chm Refer Affiliate TennLA ALA 67-68). 10: Tenn Hist Soc. 12: "Guide to the Use of Genealogical Material in the Tennessee State Library and Archives" (64). 14: Ref. 15: Tenn State Lib, Tenn State Lib and Archives, Nashville Tn 37219.

CRAMER, ALICE P(URINGTON). b Providence 23 Je 09. 4: George A Cramer. 5: Mt Holyoke 26-30 (Zool) AB; Simmons Col 40-41 (Med Lib) BS. 6: Fr. 7: Med sec orthopedic surgeon, Providence 30-33; Asst Providence Pub Lib 33-40; Libn Vick Chem Co, NY 41-42; Libn NY Orthopaedic Disp & Hosp, NYC 42-46; Libn NY State Vet Col 46-54, Asst libn 60-61; Bibliog for physician doing research, W Palm Beach Fla 62-63; Libn St Marys Hosp, w palm Beach Fla 63-. 10: Reg Conf of

Fla Med Libns. 13: Yes. 14: Med libnship. 15: Med Lib St Marys Hosp, W Palm Beach Fl 33407.

CRAMER, ANNE (OAKES). b Norman Okla 20 S 29. 5: Stephens Col 47-48; UOkla 48-51 (LS) BA, 68 MLS. 7: Asst Kan City (Mo) Pub Lib 51-58; Hdqrs libn Johnson Co Lib, Merriam Kan 59-61; Catlgr Southwestern State Col (Okla) 61-62. Libn 62-. 8: Mayors Lib Com; Okla Coun on Libs 67-. 9: ALA; OklaLA (sec 65-66); MedLA; Libs Legisl Conf Com 65-67; SWLA (sec Col & Univ Libs Div 69-70); Weatherford Lib Adv Bd 64-; Okla Coun on Libs 67-; Adv Com on Biomed Info Serv, Okla Med Program 67-. 10: AAUW. 14: Col lib, tech proc. 15: Lib Southwestern State Col, Weatherford Ok 73096.

CRAMER, KENNETH C. b Morris Twp NJ 5 Ag 28. 5: Gettysburg Col 49-52 BA; West Res 52-53 (LS) MS; Amer U 61. 7: US Navy 46-48;Lib asst Morris Co Free Lib, Morristown NJ 52; Gen asst & roving asst Enoch PrattFree Lib Baltimore 53-55; Ref dept Dartmouth Col Lib 55-60; Spec collections libn US Mil Acad Lib (W Point NY) 60-61; Col Archivist Dartmouth Col 61-. 9: SAA. 10: Fellow,soc of Antiquaries of Scotland; Viking Soc for North Research. 15: 11 Kingsford rd,hanover NH 03755.

CRAMER, ORA L. 03Reinbeck Iowa 8 F 10. 5: Iowa State Tchrs Col 28-30 (Elem Educ); Iowa State Col 38-39 & 40-41 (Home Econ, Educ) BS; UIowa 47-49 (Eng) MA; UDenver 58-59 (LS) MA. 6: Lat, Fr. 7: High sch tchr Pine Village Pub Schs, Pine Village Ind 50-52; High sch tchr Kahlotus Wash 52-53; High sch tchr Jasper PubSchs, Jasper Alta 53-54; High sch tchr Pub Schs, Langenburg Sask 54-55; High sch libn Munising Pub Schs, Munising Mich 55-57; High sch libnClarion Pub Schs, Clarion Iowa 57-58; Catlgr Creighton U 59-67; Neb Pub Lib Commsn, Lincoln Neb 68; Iowa State U Lib 68-69; Hd catlgr & hdof tech processes Peru State Col 69-. 9: ALA; NEBLA. 14: Catlg, rare bks. 15: Peru State Col, Peru Nb 68421.

CRAMER, RUTH (STEWART). b Camden NJ 19 Mr 13. 4: Edward Everett Cramer. 5: Temple U 30-34 (Lat, Eng) BS in Ed, 35-51; Drexel 64-67 MS in LS. 6: Lat, Fr. 7: Tchr Camden Evening High Sch, Camden NJ 34-35; Libn & tchr Hatboro High Sch, Hatboro Penn 35-38; Libn Gloucester High Sch, Gloucester NJ 38-40; Libn Belleville High Sch, Belleville NJ 40-42; Eng tchr Moorestown High Sch, Moorestown NJ 45-51; Asst libn Moorestown Pub Lib, Moorestown NJ summers 53-54; Hd Eng dept Elkins Park Jr High Sch, Cheltenham Twp Penn 51-52; Instr Eng methods Temple U Sch of Educ 56-57; Libn & dir lib serv Rancocas Valley Reg High Sch Mount Holly NJ 52; Instr lib sci Trenton State Col 66; Instr lib sci Glassboro Col summer 69. 8: Mem Adv Com to Princeton U Press for bks for secondary schls 64; Eval Coms for Middle States Assn, Frenchtown NJ 50, & Lenape Reg High Sch, Medford NJ 62. 9: NEA; ALA (Awards Com 68, Mem Supv Sect Com); NJSchLA (pres 60-62); Burlington Co SchLA (pres 53-55). 10: Delta Kappa Gamma; Beta Phi Mu; Alpha Sigma Alpha; AAUW. 11: Awarded fellowship to attend Inst for Media for Supvs of ESEA Title I, II & III, UColorado Grad Sch 68, II Awarded Valley Forge Found Tchrs Medal 59. 14: Sch libnship, ref. 15: 203 Colwick rd, Cherry Hill NJ 08034.

CRANDALL, ELLA (JOHNSON). b Elm Creek Neb 11 Ag 08. 4: Judge Howard E Crandall. 5: Union Col 26-30 (Com, Eng) BA; USoCal 38-40 BLS. 6: Norwegian. 7: Libn & asst in com dept Southwestern Jr Col (Tex) 30-34; Bkkeeper & registrar Seventh-day Adventist High Sch, Loma Linda Cal 34-35; Libn White Mem Med Lib, Loma Linda U 35-50; Libn Los Angeles Co Gen Hosp Med Libs, Los Angeles 50-67. 8: Lib consul to med libs. 9: MedLA (Convention Chm 56, chm Nomin Com 57-58, chm Hosp Group 61); Med Lib Group of So Cal (Org & first pres); SLA SoCal (sec 43-44, pres 43-46). 10: C of C; Bus & Prof Women; Lawyers Wives ofLos Angeles. 12: Ed & consul ed, "Nursing Literature Index (51). 13: Yes. 14: Ref, lib org. 15: 5721 Glenford st, Los Angeles Ca 90008.

CRANE, LILLY EDNA (HAMLET). b Hackensack NJ 12 S 37. 4: George L Crane. 5: IndU 55-59 (Hist) BA; UMich 65-67 MALS. 6: Ger. 7: Asst educ libn SoIllU 67-. 9: ALA. 13: Yes. 14: Ref. 15: Park Towne apts C-C RR 4, Carbondale Il 62901.

CRANE, LUCILLE G. b Cleveland 10 Ja 20. 5: Ursuline Col 38-42 (Eng) AB; West Res 42-47 BS in LS, 48-50 (Eng) MA. 6: Polish, Ger. 7: WAC (Sgt), US, ETO 43-46; Cleveland Pub Lib, Cleveland Ohio; Benedictine High Sch, Cleveland Ohio; St John Col (Cleveland); Phoenix Union High Sch System. 9: ALA; NEA; CathLA; ArizLA; arizEA. 10: Delta Kappa Gamma. 13: Yes. 14: High sch libnship. 15: 2413 N 66th st, Scottsdale Az 85257.

CRANE, SUSAN (SMYTHE). b Waxhaw NC 11 S 40. 5: Pfeiffer Col 58-62 (Eng) BA; UNC (Chapel Hill) summers 63-67 MSLS. 6: Sp. 7: Asst libn Wingate Col Lib 62-67; Asst hd tech serv Atkins Lib UNC (Charlotte) 67-. 9: ALA; SELA; NCLA; MecklenburgLA. 14: Acquis. 15: Atkins Lib Univ of NC PO Box 12665, Charlotte NC 28205.

CRANFORD, THEODORE NELSON. b Portland Ore 9 My 30. 5: UWash 48-52 (Hist) AB, 52-53 (LS) MA. 6: Fr, sp, Ger. 7: Lib asst sci div UWash Lib 49-53; Libn GS-7 Nat Adv Com Aeronautics Ames Res Center, Moffett Field Cal 54-57; Tech info libn Lawrence Radiation Lab UCal (Livermore) 57-62; Lib research analyst Space & Info Systems Div N Amer (Aviation) Rockwell, Downey Cal 62-. 8: Consul to N Amer Aviation Thesaurus Group, El Segundo Cal 65; Org & conducted employee train classes in abstracting & indexing, Downey(Cal), McGregor(Tex), & Tulsa(Okla) 65; SLA Aerospace Thesaurus group, Los Angeles 64-65; SLA Conf registration, Los Angeles 68. 9: ASIS; SLA; Lib Automation Research & Consul Serv. 10: N Amer Aviation Hiking & Mountaineering Club; Sierra Club; Downey Recreation Ctr. 13: Yes. 14: Catlg, info storage & retrieval, research & devel info syst. 15: 11931 Lakewood blvd, Downey Ca 90241.

CRANMER, MARIE B. b Newark NJ 16 Ap 21. 5: Montclair State 39-43 Eng BA; NYU 43-45 (Soc studies) MA; Rutgers 63-66 MLS. 6: French. 7: Soc studies tchr Highland Manor Sch, W Long Branch NJ 47; Eng instr Bridgewater Col 47-50; Soc studies tchr Hunter Col High 51-52; Eng tchr Tenafly High, Tenafly NJ 52-54; Eng tchr Fallsburgh High, Fallsburgh NY 54-61; Eng tchr Park Ridge High, Park Ridge NJ 61-63; Prin libn Ocean Co Lib Brick Br 63-. 9: Sullivan Co TA (sec 57-); Ocean Co LA (sec 67). 10: Sullivan Co Hist Soc Ocean Co Hist Soc 64-68. 14: Bk sel. 15: 4 Hilltop dr, Bayville NJ 08721.

CRAUMER, LUCILLE VANDER VOORT. b Camaguey Cuba. 5: Hunter Col 26-30 (Eng) BA; Columbia 43-44 BS in LS. 6: Fr, Ger. 7: Lib asst Brooklyn Pub Lib 30-43; Indexer H W Wilson Co, Bronx NY 44-52, 56-58; Ed business Periodicals Index, H W Wilson Co, Bronx NY 58-. 9: SLA; ALA; NY Lib Club. 10: DAR; NY Bot Garden; Nat Wildlife Fed; Phi Beta Kappa; Eta Sigma Phi. 14: Indexing. 15: 1055 Summit ave apt 2E, Bronx NY 10452.

CRAVEN, R JAYNE. b Chattanooga Tenn 8 N 31. 5: UChattanooga 49-53 (Music) BM; Peabody 53-54 (LS). 6: Ger. 7: Spec serv libn US Army Spec Serv, Germany 54-56; Ref libn Chattanooga Pub Lib, Chattanooga Tenn 56-57; 1st asst art & music Pub Lib of Cincinnati 57-64, Head films & recordings center 64-. 9: ALA; MusLA; OhioLA; A-V Assn of Ohio. 10: Cincinnati Mental Health Assn; Matinee Musicale Club; Commun Orchestra of Cincinnati. 14: Adult serv (fine arts & a-v). 15: Pub Lib, Cincinnati Oh 45202.

CRAVEN, RITA. b Winnipeg Can 16 Ja 43. 5: UManitoba 59-63 BA; UBritish Columbia 65-66 BLS. 7: Lib asst Winnipeg Pub Lib 64-65; Catlgr Brock U 66-68; Catlgr UManitoba Law Lib 68-. 9: ALA; CanLA; AALL; CanALL; ManitobaLA; Inst Prof Libns Ont. 15: Library Faculty of Law, Univ of Manitoba, Winnipeg 19 Can.

CRAVENS, SALLY ANN. b Paris Ark 14 My 37. 5: UArk 55-59, summers 64, 65, 66 (Bus Tchr Training) BSBA; UDenver 66-67 Libnship MA. 7: Engr records clk SWest Bell Telephone Co, Little Rock Ark 59-63; Bus tchr Paris High Sch, Paris Ark 63-66; Asst libn docs dept UFla Lib 67-. 9: ALA; FlaLA. 10: Alachua Co Assn fpr Retarded Child; UArk Alum Assn; UDenver Alum Assn; Zeta Tau Alpha Alum Assn. 14: Govt publ. 15: 1236 SW Fourth ave apt 8, Gainesville Fl 32601.

CRAVEY, WILMA (SOWELL). b Macon Ga 18 My 21. 4: Henry Oakley Cravey. 5: Mercer U 39-42 (Span) AB; Emory 42-43 AB in LS, 62-63 (LS) ML. 6: Sp. 7: Asst libn Mercer U 43-45; Research libn Fed Reserve Bank, Atlanta 45-48; Libn Reidsville High Sch, Reidsville Ga 50-55; Libn Chamblee High Sch, Chamblee Ga 55-58; Libn Cross Keys High Sch, Atlanta 58-64; Libn Oakcliff Sch, Doraville Ga 64-66; Lib Sup DeKalb Co Schs 66-. 9: ALA; NEA; SELA; GaEA (pres Lib Dept). 14: Sch libnship, lib supv. 15: 3557 Sexton Woods dr, Chamblee Ga 30005.

CRAWFORD, CAROLYN (LUCILE). b Grant Mich 16 My 11. 5: Mich State U 29-31; UMich 31-33 AB, 33-34 ABLS; West Res 34-36 (LS) MS; NYU 53. 7: Child libn Cleveland Pub Lib 34-36; Child libn Lansing Pub Lib, Lansing Mich 36-37; Child libn Akron Pub Lib, Akron Ohio 37-42; Instr & child libn Ohio U 42-47; Asst Prof UHawaii 47-59; Visiting

Lecturer West Res 54; Program spec sch libs State Dept of Educ, Honolulu 59-64, Dir sch libs & instr materials 64-. 8: Governors Study of Sch & Pub Libs in Hawaii, with R Leigh, 59-; Governors Com on Lib Serv in Hawaii, 63-64; Adv Com for a new lib educ program UHawaii. 9: ALA (Nominating Com 68; Coun 67-71); -AASchL (Bd Dirs 63-65; sec Child Sect 46); NEA-DAVI; HawaiiLA (Bd, pres 59); Hawaii A-V Assn (Bd Dirs 65). 10: ASCD; NCTE; LWV; Zonta Club; Audubon Soc. 12: Ed "Hawaii School Libraries (51, 64). 13: Yes. 14: Wk with child & ya, tech proc, educ for libnship. 15: Univ of Denver Grad Sch of Librarianship, Denver Co 80631.

CRAWFORD, CELESTE. b Jefferson Co Penn 20 S 34. 5: UBuffalo 52-56 (Eng Lit) BA; SUNY(Geneseo) 5863 MLS. 7: Elem libn Maine-Endwell Central Sch, Endwell NY 59-61; Elem libn Wilson Central Sch, Wilson NY 61-. 10: Girl Scout Leader. 14: Child wk. 15: 142 Grove st, Tonawanda NY 14150.

CRAWFORD, DUANE EDWARD. b Bowman NDak 24 N 41. 4: Janet Walsh. 5: Carroll Col Helena Mont 59-61; N Dak State U 61-63 (Social Sci) BA; UIll (Urbana) 64-66 (LS) MS. 7: Instr Churchs Ferry High Sch, Churchs Ferry N Dak 63-64; Grad asst UIll Lib (Urbana) 64-66; Union catlg libn N Dak State Lib 66-68; Catlgr Valley City State Col 68-. 9: ALA; NDLA; NDEA. 10: Kiwanis. 12: Comp, "Dakota Union List of Serials". 14: Ref, tech proc. 15: 127 Eighth ave SE, Valley City ND 58072.

CRAWFORD, ELIZABETH VALENTINE. b Spring Lake NJ 18 S 13. 4: John Alan Crawford. 5: West Car Tchrs Col 31-32; Louisburg Col 32-33; NC State U 34-36 (Eng) BS; UNC 38139 BA in LS. 7: NC State U: Asst catlg dept 36-38, 40, Hd catlg dept 40-41, Hd period dept 41-46; Chattanooga Pub Lib, Chattanooga Tenn: Ref asst 46-47, Hd med lib 47; Hd processing dir Pub Lib of Charlotte & Mecklenburg Co, Charlotte NC 48-. 9: ALA; NCLA; SELA; MecklenburgLA. 10: Quota Club. 14: Catlg. 15: 1700 Dilworth rd W, Charlotte NC 28203.

CRAWFORD, HELEN. b Sentinel Butte ND 19 Jl 06. 5: UND 23-28 (Ger) BA; Simmons 30-31 BS in LS; Chicago 44-45. 6: Ger, Fr. 7: Clsf Iowa State U 31-44; Libn, Assoc Prof Med Lib UWis(Madison) 45-. 9: ALA-AHIL (Hosp Standards Com); MedLA (past mem Exec Bd,; past chm Exchg Com; past chm Midwest Reg Group); WisLA. 10: Phi Beta Kappa; Kappa Alpha Theta; Zonta Club; AAUP. 11: Pres Citation State Med Soc Wis (62). 13: Yes. 14: Admin, rare bks, hist of med, bk sel, bldg planning, ref. 15: Univ Wis Med Lib 1305 Linden dr, Madison Wi 53706.

CRAWFORD, JOHN. b Beloit Wis 27 F 11. 4: Elizabeth Painter. 5: UWis 28-30; Northwestern 33 (Speech) BA, 35 (Speech) MA, 47 (Speech) PhD; Columbia 53-54 MLS. 7: Instr Rosary Col 34-37; Asst Prof American U 37-39; Asst Prof West Res U 40-42; (Lt Comdr) US Naval Reserve Naval Aviation: Naval aviation cadet Selection Bd, Detroit, Resident naval Off-inchg V 5, Kalamazoo & Columbus Ohio, Asst educ off NAS, Minneapolis, Civilian personnel off NAS, New Orleans, Admin off Squadron VC 5, Pacific, 42-46; Assoc Prof Eng Wesleyan U (Middletown Conn) 47-53; Ref libn New Britain Pub Lib, New Britain Conn 55-57; Libn New Britain Sr High Sch, New Britain Conn 55-57; Libn New Britain Sr High Sch, New Britain Conn 57-66; Sch Lib Consul Staff Dept Educ Hartford Conn 66-. 9: NEA; ALA; ConnEA; NELA; ConnLA (pres 57); ConnSchLA (Pres 62-64); NESchLA (chm Pub Rel Com); NEA-DAVI; CAVEA; NEREADA; Comm ASCD. 10: NE Speech Assn; NE Forensic Assn; Conn Lib Found Inc. 15: 72 Roslyn dr, New Britain Ct 06052.

CRAWFORD, MARIAN (SCHUMACHER). b Dansville NY 13 My 29. 4: Bert G Crawford. 5: Geneseo State Tchrs Col 46-50 (LS) BS: SUNY(Geneseo) 55-60 (Educ) MS; UR 68. 7: Libn Central Sch, Warsaw NY 50-52; Tchr Elem Sch, Nunda NY 54-56; Elem tchr Ellis B Hyde, Dansville NY 57-60, Elem libn 60-65; Libn Central High Sch, Dansville NY 65-; Primary Lib 69. 9: NEA; Internat Reading Assn; NY State Tchrs Assn (Com chm). 10: Dansville Tchrs Assn; AAUW; Womans Civic Club. 12: "Study Skills Handbook (65). 13: Yes. 14: Child bks & libs. 15: Wayland, NY 14572.

CRAWFORD, MARY FRANCES. b Cookeville Tenn 1 My 32. 5: Tenn Polytech Inst 49-53 (Eng) BS; UKy 55-56 MS in LS. 7: Info desk asst libn Pub Lib of Cincinnati & Hamilton Co, Cincinnati 56-59; Home econ libn Drexel Inst of Tech 59-65; Asst undergrad libn UTenn 65-. 9: ALA-ACRL; SLA; PennLA (Scholarship Com 63-64); TLA. 14: Ref. 15: Apt H-7, 1172 Keoweeave, Knoxville Tn 37919.

CRAWFORD, MARY-CARTER. b Detroit Mich 5 My 43. 5: Manhattanville 61-65 (European hist) AB; Columbia 66 (Lib serv) MS. 7: J M Mathes Inc, NYC; Asst libn 65-66, Libn 66. 9: ALA; SLA. 14: Bus ref. 15: 340 E 80 st, New York NY 10021.

CRAWFORD, (MARY) HELEN (BAILEY). b Vardaman Miss 2 Ag 34. 4: Raymond Edward Crawford. 5: Wood Jr Col 51-53 (Liberal Arts) AA; Delta State Col 53-55 (Eng, Music) BS in Ed; UMiss 63-64 MLS. 7: Eng tchr Okolona High Sch, Okolona Miss 55-56, Music tchr 56-58; Eng tchr Brunswick Ga 58-59; Libn & choral dir Hernando High Sch, Hernando Miss 59-62; Eng tchr Water Valley High Sch, Water Valley Miss 62-63; Assoc law libn UMiss 63-. 9: MissEA. 10: Womans Soc of Christ Serv; Miss Music Assn; PTA; AALL. 14: Ref, circ, periods, acquis. 15: Box 18, Philip rd, Oxford Ms 38655.

CRAWFORD, MIRIAM ISABEL (WEXNER). b Brooklyn NY 3 Jl 16. 4: William H Crawford. 5: Brooklyn Col 33-37 (Hist) BS in Soc Sci; Columbia 37-40 BS in LS, 41-47 (Adult Educ) MA. 6: Fr, Ger. 7: Catlg asst Brooklyn Pub Lib 37-39, Br lib asst 39-41, Soc sci libn 41-43; Psych asst & educ rehabilitation Med Serv US Army WAC 43-46; Adult educ dir New Rochelle Pub Lib, New Rochelle NY 46-49; Temple U: Catlg asst & asst head catlg div 58-64, Ref asst 64-65, Curator Templana collection 65-. 9: ALA-ACRL; SAA; PennLA. 10: AAUP. 13: Yes. 14: Archives, ref. 15: Temple Univ, Phila Pa 19122.

CRAWFORD, PAUL RUSSELL. b St Ignatius Mont 16 Je 19. 4: Patricia Sutton. 5: UWash 38-42 (Hist) BA, 47-49 (Hist) MA; UCal(Berkeley) 49-52 BLS. 7: (Cpl) Meteorology USAF, Europe 43-46; Ref libn humanities San Jose State Col 52-54; Ref libn Ventura Col 54-61; Dir of co schs lib serv Co Schs Off, Ventura Cal 61-. 9: ALA; CalLA; CalASchL; Cal Tchrs Assn; Co Schs Lib Serv Com (Cal State Chm); CalSCD. 10: Adv Coun, Boy Scouts; Phi Alpha Theta. 14: Ref, intel freedom. 15: 145 Stadium ave, Ventura Ca 93003.

CRAWFORD, SUSAN YOUNG. b Vancouver Can. 4: James W Crawford. 5: UBC 48 (Liberal Arts) BA; Toronto 50 (LS) MA; Chicago 55 (Physiology, Psych) MA, 63- (LS). 6: Fr. 7: Chief catlgr Amer Dental Assn, Chicago 54-55; Asst to exec v-pres Amer Med Assn, Chicago 55-59, Dir archive-lib dept 59-. 8: Numerous projs: AMA; NLM; NSF. 9: SLA; ALA; MedLA (chm Com on Surveys & Statistics); ASIS. 12: "AMA Digest of Official Actions, 1846-1958 (59); "Index to Medical Socioeconomics Literature, weekly & annually. 13: Yes. 14: Admin, research. 15: 535 N Dearborn st, Chicago Il 60610.

CRAWLEY, GLORIA (JOY). b Long Branch NJ 19 Ja 47. 5: Middlebury Col 64-68 (Fr) AB; Simmons 68-69 (LS) MS. 6: Fr, Sp. 7: Jr asst Hingham Pub Lib, Hingham Mass 63-69; Prof lib asst in resources & proc serv Boston Pub Lib 69-. 14: Catlg, ref. 15: 4 Riverview rd, Hingham Ma 02043.

CREAGER, JOHN (WILFRED). b Merom Ind 25 Ja 08. 4: Inez Paff. 5: Defiance Col (Ohio) 25-29 (Eng, Hist) AB; UIll 32-37 BS in LS. 6: Fr, Ger. 7: Asst in lib Defiance Col 26-29; Libn R B Hayes Sch, Youngstown Ohio 29-43; Libn South High Sch, Youngstown Ohio 43-64; Prin Youngstown Night High Sch, Youngstown Ohio 55-64; Act libn, Instr Glenville State Col summer 54; Libn Ohio Conservation Lab, Camp Muskingum Ohio summer 46-47; Visiting Instr Kent State U Lib Sch summer 63; Ref libn Curriculum Center Youngstown U Lib 64-67; Libn Girard Free Lib 67-. 9: NEA (Life mem); ALA; AASchL (State Dele 48); OhioEA (dele 51); OhioASchL (sec 47-49, Program Chm 51-52, pres 52-53). 10: Phi Delta Kappa; Downtown Kiwanis; Org of Protestant Men; C of C; Girard C of C. 14: Ref, educ, travel, photography. 15: "Fernwood, Rt 4 Raccoon rd, Canfield Oh 44406.

CREAGER, WILLIAM ARTHUR. b Columbus Ohio 26 Ap 32. 4: Marilyn Jordan Creager. 5: US Naval Acad 50-54 (Marine Eng) BS; Carnegie 55-59 (Ind Mgt); George Washington U 60-64 (Eng Admin) MEA. 7: Systems & methods analyst Westinghouse, Pittsburgh 55-56, Supv Tech Info Off 56-59; Asst program dir NSF, Wash DC 59-62; V-pres Herber & Co, Wash DC 62-64; Dir Wash Off Info Dynamics, Wash DC 64-; V P Wolf R&D, Wash DC 64-68; V-pres MSA, Wash DC 69-. 9: ASIS; TIMS; ORSA. 13: Yes. 14: Info program analysis, systems design, spec info centers. 15: 11200 Lukmaner rd, Rockville Md 20852.

CREASY, MARY (JACQUELIN HIGHT). b Roseland Va 25 D 09. 4: Henry Peyton Creasy. 5: Madison Col 27-29 & 56 (Elem Educ) BS; UVa 65 Certif for Libn. 7: Tchr, Amherst Co Va 29-40, Warwick Co Va 40-44, Lynchburg Va 45-62; Sch libn Lynchburg Va 62-. 9: ALA; NEA; VaLA (chm Sch Lib Sect);

VaEA (Libns Dept: pres Dist F). 13: Yes. 14: Child bks & serv. 15: 1024 New Hampshire ave, Lynchburg Va 24502.

CREECH, CHLOE ROBERTS. b Tina Ky 28 O 37. 5: Alice Lloyd Col 56-57; UKy 58-65 (Eng, LS) BA. 6: French. 7: Elem tchr Knott Co Bd of Educ, Bearville Ky 58-64; Libn Perry Co Bd of Educ, Jeff Ky 64-. 9: ALA; -AASchL; NEA; KyEA; KyLA; KyASchL; Perry Co EA. 14: Sch libs, YP. 15: Box 12, Bulan Ky 41722.

CREEK, LEON J. b Rochester NY 18 D 36. 5: St John Fisher Col Rochester NY (Ed, Phil) BS; Syracuse 64-67 (LS) MS. 6: German. 7: Tchr USA 41st Civil Affairs Co, Ft Gordon Ga (E5, Sp5) 60-62; Tchr Rochester City Schs, NY 63; URochester: Lib clk engineering lib 63-64, Prof trainee engineering lib 64-65, Prof trainee physics & math lib 65-67, sci & engineering lib & asst supv sci libs 67-. 9: ALA; SLA; Phil of Sci Assn; Amer Cath Philos Assn. 10: Rochester Acad of Sci; Friends of the Rochester Pub Lib; AAAS. 12: Ed "Consolidate Short Title Catalog of Books of the University of Rochester Science Libraries" (4th ed 69). 14: Sci & spec libs, personnel. 15: Rush Rhees Library, River Campus, Univ of Rochester, Rochester NY 14627.

CREELMAN, KATHERINE G. b NY 18 Ja 41. 5: Vassar 58-62 (Music) AB; Columbia 62-64 (LS) Ms; NYU 66-67; Brooklyn Col 67-. 6: Fr, Ital, Ger. 7: Fellow City Col (NY) 62-64; Instr catlgr Brooklyn Col 64-; Acting mus libn Brooklyn Col 69. 9: MusLA. 10: Amer recorder Soc; Country Dance Soc. 12: Comp Index to "Notes of the MusLA v 19-20. 14: Catlg, music, child lit. 15: 221 - 8th ave, Brooklyn NY 11215.

CREIGHTON, ALICE STARKEY. b Annapolis Md 9 Ja 35. 5: Col of William & Mary 52-53; Simmons 53-54; UMe 54-56 BS; UPittsburgh 62-64 MLS. 6: Fr, Ger. 7: Research med tech UPittsburgh Med Sch 58-63; Grad asst Grad Lib Sch UPittsburgh 63-64; Med lib intern Biomed Lib UCLA 64-65; Hist of Med Libn URochester Edward G Miner Med Lib 65-. 9: MedLA. 10: Beta Phi Mu; Omicron Nu; Phi Kappa Phi. 14: Hist of med, rare bks. 15: Apt 180, 400 Kendrick rd, Rochester NY 14620.

CRENSHAW, JAN (CAROL). b Odessa Tex 1 My 45. 5: Tex Woman's U 63-67 (LS) BABS, 67-68 MLS; Brite Divinity Sch TCU 68-69 (Mission Training). 7: Grad asst Col of Educ TWU Curriculum Ctr 67-68; Clerical Texas Christian U Lib ser 68-69; Libn Lon Morris Jr Col 69-. 9: SLA. 10: Relig Educ Assn of the US & Can; Beta Phi Mu. 14: Museum libs. 15: 132 Greenlawn, San Antonio Tx 78201.

CRENSHAW, MRS MARGUERITE (VANDERCLOCK). b Passaic NJ 29 Je 03. 5: Montclair Normal 21-23 Gen Diploma; Columbia 24-25 (Eng), Rutgers summer 30 (Hist) MA 36, post grad 37, 44-45; AB (Eng) UMich 27; Trenton State Col summers 47-50 BLS 51. 6: Lat, Fr, Sp. 7: Elem tchr Bd of Educ, Garfield NJ 23-25; Elem tchr Bd of Educ, Passaic NJ 27-32; Instr adult educ Bd of Educ Adult Ed Proj WPA, NYC 34-39; Coun employee rel, tech asst Wright Aeronautical Corp, Paterson NJ 42-46; High sch Eng tchr-libn Bd of Educ, Flemington NJ 46-48; Libn Averett Jr Col 49-53; High sch libn Bd of Educ, Boonton NJ 53-55; Asst prof asst dir lib sci dept A-V Coord, E Carolina Col, Greenville NC 55-63; Assoc prof bibliogr, Readers Adv 63-68; Emeritus 68-; Res consul in humanities and soc scis 68-. 8: Contb mem NCLA Sch Lib Bk Rev Proj 56-59. 9: NEA (Dele to 65 Convention); ALA; NCLA; NCEA; SELA. 10: AAUW; Amer Acad Pol & Soc Scis; Nat Trust Hist Preserv; Pitt Co Mental Health Assn. 14: Bibliog, readers adv, humanities. 15: 1701 Beaumont rd, Greenville NC 27835.

CRENSHAW, TENA L. b Coleman Fla 15 D 30. 5: Fla So Col 48-51 (Secondary Educ) BS; UFla 54-56 (Educ); UTampa summer 53 (Educ); UOkla 59-60 MLS. 6: Sp. 7: Elem & jr high tchr Coleman Elem Sch, Coleman Fla 51-55; Elem sch tchr NorthWard Elem Sch, St Petersburg Fla 55-57; Elem sch tchr Housman Elem Sch, Houston57-59; Tech libn Army Rocket & Guided Missile Agency Tech Lib, Huntsville Ala 60-61;Acquis libn Martin Co, Orlando Fla, Research libn 61-64; Reader serv libn Ling-Temco-Vought NASA Lib, Kennedy Space Center Fla 64-66; Research info specialist LockheedMissiles & Space Co, Palo Alto Cal 66-68; Hd pub serv Emory U A W Calhoun Med Lib69-. 9: SLA; MedLA. 10: Alpha Delta Pi; Kappa Delta Pi. 14: Ref, bibliog, info retrieval. 15: A W Calhoun Med Lib, Emory Univ, Atlanta Ga 30322.

CRESAP, ANNE (HUTCHINS). b Baltimore Md 20 My 16. 5: Goucher 34-38 (Eng) AB; UMich (Ann Arbor) 43 (LS); Drexel 44-45 BSLS. 6: Fr. 7: Research asst to Eng dept chm johns HopkinsU 39-42; Catlg asst Peabody Inst Lib, Baltimore 42-44; Asst libn Harvard's Dumbarton Oaks Research Lib, Georgetown DC 45-46; Hd catlg dept Union Theol sem Lib (Richmond Va) 61-65; Asst catlg libn Richmond Pub Lib, Richmond Va 66-67, Hd catlg dept 67-. 8: Trustee Wilmington Pub Lib, Wilmington NC 53-56. 9: VaLA. 10: Va Mus of Art; Phi Beta Kappa. 14: Catlg, mus libs. 15: 3704 Patterson ave, Richmond Va 23221.

CRESCENZI, JEAN DORIS. b Phila 21 F 36. 5: St Josephs Col 60-64 (Hist) BS Soc Sci; Rutgers 64-65 MLS; Temple 65-69 (Hist). 6: Sp. 7: Lib asst Free Lib of Phila 53-59; Lib asst Naval Air Engnr Center, Phila 59-62; Prof asst ref dept Temple U Lib 65-66; Acquis ref libn Col of S Jersey-Rutgers 66-. 9: NJLA. 10: AAUP. 14: Ref,bibliog, bk sel. 15: 2223 S 13th st, Phila Pa 19148.

CRESSATY, MARGARET DOUMAR (MARY). b Pasadena Cal 16 D 05. 5: Pasadena Jr Col 25-27 Certif; Occidental Col 27-29 (Educ, Eng) BA; Lib Sch of Los Angeles Pub Lib 29-30 Certif Sch of LS USC 67-68. 7: Sr asst Pasadena Pub Lib, Pasadena Cal 30-37; Sr asst von KleinSmid Lib of World Affairs, Los Angeles 37-39; Libn von KleinSmid Lib USoCal 39-43; Libn John Rndolph Haynes & Dora Haynes Found, Los Angeles 43-47; Libn Col of Osteopathic Physicians & Surgeons, Los Angeles 47-61; Libn Cal Col of Med (Los Angeles) 62-66, Archivist Cal Col of Med (Los Angeles) 67-68;Exchange libn, UCal (Irvine) 68-. 8: Cal State Chm, Amer Bk Center for War-Devastated Libs Inc, 46-47; Trade Adv Com for Lib Sci, Los Angeles Trade-Tech Col, 58- Hon mem, Lib Comm, Col of Veter Scis,kitasato U Japan. 9: Osteopathic Libs Assn (pres 61); SLA (Biol Scis Div; sec-treas51-52, Memb chm 52-56; pres So Cal Chap 55-56); CalLA (chm hosp & instituts roundtable 56-59). Med Lib Group of SoCal (pres 61-62). 12: Bk review ed "The WorldAffairs Interpreter" (39-43); Bk review ed "California Clinician, ClinicalOsteopathy" (47-66); Ed "Reminder," SLA, Biol Scis Dir 50-51. 13: Yes. 14: Exch, ref,archives. 15: 1401 N Holliston ave, Pasadena Ca 91104.

CRETINI, BLANCHE M. b New Orleans 16 My 29. 4: Gene J Cretini Jr. 5: H Sophie Newcomb Mem Col 46-50 (Sociol) BA; LSU 60-61 MS in LS. 6: Sp. 7: Ref La State Lib 61-. 9: ALA; LaLA; SWLA. 14: Ref. 15: 7277 Perkins rd, Baton Rouge La 70808.

CREWS, DOROTHY. b Ft Myers Fla 28 Ag 15. 5: FSCW 33-37 (Soc Sci) AB in Educ; UVa summer 37 (LS); UNC summers 38-41 BS in LS. 6: Fr, Sp. 7: Libn Fletcher High Sch, Jacksonville Beach Fla 37-42; Base libn EglinField, Eglin Field Fla 42-44; Asst libn Naval Air Station, Jacksonville Fla 44-45;Asst libn Willow Br Lib, Jacksonville Fla 45-49; Catlgr UFla 49-; Br libn Willow Br& Southside Br Libs, Jacksonville Fla 50-64; Head circ Jacksonville Pub Lib,Jacksonville Fla 64-66, Hd gen serv dept 66-. 8: Visiting Instr in lib sci: UNC, winter, spring 47; Fla State U, summer 52; UFla, spring 53; Consul Gulf Life Insurance Co Lib, Jacksonville Fla, 62-63. 9: ALA; SELA; FlaLA (treas 62-64, chmpub Libs Sect 55-56, v-chm-chm-elect Ref RT 69-70); DCLA (treas 68-69). 10: AudubonSoc; Jacksonville Hist Soc; AAUW; Jacksonville Pub Lib Staff Assn; Fla Hist Soc. 13: Yes. 14: Circ, br wk, ref. 15: 3917 Jean st, Jacksonville Fl 32205.

CREWS, ESSIE JANE (RAULERSON, JOHNSON). b Mayo Fla 12 Ja 12. 4: Jewell A Crews. 5: UFla summers 35-54 (Soc Studies, Eng, Supv, Admin) BAE, MAE, APG; Fla State U summers 54-59 (Elem Educ, LS) MS. 6: Sp. 7: Tchr Dixie Co Sch Bd, Cross City Fla 31-32; Tchr Taylor Co Sch Bd, Perry Fla 32-38; Tchr Nassau Co Sch Bd, Hilliard Fla 38-50; Duval Cotchr Duval Sch Bd, Baldwin Fla 50-53; Duval libn, Jacksonville Fla 54-56; Libn Duval Sch Bd 56-69; Pt time UFla Ext Lib, Jacksonville 67-69. 9: ALA; NEA; FlaLA; Nassau Co (Fla) TA (past pres); FlaEA; DuvalTA (various duties). 10: PTA; Red Cross; Comm Chest; Alpha Delta Kappa. 13: Yes. 14: Col & sch libn, circ, ref. 15: Rt 1 Box 322, Hilliard Fl 32046.

CREWS, SARAH (WOOD). b Wingina Va 20 O 24. 4: Jesse A Crews. 5: Longwood Col 41-45 (Eng) BA; Syracuse 45-46 BS in LS. 6: Sp. 7: Sr libn ref & circ Richmond Pub Lib, Richmond Va 46-48; Catlgr Va State Lib 50-56; UVa Lib: Ser catlgr 56-62, Catlg consul 62-63, Ser sect head 63-64, Catlg dept head, Asst Prof 64-66; Hd sers sect Va State Lib, Richmond 66-. 9: ALA; VaLA; Potomac Tech Libns. 14: Catlg. 15: 6213 Shannon rd, Mechanicsville Va 23111.

CRIBBEN, SISTER MARY MARGARET RSM. b Ambler Penn. 5: Villanova 34-40 (Educ) BS; Drexel 46-49 (LS) BS; Villanova 63-; West Res U 66. 6: Fr, Lat. 7: Tchr elem schs, Phila & vicinity 35-52, Libn 46-52; Libn Master Misericordiae

Acad, Merion Station Penn 52-; Faculty Gwynedd Mercy Col 58-63; Faculty Dept of Ed Villanova U 56-; Faculty Dept of Lib Sci Villanova U 63-. 8: Com mem Cath Sup, standard catalog for High School Libraries 61-. 66; Lib consul elem schs of Srs of Mercy 52-. 9: ALA-AASchL; CathLA (Adv Bd 59-62, Conv Pub Chm 54-65; East Penn Unit: chm 59-62, Exec Coun 62-; Phila Area Unit: sec 49-52; chm Elem Sect 49-52; sec High Sch Sec 54-56); NEA; Nat Cath EA; Priv Schs Tchrs Assn; Nat Assn Indep Schs; LPRC (Exec Coun 66-67). 12: Ed "Newsletter, East Penn Unit CathLA (59-62); Ed "News & Viws column in "Catholic Library World (62-)67). 13: Yes. 14: Wk with child & ya, tchg lib sci. 15: Mater Misericordiae Acad 515 Montgomery ave,Merion Station Pa 19066.

CRIDLAND, NANCY (CROOKS). b Terre Haute Ind 13 F 32. 5: IndU 50-66 (Hist) AB, 66-67 (LS) MA. 6: Fr, Ger. 7: Libn for hist IndU Lib (Bloomington) 67-. 9: AHA; ALA. 10: Phi Beta Kappa. 14: Bibliog of Amer & W European hist. 15: Indiana Univ Lib, Bloomington Ind.

CRIMMIN, WILBUR BRUCE. b Seattle 3 D 18. 4: Margaret Griffeth. 5: UWash 46-50 (Music) BA; UCal(Berkeley) 50-54 BLS. 7: Free Lib of Phila: Asst music 54-56, Asst bus sci ind dept 57-60, Admin asst bus sci ind dept 61; Head bus sci tech dept Hartford Pub Lib, Hartford Conn 61-. 8: Curator, Thomas McKean Automobile Ref Collection, Free Lib of Phila 57-61. 9: SLA (sec & dir of Conn Chap); ConnLA (Exhibits Chm 64-66; treas 66-69); Hartford (Conn) Lib Club; ASIS; ALA-RSD (Bus Ref Serv Com 67-70); -PLA (Starter List Com 67-). 10: Conn Hist Soc; Wadsworth Atheneum; Beta Phi Mu; Phi Beta Kappa. 14: Ref, bk selection. 15: 11 Arapahoe rd, W Hartford Ct 06107.

CRIPPEN, RODNEY (CUTTLESTON). b Southampton NY 8 D 31. 5: Columbia 54-59 (Eng Lit) BS, summer 61-63 MLS. 7: (Pfc) 120th Engr 40th Inf Div, Korea 53-54; Asst Foreign Missions Lib, U P Church in the USA, NYC 59-60; Queens Borough Pub Lib, Jamaica NY: Libn-trainee 60-63, Libn 63-64, Sr libn 64-66; Supv libn 66-. 9: NY Lib Club. 15: 156 E 61st st, New York NY 10021.

CRISMON, LEO TAYLOR. b Iberia Mo 24 F 06. 4: Viola Fowler. 5: William Jewell Col 27-30 AB; So Baptist Theol Sem 30-35 ThM, PhD; Columbia 45, 55-56 BS in LS. 6: Lat, Ger, Gk. 7: Pastor Glasgow Baptist Church, Glasgow Mo 35-37; So Baptist Theol SEm (Ky): Asst libn 37-41, Assoc libn 41-49, Act libn 49-51, Libn 51-. 8: Lib Consul in use of Dewey Decimal Clsf for theol libs. 10: Filson Club; Torch Club. 13: Yes. 14: Catlg. 15: 404 Pleasantview ave, Louisville Ky 40206.

CRISPEN, JOANNE (LINDENFELSER). b Miami Fla 9 Ja 28. 4: Ray G Crispen. 5: Chatham 50-53 (Eng) BA; upittsburgh 53-56 (Sociol); Rosary Col (LS). 7: Libn instr St Johns Gen Hosp Sch of Nursing, Pittsburgh 53-56; Receptionist Dr v c malloy, Akron Ohio 57; Asst libn Evanston Hosp Assn, Evanston Ill 63-66; Libn Lutheran Gen Hosp, Park Ridge Ill 66-. 9: SLA (Biol Div); MedLA; ALA. 13: Yes. 14: Ref, med research. 15: 2615 Colfax st, Evanston Il 60201.

CRISS, ESTHER (BRADLEY) (MRS). b Bay City Mich 11 Ap 08. 5: Olivet Col 24-26 (Educ); UMich 26-28 AB in LS, summer 28 Tchrs Life Certif, -62 MA in Ed, 66 (Curriculum) Educ Spec. 6: Fr, Sp. 7: Lib asst UMich Gen Lib (Ann Arbor) 44-47; Libn niv Jr/Sr High Schs, Ann Arbor Mich 47-49; Lib coord Plymouth Pub Schs, Mich 49-52, 52-64; Libn Thomas A Edison Sch, Dearborn Mich 64-68; Lib serv adv USAID/Liberia, Zorzor & Kakata Rural Tchr Train Insts; Catlgr ULiberia, Monrovia, W Africa 68; Hd libn Pioneer High Sch, Ann Arbor Mich 68-. 8: Instr lib sci Central Mich U summer 48; Mich State Instr Materials Com, Lansing Mich 62-64. 9: ALA-AASchL; NEA-DAVI; MichLA; Mich A-V Assn; ASCD; MichASchl. 10: AHA; Mich Hist Assn; NAACP; AAUW; Friends of Ann Arbor Pub Lib; Ctr for Study Democratic Insts; Nat Wildlife Fed; Washtenaw Hist Assn; UMich Alumni Assn. 14: Admin media ctrs. 15: 2916 Birch Hollow dr apt 1B, Ann Arbor Mi 48104.

CRISWELL, MRS KATHLEEN (HARRINGTON). b Throckmorton Tex 25 Je 22. 4: Dalton L Criswell. 5: No Tex State U 40-43 (LS) BS; Washburn U summer 59 N Tex State U, summer 67. 7: Libn High Sch, Henrietta ex 43-44; Libn High Sch, Hereford Tex 44-56; Libn San Andres Elem Sch, Andrews Tex 56-. 8: Mem of eval team for So Assn, 65,66. 9: NEA (Life Mem); TexASchL (treas62-63); Tex State Tchrs Assn (Life Mem). 10: Delta Kappa Gamma. 14: Child bks. 15: Box 902, Andrews Tx 79714.

CRITCHLOW, THERESE E. b Princeton NJ. 5: Trinity Col (Wash DC) 43 (Fr) BA; Columbia 56 (Fr) MA; Rutgers 63 (LS). 6: Fr, Sp. 7: Asst Amer Aid to France 46-50; Tchr Caldwell Col for Women 54-55; Tchr Solebury Sch, New Hope Penn 55-56; Searcher Firestone LibPrinceton U 61-64; Ref libn Princeton Pub Lib, Princeton NJ 64-. 9: NJLA (Ref Sect); ALA. 10: Princeton Hosp Women's Auxiliary, CercleFrancais de Princeton; Princeton Col Club; AAUW. 15: 11 Westcott rd, Princeton NJ 08540.

CRITTENDEN, SARA N. b Nova Ohio 3 O 17. 5: Blackburn Col 35-37 AAB; Fla State U 48-51 AB, MA. 7: Asst libn Willard Mem Lib, Willard Ohio 37-42, Head Libn 42-49; Libn acquis dept & period Fla State U 51-55; Head Libn St Petersburg Jr Col 55-63; Dir of Lib Serv, St Petersburg Campus Lib 63-. 9: ALA; SELA; FlaLA. 10: Beta Phi Mu. 12: "Essay and General Literature Index, an Evaluation, with Analysis of the Books for 1936 Indexed Therein, ACRL Microcard Series No 24 (54). 13: Yes. 14: Admin, ref. 15: 4542 Fourth ave N, St Petersburg Fl 33713.

CROCE, CARMELA. b Providence RI 12 Je 08. Worcester State Col 28 & 42 (Ed) BS Ed; Simmons 47 (LS). 6: Ital, Fr. 7: Worcester Pub Lib, Worcester Mass: Br lib asst 26-42, Children's libn 42-45, Hd sch div 45-49; Worcester Pub Schs; Sch libn 49-58, Hd libn 58-64, Dir sch lib serv 64-. 8: Instructor, Summer session, Simmons College 56; Instructor, Summer session, Anna Maria College, 58 & 59. 9: MassLA (planning Com); MassSchLA (Standards Com); Bay Path Lib Club (pres). 11: Essay award, Mass Ital Hist Soc. 14: Sch lib wk. 15: 716 Pleasant st, Worcester Ma 01602.

CROCKETT, FRANCES (WOOD). b Chesterfield Co Va 17 Ja 12. 4: David Edward Crockett. 5: Madison col 28-32 (Eng, Math) BS; William & Mary summer 35; George Washington U 37-38; Emory 38-39 AB in LS. 7: Tchr Midlothian High Sch, Midlothian Va 32-37; Tchr Washington-Lee High sch, Arlington Va 37-38; Libn Lunenburg Pub Lib, Lunenburg Va 39-40; Lib supv Ga Lib Commsn, gainesville 40-43; US Naval Reserve (WAVES) (Lt), Norfolk Va 43-47; Libn Walter Cecil Rawls Lib & Museum, courtland Va 62-. 9: VaLA (chm Pub Libs Sect). 10: Suffolk-Nansemond Hist Soc; AAUW; Womans Club; Louise Obici Memorial Hosp Aux; Kappa Delta Pi. 14: Admin. 15: 522 Butler ave, Suffolk Va 23434.

CROFT, BETTY MARY ELLEN. b Leaf River Ill 23 N 26. 5: UIll 44-47 (Lat) BA, 47-48 (Lat) MA, 48-51 (LS) MS. 6: Lat, Ger. 7: Catlgr UIll(Urbana) 51-62, Head catlgr 62-. 9: ALA; IllLA. 10: Beta Phi Mu; Phi Beta Kappa; Phi Kappa Phi. 14: Catlg. 15: 708 S Maple, Urbana Il 61801.

CROFT, CAROLYN JUNE (BAUER). b Enid Okla 8 Je 39. 4: Jerry D Croft. 5: Okla State U 57-61 (Elem ed, Lib) BS, 62 (Elem ed, Lib) MS, 66-69 (Lib ed); Kan StateU 58 (Elem ed); Kan State Tchrs Col 62. 7: Tchr & libn pub schs, Topeka Kan 61-62; Tchr pub schs, Manhattan Kan 62-63; Pub schs, Anthony Kan: Tchr 63-64, Tchr & libn 65-66; Instructor lib educ dept Okla State U 66. 9: ALA; NEA; OklaLA; OklaEA; Kans State TA. 10: PEO Sisterhood; Chi Omega; Alpha Beta Alpha; Outstanding Young Women of America 67; Phi Kappa Phi; Kappa Delta Pi. 14: Child lit, storytelling, sch libs. 15: 728 Lake Shore dr, Stillwater Ok 74074.

CROFT, (MARGARET) RUTH. b Omaha Neb 26 Jl 38. 5: UNeb 56-57; Ferris State Col 57, 61-62; Central Mich U 62-64 (Eng) AB; West Mich U 64-66 MSLS. 7: Journalist 2nd class USN, Corpus Christi Tex 58-61; Stud asst ref Central Mich U lib 62-64; Grad asst ref West Mich U lib 64-66; Asst children libn Pub Lib, Grand Rapids Mich 67-. 9: ALA; NCTE; MichLA. 10: Grand Rapids Libns Club; Nat Wildlife Fed. 14: Child wk, catlg. 15: 510 Woodridge NE, Grand Rapids Mi 49505.

CROISSANT, PHYLLIS. b Bradford Penn 30 J 28. 5: Dickinson Col Carlisle Penn 45-49 AB; UPittsburgh 63-64 MLS. 7: Libn West Res Acad, Hudson Ohio 65-67; Libn Moore Col of Art, Phila 65-68; Ref libn Amer Phil Soc Phila 68-. 9: ALA. 10: Phila Art Alliance; Penn Acad of Fine Arts. 15: American Philosophical Society Lib, 105 S Fifth st, Philadelphia Pa 19106.

CRONEBERGER, ROBERT B JR. b Pottsville Penn 19 Ja 37. 4: Ellen Jane Fegley Croneberger. 5: Lehigh U 54-58 (Classical Lang) BA; UPenn 59-61 (Classical Lang) MA; Drexel 62 (LS) MS. 7: LC: Lib sch grad recruit program 62-63, Asst head European Exch Sect 63-64, Admin off proc dept off 64-65, Exec asst processing dept off 65-66; Asst chief card div 66-67; Asst chief ser record div 67-. 9: DCLA. 10: Phi Beta Kappa; Omicron Delta Kappa. 14: Tech serv. 15: 6851 Strata st, McLean Va 22101.

CRONEMILLER, GEORGE R. b Savannah Ga 12 Ag 20. 5: NYU 45-46 (Eng) AB; Columbia 46-47 (Philos), 49-50 (Music) MA, 53-55 MSLS. 6: Fr, Ger, Sp. 7: Manager R Geisler Church Arts, NYC 47-49; Dir of music Kew-Forest Sch, NYC 50-52; Pre-prof libn NYU 52-53; Pre-prof libn Music Br NY Pub Lib 53-55; Music catlgr Brooklyn Pub Lib 56-. 10: Prof chorister in NYC, 45-. 14: Catlg of music & phonorecords. 15: 115 Perry st, New York NY 10014.

CRONIN, JOHN RICHARD. b Cambridge Mass 12 N 38. 4: Carol Luti. 5: St John's (Boston) 57-61 (Philos) BA; CatholicU 64-66 (LS). 6: Fr. 7: Lib asst Widener Lib HarvardU 62-63; Com teller First Natl Bank, Boston 63-64; Grad lib asst CatholicU 64-65; Assoc libn Applied Physics Lab, Silver Spring Md 65-67; Info syst analyst E R Squibb & Sons Inc, New Brunswick NJ 67-69; Info syst eng Info Dynamics Corp, Reading Mass 69-. 8: Consul Kan State Libs for cost study of interlib loan serv 69; Participant in Proj LEX for creation of thesaurus of engring & sci terms 66. 9: ASIS; SLA. 13: Yes. 14: Lib automation & mechanization, info retrieval. 15: 39 Lockeland ave, Arlington Ma 02174.

CRONIN, JOHN WILLIAM. b Lewiston Me 10 F 05. 4: Esther Johnson. 5: Bowdoin Col 21-25 (Govt) AB; Georgetown Law Sch 25-29 JD. 6: Fr, Ger. 7: LC: Asst Card Div 25-26, 28-32, Asst chief Card Div 32-38, Act chief Card Div 38-40, Chief Card Div 40-44, Asst dir Proc Dept 44-52, Dir Proc Dept 52-68; Lib Consul & Research Serv 68-. 9: ALA; BSA; CathLA; DCLA. 11: Margaret Mann Citation, 61; Melvil Dewey Award, 64; LC Distinguished Serv Award, 65. 13: Yes. 14: Acquis, catlg. 15: 2129-32nd pl SE, Wash DC 20020.

CRONISE, RUTH MARIE. b Botetourt County Va 8 D 33. 5: Radford Col 51-55 (Fr, Sp) BA in Ed; George Peabody Col 58-62 MALS; UVa 58; UOkla 67. 6: Sp, Fr. 7: Tchr (Eng, Sp, Lat) Buchanan High Sch, Buchanan Va 54-56; Tchr (reading improvement & Eng) Roanoke City Schs, 56-63; Hd of circ & asst ref Hollins Col 63-64; Libn Roanoke Co Schs, Salem Va 64-68; Libn Northside High, Roanoke Va 68-. 9: NEA; ALA; VaEA; VaLA; RoanokeCoEA; RoanokeCoSchL (chm 65-69). 10: AAUW; Fincas the Woman's Club; Beta Phi Mu. 14: Sch libnship. 15: Fincastle Va 24090.

CROOK, LOUISE MARIAN (EISENHOWER). b Hecker Ill 8 Jl 42. 4: Eugene Joseph Crook. 5: Fontbonne Col 60-62; UIll 64-66 (Eng) BA, 66-69 (LS) MS. 6: Lat. 7: Clk typist May Dept Stores, St Louis 60-62; Tchr SS Peter & Paul Grade Sch, Waterloo Ill 62-63, 65; Lab asst Mo Research Labs Inc, St Louis 64; File clk UIll Lib (Urbana) 65, Grading asst Grad Sch of Lib Sci 68. 10: Beta Phi Mu. 14: Catlg, rare bks. 15: 401 Avondale, Champaign Il 61820.

CROOKSTON, MARY EVALYN. b Thayer Ill. 5: Eureka Col 27-29 (Eng); West Res U 30-31 Certif in Lib Sci; Eureka Col 39-40)Eng) AB; George Washington U 40-41 (Eng). 6: Fr. 7: Chief circ dept Lincoln Pub Lib, Springfield Ill 31-39; ALA fellow, US Off of Educ, Wash DC 40-41; Camp libn US Army, Ft Eustis Va 41-42; Serv command libn US Army (3d serv cmd), Baltimore 42-44; Ref asst Cleveland pub Lib, Cleveland 44-46; Research libn Meldrum & Fewsmith Adv, Cleveland Ohio 46-. 8: Lectr on advertising libs Case West Res U 47-. 9: SLA (pres Cleveland Chap 48-49; Nat Advertising Div 50-51). 11: Citation for outstanding and meritorious serv US Army 44. 13: Yes. 14: Ref & research in adv. 15: Meldrum and Fewsmith Inc 1220 Huron rd, Cleveland Oh 44115.

CROPPER, ELIZABETH ANNE. b Newport News Va 13 My 41. 5: Madison Col 59-63 (LS, Soc Sci) BS; Col of William & Mary summer 60. 7: Lib asst US Dept of the Army Post Lib, Ft Eustis Va 62, Asst libn (GS-7) 63-, (GS-9) 67-. 8: Lib Career Program Coordinator, Ft Eustis Va 67-. 9: VaLA. 10: Alpha Beta Alpha; Ft Eustis (Va) Hist & Archeolog Soc; Sigma Sigma Sigma; Carrollton Womans Club (treas). 14: Ref, info retrieval. 15: Box 207 Pointe OView, Carrollton Va 23314.

CROPPER, EVELYN (GILLESPIE). b Mayslick Ky 17 Ja 29. 4: Clarence Cropper. 5: UKy 47-51 (LS) AB; UKy 64. 6: Sp. 7: Stud asst catlg dept Margaret King Lib UKy 48-51; Head of child dept Brumback Lib, Van Wert Ohio 51-54; Asst in adult circ dept Delaware Co Lib, Delaware Ohio 56-57; Sch libn Van Wert High Sch, Van Wert Ohio 59-67; Libn Lima Sr High Sch, Lima Ohio 67-68; Libn Clermont Northeastern High Sch, Batavia Ohio 68-69. 09: NEA; OhioLA; OhioASchL. 10: AAUW; Womens Club. 14: Serv to readers, catlg. 15: 1596 Turquoise dr, Cincinnati Oh 45230.

CROPPER, MARY BESS. b Burlington Ky. 5: Judson Col 21-22; Georgetown Col (Ky) 22-23; UKy 25-27 (Lat) AB, BS in LS; UMich 49-50 MALS. 6: Lat, Fr. 7: Tchr Verona Sch, Verona Ky 24-25; Tchr Burlington High Sch, Burlington Ky 27-29; Tchr Jackson High Sch, Jackson Ky 29-30; Libn Hebron High Sch, Hebron Ky 30-44; Sch lib supv (co), Burlingto Ky 44-47; Asst Prof Lib Sci Murray State Col 47-49; Instr Lib Sci Mankato State Col 50-68, Asst Prof 68-. 8: Pres Sch Lib Assn of Ky 46. 9: ALA; NEA; KyLA (pres 46); MinnEA. 10: Eta Sigma Phi; Beta Phi Mu. 14: Child & yp wk (bk sel). 15: Mankato State Col, MankatoMn 56002.

CROPSEY, HELEN M (WEBB). b Ft Atkinson Wis 4 S 08. 4: Myron G Cropsey. 5: UCal 29-33 (Bus Admin) BS. 6: Sp. 7: Spec libn No Amer Investment, San Francisco 34-35; Ed & publ Index of "The Christian Science Monitor, Corvallis Ore 59-. 9: SLA; ALA. 10: LWV. 12: Comp "Index of "The Christian Science Monitor, monthly & cumul v 1- (60-). 14: Ref. 15: 1725 Kings rd, Corvallis Or 97330.

CROSBY, A(RMINA) ELIZABETH. b Easton NY 29 F 20. 5: Dickinson Jr Col 35-37 (Hist) Academic Certif; Col of William & Mary 37-39 (Hist, LS) ABLS. 6: Fr, Sp, Ger. 7: Libn Oceana High Sch, Oceana Va 39-40; Asst libn West Side High Sch, Newark NJ 40-42; Instr Dept of Lib Sci Col of William & Mary 43-46, Instr Hist Dept 43-44; Asst libn Mohawk Col 46-48; Asst acquis libn Cornell U 48-49, Head Libn ser & bind dept 49-. 9: ALA (Adv Com Lib Tech Proj 62-66) -RSTD (Bkbinding Com 62-68, Ad hoc Com on Acquis Textbk 68-69); NYLA (RTSS Memb Com 64-68; v-pres & pres-elect Resources & Tech Serv Sect 68-69). 14: Acquis, catlg of ser. 15: 3 Pleasant st, Dryden NY 13053.

CROSLAND, DOROTHY M(URRAY). b Stone Mountain Ga 13 S 03. 4: James Henley Crosland. 5: Atlanta 23 (LS) Certif. 7: Catlg asst Atlanta Pub Lib 23-25, Br libn 25; Asst libn Ga Sch of Tech 25-26; Libn Ga Inst of Tech 27-53, Dir of Libs 53-. 8: Consul Aeronaut Lib, Arnold Engnr Devel Center, Tullahoma Tenn 52; Lib Bldg Consul, Carnegie 56; Lib Bldg Consul UIll Chicago Undergrad Div 59; Spec Invest for NSF Study on Train Sci Info Specs 61-62 Mem of Eval Comm for So Assn of Cols & Schs,Comm on Cols; Arlington U, Arlington Tex 64; Nova U of Adv Tech, Ft Lauderdale Fla,68; Fla Tech U, Orlando Fla 69. 9: ALA-ACRL; SLA; Amer Soc Engnr Educ (Lib Com 49-); ADI; Amer rep to IATUL 63-; SELA (Exec sec 50-52, pres 52-54); GaLA (pres 49-51); Atlanta Lib Club (pres 38). 10: Trustee, Atlanta Art Assn (56-62). 11: Atlantas Woman of the Year in Educ, 45. 13: Yes. 14: Acquis of outstanding collection in sci & engnr, lib bldgs. 15: Ga Instof Tech Lib, 225 North ave NW, Atlanta Ga 30332.

CROSMAN, ALEXANDER CAMERON JR. b Philadelphia Penn 9 Mr 40. 4: Eloise Anderson. 5: UVa 58-62 (Hist) BA; WVaU 67 (Educ); UKy 67-68 MSLS. 7: Lt Supply USAF, Cal & Formusa 62-66; Circ Alderman Lib UVa (Charlottesville) 68-. 9: ALA (Jr Mems RT); VaLA (Jr Mems RT). 10: Beta Phi Mu. 14: Ref, circ. 15: 211 Alderman rd, Charlottesville Va 22903.

CROSS, CATHARINE S. b Denver Col 22 S 18. 5: UColo 41 (Geol) BA; UDenver 66 (Libnship) MA. 6: Fr, Sp. 7: Acquis lobn Col Sch of Mines 66-. 9: ALA; SLA; ColoLA. 14: Geol collections, t4ch lit. 15: Thirteen Mines Park, Golden Co 80401.

CROSS, DOROTHY A. b Van Buren Co Mich 9 S 24. 5: Wayne State U 42-56 (Mus) BA; UMich 56-57 MALS. 6: Fr, Ger. 7: Libn I Detroit Pub Lib 57-59; Admin libn USA Spec Serv: Braconne France 59-61, (Main Army) Poitiers France 61-62, Area supv, Poitiers France 62-63, Area supv, Kaiserslautern Ger 63-67, Aquis, Aschaffenburg Ger 67, Aquis, Munich ger 67-. 9: ALA (Organ Com 66-67, co-chm Memb Com 67-68); MichLA; Soc for Personnel admin, Ger Chap; AFLS; Europ Subsect. 11: Certifs of Serv, USAREUR Spec Serv; Certif of Achievement, USAREUR 67. 14: Admin, acquis, personnel. 15: Lib Div US Army Spec Serv Agency, Europe APO NY 09184.

CROSS, JENNIE (SCHOOLFIELD). b Wichita Falls Tex 12 Ja 35. 4: Robert M Cross. 5: Harding Col 52-55 (Journalism) BA; UMich 65-68 AMLS. 7: Lib asst Wichita Falls (Tex) Sr High Sch 50-52; Asst Beaumont Mem Lib Harding Col summer 54; Off clk Harding Col Press 55; Bkmob libn Tulsa Pub Lib, Tulsa Okla 55-57; Paleonthological libn & lab asst Jersey Production Research Corp, Tulsa Okla 57-59; Stenogr Carter Oil Co, Shreveport La 59; Sub tchr Caddo Parish Bd of Educ, Shreveport La 60-61; Asst libn Engrg Lib Tex Easter Gas Transmission Corp, Shreveport La 61; Sub tchr St Landry Parrish Bd of Educ, Opelousas La 61-62; Asst libn Mich Christian Jr Col 62-67, Act hd libn 65-66; Doc libn Oakland U 67-. 9: ALA; MichLA (corr sec Jr Mem RT); Mich Archivists. 10: AAUP. 14: Govt docs. 15: 3871 Aquarina, Drayton Plains Mi 48020.

CROSS, LUTHER L. b Oneida Tenn 18 D 14. 4: Stella Maxine Byrd Cross. 5: Lincoln Mem U 34-35; E Tenn State U 36-40 (Hist, Eng) BS, 52-53, 60 (Hist, Econ, LS) MS PP High Sch & Elem Certif, Supv & Supv Certif. 7: Tchr Scott Co Bd of Educ, Huntsville Tenn 35-39; PRIN Scott Co Sch Bd, Winona Tenn 39-41; US Army 41-45; Clerk DA Civ EUCOM, Frankfurt a/m Germany 45-53, Libn EUCOM 50-53; Libn Oneida High Sch, Oneida Tenn 53-55; Libn Huntsville High Sch, Huntsville Tenn 56-. 8: Chm Nat Lib Week, Scott Co (Tenn) 62-63. 9: TennEA; TennLA; ETennEA;NEA. 10: Buffalo Commun Club; PTA; Develop Club; Dir Title I Summer Reading Inst,Huntsville 57. 14: Cat, ref. 15: Box 76, Huntsville Tn 37756.

CROSS, PEARL (ACRES). b Oneida Tenn 22 Jl 17. 4: Harrison Cross. 5: UTenn 55, 57, 66 (Lib serv, Eng) BS. 6: Fr. 7: Elem tchr Scott Co Schs, Oneida Tenn 40-55; Libn Oneida High Sch, Oneida Tenn 55-. 9: NEA; TennLA; TennEA. 10: Delta Kappa Gamma. 15: Rte 1 Box 87, Oneida Tn 37841.

CROSS, REGINA VACHON (MRS HARRY K). b Newton Centre Mass 9 Ag 02. 4: Harry King Cross. 5: Trinity Col Wash DC 25 (Eng) AB; Harvard 30 (Ed) Ed M; URI MLS. 6: Fr. 7: Math & Eng tchr Meadowbrook Sch, Weston Mass 26-30; Hd clinic secs Mass Gen Hosp, Boston 30-34; Volunteer libn St Grancis Chapel Lib Providence RI 56-. 9: ALA; CathLA. 10: Providence Athenaeum; Providence Preserv Soc; Museum of Fine Arts Boston; Providence Dist Nursing Assn Bd; RI Hist Soc; RI Sch of Design Museum; Audubon Soc; RI & Prov Co Garden Club. 11: Citation from RI League for Nursing 62. 14: Catlg, ref. 15: 44 Stimson ave, Providence RI 02906.

CROSS, ROBERT JOHN. b Chicago 23 O 22. 4: Elizabeth Thale Cross. 5: Carleton Col 40-43, 46-47 (Geog) BA; UColo 48-49 (Hist); UWash 49-52 (Chinese Hist & Lang), 54-55 (LS) ML. 7: US Navy (Lt jg) Naval Group, China 43-46; Research analyst US Govt, Wash DC53-54; Ref libn Tacoma Pub Lib, Tacoma Wash 55-56; Ser libn UWash 56-59; Engnr libnOre State U 59-60; Asst libn Boeing Sci Research Labs, Seattle 60-63; Assoc libnSeattle U Lib 63-64, Head libn 64-69; Asst dir pub serv West Wash State Col Lib 69-;Visiting lecturer UWash Sch of Libnship 68, 69, summer 67. 9: ALA-ACRL;-RSTD;PNLA; WashLA (dir 67-69). 15: 602-36th ave, Seattle Wa 98122.

CROSS, SUZANNE R(IDGWAY). b Jenkintown Penn 24 Je 06. 5: Rockford Col 52 (Chem) BA; Carnegie InstMLS;53 MLS; Drexel 60 Med Libn Certif Grade 1. 6: Fr. 7: Asst supv inspection Brewster Aeronautical Corp, Johnsville Penn 42-44; Lib asst Bryn Mawr Col 47-48; Lib asst Haverford Col 48-51; Lib asst Rockford Col 51-52; Libn Sch of Veterinary Med UPenn 53-64; Sci coordinator Milwaukee Pub Lib 64-. 9: ALA; Sla (Wis Chap: sec-treas 65-66, pres-elect 68); WisLA. 14: Pub serv, admin. 15: 9029 W Mt Vernon ave, Milwaukee Wi 53226.

CROSSMAN, MURIEL (COX). b Quincy Mass 22 Ja 13. 7: Br libn Thomas Crane Pub Lib 31-35; Newspaper correspondent & garden writer "Patriot Ledger, Quincy Mass 58-62; Libn Mass Horticultural Soc, Boston 62-. 13: Yes. 14: Admin. 15: 300 Massachusetts ave, Boston Ma 02115.

CROTEAU, DANIEL (REV). b Black Lake Quebec Can 7 Mr 31. 5: Sem St Charles 44-51 BA; Grand Sem 51-55 (Theol); UMontreal summers 52-53 (LS) Diploma. 6: Fr. 7: Tchr (Fr & gr) Sem St-Charles 55-57; Vice-chancelor Diocesan Chancery, Sherbrooke Que Can 57-59; Ed "Messager" (weekly), Sherbrooke Que Can 59-62; Dir stud housing USherbrooke 62, Dir libs 62-. 8: USherbrooke: Asst acad v-rector 63-65; Asst rector stud affairs 65-68; Mem bd of governors 65-; Mem Univ Senate 65-; Mem bd of trustees 65-. 9: Assn Canadienne des bibliothecaires de langue francaise (chm Sherbrooke Sect 67-68); CanLA; QueLA (chm Col & Research Sect 67-69);Sherbrooke City Lib Com (67-); Univ Libs Com (Que 67-). 14: Admin. 15: University, Sherbrooke Quebec Can.

CROTEAU, MARY H. b Hancock Mich 26 Je 36. 5: UMich 54-58 (Psych) BA, 59-60 AMLS. 7: Ref libn Escanaba Pub Lib, Escanaba Mich 60-61, Libn 61-63; Consul Mich State Lib Upper Peninsula br, Escanaba Mich 63-65; Consul MichState Lib 65-68; Dir Iowa City Pub Lib & Seven Rivers Lib Syst 68-. 11: Loleta Fyan Award, 63. 14: Admin, ext. 15: Iowa City Pub Lib, Iowa City Ia 52240.

CROUCH, (NORA) JOSEPHINE. b Hereford Tex. 5: Ga Col 42 (Eng, Soc Sci) BS; Peabody 50 MA in LS. 6: Sp, Fr, Lat. 7: Libn Boys High Sch, Rome Ga 42-44; Libn Parker High Sch, Greenville SC 44-46; Lib supv Bartow Sch System, Bartown Fla 46-47; Libn Aiken High Sch, Aiken SC 50-53; Chief Libn Aiken Co Pub Lib, Aiken SC 54-58; Dir Aiken-Bamberg-Barnwell-Edgefield Reg Lib, Aiken SC 58-. 8: SC Governors Conf onbus, Ind, Educ & Agric, 60-68; SC Governors Conf on State-Wide Traffic Safety, 61-69;Spec Com SC Progress, 62; SC Governors Conf on Pub Libs, 65; Sec SC Coun for theCommon Good 68-69. 9: ALA; Fed Rel Coord for SCLA 63-65; -LAD (Recr Netwk 62); SCLA(pres 66-67; chm &/or mem 4 coms 56-66); chm Const & By-Laws Com 69-72; chm Nom Com68-69; mem Rev Com Standards for SC Pub Lib 66-69; CSRA LA. 10: AAUW; Aiken Co (SC)Commun Serv Leaders Assn; Pilot Club; Aiken Co Hist Soc; Friends Aiken Co Pub LibAssn; Alston Wilkes Soc. 11: Appointed Dir to establish first SC Reg Demonstration Lib, 58. 13: Yes. 14: Admin, ref. 15: PO Box 909, Aiken SC 29801.

CROUCH, JAMES ALBERT JR. b Columbus Ga 27 Ag 40. 5: UNC 59-64 (Eng) BA, 66-68 MSLS. 6: Fr. 7: UNC Lib at Chapel Hill: Student asst circ dept 60-61, Undergrad lib night supv 61-62, Statistics & inventories supv circ dept 62-63, Hd order sect 65-67, Adaptive catlgr 67-68; Libn UAlaska Juneau-Douglas Commun Col 68-. 9: ALA; AlaskaLA. 12: Jt ed "Periodical Holdings in Southeast Alaska Libraries" (69). 14: Tech serv. 15: 129 Seventh st, Juneau Ak 99801.

CROUCH, LORA (ELIZABETH). b Dallas Co Iowa 18 Ja 07. 5: Dakota Wesleyan U 28-33 (Eng) BA; UIll 34-39 BS in LS. 7: Child libn Mitchell (SD) Pub Lib 28-33, Head Libn 33-44; Cith Libn Carnegi Lib, Siox Falls SD 44-60; Libn Forest Lib, Lake Placid Club NY 60-63; Head of adult serv Pub Lib, Rochester Minn 63-64; Head of acquis Salt Lake Co Lib System, Midvale Utah 64-. 8: Chm Coun of Rocky Mountain Bibliog Center for Research 54; Mem Com on Publs, Dakota Tercent Commsn, 59-60; Adv Com for Sch Libs of Utah Dept of Educ 66-68. 9: ALA (Coun 55-59); MPLA (sec 54, pres 59); SoDakLA; NYLA; MinnLA; UtahLA. 10: Commun Theater; West Hist Assn; Utah Hist Soc. 12: "Hamlin Garland, Dakota Homesteader (61). 13: Yes. 14: West Americana, bk sel. 15: 66 West Wasatch st, Midvale Ut 84047.

CROUCH, MILTON HARLEY. b Martinsville Va 25 O 37. 5: Birmingham-Southern 56-60 (Zool) BA ; LSU 60-6 1 (LS) MS; Penn State U 63- (Hist) MA. 6: Fr, Ger. 7: Asst soc sci reading rooms libn UFla 61-63; Undergrad libn Penn State U 63-. 9: ALA; PennLA. 10: AAUP; AHA; Phi Alpha Theta. 14: Ref. 15: 127 E Hamilton ave #17, State College Pa 16801.

CROUSE, (ALBERTA) LORRAINE. b Crete Neb 19 O 21. 5: UNeb 43 (Philos) BA; UDenver 44 BS in LS, 58 (LS) MA. 6: Fr, Ger. 7: Page Lincoln City Lib, Lincoln Neb 41-43, Apprentice 44; Kansas City (Mo) Pub Lib: Child asst 44-45, Child libn Swinney Br 45-47, Child libn East Br 47-56, Child libn Northeast Br 56-. 9: ALA-CSD; MoLA. 13: Yes. 14: Child & sch libs. 15: 9853 Winner rd, Independence Mo 64052.

CROUSE, MARIAN B(ARMONT). b Clearfield Penn 10 Jl 38. 5: Ind U of Penn 56-60 (Music, Elem Educ, Eng) BS in Educ; Penn State U summers 60-61 (Educ) State Certif (MA) 67; Shippensburg State Col 62-65 (LS). 6: Lat, Fr. 7: Elem tchr Chambersburg (Penn) Sch Dist 60-62; Libn Faust Jr High, Chambersburg Penn 62-67; Elem libn, Chambersburg Penn 67-. 67; Elem libn, Chambersburg Penn 67-. 9: ALA; NEA (life mem); PennStateEA (life mem). 10: Commun Chorus; Conococheague Naturalists; Chambersburg Hosp Aux. 15: 965 Leidig dr, Chambersburg Pa 17201.

CROUSE, RUTH ANNE (BARMONT). b Chambersburg Penn 1 S 07. 4: Mervin W Crouse. 5: Wilson Col 27-31 (Span) AB; Drexel 31-32 BS in LS;Shippensburg State Col 32-33 (Educ); Penn State U 34 Master's Equivalent. 6: Sp, Fr, Ger, Lat. 7: Libn & tchr Sch for Veterans Child, Scotland Penn 33-37, 45-49; Sub tchr & libn Chambersburg (Penn) Schs 55-60; Libn Chambersburg (Penn) Jr High Sch (Faust) 60-63; Libn Chambersburg (Penn) Sr High & Elem Schs 63-. 9: PennSta EA; NEA. 10: Chambersburg Area Educ Assn. 12: "Library Helps" (37). 14: Catlg, ref. 15: 965Leidig dr, Chambersburg Pa 17201.

CROW, ROCHELLE. b Johnson City Tenn 22 Ap 36. 5: Birmingham-Southern Col 54-58 (Fr) BA; UDenver summers 59-62 MA in Libnship. 6: Fr. 7: Elem tchr City of Birmingham Ala 59-62; Ref libn Birmingham-So Col 62-65, Head of pub serv 65-66, Hd catlgr 66-68; Hd Catlgr Col of Gen Studies UAla 68-. 9: ALA; AlaLA; Birmingham Lib Club (sec, v-pres). 10: AAUW; Birmingham Art Assn; Bus & Prof Women. 14: Govt docs, catlg, ref. 15: Library College of Gen Studies Univ of Ala, Birmingham Al 35233.

CROW, ROMILDA (FRAZIER). b Ashville Ala 16 N 15. 4: Collis Cunningham Crow. 5: UAla 51-52 (Ed); Howard Col

52-54 (Ed). 7: Bkkeeper Singer Co Birmingham Ala 46-47; Purchasing dept Genuine Parts Co Birmingham Ala 48-50; Libn Hayes Internat Corp Birmingham Ala 53-. 9: SLA (Ala Chap, Hospit Com, Nomin Com, sec, v-pres & pres-elect). 10: Bus & Prof Women; PTA; Quota Club. 14: Sci research, tech, engrg. 15: 1804 Oak st NW, Birmingham Al 35215.

CROWDER, DOROTHY (VERNON). b Ohio Co Ky. 5: Murray State Col 40 (Langs) AB; UNC 45 BS in LS; USoCal 59 (Communications); Colo State U 61 (Communications). 6: Fr, Swedish. 7: Libn Ky & Tenn high schs 40-43; Co Libn Murray State Col Reg Lib Serv, Mayfield Ky 43-44; Asst circ & ref libn Vassar Col Lib 45; Head circ dept & Instr in Lib Sci Berea Col Lib 46-48, Head ref dept & Instr in Lib Sci 48-53; Pub rel & educ dir Fresno Cal 54; 1st asst ref libn Edward L Doheny Jr Mem Lib USoCal 55-56, Head circ dept 56-57; Libn Sch of Engnr USoCal 57-62; Tech libn Arthur D Little Inc, Santa Monica Cal 62-64; Libn Security-First Nat Bank, Los Angeles 64-65; Tech libn & consul Booz-Allen Applied Research Inc, Los Angeles 65-67; Asst libn, Asst Prof Lib Sci Berea Col Lib 67-. 8: Participant in survey of mechanization in DoD Info centers & libs, 65-66. 9: SLA; CalLA: SELA; KyLA. 10: LWV; AAUP. 13: Yes. 14: Sci & tech bibliog, info retrieval, tchg lib sci, personnel. 15: CPO Box 336, Berea Ky 40403.

CROWDER, RUBY JO (SATTERWHITE). b Sherman Tex 8 O 18. 4: James M Crowder. 5: Tex Womans U 36-40 (LS) BA. 7: Libn Dickinson High Sch, Dickinson Tex 40-43; Lib asst Mont State Col 44; Child libn Sioux Falls Pub Lib, Sioux Falls SD 44-45; Asst in tech div & lib Mrs Tuckers Foods, Sherman Tex 49-51; Files & records, sales div Gaylord Mfg, Dallas 52-53; Libn The St Michael Sch, Dallas 61-. 9: TexLA (Sch lib div & child round table);Dallas Co LA. 10: Book Club; China Painters Soc; Dites Moi French Club. 14: Ref, elem libs. 15: 3200amherst, Dallas Tx 75225.

CROWDES, MRS ANITA JANE (LARSON). b McPherson Kan 28 Mr 38. 4: Harold W Crowdes Jr. 5: Bethany col 55-59 (Eng) BA; UUtah & UMo correspondence (LS). 7: Eng tchr High Sch, Munden Kan 59-60; Eng & libn High Sch, Little River Kan 61-62; Eng & libn High Sch, Bazine Kan 63-64; Eng & libn High Sch, Windom Kan 64-66; Eng Tchr High Sch, Lyons Kan 66-67; Libn 67-. 9: NEA; KanASchL; Kan State Tchrs Assn. 10: Kan EHU LAL Club. 15: P O Box 82, Windom Ka 67491.

CROWE, SUSAN (BRENNAN). b Kan City Mo 30 Jl 34. 5: Mt St Marys Col (Los Angeles) 53-57 (Eng) BA; USoCal 57-58 MS in LS. 7: Libn US Army Spec Serv, Darmstadt Germany 58-60; Catlg libn Hughes Aircraft Co, Culver City Cal 61-62; Asst libn Northrop Space Labs, Hawthorne Cal 63-64, Libn 65-67; Supv acquis, Aerospace Corp, Los Angeles 67-. 9: ALA; SLA; -So Cal Chap (pres 69-70); ASIS; CalLA. 14: Ref, admin, acquis. 15: 12415 Texas ave, Los Angeles Ca 90025.

CROWELL, VILLA BAILEY. b Medford Mass 12 F 16. 4: Prince Sears Crowell Jr. 5: Oberlin Col 37 AB; Ind U 62 AM. 7: Asstlibn Halls of Residence Libs Ind U 62-. 9: ALA. 10: Beta Phi Mu. 14: Tech serv. 15: 1717 Ruby lane, Bloomington In 47403.

CROWERS, CLIFFORD P. b Collingdale Penn 31 O 21. 5: UMd 46-50 (Hist) BA; Drexel 51-54 MSLS. 7: Lib asst Quartermaster Res & Devel Tech Lib, Phila 51-53; Asst dept head Pub Documents Dept Free Lib of Phila 53-. 8: Adjunct Instr, Grad Sch of Lib Sci Drexel, 62-. 9: ALA; PennLA; SLA. 14: Ref, catlg govt docs. 15: 1736 Addison st, Phila Pa 19146.

CROWL, VIRGINIA DARE. b Oneida Ohio 11 F 12. 5: Flora Stone Mather Col 30-31; Kent State 31-34 (Eng, Fr) AB, BS in Ed, summers 40-44 (Eng) AM; West Res 46-47 BS in LS. 6: Fr. 7: Tchr Augusta High Sch, Augusta Ohio 35-36; Tchr Pamyra High Sch, Palmyra Ohio 36-43; Tchr Stow High Sch, Stow Ohio 43-45; Kent State U: Asst order libn 47-56, Ser libn 56-62, Documents libn 62-. 9: ALA. 10: Bus & Prof Womens Club. 14: Docs, ref, acquis. 15: 125 N Freedom st, Ravenna Ohio 44266.

CROWLEY, CHARLENE (STEPHENS). b Jackson Mich 4 Ag 40. 4: Stephen H Crowley. 5: Pembroke Col (Providence) 58-61, 62-63 (Art hist) AB; UMich summer 61; RI Sch of Design summer 62; URI 64-65 MLS. 6: Fr. 7: BrownU: Priv sec 61-63, Asst to humanities libn 63-65, catlgr art bks 65-. 9: RILA. 10: RI Civic Chorale (59-64). 11: Phoebe Parker Scholarship 65; RILA 65. 14: Subj specialist in art. 15: 66 Larch st, Providence RI 02906.

CROWLEY, RUTH ANNE (ZEFFIRO). b Pittsburgh. 5: Mt Mercy Col 4549 (Hist) AB; Carnegie 54-56 MLS. 7: Visitor Dept Pub Assistance, Pittsburgh 49-50; Tchr Pittsburgh Pub Schs, Pittsburgh 50-5; Recreation leader Bur of Parks & Recreation, Pittsburgh 53-56; Pittsburgh Pub Schs: Asst libn 56-5, Jr high libn 58-64, Sr high libn 64-; Libn coordinator Neighborhood Youth Corps, Pittsburgh summer 64. 9: NEA; ALA; PennLA; Penn State EA; Pittsburgh EA (sec 64-66). 10: Boy ScoutsDen Mother; Alpha Delta Kappa. 14: Sch libnship. 15: 3527 Beechwood blvd, Pittsburgh Pa 15217.

CROWLEY, TERENCE. b Chicago 29 My 35. 4: Jane McCormick. 5: UNotre Dame 53-57 (Humanities) BA; Rutgers 60-62 MLS, 65-68 (LS), PhD. 7: Supply off US Navy 57-61; Ref libn Orange Co Lib, Orange Cal 62-64, Head adult ref center 64-65; Grad asst Rutgers Grad Sch of Lib Serv 65-66; Grad Fellow 66-68; Res dir Chicago Pub Lib Survey, Chicago 68-69; Res Asst Prof & Dir Lib Res Ctr UIll 69-. 8: Research assoc Penn Lib Re-survey 66. 9: ALA; CalLA; IllLA. 10: Cath Human Rel Coun of Orange Co (Cal); US Naval Reserve; AAUP. 14: Ref, pub libs, measurement & eval. 15: 428 Library Univ of Ill, Urbana Il 61801.

CROWNFIELD, ELEANOR (BOSTWICK). b New Haven Conn. 4: David Ring Crownfield. 5: Smith 47-51 (Eng) BA; Simmons 52-54 MS in LS. 7: Govt documents asst Yale U Lib 51-52; Monograph catlgr Yale Divinity Lib 53-55; Monograph catlgr Ind Rel Lib Harvard U 56-57; Res desk attendant Middlebury Col Lib 61-62; Sub libn High Sch-Jr High Lib, Alma Mich 63-64; Catlgr UNoIa Lib 64-. 9: ALA. 14: Catlg. 15: 2303 Iowa st, Cedar Falls Ia 50613.

CROXTON, FRED E. b Columbus Ohio 14 O 23. 4: Dorothy Duboise. 5: Columbia summers 40, 42 (Statistics); Oberlin Col 41-44 (Chem) BA; UTenn even 50-51 (Chem); Columbia summers 50-52, 60 (LS) MA. 7: Tech Inspector The Kellex Corp, NYC 44-45; US Army Corp Engnrs Manhatten Dist 45-46; var positions in lab & info work Carbide & Carbon Chemicals Corp, Oak Ridge Tenn 46-49; Chief catlg br, chief spec proj br, cheif bibliog unit Tech Info Serv Ext USAEC, Oak Ridge Tenn 49-53; Supt info & records Goodyear Atomic Corp, Piketon Ohio 53-62; Dir Redstone Sci Info Center US Army Missile Command, Redstone Arsenal Ala 62-68; Exec VP Tech Info Serv Co & Dep Dir NASA Scientific and Tech Info Facility, Col Park Md 68-. 8: Mem Raymond Com to Review Tech Info Mgt, Dept of Defense 67; Mem Task Force on Automation of Fed Lib Com 66-68; Memb Chemical Abstracts Adv Bd Libr Panel 67-69. 9: ACS; SLA. 10: AAAS; Assn of the US Army; Red Cross, etc. 12: Many technical papers and bibliographies. 13: Yes. 14: Mechanized proc. 15: Technical Info Services Co 5001 Calvert rd, College Park Md 20740.

CROZER, MARY ALBERTSON. b Collingswood NY 20 Ag 18. 5: UPenn 36-40 (Eng) BA; Drexel 40-41 (LS) BS. 7: Catlgr UPenn 41-46, Head ser det 46-. 14: Ser. 15: 213 New Jersey ave, Collingswood NJ 08108.

CROZIER, RICHARD JOSEPH. b Altoona Penn 2 S 19. 4: M Dorothy (McDowell). 5: Reformed Episcopal Sem 45-48 (Theol) BD; Temple 49-52 (Philos) BS in Ed; Faith Theol Sem 52-54 (Hebrew, Old Testament) STM; Drexel 56-59 (LS) MS. 6: Hebrew, Bibl Gk. 7: Libn Pine Crest Bible Inst, Salisbury Center NY 59-62; Libn Northeast Bible Inst, Green Lane Penn 62-64; Head Libn So Cal Col 64-66; Hd catlgr Oral Roberts U, Tulsa Okla 66-67; Hd libn Geneva Col (Penn) 67-. 8: Minister, Assemblies of God; Presbyter, Italian Assemblies of God, 63-64. 9: Evangel Theol Soc; ALA; Christ Libns Assn; Christ Lib Fellowship; CalLA; AAUP; NEA; Penn State Higher EA. 12: Ed "Christian Librarian (62,65). 14: Admin, tech serv, statistics, info sci & automation. 15: McCartney Lib Geneva College, Beaver Falls Pa 215010.

CROZIER, RUTH SYNNOTT. b Hemphill Tex 18 Ap 07. 4: George A Crozier. 5: So Methodist U 24-28 (Eng) BA; Tex Womans U 58-62 MLS. 6: Lat, Fr, Sp, Ger. 7: Sec Gen Motors Acceptance Corp, Dallas, NY 28-40; Lib clerk Highland Park Jr High Sch, Dallas 56-60; Libn Dallas Ind Sch Dist 60-61; Catlg libn Law Sch So Meth U 61-. 9: ALA; AALL; SWLA. 10: Beta Phi Mu; Mortar Board; Zeta Phi Eta; Kappa Delta. 14: Catlg. 15: 3828 Stanford, Dallas Tx 75225.

CROZIER, VIRGINIA (LAYTON). b Los Angeles 16 Jl 09. 5: Pomona Col 27-31 BA; Emory 31-32 BA in LS. 7: Ref asst, 1st asst in ref Pub Lib, Pasadena Cal 32-42; Lib asst tech dept Pub Lib, Seattle 42-45; Ref asst Pub Lib, Minneapolis 45; Tech libn Lib of Hawaii, Honolulu 45-58, Head main adult div 58-63; Sci ref libn UHawaii 63-68; Hd Pub Serv Hamilton Lib 68-. 9: ALA; SLA; HawaiiLA (past pres). 10: AAAS. 14: Ref. 15: 320 Poopoo pl, Kailua Hi 96734.

CRUGNOLA, MRS NELLA (TONETTI). b NYC. 4: Eugene Crugnola. 5: Hunter Col 37-41 (Ital) BA; Pratt 41-42 BLS; UConn 59-61 (Educ). 6: Ital, Fr, Sp. 7: NY Pub Lib Brs 42-43; Art sch libn The Cooper Union 43-52; Asst head info serv Ferguson Lib, Stamford Conn 58-67; Br libn 67-. 9: WestchesterLA; ConnLA. 10: North Country Players. 14: Ref. 15: 34 Wake Robin lane, Stamford Ct 06903.

CRUM, MARK. b Pittsburgh 28 My 22. 4: Margaret Ellen Peterson Crum. 5: U Pittsburgh 39-43 (Eng) BA; Carnegie 47-48 BS in LS; West Mich U 63-66 (Mgt) MBA, 66- (Educ Leadership).07: Br asst Carnegie Lib, Pittsburgh 48, Admin asst 49-50; Libn & lib off (1st Lt) Antiaircraft & Guided Missiles Sch, Ft Bliss Tex 51; Asst lib off (1st Lt) Army War Col, Carlisle Barracks Penn 52; Head Libn Kanawha Co Pub Lib, Charleston WVa 53-56; Dir Kalamazoo Lib System, Kalamazoo 56. 9: ALA; MichLA. 10: Rotary Internat; Kalamazoo Mgt Assn. 14: Mgt, grad lib educ. 15: 315 S Rose st, Kalamazoo Mi 49001.

CRUM, NORMAN JAMES. b Waverly Ill 5 S 26. 4: Le Vere Linnerson. 5: UIll 46-50 (Econ) BS High Honors, 51-53 (LS) MS; Columbia summer 55 (LS); Santa arbara City Col even 62-65 (Sci). 7: US Navy electronics tech 44-46; Std asst Com & Sociol Lib UIll(Urbana) 51-52; 1st asst sci & ind dept Pub Lib of Youngstown & Mahoning Co, Youngstown Ohio 53-56; Head bus & ind dept Omaha Pub Lib 56-62; Tech info analyst Gen Electric TEMPO, Santa Barbara Cal 62-66, Tech info spec 66-. 9: SLA; ADI. 10: Toastmasters; Beta Gamma Sigma; Beta Phi Mu; Phi Eta Sigma. 13: Yes. 14: Ref, info utilization by scientists & businessmen,info ctr mgt. 15: 512 N Soledad, Santa Barbara Ca 93103.

CRUMB, LAWRENCE N(ELSON). b Palo Alto Cal 19 My 37. 4: Ellen Adele Locke. 5: Pomona Col 54-58 (Eng lit) BA; Nashotah House 58-61 (Relig) BD; Gen Theol Sem 61-62 (Church hist); UWis 66-67 (LS) MA. 6: French, Latin, Greek. 7: Curate St John's Episcopal Church, Elkhart Ind 62-64; Curate St John's Episcopal Church, Lafayette Ind 64-65; Asst libn & instr New Testament Greek Nashotah House 65-. 8: Libn Observer, Princeton Theol Sem, 68. 9: ALA; ACRL; ATheolLA; WisLA; Waukesha Acad Lib Union; Chicago Area Theol Libns. 10: Beta Phi Mu; Phi Beta Kappa; Bel Canto Chorus, Milwaukee. 14: Catlg, ref, acad libnship. 15: Nashotah House, Nashotah Wi 53058.

CRUMP, MARCELLA CLAIRE. b Amory Miss 30 N 15. 5: Memphis State U 33-37 (Eng, Lat, Hist) BS; UGa summers 48-52 (Eng) MA; Peabody 54-55 MALS. 7: Tchr Memphis City Schs, Memphis Tenn 37-53; Tchr New Smyrna (Fla) Beach Schs 53-54; Libn Los Alamos (NM) Schs 55-56; Libn Memphis City Schs, Memphis Tenn 56-. 8: Tchr, Lib Sci Memphis State U, summer 64; Substitute Lib Supv, Rialto Cal Sch Dist, summer 58. 9: ALA; TennEA (chm Lib Sect); TennLA (chm Sch Sect). 10: AAUW; Delta Kappa Gamma; Beta Phi Mu; Phi Beta Kappa. 15: 3227 N Waynoka circle, Memphis Tenn 38111.

CRUMRINE, KATHERINE E. b Pittsburgh Pa 6 O 05. 5: UPittsburgh 32 (Eng) AB; Carnegie- Mellon U 33 BS in LS. 7: Asst Lenox Lib Lenox Mass 33-34; Carnegie Lib of Pittsburgh: Ref asst Wylie ave br 34-36, First asst Brookline br 36-38, Br libn Knoxville br 38-43, Br libn downtown br 43-45, Hd central lending dept 45-57, Personnel dir 58-. 9: ALA (chm Notable Bks Com 48); PennLA (sec 62-63, chm Memb Com 61, chm Awards Com 66-67, pres SW Dist 61); Pittsburgh Lib Club. 10: Altrusa Club; Assn of Pittsburgh Bus Women's Clubs. 11: Distinguished Alumna Award; Carnegie Lib Sch Alum Assn 68. 14: Personnel admin. 15: 2424 Beaufort ave, Pittsburgh Pa 15226.

CRUTCHER, ANNETTE (VREELAND). b Henry Co Ky 20 O 05. 5: Sherwood Music Sch 22-24; UKy ext 28; Columbia (correspondence) 29; Catherine Spalding 30-41; ULouisville 41. 7: Letter stuffer Converse Printing Co "Christian Observer, Louisville Ky 24; Ref asst Louisville Free Pub Lib, Louisville Ky 25-. 9: ALA; KyLA (Publs Chm); SELA; Louisville Lib Club. 10: Soroptimist Club; Christian Womens Fellowship; YWCA; Moral Rearmament; StaffAssn Louisville Free Pub Lib. 11: Meritorious serv award, 57. 13: Yes. 14: Ref, geneal, Ky & Louisville hist, rare bks. 15: 1133 Cherokee rd, Louisville Ky 40204.

CRUTCHFIELD, ANNE GREEN. b King George Co Va 23 O 04. 4: Angus L Crutchfield. 5: Mary Washington Col 22. 7: Lib asst Tidewater Reg Lib, Va 38-41; Aberdeen Proving Ground, Md: Personnel clerk 42-46, Libn catlgr Tech Lib 46-48, Libn ref Tech Lib 48-52, Libn Ballistic Research Labs 52-. 9: SLA; ALA-RSD. 14: Ref. 15: Aldino Rt 1, Churchville Md 21028.

CRUTCHFIELD, BENJAMIN F(RANKLIN) JR. b Durham NC 25 Ag 40. 4: Jane Folger. 5: UNC 58-62 (Fr) BA, 66-67 MS in LS. 6: Fr, Ger. 7: Specialist 5 USA, Philippines, Vietnam, Dominican Republic 63-66; Lib asst Wilson Lib UNC 67; Libn sci & tech div Queens Borough Pub Lib Central Bldg tech 67-68; Ref libn Queens Borough Pub Lib Jackson Heights Br 68-. 10: United Methodist Church Young Couples' Club. 14: Info retrieval, bibliog, govt docs. 15: 1111 Johnson st High Point NC 27262.

CRUTCHFIELD, MARY JANE. b Sutton W Va 5 O 25. 5: W Va U 43-47 BS Ed; UNC 53-55 BSLS; Emory 64 Med Libnship Certif. 6: Sp, Fr. 7: Asst libn pub lib, Westerville Ohio 47-49; Libn Montverde Sch, Montverde Fla 49-50; Libn Fairfax Hall, Waynesboro Va 50-55; Libn Post High Sch Marine Corps Quantico Va 55-57; Ref libn pub lib, Chula Vista Cal 57-59; Br libn Miami Pub Lib 59-61; Asst libn Fairchild Stratos Corp Engineering Lib Hagerstown Md 61-62; Ref libn pub lib, Silver Spring Md 62-64; Bio-med libn & doc film libn Armed Forces Radiobiology Research Inst Bethesda Md 64-66; Br libn Duke U Med Ctr Lib 67-. 8: Served with first group on Lib 21 Proj at Seattle World's Fair 62. 9: MedLA; SLA. 15: 56B Colonial apts, Durham NC 27707.

CRUTE, MARTHA (BINGHAM). b Chamberlain SD 24 My 11. 4: Joseph P Crute. 5: Yankton Col 30-34 (Langs) BA; Drexel 34-35 BS in LS; C W Post Col 59-60 NY State Sch Libn Certif. 7: Child libn Pub Lib, Rapid City SD 35-37; Libn Boys Sch, Stony Brook NY 38-45; Sch libn Co-Op Educ Servs, Suffolk Co NY 59-63; Sch libn J A Edgar Pub Sch, Rocky Point NY 63-. 9: NY State Tchrs Assn; Suffolk Co Lib Assn. 10: Girl Scout Leader; OES. 14: Child wk. 15: R I Box 47, Rocky Point NY 11778.

CRUZ, HONORIO P. b Apalit Pampanga Philippines 11 Ag 31. 4: Carmen Macalino. 5: U St tomas 57 (LS) BSE; Ateneo de ManilaU 60-61 (Econ, Educ); CatholicU 68 MSLS. 6: Sp, Fr, Tagalog. 7: Circ asst USto Tomas Lib, Manila 54-56; Asst to registrar Lourdes Sch, Quezon City Philippines 56-57; Hd libn 57-64; Ref & circ libn Ateneo de ManilaU 57-64; Act asst circ libn CatholicU 64-65; Hd interlib loan 65-66; Asst ref libn AmericanU 67-68; Ref libn Fairfax Co Pub Lib, Fairfax Va 68-69; Hd br libn 69-. 8: Technical Adviser Lourdes Convent Lib Quezon City 61-63. 9: PhilippineLA; VaLA; DCLA. 10: Alpha Lambda Epsilon; Lib Sci Student Assn; LSFC; Filipino Stud Assn; CatholicU. 14: Ref, admin. 15: 10324 Layton Hall dr 214, Fairfax Va 22030.

CRUZAT, MRS GWENDOLYN (STIGGINS). b Chicago 30 Mr 32. 5: Fisk U 47-51 (Math) BA; Atlanta 51-52 MSLS; Columbia 62 MedLA Certif. 6: Sp, Fr. 7: Child libn Los Angeles Pub Lib 52-53; Ref libn Fisk U 54-60; Asst libn Harper Hosp, Detroit 60-64; Ref libn Wayne State U Med Lib 64-. 8: Chm Tri-State Hosp Assembly Conf on Lib Serv 68; Research asst Univ City Sci Ctr& Inst for Advan of Med Communication, 66-68; Assoc dir, Fellowship Prog in Med Libnship, Wayne State U Med Lib 67-. 9: MedLA (Instr Contin Educ Courses 68-). 10: Beta Phi Mu. 13: Yes. 14: Ref. 15: 1 Lafayette Plaisance, Apt 1017, Detroit Mi 48207.

CRYDER, ROBERT W. b Joliet Ill 25 My 22. 4: Joanne Sloan. 5: UIll 48 (Hist) AB, 49 (Amer Hist) MA; Chicago 54 (LS) MA. 6: Fr. 7: Admin asst UOre Lib 51-53; Lib asst (UGL) Lib UIll 53-55, Lib asst Law 55-60; Asst circ libn UWash Lib 61-64, Spec asst to dir 64-65; Head Med Libn UIowa 65-. 9: MedLA; IowaLA. 10: UIowa Friends of the Lib; Optimist Club. 14: Med libs. 15: 1421 Buresh ave, Iowa City Ia 52240.

CRYMES, MARY FRANCES (RICH). b Wake County NC 24 F 35. 4: John James Crymes. 5: Appalachian State Tchrs Col 53-56 (LS). 7: Y-a libn Pub Lib of Charlotte & Mecklenburg Co, Charlotte NC 56-66, Ref asst 67-. 9: NCLA (sect chm Jr Mem RT 61-63). 12: "Books for Young Adults: A Selected, Annotated Bibliography" (60 & 61). 14: Ref. 15: 5729 Linford dr, Charlotte NC 28210.

CRYSTAL, BERNARD ROBERT. b Minneapolis Mn 18 Je 37. 5: UMinn 55-59 (Fr) AB, 59-61 (LS) MA; Columbia 62-. 6: Fr, Ger. 7: Non-prof lib asst Hennepin Co Lib, Minneapolis53-60; Ref libn Ind U Libs 61; Ref libn spec collections Columbia U Libs 61-66, Catlgr spec collections 67-68. 9: ALA; NYLA. 10: Phi Beta Kappa. 14: Rare bks, mss. 15: 100 Cooper st 3F, New York NY 10034.

CSABA, MARGARET JACKSON. b No Ireland 25 Jl 11. 4: Louis Csaba. 5: Loughry Agric Col (N Ireland) 32 Col Certif; Queens U (Belfast) 38 (Chem) BS; Toronto59 BLS. 6: Fr. 7: Agric chem & bacteriologist, Eng & Can 39-58; Can Dept of

Agric: Catlgr 59-62, Acquis libn 62-63, Head field lib serv 63-65, Asst libn 65-. 9: CanLA; Internat Assn of Agric Libns & Documentalists. 10: Prof Inst of the Pub Serv of Can. 15: Dept of Agric Lib, Ottawa Can.

CSAKY, SUSAN (DISCHKA). b Budapest Hungary 25 Jl 26. 4: T Z Csaky. 5: Peter Pazmany U(Budapest) 45-47 (Law); UGa 48 (Econ) AB; Johns Hopkins 48-53 (Pol Sci) MA; UNC 59-61 MSLS. 6: Ger, Fr, Hungarian. 7: Sec & foreign correspondent Hungarian Com of FAO of UN; Clerk Dept of Agric, Budapest Hungary; Research asst Dept of Pol Econ Johns Hopkins U; Bibliogr UNC Med Sch Lib; Lecturer & Libn UNC Sch of Lib Sci; Bibliogr UKy Libs, Law lib catlgr, Asst law libn. 8: Lectr Col of Law UKy 67-68. 10: Beta Phi Mu. 12: "The History of Printing in Hungary, 1600-1711,ACRL Microcard Ser. 13: Yes. 14: Ref, tchg. 15: 1032 The Lane, Lexington Ky 40504.

CSICSERY-RONAY, ISTVAN. b Budapest Hungary 13 D 17. 4: Elizabeth Tariska Csicsery-Ronay. 5: Royal Hungarian U (Budapest) 35-40 (Pol Sci, Law) PhD; Konsular Akademie (Vienna) 37-39 (Diplomacy) Diploma; Tech U (Budapest) 39-43 (Agric) Certif; Catholic U 53-57 MSLS. 6: Hungarian, Ger, Fr, Russian, Lat. 7: (1st Lt) (Reserve) Hungarian Army Artillery 38-39, 42-43; Anti-Nazi Resistance Movement 44-45; Ministerial sec Hungarian Foreign Ministry, Budapest 45-47; Pol analyst Free Euope Com, NYC 49-56; Ed Occidental Press & Adv Records, Wash DC 54-; Assoc libn II McKeldin Lib UMd 56-. 10: Internat Pen Club; Amer Acad of Pol &Soc Sci; Phi Kappa Phi. 12: "Russian Cultural Penetration in Hungary" (3d ed 52)"Koltok forradalma" ("Poets Revolution") (57); "First Book of Hungary" (67); Ed-bibliografia," a Hungarian lang quarterly publ in Wash DC (57-65). 13: Yes. 14: Catlg. 15: 2321 NWakefield st, Arlington Va 22207.

CSUROS, BARNA. b Debrecen Hungary 15 Je 24. 4: Eva A Csuros. 5: UBudapest 42-50 (Jurisprudence) Dr Jur;Columbia 60-61 (LS) MS. 6: Hungarian, Ger. 7: Asst br libn NY Pub Lib 60-65; Acquis libn Wagner Col 65-66; Hd libn 66-. 15: 55 Bristol ave, SI NY 10301.

CUBBEDGE, FRANKIE (HOLLEY). b Graniteville SC 20 Ja 37. 4: Atys B Cubbedge. 5: Winthrop Col 55-59 (LS) AB; Emory summer 61 (LS); UNC summers 63-66 MSLS. 6: Fr, Ger. 7: Libn Hamilton Elem Sch, Beaufort SC 59-61; Supv of 5 elem sch libs, Savannah Ga 61-62; Libn NC Collection E Carolina Col Lib 62-63, Head spec collections dept 63-66; Hd libn Edmunds High Sch, Sumter SC 66-67; Instr USC Ext 68; Libn WillowDr Sch, Sumter SC 68-. 9: NCLA; SCEA; ScASchL. 10: AAUW. 14: Org libs & collections. 15: PO Box 871, Sumter SC.

CUDD, BERNICE (EMRIV). b Racine Wis 27 D 32. 5: UWis 50-54 (Hist) BS, 57-58 (LS) MS. 7: Bkmob libn Rapid City (SD) Pub Lib 55-56; Asst circ desk libn Ohio State U 58-59, Gen catlgr 61-63; Ref asst Worthington (Ohio) Pub Lib 63-65; Pub serv Ohio State Univ Libs 65-66, Asst personnel libn 66-67; Hd libn Worthington Pub Lib 67-. 9: ALA; OhioLA (chm Recruit Com). 10: UWis Lib Sch Alumni; Beta Phi Mu. 15: 100 E North st, Worthington Ohio 43085.

CUDD, KERMIT GEORGE. b Rice Lake Wis 14 Mr 31: 04: Bernice Emerich. 5: UWis 49-53 (Econ) BA, 57-58 (LS) MA; Ohio State U 62-63, 66-69 (Bus Admin) PhD. 7: Navigator USAF (Capt) 53-57; Bibliog Ohio StateU Libs 58-59; Tech libn AC Spark Plug Div of GM Corp, Milwaukee 59-61; Com libn Ohio tate U Libs 61-63, Head acquis dept 63-66, Off of Acad Affairs 66-69. 8: Consul Inst for Educl Devel, NYC. 9: ALA; Ohio Valley Group Tech ServLibns (vm Nomin Com 64-65). 10: UWis Lib Sch Alumni Assn; Beta Phi Mu. 13: Yes. 14: Acquis. 15: Dept of Bus Admin, Univ of Delaware, Newark De 19711.

CUDE, OBERA (RICHEY). b Roscoe Tex 12 O 15. 4: George K Cude. 5: Southwestern U 33-37 (Eng) BA; N Tex State Tchrs Col summer 38; Tex Womens U summer 40-43 BS in LS. 7: Tchr of lang arts Elem Sch, Hamilton Tex 37-42; Tchr of lang arts Jr High Sch, Angleton Tex 42-43; Libn Sr High Sch, Angleton Tex 43-44; Asst libn Houston Ind Sch Dist 4461; Asst libn Northeastern State Col (Okla) 61-. 8: Summer lib wk at var places. 9: NEA; OklaEA; OklaLA; AHA. 10: AAUW; Delta Kappa Gamma. 14: Ref, rare bks. 15: Rt 3, Tahlequah Okla 74464.

CUEBAS-IRIZARRY, ANA E. b Mayaguez PR 29 Ap 44. 5: Col of Agric & Mech Arts 61-65 (Soc Sci) BA, 67- (Pub Admin); Pratt Inst 66-67 MLS. 6: Sp. 7: Lib asst Col Agric & mech Arts, Mayaguez PR 63-65, Catlgr 67-68, Tchr Bibliog & ref summer 68, Ref libn 68-. 8: Tchr sch lib admin UPR ext (Ponce) 68. 9: Assn of PR Pub Adminis; PR Libn Assn (coord). 14: Ref. 15: Pirinola #6, Mayaguez PR 00708.

CULBERTSON, DON STUART. b Detroit Mich 12 Ja 27. 4: Lillian Dallas Williams. 5: Albion Col 44-50 (Psych) AB; UDenver 56-58 (LS) MA. 7: Tchr Reese Pub Sch, Reese Mich 50-52; Tchr Milford Pub Sch, Milford Mich 52-57; Circ libn UWichita 58-69; Hd data proc UIll (Chicago) 60-64; Libn for research & devel Colo StateU 64-67; Exec sec ALA-ISAD, Chicago 67-. 8: Asst dir Univ Lib Info Syst Proj UIll (Chicago) 61; Dir program for implementation testing & eval UIll (Chicago). 09: ALA; ASIS; Chicago Lib Club, Chicago Reg Gp. 12: Co-auth ""Advanced Data Processing in the University Library (62). 13: Yes. 14: Automation, prof lib mgt. 15: 510 Sheridan rd #311, Evanston Il 60202.

CULBERTSON, KATHERYN C. b Coeburn Va 14 Ag 20. 5: E Tenn State U 37-40 (Eng, Lat) BS; Peabody 41, 42 BS in LS; YMCA Night Law Sch 62-68 LL.B. 6: Lat, Fr. 7: Ref libn, catlgr US Bur of Ships Tech Lib, Wash DC 45-49, 51-53; Sch libn Kingsport Pub Schs, Kingsport Tenn 49-51; eg libn Tfn Sate Lib & Archives 53-61; Dir ext serv Pub Lib of Nashville & Davidson Co, Nashville 61-. 8: Former Tenn State Exec Dir, Nat Lib Week. 9: ALA; SELA; TennLA (past sec & parliam); Nashville Lib Cl0 (pres). 10: Bus & Prof Womens Club; Zonta Internat. 14: Ext wk (brs, bkmob program). 15: Lib Ext Div, Gallatin rd at Main st, nashville Tenn 37206.

CULLEN, DOROTHY A. b Sherwood PEI Can. 5: Prince of Wales Col 30-33; Pratt 35-36 BLS; Dalhousie U 46- 48 (Eng, Hist) BA. 7: Asst libn Prince Edward Island Libs, Charlottetown 36-56, Libn 56-. 9: CanLA (2n v-pres 50-51); Atlantic prvince LA (pres 52-53 & 61-62). 10: Bus & Prof Womens Club; Prince Edward Island Music Festival Assn. 12: Ed APLA ""Bulleti (44-52). 15: Prince Edward Island Libs, Charlottetown PEI Can.

CULLEN, LAWRENCE REARDON. b St Paul I4 N 39. 4: Nancy Ryan. 5: Col of St Thomas)t Paul)68-62 58-62 Lit) BA; Catholic U 62-64 MS in LS; UMinn 64-. 6: Fr, Ger. 7: Grad lib asst Catholic U 62-63; Libn Xaverian Col 63-64; Libn St Cloud State Col 64-67; Dir of Educ Resources No Hennepin State Jr Col 69. 9: MinnLA; A-V Coordinators Assn of Minn; Minn State Jr Col Fac Assn. 10: Brooklyn Park Human Relations Commsn; League of Minn Municipalities; Human Rights Com. 14: Ref, data processing, lib tech, admin, instr. 15: 2216 Laramie Trail, Brooklyn Park Mn 55430.

CULLERS, MARY ALICE (MARQUES). b Anciao Portugal 22 O 30. 4: James Barnett Cullers. 5: Mt Holyoke 48-52 (Fr) AB; UMass summer 59 (Educ); Westfield State Col 67 (LS). 6: Fr, Sp, Portu. 7: Lib asst Hampshire Inter-lib Ctr, So Hadley Mass 56-57; Actuarial asst Mass Mutual Life Ins Co, Springfield Mass 57-59; Engring lib recs supv monsanto Co, Springfield Mass 59-64; Research libn Tecnifax Plastic Coating Corp, So Hadley Mass 65-67; Libn Tantasqua Reg High Sch, Sturbridge Mass 67-68; Asst libn corp lib Combustion Engring Inc, Windsor Conn 68-. 9: SLA. 14: Catlg, ref. 15: 133 Longmeadow st, Longmeadow Ma 01106.

CULLEY, PAUL T(HOMAS). b Lackawanna NY 8 Ja 38. 4: Cynthia Ann Haskins. 5: Alfred U 5661 (Ceramic Engnr) BS; State U Col (Fredonia NY) 61-62 (Liberal Arts); State U Col (Geneseo NY) 63-64 MLS. 7: Sci catlgr Brandeis U 64-65; Monograph catlgr USAF Cambridge Res Labs 65-67; Asst libn SD Sch of Mines & Tech 67-. 9: ALA; SLA. 10: Keramos; ACLU. 14: Catlg. 15: 436 E College, Rapid City SD 57701.

CULLY, JOHN W. b Jacksonville Ill 12 Jl 27. 5: Ill Col 44-45, 47-50 (Eng) BA; UCal 9berkeley) 57-59 MLS. 6: Fr. 7: X-ray tech T-4 US Army Med Dept 45-47; Reservations agent Air France, NYC 52-54; Sales rep Swissair, NYC, San Francisco 54-57; Lib asst UCal Lib (Berkeley) 57-59; Libn I Brooklyn Pub Lib, Brooklyn NY 59-61; Ref libn Berkeley Pub Lib, Berkeley Cal 61-66; Ref libn Cal State Lib, Sacramento 66-67, Research libn 67-68, Ed libn 68-. 9: CalLA. 10: Phi Beta Kappa. 12: Ed "News Notes of California Libraries" (68-). 14: Ref. 15: California State Lib PO Box 2037, Sacramento Ca 95809.

CULP, CAROL ANN. b Edgewood Arsenal Md 2 F 43. 5: Miami U 61-65 (Ger) AB; West Res 65-66 MSLS. 6: Fr, Ger. 7: Cuyahoga Co Pub Lib: Asst catlgr Cleveland 66-67, YA libn Brook Park 68, YA & adult serv libn Brook Park 69-. 9: ALA; OhioLA; No Ohio Tech Serv Libns. 10: Delta Phi Alpha; Pi Delta Phi. 14: Catlg, YA serv. 15: 11801 N Lane dr 7, Lakewood Oh 44107.

CULVER, VIRGINIA (NAGEL). b Knoxville Tenn 10 O 45. 4: David Alan Culver. 5: Cornell U 63-67 (Eng) AB; UWash 67-69 MLib. 7: Child libn Seattle Pub Lib 69-. 14: Child serv. 15: 106 16th ave So apt 1, Seattle Wa 98144.

CULVER, WAVE ELAINE. b Milan Mich 16 Ja 05. 5: UMich 24-28 (Pre-med sci) BA, 42-47 (Med Bacteriology, Biol Chem) MA. 6: Fr. 7: Admin sec UMich Dean's Off Lit Col 28-41; Tchr asst & lab asst UMich Med Sch44-47; Research asst Brookhaven Nat Lab, Upton LI NY 47-49; Research assoc Nat ResearchCoun Wash DC 49-52; Bibliog & sci spec LC 52-57; Info specialist Nat Air PollutionControl Admin, Off of the Dir Div of Health Effects Research. 9: SLA (Program Chm Nat Meeting 62; chm Biol Scis Group 60-61; Hospitality & Pub Chm DC Chap 64-65); Amer Med Writers Assn; SCLA. 10: Phi Sigma; Action Com for DC Sch Libs; Nat Lib Com for DC; Capitol Hill Commun Cou; Arts Club of Washington; Red Cross Gray Lady. 11 Comp "The Air Pollution Bibliography, v 1 & 2 with others (57, 59); Comp "The Polar Bibliography, v 3, with others (59); Assoc ed "APCA Abstracts in J Air Pollution Control Assn. 13: Yes. 14: Bibliog. 15: 1100 Leon st,apt 17, Durham NC 27704.

CULVERHOUSE, GERTRUDE (BAUSH). b Allentown Penn 27 F 26. 4: John B Culverhouse Jr. 5: Ursinus Col 43-47 (Bus Admin) AB; Drexel 49-50 MSLS. 7: Ref libn Enoch Pratt Free Lib bus & econ dept, Baltimore 50-60; Chief ref & circ US Soc Security Admin, Baltimore 60-. 9: SLA. 14: Ref. 15: 414 Nottingham rd, Baltimore 21229.

CUMER, GERALD L. b Washington Penn 16 Ag 42. 5: Cal State Col (Cal Penn) 60-64 (Biol sci) BS in Ed; UPittsburgh 67 (LS); UMich 66-68 AMLS. 6: Ger. 7: Sci tchr Post Junior High School Detroit Michigan 64-65; Biol tchr Northwestern High School Detroit Michigan 65-66; Cal State Col, Cal Penn: Sci libn instr 66-68, Chief catlgr instr 68-. 9: MedLA; ALA. 10: AAUP; Assn of Penn State Col & Univ Faculties. 14: Life sci, med, catlg. 15: RD 1 Box 318, Washington Pa 15301.

CUMMINGS, CHARLES F. b 27 Je 37. 5: UAla (Hist) AB; Vanderbilt (Hist) MA; Rutgers MLS. 6: Sp. 7: Fellow Dept of Hist Vanderbilt U; Prin libn NJ Div Newark Pub Lib 65-. 9: Nat Trust; Victorian Soc; Eng-Speaking Union; NJLA (Hist & Bibliog Com, subcoms on Negro Hist, Oral Hist, Revol War; chm Graphic Com). 10: NJ Hist Soc; Newark Museum Assn; South Street Seaport Museum (NYC). 14: Local hist, urban affairs, oral hist, air & water pollution, indexing. 15: NJ Ref Div Newark Lib, 5 Washington st, Newark NJ 07104.

CUMMINGS, MRS ELIZABETH W (DOOLITTLE). b New Bedford Mass 17Jl 13. 4: Frank A Cummings. 5: Bates Col 32-36 (Eng) AB; Simmons 36-37 (LS) BS; UMich summers 47, 49. 7: Providence Pub Lib 37-40; Libn Plymouth Tchrs COL 40-54; Libn (volunteer) Oracle Pub Lib, Oracle Ariz 56-63; Asst (volunteer) San Manuel Pub Lib, San Mauel Ariz 63-66; Volunteer, Nursing Home Lib Serv (Tucson Pub Lib) 66-. 8: Peace Corps tchg, UAriz, lib wk for Commun Devel Program n Panama 64. 9: ALA; Ariz State LA. 10: Delta Kappa Gamma; LWV. 11: Ariz Libn of the Year 58. 13: Yes. 14: Bk reviewing. 15: 5833 East 18th st, Tucson Az 85711.

CUMMINGS, HELEN HOWARD. b Stellarton Nova Scotia. 5: Tchr's Col 32 License; Acadia 34-37 (Eng, Hist) BA; McGill 42 BLS; Sch Lib Sci at Urbana Ill 62 MS in LS. 7: Asst librarian & catlgr Mount Allison U 46-47; Acquis & gen Provincial Lib, Halifax NS 48-50; Br libn Reg Lib, Sydney NS 50-55; Catlgr pub lib, Sudbury Ont 55-56; Chief libn pub lib, Moose Jaw Saskatchewan 56-59; Field consul State Lib, Salem Ore 59-61; Supv pub libs Provincial Lib, Halifax NS 62-63; Reg libn St Reg Lib St John NB 63-. 8: Field Consultant in Oregon assisted in Coos County demonstration and in Eastern Oregon demonstration for county libraries. 9: ALA; CanLA; APLA. 14: Admin of co & reg libs. 15: Apt 23 Low Wood Rothesay, New Brunswick Can.

CUMMINGS, JOHN M. b Calgary Alta Can. 5: UAlta 52-56 BA; McGill 61-62 BLS. 7: Chief Libn UBC Med B Lib at Vancouver Gen Hosp 62-. 9: ALA; MedLA; BCLA. 14: Ref (med), tech proc, catlg. 15: Univ of BC Med Br, Vancouver Gen Hosp, Vancouver 9 BCCan.

CUMMINGS, JOHN PATRICK. b Scranton Penn 29 D 41. 4: Kathryn McAndrew. 5: St Charles Col 59-62 (Lib Arts) AA; UScranton 63-64 (Hist) BA; Catholic U Wash DC 64-68 MSLS. 6: Sp, Fr. 7: Johns Hopkins U Applied Physics Lab, Silver Spring Md: Doc Indexer 64-66, Hd Tech Serv 66-67, Hd Readers Serv 67; Ref Libn Booz Allen Applied Research, Bethesda Md 67-68; Acquis Libn US Naval Acad 69-. 9: SLA (see DC Chap Documentation Gp 67-69). 14: Tech serv, automation. 15: 8807 Plymouth st, Silver Spring Md 20901.

CUMMINGS, LAURA. b Toledo Ohio. 5: UToledo 36 AB; UMich 37 AB in LS; Columbia 50 MS in LS. 7: Gen asst Agnes Scott Col 37-38; Catlgr Toledo Pub Lib, Toledo Ohio 38-46; Catlg ed Pacific Northwest Biblio Center, eattle 46-48; Sr catlgr Columbia U 48-51, Head ser catlg sect 51-. 9: ALA (Rep to ASA Z39, chm Ser Policy & Res Com (Mem-at-Large, Ser Sect, Exec Com); NY Tech Serv Libns (sec, pres); NY Lib Club. 14: Catlg, ser. 15: 615 W 113 st, NYC 10025.

CUMMINGS, MARTIN MARC. b Camden NJ 7 S 20. 4: Arlene Sally Avrutine Cummings. 5: Bucknell U 37-41 BS; DUKE U Sch of Med 41-44 MD. 7: Commsnd Off US Pub Health Serv (1st Lt to Maj) 46-49; Dept of Med & Surgery USVA: Chief Tuberculosis Sect & Dir Tuberculosis Res Lab, VA Hosp, ATLANTA $(#, Dir Res Serv VA Central Off, Wash DC 53-59; Emory U Sch of Med: Instr in med 48-50, Assoc in med 50-52, Asst Prof of med 53, Assoc Prof of Bacteriology 52-53; Spec Lecturer in Microbiol George Washington U Sch of Med 53-59; Chm & Prof Dept of Microbiol UOkla Sch of Med 59-61; Dir NLM 64-. 8: Chm Com on Med Res Nat Tubercul Assn 58-59; VA rep on NRC 56-59; VA rep on Nat Adv Health Coun, Surg Gen, US Pub Health Serv 56-59; Chm Panel on Sarcoidosis NRC Nat Acad of Scis 58-; Consul to Dept of Med & Surgery, VA 59-60; Consul Off of Dir, NIH USPHS, Bethesda Md 60-61;Chief Off of Internat Res NIH, USPHS, Bethesda Md 61-63; Assoc Dir for Res rants NIH, USPHS, Bethesda Md 63-. 9: Amer Soc for Clinical Investigation (Sr mem); Amer Fed for Clinical Research;Amer Thoracic Soc; Assn of Amer Med Cols; Amer Clin & Clim Assn; MedLA. 10: Cosmos Club (Wash DC). 11: DSc9hon) Bucknell U 68; Exp Serv Medal, VA; Dist, serv award DHEW. 12: "Tubercle Bacilli in "Diagnostic Procedures and Reagents (50); "Diagnostic Methods in Tuberculosis in "World Health Organization Publications (50);"Diagnostic and Experimental Methods in Tuberculosis, with H S Willis (52); A survey of medical tchg & hosp facilities in Central Amer (with Dr Harold Hinman & Anthony J Rourke) for Internat Coop Agency & State Dept (52); "Laboratory Diagnosis of Tuberculosis in "Diagnostic Standards and Classification of Tuberculosis (55); "Laboratory Diagnosis of Tuberculosis and Leprosy in "Diagnostic rocedures and Reagents (66); Foreward "Bibliography on Sarcoidosis, 1878 to 1961 (66). 13: Yes. 14: Med libnship,commun tech. 15: Nat Lib of Med, Bethesda Md 20014.

CUMMINGS, MOZELLE BROWN. b Oakman Ala 11 F 13. 4: Truman Cummings. 5: Athens Col 28-31 (Eng) AB; Auburn U 37 (Eng) MS; Peabody 57 MS in LS. 7: High sch tchr Eng Ala, SC, G 31-50; Sch libn Montgomery Co Ala 50-61, Bkmob libn summers 55-56; Field rep Ala Pub Lib Serv, Montgomery Ala summers 56-60, Head of field serv 61-. 9: ALA; SELA; AlaLA (pres, var coms). 10: Alpha Delta Kappa. 14: Lib org & devel. 15: Ramer Al 36069.

CUMMINGS, SONYA (FAGIN). b Brooklyn NY 1 F 10. 4: Lewis V Cummings. 5: Hunter Col 27-30 (Fr) BA; Columbia 30-33 (Fr); Lib Sch of Queens Borough Publib 30-31 certif; Columbia 37-45 (LS); New Sch for Soc Research 60- (Psych). 6: Fr. 7: Queens Borough Pub Lib: Grade 2 libn 31-36, Grade 2 & grade 3 ref libn, br ref inter-lib loan 36-39, Grade 3 ref libn br 39-40; Sc libn F K Lane High Sch Bd of xduc, NYC 40-56; Libn in chg Prof Lib Bd of Educ, NYC 56-66, Consul 66-. 8: Ref Staff Lib, USA World's Fair 64; Com on Wilson Indexes60-67. 9: ALA; NYLA; NY Lib Club; NYC SchLA. 10: Phi Beta Kappa. 14: Ref, wk with studs & tchrs. 15: 301 E 21 st, New York NY 10010.

CUMMINS, A(LVIN) BLAIR. b Indiana Penn 6 F 38. 4: Julia A Fulmer. 5: Mt Union Col 56-60 (Hist) BA; SUNY Col (Geneseo) 67-68 MLS. 6: Sp. 7: Sales Remington-Rand Syst div, Pittsburgh Penn 60-61; Claims adjuster Liberty Mutual Ins Co, Rochester NY 61-67; Dir Wood Lib, Canandaiqua NY 68-. 9: ALA; NYLA. 13: Yes. 14: Admin, lib planning. 15: 29 Weicher st, Rochester NY 14606.

CUMMINS, JULIA A (FULMER). b Mansfield Ohio 15 N 39. 4: A Blair Cummins. 5: Mt Union col 67-61 (Eng, Drama) BA; UWis (Madison) 61-62 (Drama); Syracuse 62-63 MSLS. 7: Child libn Rochester Pub Lib, Rochester NY 63-. 8: Storyteller for children's TV program 67-68. 13: Yes. 14: Child lit, storytelling. 15: 29 Weicher st, Rochester NY 14606.

CUNKLE, ELISABETH (CLARK). b San Francisco. 5: Marin J Col 27-29; UCal 29-31, 48-49, 65 (Eng) AB; Columbia 31-32 BSLS; Chico Sate Col 65; UNev 65. 6: Fr. 7: Page San Francisco Pub Lib 30; NY Pub Lib 31 32; Beverly Hills Pub Lib 32; Sales clerk bk dept J W Robinson Co, Los Angeles 32; Legal sec Randles & Risdon, Los Angeles 33-37; Free-lance writer, newspaper columnist 40-52; San Diego State Col:

Reserve libn 48-49, Asst Campus Lab Sch Libn, ref libn, catlg libn 49-55, Head of catlg dept 56-61; Asst br libn child San Diego Pub Lib 61-62; Humanities libn Chico State Col 62-68; Libn San Francisco Art Inst 69-.09: CalLA (sec Mt Shasta Dist 65-66); SLA; Coun of Planning Libs. 9: ALA; CalLA (sec Mt Shasta Dist 65-66). 10: State Employees Assn; Soc of Arch Histns; Natl Trust for Hist Preservation; California Tomorrow; Sierra Club; Nat Audubon Soc; Cal Roadside Coun; UN Assn; United World Federalists; Nature Conservancy; Cal Native Plant Soc; SPUR; Cal Histl c; Eng Speaking Union; Cal Heritage Coun; World Affairs Coun. 14: Spec libs, art, arch, design, planning. 15: 2355 Leavenworth st apt 305, San Francisco Ca 94133.

CUNNIFF, CAROL ANN. b Milford Mass 28 F 39. 5: Anna Maria Col 57-61 (Hist) BA; Simmons 62-64 MSLS; Assumption Col 65 (Psych). 6: Sp. 7: Sub tchr Nipmuck Reg High Sch, Mendon Mass 61; Apprentice libn Worcester FreePub Lib, Worcester Mass 61-64, Prof asst 64-65, Bkmob libn 65-69; Reg Coord Islandinterrelated Lib Syst RI 69-. 9: MassLA; ALA; YA Bk Review Coop of Mass. 10: YWCA; Bus & Prof Womens Club. 14: Ref, wk wth yp. 15: Barrington Pub Lib, Barrington RI.

CUNNINGHAM, CHARLES T. b Pittsfield Mass 22 Je 17. 5: St Michaels Col (Winooski Vt) 35-37, 40-42 (Phil) PhB; Drexel 49-50 MSLS; Trinity Col (Conn) 56-60 (Hist). 6: Fr, Ital. 7: Prof asst Jackson Pub Lib, Jackson Mich 50-51; Prof asst Hartford Pub Lib, Hartford Conn 52-61; Prof asst Springfield City Lib, Springfield Mass 61-62; Ref libn Framingham Pub Lib, Framingham Mass 62-. 9: CathLA; NELA; MassLA. 14: Ref. 15: 135 Pearl st, Framingham Mass.

CUNNINGHAM, JAY L. b Ithaca NY 8 N 36. 4: Marcia McElderry. 5: Cornell U 54-58 (Soc Sci) BA; UCal (Berkeley) 62-64 MLS. 6: Fr, Ger. 7: Stud asst Cornell U Lib 52-58; Air Defense Off USAF Air Defense Command (1st Lt) 58-62; Trainee LC 64-65, Systems research assoc65-67; Research specialist Inst Lib Res UCal(Berkeley) 67-. 9: ALA; SLA; ASIS (chm San Francisco Chap 68-69); Amer Mgt Assn; Assn for Comp Mach; CalLA (treas 68-69); Soc for Info Display. 10: Air Force Assn; Beta Phi Mu. 11: LC Train Program for Outstanding Grads of Lib Schs, 64-65. 13: Yes. 14: Lib automation & systems analysis, catlg, info retrieval. 15: 225 Columbia ave, Kensington Ca 94708.

CUNNINGHAM, JOSEPH C(ONRAD). b Asheville NC 10 Ja 25. 5: UOre 46-49 (Eng) BA; UCal 49-50 BLS. 6: Fr, Sp, Portu. 7: Steno T-3 US Army, ETO 43-46; Libn I catlg Fresno State Col 50-51; Libn I catlg Los Angeles State Col 51-54; I, II, & III II UTex 54-. 9: ALA. 10: AAUP. 14: Catlg Latin Amer materials. 15: Box 8089, Austin Tex 78712.

CUNNINGHAM, JULIA (MOORHEAD). b McDonald Penn 16 Ap 09. 5: Muskinlum Col 26-30 (Hist) BA; Carnegie 30-31 BS in LS. 7: Carnegie Lib of Pittsburgh: South Side Br 31-36, Ref dept 36-40, 54-58, Pennsylvania Div 59-, Head Pennsylvania Div 63-. 9: ALA; SLA; PennLA. 10: Amer Assn State & Loc Hist. 14: Lo hist, ref. 15: 4733 Centre ave, Pittsburgh 15213.

CUNNINGHAM, KAREN L (FROYD). b Kearney Neb 3 Ap 38. 4: David L Cunningham. 5:Hastings Col 56-60 (Elem Educ, Speech) BA; UColo 60; UErlangen (Nurnberg Germany) 62-63; UWash 64-65 M Libnship. 6: Ger. 7: Asst Libn II I lit dept, Seattle Pub Lib 65-. 9: ALA. 14: Ref, child wk. 15: 6292 NE Radford dr, Seattle Or 98115.

CUNNINGHAM, LARRY L. b Logansport Ind 26 Ja 39. 4: Theresa Damaris. 5: Allegheny Col 57-59 (Hist); Valparaiso U 59-61 (Hist, Philos) AB; Ind U 61-62 (LS) MA, 63- (Adult Educ). 6: Lat. 7: Ref asst Ind U 61-62; Acquis, ref DePauw U 62-63, Period serv libn 63-65; Libn Ind U Northwest Campus (Gary) 65-67; Asst prof of LS, Ind State U 67-68; Dir info serv Bank PRMA, Chicago 68-69; Info serv mgr Cummins Engine Co, Columbus 69-. 9: SLA; ASIS; IllLA. 10: Phi Beta Mu. 12: Ed "Flame" Adult Educ Coun Newsletter, Gary Ind (66-67). 13: Yes. 14: Info center admin, indexing, user studies. 15: Technical Center, Cummins Engine Co Inc, Columbus In 47201.

CUNNINGHAM, LUCILE (FAITH WHITE). b Mobile Ala 12 Ja 05. 5: UCincinnati 23-27 (Math) BA. 7: Br libn Cincinnati Pub Lib 27-31; Circ asst Warder Pub Lib, Springfield Ohio 50-52; Tech libn RCA Home Instruments Lib, Indianapolis 62-. 9: SLA. 10: Indianapolis Art League. 14: Sci & tech, catlg, ref. 15: RCA Consumer Electronics Lib, Bldg 6-223, 600 N Sherman dr, Indianapolis In 46201.

CUNNINGHAM, MYRA (GRACE MOBLEY). b Comanche Okla 27 Ag 25. 4: James R Cunningham. 5: Cameron Jr Col 43-45; Central State Col (Okla) 45-46 (Eng, Hist) BA in Educ; UDenver 4; Sam Houston State 57; UOkl 59-61 MLS. 6: Fr. 7: Libn Duncan High Sch, Duncan Okla 47-48; Tchr Mountain ome High Sch, Ringling Okla 48-49; Tchr Elk City Pub Schs, Elk City Okla 51-52; Asst libn Bryan AFB, Bryan Tex 56-57; Libn Capitol Hill Sr High Sch, Okla City Okla 59-62; Asst Prof of Lib Sci Central State Col (Edmond Okl) 62-. 9: OklaLA (chm Lib Educrs Div 3 yrs); OklaEA. 10: Phi Theta Kappa; Alpha Phi Sigma; Alpha Beta Alpha. 12: "Library Education in Oklahoma (62). 14: Lib educ, sch libnship, instrnal materials centers. 15: 320 Hardy dr, EdmondOk 73034.

CUNNINGHAM, NANCY JEAN (REIDY). b Providence RI 1 Ag 31. 4: John Timothy Cunningham. 5: URI 49-53 (Bus admin) BS, 65-67 MLS. 7: Med sec Providence RI 53; Social wkr State of RI Cranston RI 54; Sch libn Town of N Kingston Elem Schs 66-. 9: ALA; RILA; RISchLA. 14: Sch libnship. 15: PO Box 9, North Kingstown RI 02852.

CUNNINGHAM, VIRGINIA (ADELAIDE). b Bridgeport Ill 23 Ag 10. 4: Charles Howard Cunningham. 5: Stephens Col 28-30 (Eng) AA; UWis 30-32 (Eng) AB, Certif in LS; Columbia 36-40 (Musicology). 6: Fr. 7: Asst City Lib, Wichita Kan 32-33; Asst music div NY Pub Lib 33-34; Asst catlgr & ref libn Columbia U Music Lib 34-40; LC: Catlgr, reviser Descr Catlg Div 42-46, Head Music Sect Copyright Catlg Div 46-56, Head Music Sect Descr Catlg Div 56-. 9: MusLA (pres 56-58); ALA; Internat Assn of Mus Libs (Internat Catlg Code Commsn 52-, chm Catlg & Clsf Com 58-); DCLA67; DCLA. 10: LWV. 12: "Rules for Full Cataloging v 3 in "Code International de Catalogage de la Musique (69) Contrib to & tr of v 1-2. 13: Yes. 14: Catlg & clsf of music. 15: Descr Catlg Div LC, Wash DC 20540.

CUNNINGHAM, WILLIAM DEAN. b Kansas City Mo 9 Ag 31. 4: Mary P Carson. 5: UKan 56-59 (Psych) BA; UTex 61-63 MLS. 6: Fr. 7: Med admin specialist (S/Sgt) USAF 52-56; Libn undergrad lib UKan 59-60; Ser libn Topeka Pub Lib, Topeka Kan 60-61, Hd ext serv 63-64; Chief lib serv FAA Reg Lib, Kan City Mo 64-66; Dir adult serv Topeka Pub Lib, Topeka Kan 66-68; Lib serv program off US Off of Educ, Kan City Mo 68-. 9: ALA; CathLA (Legis Chm MidW Unit 67); KanLA (Exec Coun 67); MoLA (Federal Lib Com Recruitment Task Force 65-66). 13: Yes. 14: Adult serv, ref, y-a serv. 15: 7711 E 90th, Kansas City Mo 64138.

CUPRYS, GRACE M. b Camden NJ 17 Je 43. 5: Rutgers 61-65 (For lang) BA, 65-66 MLS. 6: Ger. 7: Catlgr E Stroudsburg State Col 66-. 9: ALA. 10: AAUP. 14: Catlg. 15: 420 N 27th st, Camden NJ 08105.

CURLEY, ARTHUR V. b Boston 22 Ja 38. 4: Dorothy Nyren. 5 Harvard 55-59 (Govt) BA; Simmons 60-61 (LS) MS. 7: Adult Serv Wker Boston Pub Lib 59-61; Dir Avon Pub Lib, Avon Mass 61-64; Dir Palatine Pub Lib, Palatine Ill 64-68; Dir Montclair Pub Lib, Montclair NJ 68-. 8: Dir, Survey of Mass lib resources, 63-64; Exec dir, Nat Lib Week, Mass 64; Planning Coord, Ill Reg Lib System No 5, 65; Reviewer, Library Journal, 65-. 9: ALA-PLA (Cost of Lib Serv Com 67-68); MassLA (Exec Bd 63-64); Mass Pub Lib Adminrs (chm Standards Com 62-64); IllLA (Exec Bd 66-67, Coord Fed Legisl 66-67); Lib Admin Coun No Ill; NJLA; NYLA. 10: Urban Coalition; ACLU. 11: Dorothy Canfield Fisher Award, 64. 12: "Modern Romance Literatures; A Library of Literary Criticism" (67). 13: Yes. 14: Admin, reg planning, bk sel, intel freedom. 15: Montclair Pub Lib, 50 S Fullerton, Montclair NJ 07042.

CURLEY, DOROTHY NYREN. b Portland Me 29 S 27. 4: Arthur Vincent Curley. 5: Boston U 47-52 (Romance Lit) BA, 53-54 (Amer Lit) MA; Simmons 60-62 MS in LS. 6: Fr. 7: Head serv dept Ginn & Co, Boston 53-54; Dir S Cornelia Young Lib, Daytona Beach Fla 55-57; Br libn Newton Free Lib, Newton Mass 58; Town Libn Concord Free Pub Lib, Concord Mass 59-64; Asst to the dir publ dept ALA, Chicago 64-65; ChiefLibn Northbrook Pub Lib, Northbrook Ill 65-68; Coord Adult Serv Brooklyn Pub Lib, Brooklyn NY 68-. 9: ALA; Ill LA; MassLA; NYLA; Mass Lib Admins (pres 62-63); Charles River Lib Club (pres 63). 10: Phi Beta Kappa. 12: "A Library of Literary Criticism: Modern American Literature (1st ed 60, 2nd ed 61, 3rd ed 63); Ed "Bay State Librarian (60-61); "A Library of Literary Criticism; Romance Literature" (67). 13: Yes. 14: Admin, bk sel. 15: Brooklyn Pub Lib, Grand Army Plaza, Brooklyn NY 11238.

CURLEY, ELMER F. b Frankford Springs Penn. 5: UPittsburgh 61 (Music, Hist) BA; Carnegie 62 MLS;

UPittsburgh 64 (LS) Advanced Certif. 6: Fr, Ital. 7: Ref asst UPittsburgh 62-64; Ref libn SUNY(Stony Brook) 64-. 8b Frankford Springs Penn 13 Ja 29. 07: 67; Hd pub serv UNev (Las Vegas) 67-, TchrLib Sci Sch of Educ. 9: ALA; NevLA; Amer Musicological Assn. 10: Medieval Acadof Amer; AAUP. 14: Ref, tchg. 15: 1170 Maryland cl apt 4, Las Vegas Nv 89109.

CURLEY, WALTER W. b Boston 29 Mr 23. 4: Marie T Sullivan. 5: Northeastern 40-47 (Bus Admin) BS; Simmons 49-50 MSLS. 7: Providence Pub Lib: Ref libn 50-55, Bus manager 56-60, Asst Dir 60-61; Dir Suffolk Coop Lib System, Patchogue NY 61-66; Consul Arthur D Little Inc, Cambridge Mass 67-. 8: Consul on 14 lib bldgs (assisted Nelson & Assocs of Mich); Guest Lecturer Simmons 55-; Consul State Libraries Ky, NC, Va, Mass, VT, NH, NY & Fla. 9: ALA (chm Insur Libs Com 60-65, sec Exhib Round Table 64-66; RILA (chm Lib Devel Com 55-60, pres 56-58): NELA (pres 60); NYLA (chm Lib Devel Com 64-66). 10: Rotary; Jr C of C; US Army Reserve (Maj). 13: Yes. 14: Data proc, lib devel, bldg consul. 15: 270 Pelham Island rd, Wayland Ma 01778.

CURRAN, CHARLES C. b Pittsburgh Penn 21 Je 34. 4: Roseann Cappella. 5: Duquesne 52-56 (Pol Sci) BEd, 59-62 (LS) MEd; Rutgers 64-67 MLS, 67 (LS). 7: Infantryman US Army Presidential Honor Guard, Arlington Va 57-58; Tchr Montour Jr-Sr High Sch, McKees Rocks Penn 58-61; Libn & asst coach Snowden High Sch, Library Penn 61-63; Libn Hanover Park High Sch, Hanover NJ 63-65; Ref libn E Stroudsburg State Col 65-. 8: Visiting instr dept of Libnship West MichU summer 68. 9: ALA; NJSLA (recruitment chm 65); MorrisCoSchLA (chm, NJ 65). 10: E Stroudsburg State Col Faculty Assn. 13: Yes. 14: Reader serv. 15: 600 Clearview ave, Stroudsburg Pa 18360.

CURRAN, NANCY (RIEDEL) . b Milwaukee 21 Ja 31. 4: Carleton Edgar Curran Jr. 5: UWis ext 48-50; UWis (Madison) 51-53 (Eng) BS in Educ, 54 (LS) MS; Educ Media Inst East Ill U summer 67. 6: Sp. 7: Libn I UWis Lib Madison) 54-56; Libn Ozarks Reg Lib, Clarksville rk 56-57; Asst libn Ark Polytech Col 57-66; Elem unit libn Charleston Comm Unit C-1 66-. 9: ALA; ArkLA; IllASchL; IllLA; IllEA. 10: Wis Lib Sch Alumni Assn. 13: Yes. 14: Ref, lib educ, sch libs. 15: 2119 Reynolds dr, Charleston Il 61920.

CURRAN, ROSEMARY C. b NYC 16 D 06. 5: Rutgers 25-29 (Lat, Span) BA; Middlebury Col summers 29-32 (Span) MA; St Johns U 51-55 MLS; C W Post (Guidance, LS). 6: Sp, Fr, Lat. 7: Span tchr Leonia High Sch, Leonia NJ 41-43; Sec Chile Amer Asso, NY 44- 46; Span-Lat tchr Elmsford (NY) High Sch 46-48; Libn Central Islip (NY) High Sch 48-. 9: NYLA; NY Tchrs Assn; Nassau-Suffolk Sch Libns. 10: AAUW: Sigma Delta Pi. 15: 72 Calton ave, Central Islip NY.

CURRIE, CLIFFORD. b Ramsgate Kent England 24 N 18. 5: LondonU 36-39 (Mod Lang) BA, 45-46 (Libnship) Diploma, FLA; Cambridge 47-50 (Law) BA, LLB, MA; Harvard 50-51. 6: Fr, Ger, Ital. 7: Staff interpreter War Off (Intelligence Corps), London & In Field 39-45; Ref libn St Pancras Pub Libs, London England 46-47; Deputy city libn Cambridge City Libs, Cambridge England 47-53; Libn Bromley Pub Libs, London England 53-59; Libn Imperial Col of Sci & Tech, London England 59-68; Exec dir Canadian Lib assn, Ottawa Ont 68-. 9: The Lib Assn, London (sec Univ & Res Sect 60-65; chm East Br 53); Sec, Intl Assn Tech Univ Libs (sec 63-67). 10: Soc of Bkmen, London; Authors' Club, London. 12: "Be a Librarian" (58); "Prospects in Librarianship" (63); Ed -canadian Library Journal". 13: Yes. 14: Lib arch and relationship of planning to wk organ. 15: Canadian Library Assn 63 Sparks st, Ottawa 4 Ont Can.

CURRIE, HILDEGARD I. b Bernburg Germany 20 Je 23. 4: Harold G Currie. 5: Lib Sch (Leipzig Germany) 43- 45 Lib Sci degree; UAriz 59- (Educ) Ed. 6: Ger. 7: Lib asst Pub Lib, Leipzig Germany 44-45; Libn Spec Serv, Okinawa 53-56; Libn Ft Huachuca Acc Schs, Ft Huachuca Ariz 59-66, Libn (Phy Sci & Eng) Tech Lib 66-. 8: Transl of tech materials from German into English, Ft Huachuca Ariz. 9: ALA; Ariz State LA. 14: Ref, catlg, readers serv. 15: Box 1317, Sierra Vista Ariz.

CURRIER, GERTRUDE A (EPPING). b Days Creek Ore 6 Jl 16. 4: Roy D Currier. 5: Walla Walla Col 35-37 (Ed); UOre 68 (Libnship). 7: Off mgr Star Plumbing & Heating, N Bend Ore 51-54; Nursing companion Priv, N Bend 55-57; Farmer's Ins Group, N Bend: Off mgr 57-60, Ins agent 57-60; N Bend Pub Lib: Lib asst 61-63, Children's libn 63-65, Libn 65-. 8: Grant from Ore State Lib on a commun lib improvement prog as a spec student 68. 9: ALA; OreLA; PNLA. 10: Zonta International; Bus & Prof Women; Grange; First Christian Church of North Bend (Fin sec 50-55, hd of child dept 46-50); Deaconess 50-. 14: Admin. 15: PO Box 643, North Bend Or 97459.

CURRIER, LURA (GIBBONS). b Erie Kan 28 S 12. 5: USo Miss 37 (Eng, Soc Studies) BS; Tex Woman's U 40 BLS. 7: Tchr Miss Pub Sch 32-39; Ref catlg libn Laretama Pub Lib, Corpus Christi Tex 40-43; Asst libn Tom Green Co Lib, San Angelo Tex 43-45; Asst libn Snohomish Co Lib, Everett Wash 45-47; Libn Pub Lib, Mt Vernon Wash 48-49; Field Rep miss Lib Commsn, Jackson Miss 50-54, Dir 55-67; Lib consul 68; Vis Lect UWash summers 67, 68, 69; Lib Specialist Wash State Lib 69-. 8: Lib Survey of Spokane and Spokane Co Wash in collab with Pub Admin Serv 68; Fiscal Analy of Tacoma-Pierce Co Surveys, Wash State 67-68. 9: ALA; (var coms); -PLA (pres 59); -AHIL (chm Research Com 67-68). 11: John Cotton Dana Award 49. 14: Lib devel, pub rel, lib educ, admin. 15: 316 cooper rd, Jackson Ms 39212.

CURRIER, MARGARET. b Cambridge Mass 8 Jl 10. 5: Mt Holyoke 27-31 (Ger) AB; UMich 34-35 ABLS. 6: Fr, Ger, Sp. 7: Catlgr Yale U Lib 31-39; Curator of the catalogue Harvard Col Lb 39-45; Peabody Museum of Archaeol & Ethnol Harvard U: Catlgr 45-46, Act libn 46-48, Libn 48-. 9: ALA; SLA (Boston chap; pres 57-58, Advis Coun 66-67); NELA; NE Tech Serv Libns. 10: Appalachian Mountain Club; Mass Audubon Soc. 13: Yes. 14: Acquis, catlg, ref, bibliog. 15: 19 West st, Belmont Ma 02178.

CURRIER, NELL. b Paris Tenn 21 Je 14. 5: Randolph-Macon Womans Col 32-36 (Math) AB; UIll 46-47 BSLS. ; NDEA Inst USC summer 66. 7: Eng tchr Grove High Sch, Paris Tenn 41-43; Eng tchr Brooke Hill Sch, Birmingham Ala 43-45; Libn Swanson Jr High Sch, Arlington Va 47-50; Libn Washington-Lee High Sch, Arlington Va 50-56; Eng tchr Grove High Sch, Paris Tenn 56-57, Math tchr 57-58; Libn Grove Jr High Sch, Paris Tenn 58-. 9: ALA (Life mem); NEA; TennEA (chm Lib Sect 68-69); W TennEA (chm Lib Sect 62-63). 10: Delta Kappa Gamma; Beta Phi Mu; Tenn Hist Soc; Henry Co Hist Soc. 14: Reading guidance for yp. 15: 317 Walnt st, Paris Tenn 38242.

CURRY, ADELE ELIZABETH GAYLORD. b Winnipeg Man Can 2 D 11. 5: Toronto 34 (Eng, Hist) BA; UMan 36 (Hist) MA; Toronto 41 BLS. 7: UTronto: Circ 41-51, Ref 52-56, Sci & med 56-65; Ontario Cancer Inst Lib, Toronto 64-. 9: CanLA; MedLA; SLA. 15: Ontario Cancer Inst Lib, 500 Sherbourne st, Toronto 5 Can.

CURRY, EMILIE S (DONALD) (MRS). b Irvington NJ 9 N 10. 5: Douglass 29-30. 7: Child libn Verona Pub Lib, Verona NJ 31-40; Sch libn Kimberley Sch, Montclair NJ 45-53; Dir Cedar Grove Pub Lib, Cedar Grove NJ 54-. 9: ALA; NJLA. 10: Nat Trust Hist Preservation; British Nat Trust; NJ Hist Soc; Essex Co Dirs Gp. 15: Cedar Grve Pub Lib, Municipal Plaza, Cedar Grove NJ.

CURRY, MAUREEN ELLEN. b Hornell NY 13 Ag 33. 5: SUNY at Geneseo 50-54 (Lib) BS; Syracuse 55-57 (LS) Certif; Public Librarian's Professional Certificate 62. 7: Sch libn N Syracuse Central Schs 54-57; Ref libn Main Lib Syracuse U summers 56-57; Sch libn Orchard Park Central Schs 57-59; 4th gr tchr Long Beach Unified Schs, Long Beach Cal 59-60; Children's libn Long Beach Pub Lib, Long Beach Cal 60-62; Field serv libn Chautauqua-Cattaraugus Lib Sys, Jamestown NY 62-67; Asst dir Chautauqua- Cattaraugus Lib Sys, Jamestown NY 67-. 9: ALA; NYLA (treas child & YA Serv Sec). 10: Fortnightly Cath Daughters of Amer; Delta Kappa Gamma. 14: Child serv, consul to mem libs of pub lib system. 15: 632 Prendergast ave, Jamestown NY 14701.

CURRY, NANNIE (DAVIS). b Crossville Ala 8 Ag 26. 4: Donald Ray Curry Sr. 5: State Tchrs Col (Jacksonville Ala) 43-46 (Math, Sci) BS; Peabody 46-47 BS LS. 7: Asst libn State Tchrs Col (Jacksonville Ala) summer 46, 47-48; Catlgr Ala Polytech Inst 48-53; Ref asst Carnegie Inst of Tech 54-55; Tech serv libn Coleman Lib Callaway Mills Co, LaGrange Ga 55-59, 60-68; Libn Troup High Sch, LaGrange Ga 68-. 9: GaLA; SELA. 10: Pi Gamma Mu; Kappa Delta Pi. 14: Catlg, ref. 15: 201 N Lee st, LaGrange Ga 30240.

CURRY, SONIA (LISSEY). b Regina Sask Can 19 S 24. 5: USask 40-44 (Eng) BA (cum laude); Toronto 44-45 BLS. 6: Fr, Ger, Ukrainian. 7: Catlgr Pub Lib, Saskatoon Sask 45-46; Chief Libn Pub Lib, N Battleford Sask 47-. 9: CanLA; SaskLA. 10: Univ Womans Club. 14: Catlg, high sch libnship. 15: Pub Lib, No Battleford Sask Can.

CURTIS, ANNE MARY KATHLEEN (PEPALL). b Arvida PQ Can 5 Jl 42. 4: John Margeson Curtis. 5: Neuchatel Jr Col (Neuchatel Switzerland) 59-60; Queen'sU 60-63 (Pol Sci) BA; McGill 63-64 BLS. 6: Fr. 7: Teller Bank of Nova Scotia, Montreal summers 61-63; Docs libn Harvard Col Lib 65-67, Chief docs libn 67-. 14: Govt docs, ref. 15: 359 Harvard st, Cambridge Ma 02138.

CURTIS, GEORGE A. b Indianapolis 16 Ja 17. 4: Jean Adams. 5: Btler U 35-40 (Eng, Speech, Religion) AB; Wabash Col 43 (Speech); Chicago 48 BLS, 51 (LS) MA. 7: Various duties Indianapolis Pub Lib 35-42; Asst stacks supt UCicago Lib 47-48; Chief f bk serv John Crerar Lib, Chicago 49-50; Asst libn E Chicago Pub Lib, E Chicago Ind 50-51; Head Libn LaPorte Pub & Co Libs, LaPorte Ind 52-62; Dir Washtenaw Co Lib, Ann Arbor Mich 62-63; Head of personnel & commun rels Wayne Co Lib, Wayne Mich 63-66; Dir River Bend Lib Syst, Moline Ill 66-. 8: Bldg consul for 8 libs; Made one general lib survey. 9: ALA; IllLA. 10: Rotary Club. 12: Ed "Focus on Indiana Libraries (54-55). 14: Pub lib admin. 15: 2503 29th ave, Rock Island Il 61201.

CURTIS, MARY ALZOA. b Trempealeau Wis 25 My 14. 5: UWash 33-37 (Gen Lit) BA, 37-38 (LS) BA. 7: 1st asst Puyallup Pub Lib, Puyallup Wash 38-40; Chief Libn VA Hosp Lib, American Lake Wash 40-. 8: Mem Statewide Advisory to Wash State Lib Commsn 68. 9: ALA; PNLA; WashLA (Hosp & Institution Lib Com 67-68; Subcom on Educ & Training 67); MedLA. 10: Snohomish Co Museum Assn; Tacoma-Pierce Co Lib Coun. 14: Hosp libs. 15: Va Hosp Lib, American Lake Tacoma Wa 98493.

CURTIS, RONALD ALLEN. b Tulsa Okla 7 Ap 40. 4: Gloria Jean Hockett Curtis. 5: Northeastern State (Okla) 58-62 (Soc Studies) BA in Educ; Okla State U 62 (Amer Hist); UOkla 62-63 MLS. 6: Sp. 7: Stud libn Tulsa Pub Lib, Tulsa Okla 54-58; Stud libn Northeastern State Col Lib (Okla) 58-62; Stud libn Okla State U Lib 62; Stud libn Tulsa Pub Lib, Tulsa Okla summer 62; Asst libn Central State Col (Okla) Lib 63-68, Automation libn 68-. 9: OklaLA; OklaEA. 12: 'Oklahoma Books & Oklahoma Authors' in "Oklahoma Librarians" 64-67. 14: Acquis, govt docs, automation, ser. 15: 406 Winding lane, Edmond Okla 73034.

CURTISS, JULIANNE L. b New aven Conn 16 D 26. 5: Colby Jr Col 44-46 (Liberal Arts) AA; So Conn State Col 53-56 BS in LS. 7: Sec ed off ""Jour of Studies on Alcohol Yale U Dept of Applied Physiol 49-53; Pub Lib, W Haven Conn: Ref asst 56-57, Br libn 57-58, Catlgr 58-63, Asst libn 60-63; Asst libn & catlgr New Col 63-66; Elem sch libn Bd of Pub Instr, Sarasota 63-. 9: FlaLA; Sarasota City TA. 14: Catlg. 15: 2155 Wood st apt B9, Sarasota Fl 33577.

CURTSINGER, EULA B. b Randlett Okla 28 D 14. 5: UArk 59-62 (Eng) BS Ed; Tex Womans U 62-65 MLS. 6: Sp. 7: Sales clerk Sterling Drug Co, Prairie Grove Ark 50-62; Libn Prairie Grove Sch Dist, Prairie Grove Ark 62-68; Asst libn 4th Army SpSer Div, Ft Walters Tex 68-. 9: ALA-AASchL; NEA; ArkLA. 10: AAUW. 14: Wk with yp & child, admin. 15: 505 N W3rd ave, Mineral Wells Tx 76067.

CURVEY, MARY FRANCES. b Portland Ore 26 D 44. 5: SW Baptist Col 62-64 (Liberal Arts) AA; Central Mo State Col 64-66 (Educ, Bio) BS in Ed; UIll 67-68 (LS) MS. 6: Sp. 7: Tchr Raytown Pub Sch, Raytown Mo 66-67; Asst ref libn UKan Med Ctr (Kan City) 68-. 9: MedLA. 10: Beta Phi Mu. 13: Yes. 14: Ref, rare bks. 15: 3749 Booth 3, Kansas City Ks 66103.

CUSEO, ALLAN A. b Rochester NY 9 N 40. 5: Brockport State Col 59-61 (Lang Arts); Geneseo State Col 61-63 BLS, 65-69 (LS) MLS. 6: Fr, Ital. 7: Asst libn Rochester Pub Lib, Rochester NY 63-65; Head Libn Sr High Sch Gates Chili Sch Dist, NY 65-. 8: Drama dir Gates Chili Central Sch. 9: ALA; NYLA. 10: PTA; Rochester Commun Players; Irondequoit Commun Theatre; Rochester Repertory Co. 14: Arts, theatre, bks, sch libs. 15: 260 Ballad ave, Rochester NY 14626.

CUSHMAN, JEROME. b Chicago 1 Je 14. 4: Hannah Trilinsky. 5: St Joseph (Mo) Jr Col 32-33; Park Col 38-40 (Eng Lit) AB; LSU 41 BS in LS. 7: Manager travel libs Mo State Lib 41, Ref libn 42; Chief Libn Salina Pub Lib, Salina Kan 46-61; Chief Libn New Orleans Pub Lib 61-. 8: Lecturer in Child Lit, Sch of Lib Serv, UCLA Eng Dept, Los Angeles 65-. 9: ALA (Exec Bd); CalLA. 10: ACLU; Bnai BRith. 12: Juvenile fiction, "Marvellas Hobby (62). 13: Yes. 14: Pub lib admin, tchg child lit. 15: 7447 Sausalito ave, Canoga Park Cl 91304.

CUSTER, ARLINE (KERN). b Billings Okla 27 S 09. 4: Benjamin Allen Custer. 5: UCLA 28-30 (Amer Hist) BA; UCal(Berkeley) 30-31 Certif in LS; Columbia summer 41 (LS); Claremont Col 34-41 (Comparative Lit). 7: Catlgr Claremont Col Lib 31-42; Catlgr UCLA Lib 43; Catlgr & accessioner UCal Lib (Berkeley) 43-44; Research-ref spec Off of Strategic Serv, Lat Amer Div, Wash DC 44-46; Chief catlgr US Dept of State Intelligence Ref Div, Wash DC 46; Libn Detroit Inst of Arts Lib 47-56; Achivist Archives of Amer Art, Detroit 54-56; Spec projs catlgr US Dept of the Interior Lib, Wash DC 57-58; Researcher & indexer US Lincoln Sesquicentennial Commsn, Wash DC 58-60; Ed LC Presidential Papers 60; Catlgr US Post Off Dept Lib, Wash DC 61-62; Indexer & head Mss Sect LC Descr Catlg Div 63-. 9: ALA-RTSD (Catlg & clsf sect; chm bylaws com 65-67; chm Margaret Mann Citation Com 68-69);-RSD (Bd mem Hist Sect 68-71); ACRL (Rare Bks Sect chm Mss collection com); Manuscript Soc; SAA; DCLA; Los Angeles Reg Group of Catlgrs (chm 40-41); Mich Reg Group of Catlgrs (chm 55-56); Potomac Tech Proc Libns; DCL 10: AHA; Amer Assn State & Loc Hist; West Hist Assn; Oral Hist Assn; Org Amer Histns. 12: Comp Index to "Lincoln Day by Day; Ed "National Union Catalog of Manuscript Collections (62-). 13: Yes. 14: Catlg, org of mss, art libnship, indexing. 15: 9305-20th ave, Adelphi Md 20783.

CUSTER, BENJAMIN A(LLEN). b Lima Ohio 16 Ja 12. 4: Arline Kern. 5: Oberlin Col 27-31 (Eng) AB (magna cum laude); West Res 31-32 BS in LS; UCal(Berkeley) 43-44 (Area & lang). 6: Fr, Ger, Ital, Russian, Sp. 7: Catlgr & clsf NY Pub Lib 32-39; Head of catlg dept UCLA 39-43; US Army Signal Corps Cryptanalysis 43-44; Head Slavic Catlg Proj LC 44-46; Processing dir Detroit Pub Lib 46-56; Ed Dewey Decimal Clsf LC 56-. 9: ALA (numerous assignment in ALA & its divs as div pres & chm &/or mem of bds & coms, etc); ASIS; SLA; Lib Assn (Gt Brit); CalLA; MichLA; DCLA; etc. 10: Phi Beta Kappa. 11: Melvil Dewey Medal, 59. 12: Ed "Dewey Decimal Classification 16th & 17th ed (58, 65); abridged 8th & 9th ed (59, 65). 13: Yes. 14: Clsf, catlg, tech serv. 15: 9305-20th ave, Adelphi Md 20783.

CUSTER, CHARLES D. b Waynesburg Penn 4 N 37. 5: Waynesburg Col 56-60 (Hist) AB; Carnegie 60-61 MLS. 6: Sp. 7: Ref libn Washington & Jefferson Col 61-65; Libn Ind-Purdue Reg Campus, Ft Wayne Ind 65-68; Exec dir Capital Dist Lib Coun, Schenectady NY 68-. 9: ALA; NYLA. 10: AAUP; AHA; Beta Phi Mu; Allen Co-Fort Wayne Hist Assn; Lepidopterists Soc. 14: Readers serv, interlib loans, archives, consortia, admin. 15: 175 S Richhillst, Waynesburg Pa 15370.

CUTCHER, DANIEL JOSEPH. b Detroit 26 O 39. 5: St Michaels Col of UToronto 58-63 (Classics, Fr) BA; West Mich U 63-65 (LS) MA; Wayne State U summer 65. 6: Fr, Lat, Gk. 7: Catlg, ref, order Oakland U Lib 65-67; Ref Cal State Poly Col 67-, admin asst 67-68, Instr 68-69. 9: ALA; MichLA (Jr Mem Round Table). 10: Dramatic Arts Film Soc; AFT; Adv Col Union Fine Arts Coun. 14: Ref. 15: c/o 18441 Lahser rd, Detroit 48219.

CUTHBERT, EVELYN R. b Sumter SC. 5: Allen U 31 (Educ) AB; NC Col (Durham) 46 BLS; Rutgers 61 (Human Rel). 6: Fr, Ger. 7: Tchr Whittemore High Sch, Conway SC 33; Tchr Lincoln High Sch, Sumter SC 34,libn 42; Libn Lincoln Pub Lib, Sumter SC 43-66; Libn Lincoln High Sch, Sumter SC 69. 9: ALA; NEA; SELA; SCLA; SCEA; Sumter CoLA; Sumter Co TA. 10: Mem of Religious &charitable Orgs; YWCA. 14: Catlg, ref, wk with yp. 15: 502 N Main st, Sumter SC 29150.

CUTLER, CAROL (COMBS). b Columbia NC 20 F 44. 4: Guy A Cutler. 5: E Car Col 62-65 (Primary Educ) BS; UNC (Chapel Hill) MS in LS. 6: Fr. 7: Libn Peace Col 66-68; Asst catlg libn D H Hill Lib NC StateU 68-. 10: Beta Phi Mu. 12: Ed UNC Sch of Lib Sci Alumni Assn Bulletin. 13: Yes. 15: Rt 1 Box 638-10, Cary NC 27511.

CUTLER, DOROTHY RUTH. b Hood River Ore 5 N 17. 5: Willamette U 36-40 (Amer Hist, Pub Admin) BA; UWash 41 (LS) BA; UIll 52 (LS) MS. 6: r. 7: Lib asst Salem Pub Lib, Salem Ore 41-43; Libn Spec Serv US Army, Pacific Theatre 43-46; Ref libn Contra Costa Co Lib, Martinez Cal 46-51; Ref libn UIll Lib (Urbana) 51-52; Lib consul Wash State Lib, Olympia Wash 52-57; Demonstration dir Columbia River Reg Lib, Wenatchee Wash 57-61; Dir lib development Wash State Lib 61-. 9: ALA (Coun);-AAStateL (Standards Revision Com); PLA (Adv Com; Syst Study); WashLA (Lib Devel Com); PNLA. 10: AAUW; LWV. 11: Soroptimist Club Distinguished Serv Award, 61. 13: Yes. 14: Lib devel, interlib coop, info netwk. 15: Washington State Lib, Olympia Wa 98501.

CUTLER, KARAN DAVIS (ELIZABETH). b 1 O 42. 4: Stephen Joel Cutler. 5: SoIllU 60-63, 64-65 (Govt) AB; UMich 65- AMLS; (Amer Culture) AM. 6: Sp, Fr. 7: Resident fellow UMich Pilot Project 65-67, Resident fellow Residential Col 67-68, Asst Dpt of Eng 67-69; Instr East Mich U Dept of Eng 68-69; Oberlin College Lib, Oberlin Ohio 69-70. 9: ALA. 10: UMich Lib Sci Alumni; Beta Phi Mu; Pi Sigmo Alpho; Amer Studies Assn. 14: Bibliog, rare bks. 15: Oberlin Col Lib, Oberlin Oh 44074.

CUTLIP, ARTHUR. b Cleveland Ohio 30 O 13. 4: Florence De Luca. 5: Adelbert Col West Res U 31-37 (Eng) BA; West Res 38-40 (Eng) MA, 50-52 MLS. 6: Sp, Fr, Ital, Portu. 7: (M/Sgt) US Army Infantry, US & Europe 41-45; Ref documents asst West Res U Lib 50-53; Chief documents div Miami Pub Lib, Miami Fla 54-. 9: FlaLA. 13: Yes. 14: Govt publs, ref, bibliog, maps. 15: Documents Div Miami Pub Lib, 1 Biscayne blvd, Miami Fla 33132.

CUTTER, REV JAMES RAYMOND OSFS. b Lockport NY 20 Jl 37. 5: Catholic U 62 (Philos) AB; De Sales Hall Sch of Theol 62-66 (Theol); Villanova summers (LS). 6: Fr, Lat. 7: Tchr & libn Father Judge High Sch, Phila 58-60; Head Libn De Sales Hall Sch of Theol Lib 62-66; Libn NE Cath High Sch, Phila 66-67; Tchr and libn St Francis De Sales High Sch, Toledo Ohio 67-69. 9: CathLA (High Sch Lib Div). 14: Admin. 15: 5001 East ave, Hyattsville Md 20782.

CVELJO, KATHERINE. b Farrell Penn. 5: Gymnasium (Sibenik Yugoslavia) 42 Diploma; UZagreb Faculty of Econ & Bus Admin (Yugoslavia) 46-51 MS; West Res 58-59 MSLS, (Slavic Langs & Lit) MS, 69-. 6: Croatian, Ital, Fr, Russian. 7: GlavnaprodKnin-Zagreb Acct 44-47; Ref libn sci tech dept Detroit Pub Lib 59-60; Head Libn DeptLibs Ohio State U 60-63; Ref libn Bus Info Dept Cleveland Pub Lib 63-65; Ref libn WestRes U 65-67; Visiting Prof Sch of Lib Sci SUNY (Geneseo) summer 68; Lecturer West Res68, summer 69. 9: ALA; SLA. 10: Phi Beta Mu; Phi Delta Gamma; Amer CROATIAN Acad Club. 14: Ref, bibliog, Slavic & East European area studies, Comp, Lib,Educ. 15: 2034 Cornell rd No. 25, Cleveland Oh 44106.

CYBULSKI, MARLYS (ANDING). b Eden Prairie Minn 3 F 33. 4: John Cybulski. 5: John Muir Jr Col 50-52 (Fine Arts) AA; UCLA 52-55 (TA-Motion picture production) BA; UCLA 60 (Info storage & ret); USoCal 60-61 (LS). 7: Stud asst UCLA Lib 54-55; Douglas Aircraft & Co, El Segundo Cal: Engr, adm libn, ref libn, catlgr 56-59, Hd libn 59-62, Hd libn Long Beach Cal 62-67; NAmer Rockwell Autonetics Div, Anaheim Cal: ERIC lexicrographer, index abstractor 67-68, Lib automation rep 68-. 8: Divisional admin of design, devel, implementation of Douglas Company de Automated Info Retrieval System 59-67; Panel member l-v presentation on spec libs 65; panel member on lib automation, STWP 11th annual meeting 64; lecturer on lib automation STWP writers' wkshop, Long Beach Cal 63; guest lecturer Lib Sch USoCal 61. 9: SLA (Nat Recr Com 69-71; SoCal Chap chm Hospit Com 68-69, chm Recruitment Com 66-68, mem-Hospitality Com 65-66; Aerospace Div: Aerospace Thesaurus Eval Gp 64-65); ASIS; SoCal Interorg Com for Libnship Recr at annual Los Angeles Career Guidance Ctr 66-68. 10: Nat Mgement Assn; Delta Kappa Alpha. 14: Lib & info ctr automation, systems analysis & eval info retrieval, netwks, interactive systems, lit search, pub relations. 15: 1977 Kornat dr, Costa Mesa Ca 92626.

CYLKE, FRANK KURT. b New Haven Conn 13 F 32. 4: Mary Zembroski. 5: UConn 49-53 (Eng) BA; Pratt 54-57 MLS; FairfieldU 61 (Educ); So Conn State Col 62 (Eng); AmericanU 68-69 (Operations Research). 6: Sp. 7: Asst YaleU Lib 48-54; Trainee NY Pub Lib 55-56; Fellow CCNY 56-57; Libn Graham-Eckes Sch, Palm Beach Fla 57-58; Ref asst pub lib, Bridgeport Conn 58-61; Hd ref & readers serv Free Pub Lib, New Haven Conn 61-65; Chief pub serv pub lib, Providence 65-66; Asst libn 66-68; Research assoc & act chief US Off Educ Lib & Info Sci Research Program, Wash DC 68-. 8: Instr; URI Grad Lib Sch 67-68, US ADP Mgt Train Ctr 68-69; Mem, Corp, East Greenwich (RI) Free Lib 66-68. 9: Internatl Fed for Documentation; ALA; US Com on Sci & Tech Info (Exec sec Panel on Educ and Training); ConnLA; DCLA; MassLA; NELA; RILA (v-pres 66, pres-elect 67); Priv Libs Assn. 10: C of C; Torch Club; Turks Head; Branford Yacht Club; Marine Hist Assn; Dinghy Cruising Assn; RI Marine Soc. 12: Ed ""Rhode Island Marine Association Newsletter (66-68); Ed Captains Shelf ""Soundings (64-66). 13: Yes. 14: Ref, research, admin, rare bks. 15: 400 Maryland ave SW, Wash DC 20202.

CYPHER, PRISCILLA (WEEKS FOSTER). b Boston 23 D 8. 4: Stanley J Cypher. 5: Wellesley 36-40 (Eng Lit) BA; Columbia 40-42 (Eng Lit) MA; Pratt 59-61 MLS; Teachers Col Columbia 59-69, NYU 69-. 7: Proofreade Westminister Press, Phila 42; Copy ed E P Dutton Co, NY 42-45, 42-59 free lance; Sch libn Armonk Schs K-9, Armonk NY 59-63; Hd Secondary Libs, Byram Hills Central Schs, Armonk NY 64-. 9: ALA; NYLA; Sch Libns of Southeast NY (pres 68-70, regl rep Exec Bd 68-69, chm Nomin Com 69). 14: Sch libs. 15: 2 Maryland ave, Armonk NY 10504.

CYR, BETTY CECILE. b Flint Mich 30 My 36. 5: Flint Jr Col 55-57 (Eng) AA; UMich 57-59 (Eng) AB; UMich 61-64 AMLS. 6: Fr. 7: Circ clerk UMich Flint Col Lib 59-61; Catlgr C S Mott Lib, Flint Mich 61-63, Head catlgr 64-68, Hd spec serv 68-. 9: Flint Lib Club; MichLA. 10: Urban League of Flint. 14: Catlg, ref, pub serv. 15: 2300 Snover rd, Mayville Mi 48744.

CYR, MRS HELEN LOUISE (WHEELER). b Oakland Cal 18 N 26. 4: Gordon Conrad Cyr. 5: UCal(Berkeley) 47 (Music) AB, 48 (Educ) Gen Secondary Credential, 54 BLS. 6: Fr. 7: Oakland Pub Schs, Oakland Cal: Tchr 49-53, Libn 54-63, Dir of Lbs 63-65, Dir of Instrl Media 65-. 8: Consul ESEA Title II Wkshop, Cal State Dept of Educ, Bur of A-V & Lib Educ 69;Cal State Advis Coun for ESEA Title II; UCal Advis Coun on Educ for Libnship. 9: ALA-AASchL (Best Bks for YA Com); NEA-DAVI; CalLA (Lib Careers Com); CalASchL(pres No Sect); A-V Educ Assn Cal. 10: Delta Kappa Gamma. 13: Yes. 14: dmin, bk sel, a-v materials sel. 15: Oakland Pub Schs, 1025 Second ave, OaklandCa 94606.

CZAPIEWSKI, SISTER MARY BEATRICE CSFN. b Pittsburgh 7 D 1890. 5: Ursuline Col 24-25; Duquesne U 38-42 BE; Catholic U 2-43. 6: Fr, Ger, Polish. 7: Tchr-libn Mt Nazareth Acad, Pittsburgh 39-65, Libn 65-. 9: CathLA. 15: 285 Bellevue rd, Pittsburgh 15229.

CZERNICKI, NORMA (McCARTY). b Lumberport WVa 27 Jl 34. 4: Edward E Czernicki. 5: Gallaudet Col 50-55 (LS) BS, summer 65 (LS). 7: Catlgr Great Falls Pub Lib, Great Falls Mont 55-66; Catlgr & adv Columbus Sch ofNursing Lib, Great Falls Mont 55-66; Catlgr TVA Tech Lib, Knoxville Tenn 66-. 10: Tenn Assn of the Deaf; Knoxville Athletic Assn of the Deaf. 14: Catlg, lib wk with the deaf. 15: 3374 Coffmandr SE, Knoxville Tn 37920.

CZIKE, STEPHEN. b Sopron Hungary 8 My 20. 5: Pazmany U (Budapest) 38-43 (Law) Dr JUR: Rosary Col 63-64 MLS. 6: Hungarian, Ger. 7: Clerk Northwestern U Law Lib 60; Catlgr Chicago Bar Assn Law Lib 64; Libn Valparaiso U Law Sch 65-67; Exec libn, Chicago Bar Assn 67-. 15: Valparaiso U Law Sch, Valparaiso Ind 46383.

D

D'ALESSANDRO, EDWARD ANTHONY. b Cleveland 11 Mr 13. 4: Grace Musche3. 5: John CarrollU 33-37 (Hist) BA (magna cum laude); West Res 37-38 (LS) BS. 6: Ital. 7: Page Brownell Jr High Sch Lib 27-28; Cleveland Pub Lib: Page Rice Br Lib 28-34, Page Main Lib 34-36, Head page Main Lib 36-37, Stud asst Main Lib sociol div 37-38, Jr asst libn Main Lib sociol div 38-41, Asst br libn Euclid 100th Br Lib 41-42, Br libn Woodland Br Lib 42-43; Lib asst Spec Serv USAAF Drew Field Fla 43-45; US Army Infantry & Quartermaster Serv, Korea 45-46; Cleveland Pub Lib: Prof asst pub rel & exhibits dept 46, Br libn Fleet Br Lib 46-49, Br libn Eastman Br Lib 49-51, Chief bk repair div 51-54, Asst head Main Lib 54-56, Bus manager Main Lib 56-59, Asst dir 59-66, Deputy dir 67-68, Act dir 68-69, Dir 69-. 9: ALA (past mem Lib Bldgs & Equipment Com); OhioLA (Exec Bd 63-66; Lib Devel Com 65-, chm 66-; Legis Com 68-; Steering Com on Ohio Lib Devel Plan 67-). 10: Univ Circle Bd of Com; X-Ray Survey, SE Cleveland; Cleveland Univ Settlement; Citizen's League of Cleveland; Friends of the Cleveland Pub Lib; Cleveland Power Squadron; West ResU Lib Sch Alumni Assn; United Appeal Campaigns. 13: Yes. 14: Admin, bk binding, biogr, data proc, lib bldgs, br lib serv. 15: 4115 W 145th st, Cleveland Oh 44135.

D'ALESSANDRO, JANE (DORN). b Waconia Minn 3 Ja 41. 4: Paul D'Alessandro. 5: Wartburg col 58-60; UMinn 60-62 (Eng) BS, 65-66 (LS) MA. 6: Ger. 7: Tchr & libn Lyle Pub Schs, Lyle Minn 62-64; Tchr & libn Howard Lake Pub Schs, Howard Lake Minn 64-65; Catlgr Baker Lib HarvardU 66-. 14: Catlg. 15: 72A Cushing st, Cambridge Ma 02138.

D'ARCY, GRACE AGNES. b Calgary Alta 3 Ag 09. 4: Geoffrey Conyers D'Arcy. 5: UBC 26-29 (Eng) BA, 30 Perm Acad Tchg Certif; UWash 62 MLS; Stanford summer 60 (Field Wk). 6: Fr. 7: Sch libn Dist 69, Parksville BC 52-60; Dist Libn Dist 69 Qualicum Beach BC 60-65, Dist lib consul 65-. 67; Supv sch libs Prov of Man, Winnipeg Man 67-. 8: Lecturer in Educ, UBC summers 63-65, UAlta summer 66; Mem, Curr Coms for basic bk lists, BC 62-64. 9: ALA; CanLA (Coun); PNLA; BCLA; BCASchL (pres 63-64); ManLA. 10: Altrusa Club. 11: Can Coun Award 60. 12: Ed BCASchL "Newsletter (62-63). 14: Admin, ref. 15: 913-200 Ronald st, Winnipeg 12 Manitoba Can.

DAANE, BETH. b Stillwater Okla 16 Ap 16. 5: Fla State Col for Women 33-37 (Health & Phys Educ) BS; Columbia 40-42 (Health & Phys Educ) MA; Fla State U 59-60 (LS) MS. 7: Eng & Health Educ tchr High Schs, Orlando & Jacksonville Bch Fla 37-43; Program dir, club dir Amer Nat Red Cross, Africa Italy Japan 43-47; Health Educ dir YWCA, Houston Tex, Phoenix Ariz 47-53; Post serv club dir, area club supv, club dir, program dir: Army Spec Serv in Alaska, Korea, La 53-59; Grad ref ast Fla State U Lib 59-60; Ref libn Santa Fe Reg Lib, Gaiesville Fla 60-61, Dir Libs 61-. 9: ALA; NASW; FlaLA; Fla Coun on Aging. 10: Altrusa Internat; PEO; LWV; Gainesville Fine Arts Assn; Gainesville Womans Club; UN Assn; Alachua Co Assn for Mental Health; Friends of the Library; Inter-Club Coun; Kappa Delta Pi; Beta Phi Mu. 11: Phillip Wylie Award. 13: Yes. 14: Ref, adult educ, serv to handicapped & elderly. 15: 1402 N W th ave, Gainesville Fla 32601.

DABNEY, MILDRED APPERSON. b Yancey Mills Va 3 Ap 13. 4: John Humphrey Dabney. 5: Col of William & Mary 30; Brooklyn Pub Lib Sch 30-31 NY State Certified Pub Libn; UVa 55; Lynchburg Col 63-65 (Hist) BA; UNC(Chapel Hill) 65- (LS); Certif Sch Libn State of Va, Certif Hist Second Schs Va. 6: Fr. 7: Libn Brooklyn Pub Lib 31-37; Libn E C Glass High Sch, Lynchburg Va 52-63; Libn Admin Lynchburg Pub Schs Va 65-. 8: Consul new elem & jr high sch libs, Lynchburg Va 65-. 9: ALA; NEA; VaLA; VaEA; VEA Lib Div Lynchburg EA; Lynchburg Sch LA; Dist "F" Libns. 10: Kappa Delta Pi. 14: Admin, yp & child libs, acquis, tech serv, Va hist. 15: 20 Easton ave, Lynchburg Va 24503.

DACEY, BARBARA ELAINE (MacKINNON). b Halifax NS Can 20 Je 38. 5: Dalhousie U 56-60 (Psych) BA; Toronto 61-62 BLS. 6: Fr. 7: Sub-prof Halifax Mem Lib, Halifax NS 60-61; Bkmob libn Halifax Co Reg Lib, Halifax NS 62-63; Child libn Halifax Mem Lib, Halifax NS 63-66; Ref libn UNB (Fredericton) 66-. 9: CanLA; APLA; HalifaxLA. 10: Univ Women's Club; Heritage Trust of NS. 14: Child lit, ref. 15: 5677 Fenwick st, Halifax NS Can.

DACUS, CAROLYN RUTH. b Rock Hill SC. 5: Winthrop Col 35-39 (Hist, Eng) AB; Peabody 41-42 BS in LS. 6: Fr. 7: Libn Goldsboro High Sch, Goldsboro NC 42-43; Lib asst Atlanta Pub Lib 43-46; Replacement Train Centerlibn, Ft Knox Ky 46; Lib asst Winthrop Col 47; Asst libn Florence State U 47-51, Head libn 51-. 8: Consul St Bernard Col 64. 9: AlaLA (chm Col & U Sect 64-65); SELA; AlaEA. 10: Alpha Beta Alpha; AAUW; Wesleyan Serv Guild; Hon Soc, Florence State U. 13: Yes. 14: Acquis, ref, admin. 15: Box 626, Florence State Univ, Florence Al 35630.

DADE, MARY JUDITH (BATES). b Hebron Ohio 14 Jl 18. 4: Merrell Elliman Dade. 5: Hiram Col 36-43 (Hist) BA; West Res 45-46 BS in LS. 7: Clerk-act libn Cleveland Pub Lib, Schs 43-49; Libn George Fox Col 51-56; Asst libn Seattle Pacific Col 56-59; Eng Dept Lib Assoc of Portland, Portland Ore 60; Asst libn Pacific Power & Ligt Co, Portland Ore 60-. 9: SLA; OreLA. 14: Ref, doc catlg. 15: Pacific Power & Light Lib Room 908 Pub Serv Bldg, Portland Or 97204.

DAETSCH, DOROTHY ANNE. b Arlington Mass 11 F 28. 4: Willard Ticknor Daetsch. 5: Radcliffe 45-49 (Eng Lit) AB; Simmons 54-55 (LS) MS. 6: Fr, Ger, Lat. 7: An asst to Dean New England Conservatory, Boston 50-53; Music libn Robbins Lib, Arlington Mass 54; Circ ref libn Free Pub Lib,Concord Mass 57-58; Ref libn Humanities Div UNC Lib (Chapel Hill) 60-65; Asst libn Uris Undergrad Lib Cornell U 65-67; Ref libnIthaca Col Lib 67-. 9: NCLA; ALA; So Central Research Lib Coun (NY State, chm Interlib Loan Com). 12: Contrib "Medieval and Renaissance Studies, a Location Guide to Selected Reference Works in the Libraries of the University of North Carolina at Chapel Hill and Duke University" (rev ed 67).5 14: Ref, bibliog. 15: 1344 Dan rd RFD 4, Ithaca NY 14850.

DAGG, CAROLE LEE (ESTBY). b Kansas City Mo 25 Ag 44. 4: Gosta Emil Dagg. 5: UWash 61-65 (Sociol) BA 67 (Ed); UBritish Columbia 65-66 BLS. 7: Clk Seattle Pub Lib 62-65; Children's libn Burnaby Pub Lib, Burnaby BC 66; Children's libn Seattle Pub Lib 67-. 14: Child wk (puppetry etc). 15: 2722 - 11th East, Seattle Wa 98102.

DAGGER, WILLIAM P. b Birmingham Eng 6 Jl 18. 4: D Joan Booth. 5: Manitoba U (St Johns Col) 37-40, 45-47 BA; McGill 47-48 BLS; Ottawa U 53-54. 6: Fr, Portu, Ital. 7: Royal Canadian Air Force Canada, Ireland 40-45 Clerk Prov Lib, Winnipeg Man 46-47; Clerk Ft William Pub Lib, Ft William Ont 46, Catlgr 48-51; Documents libn Directorate of Sci Info Serv 51-64; Dept dir Admin Defence Research Bd, Ottawa 65-67; Sci & Engnr libn McMaster U, Ont 67-. 8: Mem, Agard Tech Info Panel 56-67; Adv, ACEL lib reorgan, Chalk River Ont 54-; Consul & adv, establishment of libs of DRB in Can 51-67. 9: SLA; ASIS; OntLA. 14: Admin, ref, pub serv. 15: 10 Crystal ct, Dundas Ont Can.

DAGNESE, JOSEPH MARTOCCI. b Worcester Mass 10 O 27. 4: Doris Busi. 5: Boston Col 47-49 (Eng Lit) AB; Catholic U 49-51 (Eng Lit) MA, 51-52 MSLS; Heidelberg U (Germany) 54-55 (Ger Lang & Lit). 7: Lib asst Catholic U 51-52; US Army Ordnance Personnel Clerk (Cpl) 52-54; Catlgr Catholic U 55-57; Libn Nuclear Metals Inc, W Concord Mass 57-60; Head of acquis MIT 60-62, Sci libn 62-65, Asst dir for Tech Serv 66-. 8: Lib consul Birla Inst of Sci & Tech, Pilani (Raj) India 66-67. 9: SLA (Boston Chap Educ chm, Sci-Tech Sect 62-64, program chm 63-64, pres 64-65, Chap Relat Com 69-71); ALA; NMA. 14: Admin, tech serv, automation. 15: 47 Samoset rd, Winchester Ma 01890.

DAHL, JOYCE K. b Hackensack NJ 2 Jl 9. 4: Haakon M Dahl. 5: Mt Holyoke 36-37; Barnard 37-40 (Aesthetics) BA; Columbia 44-45 (Eng Secondary Sch) MA, 59-61 (LS) MS. 6: Fr, Norwegian. 7: Ref libn Avery Lib of Arch, ColumbiaU 61-65; Spec collections libn Brooklyn Col 65-67, Chief soc sci-educ div 67-. 8: Art Consul Rider Col, 65. 9: ALA; -LAD; -RSD. 10: AAUP; Girl Scouts; Ctr for Migration Studies, Brooklyn Col; Beta Phi Mu; Pi Lambda Theta. 14: Ref, rare bks, archives, mss, soc scis, educ, lib admin. 15: 4115 Hubbard pl, Brooklyn NY 11210.

DAHL, MAE E(MELIA). b Ely Minn 2 Ag 11. 5: Ely Jr Col 28-30; UMinn 30-33 LS BS. 6: Fr, Sp, Ger. 7: Libn catlgr (FERA) St Paul Dept of Educ 33-34; Libn asst Minn Hist Soc, St Paul 34-35; Asst catlgr UMinn 35-37; Catlgr & Asst libn Eveleth Pub lib, Eveleth Minn 37-40; Co libn Va Pub Lib, Va Minn 40-42; Hd libn Internat Falls Pub Lib, Internat Falls Minn 42-45; Catlgr Army Med Lib, Wash DC 45-46; Catlg libn Joint Bank Fund Lib Internat Monetary Fund, Wash DC 47-. 9: ALA; DCLA. 14: Catlg, admin. 15: Joint Bank-Fund Lib, International Monetary Fund, 19th & H sts NW, Washington DC 20431.

DAHL, PATRICIA MIRIAM. b Los Angeles Cal 10 Jl 24. 5: UMinn 42-46 (Hist) BS, 49-50 BS in LS. 7: Tchr Montevideo Pub Schs, Montevideo Minn 46-49; Minneapolis Pub Lib: Children's libn 50-56, Classroom libn 56-58, Asst to coordinator children's serv 58-60, Commun libn & children's libn 60-. 9: MinnLA (chm Child Div). 14: Wk with child. 15: 4524 Vandervork ave, Minneapolis Mn 55436.

DAHL, RICHARD CHARLES. b San Francisco 25 N 21. 4: Grace Field. 5: UCal 39-42 (Philos), 47 (Law) BA; UCal Law Sch 52 (Law); UNeb Law Sch 54-55 (Law); CatholicU 58 LLB. 7: T-5 Quartermaster Corps Army 42-46; Law Libn UCal (Berkeley) 51-53; Law Libn UNeb 53-55; Civil div libn Dept of Justice, Wash DC 56; Law Libn ffice of Judge Adv Gen Navy, Wash DC 56-61; Libn US Treasury Dept, Wash DC 61-63; State Law Libn Wash State Law Lib 63-66; Dir Law Lib Arizona State U 66-. 9: Fed Bar Assn; C Bar Assn. 12: "Military Law Dictionary (60; Ed "Law Library Journal (65). 13: Yes. 14: Admin. 15: Col of Law, Arizona State Univ, Tempe Az 85281.

DAHLBERG, MILDRED C. b Rock Island Il 9 Je 08. 5: Augustana Col 28 (Eng) AB; West Res 35 BSLS; IndU 39 (A-v, guidance); ButlerU 45 (A-V). 6: Swedish. 7: Libn Elston Sr high Sch, Mich City Ind 28-. 9: NEA; ALA; ISLA (scholarship chm; histn). 10: Beta Pi Mu; AAUW; Delta Kappa Gamma; Girl Scout Coun; PTA; Bk Club. 13: Yes. 14: High sch. 15: 306 Garden trail Pottawattamie Pk, Michigan City In 46360.

DAHLGREN, EDITH WILSON. b Washburn Me 30 N 20. 5: Bates Col 39-43 (Hist, Govt) AB; URI 57-60 (LS) MA. 7: Tchr Chapman Tech High Sch, New London Conn 43-47; Sch libn

Samuel Gorton Jr High Sch, Warwick RI 48-. 8: Co-chm, 2 week sch lib wkshop, Warwick RI summer 65. 9: ALA; NELA (Dir from RI 63, Educ Com); NESchLA (pres 60-62); RISchLA (sec-treas 2 terms); RILA (Educ Com); RIEA; Warwick EA. 10: Phi Beta Kappa; Phi Kappa Phi. 13: Yes. 14: Sch lib wk. 15: 194 Samuel Gorton ave, Warwick RI 02889.

DAHLIN, THELMA C(LARK) (MRS). b Hornsby Ill 10 Ap 03. 5: Pomona Col 22-26 (Hist) AB; UCal(Berkeley) 28-29 (Libnship) Certif. 6: Sp. 7: Tchr-libn Pomona City Schs, Pomona Cal 26-28; Asst libn Pub Lib, Burlingame Cal 29-44; Head schs dept Contra Costa Co Lib, Martinez Cal 44-53; Coordinator lib serv Mt Diablo U Sch Dist, Concord Cal 53-. 9: ALA; NEA; ASCD; CalLA; CalSchL; CalASCD; A-V Assn Cal; NEA-DAVI. 10: AAUW; Delta Kappa Gamma. ; Key Democr Women. 13: Yes. 14: Sch libs. 15: 2603 Vargus ct, Concord Cal 94520.

DAHLSTROM, NANCY LEA (ROSS). b Freeport Ill 25 O 43. 4: Charles M Dahlstrom. 5: N Park Col 61-66 (Fr) BA; Rosary Col 66-67 MALS. 6: Fr, Sp. 7: Sci libn Rosary Col summer 67; Asst libn Oak Park & River Forest High Sch 67-. 9: NEA; ALA; IllEA. 14: Schs, ref. 15: 427 S Elmwood ave, Oak Park Il 60302.

DAHM, SISTER MARY THERESE C SJ. b Truman Minn Jl 03. 5: Col of St Catherine 22-27 (Eng) BA; UMinn 36-39 (Eng) MA; Columbia summer 38; Col of St Catherine 42-43 BS in LS; UMinn summers 41, 46; UNotre Dame summers 52, 57. 6: Fr, Ger. 7: Tchr: Derham Hall High Sch, St Paul 26-28, St Marys High Sch, Waverly Minn 28-30, St Johns Acad, Jamestown ND 30-34, St Marys High Sch, Waverly Minn 28-30, St Johns Acad, Jamestown ND 30-34, St Marys High Sch, Waverly Minn 34-37, St Anthony High Sch, Minneapolis 37-38 Instr of Eng Col of St Catherine 38-43, Catlgr 43-44; Libn-tchr St Margarets Acad, Minneapolis 46-51; Libn Acad of the Holy Angels, Minneapolis 51-55; Libn-tchr Derham Hall High Sch, St Paul 55-62; Res libn Col of St Catherine 62-. 8: Eng instr Col of St Catherine summers 56, 58, 62. 9: ALA; CathLA (Minn-Dakota Unit: v-chm & chm 47-49 & 52-54); MinnLA. 10: Delta Phi Lambda; St Paul Audubon Soc. 11: Butler Scholarship for Study & Travel in Europe, summer 63. 13: Yes. 14: Bk sel, rare bks. 15: Col of St Catherine, St Paul 55116.

DAHM, MINNIE JULIA (VAN GORP). b Mahaska County Iowa 1 O 06. 4: . 5: William Penn Col 48-56 (Eng) BA; StateU Iowa summer 57; State Col Iowa summers 59, 60 (LS. 6: Dutch. 7: Elem tchr Christian Grade Sch, Pella Iowa 24-29; Elem tchr Evergreen Park Chr Sch, Chicago 29-34; Rural tchr elem Mahaska Co, Oskaloosa Iowa 48-57; Eng chr-libn Christian High Sch, Pella Iowa 57-59; Libn Jr High Sch, Oskaloosa Iowa 59-. 9: NEA; ALA; NCTE; IowaEA; IowaASchL (asst treas, chm Audit Com; em Com). 10: Bus & Prof Womens Club; William Penn Col Womens Auxiliar; Better Reading Coun; Travel Club of Amer. 13: Yes. 14: Catlg, ref. 15: 1349 N Main st, Pella Iowa 50219.

DAHMS, BRUCE GRANT. b San Diego Cal 27 D 39. 4: Salene Hull. 5: Cal Concordia Col 58-60; Concordia Sr Col 60-62 (Pretheol) BA; Concordia Sem 62-66 (Theol) BD; Columbia 66-68 (LS) MS. 6: Ger. 7: Libn Concordia Col Inst Bronxville NY 66-. 9: ALA; NYLA; WestchesterLA. 14: Admin, catlg. 15: 216 Midland ave, Tuckahoe NY 10707.

DAILEY, DOROTHY (MANNING). b Mt Vernon NY 28 Ag 10. 4: H Warner Dailey. 5: Wellesley 28-32 (Eng Lit) BA; Columbia 32-35 BS in LS. 6: Fr. 7: Lib asst Mt Vernon Pub Lib, Mt Vernon NY 32-35; Lib asst ColumbiaU Lib 35-36; Ref libn Col of New Rochelle 36-38; Catlg dept & central circ NY Pub Lib 38-41; Lib asst Navy Dept Lib Sect, Wash DC 2-43; Catlgr Basking Ridge Pub, Basking Ridge NJ 50-59; Libn St Bernards Sch, Gladstone NJ 5963; Libn Short Hills Country Day Sch, Short Hills NJ 64-66; Libn Tewksbury Twsp Elem Sch, Lebanon NJ 66-. 9: ALA; NEA; NJEA; Hunterdon Co EA. 10: PTA. 14: Secon Schs, child wk, catlg. 15: RD 2, Far Hills NJ 07931.

DAILEY, MARY MARGARET. b Ottawa Ill. 5: Col of St Francis (Joliet Ill) (Chem) BS; Rosary Col 65 BA in LS. 7: Libn Corn Products Co, Argo Ill 48-63, Lit analyst 63-67; Ref consul Bur Oak Lib Syst 68-; Hd ref dept Joliet Pub Lib, Joliet Ill 9: ACS; SLA; ALA; IllLA; ASIS; Chicago Lib Club. 10: Iota Sigma Pi. 14: Documentation, lit analysis, ref. 15: 18 S Prairie ave, Joliet Ill 60436.

DAILY, JAY E(LWOOD). b Pikeview Colo 17 Je 23. 4: Jennifer Mary Hole. 5: Army Specialized Train Program Grinnell Col 43-44 (Span) Certificate; NYU 49-51 (Span) BA; Columbia 51-52 (LS) MS, 55-57 DLS. 6: Lat, Span, Fr, Ital, Ger, Dutch. 7: (T/4) Psychiatric Soc Wkr, US Army 43-46; Eng tchr Amer Lang Inst Seoul Korea 46-48; Admin Off Unitarian Serv Com Team, Seoul-Pusan 52-53; Head libn Wagner Col 54-55; Libn Paula K Lazrus Lib NCCJ, NYC 55-57; Consul libn Inst of Pub Admin, Rangoon Burma 57-59; Adv libn UMandalay, Mandalay Burma 59-62; Lib consul Franklin Book Programs, NYC 62-65; Asst dir for tech serv UPittsburgh 65-68; Assoc Prof GSLIS UPittsburgh 67, Prof 68-. 8: Consul libn Coun for Financial Aid to Educ 54-57; Spec consul for Argentina & Chile Ford Found 63; Dir Feasibiity Study Rockefeller Found & Franklin Book Programs 64; AID Bk Survey, Peru 66. 9: SLA; PennLA; AAUP; ALA (Exec Bd Catlg & Clsf Sect 67-70). 11: Paula K Lazrus Mem Fellowship 55-57; Hon Tchr of Korea 48. 12: "The Grammar of Subject Headings (57); Ed "Pittsburgh Studies in Library and Information Science". 13: Yes. 14: Tech serv, comparative libnship, bk sel. 15: 709 South Negley ave, Pittsburgh 15232.

DAIN, PHYLLIS (SEGAL). b Brooklyn NY 29 N 29. 4: Norman Dain. 5: Brooklyn Col 46-50 (Hist) BA; Columbia 52-53 (LS) MS, 51-52, 54-57 (Hist) MA, 57-66 DLS. 6: Fr, 07: ColumbiaU Sch of Lib Sci: Reviser 56-58, Catlgr Libs 53-58, Asst catlg libn in chg Med Lib Catlg Dept 58-60, Lecturer Sch of Lib Serv 60-66, Asst Prof 66-. 9: ALA; AALS; NY Tech Serv Libn. 10: Phi Beta Kappa; AAUP. 13: Yes. 14: Catlg, lib hist, hist, soc sci lit. 15: 110 Crescent ave, Leonia NJ 07605.

DAKAN, NORMAN E. b Beaver City Neb 16 S 26. 4: Miyoko Muranaka. 5: UCal (Berkeley) 51-53 (Eng) BA, 53-54 BLS. 7: Asst libn Cal State Polytech Col Lib 54-56; Base libn USAF: Ashiya AFB Japan 56-58, 648 6th ABW, Hickam AFB Hawaii 60-62, 68-; Chief libn USAF: Itazuke AFB Japan 58-60, 6114th CSG, Fuchu AS Japan 62-66, 824th CSG, Kadena AFB Okinawa 66-68. 9: HawaiiLA. 12: "PACAF Basic Bibliography: Intelligence". 14: Ref, admin. 15: 99-250 Ohenana Loop, Aiea Hi 96701.

DAKIN, (EMILY) ELIZABETH. b Valley Park Miss 28 Jl 09. 5: Whitworth Col 26-27; Delta State Col 27-28; Randolph-Macon Womans Col 28-30 (Fr) AB; UMiss summer 29; Peabody summers 35-36 (Lang), 37-40 BS in LS, summers 45, 47, 53. 6: Fr. 7: Tchr Cleveland High Sch, Cleveland Miss 30-40, 41-42; Instr modern langs Delta State Col 40-41; Libn Cleveland High Sch, Cleveland Miss 42-45; Act libn Delta State Col 45-46, Staff mem Delta State Col 46-, acquis libn 59-. 9: ALA; SELA; MissLA (sec-treas 52-53); NEA; MissEA. 10: AAUW; Delta Kappa Gamma. 14: Acquis. 15: Roberts Lib Delta State Col, Cleveland Ms 38732.

DALE, BRIAN. b Waterford England 26 F 32. 4: Mary Johansson. 5: UToronto 62-67 (Hist) BA; UBritish Columbia 67-68 BLS. 7: Cost Accountant Kodak, Eng 48-50; Tech libn RAF 50-52; Personnel wk GE, Toronto 53-54; Advertising Dyment Ltd, Toronto 54-58; Bk publishers rep Copp Clark Publng Toronto 58-67; Chief libn Moose-Jaw Pub Lib, Sask Can 68-. 9: CanLA; SaskLA. 10: Rotary. 14: Music, admin. 15: Moose Jaw Pub Lib, Moose Jaw Sask Can.

DALE, CHARLES F. b Atlantic city NJ 8 O 24. 4: Connie L (Ogg) Dale. 5: Rutgers 46-49 (Pol sci) BA; Amer U 49-52 (Intl rel); St Jerome's Col 57-59 (Phil) Certif; Catholic U 59-60 (Theol); Drexel 63-64 MLS. 7: Sgt tech USA, US & Europe 43-45; Survey statistician US Census Bur, Suitland Md 49-51, 55; Survey statistician US Dept of State, Wash DC 51-52; Consumer salesman Renaire Corp, Wash DC 52-54, 56; Soc wkr Catholic Soc Serv, Wilmington Del 60-63; Spec serv libn Dela State Lib, Dover Dela 64-66; Hd tech processes PMC Col Lib, Chester Penn 66-. 9: -ACRL; ASIS; Amer Soc for Info Sci. 14: Admin, catlg systems, ref, bk sel. 15: 1105 Steven place, Valley Run, Wilmington De 19803.

DALE, CHARLOTTE J. b Harrison Ohio 1 N 17. 5: IndU 63 (LS) MA; UCincinnati 41 (Applied Arts) BS; DePauw 35-37 (Liberal Arts). 6: Fr. 7: Ed asst "Child Life Magazine" Cincinnati 42-46; Sec news & PR L B Wilson Inc, Cincinnati 46-49; Admin asst Taft Broadcasting Co, Cincinnati 49-60; Clk Cincinnati & Hamilton Co Pub Lib 61-62; Asst libn Wayne Co Pub Lib, Wooster Ohio 63-64; Consul State Lib of Ohio, Columbus 64-. 8: State Lib liaison with Ohio State Admin on Aging; Consul on Mercer Co (Ohio) Survey of Libs. 9: ALA; OhioLA. 10: Franklin Co Libns Assn (Columbus Ohio). 14: Adult serv, art ref. 15: 645 Neil ave apt 302, Columbus Oh 43215.

DALE, COUDOASHIA BERNICE (WATTS). b Mexia Tex 26 F 21. 4: Luther William Dale. 5: Tillotson Col 37-41 (Home Econ) BS; DenverU 52-58 (LS); Kan State Tchrs Col 59-61 (LS) MS, 67-69 (Lib Supv) Certif. 6: Fr. 7: Asst libn Tillotson

Col 42; Tchr Douglass Elem Sch, Parsons Kan 45-58; Asst libn Parsons Jr Col 58-59; Libn E Jr High, Parsons kan 59-62; Libn Parsons Jr High, Parson Kan 62-. 9: ALA; KanStateTA; KanLA; KASchL. 10: League of Women Voters; AAUW; Pub Lib Bd; Delta Sigma Theta; Federated Clubs; Faculty Wives; YWCA Exec Bd. 14: Catlg, ref. 15: 2710 Appleton, Parsons Ks 67357.

DALE, DORIS (CRUGER). b Madison Wis 22 Jl 27. 4: Richard Dale. 5: UWis(Madison) 45-50 (Span) BA, 52-54 MALS; Columbia 66-68 DLS. 6: Sp, Fr. 7: Ref libn Madison Pub Lib, Madison Wis 54-57, Br libn 57-58; Circ libn Appleton Pub Lib, Appleton Wis 58-59; Bus libn Rockford Pub Lib,Rockford Ill 59-62; Ref libn UWis(Milwaukee) 62-64; Ref libn No Ill U 64-66; Tchg asst Columbia U Sch Lib Serv 66-67; Asst Prof SoIll U DeptInstr Materials 69-. 9: ALA (Subs Bks Bul Com 65-67); SLA; IllLA. 10: Delta Kappa Gamma; Beta Phi Mu. 12: Comp: "A List of American Doctoral Dissertations on Africa, France, Italy (67); "A List of Doctoral Dissertations on New Zealand, Australia, Canada; Auth "The Origin and Development of the United Nations Library (diss 68). 13: Yes. 14: Ref (bus & law collections), govt docs. 15: Parke Towne Garden Apt F-C, Carbondale Il 62901.

DALE, HESTER L(OUISE). b Mont 20 N 12. 4: Thomas R Dale. 5: USoCal 52 (Econ) BA, 55 (LS) MS. 6: Ger. 7: Chem Richfield Oil Corp, Wilmington Cal 43-48, chem-libn 49-68, Supv Tech Info Ctr 68-. 8: Amer Petroleum Inst Central Abstrcting & Indexing Serv 65-, Task Force, Thesaurus control. 9: SLA (Sci-Tech Div); ACS (Lit Div); ASIS; CalLA. 10: Phi Beta Kappa. 13: Yes. 14: Ref, processing systems, lit searching, info retrieval, manual & computer, corporate netwk info serv. 15: Atlantic Richfield Co Box 787, Wilmington Ca 90746.

DALEY, JOHN GRANNIS. b Springfield Mass 21 F 24. 4: Norma Mattoon Daley. 5: UDetroit 42-48 (Zool) BS; UMich 48-53 (Piano) B of Music, 56-57 MA in LS. 6: Fr. 7: US Army ASTP 43-45; Piano tchr, Ann Arbor Mich 53-56; Music libn UMich (Ann Arbor) 55-56; Ref libn Detroit Pub Lib 57-60; Sci libn Swarthmore Col 60-63; Instr Drexel Inst 63-65; Asst Prof Simmons Col 65-. 8: Exhibits Chm SLA Convention 65 Phila. 9: SLA (Sci-Tech Div); AALS; MassLA; NELA; ALA-ACRL; PennLA. 10: AAUP; Appalachian Mountain Club; Mass Audubon Soc; Wilderness Soc. 14: Basic & sci ref, catlg, hist of libs. 15: 14 Marshal st, Brookline Ma 02146.

DALEY, NORMA (MATTOON). b Springfield Mass 27 Je 35. 4: John Grannis Daley. 5: Mt Holyoke 53-57 (Eng Lit) AB; Simmons 66-67 MLS. 6: Fr, Sp, Lat. 7: Ref asst Springfield 9mass) City Lib 57-66; Ref libn Bentley Col 67-68; Ref asst Brookline (Mass) Pub Lib 68-. 9: MassLA. 10: Appalachian Mtn Club; ,ass Audubon Soc; Wilderness Soc. 13: Yes. 14: Ref. 15: 14 Marshal st, Brooklyne Ma 02146.

DALGLISH, PATRICIA SUE (MERSMAN). b Sacramento Cal 25 Ap 42. 4: Thomas K Dalglish. 5: Stanford 59-63 (Music) AB; UCal (Berkeley) 63-64 MLS. 6: Sp, Ital, Fr, Ger. 7: Libn Undergrad Lib UWash 64; Music libn UWash 65-66; Libn S Puget Sound Reg Lib, Olympia Wash 66-67; Catlgr Central Wash State U 67-68; Hd libn Ellensburg Pub Lib, Ellensburg Wash 68-. 9: MUSLA. 10: Mu Phi Epsilon. 14: Ref. 15: 900 E Fourth ave, Ellensburg Wa 98926.

DALKEY, BARBARA JEAN (JESKALIAN). b Oakland Cal 12 Ap 36. 4: Franklin R Dalkey. 5: UCal (Berkeley) 54-58 (Eng) AB; USoCal 58-59 MSLS. 6: Fr, Armenian. 7: Libn Parkside Br San Francisco Pub Lib 60; Hd child libn Main Post Lib Presidio of San Francisco 60-62; Ref & order libn Sunnyvale Pub Lib, Sunnyvale Cal 63-64; Catlg libn 6th Army Ref Lib Presidio of San Francisco 65; Circ libn Col of Holy Names (Oakland Cal) 65-66; Libn Santa Clara Co Lib Syst Milkitas Brs 66-67; Ref libn San Jose State Col Lib 67-. 9: CalLA. 14: Readers' adv wk, spec current collections. 15: 717 Palm st, San Jose Ca 95110.

DALLAS, ZELLA (GWIN ROGERS). b Speedwell Tenn 6 Ap 10. 4: Donald Edward Dallas. 5: West Res 57-59. 6: Lat. 7: Tchr adult home sewing Singer Sewing Machine Co, Cleveland Ohio 30-33; Private tchr adult home sewing, Euclid Ohio 46-50; Exec sec A W Hecker Co, Cleveland 51-53, Production control asst 54-56; Libn Preformed Line Products Co, Cleveland 56-. 9: SLA (sec Cleveland Chap; Pub Util Sect; Bull ed); ASIS; Amer Soc for Testing Materials. 10: Frinds of Cleveland Pub Lib; Cleveland Commun Fund; DAR; Amer Bus Women's Assn. 13: Yes. 14: Catlg, indexing, research reports. 15: Preformed Line Prod Co, 5300 St Clair ave, Cleveland Oh 44103.

DALLAVALLE, CAROLYN (BLACK). b Dalton Ga 18 N 12. 5: Ga Col (Milledgeville) 30-34 9eng, Hist) AB; UNC 38-39 AB in LS. 6: Fr. 7: Ref NYC Pub Lib summers 39-40; Jr high sch libn Greensboro Pub Schs, Greensboro NC 39-42; Period of ref libn Agnes Scott Col 42-46; Period-ref Ga Inst Tech 46-49, Acquis libn 58-. 14: Period acquis, ref, col libs. 15: 570 Wimbledon rd NE, Atlanta Ga 30324.

DALLIGAN, ALICE GRACE (COOK). b Detroit 28 Ap 23. 4: Carl J Dalligan. 5: Wayne State 41-45 (Educ) BA; UMich 46-48 (Hist) MA, 49-50 MA in LS; Wayne State 64-65 (Archival Admin). 6: Fr, Sp. 7: Tchr Detroit Pub Schs 46-49, Libn 49-64; Curator of Mss Burton Hist Collection Detroit Pub Lib 64-. 9: ALA; MichLA; Mich Hist Soc; Detroit Hist Soc; SAA. 10: LWV; Detroit Internat Inst; Alpha Beta Pi; Wayne State U Alumni; Reserve Off Assn Ladies. 14: Local hist, hist mss, archives, rare bks, ref. 15: 2101 Fleetwood, Grosse Pointe Woods Mi 48236.

DALLMAN, GLENN R. b Oconomowoc Wis 31 Jl 27. 4: Charlotte Frank Dallman. 5: Northland Col 47-50 (Eng) BA; UWis(Milwaukee) 53-54 (Educ) ME; West Res 60-62 MSLS. 7: SK3C US Navy Reserve 45-46; Tchr Trinity High Sch, Ft Lauderdale Fla 50-51; Tchr-prin Lutheran Tchrs Train Col, Nigeria Africa 51-57; Tchr-libn Concordia Col (Portland Ore) 57-8; Tchr Lutheran High Sch, Cleveland 59-61; Libn Cleveland Heights Pub Lib, Cleveland Heights Ohio 61-62; Dir Indian River Jr Col 62-66; Dir St Petersburg Jr Col (Clearwater) 66-. 9: ALA; NEA; SELA; FlaLA; FlaEA; AAUP; Fac Assn Petersburg Jr Col. 15: 1740 Harmony dr, Clearwater Fl 33516.

DALPHIN, GEORGE R. b Malone NY 30 Jl 26. 5: Dartmouth 44-47 (Eng) AB; UNM 64- (Art). 7: Map libn Dartmouth Col 47-63; Staff libn Sandia Corp, Albuquerque NM 63-. 9: SLA (past chm Geog & Map Div). 12: Ed "Geography & Map Division BULLETIN" SLA (56-62); Ed "Dartmouth College Library Bulletin (57-59); "Marine Atlases in the Dartmouth College Library (50); Co-ed SW Union List of Serials (65). 13: Yes. 14: Cartography, Americana, motion pictures, fine arts, earth scis. 15: 1709 Anderson pl SE, Albuquerque NM 87108.

DALQUIST, JANET (ANUTA). b Menominee Mich 2 My 28. 4: Lloyd John DALQUIST. 5: Macalester Col 46-50 (Sociol) BA; McCormick Theol Sem 50-53 (Christian Educ) MA; UMich(Ann Arbor) AMLS. 6: Ger. 7: Asst catlg libn NY State U Col at Cortland 65-; Asst libn acquis No Mich U 66-67, Asst libn catlg 67-68; Dir lib Suomi Col 9: ALA. 14: Catlg, acquis. 15: 208 Prospect st, Houghton Mi 49931.

DALRYMPLE, CHARLES E(VERET). b Topeka Kan 29 Je 15. 4: Barbara Yeager. 5: UKan 33-39 (Soc, Pol Sci) AB; UIll 41 BS in LS. 6: Ger, S, Fr. 7: Lib asst KanU Lib 35-39, Biol libn 39-40; Circ libn UIll (Urbana) 40-41; Geologist div of sanitation Kan State Bd of Health, Lawrence Kan 41-46; Libn Manhattan Pub Lib, Manhattan Kan 46-49; Director Lincoln City Libs, Lincoln Neb 49-. 9: ALA; NebLA; MPLA (pres 47-49, treas 54). 13: Yes. 14: Bldgs & equipment. 15: Lincoln City Libs 136 S 14th st, Lincoln Neb 68508.

DALTON, CHESTER A. b Douglas Wyo 8 Ap 38. 4: Carol Clark. 5: Ottawa U (Kan) 56-60 (Bus, Econ) BA; Kan State U 60-62 (Educ, Soc Sci) MS; UDenver 63-64 (LS) MA. 6: Ger. 7: Tchr Shawnee Mission E High Sch, Shawnee Mission Kan 60-63; Ref libn Fullerton Jr Col 64-66; Head libn Cypress Jr Col 66-. 9: CalLA; Cal Tchrs Assn; Cal Jr Col Faculty Assn; NEA. 10: Phi Delta Kappa. 14: Ref, tech serv, admin. 15: Cypress Jr Col Lib, 9200 Valley View, Cypress Ca 90630.

DALTON, JACK. b Holland Va 21 Mr 08. 4: Mary Gochnauer. 5: Va Polytech Inst 24-27 (Chem Engnr); UVa 27-30 (Eng Lit) BS, MS; UMich 35-36 (LS). 7: Instr Eng Va Polytech Inst 30-34; Ref libn UVa 34-35, 36-42 Assn libn 42-50, Libn 50-56; Director Internat Rel Off ALA, Chicago 56-59; Dean Sch of Lib Serv ColumbiaU 59-. 8: Consul & adv to var institutions & foundations. 9: ALA; BSA; Bibliog Soc (London); NYLA. 10: Grolier Club. 13: Yes. 14: Educ for libnship. 15: 445 Riverside dr, NYC 10027.

DALTON, PHYLLIS I (BULL). b Marietta Kan 25 S 09. 4: Jack M Dalton. 5: UNeb 28-31 (Hist) BS in Ed; Washburn U 31; UNeb 40-41 (Eng Lit) MA; UDenver 42 BS in LS. 6: Sp, Fr, Ger. 7: Elem tchr Dist 69, Marysville Kan 27-28; Elem tchr Central Sch, Marysville Kn 31-32, Jr high sch tchr 32-33, High sch Eng tchr 33-40; Ref libn Lincoln Pub Lib, Lincoln Neb 40-41; Ref libn UNeb 42-44, Div lib in the humanities 44-48; Cal State Lib: Ref libn 48-51, Prin libn reader serv bur 51-57, Asst state libn 57-. 9: Adult Educ Assn; Amer Soc Pub

Admin; ALA (Coun, Cal Rep 63-); AAStateL (pres 64-65); CalLA (pres 69, Golden Empire Dist; pres 52-53); CalASchL; SLA. 10: West Govtal Research Assn; Beta Phi Mu. 12: "Library Service for All Alaskans" Admin Serv (69). 13: Yes. 14: Ref, admin. 15: 2589 Garden hwy, Sacramento Ca 95833.

DaLUISO, FLORENCE S. b Buffalo NY 5 Mr 15. 4: Gustave A DaLuiso. 5: Rosary Hill 62 (Mus) BA; SUNY (Geneseo) 64 (LS) Master; SUNY (Buffalo) 68 (Humanities) Master. 6: Fr, Ital, Sp. 7: Art libn SUNY (Buffalo) 64-. 8: Dir Institute in Art Libnship USOE Title II Grant. 9: ALA (Art Subsect: ed papers on art libnsip to be published in CRL Newsletter); Col Art Assn; NYLA. 14: Intl libnship. 15: 2660 So Park ave, Buffalo NY 14218.

DALY, ELIZABETH T. b NYC 6 Mr 13. 5: Rosemont Col 32-36 (Eng) BA; Columbia 41-43 (LS) MS. 7: Sales Clerk R H Macy & Co, NYC 36-39; Asst libn Brnxville Pub Lib, Bronxville NY 39-42; Purchase searcher NY Pub Lib 43-44; Libn (civilian) US Armed Forces, Germany 45-47; Libn US Dept of State, Wash DC 51-52; Libn (civilian) USAF, France 52-54; Head libn Lenox Lib Assn, Lenox Mass 56-. 9: ALA; MassLA (Adult & Educ Com 60-62); West Mass Lib Club; Berkshire LA; Mass Pub Lib Admin (sec 67-). 10: Colonial Dames of Amer; Mass Audubon Soc; Victorian Soc of Amer; DAR; Berkshire Co Hist Soc; Berkshire Garden Ctr; Oblates of St Benedict, Wash DC; Melville Soc. 14: Ref, private presses. 15: Maple ave, Sheffield Ma 01257.

DALY, SISTER LOUISE L IHM. b Jackson Mich 7 N 19. 5: Marygrove Col (Detroit) 54 (Biol) BS; Marywood Col (Scranton Penn) 68 MSLS. 6: Fr. 7: Elem tchr, Detroit & Fla 41-59; Jr high tchr Detroit 60-67; Asst catlgr Marygrove Col 68-. 9: CathLA. 14: Catlg, archives. 15: Marygrove Col Lib, 8425 W McNichols, Detroit Mi 48221.

DALY, REV SIMEON OSB. b Detroit 9 My 22. 5: ST Meinrad Col 41-45 (Philos) BA; St Meinrad Sem 45-48 (Theol); Catholic U 48-49 (Theol) STL, 50-51 MS in LS. 7: Instr St Meinrad Sem 49-50, Libn 51-. 9: ALA; CathLA; Amer Benedictine Acad; IndLA. 14: Admin. 15: Archabbey Lib St Meinrad Archabbey, St Meinrad Ind 47577.

DAMAS, JAMES J. b Charleston WVa 22 Ap 15. 4: Helen Margaret Swaya. 5: U Toledo 33-37 (Educ, Lit) BA in Ed; UMich 37-38 (Lit) MA; Columbia 39-42 BS LS. 7: Sch libn Macomber Voc High Sch, Toledo Ohio 38-; Prof asst Toledo Pub Lib tech dept 58-. 9: OhioASchL (rec sec 64-65). 10: To Library-Treasure Island (61). 14: Catlg, ref, pub, ya lit, a-v. 15: 1410 Juliet dr, Beverly Downs, Toledo Ohio 43614.

DAMASKOS, JAMES CONSTANTINE. b Newport RI 22 F 24. 4: Antonia Gerotheou. 5: Harvard 42-46 (Psych) AB; Simmons 48-50 MS in LS. 6: Ancient & Modern Gk, Lat, Ger. 7: Circ asst Boston U Chenery Lib 47-50; Catlgr Yale U Lib 50-53, Sr subj catlgr ref asst 53-56; Head humanities div Worcester Free Pub Lib, Worcester Mass 56-58; Admin asst for catlg Widener Lib Harvard 58-63; Libn Littauer Lib Harvard 63-. 14: Catlg. 15: 13 Follen st, Cambridge Mass 02138.

DAMASO, CAROL J (SENDA). b Youngstown Ohio 30 My 44. 4: Donald P Damaso. 5: St mary's Col (Notre Dame Ind) 62-66 (Elem Educ) BA; UMich 66-67 MALS. 7: Lib aide Shaker Hts Pub Lib, Shaker Hts Ohio summers 62-66; Hd child libn Fairfax Co Pub Lib, Fairfax Va 67-68; Hd child programs & serv Prince George's Co Mem Lib 68-. 8: Conducted three storytelling wkshops for Prince George's Co (Md) Mem Lib 68-69. 9: ALA; -CSD; -PLA; MdLA. 11: Frederick G Melcher Scholarship Award 66. 14: Child serv. 15: 8150 Lakecrest dr apt T 02, Greenbelt Md 20770.

DAMASO, CONSUELO. b Iloilo City Philippines 21 Ja 13. 5: Central Philippine Col 30-32 (Eng) AA; Silliman Inst 32-34 (Eng) BS in Ed (magna cum laude), 35-37 (Educ); UMich 46-49, 50, 51-53 (Eng) MA (Eng) AMLS; Columbia 50; Harvard summer 57; Radcliffe summer 60- Certif in Hist & Archival Mgt. 6: Bisayan, Sp, Fr, Ital, Port, Tagalog, Ger. 7: Libn Silliman U 35-37; Secondary sch tchr Phil Bur of Pub Schs 37-46; Catlgr UN Lib 49-0; Catlgr Harvard Col Lib 50-51; Serv asst UMich Lib rarebk rm; Libn UP Inst of Pub Admin (Manila) 53-56; Catlgr Off of Admin Harvard Col Lib 56-60; Assoc Prof Act Dir UP Inst of Lib Sci (Quezon City Phiippines) 61-66; Assoc Prof Dept of Eng & comp lit Col of Arts & Sci U of the Philippines 67-, In charge of dept lib 68-69. 8: Program Consul 4th Reg Conf-Wkshop for Libns March 25-April 1 63; Lib consul Nat DEFENSE Col of the Philippines 64-65; Program consul Sixth Reg Wkshop-Conf for Libns Dec 64. 9: ALA; Philippine LA (v-pres 53-54, chm Lib Train Com 54, v-chm Conf Com 54, pres elect 63-65, chm Program Com 65); Biennial Conf (pres 65-67); ASL of Philippines (pres 54); Bibliog Soc Philippines; UNESCO Nat Commsn of the Philippines 66-68. 10: Phi Kappa Phi; Pi Lambda Theta; Philippine Bklovers Soc. 12: Ed "Reaching Readers: The Librarys Responsibility and Opportunity (66); Ed "Bulletin of the Phiippine Library Assn (D 65 issue). 13: Yes. 14: Educ for libnship, lib resources, Philippine bibliog. 15: Univ of the Philippines, Inst of Lib Sci, UP PO Diliman Quezon City Philippines.

DAMBEKALNS, VOLDEMARS. b Latvia 14 Ap 11. 4: Lucy Clarke. 5: Tchrs Col (Jelgava Latvia) 32-36 (Educ) Diploma; URiga (Riga (Riga Latvia) 37-43 (Law, Econ) Mag iur & Mag oec; UWis 51-52 MA in LS. 6: Latvian, Russian, Ger. 7: Tchr Sch Prin, Lawyer, Dist Atty, Latvia 36-44; Catlgr NLM, Bethesda Md 52-59, Supv libn 59-. 8: Legal & lang consul for Internat Refugee Org, Germany 47-49. 9: ALA; DCLA; Potomac Tech Proc Group; Wash DC Area Med Lib Group. 10: Sigma Tau Delta. 13: Yes. 14: Subject analysis. 15: 5716 Arlington blvd, Arlington Va 22204.

DAMERON, LOGAN DOUGLAS. b Phoenix Ariz 11 S 33. 4: Frances Barnes. 5: Stanford 51-55 (Psych) AB; UMinn 55-65 (Psych, Ed), 65-66 (LS) MA. 7: Research fellow UMinn Bur of Inst Research 60-66; Circ libn Phoenix Col Lib 66-. 9: ALA; Ariz State LA. 10: Beta Phi Mu; Ariz Archaeol Soc. 14: Circ, ref. 15: 5756 West Pierson st, Phoenix Az 85031.

DAMICO, JAMES A. b Syracuse 22 My 32. 4: Kathryn E Briwa. 5: C W Post Col LIU 55-59 9bus Admin) BS; Rutgers 59-61 (LS) MSLS. 6: Ital, Sp. 7: Aviation Electronicsman 3rd US Navy 51-55; Stud asst C W Post Col Lib 58-59; Libn trainee Plainfield Pub Pub Lib, Plainfield NJ 59-61;Indexer AIAA, NYC 61-63; Br libn Gen Precision Inc, Little Falls NJ 63; Sr libn Thiokol Chem Corp, RMD, Denville NJ 63-64; Mgr Tech InfoCenter Gen Precision Inc, Little Falls NJ 64-67; Assoc research documentalist UDayton 67-68, Lib systs spec 68-. 9: SLA (chm Govt Info Serv 69-71; Dayton Chap: pres 69-70); ASIS. 10: Knights of Columbus, Council 3754. 12: "Establishment of a STINFO Program for the a f aero Propulsion Laboratory, Final Report, October 1967". 13: Yes. 14: Lib automation, systems & procedures, mgt. 15: 5989 Rosalie rd, Dayton Oh 45424.

DAMRON, MARIE G (O'CONNOR). b Auburn NY 16 My 26. 5: SUNY (Geneseo) 45-49 (Ed, LS) BS; Syracuse 58-59 (LS) MS. 7: Port Byron Central Sch, Port Byron NY: Elem sch tchr 49-50, High sch libn 50-51, 62-65; Spec serv libn USA Europe 51-53; Alexandria Pub Schs, Alexandria Va: Elem sch tchr 53-54, 55-56, Elem sch libn 56-57; Elem sch libn Waterloo Pub Schs, Waterloo NY 57-58; Wells Col: Ser libn 59-62, Hd libn 65-. 9: ALA; NYLA. 10: Kappa Delta Pi; Beta Phi Mu. 14: Ref, readers serv, lib admin. 15: RD 3, Auburn NY 13021.

DANA, D(AVID) BROWNELL. b Fond du Lac Wis 4 O 18. 5: Wis State U (Oshkosh) 36-40 (Eng) BS;UWis 40-41 (eng) MPh, 46-47 BLS. 6: Ger, Fr. 7: USAF Personnel (Capt) 42-46; Asst libn Ripon Col 47-50; Head tech serv State Hist Soc of Mo, Columbia Mo 50; Head libn Ripon Col 50-51; Head libn Wis State U (Oshkosh) 51-52; Head catlg dept Colgate U 52-61, Head tech serv 61-. 9: NYLA. 14: Clsf, catlg. 15: Box 207, Hamilton NY 13346.

DANA, MARY H. b Portland Me 20 Je 13. 5: Westbrook Jr Col 34-36 (Med sec) Certif; NJ Col for Women 40-42 (LS) BA. 7: Ward sec Mass Gen Hosp, Boston 36; Sec-clk Portland Pub Lib, Portland 37-40; NY Pub Lib: Gen asst 42-43, Asst br libn 44-47, Br libn 48-61, Chief bk ordering off 62-63, Asst chief libn 64-. 9: ALA; NYLA. 10: NY Lib Club. 14: Adult services. 15: 118 Waverly place, New York NY 10011.

DANCE, JAMES CALVIN. b Knoxville Tenn 30 My 29. 5: Maryville Col 47-51 (Eng Lit) BA; Columbia 51-52 MS. 7: Libn Psych Lib Columbia U 52-54; Press relations Detroit Pub Lib 55-56, Asst coordinator commun & group serv 56-63, Asst to coordinator bk sel 63-68, Chief commun & group serv 68-. 9: ALA (life mem); MichLA; Adult Educ Assn of Metropolitan Detroit; LPRC. 10: Friends of the Detroit Pub Lib. 11: Detroit Pub Lib Staff Memorial & Fellowship Award 66. 12: Book reviewer Detroit Free Press; Ed "Among Friends," quarterly, Friends of the Detroit Pub Lib. 13: Yes. 14: Pub rels, adult educ. 15: 2405 Carson, Detroit 48209.

DANDRE, CARMEL (SIMONETTI) (MRS). b Akron Ohio 18 My 21. 5: UAkron 38-42 (Eng) BA; Drexel 42-43 BLS. 6: Fr, Ital, Ger. 7: Circ libn Enoch Pratt Free Lib, Baltimore 43-44; Eng Instr UAkron 45-48, Order libn 44-45; Libn Akron S Sr High Sch, Akron Ohio 56-68; Libn Akron E Sr High Sch

68-. 9: NEA; OhioLA; OhioEA; OhioASchL (Dist Hospitality Chm); Akron Area Lib Assn (charter mem, sec-treas 69-); Akron EA. 10: Col Club. 14: Yp, ref. 15: 3066 Kent rd apt 208-B, Stow Oh 44224.

DANDRIDGE, PHYLLIS (WOLSEY). b Sunset Tex 25 Ja 30. 4: Glyn E Dandridge. 5: Midwest U 46-48 (Bus); N Tex State U 66-68 (Lib serv) BA, 68-69 MLS. 6: Fr. 7: Libn Tex Research Foundation, Renner Tex 68-. 9: SLA: Dallas Co TA. 10: Alpha Lambda Sigma. 14: Rare bks, sci bks: acquia, catlg, exchange. 15: 12131 High Meadow dr, Dallas Tx 75234.

DANE, WILLIAM JERALD. b Concord NH 8 My 25. 5: UNH 42-47 BA; UNancy (France) 45 Diplome; UParis 49-50 Diplome; Harvard 51-52; Drexel 50-51 MLS; Inst of Fine Arts NYU 52-59. 7: US Army, Europe 43-46; Lib asst art & music dept Newark Pub Lib, Newark NJ 47-51, Prin art libn art & music dept 57-68, Supv art & music libn 69-. 9: ALA-ACRL (chm Art Subsect 64-65). 10: Grolier Club NYC; Victorian Soc in Amer (chm Publ Com 67-). 12: "Picture Collection Subject Headings" (68). 13: Yes. 14: Art & music libs, rare bks, hist of printing. 15: Newark Pub Lib, Newark NJ 07108.

DANES, DORIS L (RUSSELL). b Post Falls Idaho. 4: Lewis E Danes. 5: Wash State U 35-39 (For Langs) BA; Catholic U 58-61 (LS) MS. 6: Sp. 7: Asstlibn Annandale High Sch, Annandale Va 60; Libn Mainland Reg High Sch, Linwood NJ 61-65; Ref libn Fairfax Co Libs, Fairfax Va 65-. 10: Beta Phi Mu. 14: Ref. 15: 4108 Mangalore dr, Annandale Va 22003.

DANFORD, ARDATH (ANNE). b Lima Ohio 11 F 30. 5: Fla State U 47-52 (LS) BA, MA. 6: Fr, Sp. 7: Bkmob libn Lima Pub Lib, Lima Ohio 52-55; Psychiatric libn UMd 55-56; Head acquis & tech proc Lima Pub Lib, Lima Ohio 56-60; Libn Way Pub Lib, Perrysburg Ohio 60-. 9: ALA; OhioLA (State chm Dist Meetings 63). 10: LWV; Amer Field Serv; Zonta. 12: "The Perrysburg Story" (66). 14: Adult serv. 15: 616 Louisianna ave, Perrysburg Oh 43551.

DANIEL, A(LLEN) MERCER. b Rochester NY 27 My 1887. 4: Portia E Daniel. 5: Storer Col 01-03 (Eng); Howard U 03-04 (Eng), 04-06 (Bus), 06-09 LLB. 6: Lat. 7: Govt Prin Clerk War Dept, Chief of Finance 14-23, Libn 23; Asst aw Libn Howard U 23-29, Act law libn 29-40, Asst Prof of Law & law libn 41-52, Assoc Prof of Law & law libn 52-56, Assoc Prof of Law & Librarian Emeritus 56-. 8: Mem Com "Law Library Journal; Trustee of Legal Aid Soc DC. 9: ALA; DCLA; Law Soc DC; Amer Bar Assn; AALL (life mem); Amer Judicature Soc (Emeritus mem); AALL (life mem). 10: AAUP (Emeritus mem). 13: Yes. 14: Legal bibliog, rare bks. 15: 654 Girard st NW apt 204, Wash DC 20001.

DANIEL, CHARLES M JR. b Dallas 13 Mr 25. 5: N Tex State U 42-48 (Eng) BA; UIll 48-49 MS in LS. 6: Sp. 7: Order libn Jefferson Parish Lib, Gretna La 50-53, Asst libn 53-54; Head of ext dept Mobile Pub Lib, Mobile Ala 54-55, asst libn 55-59; Head info & ref dept New Orleans Pub Lib 60-67; Acquis libn Bishop Col (Dallas) 69-. 9: ALA; TexLA. 10: Beta Phi Mu. 13: Yes. 14: Ref, acquis, ser, ext. 15: 5317 Mercedes, Dallas Tx 75206.

DANIEL, DONNA MARY. b Galion Ohio 19 O 32. 5: OhioU 52-56 (Hist, Govt) BS in Educ; Ohio State U summer 56; Miami U (Dayton Center) 58-59; West Res 59-64 MS in LS. 7: Sch libn Galion Jr & Sr High Sch, Galion Ohio 56-57; Tchr Northridge High Sch, Dayton Ohio 57-59; Sch libn Madison High Sch, Mansfield Ohio 59-66; Asst libn Ohio State U (Mansfield) 66-67; Sch libn Shelby Jr High, Shelby Ohio 67-. 9: NEA; ALA; OhioLA; OhioASchL (reg dir 65); OhioEA. 13: Yes. 14: Ref. 15: 406 Fairview ave, Galion Ohio 44833.

DANIEL, KATHERINE DUSENBERRY. b Due West SC 29 Jl 12. 4: David Oscar Daniel Jr. 5: Erskine Col 34 (Math, Eng) AB; Winthrop Col summer 37 (LS); UNC 43 BS in LS, 62-(LS), 69 MS in LS. 7: Tchr of Eng Honea Path High Sch, Honea Path SC 34-36; Tchr of Eng & libn Pendleton High Sch, Pendleton SC 36-42; Tchr of Eng Easley High Sch, Easley SC 42-43; Documents libn Clemson Col Lib 43-44; Documents libn Va Polytech Inst 44-45; Catlgr Winthrop Col Lib 45-46; Period libn NC State Lib 46-47; Ref libn atlgr chief of readers serv Engnr Sch Lib, Ft Belvoir Va 52-62; Catlgr UNC Lib (Chapel Hill) 62-. 9: ALA; LA; NCLA. 10: PTA. 14: Catlg, ref, docs. 15: 4012 Bristol rd, Hope Valley Durham NC 27707.

DANIEL, WENDELL BUTLER. b Floydad Tex 2 F 28. 5: UTex 52-54 (Eng) BA; Tex Tech Col 56-57 (Eng) MA; IndianaU 60-61 (LS) MA. 6: Fr, Ger. 7: 1st Lt Pilot USAF 46-52; Eng instr High Sch, Flogdada Tex 55-56; Eng instr Tex Tech Col 57-59; Libn Queens Borough Pub Lib, NYC 61-65; Hd lang & lit lib Queens Col 66-. 8: Guest lectr in Lib Sci: Ind U 67; Queens Col 68. 9: ALA. 10: Phi Beta Kappa; Beta Phi Mu. 14: Pub serv & collection bldg in acad libs. 15: 10 Land lane, Westbury NY 11590.

DANIELLS, LORNA M. b Toledo Ohio 13 Jl 18. 5: Miami U (Oxford Ohio) 36-40 (Hist) AB; Columbia (LS) BS. 7: Asst catlg dept Vassar Col 41-43, Ser catlgr 43-46; Catlgr Harvard Bus Sch 46-49, Ref asst 49-57, Ref libn 58-. 9: SLA (chm Advis Coun 64-65, chm Admissions Com 68-69, Ed; Business Division Bulletin, 57-58, chm Bus-Finance Div 58-59, Program chm Boston Chap 59-60, Hospitality chm Boston Chap 61-62; Preselect and prog chm, Boston Chap 67-68; Pres Boston Chap 68-69). 12: "Studies in Enterprise; A Selected Bibliography of American and Canadian Company Histories and Biographies of Businessmen (57), and 6 annual supps to above in "Business History Review (59-64); Baker Lib "Reference Lists, No 20 (60), No 21 (63), No 24 (65); Coll "Sources of Commodity Prices" (SLA 59); "Literature of Executive Management" (SLA 64). 13: Yes. 14: Ref. 15: 26 Concord ave apt 511, Cambridge Mass 02138.

DANIELS, EDWARD BERNARD. b MarbleheadMass 19 F 21. 4: Edith Dorothy Daniels. 5: Boston U 46-48 (Amer Lit) AB; Simmons 49-50 MLS. 7: (QM 1st class) USN 39-46; Asst libn in bus & tech & young adult libn, br libn, admin asst in area br, Enoch Pratt Free Lib, Baltimore 50-55; Head of adult serv Worcester Free Pub Lib, Worcester Mass 55-56; Chief libn Dearborn (Mich) Pub Lib 56-62; Libn Columbus (Ohio) Pub Lib 62-. 9: ALA; OhioLA (v-pres 66-67, pres 68-69). 10: Rotary Club; 4-H advis. 14: Admin, Spanish & Spanish-Amer lit. 15: 4200 Rudy rd, Columbus Ohio 43214.

DANIELS, ESTRILLA MYRTLE. b Grand Rapids Ohio 21 S 06. 5: Bowling Green State U 24-29 (Eng) BS in ED; Ohio StatU 30-38 (Eng, Educ); UIll 37-38 BS in LS. 6: Sp. 7: Tchr Country Sch, Henry Co Ohio 26-28; Tchr- Eng & Hist Liberty Center High Sch, Liberty Center 29-34; Libn Pub Lib, Pomeroy Ohio 38-39; Libn Pub Lib & High Sch, Mentor Ohio 39-44; Libn Pub Lib, Ravenna Ohio 44-. 9: ALA; OhioLA. 10: Bus & Prof Womens Club; Nature Club; Brooks Bird Club; Wilson Ornith Soc; Nature Conservancy; Thursday Literary Club. 14: Admin, ref. 15: Reed Mem Lib, 167 E Main st, Ravenna Oh 44266.

DANIELS, JANE (WILHELM). b Baltimore 25 Jl 28. 4: Worth B Daniels Jr. 5: Stratford Col 46-48; Goucher Col 48-50 (Eng) BA; Simmons 51-52 (LS) MS. 7: LP 1 Enoch Pratt Free Lib, Baltimore 52-54; Sr asst Croydon Pub Lib, Surrey Eng 54-55; LP 2 Enoch Pratt Free Lib, Baltimore 55-58, LP 3 58-61; Coordinator of spec lib serv, Baltimore Co Pub Lib, Towson Md 61-63. 8: Jinx and Jane Associates (free lance, primarily in field of publns) 63-. 9: ALA; MdLA. 12: "HLM The Mencken Bibliography, Comp by Betty Adler with the asst of Jane Wilhelm" (61). 13: Yes. 14: Spec collections, exhibits & displays, publ, publicity. 15: 210 Ridgewood rd, Baltimore 21210.

DANIELS, JEROME P. b Greensburg Penn 12 Mr 34. 4: Annette Schmidt. 5: UWis 53-57 (Speech) BS, 62-65 (LS) MS. 6: Ital. 7: Army (SP-4) Signal Corps Ga & Tex 57-59; Lib asst State Hist Soc of Wis, Madison 60-65; Asst dir Wis State U(Platteville) 65-. 9: ALA; WisLA. 10: Beta Phi Mu; Assn Wis State U Fac. 14: Admin, automation, tech serv. 15: 1125 Hollman st, Platteville Wi 53818.

DANIELS, LOUISE ANN (FOLLIOT). b NYC 25 Mr 22. 5: Hunter Col 38-42 (Fr) BA; Tex Christian U 48-52 (Eng Lit); Queens Col (NYC) 64-68 MLS. 6: Fr, Sp, Ital. 7: Mail clerk file clerk US Army (WAC) (Sgt), Ft Benning Ga & Sothwest PACIFIC Area 43-45; File clerk M W Kellogg Co NYC 42-43, 46-47; File clerk & records clerk USAF (Civil Service) Carswell AFB, Ft Worth Tex 50-54; Tech libn Greer Hydraulics Inc, NYC 54-58; Tech libn Loral Electronics Systems, Bronx NY 58-67; Tchr of lib JHS 117, Bronx NYC 67-. 9: . 14: Tech lib wk, sch lib wk. 15: 1546 E 172nd st, Bronx NY 10472.

DANIELS, MINA (HAYES). b Trenton NJ 23 Ap 27. 4: Boyd Lee Daniels. 5: Col of Wooster 45-49 (Eng, Hist) BA; Duke 59-60; UNC 64-65 MS in LS. 6: Ger. 7: Bibliog Duke U Lib 50-53; Tchr Holton Jr High, Durham NC 59-60; Libn Durham Acad, Durham NC 64-65; Ser Catlgr Duke Lib 65-67; Catlg libn UTenn Lib 68, Asst Prof Dept of Lib Serv 68-. 9: ALA; Southeastern Lib Assn; TennLA. 10: Phi Beta Kappa; Delta Phi Alpha; Phi Alpha Theta; AAUW; LWV; Beta Phi Mu. 14: Catlg, ref, adult lit. 15: PO Box 482, Maryville Tn 37801.

DANIELS, RONALD B. b Jamaica NY 25 Jl 35. 4: Sieglinde Keil. 5: Harvard 49-56, 57-58 (Eng) BA; Columbia 59-60 MLS; USussex (Englanf) 65-66 MA. 7: Asst catlg libn Cornell U Libs 60-62, Asst circ libn 62-65; Dist ref libn London Borough of Ealing Libs, London England 66-68; Asst acquis libn VPI 68-. 14: Acquis, ref. 15: 526 Edgewood lane, Blacksburg Va 24060.

DANIELSON, ROSAMOND HARRIETT. b Plainfield Conn 25 O 10. 5: Pembroke 31 (Lit) AB; Columbia 37 BS in LS 06: Fr. 7: Asst circ dept NY Pub Lib 3738; 1st asst catlg dept Pub Lib, Providence 39-44, Head catlg dept 45-48; Head ser dept UMo Lib 49-52, Head catlg dept 51-54; Asst catlg libn Cornell U ib 54-58, Assoc catlg libn 58-68, Libn catlg dept 68-. 8: Instr in LC Clsf UToronto Lib 59. 9: ALA-RTSD (Catlg & Clsf Sect: chm Subject Headings Com 62-66; Ser Sect: chm ad hoc com for ser Holdings Info Survey 64-66). 10: Phi Beta Kappa. 13: Yes. 14: Catlg, staff devel, reclsf. 15: 208 Cornell st, Ithaca NY 14850.

DANKERT, PHILIP ROWEN. b Hanover NH 29 O 35. 4: Virginia Rooney. 5: Colby Col 54-58 (Econ) BA; Simmons 61-63 MS in LS. 7: USA SP4 59-60; Cornell U Lib: Asst acquis libn 63-67, Assoc acquis libn 67-68; Ref libn Ind & Labor Rel Lib 68-. 9: ALA. 10: Jr C of C. 14: Ref, acquis. 15: 4 Candlewyck dr apt A-2, Ithaca NY 14850.

DANKEWYCH, MICHAEL. b Ukraine 8 S 25. 4: Katherine Chudzei. 5: Columbia 54-59 (Public Law & Govt) BS; NYU 59-60 (Pol Sci) MA; Columbia 60-62 (LS) MS; Georgetown 63-69 (Russian Area Studies) PhD. 7: US Army 49-52; Asst catlgr Columbia U Law Lib 60-62; Asst to libn Brooklyn Col Lib 62-63; Catlgr NLM, Bethesda Md 63-66; US Army Topographic Command, Washington DC 69. 12: "Future Potentialities of Siberia (65); "Siberia in Global Power Politics" (69). 13: Yes. 14: Catlg. 15: 5802 Kingswood rd, Bethesda Md 20014.

DANN, EVERETT REYNOLDS. b Jamaica NY 10 O 13. 4: Charlotte Patmor Dann. 5: Dartmouth 31-35 (Hist BA; Columbia 39-40 (Hist) MA, 63-65 MLS. 7: Accounting prod control Lederle Labs Div Amer Cyaamid Co, Pearl River NY 45-62; Asst libn Rockland State Hosp, Orangeburg NY 62-. 14: Bibliotherapy. 15: 76 New Valley rd, New City NY 10956.

DANOFF, FRANCES EVELYN (COLKER). b Phila 14 S 42. 4: I Michael Danoff. 5: UPenn 60-63 (Eng) BA; UNC 63-65 (LS) MS. 6: Sp. 7: Asst libn NC Wesleyan Col 64-66; Asst ref libn Soc Sci Dept Syracuse U Lib 67-. 9: ALA. 10: Phi Beta Kappa; Beta Phi Mu. 14: Ref. 15: Bldg 18 apt 6 New Slocum Hts, Syracuse NY 13210.

DANTON, J PERIAM. b Palo Alto Cal 5 Jl 08. 4: Lois King. 5: Oberlin 24-25, 26-28 (Ger) BA; U of Leipzig 25-26; Columbia 28-29 BLS; Williams 29-30 (Ger) MA; Chicago 33-35 (LS) PhD. 6: Ger, Fr. 7: Ref asst Williams Col 29-30; Asst ALA, Chicago 30-33; Libn Colby Col 35-36; Libn Temple U 36-42; Lt(jg), Lt, Lt Cdr USNR Pacific Area 42-45; Dean Sch of Libnship UCal(Berkeley) 46-61, Prof 47-. 8: Nat Lib Consul WPA 37; ALA "Booksfor Europe Program 39; Visiting Prof Chicago 42, Columbia 46; Amer SpecEthiopia 41; Ford Found Consul on Libs in Southast Asia 43; Dir US Dept of State-ALA Multi-Area Group Libn Program 63-64. 9: ALA (chm var coms 36-);-ACRL (treas 38-40, chm var coms 37-); AALS (pres 49-50); CalLA (var coms 46-); IFLA (chm Com on Lib Educ 67-). 11: Fulbright Research Scholar Germany 60-61, Austria 64-65. 12: "Book Selection and Collections: A Comparison of German and American University Libraries (63); Ed "The Climate of Book Selection: Social Influences on School and Public Libraries (58, 59); "Education for Librarianship (UNESCO 49; also French, Spanish, and Arabic eds); "Education for Librarianship: Criticisms, Dilemmas and Proposals (46); "United States Influence on Norwegian Librarianship, 1890-1940 (57); "Jamaica; Library Development," UNESCO (68); Ed Bd ACRL Monographs (66-); Bd Eds "Library Quarterly" (68-); Ed Bd "International Library Review" (68-). 13: Yes. 14: Internat libnship, lib educ, scholarly lib hist & admin. 15: School of Librarianship UCal, Berkeley Ca 94720.

DARCY, KATHLEEN MARY. b Evanston Ill 2 F 44. 5: Col Mt St Joseph on the Ohio 62-66 (Hist) AB; West Res 66-67 MSLS. 7: YA libn Lakewood Pub Lib, Lakewood Ohio 67-. 9: ALA; OhioLA; Young Libns Assn. 10: Beta Phi Mu; Women's Nat Bk Assn; Case West Res U; Sch of Lib Sci Alum Com. 11: H W Wilson Scholarship. 14: YA wk. 15: Lakewood Pub Lib 15425 Detroit ave, Lakewood Oh 44107.

DARDARIAN, GLORIA L (MELE). b Detroit Mich 13 D 32. 5: Wayne U 50-55 (Humanities) BA; UMich 55-56 (LS); Wayne State 66 MSLS, 62 Tchr Certif. 6: Albanian. 7: Sec Mich Mgt Corp, Detroit 55-59; Libn-sec Bower Div Fed Mogul, Detroit 59-61; Sch libn Detroit Pub Schs 61-64; Wayne State U: Research asst Ctr Applic of Sci & Tech 64-65, Instr Dept of Lib Sci 66-67, Asst libn Educ Lib 67-. 8: Consul Wayne State U, Dept of Bus Educ 68 develop an index to dissertations in bus educ; Consul Mich-Ohio Reg Educ Lab 68-69 develop an index to their lib resources; Consul Wayne State U Center for Urban Studies 67-68 develop an index to riots; "Document and Reference Text, An Index to Minority Group Employment Information" 67. 9: SLA; ASIS; Women's Nat Bk Assn. 10: Detroit Child Bk Fair; Wayne State U Soc Affairs Com. 12: "Culturally Disadvantaged, A Keyword-Out-Of-Context, Index and Bibliog" (66); "Sources in Educational Research" (69); Jt comp "Keyword-In-Context Index to the Educ, Res, Info Center Material Publoshed by the US Off of Ed" (66); Jt comp "Annual Index to Poverty, Human Resources and Manpower Information" (66). 14: Ref, indexing, children's books. 15: 29 Collingwood apt 305, Detroit Mi 48202.

DARLING, BARBARA C. b Natick Mass 19 Jl 11. 5: NJ Col for Women (Douglass Col) 31-35 9ls0 ab. 7: Asst NYC Pub Lib 35; Jr asst Robbins Memorial Lib, Arlington Mass 36; Libn MIT Aeronautics & Astronautics Lib 42-. 9: SLA. 10: Mass Horticultural Soc. 14: Mgt small br lib. 15: 110 Edgemere rd, W Roxbury Ma 02132.

DARLING, (MIRIAM) DORETTE. b Brainerd Minn 9 O 12. 5: East State Tchrs Col 28-31; Sioux Falls Col 31-32 (Eng, Educ) BA; UColo summers 38-41; U Denver 49 BS in LS. 6: Fr. 7: Eng tchrWhite Lake High Sch, White Lake SD 33- 38; Eng tchr Lead High Sch, Lead sd 38-42; Libn Lead High Sch, Lead SD 42-47;Lead Homestake Mining Co, Lead SD 47-63; Asst libn No State Col 67-. 8: SD State Lib Commsnr 55-; Chm SD Nat Lib Week 61. 9: ALA; MPLA; Bibliog Center for Research, Denver (Bd Dirs 60-67; SDLA (sec-treas 43-50, pres 53). 10: Dlta Kappa Gamma; PEO. 11: SD Libn of the Year, 57. 13: Yes. 14: Ref. reg hist. 15: 117 Fourteenth ave SE, Aberdeen SD 57401.

DARLING, EMILY (HOWLAND). b Philadelphia. 5: Swarthmore Col 33 Hist) AB; Drexel 65- (L). 7: Social wker Commonwealth of Penn, Phila 34-39; Sec Associated Mgt Consultants, Cleveland 56-58; Sec Scott Paper Co, Phila 58-60, Libn Marketing Lib 60-. 9: SLA. 10: Beta Phi Mu. 14: Ref. 15: Scott Paper Co, Phila Pa 19113.

DARLING, LOUISE (MARIE). b Los Aneles 3 Ag 11. 5: UCLA 33 (Bot) BA; UCal (Berkeley) 35 (Bot) MA, 36 Certif in Libnship; UCal (Berkeley) 40 (LS) Special Secondary Credential; Columbia 49 (Med Libnship). 6: Fr, Sp, Ger. 7: Asst libn Giannini Foun, U Cal (Berkeley) 36-39; Libn Acalanes Union High Sch, Lafayette Cal 40- 41; Ref asst UCLA 41-44; Area supv Army Lib Serv, Hawaii & Philippines 44-47; UCLA: Biomed libn 47-, Lecturer Div of Med Hist Sch of Med 58-, Lecturer Sch of Lib Serv 60-. 8: PHS Adv Com for Sci Publs 62-65; Consul to the Facultad de Ciencias Medicas Universidad Nacional de Honduras Tegucigalpa, Honduras 62, on Rockefeller Found Grant; On short-term assignments for SPHS: UHawaii, Harvard Med Lb, & loc institutions; Dir PHS grant to support rogram for train med libns 60-. 9: MedLA (chm Com on Internat Coop 59-62 & other coms, Bd Dirs 61-62 & 64-65, pres 63-64); ASIS; ALA-ACRL (chm Agric & Biol Scis Subsect 68-69); Amer Assn Hist Med (Coun 61-63, 68-71); CalLA; Med Lib Group of So Cal (sec 49, pres 50-51); Amer Assn of Dental Schs. 10: AAAS. 11: Golden Bruin Award 61. 13: Yes. 14: Med libnship (admin), reg serv, hist of med. 15: Biomed Lib UCal Center for the Health Scis, Los Angeles 90024.

DARLING, RICHARD LEWIS. b Great Falls Mont 19 Ja 25. 4: Persis Williams. 5: UMont 43, 46-48 (Eng) BA; 49-50 (Eng) MA; UMich 52-54 AMLS, 54-56, 59-60 (LS) PhD. 7: T/Sgt US Army 43-46; Eng tchr Choteau Pub Schs, Choteau Mont 50-51; Libn University High Sch UMich (Ann Arbor) 51-56; Asst Prof UMont 56-59; Coordinator of Lib Serv Livonia Pub Schs Mich 59-62; Sch lib spec US Off of d, Lib Serv Br Wash DC 62-64; Supv of lib serv Montgomery Co Pub Sch, Rockville Md 64-65; Asst Dir Dept of Instrl Materials Montgomery Co Pub Sch 65-66, Dir Dept of Educ Media & Tech 66-. 8: PNLA Lib Development Proj 57-58; Sch lib consul ALA Nat Lib Statistics Coord Proj Wash DC 64; Sch Lib Consul "City of Columbia Lib Feasibility Study 65; Lecturer. 9: ALA;-LAD (var coms);-CSD (var coms); AASchL (pres 66-67); ACEI (Child bk res ed, childhood education 65-68); Pacific NWLA (Sec Lib Educ Div 58-59); MontLA; MichLA; MichASchL; MdLA; MdASchL; Md Sch Media Assn; NEA-DAVI; NAEB. 11: ALA E P Dutton-John McRae

Award 59. 12: "Survey of School Library Standards (64); "Public School Library Statistics, 1962-63 (64); "The Rise of Children's Book Reviewing in America, 1865-1881" (68); Child Bk Ed "Childhood Education" (65-68). 13: Yes. 14: Sch libs, lib educ, tech serv, non-bk materials, book sel. 15: 5012 Barkwood pl, Rockville Md 20853.

DARLINGTON, ALBERT CHRISTOPHER JR. b Swedesboro NJ 5 Jl 34. 5: E Baptist Col 53-57 (Hist) BA; Drexel 57-58 BSLS. 7: Assoc libn E Baptist Theol Sem 58-68, Act libn 66-67; Tech serv libn Moorestown Free Lib, Moorestown NJ 68-. 9: ALA. 14: Tech serv, catlg, ref. 15: 1 East Main st, Moorestown NJ 08057.

DARNELL, EDNA E (BURNLEY). b Rossington Ky 4 Mr 25. 4: Willie Darnell. 5: Murray State Col 56-60 (LS Eng) BS, 65-67 MA in Ed; Peabody Grad Sch 69-. 6: Fr. 7: Tchr Elem Sch, Hardin Ky 60-61; Reg libn Ky State Dept of Libs, Murray Ky 61-64; Asst libn Murray State Col 64-66, Asst Prof Lib Sci Dept Murray State U 67-. 8: Consul Head Start Prog, ACEI Com consul Wkshop summer 69. 9: NEA; KyLA; KyEA; FDLA; ABA. 10: Murray Womans Club; Alpha Beta Alpha (sponsor); Kappa Delta Pi; Alpha Delta Kappa. 14: Catlg, a-v, child lit. 15: Rte 2, Murray Ky 42071.

DARRAH, JANE. b Leavenworth Kan 17 Ja 09. 5: Monticello Col 27-29; West Res 29-31 (LS) BS. 7: Asst Leavenworth Pub Lib, Leavenworth Kan 26-27; Asst Cleveland Pub Lib 29-31; Child libn Kansas City Pub Lib, Kansas City Mo 31-40; Asst dir-child wk Enoch Pratt Free Lib, Baltimore 40-44; (Lt) WAC US Army 44-45; Dir child wk Youngstown Pub Lib, Youngstown Ohio 46-56; Supt child wk Seattle Pub Lib 56-. 9: ALA-CSD (pres 55-56, chm Newbery-Caldecott Comm 54-55); Pacific NWLA (Chm Child Div 63-65). 14: Wk with child.

DART, EUGENIE LOUISE. b New Orleans La 13 O 18. 5: H Sophie Newcomb Col 35-40 (Fr) BA; Simmons 58-60 MSLS. 6: Fr, Sp. 7: Assoc libn Ins Lib Assn Boston 61-62; Assoc libn US Steel, NYC 64-67; Assoc libn Sch of Law Loyola U New Orleans 68-. 9: SLA. 10: Jr League of New Orleans. 14: Ref. 15: 1658 Joseph st, New Orleans La 70115.

DART, J DORIS. b St Lambert Que Can 19 My 1900. 5: McGill 16-21 (Geol) BA; Yale 21-23 (Geol); Pratt 24-25 Certif; Columbia 41-42. 6: Fr, Ger. 7: Tech asst Peabody Museum Yale U 23-24; Catlgr Henry L Doherty Co, NY 25-26; Catlgr Yale U 26-29; Asst libn & hed catlgr UNH 29-43; Libn ChemistsClub, NY 43-48; Assoc ed of sci indexing H W Wilson Co, NY 48-56, Ed "Social Sciences & Humanities Index 56-. 9: ALA; NYLib Club. 14: Subj catlg. 15: 950 University ave, Bronx NY 10452.

DAS, JEAN K. b Braintree England 2 Ag 24. 4: Kamleshwar Das. 5: Lond Sch of Econ LondU 42-45 (Econ geog) B Sc econ; Columbia 63-66 MLS. 6: Fr, Ital. 7: Libn Queens Borough Pub Lib Bayside Br 66-. 9: ALA; Great Neck LA. 10: Great Neck Com for Human Rights. 14: Wk with child. 15: 21 Allenwood rd, Great Neck NY 11023.

DASHIELL, EUNICE LEONA (MARTIN). b Boston 1 O 17. 5: Simmons 36-40 BLS. 6: Sp, Fr, Ger. 7: Ref libn NY Pub Lib 42-47; Catlgr Harvard U 47-48; Catlgr Temple U 50-53; Catlgr Boston U Chenery Lib 53-56; Head tech serv Mass Lib Ext Div, Boston 56-60; Head tech serv Brookline Pub Lib, Brookline Mass 60-. 9: ALA; MassLA; NE Tech Serv Libns (pres 66-67). 10: AAUW. 13: Yes. 14: Catlg, ref. 15: 24 Holborn st, Boston 02121.

DASSISI, SISTER CLARE SCH. b Boston 19 F 1900. 5: Mt St Vincent (Halifax NS) 26 (Educ); Fordham 26-2 BA; Emerson Col 36 (Speech); MSV Sch Lb Sci 49 BLS. 7: Tchr Our Lady of Angels Sch, Brooklyn NY 26-39; Tchr Seton Hall, High Sch, Patchogue NY 39-41; Tchr libn MT St Agnes Acad, Bermuda 41-44; Tchr-libn esurrection-Ascension Sch, Rego Park NY 44-48; Tchr-libn St Patricks High Sch, Lawrence Mass 48-52; Tchr St Margarets St Kevins, Dorchester Mass 52-57; Tchr libn John F Kennedy Youth Lib St Peters Sch, Dorchester Mass 57-. 8: Elem Sch Lib consul; Libn of Demonstration Lib, JFK Youth Lib. 9: CathLA (chm Elem Sect NE Unit); ALA; Nat Womens Bk Assn; NELA (chm Exec Bd). 11: Partic Phase I Sch Lib Manpower Proj, Knapp Foun. 14: Libn, catlg. 15: 307 Bowdoin st, Dorchester Mass 02122.

DAST, JAMES CHRISTIAN. b Bay City Mich 15 F 39. 4: Nancy Perkins. 5: Mich State U 60-64 (Botany) BS; UWis 65-68 (LS) MS. 6: Fr. 7: UWis at Madison: Aircraft electrical specialist USA 57-60, Lab tech McArdle Lab 65-66, Exch clk Middleton Med Lib 66-68, Bibliogr Hepatoma Info Exch 67-68, Libn Middleton Med Lib 69-, Ed Hepatoma Info Exch 69-. 9: ALA; Amer Inst of Biol Scis; WisLA. 14: Book sel & bibliog (biolog scis); rare bks. 15: 630 Spruce st, Madison Wi 53715.

DAUB, DOROTHY. b San Francisco 26 O 1899. 5: Denison U 18-22 (Eng) PhB; UParis 29; West Res 31 B in LS. 6: Fr, Ger. 7: Eng tchr Middletown High Sch, Middletown Ohio; Libn Spec Serv Camp Atterbury Ind 42; Libn Open Shelf Room Oberlin Col Lib 31-. 8: Volunteer Hosp Libs, Oberlin Ohio 65-. 9: ALA; OhioLA; Lorain Co LA. 14: Readers advis. 15: 145 West Lorain st, Oberlin Oh 44305.

DAUGHERTY, LYNN E (SIGNORINO). b Berwyn Ill 19 S 40. 4: E Duane Daugherty. 5: Earlham Col 58-62 (Family rel) AB; Ind U 65-65 MLS. 7: Employment interviewer Cook Co Sch of Nursing, Chicago 62-64; Hd libn Martinsville Pub Lib, Martinsville Ind 65-68; Libn Danville Pub Lib, Danville Ill 68-. 9: ALA; IndLA; IllLA. 10: AAUW. 14: Child serv, ref. 15: 614 - 7th st, Covington In 47932.

DAUGHTRY, BESSIE (MILLER). b Geneva Ala 9 N 12. 4: J B Daughtry. 5: Ala Col 38 (Bus Ed, Eng, Hist, Educ) AB; Fla State U 48 (LS) MA; Midwestern U 58 (Educ-Admin, Bus Educ) MEd; SW Tex State 66 (Psych, Hist). 6: Sp. 7: Tchr Geneva (Ala) Co Schs 34-8; Tchr Leonia High Sch, Dady Fla 38-41; Com tchr for enlisted personnel, Eglin AFB Fla 41-42, sec & admin asst 42-45; Tchr Glenmont Elem Sch, Motgomery Co Md 44; Asst catlg dept & circ dept Fla State U Lib 48, Libn of Lib Sch & Materials Center 49-52, 53-55; TchrElem Sch Pepperrell AFB, St Johns Newfoundland 52-53; Base libn Sheppard AFB, Wichita Falls Tex 56-59; Tchr Balboa Elem Sch, Balboa CZ 60-62; Instr Lib Sch Fla State U 62-63; Asst Dir Air Force Libs HQ USAF, Randolph AFB Tex 63-. 9: ALA-PLA; Tex State LA; SWLA; Bexar LA. 10: Beta Phi Mu; Zonta. 12: Ed "Newsletter" PLA Armed Forces Libns Sect (66-69). 14: Acquis, admin. 15: 262 Sherri dr, Universal City Tx 78148.

DAUME, MARY KATHERINE (ROSSITER). 4: Karl W Daume. 5: Col of Wooster 30-34 (Eng) AB; West Res 35 BLS; Wayne State 47 (A-V Admin). 6: Ger, Fr, Sp. 7: High sch libn Fairmont High Sch, Dayton Ohio 35-36; City Libn St Marys Pub Lib, St Marys Ohio 36-37; Asst circ libn Dorsch Mem Lib, Monroe Mich 44-46; County libn Monroe Co Lib, Monroe Mich 47-63; Dir Monroe Co Lib System, Monroe Mich 63-; Lib serv consul (privately employed), Monroe Mich 63-; Prof Wayne State U Sch of Lib Sci 65-67; Prof UMich Sch of Lib Sci 68. 8: Consulbkmob problems 50-; consul on library admin, lib-community relations, tech processing 63-; consul pub lib & sch cooperation 60-; mem Mich State Bd for Libs 60-65. 9: ALA (Coun, chm & mem of var coms); -ALTA (2 coms); AEA; NAVA; DAVI; MichLA (chm & mem var coms); MichASchL (Legis chm); MichAVA; MichEA; Mich Hist Soc; Monroe County Hist Soc. 10: Bus & Prof Womens Club; Altrusa; AAUW. 11: Woman of the Year Monroe Rotary Club 54; Silver Book Award LBI 63; Govs Award, Mich Minuteman 67. 2: "Library Cooperation in Port Huron and the St. Clair County Area, with Recommendations for Immediate Action and for Long Range Planning (64). 13: Yes. 14: Pub rels, ref, admin, planning serv & bldg programs, a-v. 15: 102 East Grove st, Monroe Mi 48161.

DAUTRICH, ELISABETH C (KERLING). b Reading Penn 24 Mr 16. 5: Ithaca Col 34-38 (Music Educ) BS; Drexel 62-63 MSLS. 6: Ger. 7: Music supv Senec-Gorham-Potter, NY; Music supv Mt Penn Pub Schs, Penn; Pub rel Mary Mac-Intosh Assn, Reading Penn; Reading Pub Lib, Reading Penn 57-63; Dir Hazleton Pub Lib, Hazleton Penn 63-. 8: Asst Prof of Lib Sci Penn State U 64-. 9: LA; PennLA. 10: AAUW; Commun Wkers of Hazleton; Hazleton Art League. 15: 417 W Diamond ave, Hazleton Penn 18201.

DAVENPORT, JEAN Z. b Cleveland 4 Jl 33. 4: Frederick B Davenport. 5: OhioU 51-55 (Eng) BA; West Res 55-57 MSLS. 6: Fr. 7: Desk asst Ohio U Lib 54-55; Lib asst West Res U 55-57, Lit searcher Documentation Center 61-62; Tech libn Cleveland Pub Lib 57-. 9: SLA; ALA; OhioLA. 10: OhioU Womens Club; Cleveland Museum of Art; West Res Hist Soc. 14: Sci & tech ref. 15,; 2835 S Moreland blvd, Cleveland Oh 44120.

DAVIDOFF, MARCIA. b NY 21 N 32. 5: Keuka Col 54 (Sociol) BA; West Res 55 (Soc Sci, Group Wk); SUNY (Albany) 57 MSLS; Drexel 62 (Med Libnship). 6: Sp. 7: Asst serv club dir, Ft Slocum NY 55; Teenage program dir YWCA, Paterson NJ 56; Ref asst Schenectady Co Pub Lib, Schenectady NY 56-61; Asst libn Sterling Winthrop Research

Inst, Rensselear NY 59-61; Ref circ libn Col of Physicians of Phila 61-63; Circ libn Upstate Med Center, Syracuse NY 63-66; Ref libn 66-67; Asst libn etramural progs & Asst Prof UNeb Col Med (Omaha) 67-68; Med libn Ellis Hosp, Schenectady NY 68; Sr libn NY State Med Lib, Albany NY 68-69; Libn 69-. 8: Participant in several colloquia & insts on med lib practices and admin. 09: MEDLA (Com & chm Cert Com 63-68; Upstate (NY) Reg Gp: Nomin Com 69; Phila Reg Gp Memb Chm 62); SLA (Sci-Tech Div: Bylaws Revis Com of Pharmaceut Sect 63); NYLA (Hospitality Com 66); Hudson-MohawkLA; CapitalDistLA. Omaha-Council Bluffs Lib Club; AAAS; LWV. 14: Ref, med libnship. 15: 27 Washington rd, Scotia NY 12302.

DAVIDSON, CHALMERS GASTON. b Chester SC 6 Je 07. 4: Alice Graham Gage. 5: Davidson Col 24-28 (Hist) AB (summa cum laude); Harvard 29-30 (Hist) MA, 42 (Hist) PhD; UChicago 35-36 MS in LS. 6: Fr, Ger. 7: Instr Chamberlain-Hunt Military Acad, Miss 28-29; Instr Blue Ridge Sch for Boys, NC 33-34; Instr The Citadel 34-35; Prof of hist & dir Grey Mem Lib Davidson Col 36-; Armed guard comdr (Lt jg) USN, Pacific area WWII. 10: Mecklenburg Hist Assn; NC Writers Conf; NC Lit & Hist Assn; Hist Soc of NC; Phi beta Kappa; Omicron Delta Kappa; Sigma Upsilon; Beta Theta Pi; Soc of the Cincinatti. 11: Charles A Cannon Award for NC Hist. 12: "Rural Hill" (43); "Cloud over catawba" (49); "Friends of the People" (50); "Piedmont Partisan" (51); "Mid-Point for 128" (53); "Gaston of Chester" (56); "Generations of Davidson College" (55, 64). 13: Yes. 14: NC hist, col lib admin. 15: Hurricane hill, Davidson NC 28036.

DAVIDSON, DONALD C(URTIS). b Vancouver BC 11 D 11. 4: June A Reynolds. 5: UBC 28-33 (Hist) BA; UCal (Berkeley) 33-34 (Hist) MA, 37 (Hist) PhD, 41 (LS) Certif. 06: Fr. 0: Tchg asst UCal (Berkeley) 35-37; Educ adviser Henry E Huntington Lib & Art Gallery, San Marino Cal 37-41; Libn & Prof of hist URedlands 41-47; Chief clerk, info & educ sect 6th Infantry Div US Army New Guinea, Luzon Korea 43-46; ULibn UCal (Santa Barbara) 47-, Act dean applied arts 56-57, Act dean letters & sci 57-59. 8: Consul: Cal Acad of Scis, San Francisco 55-56; U Alaska Lib 63-67;Fund for Advancement of Educ, to six So Cal Cols 63-64; USAF Acad Lib 59; UCal (Davis) Lib 64; UCal (San Diego) Lib 66; USN Postgrad Sch (Monterey) 68; mem 4 accred coms West Col Assn 51-55. 09: ALA (Coun 63-67); -ACRL (chm Col Libs Sect -53, chm Bldgs Com Col & Univ Libs 59-60); -LAD (chm Lib Admin Div; Bldgs & Equip Sect 65-67); CalLA (CURLS: sec, v-chm, chm So Div 49-53, chm Nom Com 59; State Aid Explor Com 49-53; State Nom Coms 49-50, 51-52; chm Lib, Hist, Bibliog & Archive Com 56; Spec Com to Recommend Master Plan Survey of Higher Educ 59; chm Lib Bldgs 64, 65; Coun 68-69. 11: Fulbright Fellowship USheffield Postgrad Sch of Libs 66-67. 12: Ed "Proceedings of 1953 ACRL Buildings Institute ACRL Monograph No 10 (53). 13: Yes. 14: Hist of bks, lib bldgs. 15: 3685 La Entrada, Santa Barbara Ca 93105.

DAVIDSON, DOROTHY (HARRIET) BURT. b Troy NY 2 O 09. 4: Paul Moody Davidson. 5: Trinity U 27-28; Park Coll 28-31 (Eng) BA; Memphis State U 65 (Eng) MA. 6: Portug. 7: Eng tchr Fortescue Consolidated High Sch, Fortescue Mo 31-32; Family coun United Charities, Dallas Tex 32-35; Missionary Evangelical Union of S Amer, Brazil 36-60; Eng prof & libn Mid-South Bible Col, Memphis Tenn 60-. 9: ALA; Christian Libns' Fellowship. 14: Motivation of student lib users, lib-faculty-student relationships. 15: 2485 Union ave, Memphis Tn 38112.

DAVIDSON, DOROTHY (IRENE) METCALFE. b Rochester NY 9 Ja 30. 5: Simmons 47-51 BS in LS; Ill State Tchrs Coll 63-65 (Ed); Bogan Jr Coll 64-66 (Ed). 7: Catlgr Chicago Pub Lib 51-53; Libn Evergreen Park Elem School Dist, Evergreen Park Ill 64-69; Asst libn Sears, Roebuck & Co, Chicago 69-. 9: ALA; IllLA; IllEA. 15: 9555 So Sacramento ave, Evergreen Park Il 60642.

DAVIDSON, ELISABETH (WENNING). b Nashville Tenn 18 Je 08. 4: John Wells Davidson. 5: Vanderbilt 30 (Eng, Ger) BA; UBerlin & UHeidelberg 30-31 (Ger lit/Amer-Ger Fellow; Catholic U 58 MS in LS. 6: Ger. 7: LC: Ref libn 59-63, Asst hd child bk sect 63; NJ State Lib, Trenton: Ref libn 64-65, Asst hd lending serv 67-; Libn Princeton Day Sch, Princeton NJ 65-67. 9: ALA; NJLA. 10: Nat League of Amer Penwomen; Wash Child Bk Guild; Princeton Hist Soc. 12: Jt comp "Children's Literature: A Guide to Reference Sources" (66); "The Christmas Mouse" (59); "A Cheese for Lafayette" (50); "Packet Alley" (51); co-auth "Plenty of Pirates" (53). 14: Hist of child lit, ref, Afro-Amer biog, early Americana, soc hist, hist research, recipes of hist interest. 15: 110 Bayard lane. Princeton NJ 08540.

DAVIDSON, ELIZABETH (STONEY). b Dillon SC 22 Ag 15. 4: John Richard Davidson. 5: Winthrop Col 32-36 (Fr, Eng) AB; UNC summers 42-44 BS in LS; UMich summers 54, 55 58 ABLS. 7: Tchr Ehrhardt High Sch, Ehrhardt SC 36-37; Tchr-libn St Stephens High Sch, St Stephens SC 37-40; Tchr-libn Gen Wm Moultrie High Sch, mt Pleasant SC 40-44; Prof of Lib Sci Southeastern La Col 44. 9: NEA; ALA; La Tchrs Assn; LaLA. 10: Phi Kappa Phi; AAUW; Delta Kappa Gamma; Beta Phi Mu; Kappa Delta Pi. 14: Tchg. 15: Box 675 College Station, Hammond La 70401.

DAVIDSON, HAROLD LAWRENCE. b Lisbon ND 21 D 28. 4: Belle Elaine Light. 5: Tchr Col (Valley City ND) 50-54 (Geog, Hist) BS; UDenver summers 61-64 MALS. 7: (Cpl) US Army (clerk-typist) US & Japan 46-47; Proprietor Davidsons Machine Shop, Valley City ND 50-54; Prin tchr Killdeer Pub Schs, Killdeer ND 54-57; Libn tchr Baker Pub Schs, Baker Mont 57-61; Lib supv Helena Pub Schs, Helena Mont 61-67; Asst Prof Lib Sci East Mont Col 67-. 8: Libn, Mont State Dept of Pub Welfare, Helena 62-67; Evaluative Criteria team of the NW Accred Assn 69-. 9: MontLA; PNLA; HelenaLA; NEA: MontEA. 10: Dir HEA IIB Inst, East Mont Col 69; Trustee Helena Pub Lib Bd ; PTA; Gamma Theta Upsilon; exchange Club; AAUP. 14: Wk with ya, bk sel, tchg lib sci. 15: 1903 - 10th st W, Billings Mt 59102.

DAVIDSON, JOHN SUMNER. b Kensington Md 6 Jl 08. 4: Hele Wilks. 5: U of the South 26-30 AB; Syracuse 33 MA, 38 BS in LS. 7: Instr Syracuse U 30-39; Assoc libn U of the South 39-40; State Supv Lib Proj WPA, Louisville Ky 40; Libn Muhlenberg Col 40-. 9: ALA-ACRL (Phila Chap: past sec-treas, Bd mem; chm Nomin Com); PennLA (Col & Res Sect). 13: Yes. 14: Admin. 15: Muhlenberg Col Lib, Allentown Pa 18104.

DAVIDSON, JOSEPHINE FRAZIE. b Hattiesburg Miss 28 S 34. 4: John Kenneth Davidson. 5: USoMiss 51-55 9ls0 bs; Fla State U 57-58 (LS) MA. 7: Asst in circ U of So Miss summer 55; Libn Clarksdale High Sch, Clarksdale Miss 55-57; Asst catlg libn UGa 58-61, 1st asst catlg libn 61-64; Catlg libn Armstrong State Col (Savannah) 64-67; Chief of tech serv Augusta-Richmond Co Pub Lib, Augusta Ga 67-. 9: SELA; GaLA. 10: Phi Mu; DAR; Pi Kappa Pi; kappa Delta Pi; Pi Gamma Mu; Phi Delta Rho. 13: Yes. 14: Catlg. 15: 1908 Valley Spring rd, Augusta Ga 30904.

DAVIDSON, LOIS MARY. b Salem Ill 15 N 07. 5: SoIllU 30-34 (Educ) BEd; UIll 41 (Educ) MA, 52 (LS) MS. 6: Sp. 7: Tchr pub schs Ill 26-44; Methodist Missionary Methodist Bd of Missions: Tchr 44-52, Libn in Union Sem (Matanzas Cuba) 52-60, Libn in Union Sem (Mexico City Mex) 61-63, 65-. 9: ALA; ATheolLA. 10: DAR; Sigma Pi Rho; Nat Retired Tchrs Assn. 14: Catlg. 15: Rte 4, Salem Il 62881.

DAVIDSON, LOIS PEARL. b Garrett Ind 25 Mr 29. 5: Messiah Col 47-49 (Educ); Goshen Col 49-51 (Elem Educ) BS in Ed; Ind U 63-65(LS) MA. 6: Ger. 7: Tchr Union Twp Schs, Nappanee Ind 51-53; Tchr Brethren in Christ Missions, Zambia Africa 56-59; Sec Brethren in ChristMissions, Rhodesia Africa 60-61; Tchr Waneecommun Schs, Nappanee Ind 62-64; Readers serv libn Messiah Col 65-. 9: ALA. 10: Beta Phi Mu. 14: Ref. 15: Messiah Col, Grantham Pa 17027.

DAVIDSON, LOUISE (SMITH). b Raceland Ky 6 My 15. 5: Morehead State Col 38 (Elrm Educ) AB; UKy 50 (LS) BS; Morehead State Col 63 (Supv) MA. 7: Elem tchr Raceland Bd of Educ, Raceland Ky 34-49, High sch libn 50-67; UKy Ashland Commun Col 67-. 8: Instr in lib sci, Morehead State Col summers 58-62, 65. 9: ALA-AASchL; NEA; KyLA; KyASchL. 10: AAUP; Raceland Younger Womans Club. 14: Ref, tchg. 15: 507 Pond Run rd, Raceland Ky 41169.

DAVIDSON, M(AE) JOYCE. b Providence 16 Jl 30. 5: Pembroke 48-52 (Psych) AB; Simmons 61-62 (LS) MS. 7: Sec Mutual Boiler & Machy Insurance Co, Providence 52-56; Ed research asst Walter V Clarke Assoc, E Providence RI 56-57; Personnel supv Providence Pub Lib 58-61; Asst personnel dir Detroit Pub Lib 62-66; Asst chief personnel off NY Pub Lib 66-69; Asst dir Lib Careers, Syracuse NY 69-. 9: ALA; MichLA; RILA. 14: Personnel admin. 15: 5790 Drexel, Detroit 48213.

DAVIDSON, MARGARET E. b Hamburg Iowa 13 Je 10. 5: Iowa StateU 26-30 (Bacteriology) BS; UWis 30-33 (Bacteriology) MS, 37-38 (LS) Certif. 6: Fr, Ger. 7: Commun libn Iowa State Travel Lib, Des Moines Iowa 38-42; Ref libn Waterloo Pub Lib, Waterloo Iowa 43-45; Libn Kendall Young

Lib, Webster City Iowa 46-63; Libn Ames Pub Lib, Ames I9a 63-. 9: IowaLA. 10: Sigma Delta Epsilon; PEO. 13: Yes. 14: Admin. 15: Ames Pub Lib, Ames Iowa 50010.

DAVIDSON, MAXINE ELIZABETH (GARRETT). b Grafton WVa 27 Jl 11. 5: Marshall U 28-2 (Span) BA; Fla state U 61-62 (LS) MS. 6: Sp. 7: Libn Sisterville High Sch, Sisterville WVa 62-64; Asst libn West Liberty State Col 64-69; Hd libn City-Co Lib 69-; Dir Miracle Valley Reg Lib, Moundsville WVa 69-. 9: ALA-Tri-State ACRL; WVaLA. 10: Alpha Xi Delta; Newman Club; AAUW; Fac Club. 14: Ref, 14: Ref, bk sel, displays, bk revs, acquis. 14: Ref, bk sel, displays, bk revs, acquis. 15: City-Co Library, Moundsville WVa 26041.

DAVIDSON, NELLE C(ATHERINE). b Greenville SC 7 Jl 08. 5: State Tchrs Coll (Tenn) 29-32 (Eng, Hist, Educ) BS; Peabody 35-37 BS in LS; UDenver summers 56-58 (LS) MA; LSU 59 (Hist). 6: Fr, Lat, Sp, Ger. 7: Libn Washington College High Sch, Washington Coll Tenn 33-37; Libn Johnson City Sr High Sch, Johnson City Tenn 37-38;Libn Carson-Newman Col 38-44; Instr in Lib Sci Kan State Tchrs Col (Pittsburgh) summer 41; Catlgr Tulane U summer 46; Headlibn New Orleans Baptist Theol Sem 44-. 9: ALA; ATheolLA; SLA (sec-treas & placement chm La Chap); LaLA (v-pres); East Tenn EA; New Orleans Lib Club (pres). 10: Altrusa. 13: Yes. 14: Admin, research, rare bks. 15: 4075 De Ment st, New Orleans La 70126.

DAVIDSON, ROSE. b Denver 10 D 14. 5: Iowa State Col 34-37 (Home Econ) BS; UWash 50-54 (LS) MS. 6: Fr. 7: Desk asst Petworth Br Lib, Wash DC; Circ desk supv Georgetown Br Lib, Wash DC; Asst libn Highland Park Lib, Des Moines Iowa 49; Bkmob libn Clatsop Co Lib, Astoria Ore 49-50; Bkmob libn King Co Lib, Seattle 52-57; Bkmob spec Ore State Lib 57-59; Admin Coos Co Demonstration (N Bend Ore) Ore State Lib 59-60; Admin Tillamook Co Lib, Tillamook Ore 60-64; Field consul Ore State Lib 64-67; Ref libn Douglas Co Lib (Ore) 67-. 8: Bkmob spec, Ore State Lib, 57-59; Exec dir, Nat Lib Week, Ore, 65. 9: OreLA (treas 60-61, mem & chm Standards Com 61-62, mem & chm Nom Com 68-69); PNLA. 10: AAUW; ABWA. 14: Ext wk, ref. 15: Ore State Lib, Salem Ore 97310.

DAVIES, BERNITA J(EWELL) (MATHEWS). b Canton Ill 5 D 01. 4: Elmer F Davies. 5: UIll 20-24 (Hist) AB, 25-28 LLB, 30-32 BS in LS, 59 LLM. 7: Tchr High Sch Canton Ill 24-25; Law practice, Canton Ill 29-30; Law libn & Prof of Lib Admin UIll(Urbana) 30-. 9: AALL (pres 42-43); Amer Bar Assn; Ill State Bar Assn. 10: Soroptomist Club; PEO; Order of the Coif; Phi Kappa Phi. 12: Ed "Law Library Journal (52, 53); "Research in Illinois Law (54); Jt author "Manual on the Use of Law Books (51). 13: Yes. 14: Law libs. 15: 703 West Green st, Urbana Il 61801.

DAVIES, JANE (BADGER). b Amboy Ill 9 S 13. 4: Lyn Davies. 5: Wellesley 31-35 (Ger) BA; Columbia 41-42 (Hist) MA, 43-44 (LS) BS. 6: Fr, Ger. 7: Hist tchr Monticello Prep Sch, Godfrey Ill 35-37; Hist tchr kent Sch for Girls Denver 37-41; Hist tchr Halsted Sch, Yonkers NY 42-43; Sr ref asst Columbia U Libs 44-50, catlgr rare bks 51-. 10: Soc of Arch Histns; Phi Beta Kappa; Nat Trust for Hist Preserv; Victorian Soc in Amer. 12: Ed asst "Journal of the Soc of Arch Histns (64-65); Intro to: Alexander J Davis "Rural Residences (1837) reprint (69). 13: Yes. 14: Rare bks, catlg, arch hist. 15: 549 W 123rd st, New York NY 10027.

DAVIES, RUTH ANN. b Pittsburgh 28 Je 15. 5: Penn Col for Women 35-39 (Lat, Hist) BA; UPittsburgh 39-40 (Amer Hist) MLitt; Carnegie 40-41 BSLS. 6: Lat. 7: Coordinator of lib serv North Hills Schs, Pittsburgh 41-65; Instr Sch of Lib Sci Carnegie Tech 47-62; Instr Grad Sch of Lib & Info Scis UPittsburgh 62-. 8: PennLA rep to Governors Com on Educ, 60. 9: NEA-DAVI; ALA (chm Penn Standards Implem 60-63); -AASchL (Legis Com 62-65); Penn StateEA; PennLA (mem-at-large 64-65). 11: Citation from Penn Dept of Pub Instr for "outstanding contribution to education. 12: "The School Library: Force for Educational Excellence (69). 13: Yes. 14: Sch libnship. 15: 156 McIntyre rd, Pittsburgh Pa 15237.

DAVIES, THOMAS E. b Akron Ohio 4 Ag 14. 5: Wayne State U 37-40 (Eng) BA; State Tchrs Col 40-41 (Educ) BS; UMich 45-46 ABLS; Colgate U 62 (Eng) MA. 7: US Army (T/S) Infantry 42-45; Libn Ionia Mich 46-48; Libn Lenawee Co Lib, Adrian Mich 48-49; Ref asst Union Col (Schenectady NY) 49-50; Order libn Colgate U 50-53; Asst dir & child libn W Orange (NJ) Pub Lib 53-55; Colgate U: Order libn 55-56; Circ libn 56-63, Acquis libn 63-. 14: Acquis, rare bks, spec collections. 15: Colgate Univ Lib, Hamilton NY 13346.

DAVIES, WILLIAM H. b Glenwood Springs Colo 4 Ap 30. 4: Carol Jean Tonner. 5: U Denver 50-52 (Soc Sci) AB, 53-56 (LS) MA. 6: Sp. 7: Tchr Lamar Union High Sch, Lamar Colo 52-54; Libn Garfield Co High Sch, Glenwood Springs Colo 54-57; Libn Tracy High Sch, Tracy Cal 57-64; Lib dir Tracy Pub Sch 64-. 9: CalTchrsAssn (pres loc unit); CalASchL. 10: Tracyun Players; Commun Action Coun. 13: Yes. 14: Ref, admin. 15: 471 Helene, Tracy Ca 95376.

DAVILA, DANIEL. b Caguas PR 22 F 38. 5: UPR 57-60 BA; Columbia 61-63 MLS, Tchrs Col MA. 6: Sp, Fr, Ital, Port. 7: Asst catlgr UPR Lib 60-61; Asst catlgr Columbia U Lib 61-62; Br libn Queens Borough Pub Lib, Jamaica NY 62-67; A-V Supv Kingsborough Commun Col 68-. 8: Ref libn, Lib/USA NY Worlds Fair 65. 9: ALA; NYLA; NAVA; NEA-DAVI; NYStateECA. 10: Columbia Sch of Lib Serv Alumni Club; Drama Club. 14: Ref, admin, educ. 15: 72 Columbus ave apt 15T, New York NY 10025.

DAVILA, NANCY IRENE (ROBERTSON). b New Albany Ind 13 S 34. 5: Indiana U 52-59 (Hist) BA, 61-63 (LS) MA. 7: Libn Ind U Southeast Campus (Jeffersonville) 60-. 9: ALA; IndLA. 10: AAUW. 14: Ref, personnel. 15: 1727 E Elm st, New Albany In 47150.

DAVIS, ADELINE (DOROTHY) THOMAS. b Benton Tenn 27 Jl 40. 5: Memphis StateU 58-59; UTenn 59-62 (Eng, LS) BA; Peabody Col 65-67 MLS. 6: Fr. 7: Libn Polk Co High Sch, benton Tenn 62-67; Circ libn Columbia Col, Columbia SC 67-. 8: Lib consul Polk Co Pub Schs under Title II ESEA 66-67. 9: ALA; SELA; SCLA. 14: Circ, catlg. 15: 607 Joan st, Columbia SC 29203.

DAVIS, AGNES MARION. b San Antonio Tex 14 Ag 23. 5: Lincoln Mem U 47-51 (Home Econ) BS; Peabody 53-54 (LS) MA. 7: Asst libn Lincoln Mem U 52-53; Reflibn Va Polytech Inst 54-. 9: ALA; SELA; VaLA. 10: AAUW; AAUP; Kappa Delta Pi. 14: Ref. 15: Drapers Meadow Terrace apt B-3, Blacksburg Va 24060.

DAVIS, ANNE M (MARIE). b NYC 5 Ag 12. 5: Barnard 28-32 (Eng) BA; Columbia 32-33 BLS; Fordham 36-40 (Eng). 6: Fr, Ger. 7: Ref & sch wk libn NY Pub Lib 33-36; High sch ref libn NY City Bd of Educ 36-40, High Sch libn 40-43; Off (Lt) US Naval Intelligence USNR, Wash DC 43-46; Libn US Naval Intelligence US Navy School, Anacostra DC 46-49; Dir lib serv USIS, Tel Aviv Israel 49-52; Dir lib serv USIS, Athens Greece 52-55; Asst chief Far East centers USIA, Wash DC 55-57; Dir lib serv USIS, Ankara Turkey 57-62; Reg libn USIS, Addis Ababa Ethiopia 63-67; Dir of lib serv USIA, Germany 68-. 9: ALA; SLA; East African LA; EthiopianLA. 10: Phi Beta Kappa. 11: Award for meritorious serv, USIA (66). 14: Lib development, area study collections, ref. 15: American Consulate Gen USIS, APO NY 09757.

DAVIS, BARBARA. b Tuscaloosa Ala 28 Ap 14. 5: UAla 32-36 (Hist) AB; Wis Lib Sch 36-37 Certif. 7: Circ asst br libn MIT 37-44; Libn Science Service Inc, Wash DC 44-45; Ref libn US Civil Aeronautics Admin, Wash DC 45-46; Ref libn, br libn Air U, Maxwell AFB 46-48; Head libn Friedman Lib, Tuscaloosa Ala 48-60; Ref libn UAla 61-62, Engnr libn Col of Engnr 62-. 9: ALA; SLA; AlaLA; Amer Soc Fledric & Electron Engrs. 10: Zonta International. 14: Ref. 15: Stoneleigh Court A4, Tuscaloosa Al 35401.

DAVIS, BARBARA ELLEN. b McKeesport Penn 14 My 25. 5: Carnegie 47-50 (Eng) BS, 50-51 MLS; UWis 55-58 (Music & Voice) BM; UIll 59 (usic). 6: Sp. 7: Clerk US Steel Corp, Duquesne Penn 43-47; Libn I Madison Pub Lib, Madison Wis 51-55; Music lib asst Music Sch UWis(Madison) 56-58; Music lib asst UIll Lib (Urbana) 58-60; Head of pub serv Cal State Col (Fullerton) 60-68, Assoc col libn pub serv 68-. 9: MusLA; CalLA; Orange Co LA (pres 68-69). 10: Choir dir, Blessed Sacrament Episcopal Church. 14: Admin, music libs. 15: 439 Me lody lane, Placentia Ca 92670.

DAVIS, BARBARA M. b Cranston RI 23 D 26. 4: John Williams Davis. 5: Pembroke Col 44-48 (Chem) BS; Simmons 53-56 (LS) MS. 6: Fr, Sp. 7: Asst research libn research & dev dept Cabot Corp, Cambridge Mass 48-57, Research libn 57-61; Research libn oxides & plastics research dept, Cabot Corp, Billerica Mass 61-68; Hd tech info serv Cabot SCorp, Billerica Mass 68-. 8: Instr in lib sci Womans Col of Ga, summers 52-53. 9: ACS-Div Chem Lit (sec 61-65, coun 66-68); SLA-Boston Chap (var offs). 10: Alumni Assn Simmons Sch Lib Sci (v-pres 65-67). 14: Ref, bibliog, abstractg, indexg. 15: 4 Euston st apt 3, Brookline Ma 02146.

DAVIS, BETTY (BARTLETT). b Wedowee Ala 1 Jl 27. 4: John Williams Davis. 5: Womans Col of Ga 46 (Eng) AB; Emory 52 (LS) MA. 6: Fr, Sp. 7: Tchr & libn pub schs, Ga 46-49; Libn Peabody Lab Sch, Womans Col of Ga 49-53; Dir Uncle Remus Reg Lib, Madison Ga 53-54; Var position Fla State U Lib 54-58; Head soc sci-hum div Clemson U Lib 58-61; Catlgr UWis Mem Lib (Madison) 61-64; Catlgr Va Polytech Inst Lib 64-68; Catlgr Frostburg State Col 68-. 8: Instr in lib sci Womans Col of Ga, summers 52-53. 14: Catlg, ref, wk in the humanities & soc scis. 15: 5 Frost ave, Frostburg Md 21532.

DAVIS, BETTYE (LOUISE) (CROUCH). b Indianapolis Ind 20 O 26. 4: John Dixon Davis II. 5: Mars Hill Jr Coll 43-45 (Mus); Wake Forest 45-47 (Eng) BA; E Carolina U 64-65 (Ed, Certif), 66-68 (LS). 6: Sp, Fr. 7: Tchr & libn Murfreesboro High Sch, Murfreesboro NC 63-. 9: NEA; ALA; NCEA; NCLA; NC High Sch Lib Assn. 14: Ref, tchg lib skills, reading guidance. 15: PO Box 354, Murfreesboro NC 27855.

DAVIS, BONNIE (MAXWELL). b Lafayette Ind 2 N 43. 4: Charles H Davis. 5: IndU 62-66 9comp Lit) AB, 66-67 (LS) MA. 6: Fr, Sp. 7: Lib asst PurdueU Libs 61-65; Stud hd libn Halls of Residence Libs IndU (Bloomington) 64-66, Grad asst 66-67; Dir documentation ERIC/CRIER IndU (Bloomington) 67-. 9: ALA; ASIS. 10: Alpha Lambda Delta; Phi Beta Kappa. 14: Documentation, tech serv. 15: 2631 E Second st apt 12, Bloomington In 47401.

DAVIS, CHARLES E. b Manhattan Kan 28 S 27. 4: Frances B Anderson. 5: Union Col 47-51 (Bio) BA; Kan StateU summers 58-61 (Hist) MA; USoCal summers 64-67 MS in LS. 6: Ger, Sp. 7: Dean men & tchr Highland Acad, Portland Tenn 51-55; Dean men - tchr Campion Acad, Loveland Colo 55-56; Tchr & libn Mt Pisgah Acad, Candler NC 56-61; Tchr & libn Bass Memorial Acad, Lumberton Miss 61-63; Tchr & libn San Pasqual Acad, Escondido Calif 63-66; Asst libn hd pub serv Loma LindaU 66-68; Hd libn assoc prof lib sci So Missionary col 68-. 9: ALA; TennLA. 14: Admin, acquis, ref. 15: Librarian So Missionary College, Collegedale Tn 37315.

DAVIS, CHARLES H(ARGIS). b Tell City Ind 23 S 38. 4: Bonnie Maxwell. 5: IndU 56-60 (Chem) BS; UMunich Ger 60-61 (Chem); IndU 65-66 (LS) MA, 66-69 (Info sci) Ph D. 6: Ger, Fr. 7: Asst ed "Chemical Abstracts," Columbus Ohio 62-65; ARAC Ind U: Staff chem 65-66, Dir of syst ERIC/CRIER 67-69; Asst Prof Grad Sch of Lib Sci Drexel Inst 69-. 9: ASIS (chm Ind Chap); ACS; ALA; Assn Comput Machinery. 10: AAAS; Phi Lambda Upsilon; Alpha Chi Sigma. 11: German Government Fellow 60-61. 14: Info sci, tech serv. 15: Sch of Lib Sci Drexel Inst, Philad elphia Pa 19104.

DAVIS, CHARLOTTE (DOYLE). b Peoria Ill 22 Je 08. 4: Joseph C Davis. 5: Bradley U 26-30 (Eng) BA; USoCal 48-50 MS in LS; UCal (Santa Barbara) 60- (Educ) Supv cred. 7: Tchr Peoria Pub Schs, Peoria Ill 29-50, Libn 47-50; Coordinator of lib serv Santa Barbara Co Schs, Goleta Cal 50-. 8: Consul; Lib wkshop USan Francisco; Tchr wkshop UCal (Santa Barbara); In-Serv Educ Santa Barbara Co Schs; Instr San Jose StateCol summer 60; Instr USA Extension in Libnship (Fall & Spring) 60-; Coun for Child Lit Award Com Pepperdine Col; Instr UWash Schof Libnship summer 67; Consul Cal State Dept of Educ, ESEA Title II. 9: ALA-AASchL (Elem Com 58-60, Instr Materials Com 63-66, Newbery-Caldecott Awards Com 68); CalASchL (State chm & var other offs);Cal Assn for Supv & Curric (chm Instr Materials Com; chm So Sect). 10: Delta Kappa Gamma; Sigma Kappa; Pi Lambda Theta. 12: Co-auth "Harbors of California (57). 13: Yes. 14: Childs lit, sch lib devel. 15: 5595 W Camino Cielo, Santa Barbara Ca 93105.

DAVIS, CHARLOTTE (MEARS). b Bloomsburg Penn 17 D 07. 4: Dr Newell F Davis. 5: Bloomsburg State Col 25-29 (Eng, SS) BS-Ed; Penn State U 63-64 Lib Certif; UUtah 62-63 Lib Certif; Penn State U 65- (LS) MA. 7: Tchr of SS music Dimock Sch Dist, Dimock Penn 29-32, Eng tchr Bloomsburg Sch Dist, Bloomsburg Penn 32-34; Eng tchr Huntington Sch Dist, Huntington LI NY 34-42; Tchr of SS Bloomsburg Penn 42-43; Tchr of Eng & lib Mifflin Twp Sch Dist, Mifflin Penn 43-62; Libn Central Jr Sr High Sch, Bloomsburg Penn 62-. 9: NEA; ALA; PennLA; PennStateEA; Penn Cong of Parents & Tchrs (State chm 54-59, pres 60-62). 10: Womans Civic Club; Nat Congress of Parents & Tchrs; Penn Congress of Parents & Tchrs (Life mem); Col Co Fed of Womens Clubs; DAR; Daughters Amer Colonists; AAUW. 13: Yes. 14: Sch lib, ref, bk sek, admin. 15: 26 W Fifth st, Bloomsburg Pa 17815.

DAVIS, CHARLOTTE GENEVIEVE. b Chicago Ill 28 Je 13. 5: Augustana Col 45-49 (Eng) BA; UDenver 50-57 (LS) MA; UNeb (Omaha) 65 (Educ) Secondary Certif. 6: Sp. 7: USN (Waves) Seaman 2/c, Great Lakes Ill 44-45; Asst libn Deane Col 50-52; Libn/journalism Webster Pub Sch, Webster S Dak 53-54; Libn Webster Pub Lib, Webster S Dak 54-56; Libn Dak wesleyanU 56-58; Asst libn Peru State Col 58-59; Libn Ft Morgan Pub Sch, Ft Morgan Colo 59-62; Libn Omaha Pub Sch, Omaha Neb 62-65; Libn John F Kennedy Col 65-67; Libn/English Yutan Pub Sch, Yutan Neb 67-. 9: ALA; NebLA; NebStateEA; SaundersCoEA. 10: Delta Kappa Gamma; Amer Legion Auxiliary; Amer Legion. 14: Catlg, ref, acquis. 15: Box 95, Yutan Nb 68073.

DAVIS, CHESTER KENT. b Long Beach Cal 22 Je 29. 5: Ariz State U 48-50 (Music Educ) BA; UAriz 50-51(Music Theory & Composition) MMusic; UDenver 55-57 MA in LS. 7: Libn & music tchr Round Valley High Sch,Springerville Ariz 54-56; Libn Raton Pub Lib, Raton NM 57-58; Tech serv libn NM Highlands U Lib 58-62;Acquis Libn NM State U Lib 62-66; Tech serv libn; prescott Col (Ariz) 66-67; Clark Co Lib, Las Vegas Nev 67-. 9: MusLA; ALA; NMLA (treas 62); NevLA. 13: Yes. 14: Music biblior, acquis, catlg,phonorecords, music of Spain & Latin Amer. 15: 1131-J East Tropicana, Las Vegas Nv 89109.

DAVIS, CLIFTON GEORGE. b Melrose Mass 30 Ag 35. 4: Janet Titus. 5: Paul Smiths Col 53-55 (Hotel Mgt) AAS; UDenver 55-57 (Bus Admin) BSBA; Bangor Theol Sem 57-61 (Biblical) BD; UMe 65-67 MLS. 6: Gr. 7: Clergyman E Congregational Ch, Concord NH 61-65; Asst libn Bangor Theol Sem 65-68, Libn 68-. 9: ATheolLA; NETheolLA; MeLA. 14: Org, admin, catlg. 15: 347 Hammond st, Bangor Me 04401.

DAVIS, DONALD GORDON JR. b San Marcos Tex 15 Ag 39. 5: UCLA 57-61 (Hist) BA; UCAL (Berkeley) 61-63 (Hist) MA, 63-64 MLS; UIll (Urbana) 68- (LS). 06: Fr. 7: Sr lib asst UCal Lib (Berkeley) 61-64; Sr ref libn Fresno State Col Lib 64-68; Hd dept of spec collections 66-68. 9: Org Amer Histns; ALA; -ACRL; ATheolLA; CalLA; (sec Yosemite Dist 67, Prog Chm State Col Libns Div 67). 10: Inter-Varsity Christian Fellowship; beta Phi Mu; UCal Lib Schs Alumni Assn; Friends of the Bancroft Lib; Amer Fed Tchrs. 13: Yes. 14: Ref, theol libnship, hist of libs, acad libs, lib assns. 15: Grad School of Lib Sci Univ of Ill, Urbana Il 61801.

DAVIS, DORIS G. b Louisville Ky 26 S 22. 4: Kenneth B Davis. 5: ULouisville 41-44 (Ed) BA; Kent State 63-65 (LS) MLS. 6: Fr. 7: Elem libn Bath-Richfield Schs, W Richfield Ohio 65-67; Libn West Res Acad, Hudson Ohio 67-. 9: NEA; ALA; OhioASchL; Summit Co. 11: Crawford Award (Kent State U). 14: Sch libnship, rare bks. 15: 271 Streetsboro st, Hudson Oh 44236.

DAVIS, DOROTHY (BURNS). b Millvale Penn 28 Ag 09. 4: Ralph Maxwell Davis. 5: UPittsburgh 27-31 BA, Lib Sci certif. 7: Carnegie Lib of Pittsburgh: Child libn 31-37, Yp libn 59-62, Asst head central lending dept 62-. 9: ALA; PennLA; Pittsburgh Lib Club. 10: South Hills Col Club, Pittsburgh. 14: Acquis, hist collections. 15: 814 Wainwright dr, Pittsburgh Pa 15228.

DAVIS, DOROTHY GAE. b Wewoka Okla 9 Jl 41. 5: Centenary Col (La) 59-63 (Eng) BA; UOkla 63-65 MLS. 6: Sp. 7: Stud asst Centenary Col of La Lib 61-63; Lib asst UOkla Lib 63-65; Asst ref libn Charles Stewart Mott Lib, Flint Mich 65-68, Docs libn 68-. 14: Govt publ, ref. 15: 2309 Dakota ave, Flint Mi 48506.

DAVIS, DOUGLAS ALLAN. b Los Angeles Cal 14 S 43. 5: San Fernando Valley State Col 62-66 (Hist) BA; Simmons 67-69 (LS) MS. 6: Sp. 7: Stack supv San Fernando Valley State Col Lib 65-66, 66-67; Intern for gift l exchange: Widener Lib HarvardU 67-68, lamont Lib 68-. 14: Tech serv, syst planning. 15: 19845 Hemmingway st, Canoga Park Ca 91306.

DAVIS, EDNA C. b El Centrol Cal 25 Je 19. 4: Oliver C Davis. 5: UCLA 37-41 AB; UCal (Berkeley) 42-43 (LS) Certif. 7: Ref & acquis libn W A Clark Mem Lib UCLA 43-. 9: ALA (Rare Bks Div); CalLA. 10: Augustan Reprint Soc. 14: Rare bks, ref serv. 15: W A Clark Mem Lib 2520 Cimarron st, Los Angeles Ca 90018.

DAVIS, ELEANOR (HARMON). b Seattle 12 O 09. 4: Carl DeVore Davis. 5: UWash 28-32 BS in LS, 32-33 Certif in Lib Wk with Child. 7: Child libn Seattle Pub Lib 33-38; Child libn Maui Co Lib, Wailuku Hawaii 38-39; Child libn Kauai Pub Lib, Lihue Hawaii 39-45; Catlgr Kauai Pub Lib, Lihue Hawaii 45-46; Ya libn NY Pub lib 46-47; Child libn Prince Georges Co Mem Lib, Hyattsville Md 47-48; Child libn Maui Co Lib,

Wailuku Hawaii 48-49; Act co libn Maui Co Lib, Wailuku Hawaii 49-50; Child libn Hawaii Co Lib, Hilo Hawaii 50-51; Co Libn Maui Co Lib, Wailuku Hawaii 51-52; Asst chief libn Lib of Hawaii, Honolulu 52-65; State adult bk sel coordinator Hawaii State Lib 65-66; Tchr-trainer refresher course for lib assts Inst for Tech Interchange E-W Ctr, Honolulu 67-. 9: ALA (State Mem Chm 54-58); HawaiiLA (pres 56-57, chm Personnel Standards Com 61-62, chm Constit Rev Com 55); HawaiiLA (hon life mem). 10: AAUW; Bishop Museum Assn; Hawaiian Hist Soc; NAACP; Amer Manchester Terrier Club; Amer Humanist Assn; Hawaiian Kennel Club; Friends of the Libn of Hawaii; Friends of the East-West Ctr. 12: "Norwegian Labor in Hawaii: The Norse Immigrants with Carl D Davis (62). 13: Yes. 14: Admin, bk sel; lib educ libs in devel countries of Asia & the South Pacific. 15: 1444 Ulupuni st, Kailua Hi 96734.

DAVIS, ELIZABETH (ELLERY ANDREWS). b Sackville NB Can 11 Je 02. 4: Edward Newton Davis. 5: UAlta 21-24 BS. 7: Lib asst Pub Lib, Regina Sask 18-20; Lib asst UAlta 23-24; Asst chief libn Sask Open Shelf Lib, Govt of Sask, Regina 24, Chief 26-29; Trustee Pub Lib, Prince Albert Sask 39-47; Trustee Pub Lib, Regina Sask 51-; Sask Lib Adv Coun 67. 9: CanLA (Coun); Can Lib Trustees Assn (pres); SaskLA. 10: Can Fed of Univ Women; Can Assn of Consumers; Regina U Womens Club; Regina Orchestral Soc; Norman Mackenzie Art Gallery Soc; Regina Womens Can Club; United Church Women. 11: Red Cross Soc Serv Medal; Can Lib Trustees Assn Award of Merit 68. 14: Catlg, ref. 15: 3120 Angus st, Regina Sask Can.

DAVIS, (MARGARET) ELOISE (MORTON). b Nashville 7 My 17. 4: (Melvin) Wilson Davis. 5: Murfreesboro (Tenn) State Tchrs Col 34-37 (Eng, Fr) BS; Peabody 37-38-39 BS in LS; Troy State Tchrs Col (Ala) summer 48; Delta State Tchrs Col 65; NDEA Inst for Sch Lib; Tex Womans U summer 66. 06: Fr. 7: Libn Eng tchr Carthage High Sch, Carthage Tenn 39-40; Lib asst Peabody Col 41; Tchr elem high sch Crenshaw Co, Luverne, Brantley Ala 47-52; Chem engnr libn UAla 54-56; Eng tchr Bolivar Co Cleveland Miss 62-63; Libn Eng tchr Bolivar Co Merigold Miss 63-68; Title II spec grant Cleveland High Sch Lib summer 68; Title I Elem lib supv Bolivar Co Dist IV Schs 68-. 9: NEA; Nat Clr Tchrs Assn; MissEA; MissLA; MissASchL. 10: Faculty Wives, Delta State Col; Womans Soc of Christian Serv; Pi Gamma Mu; Kappa Delta Pi. 14: Sch lib wk. 15: 1203 Maple st, Cleveland Ms 38732.

DAVIS, FRANCES FREEMAN. b Atlanta 18 Ag 24. 4: Clarence Brown Davis. 5: Clark Col 46-50 (Home Econ) BS; Atlanta summers 59-62 (LS); Atlanta 66 MSLS. 6: Fr. 7: Lib circ asst Tuskegee Inst 54-64; Res room libn Hollis Burke Frissell Lib, Tuskegee Ala 64-65; Engnr lib 65-66; Nurs lib Vet Med Lib 66-. 9: ALA; SELA. 10: AAUP; Alpha Kappa Alpha; Ala Coun of Human Rights; PTA; Tuskegee; Tuskegee Civic Assn; Jack & Jill of America Inc; NAACP. 14: Col & research libs, ya serv, sci-tech & med materials. 15: 1912 Washington st, Tuskegee Inst Al 36088.

DAVIS, FRANCES JOSEPHINE. b Galveston Tex 15 Ag 21. 5: Tenn State U 39-43 (Eng) BS; Atlanta 51-52 (LS) MS. 6: Ger. 7: Sub tchg pub schs, Galveston Tex 43-51; Acquis libn Fla A & M U 52-55; Catlgr spec collections Tex So U 55-57; Sch libn Galveston Ind Sch Dist, Galveston Tex 57-61; Catlgr gen collection Tex So U 61-62; Instr Lib Serv Educ Prairie View Col 62-63, 64-. 9: NEA; ALA; TexStateTchrs Assn; Tex Assn Col Tchrs; Tex Coun on Lib Educ. 10: Alpha Kappa Alpha. 14: Catlg. 15: Drawer C Prairie View Col, Prairie View Tx 77445.

DAVIS, Lt Col GEORGE B. b Hobart NY 26 D 24. 4: Marcia Thompson Davis. 5: Union Col (Schenectady NY) 42-45 (Fr) BA; Oberlin Col 45-46 (Fr) MA; Sorbonne 46-47 (Fr) Diplome; Brown 47-49, 52-49, 52-56, 58 (Fr) PhD; Chicago 59-60 (LS) MA. 6: Fr, Ger, Sp. 7: Tchg Fellow Brown U 47-49; Instr Fr UBridgeport 49-51; Ref asst Brown U Libs 52-56; Libn asst Prof of Fr Centenary Col (La) 56-59; Libn Bennett Col 60-65; Libn Va Mil Inst, Assoc Prof of Fr 65-. 9: ALA; VaLA. 10: Mod Lang Assn; SCMLA. 14: Admin. 15: 502 Pickett st, Lexington Va 24450.

DAVIS, GERTRUDE (CODDINGTON). b Roanoke Va 7 Je 15. 5: Col of William & Mary 32-33; Oberlin Col 33-36 (Eng Lit) BA; UNC 40-41 BS in LS; Columbia Sch of Lib Serv MS in LS 69. 6: Fr, Ger. 7: Sec Assn of Amer RRs, Wash DC 36-39; Sec Roanoke Va 39-40; Child asst NY Pub Lib 41-42; Act libn Staunton Pub Lib, Staunton Va 50-55; Staunton Mil Acad, & Mary Baldwin Col Staunton Va 50-55; Libn Staunton Mil Acad, Staunton Va 55-57; Libn Mary Baldwin Col 57-. 9: ALA (Memb Chm for Va 66-68); VaLA (chm Col & Univ Sect 67-68); SELA (Memb Chm for Va 66-68). 10: Augusta Co (Va) Hist Assn; Va Archaeol Assn; Kings Daughters Hosp Auxiliary;Womans Soc of Christian Serv. 13: Yes. 14: Admin, catlg, ref. 15: 315 Vine st, Staunton Va 24401.

DAVIS, HERMIA (ELFREDA) MEEDS. b Battle Creek Mich 5 Ap 23. 5: Va State Col 41-45 (LS) BS; Simmons 49-50 BLS; USoCal 62-63. 7: DC Pub Lib: Readers' adv in drama 50-53, YA libn 53-54; Catlgr Chicago Pub Lib 54-57; Sch libn Houston Ind Sch Dist 57-62; LA Pub Lib: YA libn 62-65, Reg YA libn (Fed proj) 65-. 8: Young Adult Librarian's Board; Los Angeles Pub Lib system 64. 9: ALA; -YASD (subcom chm of Com on Lib Serv to Disadvantaged Youth 67-); CalLA (v-pres & pres-elect YASD 69-70). 10: YWCA Exec Bd; Sec of Exposition Commun Coord Coun; Manual Arts High Sch Commun Adv Bd; Mayor's Adult Com on Youth. 14: YA wk, a-v wk in libs, the lib as related to commun problems. 15: 1246 S Redondo blvd, Los Angeles Ca 90019.

DAVIS, HILLIS DWIGHT. b Selma Ala 24 Ja 32. 4: Marian Anderson. 5: Johnson C Smith U 50-54 (Biol) BS; Atlanta U 57-58 MS in LS. 6: Fr. 7: (Spec 3) Army Ft Lewis Wash 55-57; Asst libn WVa State Col 58-65; Dir of Lib Hampton Inst 65-. 9: ALA; WVaLA; VaLA. 10: Omega Psi Phi. 14: Catlg, admin. 15: 113 Marshall ave, Hampton Institute Va 23368.

DAVIS, IRIS ANNE (ANDERSON). b Garland Tex 21 Ja 31. 5: E Tex State Col 49-52 (LS) BS; Tex Womans U 57-59 MS in LS; W Tex State U 59-60. 6: Ger, Swedish. 7: Libn Winnsboro High Sch, Winnsboro Tex 52-53; Libn La Joya High Sch, La Joya Tex 53; Libn Stinnett High Sch, Stinnett Tex 54-58; Catlgr West Tex State U 59-66; Sers catlgr N Tex State U 66-. 09: ALA; TexLA; SWLA; Tex Assn Col Tchrs. 10: AAUP. 14: Catlg (ser). 15: Box 5253 NT Station, Denton Tx 76203.

DAVIS, JAMES (HAROD MARX). b Newark NJ 1 O 28. 5: Drew U 46-50 (Psych) BA; UOre summer 49; Columbia 55-57 (LS) MS; Yale 60-62. 6: Ger, Sp, Dutch, Fr. 7: Ed asst Chanticleer Press, NYC 55; Asst in Prod & Sales Promotion Davis Delaney Inc, NYC 52-60; Catlgr Columbia U Law Lib 57-58;Subj catlgr Yale U 58-67; Indexer H W Wilson Co, Bronx NY 67-. 9: ALA; NY Tech Serv Libns; NY Lib Club. 14: Catlg, indexing. 15: 130 E 36th st, New York NY 10016.

DAVIS, JEWELL FAYE. b Clemmons NC. 5: UNC (Greensboro) (Educ) AB; UNC (Chapel Hill) Ext 40 (Eng); Columbia summer 45 (Eng); CatholicU 48-50 (LS). 7: Research asst ColumbiaU 34-39; Tchr Fairlington Pub Sch, Arlington Va 44-45; Sec Dept of Army-Navt, Wash DC 45-48; Catlgr Dept of Com, Wash DC 49-58, Chief tech serv br 59-. 9: DCLA; Potomac Tech Processing Libns. 14: Catlg. 15: 921 - 19th st NW, Washington DC 20006.

DAVIS, JINNIE (YEH). b Sian China 1 D 45. 4: Jerry Mallory Davis. 5: UMich 63-67 (Chinese Hist) AB, 67-68 AMLS. 6: Chinese, Sp. 7: Asst libn Freer Gallery of Art Wash DC 68-. 9: ALA. 10: Beta Phi Mu. 11: Margaret Mann Citation. 14: Catlg, ref. 15: 9493 Arlington blvd #303, Fairfax Va 22030.

DAVIS, JOAN PATRICIA. b Columbus Ohio 4 N 27. 5: Ohio State U 46-50 BS (Soc Admin); UMich 61-62 MALS. 6: Fr. 7: Asst libn Clintonville Br Columbus Pub Lib, Columbus Ohio 50-51; Med records libn St Francis Hosp, Columbus Ohio 52-54; Med research libn Ross Labs, Columbus Ohio 54-60; Asst ref libn Grandview Heights Pub Lib 60-61; Br libn Huber Heights Br Dayton (Ohio) Pub Lib 61-65; Med ref libn Northwestern U Archibald Church Med Lib 65-. 9: Ohio LA. 14: Med ref, readers adv, ref. 15: 6150 Kenmore ave apt 13A, Chicago Il 60626.

DAVIS, JO-ANN. b New Bedford Mass 28 Ja 40. 5: Boston U 58-62 (Comparative lit) BA, 62-64 (Comparative lit) MA; Simmons 64-66 (LS) MS. 6: Fr, Russian, Ger, Sp. 7: Asst libn Mass Gen Hosp Med Lib, Boston 64-66; Libn Rodman Job Corps Ctr, New Bedford Mass summer 65; Lib consul Wrentham State Sch, Wrentham Mass 66; Lib consul Educ Lib Simmons Col 66; Libn studship Chapman Col 68; Ohio State U: Libn Eng grad lib 66-68, Medlars analyst med lib 68-. 9: ALA; Mod Lang Assn; ASIS. 12: Chm Publs Com Ohio State U Libs 67-. 14: Automated retrieval systems, public serv, admin. 15: 350 So Chase ave, Columbus Oh 43204.

DAVIS, JOYCE (MARY). b Garden City Kan 1 Ap 25. 5: Kan State Tchrs Col (Emporia) 43-54 (Eng, LS) BS; UIll 58-59 MS in LS. 6: Sp. 7: Libn Garden City High Sch & Jr Col, Garden City Kan 54-55; Elem sch libn, Wichita Kan 55-58; Libn Northeastern Reg Lib, Cimarron NJ 59-63; Libn Scenic

Reg Lib, Union Mo 63-64; Br libn Phoenix Pub Lib 64-68; Admin libn SWest Kan, Dodge City Kan 68-. 9: ALA; KanLA. 10: Womens C of C, Dodge City. 14: Child, reg lib. 15: 2309 First ave, Dodge City Ks 67801.

DAVIS, KARIN K (TYLER). b Tacoma Wash 1 Jl 33. 4: Marvin K Davis. 5: U of Puget Sound 51-55 (Art) BA; UWash 61-62 MLS. 6: Fr. 7: Child libn Tacoma Pub Lib, Tacoma Wash 59-64; Child libn Olympia Pub Lib, olympia Wash 64-. 9: WashLA. 10: Southwest Wash Tennessee Walking Horse Assn. 14: Wk with child. 15: Rte 12 Box 550, Olympia Wa 98502.

DAVIS, KATHRYNE LAURENE. b Tulsa Okla 28 Ap 40. 5: UNM 58-62 (Hist) BA; UDenver 62-63 (LS) MA. 7: Asst libn in chg of child wk Mesa Pub Lib, Los Alamos NM 64-. 9: ALA; NMLA. 14: Pub serv, child wk. 15: 1075 Iris apt 16, Los Alamos NM 87544.

DAVIS, MADGE G. b Louisville Ky 28 F 21. 5: ULouisville 38-41 (Eng); Catherine Spalding Coll 59-61 (LS). 6: Fr. 7: Tube Turns, Louisville Ky: Lib clk 57-59, Libn 59-61; Tech libn Amer Standard Inc, Louisville Ky 61-. 8: Exec Com Governor's Planning Com on Libs 67-; Adv Coun LSCA, Title III on Interlib Coop 67-; Adv Com to Exec Bd; Louisville Tech Referral Ctr 68-. 9: SLA; KyLA (chm Spec Libs Sec 64, mem Survey Com of Ky Lib Resources 65). 11: Outstanding Special Librarian 66, presented by Ky Lib Trustee Assn. 14: Patents, info retrieval systems. 15: 6309 Ferncliff lane, Louisville Ky 40291.

DAVIS, MAILLY (MARY). b Wilmington Del 6 Fe 37. 5: UDel 55-57 (Hist); UNC 57-59 (Hist) BA; Drexel 66 (LS) MS. 7: Copyright catlgr LC 60, Classification rec asst 61-65; Ref & loan US Dept of Com Lib, Wash DC 67-. 9: SLA; DCLA. 14: Ref. 15: 4000 Massachusetts ave NW, Washington DC 20016.

DAVIS, MARGARET (CHAMBERLAIN). b NYC 2 Mr 40. 4: Courtney L Davis. LSA Okla 28 Ap 40. 6: Fr. 7: Child libn Mt Pleasant Br, Providence Pub Lib 62-66; Hd boys & girls dept 66-67; Child libn 67-. 9: ALA; NELA; RILA (Bull Com 64-65, Educ Com 68-69, N E RT of Child Libns, Exec Bd 68-69). 14: Child wk. 14: Pub serv, child wk. 15: Box 63, Saunderstown RI 02874.

DAVIS, MARGARET ELIZABETH. b Bradford Mass 21 Ja 04. 5: Wheaton Col (Norton Mass) 21-25 (Eng Lit) AB; Simmons 25-26 (LS) SB. 7: Asst Simmons Sch of Lib Sci 26-28; Asst in chg of Col Lib Simmons Col 27, 40-41; Instr Simmons Sch of Lib Sch 28-38; Catlgr, Supreme Coun 33d degree Masons 38-39; Clsfr Wellesley Col Lib 39; Catlgr Simmons Col Lib 39-69. 9: ALA; NE Tech Serv Libns; Boston Reg Group of Catlgrs & Clsfrs. 10: Haverhill Hist Soc; Newton Centre Neighborhood Club; Samuel Francis Smith Homestead Soc; Newton-Wellesley Hosp Aid Assn. 14: Catlg. 15: 67 Pelham st, Newton Centre Ma 02159.

DAVIS, MARIE A. b Pittsburgh Penn 29 Je 18. 5: Carnegie (Soc Sci) BS, (LS) BS. 7: Statistics Dept US Steel; Lib asst pub affairs Carnegie Lib of Pittsburgh 45-46; Pub rel dir 46-56; Coordinator wk with adults Free Lib of Phila 56-61, Coordinator wk with adults & ya 61-. 9: ALA (Ed Com: chm Subcom on Bks in Large Type 62-63; Jury of Clarence Day Award 63); -ASD (chm Com on Rel with State Assns 60-63, Com on Readg Improvment for Adults 65-, Bd mem 66-68, pres 68-69, Coun 69-72); Adult Educ Assn; PennLA (sec 57, v-pres & Conf Chm 61-62, pres 62-63; pres SW Dist 55, etc); Middle Atlantic Reg Conf (chm 67, chm Pub 53 & 58, etc); Penn Assn Adult Educ; Pittsburgh Lib Club (pres 51). 10: Zonta Club; Womens City Club of Pittsburgh; Phila Bksellers Club; Museum Coun of Phila; Alum Assn Carnegie-Mellon U; ACLU. 13: Yes. 14: Commun serv, bk sel. 15: Free Lib of Phila, Logan Square, Phila Pa 19103.

DAVIS, MARJORIE (FRIEND). b Phila 10 N 10. 5: Juniata Col 28-32 (Educ, Eng, Fr) AB (summa cum laude); UPenn 38-40; Drexel 58-61 MS in LS (Honors). 6: Fr. 7: 1st asst order dept UPenn Lib 35-40, Head ser div 41-43; Libn Lower Merion Sr High Sch, Ardmore Penn 56-50; Asst to curator Quaker Col Haverford Col Lib 60-64, Admin asst 64-66; Libn Narberth Presbyterian Church, Narberth Penn 63-66; Hd libn Montgomery Co Commun Col, Asst Prof 66-69, Assoc Prof 69-. 9: ALA; -ACRL; -RTSD; -LAD; Jr Col Lib Sect; PennLA (sec-treas Commun & Jr Col Div 68-). 10: Merion Civic Assn; Phi Kappa Phi; Beta Phi Mu; AAUP; Delta Kappa Gamma; Lib Assocs of Haverford Col. 14: Spec collections, mss, catlg, ref, admin. 15: 135 Winchester rd, Merion Station Pa 19066.

DAVIS, MARTHA EMILY (UNGER). b Renssalaer NY 22 F 11. 4: Leonard E Davis. 5: SUNY 30-34, 35 (Hist, Govt); Albany Tchrs Col BS in LS; Rutgers 57-58, 60 (LS). 6: Fr, Ger. 7: Asst libn Russell Sage Col 35; High sch libn Philmont High Sch, Philmont NY 35-37; Asst libn Jr Sr High Sch, Summit NY 50-51; Head libn Somervill Pub Schs, Somerville NJ 51-58; Coordinator Elem Sch, Summit NJ 58-60; Libn Governor Livingston Reg High Sch, Berkley Heights NJ 60-64; Dir of tech processing & lib consul Cherry Hill Pub Schs, Cherry Hill NJ 64-68; Libn & instr lib techniques Camden Co Voc & Tech Sch (Gloucester) 68-. 8: Org elem sch lib, Berkeley Heights NJ 49-50; planning bd & bd of trustees mem, Berkeley Heights NJ Free Pub Lib 50-53; adv to Corresponding Sec NJSLCA 55-57 & 68 Mem Curr planning com for Lib Techns course in Camden Co Voc & Tech Sch 67-69; Mem Com for Advancement of Better Pub Relations in Libs of Metro Phila area 67-69; Mem Steering Com for Lib System Devel, Camden Co Lib 69-. 9: ALA; NEA; NJEA; NJLA; NJSchLA (var offs 58-62); camden Co Voc & Tech TA; Camden Co LA; Camden Co Sch LA (pres 65-67). 14: Admin of sch libs, tech serv. 14: Admin of sch libs, tech serv. 15: 209 Hamilton rd, Marlton NJ 08053.

DAVIS, MARTIN (REMINGTON). b Gardner Mass 2 My 25. 4: Jane Jamison. 5: Emory Jr Col 42-43; USCar 43-44; UPittsburgh 46-47 (Psych) BS; Fla State U 52-53 (LS) MA. 6: Ger, Sp, Russian, Chinese, Hindi. 7: USNR (Active Duty) (Ensign) Stateside & Guam MI 43-46; USNR (Org Reserve) (Lt jg) Miami Fla & Cville Va 48-56; Insurance agent Life Ins Co of Ga, Miami Fla 48-49; Acquis clerk UMiami (Fla) 51-52; Asst to acquis libn Alderman Lib UVa 53-66; Preparations libn 66-. 9: ALA; SELA; VaLA; Potomac Tech Proc Libns. 10: Beta Phi Mu. 14: Catlg, lib computerization. 15: 117 E Buckingham cir, Charlottesville Va 22901.

DAVIS, MARY LUCILLE. b Sparta Wis 20 Ja 05. 5: State Tchrs Col (Whitewater Wis) 32 (Eng) BEd; UWis 33 (LS) Certif; Columbia summers 37-41 (LS) MS. 7: Tchr-libn pub schs, Mellen Wis 26-30; Tchr Jr High Sch, Chippewa Falls Wis 30-32; Rec asst Dept of Debating & Pub Discussion UWis(Madison) 33-34; Libn Sr High Sch, Rockford Ill 34-36, 38-40; Libn Wis High Sch, Madison Wis 36-38; Libn West High Sch, Rockford Ill 40-69; Bkmob libn Rockford Pub Lib 69-. 9: Amer Fed Tchrs; IllLA; Ill Fed Tchrs; Rockford Fed Tchrs (pres 59-61). 14: Ref, catlg, sch libs. 15: 2912 Summerdale ave, Rockford Il 61103.

DAVIS, MARYLYN POWEL. b Penns Park Penn 30 Ap 18. 5: Temple U 35-39 (Eng) BSEd; UPenn 39-42 (Eng) MA; Columbia 40-43 BSLS; NYU 55-56 (Educ). 6: Fr, Ger. 7: Asst libn George Sch, George School Penn 39-42; Lib asst NY Pub Lib 42-43; Libn High sch, E Rutherford NJ 43-44; Assoc libn High Sch, S Orange NJ 44-48; Libn High Sch, Greenwich Conn 48-63; Lib Coordinator Pennsbury Schs, Fallsington Penn 63-67; Libn Pennsbury High Sch, Fairless Hills Penn 67-. 8: Instr Simmons Col summer 56. 9: NEA; ALA;-LAD (com sec);-YASD (com); AASchL (Bd, coms); NESchLA (sec, v-pres); Com SchLA (Hon life mem) (pres coms); PennLA; Penn Sch LA; PennEA (coms); Phila Area SchL; NEA-DAVI; PennStateEA; PennsburyEA; Bucks Co SchLA (sec com). 10: Soroptimist Club; Delta Kappa Gamma; Amer Field Service. 14: Sch libs. 15: R D 1, Newton Pa 18940.

DAVIS, MAUREEN P J (BURRELL). b England 20 D 29. 4: Robert H Davis. 5: NW Polytech (London England) 53-58 British ALA; Queen'sU 59-61 BA. 7: Tchr London Co Coun, Lond england 50-53; Lib asst Holborn Borough Libs, London England 53-55; Asst libn battersea Pub Lib, London England 55-58; Asst libn Galt Pub Lib, Galt Ont Can 58-60; Asst libn Redpath Lib McGillU 61-62; Sect libn London Pub Lib, London Ont Can 62-64; Libn Stratford Tchrs Col, Stratford Ont Can 64-. 9: CanLA; OntLA. 15: RR 2, Stratford Ont Can.

DAVIS, MIKE. b Terre Haute Ind 25 Ag 39. 5: Ind StateU 57-61 (Philos) AB; UItaliana per Stranieri 65 (Ital) Certif; IndU 65-68 (LS) MA. 6: Fr, Russian, Ital. 7: Tr (E-5) US ASA (Army), Monterey & Frankfurt 62-65; Asst libn Lincoln Land Commun Col 68-. 9: ALA. 10: Phi Sigma Iota. 14: Acad libs. 15: 1435 Stevenson dr, Springfield Il 62703.

DAVIS, MILDRED W(INSOR). b Covington La 17 Je 08. 5: LSU 31 (Eng) BA; UNC 36 AB in LS. 7: Tchr-libn Charlotte High Sch, Punta Gorda Fla 31-34; Catlgr UVa 36-38; Asst period lib act head UNC(Chapel Hill) 38-42; Army libn 3d Serv Command Camp Pickett Va, Camp Reynolds Penn 42-44; Ser libn UNC(Chapel Hill) 44-50; Period catlgr Ga Inst of Tech 51-52; Period libn acquis libn UMiss 52-54; Catlg libn McNeese State Col 54-. 9: ALA; SWLA; LaLA; LaTA. 10: Phi Kappa Phi. 14: Catlg, ser. 15: 712 Iberville st, Lake Charles La 70601.

DAVIS, NANCY (BRAWLEY HOWARD). b Mooresville NC 9 D 10. 4: Benjamin Cummings Davis. 5: UNC (Greensboro) 27-29 (LS) AB, summer 30, 30-31, summer 31; Peabody 42 (LS). 6: Lat, Fr, Sp. 7: Stud asst UNC (Greensboro); Tchr & libn, Taylorsville NC 33-35; Libn Hugh Morson High Sch, Raleigh NC 35-36; Supv WPA Lib Proj, Mecklengurg & Stanley Cos NC; Libn Harding High Sch, Charlotte NC 38-40; Libn So Pines (NC) Schs 42-43; Child libn Greensboro (NC) Pub Lib 43-44; Libn Mooresville (NC) High Sch 44-46; Catlgr Mooresville (NC) Pub Lib 46-47; Elem libn, Charlotte NC 47-49; Libn Harding High Sch, Charlotte NC 49-55; Tchr Mooresville Jr High Sch 55-57; Libn Iredell Co Pub Lib, Statesville NC 57-59; Ref & circ libn Davidson Col Lib 59-60; Libn Kenly Elem Sch Lib Hillsborough Co Sch System, Tampa Fla 60-61; Libn John McKnitt Alexander Jr High Sch, Huntersville NC 61-. 9: ALA; NEA; NCLA; NCEA; SELA. 10: Mooresville Community Fund; Iredell Co Cancer Soc; Mooresville Womans Club 14: Org of sch libs, catlg. 15: 313 W McLelland ave, Mooresville NC 28115.

DAVIS, NANCY (HEATER). b Urbana Ill 15 D 31. 4: Edward L Davis. 5: UIll 49-53 (Hist) AB, 57-58 (LS) MS. 7: UIll(Urbana); Arch lib asst 58-60, Engnr lib asst 60-63, Asst agric libn 63-. 8: Urbana(Ill) Free Lib Bd Trustees 68-. 9: ALA. 12: Comp "Commodity Futures Trading; a Bibliography" (66). 15: 701 W Vermont, Urbana Il 61801.

DAVIS, RICHARD ALBAN. b Pasadena Cal 26 Ap 23. 4: Mary Hammel. 5: UCal (Berkeley) 46-47; Chicago 59 (LS) MA. 7: LCdr US Navy (Patrol Plane Commander) 42-46; Chief Tech Dept John Crerar Lib, Chicago 56-58, Chief Translation Center 58-59; Libn Labs for Applied Sci UChicago 59-60; Asst Prof Grad Sch of Lib Sci Drexel Inst 60-67; Instr Grad Lib Sch UChicago 67-; Asst libn John Crerar Lib; Dir Midwest Reg Med Lib Servs 68-. 9: SLA; MLA; ASIS; CathLA; AALS; Aslib. 10: Phi Beta Kappa; Phi Kappa Phi. 12: "Bibliograph of Use Studies (64). 13: Yes. 14: Info sci, spec libs. 15: 1451 E 55th #318, Chicago IL 60615.

DAVIS, RICHARD ALLEN. b Binghampton NY 15 ap 23. 4: Sonia Morck. 5: Albion Col 41-48 (Art) AB; State U of Iwa 48-50 (Art) MFA; UMic(Ann Arbor) 59-60 MLS. 6: Ger. 7: Army, European Theatre 43-45; Dir Saginaw Mus, Saginaw Mich 53-56; Curator of Art The SI Inst of Arts & Sci 56-59; Chief bus & tech Saginaw Pub Lib, Saginaw Mich 60-62; Head fine arts dept Cleveland Pub Lib 62-67; Assoc libn Butler U 67-68; Hd libn 68-. 9: SLA. 13: Yes. 14: Rare bks, bibliog, ref, admin. 15: 5047 N Capitol, Indianapolis In 46208.

DAVIS, RUSSELL L. b Blackfoot Id 25 O 24. 4: Emma Lou Barnes. 5: Weber Jr Coll 48-50; Utah State U 50-52 (Pol sci, hist) BS; UMich 52-53 (LS) AM. 7: Ship's cook 1st class USN S Pacific 43-46; Utah State U: Engineering libn 53-55, Circ libn 53-57, Prof of lib sci 53-57; Dir State Lib Comsn of Utah 57-. 9: ALA; MPLA (pres 60-61); UtahLA (pres 63-65). 12: Utah Ed, Merit Student Encyclopedia. 14: Admin. 15: 2150 S 2nd W, Salt Lake City Ut 84115.

DAVIS, SALLY (ANN). b Chicago 28 F 29. 505: Carroll Col (Waukesha Wis) 47-51 (Hist) BA; UWis (Madison) 53-54 (LS) MA. 6: Sp. 7: Tchr-libn Edgar (Wis) Pub Schs 51-53; High sch libn Winnetka Pub Schs, Winnetka III 54-58; High sch libn Oconomowoc Pub Schs, Oconomowoc Wis 58-60, Dir of sch libs 60-. 9: NEA; ALA; WisLA (sec 65-66); WisEA; SWisEA; MetroSchLA; Waukesha County LA (pres 62-63); WisLA (dir 67-68, v-pres & pres-elect 68-69); OconomowocEA. 10: AAUW; Tech Adv Com on Libs, SEast Wis Reg Planning Com 68-69. 14: Tech processe, sch libs, instrl materials centers. 15: 641 Forest st, Oconomwoc WI 53066.

DAVIS, SAMUEL A(UGUSTUS). b Oliveira Minas Brazil 17 F 24. 4: Arlene Powers. 5: Seminario Theol Presbyteriano (Campinas, Sao Paulo Brazil) 42-44; Presbyterian Col of SC 45-46 (Bible) BA; Union Theol Sem (Va) 46-48; Emory 51-52 (LS) MS. 6: Portu. 7: Ref libn Med Col of Va 53-55; Libn Albany Med Col 55-58; Asst libn Jefferson Med Col 58-66, Assoc libn 66-. 9: MedLA-Phila Reg Group (pres 62-63); Pennsauken (NJ) LA(v-pres 63, treas 65). 14: Ref, admin. 15: 5536 Cedar ave, Pennsauken NJ 08109.

DAVIS, SARAH MARIE. b Washington Iowa 13 F 16. 5: Coe Coll 34-38 (Hist) BA; UIowa 38-39 (Amer hist) MA 48; UMich 47-48, 48-49 AMLS; American U 52 Archives Certif. 6: Fr. 7: Hist, govt, econ, Eng, Latin & mus tchr high sch, Steele City Neb 40-42; Hist & govt tchr high sch, Woodbine Iowa 42-44; Hist tchr high sch, Sycomore Ill 43-45; Hist tchr high sch, Mt Clemens Mich 45-47; Grad asst circ dept UMich Lib 47-49; Detroit Pub Lib: Asst ref libn soc sci dept 49-50, Asst ref libn Burton Hist Collection 50-52; Swen Franklin Parson Lib No Ill: Hd libn res dept 52-68, Research & development libn 68-. 8: Lib Adv Com, Ellwood House, De Kalb Ill 68-. 9: ALA; -ACRL; NEA; Amer Assn Higher Educ; Organ Amer Histns; IllLA; IllEA. 10: AAUW: UMich Lib Sci Alum; Pi Gamma Mu; Phi Kappa Phi; De Kalb Co Fine Arts Assn; Ellwood House; Family Serv Agency, De Kalb; Art Inat of Chicago; Lyric Guild of Chicago; Chicago Educ TV Assn; Fac Club; Dames Club; Booster Club of NIllU. 11: Phi Sigma Iota Essay Award, Coe Coll 38. 14: Ref, research. 15: 143 1/2 John st, De Kalb Il 60115.

DAVIS, SHARON ANN (YORK). b Logan Utah 29 D 37. 5: Clarinda Jr Col 55-56 (Arts & Sci); UColo 56-58 (Psych) BA, MPS; DenverU 67-68 (Libnship) MA. 7: Casewkr I co pub welfare dept, Bonkler Colo 59-63; Casewkr II co pub welfare dept, Denver 63-64; Quality control reviewer State Welfare Dept, Denver 64-65; Search analyst UColo Med Ctr Lib 68-. 9: ALA. 10: Beta Phi Mu. 14: Ref, MEDLARS searching. 15: 3130 26th, Boulder Co 80302.

DAVIS, VIRGINIA (RODGERS). b Corbin Ky 10 Je. 4: Charles Martin Davis. 5: UTenn 30-34 (Eng) BA; Uky summers 45-51 (LS) MS. 7: Elem tchr Sough Ward Sch, Corbin Ky 34-42; Eng tchr Middlesboro High Sch, Middlesboro Ky 42-43, Libn 43-46; Libn Elizabethton High Sch, Elizabethton Tenn 46-. 9: NEA; ALA; SELA; TennEA; TennLA; East Tenn EA; Boone Tree Co Lib Bd. 10: Delta Kappa Gamma; Bus & Prof Womens Club; Womans Club; PTA; Elizabethton Bk Club; Hosp Auxiliary; Alpha Delta Kappa. 14: Ref. 15: 300 Holston ave, Elizabethton Tenn 37643.

DAVIS, WILLIAM NEWELL JR. b Kingsburg Cal 29 Ja 15. 4: Ruth Maudlin Davis. 5: Fresno State Col 32-36 (Hist) AB; UCal(Berkeley) 37-38 (US Hist) MA, 40-42 (US Hist) PhD. 7: US Army Air Force Compat Intel Off, Southwest Pacific 42-46; Capt Ed Hqrs 13th Air Force Intel Publs; Historian Cal State Archives, Sacramento Cal 55-56; Chief of Archives State Archives, Sacramento Cal 66-. 8: Sec Cal Heritage Preservation Commsn 63-. 9: AHA; Org Amer Histns; Amer Soc for Legal Hist; SAA; Hakluyt Soc; Selden Soc; West Hist Assn; Conf Cal Hist Socs; Cal HS. 11: State Bar of Cal, Sac Co Bar Assn, Amer Bar Assn, Commonwealth Club of Cal; Native Sons Fellow in Pacific Coast History UCal(Berkeley) 41-42; Award of Merit of Cal HS 69. 13: Yes. 14: Hist of Amer law & Amer West. 15: 4440 Sycamore ave, Sacramento CA 95841.

DAVISH, REV WILLIAM (MARTIN). b Philadelphia 1 F 13. 5: Georgetown 35-39 (Ed) AB; Woodstock Col 39-40, 43-47 (Philos, Theol) PHL, STL Catholic U 46-48 MS in LS; Inst Catholique (Paris) 61-62 (Theol). 6: Fr, Ger, Lat. Gk. 7: Tchr of Lat, Gk, Eng St Josephs High Sch, Phila 40-43; Ed asst Theol Studies, Woodstock Md 44-47; Loyola Col (Baltmore): Libn Instr in Theol 49-52, Even Dean Asst Prof in Theol 52-57, Libn Prof of Theol 57-66, Asst to pres, Dir col research, Prof of Theol, Dept chm 67-. 8: Entered Soc of Jesus 33; Ordained a Cath Priest 46. 9: ALA; Cath Theol Soc; Col Theol Soc; Assn of Univ Even Cols (Off); CathLA; MdLA. 12: "Woodstock College, 1869-1944". 13: Yes. 14: Ref, col admin, systematic theol. 15: Loyola Col, Baltimore MD 21210.

DAVISON, MARTHA A. b Northville NY 20 D 24. 5: NY State Tchrs Col 43-47 (Soc Studies, Eng) BA, summers 47-52 BSLS. 7: Eng tchr-libn Northville Central, Northville NY 47-50; Soc Studies Tchr-libn Milford Central, Milford NY 50-52; Elem libn So Colonie Central Sch, Albany NY 52-. 10: OES. 15: 622 Bridge st, Northville NY 12134.

DAVISON, RUTH M. b Columbus Ohio. 5: Ind U 53-57 Eng AB, 60-61 (LS) MA. 7: Bkmob libn Clermont Co Pub Lib, Batavia Ohio 57-60; Field consul Ind State Lib 61-67; Asst doc libn Ind U Lib 67-. 9: ALA; IndLA. 14: Govt docs. 15: RR 10 Box 210, Bloomington IN 47401.

DAVISSON, DONALD. b Sacramento Cal 2 N 28. 5: UCal (Berkeley) 48-52 (Eng Lit, Hist) BA, 53-54 BLS. 6: Fr, Ger, Sp. 7: Cryptographer US Army, Kyoto Japan 46-48; Prin lib asst UCal (Berkeley) 50-53; Asst creative arts libn San Francisco State Col 54-57, Head catlg dept 57-. 8: Lib adv, Cal Hist Soc 55-61. 9: ALA; (Conf Planning Com 66; Insts on Catlg Code Rev; Inst on Use of LC Clsf); MusLA; CalLA (Nomin Com 58-60, chm Publ Com 66-68); Cal State Col Libns RT (chm Organ Com 66, Col Rep 66-69); No Cal Tech Proc Gp (v-pres 61). 10: Assn Cal State Col Profs; Amer Fed of Tchrs; Cal Acad of Scis; Cal Hist Soc; Amer Museum of Nat Hist Assn; ACLU; AAAS; UCal Sch of Libnship Alum Assn; Audubon Soc Bureau of Amer Indians Affairs; Friends Com on Legis; NAACP; Student Non-Violent Coord Com. 12: Assoc ed "Union Review (61-62); Chm Publ Com, CalLA

(66-68). 13: Yes. 14: Catlg, clsf, music libnship. 15: 898 Green st, San Francisco Ca 94133.

DAW, MAY JOAN (BATES). b Wash DC 14 S 43. 4: Carl P Daw Jr. 5: Duke 60-64 (Fr) AB; Columbia 64-65 (LS) MS. 6: Fr. 7: Catlgr Alderman Lib UVa 65; Libn Nat Radio Astronomy Observatory, Charlottesville Va 66-. 9: ALA; SLA (treas Va chap 69-70); VaLA. 14: Local union lists of serls. 15: National Radio Astronomy Observatory Edgemont rd, Charlottesville Va 22901.

DAWKINS, MARY CATHERINE (SAUNDERS). b Flemingsburg Ky 19 S 22. 5: Morehead State Tchrs Col 41-42 (Home Econ); UKy 42-45 (Home Econ); Morehead State Tchrs Col summer 63 (LS); UKy summer 64 (Home Econ, LS) BS. 7: Libn Fleming Co, lemingsburg Ky 62-63; Reg libn Dept of Libs, Carlisle Ky 64-. 8: KyLA; SELA. 10: CYF Youth Leader, Homemaker's Club; Bus & Prof Woman's Club; Friends of Ky, Libn; Kappa Delta; U Ky alum assn. 14: Pub rel. 15: 120 Pumphrey ave, Flemingsburg Ky 41041.

DAWSON, BEATRICE (BOWEN). b Duryea Penn 1 D 05. 4: Robert E Dawson. 5: Penn State 22-26 (Soc Studies) BA; Columbia summers 28-31 (Supv, Admin) MA; Marywood Col summers 61-63 MS in LS. 7: Tchr Jr High Sch, Lancaster Penn 26-27; Prin Jr High Sch, Duryea Penn 27-34; Teller NE Nat Bank & Trust Co, Scranton Penn 56-60; Libn West Scranton High Sch, Scranton Penn 61-; Libn Tech High Sch, Scranton Penn 67-. 9: PennLA; Penn StateEA. 10: Penn State Alum Assn; Chi Omega; Delta Kappa Gamma; AAUW; Womens Tchrs Club of Scranton; PTA (Life mem). 13: Yes. 14: Ref. 15: 424 New st, Scranton PA 18509.

DAWSON, CHARLOTTE M. b Beaver Falls Penn 11 My 32. 5: Geneva Col 59-66 (Elem Educ) BSEd; UPittsburgh 66-67 MLS. 7: Exec sec Investors Diversified Serv Inc, Beaver Falls Penn 55-58; Exec sec H H Robertson Co, Ambridge Penn 59-64; Elem libn & a-v coord NEast Beaver Co Sch Dist, Beaver Falls Penn 66-. 10: AAUW; Beta Phi Mu. 14: Child lit, a-v materials. 15: 110 Bradmore st, Beaver Falls Pa 15010.

DAWSON, CORNELIA MARY. b Green Bay Wis 25 S 06. 5: Smith 23-24; Lake Erie Col 25-28 (Zool & Gk) BA; West Res 28-29 BS in LS; UMich 40-41 MA in LS. 6: Fr, Ger, Sp. Lat, Gk. 7: Asst jr libn Buffalo Pub Lib, Buffalo NY 29-32; Catlgr UCicinnati Lib 3238; Act libn Central Col (Fayette Mo) 38-40; Catlgr Pub Lib of Cincinnati 41-42; Catlgr Carnegie Endowment for Internat Peace, Wash DC 42-43; Catlgr State Hist Soc of Mo, Columbia Mo 43-49; Br libn ept of educ sociol philos & relig Buffalo & Erie Co Pub Lib, Buffalo NY 50-, Head 63-. 9: ALA; NYLA. 10: Grosvenor Soc. 14: Ref, catlg. 15: 246 Bryant st, Buffalo NY 14222.

DAWSON, DOROTHEA (STEFFAN). b Augusta Ga 2 Ap 17. George L Dawson. 5: Jr Col of Augusta 32-33; UGa 33-35 (Fr) AB; Emory 38-39 (Fr) MA. 6: Fr, Ger. 7: Fr & Lat tchr Jefferson Co Schs 37-38; Fr, Eng tchr High Sch, Manchester Ga 39-41; Sec Med Col of Ga, Augusta Ga 41-46, 49-51; Sec Chicago 46-49; VA Hosp, Augusta Ga: Sec 51-60, Libn 60-. 8: Augusta Richmond Co Pub Lib volunteer for pub, assistance with spec prog; Friends of the Lib for Augusta area; Bd of Augusta Richmond Co Pub Lib (1 yr). 9: ALA; GaLA. 10: Central Savannah River Area Libns G- in Augusta Ga; Friends of the Lib. 14: Ref publ, displays, & bk reviewing. 15: 3133 Richmond Hill rd, Augusta Ga 30906.

DAWSON, ETTA MAE (JACKSON). b Beulah Miss 5 My 19. 4: Sidney L Dawson. 5: UKan 38-40 (Eng) MA; UDenver 65 (LS) MA. 7: Tchr Prim & Jr High Sch, Kan City Kan 40-48; Tchr Jr High Sch, Tucson 48-51; High Sch, Tucson: Tchr 51-, Lib asst 57-63, Libn 64-. 8: Prof Practices Ado Coun, Ariz State Bd Educ 68-. 9: ArizStateLA (past chm Scholarship Chm). 10: Alpah Kappa Alpha; Delta Kappa Gamma. 14: Sch libs. 15: 516 E Lee st, Tucson AZ 85705.

DAWSON, JOHN MINTO. b Alva Scotland 4 Jl 17. 4: M Marcene Madden. 5: Tulane 36-40 (Eng) BA; LSU 40-41 BS in LS; UChicago 47-48 (LS) PhD. 6: Fr, Ger. 7: Bus manager UAla Lib 4-42; US Army Port Off (1st Lt) 42-45; Asst dir Tulane U Lib 45-47; Asst dir UChicago Lib 48-58; Lecturer Grad Lib Sch UChicago 53-58; Dir of Libs UDel 58-. 8: Library bldg consul; consul to ARL on Study of Centralized Catlg; Lib Surveyor; Chm adv com on lib survey to Del State Lib Commsn 64-. 9: ALA (Coun 58-69, Exec Bd 65-69, Pub Bd 67-69, Sect chm 63-64);-ACRL (chm U Lib Sect 66-67, chm & mem var coms); DelLA (pres 64-65, Com chm 60-63). 10: Newark (Del) Lib Commsn; Phi Beta Kappa; Beta Phi Mu; Beta M. 12: Ed Bd "College & Research Libraries" 63-69. 13: Yes. 14: Centralized catlg, acad lib admin, lib bldgs. 15: U Del Lib, Newark DE 19711.

DAWSON, PATRICIA (NEWELL). b Red Oak Iowa 23 S 45. 4: Douglas A Dawson. 5: UIowa 63-67 (Psych) BS, 67-68 (LS) MA. 7: Libn Harding Jr High, Des Moines Iowa 68-. 9: ALA. 12: "History of Institutional Libraries in Iowa". 15: 4837 NW 62nd ave, Des Moines Ia 50323.

DAX, EDWARD ROBERT. b Milwaukee 18 O 15. 4: June Bemis Dax. 5: Marquette U 46-49 (Hist) PhB; West Res 49-50 MSLS. 7: Clerical asst Milwaukee Pub Lib 37-42; Libn I Cincinnati Pub Lib 50-52; Libn maysville Pub Lib 52-55; Libn Vaughn Pub Lib, Ashland Wis 55-57; Libn Lancaster Free Pub Lib, Lancaster Penn 58-62; Assoc Dir Lane Pub Lib, Hamilton Ohio 62-. 8: Instr Wis Free Lib Commsn UWis Ext Div 55-56. 9: OhioLA (Co-chm Ref Wkshop 65). 13: Yes. 14: Admin, bk sel, ref, local hist. 15: Lane Pub Lib N 3d & Buckeye sts, Hamilton Oh 45011.

DAY, DOROTHY LAVERNE. b Louisville Ky 3 D 25. 4: Ruth Busby Day. 5: ULouisville 44-48 (Eng) BA; UKy 48-49 BL in LS. 6: Fr. 7: Stud asst Louisville Free Pub Lib Jefferson br 42-45, Clk 45-48, Br libn Iroquois br 49-51, A-v catlgr 51-52, Asst hd of a-v dept 52-57, A-v Dept hd 57-. 8: A-v aid instr Catherine Spalding 59-62. 9: ALA;NEA-Div of A-v Instr; Nas Assn Educ Broadcasters; SELA; KyLA; Louisville Lib Club; Ky A-V Assn. 10: J B Speed Museum Assoc. 14: Radio, films, records, tape recordings. 15: 929 Audubon pkwy, Louisville Ky 40213.

DAY, DOROTHY LYNN (AUTENRIETH). b Omaha Neb 30 Je 43. 4: Mark Tyler Day. 5: UChicago 61-65 (Pol Sci) BA, 66-68 (LS, Far East Studies) MA. 6: Fr, Chinese. 7: Stud asst uchicago Lib 62-66, Grad research asst Grad Lib Sch NSE Catlg Proj 66-68; Catlgr UNB 68-69; Asst ref libn PrincetonU 69-. 9: ALA; Assn Asian Studies (Com on East Asian Libs). 13: Yes. 14: Ref, soc sci bibliog. 15: 123 Bayard lane, Princeton NJ 08540.

DAY, DUANE (ROBERT). b Albert Lea Minn 29 O 23. 4: Ruth Busby Day. 5: Hamline U 42; UMinn 46-50 (Eng) BA, 50 BS in LS. 7: Asst libn VA Hosp, Fargo ND 50; Asst libn Brown & Bigelow, St Paul 51-52; Libn Campbell-Mithun Inc, Minneapolis 53-65; Libn Gen Mills Inc, Minneapolis 65--66; Mgr Lib Serv 67-. 8: Guest lecturer t Catherines Col 64 and UMinn seminar sssion in Grad Sch of Journalism, Sources in Advertising & Marketing 5; Founded reciprocal bus lib cooperative effort in US 63. 9: SLA-Adver & Marketing Div (chm var coms)-Minn Chap (Bulletin ed & var offs). 14: Spec libs. 15: 2233 Merrill st, St Paul 55113.

DAY, FERN (SLATER) MRS. b Esmond ND 28 N 04. 5: UND 22-25 (Commerce) BS in Ed. 7: High sch tchr pub schs, Alexander ND 25-27; High sch tchr pub schs, Spearfish SD 27-29; Law libn UND 57-. 10: Bus & Prof Womens Club; AAUW; Pi Lambda Theta. 15: 203 Park ave, Grand Forks ND 58201.

DAY, JOYCE. b Waltersville Miss. 5: UMiss 40-44 (Chem) BA. 7: Analytical chem Texaco Inc, Port Arthur Tex 44-45, Research libn 45-. 9: ACS-Div Chem Lit; SLA. 10: Photographic Soc of Amer. 14 Petroleum & petrochemical lit. 15: 2049 Rosedale, Port Arthur Tx 77642.

DAY, KATHARINE B(OLT). b Pendleton SC 27 S 06. 5: Furman U 24-27; Simmons 27-28 BS in LS. NDLETON SC 27 S 06. 9: AALL; ALA; SELA; NCLA. 12: Co-ed "Current Publications in Legal and Related Fields (53-). 13: Yes. 14: Catlg, acquis. 15: Duke U Law Lib, Durham NC 27706.

DAY, MARIE (TURNER). b Phila 18 O 24. 5: Temple U; Drexel. 6: Ger, Fr, Sp. 7: Supv LA Free Lib, Phila 55-59; Act ser libn Drexel Inst 59-60; Music catlgr West Chester State Col 61-62; Music catlgr UPenn 62-64; Chief tech data lib Defense Dept Contract Admin, Phila 64-66; Hd libn USNaval Shipyard, Phila 66-67; Chief NAS Documentation Facility NAFEC 67-68; Hd libn USNaval Hosp, Phila 68-. 8: Compiled DSA a complete bibliog of sources of tech data in US; Pub Computer Prog of NAS Documentation for FAA. 9: SLA; MedLA. 14: Catlg, admin. 15: The Drake Box 46, Phila Pa 19102.

DAY, MARK TYLER. b Chicago Ill 3 D 42. 4: Dorothy Lynn Autenvieth. 5: UChicago 60-64 (Pol Sci) BA, 64-66 (Soc Studies) MAT, 66-68 (LS, Middle East Studies) MA. 7: MAT tchr New Trier Twp High Sch West, Northfield Ill 65-66; Stud asst Oriental Inst UChicago Libs 67-68; Asst ref libn UNB Lib, Fredericton Chicago 68-69; Libn off Population Research PrincetonU 69-. 9: ALA. 10: Middle East Studies Assn; Population Assn of Amer. 14: Admin, lib sci educ, soc sci bibliog, peace research. 15: 123 Bayard lane, Princeton NJ 08540.

DAY, MARY (MORGAN). b Tallulah La 30 N 43. 5: La Coll 61-65 (Elem ed) BA; LSU 65-68 MSLS. 7: Acquis tech La Coll 65-66; Libn Gonzales Jr High, Gonzales La 66-68; Libn Cane Run & Wellington Elem Sch, Louisville Ky 68-. 9: NEA; ALA; KyWA; KyLA. 14: Acquis, catlg, ref. 15: 222 S Peterson, Louisville Ky 40206.

DAY, NANCY JANE. b Pendleton SC 1 My 05. 5: Furman U 25 (Hist) BA; Columbia 33 (LS) BS; UMich 43 MA LS. 7: Tchr pub schs, Winston-Salem NC 25-30; Asst libn Reynolds High Sch, Winston-Salem NC 30-33; Libn Womens Col (Greenville SC) 33-34; Asst Pub Lib, Greenville SC 34-35; Asst libn Furman Col 35: Asst Fla State 35-39; Instr in Lib Sci Winthrop Col 39-43; Asst Prof Emory U 43-46; Supv of Lib Serv State Dept of Educ, Columbia SC 46-. 8: Fulbright Grant (Lecturer), Chulalongkorn Univ, Thailand, 53-54. 9: ALA (Coun 49-53, 61-65, Bd of Educ for Libnship 52-58, ALA-NEA Jt Com 60-65); -AASchL (pres 54-55); NEA; ASCD (pres 66-67); SELA (pres 54-56); SCLA (sec 47, pres 61); SCEA. 10: AAUW; LWV; Delta Kappa Gamma. 13: Yes. 14: Sch libs, ref, child & yp lit. 15: 3210 Duncan st, Columbia SC 29205.

DAY, ROWENA WISE. b Emeryville Cal 12 S 13. 4: Charles R. Day. 5: UCal (Berkeley) 30-32 (Econ); Sacramento State Col 56-61 (Hist) BA; UCal (Berkeley) 61-62 MLS. 7: Lib clk Sacramento City Lib, Sacramento Cal 57-60; Libn I Cal State Lib 62-63, Libn II 63-. 9: ALA; CalLA. 10: Beta Phi Mu. 12: "Carnival of Light; the Story of Electric Light and Power in Sacramento, 1879-1895 (57). 14: Govt docs. 15: 933 54th st, Sacramento Cal 95819.

DAY, THOMAS LEE. b Ypsilanti Mich 16 Ag 40. 5: EastMichU 58-62 (Math) BS; UMich 67-68 AMLS. 6: Ger, Lat. 7: Boston Pub Lib W End Br 68-. 10: Boston YMC Union. 14: Ref, home reading, a-v, loc hist. 15: Suite 208 (Coolidge) 9 Sewall ave, Brookline Ma 02146.

DAY, VIOLA (SARAH) NORTHRUP. b NYC 24 Jl 45. 5: UBridgeport 63-67 (Eng) BA; Rutgers 67-68 MLS. 6: Sp. 7: Stud asst Carlson Lib UBridgeport 64-67; Volunteer Head Start, bridgeport Conn 65-67; Libn Coop ext serv on Air Pollution RutgersU 68; Order libn Yale Divinty Sch Lib 68-. 9: ALA. 14: Ref, child wk, bk selection. 15: 100 Westford dr, Southport Ct 06490.

De BRUIJN, ELSIE CATHERINE (WOLLASTON). b Vancouver BC Can 31 D 43. 4: J Erik de Bruijn. 5: UVictoria 61-65 (Eng, Sociol) BA; UToronto 65-66 BLS. 6: Ger, Fr. 7: Ref libn Queen'sU 66-68; Info libn UBC Lib 68-. 9: CanLA; CACUL; BCLA. 12: Ed "UBC Library News". 13: Yes. 14: Ref, info serv. 15: Information & Orientation Div'n UBC Lib, Vancouver 8 BC Can.

De BRUIJN, (JOANNES) ERIK. b Amsterdam Holland 10 D 43. 4: Elsie Wollaston. 5: UVictoria 61-65 (Pol Sci, Russian) BA; UBC 68-69 BLS. 6: Dutch, Ger, Fr, Russian. 7: Capt Canadian Intelligence Corps Canadian Army, Kingston Ont 65-68; Catlgr UBC Lib 69-. 9: ALA; CanLA; CACUL; BCLA; Assn BC Libns. 10: Beta Phi Mu. 14: Catlg, info retrieval, lib admin. 15: Lib Univ of British Columbia, Vancouver 8 BC Can.

DeBRULER, OLIVE CLEO. b Dubois Co Ind. 5: IndianaU 30-35 (Eng) AB; UIll summers 40-44 BSLS, 60 (Ed); UChicago summers (LS) MA. 7: Tchr pub schs, Huntingsburg Ind 35-36; Tchr-libn pub schs, Beech Grove Ind 36-37; Libn, Ind pub schs: Peru 37-40, Effingham 40-43; Chm libs & a-v serv high sch & jr cols, Joliet Ill 43-58; Ext instr Grad Sch Lib Sci UIll(Urbana) 58-61; Supv dir lib sci DC Pub Schs 61-. 8: Instr & asst prof lib sci in summer session: IndU, Madison Col, Ball State Teachers Col, Rutgers U, UMinn. 9: ALA-AASchL (chm A-V Com 56; advertising mgr "School Libraries" 56-62; sec lib supv sect, 64); NEA; IllASchL (sec 60-61, chm Standards Com 61). 10: Delta Kappa Gamma; Beta Phi Mu; Coun on Admin Women in Educ; Child Bk Guild of Wash DC. 13: Yes. 14: Sch libs, lib educ. 15: 4201 Massachusetts ave NW, Washington DC 20016.

DE COITO, BONNIE (HECKMAN). b Indianapolis 11 O 25. 4: Alfred De Coito Jr. 5: IndU 43-44 & 57-59 (Home Econ) BS in Educ. 7: Jr draftsman Hoffman Spec Co, Indianapolis summers 43-44; Telephone oerator Ind Bell Tele, Indianapolis 7, 48; Fatory line Sarke-Tarzian, Bloomington Ind 54-56; Indianapolis Pub Lib: Asst to child libn Brown Br 60-61, Child libn E Wash Br 62-64, Br libn Brightwood Br 64-68; Br libn Spades Park Br 68-. 9: ALA; IndLA. 10: Indianapolis Marion Pub Lib Staff Assn. 14: Pub lib wk (child & elderly people). 15: 60 N Ritter ave, Indianapolis IN 46219.

de CORDOVA, DIANE J (STEVENS). b NYC 15 F 34. 4: Donald W de Cordova. 5: Trenton State Coll 52-56 (Eng) BS; Rutgers 68-69 MLS. 6: Fr. 7: Elem sch libn Bd of Educ, Arlington Va 56-58; Elem sch libn Bd of Educ, River Edge NJ 58-68. 9: ALA; NJSLA (Exec Bd 68-69); Bergen Co Sch LA (pres 66-69). 10: Delta Kappa Gamma; Girl Scouts. 14: Elem sch libnship, media spec. 15: 119 Elm ave, Bogota NJ 07603.

De COSTER, BARBARA LOU (GRAY). b Salt Lake City Utah 22 D 32. 4: Don Theodore DeCoster. 5: MIT 50-51; (Arch Engr); Amarillo Jr Coll 51-52 (Math); W Tex State U 51-54 (Eng); UTex (Austin) 57-58 (Eng); Arizona State U 60-61 (Eng); UWash 62-67 (Eng) BA 65, (Libnship) MLS 67. 7: Tchg asst Sch of Libnship 66-67; Consul A-V Ctr UWash 67; Catlgr Lib-Med Ctr, Bellevue Commun Coll 67-. 9: ALA. 10: Alum Assn; Sch of Libnship; UWash. 14: Catlg. 15: 6343 NE 156th, Bothell Wa 98011.

De DORY, KATHERINE MARIA. b Budapest Hungary 6 Ja 23. 5: Bartok Bela Col Conservatory 46-50 (Music, Art) BA; UKy 59-61 (LS) MS; NY State Prof Libn Certif 62. 6: Fr, Ger, Hungarian, Lat, Ital. 7: Libn asst period dept UK y 58-62; Choir dir organist VA Hosp, Lexington Ky 58-62; Libn adult serv rooklyn Pub Lib 62-64; Ref libn US Mil Acad (W Point) 64- 18 month airf libn, Bien Hoa Airbase S Vietnam. 9: MusLA; NYLib Club. 10: West Point Offs Club; Metropo Museum of Art; Alliance francaise. 11: Vietnam SVC medal, 3 other mil awards. 14: Ref, lit, for langs, hist. 15: 287 Main st, Highland Falls NY 10928.

DeFATO, JOAN. b Brooklyn NY 23 Ap 35. 5: Barnard 52-56 (Botany) AB; Columbia 56-57 (LS) MS. 6: Fr. 07: Asst libn Med Lib Equitable Life Assurance Soc, NYC 57-59; Libn Boyce Thompson Inst for Plant Research, onkers, NY 59-. 9: SLA. 10: Torrey Botanical Club. 15: 1086 North Broadway, Yonker NY 10701.

DE FOREST, MARJORIE (DE ERDOS). b NYC 30 My 21. 5: Hunter Col 41 (Eng) BA; USoCal 47 (LS). 6: Fr. 7: Lib cleark NY Pub Lib; Circ & ref Camp Coles Signal Lab, Ft Monmouth NJ 42-45; Ref libn Hughes Aircraft Co, Culver City Cal; Libn Rexall Drug Co, Los Angeles 48-49; Ref libn NY Acad of Med, NYC 50-58; Libn Jewish Mem Hosp, NYC 58-64; Libn Montefiore Hosp & Md Center, NYC 65-. 9: SLA; MedLA. 10: PTA. 13: Yes. 14: Ref. 15: Montefiore Hosp & Med Center, 210 st & Bainbridge, Bronx NY 10467.

DE GENNARO, RICHARD. b New Haven Conn 2 Mr 26. 4: Birgit Erickson. 5: Wesleyan U 47-51 (Govt) AB; UParis 51-52 (Fr) Diplome dEtudes: Wesleyan U 54-55 (Hist) MA; Columbiz 55-56 MS in LS. 6: Fr, Sp, Ital, Swedish. 7: Ref libn NY Pub Lib 56-58; Asst ref libn Harvard Col Lib 58-61; Admin asst Harvard U Lib 61-63, Asst dir 63-64, Asst U Libn 64-66, Assoc U Libn for systs devel 66-69, Sr Assoc U Libn 69-. 8: Vis Prof, Lib & Info Sci, USoCal fall 68; Asst dir Inst for Educ and Train of Info Sci Fac, USoCal spring 69; Chemical Abstracts Serv Adv Bd 67-; IEEE, Info Proc Com 66-67 & Info Systems Adv Com 67-; arl microform Tech Proj Consul Panel 68-69; Var bldg & automation consultations. 9: ALA; ISAD (Planning Com 68-); -RTSD (Bk Catlgs Com 67-); -LTP Adv Com 68-); ASIS (SIG/LA Chm 69); NMA; Com on Lib Automation 65-. 12: Ed "Widener Library Shelflist, series (65-). 13: Yes. 14: Admin, automation, bldgs, reprography. 15: Harvard U Lib, Cambridge Ma 02138.

DE GRUMMOND, LENA (YOUNG). b Centerville La. 5: Southwestern 26-29 (Eng, Hist, Span) BA; LSU 36-37 BS in LS, 53-56 Admin PhD. 7: Clerk ref & research La Dept of Educ, Baton Rouge La 29-34; Staff La State Lib 37-38; Libn tchr Centerville High Sch, Centerville La 38-44; Libn Sulphur High Sch, Sulpur La 44-47; Libn Terrebonne High Sch, Houma La 47-49; State supv of sch lib La Dept of Educ, Baton Rouge La 50-61; Prov of Lib Sci USoMiss 65-. 8: Orig & developer of child's spec collection of orig illus & ms of contemp child's bks, USoMiss; Rep to SWLA 9: ALA (Coun mem rep AASchL); -AASchL; NEA; NCTE; LaLA; LaASchL; LaCTE. 10: Delta Kappa Gamma; Theta Sigma Phi; Crescent City Pen Women; Phi Kappa Phi; Gamma Mu; AAUW; La Geneal & Hist Soc; La Hist Assn; So Hist assn; La Hist Soc; Miss Folklore Soc; La Folklore Soc. 12: "Jeff Davis, Confederate Boy" (61); "Jeb Stuart" (62); "Babe Didrikson, Girl Athlete" (65); Jean Piccard, Box Balloonist (68). 13: Yes. 14: Child bks, sch libs. 15: 209 S 29th ave, apt 216, Hattiesburg MS 39401.

De HART, FLORENCE E. b Plainfield NJ 15 D 30. 5: Seton Hall 62 (Fr) MA; Rutgers 64 (LS) Ph D. 6: Fr. 7: Hd catlg dept Seton Hall 59-64; Hd ref dept 64-65; Assoc Prof & Prof Wis State U (Whitewater) 65-67; Asst Prof Sch Lib Sci UWis (Milwaukee) 67-. 8: Dir Institute on Nonbk Materials, UWis

(Milwaukee) 68. 9: ALA; Lib Coll Assocs; WisLA (chm IF Com 68-69). 10: Delta Kappa Gamma. 14: Catlg, reader serv in the acad lib, intell freedom. 15: School of Lib and Info Sci Chapman 309 Univ of Wis, PO Box 413, Milwaukee Wi 53201.

DE JARNATT, JAMES RALPH. b Ft Smith Ark 16 My 40. 5: Hendrix Col 58-62 (Eng) BA; Emory 62-63 MLS. 7: Asst ser libn USoFla 64-65; Asst spec collections libn 65-66; Asst libn & sers libn New Col (Sarasota Fla) 66-68; Sers catlg Ga Tech 68-. 9: ALA. 14: Tech proc. 15: 343 - 8th st NE, Atlanta Ga 30309.

DE JONG, ANN A. b Traverse City Mich 2 Mr 37. 4: John H De Jong. 5: Wayne State 61-66 (Hist) BA; UMich 66-67 (LS) MA. 6: Fr. 7: Staff nurse Henry Ford Hosp, detroit 58-59; Nurse pediatrician's off, Detroit 59-61; Bibliogr Lib of Med Sci UIll Med Ctr 68-. 9: MedLA. 10: Pub Rel Com SCLC Operation Breadbasket, Chicago. 14: Bibliog, ref searches. 15: 496 Old Surrey rd, Hinsdale Il 60521.

DE KLERK, ANN (MARGARET). b Eng 10 D 32. 4: John De Klerk. 5: ULondon Bedford Col 50-53 (Modern Langs) BA; ULondon 53-54 (Educ) Post Grad Certif in Educ; UPittsburgh 63-65 MLS. 6: Ger, Fr. 7: Ref asst Hunt Lib Carnegie-Mellon 65-66; Asst ref libn 66-. 9: ALA-ACRL;-RSD;-CSD; PennLA. 10: LWV; Beta Phi Mu. 14: Ref. 15: 5410 Wilkins ave, Pittsburgh Pa 15217.

de LA GARZA, PETER JACK. b San Antonio Tex 12 My 26. 5: UWash 47-51 (Hist) BA; UCal (Berkeley 51-52 (Hist); UWash 58-59 MALS. 6: Sp, Port, F. 7: US Navy Sonarman 2/c, Pacific Theatre 43-46; Manager bk depts Lowman & Hanford C, Seattle 53-54; Asst manager bk dept U Bk Store, Seattle 54-56, Manager trade bk dept 56-58; Head Order Prep Sect LC 59-60; Head acquis Columbus Mem Lib Pan American Union, Wash DC 60-68; Asst operations off order div LC 68-. 8: Spec recruit LC 59-60; Visiting lecturer on Latin Amer acquis Peace Corps Trainee group, Georgetown U summer 64. 9: ALA (Mem Com chm for DC 61-63, Hammond Map Award Com 65-); -RTSD (Acquis Sect: Policy & Research Com 65-); Seminars on the Acquis of Latin-American Lib Materials (Rapporteur-Gen 62-, mem Acquis Com 61-); DCLA; Potomac Tech Proc Libns; Wash DC Inter-gency Lib Group. 10: Phi Alpha Theta; Beta Phi Mu; Latin Amer Studies Assn; Latin Amer Com of Wash DC. 12: Contrib 18 Chapters on Latin Amer to "International Guide to Educational Documentation 1955-1960" (Paris, UNESCO 63); Final Reports of Seminars on the "Acquisition of Latin American Library Materials" (63-67). 13: Yes. 14: Acquis, docs of internat orgs, current Latin Amer bibliog, Latin Amer official publs. 15: 122 10th st SE, Wash DC 20003.

de la HERRAN, REBECA MARIA (BATISTA). b Camaguey Cuba 8 N 18. 4: Isidro de la Herran. 5: Instituto Camaguey (Cuba) 36-39 BA & BS; UHavana (Cuba) 39-43 Doctor of Law; Kan State Tchrs Col 65-66 MLS. 6: Sp, Ital, Portu. 7: Lawyer private office, Camaguey Cuba 43-59; Soc wkr Fla State Welfare Dept, Miami 63-64; Libn Arickaree High Sch, Anton Colo 64-65; Asst period dept Kan State Tchrs Col 66; Ref libn pub lib, Kan city Kan 66-. 9: ALA. 10: Kan State Tchrs Col Alumi Assn. 14: Ref. 15: 2924 Freeman ave, Kansas City Ks 66102.

De LANCEY, JAMES F. b Cedar Rapids Iowa 16 Jl 33. 5: UIowa 52-56 (Music) BM; Rutgers 59-60 MLS. 7: Draftsman & illus Universal Engnr Corp, Cedar Rapids Iowa 51; Bandsman US Army, Fr Chaffe Ark 56-58; Lib trainee NY Pub Lib 58-59; Trainee & music libn Newark Pub Lib, Newark NJ 59-61; Circ libn Georgetown U Lib 62-67, Asst libn 67-. 9: DCLA. 10: . 14: Circ, music, admin. 15: 2723 36th pl NW, Wash DC 20007.

de LERMA, DOMINIQUE-RENE (SEBASTIEN). b Miami Fla 8 D 28. 5: UMiami 46-49, 50-52 (Composition) BM; Curtis Inst of MVUSIC $() (Oboe); Ind U 56-58 (Musicology) PhD; UOkla 62-63 (LS). 6: Fr, Ital, er. 7: Assoc Prof musicology UMiami (Fla) 51-62; Lecturer in musicology Ind U 61-62; Assoc Prof Musicology UOkla 62-63; Asst Prof musicology & music libn IndU 63-68, Assoc Prof Musical & Mus libn 68-. 8: Music consul for "Choice. 9: MusLA (Bd Dirs, Program Com Midwest Chap); Musicological Soc; Internat Musicological Soc; Deutsche Mozart-Gesellschaft; Gesellschaft fur Musikforschung; Internat Asso of Music Libs; Instituto de Cultura Hispanica. 11: Ind U Found Research Grants 65-; Chapelbrook Found Grant 68-; Svenska Institutet Grant 68-; Foundation Pro Helevtia Grant 68-; Emmy Strong Award 68-; Nat Endowment for the Humanities Grant 69. 12: "An Outline-Guide to Music Literature (55); "Wolfgang Amadeus Mozart; The Influences of His First Ten Years" (58); "Music and Ideas" (62); "Black Music Now" (69); "Charles Ives Bibliography" (69). 13: Yes. 14: Music lib acquis & bibliog, phonorecord catlg; music periodicals. 15: Ind U Sch of Music, Bloomington ID 47401.

de LIAMCHIN, SVETLANA (LANA). b Czechoslovakia 16 D 44. 5: Sir George Williams U 62-66 (Philos) BA; McGill 66-68 (LS) MLS. 6: Slovak, Russian, Fr. 7: Catlg Montreal Mus of Fine Arts 67-68; Libn Dunton High Sch Protestant Sch Bd of Greater Montreal 68-. 9: QueLA; QueASchL. 14: Catlg, admin, art libs. 15: 3744 Cote des Neiges, Montreal Can.

DE LORENZO, ANNETTE MARIE. b Detroit Mich 10 N 41. 5: Manhattanville Coll 59-63 (Govt) BA; Columbia Sch of Lib Serv 63-64 (LS) MS. 6: Ital, Fr. 7: Asst libn Campbell-Ewald Co Advertising, Detroit 64-. 9: SLA. 14: Ref. 15: Campbell-Ewald Co Advertising, 3044 W Grand blvd, Detroit Mi 48202.

De MANGE, KATHERINE K(ING). b Maud Okla 8 Ag 12. 5: William Woods Col 31-32 (Art, Educ) AA; Fresno State Col 52-57 (Art, Educ) BA; UMd (College Park) 66-67 (LS) MA. 6: Sp. 7: Draftsman American Potash & Chem Corp, Trona Cal 46-52; Art & crafts tchr Sequoia Jr High Sch, Fresno Cal 55-57; Sub tchr Stockton Unified Schs, Stockton Cal 57-59; Mgr US Embassy Commissary, Guatemala City Guatemale 60-62; Libn Navy Logistics Research project George WashingtonU 67-68; Acquis libn Health Sci Lib UMd 68-. 9: SLA; MedLA. 15: 719 N Charles st, Baltimore Md 21201.

DE MEYER, HAZEL M(AY). b Kalamazoo 3 Mr 08. 5: West Mich U 25-29 (Soc Sci) AB; Columbia summers 36-39 (LS) BS. 6: Fr. 7: Libn High Sch pub schs, Holland Mich 29-43; Libn J W Sexton High Sch, pub schs, Lansing Mich 43-46; Order libn West Mich U 46-64, Educ libn Educ Resources Center 64-. 8: Consul Bronson Hosp Sch of Nursing Lib Kalamazoo 50-53; Com on Statewide Plan for Lib Devel (Mich) 58-60; Planning Com & Discussion Leader (Mich) Governors Conf on Libs 62; Consul numerous high sch Career Day Conf. 9: ALA (mem var coms in 40's);-RTSD (2 coms on acquis 60-62, 64-); NEA (mem & sec Jt Com on Lib Wk as a Career 54-57; Fin Admin Sect; Purchasing Policy Com 58-60); MichLA (Exec Bd 43-46 & 62-64, sec 45-46, chm &/or mem 5 coms during 40's & 64; Col Sect; chm &/or mem 3 coms 57-62; Tech Serv Sect; chm Com on Cost Acctg 62-63; Bd of Tech Proc Sect 65); MichEA (Life mem); Mich Assn of Higher Educ (pres 59-60, chm &/or mem several coms 56-. 10: AAUW; Nat Bus & Prof Womens Club; Mich Coun on Women in Bus & in Kalamazoo Citizens Bus Study Com; Coun on Employment Problems of Wking Women. 12: "A Basic List of Books for Boys & Girls in the Schools of State of Michigan (44, suppl 45); "Dear Mr. Architect ALA (46); "The Punched Card Data Processing Annual #2 Order Proc (60). 13: Yes. 14: Acqui, educ. 15: 801 Piccadilly rd, Kalamazoo MI 49007.

DE MOOY, CLAIRE (PLANTINGA). b Netherlands. 4: Adrian De Mooy. 5: Calvin Col 37-40 (En, Soc Studies) AB; Northwestern 40-41 (Eng Educ) MA; Rosary Col 62-64 (LS) MA. 6: Ger, Dutch. 7: Music & reading tchr Dist #99, Berwyn Ill 42-43; Asst ed house organ A B Dick & Co, Chicago 44-45; Res tchr & tchg asst Sch Dist #90 & #91 River Forest, Oak Park Ill 56-62; Sch libn Sch Dist #10, La Grange Ill 62-63; Jr high sch libn Sch Dist #90, River Forest Ill 63-64, Head Libn 64-. 8: Bd mem, Friends of the Lib, Oak Park Ill 55-59. 9: NEA; ALA-AASchL; IllASchL; IllEA; IllLA. 10: Beta Phi Mu. 14: Sch libnship, elem sch libs. 15: 5117 Lawn ave, Western Springs IL 60558.

DE MORELOS, MARY E. b Stockton Cal 27 O 13. 4: Leonardo C De Morelos. 5: UCal 31-35 (Eng) AB; Columbia 55-56 (LS) MS. 7: Ser libn Hispanic Soc of Amer, NYC 56-59; Ref libn Teachers Col Lib, NYC 59-62, Supv libn soc sci reading room 62-. 15: Tchrs Col Lib 525 W 120th st, New York NY 10027.

De PEW, JOHN NELSON. b Akron Ohio 18 N 34. 4: Joan Geisinger. 5: Bethany Col (WVa) 52-56 (Hist) BA; UAkron summer 55; West Res 56-58 MSLS; UPittsburgh 64- (LS0. 6: Fr, Sp. 7: Supv & clerk Bethany Col Lib (Bethany WVa) 52-56; Asst to asst dir West Res U Lib 56-58; Gen asst Libn NY Pub Lib 58; LCdr USNR Air Intel 58-67; Asst libn Bethany Col Lib (Bethany WVa) 64-65; Head acquis libn Duquesne U Lib 65-67; Coord of acquis, UPittsburgh 67- 9: ALA- ACRL. 13: Yes. 14: Acquis, acad lib admin. 15: 812 Redstone dr, Allison Park PA 15101.

De PRISCO, ROBERTA PAISLEY. b Sharon Penn 27 F 20. 4: A Walter DePrisco.05: /21/52-53 MSLS;/22/ 5: State Col

Clarion Penn 38-42 (LS, Eng, Soc Studies) BS in Ed; UPittsburgh 44-48 (Secondary Educ) EdM; West Res 52-53 MSLS; Penn State U summer 58 (Educ); Syracuse summer 59 (LS); Temple summer (Educ); West Res 63-65 (Supv, Curriculum). 7: Asst libn pub lib, Sharon Penn summers 40-42; Jr High libn pub schs, Arnold Penn 42-45; Head Libn pub schs, W Mifflin Penn 45-54; Catlgr Chautauqua (NY) Inst summer 53; Ref libn Tech Dept Carnegie Lib of Pittsburgh 54-55, summer 56; Head Libn High Sch, Bethel Park Penn 54-61; Assoc Prof & asst libn State Col, Indiana Penn61-63; Assoc libn Secondary Pub Schs, Shaker Heights Ohio 63-64; Asst libn Cuyahoga Community Col, summer 65; Head Libn Shaw High Sch, E Cleveland Ohio 65-. 8: Chm lib sect West Penn Educ Conf; Eval Com Commsn on Secondary Schs, Middle States Assn, 58. 9: ALA; NEA (Life mem); Penn State EA (Life mem); OhioEA (Life mem); PennLA; OhioASchL. 10: Cleveland Mus of Art.5 14: Ref, admin (sch system or tchr train col or univ). 15: 502 Logan ave, Sharon Penn 16146.

deRONDE, LOUISE. b Orange NJ 11 Ja 14. 4: Albert G deRonde. 5: Upsala Col 32-36 (Ger) AB. 6: Ger. 7: Asst libn Schering Corp, Bloomfield NJ 54-56; Ed asst advertising Winthrop Labs Inc, NYC 56-58; Libn Wallace & Tiernan Inc, Belleville NJ 58-66; White-Pharmaco Lib Div of Schering Corp, Kenilworth NJ 66-. 9: ALA; SLA. 14: Ref, research (chem & med). 15: 483 N Grove st, E Orange NJ 07017.

DE RUVO, MICHAEL GUY. b NY 8 Ja 31. 5: City Col (NY) 50-54 (Educ, Eng) BS; Columbia 54-55 (Educ, Eng) MA; Rutgers 60-63 MLS. 6: Ital. 7: Eng tchr Wellington C Mepham High Sch, Bellmore LI NY 55-58; Eng tchr Garden City Sr High Sch, Garden City LI NY 58-62, Asst libn 62-63; Libn Roslyn Jr High Sch, Roslyn LI NY 63-. 9: ALA; NYLA (NYLA/SLS pres 68); NEA; NYState Tchrs Assn; NYL Club (Coun 68-69, sec 69-). 14: Sch libs. 15: 248 E 58 st, New York NY 10022.

DE SCIORA, EDWARD A. b Chicago 17 Mr 28. 4: Anne Romano. 5: Bethany Col (WVa) 46-51 (Econ) BA; Columbia 51-54 MSLS. 7: Brooklyn Pub Lib 51-59; Dir Port Washington (NY) Pub Lib 59-. 8: Adj Asst Prof, Palmer Lib School LIU. 9: ALA; LPRC (sec); NYLA (mem chm); Nassau Co (NY) LA (pres); NY Lib Club (v-pres & pres-elect). 10: Rotary Club; C of C; North Shore Jr Sci Mus; Trustee LI Lib, Res, Coun 67. 14: Admin, lib bldgs. 15: 482 Thirteenth st, Brooklyn NY 11215.

DE STEPHEN, ANTHONY. b Canton Ohio 13 D 36. 5: Kent State 55-58 (Math) BSED, 59-64 (LS) MA. 7: Math tchr Canton Central Catholic, Canton Ohio 58-59; Math tchr Green High Sch, Greensburgh Ohio 59-62; Head bus & tech Canton Pub Lib, Canton Ohio 62; Assoc libn Goodyear Aerospace Corp, Akron Ohio 62-65; Manager info serv Harshaw Chem Co, Clevelan 65-68; Admin tech info serv RCA, Camden NJ 68-. 9: ASIS; SLA. 14: Info sci. 15: Haddon View apt 913S, Westmont NJ 08108.

de TEMPLE, JEAN M. b Canada. 5: McGill 50 BA, 51 BLS. 7: Asst dir Ottawa Pub Lib 61-. 15: Ottawa Pub Lib, 114 Metcalfe st, Ottawa Can.

DE VARENNES, KATHLEEN MENNIE. b Hull Que Can 10 My 31. 4: Rosario de Varennes Jr. 5: Ottawa U 50-53 (LS). 6: Fr, Eng. 7: Lib clerk Ottawa U 48-54, Lib clerk Med Lib Ottawa U 54-57; Catlgr Juniorat du Sacre-Coeur, Ottawa 57-summer 62; Spec asst Inventory of Period Laval U (Que) 63-68; Hd Lib of the Dept of Lands & Forests Prov Govt Que 68-. 9: CanLA; ACBLF; ALA; SLA; Assoc; Intern; De Documentation. 10: Societe Genealogique Canadienne-francaise; Societe de Genealogie d'Ottawa-Hull; Societe canadienne de Genealogie (Quebec; Societe Hist Acadienne. 12: "Genealogical Materials Compliled from "Canadiana (62); "Annotated Bibliography of Genealogical Works in the Library of Parliament (63); "Repertoire des Mariages de Gracefield (Comte de Gatineau) 1868-1960 (65); Ed "Cahiers de la Societe de Genealogie DOtawa-Hull v 1 No 1 v 2 No 1 (62-63). 13: Yes. 14: Ref, period, catlg. 15: 3362 ave Lambert-Closse, Ste-Foy Que Can.

de VARENNES, ROSARIO JR (JL). b Quebec 26 F 25. 4: Kathleen Mennie. 5: Petit Sem de Quebec 37-44 BA; Ottawa U Philosophical Inst 45-48 BPh, LPh, 48-50 (Theol) BTh, 48-50 (music) Dipl sup mussac, 51-54 BLS. Ext Laval U 63-64, 67-68. 6: Eng, Fr, Ital. 7: Lib clerk Ottawa U 51-54; Catlgr & ref Lib of Parliament, Ottawa 54-61, Asst-chief catlgr 61-63; Chief-catlgr Laval U (Que) 63-64, Dir of tech serv 64-68, Dir analysis lib automation 67-. 9: ALA; Bibliog Soc Can; Association canadienne des Bibliothecaires de langue francaise. 10: Societe d'Archeologie de Quebec; Inst of pub admin Can; alum assn Ottawa U; Foundation Univ Laval; societe artistique univ laval. 13: Yes. 14: Catlg, acquis, ref, period, automation in libs. 15: 3362 Lambert-Closse Ste-Foy Que Can.

DeVAUGHAN, SHERROW (DOROTHY). b Decatur Ala 13 Jl 39. 5: Sacred Heart Col (Belmont nc0 59-60 (Liberal Arts) AA; Spring Hill Col 61-63 (Sp, Secondary Educ) BS (cum laude); LSU (Baton Rouge) 67-69 (LS) MS. 6: Sp. 7: Tchr: Our Lady of Sorrows Sch, Birmingham Ala 60-61, Costner Sch, Gaston Co NC 64-65; Lib trainee LSU Lib 67-68; Gifts & exchange libn UNC (Charlotte) 69-. 9: ALA; SELA; NCLA; MecklenburgLA. 14: Acquis, ref. 15: 204 Ridge st, Dallas NC 28034.

de VAUX, PAULA (TURNER). b Bridgeport Conn 28 Ap 43. 4: Peter Fordney de Vaux. 5: Hiram Coll 61-65 (Eng) BA; UMich 65-67 (LS) AMLS. 6: Sp. 7: Wk-stud scholar Undergrad Lib UMich 65-67; Post libn Fort Clayton Post Lib Canal Zone 67-68; Period Libn Undergrad Lib UMich 68-. 14: Ser, acquis. 15: 2005 Huron Parkway apt 10, Ann Arbor Mi 48104.

DE VRIES MARY K(ATHERINE) (ORR). b North Branch Mich 6 Jl 08. 4: Harry De Vries. 5: UMich 26-30 AB, 30-31 ABLS, summers 34, 35 (LS). 6: Fr, Ger. 7: Catlgr Kalamazoo Col 31-33; Catlgr DePauw U 33-36; Libn Buena Vista Col 36-37; Ref asst UMich 37-40, Ref libn 56-. 9: ALA. 10: AAUW; PEO; Internat Rel Group (YPSILANTI Mich); Phi Beta Kappa; Phi Kappa Phi. 14: Ref maps, catlg. 15: 2209 Independence, Ann Arbor MI 48104.

DE WITT, BENJAMIN (LAWRENCE). b E Orange NJ 21 Ag 27. 4: Ann Maher. 5: Drew U 46-51 (Philos) AB; Columbia 56-59 (LS) MS. 6: Ger. 7: Ed asst Gen Cable Corp Research Labs, Bayonne NJ 51-52, Libn at present. 9: SLA (NJ Chap: chm memb Com 61-62, chm Bylaws Com 66-67, mem Central Stor Com 60-64); Aslib; ASIS. 10: General Cable Corp Bayonne Mgt Club (pres 65-66). 12: Inst Electr & Electron Eng, "Bibliography on High Temperature Electrical Insulation for Flight Vehicles (68). 14: Catlg, ref, abstracting, acquis. 15: 1341 North ave, Elizabeth NJ 07208.

De WITT, CAMILLA JANE. b Kingston NY 3 D 27. 5: Geneseo State Col 46-50 (LS) BS; Syracuse -57 (Educ); Oneonta State Col 58 (Educ); Albany State Col 59 MS in LS. 7: Libn Fallsburgh Central Schs, Fallsburgh NY 50-51; Libn Scotia-Glenville Central Schs, Scotia NY 51-60; Libn Kingston High Sch, Kingston NY 60-63; Libn J Watson Bailey Jr High Sch, Kingston NY 63-. 9: ALA; NY State Tchrs Assn; NYLA; Sch Libn SEast NY. 14: Ref, sch libnship. 15: 6 Saccoman ave, Kingston NY 12401.

De WITT, GRETCHEN. b Wisconsin Dells Wis 9 N 12. 5: Wis State Col 29-31 (Hist); Carroll Col 31-33 (Hist) BA (cum laude); Columbia 44-45 BS in LS; Wayne U 50-54 (Pol Sci) MA. 6: Fr, Sp. 7: Asst ref dept Milwaukee Pub Lib 40-48; Head ref dept Bryn Mawr Col Lib 48-49; Asst soc sci dept Detroit Pub Lib 49-57; Head ref dept Warder Pub Lib, Springfield Ohio 57-61; Head ref dept Columbus Pub Lib, Columbus Ohio 61-. 9: ALA (Ref Subs Bks Rev Com 64-); -RDS (New Ref Tools Com 63-65); OhioLA (chm Ref Serv Round Table 62-63, Scholarship Com 68-69). 10: Beta Phi Mu; Zonta; Ohio State Off Club; DAR; LWV. 13: Yes. 14: Ref, loc hist. 15: Columbus Pub Lib, 96 S Grant ave, Columbus Oh 43215.

De WITT, ROBERT H(ENRY). b Manitou Okla 26 Jl 17. 4: Shirley Nienhuis. 5: Iola Jr Col 33-35; Baker U 35-37 (Eng) BA; Kan State Col 37-38 (Eng) MS; UChicago 47-48 BLS. 7: Tchr-libn Greeley (Kan) High Sch 39-40, Tchr-prin-libn 40-42; Cryptographic clerk (Tech 4th grade) US Army 42-45; Tchr-libn Garnett (Kan) High Sch 46-47; Asst acquis dept UMo 48-49, Asst ref dept 49-51, Asst circ dept 52; Circ libn UNeb 52-61; Asst dir libs (pub serv) Colo State U 61-68; Asst dir libs (personnel serv) 68-. 9: ALA; Amer Soc for Personnel Admin. 10: Mens Garden Club; AAUP. 13: Yes. 14: Personnel admin, pub serv. 15: 2412 Mathews st, Fort Collins Co 80521.

DE YOUNG, CHARLES DANIEL. b Chicago 1 Je 21. 4: Margaret Wilson. 5: Central YMCA Col 40-43 (Educ, Hist); UWis(Madison) 46-48 (Hist) BS Educ, 48-49 (Amer Hist) MS; UMich(Ann Arbor) 49-50 (LS) MA. 7: Army Signal Corps teletype operator & libn in Spec Serv (Sgt) 43-46; Staff mem recreational browsing room lib, Mem Union UWis(Madison) 47-49; Staff mem film sound dept Milwaukee Pub Lib 49, Asst to Dept Head art & music dept 50-53; Dir of pub rel & coordinator of ref serv, Grand Rapids (Mich) Pub Lib 53-56; Head of circ UIll (Chicago) undergrad div 56-60; Dir of Libs Proviso Twp High Schs, Maywood Ill 60-68; Dir Bur Oak Lib

Syst, Joliet Ill 68-. 8: Mem No Central Eval Com (high sch libs) 67, 68; Mem Adv Com, Grad Lib Sch, UIll 65-67. 9: ALA;-LAD (chm & mem 4 coms & gps 61-64); NEA; IllLA (pres 64-65, chm A-v Com 59-62); MichLA (chm Pub Rel Com 56); Chicago Lib Club; IllEA; Ill A-V Assn. 10: PTA; Rotary; Phi Delta Kappa; Amer Legion; Boy Scouts; Mgr Little League & Pony League Baseball; Pub Lib Bdm Hillside Ill. 13: Yes. 14: Admin, a-v, pub rel, circ. 15: 150 N Ottawa st, Joliet Il 60431.

DEADERICK, LUCILE (ELIZABETH). b Knoxville Tenn 22 Je 14. 5: UTenn 3034 (Hist) BA; UIll 3637 BS in LS. 6: Fr. 7: Asst catlg & circ depts Lawson Mcghee Lib, Knoxville Tenn 29-36, Hd McClung hist collection 37-40; Ed asst & ed ALA Bulletin ALA, Chicago 40-47; Reg libn State Lib, Lenoir City Tenn 47-51; High sch libn Karns High Sch, Knoxville Tenn 51-68; Asst Prof Dept of Lib Serv UTenn 68-. 8: Vis lectr Dept of Lib Serv UTenn symmers 67, 68. 9: ALA; NEA-DAVI; TennLA. 10: Knox Co (Tenn) Lib Bd; Karns Commun Club; Bd of Pub Lib of Knoxville & Knox Co. 14: Sch libs, lib educ, av. 15: Rte 17, Knoxville Tn 37921.

DEAKIN, BARBARA JEAN. b Pacific Grove Cal 15 Ja 32. 5: Monterey Peninsula Col 49-51 AA; Cal State Col at Los Angeles 56-59 (Sociol) BA; Immaculate Heart Col 60 (LS) Sch lib credential, 65 MALS. 6: Sp. 7: Libn Los Angeles City Schs Hamilton High Sch 60-65; Asst libn Santa Ana Bd of Educ Santa Ana Col 66-67; Asst libn Orange Coast Col Dist Golden West Col 67-. 8: Consul & bibliog spec Los Angeles City Schs Admin Off 63-64. 9: ALA; CalLA; CalASchL; CalTA. 12: Spec bibliogs prepared for and printed by Instructional Materials Center Los Angeles City Schools (63-64). 14: Ref. 15: 2453-G Orange ave, Costa Mesa Ca 92627.

DEAKYNE, WILLIAM JOHN IV. b Harrisburg Penn 25 Je 36. 5: UHartford 57-61(Church Music) BMus Villanova 61-62 MSLS. 6: Fr. 7: Lib trainee Penn State Lib 61-62; Dir Mary Meuser Mem Lib, Easton Penn 62-64; Dir Coyle Lib, Chambersburg Penn 64-65; Dir Free Lib of Springfield Twp, Montgomery Co Penn 65-68; Dir Darien Lib, Darien Ct 68-. 8: Chm, Cumberland Valley Dist Adv Coun 65. 9: ALA; NELA; ConnLA. 10: Les Amis de Grands Orques, France; International Harpsichord Soc; Concert Harpsichordist; Concert Harpsichordist. 11: Certificate of Appreciation, City of Phila Personnel Dept - 1967. 13: Yes. 14: Admin, internat lib coop. 15: 35 Leroy ave, Darien CT 06820.

DEAL, CARL W. b Hickory NC 15 S 30. 4: Yolanda Greco Deal. 5: Lenoir-Rhyne Col 48-50; Kan State Tchrs Col (Emporia) 52 (Soc Sci) BA; Mexico City Col 54-56 (Latin Amer Studies) MA; Kan State Tchrs Col (Emporia) 58-59 (LS) MS. 6: Sp, Portu. 7: Clerical (S/Sgt) USAF, Ft Worth Tex 50-54; Asst archivist Kan State Hist Soc, Topeka Kan 56-58; Admin aide Wichita City Lib, Wichita Kan 59-61; Asst head acquis dept UKan Lib 61-63; Dir UKan Jr Year Program Costa Rica, San Jose Costa Rica 63-64; Latin Amer bibliog UKan Lib 64; Latin Amer libn & assoc dir Center for Latin Amer Studies UIll Lib (rbana) 65-. 8: Consul for a Survey of Central Amer Univ Libs for the Reg Off for Central Amer & Panama, Agency for 'nternat Devel & the Superior Coun of Central Amer Univs, 66; Consul Lib Devel Proj, Organiz of Amer States at the Colegio de Mexico, Mexico City 67. 9: ALA; IllLA. 14: Acquis of Latin-Amer lib materials, lib devel in Latin Amer, Latin-Amer bibliog. 15: 2005 Boudreau, Urbana IL 61801.

DEAL, N(EWTON) HARVEY. b Elizabethtown NC 4 Ag 19. 4: Alice Boyd. 5: E Carolina Col 36-40 (Eng, Fr) AB; Peabody 40-41 (Eng) MA, 46-47 BSLS. 6: Fr. 7: US Army 1st Lt Intelligence Order of Battle Spec 41-45; Libn Eng Prof State Tchrs Col (Bloomsburg Penn) 46-48; Asst libn Baylor U 48-49; Asst circ libn UIll (Urbana) 49-51; Ref libn UVa 51-65; Asst Unive libn UCincinnati 65-68; Dir Libs Va Commonwealth U (Richmond Va) 68-. 9: ALA (Subsc Bks Com 64-66); -ACRL; -RSD (sec-treas 62-64); SELA (Chap Chm, cm Nomin Com of Col & Univ Sect 62-64); VaLA (chm ALA Mem Com 52-57; chm Col & Univ Sect 55-57; 1st v-pres & Exec Com 63, pres 64). 10: Va Place Name Soc; Torch Club; Colonnade Club (UVa); Beta Phi Mu; Phi Delta Kappa; Pi Gamma Mu. 12: Ed "Selected Recent cquisitions UVa Lib (51-56); Ed "Virginia Librarian (57-60); Ed "Occaional Papers Va Place Name Soc (60-65); Ed Com "Southeastern Librarian (53-55). 13: Yes. 14: Ref, rare bks. 15: Virginia Commonwealth Univ-Lib, Richmond VA 23220.

DEALE, H(ENRY) VAIL. b Baltimore 14 My 15. 4: Jane Niehaus Deale. 5: Dickinson Col 31-33 (Eng); DePauw U 34-36 (Eng) BA; UIll 36-37 MLS; DrakU 47-50 (Eng) MA. 6: . 7: Circ asst Northwestern U Lib 37-39; Pub rel asst Withers Pub Lib Bloomington Ill 39-41; Civilian Pub Serv libn World War II 41-45; Asstlibn Ripon Col 45-46; Ref libn Drake U 46-48, Humanities libn 48-51; ULibn Ill Wesleyan U 51-53; Dir of Libs Beloit Col 53-. 8: Fulbright grant to Pahlavi U Shiraz Iran, 65-66; Lib consul. 9: ALA (Life mem); -ACRL (Col Sect, sec 57-59, chm 64-65, Var com assignments); IllLA; IowaLA; WisLA (treas 57-59; pres 60-61 chm &/or mem var coms). 10: AAUP; Beloit Commun Coun on Human Rights; UN Week Chm, Beloit; Wis dir, Nat Lib Week; Brotherhood Week. 11: Nat Conf Christians & Jews Brotherhood Week Award. 13: Yes. 14: Acad lib admin, prof pub rel. 15: 1427 Chapin st, Beloit WI 53511.

DEALY, THELMA ATHOLINE (THOMAS). b Long Beach Cal 6 Jl 24. 4: John Robert Dealy. 5: UCal (Santa Barbara) 46-50 (Eng) BA; USoCal 56-57 MSLS. 7: Catlgr Libn II USoCal 57-. 8: Registration Chm CalLA Conf, 64. 9: CalLA; SoCal Tech Proc Group. 10: AAUP; Beta Phi Mu; USoCal Sch Lib Sci Alumni Assn; USCAL Friends of the Lib. 14: Catlg. 15: 20112 S Dalfsen ave, Compton CA 90220.

DEAN, CROWELL O. b Whiteville NC. 5: UNC (Chem) BS; UDenver (LS) MS. 6: Ger. 7: Head Main Lib Los Alamos Sci Lab Lib 55-57; Supv tech info center A E Staley Mfg Co, Decatur Ill58-59; Head ref circ & brs Sandia Lab Tech Lib, Albuquerque NM 0-65, Supv info serv 65-; Mgr Fused Salts info ctr (AEC) 64-; Mgr Simulated Environments Info Ctr (AEC) 1965-. 9: ACS; NMLA; SLA. 10: AAAS. 12: "Southwestern Union List of Serials" (65); "Physical Properties of Fused Salt Mixtures" (65); "The Literature of Nuclear Science, Its Management and Use" (62); "Fused Salt mixtures eutectic compositions and melting points" (680. 13: Yes. 14: Systems design, info retrieval, communication theory. 15: 709 Fairway NW, Albuquerque NM 87107.

DEAN, DORA. b Pittsburgh Penn 24 F 11. 5: DePauw U 29-30; Ind U Ext (Ft Wayne) 31-34; WVa U 34-36 (Educ) BS; Columbia summers 40-44 BSLS. 6: Fr. 7: Libn Weir High Sch, Weirton WVa 36-43; Libn Engnr Research Off, NYC 43-45, Libn Engnr Research Off, Wash DC 45-57; Libn American U Grad Sch 47-48; Libn ORO John Hopkins U (Wash DC) 48-49; Libn SCAP CIE, Tokyo 49-52; USIS: Libn, Tokyo 52-56, Karachi Pakistan 56-58, Wash DC 58-60, Bangkok Thailand 60-, Cairo Egypt 66-67, Bk reviewer Wash DC 67-. 8: Seminar for USIS, Seoul Korea, Oct 55; Consul USIS, Kabul Afghanistan, Oct 57; Instr, UKarachi Lib Sch, 56-57. 9: ALA. 14: Admin, catlg. 15: Foreign Ser Mail Room USIA, Washington DC 20547.

DEAN, DORIS (WHITWELL). b Cleveland Ohio 16 Ap 23. 4: Albert Dean. 5: Baldwin Wallce Col 41-45 (Eng) BA; West Res 46 BS in LS. 6: Sp. 7: Yp libn Cleveland Pub Lib 46-47; Ref libn Ariz State Col (Tempe) 47-51; Bkmob libn LaGrange Mem Lib, La Grange Ga 52-57, Dir 57-. 9: ALA; GaLA (sec Publ Lib Sect); SELA. 14: Admin, catlg. 15: Troup Harris Coweta Reg Lib 114 Church st, La Grange Ga 30240.

DEAN, ELVA (CROSBIE). b Salt Lake City 8 Ag 03. 5: Brigham Young U 21-24, 31-32 (Educ) BS; USoCal 47-48 BSLS; Utah State U 52-53 (Hist). 7: Tchr Dixon Jr High Sch, Provo Utah 31-46; Doc libn Utah State U 48-53; Ref libn & Head of Ref UUtah 53-67; Libn West Americana Mss 68-. 9: ALA; MPLA; UtahLA. 10: AAUP. 14: Ref, mss, catlg. 15: 1816 Severn dr, Salt Lake City UT 84117.

DEAN, GRANT TALBOT. b Alma Mich 14 Mr 23. 5: Alma Col 41-42; Mich State Col 42-43, 45-46 (Hist) AB; Chicago 47-48 BLS. 7: Catlgr Stanford U 48-49; Catlgr Chicago Hist Soc 49-54; Catlgr Carnegie Endowment for Internat Peace, NYC 54-57; Catlgr Chicago Hist Soc 58-. 9: SLA; ALA; MusLA; Chicago Reg Group of Catlgrs (sec-treas 51-52, pres 52-54); NY Reg Group of Catlgrs (sec-treas 55-57). 10: Caxton Club (Chicago), Cliff Dwellers (Chicago). 13: Yes. 14: Rare bks, loc hist, catlg. 15: 1964 N Burling st, Chicago Il 60614.

DEAN, HELEN ELISABETH. b Manhattan Kan 3 N 05. 5: Kan State U 24-28 (Eng) BS; UIll 28-29 BS in LS; Columbia U summers 34, 36 (LS). 6: Fr, Ger, Sp. 7: Act ref libn Lawrence Col 29-30; Asst catlgr UMo 30-45; 1st asst catlgr 45-46; Ohio State U; Catlgr 46-49, Catlg reviser 49-50, Asst Prof & Asst hd catlg dept 51-65, Assoc Prof & Asst hd catlg dept 65-. 9: ALA-RTSD; -ACRL; MoLA (treas 44-46); Ohio LA; Ohio Valley Group Tech Serv Libns (sec-treas 52-53). 10: Amer Inst of Archael; Phi Kappa Phi; Faculty Women's Club; Beta Phi Mu. 12: Ed Index to "Missouri Historical Review v 1-25 (34). 13: Yes. 14: Catlg. 15: Ohio State Univ Lib, 1858 Neil ave, Columbus OH 43210.

DEAN, KATHRYN FRANCES. b Calgary Alberta Can 13 O 17. 5: UToronto 49-53 (Mus) LRCT; The Catholic U 59-60 MS in LS. 6: Fr, Ger. 7: Ref Catholic U 60-61; Gen ref Enoch Pratt Free Lib, Baltimore 61-67, Admin asst co serv 67-68, Asst hd humanities div 68-. 9: ALA; SLA; MedLA; MdLA. 11: Can Coun Award for "A Study of Four Canadian Music Libraries" 60. 14: Ref. 15: Apt 809, One University Parkway E, Baltimore Md 21218.

DEAN, ROSALIND M. b St Louis Mo 5 N 23. 5: WashU 41-45 (Chem) AB, 50-55, 62-63, 69- (LS). 6: Ger. 7: Control chem Cole Chem Co, St Louis 45-47; Anheuser-Busch Inc St Louis: Analytical chem 47-56, Libn 56-62; Libn Falstaff Brewing Corp, St Louis 62-68; Libn USA Engr Dist St Louis 68-. 9: SLA (Greater St Louis Chap: pres 68-69, Program Chm, Employment Chm, chm Tours & Transportation Com 64); ASIS; St Louis Lib Club. 10: Delta Phi Alpha; Adelphi Toastmistress Club; Henry Shaw Cactus and Succulent Soc. 14: Ref. 15: 1141 Albany ct, Webster Groves Mo 63119.

DEAN, WINIFRED FAY (SPOONER). b Cleveland 24 Jl 30. 4: Leslie Scott Dean II. 5: Hiram Col 47-51 (Span) BA; West Res 0-61 MSLS. 6: Ital. 7: eller & bkkeeper Southwestern Savings & Loan Co, Cleveland 51-60; Adult serv libn Cuyahoga Co Pub Lib, Cleveland 61-63; 1st asst libn bus & sci dept Atlanta Pub Lib 63-65; Hd bus & sci dept Atlanta Pub Lib 65-66; Econ bibliogr LC leg ref serv 66-67; Soc sci sel libn West Res Libs 68-. 9: ALA; SELA. 14: Ref, bibliog. 15: 4015 W 213 st, Fairview Park OH 44126.

DEANE, (JOHN) PETER S J. b Detroit 24 F 34. 5: Xavier U 53-57 (Classics) Litt B; Loyola U (West Baden Col) 57-60 (Philos & Math); West Res 62-63 MS in LS; Bellarmine Sch of Theol of Loyola (Chicago) 63- (Theol). 6: Lat, Gk, Fr, Ger. 7: Asst libn Milford Novitiate, Milford Ohio 55-57; High sch tchr St Ignatius High Sch, Cleveland 60-62; Ref staff John Carroll U (Cleveland) 62-63; Asst libn Bellarmine Sch of Theol, N Aurora Ill 63-67; Libn St John's High Sch 67-. 8: Consul for lib construction & design & collections of new high schs in Toledo & Cuyahoga Falls Ohio 64-65; Instr in use of lib & bibliog Colombiere Col summers 60-63. 9: ALA; CathLA (chm Catlg & Clsf Sect 67-69, treas High Sch Sect 69-71); IllCathLA (chm 66-67). 10: Beta Phi Mu. 11: August Alpers Award, West Res U 63. 13: Yes. 14: Catlg, clsf, ref. 15: St John's High Sch, 5901 Airport hwy, Toledo Oh 43615.

DEANE, SHIRLEY (PARK). b Richmond Ky 8 Jl 36. 4: Daniel Richard Deane Jr. 5: UKy 54-58 (Eng) BA, 58-59 MSLS. 7: Ser libn UKy Med Lib 59-62; Instr of lib sci East Ky U 65; Catlgr City Co Lib, Richmond Ky 62. 8: Instr: East Ky U; Title II Inst, Training for Libnship; Organ & Admin the Newer Media summer 68; Dir of Inventory, East Ky U Lib 63. 9: ALA. 10: Beta Phi Mu; Phi Beta Kappa. 14: Catlg, ser. 15: Rt 2 Lancaster Woods, Richmond Ky 40475.

DeANGELIS, LINNEA B(RANDIN). b NYC 16 Ap 14. 5: NYU 36-40 (Accounting) AS; Goddard Col 65-67 BA; Pratt Inst 67-68 MLS. 6: Swedish. 7: Asst registrar Health Ins Plan, NYC 47-48; Acct & analyst Albert Pleydell Assoc, NYC 49-54; Acct Rogers, Slade & Hill, NYC 54-61; Admin asst Soc for Savings, Hartford Conn 62-65; Br libn Hartford Pub Lib, Hartford Conn 66-. 9: ALA. 14: Child wk. 15: Holly dr, East Hampton Ct 06424.

DEARBORN, EVELYN (ELLSWORTH). b East Wilton Me 9 S 26. 4: Vance E Dearborn. 5: UMe 45-49 (Sociol) BA; UPittsburgh 62-64 MLIS. 7: Tchr Ashland Commun High Sch, Ashland Me 49-51; Catlgr Raymond H Fogler Lib UMe 64-. 10: Phi Betta Kappa; Phi Kappa Phi; Beta Phi Mu. 14: Catlg. 15: 5 Charles st, Orono Me 04473.

DEARDEN, AMY. b England 19 O 12. 5: UMass 31-35 (Eng) BS; Drexel 49-50 MLS. 7: Hartford Pub Lib, Hartford Conn: Lib asst 41-58; Act head bus sci & tech dept 58-61, Admin asst bus sci & tech dept 61-. 9: SLA (Memb Chm Com Valley Chap 65-66); Hartford (Conn) Libns Club. 10: Wadsworth Atheneum, Hartford Conn. 15: 1096 Farmington ave, West Hartford CT 06107.

DEARDORFF, JOHN H. b Chicago 6 Jl 33. 4: Mary C Adkison. 5: Mankato State Col 51-54 (Hist) BA; UMinn 54-55 (Hist) MA; Mankato State Col 55-56 (Educ) BS; UMinn 63-64 (LS) MA. 7: Jr High Sch tchr, Winnebago Minn 56-57; US Army Infantry (Pfc), Kan & Germany 57-59; Jr high sch tchr Central Jr High Sch, Albert Lea Minn 59-63; Ref libn Ohio State U Lib 64-66; Hd Docs Div 66-68; Ref libn Slippery Rock State Col 68-. 9: ALA; PennLA. 10: Assn Penn State Col & Univ Facs. 14: Ref, govt docs. 15: Maltby Lib Slippery Rock State Col, Slippery Rock Pa 16057.

DEASON, HILARY J(OHN). b Park City Utah 21 My 03. 5: UMich 23-27 (PhilosX AB, 27-28 (Philos) AM, 29-36 (Zool) PhD. 6: Fr, Sp. 7: Aquatic biol US Bureau of Fisheries, Ann Arbor ich 28-41; Research biologist US Fish & Wildlife Serv, Wash DC 41-45, Dir foreign activities 45-51; Research consul Episcopal Diocese of Wash, WASH DC 52-55; Dir lib program Amer Assn for the Advancement of Sci, Wash DC 55-. 8: Bibliog consul Grolier Inc NYC 59-; Bibliog consul Comptoms Encyclopedia 63-; Sec Episcopal Diocese of Wash 55-; Deputy US Commissioner Internat Whaling Commsn 50-51; US Commissioner NW Atlantic Int Fisheries Commsn 50-51. 9: ALA; NEA; Nat Sci Tchrs Assn; Amer Soc Zoologists; Amer Fisheries Soc; Ed "Transactions 40-46". 10: AAAS (Fellow); Cosmos Club (Wash DC); Diocesan Council Episcopal Diocese of Wash 55-; Sigma Xi. 12: "AAAS Science Book List" (59); "AAAS Science Book List for Children" (60,63); "AAAS Science Book List for Young Adults" (64,69); "A Guide to Science Reading" (63,64,66); "An Inexpensive Science Library" (Annual ed 57-61); Ed "Science Books, A Quarterly Review" (65). 14: Sci educ, sci bibliogs. 15: 4000 Massachusetts ave, Wash DC 20016.

DEATON, WOODROW W. b Beech Ky 24 Ag 20. 4: Edna Faye Mosley. 5: Lees Col 46-48 Diploma; UKy 49-51 (Agric) BS; UKy 59-60, summers 62-63 (LS) MS 65. 6: Fr. 7: Pvt Cpl & Sgt US Army, US & France 42-46; Documents erv wk Ky Dept of Econ Security, Jackson Ky 51-52; Asst & co agric agent UKy (Hazard & McKee Ky) 52-59; Asst catlgr & ext libn Berea Col 60-63; Libn UKy Ashland Commun Col 63-66; Asst chief libn & chief libn VA ctr, Dayton Oh 66-. 9: SLA. 14: Ref, catlg, admin. 15: 134 W Goodman dr, Fairborn Oh 45324.

DEAY, JAMES M. b Eudora Kan 19 My 21. 4: Velma Lee Robison. 5: Baker U 41-42 (Eng); UAla 46-48 (Eng) AB; Kan State Tchrs Col 49-56 (Speech-Eng) MS, 57-60 MS in LS. 6 Sp. 7: Tech Sgt US Army Med Corps, US, ETO 4245; Tchr Norton Commun High Sch, Norton Kan 49-51; Program dir Radio Station KTSW, Emporia Kan 52-53; Tchr Laguna Salada Union Elem Sch, Pacifica Cal 53-56; Tchr-libn Hamilton Rural High Sch, Hamilton Kan 56-59; Head Libn Emporia Pub Lib, Emporia Kan 59-62; Acquis libn East NM U 62-67, Dir of libs Baker U 67-. 9: ALA; KanLA. 14: Acquis, rare bks (Southwest). 15: P O Box 124, Baldwin City KS 66006.

deBEDTS, ELIZABETH (MUNRO) SEELINGER. b Norfolk Va 8 My 25. 4: Dr Ralph F deBedts. 5: Col of William & Mary (Norfolk) 45-47; Mary Washington Col 47-49 (Biol) BS; UNC 51-52 (LS) BS, 59-60 (LS) Med Lib Certif; Va Lib Certif 60. 6: Sp. 7: Lib asst US Na val Air Station, Norfolk Va 49-51; Asst circ libn UNC Lib (Chapel Hill) summer 52; Acquis libn Gifts & Exch UOre Lib 52-57, Catlg libn 57-59; Acquis libn bibliog sect UNC (Chapel Hill) 59-60; Ref libn Hughes Lib Col of William & Mary (Norfolk) 60-61; Circ libn Hughes Lib Old Dominion Col 61-, Lecturer in lib sci catlg & child lit evening & summer col 66-69. 10: UNC Lib Sch Alumni Assn; O ld Dominion Col Faculty Club; ODC Faculty Wives Club; Va Ornithology Assn. 14: Circ, tchg lib sci, ref, med libnship, recr. 15: 1123 Manchester ave, Norfolk Va 23508.

DEBENHAM, WILLIAM STUART JR. b Danville Ill 30 Ag 37. 4: Adaria Ruey Debenham. 5: UPittsburgh 56-60 (Philos) AB, 62-63 MLS. 6: Fr. 7: Ref libn Harvard U 63-64, Spec asst 64, Gift & Exch libn 64-65, Ser libn 65-66; Hd acquis dept Yale Lib 66-, Act hd bibliog dept 68-. 9: ALA; AHA. 13: Yes. 14: Bibliog, automation. 15: Acquis Dept Yale Univ Lib, New Haven Ct 06520.

DeBERNARDI, MRS WILMA (DEPUY). b Shadyside Ohio 30 Je 17. 4: Angelo P DeBernardi. 5: Wilson Col 34-38 (Soc Studies) AB; Drexel summers 59-64 MS in LS. 6: Fr. 7: Sec Amer Bitumulus Co, Baltimore 40-44; Tchr Quincy High Sch Quincy Sch Dist, Quincy Penn 47-51; Sec to the pres Nat Valley Bank & TrustCo, Chambersburg Penn 51-59; Libn head Chambersburg Area Sr High Sch, Chambersburg Penn 59-66; Asst lib coord Chambersburg Area Sch Dist 66-67, Lib coord 67-. 9: ALA; NEA; PennLA; PennSchLA; PennStateEA. 10: Bus & Prof Women's Club; Wilson Club of Franklin Co (Penn); AAUW. 14: Ref. 15: 455 Highland ave, Chambersburg PA 27201.

DeBERRY, MAURVENE. b Raleigh NC 13 O 44. 5: St Augustine's Col 62-66 (Eng) BA; AtlantaU 66-67 MSLS. 6: Fr, Ger. 7: Libn (staff) Queens Borough Pub Lib, Jamaica NY 67-68; Asst hd & asst ed US Govt Pub Bibliog Project, LC 68-. 9: ALA. 10: Delta Sigma Theta. 11: Rockefeller scholar (lib sch). 14: US Govt publ (acquis, prep of bibliog, ref). 15: 2620 Sixteenth st NW, Washington DC 20009.

DeBOARD, JUDITHA. b Charleston W Va 29 N 38. 5: Morris Harvey Col 56-60 (Ed) BS; UPittsburgh 65 MLS; W Va U 68- (Ed). 7: Tchr Anne Arundel Co Bd of Educ, Annapolis Md 60-63; W Va Lib Commsn, Charleston W Va 64; Lib asst Educ Lib UPittsburgh 65; Hd catlgr & archivist Morris Harvey Col 66-. 9: ALA; WVaLA. 10: AAUP. 11: Godfrey Cabot Scholarship 57-60. 14: Catlg, bibliog. 15: 1800 Roundhill rd, Charleston W Va 25314.

DeCAMPS, ALICE LORRAINE. b Richmond Va 22 D 42. 5: Randolph Macon Women's Coll 60-61; W Hampton Coll U Richmond 61-64 (Econ) BA; UNC 66-67 MLS. 6: Ger. 7: Asst circ libn URichmond 65-66; Ref asst Richmond Pub Lib, Richmond Va 67-. 9: ALA (Jr Mem RT); VaLA. 14: Govt docs, bus libnship, law libnship, info sci. 15: 2006 Hanover ave, Richmond Va 23220.

DeCAPRIO, ALBERT A. b Newton Mass 3 Ap 26. 4: Rita C Weber. 5: Harvard 46-48 (Eng Lit); Kenyon Col 50-52 (Eng Lit) BA; Simmons 55-56 (LS) MS. 7: (Pvt) US Army 43rd Calvalry Recon Sqdn 44-46; Ref libn Providence Pub Lib 56-58; Subj spec in psych philos & religion, & Head humanities div Worcester Pub Lib, Worcester Mass 58-59; Catlgr bus libn & head admin serv Miami Pub Lib, Miami Fla 60-69; Admin Cambria Pub Lib, Johnstown Penn 69-. 9: ALA; FlaLA; Dade County LA. 14: Admin, personnel, bus ref. 15: Cambria Public Lib, Johnstown PA 15901.

DeCHARMS, (JOAN) DESIREE. b Abington Pen 25 Mr 25. 5: Eastman Sch of Music of Rochester 43-47 (Piano) B of Music; Chicago 50-54 MLS; UIll 65- (Musicology). 7: Music catlgr UPnn 48-51; Music libn & a-v dir Roosevelt U 51-55; Asst music & drama dept Detroit Pub Lib 55-61; Asst music libn UIll (Urbana) 61-65; Msic & humanities libn Oakland U (Rochester Mich) 65-67; Mus libn Kent State 67-. 9: MusLA (chm catlg & clsf com - Midwest Chap); Amer Musicol Soc-Midwest Chap; Internat MusLA; ALA. 12: "Songs in Collections: an Index, (65). 14: Music libnship. 15: 140 Ernest dr, Tallmadge OH 44278.

DECHENE, VERONA MAY. b Winnipeg Can 2 My 32. 5: UManitoba 50-54 BA; McGill 58-59 BLS. 7: Catlgr Elizabeth Dafoe Lib UMan 59-60, Arch libn 60-61, Asst order libn 61-64, Order libn 64-. 8: Manitoba Union List of Serials 61. 9: ManLA; CanLA; ALA. 14: Acquis. 15: Box 1, Starbuck Manitoba Can.

DECHERT, DOROTHY (FULKERSON BOWER). b Chillicothe Ohio 28 Ag 06. 4: H Vergil Dechert. 5: Oberlin Col 23-27 (Eng Lit) AB; UIll 27-28 (LS) BS; Columbia 42 (LS) MS. 6: Fr, Ger, Lat, Sp, Russian. 7: Asst catlgr Peoria Pub Lib, Peoria Ill 28-35; Ref asst & spec catlgr Avery Arch Lib Columbia U 35-42; Libn Maitland Pub Lib, Maitland Fla 60-61; Head of acquis & ext Albertson Pub Lib, Orlando Fla 61-62; Catlgr & ref asst Winter Park Pub ib, Winter Park Fla 62-. 8: Bk review ed "Monthly Bulletin"; chm book selec coms for annual bk fairs, parents asson, Hunter Col elem sch 48-53; (Assoc mem); Friends of the Osborne & Lillian H. Smith Collections, Toronto, Can, Internat Inst for Child, Juv & Pop Lit, Vienna Aus; early child bks & magazines. 9: ALA; FlaLA. 14: Ref, bibliog, catlg. 15: 350 E Kings way, Winter Park FL 32789.

DECHIEF, HELENE. b Can. 5: UOttawa BA; U MONTREAL BLS. 6: Fr. 7: Research asst dept trade & com Can Embassy, Brussels Belgium 48-51; Libn Can Nat RR, Montreal 51-62, System libn 62-. 8: Tch in Special Libs, U Montreal, Ecole de Bibliotheconomie. 9: SLA. 15: 8003 Rousselot st, Montreal Can.

DECKER, CORA BUTTERFIELD. b Chicago 25 N 1900. 4: William E Decker. 5: Westhampton Col URichmond 19-23 (Hist) BA; Richmond Pub Lib Training Sch 24-25 Lib Certif; Columbia 36 (Advertising Copy); Rutgers 58-59 MSLS. 7: Richmond (Va) Pub Lib 24-26; Br libn URichmond Lib 31-36; Libn Va Mechanics Inst 36-38; Sub-br libn NY Pub Lib 38-42; Libn Nat Safety Coun, NYC 42; Ref libn Melrose Pub Lib, Melrose Mass 43-48; Coordiantor of brs Plainfield Pub Libs, Plainfield NJ 56-59; 1st asst Libn Bound Brook Pub Lib, Bond Brook NJ 59-61; Lib Dir N Arlington (NJ) Pub Lib 61; Ref dept Wilmington Inst Free Lib, Wilmington Del 62- Libn Bucks Co Hist Soc, Doylestown Pa. 9: ALS; DelLA. 14: Ref, circ, ext serv. 15: 129 E Ashland st, Doylestown PA 18901.

DECKER, GERI L. b Chicago 20 Ag 22. 5: Rosary Col 40-45 (LS) BA, MA. 6: Fr, Sp. 7: Libn Rosary Col 44-45; Libn Ill State Lib Ext Div, Chicago 47-4; Libn La Porte Pub Lib, LaPorte Ind 48; Libn La Porte City Schs, La Porte Ind 56-63; Libn Opinion Research Corp, Princton NJ 58-63; Head sociol dept Notre Dme Lib, UNotre Dame Ind 63-65, Head arch lib 65-. 9: Midwest Acad Libns. 10: AAUW; AAUP; Amer Soc Assn; Civic Music; Fine Arts Assn. 13: Yes. 14: Ref. 15: 109 Franklin ct, La Porte IN 46350.

DECKER, LELANE (KILMER). b Woodhull NY 30 S 47. 4: Marvin Decker. 5: Elmira Col 64-67 (Eng Lit) BA; USwansea (Wales) 65-66 (Eng Lit); Columbia 67-68 (LS) MS. 6: Fr. 7: Jr libn NY State Lib Div of Lib Development 68-. 13: Yes. 14: Ref, publ. 15: 14 Lakeview ave, Rensselaer NY 12144.

DECKER, MARIAN (BELLOWS). b Waukegan Ill 13 S 09. 5: Amer Conservatory of Music 28-32 (Piano, Organ) BMus; Northwestern U Medill Sch of Journalism 28-33; UChicago 48-50 MLS. 6: Fr. 7: Sch libn Warren Twp High Sch, Gurnee Ill 49-61; Sch libn Waukegan Twp High Sch, West Campus 61-67; Ref libn Waukegan (Ill) Pub Lib 67-. 9: ALA; IllLA. 10: . 14: Ref, display wk. 15: 28 N Chapel st, Waukegan IL 60085.

DECKER, MARY E (HARDIE). b Rhinebeck NY 22 Je 18. 4: Robert L Decker. 5: Cooper Union Day Art Sch 35-36 (Art); NY State Col for Tchrs (Albany) 36-40 (Eng) AB; Bard Col 62,68; SUNY (Albany) 59-65 MLS; NDEA Inst for Sch Libns, SUNY (Albany) 65. 6: Sp. 7: Eng tchr Escuela Santiago Iglesias Pantin, Ceiba PR 40-42; Chief clerk US Naval Drydock & Repair Facity, San Juan PR 42-43; Supply Off Naval Supply Depot, Norfolt Va (Ensign SC USNR) 43-45; High Sch Eng tchr Rhinebeck Central Sch, Rhinebeck NY 45-47, Elem libn 59-67; Libn supv Spackenkill Sch Dist, Poughkeepsie NY 67-. 9: ALA; NYLA; NY State Tchrs Assn; Dutchess County LA (pres); Dutchess County Tchrs Coun. 10: PTA. 13: Yes. 14: Child serv, curriculum development, instrl materials. 15: 110 E Market st, Rhinebeck NY 12572.

deCORDOVA, MRS FRANCES (MYERS). b Gordonville Tex 14 Je 19. 4: Jack M deCordova. 5: Tex Womans U 41 (LS) BA, 51 MLS. 6: Sp. 7 Elem tchr Gordonville Pub Sch, Gordonville Tex 39-41: Libn Blackland Army AF, Waco Tex 45; Asst libn Waco Pub Lib, Waco Tex 42-45, 46: Libn T W U Demonstration Sch, & Instr Sch of Lib Sci Tex Womans U 46-59; Asst Prof Sch of Lib Sci, Tex Womans U 59-. 8: Asst dir NDEA Inst Tex Womans U 65; Adv Com for "Standards for School Library Programs 62 Adv Bd Proj Impact, Lubbock Tex 67-69. 9: ALA; AALS; TexLA (Represent-at-Large 66-69, State Represent SWLA 67-69, mem chm Dist 7 60-61); Tex Coun of Lib Educ; Tex Assn of Col Tchrs; TexASchL (chm 62-63). 10: Alpha Beta Alpha. 14: Wk with child, sch libs. 15: 1214 Emerson lane, Denton TX 76201.

DEDE, BONNIE AILEEN (ROEBER). b Racine Wis 21 Mr 42. 4: Metin Dede. 5: UMich 60-63 (Russian Lang & Lit) BA, 63-66 (Gen Ling) MA, 66-68 AMLS. 6: Russian, Turkish, Ger, Czech, Serbo-Croatian, Church Slavonic, Fr, classical Gr. 7: Bibliog UMich (Ann Arbor) 68, Tech serv libn III-A 68-69, Tech serv libn III-B 69-. 10: Beta Phi Mu; Alpha Lambda Delta. 14: Catlg, acquis, E European catlg. 15: 1634-5 Murfin, Ann Arbor Mi 48105.

DEE, MATHEW F. b Cleveland 16 My 31. 5: West Res 49-54 (Eng, Fr, Hist) BA, 58-61 MSLS. 6: Fr. 7: Tchr Cleveland Pub Schs, 54-60; Tchr Rocky River Pub Schs, Rocky River Ohio 59-60; Law libn Jones, Day, Cockley & Reavis, Cleveland 61-63; Asst personnel libn Ohio State U 63-65, Asst head Dept Libs 65, Act personnel dir 65-66, Asst dir law lib 66-, 9: ALA; SLA; aall; OhioALL; OhioLA. 12: Ed "Ohio Association of Law Libraries Bulletin. 14: Ref, acquis. 15: 1659 N High st, Columbus Oh 43229.

DEERING, EDITH ANN (PROCTOR). b Elkhorn Wis 8 N 43. 4: Ronald F Deering. 5: UWis 61-65 (Eng) BS Ed; Catherine Spalding Coll 67-69 MSLS. 6: Fr. 7: Eng tchr Delavan-Darien High Sch, Delavan Wis 65-66; Ref asst Columbia U Soc Wk Lib 67; Asst Ref Ctr Kentuckiana Metroversity 69-. 9: ALA. 10: Phi Kappa Phi; Nat Grange. 14: Mechanized lib serv. 15: 3803 Layside dr, Louisville Ky 40220.

DEERING, G HELEN (FORSMAN). b Stensele Sweden 13 Jl 13. 4: Joseph W Deering. 5: Itasca Jr Coll 29-31 AA; UMinn 31-34 (Home Econ) BSE; E Tex 58-60 MLS. 7: Home econ tchr Hermitage High Sch, Hermitage Ark 51-53; Sci tchr Camden Jr High Sch, Camden Ark 53-56; Richardson Ind Sch Dist, Richardson Tex: Sci tchr 56-60, Libn 60-. 9: ALA; NEA; TexEA; TexStateLA; RichardsonEA. 10: AAUW; Alpha Delta Kappa. 14: YA. 15: 435 Terrace dr, Richardson Tx 75080.

DEERING, RONALD FRANKLIN. b Ford County Ill 6 O 29. 4: Edith Ann Proctor. 5: Georgetown Col 47-51 (Hist, Religion) BA (summa cum laude); So Baptist Theol Sem 51-55 (Divinity) BD, 55-61 (New Testament) THD; Catherine

Spalding Col 62, 64-65 (LS); Columbia 63, 67 MSLS. 6: Ger, Gk, Hebrew. 7: Bible Instr Georgetown Col (Gerogetown Ky) 50-51; Pastor College Hill Baptist Church, Cincinnati 51-53; Pastor Blue River Baptist Church, Salem Ind 54-58; Instr Gk New Testament So Baptist Theol Sem 58-60; Research libn So Baptist Theol Sem 60-67, Asso libn & dir readers serv 67-. 9: ATheol LA; Amer Acad Religion; A L A; Soc of Bibl Lit. 10: Beta Phi Mu; Sigma Tau Delta; Phi Alpha Theta. 11: Amer Theol LA Scholarship, 67. 14: Acad libnship, admin, research, ref, theolo libnship. 15: 3803 Layside dr, Louisville Ky 40220.

DEERY, THOMAS J. b Reading Penn 28 Ag 35. 4: Joanne Walsh. 5: Franklin & Marshall Col 53-57 (Geol) BS; Villanova U 61 (LS); Drexel 62-65 MS in LS. 6: Ger. 7: Geol Newfoundland & Labrador Corp Ltd, Newfoundland 56; Geol Kennecott Copper Corp, Nev 57; High Sch sci tchr Manheim TWP High Sch, Neffsville Pa 58-61; Asst tech libn Armstrong Cork Co, Lancaster Penn 61-65, Research info supv 65-. 9: SLA; ASIS. 14: Info retrieval systems, tech lib mgt. 15: 2705 Kimberly rd, Lancaster PA 17603.

DEES, ELLA MARJORIE. b Hamilton Co Fla 8 Je 39. 5: Berry Col 56-60 (Eng) AB; Fla StateU 66-67 (LS) MS. 7: Tchr Duval Co Bd Pub Instr, Jacksonville Fla 60-66; Libn Ga State Col 67-. 14: Ref. 15: 1420 Foxhall lane SE, Atlanta Ga 30316.

DEES, JULIA IDA LaMOTHE. b Annapolis Md 17 Mr 28. 5: Vassar 46-48 (Art-Arch); URI 54-55, 57-58 (Fr) BA; UParis 55-56 (Fr Civilization); UDenver 59-60 (LS) MA Drexel U (Docs workshops) 60, 65; Bowling Green State 67; UMinn 68. 6: Fr. 7: Army WAC (Active Duty) Troop cadre train & admin (1st Lt) 49-53; Army WAC (Reserve) Admin (Capt) 53-65; Lib asst stud & perm staff URI Lib 57-59; Lib asst I Art & Music Dept Denver Pub Lib 59-60, Libn I brs 61-63; Readers' serv libn & Asst Prof of Lib Sci Concord Col Lib 63-68; Ref libn Wisconsin State U (River Falls) 68-69. 8: Spec proj libn for gifts & exch Denver Med Soc Lib 63. 9: ALA; MusicLA. 10: Eng-Speaking Union; Mercer-Tazewell Human Rel Coun; Metro Opera Guild; AAUP; Nat Geog Soc. 14: Ref in acad or art/music libs, admin, reorgan. 15: 812 S Fillmore st, Denver CO 80206.

DEES, MARGARET (NYHUS). b Dupree SD 5 Mr 17. 4: Denzil Ellis Dees. 5: UIll 39 (Eng, Hist) BS, 50 (Elem Educ) MA, 57 (LS) MS. 7: Eng, hst tchr Milton High Sch, Milton Ill 40-43; Communications off 11th Naval Dist Hdqs, San diego Cal 44-46; Tchr Mentone Elem Sch, Redlands Cal 49-50; Tchr Miami Shores Elem Sch, Miami Fla 52-53; Libn Champaign Sr High Sch, Champaign Ill 57-58; Coordinator of libs Urbana Community Schs, Urbana Ill 58-. 8: Consul Title II ESEA, Off Supt of Pub Instr 65-66; Summer inst, NE State Col 69 Lib Desel Com 67-68. 9: NEA; ALA; AASchL; DAVI; ACEI; IllLA (Bd 64-66); Lib Desel Com 67-68); IllEA; IllASchL (Conf chm 66, pres 67-68); Ill Assn Childhood Educ (Publ chm 64-66); IllAVI. 10: LWV; Kappa Delta Pi; Beta Phi Mu; Delta Kappa Gamma. 13: Yes. 14: Sch libnship. 15: 2016 Boudreau dr, Urbana IL 61801.

DEEVER, GLADYS (MARGUERITE). b Kan City Mo 26 Sp 15. 5: Independence Kan Jr Col 32-34 (Eng); York Col (Neb) 34-36 (Eng) AB; UDenver 40-41 BS in LS. 7: Tchr high sch, Odell Neb 36-38; Tchr Jr high sch, No Platte Neb 38-39; Child libn Abilene Kan Pub Lib, Abilene Kan 41-43; Pub Lib, Kan City(Mo) Child libn Main Br 43-49, Child libn Main Br 49-50, Child in chg of schs div 50-68, Supv ext serv 68-. 8: Lib Com of Presidents Com for Employment of Handicapped 59-; Lectr in Wkshop for Tchrs of Deaf, NDEA, UKan Med Ctr Jl 66. 9: ALA; -PLA Sub-Com on Standards for Child Wk; ACEI; NCTE; MoLA. 10: United Church Women; Altrusa Club; Delta Kappa Gamma. 14: Child & yp bks, human rel. 15: 4227 Oak, Kansas City Mo 64111.

DEGANI, EDITH (SCHUMACHER). b NYC 12 Ap 22. 4: Meir H Degani. 5: Queens Col 38-42 BA; Pratt 42-43 BLS; NYU 45-48. 6: Fr, Hebrew. 7: Catlgr NY Pub Lib 43-44; Head catlgr Pratt Inst 44-47; Asst libn NY State Maritime Col 47-49; Catlgr Yeshiva U 56-57; Catlgr Carl H Pforzheimer Lib, NYC 59-66; Tech serv libn, Jewish Theol Sem 66-. 9: NYLib Club (sec 47-48); ALA; Jewish LA. 14: Catlg, tech serv. 15: Ft Schuyler, Bronx NY 10465.

DEGARA, JOHN. b Debrecen Hungary 9 F 01. 5: Handelshochschule & Univ (Munchen) 19-21 Diploma: UBerlin (Germany) 21-23 (Econ); UHamburg (Germany) 23-24 (Econ) PhD; indU 55-57 (LS) MA. 6: Ger, Fr, Hungarian. 7: Self employed agriculturist, Hungary 26-44; Civil serv Hungarian Ministry of Agric 45-48; French High Commissioner in Germany 49-51; Self employed interpreter & tr, Wash DC & NY 51-54; Instr IndU 55-56; Libn Head Agric Lib, Ohio StateU 57-. 9: Internat Assn Agric Libns & Documentalists; ALA; Asociacion Interamericano de Bibliotecarios y Documentalists Agricolas. 13: Yes. 15: 165 W Patterson ave, Columbus Ohio 43302.

DeHAY, DELL (MARKWARD). b Miami Ariz 26 O 18. 4: Larry C DeHAY. 5: Tex Wesleyan Col 40 (Eng) BA; N Tex State U 69 MLS. 7: Libn Tarrant Co Law Lib Ft Worth 62-. 9: AALL (sec-treas SWest Chap). 10: Bus & Profess Women's Club; Alpha Lambda Sigma. 14: Ref. 15: 6820 Jewell ave, Fort Worth Tx 76112.

DEIBEL, FRANCIS ALOYSIUS (SM). b Columbus Ohio 13 Ag 08. 5: UDayton 25-29 (Eng) BA; West Res summers 39-43 BSLS. 7: Tchr: Catholic High Sch, Hamilton Ohio 29-30, cathedral Latin Sch, Cleveland Ohio 30-41; Tchr & libn Purcell High Sch, Cincinatti 41-45, Libn 45-52; Libn St Joseph High Sch, Cleveland Ohio 53-54; Libn (asst hd circ dept) UDayton 54-. 9: CathLA (v-pres Cincinnati Unit 48-49). 14: Circ, stud lib personnel. 15: Albert Emanuel Lib Univ of Dayton, Dayton Oh 45409.

DEIBLER, BARBARA E. b Pottsville Pa 11 Ag 43. 5: Penn State 62-65 (Arts & Letters) BA; Drexel 65-66 MSLS. 6: Ger. 7: Catlgr Penn State Lib 66-. 9: ALA; 14: Rare bks, catlg. 15: 2285 W Norwegian st, Pottsville Pa 17901.

DEICHERT, LILLIAN CAROL (FLEISCHER O'BRIEN) (COOK). b NYC 27 S 12. 4: William George Deichert. 5: Hunter Col 29-33 (Pol Sci) AB; NYU 3537 (Educ); Pratt 58-60 MLS. 6: Ger. 7: Elem tchr NYC Bd of Educ 33-43; Club Dir Amer Red Cross, overseas program 43-50; Girl Scout Exec, Rapid City SD 50-51; Ref libn asst Brooklyn Pub Lib 60; Elem tchr Amer Sch, Bandung Indonesia 63-64; Asst loan libn UNH 64-68; Loan libn 68-. 9: NHLA; ALA; NELA. : AAUP; LWV; Beta Phi Mu. 14: Ref, spec collections, rare bks. 15: 17 Davis ave, Durham NH 03824.

DEILY, ELIZABETH (WORCESTER). b Media Penn 19 D 15. 4: Robert H Deily. 5: Simmons 33-37 (LS) BS; Columbia 41, 42, 43 (LS); SUNY (Albany) 66. 7: Child libn Brooklyn Pub Lib, Brooklyn NY 38-43; Libn Bruns Hosp (US Army), Santa Fe NM 44; Instr child lit suny 9albany) 57-58; Libn NY State Sch Bd Assoc, Albany 64-66; Libn Albany Inst of hist & Art 64-66; Libn NY State Hosp Assn, Albany 65-66; Elem sch libn Bethlehem central Schs, Delmar NY 66-. 10: Theatre Program, Bethlehem Ctr Sch Dist; Reg 14 Amer Educ Theatre Assn. 14: Child wk. 15: 1584 New Scotland rd, Slingerlands NY 12159.

DEILY, ROBERT HOWARD. b Bethlehem Penn 20 Ag 09. 4: Elizabeth Worcester. 5: Muhlenberg Col 27-31 (Eng Lit) AB; Columbia 31-32, 36-37 BLS, MLS; Lehigh U 32-33 (Eng Lit) MA; Chicago 39-41 (Libnship) PhD. 6: Ger. 7: Page Bethlehem (Penn) Pub Lib 25-27; Stud asst Muhlenberg Col 28-31; Catlg asst LeHigh U Lib 32-33, Ref asst 33-34; Libn Wagner Col 34-37; Asst supt order dept Brooklyn Pub Lib 37-39; Jr Col libn Englewood Jr Col 40-41; Br libn Brooklyn Pub Lib 41-42; US Army (Air Force & Military Intel) Capt (Asst to Area Intel Off) Manhattan Engnr Dist, Los Alamos NM 42-46; Prof & Head Lib Sch UKy 46-48; Prin libn State Lib, Albany NY 48-62, Act State Libn 62-63; Assoc for lib serv SUNY(Albany) 63-. 8: Present position is that of consul to 63 campus libs which comprise The Lib System of SUNY, Faculty Sch Lib Serv SUNY(Albany); Consul and surveyor of libs in private col in NY State. 9: ALA; BSA; NYLA. 10: AAUP. 12: "Bibliographies of Twelve Victorian Authors with 2 co-authors (36). 14: U & col lib admin, acquis, lib educ. 15: 1584 New Scotland rd, Slingerlands NY 12159.

DEININGER, DOROTHY F(RITCH). b Phila 9 D 09. 5: Swarthmore 28-32 (Eng) AB; Drexel summer 30, 31, 32-33 BS in LS; Columbiz 37-38 (LS) MS. 7: Lib asst Drexel Inst 33-34, 35-37; Libn High Sch, Ridley Park Penn 34-35; Lib asst Vassar Col 38-40; Libn Jones Jr High Sch, Phila 40-41; Head educ dept Pub Lib, Newark NJ 41-42; Asst head lib serv Br Bur of Naval Personnel 42-46; Head Lib Serv Br Navy Dept, Wash DC 46-. 66; Assoc Prof Grad Sch of Lib Serv Rutgers. 8: . 9: ALA (Coun 56-57);-LED (pres 54-55);-PLA (chm Armed Forces Lib Sect 50-51); SLA; Adult Educ Assn; NJLA; AALS. 10: AAUW; AAUP. 13: Yes, 14: Admin, bk sel. 15: Grad Sch of Lib Serv, Rutgers The State Univ, New Brunswick NJ 08903.

DeJONG, HELEN ELIZABETH (MOFFITT). b Greenville RI 24 O 10. 4: David Cornel DeJong. 5: Pembroke Col 28-32 (Eng) PhB. 6: Fr. 7: Asst lib RI Med Soc Lib, Providence 30-32, Asst libn 32-45, Libn 45-. 8: Consul libn RI Med Center, Howard RI 61-. 9: MedLA; NE Reg Med LA; RILA;

RI Group of Med Libns. 10: Museum ember RI Sch of Design; Phi Beta Kappa. 11: Honorary member RI Med Soc. 13: Yes. 14: Hist of med. 15: 106 Francis st, Providence RI 02903.

DEKKERS, PIETER. b Den Helder Netherlands 29 N 30. 4: Margarete Schneider. 5: Cal State Col (Los Angeles) 56-61 (Hist) BA, MA; USoCal 63-64 MALS, 67-68 (LS). 06: Ger, Dutch, Afrikaans, Fr. 6: Ger, Dutch, Afrikaans, Fr. 7: Clerk Vromans Cal Sch Bk Depository, Pasadena Cal 53-63; Catlgr Occidental Col 64-67; Catlgr UCal (Irvine) 68-. 9: ALA; CalLA; So Cal Proc Gp. 10: Libraria Sodalitas; Phi Alpha Theta. 15: 2700 Peterson pl apt 47-D, Costa Mesa Ca 92626.

DeKLERK, PETER. b Amsterdam 15 Ap 27. 5: Calvil Col 52-56 BA; Calvin Theol Sem 56-59; Westminster Theol 62-63 BD, 63-65; Emory 65-68 MLS. 6: Dutch, Fr, Ger, Hebrew, Lat, Gr. 7: Night circ & in charge stocks Candler Sch of Theol Emory U 65-68, Catlgr 68-69; Theol libn Calvin Theol Sem (Grand Rapids Mich) 69-. 9: ATHEOLLA. 14: Catlg, ref. 15: Knollcrest Calvin Lib, Grand Rapids Mi 49506.

DEKOSTER, LESTER RONALD. b Zeeland Mich 21 Ap 15. 4: Ruth Jane De Vries. 5: Calvin Col 33-37 (Eng) BA; UMich summers 40-42 (Philos) MA, 51-55 (LS) MA, 55-64 (LS) PhD. 6: Dutch, Ger, Fr. 7: Tchr & speech South High Sch, GRAND Rapids Mich 37-47; US Naval Res Air Transport Communication, Pacific 43-45; Dept of Speech Calvin Col 47-; Dir of Lib Calvin Col & Sem 51-. 9: ALA; MichLA; Grand Rapids Libns Club; Soc Reformation Research. 12: "All Ye That Labor" (56); "Communism and Christian Faith" (62); "Vocabulary of Communism" (64); "Christian and The John Birch Society" (66); "Citizen and The John Birch Society" (68). 13: Yes. 14: Admin. 15: 2800 Thornapple river dr SE, Grand Rapids MI 49506.

DEKSNIS, ALMA (KARKLINS). b Latvia 8 N 05. 4: Karlis Deksnis. 5: ULatvia 30-40 (Philos) BS; SoConn State Col 56-59 MSLS; UConn 61-65 (Educ) Diploma in Prof Educ. 6: Fr, Ger, Latvian, Russian, Sp. 7: Catlg libn Willamatic State Col 57-59; Ser libn Central Conn State Col 59-61, Chief catlg libn 62-67, Readers' adv libn 68-. 9: Conn LA. 10: Amer-Latvian Assn; New Britain Ski Club; AAUP; Faculty Assn Conn State Cols; Amer-Latvian Choral Club. 13: Yes. 14: Bks in for langs, ref research. 15: 63 Dudley st, New Britain CT 06053.

DEL CASTILLO, MIREYA (ALVAREZ). b Camaguey Cuba. 4: Eduardo del Castillo. 5: Inst of Camaguey (Cuba) 36-37 BA; UHavana (Cuba) 37-41 LLD; Kan State Tchrs Col (Emporia) 64-65 MS in LS. 6: Fr, Sp, Lat, Ital, Portu. 7: Head catlgr Rockhurst Col 65-69; Catlgr UMo 69-. 9: ALA. 14: Catlg. 15: 304 Jefferson st, apt B-6, Warrensburg Mo 64093.

DEL FRATE, ADELAIDE A. b Somerville Mass 28 D 24. 5: Simmons 43-47 (LS) BS. 6: Ittal, chem Ger, Fr. 7: Abstractor, ed MIT Project Meteor 47-49; Patent libn Dewey & Almy Chem Co, Cambridge Mass 49-52; Libn div head Jackson & Moreland Inc, Boston 52-56; Supv central tech files, & patent libn WQ R Grace & Co, Clifton NJ & Clarksville Md 56-62; Libn gov marketing Raytheon Co, Lexington Mass 63; Supv tech info Mobil Chem Co R&T Div, Metuchen NJ 63-65; Libn NASA, ERC, Cambridge Mass 65-69; Hd Lib Br Nasa Goddard Spac Flight Ctr, Greenbelt Md 69-. 9: SLA; ASIS; ACS. 13: Yes. 14: Lib admin, lib automation. 15: NASA Goddard Space Flight Center, Greenbelt Md 20771.

DEL MAR, PATRICIA (FEENY). b Albany NY 25 D 33. 4: Don Del Mar. 5: Bryn Mawr 51-55 (Archaeology) AB; Columbia 55-56 MSLS. 7: Catlgr Harvard U Grad Sch of Design 56-59; A-v libn Boston Pub Lib 59-62; Tech libn Boston Naval Shipyard, Boston 63-64; Ref libn Long Beach Pub Lib, Long Beach Cal 64-65, Film libn 65-. 9: SLA; CathLA; CalLA (v-pres & pres-elect a-v Div). 14: A-v, catlg. 15: 611 Linden ave apt 7, Long Beach Cal 90812.

DEL TORO, JOSEFINA. b San Juan PR 23 My 01. 5: Simmons 22-25 BLS;Columbia 36-37 MLS. 6: Sp, Eng, Fr. 7: UPR(Rio Piedras): Asst libn 25-41, Act libn 41-43, Assoc libn in chg of ref 43-59, Dir of pub rel depts 59-64, Assoc Prof of bibliog & ref 60-64, Dir of Libs 64-. 9: ALA; Sociedad de Bibliotecarios de Puerto Rico (pres 63). 10: Altrusa Club; YWCA; Ateneo Puertorigueno; Colegio Puertoregueno de Ninas. 11: Piaques of Merit; SBPR 65; APUPR 68. 12: "A Bibliography of the Collective Biograpy of Spanish-America (38); "A Bibliography of Puerto Rico for 1939 (41). 13: Yes. 14: Ref, admin. 15: Olimpio ave, Miramar San Juan PR 00907.

DELANA, GENEVIEVE A. b Chicago 30 Mr 27. 5: Mundelein Col 44-48 (Hist) BA; Rosary Col 48-49 BA in LS. 7: Lib asst Mundelein Col summer 48; Libn De Paul U 49-50; Assoc libn Loyola U (Chicago) 50-. 9: ALA; CathLA. 14: Catlg. 15: 112 Austin st, Evanston IL 60202.

DELANEY, JACK J. b Great Falls Mont 2 Mr 21. 5: Col of Great Falls 40-46 (Eng) BA; Our Lady of Lake Col 52-53 (LS) MS; Columbia 60; Harvard 62. 7: Soc wker Mont Dept of Pub Welfard 49-50; Psychiatric soc wker, Ft Riley Kan 50-51; Order libn Tex Tech 54-56; Libn Mary B Smiley High Sch, Houston 57; Libn Ball Hish Sch, Galveston Tex 58; Libn Centereach Pub Schs, Centereach NY 59-. 9: ALA-AASchL; Suffolk Co (NY) SchLA (pres 59-61); Amer Acad of Polit & Soc Sci. 10: . 12: Ed "The School Librarian" (61); "The New School Librarian" (68). 13: Yes. 14: Sch libs. 15: Stony Brook Lodge, Stony Brook LI NY 11790.

DELGADO, (CARRION) RAFAEL R. b Rio Piedras PR 18 O 37. 4: Forastieri de Delgado monsita. 5: UPR 58 (Educ) BAEd; Syracuse 60 MSLS. 6: Sp. 7: Libn I Dept of Educ, San Jaun PR 58-59, Libn II 60-62; Libn III Reg Col UPR (Humacao) 62-64, Lib dir 64-66; Lib dir Gen Lib (Mayaguez) 66-. 8: State exec dir Nat Lib Week 55; Ex-oficio mem Acad Seante UPR (Mayaguez Campus) 66-; Mem Adv Bd Tech Info Ctr of PR 68-; Dir Mayaguez Campus Gen Archives 69-.) 09: ALA; Sociedad de Bibliotecarios de PR (off 62-64; v-pres 64-65); Sem on the Acquis of Latin Amer Lib Materials 68-. 10: Asociacion interamericana de Bibliotecarios y Documentalistas Agricolas 68-; Rotary Club. 14: Lib admin. 15: Box 5202 College Sta, Mayaguez PR 00708.

DeLISLE, MARGARET M. b St Louis 13 S 10. 5: Webster Col 27-31 (Lat) BA; Washington U 34-35 (LS); St Louis U 34-38 (Lat) MA; Catholic U 49-50 MLS. 6: Lat, Fr, Sp. 7: Head libn Fond du Lac (Wis) Sr High Sch 53-54; Dir lib serv Catholic Hosp Assn, St Louis 54-57; Libn Grad Sch of Nursing Catholic U 57-60; Head libn St Louis Med Soc, St Luis 60-63; Catlgr St Louis U 64, Ref libn 64-65; Head libn Kenrick Sem 65-. 9: ALA (ALA-AHA Com on Indexing Hosp Lit 54-57); CathLA (chm Hosp Lib Sect 36-44); Classical Assn of Middle West; MedLA; NEA. 12: Editorial stff "Hospital Progress (54-57); "The Medical Library (57). 13: Yes. 14: Admin, asst to readers, catlg. 15: 842a Diehmoells dr, St Louis Mo 63119.

DELL, JOHN OLIVER. b Victoria BC 16 Jl 37. 5: Victoria Coll 55-58 Secondary Tchg Certif; UBC 58-60 (Hist, Eng) BA, 62-63 BLS. 6: Fr. 7: Catlgr UVictoria Lib 63-. 9: CanLA; BCLA; Assn BC Libns; Inst of Victoria Libns. 10: Maritime Museum of BC Soc. 12: Ed "Adlib" (UBC Lib School newsletter) 62-63; Ed IVY-EL newsletter 64-65; Ed KUMTUKS (UVictoria Lib newsletter) 65-68; Bk rev ed "BC Library Quarterly" 67-68. 14: Catlg (Ser & Docs). 15: Apt 306 1526 Cedar Hill Cross rd, Victoria BC Can.

DELLA PIETRA, ELEANOR MARIE. b NYC. 4: John J Della Pietra. 5: CityU (NY); Columbia 43-45 MLS. St Johns U Tchrs Col 53; LIU 59. 6: Ital, Sp, Fr. 7: NY Pub Lib: Filer 28-35, Indexer in chg 35-45, Sch & ref libn 96th St Br 45-46; NYC Bd of Educ: Sch libn in chg Clara Barton High Sch 47-52, Sch libn in chg Grover Cleveland High Sch 52-64, Sch libn Grover Cleveland High Sch 64- Recatlgr for Nat Econ Res Asso 68. 8: Consul & adv to Coun for Intercultural Books for YP. 9: NYLib Club; NYSchLA. 14: Catlg, ref. 15: 63-15 Forest ave, Ridgewood NY 11227.

DELLER, A MICHAEL. b Highland Pk Mich 8 Jl 41. 5: Oakland U 59-63 (Russian) BA; NWest U summer 63 (Russian); Ind U summer 64 (Russian); UMich 66-68 MALS. 6: Eng, Russian. 7: Tchr Unified sch dist Long Beach Cal 63-65; Tchr St Mary of Redford Jr High Sch Detroit 65-66; Libn Detroit Pub Lib 66-. 9: ALA (Jr Mem RT Bd mem); MichLA; Assn Prof Libn (Detroit Pub Lib). 10: Internat Inst of Metro Detroit; Detroit Puppeteers Guild. 14: YA, child wk. 15: 16563 Marlowe, Detroit Mi 48235.

DELMAGE, REV LEWIS S J. b Fall River Mass 3 Mr 17. 5: Georgetown U 40 (Classics) AB; Woodstock Col 41 (Ethics) PHL; Weston Col 49 (Pastoral Theol) STL. 6: Sp, Fr, Lat. 7: Period libn Sem. Manhasset NY 38-39; Instr of langs Regis High Sch, NYC 41-45; Stud coun Scranton Prep Sch, Scranton Penn 50-51; Instr of Philos Georgetown U 51-52; Asst Prof of Theol St Joseph's Col (Phila) 52-58; Dir of Reg Serv Center Christian Life Communs & its lib, Phila 56-. 8: Mem of Episcopal Adv Com Nat Fed of Sodalities; convention spkr Nat Coun of Catholic Men; Nat Fed of Christian Life Communs (Org & Dev Com). 9: SLA; Spec Libns Group of Phila Area. 10: Nat Federation of Christian Life Communs; Xavier-Damians Profes CLC for Men (dir); conducting of closed retreats for laymen (6 to 8 days). 12: Tr "Achieving Peace of Heart" by Narciso Irala SJ (54, revised 64, 69), Tr "Spiritual Exercises of St Ignatius Loyola" (68). 13: Yes. 14:

Info retrieval, catlg, ref, filing systems. 15: C/O St Josephs Col, Phila PA 19131.

DELMAN, EDITH (WECHSLER). b Boston Mass 29 D 14. 4: Louis Delman. 5: Cornell 31-32; NYU 32-35 (Math) BA; Rutgers 62-65 MLS. 6: Fr, Yiddish. 7: Sch libn S Plainfield High Sch, S Plainfield NJ 65-. 9: ALA; NEA; NJSchLA; NJEA. 14: Sch libs. 15: 418 Parkside rd, Plainfield NJ 07060.

DELMORE, ELIZABETH. b Roseau Minn 11 Sg 21. 5: Col of St Catherine 39-43 (Eng, LS) BS, summers BA; UMinn summers 63-66 (LS) MA. 6: Fr, Ger. 7: Tchr & libn: St Mary's High Sch, Bird Island Minn 45-48, Acad of the Holy Angels, Minneapolis 48-51, St John's Acad, Jamestown N Dak 51-56, St James High Sch, Grand Forks N Dak 56-59; Ref libn Col of St Catherine 59-. 9: ALA; CathLA; MinnLA. 10: Cath Interracial Coun. 14: Ref, rare bks. 15: 2004 Randolph, St Paul Mn 55116.

DELOE, VIRGINIA MAXINE. b Tyro Kan 11 N 12. 5: UOkla 30-31, 32-33; UMd 52-57 (Elem Educ) BS; UOkla 59-60 MLS. 7: Sec to Supt of Schs, Sapulpa Okla 35-52; Var positions Montgomery Co Bd of Educ, Montgomery Co Md 52-57, 58-59; Tchr Sand Springs Okla 57-58; Jr catlgr Okla StateU Lib 60-. 9: ALA; OklaLA. 14: Catlg. 15: 239-1/2 S Duck, Stillwater Okla 74074.

DeLONG, DIANNE (SOPP). b Ann Arbor Mich 5 Je 42. 4: Douglas A DeLong. 5: Kalamazoo Col 60-64 (Ger) BA; UMich 64-65 MALS. 6: Ger. 7: Spec serv libn US Army, Europe, Nurnberg W Germany 65-67; Libn Univ High Sch Ill StateU 67-. 9: McLeanCoLA. 14: Ref, pub serv. 15: 35 Payne pl, Normal Il 61761.

DeLONG, DOUGLAS ATTEBERY. b Urbana Ill 11 Ag 39. 4: Dianne Sopp. 5: Knox Col 57-61 (Hist) BA; UIll(Urbana) 61-62 MSLS. 7: Supply Off US Army Qtmr Corps (1st Lt), Ft Sheridan Ill 62-64; Army libn US Army, Europe Nurnberg Germany 64-67; Periods libn Milner Lib Ill State U (Normal) 67-68; Sers libn 68-. 9: ALA; IllLA; McLean CoLA. 14: Tech proc (ser). 15: 35 Payne pl, Normal Il 61761.

DELOUGAZ, NATHALIE (POLIAKOFF). b Leningrad Russia 13 N 10. 5: UParis 29-32 (Law) licence en droit, 33-35 (Law) diplome detudes superieurs, 39-40 (Eng) licence es-lettres; Chicago 43-44 BLS, 45-48 (LS) MA. 6: Fr, Russian, Ital, Hebrew, Ger, Sp. 7: Catlgr UChicago Lib 44-50; Head Slavic Lang Sect Descr Catlg Civ LC 50-52; Expert in lib sci Tech Asst Prog Unesco on a mission to Israel to org Lib Sch at Herew U 55-57; Head catlgr & Instr in Lib Sci Hebrew U (Jerusalem Israel) 58-65; Descr Catlg Div, Foreign Langs LC 65-66; In Charge of Setting-up LC off in London & Paris 66-67, Chief shared catlg div 67-. 9: ALA; DCLA; OTOMAC Tech Proc Libns. 13: Yes. 14: Catlg, ref. 15: 1401 N st NW, Wash DC 20005.

DELWICHE, FRANCES (LAMB). b Oakland al 22 S 08. 5: UCal (Berkeley) 25-29 (Hist) AB, 29-30 (En) MA, 30-31 Gen Secondary Certif, 34-35 Certif in Libn-ship. 6: Ger, Fr. 7: Tchr Eng, Lat ESCONDIDO Union High Sch, Escondido Cal 31-33; Libn jr grade UCal Lib (Berkeley) 35-38; Santa Clara Co Lib, San Jose Cal: Libn I 57-60, Reg libn II 60-62, Supv libn 62-. 9: ALA; CalLA; Pub lib exec Central Cal; Bay area Y A Libns. 10: Sierra Club. 14: Ref, bk sel. 15: 1140 Clark way, San Jose al 95125.

DELZELL, ROBERT FREDRIC. b Independence Kan 4 S 18. 5: Drury Col 36-40 (Fr) AB; Northwestern U 40-41 (Fr); Wash U (St Louis) 49-50 (LS) BS; UIll 50-51 (LS) MS. 6: Fr. 7: US Army Field Artillery (Supply Sgt, Staff Sgt), US, Europe 41-45; Asst to ed libn Prentice-Hall, NYC 46-48; Acquis asst ashington U 48-49, Ref asst 49-50, Chief acquis dept 51-53; Chief acquis br Air U Lib (Maxwell AFB Ala) 53-54, Asst to dir 55; Admin asst UIll Lib 55-67, Personnel libn 67-68, Dir of personnel & Prof of Lib Admin 68-. 8: Consul to Air U Lib (Maxwell AFB) 52, 53, 56; Asst Dir, orientation prog for 11 univ libns from India; mem of survey team, col and univ libs in 66; Compil & abstract of questionnaires on Canad univ and col libs 67. 9: ALA (Life mem);-LAD (chm Budgeting, Accounting & Costs Com 62-63, Personnel Admin Sect); IllLA (for Exch Libns Com 64-, chm 66-67, sec Col & Research Libs Sect 61-62); MoLA; AlaLA; SLA (sec-treas Soc Sci Div 53-54). 10: Faculty adv UIll Film Soc 61-63; Mem University Theatre Bd (UIll) 63-; Beta Phi Mu (var Nat & Chap offs); Bd Dir Campus RT; UIll Nomacad Personnel Adv Com; (var Nat & Chap offs); AAUP. 12: Ed "The Book of Beta Phi Mu (57); Ed "News Letter UIll Lib Sch Assn, publ as a UIll Bulletin twice yearly (56-). 13: Yes. 14: Admin, personnel. 15: 1506 S vine, Urbana IL 61801.

DEMARST, ROSEMARY REGINA. b NYC 20 Ja 14. 5: Sarah Lawrence 0-34 (Philos) AB. 7: Asst libn The Hanover Bank NYC 40-43; Researcher US Off Strategic Serv, Wash dc 7 london 44-45; Libn The Hanover Bank, NYC 45-53; Libn Price Waterhouse & Co, NYC 53-. 10: Jr League; Royal Soc of Lit. 14: Admin. 15: 430 East 86th st, New York NY 10028.

DeMAURO, PATRICIA ANNE. b Canastota NY 18 Ap 44. 5: Col of New Rochelle 62-66 (Eng Lit) BA; Syracuse 66-67 MLS. 6: Sp. 7: Jr libn (child dept) Buffalo & Erie Co Pub Lib, Buffalo NY 67-. 9: Buffalo & Erie Co Pub Lib Staff Assn. 10: Beta Phi Mu; Child Aid Soc (Buffalo); Neuman Exec Coun (SUNY Buffalo). 14: Child & ya wk. 15: 869 Delaware ave, Buffalo NY 14209.

DEMENT, ALICE ROBERTA (WOOD). b Raton NM 11 S 30. 5: UNM 48-51 (Mus); Cal State Col at Fullerton 63-65 (Eng) BA; USoCal 65-66 MLS. 7: Br libn San Bernardino Co Lib Rialto Br 66-. 9: ALA; CalLA. 15: 571 No Riverside, Rialto Ca 92376.

DEMERS, HENRI. b Quebec Can. 5: Montreal U (B Bibl) BA. 6: Fr. 7: Econ Dept of Trade & Comm, Quebec & Montreal 43-56; Libn Dept of Trade & Commerce, Quebec 56-. 9: Association canadienne des bibliothecaires de langue francaise (pres 62-63); SLA; CanLA. 10: C of C, Ste-Foy. 14: Ref. 15: 788 Place Philippe, Ste-Foy Quebec 10 Can.

DEMES, STANLEY BERNARD. b Keddie Cal 11 Jl 21. 4: Corinne Fleming. 5: UCal at Santa Barbara 46-47 (Eng) BA; WashU St Louis 48-49 (Eng) AM; Sacramento State Col 49-50 (Ed) Sec cred; USoCal 51-52 MSLS. 7: Asst ref libn Sacramento State Col 53-55; Libn Taft Col 55-56; Asst ref libn Kern Co Lib, Bakersfield Cal 57-58; Highes Aircraft Co, Fullerton Cal: Ref libn 59-66, Chief libn 67-. 9: Orange Co LA (sec-treas 63). 10: AIAA; AMA; ACM. 12: Past ed "Science-Technology Bulletin", SLA SoCal Chap (62). 14: Ref. 15: 424 N Locust st, Fullerton Ca 92633.

DEMETER, BELA JOSEPH. b Nyiregyhaza Hungary 12 F 19. 4: Elizabeth Lia Schoenfeld. 5: Educated in Europe; San Jose State Col 59-63 (LS) BA. 6: Hungarian, Fr, Ger. 7: Staff Stanford U Libs 64-67; William Marsh Rice U, Houston, Tex 68. 9: CalLA. 14: Catlg, ref, rare bks. 15: 615 Marsh rd, Menlo Park CA 94025.

DeMIRTAS, GAIL KATHRYN (CLAXTON). b Adrian Mich 17 D 35. 4: Resat T Demirtas. 6: Ger. 7: Libn art, mus & sports dept Toledo Pub Lib, Toledo Ohio 59-61; Libn ref dept Seattle U 61-. 14: Ref (bus, langs, music). 15: 9007-229th SW, Edmonds Wa 98020.

DeMORE, SANDRA L. b Duluth Minn 15 Je 43. 5: UMinn 63-66 (Hist) BA, 67-68 (LS) MA. 6: Fr, Polish. 7: Ref libn UMinn (Minneapolis) 68-. 9: ALA. 14: (Slavic langs & lits), Central Europ hist. 15: Ref Rm Wilson Lib Univ of Minn, Minneapolis Mn 55455.

DEMOS, HELEN MARIE. b Berwyn Ill 30 N 36. 5: Morton Jr Coll 54-56 (Liberal arts) AA; Rosary Col 58-59 (Amer studies) BA, 64-65 MALS, Ind U 58-59 (Soc studies) MAT. 6: Fr, Sp, Greek. 7: Libn I Chicago Pub Lib 65-. 9: ALA; ChicagoLA. 10: Staff Assn of Chicago Pub Lib; YWCA. 15: Rm 119 YWCA 31 E Ogden, La Grange Il 60525.

DEMOS, JOHN THEODORE. b NYC 24 Mr 27. 4: Shirley Myers. 5: NYU 47-48 (Eng); UCLA 48-49 (Eng); UCal 49-51 (Eng) BA, 51-53 (Eng) MA, 55-56 MLS; Title IIB Fellow Case-West 67-68. 6: Ital. 7: Seaman 1/c US Navy, Philippines 44-46; Lt jg US Navy, Japan, Korea, Forosa 53-55; Libn Hayward Union High Sch, Hayward Cal 56-57; Libn Eastside Union High Sch Dist, San Jose Cal 57-59; High sch libn Dept of Defense, Italy (4 yrs), Germany (1 yr) France (1 yr) 59-65; Head Physics & Math Libs Ohio State U 65-66, Hd dept libs 66-67, Asst dir tech servs 68-. 9: ALA; OhioLA. 10: Exec Bd Ohio Poetry Day. 14: Admin. 15: 215 Piedmont rd, Columbus OH 43214.

DEMOSS, ESTHER. NYC. 05: UWash 31 (Philos) AB, 33 (Philos) MA; USoCal 63-65 (LS). 6: Fr. 07: Research analyst MGM Pictures, Culver City Cal 55-60; Ref libn Space Tech Labs, Los Angeles 60; Lib supv Aerospace Corp, Los Angeles 60-66; Lib supv Northrop Corp, Hawthorne 67-. 8: Vis assoc prof USoCal Lib Sch 68. 09: SLA; CalLA; ASIS. 10: Lib sch rep, USoCal General Alum Adv Bd; Mem Adv Bd; Mem Adv Bd Libraria Sodalitas. 15: 440 S Bedford dr, Beverly Hills Ca 90212.

DEMPSEY, FRANK JOSEPH. b San Francisco 8 N 25. 5: UCal(Berkeley) 46-50 (Hist) AB, 52-53 BLS. 6: Sp. 7: Radio traffic clerk Off of War Info, San Francisco 44-45; Claims investigator Amer Pres SS Lines, San Francisco 45-46; Page, photostatician UCal Lib (Berkeley) 46-50; Yeoman 3/C US Navy 50-52; Ref libn Newark (NJ) Pub Lib 53-54; Libn US Naval Supply Center, Oakland Cal 54-58; Asst libn Berkeley Pub Lib, Berkeley Cal 58-62, Chief Libn 62-. 8: Train Off Naval Supply Center, instr reading improvement & vocabulary bldg Oakland Jr Col; Librar/USA NY Worlds air 64. 9: ALA (mem Recruitment Com, chm Friends of Libs Com 68-69); CalLA; Pub Lib Execs of Central Cal (pres 63-64); EBay Lib Coun (chm 64-65); Friends of the Berkeley Pub Lib; Friends of the San Francisco Pub Lib, Friends of Cal Lib (Bd Dirs 66-69). 10: Cal Alumni Assn; Urban League; Berkeley City Commons Club; Coun of soc Planning; Berkeley Workreation Coun, Amer Red Cross. 12: "A Review of Library Administration, with C McMicken (61). 13: Yes. 14: Admin, regional planning, wk with the underprivileged. 15: 3456 16th st, San Francisco CA 94114.

DEMPSEY, LAURENCE F. b NYC 29 My 29. 5: Hunter Col 51-56 (Hist, Pol Sci) BA; Columbia 56-59 MS. 6: Sp, Ital. 7: Tech serv Hunter Col 59-65; Asst dir & ref libn Freeport Mem Lib, Freeport NY 65-. 9: ALA; NYLA; CathLA. 14: Ref, tech serv (periodicals, govt publ). 15: 119 Pine st, Freeport NY 11520.

DEMPSEY, SISTER MARY GREGORY. b Brooklyn NY 14 Ja 25. 5: Manhattan Col 49-55 (Ital) BA; St John'sU 59-62 MLS. 6: Sp. 7: Tchr Diocese of Brooklyn, Brooklyn NY 44-66; Libn St John's Hosp, Elmhurst LI NY 66-. 9: ALA; CathLA. 14: Nursing lit. 15: 23-18 44th dr, Long Island City NY 11101.

DEN, MARY ELLEN (KAUFFMAN). b Lititz Penn 8 Ap 29. 4: Richard S E Den. 5: Millersville State Col 47-51 (LS) BS in Educ; Drexel 53-54 MS in LS. 7: Child libn Free Lib of Phila 55-58; Child libn Rockville Centre Pub Lib, Rockville Centre LI NY 58-62;Child libn City Hall Lib, Hong Kong BCC 63-64; Asst child libn Northeast Reg Lib Free Lib of Phila 64-65, Head of child dept 65-. 9: PennLA. 10: Alpha Beta Alha. 14: Child wk. 15: 7151 Eastwood st, Phila PA 19149.

DENDY, EMMA (STRIBLING). b Walhalla SC 14 Ag 07. 5: Flora Macdonald 25-29 (Hist) BA; Peabody 35-36 BS in LS; UNC 55-56 MS inls. 7: Highsch libn, Selma Ala 36-43; Eng tchr & libn, Tamas Berry Schs, Mt Berry Schs Ga 44-47; Catlgr Ala Col 47-60; Catlgr Auburn U 60-. 14: Catlg. 15: 233 Marion cir, Auburn AL 36830.

DENECKE, DOROTHY M BYNUM. b Waxahachie Tex 9 Ap 23. 4: George A Denecke. 5: Trinity U 40-42; Tex Womans U 42-44 (LS) BA, summers 50-53 (LS). 7: High sch libn pub schs, Mexia Tex 44-45; Period libn Baylor U summer 45; Jr high sch libn pub schs, Corsicana Tex 45-47; High sch libn pub schs, acogdoches Tex 47-51; Ref & circ libn Stephen F AustinCol summer 48; High sch libn pub schs, Denver City Tex 51-55; Elem sch libn pub schs, Goldsmith Tex 56-. 9: Tex State Tchrs Assn; (co-chm Lib Sect Dist 18 66-67); TexLA. 14: Child & yp. 15: Box 712, Goldsmith TX 79741.

DENEROFF, THEODORA (YOSPIN). b Elizabeth NJ 10 Je 19. 4: Paul Deneroff. 5: New Jersey State Tchrs Col 37-41 (Elem ed) BS Ed; CUNY (Queensborough) 62-66 MLS. 7: Elizabeth Elem Sch, NJ: Dy sub 41-42, Tchr 45-48; Sci expt tchr Union Township NJ 42-45; Per diem sub NY Schs, Bronx 64-65; Sub elem schs, Bronx NY 66; Tchr lib Pub Sch 122, Bronx NY 66-. 9: ALA. 14: Child lit. 15: 2705 Bainbridge ave, Bronx NY 10458.

DENERSON, ELIZABETH H(IGHT). b Bluefield WVa 11 S 30. 5: Bennett Col 48-52 (Eng) BA; Atlanta 52-53 MSLS. 6: Fr. 7: Libn Morristown Col 53-54; Asst libn Ft Valley State Col 54-57; Libn P G Appling High Sch, Macon Ga 58-62; Asst libn WVa State Col 62-. 8: taff, Juvenile Citizenship Sch, Macon Ga 60-62. 9: ALA; WVaLA. 10: Delta Sigma Theta. 12: "A Study of the Pattern of Advertising in Four Selected Negro Newspapers, 1948-5 (55). 14: Ref, govt docs, period. 15: P O Box 275, Institute WV 25112.

DENGEL, RAY E. b Pittsburgh Pa 20 Jl 38. 5: UPittsburgh 56-61 (Geog) BA, 65-66 MLS. 7: Sp/4, USA Chem Corps Tech Escort Unit ABC warfare Edgewood Arsenal Md 62-63; Quality control US Steel Corp Homestead Works metalurgical dept 65-65; Asst libn ref & interlib loan Thiel Col 66-69; Ref libn Edinboro State Col 69-. 9: ALA; PennLA. 14: Ref. 15: 18 Ridge ave, Greenville Pa 16125.

DENGLER, NADINE. b Rochester NY 29 Ag 17. 5: Keuka Col 40 (Span, Fr) BA; Simmons 41 BLS; Central Bus Col 64-65 (Journalism, Pub Rel). 6: Fr, Sp. 7: Libn Rochester Pub Lib, Rochester NY 41-50; Libn Northeastern U Lib 50-51; Ref & publicity Lucius Beebe Mem Lib, Wakefield Mass 51-53; Denver Pub Lib: Ref Div 54-56; Phil psych & religion div 56-58, Head sociol & documents 59-61, Bus div 61, Head sociol area 61-. 9: ColoLA. 10: ACLU; Japan Soc of Colo. 13: Yes. 14: Ref, philos, religion. 15: 330 E 10th ave, apt 311, Denver, CO 80203.

DENHAM, BERNARD JAMES. b London England 6 F 29. 4: Jo Patrick. 5: ULondon (England) 53-54; San Francisco State Col 63-66 (Hist) BA, 68-69 (Hist); UCal (Berkeley) 66-67 mls& stanford 68 (Hist). 7: Finance clk Middlesex Co Coun, London England 45-47; Writer Royal Navy, England 47-49; Orchestra mgr Harold Davison Ltd, London England 49-52; Teller Barclays Bank Ltd, London England 52-57; Shipper Asbestonos Corp Ltd, toronto Can 57-59; Machine operator Amer Can Co, Hoboken NJ 60-61; Warehouse supv Amer Cancer Soc, San Francisco 62-63; Ed computer print-out Wells Fargo Bank, San francisco 64-67; Ref libn Stanford U Libs 67-69, Asst to dir 69-. 9: ALA-LAD (Staff Devel Com Personnel Admin Sect 69-71); CalLA. 14: Ref, admin, bibliog. 15: Stanford Univ Libraries, Stanford Ca 94305.

DENIS, LAURENT G. b Montreal 21 F 32. 5: Loyola Col (Montreal) 51-54 (Pre-Med) BA; McGill 54-55 BLS, 58-60 MLS; Rutgers 65-67 (LS). 6: Fr, Ger. 7: Catlgr Nat Lib of Can, Ottawa Ont 55-56; Asst chief Col Militaire Royal De Saint-Jean, St-Jean Que 56-61; Dir Ecole De Bibliotheconomie U Montreal, Montreal 61-. 8: Research Assoc, Penn Re-Survey of Libs 66. 9: ALA; CanLA (Counc 63-65, chm Resol Com); Assn Canadienne Des Bibliothecaires de Langue Francaise (chm several sect & numerous coms); Quebec LA (coun, pres 69-70); Inst of Prof Libns of Ontario. 10: Can Assn Univ Tchrs; Assn canadienne des educateurs de langue francaise. 12: "Library and Community Survey Institute Proceedings (65); "La Bibliotheque de la Cite Des Jeunes (64); Co-ed Inst on Automation in Large Libs 69. 13: Yes. 14: Col & U lib admin, educ for libnship. 15: Ecole de Bibliotheconomie Univ of Montreal CP 6128, Montreal 101 Que Can.

DENISON, BARBARA. b Cleveland 12 D 26. 5: Radcliffe 44-48 (Hist, Lit) BA; West Res 48-49 (Hist) MA; Katharine Gibbs Sch (NY) 49-50 Merit Certif; West Res 62-65 MS in LS. 7: Sec US Govt Wash DC 50-53; West Res U; Sec to dean Sch of Bus 53-55; Sec to dean Sch of Lib Sci 55-56, Research assoc Sch of Lib Sci 56-60, Admin asst Sch of Lib Sci 60-65, Research asst to dean Sch of Lib Sci 65-; Asst curator, SLA Loan Collection 56-63; Dir SLA Spec Clsf Center 63-66; Exec sec training progr in med libnship 67-. 8: Consul Lib Serv Br US Off of Educ 62. 10: Archaeol Inst of Amer; Cleveland Soc; Eng-Speaking Union US. 12: Managing ed "Encyclopedia of Librarianship and Documentation" (61-66) "Selected materials in Classification; A Bibliography (SLA 68). 13: Yes. 14: Theory of clsfn, lib educ. 15: 12700 Shaker blvd, Cleveland OH 44120.

DENMAN, (RUBY) OTHELLA. b Iola Tex 16 D 08. 5: Baylor 26-31 (Educ, Eng) BA; UTex summers 37-39 (Educ, Eng) MA; Tex Womans U summers 41, 42, 54 MS in LS. 7: Primary tchr Willow Hold Pub Sch, North Zulch Tex 30-31; Head Eng dept & lib Garden City High Sch, Garden City Tex 31-36; Head Eng dept & lib Elkhart High Sch, Elkhart Tex 36-38; Head Eng dept & lib La Vega High Sch, Bellmead Tex 38-42; Catlg asst Off for Emergency Mgt Lib, Wash C summer 43; Staff Waco Pub Lib, Waco Tex summers 43, 45: Head libn Waco High Sch, Waco Tex 42-. 8: Tchr of lib sci E Tex State Col summer 52; Tchr of lib sci Tex Womans U summers 58-60; Staff Mem Lib 21 Project Seattle Worlds Fair summer 62; Tchr of lib sci Baylor U (Waco) summer 65, evening div 66-67. 9: ALA (Coun 55-57);-AASchL (chm & mem 2 coms 57-62);-LAD (Com 57-63);-YASD (Asia Proj 60-62); SWLA (Exec Bd 57-61, Scholarship Com 58-59); TexLA (var offs & com 54-69); TexASchL (sec 48-49, treas 68-69). 10: Delta Kappa Gamma; AAUW; NEA; Tex State Tchrs Assn; Tex Classroom Tchrs ssn; Wac Classroom Tchrs Assn; Waco Lib Club; Beta Phi Mu. 11: John Cotton Dana Publicity Award for Waco Hish Sch Lib Scrapbook 56. 12:"Librarianship as Revealed in Teen Age Fiction (54); Consul for "Junior Libraries (now "School Library Journal) 54-63. 13: Yes. 14: High sch libs. 15: 2912 Fort ave, Waco TX 76707.

DENNEY, JESSIE (LAWRENCE). b Toccoa Ga 16 F 12. 5: UGa 32-35 (Eng) AB; Emory 35-36 BS in LS; Auburn 63 (Elem Educ) 6th yr State Certif. 6: Fr, Lat. 7: Libn Atlanta Carnegie System, Atalana 36-42; Jr high sch tchr Heard Co, Franklin Ga 49-52; Jr high sch tchr & libn Troup Co, La Grange Ga 54-. 8: Dir of 4th Dist, ACE 4 yrs Troup Co 4-H

Adviser 54-69. 9: NEA; ACE; GAEA TennEA; Troup Co EA. 10: Delta Kappa Gamma. 15: Box 185, Franklin GA 30217.

DENNIN, MARJORIE CATHERINE (WILKINS). b Barnesville Ohio 5 O 18. 4: John H Dennin. 5: Mt Union Col 36-40 (Eng) AB; Ohio State U summers 42 0(Educ); Catholic U 60-64 MS in LS, 69 (Educ Tech). 6: Fr. 7: Tchr pub schs, Pierpont Ohio 40-42; Tchr pub schs, Dover Ohio 42-44; Recreation dir Amer Red Cross, India & China 44-46; Libn Edison Electric Inst, NYC 46-56; Libn Amer Automobile Assn, Wash DC 60-64; Catlg libn Va Theol Sem 64-65; Libn No Va Tech Col 65-66; Coord of lib serv, No Va Commun Col 66-68, Dir of learning resources 69-. 9: SLA; VaLA; DCLA. 10: CathU alum LA. 14: Media ctr mgt. 15: 4320 Old Dominion dr, Arlington Va 22007.

DENNIS, (ANNA) EUNICE. b Campbell Tex 18 Ag 06. 5: Tex Womans U 24-26; So Methodist U 26-28 (Eng) AB; UTenn 36-39 (Eng) MA; ETex State U summers 44-51 BSLS. 6: Fr. 7: Eng tchr Nacogdoches High Sch, Nacogdoches Tex 28-44; Asst libn UTex Med Br (Galvesto) 44-50; Asst libn UTex Southwestern Med Sch (Dallas) 50-68; Hd ref libn E Tex State U 68-. 9: ALA; TexLA. 10: AAUW; Phi Kappa Phi. 14: Circ, ref. 15: E Texas State Univ, Commerce TX 75428.

DENNIS, DAMRON (STATON). b Grand Saline Tex 2 N 18. 5: Tex State Col for Women 36-39 (Home Econ) BS; N Tex State Tchrs Col summer 37; UTex summer 42; Tex Woman's U 60-62 MLS. 7: Tchr Texline High Sch, Texline Tex 39-40; Dir NYA resident center, Terrell Tex summer 40; Dept head homemaking Allan Jr High Sch, Austin Tex 40-45; Supt Texline Pub Schs, Texline Tex 45-46; Tchr Klein High Sch, Klein Mont 51; Tchr Musselshell High Sch, Musselshell Mont 56-57; Interlib loan & document libn Tex Womans U 62-68; Ser libn U Tex SWest Med Sch 68-. 9: ALA; SWLA; TexLA; Dallas CLA. 10: Alpha Beta Alpha. 14: Ser, govt docs. 15: 2729 Milton, Dallas TX 75205.

DENNIS, DONALD D. b Paris France 21 D 28. 4: Mary Lou Hartig. 5: Bowdoin Col 47-51 (Eng) BA; UCal 55-56 (Hist) BA, 56-57 MLS. 6: Fr, Ger. 7: Communications off (Lt jg) US Navy 51-55; Asst br lib, asst soc sci & hist dept, asst pub documents dept Free Lib of Phila 57-60; Head of ser dept Drexel Inst 60-62; Head Libn Cedar Crest Col 62-. 9: ALA; SLA; ADI; PennLA. 10: AAUP. 12: "Simplifying Work in Small Public Libraries (65). 13: Yes. 14: Admin, lib bldgs, wk simplif. 15: 34 Trexler rd, Schnecksville Pa 18078.

DENNIS, GLADYS (MEECE). b Tonkawa Okla 12 F 15. 5: OklaU 35-38 (Eng, LS) BA, summers 62-67 MLS. 7: Tchr-libn Perry High Sch, Perry Okla 38-40; Tchr Winfield Pub Sch, Winfield Kan 60-62; Lib catlgr Southwestern Col 62-66; Lib catlgr NEast State Col, Tahlequah Okla 66-. 14: Catlg, clsf. 15: 611 Victor, Tahlequah Ok 74464.

DENNIS, MARGARET LINN. b Foochow China 17 Mr 17. 5: Allegheny Col 35-39 (Fr) BA; Syracuse 39-40 BSLS. 7: Libn Harding High Sch, Marion Ohio 40-42; Asst circ libn UKan 42-43, Period libn 43-44; Denver Pub Lib; Ref asst 44-51, 1st asst Ref Dept 51-53, Act 1st asst Sci & Engnr Dept 53); Asst ref libn Lehigh U 53-54, Ref libn 54-68, Asst libn Reader's Serv 68-. 14: Ref. 15: 530 High st, apt 5, Bethlehem PA 18018.

DENNIS, RAMONA JUNE. b Woodward Okla 19 F 44. 5: Okla Col for Women 62-63; SWest State Col 63; NWest State Col 64-66 (LS) BS. 7: Stud asst NWest State Col, Alva Okla 64-65, Asst libn 65-66; Sch libn Seiling Pub, Seiling Okla 66-. 8: Trustee Seiling Pub Lib Bd; Sec Seiling Pub Lib. 9: NEA; OklaLA; OklaEA. 10: Kappa Kappa Iota. 13: Yes. 14: Pub sch. 15: Seiling Ok 73663.

DENNIS, WILLARD KELSO. b Odebolt Iowa 21 Ap 16. 4: . 5: Southwest Mo STATE Col 34-37 (Hist) AB, UIll 38-39 BS in LS. 7: Tchr Stockton (M0) High Sch 37-38; Asst adult educ Ill State Lib 39-40; Libn Parks Air Col 40-45; Libn Beech Aircraft Corp, Wichita Kan 45-47; Libn Southwest Reg Lib, Bolivar Mo 47-63; Dir of Libs Kan City (Kan) Pub Lib 63-. 8: Consul to Manhattan (Kan) Pub Lib 64; Mo Libs Planning Commsn 3-54; Kan Lib Survey Com 63-; Adv Com Metro Lib Survey. 9: ALA-RTSD (Proc Com 60-); Mo Libs Film Coop (dir 52-63, sec-treas 54-63); KanLA; MoL (pres 54, chm Legis Com 55); NCET; KanSchLA. 10: Jr Col Com; Civic Arts Coun; Kiwanis Club; Commun Studies, Inc; SWMoLib Serv, Inc. 13: Yes. 14: Admin, tech serv. 15: 625 Minnesota ave, Kansas City KS 66101.

DENNIS, WILLYE F(RANK). b Jacksonville Fla 14 Mr 26. 4: Leo Dennis. 5: Walkers Col 44-45 (Bus) Diploma; Edward Waters Col 50-51 (Bus Admin); Clark Col 51-52, 52-53 (Bus Admin) BA; Atlanta 54 MSLS. 7: Libn Edward Waters Col 55-61; Jr libn Wilder Park Br Jacksonville (Fla) Pub Lib 58-61; Br Libn Eastside Br 61-. 68; Br libn Northside Br 68-. 8: Dir, Deltas Proj Headstart summer 65. 9: FlaLA; SELA. 10: Jacksonville Pub Lib Staff Assn; Delta Sigma Theta; YWCA; West Union Baptist Church (dir of youth activities); LWV. 11: Awards for commun serv from Johnson Branch, YMCA; Chi Eta Phi. 14: Child wk, adult educ. 15: 3111 Woodlawn rd, Jacksonville FL 32209.

DENNY, MRS FREDERICK M (ALEXANDRA IVANOFF). b Elizabeth NJ 2 N 39. 4: Frederick M Denny. 5: Col of William & Mary 57-61 (Eng) BA; Simmons 61-62 MS in LS. 7: Typist US Govt Pentagon Br. Wash DC summer 57; Pub rel Nat State Bank, Westfield NJ summer 58; Lib asst Mem Lib, Westfiel NJ summer 59; Stud lib asst Col of William & Mary 59-60; Lib asst Simmons Col 61-62; Br libn Newton Free Lib, Newton Mass 62-64; Asst ref libn NH State Lib 64-66; Ref libn Colby Jr Col 66-67; Circ libn Oriental Inst Lib UChicago 67-69. 9: ALA; NELA. 13: Yes. 14: Adult serv. 15: 7751 S Clyde ave, Chicago Il 60649.

DENNY, MARY HARLINE (KNOX). b Clarendon Tex 6 N 24. Lowell Otis Denny. 5: Clarendon Jr Col 42-44; Tex Womans U summers 44, 45, 65; St Michaels Col 57-59 (Secondary Educ) BA; UNM 62; Adams State Col summer 63 Texas Woman's U 68 MLS. 6: Sp. 7: Tchr Vega Hish Sch, Vega Tex 44-45; Tchr Skellytown Elem Sch, Whitedeer Tex 45-46; Sub tchr, Santa Fe, Rio Arriba & Los Alamos Counties 50-57, 58-61; Tchr Alcalde Elem, McCurdy Schs, Santa Cruz NM 57-58; Libn Espanola Jr High Sch, Espanola MN 61-. 9: NEA; ALA; NMEA; NMLA (sec Child YP & Sch Libs Sect 65); Espanola EA. 10: PTA. 14: Sch libs. 15: Box 62, Santa Cruz NM 87567.

DeNOBLE, AUGUSTINE (DONALD JOSEPH) (REV). b Hartford Wis 25 O 25. 5: Mt Angel Sem 46-52 (Philos) BA; Mt Angel Sem Sch of Theol 52-56 (Theol); Mt Angel Sem 58-59 (Fr); UWash summers 58-63 (Libnship) MA. 6: Lat. 7: Libn Mt Angel Prep, St Benedict Ore 56-57; Lib wk tchr of Lat, mod prob 57-59; Libn 59-60; Lib wk tchr Lat World Hist Relig Mt Angel Sem High Sch 59-64; Libn John F Kennedy High Sch, Mt Angel Ore 64-65; Libn tchr of Lat Mt Angel Sem 65-67; Asst libn & ref Mt Angel Abbey Lib 67-. 9: ALA; OreLA. 14: Ref, catlg. 15: Mt Angel Abbey, St Benedict Or 97373.

DENSKY, MARGUERITE (HUEBSCH). b Bratislava Czechoslovakia 29 Ap 09. 4: Paul Densky. 5: UComenius (Bratislava 31 MA, 32 Dr phil; U Geneve (Switzerland) 49 Dipl LSc. 6: Fr, Eng, Czech, Ger, Hungarian. 7: Circ & ref libn UN; Geneva 49-51; Catlgr MCGill Med Lib 53-56; Catlgr Redpath Lib McGill U 57; Dept head ref UMontreal 57-64, Chief Libn 64-68; Prof, Ecole de Bibliog 68-. 9: CanLA; Association cannadienne des bibliothecaires de langue francaise; QueLA. 14: Ref, bibliog, libr admin, lib educ. 15: 45 Courcelette ave, Montreal Can.

DENSON, ROBERTA FINDER. b Jersey City NJ 4 N 24. 5: Asst libn Interchem Corp, NYC 47-51; Head libn Interchem Corp, Clifton NJ 58-67; Hd libn J P Stevens & Co Inc 67-. 9: ACS; SLA. 14: Lit searching, abstracting, indexing, ref, central files. 15: 478 Maywood ave, Maywood NJ 07607.

DENTON, ALICE DEATHERAGE. b Denver Colo 12 Je 25. 4: Jesse Cameron Denton. 5: Swarthmore 43-47 (Humanities) BA; Tex Woman's U 64-67 MLS. 7: Ref libn Dallas Pub Lib science & ind dept Tex 67-68; Ref libn US Geol Survey Lib, Wash DC 68-. 9: ALA. 14: Ref, pub relations, pub. 15: US Geological Survey Library, Washington DC 20242.

DENTON, ELEANOR (OMER). b Evanston Ill 23 Ag 10. 4: Clark Wells Denton. 5: Carthage Col 27-31 (Chem) AB; UNeb 31-36 (Chem) MS, PhD; UIll 38-39 BLS. 6: Ger, Fr. 7: Libn research & development div Wyandotte Chem Corp, Wyandotte Mich 39-46, 48-. 9: ACS; SLA; Sci Res Soc Amer. 10: Bus & Prof Womens Club. 14: Ref, chem lit. 15: 645 Emmons blvd, Wyandotte Mich 48192.

DENTON, PATRICIA (HARTLEY). b Newark NJ 13 Ja 41. 5: Syracuse 58-62 (Chem, LS) BA; Columbia summer 62 (LS); West Res 62-63 MS in LS. 6: Mala. 7: Libn Lederle Labs, Pearl River NY summer 62; Libn's asst Syracuse U 58-62; Tchr-libn Peace Corps Volunteer Clifford Secondary Sch, Kuala Kangsar Perak Malaysia 63-66; Ref Libn Bell Tel Labs, Naperville Ill 66-67; NASA Electronics Res Ctr 67-. 10: Beta Phi Mu. 14: Infor retrieval. 15: co R A Denton, Box 04, Marlton NJ 08053.

DENTON, SUE ROBERTSON. b Onancock Va 30 My 15. 4: C. Hoyt Denton. 5: Wellesley 33-37 (Math) AB; Drexel BS in LS. 7: Libn Ellsworth High Sc, Ellsworth Penn 38-40; Libn Sparrows Point High Sch, Sparrows Point Md 40-43; (Lt jg) Publs Off WAVES US Navy 44-46; (Civilian) Publs Off US Navy Dept 46-55; Libn US Naval Air Station, Chincoteague Va 55-59; Libn Tech Nat Aeronautics & Space Admin, Wallops Station Wallops Island Va 59-. 14: Catlg, ref, tech bks (space tech). 15: Rt 1, Box 346-A, Onancock Va 23417.

DENTON, WILLIAM RICHARD. b Seattle 17 Jl 29. 4: Margie McQuerry. 5: Whitworth Col 47-51 (Christian Educ) BA; San Francisco Theol Sem 51-55 (Christian Educ) BD, MA; USoCal 59-63 MS in LS. 7: Minister of Educ St Johns Presbyterian Church, Reno Nev 54-57; Minister of Educ First Presbyterian Church Oakland Cal 57-59; Acquis libn Sch of Theol at Claremont (Claremont Cal) 59-. 9: ATheolLA; West Theol LA (pres 66-67); Christian LA (So Cal pres 64-66). 10: Amer Guild of Eng Handbell Ringers; Amer Bell Assn. 12: "Bells and Their Use as a Means of Christian Education" (61); Ed "Union List of Continuations". 14: Acquis, periodicals, computers & the lib. 15: 352 S Annapolis dr, Claremont Ca 91711.

DENUES, ELIZABETH H(AY). b Somerset Penn 13 Je 02. 5: Hood Col 20-25 (Hist) AB; Drexel 25-26 BS in LS. 7: Circ desk Lehigh U Lib 26-37; Engnr libn John Hopkins U 47-54; Bibliog tech lib Ft Detrick, Frederick Md 54-59, Ref 59-. 9: ALA. 10: AAUW; Frederick Mem Hosp Auxiliary; Hood Col Alumnae Assn. 14: Ref. 15: Watkins Acres-9E, Frederick Md 21701.

DEODENE, FRANK XAVIER. b Brooklyn Ny 14 Jl 34. 4: Carolyn Jupenlaz. 5: Drew U 52-56 (Hist) AB; Columbiz 58-59 MSLS. 7: Asst in circ & ref dept Drew U Lib 58-59; Asst in educ & rel dept Pub Lib of Cincinnati 59-60, Asst in sci & ind dept 61; Dire Lebanon Community Lib, Lebanon Penn 61-65; Dir Chatha Pub Lib, Chatham NJ 66-. 9: ALA; BSA: Private Lib Assn (Gt Brit); PennLA. 10: ACLU; Bk Club of Cal. 11: Joseph Towne Wheeler Award. 15: 38 Maple st, Chatham NJ 07928.

DePASS, ALICE (PRIOLEAU). b Columbia SC 9 D 09. 4: Harry Elliott DePass Jr. 5: Winthrop Col 27-28; USoCar 28-31 (Hist) AB; UNC 31-32 AB in LS. 7: Y-p libn Richland Co Pub Lib, Columbia SC 32-33; Sch libn Richland Co Pub, Columbia SC 45; Libn Park Hills Elem Sch, Spartanburg SC 54-65; Hd libn Spartanburg High Sch, Spartanburg SC 65-68; Ref libn Converse Col 68-. 8: Lecturer child lit Converse Col 62-; Instr LS Winthrop Col summer 64, 65; Asst Prof LS FurmanU summer 68. 9: ALA; SELA; SCLA. 10: Assn of Jr League of Amer; Nat Soc of Colonial Dames of Amer; Delta Delta Delta. 14: Ref, reader's adv, child lit, yp lit. 15: 104 Canterbury rd, Spartanburg SC 29302.

DEPIRO, PASQUALE S. b NYC 4 Ja 22. 4: Alma H D'Epiro. 5: Hunter Col 46-50 (Music) BA; U Denver 52-53 MALS; San Francisco State Col 61-63; Col of San Mateo 63-65. 6: Ital, Fr. 7: T/3 Internat Morse, Jap Intercept Operator US Army Signal Corps, Southwest Pacific 43-46; Catlgr Brooklyn Pub Lib 53-55; Ref libn Newark Pub Lib, Newark NJ 56-59; Catlgr Inst of Aero/Space Sci, NYC 55-59; Indexer applied sci & tech H W Wilson Co. NYC 59-61; Catlgr & ref libn Polytech Inst (Brooklyn) 59-61; Ref & a-v libn Col of San Mateo 6-. 9: Cal Tchrs Assn; CalLA; CalASchL. 14: A-v, music, catlg. 15: 1202 Cobb st, San Mateo CA 94401.

DEPLAZES, SISTER EDWARD SCL. b Helena Mont 25 Je 06. 5: UKan 28-32 (Romance lang) AB, 34-37 (Romance lang) MA; UDenver 38-40 MS in LS; UChicago 50-52 (Libnship). 6: Fr, Sp. 7: Tchr Ward High Sch, Kan City Kan 30-37; Tchr Immaculata High Sch, Leavenworth Kan 38-40; Libn Ward High Sch, Kan City Kan 40-44; Tchr Girls Central High Sch, Butte Mont 44-45; Tchr Bishop Hogan High Sch, Kan C High Sch, Butte Mont 44-45; Tchr Bishop Hogan High Sch, Kan City Mo 45-50; St Mary Col, Xavier Kan: Acquis libn 52-53, Assoc libn 53-60; Libn Central Catholic High Sch, Billings Mont 60-66; Libn Hayden High Sch, Topeka Kan 66-. 8: Adv Sch Publ Ward Immaculata Hogan High Schs; Organ St Daniel the Prophet Parish Chicago 51; Lib consul Sacred Heart High Sch Falls City Neb 54; Lib consul St Vincent Hosp Sch of Nursing, Billings Mont 66. 9: CathLA (Adv Com 67-70, Adv Bd High Sch Lib Sect 69-70; chm Midwest Unit 67-70); ALA; MontLA; KanLA; KanSchLA. 10: Topeka Area Libns; Quill and Scoll. 12: Ed News and Views "Catholic Library World" (54-62). 14: Sch libnship. 15: Hayden High School 401 Gage blvd, Topeka Ks 66606.

DePROSPO, ERNEST R JR. b Worcester Mass 10 Ja 37. 4: Joyce R (Smith). 5: ClarkU 55-59 (Govt) BA; NortheasternU 59-61 (Pol Sci) MA; Penn StateU 61-67 (Pol Sci) PhD. 6: Sp. 7: Tchg fellow NortheasternU 59-61; Asst town mgr Wilmington Mass 61; Research analyist Penn StateU (State Col) 64-65; Research consul IPA/NY, Lima Peru 64-65; Instr & research assoc, Penn StateU 65-67; Assoc prof Grad Sch Lib Serv RutgersU 67-. 8: Lib consul (syst-admin); Consul on Lat Amer admin problems (also manpower & policy). 9: Amer Soc Pub Admin (Exec Com Latin Amer Devel Admin; chm Panel on Admin and Latin Amer Land Reform); Amer Pol Sci Assn; ALA; NJLA (Co-chm NJ Lib Devel Com). 10: AAUP. 12: Co-auth "Inter-local Cooperation: Laveron County Library" (64); "Emerging trends in State Departments of Administration" (62); Co-auth "Consolidation and Cooperation of Public Library Systems" (69). 13: Yes. 14: Admin, research methods and tech, planning lib serv. 15: 189 College ave, New Brunswick NJ 08903.

DEPTA, PAWEL JOZEF. b Bydgoszcz Poland 30 Jl 27. 5: Trinity Col 55-59 (Bus Admin) B Com, (Geog, Hist) BA; IndU (Bloomington) 61-63 (Govt) AM; Simmons 64-65 MSLS. 6: Ger, Polish, Russian, Czech, Fr. 7: Warsaw Poland: Hilfsarbeiter Frontreperaturbetrieb Junkers Verke 43-44, Vol Pol Underground Movement 43-44; RiflemanPol Home Army Warsaw Uprising 44; Germany: POW Stalag II B Falling bostel 44-45, Priv British Army of the Rhine 1st Pol Armoured Div 45-47; Dispatch rider Pol Resettlement Corps, GB 47-48; Clk J Lyons & Co Ltd, London GB 50-51; Sales rep Sparkstone Med Supplies, London GB 52-55; Dealer Rocky Mt Filter Queen Inc, Denver 60-61; Ref asst Widener Lib HarvardU 63-65, Ref libn Col Lib 65-. 8: Tchg fellow Dept of Govt IndU 62-63, Grad wk, Russ and East European Inst. 9: ALA. 10: Mass Republ State Com; POLISH Veterans of WWII; Polish Amer Citizens Assn; Irish Univs Grads; Polish Krakowiak Dancers of Boston; Intl Inst of Boston; Friends of Polish Cult. 11: British Ministry of Educ Scholarship, London 55-59; IndU Scholarship 61; Tchg asstship, I U 62-63; Ford Foundation Grant, I U 62; Orders and Decorations: Cross of AK (Polish Home Army); War Medal, British Army. 13: Yes. 14: Ref. 15: 320 Harvard st, Cambridge Ma 02139.

DERBYSHIRE, JOSEPH JENSEN. b Salt Lake City 29 Ag 32. 4: Glenda Bonneru. 5: UUtah 51-55 (Eng) BA, 55-59 (Eng) MA; UWash 61-63 (LS) ML. 6: Fr, Sp. 7: UUtah: Tchg asst 55-62, Circ libn 59-61, Ser libn 61-63; Tchg asst UWash 63; Asst Prof of Lib Sci UUtah 63; Acquis libn Bowdoin Col 64, Catlgr 64-67; Dir catlg 67-. 9: ALA (Recr Com Utah 62-63); -ACRL (Union List of Ser Com Utah 61-63); MeLA. 10: Beta Phi Mu; Demo Town Com. 12: "Book Selection; a Manual for Students (62); "Arrangement of the Dictionary Catalog at Bowdoin College Library (68). 14: Catlg, acquis, ser. 15: Bowdoin Col Lib, Brunswick Me 04011.

DERER, BOHUSLAV. b Czechoslovakia 16 Ag 24. 4: Suzanne Derer. 5: Law Sch U Bratislava 43-48 (Law) Dr Jur; Brussels U 48-51 Licencie en sciences politiques et diplomatiques; Toronto 53-54 BLS. 6: Slovak, Ger, Fr. 7: Libn Toronto Pub Lib 54-56; Bkmob libn N York Pub Lib, Willow Dale Cn 56-58, Head of bkmob div 58-61; Head of Downsview Reg Br Lib, N York Pub Lib Downsview Ont 61-65; Chief Libn E York Pub Lib, Toronto 65-. 9: CanLA (Com mem); OntLA (chm Circ Sect 64); Inst Prof Libns Ont. 10: Soc of Czechoslovak Artists & Scientists of Amer; Masaryk Mem Inst; Kiwanius. 14: Admin. 15: 94 Plateau Crescent, Don Mills Ont Can.

DERNBERGER, IRENE (JACKMAN). b Holland Vt 11 Je 34. 4: Robert F Dernberger. 5: Stephens Col 52-54 AA; UMich 54-56 (Elem Educ) BA, 67-69 (LS) MA. 6: Fr. 7: Elem tchr: Van Buren Twp Schs, Belleville Mich 56-58, Lexington Sch Syst, lexington Mass 58-60. 10: LWV; Beta Phi Mu. 14: Sch libs. 15: 10 Heatheridge, Ann Arbor Mi 48104.

DERNER, CAROL ANN (NIEDHAMMER). b Evansville Ind 12 My 34. 4: George B Derner. 5: Ind U 52-56 (Amer Lit) AB, 57-58 (LS) MA. 7: Bkmob libn Gary Pub Lib, Gary Ind 56-57; Child libn Bloomington Pub Lib, Bloomington Ind 58-59;Child libn Pub Libs of Lake Co, Crown Point Ind 59-60; High sch libn Valparaiso High Sch, Valparaiso Ind 60-63; Gary Pub Lib, Gary Ind: Young adult libn 63-64, Head popular lib dept 64; Head ext dept 64-67; Hd libn Elmwood Pk Pub Lib Elmwood Pk Ill 68-. 8: Staff, Lib 21 Seattle Worlds Fair 62. 9: ALA-CSD;-YASD;-PLA; IllLA. 10: Beta Phi Mu; LWV. 13: Yes. 14: Child wk, admin. 15: 2439 N 77th ave, Elmwood Park IL 60635.

DERRICK, (MILDRED) NAOMI. b Chapin SC 17 F 09. 5: USC 28-32 (Eng) AB in Ed, summers 37-40 Lib Sch Certif;

Emory summers 44-49 BALS; USC summer 55 (L) USC Lib NDEA Inst summer 67. 7: Tchr Brookland Grammar Sch, West Columbiz SC 33-34; Tchr Chapin Grammar Sch, Chapin SC 34-40; Eng tchr-libn Inman High Sch, Inman SC 40-42; Eng tchr-libn Macon High Sch, Franklin NC 42; Tchr Chapin Grammar Sch, Chapin SC 43; Libn Chicora High Sch, Charleston Heights SC 43-59; Libn Gordon H Garrett High Sch, Charleston Heights SC 59-. 9: ALA; NEA; SELA; SCLA (pres 50); SCLA; SCEA; Charleston County EA. 11: Teacher of the Year Charleston CountySC 62. 14: . 15: Gordon H Garrett Hish Sch, Charleston Heights SC 29405.

DERRICK, WAYNE EUGENE. b Puyallup Wash 20 Jl 23. 4: Anya Sergeevna Derrick. 5: UWash seattle 46-62 (Fr) BA, 65-66 MLS; Sorbonne 48-49 (Fr Lit) Certif; UVienna 51-52 (Ger, russian), Standard Fr tchg certif. 6: Fr, Ger, Russian. 7: Admin off US For Serv, Indo-China, Hanoi 45; Supv br libs Boeing Com Airplane Div, Renton Wash; Educ libn Penn StateU. 9: ALA; SLA (Planning Com, Seattle); PennLA. 10: Boy Scouts. 14: Lib planning & facilities, acquis. 15: 445 Waupelani dr M-16, State College Pa 16801.

DERRICKSON, (MABEL) WINIFRED (COX). b Gentry Ark 11 F 16. 4: Howard Sickel Derrickson. 5: Central State Tchrs (Edmond Okla) 33-35; Okla City U 35-36; UOkla 36-37 BA in LS; Central State Tchrs (Edmond Okla) summer 37 Tchrs Certif UMo S L summer 68 Life Tchrs Certif. 7: Libn High Sch, Pryor Okla 37-38; Libn Pub Lib, Seminole Okla 38-41; Libn Pub Lib, Wewoka Okla 41-44; Air base libn US Govt Richmond Fla 44-45; 7th Naval Dist libn US Govt, Miami 45; Asst head dept Washington U (St Louis) 46-47; Libn St Louis Country Day Sch, St Louis 58-. 9: MoLA; Greater St Louis Lib Club (treas 63-66, pres 66-67, Coun 67-68). 13: Yes. 14: Admin. 15: 6312 Pershing ave, St Louis MO 63130.

DERRICKSON, NANCY LOUISE (ESHELMAN). b Lancaster Penn 21 Ap 37. 4: John A Derrickson. 5: Millersville State Col 55-59 (LS) BS; Ariz State U 62-66 (Eng) MA. 6: Lat, Sp, Ger. 7: Libn Del Rio High Sch, Del Rio Tex 59-60; Hd libn Ernest Harmon AFB Schs, Newfoundland 61-62; Elem lib coord Lancaster City Schs, Penn 62-63; Libn (catlgr & adult serv) Phoenix Pub Lib 63-64; Hd libn Tempe High Sch, Tempe Ariz 64-67; Humanities libn & rare bks curator San Antonio Col, San Antonio Tex 67-. 8: Lib consul to Val verde Co Lib 59; North Central Assn eval com Ap 67. 9: NCTE (Com on compar & world lit 69-70); ArizStateLA (Memb Chm 65-67, Second Sch Libs Chm 64-67, Prog Chm for Sch Libs Div 66-67, Nat Lib Week Com 63-67); TexLA; Tex Jr Col Assn. 10: English Club of San Antonio; Friends of the Lib, Tempe Ariz. 13: Yes. 14: Ref, rare bks, tchg. 15: 202 Bergstrom ct, San Antonio Tx 78236.

DERTIEN, JAMES (LeROY). b Kearney Neb 14 D 42. 5: USDak 61-65 (LS, Eng) AB; UPittsburgh 65-66 (Libnship) MLS. 6: Chinese. 7: Hd libn Carnegie Lib Mitchell SDak 66-67; Hd libn Sioux Falls Col 67-. 8: Mem Finance Com, Bibliog Ctr for Research, Denver; Exec dir Nat Lib Week, SD, 69. 9: ALA; SDLA; MPLA. 10: Beta Phi Mu; AAUP. 14: Admin, bibliog. 15: 2613 S Blauvett ave, Sioux Falls SD 57105.

DES BRISAY, GEOFFREY REX. b Vancouver BC Can 26 O 28. 5: UBC 47-50 (Fr, Eng) BA, 50-51 (Educ) Secondary Sch Tchg Certif; UWash 55-56 (LS) MS. 6: Fr. 7: Tchr Vancouver Sch Bd, Vancouver BC 53-55; Libn Puget Sound Jr High Sch, Highline Sch Dist Seattle 56-57; Ref libn lang & lit div Vancouver Pub Lib, Vancouver BC 57-58, Libn Dunbar Br 58-59, Deputy head acquis div 59-62, Head acquis div 62-65, Head catlg div 65: CHIEF Libn Burnaby Pub Lib, Burnaby BC 65-. 9: CanLA; ALA; BCLA (bus mgr "BC Library Quarterly" 58-62; treas 62-64); Pacific NWLA (com), BC rep to PNLA (65-); Assoc of BC Libs (treas 66-67, pres 67-68). 10: Beta Phi Mu. 14: Catlg, acquis, ref, readers advis, bk sel, admin. 15: 7052 Linden ave, Burnaby 1 BC Can.

DES CHENE, DORICE MARIE (ANDERSON). b Warren Minn. 4: Raymond J Des Chene. 5: Gustavus Adolphus Col 39-41 (Pre-Med Tech); UMinn 41-43 (Med Tech) BS; UCincinnati Evening Col 57-59 (LS); UWash 66-67 (Libnship) ML. 6: Ger, Swedish. 7: Med technologist: Child Hosp, Pittsburgh Penn 43-44, Manhattan Proj, Oak Ridge Tenn 44-45, Warren Hosp, Warren Minn 45-46, St Mary's Hosp, Minneapolis Minn 45-46; Chief technician hematology St John's Hosp, Springfield Ill 47-49; Med Technologist Decatur & Macon Co Hosp, Decatur Ill 51-53; Chief Technician Holmes Hosp, Cincinnati 54-55, 57,59; Research libn Wm S Merrell Co, Cincinnati 59-60; Electron Microscopy Technician UND 64-65; MEDLARS Search Analyst UWash 68-. 9: MedLA; SLA. 14: Bibliog, info sci. 15: 2520 166th ave SE, Bellevue Wa 98004.

DES JARDINS, MARY (RASMUSSEN). b Eagle Grove Iowa 21 J 28. 5: U No Iowa 46-48, 63-65 (LS) BA. 7: Tchr Goldfield Pub Sch, Goldfield Ia 48-49; Asst libn Kendall Young Lib, Webster City Ia 49-52; Asst catlgr Albuquerque Pub Lib, NM 54-55; Asst libn Roy J Wasson High Sch, Colorado Springs 58-61; Libn NE Hamilton Sch, Blairsburg Ia 65-. 9: NEA; ALA; Iowa State EA; NE Hamilton EA (treas). 10: Delta Kappa Gamma; Kappa Delta Pi; Women's Club. 14: Sch libs. 15: 1102 Bank st, Webster City Ia 50595.

DESAUTELS, SISTER MARIE NOE SSA (NORA). b Greenfield Mass 25 Ap 01. 5: Catholic Tchrs Col 46 (Educ) BS in Ed; Boston Col 49 (Educ) MEd; Anna Maria Col 60 (LS); Accredited by Mass Educ Dept for Lib Sci 63. 6: Fr. 7: Tchr Sisters of St Anne, Mass, RI & NY: Elem sch 24-54, Jr & sr high 54-56, Col 56-60; High sch libn Sisters of St Anne, Marlboro Mass 60-. 9: ALA; CathLA (Reg Adv Bd 69-73); NELA. 15: 22 Broad st, Marlboro Ma 01752.

DESHAIES, (BLANCHE) LOUISE THOMPSON. b Raleigh NC 13 Ap 20. 5: Peace Jr Col 36-38; Meredith Col 38-40 (Eng) AB; UNC 63-66 (LS) MS. 6: Fr, Sp, Ger, Russian. 7: Tchr Chatham Co Schs, Bells NC 41-44; Asst lab tech NC State Lab of Hygiene, Raleigh NC 44-46; Museum asst RISD Mus of Art, Providence RI 46-48; Lib asst Ind U Lib, Bloomington Ind 51-4; Tchr Sampson Co Sch, Clinton NC 54-56; Tchr Wake Co Sch, apex NC 56-59; Lib asst NC State U Lib 59-63; Lib asst UNC Lib, Chapel Hill 63-66, Hd desc cat unit UNC Lib 66-. 9: ALA; NCLA; SELA. 10: Beta Phi Mu; UNC Sch of Lib sci Alum Assn; UNC Lib Staff Assn; NCSU Lib Staff Assn; Friends if the Chapel Hill Pub Lib. 14: Catlg. 15: 125 Hamilton rd, Chapel Hill NC 27514.

DESHPANDE, GANGADHAR RAGHUNATH. b Wai Dist Satara India 29 Mr 33. 4: Nisha Uttara kelkar. 5: Fergusson Col (Poona) 49-52; BombayU Lib 55-57 Diploma in Libnship; Kirti Col (Bombay) 60-62 BA. 6: Marathi, Hindi, Sanskrit. 7: Libn D E Society's Bonbay Col 54-57; Libn Technical Lib Air-India, Bombay airport 57-63; Asst libn British Coun, Bombay 63-65, 66-67; Intern libn Croydon Pub Libs, Croydon England 65-66; Asst ref libn Sudbury Pub Libs, Sudbury Ont Can 67-69; Ref libn Chinguacousy Pub Lib, Bramalea Ont Can 69-. 8: Tchr lib admin MaharashtraLA, Poona India 64-65. 9: OntLA. 10: Sudbury & Dist Citizenship Coun; India-Can Assn. 13: Yes. 14: Ref wk. 15: 501 Balmoral dr apt 207, Bramalea Ont Can.

DESJARDINS, ALVINA A. b Cheyenna Wyo. 5: Colo StateU 35-39 (Sociol) BS; UColo summers 47, 48, 54; UDenver 56-57 (LS) MA. 6: Fr, Sp. 7: Rural & high schs in Colo & Wyo 40-44; Tchr Kimball Co High Sch, Kimball Neb 40-53; Torrington High Sch, Torrington Wyo 53-56; Catlgr Univ Lib Colo StateU 57-. 8: Tchr libnship ColoStateU summers 59, 61; Wkshop on catlg & clsf sponsored by Colo State Lib summer 62. 9: ALA; Mt PlainsLA; ColoLA. 10: Nat Fed of Bus & Prof Women; AAUW; Phi Kappa Phi. 14: Catlg. 15: 431 N Whitcomb st, Fort Collins Co 80521.

DESMARIAS, LILLIAN. b Grundy Center Iowa 7 Ag 13. 5: Cornell Col 31-33; U Iowa 33-35 (Com) BS; UDenver 50-51 (LS) MA. 7: Asst catlgr Drake U 51-53; A-v & order libn Jackson Co Lib, Independence Mo 53-55; Asst libn Boonslick Reg Lib, Sedalia Mo 55-57; Demonstration libn Mo State Lib Demon Area, Warren Franklin & Gasconade Cos Mo 57-58; Reg libn Little Dixie Reg Lib, Moberly Mo 58-62; Admin libn Northeast Mo Lib Serv, Kahoka Mo 62-. 9: ALA; MoLA. 10: Bus & Prof Women. 15: Kahoka Mo 63445.

DESMOND, JOSEPH PAUL. b Buffalo NY 18 F 07. 5: Canisius 24-28 (Eng) BA; Harvard 28-30 (Eng) MA; UMich 35-37 ABLS. 6: Fr. 7: Assoc libn Canisius Col 34-42; Major USA Transportation Corps, US, Britain, France 42-46; Partner Desmond & Stapleton, Buffalo NY 46-50; Cornell Aeronautical Lab, Buffalo NY: Contract admin 50-55, Hd libn 55-. 8: Consul NY Educ Dept; mem NY State Commsnr of Educ's Com on Lib Devel 67-. 9: ALA; SLA; West NY Lib Res Coun (pres 67, 68). 10: Bd Buffalo & Erie Co Lib 51-58; Cnisius Col Alum Assn. 14: Ref, indexing, abstracting. 15: 68 Colonial Cir, Buffalo NY 14213.

DESMOND, WINIFRED (FRICK). b New Orleans 14 My 04: Robert D Desmond. 26. 4: Robert D Desmond. 5: Tulane 49-54 (Foreign Langs) BA; LSU 57-59 MS in LS; Amer U 63-. 7: Ref libn sci & tech div LSU 59; Intern LC 59-60, Ref libn sci & tech div 60-62; Referral spec Nat Referral Center LC 62-63; Ref libn sci & tech div LC 63-64; Asst Chief ref sect Clearinghouse for Fed Sci & Tech Info, Springfield Va 64-66; Chief Ref Unit Sci & Tech Div LC 66-67; Chief libn Nat Highway Safety Bur, Wash DC 67-. 8: Library/USA NY

Worlds Fair 65; Mem, COSATI Panel 2, Info Scis Tech 67-68. 9: SLA; ala; ASIS. 12: Comp: "Worldwide Census of Scientific and Technical Serials, in American Documentation (63); "Classification and Indexing: A Selected Bibliography (64). 14: Ref, admin. 15: 324 M st SW, Washington DC 20024.

DESOER, JACQUELINE (JOHNSON). b Barranquilla Colombia SA 13 Mr 31. 4: Charles A Desoer. 5: McGill 49-52 (Bacteriology) BS; Case West Res 61-62 MSLS. Bacteriologist Sunnybrook Veterans Hosp, Toronto Can 52-54; Ref libn Imperial Oil Ltd, Toronto Can 55-61; Ref libn Engring Lib ColumbiaU 62-64, Asst engring libn 64-65; Ref libn Standard Oil Co of Cal, San Francisco 65-. 9: SLA; ALA. 10: Sierra Club. 14: Ref. 15: 2589 Hilgard ave, Berkeley Ca 94709.

DESROCHERS, EDMOND ERNEST SJ. b Boston 12 S 16. 5: UMontreal 42 (Fr) BA; Immaculate Conception 42 (Philos) Licence, 47 (Theol) Licence; Columbia 51 MLS. 6: Fr. 7: Chief Libn Maison Bellarmin (Montreal) 51-. 8: Part-time tchr UMontreal Lib Sch 52-55, & 61-69; Pres, Que Pub Lib Commsn 65-66. 9: Association canadienne des Bibliothecaires de langue francaise (pres 53-54); CanLA (pres 63-64); CanALS (pres 67-68). 12: "Programme Pour Une Bibliotheque Collegiale (61). 13: Yes. 14: Lib sci tchg, sch libnship. 15: 25 Que St Rue Jarry, Montreal 351 Can.

DESROCHES, JEAN-GUY. b St-Michel-Des-Saints Que Can 25 F 34. 4: Evangeline Landry. 5: Sem de Joliette 46-53 BA; UMontreal 53-55 (Philos) BPh, 60-62 BLS. 6: Fr. 7: Libn Central Lib Serv Dept of Educ, Fredericton NB Can 62-65; Documentalist Service des Bibliotheques publiques Ministere des Affaires culturelles, Que Can 65-. 8: Consul for Unesco, Phnom-Penh Cambodia 68. 9: Association canadienne des bibliothecaires de langue francaise. 15: 1407 des Pionniers, St Nicholas Cte Levis Que Can.

DESROCHES, JEANNETTE. b Montreal Can 29 S 39. 5: Ecole Normale Cardinal Leger 60 Bacc en pedagogie; Col Sainte-Marie 66 Bacc es arts; UMontreal 68 Bacc en bibliotheconomie. 6: Fr. 7: Enseignement Comm Ecoles Catholiques de Montreal 60-66; Bibliothecaire USherbrooke 68-. 9: Assn Canadienne des bibliothecaires de langue francaise; ABQ. 13: Yes. 14: Ref. 15: 1450 Laterriere 16, Sherbrooke P Que Can.

DESROSIERS, JEANNE MARIE. b Providence 9 My 38. 5: Goucher 56-60 (Hist) AB; Radcliffe Inst of Hist & Archival Mgt summer 60 Certif; Drexel 64-65 MS LS. 6: Fr. 7: Serv rep N E Tel & Tel Co, Boston 60-62; Jr asst high sch br Brookline (Mass) Pub Lib 62-63; Dir Gladwyne Free Lib, Gladwyne Penn 65-. 9: PennLA. 10: Longwood (Mass) Cricket Club. 14: Readers adv serv, yp, bk sel. 15: 275 Bryn Mawr ave, Bryn Mawr PA 19010.

DETLOFF, VIRGINIA (ALLAN). Port Chester NY 27 Jl 18. 4: Dr Wayne K Detloff. 5: Barnard 35-39 (Hist) BA; Syracuse 40-41 BLS; Columbia summer 42 (Med Ref). 6: Fr. 7: Libn Rye Sch, Rye NY 41-42; (Lt) WAVES, NYC 42-46; Ref asst Columbia U Sch Physicians & Surgeons 46-47; Libn Frederick Burke Sch, San Francisco 47-48; Head libn State Dept Pub Health, San Francisco 48-50; Head libn UArk Med Center 56-60; Ref asst UCal Med Center (San Francisco) 60-61; Med bibliog (private) 65-. 9: MedLA. 12: "Utilization of Health Facilities and Services, 1950-63; An annotated selected bibliography" (64). 14: Med ref, bibliog. 15: 8155 Terrace dr, El Cerrito Ca 94530.

DeTOMA, JANICE (BOWLES). b Worcester Mass 19 Ap 40. 4: Francis James De Toma. 5: Clark U 58-62 (Sociol) AB; Simmons 62-63 (LS) MS. 6: Fr, Ger. 7: Ref libn Worcester Pub Lib, Worcester Mass 62-63, Yp libn 62-63; Geog & geophysical sci libn UChicago 64-68; Asst lib Babson Inst of Bus Admin, Babson Park Mass 68-. 9: ALA; NELA. 10: Simmons Col Grad Alumni Coun; Babson Inst Women's Club. 13: Yes. 14: Bk sel, admin, catlg. 15: 56A Charlesbank way, Waltham MA 02154.

DeTONNANCOUR, ROGER G. b Fall River Mass 22 My 26. 4: Mary Fenno. 5: Providence 48-52 (Letters) AB; Simmons 52-53 (LS) MS. 6: Fr, Sp, Portu. 7: Communications US Navy 43-46; Adm asst Latin Amer Exp Co, NYC & South America 46-48; Lumberman Weyerhaeuser, Northeast 48-50; Fisherman, New England 50-51; Psychiatric aide Taunton (Mass) State Hosp 51-52; Gen asst Enoch Pratt Free Lib, Baltimore 53-54; Chief libn Armco Steel Corp, Baltimore 54-56; Manager tech info serv Gen Dynamics Corp, Ft Worth Tex 56-, Dir Eng & sci info programs 68-. 9: ALA; ASIS; SLA (chm Engnr Sect 61, chm-elect aerospace div 68-69); TexLA; MPLA; ASLIB; SDT; APMI. 10: AAAS; Cosmopolitan Internat, Vestryman Epis Church; United Fund budget chairman; Big Bros of Amer; Delta Epsilon Sigma. 11: . 13: Yes. 14: Behav scis, ref, admin computer applications. 15: 6332 Genoa rd, Ft Worth TX 76116.

DETWILER, MARGARET MARY. b Wash DC 6 Je 44. 5: Earlham Col 62-66 (Hist) BA; Drexel 66-67 MLS. 6: Ger, Fr. 7: Catlgr LC 67-. 10: Beta Phi Mu. 14: Catlg, child wk. 15: 4201 S 31st st apt 949, Arlington Va 22206.

DETZKER, IRVING. b Brooklyn NY 9 D 30. 5: CUNY 49-53 (Eng, Chem) BA; Columbia 56-59 (LS, Physiol Sci) MS. 6: Ger. 7: Lib asst NY Acad of Med NYC 54-56; Med info sci Hoffmann-LaRoche, Inc Nutley NJ 60-. 9: Research Soc of Amer; Amer Med Writers Assn; Drug Info Assn. 10: AAAS. 13: Yes. 14: Abstracting, coding, & transl med info, lit searching. 15: 1470 St John's place, Brooklyn NY 11213.

DEUBACH, VILA APRILL. b Greeley Colo 5 Ap 09. 5: Colo State Col 29-35 (Music in elem educ) AB, (Guidance & second educ) MA; UColo 36-49 (Eng & Amer Lit) PhD; UCal (Berkeley) 51-52 (LS) BLS. 6: Lat, Ger, Fr, Old Eng, Middle Eng. 7: Tchr Sargent Consolidated Sch, Monte Vista Color 34-35; Anderson Cl: Dean of Women 35-45, Co-ordinator of stud personnel 45-58, Head Libn & chm Eng Dept 58-. 9: ALA; IndCol Eng Assn; (pres 54); Midwest Eng Conf (sec 49). 10: Ind Institutional Placement Assn; Mod Lang Assn; Urban League; Altrusa Internat; AAUW. 12: "The Social Conscience in the Short Story of American Magazines, 1890-1930 Abstract of PhD diss. 14: Admin, acquis. 15: 705 High st, Anderson IN 46012.

DEUSS, JEAN. b Chicago 6 D 22. 5: UWis 40-44 (Hist) BA; Columbia 57-59 (LS) MS. 6: Ger. 7: Gen bus & personnel experience; Sec Coun on Foreign Rel, NYC 57-59, Catlgr 59-61; Head catlgr Fed Reserve Bank of NY 61-69, Asst Chief 69-. 9: SLA (treas 67-68, 69-70; sec-treas Soc Sci Div 62-64, v-pres NY Chap 62-63). 14: Catlg. 15: 94 Bank st, NYC 10014.

DEUTSCH, HERBERT. b Brooklyn NY 8 D 29. 4: Myrna Flinder. 5: Brooklyn Col 47-51 (Soc Studies, Educ) BA; Columbia 52-54 (LS) MS. 7: Libn Brooklyn Pub Lib 52-55; Lib tchr Mid-Island ooperative Summer High Sch, Nassau County NY 60-; Adjunct Asst Prof C W Post Grad Lib Sch 62-; Lib tchr Wicksire Sch, New Hyde Park NY 55-66; Coord of sch lib & a-v serv Lindenhurst Pub Schs 66-68; Dir of media Hauppauge Pub Schs, Hauppauge NY 68-. 8: Consul Tchr Wkshop Rotterdam NY 63; Consul "Booklist" nonprint reviewing prog 68-. 9: NEA; NYLA; (NYLA/SLS v-pres 68-69) NY State Tchrs Assn; Nassau-Suffolk Sch LA; NEA-DAVI. 10: Nat Cong Parents & Tchrs; Columbia U Alumni Assn; Columbia Scholastic Press Advis Assn; Friends of So Huntington pub lib. 13: Yes. 14: Sch libs, a-v materials. 15: 21 Burns ave, Melville NY 11746.

DEVAN, CHRISTOPHER (BARTRAM). b Plaifield NJ 15 N 26. 4: Margaret Brice. 5: UMd 44 (Engnr); George Washington U 46-50 (Sociol) AB; UIll 3-54 MSLS. 6: Fr. 7: US Army 45-46, 50-51; Asst field dir Ame Red Cross, Camp Breckinridge Ky 52-53; Br asst, br head, fiction libn Milwaukee Pub Lib 54-57; Libn Greene County Lib, Springfield Mo 57-60; County & Ext libn pub libs of Springfield & Greene County, Springfield Mo 60-61; Coordnator of pub lib serv Chester County Lib, West Chester Penn 61-63; Asst dir Wilmington Inst Free Lib, Wilmington Del 63-64; Dir of Libs Wilmington Inst Free Lib & New Castle County Free Lib, Wilmington Del 64-. 9: ALA (Coun 65-69, Life mem); DelLA (pres 68-69); Middle Atl Reg Lib Fed (bd Dirs 69-72). 10: Rotary Club 14: Admin, ref serv, reg pub lib development. 15: Wilmington Inst Free Lib, Wilmington DE 19801.

DEVENDORF, HELEN R. b Ridgewood NJ. 5: Syracuse AB; Columbia MA; USo Cal MS in LS. 7: Eng tchr High Sch, Kingston Penn; Libn Schuylkill Campus of Penn State U 59-67; Peirce Jr Col 68-. 9: PennLA. 10: . 15: 1316 Pine st, Philadelphia PA 19107.

DEVEREAUX, KATHRYN (ADAMS). b Hot Springs Ark 29 Jl 07. 5: Rockford Col for Women 25-26; Northwestern U 26-29 (Eng Lit) BS; UIll 29-30 BS in LS. 7: 1st asst order dept Northwestern U (Evanston) 30-36; 1st asst order dept Kansas City (Mo) Pub Lib 36-40; Circ & ref libn UKansas City (Kansas City Mo) 40-41; Libn Unity Sch of Christianity, Kansas City Mo 41-42; Libn Transworld Airlines, Kansas City Mo 42-43; 1st asst order dept Kansas City (Mo) Pub Lib 43-44; Libn Legis Ref Lib, Jefferson City Mo 44-47; Head order & bk sel St Louis County Lib, Overland Mo 47-48; Libn Livingston County Mem Lib, Chillicothe Mo 48-52; Libn Moline Pub Lib, Moline Ill 52-63; Libn Florissant Pub Lib, Florissant Mo

63-64; Consul Ill state Lib, Springfield Ill 65-67; Hd tech serv Ill Valley Lib Syst 67-. 9: ALA; MoLA; IllLA (chm A-V Comm). 10: AAW; DAR; C of C; Zonta Internat; Mem & off of 6 civic org. 12: Jt author with Hoyt Galvin "Planning A Library Builddng (55); Ed "XX Building (55); Ed "Missouri Library Assn Quarterly (44-46). 13: Yes. 14: Admin, pub serv. 15: 2511 W Westminster, Peoria Il 61604.

deVERGIE, ADRIENNE (CONSTANT). b Boston Mass 23 Mr 36. 5: BostonU 54-59 (Romance Lang) BA; Simmons 61-62 MLS. 6: Fr. 7: UTex (Austin): Catlgr undergrad lib 62-63, Ref libn undergrad lib 63-66, Tech serv libn Tarlton Law Lib Law Sch 66-. 9: AALL. 10: Phi beta Kappa. 11: Ed & comp "Notes from the Tarlton Law Lib" (UTex Sch of Law) (66-). 13: Yes. 14: Catlg, ref. 15: 500 W 34th st, Austin Tx 78705.

DEVERS, CHARLOTTE M(ADISON). b NYC 10 Ag 23. 4: William P Devers. 5: Cornell U 41-44 (Zool) BA; Columbia 56-58 (LS) MS; Monroe Commun Col 64. 6: Fr. 7: Research libn American Weekly, NYC 54-56; Libn Television Bur of Advertising, NYC 56-58; Head Libn Compton Advertising Inc, NYC 58-63; Tech libn Gen Dynamics/Electronics, Rochester NY 63-65; Lib supv Curtiss-Wright Corp Wright Aeronautical Div, Wood-Ridge NJ 65-66; Mgr info serv 66-67; Asst dir info serv 67-68; Dir No Castle Pub Lib, Armonk NY 68-. 9: SLA (pres NY Chap, chm Adver Div); ASIS. 10: Aesculapius. 12: Co-ed "Guide to Special Issues and Indexes of Periodicals," SLA (63). 13: Yes. 14: Admin. 15: 900 Warren ave, Thornwood NY 10594.

DeVILLIERS, ANN M (BIXBY). b St Joseph Mich 17 My 44. 4: Andre L DeVilliers. 5: Central Mich U 62-63 (Bio); UMich 63-66 (Med Tech) BS, 66-67 MALS. 6: Sp. 7: Tech info specialist & indexer Parke-Davis & Co, Ann Arbor Mich 68-. 9: ASLS. 14: Documentation (biomedical), ref. 15: 11792 Lesia dr, Whitmore Lake Mi 48189.

DEVINE, ELIZABETH A. Milwaukee Wis 10 Ag 27. 5: Marquette 45-49 (Eng, Phil) PhB, 49-51 (Eng) MA; UWis 59-60 MSLS. 7: Recreation dir spec serv, Ger 51-56; Tchr Spenserian Col 57-58; Hd catlgr pub lib, Highland Park Ill 60-65; Ref libn MarquetteU 66-. 9: ALA. 14: Ref, interlib loan. 15: 1732 N Prospect ave, Milwaukee Wi 53202.

DEVINE, GLORIA MARGARET. b Ottawa Ont Can 19 Ap 41. 5: St Patrick's Col 59-62 (Fr) BA; Ottawa U 63-68 BLS. 6: Fr, Sp. 7: Lib clk Bk of Can Ottawa 63-65; Asst libn Metropolitan Life Ins Co Canadian Hd Off, Ottawa 65-. 9: OttawaLA. 14: Ref. 15: 182 Fourth ave, Ottawa Ont Can.

DEVINE, JUDITH ANN (SNIDER). b Long Beach Cal 22 Mr 45. 4: John W Devine III. 5: Long Beach City Col 62-64 (Liberal arts) AA; Cal State Col at Long Beach 64-66 (Eng) BA; USoCal 66-67 MS in LS. 6: Sp. 7: Elem sch libn Norwalk-La Mirada USD Grayland Elem Sch 67-. 8: Mem ESEA Sch Dist Adv Comm 67; ESEA Eval Com 67-. 9: ALA; NEA; CalASchL; CalTA; Tchrs Assn of Norwalk-La Mirada. 10: So Cal Coun on Lit for Child & YP. 14: Child lit. 15: 9330 Telegraph rd 202, Downey Ca 90240.

DEVINE, NANCY MARIE. b Bellevue Penn 17 S 31. 5: Flora Stone Mather Col 49-53 (Fr) BA; West Res 53-54 MS in LS. 6: Fr, Sp, Ger, Ital. 7: Asst Cuyahoga Co Lib, Cleveland 53-54; 1st asst readers serv Mt Holyoke Col Lib 54-60, Ref libn 60-65, Asst libn in chg of ref 66-. 8: Consul, For Area Materials Ctr Bibliog Proj (African Bibliog) 67-. 9: ALA. 10: AAUP. 14: Ref, bibliog, bk sel. 15: 1 Burnett ave, South Hadley Ma 01075.

DeVINNEY, CORA ELLEN (ANTHONY). b. Towanda Penn 17 S 27. 4: Clarence R Devinney. 5: Bob Jones U 45-49 (Music) BA; Peabody 52-53 (LS) MA. 7: Music supv Brown Military Acad, Sulphur Springs Ark 49-50; Asst regisrar Lee Col 50-52; Ref asst Allentown Free Lib, Allentown Penn 53-56; Home reading serv Detroit Pub Lib 56-61; Readers adv Macomb County Lib, Mt Clemens Mich 61-62, Head processing 62-65, Asst dir 65-. 9: ALA; Mich LA. 10: Delta Kappa Gamma. 14: Tech processes, admin. 15: 58816 Main st, New Haven MI 48048.

DeVITA, HELEN. b Newark NJ 2 Ja 04. 5: Newark State Normal Sch 21-23; Columbia 30 Certif. 6: Sp, Ital. 7: Clerk Pub Lib, Newark NJ 21-23, Child libn 23-29, Head of Registration Dept 29-32, Ref libn Lending & Ref Dept 32-, Ref libn in chg of US Documents 42-63, Supv ref libn 63-68; Ref libn Upsala Col Lib 68-. 8: Consul, Philipsburg Pub Lib 68, 69. 9: ALA; SLA; NJLA. 10: Pilot Club. 14: Ref, admin, US Docu. 15: Newak Pub Lib 5 Washington st, Newark NJ 07101.

DEVLIN, ELEANOR RUTH. b Boston 23 F 13. 5: Albertus Magnus Col 32-35 (Eng Lit) BA; Simmons 42-44 BSLS; UPenn (Eng Lit) MA. 6: Fr, Ger. 7: Ref asst Boston Pub Lib 37-46; Libn USVA Lib, Bedford Mass 46-47; Catlg ed & reviser UPenn Lib 47-55; Asst libn in chg of ref Ohio U 55-59; Asst head ref dept Ohio State U 59-63; Head ref div Temple U Lib 63-68; Hd ref dept Ohio State U 68-. 8: Instr Drexel Grad Sch of Lib Sci 68. 9: ALA-ACRL; -RSD. 10: Theta Phi Alpha. 13: Yes. 14: Col & univ libs, ref, bibliog, catlg. 15: 393 Alexandria Colony E, Columbus OH 43215.

DEVLIN, EUGENE JAMES. b Woburn Mass 7 My 36. 4: Bonnie Bergstrom Devlin. 5: Tufts U 53-57 (Hist) AB; Simmons 61-62 MLS. 7: Personnel spec US Army Personnel Center, Ft Dix NJ 58-60; Asst ref libn WHartford Pub Lib, W Hartford Conn 61-63, Ya libn 63-67; Dir Peck Mem Lib, Kensington Conn 67-. 9: ConnLA; NELA; YA Wkshops; child RT. 10: Tufts Club, Boston; Cath Graduates Club, Boston. 14: Ref. ya. 15: 7 Brightwood rd, Unionville CT 06085.

DEVORE, HELEN (LAWTON). b Trenton NJ 14 Ap 11. 4: Charles DeVore. 5: Rutgers 39 BS, 56 MLS. 7: Libn Evans Signal Lab, Belmar NJ 42-52; Libn Signal Corps Engnr Lab, Ft Monmouth NJ 52-55; Catlgr & ref libn Dept of Agric, Wash DC 56-57; Ref libn Naval Research Lab, Wash DC 58; Libn Naval Oceanographic Off, Wash DC 60-68; Asst libn Geophys Sci Lib Environmental Sci Serv Admin, Rockville Md 68-. 9: SLA; ASIS. 15: 2243 N Trenton st, Arlington Va 22207.

DeVOS, LAWRENCE (JOHN). b Detroit Mich 5 Ja 25. 4: Delores Yonkers. 5: Calvin Col 43-48 (Greek, Eng, Speech) AB, 54-55 (Hist) Tchg Certif; Calvin Theol 48-49, 50-52 (Theol, Philos) Certif; UToledo 58-59; Bowling Green State U 60; UMich 61-64 MALS; Fla Atlantic U 66; Ball State 68. 7: Plastic tooling maker Fisher Body, Wyoming Mich 52-55; Tchr: Rogers High Sch, Wyoming Mich 55-58, Swanton High Sch, Swanton Ohio 58-60; Libn Pettisville High Sch, Pettisville Ohio 60-61; Ref libn Ryerson Pub Lib, Grand Rapids Mich 61-62, br hd 62-63; Hd printing sect State Lib, Lansing Mich 63-64, asst dir admin serv 64-65, State docs libn 65; Asst catlgr Fla Atlantic U 65-67; Admin asst Ball State U 67-. 8: 54-65 Free-lance photographer, part time; 58-61 Printer, part time; 56-61 Newspaper photo-writer, part time. 9: ALA; ASIS; Assn for Computing Machinery. 14: Automation, mechaniz, systems. 15: 2304 Twickingham dr, Muncie In 47304.

DEVYATKIN, PAUL. b Winnipeg Can 3 F 22. 4: Vita Rudikoff. 5: NYU 57-62 (Classics) BA; Columbia 62-64 MLS. 7: Asst libn Grad Center Yeshiva U 64-. 15: Grad Center Lib 55 Fifth ave, New York NY 10003.

DEW, MARJORIE. b Latta SC. 5: Furman U 24-28 (Lat) AB; Peabody 29-30, Certif in LS, 34 BS in LS, 41 MA in LS. 7: Libn Crescent Jr Col 30-33; Dickson Pub Lib, Dickson Tenn 33-34; Libn pub schs SC, NC,La, Fla, col lib wk SC, NC, La 34-; Libn Southwood Col 62-66; Asst libn Gardner-Webb Col 66-67; Libn Graham-Eckes Sch, Palm Beach Fla 67-68; Libn Fairfax Hall, Waynesboro, Va 68-. 9: NEA; ALA; SELA; NCLA; VaLA. 10: DAR. 14: Ref, period, sch, col. 15: Zelle & King st, Latta SC 29565.

DEWALD, EDNA (KUMMER). Uhrichville Ohio 3 D 07. 4: ERNEST L Dewald. 5: Ohio Wesleyan U 25-27; Ohio State U 27-29 (Eng) BS in Educ; West Res 60-62 MS in LS. 6: SP. 7: Tchr-libn Stone Creek High Sch, Stone Creek Ohio 2932; Tchr-libn Tuscarawas-Warwick High Sch, Tuscarawas Ohio 32-35; Libn gen ref dept Cleveland Pub Lib 62-64, Libn GESS dept 64-. 9: ALA; OhioLA. 10: United Church Women of Greater Cleveland; YWCA; Beta Phi Mu; Cleveland Pub Lib Staff Assn; College Club of Cleveland; Cleveland Coun on World Affairs Womens City Club of Cleveland. 12: "Landscape Architecture and Related Subjects Found in United States Government Publications 49-63 (63). 14: Ref, rare bks. 15: 12910 Fairhill rd, Shaker Heights OH 44120.

DEWAR, ETHEL (MAY). b Belleville Ont Can 8 S 09. 5: Queens U 32 BA; Toronto 39 BLS. 7: ChiefLibn Parry Sound Pub Lib 49-51; Chief Libn Victoria Co Lib Co-operative 51-53; Chief Libn Cornwall Pub Lib 53- 63; Chief Libn Oakville Pub Lib 63-65; CHIEF OF REF Chatham Pub Lib, Chatham Ont 65-67; Supv Resource Ctr Lambton-Kent Composite Sch, Dresden Ont 67-. 9: CanLA; OntLA; Inst Prof Libns Ont. 14: Admin, ref. 15: 51 Water st, Chatham Ont Can.

DEWAR, JO (ELLER). b Wilkesboro NC 9 N 25. 4: Donald N Dewar. 5: Brevard Col 42-44 Jr Col Diploma; Berea Col 44-46 (Eng) AB; UNC 47-48 BS in LS; Barry Col summer 56 (Educ); UFla ext 56, 57, 63 (Educ). 7: Chief libn Tenn Wesleyan Col 48-50; Head undergrad & popular reading dept

UTex Lib (Austin) 51; Br libn Post Lib System US Army Spec Serv, Ft Jackson SC 51-52; Chief Post Lib System US Army Spec Serv, Ft Stewart Ga 52-54; Libn Olsen Jr High Sch, Dania Fla 55-56; Libn Lauderdale Manors Sch, Ft Lauderdale Fla 56-63; Head readers' serv dept Miami-Dade Jr Col Lib, Miami Fla 63-. 8: Fla Sch Lib Adv Com 62-; State Assembly Rep to AASL 60-63; So Assn of Col & Secondary Schs Visiting Com 61; Fla Educ Assn Program Action Com Legis Planning 61-63; Co-exec Div Natl Lib Week in Fla 65; Visiting instr UGa Grad Sch Educ summer 68. 9: ALA (var coms); Fla Assn Sch Libns (pres 61-62); Fla A-V Assn; FlaLA; FlaEA. 10: Delta Kappa Gamma; AAUW; AAUP. 13: Yes. 14: Ref, pub serv. 15: 3520 Crystal View court, Coconut Grove Fl 33133.

DEWDNEY, PATRICIA HELEN (PEGG). b Tonbridge Kent England 8 My 42. 5: UWest Ontario 60-64 (Eng lang & lit) BA; UMich 66-67 MLS. 7: Communications Off Nat Research Coun, Ottawa Ont 64-65; Ref Libn Ann Arbor Pub Lib Mich 67-68; Adult Educ Offr Lond Pub Lib & Art Mus, London Ont 68-. 9: CanLA (Adult Serv). 14: Adult Educ, Programming, Pub Relations & Display. 15: Community Relations London Public Lib & Art Museum, London Ont Can.

DEWEES, MARY KATHERINE. b Los Angeles 12 Ag 41. 5: Swarthmore Col 59-63 (Pol Sci, Internat Rel) BA; UWash 64 MLibn. 7: Off girl Friends Com on Nat Legis, Wash DC summer 62; Sec UWash 63-65; Libn trainee LC 65-66; Subj catlgr 66-. 9: ALA. 10: Leader & instr, Israeli Dance Gp of the Jewish Commun Ctr. 14: Subj catlg. 15: 404 A st SE, Wash DC 20003.

DEWEY, GENE L. b Malone NY 19 Jl 38. 4: Beatrice F Dewey. 5: State U Col (Geneseo NY) 55-59 (LS) BS; UIll 59-60 (LS) MS. 7: Jr libn Buffalo & Erie Co Pub Lib, Buffalo NY 60-62; Asst circ libn SUNY(Buffalo) 62-64, Acquis libn 64-69; Chief of Acquis Univ Wis Lib, Madison 69-. 9: ALA. 14: Acquis, tech serv. 15: 471 Highland ave, Kenmore NY 14223.

DEWEY, HARRY (TILLINGHAST). b Cebu City Phillipines 29 F 20. 5: UNC at Chapel Hill 36-41 (Amer hist) AB; UWash 41-43; Columbia 43-46 MS in LS; UChicago 49. 6: Fr. 7: Chief catlgr John Crerar Lib, Chicago 46-49; Asst dir tech serv So Ill U Lib 50-53; Asst prof UWis Lib Sch 53-56; Assoc prof & libn Drexel 56-58; Assoc prof Pratt Inst Lib Sch 58-62; Lecturer UMd Lib Sch, 66-67; Act asst dir Birmingham So Cal 68-. 8: Survey of tech serv, UMich Lib 54; Bldg consul Drexel U 56-58; Ed com "Who's Who in Library Service" 4th ed. 9: ALA (var off 44-). 10: Beltsville Garden Club; Riverton Yacht Club; Art Inst of Chicago. 11: Univ fellow, UChicago 49. 12: "Introduction to Library Cataloging and Classification" (4th ed 56); "Specialized Library Cataloging and Classification" (3rd ed 56); Ed "ILA Record" (52-53). 14: Catlg, clsf. 15: 4605 Brandon lane, Beltsville Md 20705.

DEWEY, MARGARET (RESCHLEIN). b LaCrosse Wis 26 Je 37. 4: Carlyle Conrad Dewey. 5: Northwestern Col 55-59 (Eng, Speech) BA; UMinn 60-61 (LS) MA; UMo 67; UMinn 67. 7: Asst libn Northwestern Col (Minneapolis) 62-63, Act head libn 63-64; Asst head circ UMo Lib 64-65; Libn Florissant Valley Community Col Lib 65-66; Hd libn Bethel Col (St Paul) 68-. 9: MinnLA. 10: Beta Phi Mu. 14: Ref, admin. 15: 1480 N Snelling ave, St Paul MN 55101.

DEWEY, RICHARD H. b Duluth Minn 5 S 34. 4: Judith Granada. 5: USan Francisco 56-60 (Philos) BA; UParis 57-58 (Cours de Civilisation francaise) Certif; San Jose State Col 61-63 (LS) MA. 6: Fr. 7: Bks for Asian stud Asian Found, San Francisco 57, 58-61; Libn Instrl TV Center San Jose State Col 62, Asst ser libn, asst circ libn 62-63; Libn World Affairs Coun of NoCal, San Fransco 63-65; Readers serv libn American U(Beirut Lebanon) 65-68; Lib U Manitoba, Chief Bibliog 68-. 9: ALA. 12: "Bibliographies and Cataloging System for Instruction TV Center (62); Ed "New Books in World Affairs, monthly. 14: Ref, bibliog. 15: Dafoe Library, Univ of Manitoba, Winnipeg Can.

DEWTON, JOHANNES L(EOPOLD). b Vienna 27 S 05. 4: Hedwig Strauss. 5: UVienna 23-27 (Law, Pol Sci, Econ) Juris D; UIll 40-44 BS in LS, MS. 6: Fr, Ger. 7: Court sec & lawyers asst, Vienna 28-34; Lawyer, Vienna 35-38; Research asst Eng Dept UIll 44-45; Tech adv (Assim rank Col) US Army Air Force, Air Research Center London 45; Catlgr & reviser Descr Catlg Div LC 45-49; Head Cumulative Catlg Sect & Ed Catlg Publ, Catlg Maint Div LC 49-57; Asst chief Union Catalog Div LC 57-66; Chief Shared Catlg Div 66-67; Hd Nat Union Catlg Publn Project 67-. 8: Mem, Bd Dirs, Coun on Research in Bibliog 65-. 9: ALA; DCLA. 10: Beta Phi Mu. 12: Ed-in-chief "National Union Catalog, Pre-1956 Imprints. 13: Yes. 14: Catlg, union catalogs, ref. 15: 4201 7th rd So, Arlington Va 22204.

DEY, WINIFRED BOYD (GUNTLE). b Walla Walla Wash 10 Ja 27. 4: Ross B Dey. 5: Cntral Wash Col 45-47 (Educ); UOre 55-56 (Educ) BS; UWash summers 58-62 (LS) ML. 7: Libn Elmira High Sch, Elmira Ore 56-58; Ref libn S Eugene High Sch, Eugene Ore 58-64; Lib consul Lane Co Sch Dist, Eugene Ore summer 62; Lib consul SLane Sch Dist, Cottage Grove Ore summer 63; Head instr materials center S Eugene High Sch, Eugene Ore 64-. 9: NEA-DAVI; ALA; AASchL; OreEA; Ore A-V Assn. 10: Delta Kappa Gamma. 14: Educ libnship. 15: Lorane route, Box 356,Lorane Or 97451.

DEYA, LOURDES (LENDIAN). b Habana Cuba 23 O 25. 4: Jose Miguel Deya. 5: Randolph-Macon Womans Col 43-46 (Eng); UHabana 59-61 (Langs); LSU 61-62 (Span) BA, 62-63 MLS LSU 66-67 (LS), 65- (Sp, Portu, Fr). 6: Sp, Fr, Ital, Portu. 7: Lang tchr Cuban Educ Dept, Habana Cuba 49-59, Elem tchr 59-61; Asst catlgr La State Lib 64-66; Instr catlg & clsf LSU 67-. 9: SWLA; LaLA; Iota; Alpha Beta Alpha; LaTA; AALS. 10: Asociacion de Profesoresde Ingles, Havana Cuba; Asociacion Nacional de Maestros, Havana Cuba; AAUW; KappaDelta; Phi Lambda Pi; Phi Sigma. 11: US Off Educ AAUW; Baton Rouge Lib Club; SacredHeart Alumn Assn; mod lang assn. 13: Yes. 14: Catl, ref, young adult, tchg lib sci. 15: 5785 Glenwood dr, Baton Rouge La.

DI CANIO, FRANK. b Chicago 11 Ag 08. 4: Mary Grangeras. 5: De Paul Col of Com 25-30; De Paul U 30-33 (Pre-Law). 6: Eng, Ital. 7: Page Chicago Law Inst Lib 23-30, Ref libn 31-37, Asst libn 37-43, Exec libn 44- 62; Libn Judges Gen Lib US Dist Court, Chicago 62-65; Libn Lib of the US Courts, Chicago 65-. 9: AALL (chm Com Elections 60-64); Chicago ALL (Charter mem 47, pres 48-49, chm var coms). 12: "Check-List of the Holdings of te Four Major Law Libraries in the Chicago Area, with Kurt Schwerin. 13: Yes. 14: Catlg, ref. 15: Library of the US Courts, 219 S Dearborn st room 1448, Chicago Il 60604.

DI DURO, MICHELA R (MARINO). b Geneva NY 23 O 29. 4: Joseph John Di Duro. 5: SUNY (Geneseo) 48-52 (G Ed) BS, 56-60 (LS) MS. 6: Fr, Ital, Danish. 7: Tchr Canastota Central Sch, Canastota NY 52-54; Tchr Romulus Central Sch, Romulus NY 54-55; Tchr San Bernandino Schs, San Bernardino Cal 55-56; Tchr Waterloo Central Sch, Waterloo NY 56-61; Libn Hobart & Wm Smith Colleges, Geneva NY 62; Tchr-libn Geneva City Schs, Geneva NY 63-65; Tchr-libn Waterloo Cenral Schs, Waterloo NY 65- Libn Boces-Finger Lakes Occupational Ctr 68-69. 8: Experiment in Internat Living, Denmark 53-, S Amer & Dutch Antilles 69. 9: NY State Tchrs Assn; Cal Tchrs Assn. 10: Experiment in Internat Living Alumni Assn; PTA; Geneseo Alumni Assn, Geneva Hist Soc. 14: Ref. 15: 478 Castle st, Geneva NY 14456.

DI IORIO, MARY C. b Painesville Ohio 27 F 35. 5: Duquesne U 52-56 (Pharmacy) BS, 56-59 (Pharmacy) MS; West Res 62-63 (LS) MS. 6: Ital, Fr. 7: Residue analyst Diamond Alkali Co, Painesville Ohio 59-62; Research asst Chem Abstract Serv, Columbus Ohio 64-65; Libn IRC Fibers Div Midland-Ross Corp, Painesville Ohio 65-67; Pharmacist-Manager Mentor Pharmacy, Mentor Ohio 60-66; Res libn AM Corp, Cleveland Ohio 68-. 8: Registered pharmacist in Penn & Ohio. 9: SLA. 10: Rho Chi; Amer Mgt Club. 14: Documentation, ref. 15: 849 S State st, Painesville Oh 44077.

DiLISIO, ROCH-JOSEF. b Derby Conn 11 Ja 33. 5: St Thomas Sem (Liberal Arts) AA; St Marys Sem & U (Philos) BA; ULouvain(Belgium) (Philos, Langs); UEdinburgh (Lit); UFlorence (Ital Lang & Lit); Simmons (LS) MS. 6: Lat, Fr, Ital. 7: Catlgr Boston Pub Lib 61-63; Rare bks catlgr Yale U 63- Acquis libn Sacred Heart U 68-. 14: Catlg, bibliog, rare bks. 15: Hermitswood, Taunton Hill rd, NewtownCt 06470.

DI MASI, ELIZABETH (BARRETT). b Detroit 26 Ap 08. 4: Vincent P Di Masi. 5: Radcliffe 27-30(Hist) BA; Simmons 30-31 (LS) BS; USoCal 57-65 (Educ & Educ Guidance) MEd. 6: Fr. 7: 1st asst catlg dept Binghamton Pub Lib, Binghamton NY 31-32; 1st asst circ dept Toledo Pub Lib, Toledo Ohio 32-38, Head circ dept 38-48; Head adult serv Akron Pub Lib, Akron Ohio 48-54; Asst San Diego Pub Lib 54; Libn Lennox High Sch, Lennox High Sch, Lennox Cal 57-. 9: ALA; NEA; CalASchL; Cal Tchrs Assn; CalVSTA; APGA; CPGA; ASCA; CSCA. 12: "Man Alive, a Bibliography of Fiction and Biography Related to World History". 14: Couns individuals & groups. 15: 1916 Pescadores ave, San Pedro Cal 90732.

DI MUCCIO, SISTER MARY-JO. b Hanford Cal 16 Je 30. 5: Immaculate Heart Col 48-52 (Eng) BA, 58-60 LS) MA. ; US Intl U (Educ) 68-. 7: Tchr Sisters of the Immaculate Heart 48-60; Asst libn Immaculate Heart Col 60-62, Head libn 62-. 8: Sch Lib Supv, Sisters of the Immaculate Heart of Mary, 60-. 9: ALA-ACRL; CathLA; CalLA; CalASchL; LARC; SoCal Tech Processes Group; SLA. 12: Library Informational Handbook (61). 13: Yes. 14: Admin. 15: 2070 E Live Oak dr, Los Angeles 90028.

DI PIETRO, LAWRENCE N(ICHOLAS). b Philadelphia 9 My 26. 4: Helen Parker Di Pietro. 5: Rutgers 48-51 (Hist) AB; Drexel 51-52 MSLS. 6: Ital, Ger. 7: US Army Corp of Engnrs (S/Sgt) 44-46; Page Free Lib of Phila 47-50; Admin asst bk stacks Free Lib of Phila 50-52; Child libn Enoch Pratt Free Lib, Baltimore 52-53; Free Lib of Phila: Catlgr 53-55, Bkmob libn 55-57, Admin asst ext 57-59; Co-ordinator adult Dallas Pub Lib 59-65; Dir Topeka Pub Lib, Topeka Kan 65-67; Libn El Centro Col (Dallas) 67-. 9: ALA; TexLA; DallasCoLA. 13: Yes. 14: Automation, info retr, documentation. 15: 3850 Antiqua dr, Dallas Tx 75234.

DIAL, CLARENCE MILTON. b Manhattan Kan 8 Ag 24. 4: Zona Permelia Zerba. 5: Wash State U 46-50 (Mus ed) BA Mus, BEd; UOre 52-53 (Mus) M Mus; Lewis & Clark Col 58 (Mus); UDenver 65-66 MALS. 7: Chief admin clk S/Sgt USA, S Pacific Area 43-45; Vocal mus tchr Mead High Sch, Mead Wash 50-52; Vocal mus tchr Myrtle Creek Schs, Myrtle Creek Ore 53-55; Mus dir Brookings-Harbor High Sch, Brooksings Ore 55-57; Vocal mus dir Hood River Co Schs, Hood River Ore 57-59; Mus dir Marana High Sch, Marana Ariz 59-65; Ref libn Mesa Commun Col, Mesa Ariz 66-69; Dir Mesa Pub Lib, Mesa Ariz 69-. 9: ALA; MENC; NEA; ArizEA; ArizStateLA (69 Conf Prog Chm); AMEA (treas 63-65, sec Choral Sect 59-62). 10: Served as choir director and organist for var churches. 11: Bronze Star Medal for service in WW II. 14: Ref, admin. 15: 106 Madrid Plaza, Mesa Az 85201.

DIAL, ZONA PERMELIA (ZERBA). b Milton-Freewater Ore 11 N 30. 4: Clarence M Dial. 5: Wash State U 48-50 (Pre-nursing); Portland State U 58-59 (Ed); UAriz 61-63 (Liberal arts) BA; UDenver 65-66 MALS. 7: Res bk room asst UAriz 63-65; Ariz State U: Sci ref libn 66-67, Hd humanities ref 67-68, Ref serv coord 69-. 8: Lib consul Litchfield Park Campus, Ariz State U 69. 9: ALA; ArizLA (chm Arizona Highways Index Comm). 10: AAUP. 12: Co-auth "Know Your Library", No 2 "Guide for English Students". 14: Ref, admin. 15: 106 Madrid Plaza, Mesa Az 85201.

DIAMOND, HAROLD JAMES. b NYC 16 F 34. 5: Hunter Col 52-56 (Music) BA; Columbia 56-58 MS; NYU 62-65 (Music) MA. 6: Ger. 7: Libnmusic ref NY Pub Lib 56-59; Libn fine arts Hunter Col 59-66; Hd ref div Asst ProfLehman Col 66-. 9: MusLA; Amer Musicological Assn; NY Lib Club. 14: Ref. 15: 8825 240 st, Bellerose NY 11426.

DIAMOND, RUTH ELLEN (YARGER). b Swengel Penn 17 Je 18. 4: David Diamond. 5: Susquehanna U 35-39 (Hist, Pol Sci) AB; Drexel 41-42 BS in LS. 7: Asst catgr Col of Physicians of Phila 42-44; Asst libn Upper Darby Free Pub Lib, Upper Darby Penn 45; Libn Wistar Inst of Anatomy & Biology, Phila 45-46; Libn US Naval Hosp, Phila 46-48; Libn Temple U Sch of Med 48-. 9: MedLA; SLA. 14: Med libs. 15: 2517 Bleigh ave, Phila Pa 19152.

DIAZ, ALBERT JAMES. b Phila 17 O 31. 4: Karen Blomholm. 5: Swarthmore 48-52 (Hist) BA; UNC 54-56 MS in LS. 6: Sp. 7: US Navy 52-54; Spec collections libn UNM 56-58; Sales & promotion mgr Microcard Found, Madison Wis 58-69; Exec dir Microcard Editions Inc, Wash DC 60-. 8: Visiting lecturer UMd Grad Lib Sch 66. 9: ALA; ASIS; Amer Hist Assn; Nat Microfilm Assn; Latin Amer Studies Assn; DCLA. 10: Sec-treas Sem on the Acquis of Latin Amer Lib Materials 68-69; ASIS LiaisonRepres to the Nat Microfilm Assn 66-. 12: "Guide to Microforms in Print (61); "Guide to the Microfilm of Papers Relating to New Mexico Land Grants (60); "Manuscripts and Recods in the U OF NM Lib (57); "Subject Guide to Microforms in Print (63-). 13: Yes. 14: Tech serv, microreproduction. 15: 901 26th st NW, Wash DC 20037.

DIAZ, DANIEL J. b Freeland Penn 1 D 32. 4: Dorothy Fauver. 5: St Bonaventure U 50-54 (Philos) BA; Catholic U 57-59 (LS) MS. 7: Asst supv IBM Div Swift & Co, Phila 55-57; Ref asst Catholic U 57-59; Libn II humanities & soc sci div Stanford U Libs 59-62; Chief bibliog acquis UConn Lib (Storrs) 62-68; Hd acquis dept USan Francisco Lib 68-. 9: ALA. 14: Acquis, ref. 15: 543 Everett ct apt 3, Palo Alto Ca 94301.

DIAZ, DOROTHY (FAUVER). b W Hartford Conn 29 My 29. 4: Daniel Diaz. 5: Central Conn State Col 47-51 (Eng) BS; CatholicU 57-59 MSLS. 6: Fr. 7: Tchr Windsor Jr High Sch, Windsor Conn 51-53; Lib asst MIT Libs 53-55; Lib asst US Dept of Army Spec Serv, Japan 55-57; Lib asst CatholicU 57-59; Libn II StanfordU Libs 59-62; Libn II UConn Lib (Storrs) 64-68; Libn II StanfordU 68-. 10: Beta Phi Mu. 14: Catlg. 15: 543 Everett ct apt 3, Palo Alto Ca 94301.

DIBLE, JOAN (BRAIN). b Upland Penn 22 Mr 37. 5: UDel 54-58 (Biol) BA; Simmons 59-60 (LS) MS; Harvard U Ext 60-62 (German); Stanford summer 64 (Russian), summer 65 (Econ). 6: Fr. 7: Blood Bank Tech NE Deaconess Hosp, Brookline Mass 58-59; Ref libn Harvard Med Lib, Boston 60-61, Jr catlgr 61-62; Tech reports catlgr Lockheed, Palo Alto Cal 62-63; Jr catlgr UCal Med Center Lib (San Francisco) 63; Documents custodian Stanford Research Inst, Menlo Park Cal 65-66; Hd sci catlgr Stanford U Main Lib 67-. 9: ALA; MedLA; SLA. 10: LWV; Fremont Friends of the Library. 12: Main ed staff "Library Bulletin," Stanford U 68-. 14: Catlg, spec libs. 15: PO Box 2997, Stanford Ca 94305.

DIBLEY, SISTER ALICE MONICA. b Spokane Wash 27 Mr 08. 5: Holy Names Normal 25-27 Educ life Tchg Certif; GonzagaU 30-45; Siena Hts Col 45-47 (Hist) PhB (LS); CatholicU 47-53 9hist) AM. 6: Fr. 7: Dept hd film libn Army AF, Spokane Wash 34-45; Tchr SW States 47-62; Med libn Rose de Lima Hosp, Henderson Nev 62-64; Libn Dominican High Sch, Detroit 64-65; Libn Hoban High Sch, Cleveland Ohio 65-66; Libn & admin Siena Hts Col 66-. 8: Dept of Educ, San Francisco; Soc Studies Com, Mus Com. 9: CathLA; MichLA. 14: Ref, admin, bk selection. 15: Siena Heights College Lib, Adrian Mi 49221.

DICHEK, SHIRLEY (BERNSON). b NY 18 Mr 26. 4: Leonard Jay Dichek. 5: Brooklyn Col 43-47 (Eng) BA (cum laude); Immaculate Heart Col 65-68 MALS. 6: Ger. 7: Libn Corvallis High Sch, Studio City Cal 68-. 8: Consul in organ St Brendan's Sch Lib 67-68; Tech asst reclsfg Art Research Lib of Los Angeles Co Museum of Art 66-. 9: ALA; CalLA. 10: So Cal Coun on Lit for Child and Young People; Museum Serv Coun (Los Angeles Co Museum of Art). 11: Hon life memb in PTA for improving sch lib. 14: Child lit. 15: 11451 Dona Cecilia dr, Studio City Ca 91604.

DICK, ESME (J). b England 14 Je 33. 4: William Dick. 5: Mansfield Tech Col Eng 49-51 (LS); Chesterfield Tech Col Eng 51-53 (LS). 6: Fr. 7: Libn St Mary's in the Mts Sch, Littleton NH; Greenwich Lib, Conn: Ref libn 60-65, Film serv coord 65-69; Festival coordinator Amer Film Festival, NYC 69; Admin dir EFLA, NYC 69-. 9: ALA (subcom for "Booklist" reviews); FLIC (Bd sec); NELA. 10: NY Film Coun (Board mem). 12: Man ed, "Film Library Quarterly". 14: Film ref. 15: Educational Film Lib Assoc, 250 W 57th st, New York NY 10019.

DICK, EVELYN VIRGINIA (HAUSER). b Lyons Ind 4 Mr 14. 4: Max K Dick. 5: Vincennes U Jr Col 31-33; Ind U 36-38 (Eng) AB; Peabody Col summers 40-42 BS in LS. 7: Tchr & libn Crown Point High Sch, Crown Point Ind 38-40; Libn Bloomington High Sch, Bloomington Ind 40-45; Libn Burris Sch Ball State Tchrs Col 45-47; Bkkeeper & sec (Husband's firm) 47-63; Libn Speedway Jr High Sch, Speedway Ind 63-. 8: State repres to ALA 66-69; Past pres Hoosier Library Transparencies, Inc; Helped prepare transparencies publ by Tecnifax Corp. 9: ALA; -AASchL; NEA; IndSchLA; IndStateTA. 10: Assoc libn Speedway Christian Church. 12: Ed "Hoosier School Libraries" IndSchLA (64-66). 14: Sch libs. 15: 8729 Johns dr, Indianapolis In 46234.

DICK, JO ANNE. b Seattle Wash 23 My 46. 5: UWash 64-68 (Geog) BA, 68-69 M Lib. 7: Stud page UWash Lib 64-68; Child libn Seattle Pub Lib 69-. 14: Child serv. 15: PO Box 204, Keyport Wa 98345.

DICKAU, NORMA JEAN. b Albany Cal 16 Mr 43. 4: Bruce E Dickau. 5: Adams State Col 61-62; Tex West Col 62-64 (Psych) BA; UWash 64-65 M Lib; Fla State U 67-68 6th yr certif. 6: Sp. 7: Catlgr Tex West Col Lib 65-, Head catlgr El Paso Pub Lib; Libn Strozier Undergrad Lib Fla State U. 8: Consul Jesus & Mary High Sch, El Paso Tex 67. 9: ALA (JMRT); FlaLA; SWLA; Border Reg LA (corresp sec). 12: Contrib Ed; "Continuing Education," "Professional Education Library." 14: Pub serv. 15: 3614 Thomasville rd, Tallahassee Fl 32301.

DICKERMAN, DELIGHT. b Hammonton Cal 8 Jl 10. 5: UCal (Berkeley) 2729 (Eng); UPoitiers 29-30 (Fr); Columbia 30-31 (Journalism); Geo Washington U 37-42 AB in LS;

USoCal fall 58 (LS); Drexel 60-61 (LS). 6: Fr. 7: Adjutants libn (gt) Hdqrs Air Transport Command, Wash DC 44-46; Chief Libn Tech Intel Lib ERDL, Ft Belvoir Va 50-51; Libn Freer Gallery of Art, Wash DC 51-52; Chief Libn Japan Air Defense Force, Misawa, Johnson & Iazuke 52-55; Ref & child libn Co & City libs, Los Angeles 55-59; Catlgr Free Pub Lib, Moorestown NJ 60-61; Chief Libn Lemoore Naval Air Station, Lemoore Cal 62-64; Catlgr Tulare Co Lib, Visalia Cal 65-. 67; Readers adv Fresno Co Cal 67-68; Ext libn Humbolt Co Lib, Eureka Cal 68-. 9: ALA; SLA: CalLA. 14: Ref. 15: 1314 E st, Eureka Ca 95501.

DICKERSON, IRENE. 5: Centre 33-36 (Hist, Pol Sci) AB; UKy summers 37, 55-57 (LS). 6: Lat, Fr. 7: Eng tchr & libn Salvisa High Sch, Mercer Co Ky 36-40; Personal dirSportleigh Hall, Harrodsburg Ky summer 38; Eng tchr, libn & glee club dir Fairview High Sch, Mercer Co Ky 40-55; Libn & Music Dir Mercer High Sch, Mercer Co Ky 55-59, Libn 59-. 9: KyEA; KyASchL. 14: Bk sel, research. 15: Route 5, Harrodsburg Ky 40330.

DICKERSON, JESSIE MAE. b Clanton Ala 21 Jl 33. 4: Flix Earl Dickerson. 5: Ala State Col 52-55 (Eng) BS; Atlanta 62-63 MS in LS. 6: Fr. 7: Tchr-libn Laurel High Sch, Alexaner City Ala 55-62; Libn Morris Col 63- 64; Asst catlgr Atlanta U 64-68; Hd of tech serv Essex Commun Col 68-. 10: Beta Phi Mu. 14: Catlg. 15: EssexCommun Col, Baltimore Md 21237.

DICKERSON, RUBY ELIZABETH. b Blacksburg Va 8 Ag 11. 5: Va Polytech Inst 32-36 (Bus Admin) BS; Peabody 62 (LS) MA. 7: Head acquis dept Va Polytech Inst 47-. 9: VaLA; SELA. 10: AAUW. 14: Acqu, catlg. 15: 509 Lee st, Blacksburg Va 24060.

DICKEY, JACK (WITTEN). b Durant Okla 30 Ap 24. 4: Janet Stuart. 5: UOkla 46- 49 (Chem) BS, 49-51 (Educ) Ed M, 53-55 MLS. 7: US Navy (Seabees) Carpenters Mate 2d Class 43-46; Asst ref libn Okla State U 55-56; Geol libn UOkla 5660; Asst acquis libn UNM 60-61; Physics libn UIowa 62-. 9: ALA; IowaLA. 10: Beta Phi Mu; Alpha Chi Sigma. 14: Ref, sci libs. 15: 1425 Sycamore, Iowa City Ia 52242.

DICKEY, JULIA (EDWARDS). b Sioux Falls SD 6 Mr 40. 4: Joseph E Dickey Sr. 5: De Pauw U 58-59 (Hist); IndU 60-62 (Eng lit) AB, 64-67 MLS, 67 (LS). 6: Sp. 7: Asst acquis lib IndU Reg Campus Libs 65-67; Hd tech serv Bartholomew Co Lib Columbus Ind 67-. 9: ALA; IndLA (chm non-profess RT); Ohio Valley Gp Tech Serv Libns. 10: AAUW; Psi Iota Xi. 14: Tech serv. 15: Bartholomew County Lib 5th at Lafayette, Columbus In 47201.

DICKEY, LOUISE F (FORT). b DeWitt County Ill 14 Je 08. 4: A W Dickey. 5: Ill State U 41 (Eng) BEd; UIll 46 (Educ) MA, 68 (LS) MS. 6: Lat. 7: Tchr: Piatt Co Schs, Monticello Ill 28-29, Clinton Elem Schs, Clinton Ill 29-41, Clinton Jr High, Clinton Ill 41-42, Clinotn Commun High Sch, Clinton Ill 42-59; Asst co supt of schs, DeWitt Co Clinton Ill 59-64; Lib supv Off of State Supt of Pub Instr, Springfield Ill 65-67; Instr (Eng) Eureka Col 67, Asst libn & Asst Prof Melick Lib 67-. 8: State sponsor, ill Assn of Future Tchrs of Amer. 9: IllEA; NEA; IllEA (v-pres Central Div); IllLA. 10: Kappa Delta Pi; Delta Kappa Gamma; Beta Phi Mu; AAUW; AAUP. 13: Yes. 14: Ref. 15: 320 S Monroe st, Clinton Ill 61727.

DICKINSON, ARTHUR (TAYLOR) JR. b Montgomery Ala 5 D 25. 4: Marjorie Sutton Dickinson. 5: Huntingdon Col 50-53 (Hist, Eng) BA; UChicago 53-54, 57 (LS) AM. 7: Mechanical inspector Nat Cash Register Co, Montgomery Ala 44-47; Salesman Sears Roebuck & Co, Montgomery Ala 47-50; Clerk Midwest Inter-lib Center, Chicago 54; Mansfield Pub Lib, Mansfield Ohio: Ref libn 54-56, Br supv 55-56, Head co dept 56-63, Asst libn & head co dept 57-63, Head Libn 64-. 8: Bldg consul - Chillicothe (Ohio) Pub Lib 67-68; Consul on consolidation,Chillicothe Pub Lib & Ross Co Lib, 68-69; Lib Devel Com 67-, chm sub-com on salaries 69. 9: ALA; OhioLA (chm Ext Serv Round Table 60-61, mem Memb Com 64,mem Sub-prof Train Wkshop Com 64, chm Dist Meetings Com 65; Mem Ohio State LibAdv Com on Salary Survey. 10: Ohio Geneal Soc; Kiwanis Club. 12: "American Historical Fiction (58, 2nd ed 62). 13: Yes. 14: Ref, admin. 15: 105 Sunset rd, Mansfield Oh 44906.

DICKINSON, BONITA JEAN. b St Louis Mo 12 F 44. 5: St LouisU 62-66 (Hist) BA; UIll 66, 67, 67-68 MLS. 7: Y-a libn St Louis Pub Lib 68-. 9: ALA (Jr Mem RT); MoLA; Greater St Louis LA. 10: AAUW. 14: Ya, pub lib. 15: 2327 Switzer, Jennings Mo 63136.

DICKINSON, CAROLYN HUSKEY. b Columbus Ohio 3 Je 41. 4: William Joseph Dickinson. 5: UCal 59- 63 (Art Hist) BA, 63-64 MLS. 6: Sp, Fr. 7: Catlgr San Francisco State Col 64-65; Reviser-catlgr Johns Hopkins U 65-67, Asst ref libn Sci & Eng Lib 68-. 9: ALA;J Mem RT. 14: Catlg, ref. 15: 218 McCoy Hall 3401 N Charles st, Baltimore Md 21218.

DICKINSON, DONALD C. b Schenectady NY 9 Je 27. 4: Colleen (Schindler). 5: SUNY (Albany) 45-49 (Eng) AB; UIll 49-51 MS in LS; UMich 54-64 (LS) PhD. 6: Sp. 7: Ref libn Central Mo State 51-53; Asst ref libn East Mich U 53-56; Asst acquis libn UKan 56-58; HeadLibn Bemidji State Col 58-66; Dir reader serv UMo 66-. 9: ALA; MoLA; BSA. 10: NAACP. 11: Amer Philos Assn grant 68. 12: "Bio-bibliography of Langston Hughes 1902-1967," (67). 13: Yes. 14: Acquis, col& univ admin, bibliog, hist of bks & printing. 15: 1905 Iris dr, Columbia Mo 65201.

DICKINSON, HELEN (ELIZABETH). b Manilla Ont Can 23 S 20. 4: Geoffrey Dickinson. 5: UAlberta 38-42 (Fr, Lat) BA; USask 49-50; UBritish Columbia 61-62 BLS. 6: Fr, Lat. 7: Sec Wartime Prices & Trade Bd, Ottawa 43; Confidential sec Minister of Trade & Com, Ottawa 43-45; Sec Can House, Lond Eng 45-46; Libn Union Theol Col, Vancouver 62-64; Hd catlgr Dist of N Vancouver Mun Pub Lib, N Vancouver 64-. 8: Prepared 2 correspondence courses on catlg for Lib Devel Commsn of BC 69. 9: BCLA (Const com). 10: Weavers Square Dance Cub. 14: Catlg. 15: 1041 Kennedy ave, North Vancouver BC Can.

DICKINSON, LENORE M. b W Pittston Penn 5 Mr 19. 4: John Kellogg Dickinson. 5: Wayne State U 38-43 (Fr); Boston U 58-65 (Ger) AB; Simmons 65-67 (LS) MS. 6: Ger, Fr, Lithuanian, Ital, Dutch. 7: Clerk Detroit Ordnance Dist 42-43; Bkkeeper, bkseller Personal Bk Shop, Boston 43-49; Catlgr & bkseller Phillips Bk Store, Cambridge Mass 54-61; Catlgr Andover Harvard Theol Lib, Cambridge Mass 61-65, Hd catlg 65-. 9: ATheolLA; ALA; Guild of bk workers. 10: Amer RecorderSoc (past pres Boston Chap; Boston Mycological Club). 11: Lilly Endowment scholarship 65. 14: Catlgr, rare bks, book preservation. 15: 4 Humboldt st, Cambridge Ma 02140.

DICKINSON, NANCY (CARY). b Scottsville Va 26 S 12. 5: Col of William & Mary 29-34 (LS) BA. 7: Tchr-libn Pittsylvania Co Schs, Whitmell Va 34-35; Tchr-libn Powhatan Co Schs, Powhatan Va 35-38; Sch libn Fairfax Co Schs, Fairfax Va 38-39; Co sch libn Louisa Co Schs, Louisa Va 3943; Sch libn Norfolk Co Schs, Portsmouth Va 43-50; Libn Naval Station, Norfolk Va 50-59; Dist Libn Fiftm Naval Dist, Norfolk Va 59-. 9: ALA; SELA; VaLA. 15: 1803 Gifford st, Norfolk Va 23518.

DICKINSON, (O) PAUL. b Wilson NC 31 Ja 15. 4: Bessie Geanacopoulou. 5: Atlantic Christian Col 33-35; UNC 35-37 (Eng) AB, 37-38 AB in LS;Brooklyn Col 54 (Eng) AM. 6: Fr. 7: Eng tchr Alexander Wilson High Sch, Graham NC 37-38; Stud asst Ref Dept UNC Lib 38-39; Asst circ dept Central Lib Dist of Columbia Lib 40; Asst ref dept Wash Sq Lib NYU 40-41; Circ & ref libn Brooklyn Col 42-46, ref libn 46-59, humanities libn 59-, Asst prof 68-. 9: ALA-ACRL; Mod Lang Assn. 10: AAUP. 14: Ref. 15: 129 Lexington ave, New York NY 10016.

DICKISON, RAYMOND R. b Colorado Springs Colo 9 Mr 19. 4: Ruth Lien. 5: Colo Col 36-40 (Chem) BA; West res U 40-41 BS in LS; Penn State U 43-47 (Chem) MS. 6: Portu. 7: Chem libn Penn State U 41-47; Asst dir of lib UFla 47-51; Hd libn Colo Sch of Mines, Golden Colo 51-55; Chief libn Oak Ridge Natl Lab, Oak Ridge Tenn 55-. 9: SLA; ACS. 13: Yes. 14: Admin. 15: Box X, Oak Ridge Tn 37830.

DICKMAN, DOROTHY DALTON. b San Francisco 20 Jl 10. 4: Kenneth William Dickman. 5: San Fracisco State Col 26-31 (Educ, Gen Sci, Soc Sci) AB; UCal (Berkeley) 34, 57 (Educ) MA; Cornell U 40; USoCal 62-64. 6: Fr. 7: Tchr Albany City schs, Albany Cal 31-35; Statistics file sec Adolescent Study Rockefeller Found, Oakland Cal 35-36; Sec, aide Oscars Off Waldorf Astoria, NYC 36-41; Superv of operations Sch Lunch Program WPA Bd of Educ, NY 41-42; US Army WAAC 42, WAC 43-4, Army Emergency Relief (Capt) 43-46; Tchr Remedial reading Belot Col 51-53; Tchr Syracuse Reading Clinic, Syracuse NY 52-55; Tchr Los Angeles City Schs 55-64; Sch libn Los Angeles Unified Schs 64-. 8: Organizer of communal Feeding Program AWVS NY 40- 42; Lecturer, Banquet Dept Waldorf-Astoria, at Simmons Col, Cornell U, NY City Schs. 9: SLA; CalASchL; Cal Tchrs Assn; Los Angeles Sch LA. 10: Libraria Sdalitas. 13: Yes. 14: Sch libnship. 15: 11601 Ruffner ave,granada Hills Ca 91344.

DICKMAN, EMMA JANE (HAZZARD). b St Louis Mo 10 D 11. 5: UEvansville 28-31; UWis 33-34 (Eng) AB; IndU 60-62 (LS) MA. 6: Fr, Lat. 7: Br libn Pub Lib of Cincinnati 62-. 9: ALA; OhioLA. 10: Staff Assn of the Cincinnati Pub Lib; Beta Phi Mu; Hyde Park Lit Club; Suburban Symphony Club. 14: Ref. 15: 7548 Kirtley dr, Cincinnati Oh 45236.

DICKMAN, FLOYD CLARENCE. b Ottoville Ohio 15 My 39. 4: Stella Todd. 5: Miami U (Oxford Ohio) 67 (Elem Educ) BS in Ed; UMich (Ann Arbor) 67-68 (LS). 7: Hd ref libn Worthington Pub Lib, Worthington Ohio 68-; Prof child libn Ohio Dominicab Col 69-. 9: OhioLA; FranklinCoLA. 13: Yes. 14: Ref, child lit. 15: 860 Wetmore rd, Columbus Oh 43229.

DICKMAN, STELLA (TODD). b Columbus Ohio 12 D 41. 4: Floyd C Dickman. 5: St Mary of Springs 59-62 (Elem Educ) BS in Ed; UMich (Ann Arbor) 65-66 MALS. 6: Fr. 7: Ya libn Columbus Pub Lib, Columbus Ohio 66-67; Ya libn Bexley Pub Lib, Bexley Ohio 67-. 9: OhioLA; FranklinCo(Ohio)LA (v-pres 68-69). 14: Ya serv. 15: 860 Wetmore rd, Columbus Oh 43229.

DICKSON, JAMES KELLOGG. b Galva Ill 16 Jl 16. 5: Knox Col 34-38 (Eng) BA; Columbia 39 (LS) BA. 6: Fr. 7: Ref asst NYC Pub Lib 39; Ref asst Williams Col Lib 39-45; Acquis asst LSU 45-47; Enoch Pratt Free Lib, Baltimore: Fine arts dept asst 47-52, Fine arts dept hd 52-. 9: ALA (Art Subsection Chm 68); MusLA; Soc of Arch Histns; MdLA. 14: Ref. 15: Enoch Pratt Free Lib 400 Cathedral st, Baltimore Md 21201.

DICKSON, JANET S. b Niagara Falls Can 28 F 03. 5: Toronto 22-26 (Eng, Hist) BA; Simmons 33-34 (LS) BS; Columbia summers 39, 40, 43; 41, 46 (LS) MS. 6: Fr, Sp. 7: Circ child br ref Utica Pub Lib, Utica NY 28-33, 34-35; Head catlg dept pub lib, Des Moines Iowa 36-40; Instr clsf Simmons 40-41; Head tech processes Free Pub Lib, Worcester Mass 41-44; Head catlg dept NJ Col for Women Lib 44-45; Order-catlg libn Pub Lib, Providence 45-47; Head catlgr State U of Iowa Lib 47-50; Catlg libn Penn State U Lib 50-59; Chief catlg sect Smithsonian Inst Lib 59-64; Asst chief Tech Dept of Health & Welfare Lib 64-67; Nat Union Catlg Pub Project LC 67-69; Hd Post 1951 Imprints Sect LC 69-. 8: Decimal Clsf Ed Policy Com 53-58; Adv Com on Catlg & Clsf for Bookings Institution Fed Lib Survey 61-62; Civil Serv Commsn Com on Catlg & Clsf 61-62. 9: ALA (Com on Statistics 51-53); -DCC (Exec Bd 48-51, chm & mem 3 coms 43-58); -RTSD (Dir-at Large 58-60); DCLA; Potomac Valley Tech Proc Libns (Advis Coun, Nomin Com 64). 10: AAUW; LWV. 11: Melvil Dewey Award 58. 13: Yes. 14: Tech serv. 15: 2500 Wisconsin ave NW apt 718, Wash DC 20007.

DICKSON, KATHERINE MURPHY. b Boston Mass 13 Jl 32. 4: William Howard Dickson. 5: Simmons 50-54 (LS) BS; Columbia 56-58 (Eng Lit) MA (cum laude); NY State Libn Certif 58. 6: Fr, Ger, Lat. 7: Libn NY Pub Lib 54-58; asst ref libn Mass Inst Tech 58-61, Assoc ref libn 61-62, Act ref libn 62-63, Rotch arch & planning libn 63-65; Bibliogr & sci ref libn LC 66-. 8: Exchange libn Research Lab Assoc Electrical Inds, Aldermaston Court, Aldermaston Berkshire England 61-62; Library/USA Exhibit, Worlds Fair NY 64. 9: SLA; ALA; Coun Planning Libns (v-pres 64-66). 12: ""History of Aeronautics; A Preliminary Bibliography (67); ""Scientific and Technical Literature in England (62); ""Planning Your Career; A Selection from the Career Literature Available in the MIT Libraries (60). 13: Yes. 14: Ref, bibliog, admin, sci & tech, fine arts, lit. 15: 3961 Warner ave, Hyattsville Md 20784.

DICKSON, MARGARET ASHER. b Smithville Okla 9 N 21. 4: George H Dickson. 5: Tex Tech Col 39-43 (Home Econ) BS; Tex Womans U 63-64 MLS. 6: Sp. 7: Tchr Bovina High Sch, Bovina Tex 43-45; Period clerk Tex Tech Col 57-63, Assoc ref libn 64-65, Asst catlg libn 65-. 9: Tex Assn Col Tchrs. 10: Phi Upsilon Omicron;Friends of the Lib. 11: Tex Tech Lib of the yr, 68-69. 14: Catlg, ref. 15: Rt 5, Box 20, LubbockTx 79401.

DICKSTEIN, MARTIN HERMAN. b Brooklyn NY 27 Mr 25. 5: Brooklyn Col 43-55 (Music) BA; Columbia 57-58 (LS) MS. 6: Fr, Ger, Ital. 7: Auditor Navy Reg Accounts Off, NY 45-57; Lib Fellow Col of the City of NY57-58; Catlgr NY Pub Lib 58-59; Acquis libn UNev 59-69. 9: NevLA (Chm Acad &Spec Libs Sect). 14: Tech serv. 15: 5 Restone dr, Reno Nev 89501.

DIECKMAN, REV VINCENT. b Cincinnati 5 S11. 5: Duns Scotus Col 31-35 (Philos) AB; Holy Family Theol Sem 35-38 (Theol); Catholic U 40-41 BS in LS. 6: Lat, Ger. 7: Libn Duns Scotus Col 41-52; Libn St Leonard Col 58-68; Prov libn Cincinnati Franciscan Prov 50-. 8: Chaplain, VA Center, Dayton Ohio 58-. 9: CathLA; FranciscanEducConf (Lib Sect). 13: Yes. 14: Catlg. 15: 8100 Clyo rd, Dayton Oh45459.

DIENSTAG, JACOB I. b Austria. 1 S 15. 4: Claire B Levine. 5: Yeshiva Col 29-35 (Lit) BA; Columbia 49-51 MLS. 6: Hebrew, Fr, Ger, Aramaic, Yiddish. 7: Yeshiva U Lib: Lib asst 31-35, Chief semitics div 35-, Lecturer in bibliog & ref 59-, Assoc Prof of Bibliog 67-. 9: ALA; SLA; ewishLA (v-pres). 10: AAUP; Amer Acad for Jewish Research; Soc of Jewish Bibliophiles. 12: "Elijah Gaon" (49); EnHa-Mizwot; Bio-Bibliographical Lexicon of the Scholarship pertaining to the Seferha-Mizwot of Moses Maimonides (68). 13: Yes. 14: Ref, bibliog. 15: Yeshiva Univ, Amsterdam ave & 186th st,New York NY 10033.

DIERDORFF, MARIAN ELIZABETH. b Franklin Grove Ill 2 O 07. 5: Okla City U 25-28 (Pub Sch Music) BFA; UOkal (Educ) EdM; UIll summers 47-50 BLS. 7: High sch music Pub Sch, Cushing Okla 28-29; Elem & high sch music & elem subjPub Sch, Oklahoma City Okla 29-50; Elem subj & elem libn Pub Sch, Oklahoma CityOkla 50-53; Jr-sr high sch lib Pub Sch, Oklahoma City Okla 53-65; Head Libn JohnMarshall Jr-Sr High Sch, Oklahoma City Okla 65-67; Hd libn John Marshall Sr HighSch 67-. 8: Tchr of summer courses in lib sci, UOkla & Okla State U, 52-55. 9: ALA-YAD (Nomin Com 65); NEA; OklaLA (sec 56-57, treas 60); OklaEA;Okla ClrTA; NEA-DAVI. 10: AAUW; Sigma Alpha Iota; Delta Kappa Gamma; Kappa DeltaPi. 14: Sch libs; Catlg bks for YA. 15: 1205 NW 89, Oklahoma City Ok 73114.

DIERLAM, MAXINE T(HOMPSON. b Overland Mo 27 S 13. 4: Robert Jackson Dierlam. 5: Drury Col 34 (Eng Lit) BA; UColo 42 (Eng Lit) MA; Chicago 44 BLS. 7: Elem sch tchr pub schs, Springfield Mo 35-42; High sch Eng tchr pub schs, Clayton NM 42-43; Research asst Dept of Educ, UChicago 43-44; Humanities libn UColo 44-46; Asst libn Sampson Col 46; Catlgr NY State Ind & Labor Rel Lib Cornell U 47-48; Catlgr Queens Col Lib (NY) 60-. 9: TheatreLA; NY Resources & Tech Serv Libns. 13: "Bibliography on The Group Theatre," Exhibition catalog (69). 14: Catlg, theatre libs. 15: 72 Forest Row, Great Neck NY 11024.

DIETERICH, MARY. b Marengo Iowa 16 F 02. 5: Grinnell Col 21-25 (Fr) AB; Columbia 28-29 (LS) BS. 7: Tchr Brookings High Sch, Brookings SD 25-28; Act ref libn Grinnell Col Lib 29-30; Asst catlgr Iowa State Tchrs Col Lib 30-46, Ref libn 46-64; Ref libn & Archives libn State Col of Iowa 64-67; Ref libn & Archives libn UNo Iowa 67-. 9: ALA;-ACRL; NEA; IowaLA; Iowa State EA. 10: United World Federalists; AAUW; Fac Womens Club; UN Assn; Phi Beta Kappa. 14: Ref, archives. 15: Univ of Northern Iowa Lib, Cedar Falls Ia 50613.

DIETZ, (FRANCES) ANN (FRAZIER). b Utica NY 3 Mr 39. 4: Franklin M Dietz Jr. 5: Syracuse 56-60 (Home Econ) BS, 66-67 MLS. 6: Fr. 7: Sec to asst dir CornellU Lib 60-62, Searcher acquis 62-65, Catlgr 65-67; Indexer readers guide H W Wilson Co, Bronx NY 67-. 9: ALA; NY Lib Club. 10: Beta Phi Mu; Pi Lambda. 12: Ed "Science Fiction Times" (68-69); Ed "Luna" (69-). 14: Catlg, ref. 15: 655 Orchard st, Oradell NJ 07649.

DIETZ, CHARLES RAYMOND. b Brooklyn NY 31 Ag 34. 4: Dorothy Kvalheim. 5: Wagner Col 52-56 (Amer Hist) AB; Lutheran Theol Sem 56-57 (Theol); Pratt 59-60 MLS; IBM Systs Research Inst (NYC) 65; UMd 67 Sr Lib Adm Dev Program Certif. 6: Fr, Gk. 7: Co Clerk Pfc USA NYANG 69th Battle Group 57-61; Tchr Immanuel Lutheran Sch, Whitestone NY 58-59; Br libn Queens Borough Pub Lib, Jamaica NY 59-61; Lib Dir Pequannock Twp Pub Lib, Pompton Plains NY 61-63; Lib Dir Warner Lib of the Tarrytown NJ 63-66; Dir libs Abington Twp Pub Lib & Old York Road Coop Lib Syst 66-69; Dir Altoona-Blair Co Lib Syst 69-. 8: Consul: Pequannock Twp Pub Lib 61; "New American Guide to Scholarships, Fellowships, and Loans. 09: ALA;-Lad (In-Serv Train Com 65); westchester LA (Admin Sect); NJ Lib RT 61-63; NJ Lib Development Com (sec 61-62); LPRC. 10:Phi Mu Alpha; Phi Alpha Eta; Kappa Sigma Alpha. 11: ALA Scholarship for Worlds Fair Exhibit 65. 12: "Quality Library Service for a First-Class Township (66). 13: Yes. 14: Admin, pub rel, coop lib wk. 15: Sixth ave & 15th st, Altoona Pa 16603.

DIETZ, PAUL T. b Milwaukke 7 S 22. 4: Corinne Braeger. 5: Concordia Col (Milwauee) 40-42; Concordia Theol Sem 43-49 (Theol) BA, BD; Marquette U 47-51 (Hist) MA; UWis (Madison) 53-57 MALS. 7: Pastor St Pauls Lutheran Church, Colby Wis 50-52; Libn Concordia Col (Milwaukee) 52-. 8: Archivist So Wis Dist The Lutheran Church-Mo Synod; V-chm Adv Coun on LibDevel, State of Wis 69-. 9: WisLA (Intell Freedom Comm 68-). 15: W158 N6301Cherry Hill dr, Menomonee Falls Wi 53052.

DIFLOURE, ESTHER EVANGELINE (NICHOLS). b Frewsburg NY 23 Ap 07. 5: Otterbein Col 26-30 (Educ) AB; Bonebrake Theol Sem 30-36 (Old Testament) BD; UIll 36-39 BS in LS. 7: Stenogr Christian Publ Co, Dayton, Ohio 25; Dayton & Montgomery Co Pub Lib, Dayton, Ohio: Clerical asst 25-39, Sr asst acquis dept & regbr 51-56, Ref dept asst 57-61, Bibliogr serv libn in soc sci div of ref dept 62-. 9: ALA; OhioLA. 10: Dayton Music Club. 14: Ref, bibliog. 15: 6780 Brantford rd, Dayton Oh 45414.

DIKEMAN, HELEN G. b Bridgeport Conn 13 Mr 13. 5: Jr Col of Conn 30-32; Duke 32-34 (Zoology) AB. 7: Statistical clk McKesson & Robbins Fairfield Conn 34-39; Jr lib asst Bridgeport Pub Lib, Conn 39-43; Monsanto Co, Indian Orchard Mass: Asst libn 43-44, Libn research dept 44-. 9: SLA (chm Nat Chem Sect 52-53; pres Conn Valley Chap 48-49); ACS; SPE; ASI. 14: Documentation (plastics & polymer chem). 15: Monsanto Co 730 Worcester st, Indian Orchard Ma 01051.

DIKEMAN, ROBERT K. b Dunkirk NY 11 My 40. 4: Roxane N Norris. 5: West Res 66-67 MSLS; UNeb 62-66 (Chem) MS; SUNY (Binghamton) Harpur Col 58-62 (Chem) BA. 7: Adult ref asst Cuyahoga Co Pub Lib, Parma Ohio 66-67; Ref libn Chem Abstracts Serv, Columbus Ohio 67-. 9: ACS; ASIS. 10: Phi Lambda Upsilon; Beta Phi Mu. 14: Ref serv, lib automation, lib admin. 15: 88 Tulane rd, Columbus Oh 43202.

DIKIJIAN, ARMINE. b Chicago 4 N 14. 5: Barnard Col 31-35 (Fr) BA; Columbia 35-36 (Music, LS) BS. 6: Fr, Armenian. 7: Libn Brooklyn Pub Lib 36-37, Music catlgr & asst in music div 37-46, Asst supt catlg dept 46-55; Libn Nat Coun on Crime & Delinquency, NYC 56-. 8: Music LA & ALA Com on code for catlg music & records. 9: SLA; MusLA NY Chap (past sec, past pres). 13: Yes. 14: Catlg. 15: 125 Senator st, Brooklyn NY 11220.

DILIBERTO, HELEN (BRATNEY). b Newark NJ 9 Je 20. 4: Stephen P Diliberto. 5: NJ Col for Women 37-38, 42-43 (LS) AB; Upsala Col 38-42 (Hist); UCal 58-61 (Hist) AB; UColo summer 63. 6: Fr, Russian. 7: Lib asst E Orange Pub Lib, E Orange NJ 38-42; Asst libn League of Nations Lib, Princeton NJ 43-45; Tchr Berkeley Unified Sch Dist, Berkeley Cal 61-66, Sch libn 66-. 8: Memb group to develop lib curriculum for berkeley Unified Sch Dist summer 67; Curriculum development for high potential studs (material consul) summer 68; Personnel Policy Commsn Bd of Educ, Berkeley Cal. 9: NEA; ALA; Rutger'sLA; CTA; BEA; CalLA. 10: AAUW. 14: Child lit. 15: 769 Balra dr, El Cerrito Ca 94530.

DILL, CHARLOTTE ELVA. b Vancouver BC Can 13 Jl 14. 5: UBC 31-35 (Bot) BA, 35-39 (Bot) MA; Cornell U 40-43; Plant pathology Toronto 44-45 BLS. 6: Fr, Russian. 7: Lab asst UBC Bot Dept 35-40; Lab asst Cornell U Plant Path Dept, Ithaca NY 40-43; Lab asst UToronto Bot Dept 43-44; Libn Nat Res Coun Lib, Ottawa 45-64, Acquis libn Nat Sci Lib 64-. 9: CanLA; Lib Assn Ottawa; ALA; SLA. 10: Color Photographic Assn of Can; Ottawa Field-Naturalists Club. 13: Yes. 14: Acquis. 15: 7 Arundel ave, Ottawa 7 Can.

DILL, CLARA ROSELLE. b Hendersonville NC 6 Mr 26. 5: Furman 43-47 (Eng) BA; Peabody Col 47-49 BSLS, 59-60 MALS. 6: Fr, Ger. 7: Catlg libn FurmanU Lib, Greenville SC 47-53; Libn US Army Libs, Bad Toelz Germany 53-54; Supv libn lib depot US Army, Kaiserslautern Germ 54-56; Supv libn lib serv ctr US Army, Dachau Germany 56-59; Area lib US Army, Zama Japan 60-. 10: Ikebana Intl Org Soc. 14: Mil libs, catlg & clsf rare bks. 15: Camp Zama Lib Hqs USAGCJ, APO San Francisco Ca 96343.

DILLARD, GEORGIA (MAE DETERS). b Minn 5 D 38. 5: St Olaf Col 55-57 (Eng); Macalester Col 57-59 (Intl Rel) BA; UWash 60-61 MLS. 7: Libn Padelford (Eng & speech) Br UWash 61-63; Libn loan dept UCal (Berkeley) 64-66; Libn art & philos sect Phoenix Pub Lib 667; Period & circ libn Instr Materials Ctr Glendale Commun Col 67-. 9: ALA; AAUP; ArizStateLA. 10: Glendale Commun Col Faculty Senate. 15: 1533 W Missouri ave apt 22, Phoenix Az 85015.

DILLENBECK, JANE (GRAY). b Oak Park Ill 5 Ja 28. 4: Lee E Dillenbeck. 5: Elmhurst Col 45-49 (Eng) BA; URI 66-68 MLS. 6: Sp. 7: Asst libn Cumberland High Sch, Cumberland RI 66-67; Hd Adult Serv Pawtucket Pub Lib, RI 67-68; Asst Acquis Libn No Ill U 68-. 9: ALA; RILA; IllLA. 14: Acquis. 15: 1028 N Spring st, Elgin Il 60120.

DILLEY, RICHARD ALLEN. b Soldiers Grove Wis 29 Je 36. 5: Wis State Col (La Crosse) 52-54; UWis 57-59 (Fr Lit) BA, 60-61 (LS) MA. 6: Fr, Ital, Sp. 7: Personnel spec SP3 US Army, Walters AFB Tex 54, 56; UIowa: Asst acquis libn 61-62, Ref libn 62-64, Ser catlgr 64-65, Head ser dept 65-67; Acquis libn Grad Sch of Bus Stanford U 68-. 9: ALA (sec-treas Jr Mem Round Table 63-64). 14: Ser,bibliog, catlg, acquis. 15: 1777 Woodland ave, Palo Alto Ca 94303.

DILLINGER, FRANCES JANE. b Richwood WVa 12 Ja 29. 5: Morris Harvey Col 46-50 (Eng) AB; Pratt 53-54 MLS. 6: Fr. 7: Stud asst Morris Harvey Col Lib 47-50; Clerical asst Kan Co Pub Lib, Charleston WVa 49-41; Research libn McCall Corp, NYC 51-53; 1st asst & ya libn, adult serv head Brooklyn Pub Lib 54-61; Circ libn Kanawha Co Pub Lib, Charleston WVa 61-. 9: ALA; WVaLA. 10: YWCA, Kanawha Co Pub Lib Staff Assn; Zeta Mu Epsilon; Pratt Inst Lib Sch AlumAssn; Morris Harvey Col Alum Assn. 14: Circ, ya, picture collections, admin. 15: 406 Elm st, S Charleston WV 25303.

DILLON, BETTY JANE (BARRETT). b Edinburgh Ind 2 Ja 10. 4: Albert L Dillon. 5: Wellesley 27-29 (Eng); Butler U 29-31 BS in Journalim; Catholic U 46-48 BS in LS. 6: Fr. 7: Trainee Indianapolis Pub Lib 31-32; Org of filing system Fed Home Loan Bank, Indianapolis 33; Jr libn Indianapolis Pub Lib 33-35; Catlgr US Govt Pring ff, Wash DC 40-47; Catlgr US Pub Roads Admin, Wash Dc 47-50; Documents libn UPittsburgh 5056, Ser libn 57-66, Head of Central Serials 66-67, Orig catlgr 67-. 10: Beta Phi Mu; Theta Sigma Phi. 14: Tech serv. 15: 8109 Peebles rd,Pittsburgh Pa 15237.

DILLON, HOWARD W(ENDELL). b Green Valley Ill 5 N 37. 4: Ruth Marie Sherwood. 5: Knox Col 55-59 (Music) BA; Ind U 59-61 (LS) MA. 7: Intern Ohio State U Libs (Columbus) 61-62, Hd docs div 62-63, Automation & info sci libn 63-65; Assoc libn Harvard Grad Sch of Educ 65-67, Act libn 67-68, Libn 68-. 9: ALA-ISAD (provisional sec 67); ASIS (coun 67-68; chm New England Chap 68). 14: Admin, lib automation. 15: 15 Fernald dr, Cambridge Ma 02138.

DILLON, M PATRICIA (DOYLE). b Boston 1 My 23. 4: Thomas E Dillon. 5: Simmons 42-46 (LS) BS; BOSTON U summer 65 (LS). 6: Sp, Fr. 7: Circ libn MIT 46- 52; Catlgr Thomas Craine Pub Lib, Quincy Mass 53-54; Libn Endicott Jr Col 54-56; Libn Beverly Hosp Sch of Nursing, Beverly Mass 56-58; Libn-bkmob Beverly Pub Lib, Beverly Mass 59-60; Child & Jr High libn Everett Pub Lib, Everett Mass 64; Libn Hamilton-Wenham Reg High Sch, Hamilton Mass 64-. 9: ALA; SLA; NESchLA; North Shore High Sch Lib Assn; MassLA; NEA. 10: BeverlyCol Club; North Shore Simmons Club; Mass Tchrs Assn. 13: Yes. 14: High sch libs, catlg, ref. 15: Hamilton-Wenham Reg HighSch, 775 Bay rd, Hamilton Ma 01936.

DILLON, SISTER MARIE MONICA. b Chicago Ill 29 Mr 31. 5: Barry Col 52-54 (Eng); Siena Heights Col 54-57 (Eng) BA; UChicago summers 61-67 (LS) MA. 6: Lat, Sp, Fr. 7: Tchr Chicago Parochial Schs, 58-64; Libn St Edward High Sch, Elgin Ill 64-. 9: ALA; CathLA; DAVI; AASL; IllLA; IASL; NIUCLA (Memb Chm); IAVA. 14: Lib serv to ya. 15: 335 Locust st, Elgin Il 60120.

DILLON, MRS MARY (PARKER). b Clinton NC 25 N 26. 4: John Luther Dillon. 5: Flora Macdonald Col 43-47 (Soc Sci, Eng) BA; UNC 47-48 BS in LS. 6: Sp, Fr, Lat. 7: Catlgr Duke U 48-53; Head catlgr UMiami Sch of Med (Miami Fla) 53-63, Head reader serv 63-65, Research assoc 65-. 8: Org N Shore Hosp Lib 61; Consul & org N Miami Gen Hosp 63-. 9: MedLA; FlaLA; Dade County LA. 14: Catlg, pub rels, circ, ref. 15: 2025 Keystone blvd, N Miami Fl 33161.

DILLON, RICHARD H. b Sausalito Cal 16 Ja 24. 4: Barbara Sutherland. 5: UCal (Berkeley) 41-43, 46-50 (Hist) AA, AB, MA, BLS. 7: Infantryman (Pfc) USA, France & Germany 43-46; Catlgr Sutro Lib, San Francisco 50-52, Libn 53-. 8: Tchr UCal Ext Div, Col of Marin, USan Francisco, UCLA, UHawaii 59-69. 9: ALA; Cal State Employees Assn; Cal Hist Soc; West Hist Assn; CalLA. 10: Phi Beta Kappa. 11: Purple Heart; Gold & Silver Commonwealth Club Medals; Phelan Award. 12: Auth "Embarcadero", "Shanghaiing Days", "The Hatchet Men", "The Gila Trail", "Legend of Grizzly Adams", "Califronia Trail Herd", "Meriwether Lewis", "Fool's Good", "Wells Fargo Detective", "Humbugs and heroes". 13: Yes. 14: Hist, rare bks, mss. 15: Sutro Lib 2130 Fulton st, San Francisco Ca 94117.

DILLON, WILLIAM A. b Pittsburgh 2 O 22. 4: Barbara Harlow. 5: Mt St Marys Col (Emmitsburg Md) 40-41; UPittsburgh 46-48 (Eng) BA; Columbia 52-53 MSLS. 7: (T/Sgt) US Army Infantry Rifle Platoon sgt Pacific Theater 42-45; Spec Agent Carnegie Hero Fund Commsn, Pittsburgh Penn 48-50; Gen asst, stacks curator, br libn Brooklyn Pub Lib

53-58; Lib Dir Jervis Lib, Rome NY 58-. 9: ALA; NYLA. 13: Yes. 14: Admin. 15: 1216 N James st, Rome NY 13440.

DiMATTIA, ERNEST ANTHONY JR. b Boston 9 Ja 40. 4: Susan E Smith. 5: Boston Col 57-61 (Mat) AB; Simmons 62-65 (LS) MS. 6: Fr, Ger. 7: Stud asst Boston Pub Lib 57-61, Pre-prof libn 61-62; Massarmy Nat Guard, Ft Dix NJ & Ft Bliss Tex 62; (Sgt) Mass Army Reserve Nat Guard,charlestown Mass 62-68; Asst libn Monsanto Research Corp, Everett Mass 62-64; Proflibn Boston Pub Lib 64-65; Dir Salem Pub Lib, Salem Mass 65-. 9: ALA; SLA; MassLA; NELA; Greater Boston Pub Lib Admins (pres 68-69). 10: Rotary Club; Amer Red Cross. 14: Lib admin, Lib Pub Rels. 15: 346 Essex st, Salem Ma 01970.

DiMATTIA, SUSAN (SMITH). b Neptune NJ 28 Jl 42. 4: Ernest Anthony DiMattia Jr. 5: Wilson Col 60-64 (Eng, Econ) BA; Simmons 64-65 MS in LS. 6: Fr. 7: Hd libn New England Merchants Nat Bk, Boston 65-. 9: SLA (Boston Chap treas). 14: Ref, admin. 15: 345 Essex st, Salem Ma 01970.

DIMITRY, BETTY RUTH (CHAPMAN). b Phila 19 Ap 26. 4: Douglas Donald Dimitry. 5: Highland Park Col 61-63 (Liberal Arts); Wayne State U 63-65 (Educ) AB; UMich 65-(LS). 6: Ger. 7: Lib asst Henry Ford Hosp Med Lib, Detroit 59-61; Libn Austin Catholicprep Sch, Detroit 65-67; Asst Prof Oakland Commun Col (Farmington Mich) 67-. 9: ALA; MichASchL; Coun on Lib Tech. 10: Pi Lambda Theta; Pres of Alpha Pi Chapter; UMich Lib Sci Alumni Assn; Wayne State U Lib Sci Alum. 14: Lib tech. 15: 126 Maplefield, Pleasant Ridge Mi 48069.

DIMMICK, MARY LAVERNE (GUSWILER). b Charleroi Penn 13 Jl 30. 4: Edgar L Dimmick Jr. 5: Cal State Col 48-52 (Eng) BS in Ed; Carnegie 57-58 MLS. 7: Jr libn Buffalo & Erie County Pub Lib, Buffalo NY 58-59; Asst ref libn Great Neck Lib, Great Neck NY 59-63; Period libn American U 63-65; Documents libn UPittsburgh 65-66, Supv lending serv 66-68, Sr infolibn 68-. 9: ALA; PennLA. 10: Beta Phi Mu. 14: Ref, admin. 15: 205 N Homewoodave, Pittsburgh Pa 15208.

DiNAPOLI, JOHN FRANCIS. b Woburn Mass 2 D 12. 4: Dorothea A Dunigan. 5: Boston Col 36-50 (Secondary Educ) AB, M Ed. 6: Fr, Lat, 07: Ref libn Boston Col Lib 36-42; US Army Clsf & Voc & Ed Spec 42-46; Head ref Boston Col Lib 46-47; Libn US Naval Line Sch, Newport RI 47; Libn Naval War Col Logistics Lib 47-51; Ref libn Mahan Lib 51-56; Dir of Libs Naval War Col (Newport RI) 56-. 9: SLA (Mil Libns Group); ALA. 10: Oral Hist Assn. 14: Admin, rare bks. 15: 11 Morton ave, Newport RI 02840.

DINGMAN, A KATHARINE (DAVIS). b Portland Me 19 S 12. 4: Gerald F Dingman. 5: UMich 30-34 (Sociol) BA; Columbia 36 (LS) BS; UChicago 43 (LS) MA. 6: Fr. 7: Ser catlgr Columbia U 36-39; Head sociol div DC Pub Lib 39-44; Asst libn OWI, Wellington NZ 44-46; Asst libn head of adult serv, Worcester Mass 47-49; Dir US Info Lib, Brussels 49-51; Child libn Pine Point Br, Springfield (Mass) City Lib 51-59; Dir Wilbraham (Mass) Pub Lib 59-65; Asst libn ref IIL govt documents Bates Col Lib 65-67; Libn Oxford Hills High Sch, S Paris Me 68-. 9: ALA; MassLA; NELA; Westreg Pub Lib System; West Mass Lib Club; MeSchLA. 14: Pub lib advis serv, ref, schlibs. 15: RFD 2, Turner Me 04282.

DINGMAN, JOHN DONALD. b Macon County Ill 9 Ja 07. 4: Elsie Mae Michael. 5: UIll 26-41 (Ed) BA, 46 (Ed) MS 55-57 (LS); DenverU 54, 59 (LS); MillikinU 60 (LS). 7: Tchr Macon Co Schs W Stringtown Sch 28-31; Prin & tchr Niantic Grade Sch, Niantiac Ill 31-42; Centennial Jr High Sch, Decatur Ill: Tchr 42-49, Libn 49-64; Ref dept Decatur Pub Lib 56-61; Ref dept MillikinU 61-63; Consul & hd educ & train Ill State Lib Springfield 64-. 8: Com mem Nat Lib Week Ill 65. 9: Phi Delta Kappa; ALA; Nat Retired Tchrs Assn; IllASchL (treas 60-61, pres 62-63); IllLA. 14: Lib devel, ref. 15: 1065 West View st, Decatur Il 60018.

DINKIN, JOAN (PALESTINE). b Brooklyn NY 13 S 42. 4: Robert J Dinkin. 5: Brooklyn Col 59-63 (Hist) BA; Middlebury Russian Sch summer 62(Russian); Columbia 65-66 (LS) MA. 6: Russian, Fr, Sp. 7: Libn Devenco Inc NYC 64-65; Ref libn NYC Pub Lib 66; Sch libn Fair Lawn Pub Sch, Fairlawn NJ 66; Catlgr Tchrs Col Lib ColumbiaU 66-68; Catlgr Fresno State Col Lib 68-. 9: ALA; NY Tech Serv Libns. 10: La Leche League. 11: Brooklyn Col Stud Activities Award. 14: Catlg. 15: 2036 No Angus, Fresno Ca 93703.

DINNAN, LEO T. b Pontiac Mich 21 Ap 23. 4: Mary Shawley. 5: UMich 46-49 (Eng) AB, 49-50 AMLS. 6: Ger, Sp. 7: Page Pontiac City Lib, Pontiac Mich 41-43; US Army Infantry, Europe 43-46; Asst in order dept UMich Law Lib (Ann Arbor) 49-50; Lib asst Detroit Pub Lib 50-51; Head Libn Morley Lib, Painesville Ohio 51-56; Head Libn Oak Park Pub Lib, Oak Park Mich 56-62; Head of pub serv Wayne County Lib, Wayne Mich 62-63, Asst county libn 63-. 8: Lecturer in Lib Sci UMich Ext Dept 58-; Bldg consul Lapeer (Mich) Lib BD & Romeo (Mich) Lib Bd64 Consul to Bd of Herrick Pub Lib, Holland Mich 68. 9: ALA (Life Mem); MichLA(2nd v-pres 67). 10: Phi Beta Kappa. 13: Yes. 14: Pub lib admin. 15: Wayne County Lib Hdq, 33030 Van Born rd, Wayne Mi 48184.

DINNEEN, RITA MARIE (DESAULNIERS). b Boston 9 O 18. 4: Edward G Dinneen. 5: Emmanuel Col 36-40 (Hist) AB; Simmons 40-41 (LS) BS. 6: Fr. 7: Asst Boston Pub Lib Kirstein Bus Br 41-56, Bus br libn 56-. 9: ALA; SLA. 14: Ref, bus libs. 15: 205 Kent st, Brookline Ma 02146.

DINTRONE, CHARLES VINCENT. b NYC 16 My 42. 5: UCLA 60-66 (Hist) BA, MA; UOre 66-67 (Hist); UCal 67-68 MLS. 6: Fr, Ger. 7: Libn II Govt Publ Fresno State Col 68-. 9: ALA; CalLA. 14: Govt, publ. 15: Lib Fresno State College Shaw & Cedar, Fresno Ca 93726.

DiPESA, CAROL ANNE (PRESSEY). b Medford Mass 16 Jl 28. 4: Anthony P DiPesa. 5: Simmons Col 46-50 (LS) BS. 6: Fr, Sp. 7: Lib asst Boston U Col of Bus Admin 46-50; Libn grade I Detroit Pub Lib 5-51; Libn grade II Brooklyn Pub Lib 51-53, Yp libn 53-55; Head of circ Robbins Lib, Arlington Mass 55-57, Ya libn 63-64. Trustee Saugus Pub Lib, Saugus Mass 69. 14: Ya wk. 15: 16 Gilway, Saugus Ma 01906.

DIRKS, MARTHA (WOODS). b Newton Kan 28 Jl 22. 4: Arthur W Dirks. 5: Hamilton Col McGill Fr Inst (NDEA) summer 65 (Fr); DenverU summer 66 (LS); Wayne State 66-67 MSLS. 6: Fr. 7: Optometric tech, Ness City & WaKeeney Kan 50-59; Libn & tchr Quinter High Sch, Quinter Kan 63-66; Instr & adv (lib) Unified Sch Dist 208, WaKeeney Kan 67-69; Instr in lib sci Ft Hays Kan State Col 69-. 8: Adv Elem Sch Lib, WaKeeney Kan 67-69, Supv centralization (USD 208) summer 68. 9: NEA; NCTE; ALA; Kan StateTA; KSA; KanLA. 10: Phi Kappa Phi; Lambda Iota Tau; Alpha Psi Omega; Kan Coun Women; Lit Club (Federated). 13: Yes. 14: Lib sci instr for sch libs. 15: 332 North Tenth, WaKeeney Ks 67672.

DIRLIK, RAJA (GHANDOUR). b Beirut Lebanon 16 Ag 34. 4: Dirlik, Andre. 5: American U (Beirut) 55-61 (Pol Sci) BA; McGill 61-63 (Pol Sci) MA, 63-64 BLS, 67-69 MLS. 6: Fr, Arabic. 7: Catlgr McGill U Redpath lib 64-66, Reserves libn 66-68, Asst hd circ dept68-. 14: Catlg, ref, admin, circ. 15: 418 ouest ave des Pins, apt 20, Montreal130 Quebec Can.

DiROMA, EDWARD. b NYC 26 Je 19. 4: Dorothy Gallagher. 5: City Col of NY 37-41 (Eng) AB; Columbia 43-44 BLS; New Sch 55-58 (Labor Econ) MA. 7: Ref asst Econ Div NY Pub Lib 44-48, Spec Ind Rel Lit Econ Div 49-64, Documents libn 64-65, Exec asst ref dept 65-67, Chief econ div 67-. 8: Instr Grad Sch of Lib Serv Rutgers U 63-67. 9: ALA; NYLA; NY Lib Club. 10: Phi Beta Kappa. 14: Ref. 15: Res Libs NY Pub Lib, NYC 10018.

DIRTADIAN, HELEN H. b Utica NY 9 Ja 26. 5: George Washington U 46-48 AA, 48-50 (Govt) BA; UDenver 57-58 (LS) MA. 7: Libn Spec Serv Dept of Army, Okinawa 52-53; Asst dir State Lib, Juneau Alaska 58-59, State Libn 59-67; Dir Pub Lib, Utica NY 67-. 9: ALA; NYLA; Centr NYLA. 10: AAUW. 15: 916 Arnold ave,Utica NY 13502.

DiRUSSO, BENEDETTO. b Brooklyn NY 15 Mr 36. 4: Carol Ann DiRusso. 5: St Johns Col, St Johns U 54-57 (Chem) BS; Pratt 61-63 MLS. 6: Fr, Ger, Ital. 7: Sci & engnr aide USAF Holloman AFB NM 58-61; Adult serv libn Booklyn Pub Lib 61-64; Sci libn St Johns U (Queens NY) 64-67; Ref libn CUNY (York Col) 67-. 8: Free-lance research ed Grolier Infor Serv 63. 9: SLA; CathLA; Metropolitan Cath Col Libns; Lib Assn CUNY. 14: Ref, info retrieval systems. 15: 214-04 46th ave, Bayside NY 11361.

DISBROW, RUTH C. b Elmira NY 27 F 04. 5: SUNY (Albany) 23-27 (Eng) BA; Columbia summers 49-52 (LS) MS. 6: Fr. 7: Eng tchr, Germantown NY 27-29; Eng tchr, Ballston Spa NY 29-30; Tchr of Oral Eng, Yonkers NY 30-32; Tchr of Eng in immigrant educ, Binghamton NY even 35-44, Binghamton NY: Eng tchr 47-49, Tchr of soc studies 49-51, Assoc libn North Sr High Sch 49, & 51-. 9: NEA; ALA; NYLA; NYStateEA (past treas Sch Libns Sect); Sch Libns Assn So Tier (of NY counties). 10: AAUW; Women's Nat Bk Assn. 15: 30 New st, Binghamton NY 13903.

DIVELBISS, JOHN EDWARD. b Kansas City Mo 7 Ja 33. 4: Lois E (Austin). 5: Ottawa U Ottawa Kan 51-55 (Sociol) AB; Central Baptist Theol Sem 58-62; UMinn 62-63 (LS). 7: Radar control off (Lt) USN Res (active duty) 55-58; Catlgr Central Baptist Theol Sem 60-62; Circ asst Augsburg Col 62-63; East Baptist Theol Sem: Asst libn 63-64, Sct libn 64-65; Asst libn tech serv Westmont Col 65-. 9: So Cal Tech Proc Gp. 10: Deacon, 1st Cong Church, Santa Barbara Cal. 14: Ref, govt docs, catlg. 15: 23 San Dimas, Santa Barbara Ca 93105.

DIVELEY, RUTH ANNA. b Geary Okla 22 Mr 08. 5: Puget Sound 28 (Eng) AB; U Wash 29 (Eng) MA, 36 (LS) AB. 6: Fr. 7: Libn Multnomah Col 36-39; Acquis libn Occidental Col 39-. 9: ALA-ACRL; CalLA; Col & Univ Libns So Cal (pres 46); So Cal Tech Proc Gp. 10: AAUW. 14: Acquis, bibliog. 15: 2046 Addison wy, Los Angeles Ca 90041.

DIVETT, ROBERT THOMAS. b Salt Lake City 4 N 25. 4: anet Barben. 5: UUtah 43 (Arc) Brigham Young U 48, 50-53 (Hist) BS; Peabody 54-56 (LS) MA; Emory 56 (LS) ; UUtah 59-63, 67-68 (Educ Admin) ED. 7: Administrative Sgt US Marine Corp, Pacific Theater & China 44-47; Missionary Church of Jesus Christ of Latter-day Saints, N Cal 48-50; Tchr-libn Burley Jr High Sch, Burley Ida 53-54; 1st asst Vanderbilt U Sch of Med Lib 54-56; Med libn & Asst Prof Lib Sci UUtah 56-63; Assoc Prof med bibliog & Libn Sch of Med UNM 63-. 8: Consul lib automation,Mayo Clinic, 68. 9: MedLA (chm Memb Com 65-66); SLA (Biol Scis Div: chm Nomin Com 65-66). 11: Murray Gottlieb Prize for Hist of Med, 59 & 62. 12: "Classification Schedule and Subject Headings for Mormon Literature" (60, 2d ed 62). 13: Yes. 14: Admin, mechanization of libs, hist of med, med communications. 15: Med Sciences Lib, Univ of NM, Albuquerque NM 87106.

DIX, WILLIAM SHEPHERD. b Winchester Va 19 N 10. 4: Jane Griffin. 5: UVa 31 (Eng) BA, 32 (Eng) MA; Chicago 46 (Eng) PhD. 6: Fr, Ger, Sp, Lat. 7: Master Darlington Sch for Boys, Rome Ga 32-39; Instr West Res 40-42; Instr Williams Col 42-44; Research assoc Radio Research Lab, Harvard U 44-46; Instr Harvard U 46; Assoc Prof & libn Rice Inst 46-53; Libn Princeton U 53-. 8: Mem & chm, US Nat Commsn for UNESCO 55-61; Mem & v-chm US Del to UNESCO Gen Conf, Paris, 58 & 60; US Del to Conf of Asian Nat Commsns for UNESCO Manila, 61; Mem, Asian-Amer Assembly, Kuala Lampur, 63; Consul to Ford Found, Baghdad 58; Mem Bd of Dirs, Franklin Bk Programs, 65- & Clr 66-; Mem currently of Adv Coms of NJ State Lib, Duke U Lib, Harvard U Lib, Assn of Amer Univ Presses; Pres, Princeton U Chap AAUP 65-67; Consul to var cols & univs on lib arch, etc; Mem Govt Adv Com on Internat Bk & Lib Programs State Dept 67-69; Mem Adv Coun on Grad, Ed (US Off of Educ) 69-. 9: ALA (pres-elect 68-69; Coun mem-at-large 58; chm Intel Freedom Com 51-53; chm Internat Rel Com 55-60);-ACRL (Bd Dirs 55-58);ARL (Exec Sec 57-60, chm 62-63; chm Shared Catlg Com 64-68); TexLA (treas 50-52, pres-elect 52-53); NJLA (Exec Bd mem-at-large 55-57); SWLA (chm Col Libs Sect 49). 10: Phi Beta Kappa; Grolier Club (NY). 12: "The Amateur Spirit in Scholarship" (40). 13: Yes. 14: Univ lib admin. 15: Princeton Univ Lib, Princeton NJ 08540.

DIXON, D GENEVIEVE. b Buckingham Ill 29 S 09. 5: UIll 27-31 (Educ, Eng) BS, 35-37 BS in LS; Chicago 49-53 (LS) MA. 6: Fr, Sp. 7: Tchr-libn High Sch, Winnebago Ill 31-35; Asst libn New Trier Twp High Sch,Winnetka Ill 37-42; Libn Lab Sch UChicago 42-47; Lib consul Twp High Sch & Jr Col, joliet Ill 48-49; Instr in Lib Sci Kan State Tchrs Col (Pittsburg) 50-53; Dir Schof Lib Sci Texas Woman's U 53-. 9: ALA; AALS; NEA; SWLA; TexLA; Tex State Tchrs Assn; Tex Assn Col Tchrs. 10: AAUP; Altrusa Internat; Denton Friends ofLibrary; Delta Zeta. 13: Yes. 14: Adolescent lit, materials sel. 15: 423 Woodland, Denton Tx 76201.

DIXON, DOROTHY LILLIAN. b Montreal Can 18 F 16. 5: McGill 37 BA, 38 BLS. 7: Circ asst Ottawa Pub Lib, Ottawa Can 38-39; Libn Imperial Tobacco Co, Montreal 39-42; Lt WRCNS, Canada 42-45; Stills libn Nat Film Bd, Ottawa Can 46; Ref asst Ottawa Pub Lib, Ottawa Can 46-57; Asst to chief libn Windsor Pub Lib, Windsor Can 57-59; Br hd Etobicoke Pub Lib, Etobicoke Can 59-. 15: 90 Cordova ave apt 1103, Islington Ont Can.

DIXON, EVA (JOHNSON). b Evinston Fla 28 Ag 09. 5: UFla 28-37 (Sociol, Eng) ABE, 46-48 (Eng, Educ) MA; Fla State U 49 (LS); UFla 51-54 (LS); Appalachian Tchrs Col 55 (LS). 6: Sp. 7: High sch Eng tchr, Okeechobee Fla 40-42; Tech 5th Grade WAC, Camp Pickett Va 43-45; Eng tchr-libn Jefferson High Sch, Monticello Fla 45-47; A-v dir Jefferson County Schs, Monticello Fla 48-50; Eng tchr-libn Meigs High Sch, Meigs Ga 54-55; Libn Chipola Jr Col 55-57, Dir eng tchr-libn Meigs High Sch, Meigs Ga 54-55; Libn Chipola Jr Col 55-57; Dir of Lib Serv 57-. 8: Area chm NLW 65-68; Chm stud aid & scholarship com Chipola Jr Col 61-62. 9: NEA; ALA; JeffersonCoEA (pres 48-50); FlaEA (socs chm 50-51); FlaLA; FlaASchL; Fla Assn Pub Jr Cols. 10: Kappa Delta Pi; Fla Fed Bus & Prof Women's Club. 13: Yes. 14: Ref, bk talks, admin, catlg. 15: Chipola Jr Col Lib, Marianna Fl 32446.

DIXON, HELEN (STARKEY). b New Britain Conn 2 S 17. 4: William James Dixon. 5: Chatham Col 35-39 (Eng) BA; Rosary Col 67-69 (LS) MA. 6: Fr, Sp, Lat. 7: Methods engr Remington Rand Inc, NY, Conn, Mass & Md 41-50, 51-52. 10: AAUW; Col Club of baltimore; Chatham Col Alumnae Club; Parish Players; Vagabonds. 14: Lib automation. 15: 610 Sunrise, Lake Bluff Il 60044.

DIXON, MADGE CARROLL NANCE. b West Green Ga 19 N 21. 4: James Hansford Dixon Jr. 5: SGa Col 37-39 Diploma; Ga State Col for Women 39-41 (Eng) AB; Peabody 41-42 BS in LS. 6: Fr, Sp, Ger, Lat. 7: Circ & ref asst Kanawha County Pub Lib, Charleston WVa 43; Asst period libn Ga Tech Lib 44-45; Libn Jacksonville Jr Col 45-49, 53, 54; Libn W Fulton High Sch Lib, Atlanta 49-50; Period libn Stetson U 50-52; Ref & circ asst Jacksonville Pub Lib, Jacksonville Fla 52; Assoc libn Landon High Sch, Jacksonville Fla 54-57; Head libn Englewood High Sch, Jacksonville Fla 57-. 8: Lib Evaluation Coms for Robert E Lee High Sch, Jacksonville 61, & Paxon Sr High Sch 63; Libn St Pauls Episcopal Church 63; Censorship Com for Duval County Bd of Pub Instr; Coordinating Coun for Delta Kappa Gamma in Duval County; Lib Eval Com for Baldwin High Sch, Duval Co Fla 67. 9: FlaEA; FlaASchL; Duval County LA (pres 59-60); Duval County ASchL. 10: Delta Kappa Gamma; PTA. 13: Yes. 14: Catlg, ref. 15: 1361 River Hills ct, Jacksonville Fl 32211.

DIXON, RICHARD KEMP. b Dalton-in-Furness, Lanc Eng 17 Je 04. 5: Columbia 25-29 (Eng, Fr) AB, 29-30 (Fr, Educ) MA, 40-42 BLS. 6: Fr, Sp. 7: Supv libn Columbia U TC 33-. 10: Phi Delta Kappa. 14: Res bk serv, bk sel. 15: 527 W 121 st, apt 54, New York NY 10027.

DJONOVICH, J DUSAN. b Belgrade Yugoslavia 17 My 20. 4: Maria Romanov. 5: University of Belgrade Law Sch 38-42 (Pub Law, Govt) Diploma; Columbia 63-64 (LS) MS, 65 (LS). 6: Fr, Ital, Serbo-Croat, Slovene, Russ. 7: Foreign Law libn Sch of Law NYU 64-. 9: AALL; Law Lib Assn Greater NY; Internat Law Lib Assn. 10: Beta Phi Mu. 12: Ed-in-Chief & Comp "Current Publication in Legal and Related Fields" (65-66). 14: Ref. 15: 100 Bleecker st apt 9B, New York NY 10012.

DOAK, MARY MEVELLYN. b Belton Mo 17 Ap 21. 5: Central Mo State Col 39-41 (Soc Studies) BS in Educ; Chicago 44-45 BLS; UNeb -56 (Amer Hist) MA. 6: Fr. 7: chr Hughesville (Mo) High Sch 41-43; Res libn Central (Mo) State Col summers 42-43, Asst libn circ dept 43-44; UNeb: Asst libn in humanities & soc studies 4546, Asst libn in soc studies 46-48, Soc studies libn 49-61, Pub serv libn 62-. 9: ALA; NebLA (Conv Chm 64); LincolnLA; MPLA. 10: AAUP; Neb Hist Soc. 14: Circ, ref. 15: 1215 G, Apt 1, Lincoln Nb 68508.

DOAK, WESLEY ALLEN. b Oberlin Ohio 19 Ja 39. 4: Patricia Jean MacFarlane. 5: Iowa State Tchrs 56-58 (Mus); Yankton Col 58-60 (Mus); UMass 60-62 (LS). 6: Ger. 7: AOU3 USNAR 56-61; A-v Fine Arts Libn Cary Mem Lib, Lexington Mass 60-63; NSCR. 14: A-v, YA, admin, rare bks, systems analysis. 15: 5305-C Denny ave, North Hollywood Ca 91601.

DOAN, PATRICIA (ROGERS). b Fayetteville Ark 27 O 30. 4: John Cannon Doan. 5: UArk 47-51 (Sp) BA. 6: Sp, Fr. 7: Dir Okmulgee Pub Lib, Okmulgee Okla 67-. 9: ALA; OklaLA; SWLA. 10: Okmulgee Art Guild; PTA; Okla Writer's Assn. 14: Catlg, Okla rare bks, writing. 15: 540 N Morton, Okmulgee Ok 74447.

DOBB, BARTLEY. b Seattle 12 Ap 24. 5: UWash 42-46 (Pol Sci) BA, 47-50, 51-53 Wash State Tchg Certif, 55-59 M Libr,67 MA. 6: Sp, Fr. 7: Off candidate US Navy 43-45; Off asst Metropolitan Building C, Seattle 46-47; Tchg fellow in poli sci UWash 48-50, Br libn 53-. 9: PNLA; SLA. 10: Puget Sound Railway Hist Assn; Phi Beta Kappa Mountaineers. 12: "A Study of the King County (Washington) Rural LibraryDistrict" (67). 14: Ref, catlg, libs & govt. 15: 1303 NE Campus pky, Seattle Wa 98105.

DOBBERFUHL, ALMA (MULLER). b Salem Ore 12 My 22. 4: Reinhold F Dobberfuhl. 5: Centralia Jr Col 39-40; Concordia Col (River Forest Ill) 40-43 (Eng) BSE; Rosary Col

46-48 BLS; UPortland 62-65 MLS. 6: Ger. 7: Tchr Trinity Lutheran Sch, Portland Ore 43-45; Asst libn Concordia Col (River Forest Ill) 46-48; Sel & Searching Army Med Lib, Wsh DC 48-49; Head telephone ref USDA Lib, Wash DC 49-50; Tchr Trinity Lutheran Sch, Oregon City Ore 53-58; Libn Concordia Col (Portland Ore)61-. 9: ALA; OreLA (chm Const Com 68-); Portland Area Spec Libns; Willamette ChristianCols Libns. 14: Admin, ref. 15: 2811 NE Holman, Portland Or 97211.

DOBBERT, IRENE A. b Kewaunee Wis 17 D 19. 5: UWis at Madison 60 (European hist) BS, 61 MSLS. 6: Fr. 7: Priv sec Heronymus & Co, Sheboygan Wis 38-52; Licensed securities saleswoman, Sheboygan Wis 53-56; Asst to libn UWis Lib Sch & to act libn UWis Sch of Com 60; Libn Sentry Ins, 61-. 9: SLA (Ins & Bus Div); WisLA. 10: AAUW. 14: Ref, research. 15: Aldo apts 8 1579 Strongs ave, Stevens Point Wi 54481.

DOBBIN, GERALDINE F. b Nakuru Kenya 1 Je 29. 5: Victoria Col 47-49; UBC 49-51 (Eng, Math) BA, 51-52 Tchr Training; Toronto55-56 BLS. 6: Fr. 7: Catlgr UBC Lib 56-62, Head catlg div 62-67, Syst & info sci libn 67-. 9: CanLA; ALA; BCLA; PNLA; ASIS. 14: Catlg, lib automation. 15: Univ of BC Lib, Vancouver 8 BC Can.

DOBBIN, PATRICIA ANN. b Phila Penn 18 N 27. 5: Temple 66 (Hist) BA; Drexel 66-67 MSLS. 7: Interlib loan libn Montgomery Co Norristown Pub Lib 67-. 15: N Lane & Hector st, Conshohocken Pa 19428.

DOBBINS, FREDA J STAUFFER. b Hutchinson Kan 1 Je 40. 4: James R Dobbins. 5: Southwestern Col 58-62 (Eng) BA; UDenver 62-63 (LS) MA. 7: Head of adult serv Hutchinson Pub Lib, Hutchinson Kan 63-67; Consul S Central Kan Libs 67-68; Ref libn Post Lib, Ft Knox Ky 68-. 9: ALA; memb Com Mont chm (chm Mont Intellectual Freedom Com); MontLA (past pres); PNLA (var coms). 14: Ref. 15: Box 144, Muldraugh Ky 40155.

DOBBS, VIVIAN LYNN. b Dayton Tex 27 O 21. 5: Sam Houston State Col 39-41 (Sociol); Tex Womans U 41-42 (Sociol) BA; Emory 46-47 BALS; Tex Tech 48-49 Emory 67 MLA Certif. 7: Documents libn Tex Tech, Lubbock Tex 47-49; Libn Post Lib US Army, Okinawa 49-40; Post libn US Army, Europe 50-52; Field libn US Air Force, Korea 53-54; Area supv US Army, Korea 54-55; Base libn US Air Force, Victoria Tex 56-58; Base libn US Air Force, Lake Charles La 58-60; Base libn US Air Force, Austin Tex 60-64; Ref libn med & bio sci Brooke Gen Hosp, Ft Sam Houston Tex 64-. 15: 4134 Monaco dr, San Antonio Tx 78218.

DOBER, VIRGINIA DARLENE. b Columbis Ohio 28 My 27. 5: AYLOR U 45-49 (hist) BA; UNC 55-56 (LS) MS. 7: Tchr Vashti Sch, Thomasville Ga 49-50; Tchr-libn Alleghany Dist Hish Sch, Shawsville Va 50-55; Asst Prof-asst libn Radford Col 56-58; Sch libn Pearisburg High Sch, Pearisburg Va 58-61; Asst Prof E Carolina Cl 61-62; Spec Sch Libs WVa State Dept of Educ, Charleston WVa 63-67; Assoc Prof Lib Sci Chm Lib Sci Dept Concord Col. 9: ALA; NEA; AASchL;WVaLA; SELA; MidAtlLA; WVaEA; WVaAHE. 10: AAUP. 14: Sch libs. 15: Lib Sci Dept, Concord College,Athens WV 24712.

DOBRUNZ, SALLY JEAN. b St Louis 27 O 40. 5: Washington 58-62 (Eng) BA; UWis 63-64 MS in LS. 6: Fr. 7: Page Ridgely Lib, St Louis 60-62: Libn Crestview Jr Hish Sch, Eureka Mo 62-63; Lib aid UWi(is(Madison) 63-64, Tchg asst summer 64; Asst libn Webster Groves Sr High Sch, St Louis 64-. 9: NEA; ALA; MoASchL; MoState Tchrs Assn; Tchrs Assn; St Louis Suburban LA; St Louis Sub Tchrs Assn. 14: Young adult sch lib. 15: 4307 Melba ave, St Louis Mo 63121.

DOBSON, CYNTHIA (ANN)(DAVIS). b San Jose Cal 27 Mr 42. 4: John McCullough Dobson. 5: Wellesley Col 59-61 (liberal Arts); UWis 61-63 (Sociol) BA, 63-64 (LS) MA, 64-66 (Socio) MA. 6: Fr. 7: Rare bk dept UWis (Madison) Mem Lib 65-66; ChicoState Col Lib 66-67; Jt Atomic Info Exchange Group Lib Wash DC, 67-68; Iowa StateU Lib (Ames) 68-. 10: Phi Beta Kappa; Beta Phi Mu. 14: Ref. 15: 2221 Donald st, Ames Ia 50010.

DOBSON, JOHN H. b Greeneville Tenn 1 Je 24. 5: UTenn 46-48 (Hist) BA; Columbia 50-51 (LS) MS. 6: S. 7: Libn Greeneville High Sch, Greeneville Tenn 51-53; Libn Tusculum Col 53-54; Sr catlgr UTenn 54-59; Spec collections libn UTenn 59-, Curator Estes Kefauver Lib 66-. 8: Trustee Greeneville-Greene County (Tenn) Pub Lib 54-56. 9: ALA; TennLA (Exec Bd 62-67); SELA. 12: Ed "Tennessee Librarian" (62-67); "Tenn State Reporter"; "Southe astern Librarian" 62-67; Ed UTenn Lib Occasional Publications 69-. 13: Yes. 14: Rare bks, mss, archives, catlg. 15: UTenn Lib, Knoxville Tenn 37916.

DOBSON, MARJORIE L. b Osgood Ind 6 My 22. 5: Butler U 40-44 (Eng, Hist) BS; Carnegie 45-46 BS in LS. 7: Child libn Indianapolis Pub Lib, Indianapolis 41-56; Child libn Pub Lib, Pasadena Cal 57-58; Child libn Indianapolis Pub Lib, Indianapolis 58-59; Coordinator of Elem Sch Libs Metro Sch Dist of Wash Twp Indianapolis 59-. 8: Storyteller at ALA Storytelling Festival Miami Beach 55; Coord Knapp Sch Lib Proj Demonst Lib, Dist Allisonville Elem Sch 64-67. 9: ALA-CSD; -AASchL; SLA; NEA; IndSchLA; Ind State Tchrs Assn; Classroom Tchrs Assn. 10: Indianapolis Coun of Admin Women in Educ. 13: Yes. 14: Child sch libs, child lit, storytelling. 15: 1052 Ruth dr, Indianapolis In 46240.

DOCKERY, DAISY. b Laurinburg NC 09 O 43. 5: Livingstone Col 60-61; NC Col 61-64 (Bus) BS; Atlanta U 65-66 MSLS. 6: Fr. 7: Ref libn asst NC Col 64-65; Asst libn & hd catlgr Benedict Col 66-. 9: ALA; SCLA; SELA. 10: Beta Phi Mu; YWCA; Delta Sigma Theta. 11: Rockefeller Found Fellowship. 14: Catlg. 15: 1622-C Oak st, Columbia SC 29204.

DODD, GEORGINA ANNE. b Victoria BC 1 Mr 43. 5: UAlberta 61-64 (European Hist) BA; McGill 64-65 BLS. 7: Ref libn Glenbow Found, Calgary Alta Can 65-66; Sr Asst lending Kensington Pub Lib, London Eng 66-67; Deputy libn Metalbox Co, London Eng 68; Instr lib arts So Alberta Inst of Tech 68-. 9: ALA; CanLA; AltaLA. 14: Ref. 15: 2120Victoria Crescent NW, Calgary 43 Alta Can.

DODD, JAMES ARTHUR. b NYC 17 F 25. 4: Nancy Hoecker. 5: Northland Col 46-50 (Chem, Biol) BA; UWis 50-51 MS in LS; Wayne State U 53-54, 58- (Comparative Educ). 7: Wis Nat Guard Battalion Clerk S/Sgt 48-51; Youth libn Detroit Pub Lib 51-53, Adult asst libn II 53-55, 1st asst to Br Libn 55-59; Br libn Grosse Pointe Lib, Grosse Pointe Mich 59-64; Dir of Lib Adrian Col 64-. 8: Consul mem of Pub Lib Adv Bd, Eagle River Wis 64-. 9: ALA (Life Mem); MichLA (chm recruiting com 54-56, chm Newcomers Com 64-66,chm Memb Com 67-68). 10: Kiwanis; Econ Club; Lenawee Country Club. 11: KiwanisOutstanding Serv Award, Grosse Pointe 64. 13: Yes. 14: Ref, col lib, admin. 15: 4771Devonshire dr, Hooks Mill, Adrian Mi 49221.

DODD, JAMES BEAUPRE. b Eldorado Ill 21 S 26. 4: Betty Barcroft. 5: Vanderbilt 43; So Ill U 43-48 (Eng) BS in Ed, 48-50 (Eng, Educ Admin) MS in Ed; UIll 51-52 MS in LS. 7: Tech Sgt US Army Corps of Military Police 45-46; Instr & Head lang arts dept E Richland Pub Schs, Olney Ill 48-51; Asst libn AEC Nat Reactor Testing Station Lib, Idaho Falls Idaho 52-54; Libn Nat Reactor Testing Station Lib Phillips Petroleum Co Atomic Energy Div, Idaho Falls Idaho 54-55; Instr in Lib Sci UVa(Lynchburg) Div of Ext & General Studies 61-62; Head info serv sect abcock & Wilcox Co Atomic Energy Div, Lynchburg Va 55-62; Sci libn & Asst Prof No Ill U 62-67; Grad libn & Assoc Prof Ga Inst of Tech 67-68, Hd tech info serv & AssocProf 68-. 8: Sr Instr NS Savannah Deck Off TrainProgram US Maritime Commsn, Lynchburg Va 59; Tech Info Panel AEC 57-62; Va State Com for Nat Lib Week 60 & 61: Interim Com for City-Wide Lib Serv, Lynchburg Va (chm) 61-62; Prof consul SLA 65-; Consul to No Ill Gas Co 65; Consul to De Kalb Agric Assn Inc 65 Field consul to Ill State Off of Supt of Pub Instr 66; Info consulto Ga State Off of State Tech Serv 68-. 9: SLA (chm Metals Div 61-62, pres-electSo Atl Chap 69-70); ALA; IdahoLA; VaLA (chm Spec Libs Sect 60-61); IllLA (chm Coll& Res Libs Sect 65-66); GaLA; SELA. 10: AAUP. 12: "Directory of Libraries andLibrary Personnel in and Around Lynchburg Va" (60); Ed "Metals Division News" SLA(58-61); Asst ed "The Generator" Babcock & Wilcox Co (59-60); Assoc ed "IllinoisLibraries" (66-67). 13: Yes. 14: Pub rel, tech & bus libs. 15: 2898 Rockingham dr NW, Atlanta Ga 30327.

DODD, MELVIN JOE. b Fort Worth Tex 17 Jl 35. 4: Sherry Hancock. 5: Tex Wesleyan Col 54-58 (Eng) BA; N Tex State U 65-67 MLS. 6: Fr. 7: Pub sch tchr Castleberry Independent Sch Dist, Ft Worth 61-67; Libn Texas A&M U 67-. 9: ALA. 10: Alpha Lambda Sigma. 14: Gifts & exch. 15: 1207 Haines, College Station Tx 77840.

DODDS, MARY (ISABEL). b Toronto Can 14 Je 17. 5: UAlta 33-37 (Com) BCom; Columbia 54-55 (LS) MS. 6: Fr, Ger. 7: UAlta; Sec to the pres 42-54, Asst libn Ext Lib 55-56, Head Libn Ext Lib 56-. 9: ALA; CanLA; AltaLA. 10: Delta Kappa Gamma; Altrusa Club. 14: Adult educ, pub lib serv. 15: 14220-92A ave, Edmonton Alta Can.

DODGE, ALICE CYNTHIA. b San Francisco Cal 13 Je 02. 5: Mt Holyoke 21-25 (Botany) BA; Columbia 29-33 BLS; UChicago 38-40 (Pub lib) MA. 7: Utica Public Library, NY: Sr asst 25-32, Br libn 33-35, Hd central adult circ 35-45, Dir 46-68; Sr libn (spec) N Country Lib Syst, Watertown NY 68-. 8: NY Exam Com for Pub Libs 51-57 (chm 53-57). 9: ALA; NYLA (v-pres 51-52, pres 52-53). 10: AAUW; Oneida Hist Soc; Zonta Club; Senior Day Ctr. 14: Ref, admin. 15: 1050 Arsenal st, Watertown NY 13601.

DODGE, MILDRED (GAVITT). b Newton Kan 16 Ag 04. 4: Fred C Dodge. 5: Fairmount Col (now Wichita State U) 22-26 (Eng) AB; UKan 26-27 (Eng) MA. 7: Libn Wichita Elem Schs, Wichita Kan 49-52; Libn Beech Aircraft Corp Engnr Lib, Wichita Kan 52-. 9: SLA; ALA (Wichita Br). 10: Urban League Guild. 15: 452 S Holyoke, Wichita Ks 67218.

DODGE, NANCY LINDA (FRENCH). b Laconia NH 28 Ag 43. 4: David M Dodge. 5: Middlebury Col 61-62 (Sociol); UNH 62-65 (Sociol) BA; Simmons Col 65-66 MLS. 7: Ser asst UVt Lib 66-67; Hd ref St Michael's Col Lib, Winooski Vt 68-. 9: ALA-ACRL; VtLA; Champlain Valley LA. 10: Altrusa Internat; Sigma Kappa; Phi Beta Kappa; Phi Kappa Phi; Pi Gamma Mu; Alpha Kappa Delta. 14: Ref. 15: 40 East st, Essex Junction Vt 05452.

DODONAY, GEORGE ROBERT. b BudapestHungary 8 Ap 16. 5: Sch for Modern Langs (Budapest) 2335 (Ger, Fr) MA; Pazmany Peter U(Budapest) 35-40 (Econ) PhD, 40-44 (Law) LLD; Columbia 59-61 mls. 6: Hungarian, Ger, Fr, Russian, Lat. 7: Consul Prime Ministers Off, Budapest 43-57; Audit clerk Schroder Banking Corp, NY 57-60; Asst libn II NY Pub Lib 60-61; Indexer H W Wilson Co, NY 61-62; Catlgr Freeport Mem Lib, Freeport NY 62; Catlgr Cardinal Hayes Lib, Manhattan NY 62-64; Asst Prof CUNY (Manhattan Commun Col) 64-. 9: ALA; SLA; NYLA; LACUNY. 12: "Rationalization and Simplification of the Public Administration in Hungary (Budapest 45). 14: Catlg, acquis. 15: 35-55 73rd st, Apt 526, Jackson Hts NY 11372.

DODSON, JAMES T. b Cambridge Ohio 4 Je 32. 4: Ann Thompson. 5: Denison U 50-54 (Hist) BA; Ohio State U 54-55 (Hist) MA; West Res 61-62 MSLS, 68-69 (LS). 6: Sp. 7: Rep World Coun of Churches, Johannesburg SA 55-56; Instrspec US Army Ordnance Corps, Aberdeen Proving Grounds Md 56-58; Inspector State ofOhio, Columbus Ohio 58-61; Ref libn Ohio State U 62-63, Assoc libn Educ Lib 63-64;Hd libn Wright State U 64-. 9: ALA; OhioLA. 10: Beta Phi Mu. 14: Admin, lib educ. 15: 233Canterbury dr, Dayton Oh 45429.

DODSON, SUZANNE CATES. b N Vancouver BC 3 F 33. 4: Earl David Dodson. 5: UBC 50-54 (Zool) BA, 6263 BLS. 6: Fr, Swedish. 7: Libn, head of govt publ div UBC, Vancouver 63-. 9: BCLA. 11: The Marian Harlow Prie in Libnship. 14: Govt publs. 15: Univ of BC Lib, Vancouver 8 BC Can.

DOEHNER, THEODORE PHILIP. b Syracuse NY 4 Jl 28. 5: Syracuse 47-51 (Eng Lit) AB, 51-52 (LS) MA. 7: Bkseller Economy Bkstore, Syracuse NY 47-55; Sales rep Gaylord Bros Ind,tenn-Ky 55-57; libn Queens Borough Pub Lib, NYC 57-67, Departmental asst ext serv67-. 69, Ya br specialist 69-. 9: United Staff Assn NYC Pub Libs (var coms). 10: Rho Delta Phi. 14: Ref, admin. 15: 102-40 67th rd, Forest Hills NY 11375.

DOELL, DANIEL WILLIAM. b Rochester NY 8 Je 41. 5: Boston Col 59-63 (Ger) AB; Simmons 64-66 MS in LS. 7: Catlgr Newton Free Lib, Newton Mass 64-66; UMo Lib 66-. 9: ALA; MoLA. 14: Tech serv, lib automation. 15: 1502 Sylvan lane, Columbia Mo 65201.

DOERING, DOROTHY DOLORES. b St Louis 3 Je12. 5: Southwest Mo State 49-53 (Eng) BS; Ariz State Col (Tempe) summer 50; UIll 54-57 (LS) MS. 7: Clerical asst Drury Col Lib 53-57, Ref libn 57-67, Act libn 67-. 9: ALA; MoLA; Springfield Libns Assn. 10: Wilderness Soc;Audubon Soc; Renaiss Soc of Amer. 14: Ref, art. 15: Drury Col Lib, Springfield Mo 65802.

DOERRER, DAVID H. b Rochester NY 16 Ap 37. 4: Dorothy M A Upson. 5: UBuffalo 56-58 (Hist); Syracuse 63-65 (Hsit) AB, 65-66 MSLS. 7: SP5 E-5, MOS 717 (admin sp) USA USASETAF Italy 59-62; Asst circ libn Cornell U Olin Lib 66-. 9: ALA-ACRL; NYLA. 10: Beta Phi Mu. 12: News ed "C&RL". 14: Circ, admin. 15: 1257 Warren rd, Ithaca NY 14850.

DOERRER, DOROTHY (UPSON). b Cambridge Mass 22 F 40. 4: David Herbert Doerrer. 5: UBuffalo 57-62 (Hist, Govt BA; Inst for mer U(Aix-en-Provence France) 59-60; Syracuse 63-64 MS(LS). 6: Fr. 7: Libn trainee Rochester Pub Lib, Rochester NY 62-63; Catlg libn Syracuse U64-66; Catlg libn Cornell U 66-68. 14: Catlg. 15: 1257 Warren rd, Ithaca NY 14850.

DOERSCHUK, ERNEST EDWIN JR. b Sugarcreek Ohio 14 D 14. 4: Helen Monks. 5: Oberlin Col 33-37 (Hist) AB; West Res 37-38 BS in LS. 7: Lib asst NY Pub Lib38-42; US Army Air Corps, African Theatre 43-45; Asst br libn NY Pub Lib 46; LibnBr Off VA, NYC 46-48; Libn Lancaster Free Pub Lib, Lancaster Penn 48-57; Penn StateLib; Ext dir 57-62, Lib development dir 62-64, State Libn 64-. 9: ALA; AEAUSA;PennLA (pres 55-56); Penn Assn Adult Educ (pres 62-63). 10: Reserve Offs Assn; PhiBeta Kappa. 13; Yes. 14: Pub lib admin. 15: 145 Kready ave, Millersville Pa 17551.

DOHERTY, SISTER ALICE. b Chicago Ill 6 S 08. 5: Rosary Col 26-30 (Hist) BA; UIll summers 39-42 (Hist) MA; Rosary Col 55 M in LS; UWis summer 66, NDEA Inst Lib Personnel; Immaculate Heart Col (Los Angeles) summer 68 HEA Inst. 6: Fr. 7: Libn & tchr Trinity High Sch, Bloomington Ill 41-50; libn & tchr Visitation High Sch, Chicago 50-53; Libn & tchr St Thos Apostle High Sch, Chicago 53-54; Libn & tchr St John Cathedral High Sch, Milwaukee 54-56; Libn & tchr Aquin High Sch, Freeport Ill 56-57; Circ & ref libn Rosary Col 57-60; Libn Edgewood High Sch, Madison Wis 60-. 8: Mem N Central Assn Evaluating Com; Holy Name Sem 68, Mt Horeb High Sch 69; Adv Bd Mem Stud Lib Assts Wis 66-68. 9: ALA; CathLA (Adv Bd High Sch Sect 63-67, chm Ill Unit High Sch Sect 52-54, chm Madison Wis Diocese 63-65, Nat Memb Com 67-69, Nat Nomin Com 68); WisLA (mem Planning Com Stud Lib Inst 66, mem Scholarship Com 67, mem Honors Awards Com 68, mem Recruitment Com 68-69). 13: Yes. 14: Catlg, ref, instr materials. 15: Edgewood High Sch Lib 1000 Edgewood ave, Madison Wi 53711.

DOHERTY, EDMOND JOHN. b NYC 9 D 33. 4: Frances C Jeffreys. 5: St Martins Col 51-55 (Philos) BA; Rutgers 58-60 MLS. 7: Clerk Wash State Law Lib summer 51; Lib asst St Martins Col 49-55; Lib page Wash State Lib summers 52-55; Admin spec US Army, US, Europe 55-57; Lib clerk Columbia River Reg Lib, Wenatches Wash 57-58; Lib trainee Main Lib E Orange (NJ) Pub Lib 58-59, Adult libn Park ave Br 59-61; Free Lib of Phila: Adult serv libn Holmesburg Br 61, Br libn S Phila 61-63, Br libn Bushrod 63-64, Br lib Winnefield 64-66; Dir Reading Pub Lib, Reading Penn 66-. 8: Del to Penn Governors Commonwealth Conf on Human Serv 63; Adjunct instr Drexel Inst summers 68, 69. 09: ALA; -ASD (Subcom on Legis 68-); PennLA (chm Adult Serv Com 62-64, chm Lib Devel Com 66-68; pres Co-Pub Lib Div 68-69). 10: Commun Welfare Assn; EOC Reading Berks Co; United Commun Serv; For Affairs Coun; Am Soc Pub Admin; NAACP. 13: : Yes. 14: Admin, pub serv. 15: 733 N Fourth st, Reading Pa 19601.

DOHERTY, JEANNE ELIZABETH. b Needham Mass 8 Ap 39. 5: State Col at Bridgewater 57-61 (Eng) BS MEd; Simmons 64-65, 66-69 (LS) MS. 6: Fr. 7: Lib asst Needham Free Pub Lib, Needham Mass 61-62; Bibliog searcher order dept Wellesley Col Lib 62-67, Docs libn 67-. 14: Govt docs, ref, bk arts. 15: 80 Pickering st, Needham Ma 02192.

DOHERTY, JOSEPH H. b Boston 19 D 23. 4: Katherine Spencer. 5: Fordham Col 46-48 (Eng) AB; Columbia 48-51 (Eng) MA, 55 MLS. 7: Photographer US Army Air Corps 43-46; Eng tchr Hatch Prep Sch, Newport RI 1-53; Ref libn St Agnes Br NY Pub Lib 56, Relibn Donnell Lib Center 57, Asst curator Schomburg Collection 58-61, Supv asst Grand Concourse Br 62-65, Br libn Hudson Park Br 65- Lib dir Providence Col Lib, 67-. 8: Bk Discussion Program "SignificantModern Bks" NY Pub Lib 63. 9: SLA (NY Chap); ALA; United Staff Assn NYC Pub Libs (past pres NY Chap). 10: Friends of the Newport Pub Lib. 14: Adult serv, lib exhibits. 15: Wellington ave,Newport RI 02840.

DOIG, ZELMA (CAREY) MORGAN. b Coos Bay Ore 29 Ja 12. 4: Lawrence Thompson Doig. 5: Whitworth Col 29-33 (Hist) BA, 34; Wash State U summer 34 Secondary Tchg Certif; NY Theol Sem 36-37; UWash summers 64, 66, 68. 7: Tchr & libn Ewan Pub High Sch, Ewan Wash 34-35; Tchr & libn Cathlamet High Sch, Cathlamet Wash 35-36; Housemother Raymond B Goddard Home & Commun Ctr, N Fork Cal 37-39; Libn Sheldon Jackson High Sch, Sitka Alaska 62-67; Libn Sheldon Jackson Col, Sitka Alaska 67-. 9: ALA; AlaskaLA. 10: Alaska Hist Assn; Sitka Hist Assn. 14: Admin, bks on Alaska. 15: Sheldon Jackson College Box 479, Sitka Ak 99835.

DOIRON, PETER MICHAEL. b Boston 5 Ap 34. 4: Martha Holbrook. 5: UMass 57-60 (Eng) AB; Syracuse 61-62 MSLS. 6: Fr. 7: Ammo cpl US Army Artillery, Germany 54-56; Copy ed Court Square Press, Boston60-61; Asst acquis libn Oakland U 62-64; Bk review ed "Choice; Books for CollegeLibraries," Middletown Conn 64-. 9: ALA. 10: PTA; Acquis adv, Haddam Conn Pub Lib. 12: Ed & auth of editorials & bk reviews; Ed "Choice" 66-. 14: Acquis, hist of bk & printing, educ for libnship, intell freedom. 15: Town st, East Haddam Ct 06423.

DOLAN, ALICE M (ANDERSON). b Medford Mass. 4: Edward V Dolan. 7: Jr libn Thomas Crane Pb Lib, Quincy Mass 48-53; Libn Bethlehem Steel Co Shipbldg Div, Quincy Mass 53-64; Libn Gen Dynamics Electric Boat Div, Quincy Mass 64; Libn Northrop Nortronics, Needham Heights Mass 64-67; Libn Northrop Corp precision products dept,Norwood Mass 67-. 9: SLA. 10: Hanson Riding Club; Mass Audubon Soc. 15: Northrop Nortronics 66 B st, Needham Heights Ma 02194.

DOLAN, BROTHER JAMES JOEL FSC. b Chicago 6 Ap 26. 5: St Marys Col (Winona Minn) 45-48 (Commerce) BSS, 49-54 (Edu) MEd; Col of St Catherine 54-58 BS LS; Rosary Col 64 (LS) MA. 7: Tchr De La Salle High Sch, Kansas City Mo48-50; Tchr St Patrick High Sch, Chicago 50-53; Tchr Cretin High Sch, St Paul 53-54;Tchr Helias High Sch, Jefferson City Mo 54-57; Tchr-libn Benilde High Sch, St LouisPark Minn 57-63; Libn St Patrick High Sch, Chicago 63-. 9: CathLA (pres SeconSect 67-68); Minn-Dakota CathLA (publ chm 61-63). 14: Young adult serv. 15: St Patrick High Sch, 5900W Belmont ave, Chicago Il 60634.

DOLAN, PHILIP HILARY. b Cambridge Mass 5 Jl 14. 5: Harvard 31-35 (Hist, Govt, Econ) B, 35-37 (Educ) EdM; Columbia 41-42 (LS) BS. 6: Fr, Sp. 7: Asst libn Newton (Mass) Free Lib 37-41; (Mjr) US Army 42-46; Chiefcirc Harvard Col Lib 46-49; Dir Cambridge (Mass) Pub Lib 49-. 8: Lib & educ consul. 9: ALA; NEA; AEAUSA; Mental Health Assn; NELA; MassLA (treas 53-56); Coun onYouth & Leisure Time; Metro Boston Lib Planning Coun (co-founder & chm); East RegLib Adv Coun (Exec Bd). 10: Reserve Off Assn; Phi Delta Kappa; Faculty Club;Harvard Club; Nalod Assocts. 12: Ed & comp of Municipal Annual Reports. 13: Yes. 14: Admin. 15: 2Lowell ave, Newtonville Ma.

DOLBEAR, INEZ (LOURENZO). b San Rafael Cal 13 Ag 20. 4: William C Dolbear. 5: Marin Jr Col 39-41 (Liberal Arts) AA; UCal 41-43 (Span) AD; UCal 43-44 (LS) Certif. 6: Sp, Portu. 7: Libn Hosp, Med & Nursing St Marys Hosp, San Francisco 44-47; Libn ref dept San Francisco Pub Lib 47-50; Head loan desk libn Lib of Hawaii, Honolulu 50-55; Asst ya libn Kern Co Lib, Bakersfield Cal 56-57; Ref libn Contra Costa Co Lib, Pleasant Hill Cal 58-63, Act head ref sect 63- , Hd ref sect 64-. 9: ALA; CalLA; SLA. 13: Yes. 14: Ref, ya. 15: Contra Costa Co Lib, 1750 Oak Park blvd, Pleasant Hill Ca 94523.

DOLCE, DOROTHY J. b NYC 13 My 20. 4: James A Dolce. 5: NYU 36-40 (Eng) BA; Pratt 40-41 BLS. 6: Ital. 7: Lib asst Brooklyn Pub Lib 41-42; Asst libn NYU Com Lib 42-44; Map libn USAFArctic Desert & Tropic Survival Center, NYC 44-46; Libn Geneva High Sch, Geneva NY46-47; Libn Bennett Elem Sch, Boiceville NY 55-56; Libn King Hosp Sch of Nursing,Kingston NY 56-. 9: ALA; SLA; MedLA; CathLA. 14: Med ref. 15: Sunkist Lane, Ashokan NY 12481.

DOLE, GRACE FULLER. b Cambridge Mass. 5: Bryn Mawr Col 0-44 (Hist, Playwritin) BA; Radcliffe summer 43 (Hist); Middlebury Col summer 49 (F); Columbia 50-54 MLS. 6: Fr, Sp 07: Fr tchr Low Heywood Sch 48-49, Hgh sch libn 49-50; Greenwich Pub Lib 50-53; Ref dept local hist & genal div, Amer hist div, sci & info div NY Pub Lib 54-56; Asst libn Benton & Bowles Inc, NYC 56-58, Libn 58-62; Ref dept The Ferguson Lib, Stamford Conn 62-64; Libn UConn(Stamford) 64. 9: SLA (chm New Lib Devel Com 62-63); Lib Group SW Conn. 10: Jr League; Daughters of the Amer Colonists; DAR; Cntemporary Art Club of Greenwich (Conn). 13: Yes. 14: Admin, ref, catlg. 15: 124 Ritch ave, Byram Ct 10573.

DOLGIN, JEANNE (RYDELL). b NYC 3 Je 21. 4: Martin Dolgin. 5: Brooklyn Col 39-44 (Philos) BA; Columbia Grad Sch of Philosophy 44-50; Columbia 60 64 MLS. 6: Fr. Ger. 7: Copy desk asst Time In NYC 45-51; Ref clerk White Plains Pub Lib summer 62; Ref libn Scarsdale (NY) Pub Lib 64-. 9: ALA; Westchester LA. 10: Beta Phi Mu. 14: Ref, bk sel, bibliog. 15: 32 Mt View ave, Ardsley NY 10502.

DOLLEN, BERNARD H(ALLORAN). b Rochester NY 28 S05. 4: Julia Laties. 5: U Rochester 23-27 (Fr, Geol) AB, 27-31 (Geol) AM; Columbia 38-39 BS in LS. 6: Fr, Ital, Sp, Lat. 7: Asst in geol dept URochester 28-33, 37; Geologist Ground Water Survey MonroeCo Reg Plan Bd, Rochester NY 33-35; Map wk, civilian Pub Serv, Dept of the Interior,Portland Ore 43-45; Libn Niagara U NY 39-43, 46-, Dir 57-. 8: Geol consul wk, Rochester Ny 33-37. 9: ALA; CathLA (chmCol & Univ Sect 61-64); NYLA; West NY Cath Libns Conf. 12: Co-auth "Ground Water Resources of Monroe County, New York (35); Co-auth "Geology of the Clyde and Sodus Bay Quadrangles, New York (40); Ed"CULS, a quarterly paper of the Col & Univ Sect of the CathLA (61-62). 13: Yes. 14: Admin. 15: Niagara Univ Lib, Niagara University NY 14109.

DOLLEN, CHARLES JOSEPH (REV). b Rochester NY 14 Ap 26. 5: St Bernard"s 45-49 (Philos) BA; Immaculate Heart Sem 49-54 (Theol) Ordination; USoCal 56-57 MS in LS. 6: Lat, Gk, Hebrew, Sp. 7: Asst pastor Blessed Sacrament Ch, San Diego 54-64; Lib dir USan Diego 55-, Asst Prof theol 55-; Chaplain (Lt) USN Res, San Diego 60-66; Pastor St Louise de Marillac, Crest Cal 56-58. 8: Chaplain: Cath Interrac Coun of San Diego 59-64, Sisters of Soc Serv (San Diego) 55-65; Bk Rev Ed "The Priest 68-. 9: ALA; CathLA (chm Col Sect 64-65); CalLA (Intel Freedom 63-65). 12: Comp: "Marine Corps Bibliography (63); "Civil Rights, A Source Book (64); "Marmion: Fire of Love (64); "Index to The Sixteen Documents of Vatican II (67); "Ready or Not (68). 13: Yes. 14: Admin, catlg. 15: Alcala Park - USD Lib, San Diego Ca 92110.

DOLLERSCHELL, ALLEN L. b Litchfield Minn 17 Jl 38. 4: Marcia G Landeen. 5: St Cloud State Col 55-59 (Hist) BS; UHawaii summer 60; UMinn summers 61-63 (LS) MA; Winona State Col 66-67. 7: Asst libn Edina Jr High Sch, Edina Minn 59-62; Asst libn St Louis Park Sr High Sch, St Louis Park Minn 62-64; Hd libn Rochester State Jr Col, Rochester Minn 64-. 8: Instr Info Media St Cloud State Col summer 67; Instr Lib Sci; UMinn Ext Ctr, Rochester 67-69. 9: ALA; MinnLA. 10: Minn Jr Col Fac Assn. 15: 1559 7th ave NE, Rochester Mn 55901.

DOLPHUS, ROBBIE (GRANT). b Greenville SC 2 O 33. 5: Bennett Col (Greensboro NC) 51-52, 55-58 (Com ed) BS. 7: TV sec W Charlotte Sr High Sch, Charlotte NC 59-60; Bkmob libn Pub Lib of Charlotte 61; Br libn Pub Lib of Charlotte & Meckle 63-. 9: ALA; NCLA; Mecklenburg LA. 10: Staff Organ of Charlotte & Mecklenburg Co. 14: Br lib wk. 15: 410 E 9th st, Charlotte NC 28202.

DOMAN, LOIS ANN. b Cedar City Utah 22 F 44. 5: Col San Mateo 62-64 AA; San Jose State Col 64-66 (Eng) BA; UDenver 66-67 MLS. 6: Sp, Ger. 7: Stud asst San Mateo Pub Lib, San Mateo Cal 61-64; Stud asst San Jose State Col Lib 65-66; Subj catlgr LC 67-. 9: ALA. 11: Spec Recr Prog LC. 14: Catlg, child libnship. 15: 2300 S 24th rd 933, Arlington Va 22206.

DOMENECH, HELEN J. b Cardiff Md 14 My 09. 5: TempleU 27-30 BS in Ed; Drexel BS in LS. 6: Fr, Sp. 7: Libn Eddystone Jr & Sr High Sch 31-43; PMC Col: Readers' serv libn 61-66, Asst libn 66-. 8: Tutor of underprivileged child. 9: ACRL; PennLA. 10: Zonta Intl; Girl Scouts. 15: 151 Rockland rd, Havertown Pa 19083.

DOMITZ, GARY (LeROY). b Joplin Mo 27 Ap 43. 4: Carla (Annette) Hooper. 5: Kan State Tchrs Col 61-66 (Soc Sci) BA, 66-67 MLS. 7: Asst docs libn Kan StateU Farrell Lib 67-. 9: ALA; KanLA. 14: Govt docs, gen ref. 15: 900 Garden way apt 7, Manhattan Ks 66502.

DOMOWNE, SYLVIA. b Brooklyn NY 13 Ja 33. 4: Mark M Domowne. 5: Brooklyn Col 51-55 (Lit) BA; Rutgers 55-56 MLS.06: Sp, Fr. 7: Sr libn Brookln Pub Lib 56-61; Asst libn Lybrand, Ross Broth, & Montgomey, NYC 61-63; Asst dir Wantagh Pub Lib, Wantagh LI NY 63-66; Sch libn Birch Lane Sch, Mass Sch Dist #23 LI 66-. 8: Research consulPath Comp (consuls to business and industry) 64-. 9: SLA; Nassau Co NY LA; NY State SchLA. 10: Amer Leg Aux, Kings Cty NY; Rutgers Grad Sch Lib Serv Alum Assn; BrooklynCol Alumni Assn. 14: Pub serv, mgt & admin of libs. 15: 110 Booklyn ave, Freeport LI NY 11520.

DOMS, KEITH. b Endeavor Wis 24 Ap 20. 4: Margaret Ann Taylor. 5: UWis 38-42 BA; Harvard 44-45 (Far Eastern Area-ASTP); UWis 46-47 BLS. 6: Fr. 7: T/4 AUS Signal Corps-Intelligence 42-46; City libn Pub Lib, Concord NH 47-51; City libn Pub Lib, Midland Mich 51-56; Asst dir Carnegie Lib of Pittsburgh 56-62, Assoc dir 62-63, Dir 64-69; Dir Free Lib, Phila 69-. 8: Dir of Seminar on "Role of Lib in Development of Community" Karachi Pakistan 64; Mem

(Penn) Governor's Adv Coun on Lib Devel 68-; Bd pittsburgh 68-; Consul of lib bldgs & pub lib planning and devel; Pres Pittsburgh Reg Lib Ctr Inc, 67-69. 9: ALA (chm Lib Tech Proj Advis Com 59-62, Coun-at-Large 60-64, Exec Bd 63-67; Chm ALA Coun on Freedom on Access to Libs 66-68, chm Coord Com on Lib Serv to the Disadvantaged 68-); ALA-PLA (chm Spec Pub Lib Study Com 68-);-PLD (chm Lib Arch Com 54-57);-LAD (chm Bldgs & Equipt Sect 58-60, pres 63-64); Middle Atl Reg Lib Conf (chm 57); NELA (sec 47-49); NHLA (v-pres 49-50); MichLA (v-pres 55-56); PennLA (pres 60-61, chm Lib Development Com 61-62, 65-67). 10: Bd of Dir WQED-WQEX TV Sta Pittsburgh; Pittsburgh World Affairs Coun; West Penn Hist Soc; Phila Penn Union Lib Catlg & Penn Mental Health Assn; Beta Phi Mu (pres 62-64); Pittsburgh Bibliographiles. 11: Certif of Merit PennLA (61). 12: Chapters on lib bldgs in "Local Public Library Administration" (64) and "The Library Trustee" ed by Virginia Young (64). 13: Yes. 14: Admin, adult educ. 15: 4400 Forbes ave, Pittsburgh Pa 15213.

DONAGHY, MERRITT (MARTHA). b Cleveland Ohio 4 Je 40. 5: Vassar 58-60; StanfordU 60-62 9sp & Drama) BA, 62-64 (Eng Ling); Kent State 66; Simmons 67-68 MS in LS. 6: Fr. 7: Hd child dept Orlando Pub Lib, Orlando Fla 68-. 9: ALA; FlaLA. 10: Phi Beta Kappa. 14: Child lit & serv. 15: 754 Antonette, Winter Park Fl 32789.

DONAHUE, ERANA STADLER. b Oconomowoc Wis 13 O 08. 4: Willard J Donahue. 5: Whitewater (Wis) State Tchrs Col 26-28 (Educ); UWis 30-32 (Ger) PhB, 34-35 (LS). 6: Ger. 7: Tchr Waukesha Pub Schs, Waukesha Wis 30-32; Child libn W Allis Pub Lib, W Allis Wis 36-38; Libn Bismarck Pub Lib, Bismarck ND 38-51; Head circ Great Falls Pub Lib, Great Falls Mont 51-52; Libn Fergus Falls Pub Lib, Fergus Falls Minn 52-53; Libn Owatonna (Minn) Pub Lib 53-. 8: Exec dir, Nat Lib Week, Minn 62; Chm State Bd of Educ Adv Com on Pub Libs 66-68. 9: ALA (Coun 59-63);MinnLA (pres 56). 10: AAUW; LWV; Womans Club of Owatonna. 11: Librarian of the Year Award MinnLA (65). 13: Yes. 14: Admin, adult educ. 15: 208-4th ave NW, Waseca Mn 56093.

DONAHUE, MARGARET M(AUDE). b Wash DC. 5: Trinity Col Wash DC 38-42 (Hist) BA; CatholicU 43-45 (LS) MS. 6: Fr, Sp, Lat. 7: Asst hd of lib Water Reed Army Med Ctr Wash DC 51-54; UMd: Sci catlgr 54-57, Asst hd catlg dept 57-60, Hd catlg dept 60-68, Asst dir libs tech serv 68-. 9: ALA; CathLA; NEA; MdLA; DCLA. 10: AAUP. 14: Tech serv. 15: 10205 Lorain ave, Silver Spring Md 20901.

DONAHUE, MARY MARTHA. b Danville Ky 5 Ja 36. 5: Centre Col of Ky 54-58 (Eng) BA; Ind U 60-61 (LS)ma. 6: Fr. 7: Tchr Jr High Sch Pompano Beach Fla 58-60; Libn Spec Serv US Army Bad Tolz, Bad Aibling & Lenggries Germany 61-65; Ref libn Centre Col 66-67; Ref libn Wis State U (Whitewater) 67-. 9: ALA; WisLA. 10: Vagabonds of Milwaukee; AAUP; Mod Lang Assn. 14: Ref. 15: 314 N Prairie, Whitewater Wi 53190.

DONAHUE, MILDRED (ADAMS). b Deer Creek Ind 5 Ap 04. 4: Claude M Donahue. 5: Ind Bus Col 20-21 (Typing, Bkkeeping); Butler U 52-56 (Eng Lit) BS; Ind U 56-58 (LS) MA; UHawaii 61 (LS). 6: Fr. 7: Gen off wk Credit Exch Off, Loganport 21-23; Bkkeeper Ind Wheel & Rim Co, Indianapolis 24-27; Libn Indianapolis Pub Lib 54; Libn Carmel Pub Lib, Carmel ind 55; Lib coordinator Carmel-Clay schs, Carmel Ind 56-. 9: IndSchLA. 10: Bus & Prof Womens Club; AAUW; Delta Kappa Gamma. 14: Supv wk. 15: 140 EMain st, Carmel In 46032.

DONAHUGH, ROBERT H. b St Paul 20 My 30. 5: Col of St Thomas 48-52 (Eng) BA; UMinn 52-53 (LS) MA. 7: Tchg asst UMinn (Minneapolis) 53; Catlgr UFla 54; US Army SP3 CriminalInvestigation, Frankfurt Germany 54-56; Instr End UMd, (Frankfurt Ger) 56; InstrEng & speech Robert Col (Istanbul Turkey) 56-57; Head tech serv Canton Pub Lib,canton Ohio 57-62; Asst libn Pub Lib of Youngstown, Ohio 62-. 8: Tchr Negro hist,YWCA 68. 9: ALA; OhioLA (chm Tech Proc Round Table 64-65; sec 68-). 12: Ed"OhioLA Bulletin" (68-); Ed "Youngstown Library Staff Bulletin" (67-). 13: Yes. 14: Bk sel,tech serv, admin, pub rel. 15: 509 Ferndale ave, Youngstown Oh 44511.

DONALDSON, DAVID STUART. b Detroit 2 D 25. 4: Marion Fleming Donaldson. 5: Wayne State U 52-56 (Bus Admin); West Mich U 57-58 (Bus Admin, Speech) BS, 58-59 (LS); Peabody Col 63-64 MALS East Mich U 68 (Educ Admin). 9: ALA; WisLA. 14: Admin, lib bldg design & equipment. 15: 202 Euclid ave, Royal Oak Mi 48057.

DONALDSON, MARION (FLEMING). b Pontiac Mich 14 D 28. 4: David Staurt Donaldson. 7: Hd ref dept Birmingham Pub Lib, Birmingham Mich 50-56; Asst co libn Van Buren Co Lib, Paw Paw Mich 57-59; Hd bkmob dept Kalamazoo Pub Lib, Kalamazoo Mich 59-60; Dir Ingham Co Lib Syst, Mason Mich 60-62; Dir Macomb Co Lib Syst, Mt Clemens Mich 62-63; Hd libn Peabody Demonstration Sch, Nashville 63-64; Hd libn Mercy Sch of Nursing, Janesville Wis 65-66; Dir Lenawee educ Film Lib, Adrian Mich 67-68; Instr lib sci Edinboro State Col 68-. 9: MichLA (chm Co & Reg Lib Sect 62-63). 14: Lib admin, lib sci instr. 15: 202 Euclid ave, royal Oak Mi 48057.

DONALDSON, MARJORIE C. b Milwaukee 15 Je 11. 5: Rutgers U Douglass Col 29-33 (LS) BA. 7: Catlgr Pub Lib, Corning Iowa 33-34; Lib asst Iowa Travel Lib, Des Moines 34-38; Dir State WPA Lib Proj, Des Moines 38-39; Asst libn Pub Lib, Ames Iowa 39-44; Pub Lib, Pasadena Cal: Libn 44-50, Asst city libn 51-56, City libn 56-. 8: Fiscal off Metropolitan Coop Library Syst 65-69. 9: ALA; CalLA (pres Pub Lib Sect, pres So Dist); Pub Lib Execs So Cal (pres). 10: Women's City Club; Zonta Serv Club; C of C. 11: Woman of the Year Award, 63. 14: Admin, personnel. 15: 1183 Romney dr, Pasadena Cal 91105.

DONALDSON, MRS HELEN E J (EAKIN). b Imperial Sask 4 S 14. 5: Queens U (Kingston Ont) 33-36 (Hist) BA; Ontario Col of Educ 36-37 High Sch Tchg Certif; Toronto 53 MA; USoCal 56-57 (LS) MS. 7: Tchr Lord dufferin Pub Sch, Toronto 37-44; Tchr-libn Oakwood Collegiate Inst, Toronto 44-Lib consul for the E York Bd of Educ, Toronto 66-. 8: Summer sch lecturer in Ref UToronto 62; Sch Lib Standards Com for Can (chm 61-65); summer sch lecturer in sch lib admin 65. 9: CanLA; CanSchLA (chmTech Serv Com, chm Com for a Handbk on Catlg of Non-Print Materials); ALA. 13: Yes. 14: Sch libs. 15: E York Bd of Educ, 670 Cosburn ave, Toronto 13 Ont Can.

DONART, MARTHA HELEN. b Stillwater Okla 29 Jl 09. 5: Okla State U 26-30 (Amer Hist & Lit) BS; Peabody 37-38 BS in LS. 6: Fr. 7: City Libn Mangum Pub Lib, Mangum Okla 30-37; County Libn Darlington Co Lib, Darlington SC 38-42; Braille & individual loans libn Okla Lib Commsn, Okla City Okla 42-46; City Libn Stillwater Pub Lib, Stillwater Okla 46-57; Humanities libn Okla State U Lib 57-. 9: ALA; SWLA (Okla rep); OklaLA (Bd). 10: Delta Kappa Gamma; Bus & Prof Womens Club. 14: Ref. 15: 1710 Arrowhead pl, Stillwater Ok 74074.

DONEGAN, OLGA MARIE (MAHOMED). b Richmond Cal 9 Jl 15. 5: UCal (Berkeley) 33-37 (Fr) AB, 50 (Fr) MA; Stanford 52 (Educ T); San Francisco State Col 52, 57 (Remed Reading, lib resources); Nat U of Mex 54, 55 (Adv Span); UCal (Berkeley) 59 MLS. 6: Fr, Sp, Russian, Ukrainian. 7: Tchr of Fr, Span Americanization Richmond Pub Schs, Richmond Cal 38-46; Tr US Govt (G-2 sect), San Francisco 41-45; Supv tr sect US Govt (G-2 sect), Tokyo 46-50; Visiting home tchr Richmond pub schs, Richmond Cal 50-59; Sch libn Richmond Unified Dist, Richmond Cal 59-. 9: CalASchL. 10: Beta Phi Mu; Pi Delta Phi. 14: Ref, catlg,lib admin. 15: 326 31st st, Richmond Ca 94804.

DONEGHY, (FRANCES) VIRGINIA. b Macon Mo 12 O 1900. 5: UMo 23 AB; UIll 29 BS in LS; Columbia 40 MS in LS; Yale 41 MA. 7: Catlg asst UMo 23-25; Asst catlgr Kan City (Mo) Pub Lib 25-26; Catlgr UMinn (Minneapolis) 26-. 9: ALA; SLA. 15: 532 5th st SE, Minneapolis Mn 55414.

DONLEY, ALBERT MURRAY JR. b Melrose Mass 16 O 19. 4: Louise Emery. 5: Amer Internat Col 46-49 (Hist, Eng) AB; Syracuse 50-51 (LS) MS. 6: Sp, Fr. 7: Clerk NY New Haven & Hartford RR, Boston 39-41; (Cpl) USMC 9th Marines 3rdMarine Div small arms spec, So-Central Pacific 42-45; Lib asst Holyoke Pub Lib,Holyoke Mass 46-49; Libn-Dir Dedham Pub Lib, Dedham Mass 51-53; Assoc dirNortheastern U Libs 53-. 9: ALA-(ACRL, RSTD, LED, LAD, RSD, ISAD); AEAUSA; ASIS;NE Reg LA (Reg Planning Chm); MassLA (chm Legis Com & Publ Com 51); Mass Adult EducAssn (charter mem). 12: "Proposal for an Integrated Study of Cooperation and Coordination in Acquiring, Cataloging, Storing and Disseminating Multi Mediaresources" (59); "Marginal Libraries and Information Agencies" (61); "LearningResources" (65); "Learning Resources Centers" (65); "Library Systems" (65);"General Literature" (54); "Business Literature" (54); "Accounting Literature" (55);"Chemical Literature" (54); "Electrical Engineering Literature"; "Marketing ResearchLiterature"; (The last 5 are rev annually). 13: Yes. 14: Lib systems planning, reg & national cooperation, info & document storage, retrieval, &

dissemination, acquis, lib educ. 15: 84 Millwood st, Framingham Ma.

DONLEY, MARY R. b Minneapolis 18 Ja 28. 5: UMinn 46-55 (Pol Sci) BA, 55-56 (LS) MA: Columbia summers 62, 63 (LS, Hist). 6: Fr. 7: Sec Minneapolis Pub Schs 46-54; Asst libn No State Tchrs Col 56-59; Head ofcatlg & asst prof Stout State U 59-. 9: ALA; SLA; Acad Pol Sci; NEA; Assn HigherEduc; WisLA; WisEA; Assn Wis State U Faculties. 10: AAUP; AAUW; Bus & Prof WomensClub; Beta Phi Mu; Wis Hist Soc. 14: Tech serv, info retrieval. 15: Pierce Lib Stout State Univ, Menomonie Wi54751.

DONNELL, ROBERT MAXWELL. b Phoenix 6 F 28. 4: Mary Ann Chase. 5: Ariz State U 50 (Econ) BS; UDenver 62 (LS) MA. 7: Asst order libn Cal State Col(Fullerton) 62-63, Period & documents libn 63-64; Libn UOre Dental Sch 64-. 9: ALA; PNLA; OreLA. 15: 1240 SW Hillcroft ave, Portland Or 97225.

DONNELLY, ANNA M. b NYC 25 My 34. 5: St Johns U (NY) 52-56 (Eng, Langs) BA; Columbia 56-58 (LS) MS NYU 58-61. 6: Fr. 7: Page Brooklyn Pub Lib 53-56, Pre-prof child libn 56-57; Sub-proflibn St John's U (Jamaica NY) 57-58, Asst libn 58-. 9: ALA; AEAUSA. 10: Nataudubon Soc; Amer Teilhard de Chardin Assn; Liturgical Conf. 14: Ref. 15: St Johns U Lib, Jamaica NY 11432.

DONNELLY, FREDERIC D(IXON) JR. b Springfield Mass 12 D 28. 4: Caroline Hoefler. 5: LoyolaU (Chicago) 46-50 (Eng) PhB; CatholicU 50-51 MS in LS. 7: Wk fellow CatholicU 50-51; Libn I Milwaukee Pub Lib 51-53; Asst law libn LoyolaU Sch of Law (Chicago) 53-56, Law libn 56-66; Asst Prof of Lib Sci Rosary Col 66-. 9: AALL; SLA; ALA (coun 65-69); Chicago Assn of Law Libns (pres 61-62). 12: Ed AALL 6th Biennial inst "The Law Library: a Living Trust" (63). 14: Spec libs, ref, admin, lib educ. 15: 5223 N Magnolia ave, Chicago Il 60640.

DONNELLY, MARGOT (JEAN). b Canada 28 O 44. 5: McGill 61-65 (Hist) BA, 67-69 MLS. 6: Fr. 7: Imperial Tobacco, Montreal: Asst libn 65-67, Corporate libn 69-. 9: SLA. 14: Ref, admin. 15: Lib Imperial Tobacco Co of Can, PO Box 6500, Montreal 101 PQ Can.

DONNELLY, MARY ELIZABETH. b Flushing NY. 5: Hunter Col 49 (B us) BA, 53 (Elem Educ) MA; Queens Col 65 MLS. 7: Tchr PS 2 Q, E Elmhurst NY 50-62; Libn PS 7 Q, Long Island City NY 62-66; Libn PS 17 Q, Long Island City NY 67-. 9: ALA; NYLA; NYSchLA; NY Soc for Exper Study of Educ; Cath Tchrs Assn. 14: Child wk. 15: 144-04 37th ave, Flushing NY 11354.

DONNELLY, MARY JANE CHRISTINE. b Scranton Penn30 Ag 38. 5: Marywood Col 56-60 (Biol) BS, 61-62 MSLS. 7: Bio research asst Charles Pfizer, Maywood NJ 60-61; Acquis libn Kings Col(Wilkes-Barre Penn) 62-. 9: ALA; PennLA (NE Chap; v-chm 67-68, chm 68-69). 10: AAUP. 13: Yes. 14: Acquis. 15: 1101 Clover st,Scranton Pa 18508.

DONNELLY, WARD. b Philadelphia 1 Je 19. 4: Margaret Peyton. 5: St Josephs Col 45-49 BS; Drexel 58-61 MSLS. 7: Asst br libn Free Lib of Phila 58-62; Ref libn Villanova U 62-63, Microforma & av libn 64, Pub serv dir 65-66, Asst Prof Grad Sch of Lib Sci 66-. 12: Managing ed CathLA, East Penn Chap ""Newsletter (64-65). 14: Ref, admin. 15: 1536 Vernon rd, Phila Pa 19150.

DONOHUE, JOSEPH CHAMINADE. b Baltimore 26 N 30. 4: Betty C Harrison. 5: Oakland City Col 55-56; UCal(Berkeley, Santa Barbara) 56-58 (Div Tutorial) BA; Claremont Grad Sch 58-59 (Amer Studies); Simmons 59-60 (LS) MS; UCal 65-66 (LS); Case West Res 67-69 Lib & Info Sci 67-69. 6: Russian, Ger. 7: EAM operator Safe Dep & Trust Co, Baltimore 48-50; Prod expediter Westinghouse Elec, Baltimore 50-52; Info analyst & (cpl) US Army US & Europe 52-55; Adult serv libn NY Pub Lib 60-61; Ref libn Gen Elec-Tempo, Santa Barbara Cal 61-64; Asst libn Rand Corp, Santa Monica Cal; Member Tech Staff Informatics Inc, Sherman Oaks Cal & Bethesda Md 65-66; Consul Info Serv, Cleveland Ohio & Wash DC 67-; Asst Prof UMd Sch of Lib & Info Serv (College Park) 69-. 8: Consul to libs, info ctrs & serv in govt and indus; liaison between system operators and system designers; consul to publrs regarding devel plans, in lib and info sci area. 9: ASIS (Com chm Los Angeles Chap 65-66, Press & Publ Com 66 Conv); SLA (chm Educ Com SoCal Chap 65-66). 10: Los Angeles County Museum of Art (Chapter mem). 13: Yes. 14: Info systems analysis, computer applications, hueristic processes. 15: Sch of Lib & Info Serv Univ of Md, College Park Md 20742.

DONOHUE, MARY JOYCE. b Phila Penn 24 My 39. 5: Millersville State Col 57-61 (LS) BS. 7: Asst law libn US Soc Security Admin, Baltimore 62-66, Law libn 66-. 14: Law. 15: 14 E Franklin st, Baltimore Md 21202.

DONOHUE, MILDRED DOROTHIEA. b Baltimore 6 S 15. 5: UMd 34-38 (Zool) BS; Columbia 34-44 BS in LS; UIll 56-59 MS in LS. 6: Fr, Ger, Russian. 7: Lab tech UMd Med Sch-40; Asst Sci & Tech Div Enoch Pratt Free Lib, Baltimore 40-44; Nursing libn St Lukes Hosp, NYC 43-44; Prof libn I Surg General's Lib, Wash DC 44-45; Med libn Mead Johnson Co, Evansville Ind 45-47; Chem libn Glenn L Martin Co Plastic Div, Baltimore 47-49; Med libn Amer Cancer Soc, NYC 49-55; Med libn Ohio State U 55-59; Head libn tech & sci dept UMd Lib 59-. 9: ALA;-RSD; MedLA; SLA (various assignments); Internat Assn of Agric Libns & Documentalists; MdLA; DCLA; ASIS. 10: AAUW; Staff Alliance UMd; Beta Phi Mu. 11: UMd Gen Serv Bd Grant 65; Dept of Interior Water Resources Grant 69. 12: Ed "Cancer Current Literature" (50-55); Ed "Reminder, SLA Biol Div" (62-64); "Fossil Finds in Maryland," with Norma Gordon (67). 13: Yes. 14: Med & sci ref. 15: 4330 Hartwick dr apt 507, College Park Md 20742.

DONOHUE, SISTER MARY TIMOTHY. b Rochester NY 1 S 17. 5: D'Youville Col 42 (Educ) BS; CatholicU 63 (LS) MS. 6: Fr. 7: Tchr: Parochial Sch, Buffalo & Atlanta 37-44, Parochial Sch, Atlanta 44-52, Diocesan High Sch, Ogdensburg NY 52-53, Parochial Sch, Jackson Hts NY 53-55, Archdiocesan High Sch, Little Flower Phila 55-58; Superior & prin Parochial Sch Christ the King 58-64; Superior & tchr-libn Catholic Acad D'Youville Academy 64-. 8: Curriculum revision wk elem sch: St Augustine Fla summer 48, Mobile Ala summers 62-63. 9: ALA; CathLA. 10: Nat Assn of Secondary Soc Studies Tchrs. 14: Bk selection for ya. 15: D'Youville Academy 4146 Chamblee-Dunwoody rd, Chamblee Ga 30341.

DONOVAN, DAVID GERARD. b Boston 27 My 21. 4: Katharine Hickey. 5: Boston U 47-49 (Ger Lit) AB; Simmons 49-50 (LS) MS. 6: Ger. 7: Radio off US Merchant Marine 44-47; Libn various US Govt Agencies, Wash DC 50-60; Libn Gen Electric Mgt Research Serv, Ossining NY 60-62; Dir USIS Lib Serv, New Delhi India 62-65; Field dir LC Programs, Karachi Pakistan 65-67; Project off ALA Intl Rel Off, Wash DC 67-68, Dir 68-. 8: Consul; Sub-com on Libs, Planning Commsn, Govt of India, New Delhi 65; Selection Panel US Educ Found in India, New Delhi 64-65; Library consultant USAID 67-. 9: ALA; IndianLA (Life mem); Pakistan LA; New Delhi LA. 10: Pakistan Linguistic Group(Lahore Pakistan); Phi Beta Kappa; Delta Phi Alpha. 14: Acquis, ref. 15: American Lib Assn, 1420 N st NW, Wash DC 20005.

DONOVAN, KATHRYN MARY. b Phila 24 N 35. 5: East Baptist Col 53-57 (Chem) BA; Drexel 57-58 MSLS. 7: Lib internship Eli Lilly Co, Indianapolis 57; Libn I Free Lib of Phila 58-59; Ref libn Pennsalt Chem Corp, King of Prussia Penn 59-67, Libn 68-. 9: SLA (Phila Chap: chm Sci-Tech Gp 67; chm Hospitality 68); ACS; Spec Libs Coun of Phila & vicinity (Sci-Tech Group: Pub Chm 60-62, sec 62-63, adv-at large to Exec Com 64-65). 10: Amer Forestry Assn; Nat Parks Assn; AAAS; Tech Assn of Pulp & Paper Ind. 14: Ref, lit searching, indexing, admin. 15: Pennsalt Chemicals Corp, 900 First ave, King of Prussia Penn 19406.

DONOVAN, PAUL THOMAS. b Daytona Beach Fla 17 S 44. 4: Pamela Fannin. 5: Daytona Beach Jr Col 62-64 AA; Fla State U 64-66 (Eng) BA, 66-67 (LS) MS. 6: Sp, Russian. 7: Asst ref libn U S Fla Lib 67-. 8: Lib Systems Coord USFla 68-. 9: ALA; -RSD (Info Retr Com 68-); -ISAD (Computer Progr Com 69-); SELA; FlaLA (Resolutions Com 68-69, Memb Com 69-). 14: Ref, lib automation. 15: 4609 Shad st, Tampa Fl 33610.

DONOVAN, RUTH H (HADLEY). b Lincoln Neb 1 D 27. 4: Richard T Donovan. 5: UWis (Madison) 45-49 (Eng) BA, 49-50 BLS. 7: Asst soc studies libn UNeb Libs (Lincoln) 50-54; Ref libn UNev Lib (Reno) 54-62, Asst dir 62-63, 69-, Bibliog 67-69. 8: Taught 3 week wkshop on ref UNev summer 66. 9: NevLA. 10: Friends of UNev Lib; YWCA; Beta phi Mu. 14: Ref, bibliog, acquis. 15: Box 8352 University Sta, Reno Nev 89507.

DOOE, FREDERICK C. b Somerville Mass 2 Ap 42. 5: NEast 59-65 (Pol sci) BA; URI 65-69 (LS). 7: Robbins Lib, Arlington Mass: Reader's adv 65-66, Asst ref libn 66-67, Hd circ 67-68; Dir Boyden Lib, Foxborough Mass 68-. 9: ALA; NELA; MassLA. 10: Jr C of C. 14: Admin. 15: 175 Park ave, Arlington Ma 02174.

DOOLEY, HELEN A(NNE). b Bloomington Ill 10 My 03. 5: Ill Wesleyan U 21-25 (Eng Lit) AB; UWash 26-27 (Eng & Amer Lit) MA, 29 (LS) BS; Columbia 36-37, summers 41, 42. 6: Fr. 7: Eng tchr Marshall (Ill) Twp High Sch 25-26; Eng tchr El Paso (Ill) Twp High Sch 28-30; Tchr of Eng & Journalism Oshkosh Wis High Sch 30-34; Instr Eng & Journalism Southwestern Col (Winfield Kan) 37-38; Gen asst Withers Pub Lib, Bloomington Ill 34-3 asst Columbia U Undergrad Mens Browsing Room 36-37; Libn Southwestern Col (Winfield Kan) 42-44; Gen asst El Paso Pub Lib, El Paso Tex 44-45; Libn Monticello Col 45-47; Asst libn Ill State U 47-60; Libn Clermont (Fla) Pub Lib 62-65; Volunteer libn St Petersburg (Fla) Museum of Fine Arts 65-. 10: Phi Kappa Phi; Pi Gamma Mu; Alpha Beta Alpha; Kappa Kappa Gamma; St Petersburg Museum of Fine Arts; Easter Seal Guild; Garden Club; Panhellenic Assn. 14: Admin, ref, readers adv. 15: 105 Second ave, St Petersburg Beach Fl 33741.

DOOLEY, JO ELLEN (LUCE). b Wichita Falls Tex 5 S 20. 4: Emmett Francis Dooley. 5: Hardin Jr Col 37-39 (Bus); Stephen F Austin 39-40 (Bus); UOre 48-49 (Eng Lit) BA; UDenver 58-59 (Libnship) MA. 7: Tchr Fed Civil Serv Luke AFB, Arizona; Sec Fed Civil Serv Sheppard AFB & Wheelus AFB, Libya; Libn Polytech High Sch, Riverside Cal 61-64; Libn Golden Valley Jr High Sch, San Bernardino Cal 64-65; Ref libn UAlaska (Fairbanks) summers 67, 68; Ref libn Riverside City Col 68-. 8: Sponsor Student Lib Assts Assn So Cal 64-65. 9: NEA; ALA; CalTA; CalLA. 10: AAUW; Jr Col Fac Assn; Alum UDenver; Alum UOre; Delta Kappa Gamma. 14: Ref, reader guidance. 15: Riverside City College, Riverside Ca 92506.

DOOLEY, JOHN (PATRICK). b Philadelphia Pa 17 Ag 43. 5: La Salle 61-65 (Eng) BA; McGill 65-67 MLS. 6: Sp, Fr. 7: Asst stage mgr Music Fair Enterprises, Phila summer 65; Asst ref libn McGill U summer 66; Peace Corps vol Hd tech processes & ref depts U del Norte Antofagasta, Chile 67-69. 9: ALA. 15: 5310 N Camac st, Philadelphia Pa 19141.

DOOLEY, JOHN BERNARD. b Newark NJ 24 N 13. 4: Elaine Bailey Dooley. 5: U Cal(Berkeley) 30-36 (Eng) BA, 47-50 (Eng) MA, 51-53 BLS. 6: Fr. 7: Libn & Eng tchr various high schs, Cal 41-47; Eng tchr Hayward Union High SchDist, Cal 47-51, Libn 51-60; Head Libn Chabot Col 61-63; dir lib serv Col of SanMateo 63-. 8: Coord Coun for Higher Educ-Lib Resources study (Cal); Cal Jr ColAssn (chm State Jr Col Lib Com 64-). 9: CalLA; ALA. 14: Admin, bk sel, ref. 15: 1715 Lexington ave, SanMateo Ca 94402.

DOOLEY, LEOTA E (HERREN). b Hutchinson Kan 16 D 22. 4: George D Dooley. 5: Hutchingson Jr Col 40-42 Certif; Kan State Tchrs Col 42-44 (LS, Educ) BS Libnship UDenver 67 (Catlg); UOre 68 (Lib Automation). 6: Sp. 7: Circ libn TopekaFree Pub Lib, Topeka Kan 44, Child libn 45-46; Lib asst Beech Aircraft Corp,wichita Kan 46-47, Act libn 48; Head readers serv Wichita div Boeing Airplane Co,Wichita Kan 48-55, Lib supv 55-56; Head retrieval unit UDenver div Martin Co,denver 56-58; Asst libn Marathon Oil Co, Denver 58-63, Libn 63-. 8: Panel memfor UColo/SLA wkshop on Lib Automation Principles & Applications 69. 9: SLA(Loc Arrs Chm for 63 Conv; Chapt sec 58-59, chapt v-pres & program chm 62-63);MPLA; Colo Lib Devel Com 64; ColoLA. 10: Sigma Sigma Sigma. 14: Ref. 15: 2564 S Vrain, Denver Co 80219.

DOOLEY, VIRGINIA (CORTTIS). b Dudley Mass 20 My 08. 5: Wheaton Col 27-31 (Hist) AB; Newark Museum Apprentice Col 31-32 Certif; Simmons summers 44-48 (LS) BS. 6: Fr. 7: Tchr-Libn Bartlett High Sch, Webster Mass 33-43; Libn Concord Sr High Sch,Concord NH 44-46; Libn Lyman Hall High Sch, Wallingford Conn 46-. 8: Consul Bur ofLib Serv summers 59-63. 9: ALA-AASchL (Planning Co 60-66); NESchLA (past pres);Conn Sch LA (past pres); ConnEA. 10: Delta Kappa Gamma; AAUW. 14: Sch libs. 15: 240 S Main st, Wallingford Ct 06492.

DOONER, PHYLLIS (MILLER). b Ransom Kan 7 Ag 16. 5: UKan 33-37 (Hist) BA; USoCal summer 37; Colo State Col 39-42 (Eng) MA; UDenver 51-55 MALS. 7: Eng instr & libn Utica Rural High, Utica Kan 37-42; Eng instr Central High Sch, Pueblo Colo 42-52; Libn Centennial High Sch, Pueblo Colo 52-61; Docs libn McClelland Pub Lib, Pueblo Colo 66; Catlg libn So Colo State Col 66-. 8: Instr Lib Sci (catlg, clsf 68-69. 9: ALA; NEA (life mem); MPLA; ColoLA (pres So Div 55-56). 10: AAUW; Delta Kappa Gamma; Friends of McClelland Pub Lib; Pueblo Symphony Guild; Pueblo Museum Assn. 14: Catlg, lib educ, research. 15: 26 Villa dr, Pueblo Co 81001.

DORAN, MARGARET (LUCILE) CAMERON. b Auburn RI 19 Ja 13. 4: Harold Ernest Doran. 5: Simmons 31-35 BS in LS; Loyola U(Los Angeles) 61-62 (Educ) MA. 7: Lib asst Framingham (Mass) Town Lib 35-36; Asst libn Saugus Pub Lib, Saugus Mass 36-37, Libn 37-41; Libn Palms Jr High Sch, Los Angeles 57-; Vis lectr Loyola U of Los Angeles. 9: ALA (sec 57); AASchL (Rep to CalASchL 59-60); CalASchL (sec 62-63, Mem Standards Com 63-66); MassLA (sec Jr Mems 37-38). 10: Westchester Friends of the Lib; Amer Field Serv; PTA (Life mem). 13: Yes. 14: Sch libs. 15: 8026 Loyola blvd, Los Angeles Ca 90045.

DORAN, MERLE (SOUTER). b Quitman Ga 31 My 21. 4: Michael Desmond Doran. 5: Fla State Col for Women 39-43 (Psych, Elem Educ) AB; Fla State U 48-49 (LS) MA. 6: Sp, 07: Asst libn circ Fla State U 49-56; Asst to Libn Mt Holyoke Col 56-58; Ref libn Fla Presbyterian Col 60-61, 63-65; Asst Prof Fla State U Lib Sch 61-63; Asst Prof Lib Sci Est Tenn State U 65-. 9: ALA; FlaLA. 10: Beta Phi Mu. 14: Ref, sch libs, col libs. 15: 1610 Seward dr, Cherokee Hills, Johnson City Tn 37601.

DORBIN, SANFORD M. b Salina Kan 8 D 32. 4: Frances Singer. 5: Tex ChristianU 50; UCLA 53-58 (Eng) AB, 64-65 MLS. 6: Fr, Sp. 7: Coal mine labor, Millein-Heiken Germany 58-59; Cab driver Yellow Cab, LA 61-62; Diaper deliveryman Infant serv, LA 63-64; Lib asst Clark Memorial Lib, LA 64-65; Libn UCal (Santa Barbara) 65-. 9: ALA (Area recruiter 65-); UCAL (Santa Barbara) LA (pres 65). 10: Pres, Libns Assn, UCSB, 65. 12: "Family Life and Others" (poems) (68); "Persona" (poems) (69). 13: Yes. 14: Bibliog of contemporary Anglo-Amer lit, rare bks, ref serv. 15: 2571 Puesta del Sol, Santa Barbara Ca 93105.

DORFLER, MELAYN (MARION ELAYN). b Bay Shore LI NY 20 S 41. 5: Denison U 59-63 (Biol) BS; UMich 63-65 AMLS; UMich summer 66 med Bibliog & Med Lib Admin). 6: Sp, Ger. 7: Herbarium asst Denison U 61-63; Ser & documents recorder Gen Lib UMich 63-65; Asst ser libn Health Scis Lib UMd 65-67; VISTA volunteer, Knox Co Ky 67-68; Docs libn Health Scis Lib UMd 69-. 9: ALA (Md RSD). 10: Delta Phi Alpha. 14: Ref, bk sel, govt docs. 15: 515 Anneslie rd, Baltimore Md 21212.

DORMIRE, KORNELIA M (MARSHALL). b Budapest Hungary 10 Ag 41. 5: Nazareth Col (Rochester NY) 60-64 (Hist) BA; Columbia 64-65 MLS. 6: Hungarian, Ger. 7: Staff libn Coun on Foreign Rel, NYC 65-. 9: SLA. 10: Rochester (NY) Fencers Club. 14: Ref, US govt docs. 15: 210 E 15th st apt 8M, New York NY 10003.

DORNFEST, WALTER THEODORE. b Brooklyn ny 16 Mr 40. 4: Wilma Hawkins Dornfest. St John's U 59-62 (Hist) BA, 62-63 (Amer hist) MA; Pratt Inst 64-65 MLS. 6: Fr. 7: Pub Lib, Brooklyn NY: Libn trainee 63-65, Libn 65; Asst libn St John's U, Jamaica Queens NY 65-67; Instr (libn) Staten Is Commun Col 67-. 9: ALA. 10: AHA; AAUP; NY Hist Soc; Co Mil Histns; Soc Army Hist Research; Nat Geog Soc. 14: Ser, period, govt, docs, acquis. 15: 129012 Richmond ave, Staten Island NY 10314.

DORNFEST, WILMA ELIZABETH. b SI NY 14 F 42. 4: Walter T Dornfest. 5: Syracuse 59-63 (Amer Studies) AB, 63-64 (LS) MS; NYU 66- (Amer Hist). 6: Ger. 7: Asst Prof SI Community Col 64-. 9: Lib Assn City U NY (sec 67-69); ALA. 14: Catlg. 15: 1290-2 Richmond ave, SI NY 10314.

DORO, EDWARD. b Dickinson ND 3 F 10. 5: UAriz (Mus); USoCal (Eng Lit) BA; UPenn (Eng Lit) MA; U of Paris (Fr Lit); UCal(Berkeley) MLS. 7: Research asst in libnship UCal(Berkeley) 57-58; Sr asst rare bks Yale U 58-59; Curator of rare bks Northwestern U 59-62; Tchr The New Sch, NYC 62-63; Head libn-lecturer Museum of Fine Arts, Houston 64-65; Libn-tchr Franconia Col 65-67; U Libn & Prof humanities J F Kennedy Univ (Cal) 67-69; Hd libn & Prof lit Monterey Inst of For Studs (Monterey Cal) 69-. 9: ALA (Life mem). 10: Caxton Club (Chicago) etc. 11: Guggenheim Fellow. 12: Auth; "Alms for Oblivion"; "The Boar & Shibboleth"; "Shiloh"; "Mr Zenith"; "Parisian Interlude"; "The Furtherance". 14: Admin, rare bks. 15: 1275 Vallejo st, Seaside Ca 60801.

DORR, MARY L. b Buffalo NY 1 N 04. 5: Cornell U 23-27 (Eng) AB; Columbia 43-45 (LS) BS. 6: Fr, Sp. 7: Cornell U Lib; Catlgr 27-34, Reviser in catlg dept 34-46, Head catlg dept Sch of Ind & Labor Rel 46-50; Head catlgr Denison U Lib 50-58; Head catlgr Beloit Col Lib 58-. 9: ALA; WisLA; Midwest Acad Libns Conf. 10: ELOIT Col Womens Club; Art League of Beloit. 14: Catlg. 15: 629 Park ave, Beloit Wi 53511.

DORRANCE, DON. b Detroit Mich 16 D 25. 5: UMich 46-50 (Eng) BA, 60-62 (Ed) MA, 64-65 (LS) MA. 7: (Priv) USA Inf, Europe 44-46; Libn MichHosp Serv (Blue Cross), Detroit 52-54; Tchr Whitmore Lake Pub Sch, Whitmore Lake Mich 60-61; Tchr Ypsilanti Pub Sch, Ypsilanti Mich 61-63; Libn Washtenaw Co Lib, Ann Arbor Mich 63-66; Libn Bendix Aerospace Syst Div, Ann Arbor Mich 66-. 8: Consul for small libs, Washtenaw Co Lib System, 65-66; Member editorial board, Mich Chapter SLA 67-. 9: SLA (Ed Bd Mich Chap 67-). 12: Assoc ed "Overflow Magazine". 15: Bendix Corporation, Aerospace Systems Division, 3300 Plymouth rd, Ann Arbor Mi 48107.

DORREL, RUTH (LATHOM). b Perry County Ind 26 Ja 36. 4: Warren W Dorrel. 5: Evansville Col 53-57 (Hist) BA; Ind U 57-58 (LS) MA. 7: Asst loan lib Ohio Wesleyan U 58-61; Libn Inlow Clinic, Shelbyville Ind 61-63; Libn Shelbyville Jr High Sch, Shelbyville Ind 63-68; Bk catlgr Ind Hist Soc Lib 68-. 5 15: R 1, St Paul Ind 47272.

DORSETT, CORA (MATHENY). b Camden Ark 15 Jl 21. 4: George L Dorsett. 5: Centenary Col (Shreveport La) (Educ) BSE; UMiss MLS. 7: Currently Head libn Pub Lib of Pine Bluff & Jefferson County, Pine Bluff Ark. 9: ALA; ArkLA (chm Pub Lib Div); SWLA. 10: Alpha Chi; DAR; Zonta Internat; AAUW;Jefferson Co Restoration & Preserv Commsn. 11: Chi Omega Social Science Award. 14: Admin. 15: Pub Lib, Pine Bluff Ar 71601.

DORSEY, BERNICE (AMSTUTZ). b Bluffton Ohio 15 Ap 06. 5: Bluffton Col 23-27 (Eng) AB; Carnegie 29-30 BS in LS. 7: Tchr New Miami Ohio 27-29; Libn Ceredo (WVa) Dist High Sch 30-34; Asst libn Marshall U 34-49; Libn Enslow Jr High Sch, Huntington WVa 48-55; Libn Beverly Hills Jr High Sch 55-; Instr in lib sci Marshall U summers, Asst col lib libn 68-. 9: WVaLA. 10: AAUW; Cabell-Huntington Hosp Auxiliary; Delta Kappa Gamma. 15: 1406 Fifteenth st, Huntington WV.

DORSEY, VIRGINIA DICKEY. b 15 Ag 16. 4: Eugene A Dorsey. 5: UKy 35-39 (LS) AB. 6: Fr. 7: Tchr Fleming Co Bd of Educ, Flemingsburg Ky 39-41;Tchr Bourbon Co Bd of Educ, Paris Ky 41-45; Libn Bourbon Co Bd of Educ, Paris Ky55-69. 9: NEA; ALA; KyLA; KyASchL; KyEA. 10: Garden Club; Lioness Club; Phi Beta Kappa; Phi Alpha Theta. 15: Bourbon Co High Sch, Paris Ky 40361.

DOSA, MARTA LESZLEI. b Szekszard Hungary 20 My 23. 5: UBudapest 41-44 (Comparative Lit) MA; Syracuse 57 MSLS. 6: Fr, Ger, Hungarian. 7: Syracuse U; Asst ser libn, U Lib 57-58, Catlgr 58-60, Libn Metallurgical Lib 60-63, Mathematics libn 60-65, Lecturer & instr Sch of Lib Sci 61-, Asst Prof 67-. 9: SLA; AALS; NYTA. 10: Americanization League. 12: 2 bks of short stories & a novel in Hungarian, Munich & Brussels (52, 56, 58). 14: Nat & internat bibliog, govt docs. 15: 521 Thayer st, Syracuse NY 13210.

DOSZPOLY, DEZSOE. b Nagyvarad Hungary 16 My 17. 4: Irene Jambor. 5: Royal Hungarian Pazmany 41 (Pol Sci) PhD; Peter Univ of Sciences (Budapest) 43 (Law) JSD; Supreme Court 9hungary) 48 Unified Diploma for Judges & Attorneys at Law; Rutgers 63 MLS. 6: Hungarian, Kat, Ger. 7: Ref asst Free Pub Lib, Elizabeth NJ 61-63; Govt docs libn Rutgers U Lib (New Brunswick) 63-66; Dir lib serv & assoc prof Phila Col of Textiles & Sci 66-. 8: Member: Philadelphia Ad Hoc Library Council. 9: ALA; SLA; PennLA. 10: AAUP. 11: Intercoll World Champion in Swimming, Paris 37. 13: Yes. 14: Admin, govt docs. 15: School House lane & Henry ave, Philadelphia Pa 19144.

DOTE, JEAN (OSUGA). b San Jose Ca 11 Ap 36. 4: Sam S Dote. 5: Lewis & Clark Col 54-58 (Hist) BA; UWash 58-59 M of Lib. 7: Libn popular lib Lib Assn of Portland, Ore 59-60, Libn lit & hist 60-61; Asst soc sci ref libn & interlib loan libn Cal State Col (Long Beach 61-67; Hd soc sci ref dept 67-. 9: ALA; CalLA; CalStateEA. 10: AAUP; Acad Senate Cal State Col (Long Beach) 66-68. 14: Ref. 15: 11908 S Traro ave #2, Hawthorne Ca 90250.

DOTSON, VELMA (PEARL) VAN HORN. b Tulsa Okla 5 Mr 16. 4: Jasper William Dotson. 5: Northeastern State Col(Okla) 34-38 (Elem Educ, Span) BS; UHouston 51-52 (Secondary Educ); Tex A&I Col 57 (Supv); Sul ROSS Col 58 (LS); Tex Womans U 59-63 MLS. 6: Sp. 7: Tchr pub schs, Vinita Okla 38-40; Tchr pub schs, Knosville Tenn 44-45; Tchr pub schs, Corpus Christi Tex 49-50; Tchr pub schs, Browsville Tex 50-53; Tchr pub schs, Los Fresnos Tex 53-59, Libn 59-. 9: ALA; Tex State Tchrs Assn; TexLA. 10: Alpha Sigma Alpha; Kappa Kappa Iota;Delta Kappa Gamma. 14: Ref, circ. 15: PO Box 61, Los Fresnos Tx 78566.

DOTY, CONSTANCE SHIRLEY (CLARKE). b Barnesville Minn 27 Ag 18. 5: Moorhead State Tchrs Col 36-41 (Elem Educ) BA; St Olaf Col 62-63; UMinn summers 64-67 (LS). 7: Tchr minn Pub Sch: Ada 41-45, Randolph 48-55; Asst libn Pub Lib, Northfield Minn 61-66, Hd libn 66-. 9: ALA; MinnLA; MinnTA. 10: Northfield Arts Guild; Northfield Parent-Teachers Org; Bus & Prof Women's Club. 14: Admin, child bks. 15: 312 Washington st, Northfield Mn 55057.

DOTY, MADGE R. b Holland Mich 25 Ag 07. 5: Hope Col 24-27 (Eng); Mich State 27-28 (Eng) AB; West Res 48-49 MS in LS. 6: Fr. 7: Tchr Mackinaw City High Sch, Mackinaw City Mich 30-31; Tchr Davison High Sch,Davison Mich 31-37; High sch libn Lansing Mich 45-51; Circ libn, Pub Lib LansingMich 51-55, ref libn 55-64, dir of adult serv 65-66, ref libn 66-. 8: Tchr of Lib Tech, Lansing Community Col. 9: ALA-LAD(com chm 64-66)-SORT (treas 65-67); MichLA; MichEA; NEA. 14: Pub rel, ref. 15: 210 E Mt Hope ave,Lansing Mi 98910.

DOTY, ROSAMOND (CLARK). b Kellhier Minn 22 F 17. 4: Robert Earl Doty. 5: Bemidji State Col 35-39 (Eng); St Cloud State Col 56-57 (Lang Arts) BA; UMinn 65-67 (LS) Masters. 6: Ger, Fr. 7: Legal sec, Monticello Minn 49-56; Instr Elk River Sr High Sch, Elk river Minn 57-60, Libn 66-; Organizer & admin elem libs, Elk River Minn 60-66. 8: Organist St Peter Lutheran Ch 48-; Libn Big Lake-Monticello Commun Hosp. 9: Central div of Sch Libns (chm). 15: 225 E River st, Monticello Mn 55362.

DOTZMAN, ISABELLE MANGELSDORF. b Ellinwood Kan 27 Je 10. 4: John G Dotzman. 5: Mt St Scholastica Col 29-31. 7: Ref libn "St Louis Post-Dispatch" 35-39; Asstmss libn Mo Hist Soc, St Louis 61-. 15: Mo Hist Soc, Lindell at DeBaliviere,St Louis Mo 63112.

DOUCET, YOLANDE. b Ottawa Can 2 Mr 17. 5: Carleton U (Ottawa) 54 BA; UMontreal 41 (LS) Diploma; UOttawa 55 BLS. 6: Fr, Eng, Sp. 7: Gen libn Bibliotheque St-Sulpice, Montreal 42-49; Libn Royal Commsn Arts, Letters, Sci (Can), Ottawa 49-51; Chief libn Can Broadcasting Corp, Montreal 54-. 9: ALA; CanLA; SLA; QuebecLA. 15: Canadian Broadcasting Corp Ref Lib, PO Box 6000, Montreal Que Can.

DOUDNIKOFF, BASIL. b NYC 19 Ap 33. 4: Betty Barry. 5: UFla 55-59 (Ind Engnr) BS; George Washington U 60-64 (Engnr Admin) MS. 6: Russian. 7: Info systems analyst Westinghouse Electric Corp, Baltimore 59-62; Dir info systems div Jonker Bus Mach In, Wash DC 62-66; Market Planning Doc Inc, Bethesda Md 66-67; Pres Dataflow Systs Inc,Rockville Md 67-. 8: Visiting lecturer, UMd Lib Sch 66-. 9: Potomac Tech Proc Libns; ASIS. 12: Jt auth ""A Practical Approach to Information and Data Retrieval (65). 13: Yes. 14: Research in info systems desig. 15: 12911 Margot dr, Rockville Md 20850.

DOUGAN, ROBERT ORMES. b Ilford Essex Eng 21 Ag 04. 4: Margaret Truax. 51: Lecturerfor Foras Eireann, on "The Book of Kells," Dublin 55-58. 6: Lat, Fr, Ger, Ital. 7: Libn Royal Hist Soc, London 25-35; Bibliog research wker & catlgr E Ph Goldschmidt& Co Ltd, London 26-40; Adjutant & admin off (Flight Lt) Royal Air Force Station,Perth Scotland 41-45; Libn Sandeman Pub Lib, Perth Scotland 45-52; Deputy libnTrinity Col (Dublin) 52-58; Libn Henry E Huntington Lib & Art Gallery, San Marinocal 58-. 8: Org of two Scottish Bk Exhibitions, Festival of Britain, 9: ALA (chm Rare Bks Sect 64-65); Lib Assn (Gt Brit) Fellow; Bibliog Soc(London); Lib Coun of Ireland. 10: Grolier Club;Internat Bibliophile Assn. 12: Two illustrated Catalogues of Festival of Britain,51, Scottish Books Exhibitions. 13: Yes. 14: Rare bks. 15: 855 S Orange Grove blvd, Pasadena Ca 91105.

DOUGHERTY, ANNA ELIZABETH. b Wilmington Del 8 N 10. 5: UDel 28-32 (Lit) AB; Drexel 32-33 BS in LS; Columbia 42-43, 48 (LS) MS. 6: Fr, Sp. 7: Stud asst UDel 29-31; Temp govt publ libn Wilmington Inst Free Lib, Wilmington Del 34; Lib asst Del Acad of Med 34-35; Asst libn E IDuPont de Nemours Jackson Lab Patent Lib, Deepwater NJ 35-37; Bucknell U: Ref libn 38-40, Head ser dept 40-43, Head catlg dept 43-44; Asst head catlgr Bryn Mawr Col Lib 44-48; Assoc libn catlg UMich Law Lib 48-49; Clsfr Brooklyn Col Lib 49-51; Catlg reviser NLM, Wash DC 51-58, Head spec langs unit catlg 58-59; NIH Lib, Bethesda Md; Asst libn 59-63, Asst libn & act chief ref sect 60-61, Asst to the chief for program planning 63-65, Asst libn 65-. 8: US Armed Forces Med Lib Exhibit Com for the First Internat Congress on Med Libnship, London 53; Publ Com 2d Internat Congress on Med Libnship, Wash DC 63; US Civil Serv Commsn, Bur of Programs & Standards, Standards Div, Test Devel & Occupatl Research Sect, Lib Com 61-62. 9: ASIS; ALA; -ACRL (Subj Spec Sect,

Agric & Biol Scis Subsect, sec-treas 68-69); -DCC (Memb (Memb Com DC rep 54-56); -RTSD (Wash rep ALA Meeting); MedLA (Publ Com 52-56, co-chm on Convention Facilities 54 Meeting, Com for Advanced Sem in Med Libnship 61 Meeting, Ed Com Vital Notes on Med Periods 64-65, Ida & George Eliot Prize Essay Com 65-66); Jt Com on Lib Educ (CNLA), MedLA repres 66-68, sec-treas 67-69); SLA (Wash DC Chap; corr sec 57-58, Exec Bd 57-58, Adv Coun 57-59, mem 6 coms 53-59, 66-69; Biol Scis Group: chm 58-59, v-chm 57-58, Hospitality Chm 53-54, Memb Chm 59-60); DCLA (mem 3 coms 53-54 wbg (Adv Coun DC rep 56-58, Program Chm 58 Meeting); Wash DC Area Med Lib Group (chm 4 coms); Lib Assn of the Four City Col libs of NY (Exec Coun Brooklyn Col Lib Del 50-51); PennLA (sec Col Lib Sect 40-41); Phila Reg Catlgrs Group (pres 47-48). 10: YWCA; Beta Phi Mu. 12: Assoc ed "Bulletin, MedLA (52-56); Assoc ed "Chapter Notes, Wash DC Chap SLA (58-59); Asst ed "The Reminder, SLA Biol Scis Div (62-63); Jt ed "Proceedings, 2d Internat Congress on Med Libnship (63); Contr: "The Literatures of the World in English Translation, A Bibliography v 1 (68-). 13: Yes. 14: Admin, bibliog, research. 15: 3001 Veazey terrace NW apt 815, Wash DC 20008.

DOUGHERTY, BETTIE JANE. b Ft Bragg NC. 5: E Carolina Col 51-54 (Hist) BS; UNC 57-58 LS); Columbia 60-62 MLS. 6: Fr. 7: Asst libn Burlington High Sch, Burlington NC 54-55; Libn New Bern High Sch,New Bern NC 55-56; Asst documents libn UNC Chapel Hill 56-57; Ref libn Nat City Bankof NY, NYC 59-60; Libn Operations Research Gen Electric Co, NYC 60-62; Acquis libnPort of NY Authority, NYC 62-63, chief libn 63-. 9: ALA; SLA (chm Transportationdiv, treas NY Chap Document Gp); ASIS (1967 Consul Hostess, NY Chap; sec 65-67,memb chm); Amer Soc of Indexers. 14: Documentation. 15: 10 W 15th st, NYC 10011.

DOUGHERTY, MARY JOSEPHINE (SULLIVAN). b Visalia Cal 13 N 21. 4: Wienford N Dougherty. 5: Visalia Jr Col 39-41. 7: Sec-radio dispatcher Visalia Police Dept, Visalia Cal 41-42; Priv sec & libn Dist Attorneys Off Tulare Co, Visali Cal 42-54; Jury Commissioner & law libn Tulare Co, Visalia Cal 56-. 9: Cal Jury Commissioners/ Assn (past sec). 10: Visalia Coin Club; Tulare Co Employees Assn. 11: Charte certificate, AALL. 15: Tulare C Law Lib Rm 305, CountyCivic Center, Visalia Ca 93277.

DOUGHERTY, RICHARD M. b E Chicago Ind 17 Ja 35. 4: Carole Mary Low. 5: Purdue U 53-54, 57-59 (Forestry) BS; Rutgers 59-61 MLS, 61-63 (LS) PhD. 7: Laborer & 3rd Helper (Open Hearth) Inland Steel Corp, E Chicago Ind 53-57; YNT3 US Navy Nat Sec Agency Lib 54-56; Stud asst Purdue U 57-59; Libn-trainee Linden Pub Lib, Linden NJ 59-61; Research Assoc Rutgers 61-63; Chief acquis dept UNC (Chapel Hill) 63-66; Assoc dir of libs UColo 66-. 8: Tchg Grad Lib Sci courses var terms at Rutgers, UNC, USoCal, Syracuse &Wisconsin, Library Management and Building Consultant (ten libraries). 9: ALA;MPLA; ColoLA; ALA-RTSD (chm tech serv coord routines survey com 64-66); Chm, ISADCommittee for Dissemination of Information (68); Member, RTSD Committee on Costs(67-). 10: Xi Sigma Pi; Alpha Zet; Beta Phi Mu. 12: "Scientific Management of Library Operations" (66); "Colorado AcademicLibraries Processing Ctr, Final Report" (68); Asst ed for acquis "LRTS" (64-69) Edbd; "Journal of Library Automation" (68); Ed "CRL" (69-). 13: Yes. 14: Tech serv, admin, mgt, automation, bldg arch. 15: Univ of Colo Lib, Boulder Co 80302.

DOUGHERTY, RUTH ALICE. b Patriot Ind 18 Ja 31. 4: James Edward Dougherty. 5: Hanover Col 48-52 (Lang Arts) AB; Ind U 52-54 (LS) MA. 6: Sp. 7: Libn Danville High Sch, Danville Ind 52-53; Libn Franklin Twp High Sch, Wanamaker Ind 53-57; Asst libn Lawrence Central High Sch, Indianapolis 57-62; Libn MSD Lawrence Twp Lib Serv Center, Indianapolis 62-. 9: ALA (State Assembly 58-59, 68-70); NEA-DAVI; IndSchLA (chm Research Com 54-55, v-pres & Program Chm 57-58, pres 58-59, chm Nomin Com 59, chm Nat Lib Week 60); Coun 68-70; Ind Supv Instr Mats Ctrs (chm Reg Proc Com 66, sec-treas 67, pres 68); IndStateTA. '10: Beta Phi Mu; Sch Libns Discussion Club; Classic Car Club of Amer; Hoosier Lib Transparencies Inc. 12: Ed "News Noser, IndSchLA (55-56, 58-60). 13: Yes. 14: Central proc of materials, a-v catlg, sch lib research & devel, instr tech. 15: 6423 S Arlington ave, Indianapolis In 46227.

DOUGHTY, RUTH (LIVINGOOD). b Myerstown Penn 10 Mr 07. 5: Albright Col 24-28 (Eng) BS in Ed; Drexel smmer 32 (LS) Sch Libn Certi, summer 39, 42-43; Sch of Eng, Middlebury tvt Augut 45. 7: Tchr Cherr Tree High Sch, Cherry Tree Penn 28-31; Tchr E Lampeter High Sch, Lancaster Penn 31-38; Tchr-libn Myerstwn High Sch, Myerstown Penn 38-43; Tchr-lib Warwick Town Sch, Rothsville Penn 43-45; Pub libn Pub Lib, Myerstown Penn 46-52; Head interlib loan Penn State Lib 52-68; Child libn Lebanon Commun Lib, Lebanon Pa 68-. 9: ALA; PennLA. 14: Child lit, pub lib wk,ref, bkbinding. 15: 118 Sioux ave, Lebanon Pa 17042.

DOUGHTY, SHIRLEY. b Winnipeg Man Can 6 Mr 35. 5: UMan 52-56 (Eng) BA; Toronto 60-61 BLS. 6: F. 7: Systems & procedures Philips Electronics, Toronto 56-57; Asst personnel manager Rowntree Co Ltd, Toronto 57-59; Circ & ref lin York U(Toronto) 61-65, Humanities bibliogr 65-68, Hd Coll Development Sect 68-. 14: Bk sel. 15: 89 Douglas cres, Toronto 5 Can.

DOUGLAS, ALVERA L (MARCON). b Sopris Colo 16 Ag 24. 5: Adams State Col 41-45 (Eng) BA; Rosary Col 49-50 BA in LS; Washington U 51-52; UNM summer 60. 6: Sp, Ital. 7: Asst libn Adams State Col 45-49; Asst chief ref Washington U 51-53; Libn US Army (USAEUR) Spec serv, Germany 53-56; Libn Taft Jr High Sch, Albuquerque NM 59-66; Libn Manzano High Sch, Albuquerque 66-. 8: NMEA Sch Libns Child & YP Div (v-chm) 61-62, 62-63 Greater Albuquerque LA (sec68-69). 9: NMEA; NMLA; Albuquerque LA; Albuquerque Sch Libns; NEA; AlbuquerqueClrm TA. 14: Reading guidance, ref. 15: 11320 Mahlon NE, Albuquerque NM 87112.

DOUGLAS, ALYCE (MOEHN). b Chicago. 5: Chicago Normal Sch of Phys Educ 22-24 Phys Educ Tchg Certif; Rosary Col50-53 (Eng) BA, 53-54 (LS) MA. 6: Ger, Fr. 7: Libn I Legler Br Chicago Pub Lib 54-59, Asstlibn & act libn Westtown Br 59-60, Libn II Austin Br 60-66, Hd libn Toman Br 66-. 9: ALA; IllLA. 10: Ill Athletic Club. 13: Yes. 14: Admin. 15: 1434 Jackson ave, River Forest Il 60305.

DOUGLAS, BARBARA (JOY). b Warner NH. 4: Howard W Douglas. 5: Middlebury 27-31 (Amer & Eng Lit) AB; Columbia 31-32 (LS) BS, 49 MA. 6: Fr. 7: Catlgr & child libn Kellogg-Hubbard Pub Lib, Montpelier Vt 33;1st libn Gary Lib Montpelier Sem 33-35; Assoc libn NH Trav Libs Plymouth State Col35-36; Church sch libn 47-54; Child libn Rutland Free Pub Lib, Rutland Vt 53-66,Libn Elem Sch Libs, Dana Area, Rutland Pub Schs, Rutland Vt 66-. 8: Vt Congress P & T corr sec, Reading & lib serv (chm) 49-54; NE Reading Assn; VCPT Bd of Managers State Convention Chm. 9: ALA; VtLA;VtSchLA; NESchLA. 11: Freedoms Foundation Award; VtEA; Lay Citation 66. 14: Child serv, writing for child, ref. 15: 54North st, Rutland Vt 05701.

DOUGLAS, CAROLYN JOYCE (TEMPLE). b Los Angeles Cal 9 S 34. 4: Robert R Douglas. 5: USoCal 51-55 (Eng) AB (Magna Cum Laude), 55-56 (Eng) MA, 65-67 MSLS. 7: LA City Schs: Tchr 56-67, Lib coordinator a-v sect 67-. 9: ALA; NEA-DAVI; CalASchL; A-V Assn Cal. 10: Phi Beta Kappa; Phi Kappa Phi; Beta Phi Mu. 14: Catlg, sch libs. 15: 8402 Coreyell pl, Los Angeles Ca 90046.

DOUGLAS, JOHN R. b Waukegan Ill 1 Ja 33. 4: Ardis Ault. 5: Earlham Col 51-52; UDenver 56-58 (Sociol) BA, 58-59 (LS) MA. 6: Sp, Ger. 7: Map & chart libn USAF, Shreveport La, Korea 52-56; Educ libn San Jose State Col 59-61, Sci-tech libn 61-65, Circ libn 65-67, Lib publns off 67-68, Libn-tutor New Col Excptl Program 68-. 9: ALA; CalLA. 10: Amer Fed of Tchrs; ACLU; Sierra Club; Point Reyes Bird Observ. 14: Ref, bibliog, lib-campus rel. 15: 139 Senter rd, San Jose Ca 95111.

DOUGLAS, JUDY ANN. b Whitstable England 29 O 41. 5: UWest Ont 61-64 (Eng/Hist) BA; UToronto 64-65 BLS. 7: Catlgr UWest Ont (London) 65-68; Asst hd of Catlg Mem U of Newfoundland 68-. 9: CanLA. 14: Catlg. 15: 279 Freshwater rd apt 209, St John's Newfoundland Can.

DOUGLAS, LEONA (DISHON). b Crab Orchard Ky 19 O 11. 4: Clifford Douglas. 5: East Ky State Col 41 (Eng, Hist) AB; UKy 63 MS in LS. 6: Lat, Fr. 7: Tchr High Schs, Whitley Co Ky 41-59; Libn McCreary High Sch, Whitley City Ky 59-61: Libn Liberty High Sch, Liberty Ky 61-63; Libn Berea Col 63- Walton-Verona High Sch 63-. 9: ALA; Ky LA. 10: AAUW. 14: Ref. 15: 156 N Main st, Walton Ky 41094.

DOUGLAS, MARY TERESA PEACOCK. b Salisbury NC 8 F 03. 4: Clarence DeWitt Douglas. 5: UNC (Greensboro) 19-23 (Eng) AB; Columbia 28-31 BS in LS. 6: Fr. 7: Tchr pub schs, Salisbury NC 23-26, Libn 26-30; Lib supv NC State Dept of Pub Instr, Raleigh NC 30-47; Lib supv pub schs, Raleigh NC 47-68, Consultant 69-. 8: Summer Instr in Lib Sci in 15 institutions; Speaker at lib & educ meetings & at nat assns in more than 30 states. 9: AALA (chm & mem var coms); NEA; SELA (chm Sch Lib Sect 38-38); NCLA (pres 39-41, chm Sch

Lib Sect); NCEA (chm Sch Lib Sect). 10: DAR; Delta Kappa Gamma; Phi Beta Kappa. 11: ALA Grolier Award 58; Recipient Mary P Douglas Award, establ by NCASchL 68. 12: "NC Sch Lib Handbook (5th ed 53); "Planning & Equipping the Sch Lib (2nd ed 49); "Teacher-Librarians Handbook ALA (2nd ed 49), "The Pupil Assistant in the Sch Lib ALA (57); "The Primary Sch Lib and Its Services UNESCO (61). 13: Yes. 14: Sch lib. 15: 2621 Dover rd, Raleigh NC 27608.

DOUGLASS, ADELE SCHULER (BARBARA). b NYC 10 O 38. 4: Edward Fenner Douglass. 5: UWis (Madison) 57-61 (Fr) BA; Westminster Col 61-62 (Educ) Tchg Certif; UIll 66-67, 68-69 (LS) MS. 6: Fr, Ger. 7: Tchr Peace Corps vol, Republic of Cameroon 62-65; Clk II Engring Lib UIll 65-66; Asst libn Ill State Water Survey, Urbana 68-. 9: ALA. 10: Beta Phi Mu. 14: Spec libs. 15: 412 Hessel blvd, Champaign Il 61820.

DOUGLASS, KATHERINE (MOONEY). b Huntington Ind 26 Ag 10. 4: Harold E Douglass. 5: Ind U 29-34 (Educ) BS; UWis summer 37 (Eng); Purdue U summer 39 (Lib Educ); Manchester Col summers 40, 41 (LS, Home Econ); UKy 47-48 BLS; UDenver NDEA Inst summer 66 (LS); UColo 68 (A-V). 07: Eng tchr Shawswick Twp Sch, Bedford Ind 35-39; Libn-Eng tchr Madison Twp Sch, Mishawaka Ind 39-42; Libn US Naval Air Station (Ward Island), Corpus Christi Tex 42-46; Clerk-typist Los Angeles Pub Lib 46-47; Libn Indianapolis Pub Lib 48-50; Post Libn, Ft Knox Ky 50-51; Libn Ill State Water Survey, Urbana Ill 60-64; Libn Harrison High Sch, Colorado Springs Colo 65-; Libn N Jr High Sch, Colo Springs 66-68; Libn Oliver Wendell Holmes Jr High Sch, Colo Springs 68-69. 9: ALA; Colo State Tchrs Assn. 10: YWCA Coun; Beta Phi Mu. 14: Ref, spec libnship, sch libs, pub libs. 15: 2011 Bryant ave, Colorado Springs Colo 80909.

DOUGLASS, ROBERT (RAYMOND). b Florence Ala 30 O 01. 5: UAla 18-21 (Econ) AB; Peabody 34-35 BS in LS; Colo State Col 39 (Educ Admin)MA; Chicago 46-48, 57 (LS) PhD. 6: Fr, Sp. 7: Prin High Sch, Grenola Kan 21-22; Lat tchr pubschs, Atlanta 22-25; Tchr-libn pub schs, Weslaco Tex 26-28; Libn high sch, MercedesTex 28-34; Asst libn NM Mil Inst, Roswell NM 35-39; Lib Sci Instr N Tex State Col39-41; Asst, Assoc Prof, Act Dir Peabody Lib Sch 41-47; Dir, Prof Grad of Lib Sciutex 48-68, Prof 68-. 9: ALA-LED (pres 61-62); SLA; AALS (Exec Bd 47-49); SWLA (chm Com on Lib Educ 59-62); TexLA (Exec Bd 55-56 & 61-63, pres 62-63); Tex Coun on Lib Educ (chm 48-51). 10: AAUP; Phi Kappa Sigma; Phi Kappa Phi. 11: TexLA Distinguished Service Award, 64. 13: Yes. 14: Ed for libnship, research methodology. 15: 1707 Westoverrd, Austin Tx 78703.

DOUTHIT, RUTH L(ONG). b Decatur Ill 20 Jl 09. 4: Henry) Davis Douthit. 5: James Millikin U 27-31 (Eng) AB; UMinn 49-50 BS in LS. 7: Asst ref dept Minneapolis Pub Lib 50-53; Asst ref dept Columbus Pub Lib, Columbus Ohio 53-55; Head ref dept Ohio State Lib 55-68. 9: ALA; ACRL; OhioLA. 12: "Ohio Resources for Genealogists" (60,62). 14: Ref, geneal, hist, rare bks. 15: 2926 E Moreland dr, Columbus Oh 43209.

DOUTHWAITE, MARY LOUISE (SOMERVILLE). b Portland Ore 7 S 30. 4: Geoffrey K Douthwaite. 5: Lewis & Clark Col 47-51 (Eng) BA; UWash 67-69 MLib. 15: 5518 31st NE, Seattle Wa 98105.

DOW, CAROLYN FRANCES. b Bridgton Me 26 Jl 18. 5: Randolph-Macon Womans Col 36-40 (Ger) AB; Boston U 44-45 (Hist) MA; Simmons 56-57 (LS) MS. 7: Tchr Rockport High Sch, Rockport Me 42-44; Tchr Cape Elizabeth High Sch, Cape Elizabeth Me 45-46; Tchr Stearns High Sch, Millinocket Me 46-49; Tchr Waynflete Sch, Portland Me 50-52; Tchr Kennebunk High Sch, Kennebunk Me 52-53; Libn Boulder City High Sch, Boulder City Nev 53-56; Libn Sayville High Sch, Sayville NY 57-. 9: NEA; NY State Tchrs Assn; NYLA; Nassau-Suffolk SchLA. 10: AAUW; Friends of te Adelphi Suffolk Lib. 14: Sch libnship, ref, a-v materials. 15: 60 Colony dr, W Sayville NY 11796.

DOW, GAIL MARIE (STROMSMOE). b Roseau Minn 9 Ag 45. 4: G Murray Dow. 5: Augsburg Col 63-67 (Eng) BA; UMinn 65-67 For Research Scholar; UDenver 67-68 (LS) MA, 69- (Eng). 6: Norwegian, Modern Gr, Lat, Ger. 7: Stud asst Carnegie Pub Lib, Thief river Falls Minn 62-63; Acquis asst Augsburg Col Lib 63-67; Grad asst UDenver Lib 67-68, Ref libn 68-. 8: Eng Dept liaison lib, interlib loan co-ord UDenver. 10: Lambda Iota Tau. 14: Ref, bibliog. 15: 195 Laurel apt 103, Broomfield Co 80020.

DOWCETT, MITZI L (HOLMES). b Montreal 23 F 17. 4: Joseph P Dowcett. 5: U SoCal 47; San Jose State Col summers 64, 65 (LS). 7: Personal affairs consul US Air Force 44-46; Press agent Universal Pictures, NY 38-43; Libn Meadows Sch, Millbrae Cal 60- Assoc libn Taylor Intl Sch, Millbrae Cal. 9: ALA; CalASchL. 13: Yes. 14: Child libn. 15: 1146 Fernwood dr, Millbrae Ca94030.

DOWD, BROTHER PHILIP M FSC. b NYC 17 Ag 15. 5: Catholic U 36 (Liberal arts) AB, 60 MSLS, 63 (Mus) M Mus, 69 (Musicology) Ph D. 6: Fr, Sp, Ger, Lat. 7: Tchr & prin St Joseph's Juniorate, Barrytown NY 36-48; Tchr La Salle Acad, NYC 48-51; Stud Casa La Salle, Rome 51-52; Tchr De La Salle Inst, NYC 53-54; Tchr St Joseph's Novitiate, Barrytown NY 52-53; Libn De La Salle Col, Wash DC 57-69; Libn Manhattan Col, NYC 69-. 8: Music dir: De La Salle Col 57-67; St Paul's Col Wash DC 66-69. 9: CathLA (Col Sect: sec, chm; Wash - Md Unit: past chm); ALA; MusLA. 10: Amer Musicol Soc; Church Mus Assn. 12: Ed "Hymns and Psalms of Lucien Deiss" (World Lib Sacred Mus). 14: Lib admin. 15: Manhattan College, Bronx NY 10471.

DOWD, FRANCES (CONNELLY). b Newburyport Mass 9 D 18. 5: Wellesley 37-41 (Span) AB; Columbia 54-55 (LS) MS. 6: Fr, Sp. 7: Lib asst Larchmont Pub Lib, Larchmont NY 50-54; Asst catlgr OliverWendell Holmes Lib Phillips Acad, Andover Mass 55-57; Asst libn Wheelock Col Lib57-60; Head circ dept URI 60-63; Head Libn Insur Lib Assn of Boston & Registrar ofThe Sch of Insur 63-66; Dir of Tech Info Ctr, Nat Research Corp, Cambridge Mass66-67; Hd bus ind & sci dept, Providence Pub Lib, Providence RI 67-. 8: Indexer, "Insurance Periodicals Index, SLA 965). 9: SLA; NELA;RILA. 10: Mass Assn of Insur Women; LWV; Larchmont Shore Club; Wellesley Col Club;Boston Abbot Club; Rolling Green Swimming Club. 12: URI "Library Handbook(62). 14: Ref. 15: 140 Lovejoy rd, Andover Ma.

DOWDEN, KEITH. b Bristol Eng 26 My 20. 4: Ruth E Kenny. 5: Bowdoin 46-49 (Hist) BA; Columbia 49-50 MS in LS. 6: Ger. 7: Sgt US Army Air Forces 42-45; Ref asst Columbia U Libs 50-51; Ref asst Purdue U Libs 51-53, Head ref serv 53-63, Asst dir for reader serv 63-. 8: Visiting Lecturer, UIll Grad Sch of Lib Sci summer 59, 61; Visiting Lecturer UWash Sch of Libnship summer 63; Visiting Lecxturer UWis Lib Sch summer 65. 9: ALA Subs Bks Com (63). 10: Phi Beta Kappa. 13: Yes. 14: Ref. 15: 1820 Sheridan rd, West Lafayett Ind 47906.

DOWDEY, MARGARET WILCOXEN. b Huntington WVa 2 Ap 29. 4: Dr A Ben C Dowdey. 5: Tex State Col for Women 46-48 (Eng); UTex 49-51 (Eng) BA, summer 53 (LS); LSU 54-55 MLS. 7: Asst libn UTex Me Br(Galveston) 51-54; Stud asst ref LSU 54-55; Libn Kohfeld Elem Sch, Texas City Tex 55-56; Asst libn ref dept LSU summer 56; Libn Kohfeldt Elem Sch, Texas City Tex 56-57; Asst child libn Detroit Pub Lib 57-58; Libn I UTx Southwestern Med Sch(Dallas) 58-67. 9: ALA; MedLA; TexLA. 10: AAUW; Nat Soc of Women Descendents of the Ancient and Hon Artillerycomp of Mass; Woman's Aux Dallas Co Med Soc; PTA. 14: Catlg. 15: 3846 Crest Cove cir, DallasTx 75234.

DOWDY, JULIA (YANCEY). b Charlotte NC 16 F 06. 4: William H Dowdy. 5: UNC (Greensboro) 27 (Music) BS Mus; William & Mary Col summers 37-42 Lib Sci Certif; Fla State U summers 47-48 Lib Sci Certif. 6: Fr. 7: Music tchr Lewisburg (WVa) Sch System 28-30; Music tchr Bryan Col 30-35, Libn 35-43; Tchr-libn Sch system, Marion Co Fla 43-62; Libn Lake Weir High Sch, Marion Co Fla 63-. 14: Ref. 15: PO Box 65, Weirsdale Fla 32695.

DOWELL, ARLENE (GRACE) TAYLOR. b Iola Kan 22 D 41. 4: David Ray Dowell. 5: Okla BaptistU 59-63 (Eng) BA; UIll 65-66 (LS) MS. 6: Sp, Portu. 7: Tchr Tulsa Independent sch Dist #1, Tulsa Okla 63-64, Jr high sch libn 64-65; Tchg asst UIll (Urbana) 66; Desc catlgr LC 66-67; Asst libn Christopher Newport Col 67-. 9: VaLA. 10: Mortar Bd; Beta Phi Mu. 11: Shapiro Award for scholarship & promise UIll Lib Sch. 14: Catlg. 15: 15 Robinson dr, Newport News Va 23601.

DOWELL, GAIL R(ENTON). b Pittsburgh Pa 20 N 42. 4: Michael B Dowell. 5: Miami U (Oxford Ohio) 60-65 (Hist) BA; West Res 65-66 (Pub libs) MSLS. 6: Fr. 7: Asst catlg libn Penn State U 66-68; Catlg libn II Free Lib of Phila 68-. 9: ALA; PennLA. 11: Penn State L trainee 65-66. 14: Catlg, clsf. 15: Bldg 14 apt E, Frankford Arsenal, Philadelphia Pa 19137.

DOWLIN, (CHARLES) EDWIN. b Laird Colo 3 Je 33. 4: May Nichol. 5: UColo 51-55 (Mgt) BS(Bus), 55-56 (Ind Train) MPS; UDenver 62-63 (LS) MA. 07: Personnel spec US Army, Camp Wolters Tex 56-59; Prod control clerk Sundstrand Aviation, Denver 59-61, Statistician-qual control 61-62; Lib intern US VA Hosp Lib, Denver 62-63; City Libn Provo Pub Lib, Provo Utah 63-67; Hd catlg ctr State Lib Ohio, Columbus Ohio 67-68; Hd devel div 68-. 9: ALA (var coms); MPLA; UtahLA (chm Pub Lib Sect 64-65); OhioLA. 10: Rotary Club. 13: Yes. 14: Admin, adult educ. 15: 2540 Woodstock rd, Columbus Oh 43221.

DOWLIN, KENNETH EVERETT. b Wray Col 11 Mr 41. 4: Janice Simmons. 5: UColo 59-63 (Hist) BA; UDenver 63-66 (LS) MA. 6: Fr. 7: Bkmob libn Adams Co Pub Lib, Westminster Colo 61-63; Lib asst II Denver Pub Lib, 63-64; Hd libn Arvada Pub Lib, Arvada Colo 64-68; Admin asst Jefferson Co Pub Lib, Golden Colo 69-. 8: Chm Reg Libns Com Denver Reg Coun of govts. 9: ALA (-LAD/LOMS Com on Ref Statistics); ColoLA (chm Pub Lib Div, chm Memb Com, pres). 10: C of C. 14: Admin utilization of EDP. 15: 7391 W 68th ave, Arvada Co 80002.

DOWLING, ELEANORE CASSIA. b Chicago Ill 3 N 22. 5: UIll 46 BMus, 52 M Mus; UChicago 69 MLS. 6: Fr, Lat, Ital, Ger. 7: Chicago Pub Lib 61-66; WashU (St Louis) 66-68; suny 9stony Brook) 68-. 9: MusLA. 10: Sigma Alpha Iota; Amer Musicological Soc. 14: Mus libnship. 15: 82 Christian ave, Setauket LI NY 11785.

DOWNEN, MADELINE ELIZABETH (MORGAN). b Pontiac Mich 17 Ag 30. 5: Ind U 48, 49, 65 (EDUC). 6: Lat. 7: Supv The McGuire Mem Lib; St Catherine Hosp Med Staff of Paramed depts,East Chicago Ind 47-50, Med Libn 62-. 8: Ed "Hosp Newsletter St Catherine Hosp, Est Chicago Ind 64-67. 9: ALA; MedLA; IllLA. 10: East Chicago Mothers Assn. 14: Ref. 15: StCatherine Hosp, E Chicago In 46312.

DOWNES, VALERIE JEAN. b Chicago Ill 7 Ap 38. 5: UIll 56-60 (Eng tchr train) BA; San Jose State Col 60-65 (Instr Materials) MA. 7: Jr high libn Santa Clara Sch Dist, Santa Clara Cal 60-63; Elem libn Jefferson Elem Sch, Daly City Cal 63-66; Coord instr materials Sch Didt 110, Deerfield Ill 66-. 8: Project Discovery libn Daly City Cal 65-66; NDEA wkshop consul UWis (Superior) 65; Speaker, Spring Conf IllLA 68; Speaker Lake Co (Ill) Tchrs Inst spring 69. 9: ALA; IllLA; IllEA; Cal Assn of Sch Libns; Assn Child Libns. 10: Delta Kappa Gamma. 13: Yes. 14: Admin elem sch IMCS. 15: 6101 N Sheridan rd, Chicago Il 60626.

DOWNES, VELMA (HARRIS). b Jennings La 5 Jl 40. 4: Michael J Downes. 5: McPherson Col 58-62 (Elem Educ) AB; US West La summer 61; UChicago 65-66 (LS). 6: Ger. 7: Lib stud asst McPherson Col Lib 59-62; Vol wkr Brethren Serv Commsn, Germany & Austria 62-64; Research asst Grad Lib Sch UChicago 65-66; Tchr & libn UChicago Lab Schs 67-. 9: ALA. 14: Child lit. 15: 1129 Bonnie Brae, River Forest Il 60305.

DOWNES, VIRGINIA (MYERS). b NYC 21 O 06. 5: Columbia summer 57 (LS). 7: Censor US Censorship Div of Counter-Espionage, NYC 44-47; Records analystMotion Picture Export Assn, NYC 47-50; Libn Nat Coun of YMCAs, NYC 50-57, Hd libn57-. 8: V-pres & treas "Three Crowns Productions, Inc;" NYC. 9: SLA. 10: Amer Fed of Artists; YMCA Assn of Secs. 13: Yes. 14: Admin, fine arts,hist archives. 15: YMCA Hist Lib, 291 Broadway, NYC 10007.

DOWNEY, BARBARA S(HELLY). b Doylestown Penn 9 Ap 33. 4: H Fred Downey. 5: Cedar Crest Col 51-55 (Hist) BA; UIll summers 56-61 (Educ) MEd, summers 62-65 (LS) MS. 7: Eng tchr-libn Bismarck Twp High Sch, Bismarck Ill 55-62; Libn Central Bcks High Sch, Doylestown Penn 63-65; Libn Danville High Sch, Danville Ill 65-66; Libn Unity High Sch, Tolono Ill 66-67, 68-69. 9: NEA; IllEA. 15: 1101 E Washington st,Urbana Il 61801.

DOWNEY, BERNARD FRANCIS. b Boston 17 Ag 21. 4: Gloria Kachdorian. 5: Boston Col 39-43 (Eng Lit) BA; Simmons 46-47 (LS) BS. 6: Fr. 7: Aircraft Armorer US Army Air Corps (gt) 43-45; Ref libn Harvard U Grad Sch Pub Admin 47-49; Jr libn Bus Lib Pub Lib, Newark mnj 49-51; Head bus tech dept Pub Lib, Trenton NJ 51-57; Libn Rutgers U Inst of Mgt & Labor Rel, New Brunswick NJ 57-. 9: ALA (mem 3 com 53-65); SLA; Com U Ind Rel Libns;NJLA (chm recruiting com 53-54); AEAUSA; NJ Adult Educ Assn; Middlesex Co LA. 10: NJ Assn Adult Educ. 12: Comp "Library Service to Labor, with Dorothy Kuhn Oko (63); Ed "Library Service to Labor Newsletter (61-63). 14: Ref, spec lib admin, info serv in indus relations. 15: 3 Goodale Circle, New Brunswick NJ 08901.

DOWNEY, HOWARD R. b Spokane Wash 22 S 38. 4 Ann L. Purvis. 5: Seattle Pacific Col 56-58; UWash 59-60 (Geo) BA, 61-62 MLS; UCal 64-66 (LS). 6: Sp, Fr. 7: Train Sgt State of Wash Nat Guard 56-64; Page Seattle Pub Lib 56-58, Clerical58-61, Pre-prof libn 61-62; Ref libn West Wash State Col 62-64; Doctoral stud & refasst UCal (Berkeley) 64-66; Asst libn Bellingham Pub Lib 66-67, Libn 67-. 9: ALA-ACRL; WashLA (treas 67-); PNLA. 10: Beta Phi Mu; Lions Club. 13: Yes. 14: Ref, admin. 15: Bellingham Pub Lib Box 1197, Bellingham Wa 98225.

DOWNEY, LAWRENCE J. b Indianapolis Ind 1 S 31. 5: Butler U 49-54 (Sp) BA; Ind U 56-58 (LS) MA. 6: Sp. 7: Clerical asst Indianapolis Pub Lib 51-54; Records mgt spec US Army 54-56; Prof asst Indianapolis Pub Lib 56-61, Br libn 61-62, Coordinator tech serv 63-65, Coordinator Personnel Serv 65-68, now Coord tech serv Indianapolis-Marion Co Pub Lib 68-. 9: ALA (chm 3 coms 58-64); IndLA. 10: Beta Phi Mu. 13: Yes. 14: Admin, personnel mgt. 15: Indianapolis Pub Lib 40 E St Clair st, Indianapolis In 46204.

DOWNING, BERNAS (SHARP). b Sharp's Chapel Tenn 12 Ja 33. 4: Jean F Downing. 5: UTenn 51-55 (Agric) BS, 55-57 (Agric) MS. 7: Eli Lilly & Co, Ind: Asst libn Indianapolis 57-58, Assoc libn Greenfield 58-60, Supv agric inst serv Greenfield 60-. 9: Amer Soc of Animal Sci; SLA. 14: Lit searchg, ref, (info retr), catlg. 15: Eli Lilly & Co, Lib Agri Ser, Greenfield Laboratories Box 708, Greenfield In 46140.

DOWNING, MERLE ELLEN (BURBACH). b Milwaukee Wis 28 F 42. 4: Paul Butler Downing. 5: UWis (Milwaukee) 59-63 (Eng) BS; UWis (Madison) 65-66 (LS) MS. 7: Jr libn Milwaukee Pub Lib 63-65; Libn Dept of Res Development, Madison Wis 66; Libn (acquis dept) UWis Lib at Madison 66-67; Libn (ref & YA) Arlington Co Lib, Arlington Va 67-69. 9: ALA. 14: Acquis, ref. 15: 5325 Carmel way, Riverside Ca 92506.

DOWNING, MILDRED (HARLOW). b Wash DC 30 Ap 29. 5: UPenn 48-52 (Psych) BA; Drexel 57-58 (LS) MS. 6: Fr, Ger. 7: Personnel interviewer Fidelity-Phila Trust Co, Phila 52-57; Drexel: Research asst lib sch 58, Instr 68-; Research asst dept of psych UPenn Med Sch 61-64; Libn Arch Research Unit, Phila 66-67. 9: ALA; ASIS. 10: Delta Phi Alpha; National Aid to Visually Handicapped. 14: Catlg, info sci, research in lib methods. 15: 451 Oak lane, Moylan Pa 19065.

DOWNS, ALICE (DAIGRE). b Alexandria La 11 Mr 14. La Col 32-33, 57-58 (Elem ed) BA; LSU 63-64 (LS) MS. 7: N Bayou Rapides Elem Alexandria La: Tchr 59, Libn 60-62; State Dept of Educ Baton Rouge La: Staff libn 63-64, Consul 65-. 8: La Lib State Bd of Commsnrs 64 (pres 67-68); La Lib Devel Com 65; La Sch Lib Stand Com 66-67; La State Lib Fed Rel Com 69. 9: ALA; LaLA; La Sch Supvrs Assn. 10: Alexandria Serv League; DAR; Deep South Garden Club; Kent Plantation House; La Colonial Member. 11: Modisette Lib Award 60; State Del Nat Democ Conv 64. 14: Elem sch libs. 15: Alexandria La 71301.

DOWNS, MARY LEONA (WALLS). b Damascus Va 1 Ap 37. 4: Charles F Downs. 5: Madison Col 54-58 (LS, Hist, Soc Studies) BS in Ed; Colof William and Mary 61. 7: Libn Fairfield Jr High Sch, Richmond Va 58-63; Libn Brookland Jr High Sch, Richmond Va 63-64; Libn Meriwether High Sch, Woodbury Ga 64-67; Warm Springs Elem Schs 67-68; Beverley ManorIntermed Sch 68-. 9: NEA; VaEA; VaLA; SELA. 10: Zeta Tau Alpha. 14: Ref. 15: 2437 Mt Vernon st, Waynesboro Va22980.

DOWNS, ROBERT BINGHAM. b Lenoir NC 25 My 03. 4: Elizabeth Crooks. 5: UNC 22-26 (Hist) AB; Columbia 26-29 (LS) BS, MS. 7: Ref libn NY Pub Lib 27-29; Libn Colby Col 29-31; Asst libn UNC(Chapel Hill) 31-32, Libn 32-38; Dir NYU Libs 38-43; Dir Lib & Lib Sch UIll(Urbana) 43-58; Dean of Lib Admin UIll(Urbana) 58-. 8: Consul SCAP, Japan 48, 50; Adv Nat Lib & Nat U, Mexico 52; Lib Adv Turkish Govt 55, 68; Rep US State Dept, Brazil 61; Adv Govt of Afghanistan 63; Adv UPR 64-65. 9: ALA (First v-pres 51-52, pres 52-53); ACRL (pres 40-41); IllLA (pres 55-56); BSA. 10: Midland Authors; Phi Beta Kappa; Phi Kappa Phi; Beta Phi Mu; Rotary Club; Caxton Club (Chicago); AAUP. 11: Clarence Day Award 63; Joseph W Lippincott Award 64; honorary doctorates from Colby Col, UNC, UToledo, & Ohio State U. 12: "Resources of Southern Libraries (38); "Resources of New York City Libraries (42); "Union Catalogs in the Unitefstates (42); "American Library Resources, 1951-62; "Books that Changed the World (56); "The First Freedom (60); "Molders of the Modern Mind (61); "Famous Books (64); "Bear Went Over the Mountain (64); "How to Do Library Research (66); "Resources of Canadian University and Research Libraries (67); "Bibliography, Present State and Future Trends, with

Frances B Jenkins (67). 13: Yes. 14: Lib research, resources, intellectual freedom, status of libns, influence of bks. 15: 708 W. Pennsylvania ave, Urbana Il 61801.

DOWNUM, EVELYN R (BENSON). b Chicago 21 Ja 16. 4: Garland Downum. 5: Wisconsin State Tchrs Col(Oshkosh) 33-35; UIll 35-37 (Hist) AB; UTex 38-39, summer 41 (Hist) MA; Ariz StateCol 55, 59, 63; UDenver 65 (LS). 6: Fr, Sp. 7: Hist instr Ariz State Col 49,Asst libn 56-59; Libn Univ Elem Sch No Ariz U 59-66, 67-; Libn Flagstaff Pub Schs,Flagstaff Ariz 66-67. 9: ALA; Ariz State LA. 10: AAUW; Pi Lambda Theta; Kappa Delta Pi; Commun Concert Assn;Beta Sigma Phi; LWV; Mental Health Assn; Delta Kappa Gamma; Friends of the Smithand Osborne Collections, Toronto Pub Lib. 13: Yes. 14: Child bks, Southwest bks. 15: 1609 N Aztec st, Flagstaff Az 86001.

DOWTIN, MAUDE CHILES. b Troy SC 27 O 12. 5: Winthrop Col 30-32 (Hist); USCar 32-34 (Hist) AB; Emory38-39 AB in LS. 7: Tchr Bold Spring Sch, Greenwood SC 36-37; Tchr York High Sch, Yrk SC 37-38; Catlgr Statewide Lib Proj, Columba SC 39-41; Libn Post Lib 4 & 5, Ft Jackson SC 41-46; Chief Libn Post Lib System, Ft Jackson SC 46-. 9: SCLA (chm Spec Libs Sect 65, State Dir Nat Lib Week 63). 14: Catlg, admin. 15: 14-B B-4 Myron Manor Apts, Columbia SC 29209.

DOYLE, DOROTHY. b Roxbury Mass 16 Jl 15. 5: Simmons 33-37 (LS) BS. 7: Child libn NY Pub Lib 37-39; Child libn The Jones Lib, Amherst Mass 39-41; Field libn Cuyahoga County Lib, Cleveland 41-44; Navy libn US Navy Dept, Bainbridge Md, Ottumwa Iowa, San Bruno Cal, Guam, Mariana Islands 44-47; Couty Libn Tillamook County Lib, Tillamook Ore 47-50; Army libn US Army Spec Serv, Germany, France 50-55; Library consul Wash State Lib 56-. 9: ALA; PNLA; WashLA. 10: AAUW; LWV; ACLU; Wash Assn for Retarded Child; Simmons Col Alumnae Assn; NWAdult Educ Assn. 12: "An Evaluation Study of the Okanogan Public Library" (64);"Reporton a Survey of the Buckley Public Library" (64); "Survey Report on thekirkland Public Library" (63); "Report on a Survey of Renton's Public LibraryService" (62); "Report on the Survey of the Pasco Public Library" (59); "The Selahpublic Library, an Evaluation of Its Services". 13: Yes. 14: Lib development. 15: Wash State Lib,Olympia Wa 98501.

DOYLE, JAMES McGOVERN. b Johnstown Penn 11 Ap 44. 5: Macomb Co Commun Col 62-64 (Liberal Arts); Wayne State 64-67 (Ed) BS in Ed, 67-68 MSLS. 7: Info Serv Specialist Mich-Ohio Reg Educ Lab, Detroit 67-. 9: ALA (Jr Mem RT); SLA; MichLA; MichASchL; Mich A-V Assn. 11: Co-auth The Morel Information System: An Operational Handbook (69); Co-auth Information Sources Related to Education: A Searcher's Manual (69). 14: Info serv. 15: 8366 Helen ave, Center Line Mi 48015.

DOYLE, LEILA ANN. b Gary Ind. 5: Geneseo State U (LS); Buffalo State U(Eng) BS; Ind U (AV) MS. 7: Libn AV Emerson Elem Sch, Gary Ind; Instr lib sci Ball State Tchrs Col, Purdue summers 12 yrs; Med soc worker ARC ETO 45-46; Libn AV Froebel High Sch, Gary Ind 47-61; Asst dir Sch Lib Development Proj AASL-ALA 61-62; Libn AV Bailly Jr High Sch, Gary Ind 62-64; Consul for sch lib serv, Gary(Ind) Pub Schs 64-. 8: Nat Com DAVI-AASL (chm 65-); A-D Conf Lake Okoboji; var coms. 9: ALA, Ed Subcom (Coun); -AASchL (Bd Dirs); Ind Sch LA; AVID (Bd Dirs); NEA-DAVI (mem 2 coms); A-V Dirs of Ind (charter mem). 10: Delta Kappa Gamma; Assn Supv & Curr Devel; Art Festival Com (Internat Falls). 11: Ford Found Fellowship. 13: Yes. 14: Libs program in schs (elem & sec), lib as an instr materials center. 15: 620 E 10th pl, Gary In 46402.

DOYLE, PATRICIA (LOUISE) (HUCKLEBERRY). b Wewoka Okla 17 Je 39. b Wewoka Okla 17 Je 39. 4: Jack E Doyle. 5: Abilene Christian Col 57-60; Tex Womans U 60-61 (LS) BS. 7: Cushing Mem Lib Tex A&M U: Arch libn, hea 61-62, Jr ref libn 62-63, Jr ref libn interlib loans 63-64, Jr ref libn 64-65, Sr circ asst 65-66, Jrcirc libn 66-. 10: Statistics Wives Club; Tex Womans Alum Assn. 14: Circ, ref. 15: Box 1371,College Station Tx 77041.

DOYLE, RUTH M(AXWELL). b Greensburg Penn 15 Jl 13. 4: Matthew E. Doyle. 5: Allegheny Col 31-32; Chatham Col 32-34 (Eng Com) BA; Penn State U 36 (Journalism); Carnegie 50 MLS. 6: Fr. 7: Asst libn The Greensburg Lib, Greensburg Penn 36, Libn 37-44; Readers asst Carnegie Lib of Pittsburg 50-56, Ref libn 57-59; Circ libn Seton Hill Col 59-. 9: ALA; PennLA. 14: Ref. 15: Box 63 RD 3, Greensburg Penn 15601.

DOYLE, THOMAS. b Detroit 31 Ja 26. 5: Sacred Heart Sem (Detroit) 44-47 (Philos) AB; Mt St Mary's (Norwood Ohio)47-49 (Theol); St John's Prov Sem (Mich) 49-51 (Theol); St Mary's Sem & U(Baltimore)56-57 (Theol) STB; Angelicum U (Rome) 57-58 (Theol) STL; UMich 58-64 MALS; MarquetteU 61-65 (Theol) MA; U of Ottawa (Ottawa Can) 67-69 (Theol). 6: Ital, Lat, Fr. 7: Asst pastor St James Church, Ferndale Mich 51-55; Prof St Josephs Col (Mt View Cal) 55-56; Lib admin & Prof St Johns Prov Sem (Plymouth Mich) 58-. 9: Cath Bibl Assn;Amer Cath Theol Assn; Cath Liturg Conf; CathLA; Cath Homiletics Soc. 14: Admin. 15: PO Box 298,Plymouth Mi 48170.

DOZIER, ETRULIA P (MANCE PRESSLEY). b Anderson SC 23 S 30. 4: Gibb Alva Dozier III. 5: Benedict Col 49-53 (Eng) AB; Atlanta 53-58 MSLS. 6: Fr. 7: Asst libn Atlanta U Lib Sch Lib 58; Libn Whittemore High Sch, Conway SC 54-. 9: NEA. 10: Kinston Lake Young Womans Convention; Chrysanthemum Home and Garden Club. 13: Yes. 14: Ref. 15: 1915 Racepath ave, Conway SC 29526.

DRAGANSKI, DONALD C. b Chicago Ill 22 S 36. 4: ntje Sievers. 5: DePaul 54-58 (Mus) BMus; Rosary Col 65-66 MALS. 6: Ital, Ger. 7: Instrumental mus adv Educ Mus Bur, chicago 56-60; Orchestral musician US Army 7th Army Symphony in Europe 60-62; Elem tchr chicago Pub Schs 62-64, Tchr & libn 65; Asst ref libn UIll (Chicago Circle) 66-67, Asst acquis libn 68-. 9: MusLA; Amer Musicological Soc; Intl Soc ofr Contemporary Mus. 12: Ed (18 mos) of "Call Number". 13: Yes. 14: Mus libnship. 15: 7064 N Ashland blvd, Chicago Il 60626.

DRAGONETTE, DOROTHY BANDEL. b Wash DC 10 Ag 09. 5: UAriz 25-29 (Eng) AB in Ed; USoCal 48-49 MS in LS. 6: Fr. 7: Sub-prof in Catlg dept LC 30-31; Sec to libn UVt 48; Catlgr USoCal 49-51, LibnDental Sch 51-55; Ref libn Biomed Lib UCLA 55-58, Head acquis div 58-60; Head medlibn San Francisco Gen Hosp 61-. 9: MedLA; SLA; NoCal Med Lib Gp (pres 63-64). 13: Yes. 14: Med libs, catlg. 15: Med Lib San Francisco General Hosp, San FranciscoCa 94110.

DRAGONETTI, ALICE M. b Phila Pa 14 My 07. 7: Free Lib, Phila: Asst circ dept, 1st asst dept, Br libn 63-. 9: ALA; PennLA. 10: Houston Commun Ctr; Southwark Commun Coun Exec Bd. 14: Adult pub lib serv. 15: 1443 S Broad st, Phila Pa 19147.

DRAKE, CAROLINE C. b Hoosick Falls NY 22 Mr 15. 5: Oberlin Col 33-37 (Hist) AB; West Res 37-38 BS in LS; UMich summers & 55 AMLS. 6: Fr. 7: Ref asst Troy Pub Lib, Troy NY 38-44; Ser libn Russell Sage Col 44-48; Asstlibn Rensselaer Polytech Inst 48-54; Engnr libn UNotre Dame 55-61; Circ libnWilliams Col 61-62; Asst libn Sterling-Winthrop Research Inst, Rensselaer NY 62-66,Libn 66-. 9: ASIS; SLA; MedLA; Capital Dist Lib Coun. 10: AAAS; Drug Info Assn. 14: Admin, ref. 15: Bovie rd, Hoosick Falls NY 12090.

DRAKE, DOROTHY (MAY). b Hailey Ida 22 My 10. 5: UCal 28-32 (Econ) BA, 33 Certif of Libnship. 7: Staff aide Amer Red Cross, (Eng) 43-44; Pub Lib, Sacramento Cal: Asst ref dept 33-36, Supv bus & mun dept 36-44, 45-46, Asst city libn 46-58, City Libn 58-67; City-Co Libn Sacramento City-Co Lib 67-. 8: Amer Red Cross (Eng), 44-45; Visited German libs under auspices of the Fed Rep of Germ (63). 9: CalLA (2nd v-pres 55). 10: Zonta; Womens Overseas Serv League; Travelers Aid Soc; C of C; Reg Arts Coun; Adv Coun UCal Lib Schs. 14: Admin, serv to bus. 15: 2516 - 52nd st, Sacramento Ca 95817.

DRAKE, DOROTHY MARGARET. b Canton Ill 14 Ap 04. 5: Knox Col 21-25 (His) AB; Claremont Grad Sch 49 (Bibliog) MA. 7: Libn Los Angeles High Schs 25-30; Act libn Knox Col 30-31; Libn Los Angeles High Sch 31-38; Libn Scripps Col 38-. 8: Lectr San Jose State U summer 39; Deptl Libn UN (NY) 49; Adv Coun Lib Sch UCLA,UCal (Berkeley), USoCal 61-64. 9: ALA (coun 53-56); -ACRL (Exec Bd 60-64, ConsulNon West Resources Com 66-); CalLA (past pres & chm So Dist 45, chm Publ Com 59-62,chm Spec Memor Scholarship Com 66-). 10: AAUP; Pacific Coast Browning Foun; MayorsCom on City Library Study; Phi Beta Kappa; Delta Sigma Rho; San Antonio Lib Club;Claremont Sister City-Kumasi-Town Affiliation. 11: Knox Col Alum Achievement Award. 13: Yes. 14: Ref, rare bks, hist of fine bks. 15: 1030 N College ave, Claremont Ca 91711.

DRAKE, ELEANOR ANNE. b Jackson Tenn 29 Ja 31. 5: Miss State Col for Women 50-54 (LS) BS; Fla State U summer 57 Miss State U Ext Ctr 67-68. 7: Libn & speech tchr DeSoto Co High Sch, ArcadiaFla 54-55; Libn Jackson Mun Lib,

Jackson Miss summers 53, 58, 59; Libn US Armyengnr Waterways Expt Station, Research Center, Vicksburg Miss summer 62; Libn Miss Lib Commsn summers 64-68; Libn Peeples Jr High Sch, Jackson Miss 55-. 8: Exec dir, Nat Lib Week, Miss 65. 9: ALA; MissEA;MissLA (chm several coms); MissASchL (sec-treas, v-pres 67-68, pres 68-69). 10: Jackson Little Theatre. 14: Child lib wk. 15: 276 Rosslyn ave, Jackson Ms 39209.

DRAKE, ELIZABETH (MOERMAN). b Batavia Indonesia 14 Ja 37. 4: Marvin David Drake. 5: Goucher 57-60 (Modern Langs) AB; Drexel 62 MLS; John Hopkins 63-64 (RussianLit). 6: Dutch, Fr, Ger, Malayan, Russian. 7: Soc worker Travelers Aid Soc, Baltimore 58-60; Searcher acquis dept Johns Hopkins U 60-61; Asst libn McDonogh Sch, McDonogh Md 63-64; Asst libn Baltimore County Pub Lib, Towson Md 65-66, Br libn Cockeysville Md 66-. 9: ALA-RSD(Md). 10: LWV. 13: Yes. 14: Adult serv, ref. 15: 4648 Rokeby rd, Baltimore Md 21229.

DRAKE, GRADY. b Lake Worth Fla 7 Ja 22. 5: UFla 40-43, 46-47 (Psych) BS; Columbia 47-48 (LS) BS; UEdinburgh 50-53 (Soc Anthropology). 7: EM US Army ETO 43-46; Ref asst UCal (Santa Barbara) 48-50; Sci libn Northwestern U(Evanston) 54-56; Base libn US Air Force, France, Germany 57-59; Interlib loans UFla 59-60; Dir lib serv Jr Col Broward County (Ft Lauderdale Fla) 60-. 9: ALA; SELA; FlaLA (chm Col & Spec Libs Div 66). 10: AAUP; ACLU; Friends of Fort Luaderdale Pub Lib. 14: Admin, pub serv. 15: Broward Jr Col 3501 SW Dauierd, Ft Lauderdale Fl 33314.

DRAKE, HAROLD JOSEPH SJ. b Guelph Ont Can 27 S 15. 5: Ignatius Col Guelph Ont 37-39 (Classics); Regis Col 39-42 (Phil) BA; Catholic U of Amer 66 MS in LS. 6: Fr, Lat. 7: Libn St Paul's Col Winnipeg Can 59-. 9: ALA; CathLA; CanLA; ManitLA. 15: St Paul's College, Univ of Manitoba, Winnipeg 19 Can.

DRAKE, JAMES HARRY. b Louisville Ky 19 Ap 14. 5: East Ky State Col 31-36 (Hist)AB; Peabody 36-37 BS in LS, summers 40-42 (Hist) MA. 7: Circ libn Stetson U 37-39;Circ libn Purdue U 39; Ref libn NY Pub Lib summers 43-53; Ref libn Louisville PubLib, Louisville Ky summers 53-66; Libn Louisville Male High Sch, Louisville Ky 39-;Libn Shawnee High Sch, Louisville Ky summers 67, 68; Libn Ahrems Nigh Sch, Louisvilleky 67-68, 68-69. 14: Ref. 15: 328 N Bonner, Louisville Ky.

DRAKE, MARJORY H(ORTENSE). b Ann Arbor Mich 24 N 1900. 5: UMich 19-24 (Eng) AB, 26-27 (Fr) AM, USoCal 27 (Educ); UMich 29-30 ABLS, 31-37, 38 AMLS. 6: Fr. 7: Eng tchr High Sch, Charlotte Mich 24-26; Head Eng Dept High Sch, St Joseph Mich 28-29; Gen lib UMich; Gen serv asst 30, Asst ref dept main reading room 31-32, Sr asst circ dept 32-36; Libn Tusculum Col Lib 36-43; Asst libn & tchr of lib sci, Asheville Tchrs Col summer 40; UMich; Asst in chg lib sci study hall summer 43, Asst in chg Math-Econ Lib 43-44, Assoc ref libn Gen Lib 44-49, Part-time lecturer in Lib Sci Lib Sci Dept 49-59, Assoc div libn in chg Lib Sci Study Hall 49-54, Assoc div libn in chg LibSci Lib 58-63, Asst head Rare Bks Dept U Lib 63-64, Asst head Dept of Rare Bks & Spec Collections U Lib 64-. 9: ALA-ACRL (sec rare bk sect); MichLA. 10: Ann Arbor Lib Club; AAUW; Mich Audubon Soc; Washtenaw Audubon Soc; Mich Botanical Club; Mich Natural Areas Coun; Clements Lib Assocs; Phi Beta Kappa; Delta Kappa Gamma. 14: Rare bks, mod mss. 15: 332 E Willia, Apt 308, Ann Arbor Mi48108.

DRAKE, MAYO. b Tallahassee Fla 9 Je 24. 5: Fla State U 50-53 (Pub Admin) BS, 54-57 (LS) MS. 7: US Army Engnrs 44-46, Demolition Expert-South Pacific 50-51, Personnel Sgt (Staff/Sgt) Korean Conflict; Acquis asst libn Fla State U 55-56, Asst soc sci ref libn 56-57; Acquis libn UFla Med Lib 57-64, Act head libn 65-67; Libn & Prof of Med Bibliog, LSU Sch of Med (Shreveport) 68-. 9: MedLA; So Reg Med Lib Group (chm 63); Louisiana Library Assoc. 10: Game & Fish Sportsmen Club; Toastmasters Club; Fla Farm Bureau. 12: "Checklist of Periodicals Titles Currently Received by Medical Libraries in the Southern Region (3rd ed). 14: Acquis, admin. 15: LSU Sch of Med Library 510 E Stoner ave, Shreveport La 71101.

DRAKE, VIVIAN L(OUISE). b Hamersville Ohio 28 Je 10. 5: Miami U(Oxford Ohio) 26-30 (Eng, Lat) BS in Ed; Columbia 42 (LS) BS; UMich 51-52 AMLS. 7: Tchr Ohio Pub Schs 30-32; Cashier Rosenook Tearoom, Cincinnati 33-36; Asst period & ser dept Cincinnati Pub Lib 36-40; Asst libn Bard Col 42-43; Acquis libn Vassar Col 43-46; Head acquis dept UCincinnati Lib 46-50; Head order dept USoIll 50-51; Dir of adult wk Lucas Co Lib, Maumee Ohio 52-57; Libn Monessen Pub Lib, Monessen Penn 57-64; Asst head catlg dept Carnegie Lib of Pittsburgh 64-66; Hd Reg Film Ctr 66-. 9: ALA; PennLA (chm Pub Lib Sect 63-64). 14: Admin, a-v, films. 15: 5440 Fifth ave, Apt 11, Pittsburgh Pa 15232.

DRAPER, EDITH ROSE. b Marquette Mich 20 Ap 06. 4: William Hill Draper. 5: No State Tchrs Col 25-26; UWis 26-27; UMich 27-29 (Eng) BA; Drexel 61-63 (LS). 7: Tchr-libn Dade County Pub Schs, Miami Fla 59; Libn Brandwind Area Schs, Coatsville Penn 60; Libn Defiance Pub Schs, Defiance Ohio 61-64; Asst libn Defiance Col 64-. 8: Toledo Girl Scout Coun (pres 47); Farm Bureau Women, Monroe County Mich (pres 46-48); Christian Educ, Diocese of Ohio (sec 53-55). 9: ALA; OhioLA. 10: AAUW. 14: Ref, acquis. 15: 672-1/2 Jefferson ave, Defiance Ohio 43512.

DRAPER, EVELYN (JENSEN). b Watertown Mass 6 Je 08. 4: William Hill Draper. 5: Simmons 27-31 BS in LS. 7: Catlgr Duke U 31-36; Catlgr Harvard Grad Sch of Bus Admin 37-42, 55-56; Asst archivist Rollins Col 57-60, Archivist 60-. 9: SAA 12: Jt ed "Kress Library of Business and Economics, Catalogue Through 1776" (40); Ed "Kress Catalogue Supplement" (55); Ed "Kress Catalogue, 1777-1817" (57). 14: Archives. 15: 2901 Pembrook dr, Orlando Fla 32810.

DRAPER, GRETA H (BALFOUR). b NYC 5 Ag 15. 4: Harry R Draper. 5: Howard U 42 (Hist) BA; Catholic U 46 BS in LS, 62 MS in LS. 6: Fr. 7: Lib clerk Howard U 43, Ref asst 44; Asst dir of bind Catholic U 46, Dir of bindery 53-. 9: ALA; CathLA. 10: Tri Area Civic Assn (Prince Georges Co, Md); Girl Scout Leader & Del. 14: Rare bks. 15: 7271 Kolb st, Wash DC 20027.

DRAPER, WESLEY (BRIGHT). b Iowa 2 Jl 1900. 5: Taylor U 25-29 (Eng, Speech) AB; Columbia U Ext 30-31; Rutgers 57-58 (LS). 7: Asst in lib Med Soc of County of Kings & Acad of Med of Brooklyn 29-46, Libn 47-. 9: MedLA (pres 55-56, var coms 47-62); SLA; Amer Med Writers Assn; NYLA; NY Lib Club; MedLA-NY Reg Group (chm 54-55). 10: AAAS; NY Acad Sci. 11: Taylor University Alumni Merit Award 63; American Medical Writers Association, NY Chap Award 63. 13: Yes. 14: Admin. 15: 6 Wilbur pl, Bellmore NY 11710.

DRAZ, PETER. b Cleveland 21 Ja 24. 4: Beverly Antrim. 5: Denison U 42-43, 46-48 (Hist) BA; Penn Mil Col (ASTP) 43-44 (Basic Engnr) ASTP Certif; UPenn 49-54 (Hist) MA; West Res 55-56 MSLS. 6: Fr, Sp, Ger. 7: Circ dept staff UPenn Lib 53-55; LC: Recruit Program 56-57, Ref libn pub ref sect GR&B 57-58, Head reader serv sect Mss Div 58-59; Asst libn NY Times Washington Bur, Wash DC 59-62; Head pub ref sect GR&B LC 62-65; Chief Bur of Ed Ref Time Inc, NYC 65-. 8: Bd of Trustees, Jack K Burness Mem Award Inc for outstanding news-paper libnship, 64-; Visiting Com to Sch of Lib Sci West Res, 59-61; Foun Lib Com, Bus & Prof Womens Foun 65-. 9: ALA-RSD (chm New Ref Tools Com 64); SLA (Wash DC Chap: chm Soc Sci Group 64-65). 10: Beta Phi Mu; Kappa Sigma; Cosmos Club, Wash DC. 13: Yes. 14: Ref serv, newspaper libnship, British hist, Amer hist. 15: 318 Wagner ave, Mamaroneck NY 10543.

DRAZIC, MILIMIR. b Kikinda Yugoslavia 22 Ap 26. 4: Milana Preradov. 5: UBelgrade (Yugoslavia) 45-50 (Ger Langs & Lits) MA; UCopenhagen 53-54 (Scandinavian Langs & Lits) Diploma; UUppsala (Sweden) 54-5 Scandinavian Langs & Lits) Diploma; UKy 56-58 MS in LS; UChicago 59-61 (LS). 6: Serbo-Croat, Ger, Russian, Fr, Danish, Norwegian, Swedish. 7: Yugoslav Army, Yugoslavia 44-45; Libn Eng Seminar UBelgrade Yugoslavia 48-53; Lang tchr High Sch, Sweden 55-56; Order asst UKy Lib 56-57; Catlgr Northwestern U Lib (Evanston) 57-60; Head libn Glencoe Pub Lib, Glencoe Ill 61-66; Dir lib serv Manchester Commun Col (Conn) 66-. 9: ALA (life mem); IllLA; LACONI (chm 65-66). 13: Yes. 14: Admin. 15: Manchester Community Col Lib, PO Box 1046, Manchester Ct 06040.

DRAZNIOWSKY, ROMAN. b Chortkiv Ukraine 13 Ag 22. 4: Nina Jarmoluk. 5: Graz U(Austria) 47-50 (Geog); Innsbruck U(Austria) 53-57 (Geog, Cartography) PhD; Columbia 58-59 (LS). 6: Ger, Polish, Russian, Ukrainian, Slovak. 7: Map room supv Columbia U 58-62; Map curator Amer Geog Soc, NY 62-. 9: Amer Assn Geographers; SLA. 10: AAAS. 12: "Cataloguing and Filing Rules for Maps and Atlases in the Societys Collection, Amer Geogr Soc, Publ No. 4 (64). 13: Yes. 14: Map catlg, bibliog. 15: 156th st & Broadway, NYC 10032.

DREBERT, ELLEN HANNA (CHRISTENSON). b Vancouver NC Can 21 Ap 13. 4: Lynn Clinton Drebert. 5: San Diego State Col 34 (Educ, Soc Sci) BA; USoCal 41 BS in LS.

6: Swedish. 7: Child libn San Diego Pub Lib E San Diego Br 41-43, Br libn Logan Hts Br 43-48, Hd of brs 49-52, Prin libn ext div 52-. 9: ALA; CalLA. 10: Altrusa Club of the Heartland; Beta Phi Mu; Phi Kappa Phi; Pi Gamma Mu; Kappa Delta Pi. 14: Pub lib serv, lib bldgs, ref. 15: 425 Aldwych rd, El Cajon Ca 92020.

DREFFS, NORRENE MILDRED (OFLAHERTY). b Kalamazoo Mich 1 S 18. 4: Harry Dreffs. 5: Marygrove Col 36-40, 41 (Hist, Pol Sci) AB, Tchng Certif; Wayne State U 40-41 (Hist); UDetroit 47-48 (Hist); Mich State summer 52 (Educ); UMich 52-55, 61-62 AMLS. 6: Lat, Fr. 7: Eng tchr St Martins High Sch, Detroit 40-41; Teller The Detroit Bank, Detroit 42-44; Remedial tchr Fitzgerald Pub Schs, Warren Mich 44; Disbursing Storekeeper (SKD3c) USNR (WR) 11th Naval Dist Hdqtrs, San Diego 44-46; Elem tchr Fitzgerald Pub Schs, Warren Mich 46- 49; Tch-libn Gaylord Community Schs, Gaylord Mich 49-55; High sch head libn consul in lib serv Wayne Community Schs, Wayne Mich 55-63, Head Coordinator of lib serv 63-66; Jr High Sch Libn Livonia Pub Schs, Livonia Mich 66-. 9: NEA; MichLA; MichASchL (Supv Sect, past chm var coms); MichEA; WayneEA (Delegate to MichEA); LivoniaEA; MichAVA; MichASCD. 10: AAUW; Marygrove Lib Guild; Wayne-Westland Lib Bd. 14: Sch lib serv, ctlg. 15: 36723 Greenbush rd, Wayne Mich 48184.

DREHER, CORA LEE. b Shreveport La 8 Mr 41. 5: LSU 59-63 (Chem) BS, 63-65 MS. 6: Fr, Ger. 7: Asst libn Northeast La State Col 65-. 9: ALA; LaLA. 14: Ref. 15: PO Box 4513, Monroe La 71201.

DRENGA, JOAN M (MARIE). b Baltimore Md 13 N 43. 5: Col of Notre Dame of Md 61-65 (Eng & Hist) BA; Rutgers 66-67 MLS. 6: Fr, Lat. 7: Enoch Pratt Free Lib, Baltimore: Children's libn 65-66; YA libn (sr) 67-. 9: ALA; MdLA (YAD; RSD). 10: Delta Epsilon Sigma; LWV. 14: YA serv, admin, ref. 15: 1018 Green Acre rd, Towson Md 21204.

DRENNAN, HENRY (THOMAS). b Portland Ore 24 D 13. 4: Milda P Cull. 5: U Wash 48-50 (Hist) BA, 50-51 BAL; American U 62-65 (Pub Admin) MPA, 64-(Pol Sci). 7: Hood Rive Co Libn, Hood River Ore 50-53; Umatilla Co Libn, Pendleton Ore 53-56; Asst dir PNLA Lib Development Proj 56-58; Coordinator of Slavic Bibliog, UWash 58-59; Ida State Libn, Boise Ida 59-60; Pub lib spec, US Off of Educ 60-63, Coordinator of pub lib serv 63-. 8: Adv, US Off of Educ, Civil Rghts Act of 1964, 65; Consul, Washington Ctr for Metro Studies, APT Manpower Survey. 9: ALA (chm Metro Area Serv Com); Metro Washington Coun of Govts (chm Lib Tech Com). 10: Amer Soc Pub Admin; Pi Sigma Alpha; Phi Beta Kappa. 12: "Statistics of Public Libraries, 1962, with D C Holladay (65);"Statistics of Public Library Systems Serving Populations of 35,000 to 49,999, 1960, with D C Holladay (62); "Library Manpower; Occupational Characteristics of Public and School Librarians," (66); "Public Library Service for the Functionally Illiterate; A Survey of Practice" (67). 13: Yes. 14: Admin. 15: 138 E st SE, Wash DC 20003.

DRENNAN, MILDA PATRICIA (CULL). b Arlington Wash 1 F 08. 4: Henry T Drennan. 5: UWash 26-30 (LS) BS. 7: Catlgr Wash State Lib 31-36; Supr WPA Proj, Spokane Wash 37; Head libn Camas Pub Lib, Camas Wash 38-42; Lib asst Seattle Pub Lib 42-45; Libn Oregon Hist Soc, Portland Ore 46-49; Libn Ida Hist Soc, Boise Ida 58-60; Head tech serv Arlington County Pub Lib, Arlington Va 63-. 9: ALA; VaLA; SELA; DCLA. 10: AAUW. 14: Tech serv, ref. 15: 138 E st SE, Wash DC 20003.

DRENNER, DONALD VON RUYSDAEL. b Mound Valley Kan 17 N 15. 4: Anna Augusta Davenport. 5: Parsons J Col 33-35 (Chem), 37-38 (Eng). 6: Fr. 7: Engnr KGGF, Coffeyville Kan 39-41; Aircraftsman Royal Air Force, Eng 41-43; OB, Feature & Drama, British Broadcasting Corp, London 42-43; Off War Inf London & Psych Warfare Div SHAEF ETO, Chief Engnr AFN-London, Chief Engnr Radio Luxembourg, SHAEF Mission Netherlands, State Dept, West Germany 43-45; Libn Carnegie Pub Lib, Coffeyville Kan 58/59-61-. 8: Nat Lib Week, Kan Com 60-65; Org Com, SEKan Reg Lib System 65; Owner/Operator of The Zauberberg Press. 9: ALA; KanLA (Life mem). 10: Coffeyville Sch Com (chm 58-60); Coffeyville Col Advis Com; Truste, Coffeyville Lib 50-58. 11: Citation, Govt of the Netherlands; Commendation, Ardennes Offensive. 12: "The Vault of Nigh, a novel (52, 65); 7 vols of poetry. 13: Yes. 14: Admin, rare bks. 15: 503 Highland rd, Coffeyville Kan 67337.

DRENOWATZ, MARGARET C. b Paterson NJ 18 S 27. 5: Jersey City Jr Col 48-50 (Eng); Central Col(Pella Iowa) 51-53 (Eng); Douglass Col 53-54 (Eng) AB: Rutgers 54-56 MLS. 6: Ger, Fr. 7: Wk-study stud Linden (NJ) Free Pub Lib 54-56; Head Tobacco Lit Serv NC State U 56-62; Ed Wheat Abstracts Serv UNeb 62-65; Tech Info Specialist med & biol sci Food & Drug Admin, Wash DC 65-69; Catlg libn Bucks Co Comm Col 69-. 9: ALA; SLA. 12: Ed asst FDA "Clinical Experience Abstracts" (65-); Ed "Wheat Abstracts (62-65); Ed "Tobacco Abstracts (56-62). 14: Abstracting & indexing, biol scis, catlg. 15: W Trenton ave apt A213, Morrisville Pa 19067.

DRESANG, ELIZA CAROLYN (TIMBERLAKE). b Atlanta Ga 21 O 41. 4: Dennis Lee Dresang. 5: Emory U Ga 59-63 (Fr) BA; UCLA 65-66 MLS. 6: Fr, Sp. 7: Eng tchr Cross Keys High Sch, Atlanta 63; Sp tchr Lake Mills Jr/Sr High, Lake Mills Wis 63-64; Fr & Sp tchr Van Nuys High Sch, LA 64-65; Hd children's dept Encino-Tarzana Br of LA Pub Lib 66-67; Hd children's dept Ida Williams Br of Atlanta Pub Lib 67-68. 9: ALA. 10: Beta Phi Mu; Phi Beta Kappa. 14: Child wk, ref. 15: 1439 Alleghehny st SW, Atlanta Ga 30310.

DRESCHER, MILTON A(DOLPH). b Milwaukee 28 Je 04. 5: UWis(Milwaukee) 22-23 (Chem); Oberlin Col 25-26 (Chem); UWis(Madison) 26-27, 30-31 (Ger) BA; UIll 31-32 BSLS; UMich 37-38 AMLS. 6: Ger, Fr. 7: Lab asst Phoenix Hosiery Co, Milwaukee 23-25, 27-30; Researcj cje, A O Smith Corp, Milwaukee 30; Lib asst Milwaukee Pub Lib 31, Libn IV 32-41, Libn IV (new schedule) 41-, Chief of dept si & ind dept 41-. 9: ALA. 10: ACS. 14: Sci & tech lib serv. 15: 2811 N 73d st, Milwaukee Wis 53210.

DRESEN, HELEN (GRIFFIN). b Newport Wash 16 Ag 11. 5: West Mont Col 53-56 (Eng) BS in Ed; UWash summers 57, 59, 60, 61, 63 MLS; Ore State U summer 67 NDEA Inst Educ Media Specialist. 6: Ger. 7: Eng tchr libn Cut Bank Pub High Sch, Cut Bank Mont 56-67; Instr in lib sci & ref libn Mont State U 67-. 8: Ranch owner Glacier County Cut Bank, Montana 52-; ESEA Title II adv to rural tchrs in bk sel in 3 counties 67; Exec bd Mont Student Libns Assn 67-. 9: ALA; MontLA. 10: AAUP; AAUW; Delta Kappa Gamma; PEO; Mont Inst of the Arts. 14: Ref, curr lab, instr lib sci. 15: 703 South 16th, Bozeman Mt 59715.

DRESP, DONALD FRANCIS. b Omaha 17 F 36. 5: Creighton U 54-60 (Hist) AB; UOmaha summers 61, 62 (LS); UDenver summers 63-65 (LS) MA. 6: Lat. 7: Tchr-libn Valley High Sch, Valley Neb 60-62; Tchr-libn Berthoud High Sch, Berthoud, Colo 62-64; Libn Loveland High Sch, Loveland Colo 64-65; Educ ref libn Ariz State U 65-67; Coord serv Scottsdale Pub Lib Scottsdale Ariz 69-. 9: ALA (Jr Mems RT); Ariz State LA (Exh Chm 67); SWLA; Salt River Valley LA (v-pres 68-69). 10: Cath Alumni Club. 14: Sch libnship, ref, admin, pub rel. 15: 913 N 42nd st, Omaha Nb 68131.

DRESSER, ALICE (GENEVIEVE). b Madison Wis 31 Ag 11. 5: UWis 29-33 (Fr) BS, 33-34 (LS) MA. 6: Fr, Sp. 7: Child libn Detroit Pub Lib 35-47; Sch libn Madison pub schs, MdisonWis 47-59; Head of child wk Appleton Pub Lib, Appleton Wis 59-62; Br libn Dayton and Montgomery Pub Lib, Dayton 62-. 9: AL; OhioLA. 10: C of C. 15: 64 Elm st, Dayton Ohio 45415.

DREW, FRANCES K. b Jacksonville Fla 4 D 28. 5: Mt St Joseph(Maple Mount Ky) 47-48; Wesleyan Col (Macon Ga) 48-51 (Eng) AB; Wesleyan Conservatory (Macon Ga) 51-52 (Speech); Emory 52-54 (Educ) MEd, 57-59 (LS) MLn. 6: Fr, Russian. 7: Tchr Chatham Jr High Sch, Savannah Ga 55-57; Jr libn Savannah Pub Lib, Savannah Ga 57-58; Asst catlg libn UGa Lib 59-63; Head catlg dept LSU New Orleans 63-65; Catlg libn Ga Tech Lib 66-. 9: ALA; SELA; GaLA (sec Spec Libs Gp 65-67); CathLA; Metro Atlanta LA. 10: AAUP; Poetry Soc of Ga; Atlanta Lib Club. 13: Yes. 14: Catlg. 15: 710 Peachtree st NE, apt 1504, Atlanta Ga 30308.

DREW, HOWARD P. b Hartford Conn 5 Ja 25. 5: Howard U 46-49 (Govt). 7: Sgt USA 333 Field Artillery, ETO 43-45; Lib asst Nat Lib of Med Doc Sect Ref Div 48-59, Lib asst Ref Sect Ref Serv Div 59-65, Libn (Staff) 65-. 9: MedLA. 10: Disabled Amer Veterans; Airborne Assn. 11: Soldier's Medal for Valor. 13: Yes. 14: Med ref. 15: National Lib of Med 8600 Rockville pike, Bethesda Md 20014.

DREW, JEANNETTE E (PETTERS). b Antigo Wis 5 N 17. 4: Donald L Drew. 5: Milton Col 36-39 (Hist-Eng) BA; UWis 65- (LS). 6: Fr, Sp. 7: Ad-writer "Janesville Gazette, Janesville Wis 39-43; Pub rel AAFBU, Scott Field Ill 43-45; Interviewer OPA Rent Off, Beloit Wis 45-47; Asst libn Milton Col Lib 56-65, Act libn 65-67, Assoc libn 67-. 9: ALA; WisLA. 14: Ref, rare bks, bk sel. 15: 120 E Madison ave, Milton Wi 53563.

DREW, LAUREL ELAINE. b Alliance Ohio 13 Ap 41. 5: UNM 59-63 (Eng) BA; UDenver 63-64 (LS) MA. 6: Sp. 7: Ref libn Ida State Lib 64-66; Lib Dir Nampa Pub Lib, Nampa Ida 66-. 8: Member; LSCA Title IV Advisory Council. 9: ALA; PNLA; IdaLA (chm Pub Lib Div, Lib Week Com, Pub Com, PNBC Repres). 10: Valley Dramatic Readers; Lizard Butte Kennel Club. 13: Yes. 14: Ref wk, pub lib admin. 15: Nampa Pub Lib, 101 11th ave S, Nampa Id 83651.

DREWES, ARLENE (TORGERSON). b Denver Colo 12 F 28. 4: Wolfram Drewes. 5: UColo 46-51 (Geog) BA; Syracuse 51-54 (Geog); Catholic U 63-64 (LS); UMd 64-68 MLS. 6: Sp. 7: Sec; Air line hostess Cordova Air Lines, Alaska 54-55; Geog research; Catlgr Nat Geog Soc, Wash DC 68-. 9: ALA. 14: Catlg. 15: 5014 River Hill rd, Washington DC 20016.

DRICKAMER, JEWEL (ANNETTE). b Milwaukee 10 O 17. 5: West Col 34-36, 37-38 (Eng Lit) BA; UMich 36-37; West Res 39-40 BS in LS; Providence Hosp Catholic U 48 (Nursing). 7: Lit div Main Lib Cleveland Pub Lib 38-45; Traffic mgr Radio Station WJW, Cleveland 45-46; Ref room Hartford Pub Lib, Hartford Conn 46-47; Libn Nat Assn of Broadcasters, Wash DC 47-48; Libn Falls Church Pub Lib, Falls Church Va 49-51; Libn Riverdale Neighborhood & Lib Assn, NY 52-54; Supv br libn NY Pub Lib 54-59; Dir Lib Serv Center, Middletown Conn 59-63; Libn Peck Mem Lib, Kensington Conn 63-64; Deputy dir RI Dept of State Lib Serv, Providence 64-. 8: Exec dir Nat Lib Week, RI, 65. 9: ALA (Coun 65-); NYLA (past pres Child & YA Libns Sect); NELA (pre 63-64) RILA. 13: Yes. 14: Statewide planning of lib serv, pub lib serv, ya serv. 15: 1180 Narragansett blvd, Cranston RI 02905.

DRIES, LINDA R. b Juanita ND 29 Ja 38. 4: Carson E Dries. 5: UND 55-59 (Journalism) BA; UWis 59-60 MSLS. 6: Fr. 7: Analyst US Govt, Wash DC 60-62; Readers adv phil dept DC Pub Lib 62-63; Asst ref libn Chester Fritz Lib UND 63-6, Period libn 65-. 9: NDak State LA. 13: Yes. 14: Ref, serials. 15: Chester Fritz Lib UNDak, Grand Forks ND 58201.

DRIES, LUCILLE M. b Kutztwn Penn. 5: Kutztown State Col 51-54 (LS) BS; Queens Col 56-58; Syracuse 64. 7: Libn Lindenhurst Jr High Sch, Lindenhurst NY 54-56; Libn New York Ave Jr High Sch, Smithtown NY 56-58; Elem lib supv Smithtown Central Sch Dist #1, Smithtown NY 58-. 9: ALA; Suffolk Co(NY) LA; NYLA. 14: Lib serv to child. 15: 355 Route 111, Smithtown NY.

DRISCOLL, FRED HENRY. b Taunton Mass 2 F 09. 5: Brown 30 (Econ, Eng) AB; Columbia 31 BS in LS, 41 (Eng) MA. 6: Fr, Sp. 7: City Col(NYC): Lib ast order & catlg div 32-33, Lib asst circ div 33-52, Asst to libn Engnr & Sci Lib 53-, Asst Prof & ref & circ libn Engnr Lib 68-. 9: NY Lib Club; CUNY LA. 15: 316 W 101 st, New York NY 10025.

DRISCOLL, MICHAEL (NORBRT). b Minneapolis 18 Ja 40. 5: Rockhurst Col 58-60; Southwest Mo Sate Col 60-62 (Hist) BS in Ed; UOkla 62-64 MLS. 7: Ref libn Dayton and Montgomery C Pub Lib, Dayton Ohio 64-. 9: ALA; OhioLA. 14: Ref. 15: 617 W Riverview ave, Apt 205, Dayton Ohio 45406.

DRISKELL, HERMIONE (MARIE). b Louisville Ky 16 F 22. 5: La Polytech Inst 42-44 (Pub sch Mus) BA; UMich summers 53, 55, 56, fall 57 (Educ) MA; LSU summers 64, 65, fall 66 9ls0 ms. 7: Vocal mus: Arcadia Elem High Sch, Arcadia La 44-45, Elem High Sch, Gilbert La 45-50, City Sch Syst-Elem, Monroe La 51-66; Libn Wossman High Sch, Monroe la 66-. 8: Tchr ref, guidance in adolescent lit La Polytech Inst summer 69. 9: MENC; ALA; LaTA; LaLA; LaASchL (chm Publicity Com). 10: Beta Phi Mu; Delta Kappa Gamma; Kappa Kappa Iota. 12: Ed nat songbk for Kappa Kappa Iota. 14: Ref & adolescent reading. 15: 804 McGuire, Monroe La 71201.

DRIVER, ANN (CHERRINGTON). b Westerville Ohio 19 Mr 17. 4: Russell Broyles Driver. 5: Ohio State U 34-36 (Educ); American U 37-39 (Pol Sci) BA, 39-40 (Pol Sci); UMich 67-69 AMLS. 6: Fr, Ger. 7: Libn VA Hosp, Saginaw Mich 67-. 10: Pi Gamma Mu; PTA. 14: Child lit. 15: 2515 Willard st, Saginaw Mi 48602.

DRIVER, BEN CARL. b Midland Tex 16 My 16. 5: Tex Tech Col 34-38 (Bus Admin) BA; LSU 40-41 (LS) BS; UMich 43-45 (LS) MS; Columbia 48-50 (Adult Educ) MS. 7: High sch tchr Big Spring Tex 38-40; Asst in archives Tex State Lib 41-42; Physics libn UMich 43-45; Tchr & libn Mico Train Col(Kingston, Jamaica) 45-47; Physics libn Columbia U 47-51; Bio-med libn UChicago 52-58; Bus libn Columbia U 58-. 9: ALA; SLA. 14: Bus. 15: Apt 61 39 Claremont ave, NYC 10027.

DROMEY, BROTHER JEREMIAH CFX. b Boston 30 Ag 16. 5: Catholic U 35-39 (Eng) AB; John Hopkins U 39- 40 (Educ); Catholic U summers 49 (Eng) MA; St JohnsU summers 50-54 BLS. 6: Fr. 7: Tchr Mt St Joseph High Sch, Baltimore 39-47; Tchr St Joseph Prep Sch, Bardstown Ky 47-52; Tchr & libn St Johns Prep Sch, Danvers Mass 52-63; Tchr & libn Xavier High Sch, Middletown Conn 63-. 8: em of the Xaverian Brothers. 9: CathLA (sec Conn Unit); ConnSchLA; NELA; ALA. 14: Ya, high sch libs. 15: Xavier High Sch, Randolph rd, Middletown Conn 06457.

DROSTE, GEORGE HOBURG. b Fairmont Minn 20 Je 20. 5: UWash 3-41, 46-47 (Hist) BA, 47 BLS. 6: Fr, Ger. 7: US Army, Euope 42-46; ct acquis libn Cornell U Lib 47-49; Chief processing div Hoover Inst & Lib on War Revolution & Peace, Stanford Cal 50-51; Staff libn & base libn USAF Lib Serv, Guam, MI & France 51-54; Libn Whitman Co Pub Lib, Colfax Wash 55-57; Lib asst Chicago Pub Lib 57-58; Dir Wheeler Basin Reg Lib, Decatur Ala 58; Dir Pub Libs of Lake Co, Crown Point Ind 58-61; Lib asst Lib of Hawaii, Honolulu 62; Chief Libn Govt of Guam, Agana Guam 62-65; Libn Bellingham Pub Lib, Bellingham Wash 65-67; V-pres Bk Jobbers Hawaii Inc, Honolulu 67-. 14: Lib devel & ext, adult serv. 15: 11704 Durland ave NE, Seattle Wa 98215.

DROUIN, REV PAUL. b Trois-Rivieres Que Can 27 My 15. 5: UMontreal 48 (Mediaeval Studies) MA; Columbia 57 MLS. 6: Fr, Ital. 7: UOttawa: Asst libn & lecturer in hist St Pauls Sem 41-50, Med libn UOttawa Faculty of Med 50-65, Dir of Libs 59-. 9: CanLA; Association canadienne des bibliothecaires de langue francaise; MedLA; SLA; Can Assn Col & Univ Libs; OntLA; OttawaLA. 14: Admin. 15: Univ of Ottawa, 550 Cumberland st, Ottawa Can.

DROWNE, BROTHER LAWRENCE A OSF. b Malone NY 21 Ja 16. 5: St Francis Col (NY) 47 (Fr) AB; St Johns U (NY) 56 MLS. 6: Fr. 7: Tchr St Francis Prep, Brooklyn NY 46-50; Tchr St Anthonys Juniorate, Smithtown LI NY 50-54; Catlgr St Francis Col (NY) 55-57, Head Libn 57-. 9: CathLA CHM Coll Sect, chm Brooklyn-LI Unit). 14: Catlg, admin. 15: 180 Remsen st, Brooklyn NY 11201.

DRUCKER, ROSLYN (GISNET). b NYC 7 My 22. 4:Gary Drucker. 5: Brooklyn Col 39-40; Hunter Col 40-43 (Pre-Soc Wk) BA; Columbia 61-64 MLS, 67-68 (Med Bibliog & Libnship). 6: Fr, Ger. 7: Lib trainee in circ, child, bkmob & ext depts, Yonkers Pub Lib, Yonkers NY 62-64, Jr libn circ dept 64-66, Asst hd circ dept 66-67, 68-69, Act hd New Hudson River Br 69, Hd fine arts dept 69-; Asst dir Lib of Albert Einstein Med Sch, NYC 67-68. 9: NY Lib Club; WestchesterLA. 10: Phi Beta Kappa; Beta Phi Mu. 14: Pub lib serv for child & adults, a-v serv. 15: 37 Ridgeland rd, Yonkers NY 10710.

DRUMMOND, FORREST S(TUART). b Chicago 5 N 10. 4: Helen I Prime. 5: UChicago 28-32 (Law) PhB, 31-34 (Law) JD. 7: Attorney at Law priv practice, Chicago 34-37; Asst Prof of Law & Law LibnUChicago Law Sch 37- 46; Communications Off during WWII, LCDR (now Capt) US Naval Reserve USS Tex 42-45; Asst libn Assn of the Bar of the City of NY 46-50; Libn Los Angeles Co Law Lib, Los Angeles 50-. 8: Adv Bd USoCal Lib Sch 57-67; Consul, Alaska Court System for lib system 61. 9: SLA; ALA; Internat Assn of Law Libs; AALL (pres 52-53, chm Index to LegalPeriods 49-); CalLA; SoCal Assn Law Libs. 10: Assn of the Bar of the City of NY. 13: Yes. 14: Admin. 15: 301 W First st, Los Angeles Ca 90012.

DRUMMOND, HERBERT WILLIAM JR. b Big Lake Wash 2 Ja 24. 5: Mt Vernon Jr Col 41-43 (Hist); UWash 43- 45 (Hist) BA, 46-47 (Educ) Secondary Tchg Certif; UCal 50-52 (Hist) MA, 53-54 BLS. 7: US Army (Sgt), US 45-46; Tchr Lakeside Sch,Seattle 47-50; Sacramento State Col Lib: Circ libn 54-55, Asst order & catlg libn 55-58, Gen ref libn 58-59, Soc sci & bus admin ref libn 59-65, Asst col libn-ref serv 63-67, Asst Col libn Pub Serv 67-. 9: CalLA. 10: Amer Assn State & Loc Hist; Sacramento Bk Collectors Club; ACLU; Sigma Alpha Epsilon. 14: Ref, admin. 15: PO Box 443, Sacramento Cal 95802.

DRUMOND, DONALD (RYAN). b Midlnd Tex 26 Ag 33. 5: UTex 51-56 (Applied Art) BFA, 61-64 MLS. 7: Counter Intelligence Corps US Army, Ft Sam Houston Tex 56-58; Commercial artist, Odessa Tex 58-59; Lib asst San Antonio(Tex) Pub Lib 60-61; Academic asst Grad Sch of Lib Sci UTex 61-63; Lib asst Undergrad Lib UTex 63-64; Libn I Bridgeport (Conn) Pub Lib 64-67; A-v coord San Antonio Col Lib 67-. 8: NEA-DAVI; Nat Assn Lang Lab Dirs; Tex Assn Educ Tech; Tex Jr Col TA. 14: A-v materials. 15: 303 E Kings Highway, San Antonio Tx 78212.

DRURY, BARBARA (HEATH). b Trinidad British W Indies 9 Ja 09. 4: John Jay Holmes Drury. 5: Salem Col 25-27 (Eng); Moravian Col 27-29 (Eng Hist-Soc) AB; Columbia 30-31 BSLS; Rutgers summer 62 (Bk Sel Young Adults), summer 68. 6: Lat, Fr, Ger. 7: Circ asst adult & child Bethlehem Pub Lib 29-30; Head catlgr Lafayette Col Lib 31-32; Foreign period dept asst UPennLib 32-33; Head Libn Moravian Col for Women 33-36; Sr asst circ dept Princeton U Lib 36-39; Adult circ dept, sr asst & readers adv serv Trenton Pub Lib 41; Staff Dir Off of Volunteers New Brunswick CHAPTER Amer Red Cross 60; Ref & yp libn Somerset Co Lib, Somerville NJ 61-63; Libn St Bernards Sch, Gladstone NJ 63-65; Asst libn Hanover Pk Reg High Sch 66-67; Hd ref dept Springfield Pub Lib NJ 68-. 9: NJLA; NJ Indep Schs Assn; NJSchLA. 10: AAUW; LWV; Martinsville Commun Club. 12: Ed "N.J. State Bulletin, AAUW (51-53). 14: Ref, adult & ya serv. 15: Ridge rd, Spring Run, Martinsville NJ 08836.

DRURY, ROBERT MERRILL. b 8 Je 25. 4: Gloria Wilson. 5: UCal(Berkeley) 42-43, 45-49 AB; UIll 56-58 (LS) MS. 7: Asst ref libn Purdue U Libs 58-61;Libn Central Baptist Theol Sem (Kan City Kan) 61-. 9: ATheolLA (chm Period Exch Com 64-). 10: Kansas City Posse of the Westerners. 13: Yes. 14: Acquis, bibliog. 15: 2521 Washington ave, Kansas City Kan 66102.

DRYNAN, THOMAS ROBERT. b Toronto Can 1 Jl 36. 4: Marion Creery. 5: UWest Ont 58-63 (Hist) BA, 67-68 MLS. 6: Fr. 7: Tchr: Forester C I, Windsor Ont Can 63-64; H B Beal S S, London Ont Can 64-65; Bibliog UWest Ont 66-68; Admin asst McMasterU Lib 68-. 8: Interim planning off Ont Univs Bibliog Ctr, Toronto Can 69-. 9: CanLA; ALA. 14: Admin, tech serv, automation. 15: 1854 Main st W apt 104, Hamilton Ont Can.

DRYSDALE, RICHARD M. b Newark NJ 6 Je 31. 5: Lafayette Col 49-53 BA. 6: Sp, Fr. 7: Infantry US Army 53-54; Sales mgr Duradex Inc, Clifton NJ 54-59; V-pres & salesmgr Bro-Dart, Newark NJ 59-65; Pres Prof Lib Serv & L J Cards R R Bowker Co, NYC 66-. 8: Catlg automation adv LC; Com lib activities consul ALA; Lib automation consul to Harvard Grad Sch of Educ; Consul with Lib USA at World's Fair. 9: ALA (chm spec com; v-chm Exhibits Round Table); NYStateLA; CalSLA; CathLA; ASIS. 10: Bd of Trustees, montclair Acad; Cal Forum; NY Athletic Club; Bay Head Yacht Club. 13: Yes. 14: Lib bks serv. 15: 70 Bowker Co 1180 Avenue of Americas, New York NY 10036.

DRZEWIENIECKI, ZOFIA ANNA. b Warsaw Poland 1 Mr 10. 4: Walter M Drzewieniecki. 5: UWarsaw Law Sch 28-34 (Law) LLM; Syracuse 63 MS in LS. 6: Fr, Ger, Ital, Polish. 7: SEC Off of the Polish Consul Gen, Polish Foreign Off Gen Consulate, Berlin Germany 30-36; Head cultural activities Polish YMCA with Polish Forces, Palestine, Egyt, Italy, Gr Brit 41-47; Ed Polish Weekly Magazine ""Gwiazda Polarna, Stevens Point Wis 56-58; Lib traineeSUNY Col (Oswego) 60-62; Asst libn catlg dept SUNY (Buffalo) 63-64, Asst ref libn 65-, Assoc libn & Curator of Polish Room Collection 66-. 9: ALA; Assn of Libns SUNYAB; State Assn of Libns (NY). 10: Beta Phi Mu; AAUP; AAUW; Polish Arts Club, Buffalo NY; Polish Womens Alliance of Amer; Polish-Amer Coun on Cultural Affairs, Buffalo NY. 14: Ref, interlib loan, catlg, Polish lang, lit & culture. 15: 337 McKinley ave, Kenmore NY 14217.

DUANE, (EMILY) CAMILLE (ROSENGREN). b NYC 28 S 26. 4: Frank Duane (Rosengren). 5: Incarnate Word Col 44-48 (Mus, Lit) BA; Our Lady of the Lake Col 50-51 (LS) MA. 6: Fr, Sp. 7: Script reader NYC 54-58; Ref libn & catlgr Metropolitan Mus of Art, NYC 59-61; Asst Rosengren's Bkshop, San Antonio Tex 61-63; Circ & ref libn San Antonio Col 64-67; Registrar libn hd a-v dept Inst of Texan Cultures, San Antonio Tex 68-. 9: ALA; SPA; TexLA. 10: AAUP; San Antonio Symphony Soc; San Antonio Press club; San Antonio Conserv Soc; San Antonio Literacy Council. 14: Ref, catlg. 15: 801 Garraty rd, San Antonio Tx 78209.

DUBBERLY, RONALD ALVAH. b Jacksonville Fla 25 O 42. 4: Bonnie Bazemore. 5: Jacksonville U 60-64 (Hist) BA; Fla State U 64-65 MSLS. 7: Baltimore Co Pub Lib Towson Md: Ref asst 65-66, Br libn 66-67, Admin asst to dir 67-. 9: ALA; MdLA. 10: Ed Com "Maryland Libraries" (Adv Mgr). 14: Ref, Automation, admin. 15: 5933 Schering rd, Baltimore Md 21204.

DUBESTER, HENRY J. b Germany 8 N 17. 4: Dorothy Ennis. 5: City Col of NY 33-39 (Psych) BSS; Columbia 39-40 (Psych) MA. 6: Ger, Fr. 7: Chief Census Lib Proj LC 45-50, Asst Chief Gen Ref & Bibliog Div 50-54, Chief 54-64, Inf System Spec 61-62; Head Sci Info Coord Sect NSF 64, Deputy Head Off of Sci Info Ser, 65-; Adj lecturer UMd Sch of Lib & Info Sci 67-. 8: Adjunct Lecturer Ref & Bibliog Grad Lib Sch UMd 65-. 9: ALA; ASIS. 10: AAAS Internatl Com Soc Sci Documentation. 12: "National Censuses and Vital Statistics in Europe, 1918-1939, an annotated bibliography (48) suppl (48); "State Censuses: AN Annotated Bibliography of Censuses of Population Taken after the Year 1790 by States and Territories ofthe United States (48). "Catalog of United States Census Publications, 1790-1945 (50); "Population Censuses andOTHER Official Demographic Statistics of British Africa; an Annotated Bibliography (50); "Population Censuses and OTHER Official Demographic Statistics of Africa, not including British Africa (51); "Guide to Color Prints, with Milton Brooke (53). 13: Yes. 14: Ref, lib automation. 15: 6531 Elgin lane, Bethesda Md 20034.

DUBESTER, NATHAN. b Ukraine 10 O 12. 4: Pearl Lavin. 5: Oshkosh State Tchrs Col 31-36 (Hist) BEd; UWis 37-38 (LS) Certif. 7: Libn Jr Col, Marshalltown Iowa 38-40; Libn Educ Lib UWis(Madison) 40-41; Libn Central High Sch, Lima Ohio 41-42, 45-47; US Navy (PhM 1/c) US, India, Far East 41-45; Libn Horlick High Sch, Racine Wis 47-48; Libn Geo Washington High Sch, Phila 47-. 9: ALA; PhilaLA. 15: 9713 Fulmer st, Phila Pa 19115.

DuBOIS, HENRY JOSEPH. b Anaheim Cal 17 Ap 43. 4: Judith (Pacheco). 5: Cal State Col at Long Beach 61-65 (Eng) AB; U Cal at Berkeley 65-66 MLS. 6: Sp. 7: VISTA volunteer US Off Econ Opportunity, Erie Penn 66-67; Asst humanities libn Cal State Col at Long Beach 67-. 9: MusLA. 10: AAUP; Cal State Employees Assn. 14: Ref. 15: 1602 N King st apt G1-, Santa Ana Ca 92706.

DuBOIS, PAUL Z. b Ravenna Ohio 5 Ja 36. 4: Carol Johnson. 5: Antioch Col 54-55; Hiram Col 55-59 BA; Kent State 59-60 (LS) MA; West Res 60-62 (Amer Studies) MA, 68 PhD. 6: Fr, Ger. 7: Trade bk manager DuBois Bk Store, Inc., Kent Ohio 57-60; Lib coordinator Mentor Pub Sch System, MENTOR Ohio 63; Libn NY State Hist Assn, Cooperstown NY 64-. 8: Fellow Seminar for Hist Admins, Williamsburg Va summer 63; Consul to loc histl socs & to NY State Coun on Arts; Mem Adv Coun Proj Pride; Trustee Cooperstown Pub Lib. 9: ALA; BSA; SLA (Upstate NY Chap; Program Chm, pres-elect 69-70); NYLA. 10: Amer Studies Assn; Organ Amer Histns; Phi Alpha Theta. 13: Yes. 14: Admin, archives, rare bks. 15: 07: Leatherstocking st, Cooperstown NY 13326.

DUBOIS, PAUL. b Timmins Ont Can 2 Ja 40. 5: UOttawa 59-62 (Fr Lit) BA, 63 BLS; McGillU 67 MLS. 6: Fr. 7: Hd catlgr UOttawa 63-65; Catlgr Sir George WilliamsU 66-68; Asst libn & hd tech serv CEGWP du Vieux Montreal (Col) 68-. 15: 244 est rue Sherbrooke, Montreal 129 Que Can.

DuBOIS, PHYLLIS MARIE. b Poughkeepsie NY 5 Je 33. 5: Goucher 50-54 (Eng) BA; Pratt Inst 64-67 MLS. 7: Import mgr Macmillan Co NYC 54-66; Ref libn Hunter Col 67; Circ libn SUNY at New Paltz 67-. 10: Phi Beta Kappa. 15: 460 Dutchess tpke, Poughkeepsie NY 12603.

DUBOW, SYLVAN MORRIS. b Baltimore 24 D 21. 5: Amer U 45-51 (Communications) AAdmin. 7: Clerical in War Dept records War De, Wash DC 41-60; Archives ast Nat Archives 60-68, Archives tech 68-. 9: Amer Jewish Hist Soc; Archivist Jewish Hist Soc Greater Wash; SAA; Amer Assn State Local Hist; Md Hist Soc; Jewish Hist Soc of Md. 13: Yes. 14: Ref. 15: 5563 Chillum pl NE, Wash DC 20011.

DUBROWSKY, IVAN. b Ukraine 15 D 12. 4: Maria Hudzenko. 5: Tech Engring Sch (Ukraine) 29-32 (Mech) Engineer; Tchrs Inst (Ukraine) 38-41 (Lang) Tchr; LC train course (descr catlg) 65 Tain certif. 6: Ukrainian, Russian, Bulgarian, Byelorussian, Serbian. 7: Engr machino-tractors stas, Ukraine 33-38; Tchr, dir & sch insepctor, Ukraine & DP camps in Germany 38-49; Supv of machine shop: Australia 49-56, USA 56-62; Descr catlgr lc 62-. 10: Ukrainian Assn, Wash DC. 12: Ed "Vil'na Dumka," The Free Thought (Ukranian weekly in Australia 49-55); Freelance corr for Ukrainian Press in Australia. 14: Catlg. 15: 9510 Saybrook ave, Silver Spring Md 20901.

DUCHAC, JOSEPH ALLEN. b Antigo Wis 23 D 32. 5: Pomona Col 51-55 (Eng) BA; NYU 60-63 (Eng) MA; Columbia 61-64 MLS. 6: Fr. 7: Personnel clerk US Army, US 55-57; Headof ofc svcs Presbyterian Bd of Nat Missions, NYC 58-59; Asst ref libn NYU(Wash Sq) 60-63; Asst to libn NYU(U Heights) 63-64; Period libn LIU(Brooklyn) 64-. 10: AAUP. 14: Ref, period. 15: 104 Perry st #4A, New York NY 10014.

DUCHAC, KENNETH FARNHAM. b Wis 8 Ja 23. 4: Gretchen Nommensen. 5: Carroll Col 40-43 (Eng) AB; Chicago 46-47 BLS, 47-48 (Hist). 7: Libn I Detroit Pub Lib 49; Asst libn Decatur Pub Lib, Decatur Ill 50-53; Dir Kingsport Pub Lib, Kingsport Tenn 53-57; Consul Wis Free Lib Commsn, Madison Wis 57-60; Supr pub libs Dir of Lib Ext State Dept of Educ, Baltimore Md 60-68; Dir Suburban Md Lib Project, Baltimore Md 67-68; Dp dir Brooklyn Pub Lib, Brooklyn NY 69-70, Dir 70-. 8: Consul US Dept of State, Jordan 60; Catawba Co Pub Lib (NC) 65; Nioga Lib System, Niagara Falls NY 67; NJ State Lib 68. 9: ALA; MdLA; NYLA. 10: Melvil Dui Chowder & Marching Assn. 12: "Extension Services in the Nioga Library System" (67); "A Library Service Center for Suburban Maryland Public Library Systems" (68). 13: Yes. 14: Admin, processing. 15: 3621 Sylvan dr, Baltimore Md 21207.

DUCHARME, YVES. b Berthier-en-haut Que Can 14 My 35. 5: Institut Mongeau-St Hilaire (Montreal) 50-56 BA; Ecole des Hautes Etudes Commerciales(Montreal) 57-59 (Bus admin); UMontreal 60-61 BBibl. 6: Fr, Eng, Ital, Ger. 7: Catlgr clsfr Central Lib UMontreal61-62, Chief libn period div 63-65, Chief libn catlg div 65-. 66, Chief libn pub doc div 66-67, Chief libn acquis div 67-. 8: Permanent Adv Com of "La Centrale de catalogage de la Federation des colleges classiques (Montreal); Official Can del to the "Collogue de l AUPELF a lintentiondes bibliothecaires, France, Belgium, & Switzerland, 65. 9: CanLA; Association Canadienne des Bibliothecaires de Langue Francaise; QueLA (Coun Univ Sect 65-66); SLA (Montreal Chap; Documentation Div). 12: Ed "Bulletin de l ACBLF (62-); Chief ed "Nouvelles de l ACBLF (65-). 14: Documentation, communication research. 15: Univ of Montreal Lib CP 6128, Montreal Can.

DUCHIN, DOUGLAS. b NYC 8 Je 39. 4: Marilyn Sharnik. 5: UNev (Las Vegas) 66 (Eng) BA; USoCal 67 MSLS. 7: USAF 58-62; Catlgr Harvard law sch lib 67-. 10: Beta Phi Mu. 15: 133 Forest Hills st, Jamaica Plain Ma 02130.

DUCHOW, SANDRA R. b Montreal 26 D 37. 5: McGill 54-58 (Sociol) BA, 61-62 BLS, 66- (LS) MS. 7: Ref, Interlib loan libn, Catlg inf libn McGill U 62-64; Libn Montreal Neurological Inst 64-. 9: MedLA; SLA; QueLA. 14: Medicine, ref. 15: 4850 Cote des Neiges rd 1208, Montreal Que Can.

DUCKETT, KENNETH WAYNE. b Colo Springs Colo 26 Je 24. 4: Alma Rasmussen. 5: UDenver 46-50 (Soc Sci) BA; UWis 50-51 (Hist) MA. 7: (S/Sgt) US Army, US & Europe 43-45; Asst curator of mss Wis Hist Soc, Madison Wis 51-53, Curator of educ serv 53-56; Libn Ore Hist Soc, Portland Ore56-59; Curator of mss Ohio Hist Soc, Columbus Ohio 59-65; U Archivist SoIllU 65-. 9: Manuscript Soc (exec sec 63-); Ohio Acad Hist (sec-treas 60-61). 12: "Moses M Strong, Frontiersman of Fortune (55); "Hist ed "Creative Wisconsin (54); Ed "A Guide to the Care and Adminitration of Manuscripts (60). 13: Yes. 14: Mss collecting. 15: 109 S Maple st, Carbondale Ill 62901.

DUCOTE, JACKLYN (HOFFPAUIR). b Rayne La 15 Mr 42. 4: Glenn Ronald Ducote. 5: LSU 60-64 (Journalism) BA, 64-65 (LS) MS. 6: Russian. 7: Pub rel NDEA Inst for Elem Sch Libnship LSU 65; Research libn & Pub info dir Pub Affairs Research Coun, Baton Rouge La 66-; Free lance art work. 8: Wrote & produced color film on "Use of the Card Catalog in the LSU Library"; LaLA (Bulletin ed); Lib Devel Com of La; Baton Rouge Lib Club (treas). 10: Beta Phi Mu; Phi Kappa Phi; Zeta Tau Alpha. 14: Spec libnship, soc scis. 15: PO Box 3118, Baton Rouge La 70821.

DUDA, HEIDI ELISABETH (MEYER-BAHLBURG). b Hamburg Germany 31 D 28. 4: Gerhart Anton. 5: UHamburg 49-51 (Med); BostonU 61-64 (Sociol, Phil) BA; Simmons 64-66 MS in LS. 6: Ger. 7: Countway Lib, Boston: Biochem research tech 53-61, ref libn 66-67, catlgr 67-68; Medlars trainee Nat Lib of Med, Bethesda Md 68; Medlars search analyst Countway Lib, Boston 68-. 9: SLA. 10: Phi Beta Kappa. 14: Ref, computer applic. 15: 10 Shattuck st, Boston Ma 02115.

DUDECK, M PATRICIA. b S Langhorne Penn 12 Ja 26. 4: Carl Dudeck. 5: Rutgers 64 (Hist) BA, 66 MLS. 7: Lab tech organic chem Johns Manville, Manville NJ 44-47; Sn lab tech microbio Ethicon Inc, Somerville NJ 57-65; Libn med research Esso Research & Engineering Co, Linden NJ 66-. 9: SLA (NJ Chap Dinner-Hosp Chm); ASIS; MedLA. 10: Beta Phi Mu. 14: Toxicology, indust med, indust hygiene. 15: Esso Research & Eng Co, Med Res Div Lib, PO Box 45, Linden NJ 07036.

DUDGEON, EDITH M(AY). b Madison Wis 20 Ja 12. 5: Swarthmore 30-32; Lawrence Col 32-34 (Eng Lit) BA; Emory 34-35 AB in LS. 7: Circ asst DePauw U 35-38; Inf & catlg asst Gary Pub Lib, Gary Ind 38-40; Art & music ast Milwaukee Pub Lib 41-43; Lib asst US Navy Dept, Wash DC 43-46, 49-50; Ref asst US State Dept Wash DC 46-49; Bk sel & catlg Door-Kewaunee Reg Lib, Sturgeon Bay Wis 50-53; Head libn T B Scott Pub Lib, Wi Rapids Wis 53-. 9: ALA; WisLA. 14: Admin, adult serv. 15: 341 15th st N, Wisconsin Rapids Wis 54494.

DUDGEON, LUCILE. b Madison Wis 12 S 04. 5: UWis 25-27 (Econ) BA; London Sch of Econ 30-31 (Labor); UWis 31-32 (Labor) MA; Columbia 36-37 BS in LS. 7: Prompter of reading interest Milwaukee Vocational & Adult Ed Sch 27-30, 32-36, 37-39; Dir of train class Enoch Pratt Free Lib, Baltimore 39-44; US Off of War Inf Lib, Bombay India 44-46; Program off Div of Lib & Inst Dept of State, Wash DC 46-50; Dir of Liv US Inf Agency, Cairo Egypt 50-52; Program off Inf Center Serv USIA, Wash DC 53-64; Field libn Wis Lib Commsn, Madison Wis 64-65, Pub lib consul div for lib serv 65-. 9: ALA; Middle East Inst; SLA (Internat Rel chm 55-61); WisLA; DCLA (pres 58-59). 10: AAUW; LWV. 12: Special issues of "Wisconsin Library Bulletin". 13: Yes. 14: Adult serv. 15: 1347 North Wingra dr, Madison Wis 53715.

DUDLEY, CRAYTON THOMAS. b Atlanta 23 F 28. 4: Allegra Lewis. 5: Clark Col 48-50 (Religious Educ) AB; Gammon Theol Sem 59-61 (Theol) BD; American U summer 63 (Archives) Diploma; UPittsburgh 64-65 MLS. 6: Fr, Gk. 7: US Army 46-47, 50-53; Assembler installer Lockheed Aircraft, Atlanta 53-56; Mail clerk US Post Off, Atlanta 56-59; Asst libn Interdenominational Theol Center, Atlanta 61-64; Subj spec religion & philos humanities dept Enoch Pratt Free Lib, Baltimore 65-68; Coppin State Col Ref Lib (Baltimore) 68-. 9: ALA; ATheolLA. 10: Phi Beta Sigma. 13: Yes. 14: Relig, philos. 15: 4902 Belle ave, Baltimore Md 21207.

DUDLEY, DURAND STOWELL. b Cleveland 28 F 26. 4: Dorothy L Wolworth. 5: Oberlin 44-48 (Econ) AB; Wes Res 49-50 MS in LS; Ohio U (Athens) 52-53 (Eng Lit). 7: Ref staff libn Canton Pub Lib, Canton Ohio 50-53; Ref libn Marietta Col Lib 54-55; Staff libn Akron Pub Lib, Akron Ohio 55-58; Head libn Marathon Oil Co, Findlay Ohio 60-. 9: SLA (sec, Prog Chm; chm Petrol Div; Cleveland Chap; treas, Memb chm, Recr chm). 14: Ref, lib admin. 15: Marathon Oil Co Lib Rm 312-M 539 South Main st, Findlay Ohio 45840.

DUDLEY, FLORA HELEN (EHRSAM). b NYC 13 Ap 19. 4: John Chapman Dudley. 5: Barnard 36-40 (Ger) BA; Columbia 62-64 MSLS. 6: Ger, Fr, Sp. 7: Lib clerk Mamaroneck Free Lib, Mamaroneck NY 61-64, Adult serv libn 64-66, Asst dir 66-. 9: ALA; LPRC; NYLibClub; WestchesterLA; NYLA. 10: Columbia Sch of Lib Serv Alumni Assn; LWV; UN Assn; Bus & Prof Women's Club. 14: Lib pub rel, readers adv serv, ref. 15: 437 Melbourne ave, Mamaroneck NY 10543.

DUDLEY, LAURA (ELDRIDGE). b Levant Me 21 S 16. 4: Kenneth Dudley. 5: Simmons 35-39 (LS) BS; Columbia summer 48. 7: Gen asst Providence Pub Lib 40; Asst catlgr UMe 41-43; Catlgr Concord Pub Lib, Concord NH 43-46; Ref libn Portland Pub Lib, Portland Me 46-49; Asst acquis Wellesley Col 54; Order libn Hofstra U Lib 56-. 9: ALA; NY State LA (Ad hoc Com on Acquis); NassauCoLA (Col & Univ Div; corr sec 69). 14: Acquis. 15: 1353 Harvey ct, Baldwin NY 11510.

DUDLEY, LAURIE. b Abilene Tex 19 My 28. 5: Baylor U 45-49 (Span, Eng) BA; N Tex State U 63-65 MLS. 6: Sp. 7: Tchr Maverick Co Ind Sch Dist, Eagle Pass Tex 49-50; Tchr Big Spring Ind Sch Dist, Big Spring Tex 50-51; Tchr Dallas Ind Sch Dist 52-58, Sch libn 58; Child libn Dallas Pub Lib West Br 59-61, Child libn central child dept 61-65, Coord child serv 65-. 9: ALA; TexLA (chm Child Round Table 65-66). 10: Dallas Civic Opera Guild; Tex Folklore Soc. 13: Yes. 14: Child serv. 15: 6827 Case Loma, Dallas Tx 75214.

DUDLEY, MABEL. b Richmond Ky 28 Ja 09. 5: East Col (Ky) 26-30 (Eng) AB; Jordan Conservatory summers 31-36 (Piano) BMusic; Columbia summers 39, 42 (Educ) MA; UKy summers 45-48 BSLS. 7: Tchr city sch, Richmond Ky 30-44; Tchr city sch, Covington Ky 44-48; Libn Chandler High Sch, Chandler Ariz 48-. 8: Supr of Chandler sch libs, Chandler Ariz 48-54. 9: ALA; ArizLA (chm Sch Lib Div); Salt River Valley LA (v-pres). 10: Bs & Prof Womens Club; Phoenix Musicians Club; Junior Womens Club. 15: 628 Sunland dr E, Chandler Az 85224.

DUDLEY, NORMAN HOUSTON. b Los Angeles 24 Je 23. 4: Miriam Sue Fine. 5: Harvard 45-48 (Eng) AB; UCLA 63-64 MLS. 7: Vice-pres Cal Mercury Record Distributors, Los

Aneles 55-63; Admin interne UCLA Lib 64, Ref libn Col Lib UCLA 64-65, Head acquis dept UCLA Lib 65-. 9: ALA; CalLA. 14: Acquis, ref. 15: 3127 Barbara ct, Los Angeles Ca 90028.

DUDZIK, NAOMI C. b NYC. 5: Long Beach State Col 57-60 (Hist, Soc Sci) BA, 61-63 (Hist) MA; UCLA 65-66 MLS; Med Lib Intern NIH 66-67 Med Libnship Certif. 6: Sp. 7: Personnel-payroll rec West Electric, LA 49-53; IBM tab operator N Amer Aviation, LA 53-55; Research asst UCLA Neuropsychiatric Inst 65-66; Biomed lib intern UCLA Biomed Lib 66-67; Ref & acquis libn USoCal Sch of Med 67-68; Libn Child Hosp of LA 68-. 8: Inter- NIH Grant as Postgrad Med Lib Intern at UCLA 66-67. 9: MedLA; Med Lib Group of So Cal. 10: Pi Gamma Mu. 11: NIH Grant 66. 13: Yes. 14: Ref, hist of med. 15: 552 Midvale ave, Los Angeles Ca 90024.

DuFAULT, SUZANNE. b Trenton NJ 7 My 43. 5: Ursinus Col 61-65 (Hist) BA; Rutgers 65-68 MLS. 7: Catlgr Rutgers 65-68; Hd catlgr Mem U of Newfoundland 68-. 9: CanLA. 14: Catlg. 15: 63 Le Marchant rd, St John's Newfoundland Can.

DUFF, KENNETH (MAURICE) M(cCLELLAND). b Ludhiana Punjab India 18 Ja 32. 4: Mary Lou (Griesinger). 5: Col of Wooster 49-53 (Hist) BA; Rutgers 57-60 MLS. 7: Sp/3C US Army Corps of Engnrs 53-55; UPenn Lib: Clerical asst 56-57, Stack supv 57-58, 1st asst ser dept 59-60, Head Undergrad Lib 60-65; Chief Libn UNB(ST John NB) 65-. 9: CanLA; Atlantic Assn of Univs (Libns Com); APLA. 14: Admin. 15: 40 Deveber terr, St John NB Can.

DUFF, MARGARET (KAPP). b Walton Ind. 4: Cloyd E Duff. 5: Butler U (Eng, Econ) AB; West Res 63-66 MLS. 7: Child libn Cuyahoga Co Lib, Solon Ohio 66-. 14: Wk with child. 15: 2911 Weymouth rd, Shaker Hts Oh 44120.

DUFFIELD, PAULINE. b Sutton WVa 30 Ja 10. 5: Chicago Normal Sch of Phys Educ 29 Diploma; Peabody 36 (Phys Educ) BS, 40 BSLS. 7: Libn Richwood High Sch, Ricwood WVa 36-41; Libn Parker Dist High Sch, Greenville SC 41-43; Asst libn Med Sch Vanderbilt U 44-45; Libn Med & Chirosurgical Faculty of Md, Baltimore 45-52; Libn Tex Med Assn, Austin Tex 52-. 8: Sec-Treas, Tex Coun of Health Science Libs 68; Chm Nomin Comm, MedLA 68-69. 9: MedLA (treas 54-58, chm Recruitmt Com 62-64, chm Awards Com 64-65); SLA; MedLA (chm Nomin Com 68-69); Tex Coun of Health Sci Libs (sec-treas 64-). 10: Zonta Club. 11: Hon Mem Tex Med Assts Assn. 13: Yes. 15: 1219 Castle Hill, Austin Tex 78703.

DUFFY, (THOMASINE) ANNETTE (COOK). b Ponca City Okla 31 Mr 38. 4: Donald D Duffy Jr. 5: Central State Col 55-59 (Elem ed) BS Ed; UOkla 66-67 MLS. 7: Tchr Ponca City Pub Schs, Ponca City Okla 59; Tchr Pub Sch Syst, Okla City 59; Tchr Meadows Union Sch, El Centro Cal 61-62; Libn (staff) Okla State U 67-69. 9: ALA; OklaLA. 14: Catlg. 15: 136 N Duncan, Stillwater Ok 74074.

DUFFY, ESTHER (RODGERS). b Pittsburgh Penn 14 Ag 11. 4: Roger F Duffy. 5: Seton hill 28-32 (Mus) BMus, BS; UPittsburgh 34-35 Elem Educ Certif; Simmons 41-42 LS. 7: Instr in mus Col Misericordia 32-33, 35-36; Tchr Vandergrift Sch, Vandergrift Penn 33-35; Mus libn CornellU 37-41; Asst mus libn ColumbiaU 42-43; OSS, OWI, Dept of State, NY & Wash DC 43-46; Asst to the Pres Juillard Sch of Mus 46-49; Fine arts libn greenwich Lib, Greenwich Conn 61-. 9: MusLA; ConnLA. 10: Kappa Gamma Pi. 14: Phonograph rec catlg, mus catlg. 15: 2 Peters rd, Riverside Ct 06878.

DUFFY, MARY FRANCES (HICKEY). b Jersey City NJ. 4: Paul J. Duffy. 5: Seton Hall U 50 BS; Columbia 53 MSLS. 7: Lib asst Jersey City Pub Lib, Jersey City NJ 36-43, Sch libn 43-52, Prin libn bk sel 52-53, Supr libn br & ext 53-55, Asst dir 55-. 9: ALA; NJLA; Hudson County LA. 10: Jersey City Womens Club; Girl Scout Coun; LWV. 15: Jersey City Pub Lib 472 Jersey ave, Jersey City NJ 07302.

DUFFY, ROSE ELIZABETH. b Chicago Ill. 5: Rosary Col 37-42 (LS). 9: ALA; IllLA; Chicago Lib Club. 10: Chicago Art Inst; Chicago Museum of Contemp Art. 14: Ref, art bks. 15: 342 Gale ave, River Forest Il.

DUGAN, JOHN FREDERICK. b Alton Ill 2 My 38. 5: Pan American Col 56-59 (Eng, Soc Sci) BA; UTex 59-62 MLS. 6: Fr. 7: Page Pan American Col Lib 57-59; Page Lib Sch Lib UTex 59-60; Clerk-typist UTex Lib 60-62, Libn I catlg dept 62-. 14: Catlg. 15: 910 W 22nd st, Apt A, Austin Tex 78705.

DUGGAN, REV DONALD J SJ. b San Francisco 12 My 24. 5: USanta Clara 44-46; Gonzaga U 46-48 (Philos) BA; Alma Col 52-56 (Theol) STL; UCal (Berkeley) 57-58 MLS. 7: Libn Novitiate of Los Gatos, Los Gatos Cal 58-62; Asst libn USanta Clara 62-. 15: Univ Santa Clar, Santa Clara Cal 95053.

DUGGAN, JESSE EDWARD. b Ponca City Okla 16 Ap 36. 5: San Angelo Col 54-56 (Eng); UTex 56-58 (Eng) BA, 58-60 LS; UTex (El Paso) 69 (Eng) MA. 6: Sp. 7: Lib asst UTex Lib 56-59, Libn I order 59; Clerk US Army 2d Infantry Div, Ft Benning Ga 59-62; Asst acquis libn Arlington State Col 62-63, Acquis libn 63-64; Chief catlgr UTex (El Paso) Lib 64-65, Chief tech serv 65-69, Assoc Univ libn 69-. 9: TexLA; Border Regl LA (pres 68-69). 14: Tech serv. 15: 5216 Carousel, #30, El Paso Tex 79912.

DUGGAN, JULIA (MUSE). b Covington Ga 15 O 06. 4: Roy L. Duggan. 5: Converse Col (SC) 27-28; Ga State Col for Women 29 (Eng) BA; Emory 43 BA in 6: Fr, Lat. 7: Readers adv Tyrrell Pub Lib, Beaumont Tex 43-45; 1st asst Central Br, Kansas City Mo 45-46; 1st asst Fulton County Dept Atlanta Pub Lib 46-51, Head 51-59; Asst dir in chg of Ext Serv Flint River Reg Lib, Griffin Ga 60-. 9: ALA; SELA; GaLA. 14: Ext serv, ref. 15: Rt 2 Box 418, Jackson Ga 30233.

DUGGAN, MARYANN. b Lubbock Tex 25 O 25. 5: N Tex State U 42-45 (Biol-Chem) BA; So Methodist U 45-65; UTex(Ext) 55-57 (LS); Columbia summer 55 (LS); UDenver 59-60 (LS) MA. 6: Fr. 7: Lab asst N Tex State U 43-45; Analytical Chem Socony Mobil Oil Co, Dallas Tex 45-47, Research Chem 47-55, Supr Tech Lib 55-; Visiting Prof UTex Grad Sch of Lib Sci 65-66; Dir So Meth U ind info serv & asst prof 66-. 8: Adv Com Petrol Abstract UTulsa; Wking Com NTex Interlib Assn Proposal; Chm Goals for Dallas Libs 68; Consul; Ark Lib Commsn, Mobil Oil Comp, Tex A&M U; John Cotton Dana lectr, SLA 65; Spec Proj Dir LSCA Title III 68-69. 9: SLA (Consul Nat Com on Educ; Tex Chap; Proj Chm, Employment Chm, chm Educ Com); ALA-RSD (Coop Ref Serv Com); ASIS; ACS; AGI; TexLA (mem Lib Devel Com, chm Ref RT); Dallas Co LA (chm Educ Com). 10: LWV; AAAS. 11: John Cotton Dana Lecturer, SLA 65. 12: "Field Kit for Chemical Analaysis of Oil Field Brines (48). 13: Yes. 14: Sci ref, documentation, reg lib development & cooperation, info scis; lib, automation, lib netwks, lib educ. 15: 1416 Wentwood, Irving Tx 75060.

DUHART, EVELINE. b Tallahassee Fla 5 Jl 39. 5: Fla A&M U 60 (LS) BS. 6: Sp. 7: Libn Suwannee Co Douglass High Sch, Live Oak Fla 60-. 9: NEA: Fla State Tchrs Assn; FlaSchLA; FlaLA; FlaA-V Assn; FlaEA (Fac Repr). 10: Modernistic Club. 14: Ref, sch libn. 15: PO Box 92, Live Oak Fla 32060.

DUKE, FLORENCE (BYRD). b Norfolk Va. 4: Curtis C Duke. 5: Tufts U 24-28 (Hist) BS; Hampton Inst 30-31 BLS; Columbia 51 (LS) MS. 6: Fr, Sp. 7: Libn Agric & Tech Col (Greensboro NC) 31-38; Libn William Penn High Sch, High Point NC 38-43; Instr Lib Sci Dept VA State Col 43-52, Head Lib Sci Dept 52-. 8: Mem High Sch Materials Eval Com Va State Dept of Ed 54-. 9: ALA; VaLA; SELA. 10: AAUP; Assn for Student Tchg. 14: Sch libnship, catlg, child lit. 15: Route #1, Oakland ave, Colonial Heights Va.

DUKE, JULIA L. b Richmond Va 27 Ap 11. 5: Madison Col Harrisburg Va 28-32 (Ed) BS; Peabody Col Nashville Tenn 35-36 (Ed) MA; LSU 48-49 BS in LS. 6: Fr. 7: Bio lab asst Madsino Col, Harrisonburg Va 32-35; Asst prof health & PE NM State Tchrs Col 36-38; Prof health & PE La Polytech Inst 38-49; Circ libn NWest State Col 50-52; Ser libn U SWest La 52-. 9: ALA; LaLA; LaTA. 10: Phi Kappa Phi; Beta Phi Mu. 14: Ser. 15: 1011 Auburn ave, Lafayette La 70501.

DUKE, LUCY L. b Eatonton Ga 21 N 21. 5: Womans Col of Ga 41 AB; Emory 45 (LS) AB, 66 M Libnship. 7: Asst in chg of serv to pub A W Calhoun Med Lib Emory U 45-48; Catlgr & asst ref libn GA State Dept of Educ Lib Ext Serv, Atlanta 49-57; Libn Sch of Bus Admin Emory U 57-66, Libn Emory U Sch of Dentistry 66-. 9: SLA (S Atlantic Chap; past sec & treas); GaLA; Metro-Atlanta Lib Club (past v-pres); MedLA. 10: Beta Phi Mu. 14: Admin, ref. 15: Apt 3 18 Collier rd NW, Atlanta Ga 30309.

DUKE, TUTTAN (LARSON). b Hot Springs Ark 10 Mr 36. 4: James W Duke. 5: Henderson State Tchrs Col 54-56 (Bus Educ) BSE; Peabody 56-57 (LS) MA in LS. 6: Swedish. 7: Circ libn Peabody Col 57-59; Lib Dependents Schs, Ft Benning Ga 59-60; Ref asst UArk 60-62; Asst libn Chadron State Tchrs Col 62-63; Asst in ya dept Chicago Pub Lib 63-5, 2nd asst humanities dept 65-. 8: Chicago Pub Lib rep to Ill Governors Conf on Child & Youth, 64. 9: ALA; ArkLA. 10: Beta Phi

Mu; Pi Gamma Mu; AAUW. 14: Wk with yp, readers adv. 15: 5632 Primrose ave, Indianapolis In 46220.

DUKER, ABRAHAM G(ORDON). b Rypin Poland 27 S 07. 4: Lillian Miriam Sandrow. 5: Col of the City of NY 26-30 BA; Columbia 30-34, 56 PhD. 6: Hebrew, Yiddish, Polish, Ger, Russian, Fr. 7: Research libn Grad Sch for Jewish Soc Wk (NYC) 34-38; Instr of Lecturer in Hist, Sem Sch of Jewish Studies, Hebrew Union Col Sch of Educ, New Sch for Soc Research, Columbia U 41-43, 46-55; Assoc Train Bur for Jewish Communal Serv, NYC 47-49; (Sgt) pol analyst, ff of Strategic Serv US Army 43-45; Visiting Prof Wayne State U 55; Pres Col of Jewish Studies(Chicago) 56-62; Dir of Libs & Prof of Hist & Soc Institutions Yeshiva U 62-; Vis Prof in Hist Columbia U 66-67. 8: Consul: Amer Jewish Congress 52-55; Amer Jewish Tercentenary Com 53-54; Theodor Herzl Inst 55-56; Panel of Experts, Mem Foun for Jewish Culture. 9: ALA; SAA; AHA; YIVO Inst for Jewish Research (Bd 48-); Conf on Jewish Soc Studie; Amer Jewish Hist Soc; Jewish Bk Coun of Amer; Nat Conf of Jewish Communal Serv; Jewish Acad Arts & Scis; Histadrut Cultural Exch Inst. 10: Jewish Hist Soc of Eng; Polish Inst of Arts & Scis in Amer; Nat Coun for Jewish Educ; Amer Acad for Jewish Research; Soc of Jewish Bibliophiles; Assn for Jewis Demography and Stat; Brit Rishonim. 11: Fellowships & Grants; Amer Coun of Learned Socs; AM Philos Soc; Wurzweiler Foun 67. 12: Ed "Jewish Social Studies; Contrib ed "Jewish Educ; Ed & Contrib "Contemporary Jewish Record (now Commentary), 38-43); Ed "The Day (45-59); Auth "The Situation of the Jews in Poland (36): "Jewish Survival in the World Today (39-41); "Jews in the Post-War World, with Gottschalk (45); "The Polish "Great Emigration and the Jews, Univer Microfilms (56); "Jewish Community Relations" (52). 13: Yes. 14: Bibliog. 15: 90 Laurel Hill ter, NYC 10033.

DUKES, WILLIAM HENRY. b Charleston SC 13 Ap 22. 4: Elizabeth McCarthy. 5: The Citadel 46-49 (Eng) BA; Emory 52-54 (LS) MS. 7: Catlgr US Army War Col (Carlisle Penn) 54-58; Catlgr Chance Vought Aircraft Inc, Dallas 58-59; Catlgr Chrysler Corp Missile Div, Detroit 59-60; Libn Giffels & Rossetti Inc, Detroit 60-. 9: SLA. 14: Catlg, engnrg libs. 15: Giffels & Rossetti Inc, Marquette Bldg, Detroit Mi 48226.

DULANEY, MILDRED. b Mart Tex 18 Ag 09. 5: Tex State Col for Women 27-29; UTex 29-30, summer 30; Tex State Col for Women 30-31 (LS) BS, 58-59 (LS) MA. 7: Asst Waco Pub Lib, Waco Tex 32-41; Libn Camp Wolters Lib, Mineral Wells Tex 41-44; Libn Hockley Co Lib, Levelland Tex 45-46; Circ head Tex Tech Col 46-47; Head circ & ref Waco Pub Lib, Waco Tex 47-52, Libn 52-58; Gen dept Ft Worth Pub Lib, Ft Worth Tex 59-60, Admin asst for pub serv 60-. 9: ALA; SWLA; TexLA (chm Pub Lib Div 53-54). 10: Bus & Prof Womens Club; Central Tex Geneal Soc; E Ala Geneal Soc; Fort Worth Geneal Soc; Tex Geneal Soc; Ga Geneal Soc. 12: Ed "Stirpes, Tex State Geneal Soc quarterly (61); Cont "Fort Worth Genelogical Society Bulletin. 13: Yes. 14: Admin. 15: 1404 S Lake, Ft Worth Tex 76104.

DULKA, JOHN. b Milwaukee 19 Je 11. 4: Sonia Milavsky. 5: Milwaukee State Tchrs Col 34 (Eng) BE; Wis Lib Sch 36 Certif; Columbia 47 (LS) MS; Chicago 48-53 (LS). 6: Polish. 7: Milwaukee Pub Lib: Br asst 36-37, Head gen ref asst 37-41, Dir war info center 41-42; US Army AAA (1st Lt) 42-46, Sr ref asst Milwaukee Pub Lib 46, Asst ref libn 47; Ref libn UWis(Milwaukee) 47-68; Asst dir Lib for Pub Serv 68-. 9: ALA-ACRL (Ref Div); WisLA. 10: NAACP; UN Assn; AAUP; Amer Fed of Tchrs; ACLU. 14: Ref. 15: 1100 E Bywater lane, Milwaukee Wi 53217.

DULL, MAXINE ALICE. b Kremlin Mont 3 Jl 14. 5: UCal 43 AB, 44 (LS) Certif. 7: Libn Anaheim Sch Dist, Anaheim Cal 36-4; Order dept libn Ore State Col 44-46; Order dept head Lansing Lib Serv, Oakland Cal 46 Catlgr Mann Lib Cornell U 47-63, Head catlg dept 63-. 9: ALA. 14: Catlg. 15: 201 DeWitt pl, Ithaca NY 14850.

DULLEA, BARBARA A. b Brooklyn NY 31 O 28. 5: SUNY Col at Potsdam 45-49 (Ed) BEd; URochester 52-57 (Ed) MEd; Syracuse 64-65 MSLS. 7: Tchr Elem Schs, Amityville NY 49-51; Tchr Elem Schs, Rochester NY 51-55; Tchr USA Dependents Sch, Baumholder Ger 55-56; Tchr Madison High Sch, Rochester NY 56-61; Tchr Potsdam Jr High Sch, Potsdam NY 61-64; Catlgr SUNY Col at Potsdam 65-66; Ref bibliog SUNY at Buffalo 66-. 9: ALA; NYLA; SUNY Assn of Libns. 10: Beta Phi Mu. 14: Ref. 15: 188 Callodine ave, Buffalo NY 14226.

DUMAINE, MAURICE. b St-Guillaume Cte Yamaska PQ 21 Jl 16. 5: Sem Montfort 31-36; Scolasticat St-Jean 37-43 (Phil & Theol); Sem St Paul 61-63 (Canon law); U Ottawa 64-65 (LS) BBl. 6: Fr, Sp. 7: Libn Cetnre marial montfortain, Montreal 65-. 8: Missionary in foreign Countries 43-50; Teacher in Moral heology and Canon Law 50-64; Advocate in Religious Matrimonial Court 65-. 9: Association des Bibliothecaires de langue francaise; CathLA; CanLA. 14: Ref, hosp libs, Marian lib. 15: 4000 rue Bossuet, Montreal 431 P Que Can.

DUMAN, ROBERT J. b Buffalo NY 24 F 33. 4: Esther (Ratajczak) Duman. 5: UBuffalo 55-58 (Evening Division); UArizona 59-63 (Pol sci) BA, 63-65 (Pol sci) MA; UDenver 65-66 (Libnship) MS. 6: Sp. 7: Yeoman 3rd USN Key West Fla & Annapolis Md 51-55; Teach asst dept of Govt UAriz 63-64; Asst Inst of Govt Research UAriz 63-64; Congressional intern Off of Rep Morris Udall, Wash DC 64; Asst docs libn UAriz Lib 64-65; Hd acquis libn San Jose State Col 66-. 9: CalLA. 10: Amer Acad Pol & Soc Sci; Amer Fed Tchrs; Amer Pol Sci Assn. 14: Acquis, ref, admin. 15: 7070 Rainbow Dr #13, San Jose Ca 95129.

DUMARESQ, FRANCES. b Montreal 9 Ap 09. 5: McGill 28-31 (Eng) BA, 31-32 BLS, 34 (Eng). 6: Fr. 7: Libn Law Lib McGill U 33; Libn Fraser Inst Pub Lib, Montreal 35-37; Sch libn Protestant Sch Bd of Greater Montreal 37-52, Lib consul 52-. 9: CanLA (Life mem, chm YP Sect, past mem Coun); ALA; QueLA (past mem Coun). 11: Order of Scholastic Merit, Que Dept of Educ. 13: Yes. 14: Child bks. 15: 10658 Delorimier ave, Montreal 360 Can.

DUMAS, ROBERT HUGH. b Presque Isle Me 5 Ag 26. 4: Barbara Morrison. 5: UMe 4448 (Eng) AB, 4849; Boston U 5253; Simmons 5354 (LS) SM. 7: Br asst Enoch Pratt Free Lib, Baltimore 5457; Ref libn Los Angeles Pub Lib 57; Coord YA serv Dallas Pub Lib 5862; Lib dir Dedham Pub Lib, Dedham Mass 6266; City libn Decatur Pub Lib, Decatur Ill 66. 9: ALA; IllLA. 13: Yes. 14: Bks, adult serv, catlg, wk simplification. 15: Decatur Pub Lib 457 N Main, Decatur Il 62523.

DUMBAULD, BETTY. b Brooklyn Iowa. 5: Marshalltown(Iowa) Jr Col 35-37; Simmons 37-39 (LS) BS. 7: Circ libn Denison U 40-45; Ref libn Waterloo(Iowa) Pub Lib, Waterloo Iowa 46; Libn Meredith Publishing Co, DesMoines Iowa 46-55; Libn Needham Harper & Steers Inc, Chicago 55-68; J Walter Thompson Co 68-. 9: SLA (chm Adv & Marketing Div 65-66). 10: Alpha Omicron Pi. 15: 410 N Michigan ave, Chicago Il 60611.

DUMONT, NORMAND E. b Haverhill Mass 9 F 24. 5: UNH 44-48 (Econ) BA; SUNY(Albany) 54-55 MS in LS. 6: Fr. 7: Asst manager J J Newberry Co, NYC 48-51; Asst manager Lincoln Stores, Qunicy Mass 51-52; Purchasing dpt asst GEN Railway Signal Co, Rochester NY 52-54; Asst libn Albany Med Col Lib 54-55; Supr libn Brooklyn Pub Lib 55-65; Admin off UHawaii Lib 65- ; Assoc Prof UHawaii Sch Lib Stud 65-68; Asst dir Clinton-Essex-Franklin Lib Syst, Plattsburgh NY 68-. 9: ALA (chm Memb Com, Brooklyn Chap 61-65); NYLA (chm Publishers Liaison Com 65). 10: NY Lib Club; Booksellers League of NY. 14: Admin. 15: 57 Altamont st, Haverhill Mass.

DUMONT, PAUL EMILE. b Sanford Me 21 Ag 43. 5: St Francis Col (Biddleford Me) 63-67 (Econ) AB; CatholicU 67-69 MSLS. 6: Fr. 7: Lib asst St Francis Col (Biddleford Me) 64-66; Grad lib asst CatholicU 66-68; Ref libn St Francis Col 68-69; Jr libn San Antonio Col 69-. 9: ALA; MeLA; TexLA. 14: Ref, automation. 15: 24 Charles st, Sanford Me 04073.

DUNCAN, CYNTHIA B. b Madison Penn 26 Ap 32. 5: Cal State Col Cal Penn 50-53 (Speech) BS; UPittsburgh 55-58 (Lit) ML; Fla State U 64-65 (LS) MS. 7: Pub speaking tchr Gateway Union Schs, Monroeville Penn 53-64; Fla State U: Instr lib sci 65, Staff asst (spec) summer 66, Act libn materials ctr summer 67; Hd ref Mansfield State Col 66-67; Assoc Prof lib sci Winthrop Col 67-. 9: ALA; -AASchL; -ACRL; SELA; SCLA. 10: Beta Phi Mu; Alpha Psi Omega. 14: Lib admin, ref. 15: Rte 3 Box 202E, Rock Hill SC 29730.

DUNCAN, DONALD P. b Webster SD 31 Ag 36. 4: Hope Wellenreiter. 5: USD 54-58 (Pol Sci) BA; UOre 58-60 (Hist) MA; UMinn 60-66 (LS) MA. 7: Jr libn UMinn Lib (Minneapolis) 62-64; Libn UMinn Law Lib (Minneapolis) 64-66; Libn Wash State Lib 66-68, Sr libn 68-. 8: Grad asst in Hist UOre 58-60; Grad lib asst UMinn Lib 61-62. 9: AALL; Amer Pol Sci Assn; Amer Soc Public Admin; PNLA; WashLA. 10: Phi Alpha Theta; Pi Sigma Alpha; Omicron Delta Kappa. 14: Ref, publc serv. 15: 418 E X st, Tumwater Wa 98501.

DUNCAN, DONNA (NOREEN). b Montreal 19 S 40. 5: Marianopolis Col 57-58, 60-61 (Eng) BA; McGill 61-62 BLS, 68 MLS. 06: Fr. 7: Catlgr Redpath Lib McGill 62-66, Supv catlg sect catlg dept McLennan Lib 67-. 8: Chm prof position clsf com McGill U 69. 9: ALA; CanLA; QuebecLA. 10: Marianopolis Col Alumnae Assn. 14: Catlg. 15: 5240 Byron st, Montreal 248 Que Can.

DUNCAN, LESTER EDMOND JR. b Charleston SC 12 S 38. 4: Margaret Carter Duncan. 5: SoCar 60-64 (Intl Studies) AB; UNC 66-68 MSLS. 7: Air traffic controller 1272-1 Det (USAF) 56-60; Program rep SC State Bd of Health, Columbia 64; Sales rep US Vitamin & Pharmaceutical Corp, NYC 64-66; Lib asst Undergrad Lib UNC (Chapel Hill) 66-67; Circ libn McKissick Lib USoCar 67-. 9: SCLA; SELA. 10: SC State Employees Assn. 14: Docs. 15: McKiddick Lib Univ South Carolina, Columbia SC 29208.

DUNCAN, LILLIAN (PERKINS). b Manchester NH 2 Ag 10. 4: John M Duncan. 5: UNH 29-32 (Eng); UOkla 32-33 BA in LS. 6: Fr. 7: Gen asst UNH Lib 34-38; Hd circ City Lib, Manchester NH 38-45; Loan libn UNH Lib 45-47, 48-68; Pub servs libn 68-. 9: ALA; NELA; NHLA (sec 47-48). 10: AAUP. 14: Pub serv. 15: Box 404, Durham NH 03824.

DUNCAN, MARGARET (BEATON). b Portchestr NY 29 Je 30. 4: Peter Duncan. 5: New Haven State Tchrs Col 48-50; San Diego State Col 60-63 (Eng) AB; UCal (Los Angeles) 63-64 MLS. 6: Fr. 7: Catlgr & ref libn US Naval Electronics Lab Ctr Lib, San Diego 64-. 9: SLA; CalLA. 14: Catlg, ref. 15: 826 Moana dr, San Diego Ca 92106.

DUNCAN, MARIAN (H(ANE) (MacNISH). b Toronto 15 Je 24. 4: Frederick R Duncan QC. 5: Sarah Lawrence 42-46 (Econ) AB; Toronto 63-64 BLS; URochester 60-65 (Can Hist) AM. 7: Bus ref libn Toronto Pub Lib 65-. 66; Ref libn Legis Lib, Ont 66-67; Dir Central Lib Ind training lib & safety & tech lib, Ont Dept of Labour 67-. 14: Ref. 15: 21 Eastbourne ave, Toronto 7 Can.

DUNCAN, MARY RUTH (YOW). b Raleigh NC 12 F 31. 4: Walter William Duncan. 5: UNC at Greensboro 49-50; Appalachian State Tchrs Col 50-53 (Primary ed) BS; UWash summer 57; UMd summer 68. 7: Sec Lib Sci Dept Appalachian State Tchrs Col summer 53; Bkmob libn P Billings Pub Lib, Billings Mont 53-54; Libn (br) Jacksonville Pub Lib, Jacksonville Fla 55; Libn Duval Co Pub Schs, Jacksonville Fla 55-56; Walla Walla Co Schs, College Place Wash: Tchr 56-57, Libn 57-58; Tchr All-Saints Episcopal Church, Anchorage Alaska 64-65; Libn Anchorage Borough Sch Dist, Anchorage Alaska 66-. 9: ALA; NEA; AlaskaLA; AlaskaSchL. 10: Anchorage Borough Sch Dist Lib Vertical Com. 14: Reader guidance, storytelling, bk sel, nonbook material for ref. 15: 1620 Stanford dr, Anchorage Ak 99504.

DUNCAN, NINA (KATHARINE) BALDWIN. b Cleveland Ohio 7 Je 07. 4: Robert Manly Duncan. 5: Oberlin 25-28 (Fr) BA; West Res 28-29 BS in LS. 6: Fr, Sp. 7: Catlgr Lorain Pub Lib, Lorain Ohio 29-31; Circ libn Madison Free Lib, Madison Wis 31-32; Ref libn Traveling Lib Wis Free Lib Commsn, Madison 32-35; Libn Wis Legisl Ref Lib, Madison 35-39; Catlgr Atomic Energy Lib Kirtland AFB, Albuquerque 49-50; Libn Bernalillo Co med Soc Lib, Albuquerque 50-64; Catlgr UNM Law Lib 65-. 8: Co-ed Union List of Ser, Albuquerque 54. 9: SLA; AALL; SWLA; Greater Albuquerque LA (Charter mem; treasurer 51 & 61; chm Scholarship Com); NMLA (chm Scholarship Com 55-56, 67-69). 10: League of Women Voters; Pan Amer RT. 13: Yes. 14: Catlg. 15: 1919 Las Lomas rd NE, Albuquerque NM 87106.

DUNGAN, RUTH (EVANS). b Kingston Penn 16 Ag 12. 5: Syracuse 30-34 (Int dec) BFA; Misericordia 58; UMd 62-68; Rutgers 62-66 MLS. 7: Interior decorator B Altman, NYC 36-38, 41-43; Interior decorator Kresge, Newark NJ 38-41; Lib aide Hoyt Lib, Kingston Penn 55-57; Art tchr Pub Schs, Tunkhannock Penn 57-58; Lib asst Osterhout Lib Wilkes-Barre Penn 58-62; Sch libn Montgomery Co Bd of Educ, Rockville Md 62-. 9: PennLA; MdLA; MontgomeryCoSchLA (treas 65-66). 10: AAUW. 14: Ref, child wk. 15: 3320 Toledo pl apt H, Hyattsville Md 20782.

DUNHAM, JANET. b Geneseo NY 7 Jl 16. 5: State U Col of Educ (Geneseo NY) (LS) BS. 7: Clerk Gleason Works, Rochester NY 40-42; Sec IBM, Rochester NY 42-45; Libn Eastman Kodak Co, Rochester NY 45-. 9: SLA. 10: AAUW; Print Club of Rochester; Green Hills Golf Club. 13: Yes. 14: Admin (sci & tech libs). 15: Eastman Kodak Co Engr Div, Kodak Park Rochester NY 14650.

DUNHAM, MARY. b Charles City Iowa 24 S 21. 4: Richard J Dunham. 5: Iowa State Col 39-43 (Landscape Arch) BS; SUNY(Albany) 60-63 MLS. 7: Lib asst Pub Lib, Charles City Iowa 43-44; Engnrs asst Gen Electric, Schenectady NY 44; Research asst Chicago Plan Commsn 44-45; Sch libn Schenectady Pub Schs 63; Sch libn Mohawk Sch, Scotia NY 63-. 9: East NY Sch Libns Assn. 15: RD 3, Amsterdam NY 12010.

DUNHAM, PHYLLIS L. b Boulder Colo 28 My 09. 5: UColo 2731 (Romance Langs) BA, 32 (Romance Lans) MA; UDenver 41 BS in LS; UMexico 37 (Spanish); NorthwesternU 38 (Music). 7: Tchr; Eagle Co High Sch, Gypsum Colo 3436;, Alamosa High Sch, Alamosa Colo 3640; Asst ser libn Iowa State Col 4142; Censor US Off of Censorship, San Antonio Tex 4243; Libn acquis & docs div UMo (Columbia) 4347; Libn docs div UColo 4749; Asst libn Adams State Col 4954; Hd libn 54. 8: Tchr lib sci Adams State Col 49. 9: ALA (Colo Recruitment Chm); MPLA; MoLA (sec 47); ColoLA (treas 5354; chm So Div 56); Colo Coun Libns (sec & vpres). 10: Alamosa City Lib Bd; AAUW; AAUP; Phi Beta Kappa; Kappa Delta Pi; Alpha Zeta Pi; Sigma Epsilon Sigma; Delta Kappa Gamma. 14: Ref. 15: 1424 Second st, Alamosa Co 81101.

DUNIN-BORKOWSKI, PETER. b Mlyniska (Poland) 1 Mr 19. 5: Jan Kazimierz U Lwow Poland 36-37 (Hist); Jagiellonski U Poland 37-39 (Hist); Ecole Superieure des lettres Beirut Lebanon 45-47 (Fr lang & lit); U Paris 48-52 (Hist) Certif, 53-55 (Hist); Columbia 56-57 (Hist) (Polish studies), 5''' (Hist), 61-64 (Lib serv) MS in LS; U Mass 64-66 Ital. 6: Fr, Polish, Ger, Ital, Sp, Lat. 7: Press Off Polish Embassy Press Off, Bucharest 39-40; Priv Polish Army Inf under British command, Palestine, Egypt, Libya, Iraq 41-42; Ed "Kurjer Polski" (Polish newspaper), Baghdad 42-43; Proofreader "Gazeta Polska", Jerusalem 43-44; Researcher Polish Info Ctr Studies Off, jerusalem 44; Asst Polish Press Attache, Beirut Lebanon 45; Columbia Libs: Accesioner 56-57, Searcher 57-64; UMass Lib: Bibliogr 64-65, Catlgr 66-67; Descr catlgr LC Romance lang sect 67-. 9: ALA. 10: Amer Assn Advanc Slavic Studies. 14: Catlg, acquis. 15: 223 Fifth st SE, Wash DC 20003.

DUNKEL, BEATRICE VERONICA. b NYC 31 Ag 10. 5: Hunter Col 27-31 (Classics) AB; Columbia 41 LS. 7: Tchr St Barnabas Sch, Bronx NY 31-33; Lib asst NY Pub Lib, NYC 37-4; Libn US Naval Hosp, Brooklyn NY 42-46; Libn The Seton Inst, Baltimore 46-52; Libn Brooklyn Prep SCH, Brooklyn NY 53-60; YP libn Linden Pub Lib, Linden NJ 60-61; Asst catlgr Newark State Col 61-65; Dir Crowell Colliers Ref Serv, NYC 65-. 9: SLA. 13: Yes. 14: Ref. 15: 2209 Light st, Bronx NY 10466.

DUNKELBERGER, ELAINE (JERVIS). b Steubenville Ohio 19 S 22. 4: Harold F Dunkelberger. 5: W Liberty State Col 41-44 (Eng) AB; UMich 59-61 (LS) MA. 6: Fr. 7: Tchr Linden High Sch, Linden Mich 44-45; Tchr Bangor High Sch, Bangor Mich 45-52; Tchr Greenville High Sch, Greenville Mich 52-54; Tchr Romeo High Sch, Romeo Mich 54-60; Libn Flushing Central Elem Sch, Flushing Mich 60-. 14: Catlg, bk talks. 15: 221 W Lorado, Flint Mich 48505.

DUNKIN, PAUL S. b Flora Ind 28 S 05. 4: Gladys Hammond. 5: DePauw U 29 (Eng, Classics) AB; UIll 3 (Classics) AM, 35 (LS) BS, 37 (Classics) PhD. 6: Fr, Ger, Lat. 7: Catlgr UIll Lib(Urbana) 35-37; Sr catlgr Folger Shakespeare Lib, Wash DC 37-50, Chief tech serv 50-59; Prof Grad Sch of Lib Serv Rutgers U 59-. 8: Asst ed "Library Resources & Technical Services," ALA-RTSD 57-60, 67-. 9: ALA (var coms); -RTSD (pres 64-65); DCLA (ed "DC Libraries 2 yrs); NJLA; Bibiog Soc (London); BSA; Bibliog Soc UVa. 10: Phi Beta Kappa; Beta Phi Mu. 11: Recipient Margaret Mann Citation 68. 12: "Post Aristophanic Comedy (48); "How to Catalog a Rare Book (51); Commentary for: Seymour Lubetzkys "Code of Cataloging Rules (60); "Cataloging USA" (69). 13: Yes. 14: Catlg, clsf, rare bks, hist bks & libs. 15: Grad Sch of Lib Serv Rutgers U, New Brunswick NJ 08903.

DUNKLE, DOROTHY (PATTON). b Higgins Tex 26 Je 17. 4: O W Dunkle. 5: Park Col 34-35; W Tex U 35-38 (Eng) BA; Highlands U summer 42; N Tex U 60-63 BS in LS. 6: Sp. 7: Language arts tchr Perryton Jr High Sch, Perryton Tex 38-43; Elem tchr Texline Pub Sch, Texline Tex 43-44; Elem tchr NOTS, Inyokern Cal 44-45; Language arts tchr Perryton Jr High Sch, Perryton Tex 51-60, Libn 60-. 9: NEA; Tex State Tchrs Assn. 14: Ref, sch libs. 15: 701 S Fordham, Perryton Tex 79070.

DUNKLEY, GRACE (CROOM). b Kinston NC 19 N 18. 4: Malcolm D Dunkley. 5: Campbell Col 35-37; Meredith Col

37-39 (Hist) AB; Madison Col summers 54-56 Certif in LS; UNC summers 59-65 MS in LS. 6: Fr. 7: High sch tchr Va & NC pub schs 39-58; Libn Great Bridge High Sch, Chesapeake Va 58-. 9: NEA; ALA-AASchL; VaEA; VaLA. 10: Kappa Delta Pi. 14: Ref, reading guidance in high sch. 15: 324 Briarfield dr, Chesapeake Va 23320.

DUNLAP, CONNIE (ROBSON). b Lansing Mich 9 S 24. 4: Robert Bruce Dunlap. 5: UMich 42-46 (Geog, Geol) AB, 52 AMLS; UParis summer 67 Certif. 6: Fr, Ger. 7: UMich: Jr circ libn 46-52, Sr circ libn 52-54, Assoc circ libn 54-61, Act head order dept 61-62, Head order Dept 62-64, Head acquis dept 64-67, Hd Grad Lib 67-. 8: Guest lectr, Dept Lib Sci 65-68; Consul; No Mich U 66, Centre International de Perfectionnement Professionnel et Technique 67, USC 69. 9: ALA (Acquis Sect; v-chm 69-70, chm 70-71);-ISAD (chm Com on Curr Devel 69-70, sec Com on Lib Automation 66-); MichLA (chm Nomin Com 61). 10: Forewoman, Grand Jury, US Dist Court (18 months). 11: Nat Hon Soc. 13: Yes. 14: Acquis, pub serv. 15: 1570 Westfield, Ann Arbor Mich 48103.

DUNLAP, JOSEPH R(IGGS). b Weihsien Shantung China 8 F 13. 4: Leonie Coan. 5: Col of Wooster 32-36 (Hist, Eng) AB; Columbia U 36-37 (LS) BS; Columbia 37-42 (Hist) AM; Columbia U 48-56 (LS). 6: Fr. 7: Asst City Col of NY Lib 37-38, Reserve asst 38-41, Catlgr 41-43, 46-47; US Army (Pfc) ASTP 43-44, Med Corps 44-46; Ref libn City College of NY Lib 47-61, Assoc libn 61-68, Bibliogr 68-. 8: ALA Com on Interlib Loans 54-58. 9: ALA-ACRL; NY Lib Club; Lib Assn City U NY (pres 51-53). 10: William Morris Soc (Eastern Sec); NY Shavians (treas); Kipling Soc; English Neighborhood Hist Soc (NJ); Friends of Freedom Lib (chm); Leonia (NJ) Civic Conf (chm 61-64); Leonia Citizens for Pub Schs; Victorian Soc in Amer (pres 66-67). 12: "Out of a Medics Kit (45); Co-comp "Debate Index, 2nd Sup (64); "William Caxton & William Morris (64); Ed "News from Anywhere, Asst ed "Independent Shavian. 13: Yes. 14: Bk hist, ref. 15: City Col Lib, 135th st & Convent ave, New York NY 10031.

DUNLAP, LESLIE W(HITTAKER). b Portland Ore 3 Ag 11. 4: Marie Gladys Neese. 5: UOre 29-33 (Eng) BA; Columbia 34-35 (Eng) AM, 35-38 (LS) BS, 39-42 (Hist) PhD. 6: Ger, Fr, Sp. 7: Ref & gen asst NY Pub Lib 36-41; Head acquis dept UWis Lib(Madison) 42-45; Asst cief chief Ref & Bibliog Div LC 45-48, Asst chief Mss Div 48-49; Libn UBC 49-51; Assoc dir UIll Lib(Urbana) 51-58; Dir UIowa Libs 58-. 8: Lib adv Nat UMexico 48; bldg consul Northwestern Col 61-63; consul-examiner N Central Assn 65; Lib Adv Bd "Collier Encyclopedia 61-; Chm Bd of Dir Center for Research Libs 64-65. 9: ALA-ACRL; MssSoc; ARL (chm Com Microfilming Dissertations 63-64); Adv Com, Nat Union Catlg of Mss Collections 65-68; IowaLA (pres 68-69); Adv Com Ctr for Microfilming Foreign Manuscripts 67-. 10: Caxton Club (Chicago); Phi Beta Kappa. 11: ALA Fellowship; Distinguished Serv Citation, Northwestern Col. 12: "Letters of Willis Gaylord Clark and Willis Gaylord Clark (40); "American Historical Societies, 1790-1860 (44); article on "Libraries in Colliers Encyclopedia (30,000 words). 13: Yes. 14: Admin, bldgs, mss. 15: 326 Hutchinson ave, Iowa City Iowa.

DUNLAP, MARY JEAN. b Dallas Tex 27 O 37. 5: So MethodistU 55-59 (Elem Educ) BA; N Tex StateU summer 60; Tex Woman'sU summers 61-65 MLS. 7: Kindergarten helper Preston Hollow Presbyterian Ch, Dallas Tex 59; Tchr Mesquite Pub Schs, Mesquite 59-60; Libn Highland Park Pub Schs, Dallas Tex 60-. 8: Lib chm Highland Park Curriculum Coun 63-65; Chm summer reading lists for Highland Park Schs 65. 9: ALA; Amer Assn for Childhood Educ; TexLA; ClrTA; Tex Internationl Reading Assn. 10: Highland Pk Assn for Childhood Educ; Highland Park ClrTA; Delta Zelta. 14: Elem sch libs. 15: 3624 Centenary, Dallas Tx 75225.

DUNLEAVY, CLARA (NEWMAN). b NYC 23 Jl 23. 4: Martin P Dunleavy. 5: CCNY 50-54 (Eng Lit) BA; Columbia 55-56 MLS. 6: Ger. 7: Catlgr ColumbiaU Col of Physician & Surgeons 56-62; Ref libn NY Acad of Med, NYC 62-. 9: MedLA (NY Reg Group Memb Com); SLA (sci/ tech div). 10: Phi Beta Kappa. 14: Ref. 15: 2 East 103 st, New York NY 10029.

DUNLOP, KATHERINE MILLS. b Chillicothe Ohio 4 O 08. 4: Charles L Dunlop. 5: Wellesley 26-30 (Hist) BA; West Res 59-60 MLS. 6: Fr. 7: Educ dept Cincinnati Art Museum 34-36; Lib asst Shaw High Sch, Cleveland 60-61; Libn Hawken Upper Sch, Lyndhurst Ohio 60-. 8: Selected bks for Young Adult Rm, Shaker Heights (Ohio) Pub Lib summer 65. 9: ALA; OhiLA; OhioASchL. 10: Wellesley Club. 14: Sch libs. 15: 3120 Coleridge rd, Cleveland Heights Ohio 44118.

DUNMIRE, RAYMOND VERYL b Vandergrift Penn 17 D 25. 4: Ruth March Dunmire. 5: Thiel Col 46-50 (Eng) BA; Fla State U summers 53-57 (Lib serv) MA. 7: Army Airways Communication Syst USAF Sgt 43-46; High Sch Elderton Penn 51-52; Thiel Col: Asst libn 52-57, Libn (on leave part time) 57-65; UFla: Hd Inter-lib loans 60-61, instr 61-62; Dir learning ctr SEast Commun Col 65-. 8: Eval: Middle States Assn of Secon Schs & Cols; So Assn of Sec Schs & Cols; Consul: SW Va Commun Col 68; Riegel Paper Co 69. 9: ALA (life mem); NEA-DAVI; NCLA; SELA; North Carolina Historical Society; NC Commun Col LA. 10: Cub Scouts; Delta Sigma Phi; Beta Phi Mu; Phi Alpha Theta; NC Hist Soc. 12: Produced, wrote, and edited sound films and filmstrips. 14: A-v, acquis, admin, tchg. 15: Country Club dr (Box 243), Whiteville NC 28472.

DUNN, CAROLINE. b Indianapolis Ind 21 Ja 03. 5: Butler U 19-23 (Eng) AB; Columbia 27-28 BS in LS. 6: Fr, Ger. 7: Asst Pub Lib, Indianapolis 23-27; Libn Pub Lib, Connersville Ind 28-36; Ref libn Ind Div State Lib, Indianapolis 36-39; Libn Ind Hist Soc Lib, Indianapolis 39-. 9: ALA; IndLA (Life mem, coms, past treas). 10: Organiz Amer Histns; Pi Beta Phi. 13: Yes. 14: Ref, documents, mss, rare materials. 15: 140 N Senate ave, Indianapolis In 46204.

DUNN, CHLORA (CURTIS). b Haleyville Ala 10 Ja 09. 4: Floyd R Dunn. 5: Birmingham So Col 34 (Eng, Soc Studies) BA; UChattanooga summer 50; Peaody summers 51-54 MA in LS. 6: Sp. 7: High sch Eng tchr co sch systems in Ala: Arley Ala 25-28, Lynn Ala 28-36, Autaugaville Ala 36-37; Elem tchr Hamilton Co Schs, Chattanooga Tenn 48-52; Libn Chattanooga (Tenn) Pub Schs, Chattanooga High Sch 52-60, Libn Brainerd High Sch 60-; Ext tchr UTenn Ext Serv, Chattanooga Area, Dept of Lib Serv 62-68; Libn in charge of A-V Chattanooga State Tech Inst 69-. 8: Visiting tchr UTenn Sch of Lib Serv, summers 59, 60, 64; Assoc dir, DEA Lib Inst, E Tenn U summers 65-66. 9: NEA; ALA; TennEA (var offs in Libns Sect 59-62); TennLA (Recr Chm, rep to ALA convention 61). 10: Alpha Delta Kappa. 13: Yes. 14: Sch libnship. 15: 306 La Verne dr, Chattanooga Tenn 37421.

DUNN, ELIZABETH K. b Lawrence Kan. 5: UKan 28-32 (Span) AB; UDenver 51-52 MA in LS. 6: Sp. 7: Rural sch tchr Douglas Co Schs, Douglas Co Kan 33-38; Elem tchr Bucklin Pub Schs, Bucklin Kan 38-42; High sch tchr Augusta Pub Schs, Augusta Kan 42-46; Catlgr UKan Libs 48-55; Libn Haskell Indian Inst, Lawrence Kan 55-58; Tech processes libn US Armys Dependents Schs, Karlsruhe Germany 58-63; Catlgr US Mil Acad(W Point) 63-. 66; Libn Haskell Indian Inst 66-. 9: ALA; KanLA; KanASchL. 10: Bus & Prof Women's Club; AAUW; Altrusa Internat; Color Camera; Delta Kappa Gamma. 14: Centralized catlg. 15: 901 Kentucky st apt 306, Lawrence Ks 66044.

DUNN, GLADYS MAE. b New Brunswick NJ 3 O 17. 5: Douglass 35-39 (LS) AB. 7: Org asst Chloe Morse Inc, NYC 39-40; Sr lib asst catlg Pub Lib, Bridgeport Conn 40-43; Sr lib asst catlg Pub Lib, Paterson NJ 43-46; Managing ed, assoc ed Book Review Digest H W Wilson Co, NYC 46-50; Asst Staff libn of NY Authority, NYC 50-. 9: SLA; Women;s Nat Bk Assn; NY Lib Club. 10: Bus & Prof Womens Club, NYC; Eng Speaking Union; NJ Hist Soc. 12: Ed "New York Library Club Bulletin (48-49). 14: Catlg, index. 15: 146 New st, New Brunswick NJ 08901.

DUNN, JAMES TAYLOR. b St Paul 28 F 12. 4: Maria-Catherine Bach. 5: Hamilton Col 32-36 (Eng Lit) AB; Syracuse 38-39 BS in LS (cum laude). 6: Fr. 7: Asst ed Globe Travel Magazine, St Paul 36-38; Libn Chemung Co Lib, Elmira NY 39; Head libn Olean Pub Lib, Olean NY 40-48; 1st Lt Anti-Aircraft Artillery, European Theatre 42-46; Libn NY State Hist Assn, Cooperstown NY 48-55; Chief libn Minn Hist Soc, St Paul 55-. 9: MinnLA (chm Ref Sect 64, chm Resols Com 65). 10: Ft Snelling State Park Assn; AM Assoc for State & local hist (Bd mem); St Croix River Assn (secty); AM Interprofessional Inst. 11: Pi Lambda Sigma (Hon Lib Frat). 12: "The St Croix: Midwest Border River (65); Co-ed "The Gopher Reader (58); Ed "Choice Nook of Memory (50); "Marine Mills; Lumber Village" (63); "Marine on St Croix; From Lumber Village to Summer Haven" (68). 13: Yes. 15: Minn Hist Soc, St Paul Mn 55101.

DUNN, JOAN (CAHILL). b NYC 4 Ja 44. 4: Thomas W Dunn. 5: Barnard 61-65 (Zoology) AB; RutgersU (New Brunswick) 67-68 MLS. 7: Lit biologist Lederle Labs, Pearl River NY 67-68; Sr libn Johnson Pub Lib, Hackensack NJ 68-. 14: Ref. 15: 29 Karen dr, Mahwah NJ 07430.

DUNN, KATHLEEN (KELPIEN). b Los Angeles 11 D 41. 4: Robert Paul Dunn. 5: Pacific Unio n Col 59-64 (Eng) BA;

UWis 64-65 (LS) MA. 7: Stud catlgr rare bk dept UWis Mem Lib 65; Asst libn Lib Sch Lib UWis 65-. 10: Beta Phi Mu. 14: Col libnship, child lit, info retrieval. 15: 3734C W Karstens dr, Madison Wis 53704.

DUNN, MARGARET L. b Burlington NJ 23 Ja 01. 5: Illman Sch for Kindergarteners Phila 23-24; NJ State Tchrs Col(Trenton) (LS) 45. 7: Tchr Private Sch Kindergarten, Burlington NJ 25-32; Libn Lib Co of Burlington Burlington NJ 42-. 8: Burlington County Lib Commsn 59-64; 09: ALA; NJLA. 15: Beverly rd, Burlington NJ 08016.

DUNN, MARY LOIS. b Uvalde Tex. 5: Stephen F Austin STATE Col 48-51 (LS) BA; LSU 53-57 (LS) MS. 7: Asst libn Burbank Jr High Sch, Houston 51-57; Libn Black Jr High Sch, Houston 57-. 8: Consul Tex Educ Agency on Title II ESEA summer 65. 9: TexLA. 10: Phi Beta Mu. 12: "The Man in the Box; A Story from Vietnam" (68). 14: Sch libs, young adults. 15: 4301 Bissonnet Apt 44, Bellaire Tex 77401.

DUNN, MARY. b Branchville Md 28 S 22. 5: UMd 39-43 (US Hist) BA; Catholic U 45-48 (US Hist) MA; USoCal 55-57 (LS); Catholic U 58 (LS), UHawaii 67 (Hawaiian Hist). 6: Fr, Sp. 7: Tchr Md Park Jr High Sch, Seat Pleasant Md 44-51; Tchr Dept Army, Tokyo 51-53; Libn Md Park Jr Hgh Sch, Seat Pleasant Md 54-58; Libn DeptArmy, Paris 58-61; Libn Northwestern High Sch, Hyattsville Md 61-. 9: ALA; MdLA; Md State Tchrs Assn: AssnSchLibns, Md (pres). 10: Delta Kappa Gamma. 13: Yes. 14: Wk with ya. 15: 6700 Belcrest rd, Apt 608, Hyattsville Md 20782.

DUNN, OLIVER (CHARLES). b California 10 Ag 09. 4: Jane Lee. 5: Stanford 26-30 (Phil) AB, 31-33 (Law, Phil) MA; Harvard 30-31 (Phil); Cornell 34-37 (Phil) PhD; UCal (Berkeley) 48-49 BLS. 6: Fr, Sp. 7: Lockheed Aircraft Corp, Burbank Cal 40-45; Assoc dir Cal Tech Lib 49-53; Purdue U Lib: Asst dir 53-60, Assoc dir 60-. 8: Consul: Universidad Agraria La Molina Lima Peru (Rockefeller Foun) 62-63, 67; Indian Inst of Techn Kanpur India (USAID) 62, 64, 66, 68; Universiad Del Valle, Cali Columbia (Rockefeller Foun) 65-66; Universidad Nacional, Bogota Colombia (Ford Found) 67; Heidelberg Col Tiffin Ohio 66-67. 9: ALA; -ACRL. 10: Soc Hist of Discoveries; Hakluyt Soc; Soc Nautical Research; Sigma Delta Chi. 12: "A Library Development Plan for the Indian Institute of Technology Kanpur" (62); "Progress Report on the Library" (64); "The Past and Likely Future of 58 Research Libraries, 51-80: s Statistical Study of Growth and Change" (65); "The IIT/K Library March 1966: Two years' progress, present problems and a Five-Year Plan (66); Co-auth "Report of a Survey of the Biblioteca Agricola Nacional del Peru la Molina" (67). 14: Devel, admin, bldgs. 15: Purdue Univ Lib, Lafayette In 47907.

DUNN, PAULENE M. b W Gouldsbor Me 20 My 09. 5: UMe 26-30 (Eng) BA; Columbia U 49 BS in LS. 6: Fr. 7: Asst tchr in small high schs, Me 34-38; Libn Bangor High Sch, Bangor Me 38-. 9: NEA; MeTchrsAssn; NESchLA; MeSchLA (treas 62-64). 10: AAUW. 15: 135 Forest ave, Bangor Me 04401.

DUNN, ROBERTA ANN (POYNTER). b Detroit Mich 31 O 36. 4: George Robert Dunn. 5: West MichU 54-58 (LS) BS. 6: Sp. 7: Circ clk West Mich U 54-58; Bkmob & child libn St Clair Co Lib, Port Huron Mich 58-63; Asst dir Washtenaw Co Lib, Ann Arbor Mich 63-. 9: MichLA; Washtenaw Area Lib Syst. 10: Washtenaw Lib Club. 14: Bkmob, ref, child & ya, catlg. 15: 126 College pl apt 4, Ypsilanti Mi 48197.

DUNN, ROY SYLVAN. b Nixon Tex 29 Mr 21. 4: Elaine McCoy. 5: UTex 48 (Pol Sci) BA, 51 (Socil, Hist) MA; American U 50 (Archival Mgt). 7: Tex State Lib: Asst in archives & asst state archivist 47-50, Coordinator reorg & renovation 50-51, State Libn 51; Records examiner 52-53; Auditor State Comptroller, Austin Tex 53-56; Archivist Southwest Collection & Asst Prof of Sociology Tex Tchr 56-63., Dir Soutwest Collection 63- & Assoc Prof of Sociol 63-. 9: Tex State Hist Assn (Fellow); SAA (Comm on Col & Univ Archives); Amer Sociol Assn; West Tex Hist Assn; So Sociol Soc; SW Sociol Assn. 11: H Bailey Carroll Award 1967. 13: Yes. 14: Sociol Use of hist materials. 15: Box 4559, Lubbock Tx 79409.

DUNN, WILLIE MAE (SEAB). b Holden La 10 Mr 25. 4: Lemuel A Dunn III. 5: Southeastern La Col 41-44 (Hist) BA; LSU 46-47 BS in LS. 7: Br libn Wash Parish Lib, Bogalusa La 47-48; Act libn Livingston Parish Lib, Livingston La 48-49; Asst libn Vermilion Parish Lib, Abbeville La 49-50; Libn Terrebonne Parish Lib, Houma La 50-55; Libn Caldwell Parish Lib, Columbia La 55-60; Libn Tensas-Tallula h Parish Lib, Tallulah La 60-61; Libn Braden Elem Sch, Natchez Miss 61-64; Libn Morgantown Jr High Sch, Natchez Miss 64-. 9: ALA; LaLA; MissLA. 15: Rt 4 Box 311, Natchez Ms 39120.

DUNNE, ELIZABETH (KELLOGG). b Orange Mass 29 D 10. 4: James P Dunne. 5: Conn Col 27-29; NYU 36-39 BA: Columbia 39-42 BLS. 7: Subprof catlgr NY Pub Lib 37-39; Managing ed "Education Index H W Wilson Co, NY 39-42; Catlgr Hunter Col 42-46; Catlgr, asst sect head, sect head Copyright Off Catlg Div, LC 46-57, 61-. Rsearch analyst 57-61, Sect hd 61-66, Asst chief copyright off catlg div 66-68; Chief 68-. 9: ALA; DCLA. 13: Yes. 14: Catlg. 15: 1734 P st NW, Wash DC 20036.

DUNNING, ALMA (LOUISE). b Oneida NY 16 My 08. 5: Smith 26-30 (Fr Lit) AB; Syracuse 31-32 BS in LS, 56 MS in LS. 6: Fr. 7: Libn Goodyear-Burlingame Sch, Syracuse NY 33-36; Libn Skaneateles High Sch, Skaneateles NY 37-39; Libn Sch of Lib Sci, Syracuse U 47-50; Asst libn Natural Sci Lib, Syracuse U 56-. 9: ALA. 10: Beta Phi Mu; Gamma Phi Beta. 14: Ref. 15: 712 Lancaster ave, Syracuse NY 13210.

DUPONT, JULIE ANDREE. b Wash DC 25 F 39. 5: Dunbarton Col of Holy Cross Wash DC 57-61 (Hist) BA; Catholic U Amer 64-65 MSLS. 6: Fr, Lat, Greek. 7: Research grants asst Nat Inst Health Bethesda Md 62-64; US Dept Labor, Wash DC: Ref libn 65-68, Ref libn & bibliogr 68-. 9: SLA; DCLA. 10: Pi Gamma Mu; Beta Phi Mu. 14: Ref, bibliog. 15: 4455 Springdale st NW, Washington DC 20016.

DUPPSTADT, MARY ANN (MILLER). b Somerset Penn 22 S 16. 4: J Robert Duppstadt. 5: Hood Col 34-38 (Eng) BA; Carnegie 38-39 BLS. 6: Ger, Fr. 7: Child libn Lima Pub Lib, Lima Ohio 39-41; Libn Period Dept Penn State U 42; Ref libn Grosvenor Ref Lib, Buffalo NY 43-48; Sr libn Erie Co Lib, Buffalo NY 49-52; Asst libn Arlington State Col 53-56; Catlgr LTV Aerospace Corp, Dallas Tex 57-59, Indexer 59-61, Asst chief catlgr 61-. 15: 921 E Mitchell st, Arlington Tx 76010.

DUPREE, EULAVA (SLEDGE). b Coushatta La 28 O 15. 4: David Vernon Dupree. 5: NWest State Col 32-35 (Com) BA; LSU 40-45 BLS; UAriz 43. 6: Fr. 7: Red River Parish Sch Bd, Coushatta La: Tchr 35-39, Supv instr 40-43; Libn Our Lady of the Lake Sch of Nursing, Baton Rouge La 54-59; Ser rec libn LSU Lib 60-. 9: ALA; SWLA; LaLA. 10: Baton Rouge Gem & Min Soc; Four O'Clock Garden Club. 11: Delta Kappa Gamma. 14: Ser. 15: 4239 Sweetbriar st, Baton Rouge La 70808.

DUPREY, WILSON G. b Van Wert Ohio 21 Je 24. 5: Ohio State U 42-44; George Washington U 44-46 (Foreign Serv) AB; Columbia 48-49 (LS)MA. 6: Fr, Sp, Portu. 7: Searcher Card Div & Photographic Serv LC 44-48; Ref asst Stanford U Lib 49-51; Spec collections libn 51-53; Ref asst prints div NY Pub Lib 53-66; Curator map & print rm NY Hist Soc 66-. 10: Metro Mus of Art; Brooklyn Mus; LI Hist Soc; Van Wert Co (Ohio) Hist Soc; Walters Art Gallery. 14: Rare bks, mss, art prints, maps. 15: 48 Pierrepont st, Brooklyn 1 NY.

DUPUIS, LORRAINE W. b Milwaukee Wis 9 S 26. 5: Marquette U 44-48 (Chem) BS, MS, UWM 62-65 (LS). 7: Lab A O Smith Corp, Milwaukee 53; Chem instr Marquette U 53-57; Chem instr UWis(Milwaukee) 57-59; Ed "Chemical Abstract" Columbus Ohio 59-60; Chem instr UWis(Milwaukee) 60-63; Tech libn Lakeside Labs, Milwaukee 63-66; Chem instr Broward Jr Col 67-68; Info sci Wm S Merrell, Cincinnati 68-. 9: ACS; ASIS; DAR. 10: Sigma Gamma Chi. 14: Documentation. 15: Wm S Merrell, 110 Amity rd, Cincinnati Oh 45239.

DUREE, BARBARA JOYCE. b Las Vegas NM 9 Mr 22. 5: UKan 40-44 (Eng) AB, 46-49 (Eng) MA; West Res 52-53 (LS) MS. 7: Eng tchr Council Grove High Sch, Council Grove Kan 44-46; Eng tchr UKan 46-48; Copywriter Hall Brothers, Kansas City Mo 49-50; Ext libn, Topeka Pub Lib, Topeka Kan 51-53, Readers adv 53-54; Ed ya bks "The Booklist" ALA, Chicago 54-. 9: ALA; IllLA. 10: Phi Beta Kappa. 14: Ya bk sel. 15: 8053 S Throop st, Chicago 6020.

DUREN, ANNIE SCOTT (GUNTER). b Griffin Ga 19 Ja 17. 5: Womans Col of Ga 33-37 (Eng) Bs; Emory 59-60 (LS) ML; UGrenoble summer 66; UStrasbourg summer 63. 7: Tchr Griffin Pub Schs, Griffin Ga 37-45; Recreation wker Amer Red ross, Germany, Austria 45-48; Catlgr Manhattan Pub Lib, Manhattan Kan 52-54; CATLGR Q M Sch Lib, Ft Lee Va 56-58; Libn Griffin High Sch, Griffin Ga 59-62; Catlgr Robert Col Lib (Istanbul Turkey) 62-63, Acquis libn 63-. 9: ALA. 10: AAUP; Turkish- Amer Univ Assn. 14: Acquis, child bks, sch libs. 15: Robert Col, Bebek PK 8, Istanbul Turkey.

DURHAM, JOANNE RUTH. b Kamiah Ida 8 F 40. 5: George Fox Col 59-63 (Soc Studies) BA; UWash 63-64 M Lib. 7: Circ libn Seattle Pacific Col 64-65; Asst libn 65-67; Ref libn Tucson Pub Libn, Tucson Ariz 67-68; Hd adult serv 1st Ave Br 68-. 9: ArizStateLA. 14: Ref. 15: 3703 N 1st ave 25, Tucson Az 85719.

DURHAM, LAURA (WHITAKER). b Evarts Ky 27 Jl 32. 4: H Lee Durham. 5: Campbellsville Jr Col 50-51 (Elem Ed); Georgetown Col 52 (Elem Ed); East Ky U 55-56 (Elem Ed) BS; UKy 60 (LS) Certif. 7: Lincoln Cp Bd of Educ Lincoln Co Ky: Mus tchr & libn 52-53; Mus tchr 53-54; Pub sch mus tchr Madison Co Bd of Educ, Kirksville Ky 54-56; Tchr Berea Bd of Educ, Berea Ky 56-57; Rockcastler Bd of Educ, Livingston Ky: Pub sch mus tchr 58-59, Libn 59-. 9: KyASchL (Bd 65-66); Central Ky ASchL (pres 67-68; Rockcastle CTA (pres-elect 68-69). 10: Delta Kappa Gamma. 14: Ref, wk with tchrs & students. 15: Jones st, Mt Vernon Ky 40456.

DURHAM, MAE J. b Albany NY. 5: Russell Sage Col 36-40 (Fr) BA; SUNY(Albany) 40-41 BLS; Columbia 42; New Sch for Soc Research 43-45; UCal 59-60. 6: Fr. 7: Child libn NY Pub Lib 4147; Child libn Redwood City 9cal) Pub Lib 47-48; Child libn San Francisco State Col 48-59; Lecturer Sch of Libnship UCal (Berkely) 59-. 9: ALA-CSD (pres 68-69, mem Publs Com, chm Newbery-Caldecott Awards Com 68); CalLA; CalASchL; Assn of Child Libns No Cal. 10: AAUP. 12: "Literature Sampler: Junior Ed (64); "Tit for Tat and Other Latvian Folk Tales (67). 13: Yes. 14: Child & ya lit, sch libs. 15: Sch of Libnship, Univ of Cal, Berkeley Ca 94720.

DURHAM, MARY JOINES. b Sale City Ga 2 M 21. 5: Tift Col 38-42 (Eng) AB; Fla State U 59 (LS) MA. 6: Fr. 7: Instr Tift Col 42-44; Visiting tchr Co Educ Bd, Camilla Ga 46; Libn Norman Park High Sch, Norman Park Ga 52-56; Libn Norman Col 56-68; Acquis libn Valdosta State Col, Valdosta Ga 68-. 9: ALA; GaEA; SELA; GaLA. 10: Delta Kappa Gamma; Beta Phi Mu. 12: Thesis: "Study of Junior Colleges in Georgia. 14: Admin. 15: 2207 Park lane, Valdosta Ga 31601.

DURIS, RICHARD MARTIN. b North Braddock Penn 28 Ja 31. 4: Jacqueline Louis Kalebain. 5: Ind U (Penn) 49-53 (Music Educ) BS Music Ed; Carnegie 58-59 MS in LS; UPittsburgh (Educ); Carnegie-Mellon 66-68 (Musicology) MFA. 7: Music tchr Warriors Mark Sch, Warriors Mark Penn 53-54; Music tchr Cresson Joint Schs, Cresson Penn 55-56; Music & Eng tchr West Homestead Schs, West Homestead Penn 56-58; Libn Art div Carnegie Lib of Pittsburgh 59-61; Libn art & music dept Cincinnati & Hamilton County Pub Lib 61-66; Hunt Lib Carnegie-Mellon U 66-67; Hd libn Commun Lib of Castle Shannon, Pittsburgh Penn 67-68; Asst hd Mus Lib Ohio State U Libs, Columbus Ohio 68-. 8: Choir director and organist. 9: ALA; MusLA; OhioLA. 10: Kappa Delta Pi; Phi Mu Alpha; Delta Sima Phi. 14: Ref, catlg. 15: 162 S Powell ave, Columbus Oh 43204.

DURKAN, MICHAEL JOSEPH. b Louisburgh co Mayo Ireland. 4: Yvonne Marie Walsh. 5: St Patricks Col (Maynooth Ireland) 44-49 (Lat, Irish) BA; University Col(DUBLIN) 49-50 Diploma in Lib Sci. 6: Irish, Lat. 7: Lib asst Bray Urban Dist Corp, Bray Ireland 50; Lib asst Meath Co Coun, Navan Ireland 50; Libn US Inf Agency, Dublin Ireland 50-56; Asst libn Longford-Westmeath Co, Athlone Ireland 56-58; Wesleyan U(Middletown Conn): Catlgr 58-60, Head catlg dept 60-63, Asst libn 63-. 9: Lib Assn of Ireland; BSA; Bibliog Soc of Ireland; ConnLA (chm Resources & Tech Serv Sect 61-62; chm Col & Univ Sect 63-64). 10: Amer Com for Irish Studies; Circle Theater (Middletown). 13: Yes. 14: Catlg, rare bks. 15: Olin Lib Wesleyan Univ, Middletown Conn 06457.

DURKEE, DOUGLAS WILLIAM. b Windsor Vt 23 O 25. 4: Barbara Sayre. 5: UVt 46-49 (Eng) BS; Harvard 56-59 Ed M. 6: Fr. 7: Navigator (Capt) USAF 43-46; Eng tchr Fair Haven High Sch, Fair Haven Vt 49-55; Eng tchr Hudson Falls High Sch, Hudson Falls NY 55-59; Green Mt Col: Eng prof 59-61, Dir independent reading program 61-66, Hd libn 66-. 9: NELA; VtLA. 10: Fair Haven (Vt) Sch Bd; chm Fair Haven Union High Sch; Vt Bd of sch Dirs; chm Addison-Rutland Supvy Union Sch dirs. 14: Bldg col, archives, interstaff particip. 15: Sheldon rd, Fair Haven Vt 05743.

DURKIN ROBERT E. b Fargo ND 5 D 23. 4: Audrey J Wilman. 5: St Johns U Collegeville Minn) 46-50 (Eng) BA; UMinn 52-53 (LS). 7: Radio operator T/4 US Army 43-46; Eng tchr high sch, Frazee Mn 50-51; Asst engnr libn UMinn 52-53; Asst engnr libn UWis(Madison) 53-55; Asst chief libn Chance Vought Aircraft Inc, Dallas Tex 55-57; Supv engnr lib Temco Aircraft Corp, Garland Tex 57-60; Proj manager Lab Libs IBM Data Systems Div, Kingston NY 60-65; Asst dir NASA Sci & Tech Info Facility, Documentation Inc, Bethesda Md 65-68; Sr spec Tech Info Servs Co 68-. 8: AFIPS Info Dissem Com 67-. 9: SLA; ASIS. 13: Yes. 14: Data processing, info retrieval, lib automatio. 15: 12905 Bluet lane, Silver Spring Md.

DURKIN, MARY LUCILE. b Battle Creek Mich 2 Ag 14. 5: UChattanooga 32-35, 43 (Eng & Music) BA; Simmons 35-36 (LS) BS in LS; Columbia 54-55 (Educ Admin & Adult Educ) MA in ED; UMich summer 67, 68 (LS). 6: Fr, Sp. 7: Libn city & county sch systems, Chattanooga Tenn 36-3; Field libn Hamilton County sch system, Chattanooga Tenn 38-41; Dist supv WPA Statewide Lib Program, Chattanooga Tenn 41-42; Supv sch libs City Dept of Educ, Chattanooga Tenn 42-44; Club dir Amer Red Cross, Euroe 44-45; Reg dir Tenn State Lib Program, Jackson Tenn 47-48; Dir USIA Libs, Cairo, Morocco, Greece 48-58; Chief Libn US Army Aviation Sch Lib, FORT Rucker Ala 59-. 8: Wrote 4 bks with reduced vocabularies for use in USIA programs overseas. 9: SLA (Mil Libns); AEAUSA. 10: AAUW; Federally Employed Women. 14: Admin, regl/co devel. 15: P O Box 94, Ft Rucker Al 36362.

DURNELL, JANE (BILLIE) (BALLARD). b Kokomo Ind 26 Jl 16. 5: State UIowa 34-38 (Eng) BA; UOre 63-68 MLS. 7: Stud lib asst State UIowa Lib (Iowa City) 35-39; Serv rep ill Bell Tele Co, Chicago 39-42; Aviation machinist's mate 2/c USN 42-44; Sec-hostess Westminster House, Eugene Ore 58-62; Lib asst Bur Municipal Res & Serv UOre (Eugene) 62-66; Docs room supv Computing Ctr UOre (Eugene) 66-68; Ref libn UOre Lib (Eugene) 68-. 9: PNLA; OreLA. 14: Ref. 15: 2074 Onyx st, Eugene Or 97403.

DURR, BETTY JEAN. b McRae Ga 30 D 36. 5: Ft Valley State Col 54-59 (Eng) BS; AtlantaU summers 60, 61, 67, 68 MSLS. 6: Fr. 7: Bkmob libn Ocmulgee Reg Lib, Eastman Ga 59-. 9: GTEA (Lib Sect); GaLA. 10: Ladies of Prof Club, McRae Ga. 15: 317 N 3 ave, McRae Ga 31055.

DURRANCE, JOAN (COACHMAN). b Miami Fla 20 Ap 37. 4: Raymond Edward Durrance. 5: UFla 59 UNC 59-60 MSLS. 6: Sp. 7: Asst br libn Shenandoah Br Miami Pub Lib, Miami Fla 60-61, Asst libn Young Moderns Dept 61, Br libn S Miami Lib 61-62; Internat Documents libn UNC(Chapel Hill 63-65). 9: . 10: Phi Kappa Phi. 14: Ref, reader sev. 15: 12051 8th NE, Seattle 98125.

DURRANCE, RAYMOND E. b W Palm Beach Fla 7 D 36. 4: Joan M Coachman. 5: UFla 59 (Zool) BS; UNC 65 MSLS. 6: Ger. 7: Lab asst UMiami(Miami Fla) 60-62; Bioanalyst SE Fla Tuberculosis osp, Hosp, Fla 62-63; Fisheries-Oceanography Libn UWash 65-68; Planning asst UWash 69-. 8: UOre Lib Mechanization wkshop 68. 9: ALA; PNLA. 10: Beta Phi Mu; Toastmasters; PTA. 14: Sci libnship. 15: 12501 8th NE, Seattle Wa 98125.

DURRANT, RANDOLPH ALLAN III. b Phila Penn 20 Je 36. 5: La Salle 54-58 (Hist) BA; Marquette 60-65 (Slavic Hist) MA; Rutgers 66-68 MLS. 6: Ger. 7: Tchr pub sch syst, Phila 58-59, 64-66; Platoon comdr (1st Lt) USA Artillery 59-61; Lib asst Milwaukee Pub Lib 61-64; Asst catlgr Educ Testing Serv, Princeton NJ 66-68, Catlg libn 68-. 9: Amer Assn for Advancement of Slavic Studies; AHA; Acad of Pol Sci; Amer Acad Pol & soc Sci; NJLA. 10: Ctr for Study of Democratic Inst; ACLU. 13: Yes. 14: Catlg, ref, rare bks, maps. 15: Brookwood Gardens apt 908 Hickory Corner rd, Hightstown NJ 08520.

DURSO, ANGELINE M. b Ohio 23 D 21. 5: Ohio Dominican Col 44-47 (Bio sci, Nursing) BS; Case-West Res 55-56 (Admin in Schs of Nursing) MS, 66-67 (LS) MS. 6: Fr, Sp, Ital. 7: Sci instr Mercy Hosp Sch of Nursing, Canton Ohio 47-49; St John Col, Cleveland Ohio: Sci nursing instr 49-51, Med surg nursing instr 56-61, Pediatrics nursing instr 61-66; Surgical nursing instr St Luke Hosp, Cleveland Ohio 52-55; Cleveland Pub Lib; Pre-prof asst summers 61-66, Lib trainee 66-67; Libn Life sci research lib UNotre Dame, Ind 67-. 9: ALA; MedLA; SLA; ASIS; IndLA. 10: AAUP; AAUW; Beta Phi Mu; Coun for the Retarded of St Joseph Co; L'Alliance Francaise de South Bend. 14: Ref, admin (biol scis). 15: 407 S 26th st, South Bend In 46615.

DURY, MURIEL (GOLDMAN). b NY 20 D 16. 4: Abraham Dury. 5: Brooklyn Col 33-37 (Biol) BA; Columbia 39-40 (Pub Health Engnr); Carnegie 61-62 (LS); U Pittsburgh 62-63 MLS. 6: Ger, Fr. 7: Fellowship Biol Dept Brooklyn Col 37-40; Assoc biochem Dorn Lab for Med Research, Bradford Penn 53-59; Fellow Falk Med Lib, Pittsburgh Pa 62-63; Ref libn NLM, Bethesda Md 63-. 9: MedLA. 10: Beta Phi mu. 14: Ref, automation, info retrieval. 15: 5510 Cornish rd, Bethesda Md 20014.

DUSTIN, MURIEL (ROSSMAN). b Canal Zone Panama 9 Ag 43. 4: William K Dustin. 5: Gettysburg Col 61-65 (Pol Sci) BA; Syracuse 66-68 MSLS. 7: Analyst Defense Dept, Ft Meade Md 65-66; PHS Trainee WashU Sch of Med Lib (St Louis) 68-. 9: ALA; MedLA. 10: Beta Phi Mu. 15: 6605 Clayton ave, St Louis Mo 63139.

DUTELLE, THOMAS E. b Peterboro Can 30 Je 19. 4: Anne Kaufmann. 5: Brooklyn Col 38-41 (Hist); NYU 46 (Fr) BA; Columbia 47-48 (LS) BS, 50-51 (Anthropology) MA. 6: Fr. 7: Jr libn circ dept Yonkers Pub Lib, Yonkers NY 48-49, Head ref dept 49-55; Dir East Meadow Pub Lib, East Meadow NY 55-. 9: ALA; NYLA; Nassau County LA (pres 57-59). 10: Rotary Club. 14: Admin, personnel, bldgs. 15: East Meadow Pub Lib, East Meadow NY 11554.

DUTKA, JUNE (DOROTHY). b Winnipeg Manitoba Can 7 Je 43. 5: UManitoba 61-64 (Eng) BA; UBC 65-66 BLS. 6: Ukrainian, Fr. 7: Lib asst (boys & girls dept) St James Pub Lib, Winnipeg Manitoba Can 64-65; Ref libn UManitoba Elizabeth Dafoe Lib 66-68; Docs libn UManot UManitoba 69-. 9: CanLA; ManLA (memb chm). 14: Ref, govt docs. 15: 728 Pritchard ave, Winnipeg 4 Manitoba Can.

DUTKA, OREST JAROSLAV. b Matyivci Ukraine 16 O 23. 5: Ludwig-Maximilian U(Munich Germany) 45-49 (Forestry) Dipl Forst; NC State Col 52-53 (Forestry) BFM; Rutgers 54-56 MLS. 6: Ukrainian, Ger, Polish, Russian. 7: Queens Borough Pub Lib, Jamaica NY 56-57, Asst br libn 58-59, Br libn 60-62, Asst reg libn 63, Head art & music div of central lib 64-68; Asst libn Central 68-. 15: 42-25 80th st, Elmhurst NY 11373.

DUTTON, JOHN (EDGAR). b Leithbridge Alberta Can 30 Ag 24. 4: Helen Stapley. 5: UAlberta 46-50 (Hist) BA; UToronto 50-51 BLS. 6: Fr. 7: Cpl RCAF Wireless mechanic 43-46; Jr Libn UAlta 51-53; Chief Libn Lethbridge Pub Lib (Leithbridge) 53-63; Chief Libn N York Pub Lib, Willowdale 63-. 9: CanLA; OntLA (pres 69-70). 14: Pub rel, admin. 15: 5126 Yonge st, Willowdale Ont Can.

DUTTON, LEE SUMMERS JR. b Cincinnati Ohio 23 F 41. 5: MiamiU 60-64 (Pol Sci) BA; UHawaii 64-67 (Asian Studies) MA; UMich 67-68 MALS. 6: Fr, Indonesian, Japanese. 7: SE Asia libn Parson Lib NoIllU 69-. 9: ALA; Assn for Asian Studies. 14: Bibliog, ref. 15: Southeast Asia Collection Parson Lib Northern Ill Univ, DeKalb Il 60115.

DUTTON, LELAND SUMMERS. b Lorain Ohio 9 Mr 05. 4: Ruth Clitty. 5: Miami U(Oxford Ohio) 25-29 (Hist) BA; Columbia 31-32 BSLS, summer 39 (Advanced Ref). 6: Ger. 7: Loan desk asst Miami U Lib 29-31; Asst genealogy div NY Pub Lib 31-34; Miami U Lib(Oxford Ohio): Loan libn 34-38, Ref libn 38-56, Act dir of libs 56-57, Dir of Libs 57-. 9: ALA-ACRL; OhioLA (pres 40-41); Ohio Col Assn (sec-treas Col Lib Sect). 10: Deacon & Elder, Presby Church. 13: Yes. 14: Ref, bibliog. 15: 350 Patterson ave, Oxford Ohio 45056.

DUVA, ALICE M. b Pittsburgh 1 My 14. 4: Charles Duva. 7: Nursing libn Jackson Mem Hosp, Miami Fla 58-63; Med libn Halifax Dist Hosp, Daytona Beach Fla 63-. 8: Revision of Poison Control Center 65; mem tchg fac ICCU classes, Halifax Dist Hosp. 9: MedLA; Reg Conf Fla Med Libns. 10: Amer Heart Assn; Canaveral Heart Assn. 14: Catlg, med lib wk. 15: 1215 Volusia ave, Daytona Beach Fla 32014.

DUVALL, BETTY. b Dade County Mo 29 N 39. 4: Richard Duvall. 5: Southwest Mo State 57-60 (Speech) BS in Educ; UMo summer 61 (Journalism); UDenver summers 64, 65 (LS); St Louis U 65 (Speech). 7: Libn Wash (Mo) High Sch 60-61; Libn McClure High Sch, Ferguson Mo 62; Asst libn Florissant Valley Community Col, Jr Col Dist, St Louis 63-; Instrl Resources, St Louis 63-. 8: Consul exam N Central Assn of Cols & Univs. 9: ALA-ACRL (Instr/use Com); MoLA; Mo Assn Jr Cols (chm Lib Div). 10: Alpha Psi Omega; Hawthorne Players. 11: Fellowship "Wall Street Journal" 61. 13: Yes. 14: Admin, educ. 15: Foorissant Valley Commun Col, 3400 Pershall rd, St Louis Mo 63135.

DUVALL, ELIZABETH SEDGWICK. b Wash DC 31 Mr 03. 5: UMd 21-25 (Eng) AB; Columbia 29-30 BS in LS. 6: Fr. 7: Tchr Hyattsville High Sch, Hyattsville Md 25-28; Asst DC Pub Lib 28-29, Readers adv 30-39, 41-51; Ed H W Wilson Co, NYC 40-41; Catlgr Forbes Lib, Northampton Mass 51-57; Bibliogr Sophia Smith Collection Smith Col Lib 57-59; Curator 60-69, Consul 69-. 8: Tchr of lib sci, UNH, summers 54-57, UConn Contg Educ 67-69. 9: NELA; MassLA. 12: Subject Ed of 1941 Ed of "Fiction Catalog; Ed series unpub mss in Sophia Smith Collection, 63-69. 14: . 15: 222 Elm st, Northampton Mass 01060.

DWORKIN, RITA (SOKOLOV). b Brooklyn NY 28 D 28. 4: Paul Dworkin. 5: UCLA 46-47; Brooklyn Col 47-49 (Eng) BA; C W Post Col 61-64 (LS) MS. 7: Clerk-typist Pace Col 49-50; Receptionist-typist Associated Hosp Serv of NY 50-51; Trainee E Meadow Pub Lib, E Meadow LI NY 63-64, Asst ref libn 64-67; Adult serv libn 67-. 10: PTA. 12: "Modern Drama: a Checklist of Critical Literature on 20th Century Plays" (67). 14: Ref. 15: 12 McLane dr, Dix Hills NY 11746.

DWYRE, KATHERINE CLAIRE. b Canaan NH 2 Jl 09. 5: UNH 26-30 (Eng) AB; Simmons 30-31 (LS) BS. 7: Asst catlgr Penn State Col 31-34, Order libn 34-44; Asst accession libn Ohio State U 44-47; Acquis libn WVa U, Morgantown W Va 47-55; Head processing dept Worcester Pub Lib, Worcester Mass 55-62, Asst libn, Processing & personnel 62-. 9: ALA; MassLA; NELA; NE Tech Serv Libns (corr sec 65-67. 15: Pub Lib Salem Square, Worcester Mass 01608.

DYAR, MARY LESLIE. b DeSmet SD 17 My 14. 5: Carleton Col 32-36 (Zool) BA; UMinn 37-38 BS in LS. 7: Prof asst Minneapolis Pub Lib 38-45, Spec asst personnel 45-48; Libn Minneapolis Athenaeum 48-54; Admin asst personnel Minneapolis Pub Lib 55-59, Personnel off 59-, Admin off 66-67, Assoc dir 68-. 9: ALA (Life mem); (chm Personnel Admin Sect 67-68); MinnLA (sec 50-56). 10: Minneapolis Pub Lib Staff Assn; UMinn Lib Sch Alumni Assn; 14: Personnel admin, pub libs. 15: 89 Walden, Burnsville Mn 55378.

DYBDAHL, RUSSELL E. b Chicago Ill 27 Ag 14. 5: Union Col (Lincoln Neb) 32-37 (Hist) BA; UNeb summer 39; USDak 46-47 (Hist) MA; Augustana Col spring 49; State UIowa 50-54 (Pol Sci). 7: Prin: Lakeland High Sch, Ainsworth Neb 37-38, 39-41, Cottonwood High Sch, Koshopah Neb 38-39; Depot supply off & co cmdr USA, QMC, US & Europe 41-46; Tchr valentine High Sch, Valentine Neb 46; Prin Donnybrook High Sch, Donnybrook N Dak 47-48; Salesman Merit Stores & Johnson Hdwe, Sioux Falls S Dak 48-50; Libn IV (docs) State UIowa (Iowa City) 53-56; Docs libn (MUW) WichitaU 56-62, Docs & hist libn 62-. 8: Mem Kan Higher Educ Facilities Commsn's Lib Survey Com 65; Wichita State Curriculum Com 65-68; Wichita StateU Faculty Violations Appeals Com 67-69; Wichita StateU Senate 67-69. 9: KanLA (mem Exec Com 65; mem NLW Steering Com 65-69; sec Spec Libs Sect 62-63; V-chm 63-64; chm 64-65). 10: Knights of 72; USDak Grad Club; Phi Sigma Alpha. 14: US Govt docs, soc sci ref. 15: 2319 N Yale, Wichita Ks 67220.

DYCK, LINDA GAIL (STANLEY). b Edinburg Tex 4 Je 44. 4: Raymond Lee Dyck. 5: Sch of the Ozarks Jr Col 62-64 (Eng) AA; UMo 64-66 (Animal Husbandry) BS; Rutgers 67-68 MLS. 7: Stud libn Sch of the Ozarks Lib 59-61, Clerical off girl newspaper off 61-64; Stud libn UMo Lib (Columbia) 64; Housewkr private home, Columbia Mo 64-65; Research libn UMO Entomology Dept & Biological Control Lab of ARS-USDA (Columbia) 65-67; Research libn UArk Entomology Dept 67; Asst libn Smith, Miller & Patch, New Brunswick NJ 68-. 10: Gamma Sigma Delta; Rutgers Grad Sch of Lib Sci Alumni Assn. 14: Ref. 15: 261 Redmond st, New Brunswick NJ 08901.

DYE, SANDRA JEAN. b Omaha 18 Je 38. 5: Colorado Col 57-61 (Zool) BA; UCal (Berkely) 61-63 MLS. 6: Fr, Ger. 7: Res bks Colroado Col 58-61; Libn Nat Park Serv, Yosemite Nat Park summers 62-63; Ref San Rafael City Lib, San Rafael Cal 62-63; Catlgr UWash 64-. 9: ALA; SLA; PNLA. 10: Nat Parks Assn; UCal Lib Sci Alum Assn. 14: Nat hist, zool, med. 15: 2310 NE 48th, Apt 704, Seattle 98105.

DYER, JEAN E (HAWK). b Allentown Penn 8 F 28. 4: Pamer E Dyer. 5: Kutztown State Col 45-48 (LS) BS in Ed; Penn State Col 49, Temple U 68, 69. 6: Sp. 7: Libn Sunbury High Sch, Sunbury Penn 48-52; Libn Greenwood High Sch, Millerstown Penn 56-57; Catlgr Bucks Co Free Lib, Doylestown Penn 58-60; Libn Pennridge High Sch, Perkasie Penn 60-. 9: NEA; PennStateEA; Bucks Co (Penn) LA, BucksCoSchLA (v-pres). 15: 102 Walnut st, Sellersville Pa 18960.

DYER, MARY MARGARET. b Sioux City Iowa. 5: Briar Cliff Col 30-32 (Eng); Morningside Col 32-36 (Eng, Hist) BA; UIll 40 BLS; UDenver summer 46. 6: Sp. 7: Ref dept pub lib, Sioux City Iowa 40-43; Adult lib dept Kean Co Free Lib, Bakersfield 43-44; Children's lib Santa Monica Pub Lib, Santa Monica 44-. 9: ALA; (many State Committees, Standard Committee); CalLA (pres Child & YA Sect, mem var coms).

10: (Altrusa Internat); Hon life mem PTA. 14: Child wk. 15: Santa Monica Pub Lib, Santa Monica Ca 90401.

DYESS, DESSIE MAE (VOTAW). b Smithville Tex 3 O 23. 4: Stewart Wood Dyess. 5: UTex 41-44 (Eng); N Tex StateU 44-45 (LS) BS; E Tex StateU 65-66 (LS) MS in LS. 6: Sp. 7: Hd libn Austin Presbyterian Theol Sem 54; Catlgr & asst ref & libn Tex State lib, Austin Tex 54-63; Ser catlgr Dallas Pub Lib, Dallas Tex 64-68; Hd catlg dept W Tex StateU 68-. 9: TexLA; SWLA; Friends of Tex Libs. 10: Austin Lib Club. 14: Catlg. 15: 500 Holman lane, Canyon Tx 79015.

DYESS, STEWART W. b Holland Tex 25 D 33. 4: Dessie Mae (Votaw) Dyess. 5: St Edwards U 52-54 (Econ); UTex 54 (Govt, Econ); E Tex State U 65 (Govt, LS) BS, 65-66 MS in LS. 7: Lib & licensing wkr Tex Dept Pub Welfare, Dallas 62; Hd libn N Br Lib, Ft Worth 66; Asst to the libn W Tex State U Lib 68-. 9: ALA; SWLA; TexLA (Memb Chm Dist 1 #68-69). 10: Friends of Tex Libs; Senate Club; Dallas Tex. 14: Admin. 15: 500 Holman lane, Canyon Tx 79015.

DYGERT, MICHAEL HOWARD. b Burlington Vt 15 N 38. 4: Joan Sylvester. 5: Worcester Jr Col 57-59 (Lib arts) AA; Northeastern U 59-62 (Hist) AB; URI 64-66 MLS. 7: Lib aid Boston Pub Lib 60; Lib asst Northeastern U Lib 60-62; Tchr Greenville Pub Schs, Greenville NH 62-63; Ref asst & br libn Malden Pub Lib, Malden Mass 63-65; Ref libn catlgr Saugus Pub Lib, Saugus Mass 65-67; Dir Winthrop Pub Lib, Winthrop Mass 67-. 8: Consul URI Lib 66. 9: ALA; NELA; MemLA (treas Pub Lib Adminrs Sect 68-69); Greater Boston Pub Lib Adminrs. 10: N Shore Lib Club. 13: Yes. 14: Ref, admin, pub rel. 15: Winthrop Pub Lib, Winthrop Ma 02152.

DYKE, MARGARET KATHLEEN (GORDON). b Toronto 24 My 33. 4: Chesley R Dyke. 5: UToronto 52-56 (Fr, Ger) BA, 56-57 BLS. 6: Fr. 7: York Pub Lib, Toronto: Bkmob Libn 57-58, Asst Br Libn 59-61, Catlgr 61-64, Hd Tech Serv 64-. 9: CanLA; OntLA (chm of Ont Lib Rev Adv Com 67-68). 14: Catlg. 15: 2 Bloomington Crescent, Downsview Ont Can.

DYKES, ELIZABETH (PANKRATZ). b Cordell Okla 20 O 10. 4: J Harvey Dykes. 5: Okla State U 56 (Humanities) BA; Tex Woman's U 68 MLS. 6: Ger. 7: Instr Okla State U 56-57; Ref libn Okla Christian Col 62-66; Ref libn Harding Col 67-. 9: ALA; SWLA; ArkLA. 10: Beta Phi Mu; AAUW. 14: Ref. 15: Harding College Box 612, Searcy Ar 72143.

DYKSTRA, STEPHANIE (MacGREGOR-GREER). b London 1 Je 40. 4: Aldert Dykstra. 5: Carleton U Ottawa (Eng) BA; McGill 62-63 BLS. 6: Fr. 7: Ref libn Redpath Lib McGill U 63-65; Interlib loans Can Dept of Agric, Ottawa 65-67; Asst ref libn 67-. 10: Film Soc; Profess Inst Pub Serv. 14: Ref. interlib loans. 15: 227A First ave, Apt 3, Ottawa 1 Can.

DYMENT, ALAN REGINALD. b London England 21 Ja 42. 5: Kingston Tech Col, Croydon Tech col, Ealing Tech Col 58-64 British ALA. 6: Fr. 7: Lib asst Sutton & Cheam Pub Libs 58-62; Film lib asst BBC 62-64; Br libn Surrey Co Lib Serv 64-66; Catlgr Coop Bk Centre of Can 66-68; Asst libn Centennial Col 68-. 10: Sutton Film Soc. 13: Yes. 14: A-v & other non-book materials. 15: 544, Birchmont rd apt 910, Scarborough Ont Can.

DYSINGER, ROBERT EDWIN. b Owls Head Me 30 Je 24. 4: Helen athaway. 5: Bowoin 4-42, 45-46 (Hist) AB; UMich 48-49 (Eng) MA; U of State of NY 54-55 MS in LS. 7: (T/Sgt) USAAF 43-45; Ref libn Colby Col Lib 55-57; Asst libn Bowdoin Col 57-60; Libn Alton Lib So Ill, Alton Ill 61-62; Sr catlgr UNH Lib (Durham) 62-64, Br libn 64-69; Libn St Mary's U Halifax NS 69-. 8: Tchr of ref Colby Col 55-57; Tchr, catlg & ref UNH 63-69. 10: AAUP. 13: Yes. 14: Admin, tech processes, ref. 15: Lib St Mary's U, Halifax NS Can.

DYSON, ALLAN JUDGE. b Lawrence Mass 28 Mr 42. 4: H Judith Weinstein Dyson. 5: Harvard 60-64 (Govt) BA; Simmons 66-68 (LS) MS. 7: Chief admin serv off (1st Lt) USA, Watertown Arsenal Mass 64-66; Grad asst Simmons Col Lib 66-68; Asst to dir Columbia U Libs 68-. 9: ALA. 14: Admin. 15: 39 Claremont ave, New York NY 10027.

DYSON, ANNE JANE (HOLTON). b Amite La 5 Mr 12. 4: Harold F Dyson. 5: LSU 29-34 (Eng) AB, 34-35 BS in LS. 7: Gen asst LSU 35-37, 1st asst ref dept 37-42, Chief ref libn 42-45, Sr ref libn interlib loans 45-62, Asst libn humanities div 62-. 9: ALA; LaLA. 10: Baton Rouge Little Theatre; AAUW. 12: Comp, with H H Palmer; american Drama Criticism (67), "European Drama Criticism (68). 14: Ref. 15: 7575 Jefferson Highway, Baton Rouge La 70806.

DZIURA, WALTER T. b New Bedford Mass 11 N 30. 5: Boston U 48-52 (Eng) BA; Simmons 52-53 (LS) MS. 6: Polish. 7: US Army 53-55; Research asst Bibliog of American Literature Harvard U 55-58; Dir Hingham Pub Lib, Hingham Mass 58-. 8: Lecturer, Lit of the Humanities, Simmons 62-. 9: MassLA; Old Colony Lib Assn; Greater Boston Pub Lib Admins. 12: Ed bulletin of Bibliography and Magazine Notes (64-). 14: Admin. 15: 143 Ft Hill st, Hingham Ma 02043.

DYSON, (SAM) SAMUEL ARCHER. b Shreveport La 3 S 28. 4: June Wallace. 5: Tulane U 45-46 (Pre-Med); Northwestern State Col 47-50 (Biol) BS; Southwestern Baptist Theol Sem 50-52 9homiletics); N Tex State U 51-52 (LS); LSU 52-53 (LS) MS. 6: Ger, Hebrew, Fr, Gk. 7: Midshipman US Navy Air Corps, Pensacola Fla 48; Stud asst in Lib Northwestern State Col, Southwestern Baptist Theol Sem, & LSU 47-51, 52-53; Head Libn Assoc Prof of Libnship La Col 53-60; Assoc libn, Assoc Prof La Polytech Inst 60-66; Dir of libs, Assoc Prof 66-. 8: Pastor of Angola Mission, La State Penitentiary 54-58; Pastor New Sunrise Baptist Church, Otis La 58-59; Chaplain at La State Indl Sch for Girls, Pineville La 59-60; Pastor of First Baptist Church, Vienna La 60-63; Pastor, Corinth Baptist Church, Dubach La 67-. 9: ALA; LaLA (chm Col & Ref Sect 58-61 & 64-65, chm Convention Commercial Exhib Com 56, chm Legis Com 57-61, Recr Com 60-63, Rep to SWLA 61-63, La Col Conf, chm Lib Sect 57-58 & 63-64; Parliamentarian, chm 63-64, chm Aud Com 65-67; 2nd v-pres, 67-68; chm Finance Sub-com of Col & Ref Sect Study Com 68-69. 10: Lions Club; YWCA; Boy Scouts of America; Nat Rifle Assn; Civil Air Patrol; CB Radio. 13: Yes. 14: Admin, pub serv, automation. 15: 2 Westwood Hills, Ruston La 71270.

DZMURA, ELIZABETH A. b Pittsburgh 27 Ap 17. 5: Seton Hill Col 34-38 (Sociol) BA; UPittsburgh 63-65 MLS. 6: Fr. 7: Quartermaster Corps USMC Womens Reserve (Cpl) 44-45; Sec-stenog US Steel Corp, Pittsburgh 46-47, Sec 48-52; Sec Pittsburgh Outdoor Advertising Co, Pittsburgh 53; Sec Union Switch & Signal Div Westinghouse Air Brake Co 53-64; Lib asst UPittsburgh 64-65; Acquis libn Hunt Lib Carnegie Inst of Tech 65-. 67; Asst catlgr 67-. 9: ALA; ACRL Tri-State Chap. 10: Bus & Prof Womens Club, AAUW; Beta Phi Mu. 14: Catlg, acquis. 15: 1212 Macon st, Pittsburgh 15218.

DZURINKO, MARY K. b N Charleroi Penn 21 O 43. 5: Cal State Col (California Penn) 62-65 (Ger) BA; Rosary Col 67-69 MALS. 6: Ger, Lat. 7: Tchr: St Philip Grade Sch, Donora Penn 65-66, Bishop Kenny High Sch, Jacksonville Fla 66-67; Grad asst Rosary Col Lib 67-. 9: ALA. 10: Kappa Delta Pi. 14: Catlg, acquis. 15: 574 Sixth st, N Charleroi Pa 15022.

E

EAGER, NANCY (WALTON). b Bellingham Wash 18 S 37. 4: Donald R Eager. 5: Westmont Col 55-59 (Eng Lit) AB; UCal (Berkeley) 63-64 MLS. 7: Sec Tech Mil Planning Operation, Santa Barbara Cal 59-60; Engnr asst Cal Advanced Propulsion Systems, San Ramon Cal 60-61; Sec Thompson-Ramo-Wooldridge, Sierra Vista Ariz 61-63; Child libn Hayward Pub Lib, Hayward Cal 64-. 9: ALA. 14: Child wk. 15: 1519 Riegerave, Hayward Ca 94544.

EAGLE, OPAL (COLE). b Vermillion Grove Ill. 4: I Orval Eagle. 5: DePauw U 22-26 (Eng Lit) AB; St Louis lib Sch 30-31 Lib Certif. 6: Fr. 7 Tchr Madison High Sch, Madison Ind 27-29; Asst child libn Travel Libs St Louis Pub Lib 31-32, Asst child libn Divoll Br 32-36, Asst child libn Carondelet Br 36, Child libn Gravois Br 37-53, Chief ya dept 53-58, Coordinator of ya serv 58-. 8: Lecturer on ya wk in libs at Inst, Mo U, 60; Adv Com of Mo for White House Conf on Child & Youth, 60; Adv Com for survey of Mo pu libs, 62; Chm Nat Lib Week 59-62. Lect on YA wk at Washington U 53-; Leader of wkshops on YA wk Ill State Lib &Mo State Lib 68. 9: ALA (Coun-at-Large 57-61, Coun 65-66, Reg Chm Memb Com 62-64)-YASD (dir 56-62, pres 65-66); MoLA (Chm Child Libns Sect 49). 10: Bus & Prof Womens Club; Soroptimist Club; AAUW. 11364 07: Eng tchr Madison High Sch, Madison Ind 27-29; Asst child libn Travel Libs Stlouis Pub Lib 31-32, Asst child libn Divoll Br 32-36, Asst child libn Carondelet Br36, Child libn Gravois Br 37-53, Chief ya dept 53-58, Coordinator of ya serv 58-. 13: Yes 14: Child & ya serv. 15: 4058 Magnolia pl, St Louis Mo 63110.

EAGLEY, MONA (MARGUERITE). b Merrickville Ont Can 10 Ap 05. 5: Queens U summers (Eng) BA; Ottawa U BLS; Ontario Col of Educ Perm High Sch Assts Certif; Spec in Sch Libnship (Ont), Spec in Art (Ont). 7: Eng tchr St Carleton Dist

High Sch; Tchr-libnFisher Park High Sch & Laurentian High Sch Ottawa Ont 51-61; Libn CedarbraeCollegiate Inst, Scarborough Ont 61-65; Lecturer Sch Libnship Col of Educ UToronto65-67; Asst supt curriculum & sch libs Ont Dept of Educ 67-68. 9: CanLA; ALA;OntLA; OntEA. 10: Art Gallery of Toronto; Royal Commonwealth Soc. 11: CentennialMedal (Can) 67. 13: Yes. 14: Sch libnship, bk reviewing. 15: 112 Ruscica dr, Toronto 16 Can.

EAGON, CARRIE (WILSON). b Chattanooga Tenn 19 Ag 20. 4: Bruce D Eagon. 5: UTulsa 39-42 (Liberal Arts) BA; LSU summers 46, 47, 49, 50 (Scis) BLS. 7: Lib asst Tulsa PubLib, Tulsa Okla 42-43; Prod & planning libn Douglas Aircraft, Tulsa Okla 43; Circlibn UTulsa 45-50; Libn Jersey Prod Rsch Co, Tulsa Okla 55-64; Chief Libn Esso Prod Research Co, Houston 65-. 8: Records Mgt Study 69. 9: ACS (Lit Div); SLA (chm Petrol Sect 62, Nat Recr Com 63-65 & 68-70; Okla Chap Consul Com chm 58-64, Dir 60-64, v-pres & program chm 61-62, pres 62-63, Liaison off 64-65; Tex Chap, chm Consul Com 65); Houston Lib Club (pres 70); Geo Sci Info Soc. 10: Arithritic Assn; Hemophilia Assn. 11: SLA John CottonDana Lecture; UDenver 69. 13: Yes. 14: Ref, admin. 15: 3120 Buffalo Speedway, Houston Tx 77001.

EAKIN, LAURABELLE. b New Castle Penn. 5: Grove City Col 34-38 (Eng) AB; West Res U 42-46 BSLS. 7: Sch libn Verona Sch Dist, Verona Penn 41-44; Sch libn E Dear Sch Dist, Creighton Penn 44-49; Med libn VA Hosp, Aspinwall Penn 49-50; Chief libn VA Hosp, Pittsburgh Penn 50-57; Ref libn Falk Lib Sch Health Prof UPittsburgh 58-. 8: Instr, Course in Med Libnship, UPittsburgh Grad Sch of Lib & Info Sci 68-69. 9: MedLA; SLA. 10: AAUW; ACLU. 12: "Good Books for Children (59, rev ed 62, 3d ed 66); "Subject Index to Books for Intermediate Grades (ed ed 63); "Subject Index to Books for Primary Grades, with Eleanor Merritt (2d ed 61; 3d ed 66); Co-comp "A Bibliography of the History of Rheumatic Diseases, 1940-1960. 13: Yes. 14: Ref. 15: 5300 Fifth ave apt B1, Pittsburgh Pa 15232.

EAMES,ROBERT W(ALLACE). b Canastota NY 21 My 28. 5: Hartwick Col 48-50, 51-53 (Eng)BA; Columbia 53-54 (LS) MS. 7: US Army (Sgt) 46-48, 50-51; Rochester Pub Lib, Rochester NY: Asst lit & biog div 54-56, Asst art div 56-58, Act head gen ref div 59-60, Head info serv div 61-. 8: Staff, Lib/USA, NY Worlds Fair, 64. 9: ALA; NYLA. 10: ACLU. 14: Ref. 15: 5 Arnold Park, Rochester NY 14607.

EARLE, ELINOR S. b Union City Ind 24 Mr 21. 5: UKy 38-42 (Eng) AB; Ohio State U 46 (Eng) MA; UIll 46-47 BS in LS. 6: Fr. 7: Aer Mate 2/c US Women's Nav Reserve 44-45; Ref asst Lincoln Lib, SpringfieldIll 47-48; Asst in ref Akron Pub Lib, Akron Ohio 48-51, Head gen ref 51-57; Baselibn USAF, Phalsbourg France 57-59; Asst in ref Akron Pub Lib, Akron Ohio 59-61, Brlibn Kenmore Br 61-. 9: ALA; OhiLA. 10: AAUW; DAR; DAC; Prof & Bus Women; Phi Beta Kappa. 13: Yes. 14: Ref, adult reading adv. 15: 77 Fir Hill, apt 5B11, Akron Oh 44304.

EARLE, MARY ELIZABETH. b Mattoon Ill 19 O 14. 5: UKy 32-36 (LS) AB; UIll 42 BS in LS. 6: Fr. 7: Tchr-libn Kings Mountain High Sch, Kings Mountain Ky 36-37; Libn Pikeville Col 37-40; Ref libn Lib Ext Div, Frankfort Ky 40-43; Hosp libn Darnall Gen Hosp, Danville Ky 43-44; Ext libn Lib Ext Div, Frankfort Ky 44-45; Libn John McIntire Pub Lib, Zanesville Ohio 45-48; Head order catlg dept Lima Pub Lib, Lima Ohio 48-53; Head tech processes Akron Pub Lib, Akron Ohio 53-. 9: ALA; OhioLA; No Ohio Tech Serv Libns. 10: Ohiana Lib Assn; AltrusaInternat; DAR; DAC; UDC; Huguenot Soc of Ohio. 14: Tech serv, ref. 15: 77 Fir Hill,apt 5B11, Akron Oh 44304.

EARLEY, ELLEN (MACK). b Carthage Ill 25 O 15. 4: George E Earley. 5: Carthage Col 33-37 (Eng) AB; UMich 37-38 ABLS. 7: Asst Earlham Col Lib 38-42; Asst in educ dept Newark Free Lib, Newark NJ 42-44; 1st asst lending dept E Orange Free Lib, E Orange NJ 44-45; 1st asst Great Neck Lib, Great Neck NY 46-47; Br libn Newton Free Lib, Newton mass 47-54; Lecturer So IllU 61-63; Libn Kemper Hall, Kenosha Wis 68-. 10: League of women Voters; Commun Concerts. 15: 7321 5th ave, Kenosha Wi 53140.

EARLEY, GEORGE E. b Revere Mass 22 S 16. 4: Ellen Mack. 5: Bentley Sch of Accounting (Boston) 35-39 Diploma; Pratt 46-47 BLS; Boston U 47-50 (Hist) BA. 6: Fr. 7: Asst Boston Pub Lib 36-42; US Navy 42-45; Asst NY Publib 46; Ref asst Boston Pub Lib 47-56; Asst lib dir Freeport Mem Lib, NY 56-58; Headlibn Wallace Mem Lib, Hastings Mich 58-59; Head libn Hayner Pub Lib, Alton Ill 59-63;Dir GM Simmons Pub Lib, Kenosha Wis 63-. 9: ALA; WisLA (var coms); Kenosha LA (pres66); SE Wis Reg Lib Conf (chm 69). 10: Rotary. 13: Yes. 14: Admin. 15: 7321 5th ave, KenoshaWi 53140.

EARNSHAW, VIRGINIA (WATSON). b Cameron WVa. 5: Western Col for Women 30-31 (Eng); Ohio State 31-33 (Eng) BS in Ed; WVA U 44 (Ed); Catholic U 53 MS in LS. 7: Eng Tchr Marshall County Schs, Sherrard WVa 34-35, 43-45; Lib asst Dept of State Lib, Wash DC 45-47; Supv of clerical wk Catalog Dept DC Pub Lib 47-5; Catlgr Bureau of Ordnance Lib Navy Dept, Wash DC 53-57; Asst chief Processing Unit & chief catlgr Off of Tech Serv, Wash DC 57-58; Chief tech processing br Fed Aviation Agency Lib, Wash DC 58-66; Hd catlg br Nav Air Systs Command Lib, Wash DC 66-. 8: Act Chief Lib Serv Div Fed Aviation Agency 65-. 9: SLA; DCLA; Potomac Tech Processing Libns. 11: Sustained Superior Performance Award (65). 12: Comp; "SubjectHeadings Used in the Federal Aviation Agency Library System"; Contributor "Classification; Subclass TL, Aeronautics"; "Aviation Subject Headings and Classification Guide," comp with Agnes A. Gautreaux (SLA 66). 14: Tech serv, info retrieval,thesauri. 15: 1602 Abingdon dr, Alexandria Va 22314.

EASON, HELGA HALVORSEN. b Nebraska City Neb 31 Ja 08. 4: Morris Jackson Eason. 5: Ohio Wesleyan U 27 AB; Simmons 29 BS. 7: Circ asst NY Pub Lib 30-39; Br libn Evansville Pub Lib, Evansville Ind 41-45; Ref libn Miami Pub Lib, Miami Fla 47-52, Community rel dept 52-. 8: Bd WTHS-TV (educ V sta). 9: ALA-LAD (dir Pub Rel Sect 63-66, chm Leaflets Com 59-62); -ASD (chm Nat LibWeek 63-66, 2nd v-pres 68-69; FlaLA (chm Pub Lib Sect 58-59, chm Pub Rel Com 64-66& 67-68); Dade County LA (pres 56-57); SELA (chm Pub Rel Com 68). 10: LWV; NatLeague Amer Pen Women; Welfare Planning Coun of Dade Co; C of C; Miami Fin WelfareEmployees Fed Credit Union; City of Miami Pub Lib Staff Assn. 11: John Cotton DanaPublicity Awards 52, 53, 54, 55; Art Directors Club of Greater Miami, Display andindustrial Booklet (art) 54; FLA Fed of Women's Clubs, certificate of merit by Epsilon Sigma Omicron, 63-64; FLA, Nat Lib Week Award, 66. 13: Yes. 14: Adult educ, pub rel. 15: Miami Pub Lib 1 Biscayne blvd, Miami Fla 33132.

EASON, SUE ANN. b Ennis Tex 3 S 40. 5: Jacksonville Bapt Col 58-60 (Educ) AA; E Tex State Col 60-62 BS in LS; E Tex StateU 62-68 MS in LS. 7: Lib coord Corsicana (Tex) Elem Schs 62-63; Libn Collins Jr High Sch, Corsicana Tex 63-68; Asst catlg libn Stephen F Austin State Col 68-. 9: AAUW; TexLA. 14: Child & ya lit, catlg. 15: 214 Carolyn st apt B, Nacogdoches Tx 75961.

EAST, CATHERINE (ROMBACH). b St Louis Mo 04: Robert D East. 5: Rutgers 64-66 (Eng lit) AB; Drexel 66-68 MSLS. 6: Ger. 7: Correspondent Curtis Publishing Co, Phila 56-58; Asst to Ser Libn Drexel Lib 66; Acting Ser Libn Phila Col of Textiles & Sci Lib 66-68; Ref Asst Cherry Hill Pub Lib, Cherry Hill NJ 68; Catlgr Glassboro State Col Lib 69-. 9: ALA. 10: Beta Phi Mu. 14: Ref, catlg. 15: 511 W Evesham ave, Magnolia NJ 08049.

EAST, MONA. b Worthington Ind 22 Ap 20. 5: Chicago 41-44 (Hist); UMich 46-49 (Hist) AB, 49-52 AMLS. 6: Ger, Fr, Ital, Lat. 7: Subprof UChicago Libs 41-45; Jr order libn UMich Lib(Ann Arbor) 45-52, Sr order libn 52-53, Sr bibliog 53-54, ssoc bk sel libn 55-64, Asst head acquis dept & sel off 64-67, Asst head & Sel off tech serv dept 67-. 9: ALA. 14: Bk sel, acquis. 15: PO Box 1688, Ann Arbor Mi48106.

EASTER, RUTH (HILL). b High Point NC 5 Mr 25. 4: Edwin H Easter. 5: Mitchell Jr Col 43-44; Greensboro Col 44-47 (Eng) BA; Emory 47-48, 49 BS in LS. 7: Asst libn Davidson Co Pub Lib, Lexington NC 48-51, 53-56, Catlgr 58-59; Asst libn sch of lib serv lib columbiaU 51-52; Coord child serv Pack Mem Pub Lib, Asheville NC 68-. 10: Delta Kappa Gamma; AGO. 14: Child serv, catlg, ref. 15: 6 Baird lane, Asheville NC 28804.

EASTERLY, AMBROSE. b Tenn 4 Ja 20. 4: Rubye Robinson Easterly. 5: Berea Col 38-42 (Fr) AB; Peabody 48-49 (LS) MA, 50-54 MS in LS; Chicago 54-56 (LS). 6: Fr, Sp. 7: Stud asst Berea Col Lib 39-42; (Pvt to Maj) USMCR 42-45; V D Control Tenn Dept of Pub Health 45-48; Ref asst Peabody Col 48-49; Catlg libn Middle Tenn State Col 49-55; Gifts & exch asst UChicago Lib 55-56; Assoc libn UMo 56-65; Libn Murray State Col 65-67; Dir Lib Serv W R Harper Col 67-. 9: ALA; SELA; TennLA; KyLA; MoLA; IllLA. 10: State Hist Soc of Mo; Phi Kappa Phi. 13: Yes. 14: Admin, lib educ, recr, lib hist. 15: 269 Eggleston, Elmhurst Il 60126.

EASTERLY, JOE A. b Big Sandy Tex 31 My 07. 4: Ruth Pope. 5: E Tex StateU 28-32 (Hist) BA; UTex 32-33 (Hist) MA; Peabody Col 38-40 BS in LS. 6: Fr, Sp, Ger. 7: Prin elem sch, Garland Tex 33-35; Tchr & libn Union Grove High Sch, Gladewater Tex 35p39; Docs & period libn E Tex StateU 39-43, 45-46; Personnel clsf US Army AF, Amarillo Tex 43-45; Engring libn Ordnance Aerophysics Lab, Daingerfield Tex 46-65; Ref & circ libn McMurry Col 65-68, Lib dir 68-. 9: ALA; TexLA; AbileneLA. 10: Phi Beta Kappa. 14: Ref, admin. 15: 1026 Westridge dr, Abilene Tx 79605.

EASTLICK, JOHN TAYLOR. b Norris Mont 28 Ap 12. 5: Ariz State Tchrs Col 34 (Educ, Music, Eng) AB; Colo State Col 39 (Educ) MA; UDenver 40 (LS) BS. 7: Instr Yuma (Ariz) High Sch 34-38; Circ dept Denver Pub Lib 39-40; Libn UWis, Wisconsin High Sch (Madison) 40-42; (Capt) USAAF Instr personnel adj 42-46; Chief Lib Div VA, Denver 46-48; Asst to Malcolm G Wyer Denver Pub Lib 48-51; Libn Denver Pub Lib 51-69; Prof Grad Sch of Libnship, Univ Denver 69-. 8: Consul to Sec of the Army, instr Japanese educs in reorg of Japanese educsystem (Tokyo) 48-49; Lib Bldg Consuls, Glenview Ill 60-; Francis R St John LibConsuls Inc, NYC 65; Adv Com on Curr UDenver Grad Sch of Libnship 56-, & AdjunctProf; var reg lib surveys 60-68. 9: ALA (2nd v-pres 59-60); PLD (pres 56-57); Colo LA; MPLA; Bibliog Center for Research Inc (Rocky Mtn Reg; Recording for the Blnd (Exec Com, Denver Unit). 10: City Club; Adult Educ Coun of Metro Denver; Denver Coun for Educl TV (pres 54-56). 11: Exceptional Serv as Libn of the City & Co of Denver, 55; Mayors Award of Honor, 62; Outstanding Alumnus Award, Colo State Col, 62. 12: Comp "The Sixties and After," ALA-LAD (60);Co-auth; "The Chattanooga Public Library, A Survey (ALA 58); "Pikes Peak Regionaldistrict Library, A Survey," (ALA 67). 13: Yes. 14: Lib bldg construction, equip, furnish, rare bks, conserv, fine printin. 15: U Denver Grad Sch, Denver Co 80210.

EASTON, MYRTLE (HELMS). b Penn 20 O 06. 4: Virgil J Easton. 5: Moravian Col 25-29 (Eng) BA (cum laude); Lehigh 30-35, 57 (Eng); Colu 9eng) BA (cum laude); Lehigh 30-35, 57 (Eng); Columbia summers 30, 31, 34, 35 (Col & Univ libs) BS. 6: Ger, Fr. 7: Stud asst Bethlehem Pub Lib Bethlehem Penn 25-29; Catlg typist LehighU Lib 29-30, Asst circ libn 30-35, Circ libn 35-43; Consul V J Easton Bkbinding Co, Nzareth Penn 46-; Libn Pen Argyl High Sch, Pen Argyl Penn 55-57; Libn Nazareth Area Jr High Sch, Nazareth Penn 57-. 9: NEA; PennEA; NazarethAreaEA; PennLA. 10: Nazareth Sr Woman's Club. 14: Ref, lib instr, recruiting. 15: 459 E Center st, Nazareth Pa 18064.

EASTON, WILLIAM WONCH. b Grand Rapids Mich 23 N 19. 4: BEULAH May Ely Easton. 5: Grand Rapids Jr Col 37-39 (Eng) A; UMich 39-41 (Hist) AB, 49-52 (Geol) MS; Ariz State U 62 (Secondary Educ) Cal Certif UDenver 63-64 (LS) MA. 6: Sp, Fr. 7: (Pvt to 1st Lt) USMC, US & Pacific 42-45; Contractor Smith Easton Smith &Wohlferd, Grand Rapids Mich 46-50; Paleontological field asst Smithsonian Inst,Missouri River 50-52; Geologist Mich Geol Survey, Allegan Mich 52-53; UraniumGeologist US AEC, Grand Junction Colo 53-58; Exploration geol Pan Amer Petroleum,Alta & Alaska 58-60; Field reviewer US Census Bur, Minneapolis 60; ConstructionInspector Comstock & Davis, Minneapolis 60; Soil mechanic Ariz Highway Dept,Safford Ariz 60-62; High sch sci tchr, Carlsbad Cal 62-63; Construction inspectorDresselhaus Engnrs, Oceanside Cal 63; Grad asst Sci Lib UDenver 63-64; Geol libnGeophoto Serv, Denver 64; Map libn Ill State U 64-. 8: Advance man for Geol Conf covering Colo Plateau Consul US NavalOceanographic Lib. 9: Geol Soc Amer; Soc of Vertebrate Paleont; SLA; IllLA; GeoSci Info Soc. 10: Alpha Beta Alpha; Indian Guides; Marine Mem Assn. 11: MeritoriousServ Award, USAFC, 56. 12: "Correlation of Stratigraphy and Vertebrate Faunal Distribution of Continental Oil gocene of North America," 6 reports on geol surveyssponsored by AEC & Pan Amer Petrol; "Automating the Illinois State University Maplibrary". 14: Maps, sci, ref, automation, Colo. 15: 14 McCormick blvd, NormalIl 61761.

EASTTY, JOHN R. b New Rochelle NY 12 Ag 31. 4: Barbara Rizzo. 5: Lycoming Col 49-51 (Hist); Bucknell 53-55 (Hist) BA; Hofstra 55-57 (Educ) MS in Ed; C W Post Col 63-69 mls. 6: Ital. 7: Airman 2nd class USAF 51-52; Tchr: Roosevelt Pub Schs, Roosevelt NY 56-57, NYC Pub Schs 58-59, E Meadow Pub Schs, E Meadow NY 59-63; Libn E Meadow Pub Schs 63-; Libn Plainview-Old Bethpage Pub Lib, Plainview NY 63-. 9: Nassau-SuffolkLA. 14: Ref, reading guidance. 15: 5 Gnarled Oak dr, E Setauket NY 11733.

EATENSON, ERVIN. b Dallas Tex 18 Ap 24. 5: So MethodistU 42-46 (Journalism) BS; Columbia 51-55 (LS) MS. 7: Asst Grad Psych Lib ColumbiaU 49-51, Hd Optometry Lib 51-56; Hd sci tech div San Jose State Col Lib 56-62; Hd commun living dept Dallas Pub Lib, Dallas Tex 62-68; Coord adult serv 68-. 8: Consul Dallas Morning News Lib 67. 9: ALA-ACRL (Bd Dirs 61-62; v-pres Tchrs Educ Sect 61-62); -ASD (Notable Bks Coun Participating Lib 65-67; Notable Bks Coun 68-70; chm 69); TexLA (Publicity Com 64-66); SWLA (Conf Publicity Com 66); DallasCo(Tex)LA (Directory Com 67; Projs Com 68). 10: Dallas Pub Lib Staff Assn; Commun Coun of Greater Dallas (Panel on Aging 64-66); Sigma Delta Chi. 12: Ed Dallas Pub Lib Staff Assn "Outline" (64-). 13: Yes. 14: Adult serv, pub rel. 15: 1954 Commerce st, Dallas Tx 75201.

EATON, ANDREW (JACKSON). b Holley NY 5 Jl 14. 4: Mary Emeline Eaton. 5: Col of Wooster 31-35 (Hist) BA; UMich 35-36 ABLS; Chicago 40-44 (LS) Phd. 6: Fr, Ger. 7: Sr asst hist & travel div Rochester Pub Lib, Rochester NY 36-39; Research asst Grad Lib Sch UChicago42-43; Ref libn Lawrence Col 44-45; Chief ref libn LSU 45-46, Assoc dir of libs 46-53; Dir of Libs Washington U 53-. 8: Faculty Sch of Lib Srv Columbia U summer 47; Sch of Lib Sci UNC summer 52. 9: ALA (Coun 67-71); -ACRL (Exec Bd 52-53, 63-66,67-71, chm U Libs Sec 64-65); MoLA (pres 65-66); ARL (pres 68). 10: AAUP; Phi Beta Kappa. 11: Coun on LibResources Fellowship 69. 13: Yes. 14: Admin, lib coop. 15: Olin Library Washington U, St Louis Mo 63130.

EATON, CASINDANIA PRATT. b Bridgewater Mass 16 F 07. 5: Simmons 25-29 (LS) BS. 6: Fr, Ger. 7: Libn Walpole (Mass) Pub Lib 29-31; Libn Mass State Cancer Hosp, Pondville Mass 30-31; Readers adv Osterhou Free Lib, Wilkes Barre Penn 31-40; NY Pub Lib: Libn 41-42, Asst br libn 42-46, Br libn 46-58, Coordinator Manhattan Brs 58-. 9: ALA; NYLA; NY Lib Club. 14: Admin. 15: 20 W 53 st, New York NY 10019.

EATON, DEBORAH ANN. b Concord NH 6 N 45. 5: Colby Jr Col 63-65 (Liberal Arts) Assoc BA; UDenver 65-67 (Eng) BA, 67-68 (LS) MA. 6: Sp. 7: Stud asst UDenver Lib period 66-67; Libn Bur Sport Fisheries & Wildlife, Denver 68-. 9: ALA; SLA. 14: Ref (bio sci). 15: 2236 S Franklin st, Denver Co 80225.

EATON, ELIZABETH (SHELBY). b Paducah Ky 16 Jl 10. 5: Randolph-Macon 28-29; UKy 29-32 (Math) AB; UIll 45-46 BLS; Chicago 50-53 (LS) MA. 6: Fr. 7: Deputy collector US Internal Revenue, Louisville Ky 33-40; Chief clerk US Surgeon Generals Off, Fort Knox Ky 40-45; Asst libn US VA, Hines Ill 46-54; Lib dir Mead Johnson Res Center, Evansville Ind 54-62; Asst libn Health Center UFla 62-. 8: Lib consul Alachua Gen Hosp, Gainesville Fla 62-. 9: SLA (chm Pharmaceut Sect 64-65, Bus manager "Unlisted Drugs" 59-62); MedLA(Publ Com 62-65); ACS (lit sect). 10: Beta Phi Mu; Pi Mu Epsilon; Phi Mu; Kappa Delta; PEO. 13: Yes. 14: Ref. 15: 1020 South West Third ave, Gainesville Fl32601.

EATON, JEANNINE (TODD). b Ellisville Miss 18 F 31. 4: Henry J Eaton. 5: Miss State Col for Women 48-52 (LS) BS; UMiss 65; USo Miss 66; Miss State U 69. 7: Libn Leland High Sch, Leland Miss 52-53; Asst Libn Lee Co Lib, Tupelo Miss 53-55; Staff Pub Lib, Memphis Tenn 55-58; Tchr Memphis City Schs, Memphis Tenn 58-60; Libn Whitten Jr High Sch, Jackson Miss 61-65; Libn Provine High Sch, Jackson Miss 65-. 9: ALA; -AASchL; NEA; MissLA; MissASchL; MissEA. 15: 3448 Janet st, Jackson Ms 39208.

EATON, NANCY RUTH (LINTON). b Berkeley Cal 2 My 43. 4: Stanford 61-65 (Eng Lit) AB; UTex (Austin) 66-68 MLS. 6: Ger. 7: Catlgr (libn I) UTex Lib (Austin) 68-. 9: ALA; TexLA. 13: Yes. 14: Catlg. 15: 2207B W 12th st, austin Tx 78703.

EATON, ORVILLE L. b Thayer Kan 15 Jl 12. 4: Alta Moynihan. 5: Kan State Col (Pittsburg) 30-38 (Eng) BS, 38-40 (Eng) MA; UKan 40-46 (Educ,Eng) Phd; Chicago 46-48 BLS. 6: Fr, Ger. 7: Elem tchr, Kan 30-35; Eng tchr Joplin Pub Schs, Joplin Mo 38-40; Instr UKan 40-42; Ed & writer Command & Staff Sch, Ft Leavenworth Kan 43-46; Dir of Libs UKan City 46-50; Libn, Head Lib Sci Kan State Tchrs Col (Emporia) 50-58, Grad chm 53-58; Chm Dept of Lib Central Mich U 58-. 9: ALA-ACRL (chm Educ Libns Sect 64-65); MichLA; Mich Assn Higher Educ. 13: Yes. 14: Educ, admin, sch libnship. 15: Rt 3, Mt Pleasant Mi 48858.

EAVES, EDNA (BROWN). b Limestone Co Ala 23 Ag 08. 5: Athens Col 27-30 (Home Econ) BS; Carver Sch of Missions (Louisville Ky) 34-36 (Religious Educ) MRE; Peabody 48-49 BS in LS, 54, 57 MS in LS. 7: Home econ tchr Tanner High Sch, Tanner Ala 30-33; S S field wker Baptist St Dept,

Montgomery Ala 36-38; Church sec First Baptist Church, Ashland Ky 38-40; Promotional sec First Baptist Church, Laurens SC 40-43; Religious Educ dir First Baptist Church, Jefferson City Mo 44-45; Ky Ch Lib Sec Baptist Bk Store, Louisville Ky 46-48; Circ libn Howard Col 50-52; Lib supv Jefferson Co Schs, Birmingham Ala 52-57; Head Libn Mars Hill Col 57-62; Head Libn Mobile Col 62-64; Catlgr asst libn Furman U 64-. 9: SELA; ScLA. 10: Delta Kappa Gamma. 14: Catlg. 15: Furman Univ Lib, Greenville SC 29613.

EBAUGH, LAURA SMITH. b Greenville SC 12 Ap 1898. 5: Goucher Col 15-19 (Hist) AB; Columbia 19 (Sociol) MA; UChicago of Soc Wk 38; UNC 41 (SS). 7: Greenville Co home serv Amer Red Cross, Greenville SC 19-22; Tchr-head of highsch hist dept City Schs, Greenville SC 22-33; Soc wk tchr USCar summer 34; Co dirsoc serv ERA, Columbia SC 34-35; Assoc Prof of sociol Furman U 35-63; Adult educ assocgreenville Co Lib, Greenville SC 63-.11394 8: Assoc dir SC Nat Lib Week, 65; Exec dir SC Nat Lib Week, 66; Chm Area Leadership Conf, 65; Merit Coun SC State Dept of Pub Welfare 41-. 9: So Sociol Soc (v-pres). 10: AAUW; Womans Club; Thursday Club; Greenville Co Hist Soc (Founder mem); YWCA; var Greenville Co (SC) soc welfare groups. 11: Soc wker of the year, No Greenville Jr Col 63; Grenville Commun Woman of the Year Award, 65. 12 Contrib to "Experiment in Adult Education (41); Co-auth "Arts in Greenville (60); Co-auth "Horticultural Gardening in Greenville (62). 13: Yes. 14: Adult educ. 15: 311 Pettigru st, Greenville SC 29601.

EBELING, ELINOR (HODGES BAKER). b Detroit Mich 23 Ag 32. 5: Albion Col 50-52 (Liberal Arts); Wayne State 52-54 (Eng, Hist) BA; UMich 54-57 (LS) MALA; West Mich U 67-68 (LS). 6: Sp. 7: Libn Fordson High Sch, Dearborn Mich 54-61; Catlgr Henry Ford Community Col Lib, Dearborn Mich 61-65, Head tech serv 65-67; Asst Prof Lib Sci Ill State U 68-. 9: ALA (Jr Col Lib Sect; com on Instr and Use 64-); IllLA; IllASchL (Profess Rel Com 68-). 10: Delta Zeta; Alpha Beta Alpha; Beta Phi Mu; Pi Lambda Theta. 12: "Tech Processing Manual for Henry Ford Commun Col (64). 13: Yes. 14: Catlg, automation, lib educ, sch libnship. 15: 322 E Vernon ave, Normal Il 61761.

EBERHARDT, JAMES G(LENN). b Athens Ga 7 Mr 17. 4: H(elen) Alberta Stackhouse. 5: UFla 40 (Educ) BAE; Peabody 41 BS in LS, 48 MS in LS, 57 (Educ Admin) EdD. 7: Libn Brevard Co High Sch, Titusville Fla 41-42; US Army USAAF, AAA, INF, US & europe 42-46; Off mgr G A Stackhouse Inc, Hyannis Mass 46-47; Asst libn Tchrs Col of Conn 47-48; Prof of lib sci East Ill State Col 49-54; Act dir of lib 58-59; Libn SUNY Col (Geneseo) 60-67; Dir lib serv Fla Keys Jr Col 67-. 15: 2 Amaryllis dr Key Haven, Key West Fl 33040.

EBERHART, (MARY) EMILY. b Youngstown Ohio. 5: Flora Stone Mather Col West Res (Eng) AB; West Res 38-42 BS in LS; Ohio State U Summer 37 (Eng). 6: Fr, Lat. 7: Libn Chaney High Sch, Youngstown Ohio 33-. 9: NEA; OhioEA; NE Ohio Tchrs Assn; OhioASchL. 14: Ref. 15: 2119 Ohio ave, Youngstown Ohio 44504.

EBERHART, W(ILBUR) LYLE. b Topeka Kan 30 My 22. 4: Louise Tamura Eberhart. 5: Washburn Mun U 41-45 (Hist) AB; UWis 45-48 (Amer Hist) 50-51 MS in LS. 7: Br asst libn I Detroit Pub Lib 51-53, Ref asst libn II 53-54, Br asst libn III54-58, Chief of lib div 59-62; Field libn Wis Free Lib Commsn, Madison Wis 62-64,Adult serv consul 64-65; Dir, asst supt Div for Lib Serv Wis Dept of Pub Instr,Madison Wis 65-. 9: ALA-AASchL (chm Legis Liaison Com 69-70); AEA; WisLA. 10: UWis Lib Sch Alumni Assn (pres 64-66). 13: Yes. 14: Adult serv, lib ext, admin. 15: 903 State Office Bldg, Madison Wi 53702.

EBERSOLE, (WILLIAM) DALE JR. b Findlay Ohio 17 N 39. 5: Wittenberg U 57-61 (Math) BS; N Tex State U 65-66 MLS. 7: Deputy missile combat crew commander (1st Lt) USAF 61-65; Asst sci libn UHouston 66-68; Asst ref libn UToledo 68-. 9: SLA. 10: AAUP; Beta Phi Mu; Gamma Theta Upsilon; Alpha Lambda Sigma. 14: Maps, sci ref, ser. 15: 215 Islington apt W, Toledo Oh 43610.

EBERT, ELOISE Q(UEEN). b Scottsbluff Neb 17 Ag 11. 5: Park Col 29-31; UMinn 36 (LS) BS; UIll 56-57 (LS) MS. 7: Lib asst Pub Lib, Council Bluffs Iowa 31-35; Libn Pub Lib, Sauk Centre Minn 36-37; Libn Pub Lib, Falls City Neb 37-42; Post Libn, Ft Francis E Warren Wyo 42-45; US Army Lib Serv, European Command 45-49; Chief Libn, European Command 47-49; Asst state libn Ore State Lib 49-59, State Libn 59-, 8: Adv Com Nat Stat Coord Proj, 63-64. 9: AAState L (pres 63-64); ALA (Coun rep Ore 51-57); PNLA (pres 61-62); OreLA (Exec Bd 51-). 10: Ore Hist Soc; Amer Soc Pub Admin; Salem Art Assn; Ore UN; AAUW; LWV; Chemeketans; Beta Phi Mu; Theta Sigma Phi; Delta Kappa Gamma. 11: Ore Woman of Achievement, 65. 13: Yes. 14: Admin, lib devel, legis ref. 15: Ore State Lib, Salem Ore 97310.

EBERT, MYRL L-F. b Louisville Ky 20 O 13. 5: Peabody 39-43 (Phys Educ, Eng) BS; Vanderbilt 40; Peabody 43-45 BS in LS; Columbia 48-51 (LS) MS. 7: Clerical asst Vanderbilt MedLib 42-45; Ref asst Columbia U Med Lib 45-46; NY Acad of Med, NYC; Ref asst 46-47,Asst ref libn 47-49, Period libn 49-51; Assoc libn NYU Bellevue Med Center 51-52;Assoc Prof & Chief Libn Div of Health Affairs UNC (Chapel Hill) 52-. 8: Assoc Prof, UNC Sch of Lib Sc 58-; Consul, hosp & med libs in NC, SC, & Ky 57- Specconsul AMA & USaigon Med Sch, S Vietnam 66-68; Consul MEDLARS,NLM, 65-. 9: MedLA(sec 62-64, chm Nomin Comm 66-67, chm SE Reg Group 53-54); SLA; NCLA (rec sec 57-59;chm Spec Libs Div 53-55). 10: Amer Assn Hist Med; Piedmont Craftsmen; Amer AssnDental Schs; Assn Amer Lib Schs. 12: "Introduction to the Literature of the Medicalsciences" (2d ed 67); Ed "North Carolina Libraries" (fall 62); "Guide to theLiterature of Science" (68). 13: Yes. 14: Admin, ref, med lib educ, med lib hosp bk sel. 15: Div of Health Sciences Lib UNC, Chapel Hill NC 27415.

EBETINO, SHIRLEY (MORGAN). b Schenectady NY 8 Jl 32. 4: Charles A Ebetino. 5: State U Col (Oswego NY) 50-54 (Elem Educ) BS magna cum laude; SUNY(Albany) 60-64 MLS; Syracuse summer 62, 65 (LS, Math). 6: Sp. 7: Elem sch tchr Schenectady Pub Schs. Schenectady NY 54-57; Elem sch tchr US Dept of Navy, Guantanamo Bay Cuba 57-59; Elem sch tchr Ichabod Crane Central Sch, Kinderhook NY 59-61; Elem sch tchr Guilderland Central Schs, Guilderland NY 61-62; Elem sch libn & catlgr Schenectady Pub Schs, Schenectady NY 62-65, Apprentice lib coordinator 65- Lib coord 66-, Dir Reg Ctr for Instrl Materials Serv 68-. 8: Faculty of NDEA Inst in Sch Libnship State U Col (Geneseo NY) 65; Consul in the prep of bibliogs for NY State Dept of Educ 64-65 Coord NDEAInst Lib Serv to Deaf, Gallaudet Col Wash DC 66. 9: ALA;-AASchL (sec-treas SchLib Supv Sect); ENY Sch LA (pres 66-68); NY State A-V Assn; Hudson-Mohawk LA (treas66-); NY State Tchrs Assn; Schenectady County Reading Assn; Assn Childhood Educ. 10: Kappa Delta Pi. 14: Sch lib admin, reading guidance, automated tech serv. 15: 137 Main st,Altamont NY 12007.

EBINGER, M(EADA) GALATRO. b Hartford Conn 16 N 27. 4: Joseph C Ebinger. 5: St Joseph Col (West Hartford) 45-49 (Eng Lit) BS; Syracuse 54-55 MLS. 7: Tchr St Peter's Sch, hartford Conn 49-51; Lib asst child dept Hartford Pub Lib, Hartford Conn 51-54; Child libn Albany br 55-57, Br libn 57-63; Consul Little Peoples' Day Sch, Wallingford Conn 67-. 10: Conn Hist Soc; Conn Antiqu & Landmark Soc; Mark Twain Assn; AAUW; Chesire Philat Assn. 14: Ref, child. 15: 111 Mohawk dr, Wallingford Ct 06492.

EBLE, JEANNE (SHARPE). b Syracuse NY 23 F 20. 4: Louis B Eble. 5: URochester 38-42 (Hist) BA; West Res 42-43 BS in LS; Wayne State 48-51 (Admin) MEd UMichigan 64-66 AMLS. 6: Ger. 7: Sr asst I Rochester Pub Lib, Rochester NY 43-44; Head Libn Baldwin High Sch, Birmingham Mich 46-48; Sr libn II Detroit Pub Lib 49; Head Libn Highland Park High Sch, Highland Park Mich 49-54; Elem libn E Detroit Pub Schs, E Detroit Mich 57-58; Head Libn Highland Park Col 58-67; Hd lib & chm of fine arts dept Fraser HighSch, Fraser Mich. 8: Library Consultant: Detroit U Sch & Grosse Pointe Country Day Sch 51, and Mich Lutheran Col 64, 68. 9: MichLA (sec-treas Jr Col sect; NEA. 13: Yes. Author-contrib "Basic Books for Junior Col Lib (61). 14: Admin, ref, readers adv. 15: 12490 EastOuter dr, Detroit Mi 48224.

EBLE, MARY M (COATES). b Akron Ohio 6 D 17. 4: John F Eble. 5: Notre Dame Col for Women 35-39 (Eng, Econ) BA; Case west Res 63-67 MSLS. 6: Lat, Fr. 7: Lib clk Cleveland Hts Sch Lib, Cleveland Ohio 39; Bkmob libn Cuyahoga Co Lib, Fairview Park Ohio 63; Elem sch libn Fairview Park Schs, Fairview Park Ohio 63-, High sch libn & lib coord 68-. 9: ALA; -AASchL; NEA; OhioASchL; OhioLA; OhioEA & Educational Media Council of Ohio. 10: Beta Phi Mu; Chrsit Child Soc. 14: Child & ya & sch libnship. 15: 3479 Colletta lane, Cleveland Oh 44111.

EBRIGHT, ELIZABETH (JOAN). b Baldwin Kan 1 D 11. 5: Baker U 29-33 (Eng) AB; UKan 34-36 (Eng) MA; UIll 37-38 (LS) BS. 7: Ref libn Kewanee Pub Lib, Kewanee Ill 38-41; High Sch libn Kewanee High Sch, Kewanee Ill 38-42; Asst libn Washburn U 42-45, Hd libn 45-65; Spec instr Eng Baker U 66-. 8: Trustee, Baldwin City Library. 9: ALA; NCTE; KanLA.

10: Nat League Amer Pen Women; AAUW; Wesleyan Serv Guild. 11: Alpha Chi Omega; Phi Beta Kappa; Beta Phi Mu. 14: Ref. 15: 613 8th st, Baldwin Ks 66006.

EBRIGHT, MADGE (CONWAY CHILCOTE). b Menominee Wis 1 Je 18. 4: Neale Ebright. 5: UOre 35-41 (Mus) BA; UWash 41-42 BLS; UCal (Long Beach) 58; USoCal 63-67 MLS. 7: Jr catlgr UOre 42-44; Period libn 45-46, Sr Ref libn summer 53; Sch lib supv Klamath Co Lib, Klamath Falls 49-53; Libn Eugene Pub Schs, Eugene Ore 53-57; Libn inglewood Unified Sch Dist, Inglewood Cal 58-63; Libn Palos Verdes Pen Unified Sch Dist, Palos Verdes Cal 63-68. 8: ESEA, Title II, Phase II proposal for demon ctr, ridgecrest Intermed Sch, Palos Verdes Cal 66-67; Sch Lib Wkshop for Leadership Personnel, Monte Corona Cal 67. 9: ALA; NEA; CalSchoolLA. 10: Phi Delta Gamma; PTA; Mu Phi Epsilon. 14: Sch libs, a-v, ref. 15: 3220 Merritt dr, Torrance Ca 90050.

EBRO, DIANA CAROLE (PICCIO). b Bacolod City PI 20 D 38. 5: UPhilippines 54-58 (LS) BA; Simmons 64-65 (LS) MS. 6: Eng, Filipino, Sp, Ger. 7: Clerk Veterans Claims Commsn, Quezon City PI 58-59; Libn Pacifica Inc (Petroleum & Mining Co), Manila PI 59; Cashier Visavan Packing Corp, Bacolod City PI 60-61; Libn I UPhilippines Grad Sch of Pub Admin Lib, 61-62, Col of Med Lib 62-64; Catlgr L-7 Sch of Med Lib Yale U 65- Sr catlgr L-8 Sch of Med Lib Yale U 65-67;Fachreferentin Universitat Ulm Med-Naturwiss Hochschule, Germany 67-. 8: Fulbright- Hays Travel Grant 64-65;Simmons Col Foreign Scholarship Award 64-65; Philippine rep Boston Area Seminar for Internat Stud 64. 9: MLA;SLA; PhilippineLA Assn Spec Libs Philippines; ALA; UPhilippinesLA. 10: Sigma Delta Phi; Fulbright Assn of the Philippines. 11: Fulbright-Hays Grant. 14: Catlg,ref, indexing. 15: Universitatsbibliothek Ulm, Medizin-Naturwiss Hochschule, 79Ulm Germany Postfach 1304.

EBY, JOAN (SHAEFFER). b Lancaster Pa 9 My 42. 4: Donald C Eby. 5: Millersville State Col 60-64 (Elem Educ) BS in Ed; Drexel 67-69 MSLS. 7: Elem tchr Donegal Union Sch Dist, Mt Joy Penn 65-66; Elem libn Pennsbury Schs, Fallsington Penn 66-68; Child libn Glenside Free Lib, Glenside Penn 69-. 14: Child libn. 15: Graber rd, Redhill Pa 18076.

ECHELMAN, SHIRLEY. b Omaha Neb 7 O 34. 4: Elliott Jacob. 5: UWis 52-54 (Econ); UOmaha 54-56 (Econ) BA; Rutgers 65-66 MLS. 7: Libn Basic Econ Appraisals Inc, NY 60-65; Research libn Chem Bank, NY 66-. 9: SLA (NY Chap; 2nd v-pres 68-70). 10: Pi Gamma Mu; Beta Phi Mu. 12: Ed "Chapter News", SLA NY Chap (68-70). 14: Ref, admin. 15: 760 W End ave, New York NY 10025.

ECKARDT, GLADYS BEACH. b Hartland NY 7 S 12. 4: Karl Paul Konrad Eckardt. 5: URochester 30-34 (Eng Lit) AB; Rutgers 57-58 MLS. 6: Fr. 7: Lib Dir Wood Ridge Pub Lib, Wood Ridge NJ 56-58; Lib Dir Rutherford Pub Lib, Rutherford NJ 59-. 9: ALA; NJLA (sec); Bergen-Passaic LA (pres). 10: Womans Col Club of Rutherford. 13: Yes. 14: Admin. 15: Rutherford Pub Lib, Rutherford NJ 07070.

ECKEL, VIRGINIA ELAINE. b Anderson Ind 20 D 24. 5: Ball State U 42-46 (Bus, Soc Sci BS in Ed; Peabody (LS) MA. 7: Libn Sinclair Col 46-52; Libn Wright Patterson Air Force Base Br Lib 52-61;Catlgr Air Force Inst of Tech 61-64; Chief libn Air Force Inst Tech DWSMC Br,Wright Patterson Air Force Base (Ohio) 64-. 8: Bus tchr Sinclair Col 52-60 Instr in Lib Sci Wittenberg U66-; Guest instr for Sci Tech Info courses, Sch of Systems & Logistics, AFIT. 9: SLA (treas Dayton Chap 68-69); Miami Valley LA (past chm). 14: Admin, ref. 15: 2993 Westcott dr, Kettering Oh 45420.

ECKERT, DANIEL LEE. b Milwaukee 23 Ja 36. 5: La Crosse State U 58-60 (Hist, Geog) BS; Clark U 60-61 (Geog); LSU 63-64 (LS). 7: Lib asst adult serv Milwaukee Pub Lib 61, 62; Lib aide LSU Lib 64; Libn I Milwaukee Pub Lib 64; Reader serv libn, gifts 7 exch libn Marquette Mem Lib, Milwaukee 65-66; Dir Cedarburg Pub Lib, Cedarburg Wis 66-68; Dir Whitewater Pub Lib, Whitewater, Wis 68-. 8: Adv Lib Com SEWRPC 66-68. 9: ALA; WisLA. 14: ref,admin. 15: RT 3, Kewaunee Wi 54216.

ECKERT, ELIZABETH (WOODMAN). b Middletown NY 26 N 09. 4: John N Eckert. 5: Swarthmore 27-31 (Eng, Hist) AB; Columbia 32-33 (LS) MS. 7: Libn Middletown State Hosp 34-65 (ret). 8: Consul Horton Mem Hosp Med Lib, Middletown NY 62-65. 9: MedLA; NYLA. 10: Horton Mem Hosp Bd (Middletown NY) 65-. 13: Yes. 14: Small hosp libs. 15: 08 Coolidge ct, Middletown NY 10940.

ECKES, HAROLD JOHN. b New Hampton Iowa 6 Ag 38. 5: UNoIowa 56-60 (Soc Sci) BA; UDenver 61- (LS, Educ) MA; San Francisco State Col 64; UCLA 67. 7: Libn: Eldora High Sch, Eldora Iowa 60-61, Mt Pleasant High Sch, Mt Pleasant Iowa 61-62, St Francis High Sch, Milwaukee 62-65; Acquis libn Wis StateU (Whitewater) 65-66, Instr of lib sci 67-, Libn Whittier High Sch, Whittier Cal 66-67. 8: Consul: N Central Assn Accreditation Team 62, West Assn Accreditation Team 66. 9: AAUP; WisEA; WisASchL; Wis A-v Inst; Assn Wis State U Faculties. 10: Phi Delta Kappa; Alpha Beta Alpha. 14: Lib sci instr, media ctr concept, ya lit. 15: Dept of Lib Sci Wisconsin State Univ, Whitewater Wi 53190.

ECKMIER, (ROBERT) GLENN. b Huron Co Ontario 26 N 09. 4: Alice Jean Barr. 7: Asst libn Huron Co Lib, Goderich Ont 45-61; Clk-driver Scarborough Tp Lib, Scarborough Ony 61-67; Acquis supv Algoma Col Lib, Sault Ste Marie Ont 67-. 9: CanLA; OntLA. 15: 40 Tadcaster pl, Sault Ste Marie Ont Can.

ECKMIER, ALICE JEAN (BARR). b Ethel Ont Can 21 Ag 06. 4: Robert Glenn Eckmier. 5: UBC 25-29 (Psych); McGill 29-30 (LS) Certif. 6: Fr. 7: Asst Pub Lib, Vancouver BC 27-30, Prof asst 31-33; Accountant Nesbitt Thompson, Vancouver BC 33-36; Accountant Colpitts Bros, Calgary Alta 36-40; Chief Libn Pub Lib, Ethel Ont 41-45; Chief Libn Huron County Lib, Goderich Ont 45-61; Br libn Scarboro Pub Lib, Scarboro Ont 61-63; Sr acquis libn York U(Toronto) 63-67; Chief libn Algoma Col Lib 67-. 9: CanLA; ALA; OntLA (exec bd 6 yrs);Inst Prof Libns Ont. 10: Bus & Prof Womens Club. 13: Yes. 14: Canadiana. 15: 40 Tadcaster pl, Sault Ste Marie Ont.

EDACK, MARGARET HARDER. b Phila Pa 17 Jl 22. 4: John P Edack. 5: Susquehanna U 39-40 (Sci); Upsala 59-62 (Elem Educ) BA; Rutgers 63-66 MLS. 6: Fr. 7: Sec-advertising US Coast Guard Magazine, NYC 41-45; Tchr Gould Ave Sch, N Caldwell NJ 62-66; Sch libn Grandview Sch, N Caldwell NJ 66-. 9: NEA; NJSchLA; NJEA; EssexCoLA; North Caldwell EA (pres 67-68). 15: 62 Wynnewood rd, Livingston NJ 07039.

EDDY, REV CLYDE E. b Minot ND 20 F 16. 5: Col of St Thomas 34-38 (Fr) BA (summa cum laude); St Paul Sem 46-51 (Theol); UMinn 58-63 (LS). 6: Fr, Sp, Lat. 7: Tchr Lakeville Pub High Sch, Lakeville Minn 38-41; Tchr Robbinsdale Pub High Sch, Robbinsdale Minn 41-44; Tchr St Thomas Mil Acad, St Paul 51-58; Libn Col of St Thomas (St Paul) 58- Libn St Paul Sem 68-. 9: ALA; CathLA; DakCathLA (pres). 13: Yes. 14: Admin. 15: Col of St Thomas, St Paul Mn 55101.

EDDY, HARRY L. b Marietta Ohio 1 S 06. 4: Elizabeth Tope. 5: Grand Junction Jr Col 24-25 (Liberal Arts); UDenver 35-36 (Educ, Botany) AB; George Washington U 39-40 (Bot) MA. 6: Fr. 7: High sch tchr, Cotopaxi Colo 37-38; AAR Bur of RR Econ Lib, Wash DC: Entered service Oct 1940, beginning as Custodian of Shelves & in chg of ser & correspondence files, advanced thru Ref asst, ref libn to Libn 1960-. 9: SLA. 10: Sigma Xi. 15: AAR Bur of Railway Econ Lib, Rm 1002, Transportation Bldg, Wash DC 20006.

EDDY, LEONARD MAX. b Stamps Ark 26 Ap 32. 4: Marjorie JoAnn Bristow. 5: So State Col 50-54 (Secondary Educ) BSE; Henderson State Tchrs Col 54; UOkla 59-61 MLS. 7: Tchr-libn Mt Holly Pub Schs, Mt Holly Ark 54-55; Clerk-typist US Army (Spec 3rd Class) 55-57; Libn A C F Industries, Albuquerque NM 57-59; Lib fellow UOkla(Norman) 59-61, Sci area libn 61-62; Libn UOkla Med Center (Okla City) 62-. 9: MedLA; OklaLA; Amer Assn Hist of Med. 14: Admin, med libnship. 15: 113 Kelley dr, Moore Ok 73060.

EDDY, WARREN S(UTHERLAND). b Niagara Falls NY 9 Mr 37. 4: Joanne (Adsit) Moore. 5: URochester 55-59 (Hist)BA High Honors; Syracuse 60-61 MS LS. 7: Clerk Niagara Falls (NY) Pub Lib 58-61,Libn ref dept 61; Asst libn Cortland (NY) Free Lib 61-64, Lib dir 64-. 9: ALA; NYLA. 10: Cortlandco (NY) Hist Soc; Phi Beta Kappa; Beta Phi Mu; Rotary Club. 14: Admin, adult serv. 15: Box 421,Cortland NY 13045.

EDELEN, JOSEPH R JR. b Belleville Ill 5 S 44. 4: Mary M Beaty. 5: St Mary's Col (St Mary Ky) 62-66 (Phil) AB; St Mary's U (San Antonio Tex) 66-67 (Hist) AB; Catholic U 67-68 MSLS. 6: Lat. 7: Clk typist St Mary's Col (St Mary Ky) 62-65, Hd libn 65-66; Clk SW Research Ctr, San Antonio Tex 66; Asst to ref libn Trinity U 66-67; Searcher LC 67; Catlg libn U SDak 68-69; Hd catlg 62-. 8: Instr Catlg & Clsfn, US Dak spring 69. 9: ALA; SLA; ASIS; CathLA; SDakLA. 10: Beta Phi Mu; Phi Alpha Theta; Clay Co Hist Soc. 14: Catlg, admin. 15: 301 Lewis st, Vermillion SD 57069.

EDELMAN, HENDRIK. b Wageningen Netherlands 27 N 37. 4: Annekee Witte. 5: Peabody Lib sch 67-69 MLS. 6: Dutch, Fr, Ger. 7: Asst export mgr Martinus Nijhoff, The Hague 58-65; Sales mgr D Reidel Pub Co, Dordrecht 65-67; Univ Ctr bibliog Joint Univ Libs Nashville 67-. 8: Consul NY Metro Ref & Research Lib Agcy Inc 68. 9: ALA; BSA; TennLA. 12: "Shared Acquisitions and Retentions (SHARES) in the New York Metropolitan Area" (69). 13: Yes. 14: Collection dev. 15: Joint Univ Libs, Nashville Tn 37203.

EDELSON, ALAN MARTIN. b NYC 17 Mr 39. 4: Carol Marcia (Herman). 5: URochester 55-59 (Phys Chem) BS; Columbia 63-64 (LS) MS. 7: Staff Parkinsons Disease Inf and Research Center Columbia U Col of Physicians and Surgeons 64-. 8: Owner 7 Publisher of Raven Press 62-. 9: SLA; MedLA. 10: Phi Beta Kappa; Beta Phi Mu. 11: ACS gold medal URochester; Stoddard Prize in Mathematics URochester. 14: Documentation, develop of biomed info media. 15: Parkinsons Disease Informationand Research Center, Black Research Bldg, 650 W 168th st, New York NY 10032.

EDELSTEIN, J M. b Baltimore 31 Jl 24. 4: Eleanor Rockwell. 5: Johns Hopkins 42-43, 46-47 (Hist) AB, 47-49 (Hist); UFlorence(Italy) 49-50 (Hist); UMich 52-53 (LS) MA. 6: Ital, Fr. 7: (Pfc) US Army, US & Italy 43-46; Hist tchr, various 46-52; Asst serv libn Legis Ref Serv LC 54-55, Ref libn RARE Bk Div 55-62; Bibliog UCLA 62-64; Libn for spec collections NYU 64-66; Bibliog & lecturer UCLA 66-. 9: ALA-ACRL (chm Rare Bks Sect 68-69); BSA. 10: Phi Beta Kappa; Grolier Club (NY); Rounce & Coffin Club (Los Angeles); MS Soc;Renaissance Soc. 11: Fulbright Award to Italy. 12: "A Bibliographical Checklist of the Writings of ThorntonWilder" (59); "A Garland for Jake Zeitlin on the Occasion of his 65th Birthday &the Anniversary of his 40th Year in the Book Trade" (67); "A Selected Catalog of Booksfrom the Library of Don Cameron Allen" (68); Ed 'News & Notes' in "Papers of thebsa-. 13: Yes. 14: Rare bks , mod first eds, Eng & Amer Lit, bibliog, bk trade, pub. 15: Univ Research Library UCLA, Los Angeles Ca 90402.

EDENS, MARIETTA HANCOCK. b Green Forest Ark. 5: UArk 49 (Eng) BSE; LSU 54 (LS) MS. 7: Libn Berryville Pub Schs, Berryville Ark 46-52; Libn Ozarks Reg Lib, Clarksville Ark 52-54; Libn Terrebonne Parrish Lib, Houma ouma La 54-55; Instr in Lib Sci Kan State Col (Pittsburg) 55-57; Libn Allen Parish Lib, Oberlin La 57-59; Asst dir of lib serv Ventura Co Lib, Ventura Cal 59-64; City Libn Oceanside Pub Lib, Oceanside Cal 64-68; Dist libn Green Forest Schs, Green Forest Ark 68-. 8: Staff, Lib 21, Seattle Worlds Fair. 9: ALA; NEA; ArkLA; ArkEA. 14: Admin, ref. 15: Rte 3 Box 16B,Berryville Ar 72616.

EDGAR, NEAL LOWNDES. b NYC 21 Je 27. 4: Susanna Capper. 5: Trinity Col(Hartford Conn) 46-50 (Econ) BA; SUNY(Albany) 56-58 (Educ, LS) MA, MSLS; UMich 61-65 (LS) AMLS, PhD. 7: Prof radio in NY, Mass 50-55; High Sch Eng tchr, NY State 55-57; Pre-prof NY Academy of Med Columbia U Med Lib, & Dept asst SUNY(Alany) 58; Asst libn SUNY(Albany) 58-61; Coordinating libn Residence Halls UMich 61-65; Ser catlgr LC 65-66; Acquis libn Kent State U 67; Ser libn 68-. 9: ALA; OhioLA. 12: "A History and Bibliography of American Magazines, 1810-1820. 13: Yes. 14: Tech serv. 15: 551 Cuyahoga st, Kent Oh 44240.

EDGE, STELLA L (VANDIVER). b Pangburn Ark 9 D 18. 4: Thomas S Edge. 5: Col of the Ozarks 36-37; Okla Baptist U 38-41 (Eng) BA (magna cum laude); Madison State Tchrs Col (Va) summer 54; UDenver summers 59-61, 62-63 (LS) MA; UColo eves 65, 66, 68. 6: Fr. 7: Instr Eng Okla Baptist U 43-46, 52-53; Manager, instr Priv Kindergarten, Fairfax Co Va 51-52; Elem tchr Fairfax Co (Va) Schs 54-55; Elem tchr Cherry Creek Dist No 5, Englewood Colo 55-60, Elem libn 60-. 8: Res asst Colo U Med Sch 63-66; Vis asst prof of lib sci, Highlands U, NM summers 67, 68. 9: NEA-DAVI; ALA; ColoLA; ColoASchL (pres 67-69); ColoEA (sec-treas, chm Libns Group of East Div 67). 10: LWV. 13: Yes. 14: Wk with child, curr devel, programmed learning. 15: 2512 S Univ blvd 806, Denver Co 80210.

EDGINGTON, VIRGINIA J (JOHNSON). b St Louis Mo 21 Ap 10. 5: WashU (St Louis) 28-31 (Econ, Educ) BA; Miss State Col for Women 49-51 (LS) BS; UFla 54-59 (LS). 7: Libn Gulf High Sch, New Port Richey Fla 54-55; Libn Taylor Co High Sch, Perry Fla 55-56; Asst libn Fla State U 56-59; Libn Ga Power Co, Atlanta 59-. 9: SLA; SELA. 10: Alpha Delta Pi. 15: PO Box #4545, Atlanta Ga 30302.

EDKINS, DOROTHY L. b Minneapolis Minn 2 S 22. 5: Wis StateU (River Falls) 39-43 (Eng) BS; Wis StateU (Oshkosh) summers 54-55, 60-63 (LS). 7: Vocal mus tchr Bd of educ, New London Wis 43-45, Eng tchr & libn 45-55, Libn 55-. 8: Dean of Girls 55-61. 9: ALA; NEA; WisEA; NEastEA (Resolutions Com); WisLA. 10: Bus & Prof Women; New londonEA; Girl Scout leader; Delta Kappa Gamma. 13: Yes. 14: Ya, ref. 15: 608 Nassau st, New London Wi 54961.

EDLHAUSER, JUNE MARIAN (HELGASON). b Milwaukee. 4: Ernst Edlhauser. 5: Milwaukee-Downer Col 36-40 (Fr, Eng) BA; UWis 40-41 BLS; UParis 50 (Fr). 6: Ger, Fr. 7: Asst libn S Milwaukee Pub Lib, S Milwaukee Wi 41-42; Asst libn Milwaukee-Downer Col 42-43; Asst art & music dept Milwaukee Pub Lib 43-48, Lib in chge Allis Art Lib 48-53; Dir US Info Center Lib USIS, Vienna 53-57; Neighborhood lib head, lin IV Milwaukee Pub Lib 58-. 9: ALA; WisLA. 14: Pub lib serv. 15: 2706 N Farwell ave, Milwaukee 53211.

EDLUND, PAUL ERIK. b Cortland NY 11 My 22. 4: Mary Jane Wells Edlund. 5: Central City Bus Inst 40-41 (Bus Admin) Certif; Yale U 45-48 (Hist) BA; UVa49-50, 53-54 (Hist) MA; UMich 54-55 (LS) MS. 7: US Air Force (2nd Lt) Bombardier15th AF 42-45; Hist tchr Cooperstown (NY) Acad 48-49; Hist tchr City of AttleboroMass Jr High & High Sch 50-53; Circ asst UVa Alderman Lib 53-54; LC; Lib recruit 55,Asst documents expediter, Asst head Gift Sect, Admin asst Processing Dept, Prinevaluations officer, Head Orientalia Exch Sect, Head Gift Sect, Head E EuropeanAccessions Index Proj, Head Prep Sect Ms Div, Collections maintenance & preservationofficer, Asst chief Exch & Gift Div; Exec off processing dept 68-. 9: ALA. 13: Yes. 14: Acquis, preserv. 15: 11210 Kenilworth ave, Garrett Park Md 20766.

EDMONDS, ELIZABETH ANN. b Carlsbad New Mexico 17 D 45. 5: UNDak 63-66 (Eng) BA; UDenver 66-67 (Libnship) MA. 7: Child libn Howard Whittemore Memorial Lib, Naugatuck Conn 66; Libn Seattle Pub Lib hist dept 67-. 9: PNLA. 14: Ref. 15: 538 Lakeside S apt 404, Seattle Wa 98144.

EDMONDS, MAY H(ARNDEN). b Firest Park Ill 9 My 13. 4: Charles A Edmonds. 5: Ill Inst of Tech 31-36; Carnegie Tech 37-38 Certif in LS; UMiami (Fla) 47-50 (Educ) BEd, 50-57 9reading) MEd. 7: Clerical asst Oak Park Pub Lib, Oak Park Ill 30-37, Br & child asst 38-43; Asst libn (US Coast Guard W R Spar) Air Sea Rescue Tech Lib, Wash DC 44-45; Catlgr UMiami Lib (Fla) 47-52; Coord wk with child & yp Miami Pub Lib, Miami Fla 52-. 8: FlaLA rep to White House Conf on Child & Youth 60; Co-chm & ed Jt Bk Selection List of Miami Pub Lib & Dade Co Sch Libs 55-. 9: ALA (Spec Com to US Jaycees Gooding Reading Program chm 65-); -CSD (2nd v-pres 69-70; chm Adv Com to US Jaycees Good Reading Program 64-67; Newbery-Caldecott Awards Com 63-64, 67-68); -LAD (Recruiting Com 58-61); FlaLA (sec 60-61; chm Sch & Child Sect 54-55; Recruitment Com 58-66); DadeCoLA (pres 59-60). 10: Kappa Delta Pi. 13: Yes. 14: Child & ya serv, recruitment. 15: Miami Pub Lib 1 Biscayne blvd, Miami Fl 33132.

EDMONSON, MRS JOHN H (EVELYN CLIFFORD). b Pine Bluff Ark O 29. 4: John H Edmonson. 5: Ark State Tchrs Col 47-51 (Eng) BSE; Ark A&M summer 57; UUtah Correspondence 65 (LS). 6: Sp. 7: Tchr Brinkley High Sch, Brinkley Ark 51; Tchr Sherrill Jr High Sch, Sherrill Ark 51-52; Watson Chapel High Sch, Pine Bluff Ark: Tchr-libn 52-61, Tchr 62-65, Libn 65-. 9: ArkLA. 10: Delta Kappa Gamma. 15: RT 7 Box 500, Pine Bluff Ar 71601.

EDSALL, SHIRLEY ANN. b Bath NY 16 Ja 33. 5: State U (Albany NY) 50-54 (Math, Biol) AB (signum laudis), 55 MSLS, Rutgers U spring 68. 6: Fr. 7: Sch libn Campbell Central Sch, Campbell NY 55-61; Libn Corning Community Col 61-. 8: Ref libn, Lib/USA NY Worlds Fair 64; Instr Mansfield State Col Lib Sch, summer 62. 9: ALA-Jr Col Libns Sect;Sec 63-64, chm Nomin Com 64-65, chm Bibliog Com 65-68; chm 68-69; -RSD (Chapts Com64-67, Exec Bd Jr Mem RT 64-67); -ACRL (Planning & Action Com 68-69; Ed Com Sub-Comon Voc/Tech Lists 67-); NYLA Bd of Dirs Col & Univ Sect 67-69; SUNY Two-Year LibnsGroup (chm 66-67), Head Libn, Conf Sect 68-69, Chancellors Advis Com on Lib, 68-69. 10: AAUW; AAUP; Friends of Corning Pub Lib; Beta Phi Mu; AAJC; NYState Col Assn. 12: Ed "SUNY Two-Year College Libraries Union List of Periodicals (2nd ed 64). 14: Ref, admin. 15: Rt 1, Campbell NY 14821.

EDWARDS, ANNE (GRAVER). b Atlanta Ga 2 Ja 43. 4: Donald Clark Edwards. 5: Wis StateU (Stevens Point) 63-66 (Eng) BS; UIll 66-67 (LS) MS. 6: Ger. 7: Sec & clk City News Serv, Stevens Point Wis 63-65; Jr catlgr UMo, Columbia Mo 67-68; Asst catlg libn Macalester Col 68-. 8: Stud tchr DC Everest High Sch, Schofield Wis 66. 9: ALA; MinnLA. 14:

Catlg, ya serv. 15: 1520 Charleton apt 210. W St Paul Mn 55118.

EDWARDS, (EMMA) FRANCES. b Chatham Va 2 Ja 12. 5: Longwood Col 28-32 (Hist) BS in Ed; Peabody Col summers 39-41 BS in LS. 7: Tchr & libn Chatham High Sch, Chatham Va 32-40; Lib supv Loudoun Co, Leesburg Va 40-41; Libn Gastonia Sr High, Gastonia NC 41-42; Army libn, Camp Normoyle, San Antonio & Camp Swift Tex 42-46; Chief & med libn VA, Perry Point Md, Camp Moore & Asheville NC, Ft Benjamin Harrison & Indianapolis Ind 46-48; Dir pub lib, Norwalk Ohio 48-63; Dir Wash Co Pub Lib, Marietta Ohio 63-68; Personnel libn ohioU Lib (Athens) 68-. 8: Pub Lib Bldg consul & inter decor: Norwalk 48-63, Washington Co (Marietta) Ohio 63-68, Jackson Ohio (68-), Logan Ohio 69-, Steubenville Ohio 69-. 9: ALA; OhioLA (Exec Bd 66-68, Devel Com 65, Spec Com to Establish Standards for Small Lib Bldgs, Com to Certify libns for Co Dist Libs 67-70). 10: AAUW; LWV; Book clubs; Shakespeare Club; Travel Club; Bus & Profess Women; Zonta. 11: Recipient of ALA1S first Radio Award 67; Accredited reporter, by NASA, to attend G-9 shoot May 66 & Apollo 8 Dec 21 68. 14: Admin, bldgs, pub rel (radio, TV & talks), rare bks, reg lib organ, surveys. 15: 10-202 Monticello dr, Athens Oh 45701.

EDWARDS, MRS BERTHA WINBORNE. b Portsmouth Va 8 Je 20. 4: George Isiah Edwards. 5: Hampton Inst 38-42 (Educ, LS) BS. 7: Clerk-typist Naval Operating Base, Norfolk Va 42-43; Tchr Zion Baptist Church Kindergarten, Portsmouth Va 44-45; Libn Portsmouth Commun Lib, Portsmouth Va 45-62; Libn asst ref dept Portsmouth Pub Lib, Portsmouth Va 62-. 9: ALA; SELA; VaLA. 10: Portsmouth Mental Health Assn; YMCA; Merry Makers Club; Delta Sigma Theta.11432 13: Yes. 14: Ref. 15: 1115 Wilcox ave, Portsmouth Va 23704.

EDWARDS, DOROTHY MAI. b Trezevant Tenn 16 N 13. 5: Murray State Col 31-33; UTenn 36 (Eng-Latin) AB; Peabody 41 BS in LS. 7: Tchr High Sch, Huntingdon Tenn 33-41, Libn 39-41; Dist Supv Ky Statewide Lib Proj, Louisville Ky 41-42; Libn Camp Breckinridge Ky 42-43; Asst libn Allentown Free Lib, Allentown Penn 43-63; Asst dir White Plains Pub Lib, White Plains NY 63-. 8: Planning, supv, & coordinating county bkmob & br operation; Consul on establishment of community libs. 9: ALA; NYLA; Westchester LA. 10: College Club. 13: Yes. 14: Admin, personnel, bk sel, tech processing. 15: 10 Nosband ave, Apt 6F, White Plains NY 10605.

EDWARDS, ELIZABETH (ROBINSON). b Chattanooga Tenn 26 Ap 07. 5: UChattanooga 24-27 (Eng Lit) AB; Columbia 29 BS. 7: Catlgr Chattanooga Pub Lib, Chattanooga Tenn 29-30; br asst Queensboro Pub Lib, Jamaica NY 30-31; Br asst NY Pub Lib 31-33, Sub-br libn 33-36, Asst supt ext div 36-43, Br libn 43-44; Org & dir Oak Ridge Pub Lib, Oak Ridge Tenn 44-46; Head Libn Chattanooga Pub Lib, Chattanooga Tenn 46-66; Dir Rolling Prairies Libs Syst, Decatur Ill 66-. 9: ALA (var coms); SELA (pres 47-49); IllLA. 10: Adult Educ Coun; Commun Rel Conf. 13: Yes. 14: Admin, adult educ. 15: Rolling Prairies Libs, 345 W Eldorado, Decatur Il 62522.

EDWARDS, GERTRUDE DORIS. b Ashley Penn 28 Mr 09. 5: UWash 26-32 BS in LS, 42 (Eng) BA. 7: Reviser UWash Sch of Libnship32-42, Instr summers 38-41; 1st asst Everett Pub Lib, Everett Wash 42-43; Catlgr Tech Lib Bonneville Power Admin, Portland Ore 44-45; Catlgr Lib Assn of Portland, Portland Ore 46-48, Head catlg dept 48-. 9: ALA; PNLA; OreLA. 10: Ore Hist Soc; ACLU. 14: Catlg. 15: 2545 SW Terwilliger blvd, apt 819, Portland Or 97201.

EDWARDS, GRACE (COLEMAN). b Charlotte NC 30 D 35. 4: Bobby L Edwards. 5: Bennett Col (NC) 53-57 (Eng) BA; Ind U summers 58-60, 62 (LS) M AT. 7: Elem libn Bd of Educ, Lynchburg Va 57-59; Libn Marie Davis Elem Sch, Charlotte NC 59-61; Eng tchr Central High Sch, Louisville Ky 64-65, Libn 65-. 9: KyEA; NEA; Louisville EA. 10: Delta Sigma Theta; YWCA. 14: Catlg, ref. 15: 1307 S 45th st, Louisville Ky 40211.

EDWARDS, LENEIL. b Bell Buckle Tenn 16 My 09. 5: Randolph Macon 27-31 (Lat) AB; Peabody 39-41 BS in LS. 7: Tchg Bell Buckle High Sch, Bell Buckle Tenn 32-41; Libn HAYWOOD Co High Sch, Brownsville Tenn 41-50; Libn Isaac Litton High Sc, ashville 50-53; Head Dept of Lib Serv Middle Tenn State U 53-. 9: ALA; NEA (Life mem); SELA; TennLA (chm Sch Lib Sect 64-65); TennEA (chm Sch Lib Sect 64-65). 10: Delta Kappa Gamma; AAUW. 15: 1135 East Clark, Murfreesboro Tn 37130.

EDWARDS, MARGARET A. b Childress Tex 23 O 02. 4: . 5: Trinity U 19-22 (Eng) AB; Columbia 26-27 (Lat) AM, 37 (LS) BS. 07: Eng & Lat tchr Forney High Sch, Forney Tex 22-24; Eng tchr Vernon High Sch, Vernon Tex 24-26; Lat tchr Towson High Sch, Towson Md 27-32; Asst circ, ya libn, coordinator of wk with ya Enoch Pratt Free Lib, Baltimore 32-62. 8: Visiting tchr, Lit for Adolescents: UAriz 63, Rutgers U 62-, McGill U 67-; Catholic U 63-; Conducted wkshops UDenver 62, UTex 65, St Catherines (Minn) 64, UMont 66, 67, UTenn 68. 9: ALA (past mem Coun)-Div Child & YP (sec 41; mem Com to Ed ""Public Library Prepares for the Teen Age); MdLA (past pres). 10: LWV; ACLU; ADA. 11: Grolier Award, 57. 12: "The Fair Garden and the Swarm of Beasts" (69). 13: Yes. 14: Wk with ya. 15: Box 59 Rt 3, Joppa Md 21085.

EDWARDS, OLGA (DAUPHINE). b New Orleans La 28 F 20. 4: Andrew S Edwards. 5: Xavier U 38 (Educ) BA; SUNY(Geneseo) 60 (LS) MS. 7: Elem tchr Catholic Sch, New Orleans -48; Libn pub sch, Opelousas La 49-54; Sr lib clerk Pub Lib, Endicott NY 54-59; Libn Pub Lib, Rochester NY 60-, Ext dept hd 64-. 8: Story-teller on Storyland (Educ TV program). 9: NYLA; Amer Soc Pub Admin. 10: Alpha Kappa Alpha. 11: AKA Citation Award for Outstanding Commun Serv. 14: Child serv. 15: 323 Jefferson ave, Rochester NY 14611.

EDWARDS, RITA LILIAN (DANBY). b Toronto 5 Ap 28. 4: John Edwards. 5: UToronto 47-51 (Arts) BA; Ontario Col of Educ 52-53 (Latin & Eng) HSA Certif; UOttawa 57-62 BLS; UToronto 63-64 (Educ) BEd, 64-68 (Adult Educ) MEd. 6: Lat, Fr. 7: Tchr Loretto Abbey Col Sch, Toronto 51-52; Tchrledbury Park Elem Sch, North York Can 53-54; Tchr Cobden Dist High Sch, Cobden Can54-55; Tchr libn Nickel Dist High Sch, Sudbury Can 55-57; Tchr N Toronto Collegiate,toronto 58-59; Tchr-libn Laurentian High Sch, Ottawa 60-63; Lib Head Bathurst HeightsSecondary Sch, North York Can 63-68; Chief libn George Brown Col of Applied Arts &Tech, Toronto 68-. 8: Subst lectr in clsf Ryerson Polytech Inst, Toronto 68-. 9: CanLA; ALA. 10: Can Audubon Soc, Can Assn Adult Educ, Ont Assn Continuing Educ. 14: Adulteduc, tchg & training of lib technicians, rare bks. 15: Apt 102, 34 Carscadden dr,Willowdale Ont Can.

EDWARDS, SAMUEL EUGENE. b Roanoke Va 21 O 41. 5: Gallaudet Col 60-65 (LS) BS. 6: Fr, Lat. 7: Lib asst Md Inst Lib Col of Art summer 64; Lib asst Gallaudet Col Lib 64-65; Lib asst Md Inst Lib Col of Art summer 65; Lib asst Gallaudet Col Lib 65; Lib Bind asst Smithsonian Lib, Wash DC 65-68; Lib order asst II Catholic U 68 10: Wesley Club, Gallaudet Col; Dance Com of Cultural Arts, Gallaudet Col. 11: Dance Honor Award 62; Nanette Fabray Scholarship (for Conn Col Sch of Dance) 63 (Has had dancer-actor roles in col performances in the East 68). 14: Bind, rare bks, catlg,acquis. 15: 4602 Linden rd, Baltimore Md 21227.

EDWARDS, WILLIE M. b Winston Salem NC. 4: Alfred L Edwards. 5: Livingstone Col 48 (Sociol, Econ) BA; Atlanta 52 MS in LS. 7: Instr in Lib Sci Southern 51-55; Ref libn Iowa City Pub Lib 55-57; Asst Dival Libn Mich State U 57-60; Catlgr UNigeria 61-62; Subj bibliogr agric econ dept Mich State U, East Lansing Mich 62-64; Chm Georgetown Day Sch Parent Volunteer Com 65-66; Libn Tylar Elem Sch 67-. 9: ALA-RSD; Internat Assn of Agric Libns &documentalists; DC Sch LA; DCLA. 10: AAUW; LWV. 14: Child lit ref. 15: 819 6thst SW, Wash DC 20024.

EFFERTS, MARA. b Riga, Latvia 11D21. 5: Heidelberg Musik-Hochschule 48-49 (Piano) Tchrs Diploma; New Eng Conservatory of Music 49-51 (Piano) BM, 52-54 (Piano) MM; Simmons 59-61 MS in LS. 6: Latvian, Ger, Fr. 7: Interpreter tr UNNRA & IRO, Fulda Germany 46-48; Piano tchr Heidelberg Konservatorium, Heidelberg Germany 48-49; Priv music tchr, Greater Boston 49-59; Stud asst Simmons Col Lib 60-61; Catlgr Harvard Law Lib 61-. 9: NE Tech Serv Libns. 10: Harvard Lib Club. 14: Catlg. 15: 62 Toxteth st, Brookline Mass 02146.

EFTEKHARI, LUZ (CARMONA) MRS. b Medellin Colombia 4 O 35. 4: Qasem Eftekhari. 5: U Pontificia Bolivariana (Colombia) 56-59 (Phil & Letters) Licentiate; Inter-Amer Sch of Lib Sci (Colombia) 60-61 (LS) Licentiate; Catholic U 63-64 (LS) Master. 6: Sp, Fr. 7: Ref libn med lib UAntioquia, Medellin Colombia 62-63; Instr Inter-Amer Lib Sci Sch, Medellin Colombia 64-65; Specialist Pan American Union Lib, Wash DC 66-67, ref libn 67-. 9: ALA; Asociacion Colombiana de Bibliotecarios (v-pres 63); Asociacion de Egresados de la Escuela Intermaricana de Bibliotecologia. 14: Ref, admin. 15: 2400 Queens Chapel rd Apt 912, Hyattsville Md 20782.

EGAN, ELIZABETH (BEAMER). b Baldwin Kan 12 Ap 14. 5: Baker U 32-36 (Eng) AB; Ind U 58-60 (LS) MA. 6: Fr. 7: Libn Inst for Sex Research Ind U 60- Libn optometry br lib, IndU 67-. 9: ALA; SLA. 10: Alpha Delta Sigma;MedLA. 14: Clsf, catlg, clandestine bks. 15: 600 S Woodlawn, Bloomington In 47403.

EGAN, SISTER M FRANCIS JOSEPH OP. b Quincy Mass 12 O 11. 5: Villanova summers 47-51 bs in LS; CatholicU summers 54-58 MS in LS; Providence Col of Theol summers 60-62 Certif. 6: Fr. 7: Br libn Thomas Crane Pub Lib, Quincy Mass 29-32; NY Archdiocese schs 33-48; Libn St Mary's High Sch, Paterson NJ 48-56; Libn Mt St Mary Acad, Newburgh NY 56-65; Prin St Joseph High Sch, Toms River NJ 65-67; Dir Mt St Mary Col Lib 67-. 9: ALA; CathLA; NYLA; SEast NY Lib Resources Coun (trustee). 14: Catlg, ref. 15: Mount Saint Mary Col, Newburgh NY 12550.

EGAN, MARGARET L (DONNELL). b Asheville NC 16 N 09. 4: Irwin P Egan. 5: NC Col for Women 27-31 (Eng) AB; Columbia 32 BS in LS. 7: Order clerk Ind State Lib 34-36, Asst ref div 36-44; Asst ref div Cincinnati Pub Lib 44-46; 1st asst ref div Ind State Lib 46-48, Chief ref div 48-. 9: ALA; IndLA. 14: Ref. 15: Ind State Lib, Indianapolis In 46204.

EGAN, MARY DELAMAR. b Raleigh NC 12 D 11. 4: Theodore Matthew Egan. 5: Peace Col 28-30 (Eng); Womens Col UNC 30-32 AB; UNC 32-33 AB in LS; Columbia summer 38 (LS). 7: Sch libn Hendersonville High Sch, HENDERSONVILLE NC 35-36; Sch libn Mullins High Sch, Mullins SC 36-38; Asst libn Worth Elliot Carnegie Lib, Hickory NC 38-41; Libn Quartermaster Sch Tech Lib, Ft Lee Va 41-43; Chief Catlgr Jacksonville Pub Lib, Jacksonville Fla 45-. 9: SELA; Fla LA. 115: 5223 Vassar rd, Jacksonville Fl 32207. 14: Catlg. 15 5223 Vassar rd, Jacksonville Fla 32207.

EGAN, MARY JOAN (KOONZ). b Albany NY 22 Je 19. 4: William Wilson Egan. 5: SUNY(Albany) 36-40 BSLS, 46-47 (Eng), 58-62 (Educ) MSEd; Ithaca 58-59 (Educ); Columbia 62 (Programmed Instr-CPI); SUNY(Oneonta) 64 (Guidance). 6: Fr. 7: Sub libn Albany Med Col Lib summer 40; Libn Albany Pub Lib, Albany NY 40-41; Libn k-12 Burnt Hills-Ballston Lake Central Schs, Scotia NY 41-43; Head tchr Schenectady Child Care Center, Schenectady NY 44-47; Jr high libn Schenectady Pub Schs, Schenectady NY 43-46; Libn Shenendehowa Central Sch, Elnora NY 57; Elem libn Burnt Hills-Ballston Lake Central Schs, Scotia NY 58-61, Lib dept chm 61-, Proj dir 66-. a08: Assoc Prof in Sch of Lib Sci SUNY summer 65; Knapp Proj Team leader 65; Consul NDEA Inst on Sch Libs summer 65, spec in multi-media approach to lib instr prog; Consul SUNY(Oneonta & Albany) & NYLA wkshops; Taught television series of 16 lessons on lib skills. 9: ALA (Ad hoc com on lib instr 64-);-AASchL (Com on Educ Media 66-67, Publ Com 69; sec-elect 69); NEA-DAVI; NYLA (chm Personnel Com RTSS 63-); NY State TA; NY A-V Assn; Burnt Hills-Ballston Lake TA. 10: Capitol Dist Reg Educ Ctr (Steering Com in Devel 65-66, chm Com Title III 65-67); East NY SchLA; Cath Daughters of Amer; SUNY Lib Sci Alumni Assn; SUNY Theatre Alumni Assn; Confraternity of Christ Doctrine. 11: Brittanica Award 65; Outstanding Sch Devel Award, NYLA 68. 13: Yes. 14: Sch libs, multi-media approach to libs & lib instr, central processing, catlg, ref. 15: 2 Midline rd, Ballston Lake NY 12109.

EGELSTON, MARGUERITE (NORDYKE). b Springbrook Ore 8 Mr 14. 4: Elwood Franklin Egelston. 5: Pacific Col 46 (Eng) BA; Ore Col of Educ 55 (Elem Educ) BS; PortlandU 61 MLS. 7: Elem tchr Ore schs 51-58; Libn St Helens (Ore) Jr High Sch 58-61; Libn State Farm Mutual Auto Ins Co, Bloomington Ill 62-. 9: SLA; AALL; IllLA; McClean Co Libns. 14: Ref. 15: 8 Briarwood ave, Bloomington Il 61701.

EGGEN, J(OHN) ARCHER. b Virginia Minn 4 My 15. 4: Trueda Monson. 5: UMinn 37-40 (LS) BA. 7: Design engr & co-libn Cont Machines Inc, Minneapolis 41-45; Libn pub lib, Fergus Falls Minn 45-49; Dir pub lib, Cedar Rapids Minn 49-56; Dir pub lib, St Paul 56-. 8: Lib bldg consul 50-58. 9: ALA; MinnLA. 10: St Paul Rotary Club; St Paul Univ Club. 13: Yes. 14: Admin. 15: 90 W Fourth st, St Paul Mn 55102.

EGGERT, MERIS MORRISON. b Topeka Kan 7 S 38. 5: So MethodistU 56-57 (Mus); IndU 57-60 9speech, Theater) BS of Ed, 61-64 MA in LS. 7: Ref libn (stud) IndU (Bloomington) 61-64; Libn for anthrop folklore research ctr 62-63; Catlgr SoIllU 67-68; Curriculum educ libn Tex SoU 68-. 8: Lib consul Sch of Educ Tex So 68-69. 9: ALA; Tex Assn Col Tchrs; TexLA; Tex So U Faculty Forum. 10: Sigma Kappa; AAUW; Commun Relations Com. 12: Ed "New Voices" (68). 14: Curriculum & educ ref, spec wks on or by Negroes, catlg, bibliog. 15: 6922 Holmes rd #50, Houston Tx 77017.

EGOFF, SHEILA A. b Auburn Me 20 Ja 18. 5: UToronto 38 Diploma in Libnship, 48 (Eng) BA; ULondon 49 Diploma in Libnship; BritishFLA 50. 7: Gen libn Galt Pub Lib, Galt ont Can 38-42; Child libn Toronto Pub Lib, Toronto Can 42-52, Ref libn 52-57; Ed CanLA Ottawa 57-62; Assoc Prof UBC Sch Libnship 62-. 9: CanLA; ALA; BritishLA; BCLA; Assn BC Libns. 12: "The Republic of Childhood: A Critical Guide to Canadian Children's Books in English" (67). 13: Yes. 14: Child & yp lit, lib wk with child & yp, sch libs. 15: School of Librarianship Univ of British Columbia, Vancouver 8 BC Can.

EHLERT, ARNOLD DOUGLAS. b Mondovi Wis 22 Ap 09. 4: Thelma A Adolphs. 5: John Fletcher Col 27-32 (Gr) AB; Dallas Theol Sem 38-45 (Theol) ThM, ThD; USoCal 49-53 MSLS. 6: Ger. 7: Off Volunteers of Amer Rockford Ill 32-38; Libn Dallas Theol Sem 42-48; Libn Fuller Theol Sem 48-55; Hd libn Biola Schs & Cols, La Mirada Cal 55-69; Gerzd studies libn 69-. 9: Amer Theol LA; Natl Assn of Evangelicals; Evangelical Theol Soc; Christian Brethren Research Fellowahip; Victoria Inst of Gt Brit; Internat Soc of Bible Collectors (founder & pres); World Future Soc; Christian LA. 10: Beta Phi Mu. 12: Auth: "The Biblical Novel, a Checklist" (60); "Bibliographic history of Dispensationalism" (65); "Brethren Authors: a Checklist, with an introduction to Brethren Literature," (69); Bk ed "The King's Business"; Ed "The Bible Collector". 13: Yes. 14: Theol bibliog, catlg; internat bibliog for the Plymouth brethren lit and for the lit of Jewish-Christian relations. 15: 1327 Ferndale st, Anaheim Ca 92801.

EHRESMANN, JULIA (MOORE). b New Orleans La 12 Ap 39. 4: Donald L Ehresmann. 5: Pomona Col 57-61 (Hist of art) BA; NYU Inst of Fine Arts 61-66 (Hist of Art) MA; Rutgers 66-67 MLS. 6: Ger, Ital, Fr. 7: Lib asst Ford Foundation, NYC 62-64; Guest libn Germanisches National Mus, Nuremberg W Germany 67-68; Sr libn Bloomfield Pub Lib bloomfield NJ 68-. 9: ALA; SLA; NJLA. 10: Beta Phi Mu; Guest libn, 67-68, germanisches National Museum, Nuremberg, Germany. 13: Yes. 14: Art libnship, ref, acquis. 15: 711 Greenwood rd, Union NJ 07083.

EHRHARDT, ALLYN (KEITH). b Columbus Ohio 13 Ap 40. 5: Ohio State 58-62 (Eng) BA; UIll 64-65 (LS) MS. 7: Asst ref dept Columbus Pub Lib, Columbus Ohio 60-64, 65-66; Asst sci lib UIll (Urbana) 64-65; Hd libn FranklinU Lib 66-. 9: ALA; OhioLA; Franklin Co (Ohio) LA (pres 67-68). 14: R ef. 15: 637 S Third st, Columbus Oh 43206.

EHRHARDT, MARGARET (WRIGHT). b Orangeburg SC 17 S 18. 4: Benedict G Ehrhardt. 5: Duke 35-39 (Hist) BA; Emory 45-49 BALS. 6: Fr. 7: Asst libn Orangeburg Co Pub Lib, Orangeburg SC 42-44; Libn Orangeburg City Schs, Orangeburg SC 44-51, Lib supv 50-51; Child libn Richland Co Pub Lib, Columbia SC 52-58; Asst order libn USoCar (Columbia) 60-64; Order libn Wofford Col 64-65; Supv State Dept of Educ, Columbia SC 65-. 9: ALA; SELA; SCLA; SCEA; ASCD. 10: Delta Kappa Gamma; AAUW. 13: Yes. 14: Child lit. 15: 227 LaWand dr, Columbia SC 29210.

EHRLICH, EVELYN (TALVITIE). b Detroit Mich 13 F 29. 4: Robert E Ehrlich. 5: Wayne state 47-51 (Chem) BS; SUNY (Geneseo) 65-67 MLS. 6: Sp, Fr, Ger. 7: Instr (chem) Hobart Col 51-54; Catlgr AlfredU 67-. 9: ALA; NYLA. 10: Friends of the Alfred Mobile lib. 14: Catlg, ref. 15: RD 1, Alfred Sta NY 14803.

EHRLICH, MATHILDE (WILHELMINE AUGUSTE GEIS). b Duelmen Germany 16 F 15. 4: Frank Ehrlich. 5: Marienschule-Oberlyzeum (Germany) 30-34 (Eng, Biol) Abitur; Padogogium Dr Nagel (Leipzig Germany) 35-36 (Eng) Certif; St Peter's Col 62-66 (Philos) BA; Pratt 67-69 MLS. 6: Ger, Fr, Lat. 7: St Elizabeth's, London England 34-35; Foreign Lang Inst (Koblenz Germany) 36-38; Ger-Amer Schulverein, NYC 44-45; Holy Rosary Acad high Sch, Union City 62-68. 9: ALA; NEA; NJLA; NJSchLA. 10: Beta Phi Mu. 11: Philosophy medal 64-65, St Peter's; Middle States Certif of merit for outstanding serv to second educ. 14: For bks, lib serv to child & ya. 15: 1606 Palisade ave, Union City NJ 07087.

EHRMANN, MARIE (SCIALABBA). b Brooklyn NY 28 Jl 22. 4: Rolf H Ehrmann. 5: Brooklyn Col 39-43 (Chem) BA; Brooklyn Polytech Inst 43-44 (Chem); NY Law Sch 47 (Law); St John's U 50-51 (LS). 6: Ital, Fr. 7: Chem H D Roosen Co, Brooklyn NY 43-45; Chem W J Bush Corp, Linden NJ 45; Libn Chilean Iodine Educ Bur, NYC 51-56; Libn US Gypsum Co, Des Plaines Ill 61-. 9: SLA; ACS; ASIS. 14: Info retrieval systems. 15: 1446 Garden st, Park Ridge Il 60068.

EIBERSON, HAROLD. b NYC 5 S 13. 4: Rosalyn Feinberg. 5: CCNY 29-33 (Hist) BSS; Columbia 34-36 (Hist) MA, 34-37 BLS. 7: Ref asst CCNY Lib 33-43, Catlgr 43-50, Pub admin libn 50-63, Libn in charge Baruch Sch Lib 63-68; Act chief libn Baruch Col 68-. 8: Adv Woodrow Wilson Foundation Lib 42. 9: ALA; BSA. 10: Amer Pol Sci Assn. 12: "Sources for the Study of the New York Area" (60). 15: 114-114 228 st, Cambria Hts NY 11411.

EICKMEYER, ALICE JUNE. b Lakeview Ore 4 My 42. 5: UOre 62-68 (Hist) BA, 68-69 MLS. 6: Fr. 7: Stud asst (circ dept) UOre (Eugene) 64-68, Stud asst (doc dept) 68-69; Hist & lit ref libn Portland Pub Lib, Portland Ore 69-. 9: ALA. 14: Ref, govt docs. 15: 245 Kourt dr, Eugene Or 97402.

EIFERT, PHILLIP MICHAEL. b Covington Ky 11 D 45. 5: UDayton 63-67 (Hist) BA; West Mich U 67-68 MLS. 6: Sp. 7: Lib asst West Mich U Lib 68; Libn I Dayton Pub Lib, Dayton Ohio 68-. 10: Beta Phi Mu. 14: Ref. 15: 215 E Third st, Dayton Oh 45402.

EILTS, JOHN A(LVIN). b Hillsboro Ore 12 My 42. 5: Portland State Col 60-64 (Pol Sci) BA; Harvard summer 63 (Arabic); American U (Cairo Egypt) 64-66 (Arabic Studies); UMich 68-69 AMLS. 6: Arabic, Turkish, Fr. 7: Personnel mgt clk (Sp4) US Army, Turkey 66-68; Stud asst UMich Dept of Lib Sci 69. 14: Near East bibliog, ref. 15: 307 Thompson #210, Ann Arbor Mi 48108.

EIMAS, EVELYN (MARIE) (HOSAFROS). b Mt Blanchard Ohio 18 Ja 14. 4: Marcus Eimas. 5: Findlay Col 32-36 (Eng) BA; UDenver 57-62 (Libnship) MA. 7: Tchr high sch; Crestview Fla 49, Aurora Colo 53-58; Libn sr high, Aurora Colo 58-. 8: Standards for Sch IMC State Com 65. 9: NEA; NCTE; ALA; ColoEA; ColoASchL; Colo A-V Assn; ColoLA (v-chm Sch Div 69). 10: Delta Kappa Gamma; AAUW. 14: Ref. 15: 482 Jamaica st, Aurora Co 80010.

EIMAS, JOAN (DOPPENBERG). b Orange City Iowa 30 N 42. 4: Richard Eimas. 5: Northwestern Col 60-64 (Eng) BA; UDenver 64-65 (LS) MA. 6: Ger, Dutch, Fr. 7: y-a libn Arlington Co Pub Lib, Arlington Va 65-66; Catlgr Georgetown U Lib 66-67; Catlgr margret I King Lib UKy 67-. 9: KyLA; Ohio Valley Group Tech Serv Libns. 10: AAUP. 14: Catlg, ref. 15: 1012 Merrick dr, Lexington Ky 40502.

EIMAS, RICHARD. b Portsmouth Ohio 14 My 38. 4: Joan Eileen Doppenberg. 5: UColo 56-60 (Zoology) BA; UDenver 64-65 (LS) MA. 6: Fr, Ger. 7: Lt (jg) USN Communications 61-64; Libn div research serv NIH, Bethesda Md 65-66, Libn div computer research & tech 66-67; Asst libn Med Ctr Lib UKy (Lexington) 67-69, Assoc dir 69-. 8: NIH Med Lib Internship Program 65-66; Visiting lecturer Sch Lib Sci UKy 68-. 9: MedLA (Com on Continuing Educ); SLA; ASIS; SELA; KyLA (bus mgr Bulletin). 10: Phi Delta Kappa; Naval Res Assn; US Naval Inst; Alpha Phi Omega. 14: Admin, automation, documentation. 15: 1012 Merrick dr, Lexington Ky 40502.

EINHORN, NATHAN R. b York Penn 15 Ja 23. 5: Penn State 41-43, 45-47 (Hist) BA; Harvard 47-49 (Hist) MA; Columbia 49-50 (LS) MS. 7: US Army, US & Europe 43-45; LC: Spec recruit 50-51, Asst hd gift sect 51-54, Hd Orientalia exchange sect 54-56, Hd Amer & British exchange sect 56-58, Asst chief exchange & gift div 58-64, Asst chief order div 64-68, Chief exchange & gift div 68-. 9: ALA; DCLA. 14: Acquis. 15: 3507 DePauw pl, College Park Md 20740.

EISEN, MARC M. b NYC 12 Ap 40. 4: Emily Mitnick. 5: Syracuse 56-60 (Eng) AB; Brooklyn Col 60-61 (Amer Lit); Rutgers 63-65 MLS. 7: Trainee Brooklyn Pub Lib, Brooklyn NYC 63-65; Hd adult serv & ref Piscataway Pub Lib, NJ 65-66; Hd ref dept E Orange Pub Lib, NJ 66-. 8: Led NJ State Lib wkshop for small pub libs, Cumberland Co NJ 69; Act Sgt (tank commander) NY Nat Guard & US Army Res 62-68. 9: ALA; NJLA (Memb Com). 10: Beta Phi Mu; Jaycees; B'nai B'rith. 14: Ref. 15: 205-13 Lexington blvd, Clark NJ 07066.

EISENBACH, ELIZABETH (RAFFIN). b Terre Haute Ind 24 D 19. 4: Robert Eisenbach. 5: Stanford 35-39 (Econ) AB; UCLA 60-62 (LS) Masters. 6: Fr. 7: Libn UCLA Sch Lib Serv 62-, Lecturer 66-. 9: ALA; CalLA. 10: UCLA Libns Assn. 14: Ref, bibliog. 15: 330 S B undy dr, Los Angeles Ca 90049.

EISENHART, ELIZABETH JANE. b Binghamton NY 20 D 17. 5: Skidmore 39 (Fine Arts) BS; Columbia 41; NY City Col 52-54 (Sp, Ital). 6: Fr, Ital, Sp. 7: Staff picture collection NYC Pub Lib 41-43; Press agent, writer 20th Century-Fox Film Corp, NYC 43-59; Asst to pres Geo-Physical Maps Inc NYC 59-60; Libn chief Amer Bible Soc, NYC 60-. 9: ATheolLA; SLA; NY Lib Club. 12: Ed "Scriptures of the World" (65). 14: Rare bks. 15: Amer Bible Soc Lib 1865 Broadway, New York NY 10014.

EISENHART, RUTH C(ECILIA). b Binghamton NY 28 S 09. 5: Mt Holyoke 28-32 (Eng Lit) BA; Columbia 35-38 BS in LS. 6: Fr, Ger, Swedish. 7: Catlgr YaleU Lib 32-40; Hd catlgr Union Theol Lib, NYC 40-67; London ed Nat Union Catlg Publ Proj ALA, London England 67-69; Assoc catlg ed Pre-1956 Nat Union Catlg Publ Proj LC 69-. 8: Prepared wking paper & attend Intl Conf on Catlg Principles, Paris 61; Conducted wkshops on theol clsf & catlg Protestant theol sem libs, SE Asia 66; ATheolLA consul to ALA Catlg Code Revision Com 61-62. 9: ALA-RTSD (chm &/or mem 2 coms 62-69); ATheolLA (chm &/or mem 3 coms 62-67); NY Tech Serv Libns; NY Area Relig Libns Gp (chm 44-45 & 59-60. 10: Phi Beta Kappa. 12: Ed "Classification of the Library of Union Theological Seminary Revised" (67). 13: Yes. 14: Catlg & clsf, tchg. 15: 2500 Wisconsin ave NW, Washington DC 20007.

EISENLOHR, EUGEN (BIGELOW). b Berlin Germany 15 My 16. 4: Ruth Kaempfer. 5: Columbia 36-40 (Ger) BA; Pratt Inst 48-49 BLS. 6: Ger. 7: Chief clk recreation & info off YMCA Wm Sloane House, NYC 41-47; Grade libn br circ NYC Pub Lib 47-49; Ref asst NorthwesternU 49-51; Jr, Sr & prin ref libn Newark Pub Lib, Newark NJ 51-59; Ref libn Trinity Col 9hartford Conn) 59-63; Asst instr So Conn State Col 60-63; Hd ref libn RutgersU (Newark) 63-67; Sr ref libn hd ref dept Plainfield Pub Lib, Plainfield NJ 67-. 9: ALA (treasurer Essex Co Ref Serv Div 64-66); NJLA. 10: Nutley (NJ) Adult Sch (Bd of Trustees 57-60); Plainfield (NJ) Health Coun. 14: Ref. 15: 975 Park ave, Plainfield NJ 07060.

EISENMAN, DAVID. b Midland Mich 12 Mr 36. 4: Marie Jeanne Beullay. 5: UMich 54-58 (Hist of Art) AB, 61-62 AMLS. 7: PFC US Army 59-60; Libn So Sem Jr Col 62-64; Catlgr Norfolk Pub Lib, Norfolk Va 64-68; Hd of processing Macomb Co Lib, Mt Clemens Mich 68-. 14: Catlg. 15: 21930 Dunham rd, Mt Clemens Mi 48043.

EISNER, JOSEPH. b NYC 14 My 29. 4: Naomi Leff. 5: Syracuse 46-50 (Ger) BA (cum laude), 50-51 (LS); Columbia 53-54 (LS) MS. 6: Ger, Sp. 7: Lt (jg) US Naval Res, USS Yellowstone 51-53; Ref libn Hicksville Pub Lib, Hicksville NY 54-55; Dir Plainview-Old Bethpage Pub Lib, Plainview NY 55-68; Dir Assn NY Libs for Tech Serv, Garden City 68-. 8: Consul; St legis com to revise & simplify educ law 69, NJ State Lib 68; Ramapo-Catskill Ref Survey 65; Var survey assignments 62-69; Commsner on Educ's Com on Lib Devel 67-; Lecturer C W Post Lib Sch 61-67, Adjunct asst prof 68-. 9: NYLA (Lib Standards 58-63; Legis Com, mem 58-63, chm 64-69; chm Fed-State Lib Com 60-61); Nassau Co (NY) LA (pres 59-61; chm Legal Problems Com 58-59 & 61-63); Lib Trustees Foundation of NY; Nassau Lib Syst (Contract Rev Com 63; Central Ref Bldg Com 63-64, Goals & Objectives Com 67-68). 12: Comp "Handbook of Laws and Regulations Affecting Public Libraries in NY State" (63). 13: Yes. 14: Admin, info sci. 15: 54 Nassau ave, Plainview NY 11803.

EITEL, LAURA DOROTHY. b Berlamont Mich 15 Ag 10. 5: West Mich U 40 (Eng) AB; West Mich U 50 (Libnship). 7: Catlg & ref libn Ingham Co Lib, Mason Mich 51-52; Br asst & br libn Wayne Co Lib, Wayne Mich 52-56; Libn Hall-Fowler Memorial Lib, Ionia Mich 56-59; Libn S Haven Memorial Lib, S Haven Mich 59-. 9: ALA; MichLA. 10: AAUW; South Haven Art League. 15: R 1, Grand Junction Mi 49056.

EK, JACQUELINE (ELIZABETH HELEN). b Chicago Ill 23 Ja 31. 5: Le Clair Col 48-49; Col of St Francis 49-52 (Sp) AB; UIll 52-53 MS in LS. 6: Sp. 7: Adult activities dept, Gen adult dept, Arts div a-v sect, Hd films div Indianapolis-Marion Co Pub Lib 53-. 9: ALA; FLIC; EFLA; IndLA. 10: Indianapolis-Marion Co Pub Lib Staff Assn. 11: Indianapolis-Marion Co Pub Lib Distinguished Serv Award 68. 14: Film, a-v. 15: Indianapolis-Marion County Pub Lib 40 E St Clair st, Indianapolis In 46204.

EKDAHL, JANIS KAY. b Topeka Kan 7 D 46. 5: Occidental 64-68 (Art Hist) BA; Columbia 68-69 MLS. 6: Fr. 7: Summer trainee Topeka Pub Lib, Topeka Kan summers 68-69. 9: ALA; SLA. 14: Fine arts. 15: 521 W 122nd st 64, New York NY 10027.

EKSTROM, DOROTHY ANN (NA PIER). b Lima Ohio 20 Ja 24. 4: E Ross Ekstrom. 5: Bluffton Col 41-42 (Music); Cincinnati Conservatory of Music 43-45 (Voice); NorthwesternU 46-53 (Voice) B Mus; IndU 55-59 Lib Sci MS in LS. 7: Instr in voice Anderson Col 52-54, Asst to libn 53-55;

Asst to educ libn IndU (Bloomington) 55-58, Catlgr 58-59, Music libn 59-63; Asst libn Wilmington Col (Wilmington Ohio) 63-. 9: ALA; OhioLA. 10: Beta Phi Mu. 14: Catlg, circ. 15: Wilmington College, Wilmington Oh 45177.

EKSTROM, ROXY LEE (EHLERT). b Chicago Ill 2 Ag 44. 4: Richard Ekstrom. 5: NEast State Col 62-65 (Educ) BA; Rosary Col 66-69 MALS. 6: Sp. 7: Receptionist, Chicago 60-63; Lib aide NEast State Col (Chicago) 63-65; Tchr Chicago Bd of Educ 66; Libn trainee Chicago Pub Lib 66-69, Child libn NW Br 69-. 10: Beta Sigma Phi. 14: Child serv. 15: 251 Milton lane, Hoffman Estates Il 60172.

EL-HADIDY, BAHAA. b Cairo Egypt 21 Je 31. 4: Lily El-Hadidy. 5: Fac of Sci CairoU 49-54 (Chem, Geol) BS; Rutgers 61-63 MLS; West ResU 63-65 (Info Sci); UPittsburgh 65- 9info Sci). 6: Arabic, Fr. 7: Documentalist Nat Documentation Ctr, Cairo Egypt 55-61; Info analyst KAS Ctr, Pittsburgh Penn 67-69; Chem info specialist Pittsburgh Chem Info Ctr 69-. 9: ALA; ASIS (v-pres UPittsburgh Stud Chap). 14: Info sci. 15: 4628 Bayard st apt 107, Pittsburgh Pa 15213.

ELAZAR, DAVID HERZL. b Denver Colo 31 Jl 41. 4: Ruth Klestadt. 5: Wayne State U 59-64 (Chem) BA; UMich 64-65 MALS. 6: Hebrew. 7: Hd libn United Hebrew Schs, Detroit 62-; Ref libn Wayne StateU Sci Lib 65-. 8: Consul to small & medium size libs of Judaica. 9: Geosci Info Soc; Assn Jewish Libs. 12: Co-auth " A Classification for Libraries of Judaica" (68). 14: Ref, lib orientation programs. 15: 19380 Sussex, Detroit Mi 48235.

ELBAUM, ESTHER HIANNY. b Milwaukee Wis 12 Ap 17. 4: Louis Elbaum. 5: UWis (Milwaukee) 33-37 (Educ, Soc Sci) BE; UWis (Madison) 39-40 BSLS. 6: Ger, Fr, Hebrew, Yiddish. 7: Jr libn publicity asst Madison Free Lib, Madison Wis 40-43; Jr asst circ Seattle Pub Lib 43-44; Managing ed of Newsletter Hadassah, NYC 44-47; Catlgr Bd of Jewish Educ, milwaukee 62-64; Asst catlgr MaruqetteU 64-. 9: ALA; WisLA. 10: Wis Acad of Sci, Arts & Letters; Wis Soc for Jewish Learning; Kappa Delta Pi. 14: Catlg, readers serv. 15: 3717 N 51 blvd, Milwaukee Wi 53216.

ELBERT, CAROL ANN (HAUPT). b Des Moines Iowa 7 O 45. 4: Stephen Thomas Elbert. 5: Tarkio Col 63-64; UNoIowa 64-66, 67-68 (Fr, LS) BA; UGrenoble (France) winter 66 (Fr); UWash 68-69 (Libnship) MA. 6: Fr. 7: Sch libn Briarwood Elem Sch, Issaquah Wash 69-. 14: Sch libs. 15: 701 Ridgewood ave, Ames Ia 50010.

ELDER, DONALD JOHN. b Miles City Mont 24 D 41. 4: Stephanie Jane Johnson. 5: UMont 60-65 (Pol Sci) BA; UMich 66 AMLS. 6: Russian. 7: Catlgr Iowa StateU (Ames) 67-68; Hd reclsf project No IllU 68-. 9: ALA. 14: Tech processes. 15: 808 Ridge rd apt 201, DeKalb Il 60115.

ELDER, JANE (DOWLER). b Crafton Penn 4 S 14. 5: Chatham Col 32-36 (Eng) BA; Drexel 51-52 (LS) MS. 6: Fr. 7: Libn Central High Sch, Hopewell Twp NJ 53-55; Libn Ewing twp Schs, Trenton NJ 55-61; Libn Ridgewood Pub Schs, NJ 62-64; Reader's asst Carnegie Lib of Pittsburgh. 9: ALA. 10: 20th Century Club of Pittsburgh; Col Club of Pittsburgh. 15: 4716 Ellsworth ave, Pittsburgh Pa 15213.

ELDER, JOYCE D. b Montreal Can 7 Ag 25. 5: McGill 42-46 (Psych) BA, 48-49 BLS. 7: Ref libn Engring Inst of Can Montreal 49-51; Asst libn Bank of Montreal 55-58; Ref libn Fraser Hickson Inst, Montreal 59-60; Bkkeeper & Off Mgr J A Elder & Co, Montreal 52-54, 60-63; Libn Verdun High Sch, Montreal 64-68; Dir Lib Serv Lennoxville Reg Sch, Lennoxville PQ 69-. 9: CanLA; SLA; Montreal SchLA. 14: Ref, admin. 15: RMD 1, Beebe PQ Can.

ELDER, MARGARETTA ALEXANDER. b Reedsville Penn 28 N 18. 5: Penn State U 37-41 (Educ) BA; Drexel 46-47 (LS) BS. 7: Elem tchr Lewistown Sch Dist, Lewistown Penn 41-46; Asst libn Mifflin Co Lib, Lewistown Penn 47-. 10: AAUW; Penn State Alum Assn. 14: Child & YA, film serv. 15: 116 Logan st, Lewistown Pa 17044.

ELDER, RICHARD HARRY. b Philadelphia Penn 7 D 27. 5: UMd 59-64 (Bus) BA, 65-66 (LS) MS. 7: Pfc USA Airborne pub info off 50-52; Sales coord Crown Cork & Seal Co 56-59; Tchr City of Baltimore 60-62; Clerical asst Enoch Pratt Free Lib, Baltimore 63-64, Sr catlgr 66-67, Asst hd catlg dept 67-. 9: ALA; MdLA. 14: Catlg. 15: 4505 Prospect cir, Baltimore Md 21216.

ELDRED, HEATHER ANN (ELSMO). b Racine Wis 4 S 42. 4: John W Eldred. 5: UWis 60-64 9eng Lit) BA, 64-65 MA in LS; Marquette 66. 6: Fr, Ger. 7: Sec-registrar Racine Co Hist Mus, Racine Wis 61-62; Dir child & y-a serv Cudahy Pub Lib, Cudahy Wis 65-66; Asst libn & catlgr Marquette U Law Lib 66-. 8: Act hd Marquette U Law Lib 69-70. 9: AALL; WisLA. 13: Yes. 14: Child serv, catlg in law lib. 15: 816 E Glen ave, Milwaukee Wi 53217.

ELDREDGE, LUCILE MILDRED. b Sturgis SD. 5: Colo STATE Col of Educ 39 (Hist) BA; UDenver 45 BSLS, 62 (LS) MA. 7: Tchr pub schs, Pierre SD 21-42; Tchr-libn High Sch, Winner SD 42-45; Libn Yankton Col 45-66; Dir libs Ingleside, Hastings Neb 66-69; Libn, Broken Bow Neb 69-. 9: ALA; SDLA; Mountain Plains LA. 10: State and county hist societies; DAR (state and nat offs); Bd St Mary;s Sch for Indian Girls; Phi Alpha Theta; AAUW; AAUP. 13: Yes. 14: Reg hist. 15: Carnegie Lib, Broken Bow Nb 68822.

ELDRIDGE, DOROTHEA HELENE. b Kansas City Mo 27 O 22. 5: Drury Col 40-43; UKan City Mo 43-44 (Art Hist); UColo 44-45 (Interior Decor) BFA; UDenver 62-63 MS in LS. 7: Gen off wk Kan City Mo & Denver Colo 45-51; Comptometer operator & jr accountant TWA, Kan City Mo 51-56; Comptometer operator Bay Petroleum Co, Denver 56-57; Comptometer operator Colo & So RR, Denver 57-60; Lib asst Johnson Co Lib, Merriam Kan 61-62; Readers adv fine arts dept Topeka Pub Lib, Topeka Kan 63-66; Period libn & catlgr Johnson Co Lib, Merriam Kan 66-68; Asst acquis libn UMo Kan City 68-. 9: ALA; KanLA; MPLA. 10: Delta Phi Delta& ywca& zeta Tau Alpha. 14: Acquis, catlg. 15: 5300 W 66th terr, Shawnee-Mission Ks 66208.

ELFTMANN, ROBERT ARCHIBALD. b Minneapolis 28 My 01. 4: Marguerite Starkey Elftmann. 5: UMinn 49 (Educ) BS, 53 (LS) MA. 6: Swedish, Ger. 7: US Naval Reserve, Trinidad BWI, Gulfport Miss 42-45; Libn Ellendale State Normal & Ind Col 51-53; Asst libn Stout State Col 53-54; No State Col (Aberdeen SD): Head Libn & Asst Prof 54-58, Head Libn & Assoc Prof 58-59, Dir of Lib 59-66; Asst Prof lib sci div Clarion State Col 66-. 9: ALA-ACRL; NEA; Assn for Higher Educ; SDLA; SDEA; MPLA; PennLA; PennASchL. 10: Phi Delta Kappa; Rotary. 13: Yes. 14: Lib bldgs, acquis, standards, bibliog, admin. 15: 83 N 5th ave, Clarion Pa 16214.

ELGIN, LILLIAN (COLEMAN). b Ira (Buchanan Co) Va 16 F 14. 5: Berea Col 31-37 (Chem) BA; UVa summer 40 (LS); Madison Col summer 50 (LS); Peabody Col summers 54, 58, 59. 7: Tchr & libn Hurley High Sch, Hurley Va 37-44, 47-52; Libn Grundy High & elem schs, Grundy Va 52-59; Asst libn Union Col (Barbourville) 59-61; Libn Buchanan Co Pub Lib, Grundy Va 61-. 9: ALA; VaLA. 10: Delta Kappa Gamma; Buchanan Co Lib League. 14: Catlg. 15: Box 58, Grundy Va 24614.

ELGOOD, WILLIAM R. b Richmond Que Can 22 O 22. 4: Ann Drew. 5: UVt 46-50 BA; UMich 51 MA, 64 MALS. 6: Fr, Ger. 7: Gunnery instr Royal Canadian Air Force 41-45; Tchgfellow & debate coach UMich 50-52; Speech Instr General Motors Inst, Flint Mich 53-58, Dir of Lib 58-. 9: SLA (sec Mich Br 65); Amer Soc Engrg Educ (Lib Com 65-67); Flint Lib Club(pres 65); Inter-Assn Lib Scholarship Fund (treas 66-69). 10: Bd Flint IndusExecutives Club; Flint Com to Welcome Foreigners. 13: Yes. 14: Admin. 15: 1615 E Court st, Flint Mi48503.

ELIAS, ARTHUR WILLIAM. b NYC 21 F 27. 4: Norma Segal. 5: UBuffalo 46-48 (Biol); UAlabama 48-50 (Biol) BS; Rutgers 54-55 (Med Sci) MS. 6: Ger. 7: Med resarch tech USN, Camp Lejeune NC 50-52; Pharmacologist Maltbie Labs, Hanover NJ 52-54; Pharmacologist Warner-Lambert, Morris Plains NJ 54-59, Manager sci info serv 59-62; Manager sci info sect Wyeth Labs, Radnor Penn 62-64; Dir Publ Inst Sci Info, Philadelphia 64-66. v-pres 66-68; Exec dir Infoco America 68-. 8: Assoc Prof (Info Sci) Drexel Inst Grad Sch Lib Sci. 9: ASIS(chm Placement Serv & chm local chaps). 12: Ed "Proceedings" ADI (Parameter of InfoSci) (54); Ed "Tech Info Center Admin" 3 vols (64-66); Ed "American Documentation"(64-). 13: Yes. 14: Indexing info, sci, info retrieval, lib educ. 15: 225 S 15 st, Phila Pa 19102.

ELISON, GAR THYNE. b Sublette Ida 22 Jl 40. 4: Marilyn Durfee. 5: Utah State U 58-60 (Bus); Brigham Young U 63-65 (Pol Sci) BA; UOkla 65-66 MLS. 6: Ger. 7: Docs libn Idaho State U, Pocatello Idaho 66-68, Act hd of readers serv 68-69; Assoc libn UNM Med Lib 69-; Asst dir RMP Health Info Ctr NM Reg Med Progeam, Albuquerue 69-. 9: NMLA (chm Com on State Docs). 14: Docs, multi-media in libs, computers in libs. 15: 4312 Ponderosa NE, Albuquerque NM 87110.

ELISON, MARILYN (DURFEE). b Rupert Ida 20 N 41. 4: Gar Thanye Elison. 5: Brigham Young U 60-64 (Mus) BS; UOkla 65-66 MLS. 7: Mus tchr Farrer Jr High, Provo Utah 64-65; Humanities libn Ida State U 66-68. 14: Ref & bibliog (univ level). 15: 4312 Ponderosa NE, Albuquerque NM 87110.

ELKIN, BETTY LEE. b Cincinnati Ohio 2 Je 19. 5: UCincinnati 42-44 (Fr); Columbia 66 (LS) MS. 6: Fr, Sp. 7: Tchr Mark Twain High Sch, Statesburg WVa 40-42; Clk & machine operator Tool Steel Gear & Pinion Co, Cincinnati 43-44; Prod dept advertising Stockton West Burkhardt Ralph Jones, Cincinnati 45-46; Phonograph rec buyer: Steinberg's Inc, Cincinnati 47-50, Notes Inc, Cincinnati 50-53, Higbee Co, Cleveland Ohio 53-61; Exec sec Call Assoc, NYC 63-65; Asst acquis libn SUNY (Stoney Brook) 67-. 9: ALA; NY Mus LA. 14: Latin Amer area collections, acquis. 15: 49-66B Piedmont dr, Port Jefferson Station NY 11776.

ELKINS, THELMA LOUISE. b Crayne Ky 21 D 26. 5: UnionU 47-51 (Eng) BA; SWest Sem 52-54 9youth Wk) MRE; USoCal 60-63 MSLS. 7: Bkkeeper UnionU 51-52; Youth dir First So Baptist Ch, San Francisco 54-57; Dir campus activities Cal Baptist Col 57-60, Pub serv libn 60-65; Ref libn Cal WestU 65-66; Asst ref libn Colo State Col 66-68; Libn Baptist Col (Charleston SC) 68-. 9: ALA; SELA; SCLA. 14: Ref. 15: 4 Capitan ct, Charleston Heights SC 29405.

ELKOURI, JIM R. b Chickasha Okla 7 Ag 38. 5: UOkla 56-60 (Letters) BA, 60-62 MLS. 7: Jr documents libn Okla State U Lib 2-63; Documents & gifts libn Okla City U Lib 63-65; Catlg libn 65-. 9: ALA; NEA; SWLA; OklaLA (chm Inte Freedom Com 64-65). 10: Phi Beta Kappa; Phi Alpha Theta; Beta Phi Mu. 14: Catlg (humanities). 15: 2332 NW 16, Oklahoma City Okla 73107.

ELLEBRACHT, ELEANOR (VIOLA). b Ft Sam Houston Tex 23 Ap 37. 4: Pat Ellerbracht. 5: Ark Col 54-58 (Eng) BA; UArk summer 58 (LS); Peabody 59-60 (LS) MA. 6: Sp. 7: Stud lib asst Ark Col 55-58; Tchr-libn Sulphur Rock High Sch, Sulphur Rock Ark 58-59; Stud lib asst ref Joint U Lib Nashville 59-60; Asst libn Ark State Col 60-67; Ref libn NE Mo State Col 67-. 09: ArkLA; ArkEA; MoStateTA; MoLA. 10: AAUW; Ark State Col Faculty Assn. 14: Ref, interlib loans, govt documents, ser, tch lib sci. 15: Box 347, Kirksville Mo 63501.

ELLEN, SISTER MARY (HOY) CSJ. b Cleveland 24 My 04. 5: St Jt John Col (Cleveland) 28-37 (Educ) BS in Educ; John Carroll U 39-45 (Rel,Guidance); West Res 44-47 BS of LS, 57-58 MS of LS. 6: Fr. 7: Jr high Eng tchr St Vincentde Paul, Cleveland 24-45; Jr high Eng tchr St Colman Sch, Cleveland 45-49; Jr highEng tchr St Clement Sch, Cleveland 49-55; Jr high Eng tchr St Thomas Aquinas Sch,cleveland 55-57; Jr high Eng tchr St Aloysius Sch, Cleveland 57-58; High sch libnNazareth Acad, Parma Heights Ohio 58-. 8: Asst libn, St John Co (Cleveland) summers 56, 60-62. 9: CathLA; OhioASchL. 14: Wking with yp, ref. 15: Nazareth AcadLib, 6000 Queens Highway, Parma Heights Oh 44130.

ELLENBERGER, JACK S. b Lamar Colo 5 S 30. 5: Georgetown U Sch of Foreign Serv 55-57 (Internat Rel) BSFS; Columbia 57-59 MSLS. 6: Fr. 7: Law libn US Dept of Health Educ & Welfare, Wash DC 57; Libn Carter Ledyard & Milburn, NYC 57-60; Libn Jones Day Cockley & Reavis, Cleveland 60-61; Libn Bar Assn f the Dist of Columbia, Wash DC 61-63; Libn Covington & Burling, Wash DC 63-. 8: Instr Law Libnship US Dept of Agric Grad Sc(Wash DC) 63-. 9: AALL (chm &/or mem 3 coms 59-69); SLA (pres Wash DC Chap 68-69); DCLA. 13: Yes. 14: Ref & bibliog of law libnship. 15: 888 Sixteenth st NW, Wash DC 20006.

ELLERBE, HELEN (CUBBERLY). b Cedar Key Fla 29 Jl 06. 5: Randolph Macon Womens Col 24-25; Fla State Col for Women 25-28 (Eng) AB; Emory 40-41 BA LS; UFla 59-60 (Educ) M Ed; Emory 57 (LS); Appalachian State U 67 (LS). 7: Asst in Theol Lib Emory U 40-41; Libn US Army, Camp Murphy Fla 42-44; Libn UFla41-42, 50-60; Libn Westwood Sch, Gainesville Fla 60-68; Libn Cultural Enrichment Ctr, Gainesville Fla 68-. 9: FlaLA; FlaASchL; FlaEA. 10: Fla HistSoc; Alachua Co (Fla) Hist Commsn; Alachua Co Hist Soc; Gainesville Centenn Commsn 69. 12: Index "Proceedings of the Florida Horticultural Society" (54); "Historywalk Around Downtown Gainesville." (69). 15: 918 SW 8 lane, Gainesville Fl 32601.

ELLINGER, WERNER B(RUNO). b Heidelberg Germany 28 Ag 08. 4: Lucile Morsch. 5: Heidelberg 27-28, 29-31 (Law) DrJur; Berlin 28-29; Columbia 39-40 (LS) BS. 6: Ger, Fr. 7: Legal counsel Dept store chain, Baden-Baden Germany 34-37; Gen office wk, NYC 37-39; Asst libn Inst for Advanced Study, Princeton NJ 40-41; Catlgr LC 41-42, Subj catlgr LC42-51, Sr subj catlgr 51-69, Spec in law clsif 69-. 8: In chg of developing LC clsf for law 52- Consul UCal (Davis) 67, dir of wkshops,Phila 68, Wash 69 on application of LC law clsf. 9: AALL (chm &/or mem 3 coms 52-63); ALA-ACRL (chm &/or mem 3 coms 57-62); ALA-RTSD (chm &/or mem 2 coms 46-); Internat Assn Law Libs (Delegate to Internat Conf on Catlg Principles, Paris 61); DCLA (pres 62-63); Ptomac Tech Processing Libns (chm 46-48); Law Libns Soc Wash DC; Amer Soc Internat Law. 11: Carnegie Fellowship 39. 12: "Der Rechtsschutz derKunstlerischen Darstellung" (34), "Sea Power in the Pacific; a Bibliography,"with H Rosinski (42), "Subject Headings for the Literature of Law andinternational Law" (63, 2d ed 69) Ed "DC Libraries" (58-60). 13: Yes. 14: Catlg, & clsf (esp of legal lit). 15: 4701 Willard ave,Chevy Chase Md 20015.

ELLINGWOOD, BEVERLY (GOEBEL). b Rochester NY 21 Mr 29. 4: Franklyn Kelley Ellingwood. 5: URochester 46-50 (Sociol) AB; Drexel 50-51 (LS) MS. 7: Adult asst Rochester Pub Lib, lincoln Br, Rochester NY 51-53; Asst Eastman Kodak Co, Research Lib, Rochester NY 53-57; Case Wker Dept Soc Welfare, Rochester NY 57-59; Lib Dir Webster Pub Lib, Webster NY 59-66; Sr libn E Rochester Pub Lib, Rochester NY 68-. 9: NYLA. 15: 195 Longview dr, Webster NY 14581.

ELLINWOOD, LEONARD WEBSTER. b Thomaston Conn 13 F 05. 4: Lera Slayback. 5: Aurora Col 23-26 (Philos) BA; Eastman Sch of Music URochester 33-34 (Musicology) MMus, 34-36 (Musicology) PD. 6: Ger, Lat. 7: Music instr Mt Hermon Sch, Mass 27-33; Tchg Fellow Eastman Sch URochester, NY 34-36; Instr I Musicology Mich State Col 36-39; Sr subj catlgr humanities LC 40; Sr catlgr humanities 62-. 8: Asst minister Wash Cathedral DC 48-; Instr Col of Church Musicians, DC 63-. 9: Amer Musicological Soc; Mediaeval Acad Amer; Renaissance Soc of Amer; Hymn Soc of Amer (Fellow); MusLA; Organ Hist Soc. 10: Trustee, Wash Cathedral Choral Soc. 12: Ed ""Dictionary of American Hymnology (55-); ""Musica Hermanni Contracti (36); ""Works of Francesco Landini (39); ""History of American Church Music (53); Ed ""Bio-Bibliog Dictionary of Amer Musicians (41); ""Hymnal (40); ""Companion (49); etc. 13: Yes. 14: Subj control of info. 15: 3724 Van Ness st NW, Wash DC 20016.

ELLIOTT, AGNES (SKOLOUT). b Beardsley Kan 18 Mr 13. 4: Donald Bruce Elliott. 5: UKan 35-39 (Journalism) BA; Kan State Tchrs Col 58-59 (LS) MS. 6: Czech. 7: Sec US Military Serv 58; Catlgr engnr lib Boeing Co, Wichita Kan 59-61; Libnwichita Bd of Educ, Wichita Kan 61-. 9: Wichita Lib Club (pres 63); Wichita City Tchrs Assn (Legis Com). 10: Wichita Rose Soc; Rose Shaw Judge, AmerRose Soc. 13: Yes. 15: 623 N Hampton rd, Wichita Ka 67206.

ELLIOTT, BARBARA BLANCHE. b Baltimore Md 14 S 36. 5: Smith 54-58 (Zool) BA; Drexel 59-60 MSLS. 7: Case wker Welfare Dept Child'sdiv, Baltimore 58-59; Pre-prof Baltimore Co Pub Lib, Pikesville Br 59-60, Gen asstCatonsville Br 60-61, Gen asst Pikesville Br 61, Br libn Reisterstown Br 61-62; Genref asst Welch Med Lib, Baltimore 62; Gen asst Baltimore Co Pub Lib, Parkville &reisterstown Brs 62, Interlib loan libn Admin Off 62-67, Asst br libn Randallstownbr 67-. 9: ALA-RSD (Md Affiliate); MdLA. 10: Phi Kappa Phi; Beta Phi Mu; SmithCol Club. 14: Ref, adult serv. 15: 1034-C Woodson rd, Baltimore Md 21212.

ELLIOTT, DOROTHY EVELYN (HUFFORD). b Crawfordsville Ore 9 D 8. 4: Edward Carl Elliott. 5: Ore Col of Educ 38-40 (Educ) diploma; East Ore Col 42-44 (Educ) BS; Ore State Col 44-47 (Educ) MEd; UOre 51-53; (Educ); UPortland 59-61 (LS) MS. 7: Elem tchg pub schs, Condon, Pendleton, Union Ore 40-44; Secondary tchg pub schs, Umatilla Ore 45-51; Elem tchg Portland Pub Schs 55-62; Head libn Cleveland High Sch 62-. 8: Tchr, ref & bibliog, Portland State Col, Cont Educ Div; Dir wkshop in elem libnship UPortland; Tchr in-serv class, Portland Pub Sch. 9: NEA; ALA; OreASchL. 10: Delta Kappa Gamma; Kappa Delta Pi. 14: Ref. 15: 725 SE Rhone, Portland Ore 97202.

ELLIOTT, EDWARD H(AROLD). b Brooklyn NY 20 Ja 07. 4: Caroline Stabler. 5: Brooklyn Polytech Inst even24-28; UWis 28-31 (Physics) BA; Pratt 32-33 (LS) Certif. 6: Fr, Ger. 7: Lab asst Bell Tel Labs, NYC 24-28; Ref asst NY Pub Lib 33-35; Abstractor & ref libn Standard Oil Dev Co, Elizabeth NJ 35-38; Head sci & tech ref dept Pratt Inst Free Lib, Brooklyn NY 38-44; Patent analyst Hercules Powder Co, Wilmington Del 44-45; Ref libn, manager Main Lib Gen Electric Co, Schenectady NY 45-61; Sci libn Union Col Lib (Schenectady NY) 61-. 9: ALA; SLA. 10: Edison Club; Adirondack

Mountain Club. 12: Contrib to ""Industrial Electronics Handbook (48). 13: Yes. 14: Ref, admin. 15: 1372 Clifton Pak rd, Schenectady NY 12309.

ELLIOTT, ELLA MARIAN. b New Haven Conn 27 Ag 05. 5: Mt Holyoke 23-27 (Eng Lit) BA; Columbia 28-29 BLS; Chicago 41-42 MA. 7: Br asst New Haven Pub Lib, New Haven Conn 27-28; Catlgr NYU Wash Sq Lib 29-31;Catlgr Harvard U Grad Sch of Bus Admin Lib 31-39; Hd Catlgr Hamilton Col Lib 39-41;Catlgr UCal Lib (Berkeley) 42-46; Head acquis libn Vassar Col Lib 46-. 15: VassarCol, Poughkeepsie NY 12601.

ELLIOTT, HAZEL ELIZABETH (HENDERSHOT). b Waverly WVa 22 D 12. 4: James C Elliott. 5: Marshall U 30-34 (Eng) AB; WVa U summers 35-40 (Educ) MA. 7: Libn Williamstown (WVa) High Sch 35-42; Clerk US Govt OPA, Charleston WVa42-44; Clerk US Govt OPA, Wash DC 44-46; Libn High Sch, Williamstown WVa 60-62;Asst libn High Sch, Parkersburg WVa 62-65& head Libn 65-. 9: ALA; NEA; WVaEA;WVaSchL (v-pres 67-68); WVaLA. 14: Ref, admin. 15: 2518 Liberty, Parkersburg WVa 26101.

ELLIOTT, JEAN ANN. b Martinsburg WVa 18Ja 33. 5:Shepherd Shepherd 50-54 (Educ) AB; Syracuse 55-57 MS in LS; Shippensburg State Col 66- (Hist). 7: Grad asst Syracuse U 55-57; Asst libn Fairmont State Col 57-60: Ref asst UPittsburgh 60-61; Acting libn Shepherd Col 61-62; Asst libn 62-. 8: WVa Cm for Lib Sci Currs to Certify Sch Libns, 61. 9: ALA-ACRL (Tri-State Chap; sec-treas 68-69); WVaLA (chm Col Sect 68-69); CumberlandValleyLA. 10: Alpha Beta Alpha; AAUP; Jefferson Co Hist Soc. ; AAUW; Shepherd Col Alumni Assn. 14: Ref, loc hist. 15: 414 S Rosemont ave, Martinsburg WVa 25401.

ELLIOTT, LLOYD GENE. b Charleston W Va 16 Je 40. 5: UMe 60-63 (Zoology) BA; West Res 65-66 MS in LS. 7: 1st Lt USA, Ft McClellan Ala 63-65; Ref libn & bibliog UMe 66-68, asst Prof of lib serv 68-. 9: ASIS. 15: Fogler Lib Univ of Maine, Orono Me 04473.

ELLIOTT, M MARGARET DRAKE. b Breckenridge Mich 31 Ag 04. 4: Paul A Elliott. 5: Albion Col 24 (Sci Liberal Arts) AB; UMich 25 (Sci) MS; West Mich U & UMich 52-60. 6: Ger, Sp, Fr, Hebrew, Lat. 7: Instr Albion Col 25-27; Instr Bay View Summer U 27-37; Lib asst, br libn,hackley Pub Lib 28-32; Instr Muskegon Pub Schs, Muskegon Mich 32-48; Libn MuskegonHigh Sch, Muskegon Mich 50-. 8: Comp "Books and Brochures of Poetry by Mich Poets, for Bk ed com of Mich Assn of Sch Libs for "Michigan Authors, (60) and "Michigan Poets (64); free lance writer 30-. 9: ALA; NEA; Nat League Amer Pen Women; MichEA; MichLA;Mich Assn Sch Libns; Lakeshore LA; Muskegon Tchrs Club; Outdoor Writers of Amer;Assn of Amer Bk Women; Mich Acad of Sci, Arts & Letters. 10: AAUW; PEO; MuskegonWoman's Club (past pres); YWCA (past pres); Delta Kappa Gamma; Alpha Xi Delta; PoetrySoc of Mich (past pres); Mich Fed Garden Clubs; Herb Soc of Amer; Penn Folklife Soc;Mich Audubon Soc (pres 5 terms); Writers Group (charter mem, past chm); JuvenileWriters Workshop; Muskegon Co Mus (Bd 37-); Grand Rapids Mus Assn; Urban League; MichFolklore Soc. 11: Career Woman of Year (Lib Week 63). 12: Weekly outdoor column in "Muskegon Chronicle" 30-; Monthly columnon Herb-gardening "Ozark Gardens" 55-; 36 juvenile stories (38-42); about 300 publpoems; ABC of Herbs; Christmas Again; Round and Round- A year (with husband). 13: Yes. 14: Sch & child lit, poetry, nat sci, folklore. 15: 1513Nelson st, Muskegon Mi 49441.

ELLIOTT, MARGARET (HACKER). b Decatur Ala 22 My 18. 5: UAla 34-37 (Chem, Pre-Med) AB, 51-53 (LS) BS Ed. 6: Lat, Ger. 7: Asst libn Birmingham (Ala Pub Lib, Eastlake Br 53-54; Libn Baroness Erlanger Hosp Med Lib, Chattanooga Tenn 54-63; Libn Baroness Erlanger Hosp Patients Lib, Chattanooga Tenn 54-63; Libn Doctors Lib TC Thompson Childs Hosp, Chattanooga Tenn 54-; Libn Baroness Erlanger Hosp & Chattanooga- Hamilton Co Med Soc, Jt Med Lib, Chattanooga Tenn 63-. 8: Consul, Nurs Sch Lib Baroness Erlanger Hosp, Chattanooga Tenn 53-. 9: MedLA; ALA; SELA; TennLA. 10: Kappa Delta Pi. 14: Ref, catlg. 15: 208 Booth rd. Chattanooga Tenn 37411.

ELLIOTT, MARIA ESTHER (VEGA). b Naranjito PR 7 F 33. 4: William M Elliott. 5: UPR 49-51 (Eng); Cardinal Stritch Col 51-53 (Eng) BA; UKan City Sch of Law 59-60 (Law); UDenver 63-64 MA LS. 6: Sp, Ital, Portu. 7: Govt of PR: Tchr Naranjito 53-54, Soc wker 54-55, Tr, San Juan 55-56, Libn, San Juan 56-59; Head Libn Huntington Woods Lib, Huntington Woods Mich 65-68; Hd child serv Santa Ana Pub Lib, Santa Ana Cal 69-. 15: 15782 Clarendon,Westminster Ca 92683.

ELLIOTT, MAUDE (SISTER). b Montreal Can 23 Ja 13. 5: UMontreal 29-33 (Latin, Phil) BA, 40-41 (Eng) MA; UBC 64-65 BLS. 6: Fr. 7: Tchr Convent of the Sacred Heart: Montreal 37-44, 51-53, halifax Can 44-51, 65-, Winnipeg Can 53-55, Vancouver Can 55-64; Libn Jr Col of the Sacred Heart, Halifax Can 65-. 8: Dean of Studies: Convent of the Sacred Heart, Montreal 37-43; Convent of the Sacred Heart, Halifax 44-51; Chm French Dept Convent of the Sacred Heart Vancouver 55-64. 9: CanLA; APLA; HalifaxLA. 15: Convent of the Sacred Heart, 5820 Spring Garden rd, Halifax NS.

ELLIOTT, NANCY L (MEDLAND). b Spokane Wash 30 N 43. 4: Harold M Elliott. 5: Chabot Col 62-63 (Fr); San Francisco State Col 63-66 (Fr) BA; Simmons 66-67 (LS) MS. 6: Fr. 7: Asst city libn San Bruno Pub Lib, San Bruno Cal 67-. 9: Peninsula LA (Prog Chm). 14: Ref. 15: 111 S Mayfair, Daly City Ca 94015.

ELLIOTT, RICHARD G(ARDNER). b Wheeling WVa 23 Ja 23. 4: Olive Schroyer. 5: Clarion State Col 45-57, 49-50 (Eng) BS; Syracuse 50-51 (LS) MS; USoCal 69 Info Sci Inst. 7: Libn I State Col of Wash 51-54; Ref libn Cedar Rapids Pub Lib, Cedar Rapids Iowa 54-56; Libn Fairmont State Col 56-58; Libn Col of Ida 58-. 9: ALA-ACRL; PNLA; IdaLA. 10: AAUP. 13: Yes. 14: Lib admin, lib bldg construction, info sci. 15: 2307 Colorado ave, Caldwell Id 83605.

ELLIOTT, RICHARD JAMES. b Windsor NY 07. 5: Dartmouth 30 AB; UPenn 31 (Eng) MA; Columbia 40 BS. 7: Clerk & libn bk order off, div head lang & lit, asst supt of central serv Brooklyn Pub Lib 37-46; Libn soc sci div, div head lang & lit Brooklyn Pub Lib 48-50; Ref libn Brooklyn Col Lib 50-60; Catlgr & ref libn Harpur Col 60-. 13: Yes. 14: Ref. 15: 13901 Harpur Col, Windsor NY 13865.

ELLIOTT, SHARLENE RAE. b Lampasas Tex 11 Jl 46. 5: San Antonio Col 64-66 AA; SW Tex State Col 66-68 (Elem Educ) BS in Ed; N Tex StateU 68-69 MLS. 7: Jr libn San Antonio Col 69-. 9: ALA. 14: Ref. 15: 146 Oxford dr, San Antonio Tx 78213.

ELLIOTT, SHIRLEY BURNHAM. b Wolfville NS 4 Je 16. 5: Acadia 33-37 (Eng) BA; UToronto 37-38 (Eng); Acadia 38-39 (Eng) MA; Simmons 39-40 (LS) SB. 6: Fr. 7: Gen asst Brookline Pub Lib, Brookline Mass 40-42, Ref asst 42-46; Asst libn URI (Kingston) 46-49; Asst ed Canadian index Canadian Lib Assn Ottawa Ont 49-50; Chief libn Colchester-E Hants Reg Lib, Truro NS 50-54; Leg libn Province of Nova Scotia, Halifax NS 54-. 8: Libn on the Staff of the Duke of Edinburgh's Second Commonwealth Conf Canada May-June 62. 9: CanLA (Counc 64-67); APLA; HalifaxLA. 10: Can Club of Halifax; Halifax Univ Women's Club; Royal Commonwealth Soc; Senate of Acadia U. 12: Ed "Atlantic Provinces Checklist" (57-65); Ed "Nova Scotia in Books, 1752-1967" (67). 14: Ref Canadiana. 15: Province House, Halifax NS Can.

ELLIOTT, WILLIAM. b NYC 8 S 21. 4: Annette Dyar. 5: City U of NY 38-42 (Econ) BA; Pratt 42-43 BLS; NYU 51-54 (Public Affairs) MA; Sorbonne 45 (Linguistics) Certif. 6: Fr, SP, Ger. 7: Cryptanalyst specialist US Army Intelligence, England, France 43-44; Catlgr & acquis asst NYU 46-52; Head acquis dept Colgate U 53; Field rep Electric & Musical Industries, NYC & NJ 54-61; Tech libn & tech ed Vitro Corp, NYC & Wash DC 62-63; Mgr lib serv Pepsico, NYC 64-66; Chief libn Nat Industrial Conference Bd, NYC 67; Libn USA Standards Inst, NYC 68; Libn Haskins & Sells, NYC 69-. 8: Consul (Detached Serv) US Army Lib Serv Train Within Civilian Agencies PROGRAM (46); Mem Z-39 Com on Lib Performance Standards; Mem Z-85 Com on Lib Equipment. 9: SLA; ALA; NY Lib Club. 10: Audio Engnring Soc; Lions Club; Churchill Club (London); Koscinogko Found; Woodrow Wilson/FDR Soc; NYU Alumni. 12: "Russo-Polish War, 1919-1922 (54). 13: Yes. 14: Admin. 15: 38 W 95th st, New York NY 10025.

ELLIS, AILEEN VIRGINIA. b Cranberry NC. 5: Milligan Col (Hist) AB; Peabody BS in LS, MA; Fla State U 66-68 (Mgt). 6: Fr, Ger, Sp. 7: Libn Vet Hosp, Waco Tex, Libn Vet Hosp, Oleen NC, Libn Phil Ry Com, Manila PI, Libn Ernie Pyle Lib, Tokyo, Catlgr UTenn, Libn-archivist Air U, Maxwell AFB Va, Staff libn Continental Air Command, Robins AFB Ga 63-66; Libn Base Lib Eglin AFB, Fla 66-. 8: Lib/USA, NY Worlds Fair, 65. 9: ALA; SLA; ALA Chap; sec-treas 60-61, Histn 63; Sela; FlaLA; AlaLA. 10: AAUW; DAR; Little Theatre. 12: Assoc ed "Alabama Librarian (63). 13: Yes. 14: Catlg, ref, admin. 15: P O Box 1732, Eglin AFB Fl 32542.

ELLIS, DOROTHY ANN (NAIDEN). b Indianapolis Ind 10 Jl 18. 4: William Donohue Ellis. 5: Pembroke Col 36-40 (Lat) BA; Case-West Res 47-68. 6: Fr, Sp. 7: Tchr LaGrange High Sch, LaGrange Ohio 41-42; Tchr Rocky River High Sch, Rocky River Ohio 44-45, Libn 46-51, 61-. 8: North Central Evaluation Team 66; State-wide survey on integrated (prinr and non-print) libs. 9: ALA; NEA-DAVI; OhioASchL (chm a-v com); Educ Media Coun; OhioEA. 10: College Club; Aircraft Owners Pilots Assn. 14: Sch libs, educ media co-ord. 15: 1060 Richmar dr, Westlake Oh 44145.

ELLIS, ELINOR VIVIAN (WALL). b Charleston Miss 8 O 24. 4: Richard Ellis II. 5: Tuskegee Inst 41-45 (Elem Educ) BS Elem Ed; Atlanta 57 (LS) MSLA. 6: Fr, Sp. 7: Dir of Lib Selma U 46-57; Catlg & ref libn Ala A&M Col 58-62; Tchr libn Brantley High Sch, Selma Ala 62-63; Period libn Fla A&M U 63-65, Asst dir Curriculum Lab Sch of Educ 66-. 8: Lib consul for high schs, 62; Readers adv for col commun 63; Libns consul for PTA 64; Faculty Senate 65. 9: ALA; AlaLA; FlaLA. 10: Delta Sigma Theta. 13: Yes. 14: "The Role of The Curriculum Laboratory In The Preparation of Quality Teachers"(69). 15: 713 Stafford st, Tallahassee Fl 32307.

ELLIS, JACK D. b Morehead Ky 10 Ja 27. 4: Janis Caudill. 5: Morehead State Col (LS) AB; Peabody (LS) MA; Fla State U (Educ); UFla (Educ); USoMiss (Educ). 6: Ger. 7: Tchr Morehead(Ky) schs 50-53, Bkmob libn 53-57; Libn-AV Coordinator St Petersburg(Fla) schs 57-58; Libn-AV Dir St Petersburg Jr Col 58-60; Supv Inst Materials Pinellas Co Fla schs 60- Consul Coronet Films Dir of Libs Morehead St U. 8: Governors (Fla) Adv Com on Libs; Consul Manpower Development Train Center; Consul Womens Job Corps; Consul Electronic Industries Libn; Consul NDEA Insts. 9: ALA; NEA;KyLA. 10: AAUP; Phi Delta Kappa. 12: Ed "Bookcase, off publ of FlaASchL. 13: Yes. 14: Admin. 15: Director of Libraries MSU, Morehead Ky 40351.

ELLIS, JEAN (REVA). b Marion NC 9 S 20. 5: Meredith Col 37-41 (Math) AB; UNC 41-42 (LS) BS. 7: Mathematician Nat Advisory Committee for Aeronautics, Langley Field Va 42-45; Asst ext libn Durham Pub Lib, Durham NC 46-47; Asst libn Spartanburg Pub Lib, Spartanburg SC 47-54; Libn Leesburg Pub Lib, Leesburg Fla 54-57; Circ libn Greensboro Pub Lib, Greensboro NC 57-59, Asst libn 59-. 9: ALA; SELA; NCLA; Greensboro Lib Club. 10: Bus & Prof Womens Club. 14: Admin. 15: 802 N Eugene st, Greensboro NC 27401.

ELLIS, JOYCE PAULA (SILHAVY). b Saginaw Mich 16 D 27. 4: A Harlow Ellis. 5: Conn Col 45-49 (Eng Lit) BA; Simmons 64-67 MLS. 7: Lib asst Soc Law Lib, Boston 49-50; Prof asst Boston Pub Lib 50-56, Child libn 57-61; Child libn Edgell Lib, Framingham Mass 62-63; Br libn Merriam Br Lib, Framingham Mass 63-66; Br libn Centre Lib, Framingham Mass 66-68; Dir libs Framingham Pub Lib, Framingham Mass 68-. 9: ALA; MassLA; Charles River Lib Club. 14: Admin. 15: 1041 Grove st, Framingham Mass 01701.

ELLIS, JUDITH ANN. b St Charles Mo 21 Je 36. 5: Col St Teresa 54-55 (Liberal Arts); UNor Iowa 55-58 (Bus Educ) BA; UColo summer 62; UIowa 66-69 (LS) MA. 6: Sp. 7: Secondary tchr Keota Commun Schs, Keota Iowa 58-64; Admin libn Davenport Pub Lib, Davenport Iowa 64-. 9: ALA; IowaLA. 10: Pi Lambbda Theta; Pi Omega Pi; Bus & Prof Women. 14: Pub lib admin, adult serv. 15: 413 W 6th st, Davenport Ia 52803.

ELLIS, MARIE CAROL. b Tallahassee Fla 10 N 43. 5: Fla StateU 61-64 (Eng) BA, 65 (LS) MA. 6: Fr. 7: Asst ref libn Col of William & Mary 66-. 9: ALA; VaLA. 10: Phi Beta Kappa; Phi Kappa Phi; Beta Phi Mu. 12: "A Guide to Historical Materials in the Swem library". 14: Ref. 15: 210 Nelson ave, Williamsburg Va 23185.

ELLIS, MARY ANN (STEINMANN-RAKER). b St Louis Mo 24 S 26. 4: John H Ellis. 5: Harris Jr Col 45-47 AA; Wash U 47-49 BSLS. 7: USAF: Base libn, Okinawa 49-51, Japan 52-54, supv libn, Germany 54-57, Ref libn St Louis 58-; Catlgr pub lib, St Louis 58. 8: Ref Libn, Lib/USA Exhibit, NY World's Fair 64. 9: ALA. 10: Greater St Louis Lib Club. 14: Ref. 15: 1943 Missouri State rd, Arnold Mo 63010.

ELLISON, SUZANNE (BRADWAY). b Bremerton Wash 5 My 44. 4: James Ellison. 5: UOre 62-66 (Math) BA, 66-67 MLS. 6: Ger. 7: Asst libn UNeb Libs (Lincoln) 67-. 14: Sci ref, catlg. 15: 1338 B st, Lincoln Nb 68502.

ELLISON, THELMA (BYRD). b Williamsburg Ky 16 Je 13. 4: Green C Ellison. 5: Union Col 54 (Educ) BS; Peabody 55-57 (LS) MA. 6: Fr, Sp. 7: Tchr Loyall High Sch, Loyall Ky 32-44; Tchr Black Star High Sch, Alva Ky 44-52, Libn 52-60; Libn Mainland Jr High Sch, Daytona Beach Fla 60-65, Head libn 65-69. 8: Group Leader for HARLAN Co (Ky) Guidance Program Inst, 50-55; In-Serv Train Coun for Harlan Co Schs, 55-60; Chm, Lib Facility Planning in Volusia Co (Fla) Schs. 9: NEA; KyEA; FlaEA. 10: Delta Kappa Gamma. 13: Yes. 14: Bk sel for sch libs, ref wk with pupils. 15: 2222 S Peninsula dr, Daytona Beach Fl 32018.

ELLISON, VIRGINIA (NOLAN). b NYC 4 O 23. 4: John L Ellison. 5: Hofstra Col 40-45 (Bus Admin) BS; Long Island U 65-67 MSLS. 7: Ref/ya Hicksville Pub Lib, Hicksville NY 67-69; Ref libn HofstraU 69-. 9: ALA. 10: AAUW. 14: Ref. 15: 9 Intervale, Rockville Ctr NY 11570.

ELLISOR, PAGE. b Beaumont Tex 7 O 24. 5: UHouston 43-47 (Music, Psych, Educ) BS, MS; UBC summers 49, 54 (Bacteriology); UTex 54-55, summers 55, 56, 58 (LS); UColo summers 57, 60-62 (LS, AV); Utah summer 59 (Psych) Brigham Young U summer 68 (LS). 7: Coun & psych tech UHouston 46-48; Banking First St Bank of Bellaire, Bellaire Tex 53-54; Bkkeeper-cashier Kelly Springfield Tire Co, Houston Tex 50-51; Elem sch tchr Houston Pub Schs, Houston Tex 55-59, Elem sch libn 59-. 8: -65. 9: ALA; NEA;TexLA; Tex State Tchrs Assn; HoustonASchL (v-pres 64, treas 66). 14: A-V, fine arts. 15: 1132 W Cottage ave, Houston Tx 77009.

ELLISTON, GRAHAM (NIGEL TORQUIL). b Gibraltar 23 O 34. 5: UVictoria 53-54, 56-57; UBC 57-59 (Psych, Criminology) BA; UWash 60-61 Master of Libnship. 6: Fr. 7: Lab asst Sidney Roofing, Victoria BC 55-56; Lib asst UVictoria 59-60; Catlgr (ser) UBC 61-64, Ser libn 65-67, W European bibliog 67-69, Ser bibliog 69-. 10: BC Civil Liberties Assn. 12: Ed "Democratic Commitment" (Newsletter of BC Civil Liberties Assn 67-68). 14: Ser backfiles. 15: 4 3624 W 14th ave, Vancouver 8 BC Can.

ELLSWORTH, RALPH E. b Forest City Iowa 22 S 07. 4: Theda Chapman. 5: Oberlin Col 25-29 (Pre-Journalism) AB; West Res 30-31 BS in LS; Chicago 34-37 (LS) PhD. 6: Ger, Fr. 7: Libn Adams State Col 31-34; Dir of Libs, Prof UColo 37-43; Dir of Libs, Prof UIowa 44-58; Dir of Libs, Prof UColo 58-. 8: Consul more than 90 col & univ lib bldgs, 44-. 9: ALA-ACRL (pres); ARL (Bd Dirs); ColoLA (pres 37-38 & 65). 10: Cactus Club (Denver). 11: LLD (hon) West Res U, 56. 12: "Modular Planning forCollege and Small University Libraries," with Donald E. Bean (48); "The State ofthe Library Art; Buildings" (60); "Planning the College and University LibraryBuilding" (60, 2nd ed 68); "The American Right Wing," with Dr. Sarah Harris (61);"The School Library; Facilities for Independent Study in the Secondary School," withhobart D. Wagener (63); "The School Library," (65). 13: Yes. 14: Planning lib bldgs. 15: 860 Willowbrook, Boulder Co 80302.

ELLSWORTH, RUDOLPH CHARLES. b Allegan Mich 23 Jl 20. 5: St Johns Col (Annapolis Md) 46-49 (Liberal Arts) BA; Columbia 49-50 (LS) MS; Uppsala U (Uppsala Sweden) 59-61 (Hist of Art) Filosofie Licenciat U Chicago 65-(LS). 6: Lat, Fr, Ger, Danish, Swedish, Norwegian. 7: (1st Lt) US Army Signal Corps, European & Pacific Theaters, World War II; Searcher LC Coop Acquis Proj, Wash DC 46; Stud asst Columbia U Libs 49-50; Lib asst City Col Baruch Sch of Bus (NY) 50-51; Coord of refugee resettlement in Scandinavian area for internat voluntary welfare agency & correspondent for internat news serv, Stockholm, Scandinavian area & west Europe 55-59; Ref libn Newberry Lib, Chicago 62-67; Hd ref & res div Douglas Lib Queen's U, KingstonOnt 67-. 8: Consul in Amer bibliog, Royal Lib, Stockholm & Uppsala Univ Lib, Uppsala Sweden, 54; Consul on mgt studies of German & Scandinavian libs, ALA Lib Tech Proj, Chicago 64-. 9: ALA; CanLA (CACUL Subcom Lib Orientation); Inst Prof Libns Ont (ProgCom). 10: Academicum Catholicum Suecium (Stockholm); Amer-Scand Foun (Chicago);Caxton Club (Chicago); Soc of Typographic Arts (Chicago), Pi Kappa Alpha, NewmanAlum Kingston, Foreningen for Bokhantverk, Stockholm. 11: Amer-Scand Fellowship toSweden to study univ libnship, 51-52; Wessen Foun (Stockholm) & Swedish Inst9stockholm) fellowships to complete study of Swedish bk designer Akke Kumlien, 60;Can Nat Comm for UNESCO travel grant, 68; Queen's U Arts Research Com award 68. 13: Yes. 14: Ref, rare bks, tchg libnship, hist of libs, printing, lit of art hist; hist ofscholarship, Can-Amer rel, libnship in Scand countries & Germany. 15: 241 Alfredst, Kingston Ont Can.

ELMAN, STANLEY A. b Buffalo NY 24 Ap 28. 5: U for Foreigners (Perugia Italy) 48 (Ital Lang, Hist, rt) Certif of Prof; Notre Dame U 49-53 (Biol & Chem Sci) BS; UBuffalo 53-58 (Sci Educ) ED M; SUNY (Geneseo) 59-61 MLS; Columbia 63-65 (LS). 6: Polish, Ital, Russian. 7: US Army

46-49; Spec Instr Park Sch, Snyder NY 55; Chem NUKEM Prod, Buffalo NY 56-57; Tech abstracter indexer Cornell Aero Lab of Cornell U 57-62; Ref libn John Hopkins U APL, Silver Spring Md 62; Chief tech abstracter tr AIAA Internat Aerospace Abstracts, NYC 62-63; Supv lib serv Thiokol Chem Corp Reaction Motors Div, Denville NJ 63-67; Group supv & acting mgr Jet Propulsion Lab Lib Cal Inst of Tech 67-. 9: SLA; ALA; ASIS; CalLA. 10: USAF Reserves (Major). 14: Spec libs, info retrieval systems, acad libs. 15: 276 S El Molino ave apt 27, Pasadena Ca 91106.

ELMORE, BETTY LEE. b Puyallup Wash 11 O 23. 5: UMiss (LS) BAE. 7: Seaman 1st class 9waves0 usn 45-46; Sec Dept Lib Sci UMiss (University) 64-67; Asst br libn 1st Reg Lib, Oxford Miss 67-68, Br libn (temp) 68; Jr catlgr UMiss (University) 68-. 14: Catlg, pub libs. 15: 208 Chandler ave, Oxford Ms 38655.

ELROD, J McREE. b Gainesville Ga 23 Mr 32. 4: Norma Cummins. 5: UGa 49-52 (Hist) AB magna cum laude; Peabody 52-53 (LS) MA; Scarritt Col 53-54 (Christian Life & Thought) MA(CLT); Yale Inst of Far East Studies 54-55 (Korean) Certif; Peabody 60 MSLS. 6: Korean. 7: Asst libn Belmont Col 53-54; Assoc libn Yonsei U (Seoul Korea) 55-60; Visitingprof Peabody Lib Sch 60; Libn Central Col (Fayette Mo) 61-63; Supv catlg dept OhioWesleyan U 63-67; Hd catlg div UBC 67-. 8: Catlg consul Defiance Col 65-67; Catlg consul Ashland Theol Sem66-67. 9: KoreanLA; CanLA; BCLA; ALA. 10: CAUT; BCAACP; BC Civil Liberties Assn;Phi Beta Kappa; Phi Kappa Phi; Omicron Delta Kappa. 12: "Index to English languagePeriod Local Literature Published in Korea 1890-1940" (60); "Filing in the PublicCatalog and Shelf List" (66); other indices and programmed instr units. 13: Yes. 14: Tech processing, lib educ, programmed instr in lib tech serv. 15: 2012Dollarton Hwy, N Vancouver BC Can.

ELROD, MIRIAM ALICE. b Walhalla SC 7 S 33. 5: Withnrop Col 51-55 (Sp) AB; UTenn 61 (Sp); American Inst for For Trade 62 (Sp); Rutgers 64-66 MLS. 6: Sp. 7: Cryptanalyst Nat Security Agcy, Wash DC 55-58; Tchr & libn Seneca High Sch, Seneca SC 58-62; Tchr Surrattsville High Sch, Clinton Md 62-63; Clk-typist State-Record Newspaper, Columbia SC 63-64; Libn Somerset Co Lib, Somerville NJ 64-68; Libn Hillsborough High Sch, Belle Mead NJ 68-. 14: Child libn. 15: Apt K 1450 Oak Tree dr, N Brunswick NJ 08902.

ELROD, (SELMA) FRANCES. b Tarboro NC 5 Mr 26. 5: Meredith Col 43-47 (Hist) AB; Drexel 47-48 (LS) BS. 6: Fr. 7: Asst libn in chg child dept Portsmouth Pub Lib, Portsmouth Va 48-51; Head child dept Greensboro NC 51-56; Head child dept Mt Vernon Pub Lib, Mt Vernon NY 56-. 9: ALA; NYLA; Westchester LA; Westchester YA & Child Libns (pres). 10: Westchester Womans Club; Mt Vernon Coun of Commun Serv. 13: Yes. 14: Child serv. 15: 753 Gramatan ave, Mt Vernon NY 10552.

ELSE, MRS CAROLYN J (WAHLBERG). b Minneapolis 31 Ja 34. 5: Stanford 52-56 (Psych) BA; UWash 56-57 MLS. 7: Libn I br wk Queensborough Pub Lib 57-59; Field libn US Army Spec Serv, Germany & France 59-62; Chief info serv Bennett Martin Pub Lib, Lincoln Neb 62-63; Br libn Pierce Co Pub Lib, Tacoma Wash 63-65, Dir 65-. 9: ALA; PNLA; WashLA. 14: Admin. 15: 2356 Tacoma ave So, Tacoma Wa 98402.

ELSE, JAMES P(RENTISS). b Pueblo Colo 9 O 20. 4: Peggy Nicholls. 5: Pueblo Jr Col 39-40 (Eng) AA; UDenver 38-39, 42-43, 46 (Eng) ab: Iliff Sch of Theol 46-50 (Theol) ThM; UDenver 57 (LS) MA. 7: US Army 96th Evac Hosp (Cpl), ETO 43-45; Minister Methodist Church, Wyoming, Mont 47-56; Catlg libn Sch of Theol at Claremont (Cal) 57-. 9: ALA; ATheolLA. 14: Catlg, ref. 15: 187 Brown dr, Claremont Cal 91712.

ELSER, GEORGE CARLTON. b Los Angeles 22 Ap 24. 4: Cristina Martinez. 5: UCLA 42, 46-48 (Span) AB; Middlebury Col summers 48-50 (Span) MA; UMadrid 51-52 (Span Lit); USoCal 54-55 MS in LS. 6: Sp, Fr. 7: Instr of For Lang Ursinus Col 48-50; Instr of For Lang Valparaiso U 50-54; Libn El Camino Col 55-57; Dist libn Palos Verdes Sch Dist, Palos Verdes Cal 57-58; Head Libn Chaffey Col 58-. 8: Ref libn LIBRARY/USA, NY Worlds Fair 64. 9: ALA-ACRL (com on Commun Use of Acad Libs); NEA; DAVI; Cal LA; Cal Tchrs Assn; CalASchL; Cal A-V EA; San Antonio Lib Club (pres 62-63). 10: Kiwanis; Beta Phi Mu; Sigma Delta Pi; Phi Kappa Phi; Libraria Sodalitas.13: Yes. 14: Ref. 15: 5885 Haven ave, Alta Loma Ca 91701.

ELSHOFF, SISTER DOLORES. b Milwaukee Wis 20 Mr 15. 5: Mt St Mary Col 33-37, 44-45, 55, 65, 67 (Math) BA (magna cum laude); WayneU summer 37; Marquette 37-39, 41-42, summers 64, 69; Milwaukee State Tchrs summers 38, 41; UWis ext div 43-44 MALS. 6: Ger. 7: Tchr Mercy High Sch, Milwaukee 38; Sch sec Milwaukee Pub Schs, 39-42, Tchr 42-43; Tchr Acad of Our Lady, Chicago 43-44; Tchr & libn St Marys Acad, Frainie du Chief 45-49; Tchr & libn Caroline Acad, Nequon 59-68, Directress 52-68; Asst catlgr MarquetteU 68-. 9: ALA; CathLA. 10: AAUP. 13: Yes. 14: Catlg. 15: 923 N 14th st, Milwaukee Wi 53233.

ELSON, (E) JEAN. b Guelph Ont 25 My 09. 5: UWest Ont 29-34 BA; McGill 45-46 BLS. 7: Lib asst UWest Ont 46-61, Hd catlg dept 61-. 9: CanLA; OntLA. 14: Catlg. 15: U of West Ont Gen Lib, London Ont Can.

ELSTEIN, ELLA. b 14 Ap 05. 4: Daniel Elstein. 5: Lib Inserv Train at Columbia U Sch of Soc Wk Lib 56. 7: Libn Marks & Clerk, NYC 37-40; Libn Child Welfare League of AMER, NYC 40-. 9: SLA. 15: 44 E 23rd st, NYC 10010.

ELSTEIN, HERMAN. b New York, NY 6 N 38. 4: Judith Alberstein. 5: Brooklyn Col 57-60 9eng) BA; Rutgers 65-66 MLS. 6: Hebrew. 7: Adult serv libn Brooklyn Pub Lib, NYC 65-66; Reader serv libn Rider Col 66-67, Acquis libn 67-. 9: ALA. 10: AAUP. 14: Acquis, Amer lit orientat methods. 15: 150 Bell ave apt 3, Yardley Pa 19067.

ELVESON, LEON. b Bronx NY 27 Je 20. 4: Sylvia Schaffer. 6: Yiddish. 7: Circ libn William Douglas McAdams Inc, NYC 53-58, Act libn 58-60; Research asst The Medimetric Inst, NYC 60-65; Med libn The Jewish Hosp of Brooklyn Greenpoint Div, Brooklyn NY 65-. 8: Consul on period The Medimetric Inst, NYC 60-65; Free lance med bibliogr 60-. 9: MedLA-NY Reg Group; SLA; 10: Victory Day Care Center Inc (Bd); PTA. 14: Med bibliog. 15: 1870 Schieffelin ave, Bronx NY 10466.

ELVOVE, ETHEL. b Paris Ky 6 Je 13. 5: UKy 31-32; George Washington U 37-41 (LS) BA. 6: Fr, Sp. 7: Lib asst US Army Map Serv Lib, Wash DC 42-43; Lib asst US Govt OPA, Wash DC43; Lib asst US Dept of Agric Lib, Wash DC 43-44; Asst libn US Bur of Mines Lib,Wash DC 44-45; Libn US Bur Reclamation, Wash DC 45-47; Libn Sci Serv Lib, Wash DC47-48; Catlgr NLM 48-. 9: SLA (chm &/or mem 5 coms of Biol Sci Div 52-65); -DC Chap (memb chm 57-58); DCLA; Md,Va,&DC Reg Catlg groups; Potomac Tech Processing Libns; DC Area Med Lib Group. 14: Catlg. 15: 4725 8th st NW, Wash DC 20011.

ELY, ETHEL (NORMAN). b Brookline Mo. b Brookine Mo. 4: Robert Andrew Ely. 5: Southwest Mo State Col 28 (Soc Sci) BS; So Bapt Sem Train Sch 32 (Religion) MA. 7: Elem tchr rural sch, Greene Co Mo22-25; High sch tchr & libn high schs, Richey, Conway, Granby, Peace Valley Mo37-44; Asst libn State Col (Springfield Mo) 28-30, 44-46; Asst ref & ref br libnPub Lib, Springfield Mo 48-63; Asst libn Southwest Bapt Col 63-. 14: Ref, circ,catlg, admin. 15: Southwest Baptist Col, Bolivar Mo 65613.

ELY, MYRTLE HOVERSON (MILLER). b Rolette ND 28 D 11. 5: Duluth State Tchrs Col 26-29 (Kindergarten, Primary) Certif; UMinn 29-37 (Intermediate) BA, 54 (LS) BS; UWis summers 60-66 ME(Jan 66). 6: Fr. 7: Kindergarten tchr pub schs, Nashwauk Minn 28-30; Nursery sch tchr, Owatonna Minn 32; Prim tchr & libn pub schs, Munger Minn 45-48; Prim tchr pub schs, Proctor Minn 48-49, Libn 49-50; Head Libn & AV dir Proctor Consolidated Schs 50-61; Libn pub schs, Madison Wis 61-. 9: ALA; NEA-DAVI (var coms); Minn A-V Assn; MinnEA; WisEA. 10: (Minn) Lib Reading Club (pres). 11: Certif of Leadership in Audio-Visual from State Assn of Minn. 13: Yes. 14: Instr materials. 15: 917 Laurie dr,Madison Wi 53711.

EMBER, GEORGE. b Budapest Hungary 21 N 17. 4: Violet Leichner. 5: Sir George Williams U 62-65 (Philos, Psych) BA; West Res 65-67 MSLS. 6: Ger,Hungarian. 7: Libn UMontreal 60, Chief documentation serv 61-65; Lecturer &project Mgr, Center for Documentation & Communication Research, Sch of

Lib Sci WestRes U 65-68; Sr member health scis resource ctr Nat Sci Lib of Can 68-; LecturerOttawa U 68-. 9: ASIS; MedLA. 12: "Symbolic Shorthand System for Physiology andmedicine," with Hans Selye (64); "Medical Librarian's Role in Diagnostic JudgmentProcesses (68). 13: Yes. 14: Med info systems & libnship. 15: National Science Lib,Ottawa 2 Can.

EMBREE, RUTH (GRAHAM). b Duluth Minn 30 N 09. 4: Donnelley S Embree. 5: Los Angeles Pub Lib Sch 27 Certif; USoCal 29-31 (Psych); UCal 40; UHawaii 40-41. 7: Lib asst Los Angeles Pub Lib 27-31; Lib asst Lib of Hawaii, Honolulu 31-34, 37-39; Libn US Navy Missile Test Center, Pt Mugu 53-55; Libn Dept of the Army, Army Lib, Pentagon 55-56; Libn Dept of Commerce US Census Bureau Lib 56; Tech libn US Navy Electronic Supply Off 58-60; Base libn Air Force, Wheeler AF Base 61-66; Base libn Hickam AF Base 66; Lib tech UHawaii 66-. 9: ALA; HawaiiLA (prog chm 65-). 10: Wheeler Federal Credit Union (dir); Zeta Tau Alpha (pres Hawaii Alumnae Chap). 14: Child wk. 15: 1001 Wilder ave,apt 906, Honolulu Hi 96822.

EMBS, ARDITH HELEN (BOEKELOO). b Kalamazoo Mich 26 Mr 22. 4: Robert Alfred Embs. 5: Kalamazoo Col 39-43 (Biol) BA; West Mich U 66 MSL. 7: Admin asst West Mich U dept of libnship 66-. 9: ALA; AALS; MichASchL; MichLA. 10: AAUW. 14: Lib educ, sch libnship. 15: 1008 Par 4 cir, Kalamazoo Mi 49001.

EMBURY, MARGARET W (WANDERER). b Philadelphia 17 My 14. 4: Jerome L Embury. 5: Washington Col 35 (Econ) BA. 7: Sec E I dPont de Nemours & Co, Chambers Works 36-50, Libn, Carneys Point NJ 54-. 10: YMCA. 15: E I duPont de Nemours & Co, Carneys Point Development Lab, Carneys Point NJ 08069.

EMCH, LUCILLE B(ERTHA). b Toledo Ohio 30 Ap 09. 5: UToledo 26-30 (Amer Lit) BA, 37-39 (Amer Lit) MA; UMich 41 AB in LS. 6: Lat, Fr, Ger. 7: Asst libn UToledo Lib 29-40;Assoc libn 40-, Asst Prof of Lib Sci 46-53, Assoc Prof of Lib Sci 53-. 9: ALA;Gutenberg Gesellschaft (Mainz Germany); OhioLA; Printing Hist Soc, London; AmerInst Oriental Research. 10: Beta Phi Mu; UMich Lib Sci Alumni Assn; Womes Nat Bk Assn; AAUW; Phi Kappa Phi; Delta Kappa Gamma; Chi Omega; Archaeol Inst Amer. 13: Yes. 14: Hist of bks & printing, catlg, acquis, admin (univ libs). 15: 752 Alvison rd, Toledo Ohio 43612.

EMELE, RUSSELL J. b Belvidere NJ 17 F 25. 4: Carol Boylhart. 5: Dickinson Col 46-49 (Hist) AB; NYU 48-49 (Hist) AM; Trenton State Col 53 BLS; Columbia 56-57 (Instr Materials); Rutgers 63-64 (LS). 6: Sp. 7: (Cpl) US Army, USA, Europe 43-45; Libn Belvidere (NJ) pub schs 50-53; Libn,assoc Prof East Stroudsburg State Col 53-60, Head Libn, Assoc Prof 60-66; Prof 66-. 8: Consul to University Microfilms, Ann Arbor Mich 65-67; Penn Adv Com On Title II Programs; Com on Interlib Coop in Penn. 9: ALA;AHA; Miss Valley Assn; Agric Hist Assn; NEA; PennLA (chm Col & Research Sect 67);Penn State EA. 10: AAUP; Goodwill Fire Co; Bd of Educ, Belvidere NJ; Deputy CivilDefense Dir, Belvidere NJ; Munic Planning Bd. 12: "Curriculum Material Centers, Commonwealth of Pennsylvania (62). 14: Bibliog, ref, acquis, admin, a-v, microforms. 15: East Stroudsburg State Col, EastStroudsburg Pa 18301.

EMERICK, KENNETH F. b Brookville Penn 19 Jl 25. 4: Leona Rice. 5: Clarion State Col 47-50 LS BS in Ed; Rutgers 57-60 MLS. 7: Catlgr E Liverpool Pub Lib, E Liverpool Ohio 50-55; Co libn Mansfueld Pub Lib, Mansfield Ohio 56-57; Catlgr Massillon Pub Lib, massillon Ohio 58-60; Libn Wadsworth Pub Lib, Wadsworth Ohio 61-62; Catlgr Clarion State Col 63-. 9: PennLA. 10: SANE; ACLU; Fellowship of Reconcilation. 14: Catlg. 15: 26 S 2nd st, Clarion Pa 19610.

EMERICK, RALPH STEPHEN. b Franklin Ohio 6 Ja 28. 5: Xavier 51 (Eng) BA; UCincinnati 53 (Eng) MA; UMich 56 MLS. 6: Ger, Fr. 7: Assoc libn Lawrence U 56-64; Dir Stephens col Lib 64-67; Libn Hobart & William Smith Col 67-. 9: ALA; NYLA. 10: Mod Lang Assn; AAUP. 12: Ed "Guidelines for Audio-Visual Services in Academic Libraries", ALA (68). 14: Admin. 15: PO Box 302, Geneva NY 14456.

EMERICK, TYRON DAVID. b Modesto Cal 30 Je 37. 4: Margaret Ann Propst. 5: Graceland Col 56-57; San Jose State Col 57-58; Fresno State Col 58; NWMo StateCol 59-60 (Hist) BS in Educ; Kan State Tchrs (Emporia) summers 63-66 (Libnship) MS. 7: Soc studies tchr Worth Co R-1 High Sch, Grant City Mo 60-61; Tchr-libn Avohahigh Sch, Avoca Iowa 61-62; Tchr-libn Exira High Sch, Exira Iowa 62-63; Sch libnmilford Comm Schs, Milford Iowa 63-65; Head Libn Newton Sr High Sch, Newton Iowa65-67; Dir N Platte Pub Lib, N Platte Nb 67-. 8: Exec Bd Adv Iowa Stud Libns Assn64-65, 66-67; Lib Consul McPherson Co High Sch (Tryon NB) 67. 9: ALA; NEA-DAVI;IowaASchL (exec bd 65); NebLA (public lib sect; sec 67-68, v-chm 68-69). 10: ACLU;Optimist Club; Y Advis Bd; Citizen's Planning Com for Recreation. 14: Admin, bksel, soc sci ref, a-v. 15: 406 Hahn ave, N Platte Nb 69101.

EMERSON, KATHERINE T(ERRELL). b Jacksonville Fla 2 Ap 27. 4: Everett H Emerson. 5: Duke 44-49 (Hist) BA, MA; LSU 52-53 (LS) MS; Lehigh U 55-58 (Eng). 6; Sp, Fr. 7: Catlgr LSU Lib 53-55; Catlgr Moravian Col 55-56; Lehigh U Lib: Catlgr 56-57, Act head catlgr 57-58, Head catlgr & asst libn 58-60; Catlgr St Petersburg Pub Library, St Petersburg Fla 63-65; Asst head monographic catlg UMass Lib 65-67; Asst to Dir 67-. 9: ALA. 10: LWV; ACLU; Phi Beta Kappa; Tau Psi Omega;Sigma Delta Pi; Danforth Assoc. 12: Bk review ed "Lehigh University Alumni Bulletin (57-60). 13: Yes. 14: Admin, tech proc. 15: 109 Chestnut st, AmherstMa 01002.

EMERSON, MARGARET L. b Baltimore 8 O 19. 5: Antioch Col 36-38 (Eng); Cornell U 38-41 (Comparative Lit) AB; Columbia 41-43 BLS. 7: Libn NY Pub Lib 41-43; Analyst Dept of the Army, Wash DC 43-49; Libn Operations Research Off Johns Hopkins U, Wash DC 49-61; Libn Research Analysis Corp, McLean Va 61-. 9: SLA. 10: Phi Beta Kappa. 14: Tech lib mgt. 15: 4317 Glenridge st, Kensington Md 20795.

EMERSON, VIRGINIA. b Somerset Penn 8N 27. 4: S Jonathan Emerson. 5: UMich 45-49 (Eng) BA; UCal 53-54; Drexel 59-61 (LS) MS. 6: Fr. 7: City Ed Somerset Co, Somerset Penn 49-50; Sec E P Dutton, NYC 50-51; Exec sec Christian Democratic Union, NYC 51-53; Lib asst UMich Law Sch (Ann Arbor) 55-57; Research asst Drexel Inst 62; Libn Phila Musical Acad, Phila 62-64 Libn New Sch of Mus 69-. 15: 3206 Midvale ave, Phila Pa 19129.

EMERSON, WILLIAM L. b Los Angeles 20 S 20. 5: UCLA 46-49 (Eng) AB; UCal (Berkeley) 49-50 (Eng) MA; USoCal 52-53 MSLS;Columbia 54-57 (LS). 7: Circ libn Cal State Col (Los Angeles) 53-54; Ref libnEngnr Lib Columbia U 54-56; Libn Math Lib Columbia U 56-57; Head sci ind dept LongBeach Pub Lib, Long Beach Cal 57-62; Dist Libn Palos Verdes Lib Dist, Palos VerdesPeninsula Cal 62-. 9: ALA; SLA (Exhib chm Nat Conv 68); CalLA (v-pres & pres-electSo Dist 69); Pub Lib Execs Assn of SoCal; Los Angeles LA; SoCal Tech Proc Gp. 10: Peninsula Coun for Youth; C of C; Peninsula Friends of the Lib; Palos Verdes Commun Arts Assn. 13: Yes. 14: Ref, admin. 15: 650 Deep Valley dr, Palos Verdes Peninsula Ca 90274.

EMERT, FLORENCE A(MELIA). b Miamisburg Ohio 8 My 21. 5: Otterbein Col 38-42 (Chem) BS; West Res summers 47-52 MS in LS. 7: Chem WVa Ordnance Wks, Pt Pleasant WVa 42-44; Catlgr Dayton Pub Lib, Dayton Ohio 50-52; Catlgr UAriz 52-55; Catlgr LSU 55-56; Catlgr Battelle Mem Inst, Columbus Ohio 56-. 9: SLA (sec Dayton Chap 64-65); ASIS; ACS. 14: Catlg (espec tech reports). 15: 1225 King ave, apt 2-A, ColumbusOh 43212.

EMERY, ADELE (KOHN). b San Francisco 24 O 13. 4: Clark Emery. 5: UCal (Berkeley) 31-35 (Eng) AB, 35-36 Certif in Lib Sci. 7: Asst order dept Ore State System of Higher Educ, Corvallis Ore 36-39; UMiami Lib (Coral Gables Fla): Jr catlgr, Instr 46-49, Sr catlgr, Asst Prof 49-60, Head catlg dept, Asst Prof 61-, Assoc Prof 62-. 9: FlaLA. 14: Catlg. 15: Univ of Miami Lib, Coral Gables Fla 33124.

EMERY, CHARLES DAVID. b Newcastle Upon Tyne England 25 Ag 34. 4: Enid Elizabeth guthrie. 5: King's Col UDurham England 53-57 (Lat, Greek) BA (Honours). 6: Fr, Lat, Greek. 7: Lib asst Newcastle Upon Tyne City Libs, Newcastle Upon Tyne England 57-60; Asst libn UEdinburgh 61-67; Hd bk order dept UAlta 67-. 9: Assoc The Lib Assn (Gt Brit); CanLA; AltaLA (chm Memb Com); EdmontonLA (pres 69-70). 10: Assn Profess Libns ualta (treas 67-68, pres 68-69); Can Assn Univ tchrs; Assn of Acad Staff UAlta. 14: Acquis, analyt bibliog. 15: 11727-43 ave, Edmonton 73 Alta Can.

EMERY, MARY BIRMINGHAM. b San Jose Cal 26 N 37. 4: John F Emery. 5: San Jose State Col 56-60 (Pol Sci) BA; USanta Clara 60-63 JD. 7: Asst Prof of Law & law libn USanta Clara 63- AssocProf of Law & Law libn 67-. 9: AALL; Cal State Bar Assn. 10: Santa Clara CoDemoc Centr Com; World Affairs Coun; ABA; AAUP. 14: Law lib ref wk. 15: USanta Clara Law Lib, SantaClara Ca 95053.

EMIGH, BARBARA (GROCE). b Waller Tex 24 F 10. 5: Our Lady of the Lke Col 27-30 (Eng) AB, 52-55 MS in LS. 6: Fr. 7: Libn Post Lib, Ft Sam Houston Tex 56-57; Lecturer Dept of Libnship Our Lady of the Lake Col 56-59, Instr 60- Asst Prof 66-. 9: ALA; CathLA; TexLA. 14: Catlg, child serv. 15: 531 Ogden lane, San Antonio Tx 78209.

EMMA, SISTER M (HVOZDOVIC) SSCM. b Wilkes-Barre Penn 5 Ag 12. 5: Marywood Col 32-51 (Sci) BA, 51-52 MA in LS. 6: Slovak, Lat, Sp. 7: Tchr St Cyril Acad, Danville Penn 32-40; Tchr St John the Baptist Sch, MtCarmel Penn 42-44; Tchr St Michael's Sch, Jessup Penn 44-46; Tchr Holy TrinitySch, Gary Ind 46-50; Tchr-libn St Joseph Jr High Sch, Hazelton Penn 52-58; Libn Andrean High Sch, Gary Indhigh Sch, Gary Ind 58-. 8: Visiting Instr Marywood Col 59-. 9: ALA; CathLA (Com for Cath Sup to "Standard Catalog forhigh School Libraries 55-65; past chm Scranton Penn Unit; IndSchLA. 13: Yes. 14: Sch lib wk. 15: AndreanHigh Sch Lib, 5959 Broadway, Gary In 46410.

EMMONS, CHARLES A. b Cornwall Conn 2 Ap 17. 4: Janet Marie Staffhorst. 5: UConn 50-54 (Hist) BA, 54-56 (Hist) MA; UWash 60-61 (LS) MS. 7: Aviation ordinanceman USN 43-46; Agric economist USDA, Burlington Vt 57-60; Libn US Naval CB Ctr, Davidville RI 61-68; Libn Mondville High Sch, Oakdale Conn 68-. 10: Phi Alpha Theta. 15: RFD, Voluntown Ct 06384.

EMPSON, DONALD LAWRENCE. b Minneapolis Minn 1 N 42. 4: MaryAnn Kronebusch. 5: UMinn 61-65 (Eng) BA, 65 (LS) MA; UIowa 68 (Educ Media). 6: Fr, Ger. 7: Dir Chippewa Co Lib Syst, Montevideo Minn 66-67; Instr Sch of Lib Sci UIowa (Iowa City) 67-. 9: ALA; IowaLA. 10: AAUP. 14: Admin, catlg. 15: 509 Garden st, Iowa City Ia 52240.

ENDERS, GERTRUDE ELSA. b Baltimore 9 Je 15. 5: Elmhurst Col 33-37 (Eng) BA; Drexel 37-38 BS in LS; UDenver 54 (LS). 6: Ger. 7: Br libn Evansville Pub Lib, Evansville Ind 39-41; Period libn US Fed Wks Agency, Wash DC 41-43; Casewkr Travelers Aid Soc, Wash DC 43-45; Examiner-Test Development US Civil Serv Commsn, Wash DC 45-47, Ref libn 47-54, Asst libn 54-61; Head acquis & binding US Patent Off, Wash DC 61; H Law libn US Dept of Commerce, Wash DC 61-64; Asst libn US Post Off Dept, Wash DC 64-, Head ref libn 64-. 9: SLA; Church & SynagogueLA; DCLA. 14: Ref, research, admin. 15: 703 N Ivy st, Arlington Va 22201.

ENDRES, DOROTHY (GOODLOE). b Canon City Colo 3 Ag 09: 04: Jacob Mihael Endres. 4: J Michael Endres. 5: Independence Jr Col (Kan) 27-29; Kan State Col(Pittsburg)29-31 (Educ) BS; UTex 67-68 Lib Certif. 7: Adult serv libn Leon Col Pub Lib, Tallahassee Fla 58-60; Asst br libn Jackson Pub Lib, Jackson Miss 60-62; Child libn Parkdale Br, Corpus Christi Tex 62-64; Supv child serv La Retama, Corpus Christi Tex 64- Sch libn Kostoryz Elem Sch, CorpusChristi ISD Tex. 9: TexLA (sec Child Round Table 64-65). 14 Child wk. 15: 6026 S Alameda, Corpus Christi Tx 78412.

ENDY, TERRY (ACKERMAN). b Phila 14 S 42. 4: Walter C Endy. 5: Kutztown State Col 60-63 (LS) BS in Ed. 6: Sp. 7: Libn Pennridge Joint Elem Schs, Perkasie Penn 63-. 9: NEA; PennStateEA. 10: appa Delta Pi; Pennridge Elem Faculty Asn; YMCA. 14: Catlg, child bks. 15: 330 Orvilla rd, Lansdale RD #1 Penn 19446.

ENEQUIST, JACQUELINE L (HELMERICHS). b St Louis 19 My 19. 4: Nils E Enequist. 5: Northwestern 36-37 (Liberal Arts); Monticello Jr Col 38-39 (Liberal Arts) AA; Chicago 39-41, 46-47 (Eng) BA; Columbia 47-48 (LS) BS. 6: Sp. 7: Libn Botetourt-Rockbridge Reg Lib, Lexington Va 48-49; Br libn of Hawaii,Wahiawa Hawaii 50-54; Hosp libn Tokyo Army Hosp Army Spec Serv, Tokyo 54-55; Supvlibn Camp McGill Army Spec Serv, Japan 55-57; Adult bkmob libn Lib of Hawaii, Honolulu57-58; Head circ dept UHawaii Lib 58-59; Head ext dept Maui Co Lib, Wailuku MauiHawaii 59-64; Pub Lib consul lib ext div NY State Lib 64-67, Assoc Pub Lib Servs DivLib Development 67-. 9: ALA (chm Recr & Mem Coms 59-64); HawaiiLA (Program Chm 58-59); NYLA (Bldg & Equip Com 65). 13: Yes. 14: Bldg, ext. 15: 71a Edgewood ave, Albany NY 12203.

ENEQUIST, ROBERT LARS. b Baltimore 7 Ja 18. 5: Syracuse 48-52 (Eng) BA, 53 (LS) MS. 7: Admin asst Enoch Pratt Free Lib, Baltimore 53-58; Chief Libn Wagner Col 58-63; Chief Libn The Col of Insurance (NYC) 65-. 9: ALA; SLA. 10: Phi Beta Kappa. 13: Yes. 14: Admin. 15: 175 Adams st, Brooklyn NY 11201.

ENGEL, HENRY WILLIAM. b Racine Wis 16 S 13. 4: Irene B Marek. 5: Carroll Col 37-41 (Biol) BA; UWis 45-46 BLS; UMich 48-53 AMLS. 7: Asst circ libn DePauw U Lib 46-48; Head circ desk UMich Lib (Ann Arbor) 48-53;High sch libn Escanaba High Sch, Escanaba Mich 53-54; Head Libn Ironwood Pub Lib,ironwood Mich 54-58; Dir of Libs Ottumwa Pub Lib, Ottumwa Iowa 58-64; Head Libnkankakee Pub Lib, Kankakee Ill 64-67; Hd libn Coldwater Pub Lib, Coldwater Mich 67-69;Dir LaPorte Pub Lib, LaPorte Ind 69-. 9: ALA; MichLA. 14: Admin. 15: 81 S Circle dr, Coldwater Mi 49036.

ENGEL, JOHN H(ENRY). b Dumont Iowa 19 Jl 41. 5: UNo Iowa 59-63 (Soc Sci, LS) BA; UIowa summer 65; UDenver summers 66-68 (Libnship) MA. 7: Jr high libn Boone Commun Schs, Boone Iowa 63-68; Jr high libn Linn-Mar Commun Schs, Marion Iowa 68-. 9: ALA; NEA; Iowa State EA; IowaASchL (chm Budget & Aud Com, 2 yrs). 10: Boone Educrs Assn Linn-Mar EA. 14: Sch libs & their devel into materials cts. 15: 475 5th ave, Marion Ia 52302.

ENGEL, MARY LOUISE. b Canonsburg Penn 30 S 28. 5: George Washington U 52-58 (Eng) BA; Catholic U 58-60 MSLS George Washington U 68- (Amer stud). 6: Fr, Ger. 7: Libn USDA Nat Agric Lib, Wash DC 60-68; Info spec US Dept of TransportationFHA 68-. 8: Consul on Dept of Defense Thesaurus of Eng & Sci Terms. 9: AmerStudies Assn. 10: Phi Beta Kappa; Beta Phi Mu; Nat Photographic Soc. 12: ContrAgric/Biol Vocabulary," Nat Agric Lib (67). 14: Thesaurus bldg, vocabulary compatibility, mechanization, hist of bks & printing. 15: 730 24th st NW, apt 211, Wash DC 20037.

ENGELBERT, LINDA (DANIELS). b Utica NY 1 Ja 47. 4: Kim B Engelbert. 5: SUNY (Geneseo) 64-68 (Lib Educ) BS. 6: Sp. 7: Elem sch libn Clinton Central Sch, Clinton NY 68-69; Child libn E Orange Pub Lib, E Orange NJ 69-. 9: ALA. 14: Child & ya. 15: 67 S Munn ave, East Orange NJ 07018.

ENGELBRECHT, LLOYD C. b St Louis 14 O 27. 4: June-Marie Fink. 5: City Col (San Francisco) 45,48, UCal (Berkeley) 48-50 AB; Columbia 50-51 MS inLS; UChicago 66-. 6: Ger, Fr. 7: (Pfc) US Army Chem Warfare Mil Police Infantry46-47; Jr libn art & music dept Newark Pub Lib, Newark NJ 51-52; Jr libn art &pictures dept Oakland Pub Lib, Oakland Cal 52-53; Proprietor Lib Music Serv, SanFrancisco 53-56; Art & music libn Forbes Lib, Northampton Mass 56-59; Fine arts libnUIll Lib (Navy Pier & Chicago Circle) 59-. 9: MusLA (sec-treas Mid-West Chap61-63); Col Art Assn of Amer. 10: AAUP; AFT; ADA; ACLU. 12: Co-auth 'Records andtapes' in "Music Librarianship" (66). 13: Yes. 14: Lib use of phonorecords & sound equip, ref & acquis (art, arch, music). 15: 2116 N Dayton st, Chicago Il 60614.

ENGELDINGER, EUGENE A. b Menomonie Wis 30 O 40. 4: Margaret L Thompson. 5: Wis StateU (Eau Claire) 61-65 (Hist) BS; UKan 65-68 (Hist) MA; UWis 68-69 MSLS. 6: Fr. 7: Aerographer's mate USN AG3 (E-4) 58-61; Asst ref libn Ind U Lib (Bloomington) 69-. 9: ALA. 14: Ref. 15: 3321 Stonetcrest rd, Bloomington In 47401.

ENGELHARDT, HILDA EVELYN. b Brooklyn NY 31 D 05. 5: Adelphi Col 22-26 (Hist) BA; Columbia 34-36 BLS. 7: Sch libn Barringer High Sch, Newark NJ 37-40; Lib asst Midwood High Sch NY Bd of Educ 41-49, Tchr of lib Stuyvesant High Sch 49-. 15: 137 Ave A, New York NY 10009.

ENGELHARDT, SARA MARLOW. b Montgomery Ala 26 Mr 44. 5: Sweet Briar Col 62-64; UAla 64-66 (Sociol) BA; Emory 67-68 Master of Libnship. 7: Child welfare wkr-in-train pensions & Security Dept Elmore Co, Wetumpka Ala 66-67; Catlgr Air U Lib, Maxwell AFB 68-. 9: SLA. 10: Jr League; Alpha Kappa Delta; Kappa Kappa Gamma. 14: Catlg, ref. 15: Air University Lib Systtems Div, Maxwell Air Force Base Al 36112.

ENGELKE, HANS. b Kirkwood Mo 11 D 27. 4: Betty McTyre. 5: Chicago Musical Col 48-51 (Composition) BM, 51-52 (Composition) MM; USoCal 53-59 (Musicology) PhD; Chicago 59-61 (LS) MA. 6: Ger, Fr. 7: US Army Finance Dept T/4 46-47; Lib asst USoCal 54-59; Lib asst UChicago 59-61; Catlgr West Mich U 61-64, Head acquis dept 64-67, Asst Dir for Resources 67-. 9: ALA; MichLA (chm Tech Serv Sect 67-68). 14: Acquis, tech serv, admin. 15: 640 Weaver ave, Kalamazoo Mi 49007.

ENGELKING, HESS (HOUGHTON). b NYC 27 Je 10. 4: Lessing L Engelking. 5: Radcliffe 28-32 (Anthropology) AB, 33-34 (Anthropology); Rutgers 57-59 MLS. 7: Head Tech Serv

Plainfield Pub Lib, Plainfield NJ 59-64, Head Ref Serv 64-65; Head Readers Serv Free Pub Lib, Madison NJ 65-, Asst dir 67-. 9: ALA; NJLA (Tech Serv Sect; pres-elect 65-66, pres 66-67). 15: 981 Leland ave, Plainfield NJ 07062.

ENGEN, SUSAN (HENKEL). b Plainfield NJ 28 S 40. 4: Richard B Engen. 5: UWis 58-62 (Amer Institutions) BA, 62-63 (LS) MA. 6: Fr. 7: Jr libn Amer Lib in Paris 63; Libn child dept Seattle Pub Lib 63-65, Libn educ sociol dept 65-66, Hd Child Lib 66-69. 8: Libn/Storyteller Lib/USA, NY World's Fair, 65; Storyteller on "Buttons & his Buddies," TV show for child (KCTS-TV) 64-65. 9: ALA (chm Memb Com Wash State 68-69; Jane Adams Bk Award Com 66-69; Newbery-Caldecott Com 69); PNLA (chm Young Reader's Choice Award Com Wash State 68); WashLA. 10: Seattle Pub Lib Staff Assn. 14: Child lit. 15: Mendenhall Apts #503 326 4th st, Juneau Ak 99801.

ENGERBRETSON, BETTY LOUISE. b Canby Minn 25 My 19. 5: Villa St Scholastica 38-42 (Hist, Eng) MA, 55. 7: Bibliogr UMinn Lib 44-45; Child libn Minneapolis Pub Lib 46-48, Ref asst 48-49, Libn Minneapolis Hist Collection 49-54, Athenaeum libn 55-, Head of adult bk sel 64-. 8: Instr in Childs Lit UMinn summer 47. 9: ALA; Womens Nat Bk Assn; MinnLA; MinnHA; CathLA. 10: Minneapolis Womens Rotary Club. 12: Children's book; "WhatHappened to George" (47,56). 13: Yes. 14: Rare bks, hist materials, adult bk sel. 15: 4120 Colorado ave S, Minneapolis Mn55416.

ENGLAND, MARY BELLE. b Decaturville Tenn 28 Ja 23. 5: Lambuth Col 41-45 (Hist) AB; Peabody Col 54-57 MA in LS, 63-67 (LS) EdS. 7: Clk: Dyesrsburg AB, Halls Tenn 43, Tenn Eastman, Oak Ridge Tenn 45-46; Tchr: Lexington High Sch, Lexington Tenn 46-50, College Park High Sch, College Park Ga 50-56; Libn Headland High Sch, E Point Ga 56-69; Dir lib serv Fulton Co Bd of Educ, Atlanta 69-. 8: Instr NDEA Inst, "The Culturally Deprived Child" AtlantaU summer 66. 9: ALA; NEA; GaEA (pres Lib Dept 67-68). 10: Delta Kappa Gamma. 11: Eng Speaking Union Scholarship for study at UBirmingham England. 14: Supv. 15: 1892 W John Calvin ave, College Park Ga 30337.

ENGLE, EMMA PEASLEE. b Wilkinsburg Penn 8 Ja 07. 5: Swarthmore 2428 (Lat) BA; Drexel 41-42 BS in LS. 6: Fr, Lat. 7: Nurse Aid Maison Maternelle, France34-35; Housemother Child Home, Mt Holly NJ 36-40; Asst libn Free Pub Lib, Bound Brook NJ 42-56, Head Libn 56-. 9: ALA; NJLA. 10: Zonta Internat; Womans Lib Club of Bound Brook. 14: Catlg, ref. 15: 224 Mountain ave, Bound Brook NJ 08805.

ENGLE, EMMA R. b Lancaster Penn 5 Ja 15. 5: Messiah Col 37-38; Elizabethtown Col 45-48 (Eng, Soc Studies) AB; Millersville State Col 65 (Lib Educ) Marywood Col 66-69 (LS). 7: Baker Engles Bakery, Bausman Penn 32-37, 40-45; Eng tchr Gordon Jr High Sch, Coatesville Penn 48-49; Instr in Eng, Col Registrar Elizabethtown Col 49-63; Libn Elizabethtown Pub Lib, Elizabethtown Penn 63-64; Libn St Josephs Sch of Nursing St Josephs Hosp, Lancaster Penn 65-. 9: CathLA. 10: Bus & Prof Womens Club. 14: Sch libnship. 15: St Josephs Hosp Sch of NursingLib, College ave, Lancaster Pa 17604.

ENGLE, LUCIA (STRAHAM). b St Louis Mo 13 Ap 17. 4: Marvin D Engle. 5: Stowe Tchrs Col 33-37 (Elem Educ) AB; Hampton Inst 37-38 BS in LS; Columbia 50, 51, 58 (LS). 7: Br libn Lincoln Lib, Springfield Mo 38-39; Elem sch tchr Bd of Educ, St Louis 39-41; Libn-in- charge Stowe Tchrs Col 41-47; Asst program dir Amer Red Cross, Burma & India 45-46; Libn NYC Pub Lib 47-49; Tchr of lib Bd of Educ, NYC 49-56, Dist libn 56-60, Supv sch lib serv 60-63, Asst dir lib serv 63-. 8: Lectr Queens Col Lib Sci Div (NY) 59. 9: ALA-CSD (Mag Evaluation Com 62-64; Local Arrangements 66 conf; Development Com 66-69; Com on child Bks in Relation to Radio & TV); -AASchL (Supv Publ Com 68-69); -CBC (Jt Com 68-70); -LED; -LAD (Women's Nat Bk Assn Bd of Mgrs 66-69); ALA (Publ Planning Com 57-60; Exhibits RT Award Com 69; mem-at-large Newberry-Caldecott Award Com 69; Aurianne Award 65-66); NYLA; NY State Eng Coun (v-pres 63); NY Lib Club; CathLA. 10: Amer Inst of Graphic Arts; Nat Coun Admin Women in Educ; Nat Assn for Aid to Visually Handicapped; CYP; NAACP; Urban League; NY Assn Black Supv & Admins; Alpha Kappa Alpha. 13: Yes. 14: Sch lib serv, child serv. 15: 2225 Fifth ave, New York NY 10037.

ENGLEMAN, LOIS E. b Burlington Ind 18 O 1899. 5: Millikin U 17-18, 19-22 (Hist & Pol Sci) AB; West Res 30-31 BS in LS; Cambridge summer 34; Columbia 38-39 (LS) MS; UEdinburgh summer 55. 6: Fr. 7: High Sch tchr, S Bend & Elkhart Ind 25-30; Libn Buchtel High Sch, Akron Ohio 31-32; Libn Shimer Jr Col 32-42; Bibliogr Amer Assn of Jr Cols, Wash DC 40; Libn Colby Jr Col 42-44; Asst to Libn Wellesley Col 44-47; Libn West Col for Women 47-48; Libn Denison U 48-64; Consul Col & Undergrad Libs, Bowling Green State U 64-66; Registrar & catlgr Denison U Art Collection 67-. 9: ALA-ACRL. 10: AAUP; AAUW. 12: "The Literature of Junior Col Terminal Education, with W C Eells (41). 14: Art (espec Burmese). 15: 1 Sheppard pl, Granville Ohio 43023.

ENGLER, LOIS (NYSTROM). b New Rockford ND 18 Jl 21. 5: Gogebic Jr Col 38-40 AA; UND 40-42 (Eng) BS; UWis summers 48-51 BLS. 7: Tchr-libn High Sch, Oklee Minn 42-43; Tchr-libn High Sch, Fertile Minn 43-46; Libn High Sch, Park Rapids Minn 46-50; Libn High Sch, Rock Springs Wyo 50-51; Libn Camp Carson Hosp, Camp Carson Colo 51-53; Tchr Devils LAKE Jr High Sch, Devils Lake ND 53-55; Libn Bismarck Jr Col 55-. 9: NDLA (sec-treas 63-64, treas 64-65; chm Col & Univ Sectsect 69-70); Bismarck-MandanLA (pres). 10: Zonta Internat. 14: Admin, ref. 15: 211 Anderson, Bismarck ND 58501.

ENGLEY, DONALD BROWN. b Stafford Springs Conn 19 Jl 17. 4: Hope Lummis. 5: Amherst 35-39 (Hist) BA; Columbia 40-41 BLS; Chicago 46-47 (LS) MA. 6: Fr, Ger. 7: Stud asst Amherst Col 36-39, Lib asst 39-40; Stud asst Columbia U Lib 40-41; Lib asst NY Pub Lib 41; (Pvt to Maj) US Army Antiaircraft Artillery; Libn US Army U Center Biarritz France 45; Libn Norwich U 47-49; Assoc libn Trinity Col Hartford Conn 49-51, Libn 51-. 8: Conn State Lib Com 59-; Mark Twain Mem(Hartford) (Trustee & Adv Bd 54-); Lib Bldg Consul 52-; Watkinson Lib Trinity Col(Conn) (Trustee 61-); Conn Governors Com on Libs (chm 62-63) Trustee Noah Webster House Found 65; Chm Capitol Region Lib Coun 69; Mem YaleU Council's Lib Com 65-. 9: ALA; ConnLA (pres 52-53); BSA. 10: Grolier Club; Conn Hist Soc (Standing Com). 11: Honorary MA Degree Amherst Col 59. 12: Ed "Trinity Col Lib Associates Gazette". 14: Rare bks, admin. 15: TrinityCol Lib, Hartford Ct 06106.

ENGLISH, DOROTHY VINCENT. b Lawrence Mass 7 Je 21. 5: Emmanuel Col 38-42 (Eng) AB; Simmons 42-44 (LS) BS; Boston Col 44-47 (Eng) MA; Albany State Col for Tchrs summer 59. 7: Libn Boston Col Lib 42-44; Libn Harvard Museum of Comp Zool, Cambridge Mass 44-45; Libn NY State Museum, Albany NY 45-46; Libn Endicott Pub Lib, Endicott NY 47-49; Libn Roosevelt Elem Sch, Johnson City NY 59-60; Libn Berkeley Pub Lib, Berkeley Cal 60-61; Head child serv Vallejo Pub Lib, Vallejo Cal 61-68; Supv child serv San Mateo Co Free Lib, San Mateo Cal 68-. 9: ALA; CalLA; Assn Child Libns No Cal (Bk Review Chm, Coun mem, pres 65-66); Bay Area Y A Libns. 10: PTA. 13: Yes. 14: Child bks. 15: 1437 Coronel ave, Vallejo Cal.

ENGLISH, JAMES DANA. b New Haven Conn 15 Mr 32. 5: Yale 50-54 (Econ) BA; UNC 65-66 MLS. 6: Fr. 7: Trust Dept Union & New Haven Trust Co, New Haven Conn 54-64; Bibliog Dept Sterling Lib Yale U 66; Period & Ser Libn Quinnipiac Col Lib 66-. 9: ALA; ConnLA. 10: New Haven Astronomical Soc; Boy Scouts of Amer; Yale Club of New Haven. 14: Periodicals. 15: 99 E Rock rd, New Haven Ct 06511.

ENGLISH, THOMAS G. b Broken Bow Neb 10 O 28. 4: Eileen Thomas. 5: Hastings Col (Hastings Neb) 46-49; UNeb 49-50 (Zool) BA; Fla State U 57-58 (LS)MS. 7: (Lt jg) US Navy 50-55; Asst sci libn UNeb 58-60; Documents analyst US NavyElectronics Lab, San Diego 60-62; Engnr libn Gen Dynamics/Astronautics, San Diego62-64; Supv of dept libs UMinn(Minneapolis) 65-. 9: ALA; SLA; MinnLA. 14: Admin. 15: 3535 Belden dr, MinneapolisMn 55418.

ENGSTROM, CAROL A. b Thompson Iowa 16 N 12. 4: Chellis G Engstrom. 5: Mason City Jr Col 31-33 (Liberal Arts); UMinn 54-59 (Eng) BS, 59-62 (LS)MA. 7: Libn Grandview Jr High Sch, Mound Minn 60-. 9: NEA; ALA-AASchL; Minn ASchL (Program Com 62-63); MinnEA. 10: Amer Field Serv; LWV; Delta Kappa Gamma. 12: Ed Minn LA "Newsletter (65). 14: Reading guidance for yp. 15: Box 104, Mound Mn 55364.

ENGSTROM, RUTH (AMOS). b Baltimore 2 O 03. 4: J Leslie Engstrom. 5: Albion Col 21-25 (Eng) BA; UMich summer 51 (LS): Swedish Inst for Cultural Rel(Stockholm)summer 56; West Mich U 58 (LS) MS. 6: Fr. 7: Tchr pub schs, Houston Tex 26; Tchr Capitol Hill High Sch, Okla City Okla 27-29; Tchr pub schs, Albion Mich 39; Tchr-libn High Sch, Vandercook Lake Mich 49-52; Sch libn Washington Gardner High Sch, Albion Mich 52-. 9: ALA; NEA; MichLA; MichASchL; MichEA; AlbionEA. 10: AAUW;

PTA; Entre-Nous (Federated) Club of Albion. 15: 420 Linden ave, Albion Mich 49224.

ENLOW, HELEN (HAHN). b Edgeworth Penn 14 D 09. 4: Frank B Enlow. 5: UAkron 28-30, 31-34 (Educ) BE; Muskingum Col 30-31; Ohio State U 44-46 (Biol). 6: Sp, Fr. 7: Clerical asst Akron Pub Lib, Akron Ohio 40-43; Sec & libn Curtiss-Wright Corp, Buffalo NY 43-44; Sec, Bk Serv Manager Friends of the Land, Columbus Ohio 44-47; Spec asst ref dept Columbus Pub Lib, Columbus Ohio 47; Libn Ohio Agric Expt Station (now The Ohio Agric Research and Development Center), Wooster Ohio 48-. 8: Mem bldg com for Auditorium-Lib-Statistics Lab Bldg, completed 68. 9: SLA (sec-treas Biol Sci Div 62-63, Ed 54-56, Adv 64-65); ALA; Internat Assn of Agric Libns & Documentalists (Bibliog Com). 10: WildernessCtr; The Nature Conservancy. 12: Ed "Reminder," Biol Sci Div SLA (54-56); Comp"Library News," monthly list of agric docs. 13: Yes. 14: Mechanized lib procedures, ref inbiol scis. 15: Lib Ohio Agr Res & Dev Center, Wooster Oh 44691.

ENNIS, LUCYANN M (METCALF). b West Reading Penn 23 D 41. 4: George Wilson Ennis. 5: Ursinus Col 59-63 (Chem) BS; Drexel 63-64 MS in LS. 7: Research libn DuPont Tech Lib, Wilmington Del 64-65; Libn Leeds & Northrup CoR/D Lib, North Wales Penn 65-68, Info Spec 68-. 9: SLA; SLCoun of Phila &Vicinity (treas 65-66); ASIS. 14: Ref, info retrieval. 15: Leeds & Northrup CoR/D Lib, Dickerson rd, North Wales Pa 19454.

ENNIS, MARY JANE (ROWLEY). b Cincinnati 11 My 20. 4: Matthew C Ennis Sr. 5: UCincinnati Evening Col 58-59 (LS), 60-61 (Span), 61 (Ger). 6: Sp, Ger, Fr. 7: Sec to tech consul & asst libn Drackett Co, Cincinnati Ohio 51-56, Sec to Research Dir 56-57, Col libn & tr (non-tech) 57-. 9: SLA (Cincinnati Chap chm &/ormem 3 coms 61-66, sec 67-69). 14: Ref. 15: 5020 Spring Grove ave, Cincinnati Oh 45232.

ENOS, MARIAN (PATTERSON). b Farmingdale NJ 27 Jl 08. 4: Frank E Enos. 5: Trenton State Col 45 (Soc Studies) BS, 49 BLS. 7: Elem tchr Englishtown Grammar Sch, Englishtown NJ 27-46; Libn High Sch, N Plainfield NJ 46-48; Libn Sr High Sch, Fair Lawn NJ 48-65; Libn N Highlands Reg High Sch, Allendale NJ 65-. 68; Adj Paterson State Col 62-; Dir lib Program Alphonsus Col 68-. 9: ALA (Life mem); NEA (Life mem); NJEA; NJLA; NJSchLA; Bergen Co Sch Libns (pres). 10: AAUW; Delta Kappa Gamma. 13: Yes. 14: Lib educ, bk sel. 15: 175 West Orchard st, Sllendale NJ 07401.

ENOS, MARY ELIZABETH. b Bronxville NY 19 O 43. 5: Mary Washington 61-65 (Hist) BA; Inst for Amer Univs Jr year abroad 63-64; Columbia 65-66 (LS) MS. 6: Fr. 7: Libn trainee New Rochelle Pub Lib, New Rochelle NY 66; Libn New Rochelle High Sch Lib 66-67; Libn San Francisco Pub Lib 67-68; Libn Sch of the Mus of Fine Arts Lib, Boston 69-. 14: Ref (art, film, drama). 15: 2 Aviemore dr, New Rochelle NY 10804.

ENSLEY, ROBERT FRANCIS. b Portola Cal 30 O 40. 5: Graceland Col 58-60 AA; UMo 60-62 (LS) AB; UDenver 63-64 (LS) MA. 7: Field libn Ida State Lib 64-68; Coord pub lib programs 69-. 8: Asst exec dir Nat Lib Week 65-68. 9: ALA; -AAStateL (Nat Adv Commsn Report Ad hoc Com 68-69); IdaLA (Recr Coun Netwk 65-, Pub Rel & NLW Com 68-69); PNLA (Recr Com 65-66, Memb Com 67-69; Prog Com 68-69). 10: Boise Commun Concert Assn. 13: Yes. 15: 517 Main st, Boise Id 83702.

ENYART, ROBERT C. b Fulton Ind 20 Ja 11. 4: Esther G. 5: Ind Central Col 29-33 (Hist, Bible) AB; Bonebrake Theol Sem 33-35; Iliff Sch of Theol 36-37, 40-41, 49 (New Testament) ThM; UDenver 55-57 (LS)MA. 7: Pastor First United Brethren Church, Denver 35-36; Tchr Dist 3, Sedgwick Co Colo 37-38; Tchr Grade Sch, Fleming Colo 38-39; Pastorates Methodist Church, Colo, NM, Tex 41-48; Tchr libn High Sch, Nucla Colo 54-56; Libn sci & engnr dept Denver Pub Lib 56-. 9: ALA. 14: Ser to pub, ref. 15: 2607 S Madison st, Denver Co 80210.

ENYINGI, PETER. b Budapest Hungary 6 O 26. 4: Etlka Bodis. 5: Pazmany Peter Tudomanyegyetem (Hungary) 44-48 (Law) DrJur Utr; Columbia 59-60MS in LS. 6: Hungarian, Ger, Fr. 7: Catlgr Cornell Law Sch Lib 60-. 67, Asst law libn 67-68; Catlgr Los Angeles Co Law Lib 68-. 9: AALL;Internat Assn Law Libs. 15: 428 S Hamel rd, Los Angeles Ca 90048.

ENZ, PHILIP I(RWIN). b Oklahoma City Okla 25 S 37. 4: Carolyn Sue (Holt) Enz. 5: Phillips U 55-58 (Chem) BA; Ind U 64-68 (LS) MA. 6: Ger. 7: Analytical chem New Eta Milling Co, Ark City Kan 59; Electrochemical engr PR Mallory & Co, indianapolis 59-63, Lib info specialist 63-67; Admin libn Larue D Carter Memorial Hosp, Indianapolis 68. 8: Adv Coun for LSCA Title IVa 68-; Conducting in-serv training for employees of state inst libs (Med and Patients Libs) May 69. 9: SLA; ACS. 12: Ed "MNEMONIC", bimonthly bull Med Lib, Larue D Carter Mem Hosp. 14: Ref. 15: 279 S Downey ave, Indianapolis In 46219.

EPPERLY, ELIZABETH (ROLLINS NORTON). b Amarillo Tex 23 Ap 21. 5: Amarillo Jr Col 39-41; USoCar 44-46 (Eng, Art) AB; UVa 46-47, 66-67 (Eng lit); CatholicU 67-69 MSLS. 7: Sec to asst dir personnel LC 66-67; Prin aide Fairfax Co Pub Lib, Vienna Va 68-69, Child libn 69-. 15: 7506 Ambergate pl, McLean Va 22101.

EPPERLY, JOYCE (VAN ROEKEL). b Iowa 18 Mr 38. 4: Edgar V Epperly. 5: Central Col (Pella Iowa) 56-60 (Math) BA; Peabody Col 65-68 MLS. 7: Jr high tchr Pella Commun Schs, Pella Iowa 60-64; Des Moines (Iowa) Independent Schs: Jr high tchr 64-65, Jr high libn 65-67; Elem libn Franklin Spec Sch, Franklin Tenn 67-. 9: NEA; ALA; TennEA; IowaSEA. 14: Child wk, catlg. 15: 2918 Hillsboro F-2, Nashville Tn 37215.

EPPES, WILLIAM DAVID. b Goodwater Ala4 Mr 18. 5: William and Mary 38-39 (Amer Hist) AB; UMiam summer40; Peabody 38-40 BS in LS; NYU 57-59 (Communications) MA Columbia U Lib Sch summer 60. 7: Ref asst Newark Pub Lib, Newark NJ 40-44;Dir Z X McCord Co, Goodwater Ala 42-45; Ref asst George Washington U 45-48; Ref asstSan Francisco State Col 49-50; Owner-Manager Sun-Tan Apts, St Petersburg Fla 51-53;Dir stack personnel Burler Lib Columbia U 54-57; Asst Prof curriculum materialsNewark State Col 57-59; Ref asst Barnard Col 59-60; Asst libn Cooper Union 61-. 8: Researcher pub rel dept motion picture div Esso Standard Oil Co 59-60; CatlgCooper Collection Cooper Union, NYC. 9: ALA; SLA. 10: NY Hist Soc; Nat Trust forHistoric Preserv. 13: Yes. 14: Ref, catlg. 15: 68 Bedford st, New York NY 10014.

EPSTEIN, DORIS EISENBERG. b Woonsocket RI 31 Ja 33. 4: Abraham H Epstein. 5: Pembroke 50-54 (Amer Civilization) AB; UWis 63-65 (LS) MA. 7: Soc Wker San Diego Dept of Pub Welfare, San Diego Cal 54-56 Order dept SUIowa 66-67, Catlg dept 68-69. 15: 612 Lynn ave, Ames Ia 50010.

EPSTEIN, ELIZABETH HELLER. b Newark NJ 26 O 36. 4: Bernard G Epstein. 5: Rutgers 9newark) 54-58 (Psych) BA; NY Theol Sem 60-62 (Relig Educ) MRE; Rutgers (New Brunswick) 59-64 MLS. 7: Lib asst USA Spec Serv, Korea 62-63; Asst br libn Hartford Pub Lib, Hartford Conn 64-65, Br libn 65-68; Sch libn Hartford Bd of Educ 68-. 9: ConnLA. 15: 102A Sherbrooke ave, Hartford Ct 06106.

EPSTEIN, JACOB S. b Tallinn Estonia 3 D 13. 4: Ruth Esther Brose. 5: UCincinnati 35-37, 40-42 (Econ) BA; Columbia 46-47 (LS) BS. 7: Asst ref dept Cincinnati Pub Lib 39-42; US Army Infantry Medic 42-46; Cincinnati Pub Lib: Asst pub documents 47-49, Asst sci & ind 49-50, Ref dept, org new bus dept 50-52, Head govt & bus dept 52-56, Admin asst to dir 56-57, Asst libn 57-. 8: Chm Nat Lib Week, Ohio 62. 9: SLA (pres Cincinnati Chap 52-53); OhioLA (Exec Bd 66, chm Admin Training Com65-66, chm Memb Com 66-67). 15: 1214 Delta ave, Cincinnati Oh 45208.

EPSTEIN, JOSEPHINE (FERNIE TROSTLER GALLO) (MRS). b Brooklyn NY 23 S 19. 5: Barnard 35-39 (Chem) BA with certif in sci; Duquesne 59-60 (LS) William & Mary 60-61. 6: Fr, Ger. 7: Lab asst Guggenheim Dental Clinic NYC 39-40; Tech asst lib Bell Telephone Labs NYC 40-43, Tech asst Radar Project 43-44; USNR (WAVES): Ens Commander-in-Chief Hdqtrs 44-45, Lt Jg bur of ships electronics & sonar, Wash DC 45-46; Hd research lib & tech files Gen Aniline & Film Corp central research labs, Easton Penn 46; Hd research lib & tech ed J & L Steel Corp, Graham research lab, Pittsburgh Penn 57-60; Hd tech lib textile fibers div Dow Chemical Co, Williamsburg Va 60-64; Hd intl info ctr Dow Chemica& Co, Midland Mich 64-68, Hd bus info ctr 68-. 9: SLA; ASIS. 14: Indexing report lit for mechan systems, ref in bus & internat bus. 15: 1109 Glendale st, Midland Mi 48640.

EPSTEIN, MARION (HILLSBERG). b NYC 9 Jl 15. 4: Milton Epstein. 5: Brooklyn Col 32-36 (Math)BA; Columbia 36-37 (Math); Queens Col 57-61 (Lib Educ) MS in Ed, Diploma in Lib Educ. 7: Sch libn Plainedge Pub Schs, Bethpage LI NY 58-. 14: Sch & child lib wk. 15: 67-31 167th st, Flushing NY 11365.

EPSTEIN, MARY ANN (WALSH). b Trenton NJ 6 Ap 28. 4: Theodore Epstein. 5:Caldwell Col 47-50 (Music) BA; Rutgers 56-58 MLS. 7: Jr libn State Lib Bur, Trenton NJ 50-51; Sr libn Trenton Pub Lib, Trenton NJ 52-58; Sr libn Mercer Co Lib, Trenton NJ 58-64; Ref libn Rider Col 64-. 9: NJLA. 14: Ref. 15: 49 Merritt dr, Trenton NJ 08638.

EPSTEIN, RHEDA. b Birmingham Ala 26 My 45. 5: UFla 63-67 (Educ, LS) BAE; Drexel 67-68 MLS. 6: Sp. 7: Asst libn USoFla 68-. 9: ALA; FlaLA. 14: Catlg. 15: 13145 N 20th st apt 211, Tampa Fl 33612.

EPSTEIN, SARAH GUNG. b Providence. 5: RI Col of Educ 43-44 (Elem Educ); UMiami 55 (Secondary Educ); URI 55-57 (Hist) BA; Pratt 57-58 MLS. 6: Ger. 7: Lib asst Providence Pub Lib 45-55; Sch libn Providence Sch Dept 58-. 9: ALA-AASchL (del State Assembly); RISchLA (treas, del to State Assembly); NESchLA (Planning Com); RILA; NELA. 10: Providence Tchrs Union; Amer Fed of Tchrs; Pratt Grad Lib Sch Alumni Assn. 14: Sch libs, child & ya. 15: 49 Savoy st, Providence RI 02906.

EPSTEIN, THEODORE. b NYC 22 D 15. 4: Mary Ann Walsh. 5: Brooklyn Col 34-38 (Psych) BA; Syracuse 50-51 MS in LS. 7: Motion picture theater manager NYC 37-41; Lib off US Army (Capt), Ill & Germany 42-50; Col Libn Rider Col 51-. 8: Consul on Bldg F F Moore Lib, Rider Col 62-64. 9: ALA; NJLA (past pres, Col & Univ Sect, treas Scholarship Funds). 10: US Army Reserves (Lt Col); Torch Club; AAUP; Beta Phi Mu; Boy Scouts. 13: Yes. 14: Bldgs, admin. 15: 49 Merritt dr, Trenton NJ 08638.

ERBES, RAYMOND GUSTAVE. b Mendota Ill 18 N 22. 5: UIll 48 (Educ) BS of d, 50 MLS. 7: US Navy pub rel dept Spec X 46-48; Tchr-prin Harding Grade Sch, Earlville Ill42-43; Tchr-libn Roosevelt Mil Acad, Aledo Ill 43-46; Libn Evanston T High Sch, Evanston Ill 48-50; Head Libn Reavis High Sch Lib, Oak Lawn Ill 50-. 8: Tchr, Rosary Col Dept of Lib Sci, 65-; Tchr of lib sci courses during summer sessions at var cols & univs for many yrs North CentralAssn consul coms. 9: ALA-AASchL (treas, Bd Dirs 57-60, chm Com on Sch Lib Quarters55-58); NEA; IllEA; IllLA (Exec Bd 53-55); IllASchL (pres 60). 10: Youth Commsn,Oak Lawn Ill; Bd Dirs Stickney Pub Lib. 12: Ed "News For You, IllASchL J (55-57). 13: Yes. 14: Sch libs. 15: 7907 S Newland, Oak Lawn Il 60459.

ERDELYI, GABOR. b Debrecen Hungary 19 Ag 27. 4: Elizabeth Vegh. 5: UDebrecen 46-48 (Philos); UBudapest 48-49 (Philos) BA (cum laude), 49-50 (Philos) MA; UMich 57-58 MLS. 6: Hungarian, Ger, Dutch; Lat, Ital. 7: Asst Prof of Philos Kossuth U (Debrecen Hungary) 51; Tchr of pol econ Economic Gynasium (Debrecen Hungary) 52-56; Catlgr libn I UColo 58-60; Stanford U: Catlgr libn II 60-62, Soc sci libn II 62-63, Curator Germanic langs 63-. 66; Hd readers serv Tufts U 66-68; Private research Cal Institutions 68-. 9: ALA. 10: Stanford Faculty Club. 12: Co-comp "German Periodical Publications (67). 13: Yes. 14: Readers serv, spec collections, automation. 15: 565 Arastradero 211, Palo Alto Ca 60301.

ERICKSON, CHERYL A. b Seattle Wash 20 Ap 44. 4: Richard H Erickson. 5: UMinn 63-66 (Sp) BA, 66-67 (LS) MA. 6: Fr, Sp, Dutch. 7: Docs libn UMinn (Minneapolis) 67-68; Child libn Fairfax Co, Fairfax Va 68-. 9: VaLA. 14: Docs, ref. 15: 8114G Colony Point rd, Springfield Va 22150.

ERICKSON, ERNST WALFRED. b Superior Wis 21 N 11. 4: Marion Ihrig. 5: Superior (Wis) State Tchrs Col 31-35 (Eng) BEd; UIowa 35-36 (Eng) MA; UMinn 45-46 BS in LS; UIll 50-52 (LS) PhD. 6: Swedish. 7: Eng tchr pub schs, Superior Wis 36-45; Asst libn State Tchrs Col, MoorheadMinn 46-47; Libn East Ore Col 47-50; Research asst UIll(Urbana) 50-51, Circ asst51-52; Head Libn East Mich U 52-69, Lib consul 69-. 8: Smith-Mundt Grantee, orgCentral Lib Kathmandu Nepal 58-59; surveyed West Wash State Col Lib & Detroit Instof Tech Lib 62, Murray State U 69; accreditation teams for Mich Commsn for Colaccreditation 63-64. 9: ALA (Coun 63-64)ACRL (var offs 56-67); MichLA (v-pres 63-64). 10: AAUP, Ypsilanti Human Relations Commission chm 6-62); Beta Phi Mu. 12: "College and University Lib Surveys 1938-1957" (61); "Reportof a Survey of the Western Washington State Col Lib," with L W Anderson (62); Co-auth"Report of a Survey of Murray State University Libraries" (69). 13: Yes. 14: Admin. 15: 1209 Whittierrd, Ypsilanti Mi 48197.

ERICKSON, ESTELLE (THELMA). b Russell ND 5 S 14. 5: Reed Col 35-39 (Lit) BA; UWash 42-43 BS in LS. 6: Fr. 7: Clerical asst sch dept Lib Assn of Portland, Portland Ore 39-42; Catlgr Seattle Pub Lib 43-45; Catlgr Lib Assn of Portland, Portland Ore 45-52, Asst head catlg dept 52-. 9: ALA; PNLA; OreLA. 14: Catl. 15: 4147 SE 64th ave, Portland Ore 97206.

ERICKSON, GERALD R. b Provo Utah 17 Ja 24. 5: Pepperdine Col (Educ, Psych) BS; USoCal 51-52 MSLS. 6: Ger, Sp. 7: Domiciliary libn VA, LA 52; USAF: Field depot libn (FEAF), Japan & Korea 52-55, Base libn (USAFE), Germany 55-57; Base libn (SAC) Spain, Morocco, & PR 58-63, Staff libn 13th AF (PACAF), Philipines 63-67; Chief info analyst & proc branch, FAA, Wash DC 67-. 9: SLA; DCLA. 14: Automatic data processing applied to info retrieval. 15: 520 N st SW, Wash DC 20024.

ERICKSON, HAROLD H J. b Point Mills Mich 22 O 31. 5: Mich State U 50-54 (Eng) BA; UMich 58-59 MALS. 7: Court reporter US Army(SP3), Japan 54-56; Eng tchr Cass City High Sch, Cass City Mich 56-58; Searcheracquis dept UCincinnati 59-61; Head gift & exch Syracuse U 61-64, Head acquis 64-65;Dir of Libs UNevada (Las Vegas) 65-. 9: ALA-RTSD; NYLA (sec-treas RTSD); NevLA. 14: Acquis. 15: UNevada Las Vegas Lib, Las Vegas Nv 89109.

ERICKSON, J IRVING. b Stambaugh Mich 19 Jl 14. 4: Myrtle A Hulting. 5: N Park Col & Sem 35-41 (Theol) Diploma; Wheaton Col 44-45 (Eng Lit) AB; Chicago 46-47 (Eng Lit) MA; Rosary Col 61-63 MLS. 6: Swedish. 7: Pastor Wiley Heights Covenant Church, Yakima Wash 41-44; Pastor Glen Ellyn Covenant Church, Glen Ellyn Ill 46-48; Chaplain N Park Col & Theol Sem 47-61; Chaplain & Dir of Mellander Lib N Park Theol Sem 61-. 8: Chm, Hymnal Com Evang Coun Church of Amer 67-. 9: Nat Assn Col & U Chaplains (55-61); ATheol LA. 10: Beta Phi Mu. 14: Ref, rare bks. 15: 3456W Berwyn ave, Chicago Il 60625.

ERICKSON, RODNEY OSCAR JOHN. b Sedan Minn 13 My 34. 5: Augsburg Col 52-56 (Hist) BA; UMinn 56-65 (LS) MA. 6: Norwegian. 7: Tchr Zumbrota High Sch, Zumbrota Minn 56-57; Sp4 Minn Nat Guard 57-58; Libn Fertile Pub Schs, Fertile Minn 58-64; Libn Moorhead Sr High Sch, Moorhead Minn 64-66; Hd libn Moorhead Pub Schs 64-66; Asst libn Moorhead State Col 66-. 8: Mem N Central Assn Visit Com 67. 9: ALA; NEA; MinnEA. 10: Phi Delta Kappa; Minn State Col Inter-Faculty Assn. 14: Acquis, ref. 15: 1010 11th st S, Moorhead Mn 56560.

ERICKSON, ROLF H. b Green Bay Wis 18 N 40. 5: St Olaf Col 58-62 (Eng) BA; UWis 9madison) 65-66 (LS). 6: Norwegian. 7: Libn Bumayong Schs Lutheran Mission territory of Papua & New Guinea 62-64; Libn Random Lake High Sch, Random Lake Wis 64-65; Admin asst Northwestern U Lib 66-. 9: ALA; Nord,amms Forbundet. 14: Ref, pub serv, admin. 15: 1940 Sherman ave, Evanston Il 60201.

ERICKSON, TURE (REXFORD). b New Westminster BC Can 26 O 36. 4: Lynn Wong. 5: UBC 54-62 (Eng, Hist) BA, 63-64 BLS. 6: Ger. 7: Asst party chief BC 57-61;Ref Libn Woodward (biomed) Lib, UBC 64-65; Hd Sedgewick Undergrad Lib, UBC 65-. 9: CanLA; ALA; BCLA. 14: Ref, circ, undergrad serv & facil. 15: Sedgewick Lib Univ of BC, Vancouver BC Can.

ERICSON, JACK TODD. b Dewittville NY 9 Jl 38. 5: Allegheny Col 57-61 (Hist, Educ) BA; UConn 61-63 (Hist) MA. 7: Penn Hist & Museum Commsn, Harrisburg summers 61-62; State Hist Soc of Wis, Madison 64-68; Hd of dept Syracuse U Lib mss div 68-. 9: SAA. 10: State & local hist socs. 14: mss admin. 15: 420 Allen st, Syracuse NY 13210.

ERICSON, MARY A (BERNAUER). b Madison Wis 18 O 42. 4: Jon Louis Ericson. 5: UWis60-64 (Russian, Fr) BA UIowa 67-68 Russian; DrakeU 68-69 English. 6: Russian, Fr. 7: Bibliog asst LC 64-65; Bibliog UConn Lib 65; Catlgr of Russian bks UWis 65-66; Catlgr DrakeU Law Lib 69-. 14: Catlg. 15: 1505 28 st, Des Moines Ia 50311.

ERIKSEN, CONRAD J K JR. b Wichita Kan 9 Ap 34. 5: Kan StateU 52-56 (Bus Admin) BS; UMo 58-60 (Hist) MA; UIll 65-66 (LS) MS. 7: Tchr St Louis Sch Syst 60-65, Dir lib serv 66-. 9: MoASchL (treas 67-68). 15: 6246 Reber pl, St Louis Mo 63139.

ERLANDSON, EILEEN M. b St Paul Minn 28 Je 20. 4: Carl E Erlandson. 5: Moorhead State Col 39-42 (Educ). 6: Ger, Norwegian. 7: Sec of translation serv Wayne State U 46-49; Libn Economics Lab Inc, St Paul 52-66; Libn Bethesda Lutheran Hosp, St Paul 66-. 9: SLA; Hosp & Med Libns ofMinn. 14: Chem, med sci, nursing, nursing educ. 15: 705 Sherwood ave, St Paul Mn55106.

ERLANDSON, NANCY ELLEN. b Hartford Conn 19 Ag 37. 5: Willimantic State Tchrs Col 55-60 (Elem Educ) BS; So Conn State Col 62-64 (LS) Certif; URI 63 (LS). 7: Tchr Montville Conn 60-64; Libn Norwich Reg Tech Sch 64-. 9: ALA; Amer Vocat Assn; ConnSchLA; Conn Vocat Assn (sec 67-69); Instr Organ of Conn Vocat Schs. 10: Mystic Seaport Marine Hist Assn. 15: PO Box 234, Gales Ferry Ct 06335.

ERLANDSON, RUTH MADELINE. b Galesburg Ill 20 Jl 07. 5: Knox Col 24-28 (Eng) AB; UIll 35-37 BS in LS, 37-43 (LS) MS; Columbia 46-48(Swedish Lit); Uppsala (Uppsala Sweden) 48 (Swedish Lit). 6: Swedish, Ger, Sp. 7: Catlg & loan asstPub Lib, Galesburg Ill 29-31, Catlgr 31-37; Catlgr UIll (Urbana) 37-38, Ref asst39-44; Chief ref libn Pub Lib, White Plains NY 44-46; Chief ref libn asst libnBrooklyn Col 46-53; Head ref dept Ohio State U 53-64; Consul for Lib Research &Lecturer in bibliog, Assoc Prof of Lib Admin Ohio State U 64-, Asst Prof of libadmin 53-59, Assoc Prof 59-66, Prof 66-. 8: Visiting lecturer UIll Grad Sch of Lib Sci summers 44, 56, 62; Lecturer Brooklyn Col Sch of Gen Stdies 47-53; Lib adv & lecturer Chulalongkorn Univ, Bangkok Thailand, 56-58 (under The Asia Foun); Lib adv, Chiengmai Univ, Chiengmai Thailand, summer 65 (under The Asia Foun). 9: ALA (Internat Rel Round Table);-ACRL(Dir-at-Large 64-68);-RSD (sec 47-48, Subs Bks Com 52-54); ThaiLA (Hon Mem); Franklinco (Ohio) LA (pres 55-56). 10: Amer-Scand Foun; Siam Soc, Bangkok Thailand; PhiKappa Phi; Beta Phi Mu. 11: Amer-Scand Foun Fellowship to Sweden, 48-49. 13: Yes. 14: Ref, subj bibliog, internat aspects of lib serv. 15: 89 E Henderson rd, apt D, Columbus Oh 43214.

ERLICH, ISABEL JOAN. b St Louis. 5: Washington U 22-25 (Eng) AB; Emory U 25-26 (LS) Certif. 7: Asst, 1st asst, Head of ref dept Atlanta Pub Lib 26-. 9: ALA; SELA; GaLA; Atlanta Lib Club. 10: Atlanta Ballet Assn; Coun Jewish Women. 15: 126 Carnegie way, Atlanta Ga 30303.

ERLICH, MARTIN. b Phila 20 Je 24. 4: Florrie Hancock. 5: Temple U 42-47 (Hist) BA; Drexel 47-48 BSLS; Wayne U48-54 (Hist) MA. 7: (Pfc) US Army Field Artillery 43-45; Asst libn Dearborn Pub Lib, Dearborn Mich 48-50; Libn US Coast Guard, Wash DC 50-53; Ref asst Detroit Pub Lib 53-56; Dir Mineola Mem Lib, Mineola NY 56-64; Co Libn Stanislaus Co Free Lib, Modesto Cal 65-66; Dir Orange Pub Lib 66-. 9: ALA; CalLA. 13: Yes. 14: Recr, admin. 15: OrangePublic Lib, 101 N Center, Orange Ca 92666.

ERMEL, GEORGE F. b Plymouth Penn 26 De 25. 5: Bucknell U Jr Col 46-48; Wilkes Col 48-50 (Soc Sci) BA; Syracuse 50, 52-53 MS LS. 6: Fr, Sp, Russian. 7: (Lt) US Navy 50-52; Asst libn Wilkes Col Lib 53-65; Supv libn Army Map Serv, Wash DC 65-68; Chief West Hemisphere Analysis, Army Togographic Command, Wash DC 68-. 9: ALA; PennLA; DCLA; SLA. 10: US Naval Reserves; Navy League; Naval Reserve Assn; Civic Club; Kiwanis; Pi Lambda Sigma; Hobby Club; US Naval Inst. 13: Yes. 14: Admin, catlg, ref. 15: 12000 Old Georgetown rd C700, Rockville Md 20852.

ERNEY, ALICE (CRAIG). b NYC 26 F 26. 4: Richard A Erney. 5: Denison U 44-48 (Sociol) BA; Columbia 48-49 (Childhood Educ) MA; UWis 59-61 (LS) MS. 7: Tchr Pub Sch No 2, Lawrence LI NY 49-52; Libn Van Hise Sch Madison Wis 61-. 9: NEA; ALA; WisLA; WisEA. 10: Kappa Delta Pi; Pi Lambda Theta. 14: Sch lib. 15: 206 Marinette Trail, Madison Wis 53705.

ERNEY, RICHARD A. b Stryker Ohio 15 D 24. 4: Alice Craig. 5: Denison U42; UVa 43-44; Denison U 46-48 (Educ) BA; Columbia 48-49 (Soc Sci) MA, 49-50, 53-57 (Hist) PhD. 7: (Cpl) US Army Air Corps 43-46; Tchr soc studies Lawrence High Sch, Lawrence NY 50-53; Instr soc studies Tchrs Col Columbia U 57; State Hist Soc of Wis, Madison Wis: Field rep 57-60, State Archivist 60-63, Assoc dir 63-. 9: SAA; Org Amer Histns; Amer Assn State & Loc Hist; Great Lakes Hist Soc; State Hist Soc Wis; Wis Acad of Scis Arts & Letters; Amer Soc Pub Admin. 12: . 13: Yes. 14: Archival admin. 15: 206 Marinette Trail, Madison Wis53705.

ERNST, WILLIAM BENEDICT JR. b Boston 17 D 16. 4: Jeannette Reed. 5: Harvard Col 35-39 (Hist of Art) AB, 39-41, 46 (Hist of Art) AM; Simmons 46-48 (LS) BS. 7: Harvard U: Catlgr 46-48, Ref asst Lamont Lib 48-51, Ref libn Lamont Lib 51-5, 1st asst Lamont Lib 53-56, Libn Lamont Lib 56-60; Asst dir SUNY (Buffalo) 60-62, Assoc dir 62-69; Dir UIll (Chicago Circle Campus) 69-. 9: ALA; NYLA (pres COL & Univ Sect 65). 14: Admin. 15: 809 Leyden lane, Wilmette Il60091.

ERSFELD, WILLIAM. b NYC 30 My 20. 4: Dorothy Taylor. 5: Adelphi U 50-54 (Eng) AB; Columbia 54-56 MSLS. 7: Air intelligence adjutant gen sect US Army Air Corps, Ala, Cal, Hawaii, Saipan, Gaum 42-46; Queens Borough Pub Lib, Jamaica NY: Br libn 58-59, Procedures writer 59-61, Asst dir pers & mgt analysis 61-63, Dir pers & mgt analysis 63-65; Asst to dir Nassau Lib System, Hempstead NY 65-67; Coord admin serv Nassau Lib Syst 67-. 9: ALA (Nomin Com); -LAD; NYLA(Com on appoint of foreign libns 68-, Personnel Admin Com 65-); NY Lib Club. 13: Yes. 14: Admin. 15: 27-27 166 st, Flushing NY 11358.

ERSKINE, STEPHEN CURTIS. b Wellesley Mass 1 F 40. 5: Middlebury Col 58-62 (Sp, Hist) BA; UMadrid 60-61 (Jr Year); Simmons 67-68 (LS) MS. 6: Sp, Fr. 7: Personnel serv off (lib) Capt USAF 62-67; Asst ref libn & docs libn Dickinson Col 68-. 9: ALA. 14: Ref, admin. 15: Box 593, Carlisle Pa 17013.

ERSTED, RUTH. b Brookings SD 17 O 04. 5: UMinn 27 (Eng) BS; Chicago 50 (LS) MA. 7: Sch libn pub schs, Hopkins Minn 27-33; Sch libn UMinn High Sch, Minneapolis33-36; Supv sch libs State Dept of Educ, St Paul 36-. 8: Tchr in lib sci summersessions at 4 univs & cols. 9: ALA (co-chm Standards for Sch Lib Programs 50);NEA; MinnEA; MinnLA; MinnASchL (Com on Standards for Sch Media Progs 69). 10: CLU; LWV. 12: Jt auth "Planning Guide for High School Libraries (54). 13: Yes. 14: Sch libnship. 15: StateDept of Educ, Centennial Bldg, St Paul Mn 55101.

ERTEL, MARGARET (PARKER). b MAdenville NC 25 Ap 07. 4: Dr L D Ertel. 5: Salem Col(Winston Salem NC) 24-28 (Eng) AB; UNC(Chapel Hill) 43-45 (Educ) MA; Appalachian State Tchrs Col summers 51-55, 57-59 (LS) 06: Fr. 7: Eng tchr High Sch, Black Mountain, Fairview, Burlington NC 30-41; Tchr-libn McDowel Co Schs, Glen Hope NC 41-45; Libn Leicester High Sch, Leicester NC 45-53; Libn Goldsboro Sr High Sch, Goldsboro NC 53-61; Lib supv Camp Lejeune Dependents Schs Marine Corps Base, Camp Lejeune NC 61-. 9: ALA; NE; NCLA; NCEA. 10: AAUW; Bus & Prof Womens Club; NC Lit & Hist Assn; UDC. 14: Catlg, bk sel, story telling, bk reviewing. 15: 3326 Hagaru dr, Tarawa Terrace NC 28543.

ERWIN, JACQUELIN R (INGLIS). b Regina Sask Can 16 D 13. 4: Richard P Erwin. 5: UWash 30-34 (Ger) BA, 34-35 BS in LS. 7: Asst libn Olympia Pub Lib, Olympia Wash 35-39; Bkmob libn Seattle Pub Lib 55-56; Catlgr UWash 57; Libn World Trade Center Lib, San Francisco 58-61; Asst libn Langley Porter Neuropsychiatric Inst, San Francisco 61-. 9: SLA; MedLA; CalLA. 15: 2063 20th ave. San Francisco Ca 94116.

ERWIN, (JOSEPHINE) DOT (WHISENANT). b Breckenridge Tex 17 My 33. 4: Robert Earl Erwin. 5: Odessa Col 51-52, 53-54 (Educ) AA; Tex Tech Col 52-53, 54-55 (Eng) BA; N Tex State Col summers 57, 65 (LS); UTex summer 60 LS Certif. 6: Sp. 7: Eng tchrbailey Co Ind Sch Dist, Muleshoe Tex 55-56; Jr high libn Crane Co Ind Sch Dist,Crane Tex 57-60; Ector Col Ind Sch Dist, Odessa Tex; Jr high Eng tchr, Hood 60-61,Elem sch libn, Lamar 61-65, Elem sch libn, Goliad 65-. 9: Tex State Tchrs Assn. 10: Ector Co ClrTA (sec68-69); Beta Sigma Phi. 14: Elem sch libnship. 15: 1718 Glenwood, Odessa Tx 79762.

ERWIN, LINDA (McINTOSH). b Austin Tex 22 Je 39. 4: Kenneth Erwin. 5: Victoria Col 57-58; UTex (Austin) 58-61 (Sp) BA, 66-68 MLS. 6: Sp, Portu, Fr. 7: Tchr: Victoria High Sch, Victoria Tex 61-62, El Campo High Sch, El Campo Tex 62-63, Del Valle High Sch, Del Valle Tex 63-66; Latin Amer catlgr UTex (Austin) 68-. 9: TexLA. 10: Phi Beta kappa. 14: Lat Amer lib materials. 15: 3902 Seiders #6, Austin Tx 78756.

ESALA, LILLIAN H(ELEN) (DUNBAR). b Toledo Ohio 16 F 23. 4: Sulo M Esala. 5: UToledo 41-44 (Hist) BA; Columbia 44-45 (LS) BS. 7: Lib asst NY Pub Lib 44-45; Co libn Va Pub Lib, Va Minn 45-46; Soc wker St Louis Co, Va Minn 55; Head Libn Hoyt Lakes Pub Lib, Hoyt Lakes Minn 59-60; Head Libn Va Pub Lib, Va Minn 61-. 9: ALA; MinnLA; ArrowheadLA. 10: Numerous local & regional societies. 11: MinnLA Certif of Merit 66. 13: Yes. 14: Ext serv, local hist, lib resources & tech, admin, ref. 15: Box 180 Route 1, Embarrass Ma 55732.

ESCH, MARTHA JOAN (ESCH). b Ann Arbor Mich 9 S 45. 5: UMich 63-67 (Pol Sci) BA, 68 9ls0 ma. 6: Sp. 7: Libn Long-Lapham Elem Sch, Dearborn Mich 69-. 9: ALA; MichASchL. 14: Sch lib wk, ref, hist collections. 15: 339 Pondview dr, Saline Mu 48176.

ESCHELBACH, MR CLAIRE JOHN. b Ann Arbor Mich 7 Mr 29. 5: UMich 47-51 (Hist) BA, 51-52 AMLS; San Francisco State Col 63-65 (Educ) Cal Libn Credential. 7: US

Army Finance Corps, US, Korea 52-54; Catlgr UCal Lib Santa Barbara, Goleta Cal 54-59, Head catlgr 59-63, Spec collections libn 59-63; Asst libn Fed Reserve Bank of San Francisco Co Research Lib 63-65; Coordinator of Tech Processing Foothill Col Lib 65-66; Catlg libn Col of Marin 66-. 9: SLA; CalLA. 10: CalTA. 12: "Aldous Huxley, a bibliography 1916-1959 (61). 14: Catlg, bibliog. 15: 514 Edgewood ave, Mill Valley Ca 94941.

ESHELMAN, GAIL (ABIGAIL IRWIN). b Toledo Ohio 1 Ja 16. 4: Ralph H Eshelman. 5: Col of Wooster 34-38 (Hist) BA; Wayne State 52-58 (LS) ME. 6: Fr. 7: Tchr of Hist, Eng, Lat & Fr Sterling High Sch, Sterling Ohio 38-40; Lib sub Dearborn Pub Schs, Dearborn Mich 51-55; Asst libn Thurston High Sch, S Redford Mich 55-59; Head Libn Pierce Jr High Sch, S Redford Mich 59-. 9: ALA; NEA; MichASchL; MichEA (var offs); SRedfordEA. 10: PEO. 14: Young adults. 15: 33870 Quaker Valley rd, Farmington Mich 48024.

ESHELMAN, MABEL S(HEARER). b Elizabethtown Penn 23 O 06. 5: Elizabethtown Col 23-25, 28-30 (Eng) AB in Ed; Drexel 54-55 MS in LS. 6: Fr, Ger. 7: Elem tchr Mt Joy Twp Sch, Mt Joy Twp Penn 25-28; Elem tchr Elizabethtown Area Sch, Elizabethtown Penn 30-59, Elem libn 59-. 9: NEA; ALA; Penn State EA; PennLA; Lancaster Co LA. 10: Bd Dirs, Elizabethtown Pub Lib; Elizabeth Hughes Soc. 14: Wk with child. 15: 250 E Orange st, Elizabethtown Penn 17022.

ESHELMAN, WILLIAM ROBERT. b Oklahoma City Okla 23 Ag 21. 4: Eve Kendall. 5: Pasadena Jr Col 39-40 (Engnr); Chapman Col 40-43 (Eng) AB; UCal(Los Angeles) 48-50 (Eng) MA; UCal(Berkeley) 50-51 BLS. 6: Fr. 7: Manager Assoc Stud Bkstore Chapman Col 41-42; Internee Civilian Pub Serv, Waldport Ore 43-46; Clerk J H Batteiger Co, Los Angeles 46-47, Sales promotion manager 47-48; Reader TA UCLA Dept of Eng 49-50; Lib asst UCLA UC(Berkeley) 50-51; Asst period libn Los Angeles State Col 51-52, Serials libn 52-53, Asst col libn 54-59, Col Libn 59-65; U Libn & Prof of Bibliog Bucknell U 65-68; Editor Wilson Lib Bulletin 68-. 8: Consul lib bldg Whittier Col 60; Consul lib serv UNevada 64; Consul lib serv UWest Fla 64; Sec Research Team "The Part-Time Professor Fund for the Advancementof Educ Los Angeles State Col 56-57; Adv Coun on Educ for Libnship UCal(Berkeley & Los Angeles) 61-64; Accreditation Teams, West Col Assn, Orange Co State 61, Upland Col 62; Consul lib serv Alderson-Broaddus Col 67-68; Consul Bowker Co; Scarecrow Press Award Jury 68. 9: ALA (Ed Com 64-66);-ACRL (2 coms 64-67);-LAD (2 coms 68-70); CalLA (Serv on coms 55-, pres S Dist 65); PennLA (Intel Freedom Com 68-69). 10: AAUP (pres 64-65: Assn Cal State Col Profs (Chapt v-pres 62-63); Los Angeles Chap Citizens Commsn for the Pub Schs (Bd 53-54); Rounce & Coffin Club (Bd 53-55, sec 53-56); Western Bks Chm 52; Judge West Bks Competition 61; West Bks Exhibitions 60-65; Typophiles 68-. 11: 1st Annual Shirle Robbins Poetry Competition UCLA 1st Prize 49; 1st ALA-H W ilson Co Lib Periodicals Award. 12: Ed "California Librarian (60-63); In prep: Typophiles Chapbook on Cal fine printers. 13: Yes. 14: Acquis, rare bks, fine printing, admin. 15: 592 Gail ct, Teaneck NJ 07666.

ESHLEMAN, GLENNA M. b Lancaster Penn 14 1 28. 5: Millersville State Col 46-50 (LS) BS in Ed; Lebanon Valley Col even 51-53 (Span); Columbia 51-54 MS in LS; UHawaii summer 65 -68 Asian & Pacific Studies; W Chester State evenings 66-69 (Geog, A-V). 7: Libn Annville Cleona Jt Schs, Annville Penn 50-54; Ed staff "Books in Print Bowker Bib Serv, Lancaster Penn summers 57-61, 63, 64; Libn Kennett Jr Sr High Sch, Kennett Square Penn 54-. 9: NEA; Penn State EA. 14: Sch lib wk. 15: Good Hope rd, Landenberg Rt 1 Pa 19350.

ESHLEMAN, J. ROBERT. b Myerstown Penn 18 Ja 09. 5: Indiana Central 25-29 (Piano) B Mus; Lebanon Valley 29-31 (Eng) AB; Bonebrake Theol Sem 31-32 (Church Hist); Columbia 32-33 (Eng); UKy 50-52 AM(LS). 7: Managing dir Associated Players, NYC 33-43; (Pfc) US Air Force 42; Organist Arcanum (Ohio) EUB Church 43-45; High sch tchr Arcanum Schs, Arcanum Ohio 45-46; Organist EUB Church, New Madison Ohio 45-56; Libn Arcanum Pub Lib, Arcanum Ohio 46-53; Music supv Russia Pub Schs, Russia Ohio 47-49; Ref libn Dayton Pub Lib, Dayton Ohio 50-55; Head Libn Franklin Pub Lib, Franklin Ohio 55-; Organist Normandy EUB Church, Dayton Ohio 61-. 9: ALA; OhioLA. 10: Amer Guild of Organists; Beta Phi Mu; Rotary; Franklin Area Hist Soc. 14: Ref. 15: Box 91, Franklin Oh 45005.

ESKEY, SUE (UNGER) (MRS). b Pecatonica Ill. 5: Cal State Col (Long Beach) 55-60 (Eng) AB; Ariz State U 63-65 (Educ, LS) MA, 67-69; UAriz 66-67. 7: Hd libn pub lib, prescott Ariz 62-63; Hd libn Phoenix Indian Sch, Phoenix 64-65; Asst libn Mesa High Sch, Mesa Ariz 65-66; Co-libn Westwood High Sch, Mesa Ariz 66-68; Hd libn Tempe High Sch, Tempe Ariz 68-. 9: NEA; ALA; ArizEA; Tempe SecondEA; Maricopa Urban TA; Ariz stateLA. 10: Kappa Delta Pi. 14: Second sch libs. 15: 849-B N Revere dr, Mesa Az 85201.

ESPELIE, ERNEST MARVIN. b Stoughton Wis 22 Je 08. 4: Mary Belle Whitten. 5: Luther Col 27-31 (Eng, Hist) AB; UMich 31-32 ABLS, 32-35 AMLS. 6: Norwegian. 7: Catlgr law lib UMich 32-37; Libn Concordia Col 37-38; Libn & commissioned prof (Commander) US Coast Guard Acad, New London Conn 38-58; Libn Augustana Col (Rock Island Ill) 59-. 9: Amer Scand Foun (pres Augustana Chap 61-63); ALA; Augustana Hist Soc; Norweg-Amer Hist Assn (mem Bd 64-); IllLA. 10: Kiwanis; AAUP. 11: Distinguished Service Award, Luther Col, 63. 12: Ed, with J I Dowie, "The Swedish Immigrant Community in Transition; Essays in Honor of Dr Conrad Bergendoff" (63); Ed "Augustana Lib Publs". 13: Yes. 14: Catlg, admin. 15: 3407 30th st, Rock Island Il 61201.

ESPENSHADE, RALPH STERLING. b Palmyra Penn 1 D 26. 5: Lebanon Valley Col 46-49 (Bio Sci); Kan State U 49-50 (Biol Sci) BS; UIll 50-51 (Zool) MS; UMich 56-57 (LS) MA. 7: (Cpl) Off of Adjutant Gen, Hdqrs Fifth Fighter Command USAF, US, Philippine Islands, Japan 44-46; Stenciler-spray painter Olmstead AFB, Midletown Penn 51-56; Ser asst, ref asst Agric Lib Penn State U 57-60; Prof asst sociol dept Minneapolis Pub Lib 60-64; Sr sci lib Sci Lib UAriz 64-. 9: ALA; Ariz State LA; SWLA. 10: Wilderness Soc; Ecological Soc Amer; Amer Inst Biol Scis; AAAS. 14: Ref, admin. 15: Sci Lib Univ of Ariz, Tucson Az 85721.

ESSICK, JAMES F. b Cleveland 20 S 34. 4: Suzanne Horth. 5: Fenn Col 58-62 (Eng) BA; West Res 62-63 MLS. 7: Electronics tech 2d class USN 53-57; Asst libn Baltimore County Pub Lib Pikesville Br 63-64, Br libn Reisterstown 64-. 9: ALA; MdLA (Adult Serv Div). 10: US Power Squadron. 14: Adult serv. 15: 1428 Burton ave, Lutherville Md 21093.

ESSICK, SUZANNE H. b Cleveland 8 Ja 39. 4: James F Essick. 5: Hiram Col 55-56 (Biol); UWyo 56-60 (Biol) AB; West Res U 62-63 MSLS; Med Lib Assn Certif 64. 6: Fr. 7: Catlgr Lib of Med & Chirurgical Faculty, Baltimore 63-. 9: . 14: Catlg. 15: 1428 Burton ave, Lutherville Md 21093.

ESSLINGER, GUENTER. b Stuttgart Germany 2 Jl 29. 4: Margaret H Bonneil. 5: Jamestown Col 57-60 (Sociol) BA; UMinn 61-63 (LS) MA. 6: Ger. 7: Jr libn UMinn (Minneapolis) 63-64; Docs libn Mankato State Col 64-67; Circ & docs libn Gustavus Adolphus Col 67-. 9: ALA; MinnLA. 10: United World Federalists; AAUP; ACLU; UN Assn of USA. 14: Govt docs, ref. 15: 5209 Irving ave S, Minneapolis Mn 55419.

ESTEP, MARIAN (THERESA). b Marion Ind 14 Ag 03. 5: Ohio State U 23-30 (Hist) BS in Ed, 34-41 (Bacteriology); UMich 49-50 AMLS. 6: Fr, Ger. 7: Clerk Bkstore, Columbus Ohio 21-28; Asst Ohio State U Lib 33-41; Tech asst Ohio State U Col of Med 41-49; Bibliogr Ohio State U Lib 50-51; Veterinary med libn UIll(Urbana) 51-. 9: ALA; MedLA; IllLA. 10: Delta Kappa Gamma; Altrusa Club; Phi Beta Kappa; Beta Phi Mu; Sigma Delta Epsilon. 14: Ref. 15: 250 Veterinary Medicine Bldg UIll, Urbana Il 61801.

ESTES, ELAINE (GRAHAM). b Springfield Mo 24 N 31. 4: John M Estes Jr. 5: Drake U 49-53 (Retailing, Bus Admin) BS, 56 Tchrs Certif; UIll 61-62 (LS) MS. 7: Detail & sales wk Yonkers of Iowa, Des Moines Iowa 54-56; Adult educ tchr Saydel & West Des Moines Sch Systems 56-60; Circ dept Pub Lib of Des Moines (Iowa) 56-60, Inf div 6-61, Libn I ref dept 62-63, Libn II circ dept 63-65, Libn II ref dept 65-. 9: ALA; IowaLA (past chm Adult Serv); Lib Assn Des Moines Metro Area (past pres). 10: Adv Coun Des Moines Dept of Adult Educ; Des Moines Chap of Links Inc (past pres); Iowa Bd of Internat Educ (Diplomatic Rel chm); Des Moines Art Center; Iowa Soc for the Preservation of Historic Landmarks (sec); Polk County Hist Soc; Beta Phi Mu; Alpha Kappa Alpha; Staff Assn Des Boines Pub Lib; Commun Playhouse Assn. 14: Ref, reader guidance. 15: 944 W9th st, Des Moines Iowa 50309.

ESTES, DAVID E. b Atlanta 23 Jl 17. 5: Berry Col 39 (Eng, Journalism, Educ) AB; Emory 46 (LS) BS, 51 (Pol Sci) MA. 7: Army libn US Army, Atlanta 42-44; Lib asst Ga Tech 45; Documents libn Emory U 46-53, Ref libn 54-62, Chief spec collections 62-.08: Consul Berry Col Lib 62; Consul Gordon Mil Col Lib 65; Lib Com Atlanta Historical Society (chm) 65-; Libn Glenn MEM Church Lib 64-. 9: ALA (Coun 68-); SAA (var coms); SELA (var coms 61-62); GaLA (var coms 57-63); Atlanta Lib Club (pres 56-57, var coms). 10: Atlanta Hist Soc; Eng Speaking Union; Pi Sigma Alpha; Amer Assn State & Loc Hist. 13: Yes. 14: Rare bks, mss, ref. 15: Emory U Lib, Atlanta Ga 30322.

ESTES, RICE. b Spartanburg SC 27 Ap 07. 4: Eleanor Rosenfeldt Estes. 5: USC 24-28 (Eng) AB; USoCal 28-29 (Eng) AM; Pratt 31-32 BLS; Columbia 44-45 (Eng). 6: Ger. 7: Evening session libn Brooklyn Col 33-35; Asst libn Stuyvesant High Sch, NYC 35-38; Ref libn Brooklyn Col 38-44; Asst Prof Pratt Inst 44-48; Asst libn USoCal 48-52; Libn Fairfield Pub Lib, Fairfield Conn 52-53; Assoc libn George Washington U 53-55; Libn & sec Pratt Inst 55-. 8: Alumni Sec Pratt Inst 44; Act Dean Lib Sch Pratt Inst 55-56; Lecturer Pratt Lib Sch 56-; Consul NY Inst of Tech 60-61; Dir Research Study of Brooklyn col libs for Coun of Higher Educ Inst of NY 62-63. 9: ALA (chm Grolier Award Com 65-66; chm Clarence Day Award Com 68-69);-ACRL; SLA; BSA; NYLA; ConnLA (sec 53); NY Lib Club (sec 56-57; pres 61-62). 10: Archons of Colophon; Conf East Col Libns (chm 65); Phi Beta Kappa; Beta Phi Mu. 12: "Study of Seven Brooklyn College Libraries and Their Cooperative Potential" (63). 13: Yes. 14: Admin, educ for libnship, bibliog. 15: 175 Steuben st, Brooklyn NY 11205.

ESTES, RUTH ELIZABETH (MADDEN). b Rochester NY D 13. 4: Cameron B Estes. 5: Albany State Col for Tchrs 31-35 (Eng) BA; State Col at Geneseo 63-65 MLS. 7: Eng tchr Mt Upton Central Sch, Mt Upton NY 35-36; Eng tchr Millbrook Union High Sch, Millbrook NY 36-39; Circ libn Rochester Inst of Tech 65-, Ref libn 67-. 9: ALA; NYLA; Monroe LA. 10: LWV; Friends of the Rochester Pub Lib; Rochester Mus Assn; Scottsville Lib Bd. 15: 1036 Quaker rd, Scottsville NY 14546.

ESTES, THELMA JONES. b Mt Victory Ky 5 O 15. 4: James Lovel Estes. 5: Sue Bennett Col 33-36 elem tchr certif; UKy 51-54 (LS) AB; Nazareth Col 59-62 MS in LS. 6: Fr. 7: Elem tchr Pulaski Co Schs, Somerset Ky 37-40; Elem tchr Ferguson City Schs, Luretha Ky 43-46; Elem tchr Crab Orchard Sch, Crab Orchard Ky 50-51; High sch libn Crab Orchard High Sch, Crab Orchard Ky, Crab Orchard Ky 51-53; Elem tchr Fort Knox Dependent Schs, Fort Knox Ky 53-54, Elem libn 54-60, Dir of lib serv 60-. 8: Consul for Wkshop in Lb Sci of the Elem Lib Nazareth Col 62; Instr of Wkshop in Use of AV Materials Nazareth Col 63; Consul Assn of Supv & Curr Devel Ky meeting 68-; Consul & leader for Fayette Co Wkshop on Materials Ctrs, Lexington Ky 68. 9: ALA (Recruitment Com 63-64); KyASchL (treas 60); Fourth District LA (pres 58-59). 10: Bus & Prof Womens Club. 13: Yes. 14: Sch libs, materials ctrs. 15: 414 E Spring rd, Radcliff Ky 40160.

ETCHISON, ANNIE LAURIE. b Cana NC 5 D 09. 5: Pineland Col 28-30 AA; Cleveland Col 30-37 BA; John Carrol U 39; West Res 39-40 BLS. 6: Fr, Ger. 7: Chief libn HQ AFWESPAC, Manila PI 46-47; Command libn HQ European Command 2d Dist, Europe 47-49; Command libn Dept of Air Force, Alaska 50-51; Libn Dept of Army, Wash DC 52-54; Staff libn Hdqrs KCOMZ, Korea 54-55; Libn Dept of Navy, Wash DC 56; Chief libn Fort Bragg NC 56-63; Staff libn Hdqrs Third US Army, Fort McPherson Ga 63-. 8: Consul, lib automation, HQ 3rd US Army 64-67; Bldg consul 64-67; Adv in planning for 5 new post libs. 9: ALA; GaLA. 10: Armed Forces Govt Employees Union. 12: "Foreign Novels in Translation" (31); "American Spirit in Fiction" (41). 13: Yes. 14: Admin, lib automation. 15: Spec Serv Div Off DCS Personnel, Fort McPherson Ga 30330.

ETHELDREDA, SISTER MARY (SMELTZER) RSM. b Loretto Penn 13 O 10. 5: Col Misericordia (Eng) BA; Villanova U MSLS; Fla State U Lib Supvrs Inst 66. 6: Lat, Fr, Sp. 7: Tchr-libn Our Lady of Lourdes Sch, Altoona Penn; Tchr-libn St Paul Sch, Butler Penn; Libn Bishop Guilfoyle High Sch, Altoona Penn; Tchr-libn Our Mother of Sorrows Sch, Johnstown Penn; Aloysius Jr Col, Hd libn 66-69. 8: Lib consul, Altoona-Johnstown Diocese 55-65; Review Bd, Harper & Row Publ, Evanstown Ill 63-69; Bk Sel Com, Penn Dept of Pub Instr; Coord of sch libs, Altoona-Johnstown Diocese; Mem Sch Lib Resource Selection Adv Com, ESEA Title II 67-69. 9: ALA; CathLA (West Penn Unit: chm Lib Recr Program 65-67); Internat Reading Assn (chm West Penn Unit 63-65); PennLA (Pub Rels Com 68-69). 13: Yes 14: Child bks, ref. 15: Mt Aloysius Jr Col, Cresson Penn 16630.

ETHERIDGE, VIRGINIA. b Miss 24 N 33. 5: Miss So Col 51-55 (Music Educ) BME; Colo State Col summer 57 (Music Supv); LSU 58-59 (LS) MS. 6: Ger. 7: Libn NY Pub Lib Music Lib 59-61, Donnell Ref Lib 61-63; Ref asst Foreign Rel Lib, NYC 63-. 9: ALA; SLA. 14: Ref. catlg. 15: 58 E 68th st, New York NY 10021.

ETKIN, ELAINE (KAY GROSSBART). b Detroit Mich 15 Je 42. 4: Asher Etkin. 5: UMich 60-64 (Anthrop) AB, 64-65 AMLS. 6: Fr. 7: Archaeological field crew wker UMich (Grand Rapids) 63; UMich (Ann Arbor): Desk clk Betsy Barbour House 63-64, Asst grad res bk room 65; Libn psych lib 65; File clk Creditor's Serv inc, Detroit 64; Staff libn NYC Pub Lib 66-67; Ref libn YaleU 67-. 9: ALA. 10: Yale Dames. 14: Adult serv, ref, intel freedom. 15: 32 Highview ter, Hamden Ct 06514.

ETTELE, EDMUND ROBERT. b Kobe Japan 20 Je 28. 5: Brown U 47-50 (Econ) AB; Harvard 53-55 MBA; West Res 62-63 MS in LS. 6: Fr. 7: (Sgt) personnel sect Hqs 12th Inf Regt, Gelnhausen Germany 51-52; Supv purchasing Westinghouse Electric Corp, Baltimore 55-61; Pre-prof Enoch Pratt Free Lib, Baltimore 61-62; Boston Pub Lib: Ref libn Kirstein Bus Br 63-64, Chief bk purchasing dept 64, Supv of gen lib operations 64-67, Supv resources & processing 67-68, Asst to Dir systems development & data processing operation 68-. 9: ALA; MassLA. 14: Automation, admin, tech serv. 15: Boston Pub Lib, Copley Square, Boston Ma 02117.

ETTER, HELEN (KOURI). b St Louis Mo 5 Ja 21. 4: Alfred G Etter. 5: Wash U (St Louis) 37-41 (Eng) AB; Columbia 41-42 BSLS. 6: Fr. 7: Asst child libn NYC Pub Lib 42-43; Research libn Ralston Purina Co, St Louis 43; Hd George W Brown sch of soc wk lib wash U (St Louis) 43-44; Libn Mercantile Lib, St Louis 45; Libn Ferguson (Mo) Pub Lib 45; Libn Aspen Pub Schs, Aspen Colo 64-68; Libn Basalt Pub Schs, Basalt Colo 68-. 9: ALA; ColoEA; ColoASchL. 10: Amer Theatre Inst, Aspen Colo. 12: Bk reviewer "Wildlife News". 14: Storytelling, child reading interests, creative dramatics. 15: Bridge House Box 117, Aspen Co 81611.

EUBANK, MARIE (GRIFFIN). b Collinsville Tex 20 Jl 06. 5: Ark Col 24-28 (Fr, Educ) AB; Peabody 49-52 (LS) MA. 6: Fr, Sp. 7: Eng tchr Marmaduke High Sch, Marmaduke Ark 41-50; Eng tchr Newport High Sch, Newport Ark 50-52, Libn 52-. 8: Instr in lib sci during summer sessions of 4 univs & Cols 53-. 3-. 9: ALA; NEA; ArkEA; ArkLA (pres Sch Div); SWLA. 10: Ark Congress Parents & Tchrs; Delta Kappa Gamma; Kappa Delta Pi. 13: Yes. 14: Serv to yp. 15: 1301 Holden ave, Newport Ark 72112.

EUBANKS, JACQUALYN K (PELDZUS). b Chicago 17 Ap 38. 4: Lloyd W Eubanks. 5: UChicago 55-59 (LS) AB, 59-63 (LS) MA; Columbia Tchrs Col 67-69 Higher & Adult Educ) MA. 7: Lib trainee Chicago Pub Lib Visual Materials Center 59-61; Grad asst UChicago catlg dept 61-63; Army libn USDA Spec Serv Br, Germany 63-65; Asst libn Amer ASSN OF Advertising Agencies, NY 65-66; Ref libn Brooklyn Col Lib 66-. 8: Consul Neighborhood Col Opportunity Program 68-69. 9: SLA; ALA (By-laws Com chm, RT on Soc Responsibilities);-ACRL (By-laws Com,Educ & Behavioral Research Subsec); LACUNY; UFCT (Brooklyn Col Chap); NY Libns RT on Soc Responsibilities). 14: Educ ref. 15: Brooklyn Col Lib, Brooklyn NY 11210.

EUREN, FLORENCE S. b Moorhead Minn 22 Ja 06. 5: Moorhead State Tchrs Col 27-37 (Hist) BE; UMinn 45-46 BS in LS. 7: Tchr Jr High Sch, McIntoch Minn 27-30; Tchr Jr High Sch, Fosstoon Minn 30-42; Tchr Jr High Sch, Thief River Falls Minn 42-43; Libn Sch System, Thief River Falls Minn 43-45; Libn circ Ore State U 46-48; Bkmob libn Pacific Co, Raymond Wash 48-57; Asst ser libn Ore State U 57-. 9: ALA; PNLA; OreLA. 10: AAUP; Delta Kappa Gamma. 14: Ser. 15: 2964 Johnson, Corvallis Ore 97330.

EURY, WILLIAM LEONARD. b Gastonia nc 16 O 04. 5: Duke 22-26 (Langs) BA; Peabody 34-37 BS in LS, 47-51 MS in LS. 6: Fr, Ger. 7: Tchr Clarkton(NC) High Sch 27-29, USAAF (Cpl), Italy 42-45; Libn Appalachian State Tchrs Col 29-. 9: ALA; SELA; NCLA; NEA; NCEA. 10: Air Force Assn; AAUP; Phi Delta Kappa. 12: "The Music Library in the Teachers College" (51). 14: Admin. 15: Box 188 Appalachian Apts, Boone NC 28607.

EUTSLER, LUELLA (SHATTUCK). b Erie Penn 9 O 11. 4: Daniel D Eutsler. 5: Edinboro State Tchrs Col 29-31 (Educ); Berea Col 31-33 (Hist & Pol Sci) BA; West Res summers 33, 34, 52-54 MS in LS. 7: Tchr-libn Berea High Sch, Berea Ky 33-36; Tchr High Sch, Metlakatla Alaska 37-39; Libn Osbourn High Sch, Manassas Va 50-55; Ref libn Wittenberg U Lib 55-. 8: NDA Inst on Asian Materials for Col Libs, UHawaii summer 68. 9: ALA; OhioLA. 10: Springfield Urban League; AAUP, Beta Phi Mu; Phi Kappa Phi. 11: Amer Theol LA Lilly Endowment study grant summer 59. 14: Ref, geneal. 15: 370 E Cassilly st, Springfield Oh 45503.

EVANS, ANNE C(ASE). b Watertown Conn 20 Ap 12. 4: Harrison L Evans. 5: UVt 30-32 (Eng); Simmons Col 32-34 (LS) BS. 7: Tchr Jamaica Vt, Newfane Vt, Putney Vt 52-58; Tchr Canal Street Sch, Brattleboro Vt 58-67, Prin 63-67; Lib consul Windham SE Supv union Brattleboro Vt 67-. 8: A-V coord for elem schs, Windham SE Supv Union 67-. 9: NEA-DAVI; ALA; AASL; VtEA; NELA; NEASchL; VtLA; VtASchL; Vt Educ Media Assn. 14: Sch lib wk, a-v wk with child. 15: 62 Canal st, Brattleboro Vt 05301.

EVANS, BEATRICE M(ARY). b Ft William Ont Can 7 O 07. 5: UMan 25-29 BA; McGill 46-47 BLS; UToronto 68 (LS). 6: Fr. 7: Asst pub lib, Winnipeg Can 29-44; Libn WRCNS (Navy), Halifax & Victoria Can 44-46; Catlgr travel libs Dept of Educ, Toronto 47; Chief libn Prov Lib Serv Dept of Educ, Toronto 60-. 8: Cadmus Ed Bd 62-; Eng Speaking Union Consul on Can bks 63-; Overseas Bk enter (Bd) Bks for developing countries 62-. 9: CanLA (var coms); ALA; OntLA (var coms); Inst Prof Libns of Ont (Bd). 13: Yes. 14: Ref, lib ext. 15: 120 Rosedale Valley rd apt 411, Toronto 5 Ont Can.

EVANS, CAROL ALICE. b St Joseph Mo 30 My 28. 5: St Joseph Jr Col 46-48 AA; Mt St Scholastica Col 48-50 AB; Catholic U 63 MSLS. 6: Fr. 7: Catlg dept Georgetown U 51-55, ref dept, ref libn 55-66, Acquis libn 66-. 9: CathLA (treas Wash DC-Md Unit 65-66); DCLA. 12: "Professionally Speaking column in "Catholic Library World occasion issues (63-65); Ed "Publications of the Faculty. . . Georgetown University (53-63). 14: Ref. 15: 3850 Tunlaw rd NW, Wash DC 20007.

EVANS, DAVID G. b Columbus Ohio 12 D 34. 4: Martha Thayer. 5: Ohio State 53-57 (Hist) BA, 57-58 (Educ) BS in Educ; Case West Res 63-65 MS in LS. 7: Tchr Mansfield Pub Schs Mansfield Ohio 58-59; Sgt USA, Intelligence Corps 59-62; Asst to asst dir Case West Res U Lib 63-64; Libn adult serv Lakewood Pub Lib, Lakewood Ohio 64-68; Libn Ohio state U (Marion) 68-. 9: ALA; OhioLA. 14: Ref, intel freedom, reader guidance. 15: 282 E Walnut st, Marion Oh 43302.

EVANS, DORIS JEAN. b Duquesne Penn 13 Je 29. 5: UWis 50-52, 60-62 (Eng)BA, 62-63 (LS) MA. 6: Fr. 7: Bkkeeper-clerk Leath & Co, Madison Wis 48-52, 54; Auditing dept Beckwith Machinery Co, Pittsburgh 53; Bkkeeper-sec Yellow Cab Co, Madison Wis 54-60; University page Madison Pub Lib, Madison Wis 61-63; Adult libn 1st asst Cleveland Heights Pub Lib Unversity Heights Br, Cleveland Heights Ohio 63-; Asst hd ref dept G M Simmons Lib, Kenosha Wis 67-69, Hd 70-. 9: ALA; WisLA; Kenosha LA. 15: 1600 60th st apt 22, Kenosha Wi 53140.

EVANS, EMMA B. b Chihuahua Mexico 10 D 10. 4: Vaughn O Evans. 5: UUtah 28-32 (Art). 7: Asst ref dept El Paso Pub Lib 63, Hd Fox br lib 64-65, Asst SW ref 66-67, Hd art ref 68-. 14: Art ref. 15: 4501 Memphis, El Paso Tx 79903.

EVANS, FRANK BERNARD. b Nesquehoning Penn 21 Ag 27. 4: Rose T DiMaio. 5: COLGATE 45-46; Penn State U 45-49 (Hist) BA; UPenn 49-50 (Hist) AM; Penn State U 50-52, 56-58, 62 (Hist) PhD. 6: Fr, Ger. 7: USNR & USN 45-48 (aviation midshipman); Faculty dept of hist Penn State U 50-52, dept of hist & pol sci 52-56, dept of hist 56-58; Assoc archivist Commonwealth of Penn, Penn Hist & Museum Commsn, Harrisburg 58-61, State Archivist 61-63; Dir Ford Film Proj Off of Civil Archives NARS, Wash DC 62-64; Asst to Exec Dir Nat Hist Publ Commsn NARS, Wash DC 64-65; Dir Archival Proj Div Off of Civil Archives NARS, Wash DC 65-66; Dir diplomatic legal & fiscal records div Off of Nat Archives NARS 66-68; Deputy asst Archivist for Pres Libs 8: Dir archival train NARS, Wash DC 63-; Dir Archives Inst 63-; Professorial lecturer in archives admin Amer U, Wash DC 63-67 Adj Prof Dept of Hist Amer U 67-; Consul Me State Cultural Bldg Author 66-; Consul on Archives to Govt of Turkey 68-; Archives consul Rockefeller Pound 69. 9: SAA (Coun 68-); AHA; Org Amer Histns; Amer Assn State & Loc Hist; Penn Hist Assn. 10: AAUP; Pi Gamma Mu; Phi Alpha Theta. 11: Fellow SAA (Certifs in ARCHIVES Admin & Record Mgt); GSA Commend Serv Award 12: "Pennsylvania Politics, 1872-1877: A Study of Political Leadership (66); "Modern Methods of Arrangement of Archives in the United States" (Coun Brussels 69). 13: Yes. 14: Admin archives & personal papers, archival principle & techniques, hist of archives admin. 15: 3102 Belair dr, Bowie Md.

EVANS, G EDWARD. b Huntingdon Penn 5 Ja 37. 4: Beverly Roe. 5: UMinn 55-59 (Anthropology) BA, 59-61 (Anthropology) MA, 62-63 (LS) MA; UAriz 61-62. 6: Fr. 7: Ser libn Cal State Col(Hayward Cal) 63-65; Catlgr Ill State U 65-. 9: ALA; Amer Anthropol Assn; IllLA; CalLA; CalTA. 10: AAUP. 13: Yes. 14: Tech processes, acquis, admin, educ for libnship. 15: Ill State U, Milner Lib, Normal Ill 61701.

EVANS, GLORIA MARYLYN (CLARKE). b Windsor Ont Can 28 Je 28. 4: Frederik O Evans. 5: Assumption U (Windsor Ont) 58 (Eng) BA; Ont Dept of Educ 53, 54 Certif Lib Sci. 6: Fr. 7: Lib clerical Windsor Pub Libs, Windsor Ont 42-53, Lib asst 53-55; Libn Prod & Engnr Div Parke Davis & Co, Detroit 55-. 9: SLA (dir 67-70, chm 1970 Conf, chm Consultation Serv Com 63-68; pres Mich Chap 65-66). 10: Altrusa Internat; Bus & Prof Womens Club; Lawyers Wives of Mich. 13: Yes. 14: Ref (bus & tech). 15: Parke Davis & Co, RPA Box 118, Detroit Mi 48232.

EVANS, ISABEL (BICKETT). b Willow City ND 17 Jl 03. 4: Floyd L Evans. 5: St Joseph Jr Col 22-24 AA. 7: Lib asst St Joseph(Mo) Pub Lib 24, Br libn 25, Asst head circ 46-52, Ref head 52-63, Act libn 63-64, City Libn 64-. 9: ALA; MoLA. 10: DAR; St Joseph Womens Press Club; Runcie Club; Duchesne Study; St Joseph Art League. 15: Pub Lib 10th & Felix sts, St Joseph Mo 64501.

EVANS, JUDITH ANN (SIMPSON). b Hamilton Ont Can 7 Je 45. 4: David M Evans. 5: Queen'sU 62-66 (Bus) BA; UToronto 66-67 BLS. 7: Govt docs libn UToronto Lib 67-68; Ref libn Provincial Lib Serv, Toronto Can 68-. 9: OntLA. 14: Ref. 15: 4 New st, Toronto 5 Ont Can.

EVANS, LOUISE. b Griffin Tex 20 Ag 19. 5: N Tex State Tchrs Col 35-38 (Bus) BS, 38-39 (Bus) MS, 39-46 Certif in Lib Serv. 7: Acquis libn N Tex State U Lib 39-. 9: ALA; TexLA. 10: Kappa Delta Pi. 12: Co-ed "Nrth Texas Regional Union List of Serials, rev ed (48). 14: Acquis, catlg. 15: Box 5032 NT sta, Denton Tex 76203.

EVANS, LUTHER HARRIS. b Sayersville Tex 13 O 02. 4: Helen Murphy. 5: UTex 19-23 (Pol Sci) AB, 23-24 (Pol Sci) AM; Stanford 24-27 (Pol Sci) PhD. 6: Fr, Sp. 7: Instr Stanford U 24-27; Instr govt NYU 27-28; Instr pol sci Dartmouth Col 28-30; Asst Prof pol Princeton U 30-35; Nat Dir Hist Records Survey WPA, Wash DC 35-39; LC: Dir Legis Ref Serv 39-40, Chief asst libn 40-45, Libn of Congress 45-53; Dir Gen of UNESCO, Paris 53-58; Proj Dir Brookings Inst, Wash DC 59-61; Proj Dir Educ Implications of Automation NEA, Wash DC 61-62; Dir of internat & legal collections Columbia U 62-. 8: Mem, Unesco Exec Bd 49-53; Mem, US Nat Commsn, 46-52 (chm 52) & 59-63; Chm, US delegation to Interamer Copyright Conf, Wash DC 46; Chm US delegation to Unesco Universalcopyright Conf, Geneva 52; Consul UTex on area studies program & lib devel, 59. 9: ALA (Life mem); Soc for Internat Devel; ADI (pres 51-52); Amer Pol Sci Assn; NEA (Life mem); NYLA. 10: Archons of Colophon; ACLU; UN Assn USA; US Com for Refugees; Popular Printing Inc. 11: Del or adv to Unesco confs 45, 47-53; hon degrees from 10 univs & cols; decorated by the govts of Brazil, France, Japan, Lebanon & Peru. 12: "The Virgin Islands from Naval Base to New Deal (45); Ed "Automation and the Challenge to Education, with G E Arnstein (62); "Federal Departmental Libraries A Summary Report of a Survey and a Conference, with others (63); "Background Book, 10th Nat Con of the US Nat Commsn for Unesco (65), & Supple (65); Ed "American Documentation (61); Ed-in-chief "Watts One Hundred Immortals of Mankind. 13: Yes. 14: Admin, lib internat rel, area studies lib programs, lib use of computers, copyright. 15: 25 Claremont ave, NYC 10027.

EVANS, LYLE (EVELYN). b Briercrest Sask Can. 5: USask 40 (Eng) BA; Toronto 42 BLS; Columbia 52 (LS) MS. 7: Elem sch tchr, Sask 0-37; Secondary sch tchr, Sask 38-39; Toronto Pub Libs 42-45; Graham-Edas Eckes Sch, Palm Beach Fla 45-46; Prov Supv of Sch Libs (First Prov Supv of Sch Libs in Can) Dept of Educ, Sask 46-62; Assoc Prof of Educ USask(Regina) 62-; Libn Regina Tchrs Col 62-64; Assoc Prof of Educ USask (Regina) 69-. 8: Sec State Supvrs of Sch Libs 58-59, chm 59-60. 9: CanLA (chm yp sect 54-55); CanSchLA (v-chm & chm-elect 68-69); ALA (Coun yrs);-AASchL (Bd dirs 2 yrs, mem Standards Com 65-); SaskLA (past pres); SaskASchL; ReginaLA. 10: Univ Womens Club; Can Assn of Univ Tchrs. 13: Yes. 14: Sch libs, educ of sch lins. 15: 17 Elizabeth Arms, 133 Proctor pl, Regina Sask Can.

EVANS, (MARGARET) MALVENA. b Chalmers Ind. 5: State U of Iowa 17-21 (Eng) BA; UIll 28-29 BS in LS; UTenn 35-36 (Fr); UMo 36-37 (Ger). 7: Asst catlgr Decatur Pub Lib, Decatur Ill 29-32; Asst catlgr State U of Iowa Lib 35; Asst catlgr UTenn Lib 35-36; Asst catlgr UMo Lib 36-38; Catlgr Tyrrell Pub Lib, Beaumont Tex 38-48; Sr catlgr Tulane U Lib 48-62, catlgr 62-. 9: New Orleans Lib Club. 10: Beta Phi Mu; Tulane U Lib St Off Assn. 14: Catlg. 15: 2817 Dublin st, New Orleans La 70118.

EVANS, MARGARET (STERLING). b Hammond Ind 11 O 40. 4: John Evans. 5: Ind U 58-62 (Hist) AB, 62-63 (LS) MA. 6: Fr. 7: Libn Bishop Noll Inst, Hammond Ind 63-.14: Catlg, ya. 15: 18104 Ridgewood ave, Lansing Il 60438.

EVANS, MARION R. b Los Abgeles Cal 3 N 29. 5: UWash 47-52 (Pol Sci) AB in Ed; Kan State Tchrs Col 53-54 MS in LS. 7: Catlgr Orange Co Lib, Santa Ana Cal 54-60, 61-67; Catlgr Portland State Col Lib 60-61; Act coord Nev Ctr for Coop Lib Serv, Carson City Nev 67-68, Catlgr 67-. 9: ALA; CalLA. 14: Catlg, acquis. 15: 701 W Telegraph #8, Carson City Nv 89701.

EVANS, MARY L (KEEPERS). b Ringsted Iowa. 4: Dr Walter B Evans. 5: Hamline U 25-29 (Eng) BA; UMinn 46 BS in LS. 6: Fr. 7: Tchr-libn High Sch, Lanark Ill 43-45; Libn Central High Sch, Peoria Ill 45-46; Libneduc & period depts U Lib USoCal 46-53; Libn ref dept Pub Lib, Alhambra Cal 53-. 10: AAUW. 14: Ref, bk review. 15: 777-6 E Valley blvd, Alhambra Ca 91801.

EVANS, MIRIAM ROBERTS. b Moorstown NJ 29 F 08. 5: Earlham Col 27-30 (Eng) BA; Drexel 31-32 BS in LS; UMich summers41-44 (LS) MA. 7: An asst libn Moorestown Free Lib, Moorestown NJ 32-33, 34-37; Libn Pocono Manor Inn, Pocono Manor Penn summers 33-34; Ref libn & head of circ dept Bucknell U Lib 37-44; Documents libn UMiami (Coral Gables Fla) 44-45; Libn Abington Lib, Jenkintown Penn 45-48; Dir Ocean Co Lib, Toms River NJ 48-. 9: ALA; NJLA (treas 52-54, 2nd v-pres 64-65, v-pres & pres-elect 66-67, pres 67-68, Exec Bd lib devel com). 10: AAUW; Ocean Co (NJ) Hist Soc; Garden State Symphony League; Commun Mem Hosp Auxiliary Assn; Zonta. 14: Ref, admin. 15: Ocean Co Lib 15 Hooper ave, Toms River NJ 08753.

EVANS, NELSON H. b Phila Pa 26 N 37. 5: Allegheny Col 55-57 (Phil); Wilmington Col (Ohio) 60-62 (Phil) BA; Drexel 63-65 MS in LS. 7: Lib asst Haverford Col 63-64; Lib asst Lippincott Lib UPenna 65; Catlg libn Trenton State Col 65-. 9: ALA; CathLA; NJLA. 14: Catlg, ref, govt docs. 15: Lib Trenton State Col, Trenton NJ 08625.

EVANS, NICOLETTE. b Brooklyn NY 18 Ap 40. 5: Queens Col(Flushing NY) 57-63 (Lib Educ) BA, MS in Ed, Certif in Lib Ed. 6: Sp. 7: Elem Sch Libn Island Park Schs, Island Park NY 62-; Libn TI reading prog, Island Pk Schs, Island Park NY summer 67. 9: ALA; NYLA; Nassau-Sufflk SchLA; Queens Col LA; NY State Tchrs Assn. 14: Child bks. 15: 178-25 Zoller rd, Jamaica NY 11434.

EVANS, PHILIP B H. b Vancouver BC Can. 5: UBC 45-49 (Hist, Eng) BA; UWash 49-50 BALS. 7: Ref asst Bellingham Pub Lib, Bellingham Wash 50-51; Map asst Brooklyn Pub Lib 51-57 Asst br libn Highlawn Br 55-57; Circ libn J Walter Thompson Co, NYC 57-59; Queens Borough Pub Lib, Flushing Br, Queens NY: Ref libn 59-61, Asst br libn Elmhurst Br 61, Asst br libn Forest Hills Br 62, Br libn Broadway Br 64-. 8: Lib/USA, Group XI, 65. 9: SLA;-ASD (Adult Materials Sel Pol, Pract & Proced Com); ALA; NYLA; NY Lib Club (Pub Rel). 10: Bksellers League. 14: Ref. 15: 205 3rd ave, New York NY 10003.

EVANS, R b Portland Ore 8 Jl 26. 5: Reed Col 49 (Lit, Lang) BA; UCal (Berkeley) 62 MLS. 6: Fr, Ger, Sp. 7: Asst Dir Berkeley Pub Lib, Berkeley Cal 62-. 9: ALA; CalLA. 14: Admin, For lang materials, pub rel, personnel. 15: Nine Gordon, Sausalito Cal 94965.

EVANS, RENEE CAROL. b Los Angeles Cal 20 D 33. 5: Whittier Col 52-56 (Chem) BA; UCLA 66-67 MLS. 6: Ger, Sp, Fr. 7: Research chem Eastman Kodak Co, Rochester NY 56-57; Research engr Rocketdyne, Canoga Park Cal 58-61; Tech libn Cal-Tech Jet Propulsion Lab, Pasadena Cal 61-62; Lit research analyst Aerospace Corp, LA 62-66, 69; Tech libn IBM-Fed Syst Div, LA Cal 67-68; Tech lit searcher Cal-Tech Jet Propulsion Lab 68-69. 9: SLA; ASIS (treas, Los Angeles Chap 65-66); CalLA. 11: S L Scholarship 66; H W Wilson Fellowship 66. 14: Ref, lit searching, info retrieval systems. 15: Aerospace Corp PO Box 95085, Los Angeles Ca 90045.

EVANS, RICHARD A. b Wilkes-Barre Penn 29 Ag 23. 4: Jane Shafer. 5: Kings Col 46-50 (Soc Sci) AB; Syracuse 50-51 MSLS. 7: Libn US Gt, Wash DC 51-57; Manager Tech Info Center HRB-Singer Inc, State Col Penn 57-63; Supv lib serv Applied Physics Lab/JHU, Silver Spring Md 63-67; Lib dir US Naval Academy, Annapolis Md 67-. 9: SLA (Documentation Gp Wash DC; treas 66, program chm 67); ASIS. 13: Yes. 14: Admin, consul. 15: 14315 Gaines ave, Rockville Md.

EVANS, ROBERT WILKINSON. b Pontiac Mich 25 Ap 30. 5: Chicago 46-50 PhB, 48-55 (LS) MA. 7: Libn U Coll UChicago 50-52; Circ libn Augustana Col 52; Army PIO (Sgt), Tokyo 52-54; Libn Muskingum Col 55-61; Head acquis dept Oberlin Col Lib 61-63, Assoc libn 63-68; Lib dir SUNY (Purchase) 69-. 8: Consul: Bethany Col(Bethany WVa) 58, Morningside Col 63; Lecturer West Res U Sch of Lib Sci 62, 64. 9: ALA-ACRL (sec Col Sect 65-66); Ohio Col Assn (chm Libns Sect 63-64); No Ohio Tech Serv Libns (chm 64-65). 10: AAUP; ACLU; Penn Genal Soc. 13: Yes. 14: Tech serv, acad libnship. 15: SUNY, Purchase NY 10577.

EVANS, RUSSEL CHRISTMAS. b Milwaukee 29 D 33. 4: Rebecca T Evans. 5: Lawrence Col 51-55 (Eng) BA; UMinn 60-65 (LS) MA. 6: Fr, Ger. 7: Insurance inspector Factory Insurance Assn, Minneapolis 55-59; Circ asst Macalester Col 59-61; Asst catlgr Beloit Col 62-65; Tech serv dept Wis State U(LaCrosse) 65-. 9: ALA. 10: AAUP; ACLU. 14: Catlg, acquis. 15: 226 S 16th st, LaCrosse Wis 54601.

EVANS, RUTH ANNE. b Schenectady NY 18 My 24. 5: Smith 42-46 (Hist) AB; Columbia 47-48 (Catlg) BS. 6: Fr. 7: Asst catlgr Colgate U Lib 48-52; Asst catlgr & ref libn Union Col Lib (Schenectady) 52-60, Asst libn 60-. 9: ALA; NYLA. 10: Phi Beta Kappa; AAUP; AAUW. 12: Comp "Catalogue of the W Wright Hawkes Collection of Revolutionary War Dicuments" (68). 14: Ref. 15: 742 De Camp ave, Schenectady NY 12309.

EVANS, SALLY (FISKE). b Flushing NY 31 Ja 43. 4: Robert Paul Evans. 5: SUNY (Geneseo) 60-64 (LS) BS; URI (LS). 7: Libn Bay Road Elem Sch, Webster NY 64-65; Libn Jenks Jr High Sch, Pawtucket RI 65-68; Catlgr Pawtucket Pub Lib, Pawtucket RI 68, Co-ord tech serv 68-. 9: RILA (chm Bulletin). 14: Tech serv. 15: 451 Broadway, Pawtucket RI 02860.

EVENSON, MARIELLEN (METTEL). b Sauk City Wis 13 O 20. 4: Donald N Evenson. 5: UWis 37-42 (Eng, Educ) BA, 56-57 (LS) MA. 6: Ger. 7: Tchr-libn High Sch, Luxemburg Wis 42-43; Tchr-libn High Sch, Medford Wis 43-46; Libn Sr High Sch, Baraboo Wis 46-55; Libn Byron Jr High Sch, Shaker Heights Ohio 57; Libn & Instr UWis (Milwaukee) 58-64; Libn in chg tech processes Milwaukee Tech Col, Milwaukee 64-. 9: SLA (treas Wis Chap 65-); WisLA. 10: Pi Lanbda Theta; Beta Phi Mu. 14: Catlg. 15: 2570 N Maryland ave, Milwaukee Wi.

EVERETT, DAVID GRAHAM. b Los Angeles 5 Mr 37. 4: Grace Kim. 5: UCLA 55-60 (Eng) AB; USoCal 64-65 MS in LS. 7: US Navy Line Off (Lt JG) 60-63; Stud libn Los Angeles Pub Lib 64-65; Libn Hughes Aircraft Co, Culver City Cal 65-66; Supv tech info ctr Northrop Ventura, Newbury Park Cal 66-68; Libn II UCal Irvine 68-. 9: SLA. 10: US Naval Res Surface Div. 15: 4622 Sierra Tree lane, Irvine Ca 92664.

EVERETT, EDNA (HAGEN). b Winger Minn 5 D 18. 4: David B Everett. 5: El camino Col 62 (Hist) AA; UMd 66 (Hist) BA; USoCal 67 MSLS. 6: Norwegian, Ger. 7: Ref libn Minot State Col 67-68; Ref libn McHenry Pub Lib, Modesto Cal 68-. 9: ALA; CalLA. 14: Ref. 15: 2377 Shaffer rd, Atwater Ca 95301.

EVERETT, ELEANOR (STRUNK). b Kingfisher Okla 3 Je 13. 5: Okla Col for Women 33-35 (Educ); UOkla 36-39 BA (Hist), BALS. 7: Asst State Supv WPA, Okla City Okla 39-41; Lib asst US Dept of State, Wash DC 41-45; Child libn Chicago Pub Lib 54-59; Libn of Child lit So Ore Col 59-. 8: Dir Storytelling Inst (HEW Higher Educ Act of 1965) 69. 9: ALA; OreLA; OreASchL. 10: ALA; OreLA. 14: Child lit, lib educ. 15: 461 Allison, Ashland Or 97520.

EVERHART, FRANCES (BURNETT). b Spartanburg SC 3 F 18. 5: Winthrop Col 35-39 (Eng, Journalism) (AB) Ind U summer 47 Certif in Elem Educ; USCar 57-58 Sch Libn Certif; UNC 63-65 MSLS. 6: Fr. 7: Tchr Newport News Va, Spartansburg Co SC; Tchr No Charleston (SC) High Sch 44-45; Tchr St Andrews, Charleston SC 47-51; Tchr Rockingham NC High Sch 53-54; Tchr Brookland-Cayce, Columbia SC 54-55; Tchr Lower Richland, Columbia SC 56-57; Tchr Forest Lake, Columbia SC 57-58, Libn 58-66; Libn Baptist Col, Charleston SC 66; Asst Prof dept of lib sci E Car U 66-. 9: ALA;-AASchL;-LED; NEA; SCEA; SELA; SCLA. 10: DAR; Town Theatre; First Nighters Drama Club; Photography Club; Poetry Club; AAUW. 14: Child libn, hist of bks. 15: 1503 Wyndham rd, Columbia SC 29205.

EVERHART, OSCAR CHARLES. b Danville Ill 2 Jl 09. 5: UMd 26-28; Ind U 46-47 (Sociol); Pomona Col 47-48 (Sociol) AB; Ind U 50 (LS) MA. 6: Fr. 7: Sales rep A C McClurg &

Co, Chicago 29-46; Radar Spec US Army 42-45; Libn Jeff Twp Pub Lib, Jeffersonville Ind48-51; Lib consul Ext Div Ind State Lib 51-53; Acquis Head asst to Dir Ind State Lib 53-58; Assoc libn Pub Lib, Miami Beach Fla 58, Chief Libn 58-. 8 Estab libs in state insts (mental, penal, etc) while lib consul for the Ind State Lib. 9: ALA (chm 2 coms 53-54, 62); FlaLA (sec 61); Dade Co LA (pres 60). 13: Yes. 14: Admin, pub rel. 15: 2100 Collins ave, Miami Beach Fla 33139.

EVERINGHAM, JOYCE DUBERT. b Hornell NY 14 My 29. 4: Neil G Everingham. 5: NY State Col for Tchrs (Albany) 46-50 (Soc Studies) BA; NY State U Col (Geneseo) 57 (LS) MA. 7: Libn Canaseraga Central Sch, Canaseraga NY 50-51; Libn Perry High Sch, Perry NY 51-55; Libn E Pembroke Elem Sch, E Pembroke NY 57-59; Libn Stevens Jr High Sch, Williamsport Penn 59-62; Libn Fairmount Sch, Syracuse NY 62-63; Head Libn Westhill High Sch, Syracuse NY 66; Coord of lib servs Westhill Sch Dist, Syracuse NY 66-. 8: Com for choosing recipient of NYLA Sch Libs Archs Award, 6566; NYLA, Vice-treas and pres of Onondaga-Oswego School Librarians Association. 9: ALA; NYLA (Recr Adv Com; Ad hoc Com for new directions of Sch Lib Sect); NY State Tchrs Assn; Onondaga-Oswego SchLA (v-pres & pres). 10: Orchard Village Assn; PTA; Castile Hist Soc; Friends of the Lib. 11 Ect of serv (pub & sch libs). 15: 152 Northwood Way, Camillus NY.

EVERITT, ROBERTA M. b Catskill NY 23 O 10. 5: NY State Col for Tchrs (Albany) 28-32 (Hist) AB, 32-33, summer 38 BS in LS; NYU 39-42, summer 53 (Human Rel) MA; Columbia summer 49 (LS); UDenver summer 62 (LS). 7: Bd of Educ, Catskill NY: Sec to supt of schs 33-35, Tchr 35-40, Asst libn 40-43; Sr high sch libn Bd of Educ, Gloversville NY 43-48; Bd of Educ, Farmingdale NY: K-12 libn & pub libn 48-53, 7-12 libn 53-57, Sch lib coordinator 57-. 8: Examiner, NYC Bd of Educ, 62-63, 65-67. 9: ALA (Life Mem);-AASchL (com chm 67, sch lib supervisor); NEA; NYLA (Sch Lib Sect); NY State TA; Nassau-Suffolk SchLA (pres 57-58, past treas, mem var coms). 10: PTA (Hon life mem); Girl Scout Leaders Assn; Boy Scout Coun; Gloversville Intercultural League; Bus & Prof Womens Club; Trustee of local histor soc; Librarian-of-the-Year Award, Nassau-Suffolk SchLA 66. 12: "We Learn from Library Books (62). 13: Yes. 14: Sch lib supv, library automation. 15: RD 1 Box 295, Catskill NY 12414.

EVERS, JACQUES J. b Willebroek Belgium. 4: Mary Jeanne Connor. 5: ULouvain 47 Candidature in Applied Econ Sci; UDetroit 61 MBA; UMich 68 AMLS. 6: Dutch, Fr, Ger. 7: Accountant Ford Motor Co, Dearborn 51-52; Supply Specialist USA Signal Corps, Ga 52-54; Export-Credit Chrysler Corp Export Div, Detroit 54-58; Statistician Automobile Manufacturers Assn, Detroit 59-. 9: ALA; SLA. 10: Dearborn Interfaith Action Coun. 12: Comp "World Motor Vehicle Data", annual. 13: Yes. 14: Stat & econ research for bibliog. 15: 26744 Constance, Dearborn Heights Mi 48127.

EVERSBERG, CAMILLE (McANDREW). b Baton Rouge La 30 Ag 43. 4: (Hervey) Wallace eversberg. 5: LSU 61-65 (Psych) BA, 65-66 (LS) MS. 6: Fr, Ger. 7: Info desk & asst interlib loan libn LSU Lib 66-67, supv order orocessing 67-68, Hd order dept 68-. 9: ALA; LaLA. 10: Jr League; Chi Omega; AAUW; Baton Rouge Lib Club. 14: Acquis. 15: 1160 Stanford ave, Baton Rouge La 70808.

EVERSON, JEAN E. b Columbia Co Wis 7 Je 36. 5: Wis State Col (La Crosse) 54-58 (Eng) BA; UWis 58-59 MA in LS. 7: Dimestore clerk SchultzBros Inc, Wisconsin Dells Wis 50-58; Lib clerk Wis State Tchrs Col (La Crosse) 57-58; Lib clerk UWis Lib Sch 59; Brooklyn Pub Lib: Libn 59-61, Sr libn 61-65, Young teens spec 65-. 8: Adv manager, "Top of the News, 63-65. 9: ALA (sec-treas Jr Mems RT 68-69); NYLA. 10: CORE; Friends of Freedom Libs. 11 Young teens. 14: Young teens. 15: Apt 4H 35 Crown st, Brooklyn NY 11225.

EVERSON, LAURA (WILSON). b Cincinnati 25 Je 2. 4: C Donald Everson. 5: Miami U(Oxford Ohio) 44-47 (Psych) AB; LSU 61-65 (LS) MS. 6: Fr, Sp. 7: Libn Our Lady of the Lake Sch of Nursing, Baton Rouge La 64-65; Sr Libn div of research Col of Bus Admin LSU 65-66; Hd libn GSR1, Baton Rouge 66-67; Lib La Law Enforcement Commsn 68-. 9: ALA; MedLA; SLA; LaLA; Baton Rouge LA. 14: Research, ref. 15: 3743 Silverside dr, Baton Rough La 7088.

EVERTS, EVELYN (CLARK). b Newcastle Wash 1 Ja 15. 4: William E Everts Jr. 5: West wash State Col 32-34; UWash 34-36 (Zool) BS, 36-36 BA in LS; Drexel Inst 67 (LS). 6: Sp, Fr, Ger. 7: Libn Wash StateU 37-39; Libn Boise State Col 57-. 9: ALA; PNLA; IdaLA. 10: AAUW. 14: Ref wk. 15: 1902 N 20th st, Boise Id 83702.

EVERTS, IRMA DEE. b Shelbyville Mo 3 Ja 21. 4: Wilson Everts. 5: UOkla 38 (Eng) BA; 39 (LS) BS. 6: Fr. 7: Libn (established lib), Pryor Okla 40-43; High sch libn, Norman Okla 43-44; Army & Navy libn 44-45; Pub lib wk, San Antonio Tex 47-55; Libn priv sch, San Antonio Tex 55; Decorator Leonard's Colonial Shoppe, San Antonio Tex 59-61; Asst libn San Antonio Col 61-. 8: "Library Hour" Radio Prog 67-. 10: Delta Kappa Gamma; Delta Psi Omega; Cosmopolitan Internat. 13: Yes. 14: Ref. 15: 11602 Intrigue, San Antonio Tx 78216.

EVETT, MARY LOUISE (SYDOW). b Denver 24 Jl 15. 4: Paul L Evett. 5: Colo State Col 32-35, 42 (Hist); Centrl Mich U 48-49 (Eng) BS; UMich 49-55 (Educ) MA. 6: Lat, Fr. 7: Mt Pleasant (Mich) Pub Schs: Tchr 49-55, Sr high sch libn 55-60, Dir of sch lib serv 60-. 8: Supv of stud tchrs Central Mich U, Mt Pleasant Mich 49-. 9: ALA: NEA: MichASchL; MichCTe. 14: Curr devel for tchrs & studs, tchr training. 15: Mt Pleasant Pub Schs, Mt Pleasant Mi 48858.

EVRAIFF, LOIS (KLEHAMER). b Rochester NY 29 Ja 31. 4: William Evraiff. 5: SUNY (Geneseo) 49-53 (LS) BS; Wayne State 57 (LS) M Ed. 7: Sch libn Allen Creek Sch, Rochester NY 53-56; Grad asst Wayne State U 56-57, Instr 57-61; Dir Educ Improvement Ctr, Detroit 61-63; Libn Nueva Day Sch, Menlo Park Cal 67-. 9: ALA; Assn of Child Libns NoCal; CalLA; Assn Supv & Curr Devel. 14: Bk sel& child lit, reading guidance, curr devel, sel & utiliz of learning materials. 15: 1976 Ticonderoga dr, San Mateo Cs 94402.

EWALD, MARJORIE (KLECKNER). b Painesville Ohio 19 Je 16. 4: Charles Richard Ewald. 5: Heidelberg Col 34-38 (Eng, hist, & educ) AB; Wes Res 40-41 BSLS. 6: Fr. 7: Eng & hist tchr Roosevelt Jr High Sch Middletown Ohio 38-40; Head Libn Tiffin Pub Lib, Tiffin Ohio 42-49; Eng tchr & sch libn Old Fort High Sch, Old Fort Ohio 56-60; Sch libn Fremont Jr High Sch, Fremont Ohio 60-. 9: OhioEA; NWOhioEA; OhioASchL. 10: DAR; AAUW. 14: Yp, sch wk. 15: Rt 5, Tiffin Ohio 44883.

EWALD, ROBERT B(YRNES). b Lexngton Va 21 N 38. 4: Linda Lovejoy. 5: Hampden-Sydney Col 57-61 (Classics) AB; Harvard 61-64 (Theol) STB; Simmons 64-66 (LS) MS; U Tubingen 67-68 Theol. 6: Ger, Fr, Dutch, Gr, Lat. 7: Asst in rare bks Harvard Divinity Sch Lib 61-64,Catlgr 64-66; Employee Otto Harrassowitz, Wiesbaden Ger 66-67; Catlgr LC 68-. 9: ATheolLA; ALA. 15: 600 G st SE, Washington DC 20003.

EWALT, MARY LEE (HARRIS). b Macomb Ill 10 Mr 17. 4: David L Ewalt. 5: WestIllU summer 35-37 (Hist); UIll 36-37 (Hist); UChicago 41 (Hist); Rockford Col 37-38 (Hist); NorthwesternU 39-40 (Hist). 7: Hd clsf dept E H Brown Adv Agcy, Chicago 40-41; Purchasing agt US Army Spec Serv, Camp Ellis 41-45; Asst to Walter M Hill (are bks), Chicago 45-48; Asst libn Arlington Hts Mem Lib, Arlington Hts Ill 61-. 14: Catlg, rare bks. 15: 500 N Dunton ave, Arlington Hts Il 60004.

EWELL, ADELE. b Romeo Mich 20 D 06. 5: UMich 24-28 AB in Ed, 30-31 ABLS, 40-41 AMLS. 7: Mich State U: Period libn 31-34, Order libn 34-41, Catlgr 41-43; Catlgr UIll(Urbana) 43-44; Catlgr UMich 44-. 9: ALA. 10: Phi Beta Kappa; Pi Lambda Theta; Phi Kappa Phi. 14: Catlg. 15: 505 Packard st, Ann Arbor Mich 48104.

EWEN, SYLVIA (Scott). b NYC 22 Jl 16. S01 J. 5: Hunter Col 32-36 (Eng) BA; Colmbia 40-41; Pratt Inst 66-68 MLS. 6: Fr. 7: Docs libn SUNY A & T Col (Farmingdale) 68-. 10: Beta Phi Mu. 14: Ref, docs. 15: 15 Dodford rd, Great Neck NY 11021.

EWICK, C RAY. b Shelbyville Ind 13 S 37. 4: Joann (Hotchkiss) Ewick. 5: Wabash Col 55-59, 62 (Eng Lit) BA; Ind U 65-66 (LS) MA. 7: Salesman Shelbyville Ind 60-62; Preprof Indianapolis Pub Lib 62-65; Consul (construction) Ind State Lib, Indianapolis 66-67, Asst dir 67-. 9: ALA; IndLA (chm Loc Arr Com 67, 68). 14: Admin. 15: 4803 Chesterfield W dr, Indianapolis In 46227.

EWING, ALICE (CAUSEY). b Cleveland Miss 30 D 25. 4: James G Ewing. 5: Delta State Col 41-45 (Eng) BS in Ed; Peabody Col 65-67 MLS. 7: Tchr Central High Sch, Jackson Miss 45-48; Libn Central High Sch, Nashville 65-. 9: ALA; NEA; TennEA; Middle Tenn EA; Metro Nashville EA. 14: Sch libs. 15: 1142 Duncanwood dr, Nashville Tn 37204.

EWING, ALISON (GOSTOW). b Detroit Mich 8 N 46. 4: Stephen Ward Ewing. 5: UWis 64-66 (Psych) ILS; UMich

66-68 (Psych) BA, MS in LS. 6: Fr, Russian. 7: Stud lib asst umich Bus Lib (Ann Arbor) 67-68; Ref libn Northbrook Pub Lib, Northbrook Ill 69-. 9: ALA; IllLA. 10: Phi Beta Phi; UMich Alumnae Assn. 14: Ref. 15: 1460 N Sandburg ter, Chicago Il 60610.

EWING, DONALD C. b Forest City Iowa 9 Ap 23. 4: Joan Gannon. 5: St Thomas Col 4650 (Hist) BA; UMinn 5052 (Hist) MA, 5354 (LS) MA; Wayne State U 6465 (Archives). 7: Staff sgt US Army, N Africa, India 4346; Catlgr Wayne State U 5455; Libn USAF, England 5556; Ref libn soc studies Wayne State U 5666, Hd soc studies div 66. 9: ALA; SAA. 14: Ref, archives, rare bks. 15: 124 Meridan, Dearborn Mi 48124.

EWING, HELEN (McLEOD). b Butte Mont 1 Je 03. 4: Robert Lee Ewing. 5: UMont 21-25 (Eng) BA; Carnegie 31-32 (LS) BS. 6: Fr, Sp. 7: Tchr-libn Crafton High Sch, Crafton Penn 32-35; Tchr-libn McKeesport High Sch, McKeesport Penn 35-37; Libn Roosevelt Co Lib, Wolf Point Mont 49-50; Libn City-Co Lib, Glasgow Mont 50-62; Asst Prof & Circ Libn Mont State U 62-. 8: Mont State Lib Commsn 53-62. 9: AL; PNLA; MontLA (pres 60-61). 10: Bus & Prof Womens Club; AAUW; AAUP. 11: Woman of the Year 58, Glasgo(Mont) Bus & Prof Womens Club. 14: Circ, personnel admin, acquis. 15: 519 W Arthur, Bozeman Mont 59715.

EWING, STEPHEN DOUGLAS. b San Leandro Cal 7 Ap 24. 4: Dorlesa Barmettler. 5: UCal 46-50 (Psych) BA, 50-51 BLS. 7: Radar mechanic USAF, US & Italy 43-45; Page & prin libn UCal(Berkeley) 47-51; Libn ref Tacoma (Wash) Pub Lib 51-53; Co libn Hardin Co Lib, Kenton Ohio 53-55; Co libn Humboldt Co Lib, Eureka Cal 55-58; Lib dir San Leandro Pub Lb, San Leandro Cl 58-. 9: ALA; CalLA (pres Pub Libs Sect 64, pres Redwood Dist 56); Pub Lib Execs Central Cal (treas 64 & 65). 13: Yes. 14: Pub lib admin. 15: 300 Estudillo ave, San Leandro Cal.

EWING, WILLIAM STERLING. b Belleville Mich 28 Ag 12. 5: UMich 30-35 (Hist) AB, 36-37 ABLS, 47-50 AMLS. 7: Jr asst Detroit Pub Lib 38-41; (Lt) US Coast Guard, Pacific Area 43-45; Ref libn UMich 41-42, 46-52, MS libn 52-. 8: UMich Assn of Lib Sci Alumni, 65. 9: SAA; Amer Assn State & Loc Hist; Manuscript Soc; Hist Soc Mich. 10: Washtenaw Co (Mich) Hist Soc; Signature Club. 12: Comp "Guide to the Manuscript Collections in the William L Clements Library, 2nd ed (53). 13: Yes. 14: Mss. 15: 555 E William st apt 25-C, Ann Arbor Mi 48108.

EYERMAN, MARY ELIZABETH. b Grove City Ohio 7 D 14. 5: Capital U 32-36 (Fr, Hist) AB; Ohio State U summers 36-37, 39-41 (Educ); UWis 50-51 (LS) MA. 6: Fr. 7: Tchr Jackson Tp Schs, Grove City Ohio 36-38; Tchr Jefferson Twp Schs, Gahanna Ohio 38-39; Tchr Logan City Schs, Logan Ohio 39-50; Libn Columbus Pub Schs, Columbus Ohio 51-. 9: ALA (life mem); OhioASchL; OhioEA; Columbus EA. 10: Delta Kappa Gamma, Bus & Profess Women's Club. 14: Ref. 15: 3597 Orchard lane, Grove City Oh 43123.

EYMAN, ELEANOR (GARDNER). b Pittsburgh 3 Ja 20. 4: David R Eyman. 5: Fla State Col for Women 37-38; UMiami 38-41 (Eng) AB; Fla State U 54-58 (LS) MA. 7: Libn Stranahan High Sch, Ft Lauderdale Fla 56-61; Libn Miami-Dade Jr Col 61-63, Act dir No Campus Lib Serv 63-66, Dir 66-. 8: Consul, Rockland Jr Col, 64; Mem, So Assn eval teams, 3 yr col lib bldgs 67-69. 9: ALA (consul Jr Col Lib Bldgs);-LED (partic Reg Manpower Conf 69); FlaLA (chm Loc Conf Com 68, Memb Com, Pub Rel Com; Jr Col Sect). 10: Beta Phi Mu; Kappa Delta Pi; Fla Resources Conf. 13: Yes. 14: Jr col admin. 15: 5305 SW 62 ave, Miami Fl 33155.

EZELL, MARTHA (McCLURE). b Grandview Wash 26 F 13. 4: James R Ezell. 5: Reed Col 30-34 (Math) BA; UWash 34; UOre 35-38 (Ger) MA; UCal(Berkeley) 39 (Ger); UWash 56-57 (LS) ML. 6: Ger. 7: Tchr Odessa High Sch, Odessa Wash 36-39; Film libn Lib Assn of Portland Ore 48-51; Films & adult serv Ft Vancouver Reg Lib, Vancouver Wash 52-56; 57-59; Assoc libn & act libn Linfield Col 59-62, Libn 61-. 9: PNLA; OreLA; Pac NW Col Lib Assn; Willamette Valley Christian Col Lib Assn (chm 64-66). 10: AAUP; Beta Phi Mu; Grange SOROPTIMIST Club. 14: Admin. 15: Rt 3 Box 398, McMinnville Or 97128.

EZZO, MARY (EMMA) ROSS. b Lancaster Pa. 19 Ja 13. 4: Stephen Alton Ezzo. 5: Millersville State Tchrs Col 30-34 (Eng & LS) BS in Educ; Johns Hopkins U 56-57; Rutgers (summers) 58-59 (LS); UMd (eve & summer) 61-65. 7: Accounting Clerk Armstrong Cork Co, (Lancaster Pa) 35-40; Accounting Clerk V-C Dry Cleaners, (Suffolk Va) 45-46; Telephone Operator Southern Bell Tel, (Fort Lauderdale Fla) 46; Accountant glenn L Martin Co, (Baltimore Md) 41-45, Sr Clerk Engineering 46-50, Engineering Libn 50-56; Libn Board of Educ Balto Co, (Towson Md) 56-. 9: ALA; NEA; MdLA; Md State TA; Tchrs Assn of Baltimore Co; Assn Sch Libns Md; Sch Libns Baltimore Co. 14: Wk with ya. 15: 719 Silver Creek rd, Baltimore Md 21208.

F

FABER, ELIZABETH MARGUERITE. b Watertown Wis 4 F 12. 5: Northwestern Col 33 Eng) BA; UWis 34 (LS) Diploma; Columbia Col(Chicago) 37 Mof Speech. 6: Ger. 7: Pub Lib, Watertown Wis 28-33, Asst 34-35; Asst Pub Lib, Cedar Rapids Iowa 35; Child libn East Side Br, Evansvile Ind 36:; Libn Pestalozzi Froebel Tchrs Col 36-40; Libn Pub Lib, Watertown Wis 40-. 9: ALA; WisLA. 10: LWV; Saturday Club; Euterpe Club; Curtain Club; Watertown(Wis) Art Assn; Watertown(Wis) Hist Soc. 14: Admin. 15: 201 W Main st, Watertown Wis 53094.

FABER, HANNELORE (FLOCH). b Germany 22 O 41. 4: Edward G Faber. 5: UMan 60-63 (Sci) BS; UBC 64-65 BLS. 6: Ger. 7: Acquis libn Atomic Energy of Can Ltd, Chalk River Ont 65-67; Libn Dunlop Research Ctr, Sheridan Park Ont Can 67-. 9: CanLA. 14: Acquis, ref. 15: Dunlop Res Cntr, Sheridan Park Ont Can.

FABER, SALAMON. b Rozdziele Gorne Poland 6 Jl 11. 4: Gertrude I Schachter. 5: Jewish Theol Sem (Breslau) 35-39 Rabbi; Friedrech WilhelmU (Brèslau) 35-39 (Philos); Queens Col 37-39 MLS; Dropsie Col 39-42 (Orientalia); Jewish Theol Sem (NY) 48-51 (Rabbinica) DHL. 6: Hebrew, Yiddish, Polish, Ger. 7: Asst to libn Jewish Theol Sem (Breslau) 37-39; Rabbi Shaare Shomayim Congrea 9breslau) 37-39; Rabbi Shaare Shomayim Congregation, Phila 40-47; Educ dir Hillel Acad, Pittsburgh Penn 47-48; Rabbi Beth Israel Temple, Warren Ohio 48-54; Rabbi Kew Gardens Anshe Sholom, Kew Gardens NY 54-; Catlgr Brooklyn Pub Lib, Brooklyn NY 69-. 8: Pub Librarian's Provisional Certif 69. 9: Rabbinical Assembly. 10: Interfaith Coun of SW Queens. 13: Yes. 14: Catlg, ref, bibliog. 15: 101-09 75th rd, Forest Hills NY 11375.

FABIAN, MERLE G. b Baltimore 21 F 38. 4: Larry L Fabian. 5: Syracuse 55-59 (Amer Studies) AB; Washington Semester Program American U 58; Harvard summer 58; Catholic U 60-62 MS in LS. 7: Research asst Bur of Soc Sci Research, Wash DC 59-60; Lib trainee Mt Alto VA Hosp, Wash DC 61-62; Ref libn San Francisco Pub Lib 62-63; Head resources off Govtl Affairs Inst, Wash DC 63-66; Senior ref libn US Civil Serv Commission 66-. 9: DCLA. 10: Phi Beta Kappa; Phi Kappa Phi; Lambda Sigma Sigma; Eta Pi Upsilon; Pi Delta Phi; Beta Phi Mu. 12: Ed "DC Libraries journal (66-67). 14: Ref, admin. 15: 5500 Prospect Place, Chevy Chase MD 20015.

FABILLI, JOSEPHINE CAROLINE. b Pacentro Italy. 5: Dominican Col, Fresno State Col 28-30; UCal(Berkeley) 30-32 (Fr) BA, 33 Certif, 37-38 (Romance Lang); USoCal 65 66 MA, 69 (Span) PhD. 6: Fr, Sp, Ital, Portu, Lat. 7: Pub sch libs -38; Catlgr Stanford U Libs 38-43; Exec asst Hispanic Found LC 43-45; Lib consul Foreign Affairs Off Dept f State USIA 45-53; Ref libn Lib Pan Amer Union, Wash DC 55-56; Head adult dept Free Pub Lib, Worcester Mass 56-59; Ref soc sci libn Los Angeles State Col 59-62; Asst libn pub serv USoCal 62-65; Ref wk Cal State Col, Los Angeles 66-. 8: Instr Escuela de Bibliotecarios, Lima Peru 44 (sent by LC); Missions for LC to nat libs of Colombia & Paraguay, 44-45; 3 tour of duty in Hispanic-Amer counries for Dept of State, USIA, as lib consul 45-53; Instr (Fr, Span, Ital), USoCal 66-; Instr summer sessions Immaculate Heart Col Los Angeles Cal (Lib Sci, Span) 66-68. 9: ALA; CalLA (sec & chm of CURLS, So Div 63-65). 10: Pacific Coast Coun on Latin-Amer Studies; AAUP. 12: "Bibliography of Works on Library Science, LC (44); Co-ed "Repertorio de Publicaciones Periodicas Actuales Latinoamericanas, Unesco & Pan Amer Union (58). 13: Yes. 14: Rom langs, humanities (ref & catlg). 15: 3789 Menlo ave, Los Angeles Ca 90007.

FABRITZE, CATHARINE M (EGAN). b Allentown Penn 4 Jl 12. 4: Albert A Fabritze. 5: Kutztown State Col 35 (Eng, Soc Studies, LS) BS. 7: Elem libn Allentown Sch Dist, Allentown Penn 35-58, Supv of elem libs 58-64; Coordinator of Elem Libs Whitehall-Coplay Sch Dist, Hokendaugua Penn 65-. 9: NEA; Penn State EA; PennLA (Eval Com 64). ; Whitehall-Coplay EA. 13: Yes. 14: Elem sch libs. 15: 516 Second st, Whitehall Pa 18052.

FACHILLA, MRS LOUISE A. b Rossville Ga 28 Je 23. 4: Nicholas Fachilla. 5: Emory & Henry Col 43-47 (Eng) BA; Vanderbilt 62-63 (Eng) MA; Peabody 63-64 (LS) MA. 7: Sec Bryan Hsiery Mill, Rossville Ga 41; Asst clerk computing sect Tenn Valley Authority, Chattanooga Tenn 41-43; Sec to treas Emory & Henry Col 43-47; Church sec Trinity Meth Chirch, Decatur Ala 47; Registrar Central High Sch, Chattanooga Tenn 48-51; Church sec Smyrna Meth Church, Smyrna Tenn 57-60; Readers serv libn Emory & Henry Col 64-. 9: ALA (Memb Com Va rep);-ACRL; TennLA; VaLA; SELA. 10: PTA; Beta Phi Mu. 14: Ref. 15: P O Box 30, Emory Va 24327.

FACKOVEC, WILLIAM MARTIN, S M. b NYC 18 Ap 25. 5: UDayton 49 (Fr) BS in Ed; West Res 59 MS in LS. 6: Fr, Sp, Latin. 7: Tchr St John Baptist High Sch, Phila 49-50; Tchr-libn North Catholic High Sch, Pittsburgh 50-57; Tchr-libn Purcell High Sch, Cincinnati 58-60; Libn UDayton 60-. 9: ALA; CathLA. 12: "Lourdes Publicatons in French in the Clugnet Collection (58). 13: Yes. 14: Catlg, clsf, rare bks. 15: UDayton, Dayton Ohio 45409.

FADDEN, ALICE ELIZABETH (McLEAN). b Seattle 10 Ag 12. 4: Gene S Fadden. 5: UWash 30-34 (Eng) BA, 34-35 (Libnship) BA. 7: Asst libn Central Wash State Col 35-37; Sec Sch of Libnship UWash 37-38; Libn Olympic Jr High Sch, Seattle 62-. 9: ALA; NEA; WashEA; Highline EA; Wash State ASCHL. 14: Sch libs. 15: 2501 SW 149th st, Seattle Wa 98166.

FADENRECHT, GEORGE H. b Kirk Colo 17 F 15. 4: Florence Blocher. 5: Saskatchewan (Prov) 38-39; Tabor Col 39-40, 46-47 (Psych) AB; UKan 47-50 (Hist) MA; UColo 49-50 (Hist); UMich 52-53, 60-61 MALS. 6: Ger. 7: Tchr Kan Schs 40-41; Civilian pub serv Mennonite Central Com 41-45; Asst Prof of hist Bluffton Col 50-52; Circ libn Kan State U 53-54, Asst dir 54-61, Assoc dir 61-64; Dir of Libs Central Wash State Col 64-. 8: Wash Higher Educ Lib Com. 9: ALA; KanLA (coun, treas); PNLA. 10: Mennonite Hist Soc; Kan Hist Soc; Phi Alpha Theta. 13: Yes. 14: Admin, acquis, catlg, personnel. 15: RFD 4 Box 120, Ellensburg Wa 98926.

FADER, EDYTHE E (ALEXANDER). b Waterville Wash 24 Je 00. 5: Skagit Valley Col 51-53 AA; West Wash Col of Educ 53-57 (Soc Sci) BA in Ed; UWash 58-61 MLS. 6: Sp. 7: Tchr & libn Madison Elem Sch, Mt Vernon Wash 54-60; Libn & a-v dir Skagit Valley col 60-62, Catlg & ref libn 62-65, Night libn (ref) 66-. 9: NEA; ALA; WashEA; WashStateASchL (sec Dist 1, 59-60); WashLA. 14: Catlg, ref. 15: 1814 Douglas st, Mt Vernon Wa 98273.

FAGAN, GEORGE V. b Phila 4 O 17. 4: Ernestine Hudak Fagan. 5: Temple 36-40 (Euc) BS, 41 (Hist) MA; UPenn 54 (Hist) PhD; UDenver 57 MALS. 6: Ger, Fr. 7: Instr hist Temple U 40-41, 46-51; (2d Lt to Col) AUS-USAF 42-51; Instr hist US Naval Acad (Annapolis) 51-54; Assoc ed Air U Press, Maxwell AFB Ala 54-55; Assoc prof of hist USAF Acad Colo 55-56, Prof of hist & dir of lib 56-69; Prof of Lib Sci & Hd libn Colorado Col 69-. 8: Exec dir, Nat Lib Week, Colo 59-62; Lecturer in hist UColo, Colorado Springs 60-. 9: ALA; AHA; Assn Amer Histns; MPLA; ColoLA. 10: Colorado Springs Fine Arts Center. 12: ""Alexander Dallas Bache, Educator (41); ""Study Guide to American History (57); ""Self Evaluation, USAF Academy Library (58); ""Geography and National Power (53); Co-auth ""The USAF Academy Site and the Pikes Peak Region (62). 13: Yes. 14: Admin, spec collections. 15: 1408 N Cascade ave, Colorado Springs Co 80907.

FAGERBURG, DOROTHY (SPENCER). b Temple Tex 6 Jl 07. 4: A Theodore Fagerburg Jr. 5: Occidental Col 31 (Eng Lit) AB; USoCal 38 BS in LS; Occidental Col 40 (Eng Lit) AM. 7: Asst libn USoCal 38-40; Asst Prof of Lib Sci Ill State U 57-. 8: Professional bk reviewer for radio & other audiences 38-; Instigator of Lib Instr via Closed Circuit TV V Ill State 60; 6; Consul in Lib Instr via Closed Circuit TV SoIll U 63. 9: ALA; AASchL; IllLA; IllASchL; IllEA; McLean Co LA; Midwest Acad LA. 10: Bloomington-Normal Art Assn (past Bd pres); YWCA; Travel Club (past pres); Longfellow Club (past pres); Second Presby Church (Bd of Deacons); Alpha Beta Alpha. 13: Yes. 14: Lib hist, hist of bks & printg, instr in use of lib. 15: 29 Norbloom ave, Normal Ill 61761.

FAGERHAUGH, KENNETH H. b Opheim Mont 14 D 14. 5: Luther Col 36 (Chem) BA; UMich 42 ABLS. 07: Chem DuPont, Kankakee Ill & Tulsa Oka 4243; Lib & supv classified files Clinton Labs, Oak Ridge Tenn 4345; Libn Rohm & Haas Co, Phila 4546; Tech libn Off of the Quartermaster, Phila 4648; Research libn John Crerar Lib, Chicago 4850; Asst libn 5052; Libn & assoc prof of lib sci Carnegie Inst of Tech 52. 7: Chem duPont, Kankakee Ill & Tulsa Okla 42-43; Lib & supv classified files Clinton Labs, Oak Ridge Tenn 43-45; Libn Rohm & Haas Co, Phila 45-46; Tech libn Off of the Quartermaster, Phila 46-48; Research libn John Crerar Lib, Chicago 48-50, Asst libn 50-52; Libn &assoc prof of lib sci Carnegie Inst of Tech 52-. 9: ASIS (Coun 54-55, treas 55-57); ALA-ACRL (Tri-State Chap);-LAD (Sect on bldgs & equip, v-chm 61-64, chm Nomin Com 63-64);-LED (Exec Bd 55-57, chm By-Laws Com 58-59); SLA (Exec Bd 51-54 Convention chm 55-56, chm 50th Anniv Com 54-59, chm Spec Clsf Com 64-66, v-chm Pittsburgh Chap 55-56); USBE (mem-at-large Exec Bd 56-62); PennLA (treas 56-57, pres 67-68, chm Const Com 54-55, chm Org Com 64-65). 10: AAAS (Fellow); Pittsburgh Bibliophiles; Phi Kappa Phi. 11: Distinguished Serv Award Luther Col 69. 14: Admin, rare bks. 15: Rt 1 Box 430A, Coraopolis Pa 15108.

FAHERTY, GLADYS (WENSEL). b Oakland Md 27 Je 33. 4: William J Faherty. 5: Frostburg State Col 51-55 (Educ) BS; Penn State U 58; UNC 63-67 (LS) MS. 6: Fr. 7: Phys educ tchr Beall High Sch Frostburg Md 55-64; Libn Mt Savage Sch, Mt Savage Md 64-. 8: Church Libn 64-69; Lib Aides Reg Sponsor 68-69; Administered Federal Funds in Demonst Sch Lib 66-68. 9: ALA; NEA; Md State TA; MdASchL. 10: Beta Phi Mu; Delta Kappa Gamma. 11: Leadership Awarf, Frostburg State Col 55. 14: Sch libnship. 15: 169 Spring st, Frostburg Md 21532.

FAHEY, REV JAMES L. b Boston Mass 30 D 32. 5: Holy Cross 50-54 (Eng) AB; St John's Sem 54-59 (Theol) MA; Simmons 65-66 MSLS. 6: Fr. 7: Libn Pope John XXIII Nat Sem, Weston Mass 67-. 9: CathLA (v-chm NE Unit 69-70). 14: Sacred scis. 15: Pope John XXIII Nat Sem Lib, 558 South ave, Weston Ma 02193.

FAHLBERG, KENNETH. 4: Doris M Fahlberg. 5: Augustana Col 47 AB; Columbia 57 MSLS. 7: Brooklyn Pub Lib 54-59; Pomona Pub Lib, Pomona Cal 59-60; Brooklyn Pub Lib 60-. 15: 67 Ferris ave, Brentwood NY 11717.

FAHNESTOCK, FRANK RUDOLPH. b Chadron Neb 6 N 23. 4: Mitsuko Fahnestock. 5: Whittier Col 4648 (Hist); USoCal 4953 (Soc Studies) BA; UTex 5960 MLS. 7: (Sgt) US Army Air Force 4245; Thermoplastics mechanic N Amer Avn Corp, Downey Ca 4852; Asst fld dir Amer Red Cross 546; Film & period libn Lib of Hi, Honolulu 6062; Catlgr UHawaii Sinclair Lib, Honolulu 6265; Dir Cen Processing Ctr Hawaii State Lib, Honolulu 65. 9: HawaiiLA (dir). 14: Catlg. 15: Hawaii State Lib 478 S King st, Honolulu Hi 96814.

FAHNESTOCK, MITSUKO MRS. b Haiku Maui Hawaii 29 O 28. 5: UHawaii 46-50 (Eng) BA; USoCal 55-56 MS in LS. 6: Japanese. 7: Base libn 5th AF, Japan 56-59; Br libn Lib of Hawaii Kailua Br 60; Station libn NAS Barber's Point USN, Ewa Oahu 61-62; Patients' libn Leahi Hosp, Honolulu 62; Naval base libn USNaval Station Pearl Harbor Hawaii 63-68, Dist libn 14th ND 69-. 9: ALA; HawaiiLA. 10: Beta Phi Mu. 14: Ref. 15: 1716 Keeamoku st, apt 806, Honolulu Hi 96822.

FAHRENBACH, BETTY L (HICKMAN). b Cedar Rapids Iowa 6 N 28. 4: Lester J Fahrenbach. 5: LA City Col 58-59 (Home Econ); Cal State Col (LA) 59-62 (Home Econ) MA; Immaculate Heart Col 65-67 MLS. 6: Sp. 7: Reservation Agt United Airlines, LA 57-62; Tchr El Monte Union High Sch Dist, Rosemead Cal 62-63; Libn I City of Alhambra, Alhambra Cal 67-. 9: ALA; CalLA. 14: Ref. 15: 606 N Nicholson ave, Monterey Park Ca 91754.

FAHRNEY, ROENNA. b Frederick Md 13 Ap 11. 5: Hood 28-32 (Eng) AB; Simmons 50-51 MLS. 6: Fr, Sp, Ital. 7: Asst Enoch Pratt Free Lib, Baltimore 33-42; Asst libn Ft Detrick Tech Lib, Frederick Md 47-57; Dir Harford Co Lib, Bel Air Md 58-. 8: Trans for Off of Censorship during WW II. 9: ALA; MdLA. 10: Soroptimist Club. 14: Admin. 15: 100 Pennsylvania ave, Bel Air Md 21014.

FAIBISOFF, SYLVIA G. b NYC 7 D 21. 4: Leon Faibisoff. 5: Hunter Col BA; West Res 41-42 BLS; UGuadelajara 63 (Sp) Certif; West Res 66-67 (Pol Sci) MLS. 6: Fr, Sp. 7: Soc sci libn Brooklyn Pub Lib; Camp libn Minidoka Relocation Ctr (Japanese-Amer camp), Minidoka Ida; Hd bkmob sch serv Framingham Town Libs, Framingham Mass; Hd of dept CSR Cornell U Libs 56-67; Exec dir S Central Research Lib Coun, Ithaca NY 68-. 8: Instr SyracuseU 68-69. 9: ALA; ASIS; NYLA. 13: Yes. 14: Govt docs, bibliog, catlg. 15: 136 Cascadilla pk, Ithaca NY 14850.

FAIGMAN, EDITH I(LSE). b Leipzig Germany 24 F 22. 5: Hunter Col 39-43 (Eng) BA; Pratt 48-49 BLS 6: Ger. 7: Writer "Current Biography, H W Wilson Co 45-48; Ref libn NY Pub Lib 49-. 9: SLA. 10: Coun for Basic Educ; Metro Opera Guild.

13: Yes. 14: Ref, catlg. 15: 226 W Tremont ave, Bronx NYC 10453.

FAIN, BUNA TURNER. b Montgomery Ala 30 Jl 05. 4: Clarence Samuel Fain. 5: Ga State Col for Women 47 (Educ) BS; Emory 52 (Libnship) ML, 63 (Libnship). 7: Libn High Sch, McRae Ga 46-51; Libn Jeff Davis High Sch, Hazlehurst Ga 52-54; Dir Okefenokee Reg Lib, Waycross Ga 54-. 9: ALA; NEA; GaLA; SELA; GaEA (dist lib chm). 10: Delta Kappa Gamma; AAUW (pres Waycross Chap); Waycross Womans Club (pres); Waycross Federated Garden Clubs (past pres Coun); DAR; UDC; Pilot Club. 14: Tchg lib sci. 15: 1004 Richmond ave, Waycross Ga 31501.

FAIN, ELAINE (FOLK). b Chicago 8 S 29. 4: Haskell Fain. 5: UIll 46-49 (Journalism) BS; UCal 51-52 BLS. ; UWis 65-66 MS. 6: Norwegian, Ger. 7: Libn UCal Law Sch(Berkeley) 52-54; Libn UCal(Berkeley) 55-56; Health educator Wis State Health Dept, Madison 56-58; Ref libn CUNA Internat Inc, Madison Wis 62-65; Tchg asst UWis (Madison) 65-66; Instr 67-. 9: . 14: Ref, spec libs. 15: 2306 Van Hise ave, Madison Wis 53705.

FAIN, ROBIN. b Jessamine Co Ky 14 Ap 12. 5: UKy 29-41 (Elem Educ) AB, 48-52 (Secondary Educ) MA, 54-58; UDenver 63. 7: Jessamine Co Schs, Nicholasville Ky: Elem tchr 30-45, 48-; Wilmore High Sch, Wilmore Ky: Tchr 46-48, Tchr & libn 48-58. 8: Consultant in various wkshops in Ky; Vis instr in Lib Sci, UKy 6-, 62, 64, 65, 66. 9: NEA (life mem); ALA; -AASchL; KyLA; KyASchL (bd mem 60-61, pres 62-63, parliament 65-68; var coms); SELA; KyEA (var coms). 10: Delta Kappa Gamma. 11: Outstanding Sch Libn (Ky) 67. 14: Sch libn. 15: Rte #2, Nicholasville Ky 46356.

FAIR, ETHEL MARION. b Carlisle Penn 15 N 1884. 5: Vassar 02-06 (Lat) AB; Lib Sch NY Pub Lib 15-16 Certif; Chicago 34-35 (LS) MA. 6: Ger. 7: Instr in priv sch for girls, Norwalk Conn 06-08; Lib asst Harrisburg Pub Lib, Harrisburg Penn 13-15; Spec Investigator US Bur of Labor Statistics 18; Spec asst Penn State Lib 19-20; Catlgr Purdue U Lib 20-2; Instr UWis Lib Sch 22-27; Act libn Wilson Col 28; Act prin Carnegie Lib Sch, Atlanta 29-30; Dir Lib Sch NJ Col for Women 30-50; Professor Emeritus, ret 50; Lib Lecturer & Consul American U(Cairo Egypt) Fulbright Award 50-52; Consul & Act Libn in various positions, 52-63; Interim exec sec LED ALA Chicago 63-64. 8: Survey of Lib Commsn, MdLA 44; Survey of Lib Ext Serv, Mass Dept of Educ 44; Mem Adv Bd Grad Sch Lib Serv, Rutgers U. 9: ALA (chm &/or mem var coms); SLA (var coms); Penn LA; NJLA (pres 45-46, mem var coms). 10: LWV; Harrisburg Col Club. 11: Doctor of Humane Letters (hon), Douglass Col, Rutgers, 59; Hon mem Alumni Assn, Grad Sch of Lib Serv, Rutgers, 64. 12: Ed"Countrywide Library Service, ALA (34); Ed "Librarianship in the Service of Youth, Tr into Arabic by Mohaded Mohamed (Cairo 50). Pul Publ Arabic only. 13: Yes. 14: Admin, catlg. 15: 3025 N Second st, Harrisburg Penn 17110.

FAIR, JUDY (HUGHES). b Rapid City S Dak 6 O 40. 5: Stanford 58-62 (Eng) AB; UCal 9berkeley) 62-63 MLS. 7: Stanford U Libs: Libn tech info serv 63-65, Intl doc libn govt docs div 65-67, Act chief govt docs div 67, Chief govt docs div 67-. 9: ALA; SLA; ASIS; Coun of Planning Libns; CalLA-CURLS (sec No Div). 10: Sierra Club; Wilderness Soc; Other Conserv Orgs. 14: Govt docs, ref, admin. 15: Box 2285, Stanford Ca 94305.

FAIR, NORMA JEAN. b Hutchinson Kan 18 Ap 42. 5: Sterling Col 60-64 (Eng) BA; Kan state Tchrs Col 65-66 (LS) MS. 6: Fr, Ger. 7: Tchr & libn high sch, Gypsum Kan 64-65; Catlgr UMo (Columbia Mo) 66-. 9: ALA. 10: AAUW. 14: Catlg, clsf. 15: 1409 University ave, Columbia Mo 65201.

FAIRBANKS, ALINE MARGARET. b Fort Collins Colo 3 Mr 24. 5: UIll (Urbana) 42-48 (Applied Mus, Mus educ) BS, BM, 64-66 (LS) MS. 6: Fr. 7: Tchr Winchester Pub Schs, Ill 48-49; Ed repr Boosey & Hawks Inc NYC 50-52; Edl research asst Field Enterprises Ed Corp, Chicago 62-64; Asst ref libn UIll (Chicago Circle) 66-67, Act hd ref libn 67-68, Head ref libn 68-. 9: ALA; IllLA. 10: Chicago Lib Club (Soc Chm 68-69). 14: Ref. 15: The Lib UIll at Chicago Circle, Chicago Il 60680.

FAIRBANKS, HELEN E. b Bainbridge NY 22 Ap 15. 5: Oberlin 33-37 (Hist) BA; Simmons 37-38 BS in LS. 7: Ref asst NY Pub Lib 38-42; Ref asst Lib Soc Security Admin, Wash DC 42-47; Lib consul Ford Founs Proj with the Sch of Pub Admin, Caracas Venezuela 63-64; Libn pub admin collection Princeton U Lib 47-64; Libn ind rel sect 69-. 9: SLA; ALA. 10: LWV. 14: Ref. 15: 70 Valley rd, Princeton NJ 08540.

FAIRMAN, WIRT. b Bellevue Ida 27 Ag 16. 4: G Maggs. 5: Gooding Col 35-37; Willamett U 37-38; UIda 39-42 BSEd; Kent State 48-50 MA; UMich summer 61. 7: Asst libn Theil Col 50-53; Tech libn Pub Lib of Fr Wayne & Allen Co, Ft Wayne Ind 53-56; Libn Inds Inst of Tech 56-59; Libn Magnavox Co, Ft Wayne Ind59-63; Libn Internat Harvestor Motor Truck Div 63-. 9: ALA; SLA. 10: Ft Wayne Libus Club; Antique Auto Club; Auburn Cord Dusenberg Club. 14: Tech ref. 15: 2026 Bayer ave, Ft Wayne Ind.

FAIRSTONE, PHILIP JAY. b Philadelphia Penn 31 My 22. 5: UPenn 40-43 (Eng) BA; Columbia 63-64 MLS. 7: Cryptanalyst USAF, China, Burma, India 43-45; Field rep Assoc Hosp Serv, nyc 46-48; Gen mgr Wilmar Co Inc, NYC 48-59; Bk traveler Columbia U Press 59-60; Reg publ mgr Pergamon Press, NYC 60-63; Dir Ridgefield Pub Lib, Ridgefield NJ 64-66; Ref libn Yeshiva U Lib 66-. 13: Yes. 15: 420 Fairview ave, Fort Lee NJ 07024.

FAIRWEATHER, JANE. b Honolulu 1 Ja 14. 5: UHawaii 31-35 (Arts, Sci) BA; Columbia 35-36, 50 (LS) MA. 6: Ital. 7: Libn Lib of Hawaii 37-4; Manager Henry M Snyder & Co, Honolulu 42-43; Army Libn in Hawaii 43-45; Exec Army Libn Hdqrs FEC, Manila 45-46; Chief Army Libn Hdqrs FEC, Japan 46-48; Adv on Japanese lib Hdqrs SCAP, Japan 49; Dir of Libs USIS, Calcutta, Baghdad, Italy 50-; Deputy chief Afr Br USIA, Wash DC 66, Chief Lat Amer Br for libs & ctrs 67-. 9: ALA (Internat Round Table); Associazione Italiana Biblioteche; DCLA. 14: Catlg, ref, lib promotion. 15: USIA 1776 Pennsylvania ave, Wash DC.

FAIST, PEARL. b Reed City Mich 1 N 14. 5: Central Mich U 40-44 (Eng) BS; UDenver summer 47; Peabody summers 52-54 (LS) MA; West Mich U NDEA Inst summer 66. 7: Ref asst Central Mich U summers 48, 50; Libn Sr High Sch, Traverse City Mich 44-. 9: NEA (Life mem); MichEA (Life mem); MichASchL. 15: 311 W Ninth st, Traverse City Mich 49684.

FAJARDO, LIESELOTTE H (WERNER). b Berlin 8 Mr 26. 5: Pacific U 47-50 (Fr, Sp) AB cum laude, 50-51 (Lit, Educ) MA; Staford U 50-53 (Span); UCal(Berkeley) 59-60 MLS. 6: Ger, Fr, Sp, Ital, Portu, Dutch, Scandinavian langs, Rumanian, Lat. 7: Sr lib asst Hoover Inst, Stanford Cal 50-54; High sch tchr Sequoia Union High Sch Dist, San Carlos Cal 54-55; Home & sub tchr Sequoia & San Maeo Union High Sch Dist, San Mateo Cal 55-57; Lib asst San Mateo Co Lib, Menlo Park Cal 57-59; Research asst UCal Lib Sch(Berkeley) 59-60; Catlgr San Mateo Co Lib, Belmont Cal 60-61; Head tech processes Varian Associates Tech Lib, Palo Alto Cal 61-66; Lib consul Tolos Assocs, Palo Alto Cal 66; Ref libn & Translator Syntex Corp, Palo Alto Cal 67; Lib consul Dalmo-Victor Corp, Belmont Cal 67-68; Libn II bibliog sect UCal (Santa Barbara) 68-. 8: Numerous tech translations contrib to chem abstracts. 9: SLA; CalLA. 13: Yes. 14: Catlg, acquis, translg, abstractg, automation of lib functions. 15: 2624 San Carlos ave, San Carlos Cal 94070.

FALARDEAU, ERNEST RENE (REV) (SSS). b Holyoke Mass 14 N 28. 5: Eymard Sem 43-49; St Joseph Sem 51-53; Pontificial GregorianU (Rome) 53-59 Doctor S Theol; West Res 61-62 MSLS. 6: Fr, Ital, Sp, Lat, Ger, Gk. 7: Prof theol & libn St Joseph Sem (Cleveland Ohio) 60-67; Rector & libn Eymard Sem 67-. 8: Chm Renewal Comm Blessed Sacrament Fathers 66-; Sec Dutchess Co Clergy Assn 68-. 9: CathLA (chm No Ohio Unit Adult Libs Sect 66-67; Local Arrangements Com 1967 Nat Convention); ALA; Catholic Theol Soc Amer. 12: "Eucharistic Service in the Writings of St Peter Julian Eymard" doctoral diss (59). 13: Yes. 14: Admin. 15: Eymard Seminary, Mansion dr, Hyde Park NY 12538.

FALBO, EDNA A. b Opeakiski W Va 16 S 14. 5: W Va U 32-33 (Soc Studies), 35-38 (LS) BS, Lib certif, summer 38-42; Amer U 46. 6: Ital. 7: US govt GS-13 Navy Dept, labor Dept & Agency for Intl Development, Wash DC 43-. 8: US Civil Serv Connsn Admin Intern 46; Records Mgt Survey, Athens, Rome, and Beirut 65-66. 9: Assn of Records Execs & Adminrs (DC Chap: sec 67-70, mem 2 coms); SLA (DC Documentat Gp). 10: Mortar Board; Quota Internat; W Va Alum; W Va State Soc; Nat League Amer Pen Women. 14: Ref ctr admin. 15: 921 - 19th st NW, Wash DC 20006.

FALCK, IRMA MARGARET. b Chatsworth Ill 29 S 11. 5: USD 29-33 (Educ) BS in Ed; UIll summers 59-63 MS in LS. 7: USD Lib; Gen asst 44-46, Res Room libn 46-49, Asst circ libn 49-54, Circ libn & Interlib Loans 54-60, Documents libn & asst ref libn 60-68; Docs libn 68-. 9: ALA; SDakLA; SDak Acad Lib Sect; MPLA. 10: AAUW; Bus & Prof Women's Club; Woman's Soc of Christian Serv; Faculty Woman's Club. 14:

US docs, UN docs, ref. 15: 712-B E Main st, Vermillion SD 57069.

FALGIONE, DONNA K(OLL). b Winside Neb 25 Ja 37. 4: Joseph F Falgione. 5: Wayne State Col 55-58 (Hist, Educ) BA in Ed; Carnegie 60-61 MLS. 7: Soc serv tech Norfolk State Hosp, Norfolk Neb 56-57; Legal sec Stewart & Hatfield, Sioux City Iowa 58-60; Readers adv Carnegie Lib of Pittsburgh 61-63, Ref asst 63-. 10: Pi Gamma Mu; Forest Hills Jr Womens Club; Forest Hills Human Relations Com. 14: Ref, bk reviewing. 15: 307 Burlington rd, Pittsburgh 15221.

FALGIONE, JOSEPH F. b Pittsburgh 4 O 31. 4: Donna Koll. 5: Duquesne U 49-54 (Music Educ) BS; Carnegie 56-57 MLS. 7: (1st Lt) US Air Force Personnel Off 54-56; Roving asst Free Lib of Phila 57-59; Head Libn Athens C Pub Lib, Nelsonville Ohio 59-60; Ref asst Carnegie Lib of Pittsburgh 61-62; Dist field rep Carnegie Lib of Pittsburgh 63-65, Coordinator dist serv 65-. 8: Lib serv consul, Greater Canonsburg (Penn) Pub Lib, 65-66; Survey of Morgantown (WVa) Pub Lib 65-; Memb Tech Adv Com Allegheny Co (Pa) OEO 65-66; Site & Bldg Survey Johnstown Penn 67; Bldg & Serv Study, Clarksburg W Va 67-68; Lib Bldg Consul, Sharon Penn 68-69; Bldg consul, Waynesburg Penn 68-69. 9: PennLA; Pub Lib Sect; 9chm-elect 65-66, chm 66-67, Exhib chm 69 Conf). 11: Distinguished Alumnns Award 69, UPittsburgh Grad Sch of Lib & Info Scis. 13: Yes. 14: Pub lib admin, adult serv. 15: 307 Burlington rd, Pittsburgh 15221.

FALKNER, ETTA. b NYC 30 My 17. 5: Hunter Col 34-38 (Bio) BA; Columbia 40-42 (Adult Educ) MA. 7: Clk NY Pub Lib 36-39; Asst lantern slide div Amer Mus of Natural Hist, nyc 39-42, Instr 42-46, Asst supv spec exhibition 46-50, Asst curator dept of educ 50-52; Publ ed & supv of educ Munson-Williams-Proctor Inst, Utica NY 52-58; Dir Old gaol Mus, York Me; Libn research lib Old Sturbridge Village, Sturbridge Mass 62-. 8: Child museum consul; Morristown NJ 48-50, Charleston W Va 49, Charlotte NC 51. 9: Amer Assn of Museums (chm several sects); Amer Assn State & Local Hist (chm Lib Tech Wkshops, Conf NE Hist Socs 65); MassLA; Soc Preserv of NE Antiq. 10: Old Gaol museum, York Me; Strawbery Banke, Portsmouth NH; Southbridge (Mass) Hist Soc; Worcester 9mass) Art Museum. 14: Catlg, NE Americana, crafts & tech, early Amer juveniles, conserv of collections. 15: 339 South st, Southbridge Ma 01550.

FALKNOR LENORE ROSS. b Dayton Ohio 13 N 09. 4: Carl L Falknor. 5: Earlham Col 27-31 (Hist) BA. 6: Ger. 7: Sr asst catlg dept Dayton Pub Lib, Dayton Ohio 31-44, Sr asst acquis dept 44-46; Catlgr Air Force Inst f Tech Lib, WPAFB Ohio 46-49; Libn Air Force Museum, WPAFB Dayton Ohio 49-55; Head tech processes Air Force Inst of Tech Lib, WPAFB Dayton Ohio 55-61; Head catlg dept Wright-Patterson Air Force Base Tech Lib, Dayton Ohio 61-. 9: ALA; OhioLA. 14: Catlg. 15: 3087 Tralee trail, Dayton Oh 45430.

FALL, ANNA LOU (LUCILE) HOUGEN. b Fertile Minn 18 D 15. 4: Clair Ellwood Fall. 5: St Cloud State 37-40 (Eng) BS, 40 (LS) Credential; USoCal 66-67 (LS). 7: Tchr US Grant Sch, Royal Oak Mich 40-42; Child libn Hunt br Fullerton Pub Lib, Fullerton Cal 62-68, Libn 68-. 9: CalLA; OrangeCoLA; So Cal Coun on Lit for Child & YP. 10: AAUW; Kappa Delta Pi. 14: Ref, child lit, art. 15: 1062 Cerritos dr, Fullerton Ca 92632.

FALLON, SISTER ANN. b Bronx NY Mr 11. 5: Villanova U 51-56 (Educ) BS in Ed; Columbia 56-59 MS in LS; Fordham 60-61 (Theol), 62-64 (Communication Arts); NYU 65- (Communication Arts Prog); Boston U 67-69 Communications in Educ CAGS Program; Simmons 66 Advanced Libnship (NDEA grant). 6: Fr. 7: Tchr Mt St Mary, Newburgh NY 43-56; Tchr Nativity Sch, Bronx NY 56-60; Libn Pope Pius XII High Sch, Passaic NJ 60-69; Ref libn Mugar Mem Lib Boston U 69-. 9: ALA; CathLA; NYLA; PassaicCoSchLA (pres 68); MassLA; NJSchLA (Exec Com 68). 10: Paterson NJ Diocesan Lib Coun. 14: Ref, ya. 15: 16 Keswick st, Boston Ma 02215.

FALLS, ANONA JENKINS. b Clarksdale Miss. 5: Goucher Col 22-25 (Soc Sci); UIll summer 38 (LS); Carnegie 39-40 Certif in Lib Sci. 7: Carnegie Pub Lib, Clarksdale Miss: Asst child libn 36-39, Child libn 40-46, Asst libn 46-48, Libn 48-. 8: Mem & sec Bd of Commsnrs, Miss Lib Com 55-58. 9: ALA; MissLA (v-pres & pres 50-53, Exec Bd 50-59; chm Adult Educ Com 60-61, & other duties); SELA. 10: Bus & Prof Women's Club; DAR; Gamma Phi Beta; Clarksdale Country Club; Little Theatre; Clarksdale Commun Concerts. 13: Yes. 14: Bks about & by Mississippians. 15: 229 Maple st, Clarksdale Ms 38614.

FALLS, W MARGRETE (GOETZE). b NYC 28 Je 41. 4: John Allen Falls. 5: SUNY (Albany) 59-63 (Eng) AB, 63-64 (Eng) MA; Columbia 65-67 (LS) MS. 6: Ger, Sp. 7: Lib aide NY State Lib, Albany NY 64; Libn Curtis Publ Co, NYC 64-65; Libn NYU 65-67; Libn NYC Commun Col 67-. 9: ALA; SLA; NY Lib Club; CUNYLA; NY State Assn Jr Col; NY State LA. 10: Columbia Alumni Assn. 14: Admin, ser. 15: 328-78th st, Brooklyn NY 11209.

FALSONE, ANNE MARIE (McMAHON). b NYC 20 My 37. 4: Pete Falsone Jr. 5: Memphis State U 55-56, 57-59 (Secondary Educ) BS, 61- (Amer Hist). 7: Tchr St Michaels Sch, Memphis Tenn 55-56; Libn White Station Jr High Sch, Memphis Tenn 59-64; Libn White Station Sr High Sch, Memphis Tenn 64-. 8: Chm Lib Sect, Memphis (Tenn) City Schs, 63-64. 9: NEA; ALA-AASchL; TennEA; TennLA. 10: Alpha Delta Pi; Phi Alpha Theta. 14: Sch lib serv, yp. 15: 1055 Wingfield rd, Memphis Tenn 38122.

FALT, MARY H(ELEN). b Northeast Harbor Me 13 Je 06. 5: Acadia U 26 (Langs) BA; Simmons 27 BS in LS. 6: Fr, Lat, Sp. 7: Circ libn UNH 27-39, Ref libn 39-41; Libn Amer Optical Co, Southbridge Mass 41-46; Libn Barrington Pub Lib, Barrington RI 46-52; Libn Welles-Turner Mem Lib, Glastonbury Conn 52-. 9: ALA; ConnLA. 10: Hist Soc of Glastonbury (Conn); Soroptimist. 15: 2407 Main, Glastonbury Conn 06033.

FAMBROUGH, (SALLY) EVELYN (WALLACE). b Woodson Tex 23 Ag 14. 4: Truman E Fambrough. 5: Tex Womens U 32-37 (Govt & Econ) BA; Tex Tech summer 50 (Educ); N Tex State U 53-55 BS in LS; UWis summer 65 (NDEA Inst). 6: Sp. 7: Tchr Seminole Pub Sch, Seminole Tex 50-53; Jr high libn Pub Sch, Mineral Wells Tex 53-5; Libn Pub Sch, Seminole Tex 55-62; Dir Tom Green Co Lib, San Angelo Tex 62-63; Libn Alhambra Sch Dist, Phoenix 63-66; Lib supv Flagstaff Sch Dist, Flagstaff Ariz 66-. 9: ALA; NEA; TexLA (chm Dist 4); ArizLA. 10: AAUW; Altrusa Club; Tex Fed Clubs; Alpha Lambda Sigma. 14: Child bks. 15: 415 W Apache rd, Flagstaff Ar 86001.

FAN, MARGARET MEI-CHIH. b Taiwan Republic of China 25 Jl 42. 5: Nat TaiwanU 60-64 9for Lang & Lit) BA; Tex Woman'sU 66-68 MLS. 6: Chinese. 7: Catlgr Taipei Med Col Lib, Taipei Taiwan 64-66; Asst catlgr Lima Pub Lib, Lima Ohio 68-. 9: ALA; OhioLA. 14: Catlg. 15: 748 W High st, Lima Oh 45801.

FANCHER, MARY DAILLY. b Cleveland Ohio 26 O 13. 4: Thomas Edward Fancher. 5: Col of wooster 32-35 (Eng) BA; West Res U 62 MSLS. 6: Fr. 7: Lib clk, Cleveland Hts Pub Lib, Cleve Hts Ohio; Asst Libn 56-61; YA Libn; Libn Euclid Pub Lib, Euclid High Sch 62-64; Lib coord Mentor Bd of Educ, Mentor Ohio 65-. 10: Phi Beta Mu 15: 1896 Hillside rd, E Cleveland Oh 44112.

FANELLI, MICHELLE B (KLAYMAN). b Detroit Mich 20 Jl 43. 4: Richard Fanelli. 5: Wayne state 61-62; UMich 62-65 (Pol Sci) BS, 65-66 MLS. 7: Libn UMich Bus Sch (Ann Arbor) 65-66; Libn Foote Cone & Belding Advertising Agcy, NYC 66-67; Ref libn Morgan Guaranty Trust Co, NYC 67-. 14: Ref (bus & econ). 15: 6515 blvd E #7Q, W New York NJ 07093.

FANG, JOSEPHINE MARIA (RISS). b Saalfelden Austria 3 Ap 22. 4: Pao-Hsien Fang. 5: UVienna(Austria) 40-47 (Eng & Amer Lit) Absolutorium; UGraz(Austria) 47-48 (Eng & Amer Lit) PhD; Catholic U 50-54 MSLS; UGrenoble(France) 60-61 (French Lang & Lit) Certif. 6: Ger, Lat, Fr. 7: Assistantship in Lib Sci Catholic U Lib 51-53; Catlgr Farmington Plan Catholic U Lib 54-60; Assoc ed "The Guide to Catholic Lit," CatholicLA, Wash DC 61-63; Research ed "The New Catholic Encyclopedia," Catholic U 63-66; Assoc ed "Corpus Instrumentorum Inc," Wash DC 66-68; Chief acquis libn Boston Col. 8: Lecturer, Ref & ibliog, Catholic U summer 64; 67; Adjunct lectr Sch of Lib & Info Servs UMd 66, 67. 9: ALA; CathLA; DCLA; AALS; MassLA. 10: AAUW. 12: Jt ed "Guide to Catholic Literature, 1961 & 1962 (62, 63). 13: Yes 14: Bibliog, ref, catlg. 15: 156 Common st, Belmont Ma 02178.

FANNING, VIRGINIA (HANNAH). b Oriskany Va 3 My 16. 4: Stuart Davidson Fanning. 5: Concord Col 34-38 (Elem Educ) BS; Columbia 41-44 BSLA. 6: Fr. 7: Tchr, Montcalm WVa 38-41; Asst libn Concord Col 41-. 9: WVaLA. 10: Alpha Beta Alpha. 14: Catlg. 15: 209 College ave, Princeton W Va 24740.

FANSHER, VIRGINIA (CLAIRE). b Edmond Okla 21 Jl 25. 5: UOkla 43-47 BA in LS; Columbia 58-59 (LS) MS. 7: Asst libn Gasoline & Gas Dept Phillips Petroleum Co, Bartlesville Okla 47-50; Asst libn Dunklin Co Lib, Kennett Mo 50-51; Br libn Youngstown Pub Lib, Youngstown Ohio 51-57; Br libn

Cincinnati Pub Lib 59-. 9: ALA; OhioLA. 10: Phi Beta Kappa. 14: Adult serv. 15: 106 Farragut rd, Cincinnati 45218.

FANSLER, ELSIE ANNE. b Frankfurt/Main Germany 29 S 03. 5: UWis 40-46 (Span) BA, MA, 46-51 MSL. 6: Ger, Sp, Fr, Portu. 7: Catlgr UWis(Madison) 48-58; Catlgr State Hist Soc of Wis(Madison 58-62; Asst Prof & catlgr UMiami (Coral Gables Fla) 62-. 9: FlaLA. 10: Sigma Delta Pi; Beta tphi Mu. 14: Catlg, indexing, translatg. 15: 6140 SW 45th st, Miami Fl 33155.

FANT, HANDY BRUCE. b Abbeville SC 21 N 03. 4: Kathleen Camp. 5: UGa 20-24 (Eng) AB; Mercr U 24-27 (Eng) AM; Harvard 28-30 (Hist) AM, 37-40 (Hist). 6: Lat, Fr, Ger, Gk. 7: Instr Lanier High Sch for Boys, Macon Ga 24-28; Act asst prof of Amer hist UMe 29-30; Instr Afton Central Sch, Afton NY 33-37; Capt to Col Infantry US Army, US & Philippines 41-46; Staff Nat Archives, Wash DC 40-41, 46-55; Staff Nat Hist Publ Com, Wash DC 55-. 9: AHA; So Hist Assn; SAA; Ga Hist Soc; Vt Hist Soc 12: Co-comp "Preliminary Inventory of the Records of the United States House of Representatives, 1789-1946, 2 v (59); News notes ed "The American Archivist (56-59). 13: Yes. 14: Archives, mss. 15: 8110 Whites Ford way, Rockville Md 20854.

FANUS, PAULINE (RIFE). b New Oxford Penn 14 F . 4: William E Fanus. 5: Penn State U 45 (Home Econ) BS; Villanova 61 MS in LS. 6: Fr. 7: Period libn Tex Col of Arts & Ind 45; Nursery sch tchr Studio Sch, Wayne Penn 52-55; Circ libn & ref The Franklin Inst, Phila 64-66; Asst libn Ursinus Col 66-; Catlg libn & Instr East Baptist Col (Pa) 66-. 14: Ref, catlg. 15: Country Club rd Rt 2, Phoenixville Penn 19460.

FAORO, MADGE (MacFARLAND). b Buffalo NY 20 S 16. 4: Victor J Faoro. 5: Milwaukee State Tchrs Col 34-38 (Secondary Educ, Soc Sci) BS; UWis summer 38 (Speech); Marycrest Col summer 56 (LS); UIll summers 61-65 MLS. 6: Fr. 7: Proofreader Gen Publ, Chicago 40; Cler-ed Rock Island Arsenal, Rock Island 43-44; Proofreader Davenport Democrat, Davenport 41-42; Eng tchr Ind Sch Dist, Davenport 44-45; Free lance market researchr, Iowa-Ill 46-56; Adult Head, Bkmob & Ext dept Head, Ya hd, Coord of adult serv, Davenport Pub Lib, Davenport Iowa 56-. 9: ALA (Recruitment Network); IowaLA (past chm 2 sect), Recr Com, (Mem Exec Bd 68-71). 10: PTA; Congreg Church (Deaconess); Mu; UWis Alun Assn; UIll Alum Assn. 14: Adult serv. 15: 2328 W High, Davenport Iowa 52804.

FARBER, EVAN IRA. b NYC 30 Je 22. 5: UNC 39-44 (Pol Sci) AB; Princeton 45-47 (Pol Sci); UNC 50-51 (Pol Sci) MA, 51-53 (LS) BS. 6: Fr, Sp. 7: Instr in Pol Sci Princeton 47; Instr in Pol Sci UMass 48-49; Asst documents dept UNC Lib 51-53; Libn State Tchrs Col (Livingston Ala) 53-55; Chief ser & bind dept Emory U Lib 55-62; Libn Earlham Col 62-. 8: Consul; foreign Area Materials Ctr Bibliog 65-, Malone Col 66-, Asbury Col 66-67; Instr in Lib Sci East Ind Ctr, Ind U (part-time) 63-, Dir Sem on Non-West Studies for Col Libns, Columbia Univ School of Lib Serv, summers 66, 68-. 9: ALA (Bldgs & Equip Com, Non-West Resources Com); -ACRL (chm Col Sect 68-69); -LED; IndLA (Legisl Com). 12: "Classified List of Periodcals for the College Library (4th ed 57); Assoc Ed "Southeastern Librarian (60-62); Assoc Ed "Explorations in Entrepreneurial History (63-); Co-auth "Student Economists Handbook (67). 13: Yes. 14: Period, admin, col libs, non-West studies, ref. 15: 331 College ave, Richmond In 47374.

FARBER, GISELA HILDEGARDE. b Vienna 20 F 23. 5: Carleton Col 44-48 (Psych) BA (magna cum laude); Stanford 48-50 (Psych); UCal(Berkeley) 53-54 BLS. 6: Ger. 7: Child nurse Nat Child Home, Eng 39-43; Tchr Del Norte Co Cal High Sch 50-53; Libn & av coordinator Ventura Union Cal High Sch 54-. 9: ALA; NEA; CalASchL; Cal Tchrs Assn. 10: AAUW; Phi Beta Kappa. 14: Sch lib wk with child & yp. 15: 1817 E Thompson blvd #8, Ventura Ca 93003.

FARDIG, ELSIE. b Chicago 14 Ap 24. 4: Glen Fardig. 5: Wilson Jr (City) Col 42-44; Northwestern 44-48, 51 (Music) BMus; Fla State U 55-58 (LS) MS. 6: Sp, Fr. 7: Periods clerk San Antonio Pub Lib 50; Ser clerk UMiami (Coral Gables) 51-57; Mus libn 57; Asst Prof 62-; Asst Prof of mus bibliog 67-. 8: Music Dir So Shakespeare Repertory Theatre, Miami Fla 65; Judge (Composition Awards) All-Miami Youth Symphony, 64, 65. 9: MusLA. 11: Compositions performed at Amer Festival of Music, Miami; Brevard NC Music Center; etc. 12: "The Music Collection of the University Library, A Study of Its Organization (Masters Thesis, Fla State U 58, ACRL microcard ser (61). 14: Music (catlg, acquis), admin, ethnomusicology. 15: 6380 SW 69 st, S Miami Fl 33143.

FARHAT, FRED E. b Inglewood Cal 24 S 25. 4: Mary Margaret Bradley. 5: Pomona Col 46-49 (Eng) BA; Syracuse 50-52 (Eng & LS) MSLS. 6: Sp, Arabic, Ger. 7: Radio operator US Marine Corps 42-46; Libn II Detroit Pub Lib 52-56; Chief libn Rocketdyne Div of NAA, Canoga Park Cal 56-59; Supv Hughes Aircraft Co Lib, Culver City Cal 59-62; Chief Libn Atomics Internat Div of NAA, Canoga Park Cal 62-. 9: ASIS; SLA. 10: N Amer Rockwell Mgt Assn. 14: Lib admin. 15: 11242 Dempsey ave, Granada Hills Cal 91344.

FARKAS, ANDREW. b Budapest Hungary 7 Ap 36. 5: U of Law (Budapest) 54-56 (Law); Occidental Col 57-59 (Fr) BA; UCal(Berkeley) 61-62 MLS; UCal(Davis) 63-65 (Ital). 6: Hungarian, Ital, Fr, Ger. 7: Stock control spec (E-4) US Army, US & Germany 59-61; Gift & exch libn UCal Lib (Davis) 62-65, Gift & exch libn & asst head acquis dept 65-66; Chief bibliog & asst Hd of Acquis Dept 66-67; Asst mgr Pub Rel Walter J Johnson Inc 9: ALA. 10: Alpha Mu Gamma. 13: Yes. 14: Acquis, admin, rare bks, a-v, record collections. 15: Box 212, New York NY 10011.

FARLEY, (ALFRED) EARL (JR). b Great Falls Mont 10 Je 29. 4: Hilde E Shuptrine. 5: UCal(Los Angeles) 47-52 (Pre-Libnship) AB; USoCal 52-53 MS in LS; UOkla summer 62 NSF Computer Sci Conf. 6: Ger, Fr, Sp, Russian. 7: Stud asst UCal(Los Angeles) 48-52; Catlgr spec collecions UKan Lib 53-55, Head catlgr prep dept 55-59, Dept Head Prep Dept 59-63, Lib systems spec 63-65, Asst dir for Research 65-67; Dir Clendening Med Lib UKan Med Ctr 67-. 8: Farmington Plan Survey, Lawrence Kan 58-59; Consul UCLA Libs on Photographic brieflisting 62; Proj Dir "Kansas Slavic Index 62-63; Proj Dir "Kansas Union List of Serials 63-65. 9: ALA-ISAD (Bd of Dirs); SLA; MedLA; ASIS; KanLA. 10: Com); UKan Computation Center Operations Com; AAUP; Phi Beta Kappa; Beta Phi Mu. 12: "He Who Destroyes a Good Booke . . ., catlg of banned books, with Joseph Rubinstein (55); "Kansas Slavic Index; Current Titles: Social Sciences, Humanities, computer index (63); "Kansas Union List of Serials (65). 13: Yes. 14: Systems analysis & automation of library procedures, technical services; info retrieval. 15: 10325 Russell, Overland Park Ks 66212.

FARLEY, JAMES VINCENT JR. b San Francisco 19 S 26. 4: Margaret Bertolli. 5: N Tex Agric Col 44-45; Tex Christian U 45; UTex 45-46 (Naval Sci) BS; USan Francisco 49- (Educ, LS) Libnship Cred & Gen Secondary Cred. 7: Cost inspector Navy Dept, San Francisco 43; Ensign USN 44-49; Asst to Dir Evening Div USan Francisco 51-56; Tchr San Francisco United Sch Dist 52-63; Libn Benjamin Franklin Jr High Sch, San Francisco 63-. 9: ALA; Cal Assn Sch Libns; CalLA. 10: Nat Coun for Geog Educ; US Naval Inst; var groups wkg for soc justice. 14: Sch libnship. 15: 21 Santa Margarita dr, San Rafael Cal 94901.

FARLEY, JOHN. b NYC 19 Mr 20. 4: Rita Johnston. 5: Catholic U 37-40 (Eng) BA (magna cum laude); Columbia 49-50 (Eng) MA, 51-53 (LS) MS; NYU 58-64 (Educ) PhD. 6: Fr. 7: Tchr various NYC schs 40-43, 46-50; US Army Air Force (Cpl) ed, writer, pub rel AAF Hq, Wash DC 43-46; Eng-soc studies tch Bedford Park High Sch, NY 50-52; Libn Cranford High Sch, Cranford NJ 52-53; Libn W Hempstead High Sch, W Hempstead NY 53-58; Curriculum coordinator Sewanhaka Central High Sch Dist, Floral Park NY 58-60; Asst Prof Lib Educ Queens Col 60-61, Chm Lib Sci Dept 61-67; Prof Lib Sci & Dean Sch of Lib Sci SUNY (Albany) 67-. 9: ALA; NYLA; NY Lib Club. 13: Yes. 14: Lib educ, sch libnship, ref, mass printing. 15: 12 Granada dr, Elnora NY 12065.

FARLEY, MARGARET (ELOISE KINKLER). b Bee Co 5 Ag 16. 5: Tex Woman's U 35-37, 38, 40-41 BA, BSLS; UTex summer 39; NTex State U summer 41. 6: Sp. 7: Tchr: Bee Co 37-38, Berclair Tex 38-40; Tchr & libn, Sanderson Tex 41-44, 54-62, Libn 62-; Libn, Beeville Tex 44-46. 8: Sect dir Reading Conf at Sul Ross, Alpine (TAIR), summer 54; Nat Lib Week Chm fpr Terrell Co 66; Governor's Conf on Libs 66; Directed organ of a pub lib for Terrell Co 67. 9: ALA; NEA; TexStateTA (Del from Trans-Pecos Dist 62); TexLA (sec YA RT 67-68); Terrell Co TA (pres 59-60); Trans-Pecos (del 60, v-chm Lib Sect 67-68, chm Lib Sect 68-69). 10: Delta Kappa Gamma; Friends of Lib, Terrell Co Pub Lib; Amer Legion Auxil; Sanderson Culture Club. 11: Tchr of the Year, Terrell Co 68. 14: Ref, wk with child & ya. 15: Box 278, Sanderson Tx 79848.

FARLEY, RICHARD ALAN. b Ashland Co Wis 17 Ja 18. 4: Mary Anne Erickson. 5: Northland Col 36-40 (Lang) BA; UWis 40-41 BLS UIll 51-52 (LS) MS, 67 (LS) PhD. 6: Fr. 7: Asst libn Beloit Col 41-42; S/Sgt Army AF, US & S Pacific

42-46; Asst circ libn & asst dor UNeb Lib (Lincoln) 46-49; Dir Drake U Lib 49-51; Assoc dir UNeb Lib (Lincoln) 54-63; Dir Kan State Tchrs Col Lib 63-66; Dir Kan State U Lib 66-. 8: Coop faculty mem, Dept of Libnship, Kansas State Tchrs Col 64-. 9: ALA; KanLA; NebLA; MPLA. 10: AAUP; Trustee william Allen White Foun (Lawrence Kan); Mem State Lib Adv Commsn (Topeka Kan); Lions Internat. 11: Beta Phi Mu. 14: Univ lib admin, personnel. 15: 227 Summit, Manhattan Ks 66502.

FARMER, FRANCES. b Keysville Va 5 D 09. 5: Westhampton Col (URichmond) 27-31 (Hist) BA; URichmond Law Sch 31-33 LLB. 6: Fr. 7: URichmond: Sec to dean law sch 31-38, law libn 38-42; Law libn UVa 42-. 8: Law lib consul: Sup Ct of Va 48, Wash & Lee Law Sch 55, La State U Law Sch 65, UGa Law Sch 66, UAla Law Sch 67, UBaltimore 67-68. 9: AALL (pres 59-60); Va State Bar (co-ed "Va State Bar News"). 10: Westhampton Col Alum; AAUW. 11: Charles T Norman medal for "Best all around Law Grad". 12: Co-auth -manual of Legal Bibliography" (46); "The Wilson Reader" (Eng & Fr ed). 13: Yes. 15: 2031 Hessian rd, Charlottesville Va 22903.

FARMER, LINDA ANNE (CASSIDY). b Toronto Ont 23 J& 41. 4: Fraser Farmer. 5: McGill 58-62 (Eng, Fr) BA; UToronto 63-64 NLS. 6: Fr. 7: Lib asst McGill Law Lib 62-63; Libn (Gen) E Tobicoke Pub Lib, Toronto 64-66; Libn (Catlg) MacDonald Col 66-67; Libn 9ref) UManitoba 67-. 9: ManLA (cor sec). 14: Ref, info sci. 15: 23 Dickens dr, Winnipeg 22 Man Can.

FARMER, MARGARET KATHLEEN. b Montreal Can 20 Mr 15. 5: Sir George WilliamsU 47-53 BA; QueensU summer 51; McGill 52-54 BLS; Columbia summer 58 MLA Certif Gr 1; McGill 68 MLS. 6: Fr. 7: Reg nurse Toronto Gen Hosp, Toronto 36-41; Clerk IBM Dept Royal Can AF, Toronto 41-42; Reg nurse Royal Victoria Hosp, Montreal 43-47; Med lib McGillU: Asst catlgr 47-51; Head catlgr 52-63; Asst libn 64-68, Act med libn 68-. 9: MedLA; CanLA; QueLA. 14: Acquis. 15: Med Lib McGill Univ 3655 Drummond st, Montreal 2 Can.

FARMER, ORTON KEITH. b Sac City Iowa 14 N 08. 4: Mary Jeannette Rainey Farmer. 5: Long Beach Jr Col 28-29, 29-30 (Bus Admin) AA; Buena Vista Col 60-62 (Bus Educ) BS; UDenver summers 61-64 (LS) MA. 7: Owner & manager Park Hotel, Sac City Iowa 3557; Coun Iowa State Employment Serv, Des Moines Iowa 57-58; Manager Corn Belt Finance Corp, Sac City Iowa 58-60; Libn Sac Commun Schs, Sac City Iowa 62-. 9: ALA; NEA; IowaASchL; Iowa State EA. 14: Ref. 15: 1002 Schaller st, Sac City Iowa 50583.

FARMER, VARELIA H(OLLETT). b Belmont Co Ohio 24 O 03. 4: Cletus A Farmer. 5: Ohio U 20-24 (Fr) AB; West Res 28-29 BSLS. 6: Fr. 7: Fr tch High Sch, Bellaire Ohio 24-27; Math tchr Joseph Welty Jr High Sch, New Philadelphia Ohio 27-28; Catlgr Cleveland Pub Lib 29-33, Asst sociol div 33-39, Asst head of main lib 39-54, Supv processing dept 54-59, Asst to Dir 59-65, Asst to Dir in Chg of main lib 65-. 9: ALA; Womens Nat Bk Assn; OhioLA. 10: Friends of the Cleveland Pub Lib; AAUW (Life mem, var offs 43-66; Cleveland Alumnae Club of Mortar Board; LWV; Tilla B Porter Parliamentary Law Club of Cleveland; Cleveland Womens Club of Ohio U Alumni Assn; Kappa Delta Pi; Mortar Board. 14: Admin, ref, catlg, pub lib serv. 15: 15617 Munn rd, Cleveland 44111.

FARMER, VIRGINIA GODDARD. b Alliance Ohio 6 Ag 19. 5: Mt Union Col 41 AB; Carnegie 42 (LS) BS. 7: Asst child dept Pub Lib, Lima Ohio 42-44; Child libn Pub Lib, Cleveland Heights Ohio 44-50; Head main child room Pub Lib, Akron Ohio 50-57; Instr storytelling Kent State U 55-57; Coordinator child serv Pub Lib, Akron Ohio 57-. 8: Chm Com to Prepare Citizenship Bibliog for "Nat Educ Journal 53. 9: ALA-CSD (Adv Com 64-65, Newbery-Caldecott AWARD Com 59-60); OhioLA (Exec Bd 49-50 & 56-57; chm Child Sect 56-57). 10: United Commun Coun; Akron (Ohio) Counc of Parents & Tchrs; Womens Auxiliary Bd, Summit Co (Ohio) Child Home; Friends of Child Hosp; Child Concert Soc; Assoc for Childhood Educ Internat Summit Co (Ohio) Pre-School Assn; Kappa delta. 14: Child wk. 15: Akron Pub Lib 55 S Main st, Akron Oh 44308.

FARNELL, MARGARET (ISABEL HAMILTON O'CONNOR). b Edmonton Alta Can 12 S 15. 4: Gerald Gordon Farnell. 5: UAlberta 32-36 (Mod Langs) BA; Simmons 36-37 (LS) BS. 6: Fr, Sp, Ger. 7: Catlgr UAlberta 37-40, Ref libn 40-42, 58-63, Undergrad libn 63-; Sec British Security Co-ordination, NY, Haiti, Montevideo 42 Buenos Aires 45. 9: ALA; CanLA; AltaLA; EdmonLA; Assn Prof Libns UAlta. 14: Ref. 15: 36 St George's Crescent, Edmonton 40 Alta Can.

FARQUHARSON, MARION W(ILBUR). b Boston 14 F 09. 5: UWash 30-34 (Fine Arts) BA, 34-35 BA in LS. 7: Child Libn Seattle Pub Lib 35-43; Head of child room variou brs of the NY Pub Lib 43-61; Head of child dept New Rochelle Pub Lib, New Rochelle NY 62-. 8: Book Review Adv Bd "School Library Journal 63-67; Child bk ed for "Christian Herald Magazine 53-. 9: NYLA; WestchesterLA. 13: Yes. 14: Child wk. 15: 70 Locust ave, New Rochelle NY 10801.

FARR, ARIE P(ORTER). b McCall Creek Miss 4 N 07. 4: Eugene I Farr. 5: Miss Womans Col 24-28 (Eng) BA; UIl summers 30, 31 (LS). 7: High sch tchr-libn, McCall Creek Miss 28-29; High sch tchr-libn, Roxie Miss 29-33; Libn Clarke Mem Col 46-51; Catlg libn Miss Col 52-. 9: MissLA. 14: Catlg. 15: POBox 74, Clinton Miss 39056.

FARR, LOUISE REVERE (MASHBURN). b Kinston NC 31 D 08. 4: George Farr. 5: Davenport col 28-30 Diploma; Atlantic Christian Col 31-32 (Eng) AB; George Washington U 32-33 ABLS; Peabody Col 63, 68-69 MLS. 6: Fr, Sp, Hindustani. 7: Catlgr Sondley Ref Lib, Asheville NC 34-35; Libn Buncombe Co Med L, Asheville NC 35-40, 53-56; Asst libn VA Patient's Lib, Oteen NC 48-53; Libn City Is Lib, Daytona Beach Fla 63; Libn Isobella Thoburn Col, Lucknow India 64-67; Catlgr E Carolina U 67-68. 8: Buncombe Co Lib Club. 9: ALA. 10: AAUW; Commun chm UNICEF, Asheville 58-62; Carolina Bird Club; Audubon soc; Girl Scout Leader. 14: Ref, rare bks. 15: c/o Mrs C B Mashburn, Farmville NC 27828.

FARRAR, GRETCHEN (WATKINS). b Estate Las Pajas Dominican R. 4: William W Farrar. 5: Douglass Col 4347 (Eng Lit) AB; Rutgers 6065 MLS. 6: Sp, Fr. 7: Exec sec to partner J H Whitney & Co, NYC 4954; Admin asst to James C Cleveland Esq, Concord NH 5456; Admin asst to vpres Internat Div Shulton Inc, Clifton NJ 5660; Tech correspondent & libn Daystrom Inc Central Research Lab, W Caldwell NJ 6062; Tech libn St Regis Paper Co Tech Center, W Nyack NJ 6268; Lib consul Tech Assn of Pulp & Paper Ind 68. 9: SLA (SciTech Div; chief teller 67; Paper & Textile Sect; Nomin Com 6567, chm Info Liaison Com 6465; NY Chap; Prog Com, Hospitality Com, chm Nat Lib Week); ASIS; Tech Assn Pulp & Paper Indus (sec Com on Info Retr); SEast (NY) Lib Resources Coun. 10: Beta Phi Mu; Sigma Delta Pi; Montclair Sky Club; Montclair Operetta Club; Richmond Co Yacht Club. 14: Info liaison, library org & admin, ref, coord indexing, av serv. 15: 7 Prospect st, Caldwell NJ 07006.

FARRELL, LOIS CARNEY (Mc CASKEY). b Indianapolis Ind 11 My 19. 5: De Pauw 36-40 (Botany) BA; UCal (Berkeley) 40-42 (Botany) MA; UMich 62-63 MALS. 7: Hd lab asst botany dept De Pauw U 39-40; Audiometrist, Montgomery Co Health Dept, Md 57-62; Sci bibliog Harpur Col Lib, SUNY (Binghamton) 63-65; Tech info specialist Lawrence Radiation Lab, Livermore Cal 65-67; Research libn Stone Marracini & Patterson, San Francisco 67; Program dir vision info ctr Countway Lib of Med, Boston 67-. 9: SLA. 14: Info retrieval. 15: Vision Info Ctr, 10 Shattuck st, Boston Ma 02115.

FARRELL, MARGARET A (HOWARD). b Nampa Ida 25 Je 23. 4: Glenn E Farrell. 5: NW Nazarene 40-45 (Hist) AB; UWash 46-47 5th year Sec Certif, 65-66 M of Libnship. 7: Tchr Quillayute Valley High Sch, Forks Wash 45-47; Recreation dir Ruth Sch for Girls, Burien Wash 47; Libn Fife Jr-Sr High Sch, Fife Wash 66-67; Ref libn Pierce Co Lib, Tacoma Wash 67-. 9: ALA; WashLA. 10: Des Moines Lib League; PTA. 14: Ref adult serv. 15: 21220 - 4th Pl S, Seattle Wa 98148.

FARRELL, MARGARET MARY. b Phila 17 S 22. 5: Rosemont Col 40-44 (Eng) AB; Drexel 44-45 BS in LS; St Josephs Col even 47-48 (Hist, Educ). 6: Fr, Lat. 7: Libn Thomas More Found, Phila 45-46; Libn Fitzsimons Jr High Sch, Phila 46-48; Asst catlgr Bryn Mawr Col Lib 48-52; Lib asst Lavoisier Lib Expt Station EI DuPont de Nenours & Co, Wilmington Del 52-63, Catlg libn 63-. 9: ALA; SLA; (Coun Phila Area Unit); CathLA. 14: Catlg, clsf, ref. 15: 179 Upland terrace, Bala-Cynwyd Penn 19004.

FARRELL, PATRICIA (CRELL). b Seattle Wash 1 S 20. 5: UWash 38-42 (Anthrop) BA; UCal (Berkeley) 65-66 MLS. 7: Hd bk catlgr tech lib Sandia Corp, Albuquerque 66-68; Supv reports sec lib serv dept Stanford Research Inst, Menlo Park Cal 68-70; Supt libn Bio-Agric Lib UCal Riverside 70-. 9: SLA; CalLA. 10: AAUW; UCal Alumn Lib Assn. 14: Ref, report lit. 15: Bio-Agricultural Lib, UCal, Riverside Ca 92507.

FARRELL, RUTH J(ANET). b Utica NY 28 My 30. 5: State UCol of Educ (Geneseo NY) 48-52 BSLS. 7: Lib asst Jervis Lib, Rome NY 52; Asst libn USNaval Train Center, Bainbridge Md 52-53; Asst libn & libn US Army Hosp, Ft Carson Colo 53-55; Asst libn Base Lib, Mitchel AFB NY 55; Base libn Base Lib, Manhattan Beach AFSta NY 55-56; Base libn & catlgr USAF, Wiesbaden, Germany 56-58; Asst libn Utica Pub Lib, Utica NY 59-60; Base libn (USAF) Kingley Field, Klamath Falls Ore 60-63; Chief catlg, Lib System, Ft Ord Calif 63-67; Bkmble libn Mid-York Lib Syst, Utica NY 67-68; Catlg FAA/NAFEC, Atlantic City NJ 68-. 9: ALA. 10: Nat Travel Club; Amer Mus Natural Hist; Nat Wildlife Fed. 14: Catlg, pub libs. 15: H-6 Champagne Apts, Somers Point NJ 08244.

FARRELL, SALLIE (JOHNSON). b Brookhaven Miss 29 D 09. 5: Miss State Col for Women 27-31 (Eng) BA; UIll 31-32 BS in LS. 7: Tchr-libn Picayune High Sch, Picayune Miss 32-33; Asst Queens Borough Pub Lib, Jamaica NY 34-36; Asst Tulane U Lib 36; Ref libn La Lib Commsn, Baton Rouge La 36-38; Parish Libn Shreve Mme Lib, Shreveport La 39; Libn Tri-Parish Lib Demonstration, Winnfield La 40; Libn Winn Parish Lib, Winnfield La 40-41; Libn Rapides Parish Lib, Alexandria La 42-43; Libn Calcasieu Parish Lib, Lake harles La 44-46; Field rep La State Lib 46-54, Dir field serv 54-62, State Libn 62-. 8: US-USSR Libn Exg Mission 61. 9: ALA (v-pres 54-55, Coun 63-67); LaLA (pres 43-44); SWLA. 10: Pub Affairs Res Coun (Bd); Nat Fed Bus & Prof Womens Clubs; Delta Kappa Gamma; Alpha Delta Kappa. 13: Yes. 14: Adult educ, pub rel. 15: 1922 Ramsey dr, Baton Rouge La 70808.

FARRIER, MARGARET A (HOLCOMB). b Ft Worth Tex 11 Ag 20. 4: Robert Farrier. 5: Tex Christian U 38-39 (Liberal Arts); Arlington State Col 39-40 (Liberal Arts); N Tex State U 40-42 BA in LS. 7: Libn Alamo Elem Sch, Wichita Falls Tex 42; Libn tech US Quartermaster Depot, Ft Worth Tex 42-43; Army libn Midland Army Air Field, Midland Tex 43-44; Army libn-Rating PO 1120-1 FW Army Air F, Ft Worth Tex 44-45; Libn Libn Lneri High Sch, Ft orth Tex 56-57; Libn Convair Engnr, Ft Worth Tex 57-58; Libn Hayden Pub Lib, Hayden Ariz 63-, Hd libn. 9: ArizLA. 10: Confraternity of Christian Doctrine. 15: POBox 466 562 Ray ave, Hayden Ariz 85235.

FARRINGTON, MARJORIE POST. b Middletown Ohio 31 MY 14. 4: Alan M Farrington (Lt Col USA Ret). 5: Miami U 31-35 (Eng) BA; Carnegie 36 BSLS; UMinn 37 (Hosp Libnship) Certif. 6: Ger, Fr. 7: Stud asst Miami U Lib (Oxford Ohio) 35; Br asst Pleasant Ridge Br Cincinnati Pub Lib 36-37; Libn SUI Hosp Libs, Iowa City Iowa 38-41; Asst libn Herman Keifer Hosp Wayne Co Lib, Detroit 41-43; Libn Spec Serv Camp Ellis Ill 43-45; Adult Supv Br Dept King Co Lib, Seattle 58-59; Chief circ El Paso Pub Lib, El Paso Tex 60-62; Pub rel libn King Co Lib System, Seattle 62-66; Coord Adult Books 66-. 9: ALA; WashLA (Conv chm 64, 65); WashStateASchL (chm Conv arrangements 69). 10: OES; DAR; Soroptimist; 15: King Co Lib System, 1100 E Union, Seattle Wa 98122.

FARRINGTON, WILLIAM H. b Fort Worth Tex. 5: Texas A & M 43-44; UTex 44-46 (Journalism) BJ, 48-49, 52-53 MLS. 7: Catlgr Okla A & M Lib 49-52; Hd ser acquis UTex (Austin) 52-53; Libn NMMI, Roswell NM 53-54; Catlgr NM State U 54-57; Hd catlgr NM State L, Santa Fe 57-58; Hd tech servs Santa Ana Pub Lib, Santa Ana Cal 58-59; Hd ref San Diego co Lib 60-63; Asst catlgr hd ser new campuses program UCal (San Diego) 63-65; Catlgr Albuquerque Pub Lib 65-66; Hd SW & rare bk room NM State Lib, Santa Fe 66-69; Coord of LSCA titles 69-. 9: ALA; SLA (v-pres Rio Grande Chap 68-69, pres 69-70); West Hist assn; Oral Hist Assn; NMexLA (Publ Chm, Publ Chm for Nat Lib Week in N Mex 69); SWLA (Awards Com 69-). 10. Hist Soc of Santa Fe; Santa Fe Commun Theatre. 14: Admin, SE hist, reg devel, fed prog. 15: PO Box 1063, Santa Fe NM 87501.

FARRIOR, GRACE (BETTS) (MRS). b Raleigh NC 7 O 17. 5: Meredith Col 34-38 (Eng) AB; UNC 55-57 MS in LS. 6: Fr. 7: Asst libn UNC (Greensboro) 57; Docs asst UNC (Chapel Hill) 56-57. 8: Survey of the Thomas F Holgate Lib, Bennett Col, Greensboro NC 62. 9: ALA; SELA; NCLA. 10: UNC Sch Lib Sci Alum Assn. 11: Beta Phi Mu. 12: Ed bulletin of the Alumni Association, UNC Sch of Lib Sci 61-63. 14: Admin, tech processing. 15: 304 Waverly way, Greensboro NC 27403.

FARRIS, DONN MICHAEL. b Welch WVa 4 N 21. 4: Joyce Lockhart. 5: Berea Col 39-43 (Philos) AB; Garrett Theol Sem 43-47 BD; Northwestern 44-47 (Philos); Yale 47-48 (Theol); Columbia 49-50 MS in L.07: Stud asst Northwestern U 43-44; Pressman Mumm Print Shop, Evanston Ill 44-47; Gen asst Yale Divinity Sch Lib 48-49; Asst catlgr Gen Theol Se(NYC) 49-50; Duke Divinity Sch: Libn 50-, Asst Prof of theol bibliog 59-64, Assoc Prof of theol bibliog 64-. 9: ATheolLA (Exec Com 53-56, pres 62-63, Adv Bd on Lib Devel Program 61-); Amer Soc of Church Hist; NCLA (chm Com on Intel Freedom 63-65), SELA. 12: Ed "Aids to a Theological School Library (58); Ed ATheolLA "Newsletter (53-); Bk rev ed "he Duke Divinity School Review (59-). 13: Yes. 14: Admin, acquis, ref. 15: 921 Buchanan blv, Durham NC 27701.

FARRIS, JAY DEE. b Green Co Mo 26 N 46. 5: Jefferson Col (Hillsboro Mo) 64-66 AA; SW Mo State Col 66-68 (Soc Sci) BS in Ed; Peabody 68-69 MLS. 6: Fr. 7: Asst to libn Jefferson Col Hillsboro Mo 64-66; Lib intern Mo State Lib, Springfield 66; Asst to libn Science Lib JointU Lib, Nashville 69-. 9: ALA; ASIS. 14: Ref, catlg, readers adv, admin. 15: 1322 South 5th st, DeSoto Mo 63020.

FARRIS, ROBERT C. b Swoyersville Penn 8 N 22. 4: Lillian Aleknavich. 5: UNC 39-43, 47 (Music) BA; Columbia 55-56 MLS. 7: Pilot US Army Air Corps 43-45; Catlgr, br asst, Hd bk receiving dept Detroit Pub Lib 56-62; Chief of Processing Grosse Pointe Pub Lib 62-64; Head card prep unit Purdue U Libs 64-. 9: ALA; -RLMS (Exec Bd); -RTSD (Exec Bd); IndLA. 14: Catlg. 15: 900 Kent ave, West Lafayette In.

FARROW, MILDRED H(AYWARD). b West Palm Beach Fla 8 Ap 19. 5: Asheville Normal & Tchrs Col 35-39 (Elem Educ) BS in Ed; Peabody 41-42 BS in LS; UNC 55-56 MS in LS; Chicago 60-62, 65-. 7: Tchr St Marys in-the-Field, Valhalla NY 40-41; Sch libn Murphy City Schs, Murphy NC 42-45; High Sch libn Tarboro City Schs, Tarboro NC 45-49; Asst libn Guilford Col 49-60; Asst libn Field Enterprises Educ Corp, Chicago 60-62; Ref libn Ind Rel Center UChicago 62-. 9: ALA; SLA; IllLA; NCLA; SELA. 10: Chicago Lib Club; ACLU; Fellowship of Reconciliation; Episcopal Pacifist Fellowship; Episcopal Soc for Cultural & Racial Unity. 14: Catlg, acquis, educ for libnship. 15: 1400 E 55th pl, Apt 909, Chicago 60637.

FARROW, RUTH (MARGARET) (DES BRISAY). b Rochester Minn 25 F 22. 4: Francis Alfred Farrow. 5: UBC 39-43 (Bacteriol) BA; McGill 67-69 MLS. 6: Fr. 7: Pub Health Labs, Vancouver BC 43-45; Vancouver Gen Hosp (TB Clinic), Vancouver BC 46-47; Lakeshore Gen Hosp, Pointe Claire Pa 65-66. 14: Med ref. 15: 207 Darwin Rive, Montreal 201 PQ Can.

FARTHING, ANTHONY WALTER. b Aldershot England 26 F 43. 4: Diana Hilary Watts. 5: 67 British ALA. 7: Asst pub lib, Aldershot England 58-61, Ref asst 61-63, Lending libn 63-68; Reg consul NWest Reg Lib, Ft William Ont 68-. 14: Pub lib serv to small communs. 15: c/o 910 Victoria ave, Ft William Ont Can.

FASANA, PAUL JAMES. b Bingham Canyon Utah 20 Jl 33. 5: UCal (Berkeley) 51, 5859 Lang & Lit, BA; UCal (Berkeley) 6061 (LS) MLS. 6: Ital, Fr. 7: Sci catlgr NY Pub Lib, NYC 6061; Systems engineer Itek Corp, Lexington Mass 6163; cChief, catlg USAFCRL Lib, Bedford Mass 6364; Asst coordinator of Catlg Col Univ Libs, NYC 6466; Asst to Dir, Col Univ Libs, NYC 66; Sec to Planning Council Collaborative Lib System Development, CU, 68. 8: Ctr for Urban Educ 6566; Metro Applied Research Ctr 68; Charge de cour, Ecole de bibliotheconomie, UMontreal 68; Lectr, Grad Sch of Lib Sci, McGillU. 12: Institute on Automation in Large Libraries-- (68); Generalized Programming Languages and Systems-- (68); Electronic Data Processing Concepts-- (68); Elements of Information Systems-- (68). 13: Yes. 14: Automation, systems analysis. 15: Columbia University Libraries, New York NY 10027.

FASS, EVELYN (MENTER). b Syracuse NY 30 Jl 22. 4: Irwin Fass. 5: Syracuse 39-43 (Eng) BA, 43-44 BS in LS. 7: (Lt) US Naval Reserve(W) Communications Officer 44-46; Interlib loan libn Army Lib, Wah Wash 46-48, Catlgr 48, Ref asst 43-53; 48-53 asst Levittown Pub Lib, Levittown NY 60-61; Ref asst Silver Spring Pub Lib, Silver Spring Md 62-63; Libn Hist Evaluation & Research Org, Wash DC 63-65; Ref libn Inst for Defense Analyses, Arlington Va 65-67; Act chief open lib 67-68; Asst libn for reader serv 68-. 9: SLA. 10: Phi Beta Kappa; Pi Lambda Sigma. 14: Ref, mil hist, soc sci. 15: Inst for Defense Analyses 400 Army-Navy dr, Arlington Va 22202.

FAST, ELIZABETH (TRYGSTAD). b Brooklyn NY 8 F 31. 4: Nicholas W Fast. 5: Radcliffe 48-52 (Eng) AB; SConn State Col 62-66 LS; URI 67-68 MLS. 7: Elem sch libn Groton Pub Schs, Groton Conn 62-65, Dir of lib serv 65-68; Dir of educl media 68-. 8: Adv Com, Lib TV Program So Conn State Col; Chm Groton Sch Lib Adv Com 60-64; Instr; conting Educ Prog UConn 68-; Consul NDEA Media Serv Course UNH 68-;

Inst Columbia U 67. 9: ALA-AASchL (var coms); -CSD (com duties); NEA-DAVI; NELA; ConnLA (com duties); ConnEA; ConnSch LA; NESchLA; ASCD. 10: PTA; LWV; Phi Beta Kappa; Alpha Delta Kappa. 11: Alternate, White House Fellows Program, 65. 13: Yes. 14: Sch libs, tech proc, child serv, lib educ. 15: 2 Chestnut Hill sq, Groton Conn 06340.

FATKA, VEDA MAE (WILSON). b Kingsley Iowa 14 Ag 19. 4: Wilbur Fatka. 5: Westmar Col 37-41 (Eng) BA; UColorado summers 58, 59; UMinn 62-63 (LS) MA. 6: Ger, Fr, Lat. 7: High sch tchr pub sch, Defiance Iowa 41-42; High sch tchr pub sch, Fairdale Ill 42-43; High sch tchr pub sch, Armstrong Iowa 55-59; Jr high tchr pub sch, Estherville Iowa 60-62, 63-65; Instr in Lib Sci State Col of Iowa 65-67; Sch libn Muskegon Pub Schsm Muskegon Mich 67-. 8: Lectr UMinn summer 67. 9: NEA; ALA; AASchL; IowaASchL (pres 65-66); Iowa State EA. 10: Delta Kappa Gamma (State corr sec 63-65); Beta Phi Mu; AAUW. 13: Yes. 14: Sch libn. 15: 1892 Crestwood lane, Muskegon Mi 49441.

FATTIG, HELEN (McNEIL). b Enterprise Ala 5 Jl 09. 4: Wilbur Leroy Fattig. 5: Howard Col 27-30 (Eng) AB; Emory 33-34 AB in LS. 7: Asst libn Birmingham Pub Lib, Birmingham Ala 27-33; Libn Ensley High Sch, Birmingham Ala 34-35; Libn Bass High Sch, Atlanta 48-56; Resource libn Area III Atlanta Pub Schs 56-. 9: ALA; -AASchL (chm Encyel Brit Sch Lib Awards Com 65-66); -LSD; NEA; City, Town & Co Lib Supvs; SELA; GaLA (2nd v-pres 61-63, pres 65-67); GaEA (pres Lib Dept 63-65); Ga Dept Distr Supvrs 9chm 5th Dist 62-63). 10: Atlanta Lib Club. 11: Delta Kappa Gamma. 12: Co-auth "Resource Librarian's Handbook", Atlanta Pub Schs (56); "Library Lessons for Atlanta High Schools" (50). 14: Sch libs. 15: 1643 N Gatewood rd NE, Atlanta Ga 30329.

FAUCHER, BLANCHE. b Montreal. 5: Montreal BA, (LS) Diploma. 6: Fr, Sp, Eng. 7: Catlgr & clsfr Montreal Civic ib 45; Ref 52. 8: Deleg to IFLA Conf 66-67; Mem Com to Establish the Corporation of Profess Libns of Quebec 66-68. 9: CanLA; Association canadiene des bibliothecaires de langue francaise (v-pres 65-66, pres 66-67); QueLA. 10: Assn des femmes diplomees dUniversites, Semaine des bibliotheques canadiennes. 12: Ed "ACBLF Bulletin. 13: Yes. 14: Catlg, ref. 15: 3460 Grey ave, Montreal 260 Can.

FAUCHER, ROSE-GRACE. b Saginaw Mich 29 O 14. 5: Brescia Hall(London Ont)32-33 (Fr); Loyola U(Chicago) 35-38 (Fr) PhB; UMich(Ann Arbor) 38-39 ABLS, 41-44 AMLS. 6: Fr. 7: Asst acquis libn UMich 39-42, Circ asst 42-43, Gen serv asst 43-44, Sr circ libn 44-46, Assoc circ libn 46-53, Div libn, Dentistry 54-61, Asst head Undergrad Lib 61-63, Head Undergrad Lib 63-. 9: ALA; MichLA; Ann Arbor LA. 10: Women of the Faculty (UMich); UMich Faculty Womens Club; Kappa Gamma Pi; Omicron Kappa Upsilon. 14: Col libs, ref, admin. 15: 601 Sunset rd, Ann Arbor Mi 48103.

FAUNCE, MARIA (CASAS). b Madrid Spain. 4: Stephen S A Faunce. 5: Inst Francaise en Espagne 43-48 (Fr) Certificat detudes de langue francaise; UMinn 57-60 (Linguistics) BA; UMich 60-61 MALS, 62-67; (Romance Lngs); UPuerto Rico 67- (Hispanic Lit). 6: Sp, R, Ital, Portu, Fr, Eng. 7: Circ libn US Info Serv, Madrid Spain 54-56; Asst curator James Ford Bell Collection UMinn 56-57; Acquis asst UMinn 57-60; Audio Visual libn UMich (Ann Arbor) 60-62; Catlg libn Slavic Sect 62-66; Hd tech serv InterAmer U (Puerto Rico) 66-68; Prof Inst of Libnship UPuerto Rico 68-. 8: Consul on spec lib problems for Fomento Cooperative 68-69. 9: Sociedad de Bibliotecarios de Puerto Rico. 14: Catlg, rare bks, tchg. 15: Palma Real II-J Madrid 2, Miramar Puerto Rico 00907.

FAUNCE, STEPHEN (SANFORD ANNIS). b Denver Col 18 Jl 33. 4: Maria Casas. 5: UMinn 55-59 (Psych) ALA, BA, MA; UMich 59-61 (Ling) AM, 61-62 (Near East Studies) AM; UMinn 64-65 MALS. 6: Sp, Fr, Arabic, Portu. 7: E-2 USA, Korea & Japan 50-54; Tchg fellow UMich (Ann Arbor) 62-64; Asst to libn WashU (St Louis) Med Sch 65-66; Hd libn Inter AmerU, Bayamon PR 66-68; Analyst IBM, San Juan PR 68-. 9: Sociedad de Bibliotecarios de PR. 13: Yes. 14: Mechanization, info retrieval. 15: Palma Real 11-J Madrid 2, Miramar PR 00907.

FAUROT, MARY RUTH. b Topeka Kan 22 Ap 46. 5: UCal (Riverside) 64-68 (Hist) AB; UCLA 68-69 MLS. 6: Lat, Fr, Ger. 7: Ser catlgr URI (Kingston) 69-. 9: ALA. 10: Phi Beta Kappa. 14: Catlg, ref. 15: 532 37th st, Sacramento Ca 95816.

FAWCETT, JOAN (SYLVIA). b Halifax Nova Scotia Can 5 Jl 19. 4: William Gordon Fawcett. 5: DalhousieU 37-40 (Eng) BA, 40-41 (Educ) BEd; UToronto 65-66 BLS. 6: Fr. 7: Prin of schs, Hantsport NS 41-42; Secondary sch supply tchg, Oakville Ont 62-65; Catlg asst mcMasterU 66-67; Ref libn Oakville Pub Lib, Oakville Ont 67-. 9: OntLA. 10: Univ Women's Club; Oakville-Trafalgar Mem Hosp Auxiliary; Oakville Hist Soc. 14: Ref. 15: 209 Morrison rd, Oakville Ont Can.

FAY, BARBARA. b Hartford Conn 4 O 41. 5: Douglass Col 59-63 (Lat Amer Studies) BA; Rutgers 63-65 MLS. 6: Sp. 7: Intern-adult serv E Orange Pub Lib, E Orange NJ 63-66; Senior libn 66-. 9: ALA; NJLA (sec Ref Sect 68-69). 10: Summit Area Douglass Alumnae Club. 14: Adult serv, ref. 15: E Orange Pub Lib 221 Freeway drive E, East Orange NJ 07018.

FAY, KATHLEEN JEANNE. b Baltimore 24 O 41. 5: Col of Notre Dame (Md) 59-63 (Hist) AB; UNC 64-65 MS in LS. 6: Fr. 7: Secondary tchr Baltimore City Sch 63-64; Ya lib Enoch Pratt Free Lib, Baltimore 65-. 67; Bkmob libn 67-. 9: ALA. 14: Ya wk, ref, adult serv. 15: 1009 F Donnington cir, Baltimore Md 21204.

FAY, KATHRYN ELLEN. b Madrid NY 31 J 12. 5: St Lawrence U 29-33 (Eng, Lat) BA; Albany State Col summers 37-42 BS in LS; St Lawrence U 60 (Admin) M in Ed. 6: Fr. 7: Eng tchr Madrid-Waddington (NY) Central Sch 33-39, Eng tchr & libn 39-43, Eng tchr, libn, vice-prin 43-57, Libn, vice-prin 57-62, Prin Jr-Sr High 62-69, Libn & dist v-prin 69-. 8: Honor Soc Adv; AFS Com. 9: NEA; NY State Tchrs Assn (No Zone, No Country Reading Coun, No Country Adminrs); NY State Second Sch Adminrs; ASDC. 10: Delta Kappa Gamma. 14: Ref, research. 15: 6 Church st, Madrid NY 13660.

FEAGIN, OBION WATSON. b Calhoun Co Miss 31 Ja 15. 4: Oscar R Feagin. 5: UMiss 32-36 (Eng) BAE, 56-59 MLS. 7: Elem tchr, Calhoun Co Miss 36-37; Elem tchr Puerto Rico 46-48; Non-prof asst Period Dept UMiss 56-59, Jr libn Period Dept 59-62, Ref libn 62-. 9: MissLA; SELA. 15: PO Box 171, University Miss 38677.

FEALY, HARRIET ELIZABETH. b Franklin Ohio 11 Ag 35. 5: Col of Mount St Josep(Ohio) 53-57 (Elem Educ) AB; UKy 57-61 MS in LS; Kent State 65 NDEA Lib Inst. 6: Fr. 7: Elem tchr Carlisle Local Sch, Carlisle Ohio 57-61, Libn 61-; Fr tchr 61-63; Summer tour escort; trailway Bus, Cincinnati 63, 64; Royal Travel Serv 67, 68. 8: Volunteer in setting up elem sch libs; st Peter, Fairborn Ohio; St Francis, Lebanon Ohio; St Susannah, Mason Ohio. 9: NEA; ALA; OhioEA; OhioASchL (chm Standard Com 67, 68; Dir 68-69); OhioLA. 10: Carlisle Federal Credit Union sec 61- 4-H Leader 57-; Franklin area Hist Soc (Chart mem, v-pres), sec Bd Dirs). 12: "Centennial History of St Mary Parish, Franklin Ohio, 1868-1968. 13: Yes. 14: Wk with sch child. 15: 430 Victoria lane, Franklin Ohio 45005.

FEARN, ROBIN ARNOLD CRAIG. b Canton Ohio 10 Ja 40. 4: Mary Elizabeth Oakes. 5: Malone Col 58-59 (Liberal Arts); Ohio U 59-64 (Liberal Arts, LS) BA; Case West Res U (Info Sci) MSLS. 6: Ger. 7: Tchr York Local Sch Dist, Buchtel Ohio 62-63; Salesman & inventory control Mathews Oil Co, Athens Ohio 61-62 & 63-64; Tech libn Babcock & Wilcox Co Research Center, Alliance Ohio 64-. 8: Info & Communication Serv consul: tech info centers; info systems analyst; oral communications; tech writing; info sci, info procg on computers. 9: ASIS; SLA. 10: Independent Order of Foresters; 14: Documentation, info center & serv systems analysis, staff train. 15: 4865 Hills & Dales rd, Canton Ohio.

FEASEL, MRS ARLENE V(INALL). b Pittsburgh Penn 4 My 41. 4: Richard McDowell Feasel. 5: Stetson U 38-40, 46-47 (Eng) AB, 63-65 (Educ) MA 68-69. 7: Assignment clerk So Bell Telephone Co, Daytona Beach Fla 40-42; Civil Serv clerical US Naval Air Sta, Daytona Beach Fla 42-45; Stetson U: Lib sec 56-58, Lib accountant 58-62, Dept head period & binding 62-64, Dept head instr materials & periods & binding 64-68; Elem sch libn 68-69. 9: NEA-DAVI; FlaLA; VolusiaCoLA. 10: Jr Womans Club; PEO; PTA; Stetson U Womans Club; Tau Beta Sigma; Phi Beta Kappa; Lake Winnemissett Civic Assn. 14: A-V, instr materials, ref. 15: 123 Lake Winnemissett dr, Deland Fl 32720.

FECZKO, DORIS ANNE. b Jersey City NJ 1 D 24. 5: Stetson U 43-46 (Soc Sci Educ) ABA (cum laude); Columbia 57-58 (LS) MS. 6: Fr. 7: Eng soc sci tchr Seabreeze High Sch, Daytona Beach Fla 45-46; Soc sci tchr Widwood High Sch, Wildwood Fla 46-47; Elem tchr Ormon Beach Sch, Ormond Fla 47-49; Asst reader serv ed "House Beautiful NYC 50-54; Gen br asst Enoch Pratt Free Lib, Baltimore 58-59; Ya libn Montclair Pub Lib, Montclair NJ 59-65; Sch libn Montclair High Sch, Montclair NJ 65-. 8: Reviewer of "Adult Books for Young People in "Lib Journal 63-64. 9: NEA; NJEA; NJLA;

NJSchLA. 10: Bus & Prof Womens Club. 13: Yes. 14: Ya wk, sch libnship. 15: 307 Hoovr ave, Bloomfield NJ 07003.

FEDDER, ALICE N(AOMI ELIZABETH). b E Wayland NY 28 Je 15. 5: Geneeo State Normal Sch 36-40 (Edu, LS) BS in Ed; Columbia 46-50, 52 MS in LS. 6: Fr. 7: Instr Lib Sci Fisk U summer 46; High sch libn York Central Sch, Retsof NY 42-46; Sch lib lab libn Tchrs Col Columbia U 46-50; Instr Lib Sci State Tchrs Col (Geneseo NY) 50-51; High sch libn U High Sch UIll (Urbana) 51-56; Lib consul to Ministry of Educ, Kabul Afghanistan 56-57; Act libn Wells Col 59; Assoc libn I Milne Lib SUNY Col (Geneseo) 59-67; Libn Commun Col of Finger Lakes, Canandaigua NY. 9: ALA. 10: AAU; Beta Phi Mu; 13: Yes. 14: Ref, readers serv, lib mgt. 15: 3706 Saddleback rd, Canandaigua NY 14424.

FEDEROWICZ, BROTHER JOHN CSC. b St Paul Minn 20 Je 22. 5: GonzagaU 46-47 (Phil, Eng) PhB; Notre DameU 40-52 (LS) Certif; Kent State 65-69 MLS. 6: Fr, Ger. 7: Tchr & libn Schs conducted by Brothers of Holy Cross, Indianapolis, Chicago, S Bend, Milwaukee 43-50; Libn Schs conducted by Brothers of Holy Cross, Cleveland & Akron Ohio 50-. 8: Adv bd Dujarie Press, Notre Dame Ind 64-67; Visiting lib sci lectr Holy Name Col Manitowoc Wis summer 69-; Corp sec Archbishop Hoban High Sch Inc 68-. 9: CathLA (Publicity Chm 67); ALA; OhioASchL; Ohio Hist Soc; DiocesanLA; Akron Area libn's Assn. 12: Ed "Book Review Bulletin of the Diocesan Library Association" (54-56); "Catholic Book Tests, series 1-4" (54). 13: Yes. 14: Lib educ, tech in sch libs. 15: 400 Elbon ave, Akron Oh 44306.

FEDIUK, SIMON. b Ukraine 15 F 101 04: Lidia Pyrozynsky. 5: The Academy of Foreign Com (Poland) 34-37 Master of Com; Central U (Madrid Spain) 48-52 (Pol) PhD; Diplomatic Sch of Foreign Off (Madrid Spain) 2-54 Sec of State; Columbia 61-66 (LS) MS. 6: Ukrainian, Polis, Russian, Sp, Ger, Portu. 7: Asst libn Geol Lib Columbia U 60-63; Catlgr Amer Geog Soc, NY 63-66; Hd libn ref lib Exec Dept, Div of Human Rights, NY 67-. 8: Supvr Special Library on Civil Rights and comp "Library Accessions Annotated. 9: SLA; Amer Geog Soc. 10: Free Ukranian Acad in the US; Shevchenko Sci Soc, NY. 11: Award "Isidro Bonsoms from "Ecma Diputacion Provincial de Barcelona, 52, for PhD diss. 13: Yes. 14: Catlg of mas & bks. 15: 160 - 1st ave, New York NY 10009.

FEDORKO, MARY ANN. b Erie Penn 9 S 43. 5: Edinboro State Col 61-65 (LS & Soc Studies) BS Educ, 65-66 (Soc Studies) M Educ; UPittsburgh 67-68 MLS. 7: Elem libn Wattsburg Jt Area Sch, Wottsburgh Pa 65-66; Elem libn Niagara Wheatfield Jt Area Sch, Sanford NY 66-67; Catlgr UPittsburgh, Pittsburgh Pa 67-68; Libn Orlando Pub Lib, Orlando Fla 68-. 9: NEA; ALA; SLA; Penn State EA; FlaLA. 14: Catlg, elem lib wk. 15: MPO PO Box 2883, Orlando Fl 32802.

FEDOROWYCZ, WASYL. b Wyszenka Ukraine 25 D 11. 4: Stefania Kunynec. 5: ULviv 31-35 (Law) LLM; UOttawa 66-67 BLS. 6: Ukrainian, Polish, Russian, Ger. 7: Court applicant Court (Sad Okregowy), Lviv 36-39; Income tax referent taxation division, Lviv 40-44; Various, Austria 45-48; Various, Canada 49-66; Catlgr civil law lib UOttawa 67-. 9: CanLA; AALL; CanALL. 10: Ukrainian Nat Federation, Canada; Assn of Ukrainian Lawyers, Canada. 14: Catlg, ref. 15: 56 Henderson ave, Ottawa 2 Ont Can.

FEDYNSKYJ, JURIJ. b Mosty Welyki Ukraine 19 S 12. 4: Nathalie Moschinsky. 5: Lvov U 30-34 Magister iuris; Innsbruck U 42-43 DrJur; Columbia 55-57 MS in LS; UNotre Dame 57-59 (Law); Ind U 63-65 DJur. 6: Ger, Ukrainian, Pol, Russ, Fr, Ital, Lat, Gk. 7: Jr mem of the Bar priv off, Lvov 34-39; Asst Prof Civil Law ULvov 39-41; Asst & Tchg Assoc UInnsbruck 43-48; Legal adv, Intern Refugee Org, Innsbruck 49; Gen sec Shevchenk Sci Soc NY 51-57; Asst law libn UNotre Dame(Notre Dame Ind) 57-59; Asst law libn Ind U 59-, Research Scholar in Law 61-66; Research scholar in law 61-; Asst prof of law 66-69; Assoc law libn 67-; Assoc prof of law 69-. 9: Internat Assn Law Libs (sec 62-65); AALL. 10: Shevchenko Sci Soc; Forschungsinstitut fur den Donauraum (Vienna); Amer Foreign Law Assn; Brit Inst Intern & Comp Law Soc de Legisl Comp, Paris. 12: "Rechtstatsachen auf dem Gebiete des Erbrechts im Gerichtsbezirk Innsbruck (43). 13: Yes. 14: Law libnship. 15: Ind U Law Lib, Bloomington In 47401.

FEELEY, CAROLYN. b Pittsburgh 4 My 41. 5: Duquesne U 59-63 (Chem) BS; UPittsburgh 63-64 MLS, UFla Ed 67-68. 6: Ger, Russian, Fr. 7: Mathematician Surgical Research Dept Montefiore Hosp 63-64; Tech libn EI duPont de Nemours & Co Ind & Biochem Dept Pharmaceutical Reearch Div 64-67; Grad asst UFla Research Lib 67-68; Ref libn Health Ctr Lib 68-. 9: SLA; Fla Med Libns (sec 69); ASIS (treas Fla-Ga Chap). 14: Reg med progs. 15: Univ of Florida Health Ctr Lib, Gainesville Fl 32601.

FEENEY, M(ARY) PATRICIA. b Philadelphia Penn 20 Je 43. 5: Mt St Mary Col 61-65 (Eng) AB; Drexel 67-68 MSLS. 6: Fr. 7: Tchr St Patrick's Convent Sch, Pelham NH 65-66; Assoc catlgr Kenyon Col Lib, Gambier Ohio 68-. 9: ALA; ASIS; OhioLA. 14: Bibliog, catlg, info sci. 15: 4 1/2 S Clinton st, Mount Vernon NY 43050.

FEENEY, MARY ELIZABETH. b Kan City Mo 15 S 18. 5: Col of St Elizabeth 36-39 (Eng), UPenn 46-47 (Sociol, Eng) AB; UPenn Lib Prof Train Program Research Libnship; Drexel 59-60 (Med Bibliog & Libnship) Med Lib Assn Grade 1 Certif. 6: Fr, Lat. 7: (Lt) USN (WR), Wash DC 424; Head res bk dept UPenn Lib 49-52; Libn Hosp of the UPen 52-62; Asst libn Lib of the Col of Physicians of Phila 62-64; Assoc libn NY Acad of Med Lib, NYC 64-. 9: MedLA (Asst Placement Adv 59-61, Com on Advanced Seminars 60-61, Com on Continuing Educ 65-69, Subcom on Curr 65-68); SLA; NYLib Club. 11: Christopher Prize Essay 51. 12: Asst ed "Catholic Library World 56-58, Consul ed (58-60). 13: Yes. 14: Admin, ref, acquis. 15: NY Acad of Med 2 E 103rd st, NYC 10029.

FEINBERG, HILDA (WARSHAW). b Atlanta. 4: Joseph Feinberg. 5: UGa (Chem) BS (summa cum Laude, MS; Columbia 63 (LS) MS, 68-69 (LS). 6: Fr, Ger. 7: Chem-libn NY Quinine Co, NY 39-41; Head research lib Revlon Research Center, NY 55-. 8: Asst consul, Survey of Chicago Pub Lib 68-69. 9: SLA; MedLA; ACS; ASIS; Soc Cosmetic Chemists; Amer Assn Textile Chemists & Colorists. 10: Phi Beta Kappa; Beta Phi Mu. 13: Yes. 14: Info sci. 15: 1685 Ocean ave, Brooklyn NY 11230.

FEINGOLD, ELIZABETH (FRENCH) (MRS). b Ilion NY 13 My 07. 4: Abraham Feingold. 5: Smith 25-29 (Eng) BA; Columbia 31-32 MS. 7: Libn Hartford Pub Lib, Hartford Conn 29-31; Libn Queens Borough Pub Lib 32-36; Sch libn Bd of Educ, NYC 36-52; Dist libn, Br libn Brooklyn Pub Lib, Brooklyn NY 59-. 9: ALA; NYLA; NY Lib Club. 10: Women's Nat Bk Assn. 11: Friends of the Lib Award 66, Brooklyn Pub Lib. 15: 64 Sterling st, Brooklyn NY 11225.

FEINMAN, VALERIE (JACKSON). b Hamilton Ont Can 28 Je 37. 4: Robert D Feinman. 5: McMasterU 56-63 (Sci Studies) BA; Syracuse 64-66 MSLS. 7: Lib trainee N York Pub Lib, Toronto Ont 62-64; Physics libn SyracuseU 64-65; Ed SUNY Union list of ser Upstate Med Ctr Lib, Syracuse NY 65-68, Subj analyst biomed communications network 68-69. 9: ASIS; MLA; CanLA; UpstateNYMedLA. 10: SyracuseU Lib Sch Alumni Assn; Beta Phi Mu. 12: Ed "Union List of Serials in the Libraries of the State University of New York" (66 & 2nd ed 67); "Central New York Union List of Serials" (68). 14: Indexing, subj analysis & clsf, automation, SDI. 15: Upstate Med Center Lib 766 Irving ave, Syracuse NY 13210.

FEINSTEIN, LEONORE H(ART). b NYC 30 Ap 15. 4: William Feinstein. 5: Hunter Cl 31-35 (Lat) BA; UCal 48-50 BLS. 7: Subj file clerk Gen Foods Corp, NYC 37-40; Clerical asst Oakland (Cal) Pub Lib 47-48, Jr libn 49, Dir wk with youth 50-51; Bibliogr lib photo serv UCal (Berkeley) 53-63, Residence halls libn 64-. 9: ALA. 10: LWV. 13: Yes. 14: Wk with y. 15: 950 Grizzly Peak blvd, Berkeley Ca 94708.

FEITH, IRENE. b Highland Falls NY 26 My 19. 5: Ladycliff Col 37-41 (Hist) BA. 7: Lib asst US Mil Acad Lib (W Point) NY 45-58, Period & document libn 58-64, Document libn 64-. 14: Docs, ref. 15: 29 Wyandotte ave, Highland Falls NY 10928.

FELD, BETTY (LYLE). b Smethport Penn 3 F 11. 4: Louis A Feld. 5: Rollins Col 28-32 (Fr) BA; Ecole Normale Superiure de Jeunes Filles, Sevres France 32-33; Columbia 34-37 BS in LS; 56-61 MS in LS. 6: Fr. 7: Stud asst Rollins Col Lib 28-32; Clerk Queens Borough Pub Lib, Jamaica NY 33-37, Catlgr 38-57, Asst supt catlg div 58-60, Asst chief tech processes 60-65; Catlg libn Hofstra U Lib 65-. 9: ALA; NY Tech Serv Libns; NYLA; NassauCoLA. 10: Beta Phi Mu. 14: Catlg. 15: 120-11 Hillside ave, Richmond Hill NY 11418.

FELDER, FELICIA VAUGHAN (HARRIS). b Knoxville Tenn 21 S 37. 5: Knoxville Col 54-58 (Eng) BS; UTenn 60 (Educ), summer 62 (Bus Admin); Atlanta U 65-66 MSLS. 6: Fr. 7: Tchr McMinn Co Pub Schs, Athens Tenn 58-60; Receptionist & asst in admin offs Knoxville Col 60-63, Asst to dir of pub rel 63-65; Grad asst Trevor Arnett Lib Atlanta U 65-66; Libn Knoxville Col 66-. 8: Represented Knoxville Col at the Nat Alum Coun Meeting of the United Negro Col Fund; Gary Ind 64, Dallas Tex 65, Charlotte NC 67, Chicago 68; Tchr-Libn Summer Study Skills Prog, Bd of Nat Missions, knoxville Col summer 67, 68. 9: ALA; TennLA; SELA. 10: Tenn Coun on Human Relations; Citizens for Justice; Knox Co Demo Women's Club; Knoxville Col Alum Assn; YWCA; NAACP; Heart Assn; Alpha Kappa Alpha. 11: Outstanding Young Women of America (67). 14: Ref. 15: 2715 Lay ave SE, Knoxville Tn 37914.

FELDER, JIMMIE (LEE) ROBINSON. b Hayneville Ala 27 Mr 25. 4: John Richard Felder. 5: Ala State Col 43-47 (Eng) BS, 49-54 (Eng, LS) MEd, summer 57 (Elem Educ) Elem certif; UAla 66 (LS) Peabody Col 66-69 MLS. 7: Tchr: Merritt High Sch, Midway Ala 47-48, Morning Star Jr High Sch, St Clair Ala 48-49, Lowndes Co Train, Hayneville Ala 49-50, Gordonville Ctr School, Hayneville Ala 50-56; Tchr & libn Lowndes Co Training Sch. Hayneville Ala 56-62; Libn George Washington Carver High Sch, Montgomery Ala 62-. 8: Chm of Oratorical Com, Lowndes Co Schs 52-59; Chm Spelling Bee Com 59-62. 9: NEA; ALA; SELA; AlaASchL; AlaLA; LowndesCoTA (sec 4 yrs). 10: Student Lib Assts of Ala; Tots and Teens; YMCA; Leukemia Soc. 14: Catlg, ref. 15: 1118 Oak, Montgomery Al 36108.

FELDMAN, GLADYS (ROSEMARIE) NAUWIRTH. b NYC 15 My 23. 4: Irving S. 5: Barnard 40-44 9eng) BA; Carnegie Inst 49-50 MLS; Newark State Col Certif in pub schs K-12. 6: Ger. 7: Yeoman 2/c WAVES, NY 44-46; Clerical asst (ref) Carnegie Lib of Pittsburgh 47-49, stud asst 49-50, Ref libn 50-51; Sch libn: Fair Haven Pub 62-63, Bayville Pub 64-65; Catlgr Ocean Co (Commun) Col 67-. 9: ALA; NJEA. 10: Phi Beta Kappa; AAUW; PTA. 14: Ref, catlg. 15: 982 President ave, Toms River NJ 08753.

FELDMAN, MARIANNE (LEHMANN). b Magdeburg Germany 30 O 27. 4: Philip B. 5: Reed 45-48 (Hist); UWash 48-49 (Educ, Hist) BA, Lib & tchg certifs; Lewis & Clark 52-60 9educ, Ger, Hist) Ore tchg certif; UPortland 64-67 MLS. 6: Ger. 7: Dist libn bellevue Sch Dist, Bellevue Wash 49; Tchr & libn, Eugene & Portland Ore 50-54; Sub libn Portland Sch Dist I, Portland Ore 64-67; Libn Roosevelt High (Knapp Foundation), Portland Ore 67; Ref & acquis libn Ore Hist Soc, Portland 68-. 9: ALA; PNLA; OreLA. 14: Research & ref in Northwest hist. 15: 6141 SW Seymour st, Portland Or 97221.

FELDMAN, MARY HELEN (KEARNEY). b Sapulpa Okla 21 Jl 20. 5: Monte Cassino Jr Col 37-39 AA; Cincinnati Conservatory of Music 39-41 (Piano); UMd 61-63 (Educ) BS in Ed; Cath U 63-64 MS LS. 6: Fr, Sp. 7: Billing clerk Anchor Petroleum Co, Tulsa Okla 42-45; Tchr Montgomery Co, Rockville Md 63; Lib asst Takoma Park Lib, Takoma Park Md; Catlgr St Marys Elem Sch, Rockville Md 64; Catlgr USBE, Wash DC 64; Indexer New Catholic Encyclopedia, Wash DC 65-66; Hd tech serv Trinity Col Lib 65-. 9: ALA (DC Memb Chm 69-71); DCLA (chm Interfaith Lib Com 68-); CathLA (sec Wash-Md Unit 67-69, Legisl Chm 69-71). 10: Phi Kappa Phi; Beta Phi Mu. 14: Catlg, indexing, art, musi, child lit. 15: 7117 Poplar ave, Takoma Park Md 20012.

FELDMAN, MONROE. b New Britain Conn 28 Ja 16. 4: Rose S Rothenberg. 5: City Col of NY 34-40 (Span); Mexico City Col 47-48 (Latin-Amer Studies) BA; UMich 57-60 AMLS. 6: Lat, Sp, Fr, Ital. 7: T/5 (cpl) Clerk Army of the US 42-45; Owner Bergen Bkshop, Brooklyn NY 48-51; Mailroom supv Guiterman Co Inc, NYC 51-52; Export manager Tann Corp, Detroit 52-59; Ref libn Ferndale Pub Lib, St Clair Shores Mich 60-63; Libn Defense Logistics Serv Center, Battle Creek Mich 63-66; Libn Phys Sci & Engin Nav Ordn Lab, Silver Spring Md 66-. 9: SLA (Pub Com Mich Chap 65-66). 10: Bnai Brith (record sec); Mich Table Tennis Assn. 14: Admin, ref, rare bks. 15: 8857 Garland ave, Silver Spring Md 20901.

FELDMAN, SUSAN ELEANOR (GOODMAN). b NYC 14 F 47. 4: Robert L Feldman. 5: CornellU 63-67 (Ling) BA; UMich 67-68 AMLS. 6: Fr, Japanese. 7: Stud asst Cornell Music Lib 66-67; Ref libn CFSTI, Springfield Va 68-. 9: ALA. 10: Fairfax Symphony Orchestra; Beta Phi Mu. 14: Ref. 15: 21 Seabrook st, Rochester NY 14621.

FELICIA, SISTER CSM. b Buffalo NY 8 D 24. 5: Stanford 42-44, 46-48 (Amer Hist) AB; UPhilippines 50-5 (Oriental Hist) MA; Columbia summers 60, 61 (Guidance & Langs); UArk Ext Div 61-62 (Principles of Secondary Educ; Tests & Measurements). 6: Fr, Sp. 7: US Army Spec Serv Div, Ed "WAC Newsletter NYC 44-46, (T/Sgt) Personnel Off OAB Orlando Fla 45; Writer-announcer Radio Statio KBIO & Burley Herald-Bulletin, Burley Ida 48-50; Instr in hist U of the Philippines 50-54; Hist & lang tchr St Marys Sch, Sewanee Tenn 58-63, Guidance Coun 61-63; Mistress of studies St Marys inthField, Valhalla NY 63-64; Rep of Community at Conf of Anglican Religious at Mendham NJ 65 & at Ecumenical Conf for Religious, Arlington Heights Mass 65; Proj coord Title III Teenagers Cultural Ctr, Valhalla NY 68-69. 9: ALA-ASD; NEA. 12: "The Majapahit and Sriv Vijayan Empires (52); Ed WAC Newsletter (45-46). 13: Yes. 14: CATLG & sch lib org, independent study programs for exceptional students. 15: St Marys in-theField, Valhalla NY 10595.

FELIX, MARY (TOUMBACARIS). b Jersey City NJ 23 Ja 16. 4: Adonis D Felix. 5: Hunter Col 34-38 (Sp) AB; SUNY(Albany) 53-59 MSLS. 6: Sp, Ital, Fr, Gk. 7: Microfilm operator NY Pub Lib 42-49; Lib asst NY State Lib 51-53, Jr libn 53-55, Asst libn 56, Order sect head 56-62, Asst ref libn 63-64, Sr ref libn 65-; Assoc libn interlib loan 66-. 9: NYLA. 14: Ref & rare bks. 15: Kinderhook NY.

FELKER, JEANNE. b Middleburg Penn 6 Mr 31. 5: Wilson Col 49-53 (Eng) BA; Columbia 55-57 (LS) MS. 7: Trainee & child libn Brooklyn Pub Lib 55-60; Child libn Allentown Pub Lib, Allentown Penn 60-62; Army libn US Army Spec Serv, Kitzingen Germany 62-64; Child libn NY Pub Lib 65-. 9: ALA. 14: Child lit. 15: 36 Hamilton ave, Staten Island NY 10301.

FELKER, WILLIAM ARTHUR. b Beavertown Pa 4 N 39. 5: Gettysburg Col 57-61 (Pol Sci) AB; Penn State U 61-62 (Hist) MA; UChicago 63 (LS); Drexel 63-66 (LS) MS. 7: Lib trainee Chicago Pub Lib 63; Lib trainee Free Lib of Phila 63-66, Libn I 66, Libn II 66-68, Libn III 68-, Hd soc sci & tech dept NE Reg Lib 67-. 9: ALA; PennLA. 14: Ref. 15: 4433 Pearson ave, Phila Pa 19114.

FELL, SAVILLA LYNN (TYLER). b Milwaukee Wis 18 F 37. 4: William Fell. 5: Penn State U 54-58 (Romance Langs & Lits) BA, 61-63 (Fr) MA; UWis (Madison) 66-67 (LS) MA. 6: Fr, Sp, Rumanian. 7: Clk-typist UN, NYC 58-60; Instr of Fr Ohio Wesleyan U 63-64, 65-66; Bilingual sec UNESCO, Paris 65; Ref libn UWis (Milwaukee) 67-. 9: ALA. 14: Ref. 15: 2722 E Hartford ave, Milwaukee Wi 53211.

FELLAND, NORDIS. b Northfield Minn 14 D 01. 5: St Olaf Col 19-23 (Eng, Hist) BA; Pratt 26-27 BLS; Columbia 31-32. 7: Libn asst Amer Geog Soc, NYC 27-43, Libn 43-. 9: ALA; SLA (chm Museum Div 46-47, chm (chm Geog & Map Div); NY Tech Serv Libns (chm 49-50). 10: Assn Amer Geogrs. 11: Distinguished Alumni Award, St Olaf Col; Honors Award, SLA Geog & Map Div. 12: Ed "Current Geographical Publications (43). 13: Yes. 14: Catlg, ref. 15: Amer Geog Soc Broadway & 156th st, NYC 10032.

FELLER, CAROLINE J. b Wash DC 12 My 35. 4: Peter A Bauer. 5: UColo 53-55; Sarah Lawrence 55-57 BA; Columbia 58 MLS. 6: Fr, Ger. 7: Libn Miss Hewitts Classes, NYC 60-61; Libn NY Pub Lib 58-60; Libn Eron Prep Sch, NYC 62-63; Libn Colo Rocky Mt Sch, Carbondale Colo 63-65; Radio announcer KSNO, Aspen Colo 64-66; Asst Prof UOre Sch of Libnship 66-. 8: TV Series, KOAC, "Carolina Folk Tales Around the World 67-68. 9: ALA; NEA-DAVI; Puppeteers of Amer; Amer Folklore Assn; OreLA. 10: Soc Amer Magicians. 11: Ersted Award for distinguished tchg, 68. 14: Child bks, storytelling. 15: School of Librarianship U of Oregon, Eugene Or 97403.

FELLER, JUDITH (MILLER). b Phila Pa 29 Ag 39. 4: Walter A Feller. 5: UPenn 57-61 (Creative writing) BA; Drexel 62-63 MS in LS. 6: Fr. 7: Ref interlib loan E Stroudsburg State Col 63-65; Ref interlib loan Temple U 66-. 9: ALA; PennLA. 12: Three Poets and an Artist (62). 14: Ref, bibliog. 15: 1139 E Mt Airy ave D-4, Phila Pa 19150.

FELLER, SIEGFRIED. b Essen Germany 15 Ja 26. 4: Karen Wynnell Bartok. 5: UMich 46-51 (Eng Lit) MA; UIll 59-60 MS LS. 6: Ger. 7: Tech/4 Radio Operator US Infantry, Europe 44-46; Manager Bob Marshalls Bookshop, Ann Arbor Mich 51-54; Owner-Manager Creative Bookmen Assoc, Riverside Cal 55-56; Traveling rep AA Lampl Art Bks, Costa Mesa Cal 56-59; Asst Order Libn S Ill U 60-61; Chief acquis libn UOkla Lib 61-64; Chief acquis libn UMinn Lib (Minneapolis) 64-67; Chief bibliog(r) & assoc dir UMass Lib. 9: BSA; Minn LA. 10: Beta Phi Mu. 13: Yes. 14: Acquis, bibliog, collection-blg. 15: RFD 2, Amherst Ma 01002.

FELLIN, OCTAVIA. b Santa Monica Cal 2 Ja 19. 5: UDenver 41 (Eng Lit, Lang) BA; Rosary Col 42 BA in LS. 6: Lat, Sp. 7: Asst libn St Mary of the Woods Col 42-44; Chief Libn Bruns Gen Hosp Gen & Med Libs,

Santa Fe NM 44-46; Libn Camp McQuade, Watsonville Cal 47; Chief Libn Gallup Pub Lib, Gallup NM 47-. 8: Lib consul NDEA Inst on Tchg a Second Lang, Chinle Ariz summers 66 & 67; Summer Insts, UCLA Ore State U Gallup 67, 68; Chm NM Com for Nat Lib Week; Chm of NMLA Com to Extend Lib Serv. 9: ALA (Mem Com NM rep, Legis coord for NMLA); NMLA (past v-pres, chm &/or mem 5 coms). 10: NM Folklore Soc; Gallup Mus Indian Arts & Crafts; AUW; Gallup Commun Concerts Assn; NMex Governors Com on Aging; Gallup Opera Guild; Organizing chm of McKinley Gen Hosp Auxil. 11: Winner of Award for Outstanding serv for mus wk from the Gallup C of C; Dorothy Canfield Fisher Award for Gallup Pub Lib, 61. 12: Sometime free-lance writer; Ed NMLA "Handbook on Historical Material. 13: Yes. 14: Rare bks on the Southwest, principally Navajo, Hopi & Zuni Indians. 15: 513 E Mesa ave, Gallup NM 87301.

FELLOWS, BARBARA (GOODWIN). b Boston Mass 20 S 27. 4: Alonzo Brown Fellows. 5: Radcliffe 45-49 (Soc Rel) AB; Sorbonne 49-50 (Fr Civilization) Certif; UPittsburgh 66-68 MLS. 6: Fr. 7: Libn (staff) Carnegie Lib of Pittsburgh 68-. 9: PennLA. 10: Beta Phi Mu. 14: Ref (Penn div). 15: 285 Old Farm rd, Pittsburgh Pa 15228.

FELO, MARY. b Flint Mich 17 Ja 32. 5: Mich State U 50-54 (Elem Educ) BA; UCal (Berkeley) 63-64 (LS) MA. 6: Ger, Fr. 7: Tchr Long Beach Unified, Long Beach Cal 54-57; Tchr US Army, Germany 57-60; Lib asst US Army, San Francisco 60-63; Libn Lawrence Radiation Lab, Livermore Cal 64-67; Libn Friden Inc, San Leandro Cal 67-68; Libn MB Assoc, San Ramon Cal 68-. 9: SLA; ASIS. 10: LWV. 14: Info retr systems. 15: 20 Casa Maria ct apt D, Alamo Ca 94507.

FELTER, JACQUELINE (ROOT) WILLIAMS. b Cleveland 26 Jl 09. 4: Irving D Felter. 5: West Res 27-31 (LS) BS. 6: Fr, Ger. 7: Branch libn Osterhout Free Lib, Wilkes-Barre Penn 31-36; Libn Kingston High Sch, Kingston Penn 36-42; Asst libn, Libn NY Post-Grad Med Sch (NYC) 43-48; Libn Memorial Sloan-Kettering Cancer Center, NY 48-49; Libn Med Soc Co of Queens, Forest Hills NY 60-61; Dir Union Catlg Med Lib Center, NYC 61-67; Act Dir Med Lib Ctr 67-. 9: ASIS; ALA; MedLA (pres 68-69); SLA; NY Lib Club. 10: Phi Beta Kappa. 12: Assoc ed "Bulletin of the Medical Librar Association, (57-62); Ed pro tem (65-66); Comp "Cumulative Indxs, 1-40 & 41-50; Co-ed "Handbook of Medical Library Practice (3d ed 69). 13: Yes. 14: Med lib admin, ref, catlg, period & sers, lib automation. 15: 115-25 84th ave, Richmond Hill NY 11418.

FELTON, GLADYS SLAUGHTER. b England Ark. 5: Ark State Tchrs Col 49-53 (Educ) BSE; Peabody 53-54 MA in LS. 7: Asst libn Henderson State Tchrs Col 54-56; Asst ref libn UArk 56-. 9: ALA; ArkLA (chm Col Div 65). 14: Ref, govt documents. 15: 309 N Washington, Fayetteville Ar 72701.

FENELON, PATRICIA SUZANNE. b Davenport Iowa 12 O 34. 5: Cardinal Stritch Col 52-56 (Hist) BA; UPenn 56-57 (Oriental Studies); Columbia 66-69 (LS) MS. 6: Fr, Sp. 7: Clerical asst UNotre Dame (Ind) 60-65, Libn 68-; Clerical asst UChicago 65-66; Clerical asst ColumbiaU 66-68. 9: ALA. 10: Ladies of Notre Dame; Gemstone Club; ADA; Delta Epsilon Sigma. 14: Ref, rare bks. 15: 301 Parkovash, S Bend In 46617.

FENG, CYRIL C(HIEN) H(WA). b Hanchow China 1 D 36. 4: Chamei Chih. 5: Tamkang Col of Arts & Sci 58-62 (Eng Lit) BA; UKy 63-65 MS in LS. 6: Chinese, Eng, Fr. 7: Br libn Sch of Med Lib, UMiami (Coral Gables Fla) 65-67; Acquis libn Sch of Med Lib UMiami 67-. 8: Mem of med sch computer com UMiami 68-; Mem of med sch curr com UMiami 69. 9: MedLA; SLA; NMA (National Microfilm Association). 14: Ref. 15: Med Lib UMiami 1600 NW 10 ave, Miami Fl 33152.

FENG, Y T. b China. 5: UShanghai 41-45 (Eng Lit) AB; L'Universite de l'Aurore 45-46 9law); Colo State Col 46-47 (English Lit) MA; UDenver 47-53 (Soc Sci) PhD; Columbia 53-55 MSLS. 6: Chinese, Fr. 7: Lib trainee NYC Pub Lib 53-55; Ref asst Harvard Col Lib 55-57, Specialist in bk selection 57-65, Asst libn 65-67; Asst dir research lib serv Boston Pub Lib 67-. 9: ALA (life mem). 15: Boston Pub Lib, Boston Ma 02117.

FENIMORE, JEAN. b Anderson Ind 24 O 16. 5: Tulane 50-53 (Hist, Soc) BA; Columbia 61-66 MLS. 6: Fr. 7: Army nurse corps (1st Lt), US & ETO 41-46; Dir nurses Ill Child Hosp Sch, Chicago 48-50; Adm asst Univ Col Tulane U 53-58; Lib tech asst I NYC Pub Lib 59; Lib & ref asst Nat Coun of Churches, NY 59-61; Asst libn Missionary Research Lib, NYC 61-65; Wk-study asst ref bus lib Columbia U 65-66; Asst libn Carnegie Endowment for intl Peace NYC 66-68; Hd adult serv Boise Pub Lib, Boise Ida 68-. 9: SLA; ALA; IdaLA; PNLA. 11: Distinguished Service Award U Col Alum Assn (Tulane) 58. 14: Ref, adult serv. 15: 500 West Franklin st, Boise Id 83702.

FENKER, JOHN ARTHUR. b LPorte Ind 16 Je 38. 5: Ind U 56-60 (Eng Lit) BA; UWis 63-65 MA in LS. 7: Sr lib asst Stanford U Lib 61-63; Proj asst UWis Med Lib(Madison) 63-65; Libn I Contra Costa Co Lib, Pleasant Hill Cal 65-67; Docs libn East Mich U 67-. 10: Beta Phi Mu. 14: Ref, govt docs. 15: East Michigan Univ Lib Documents Off, Ypsilanti Mi 48197.

FENNELL, DORIS PAULINE (CAMPBELL). b 04: Gordon Stark Fennell. 5: McMaster 48-51 (Geog) BA; UToronto 61-62 BLS. 7: Elem sch tchr Ontario; Sch libn Kipling Collegiate, Toronto Ont 62-64; Sch lib co-ord Toronto Twp Bd of Educ 64-66; Asst supt Dept of Educ, Ont 66-. 9: CanLA; Can Sch LA; ALA; OntEA; Child Recreat Reading Coun; Ont Sch Lib Supvrs Assn. 14: Sch libs. 15: 148 Princess Anne Crescent, Islington Ont Can.

FENNER, EDWARD H(AIG). b Oakland Cal 28 Ag 15. 4: Sarah Ione Gillespie. 5: NYU 35-39 (Bus Admin) BS; Columbia 41-42 BLS, 46-48, 52 (LS) MS, 52 (Personnel Admin). 6: Fr, Ger. 7: Lib asst Col of the City of NY 42; Asst libn Columbia U Sch of Bus Lib 43-44; Head sci tech dept Schenectady (NY) Pub Lib 44-46; Head libn Marvyn Scudder Financial Lib Columbia U & Asst libn grad sch of bus 46-48; Head bus & econ dept Enoch Pratt Free Lib, Baltimore 48-59; Dir Elmont Pub Lib, Elmont LI NY 59-. 8: Lib survey Johns Hopkins eco collection 49; survey UFla Bus Sch Lib 54; Consul to Dean, Grad Bus Sch, UFla on lib bldg needs for proposed new Grad Sch 54. 9: ALA (Subs Bks Com 51-53, chm Wk with Bus Group Com 53-54; chm NY Reg Group Bus & Tech Com 47-48)-RSD ("Library Journal Ref Bks Com 58-59); SLA (treas 52-54, chm Fin Com 53-54, chm Const & ByLaws Com 5-54, 53-54, Budget Com 52-54; chm Bus Div 51-52; pres Baltimore Chap 49-51 & 58-59); MdLA (treas 54-56, v-pres 58-59, chm Budget Com 54-55, chm Const & ByLaws Com 57-58, chm Intel Freedom Com 53-54); Nassau chm Bylaws Com); Co LA (pres 64-65, Memb Chm 61-62, ch Program Com 62-63); NYLA (mem var coms). 10: Kiwanis Internat; YMCA; Boy Scouts; Salvation Army; Anti-Poverty Com; Sr Citizens Com; Econ Opportunity Planning Commsn for Elmont LI NY. 11: Kiwanian of the Year 62; Amer Legion Citation of Honor as scouter of the year 68. 13: Yes. 14: Admin, ref, personnel. 15: 128 Hamilton rd, Hempstead LI NY 11550.

FENSKE, RACHEL ELIZABETH (BEARD). b Downing Wis 25 My 12. 4: H Francis Fenske. 5: UWis (River Falls) 30-32, 34-36 (Eng) BE; UWis (Eau Claire) summer 34; UMinn 38-39 (LS) BS. 7: Asst libn N Br Pub Lib, Omaha Neb 39-43; 1st asst Homewood Br Carnegie Lib, Pittsburgh Pa 43-44, Asst central lending 44; Gen asst Pub Lib, Eau Claire Wis 51-52; Child libn and asst dir Ingham Co Lib, Mason Mich 52-58, Hdq libn and asst Dir 58-60; Asst ext libn Ida State Lib 61-61, Ext libn and asst State Libn 61-65, Ext libn 65-. 9: ALA; MichLA (sec Co Lib Sect); IdaLA; PNLA. 13: Yes. 14: Readers' serv (adult & child), lib devel. 15: Box 2614 (01) Res 1111 N 7th, Boise Id 83702.

FENSKE, RUTH E(LIZABETH). b Menomonie Wis 29 S 45. 5: Willamette U 63-67 (Math) BA; UWis 67-69 (LS) MA. 6: Fr, Ger. 7: Projects asst Middleton Med Lib UWis (Madison) 67-69; Trainee WashU School of Med (St Louis) 69. 9: MedLA; SLA. 14: Catlg, bibliog of sci. 15: 103 N Randall apt I, Madison Wi 53715.

FENSTERMAKER, ELLEN PUTNEY. b State College Penn 6 Jl 17. 5: Oberlin Col 35-39 (Pre-Lib) AB; Drexel 39-40 BS in LS. 7: Sub-prof US Fed Wks Agency, Wash DC 41-42, Ref libn 42-44; Asst ref libn US Pub Rds Admin, Wash DC 44-4; Ref libn US Bur of Pub Rds, Wash DC 47-51; Ref libn Montgomery Co (Md) Dept of Pub Libs (Wheaton Lib) 55-61, Ref Libn (Bethesda Lib) 61-. 10: Quoto Internat. 14: Adult serv & ref. 15: 1715 Republic rd, Silver Spring Md 20902.

FENSTERMANN, DUANE W. b Greeley Iowa 25 Ja 39. 4: Marlene K Fiet. 5: UDubuque 56-58 (Phil); Morningside Col 58-61 (Phil) BA; Duke Divinity Sch 61-64 (Theol) BD; UNC (Chapel Hill) 64-66 MS in LS. 7: Acquis libn Luther Col Lib 66. 8: Dir NE Iowa Union List of Ser Proj 67-. 9: ALA; ASLS; IowaLA; NE Iowa Acad LA. 12: Comp "Northeast Iowa Union List of Serials", (68, 69); "Computers and Data Processing: a Bibliography of Materials Available from the Luther College Library" (68); "A Bibliography of Selected

Latin American Resources Held by the Luther College Library" (69). 14: Acquis, tech processing. 15: Luther Col Lib, Decorah Ia 52101.

FENTON, ELIZABETH ANNE. b Toronto Can 20 F 38. 5: UToronto 63-66 BA, 66-67 BLS. 6: Fr. 7: V-pres Research Canadian Tele Employees Assn Montreal 67-. 9: CanLA; MontSLA. 15: Canadian Telephone Employees Assoc Rm 1270, Place du Canada, Montreal 247 Can.

FENTON, CALVIN D. b Carthage NY 7 F 39. 5: SUNY(Albany) 58-62 (Soc Studies) AB (cum laude), 62-63 MSLS. 7: Libn Milne Sch SUNY(Albany) summer 63; Asst libn NY Mil Acad, Cornwall-on-Hudson NY 63-66; Hd libn & A-v dir NY Mil Acad Cornwall-on-Hudson NY 66-; (Sp5) NY Army Res Nat Guard 64-70. 9: NYLA; NY State TA. 10: SUNY Albany Lib Sch Alumni Assn. 14: Ref, catlg, young adult serv. 15: NY Mil Acad, Cornwall-on-Hudson NY 12520.

FENTON, PETER LOW. b Providence RI 2 N 41. 4: Anne Peyton Nicholson. 5: Bowdoin Col 60-64 (Eng, Art) BA; Columbia 65-66 (LS) MS. 6: Ger, Fr. 7: Asst in charge spec collections Bowdoin Col 64-65; Asst period libn Bucknell U 66-67; Staff assoc Coun for the Advancement of Small Cols, Wash DC 67-68; Hd libn Franklin Pierce Col 68-. 9: ALA; NELA; NHLA. 10: NH Col & Univ Coun (Libn's Policy Com). 12: Ed "Newsletter" "Membership Directory" Coun for the Advancement of Small Cols (67-68). 14: Bldg Planning, admin. 15: Box 141, Dublin NH 03444.

FENTON, YVONNE. b South Shields Eng 9 Ag 27. 5: Kings Col UDurham (Eng) 45-48 (Fr, Ger) BA; UZurich (Switzerland) summer 47; 52 Associateship of the Lib Assn Gt Brit. 6: Fr, Ger, Dutch. 7: Lib asst City Libs, Newcastle upn Tyne 48-50; Lib asst Pub Ref Lib, Liverpool 50-52, Catlgr 52-53; Catlgr UAlta Lib 53-60, Asst chief catlgr 60-. 14: Catlg. 15: 10835 65th ave, Edmonton Alta Can.

FENWICK, ELEANOR MARIE. b Leonardtown Md 2 F 38. 5: Towson State Col 55-59 (Educ) BS; Fla State U 63-64 (LS) MS; Fla State U 67-68 (LS). 7: Tchr Bd of Educ, St Marys Co Md 59-63; Libn Bd of Educ, Baltimore Co Md 64-65; Libn of elem schs Bd of Educ, St Mary;s Co Md 65-67; Supv of Libs Bd of Educ 68-. 9: NEA-DAVI ALA; Md State Tchrs Assn; MdLA; St Marys Co EA. 10: St Marys Co Hist Soc; Kappa Delta Pi, Beta Phi Mu; Colonial Dames. 14: Sch libs, wk with child. 15: Box 352, Leonardtown Md 20650.

FENWICK, SARA INNIS. 5: West Res BA; Chicago (LS) MA. 7: Asst child libn, yp libn, head of wk with child Pub Lib, Wilkes-Baree Penn 31-44; Asst to dir of wk with child Enoch Pratt Free Lib, Baltimore 44-46; Head of wk with child Gary Pub Lib, Gary Ind 46-49; Elem sch libn Lab Sch, UChicago 49-56; Asst Prof & Assoc Prof Grad Lib Sch UChicago 56-. 8: Summer sch visiting lecturer & instr in Ext Center Ind U; NEA Del to World Confed of Orgs of the Tchg Profn, Rio de Janeiro, 63; Fulbright Sr Lecturer to Australia, 64; Adv Com of "Britannica Jr Encyclopedia, Bd of Pre-Collegiate Educ; Adv Com of Reading Conf; Com on Preparation of Secon Sch Tchrs; Coun of the Grad Sch of Educ UChicago. 9: NCTE; ALAAASchL (past pres); Internat Reading Assn; NEA-DAVI; Assn for Higher Educ; Assn Supv & Curr Devel; IllEA; IllLA. 10: Pi Lambda Theta. 13: Yes. 15: Grad Lib Sch, Univ of Chicago, Chicago.

FENYO, LESLIE A(NTHONY). b Budapest Hungary 10 Ap 15. 4: Eva de Osvath. 5: Sci & LS training in Hungary (Szeged, Budapest). 6: Eng, Ger, Hungarian, Fr, Lat. 7: Gen manager First Hungarian Agric Machine Wks, Budapest 47-49; Dept chief Hungarian Nat Tech Lib, Budapest 50-56; Supv Austrian Documentation Center of Tech & Economy, Vienna 57; Catlgr MacDonald Col McGill U 59-65; Libn N Electric Co Ltd, Montreal 65-. 8: Examining Bd for tech libns in Hungary, Budapest 54-56; Lecturer Tech U(Budapest) 54. 9: CanLA; SLA (Documentation Div); QueLA; Assn International des Documentalists, Paris. 15: 4669 Cote St Catherine rd, Montreal 252 Can.

FERET, BARBARA L. b Detroit Mich 11 Ag 40. 5: UMich 57-61 (Educ) BA, 64-65 AMLS. 6: Ger. 7: Assoc libn Dutchess Commun Col, Poughkeepsie NY 65-. 9: ALA. 13: Yes. 14: Ref. 15: Netherwood rd, Hyde Park NY 13206.

FERGENSON, RUTH L(EAVITT). b St Louis Mo 25 N 07. 4: Moses C Fergenson. 5: Radcliffe 24-28 (Fr) BA; Pratt 28-29 BLS. 6: Fr. 7: Ref libn NY PubLib 96th St Br 29-30; Lib asst Julia Richman High Sch, NYC 30-4; Lib asst in chg of Lib Fores Hills High Sch, NYC 41-49, tchr of lib & libn 49-65; Libn Parkway Sch, Jamaica NY 65-66; Catlgr Nassau Central Sch Dist # 2 66-67; Libn Woodmore Acad 67-68; Asst libn Explorer's Club 68-. 8: Tchr of educ & Lib Sci St Johns U summers 50-55; Asst examiner NYC Bd of Educ 48-62. 9: NYC Sch LA. 10: Phi Beta Kappa; Radcliffe Club of NY; UN Assn; NY Lib Club. 14: Ref, sch lib wk. 15: 110-21 73d rd, Forest Hills NY 11375.

FERGUSON, DONALD WALLACE. b Ridgetown Ont Can 19 O 04. 4: Aurelie Menard. 5: UWest Ont 22-26 (Eng, Fr) BA, 26-27 (Fr) MA; UMich 30-31 (LS) BA. 6: Fr, Ger, Sp, Ital. 7: Asst libn Kenyon Col 32-43; Libn ND State Col 43-62; Catlgr St Marys Col(Winona Minn) 62-63; Asst libn Wis State U(Stvens Point) 63-. 8: Membership Com NDLA 46-54. 9: ALA; NEA; State lib & educ assns. 13: Yes. 14: Catlg. 15: 805 Prentice st, Stevens Point Wis 54481.

FERGUSON, DOROTHY G. b Seattle Wash 10 Ag 28. 4: Roland C Ferguson. 5: UWash 46-50 (Anthrop) BA, 66-69 (Libnship) Masters. 7: Sec Gen Serv Admin, Seattle 51-52; Sec aeronautical Engring Dept UWash 52-54. 9: ALA-CSD. 10: Nat Audubon Soc; Nat Conservancy; Nat Wildlife Soc. 14: Child serv, serv to unreached. 15: 14416 NE 16th pl, Belleune Wa 98004.

FERGUSON, DOUGLAS. b Detroit Mich 4 Jl 35. 5: Macalester Col 52-56 (Phil) BA; UCal 9berkeley) 66-67 MLS. 6: Fr, Ger. 7: Soc wkr Co Welfare Merit Syst, St Paul 57-61; Supv Standard Oil Co, San Francisco 61-66; Research intern Indian Nat Sci Documentation Ctr, New Delhi 67-68; Research asst UCal Inst for Lib Research 69-. 9: ALA; ASIS; CalStateLA. 10: AAAS. 11: Berkeley Prof Schs Fellow; India 67-68. 14: Ref, automation, operations research. 15: 3996 Sacramento st, San Francisco Ca 94118.

FERGUSON, ELEANOR A (ARCHER). b Indianapolis Ind 23 Mr 09. 5: Radcliffe 26-30 (Hist & Lit) AB; Simmons 33-34 (LS) BS; Columbia 48 MS in LS. 6: Fr. 7: Asst child dept Utic Pub Lib, Utica NY 34-36; Child libn Rochester Pub Lib, Rochester NY 37-40; Head Libn James Prendergast Free Lib, Jamestown NY 40-45; Head Libn Free Pub Lib, Council Bluffs Iowa 45-48; Chief Libn Dearborn Pub Lib, Dearborn Mich 46-55; Dir Lib Serv Center State Dept of Educ, Middletown Conn 55-57; Exec Sec ASL, PLA, ALA 57-. 9: AEA; ALA. 10: Soc of Ind Pioneers. 12: Articles on libs "Book of the States, "Municipal Yearbook. 13: Yes. 14: Admin, wk with child, State lib ext. 15: ALA 50 E Huron st, Chicago Il 60611.

FERGUSON, ELIZABETH. b Willoughby Ohio 27 Ja 06. 5: Middlebury Col 2325 (Music); Oberlin 2527 (Eng Lit) AB; West Res 2930 BS in LS. 7: Child dept Pub Lib, Cleveland 2930; Ref libn Pub Lib, Lima Ohio 3043; Libn Inst of Life Insurance 4469; Inst in spec libs Queens Col of Gen Studies (NYC) 5355; Lecturer in spec libs Pratt Inst 59. 8: Supv of non-prof train courses Ballard Sch YWCA NY 49-; Continuing mem of Ballard Sch Com as rep of NY Chap SLA. 9: ALA; SLA (pres 52-53, Exec Bd 51-54; chm of div & 4 coms); CNLA (chm, SLA Rep, Trustee 54-62); LPRC (pres 49-50). 12: "Creation & Development of an Insurance Library," with co-author (49); Ed "Sources of Insurance Statistics" (65); Consul ed "Insurance Literature" (monthly); Comp annual lists of specialized insurance ref bks. 13: Yes. 14: Ref, bibliog, life & health insurance, pub rel, tchg. 15: 105 E 24th st, New York NY 10010.

FERGUSON, FERN ELOIS (WILSON). b Wheeling WVa 10 Ja 13. 4: George J Ferguson. 5: Bethany Col (WVa) 30-34 (Eng) BA; UIll 35 BLS, UAriz 68-69 (Educ). 6: Fr. 7: Libn circ Northwestern U 35-37; Libn circ Ohio Co Pub Lib, Wheeling WVa 37-39; Libn Wheeling High Sch, Wheeling WVa 59-61; Ref libn Tucson Pub Lib 61-64, Wilmot Br Libn 65-. 67; Tucson Pub Schs 68-. 9: ALA; Ariz State LA; Tucson EA. 10: DAR; AAUW. 14: Ref, br lib wk, sch libs. 15: 3220 Via Celeste, Tucson Az 85718.

FERGUSON, (HELEN) ONETA (GALBREATH). b Torndale Tex 18 Ja 20. 4: Volney B Ferguson. 5: Edinburgh Jr Col(Tex) 38-39 (Eng) AA; Southwestern U 43 (Eng) BA; Southwest Tex State summer 45 (Eng); E Tex State U 60 (Eng) MA, 66 MS in LS. 6: Sp. 7: Tchr Lawrence Chapel Sch, Williamson Co Tex 40-42; Tchr Coupland High Sch, Coupland Tex 42-44; Libn Allan Jr High Sch, Austin Tex 44-45; Tchr Flour Bluff Sch, Corpus Christi Tex 45-46; Tchr Dimple High Sch, Clarksville Tex 47-48, 57-59; Tchr Detroit Tex HiSch 49; Tchr Jarrell High Sch, Jarrell Tex 59-61; Libn San Saba High Sch 61-62; Tchr Cisco High Sch 62-63, Libn 63-64; Chief libn Cisco Jr Col 64-. 9: ALA; TexLA; Tex Jr Col TA. 10: Delphian Club; Delta Kappa Gamma; Pi Gamma Mu; Phi Theta Kappa; Alpha Chi. 13: Yes. 14: Acquis, admin, Texana collection. 15: 1508 Bullard, Cisco Tx 76437.

FERGUSON, JOHN W. b Ash Grove Mo 4 N 36. 4: Nancy (Southerland). 5: Southwest Mo State Col 54-58 (Geog) BS; UOkla 61-62 MLS. 6: Ger. 7: Lib page Springfield Pub Lib, Springfield Mo 52-58, Admin asst 58-61; Assoc central libn Pub Libs of Springfield & Greene Co, Springfield Mo 62-64; Asst co libn Cass, Jackson & Platte Co Pub Libs, Independence Mo 64-66; Asst dir Mid-Continent Pub Lib 66-. 9: ALA; MoLA (sec Pb Lib Div 65, pres 68). 10: Mo Libs Film Cooperative (Bd 65-). 15: 15616 E 24 hwy, Independence Mo 64050.

FERGUSON, MALCOLM MAGOUN. b Arlington Mass 1 O 19. 4: Priscilla L Taylor. 5: Harvard 39-42, 46 (Eng Lit) AB; Simmons 60-63 MSLS. 6: Fr, Ger. 7: (S/Sgt) Med Admin Corps 42-45; Owner Brookfield Bkshop, Sanbornville NH 46-54; Libn Clarostat Mfg Co Inc, Dover NH 54-56; Ref libn MIT Lincoln Lab(Lexington Mass) 56-63; Supv lib serv Itek Corp, Lexington Mass 63-. 8: Active in out-of-print bk dealing & collecting; writing free-lance fantasy & reg lit; bk reviewing. 9: SLA (chm Aerospace Div 64-65, Boston Chap Bulletin ed). 12: Assoc ed "Proceedings in Print 64, 65. 13: Yes. 14: Ref, acquis. 15: 396 Main st, West Concord Mass 01781.

FERGUSON, RICHARD DIMITRI JR. b Richmond Ind 29 S 33. 4: Grace Hollingshead. 5: BostonU 58-61 (Sociol) AB, 61-62 (Pub Rel), (Communicational Research) MS; Simmons 66-69 MLS. 6: Fr. 7: Surgical tech HM2 USN Hosp Corps 54-58; Computer programmer tech documentation Honeywell EDP 63-67; Info specialist Bolt Beronek & newman 67-68; Systems analyst Amer Alumni Coun summer 67; Info specialist Edu Com 68-. 8: Research assoc Educ Info Netwk 68-69; Info specialist BBN/MGH hosp computer project 67-68; Research assoc Practice Oriented Info Syst Experiment & NLM; Studies & Nat Agric Lib Netwk. 9: ASIS; ALA; Soc Tech Writers & Publishers. 10: Boy Scouts Amer. 12: "Directory of Information Networks and Network Activities" (69). 13: Yes. 14: Info storage & retr syst, info netwks. 15: 314 Oakland st, Wellesley Ma 02181.

FERING, ADELE (SMITH). b Wilmington Del 21 Ag 10. 4: Arnold M Fering. 5: UDel 28-32 (Eng Lit) BA; Drexel 43 BS LS. 6: Fr. 7: Lib asst UDel 32-42; Circ asst Swarthmore Col 42-43; Catlgr US Bur Budget Lib, Wash DC 43-45; Catlgr Head of sers catlg US Dept Agric Lib, Wash DC 45-51; Head catlg sect US Patent Off Sci Lib, Wash DC 51-. 9: SLA (past corres sec DC chap); DCLA; Potomac Tech Proc Libns (sec 61-62). 11: Govt Superior Performance Award 63. , 67. 14 Catlg, tech proc. 15: 2605 Adams Mill rd NW, Wash DC 20009.

FERN, ALAN MAXWELL. b Detroit 19 O 30. 4: Lois Karbel. 5: UChicago 48-60 (Hist of Art) AB, MA, PhD; ULondon Courtauld Inst of Art 54-55 (Hist of Art). 6: Fr, Ger. 7: Faculty The Col UChicago 53-54, 55-61; Asst curator of fine prints, Prints & Photographs Div LC 61-62, Curator 62-64, Asst chief 64-. 9: SLA; Col Art Assn; Print Coun of Amer (Bd Dirs); Amer IO PHIC Arts (Bd Dirs). 11: Fulbright Grant 54-55. 12: "L Pissarro/Eragny Press" (57); Co-auth "Art Nouveau" (60); "Word & Image" (69); Bk rev ed "Art Journal". 13: Yes. 14: Hist of bks & prints, picture libnship, curatorial wk, hist of art. 15: LC, Wash DC 20540.

FERN, ANNETTE. b Detroit 13 Mr 37. 5: Reed Col 54-58 (Eng Lit) AB; San Francisco State Col 59; Drama UChicago 62- AM LS, 68. 6: Fr, Ital. 7: Asst archives Art Inst of Chicago 59-60; Sales child bks Krochs & Brentanos Chicago 60; UChicago Lib Serv asst Bus & Econ Lib 61-62, Head modern lang reading room 62-63, Asst ref & intrlib loan 64-65, Asst ref libn 65-. 14: Ref, performing arts. 15: Univ of Chicago Lib, 1116 E 59th st, Chicago Il 60637.

FERN, LOIS. b Detroit 2 O 34. 4: Alan M Fern. 5: UChicago 51-54 BA, 55-61 (LS) MA. 6: Fr. 7: Lib asst UChicago Lib 54-57; Asst managing ed "Journal of General Education, Chicago 56-59; Asst ref libn UChicago 59-61; Ref libn US Info Agency, Wash DC 63-. 8: Consul libn to Chesapeake & Potomac Telephone Cos 62; Chm Task Force on Pub Rel, Fed Lib Com 68-. 9: ALA-ACRL (Subj Spec Sect 67-70); DCLA (Prog Chm 67-68, Bd Dirs 68-71). 11: Meritorious Honor Awad,U .' 14: Ref. 15: 3605 Raymond st, Chevy Chase Md 20015.

FERNANDES, ELIZABETH (ZIEGLER). b Trenton NJ 8 Ja 09. 5: Trenton State 25-27 (Educ) Certif& rutgers ext 33-37 (Educ) BS; NJ Lib Commsn Summer Sch 28-32 (LS) Certif. 7: Gen asst Trenton Pub Lib 27-35, Sr asst circ 35-45, Act hd circ 45-46, Prin libn Cadwalader br (Trenton) 46. 8: Act Dir Trenton Pub Lib 61. 9: ALA (Notable Bks Com); NJLA (chm Human Relat Com 60-62). 10: LWV; Mercer Co Assn for Retarded Child; Trenton Hist Assn. 14: Br wk with emphasis on disadvantaged child. 15: 202 N Hermitage ave, Trenton NJ 08618.

FERNNDEZ, NORA. b Havana Cuba 22 Ja 29. 5: U de la Habana 45-49 (Estudis linguisticos-literarios) Fra; Escuela Cubana de Bibliotecarios 50-51 Bibliotecaria. 6: Sp. 7: Catlgr Sociedad Economica de Amigos del Pais, Havana Cuba 52-53; Libn Direccion Tecnica de Fiscalizacion y Sistemas de Contabilidad, Havana Cuba 53-56; Catlgr Pan American Union Columbus Mem Lib, Wash DC 56-. 8: Prof of lib sci, Escuela Cubana de Bibliotecarios 53; Beca-trabajo otorgada LC 51-52. 9: ALA; Asociacion Cubana de Bibliotecarios (sec 52-54). 14: Catlg, clsf. 15: 4201 Lee hwy apt 201, Arlington Va 22207.

FERNANDEZ-CABALLERO, CARLOS FRANCISCO SOLANO. b Emboscada Paraguay 23 F 37. 5: Facultad de DerechoU Nacional de Asuncion 56-59, 65-67 (Law); Escuela de BibliotecariosU Nacional de Cordoba (Argentina) 61-63 (LS) Mibrarian; Syracuse 67-68 msls. 6: Guarani, Castillian, Portu, Ital. 7: Paraguayan Army Inf sgt 54-56; Dir of lib Facultad de Ciencias San Luis Argentina 64-65; Chief libn Binational Ctr Lib, Asuncion Paraguay 65-67; Libn Instituto de Ciencias, Asuncion Paraguay 66-68; Catlgr LC 68-. 9: Asociacion de Bibliotecarios del Paraguay (treas). 10: Asociacion de Bibliotecarios Graduados de la Republica Argentina. 11: Fulbright Scholar 67-68. 14: Bibliog, hist of bks & libs. 15: 10 10th st SE, Washington DC 20003.

FERRAND, WILLIAM GRAMMONT. b Columbia La 14 S 10. 4: Frances Lamar Ferrand. 5: La Col 27-30 (Eng); SW La Inst 39-40 BA; West Res 40-41 BS in L Sc. 6: Fr, Sp. 7: USA Sgt 41-46; NY & Cuba Mail Steamship Co, NYC 46; Northwestern U Lib 48-52, 65-; UMo Lib (Columbia) 52-53; A C McClurg & Co, Chicago 53-64. 9: ALA. 14: Acquis. 15: 2200 Hartzell st, Evanston Il 60201.

FERRARA, MARK MICHAEL. b Bayonne NJ 15 F 35. 4: Barbara Stephen. 5: Seton Hall 57-61 9soc Studies) BS, 61-65 (Asian Area Studies) MA; Rutgers 65-67 MLS; Jersey City State Col 67 (Amer Hist). 6: Ital. 7: Specialist 3rd/cl food serv USA, Europe 54-56; Employment coun NJ State Employment Serv, Jersey City NJ 61; Tchr Dover Sr High Sch, Dover NJ 61-66; Libn Bloomfield Sr High Sch, Bloomfield NJ 66-67; Admin serv libn newark State Col 67-. 9: ALA; -ACRL (Info Sci & Automation Div); NJEA. 10: AAUP; Newark State Col Fac Assn. 14: Admin, circ, reader serv. 15: 25 Manor dr, Newark NJ 07106.

FERRELL, DOROTHY ANNE P(ERKINS). b Nicholasville Ky 6 N 14. 4: James Edwin Ferrell. 5: UKy 33-37 (LS) AB; Peabody summers 47-49 (LS) MA; Fugazzi Col of Bus (Lexington Ky) 41 (Shorthand & Typing); UVa ext 48 (A-V). 7: Supv Nat Youth Admin, Hopkinsville Ky 40-42; Sec Nat Union Fire Insurance Co, Louisville Ky 42-44; Stenographer Tobacco By Products & Chem Co, Louisville 44-45; Clerk 1105th AAF BU CRBW-ATC Miami Army Air Field, Miami Fla 45-46; Sec bkkeeper Cumberland Falls (Ky) State Park 46; Libn Versailles (Ky) High Sch 46-47; Libn Clifton Forge (Va) High Sch 47-60; Lbn Clifton Forge (Va) High Sch 47-60; Libn C & O Sch of Nurs, Clifton Forge Va 57-; Asst libn Mary Baldwin Col (Va) 60-. 9: ALA; SELA; VaLA. 10: Beta Sigma Phi. 14: Catlg. 15: 1001 Selma blvd, Staunton Va 24401.

FERRELL, EDITH (HAY). b Nether Providence Twp Penn 12 F 32. 4: William Russell Ferrell. 5: Swarthmore 50-54 (Hist) BA; Boston U 61-66 (Adult Educ) M Ed; Simmons 66-68 (LS) MS. 6: Ger. 7: Curriculum ctr lib coord Harvard Graduate Sch of Educ & Lesley Col Libs 68-. 9: ALA. 14: Educ & Behavioral Sci Libs. 15: 222 Upland rd, Cambridge Ma 02140.

FERREN, DOROTHY ADELE. b Mountain View Cal 16 S 20. 5: Pacific Union Col 38-42; Columbia Union Col 43-44 (Eng) BA; CathU 45-47 BS in LS; USoCal 56, 58 MS in LS. 7: Asst libn Seventh-day Adventist Theol Sem, Wash DC 44-47, Act libn 47-48; Asst libn Andrews U 48-54; Assoc libn Pacific Union Col 54-61, Assoc libn 61-. 9: ALA; CalLA. 14: Catlg. 15: 380 Sky Oaks dr, Angwin Cal 94508.

FERRERO, LUCIA N. b Penn 13 D 23. 5: Mt Mercy Col 41-45 (Bio) AB; De Paul 54-58 (Hist) MA; Fordham 58- (Hist); Rutgers 64-66 MLS. 6: Ital, Fr, Sp, Ger. 7: Med tech Research & Educ Hosp UIll(Chicago) 53-57; Tchr Mother of Sorrows, Blue Island Ill 57-58; Tchr Aquinas High Sch, Bronx NY 58-60; Med tech NY Hosp Cornell Med 60-66; Libn NYC Pub Lib 65-66; Libn-catlgr Yonkers Bd of Educ, Yonkers NY 66-68; Libn Scarsdale NY 68-. 9: ALA; NYStateLA. 10: Nat Audubon Soc; Nat Wildlife Fed; Sierra Club; Wilderness Soc; Defenders of Wildlife; Renaissance Soc of Amer; Cath Hist

Assn of Amer; AHA; Medieval Acad. 14: Catlg, rare bks. 15: Scarsdale High School Lib, Scarsdale NY 10583.

FERRING, (E) GERALDINE. b Dubuque Iowa 29 Mr 12. 5: Drake U 30-34 (Eng) BA; UMich 39-40 MALS; USan Francisco 50-58 (Admin & Supv) Tchg Credential. 6: Fr, Ger. 7: Tchr Patterson Schs, Patterson Iowa 34-37; Periods libn Drake U 42-43; Libn N Mich U 40-45; Libn & instr U High Sch & Dept of Libnship UMich 45-46; Libn Will Rogers Jr High Sch, Long Beach Cal 46-47; Libn Napa Jr Col 47-49; Libn Mission High San Francisco Unified Sch Dist 49-50, Libn order & dept Secondary Schs 50-58, Supv libs & textbks 58-. 8: Dir of Libs Internat Sch, Bangkok Thailand 64-65. 9: ALA (Life mem); NEA; CalLA; Cal Tchrs Assn; CalASchL (past pres); Women's Nat Bk Assn; Nat Council Administrative Women in Educ. 10: Cath Profess Women. 13: Yes. 14: Supv. 15: 405 Serrano dr apt 6-J, San Francisco Ca 94132.

FERRIS, (HOPE) DONALD. b Allentown Penn 2 O 15. 5: Lehigh 34-39 (Engnr Physics) BS; Fla State U 49-52 (LS) MS. 7: (Maj) US Army (Armor) 39-47; Tchr Dade Co (Fla) Pub Schs, Miami Fla 47-51; Libn UTenn Martin Br (Martin Tenn) 51-57; Libn Agric Lib UMinn(St Paul) 57-63; Head order unit Purdue U 63-. 9: ALA; SLA; TennLA (pres 56-57); MinnLA; IndLA; Ohio Valley Group of Teh Serv Libns. 10: AAUP; Beta Phi Mu. 14: Admin, tech serv. 15: RR10, Lafayette In 47906.

FERRIS, LENORE T(HROCKMORTON). b Seattle 3 Ag 13. 4: Charles F Ferris Jr. 5: UWash 31-35 (Arts & Sci) AB, 35-36 (LS) AB. 7: Libn Seattle Pub Lib 36-41, Libn educ, psych. sociol dept 60-68, first asst 69-. 9: Wash LA. 10: Ryther Child Care; 4 & 20 Club. 15: 2912 W Boston st, Seattle Wa 98199.

FERRIS, WILLIAM H. b Rye NY 9 D 37. 4: Judith Ann. 5: Bishop'sU 56-60 BA; UNB 65 BEduc; EmoryU 67-68 MLn. 6: Fr. 7: Tchr Bishop's Col Sch 62-67; Catlgr-collections Harriet Irving Lib UNB 68-69; Libn St Andrew's Col 69-. 9: CanLA; CACUL; APLA. 14: Sch libs (org & mgt). 15: st Andrew's College, Aurora Ont Can.

FERRY, MARY R (DEVERS). b Hazleton Penn 6 My 17. 4: Paul H Ferry. 5: Kutztown State Col 33-35 (Elem Educ) Certif; Mulhenberg Col 36-39 (Secondary Educ) BS; Temple summers 40-44 (LS) MA equivalent. 7: Tchr & libn McAdoo (Penn) High Sch 39-49; Libn & tchr Penn State U (Hazleton) 56-. 9: PennLA. 10: Penn State U Womens Auxiliary. 11860 04: Rose Scolnik. 14: Ref, tchg ref. 15: Penn State U, Hazleton Penn 18201.

FESLER, ELMA F (DAVIS). b Eugene Ore 5 O 13. 4: Chauncey Fesler. 5: Marycrest Col 64 BEd; UIll 67-69 (LS) Masters. 7: Tchr-libn Toulon Elem, Toulon Ill 51-62; Jr high tchr Colona Pub Sch, Colona Ill 62-65; Elem libn Moline Pub Schs, Moline Ill 65-68; Grad asst/tchr UIll (Champaign-Urbana) 68-69; Tchr lib sci UWest Ill 69-. 8: NDEA Lib Inst IndU (Bloomington) 65. 9: ALA; ACEI; NEA; IllEA; IllASchL. 10: Delta Kappa Gamma; Beta Phi Mu. 14: Sch libnship, tchg lib sci, multi-media materials. 15: 375-2 Eggers drm Macomb Il 61455.

FESSLER, AARON LOUIS. b NYC 2 N 17. 4: Rose Scolnik. 5: City Col of NY 36-41 (Psych) BSS; Columbia 47-50 MSLS. 6: Ger. 7: Occupational analyst US Employment Serv, Wash DC 43-47; Asst ref libn Russell Sag Found, NYC 47-49; Head ref dept Cooper Union (NYC) 49-58; Research libn Philips Labs, Briarcliff Manor NY 58-61; Chief tech libn Olin Mathieson Chem Corp, New Haven Conn 61-65; Dir of Lib Bard Col 66-. 8: Manager Reprint Expediting Serv (ALA) 55-58; Instr in Lib Sci So Conn State Col 61-. 9: SLA (chm Educ Com Conn Valley Chap 63-64); Assn for Computing Machinery. 10: Prof Consul SLA 58-; Bd of Dir No Haven Mem Lib 63-; Conn State Lib Res Adv Com 65-; Leader Great Bks Discussion Group. 12: ""Newspapers: United STATES & Foreign (57); Ed ""Reprint Expediting Servive Bulletin; Bk reviewer ""Library Journal (54-). 13: Yes. 14: Admin, educ for libnship, lit of the scis. 15: 45 Allendale dr, North Haven Conn 06473.

FETROS, JOHN G. b Billings Mont 19 Ag 32. 5: UCal (Berkeley) 50-54 (Bus Admin) BS; USoCal 63-64 MLS. 7: Supply requirements off USAF, McClellan AFB Sacramento & Norton afb san Bernardino Cal 55-63; Yeoman YN3 USN 55-57; Ref libn San Francisco Pub Lib 64-. 9: ALA (Code of Ethics Com). 10: Beta Phi Mu; Phi Beta Kappa. 13: Yes. 14: Ref. 15: 3220 24th st, Sacramento Ca 95818.

FETTERER, RAYMOND A. b Sheboygan Wis 2 Jl 03. 5: St Francis Seminary (Milwaukee) 27-31 (Philos) BA, 31-35 (Church Hist) MA; UMich summer 34 (LS); Catholic U 36-39 (Math) MS, summer 33 (LS). 6: Ger, Lat. 7: Curate St Annes Parish, Milwaukee Wis 35-36; Instr math & physics, & asst libn St Francis Seminary (Milwaukee) 39-47, Libn 47-. 9: CathLA (chm Seminary Libs Sect 56-57, sec-treas 57-66, chm Ecumenical Periodical Exch 64-; chm Wis Unit 53-55); WisLA. 13: Yes. 14: Admin. 15: St Francis Seminary, 3257 S Lake dr, Milwaukee Wi 53207.

FETTERLEY, MABLE LOUISE (McCALLA). b St Catharines Ont Can 21 F 13. 5: St Catharines Collegiate Inst; Macdonald Inst, Ont Agric Col 33 (Home Econ) Assoc. 7: Asst dietitian Peel Mem Hosp, Brampton Ont 34-35; Asst libn Norton Co, Chippawa Ont 59-65, Libn 65-. 9: SLA. 10: Imprial Order Daughters of the Empire (Regent 45-48); Can Club of the Niagara Frontier (Dir 65). 12: "Bibliography on Comminution (65). 14: Admin. 15: 424 LaMonte ave, Chippawa 101 Ont Can.

FETZ, BETTY (ESSEX). b Hope Ind 19 Ja 22. 4: Jack E Fetz. 5: IndU 40-43 (Eng) BS in Ed; Carnegie Inst 45-47 BS in LS. 7: Lib staff IndU (Bloomington) 44, 46-47, Catlgr 47-48; Libn Brownstown High Sch, Brownstown Ind 44-45; Catlgr Ball State U 65-. 9: Ind State LA; Ohio Valley Tech Serv Libns. 10: AAUW. 14: Catlg. 15: 2012 Cambridge, Muncie In 47304.

FETZ, FRANCES D (DALE). b Springfield Ohio 20 Je 11. 5: UAla 32-34, 41. 7: Spec serv libn: Ft Story Va 55-56, Redstone Ala 56-61, Camp McCoy Wis 62, Ft Benjamin Harrison ind 62-63, Yuma Proving Ground Ariz 65-68; Libn Welfare & Morale Sect, Dugway Proving ground Utah 63-65; Libn personnel serv, APO San Francisco 68-. 14: Org, planning, reader's adv serv. 15: 6112 Air Base Sq Box 108, APO San Francisco Ca 96299.

FIALA, SISTER ANNE RSM. b Karlin Mo 10 D 22. 5: Mt Mary Col (Milwaukee) (Hist) BA; Rosary Col MS in LS. 6: Czech, Fr. 7: Head libn Catherine McAuley Lib Mt Mercy Col (Cedar Rapids Iowa) 58-. 9: ALA; IowaLA; Cedar Rapids Libns. 14: Ref, catlg. 15: Mt Mercy Col, Cedar Rapids Iowa.

FIALKIN, HILDA (ZATLIN). b NYC 4 My 15. 4: Harry Fialkin. 5: Hunter Col 30-34 (Hist) BA; Columbia 35-40 (Eng) MA, 57-60 (LS) MS. 7: Tchg high schs, NYC 35-40; Libn Hauppauge High Sch, Hauppauge NY 57-. 9: ALA; SCLA; NY State TA; NEA. 15: 55 St Marks lane, Islip NY 11751.

FIANT, ELENA MARIA (DOVYDENAS). b Kaunas Lithuania 25 N 36. 4: W D Fiant. 5: Wilkes Col 55-59 (Eng) BA; Columbia 59-60 (LS) MS. 6: Lithuanian. 7: Libn E Patterson (NJ) High Sch 60-61; Child libn Brooklyn (NY) Pub Lib 61-64; Child libn Summit (NJ) Pub Lib 64-; Reg libn San Mateo Co Lib 65-. 14: Child & adult pub lib. 15: 633 Prospect, San Carlos Ca 94070.

FICHTELBERG, DORIS (VIRGINIA HORNBURG). b Wellesville NY 17 My 25. 4: Leo E Fichtelberg. 5: Julliard Sch of Mus 43-44; Hiram Col 44-47 AB; Rutgers 64-66 MLS. 6: Ger, Fr, Sp. 7: Lib Asst Rec Lib Donnell Free Pub Lib, NYC 56-60; Shelf Libn Catlg Dept Princeton U 63-64; Lib asst catlg dept Rutgers 64-66, Mus Lib PT 65-66; Acquis lib Free Pub Lib, Elizabeth NJ 66-68, Mus libn 68-. 9: ALA; NJLA. 14: Music, ctlg. 15: 307 Salem rd, Union NJ 07083.

FICHTELBERG, LEO E. b NYC 14 N 29. 4: Doris Hornburg. 5: City Col (NYC) 48-53 (Anthropology, Sociol) AB; Black Mt Col 56 (Poetry, Creative Writing); Rutgers 57-58 MLS. 7: Truck Driver (Pvt-2) US Army 53-55; Bkkeeper Excelsior Quick Frozen Meat Prods, LIC NY 55-56; Bkkeeper LF Dommerick & Co, NYC 56-57; Sr libn Brooklyn Pub Lib 58-61; Adult serv field libn NJ State Lib 61-64; Adult serv coordinator Free Pub Lib of Woodbridge (NJ) 64-66; Asst dir Free Pub Lib, Summit NJ 66; Asst libn dir Free Pub Lib, Union Twp 66-68; Lib dir Free Pub Lib, Paterson NJ 69-. 8: Nat Lib Week Coord (NJ) 61-64. 9: ALA; AEA; NYLA; NJLA (chm com on Restrict Lib Practices of Adult Serv Sect 65. 12: Ed "Newsletter Pub & Sch Lib Serv Bur, NJ State Lib (61- 64). 13: Yes. 14: Adult serv, admin. 15: 307 Salem rd, Union NJ 07083.

FICKAS, EDITH JO (SILVERSTEIN). b Detroit 25 D 40. 5: Wayne State 58-61 (LS) BS in Educ; Peabody 63-64 MA in LS. 6: Dutch. 7: Libn Adams Jr High Sch, Wayne Mich 61-62; Libn Oak Ridge Pub Lib, Oak Ridge Tenn 64-65; Child libn Glendora Pub Lib, Glendora Ca 66-69. 9: ALA. 14: Child serv. 15: 255 Spinks Canyon rd, Duarte Ca 91010.

FIDLER, (LEAH) JOSEPHINE. b Glenville WVa 23 O 32. 5: Glenville State Col 50-54 (Eng, LS) AB Ed (magna cum laude); Ind U 56-60 MA in LS. 6: Fr. 7: Libn Tygarts Valley High Sch, Mill Creek WVa 54-55; Asst libn Glenville State Col 55-57; Head Libn Alderson-Broaddus Col, Philippi WVa 57-62; Instr in Lib Sci Marshall U 62-64, Asst catlg libn 64-66, Bibliogr 66-. 8: Libn at Marshall Lab Sch & act head of Dept of LVIB Sci 62-63. 9: ALA-ACRL (Tri-State sec-treas 64-); WVaLA (chm Col & U Libs Sect 62-63); Cabell Co LA, Ohio Valley Group Technical Service Librarians. 10: AAUP; AAUW; Marshall U Faculty Womens Cl; Alpha Beta Alpha; Beta Phi Mu; Delta Kappa Gamma. 12: Asst ed "West Virginia Libraries" (67-). 14: Lib educ, admin, bibliog. 15: 423 6th ave Apt A, Huntington WVa 25701.

FIDOTEN, ROBERT EARL. b NYC 21 O 27. 4: Marsha Abrams. 5: NYU 44-49 (Radio) BA; Pratt 49-50 BLS; Sch of Educ(Harvard) 50-52 (Measurement & Exp Methods); UPittsburgh 65- (Info Sci). 7: Libn Emerson Col 50-51; Catlgr Brandeis U 51-52; Lib Supv Link Aviation Inc, Binghamton NY 52-56; Head Libn RIAS Inc, Baltimore 56; Chief Libn Republic Aviation Corp, Farmingdale NY 56-64; Manager info serv Pittsburgh Plate Glass Co, Pittsburgh Penn 64-, Asst dir of research planning & info sci 69-. 8: Appointed by Nassau Co Exec to Adv Com on a Nassau Co(NY) Ref Lib 64; Internat Commsn on Glass, Subcom A-12 (Document & Treatment of Data) 69-; Lib Technic Prog Adv Com, Allegheny Co Commun Col. 9: SLA (NY Chap Sci-Tech Group treas 64, Recruitment chm 63-64, chm Planning Com 67-69; Pittsburgh Chap H W Wilson Com chm 65-66, v-pres 66-67, pres 67-68, dir 68-69; Engrg Div chm-elect 66-67, chm 67-68); Suffolk Co LA (Col & res lib com chm 61-62, v-pres 62-64). 10: Plainview-Old Bethpage Bd of Educ (pres 64); Beta Phi Mu. 13: Yes. 14: Specialized info centers, tech writing, pub rel, research mgt & planning. 15: 118 Greyfriar dr, Pittsburgh 15215.

FIEBERT, ELYSE (EVANS). b Columbus Ohio 14 Jl 27. 4: Richard A Fiebert. 5: Ohio State U 45-48 (Personnel) BS; Drexel 63-66 MSLS; Penn State U 67-68 (Educ); Temple 67-68 (Educ). 7: Research asst Temple U Lib 63-64; Research asst Drexel Inst Lib sch 64-66; Asst libn Haverford Twp Sch Dist Jr High 67; Hd libn Haveford Twp Sch Dist Sr High 67-. 8: Coord Tchr Interaction Sch (soc studies course in urban problems). 9: ALA; NEA; Penn State LA; Penn State EA; Delaware Co Sch Libns. 10: Sponsor, Lib Club; Sponsor, Media Technicians Club; Co-sponsor, Future Tchrs of Amer. 14: YA; research methods, a-v. 15: 1604 Hampton rd, Haverton Pa 19083.

FIELD, CAROLYN W(ICKER). b Melrose Mass 5 N 16. 5: Simmons 38 (LS) BS; Boston U 42-43 (Soc Psych). 6: Fr, Ger, Sp, Lat. 7: Child LIBN NY Pub Lib 38-40; Hostess-libn Boston YMCA 40-42; Instr Sch of Lib Sci Simmons Col 42-43; Field wkr Cuyahoga Co Lib, Cleveland 43-44; Recreation wkr Amer Red Cross, Norwich Eng 44-45; Head of child wk Wilmington Inst Free Lib, Wilmington Del 46-50; Libn New Castle Co Free Lib, Wilmington Del 50-53; Coordinator Wk with child Free Lib of Phila 53-; Instr UNC(Chapel Hill) 52; Instr UDel Grad Sch of Educ 58-59; Instr Drexel Inst of Tech Grad Sch of Lib Sci 61, 63, 65-. 8: Delegate to 1960 White House Conf on Child & Youth; Consul: Penn Governors Com on Child & Youth 59-62; LC Adv Com on Selection of Child Bks for the Blind 58-; Nat Coun of Tchrs of Eng 63-70 "Our Wonderful World, "Book of Knowledge, "School Library Journal. "American Educator Encyclopedia. 09: ALA (Commsn on a Nat Plan for Lib Educ 63-64, Coun 63-67); -CSD (pres 60, chm &/or mem 10 coms 56-66); -LAD (Recruiting Com 57-64); -PLA (mem 2 coms); DelLA (sec 47-48, pres 50-53); PennLA (chm 3 coms). 10: Phila Girl Scout Coun (Program Adv Com 60-); Phila Regional Writers Conf (sec 64-66); Womens Nat Bk Assn; Penn Folklore Soc; Bksellers Assn Phila. 11: Grolier Award 63; Lib Bind Inst Silver Bk Award 63. 13: Yes. 14: Child wk, rare child bks, recruiting, lib educ. 15: 1A Manheim Gardens, Phila 19144.

FIELD, DOROTHY. b Rockville Centre NY 28 Ag 22. 5: Mt Holyoke 40-43 (Psych) AB; Columbia 46-49 (LS) BS. 6: Fr. 7: Jr statistician Guaranty Trust Co of NY 44-45; Jr lib asst, Sr libn pub lib, Rockville Centre NY 45-52, 53; Sr libn adult serv Morris Co Free Lib, Morristown NJ 52-53; Br asst Lib of Hawaii, Honolulu 54; Stat clerk Hawaiian Trust Co, Honolulu 54-55; Sr libn catlg W Orange (NJ) Pub Lib 55-57, Act dir 57; Sr libn lending & ref dept pub lib, Newark NJ 58-60; Field libn State Lib, Santa Fe NM 60-63; Ref libn sci-tech, soc-sci & bus ref div Ariz State U 63-64; Sr libn lending & ref dept pub lib Newark NJ 64-66. 9: ALA (Subs Bks Bull Com 64-65); NJLA; SLA. 14: Ref, adult serv. 15: 372 Mt Prospect ave apt F5, Newark NJ.

FIELD, JEAN. b Boston 12 Jl 36. 4: Charles L Field. 5: Wellesley 54-58 (Biblical Hist) BA; Simmons 60-62 (LS) MS. 6: Fr. 7: Catlgr MIT, Cambridge 64-66; Asst engrg libn MIT 67-68; Acquis libn Sylvania Electronic Systs, E Needham Hts Mass 69-. 14: Catlg, ref, bk sel. 15: 27 Kilsyth rd, Brookline Ma 02146.

FIELD, JOHN (LINWOOD). b Bangalore India 21 Ap 41. 5: Emmanuel Col CambridgeU 60-63 9hist) MA; Inst of Educ LondU 63-64 ELT Certif Ed; UBC 68-69 BLS. 6: Fr, Ital, Sp. 7: Tchr British Coun Eng Lang Inst, Lond 63-64; Tchr Greater Montreal Sch Bd 65-66; Tchr St Georges Sch, Vancouver BC 66-68; Soc sci div UBC 69-. 9: CanLA; ALA; CACUL; BCTF. 14: Com & bus admin, rare bks, mus. 15: 3755 W 6th ave, Vancouver BC Can.

FIELD, JUDITH (JUDY). b Bucyrus Ohio 30 S 39. 4: Nathaniel Lamson Field III. 5: UMich 57-61 (Bus Admin) BBA, 61-62 AMLS, 66- (Intl Bus). 7: Ref libn West Electric/Bell Telephone Labs Inc, Indianapolis 62-65; Libn III-A UMich Natural Sci Lib (Ann Arbor) 65-66, Assoc libn Grad Sch of Bus Admin 66-69, Intl bus libn 69-. 9: SLA; ALA; ASIS. 12: Ed "Indiana Slant" (63-65); Asst ed "Michigan Chapter Bulletin, SLA (68-). 10: Beta Phi Mu; Richmond Area Assn for Retarded Child. 14: Intl bus. 15: 1613 Brooklyn, Ann Arbor Mi 48104.

FIELD, SISTER MARY OP. b Wisconsin Dells Wis 17 Ja 18. 5: Rosary Col 35-39 (Hist) BA; UWis (Madison) 39-40 (Soc Sci) MA; Rosary Col 60 MALS; UCal (Berkeley) summer 68. 06: Fr. 7: Tchr-libn Reedsburg Pub High Sch, Reedsburg Wis 43-44; Tchr-libn Trinity High Sch, River Forest Ill 46-49; Tchr Visitation High Sch, Chicago 49-50; Tchr-libn Sacred Heart Acad, Wash DC 50-53; Tchr-libn Anaconda Central High Sch, Anaconda Mont 53-57; Libn Bishop McGuinness High Sch, Okla City Okla 57-60; Ref & circ libn Rosary Col Lib 60-64, Libn 64-. 9: ALA; CathLA (sec Ill Unit 62-64); IllLA (com mem Col & Res Libs Sect 64-, Ad Hoc Com on Coop). 10: Kappa Delta Pi. 14: Ref, bksel. 15: Rosary Col 7900 W Division st, River Forest Ill 60305.

FIELD, OLIVER THOBURN. b Aberdeen Wash 3 N 12. 4: Ruth Rutledge. 5: West Wash State Col 31-32; Reed Col 32-35 (Lit) BA; UWash 35-37 (Libnship) BA; UOre 37-41 (Lat); Columbia 56-57 (LS), 69 DLS. 6: Ger, Norwegian, Fr. 7: Curator John Henry Nash Collection UOre 37-41; Instr in ref UOre 40-41; Catlgr Dept of State, Wash DC 41-42; Head ref & circ Fed Pub Housing Authority Lib, Wash DC 43; Head circ & spot ref NLM 43-44, Catlgr 44-46; Catlgr for med bks for NLM at LC 45-46; Chief tech serv Assoc Col of Upper NY, Plattsburg NY 47-48; Chief tech serv US High Commsn for Germany (Berlin, Frankfurt, Bonn) 48-52; Lib consul US Info Centers, Bonn 52-53; Head Automotive Hist Dept Detroit Pub Lib 53-54; Chief catlg br Air U Lib(Maxwell AFB Ala) 54-58, Chief tech serv div 58-65; Asst Prof Grad Sch of Lib Sci UIll 65-69; Assoc Prof Grad Sch of Libnship UDenver 69-. 8: Mem-Sec of State for Ill Subcom on Educ Prog for LSCA Titles I & II. 9: ALA; -RTSD (chm Subject Heading Com 61-62, mem Descrip Catlg Com 67-). 10: Beta Phi Mu. 11: Jules Mauritzson Award for Scandinavian Lit 37. 12: Contrib to "American Houses a Study of the US Info Center Program in Germany (53). 13: Yes. 14: Catlg, lib educ. 15: Grad Sch of Lib Sci, UIll, Urbana Ill 61803.

FIELD, RUTH (GRAHAM). b Bowling Green Ky 7 Jl 12. 4: Theodore E Field. 5: U Louisville 31-35 (Eng) AB; UIll 35-36 BS in LS, 36-38 MA in LS. 6: Fr, Ger. 7: Asst UIll Lib Sch 36-38; Catlgr ULouisville Lib 38-39, Head catlgr 39-45, Ser catlgr 54-62, Head catlgr 62-. 9: ALA; KyLA; Ohio Valley Group Tech Serv Libns (chm 42-43). 10: Astronomical League; Phi Kappa Phi; Beta Phi Mu. 14: Catlg. 15: 3017 Sherbrooke rd, Louisville Ky 40205.

FIELDER, SYBIL (MITCHELL). b Long Beach 10 D 11. 4: . 5: Scripps Col 29-32 (Econ Geog) BA; UWash 45-46 (LS) BA; UCal 62 Col secondary tchg credential. 6: Fr. 7: Lib asst Scripps Col Lib 46-47, act libn 56-57; Ref dept UWash Lib; US Naval Hosp Lib, Seattle; Ref libn Mt San Antonio Col Lib 57-59; El Roble Jr High Sch, Claremont Cal 59-65; Asst libn Scripps Col 65-. 9: CalLA. 10: San Antonio Lib Club. 14: Ref, rare bks. 15: 1010 Oxford ave, Claremont Ca 91711.

FIELDERS, MARGARET GRANT. b Montgomery Co Penn 22 N 14. 5: Penn State Col 31-35 (LS, Eng, Hist) BS in Ed; Drexel Inst 46-47 (LS) BS in LS; Temple 52 (Educ); Bread Loaf Sch of Eng Middlebury Col summers 58-62 (Eng) MA. 6: Ger. 7: Child libn Wyomissing Pub Lib, Wyomissing Penn 37-42, 45-46; Hosp & film libn (Sgt) USA (WAC) US 42-45; Libn La Salle Col High Sch, Phila 47-54; Libn Col of St Mary of the Springs, Columbus Ohio 54-60; Chm dept of lib sci Ohio Dominican Col 60-. 8: Dir Honors Prog, Ohio Dominican Col 60-; Dir Inst Lib Inst, Title IV-A, LSCA 69; Consul Lib Tech Wkshop 67. 9: ALA; CathLA (Adv Coun 60-); OhioLA; ColumbusLA (chm 58-60, Bk Week Chm, 61-62, Memb Chm 62-64). 10: Delta Epsilon Sigma. 11: Drexel Alumni Award 47. 12: Ed "Honorable Mention", Honors Program, Ohio Dominican Col. 14: Tchg lib sci. 15: 6079 Clark State rd, Columbus Oh 43230.

FIELDS, ARCHIE REID. b Whitesburg Ky 2 S 17. 4: Dorothy Provnce Fields. 5: US Naval Acad 37-41 (Naval Sci) BS; US Naval Postgrad Sch 45-46 (Aerology); Stanford 61-62 (Educ) MA; UWash 63-64 MLibnship. 6: Fr. 7: Various (mainly aviation) US Navy (Retired in rank of Commander, USN) 41-61; Tchr jr high sci, Albany Ore 62-63; Catlgr UNC Hill) 64-66; Chief of circ UNC, Chapel Hill 66-. 9: ALA. 13: Yes. 14: Circ, tech processes. 15: Circ Dept UNC Lib, Chapel Hill NC 27514.

FIELDS, DONALD E. b Martinsburg Ohio 20 O 01. 4: Frances Twaddle. 5: Lebanon Valley Col 20-24 (Classics) AB; Princeton 25-26, 27-28 (Classics) MA; Chicago 30-31, 33-35 (Lat) PhD; UMich 46-47 ABLS. 6: Lat, Fr, Ger, Sp 07: Master in Lat Palmer Inst Starky Sem, Lakemont NY 24-25; Master in Lat Chestnut Hill Acad, Chestnut Hill Penn 26-27; Act Prof of Latin & Gk Lebanon Valley Col 28-30; Instr in Lat Iowa State Tchrs Col 31-32; Asst Prof of Lat Muskingum Col 36-42; Army Air Force Link Trainer Instr (Sgt) 42-45; Reading room asst Johns Hopkins U 46-47; Assoc libn Lebanon Valley Col 47-55, Libn 56-. 9: Amer Philol Soc; PennLA. 12: "Technique of Exposition in Roman Comedy (38). 14: Admin. 15: 46 S Lancaster st, Annville Penn 17003.

FIELDS, FRANCES TWADDLE. b Dunmore Penn 28 F 1900. 4: Donald Eugene Fields. 5: Lebanon Valley Col 24-29 (Eng) AB; Johns Hopkins 32-42 (Span); UMich 46-47 AB LS; U de San Carlos de Guatemala 57, 59-60 (Span) MA Span Lit. 6: Sp. 7: Span tchr High Sch, Galeton Penn 19-22; Eng tchr High Sch, Coamo PR 22-25; Br libn Enoch Pratt Free Lib, Baltimore 25-27; Catlgr Johns Hopkins U 27-46; Asst Prof of Span & catlgr Lebanon Valley Col 47-. 9: ALA; PennLA. 12: "El paisaje en la Obra de Gabriel Miro. 14: Catlgr. 15: 46 S Lancaster st, Annville Penn 17003.

FIEVET, YVONNE MADELEINE. b Hartford City Ind 24 Ja 09. 5: Chicago Musical Col 27-28 (Piano) Tchrs Certif; UChicago ext 38-39; Bowling Green State U 40-44, 46-47; Columbia 46-47 (LS). 6: Fr, Sp. 7: Tchr of piano, Sandusky Ohio 28-36; Receptionist & sec med off Sandusky Ohio 31-36; Lib asst Lib Assn of Sandusky Ohio 37-40, Asst libn 40-45, Asst libn & child libn 45-48, Asst libn & catlg & order libn 51-; Libn Providence Sch of Nursing, Sandusky 58-67. 9: ALA; CathLA (Mem Com on Hosp Sect); OhioLA; N Ohio Tech Serv Libns (sec 62-63). 10: Sandusky Stamp Club,; The Marian Philatelist; Coros. 14: Catlg, child bks, phono records. 15: 910 Carr st, Sandusky Ohio 44870.

FIFE, MARGARET (EWING). b Atlanta 22 My 17. 4: William M Fife. 5: Atlanta Jr Col 36-38; Womans Col of Ga 38-40 (Educ, Eng) BS Educ; Emory 63 (LS) ML. 7: tchr Atlanta Pub Sch 39-40; Coordinator defense review Fed Bur Investigation, Wash DC 41-45; Manager housing project Greenville Housing Authority, Greenville SC 46-47; Libn Atlanta Pub 56-64, 46-64, Resource libn area 5 64-. 9: NEA; ALA; GaEA; GaLA; SELA; ASCD; Metro Atlanta LA; Atlanta EA. 10: Alpha Delta Kappa; Delta Kappa Gamma 13: Yes. 14: Sch libs. 15: 1322 Breezy lane NE, Atlanta 30329.

FIGGATT, RUTH EDWINA. b Parkersburg WVa 23 D 23. 5: Averett Col 41-43 (Liberal Arts) Diploma; Marshall U 43-45 (Bot) BA; Drexel 48-49 BS LS. 7: Libn Rio Grande Col 46-48; Catlgr Fairmont Col 49-52; Asst libn ext dept Kanawaha Co Pub Lib, Charleston WVa 52-56, Asst libn circ dept 56-61, Chief circ libn 61-. 9: ALA; WVaLA (sec 62-65, chm Pub Lib Sect, 65-66, 1st v-pres 66-67, pres 67-68). 10: AAUW; Chi Beta Phi. 14: Catlg, W Virginiana. 15: 821 Hudson st, St Albans WVa 25177.

FIGUERAS, MYRIAM. b Cuba 12 D 28. 5: UHavana 46-50 (Lit, Art) Doctor in phil & letters, 59-60 (LS) Libn; Catholic U 62-67 MLS. 6: Sp. 7: Prof of Sp Escuela del Hogar, Camaguey Cuba 57-58; Indexer Columbus Memorial Lib, Pan American Union, Wash DC 61-. 9: ALA; DCLA. 10: Corcoral Gallery of Art, Wash DC. 14: Catlg, indexing. 15: 3413 Carlyn Hill dr Apt 21, Falls Church Va 22041.

FILBY, P WILLIAM. b Cambridge Eng 10 D 11. 4: Vera Ruth Weakliem. 5: Cambridge U (Eng). 6: Fr. 7: Var Cambridge U Lib (Eng) 28-38; Libn Cambridge Philos Soc, Cambridge Eng 38-40; Capt Intelligence Corps, British Army, Eng 40-46; Sr archer British Foreign Off, London 46-57; Asst dir Peabody Inst Lib, Baltimore 57-65; Libn & asst dir Md Hist Soc, Baltimore 65-. 8: Sec & amanuensis to Sir James G Frazer, auth of "The Golden Bough, Cambridge Engl 34-40; Bk appraiser 65-. 9: ALA-RSD (Hist Sect; chm Geneal Com, Indexing & Bibliog Com 63-); BSA; Private Libs Assn. 10: Grolier Club(NY); Typophiles; Baltimore Bibliophiles; Soc of Scribes & Illuminators (Hon mem); Friends of Evergreen House; Md Hist Soc; Several British Archaeol, Loc Hist, Geneal & Heraldry Socs. 12: "Cambridge Papers (36); "Calligraphy & Handwriting in America, 1710-1962 (63); Jt comp "2000 Years of Calligraphy (65); "Md Union List of Serials (61-64). 13: Yes. 14: Rare bks, bibliog, Marylandiana, exhibitions, Calligraphy. 15: 307 Madison st, Savage Md 20863.

FILION, REV PAUL-EMILE SJ. b Montreal (Colleges Grasset et Brebeuf) 39-43 BA; Col de lImmaculee- Conception 46-48 (Philos)LPh, 51-55 (Theol) LTh; Columbia 56-57 MS LS. 6: Fr. 7: Instr gen sci & head, sci Labs Tafari Makonnen Secondary Sch, Addis Ababa Ethiopia 48-51; Chief Libn Col de lImmaculee- Conception (Montreal) 57-60; Chief Libn Laurentian U Sudbury Ont) 60-. 8: Lecturer, Lib Sch UMontreal 57-60; Assoc in Survey of Laval U Lib 62 & 65; Tour of W Germ, libs on invit of Germ Govt 64; Mem Survey of Can Col & Univ Libs 67-68. 9: CanLA (2nd v-pres 65-66, Coun 68-71); Association canadienne des bibliothecaires de langue francaise (pres Reg Sect of Montreal 59-60; pres Sect of Univ govtal & spec libs 63-64); Inst of Prof Libns Ont (2nd v-pres 65-66); Nat Lib of Can Adv Bd mem repr Ont 64-67. 11: Centennial Medal 67; LLD, ULaval 69. 12: Ed "Newsletter Can Assn of Col & U Libs. 13: Yes. 14: Lib educ, coord of lib serv. 15: Laurentian U Lib, Sudbury Ont Can.

FILSINGER, BARBARA (MINA). b NJ 8 My 36. 5: Trenton State Col 54-58 (Eng) BS in Ed; Rutgers summers 59, 61, fall 60 MLS; New Sch for Soc Research even 61, 62 (Adult Educ); Trinity Col (Dublin) summer 68. 7: Libn Jr High Sch, Chatham NJ 58-60; Libn Jr High Sch, Syosset NY 60-64; Libn NY Pub Lib 62; Libn Jr High Sch, Bloomfield NJ 65-66; Libn Jr High Sch, Westfield NJ 66-& scotch Plains Pub Lib 69-. 9: ALA;NEA; Several state & local educ & lib orgs. 10: Kappa Delta Pi. 14: Sch lib wk. 15: 2268 Stocker lane, Scotch Plains NJ 07076.

FINBERG, VERA L (KAHAN). b Minneapolis 2 N 42. 4: Harvey Jay Finberg. 5: West Res 60-64 (Chem, Ger) BA; Columbia 64-65 (LS) MS. 6: Ger, Fr. 7: Lib clerk IBM, Yorktown Heights NY summer 61, 63; Ser libn Adelphi U 64-68; Child libn Fairfax Co Pub Lib, Fairfax Va 69-. 9: ALA. 14: Ref, ser. 15: 3714 N Rosser st, Alexandria Va 22311.

FINCH, EDITH W(HITE). b Phila 3 My 15. 4: David Finch. 5: UPenn 32-36 (Educ) BS, 36-38 (Hist) MA; Drexel 41-42 BS LS. 6: Fr. 7: Catlgr US Bur of the Budget Wash DC 42-44; Bus libn Temple U 44-58; Libn Amer Gas Assn, NY 58-. 9: SLA. 14: Admin. 15: Amer Gas Assn 605 Third ave, NYC 10016.

FINCH, JEAN LUANA. b Santa Monica CAL 17 N 33. 5: Lewis & Clark Col 52-54 (Art Hist); UAriz 54-55 (Art Hist) BFA; UCal 58-59 (Span); UWash 62-63 MLS; NYU 65-66 (Art Hist) IFA. 6: Sp, Ger, Fr. Ital, Portu, Dutch. 7: Chief Clerk 1 Jantzen Inc, Portland Ore 55-57; Act libn Bancroft Lib (Mss div) UCal(Berkeley) 58-62; Libn I art div NY Pub Lib 63-65, Libn II 65-; Chief fine arts catlgr Stanford U Libs 66-68, Hd art libn & libn III Nathan Cummings Art Lib 69-. 8: Consul on Establishment of AFL/CIO lib, Seattle. 9: ALA; Col Art Assn; Amer Soc Architl Histns. 12: "Some Fundamentals in Arranging Arhives & Manuscript Collections (64). 14: Ref, mss, art. 15: 878 Partridge ave, Menlo Park Ca 94025.

FINCH, MARTHA B(ELDING). b Whitehall NY 7 Mr 05. 5: Cornell U 24-28 (Classics) AB; UMich 29-30 AB LS. 6: Lat, Ger, Fr. 7: Tchr Whitehall High Sch 28-29; Circ libn Swarthmore Col 31-34; Catlgr Brown U 34-38; Head catlgr Fitchburg Pub Lib, Fitchburg Mass 38-43; Catlgr Dartmouth Col Lib 43-45; Asst head catlgr Providence Pub Lib 45-46; Libn III catlg UCal Lib (Berkeley) 47-. 9: ALA; N Cal Tech Serv Group. 10: Cornell Womens Club of N Cal; LWV; Berkeley Lawn Bowling Club. 14: Catlg. 15: 1504A Bonita ave, Berkeley Ca 94709.

FINDLAY, ELSIE (McCABE). b Little Forks, Cumb Co NS Can 12 F 04. 4: J Warren Findlay. 5: Acadia U 28 (Eng) BA, 41 (Eng) MA; Simmons 46 (LS) BS. 6: Fr. 7: Asst art dept Springfield City Lib Assn, Springfield Mass 28-34; High sch tchr & sch libn, NS 36-44; Asst ref dept Watertown Pub Lib,

Watertown Mass 45-56; Chief of bk serv div Lib ext Mass Dept of Educ, Boston 46-52; Head Libn Salem State Col 52-54; Sch libn Quincy Point Jr High Sch, Quincy Mass 54-63; Head ref dept Vaughan Mem Lib Acadia U 63-. 9: CanLA; Can Assn Col & Univ Libs; APLA. 10: Delta Kappa Gamma; Can Fed of Univ Women; Nova Scotia Hist Assn; Wolfville Hist Soc. 14: Ref, sch lib wk. 15: RR 2, Wolfville NS Can.

FINDLEY, MARCIA (McGREW). b Oklahoma City Okla 24 N 39. 4: Joe Sanders Findley Jr. 5: Okla StateU 57-60 (Hist); UOkla 60-61 (Hist) BA; Fla StateU 61-63 (LS). 7: Circ & ref libn Okla StateU 62; Grad asst govt docs Fla StateU 62; Ref & catlg libn UNotre Dame (S Bend) 63-65; Hd libn (2 libraries) US Army, Mainz Germany 66-67; Bibliog AuburnU 67; Hd tech serv Spring Hill Col 68-. 15: 6460 Stuardi ct, Mobile Al 36608.

FINDLY, ELIZABETH (SARAH). b Winfield Kan 2 Ap 08. 5: Drake U 25-29 (Hist) AB; UIowa summer 30; UIll 33-34 BS LS; UOre 39-42; UMich summers 42-44 AM LS. 6: Lat, SP, Fr. 7: Tchr jr & sr High Sch, Prin Jr High Geneva Consolidated Sch, Geneva Iowa 29-33; Circ asst UIowa summer 34; UOre: Sr asst ref dept 34-35, Sr asst circ dept 35-37, Sr asst ref dept 37-47, Head ref libn 47-50, Head ref & documents libn 50-66, Head ref libn 66-. 8: Tchr, bibliog, ref, & use of lib 35-; Tchr summer courses in lib sci U Wash & UOre 53-. 9: ALA (Ore rep on Coun 65-69)-ACRL (Bd Dirs 56-60; chm Ref Libns 51-52, mem Com on Lib Serv 67-69); 51-52); PNLA (chm Bd of Mgrs 56-60, chm Ref Div 59-61, 2nd v-pres 67-69); 56-60); OreLA (pres 50-51, chm Ref Div 61-63, chm Bibliog 63-, mem var coms) 63-). 10: AAUP; Phi Beta Kappa; Wesley Foundation; Altrusia Club. 13: Yes. 14: Ref, newspapers, interlib loan, educ for libnship. 15: 860 E 39th ave, Eugene Or 97405.

FINE, RUTH. b St Louis. 5: UMich 25-29 AB LS; AmerU 39. 6: Fr. 7: Jr ref asst to 1st asst soc sci div Detroit Pub Lib 29-37; Asst libn US Dept of Labor Lib, Wash DC 37-41; Chief Libn US Bur of the Budget, Wash DC 41-. 8: Planning Com on the Establt of a Fed Lib Com 63-64; Task Force on Mission of Fed Libs, Fed Lib Com 64-65. 9: ALA (Sub Bks Com 51-54);-LED (sec 46-49); SLA (Bus Div: chm 47-48, on Stat Lib Serv Br Off of Educ 59; chm Stat com 60-64; WashDC Chap pres 53); DCLA (pres 63). 10: Phi Beta Kappa; Phi Kappa Phi. 11: Exec Off of the Pres, Bur of the Budget Dirs Exceptional Serv Award 61. 13: Yes. 14: Admin, ref. 15: 449 Exec Office Bldg 17 & Pennsylvania ave NW, Washington DC 20503.

FINE, SHEILA LYNNE (BESSER). b Chicago 13 S 42. 4: Freddie Irvin Fine. 5: Miss State Col for Women 60-64 (LS) BS. 7: Catlgr Northwest Reg Lib, Winfield Ala 65-. 9: ALA. 10: Sulligent Pub Lib Bd; Sulligent Study Club. 14: Pub rel, catlg. 15: Box 276, Sulligent Ala 35586.

FINEGOLD, RONALD. b Montreal Can 4 Mr 38. 5: Sir George Williams 55-60 (Pol Sci) BA; McGill 65-67 MLS; Carleton U summer 68 Certif in archives principles & admin. 6: Fr, Hebrew, Yiddish. 7: Libn Jewish Pub Lib, Montreal 67-. 9: CanLA. 15: 4925 Edouard Montpetit blvd Apt 8, Montreal 248 Que Can.

FINELY, (MARIAN) JEAN (LOCKWOOD). b Portland Ore 23 Jl 29. 4: Ralph E Finely. 5: UWash 47-51 (Educ) BA, 51-54 (LS) ML. 6: Sp. 7: Com tchr Grandview (Wash) Schs 52-53; Jr high libn Seattle Pub Schs 54-55, Jr high tchr 59-61; Libn Olympia (Wash) Elem Schs 64-. 9: ALA; NEA; WashEA; WashLA. 10: Delta Kappa Gamma; Internat Reading Assn. 14: Sch libs. 15: 2138 N Milroy, Olympia Wash 98501.

FINGERSON, RONALD LEE. b Billings Mont 15 Je 33. 4: Dixie Lee Kerr. 5: UIowa 57-61 (Eng) BA; UMinn 62-63 (LS) MA; UIowa 64-68 (Creative Writing) MFA. 6: Ger. 7: Dental Tech Third Class Petty Off US Navy 51-55; Eng tchr Washington Jr High Sch, Racine Wis 61-62; Ref libn UIowa Lib 64, Spec collections libn 64-; Mss libn UIowa 66-68; Hd of ser dept UIowa 68-. 9: IowaLA. 10: Friends of the UIowa Libs. 13: Yes. 14: Rare bks, mss. collecting, bibliog. 15: 733 Highland ave, Iowa City Ia 52240.

FINK, IRENE E. b Phila. 5: Temple U 45-49 (Econ) BS (in Bus); Drexel 59-62 MSLS; Certif by MedLA-Grade I 62. 7: Asst libn Fed Reserve Bank of Phila 51-63; Asst libn Rutgers U Col of S Jersey (Camden NJ) 63-65;Market research Smith Kline French LAB, Phila 65-. 8: Free-lance research wk in child psychiatry 62-. 9: SLA ("Bulletin ed, chm Bus & Fin Div 64-65, Coun sec Phila Area 65-66). 10: Bd of Managers Bus Alumni Assn; Temple emple U; Beta Gamma Sigma; Beta Phi Mu. 11: Pub Admin Award, Temple U 49. 14: Ref. 15: Marketing Lib, Smith Kline & French Lab, 1500 Spring Garden st, Phila Pa 19101.

FINK, MARY ELLIN (McCRADY). b Wash DC 19 D 26. 4: Clinton F Fink. 5: UMich 44-48, 50-51 (Sociol) AB, 53-54 (Educ) Certif, 60-62 AMLS. 7: Libn Orthetics Research Proj Univ Hosp, Ann Arbor Mich 63; Bindery wkr Olsen's Bookbindery, Ann Arbor Mich 63-64; Catlgr Detroit Pub Lib, Detroit 64-66; Bindery wkr UMich Binding Dept (Ann Arbor) 66-. 14: Catlg, bindery prep. 15: 610 Huron View blvd, Ann Arbor Mi 48103.

FINK, RONN (RONALD). b Everett Penn 23 O 6. 5: Juniata Col 54-58 (Eng) BA. 7: News ed, reporter Bedford Co Press, Everett 50-60; Staff reporter "The Tribune Democrat, Johnstown 60-62; Pub rel dir Penn State Lib 62-. 8: Exec dir, Nat Lib Week, Penn, 66, 67. 9: ALA; LPRC (Exec Bd 67-69); Lib Pub Rel Soc Greater Phila; PennLA (Bd Dirs 65-68, Exec Com 67-68, chm Publ & Pub Del Com 67-68). 10: Penn Pub Rel Soc. 13: Yes. 14: Pub rel. 15: 712 Green s, Harrisburg Penn 17102.

FINKEL, EMANUEL. b NYC 12 Je 11. 4: Esther Kalb Finkel. 5: City Col (NY) 31-35 (Pre-Law) Law Qualifying Certif; Brooklyn Law Sch 35-38 LLB, 38-39 LLM; LIU 64-(LS), 67 MSLS. 6: Fr. 7: Salesman E J Oberlaender, NYC 29-43; Sales Manager Bennett-Lang, NYC 43-50: Sales Manager Ulster Cravat, Kingston NY 50-53; Vice-pres Westbury Cravats, NYC 53-64; Jr libn Nssau Commun Col 64-65, Tech asst 65-, Libn 66-67, Lib spec & Asst Prof 68-. 8: Private legal consul NYC 40-59. 9: Nassau Co(NY)LA. 10: AAUP; Admitted to the practice of Law 39 in NY. 14: Ref, acquis. 15: 58 Pearl st, New Hyde Park NY.

FINKELSTEIN, MILDRED (SANG). b NYC 15 F 21. 4: Howard Finkelstein. 5: Millersville State Col 62-64 (LS); Brooklyn Col 36-40 (Psych, Pol Sci) AB; 07: Libn Abraham Lincoln Jr High Sch 64-. 9: ALA; NEA; PennLA; Penn State EA. 14: Adolescent lit. 15: 43 Pilgrim dr, Lancaster Pa 17603.

FINKLER, NORMAN. b Philadelphia 20 Jl 20. 4: Etta Berg. 5: Temple 37-42 (Eng) BS Educ; Drexel 46-49 BS LS; UPenn 49-56 (Amer Civilization) AM. 6: Fr, Ger. 7: Sub tchr Bd of Educ, Phila 42; Tech 5th Grade US Army, European Theater 42-46; Libn-instr in Eng Delaware Valley Col 46-48, libn asst Prof of Eng 48-53; Free Lib of Phila: Libn II soc sci & hist dept 53-57, Br libn W Oak Lane Br 57-59, Asst coordinator wk with adults 59-62; Deputy dir Montgomery Co Dept of Pub Libs, Bethesda Md 62-. 8: Consul RR Bowker Co 68 & 69; Mem Md Spec Commsn to Review & Prepare Recommendations for Revisions of Pub Lib Law. 9: ALA (Subscription Bks Com 56-62; Notable Bks Coun: 60-64, chm 63-64);-ASD (Author Selection & Adv Com; chm Cultural Antrop 65-67); MdLA (pres 68-69; 1st v-pres 67-68; chm Ed Com 65-68); DCLA (Program Com 65-66). 12: Ed "Maryland Libraries". 13: Yes. 14: Admin, bk sel, ref, automation. 15: 6400 Democracy blvd, Bethesda Md 20034.

FINLAY, (REV) DONALD FRANCIS. b Toronto Can 6 Je 36. 5: UWindsor 58-60 (Eng) BA; U St Michael's Col 62-65 (Theol) STB; Rosary summers 63-66, fall 66 MA in LS. 6: Fr. 7: Libn Pontificial Inst of Medieval Studies, Toronto 66-. 9: ALA; CanLA. 14: Rare bks. 15: 59 Queens Park Crescent, Toronto 5 Ont Can.

FINLAY, LOIS MARIE. b Bridgeport Conn 9 Jl 44. 5: UPittsburgh 62-67 (Eng Lit) BA; UMinn 67-69 (LS) MA. 6: Sp. 7: Ref libn UVt Charles A Dana Med Lib 69-. 9: MedLA. 14: Ref. 15: 41 University ter, Burlington Vt 05401.

FINLAYSON, JANET (LOUISE). b Lennoxville Que 5 My 38. 5: Macdonald Col McGill U 55-59 9home econ tchg) BS & class 1 teaching certificate; McGill 64-65 BLS. 6: Fr. 7: Tchr: Three Rivers Protestant Sch Bd, Three Rivers Que 59-61, Hudson Protestant Sch Bd, Hudson Que 61-62; Lib asst McGill U Macdonald Col 62-64, Circ libn 65-66, Ser libn 66-67; Libn Protestant Reg Sch Bd of Chateauguay Valley, Ormstown Que 67-. 9: CanLA; Prov Assn Prot Tchrs. 14: Public serv, collection bldg. 15: RR 5, Ormstown Que Can.

FINLEY, DOLORES RUTH (TERRIO). b Portsmouth NH 11 D 27. 4: Harold Robert Finley. 5: U of NY(Geneseo) 60-64 (LS) BS; Syracuse 66-69 MSLS. 06: Fr. 7: Libn Victor Elem Sch, Victor NY 64-. 9: ALA; NYLA; NY State Tchrs Assn. 10: Supt St John's Episcopal Church Sch; 4-H club leader; Kappa Delta Pi; Finger Lakes Trail Conf. 14: Child lit. 15: 5015 North rd RD 4, Canandaigua NY 14424.

FINLEY, LUCY (SUTHERLAND) (MRS). b Anniston Ala 11 Ag 07. 5: Ark State Tchrs Col 25-28 (Soc Sci) BA; Peabody 52 (LS) MA. 6: Fr. 7: Tchr high sch, Fordyce Ark 28-32; Tchr & libn Malvern High Sch, Malvern Ark 45-52; Asst libn Henderson State Col 52-. 9: ALA; ArkLA (past treas); ArkEA (past treasurer). 10: Delta Zappa Gamma; Delta Zeta. 14: Ref. 15: 824 N Faculty pl, Arkadelphia Ar 71923.

FINLEY, THELMA. b Ottumwa Iowa 9 S 08. 5: Ottumwa Heights Col 26-28; UUtah 41-42, 43-44, 46-47 (LS); UIowa Correpondence 47, 48, 49, 59 (LS). 6: Fr. S. 7: Sch contacts libn Pub ib, Ottumwa Iowa 28-61; Sch libn Ottumwa Commun Schs, Ottumwa Iowa 61-. 9: ALA; IowLA; IowaASchL. 14: Wk with child. 15: 807 Richmond ave, Ottumwa Iowa 52501.

FINLEY, VERNON R. b Latonia Ky. 4: Nancy Norwood. 5: WashU(St Louis) AB; LSU BSLS. 7: Ref dept St Louis Pub Lib 38-42; Circ libn Cooper Union Lib (NY) 42-48; Circ div, acquis div Brooklyn Col Lib 48-. 15: Brooklyn Col Lib, Brooklyn NY 11210.

FINNAN, ANNE MARY. b Scranton Penn 11 Ja 22. 5: Marywood Col 39-43 (Soc Studies) AB, 43-44 S LS; Columbia 55-58 (Soc & Philos Found of Educ) MA; Harvard summer 68. 6: Fr, Lat, Ger. 7: Asst libn Mt St Agne Col 44-45; Libn Glen Burnie High Sch, Glen Burnie Md 45-46; Libn Loyola Col, Baltimore 46-51; Jr libn US Supreme Court Lib, Wash DC 52-54; Libn FordhamU Lib Sch of Educ 54-58; Educ spec & ref libn Fordham U Lib (Lincoln Ctr) 59-. 9: ALA; SLA; CathLA. 10: Oratoria Soc of NY; NY Prof Sodalty; Kappa Delta Pi. 14: Ref & research in the soc studies & educ, admin. 15: 714 Hawthorne st, Avoca Penn.

FINNEL, SOMA HEIMER. b Brooklyn NY 17 F 25. 4: Frank I Finnel. 5: Brooklyn Col 42-46 (Pol Sci) BA; C W Post 64-66 MS in LS. 7: Asst br libn Queensboro Pub Lib, Queens NY 64-68; Adult serv libn Merrick Lib, Merrick NY 68-. 9: ALA; NYLA. 10: W Nassau Mental Health Clinic Assn. 14: Adult serv. 15: 46 Grace ave, Great Neck NY 11021.

FINNEMORE, M ALISON. b Montreal 27 O 24. 5: McGill 46 (Eng, Sociology) BA, 47 BLS. 7: Catlgr McGill U com lib 47-48, Asst libn 48-51; Asst libn Shawinigan Water & Power Co Ltd, Montreal 51-53; Asst libn Pulp & Paper Research Inst of Can, Montreal 53-. 8: Helped establish Pub Lib in Mount Royal 53-54. 9: CanLA; SLA; QueLA (past treas). 14: Bk sel, ref. 15: 112 Balfour ave, Montreal 304 PQ Can.

FINNEY, LANCE CARL. b Wetumka Okla 24 F 29. 5: UBaltimore 56-62 (Ind Mgt) BS; UOkla 63-64 (LS) MLS. 6: Sp. 7: Asst to plant Engnr Mathieson Chem Cor, Baltimore 52-62; Libn popular lib Enoch Pratt Free Lib, Baltimore 62-63, Adult asst ind & sci dept 64, Libn Walbrook Br 65, Libn Hollins-Payson Br 66, asst 66-. 9: ALA; MdLA. 10: Admin Okla Hist Soc; Fractional Indian Soc of Baltimore; Okla State Soc of Citizens Planning & Housing Assn; Metro Civic Assn; Beta Alpha. 14: Adult serv, sci & histl (regl) collections & physically handicapped. 15: 238 Montgomery st, Baltimore Md 21230.

FINSETH, MARCIA K. b Bismarck ND 5 O 13. 5: St Olaf Col 37-39 (Sociol) BA; U Wash 47-48 (LS) BA. 7: Asst ref dept Seattle Pub Lib 48-49; Asst lib Central Wash Col Educ 49-52; Asst educ Cincinnati Pub Lib 52-55; Asst ref dept Seattle Pub Lib 56-59; Br libn Portland Pub Lib, Portland Ore 59-60; Libn for the blind Seattle Lib for the Blind-Seattle Pub Lib 60-. 9: ALA (Round Table for the Blind); WashLA. 10: Altrusa Club. 14: Wk with the blind or physically handicapped. 15: 425 Harvard ave E, Seattle Wa 98102.

FINZI, JOHN CHARLES. b Campiglia Marittima Italy 27 Mr Mr 20. 5: URome (Italy) 37-38 (Belles Lettres); UCLA 42-44 (Hist) BA, 44-45 (Eng Hist) MA, 45-50 (Eng, Hist); UCal(Berkeley) 56-57 MLS. 6: Ital, Sp, Fr, Portu, Ger. 7: Tchg asst Eng Hist UCLA 47-50, Ref asst & mss catlgr William Andrews Clark Mem Lib 51-56; Research asst UCal (Berkeley) Sch of Lib Sci 56-57; LC: intern 57, Bibliog 58, Head, Orientalia Exch Sect 58-59, Head, European Exch Sect 59-61; Dir, Pub Law 480 Programs, S Asia, LC, New Delhi 61-64, Coordinator for the development & org of the collections LC 64-66, Asst dir for the dev of collections 66-. 8: Spec consul (under ALA sponsorship) to the Nat Lib of Florence Italy Nov-Dec 67; Participant, Jointly sponsored Proj for For Libns (ALA-Dept of State) 67-. 9: ALA; IndianLA; DCLA. 10: Phi Beta Kappa; Beta Phi Mu; AHA. 12: "Oscar Wilde and His Literary Circle; A Catalog of Manuscripts and Letters in the William Andrews Clark Memorial Library" (67); "The National Central Library of Florence; Report of a Survey, Nov-Dec 1967" (68). 13: Yes. 14: Lib admin, ref, acquis, info systems. 15: 2700 Virginia ave NW, Washington DC 20037.

FIROR, MARY (CATHERINE). b Thurmont Md 4 Ap 21. 5: Beaver Col 37-41 (Fr) BA; Drexel 41-42 BS LS. 6: Fr. 7: Libn High Sch, Mt Jackson Va 42-44; Libn High Sch, Woodstown NJ 44-47; Asst libn West Md Col 47-52; Catlgr Hawaii Co Lib, Hilo Hawaii 52-54; Catlgr Denver Pub Lib 54-67; Catlgr Jefferson Co Pub Lib, Golden Colo 68-. 9: ALA; ColoLA; MPLA. 10: . 14: Catlg. 15: 3220 Fenton st, Denver 80212.

FIROR, SARAH (ELIZABETH). b Baltimore Md 12 O 11. 5: Ga State Tchrs Col 29-31; UGa 31-33 (Econ) BS in Com, 46-49 (Ceramics) BFA; Emory summers 52, 53 (LS); Fla State U (LS) MS. 7: Statistical clerk Agric Adjustment Admin, Athens Ga 33-37; Statistical clerk Malaria Research Lab (USPHS), Savannah Ga 37; Calculating machine operator Flood Control Surveys US Dept Agric, Cartersville Ga, Salisbury NC 38-41; Calculating machine oerator Agric Adjustment Admin, Athens Ga 41-47; Aerographers Mate 2/c WAVES 43-46; Supv ofCirc Berea Col Lib 49-66; Ref libn 67-. 9: ALA; SELA; KyLA (sec-treas Col & Ref Sect 55-57). 10: AAUW; Bus & Prof Womens Club; Phi Beta KAPPA: Phi KAPPA Phi. 14: Reader serv, ref. 15: Berea Col Lib, Berea Ky 40403.

FIRTH, MARGARET (ASQUITH). b Lawrence Mass 21 Mr 19. 5: UMass 36-40 (Eng, Hist) BA; Simmons 40-41 BS in LS. 6: Fr, Ger. 7: Stud asst UMass Goodell Lib 37-40; Ref asst Clark U, Worcester Mass 41-42; Libn Celanese Corp, Cumberland Md 42-45; Libn United Shoe Machinery Corp Res Div, Beverly Mass 45-. 9: SLA (sec 54-56 & many coms, Boston Chap pres 51-52 & com duties); ASIS. 10: Beverly Col Club, Guild of Beverly Artists; N Shore Mgt Club; ASLIB; Inst Info Scientists (England). 11: SLA Sci-Tech Div First Award of Merit 1960. 12: Ed "Handbook of Scientific and Technical Awards, in the US and Canada 1900-1952" SLA. 14: Ref, admin. 15: United Shoe Mach Corp, Research Div, Beverly Mass 01915.

FISCHER, JOHN. b Trencsen Hungary 3 N 10. 5: UDebrecen (Hungary) 28-32 (Law) Absolutorium; USzeged (Hungary) 32 Dr iur; George WashingtonU 49-51 M of Comp Law. 6: Hungarian. 7: Attorney, Hungary 38-43; Co commsner local govt, Hungary 44-45; Attorney, Budapest Hungary 46-47; Indexer-digester LC law lib 49-41, Acquis libn order div 52-59, Supv acquis unit order div 60-62, Subj catlgr (law) subj catlg div 62-. 8: Admitted to law practice Hungary 37, Wash DC 59. 9: Law Libns' Soc, Wash DC. 14: Clsf (law). 15: 2500 Que st NW, Washington DC 20007.

FISCHER, JULIA (STANIEL). b Newark NJ 25 A 08. 4: Joseph F Fischer. 5: Simmons 28-32 (LS) BS; Seton Hall U 53-55 (Educ). 7: Asst Newark Pub Lib, Newark NJ 25-26; Libns asst Newark Museum, Newark NJ 26-28; Asst libn State Tchrs Col(Ktztown Kutztown 32-33; Asst libn Mt Holyoke Col 33-35; Ref libn Frick Art Ref Lib, NYC 35-44; Itinerant libn Bd of Educ, Newark NJ 53-60; Libn Vailsburg High Sch, Newark NJ 60-. 8: Consul & catlgr of nursing sch lib Hartford Hosp, Hartford Conn 43. 9: Newark Sch LA (treas 2 yrs); NJEA; Newark Tchrs Ass. 10: Simmons Col Alumnae Assn; PTA; St Benedicts Mothers League 14: Ref. 15: 46 Mead st, Newark NJ 07106.

FISCHER, MARGARET MARY. b Wilkes-Barre Penn. 5: Col of New Rochelle 49-53 (Eng) BA; Marywood Col 53-54 MA in Libnship. 6: Fr, Ger. 7: Asst libn King's Col Lib 54-. 9: ALA;-ACRL; PennLA; NE Penn LA (sec-treas 64-66, chm 57-58). 10: AAUW; New Rochelle Alumnae of NE Penn; Theatre 3, Col Misercordia; AAUP; Oral Hist Assn. 13: Yes. 14: Ref, catlg, pub rel. 15: 496 S River st, Wilkes-Barre Penn 18702.

FISHER, CAROLYN (LOWRY). b Jacksonville Tex 5 O 39. 4: Kenneth E Fisher. 5: NW Mo state Col 57-61 (Elem Educ) BS; UDenver summers 63, 64, 65 (Libnship) MA. 7: Tchr, W Nodaway RI, Burlington Jct Mo 61-63; Catlgr NW Mo State Col Lib 63-. 9: MoLA. 10: AAUW. 14: Catlg. 15: Wells Lib Northwest Missouri St Col, Maryville Mo 64468.

FISHER, DOROTHY (HAGEN FRANCIS). b St Louis Mo 20 F 12. 4: Guin Menard Fisher. 5: WashU (St Louis Mo) 31-35 (Eng) AB; UIll (Champaign) 37 BS in LS; USan Francisco 66-67 (LS). 7: Asst libn Carpenter Br Lib, St Louis Mo 38-43; Off (Commdr) USN 43-67; Libn & dir lib serv Golden Gate Col 67-. 10: Pilot Club Intl. 15: 1050 N Point st apt 1602, San Francisco Ca 94109.

FISHER, ILO DOLORES. b Springfield Ohio 18 O 13. 5: Wittenberg U 31-35 (Eng) AB; UIll 40 BLS, 47-51 (LS) MS 67. 6: Fr. 7: Tchr Springfield (Ohio) Pub Schs 35-36; Catlgr Wittenberg U 36-43; Head catlg & order dept Warder Pub Lib,

Springfield Ohio 43-46; Head Libn Wittenberg U 46-64, Chief tech serv 64-68, Spec projects libn 68-. 8: Dir, undergrad lib sci program, Wittenberg Univ; Consul on Pub Schs, Springfield & Clark Cos 67-. 9: ALA (Coun 54-56);-ACRL; ATheolLA; OhioLA; Ohio Valley Regl Catlgrs Assn; OhioASchL; SLA (pres Dayton Chap 68-). 10: Womens Nat Bk Assn; Mental Health Assn; Springfield Guidance Center; Comprehensive Menal Health Com; Altrusa Internat; Beta Phi Alph. 11: AAUP; Friends of Pub Lib; Beta Phi Alpha Scholarship Award. 12: Introd to "Baltasar Gracian," by Benjamin C Vila (67); Ed SLA-Dayton Chap Bulletin (67-68). 13: Yes. 14: Tech serv, rare bks, catlg. 15: 5747 Detrick Jordan rd, Springfield Ohio 45502.

FISHER, JOHN ANDREW. b Rawlins Wyo 1 My 28. 5: UWyo 46-49 (Hist) BA; Rutgers 56-57 MLS. 7: (Sgt) US Army Co Clerk, Seattle & Korea 51-53; Clerk Doubleday Bk Shops, Phila 53-54; Lib asst Phila Free Lib 54, Supv stacks 54-57; Asst bkmob libn Colo State Lib, Las Animas Colo 59; Demonstration libn Colo State Lib, Yuma Colo 59-61; Field consul Colo State Lib, Denver 61-63; State Libn Wyoming State Lib 63-68; Lib serv prog off US Off of Educ, Region VIII (Denver) 68-. 9: ALA (Coun 65-67); SLA (v-pres 67-68); WyoLA; NEA-DAVI; NAEB; ASIS. 12: "Financial Planning in the Small Public Library," (ALA Small Libs Proj Pamphlets 18 (69). 13: Yes. 14: Adult serv, lib educ. 15: Centennial Wyo 82055.

FISHER, LILLIE (RICE). b Phila Pa 16 N 14. 4: Henry B Fisher. 5: Bryn Mawr Col 32-36 (Chem) BA; UTulsa, Okla State U, UUtah, Loyola U (Chicago) 57-65 (LS). 7: Research asst Yale U Med Sch 36-37; Tech abstractor Hercules Pow der Co Research Ctr, Wilmington Del 37-41; Clk & libn Phillips Petroleum Co, Bartlesville Okla 51-53, Lit chem 53-54; Research chem US Bur of Mines Petroleum Research Ctr, Wilmington Del 57-65, Asst libn Bartlesville Okla 65-. 9: SLA (treas Okla Chap 68-69). 15: 3420 Wildwood ct, Bartlesville Ok 74003.

FISHER, LORETTA (GAYLORD). b Albany Ore 29 My 08. 5: Willamette U 26-30 (Socol) AB; Columbia 37-38 BS LS; UWash summer 59 (LS); Georgetown U summer 61 (Mgt). 7: Clerical Ore State Lib 30-37; Stud asst Avery Lib Columbia U 37-38; Circ asst res libn & ref asst Ore State U 38-42; Ore State Lib Readers adviser 42-53, Act head of readers serv 53-54, Oregoniana libn 55-56, Head of readers serv 56-62, Asst state libn 62-68; Asst ref libn Ore State U 68-. 9: ALA; PNLA; OreLA. 10: Salem City Club. 12: Ore chm "Northwest Books; First Supplement (49). 14: Admin, pub serv. 15: 2916 NW Polk, Corvallis Or 97330.

FISHER, MARGARET. b Fountain Hill Penn 7 Ja 25. 5: Smith 43-47 (Psych) BA; Drexel 62-67 MSLS. 7: Circ desk clk Reading Pub Lib, Reading Penn 47-48; Home serv wkr Amer red Cross, Reading Penn 48-50; Field dir Camp Fire Girls, Reading Penn 50-52; Exec sec CIA, Wash DC 52-61; Libn Amer Casualty Co, Reading Penn 61-65; 1st asst ref libn Reading Pub Lib 65-. 9: ALA; PennLA. 10: Jr League of Reading Penn; Beta Phi Mu. 14: Ref. 15: 1319 Reading blvd, Wyomissing Pa 19610.

FISHER, MARSHALL. b Chicago Ill 11 O 43. 5: Wright Jr Col 62-63 AA; Chicago Tchrs Col North 63-65 (Educ) BEd; NoIllU 65 (Hist); Rosary 66-67 (LS) MA. 7: Libn Bogan City Col summer 67; Asst libn (catlgr) William Rainey Harper Col 68-. 9: NEA-DAVI; ALA; IllLA. 10: B'nai B'rith. 14: Catlg, automation in libs. 15: 5625 N Spaulding, Chicago Il 60645.

FISHER, MARSHALL H(AROLD). b Brooklyn NY 23 My 24. 4: Joan Perlman. 5: Hofstra Col 41-43, 46-48 (Biol) BA; Pratt 49-50 BLS. 7: US Army Med Dept X-Ray Tech (Tech 5th Gr) 43-46; Sublibn Grade Brooklyn Pub Lib 48-49; Period libn SUNY Col of Med (NYC) 50-51; Asst libn Forrestal Research Center, Princeton NJ 52-59; Asst libn Allison Div GM Corp, Indianapolis 59-60; Libn Tech Inst northwestern U 60-65; Chief reader serv Argonne Nat Lab, Argonne Ill 65-. 9: ALA; MedLA; SLA. 14: Admin. 15: 189 Main st, Glen Ellyn Il 60137.

FISHER, MARY ELLA (LIPCHAK). b Pittsburgn Penn 14 Mr 41. 4: Michael John Fisher. 5: UPittsburgh 59-63 (Math) BS; UMd 66-67 MLS. 7: Clerical asst Uris Lib CornellU 63-66; Machine methods libn Welch Med Lib, Baltimore 67-. 14: Electronic data proc in lib wk. 15: 1112 E 36th st, Baltimore Md 21218.

FISHER, MARY L. b Fall River Mass 1 Jl 28. 4: Robert N Fisher. 5: Radcliffe 45-49 (Govt) AB; URI 57-58 (LS) Certif; Simmons 65-67 MLS. 6: Fr, Sp. 7: Asst econ libn MIT 49-50; Acquis libn Tchrs Col of Conn 50-51; High sch libn Warren Pub Sch, warren RI 57-60; Asst to supt sch libs, Worcester Mass 60-63; Curriculum libn Lexington Pub Schs, Lexington Mass 65-66; Libn & bibliog Harvard U Press 67-. 8: Planning com for bibliog of New England hist 69-. 9: ALA; NELA. 12: "Cambodia: an Annotated Bibliography of Its History, Geography and Politics . . . 1954" (67). 14: Ref, bibliog. 15: 12 John Poulter rd, Lexington Ma 02173.

FISHER, MAUREEN. b Gary Ind 14 Ja 10. 5: Rockford Col 27-31 (Eng) BA; Columbia 31-32 (LS) BS. 6: Fr. 7: Head circ dept Hammond Pub Lib, Hammond Ind 32-39; Head Libn Niles Pub Lib, Niles Mich 40-60; Libn West nd Br, Rockford Pub Lib, Rockford Ill 50-61, Libn Rockton Centre Br 61-63, Head soc sci div 63-69, Coord Supv Main Lib & Gp Acticities 69-. 9: ALA; IllLA. 10: AAUW; Coun for Commun Serv& rockford Cultural Coun. 12: Weekly library column in 2 local newspapers (47-). 14: Supv, wk with gps. 15: 205 CARLTON TER, Rockford Ill 61103.

FISHER, PATRICIA A(TKINS). b Sault Ste Marie Mich. 4: O A Kenneth Fisher. 5: Mich Col of Mining and Tech 53-55; West MichU 55-57 (Hist) AB; UMich 60-61 MA LS; UColo (Denver) 66-67. 7: Libn Whitehall Pub Schs, Whitehall Mich 57-60; Libn Kalamazoo Pub Schs Milwood Jr High Sch 61-63; Libn I, II Hild Reg Br Chicago Pub Lib 63-64; Libn II Gen Info Detroit Pub Lib; Libn Denver Pub Schs 66-67; Ref libn UDenver 67-. 9: ALA. 10: Kappa Delta Pi; Pi Gamma Mu. ; LWV. 14: Sch libs. ref. 15: 1337 E Cornell ave, Englewood Ca 80110.

FISHER, SUSAN (SCHWARZ). b Vienna 24 S 19. 4: Paul Fisher. 5: Realgymnasium (Vienna) 29-36; Textile Col(Vienna) 37-38; UMinn summer 49. 6: Ger, Fr. 7: Lib asst Dartmouth Col 48-51; Lib asst NACA, Wash DC 51-55; Catlgr USDA, NAL, Wash DC 55-60, Catlg reviser 50-66, Asst sect hd shared cat div LC 66-. 9: ALA; Internat Assn of Agric Libns & Documentalists; DCLA. 14: Catlg. 15: 7024 Bybrook lane, Chevy Chase Md 20015.

FISHER, WILLIAM HENRY. b Sellersville Penn 30 O 25. 4: Edith Rosenblad. 5: New Eng Conservatory of Music 46-48 (Music Educ); Syracuse 48-50 (Hist, Pol Sci) BA, 50-51 MS LS; Rutgers (LS). 7: US Navy "Musician Wash DC 44-46; Ref libn & catlgr USCIA, Wash DC 51-53; Assoc libn Radio Corp of Amer, Princeton NJ 53-65; Head Libn West Electric Engnr Research Center, Princeton NJ 65-. 9: SLA (Transl Activ Com 69-71; Phila & Vicin Unit; chm Sci/Tech Sect 56-57; Princetön-Trenton Chap; pres 67-68). 10: Kappa Gamma Psi; Boy Scouts; Amer Red Cross. 14: Admin, acquis, info systems. 15: 7 Harvest dr, Pennington NJ 08534.

FISHLER, ESTHER BAKER. b Boston 25 N 06. 4: Bennett H Fishler. 5: Wellesley 25-29 (Biblical Hist) BA; Columbia 32-34 (LS) MS. 6: Fr. 7: Gen asst Albany Pub Lib, Albany NY 31-34; Field wker Mass State Lib 35; Ref libn Geo L Pease Mem Lib, Ridgewood NJ 36-40, Lib dir 40-62; Lib dir The Ridgewood Lib, Ridgewood NJ 62-. 8: NJ State chm Nat Lib Week 61. 9: ALA; MassLA; NJLA (pres 50-51, chm &/or mem 4 coms). 10: Ridgewood Adult Sch Trustee (pres 53-58); Col Club of Ridgewood Womans Club of Ridgewood; Ridgewood Art Assn; Bergen & Passaic Co Lib Club (pres 41-42). 13: Yes. 14: Admin, ref. 15: 125 North Maple ave, Ridgewood NJ 07450.

FISHMAN, JACK. b NYC 22 Ja 24. 5: UIdaho 42-43 (Educ); Wash Sq Col NYU 46-48 (Hist); UIdaho 49-50 (Socol) BA; NYU 50-51 (Sociol); Pratt 61-63 MLS. 7: US Army Air orps Clerk (Cpl) 43-46; USAF Staff Sgt Personnel Tech 51-58; Case wker NYC Dept of Welfare 58-61; Sr Brooklyn Brooklyn Pub Grand Gand Army Plaza NYC 61-66; Coord adult serv Free Pub Lib, Woodbridge NJ 66-67, Asst dir 67-. 9: ALA;-ASD (chm Conf Prog Com 69); NJLA (Prog Chm 66-67, chm Publ Com 67-, Nat Lib Week Steering Com 67-69). 12: Ed "New Jersey Libraries". 14: Adult serv, lib admin, personnel. 15: 435 W 57th st, New York NY 10019.

FISK, LOIS (CRAIG). b Arlington Mass 15 N 16. 4: Charles F Fisk. 5: Simmons 34-38 (LS) BS. 7: Circ asst Providence Pub Lib 38-41; Adult serv libn George L Pease Mem Lib, Ridgewood NJ 61-62, Br libn 62-. 9: ALA; NJLA; Bergen-Passaic Lib Club. 10: Bergen Co (NJ) Simmons Club. 14: Ref, Yp, Bk sel, readers adv. 15: 325 Monroe ave, Wyckoff NJ 07481.

FISZHAUT, GUSTAWA MARIA. b Warsaw Poland 14 Je 38. 5: UBC 56-61 (Econ) BA, 62-63 BLS. 6: Polish, Fr. 7: Libn I catlgr UToronto 63-64; Libn II slavic catlgr UBC 64-, Ref libnSp Soc sci & Slavic bibliog 66-. 9: CanLA; BCLA; Can

Assn Slavists. 14: Slav bibliog, ref. 15: 6070 Cartier st, Vancouver 13 BC Canada.

FITCH, (HARRY) GLEN. b Owosso Mich 26 Jl 12. 4: Eleanor Wilkinson. 5: East Mich U 30-43 (Fr, Ger) AB; Peabody 34-35 BS in LS; Mich State U 35-39 (Eng) MA. 6: Fr, Ger. 7: Even ref libn Mich State U 35-37, Ref libn 37-46; Libn Hillsdale Col 46-. 9: MichLA (treas 50-54; chm Dist II; sec Col Sect). 10: Phi Delta Kappa; Kappa Delta Pi. 14: Ref, admin. 15: Hillsdale Col, Carr Mem Lib, Hillsdale Mich 49242.

FITCH, DONALD EVERETT. b Miles City Mont. 4: Dorothy Ann (Lamb) Fitch. 5: Gonzaga U 49-53 (Eng) BA; UCLA 53-54, 56-58 (Eng) MA; UCal(Berkeley) 58-59 MLS. 6: Ger, Lat. 7: Mil police US Army, Europe 46-49; Personnel US Army, EuroUS 50-51; Eng faculty Coeur dAlene High Sch, Coeur dAlene Idaho 54-56; Eng faculty Santa Monica City Col 58; Catlgr UCal Lib (Santa Barbara) 59-62, Head ref dept 63-. 12: Ed "Soundings" UCal (Santa Barbara) journal). 13: Yes. 14: Ref, bibliog. 15: Univ Cal Lib, Santa Barbara Cal.

FITCH, ROBERT PAUL. b Bushnell Ill 5 Ja 36. 5: Monmouth Col 54-58 (Chem) BA; Bradley U 56; West Ill U 62-63; Peabody 63-64 (LS) MA; Ind U 64-65 (AV Communication) MS. 67: Analytical chem Victor Chem Wks, Chicago Heights Ill 58-59; (Sp4) Hosp Lab Tech & X-Ray Tech US Army, US & Europe 59-62; Med Supply Clerk A S Aloe, Seattle 62; Stud asst West Ill U Lib 63; Grad asst Ind U A-V Center(Bloomington) 64-65; Head Libn McKendree Col 65-67; Acquis libn Heterick Mem Lib Ohio Northern U 67-. 9: ALA; NEA-DAVI. 10: Rotary Internat. 14: Automated instr materials ctr concept in acad libs. 15: 204 CBI apts, 502 S Main, Ada Oh 45810.

FITCH, VIOLA K. b Steuben NY 19 Ag 07. 5: Simmons 26-30 BS, Columbia 50 (LS) MS. 7: Jr high sch libn br child libn Providence Pub Lib 30-37; Supv of wk with child Lucas Co Lib. Maumee Ohio 37-40; Supv of wk with child Wayne Co Lib, Detroit 40-45; 1st asst ref dept Utica Pub Lib, Utica NY 45; Childlibn Jervis Lib, Rome NY 46; Libn Brooklyn Child Museum, Brooklyn NY 46-47; Ref asst Sch of Lib Ser Columbia U 47-48; Child libn St Cloud Tchrs Col 48-49; Head Libn Pontiac Central High Sch, Pontiac Mich 49-59; Supv of sch libs Kalamazoo PubLib 59-62; Coordinator of instrl materials serv Livonia Pub Schs, Livonia Mich 62-. 8: Visiting instr, lib sci summer courses, 5 institutions. 9: ALA; MichLA; MichASchL; MichEA. 14: Child & sch libnship. 15: 18980 Fenton ave, Detroit 48219.

FITE, BETHEL. b Clarksdale Miss 30 D 10. 5: Miss State Col for Women 28-32 (Lat) AB; Drexel 37-38 BS in LS; Columbia 43-44 (Adult Educ) MA. 7: Tchr of Lat & Eng Duncan Consolidated High Sch, Duncan Miss 32-35; Lib asst Carnegie Pub Lib, Clarksdale Miss 35-37; Tech Supv Gulf Coast Area WPA, Gulfport Miss 38-39; Co Libn Alcorn Co Lib, Corinth Miss 39; State Supv Lib Proj WPA, Jackson Miss 39-42; State Chief War Serv Sect WPA, Jackson Miss 42-43; Reg Libn Murray State Col 44-46; Dir dept lib ext UAla 46-. 9: ALA; AlaLA (chm Com Intel Freedom 68-69); SELA. 10: AAUW; LWV. 11: Inst of Internat Educ scholarship for study in Gt Brit summer 50. 14: Ref, adult educ. 15: Drawer 2987, University Ala 35486.

FITES, GILBERT G JR. b Springfield SA 30 Je 21. 4: Grace Bosma Fites. 5: Kent State 39-41, 45-47 (Bus Admin) BS in BA; UDenver 47-48 (LS) MA; Ind U 51-52 (A-V Educ) MS in Ed. 7: 43rd Infantry Div 42-45; Stud asst Kent State U 45-47; Circ libn Kan State Col(Pittsburg) 48-51; Head libn Firmont State Col 52-56; Consul Palo Alto(Cal) Unified Sch Dist 57-59; Head Libn Ariz State Col 59-65; Head Libn Northeastern State Col 65-, Dir div of lib sci 65-. 9: ALA; OklaLA; Theatre LA. 10: Circus Hist Soc; Club du Cirque. 13: Yes. 14: Cherokee Indians, hist of Amer circus. 15: Northeastern State Col Lib, Tahlequah Okla.

FITZ, ANNE (HEITMANN). b Lincoln Ill 5 Ag 11. 4: Elmore J Fitz. 5: Rockford Col 28-32 (Hist) BA; Chicago 32-33 (Pol Sci) MA, 34-35 (Soc Serv); SUNY(Albany) 63-64 MSLS. 6: Fr. 7: Soc wker Cook Co Bureau of Pub Welfare, Chicago 35-38; Soc wker Juvenile Court, Wash DC 38-40; Soc wker Family & Child's Serv, Pittsfield Mass 57-63; Circ libn Williams Col 64-. 9: ALA. 10: Great Bks Discussion Group (past chm); LWV Discussion Program (past chm); Legis Com Pittsfield Commun Coun (past chm); ACLU; Appalachian Mountain Club; Mass Audubon Soc. 14: Ref. 15: 119 Summer st, Lanesboro Ma 01237.

FITZ, THOMAS R(ICHARD). b Laurel Ind 29 S 34. 4: Judith Ann Schwendener. 5: SWest col 52-56 (Soc Sci) AB; DrewU 56-59 (Theol) BD, 59-61 (Old Testament Hist). STM; Iliff sch of Theol 62-64 (Old Testament Hist); UDenver 65-66 (LS) MA. 6: Hebrew, Aramic, Ger. 7: Minister United Methodist Ch, Overton Neb 61-62; Supply tchr pub schs Denver 63-65; Adult serv libn pub lib, Englewood Colo 66-67; Asst libn Barron Co Campus of Stout StateU 67-. 9: Amer Acad of Relig; Assn of Wis State Univs Faculties; Heart of the North Schoolmasters Assn. 10: Ambassadors of the Rice Lake C of C; Pi Gamma Mu. 15: Rural rte 2, Birchwood Wi 54817.

FITZGERALD, ANN (LOUISE). b Chicago Ill 30 Ja 43. 5: Loretto Hts Col 61-65 (Eng) BA; UDenver 65-67 (LS) MA. 7: Catlgr Loretto Hts Col, Denver 65-67; Hd catlg dept metropolitan State Col, Denver 67-68; Tech info specialist Nat Safety Coun Safety Research Info Serv 68-. 14: Catlg, indexing. 15: 1555 N Dearborn Pkwy, Chicago Il 60610.

FITZGERALD, DOROTHY (STICKLE). b Canyon City Colo 23 F 06. 4: Harold Belden Fitz Gerald. 5: Barnard 24-28 t9eng, Fr) BS; Columbia 36-37 BS in LS, 38-40 (En) MA. 6: Fr. 7: Eng tchr Bd of Edu, Newtown Pen 28-36; Lib asst NY Pub Lib 37; Ref libn Glen Ridge Pub Lib, Glen Ridge NJ 37-43; Tchr of Lib Sci Newark State Tchrs Col 41; Libn S Jr High Sch, Bloomfield NJ43-, Chm Eng dept 58-; Supv Jr High Libs, Bloomfield NJ 65-. 8: Consul H W Wilson Co 64-65. 9: ALA; NEA Reg chm; NJLA (var coms); NJSchLA; NJEA. 10: NJ English Tchrs Assn; Banard Col Alumnae Assn; Friends of the Lib, Bloomfield NJ. 14: Sch libs. 15: 270 Ridgewood ave, Glen Ridge NJ 07028.

FITZGERALD, LOUISE (HERBERT). b Framingham Mass. 4: Edward FitzGerald. 5: Simmons 38 BLS. 7: Child libn Providence Pub Lib 38-41; Br libn Great Neck (NY) Pub Lib 41-43; Ed Staff); "Time NYC 43-46; Pub rel consul Madison (Wis) Pub Lib 59-61; Project consul Kellogg Pub Lib, Green Bay 62-65; Consul Diocesan Sch Lib Center, Green Bay 65-. 8: Adv, Contin Educ for Women, UWis 61. 15: 2702 Ravine way, Green Bay Wis 54301.

FITZGERALD, MICHAEL JOSEPH. b Providence 2 Mr 36. 5: Providence Col 53-57 (Eng) BA; Fulbright at Munich Universita2t 57-58 (Eng, Ger); Brown U 58-60 (Eng); Simmons 62-64 MSLS. 6: Ger, Fr, Lat. 7: Catlg asst Brown U 60-65; Catlgr Harvard U 65-. 9: RILA; NE Tech Serv Libns (chm 67-68). 14: Catlg. 15: 109 Oxford st, Arlington Ma 02174.

FITZGERALD, PATRICIA (GERECKE). b Toronto 19 Ag 39. 4: Maurice Pim FitzGerald. 5: UToronto, Trinity Col 58-62 (Fr, Ger) BA; UToronto 63-64 BLS; West Res 64- (LS)67 MS in LS. 6: Fr, Ge. 7: Clerk Ont Hosp Serv Commsn, Toronto summers 59-62; Clerical asst UToronto Lib 62-63; Catlgr West ResU Freiberger Lib 64-67; Asst hd catlg dept U Waterloo Lib 67-. 9: ALA; CanLA. 10: Univ Women's Club. 14: Catg. 15: 120 Longwood dr, Waterloo Ont Can.

FITZGERALD, RUTH FLORENCE (CARPENTER). b South Haven Mich 18 Ja 35. 4: Richard Lee Fitzgerald. 5: West Mich U 52-61 (Eng) BS, 64-68 MSL. 6: Fr. 7: Tchr: West Sch dist, Parma Mich 58-64, Albion Pub Schs, Albion Mich 64-66; Libn Albion Sr High Sch, albion Mich 66-68; Libn Jackson Commun Col, Jackson Mich 68-. 8: Calhoun Co Media masters, Marshall Mich 66-68; Lib Com, Albion Pub Schs 65-68; Lib Tech Adv Com, Chm Jackson Commun Col 69. 9: ALA; AASchL; NEA; MichASchL; MichEA; Jackson Commun Col EA. 10: Beta Phi Mu. 14: Ref. 15: 6900 McCain rd, Jackson Mi 41201.

FITZGERALD, WILLIAM AMBROSE. b Boston 28 Ja 06. 4: Julia F Morris. 5: Boston Col 23-27 (Langs) AB, 27-28 (Hist) MA; Fordham 30-34 (His) PhD; Columbia 35-38 BS LS, 38-39 (LS). 6: Lat, Sp, Ital, Gk. 7: Libn- archivist Brooklyn (NY) Prep 28-44; Lecturer Lib Educ Boston Col summers 33, 34, 37; Lecturer Lib Sci Georgetown U summer 36; Visiting Prof Lib Sci Villanova U summers 39, 40, 41; Instr LIB Sci & Hist St Johns U (NY) 42-45; Libn Stuyvesant Even High Sch, NYC 39-40; Libn & Asst Prof of Med Hist St Louis U 44-48; Dir of Lib Sch & Prof of Lib Sci Peabody Col 48-63; Lib Consul Republic of China, Taiwan China 56-58; Lib Sci Adv Libya, Liberia, Sierra Leone 61-63; Dir of Libs & Prof of Lib Sci Marquette U 64-. 9: ALA-LED (pres 56-57); CathLA (pres 39-41; SLA (pres Wis Chap 68-69); MedLA; SELA; WisLA. 10: AAUP; Cath Commsn of Intel & Cultural Affairs; Galery of Living Cath Authors (pres 44-49). 11: Bishops Lib Medal Mid-South Conf of CathLA 61. 12: Contrib "New Library of Catholic Knowledge, 12 v (63-65); Ed Booknotes "Peabody Journal of ducation (48-63); Ed "Current Reference Books in "Wilson Lirary Bulleti (51-52); Contrib "Catholic Encyclopedia for School and Home 12 v (65). 13: Yes. 14: Lib hist, admin. 15: 1111 N Astor st B3, Milwaukee Wi 53202.

FITZMAURICE, EDNA (MAYER). b Kenosha Wis. 5: UWis 25-26 (Libnship) Diploma; San Jose State Col 53-60 (LS) BA. 6: Sp. 7: Asst child libn G M Simmons Lib, Kenosha Wis 19-24; Br libn McKinley Jr High Sch, Kenosha Wis 26-30; Br libn Washington Jr High Sch, Kenosha Wis 30-37; Asst libn Dept of Adult Educ San Jose Unified Sch Dist, San Jose Cal 52-56, Libn 56-. 8: Parish libn St Patricks Church MLib, San Jose Cal 54-69. 9: ALA; CathLA; Cal Assn Sch Libns. 10: Intercultural Coun (San Jose Cal); The Literary Group (San Jose); The Pathfinders. 14: Ref, adult educ. 15: 55 S 6th st #307, San Jose Ca 95112.

FITZPATRICK (MARGARET) ELAINE. b Edmonton Alta Can. 5: UAlta 47-51 (Chem) BSc. 7: Sec UAlta Dept of Chem 51-52; Sec Can Industries Ltd, Toronto 52-56, Libn 56-. 9: SLA-Toronto Chap (pres, v-pres, program chm, sec). 14: Chemistry. 15: Canadian Industres Ltd, Paint Res Lab 1330 Castlefield ave, Toronto 19.

FITZPATRICK, LENA (RICCARDI). b Jersey City NJ 21 O 13. 4: Thomas Fitzpatrick. 5: Seton Hall U 62 (Soc Sci) AB. 7: Lib asst Free Pub Lib, Jerey City NJ 30-48, Prin libn art & music 48-55, Supv libn brs & exts 55-. 9: ALA; NJLA (pres Ext Sect); Hudson Co LA. 10: Bus & Profess Women's Club. 15: 154 Bowers st, Jersey City NJ 07307.

FITZSIMMONS, RICHARD. b Scranton Penn 21 Mr 43. 5: UScranton 61-65 (Bus Admin) BS; UPittsburgh 65-66 (Lib, Info Sci) MLS, 66- (Lib, Computer Sci). 6: Sp, Fr, Lat, russian. 7: Lib asst UScranton 63-65, Asst libn 66-68; Lib asst Carnegie Lib of Pittsburgh Penn 66; Hd libn Worthington Scranton Campus Lib Penn StateU (Dunmore) 68-. 8: Adv com of the Friendly Sons of St Patrick. 9: ALA; AAUP; CathLA; PennLA (state adv New Libn's Sect, sec-treas NE Chap, memb chm NE Chap). 10: Commun Concert Assn; Museum Assn; Friends of Scranton Pub Lib; Beta Phi Mu. 12: "Bibliography on the european Economic Community and Great Britain"; "Bibliography of Pierre Teilhard de Chardin". 14: Admin, ref, bldg planning, computers. 15: 746 N Webster ave, Scranton Pa 18510.

FIVASH, MARILYN V (WEIN). b Stegar Ill 29 Je 26. 4: Lawrence Weldon Fivash Jr. 5: Andrews U 44-48 (Fr) BA; UMich summers 50-5; AMLS. 6: Fr. 7: Tchr High Sch, Galien Mich 48-50; Tchr-libn High Sch, Tustin Mich 50-53; Tchr-libn High Sch, Rose City Mich 53-55; Tchr-libn High Sch, Firview Mich 55-58; Tchr- libn Acad, Broadview Ill 58-59; Libn Andrews U 59-. 8: Tchr of Lib Sci. 9: ALA; MichLA; Berrien Co Coop LA. 10: Altrusa Club. 14: Catlg, cir, ref, admin. 15: 1008 Kedhart, Berrien Springs Mi 49103.

FIX, DOROTHY DEKLE. b Birmingham Ala 23 Jl 15. 4: John E Fix. 5: Franklin Col of Ind 32-36 (Math, Bio-Chem) AB (Cum Laude); Ball State summers 67, 68 (Phys Educ) Tchg certif; Rutgers 62-65 MLS. 6: Ger. 7: Tchr Lakeview Sch, Rossville Ga 36-37; Supv elem phys educ Kokomo Elem Schs, Kokomo Ind 37-38; Tchr Kokomo High Sch 38-40; Libn So Blvd Sch of Chatham Twp, Chatham NJ 60-. 8: Selector for elem sch lib Collection 66-. 9: ALA; NJSchLA (Memb Com); NJEA; Morris Co EA; Morris Co SchLA (treas & Memb Chm). 10: Beta Phi Mu; Chatham Twp Girl Scout Assn. 14: Child lit, elem sch libs. 15: 21 Rolling Hill dr, Chatham NJ 07928.

FLACK, CHARLES R(UTHVEN). b Hagersville Ont Can 8 Ag 1896. 5: UWis 19-20 (LS) Diploma; UAlberta 21-25 (Eng, Fr, Math) BA; UIll 25-26 BLS, 28-29 (Eng) MA; UChicago 35-36, 40-41 (LS, Psych, Educ). 7: Catlgr St Benedict's Col, Atchison Kan 26-28; Libn SWest La Inst 28-38; Libn Hampton Inst 38-40; Dir of lib sci State Col, Clarion Penn 41-65; Catlgr West Col, Oxford Ohio 66-67; Libn Drake Col 67-. 9: ALA; LaLA; VaLA. 10: Nat Rifle Assn. 14: Catlg. 15: 2032 San Luis, Stockton Ca 95207

FLAGG, CEDRIC R. b Westford Vt 9 Ag 08. 4: Helen Miller. 5: Middlebury Col 27-31 (Chem) BS; Columbia 31-32 BS LS. 6: Fr, Ger, Russian, Sp, Ital. 7: Lib asst Middlebury Col 32-37; Libn Titanium Div Nat Lead Co 37-40; Libn Squier Lab, Ft Monmouth NJ 40-47; Chief Lib br Off of Asst Sec of Defense (R&D) 47-53; Chef lib br Goodyear Atomic, Portsmouth Ohio 53-55; Chief info serv Armour Research Chicago 55-56; Chief abstracter West ResU 56-59; Libn Plant 1 Boeing Airplane C, Wichita Kan 59-62; Chief documentation div Norwich Pharmacal Co, Norwich NY 62-63; Libn spec collections SUNY(Cortland) 63-64; Libn Amer Pharmaceutical Assn, WASH DC 64-. 9: ADI; SLA; MeLA. 12: "Metals Abstracts (56-59); "Searching the Government Documents & "Abstracting and Indexing the Metallurgical Literature in "Metal Abstracts (56-59). 13: Yes. 14: Pharmaceut ref, abstracting, indexing, translating, machine methods. 15: 2118 Grayson pl, Falls Church Va 22043.

FLAGG, JO ELLEN. b Charleston WVa 8 F 37. 5: WVa Wesleyan Col 54-58 (LS) BS; West Res 59-61 MS in LS; UWis 67-68 Certif in Libnship. 7: Coyle & Richardson Dept Store, Charleston WVa summers 54-58; Lib asst Case Inst of Tech 59-61; Sci libn Oberlin Col 61-. 9: ALA. 10: LWV; AAUW; ACLU; Welcome Wagon. 14: Sci (ref & catlg), automation. 15: 98 Union st, Oberlin Ohio 44074.

FLAKE, CHAD J. b Snowflake Ariz 28 D 29. 5: Ariz State Col 47-49 (Educ); Brigham Young U 51-53 (Eng) BA; UDenver 54-55 (LS) MA. 6: Sp, Fr, Lat. 7: Ref asst Brigham Young U 53-54, Documents libn 55-57, Curator spec collectins & Instr in Lib Sci 57-. 8: Com on Mormon Clsf UTahLA (chm). 9: ALA; MPLA; UtahLA (pres 64). 10: West Hist Assn; Utah Valley Hist Assn; Utah Westerners; Beta Phi Mu. 12: Classification of Mormonism," "Mormon Bibliography 1830-1930" (64-); Mormon Americana. 13: Yes. 14: Rare bks, west hist. 15: 261 S 3rd E, Provo Utah 84601.

FLAKE, MARY EVELYN (LINDERMAN). b Demorest Ga 23 Mr 19. 5: Columbia Union Col 48-51 (Eng) BA; UMd 51 (LS0; USoCal 60-65 (LS). 7: Tchr-libn Forest Lake Acad, Maitland Fla 51-52; Lib clerk Hycon Mfg Co, Pasadena Cal 55-56; Libn Stanford Res Inst So Cal Labs, South Pasadena Cal 56-. 9: SLA. 14: Ref, catlg. 15: 901 Valley View, Monrovia Cal.

FLANDERS, FRANCES (VIVIAN). b Howe Okla 18 S 08. 5: Mansfield Female Col 25-27; Northwestern State Col(La) 27-29 (Eng, Soc Sci) AB; LSU 34-36 BS in LS. 6: Fr. 7: Tchr Sabine Parsh Sch Bd, Belmont La 27-28; Tchr-libn De Soto Parish Sch Bd, Pelican La 29-35; Libn Monroe City Sch Bd, Neville High Sch 36-46; Tchr Lib Sci Southwestern La Inst summers 38-39; Asst libn La State Lib, Bossier & De Soto Parishes 41-42; Tchr Lib Sci Northwestern State Col(Natchiotoches La) summers 44-45; Head Libn Ouachita Paish Pub Lib, Monroe La 46-. 8: Lib consul for the Fayetteville Pub Lib, Fayetteville Ark 60-62; Rogers Pub Lib, Rogers Ark 63; Bldg consul La State Lib 67-. 9: ALA (past Memb Chm); LaLA (var offs 37-63, chm var coms). 10: DAR (Regent 52-54, La State Libn 54-57); AAUW; Delta Kappa Gamma; Phi Mu; Phi Kappa Phi; Daughters of Founders and Patriots of America; Colonial Dames of the Seventeenth Century; Garden Club. 11: Library received Modisette Award 49, 65; Library received John Cotton Dana Award 56; voted "Boss of the Year by Ouachita Parish OE Club 63. 12: Weekly column "Guide to Good Reading "Monroe Morning World 46-; Weekly radio program KMLB 50; Monthly television program KNOE. 13: Yes. 14: Ref, lib bldgs, geneal. 15: 1703 N Third st, Monroe La 71209.

FLANDERS, LILLIAN (FRENCH). b Ind 8 Ja 07. 4: Maxwell Flanders. 5: Whitter Col 25-29 (Eng) BA; UCal 29-30 (LS) Certif. 7: Lib asst UCal(Los Angeles) 30-35; Young Hd adult servs Whittier Pub Lib, Whitter Cal 57-.09: CalLA. 15: 6538 S Bright ave, Whittier Ca 90601.

FLANDREAU, ARTHUR (CONOVER) (JR). b Brooklyn NY 26 Ja 27. 4: Janet Elder. 5: Dickinson Col 47-50 (Hist) BA; Chicago 50-52 (LS) MA. 7: Spec agent US Army Counter Intelligence Corps, Japan 46; Libn Nat Opinion Research Center, Chicago 51-52; Ref asst Dartmouth Col Lib 52-55; Ref libn Dickinson Col Lib 55-58, Asst libn 59-61; Lib Dir Concord Col Lib 61-. 9: WVaLA. 10: AAUP; Phi Beta Kappa. 14: Acad libnship, ref, admin. 15: PO Box 726, Athens WVa 24712.

FLANIGAN, CHARLES J. b Erie Pe 16 N 06. 5: UBuffalo 29-32 (Hist) BA, 32-34 (Hist) MA, 34-35 BLS. 6: Ital. 7: Lib asst Buffalo Pub Lib, Buffalo NY 32-41, Chief adult circ 45-48; Deputy dir Buffalo & Erie Co Pub Lib, Buffalo NY 48-. 9: ALA; NYLA. 14: Admin. 15: Buffalo & Erie County Pub Lib Lafayette sq, Buffalo NY 14203.

FLANNERY, LOUIS. b Rydar N Dak 1 Ap 37. 5: PacificU 54-58 (Lit) BA; UWash 60-61 (LS) MS; UUtah 63; Portland StateU 64. 7: Tchr Roseburg High Sch, Roseburg Ore 58; Clk admin sect counter intelligence corps 112th CIC, Ft Sam Houston 60; Libn Centennial High Sch, Gresham Ore 61; Libn Tigard High Sch, Tigard Ore 62-64; Asst libn PacificU 65, Libn 66-. 9: ALA; PNLA; OreLA. 14: Admin. 15: Pacific Univ, Forest Grove Or 97116.

FLEAGLE, MARIANNE D. b Baltimore Md 3 Ja 19. 4: Robert G Fleagle. 5: Goucher 36-40 (Eng) BA; UWash 65-66 M Lib. 6: Fr. 7: Bkmob libn King Co Lib Syst, Seattle 66-67; Ref libn Bellevue Lib King Co Lib Syst, Bellevue Wash 67-. 8:

Teacher, English-Social Studies, Baltimore County Secondary Schools 40-42. 9: ALA; PNLA; WashLA. 10: Beta Phi Mu. 14: Ref. 15: 7858 - 56th pl NE, Seattle Wa 98115.

FLECK, MARY R. b Milwaukee 29 Mr 03. 4: John G Fleck. 5: Smith 20-24 (Hist) BA; Oxford U 27; SUNY 57-59 MS LS. 6: Fr, Ger. 7: Interior decorator J Wattley Inc, Cleveland 27-33; Asst br libn Buffalo & Erie Co Pub Lib, Buffalo NY 57-59; Asst circ libn Medford Pub Lib, Medford Mass 59-60; Asst libn adult serv-ref Belmont Pub Lib, Belmont Mass 60-67; Supv Pub Lib Dev Mass Bur Lib Ext 67-. 9: MassLA; Charles River LA. 10: YWCA; Buffalo Smith Col Club. 14: Ref. 15: 1 Emerson pl, Boston Ma 02114.

FLECKSTEINER, CATHERINE (RILEY). b Bethlehem Penn 19 Ap 26. 4: John W Fleckster. 7: Catlg asst Lehigh U Lib 45-60, Catlgr 60-64, Ser catlgr 65-. 14: Catlg. 15: RD 1. Saylorsburg Pa 18353.

FLEDDERUS, HELEN. b Boston 16 F 31. 4: J Dyck Fledderus. 5: Smith 51 (Hist) BA. 6: Fr. 7 Lib trainee Harvard U Lamont Lib 51-52; Libn George S. Armstrong & Co Inc, NYC 53-57; Ref libn J Walter Thompson Co Info Center, NYC 58-60; Libn Readers Digest Advertising Dept, NYC 61-. 8: Bus mgr "Whats New in Advertising & Marketing 62-63. 9: SLA (Program Chm NY CHAP 63-64). 14: Ref. 15: 10 Mitchell pl, New York N Y 10017.

FLEGAL, JEAN (ELIZABETH). b Zanesville Ohio 5: Carnegie 38-43 (Gen Stud) BS; Columbia 49-52 MLS; NYU Grad Sch of Bus 59-67, (Mgt), MBA. 6: Sp. 7: Sec to chief chem Hazel-Atlas Glass C, Zanesville Ohio 33-38; Sec, Pittsburgh 38-41; Asst to admin ESMWT Carnegie Inst of Tech 40-42; Sec to Dir Microb Res Merck & Co Inc, Rahway NJ 43-50; Sec The Amer Assembly Columbia U 50-51; Libn Gen Purchasing Dept Union Carbide Corp, NY 51-59, Libn Bus Lib 59-. 9: SLA (treas, chm Nonserial Publs Com); -NY Chap (pres); NY Lib Club. 10: Phi Kappa Phi. 14: Ref, admin. 15: 360 E 55th st, New York NY 10022.

FLEISCHER, MARY BETH. b Corpus Christi Tex 6 F 34. 5: N Tex StateU 51-55 (LS) BA; UTex 59-63 MLS. 7: Libn pub schs, Pleasanton Tex 55-57; Libn pub schs, Ft Stockton Tex 57-60; Libn UTex 61-. 9: TexLA. 14: Ref, acquis. 15: Barker Tex Hist Lib Univ of Tex, Austin Tex 78712.

FLEISHER, LISBETH DEUTSCH. b Vienna 3 Mr 17. 4: Joseph H Fleisher. 5: UVienna 37-38 (Musicology); Syracuse 57-61 MS (LS). 6: German, Fr, Ital, Lat. 7: Cornell U; Prin lib asst Rare Bk Dept 57-60, Asst libn 60-62, Asst catlg libn 62-64; Assoc Veterinary libn NY State Veterinary Col 64-67; Assoc libn Sun Oil Co, Phila 67-68; Ref libn Tech Lib, Edgewood Md 69-. 9: SLA. 10: Beta Phi Mu. 15: 8911 F Waltham Woods rd, Baltimore Md 21234.

FLEISHER, MARY-LOUISE. b Philadelphia 11 D 28. 5: Rosemont 46-50 (Soc Sci) BA; Villanova 58-60 MS LS. 6: S. 7: Sec Rittenhouse Found, Phila 53-57; Sec Amer Friends Serv Com, Phila 58-59; Res room libn VillanovaU Lib 59-60; Catlgr & clsfr VAN Pelt Lib UPenn 60-. 10: Womens Faculty Club, UPenn. 14: Catlg. 15: Suffolk Manor H414 Broad & Clearview sts, Phila Pa 19141.

FLEKSTRA, GERARD J JR. b Grand Rapids Mich 24 Ja 31. 4: Ruth M Barney. 5: Central Bible Col 56-58 (Bible) BA; Gordan Divinty Sch 58-60; So Conn State Col 67- (LS). 7: Sgt USMC 50-54; Pastor First Pentecostal Ch, Newburyport Mass 59-61; Pastor First Assembly of God, Meriden Conn 62-66; Acquis libn Central Bible Col 66-68, Libn 68-. 9: ATLA; Christians Libn Fellowship. 10: Delta Epsilon Chi. 14: Bibliog of spec areas. 15: 404 W Evergreen st, Springfield Mo 65803.

FLEMING, ANN. b Nashville 30 D 23. 4: Herman Fleming Jr. 5: Peabody 41-45 (Eng) BA; Tex Womans U 55-56 MLS. 7: Circ & ref Arlington State Col 57; Libn Arlington High Sch, Arlington Tex 58-68; Instr in Lib Sci Sam Houston State Col summers 67, 68, Instr Lib Sci 68-. 9: TexASchL (sec 67-68); Tex Teen-Age Lib Assn. 14: Catlg, ref, acquis. 15: 1319 Ave N, Huntsville Tx 77340.

FLEMING, FRANCES O. b Kelso Wash 10 Ag 24. 5: Phoenix Col 41-43; Ariz State U 45-48 (Pol Sci) BA, 48-50 (Educ) MA; USoCal 51-55 MSLS. 7: Libn Phoenix Elem Schs 48-57; Field libn US Army Spec Ser, Germany 57-58; Command libn US Army Spec Serv, Paris 58-60; Coord of libs US Air Force Dependents Sch, Wiesbaden Germany 60-62; Supv lib serv Bd of Educ of Baltimore Co, Towson Md 62-68, Coord lib serv 68-. 8: Wkshop Consul Mich State Lib, Lansng Mich 55; Plan Consul Dept DEF Dependents Sch, Karlsruhe Germany 67; Symposium Consul, Syracuse U 67; Wkshop Consul, Syracuse U 68. 9: NEA; ALA; AASchL (Index ed "School Libararies 63-65, & 66-69, chm Publ Com 65); YASD (dir 65-68); MdLA (v-pres 65); Assn of Sch Libns of Md; Ariz State LA (v-pres & ed "Arizona Libraries 52-54, pres 56). 10: Beta Phi Mu; Kappa Delta Pi. 14: Sch libs. 15: Bd of Educ Baltimore Co, Aigburth Manor, Towson Md 21204.

FLEMING, JOHN ZINN. b Lewistown Penn 5 S 41. 4: Dorothy Smith. 5: Juniata Col 59-63 (Music Educ) BS; UPittsburgh 65-67 MLS. 6: Fr, Ger. 7: Instrumental music tchr Wilmington Area Schs, New Wilmington Penn 63-64; Elem mus tchr Red Lion Area Schs, Red Lion Penn 64-66; Libn & asst mgr York Symphony Orchestra, York Penn 64-66; Asst gift libn UPittsburgh 66-67; Mus lib asst UIll (Urbana) 67-. 9: MusicLA. 10: Champaign-Urbana Symphony Orchestra; UIll Lib Staff Assn; Beta Phi Mu. 14: Acquis, catlg, phono rec, care of wind, choral & orchestral collections. 15: 708 W Springfield ave apt 6, Champaign Il 61820.

FLEMING, LOIS V DELAVAN. b Toledo Ohio 25 Ja 28. 4: Philip J Fleming. 5: Fla State U 46-50 (Journalism) BA, 64-65 (LS) MA, (LS) 67-68; UUtah 68-. 7: Research libn Fla Advertising Commsn, Tallahassee 49-52; Grad asst to Dean Louis Shore:Fla State U 64-65; Mus catlgr Strozier Lib Fla State U 65-67. 8: Circ mge "Florida Libraries 64-65. 9: ALA; FlaLA; SELA. 10: Fla Hist Soc; Beta Phi Mu; Beta Sigma Phi; Nat Assn of Parliamentarians. 14: Ref, adult serv. 15: Rt 3 Box 131, Quincy Fl 32351.

FLEMING, SISTER STELLA MARIS OP. b Somerville Mass 20 Jl 10. 5: Boston Col 42 (Eng) AB; CathU 43 BS LS. 6: Lat, Fr. 7: Libn St Catharine Col 43-66, Lecturer in Lib Sci Catherine Spalding Col, Louisville Ky summers 46; Libn Siena Col 66-. 9: ALA; CathLA. 12: Ed "The Catholic Booklist (50-56). 14: Catlg, tchg of catlg. 15: Siena Col 4405 Poplar ave, Memphis Tn 38117.

FLEMISTER, WILSON N. b Atlanta 15 Ag 39. 4: Shirley Willingham. 5: Clark Col 57-59, 61-63 (Music) BA; AtlantaU 64-65 MS in LS; Emory 67-68. 6: Fr. 7: Intl Theol Ctr, Atlanta; Asst libn 65-68, Hd libn 68-. 8: Standing com on Bibliog Resources of Commsn on Archives & Hist of Methodist Ch; Pres Methodist Libns Fellowship. 9: ATheolLA. 14: Catlg, admin. 15: 234 Napoleon dr SW, Atlanta Ga 30314.

FLENER, JANE GARDNER. b Hopkinsville Ky 3 Ja 20. 5: Bethel Womans Col 37-39 AA; Peabody 39-41 (Eng) BS, 41-42 BS in LS, 43-45 (Eng) MA; Ind U 59-63 (Higher Educ) Ed D. 7: Asst libn Tchrs Col of Conn(New Britain) 42-45; Asst libn Furman U 45-53; Asst libn Austin eay Peay Col 53-55; Educ libn Ind U Lib 55-64, Asst dir 64-. 8: Mem, Adv Coun on Col Lib Resources Prog, Higher Educ Act of 1965, Title II-A 68-70. 9: ALA (life mem); -ACRL (Nomin Com 68-69); -LAD (Exec Bd Personnel Admin Sect 66-68); SLA (Ind Chap Bd 68-69); IndLA (life mem, Bd 66-67, v-pres & pres-elect); ConnLA; SCLA; TennLA; SELA. 10: AAUW; Altrusa; YWCA (Bd); University Club. 14: Lib admin, personnel. 15: Indiana Univ Libs, Bloomington In 47401.

FLETCHER, CAROLYN T. b Lafayette Ind 6 N 28. 4: Ben C Fletcher. 5: Purdue U 46-49 (Liberal Sci) BS; UIll 49-50 MS in LS. 6: Sp. 7: Catlgr Richter Lib UMiami (Coral Gables Fla) 50-. 9: ALA; SELA; FlaLA (sec Col & Sp Sect, Recruitment Com); Memb Com 68-69); DadeCoLA. 10: Friends of the UMiami Lib. 14: Catlg. 15: 5895 SW 50th st, Miami Fla 33155.

FLETCHER, ELIZABETH CHAMBERS SULLIVAN. b Hattiesburg Miss. 4: Ibert W Fletcher Sr. 5: MissSoCol 36-41 (Soc Studies) BS, 56 (LS); USoMiss 64-65 MS in LS. 6: Sp, Fr. 7: Asst libn State Lib, Jackson Miss 40-42; Ext libn Gulfport-Harrison Co Lib, Gulfport Miss 56-57; High sch libn Long Beach Mun Sch Dist, Long Beach Miss 57-66; Supv of lib servs Long Beach Mun Sch Dist 66-. 9: ALA; SLA-REG8; MissLA; MissEA; MissASchL (v-pres 69-70). 10: YWCA (Recruit Com); AAUW; USoMiss Alum Assn. 14: Ref, young adults, child libs. 15: 4622 Lewis st, Gulfport Miss.

FLETCHER, HOMER L. b Salem Ind 11 My 28. 4: Jacquelyn Blanton Fletcher. 5: IndU 49-53 (Hist) AB; UIll 53-54 MS LS. 6: Fr, Sp. 7: Stud asst UIll Lib Sch Lib 53; Research asst UIll Lib (Urbana) 53; Tchr asst UIll Lib Sch 54; Libn I Milwaukee Pub Lib 54-56; Head libn Ashland Pub Lib, Ashland Ohio 56-59; City libn Arcadia (Cal) Pub Lib 59-65; City libn Vallejo (Cal) Pub Lib 65-. 8 Exec dir Nat Lib Week, Cal 64. 9: ALA (Intel Freedom Com 67-); CalLA (pres Pub Libs Sect 67, mem & chm Intel Freedom Com 62-68); Pub Lib Execs Assn So Cal (pres 64). 10: Major 129th Air Commando Group, Cal Air Nat

Guard; Phi Beta Kappa; Rotary Club; Assn for Neurologically Handicapped Child; elder First Christ Church. 13: Yes. 14: Intel freedom, lib admin, lib bldgs. 15: 1825 Sereno dr, Vallejo Cal 94590.

FLETCHER, KATHLEEN G. b Ruston La 13 A 13. 5: La Polytech Inst 29-32 (Eng) BA; LSU 32-33 BS in LS; UIll 46-47 MS in LS. 7: Libn Gilbert High Sch, Gilbert La 33-35; Libn University Sch FSCW, Tallahassee Fla 35-41; Army Air Force libn MacDill Field, Tampa Fla 41-46; Elem libn Froebel Sch, Gary Ind 48-51; Supv of city sch libs, High Point NC 51-55; Asst Prof SoIllU 55-. 8: Taught sch libnship courses summers, Emory U 49-54, UNC 55, San Jose State 57, Portland State Col 62-64, Ariz State U 65,66,68. 9: ALA; IllLA. ; NEA-DAVI; IllEA. 10: AAUW; Beta Phi Mu; Humane Soc. 13: Yes. 14: Sch libnship. 15: 606 Glen View dr, Carbondale Il 62901.

FLETCHER, RUTH (ANDREWS). b Pittsfield Mass 13 My 15. 4: Leo W Fletcher. 5: Wheaton col (Mass) 31-35 (Lat) AB; Simmons 64-67 (LS) MS. 6: Fr, Ger. 7: Priv tutoring Thayer Acad, Braintree Mass 57-60, 61-66; Ref libn Wheaton Col, Norton Mass 67-. 9: ALA. 10: Amer Guild of Organists; Orton Soc; Reading Reform Foun. 14: Ref, archives. 15: 42 Park st, Mansfield Ma 02048.

FLEURY, MARY GRACE. b Madison Wis 30 My 07. 5: UWis 25-29 (Eng) BA, 29-30 (LS) Certif; Columbia summers 37, 39, 40 MS L. 7: Asst educ dept Newark (NJ) Pub Lib 30-44; Kansas Cty (Mo) Pub Lib: Asst bk info 44-45, Head bk info 45-60, Catlg info libn 60-. 9: ALA; Adult Edu Assn; MoLA. 10: Womens C of C; Cath Womens Club; Patroness of Cath Commun Lib; Bus & Prof Womens Club. 14: Adult educ. 15: 115 N Bales ave, Kansas City Mo 64123.

FLICK, FRANCES JOSEPHINE. b Maryville Mo 17 Ag 16. 5: Westhampton Col 34-36 (Liberal Arts); Iowa State U 36-39 (Forestry) BS; Syracuse 41-43 (LS) BS. 6: Fr, Ger, Sp, Russian, Lat, Gk. 7: Lib asst to asst ref libn Pub Lib, Des Moines Iowa 40-44; Engnr libn La Polytech Inst 44-45; Engnr libn Carrier Corp, Syracuse NY 45-47; Forestry bibliogr at Agric Lib, Wash DC 47-56; Libn Bur of Labor & Mgt UIowa, Iowa City Iowa 5657; Ref libn UIowa Lib 57-61; Libn Nat Animal Disease Lab USDA, Ames Iowa 61-. 08: Lib adv Kentucky Proj USan Carlos, Guatemala 60. 9: SLA; ASIS; IowaLA (Fed Relat Coord); MedLA-Midwest Reg Group. 10: AAUW. 12: Special bibliographies of USDA: "Economics of Forestry (50, 55); "The Forests of Continental Latin America (52). 13: Yes. 14: Spec bibliog & documentation, estab new spec libs. 15: Nat Animal Disease Lab ARS-USDA P O Box 70, Ames Ia 50010.

FLINK, LUCILLE M. b Bessemer Mich 18 N 45. 5: Gogebic Commun Col (Ironwood Mich) 63-65; UMich 65-67 (Educ) BA, AMLS. 6: Fr. 7: Asst ext libn UMich (Ann Arbor) 68-69, Assoc ext libn 69-. 9: ALA. 14: Ref, acquis. 15: 1026 Church st, Ann Arbor Mi 48104.

FLINT, ALICE (FAUST). b Waterloo Iowa 6 Je 13. 4: Arthur E Flint. 5: UNo Iowa 31-35 (Eng) BA; UWis 35-36 Diploma in LS. 7: Libn pub lib, Clintonville Wis 36-37; Hd order dept pub lib, Davenport Iowa 37-41; Asst libn UIowa Lib (Iowa City) 41-42; Catlgr Westminster Col Lib (Salt Lake City) 59-62, Libn 62-63; Libn Chapman Col Lib 63, Hd dept of lib sci 67-. 9: ALA; CalLA; Orange Co LA (v-pres & pres-elect 68-69). 10: PEO. 14: Ref, catlg, tchg. 15: 1219 E Adams, Orange Ca 92667.

FLINT, ELAINE (NELSON). b DULUTH Minn 29 Jl 17. 4: Howard Raymond. 5: Duluth State Tchrs Col 35-38; Villa St Scholastica 38-39 (Hist) AB (cum laude); UMich 39-40 ABLS; UMont 47-54 (Hist) MA; U de San Carlos summer 47, 48. 6: Sp. 7: Doc & ser asst UMont 40-43, Circ libn 44-47; Eng tchr Instituto Guatemalteco-Americano, Guatemala 47-49; Libn Instituto Cultiral Peruano-Norteamericano, Lima Peru 49-51; Libn Centro Ecuatoriano-Norteamericano, Quito Ecuador 51-53; Catlgr & curriculum libn Phoenix Elem Schs Admin Bldg, Phoenix 54-61; Libn W High Sch, Phoenix 61-63; Catlgr lib tech serv MCJC Dist, Phoenix 63-66; Instr lib sci Ariz State U summer 66; Asst dir & hd ref serv Glendale Commun Col 66-. 8: Adv wk: Amer Sch Lib & Hospital de Maternidad Lib quito, Ecuador 51-52. 9: ALA; Ariz State LA; Salt River LA. 10: Alpha Delta Kappa; Phi Alpha Theta; AAUP. 14: Ref, Lib orient, Lib educ. 15: 6539 N 61st ave, Glendale Az 85301.

FLINT, KATHERINE (OBRIEN). b Montreal PQ Can. 4: Leroy Flint. 5: West Res 23-24 (LS) Certif, 36 BS. 6: F 7: Br libn Friendly Inn, Cleveland 26-30; Br libn Cdar Br, Cleveland 30-40; Br libn Alta Br, Cleveland 40-43; Br libn Jefferson Br, Cleveland 43-49; Br libn Hough Br, Cleveland 50-56; Br libn Wooster Br, Akron Ohio 56-58; Br libn North Br, Akron 58-. 8: Chm Lib Wk with Colored Peole, Cleveland 28-40; Radio bk reviewing, Cleveland Pub Lib 38-55. 9: ALA; OhioLA. 10: Cleveland Negro Hist Assn; Negro Welfare Assn; NAACP; CENOCOLA Ital Cultural Group; LWV; Akron Art Inst; Cleveland Mus of Art; Kent W Faculty; North Garden Club. 12: Ed Cleveland Staff Assn "News and Views" (38); Comp "The Negro; His Problems and Achievements" a bibliog (39). 13: Yes. 14: Pub lib wk (For & colored groups). 15: North Br Lib 183 E Cuyohoga Falls ave, Akron Ohio 44310.

FLINT, KATHLEEN. b Toronto Can 11 Je 46. 5: McGill 63-67 (Psych) B Sc, 67-69 MLS. 7: Catlgr Macdonald Col McGill U 68-. 9: CanLA. 14: Ref, Catlg. 15: 175 - 49th ave, Lachine 610 Que Can.

FLINTOFF, JOAN EVELYN. b Flint Mich 4 Ap 40. 5: Flint Jr Col 58-60 (Hist) AA; Flint Col UMich 60-62 (Hist) BA; UMich 62-63 AM LS. 6: Fr, Ger, Swedish. 7: Libn I catlgr UCLA 63-66, Libn catlgr 66-, mus catlgr 66-68, sers catlgr & asst hd of contin sect in catlg dept 69-. 9: ALA; CalLA (Memb Repr for UCLA); SoCal Tech Proc Gp; MusLA (SoCal Chap; memb Com 68; Nomin Com 68; Music Survey Com). 10: Pi Alpha; Beta Sigma Phi. 14: Catlg. 15: Univ Res Lib UCLA, Los Angeles Cal 90024.

FLOOD, FRANCIS JAMES. b Belfast N Ireland 17 Mr 25. 5: Siena Col 41-43, 46-47 (Eng) BA; Okla State U 44 (Electronics); SUNY (Albany) 47-48 (LS); UMich 48-51, 68-69 (Lat) AMLS, MA. 6: Fr, Ger, Lat. 7: Electronics tech ETM 1/c USN Japan, US & Pacific 43-46; Asst libn Siena Col 47-48; Lib asst lib sci lib UMich (Ann Arbor) 48-50, Instr & reviser 49-51; Asst prof dept of lib sci UMo (Columbia) 51-67, Chm 51-67, Assoc Prof Sch of lib & info sci 67-. 8: Lecturer, School of Lib Science, UMich, Ann Arbor 68-. 9: ALA; AALS; MoLA. 10: AAUP; Congress of Parents & Tchrs. 12: Ed "School Library handbook", State Dept of Educ, Jefferson City Mo (64). 14: Lib educ, ref, bibliog, lib hist. 15: Sch of Lib and Info Sci U Mo, Columbia Mo 65201.

FLOOD, SUSAN C (JOHNSTON). b Hartford Conn 22 Ap 43. 4: Clifford A Flood Jr. 5: Knox Col 61-65 (Hist) AB; Case West Res 65-66 MSLS. 6: Ger. 7: Asst order libn purdueU 66-. 9: ALA (Jr Mem RT); IndLA. 10: Beta Phi Mu; Mortar Board. 14: Acquis. 15: 2450 Sycamore A-3, W Lafayette In 47906.

FLORES, ANITA R (MAAS). b Albany NY 18 Ag 05. 5: Col St Rose 21-25 (Lang) AB; NY State Col for Tchrs 37-39 BS in LS. 7: Assoc libn Siena Col 39-57; Catlgr NY State Dept Health, Albany 59; Catlgr Albany Med Col Lib, NY 57-. 9: CathLA (Albany Unit Chm). 14: Catlg. 15: 625 Washington ave, Albany NY 12206.

FLORES, ANNIE T. b Dumaguete City Philippine. 5: St Paul Col (Philippines) 51-53 AA; U of the Philippines 53-55 (LS) BS in Educ; Cath U 60-62 MS LS. 6: Sp, Phil. 7: Libn tchr St Paul Col (Philippines) 55-60; Grad lib asst Cath U Wash DC 60-62; Bkmob libn Prince Georges Co Lib, Md 62; Asst head circ dept Cath U 62-64, Head Libn Lib Sci Lib 64-. 15: 2755 Ordway st NW, Wash DC 20008.

FLORES, ROBERT J. b Albany NY 26 Jl 27. 4: Agatha M Thomas. 5: Siena Col 45-49 (Eng) AB; NY State Col (Albany) 49-50 BS LS. 6: Sp, Fr, Lat. 7: Photographer Obenaus Studio, Albany NY 43-49; Lib asst Siena Col 45-49; Army Res Off NYNG & USAR (Capt), Albany NY 45-64; Lib asst NY State Col (Albany) 49-50; NY State Lib: Jr ref libn 50-54, Asst lib supv Ext Div 54-57, Sr lib supv Ext Div 57-64, Assoc lib supv Ext Div 64-67; Chief Bur of Pub Libs 67-. 8: Visiting instr SUNY (Albany), Lib Sch 63-64; Sec NY State Pub Libns Certifn Exam Com 64-. 9: ALA-LAD (Com on Certifn, NY chm Person-to-Person Recr Netwk 64); NYLA (chm Scholarship & Recr Co 58-59); Hudson-Mohawk LA. 10: Albany Lib Sch Alumni Assn. 12: Ed "The Bookmark, NY State Lib 64-65. 13: Yes. 14: Ext wk, ref, personnel. 15: 13 Comely lane, Latham NY 12110.

FLORIO, JANET L (SOLLERS). b Newman Ill 7 N 34. 4: Philip Florio. 7: Asst libn "Decatur Herald & Review", Decatur Ill 52-57; Hd libn "Tucson Daily Citizen", Tucson Ariz 60-. 15: 208 N Stone ave, Tucson Az 85701.

FLORY, JANET CORDELIA. b Bridgewater Va 1 N 13. 5: Bridgewater Col 30-34 (Eng) BA; UVa 36-37 (Eng) MA; Columbia 46-48 BS LS. 6: Fr, Ger. 7: Ref libn US Dept of Com, Wash DC 39-46; Stud asst Sch Lib Serv Lib Columbia U 46-48; Asst libn Bridgewater Col 48-49; Rare bk catlgr UVa 49-54; Rare bk catlgr Duke U 55-57; Ref libn CIT Financial

Corp, NYC 57-. 9: SLA. 14: Ref, rare bk. 15: 220 W 21 st, New York NY 10011.

FLORY, JOSEPHINE K. b Monticello Ind 5 My 14. 4: Rolland C Flory. 5: Manchester Col 34-38 (Hist) AB; Cornell U 45-46; Ind U 63-64 (LS) MA. 6: Sp. 7: Ref Purdue U Libs 61, Interlib loan 61-63, Asst coordinator of reg campus libs 64-. 9: ALA; IndLA. 10: AAUP; Purdue U Lib Staff Assn. 14: Ref, admin. 15: Purdue Univ Libs, Lafayette Ind 47907.

FLOWER, JANET (MARIE). b Portland Ore 28 My 24. 5: Ore Col of Educ 47 (Soc Sci, Educ) BS, 56 (Educ) MS; UOre 69 MLS. 6: Sp. 7: Materials specialist White Bear Lake Sr High Sch, White Bear Lake Minn 67-68; Reg libn NM State Lib, Belen 68-. 8: Ed bd "The Student Writer", nat period devoted to creative writing efforts of jr & sr high sch studs. 9: NEA. 14: Geneal, yp & sch libnship. 15: 107 1/2 N 3rd, Belen NM 87002.

FLOWERS, BETTY BROOKS. b NYC 13S 13 S 5: Hunter Col (Soc Sci) BA; Columbia (LS) MS. 6: Fr, Ger, Sp. 7: Acquis City Col (NY) 52-53; Lib asst Nat Recreation Assn, NYC 53-55; Catlgr & ref Columbia Sch ofSoc Wk 56-61; Supv Union Catlg, Med Lib Center, NYC 62-67; Ref libn NYU Med Ctr Lib 67-. 8: Consul, Child Study Assn of Amer 58; Consul, Div of Commun Psychiatry, Sch of Pb Health, Columbia U 62. 9: SLA (Biol Scis Div); MedLA(NY Reg Gp; sec Exec Com 68-). 10: NY Lib Club; Zool Soc of NY. 12: "Authority List of Subject Headings in Social Welfare, SLA (60). 13: Yes. 14: Catlg, ref. 15: 1553 York ave, New York NY 10028.

FLOWERS, HELEN (FOOTE). b Elizabethtown Ky 10 Ag 31. 4: E C Flowers Jr. 5: Bethel Womans Col 49-51 AA; Peabody 51-54 (Eng, Educ) BA; Columbia 61-62 (LS) MS, 64-65 (LS). 7: Asst circ libn Joint U Libs, Nashville 52-54; Libn Army Lib Serv, Ft Gordon Ga 53-54; Tchr St Andrews Parish High Sch, Charleston SC 56-61; Libn Ashley Hall, Charleston SC 62-64; Libn Bay Shore Sr High Sch, Bay Shore NY 65-. 9: ALA; NEA; SuffolkCoLA (Goals Chm 68, corr sec 69). 10: LW. 14: Wk with ya. 15: 421 E Main st apt S-2, Bay Shore NY 11706.

FLOYD, ANNE HARDING. b Henderson Ky 19 Ja 05. 4: William Burney Floyd. 5: West Col 21-25 (Lit) AB; St Louis Lib Sch 27-28 Certif. 7: Head circ Evansville Pub Lib, Evansville Ind 28-30; Libn Hinsdale (ILL) Pub Lib 30-34; Asst ref libn Louisville (Ky) Pub Lib 39-40; Coordinator of child wk Louisville Pub Lib & WPA, Louisville Ky 40-42; Dir Red Cross Blood Donor (Ky), Louisville Ky 43-47; Asst libn PAC Lib, Edinburg Tex 49-. 9: TexLA(Acquis Round Table); Tex Assn of Col Tchrs; SWLA. 10: Pan Amer Round Table; Edinburg Study PEO. Bd. 14: Catlg, ref. 15: Pac Lib, Edinburg Tx 78539.

FLOYD, DORA. b Whitesboro Tex 9 My 07. 5: N Tex State U 24-28 (Eng) BA; Chicago Musical Col 28-29, 30-31 (Piano) BMusic; Tex Womans U 34-35 (Eng) MA, 45-46 BS LS. 7: Tchr High Sch, Garland Tex 35-39; Tchr Jr High Sch, Port Arthur Tex 39-43; Tchr Highland Park Jr High Sch, Dallas 43-45; Libn Highland Park High Sch, Dallas 46-52; Music libn Tex Christian U 52-53; Catlgr Tex Womans U 53-. 9: ALA; TexLA; SLA (sec-treas Tex Gp of Catlgrs 59-60). 10: AAUW; Delta Kappa Gamma; Tex State Hist Assn; Alpha Chi; Kappa Delta Pi 14: Catlg. 15: Box 3801 TWU Sta, Denton Tex 76204.

FLUCKIGER, ADRIENNE (NORTHAM). b Branford Conn 28 Ag 26. 4: James R Fluckiger. 5: Middlebury Col 43-47 (Sociol) BA; LIU 63-67 MLS. 7: Casewkr Conn State Div Child Welfare, New Haven Conn 47-49; Trainee Seaford Pub Lib, Seaford NY 63-65; Child libn 65-68; Child libn Syosset Pub Lib, Syosset NY 68-. 9: NYLA; NassauCoLA. 13: Yes. 14: Child wk. 15: 3964 Marilyn dr, Seaford NY 11783.

FLUELLEN, GWENDOLYN F(ANNIN). b Atlanta Ga 12 Mr 35. 4: Anderson Fluellen. 5: Clark Col 52-56 (Fr AB; Atlanta 56-58 MS LS. 6: Fr. 7: Child libn NY Pub Lib 57-59; Child libn Fulton Co Bd Educ, Palmetto Ga 59-60; Br libn Atlanta Pub Lib 60-61; Child libn Atlanta Bd of Educ 61-. 9: NEA; GaTA (Libns Sect); Gate City TA. 10: YWCA; Alpha Kappa Alpha; Sparklers Bridge Club; YMCA-Ys Mennettes. 14: Child wk. 15: 520 Park Valley dr NW, Atlanta Ga 30318.

FLYNN, BETTY (M ELIZABETH WALSH). b Boston 24 Ap 27. 4: Edward F Flynn Jr. 5: Emmanuel Col 45-49 (Hist) AB; Simmons 50-51 MS LS. 6: Fr. 7: Br child libn Lynn Pub Lib, Lynn Mass 51-53, Bkmob libn 53-60; Ref & bk serv State Div of Lib Ext, Boston Mass 60-62, Supv of field serv 62-64, Supv of Pub Lib Development 64-. 8: Com on Inst Libs, Amer Correctional Assn for Rev of "Objectves & Standards For Libraries in Correctional Institutions 62; Pub lib constr consul, Mass Bureau of Lib Est 62-; Lib placement serv & recr activities, State agency 65-. 9: ALA; Recr Com Rep from Mass 67-69; -AASchL (Legis Liaison Com 67-70); -LAD; NELA (Memb Com 67-69, sec Ext Libns); MassLA (sec 67-69, coms; recr, Educ, Personnel Serv); MassTA. 10: Quota Internat; Eire Soc; Col Club, Boston. 13: Yes. 14: Lib admin, bldgs, recr & lib placement. 15: 312 Humphrey st, Swampscott Ma 01907.

FLYNN, KATHRYN JEAN. b Buhl Minn 11 D 20. 5: Milwaukee-Downer Col 38-42 (Eng) BA; UWis(Madison) 49-50 BLS. 7: Sec John N Gannon Law Firm Hibbing Minn 42-43; Sec to pres Milwaukee-Owner Col 43-49; Asst libn 50-52, Catlgr 52-53; Chief libn Shorewood Pub Lib, Shorewood Wis 53-63; Dir Neenah Pub Lib, Neenah Wis 63-. 8: Instr in lib sci even sch UWis (Milwaukee) 56-58, 60-61. 9: ALA; WisLA (Pub Lib Sect; v-pr es 67, pres 68; pres Catlg Sect 53, chm Scholarship Com 59); Fox River Valley LA (pres 65-66). 10: AAUW; Wis Lib Sch Assn; Lawrence U Alumni Assn; UWis Alumni Assn; Beta Phi Mu. 14: Admin of pub libs. 15: 628 Hansen st, Neenah Wi 54956.

FLYNN, SISTER MARY GRACE. b Wheeling W Va 16 S 27. 5: Duquesne 53-57 (Educ) BA; Catholic U summers 59-66 MS in LS. 6: Fr, Lat. 7: Libn Mt de Chantal Visitation Acad, Wheeling W Va 59-; Dir of Novices Convent of the Visitation, Wheeling W Va 67-. 8: Var offs Diocese of Wheeling W Va 67-69. 9: ALA. 12: Comp "Index of the Works of St Francis de Sales" (68). 14: Sch libs. 15: Mt de Chantal Acad, Wheeling W Va 26003.

FLYNT, MADELINE (VIRGINIA). b Laurel Miss 8 Ap 07. 5: William Carey Col 30 (Fr, Eng) BA; UAla 43 Lib Sci Certif; Peabody 50 (LS) MA. 6: Sp, Fr, Lat. 7: Eng tchr High sch in Jones Co Miss 33-37; Eng tchr Pachuta High Sch, Pachuta Miss 37-39; Eng tchr Wiggins High Sch, Wiggins Miss 39-40; Eng tchr-libn Magee High Sch, Magee Miss 40-42; High sch libn Columbia High Sch, Columbia Miss 42-44; Eng tchr Pascagoula High Sch, Pascagoula Miss 44-45, High sch libn 45-52; Asst Prof of Lib Sci USoMiss 52-. 8: Com on Miss Lib Handbook 51; Sch evaluations for Southern Assn in Miss 48-52. 9: ALA; MissLA. 14: Tchg lib sci. 15: 1029 Third ave, Laurel Miss 39440.

FOCKE, HELEN M. b Cleveland Ohio 10 Je 02. 5: West Res U 1923 (Chem) AB, 2628 (Geol) AM, 2829 BS in LS. 6: Fr, Ger. 7: Grad asst Chem & Geol West Res 2328; Lib asst Popular Lib Cleveland Pub Lib 2930, Lib asst scitech 3040, asst hd 4042; Supvg libn Case Inst of Tech 4247; Lectr Sch Lib Sci West Res U 4347, Assoc Prof 4753, Prof 5367, Prof Emeritus CaseWest Res 67. 8: Vis Prof; Japan Lib Sch, Keio U, Tokyo summer 60, Sch of Libnship UWash 68, Sch of Lib Sci UAlta spring 69, Lib consul, Amer Soc Metals 4750; Lib Adv Bd Colliers Encyclopedia-- 60. 9: ALA (Coun 5758, 6465; Awards Com 6266, Subscription Bks Com 4559, chm 4650; LED (treas 5354; chm Tchrs Sect 6364); RSD (pres 6465; Bibliog Com on Lib Wk as a Career 5254); AALS; SLA (pres Cleveland Chap 4748); OhioLA (1st vpres 3536, treas 4345; chm Jr Mems Sect 3436). 10: Soroptimist Club; PEO. 11: Distinguished Alumna Award, West Res U 66. 12: Assoc ed American Documentation (5356); Ed Clearing House Newsletter, ALA Jt Com on Lib Wk as a Career (5457). 13: Yes. 14: Ref, govt docs, documentation, scitech lit. 15: School of Lib Sci Case Western Reserve Univ, Cleveland Oh 44106.

FOCKE, MARY FRANCES. b Cleveland 13 N 10. 5: Ohio State U 28-32 (Music Educ) BS in Educ; West Res 35-36 BS LS. 6: Fr. 7: Apprentice wk Ohio State Lib 35; Ya libn & gen ref wk S Bend Pub Lib, S Bend Ind 36-47; Ref asst art & music dept Pub Lib of Cincinnati & Hamilton Co, Cincinnati 47-51, Gen catlgr 51-61, Supv of jr catlgrs 61-. 8: Lecturer on Lib Sci UCincinnati, evn Col 61-63. 9: ALA; OhioLA; Ohio Valley Group Tech Serv Libns. 13: Yes. 14: Catlg, tchg lib sci. 15: 6584 Wooster Pike, Mariemont Ohio 45227.

FOCKLER, HERBERT HILL. b Summersville WVa 18 F 22. 4: Mary Hildegarde Ziegler. 5: UPenn 40-41 (Bus Admin); WVaU 47 (Pol & Soc Sci) BA, MA: Oxford U 48 (Pol, Econ); Harvard 49 (Econ); Catholic U 50-52 MSLS. 6: Fr, Sp. 7: Statistician US Dept of Labor, Wash DC 49-50; Legis rep ALA, Wash DC 52; Lib supv Princeton U 52-54; Supv of govt ref sect LC 56-58; Ed & bibliogr White House Conf on Child & Youth, Wash DC 59-60; Res Program admin NIH, Wash DC 61-66; Training & Res Grants Admin NLM 66-. 8: Chm Fed Lib Com Task Force on Role of Libs in Info Systems 67-; Mem COSATI Panel on Educ & Training 67-; Mem Fed Lib Com Task on Training 67-; Exec sec NLM Manpower & Training Com 66-; Exec sec NLM Fellowships Review Com

67-. 9: Amer Pol Sci Assn; Amer Acad of Pol & Soc Sci; ASIS; Amer Pub Health Assn; Authors Club of Wash DC; Coun of the So Mountains; Amer Acad of Politics; ALA; SLA; MedLA; Wash Acad Sci. 10: AAAS; AAUP; Smithsonian Inst Assocs; WVa Planning Assn. 13: Yes. 14: Admin, research, educ. 15: 10710 Lorain ave, Silver Spring Md 20901.

FOECKING, CLAIRE MARIE. b Cleveland 31 O 34. 5: Ursuline Col 52-56 (Chem) BS; West Res 56-57 (LS) MS. 7: Assoc libn Union Carbide Corp Parma Research Center, Research Lib, Parma Ohio 57-64; Head Libn Union Carbide Corp Consumer Products Div, Development Lab Lib, Cleveland 64-. 9: SLA; ACS; ASIS. 14: Govt documents. 15: P O Box 6056, Cleveland Oh 44101.

FOELL, JOHN F. b Syracuse NY 1 O 30. 4: Martha Cavender. 5: Manhattan Col 48-50; UOkla 53-55 (Chem) BS; Drexel 58-59 (LS). 6: Ger. 7: Career guidance clk (A/2c) USAF 51-53; Chem analytical lab East States Petroleum Co, Houston Tex 55-57; Asst libn Armstrong Cork Co research & development ctr, Lancaster Penn 57-60; Research libn continental Oil Co research & development dept, Ponca City Okla 60-. 9: SLA. 14: Searching, trans. 15: 2136 John, Ponca City Ok 74601.

FOGELSTROM, CLARENCE J. b Perry Iowa 4 D 28. 4: Suzanne Stephens. 5: St Cloud State col 56 (Elem Educ, Speech, Mus) AA, BS, BA; UMinn 59 (LS) Lib Credential; San Francisco State Col 65 (Educ Admin) Admin Credential; Ind U 66 (A-V Educ) MS. 6: Fr, Korean. 7: Rural sch tchr Grand Forks Co Schs, Grand Forks N Dak 48-51; Classified Sgt USA, Korea 51-54; Elem tchr Minnetonka Sch Dist, Excelsior Minn 55-57; Field wkr N Dak Library Comsn 56; High Sch libn Minnetonka Sch Dist, Excelsior Minn 57-58; Dist libn San Bruno Park Schs, San Bruno Cal 58-68; Sch lib specialist div lib serv USOE, Wash DC 68-. 8: Consul to Yolo Co (Cal) Sch Off on sch lib serv; Consul & instr Cal State Dept of Educ wkshops on catlg of non-bk materials. 9: ALA; NEA; -DAVI; Assn for Supv & Curr Devel; NCTE; DCLA. 12: Co-ed 2nd ed "The Organization of Nonbook Materials in School Libraries". 14: Catlg of nonbook materials, educat media ctrs. 15: USOE Div of Lib Serv, 7th & D sts SW, Wash DC 20202.

FOGERTY, (DOROTHY) JANET. b Groveton NH 20 D 25. 5: Randolph-Macon 44-47 (Econ & Gk) BA; West Mich U 55-57 (LS) MA. 6: Fr. 7: Acquis libn Ujohn Co, Kalamazoo 53-68; Ref libn 68-. 9: SLA (sec Pharmac Div 66-68). 10: Servce Club of Kalamazoo Inc; Beta Phi Mu. 14: Acquis, ref. 15: The Upjohn Co Tech Lib 25-7, Kalamazoo Mich 49001.

FOGG, ELIZABETH CASPER. b Salem NJ 26 Mr 34. 5: Ursinus Col 52-56 (Eng) BA; Drexel 56-57 MS LS; UPenn 61-63 (Amer Civilization). 6: Fr. 7: Lib clerk Jackson Lab E I DuPont de Nemours, Carneys Point NJ summer 56; Ref asst Ref Lib Drexel Inst of Tech 57-58, Humanities libn 59-67; Humanities & soc sci libn 67-69, Princ libn Salem Free Pub Lib 69-. 8: Consul "Essay & General Literature Index 60-69; Volunteer consul & catlgr Salem Monthly Meeting of Friends 64-, Drexel Collection Libn 67-69. 9: ALA-ACRL; SLA. 10: Womens Univ Club (Phila); AAUW; Mod Lang Assn; Salem Co (NJ) Histl Soc; Salem Co Mem Hosp Womens Auxiliary; Alpha Club (Phila); Salem Country Club; Hist Soc Penn. 14: Ref, catlg, admin. 15: Salem Free Pub Lib 120 W Broadway, Salem NJ 08079.

FOGGIN, CAROL (MONROE). b Maynardville Tenn 20 O 42. 4: James H Foggin. 5: Hiwassee Col 60-62 AA; UTenn 62-64 (Eng) AB; Emory 67-69 M Libnship. 6: Sp. 7: Lib asst UTenn Undergrad Lib (Knoxville) 64-67; Lib asst EmoryU 67-68; Ref libn Ga State Col 69-. 14: Ref, catlg, computer applications to libs. 15: 1736 Fair dr, Knoxville Tn 37918.

FOGLEMAN, MARGUERITE F. b Alexandria Va 3 Jl 26. 4: Francis K Fogleman. 5: LSU 43-47 (Home Econ) BS, 47-48, BS in LS. 6: Ger, Sp, Fr. 7: Jr catlgr LSU LIB 48-50; Catlgr Cossitt Pub Lib, Memphis Tenn 50-51; Lib asst KENNEDY VA Hosp Lib, Memphis Tenn 51-52; Asst ser libn LSU Lib 57-59; Asst catlg & ref libn Wilmington Pub Lib, Wilmington NC 61-63; Asst libn Wilmington Col Lib (Wilmington NC) 63-65; Asst libn Augusta Col Lib 65-67; Assoc libn 67-. 9: ALA; SELA; GaLA; CSRA LA. 10: LSU Alumni Assn; Alpha Chi Omega; Phi Upsilon Omicron; Beta Phi Mu. 12: Ed "CSRA LA Directory (68). 14: Tech proc, ser. 15: 706 Woodlawn ave W, N Augusta SC 29841.

FOGLER, BETTY H(UNTER). b Flint Mich 20 S 22. 4: Harold M Fogler. 5: Graceland Col 40-42 (Eng) AA; UMo 43-45 (Eng) BS; UDenver 60, 62 (LS) MA. 7: Lib asst pub serv Acad Lib US Air Force Acad 57-62, Ref libn 62-. 14: Ref. 15: Box 173, Palmer Lake Colo 80133.

FOGLESONG, MARILEE ANN. b Peoria Ill 13 N 36. 5: Ill State Normal 54-58 (Eng) BS; UIll 61-62 (LS) MS. 6: Fr. 7: Fr tchr Peoria High Sch, Peoria Ill 57-59; Eng tchr LaHarpe Comm High Sch, LaHarpe Ill 59-61; Young adult libn Free Lib of Phila 62-65; Young adult libn Madison Pub Lib, Madison Wis 65-67; Commun serv libn reader development program Free Lib of Phila 67-. 8: Group wk with teenage boys on probation from Phila County Court. 9: ALA; PennLA. 14: Young adult serv, commun serv, wk with the disadvantaged. 15: Reader Dev Program 336 N 23rd st, Philadelphia Pa 19103.

FOISE, ARTHUR D. b Brooklyn NY 1 F 15. 4: Rita Sacks. 5: Brooklyn Col 33-37 (Hist) BA; Columbia 53-60 MS. 6: Fr, Sp. 7: T/4 US Army Cryptographic Tech 44-46; Prod manager Business Letter Serv, NYC 46-52; Libn Gen Soc of Mech & Tradesmen, NYC 53-57; Libn Mercantile Lib, NYC 57-61; Sr libn Brooklyn Pub Lib 63-. 9: ALA. 10: Brooklyn Lib Guild; State Co & Munic Employees Amer; Flatlands-E Flatbush Civic Improvement Assn. 14: Ref, rare bks. 15: 9720 Kings hwy, Brooklyn NY 11212.

FOLCARELLI, RALPH JOSEPH. b Phila 5 O 28. 4: Carol Field. 5: State Col (Kutztown Penn) 46-47, 49-51 (LS) BS Educ; NY State Col Tchrs (Albany) summer 53; Rutgers 55-58 MLS, 59 (LS); NYU 66- (Communications). 6: Sp. 7: US Army, Army Med Lib, Wash DC 48, summers 49, 50; Sch libn Tri Valley Sch, Grahamsville NY 51-54; Coordinator Pennsbury Schs, Fallsington Penn 54-59; Instr Lib Sci WVaU summers 59, 61; Head Libn Mansfield State Col 59-61; Lib coordinator Cold Spring Harbor (NY) Schs 61-65; Assoc Prof Grad Lib Sch LIU 62, 65-. 8: Penn Dept of Pub Instr Com to Revise Sch Lib Standards, 58; Summer wkshop dir, Syracuse U 67; Co-dir Communications Media Sem, Adelphia Suffolk - LIU summer 68; consul for several village schs. 9: NEA-DAVI; (Life mem); ALA; NYLA; Nassau-Suffolk Sch LA; Sufflk Co Lib Assn (Exec Bd 64-); LI Educl Communications Coun. 10: Harbor Tchr Assn; LI Intel Freedom Com 64-; Trustee, Levittown (Penn) Pub Lib; Kappa Delta Pi. 13: Yes. 14: Sch lib serv, lib educ. 15: 118 Bay dr, Huntington LI NY 11743.

FOLEY, JAMES. b Cohoes NY. 4: Katherine Byrne. 5: Siena Col 55-58 (Eng) BA; SUNY (Albany)58-59, 59-60 MS LS; SUNY Binghamton)63-64. 7: Catlgr U Notre Dame (S Bend Ind) 60-62; Head catlg dept SUNY,(Binghamton) 62-64; Head tech serv SUNY,(Fredonia)64-65; Catlgr LC 65-66; Hd acquis dept SUNY (Stony Brook) 66-68; Assoc libn Health Scis Lib 68-. 9: ALA; SLA; MedLA; NYLA. 14: Tech serv, automation. 15: 645-67 Belle Terre rd, Port Jefferson NY 11777.

FOLEY, MARGARET MARY. b Troy NY 21 Mr 25. 5: Col of St Rose 47 (Soc Studies) BA; SUNY (Albany) 51 MS in LS. 7: Clk Circ Desk Albany (NY) Pub Lib 47-48, Ref asst & ya libn 48-51; Br libn Schenectady Co Pub Lib, Schenectady NY 51-54, Hd circ dept 54-66, asst dir 66-. 9: ALA; NYLA; Hudson-MohawkLA (sec 59-61, v-pres 68-). 10: Watervliet Civic Ctr Lib Trustee. 15: 33 Sylvan ave, Latham NY 12110.

FOLEY, SUZANNE LOUISE. b Boston 4 O 42. 5: William & Mary 60-64 (Hist) AB; Rutgers 64-65 MLS. 7: Clerk Beacon Bk Shop, Norfolk Va summers 61-62; IBM operator Regstrars Off Col of William & Mary 63; Searcher Col of William & Mary Lib 64, Ref libn 65-. 9: ALA; VaLA. 12: "A Guide to Historical Materials in the Swem Library (68). 14: Ref. 15: Library Col of William & Mary, Williamsburg Va 23185.

FOLLAYTTAR, JOSEPH C. b NYC 25 N 10. 4: Rose Hodulik. 5: Lafayette Col 29-33 (Chem) BS; Trenton State Col 50 BLS; Montclair State Col 53 (Admin, Supv) MA; US Command & Gen Staff Col 60 (Mil Sci). 6: Fr, Ger. 7: Prin Uniontown Sch, Lopatcong Twp NJ 34-36; Libn Flemington (NJ) High Sch 37-39; Libn Teaneck (NJ) Sr High Sch 39-; US Army (Lt Col) Transportation Corps 41-47; Lib Dir Lodi Mem Lib, Lodi NJ 52-. 8: Middle States Assn Visiting Com. 9: ALA; NEA; NJLA (Intel Freedom Com, Scholarship Com); NJEA; NJSchLA; NJ Sch Lib Coun Assn; NJ Secon Tchrs Assn. 10: Marcotte Lane Civic Assn. 13: Yes. 14: Sch libs. 15: 19 Marcotte lane, Bergenfield NJ 07621.

FOLLICK, EDWIN D(UANE). b Glendale Cal 4 F 35. 4: Lorayne A Horka-Follick. 5: Pasadena City Col 52-54 (Humanities) AA; Cal State (LA) 54-57, 60-61 (Soc Sci, Educ) BA, MAEd; Pepperdine 55-57 (Soc Sci) MA; St Andrew's (Lond) 56-58 (Sociol-Relig) PhD, DTheol; USoCal 61-65, 68 MSLS, MEd; AdMEd; Blackstone (Chicago) 65-67 (Law) LLB; JD. 6: Ancient lang. 7: USA chaplain's asst Armed Forces,

Chicago Air Defense 58-60; Tchr & libn LA City Schs 57-58, 60-; Evening libn LA Pierce Col 64-69; Prof theol (Extern) St Andrew's (Lond) 61-68; Dir Lib & Instr Materials Ctr, Cleveland Chiropractic Col LA 69-. 8: Clergyman, The Ecumenical Church Foun & the Free Prot Episc Church of London (ordained 58); Research Fellow in the US, St Andrew's, London & the Free Prot Episc Sem, London. 9: ALA (life mem); -AASchL; NEA (life memb); AALL; CalASchL; Los Angeles SchLA. 10: Phi Delta Kappa; USoCal Alumi Assn; USoCal Lib Sch Alumi Assn; USo Cal Sch of Educ Alum Assn; Cal State Col at Los Angeles Alum Assn. 12: PhD Diss, "The Cultural Influence of Mormonism in Early Nineteenth Century America", Ann Arbor Univ Microfilms 58. 14: Educ libnship, law libnship. 15: Cleveland Chiropractic Col Lib, Cleveland Oh.

FOLLMER, DIANE E. b Iowa 12 O 43. 5: Luther Col 61-63; UIowa 63-65 (Eng Educ) BA, 65-66 (Data Processing); UPittsburgh 66-67 (Info Sci) MLS. 6: Fr. 7: Libn Iowa Educ Info Ctr, Iowa City 65-66; Grad asst UPittsburgh & Knowledge Availability Syst Ctr, pittsburgh Penn 66-67; Libn Pillsbury Co, Minneapolis Minn 67-68; Info syst analyst 3M Co, St Paul 68-. 9: ASIS (Sec Minn Chap); SLA. 10: Beta Phi Mu; Pi Lambda Theta. 14: Spec lib info systs. 15: 3M Company 201-2S 3M Center, St Paul Mn 55101.

FOLLSTAD, VIRGINIA P(AULINE) (MILLER). b Oakland Neb 24 My 35. 4: Merle N Follstad. 5: Luther Col 52-54 (Liberal Arts) AA; Bethany Col(Lindsborg Kan) 54-56 (Eng) BA; UMinn 59-61 (LS) MA. 7: Research asst Mt Olivet Lutheran Church, Minneapolis 56-61; Jr libn UMinn 61-62, Libn 62-64; Libn II Fresno Co Free Lib, Fresno Cal 65-66; Asst catlg libn Bradley U 68; Asst catlg libn Wis State U (White Water) 68-. 9: ALA. 10: Beta Phi Mu; AAUW. 14: Ref, catlg. 15: 320 N Tratt st, Whitewater Wi 53190.

FOLMER, (CHARLES) FRED. b Independence Ky 20 Jl 10. 5: East Ky 28-32 (Soc Sci) AB; Peabody summers 35-37 BS LS; UMich 40, 41, 46 AM LS. 6: Fr. 7: Tchr-libn Lloyd High Sch, Erlanger Ky 33-37; Asst libn Neb State Col 37-38; Supv of dept libs State U Iowa 38-41; Chief pharmacist mate US Coast Guard 42-45; Assoc libn & Lecturer in Lib Sci UTex 46-67; U Libn 67-. 9: ALA; SWLA; TexLA (pres 53-54). 10: Tex State Hist Assn; Ky Hist Soc. 14: Admin, lib bldgs, lib educ. 15: 1707 Westover rd, Austin Tex 78703.

FOLTS, STEPHEN BERTRAN. b Brooklyn NY 29 Je 38. 4: Martha C Neary. 5: Syracuse 56-60 (Eng) AB; Ind U 61-62 (Eng); Simmons 62-64 (LS) MS. 6: Ger. 7 Ref libn Simmons Col Lib 64-67; Asst to exec dir SE NY Lib Resources Coun 67-. 9: NYLA; MusLA. 13: Yes. 14: Ref, bibliog. 15: 54 Oakwood blvd, Poughkeepsie NY 12603.

FOLTZ, FLORENCE P(ICKETT). b Las Animas Colo 2 D 07. 4: Everett F Foltz. 5: Colo Col 26-30 (Eng, Hist) AB; UIll 30-31 BS LS. 6: Sp. 7: Lib asst UColo 31; Libn Fountain Valley Sch, Colo Springs Colo 31-33; Libn Cowles Commsn for Econ Research, Colo SPRINGS Colo 33-34; Libn San Luis Sch for Girls, Colo Springs Colo 34-35; Libn W High Sch, Denver 35-46; Libn S High Sch, Denver 46-. 8: Instr in Lib Sci summer courses; udenver (56), UWash (58), UColo 61-. 9: ALA-AASchL; ColoLA (pres 47); MPLA (v-pres 48); ColASchL (pres 61). 10: Comp "Colorado Library Directory (47, 50, 54, 57). 13: Yes. 14: Tchg bk sel & catlg to sch libns. , sch ref, sch lib admin, lit for ya. 15: 1886 S Federal blvd, Denver Co 80219.

FONDELL, EVANGELYN E. b Dawson Minn 11 Ag 10. 5: UMinn 29-33 (Eng, Hist) BS LS. 6: Swedish, Ger. 7: Temp asst Minneapolis Pub Lib 33-3; Ref asst UIowa Lib 35-40; Child libn New Philadelphia (Ohio) Pub Lib 40-42, Head libn 42-46; Order libn Bellingham (Wash) Pub Lib 46-47; Sr asst ref dept Seattle Pub Lib 47-60, Sr asst Hist dept 60-. 9: PNLA; WashLA. 15: Seattle Pub Lib 1000 Fourth ave, Seattle Wa 98101.

FONGER, LEE ARDON. b Superior Wis 17 My 32. 4: Carol DeBruyne. 5: Wis State Col(Superior) 50-55 (Eng) BA; UWis 57-58 MALS. 6: Fr, Ger, Turkish. 7: High sch tchr 55-57; Libn Robert Col(Istanbul TURKEY) 58-. ; Deputy libn Makerere U Col, Kampala Uganda 69-71. 8: Catlgr Gustavus Adolphus Col 63-64. 9: ALA; TurkishLA. 10: AAUP. 14: Lib devel. 15: Robert Col Lib, Bebek PK 8, Istanbul Turkey.

FONSTEIN, EVELYN. b Chicago 11 Ag 23. 5: Roosevelt U 42-46 (Psych) BA; Rosary Col 46-47 BSLS. 7: Asst catlgr Chicago Tchrs Col 47-48; Libn Childs Mem Hosp, Chicago 48-51; Libn Ill Commsn for Handicapped Child, Chicago 52-59; File clerk Exchange Nat Bank, Chicago 59-61; Asst libn Chicago Med Sch 61-62; Libn Grant Hosp Sch of Nursing, Chicago 62-66; Libn Passavant Mem Hosp James Ward Thorne Sch of Nursing 66-. 8: Hosp lib volunteer wk. 9: ALA; MedLA; SLA. 14: Med ref. 15: 5124 Dorchester, Chicago Il 60615.

FONTANA, NICHOLAS. b NYC 9 Ja 08. 4: Irma Burns. 5: Oberlin Col 27-31 (Eng) AB; Columbia 31-32 (Eng) MA, 34-35 BLS. 7: Lib interne Columbia U Lib 35-37; Lib Fellow City Col (NY) Lib 37-38; Circ libn Brooklyn Col Lib 39-; Chief circ div 64-. 15: 156 W Waterview st, Northport NY 11768.

FOOHEY, MARY ANN. b Wilmington Del 13 Jl 36. 5: Col of New Rochelle 54-58 (Eng) BA; Catholic U 58-61 MS LS. 6: Fr. 7: Lib asst Lib Col of New Rochelle 55-58; Grad lib asst Catholic U 58-60; Catlgr asst to chief catlgr Catholic U 60-62; Catlgr Lib Vitro Lab, Silver Spring Md 62-63, Supv processing sect & catlgr 63-. 8: Prepared index for papal encyclicals "Mater et Magistra and "Pacem in Terris for the Nat Cath Welfare Conf 61 & 62. 14: Catlg, acquis (spec or univ libs). 15: 13517 Georgia ave #203, Silver Spring Md 20906.

FOOS, DONALD DALE. b Chicago 11 Mr 29. 4: Ferol Ann Accola. 5: UAla(Montgomery) 52-56 (Pol Sci); UMd (Far-East, Tokyo, Japan) ' 58-61; Sci); UAla 61-62 (Pol Sci) AB; Fla State U 63-64 (LS) MS; UKy 67-68 (Pol Sci). 6: Fr. 7: Instr Aeromedical Evacuation USAF Sch of Aviation Med, Gunter AFB Ala 52-58; Instr Aeromedical Evacuation 9th AERON, Tachikawa AB Japan 58-61; Info spec Ala Pub Lib Serv, Montgomery Ala 62-63; Stud asst Fla State U Materials Center 64; Proj off LSCA Title II (Construction) Ala Pub Lib Serv, Montgomery Ala 64-. 66; Dir El Paso Pub Lib, El Paso Tex 66-67; Lecturer Sch Lib Sci UKy 67-68; Lib Consul Ky State Lib 67-68; Instr Ky State Col summer 68; Asst Prof & Admin Asst to Dean Sch Lib Sci (Geneseo) 68-69. 8: Library/USA Ref staff NY World Fair 65; Admin Coosa Valley Reg Lib 62, Autauga-Bibb-Chilton Counties LSA Demonstration 63 as staff mem of Ala Pub Lib Serv; Exec dir Nat Lib Week, Ala 65; Adv Trans-Pecos (Tex) Resource Area Survey 66; Lib consul, Radford Sch for Girls, El Paso 67. 9: ALA (JMRT Liaison to Ala, Memb Com, chm Hammond Award Jury 67-68); AALS; SWLA; SELA; AlaLA (Exhib Chm 66); KyLA (chm Legis Com 67-68); TexLA (chm-elect Pub Lib Div). 10: Civil Air Patrol; Alpha Beta Alpha; AAUP; Optimists. 13: Yes. 14: Lib educ, pub lib, research, serv to the disadvantaged. 15: Fla State U, Tallahassee Fl 32306.

FOOS, FEROL ANN (ACCOLA). b Kirksville Mo 16 S 41. 4: Donald D Foos. 5: Okla StateU 59-63 (Educ) BS in Educ; Fla StateU 63-64 (LS) MS; Amer Inst of Banking (Atlanta) 65-66 (Banking & Econ); Ga State Col 65-66 (Data Processing). 7: Stud asst curriculum lib Dept Educ Okla StateU 62; Br libn Tulsa City-Co Syst, Tulsa Okla summer 63; Grad asst Fla State U Lib Sch 64; Fed Res Bank of Atlanta Research Lib: Catlg libn 64-66; Asst libn 66-68; Independent research SUNY (Geneseo) Milne Lib 69-. 8: Verifier "Basic Book List for Technical Institutes," S Atlantic Chap SLA 66-68; Tour guide Fed Res Bank of Atlanta 65-68. 9: SLA (S Atlantic Chap: Hospitality Chm 65-66, sec 66-68); SELA; GaLA; Metro AtlantaLA. 10: Alpha Chi Omega Sorority; Amer Inst of Banking; Phi Kappa Phi; Phi Delta Kappa; Alpha Beta Alpha. 13: Yes. 14: Spec libs. 15: 37 Hopkin st, Mt Morris NY 14510.

FOOTE, JOYCE RUTH (STRYKER). b Sayville LI NY 7 My 30. 4: Donald Henry Foote. 5: State U Col(Geneseo NY) 48-52 BS in LS; Hofstra Col 53-55 (Elem Educ); State U Col(Oneonta NY) summer 60 (Elem Educ). 6: Fr. 7: Summer sch libn Sayville High Sch, Sayville NY 52-54; Lib asst Pub Lib, Sayville NY summers 52-55; Libn Bellport Union Sch, Bellport NY 52-55; Elem tchr Central Sch, Churchville NY 56-57, Elem libn 57-58; Campus Sch libn State U Col(Oneonta NY) 60-61, 63-64, 67-. 8: The Campus Sch libn serves as consul to faculty & stud of Educ Dept; MEMB Bk Sel Com,Kenyon Free Lib, Morris NY; Consul for Oneonta Consol Schs, (establ libs for 2 new elem schs) 66. 9: ALA; NEA; NY State LA; NY State Tchrs Assn. 14: Child wk. 15: 2 Grove st, Morris NY 13808.

FOOTE, MARCELLE K. b Albion Ind 12 N 10. 5: Ind U 28-32 (Eng) AB; West Res 32-33 BLS. 7: Libn Pub Lib, Albion Ind 33-37; Libn Pub Lib, Connersville Ind 37-56; Field consul Ind State Lib 56-60, Head ext div 60-67, Dir 67-. 8: Sec Ind Com on Pub Records 67-; Sec Ind Certification Bd 67-; Ind Commsn on the Aging Educ Com 69-. 9: ALA (LAD/LOM Statistics Com for Pub Libs); -ALTA (chm Trustee Citation Com 62); AAStateL (sec 63-64); IndLA (past treas & v-pres, pres 51-52); IndSchLA. 10: Altrusa International; AAUW; Delta Zeta. 11: Librarian of the Year, 66. 14: Admin. 15: Ind State Lib 140 N Senate, Indianapolis In 46204.

FORBES, C F. b Whittier Cal 29 Ap 31. 5: UBC 54-58 (Geol) BSc, 65-66 MLS. 7: Ref libn ubc 64-65, 65-68, Asst Hd Sedgewick Lib 68-. 9: CanLA. 14: Ref, spec collections, collection bldg, admin, undergrad serv. 15: Asst Head Sedgewick Lib, Univ of British Columbia Can.

FORBES, EDITH (JAMESON). b Yonkers NY 6 Jl 21. 4: Warren P Forbes. 5: Col of New Rochelle 38-42 (Eng) BA; Pratt 61-63 MLS. 6: Fr. 7: Sec Columbia U 44-49; Lib clerk Hempstead (NY) Pub Lib 55-64; Ref libn Nassau Commun Col 63-, Deputy dir 67-. 9: Nassau Co (NY) LA; NYStateLA. 14: Ref. 15: 29 Maryland ave, Hempstead NY.

FORBES, JOHN B. b Aberdeen SD 30 Ap 31. 4: Beverly Anderson Forbes. 5: Harvard 48-52 (Slavic Langs) AB; UMinn 55-57 (LS) MS. 6: Russian, Ger. 7: US Army (Cpl) 52-55; Jr libn UMinn (Minneapolis) 57-59; US Nat Agric Lib, Wash DC: Bibliog, Bibliography of Agric Sect 59-63, Chief 63-64, Chief div of indexing & documentation 64-. 9: Internat Fedn for Documentation; Internat Assn of Agric Libns & Documentalists; ASIS; SLA; DCLA. 10: Beta Phi Mu. 14: Indexing, documentation. 15: 10809 Georgia ave apt T-1, Wheaton Md 20902.

FORBIS, YATES McDONALD. b NC 28 O 29. 4: Ida Dean Cock. 5: Appalachian State Col 55 (Educ) MA; Columbia 60 MS in LS. 7: Battalion Steno US Army 3d Engnr Corp, Korea 53-54; Libn Kenmore Jr High Sch, Arlington Va 55-58; Circ asst Law Sch Lib, Columbia U 58-60; Libn St Andrews Col 60-63; Ref libn Kenyon Col 63-65; Deputy libn Dickinson Col 65-68; Hd libn 68-. 8: Ref libn Library USA NY Worlds Fair 65; Conferee Danforth Summer Campus Wkshop, Colo Springs Colo summer 62. 9: ALA. 10: AAUP. 14: Ref, admin. 15: 204 South West st, Carlisle Penn 17013.

FORCE, RONALD W. b Sioux City Iowa 7 S 41. 4: Jo Ellen Hitch. 5: Iowa State U 59-63 (Entomology) BS; UMinn 66-68 (LS) MA. 6: Ger. 7: 1st Lt (Aviator) USA 63-66; Asst hd dept libs Ohio State U (Columbus) 68-. 9: ALA; OhioLA. 14: Pub serv. 15: 2067 Harwitch rd, Columbus Oh 43221.

FORCHHEIMER, RUTH (COHNREICH). b Berlin Germany. 4: Ludwig L Forchheimer. 5: UFreiburg in Br Germany 30 (pre-med); UBerlin 31-33 (pre-med, med) BS; Pratt 61-63 MLS. 6: Ger, Fr, Sp, Lat. 7: Catlg entry investigation NY Pub Lib 63-65, Catlg rare bks 65-66; Monograph catlg 67-. 9: ALA; NY Lib Club. 14: Catlg. 15: 136-10 72nd ave, Flushing 67 NY 11367.

FORD, CAROLYN W(ALCOTT). b Tuskegee Inst Ala 18 Jl 13. 5: Tuskegee Inst 31-35 (Biol) BS; UIll 52-53 (LS) MS. 7: Instr civics & biol Tuskegee Inst High Sch, Tuskegee Inst Ala 35-38; Mgr col bkstore Bennett Col 41-42; Tuskegee Inst: Circ asst 45-46, Ser asst 47, Head ser div 48-57; Asst Prof Atlanta U,Sch Lib Serv 57-58; Asst ref libn Tuskegee Inst 58-65; Act hd ref div 66-. 9: ALA; AlaLA; SELA. 10: AAUP; Womens Internat League for Peace and Freedom; YWCA; UIll Lib Sch Ass; AAUW; Internat Reading Assn; NAACP. 14: Ref, doc. 15: PO Box 127, Tuskegee Inst Ala 36088.

FORD, CIDELLIA (REULET). b Vacherie La 11 Ja 17. 4: Kenneth Eldo Ford. 5: LSU 33-37 (Fr, Hist) BA, 37-39 BS in LS. 6: Fr. 7: Jr catlgr Dept libn Bio, Com LSU 39-44; Catlgr Catholic U 44-45; Asst Orange Pub Lib, Orange Cal 45; Dept libn agric econ & biol LSU 45-46; Sch libn Sacred Heart Sch, Griffin Ga 54-57; Asst dir & act dir Flint River Reg Lib, Griffin Ga 58-60, Libn in chg of processing 60-. 9: ALA; SELA; GaLA. 14: Tech processes. 15: 1202 E College, Griffin Ga 30223.

FORD, CONSTANCE (J). b Grubbs Ark 8 N 17. 5: Harding Col 36-41 (Fr) BA; Washington U 51-53 (LS) BS. 6: Fr. 7: Asst libn Harding Col 49-51; Circ asst Washington U Lib 51-53; Tech libn Union Electric, St Louis 53-60, Supv lib serv 60-67, Chief libn 67-. 8: SLA-St Louis Chap Lib Consul for bus and industry. 9: SLA (chm Pub Util Sect; St Louis Chap: v-pres & pres); MoLA (State Recr Com). 10: Zonta Internat; Downtown St Louis Inc. 15: 300 Mansion House ctr apt 1008, St Louis Mo 63102.

FORD, DEIRDRE (DARLING). b Lansing Mich 28 My 41. 4: William T Ford. 5: Smith 59-60; Brenau Col 60-61; Whittier Col 61-63 (Pol Sci) BA; UCal (Berkeley) 65-66 MLS. 6: Fr. 7: Credit supv Liberty Mutual Ins Co, San Francisco 63-65; Asst ref libn UIll (Cgicago Circle) 66-. 9: ALA. 10: Pi Sigma Alpha; Beta Phi Mu. 14: Ref. 15: 1400 E 55th pl apt 906, Chicago Il 60637.

FORD, FREDDIE T. b Jacksonville Fla 22 Jl 33. 4: John H Ford. 5: Carson Newman Col 51-52; Emory 63-66 (Educ) BA, 66-67 MLN. 7: Libn & materials coord Indian Creek Sch DeKalb Co, Clarkston Ga 67-. 9: ALA; GaEA (Lib Sect). 14: Child serv, sch libs. 15: 1193 Blueberry Trail, Decatur Ga 30033.

FORD, HARRIETTE J (PAULSON). b Atlantic Iowa 23 Jl 19. 4: Calvert W Ford. 5: Immaculate Heart Col 61 (LS); Santa Ana Col 68-69 (LS). 7: File clk-lib Autonetics Div of N Amer Rockwell, Anaheim Cal 56-57, Gen file clk-lib 57-58, Lib attendant 58-61, Lib asst 61-63, Br libn 63-. 9: SLA. 14: Docs, ref, circ. 15: 5925 Arbor rd, Lakewood Ca 90713.

FORD, MARGARET HELEN (DRESHER). b Lyons Kan 10 Ap 06. 4: James Ford. 5: McPherson Col 25-29 (Eng) AB U -0 BS in S39-40 (LS) MA. 6: Ger, Fr. 7: Catlgr Ft Hays Kan State Col Lib 30-39; Head Bind Mayo Clinic Lib, Rochester Minn 55-64, Chg Mayo Clinic Author Bibliog Mayo Clinic Lib 65-. 14: Catlg, ref. 15: Lower Hillside lane, Marvale Addition, Rochester Mn 55 901.

FORD, OSCAR W. b London Ohio 22 Ja 32. 4: Frieda Van Harreveld. 5: Pomona Col 57 (Psych) BA; CatholicU 63 MSLS. 6: Russian, Ger, Fr, Sp. 7: Interpreter-trans US Army 52-55; Researcher NSA, Md 57-59; Ref libn LC 59-63; Order libn Rand Corp, Santa Monica Cal 63-66; Asst supv tech doc ctr Hughes Aircraft Co, Culver City Cal 66-68; Dir spec serv Nev State Lib, Carson City Nev 68-. 9: NevLA. 14: Admin. 15: 1849 Alpine, Carson City Nv 89701.

FORD, RAMONA LOUISE (OWEN). b Kansas City Mo 29 Jl 37. 4: Arthur Morton Ford. 5: Baker U 55-59 9eng) AB; Ind U 61-62 (LS) MA; Tex Tech Col 66-67; UVienna summer 67 (Ger) Certif; New Sch for Soc Research 68- (Sociol). 6: Fr, Ger. 7: Asst archivist Indiana U (Bloomington) 59-60; Libn So Jr High Sch, Raytown Mo 60-61; Ref & acquis UKan Lib 62-65; Hd readers' serv Haille Sellassie I U, Addis Ababa Ethiopia 65-66; Ref bus lib Columbia U 67-68; Ser libn Brooklyn Col 68-. 8: Instructor, Student Asst Lib Workshop (Summer 63) Indiana U; Libn ALA Exhibit, World's Fair (Summer 64); consultant Commercial School, Addis Ababa Ethiopia (65-66); Asst Prof Extension Haille Sellassie I Univ (65-66). 9: LACUNY. 10: Pi Lambda Theta& beta Phi Mu. 11: Outstanding Young Women of Amer (67); Alpha Sigma. 14: Ref, ser. 15: 55 E 9th st apt 6-P, New York NY 10003.

FORD, STEPHEN. b Detroit 7 S 24. 4: Betty Reid. 5: Wayne State 43-48 (Hist) AB; UMich 48-49 AMLS. 6: Fr, Ger. 7: Asst libn Lawrence Col 49-53; Chief ser div SoIll U 53-54; Head order dept UMich(Ann Arbor) 54-62; Dir of Libs Grand Valley State Col, Allendale Mich 62-. 8: Dir Proj to Develop Performance Standards for Lib Bind (ALA/SLA) 60-61; Consul in lib development UBaghdad Iraq 61-62; Lectr lib sci UMich 65, 66, 68. 9: ALA; MichLA (v-pres 65-66). 10: Beta Phi Mu; Phi Kappa Phi; USA Standards Inst (chm Subcom Z39/16). 12: Ed IllLA "Record (53-54); Ed "Serial Slants (55-57); Asst ed "Library Resources & Technical Servces 57-59 (62-65). 13: Yes. 15: 3346 Coit st NE, Grand Rapids Mich 49505.

FORD, TERESA (CROCE). b Providence. 4: Paul W Ford. 5: State Col(Worcester) (Educ) BS in Ed; Simmons MS in LS. 7: Period div asst Worcester(Mass) Pub Lib 30-38, Asst Greendale Br 39-42, Child libn Quinsigamond Br 43-45, Ext serv to schs 45-47, Bkmob libn 47-48, Sch libn N High Sch Worcester Sch Dept 60, Sch libn c/o Burncoat Sr High Libs 64-68; Media Lib (Demonstration Grant - fed govt) May St School, Worcester Mass 68-69. 8: Spec proj on "Primary Sources Available for Tchrs from Grade 4 through Grade 12; Com for advance placement of stud of higher levelinto col; Libn on Speedway Prog summer 68. 9: MassTA; MassLA; WorcesterTA; Worcester Women TA (chm Nomin Com); BurncoatTA. 10: NE Folk Festival Club; Worcester Women Tchrs Assn; Burncoat Tchrs Assn. 14: Ref, tchg lib skills & use of multimedia materials. 15: 56 Claridge rd, Worcester Mass 01606.

FORD, WILLIAM THOMAS. b Buffalo Ill 19 S 39. 4: Deirdre Darling. 5: SoIllU 56-64 (Eng) BA; Rosary Col 66-68 MALS; DePaul 68- (Law). 6: Sp, Ger. 7: Circ asst UIll (Chicago Circle) 66-67; Ref asst UChicago Law Sch Lib 67-68; Humanities & ser catlgr uchicago 68-. 9: BSA; Mod Lang Assn. 14: Catlg, rare bks, law. 15: 1400 E 55th pl apt 906, Chicago Il 60637.

FORESTER, JAMES LAWRENCE. b Cord Ark 14 Ap 35. 4: Jean Martha Brouillette. 5: Arkansas Col 52-55 (Hist) BSE; Peabody 60 (LS) MA; LSU 60- (Hist). 6: Fr, Ger. 7: Tchr-libn Rison (Ark) High Sch 55-57; Libn Sarepta (LA) High Sch

57-58; Sp 4 Personnel Classification Spec US Army 58-60; Ref libn LSU (New Orleans) 60-61, Instr in bks & libs 61-64; Head, order dept LSU (Baton Rouge) 65-66; Head Libn lsu (Eunice) 66-. 9: ALA; LaLA; SWLA; New Orleans Lib Club. 10: Phi Alpha Theta; Alpha Psi Omega; La Hist Soc. 13: Yes. 14: Catlg, admin. 15: Le Douy Lib La State Univ at Eunice, Eunice La 70535.

FORESTER, JEAN MARTHA (BROUILLETTE). b Port Barre La 7 S 34. 4: James Lawrence Forester. 5: LSU 51-55 (Eng) BS, Peabody 55-56 (LS) MA. 7: Libn Howell Elem Sch, Springhill La 56-58; Asst post libn Ft Chaffee (US Army), Ft Smith Ark 58; Field libn Orleans Ara Command (US Army) Orleans,France 59; Acquis libn Northwestern State Col, Natchitoches La 60; Ser libn LSU (New Orleans) 60-66; Ser libn LSU (Eunice) 67-. 9: LaLA; SWLA; Friends LSU(E) Lib. 10: Alpha Beta Alpha; Phi Mu; Delta Kappa Gamma. 13: Yes. 14: Acquis, ser, instr in lib usage. 15: Box 304, Eunice La 70535.

FORGET, LOUIS J S. b Bearn Que Can 13 Ag 41. 4: Claudette Venne. 5: UMontreal 59-63 (Sci) BA, 63-64 BBibl. 6: Fr, Eng. 7: Libn III I Nat Lib of Can, Ottawa 64-. 9: CanLA; ALA; OttawaLA; Prof Inst Pub Serv of Can; Societe des Diplomes de LEcole de Bibliotheconomie UMontreal. 14: Subj catlg, indexing, info retrieval, mechanized lib proc. , systems anal. 15: 114 Daly ave apt 2, Ottawa 2 Ont Can.

FORLANO, ADRIENNE E(LIZABETH). b Chicago Ill 18 F 37. 5: LA Valley Col 57-58; UCLA 58-62 (Hist) BA; USoCal 62-64 (LS) MS. 6: Ger, Sp. 7: Lib clk LA Pub Lib 58-61, Libn 61-65; Asst libn Bell & Howell Research Ctr, Pasadena Cal 65-66; Tech lit analyst Aerospace Corp, El Segundo Cal 66-68; Chief libn Northrop Ventura tech info ctr, Newbury Park Cal 68-. 9: SLA; CalLA; So Cal Assn Sch & Child Libns. 10: Pierpont Bay Assn, Ventura Cal; All City Employees Assn, Los Angeles, Cal; Northrop Mgt Clb, Los Angeles, Ca&/ 14: Ref. 15: Northrop Ventura Tech Info Ctr 1515 Rancho Conejo blvd, Newbury Park Ca 91320.

FORMA, CAMILLE MARIE. b Buffalo NY 16 N 43. 5: SUNY (Buffalo) 61-65 (Sociol, Psych) BA; West Res 65-66 (Documentation) MSLS. 6: Sp. 7: Ref libn Columbia U Parkinson Disease Infor & Research Ctr 66-68; Ref libn Standard Oil Co (NJ), NYC 68-. 9: ASIS; SLA. 14: Ref, automation. 15: 300 1/2 E 65th st Apt 2A, New York NY 10021.

FORMAN, DOROTHY J. b Detroit Mich 26 Ja 19. 5: Wayne State 37-41 (Sch LS) BA. 7: Asst research labs General Motors Corp, Detroit Warren Mich 40-61, Libn Ternstedt Div, Warren Mich 61-68, Libn Fisher Body Div, Warren Mich 68-. 9: SLA (Mich Chap pres 55-56). 10: Engrg Societies of Detroit. 15: 30007 Van Dyke ave, warren Mi 48090.

FORMAN, JACK. b Rochester NY 11 O 42. 5: URochester 60-64 (Hist) AB; Rutgers (New Brunswick) 66-67 MLS. 7: Lib trainee Rochester Pub Lib, Rochester NY 65-66; Jr libn woodbridge Free Pub Lib, Woodbridge NJ 67-69, Br hd 69-. 8: Hd com providing recorded bk talks for local radio sta. 9: NJLA; MiddlesexCoLA; Woodbridge Staff Assn. 14: ya & adult programs, materials, selection. 15: 126 Montgomery st apt 3-E, Highland Park NJ 08904.

FORMAN, SIDNEY. b Brooklyn NY 16 Mr 15. 4: Belle Schaeffer. 5: City Col (NY) 32-36 (Hist) BSS; Columbia U 36-39 (Hist) MA, 49 PhD, 59 MS LS. 7: State ed, NY State Writers Proj, Albany NY 40-41; Tech ed US Army Signal Corps, Belmar NJ 41-42; US Army T-4 42-46; Archivist lib US Mil Acad (W Point) 46-54, Dir Archives 54-57, Dir LIB 57-62; Prof of Soc Sci, Ladycliff Col 46-62; Prof of Educ & Libn Teachers Col Columbia U 62-. 8: Var Middle States Accredit Teams. 9: ALA (chm John Cotton Dana Awards Com 64-66); SLA; NEA. 10: AHA. 12: "Story of the Five Towns (41); "West Point-A History of the US Military Academy (50); "Fort Sumter (60); Research ed "School Libraries (66-69). 13: Yes. 14: Admin. 15: 501 W 120 st, New York NY 10027.

FORNEY, DOROTHY JEAN. b Salem Ohio 12 My 29. 5: Youngstown U 49-53 (Eng) BA; West res 53-54 MS in LS. 7: Circ libn Youngstown U 54-56, Ref libn 56-60, Catlg libn 60-63, Acquis libn 63-66, Organizer Title 2 Project E Palestine City Schs summer 66; Prof asst Salem Pub Lib, Salem Ohio 66-67; Catlg & acquis libn Mt Union Col 67-. 9: OhioLA. 15: 325 Vincent blvd, Alliance Oh 44601.

FORNEY, MARTHA ESTELLE. b Brenham Tex 31 D 20. 4: Samuel Alexander Forney Sr. 5: Prairie View A&M Col 38-42 (Eng) BA; Emporia State Col 42-43 (LS) Certif, 56-57 MS LS. 6: Fr. 7: Libn High Sch, Webster Groves Mo 43-46; Asst libn Denver Pub Lib 48-56; Libn Carver High Sch, Waco Tex 57-; Asst libn McLennan Commun Col, Waco 66-. 9: TexLA. 10: Delta Sigma Theta; Jack & Jill Club of Amer, Inc; YWCA. 14: Ref, ya serv. 15: 4200 Orchard lane, Waco Tex 76705.

FORREST, DELLA M. b Cleveland 27 Ap 06. 5: Oberlin 23-24; UMich 24-27 (Eng) AB in Ed, 27-28 ABLS. 6: Fr, Sp. 7 Catlgr Oberlin Col 28-29; Catlgr UMich(Ann Arobr) Arbor Sr clsf 30-43, Assoc catlg libn 43-56, Asst head catlg dept 56-63, Assoc head catlg dept 63-65, Act head catlg dept 65-66; Hd catlg dept 66-67; Head tech serv dept 67-. 8: Consul; mich State U, East Lansing 58; No Mich U, Marquette 66. 9: ALA-RTSD (Catlg & Clsf Sect; com on Coop with Latin Amer catlgs & clsfrs 59-61); MichLA (sec-treas Reg Group of Catlgrs 57-58; Tech Serv Sect; dir-at-Large 60-63; Cost Acctg Study Com 62); Ann Arbor Lib Club (sec 53-54). 10: AAUW; Women of the Fac, UMich; Fac Womens Club. 14: Tech serv. 15: 1237 Island dr, Ann Arbor Mi 48105.

FORREST, FRED H(AROLD). b Blum Tex 8 N 19. 5: Columbia 45-48 (Eng) BS, 48-49 (Eng) AM, 49-52 (LS) MS. 6: Fr, Sp, Ger 07: Y 1/c US Naval Reserve 42-45; Asst circ libn Columbia U Libs 51-59; Libn in chg of pub serv C W Post Col 59-61; Libn & Prof of Eng Webb Inst of Naval Arch, Glen Cove NY 61-. 13: Yes. 14: Ref, catlg. 15: 429 W 46 st, New York NY 10036.

FORREST, KATHRYN S(NYDER). b Johnson Co Ind 9 Ja 24. 4: William M Forrest. 5: Ind Central Col 41-44 (Eng, Hist) BA; USoCal 58 MS LS. 7: Lib asst Citrus Expt Station UCal (Riverside) 53-56; Lib asst documents sect UCal (Berkeley) 56; Lib asst in chg Grad Reading rm USoCal 56-57; Acquis libn Los Angeles State Col 58-60; Acquis libn Cal Inst of Tech 60-61; Head Libn Bio-Agric Lib UCal(Riverside) 61-. 9: SLA; Internat Assn of Agric Libns & Documentalists; CalLA. 10: Beta Phi Mu. 14: Tech serv, documentation. 15: Univ of Cal, Lib, Riverside Cal 92502.

FORREST, WILLIAM M(ILLARD). b Elkhart Ind 19 S 23. 4: Kathryn Snyder Forrest. 5: UCal (Berkeley) 56 (Gen Curriculum) BA; USoCal 56-57 MSLS. 6: Ger, Sp. 7: Pilot USA Air corps 42-46; Catlgr Cal State Polytech Col 57-58, Building coord 58-64; Catlgr UCal 9riverside) 65-66; Br coord San Bernardino Pub Lib, San Bernardino Cal 66-. 8: Bldg consul Los Angeles 62-64. 9: CalLA. 14: Pub lib. 15: 4864 Mariposa dr, San Bernardino Ca 92404.

FORSHAW, WILLIAM SHERLOCK. b NYC 28 Ja 14. 5: Columbia U 30-34 (Eng Lit) BA, 56-58 (LS) MS. 6: Fr, Ger. 7: Ed asst Time Inc, NYC; Naval aviation res off (Lt comdr), Wash DC 42-46; Mgr Doubleday Bk Shops, NYC, St Louis, Detroit 47-58; Asst popular lib Enoch Pratt Free Lib, Baltimore 58-60, Hd co serv 60-62, Sr subj specialist 63-. 8: Film Histn, Baltimore Museum of Art. 9: ALA; TheatreLA (Board Memb); MdLA. 14: Rare bks, relating new media to bks. 15: 2624 St Paul, Baltimore Md 21218.

FORSMAN, CAROLYN (APPELMAN). b New York 10 D 43. 4: John Forsman. 5: NYU 60-64 (Phil) BA; UCal (Berkeley) 64-65 MLS. 7: Stud libn Richmond Pub Lib, Richmond Cal 64-65; Libn I Baltimore Co Pub Lib, Md 65-66; Libn I Contra Costa Co Lib, Cal 66-67; Sr libn hd ref Vallejo Pub Lib, Vallejo Cal 67-. 9: ALA; CalLA (sec Ref Serv Div 68-69; mem Nat Lib Week Com 68-69). 10: Bay Area YA Libns; ACLU; Beta Phi Mu. 14: ya serv, ref serv, intel freedom. 15: PO Box 823, Berkeley Ca 94701.

FORSTER, (GRACEMARY) IMOGEN. b Nottingham UK 16 My 40. 5: St Hilda's Col (Oxford) 59-62 (Eng Lit) MA; U E Anglia (Norwich) 63-64 (Eng Lit); Loughborough Tech Col 66-67 (LS) ALA. 6: Fr, Ger, Sp, Ital. 7: Admin asst UKent (Canterbury) 65-66; Asst libn leicesterU 67-68; Prof libn SyracuseU 68-. 9: TheLA (Britain). 14: Bibliog of Eng lit. 15: Room 302 Syracuse Univ Lib, Syracuse NY 13210.

FORSTER, WALTER E(DWIN). b Detroit 16 Jl 08. 4: Lorine E Walton. 5: Wayne U 29-38 (Eng) BA; Columbia 39-40 BS LS; Wayne U 41-49 (Econ) MA. 6: Ger. 7: Sec Chrysler Advisory Bd Chrysler Corp, Highland Park Mich 32-39; Ref asst Brooklyn Pub Lib 40; Ref asst Detroit Pub Lib 41-48, Chief bus & finance dept 49-. 9: ALA; SLA (chm Bus & Fin Div 59-60: pres Mich Chap 58-59. LA. 10: Amer Econ Assn; Detroit Turners; Burning Tree Country Club; Econ Club of Detroit. 13: Yes. 14: Ref. 15: Detroit Pub Lib 5201 Woodward ave, Detroit Mi 48202.

FORSYTH, FRANCES ELIZABETH (ANDREWS). b Kewannee Kewanee 14 a 10. 4: John B Forsyth. 5: Knox Col

26-30 (Hist) AB; Columbia 30-31 BS in LS; Wayne State 54-56 Tchg Certif; UMich 58-62 MALS. 7: Head ref & circ Union Theol Sem(NYC) 31-34; Libn Oakwood Jr High Sch, East Detroit Mich 54-56; Sch libn Elem Lib Off, Farmington Mich 56-67; Pioneer Middle Sch learning resource ctr Plymouth Commun Schs, Plymouth Mich 68-. 9: ALA; MichASchL; MichEA; Mich A-V Assn. 10: Phi Beta appa; Frends of Detroit Pub Lib; Founders Soc of Detroit Art Inst Women"s City Club; Assn UN; YMCA; AAUW. 14: Catlg, child bks, ref. 15: 18825 Lancashire rd, Detroit Mi 48223.

FORSYTHE, DAVID N. b McKeesport Penn 24 Jl 40. 5: Muskingum Col 58-62 (Econ) AB; UIll 62-63 (LS) MS. 6: Fr. 7: Asst ref libn Pratt Inst 63-64; Asst libn UWash bus admin lib 64-66; Acquis libn Lafayette Col 66-68; Hd bibliog serv West Mich U 68-. 8: Lib usa ny world's Fair 64. 9: ALA; SLA. 14: Acquis. 15: 11038 Portage rd, Kalamazoo Mi 49002.

FORT, GILBERTO VICTORIANO. b Havana Cuba 25 F 29. 4: Zorayda Arango. 5: Inst de la Habana 43-48 (BA) UHavana 48-57 (Dr of Law); Kan State Tchrs Col(Emporia) 64-65 MS in LS; UIll (Sp & Lat Amer Bibliogr) summer 68. 6: Sp, Eng, Portu, Lat, Fr, Ital. 7: Lawyer, Havana Cuba 57-62; Asst catlgr Kan State Tchrs Col Lib (Emporia) 64-65; Latin Amer catlgr Watson Lib UKan 65-67, Latin Amer bibliog 68-. 8: Adv Com for the Selection of Span & Portu Material to Book Reprints Internat Inc, Miami Fla. 9: ALA; Sem on the Acquis of Latin Amer Lib Materials, Inc (chm Const & By-Laws Com, mem Exec Bd). 10: Colegio Nacional de Abogados de Cuba en el exilio; AAUP; Midwest Coun; Assn Lat in Amer Studies. 12: "The Cuban Revolution of Fidel Castro Viewed from Outside; An Annotated Bibliography" (69). 14: Catlg, admin, bibliog. 15: Sunflower Apts No 18, 11th & Missouri sts, Lawrence Ks 66044.

FORT, MANDY (SIMPSON). b Nashville 31 Jl 36. 4: Dudley C Fort Jr. 5: Vanderbilt 5458 (Sp) BA; Inst Tech de Monterey (Mexico) summers 5556; Peabody summer 58 (LS); Columbia 5960 (LS) MS. 6: Sp. 7: Libn Harpeth Hall Sch, Nashville 5859; Res libn Joint U Libs, Nashville 6061; Ref libn Augusta Ga Pub Lib 62; Chem libn Joint U Libs, Nashville 6264; Asst med libn Gen Hosp, Cincinnati 6466; Head med lib 66. 15: 3203 Golden ave apt 500, Cincinnati Oh 45226.

FORTADO, ROBERT JOSEPH. b Jacksonville Ill 22 Ap 33. 5: Ill Col 56-60 (Eng) BA; UIll 60-61, 67 (LS) MS. 7: Railway agt CB&Q RR Co, Galesburg Ill 51-61; Communications tech II USN NSG 52-56; Grad asst circ dept UIll Lib 60-61; Libn Triad High Sch, St Jacob Ill 61-64; Ref & docs libn SoIllU 64-. 14: Govt publ. 15: 137 Springer ave, Edwardsville Il 62025.

FORTH, (WM) STUART. b Manistee Mich 13 Ag 23. 4: Pearl Brown. 5: UMich 48 (Hist, Eng) BA, 50 MALS; UWash 54-59 (Hist) PhD. 6: Ger, Fr. 7: (S/Sgt) US Army Air Force US & abroad 43-46; Catlg libn Ore State U 50-52, Admin asst 52-54; Tchg fellow-Hist UWash 54-56; Asst ref libn Seattle Pub Lib 56-59; Head Undergrad Lib UKan 59-61, Assoc Dir of Libs 61-65; Dir of Libs UKy 65-, v-pres stud affairs 69-. 9: ALA (chm Memb Com of Kan); -ACRL (chm Univs Sect 67-68); AHA; Org Amer Histns; BSA; KanLA; KyLA; PNLA (sec 53-54); SELA. 10: AAUP; ACLU. 13: Yes. 14: . 15: King Lib UKy, Lexington Ky 40506.

FORTIER, HARLEY L. b Ludington Mich 14 D 23. 5: UMich 43-47 (Hist) AB, 47-48 ABLS. 7: Asst researcher Universal Studios, Universal City Cal 49-57; Asst researcher MGM Studios, Culver City Cal 57-64; Libn Walt Disney Productions, Burbank Cal 64-. 9: SLA. 15: Walt Disney Productions 500 S Buena Vista, Burbank Cal 91503.

FORTIN, CLIFFORD C. b Hamel Minn 7 Ap 22. 5: UMinn 39-43 (Educ-Hist) S, 49-51 (LS) MA, 58- (Educ). 6: Ger. 7: Personal affairs coun US Army Air Force, Amarillo Tex 45-46; High sch prin, Middle River Minn 48-49; Catlg & ref libn Kan State Col 51-53, Order libn 53-55; Asst libn Wis State Col(River Falls) 55-62, Assoc Prof of Lib Sci 63-. 8: Com on Lib Educ in Wis 60-62 which planned the Oct 62 Milwaukee Inst on Lib Educ; Wkshop for Schl Libns, Riser Falls 64. 9: ALA-LED (Tchrs Sect Nomin Com 69-70); WisLA (sec Standing Com on Lib Educ 68-69). 10: AAUP. 14: Sel, ref, lib educ. 15: Route 1 Box 153C, Hamel Mn 55340.

FORTNER, DONALD DEE. b Kansas City Miss 27 Jl 35. 4: Myrtle Frances Mulnix. 5: Kan City Art Inst 59-65 (Fine Arts) BFA; UOkla 66-68 MLS. 6: Ger. 7: Adult serv libn daniel Boone Reg Lib, Columbia Mo 68-. 14: Ref, pub serv. 15: Crescent Meadows Rte 8, Columbia Mo 65201.

FORTNEY, MARY (EVAN). b LaCrosse Wis 4 N 29. 5: Milwaukee-Downer Col 47-51 (Geog- Geol) BA; UWis (Madison) 51-53 (Geog), 65-66 MALS. 7: Map libn UWis geog dept (Madison) 53-65; Map libn Northwestern U 66-. 9: SLA. 10: Assn Amer Geogrs. 15: 1509 Hinman, Evanston Il 60201.

FOSBENDER, JULE JOANN. b Paw Paw Mich 23 Ag 32. 5: West Mich U 0-54 (LS) BA. 7: Libn Tecumseh High Sch Lib, Tecumseh Mich 54-56; Ref libn Lenawee Co Lib, A Pub Lib, Tecumseh Mich 54-67. 9: ALA; MicLA (chm dist 2, 61-62, MichEA; Bus libn Kalamazoo Lib Syst 67-. 14: Admin. 15: 266 Eisenhower dr, Mattawan Mi 49071.

FOSDICK, EMMA (HASKELL). b Truro NS 3 Ja 30. 4: Sidney Fosdick. 5: Dalhousie U 46-49 (Biol, Chem) BSc UBC 63-64 BLS. 7: Tech Fisheries Research Bd, St Andrews NB 49-51; Admin Off Royal Can Air Force 52-58; Jr Biol & libn Internat Pacific Salmon Fisheries Commsn, New West Minster BC 58-63; Sci libn John Crerar Lib, Chicago 64-65; Research Assoc Archive-Lib AMA, Chicago 65-68; Libn-in-charge Can Ctr for Inland Waters Lib, Burlington Ont 68-. 9: SLA. 14: Ref. 15: 7 Elizabeth st N #801, Port Credit Ont Can.

FOSHEE, (ELLA) MARTEYNE. b Greeneville Tenn 5 Ap 28. 5: E Tenn State U 46-49 (Eng) BS, summers 51-53 (Educ) MA. 7: Greene Co(Tenn) Bd of Educ: Tchr Moseim High Sch 50-51, Tchr-libn Ottway High Sch 51-62, Libn N Greene High Sch 62-. 9: NEA; ALA; TennLA; TenEA. 10: Alpha Delta Kappa. 14: Sch libnship. 15: Rt 2, Mosheim Tenn 37818.

FOSS, LILA M. b Hope Ark 17 Ap 20. 5: SWest La U 38-42 (Eng, Hist) BA; LSU Lib Sch 42-43 BA in LS. 6: Fr, Sp. 7: Libn USAF, Lake Charles La 43-45; Asst ref libn Atlanta Pub Lib 45-46; Asst ref libn SEast La Col 46-47; Asst libn Texas A & M Col 48-51; Hd libn pub lib, Lake Charles La 51-59; Asst libn pub lib, Arlington Mass 59-60; Ser libn Brown U Lib 60-66; Libn Tex Instruments Inc, Attleboro Mass 66-. 9: SLA; MassLA. 10: Mass Hort Soc; Old Sturbridge Village Assn. 14: Admin, ref. 15: 171 Broad st, North Attleboro Ma 02760.

FOSTER, BESSIE MAE (JOHNSON). b Lowdnes Co Valdosta Ga 11 Je 38. 4: Rev James H Foster. 5: Albany State Col 55-59 (Elem Educ) BS; Ft Valley Col summer 60 (LS); Atlanta U 65-66 MSLS; UGa lib educ inst summer 68. 6: Sp, Fr. 7: Libn Cook Co Train Sch, Adel Ga 59-65; Stud asst catlg Atlanta U 65; Asst ref libn Fla A & M U 66; Acquis libn Alcorn Col 67; Libn Valdosta High Sch, Valdosta Ga 67-. 9: NEA; ALA; -ACRL; AASL; Lib Research RT; GaEA (Lib Dept); GaLA. 10: AAUW. 14: Ref, sch libs. 15: PO Box 831, Valdosta Ga 31601.

FOSTER, EDITH LENORE. b Carrollton Ga 6 Mr 06. 5: LaGrange Col 22-26 (Eng) BA; Emory 43-44 (LS) AB. 7: Tchr Buena Vista High Sch, Buena Vista Ga 26-27; Drama Coach Wayne p sewell Prod Co, Newnan Ga 27-28; Hd Eng Dept: Chocktow Co High Sch, Butler Ala 28-33, Trion High Sch, Trion Ga 33-40, Tallapoosa High Sch, Tallapoosa Ga 40-41, gordon Mem High Sch, Chickamauga Ga 41-43; Asst Prof Eng W Ga Col 44-45, Asst Prof Lib Educ 58-64; Dir W Ga Reg Lib, Carrollton 44-. 8: Consul, Fla StateU summer 55; Testified before Congressional Educ Com in behalf of Lib Serv Act 60; Exec Dir Ga Lib Week 59-60. 9: ALA (Coun 59-63; pres Adult Educ Sect 55-56; chm Coord Com Operation 58-59); SELA (chm Recr Com 52-56); Ga Pub Lib Film Com (chm 58); GaLA pres 61-63, chm Budg Com 63-65, chm Lib Devel Com 63-65, Fed Rel Com, Adv Title II Com, chm Nix-Jones Lib Award of Distinction Com, mem Intel Freedom Com 67-69). 11: Nat Lib awards 60-61; Carroll Co's outstanding citizen 50. 12: Auth, #14 of ALA "Small Libraries Project"; Auth of 2 bks of poems: "Beside the Wishing Well" and "To Wind a chain". 13: Yes. 14: Adult educ, ref, wk with area libns; reg wk in devel new libs. 15: 219 E Sims st, Carrollton Ga 30117.

FOSTER, ELSIE D (GATES). b Oklahoma City Okla 1 S 17. 4: Vearl Sanford Foster. 5: Central State Col 35-39 (Tchg Lat, Eng) AB; San Jose State Col summers 42-45 (LS); UDenver 53-54 (LS) MA. 6: Sp. 7: Tchr Waynoka (Ola) High Sch 39-41; Tchr Stockton (Cal) Unified Sch Dist 43-44, Tchr-libn 44-50, Libn 50-; Libn Stockton (Cal) Pub Lib 48; Asst libn Bus Admin Lib, UDenver 53-54; Asst ref libn San Jose State Col 57; Asst ref libn Frenso State Col 58; Libn Bullard High Sch, Fresno Cal 58; Libn Franklin High Sch, Stockton Unified Sch Dist 58-. 9: NEA; Cal Tchrs Assn; CalASchL. 10: Dlta Kappa Gamma; AAUW; Altrusa Club. 14: Sch libs. 15: 1003 S Tuxedo ave, Stockton Cal 95204.

FOSTER, F BLANCHE. b Centerville Tenn 6 Ja 19. 5: Tenn State U 35-40 (Eng) BS; Atlanta U 46-47 BLS; UMich 50-51, 58-62 AMLS; Sophia U (Tokyo) (Oriental Lit). 6: Fr, Ger. 7:

Tchr Darwin High Sch, Cookeville Tenn 42-45; Hd libn Sam Houston Col 47-50; Libn Bd of Educ Detroit 51; Instr NDEA Va State Col 66; Asst dir Afro-Amer life Program, Detroit 68. 8: Libn Internat Afro-Amer Museum; Detroit 68; Adv Bd Black Hist Proj, Wayne State U 68-. 9: ALA; WILPF; MichASchL. 10: Founders Soc; Detroit Hist Soc; Internat Afro-Amer Museum. 12: "First Book of Kenya" (69); "First Book of Dahomey" (70). 14: Readers serv. 15: 2285 Webb, Detroit Mi 48206.

FOSTER, I(DA) LOREEN (BREWER). b Gosport Ind 15 Ap1899. 4: C Holt Foster. 5: Franklin Col summers 17, 19, 20-21, 22-24 (Hist) AB; UKY SUMMERS 48-50, BS LS; UCincinnati summers (Soc Sci). 7: Elem tchr, Owen Co Ind 17-20; Elem tchr, Spencer Ind 21-22; High sch tchr, Van Buren Ind 25-27; Elem tchr, Monterey Ky 39-42; High sch tchr-libn, Kings Mills Ohio 43-5; High sch libn Green Cove Springs Fla 53-65; Jr col libn, St Johns River Jr Col 65-68; Elem sch libn, S Bryan Jennings Elem Sch 68-69. 8: Visiting Com, Sch Eval, S Assn of Cols & Schs. 9: NEA; ALA; FlaLA. 10: Study Club; Delta Kappa Gamma; Garden Club, Beta Phi Mu. 15: 426 St Johns ave, Green Cove Springs Fl 32043.

FOSTER, IMOGENE. b Adolphus Ky 10 Ag 21. 5: West Ky State Col 40-42, 53 (LS) BA; Peabody 57-59 (S) MA. 7: Tchr Allen Co Elem Schs, Scottsvile Ky 2-53; Lib asst Berea Col 53-55; Tchr Scottsville (Ky) Elem Sch 55-58; Libn Hart Mem Consolidated Sch, Hardyville Ky 58-59; Info libn UMo 59-63; Ref libn Morehead State Col 63-65; Ref libn West Ky U 65-. 9: NEA; ALA; KyEA; KyLA. 10: AAUW. 14: Ref. 15: Margie Helm Lib, Bowling Green Ky 42101.

FOSTER, IVA W. b Lewiston Me 19 Jl 09. 5: Bates Col 26-30 AB; Columbia 33-34 (LS) BS. 6: Fr. 7: Libn I & II Pub Lib, Brooklyn NY 31-33; Bates Col: Catlg libn 35-41, Asst libn 41-57, libn 57-. 9: ALA; ACRL; NELA (chm Scholarship Com 63-65); MeLA. 15: 22 Granite st, Auburn Me 04210.

FOSTER, PAULINE (McCANDLESS). b Allendale Mo 9 Ja 04. 4: Franklin J Foster. 5: Drury Col 22-26 (Eng) AB; UIll 30-31 BS LS; UAla 41-43 (Secondary Educ)MA. 7: Asst libn Drury Col 26-30; Catlgr Swarthmore Col 31-38; Chm Dept of Lib Sci UAla 38-. 9: ALA; NEA; SELA (chm Lib Educ 60-62); AlaLA (pres 42-44). 10: AAUW; Delta Kappa Gamma; Beta Phi Mu; Alpha Beta Alpha; Mortar Bd. 13: "Know Alabama (42); "Design Manual for Building and enovating School Libraries (60). 14: Lib educ, sch libnship, ref. 15: PO Box 2242, University Ala 35486.

FOTH, ELLEN K. b Brooklyn NY 3 Je 20. 4: Frederick E Foth. 5: Mt Holyoke 37-41 (Hist) AB; Columbia 47 (LS) BS. 6: Fr. 7: Clerk Atlantic Mutual Insurance Co, NYC 42-45; Storekeeper (T) Third class USNavy Wash DC 44-46; Ref asst Harvard Col Lib 47-49; Ref asst Wilmington Pub Lib, Wilmington Del 49-50; Br libn (Bellevue ave br) Montclair Pub Lib, Montclair NJ 50-. 9: ALA; NJLA. 10: North Jersey Mt Holyoke Club; Col Womens Club of Montclair. 14: Readers adv wk, bk sel, ref. 15: 100 Sherman ave, Cedar Grove Nj 07009.

FOURIER, RUTH (GASSER). b Nashville 27 Jl 20. 4: Arthur E Fourier. 5: Vanderbilt 38-42 (Eng) BA; USoCar 46-48 (Eng) MA; Vanderbilt 48-50 (Eng) PhD. 6: Ger, Fr. 7: (Lt) USNR (WR) Disbursing & Supply Off 43-46; Instr of Eng USCar 46-48; Humanities libn Auburn U Lib 62-, Act hd humanities div 67-. 9: AlaLA. 10: Phi Beta Kappa. 14: Humanities ref, bibliog. 15: Auburn Univ Lib, Auburn Al 46830.

FOURNIER, CHARLOTTE (TILTON). b Long Beach Cal 30 Ap 23. 4: Rene Paul Fournier. 5: Stanford 41-45 (Soc Sci) BA; Immaculate Heart Col 66-68 (LS) MA. 6: Fr. 7: Libn Mental Health Development Ctr, Hollywood Cal 67-68; Libn Mt Wilson Observatory Lib, Pasadena Cal 68; Libn LA Co Dept of Personnel 69-. 9: SLA; MedLA; CalLA. 10: Stanford alumni Assn; Humane Soc of the US. 14: Acquis, exchange programs, bibliog. 15: 2737 Rustic lane, Glendale Ca 91208.

FOUTZ, CHLOE V. b Vamoosa Okla 31 Mr 38. 5: Southwestern Jr Col 56-58; Union Col(Lincoln Neb) 59-61 (Home Econ) BA; UIll 61-62 (LS) MS. 6: Ger. 7: Asst libn Union Col Lib(Lincoln Neb) 62-; Asst Prof Lib Sci 62-. 9: ALA; NebLA (Col & Univ Sect; past pres, sec-treas); Lincoln Neb LA. 10: Fac Womens Club; activities connected with the Seventh-day Adventist Church, college sponsorships, etc. 14: Ref, lib bldgs. 15: 4621 Stockwell apt 6, Lincoln Nb 68506.

FOW, META Y(ARALL). b Yeadon Penn 17 Mr 1899. 5: Swarthmore Col 18-22 (Eng) AB; Drexel 24-25 (LS) MS Equiv. 6: Fr, Ger, Sp. 7: Permanent sub Jr & Sr High Schs, Phila 32-37; Catlgr Pub Lib, Brooklyn NY 38-41; Catlgr NY Hist Soc, NYC 43-45; Catlgr Amer Bankers Assn, NYC 45-51; Spec catlgr Pub Lib, Wilmington Del 52-53; Jr high sch libn Ridley Twp (Penn) 53-60; Jr high sch libn Darby-Colwyn Jt Schs, Darby Penn 60-. 9: NEA; Penn EA; Del Co (Penn) Sch LA. 10: Delta Kappa Gamma. 14: Catlg, tchr libn. 15: 100 Morton ave, Ridley Park Pa 19078.

FOWLER, HATTIE (ELIZABETH). b Georgetown Tex 3 N 04. 5: Southwestern U 21-25 (Eng)BA; Tex U summers 33, 34; Tex Womans U 52-54 MLS. 6: Sp. 7: Eng tchr Wheelock Sch, Wheelock Tex 25-26; Eng tchr Lyford High Sch, Lyford Tex 2738; Eng tchr La Feria J High Sch, La Feria Tex 26-27; Libn Port Arthur Schs, Port Arthur Tex 38-46; Libn Greiner Jr High Sch, Dallas Tex 46-57; Libn Bryan Adams High Sch, Dallas 57-. 9: ALA; NEA: Tex State Tchrs Assn; TexLA; Tex Classroom Tchrs Assn; Classroom Tchrs of Dallas. 10: Delta Kappa Gamma; AAUW; Dallas Womans Forum; Wesleyan Serv Guild. 14: Catlg, ref, wk with yp. 15: 5911 Victor st, Dallas Tx 75214.

FOWLER, JOYCE M. b Waverly NY 22 Je 42. 5: SUNY (Geneseo) 64 (Educ, LS) BS. 7: High sch libn pub sch, NY State 64-65; Elem libn pub sch, NY State 65-68; Ser libn Williams Col 68-. 8: Red Cross hosp vol. 9: ALA. 10: Old Sturbridge Hist Soc; Bennington Museum. 14: Ser. 15: 737 Main st, Bennington Vt 05201.

FOWLER, TALBERT (B) JR. b Columbia SC 12 F 20. 4: Mabel Hiatt. 5: UFla 38-42 (Psych) AB; UFla Col of Law 46-49 JD UFla 50-51 (LS). 7: Acetylene burner leaderman Wainwright Shipyard, Panama City Fla 42-43; US Army (Sgt) US Army Combat Engnrs, Cal, Tex, & Pacific 43-46; Lib ser asst UFla Main Lib spring 49; Asst libn UFla Col of Law 49-54; Law practice, Gainesville Fa 53-54; Libn & Asst Prof of Law UAla Law Sch, Tuscaloosa Ala 54-57, Libn & Assoc Prof of Law 57-59, Libn & Prof of Law 59-. 69; Libn & Prof of Law UPittsburgh Law Sch, Pa 69-. 9: AALL; Fla Bar Assn; Ala State Bar; AlaLA. 13: Yes. 14: Ref, acquis. 15: 556C Trenton sq apts, Pittsburgh Pa 15221.

FOWLER, THOMAS S. b Seattle Wash 15 F 42. 5: UPuget Sound 60-64 (Speech, Drama) BA; UWash 68-69 Master of Libnship. 6: Fr. 7: High sch tchr Hawaii Dept of Educ, Aiea 65-68; Non-print catlgr Bellevue (Wash) sch dist 68-. 9: ALA; NEA. 11: UWash Sch of libnship William E Henry Award. 14: Child, ya, catlg. 15: 3216 NW 58th, Seattle Wa 98107.

FOWLIE, FAY C. b Prince Albert Sask 25 D 46. 5: UCalgary 64-65 (Hist) BA; UBC 67-68 BLS. 6: Sp, Fr. 7: Libn I UCalgary 68-69, Hd period 69-. 9: CanLA; AltaLA. 10: Se, on Acquis of Latin Amer Lib Materials. 14: Latin Amer collection, ser. 15: 420 Trafford dr, Calgary 47 Alta Can.

FOWLIE, LES(LIE) (ELDON). b Wallaceburg Ont Can 10 F 28. 5: Queens U 49-50, 52-53 (Pol Sci) BA; UHamburg (Ger) 56-57; UToronto 59-60 BLS. 6: Fr, Ger. 7: Jr admin trainee Dept of Citizenship & Immigration, Citizenship Br, Ottawa/Edmonton 53-56; Exec asst to the sec Can Nat Com for UNESCO, Ottawa 57-59; Asst libn Ext Lib UAlberta, 60-62; Libn Assn of Universities & Colleges of Can, Ottawa 63-67; Libn The Architects Collaboratives, Cambridge Mass 67-68; Dir Niagara Reg Lib, St Catherines Ont 68; Chief libn St Catherines Ont Pub Lib 68-. 9: CanLA (chm Adult Serv Sect 66-67); Can Assn Col & Univ Libs; SLA; Niagara Coun forContg Educ (sec). 12: Ed "University-Affairs (66-67). 14: Catlg, ext activities. 15: Niagara Regional Lib Sys 59 Church st, St Catharines Ont Can.

FOX, CHARLESANNA LOUISE. b Asheboro NC 4 Ag 10. 5: UNC (Greensboro) 26-30 (Hist) AB; UNC (Chapel Hill) 38-39 ABLS. 6: Sp. 7: Tchr, Maxton NC 30-34; Typists-Stenographer DC Pub Lib 35-37; Catlgr Carnegie Pub Lib, Winston-Salem NC 39-40; Circ asst Lawson McGhee Lib, Knoxville Tenn 40-42; Camp libn, Camp Lejeune NC 42-45; Dist libn 14th Naval Dist, Pearl Harbor Hawaii 45-47; Group serv libn Lawson McGhee Lib, Knoxville Tenn 47-49; Co Libn Randlph Pub Lib, Asheboro NC 49-. 8: NC State Exec Dir Nat Lib Week 69-70. 9: Adult Educ Assn (Exec Com); ALA (var coms): NCLA (pres 53-55); NC Adult Educ Assn (pres 54-55); SE Adult Educ Assn (pres 56-57). ; SELA (NC repr on Exec Bd 66-70). 10: City of Asheboro Recr Adv Com 68-70. 14: Ref, adult serv, admin. 15: Randolph Pub Lib 201 Worth st, Asheboro NC 27203.

FOX, CONSTANCE GERTRUDE. b Weiser Idaho 1 Ja 05. 5: Idaho Tech Inst 23-25 (Civil Ennr); Fullerton Jr Col 25-26; Santa Ana Jr Col 30-33 AA; UCal 37-39 (Anthropology) AB; UWash 39-40 BA in Libnship. 7: Asst in Engnr dept Ole

Hanson Syndicate, San Clemente Cal 26-28; Map searcher Orange Co Auditors Off, Santa Ana Cal summers 28-39; Asst to reviser & to ref prof Sch of Libnship UWash 40; Libn Lincoln Pub Lib & Lincoln High Sch, Lincoln Cal 41-43; Libn Anacortes Pub Lib, Anacortes Wash 43-46; Asst libn catlgr Raymond Pub & Pacfic Co Libs, Raymond Wash 46-49; Hd Catlgr Ft Vancouver Reg Lib, Vancouver Wash 49-. 9: ALA; PNLA; WashLA. 10: Bus & Prof Womens Club; Friends of Ft Vancouver Reg Lib; Old Slocum House Theater Assn. 14: Catlg. 15: 215 E 12 st apt 106, Vancouver Wash 98660.

FOX, REV FRANCIS JOSEPH SJ. b Chicago 21 Ap 21. 5: USan Francico 39-40 (Eng); USanta Clara 40-44; Gonzaga U 44-47 (Philos) AB, 48 Educ MA; Loyola U (Los Angeles) summers 48-50; Alma Col 50-54 (Theol) STB; San Jose State Col summers 57, 58 (LS); USoCal summers 59-61 (LS) Ariz Lib Credential; Rosary Col summers 64, 65 66 (LS) MA in LS. 6: Lat, Sp. 7: Libn Brophy Col Prep, Phoenix 55-; Archivist Diocese of Tucson 67-. 8: Tchr, US hist in secon schs 55-65. 9: CathLA (SW Uni: chm Ariz Sect); ALA (Ariz State Recr repr 64-66); Ariz State v-pres (vpres 63-64, chm Recr Com 61-63 & treas 67-69); 64-66); Salt River Valley Lib Assn (pres 62-64). 13: Yes. 15: Brophy Col Prep 4707 N Central ave, Phoenix Az 85012.

FOX, GERTRUDE W(EINBERGER). b Boston 6 F 18. 5: State Tchrs Col (Boston) 36-40 (Chem) BS Ed, 41 MS Ed; Cath U 55-60 MS LS. 6: Fr, Sp, Gr, Lat. 7: Bibliogr Nat Housing Center Lib, Wash DC 60; NIH, Bethesda Md Ref libn 60-61, Engnr br libn 61-63, Ref libn 63-65; Med lit analyst NLM, Betesda Md 65-67; Tech info spec NLM 67-. 9: ALA; SLA; MedLA; ASIS. 10: Beta Phi Mu. 12: "List of Subject Headings in Homebuilding, Nat Housing Center Lib (60); "Design of Clean Rooms PHS Bibliog Ser 54 (64). 14: Ref, documentation. 15: Nat Lib of Med, Bethesda Md 20014.

FOX, HELEN ANNE. b Zanesville Ohio 2 Ja 10. 5: Ohio State U 32 (Journalism) BS; Muskingum Col 36 Educ Certif; UDenver summer 39-41 BS LS. 6: Fr. 7: Asst libn John McIntire Pub Lib, Zanesville Ohio 35-36; Libn Zanesville Sr High Sch 36; Libn Zanesville Br Ohio U 60-. 9: NEA; OhioASchL (Dist rep & var coms). ; OhioEA. 10: Delta Kappa Gamma; Pilot Internat; AAUW; Bus & Prof Women; Muskingum County Coin Club. 14: Yp wk. 15: 3120 Lookout dr, Zanesville Ohio 43705.

FOX, HERBERT (STANLEY). b Edmonton Alberta Can 11 Ap 29. 4: Virginia Clucas. 5: Concordia Sem (St Louis Mo) 49-54 BA, Theol Diploma; UBC 68-69 BLS. 6: Ger. 7: Parish minister Ch (Lutheran): Chilliwack BC 54-58, Vancouver BC 58-61; Univ chaplain Ch (Lutheran) UBC 61-68. 14: Ref, acquis. 15: 2720 Keremeos ct, ancouver 8 BC Can.

FOX, JEAN JOICEY. b Toronto 19 Ap 20. 5: UWest Ont 39-45 (Eng) BA; Toronto 45-46 BLS. 6: Fr. 7: Yp libn Enoch Pratt Free Lib, Baltimore 46-48; Br libn Portland Pub Lib, Portland Ore 48-50; Dir wk with child Conventry City Lib, Conventry Eng 50-52; Dir wk with yp Decatur Pub Lib, Decatur Ill 52-54; Campus libn De Paul U 54-59; Libn Niles Pub Lib, Niles Ill 59-62; Head research, Research Associates, Lake Bluff Ill 62-63; Assoc libn Amer Med Assn Lib, Chicago 63-. 9: ALA; MedLA; IllLA. 10: LWV. 14: Ref. 15: 2631 N Washtenaw, Chicago Il 60647.

FOX, LINDA JOAN. b Detroit Mich 29 D 41. 4: Talbert James Fox. 5: UMich 59-63 (Amer Studies) BA; Simmons 63-64 MSLS. 6: Fr. 7: Libn Order & Sci Ref San Jose State Col 64-65; Asst circ libn USoCal 65-66, Hd Col Lib 66-. 9: ALA. 14: Ref, admin. 15: 229 Sixth pl, Manhattan Beach Ca 90266.

FOX, MERLE U. b Lantz Md 5 My 20. 4: Alice B Ogline. 5: Towson Jr Col 51-53 AA; West Md Col 53-55 (Sociol) BA; Lancaster Theol Sem 55-58 (Town & Country Ch) BD; West Mich U 65-66 (Spec Libs) MSL. 6: Fr, Ger. 7: Sheet metal wker: Fairchild Aircraft Corp, Hagerstown Md 41-51, Emmert Mfg Co, Waynesboro Penn 51; Parish minister Ch of Christ 58-63; Catlgr Buffalo & Erie Co Pub Lib, Buffalo NY 66; Catlgr & pub serv libn Heidelberg Col, Tiffin Ohio 67-68; Hd libn Penn State U (DuBois) 69-. 9: ALA; PennLA. 10: Grange; Hist Soc. 14: Catlg, rare bks, archives, ref. 15: 27 3rd st, Falls Creek Pa 15840.

FOX, RUBY (HERRING). b Yolande Ala 20 S 18. 5: Massey Bus Col (Birmingham Ala) 37-38 (Sec); UAla 39-43 (LS) BS Educ. 6: Fr, Ger. 7: Libn Crossville High Sch, Crossville Ala 43-43; Lib asst US Dept of Agric Lib, Wash DC 43, Catlgr 43-49; Sub tchr Md Park High Sch, Seat Pleasant Md 54-55; Bibliog US Navy Hydrographic Off, Suitland Md 55; Catlgr US Navy Hydrographic Off Lib, Suitland Md 55-56; Catlgr US Nat Agric Lib, Wash DC 56-58, Catlg-reviser 58-67; Chief spec bibliogrs sect 67-68; Catlg-reviser 69-. 9: ALA; SLA; DCLA; Potomac Tech Proc Libns (sec 65-66). 14: Catlg. 15: 10801 Montgomery rd, Beltsville Md 20705.

FOX, VERA (C WHIPPLE). b Marathon NY29 NY 29 07. 4: Howard D Fox. 5: Cortland Normal Sch 26-29 (Elem Educ); Geneseo State Tchrs Col 44-45 (LS) BS; Cortland State Tchrs Col summers (Educ) MS. 7: Elem tchr-hist, health, penmanship, St James LI NY 29-30; Elem tchr Whipple SC, N Troy NY 30-44; Sch libn Holland Patent NY 45-46; Child libn Sierra Madre Cal 46-47; Elem tchr Horace Mann Sch, Binghamton NY 47-48; Libn elem schs, Endicott NY 48-65. 8: Bk talks & lectures to church, parent, & PTA groups, ACEI & IBM Mothers Club. 9: NEA; NY State Tchrs Assn. 10: Delta Kappa Gamma; Kappa Delta Pi. 13: Yes. 14: Catlg, ref. 15: 301 La Grange st, Vestal NY 13850.

FOX, ZEOLA (HESSELTINE-MISKIMINS). b Wayne Co Iowa 7 Je 03. 5: Centerville Commun Col 49-50 (Elem Educ); Kirksville NE State Tchrs 48, 51-55 (Elem & Secondary Educ) BS; Buena Vista summer 56 SecondaryBS Kirksville NE Mo State Tchrs Col 59 MA; Iowa state dept 61 Lib Certif. 6: Lat. 7: 4-H Club Leader, Co-chm 37-49; Elem Sch, Centerville Iowa 50-56; Phys Educ & Libn Jr High Sch, Centerville Iowa 56-57; Libn High Sch, Centerville Iowa 57-61; Libn pub sch & college, Centerville 61-64; Libn Centerville Commun Col 69-. 8: Supv for pub sch lib, Centerville Iowa 61-65. 9: NEA-DAVI; ALA; IowaStateEA; IowaLA; IowaSchLA. 10: Delta Kappa Gamma; Hon 4-H Leader; Nominated Mother of the Year50; OES; WHP White Shrine; Young Ladies Missionary Leader. 13: Yes. 14: Supv, catlg, ref. 15: R #1, Centerville Iowa 52544.

FOY, BERNARD LOUIS. b Merom Ind 19 S 11. 4: Evelyn Maudlin Foy. 5: Ind U 29-34 (Hist) AB; UIll 35-36 BS LS, 36-37 (LS). 6: Ger, Fr. 7: Chief newspaper div UIll Lib (Urbana) 36-37; Tech Lib Tenn Valley Authority, Knoxville Tenn: Order libn 37-40, Ref libn 40-41, Chief Libn 41-68; Chief readers serv Fla Tech U Lib 68-. 8: SLA Prof Consul to Ind & Tenn State Lib 67-68. 9: SLA; SELA; TennLA (pres 56). 10: Kiwanis Club; Torch Club; Tech Soc of Knoxville; Meadow Hills Commun Assn. 12: Index, "Bibliography of the Tennessee Valley Authority," annual; "A Bibliography of the TVA Program," annual. 13: Yes. 14: Admin, ref. 15: 2021 Kewenee trail, Casselberry Fl 32707.

FRAENKEL, MIRIAM. b Jerusalem 4 Jr 28. 4: Gerd Fraenkel. 5: Epstein Tchrs Sem 49-51 Tchr's certif; IndU 58-62 (Anthrop, Folklore) BA; Peabody Col 67-68 MLS. 6: Hebrew, ger. 7: Culture activities organizer Israeli Army 48-49; Tchr Israel educ ministry 51-56; Film libn IndU 57-60, Folklore libn 62; Instr Col of Jewish Studies, pittsburgh Penn 62-67; Catlg libn Jt U Libs, Nashville Tenn 67-. 9: Tenn Tech Serv Libns. 10: Beta Phi Mu. 14: Catlg. 15: 2142 Blakemore ave, Nashville Tn 37212.

FRAME, PAUL NELSON. b Tulsa Oka 22 F 19. 4: Florence Kuhn. 5: UNM 36-37 (Anthropology); UChicago 37-40 (Eng) BA; UOkla 46-49 (Hist) MA; UDenver 49-50 (LS) MA. 7: Ref libn UDenver 50-51; Ref libn Los Angeles Pub Lib 51-53; Ref libn Denver Pub Lib 53-55; Catlgr USAF Acad Lib (Denver) 55-58; UDenver Libs; Head Tech Serv Div 58-59, Asst dir of libs 59-61, Assoc prof of libnship 61-65; Lib dir Temple Buell Col 65-. 9: ALA; MPLA; ColoLA (pres 62-63); Bibliog Center for Research, Denver (Trustee 64-66); Adult Educ Coun, Denver; Colo Coun for Lib Devel 67-69. 10: Okla Hist Soc; Colo Hist Soc. 12: Ed "Mountain-Plains in Books; a Regional Bibliography (61-65). 13: Yes. 14: Admin, catlg, re. 15: 840 Magnolia st, Denver Co 80220.

FRAME, RUTH RHEA (McFALL). b Frederick Oka 19 O 16. 5: Central State Col 33-37 (Educ, Music) BA; Peabody 38-39 BS in LS. 7: Libn US Army Manila PI 46-47; Libn US Army Germany, Austria 48-51; Chief libn US Army Nurnberg Germany 52-55; Chief libn Spec Serv Lib Eng Corps, Ft Belvoir Va 56-58; Lib consul Mich State Lib 58-64, Dir prof serv 64-67; Exec sec LAD, ALA 67-. 9: ALA; MichLA. 10: Altrusa Club. 14: Admin. 15: 50 E Huron st, Chicago Il 60611.

FRANCE, CLARICE MARTHA. b Major County Okla 15 F 05. 5: Okla City U 22-27 (Fr) BA (magna cum laude); UOkla 46-47 (LS) BA. 7: Priv sch tchr Miss Pollocks, Okla City Okla 24-26; Lib asst Carnegie Lib, Okla City Okla 26-47; Libn-Stonewall Jackson Jr High High Sch, Okla City Okla 42-46; Asst catlgr Okla City Libs, Okla City Okla 47-51; Catlg libn 51-. 1-. 9: ALA; SWLA; Okla LA (sec-treas Catlg Sect). 10: AAUW; Okla Symphony Soc; Red Cross Wesleyan Serv Guild. 14: Catlg, child lib serv. 15: 115 NW 14, Oklahoma City Okla 73103.

FRANCELLA, SISTER M IHM. b Chicago 20 Jl 13. 5: Immaculate Heart Col 32-38 (Educ) BA, 38-41 (Educ) Gen Secondary Cred; 57-65 MA LS. 6: Fr, Sp, Ger. 7: Libn six elem schs, Los Angeles 34-50; Libn-tchr five high schs, Los Angeles 50-; Prin Mary Star of the Sea High Sch 68-. 9: CalLA; Sch Libns So Cal. 10: Cath Bus Educ Assn. 13: Yes. 14: Ref, circ. 15: 810 W 8th st, San Pedro Cal 90731.

FRANCIS, DEREK (RALSTON). b Winnipeg Man Can 26 S 41. 5: UMan 58-62 (Interior Design) BID; UBC 64 BLS. 06: Fr. 7: Catlgr UMan 64-65, Sci-tech libn 67-69; Colombo Plan lib adv Khon Kaen U (Bangkok Thailand) 65-66; Asst Prof UBC Lib Sch 69-. 9: CanLA; ThaiLA; ManLA; Can Assn Col & Univ Libs (dir). 10: Boy S cout Leader. 14: Catlg, admin, machine applications. 15: UBC Sch Libnship, Vancouver BC Can.

FRANCIS, ELLA STONE (GATEWOOD). b Fountain Run Ky 12 Ap 12. 4: W F Francis. 5: West Ky State Col 32-52 (Eng) BA; UKy summers 37,39; Peabody 52 (LS) MA; UFla 56-62 (Higher Educ). 7: Tchr Elem & Sec Schs, Ky 32-48; Libn high schs, Ky 48-51; Libn jr & sr high schs, Haines City Fla 52-55; Libn P K Yonge Lab Sch UFla 55-62; Dir of Lib Serv Lake City Jr Col 62-. 8: Instr in Lib Sci Appalachian State Tchrs Col summers 54, 55, 60-63; Visiting Lecturer in Lib Sci UTenn summer 62; Instr in Lib Sci UFla summers 56-59; Consul Polk County Sch Libns 58; Chm Evaluation Team Clearwater & Palmetto High Schs, Miami Fla 59, 60; Adv So Assn Lib Standards & Lib Educ 59. 9: ALA; FlaEA; FlaLA; FlaASchL (Life mem, pres 57). 10: AAUW; Woman's Club. 14: Ref, admin. 15: 401 Defender ave, Lake City Fl 32055.

FRANCIS, FRANK JR. b Weeks Island 8 S 35. 4: Willie Mae Willis. 5: Grambling 53-57 (Hist) BS; LSU 62-66 MALS. 6: Fr. 7: Tchg Polk Co Sch Bd, Gloster Miss 57; Libn US Army, Kenai Alaska 57-59; Libn Grambling Col 59-. 8: Sch wkshop for libns Rust Col 69; Consul, Org of Cook Inlet Lib for centralized acquis Kenai Alaska 58; Dir Baptist Stud Activities for no sect La. 9: ALA; LaLA; LaEA. 10: Baptist Stud Union; Le Cercle Francais; Alpha Kappa Mu; Sigma Rho Sigma; Assn of Hist Tchrs; Omega Psi Phi. 11: Omega Psi Phi's Man of the Year, Educator's Award 66. 12: "Organization of the Central Processing Center: Kenai Library" (58). 13: Yes. 14: Acquis, multimedia in lib educ, ref. 15: 325 N Main, Gramnling La 71245.

FRANCIS, GLORIA AILEEN. b Detroit 2 N 30. 5: Wayne State U 48-52 (Fr) AB; UMich 60-63 AM LS. 6: Fr, Ital. 7: 1st Lt (USAF) Spec: Ground Electronics Off 52-58; Pre-prof ref libn Dearborn (Mich) Pub Lib 60-64; Catlgr rare bk asst Detroit Pub Lib 64-66, Chief gifts & rare bks 66-. 9: ALA; Bk Club of Detroit. 14: Rare bks. 15: 461 W Savannah, Detroit Mi 48203.

FRANCIS, HELEN C. b Phila. 4: Robert H Francis. 5: Douglass Col 51 BA LS; Rutgers U 55 (LS) MS. 6: Fr. 7: Protocol asst US State Dept, Egypt & Greece 43-49; Br libn USIS Lib, Thailand 1-52; Pub rel libn Bloomfield (NJ) Pub Lib 52-54; Adult serv libn N State Lib 55-57; Libn US Dept Interior, Morristown NJ 57-58; Libn Fairleigh Dickinson U 58-60; Dir Springfield Free Pub Lib, Springfield NJ 62-. 8: Dir Amer Heritage Proj for NJ 55-57. 9: ALA; Adult Educ Assn; NJLA (chm Sub-com on Revis Employments Standards); NJ Adult Educ Assn. 10: AAUW; LWV; Springfield (NJ) Hist Soc. 11: Grant from the Fund for Adult Educ,56, for boader devel of adult lib wk in NJ. 14: Admin, ref, personnel, preserv of hist materials. 15: South & Pear st, Morriston NJ 07960.

FRANCIS, HELEN FAYE A(LSBURY). b Springfield Ill 5 Je 08. 4: Joseph O Francis. 5: Harris Tchrs Col 26-30 (Educ, Soc Studies) AB; Central Mo State Col 30-56 (LS, Fr); UDenver summers 54-57 (LS) MA; UHawaii summer 62 (Asian Studies); Portland State Col Ext 61-64; Sorbonne (Paris) summer 66 (LS). 6: Fr. 7: Tchr High Sch, Harwood Mo 31-32; Tchr High Sch, Schell City Mo 34-37; Tchr & libn High Sch, Oscola Mo 42-59; Libn Sr High Sch, Pendleton Ore 60-. 8: Ore State Dept of Educ, Com for Rev of Lib Standards, 65. 9: OreLA (sec); Central Mo LA (pres); East Ore LA (pres). 10: AAUW; LWV; Altrusa Internat; Tuesday Club. 14: Ref. 15: 319 NW Bailey, Pendleton Ore 97801.

FRANCIS, ROGER B(RYANT). b Taunton Mass 10 S 15. 4: Eleanor Stringer. 5: Brown 34-38 (Eng Lit) AB; Columbia 39-40 BS in LS. 7: Stud asst Brown 37-38, Circ asst 38-39; Stud asst Columbia Col 39-40; Ref asst NY Pub Lib 40-43; US Army Serv Forçes Chaplains Asst, US, Eng, France, Belgium 43-46; Gen asst ref dept NY Pub Lib 46-48, Exec asst 48-52; Dir Pub Lib, South Bend Ind 52-. 8: Lib Adv Com IND Legis Lib Study Com 65-66; Consul Kendallville (Ind) Pub Lib 63; Lectr Lib Mgt, Ind U (South Bend) 69. 9: ALA (Coun 57-61, Memb Com 63-69);-LAD (chm Org & Mgt Sect 59-60, chm Bldg & Equipt Sect 65-66); IndLA (pres 58-59, chm Legis Com 63-65 & 67-69, etc.). 10: Rotary Club; Ind Civil Liberties Union, Coun of Churches St Joe Co; Int Rel Coun; Urban League. 11: Award of Merit, South Bend Civic Planning Assn 60; Indiana Librarian of the Year 65. 13: Yes. 14: Pub lib admin, bldg, personnel. 15: So Bend Pub Lib 122 W Wayne st, South Bend Ind 46601.

FRANCK, ILONA MARIE (GODRY). b Buffalo NY 18 Jl 43. 4: William F Franck. 5: Rosary hill Col 61-65 (Hist, Govt) BA; Syracuse 66-67 MLS; ULouisville 68- Educ. 7: Libn trainee Bu trainee Buffalo & Erie Co Pub Lib, Buffalo NY 65-66, Jr libn 67-68; Ref libn louisville Free Pub Lib, Louisville Ky 68-. 9: ALA. 14: Ref. 15: 1108 Hilliard ave, Louisville Ky 40204.

FRANCK, JANE P(AUL). b Akron Ohio 11 Ja 21. 5: Hofstra U 38-42 (Ger & Fr Lits) BA (Cum laude); Columbia 42-43 (LS) BS, 46-49 (Musicology) MA. 6: Ger, Fr. 7: Ref & circ asst Columbia U Music Lib 43-46, 1st asst 46-49; Catlgr Cty Col Library (NY) 49-54, In chrge of sel & catlg of music materials 53-54; Archivist assembling org Inventorying the archives, the first of the City U unts, City Col (NY) 60-68; Libn Ford Foundation, NY 68-. 8: Lecturer, Lib Sch Pratt Inst 63-68; Consul archivist; NY Philharmonic 67-, MusLA 67-. 9: ALA-Div of Catlg & Clsf (JT Com on Mus Catlg 48-53); MusLA; SocAA; Amer Musicol Soc. 10: Annual Film Festival St Hildas & St Hughs Sch, NYC. 11: William Mason Scholar, Columbia U 47-48. 12: "Code for Cataloging Music & Phonorecords ALA (58)"; Ed "Circum-Spice 965-68); "Preliminary Inventories, City College Archives" (65-68). 13: Yes. 14: Archives, spec collections, ref. 15: 250 W 104th st apt 62, New York NY 10025.

FRANCK, MRS MARGA. b Berlin 24 Ap 07. 5: Westendschule 27 Certif; Heidelberg 31 PhD; Columbia 44 BS in LS. 6: Eng, Fr, Ger. 7: Stud asst Columbia U 42-43; Libn NY Psychoanalytic Inst, NYC 43-47; Libn Temple Emanuel, NYC 44-46; Sr catlgr ser div Columdia U 47-48; Ed "Union List of Serials H W Wilson Co, NYC 48-53; Ed Index, Inex, H W Wilson Co, NYC 54-. 8: Mem-at-large exec com Ser Sect RTSD 60-62; Ed com Mental Health Bk Review Index 61-; Bd of Dir Coun on Research in Bibliog Inr 65-. 9: ALA; NY Lib Club; NY Tech Serv Libns. 12: (Co-ed) Gundolf, Friedrichs "Dem lebendigen Geist: aus Reden, Aufsatzen und Buechern 13: Yes. 14: Catlg, bibliog. 15: 340 Haven ave, New York NY 10033.

FRANCKOWIAK, BERNARD M. b Pulaski Wis 2 Je 34. 4: Nancy Pichette. 5: Wis Stateu 55-59 (Bio) BS; Purdue summers 66; Peabody Col summers 65, 67, 68 MLS. 7: Libn Kimberly High Sch, Kimberly Wis 59-62; Libn Ripon High Sch, Ripon Wis 62-68; Lib supv Wisconsin Dept of Pub Instr, Madison 68-. 9: NEA; ALA; AASchL (supv sect); WisEA; WisLA; WisASchL (chm-elect 69-70). 13: Yes. 14: Sch lib supv & dev. 15: 6514 Cooper ave, Middleton Wi 53562.

FRANDO, ILDEFONSA (ABELLA). b Tacloban City Philippines 23 Ja 24. 4: Mariano A Frando. 5: Soc of the Divine WordU (Philippines) 52 (Econ) BS in Ed. 6: Sp, Tagalog. 7: Elem sch tchr, Philippines 46-48; High sch tchr, Philippines 52-55; Elem sch tchr Resurrection Elem, St Louis Mo 56-57; Clk-typist St LouisU, Pius XII Memorial Lib 57-63, Catlgr 63-. 14: Catlg. 15: 2525 Dove dr, Florissant Mo 63031.

FRANK, BEATRICE ELISE (BABUSHKIN). b NYC 25 Ap 12. 5: NYU 28-31 (Fr) BA; Columbia 32-37 (Fr) MA; U of NYC (Queens) 58-64 (LS) MS. 6: Fr, Ger, Lat. 7: Soc Wker Dept of Welfare, NYC 35-53; Tchr of Lat & Eng Bd of Educ, Lynbrook NY 56-60, Sch libn 61-. 15: 11 Evergreen ave, Lynbrook LI NY 11563.

FRANK, EMMA L(UCILE). b Jamestown NY 14 My 1900. 5: Oberlin 23-34 (Music) AB; West Res U 34-36 BS in LS; UMich 46-47 MA in LS. 7: Sec to Libn Oberlin Col 24-31, Libn tgrad Sch of Theol 31-66, Libn Emeritus 66-. 9: ATheolLA. 15: 148 North Prospect st, Oberlin Ohio 44074.

FRANK, MARINA GAIL. b Rossville Ind 16 Ap 36. 5: Purdue 54-58 (Soc Studies) BS, 58-61 (LS) MS; Ball State U 65-68 (LS). 7: Tchr-libn Carroll Cons Sch Corp, Flora Ind 58-61; Libn Lafayette Park Jr High Sch, Kokomo Ind 61-69; Head libn Kokomo High Sch, Kokomo Ind 69-. 8: Ed of A-v Handbook for Kokomo Schs 64-65; Consul on establt of libs in Kokomo 65; Libn, Profess Lib in Sch Admin Bldg 66-69. 9: NEA; IRA; ALA;-AASchL; Ind State TA; IndSchLA; Kokomo TA (corr sec 67-69). 13: Yes. 14: Sch libs, organ. 15: 1509 Pleasant dr, Kokomo In 46901.

FRANK, NATHALIE D. b Russia 28 Ja 18. 5: Barnard 35-39 (Fr) BA; Columbia 39-41 BSLS. 6: Fr, Russ. 7: Asst Columbia U Libs 39-41; Asst libn Clarke Sinsabaugh & Co, NYC 41-42; Sr Asst in chg of current corp files War Info, NYC 42-43; Head research libn Geyer Morey Ballard Inc, NYC 44-65; Dir info & lib serv Stewart Dougall & Assoc Inc, NYC 65-67; Lecturer & Assoc Prof Pratt 68-. 8: Approved lib consul SLA 58-; Amer Math Soc tr 60; Catlg Instr Ballard Sch, NYC 54-. 9: ASIS; Amer Marketing Assn; SLA (chm &/or mem var coms). 10: AATSEEL; Alumni Assn Columbia Sch Lib Serv; Amer Translators Assn; World Assn for Pub Opinion Research; Advert Club of NY; Advert Women of NY. 12: "Current Sources of Information for Market Research (54); "Market Analysis; A Handbook tf Current Data Sources (64); Ed "Whats New in Advertising & Marketing; Ed Amer Marketing Assn NY Chap "Newsletter. 13: Yes. 14: Ref, bibliog, catlg. 15: 120 Vermilyea ave, New York NY 10034.

FRANK, PETER (RUPRECHT). b Vienna Austria 7 Ap 24. 4: Anne Ruth Strauss. 5: Higher modern sch Vienna, Strassbourg, Frankfurt 34-42, 46 Matura; UVienna 46-50 (hilos) PhD. 6: GER. 7: Chief reader & ed H Luchterhand Pub House, Berlin 54-56; Chief reader & advertisin & advertising mgr Wissenschaftl Buchgesellschaft, Darmstadt 56-60; Chief reader C Hanser Publ House, Munich 60-63; Chief reader & ed H Luchterhand Publ House, Neuwied 63-67; Curator for Germanic maerials StanfordU Libs 67-. 10: Lessing Soc (Cincinnati); Maximilian Gesellschaft, Hambrg (W Germany); Gesellschaft der Bibliophilen Munich. 12: Ed F Grillparzer, "Samtliche Werke", 4 v (60-65); co-ed "Deutsche Essays", 4 v (68). 14: Ger & Aust lit and intel hist, arts of the bk, bibliog. 15: 1066 Manhattan ct, Sunnyvale Ca 94087.

FRANKE, EILEEN MARGARET. b St Louis Mo 23 F 30. 5: Webster Col 48-52 (Span) AB; st Louis U 53-55 (Span) MA (Tchg); UMich 57-59 MS LS. 7: Tchr Sacred Heart Acad, St Charles Mo 52-54; St Louis Pub Lib: Asst St Louis U Br 55-57, Asst readers adv serv 57-60, Asst ref dept 60-65, Chief educ dept 65-. 9: ALA (Steering Com Staff Org Round Table 65-66). CathLA; MoLA; Greater St Louis Lib Club (sec 60, treas 62). ; SLA. 14: Ref. 15: St Louis Pub Lib, Olive st, St Louis Mo 63103.

FRANKEL, EDITH. b NY 26 F 2. 5: Hunter Col 42-46 (Mathematical Statistics) AB; Columbia 46-48 (LS) BS. 7: Jr libn catlg dept Yonkers Pub Lib, Yonkers NY 48-51, Sr libn head of ext dept 51-52; Libn Rosenwald Lib, UChicago 52-57; Head of readers serv Brandeis U Lib summer 57-58; Tech libn Engnr Lib Republic Aviation Corp Farmingdale 58-62; Hd of ext dept Mt Vernon Pub Lib, Mt Vernon NY 62-63; Hd of adult circ dept 63-68; Assoc libn curriculum materials libn SUC, Potsdam NY 68-. 9: ALA; SLA; NYLA; SUNY LA. 10: AAUP. 14: Adult serv, admin. 15: Meadow E F3, Potsdam NY 13676.

FRANKEL, M(ARY) KATE (SPEAR). b San Francisco 26 F 26. 4: Benjamin A Frankel. 5: UCal(Berkeley) 44-49 (Eng) BA, 50-52 (Eng) Tchg Credential, 62-64 MLS. 6: Fr, Sp. 7: Ref libn San Leandro (Cal) Pub Lib 65; Libn Roosevelt Jr High Sch, Richmond Cal 65-67; Libn Franklin Elem Sch, Berkeley Cal 67-68; Libn Oxford Elem Sch, KELEY Cal 68-. 9: ALA; CalLA; CalASchL. 10: PTA Coun. 14: Wk with child. 15: #1 Rochdale way, Berkeley Cal 94708.

FRANKEL, WALTER ALBERT. b Flushing NY 20 Jl 38. 5: Concordia Collegiate Inst Jr Col 55-57 AA; Concordia Sr Col 57-58, 59-60 (Hist) BA; Concordia Theol Sem 60-62; SUNY(Albany) 62-63 MLS. 6: Ger, Lat, Gk. 7: Elem St Johns Lutheran Sch, Glendale NY 58-59; Assoc libn Hudson Valley Community Col 64-65; Period libn Russell Sage Col Lib 65-67; Libn Taft School, Watertown Conn 67-. 9: BSA; PrivateLA; Bibliogl Soc (London). 10: Printing Hist Soc; Gutenberg Gesellschaft. 14: Ser, rare bks, printing, hand bkbinding. 15: Schoolhouse rd Rt 2, Buskirk NY 12028.

FRANKENBERG, CELESTINE (GILLIGAN). b NYC. 4: Robert Clinton Frankenberg. 5: Hunter Col 42-46 (Art) BA; Pratt Inst 47-48 MLS. 6: Fr, Ger. 7: Libn (staff) NYC Pub Lib 48-50; Ref libn Hunter Col 48-49; Supv photo lib Pan American World Airways NYC 50-55; Art & picture research libn Young & Rubicam Inc NYC 55-67, Asst dir lib serv 67-. 9: SLA (Picture Div, NY Chap; helped organize Div in 52, sec-treas 56-58, 62-63, Nat chm of Div 65-66); Served on var coms of the Picture and Advtg Divs. 12: Ed "Picture Sources 2", SLA (65). 14: Picture research in lib sci. 15: 601 E 20th st, New York NY 10010.

FRANKENBERG, HERBERT BENNO. b Berlin Germany 9 My 29. 5: Sir George Williams U 55-60 BA; McGill U 60-61 BLS. 7: Clerk-payroll Montreal Gen Hosp 51-54; Personnel dept Govt of Can 55-58; Catlgr Canadair Engrg Lib 61-63; Libn St Joseph Tchrs Col 63-. 9: QueLA. 14: Ref. 15: 6060 Cote St Duc rd, Montreal 29 Can.

FRANKIE, SUZANNE (OPENLANDER). b Toledo Ohio 20 Je 35. 4: Richard J Frankie. 5: Bowling Green State U 53-57 (Sociol) AB; UMich 58-59 AML; Wayne State 63- (Art Hist). 7: Lib asst pre-prof Toledo (Ohio) Pub Lib 57-58; Lib asst pre-prof Plainfield (NJ) Pub Lib 58-59; Libn I UMich(Ann Arbor) 59-62; Libn I & II Wayne State U 62-66; Res libn Ctr for Voc & Tech Educ, Columbus Oh 66-. 9: ASIS. 14: Ref, circ, admin. 15: 2601 Charing rd, Columbus Oh 43221.

FRANKLIN, ANN (PENNINGTON) YORK. b Friendship Tenn 22 N 23. 4: Carl Franklin. 5: ULouisville 40-44 (Chem) AB; Nazareth Col 57-59 MS in LS; Catherine Spalding Col 60-61 Secondary Tchrs Certif, 65 Supervised Stud Tchg Certif. 6: Sp. 7: Church libn Christ Methodist Church, Louisville Ky 58-63; High sch libn Durrett High Sch, Louisville Ky 61-66; Visiting libn Jefferson Co Bd of Educ 66-. 8: Co-ordinator for wkshops at Catherine Spalding Col 64-65. 9: ALA; NEA; KyASchL (sec 65-66); KyLA (treas 66-68); KyEA. 10: Louisville Lib Club; Jefferson Co TA; Delta Kappa Gamma. 11: Outstanding Sch Libn of 1964 Award by Ky Trustee Lib Assn. 12: Ed var issues of KyASchL Bulletin. 13: Yes. 14: Ky materials for students from grades 1 through 12. 15: 427 Old Stone lane, Louisville Ky 40207.

FRANKLIN, MRS CATHERYNE (SETTLE). b Poplar Mont 20 Je 13. 5: Westmoreland Col 29-31 (AA); UTex 31-32; UOkla 34-35 (LS) BA; UTex 47-54, 54 MLS, UTex 56 , 57, 66, 67; Rutgers summer 63; USoCal summer 65; Case West Res summer 68. 7: High sch libn, Mercedes, Seymour, Laredo Tex 35-40; Armed Forces libn US Army Spec Serv, Ft Hood Tex 41-45; Arch libn UTex 47-54; Lecturer Grad Sch of Lib Sci UTex 54-65, Asst Prof 65 -. 9: ALA; AALS (chm State Assembly Planning 68-71, Stand Impl Com 68-70, v-pres. 68-70); SWLA; TexLA; Tex State Tchrs Assn; Tex Ass n Sch Libns (treas 65-66, v-chm 67-68, chm 68-69, State Assembly D el 67-69). 10: Austin Lib Club; Delta Kappa Gamma; Beta Phi Mu; Tex Assn of Col Tchrs; Alumni Assn Grad Sch of Lib Sci UTex (permanent treas); NEA-DAVI; Tex Assn of Educ Technologists. 13: Yes. 14: Child lit, sch libs. 15: 505 W 7th apt 212, Austin Tx 78701.

FRANKLIN, ESTHER ELIZABETH (FELKNER STAMM). b Garden City Kan 28 Jl 25. 4: Ben Franklin. 5: U Utah 41-45 (Eng) AB; UCal (Berkeley) 47- & summers (Educ) Gen Elem Cred; Chico State Col 58-60 (Educ, Pol Sci) MA; UWash summer 62-65 (Lib, Pol Sci ML. 6: Fr. 7: Adv Dept Copy "Salt Lake Trib-Telegram" 45-46; Asst promotion manager Oakland Post Enquirer, Oakland Cal 47; Tchr Richmond Cal 48-5tchr Sacramento Pub Schs, Sacramento Cal 50-51; Sub tchr Chico Pub Schs, Chico Cal 58-61; Asst humanities libn Chico State Col 61-66; Instr on bk sel Chico State Col spring 63 & 65; Dir wkshop in materials for yp Chico State Col summer 64; Lectr Sacramento State Col UCal(Davis) Ext 66-; Consul lib serv Sacramento Co Info Media Ctr 66-. 9: CalLA (Com on Intel Freedom 64-); Assn Cal State OL Prof (Com on Lib Devel); CalASchL (chm Co Sect 67-68, chm Legis Com 68-). 10: AAUW; UN Assn; LWV; PTA, Alpha Chi Omega; CASCD. 12: "Understanding World Neighbors in the Classroom (61) (Fearon); Bibliog staff "Twentieth Century Literature. 13: Yes. 14: Sch lib serv, Yp, lib instr. 15: 2278-B Shadydale ct, Sacramento Ca 95825.

FRANKLIN, GERTRUDE HOPEWELL. b Revere Mass 21 O 07. 5: Simmons 26-30 (LS) BS; Columbia 38-42, 52-58 (LS) MS. 6: Fr, Ger, Sp. 7: Student asst Simmons Col Lib 27-30; Asst libn NYC Pub Lib circ dept 30-38, Catlgr 38-42; Hd catlgr Atlanta U 42-44; Hd catlgr lincoln U (Jefferson City) 44-52, 53-57; Asst libn NYC Pub Lib ref dept 52-53; Catlgr Tchrs Col Columbia U 57-. 9: ALA; NY Tech Serv Libns. 14: Doc & ser catlg, sel & acquis. 15: Apt 13-G 156-20 Riverside dr W, New York NY 10032.

FRANKLIN, MARJORIE TALBOT. b Cumberland Md 20 S 28. 5: HowardU 46-50 (Eng) BA; Carnegie Inst 51-52 MLS. 7: Libn Carnegie Lib of Pittsburgh 52-62, Br libn 62-. 15: 1732 Brownsville rd, Pittsburgh Pa 15210.

FRANKLIN, MARY MAC (WILSON). b Knoxville Tenn. 4: Robert D Franklin. 5: UTenn 25-29 (Eng) BS in Ed; Columbia 31-32 BS in LS. 7: Schs-Bkmob libn Lawson McGhee Lib, Knoxville Tenn 29-31; Ref & schs libn NY Pub Lib 32-38; Libn Miss Hutchisons Sch, Memphis Tenn 39-43; Libn Rogers High Sch, Toledo Ohio 61-. 9: OhioLA. 15: 207 Manchester blvd, Toledo Oh 43606.

FRANKLIN, ROBERT DUMONT. b Memphis Tenn 15 S 08. 4: Mary MacFarland Wilson Franklin. 5: Southwestern Col (Memphis) 26-27 (Eng); UTenn(Knoxville)30-33 (Hist) BA; Columbia 33-34 BS in LS; Chicago 44 (LS). 6: Fr. 7: Page & asst Cossitt Lib, Memphis Tenn 25-32; Even asst Columbia U SLS Lib 33-34; Asst NY Pub Lib 34-36; Dir of Libs Amer Merchant Marine Lio Assn, NYC 37-38; Dir Shelby County Libs, Memphis Tenn 38-46; Asstdir Toledo Pub Lib, Toledo Ohio 46-55, Dir 55-; Lecturer UToledo 61-. 8: Exec Sec Fund-Raising campaign for ALA Wash Off 44; Consul in site selection for 4 pub libs 62-68; Visiting lecturer var lib schs 60-. 9: ALA (Life mem, past Coun mem & chm var coms); OhioLA (pres 55). 10: Toledo Tennis Club; Rotary Club. 12: Ed "The Tee-Pee"; Co-author of "Choral Music Published in 1955 Declaration for Peace". 13: Yes. 14: Lecturing on admin & pub rel. 15: Toledo Pub Lib, Toledo Oh 43624.

FRANKLIN, WILLIE MAUDE (MIZE). b Tula Miss 31 Jl 08. 4: Floyd Simmons Franklin. 5: UMiss 26-27, summers 27-31, 33; USoMiss 45-47 (Eng) BS; UMiss summers 57-59, 61, 63 (LS) MS. 7: Eng & Lat tchr, Hillsboro Scott Co Miss 29-30; Elem Goodhope, Scott Co Miss 32-34; Elem Pisgah, Rankin Co Miss 36-42; Elem Harperville, Scott Co Miss 4243, High sch Eng 43-47; High sch Eng, Walnut Grove, Leake Co Miss 47-49; Libn elem & high sch Eng, Redwood, Warren Co Miss 49-62; Libn, Culkin, Warren Co Miss 63-65; Libn, Warren Central, Warren Co Miss 65-. 9: ALA; SELA; MissLA; MissEA. 10: Delta Kappa Gamma; AAUW; Vicksburg Little Theatre Org; Miss Art Assn; Vicksburg Hist Soc; Vicksburg Art Assn. 14: Ref, catlg. 15: 221 First ave, Vicksburg Miss 39180.

FRANKS, ETHEL V(EAL). b Deepstep Ga 23 N 13. 4: Daniel Wells Franks. 5: Ga State Col for Women 31-35 (Educ) BS Ed, 56 (LS); UGa Ext 62. 7: Circ libn Brunswick Pub Lib, Brunswick Ga 53-. 9: ALA; GaLA; GaEA. 15: Brunswick Pub Lib, Brunswick Ga 51520.

FRANKS, HELEN (WHITE). b Knox County Ohio 29 D 07. 4: Paul C Franks. 5: Manchester Col 25-29 (Lat) BA; Kent State summers 57-62 (LS) MA. 6: Fr. 7: Tchr Hartville (Ohio) High Sch 29-32; High sch libn Marlington Local Sch Dist, Alliance Ohio 57-. 9: NEA; ALA; OhioEA, OhioASchL. 14: Ref, yp. 15: 10450 Moulin, Alliance Oh 44601.

FRANKS, ROBERT H. b Denver 5 Je 32. 4: Dorothy Franks. 5: Seattle Pacific Col 53-57 (Biblical Lit) BA; San Francisco Theol Sem 58-59; UColo 59-61 (Educ); UDenver 62-65 (LS) MA. 7: Signalman US Army, Alaska 51-53; Tchr Buena Vista (Colo) Pub Sch 61-62; Tchr Pub Schs, Otis Colo 62-63; Tchr-libn Pub Schs, Security Colo 63-65; Catlg libn Midland Col 65-69; Libn Huron Col 69-. 9: ALA; NebLA (v-chm Col & Univ Sect 68-69). 14: Catl. 15: Huron Col, Huron SD 57350.

FRANTZ, JOHN C. b Seneca Falls NY 25 Ag 26. 4: Vivien Rowan. 5: Syracuse 50 (Eng) AB, LS; AB, 52 (LS) MS. 7: Asst head bus & ind dept Omaha (Neb) Pub Lib 52, Br libn 53-55; Pub Lib consul Wis Free Lib Commsn 55-59; Dir Kellogg Pub Lib, Green Bay Wis 59-61; Lib ext spec lib serv br US Off of Educ 61-64; Chief Lit Serv & Construction Act Lib Serv Br US Off of Educ 65-67; Dir Brooklyn Pub Lib 67-. 8: Visiting lecturer, Lib Sci Syracuse U; Visiting faculty Ferris Mich Lib Tech Inst; Instr UWis Ext Dept. 9: ALA (chm Publ Com 56);-AAStateL (chm Planning Com 62, mem-at-large, Bd of Dir 65); WisLA (pres-elect 61); NYLA (chm Legis Com 69-). 12: "State Plans under the Library Services Servces Act, Suppl 3 (62); "Small Library Project Sec of "Library Administration. 13: Yes. 14: Pub lib ext & development, lib admin. 15: Brooklyn Pub Lib, Grand Army Plaza, Brooklyn NY 11238.

FRANTZ, RAY W JR. b Princeton Ky 17 Ag 23. 4: Doris Methvin Frantz. 5: Grinnell Col 41-42 (Arts & Sci); UNeb 42-43, 46-48 (Eng, Hist) AB; UIll 48-49 MS in LS, 50-55 (Eng) MA, PhD. 6: Fr. 7: ASTP & Infantry US Army European Theater 43-46; Lib asst UIll(Urbana) 49-50, Eng tchr 53-54; Libn URichmond 55-60; Asst dir Ohio State U Lib 60-62; Dir of Libs UWyo 62-67; Lib consul Proposed College at Sun City Ariz 64; Univ libn UVa 67-. 8: Consul Sun City Col 64. 9: ALA (Chicago State rep, Copyright Revision Com, Memb Com, Publ Com);-ACRL;-LAD (Recruiting Com); WyoLA (v-pres & pres-elect); VaLA; BSA; Bibliog Ctr for Res, Rocky Mtn Reg (Bd of Trustees). 10: Beta Phi Mu. 13: Yes. 14: Admin, lib hist. 15: Univ lib Univ of Va, Charlottesville Va 22901.

FRANZEL, ADELINE. b St Louis Mo 14 My 14. 5: Wayne U 30-32 (Eng); UOkla 55-56 (Educ) BA, 57-58 (LS) MA. 7: Admin off (Capt) USA & USAF 42-45; Admin off (Major) USAF 49-55; Ref libn Okla City Libs 58-59; Hd spec serv Okla State Lib, 59-61; Hd libn Free Lib of phila Lib for the Blind 62-66; Chief spec serv NJ State Lib 66-. 8: Memb of COMSTAC, Standards for Lib Serv 63-66; Adv Com Nat Aid to Visually Handicapped; Memb of Lib Sub- Coms, President's Com on Employment of the Handicapped 65-. 9: ALA (past chm RT on Lib Serv to the Blind); AAWB (past chm Lib Serv Div); NEA; NJLA; NJ Conf on the Handicapped; AEAUSA (past pres Okla Chap). 10: Nat Coun of Jewish Women Okla Alumni Assn; Zonta Nat Braille Assn; Air Force Aid Soc National Rehabiliation. 11: Argosy Club Merit Award (64); Comstac Outstanding Achievement Award (66); Abba Eban Medal (68). 14: Lib serv to blind & physically handicapped, service to individuals in inst. 15: Carteret Arms Apt 9-S 333 W State st, Trenton NJ 08618.

FRARY, MILDRED (PARTRIDGE) (MRS). b Los Angeles Cal 26 F 21. 5: UCLA 39-43 (Eng) BA; USoCal 47-48 MS in LS. 7: Catlgr LA City Schs 48-49, Elem lib coord 49-58, Supv elem lib 58-62, Dir lib serv 62-. 8: Memb President's Nat Adv Commsn on Libs 67-68; Memb Off of Educ Adv Com on Research & Institutes 69-71; Lib Adv Com, Field enterprises Educ Corp. 9: ALA-AASchL (Bd Dirs 61-63, var coms); CalASchL (pres 62-63 Bull ed 52-53). 10: Beta Phi Mu; Delta Kappa Gamma; Alpha Delta Pi. 14: Admin. 15: 3500-245 W Manchester blvd, Inglewood Ca 90305.

FRASER, CAROL E(VERETT). b Glen Ridge nj 8 S 17. 4: Ronald J Fraser. 5: Simmons Col 39 (LS) BS. 7: Br libn Brookline Mass Pub Lib 39-44; US Army libn Ft Monmouth, Ft Dix, Camp Devens, Germany & Japan 44-53; Acquis & act dir Stonehill Col 66, Dir 66-. 9: ALA; NELA; MassLA. 10: Friends of the Lib. 14: Acquis & admin. 15: 280 Lincoln st, Stoughton Mass 02072.

FRASER, DAVID ALEXANDER. b Syracuse NY 12 Ag 40. 4: Barbara Mauro Fraser. 5: Hamilton Col 58-62 (Art Hist) AB; Syracuse 62-66 (Art Hist) MA, MSLS. 6: Lat, fr. 7: Act rare bk libn Syracuse U 63-64, Rare bk biblioge 65-66; Curator Lib Co of Phila 67-. 8: Instr, Syracuse U Sch of Lib Sci (65-66); Lib Pub Rel Consult, Bucks co Free Lib (68-69). 9: BSA. 10: Amer Soc for Aesthetics; Philobiblon Club. 14: Rare bks, prints, paintings, art bks. 15: 1314 Locust st, Philadelphia Pa 19107.

FRASER, (META) DOREEN (ELIOT). b Grenfell Sask Can 8 Je 15. 5: UAlta 33-36 (Eng, Langs) BA; Toronto 36-37 BLS; Columbia 53 (Med Bibliog). 6: Fr. 7: Jr libn UAlta 37-40, Med libn 40-42; (Lt) WREN Supply Br 42-46; Sr libn BC Prov Lib Commsn, Prince George 46-47; Sr libn UBC Lib 47-50, 1st asst ser dept 50-51, Biomed libn 51-64; Lecturer UBC Sch of Libnship 61-64; Asst libn catlg proj Anglican Theol Col (Vancouver BC) 55-61; Med libn Dalhousie U (Halifax NS) 64-67, Health scis libn 67-. 8: Surveyed BC Dept of Health Lib Victoria BC 55; PNLA assignment, survey of Vancouver Med LA 56; Pacific Northwest Reg Group Med Lib Assn Study for PNLA Development Proj (chm) 57-58; BC Med Lib Serv Develop program 58-63; Consul to Col of Physicians & Surgeons of BC for BC Med Lib Serv 60-61; Study of spec libs in BC for CanLA Study Projs 61; Health Agency Lib Survey of Metropolitan Vancouver 58-59. 9: MedLA (comm chm & var other offs 57-64); SLA; BCLA (pres 62-63, chm 5 coms 54-64); PNLA; Atl Provs LA; Halifax LA (Subcm chm & mem com on lib serv to Handicapped 68-69); CanLA (chm Com on Med Sci Libs 63-65); Chm Assn Com Med Sch Libs (ACMC/AFMC) 67-69. 10: Greater Vancouver Health League (var offs); Guider in Canadian Girl Guide Assn; Can Red Cross Lodge Serv; Can Fed of UW; Pi Beta Phi. 13: Yes. 14: Ref, development of lib serv. 15: WK Kellogg Health Sci Lib, Sir Charles Tupper Med Bldg Dalhousie U, Halifax NS Can.

FRASER, EDITH (JOHNSTON). b Fort Smith Ark 6 My 18. 5: UAriz 35-39 (Educ) BA; Fla state U 59-62 (LS) MS; UIll 67-68 (LS) MAS. 7: Tchr, Tucson Ariz 48-52; Tchr Southside Elem Sch, Sarasota Fla 57-59; Libn Alta Vista Sch, Sarasota Fla 59-63; Lib admin spec serv, Germany 63-65, Korea 66; Research asst ERIC UIll (Urbana) 67; Asst area libn spec serv, Vietnam 68-. 9: ALA. 11: Beta Phi Mu. 14: Acquis, lib admin. 15: Spec Serv Off USASUPCOM, Qui Nhon APO San Francisco Ca 96238.

FRASER, HELEN A. b NYC 17 Je 02. 5: Cornell 21-26 (Eng) AB AM; NY State Col for Tchrs (Albany) 33-34 BS LS. 6: Fr. 7: Tchr Cherry Valley (NY) High Sch 26-27; Tchr Broadalbin (NY) High Sch 27-30; Tchr Pearl River (NY) High Sch 30-33; Tchr Maybrook (NY) High Sch 35-36; Asst libn Albany Med Col 42-54, Libn 54-63; Libn Trudeau Inst Saranac Lake NY 64-. 10: Abany Coun, State Commsn for Human Rights; NY Folklore Soc; NY State Hist Assn. 14: Med hist, folklore. 15: Hotel Saranac, Saranac Lake NY 19283.

FRASER, REV JEROME R. b Detroit 15 N 31. 5: Sacred Heart Sem 49-53 (Philos) BA; UMich 60-61 AMLS; UDetroit 61-62 Tchrs Certif; Wayne State 62- (Hist). 6: Sp, Lat, Fr. 7: Asst Pastor All Saints Church, Detroit 57-58; Asst Pastor St Boniface Church, Detroit 58-59; Libn Sacred Heart Sem (Detroit) 60-. 8: Archivist Archdiocese of Detroit 62-64; Jt Com for Sch Lib Development in Mich 62-65. 9: ALA; SAA; CathLA(v-chm High Sch Sect, chm Mich Unit); MichLA; MichASchL. 13: Yes. 14: Sch lib org, centralized serv, a-v. 15: 2701 W Chicago blvd, Detroit Mi 48206.

FRASER, RAYMOND JAMES. b West Hartford Conn 29 Ag 32. 4: Virginia Johnson. 5: Tri-State Col 56-59 (Chem Engnr) BS; Syracuse U 62-64 MS LS. 7: Aircraft mechanic USAF (Airman 1st class) 51-55; Catlgr United Aircraft Corp, E Hartford Conn 59-62; Catlgr Ind State U 64-66; Asst plant libn Union Carbide Oak Ridge Gaseous Diffusion Plant 66-68, Plant libn 68-. 9: SLA. 10: Carbide Astron Club. 14: Catlg, admin. 15: 124 Everest cir, Oak Ridge Tn 37830.

FRASER, ROBERT SCOTT. b Syracuse NY 15 Ap 43. 4: Elizabeth Marty. 5: Hamilton Col 61-65 (Hist) AB; Syracuse 65-66 MSLS, 66-68 (Eng) MA. 6: Lat, Ger. 7: Rare bk catlgr Syracuse U 66-68; Rare bk catlgr Princeton U 68-. 8: Grad asst Syracuse U Lib Sch Symposium on Rare Bks & Mss summer 66. 9: ALA-ACRL (Rare Bk Sect); BSA. 10: Friends of the Princeton U Lib. 14: Rare bks, bibliog, fine printing, bk illus. 15: 3M Hibben Apts Faculty rd, Princeton NJ 08540.

FRAZIER, MYRLE OWEN. b Roxton Lamar Co Tex 28 O 1899. 5: Paris Jr Col 25-26, summer 26, 27 Abilene Christian summers 28, 36, E Tex State U summers 29-31, 49, 50, & 30-31 (Hist, BA, MA, BSLS; Tex Tech ext 48-49 (A-V Educ); UTex Tele-lecture (Modern Math). 7: Elem tchr Pub Sch, Fulbright Tex 26-27; Elem tchr & Prin Pub Sch, Martin Co Sch Dist Deport Tex 27-28; Elem tchr Pub Sch, Golan Co Sch Dist Sylvester Tex 28-29; Elem tchr & Prin Pub Sch, Strayhorn Co Sch Dist Snyder Tex 29-30; tchr Pub Sch, Colorado City Tex 32-33; Nursery & off clerk CWA (US govt), Colorado City Tex 34; High sch tchr-libn Pub Sch, Roscoe Tex 34-38; Area Supv Lib Proj WPA (US govt), Spur Tex 38-39; High sch tchr Pub Sch, Avoca Tex 42-43; Jr high sch tchr Pub Sch, Sweetwater Tex 43-45; Sales clerk Sears Roebuck, Sweetwater Tex 45-46; Chief price clerk OPA (US govt), Sweetwater Tex 46; Prin & elem tchr Pub Sch, Coahoma Tex 47-49; Col sub tchr E Tex State U 49; C-op libn 3 pub schs, Taylor Co Tex 50-51; High sch libn pub schs, Winters Tex 51-65; Tech libn Kelly AFB Security Hdqrs summer 56; Jr Col Libn Southwestern Christian Col 65-67; Libn Pub Schs, Bridgeport Tex 67-69. 8: Tchr Basic Adult Educ, Bridgeport. 9: Tex State Tchrs Assn (past chm, sec, & v-pres Lib Div Dist 11). 10: Alpha Chi; Kappa Delta Pi; Teen Age LA (past loc, dist & state sponsor). 14: Ref. 15: N Main, Winters Tx 79567.

FRAZIER, PAULINE (WILKINS). b Chattanooga Tenn 15 l 17. 4: Asa Van Frazier. 5: Tenn A&I State U 53-59 (Elem Educ) BS; UTenn 61-65 (Instr Materials) MS. 7: Beautician Lidaro Beauty Salon, Chattanooga Tenn 47-51; Tchr E Fifth St Sch, Chattanooga 59-65; Libn Orchard Knob Jr High Sch, Chattanooga 65-. 9: NEA; Tenn Educ Assn Inc; E Tenn Educ Assn; ChattanoogaEA; Assn Clsrm Tchrs; ChattanoogaAreaLA; Tenn Assn Pub Sch Educrs. 10: Clair Voiyant Bridge Club; Alpha Kappa Mu; Kappa Delta Pi; Womens Soc Christian Serv; LWV. 14: Ref, cltg. 15: 2171 Shepherd rd, Chattanooga Tenn37421.

FRAZIER, SANDY. b Pittsburgh Penn 22 My 42. 5: Fairmont State Col 60-62 (Phys Ed); UPittsburgh 62-64 (Phys Educ) BS in Educ, 65-67 MLS. 6: Ital, Sp. 7: Rec analyst us steel Corp, Pittsburgh Penn 64-65; Lib trainee UPittsburgh 65-67; Soc wk libn SyracuseU 67-68; Ed NY State Union list of Ser Upstate Med Ctr Lib, Syracuse NY 69-. 9: SLA; ASIS; UpstateNYMedLA. 14: Info retrieval, ref (med & soc sci). 15: 2808 James st apt 2, Syracuse NY 13206.

FRAZIER, THOMAS. b Seattle 28 O 18. 4: Kendall Warner. 5: UWash 37-40, 46-48 BA, 48-49, 53 (Eng Lit) MA, 51-52 MLS. 6: Fr, Sp, Ger. 7: Fireman Oiler Engnr Amer Merchant Marine, N Atlantic, Medit & Pacific 42-45; Bibliog sect libn, sect head UWash Lib 52-54 Humanities libn, Act head libn Drake U Lib 54-57; Catlgr, head, original catlg sect Mich State U Lib 57-62; Catlgr U Wash Lib 62-64; Head catlgr West Wash State Col 64-. 9: ALA; PNLA. 14: Catlg. 15: 1658 Chuckanut Point rd, Bellingham Wa 98225.

FRECH, KATHERINE SUE (KENT). b Alliance Neb 22 Ag 29. 5: Casper Col 47-48, 65; UNeb 48-50; UWyo 65-67 (Fr) BA. 6: Fr. 7: Geol sec Chem & Geol Labs, Casper Wyo 47-48; Sec v-pres Nat Bank of Com, Lincoln Neb 49-50; Sec mgr KOLN Radio, Lincoln neb 50-51; Sec prod mgr Gen Petroleum Oil, Casper Wyo 52-54; Dir bkworm program natrona Co Pub Lib, Casper Wyo 64-66, Adult serv dir 68-. 8: Exec Dir Nat Lib Week, Wyo 66-68; State Adv Coun Title IV B Wyo 69. 9: ALA; NEA; WyoLA; WyoEA. 10: PEO; Kappa Alpha Theta; Phi Delta Kappa; Kappa Delta Pi; Phi Sigma Iota; Alpha Epsilon Rho; Casper Symphony Guild; Women's Coun Amer Symphony Orchestra League. 14: Child motivational reading programs, adult serv, serv to handicapped. 15: 320 College dr, Casper Wy 82601.

FRECHETTE, EDMEE. b Victoriaville 5 Je 30. 5: Coll St-Maurice 49 Baccaureat; U de Montreal 50 Bibliotheconomie. 6: Fr. 7: Bibliothecaire Ville de Montreal 59-. 9: Assn canadienne des bibliothe3aires de lengue francaise. 14: Catlg. 15: 1010 rue Cherrier app 1708, Zone 132 Montreal Can.

FRECHETTE, JAMES RONALD. b Central Falls RI 25 Ap 44. 5: RI Col 63-67 (Hist) BA; URI (Kingston) 67-69 MLS. 6: Fr. 7: Catlgr Dept of State Lib Serv, Providence RI 69-. 9: RILA. 14: Catlg. 15: 487 West ave, Pawtucket RI 02860.

FREDENBURG, VERA LOIS. b Indianapolis 30 Mr 25. 5: Butler U 43-46 (Educ) BS; Ind U summers 49-54 (LS) MA. 7: Tchr Noblesville (Ind) High Sch 46-49; Tchr-libn Millersburg (Ind) Schs 49-51; Libn Froebel, Gary Ind 51-52; Libn Plymouth (Ind) High Sch 52-56; Libn Ruley Jr High Sch, Pueblo Colo 56-60; Asst Prof & asst libn Adams State Col, Alamosa Colo 60-62; Supv lib serv Arapahoe Sch Dist #6, Littleton Colo 62-. 66; Asst dir div of instr media Off of Supt Pub Inst State of Ind, Indianapolis 66-. 8: Visiting Instr in lib sci summer courses: West State Col 59-60; Denver U, Denver 63, 65; Highlands U 65, 66. 9: ALA; -AASchL; NEA-DAVI; ASCD; ColoLA; ColoASchL (pres); IndSchLA; IndStateTA; Ind Assn Supv & Curr Devel. 13: Yes. 15: 1819 Madison Village dr 38, Indianapolis In 46227.

FREDENBURGH, MARJORIE H FOLLETTE. b Seneca Falls NY 22 Jl 04. 4: Theodore Fredenburgh. 5: William Smith Col 23-27 (Eng, Hist) BS; Columbia 31 (LS) BS. 6: Fr. 7: Lib aide Hobart Col; Lib asst NY Pub Lib; Lib asst & head libn Prospect Heights High Sch, Brooklyn; Br libn Fairfax County Pub Lib George Mason Br, Annandale 58-. 9: VaLA. 14: Ref. 15: 801 N Pitt st #1507, Alexandria Va 22314.

FREDERIC, SISTER M CATHERINE FMSC. b NYC 2 My 02. 5: Manhattan Col 35-42 (Eng) BA; Villanova U 4650 (Eng) MA; St Johns U 54-57 MLS. 7: Tchr bus subjs St Anthonys Sch, Butler NJ 27-34; Tchr bus subjs Holy Family & Alverna Bus In, Union City NJ & Yonkers NY 35-45; Tchr world hist & religion St Peters Annex Phila 45-49; Tchr world hist, relig & bus subjs Ladycliff Acad, Highland Falls NY 49-52, Tchr Eng, relig & Libn 52-58; Libn St Josephs High Sch W New York NJ 58-62; Head Libn Ladycliff Col 62-. 9: ALA; CathLA (Memb chm 61-64, chm Col & Univ Sect 66-68; chm Greater NY Unit 58-60; Metro Cath Col Unit); Franciscan Sisters Educl Conf (treas & Bd mem); Nat CathEA; NYLA; Pro Deo Assn of Cath Cols (chm Lib Sect 65-67). 12: "A Modern Flower of St Francis (39); "A. Vade Mecum for Teachrs of Religion (49); ". and Spare Me Not in the Making (52);"Beneath the Lamps Rays (61); "The Handbook of Catholic Practices (64); Ed Commun "Newsletter (49-55); Ed "Newsletter Greater NY Unit CathLA 55-58; Ed "Pro Deo Newsletter (65); Ed Col & Univ Sect Newsletter 68-. 13: Yes. 14: Bk sel, ref. 15: Ladycliff Co, Highland Falls NY 10928.

FREDERICK, ALICE F(LORENCE JOHNSON). b Alameda Cal 3 Jl 10. 5: UCal (Berkeley) 28-31 (Hist) AB, 31-32 (LS) Certif, 40 (LS) MA. 7: Libn Prescott Jr High Sch, Oakland Cal 32-35; Libn Oceanside-Carlsbad High Sch & Jr Col, Oceanside Cal 35-38; Libn & tchr in Several Cal sch dists 38-54; Dist Libn Orinda (Cal) Union Sch Dist 54-. 8: Visiting tchrs in lib sci summer courses: UDenver & SoOre Col 61-64. ; UNM 66, UOre 68. 9: NEA; Cal Tchrs Assn; CalLA; CaASchL (Program Chm 62; chm sevral coms of No Sect); Assn of Child Libns No Cal; Orinda Tchrs Org (pres 67-68). 10: PTA. 13: Yes. 14 Lib serv to child; coop beween sch & pub libs. 14: Child serv, coop between sch & pub libs. 15: 1061 Keith ave, Berkeley Cal 94708.

FREDERICKSEN, RICHARD BRUCE. b Milwaukee Wis 5 My 37. 4: Elaine Freedman. 5: UCLA 59-63 (Psych) AB; USoCal 65-67 (LS) MS. 6: Russian, Ger. 7: PBX installer Pacific Tel Co, LA 55-57; Comm sec clk (Pfc) USA 60-61, 61-62; Clk Times-Mirror Co, LA 59-66; Clk UsoCal lib 65; Ref libn LA Pub Lib 65-67; Hd catlg sect UC (San Diego) Biomed Lib, La Jolla Cal 68-. 9: SLA; MedLA; Tech Proc Gp So Cal. 10: Sierra Club. 14: Ref, tech processes. 15: 3960 Sioux ave, San Diego Ca 92117.

FREEBERN, ELEANOR P(EARSE). b Center Moriches NY 17 Jl 17. 4: Ralph Martin Freebern. 5: Cornell U 34-38 (Home Econ) BS; Columbia 46-47 (LS). 7: Reporter "The Ithaca Journal, Ithaca NY 38-39; Libn Halsted Sch, Yonkers NY 45-50; Libn Pakistan Mission to the UN, NYC 50-59; Libn Off of the Messrs Rockefeller, NYC 59-61; Ref libn J Walter Thompson C,NYC 61-63; Libn Parade Publications Inc, NYC 63-. 9: SLA. 14: Ref. 15: 82 Sherwood ave, Ossining NY 10562.

FREED, J ARTHUR. b Los Angeles 11 N 29. 4: Nancy Laubach Freed. 5: UCal 47-51 (Anthropology) AB, 52, 54-56 MA (Anthropology), MLS. 7: Cpl (E-4) US Army, US, Germany 52-54; Adult serv Libn Brooklyn Pub Lib 56-57, Sr libn 1st asst br libn 57-58; Los Alamos Sci Lab, Los Alamos NM: Asst report libn 58-59, Order libn 59-60, Libn Main Lib 60-66; Pub serv libn 66-67; Asst hd libn 67-. 8: Chm NM Lib/A-V Educ Coun 69-. 9: SLA (Rio Grande Chap; several offs & chm 4 coms 59-; chm Nuclear Sci Sect of Sci-Tech Div 64-65; Memb Chm Nuclear Sci Div 66-69); NMLA (No Reg Loc Action Com 65-67, chm Col, Univ & Spec Libs Sect 68-69). 10: Los Alamos Opera Guild. 13: Yes. 14: Ref, circ, catlg, acquis, admin. 15: Los Alamos Sci Lab Box 1663, Los Alamos NM 87544.

FREEDMAN, FREDERICK. b Newark NJ 20 D 29. 4: Jacqueline Kahane. 5: NYU 48-52 (Mus) AB; UIowa 52-54 (Piano, Musicology) MA, 56-59 (Musicology). 6: Ger, Fr. 7: Lib tech asst NYC Pub Lib 59-64; Mus libn UCLA 65-67; Mus libn & lectr in mus Vassar Col 67-. 8: Adv mus ed, Free Press of Glencoe 60-; Gen ed mus titles Da Capo Press 63-. 9: Amer Musicological Soc (sec Greater NY Chap 61-62); MusLA (chm So Cal Chap 66-67); Col Mus Soc (chm Lib Holdings Com 67-). 13: Yes. 14: Ref, rare bks, bibliog. 15: 22 Watson rd, Poughkeepsie NY 12601.

FREEDMAN, GLORIA S(ILVERSTEIN). b NYC 27 My 29. 4: Alan R Freedman. 5: State U of NY 47-52 AB, MA, 61-65 MLS. 7: Sec State U Lib Dept (Albany) 52; Tech asst in lib NY State Educ Dept, Albany 52-54; Libn St Agnes Sch, Albany NY 65-. 9: NYLA. 15: 31 Freeman rd, Albany NY 12208.

FREEDMAN, JANET LOIS (SALTZ). b Cambridge Mass 18 Jl 40. 4: Robert Freedman. 5: Simmons 62 BS in LS, 66 MS in LS. 6: Fr. 7: Young adult & ref libn Stoneham Pub Lib, Stoneham Mass 62-63; Dir Endicott Jr Col Lib 63-65; Consul to LC reclsf proj Salem State Col 67-. 9: ALA. 13: Yes. 14: Admin, ref, tech serv. 15: 5 Pond st, Marlehead Ma 01945.

FREEDMAN, JUDITH S(AFTLAS). b Philadelphia Penn 3O 44. 4: Allan Stanley Freedman. 5: Umd 62-66 (Hist) BA, 66-68 MLS. 6: Sp. 7: Legal publ specialist Off of Fed register, Wash DC 66; Lib tech US Info Agcy, Wash DC 66-68; Ref libn Inst for Defense Analyses, Arlington Va 68-. 9: DCLA. 14: Ref, readers serv. 15: 9324 Edmonston rd, Greenbelt Md 20770.

FREEDMAN, MAURICE (JULIUS). b Newark NJ 14 N 39. 4: Hermene Terry. 5: Rutgers 57-61 (Philos) BA; UCal (Berkeley) 61-63 (Philos), 64-65 MLS. 6: Fr, Ger. 7: Jr lib clerk Newark (NJ) Pub Lib 55-59; Page Bancroft Lib UCal Lib(Berkeley) 65; Acquis grad Theol Union Bibliog Center, Berkeley Cal 65; Intern LC 65-, Asst hd African-Asian exch Sect exch & gift sect 66, Admin off proc dept 66-67, Exec asst proc dept 67-68; Mgr lib processing Info Dynamics Corp, Reading Mass 68-69; Coord lib tech servs dept Hennepin Co Lib, Minneapolis 69-. 9: ALA; CalLA; DCLA, NELA; ASIS. 13: Yes. 14: Admin of large lib, automation techniques applicable to lib wk. 15: Hennepin Co Lib 300 Nicollet mall, Minneapolis Mn 55415.

FREEDMAN, MURIEL A HERSH. b NYC 9 O 41. 4: Arnold David Freedman. 5: Gallaudet Col 58-63 (LS) BS. 6: Fr, Lat. 7: Catlgr Los Angeles Co Pub Lib, Los Angeles 63-. 10: Delta Epsilon; John Tracy Clinic; Hebrew Assn for the Deaf. 14: Catlg. 15: 21014 Chase st, Canoga Park Ca 91304.

FREEDMAN, NATHAN. b Poland 10 Ja 10. 4: Helen Berdick. 5: CUNY 27-31 (Eng) BSS; UMd 66-67 MLS. 7: Deputy Dir Div of Retirement and Survivors Benefits Off of Program Evaluation and Planning Soc Security Admin, Woodlawn Md 36-66; Asst libn Lib Co of the Baltimore Bar 67-. 9: ALA; AALL; SLA; MdLA. 14: Catlg, admin, ref. 15: PO Box 144, Baltimore Md 21203.

FREEGARD, SUSAN BETH. b St Louis 21 Jl 37. 5: Lindenwood Col 55-59 (Eng) BA; UNC 59-60 MS in LS. 6: Fr. 7: Asst libn Ozark Reg Lib, Ironton Mo 60-62; Jr libn UMo(Columbia) 62-64; Act libn UMo (St Louis) 64-66, Libn 66-. 9: ALA; MoLA; Mo Assn Col & Res Libs (v-chm 69). 15: 8001 Natural Bridge rd, St Louis 63121.

FREELAND, ROBERT FREDERICK. b Flint Mich 20 D 19. 4: June Voshel Freeland. 5: East Mich U 38-42 (Music) BS; Mich State U summer 40 (Music); USoCal 47-48 (LS, Educ) MS; UMich 50-52 (LS); San Diego State Col 53-56 (Educ). 7: Music supv Warren (Mich) Consolidated Sch 46-47; Music supv Carson City (Mich) Pub Schs 48-50; Libn & av coordinator Ford Found Edison Inst, Dearborn Mich 50-52; Libn & avcoordinator Helix High Sch, La Mesa Cal 52-. 8: Instr in Eng, San Diego City Col 54; Lecturer in Lib Sci, San Diego State Col 62-. 9: ALA; NEA-DAVI; CalLA (Recr Com); CalSchLA; A-V Educ Assn Cal; Cal Tchrs Assn. 10: Friends of The Lib, San Diego State Col. 12: Bk & av review ed "School Musican magazine for 20 yrs. 14: Lib sch educ. 15: 4544 Acacia ave, La Mesa Cal 92041.

FREEMAN, ALICE VAUGHAN. b Montgomery Ala 23 O 41. 5: UAla 59-63 (LS) BS; LSU 63-64 MS in LS. 6: Sp. 7: Ref libn UAla 64-65; Libn Alexander City State Jr Col 65-. 9: ALA; AlaLA; SELA; Ala Jr Col LA (past sec-treas, v-pres, pres). 10: Alpha Beta Alpha; Alpha Delta Kappa; Bus & Profess Women; AAUW. 14: Ref, admin. 15: P O Box 29, Alexander City Al 35010.

FREEMAN, CAROL LYNNE. b Williston N Dak 25 F 44. 5: SW Mo State Col 62-66 (Hist) BS in Ed; Syracuse 68-69 MS in LS. 6: Sp. 7: Libn Camdentown Sr High Sch, Camdentown Miss 66-68. 9: ALA; MoStateLA. 14: Ref, lib educ, rare bks. 15: RR 1, Brighton Mo 65617.

FREEMAN, CLARA O. b Beallsville Penn 22 O 08. 5: Cal State Col (Penn) 25-31 (Elem Educ, Eng, Lat, Soc Studies) BS Ed; UPittsburgh 33-36 (Educ) MEd, 45-49 (Admin) Secondary Sch Prin Certif; Clarion State Teachers Col 55-56 (LS) WVaU 57 (LS); UChicago 57 (LS). 6: Lat. 7: Tchr Elem Sch, Bentleyville Penn 27-29; Tchr Elem Sch, Beallsville Penn 29-36; Music supv Elem Sch, Somerset Twp Penn 36-42; Tchr Eng & Lat Bethlehem-Center (Penn) High Sch W Betlehem Twp Penn 42-54, Tchr Eng 54-58, Libn 58-. 9: ALA; NEA; PennLA; Penn State EA. 11: Bus & Prof Womens Club. 14: Sch libs. 15: Box 133, Beallsville Penn 15313.

FREEMAN, ELLEN L(UCILLE). b Hopkinsville Ky 27 Ja 27. 5: Newcomb Col 44-46; UHouston 48-55 (Fr) BA; Columbia 57-58 MS LS. 6: Fr, Sp, Ger, Russian. 7: Sub-prof ref libn Houston Pub Lib 46-57; Geol libn Ind U Dept of Geol & Ind Geol Survey, Bloomington Ind 58-. 9: ALA; SLA (pres Ind Chap, sec-treas Geog & Map Div); ASIS. 10: AAUW; Pi Delta Phi; Beta Phi Mu. 11: Hammond Inc Lib Award (ALA) 68. 14: Ref. 15: Geology Lib, 1005 E 10th st, Bloomington In 47405.

FREEMAN, ELSA SLOANE. 4: Stuart Irvington Freeman. 5: Columbia 39-40 (LS) BA. 6: Fr, Ger. 7: Ref & sch asst NY Pub Lib 40-41; Jr libn US Bur of Agric Econ, Wash DC 41-42; Ref asst, sr ref asst, asst chief circ sect US Dept of Agric Lib, Wash DC 42-49; Asst libn US Bur of Ordnance Navy Dept, Wash DC 49-51; Head Libn US Off of Geog Dept of Interior, Wash DC 51-56; Dir Dept of Housing & Urban Developmen, Wash DC 56-. 8: John Cotton Dana Lectr, SLA 67. 9: ALA (chm Bldgs Com for Hosp Instr & Spec Libs 62-65); SLA (chm Recr Com 55-56, v-chm Member Comm 53-55, chm Convention Program Com 61-62; pres Wash DC Chap 54-55; chm Bldg & Housing Sect 65-); DCLA. 10: Phi Beta Kappa; Beta Phi Mu; No Va Fine Arts Assn; Natural Cathedral Assn; Little Theatre of Alexandria; Alexandria Coun of Church Women; Internatl Toastmasters; Natl Assn of Housing and Redevelopment Officials. 13: Yes. 14: Admin. 15: 3519 Ft Hill dr Wilton Woods, Alexandria Va 22310.

FREEMAN, INA (BENNER). b Carthage NC 21 S 27. 4: Donald McKinley Freeman. 5: Campbell Col 45-47 (Bus Admin) AA; Wake Forest 51-54 (Eng) BA; UAriz 66. 7: Baptist Bk Store, Raleigh NC 47-55; Dept sec pol sci UNC (Chapel Hill) 55-62; Asst to libn Fishburn Lib Hollins Col 62-63; Circ libn UNC Lib (Charlotte) 63-65; Supv central child Tucson Pub Lib 66-. 9: ArizLA. 14: Child wk. 15: 1425 Calle tiburon, Tucson Az 85704.

FREEMAN, KATHRYN EAVES. b Rowan Co NC 16 D 07. 5: UNC 25-29 (LS) AB. 7: Circ libn UNC (Greensboro) 29-34; Libn Peace Jr Col 34-36; Interviewer NC State Employment Serv, Durham NC 36-43; Employment dir Erwin Mills Inc, Durham NC 43-54; Off mgr UNC (Chapel Hill) 54-57, Libn sch of pharmacy 57-. 9: SLA; NCLA. 15: 365 Tenney cir, Chapel Hill NC 27514.

FREEMAN, (LOLA) LUCILE. b Pony Mont 4 F 13. 5: Phillips 48-51 (Bible, Religious Educ) AB; Butler U summer 55-58 (Christian Doctrine) MA; Mont State U 61-62 (Educ) Tchr certif; UDenver summers 63-65 MA in Libnship. 7: Tchr Weekday Religious Educ Inc, Indianapolis 51-61; Tchr & libn Rudyard Pub Schs, Rudyard Mont 62-63; Libn Greybull High Sch, Greybull Wyo 63-66; Catlg libn (hd) Cowles Lib Drake U 66-. 8: Co-tchr for course in basic catlg, Commun Col DrakeU fall 68-69. 9: ALA; IowaLA. 14: Catlg. 15: 2818 Cottage Grpve ave Apt 3, Des Moines Ia 50311.

FREEMAN, MARILYN (ROSE). b Niles Mich 3 O 40. 4: Martin. 5: Hillsdale Col 58-61 (Eng); UMich (Ann Arbor) 61-62 (Eng); UCal (Berkeley) 62-63, 65 (Eng) BA, 65-66 MLS. 7: Ser libn UBC 66-69; Libn II UCal (Irvine) 69-. 14: Tech processing, systems design & analysis. 15: Crawford Hall UCal, Irvine Ca 92664.

FREEMAN, (MARTHA) JEAN. b Spencer NC 8 g 12. 5: UNC (Greensboro) 29-33 (LS) BA; UNC (Chapel Hill) 52-58 (Hist) AB. 7: Tchr-libn High Sch, Cliffside NC 34-35; Clsfr US Farm Security Admin, Raleigh NC 35-41; Sch of Lib Sci UNC: Exec sec 41-47, Asst to the dean 47-57, Lecturer & asst to the dean 57-. 9: AALS; SELA; NCLA. 10: DAR; Beta Phi Mu; Phi Alpha Theta. 13: Yes. 14: Lib educ, admin. 15: 365 Tenney ci, Chapel Hill NC 27514.

FREEMAN, NANCY JANE. b Hibbing Minn. 5: UMinn 54-57 (Interdepartmental) BA, 57-58 (LS) MA. ; UWis 68-69 (LS). 7: Libn, sr libn NY Pub Lib 58-62; Asst to Dir Lib Sch UMinn(Minneapolis) 62-. 8: Survey team for survey of lib serv in N Dak 66. 9: ALA; AALS; MinnLA. 10: AAUP; ACLU; Phi Beta Kappa; Beta Phi Mu; Sigma Epsilon Sigma various Alumni Assns. ; AEAUSA. 12: Ed "Library Services in North Dakota (66). 14: Lib educ, sel, acquis, admin. 15: UMinn Lib Sch, Minneapolis Mn 55455.

FREEMAN, RAYMOND CARL. b Colerain NC 17 O 08. 4: Mary Adams. 5: UNC 38 (Geol) BS; East Carolina U 46; Appalachian State U 66 (LS) MA, 66 (A-V). 6: Fr. 7: Lt Col USAF Airmanitions 42-63; Asst libn Frederick Col, Portsmouth Va 65-66; A-v libn appalachian State U 66-67; Dir, learning resources Surry Commun Col 67-. 9: ALA; NAEB; NEA-DAVI; NCSchLA; NCCCLA; NCEA-NCDAVI. 10: ROA. 14: Ref. 15: Surry Commun Col, Dobson NC 27017.

FREEMAN, ROBERT G. b Monson Mass 22 Ag 26. 5: UMass 46-50 (Math) BS; Pratt 52-53 (LS) MS. 7: Tech Sgt US Army, USA, ETO 44-46; Gen asst UMass Lib 50-52; Gen asst Great Neck Lib, Great Neck NY 53-60; Indexer "Cumulative Book Index H W Wilson Co, NYC 60-62; Chief catlgr Great Neck Lib, Great Neck NY 62-. 9: NY Reg Tech Serv Libns. 14: Catlg. 15: 1737 York ave, NYC 10028.

FREEMAN, MRS THOMAS GLOVER. b Caledonia Miss 18 Mr 30. 4: Thomas Glover Freeman. 5: Miss State Col for Women 58-59 (LS) BS; Miss State U summers 61, 62; Miss State Col for Women 60-63 (LS) BS. 7: Libn Lowndes Co Lib System, Caledonia Miss Pub Lib 60-62; Libn Lowendes Co Sch System, Caledonia (Miss) High Sch 63-64; Libn Aberdeen City (Miss) Sch System, Aberdeen High Sch 64-. 9: MissEA; AberdeenEA; MonroeCoEA. 10: Civic Club; PTA; Alpha Beta Alpha. 14: Reading guidance, catlg, ref. 15: 25G Oak dr, Aberdeen Ms 39730.

FREEMAN, THOMAS JASPER. b Randolph County Ala 29 Mr 30. 4: Marian Laney. 5: Southern Union Col 53-54; Jacksonville State Col 54-56; (Hist) BS in Sec Ed; Auburn U 56-8 (Sch Admin) Ed; Peabody 59-61 MA in LS. 7: Textile wker Callaway Mills, LaGrange Ga 46-54; US Army Ordnance Cops (Cpl) 51-53; Libn Walter Wellborn High Sch, Anniston Ala 56-61; Asst libn Jacksonville State U 61-. 61-. 8: Org Lib Walter Wellborn High Sch 56; Org Parish Lib Church of St Michaels and All Angels, Anniston Ala 57; Org Calhoun Cunty Ala Tchrs Prof Lb 59. 9: AlaEA; AlaLA. 13: Yes. 14: Acquis. 15: 719 Bain ave, Weaver Al 36277.

FREEMAN, VIRGNIA (HAHN). b Everett Mass 17 S 07. 5: Simmons 24-28 (LS) BS. 7: Asst Stone & Webster Lib, Boston 28-29; Asst Harvard Landscape Arch Lib (Cambridge Mass) 29-31; Asst Parlin Mem Lib, Everett Mass 49-53; Asst Kennebunk Free Lib, Kennebunk Me 55-59, Libn 59-65, Catlgr 65-. 9: MeLA. 10: Simmons Alumnae Assn; Olympian Club (Kennebunkport Me); Kennebunkport Hist Soc. 14: Catlg. 15: PO Box 294, Kennebunkport Me 04046.

FREESE, ROBERT THEODORE. b New Brunswick NJ 20 Mr 30. 5: Rutgers 48-52 (Geog) BS; UMich 52-53 (Geog) MA, 53-55 (Geog), 59-61 AMLS. 7: Aviation storekeeper USN, Quonset Point RI 56-57; Lib asst UMich (Ann Arbor) 57-61, Engring libn 61-63, Engring- Tran transportation libn 63-. 10: Phi Beta Kappa. 15: 1310 Packard, Ann Arbor Mi 48104.

FREIBURGER, L ROBERT. b Rochester NY 19 F 39. 4: Berenice Toner. 5: State U Col (Geneseo NY) 57-61 (Lib Educ) BS; Ind U 61-62 (A-v communications) MS. 7: Film libn Rochester (NY) Pub Lib 62-63; A-v coordinator State U Col (Geneseo NY) 63-. 9: NEA-DAVI; NY State A-V Assn; Rochester A-V Assn; George Eastman House Associates. 13: Yes. 14: Materials spec. 15: 6 Prospect st, Geneseo NY 14454.

FREIDES, THELMA (KATZ). b NYC 26 F 30. 4: David Freides. 5: Hunter Col 48-52 (Pol Sci) BA; Yale 52-55 Internat Rel) MA; UMich 58-60 (LS) MA. 6: Fr, Russian, Sp. 7: Research asst Pol Sci Yale U 54-55; Libn-in-train McGregor Pub Lib, Highland Park-Mich 58-60; Ref libn Wayne State U Lib 60-66; Doc libn Emory U Lib 66-67; Assoc Prof Sch Lib Serv Atlanta U 67-. 9: ALA. 10: AAUP. 12: "Newspaper Resources of Metropolitan Detroit Libraries; a Union List, with H A Sullivan (65). 13: Yes. 14: Ref, lit & bibliog of soc sci, govt docs. 15: School of Lib Serv Atlanta Univ, Atlanta Ga 30314.

FREIFIELD, NORMA ELIZABETH. b Edmonton ALTA Can 30 Je 17. 5: UAlta 35-38 Arts BA; UToronto 39-40 BLS. 6: Fr. 7: UAlta: Circ asst 41-50; Head circ dept Rutherford Lib 50-63, Head circ dept Cameron Lib 63-. 9: ALA; CanLA (mem &/or chm several coms); AltaLA (pres 54-55, var other exec duties). 10: Can Fed of Univ Women; Delta Kappa Gamma. 13: Yes. 14: Circ, col, univ & res lib. 15: 10409 - 133 st, Edmonton 40 Alta Canada.

FREISER, LEONARD H. b NYC 9 F 25. 4: Helen Hammer. 5: Manhattan Sch of Music 45-48 (Composition) Mus Bac; Columbia 47-48 (Edu) MA, 54-55 (LS) MS. 7: Asst Prof San Jose State Col 51-52; Ref asst br lib Brooklyn Pub Lib 54-57; Assoc Prof NY State Col (Albany) 59-60; Chief Libn Crandall Lib, Glens Falls NY 57-60; Chief Libn Toronto Bd of Educ 60-68; Exec dir LI Lib Resources Coun 68-. 8: Surveyor & consul Calgary Sch Libs. 9: ALA (Cou); OntLA (pres). '): Ont Assn for Curricuum Development (Cun); U Presidents of Ontario (Spec Com on Libnship). 13: Yes. 14: Lib serv. 15: LI Lib Resources Coun 55 Vanderbilt pkwy, Dix Hills NY 11746.

FREITAG, RUTH S. b Lancaster Penn 8 Je 24. 5: Penn State Col 41-44 (Hist) AB; USoCal 58-59 MS LS. 6: Ger, Fr. 7: Womens Army Corps (SFC) hist clerk, Peiping, Nanking, Shanghai China 45-49; Communications wk in the Foreign Srv Dept of State, Amer Embassy, London, Amer Consulates-General, Geneva & Hong Kong 49-56; Underwriting approver-Prudential Ins Co of Amer, West Home Off, Los Angeles 56-58; LC: trainee libn 59, Ref asst Bibliog & Ref Correspondence Sect Gen ref & Bibliog Div 60-61, bibliog 61-63, Sr bibliog 63-65, asst sect head 65-68, Hd 69-. 9: ALA; DCLA. 10: Beta Phi Mu. 12: Comp "Agricultural Development Schemes in Sub-Saharan Africa a Bibliography (63); Comp "Union Lists of Serials; a Bibliography (64); Asst ed "D.C. Libraries (63-)67); Comp "Presidential Inaugurations, A Selected List of References, (Bd Ed 69). 13: Yes. 14: Ref. 15: 1300 S Arl Ridge rd, Arlington Va 22202.

FREITAG, WOLFGANG M(ARTIN). b Berlin Germany 27 O 24. 4: Doris Pfeil. 5: UFreiburg iB (Germany) Albert Ludwis Universitat 49 (Eng) Dr Phil; Simmons 56 (LS) MS. 6: Ger, Fr, Ital. 7: Ref libn US Info Center, Frankurt Germany 50-53; Ed Droemer/Knaur Verlag, Munich Germany 53-55; Catlgr Harvard Col Lib 55-60; Libn Gordon McKay Lib Harvard 60-62; Chief Libn undergrad bk sel Stanford 62-64; Libn Fine Arts Lib Harvard 64-65; Assoc u libn for rsources & acquis Harvard 65-67; Lectr in Fine Arts & Fine arts libn 67-. 8: Res asst to Keyes D Metcalf on "Planning Academic and esearch Library Buildings 60-64; Consul to libs and publishers. 9: ALA; -RTSD (Internat Org Publs Com 60-64); -ACRL (A-V Com 67-69; Subj Spec Sect; chm Art Subsect 69-70). 10: Col Art Assn Amer. 12: Tr into German "Alice in Wonderland (54, 2nd ed 58). 13: Yes. 14: Bk sel, documentation, mss. 15: 43 Fair Oaks dr, Lexington Mass 02173.

FRENCH, CLARICE P(AXTON. b Jester Okla 9 D 04. 4: Walton W French. 5: Central State Col 23-24; Southwestern State Col 32 (Eng) BS; UOkla 64 MLS. 6: Fr. 7: Tchr Port School, Sentinel Okla 26-30; High sch Eng tchr Westview, Hollis Okla 30-40; High sch Eng tchr Canute, Canute Okla 46-56; High sch Eng tchr, Dill City Okla 56-60; High sch libn Burns Flat (Okla) Sch 60-64; Hd col Libn Okla Christian Col 64-. 9: ALA; SWLA (chm 64); OklaLA (sec Col Div 68-69); OklaEA. 10: Delta Kappa Gamma. 14: Ref. 15: Memorial & Eastern, Oklahoma City Okla 73111.

FRENCH, ELIZABETH (HALE). b Salina Kan. 4: Merton B French. 5: Washburn Col 30-37 (Eng) AB; UIll 38 BS in LS. 7: Circ asst Topeka Pub Lib 36-39, Ref libn 50-55; Act hd Burlington (NC) Pub Lib 39-40; Period libn Washburn U Lib 63-. 9: ALA. 10: YWCA; United Fund; PEO. 14: Ref. 15: 1306 High ave, Topeka Ks 66604.

FRENCH, FRANCES (SUE). b Belzoni Miss 20 Ag 27. 5: Blue Mountain Col 44-48 (Eng) AB; Emory 4849 (LS) ML. 6: Fr. 7: Asst ref libn UGa 50-51; Jackson Mun, Jackson Miss Ref libn 51-, Act libn 59-61, Coordinator of ref serv 65-68; Info spec Miss Research & Devel Ctr 68-. 9: ALA; MissLA; SELA. 10: YMCA; Miss Art Assn; Jackson Symphony. 14: Ref. 15: Miss Research & Dev Ctr Info Servs Div P O Drawer 2470, Jackson Ms 39205.

FRENCH, GRACE MARGARET. b Midland Co Mich 5 Mr 27. 5: Messiah Col 45-47; Central Mich U 47-48; Goshen Col 50-51 (Educ) BS; UMich 56-57 AMLS. 6: Ger. 7: Elem tchr: Midland Co Rural Schs, Midland Mich 48-50, Bremen Schs, Bremen Ind 51-54, Midland Sch Dist, Midland Mich 54-56; Child libn Ferndale Pub Lib, Ferndale Mich 57-58; Libn Mt Morris Sch Dist, Mt Morris Mich 58-60; Libn Lansing Sch Dist, Lansing Mich 60-. 9: ALA; NEA; MichEA; MichASchL; LansingEA. 10: AAUW; UMich Alum Club. 14: Sch libn. 15: Rte #1, Wheeler Mi 48662.

FRENCH, HANNAH DUSTIN. b Hadlyme Conn 31 Ag 07. 5: Mount Holyoke 24-29 (Eng Li) BA; Drexel 29-30 BS in LS; Columbia 38-39 MS. 6: Lat, Fr. 7: Asst in catlg dept Wheaton Col (Norton Mass) 30-31, Asst ref & circ dept 31-33, Head of ref & circ 33-38; Act head order dept Wellesley Col 39-41, Head order dept 41-44, Research libn in chg of spec collections44-. 9: ALA-ACRL (Rare Bks Div; Act chm 56, sec 61-62); BSA; Bibliog Soc (London); Bibliog Soc UVa. 11: Scholar, Radcliffe Inst 67-68. 12: "Early American Bookbinding by Han, in "Bookbinding in America (41). 13: Yes. 14: Rare bks, bibliog, bk arts. 15: Wellesley College Lib, Wellesley Ma 02181.

FRENCH, IRENE J(OHNSTON). b Memphis Tenn 9 Ag 03. 4: Junius Butler French. 5: Wash U (St Louis) 20-24 (Eng & Fr Lit) AB; NY State Lib Sch (Albany) 24-25 Certif. 6: Fr. 7: Asst in circ dept Cossitt Lib, Memphis Tenn summers 20-24; Stud asst in catlg dept Wash U Lib (St Louis) 21-24; Stud asst Harmanus Bleecker Lib, Albany NY 24-25; Head order dept Lawson McGhee Lib, Knoxville Tenn 25-26, Head order & catlg dept 26-33; Head catlg dept Knox Co Lib, Knoxville Tenn 50-67; Hd order dept Pub Lib of Knoxville & Knox Co Tenn 67-. 9: ALA; SELA; TennLA. 10: Smoky Mountains Hiking Club; Tenn Ornithological Soc. 14: Acquis, catlg. 15: 3108 Ocoee trai, Knoxville Tenn 37917.

FRENCH, MICHAEL F. b Bath NY 6 N 42. 4: Beatrice Luther. 5: SUNY (Cortland) 59-63 9educ) BS; SUNY (Geneseo) 68-69 MLS. 7: Tchr Naples Central Sch, Naples NY 63-64; Statistical clk Erie Co He Dept, Buffalo NY 64-65; Tchr Buffalo Pub Schs, Buffalo NY 65-68; Ref asst Lorain Pub Lib, Lorain Ohio 68-. 9: ALA; OhioLA. 14: Ref, ya. 15: 1742 E Erie st, Lorain Oh 44052.

FRENCH, MURIEL R. b Greenfield Mass 12 N 18. 4: Arthur E French Jr. 5: NH 35-39 (Pre-med, Eng) BA; UPittsburgh 62-63 MLS. 6: Fr. 7: Sec Radio Station WTAG, Worcester Mass 40-45; Br libn New Castle Penn 60-62; Asst libn New Castle Free Pub Lib, New Casle Pen 63-. 9: PennLA; (Chm 4-County Chap). 10: Beta Phi Mu; LWV; Col Club of New Castle; Bus & Prof Women; Quota Club. 14: Ref, readers adv, adult serv, acquis. 15: 2308 Delaware ave, New Castle Penn 16101.

FRENCH, PAULINE. b Indianapolis 29 S 10. 5: Franklin Col 28-32 (Eng) AB; UTex summer 36; UDenver summers 37, 44-45 BLS. 7: Tchr, Tex 32-38; Asst Logansport Pub Lib, Logansport Ind 40; Indianapolis Pub Lib: Asst 40-44, Reader's asst 45, Br libn 46, Adult activities & film libn 47-57; Head gen adult dept 57-60, Supv central serv dept 60-. 9: ALA; IndLA. 15: Indianapolis-Marion Co Pub Lib, 40 E St Clair st, Indianapolis In 46204.

FRENCH, WARREN F(RANCIS). b Andover NH 5 D 20. 4: Marjorie Cooke. 5: UNH 41-45 (Psych) BA; Syracuse 49-50 MS in LS. 6: Fr. 7: Catlgr Wilkes Col 50-56; Catlgr northwesternU 56-57; Ref asst Ohio StateU 57-60; Catlgr Hartford Sem Found, Hartford Conn 60-63; Catlgr UMass 63-68, Sr catlgr 68-. 14: Catlg. 15: 22 Lexington ave, northampton Ma 01060.

FRENCH, ZELIA JANE. b Howard Kan 20 Ag 05. 5: Southwestern (Kan) 24-28 (Sociol) AB; UIll 29-30 BS LS. 7: Asst libn Pratt (Kan) Pub Lib 31-32; Catlgr Pub Lib, Hutchinson Kan 33-34; Child libn Pub Lib, El Dorado Kan 36-38; Supv WPA-Lib Proj, Topeka Kan 39-42; Tech libn N Amer Aviation, Kan City Kan 2-43; Bus & Tech dept Kan City (Mo) Pub Lib 43-45; Asst libn Jackson C Lib, Independence Mo 45-49; Sec Travel Lib Commsn, Topeka Kan 49-64; Libn Pub Lib, Miami Okla 64-. 9: OklaLA. 10: AAUW; Nat Womens Bk Assn; Kan Coun for Child & Youth; Nat Womens Press Assn; Nat Assn of en Women (Life mem); Kan Congress of Parents & Tchrs (Hon mem); Delta Kappa Gamma. 12: Ed "Kansas Library Bulletin (49-64). 13: Yes. 14: Adult educ. 15: 516 B NW, Miami Okla 74354.

FRENETTE, ROBERT A. b Swansea Mass 27 D 27. 5: Brown U 50-54 (Amer Civilization) AB; Simmons 60-62 MLS. 7: Radioman US Navy 50-54; Reporter-photographer "Coos Bay (Ore) World 57-60; Libn II Detroit Pub Lib 62-66; Libn VA 67-68; Ref libn Randolph-Macon Col 68-. 9: ALA; VaLA. 10: Phi Beta Kappa. 14: Ref. 15: 208 Maiden lane, Ashland Va 23005.

FRENETTE, THERESE. b Portneuf Que 3 N 31. 5: Bates Col 51-55 (Soc sci) BA; Pratt Inst 62-63 MLS. 6: Fr. 7: Adult serv specialist Brooklyn Pub Lib 62-66; Asst to ref dept hd Polytech Inst Brooklyn 66-67; Lobn in charge Sinclair & Valetine Co 67-. 9: SLA; ASIS. 14: Indexing. 15: 53 Jackson st, Yonkers NY 10701.

FRENIER, RICHARD (WALTER). b Montpelier Vt 8 O 37. 5: NortheasternU 55-60 (Chem) BS; Syracuse 61-63 (LS) MS; UMd 63- (Fine Arts Hist). 6: Fr, Ger, Portu. 7: Libn Allied Chem Corp Solvay Process Div, Syracuse NY 60-63; Catlgr UMd (College Park) 63-67, Hd engring & phys sci lib 67-. 8: Indexing consul for Airport Operators Coun, Wash DC 66-; Abstractor & indexer Legal Dept of Air Transport Assn, Wash DC 67-68. 10: IEEE; Amer Road Builders Assn; Amer Soc for Indexers. 14: Admin, automation. 15: 2029 Q st NW, Washington DC 20009.

FRESE, ANNE (HORVATH). b Chicago 5 Ja 21. 4: Henry C Frese. 5: U Budaest 39-40 (Liberal Arts); Bryant Stratton Bus Sch 40 (Bus); Mich State Lib Wkshops 59 Certif; Andrews U, IndU, West Mich U 60- (LS). 6: Ger, Hungarian, Serbian. 7: Priv sec U S Steel Corp, Chicago 40-45; Ref libn Niles Pub Lib, Niles Mich 58-66, Admin 66-. 8: Church Lib 58-61; Aid in sel of child bks paochial schl. 9: ALA; CathLA; MichLA; Berrien Co Coop Libs Assn (sec). 14: Ref, local hist. 15: Niles Pub Lib 3105 Creek rd, Niles Mi 49120.

FRESHLEY, RONALD SCOTT. b Alliance Ohio 13 Je 37. 4: Nancy Parkin Freshley. 5: Bowling Green State U 60-63 (Eng) BA; UDenver 64-65 (LS) MA. 6: Fr. 7: Ref libn UDenver Mary Reed Lib 65; Asst catlgr SUNY (Stony Brook) 65-67; Ref libn Hofstra U 67-. 15: 20 Felix place, Amity Harbor NY 11701.

FRETWELL, GORDON E. b Adrian Mich 16 Ja 37. 4: Sharon Lynne Wick. 5: Mich State U 54-59 (Soc Sci) BA; UMich 60-64 MALS, 65 (Pub Admin). 6: Sp, Ger. 7: Chief page Lansing Libs, Lansing Mich 59-61; Wk-study scholar UMich Gen Lib (Ann Arbor 61-62; Head circ dept UMich Law Lib (Ann Arbor) 62-65; Head pub serv UCal(San Diego) 65-. 14: Pub serv, admin. 15: 837 Ocean Crest r, Cardiff-by-th-sea, Cal 92007.

FREUDENTHAL, JUAN R. b Santiago Chile 11 S 37. 4: Patricia Miner. 5: UConcepcion (Chile) 57-60 (Journalism) Titulo de Periodista; UMunich (Germany) 62-63 (Journalism) Certification; Syracuse 65-66 MSLS. 6: Ger, Sp. 7: Research asst Thomas Y Crowell Co, NY 63; Asst to dir Goethe-Inst, Santiago (Chile) 64-65; Ref libn Hamilton Col 66-68; Spec collections libn SUNY (Binghamton) 68-. 8: Reporter for Chilean newspapers Chile 58-60; Instr in Spanish, SUNY (Binghamton) Off Cont Educ. 9: ALA; Cent NY Ref & Res Coun; Five Assocd Univs & Libs (Spec Collections Com). 11: UNESCO scholarship to study in Ecuador 59; Deutscher Akademischer Ausstauschdienst scholarship 62-63. 12: "International Information Agencies" (60). 14: Humanities, admin, spec collec. 15: 305 1/2 E Main st, Endicott NY 13760.

FREUDENTHAL, MARY ANN (MARIANNE SILBERSTEIN). b Bielsko-Bialo Bielsko-Biala 4 Je 12. 5: German U (Prague Csr 30-32 (Philol) BA; Columbia 61-63 MLS. 6: Ger, Fr, Hebrew, Ital, Polish. 7: Conference sec & asst ed Dept of Civil Engnr & Engnr Mechanics, Internat Conf on Fatigue in Flight Structures Columbia U 55-56; Asst & sec P R Dept Visiting Nurse Serv of NY, NY 56-60; Stud libn engnr Columbia U 63; Circ libn Union Theol Sem (NY) 63-64; Libn Israel Inst of Tech-Technion (Haifa) 64-65; Abstractor-Ed Engin Index Inc, NY 65-67; Ref libn NY Inst of Tech 67-68; Ed Intnl Conf on Structural Safety & Reliability, Wash DC & NY 69-.0x; 8work-study in info & bibliog servs, Dept of Rheology, Federal Standard Inst, West Berlin, Ger, summer 65. 9: Internat Fed for Documentation; SLA (NY Chap Documentation & Museums Div); NY Lib Club; NY Tech Serv Libns. 10: Alumni Fed of Columbia Univ; Internat Fed Documentation; AAUP; Matterhorn Sports Club (NYC). 12: Asst ed "Fatigue in Aircraft Structures (56). 13: Yes. 14: Ref, acquis, documentation, bibliog. 15: 4515 Willard ave, Chevy Chase Md 20015.

FREUND, ALFRED L. b Bayshore LI NY 23 D 29. 4: Elizabeth Pappas. 5: City Col (NY) 50-54 (Hist) BA; Pratt 58-61 MLS. 6: Fr. 7: Sp3 US Army Finance Corps Heidelberg Germany 54-56; Underwriter Hartford A & I Co, NYC 56-59; Lib asst "Newsweek NYC 59-61; Ref, ya lbn Hicksville (NY) Pub Lib 61-63; Lib Dir Plainedge Pub Lib, Massapequa NY 63-. 9: ALA; NYLA; NassauCoLA (chm Profess Practices Com 65-); NCLA (chm Administive Problems Coun). 10: Phi Alpha Theta; Beta Phi Mu, PTA. 14: Admin, pub libs. 15: 9 Flamingo rd, Levittown NY 11756.

FREUND, CLARE ELIZABETH. b Gleiwitz Germany 21 Ap 23. 5: UPenn 46-47 & ummers; Bucknell U 47-50 (Soc Studies) AB; Drexel 50-51 MS in LS. 6: Ger, Fr. 7: German Monitor British Broadcasting Corp, Eng 41-46; Lib asst UPenn 46-47; Dir of Ger House & housemother Bucknell U 47-50, Lib asst 49-50; Research libn Time Inc, NYC 51-62; Asst libn Eastman Kodak Labs, Las, Rochester NY 62-. 9: SLA (Recr Chm West NY Chap 64-65, Placement Chm Upstate NY Chap 65-). 10: Delta Kappa Gamma; Phi Beta Kappa. 14: Ref, catlg, computer applications. 15: 144 Westminster rd, Rochester NY 14607.

FREVE, REAY (MARY). b Glasgow Scotland 8 F 32. 4: Dorien Freve. 5: Lib Assoc Lond 56 ala. 7: Asst Surbrton Pub Lib, Surrey England, Br libn 50-56; Asst Toronto Pub Lib, Ont can 57; Asst Vancouver Pub Lib, BC Can 57-61; MIT: Asst, Asst libn Rotch Lib, Libn Rotch Lib 61-. 8: Lib Com Boston Arch Ctr 67-. 9: ALA; LA (London). 10: Citizens Housing & Planning Assn of Metropolitan Boston; Trustees of Reservations; ACLU. 14: Admin, bk selection, ref. 15: 65 Park dr, Boston Ma 02215.

FREY, AGNES LOUISE. b Norristwn Penn 8 N 21. 5: Immaculata Col 43-47 (Hist) AB; Drexel 47-48 BS LS. 7: Asst libn Norristonw (Penn) Pub Lib 48-49; Asst libn Valley Forge Gen Hosp, Phoenixville Penn 49-50; Br libn Wilmington (Del) Pub Lib 50-51; Chief period sect, ref libn, chief acquis sect US Army War Col, Carlisle Barracks Pen 51-67; Libn Spec Serv Lib, Ascom Dist Korea 67-; Libn Command Ref Lib 8th US Army, Seoul Korea 67-. 10: AAUW. 14: Acquis, ref, admin. 15: Command Ref Lib Lib Serv Ctr Spec Serv Sect Hq 8th US Army, APO San Francisco Ca 96301.

FREY, EMIL FERDINAND. b Zuerich Switzerland 0 10 27. 4: Cleo Marie Graham. 5: William Jennings Bryan U 53-57 (Hist) BA; UTenn 57-59 (Ger) MA; UNC 61-62 (LS) MS. 6: Ger, Fr, Ital. 7: Serv manager Union Trading Co, Kano Nigeria 50-52; Tech dir S A Perrot Duval, Geneva Switzerland 52-53; Asst ordr libn UTenn 59-60; Salesman Curtis 1000 Inc, Durham NC 60-61; Admin libn Duke U Med Center Lib 62-63; Assoc libn Mayo Clinic, Rochester Minn 64-69; Dir Health Sci Lib SUNY (Stony Brook) 69-. 9: MedLA; SLA; Amer Mgt Assn. 10: High Noon Toastmasters 2676; Winona Consistory; Rotary. 13: Yes. 14: Admin, rare bks, ref, computerization. 15: Health Sci Lib SUNY at Stony Brook, Stony Brook NY 11790.

FREY, JOHN ELDRED. b Racine Wis 4 F 30. 4: Carol Thompson. 5: Wis State U 57 (Eng) B Ed; UIowa 60 (Eng) MA; UIl 61 (LS) MS. 7: (Sgt/Maj) Army 51-53; Tchr Pub Schs, St Petersburg Fla 58-61; Head libn Jeffersonville (Ind) Pub Lib 62-64; Asst Dir Louisville (Ky) Free Pub Lib 64-66; Dir Jeffersonville Twp Pub Lib In 66-. 8: Instr UKy Sch Lib Sci; Cath Spalding Col Dept Lib Sci. 9: KyLA; ALA; IndLA. 10: Rotary Club; Chamber of Commerce. 13: Yes. 14: Pub lib admin. 15: Jeffersonville Twp Pub Lib, Jeffersonville In 47130.

FREY, PETER ANTHONY. b Maracaibo Venezuela 26 O 36. Marguerite Mundy. 5: UIll 56-58 (Geog) BA, 65-67 (LS) MS; UGa 62-64 (Pol Sci) MA. 6: Fr. 7: Libn Inst of Labor & Ind Rels UIll (Champaign) 67-. 9: ALA; Com of Univ Indust Relations Libns. 10: Phi Kappa Phi; Beta Phi Mu. 14: Pol sci, legisl ref, law. 15: 1816 Larch place, Urbana Il 61801.

FRICK, BERTHA MARGARET. b Rockwell City IOWA 4 a Ja 5: Grinnell Col 14-17; UIowa 17-18 (Math) AB; UColo 23 (Math); Columbia 28-29, 31-33 BS in LS, MS in LS. 6: Fr, Ger, Ital. 7: Tchr of math High cs, Iowa, Colo, Va 18-28; Catlgr Queensborough Pub Lib, Jamaica NY 29-31; Columbia U: Catlgr of rare bks 31-38, Curator of Plimpton, Smith & Dale Collection 38-45, Tchr, Asst Prof, Assoc Prof Sch of Lib Serv 31-60 ret; Vsiting Prof summer sessions Columbia U 61-64, 66-67; UCal 65-; Prof UNESCO Course in Librnship, Copenhagen, Denmark 66. 8: Mem ALA-US Army group appointed to establish Japan Lib Sch, Keio Univ, Tokyo, 51-52; Mem Dewey Dec Clsf Educ Policy Com, 53-60; Surveyor of libs in Christian Cols in Indonesia, Philippines, Hong Kong, Taiwan, Korea (United Board for Christian Higher Educ in Asia), 63. 9: ALA; NY Reg Catlgrs Group (past sec & pres). 11: Melvil Dewey Medal, 65. 12: Ed "Sears List of Subject Headings, 6th-8th eds (50, 54 59); Auth "Report of Libraries in East Asia, mimeo (64). 13: Yes. 14: Rare bks, catlg, clsf. 15: Meadow Lakes. 17/10 U, Higtstown NJ 08520.

FRICK, CLAUDETTE JOAN. b Chicago Ill 6 Ag 42. 5: Mich TechU 62-64 (Liberal) BA, 65-66 (Arts); West MichU 64-65 (Liberal Arts); Rosary 67-69 MALS. 7: Dictaphone operator Prudential Ins Co, Chicago 60-62; Libn trainee Chicago Pub Lib 66-69, Libn I 69-. 10: Mich Tech Alumni Assn; Beta Phi Mu. 14: Child wk. 15: 533 S Euclid, Oak Park Il 60304.

FRICKE, MARYANN ELIZABETH. b Phila Pa 5 Ag 44. 5: St Francis Col 62-66 (Elem Educ) BS, Catholic U 66-67 MS in LS. 6: Fr. 7: Tchr & libn Cherry Hill Pub Schs Cherry hill NJ 67-. 9: ALA; NEA; NJEA; Local & Coun Orgs. 10: Beta Phi Mu. 14: Lib admin & tchg lib sci. 15: 615 Grape st, Hammonton NJ 08037.

FRIDERICHSEN, BLANCHE (ALEXIA) (IRVINE). b Saskatoon Saskatchewan 21 Mr 25. 4: Andreas Friderichsen. 5: USask 44-48 (Hist) BA; Toronto 48-49 BLS; U Alta 59- (Educ) Tchg Certif. 6: Fr. 7: Child libn Pub Lib, Edmonton Alta 49-52; Acquis libn UToronto 52; Catlgr McGill U Lib 52-53; Child libn Bromley Lib, Bromley Eng 53; Head of circ Pub Lib, Edmonton Alta 54-58; Lib supv Co of Strathcona Schs, Edmonton Alta 59-65; Sch lib consul PROV OF Alta, Edmonton Alta 66-. 8: Lectr UAlta Sch Lib Serv summers 66, 68. 9: CanSLA (Statistics Com); AASchL; AltaTA; Sch Lib Coun (dir). 10: Alta Lib Bd; Beta Sigma Phi (Hon). 12: Auth Child Sect of Alta Govt "Library Custodians Course (59). 13: Yes. 14: Sch libs. 15: 9820 - 104 st apt 11C, Edmonton 14 Alta Can.

FRIDINGER, SUSANN MARIE. b Waynesboro Pa 4 Ag 46. 5: Shippensburg State Col 64-67 9ls0 bs, 69 (LS); West Md Col 68-69 (Educ). 6: Sp. 7: Libn Victor Cullen Sch, Cullen Md 67-. 9: ALA; MdLA; Cumberland Valley LA; Educal Media Assn Md. 10: Bus & prof Women's Club. 14: Institut schs. 15: Rte 4, Waynesboro Pa 17268.

FRIEDEN, RONALD GEORGE. b West Union Iowa 2 D 40. 5: UFla 58-63 (Bus Educ) BS, summer 64 (Lib, A-v serv) Certif, summers 64-68 (Lib, A-v serv) MS. 7: Stud asst Ft Myers Jr-Sr High, Ft Myers Fla 53-58; Stud asst Educ Lib UFla 62-63; Sch libn & a-v coord Ft Myers Jr High Sch, Ft Myers Fla 64-. 8: So Assn Evaluation Visiting Com: Charlotte Jr High, Punta Gorda Fla 65, N Shore Jr-Sr High, W Palm Beach Fla 68. 9: Clr TA of Lee Co (treas 65-66); FlaASchL; Fla A-v Assn (Lee Co Memb Com). 10: Phi Delta Kappa. 14: Ref, a-v serv. 15: 660 Marsh ave, Fort Myers Fl 33905.

FRIEDENSTEIN, HANNA (JOHANNA). b Vienna Austria. 5: Univ Col London U 38-41 (Chem) BSc; Simmons 48-50 (LS) MS. 6: Ger, Fr. 7: Research chem Phillips Electrical Ltd, Mitcham Surrey Eng 42-46; Staff intelligence off, British Oxygen Co, Morden Eng 46-47; Research libn Cabot Corp, Boston & Cambridge 47-57; Hd tech info serv 57-68; Mgr info ctr 68-. 9: ACS (chm Div Chem Lit 59); SLA (chm Chem Sect 57-58; pres Boston Chap 55-56); ASIS (chm elect NE Chap 69). 14: Info retrieval services. 15: c/o Cabot Corp 125 High st, Boston Ma 02110.

FRIEDLANDER, FLORENCE (SACKS). b Brooklyn NY 25 Ap 27. 4: Philip. 5: Brooklyn Col 42-46 (Sociol) BA; C W Post Col 62-65 MLS. 7: Child Libn Shelter Rock Pub Lib, Albertson NY 64-. 9: ALA (Jaycee Good Reading Com); NYLA; NassauCoLA. 10: Alum Assn of Palmer Grad Lib Sch; C W Post Col. 14: Storytelling a-v, ref. 15: 6 Morris Dr, New Hyde Park NY 11040.

FRIEDLANDER, JANET M(ONGAN). b NYC 14 Jl 31. 4: Frank Friedlander. 5: Cornell 49-53 (Amer Lit) BA; UTex

55-57 MLS; Case West Res (US Off Educ Doctoral Fellow) 66-. 6: Fr, Lat. 7: Admin asst Prentice-Hall NYC 53; Admin asst Harris Group NYC 53-54; Intern Austin (Tex) Pub ib 56-57; Ref asst Cleveland Pub Lib 57-58; Adult serv libn Cuyahoga Co Pub Lib, Clveland 61-62; Tech libn US Naval Ordinance Test Station, China Lake Cal 63-66. 9: ALA; SLA; ASIS; OhioLA. 13: Yes. 14: Ref, info sci. 15: 2189 Lamberton rd, Cleveland Oh 44118.

FRIEDLANDER, MICHEL OTTO. b Vienna 15 F 08. 4: Jenny Jacob. 5: UVienna 27-31 (Law) LLD; Carnegie 41-42 BS in LS. 6: Ger, Fr, Sp, Ital. 7: Ref libn Carnegie Lib, Pittsburgh 41-42; Asst libn Stevens Inst of Tech 42-46; Exec Sefri Knitwear, NYC 4657; Dir of Engnr Lib Grumman Aircraft Engnr Corp, Bethpage NY 57-. 8: Wilson Index Com. 9: SLA (chm ASTIA Coordinating Com 59-62, Lib Consul 59-, chm Aerospace Div 65-66); IEEE (Info Com); ASIS. ADI 10: Amer Astronautical Soc; Inst of Navigation. 10: Amer Astronautical Soc Inst of Navigation. 13: Yes. 14: Admin, documentation. 15: c/o Grumman A/C Engineering Corp, Bethpage NY 11714.

FRIEDMAN, ELYSE RACHEL (MARINSKY). b Oak Ridge Tenn 17 O 45. 4: Sanford R Friedman. 5: HebrewU (Jerusalem) 63-64 (Jewish Studies); URochester 64-66 (Ling) AB; CornellU 66 (Chinese); MIT 66-67 (Ling); Simmons 67-68 (LS) MS. 6: Fr, Hebrew, Sp. 7: Ref asst Pub Lib of Brookline, Brookline Mass 68-. 14: Ref, ya. 15: 1542 Commonwealth ave, Brighton Ma 02135.

FRIEDMAN, FAY B(ROCKMAN). b NYC 29 O 21. 4: Allen Friedman. 5: LSU 38-41 (Eng) BA; 41-42 BS LS; Newark State Col 63, 65 (Educ) Certif for NJ Sch system. 7: Ref & ya asst New Orleans Pub Lib 42; Got libn US Off of Censorship, New Orleans 42-45; Ref asst Youngstown (Ohio) Pub Lib 47-49; Ref libn Warren (Ohio) Pub Lib 60-62; Libn Governor Livingston Reg High Sch, Berkeley Heights NJ 65-. 8: Middlestates Eval Com, Howell High Sch, Farmingdale NJ 69; Lay Adv Com of Adult Educ Prog for Union Co Reg High Sch, District #1 69-70. 9: ALA; NJEA; NJSchLA. 14: Ref & research, wk with ya. 15: Governor Livinston E G High Sch, Berkeley Heights NJ 07922.

FRIEDMAN, HAROLD J. b Phila 25 Je 13. 4: Eleanor Myers. 5: Temple 30-38 (Bus Admin) BS Com; Drexel 61-62 MLS. 6: Fr. 7: Gen mgr Friedman Elec Supply, Phila 35-42; Seaman 1st cl US Navy-Seabees, New Guinea 43-45; Pres Friedman Elec Supply, Phla 52-61; Libn II Annenberg Sch of Communications UPenn 62-67; Hd libn Girard Col 67-68; Admin libn Dropsie Col 68-69; Catlgr Phila Col of Art 69-. 9: SLA; ALA. 10: Penn Hortic Soc; Penn Acad Fine Arts. 13: Yes. 14: Catlg. 15: 7408 Woodlawn ave, Phila 19126.

FRIEDMAN, LUCILLE (WENDROW). b NYC 25 Jl 18. 4: Stanley I Freedman. 5: UWash 36-40 (Eng Lit) BA, 40-41 (Educ) BA in Ed, 64-66 MLS. 7: Salesclk: S H Kress, Everett Wash 35-36, Sears Roebuck, Seattle 37-41; Typist UWash 38-40; Tchr Roy High Sch, Roy Wash 42; Sub tchr: Seattle Pub Schs 62-64, Belevue Pub Schs, Bellevue Wash 62-64; Libn Mercer Is Pub, Mercer Is Wash 64-. 8: Wash State Lib Reading Com. 9: ALA; NEA-DAVI; WLA; WashStateASchL (pres-elect Reg 13). 10: UWash Alum Assn; Beta Phi Mu; Seattle Symphony (Women's Div); Seattle Opera Assn; Hadassah. 14: YP lit. 15: 3789 - 79th ave SE, Mercer Island Wa 98040.

FRIEDMAN, RUTH E (LAFFITTE). b NYC 3 Ap 17. 5: Mt Holyoke 34-38 (Hist, Pol Sci) AB; Columbia 38-39 (Dept of Pub Law) MA; So Conn State Col 63-68 (LS) MS. 6: Fr. 7: Agt & reservations clk Amer Airlines, NYC 40-42, instr (agts & reservations) 42-43; Bkmob asst Ferguson Lib, Stamford Conn 62; Child libn Darien Lib, Darien Conn 63-67, 68-; Child libn S Norwalk Lib, S Norwalk Conn 67-68. 9: ConnLA. 15: 373 Main st, New Canaan Ct 06840.

FRIEND, DAVID SCOTT. b Bloomington Ind 22 My 28. 4: Janice Gillespie. 5: Ind U 46-51, 54 (Music) BM; Fla State U 54-55, 57-58 MSLS; Washburn U 60-61 (Russ Lang). 6: Ger. 7: Investigator US Army CIC 51-53; Investigator US Army & US Civil Serv, Munich Germany 55-56; Asst head adult serv Topeka Pub Lib, Topeka an 58-59, Head adult serv 60-62, Admin asst & head fine arts 62-65; Head libn Frankford Pub Lib, Frankfort Ind 65-; Dir Pocatello Pub Lib & Gateway Reg Ref Ctr, Pocatello Idaho 67-. 8: Exec dir for Kan NLW 62; LSCA Title IV Adv Com (Idaho) 68; State dir (Indiana) ALA Off for Recr 67; IndLA (Recr Com 67); IdahoLA (Legisl and Lib Devel Coms 68-). 9: ALA; IdahoLA; PNLA. 10: Topeka Inst of Internat Rel; Topeka Human Rel Com; Clinton Co Hist Soc; Rotary; Pocatello Human Rel Coun. 13: Yes. 14: Acquis, ref. 15: 320 Flamingo dr, Pocatello In 83201.

FRIEND, MYRNA MARIE FLORENCE (CAMERON). b Weston Ontario Can 1 Jl 31. 5: McGill 49-53 BA, 59-61 (Eng) MA; UToronto 64-65 BLS. 6: Fr, Ger. 7: Bibliogr dept bk selection for research UToronto Lib 65-67, Ref libn Erindale College Lib 67-68, Hd pub serv erindale Col Lib 69-. 9: CanLA; Can Assn Col & Univ Libns. 10: Beta Phi Mu. 14: Acquis, ref, admin. 15: Erindale Col Lib Mississauga rd N, Clarkson Ont Can.

FRIES, MARY A. b Chehalis Wash 13 My 24. 5: Marylhurst Col 41-45 (Hist) BA; UWash 45-46 BA in Libnship. 6: Ger. 7: Asst libn Port Angeles Pub Lib, Port Angeles Wash 46-47; Libn I Tacoma Pub Lib, Tacoma Wash 47-52, Libn II 52-58, Head child dept 58-. 9: ALA; CatLA; PNLA; WashLA; Wash State Assn Sch Libns. 14: Child wk. 15: 620 No C, Tacoma Wash 98403.

FRIESE, EUGENE HUGH. b Everett Wash 11 Ap 33. 5: West Wash State Col 53-55 (Educ) BA Ed; UWash 58-61 (LS) ML. 6: Fr, Sp. 7: Tchr Highline Pub Schs, Seattle 55-56; Surv US Army, Germany 56-58; Highline Pub Schs, Seattle: Tchr 58-60, Libn 60-62, Lib Serv Coord 62-69. Lib serv coordinator 62-. 8: Consul Higher Educ Inst, Wash State U 68; Instr Central & West Wash State Cols Ext Div 62-69; Instr in Lib Sci, Seattle U, summers 63-69. 9: NEA-DAVI; ALA; ASCD; Wash State ASchL (Conf Chm). 10: Amer Folklore Soc; Puppeteers of Amer; Shakespeare Assn; Lib Guild. 11: John Cotton Dana Award 64. 13: Yes. 14: Sch lib serv, child lit, lib educ, curriculum, admin. 15: Instr Resources Ctr, 15701 Ambaum blvd SW, Seattle Wa 98166.

FRIESEN, SUSANNE (MARIE). b Highland Il 21 Je 34. 5: Goshen Col 52-56 (Hist) BA; IndU 57-63 (LS) MA. 7: Catlgr Goshen Pub Lib, Goshen Ind 57-, Asst libn 64-. 8: Organ Akron Area LA. 9: ALA; CathLA; OhioASchL; OhioLA (chm high sch sect 60-62 & 69-; Summit Co LA. 10: Beta Phi Mu; Ind Hist Soc. ; Sierra Club; Wilderness Soc; Nat Wildlife Fel2267 14: Catlg. 15: 503 N Riverside blvd, Goshen In 46526.

FRIESS, SISTER MARY BERNARD OP. b Akron Ohio 13 Je 1893. 5: Sisters Col summers 29-31 (Educ); Akron U 38 BS in Ed; Rosary Col 38-39 (LS) AB; Siena Heights summers 40-41 (Langs); Villanova summers 41-44 (Eng, Religion); John Carroll U 42-45 (Educ); UIll summers 47-50 MS in LS; John Carroll U 60-63 (Guidance); Ohio State Perm Elem Certif 22; Permanent High Sch Certif 50. 6: Ger. 7: Elem tchr Catholic schs, NJ, Ohio 09-38; Tchr-libn Our Lady of the Elms, Akron Ohio 39-41; Tchr-libn Sacred Heart Acad, Akron Ohio 41-46; Tchr, libn St Vincent High Sch, Akron Ohio 46-49; Tchr, libn, prin St Joseph Sch, Alliance Ohio 49-50; Tchr-libn St Vincent High Sch, Akron Ohio 50-63, Libn 63-. 8: Organ Akron Area LA. 9: ALA; CathLA; OhioASchL; OhioLA (chm High Sch Sect 60-62, 69-; Summit Co LA. 13: Yes. 14: Bk reviewing, catlg, teen-age bks. 15: 22 So Walnut st, Akron Oh 44303.

FRIEZE, WILLIAM SCOTT. b Charlotte NC 25 N 14. 4: Lola Anne Sparkman. 5: Davidson Col 33-37 (Psych) AB; Columbia 37-40, summer 41 BS in LS; Chicago summer 46 (LS). 6: Fr, Ger. 7: Stud asst Davidson Col Lib 35-37, Catlgr 37-45; US Army Spec Train Units (Cpl) 42-45; Admin asst Tampa Pub Lib, Tampa Fla 46-47, Dir of Libs 47-65, Asst Dir of Libs 65-. 9: ALA; SELA; FlaLA (pres 54). 10: Kiwanis Club. 13: Yes. 14: Admin, bldgs, catlg, automation. 15: 606 Marmora ave, Tampa Fla 33606.

FRINK, BARBARA WALKER (MRS). b Springfield Ill 28 Jl 31. 5: UMiami 49-53 (Home Econ) AB; Emory 67-68 MLib; Queens Col 69. 6: Fr. 7: Sec to chm dept of home econ UMiami (Coral Gables) 52-54, Instr evening div 53-54; Instr of Eng (contract with Laos govt agy), Vientiane Laos 58; Child libn Coral Gables Pub Lib, Coral Gables Fla 60-62; Owner bkkeeping and tax serv, Miami Fla 63-67; Child commun libn Pub Lib of Charlotte & Mecklenburg Co, Charlotte NC 69-. 9: ALA; SELA; NCLA. 10: Cum Laude, Mortrar Board; Kappa Pi. 14: Admin, tech processing, child serv. 15: 1348-B Green Oaks lane, charlotte NC 28205.

FRISBIE, ELIZABETH BRUCE (FUGAZZI). b Memphis Tenn 19 S 42. 4: Douglas William Frisbie. 5: UKy 60-64 (Eng) BA, 64-65 MSLS. 6: Sp. 7: Ref libn Cincinnati Pub Lib 66; Ref & docs asst UMinn (Minneapolis) 66-68; Docs libn MiamiU (Oxford Ohio) 68-. 14: Univ & col lib ref, US & for docs. 15: 315 N Campus ave, Oxford Oh 45056.

FRISCH, SISTER ANNE MARY AQUINAS OSB. b Kenton County Ky 25 Mr 31. 5: Villa Madonna Col 50-61 (Elem Educ); Xavier U summer 61; Villa Madonna Col 63-64 Lib Sci Certif; U Dayton & Mid Tenn State U summer 67. 7: Tchr Sisters of St Benedict, Covington Ky 50-69; Libn Blessed

Sacrament Elem Sch, Ft Mitchell 68-. 9: CathLA (Bd mem Cincinnati Unit); ALA; KyLA. 14: Elem lib wk. 15: 2500 Amsterdam rd, Covington Ky.

FRISTOE, ASHBY JACKSON. b Baltimore Md 14 Jl 18. 4: San Lucas. 5: Tulane 35-42 (Eng) BA; Rutgers 63-64 MLS. 6: Fr, Ger. 7: (Lt Col) USMC (Inf) 42-63; Wk/study stud asst Linden Pub Lib, Linden NJ 63-64; Hd ser sect UNC Lib (Chapel Hill) 64-65, Hd acquis dept 65-67, Chief tech processing 67-69; Assoc libn tech serv UHawaii Lib 69-. 8: Consul on tech serv to various libs. 9: ALA-RTSD (Acquis Sect Bkdealer-Lib Rel Com 69); SELA (chm Com on Interlib Policies 68); NCLA. 10: AAUP; Kiwanis Club; Beta Phi Mu. 12: Mng ed "Southeastern Librarian" (66-69). 14: Acquis, catlg, processing, admin. 15: UHawaii Lib 2550 The Mall, Honolulu Hi 96822.

FRITSCHE, JOHANNA E(LIZABETH). b NYC 5 F 15. 5: Hunter Col 32-36 (Lat) BA; Columbia 38-39 BS LS; ULausanne (Switzerland) summer 62 (Fr). 6: Fr, Ger. 7: Reviser Columbia U Sch of Lib Serv 39-40; Libn Notre Dame Col, SI NY 40-44; Ref asst US War Dept Pentagon Lib, Wash DC 44-46; Ind rel libn Union Carbide & Carbon Corp, NY 46-50; Ref asst Safeway Stores Inc, Oakland Cal 50-53; Sr libn music dept Oakland Pub Lib, Oakland Cal 53-62; Music libn Sonoma State Col 63-. 9: Music LA; CalLA; Amer Musicol Soc. 10: AAUP; Assn of Cal State Col Profs; Phi Beta Kappa. 14: Ref, catlg music. 15: 865 Sonoma ave, Santa Rosa Cal 95404.

FRITZ, EVELYN M. b Rossville Kan 11 My 06. 5: Brenau Col 23-27 BO, 28 BA; Emory 30-31 AB in LS; UMich summers 40-42 MA. 7: Asst libn Ga State Tchrs Col (Athens) 31-35; Asst catlg & clsf UGa 35-40, Head recatlg div 40-41, Order libn 41-46, Act dir of libs 46-47, Assoc dir of libs 47-. 9: ALA; SELA (Exec Bd & var coms); GaLA. 10: Delta Zeta; Zeta Phi Eta; Pi Gamma Mu. 15: 495 Milledge Terrace, Athens Ga 30601.

FRITZ, LUCILE. b Columbus Neb 20 S 12. 5: Lindenwood Col 30-31; Nebraska Wesleyan U 31-34 AB; UWis (Madison) 34-35 (LS) Diploma. 7: Order dept UIowa Lib (Iowa City) 36-37; Ref libn Lincoln Lib, Springfield Ill 37-58, Assoc ref libn 63-; Circ libn Columbus Pub Lib, Columbus Neb 58-63. 9: ALA; IllLA. 14: Ref. 15: 719 E Jackson, Springfield Il 62703.

FRITZ, RALPH A(BNER). b Atlantic Iowa 28 Je 1893. 4: Roletta Jolly. 5: State U Iowa 13-17 (Econ) AB, 19-20 (Sociol) MA, 26-28 (Educ) PhD; Peabody 42-43 BS in LS; UColo summer 22; Harvard summer 25. 7: Tchr rural schs, Cass County Iowa 12-13; US Army 129th Inf Capt) 17-19; Tchr phys educ, Douglas Wyo 20-21; Prin Roosevelt Sch, Colo 22; Sup schs Fountain, Colo 22-24; Instr Iowa State Tchrs Col summer 24; North High Sch, Des Moines Iowa 24-25; Coun Cong Church, Iowa City 25-26; Instr to Prof Kan State Tchrs COL (Pittsburg) 28-42; Libn 42-45; Dir Lib Educ Kutztown (Penn) State Tchrs Col 45-55; Lecturer Appalachian State Tchrs Col summers 48, 49; Lecturer UWyo summer 53; Lecturer in Lib Sci Emporia (Kan) State Tchrs Col 55-59; Asst libn Hastings Col 59-64; Lib consul Guilford Col 64-66; Asst Libn Davidson Co, Commun Col 66-67, Lib Consul 68-. 9: ALA-ACRL (Bldg Com); PennLA (chm Col & Ref Sect); NCLA; SELA. 10: Kiwanis Club; Phi Delta Kappa; Amer Educ Research Assn. 12: "An Evaluation of Two Special Purposes of Junior High Schoo: Economy of Time and Bridging the Gap (28). 13: Yes. 14: Lib org, admin. 15: PO Box 8003, Guilford Col Greensboro NC 27410.

FROEHLICH, REV CANICE G OFMCAP. b Pittsburgh 19 Ag 20. 5: St Fidelis Col 38-42 (Philos); Capuchin Col 43-47 (Theol); West Res summer 48 (Educ); Cath U 48-50 MS LS. 6: Lat. 7: Instr St Fidelis Sem 47-48; Instr, registrar, libn St Josephs Mil Acad, Hays Kan 50-. 9: CathLA; KanASchL; KanLA. 15: St Josephs Mil Acad, Hays Kan 67601.

FROELICH, ANNAH MARGARET S(MITH). b Weverton Md 11 S 03: 04: Dayton E Froelich. 5: Irving Col 20-24 (Fr) AB; Drexel 26-27 BS LS. 7: Tchr Jenks Twp High Sch, Marienville Penn 24-25; Tchr Frederick (Md) High Sch 25-26; Asst catlgr UNC 27-29; Catlgr Fla State Col 29-37; Libn Indian Valley Pub Lib, Telford Penn 65-66; Catlgr Norristown Pub Lib, Montgomery Co 66-. 14: Catlg. 15: 298 Leidy rd, Souderton Penn 18964.

FROELICH, SISTER MARY FIDELIS (IDA DOROTHY FROELICH). b Noble Twp Defiance Co Ohio 26 Ja 1898. 5: Immaculate Heart Col summers 36-42 (Educ) BA; UAriz summers 45-60 (Lib); Mira Costa Col summers 66-67. 6: Ger. 7: Libn: St Mary's High Sch, Phoenix 43-60, 63-64, 68-, Immaculata Lib, Dayton Ohio 61-62, Central Catholic High Sch, Lafayette Ind 62-63; Libn & tchr San Luis Rey Acad, San Luis Rey Cal 64-68. 8: Tchr- libn: St Mary's High Sch 22-60; San Luis Rey Acad 64-68. 9: ALA; CathLA; OhioSchLA. 12: "Pleased to Meet You", textbk for lib sci classes in High Sch (58); "Library Science Program for High School" (67). 14: Sch libs. 15: Immaculata Lib 4830 Salem ave, Dayton Oh 45416.

FROHLICH, JEAN DENISON. b Sheboygan Wis 24 Jl 14. 4: Philip Frohlich. 5: Northland Col 31-35 (Eng) BA; UDenver 62 (LS) MA. 7: Libn St Johns Sch of Nursing, Rapid City SD 58-60; Libn Rapid City High Sch, Rapid City SD 61-62; Libn Md State Dept of Health, Baltimore 62-63; Chief Libn Sinai Hosp Libs, Baltimore 63-. 8 Alternate rep of MedLA to the Interagency Coun on Lib Tools of Nursing 65-66. 9: MedLA (Interagency Coun on Lib Tools for Nursing 65-; Nursing Sect; sec 68, chm 69-); SLA (Baltimore Chap; Memb Chm 63-67, Exec Bd 68-69). 10: LWV. 14: Med & nursing libnship. 15: 3214 Blue Hill rd, Baltimore Md 21207.

FROHLICHER, RUTH G(ENS). b Mankato Minn 3 S 10. 4: Stephen V Frohlicher. 5: Carleton Col 29-30 (Liberal Arts); Riverside Lib Sch 31 (LS); Intermountain Union Col 31-32 (Liberal Arts); UMinn 62-63 (LS). 7: Lib asst Gt Falls (Mont) Pub Lib 28-42 (intermittent 7 years); Head Libn Univac Div Sperry Rand Corp St Paul 57-64; Head catlgr SD State Lib 64-65; Acquis head Gt Falls (Mont) Pub Lib 65-66, Tech Proc hd 66-67, Ref asst 67-. 9: ALA; SLA; MontLA; Gt Falls Area LA. 10: PEO. 14: Ref. 15: 1216 - 6th ave N, Great Falls Mont 59401.

FROMMEYER, L RONALD. b Cincinnati Ohio 2 S 35. 4: Patricia Miday. 5: Atheneum of Ohio 53-57 (Phil, Educ) BA, 57-60 (Theol); West Res 61-65 MSLS. 7: Personnel specialist (S/Sgt) USA Res, Ft Knox, Cleveland Ohio 60-66; Cuyahoga Co Pub Lib, Cleveland Ohio: Y-a specialist 60-64, Asst hd order dept 64-65, Hd order dept 65-66; Hd tech serv UAkron Lib 66-67; Wright State U Lib: Acquis libn 67-, Act hd libn 68-69. 9: ALA; CathLA; OhioLA. 14: Acquis, ser, admin. 15: 1732 Pershing blvd, Dayton Oh 45420.

FROMMHERZ, CARL J. b Chicago 7 Ja 11. 5: UChicago 33-38 (Pol Sci) AB; Columbia 38-41 BS in LS. 7: Catlgr US Naval Acad 42-43; Catlgr Forbes Lib, Northampton Mass 46-49; Catlgr UIll (Chicago Circle) 51-. 67; Hd Tech Proc Lib Lamar, Beaumont Tx 67-. 9: Libns in Tech Serv (chm Chicago Reg Group 60-61). 10: Assn for Research & Enlightenment; Amer Fed of Astrologers. 14: Catlg, tech proc admin. 15: Box 10277 Lamar Tech Sta, Beaumont Tx 77705.

FROSCHER, JEAN (LONGDON). b Daytona Beach Fla 1 O 24. 4: James L Froscher. 5: Fla State Col for Women 42-46 (Modern Langs) BA; Fla State U 47-48 (LS) MA. 6: Fr, Sp, Ger. 7: Catlgr UFla 48-51; Libn DreamLake Elem Sch, Apopka Fla 57-59; Catlgr Fresno State Col 63-64; Catlgr Polk Jr Col 65-. 9: NEA-ALA; FlaLA; SELA. 10: Fla Assn Pub Jr Cols (Blue Ribbon Task Force). 14: Catlg, rare bks. 15: 1315 Stately Oaks dr NW, Winter Haven Fl 33880.

FROST, ANACLARE. b Chicago 2 F 42. 5: Monmouth Col (Monmouth Ill) 59-63 (Sci) AB; West Res 63-64 MS in LS. 6: Fr, Ger, Russian. 7: Ser libn Med Lib Wayne State U 64-. 9: MedLA; ALA (Jr Mems RT); MichLA (sec-treas Jr Mems RT) 10: YWCA Bd of Mgt; Beta Phi Mu. 14: Ser, catlg, bibliog, union list. 15: 1300 Lafayette E apt 309, Detroit Mi 48207.

FROST, JOHN ELDRIDGE. b Eliot Me 13 Ja 17. 5: UMe 34-38 (Hist) BA; Berkeley 38-41 (Theol) STB; UNH 46-47 (Eng) MA; Columbia 47-48 (LS) BS; NYU 50-53 (Amer PhD. PD. 6: Fr, Sp. 7: Church wk Episcopal Church, Mass, NY 41-44; Lieut (chaplain) USNR 45-46; Asst libn Drew U 49; Catlgr & asst libn NYU 50-55, Libn University Heights Lib 55-60, Libn Gen U Lib 60-. 9: ALA. 10: Phi Beta Kappa; Columbia Sch Lib Sci Alumni (pres 65-66; Me Hist Soc; NYU Soc for the Libs (pres 67-68). 12: "Colonial Village (48); "Sarah Orne Jewett (60); Ed Libraries "Bulletin (60-). 13: Yes. 14: Admin, catlg. 15: Gen U Lib NYU Washington Square, New York NY 10003.

FRY, BERNARD M. b Bloomfield Ind 24 O 15. 4: June Foster. 5: IndU 33-39 (Govt) AB, AM; Catholic U 50-53 MS in LS; Amer U 58-59 (Pub Admin). 6: Fr. 7: Libn instr Mary Washington Col UVa 39-40; Chief bibliogr leg ref serv LC 40-42; Capt USA corps of engs 42-46; Chief libn Atomic Energy Comsn Wash DC 47-55; Dir div tech info serv 56-58; Deputy hd NSF off sci info serv 59-63; Dir US Dept of Commerce clearinghouse for sci & tech info 63-67; Dean grad lib sch IndU Bloomington 67-. 8: Mem Com on Sci & Tech

Info 65-67; Info Prog Adv Com, NIH 65-; Nat Adv Com Proj URBANDOC 65-; Sr Consul Can Govt Com on Sci & Tech Info 67-69; Chm Exec Com European Transl Ctr 65-67. 9: ASIS (pres 67); SLA (chm Sci Tech & Documentation Div; pres Wash Chap 54-55); IndLA. 10: Civitan Club. 11: Phi Delta Kappa. 12: Ed "Space Science and Technology" (63); Ed "Production and Use of Technical Reports" (55); "Library Organization and Management of Technical reports Literature" (53); Ed-in-Chief "Information Storage and Retrieval" (67-). 14: Lib netwks, spec libs, info sci & tech. 15: Grad Lib Sch Ind Univ, Bloomington In 47401.

FRY, DORATHY V (EBERLY). b Clay Twp Lancaster Co Pa 23 D 14. 4: Harold R Fry. 5: Millersville State Tchrs Col 31-33; Duke summer 34-36; Millersville State Col 61-62 BS in Ed; Drexel summer 63-67 MSLS. 6: Fr, Ger. 7: Elem tchr: Clay Twp Sch Dist 34-46, Warwick Twp John Beck 46-51, Ephrata Area Fetters 51-61; Elem libn Ephrata area Ephrata 62-. 8: Elementary library Coordinator - Ephrata Area 64-. 9: ALA; NEA; PennLA; Penn State EA; Ephrata Area EA (pres 68-69). 10: Delta Kappa Gamma; Alpha Beta Alpha; 4-H Club Leader; Girl Scout Leader; Penn Soc of Farm Women; Soc #3, Lancaster Co. 11: Outstanding 4-H Leader Award 58. 14: Storytelling, folklore. 15: Rte 1, Stevens Pa 17578.

FRY, JAMES WILSON. b Canton Ohio 8 My 39. 4: Mildred H Covey. 5: Ky Christian Col 62-65 (Relig); Milligan Col 65-66 (Hist) AB; Ohio State 66-68 (Hist); IndU MLS. 6: Greek. 7: Lib asst Ohio StateU (Columbia) 67-68; Grad asst (lib sci) IndU (Bloomington) 68-69; Ref dept Ohio StateU (Columbus) 69-. 9: ALA; OhioLA. 14: Ref, lib admin. 15: 2851 Pontiac, Columbus Oh 43211.

FRY, MARY EDITH. b Prosser Wash 26 N 10. 5: Goucher Col 30-34 (Chem) BS; Womens Med Col 34-36; Columbia 37-39 (LS) BS, 51 (LS) MS. 7: Circ asst Ore State Col 37-40; Tech asst Seattle Pub Lib 41-50, Head of tech dept 51-. 9: ALA; SLA; PNLA; WashLA. 15: Seattle Pub Lib 4th & Madison, Seattle Wa 98104.

FRY, O IRENE. b Torchlight Ky 23 Jl 13. 4: Harold E Fry. 5: West Ky Tchrs Col 32-36 (Geog) BS; West Mich U 56-58 (LS) MA. 7: Tchr & sch libn Pennfield Schs, Battle Creek Mich 52-57; Sch libn Springfield Schs, Battle Creek Mich 57-. 9: ALA; MichLA; MichASchL; NEA; MichEA. 14: Child & young adult bks. 15: 333 Briarwood lane, Battle Creek Mich 49015.

FRY, ROY H(ENRY). b Seattle 16 Je 31. 5: Seattle U 49, 59 (Hist); UWash 53-59 (Anthropology, Asiatic Studies) 2 BA degrees, 59 Provisional-Gen Tchg Certif; West Mich U 64-65 (LS) MA; Lower Columbia Col 64 (Geol); UIll summer 67 (LS). 6: Fr. 7: Commissaryman Third Class (Cook) US Naval Reserve 51-52; Libn & a-v dir Zillah Pub Schs, Zillah Wash 60-61; Libn Mark Morris High Sch, Longview Wash 61-64; Ref libn Loyola U (Chicago) 65-, Doc libn 66-. 8: Consul Jr High Sch Lib, Wash 63; Loyola U (Chicago); Tchg asst in Anthropology 66, Instr in Lib Sci, Nursg Prog for Disadvantaged Students summers 68, 69. 9: ALA; PNLA; IllLA. 10: AAUP; Amer Legion; Episcopal Soc for Cultural & Racial Unity; UWash Alumni Assn. 14: Ref, govt docs, lib instr. 15: 1209 W Sherwin ave, Chicago Il 60626.

FRY, STEPHEN MICHAEL. b Boise Idaho 5 Ja 41. 4: Frances (White) Fry. 5: UCal 9riverside) 59-64 (Mus) BA; Claremont Grad Sch 64-65 (Mus) MA; Cal State Col (LA) 65; USoCal 65- MLS. 6: Ger. 7: Lib intern Pomona Pub Lib, Pomona Cal 65-66; Libn & tchr Cal Inst for Women, Frontera Cal 66-67; Mus libn UCal (Riverside) 67-. 9: MusLA; Intl Assn Mus Libs; Amer Musicological Assn. 14: Mus ref, bibliog. 15: University Lib Univ of Cal, Riverside Ca 92507.

FRYAR, LINDA (SUZANNE). b Decatur Tex 30 S 42. 5: N Tex State U 60-63 (LS) BS. 07: Libn Burkburnett Jr High Sch, Burkburnett Tex 63-65; Libn-catlgr Sheppard AFB Tex 66-. 9: ALA. 14: Admin. 15: 1511 Nunneley apt 2B, Wichita Falls Tx 76306.

FRYDEN, FLOYD NORTON. b Detroit 18 S 37. 5: Chicago 54-58 (Liberal Arts) AB, 58-60 (LS) AM, 66. 6: Fr. 7: Lib asst UChicago Lib, Chicago 58-59; Libn I adult serv Chicago Pub Lib 59, 60; Libn UChicago Lab Schs 60-. 9: ALA. 10: Beta Phi Mu; Chicago Lib Club. 13: Yes. 14: Catlg. 15: 5423 S Harper ave, Chicago Il 60615.

FRYE, LARRY J. b Middletown Ind 21 Jl 41. 4: Barbara Jean Good. 5: Bethany Col (Bethany W Va) 59-63 (Relig) BA; Yale Divinity Sch 63-64; Rutgers 65-66 MLS. 7: Bibliog searcher order dept Yale U Lib 64-65; Stud ref dept asst Rutgers U Lib 65-66; Catlgr Millikin U 66-69; Dir libs Bethany Col (Bethany W Va) 69-. 9: ALA; WVaLA. 10: AAUP; ACLU; Religious Soc of Friends. 11: Woodrow Wilson Fellow, Yale Divinity Sch 64-64. 14: Catlg, clsf. 15: PO Box Bethany Col, Bethany W Va 26032.

FRYER, KAY B(URKHART). b Pittsburgh Penn 17 Ag 40. 5: Westminster Col 58-62 (Elem Educ) BS in Ed; UPittsburgh 62-63 MLS. 6: Sp. 7: Elem sch tchr Fox Chapel Area Schs, Pittsburgh Penn 61-62; Supv Human Rel Area Files UPittsburgh 62-63; LC: Catlgr Eng lang sect descr catlg div 63-66, Catlgr Eng sect shared catlg div 66-. 10: Beta Phi Mu. 14: Catlg. 15: 3313 Stanford st, Hyattsville Md 20783.

FUCHS, JAMES R. b Akron Ohio 12 O 22. 5: UAkron 40-43, 46-47 (Hist) BA; UAriz 47-48, 51-52 (Hist) MA. 7: Tank Platoon Ldr US Army, USA & Germany 43-46; Archivist Nat Archives, Wash DC 49-54; ARCHIVIST Nat Archives, Independence Mo 54-57; Archivist, Keeper of the Archives, Harry S Truman Lib, Independence Mo 57-62, Chief, oral hist proj 62-. 9: SAA (Fellow). 10: State Hist Soc of Mo. 12: "A History of Williams, Arizona, 1876- 1951 (53). 14: Ref, mss, oral hist, acquis (mss). 15: Harry S Truman Lib, Independence Mo 64051.

FUCHS, JOSEPH L. b Fulton NY 27 Ag 30. 4: Rose-Marie Staeudinger. 5: St Bernards (NY) 48-52 (Philos) BA; UTuebingen (Germany) 57-58 (Hist, Ancient & MA); Cath U 58-59 MS LS; Amer U 60-61 (Hist, Data Processing). 6: Ger. 7: Ref & CIRC LIBN Amer U 59-61; Sr catlgr NIH, Bethesda Md 61-62; Documentation Inc (NASA Sci & Tech Info Facility) Bethesda Md: Tech indexer 62-63, Vocabulary ed 63-64, Chief linear edit br 64-65, Head tech indexing br, Navy Automated R & D Info System, Naval Ship R&D Ctr, Wash DC 65-68; Chief of Doc Ctr of Alcohol Studies Rutgers 68-. 9: SLA; ASIS. 10: Beta Phi Mu; Phi Alpha Theta. 14: Info retrieval, catlg, automation of bibliog. 15: 11400 Georgetowne dr, Potomac Md.

FUCHSMAN, EDNA B. b NYC 3 Ja 18. 4: Charles H Fuchsman. 5: Hunter Col 35-39 (Biol) AB; West Res 61-64 MSLS. 7: Catlgr Shaker Heights Bd of Educ, Shaker Heights Ohio 64-. 9: ALA. 14: Catlg. 15: 3441 Washington blvd, Cleveland Heights Ohio 44118.

FUEGLEIN, ROBERT J. b Cleveland Ohio 10 Ag 29. 4: Rita S. 5: West Res 48-50, 53-55 9eng) AB; Columbia 55-56 (Eng); Pratt Inst 60-61 MLS. 7: US Army 51-53; Soc sci ref libn City Col Lib, NYC 61-. 14: Ref. 15: 255 W 84th st, New York NY 10024.

FUENTES, IDALIA (VILLARREAL). b Rio Grande City Tex 21 Mr 26. 4: Gilbert. 5: Tex Woman's U 48-51 (Sp) BA; Drexel 67-68 MS in LS. 6: Sp, Fr, Portug. 7: Tchr McA&en High Sch, McAllen Tex 51-53; Searcher reviser Subj orders libn, Asst supv, Supv Decimal clsf specialist LC 55-. 9: ALA. 10: AAUW. 14: Clsf. 15: 1932 Merrimac dr, Adelphi Md 20783.

FUKEI, (GLADYS) ARLENE (HARPER). b Frankfort Kan 18 N 20. 4: Budd S Fukei. 5: UWash 52-57 (Educ, Journalism, Far Eastern) BA, 62-63 (LS) MA. 6: Chinese. 7: Tchr Highline High Sch, Seattle 57-58; Libn South Mercer Jr High Sch, Mercer Island Wash 63-. 9: NEA-DAVI; WashStateASchL; WashEA. 10: Girl Scouts leader. 12: "East to Freedom," A Novel (64). 14: Sch libnship. , educ media. 15: 7503 18th NE, Seattle Wa 98115.

FULCHER, MRS JANE M. b Washington Penn 26 D 16. 4: John S Fulcher. 5: Wellesley 33-37 (Econ) AB; Catholic U 51-54 MSLS. 6: Fr, Ger, Sp. 7: Tchr Perkins Inst, Watertown Mass 38-42; Instr Harcum Jr Col 42-43; Lib asst Biol Sci Lib Brown U 46-48; Lib asst Beloit Col Lib 49-51; Lib asst Geo Washington U Hosp 51-53; Libn NLM 53-58; Med libn Washington Hosp Center, Wash DC 58-. 8: Lecturer in med libnship Dept of Lib Sci Catholic U 61-. 9: MedLA; ALA; SLA; ASIS. 12: "How to Use 'Index Medicus'; A Programmed Unit for Medical Students and Physicians" (67). 13: Yes. 14: Med libs, ref, catlg. 15: 18 East Hunting Towers, Alexandria Va 22314.

FULCHER, SARAH (ALMETTA) BUNN. b Mecklenburg County NC 6 Ag 41. 4: William Freddy Fulcher. 5: Appalachian State U 59-63 (LS, Hist) BS; Davidson summer 67, 68 (Art). 7: Libn; Cotswold Sch, Charlotte 63-66, Park View Sch, Mooresville NC 66-68, Chantilly Sch, Charlotte NC 68-. 9: ALA; NEA; Internat Reading Assn; NCEA. 10: Jr Civic League. 14: Child lit, reading guidance for ya. 15: 6313 Long Meadow rd, Charlootte NC 28210.

FULFORD, JANICE W(ALTON). b Rochester NY 19 Mr 29. 4: David Arnold Fulford. 5: Houghton Col 46-50 (Hist) AB; Syracuse 50-51 MS LS. 7: Asst libn Houghton Col 51-53; Ser asst Syracuse U Lib 53-54; Jr libn & sr libn Syracuse Pub Lib, Syracuse NY 54-. 9: ALA. 10: Civil Serv Employees Assn; NY Hist Assn; Pi Lambda Sigma. 15: 311 Hutchinson ave, Syracuse NY 13207.

FULLER, (J) AMY. b Kinnickinnic St Croix Co River Falls Wis 20 Je 04. 5: Wis State Col (River Falls) 20-34 (Eng) B of Ed; Wheaton Col (Wheaton Ill) 27-28; UNC 35-37 AB in LS. 6: Fr, Sp. 7: Asst libn Wis State U (River Falls) 24-. 15: Rt 2, River Falls Wis 54022.

FULLER, DONALD F. b San Francisco 13 O 25. 4: Susan Arthur. 5: San Diego State Col 40-42; (Pre-Dental);UCal(Berkeley) 42-43, 46-47 (Hist) AB; UCal 49 BLS. 6: Fr. 7: Master sgt US Army 43-46; Asst ref libn Ore State Col 49-50; Prin libn Alameda Co Lib, Hayward Cal 50-61; Asst co libn Santa Clara Co Lib, San Jose Cal 61-68; City libn, Santa Clara Cal 68-. 9: ALA; CalLA (Bd Dirs 65-66, Golden Gate Dist; sec 63-64, pres 65-66); Pub Lib Exce Central Cal (sec 64-65, v-pres 68-69, pres 69-70); Peninsula LA (pres 66-67). 10: Sierra Club; PTA. 14: Admin, child wk, ref. 15: 2635 Homestead rd, Santa Clara Ca 95051.

FULLER, DOROTHY CLYDE. b Atkins Va 14 Je 30. 5: Emory & Henry Col 48-52 (Hist) BA; UNC 59-61 MS LS. 7: Ext asst Va State Lib 61-63, Pub lib adv 63-67; Pub lib consul 67-. 9: ALA; VaLA (treas 68-69). 14: Pub libs, adult serv. 15: Va State Lib, Richmond Va 23219.

FULLER, ELIZABETH C(ARTER). b Wash DC 4 S 18. 5: Duke 35-39 (Eng) BA; UNC 42-43 BS LS. 7: Lib asst Wash-Lee High Sch, Arlington Va 39-42; Jr statistical clerk, US Dept of Labor, Wash DC summer 42; Post libn US Army, Army Air Field, Romulus Mich 44-46; Post libn Topeka Army Air Field, Topeka Mich 46-47; Base libn Hamilton Air Force Base, Cal 47-48; Staff libn Hq 10th Air Force, Ft Benjamin Harrison Ind & Selfridge Air Force Base Mich 48-51; Command Libn Hq Tactical Air Command, Langley Air Force Base Va 51-. 9: ALA; VaLA. 15: 137 Yeardley dr, Newport News Va 23601.

FULLER, GAYLIN S. b Cedar City Utah 19 O 38. 4: Edna Bingham Fuller. 5: Weber Jr Col 57-58 (Engnr); Utah State U 60-63 (Pol Sci) BS; Pratt 63-65 MLS. 6: Sp. 7: Lib trainee Brooklyn Pub Lib 63-65; Acquis Pratt summer 65; Act libn Ricks Col 65-, Libn 67-. 9: ALA; PNLA; IdahoLA (chm Col & Res Div 67-68, v-pres & pres-elect 69-70). 10: Beta Phi Mu. 14: Admin. 15: 148 S 1st st E, Rexburg Idaho 83440.

FULLER, JOYCE (MATTSON). b Klamath Falls Ore 30 My 28. 4: Harry L Fuller. 5: UOre 48-50 (Eng) BA; UWash 50-51 (LS) BS. 7: Bkmob libn Pierce Co Lib, Tacoma Wash 51-53; Bkmob libn Mid-Columbia Lib, Kennewick Wash 53-54; Act catlgr So Ore Col 55; Asst libn Pub Lib of Medford & Jackson Co, Medford Ore 56-57, Child libn A-V Record libn Pierce Co Lib, Tacoma Wash 62-. 10: Coun on Aging; Phi Beta Kappa. 14: A-v, child wk. 15: 510 S Cushman, Tacoma Wash 98405.

FULLER, MIRIAM (DE LOIS) MORRIS. b Big Stone Gap Va 1 F 33. 5: Swift Mem Jr Col 49-51 (Liberal Arts) Diploma; Va State Col 51-53 (LS) BS; Columbia summers 56, 57 (Bus Educ); Clinch Valley Col of UVa 60-61, 63 (Bus Educ); UIll summer 65 (LS), MSLS 68. 7: Tchr-libn Bland High Sch, Big Stone Gap Va 53-64; Libn Thompson- Litton Engnr Firm, Wise Va 65; Libn Appalachia High Sch, Appalachia Va 65-67; Libn Leal Sch, Urbana Ill 67-; Faculty UIll summer 69. 9: Va Tchrs Assn; IllLA; Urbana EA; Assn Childhood Educ. 10: AAUW; Leader Girl Scout Troop. 11: Shields-Howard Poetry Award, Va State Col. 12: "Literature Appreciation Kit" (69). 14: Admin. 15: 520 Fourth ave, Big Stone Gap Va 24219.

FULLER, MURIEL LAURA. b Holmen Wis 28 S 12. 5: La Crosse (Wis) State Tchrs Col 30-35 (Eng) B Ed; UWis 42-43 BLS; UMich 55-56 (Adult Educ) MA. 7: Eng tchr Birchwood (Wis) High Sch 35-37; Eng tchr Ontario (Wis) High Sch 38-42; Asst libn Pub Lib, La Crosse Wis 43-47, Head Libn 47-53; Pub lib consul State Lib, Lansing Mich 53-62; Lecturer UWis Lib Sch 62-63, Asst Prof & Chm Dept of Lib Sci, U Ext 63-66, Assoc Prof 66-. 8: Dir, Lib Commun Proj in Mich 55-60; Consul on ND libs, for State Lib Commsn & State Hist Soc 66. 9: ALA-ASD (pres 62-63);-LED (dir 68-); AEAUSA (Publ Com 66, mem Deleg Assembly sev sessions, sec Coun of State Assn); WisLA (pres 68-69); Adult Educ Assn Wis (dir 66-67). 10: AAUW; ACLU; Altrusa. 12: "Michigan Library Community Project: Report (60); "Tri-County Lib Study: Dickinson, Menominee, Delta Counties (Michigan) (60); Ed WisLA "Newsletter" 68-69. 13: Yes. 14: Lib educ, pub lib, adult serv. 15: 1347 N Wingra dr, Madison Wis 53715.

FULLER, ROBERT STEVENS. b Phila 15 Ag 30. 5: Maryville Col 48-52 (Physics) BS; Penn State 52-53 (Meteorology); UIll 59-61 (LS) MS. 7: Radar mechanic USAF (S/Sgt) 53-57; Publ engnr IBM Corp, Kingston NY 57-58; Libn I Lib of Hawaii, Honolulu 61-62; Lib asst Penn State Lib 65; Asst in catlg Catonsville Community Col 65-66; Libn I Kutztown State Col 66-. 9: ALA. 10: SAR; Allentown Museum; Allentown Symphony Assn; Commun Concert Assn; Broadway Theatre League of Lehigh Valley. 14: Catlg. 15: Apt Plaza E-3, Kutztown Pa 19530.

FULLERTON, HELEN J(ANE). b Howes Cave NY 10 N 09. 5: Cornell U 27-32 (Math) AB 31; (Physics) AM 32; Pratt Inst 35-36 BLS. 7: Asst Wells Col 36-37; Catlgr Antioch Col 37-39; Catlgr Brown U 39-43; Hd catlgr Peabody Inst 43-45; Catlgr Vassar Col 45-47; Hd catlgr 47-. 9: ALA; NYLA; NY Tech Serv Libns; Dutchess Co LA. 10: Phi Beta Kappa. 14: Catlg. 15: Vassar Col, Poughkeepsie NY 12601.

FULLERTON, MARGARET G(RAY). b Cedar Falls Iowa 1 N 04. 5: State Col Iowa 25 (Eng, Speech) BA; Columbia 30 (Speech, Educ) MA, 38 BS LS. 7: Ref libn Grinnell Col Lib 38-44; Libn Army Air Force Lib, Sioux Falls SD 44-45; Ref libn Des Moines (Iowa) Pub Lib 45-46; Catlgr U of No Iowa Lib 47-. 9: ALA; NEA; IowaLA; Iowa State EA. 10: AAUW; AAUP. 12: "Together We Sing," Follett Sch Music Ser (50, 52, 56, 63); "Discovering Music Together" (66, 67). 14: Catlg. 15: Univ of No Iowa Lib, Cedar Falls Ia 50613.

FULLERTON, SYLVIA JEAN. b NS Can 19 N 34. 5: Dalhousie 53-55 (Zool) BS; Columbia 58-59 (LS) MS. 6: Fr. 7: Lab tech Rockefeller Inst, NY 55-58, Lib asst 58-60; Catlgr NS Prov Lib, Halifax 60-61; Sci libn Dalhousie (NS) 61-. 9: CanLA; SLA; HalifaxLA; APLA; ALA. 14: Ref, bk sel & collections. 15: Dalhousie Univ Lib, Halifax NS Can.

FULMER, MARGARET. b Concordia Kan 3 Ag 07. 5: UNeb 29 (Liberal Arts) BA; UWs 30 (LS) diploma; Columbia summer 40; UDenver 53 (LS) MA. 7: Ref libn State Lib Commsn, Bismarck ND 30-33; Chief Libn Carnegie Lib, Hastings Neb 33-36; Chief Libn Parmly Billings Mem Lib, Billings Mont 36-44; Asst to Miss Julia Wright Merrill ALA 44-45; Chief Libn Great Falls Pub Lib, Great Falls Mont 45-52; Instr Lib Sch UMinn 52-55; Chief Libn Whittier Pub Lib, Whittier Cal 55-. 9: ALA; CalLA; Pub Lib Exec Assn So Cal. 10: AAUW; LWV. 13: Yes. 14: Pub lib development & standards, planning & legis, trustees, friends groups, pub lib admin, adult educ. 15: Whittier Pub Lib, 7344 So Washington ave, Whittier Ca 90602.

FULTON, ELIZABETH WATSON. b Pittsburgh Pa 13 N 35. 5: Wilson Col 53-57 (Eng) AB; Steubenville Bus Col 57-58 (Sec Sci) Certif; UPittsburgh 65-69 MLS. 6: Fr. 7: Tchr Steubenville Bus Col 58-63; Asst libn Nat Steel Corp Research Ctr, Weirton W Va 63-. 9: SLA; WVaLA. 14: Ref. 15: 405 Colonial dr Apt 33, Steubenville Oh 43952.

FULTON, JUNE MARIE (HUFF). b Berwyn Ill 26 My 43. 4: James F Fulton III. 5: UNC (Greensboro) 61-65 (Hist) BA; UNC (Chapel Hill) 66-67 MS in LS, Certif Grade I, MLA. 6: Ger. 7: Asst acquis libn UNC (Greensboro) 67-68; Ser catlgr UAla (Huntsville) 69-. 8: Comp med bibliog Dr EE Peacock UNC Med Sch (Chapel Hill) 67. 14: Bibliog. 15: 592 Eastbrook rd, Ridgewood NJ 07450.

FUNG, RUTH (WONG). b Honolulu 26 Ag 23. 4: George K F Fung. 5: UHawaii 40-46 (Educ) Ed B; Carnegie 47 BS in LS. 6: Eng. 7: Child libn Lib of Hawaii, Honolulu 47-49; Sch libn Dept of Educ, Honolulu 49-; Bkmob libn Lib of Hawaii, Honolulu 54; Summer sch libn San Mateo City Schs, San Mateo Cal summer 65; Sch libn Lincoln Sch Dept of Educ, Honolulu 59-. 8: Child libn Library/USA NY Worlds Fair 64. 9: NEA; ALA (Mem chm Hawaii Reg 47); CathLA; Hawaii LA (dir 62, 63; var coms & offs 48-57). 10: Associated Chinese U Womens Club (Honolulu); PTA; Delta Kappa Gamma. 13: Yes. 14: Sch libs, child wk. 15: 1350 Ala Moana blvd, Honolulu Hi 96814.

FUNK, CHARLES E(ARLE) JR. b Staten Island NY 22 O 13. 4: Alma Griswold. 5: Polytech Inst Brooklyn 45-50 (Chem) BS (Magna cum laude); Columbia 53-55 (LS) MS. 6: Ger. 7: Chem Amer Cyanamid C, Stanford Conn 36-50, Group leader Tech Info 51-65; Supv Dept of Planning Evaluation &Research Conn State Lib 65-. 9: SLA (Conn Valley Chap sec 63-64, pres 64-65, Bulletin 65-66, Pub Chm 67-69); ConnLA (sec 65-66, Procedures Chm 66-69); NELA (Regl Planning Com 66-69).

65-66). 10: Lib Group of SW Conn (chm 63-65); Conn Lib Found (co-incorporator & sec pr tem 65); Capitol Reg (Conn) Lib Study Com 67-69. 12: Co-author "Horsefeathers and Other Curious Words (58); Ed "Directory of Subject Strength in Connecticut Libraries" (68). 14: Ref, lib planning. 15: Conn State Lib, 231 Capitol ave, Hartford Ct 06115.

FUNK, ELIZABETH A. b Pottstown Pa 17 Ag 38. 4: James R Funk. 5: Juniata Col 60 (Hist, Pol Sci) BA; Drexel 64 (LS) MS. 7: Sr high libn Cumberland Valley Schs, Mechanicsburg Penn 61-62; Libn II Penn State Lib Harrisburg Penn 66-. 9: ALA; PennLA; Capital Area LA. 14: Child, ya wk, recr. 15: 1916 Columbia ave, Camp Hill Pa 17011.

FUNK, GRACE EMMOLINE (TOMLINSON). b Saskatoon Sask Can 20 Ap 24. 4: Jacob A Funk. 5: USask 42-45 (Eng) BA; UAlberta 45-46 Certif in Educ; UBC 66-67 BLS. 7: High sch tchr: Aulliwach Sch Dist, Agassiz BC 47-49, Armstrong Sch Dist, Armstrong BC 49-50; High sch tchr & libn: Enderly Sch Dist, Enderly BC 57-60, Sch Dist 23 Kelauna, Rutland BC 60-66; Elementary sch libn Sch Dist 23 Kelaung, Rutland BC 67-. 9: CanLA; ALA; BCSchLA (treas 65-66, record sec 68-69); BCLA; Assn BC Libns. 10: Can Col of Tchrs; BC Tchrs Fed. 14: Child lit. 15: RR #1, Lumby BC Can.

FUNK, MARY A(MELIA). b Littlestown Penn 13 My 04. 5: Shippensburg State Tchrs Col 20-22 (Hist, Eng) Teachers Certif; Simmons 24-27 (LS) BS; Columbia 32-33 (LS) MS. 6: Fr. 7: Prin Pleasantville High Sch, Alum Bank Penn 22-23; Tchr Richland Twp High Sch, Getstown Penn 23-24; Asst libn State Tchrs Col, Kutztown Penn 27-39; Asst libn Muhlenberg Col 39. 9: ALA; PennLA (chm Dist Lib Chap 51; sec Col Div 57). 10: AAUP; AAUW. 14: Ref. 15: 521 N Leh st, Allentown Pa 18104.

FUNK, RALPH H(AMILTON). b Holdenville Okla 7 My 31. 5: UOkla 49-54 (Eng) BA, 56-58 MS LS; Okla State U 65- (Computer Tech). 7: Tchr Marshall (Okla) Pub Sch 55-56; Asst ref dept UKan Lib 58-59, Asst head acquis dept 59-60; Documents libn Okla State Lib 60, Lgis ref libn 60-67; Act dir Okla Dept of Libs, Oklahoma City 68, Dir 68-. 9: AALL. 10: Okla Health & Welfare Assn. 12: ""Who is Who in the Oklahoma Legislature 29th (63-). 13: Yes. 14: Ref, admin. 15: 109 State Capitol, Oklahoma City Ok 73105.

FUNKE, ANNELIESE (MARCKWALD). b Strasbourg 6 Je 04. 5: U of Frankfort 22-24; Simmons 43 (LS) BS. 6: Ger, Fr. 7: Asst Schekenberg Bibliothek U of Frankfort 22-24; Catlgr of rare bks at bkdealers, Frankfurt, Vienna, Berlin 24-30; Asst Friends Hist Lib, Swarthmore Penn 40-41; Catlgr Carl Schurz Mem Found, Phila 42; Catlgr Cornell U 43-45; Sr catlgr Enoch Pratt Free Lib, Baltimore 45-48; Rare bk catlgr UIowa 48-. 9: ALA; IowaLA. 10: AAUW. 12: "The Ephrata Cloisters: An Annotated Bibliography, with Eugene E Doll (44). 13: Yes. 14: Catlg, rare bks. 15: 400 N Clinton st, Iowa City Iowa 52240.

FUNKHOUSER, RICHARD LEWIS. b Lafayette Ind 13 Ap 34. 5: IndU 52-56 (Soc Sci) BS Ed, 56-57 (LS) MA. 7: Asst ref unit Purdue U Libs 57-58, Engring libn 58-. 8: Vis Prof Indian Inst of Tech, Kanpur, India 64-66. 9: SLA (Ind Chap treas 67-69); Amer Soc Engrg Educ (Engrg Sch Libs Div: v-pres Sect East 67-68); ALA. 14: Ref. 15: Box 86 RR 3, Delphi In 46923.

FURBUR, MARTHA (KRUSE). b Crosby Minn 19 Ap 14. 4: Roger Anson Furbur. 5: Col St Scholastica (Duluth) 63-64 (Liberal Arts); Kan City Jr Col 34-35 (Liberal Arts) AA; UMinn 35-37 (Liberal Arts) BA; Kans State Tchrs Col 37-38 (LS) Certif. 6: Fr. 7: Catlgr Med Lib Mercy Hosp, Kansas City Mo summer 37; Ref libn DrakeU 38-41; Supv of files No Pump Co (US Naval Ordnance) Minneapolis 41-43; Hd libn Kirksville Col of Osteopathy & Surgery 44-46; Asst (city desk) Super Value Stores Inc, Minneapolis 47-59; Hd catlgr Orange Co Pub Lib, Orange Cal 62-. 8: Resident in med lib wk Orleans Parish Med Soc, New Orleans 43-44. 9: CalLA; Orange CoLA; So Cal Tech "rocesser Group (Memb Group; Nominating Com). 10: Santa Ana Amer Legion Aux; VFW Aux. 14: Catlg, ref. 15: 1413 N Spurgeon #5, Santa Ana Ca 92701.

FURLONG, PATRICIA. b Trenton Miss 27 S 44. 5: Trenton Jr Col 62-64 AA; NW Mo State Col 64-66 (Elem Educ) BS in Ed; UMich 66-67 (LS) MA. 6: Sp. 7: Clk Grundy Co Jewett norris Lib, Trenton Mo 62-64; Child libn Daniel Boone Reg Lib, Fulton Mo 67-. 9: ALA; MoLA. 10: AAUW. 14: Child & yp serv. 15: Churchill Manor apt 1 Rte 2, Fulton Mo 65251.

FURLONG, ROBERT E. b Chicago 21 Ap 41. 4: Eileen B McNamara. 5: Bradley U 59-63 (Chem) AB; UIll 63-65 (LS) MS. 6: Ger, Sp. 7: Lib asst UIll (Urbana) 63-65; Br libn Fresno Co Free Lib, Fresno Cal 65-. 67; Libn Queen of the Valley High Sch Lib, Fresno Cal 66-68; Reg br libn III Fresno Co Free Lib 67-68; Head tech serv Riverside Co Free Lib 68-. 9: ALA (sec Staff Assn RT 67-); CalLA (sec Pub Lib Sect 66-67; Fin & Regist Chm 1967 Conv). 10: Fresno Co (Cal) Free Lib Staff Assn. 14: Pub serv, tech serv, admin. 15: 619 Massachusetts ave, Riverside Ca 92507.

FURNESS, ANNE WINSLOW. b Boston 24 D 26. 5: Bryn Mawr 44-47 (Gk); Boston U 47-50 (Eng) AB; Simmons 50-51 (LS) MS. 6: Fr. 7: Asst libn Wheelock Col 52-54; Jr lib asst W E Fernald Sta Sch, Waverley Mass 54-56; Catlgr Post Lib, Ft Devens Mass 56-59; Jr libn catlg dept White Plains Pub Lib, White Plains NY 59-60; Indexer "Readers Guide, H W Wilson Co, NYC 62-. 9: ALA; NY Tech Libns; NY Lib Club. 10: Brookline (Mass) Hist Soc; Boston Atheneum; All Souls Players (NY); Country Dance Soc, Boston; Scottish Country Dance Soc; Footlight Club, Boston; NE Folk Festival Assn. 14: Catlg. 15: 4 Channing cir, Cambridge Mass 02138.

FURNESS, REGINALD JEREMIAH. b Burlington Vt 7 Ap 28. 4: Blanche G Proulx. 5: Boston U 48-50 AA; Boston U Sch of Law 50-52 LLB. 6: Fr, Ital. 7: Sl/c (Qm) US Navy 45-47; Head stud libn Boston U Sch of Law 52-54, Asst law libn 54-68, Chief libn 68-. 9: AALL. 14: Ref. 15: 765 Commonwealth ave, Boston Ma 02215.12331

FURNEY, GRACE MARY I(NDIVINO). b Rochester NY 3 Ap 13. 4: Anthony J Furney. 5: SUNY(Geneseo) 30-33 (Educ) Teaching Certif, summer 32, 33 (LS); UVa Ext 52-53 (Amer Hist). 6: Ital, Fr. 7: Libn Rochester Collegiate Center Rochester NY 33-36; Store mgr Wholesale Candy & Tobacco Co, Rochester NY 36-37; Saleswoman Avon Products Inc, Rochester NY 39-41; Clerk Dept of the Army, Wash DC 42-44, Ser asst 44-51; Libn acquis Off of Price Stabilization, Wash DC 51-53; Ref libn Army Map Serv, Wash DC 53-60; Asst chief Lib Joint Atomic Info Exch Group, Wash DC 60-68, Chief libn 68-. 9: SLA (Memb Com 56-57, sec 57-58). 10: Shenandoah Retreat Golf & Country Club; Sleepy Hollow Woods Civic Assn; Travel Club. 14: Catlg, ref, acquis. 15: 3616 Sprucedale dr, Annandale Va 22003.

FURNIVAL, ELEANOR K (WARD). b NYC 3 Jl 69. 5: Brothers Col DrewU 51-61 (Relig) BA; Union Theol Sem 61-62 (Theol); Columbia Sch of lib serv 68-69 BS. 6: Fr. 7: Catlg dept Vassar Col Lib 66-. 9: ALA. 10: Pi Gamma Mu; Fellowship of St Alban & St Sergius. 14: Catlg, theol libnship. 15: Hoofprint rd, Millbrook NY 12545.

FURR, MARGARET (LEE) HODGES. b Roanoke Va 12 S 43. 4: Richard Michael Furr. 5: William & Mary 61-65 (Hist) AB; UNC 66-67m 68 MS in LS; UTenn 68-69. 7: Clk Sidney's, Roanoke Va summers 62 & 63; Lib asst Roanoke Pub Lib, Roanoke Va 65-66; Ref asst Pub Lib of Knoxville & Knox Co, Knoxville Tenn 67-. 9: TennLA. 10: Pi Delta Epsilon; Jr League. 14: Ref. 15: 2911 Crystal Spring ave SW, Roanoke Va 24014.

FURROW, BARBARA BESSMER (KLEIN). b Wyandotte Mich 27 My 41. 4: Roland M Furrow II. 5: Kalamazoo Col 59-63 (Eng, Biol) BA; Mich U (Ann Arbor) 63-64 (Nursing), 64-65 mals. 6: Fr. 7: Child libn Lake Forest Pub Lib, Lake Forest Ill 65-66; Adv & catlgr st Mary's Sch, Lake Forest Ill 66; Catlg libn Lake Forest Col 66-67; Asst to libn Hastings Pub Lib, Hastings Mich 67; Catlg libn hd of LC sect Mich State U (E Lansing) 67-. 9: ALA; LACONI (Child Libns Div); MichLA. 10: AAUW. 14: Catlg. 15: 2065 hamiltno st, Holt Mi 48842.

FURST, FLORENCE W(OLOVITCH). b Phila 25 My 16. 4: Arthur Furst. 5: Brooklyn Col 33-34; Los Angeles Jr Col 35-36; UCLA 36-38 (Fr) BA; UCal (Berkeley) 38-39 Certif of Libnship. 6: Fr, Ger. 7: Jr libn Oakland Pub Lib, Oakland Cal 39; Catlgr Contra Costa Co Lib, Martinez Cal 39-40, Ref libn 4041; Catlgr Palo Alto Pub Lib, Palo Alto Cal 57-58; Chem libn Swain Lib of Chem, Stanford U 59-. 9: ALA; CalLA. 10: Humanist Soc. 14: Catlg, acquis, sci ref. 15: Swain Lib of Chem, Stanford Univ, Stanford Cal 94305.

FURUYA, MRS NATSUKO (YOSHIMURA). b Kobe Japan 26 My 36. 4: Zenbei Furuya. 5: Kobe Col (Kobe Japan) 55-57 (Eng); Rockford Col 57-59 (Amer Lit) BA; UChicago 59-62 (LS) MA. 6: Chinese, Fr, Ger, Japanese. 7: Grad stud asst Far East Lib, UChicago 59-61, Catlgr 61-62; Catlgr York U Lib, (Toronto) 62-65, Act head catlg dept 65-67, Hd catlg dept 67-. 9: ALA; CanLA. 13: Yes. 14: Catlg, clsf, data processing. 15: 62 Grandview ave, Willowdale Ont Can.

FUSARO, JANIECE (BARRE). b Detroit Mich 7 F 25. 4: Ramon Michael Fusaro. 5: UMinn 42-46 (Chem) BA, 47-49 (Ger Lit) MA, 51-53 BSLS, 68 (Ger Lit) PhD; Middlebury Col summer 53 (Ger). 6: Ger, Fr, Danish. 7: UMinn (Minneapolis): Tchg asst Ger dept 48-51, Libn (acquis) 51-53; Prof Col of St Catherine 51-53; Libn Anoka-Ramsey State Jr Col 65-. 8: Consul Golden Valley Luth Col; Memb Adv Com for Lib Netwk, State Dept of Educ Minn; Mem Adv Com for Lib Survey, Minn High Educ Coord Comsn; Consul appalachian U Jr Col Libnship Inst. 9: ALA-ACRL (chm N Central Reg, Spec Proj Com 68-70); mem Bibliog Com ACRL-JCLS 68-70; NEA-DAVI-PEMS (Com for Para-prof Media Specs 69-70); MinnLA; Memb Com Chm 68. 10: CLU; Minn Tchrs of German; Fine Arts Society; Alpha Lamda Psi; Jr Col Fac Assn. 11: Minn Libn of the Year 68. 14: Communications, ref. 15: 3108 36th ave NE, Minneapolis Mn 55418.

FUSSLER, HERMAN HOWE. b Phila 15 My 14. 4: Gladys F Otten. 5: UNC 31-35 (Mat) AB, 35-36 AB LS; UChicago 38-41 (LS) MA, 46-48 (LS) PhD. 6: FR. 7: Asst sci & tech div NY Pub Lib 36; UChicago Lib: Head deptphoto reprod 36-46, Sci libn 43-47, Asst dir 47, assoc dir 47-48, Dir 48-. 8: Instr UChicago Grad Lib Sch 42-44, Asst Prof 44-48, Prof 48; Acting Dean, Grad Sch UChicago 61-3; Asst dir Sci & Tech Info Div, Metallurg Proj, Manhatten Proj 42-45; Head, demonstration of Microphotography, Paris Int Exposition 37; Consul: Ford Found, on Maison Des Sciences De LHomme, Paris 60-63; Ford Found, on Univ Sao Paulo, Brazil 62; on Libs to Chancellor of the State Cols of Cal 63; on UCal Lib Research Inst 64; Mem Amer Coun of Learned Socs (Com on Research Libs 66-67); Mem Bd of Regents NLM 63-67; Mem Nat Adv Commsn on Libs 66-67. 9: ALA (Coun 56-59, chm &/or mem var coms);-ACRL (var com assignments); ASIS; Center for Research Libs (past chm Bd Dirs); ARL (Bd dirs 62-64); AAAS (Publs Com 64-68). 10: Caxton Clu, Quadrangle Club (UChcago); AAAS (Publ Com 64-66). 11: ALA; Melvil Dewey Medal 54. 12: "Photographic Reproduction for Libraries (42); ed "Library Buildings for Library Servce (47); ed "The Function of the Library in the Modern College (54); Co-author "Patterns in the Use of Books in Large Research Libraries (61-69). 13: Yes. 14: Research lib resources & use; lib bldgs. 15: Univ of Chicago Lib, 1116 E 59th st, Chicago Il 60637.

FUZ, GEORGE C. b Plock Poland 5 Ja 25. 4: Greta M Mulder. 5: The Netherlands Sch of Econ (Rotterdam) 49-51 MA, PhD; UCLA 62-63 MLS. 6: Dutch, Ger, Polish, Fr, Russian, Czech, S Afrikans. 7: Allied Armed Forces 44-45; Banking & finance, US, Can & Europe; Trainee Los Angeles Co Pub Lib, Los Angeles 62-63; Catlgr & tr Los Angeles C Law Lib, Los Angeles 63-64; Asst Prof Loyala U (Los Angeles) 63-64; Catlgr Los Angeles State Col 65-66; Sr research analyst Blue Cross of So Cal 64-; Acquis libn & catlgr USoCal Med Ctr 67-. 9: ALA; Amer Econ Assn; Royal Econ Soc. 10: UCal Lib Schs Alumni Assn; Friends of the Royal Lib ofThe Hague (Neth). 12: "Welfare Economics in English Utopias from Francis Bacon to Adam Smith (52). 13: Yes. 14: Catlg, bk sel, rare bks, law, econ, med acquis. 15: 1525 N Sanborn ave, Los Angeles 90027.

FYFE, JANET (HUNTER). b Blantyre Scotland 29 Ap 29. 5: UEdinburgh 47-50 (Eng) MA; Scottish Col of Com 50-51; Northwestern Polytech (Lond); Ealing Tech Col (Lond) 56 ALA, 59 FLA. 6: Ital, Fr, Ger. 7: Lib asst Willesden Pub Libs, Willesden London 53-54; Br libn Osterley br Heston & Isleworth Pub Libs 55-57; Sr asst libn USt Andrews, St Andrews Fife Scotland 57-63; Ref libn USask Regina campus lib 63-65; Co-ord br libs USask Murray Memorial Lib 65-66; Hd bibliog dept 66-. 12: Co-comp "Directory of Special Collections in Canadian Libraries" 2 v, CanLA (68); Ed "Saskatchewan Library" 66-. 14: Bibliog, bk sel, rare bks. 15: 1761 Prince of Wales ave, Saskatoon Sask Can.

G

GABBAY, SUSAN (DAVIS). b Charlottesville Va 3 Jl 30. 4: Jacob N Gabbay. 5: IndU 47-51 (Fr) AB; Sy 47-51 (Fr) AB; Syracuse 65-66 MSLS. 6: Fr. 7: Clk a-v ctr IndU 50-51; Trainee Beauchamp Br Syracuse Pub Lib Syracuse NY 62-64; Trainee Liverpool Pub Lib, liverpool NY 65-66, Child libn 66-. 9: NYLA. 10: Phi Beta Kappa; Beta Phi Mu. 14: Child serv. 15: 6 Bayberry cir E, Liverpool NY 13088.

GABEL, (EMMA) MARGARET. b Perkasie Penn 10 Ag 28. 5: State Col (Kutztown Penn) 46-50 (L) BS in Ed; Syracuse 53-57 (LS) MS. 7: Libn Morrisville Sr High Sch, Morrisville Penn 50-52; Asst libn Susquehanna U 52-56; Asst libn State Col (Indiana Penn) 56-66; Hd catlgr & asst to dir Elizabethtown Col 66-. 9: ALA-ACRL; NEA; PennLA; Lancaster Co LA; Assn Higher Educ. 10: AAUP; Kappa Delta Pi; Delta Kappa Gamma; Pi Lambda Sigma; Beta Phi Mu. 14: Catlg. 15: 226 E Orange st apt B, Elizabethtown Pa 17022.

GABRIEL, SISTER MARY CAROL OP. b Brooklyn NY 10 D 22. 5: St Johns Tchrs Col 45-50 (Eng) BA; St Johns U 53-56 MLS. 7: Elem tchr Presentation Sch, Jamaica NY 43-55; Tchr & libn St Michaels High Sch, Brooklyn NY 55-61; Libn tchr St Agnes High Sch, Rockville Centre NY 61-67, IMC coord 67-68; Period libn, Molloy Col 68-. 9: ALA; CathLA (Convention Com, Nomin Com; sec-treas Brooklyn-LI Unit); NEA; NYLA; Nassau Co LA; Metro Cath Col LA. 10: Confraternity of Chrstian Doctrine; Nat Bus Assn; Columbia Year Bk Moderators. 13: Yes. 14: Ya. 15: N Village ave, Rockville Centre NY 11570.

GABRIELSON, ERNA E (HINRICHS). b St Joseph Ill 6 F 28. 4: Glen F Gabrielson. 5: Wartburg Col 45-49 (Eng, Gen Sci) BA; UIll 49-50 (LS); UWash 59-61 MSLS. 6: Ger. 7: Boeing Vo Aerospace Div, Seattle: Indexer 50-57, Hd indexer 57-68, Chief catlgr 68-. 9: ASIS; SLA (PNW Chap: pres-elect 68-69, pres 69-70. 10: AAUW; Beta Phi Mu. 14: Indexing, thesauri develop, info retrieval, systems analysis. 15: Boeing Co aerospace Lib, PO Box 3999, Seattle Wa 98124.

GABRIELSON, ORLEN NELS. b Valley Wis 13 Mr 38. 5: Modesto Jr Col 63-65; Stanislaus State Col 65-67 (Hist) BA; UCal (Berkeley) 67-68 MLS. 6: Fr, Ger. 7: Catlg libn Stanislaus State Col 68-. 9: ALA; Org Amer Histns; CalLA. 10: Cal Col & Univ Fac Assn. 14: Catlg, bk selection, fine printing. 15: 1608 N Rosemore ave, Modesto Ca 95351.

GAENSBAUER, ENA (MARJORIE) (MURPHY). b Charlottetown PEI Can 23 S 32. 4: Alfred Gaensbauer. 5: St Dunstan's U 50-54 (Hist) BA; UToronto 56-57 BLS. 7: Lib asst PEI Reg Libs, Charlottetown Csn 54-56, Asst libn 57-58; Child libn Edmonton Pub Lib, Edmonton Alberta Can 59, Br libn 60-61; Ref libn UBC Lib humanities div, 61-62, Ref libn sci div 63-64; Gen libn Vancouver Pub Lib, Vancouver Can 69-. 9: ALA; CanLA; BCLA. 14: Ref, child. 15: 3461 W 12th ave, Vancouver 8 BC Can.

GAERTNER, DONELL J. b St Louis 30 S 32. 4: Darlene Oberbeck. 5: Wash U (St Louis) 50-54 (Econ) AB; UIll 54-55 MLS. 7: US Army Anti-Aircraft Artillery (1st Lt) 55-57; Admin asst St Louis County Lib, St Louis County 57-63, Asst dir 63-68, Dir 68-. 9: ALA; SLA; MoLA (pres 64-65). 10: Beta Phi Mu. 14: Admin. 15: 1640 So Linbergh blvd, St Louis Mo 63131.

GAFFNEY, HELEN AGNES. b Clayville NY 19 Jl 05. 5: Syracuse U summers 39, 40; Catholic U summer 41; UBuffalo 39-42 (Eng) BA; Columbia 42-43 (LS) BS. 7: Ref libn Hamilton Col Lib 43-53; Ref asst Utica Pub Lib, Utica NY 54-55; Dir of Lib Mohawk Valley Tech Inst, Utica NY 55-59; Utica Pub Lib, Utica NY: Ref asst 59-60, Head child room 61-64, Head catlg dept 64-68; Catlgr Miami U Oxford Ohio 69-. 9: ALA; OhioLA& Central NY Libns Assn. 10: AAUW; Delta Kappa Gamma; Altrusa Internat. 13: Yes. 14: Catlg, ref. 15: 210 S Campus ave, Oxford Oh 45056.

GAGEN, CYNTHIA ANN. b NYC. 5: Columbia 58-61 (Eng Lit) BS, 63-67 (Admin & Ref) MLS (cum laude). 6: Sp, Ital, Fr, Lat. 7: Asst libn (ref) Tchrs Col Lib, NYC 58-60; Libn Crowell Collier Educ Corp, NYC 61-66; Deputy dir & libn Collier's Ref Serv, NYC 66; Chief corp libn Crowell Collier & Macmillan, NYC 66-. 8: Free-lance research assignments. 9: ASIS; SLA. 10: Beta Phi Mu. 12: Contrib "Merits Students encyclopedia," "Collier's Encyclopedia." 13: Yes. 14: Admin, research, lib facilities planning. 15: 306 E 96th st, New York NY 10028.

GAGLIARDI, JOAN COSGROVE. b New Haven Conn 23 F 40. 4: Alfred P Gagliardi. 5: Salve Regina Col 57-61 (Eng) AB; So Conn State Col 61-64 (LS) MS. 6: Fr. 7: Sch libn Washington Jr High Sch, Meriden Conn 63-. 14: Wk with child, catlg. 15: 47 Kensington ave, New Britain Ct 06051.

GAGNE, GERARD J. b Thompson Conn 5 Ja 22. 4: Lorraine Raboin. 5: Assumption Col (Worcester Mass) 65 (Educ) BA; UPittsburgh 65- (LS); Simmons (LS). 6: Fr. 7: Manager Hilary House Bksellers, Spencer Mass 48-58; Assoc libn Assumption Col Lib (Worcester Mass) 58-66, Dir 66-. 8: Consul for Mallet Lib Nion St Jean Baptiste d'Amerique Woonsocket RI. 9: ALA; CathLA; NELA; MassLA; Worcester Area Coop Libns; BSA; NELA. 10: Friends of Worcester Free Pub Lib; AAUP;

Rotary Internat; Beta Phi Mu. 13: Yes. 14: Admin, ref, bibliog. 15: 29 Clark st, Spencer Mass.

GAGNE, (DOROTHY) JOAN. b Hamilton Ont Can 8 D 23. 4: Raymnd Clovis Gagne. 5: Toronto 41-45 (Modern Hist) BA; Ontario Col of Educ 45-46 (High Sch Spec) Certif in Hist; McGill 63-64 BLS, 66-68 MLS. 6: Eng, Fr. 7: High sch Tchr, Chapleau Ont 46-47; High sch tchr, Dundalk Ont 47-48; High sch tchr Cochrane Ont 50-52; High sch tchr Trenton Ont 60-62; High sch tchr Eastview Ont 62-63; Catlgr Macdonald Col Lib (Ste Anne de Bellevue Que) 64-65, Order libn 65-66; Supv processing sect catlg dept McLennan Lib McGill 67-. 9: CanLA. 14: Catlg, acquis. 15: 1226 Lajoie ave, Outremont Que Can.

GAGNON, RAYMONDE. b St Francois Montmagny P Que Can 19 Ag 39. 5: Laval U 61 BA; UMontreal 62 BLS. 6: Fr. 7: Catlgr Ottawa Pub Lib, Ottawa Ont Can 62-. 9: Lib Assn of Ottawa. 14: Catlg. 15: 13 Vaudrevil, Hull P Quebec Can.

GAHAGAN, STEVEN W JR. b New Orleans 8 Mr 27. 5: LSU 54-58 (Eng) BA, 62-63 (LS) MS. 6: Fr, Sp. 7: Lib asst New Orleans Pub Lib summers 45, 46, 47-50; Med libn US Army Hosp Camp Chaffee Ark (Sgt) 50-53; Br libn & asst Jefferson Parish Pub Lib, Metairie La 54-56, Act br lib 57; Lib trainee LSU Lib 62-63; Ser & acquis libn U of the South 63-65; Asst libn & Asst Prof Francis T Nicholls State Col 65-. 9: ALA; La State LA. 10: Alpha Beta Alpha; Beta Phi Mu. 14: Ref, ser, acquis. 15: RFD Rte 2, Box 502, Thibodaux La 70301.

GAHRAN, ROBERT AUGUSTUS. b Albany NY 25 Jl 14. 4: Hazel Ward. 5: Hamilton Col 34-36; Pratt 47-48 (LS) . 6: Fr. 7: Army libn 96th Coast Art (Cpl), Hilo Hawaii 42-44; Army libn USA-4th Div (T/Sgt), Kadina Okinawa 45; Lib aide Brooklyn Pub Lib 45-47; Period libn Lib of Hawaii, Honolulu 47-54; Br libn Kapaa Br Kauai Pub Lib, Kaaa Kauai 55-57; Asst libn Kauai Pub Lib, Lihue Kauai 57-63; Asst libn Crosby Lib, Gonzaga U 63-. 9: CathLA; ALA; Hawaii LA; PNLA; Wash State LA. 14: Acquis, ref, rare bks, Hawaiiana. 15: Crosby Lib Gonzaga U, Spokane Wa 99202.

GAINES, ABNER J. b Atlantic City NJ 31 Mr 23. 4: Rosalyn Berenson. 5: UWis 40-43 (Hist); UMich 43-44 (Hist) AB; Columbia 46-47 BSLS; UPenn 48-51 (Hist) MA. 6: Fr, Ger. 7: (Cpl) US Marine Corps Reserve 43-46; Sr libn NJ State Lib 47-50, Ref libn 50-51; Libn S Asia Reg Studies Lib UPenn 52-57; Bibliog Temple U 58-63; Assoc libn URI 63-. 8: RI Governor's Com to Revise Lib Legisl 66-67; Instr in Lib Sci; URI Ext Div 66, Grad Lib Sch 68; Bibliog consul, Johnson & Wales Bus Col, Providence 68. 9: ALA; RILA (Exec Bd 68-69). 10: ACLU; Amer Acad Polit & Soc Sci; Ctr for the Study of Democ Instns; Columbia Alum Assn. 13: Yes. 14: Ref, acquis, admin. 15: 98 Biscuit City rd, Kingston RI 02881.

GAINES, ERVIN J. b NYC 8 D 16. 4: Martha Zirbel. 5: Columbia 36-42 (Eng) BS, 46-47 (Eng) MA, 47-52 (Lit) PhD. 7: Officer (Lt jg) US Navy 43-46; Instr Columbia U 46-53; Chief of train Radio Liberation Munich Germany 53-56; Train dir Teleregister Corp, Stamford Conn 56-57; Consul Elmer Davis & Assoc, NYC 57-58; Asst dir Boston Pub Lib 58-64; Dir Minneapolis Pub Lib 64-. 8: Consul Macalester Col; lectr Lib Schl UWis, UMinn. 9: ALA (Coun); MinnLA (Legisl Chm). 10: CLU; Hennepin Co Respir Diseases Assn; Hennepin Co Hist Soc. 13: Yes. 14: Pub lib admin. 15: 1813 Girard ave S, Minneapolis Mn 55403.

GAINES, JAMES E JR. b Dalton Ga 21 F 38. 4: Sally Martin. 5: Emory 57-61 (Eng Lit) BA, 62-64 (LS) ML. 6: Fr. 7: Tchr Marist Col High Sch, Atlanta 61-62; Circ asst Emory U Lib 62-63, Acquis asst 63-64; Serv libn UCincinnati Lib 64-65; Asst catlg libn Antioch Col Lib 65-66; Reclf dir 67-68; Dir Birmingham-So Col 68-. 9: ALA; SELA; AlaLA. 10: Kappa Phi Kappa. 13: Yes. 14: Pub serv, catlg, acquis, admin. 15: Birmingham-Southern Col Lib, Birmingham Al 53204.

GAINES, LUCILLE (SIMCOE). b Norfolk Va 30 Ag 19. 4: William H Gaines Jr. 5: Randolph-Macon Womans Col 7-41 (Lat) BA; Columbia 44-45 (LS) BS; Duke 45-50 (Lat). 6: Lat, Fr. 7: Soc studies tchr Granby High Sch, Norfolk Va 41-42; Lat tchr Pape Sch, Savannah Ga 42-43; Tchr-libn Mathews High Sch, Mathews Va 43-44; Ref libn Duke U Lib 45-50; Order libn Va State Lib 50-51; Catlgr Va Hist Soc, Richmond Va 56-57; Catlgr Collegiate Schs Lib, Richmond Va 61-. 10: Phi Beta Kappa; Sigma Kappa. 12: Comp "Index to Virginia Magazine of History and Biography (52); "Index to Proceedings of New Jrsey Historical Society (59, 60, 61); "Index to A Hornbook of Virgiia History, Va State Lib (65); "Index to Journals of Colonial Council & Council of State of Virginia (66, 67). 14: Catlg, ref, indexing. 15: 1814 A Hanover ave, Richmond Va 23220.

GAISER, BESSIE FRANCES. b Leavenworth Co Kan 8 N 14. 5: St Mary Col (Xavier Kan) 32-43; Kan State Col (Pittsburg) 44-46 (Educ, Eng) BS in Educ; UKan 56; Kan State Tchrs Col (Emporia) 59 MS in LS. 7: Tchr Rural schs, Leavenworth Co Kan 39-44; Tchr rural schs, Wyandotte Co Kan 44-47; Tchr rural sch, Johnson Co Kan 47-48; Supply tchr, Kansas City Mo 48-49; Rural sch & prin, Leavenworth Co Kan 49-56; Tchr, Leavenworth Kan 57-58; Libn Ruskin High Sch, Hickman Mills Mo 59-62; Libn Ridgevew Elem Sch, Prairie Village Kan 62-. 9: NEA (life mem); ALA-AASchL; Kan State Tchrs Assn; KanLA (var past duties); KanASchL (var past duties). 10: Delta Kappa Gamma. 14: Catlg. 15: 110 Sheldon, Leavenworth Kan 66048.

GAISER, MARIE AGNES. b Leavenworth Kan 4 D 10. 5: St Mary Col (Xavier Kan) 28-30 AA, summers 38, 39, 41-43, 48; Kan State Col (Pittsburg) summers 44, 45, 47 (Educ) BS; Colo State Col summers 52, 53, 55, 56 (Educ) MA; Kan State Tchrs Col (Emporia) summers 32, 60, 62, 65 (LS). 7: Rural sch tchr Pub Schs, Leavenworth & Wyandotte Cos Kan 30-44; Elem tchr & tchg prin pub schs, Leavenworth Kan 4460; Jr high sch libn pub schs, Leavenworth Kan 60-. 9: NEA (life mem); -DAVI; ALA-AASchL; Kan State Tchrs Assn; KanASchL; KanLA; mpla; KanAVCO. 10: AAUW; Delta Kappa Gamma. 15: 110 Sheldon, Leavenworth Ks 66048.

GALAWAY, WILLIAM JAMES. b Luston Neb 30 Je 39. 5: UPuget Sound 59-61; Colo State Col summer 61; UNeb 62-64 (Hist) BS; UDenver summers 65, 66, 67, 69 (Libnship) MA. 7: Chaplain's serv specialists (E-4, Alc) USAF 57-61; Lib clk Mc Chord AFB LIb (Wash) 58-61; Lib asst Greeley Pub Lib (Colo) summer 61; Lib asst Bennet Martin Pub Lib, (Lincoln Neb) 61-64; Tchr, Lincoln Ore 64-65; Libn Kimball Co High Sch Kimball Neb 65-67; Ref libn Rockford Pub Lib, Ill 67-69; Hd libn Guilford High Sch, Rockford Ill 65-. 9: NEA (life mem); ALA; Nat Coun Soc Studies; IllEA; IllLA; RockfordEA. 10: Lib bd, Driftwood Pub Lib, Lincoln City Ore 64-65; Grad Lib Student Assn (UDenver); Lincoln City Libs Staff Assn. 14: Sch libs. 15: Rte 1 Songbird lane, Cherry Valley Il 61016.

GALBAN, AGNES S. b NYC 9 Jl 29. 5: Col of New Rochelle 45-47 (Eng); Barry Col 47-49 (Eng) BA; Columbia 67- (LS). 6: Sp, Fr, Port. 7: Ref libn Amer Iron & Steel Inst, NY 59-68; Dir & chief libn Hill & Knowlton Inc, NY 68-. 9: SLA. 14: Ref. 15: 520 E 86th st, New York NY 10028.

GALBAN, VICTORIA (SUAREZ). b NYC. 5: Barry Col 50-51; Marymount Col 51-54 (Span Lit, Hist) BA; Columbia 59-60 (LS) MS. 6: Sp, Fr, Ital, Portu. 7: Catlg-ref libn Art Ref Lib Metro Mus of Art 60-65, Sr libn 65-. 9: SLA. 14: Catlg, ref. 15: Metro Mus of Art 5th ave at 82nd st, New York NY 10028.

GALBRAITH, ISABELLE (VAN TASSEL). b Watertown NY 2 S 25. 5: Geneseo State Tchrs Col 41-45 (LS) BE; Syracuse 58-62 MLS. 7: Child libn Oswego City Sch Lib, Oswego NY 45-46; Sub tchr Town of Webb Schs, Old Forge NY 57, Libn 57-60; Elem libn Marcellus Central Sch, Marcellus NY 60-62; Ser catlgr Syracuse U ib 62-64; Head catlg dept UAlaska Lb 64-. 8: Asst dir, Inst in Sch Libnship, UAlaska summer 68; Instr materials consul, Alaska Rural Sch Proj 68-69. 9: ALA (Memb Chm for Alaska 67-70); NEA-DAVI (Memb Chm Alaska Div 69-); AlaskaLA (Conf Chm 65, 67, 69; Pub Chm 67-68; Chm Lib Devel & Legis Com 68-69). 10: Alaska Instr Media Assn; Zonta Internat. 14: Catlg, serv, child wk, sch libs. 15: Box 5-782, College Alaska 99701.

GALBRAITH, LOIS ANNE. b Denver Col 9 D 42. 5: Our Lady of the Lake 61-64 (Eng, LS); Tex Tech 64-65 (Eng) BA; UTex 65-66 (LS). 7: Lib asst Daughters Republic Tex Lib, San Antonio Tex 62-64; Stud asst Tex TechU Lib 64-65; Libn I San Antonio Pub Lib, San antonio Tex 66-69, Libn II 69; Libn 65-67, Ft Sam Houston Tex 69-. 9: ALA; TexLA. 14: Automated libs, tech serv, catlg. 15: 431 Tammy dr, San Antonio Tx 78216.

GALBRAITH, MARY ELIZABETH. b Seattle Wash 19 Ap 13. 5: UWash 31-35 (Eng) BA, 59-60 MLS. 7: Sec US Govt, Seattle, South & Central Amer 41-47; Sec US For Serv US Dept of state, Bucharest Rumania 47-49, Madrid Spain 50-54; Asst to Dean Col of Arts & Sci uwash 55-60; Libn (hd circ) Mont State Col 60-62; Libn (ref) Seattle Pub Lib 62-. 10: Kappa Kappa Gamma; Beta Phi Mu. 14: Lit, ref, displays. 15: 1446 E Roy st apt 301, Seattle Wa 98102.

GALBREATH, MRS ALENE (CANTRELL). b McLeansboro Ill. 5: So Ill U 35 (Eng) B Ed; UIll 37-39 (Classic) AM, 42-47 BS in LS, 59-62 (LS) MS. 7: Tchr of Lat & libn high sch, Martinsville Ill 39-43; Tchr of Eng & Lat high sch, Marshall Ill 43-45; Libn high sch, Normal Ill 45-48; Catlgr Washington U(St Louis) summer 48; Coordinator of lib serv McLean Co Unit Dist No 5, Normal Ill 48-66; Child consul Cornbelt Lib Syst, Bloomington Ill 67; Lib Winston Churchill Col 68-. 8: State Com of Ill Curr Program, Area Consensus Study No 6, 52-53; Chm, Lib Serv Com, McLean Co Unit Dist No 5, 63-65. 9: ALA-AASchL (sec-treas City & Co Supvs Group 56-57); NEA; IllLA; IllASchL (Bd 57-59, Publ Com 2 yrs, Regist Com 2 yrs); IllEA. 10: Delta Kappa Gamma. 14: Sch libs. 15: 506 S Fell ave, Normal Il 61761.

GALBREATH, PAULINE (KINCADE). b Ashmore Ill 13 Jl 10. 4: Harold C Galbreath. 5: East Ill U 57 (Foreign Lang) BS in Ed; UIll 60 MS in LS; SoIllU summer 62 (LS), UIll summers (LS). 7: Lib clerk East Ill U 57-58; Libn Commun Unit No 2, Mat toon Ill 58-67; Instr of Lib Sci E Ill U 67-. 9: ALA-ACRL; IllEA; IllLA; IllASchL. 10: K ppa Delta Pi; Beta Phi Mu; UIll Lib Sch Assn. 14: Ref, lib sci tchr. 15: Ashmore Il 61912.

GALE, ANN JEANNETTE. b St Charles Mich 8 Ap 31. 5: UMich 48-52 (Hist) AB; Columbia summers 54, 56, 57-58 (LS) MS. 7: Jr high tchr Hartford Pub Sch, Hartford Mich 52-53; Tchr Bellevue Rural Agric Sch, Bellevue Mich 53-54; Sub tchr Mem High Sch, W New York NJ 54-55; Tchr & libn Hemlock Rural Agric Sch, Hemlock Mich 55-57; Circ asst Mercantile Lib, NYC 57-58; Asst ref libn Cornell U Lib 58-62; Ref libn UMich Gen Lib 62-. 9: ALA; MichLA, (sec-treas Acad Libs Div 68-69). 14: Ref. 15: 845 Brookwood pl, Ann Arbor Mich 48104.

GALE, FREDERICK CHARLES. b London 27 Je 22. 4: Jeryl Gale (Caruk). 5: London Col for Choirester 39; London Polytech Inst 34-41, 46-48 (Sci); La Salle Law Sch 52-55. 6: Fr. 7: Instr UCLA 51-63; Medico-Legal Analyst (private) Los Angeles 55-63; Asst libn UNev 63-65; Asst State archivist Div of Archives, Carson City Nev 65-. 8 Libn & Proj Dir Nev State Heritage Assn. 9: SAA; Soc Hist Med; NevLA. 10: Amer Soc of Criminology; Internat Assn for Identification. 12: "Union Catalog of Nevada Manuscripts, with others (63). 13: Yes. 14: Archival org. 15: Div of Archives Dept of State Capitol Bldg, Carson City Nev.

GALE, SELMA R(OBERTA KAUFMAN). b NYC. 5: UDenver 4749 BA/LSD; New Sch for Soc Research 5661 (Pol Sci). 6: Fr, Sp. 7: Libn child dept New York Pub Lib Highbridge Br 5657; Libn Milbank Lib ColumbiaPresbyterian Med Center, NYC 5762; Consul patients libs United Hospital Fund, NYC 62. 8: Consul Devel of Pediatric Patients- Lib Univ Hosp, NYC 6668. 9: ALA (Statistics Com for Hope & Inst Libs); SLA; MedLA; NYLA; NY Lib Club. 10: Altrusa; Citizen-s Union; Phi Beta Kappa. 12: Consul "Essentials for Patients' Libraries - A Guide". 13: Yes. 14: Hosp libs. 15: 600 W 218 st, New York NY 10034.

GALEJS, JOHN E. b Latvia 18 Jl 27. 4: Irma Kajaks. 5: UMinn 50-55 (Internat Rel) BA, MA, 57-58 MALS. 6: Latvian, Ger. 7: Merchandise mgr AM Martin Co, Minneapolis 53-56; Ser libn Iowa State U 58-62, Head ser dept 62-, Coord resource devel 68-69, Asst dir resources & tech servs 69-. 9: ALA-RTSD (Ser Sect Policy of Research Com: 67-, sec 69; v-chm Ser Discussion Gp I 69); IowaLA (Resources & Tech Serv Sect chm 66). 10: AAUP. 14: Ser, acquis, govt docs. 15: 332 Westwood dr, Ames Ia 50010.

GALFAND, SIDNEY. b Phila 12 S 15. 4: Rose Nemerov. 5: Temple 32-36 (Secondary Educ) BS; Drexel 37-38 BSLS; Temple 44-46 (Psych) MS. 7: Jr libn Temple U 33-38; Asst libn NY Pub Lib 38-39; Libn or lib asst var high schs 39-50; Libn Benjamin Franklin High Sch, So Phila 50-52, W Phila High Sch 52-61; Supv Central Processing Sch Dist of Phila 61-69; Instr Villanova U Grad Lib Sch 61-; Libn Standard Even High Sch, Phila 64-; Libn Frankel Lib Har Zion Temple, Phila 64-; Chm Dept of Lib Sci Villanova U Grad Sch 69-. 8: Readers consul & Lecturer Drexel Even Col 39-; Instr Drexel Lib Sch 61-63. 9 ALA; (Sch Lib TECH Serv Com 61); SLA; CathLA; Jewish Libns Assn (pres Greater Phila Unit; chm Drexel Seminars on Synagogue Libnship 62-65); Sch Libns Assn of Greater Phila (pres, sec); Phila Area Tech Serv Libns; Penn State EA (Dept of Supv & Curric); Secon Sch Tchrs Assn. 10: Phila Even Sch Assn; Schoolmens Club; Amer Fed of Tchrs; Pi Gamma Mu; BNai Brith Educators Lodge. 13: Yes. 14: Calg, lib educ, Synagogue libs. 15: 725 Yale rd, Cynwyd Penn 19004.

GALFFY, ADORJAN IMRE, DE. b Budapest Hungary 30 S 25. 04 Piroska Kardos. 5: Peter Pazmany U of Sci (Budapest Hungary) 43-48 (Jurisprudence, Pol Sci) Dr Jur Rer Pol (summa cum laude); Columbia 59-61 MS in LS. ; San Jose State Col 64-66; Cal Jr Col Tchg Certif; pol Sci, Hist, Libnship. 6: Hungarian, Ger, Russian, Fr, Sp, Lat. 7: Com correspondnt Steel & Metalfactory of Kobanya, Budapest X Hungary 49-50; Legal Advisor Hungarian State Railways, Budapest VII Hungary 50-56; Gen clerk trainee The Chase Manhattan Bank, NYC 57-59; Life insurance salesman Mutual of NY Insurance Co, White Plains NY 59; Newspaper libn NY Hist Soc, NYC 60-61; Ref libn Santa Clara Pub Lib, Santa Clara Cal 62; Libn III catlg San Jose State Col 61-. 14: Admin, tech serv, soc sci, law, pol sci, hist. 15: 677 Fremont st apt D, Menlo Park Ca 94025.

GALICK, V GENEVIEVE (BOISCLAIR). b Lynn Mass 27 F 13. 4: George Joseph Galick. 5: Simmons 30-34 (LS) BS. 6: F,Ger, Sp. 7: Head ya dept Lynn Pub Lib, Lynn Mass 34-42; Spec Instr Simmons Col 40-42; US Army libn, Ft Devens, Ayer Mass 42-44; Instr in Lib Sci Army Info & Ed Staff Sch, Oberammergau Germany 45; US Army libn ETO Hqs Lib Br, Frankfurt Germany 45; Asst Dir State Div of Lib Ext, Boston Mass 46-49, Dir 49-. 8: Spec lecturer Simmons Col 49-65; Consul, Mass Div of Civil Serv 49-68; Consul, Conn Bur of Libs 59; Lib Examr NY State Civil Serv Div 60-64; Consul USEOE Lib Serv Br 60; Consul Tex State Lib 66; Adv Com Mass Bd of Higher Educ 67-; Compact Adminr for Interstate Lib Serv, Mass 67-. 9: ALA (Life mem; Adv Com on Methods Proj for Small Libs 63-64; Lippincott Jury Award Com 64)-LAD (Com on Personnel Practices in State Libs 60);-ALTA (Spec Com on ALTA Assembly 64);-AASchL (Nomin Com 65); CathLA; SLA; Adult Educ Com; NELA (chm Nomin Com 63-64); MassLA (sec 49-50); NELA (v-pres 67-68, pres 68-69); AEASUSA. 10: Womens Nat Bk Assn. 13: Yes. 14: State level ext activities, admin, lib educ. 15: 28 Travis rd, Natick Ma 01760.

GALKOWSKI, EUGENE FRANCIS. b Worcester Mass 14 Ag 26. 4: Patricia E Murphy. 5: Holy cross 44-48 (Hist) BA; ClarkU 54-55 (Lib Techniques) Certif; Syracuse Communications Libns' Inst 61 Certif; URI 62-66 MLS; IMd Automation Bibliog Serv Inst 68 Certif; Rensselaer Inst Syst Study Related to Lib Operations 68 Certif. 6: Polish, Fr. 7: Asst libn Worcester Telegram Publ Co, Worcester Mass 48-56; Libn New Bedford Standard-Times, New Bedford Mass 56-65; Libn Fall River Div SEast Mass Tech Inst 65-66, Libn for pub serv & ref & act dir of a-v serv 66-. 9: SLA (Boston Chap, Educ Com 66-67); NELA; MassLA (Educ Com 66-68, Publ Com 66-68, Program Com 68-). 10: Old Dartmouth Lib Club. 14: Pub serv, automation, a-v serv. 15: 41 Chesworth st, Fall River Ma 02723.

GALKOWSKI, PATRICIA ELAINE (MURPHY). b Nashua NH 20 F 28. 4: Eugene Francis Galkowski. 5: Brown 45-49 (Chem) ScB; Columbia summer 52 (LS); URI 62-65 MLS. 6: Fr. 7: Asst, Phys Sci Lib BROWN U 49-63, Asst phys sci libn 63-. 9: RILA (recording sec 67-68). 14: Scis, ser. 15: 41 Chesworth st, Fall River Ma 02723.

GALLAGHER, AGNES. b Glasgow Scotland 5 My 15. 5: Tufts 33-37 (Eng) AB; Simmons 46-47 BSLS. 6: Fr. 7: Tchr Dartmouth High Sch, Dartmouth Mass 37-43; Tchr Haverhill High Sch, Haverhill Mass 43-44; Asst libn Engnr Lib Harvard U 47-49; Base libn Wheelus Field, Tripoli Libya 50-52; Base libn Mitchel Field, Hempstead NY 52-53; Base libn Laurence G Hanscom Field, Bedford Mass 54-. 9: ALA (Armed Forces Sect Mem Com 64-65; NE Tech Proc Libns. 10: Phi Beta Kappa. 14: Admin, catlg. 15: 49 Essex st, Andover Mass 01810.

GALLAGHER, REV DENNIS JOSEPH OSA. b BRYN Mawr Penn 30 Mr 35. 5: Villanova 56-60 (Philos)BA, 60-65 (LS) MS; Augustinian Col 60-65 (Theol) MA. 6: Lat. 7: Libn Augustinian Col 63-65; Libn, Dir of a-v & tchr Austin Prep Sch, Reading Mass 65-. 9: CathLA. 14: Admin. 15: Austin Prep Sch 101 Willow st, Reading Mass 01867.

GALLAGHER, JOAN L. b Wilkes-Barre Penn 1 Mr 32. 5: Col Misericordia 49-53 (Chem) BS; Rutgers 60-64 MLS. 6: Ger, Russian. 7: Organic chem Amer Cyanamid Co, Bound Brook NJ 53-60, Ref libn 60-63, Chief Libn 63-. 9: ACS; SLA(NJ Chap; sec); ASIS. 13: Yes. 14: Res lib, admin, automation, SDI, info retr systems. 15: Amer Cyanamid Co Org Chem Div, Bound Brook NJ 08805.

GALLAGHER, MARGUERITE R(EGINA). b Jackson Tenn 3 Je 13. 5: St Xavier Col 30-34 (Classics) AB; Loyola U 36-37 (Lat); Chicago 52-54 (LS) MA. 6: Ger, Lat. 7: Jr lib asst

Chicago Pub Lib 38-41; Jr lib asst Great Lakes Naval Hosp, Waukegan Ill 42-43; Sr lib asst Chicago Pub Lib 43-46, Libn I Br 46-54; Instr lib sci Marywood Col 54-55; Libn II Br Chicago Pub Lib 55-59, Libn II Br libn Walker br 59-67. 8: Visiting instr lib sci Rosary Col summer 65, 66, 67; Reg libn Southside Dist 67-. 9: ALA. 10: Chicago Lib Club. 14: Pub libs, bk sel, lib educ. 15: 1401 E 55th st apt 412, Chicago Il 60615.

GALLAGHER, MARIAN GOULD. b Everett Wash 29 Ag 14. 5: Whitman Col 31-32 (Pre-Law); UWash 32-35 BA, 37 LLB, 39 B(LS). 7: Law lib asst UWash 37-39; Law Libn & Instr of Law UUtah 39-44; UWash: Law Libn & Asst Prof of Law 44-48, Law Libn & Assoc Prof of Law 48-53, Law Libn & Prof of Law 53-, Adjunct Prof Sch of Libnship 44-. 8: Nat Adv Commsn on Libs 67-68. 9: AALL (pres 54-55); WashStateLA (2nd v-pres 67-69). 13: Yes. 15: 801 Spring st, Seattle Wa 98104.

GALLAGHER, MARTHA (RIDDELL). b Swampscott Mass 15 Ja 22. 4: John O Gallagher. 5: Tufts 39-43 (Hist) AB; Columbia 55-58 MLS. 7: Libn E Orange Free Pub Lib, E Orange NJ 58-59; Libn Washington Sch, E Orange NJ 59-. 9: NJSchLA; NJLA. 10: LWV. 15: 158 Renshaw ave, E Orange NJ 07017.

GALLAGHER, (DOROTHY) NORA. b NYC. 5: Hunter Col 37-41 (Eng) AB; Columbia 41-43 (LS) BS; Fordham 61-63 (Hist). 7: Page Queens Borough Pub Lib, Jamaica NY 36-39; Student asst Hunter Col 39-41, Lib asst 43-44; Circ libn Adelphi Col 44-45, Act libn 45-46, Libn 46-63, Dir libs 63-. 8: Lib bldg consul Mount Saint Vincent Col, NY 66. 9: ASIS; ALA; -ACRL (A-v Com 65-67); -RSD (Com on Wilson Indexes 52-; NYLA (Coun 62-63; Col & Univ libs Sect: sec-treas 55-56, pres 62-63); NassauCoLA (pres 52-54; chm Com on State Aid for Libs 51-53); Metro Col Inter-Lib Assn (v-pres elect 65-66); LI Lib Resources Coun (Trustee 67-, v-pres 69-). 10: Nassau Co Hist Soc; NY Lib Club. 13: Yes. 14: Admin, coop, bldg planning. 15: 708 Westbury ave, Westbury NY 11590.

GALLARD, MARJORIE (FRANK). b Buffalo NY 21 D 26. 5: Whittier Col 44-48 (Sociol) BA; UNM 50-53 (Educ); USoCal 56-57 (LS) MS. 6: Sp. 7: Instr US Indian Serv, Sherman Inst 48-50; Child welfare NM Dept Pub Welfare, Albuquerque NM 5051; Tchr Albuquerqe Pub Schs, Albuquerque NM 51-53; Tchr El Monte Pub Schs, El Monte Cal 53-57; Libn Los Angeles City Schs, Los Angeles 57-; Libn Harbor Col 63-. 8: Training tchr 68-69 USC Lib School. 9: ALA; CalASchL; Los Angeles SchLA. 10: Delta Kappa Gamma; Sierra Club; AAUW; UN Assn; Lib Sodalitas. 13: Yes. 14: Navajo Indian lore & folk takes. 15: 1741 W 26th st, San Pedro Cal.

GALLER, ANNE (MARIE). b Budapest Hungary 3 S 32. 4: Mark Galler. 5: Sir George Williams U 53-57 BA; Simmons 57-58 MS. 6: Eng, Fr, Ger, Hungarian. 7: Asst libn Montreal Trust Co, Montreal 58-59; Libn Canadian Marconi Co, Montreal 59-61; Assoc libn Nat Film Board of Can, Montreal 61-65; Libn Outremont High Sch, Outremont Can 65-68; Lib consul bk processing ctr PSBGM, Montreal. 9: CanLA; SLA (Montreal Chap mem chm 59-65, 69-); QueLA; QueASchL. 14: Ref, catlg. 15: 6310 Somerled, Montreal 261 Can.

GALLI, MARILYN C(ARROLL). b Hartford Conn 19 My 28. 4: John L Galli. 5: LI Agric & Tech Inst 47, Adelphi Col 55. 6: Ger, Fr. 7: Libn Brookhaven Nat Lab, Upton NY 48-. 9: SLA. 14: Period (sci & tech), circ. 15: Halsey lane, Resenburg NY 11960.

GALLIEN, PAUL WAYNE. b Springfield Vt 18 Mr 39. 5: Gallaudet Col 60-65 (LS) BS. 7: Libn (acquis) selector/searcher US tmospheric Sci Lib (ESSA) Gramax Bldg, Silver spring Md 65-. 10: Alpha Sigma Pi. 14: Acquis. 15: 4840 Eastern lane apt 203, Suitland Md 20023.

GALLINGER, JANICE. b Melrose Mass 2 S 25. 5: Tufts Jackson 44-48 (Hist) AB; Carngie 56-57 MLS. 7: Clerk Col Nat Life Insurance Co, Boston Mass 48-50; Pol asst Foreign Serv of USA, Rangoon Burma 50-55, Bonn Germany 55; Tchr Leslie-Dearborn Sch, Cambridge Mass 56; Asst libn Erie C Tech Inst, Buffalo NY 57-65; Col Libn Plymouth State Col 65-. 8: Exec dir, Nat Lib Week, NH 69; Mem, NHCUC Libns Adv Coun; NCATE Accred Team 69. 9: SLA; NELA; NHLA. 10: Beta Phi Mu; AAUP. 14: Admin, tech proc, acquis. , curr materials. 15: 11 Rogers st, Plymouth NH 03264.

GALLO, ALFRED R. b Brooklyn NY 30 Ag 42. 5: St Francis Col 60-64 (Hist) BA; Pratt Inst 64-66 MLS. 6: Fr, Lat. 7: Sr libn Brooklyn Pub Lib, Brooklyn NY 66-. 9: ALA. 10: Beta Phi Mu. 14: Wk with ya. 15: 2111 68th st, Brooklyn NY 11204.

GALLO, BELA. b Szolnok Hungary 30 Ap 34. 4: Joan Rosenberg. 5: Eotvos Lorand U 52-56 (Hungarian Lit & Lang) Diploma; UMysore 60-61 (Indology) Post-Grad Diploma; Rutgers 63-64 MLS. 6: Hungarian. 7: Asst libn Harvard U 58-60; Fellow Paderewski Found Inc, NYC 60-62; Asst area supv Housing Authority of the City of Newark NJ 62-64; Asst Libn West Md Col 64-66; Act col libn Cal State Col (Dominguez Hills Cal) 66-. 9: ALA; CalLA. 10: AAUP; Assn Cal State Col Profs. 14: Bibliog serv. 15: 3241 Bradbury rd, Los Alamitos Ca 90720.

GALLO, NORMAN J. b New Orleans La 19 S 31. 4: Reiko Orino Gallo. 5: Tulane 50-53 9journalism) BA; LSU 65-66 MSLS. 6: Fr. 7: Intelligence off USAF 57-59; Credit reporter Dun & Bradstreet Inc, New Orleans 60-61; Eng tchr Mason Eng Sch, Tokyo 61-62; Lib asst New Orleans Pub Lib 62-65; Catlgr Jefferson Parish Pub Lib, Metairie La 66-67; Hd humanities dept Worcester Pub Lib, Worcester Mass 67-68; Libn Carmichael Pub Lib, Carmichael Cal 68-. 9: CalLA. 13: Yes. 14: Ref, admin. 15: 5605 Marconi ave, Carmichael Ca 95608.

GALLOWAY, LINDA (BENNETT). b Dixon Ky 8 Ag 17. 4: E Agnew Galloway. 5: Stephens Col 34-36 AA; UIll 36-38 AB, 38-39 BSLS; Cite Universitie (Paris) summer 45; Vanderbilt U 48-49 MA; West State Col 60. ; E Car U 68; UNC 68. 6: Fr, Ger. 7: Asst libn Evanville Ind 39-41; Libn Camp Breckenridge Ky 41-44; Libn European Theatre Operations, SHEAF Europ 44-46; Libn Dixon Pub Lib, Dixon Ky 46-51; Libn coordinator Webster County Schs, Dixon Ky 60-67; Libn Goldsboro City Schs 67-. 8: Historian UF ETO & 15th Army BAD Nauheim, Frankfurt Germany 45-46. 9: ALA; NEA; KyLA; KyASchL (pres-elect 66-67); KyEA; NCEA (Loc treas). 10: Dixon Womans Club; DAR; Delta Delta Delta; WCCC1; Delta Kappa Gamma. 12: "Andrew Jackson, Jr, Son of a President (66). 13: Yes. 14: Army libs, ref, elem wk. 15: Walnut Creek Estates Rt 3, Goldsboro NC 27530.

GALLOWAY, LOUISE. b Lexington Ky 21 F 21. 5: UKy 37-41 (Hist, LS) AB in Ed; Columbia summers 44, 46, 48-50 MS in LS, summers 55, 58-60 (Curriculum, Tchg) Ed D. 7: Libn Corbin High Sch, Corbin Ky 41-42; Libn Simon Kenton High Sch, Independnce Ky 42-43; Libn U Sch, Lexington Ky 43-46; Libn Paw Paw Schs, Paw Paw Mich 46-47; State supv sch libs State Dept Educ, Frankfort Ky 47-54; Asst Prof Lib Sch Fla State U 54-61; Head Circ Dept & Assoc Prof 61-. 8: Sch libs consu, Philippine Dept of Educ, 52-53. 9: ALA; KyLA (2nd v-pres 62-63; chm Col & Ref Sect 64-65); Louisville Lib Club. 10: Delta Kappa Gamma. 12: Ed "Roads to Greatness, Colliers Jr Class Ser. 13: Yes. 14: Admin, pub serv. 15: 212 Bilmore rd, Louisville Ky 40207.

GALLOWAY, LUCILLE ELINOR (MAY). b Hamilton 18 Ag 21. 4: Leslie Charles Galloway. 5: McMaster U 39-42 BA; UToronto 42-43 BLS. 7: Libn asst Toronto Ref Lib, Toronto Can 43-46; Libn asst Hamilton Pub Lib, Hamilton Can 46-50, Hd arts & sci dept 50-57, hd tech serv 65-67; Chief libn Burlington Pub Lib, Burlington Can 68-. 9: OntLA (Coun); Ont Reg Pub Libs (Bd memb). 10: Univ Women's Club; Arts and Letters Club; Player's Guild of Hamilton. 14: Ref, tech serv. 15: 482 Elizabeth st, Burlington Ont Can.

GALLOWAY, MARGARET ELLEN (GILES). b Amarillo Tex 23 F 42. 4: James William Galloway. 5: W Tex State U 60-63 (Eng, Hist) BA, 65- (Hist); Tex Woman's U 63-64 Mof LS. 6: Sp. 7: Asst catlgr W Tex State U 64-65, Order libn 65-66, Hd catlg dept 66-67; Asst acquis libn N Tex State U 67-. 9: ALA. 14: Acquis, catlg. 15: 115 Hann st apt 6, Denton Tx 76201.

GALLOWAY, R DEAN. b Dinuba Cal 26 F 22. 4: Jenalyne Fetterhoff. 5: Humboldt State Col 41-47 (Soc Sci) AB; USoCal 49-50 MS in LS. 7: Naval aviator US Navy Ensign 42-45; Libn Humboldt State Col Lib 47-60; Libn UTehran Inst for Admin Affairs 56-58; Libn Stanislaus State Col 60-. 9: ALA; CalLA (pres Col Univ & research lib div 69). 10: AAUP; Assn of Cal State Col Profs; Cal Col & Univ & Univ Fac Assn. 12: Jt Comp "Annotated Bib liography of the History of Humboldt and Del Norte Counties Cal" (60); Ed Newberry, Homer "History of u " (64)1: Yes. 14: Standards & status of libns. 15: Stanislaus State Col, Turlock Ca 95380.

GALLOZZI, CHARLES. b Phila 12 N 11. 4: Bernice Larrabee. 5: Columbia 33 (Eng Lit) BA; Rutgers 58 MLS. 7: Lib asst Cooper Union Lib 33-36; Sr lib asst Free Lib of Phila 45-49, Head dept for the blind 49-57; Asst Chief Div for the Blind LC 58-. 8: Surveyed Atlanta Lib for the Blind 56; Adv Com Survey of Lib Serv for the Blind 56; Presidents Com on Employment of the Handicapped. 9: ALA (chm Round Table on Lib Serv to the Blind 57-58); Am Assn of Wkrs for the Blind (group chm 59-60); pres DC-Md Chap 69); Nat Soc for the Prevention of Blindness; Am Assn of Instr of the Blind; Nat Braille Assn; Am Soc for Pub Admin; DCLA; Md Assn for the Visually Handicapped (treas 69-). 10: . 11: Louis Braille Award 58; Isabel W Kennedy Award 61; Educ Week for the Blnd Award 64. 13: Yes. 14: Lib serv to the blind. 15: Div for the Blind LC, Washington DC 20540.

GALLUP, LUCY A. b Dundee Mich 30 Jl 11. 4: Louis O Gallup. 5: West Mich U 30-34 (Eng) AB, 57-58 (LS) MA. 7: Desk & ref, HS Kalamazoo Pub Lib 30-35, 58-59; Asst & ref Goshen (Ind) Pub Lib 38-41; Photostat div NY Pub Lib 43-45; Libn Sturgis Pub Lib 51-57;Libn White Pigeon Commun Sch 60-. 10: Nat Wildlife Fed. 12: Child bks: "Spinning Wings (56); "Independent Bluebird (59). 14: Ref. 15: Daybreak Hill Rt 3, Sturgis Mich 49091.

GALNEDER, MARY. b Detroit 29 Je 36. 5: Wayne State 55-59 (Geog) BA; So Ill U 60-63 (Geog) MA. 6: Ger. 7: Jr clerk Detroit Pub Lib 52-58, 59-60; Map processing asst LC summer 60; 61; libn So Ill U 61-65; 62-65; libn UWis(Madison) 65-. 9: SLA. 10: Assn of Amer Geographers. 13: Yes. 14: Maps. 15: 1667 Capital ave No 13, Madison Wis 53705.

GALVIN, HOYT R(EES). b Pleasantville Iowa 26 F 11. 4: Mary Sayre. 5: Simpson Col 28-32 (Physics) AB; UIll 33-34 BS in LS. 7: Ref libn TVA Tech Lib, Knoxville Tenn 34-35, Order libn 35-36; Dir Reg Lib Serv, Huntsville Ala 36-40; U Libn UNC (Charlotte) 67-68; Dir Pub Lib of Charlotte & Mecklenburg Co, Charlotte NC 40-. 8: Consul or instr to 6 academic institutions, 72 loc pub lib agencies, 4 state lib agencies, US Off of Educ, UNESCO; Mem Ala State Lib Bd 39-40. 9: ALA (chm Bldgs & Arch Com 50-54); -LAD (pres 65-66); AlaLA (pres 38-39); NCLA (pres 42-43); SELA (pres 62-63); NC Adult Ed Assn (pres 57-58). 10: Rotary Club; C of C; Nat Conf Christians & Jews. 11: Certif of Achievement, Brookings Inst; Young Man of the Year, Jr C of C (42). 12: "Films in Public Libraries (47); Ed "Planning a Library Building: the Major Steps (55); Author "The Small Public Library Building with M Van Buren (59); Author-ed "Proposed Outline for Public Library Building Institutes and Workshops (64). 13: Yes. 14: Lib bldg planning, lib coop, lib assn activities, lib admin. 15: Pub Lib 310 N Tryon s, Charlotte NC 28202.

GALVIN, THOMAS J(OHN). b Arlington Mass 30 D 32. 4: Marie Schumb Galvin. 5: Columbia 50-54 (Eng) AB; Simmons 55-56 (LS) MS; Boston U 62-65; Case West 66-. 6: Fr, Ger. 7: Ref libn Boston U Libs 54-56; Chief Libn Abbot Pub Lib, Marblehead Mass 56-59; Lecturer in Lib Sci Simmons Col 57-62, Asst dir of Libs 59-62, Dir of studs & Asst Prof of Lib Sci 62-67; Dir of Studs & Assoc Prof 67-. 8: Lib consul Mass Bd of Reg Commun Cols 60-61; Exec Off Multinat Seminar for Foreign Libns Simmons Col 61-62; Lib consul Salem (Mass) State Col 62; Lib adv Pierce Col (Athens Greece) 62-; Act Dir Sch of Lib Sci Simmons Col 62-63, 69-70; Lib consul Vt Tech Col 64-65; Exec Off Pub Lib Bldg, Trustee & Sch Media Spec Insts Simmons Col 65-68; Lectr Dept of Epidemiology, Harvard Sch of Pub Health 66-; Lib consul; houghton Mifflin Co 65-66, Groton Md 65-66, State St Bank & Trust Co 66, Beacon Press 66-, Duxbury Md 68Consul USOE 69. 9: ALA (Coun 64-66, chm & mem 7 coms 55-66); -RSD (dir 67-70); AALS; NEA; (chm & mem 2 coms); MasLA (treas 59-62, chm & mem 4 coms). 10: AAUP; Phi Beta Kappa. 12: "Problems in Reference Service: Case Studies in Method and Policy (65). 13: Yes. 14: Ref materils & serv, development o pub & acad lib bk collections, lib admin, lib educ. 15: Simmons Col 300 The Fenway, Boston Ma 02115.

GAMAGE, ALVIN F. b Bristol Me 22 Je 29. 4: Gay Kimball. 5: UMe 47-51 (Eng) BA; Columbia 53-54 (LS) MS. 7: Sgt US Marine Corps 51-54; Ya libn Enoch Pratt Free Lib, Baltimore 54-57, Admin asst 57-59; Dir Brattleboro Free Lib, Brattleboro Vt 60-63; Ref libn Trinity Col (Hartford Conn) 63-67; Asst libn for readers serv Skidmore Col Lib 67-. 9: ALA; NYLA. 10: Thoreau Soc. 14: Ref, admin. 15: RFD 1, Saratoga Springs NY 12866.

GAMAL, SANDRA (HODGES). b Houston 8 F 38. 4: Saad M Gamal-Eldin. 5: N Tex State Col 55-58 (Span) BA; Tex Womans U 58-59 MLS. 6: Sp, Arabic. 7: Gen catlgr UTex 59-61; Catlgr West langs American U Cairo UAR) 61-62; Libn Cairo Amer Col (Cairo UAR) 62-68; Ser catlgr Amer U, Beirut Lebanon 68-. 9: ALA; NEA; LebaneseLA. 14: Sch lib supv, catlg, ser. 15: Minkara Bldg 36 Sakiet el Janzeer, Beirut, Lebanon.

GAMBARDELLA, ELEANOR (TARBELL). b Jackson Mich 25 Ja 12. 4: Joseph R Gambardella. 5: Tri-State Col 32 (Civil Engnr) BS in CE; UMich 37 (Civil Engnr) BSE(CE), 45 ABLS, 46 AMLS; Tri-State Col 51 (Admin Engnr) BS in AdE; UOslo 46. 6: Fr, Ger, Norwegian, Sp, Danish. 7: Lib asst Jackson Pub Lib, Jackson Mich 39-41; Lib asst UMich Engnr Lib, Ann Arbor 41-42; Inspec USAAF Materiel Command, Jackson Mich 43-45; Libn Tri-State Col 47-63; Catlgr Olivet Col 63-65; Asst libn Olivet Col 65-67; Libn 67-. 9: ALA; MichLA. 10: Soc of Women Engnrs. ; Mich Acad Arts & Scis; AAUW. 14: Lib admin, lib bldgs. 15: Olivet Col Lib, Olivet Mi 49076.

GAMBEE, BUDD L(ESLIE). b Auburn NY 16 N 17. 4: Ruth Richter. 5: URochester 37-40 (Eng) BA; UMich 40-41 ABLS, 49 MALS, 63 PhD. 6: Fr. 7: Ref libn Aurora Pub Lib, Aurora Ill 41-43; Sr asst libn Detroit Pub Lib 43-48; Chief a-v aids dept WVa U Lib 48-51; Film libn Asst Prof Ball State Tchrs Col 51-58; Assoc Prof of Lib Sci SUNY (Albany) 58-61; Viiting Lecturer UMich Dept of Lib Sci (Ann Arbor) 63; Assoc Prof Sch of Lib Sci UNC(Chapel Hill) 63-. 8: Fulbright lecturer in Lib Sci, Cairo Egypt 52-53. 9: ALA; -LED (sec-treas Tchrs Sect); NEA-DAVI; NCLA; SELA. 10: Beta Phi Mu; AAUP; NC State Art Soc; Metropolitan Opera Guild;Chapel Hill Hist Soc. 11: URochester Hull Prize 40; Carles Ellis Caldwell Prize for work in English studies. 12: "Frank Leslie and His Illustrated Newspaper, 1855-1860 (64); "Non-Book Materials as Library Resources (67). 13:Yes. 14: Lib educ, a-v aids, bk sel, lib hist, art bibliog, publishing. 15: Sch Lib Sci UNorth Carolina, Chapel Hill NC 27515.

GAMBLE, CONNOLLY CURRIE JR. b Hickory NY NC O 21. 4: Melba Burgess. 5: Lenoir Rhyne Col 38-42 (Physics) BA; Union Theol Sem 42-45 (Theol) BD, 49-51 (Theol) ThM, ThD; UNC 51-52 BS in LS. 6: Gk. 7: Chaplain (Lt jg) US Naval Reserve, Bethesda Md 45-46; Pastor Presbyterian Church, Whitmire SC 46-49; Asst libn Union Theol Sem (Richmond Va) 52-56, Dir of Continuing Educ 56-. 8: Exec Bd Lib Development Program Amer Theol LA 60-69; Continuing Educ Com Dept of the Ministry Nat Coun of Churches (chm) 63-65. 9: ATheolLA (Exec Bd, pres 60-61); VaLA; SELA. 10: Ordained minister of Presbyterian Church in the US; Richmond Area Coun on Human Rel (Bd). 12: "The Continuing Education of the American Minister (60); Bk ed, "Presbyterian Survey, Atlanta; "Continuing Education and the Churchs Ministry (67); "Continuing Education for Ministry (68). 13: Yes. 14: Educ serv. 15: 3218 Chamberlayne ave, Richmond Va 23227.

GAMBLE, NAN CATHERINE (HENLEY). b McAlester Okla 12 Ap 17. 5: UOkla 36-39 (Span) BA, 63-64 MLS. 6: Sp, Fr. 7: Ref asst Amarillo Pub Lib, Amarillo Tex 59-61; UOkla Lib: Lib asst 61-64, Info libn 64-65, Humanities libn 65-. 8: Lib fellow UOkla Lib 63-64. 9: ALA; OklaLA. 14: Ref, rare bks. 15: 916 Birch, Norman Okla 73069.

GAMBLE, ROBERT A. b Duncan Okla 1 Je 40. 5: Okla State U 58-63 (Hist) BA; UKan 63-64 (Hist); UOkla 64-65 MLS. 7: Docs libn Okaland U 65-67; Docs libn UTex (Arlington) 69, 69-. 9: ALA; SLA; TexLA; Tex Assn of Col Tchrs. 14: Govt publ, ref, archives. 15: 920 Peach st apt 250, Arlington Tx 76010.

GAMBY, GLENDA (CROCKETT). b Keokuk Iowa 7 My 44. 4: John Edward Gramby. 5: UMo 62-66 (Eng, LS) BA; UIll 66-67 (LS) Masters. 7: Prof materials libn Mo State Lib, Jefferson City 67-. 9: ALA; MoLA. 10: Beta Phi Mu. 14: Ref, adult serv. 15: Mo State Lib, Jefferson City Mo 65101.

GANDT, ESTHER MARY (MORRIS). b Richland Center Wis 22 Ap 07. 4: Reuben A Gandt. 5: Wis State U (Whitewater) 24-27 (Eng) B Ed; UWis(Madison) 57-59 (Eng) BA, 59-60 MALS. 6: Fr. 07: Eng, libn pub sch, Oconto Falls Wis 27-30; Eng, libn pub sch, Oconomowoc Wis 30-34; Asst libn Wis High Sch, Madison Wis 59-60; Libn pub sch, Madison Wis 60-. 9: WisLA; MadisonLA; WisEA (sec Lib Sect). 10: State (Wis) Mental Health Assn (Bd); YWCA (Bd); Phi Delta Gamma; AAUW. 12: "Transparencies on Teaching in Library Science. 14: Child lit. 15: 2045 Dodge st, Madison Wis 53713.

GANFIELD, (ELEANOR) JANE. b Waukesha Wis 30 Ja 12. 5: Carroll Col (Waukesha Wis) 28-32 (Hist) BA; Columbia 32-33 BS in LS; Chicago summer 36 (LS); Columbia summers 37-40 MS in LS. 6: Fr. 7: Libn Carroll Col (Waukesha Wis) 33-40; Libn Riverside Pub Lib, Riverside Ill 40-41; Libn Blacburn Col Lib, Carlinville Ill 41-44; Libn Wittenburg Col Lib 44-45; Ser Libn & Asst dir for processing serv Purdue U Libs 45-. 9: ALA;IndLA. 10: AAUP; AAUW. 14: Procesing. 15: 324 W Lutz, West Lafayette In 47906.

GANNAWAY, VIRGINIA ALMIRA. b Hodgenville Ky 31 Ja 10. 5: East Ky U 30-34 (Home Econ) BS; Carver Sch So Sem 35-37 (Relig Educ) MRE; Fla State U summer 57, 59 Certif Lib & A-V Materials; U S Fla ext 68. 7: Home econ tchr: Central Park High Sch, Ohio Co Ky 34, Acadia Baptist Acad Home Missionary (SBC) La, Aucilla Fla 41-42; PhM 1c USN Med Corp, Phila, NJ 43-45; Off nurse, Lakeland Fla 45-55; Off clk registrar's off Fla So col 56; Libn Lakeland Jr High, Lakeland Fla 57-. 8: Librarian, Southside Baptist church, Lakeland Fla 56-. 9: NEA; ALA; FlaEA; FlaASchL; FlaLA; Fla A-V Assn; PolkCoEA; PolkCoSchL. 10: AAUW; Fla Bapt Conv LA; Friends of the Lib. 15: 1027 S Lincoln ave, Lakeland Fl 33803.

GANONG, HARRY WINSLOW. b Lower Gagetown NB Can 25 Je 13. 4: Agatha Covey Palmer. 5: UNew Brunswick 36-40 (BA); Acadia U 40-41; Toronto 45-46 BLS. 7: Tchr Bishops Sch, Lennoxville Que 41; Instr Classics Dept Acadia U 40-41; Royal Can Air Force Aircraftsman, overseas 41-45; Acadia U Lib; Catlgr 46-50, Act libn 50-51, libn 51-. 8: Nat Lib Adv Coun of Can 63-66. 9: Maritime LA (pres 55-56); CanLA; APLA. 12: Comp "Catalogue of Maritime Baptist Historical Collection in Library of Acadia University, Kentville NS Canada (55). 15: Fairfield st, Wolfville NS Can.

GANS, DEBORAH (RITT). b NYC 15 F 10. 5: Hunter Col 27-31 (Hist) BA; Columbia 35-38 (Socol) MA; NY Sch of Soc Wk 41; Pratt 55-56 MLS. 6: Ger. 7: Case wker Dept of Welfare, Yonkers NY 34-39; Case wker Dept of Family & Child Welfare, West Co NY 39-42; Case wker Family Serv Soc, Yonkers NY 42-43; Catlgr Pub Lib, Port Chester NY 56-60; Ya libn & br libn Pub Lib, New Rochele NY 60-62, Ref head 62-. 9: ALA; NYLA; WestchesteLA; NY Lib Club. 10: Zonta Internat. 15: 541 Pelham rd, New Rochelle NY 10805.

GANTNER, JOSEPH F. b San Francisco Cal 24 Mr 20. 4: Dolores Marcucci. 5: UCal(Berkeley) 41 (Zool, Eng) AB, 52 (Zool, Genetics) MA, 60 MLS. 6: Fr, Ger. 7: UCLA Biomed Lib: Catlg dept 60-1, Ref dept 61-63; UCal San Diego): Hd Scripps Inst of Oceanography 63-66, Ast univ libn 66-. 9: ALA; AAUP; CalLA (coun 69-70); UCal Lib sch Alum Assn (pres 69). 10: Sigma Xi; Beta Phi Mu. 11: NSF Fellowship 58-59. 12: "A Test for Recombinational Lethals in the Second Chromosomes of Drosophila Melanogaster" (41). 14: Lib admin, personnel, lib bldgs. 15: 469 Belvedere st, La Jolla Ca 92037.

GARAFOLA, GERALD A. b Newark NJ 21 N 29. 4: Rita Hilbert. 5: Seton Hall Col 47-48 (Pre-Law); UAla 48-51 (Pre-Law) BS; Seton Hall Law Sch 53-56 LLB. 7: Mgt off US Army QMC (Capt) 51-53; Law Libn Seton Hall Law Sch 61-. 15: Seton Hall Law Lib 40 Clinton st, Newark NJ.

GARBACK, MRS (KATHERINE CARROLL) KAY. b Merryville La 8 Ja 08. 5: LSU 32-37 (Eng) BA, 61-63 (LS) MS. 6: Fr, Lat. 7: Sec Receptionist Law Firm, Baton Rouge La 37-42; Cafe mgr Shirley St Cafe, De Ridder La 42-47; Club waitress Marin Country Club, Marin Co Cal 47-50; GS3 - GS5 US Army Engnrs, Anchorage Alaska 50-53; Documents asst LSU 61-63; Asst libn & instr Francis T Nicholls State Col 63-. 9: ALA; LaLA. 10: Bus & Prof Women; OES; Alpha Beta Alpha; AAUW; Thibodaux Lit Club; Nicholls Faculty Womens Club. 14: Ref, catlg, humanities libnship. 15: 111 Spruce st, Thibodaux La 70301.

GARBARINO, MRS ELIZABETH S. b Boston 24 Mr 13. 4: Dante V Garbarino. 5: Mass certif in libnship; Northeastern U 69-. 7: Sec Russell Box Co, Medford 31-35; Sr asst Medford Pub Lib 47-58; 49-58; Asst libn Sylvania Tech Lib, Waltham Mass 58-60; Asst libn Stoneham Pub Lib, Stoneham Mass 60-63, Head Libn 63-. 9: ALA; MassLA (Pub Lib Adminrs Sect); NELA; Charles River Lib Club. 10: Stoneham (Mass) Hist Soc. 14: Admin. 15: Stoneham Pub Lib, Stoneham Ma 02180.

GARBER, MARION H(ARRIETT). b Charleston SC 20 Je 21. 5: Temple 39-43 (Psych) AB; Drexel 46-47 BS in LS. 7: (Sgt) WAC 43-45; Army libn US Army Spec Serv, Germany 47-49; Libn AEC Tech Info Serv, Oak Ridge 50; Libn Oak Ridge Inst of Nuclear Studies 50-58, Assoc lib upv 58-. 9: ALA; SLA; TennLA. 10: Recording for the Blind; Nat Park Assn; Nat Wildlife Assn; Oak Ridge Reg Mental Health Assn; ACLU. 14: Ref, admin. 15: 157 N Seneca rd, Oak Ridge Tenn 37830.

GARBRECHT, DONALD LEROY. b St Paul 7 S 36. 4: Diane Horton Garbrecht. 5: UMinn 54-58 (Hist) AB, 59-61 LLB, 61-62 (LS). 7: Asst law libn UMe 62-63, Law Libn 63-. 9: Amer Bar Assn; Amer Judic Soc; AALL (chm Com on Exch of Dup Material, chm Nomin Com 68-69); NE Law Libns (dir 67-69). 13: Yes. 15: 68 High, Portland Me 04141.

GARCIA, COLLEEN (ALLEN). b Attica Kan 9 My 31. 4: Ramiro Garcia. 5: UColo 53 (Span) BA; UDenver 57 (LS) MA. 6: Sp. 7: Mountain States Telephone Co, Denver 53-57; Libn Army Spec Serv, Okinawa, Ryukyu Islands 57-60; Med libn Brooke Army Med Center, Ft Sam Houston Tex 60-61; Libn Naval Supply Center, Oakland Cal 61; Ref libn head ref serv NASA Ames ResearchCtr, Moffett Field Cal 62-. 9: SLA. 14: Ref. 15: 1145 Lexington dr, Sunnyvale Cal 94087.

GARCIA, JOSE HERNANDEZ. b San Antonio 20 My 22. 5: San Antonio Col 40-42 (Educ) AA; UReale (Perugia Italy) 44 (Ital); USoCal 46-47 (Educ) BA; URome 49; Sorbonne 50; Our Lady of the Lake Col 52-53 (Educ) MA; George Washington U 60; Our Lady of the Lake Col 62-63 BLS. 6: Sp, Ital, Fr, Portu. 7: Admissions Robt B Green Hosp, San Antonio Tex 39; Libn San Antonio Pub Lib, San Antonio Tex 40-42; Cable & radio censor US Navy (Y1C), N Africa, Sicily, Italy 42-45; Catlgr Columbia U 47-48; Research reporter Catholic Welfare Conf, Wash DC 54-55; Tchr McInney Hills Schs, Silver Springs Md 55-62; Libn Rocking Horse Sch, Rockville Md 63-. 9: NEA; Md State Tchrs Assn; MdSchLA. 10: Alpha Beta Alpha. 14: Child lit. 15: 4508 Hartwick rd, College Park Md 20740.

GARDINER, ELIZABETH (PELTON). b Lowville NY 4 S 19. 5: Radcliffe 41-43 (Fine Arts) AB; Syracuse 62-63 (LS) MS. 7: Link instr (Sgt) USMC-WR 43-46; Catlg dept SyracuseU 63-64, Asst circ libn 65-67, Journalism libn 67-. 8: Chm lib com Episcopal Diocese of Central ny 67-68. 10: Bd mem Jamesville-DeWitt Sch PTA 67-68; SyracuseU Libns Assn. 14: Journalism. 15: 6716 Kinne rd, DeWitt NY 13214.

GARDINER, ROGER FREDERICK. b London Ont Can 5 Ag 36. 4: Art bibliog & acquis, rare bks. 5: UWest Ontario 55-59 (Classical Philology) BA; Philips Universitat (Marburg W Germany) 64-65 (Classical Philology, classical Art, Archaeology); UMich (Ann Arbor) 66-67 MALS. 6: Ger, Lat, Fr. 7: Tchr Burford Dist High Sch, Burford Ont Can 59-60; Tchr Chatham Bd of Educ, Chatham Ont Can 60-66, Sch libn Chatham Collegiate Inst 62-66; Fine arts Bibliog UWest Ont 67-. 8: Organ Loan Exhibit & comp of catlg of Postian Collection: The Art of the Oriental carpet, McIntosh Gallery, UWest Ont 69. 9: ALA; Col Art Assn. 10: Arms & Armour Soc 9london). 11: Rotary Foun Fellowship for post grad study 64-65. 15: 892 Waterloo st, London Ont Can.

GARDINER, RUSSELL KENNETH. b Cal 28 Ap 31. 5: UCal (Berkeley) 52-53, 57-58 (Slavic Lang & Lot) BA, 65-66 MLS. 6: Russian, Ital, Fr, Polish. 7: Research asst UCal Machine Translation Project (Berkeley) 59-65; Libn II (catlgr of Slavic material) UCal Lib (Berkeley) 66-. 9: ALA. 14: Catlg. 15: 1930 Vine st, Berkeley Ca 94709.

GARDINER, VERNA JUNE (CARTER). b H Branch Ind 15 Je 41. 4: Robert A Gardiner. 5: Purdue U 58-63 (Bio) BS; UIll 63-64 (LS) MS. 7: Asst bio libn UIll (Urbana) 64-. 14: Sci libnship. 15: 429 Fairlawn dr, Urbana Il 61801.

GARDNER, ADELAIDE (CARTER). b E Douglas Mass 27 Ap 22. 4: Edward M Gardner Jr. 5: Wellesley 40-44 (Ital) AB; Columbia 61-65 (LS) MS. 6: Ital, Fr. 7: Communications Off USNR (WAVES), Wash DC 44-45; Asst off- in-chge WAVES USNTS, Newport RI (Lt jg) 45-46; Exec dir Girl Scout Coun, Haverhill Mass 47-49, Pittsfield Mass 49-54; Train adv Nat Staff Girl Scuts USA, Heidelberg Germany 54-55; Elem sch libn Ridgewood Pub Sch, Ridgewood NJ 65-. 9: NEA; ACE; ALA; NJEA. 10: Local Fair Housing Com . 15: 242 Highwood ave, Ridgewood NJ 07450.

GARDNER, CARROLL (SUTHERLAND). b Toledo Ohio 22 F 37. 4: Jack I Gardner. 5: U of the Pacific 55-57; UWash 57-59 (Sociol) BA, 59-60 MLS. 7: Asst libn Grays Harbor Co Lib, Montesano Wash 60-62; Asst dir Cooperative Processing Center, Nevada State Lib 64-67; Field serv libn 69-, 9: ALA; NevLA. 10: LWV; Nev State Emploees Assn. 15: 303 W Fleischmann way, Carson City Nev 89701.

GARDNER, CHARLES A. b Tucson 21 F 30. 4: Sara Jane Hepner. 5: UAriz 47-51 (Eng) BA; UDenver 52-53 (LS) MA. 6: Fr. 7: Circ libn Colo State Col 53-55; Ref libn USAF Acad 55-57; Supv of Sch Lib Tucson Pub Sch 57-62; Libn soc sci div Wash State U Lib 62-65; Libn Hastings Col (Hastings Neb) 65-. 9: ALA; NebLA; MPLA; ArizLA; ColoLA. 10: ACLU. 13: Yes. 14: Admin, ref, acquis. 15: Perkins Lib Hastings Col, Hastings Neb 68901.

GARDNER, EDWARD M. b NYC 22 S 03. 4: Marguerite Barr. 5: NYU Wash Sq Col 24-29 (Eng) BS; Columbia 33-34 BLS. 7: NY Pub Lib: Stack page 23-29, reading room asst 29-44, catlgr map div 45-68; Catlgr map dept Amer Geogl Soc 69-. 14: Catlg. 15: 160 Bennett ave, New York NY 10040.

GARDNER, GENE MARIE. b Kalamazoo 9 Jl 42. 5: Mich State U 60-64 (Zool) BS; UMich 64-65 MALS. 7: Child libn Wayne Co Lib, Plymouth Mich 65-67; Lab tech UWash Hosp 67; Volunteer Volunteers in Serv to Amer, Denver 67-68; Inst Consul Colo State Lib 68-. 9: ALA; ColoLA. 14: Child lit. 15: 1362 Lincoln, Denver Co 80203.

GARDNER, REV HAROLD BERNARD. b Fairport NY 25 S 29. 5: Toronto 51-54 (Lat) BA; U St Michaels Col 55-56, 57-60 (Theol) STB; West Res 60-61 MS in LS. 6: Lat, Fr. 7: Libn St Basils Sem (Toronto) 59-60, 61-62; 67-68; Libn Pontifical Inst of Mediaeval Studies (Toronto) 62-67; Libn U St Thomas 68-69; St Michaels Col 69-. 8: Curator Etienne Gilson Collection, Pont Inst of Mediaeval Studies 62-. 9: ALA; CanLA; CathLA. 13: Yes. 14: Catlg, rare bks, archives. , bibliog. 15: 50 St Joseph st, Toronto 5 Ont Can.

GARDNER, IDA S. b Asheville NC 17 O 18. 5: NC Col 39 (Biol) BS; Fisk U summer 42; Columbia Tchrs Col 44-45; NC Col 46 BS in LS; UMinn summer 52, LSU summer 66. 6: Fr, Lat. 7: Tchr-libn Ashland ave Jr High Sch, Asheville NC 42-45; Circ libn Southern U 46-60, Readers adv & res libn 60-, Readers Adv 66-. 9: ALA. 10: AAAS; YWCA; Girl Scout Leader; Nat Assn Col Women. 14: Circ, ref, ser, readers adv. 15: Box 9844, So Br P O, Baton Rouge La 70813.

GARDNER, JACK I(RVING). b Seattle 7 O 34. 4: Carroll Sutherland. 5: UWash 53-60 (Eng) BA, 59-60 (LS) ML. 6: Sp. 7: Warehouseman, Laborer Sears Roebuck, Seattle 51-54; (Pfc) Mechanic US Army, Cal, Tex, Hawaii 54-56; Stud lib clerk Med Lib UWash 60; Libn br & SS Div Brooklyn Pub Lib 60-62; Stud, tchr Berlitz USeville (Madrid, Seville) 62-63; Temp libn Sno-Isle Reg Lib, Everett Wash 63; Catlgr Pub Serv Lib Nev State Univ of Nev & Nev State Lib, Carson City & Reno Nev 63-67; Docs libn Nev State Lib 68-. 8: Nev State chm, Nat Lib Week, 64-65. 9: NevLA (Convention Reserv Chm 64, Exhib Chm 65, Adv Manager for "Nevada Libraries), Fin Com 68-69). 14: Reg devel. 15: 303 W Fleischmann way, Carson Cty Nev 89701.

GARDNER, KATHERINE ANN. b Wash DC 4 O 39. 5: Rollins Col 57-59 UNC 60-62 (Eng) AB, 64 MS in LS. 6: Fr. 7: Lib asst Nat Agric Lib, Wash DC summers 62-63; Trainee libn LC 64-65, Info Systems Research asst 65, Ref libn 65-67, Ref coll libn 67-. 9: ALA; DCLA. 10: Phi Beta Kappa; Beta Phi Mu. 11: Selected by LC for its annual recruitment prgram for outstanding lib sch grads. 12: "Book Reviewing in American Journals in the Physical Sciences, ACRL Microcard Ser. 14: Ref. 15: 220 C st SE apt 209, Wash DC 20003.

GARDNER, LAURA AMY (NUSSBAUM). b NYC 9 S 39. 5: City Col (NY) 55-59 (Hist) BA; Columbia 60-62 MLS. 6: Ital, Sp, Fr. 7: Libn The Population Coun Inc, NYC 59-60; Trainee at br NY Pub Lib 60-61; Asst libn NYU Inst of Fine Arts61-64; Ed libn Grolier Inc, NYC64-. 8: Lib/USA NY Worlds Fair 65. 9: SLA; ALA; NY Lib Club. 10: English Speaking Union. 14: Ref. 15: 150 W 15 st, New York NY 10011.

GARDNER, MARGARET (GREENLEAF). b Richmond Ky 24 Ap 10. 5: Vassar 27-31 (Span) AB; UKy 61-62 MS in LS. 6: Fr, Sp, Portu. 7: Instr Transylvania Col 43-44; Partner Ransdell Insurance Agency, Owenton Ky 55-61; Asst catlg dept UKy 62; Educ resources libn USFla 62-; Asst period libn East Ky U 67-; Research Spec East Ky U 69-. 9: ALA; KyLA. 10: AAUP; Madison Co (Ky) Hist Soc. 14: Periods, bibliog. 15: 213 Lancaster ave, Richmond Ky 40475.

GARDNER, RICHARD KENT. b New Bedford Mass 7 D 28. 5: Middlebury Col 46-50 (Arts) AB; Inst des Professeurs de Francais a lEtranger, Faculte des Lettres, U de Paris 53-54 (Fr Lit) Dipl Litt; Case West Res 50-51, 54-55 MS in LS, 59-(LS, Fr Lit), PhD. 6: Fr, Ital, Ger. 7: Circ asst Middlebury Col Lib 47-50; Ref & circ asst New Bedford Free Pub Lib, New Bedford Mass summers 48, 49 & 53; Ref & circ asst Case Inst of Tech Lib 50-51; US Army Mil Intelligence (Cpl) Libn 525th Mil Intelligence Serv Group, Ft Bragg NC 51-53; Libn Foundation des Etats-Unis, Cite U(Paris) 53-54; Order libn Case Inst of Tech Lib 54-55, Asst libn 55-57; Lib adv Mich State U Adv Group in Pub Admin to the Govt of Vietnam, Saigon Vietnam 57-58; Libn Marietta Col 59-3; Ed "CHOICE: Books for College Libraries, ALA-ACRL, Middletown Conn 63-66; Lecturer West Res Sch of Lib Sci 66-. 8: Consul Ashland Col (Ohio) Lib 68; Survey Loyola U (Chicago) Libs 68-69; Survey Lib Coop in 36 Tex countries 68-69. 9: ALA-ACRL; -LED; RTSD (var coms); OhioLA (Exec Bd 62-63); Ohio Col Assn; Lib Sect; (v-pres 62-63, pres 63); Mem Jt Com on Lib Coop 62-63. 10: Phi Beta Kappa; Beta Phi Mu. 12: "The Cataloging and Classification of Books, tr into Vietnamese with the VIETNAMESE Dec Clsf (Saigon 59); "Bibliography of Periodicals Published in Vietnam (Saigon 58); Ed "CHOICE: Books for College Libraries (64-66); "Opening Day Collection (67); "Education for Librarianship in France; an Historical Survey (68). 13: Yes. 14: Col libs, acquis, ref. 15: Ecole de Bibliotheconomie U of Montreal, Montreal P 2 Can.

GARDNER, ROBERTA JOAN. b YC 12 Ap 3. 4: Morris H Gardner. 5: Queens Col 49-51, 60-62 (Econ) BA; Pratt 62-64 MLS. 6: Sp. 7: Asst libn Queensboro Pub Lib, Jackson Heights Br 61-64; Ref libn Port of NY Authority 64-65; Head Libn James C Buckley Inc, NYC 65; Dir lib serv Bus International, NYC 65-. 9: SLA. 10: Beta Phi Mu. 14: Ref, admin. 15: 99-30 59th ave, Rego Park NY 11368.

GARDNER, SUZANNE (THRASHER). b Bellows Falls Vt 6 Ap 42. 4: Charles J Gardner. 5: Simmons 60-64 BLS; BostonU 68-69 (Sch Lib) MEd. 6: Fr. 7: Asst libn Maria Mitchell Assn, Nantucket Mass summers 62-63; Tchr & libn Nantucket School Dept, Nantucket Mass 64-. 9: ALA; DAVI; Amer Assn Tchrs of Fr; NESLA; Mass A-V Assn; MassSchLA. 10: Girl Scouts of Amer; DAR; Pi Lambda Theta. 14: Instr materials serv in sch. 15: Derrymore rd, Nantucket Ma 02554.

GARDNER, VIRGINIA (SUE WEBSTER). b Little Rock Ark 7 O 22. 4: (Oliver) Ray Gardner. 5: Ouachita Baptist Col 39-43 (Relig Educ) AB; SWest Baptist Theol Sem 46-48 (Adolescent Educ) MRE; UMich 62-67 MALS. 6: Fr. 7: Tchr-libn Sparkman High Sch, Sparkman Ark 43-44; Libn Central Baptist Col 48-50; Catlg Asst UArk Libs 50-51; Res bk rm Supv Purdue U Libs 51-52; Med Libn Beatty Mem Hosp, Westville Ind 52-54; Libn Davidson Jr High Sch, Southgate Mich 62-66; Elem Catlgr IMC Birmingham Pub Schs, Birmingham Mich 66-. 9: ALA; -AASchL; MichASchL; BirminghamEA. 10: Beta Phi Mu. 14: Catlg, tech proc. 15: 4197 Iverness lane, Orchard Lake Mi 48033.

GARDNER, WILLIAM MICHAEL. b Cleveland 16 D 32. 4: Betty Krug. 5: John Carroll U 51-55 (Eng) BS; West Res 59-60 MSLS. 7: US Army (Sgt) Radioman 55-57; Territory manager Wyeth Labs, Cleveland 59; Catlg-ref libn Albert R Mann Lib, Cornell U 60-63; Asst acquis libn 64; Libn Agric Lib UKy 65-; Asst dir tech serv 66-. 9:ALA;Internat Assn Agric Libns & Documentalists; KyLA. 14: Biol sci, admin. 15: 922 Wolf Run rd, Lexington Ky 40504.

GARDOS, SUSAN JO. b Newark NJ 14 Je 40. 4: George Gardos. 5: Douglass 58-62 (Hist) BA; UWis 63-65 (Russian Studies) MA; Simmons 65-68 MLS. 6: Russian. 7: Libn Russian Research Ctr Harvard 65-. 10: Phi Beta Kappa. 11: Fulbright Scholarship. 15: 49 Garfield st, Cambridge Ma 02138.

GARFIELD, ELEANOR C ATTLEY. b Swampscott Mass 26 My 14. 4: Leonard D Garfield. 5: Ohio U 34-38 (Sociol) AB; Simmons 61-63 (LS) MS. 7: Young adult libn Pub Lib, Belmont Mass 57-63; High sch libn Belmont Sr High Sch, Belmont Mass 63-. 9: ALA; MassLA; MassTA; BelmontTA. 14: Young adult wk. 15: 76 Washington st, Belmont Mass 02178.

GARGAL, BERRY (BETTE) . b Newark NJ 2 D 30. 5: Vassar 48-52 (Ger) AB; SUNY (Albany) 69 (LS) MLS. 6: Ger, Gk, Fr. 7: Tech ed Sprague Electric Co, N Adams Mass 52-55, Libn 55-69; Assoc libn Lehigh U 69-. 9: SLA. 13: Yes. 14: Sci libs. 15: Mart Lib Lehigh Univ, Bethlehem Pa 18015.

GARITANO, JUDITH JEFFREYS. b Alamance County NC 4 My 38. 5: Wake Forest 56-60 (Eng) BA; UNC (Chapel Hill) 63, 64-65 MS in LS. 7: Tchr Winston-Salem City Schs, Winston-Salem NC 60-62; Tchr & lib asst Sachem Sch Dist, Long Is NY 62-63; Tchr fayetteville City Schs, Fayetteville NC 63-64; Libn & NC Advancement Sch, Winston-Salem NC 65-66, Assoc state supv of fed programs for instr materials 66-68; State supv sch libs State Dept of Pub Instr, Raleigh NC 68-. 9: ALA; SEastLA; NCLA; NCEA; Beta Phi Mu, sec-treas of NC Chapter 69-71. 10: Kappa Mu Epsilon; Phi Sigma Iota; Phi Beta Kappa. 14: Sch libs. 15: 2016 Carroll dr, Raleigh NC 27608.

GARLAND, CHARLOTTE. b Scranton Iowa 24 F 21. 5: Drake U 42 (Eng) AB; UMich 44 ABLS. 7: Catlgr UMich Gen Lib (Ann Arbor) 44-45; Catlgr Pub Lib of Des Moines,

Des Moines Iowa 51-. 9: ALA; IowaLA. 10: Foster Parents Plan; Wesleyan Serv Guild; Phi Beta Kappa; Phi Kappa Phi. 14; Catlg. 15: 2600 Hubbell, Des Moines Ia 50317.

GARLAND, JOHN LOUIS. b Seattle 18 S 28. 4: Paula Mary Joy. 5: St Edwards 46-50 (Philos) AB; Catholic U 51-53 MSLS; Georgetown U 55-59 LLB. 6: Fr. 7: Grad Lib Fellowship Catholic U 51-53; US Coast Guard active duty 53-55, current rank Lt; Ref analyst CIA,Wash DC 55-58; Systems analyst info systems GE, Bethesda Md 58-61; Systems analyst intelligence systems IBM, Bethesda Md 61-63, Manager legal info systems 63-65; Manager corp info retrieval serv IBM, Armonk 65-67; Mgr Info Retrieval Dvlpt IBM, Armonk 67-68; Mgr Advanced Systs Techniques 68-. 10: Lib Sci Chap, Catholic U Alumn Assn. 11: IBM Outstanding Contribution Award, 63. 13: Yes. 14: Application of computers to lib info ctr functions, mgt info & systems, legal info systems. 15: Brook Farm rd, Bedford Village NY 10506.

GARLAND, VIRGINIA L. b Pittsburgh 12 D 05. 5: Wellesley 24-26; UPittsburgh 26-28 (LS) AB; Carnegie 2 (LS) Certif. 7: Asst ref dept Carnegie Lib of Pittsburgh 26-28, Br asst Homewood Br 28-32; Libn Philadelphia Co, Pittsburgh 32-51; Libn tech dept, Pittsburgh 51-. 9: SLA (past pres Pittsburgh Chap). 10: Natural Color Camera Club; Photographic Soc of Amer. 12: Ed "Science and Technology", purchase guide for pub libs (65-). 13: Yes. 14: Sci & tech ref. 15: 4601 Bayard st, Pittsburgh Pa 15213.

GARLOCH, LORENA A. b North Girard Penn 28 S 08. 4: Paul H Byers. 5: Westminister Col 24-27; UMich 27-28 AB in LS; UPittsburgh 41-43 MA in Geog; Rutgers 56. 6: Fr, Sp. 7: Catlgr Oberlin Col 28-29; Order libn Amer Lib in Paris, Paris France 30-31; Ref libn UPittsburgh 31-39, Dir of pub serv 40-46, Asst libn & Lecturer 47-51, Act U libn 52-53, U Libn 54-63; Asst Prof Rutgers 64-66; Assoc Prof SUNY (Buffalo) 66-68; Dir of instl Research La Roche Col 68-. 8: Lecturer on travel abroad UPittsburgh 60-; Conductor of European trips; Judge geog shows Buhl Planatarium Pittsburgh 58-; Evaluator of Middle States Assn var times. 9: ALA-ACRL (chm Com on Urban U Libs 59-66, Com on Nat Lib Week 62-64, pres Tri-State ACRL); Soc of Indexers (Brit); PennLA (pres 60-61). 10: Geog Club of Western Penn; AAUP; Sigma Xi; Phi Alpha Theta; Pitsburgh Lib Club. 12: Ed "Library Trends" (Ap 62). 13: Yes. 14: Ref, bibliog. 15: 1558 Graham blvd, Pittsburgh Pa 15235.

GARLOCK, NORENE L. b Oneida NY 16 D 28. 5: State U Col (Geneseo NY) 46-50 (LS) BS in Ed; Syracuse 61 MS in LS. 7: Libn St Johnsville Central Sch, St Johnsville NY 50-56; High sch libn New Hartford Central Sch, New Hartford NY 56-60, Sch lib supv 60-68; High sch libn, Oneida NY 68-69; Lib coord Oneida City Sch Syst, Oneida NY 69-. 8: Libn at Child World, Lib/USA, NY Worlds Fair 65. 9: NEA; NYLA (Sch Lib Sect; treas 63, mem Bd 67-69); (treas Sch Libs Sect 63); NY State Tchrs Assn (del 60-, chm Lis Sect 58 & 66); Central NY Libns Assn (pres 58). 10: New Hartford Tchrs Assn; Utica Educ Film Exch, Zonta. 14: Sch lpbs, a-v materials, bk rev. 15: R D 2 West rd, Oneida NY 13421.

GARMON, KAY (WINSETT). b Pamplin Va 6 S 36. 5: Del Mar Jr Col 55-56; Col of William & Mary(Richmond Prof Inst Br) even 57-65, (LS). 7: Lib clerk W B Ray High Sch, Corpus Christi Tex 55-56; Girl fridayLocal Loan Co, San Diego 56; Girl friday Walt Tufford Inc, San Diego 57; Lbn Virginia-Carolina Chem Co, Richmond Va 57-60; Libn Texaco Exp Inc, Richmond Va 60-65; Libn Xerox Corp, Rochester NY 66-. 9: SLA (Aerospace Div); AALL; MonroeCoLA. 10: Bon Air Jr Womens Club. 12: Comp 1st Ed, Coord 2nd Ed "Richmond-Hopewell Special Libraries 14: Admin. 15: 2103 East ave apt B, Rochester NY 14610.

GARNER, MARGARET (TOLIVER). b Beckley WVa 18 Ap 16. 4: Marvin P Garner. 5: Transylvania Col 32-36 (Eng) AB; Columbia 36-37 (LS) BS. 7: NY Pub Lib: Circ asst 37-41, Assoc br Libn 46-47; Asst libn Sate U Col (Potsdam NY) 53-64, Assoc libn 64-. 14: Acquis, tech proc. 15: State Univ Col Lib, Potsdam NY 13676.

GARNER, VIVIAN COCHRAN. b Walla Walla Wash 11 Jl 11. 4: Kenneth E Garner. 5: Whitman Col 29-33 (Eng) AB; UWash 33-34 AB in Libnship. 7: Asst libn & catlgr Walla Walla Pub Lib, Walla Walla Wash 34-46, 52-. 9: ALA; PNLA; WashLA. 10: AAUW. 14: Catlg. 15: 1217 Bonsella, Walla Walla Wa 99362.

GAROOGIAN, ANDREW. b Brooklyn NY 10 Ja 28. 4: Rhoda Lillian Garoogian. 5: Brooklyn Col 45-48, 58-60 (Pol Sci) BA, 67-; Pratt 60-62 MLS. 7: (Pfc) US Army Area Serv Unit, Camp Polk La 50-52; Sr libn asst div chief Soc Sci Div Brooklyn Pub Lib, Grand Army Plaza 62-66; Brooklyn Col Lib soc sci ed div 66-. 9: CUNYLA. 10: Amer Pol Sci Assn. 12: Research ed (free-lance), Grolier Soc (NY), 64-, 65. 14: Ref . 15: 200 E 17 st, Brooklyn NY 11226.

GARRALDA, JOHN C. b Elko Nev 13 S 34. 4: B Jean Boger. 5: Southwest Col (Winfield Kan) 51-52; Kan State Col (Pittsburg) 53-56 (Speech) BS; UDenver summers 59-63 (LS) MA. 7: High sch Eng & lib Severy High CH, Severy Kan 58-63; Ser, documents libn Kan State Col 63-. 67; Asst Prof lib sci 67-69; Dir lib 69-. 9: ALA; KanLA; KanASchL. 10: AAUP. 14: Lib admin. 15: Porter Lib Ks State Col, Pittsburgh Ks 66762.

GARRARD, NELL. b Durham NC 12 06. 5: Duke 24-28 (Hist) AB; Emory 28-29BLS. 7: Catlgr Pub Lib, Durham NC 29-30; Catlgr Duke U Lib 30-32; Catlgr, Libn Greenwood City & Co Pub Lib, Greenwood SC 39-47; Libn Cherokee Co Pub Lib, Gaffney Sc 47-. 9: ALA; SELA; SCLA. 10: AAUW. 15: 210 N Limestone st, Gaffney SC 29340.

GARRATT, LORIS (HUSEBOE). b Madison Wis 30 S 28. 4: Rowland M Garratt. 5: UWis 46-50 9eng) BA; UWash 64-66 MLS. 7: Asst (educ dept) Seattle Pub Lib 66-68; Asst (lit dept) 68-. 9: PNLA; WashLA. 10: Beta Phi Mu. 14: Religious & philos collections. 15: 2540 NE 106th pl, Seattle Wa 98125.

GARRAWAY, MARTHA (STENNETT) b Ellisville Miss 10 F 41. 4: Charles W Garraway. 5: USoMiss 62 (LS) BS; UMiss 64-65 (LS); USoMiss 65-66 (LS) MS in LS. 7: Libn W Tallahatchie High Sch, Webb Miss 62-63; Jr high libn Holly Springs City Sch, Holly Springs Miss 63-65; Delta State Col, Cleveland Miss 66-68. 9: ALA; MissLA; MissEA. 14: Periods. 15: Box 2380 So Station, Hattiesburg Ms 39401.

GARRETSON, GEORGE DALTON. b Roanoke Va 27 D 25. 4: Elizabeth Wheeler. 5: Roanoke 59-64 (Eng) BA; Drexel 64-65 MSLS. 7: Sgt USMC 44-46; Dept hd Roanoke Pub Lib, roanoke Va 59-63; Hd libn Memorial Lib of Radnor Twp, Wayne Penn 65-. 8: Scarescrow press Award Com 68; Proj chm Lib Pub Relations Assn of Greater Phila 67-68. 9: Nat Aid to Visually Handicapped (Adv Bd); PennLA (chm SE Chap). 14: Admin. 15: Box 55, Wayne Pa 19087.

GARRETT, (HARLEY) STUART. b Knoxville Tenn 2 F 31. 5: UTenn 49-52 (Music); E Tenn State U 52-53 (Music) BS; Peabody 59-60 (LS) MA. 6: Fr.07: Asst adv acct exec Gunn-Mears Adv Agcy, NYC 54-57; Adv acct exec Furman-Roth Agency, NYC 57-59; Catlgr Free Lib of Phila 60-63; Catlgr UTenn 63-. 9: ALA; TennLA; SELA. 10: Beta Phi Mu. 14: Catlg. 15: Rt 3, Corryton Tenn 37721.

GARRETT, MARY ELIZABETH (McDADE). b DeKalb Miss 2 D 18. 4: Edgar J Garrett. 5: E Miss Jr Col 36-38; Miss Womans Col 38-39; Miss State Col for Women 39-40 (Eng) AB; UAla summer 41 (LS). 6: Fr. 7: Eng tchr & Libn Walnut Grove High Sch, Walnut Grove 41-43; Eng tchr & libn Jett High Sch, Vicksburg Miss 44-46; Steno P P Williams Co, Vicksburg Miss 46-56; US Army Engnr Waterways Expt Station, Vicksburg Miss: Steno 56-57, Lib asst 57-60, Libn ref & bibliog 60-. 9: MissLA (sec Spec Libs Sect 60). 11: Superior Performance Award (Waterways Expt Sta) 58. 14: Ref, bibliog. 15: 127 Porters Chapel rd, Vicksburg Miss 39180.

GARRETT, NORMA JEAN. b Tuscumbia Ala 25 Ag 37. 5: Ala State Col 56-60 (Bus) BS, Lane col 67; Memphis State 66 (LS); UTenn 67, 68 (LS). 6: Fr. 7: Sec to libn Lane Col 60, Asst in catlg 60-, Acquis libn 64. 9: TennLA. 10: NAACP; Alpha Kappa Alpha; W Tenn Coop Com. 11: Citation for outstanding serv from Alpha Phi Alpha. 14: Acquis, rare bks, spec collection (Negro bks). 15: 905 Lane ave apt 4, Jackson Tn 38301.

GARRETT, ROBERTA ANNE (STEVENS). b Newark Ohio 15 S 17. 5: Muskingum Col 34-36; UTenn(Knoxville) 36-38 (Fr) BA; UMich(Ann Arbor) 41-43 ABLS. 6: Fr. 7: Asst Newark Pub Lib, Newark Ohio 38-41; Jr catlgr UMich(Ann Arbor) 41-43, Jr med-libn 43-45; Libn MIB Hosp(Cooperstown NY) 45-47; Libn Owens-Corning Fiberglas Corp, Newark Ohio 47-52; Asst catlgr Denison U & part time asst Newark Pub Lib 52-60; Ref asst Ohio State U 61-62, Head Veterinary Med Lib 62-. 8: Supv Physics Lib Ohio State U 64-65; Supv Aero-Civil & Electrical Engnr Libs Ohio State U 65. 9: MedLA. 14: Ref. 15: 2372 Swansea rd, Columbus Ohio 43221.

GARRISON, ALICE MARIE. b Smith Center Kan 20 F 14. 5: Long Beach Jr Col 31-33 (Eng) AA; UCLA 33-35 (En) BA; Pratt 37-38 MLS; USoCal 46-49 (Educ) MS Ed. 7: Catlgr Pratt

Inst 38-40; Libn Long Beach Pub Lib, Long Beach Cal 40-43; Clubmob capt Amer Red Cross, European Theater 43-45; Libn Long Beach Pub Lib, Long Beach Cal 45-46; Libn Jordan High Sch, Long Beach Cal 46-49; Libn Long Beach City Col 49-. 9: NEA; Cal Tchrs Assn; CalASchL; CalLA. 10: Cal Jr Col Faculty Assn; Tchrs Assn of Long Beach; Long Beach Sch Libns Assn; Long Beach Art Mus; Los Angeles Co Mus of Art; UN Assn. 14: Catlg. 15: 21 Via Di Roma walk, Long Beach Ca 90803.

GARRISON, GUY GRADY. b Akron Ohio 17 D 27. 4: Joanne Sergeant. 5: Baldwin-Wallace Col 46-50 (Eng) BA; Columbia 53-54 (LS) MS; UIll 58-60 (LS) PhD. 7: US Army Infantry 50-52; Stud asst Columbia U Libs 53; Trainee NY Pub Lib 54; Br libn, head of circ, asst libn Oak Park Pub Lib, Oak Park Ill 54-58; Grad Col Fellow UIll(Urbana) 58-60; Head of reader serv Kansas City (Mo) Pub Lib 60-62; Research assoc prof, Research Prof & dir LRC Grad Sch of Lib Sci Drexel, Philadelphia 68-. 9: ALA; PennLA. 10: Beta Phi Mu. 12: "A Statewide Reference Network for Wisconsin Libraries (64); "Research Methods in Librarianship (Library Trends 13:1, Issue ed) (64); Co-auth "Library Resources in the North Country Area of New York State (66); "The Changing Role of State Library Consultants (68). 13: Yes. 14: Pub libs, state libs, lib bldgs, lib educ. 15: Grad Sch of Lib Sci Drexel, Philadelphia Pa 19104.

GARST, GLENDA FAE. b Clarksdale Miss 23 Je 42. 5: Miss State Col for Women 60-64 (Eng) BA; LSU 64-65 (LS) MS. 6: Sp, Fr. 7: Asst Prof of Lib Sci U Libs U Southwestern La 65-. 9: ALA; LaLA. 10: Phi Kappa Phi. 12: "Library Handbook, USouthwest La (67); Ed "Dupre Library Newsletter. 13: Yes. 14: Ref, tchg. 15: 106 Wilcox st, Lafayette La 70501.

GARST, MARY ELIZABETH. b Clarksdale Ms 6 S 08. 5: Our Lady of the Lake Col 26-27; Miss State Col for Women 27-30 (Eng) AB; UIll 30-31 BS in LS. 7: Asst libn St Mary col (Leavenworth Kan) 32-33; Asst libn Carnegie Pub Lib, Clarksdale Miss 33-38, 43-47; Libn Col of Our Lady of the Elms 38-43; Asst libn LSU (Baton Rouge) 48-. 9: ALA; LaLA. 10: LSU Lib Staff Assn; Cath Daughters of Amer. 12: Mng ed LaLA Bulletin. 14: Ref, travel. 15: 2403 Horace st, Baton Rouge La 70808.

GARTLAND, HENRY JOSEPH. b Somerville Mass 2 Ap 13. 4: Alice Johnson Gartland. 5: Boston Col 32-36 (Soc Sci) AB; Boston Tchrs Col 36-37 (Educ) M Ed; Simmons 49-50 MS in LS. 7: Ref libn Boston Pub Lib 29-41; Lib off, Ft Lee Va 42-4; Lib off Army Serv Forces, NY 44-45; Lib off US Army-Europe, Paris, France 45; Lib off US Army Japan, Tokyo 46; USVA: Br libn, Boston 46-49, Asst dir lib serv, Wash DC 49-54, Dir Lib Serv, Wash DC 54-. 8: Chief, Army Lib Program, 49-65; Fed Lib Com (chm Physics Fac). 9: MedLA. 10: US Army Reserve, Staff Spec (Col); Assn of Mil Surgeons of US. 13: Yes. 14: Admin. 15: 4416 N 25th st, Arlington Va 22207.

GARTON, PAULINE MICCICHE. b Penn 5 F 39. 4: George E Garton. 5: UBuffalo 57-61 (Eng) BA; Canisius Col 61-63 (Teaching Eng) MS; West Res 63-64 MSLS; UMd 58 "Inst on the Automation of Bibliog Serv". 6: Fr. 7: Tchr Lockport Sch System, LOCKPORT NY 61-62; Tchr Buffalo City Schs, Buffalo NY 62; Lib asst DYouville Col 63; Bibliog UWash Lib 64, Asst ser libn 64-67; Hd per dept Fresno State Col 67-. 8: Mem Conference on Educ & Manpower for Libnship, ALA, West sts. 9: ALA (Exec Bd JMRT 69-71); ASIS; CalLA (alternate campus rep Fresno State Col Chap 68). 10: Bd Dirs UWash Lib Staff Assn; UWash Faculty Womens Club; Assn Cal State Col Profs. 13: Yes. 14: Tech serv, acquis, catlg, automation. 15: 4580 E Garland, Fresno Ca 93726.

GARTON, WILLIAM W. b Cambria Iowa 9 Ag 35. 4: (Mary) Sue Anderson. 5: Simpson Col 55-59 (Hist) BA; UIll 59-60 MSLS; Simpson Col summer Grad Program 65 (Amer Studies); UIll 68-69 (Hist). 6: Fr, Ger. 7: Grad asst UIll Lib (Urbana) 59-60; Head Libn Simpson Col 60-. 9: ALA; IowaLA. 10: AAUP. 14: Admin, acquis. 15: Dunn Library Simpson College, Indianola Iowa.

GARVER, ELIZABETH (FINCH). b Indianapolis 20 My 17. 4: Clyde L Garver. 5: DePauw U 34-38 (Lat) AB; UMich 59-63 MALS. 6: Lat, Sp. 7: Jr libn Indianapolis Pub Lib 39-44; Ref libn Kent Co Lib, Grand Rapids Mich 54-55, 57-58, Br libn 58-63; Sch libn Union High Sch, Grand Rapids Mich 63-64; Head child serv KentCo Lib, Grand Rapids Mich 65-. 9: ALA; MichLA (Com on Lib Serv to Child); MichASchL. 10: Womens Natl Bk Assn; Amer Bus Womens Assn. 14: Child serv. 15: 726 Fuller ave, Grand Rapids Mi 49505.

GARVIN, BARBARA T. b Manatee Fla 20 F 37. 4: James S Garvin Jr. 5: Fla So Col 55-59 (Eng) AB; Emory 59-60 MLS. 7: Stud asst E T Roux Lib Fla So Col 55-59; Lib asst Ocala Fla Pub Lib 56-59; Asst Union Catalogue Atlanta-Athens Area, Atlanta 59; Libn I Fine Arts Dept Atlanta Pub Lib 59-61; Asst libn Fulton Co Bd of Educ Russell High Sch, East Point Ga 61-63, Libn Jere Wells Elem Sch 64-65; Catlgr Smyrna Pub Lib, Smyrna Ga 65; Elem & Jr high lib supv Mariette Ga City Schs 68-69; Libn Hickory Hills Elem Sch 68-69. 9: NEA; GaEA (Child & YP Sect); GaLA; ALA. 10: Delta Tau Delta; Pi Gamma Mu. 14: Child & yp wk, ref, fine arts. 15: 2504 Glendale circle, Smyrna Ga 30080.

GARVIN, JEWEL H. b Ga 27 Jl 10. 5: Fla State Col for Women 28-32 Modern Langs) AB; Emory 32-33 BS in LS, summer 64 (Med Libnship). 7: Head Libn Cox Col 33-34; Head Libn org lib for Atlanta Bureau Federal Transient Prog 34-35; Clsf & catlg spec libs for: Civil War Lib Chicka & Chatta Mil Park 36, & Soc Welfare Lib for Soc Planning Coun Atlanta 39; Exec Sec Ga Conf on Soc Welfare, Atlanta 39-44; Head Libn Napsonian High Sch, Atlanta 46-48; Head Libn Ocala Pub Lib, Ocala Fla 51-60; Asst libn J Hillis Miller Health Center Lib UFla 60-. 8: Clsf, catlg, org spec lib for Ga Tax Revision Com 49; Spec assignments, Emory U Lib Sch 48, 49; Consul Venice (Fla) Pub Lib summer 63. 9: ALA; MedLA; SELA; FlaLA (chm & mem var coms, treas). 10: LWV; Springlake-Wildwood Civic Club; PTA; Beta Pi Theta; Great Bks Discussion Group. 13: Yes. 14: Pub serv, ref, rare bks, bibliotherapy. 15: University Station ox 12546, Gainesville Fla.

GARVIN, MRS LOUISE B. b Orangeburg SC 24 Ja 07. 4: John Calhoun Garvin. 5: Columbia 24-26; Randolph- Macon 26-29 (Hist) BA; Emory 30-31 BA in LS; Columbia summer 39 (LS). 6: Fr, Ger, Sp. 7: Sch libn Badin Pub Sch, Badin NC 33-35; Sch libn Wadesboro Schs, Wadesboro NC 35-36; Libn Thackson High Sc, Orangeburg SC 36-43; Libn (Civilian) Army, Ft Benning Ga 43-46; Libn Opportunity Sch, Columbia SC 46-51; Chief of tech serv Augusta-Richmod County Pub Lib, Augusta Ga 51-64; Catlgr USC 64-. 9: ALA; SELA; SCLA. 10: Bus & Prof Womens Club. 14: Catlgr. 15: 1507 12th st, Cayce SC 29033.

GARWOOD, SAM. 5: Nyack Missionary Col 54-58 (Bible) BS; NYU 60-64 (Hebrew Culture) MA; Rutgers 65-66 MLS. 6: Ger, Hebrew. 7: Catlgr Brooklyn Col Lib, Brooklyn NY 66-. 14: Catlg, reclsf, ref. 15: 697 E 22nd st, Brooklyn NY 11210.

GARYPIE, RENWICK. b Massapequa NY 21 My 32. 4: Barbara Phillips. 5: Hamilton Col 50-54 (Eng Lit) AB; UMich 55-56 MALS; Wayne State 58- (Publ Admin). 6: Sp. 7: Lib aid Wayne County Lib, Plymouth Mich 55; US Army Finance Corps Disbursing Spec (S/Sgt) 56-57; Br libn Wayne County Lib, Inkster Mich 58-59; Head a-v dept Wayne County Lib, Wayne Mich 60-62; Dir Ingham County Lib, Mason Mich 62-67; Dir Sioux City Pub Lib, Sioux City Ia 67-. 9: ALA (Life mem); MichLA (Legis chm 63-64); IowaLA (Legisl Com 68-69). 10: Amer Film Festival (Judge 60 & 61); Kiwanis Club; Amer Interprofess Inst. 13: Yes. 14: Admin. 15: 2310 E Solway, Sioux City Ia 51104.

GASKIN, MARTIN S. b NYC 10 Jl 32. 4: Helen Pessin. 5: West Mich U 56-59 (Hist) BA; UMd 59-56; UMich 59-63 MALS. 6: Fr. 7: Admin spec USAF A/1c 51-56; Libn Roseville Sch System, Roseville Mich 59-64, Tchr 64-65; Ref libn Macomb Co Commun Col 64-67; Dir Lib servs, St Clair Commun Col 67-. 8: Teach use of lib throughout Commun Col; Bldg consul to pub and med libs. 9: ALA; -ACRL (Instr & Use of Com, chm Jr Col Sect); MichLA; MSchAVA; NEA-DAVI. 10: Lib Study Commsn, Sterling Twp Mich (chm); BNai Brith. 12: "Library Handbook Macomb Co Commun Col (65); "Library Handbook St Clair Co Commun Col (67). 14: Ref, readers adv. , admin, instr materials. 15: 690 Chippewa, Mt Clemens Mi 48403.

GASTL, LeROY FREDERICK. b Lawrence Kan 17 My 25. 5: Kan State Tchrs Col (Emporia) 46-50 (Eng, Soc Sci) BS in Ed; UKan summers 51-53 (Psych); Kan State Tchrs Col (Emporia) 56-57 (LS) MS. 6: Lat, Sp. 7: Tec-5 Mil Railway Serv US Army, US & Europe 43-46; Eng tchr, libn Pawnee Rock High Sch, Pawnee Rock Kan 50-51; Eng tchr, libn Sterling City Schs, Sterling Kan 51-53; Eng tchr Junction City High Sch, Junction City Kan 53-55; Hdqrs libn Johnston Co Lib, Shawnee-Mission Kan 57-59; Owner-manager Gastls Bk Shop, Mission Kan 59-64; Assoc libn ref Chadron State Col 65-. 9: ALA; NebLA; Neb State EA; Chadron State Col EA. 10: AAUP. 14: Ref, ser, lib sci educ. 15: 120 E Tenth st, Chadron Neb 69337.

GASTON, MABLE YOUNG. b Calhoun City Miss 21 Ap 26. 5: Miss State Col for Women 44-48 (HIST) B ; UMiss 55, 57, 58 MLS. 7: Libn Forrest Co Agric High Sch, Brooklyn Miss 48-57; Libn Greenville High Sch, Greenville Miss 57-. 8: Visiting Asst Prof of Lib Sci, UMiss summers 60-. 9: ALA; NEA; ClrTA; MissLA (sec 60); MissASchL (pres 62); MissEA. 10: Delta Kappa Gamma; DAR; Alpha Beta Alpha; AAUW.14: Sch libs, rel. 15: Box 366, Calhoun City Miss.

GAT, DIMITRI VSEVOLOD. b Pittsburgh 5 O 36. 4: Margaret Moses. 5: Carnegie 54-57 (Chem Engnr); UPittsburgh 58-60 (Eng) BA, 61-62 MLS. 6: Fr. 7: Advertising asst Calgon Corp, Pittsburgh 60-61; Bus Sch Lib UPittsburgh 61-62; Descr catlgr Harvard U Widener Lib 62-63, Admin asst Dir Off 64-66; Asst libn tech serv Harvard Grad Sch Educ 66-69; Asst libn Mt Holyoke Col 69-. 9: ALA; ASIS; SLA; MassLA. 10: Harvard Lib Club. 12: Ed "The Harvard Librarian," monthly newsletter 65-66; Auth "The Shepherd Is My Lord," novel (69). 14: Catlg, small col lib admin. 15: Williston Memorial Lib Mt Holyoke Col, South Hadley Ma 01075.

GATES, BARBARA A(NN). b Worcester Mass 8 Ap 24. 5: Simmons 42-46 (LS) BS; Columbia 51-53 (LS) MS. 7: Catlgr Iowa State Col 46-49; Catlgr Vassar Col 49-52; Head tech serv Pub Lib of Brookline, Brookline Mass 53-60; Sr catlgr Boston U Libs 60-62, Head ser dept 62-. 67; Hd task force 67-69; Hd tech serv Oberlin Col 69-. 9: ALA-ACRL;-RTSD; MassLA; NELA; NE Tech Serv Libns (pres 58-59). 10: AAUW; Mass Soc for Univ Educ of Women. 14: Ser (acquis & catlg). 15: 130 Elm st, Oberlin Oh 44074.

GATES, FRANCIS. b Sacramento Cal 28 Ap 27. 5: UCal(Berkeley) 52 (Pol Sci) AB, 54 BLS; San Francisco Law Sch 63 LLB. 7: Libn soc sci ref serv Gen Lib UCal (Berkeley)54-60; Libn & research attorney Continuing Educ of the Bar, U Ext, Berkeley 60-. 9: AALL (chm Recr Com 64-66, mem Place Com 61-, chm Com on Fed Legisl 69-70; pres West Pacific Chap 69-70); State Bar of Cal; San Francisco Co Bar Assn; Alameda Co Bar Assn (Com on Legisl). 10: Phi Beta Kappa. 12: "Review of Selected 1963 Code Legislation; "Review of Selected 1965 Code Legislation; etc. 13: Yes. 14: Law lib admin, spec ref problems, law off mgt. 15: P O Box 815, Berkeley Ca 94701.

GATES, JEAN KEY. b Carthage Ark 23 S 11. 5: Hendrix Col 27-30 (Fr) BA; Ark summers 41, 43, 46, 48 (Educ Admin); Catholic U 50-51 MS in LS; George Washington U summers 56, 59 Educ Fr). 6: Fr. 7: Tchr of Fr & Eng Fourche Valley High Sch, Briggsville Ark 30-31; Tchr Thornton Elem Sch, Thornton Ark 33-34; Tchr of Fr & Eng Eudora High Sch, Eudora Ark 34-37; Co Supv of Schs, Chicot Co Ark 37-49; Libn DC Tchrs Col 51-58, Libn in chg of Lib Instr 58-63; Visiting Lecturer Col of Educ Lib Sci Educ UMd 64-66; Lecturer Col of Educ Lib a-v educ U So Fla 66-68; Asst Prof 68-69. 8: Educl adv "The College Library Series, six filmstrips correl with "Guide to the Use of Books and Libraries, McGraw-Hill Bk Co, 65; Consul ed, McGraw-Hill Ser in Lib Sci, 65-. 9: FlaEA; FlaASchL. 10: Delta KappaGamma; Beta Phi Mu. 12: "Guide to the Use of Books and Libraries (62, 2nd ed 69); "Introduction to Librarianship (68). 13: Yes. 14: Tchg, ref, instr in use of lib, hist of bks & libs. 15: 4015 Bayshore blvd, Tampa Fl 33611.

GATLIFF, JANE WANDA. b Chillicothe Ohio. 5: Wilberforce U 35-39 (Bus Educ) BS; Atlanta U 52-53 (LS) MS. 6: Fr. 7: Priv sec Phillis Wheatley Assn, Cleveland Ohio 40-42; Accounting clerk Bureau of Unemployment Comp, Columbus Ohio 42-52; Ref libn Ohio State U 53-57; Interlib loan libn Ohio State U 57. 9: ALA. 13: Yes. 14: Ref, interlib loan. 15: 2074 Greenway North, Columbus Ohio 43219.

GATLIN, PATRICIA (FULLER). b Hilton Village Va 16 Je 27. 4: Thomas W Gatlin Jr. 5: Westhampton Col URichmond 44-48 (Psych) BA; Washington U St Louis) even 63-68 (LS). 7: Hosp libn US Army, Ft Belvoir Va 49-52; Lib asst Kan City (Mo) Pub Lib 53-62; Tech libn Union Electric Co, St Louis 63-67; Supv of lib servs 67-. 9: SLA (Greater St Louis Chap: Memb Chm 65)68, employment chm 69). 14: Catlg, ref. 15: Union Electric Co Lib P O Box 149, St Louis Mo 63166.

GATNER, ELLIOTT S(HERMAN) M(OZIAN). b NYC 24 O 14. 4: Shirley Golden Gatner. 5: LIU 34-36 (Eng, Hist) BA; City Col (NY) 37-39 (Educ) MS; Columbia 39-40, 46-47 (LS) BS, 48-50, 52-54 (Ed Admin, Hist). 6: Fr, Ger. 7: US Army Artillery & Infantry (Pvt to 1st Lt) 41-46; Instr in Eng LIU 39-47, Instr in hist & govt 48-52; US Army Infantry (Capt) 5052; LIU: Asst Prof of Hist & Govt 53-56, Ref libn 53-61, Assoc Prof of hist 56-63, Asst dir of libs 61-64, Prof of hist 63-. Asst to the Provost 64-65, Assoc dir of libs 65-. 8: Dir, Veterans Affairs (LIU) 46-50; Lecturer Air Force Reserve Train Program, 55; Consul Southampton Col Lib, 62-64; Assoc Dir IU Press, 64-. 9: ALA; AHA; Mod Lang Assn; NCTE; Col Eng Assn; Acad Libs of Brooklyn (pres). 10: AAUP. 11: NY State Conspicuous Service Cross; Bronze Star Medal. 12: "Cooperatve Agreements Among Institutions of Higher Education (41); "Study Guide to English Literature, 2 v (47-48); "Handbook of Research and Report Writing, 10th ed (64); Ed "Life, Land and Water in Ancient Peru (65); Ed LIU "Library Leaves (52-); Ed LIU Official Publications (46-50 & 52-54, & occasional later issues). 13: Yes. 14: Ref, bibiog, admin. 15: 81-07 248th st, Bellerose NY 11426.

GATTINGER, (FRISTON) EUGENE. b Duff Sask Can 13 O 20. 4: Edith McAlpine. 5: Tchrs Col (Regina) 38-39 Permanent 1st Class Certif; USask 46-51 BA (Hist); MA (Eng); McGill 51-52 BLS (Eng); U West Ont 58-60. 6: Fr, Ger. 7: Tchr Loch Sloy Sch Dist, Invermay Sask 39-41; Mili serv RCAF, Canada UK 41-45; Libn Can Dept Health & Welfare, Ottawa 52-53; Libn & registrar Ont Veterinary Col (Guelph Ont) 53-63; Head Libn Mem U of Newfoundland (St Johns Newfoundland) 63-67; Asst dir libs York U, Toronto 67-69; Chief libn Toronto Bd Educ 69-. 8: Chm, CACUL (Univs) Report of Position Clsfns & Salaries, 3-yr proj with terml Report at Calgary Conf 66; Consul for Lib Devel, Can Jr Col, Lausanne, Switzerland 69. 9: ALA; CanLA; TorontoLA; Toronto Tchrs LA; APLA (pres). 10: Humanities Assn Can; Guelph Civic Symphony. 11: Can Coun Scholarship 58; Winner, Newfoundland Arts & Letters Competition (Historical Section) 65; Gold Medal for Poetry (67). 12: "The Century of Challenge (62); Ed APLA "Bulletin (63)-67. 13: Yes. 14: Univ lib admin, reclsfn of lib collections; a-v progs (lib orientation). 15: 31 George Henry blvd, Willowdale (Toronto) Ont Can.

GATTON, MRS EDNA. b Coldwater Kan 9 My 10. 4: Harlan Gatton. 5: Drury Col 53-56 (Elem Educ) AB; Kan State Tchrs Col (Emporia) summers 57-61 (LS) MS; UMo(Kan City) summer 64. 7: Libn High sch, Pierce City Mo 57-61; Asst catlgr Porter Lib Kan State Col (Pittsburg) 61-62; Asst libn Pub Lib, N Kan City Mo 63- 66, Libn 66-. 8: Instr in child lit, Park Col, 64 & 65. 9: ALA; MoLA. 14: Child serv. 15: 8103 Highway 9, Parkville Mo 64152.

GATTON, NEIL FRANKLIN. b Lansing Mich 4 Je 33. 5: Mich State U 51-55 (Hist, Eng) AB; UMich 60-64 MALS. 6: Fr, Sp. 7: Secondary tchr Lansing Pub Schs, Lansing Mich 55-56; Personnel admin spec USA, San Francisco 56-58; Secondary tchr Lansing Pub Schs, Lansing Mich 59-60; High sch libn Everett High Sch, Lansing Mich 60-65; Bus Sci & Tech Lib Lansing Pub Lib Lansing Mich 65-. 9: ALA; MichLA. 10: Internat Civitan; UMich Alumni Club; Mich State U Alumni Club; Kappa Delta Pi. 14: Ref, bus & tech serv, a-v. 15: 3330 Tecumseh River rd, Lansing Mich.

GAUCH, M LOIS. b Rochester N. 5: State U Col of Educ (Geneseo NY) 49-53 (LS) BS; URochester 53-56 (Educ) M Ed. 7: Libn Dansville Elem Sch, Dansville NY 53-54; Libn West Irondequoit Sch System, West Irondequoit NY 54-57; Libn Eastman Kodak Co-Nontheatrical Films Div, Rochester NY 57-64, Libn Bus Lib 64-. 9: ALA; SLA (Upstate NY Chap; Dir 64-65, Bulletin ed 64-65, v-pres 67-68, pres 68-69). 10: AAUW. 15: Eastman Kodak Co Bus Lib 343 State st, Rochester NY 14650.

GAUDET, GERALD. b Haverhill Mass 11 D 22. 5: Marist Col 42-44; Fordham 44-48 & 49-53 (Educ, Hist) BS in Ed; Russell Sage 58-59; Rutgers 59-60 MLS; UMd 61, 64. 6: Fr, Sp, Ital. 7: Tchr Marist Brothers, NY 44-58; Sch libn Bd of Educ of Baltimore Co 60-. 8: Libn I, Free Lib of Phila, summers 62-. 9: ALA; Md State Tchrs Assn; Assn of Sch Libns Md; TABCO. 10: Rutgers Alumni Assn Grad Sch of Lib Serv; Nat Cong of Parents & Tchrs. 15: 212 W Franklin st, Baltimore 21201.

GAUDREAULT, DELPHIS. b Rimouski Que Can. 5: Col de Jonquiere 56-63 BA; UOttawa 63-64 BLS. 6: Fr, Ital, Sp, Lat. 7: Clsf-catlgr Col de Jonquiere Lib (Jonquiere Que) 64- 67; Clsf-catlgr Sem St Georges Lib St Georges Beauce Que 67-. 9: CanLA; Assn Canadienne des Bibliothecaires de Langue Francaise. 14: Catlg, clsf. 15: Sem St Georges, St Georges Beauce Que Can.

GAULT, FLORENCE (DICKERSON). b Cuthbert S Dak 26 D 16. 4: William Sherwell Gault Sr. 5: SEast La Col 35-37 (Educ) Tch's Certif; Wayne State 63-66 BSLS. 7: Tchr: Ponchatoula Grammar Sch, Ponchatoula La 37-43, Covington Grammar Sch, Covington La 43-45; Elem sch libn Warren Consolidated Sch Dist, Warren Mich 67-. 9: ALA; NEA; MichEA; WarrenEA. 10: Northwood Meadows Homeowners

Assn, Royal Oak Mich 55-57; YWCA; Royal Oak Womans Club; Oakland Fed of Women's Clubs. 14: Child bks, hist of Fla parishes. 15: 2823 Oliver, Royal Oak Mi 48073.

GAULT, JAMES E(DWARD). b Charlottesville Va 17 Jl 20. 5: Va State Col 36-41 (Art Educ, elem Educ) BS; UCal (Berkeley) 66-67 (Libnship) MLS. 6: Fr, Ger. 7: Marine radio operator US Maritime Serv, NY 43-46; Electronics tech 2c USN 46-49; Electronics tech USNaval shipyards, NY & San Francisco 50-55; Electronics tech com & ind San Francisco Bay Area 56-66; Libn I Contra Costa Co Pub Lib, Pleasant Hill Cal 67-68; Libn I & II, UCal Lib (Berkeley) 68-. 8: YA libn Contra Costa Co Lib, Pittsburgh 67; Ethnic minorities lit adv, UCal Lib 68-. 9: ALA; CalLA. 10: Iota sigma Lambda; Alpha Phi Alpha; Palo Alto Fair Housing Coun; San Mateo Fair Housing Coun. 14: Ref. 15: 1930 Vine st apt 106, Berkeley Ca 94709.

GAUNCE, MARGARET (LONG). b Breckinridge Co Ky. 4: Stewart M Gaunce. 5: Ky Wesleyan Col 29-33 (Eng, Span, Educ) AB; UKy summers 50-55; Catherine Spalding Col 60-62 (LS) MS. 6: Sp. 7: Eng tchr Henry Co Bd of Educ, Pleasureville Ky 3943; Eng tchr Mercer Co Bd of Educ, McAfee Ky 49-50; Tchr-libn Henry Co Bd of Educ, New Castle Ky 52-60, Libn Henry Co High Sch 60-. 8: Com for Rev of Educ Bul "Library Service for Kentucky Schools 64-65. 9: NEA; KyEA; KyLA; KyASchL (treas 65-66; pres 5th Dist 64-65). 10: Bus & Profess Women's Club. 15: New Castle, Ky 40050.

GAUTHIER, JANET ANNE (DANN). b Beaverton Mich 20 J e 12. 4: Orville L Gauthier. 5: Central State Tchrs Col 28-32 (Eng) AB; UMich 38-39 (Educ Admin) MA, 58-62 MLS; Wayne State 54-58 (LS). 6: Sp. 7: Elem tchr Beaverton Pub Schs, Beaverton Mich 32-35; Eng tchr PR Pub Schs, Coamo PR 35-36; Elem tchr Milford Pub Schs, Milford Mich 36-38; Critic tchr Dillon State Tchrs Col 39-40; Elem tchr Grosse Ile Pub Schs, Grosse Ile Mich 40-41; Elem tchr Pontiac Pub Sch, Pontiac Mich 41-45, 47-54; Bus Engnr & Personnel US Coast Guard 47; Head elem libn & prof lib libn, Pontiac Mich 54-. 9: NEA; ALA; AASchL; MICHEA; MichASchL. 10: Bus & Prof Womens Club; Delta Kappa Gamma. 13: Yes. 14: Admin. 15: 110 Spokane dr, Pontiac Mich.

GAUTHIER, SISTER LILLIAN E SBS. b Chippewa Falls Wis 7 S 02. 5: Villanova 21-24 (Educ); Loyola U of the South 27-33 (Fr, Eng) AB; CatholicU 36-39 MSLS; Villanova 47-49 (Fr, lat) AM. 6: Fr, Lat, Sp, Ital. 7: Libn XavierU, New Orleans, 39-45, 53-65; Libn Blessed Sacrament, Cornwells Hts Penn 45-53; Libn Col of Pharmacy XavierU, New Orleans 67-. 8: Dir certif course in lib sci for tchrs 39-45; XavierU of La summers 53-65; Tchrs' Inst & Wkshop Blessed Sacrament Col (Penn) 58. 9: ALA; CatholicLA (chm Greater New Orleans Unit); MedLA; SLA; LaLA (sec Col Sect). 10: Beta Phi Mu. 13: Yes. 14: Ref, train of tchrllibns, med libnship. 15: Lib Col of Pharmacy Xavier Univ of La 7325 Palmetto st, New Orleans La 70125.

GAUTHIER, SISTER MARY EDMOND RSM. b Southbridge Mass 20 S 17. 5: Nazareth Col (Rochester NY) 36-39 (Eng) BA; St Johns U (NY) 40-44 BLS. 6: Fr. 7: Eng tchr Our Lady of Mercy High Sch, Rochester NY 39-42, Libn 43-54; Libn Notre Dame High Sch, Elmira NY 55-61; Libn Cardinal Mooney High Sch, Rochester NY 62-. 66; Eng tchr, libn Our Lady of Mercy High 67-. 15: 1437 Blossom rd, Rochester NY 14610.

GAUVREAU, CATHERINE M (CUMBERLAND). b Wash DC 29 F 12. 4: George P Gauvreau. 6: Russian, Fr, Ger, Sp. 7: Loans US Maritime Commsn, Wash DC 41-54; Libn Ind Col of the Armed Forces, Wash DC 55-65; Libn Naval Ship Research & Development Ctr, wash DC 65-. 9: SLA (Mil Libns, Sci & Tech Divs); DCLA. 11: Presidential Citation for work at Los Alamos NM 45-46. 14: Ref. 15: 3535 Manorwood dr, W Hyattsville Md 20782.

GAVER, MARY VIRGINIA. b Wash DC 10 D 06. 5: Randolph-Macon 23-27 (Eng) AB; Columbia 30-32 BLS, 37-38 MLS, 45-50 (Educ Admin). 7: Libn George Washington High Sch, Danville Va 27-37; Visiting Instr UVa & Emory 34-42; Tech dir WPA of Va, Richmond Va 38-39; Libn Scarsdale High Sch, Scarsdale NY 39-42; Libn & Assoc Prof State Tchrs Col (Trenton NJ) 42-54; Visiting Instr U Tehran (Tehran Iran) 52-53; Assoc Prof & Prof Rutgers U Grad Lib Sch 54-. 8: Chm Adv Com Sch Lib Development Project 60-62, Knapp Sch Libs Proj 62-65. 9: ALA (pres 66-67);-AASchL (pres 59-60);-LED (pres 48-49; chm Spec Com on Nat Manpower 67-69); NEA (Life Mem); NJLA (pres 54-55; co-chm Lib Devel Com 63-68). 10: AAUP; Zonta Internat; Phi Beta Kappa; Womans Nat Bk Assn. 11: Putnam Award 63; Rutgers Res Coun Award 63; Beta Phi Mu; Good Teaching Award 65; LLD LIU (CW Post) 66, Mt Holyoke 68-. 12: "Effectiveness of Centralized Libraries in Elementary Schools " (2nd ed 63); "The Research Manual," with Lucyle Hook (3rd ed 63); "School Libraries of Puerto Rico, with Gonzalo Velazquez" (64); "The Elementary School Library Catalog (65); "Patterns of Development in Elementary School Libraries Today" (3rd ed 69). 13: Yes. 14: Building lib collections, sch libs, child libs. 15: Grad Sch Lib Serv Rutgers U, New Brunswick NJ 08903.

GAY, ANN (HARWELL). b Meridian Miss 24 F 31. 4: Paul Laughlin Gay. 5: Meridian Jr col 49-51 AA; Miss State Col for Women 51-53 BS in LS. 7: Lib asst Gates Memorial Lib, Port Arthur Tex 53-54; Ref unit asst Purdue U Lib 54-56; Hd libn Broadview Pub Lib, Broadview Ill 56-57; Hd libn Choctaw Co Pub Lib, Butler Ala 62-. 9: ALA; AlaLA. 10: Ala Hist Assn. 14: Reader guidance, ref. 15: 308 Miller ave, Butler Al 36904.

GAY, BIRDIE (SPIVEY). b Atlanta Ga 03 Mr 18. 4: Howard Donald Gay. 5: Morris Brown Col 35-39 (Elem Educ) AB; Atlanta U summers 59-62 MSLS. 6: Fr. 7: Tchr & libn Edward r carter Sch, Atlanta 46-49, Libn 49-. 8: NDEA participant in lib wkshop. 9: ALA; NEA; GaTA; GaEA; GaLA; Gate City TA. 10: Beta Phi Mu; YWCA; Sigma Gamma Rho. 14: Ref, child serv, readers serv. 15: 1874 Penelope rd NW, Atlanta Ga 30314.

GAY, PAUL. b Lausanne Switzerland 4 D 10. 4: Katharine D Patterson. 5: Drexel 43 Certif in LS. 6: Fr, Ital. 7: Free lance hist & genealogical research 33-35; Lib asst Phila Museum of Art 35-39; Ed & catlgr Lib Co of Phila 39-43; Biddle Law Lib UPenn: Catlgr 43-46, Act libn 45-46 & 62-63, Asst libn 46-. 8: Consul on legal collections, Penn State U 65. 9: SLA (Adv Coun 40-43, treas 45-46, dir 49-50; chm Fin Com 49, chm Budget & Fin Com 49-50); AALL (chm 56 Phila Conv; served on var coms); Spec Libs Coun of Phila & Vicin (pres 40-43, dir 65; served on numerous coms). 10: Staff Assn UPenn Libs; Suburban Fair Housing Inc; Phila Art Alliance. 14: Admin, catlg, rare bks. 15: Biddle Law Lib 3400 Chestnut st, Phila 19104.

GAYLOR, ROBERT GENE. b Ardmore Okla 16 Mr 39. 5: Jamestown Col 57-60 (Pol Sci); Mich State U 60-61 (Hist) BA; UOkla 61-63 MLS, Wayne State U 67 (Educ). 6: Ger. 7: Documents libn UKan 63-64; Asst U Libn for pub serv Oakland U 65-. 8: Libn Library/ USA NY Worlds Fair 64. 9: ALA; MichLA. 10: AAUP. 14: Ref. 15: 1030 Adams rd S, Rochester Mi 48063.

GAYLORD, ANNE (CARY). b Newport News Va 9 S 13. 4: Stanley H Gaylord. 5: UTampa 31-34; Fla So Col 34-35 (Sci) BS; UNC (Chapel Hill) summers 38-40 BS in LS. 7: Tchr libn Okeechobee High Sch, Okeechobee Fla 35-39; Libn Jackson County High Sch, Marianna Fla 39-41; Libn Fayetteville High Sch, Fayetteville NC 41-42; Libn Hillsborough High Sch, Tampa Fla 59-; Supv of Secondary Libs Hillsborough Co, Tampa Fla. 9: NEA; FlaEA; FlaASchL (dist chm 63-65). 10: Delta Kappa Gamma. 15: 6701 Navin ave, Tampa Fla 33604.

GAYMON, NICHOLAS EDWARD. b Pinewood SC 8 Ap 28. 4: Marjorie Sinkfield. 5: Morehouse Col 46-50 (Biol), 55-56 (Psych) AB; Atlanta 56-59 MSS. 6: Ger. 7: (Cpl) US Army Supply Spec, US 51-53; Structural assemblyman Lockheed Aircraft, Marietta Ga 53-59; Acquis libn Atlanta U 59-65, Circ libn 65; Head libn Dillard U 65-. 8: Visiting Team, So Assn of Col & Schs. 9: ALA; LaLA; SWLA. 10: NAACP; YMCA. 14: Admin, acquis. 15: 2578 Virgil blvd, New Orleans La 70122.

GAYNOR, WILLIAM A. b New Haven Conn 27 O 23. 5 Georgetown U 46-50 (Soc Sci) BS; Fairfield U 50-52 (Educ) MA; Villanova 62-63 (LS) MS. 7: US Navy, S Pacific Area 43-46; Tchr Penn Mil Col 55-56; Libn Valley Forge Mil Acad, Wayne Penn 56-61; Libn Deptfod Twp High Sch, Deptford NJ 61-65; Libn acquis & Period libn Glassboro State Col 65-. 9: ALA; CathLA; NJLA; NJEA. 10: Glassbro State Col Faculty Assn. 14: Acquis, secon sch libs,ser, ref. 15: 215 Yale ave, Swarthmore Penn.

GAZZAWAY, DONALD HOMER. b Dallas 17 F 35. 4: Ann Jackson. 5: So Methodist U 57-60 (Philos); N Tex State U 60-61 (Eng); Arlington State Col 63 (Eng); Southwest Tex State Col 65-67 (Sociol). 7: Mail Clerk Texaco Inc, Dallas 53; I & E NCO Sp 3 US Army, United Kingdom 54-55; Warehouseman Graybar Elec, Dallas 56; Clerk Goldthwaites C, Dallas 56-57; Libn-supv Dallas Pub Lib 57-64; Libn asst Santa Clara C Lib, Campbell Cal 64; Chief Libn Mid-Tex Bkmob Lib, Lockhart Tex 65-68; Bkmob libn Monterey Co Lib, Salinas Cal 68-. 10: Dallas Jazz Soc. 14: Bkmob. 15: 282 Pingree way, Salinas Ca 93901.

GEALER, BEVERLY RUTH (GONTE). b Detroit Mich 15 Ag 33. 4: Aubrey Z Gealer. 5: Wayne state 51-52, 61-66 (LS) BS, 66 Tchr Certif (Mich), 68-. 7: Libn Detroit Pub Schs 67-. 9: ALA. 10: Hadassah, Bnai Brith, Women of Wayne State Alum Assn, Zionist Organ. 14: Sch lib, instr materials ctr. 15: 20277 Alderton, Detroit Mi 48219.

GEARIN, LOUVAN (BRABHAM). b St Louis 5 Jl 17. 5: Fisk U 33-37 (Eng) AB; Atlanta 48-49 BSLS; UMich summers 42, 52-54 MSLS; Washington U 58, 62-64. 7: Tchr Bd of Educ, Monroe City Mo 37-39; Tchr Bd of Educ, Pacific Mo 39-41; Tchr Garfield Sch, Mexico Mo 41-43; Serv rep Southwestern Bell Tel Co, St Louis 44-46; Libn Lincoln Inst, Lincoln Ridge Ky 49-53; Libn Tuskegee Inst summers 50, 56; Libn Steger Jr High Sch, Webster Groves Mo 53-. 8: Instr NDEA Inst, Atlanta U Sch of Lib Sci summer 66. 9: ALA; NEA; MoState Tchrs Assn; MoASchL; Webster Groves Commun TA (Exec Com 64); Greater St Louis Lib Club (Exec Com 60-61); St Louis Suburban SchLA (pres 61-63). 10: Alpha Kappa Alpha; NAACP. 14: Bibliog, ref, bk talks. 15: 11999 Villa Dorado dr apt C, St Louis Mo 63141.

GEARY, KATHLEEN (ANNE). b Pittsfield Mass 28 O 39. 5: Trinity Col. 57-61 (Eng) BA; Simmons 61-63 MLS. 6: Sp. 7: Circ asst St Michaels Col (Burlington Vt) 58-61; Desk asst Simmons Col 62-63; Asst libn Fletcher Free Lib, Burlington Vt 63, Act libn 63, Libn 63-. 8: Organized local libns to form Champlain Valley LA 63 (pres 64-65); organized Cooperative Purchasing program for CVLA(65). 9: NELA (Nom Com 65, 69); VtLA (v-pres & actg pres 65, pres 65-67, chm CertifStudy Com 67, pres pro-temp Pub Lib Sect 68, chm Constit Rev Com 68-69). 10: Zonta Club; LWV; Chittenden Co Hist Soc; Vt Archaeol Soc. 14: Admin, interlib cooperation, rare bks. 15: Fletcher Free Lib, 227 College st, Burlington Vt 05401.

GEBHARD, ELKE MARIA (MEWES). b Hamburg Germany 11 My 20. 4: Karl A Gebhard. 5: UBonn am Rhein & UHamburg (Germany) 40-45 (Chem & Med) BS. 6: Ger, Fr, Russ, Dutch. 7: Libn Lib Depot US Army, Nuernberg Germany 49-50; Med libn 16th Field Hosp US Army, Nuenerg Germany 50-55; Research libn Shulton Inc, Clifton NJ 59-66;Asst libn Warner Lambert Research Inst, Morris Plains NJ 66-. 8: Spec interpreter med dept BAOR, Hamburg Germany (British Occupation Forces) & supt in chg of DP Med Store. 9: SLA. 10: LWV. 14: Lit searches, transl, abstracting in med & chem field. 15: Forest Place, Towaco NJ 07082.

GECKLER, LUCIE HODGES. b Charleston SC 15 Jl 17. 5: Goucher Col 33-37 (Biol) AB; Columbia 38-40 (Bot) MA; Ind U 40-45 (Bot) PhD. 6: Fr, Ger. 7: Johns Hopkins U: Lib asst 58-61, Chem libn 61-65, Sci ref libn 65-. 10: Md Assn for Retarded Child; YMCA; United Christian Citizens; Phi Beta Kappa; Sigma Xi. 13: Yes. 14: Ref. 15: Milton S Eisenhower Lib Johns Hopkins Univ, Baltimore 21218.

GEDDES, ANDREW. b Flushing NY 2 O 22. 4: Elaine S Harrington. 5: Hofstra U 46-50 (Hist) BA; Columbia 50-51 MSLS. 7: Gen asst Brooklyn Pub Lib 51, Asst br libn 52, Br libn 52-55; Admin asst Queens Borough Pub Lib, Jamaica NY 55-56, Chief ext serv 56-60, 61-63, Act personnel dir 60-61; Deputy dir Nassau Lib System, Hempstead NY 63, Dir 64-. 8: Study of the messenger procedure of the Brooklyn Pub Lib 55; Survey of the Patchogue (NY) Pub Lib 62; Survey of Queens Communities with Recommendations for Lib Serv, Jamaica NY 63; Survey of the Finkelstein Mem Lib, Spring Valley NY 63; Survey of the Cherry Hill (NJ) Free Pub Lib 64; Survey of Gloucester City (NJ) Lib 68; Tchr Columbia 68, UKy 68. 9: ALA (chm & mem var coms & var other uties 59-)-LAD(5 coms 60-);-PLA(Nom Com 64); Lib Pub Rel Coun (treas 61-63, 2 coms 63-65); NYLA (pres 65-66, dir & chm 2 coms 62-65); NY Lib Club (treas 57-60, com chm 55-57). : Oceanside Free Lib Assn; Bksellers League of NY; Hofstra Alumni Assn; Columbia Alumni Assn. 12: Ed "Current Trends in Branch Libraries, Library Trends (Ap 66). 13: Yes. 14: Admin, personnel, lib mgt & fin. 15: 29 Patten ave, Oceanside NY 11572.

GEDDES, BRUCE (ALEXANDER). b Winnipeg Manitoba Can 27 N 39. 4: Ruth Elizabeth Howard. 5: UManitoba 61-64 (Eng) BA; UBC 68-69 BLS. 6: Fr. 7: Tchr Canadian Univ Serv Overseas, Jamaica 64-66; Libn (staff) Toronto Pub Lib, Toronto Can 69-. 9: CanLA; ALA. 14: Ref. 15: #2-2505 W 2nd ave, Vancouver 9 British Columbia Can.

GEDDES, ELAINE (HARRINGTON). b LI City, NY 3 Mr 22. 4: Andrew Geddes. 5: SUNY(Geneseo) 39-43 (Elem Educ, LS) BS in Ed, 53 (LS); Hofstra U 53-56 (Secondary Educ). 7: Elem tchr UFSD No 11, Oceanside LI NY 43-44, Libn Jr High Sch 44-. 14: Ya. 15: 29 Patten ave, Oceanside LI NY 11572.

GEEGH, MARGARET IRENE. b Prophetstown Ill 24 Mr 08. 5: Hope Col 26 (Ger); Sioux Falls Col 29-32 (Eng) AB; East Baptist Theol Sem 38-39 (Religious Educ) MRE; UMich 61 AMLS. 6 Ger. 7: Tchr Va Coun of Rel Educ 39-44; State child wkr NJ Baptist Convention, Paterson NJ 45; Clerk Holand Furnace Co, Holland Mich 46-58; Catlgr Herrick Pub Lib, Holland Mich 9-60; Young adult libn Grand Rapids Pub Lib, Grand Rapids Mich 61-, Supv Philos-Relig Dept & ya 67-. 9: ALA; MichLA. 10: Urban League; Grand Rapids Lib Club; Women's Nat Bk Assn. 15: 500 E Fulton, Grand Rapids Mi 49503.

GEER, HELEN THORNTON. b Newcastle Penn 27 Ja 03. 5: Wheaton Col (Mass) 22-26 (Eng Lit) AB; UIll 27-28 BS in LS; Columbia 29-34 (LS) MS. 6: Fr. 7: Circ asst &br libn Pub Lib, Evanston Ill 28-29; Ref libn Flushing Br Queens Borough Pub Lib, Flushing NY 29-36; 1st asst art & music div Queens Borough Pub Lib, Jamaica NY 36-42, Act head bus sci & tech div 42-44; Ref asst Harper Lib U Chicago 44-46; Ed "Bibliographic Index H W Wilson Co, NYC 46-47; Hdqrs libn ALA, Chicago 47-56; Dir The Library Mart (Manufacturers rep), Fairhope Ala 56-58; Ed "Library Literature H W Wilson Co, NY 58-62; Asst libn Wheaton Col (Mass) 62-64; Assoc Prof Grad Lib Sch URI 64-69, Ed wk & consul 69-. 9: ALA-RSD;-ACRL;-LED; SLA (chm Educ & Lib Sci Sect of Soc Sci Div 49-50); Chicago Lib Club (pres 53-54); NELA; RILA. 10: Chicago Wheaton Club. 12: "Charging Systems (55); Ed "Facts and Faces, ALA-RSD (61-). 13: Yes. 14: Ref, hist of bks & ptg, circ systems. 15: 20 Elton st, Providence RI 02906.

GEIGER, GRADY EUGENE. b Columbus Ga 19 Ag 26. 5: Auburn U 47-50 (Eng) BS; UMich 61-63 AMLS. 6: Sp, Ger. 7: Asst to overseer Pepperell Mfg C, Opelika Ala 50-55; Sales correspondent C S Martin Co, Atlanta 55-60; Circ libn Auburn U 60-61; Wk-styd scholar UMich(Ann Arbor) 62-63; Head circ R B Draughon Lib, Auburn Ala 63-. 9: AlaLA (sec-treas f div); SELA. 10: Ala Acad Sci; AAUP. 14: Circ, area bibliog, spec collections. 15: 1010 Rudd ave, Auburn Ala.

GEIL, WILMA JEAN. b Pittsburgh 24 My 39. 5: Swarthmore 57-61 (Music) BA; UIll 62-64 (LS) MS, 61-67 (Musicology). 6: Ger, Fr. 7: Asst music libn UIll(Urbana) 63-. 9: Mus LA; Amer Musicol Soc. 15: 220 Smith Music Hall Univ of Ill, Urbana Ill.

GEIMAN, ROBERT H. b Campbelltown Penn 20 Ag 37. 4: Julia A Fox Geiman. 5: Moody Bible Inst 55-58 (Gen Bible) Diploma; Mich State U 58-61 (Soc Studies) BA; Carnegie Inst of Tech 61-62 MLS. 7: Asst libn Ferris State Col 62-64; Prin-tchr Bur of Indian Affairs, Nunapitchuk Alaska 64-65; Reg Dir of Libs Bur of Com Fisheries, Auke Bay Alaska 65-. 9: PNLA; AlaskaLA. 10: Rotary; Beta Phi Mu. 14: Admin, docs, acquis. 15: Bur of Com Fisheries Box 155, Auke Bay Alaska 99821.

GEIS, ELIZABETH (SARAH) (TALLEY). b Hobart Okla 18 S 07. 4: Clarence George Geis. 5: Phillips U 25-29 (Eng) AB; Columbia 29-30 BLS. 7: Libn Enid Pub Lib, Enid Okla 25-29; Libn Garfield Col Lib, Enid Okla 30-33; Head circ dept UWyo 34-37; Libn Emerson Jr High Sch, Enid Okla 48-59; Libn DeWitt Waller Jr High Sch, Enid Okla 59-66; Asst dir lib resources div Okla State Dept Educ, Okla City, Okla 66-. 8: Instr, Lib Educ Dept, Okla State U summers 62-65. 9: NEA-DAVI; ALA; OklaEA (chm Sch Lib Div); OklaLA. 10: Delta Kappa Gamma; AAUW. 14: Catlg, bk sel, admin. 15: 731 NE 17th st, Oklahoma City Ok 73105.

GEISAR, BARBARA JEAN. b Milwaukee Wis 3 N 42. 5: Milwaukee Downer Col 60-64 (Art) BA, (Hist) BA; UWis (Milwaukee) 64-66; UIll 66-67 MLS. 6: Fr, Sp. 7: Lib stud asst milwaukee Downer Col Lib 63-64; Lib stud asst UWis (Milwaukee) 64-66; Lib intern Milwaukee Journal Co summer 66; Asst acquis libn MarquetteU Mem Lib 67-. 14: Bibliog searching, child & ya lit. 15: 603 W Apple Tree rd, Glendale Wi 53217.

GEISLER, BARBARA (REICHMUTH). b San Francisco Cal 1 Mr 44. 4: William Frederic Geisler. 5: UCal (Berkeley) 62-66 (Eng) AB, 67-68 MLS. 6: Fr, Ger. 7: Serv libn Hastings Col of Law Lib 69-. 9: AALL. 14: Tech serv, rare bks. 15: 10 Tenth ave, San Francisco Ca 94118.

GEISLER, MARY JANE (KURATLI). b Portland Ore 28 O 41. 4: David Conn Geisler. 5: UOre 59-64 (LS) BS; Portland State Col 64-68 (Educ, LS) MS. 6: Lat. 7: Instr Media Libn Beaverton High Sch, Beaverton Ore 64-68; High Sch Libn

Boise Pub Schs, Boise Ida 68-. 8: NDEA Grant, 67; Educl Media; Ore State U. 9: ALA; NEA-DAVI; Ida A-V Assn. 10; AAUW; Pi Beta Phi. 14: YA serv. 15: 1110 Warm Springs ave, Boise Id 83702.

GEISSE, HAROLD L JR. b Wausau Wis 12 D 23. 5: Princeton 46-49 (Philos) BA; Harvard 50-51 (Philos) MA; Columbia 68-69 MS in LS. 6: Fr. 7: S/Sgt USA Inf 43-46; Col textbk salesman Harcourt Brace & Co, NYC 49-50; Ed Liveright Pub Co, NYC 52-53; Copywriter Doremus & Co Advertising, NYC 53-68; Circ libn Olin Lib WesleyanU (Middletown Conn) 69-. 10: Phi Beta Kappa. 14: Circ. 15: Olin Lib Wesleyan Univ, Middletown Ct 06457.

GEIZER, NAN LATILLA (ANNIE). b Halifax NS Can 9 Mr 16. 5: Dalhousie U 32-36 (Eng) BA, MA; Mt St Vincent 57 BLS. 7: Tchr Halifax Bd of Sch Commsnrs, Halifax NS 37-41; Army (CWAC) Capt, Can & UK 42-46; Tchr Halifax Bd of Sch Commsnrs, Halifax NS 46-52, Tchr-libn 52-66; Tchr of Eng Uganda Col of Com, Kampala Uganda (under Can Intl Development Agency) 66-68; Libn Halifax Bd of Sch Commsnrs 68-69; Dir Sch Lib Serv, Dartmouth NS 69-. 9: CanLA. 10: United Serv Inst; Bus & Prof Womens Club; Credit Union; NS Tchrs Union; Can Col of Tchrs; Can Tchrs Fed. 15: 3140 Hemlock ave, Halifax NS Can.

GELBERT, MARIANNE ELISSA. b Phila 7 Jl 40. 5: Gettysburg Col 58-62 (Eng) BA; UPittsburgh 62-63 MLS. 7: Ref libn URI 63-65, Catlgr 66-67; Catlgr Muskingum Col (Ohio) 67-. 9: ALA; OhioLA. 14: Catlg. 15: 16 Wayside acres, 210 Lincoln lane, New Concord Oh 43762.

GELFAND, MELVYN WAYNE. b Phila 6 N 38. 5: Temple 57-62 (Journalism) BS; Drexel 62-63 MLS. 6: Sp. 7: Jr asst libn Bus Lib, Temple U 63-66, Sr asst libn 66-69, Sers libn 69-. 9: ALA. 10: Phi Alpha Theta; Sigma Delta Chi; Beta Phi Mu; H G Wells Soc of Eng. 14: Ref, ser. 15: 8 Wagon Bridge Run, Moorestown NJ 08057.

GELFAND, MORRIS ARTHUR. b Bayonne NJ 1 Je 08. 4: Beatrice Traube Gelfand. 5: NYU 27-33 (Econ) BS; Columbia 33-34 BS in LS; NYU 37-39 (Higher Educ)MA, 39-60 (Higher Educ) PhD. 6: Fr. 7: Asst-in-chg res reading room Washington Sq Lib, NYU 31-37; Lib asst Queens Col Lib (NY) 37-41, Asst libn 41-42; (Pvt to Sgt) US Army Air Corps 42; (2nd Lt to Maj) USAF Statistical Off Group adjutant, ETC; Lib off US Armed Forces, Pacific 42-46; Libn Queens Col Lib (NY) 46-59; Prof & libn Paul Klapper Lib Queens Col 59-69, Prof of Lib Admin 70-; Lecturer Pratt Inst Grad Sch of Lib & Info Sci. 8: Consul, Yeshiva U Libs 56-58; Fulbright lecturer & lib consul, URangoon Burma 58-59; Unesco lib bldg consul; Unesco lib expert, Thailand 62; Visit Coms Middle States Assn 49-; 12 short-term col & univ consul jobs since 55. 9: BSA; ALA (chm Com on Bk Acquis 53-54, mem Com on Rel with Publrs 55-56, chm Wilson Indexes Com 52-53, Adv com for U Brasilia proj 63-, rep to UN non-govtl orgs 62-65)-ACRL (Com on Standards 61-62, Com on Lib Surveys 62-65; Program Com for 66 conf; chm Local ArrgtsCom for 66 conf); NY Lib Club (pres 47-48). 10: AAUP; Trustee Bryant Lib Assn, Roslyn NY; Amer Field Serv; Trustee NY Metro Ref & Research Agency; Coun on Research in Bibliog; Burma Coun, Asia Soc; Grolier Club; Phi Delta Kappa. 12: "Historical Study of the Evaluation of Libraries in Higher Institutions by the Middle States Association, PhD Diss" (60); "University Libraries for Developing Countries" (Paris, Unesco 68). 13: Yes. 14: Col & univ lib admin, lib bldgs, educ for libnship, lib eval. 15: Stone House, Post dr, Roslyn Harbor NY 11576.

GELFMAN, DAVIDA (LIBERMAN). b Holyoke Mass 31 Ag 15. 4: Raymond Gelfman. 5: Simmons 32-36(LS) BS. 7: Lib asst Boston U Sch of Educ 36-38; Asst to catlg prof Simmons Col 41-42; Libn Pembroke Col 45-46; Circ libn Springfield Col 47-48; Elem libn Longmeadow Sch Dept, Longmeadow Mass 64-. 9: ALA; NEA; MassLA; West Mass Lib Club; Mass SchLA. 10: Simmons Col Club; United Hebrew Sch Bd; Bk Reviewers Club; Vis Nurse Assn. 14: Elem sch media ctrs. 15: 178 Redfern dr, Longmeadow Ma 01106.

GELINAS, JEANNE (LOUISE). b Col of St Catherine 50-54 (Fr, LS) BA; U de Poitiers 54 9fr); Case-West Res 65-66 MSLS. 6: Fr. 7: Child & ref asst Minneapolis Pub Lib 55-58; Roving br asst NY Pub Lib, Bronx NY 58-59; Ref & circ asst Marquette U Lib 59-61; Ref asst Minneapolis Pub Lib 61-62, Asst hd lit dept 62-65; Bibliog serv libn Wisconsin State Lib, Madison 66-67; Asst dir Gerguson Pub Lib, Stamford Conn 67-. 8: Coordinator of French Bk Circuit, Fairfield Co Conn 67-; Mem Adv Com, Title III LSCA, To Conn State Lib 68-. 9: ALA (Notable Bks Coun 68-72; mem Econ Status, Welfare & Fringe Benefits Com; PAS of LAD 68-); ConnLA (Repr-At-Large 68-69); NELA. 10: Phi beta Kappa; Pi Delta Phi; Kappa Gamma Pi; Beta Phi Mu; Alumnae Assn, The Col of St Catherine; Commun Coun of Stamford Conn; Minn World Affairs Ctr; Fulbright Scholarship 54-55; H W Wilson Foun Scholarship 65-66. 13: Yes. 14: Adult serv, acquis, ref 9humanities & Soc Scis), interlib loan, bibliogr, bk sel, lib educ. 15: 25 Bracewood le, Stamford Ct 06905.

GELLATLY, PETER. b Scone Scotland. 5: UBC45-50 BA; UWash 53-54 ML. 6: Fr, Ger, Sp, Ital. 7: Royal Can Air Force 43-45; Head bibliog UWash Libs 54-56, 57-59; Catlgr Lib of Parliament, Ottawa 56-57; Ser libn UWash Libs 59-. 9: ALA; PNLA. 10: Beta Phi Mu. 13: Yes. 14: Acqui, ser. 15: 5502-15th ave NE Apt 7, Seattle 98105.

GELLER, EVELYN G. b Brooklyn 5 F 33. 5: Brooklyn Col 49-54 (Eng, Philos) BA (magna cum laude); Catholic U 56-57 (Educ); Columbia 58-59 (Eng) 66 (LS). 6: Fr, Hebrew. 7: Tchr Trenton NJ & Montgomery Co Md 57-59; Asst ed gen publications, H W Wilson Co, NYC 60-61; Asst ed "Wilson Library Bulletin," H W Wilson Co, NYC 61-63; Asst dir of Research D H Blair, NYC 63-64; Ed "School Library Journal," R R Bowker Co, NYC 64-. 8: Consul "Audio visual Marketplace" 68-69; Bowker bk ed bd. 9: ALA; NEA-DAVI; NY State A-V Assn. 10: Womens Nat Bk Assn. 12: Ed "School Library Journal". 13: Yes. 14: Bk sel, censorship, ref, a-v developments. 15: School Lib Journal, R R Bowker Co, 1180 Avenue of the Americas, New York NY 10036.

GELLER, HILAIRE. b Jersey City NJ 10 S 16. 4: Eva Judith Maccoby. 5: Jersey City Jr Col 47-48; Bayonne Jr Col 48-49; Rutgers (Newark) 49-51 (Eng Lit) AB; Columbia 51-52 MLS. 6: Ger, Yiddish. 7: Laborer traffic dept asst Corona Corp, Jersey City NJ 35-40; Photographer Robert K Weitzen Studio, NYC 40-41; S/Sgt US Army Air Corps, Europe & USA 42-45; Libn, asst br libn NYC Pub Lib 52-57; Libn Wayne Jr High Sch, Wayne NJ 57-60; Libn asst dir Clifton Pub Lib, Clifton NJ 60-. 9: ALA; NJLA. 10: Bergen-Passaic Lib club. 14: Ref. 15: 265 Valley rd, Wayne NJ 07470.

GELLER, WILLIAM SPENCE. b Los Angeles 31 Mr 14. 4: Helen Hamilton. 5: USoCal 36 AB, 37 MS; UCal 53 BLS. 7: Los Angeles County: Stud research tech Bureau of Admin Research 37-38, Admin asst Health Dept 38-40, Sr admin asst Health Dept 40-44, Sr admin asst Charities Dept 44-45, Admin analyst Chief Admin Off 45-48, Bus manager Lib 48-53, Asst to County Libn 53-56, Asst county libn 56-63, County libn 63-. 8: Bldg consul; Adv Coun USoCal Sch Lib Sci 65-68; Adv Coun Educ for Libnship UCal Schs Lib Serv 65-68; Lib Adv Com Co Supvs Assn Cal 64-; State of Cal Pub Lib Devel Bd 66-70; Adv Com Cal Statewide Survey Pub Lib Serv; Hist Landmarks Adv Com Co of Los Angeles. 9: ALA (Coun 69; Interlib Coop Com: 63-67, chm 66; chm Study of Pub Lib Syst Com 67-68; reg chm Memb Com 62);-PLA (Bd Dir 69);-LAD (Equipment Com 58-, chm 62, chm Nominating 65); Admins Large Pub Libs; Amer Soc Pub Admin; CalLA (v-pres & pres-elect 69; Coun 68; Long Range Planning Com; 68-69, chm 69; treas 67; pres So Dist 66; Legis Com 65-67; chm Finance Com 65; Lib Devel & Standards Com 62-63, 67; chm Constitution Revision Com 55; chm Exhibits Com 54); West Governmental Research Assn. 10: Pub Lib Execs SoCal; UCal (Berkeley) Alumni Assn; Pi Sigma Alpha; Scapa Praetors (USoCal); Speechcrafters; Mgt Coun (Co of Los Angeles). 13: Yes. 14: Bldg consul, lib mgt & finance, admin. 15: Post Office Box 111, Los Angeles Ca 90053.

GEMME, IMOGENE EDNA. b Englewood NJ 6 O 23. 5: Northland Col 41-42; UCLA 43-44, 46-48 (Hist) BA; USoCal 58-61 MS in LS. 7: Libn officers mess, Navy Yard, Wash DC USNR-WAVES-S 1/c 44-6; Lib asst Alhambra Pub Lib, Alhambra Cal 46; Typist A C Vromans Wholesale, Pasadena Cal 48-49; Lib asst Arcadia Pub Lib, Arcadia Cal 49-50; Lib asst CalTech Jet Propulsion Lab, Pasadea Cal 51-60; Libn Electro-Optical Systems Inc, Pasadena Cal 60-61, Co libn 61; Research libn Aeronutronic Div Ford Motor Co, Newport Beach Cal 61-66, Ref libn 66-. 8: Consul Electro-Optical Systems Inc Lib, Pasadena Cal 61. 9: SLA. 12: "A Selective Bibliography of Government Publications on Solar Energy (61); "Thermal Diffusion & Soret Coefficients (62); "Isothermal Diffusion in Liquids (63). 14: Ref, lit searching. 15: 239-B Elden ave, Costa Mesa Cal 92627.

GEMMELL, H(ORTENSIA) TYLER. b Pulaski Va 4 N 04. 5: Randolph-Macon 22-26 (Eng) AB; Columbia summers 27, 29-31 (LS) BS, 38-39 (LS) MS. 6: Fr. 7: Lib asst Randolph-Macon Womans Col 26-38; Catlgr Bedford (Va) Lib summer 36; Org Pulaski County Pub Lib, Pulaski Va summer 37; Asst catlgr Vassar Col Lib 39-45; Head catlgr NJ Col for Women 45-47; Head libn Mary Helen Cochran Lib Sweet Briar

Col 47-. 69; Visiting catlgr Washington & Lee Univ, Lexington Va 69-70. 8: Visiting Prof Peabody Grad Lib Sch summers 49, 58-59; Visiting Prof Trenon (NJ) State Tchrs Col, summers 50-52, 54; Fulbright Lectureship Mandalay Burma 55-56; Lectr & consul US-India Women's Col Exch Prog (India) 66-67. 9: ALA; SELA; VaLA; Bibliog Soc, Va. 10: Phi Beta Kappa; Lynchburg Hist Soc; AAUP. 14: Catlg. 15: Sweet Briar, Va 24595.

GENAWAY, DAVID C. b Elmira NY 29 Ny 37. 4: C Inez Travis. 5: Atlantic Union Col 55-60 (Theol) BA; Andrews U 60, 62-64 (Applied Theol) MA; UMich 64-65 AMLS. 7: Elem tchr Flint Jr Acad, Flint Mich 60-61; Spec educ tchr Niles Exceptional Sch, Niles Mich 61-62; Descr catlgr Andrews U Lib 63-64; Catlg libn Central Wash State Col 65-67; Asst Prof Peabody Lib Sch 67-. 8: Consul; Country Music Hall of Frame Lib, Nashville 68-; Baptist Sch of Nursing Lib, Nashville 67-. 9: ALA; -AASchL; -ACRL; -RTSD; -LED; -ISAD; AALS; TennLA. 10: AAUP; Ski Club. 13: Yes. 14: Catlg, tchg, admin, automation, tech proc. 15: Peabody Lib School, Nashville Tn 37203.

GENEVIEVE, SISTER MARY (BAKER) SND. b Toledo Ohio. 5: Notre Dame Col 26 (Eng) AB; West Res 30 (L) BS; Columbia MS in LS. 6: Ger, Sp, Ital. 7: Tchr Notre Dame Acad, Cleveland 18-25; Libn Notre Dame Col (leveland) 26-. 9: CathLA. 13: Yes. 14: Ref. 15: 4545 College rd, Cleveland 44121.

GENNETT, ROBERT G. b Queens NYC 1 Mr 37. 5: Queens Col (NY) 54-59 (Hist) BA; Columbia 61-62 MLS. 6: Fr. 7: NY Pub Lib; Lib asst mss 60, Lib asst Amer Hist 61, Ref libn Info Div 61-64; Acquis libn Fordham U Law Sch 64; Head of ref serv Lafayette Col 65-68, Asst libn 9: SLA; PennLA. 10: Amer Friends of Lafayette; Phi Alpha Theta. 14: Ref, rare bks, admin. 15: 3649 Chipman rd, Easton Pa 18042.

GENTHNER, FREDERICK LUDWIG. b Delaware Ohio 12 Ja 19. 4: Sarah Loretta Boss. 5: Ohio Wesleyan 36-40 (Fr) BA; Peabody Col 40-41 BS in LS; UMich summers 48-50 (LS) AMLS. 6: Fr. 7: Enlisted man Coast Artillery (Basic train & libr assignment), Camp Callan Cal 41-42; Capt ordnance cept, US, North Africa 42-46; Asst ref libn Ohio StateU (Columbus) 46-48; Period libn (asst prof) Ball State Tchrs Col 48-51; Period & ser libn Cal State Polytech Col 51-65, Spec collections (docs) libn 65-. 8: Prof libn in Army camp lib 41-42. 9: ALA; CalLA. 10: Kappa Phi Kappa; Phi Mu Alpha; Elks. 14: Period, ser, docs, maps. 15: 15 Elm ct, San Luis Obispo Ca 93401.

GENUNG, LENA HARRIETT. b Pomona 9 D 09. 5: Pomona Col 32 BA; UWis 33 MA; UCal (Berkeley) 46 Lib Certif; USoCal 39. 7: Instr Claremont Grad Sch 39-40; Tchr & libn Corona High Sch, Corona 41-45; Dn of lib & a-v Mt San Antonio Col, Walnut Cal 46-. 8: Adv Com on Microforms in Commun Col Libs, AAJC USOE Consul, AAJC Prog with Devel Instns 69-70; Cal Adv Com on Lib Schs 69. 9: ALA (A-V Com 67-70; AAJC/ALA Jt Com 65-69); chm JCLS, ACRL, 66-67 -ACRL (A-V Com 65-69, Com on Legisl 68-69); CalLA; (Co-chm Standards Com Jr Col RT 65-68, chm Com on Commun Col Coop 69, Lib Devel & standards Com 69). 10: Phi Beta Kappa; Pi Lambda Theta; Phi Delta Gamma; Delta Kappa Gamma; Soroptimist Club; Bus & Profess Womens' Club; Coun of Campfire Girls. 11: Women Achievers Award 67, Pomona Service Club. 12: Co-auth "Language for Literature," (55). 13: Yes. 14: Admin. 15: 1390 W 15th st, Upland Ca 91786.

GEORGE, HARRY C III. b Pittsburgh Penn 6 Jr 44. 4: Laurel D George. 5: Clarion State Col 62-66 (LS) BS; UPittsburgh 68- MLS. 7: Libn Penn Hill Sch Dist, Pittsburgh Penn 67-. 9: ALA; ASIS. 14: Lib automation of tech proc. 15: 26 Sierra dr, Pittsburgh Pa 15239.

GEORGE, JOHN E. b Port Arthur Tex 15 My 24. 4: Catherine May Garrison. 5: N Tex U 48-49 (Econ) BA, 49-50 (Econ) MA, 55-56 BSLS. 6: Ger, Fr. 7: Page Ft Worth Pub Lib, Ft Worth Tex 51-52, Head Tex hist 52-54; Head govt documents Dallas Pub Lib 55-. 9: Tex State LA. 14: Govt docs. 15: 6407 Howard, Dallas 75227.

GEORGE, MARJORY (BROADHEAD). b Hamilton Ont Can 14 O 13. 4: T E Lloyd George. 5: McMaster U (Hamilton Ont) 31-35 (Eng) BA; Toronto 35-36 Diploma in Libnship, summer 39 BLS. 6: Fr. 7: Asst circ dept Pub Lib, Hamilton Ont 37-40, Asst ref dept 39-41; Catlgr Ont Col of Educ 43-45; Catlgr UToronto 47-49; Catlgr Pub Lib, Chatham Ont 50-60; Asst chief libn & head catlgr Pub Lib, Chatham Ont 60-. 9: Inst Profl Libns Ont (dir 67-69); OntLA. 10: Can Fed Univ Women. 14: Catlg. 15: 76 Willowmac ave, Chatham Ont Can.

GEORGE, (SIM) MARY. b Hong Kong 26 S 38. 4: William George. 5: Hong Kong U 59-62 9geog & Geol) BA; Tex Woman's U 62-64 MLS; Columbia 66 Med (Libnship) AMLA; New Sch of Soc Research 68- (Sociol). 6: Chinese. 7: Sr libn Jersey City Pub Lib, Jersey City NJ 64-67; Asst libn St Peter's Col Lib 67-. 9: MedLA. 10: Trustee, Internat Inst. 14: Ref. 15: 201 St Pauls ave, Jersey City NJ 07306.

GEORGE, MELVIN R. b Grove City Min 20 F 37. 4: Shirley Hattendorf. 5: St Cloud State Col 55-59 (Lang Arts) BS, 59-60 (Eng) MS; UMinn 62-65 (LS) MA. 6: Fr. 7: Eng tchr Pub Schs, St Louis Park Minn 60-63, Libn 63-65; Libn Elmhurst Col 65-; Visiting instr Rosary Col Grad Lib Dept 67-. 9: ALA; IllLA. 14: Admin. 15: 580 Mitchell st, Elmhurst Il 60126.

GEORGE, VIRGINIA R STRATFORD. b Chicago. 4: Edward George. 5: Northwestern 45-47 (Mech Engnr); UKY (50) (Mech Engnr) BSME; UWash 62-64 (LS) ML. 7: Staff lbn Boeing Sci Research Labs Lib, Seattle 64-. 9: SLA; ASIS. 10: LWV; Beta Phi Mu. 13: Yes. 14: Computer catlg, computer-prduced bk catlgs. 15: 22608 90th W, Edmonds Wash 98020.

GEORGESON, PATRICIA ANN. b Madison Wis 25 My 34. 5: UWis 52-57 (Amer Inst) BS, 57-58 (LS) MS. 6: Fr. 7: Libn I Madison Pub Lib, Madison Wis 58-59, Br libn Lakeview Br 59-66, Br libn S Madison Br 67, Supv libn Tech Processes Div 67. 9: ALA; WisLA (chm-elect Tech Serv Sect 68-69). 10: LWV; UWis Lib Sch Alumni Assn. 14: Catlg. 15: 4218 Bagley Pkwy, Madison Wis 53705.

GEORGI, CHARLOTTE. b Pittsburgh. 5: UBuffalo 42 BA (magna cum laude), 43 MA; UNC 56 MS in LS. 6: Fr, Ger. 7: Instr Army Air Forces 23rd Train Div SUNY(Buffalo) 42-43; Asst Prof humanities dept Stephens Col 4354; Head bus admi lib UNC 55-57, Chief bus admin lib & soc sci div 57-59; Head bus admin lib UCLA 59-. 8: Consul; Bank of Amer 66-68; Cantor, Fitzgerald 68; Cal State Lib for State Technical Serv Act 68-. 9: ALA; CalLA; SLA (Bus & Fin Div; sec 61-62, v-chm 62-63, chm 63-64, Bd Dirs 66-69). 10: AAUP; Phi Beta Kappa; Pi Lambda Theta; Beta Phi Mu; Phi Chi Theta. 12: "The Novel and the Pulitzer Prize, 1918-1958 (58); "The Businessman in the Novel (59); Co-comp "Sources of Commodity Prices (60); Co-ed "Statistics Sources (2d edn 65); Ed "The Literature of Executive Management (63); Co-ed "Encyclopedia of Business Information Sources" (69-). 13: Yes. 14: Bibliog, ref, admin. 15: 328 N Bowling Green way, Los Angeles Ca 90049.

GEPPERT, ALIDA L. b Mitchell SD 21 Ap 42. 5: Mt Marty Col 60-63; So State Col 64-65 (Eng) BS; West Mich U 66-67 MLS. 6: Fr. 7: Tchr & libn Lynch Pub Sch, Lynch Neb 65-66; Libn Neb State Lib, Spencer 66; Asst libn & assoc prof So State Col (S Dak) 67-. 8: Lib consul, Lynch Pub Sch 67-68. 9: ALA; -AASchL; NEA-DAVI; MPLA; S Dak LA. 10: Beta Phi Mu; AAUW; AAUP. 14: Sch libnship, educ tech. 15: Southern State Col, Springfield SD 57062.

GERARD, DORA M. b Reigate England 12 Ag 10. 5: UCLA 30-35 (Eng) BA; Pratt Inst 35-36 (Lib) MS equiv. 6: Fr, Ger. 7: Circ dept UCLA Lib 36-43, Acquis dept 43-48, Agric libn 48-60, Biomed lib hd acquis div 60-68, Geol-Geophys libn 68-. 9: Geosci Info Soc. 14: Acquis, ref. 15: Geol-Geophys Lib, Univ of Cal, 405 Hilgard ave, Los Angeles Ca 90024.

GERARDI, FLORENCE RITA (PAGANINI). b Brooklyn NY 16 Mr 24. 5: St Josephs Col for Women 42-45 (Chem) BA; Brooklyn Col 51-52 (Educ); Rutgers 62-65 MLS. 6: Fr, Ger, Ital, Sp. 7: Chem Hoffman LaRoche, Nutley NJ 46-48; Tchr Pequannock Twp Bd of Educ 57-62; Lit sci Amer Cyanamid, Princeton NJ 62-64; Lit chem UOP Chem Co, E Rutherford NJ 64-. 8 Punch card retrieval system for odiferous organic chemicals, UOP Chem Co 1965-. 9: ASIS; SLA. 10: Kappa Gamma Pi. 14: Chem lit, retrieval systems, ref. 15: Rt 17, E Rutherford NJ 07073.

GERBER, MARILYN (FARLEY). b Hutchinson Kan 27 Jl 39. 4: Homer C Gerber. 5: Ohio wesleyanU 57-59 (Eng); Bluffton Col 59-61 (Eng) BA; Kent StateU 63-65 (LS); Fla StateU 65-68 (LS, Educ Admin) MS. 7: Lib asst Bowling Green StateU 61-62; Lib aid Dayton & montgomery Co Pub Lib, Dayton Ohio 62-63; Libn Triway High Sch, Wooster Ohio 63-64; Libn St Joseph-Ogden High Sch, St Joseph Ill 64-65; Libn N Fla Jr Col 66-68; Y-a libn Orlando Pub Lib, Orlando Fla 68-. 9: ALA; ASCD; NEA-DAVI; FlaLA. 10: Beta Phi Mu; Kappa Delta Pi. 14: Ya serv. 15: 937 Barbados ave, Orlando Fl 32807.

GERBEREUX, ROBERT LOUIS. b Yonkers NY 1 Ap 43. 4: Carolyn Simpson. 5: NYU 60-64 (Eng) BA; Pratt Inst 64-66 (Ref Serv) MLS; LIU 67- (Educ). 7: Asst ref & catlg libn Southampton Col LIU 65-66, Asst ref libn & hd period dept 66-67, Act hd ref dept 67; Hd ref libn 67-. 8: Instl rep to LI Lib Resources Coun. 9: ALA; NY State LA. 10: AAUP; NY Pub Lib Assn. 14: Ref, periods. 15: Seven Country Club dr, Southampton NY 11968.

GERBOTH, WALTER. b Flushing NY 27 F 25. 4: Janice Lake. 5: Queens Col 46-50 (Music) BA; Columbia 51-53 (LS) MS. 6: Ger. 7: Asst libn Equitable Life, NY 52-56; Music libn Brooklyn Col 56-. 8: NY State Dept of Educ, Off of Area Studies, Dir of Musical Projs, summer 63. 9: MusLA (pres, chm Publns Com; past chm NY Chap); Amer Musicological Soc (Jt AMS: MusLA Reprints Com); Soc for Ethnomusicology; Soc for Asian Music (NY), Internat Assn Mus Libns. 12: "Index of Music Articles in Festschriften In Medieval and Renaissance Music" (66); "A Selected Bibliography of Books, Pamphlets and Articles about African Music, NY State Dept of Educ" (63); "Music of East and Southeast Asia; A Selected Bibliography of Books, Pamphlets, Articles and Recordings NY State Dept of Educ" (63). 13: Yes. 14: Bibliog. 15: 1156 E 43rd st, Brooklyn NY 11210.

GERCKEN, RICHARD. b Jacksonville Fla 15 Ja 33. 4: Barbara Kubie Gercken. 5: Oberlin 50-51 (Mod Lang); UNotre Dame 51-54 (Mod Lang) AB; UCLA 57-59 (Mod Lang, Cinema); MLS. 6: Fr, Sp. 7: Code clk US Inf, Germany 55-57; Ref libn NYC Pub Lib 64, Asst br libn 67-69; Hd ref libn UMont Missoula Mt 69-. 9: ALA. 14: Ref, child lit, Amer letters, Eng letters, West Americana. 15: 175 Pinehurst ave 5C, New York NY 10033.

GERE, SARA B. b Reading Penn 18 Ap 09. 5: Syracuse 30 (Eng) AB, 41 (Eng lit) MA, 51 MLS. 7: Info & educ off WAC, Ft Des Moines Iowa 45-46; Hd ref dept Eau Claire Pub Lib, Eau Claire Wis 52-53; Br child libn Cuyahoga Co Pub Lib, Cleveland Ohio 53-55; Coord ref serv Decatur Pub Lib, Decatur Ill 55-59; Hd jub dept Wilmington Inst Free Lib, Wilmington Del 59-63, Hd circ dept 63-65, Asst dir 65-. 9: ALA; DelLA. 10: Beta Phi Mu; Bus & Profess Women's Club. 14: Ref, readers adv, personnel. 15: 207 Claymont gardens, Claymont De 19703.

GERGELY, EMMA. b NJ 30 O 29. 5: Douglass 54 (Bacteriology) BS; Rutgers 57 MLS. 6: Hungarian. 7: Lab asst Heyden Chem Corp, Penns Neck NJ 48-49; Lab tech E R Squibb, New Brunswick NJ 49-52; Research asst Rutgers U 54-55, Lib asst 56-57; Ref libn Bell Telephone Labs, Whippany NJ 57-61; Libn Rutgers U Inst of Microbiology, New Brunswick NJ 61-. 9: ALA; SLA (NJ Chap; Bulletin ed 62-63); Amer Soc Microbiol (Archivist NJ br). 10: Recording for the Blind Inc. 14: Ref. 15: Rutgers Univ Inst of Microbio, New Brunswik NJ 08903.

GERHARDT, LILLIAN NOREEN. b New Havn Conn 28 S 32. 5: So Conn State Col 50-54 (LS) BS; Chicago 61-62 (LS). 6: Sp. 7: Storyteller New Haven Pub Lib, ew Haven Conn 54, Asst ref libn 55; Asst ref libn Curtis Mem Lib, Meriden Conn 56-58, Head ref libn 58-61; Assoc ed Virginia Kirkus Serv Inc, NYC 62-66; Exec ed School Library Journal "Book Review" & R R Bowker juvenile projects 66-. 9: ALA; NYLA; WNBA; NYLC. 12: Supervisor of juvenile & young adult reviewing, Va Kirkus Service Inc (62-66). 13: Yes. 14: Bk sel. 15: 82 Irving Place No 1c, NYC 10003.

GERITY, LOUISE P. b Honolulu Hawaii 29 Jl 33. 4: Thomas W Gerity. 5: Reed Col 51-5 (Lit) BA; Columbia 55-57 (LS) MS; UMich summer 62. 6: Fr. 7: Trainee NY Pub Lib 55-58; Child libn Lib of Hawaii, Honolulu 59-62; Catlgr Portland State Col Lib 62-63; Ref libn Lewis & Clark Col 63-. 9: OreLA; ALA. 15: 5717 SW Washington Ct, Lake Oswego Ore.

GERITY, THOMAS W. b Wamic Ore 30 D 19. 4: Louise Gerity. 5: Ore Col of Educ (39). 6: Fr, Sp. 7: Trainee UMich Dental Sch Lib 50-51; Asst ref libn UNM Lib 51-55; Asst tech dept Portland Pub Lib55-56; Asst soc sci dept Detroit Pub Lib 56; 1st asst lit & hst dept Portland Pub Lib 56-59; Head sci-soc sci dept Portland State Col Lib 59-67; Hd Bus & Econ Dept Portland State U Lib 67-. 8: Tchr of lib sci course: UPortland 61, UOre Exten Div 65; Mem Grad Coun, Portland State U 67-70. 9: ALA; PNLA. 14: Ref, spec libs. 15: 5717 SW Washington ct, Lake Oswego Ore.

GERMOVNIK, REV FRANCIS. b Vodice Yugoslavia 27 S 15. 5: Classical gymnaium (Ljubljana Yugoslavia) 30-35; ULjubljana 36-42 (Theol); Angelicum (Rome) 42-45 Dr in Canon Law; Our Lady of the Lake Col 48-50 (BS in LS); Rosary Col 65- (LS). 6: Slovenian, Serbian, Ger, Ital, Fr, Eng, Lat, Gk, Sp. 7: Prof & ibn St Johns Sem 46-52; Prof & Libn Assumption Sem 52-54; Prof & Libn St Marys Sem (Perryville Mo) 54-64; Prf & Libn De Andreis Sem 64-. 9: ALA; CathLA. 10: Canon Law Soc of Amer. 14: Catlg, rare bks. 15: De Andreis Sem 11 E 127th st, Lemont Ill 60439.

GERON, CARY ANN. b Dallas Tex 30 Ja 38. 5: Tex Womens U 56-61 (LS) BS. 6: Sp. 7: Head libn Terry County Lib, Brownfield Tex 61-65; Asst libn Baptist Theol Sem (Ruschlikon-Zurick Switzerland) 65-67; Circ libn Golden Gate Bapt Theol Sem, Mill Valley Cal 67-. 9: ALA; TexLA; CalLA. 14: Catlg, child wk. 15: Golden Gate Bapt Theol Sem, Mill Valley Ca 94941.

GEROULD, ALBERT C(HAMBERLAIN). b Minneapolis 8 Ap 10. 4: Alberta Wright. 5: Dartmouth 32 (Mod Eur Hist) AB; UMunich 32-33 (Ger & Lit); Columbia 35 BS in LS. 6: Fr, Ger. 7: Hist master Mohonk Sch, Lake Mohonk NY 33-34; Temp asst NY Pub Lib 35; Asst ref libn Stanford U 35-38; Libn Col of Pacific 39-46; Interrogator of POWs 30th Inf Div & Libn, Document Center US Army, Berlin 42-45; Asst libn UN, Lake Success NY; Libn Clark U 47-53; Chief central pub depts Free Lib, Phila 53-. 9: ALA-LAD (chm Lib Org & Mgt Sect 65-66);-ACRL; SLA (pres Phila Chap 63-64); PennLA (chm Com on Preserv of Lib Materials 60-63); BSA (repres on Jt Com on Union List of Serials 69-). 10: Philobiblon Club; Sierra Club; Appalachian Mountain Club; US Army Reserves (Lt Col). 15: 6923 Greene st, Phila Pa 19119.

GERRITY, MARLINE (R). b Omaha 11 Je 23. 4: James J Gerrity. 5: Webster Col 40-44 (Chem) BS; Immaculate Heart Col 62-63 (LS) MA. 6: Fr. 7: Control tower operator USNR(WR), Patuxent River Md 44-46; Ref & circ libn Cal Inst Tech 63-64; Libn Carnegie Inst Mt Wilson Observatory, Pasadena Cal 65-68; UNeb Col of Med Eppley Inst Libn 68-. 10: Kappa Gamma Pi. 14: Ref. 15: 9415 Mayberry st, Omaha Nb 68114.

GERRITY, SISTER ROSANNE OSU. b Youngstwn Ohio 1 Jl 07. 5: Trinity Col (Wash DC) 30 (Hist, Pol Sci, Eng) BA; Catholic U 43 BSLS. 6: Fr. 7: Libn Ursuline High Sch, Youngstown Ohio 32-64; Libn Ursuline Motherhouse & Educ Center, Canfield Ohio 64-. 9: CathLA (v-chm No Ohio Unit). 12: Ed CathLA, No Ohio Unit "Book Review Bulletin". 14: Catlg. 15: Ursuline Motherhouse & Educ Center, 4250 Shields rd, Canfield Ohio 44406.

GERSACK, DOROTHY (JEANNE) (HILL). b Lvingston Ill 24 O 10. 4: Joseph Robert Gersack. 5: Wittenberg Col 28-29, 30-31 (Educ); West Col for Women 29-30 (Eng, Hist); UIll 31-37 BS, BS in LS, MS in LS; George Washington U Law Sch 40-41. 6: Lat, Ger, Fr. 7: Lib asst Danville (Ill) Pub Lib 27-28, 33; Asst child libn Warder Pub Lib, Springfield Ohio 30-31; Catlgr UIll Lib (Urbana) 34-36; Catlgr Nat Archves 36-41; Archivist & asst chief Div of Veterans Records Nat Archives 41-49; Mgt analyst Div of Records Mgt 50-58; Archivist Mil rec 59-61; Archivist Off of Records Appraisal 62-. 8: Staff, Extraord Cong of the Internat Coun on Archives, US Dept of State, 66; Team mem, Prog Eval of paper wk mgt operations, US Bur of Prisons & Prison Indus 66-67 and Bur of Pub Debt 68-69; Partic in Conf on the Nat Archives and Statist Res, May 68; "National Crime Reporting, 1930-67". 9: ALA-RSD (Hist Sect; Conf Prog Com); DC, Md & Va Reg Catlgrs; SAA (Fellow). 10: Adv Com Davis Lib (Montgomery Co MD); AAUW; Beta Phi Mu; UIll Lib Sch Alumni; Phi Gamma Psi; Delta Zeta; Bethesda Fire Bd; Old Georgetown Rd Citizens Assn. 12: News Notes Ed "The American Archivist" (60-68); "Federal Court Records" (51); "Management of Records in the Federal Courts" (52); "Disposal of Federal Court Records" (53); "Records of the Federal Courts" (55). 13: Yes. 14: Catlg, ref, pub archives and mss. 15: 5600 Oakmont ave, Bethesda Md 20034.

GERSH, JONAS. b NYC 18 Ap 30. 5:NYU 52-54 (Pre-Prof Soc Wk) BS; Columbia 56-58 MLS. 6: Sp. 7: Libn Queensborough Pub Lib, NYC 58-63; Ref libn Elmont Pub Lib, Elmont NY 63-65, Br libn 65-67; Ref libn Rockville Ctr Pub Lib, Rockville Ctr NY. 14: Admin, ref. 15: 87-25 169th st, New York NY 11432.

GERSON, ELLEN. b NYC 22 Ja 44. 5: CCNY 64 (Educ) BS; Rutgers 65 MLS. 6: Braille. 7: Sr libn Free Lib of Woodbridge, Woodbridge NJ 65-67; Supv libn Inst of Rehabilatory Med, NYC 67-68; Commun serv rep NJ Lib for the Blind, Trenton 68-. 8: Research asst Rutgers U 64-65. 9: ALA; NJLA. 10: Nat Braille Inst. 14: Child & ya wk. 15: 475 FDR dr, New York NY 10002.

GERTLER, PAULINE (ZUCKERMAN). b Montreal Can 13 Je 36. 4: David Gertler. 5: McGill 53-57 (Pol Sci, Econ) BA, 57-58 BLS. 6: Fr, Sp, Hebrew. 7: Libn Engnr Inst of Can, Montreal 58-60; Libn CIL, Montreal 60-61; Libn Alsec, Montreal 61-63; Libn YM-YWHA, Montreal 63-64; Libn McGill U 64-. 14: Catlg, ref. 15: 4941 Jean Brilliant, Montreal Can.

GERTZOG, ALICE (SOLOMON). b Brooklyn NY 30 Ap 34. 4: Irwin N Gertzog. 5: Antioch 52-56 (Lit) AB; CatholicU 58-60 MS in LS. 7: Ref libn UNC (Chapel Hill) 60-62; Consul NASA, Wash DC 62-63; Instr in lib sci So Conn State Col 64-65; Chief bibliogr New Haven Col Lib 65-67; Ref libn New Haven Pub Lib, New Haven Conn 67-. 14: Ref. 15: 63 Forest Hill rd, North Haven Ct 06473.

GERULAITIS, LEONARDAS VYTAUTAS. b Kaunas Lithuania 6 N 28. 4: Renate S Keppler. 5: UMich 55-56 (Hist) AB, 56-57 (hist) AM, 63 MALS, 69 (Hist) PhD. 6: Lithuanian, fr, Ger, Russian, Ital, Lat, Sp. 7: Asst Prof OaklandU 63-. 10: AAUP; ACLU; AHA; Renaissance Soc of Amer; Mediaeval Acad of Amer; Phi Kappa Phi; Beta Phi Mu. 13: Yes. 14: Hist, rare bks. 15: 388 W Maryknoll, Rochester Mi 48063.

GERVASI, MRS MILDRED I (QUILLIN). b DeQueen Ark. 5: N Tex State U 38-42 (LS) Educ (BS); Peabody 59 MA in LS. 7: Act hd of music lib N Tex State U summer 42; Head libn Midwestern U 42-45; Head of Catlg Dept N Tex State U 45; Continuations catlgr URochester 51-54; Head libn Southwestern U 57-. 9: ALA; SWLA; NEA-Assn for Higher Educ; TexLA (chm Archives Hist & Loc Hist Round Table 65-66; Dist 8: sec-treas 62-63, v-chm 63-64, chm 64) College & Univ Div TLA; sec-treas 67, v-chm 68, chm 69. 10: AAUW; AAUP; Kappa Delta Pi; Alpha Lambda Sigma. 14: Admin, catlg, rare bks. 15: 1612 Williams dr, Georgetown Tex 78626.

GERWING, HOWARD BERNARD. b Kelowna BC Can 24 My 32. 4: Marina Sissojew. 5: UBC 50-54 (Hist, Eng) BA, 62-63 BLS. 7: Tchr Corona Stage Acad, London 57-58; Lib asst ser UBC 60-62; Libn ref UVictori(BC) 63-66, Spec collections 66-. 9: BCLA (pres 67-68); Inst of Victoria Libns (program chm). 10: Victoria Rugby Union. 12: Ed "BC Library Quarterly". 13: Yes. 14: Ref, rare bks, mss. 15: Univ of Victoria, Victoria BC Can.

GERYCH, GEORGE. b Ukraine 9 Ja 11. 4: Christina Kolessa. 5: ULviv 31-34 (Law), 35-36 (Com), 36-38 (Theol); Karls U (Prague) 41-45; Ukr U (Prague) 40-41 (Law) LLD; UOttawa 59-60 BLS, 60-61, 65 MLS. 6: Ukrainian, Ger, Polish, Czech, Russan. 7: Asst Prof Ukrainan Free U (Munich) 46-48; Catlgr UOttawa Lib 60-61; Lecturer UOttawa Lib Sch 61-, Asst Prof 65-. 9: CanLA; Association canadienne des bibliothecaires de langue francaise; OttawaLA; OntLA. 10: CAUT; APUO. 12: "Exegesis Silvestri Kossiv, 1634 (61); "Theologico-Literary Activity of J Kuntsevych(60); "Canonical Aspects of the Anathema Against Mazeppa (60); "Transliteration of Cyrillic Alphabets, LLD MLS (65); "Bibliographical Critical Analysis of Tthe Works of J Kuntsevych" (67). 13: Yes. 14: Ref, catlg. 15: 236 Mountbatten ave, Ottawa 8 Can.

GESCHWINDT, JOHN E(DWARD). b Port Clinton Penn 2 D 41. 5: Kutztown State Col 59-64 (LS) BS in Ed; Syracuse 65-68 MS LS. (LS). 7: Jr-sr high sch libn Big Spring Sch Dist, Newville Penn 64-68; Libn York Co Voc Tech Sch 68-69; Ref dept Penn State Lib 69-. 9: NEA; ALA; Penn State EA; PennLA; PennASchL. 10: Jr C of C; Beta Phi Mu. 14: Sch lib wk, ref. 15: RD #1, Dillsburg Pa 17019.

GESKE, JANE (POPE). b Sutton Neb 27 N 18. 4: Norman A Geske. 5: UNeb (Omaha) 37-41 (Speech, Eng) BA; UDenver 43-44 (LS) BS. 6: Fr. 7: Asst libn UNeb (Omaha) 44-45; Ser records libn LSU 45-46; Head ser dept UDenver 47-53; Head ser dept UChicago Supv 53-60; Consul NEB Pub Lib Commsn, Lincoln Neb 60-. 8: Chm Downtown Lecture Series on Technical Services, UChicago Grad Lib Sch, 57-58. 9: ALA (pres Ser Round Table 55-56); NebLA pres 66-67; MPLA (Com on the Bibliog Center 62-)66). 10: Neb Arts Coun; Neb Art Assn. 13: Yes. 14: Ext of lib serv. 15: 2628 High st, Lincoln Nb 68502.

GESTERFIELD, KATHRYN (JENSEN). b Minatare Neb 3 Ap 15. 4: Arnold D Gesterfield. 5: Neb State Col (Chadron) 33-35; Neb State Col (Kearney) 37-38; U Denver 38-39 (LS) AB; UIll 60-61 (LS) MS. 7: Br asst Denver Pub Lib 39-42; (M/Sgt) WAC 42-45; Libn Scottsbluff Pub Lib, Scottsbluff Neb 46-60; Asst in ref UIll (Urbana) 60-61; Libn Champaign Pub Lib, Champaign Ill 62-69; Consult, Lib Devel Br, Ill State Lib 70-. 8: Research asst, "Nebraska Libraries Face the Future, a Report of a Comprehensive Survey, 61. 9: ALA; IllLA (2nd v-pres 68-69, chm pub lib sect 63-64); NebLA (pres 51-52). 10: LWV; AAUW; Delta Kappa Gamma; Zonta. 14: Admin, ref. 15: 306 W Church st, Champaign Ill 61821.

GEVERDT, LOUELLA G. b Orchard Park NY 24 Ap 42. 5: State U Col (Geneseo NY) 60-64 (LS) BS; USoCal 64-65 MSLS. 7: High sch lbn Clarence Central High Sch, Clarence NY 65-. 9: ALA; NYLA (Ad hoc Com mem SLS-NYLA 67-69); NY State Tchrs Assn. 10: Kappa Delta Pi; Beta Phi Mu. 14: Sch libnship, young aults. 15: S6377 Bunting rd, Orchard Park NY 14127.

GHEBELIAN, CAROLINE (SPROUSE). b Staunton Va 2 Ap 29. 4: Oscar Ghebelian. 5: Mary Baldwin Col 45-49 (Music) BA; Col of William & Mary summer 47, 49. 7: Asst to libn Mary Baldwin Col 49-51; LC: Searcher Card Div 51, Prelim catlgr Descr Catlg Div 52, Music catlgr Copyright Off 52-57, Asst head Music Sect Copyright Off 57-62, Asst head Ed & Publ Sect Copyright Off 62-63; Head LibDiv US Naval Explosive Ordnance Disposal Facility, Indian Head Md 63-. 8: Navy Rep, Fed Lib Com Task Force on Recr 68-. 9: SLA; Coun of Libns; East Coast Naval Labs (chm Training Co 67-). 14: Catlg (music, ordnance). 15: Cogs Doon, Indian Head Md 20640.

GHOLSTON, (HOWARD) DONALD. b Lorenza Tex 20 Ag 27. 5: San Angelo Col 44-46 (Chem) AA; UTex 48-50 (Chem) BS, 50-53 (Biochem) MA, 53-54 (LS). 6: Fr, Ger. 7: Lib intern E R Squibb, New Brunswick NJ 54-55, Asst libn 55-61; Libn Chevron Research Co, Richmond Cal 61-. 9: SLA (dir San Francisco Bay Reg Chap 64-66); ACS. 12: Asst ed "Unlisted Drugs (55-59); Ed "Unlisted Drugs (60-61); Co-ed "Dictionary of German Chemical Abbreviations (66). 13: Yes. 14: Admin. 15: Chevron Research Co 576 Standard ave, Richmond Cal 94802.

GHOLZ, CHARLES ARTHUR. b Worthington Minn 23 Mr 15. 4: Renee Charpentier Gholz. 5: Winona State Col 35-38 (Music Educ, Soc Sci) BE; UMinn 45-46 (Music Educ, Soc Sci) BS, 46-47 (Music Educ, Soc Sci) M Ed; LSU 64-65 (LS) MS. 6: Sp. 7: High sch bandmaster 38-43; Armed Forces 43-45; High sch bandmaster 47-60; Sch libn Lydia Patterson Inst, El Paso Tex 60-61; Ref asst Austin Pub Lib, Austin Tex 61-62; Field consul Tex State Lib 62-64; Dir St Charles Co Lib, St Charles Mo 65-; Asst dir Col Lib Ft Lewis Col, Durango Colo 66-67; Asst libn LSU (New Orleans) Libn 67-. 9: ALA; LaLA. 10: AAUP. 11: Man of the Year, Nogales Ariz 49. 13: Yes. 14: Admin, ref. 15: 5510 Warrington dr, New Orleans La 70122.

GIARDINO, MARY K. b WesterlyRI 22 Je 08. 5: Bryant Col 28-30 (Secretarial) Diploma; URI 62-64 (LS) Certif; Brown 62-64 (Hand bk bind) Certif. 6: Ital. 7: Eve Evans Shop, Westerly RI 37-50; Hosp clerk RI Med Center, Howard RI 53-60, Med libn 61-. 9: MedLA. 10: Bus & Prof Womens Club; RI State Employees Assn. 15: RI Med Center Lib Box 5, Howard RI 02834.

GIBBENS, JERRY D. b Imboden Ark 20 Ag 42. 4: Barbara (Mitchell). 5: Ark State Col 61-63 (Eng) BSE; Ind U summers 66, 67 (LS); Ark State U 68-69 (Eng) MSE. 6: Fr. 7: Eng tchr Arcadia Valley High Sch, Ironton Mo 63-65, Libn & tchr 65-67; Asst libn & instr in Eng So Baptist Col 67-. 9: ALA; NCTE; NEA; ArkLA; Ark Coun Tchrs of Col Eng. 10: Ark Hsit Assn; Great Bks Club; Mod Lang Assn. 14: Catlg, ref. 15: 307 Faculty dr, Walnut Ridge Ar 72476.

GIBBON, ANNETTE. b Marion Ohio 16 F 45. 5: Heidelberg Col 63-67 (Hist, Eng) AB; UMich 67-68 AMLS. 6: Sp. 7: Ref libn State Lif of Ohio, Columbus 68-. 9: ALA. 10: Phi Alpha Theta. 14: Ref. 15: 303 Executive dr AS, Marion Oh 43302.

GIBBS, ANNE LOUISE. b Yazoo City Miss 14 Ap 45. 5: USoMiss 63-67 (Eng) BA; Fla StateU 67-68 (LS) MS. 6: Fr. 7: Clk Richs Memorial Lib, Yazoo City Miss summer 65; Pre-catlgr stud asst USo Miss Lib 66-67; Planimeter operator Agric Stabilization & Conservation Serv, Yazoo City Miss summer 66-67, Asst libn Fla TechU 68-. 9: SLA; FlaLA. 14: Catlg, bibliog. 15: PO Box 217, Oviedo Fl 32765.

GIBBS, SISTER BERNARD JOSEPH. 5: St John'sU BA (magna cum laude), MLS. 6: Fr. 7: Libn Mt Saint Mary Acad, Newburgh NY; Libn Mt Saint Mary Col, Newburgh NY 65-. 8: Org: Cathedral High Sch Lib, Raleigh NC, Mt St Mary Acad Lib, Newburgh NC, Mt St Mary Col Lib, Newburgh NY. 9: ALA; ALA-ACRL; CatholicLA; NYLA. 15: Mount St Mary Col, Newburgh NY 12550.

GIBBS, BERTHA (WHITTINGTON). b Goldsboro NC 19 O 18. 4: James A Gibbs. 5: Fisk U 34-38 (Math) AB; UIll 40-41 BSLS. 6: Fr, Sp, Ger. 7: Asst libn Ky State Col 40-42; Ref libn Hampton Inst 43; Circ libn Fisk U 44; Libn Va Union U 44-46; Catlgr Harvard U 46-47; Ref libn Boston U Sch Theol 56-57; Ref libn Armour Research Inst Div of Weapons Evaluation Ill Inst of Tech 58-60; Catlg asst Field Mus of Natural Hist 60-64, Ref libn 64-. 9: SLA. 10: Alpha Kappa Alpha; Girl Scouts; United Negro Col Fund. 14: Ref, catlg. 15: 8242 S Langley ave, Chicago 60619.

GIBBS, DONALD TAYLOR. b Newton Lower Falls Mass 3 Mr 18. 4: June Nesbitt. 5: Williams Col 37-41 (Eng) AB; Simmons 46-47 (LS) BS. 7: US Army 42-45; Sr lib asst Rochester (NY) Pub Lib 47-49; Catlgr Redwood Lib & Athenaeum, Newport RI 49-52, Libn 52-. 8: V-chm Adv Commsn RI Dept of Lib Serv, 64-. 10: Rotary Club. 14: Ref, admin. 15: Redwood Lib Bellevue ave, Newport RI 02840.

GIBBS, JANE FRANCES. b Lincoln Neb 6 Mr 13. 5: Miami U (Oxfod Ohio) 31-35 (Hist) AB; West Res 35-36 BS in LS. 6: Fr. 7: Catlgr, asst ref libn Canton Pub Lib, Canton Ohio 36-40; Gen asst Cleveland Heights Pub Lib, Cleveland Heights Ohio 40-44; Catlgr NLM hist of med div, Cleveland 44-62; Libn Cleveland Museum of Nat Hist 62-. 9: Amer Assn Hist Med; ALA; (Div of Catlg & Clsf: chm &/or mem var coms SLA; 49-51); OhioLA; No Ohio Tech Serv Libns (chm 52); Lib Club of Cleveland (v-chm 51). 10: Bus & Prof Womens Club. 14: Rare bks, catlg, ref, mus libs. 15: 2600 Traymore rd, Cleveland 44118.

GIBBS, MARGARET. b Onalaska Tex 3 F 14. 4: Fred C Gibbs. 5: Decatur Baptist Col 55 AS; N Tex State U 57 BS in Ed; Tex Woman's U 59 MLS. 7: Exec sec Decatur Baptist Col 57-58; Dir Decatur Baptist Col Lib 58-65; Dir Dallas Baptist Col Lib 65-. 9: ALA (chm Spec Proj Com 67-68); TexLA; SWLA; Tex Jr Col TA; DallasCoLA. 10: International Platform Assn; AAUP; Delta Kappa Gamma; Kappa Delta Pi; Alpha Beta Alpha; Dallas baptist Col Woman's C&ub. 14: Admin, ref, reading guidance. 15: 3706 Kimballdale dr, Dallas Tx 76201.

GIBBS, NANCY JEAN (LANE). b Brooklyn NY 17 D 42. 4: Robert C Gibbs. 5: Madison Col 60-63 (Elem Educ) BS; UDenver 65-66 MSLS. 6: Fr. 7: Tchr Morrisville Bd of Educ, Morrisville Penn 63-65; Ref libn Penn StateU (Univ Park) 66-67, Personnel libn 67-68; Catlg libn AuburnU 69-. 9: ALA. 10: Zeta Tau Alpha. 14: Ref, personnel. 15: 420 N Dean rd Patio apts 138, Auburn Al 36830.

GIBBS, PHYLLIS ANN (MADDEN). b Bloomington Ill 12 Jl 27. 4: Richard Elmer Gibbs. 5: Rosary Col 45-49 BLS. 7: Asst libn Chicago Pub High Schs 49-51; Tech info specialist Off of Naval Research, Chicago 51-56; Asst libn Naval Train Ctr, Great Lakes Ill 57-59; Med libn Naval Hosp, Great Lakes Ill 59-. 15: 36 S Wheeling ave, Wheeling Il 60090.

GIBBS, ROBERT COLEMAN. b Bath NC 27 Ag 30. 4: Nancy Jean Lane Gibbs. 5: Duke 48-52 (Hist) AB; UNC 57-58 MSLS. 7: Gifts & exch libn Penn State U 58-60; Acquis asst UFla 60-64; Ser acquis libn Penn State U 64-68; Asst to the dir of libs Auburn U 68-. 9: ALA; PennLA; AlaLA. 10: AAUP; Beta Phi Mu; Soc Study So Lit. 14: Acquis, ser, bibliog, admin. 15: Patio apts #138, 420 N Dean rd, Auburn Al 36830.

GIBEAU, PATRICIA LOUISE (BELLAZZI). b Port Colbourne Ont Can 24 Jl 18. 4: Fernand L Gibeau. 7: Clk-lib asst Canadair Ltd, Montreal 53-61; Libn Canadair Ltd Plant 4 Engring Lib, Montreal 62-. 9: SLA; QuebLA. 14: Ref. 15: Canadair Limited PO Box 6087, Montreal 101 Queb Can.

GIBSON, ANNE (DUCKWORTH). b Clinton Mass 1 Ap 43. 4: William F Gibson. 5: UFla 60-64 9educ) BAE; URI 65-67 MLS. 7: Tchr Knotty Oak Sch, Coventry RI 64-66; Libn Coventry High Sch, Coventry RI 66-. 8: Libn Title II Mus Program 66-. 9: NEA; ALA; RIEA; RISchLA. 10: Zeta Phi Eta; Jr Women's Club. 15: Liberty lane, West Kingston RI 02892.

GIBSON, BARBARA CATHERINE (BAIRD). b Vancouver BC Can 17 N 15. 4: William Carleton Gibson. 5: UBC 32-36 (Eng, Hist) BA, 53-55 (Nursing) BSN, 62-63 BLS. 6: Fr, Ital, Lat. 7: Grad nurse (RN) Herbert Reddy Mem Hosp, Montreal 39-40; Grad nurse (RN) Shriners Hosp for Crippled Children, Montreal 40-41; Grad nurse RCAMC Can Army Nursing Sister (Capt) 41-46; Grad nurse (BSN) UBC Sch of Nursing Instr 55-58; Libn catlgr med materials, Ital, rare bks UBC Lib 63-67; Asst Prof Sch of Libnship UBC 67-. 13: Yes. 14: Catlg, rare bks. 15: 5516 NW Marine dr, Vancouver BC Can.

GIBSON, CLAUDE EWING. b Tuskegee Ala 25 Ap 35. 5: Rensselaer Polytech Inst 53-57 (Chem) BS; USoCal 58-65 (LS) MS. 6: Fr. 7: Tech reports analyst Goodyear Atomic Corp, Portsmouth Ohio 57-58; Asst libn Ryan Aeronautical Co, San Diego 58-61, Lit research spec Space Tech Labs, Redondo Beach Cal 61-63; Asst chief libn Grumman Aircraft Eng Corp, Bethpage NY 63-68, Dir of Libs 68-. 9: ASIS; SLA (treas So Cal Chap 62-63); IEEE; Nat Security Indus Assn (Tech, Info, Adv Com). 14: Admin, lib automation. 15: 41 Landing rd, Huntington NY 11743.

GIBSON, COLLEEN (CAROLYN). b Winnipeg Manitoba Can 8 O 40. 5: UBC 58-62 (Eng) BA, 65-66 BLS. 7: High sch tchr, Hazelton BC 62-63, Chilliwack BC 65; Ref libn UCalgary 66-67, Circ libn 67-68, Hd circ dept 68-. 9: ALA; pARCL (Readers Serv Div); CanLA (chm com on Interlib Loans Procedures Manual, Info Serv Sect; mem Biennial Structure Study Com; chm Info Serv Sect; mem Can Assn of Col and univ Libs Sect; mem Tech Serv Sect). 10: Calgary Choral Soc; Mac Wkshop (Theater Group, Amateur). 14: Ref, guidance serv, (A-V orient for Students), automation. 15: Univ of Calgary Lib, Calgary 44 Alberta Can.

GIBSON, DAN MARTIN. b San Fernando Cal 22 Jl 27. 4: Helen Lee Gibson. 5: Los Angeles City Col 46-48 (Eng) AA; Pomona Col 48-50 (Eng) BA; UCLA 50-52 (Educ); USoCal 53-54 MSLS. 7: Tchr Los Angeles City Schs 52-53; Libn Roosevelt Jr High Sch, San Diego 54-55; Libn Marston J High Sch, San Diego 55-58; Libn Clairemont High Sch, San Diego 58-60; Libn Admin Off San Diego City Schs 60-63; Supv of Sch Libs Beverly Hills Unified Sch Dist, Beverly Hills Cal 63-64, Dir of Instr Materials 64-. 8: Consul, Sch Lib Facilities & Programs 67-. 9: NEA-DAVI; CalASchL (treas 61-62, pres-elect 69-70, sect pres 65-66); CalLA; Cal Tchrs Assn. 13: Yes. 14: Unified instr materials programs. 15: 255 S Lasky dr, Beverly Hills Cal 90212.

GIBSON, E(LLEN) BERNICE. b Chicago 30 Ap 06. 5: Milton Col 27 (Lat) BA; UWis 29 (LS) Diploma. 7: UWis Lib Sch: Asst & reviser 29-39, Instr & reviser 39-45, Instr & Libn 45-, Libn 64-. 9: ALA; WisLA (chm Catlg Sect 51-52, chm Tech Serv Sect 63-64). 14: Catlg. 15: 425 Henry Mall, Madison Wis 53706.

GIBSON, ELEANOR BEATRICE. b London 8 Mr 05. 5: Cornell U 23-28 (Fr) AB; St Josephs Col (Conn) 37-38 (LS); Syracuse 54-57 MS in LS. 6: Fr. 7: Policy dept Aetna Life Insurance Co, Hartford Conn 28-33; Libn research dept Aetna Life Affiliated Cos, Hartford Conn 33-42; Auxiliary (1st Lt) WAAC, WAC AU Australia, New Guinea, Manila 42-46; Libn Carrier Corp, Syracuse NY 47-67, Lib adv 67-68; Tech Supv Union Catlg Conn State Lib 68-. (Capt) WAC AUS Japan 50-51. 8: John Cotton Dana Lecture UToronto Lib Sch 62. 9: ASIS; ASLib Brit; SLA (Life member, PRES WNY Chap, Nat chm Metals Div); ConnLA. 10: Womens Nat Bk Assn; Central & No NY Lib Resources Project ad hoc Com (sec 64-); Pi Lambda Sigma; Beta Ph Mu; Col Art Assn Amer. 11: SLA (Hall of Fame, elected 68; Honors Award Metals/Materials Div 68). 12: Ed "Guide to Metallurgical Information, with E W Tapia" (2nd ed 65); Ed var bulletins. 13: Yes. 14: Admin, spec lib on air conditioning. 15: 23 Fernridge rd, W Hartford Ct 06107.

GIBSON, ELIZABETH ANNE. b Sherbrooke 19 S 41. 5: Bshops U 60-64 (Hist, Eng) BA; McGill 64-65 BLS. 6: Fr. 7: Asst libn Aluminum Co, Montreal 65-. 9: CanLA. 14: Catlg. 15: 1340 St Croix, St Laurent Que Can.

GIBSON, ELSIE O. b Belleville NJ 12 Je 16. 5: Syracuse 34-38 (Hist, Eng) AB; Radcliffe 39-41 (Hist) MA; Rutgers 55-56 MLS. 7: Assoc libn Bloomfield Col 56-57; Libn Panzer Col 57-58; Acquis libn Montclair State Col 58-65, Lib sci coordinator 62-. 9: NEA; NJLA; NJEA; ALA. 10: AAUP; Coun of State Employees; NJ State Cols Faculty Assn; Womens Univ Club, NYC. 14: Lib educ. 15: 192 Inwood ave, Upper Montclair NJ 07043.

GIBSON, FRANK E(VERETT). b Des Moines Iowa 30 My 13. 4: Bette Beckett Gibson. 5: Drake 48 (Hist) BA; UMinn 49 BS in LS, 52 (LS) MA. 6: Fr. 7: Accountant Iowa Power & Light, Des Moines Iowa 32-42; US Army 42-46; Acquis libn UMinn St Paul 49-52; Assoc libn Omaha U 52-53; Asst dir Omaha Pub Lib 53-57, Dir 57-. 8: Lib bldg consul. 9: ALA (Coun 63-66, chm & mem 3 coms 56-64); NebLA (pres 56-57). 10: Kiwanis; Phi Beta Kappa. 13: Yes. 14: Admin, lib bldgs. 15: 6802 N 41st st, Omaha 68112.

GIBSON, HELEN (PARKER). b Ogden Utah 28 O 04. 5: West Res 26-27 (LS) Certif; UUtah 27- (LS) sch lib Certif. 6:

Fr. 7: Child libn Ogden Pub Lib, Ogden Utah 23-26, 28-29; Child libn Cleveland Pub Lib, Cleveland Ohio 26-27; Child libn Seattle Pub Lib, 30-32; Libn E High Sch, Salt Lake City 33-44; Libn Salt Lake Co Lib, Midvale Utah 44-45; Dir of libs Davis Co Lib, Farmington Utah 45-. 8: Wkshops with Utah State Agric Col in bk sel 46-49; Consul: Kamas High Sch Kamas Utah 51, Wasatch Co Lib Devel Com 50, Pub lib Nephi Utah 52. 9: ALA (Coun; Memb Chm for Utah); MPLA (chm Pub Lib Sect); UtahLA (pres; chm Sch Lib Sect). 10: Humane Soc; PTA. 13: Yes. 14: Child wk, admin. 15: 10 South 1st W, Kaysville Ut 84037.

GIBSON, IMOGENE (WYATT). b Olney Tex 14 Jl 26. 4: Paul Gibson. 5: UTex 43-45 (Biol); UChicago 46-47 (Bacteriology) BS; Tex Woman'sU 66-69 MLS. 7: Tech Nalco Chem, Chicago 48-51, 54-56; Tchr: Chicago Hts School Dist, Chicago Hts Ill 61-62, Edison Sch Dist, Edison NJ 62-63; Catlgr Austin Col 65-. 10: Beta Phi Mu. 14: Catlg, ref. 15: 1125 Western Hills dr, Sherman Tx 75090.

GIBSON, LINDA N(ANCE). b Victoria BC Can 3 Ag 40. 4: Hughes Gibson. 5: Acadia U 57-61 (Philos) BA; McGill 62 BLS. 7: Libn UToronto Lib 63-. 9: CanLA. 14: Ref. 15: 171A Madison ave, Toronto 5 Canada.

GIBSON, MARGARET GEISSINGER (NOSS). b Tokyo Japan 19 My 22. 4: Wallace Gibson. 5: Berea Col 40-44 (Home Econ) BS; Wayne State U 60-61 (LS); UMich 61-63 AMLS. 6: Fr, Ger, Japanese. 7: Dietitian St Josephs Infirmary, Louisville Ky 44-45; Tchr Richmond Schs, Richmond Mich 59-62; TchrLAnse Creuse Schs, Mt Clemens Mich 63, Libn 63-; Libn Macomb Co Lib, Mt Clemens Mich 64; Coord Elem Sch Libs & Dir Centralized Processing Lanse Creuse Schs Mt clemens Mich 68-. 9: ALA; NEA; MichASchL; Mich A-V Assn. 14: Elem sch libs. 15: 9004 Gratiot, Richmond Mi 48062.

GIBSON, NORMA JEAN. b Lexington Ky 27 Jl 30. 5: UKy 50-54 (LS) BA. 7: Libn Educ Lib UKy 54-59, Libn Fine Arts Lib 59-. 9: ALA; KyLA. 14: Pub serv. 15: 670 Springridge dr, Lexington Ky 40503.

GIBSON, ROBERT STANSILL. b Richmond County NC 1 Ag 25. 4: Janie Edwards. 5: High Point COL 46-48 (Eng); Duke 48-49 (Educ) AB; Duke Divinity Sch 49-53 (Res & Tchg) BD; Fla State U 60-61 MA in LS. 7: Yeoman 2d class US Naval Res 44-46; Instr Spartanburg Jr Col 49-50; Pastor NC Methodist Conf 52-58; Dir Appalachian Wesley Found, Boone NC 58-60; Asst soc sci & asst catlg libn UGa 61-62, Asst soc sci libn 2-63; Assoc libn Louisburg Col 63-64; Pub serv libn Radford Col 64-. 9: ALA; SELA: VaLA. 10: Civitan Club; Beta Phi Mu. 14: Ref, admin. 15: 602 Vienna ave rte 1, Radford Va 24141.

GIBSON, ROBERT W JR. b Canova SD 15 Mr 23. 4: Wilma Jeanne Caster Gibson. 5: Yankton Col 41-44 (Chem) BA; Ohio State U 45-49 (Educ) (intermittently). 7: Chem Maytag Washing Machine, Newton Iowa 44; Ass supv-libn Battelle Mem Inst, Columbus Ohio 44-62; Asst libn IBM-Thos J Watson Research Center, Yorktown Heights NY 62-65; Libn Res Labs Gen Motors Corp, Warren Mich 65-. 8: Pres Kresge Sci Lib Assn 68-; Lib consul SLA Mich Chap 66-68; Mem Steering Com, Mich Ref & Research Resources. 9: ALA; SLA (Bd, chm & mem var coms, pres-elect 68-69, pres 69-70, chm Metals/Materials Div; past pres Cleveland Chap); ASIS; ACS. 10: Engnr Soc of Detroit; AAAS; NY Acad Sci; Engnrs Jt Coun; Macomb Co Commun Col Lib Adv Com; Oral Hist Assn. 13: Yes. 14: Admin, application of machines to lib procedures, personnel. 15: Res Labs General Motors Corp 12 Mile & Mound rds, Warren Mich 48090.

GIDDINGS, CLIFFORD F(REDERICK). b E Dorst Vt 28 My 36. 5: UVt 54-58 (Fr) BA; UGrenoble(France) 58-59 2 Certificats detudes francaises; UWis 59-61 (Fr) MA; Chicago 63- (LS). 6: Fr, Sp, Ital. 7: Fr Master Lake Forest Acad, Lake Forest Ill 61-63; Ref libn Newberry Lib, Chicago 64-65, Head ref & circ 66-. 66; Dir lib serv Scott, Foresman & Co, Glenview Ill 68-. 8: Bibliogr in hist linguistics, The Newberry Library, Chicago 65-68. 9: ALA; SLA; ASIS. 10: Caxton Club(Chicago); The Executive's Club (Chicago); ACLU; Amer Mgt Assn. 11: Fulbright stud to France 58-59. 14: Hist lings, ref. 15: 1900 E Lake ave, Glenview Il 60025.

GIEBEL, MIRIAM CATHERINE (DONAHOE). b Williamsburgh Iowa 10 O 34. 4: William Giebel. 5: Marquette U 52-56 (Sociol) BS; Rosary Col 59-60 MSLS. 7: Order dept asst Marquette U Lib 56-58; Catlg dept asst Rosary Col Lib 58-59; Head tech processes Chicago Heights Pub Lib, Chicago Heights Ill 59-63; Libn Little Company of Mary Sch of Nursing, Evergreen Park Ill 63-64; Asst to the libn Hdqrs Lib ALA, Chicago 64-67; Libn Markham Pub Lib 68-. 9: ALA; IllLA. 15: 234 Tahoe dr, Chicago Heights Il.

GIERYIC, MICHAEL DONALD. b Sheboygan Wis 9 S 36. 4: Jane VandeBoom. 5: Wis State U (Oshkosh) 54-58 (Elem Educ) BS; UWis 62-63 MS in LS. 6: Ger, Fr. 7: Soc studies tchr Jr High Sch, Grafton Wis 58-60; Libn High Sch, Port Wash Wis 60-62; Asst ref libn Colgate U Lib 63-65, Catlg libn 65-68; Hd libn SUNY at Morrisville 68-. 10: AAUP. 14: Catlg. 15: 10 Milford st, Hamilton NY 13346.

GIESBRECHT, JOSEPHINE (CHAMBERLAIN). 5: UBC 50-52 (Hist) BA; McGill 53-54 BLS. 7: Catlgr Lib Parliament, Ottawa 54-56; Catlgr UBC 57-59; Catlgr Nat Lib, Ottawa 60-. 9: CanLA. 15: Nat Library, Ottawa Can.

GIFFORD, HILDA GORHAM. b Montreal Can 22 S 15. 5: McGill 34-38 (Fr, Ger) BA, BLS. 6: Fr, Ger. 7: Catlgr Dalhousie U (Halifax) 38-43; Postal censorship Civil Serv, Ottawa 43-45; Period libn ILO, Montreal 45-46; Catlgr Dartmouth Col 47-48; Chief Libn Carleton U (Ottawa) 48-. 9: CanLA (var offs); OntLA; Lib Assn of Ottawa; Inst Prof Libns Ottawa (var offs); Can Assn of Col & Univ Libs (var offs). 10: University Womens Club. 13: Yes. 14: Admin, bk sel. 15: 57 Wilton Crescent, Ottawa 1 Ont Can.

GIFFORD, OLIVE R(UTH VENN). b N Bloomfield Ohio 3 N 11. 4: Herbert E Gifford. 5: Youngstown U 29-33 Tuba) BM; Kent State 34-36 (Music, Educ) BS in Educ; UDenver 53-55 (LS) MA. 7: Vocal music Jefferson High Sch, Jefferson Ohio 36-40; Co-owner Giffords Music Store, Ravenna Ohio 0-52; Jr high tchr Garfield Sch; Garrettsville Ohio 52-53; Libn Iliff Sch of Theol 55; High sch libn Canon City High Sch, Canon City Colo 55-61; Catlg libn Willamette U 61-63; Asst libn Northeastern Jr Col (Sterling Col) 63-64; Circ documents libn West State Col (Gunnison Colo) 64-68, Circ-res libn 64-. 9: ALA (Life mem); NEA; MPLA; ColoLA; ColoASchL (Constit Com); ColoEA. 10: AAUW; AAUP. 14: Catlg, circ, pub sch libnship. 15: P O Box 843, Gunnison Colo 81230.

GIFFORD, ROGER G(AILLARD). b Brooklyn NY 6 Je 14. 4: Lorraine Benson. 5: Clark U 32-36 (Hist) AB; Columbia 39-41 (LS) BS. 7: Clerk G M-P Murphy Co, NYC 36-37; Claims adjustor Liberty Mutual Insurance Co 37-39; Stud asst libn Columbia U 39-41, Nigh supv circ dept 41-42; Ref libn Cooper Union, NYC 42-43; (M/Sgt) US Army 43-45; Sr libn Newark Pub Lib, Newark NJ 45-46; Lib Div US Dept of State, Wash DC: Ref libn 46-47, Asst chief bibliog 47-48, Chief sel & record sect 48-53, Chief tech serv br 53-58; Reg foreign publ procurement off Amer Embassy, New Delhi India 58-60, Officer in chg Consular Sect 60-63; Consular Off Amer Embassy, London 63-64; Bibliog for S Asia Mich State U Lib 64-65, Acquis libn 65-. 9: ALA. 10: Amer For Serv Assn. 14: Acquis, tech serv, S Asia. 15: 2881 Crestwood dr, East Lansing Mich 48823.

GIFFORD, VIRGINIA (SNODGRASS). b Cottonwood Idaho 15 Je 36. 4: Guy A Gifford. 5: Central Wash State Col 53-57, summers 58-59 (Music Educ) BA, MEd; Wash StateU summers 56-57 (Music Educ); Eastman Sch of Music 59-60 (Music); CatholicU 65, 66, 68-69 MSLS. 6: Ger. 7: Tchr: Garrison Jr High Sch, Walla Walla Wash 57-59, Wheaton high Sch, Montgomery Co Md 61-62; Reviser-reviewer & music catlgr LC Copyright Off 63-. 9: ALA; MusicLA; DCLA. 10: Kappa Delta Pi. 14: Catlg, music. 15: 720-9th SE, Washington DC 20003.

GIGLIO, RUDOLPH GEORGE. b Boston 20 S 22. 5: Boston U 47-51 (Psych) AB; Simmons 51-52 (LS) MS; UHartford 55-58 (Engnr) BS. 7: Army of the US 43-46; Lib asst Boston Pub Lib 49-52; Lib asst Boston U 51; Lib asst Harvard U 52; Catlgr Boston U 52; Catlgr Yale U 52-53; Catlgr Free Lib of Phila 53-54; Pratt & Whitney Aircraft, E Hartford Conn; Draftsman 55-56, Design engnr 57-60; Indexer "Applied Science & Technology Index," H W Wilson Co, Bronx NY 62-. 9: ALA; SLA; ASIS; NY Tech Serv Libns; NY Lib Club. 10: AAAS. 14: Indexing, catlg, clsf, theory of info systems. 15: 930 Ogden ave apt 63, Bronx NY 10452.

GIL, OLGA JOAN. b Winnipeg Man Can 10 F 39. 5: UMan 56-59 (Hist) BA; McGill 59-60 BLS. 6: Fr, Ukrainian. 7: Circ libn UToronto 60-61, Ref libn 60-65; Documents libn Sir George Williams U 65-68; Docs libn York U (Toronto) 68-. 8: Guest lectr in Govt Pubs, McGill Lib Sci 68. 9: CanLA (sec Info Serv Sect); ALA;-ACRL; Inst Prof Libns Ont; OntLA (chm &/or mem 4 coms 62-); Inst Profess Libns Ont; QueLA. 10: Beta Phi Mu. 12: "A Guide to the Use of Uncatalogued Materials and of Material Requiring Special Handling in its Use in the University of Toronto Library (63); "A Guide to the

Use of Government Publicatins and United Nations Material (64); Contrib "Bibliographia historae rerem rusticarum internationalis, 1962- (64); 64. 14: Ref, govt docs. 15: 50 Ruddington dr apt 808, Willowdale 433, Ont Can.

GILB, NOREEN S. b Sacramento Cal 8 Ap 39. 4: Thomas J Gilb. 5: Bakersfield Jr Col 57-58; Mt St Marys Col 58-61 (Eng Lit) BA; Columbia 62-65 (LS) MS. 6: Fr. 7: Asst film libn NY Pub Lib 63-65; Asst ref libn UNev 65-66, Libn Desert Research Inst 66-. 9: ALA; NevLA; SLA. 13: Yes. 14: Spec libs. 15: P O Box 8573 Univ Sta, Reno Nev 89507.

GILBERT, BELLE (GREENFIELD). b NYC 23 Ja 22. 4: Emanuel Gilbert. 5: Hunter Col 38-42 (Hist) BA; Simmons 65-69 MLS. 7: Libn Newton High Sch, Newton Mass 67-. 9: MassSchLA. 10: LWV; Hunter Alumni Assn. 14: Sch libs. 15: 55 Hinckley rd, Waban Ma 02168.

GILBERT, CHRISTINE B. b Brooklyn NY 30 Je 09. 5: Mt Holyoke Col 28-32 (Religion, Hist) BA; Columbia 33-34 BLS, 45 (Educ) BA. 6: Fr. 7: Asst libn Lincoln Sch of Tchrs Col Columbia U 34-39; Libn Sch Lib Lab Tchrs Col (NY) 39-45; Lib Lincoln Sch Tchrs Col 45-46; Lib Munsey Park Sch, Manhasset NY 47-49; Dir Sch Commun Rel Manhasset (NY) Pub Schs 50-62; Assoc Prof of Lib Sci LIU Grad Lib Sch 55-; Libn Plandome ROAD Sch, Manhasset LI NY 62-68; Assoc Prof Grad Lib Sch LIU 68-. 9: ALA;-CSD (Newbery-Caldecott Com 63-64); NEA; NYLA; NY State EA; Nassau-Suffolk SchLA. 12: Co-auth, with Ruth Strang, "Gateway to Readable Books. 13: Yes. 14: Bk reviewing, child lit, sch libs, sch media ctrs. 15: Post apt AE9, Greenvale NY 11548.

GILBERT, ELIZABETH (DINWIDDIE). b Madison C Ky 15 Ap 07. 5: Berea Col 26-30 (Home Econ) AB; West Res summers 33-38 BS in Lib Sci; Columbia summer 49 (Col libnship); West Res summer 55. 6: Lat, Fr. 7: Supv of circ Berea Col 30-44, Libn 44-, Chm Dept of Lib Sci 44-, Prof of Lib Sci 65-. 8: Ky Bd for Certif of Libns 57-. 9: ALA; SELA (Ky rep on Bd 67-, planning bd 65-66); KyLA (pres 45-46). 10: Berea Progress Club; AAUW; AAUP; Friends of Ky Libs; Phi Kappa Phi; Kappa Delta Pi. 11: Outstanding Col & Univ Libn, KyLA 66. 13: Yes. 14: Admin, lib educ, rare bks. 15: Rt 1, Berea Ky 40403.

GILBERT, HARRIETT JOAN. b Grinnell Iowa 13 Ag 34. 5: Amer Inst Bus 53 (Bus Machines). 7: Sec Newton Pub Lib, Newton Iowa 62; Sec Newton Mfg Co, Newton Iowa 53-54; Sec jasper Co Lib, Newton Iowa 54-56, Asst libn 56-60; Sec Newton Pub Lib, Newton Iowa 62, county libn 60-64; Child libn & dir sch serv Oskaloosa Pub Lib, Oskaloosa Iowa 64-. 9: ALA; IowaLA (Ext Sect: sec 62-64). 10: Bus & Profess Women's Club; Altrusa; Delta Kappa Gamma. 14: Child & ya serv. 15: 308 First ave E, Oskaloosa Ia 52577.

GILBERT, HARRY (CHARLES). b Paducah Ky 11 F 31. 4: Mary Alice Carter. 5: Murray State Col 55-59 (Hist) AB; Miami U 59-60 (Hist) MA; UDenver 62-63 (Libnship) MA. 7: Disbursing Clerk 3d Class US Navy Atlantic Fleet 51-55; Instr in hist Southwestern Col (Winfield Kan) 60-62; Act dir of the Lib Rose Polytech Inst 63-65; Asst order libn Ind State U 65-67; Asst hd acquis UKy (Lexington) 67-. 9: ALA; KyLA; Ohio Valley Tech Serv Group. 10: Optimist Club. 14: Acquis. 15: 925 Lane Allen rd, Lexington Ky 40504.

GILBERT, LAURA M. b Grafton Wis 12 O 17. 5: UWis(Milwaukee) 35-39 (Secondary Educ, Math) BS; Chicago summers 45-48, 58 BLS. 6: Fr, Ger. 7: Libn Henry Clay Sch, Whitefish Bay Wis 39-42; High sch libn Central High Sch, Sheboygan Wis 42-60; Sr high sch libn & dept chm & mem of Faculty Coun South High Sch, Sheboygan Wis 60-. 9: NEA; WisEA. 10: Sheboygan Mem Hosp Corp; Nat Audubon Soc; Kappa Delta Pi. 14: Yp, ref, a-v. 15: 2609 N 5th st, Sheboygan Wis 53081.

GILBERT, NANCY LOUISE. b Norfolk Va 3 N 38. 5: Greensboro Col 57-61 (Sp) AB; UNC (Chapel Hill) 66-68 MLS. 6: Sp. 7: Claims examiner Soc Security Admin, Baltimore 61-62; Lib asst Amer Auto Assn, Wash DC 62-64; Computer programmer US Coast Guard, Wash DC 64-65; Asst libn Amer Auto Assn, Wash DC 65-66; Lib tech Defense Supply Agcy, alexandria Va 67; Stud ref asst Humanities Div Wilson Lib UNC (Chapel Hill) 66-67, 67-68; Ref libn Va Beach Pub Lib, Va Beach Va 68; Army libn Spec Serv, Worms Germany 68-69, Crailsheim Germany 69-. 9: ALA (European Armed Forces Libns Subsect); VaLA. 14: Ref. 15: 3872 Jefferson blvd, Virginia Beach Va 23455.

GILBERT, RACHEL MARY (HARKEMA). b NYC 1 Jl 28. 4: A Edward Gilbert. 5: Hunter Col 43-47 (Speech) BA; Immaculate Heart Col 67-68 MLS. 6: Ger. 7: Real estate broker, los Angeles 55-67; Dir music St Paul's Lutheran Ch, Santa Monica Cal 59-68; Libn-in- charge Los Angeles Co Pub, S Gate Cal 68-. 9: CalLA. 10: Amer Guild of Organists; Choral Conductor's Guild. 14: Admin, ya serv. 15: 552 Stassi lane, Santa Monica Cyn Ca 90402.

GILBERT, VICTORY (KAUFMAN). b Brooklyn NY 11 N 18. 4: Morton R Gilbert. 5: NYU Wash kSq Col 35-39 (Retailing) BA; C W Post Col of LIU 61-65 (LS) MS. 6: Fr. 7: Resident Buyer Ouida Browne Inc, NYC 39-41; Sch libn Ralph J Osgood Jr-Sr High Sch, Kings Park NY 62-65; Sch libn Kings Park High Sch, Kings Park NY 65- 66; John F Kennedy High Sch, Bellmore NY 66-. 9: NEA; NY State Tchrs Assn; NYLA; ALA. 15: 111 Sprucewood dr, Levittown NY 11756.

GILBORNE, JEAN E. b Bonfield Ill 21 Je 10. 5: Ill State Normal U 37 (Eng) B Ed; UIll 44 (Eng) MA, 51 MS in LS; UCal (Berkeley) summer 56 LS. 6: Fr. 7: Tchr Rural Schs Kankakee Co 28-38; High Sch tchr Pub Sch Sheridan, LaSalle Co 38-39; High Sch tchr Pub Sch Fillmore, Montgomery Co 39-40; High Sch tchr Pub Sch Ashmore, Coles Co 40-42; High Schana Ill 50-51 High sch libn Geneseo High Sch, Geneseo Ill 51-54; Unit libn Geneseo Commun Unit 54-. 8: Lib Staff Wis State Col (Plattville) summer 59; Instr ext class UIll(Princeton, Ill) 53-54. 9: ALA; NEA; IllLA; IllEA; IllASchL (Reserv Chm for 2 confs). 10: Bus & Prof Womans Club; Blackhawk Libns Group (pres, sec); wk with Ill Stud Libns Assn as sponsor; Wesleyan Serv Guild; Beta Phi Mu. 14: Wk to coordinate sch instrl materials. 15: 607-1/2 S Center st, Geneseo Ill 61254.

GILCHRIST, BESSIE B. b Rehoboth SC 16 S 03. 5: UGa 23-27 (Eng, Hist) AB (magna cum laude); Emory 31-32 AB in LS; UIll summer 39 (LS). 6: Fr. 7: Tchr-libn Jesup High Sch, Jesup Ga; Libn Wingate Jr Col; Libn Middle Ga Col; Libn Augusta Pub Lib, Augusta Ga 43-47; Lbn VA Hosp Lenwood Div, Augusta Ga 47-62; Chief Lib Serv VA Hosp orest Hills Div, Augusta Ga 62-. 9: ALA; Central Savannah River Area LA (sec-treas 63-64). 10: AAUW; Augusta Kennel Club Inc; Augusta Rose Soc. 14: Catlg. 15: 1209 Stovall st, Augusta Ga 30904.

GILCHRIST, MARTHA (SCOTT). b Indianapolis 12 Ja 12. 4: George E Gilchrist. 5: Butler U 31-35 (Journalism); Columbia summer 44 (LS). 7 Clerical asst catlg dept Indianapolis Pub Lib 27-37; Clerical asst Joint Ref Lib of Pub Admin Serv, Chicago 39-43; Asst order dept Post Lib US Army, Ft Monmouth NJ 44; Catlgr & ref asst Joint Ref Lib of Pub Admin Serv, Chicago 45-63, Libn 63-67, Assoc libn 67-. 9: SLA. 12: Ed (with Marianne Yates) "Administrative Reorganization of State Governments (48). 14: Catlg. 15: 1313 E 60 st, Chicago Il 60637.

GILDEN, WILLIAM K. b Anacortes Wash 27 Mr 33. 5: Carroll Col (Helena Mont) 51-55 (Philos) AB; UWash 55-56 (LS) ML. 7: Tchg asst Sch of Libnship UWash 56; Chaplains asst US Army Presidio of San Francisco 57-59; Jr libn catlg dept San Francisco Pub Lib 59-62, Br libn Golden Gate Valley Br 62-63, Head catlgr 63-64; Asst sup catlg libn Cal State Lib 64-65, Supv catlg libn 65-66, Chief tech serv 66-. 8: Gen libn Library 21 Seattle Worlds Fair 62. ; Inst Educ & Training of Info Sci Fac, USoCal 69. 9: ALA-RTSD;-ISAD; Amer Assn State Libs; CalLA; No Cal Tech Processes Gp; So Cal Tech Processes Gp; ASIS. 11: Delta Epsilon Sigma. 14: Catlg, wk simplification in bk processing, lib automation. 15: 4040 T st, Sacramento Cal 95819.

GILDERSLEEVE, PATRICIA (MOORE). b Lincoln Neb 3 Ja 30. 4: Hallet Gildersleeve. 5: UNeb 48-52 (Eng, Hist) BSc; UIll 57-58 (LS) MSc. 7: Libn Ill State Water Survey, Champaign 57-60; Catlgr Neb Pub Lib Commsn, Lincoln 68-. 10: Great Books. 14: Catlg. 15: 1861 Dakota, Lincoln Nb 68502.

GILES, CLIFTON F JR. b Marlboro Mass 29 N 35. 4: Joan E Fyle. 5: UMass 57-60 (Hist) BA; UIll 61-63 MLS; UMo 68 (Comp Inst). 6: Fr. 7: Shop supv US Army Signal Corps (E-5) 54-57; Circ & ref Univ of Mass Lib 60-61; Circ UIll 61-63; Ref UMd 63-64; Catlgr UNH 64-66; Asst to dir UDel 66-67, Asst dir 67-. 8: Consult Adv Com Lib Tech, D el Tech & Commun Col 69. 9: ALA (Del Memb Chm 67-69); NELA; NHLA (treas 65-66); DelLA (Memb Chm 67-69). 10: AAUP. 13: Yes. 14: Admin, tech serv. 15: 384 S Col ave, Newark De 19711.

GILES, FLEETWOOD JR. b Brandon Tex 17 My 29. 5: UTex 46-50 (Pre-Med) BA, 51-52 (Educ), 54-58 MLS. 7: Seaman apprentice US Navy San Diego 51; Pricing clerk Milstead Co, Austin Tex 52-54; Catlgr UTex Lib (Austin) 54-.

9: ALA; TexLA; SWLA. 12: "Texas Librarians; A Study Based on Who's Who in Library Service" (3d ed 1955, No 113 in ACRL Microcard Ser, Publ 1960). 15: 5701 Wynona ave, Austin Tx 78756.

GILES, GERTRUDE (ANDERSON). b Hawkinsville Ga 14 My 1898. 4: Reuben W Giles. 5: Womans Col of Ga 16-21 (Eng) AB; Appalachian Tchrs Col 58 (LS) MA. 7: Libn Womans Col of Ga 21-30; Tchr Washington Co Bd of Educ, Sandersville Ga 44-45; Libn Baker Co Bd of Educ, Newton Ga 52-69. 9: ALA; NEA; GaLA (chm 2nd Dist). 10: AAUW; Delta Kappa Gamma. 14: Sch libs. 15: P O Box 46, Newton Ga 31770.

GILES, LOUISE (JONES). b Aragon Ga 20 Ap 30. 4: Edwin C Giles. 5: UAkron 48-52 (Modern Langs) BA; Drexel 52-53 (LS) MS; West Res summer 51 (Span); Independent study in Honduras, Central Amer on exch fellowship 53-54. 6: Sp, Fr. 7: Detroit Pub Lib: Libn I, II 53-59, Foreign lang spec in chg of foreign lang collection 59-60, 1st asst 60-65; Asst Prof-Libn Oakland Commun Col 65- 09: ALA; MichLA (Memb Com 61-62). ; Assoc dean Learning Resources Ctr Oakland Commun Col 68-. 9: Mich Commun & Jr Col Lib Adminrs (chm). 10: Detroit Pub Lib Staff Assn; Pi Sigma Alpha; Phi Sigma Alpha. 12: "Aspects of the Communtycollege Fiel; a Bibliography" (69). 13: Yes. 14: Ref, bk sel, admin. 15: 19769 Steel ave, Detroit Mi 48235.

GILES, MARTHA ANN (MARTIN). b Birmingham Ala 27 N 27. 4: Ted A Giles. 5: Ala Col 45-48 (Eng, Hist) AB; Emory 48-49 (Libnship) ML. 7: Atlanta Pub Libn Atlanta Pub Lib 50-53, 62-67; Asst libn Kennesaw Jr Col 67-. 9: ALA; SELA. 10: Kennesaw Jr Col Women's Club. 14: Ref. 15: 250 Alpine dr, Roswell Ga 30075.

GILFOYLE, PHYLLIS J. b George B Gilfoyle. 5: UChicago BA, (Phil) MA. 7: Lib asst Country Club Hills Pub Lib, Country Club Hills Ill 64, Hd libn 65-. 9: ALA; IllLA; LACONI. 10: Sch Bd mem; Commun Chest; Girl Scout Neighborhood Com; PTA IDC; ACLU; IASB. 14: Pub lib serv. 15: Country Club Hills Pub Lib, 18630 Baker ave, Country Club Hills Il 60477.

GILHEANY, ROSARY (SCACCIAFERRO). b NYC 2 O 29. 4: Thomas Joseph Gilheany. 5: Barnard 45-49 (Hist) AB; Columbia 49-51 (LS) MS; 67 MedLA Med Lib Certifn. 6: Sp, Fr, Ital. 7: Asst Lib Sch of Bus City College (NY) 50-51; Catlgr NY Hist Soc, NYC 51-53; Libn Regis High Sch, NYC 53-54; Asst libn Continental Insurance Cos, NYC 54-61; Ref libn & catlgr Acad of Med, Bloomfield NJ 62-. 8: Consul catlg & clsf wkshops for hosp lib personnel. 10: NJ Hist Soc; Barnard Col Club No Central NJ; AAUW; LWV Bd. 13: Yes. 15: 21 De Vausney pl, Nutley NJ 07110.

GILL, BERNARD I(VES). b Rockford Ill 16 My 21. 4: Dorothy Hovde. 5: Beloit Col 39, 42; UIll 40-43 (Sociol) BA, 48-49 (LS) MS; UMinn 63-64 (Amer Studies). 6: Fr, Ger. 7: (Lt jg) USNR, Mediterranean & Pacific 43-45; Tchr soc studies Bensenville Jr High Sch, Bensenville Ill 46-47; Ref asst Milwaukee Pub Lib 49-50; Head Libn Moorhead State Col 50-. 9: NEA; ALA; Amer Studies Assn; MinnEA; Minn LA. 10: AAUP. 14: Admin, tech proc, ref collection, bldgs & equipment. 15: Moorhead State Col, Moorhead Mn 56560.

GILL, GLADYS LILLIAN. b Bell Cal 13 je 06. 5: UCLA 26-29 (Hist); UCal(Berkeley) 29-30 (Hist) BA; UIll 30-31 BS in LS. 7: Kern Co Free Lib, Bakersfield Cal: Asst libn Baker St Br 31-33, Br libn baker St Br 33-39, Asst br supv 39-40; Br libn Delano Br Kern Co Free Lib, Delano Cal 40-41; Camp Libn 9th Corps US Army, Camp San Luis Obispo Cal 41-45; Camp Libn Camp New Orleans AAC US Army, Mailly le Camp France 45; Area Libn Nancy Garrison Area AAC US Army, Nancy France 45-46; Area Libn Metz Garrison Area West-Base Sect US Army, Metz France 46; Libn Reims Garrison Area West Base Sect US Army, Reims France 46; City Libn Wenatchee Pub Lib, Wenatchee Wash 47-48; OCSS, US Army: Field libn, Post libn, & Command libn, various cities in Germany 48-64, Command Libn USA Communications zone, Europe, Orleans France 64-67; Asst chief lib div USA Spec Serv Agency EUR Munich Germany 6769; Dist Lib supv Baden Wuerttemberg SUPDIST, Ludwigsburg Germany 69-. 9: ALA (Life Mem, Armed Forces Libns Sect, Overseas Subsect). 10: AAUW (Life mem); Bus & Prof Womens Club. 14: Admin, personnel, ref, ya, reg & co libs. 15: Lib Br Spec Serv Div, US Forces Support Dist Baden Wuerttemberg, APO NY 09154.

GILL, JAMES WILSON. b Ottawa Can 6 Ja 41. 5: UWash 59-63 (Far East) BA; UBC 63-64 BLS, 66-69 (Law) LLB. 6: Japanese. 7: Ref libn Vancouver Pub Lib, Vancouver BC 64-66; Libn Russell & DuMoulin, Vancouver BC 68-. 8: Law lib consul wk 67-. 9: ALA; CanLA; CanALL; BCLA. 10: Assn BC Libns. 12: Ed BCLA "Reporter 64-. 14: Law libnship. 15: 3267 Point Grey rd, Vancouver 8 BC Can.

GILL, JOHNOWEEN. b Sulphur Springs Tex 6 D 24. 5: E Tex State U 41-44 (Eng) BA; Tex Woman's U summers 51-54, 58 MLS. 6: Sp. 7: Tchr: Winnsboro High Sch, Winnsboro Tex 44-45, Sulphur Springs High Sch, Sulphur Springs Tex 45-46; Correspondent Sears Roebuck, Dallas Tex 47-52, Libn Katy High Sch, Katy Tex 52-61, Asst ref libn Tex Christian U 61-. 9: ALA; TexLA. 10: Delta Kappa Gamma; Alpha Chi; Sigma Tau Delta. 14: Interlib loan, ref. 15: 7109 Dalewood lane, Dallas Tx 75214.

GILL, LINDA (SMITH). b Chattanooga Tenn 4 Ap 39. 5: Martin Col 57-59; Peabody Col 59-61 (Soc Sci) BA, 61-62 (LS) MA. 7: Circ libn Joint Univ Libs (Peabody), Nashville 62-63; Ref libn ClemsonU 63-64, Govt docs libn 64-66; Period libn Middle Tenn StateU 66-. 9: ALA; SELA; TennLA; TennEA. 10: Alpha Gamma Delta& delta Kappa Gamma; Wesleyan Serv Guild. 14: Period, govt docs. 15: 802 E Main st apt 20 Riviera apts, Murfreesboro Tn 37130.

GILL, LOUIS J. b Shenandoah Penn 24 Ja 27. 4: Joan Gernon Gill. 5: State Tchrs Col (Kutztown Penn) 48-52 (LS) BS; Seton Hall U 55-57 (Admin, Sup on Sec Level) MA; Rutgers 62-65 MLS; UWis summer 66; Wayne State U summer 67-. 7: US Navy 45-46; Sr high libn Rutherford High Sch, Rutherford NJ 52-55; Sr high libn Wayne High Sch, Wayne NJ 55-57; Jr high libn River Dell Reg Sch, River Edge NJ 57-65; Dir of IMC 65-67; Dir of sch libs, Madison Twp Sch Dist, Old Bridge NJ. 8: Head varsity football coach for 2 yrs at Rutherford High, 3 yrs as asst coach of football at Rutherford & Wayne, and 8 yrs as freshman football coach at present position, head basketball coach 2 yrs and asst for 1 yr. 9: NEA (Life mem); ADI; NJEA; NJSchLA (Recr Com). 10: NJ Inter-Scholastic Athletic Assn. 14: Development of modern lib concepts in pub sch libs. 15: 30 Fairpark pl, Wayne NJ.

GILL, MATTIE (MASHAW). b Ala 19 Ja 19. 4: Theodore Douglas Gill. 5: Miles Col 36-40 (Eng) AB; UDenver summer 53-56 (LS) MA. 6: Fr. 7: Elem sch tchr, Birmingham Ala 43-52; Elem libn, Birmingham Ala 53-59; High sch libn, Birmingham Ala 60-; Asst col libn evenings, Birmingham Ala 63; Libn Wenonah State Jr Col 66-; Asst col libn evenings Miles Col 67-. 9: ALA; NEA; Ala State Tchrs Assn; Ala Sch Libns. 10: Fairfield Civic League; LEtude dArt Soc & Civic Club; Phi Delta Kappa. 15: 5508 Court G, Fairfield Ala 35064.

GILL, MRS MILDRED (LUKER). b E Bernstadt Ky 1 O 14. 4: Glenn B Gill. 5: Sue Bennett Col 32-34; Berea Col 34-36 (Eng) AB; UKy summers 57-60 MS in LS; Newer Media Inst E Ky U summer 68. 7: Sec Brock-McVey, Lexington Ky 41-45; Exec sec to state libn, Commonwealth of Ky, Frankfort 45-47; Bkmob Libn Franklin County, Frankfort Ky 56-57; Libn Elkhorn High Sch, Frankfort Ky 57-58; Libn Franklin County High Sch, Frankfort Ky 58-; Visiting Prof UKy 66; Tchr Inst for Train in Libnship E Ky U 69. 8: Org Franklin Co High Sch Lib 58; Org First Baptist Church Lib 60; Head libn First Baptist Church Frankfort Ky 60-69; Evaluated Jessamine Co High Sch Lib; So Assn Evaluation Com 62; Sponsor of Stud Libn Assn of Central Ky 63-65; Mem Sch Lib Ed Adv Com, UKy 67-. 9: ALA (NEA del 69); KyLA; KyASchL (chm Stand Com, Nomin Com; KyEA del 68-70); KySchL (chm 69-70); KyEA; FCASchL (chm 68-69); FCEA (pres 69-70). 10: Beta Phi Mu; LWV. 14: Sch libs. 15: 325 Cardinal ave, Frankfort Ky 40601.

GILL, SUZANNE (LUTZ). b Quincy Ill 30 Je 41. 4: James H Gill. 5: Fontbonne Col 59-63 (Hist) BA; UMich (Ann Arbor) 66-67 MA in LS. 6: Sp. 7: Libn Parkway Central Jr High, chesterfield Md 63-66; Libn Commun & Tech Col of UToledo 67-68, Co-ord Lib Tech Aide Program 68-. 8: Mem Coun on Lib Tech. 9: ALA; OhioLA. 10: AAUP; Amer Leg Aux; Pi Gamma Mu. 14: Tchg. 15: 2621 Whiteway, Toledo Oh 43606.

GILLARD, WILLIAM A(NTHONY). b Scranton Penn 22 O 04. 5: St Thomas Col UScranton 21-25 AB; St Johns U 29-32 LLB; Columbia 33-36 BLS; Tchrs Col Columbia U 40-41. 6: Fr. 7: Instr St Thomas High Sch, Scranton Penn 25-27; Instr St Thomas Col (Scranton Penn) 27-29; St Johns U (NY); Instr 29-36, Asst libn, Libn 30-36, Act dir 36-42, Dir of libs -, Prof lib sci 49-68. 8: Served on several Middle States Eval Coms. 9: CathLA (Exec Bd 55-57 & 61-66, pres 63-65); ALA; CNLA (sec 61-63) ; Jt Com on Lib Educ (sec 59-61); NYLA. 13: Yes. 14: Ref, lib educ. 15: 9005 210 pl, Bellaire LI NY 11428.

GILLESPIE, CONSTANTINE JOHN. b Washington DC 9 N 28. 4: Louise Meyer. 5: George WashingtonU 47-52 (Zool) AB; UMd 66-68 MLS. 6: Grk, Fr, Ital, Sp. 7: Indexer med lit for "Index Catalogue of the Library of the Surgeon General's Office" Army Med Lib, wash DC 48-50; Indexer & reviser of med lit for "Current List of Medical Literature" Armed Forces Med Lib, Wash DC 50-56; Corp president Record Sales Co Inc, Arlington Va 56-58; Indexer & reviser of med lit for "Current List of Medical Literature" & "Index Medicus" Nat Lib of Med, Wash DC 58-61; Hd index sect bibliogr serv div ("Index Medicus" & MEDLARS System) Nat Lib of Med, Bethesda Md 61-67; Mem task force new computer implementation (MEDLARS II) 67-68; Hd MEDLARS mgt sect bibliog serv div 69-. 8: Official rep Nat MEDLARS quality control staff bibliog serv div 68-69; Hd Lib Med on Wking Gp on Bibliog Codes of US Nat Lib Task terminology US Dept Agric Grad Sch, Wash DC. 9: ASIS; Force on Automation & Other Coop Serv; Instr med MedLA. 14: Computer methods of info storage & retrieval, indexing of biomed materials. 15: 9817 Belhaven rd, Bethesda Md 20034.

GILLESPIE, JOHN THOMAS. b Ft William Ont Can 25 S 28. 5: UBC 44-48 (Eng) BA, 48-49 (Educ) Tchrs Certif; Columbia 55-57 (LS) MS. 7: High sch tchr BC schs 49-54; Trainee NY Pub Lib 55-56; Libn Hicksville High Sch, Hicksville NY 56-57; Libn Roslyn Jr High Sch, Roslyn NY 57-62; Circ libn Hunter Col Lib 59-61; Asst Prof adjunct LIU C W Post Col 60-62, Assoc Prof Grad Lib Sch 62-. 8: Bk adv com ""School Library Journal 62-. 9: ALA-AASchL (Memb Com); NYLA (Sch Lib Sect; Bd mem, pres); Nassau-Suffok SchLA (pres). 10: NY Lib Club; AAUP; Melvil Dui Chowder & Marching Assn; Kappa Delta Pi; Phi Kappa Delta. 12: "Juniorplots" (67); "Library Learning Laboratory" (69); "Introducing Books" (69). 13: Yes. 14: Sch libs. 15: Grad Lib Sch LIU, Greenvale NY 11548.

GILLESPIE, SISTER MARGARET/JANE OP. b Portland Ore 21 Je 22. 5: Marylhurst Col 41-44 (Eng); Rosary Col 44-45 (LS) BA, summers 55-60 (LS) MA; UDenver summer 65 (NDEA). 7: Libn Trinity High Sch, River Forest Ill 47-61; Libn St John Cathedral High Sch, Milwaukee 61-. 8: Nat Def Educ Act fellow, UDenver 65. 9: ALA-AASchL; CathLA; WisLA; NCTE; Wis Cath LA; Ill Cath LA (chm High Sch Unit 58-59). 14: Lit for ya. 15: 830 N Jackson st, Milwaukee Wi 53202.

GILLESPIE, SARAH (SHERRILL) (CALHOUN). b Clio SC 26 F 37. 4: Neal C Gillespie. 5: Columbia Co (Columbia SC) 55-59 (Hist) BA; Duke 59-62 (Hist) MA; Emory 64-65 (LS) ML. 7: Bibliog Duke U 60-61, Catlgr 61-63; Catlgr GaState Col 64, 65-67; Libn Atlanta Hist Soc 67-68; Ref Archivist Emory U 69-. 9: ALA; SELA; GaLA. 14: Catlg, mss. 15: 2498 Joiner ct, Decatur Ga 30033.

GILLETT, VERA (DE OREO). b London Eng 24 O 15. 4: John Kenneth Gillett. 5: Dyke Col of Com 30-32 (Bus Admin); West Res Cleveland Col 31-33, 39-40. 7: Lib research & sec E C Prior Assocs, Cleveland 34-39; US Rep Allied Eng Co, Buenos Aires Argentina 40-51; Spec lib materials TENAFLY Pub Schs 53-61; Libn Englewood Hosp Sch of Nursing, Englewood NJ 60-. 8: Hosp admin & med research, Englewood Hosp 60-. 9: ALA-AHIL. 14: Analytical catlg for research libs. 15: 3 Byrne lane, Tenafly NJ 07670.

GILLETTE, GERALD WAYNE. b Labette Kan 17 F 28. 4: Louise C Calvin. 5: Park Col 50 (Soc Sci) AB; Princeton Theol Sem 53 (Theol) BD; UChicago Divinity Sch 59 (Church Hist) MA; Rutgers 61 MLS. 7: Asst libn res dept UChicago 54-57; Ref libn Princeton Theol Sem 58-63; Research historian Presbyterian Hist Soc, Phila 63-. 9: ATheolLA; Presby LA; SAA. 10: Ordained minister, United Presbyterian Church USA. 12: Assoc ed "Journal of Presbyterian History. 13: Yes. 14: Theol libnship, church archives. 15: 1362 Paddock way, Cherry Hill NJ 08034.

GILLETTE, VIRGINIA L(OUISE). b Toledo Ohio 6 Mr 36. 4: William Benjamin Gillette. 5: Ohio State 54-58 (Eng) BA; Pratt Inst 65-67 MLS. 6: Ger. 7: Tchr Parma Pub Schs, Parma Ohio 63-64; Acquis libn IndU Sch of Med Lib (Indianapolis) 67-. 9: ALA. 10: Beta Phi Mu; Alpha Lambda Delta. 13: Yes. 14: Acquis, catlg. 15: 501 W Ninety-second st, Indianapolis In 46260.

GILLEY, RUTH E(VELYN). b Russell Ky 19 O 04. 5: Olivet Nazarene Col 22-26 (Hist) AB; UKy 26 (Educ, Mus); Cincinnati Conservatory of Mus (Mus); Ohio State 30-32 (Hist) AM, 39; UIll 45-46 BS in LS. 7: Tchr pub schs: Russell Ky 26-29, 31-37, Reynoldsburg Ohio 37-38; Libn Olivet Nazarene Col 39-67, Assoc Prof Lib Sci 50-67; Lib consul tech serv 67-. 9: ALA; -ACRL; Christ Libns Fellowship; OhioLA. 10: Pi Lambda Theta; Phi Delta Lambda; Beta Phi Mu. 14: Catlg. 15: 2 Dixie dr RFD 4, Mount Vernon Oh 43050.

GILLFILLAN, NANCY ANNE (MILES). b Robinson Ill 8 Ja 42. 4: Richard Allen Gillfillan. 5: UIll 60-64 (Eng) AB, 64-66 (LS) MS. 7: Asst (soc sci dept) Kan City (Mo) Pub Lib 64-66; Extended serv libn Ind State U (Terre Haute) 66-67, Instr of lib sci & extended serv libn 67-. 9: ALA (Ext Lib Serv Com); Assn of Field Serv in Tchr Educ (Publ Com); Adult Educ Assn of Ind (Bd Dirs 67-). 10: Marhsall (Ill) Pub Lib Bd of Trustees. 12: Ed "Adult Horizons," of Adult Educ Assn Ind (67-). 13: Yes. 14: Lib educ, adult educ, ref. 15: rr 2, Marshall Il 62441.

GILLHAM, MARY (ALICE). b Princeton Ill 1 Mr 16. 5: Monmouth Col 35-39 (Speech) AB; UIll summers 40, 44, 45, 49, 50-52 (LS) MS; UDenver summer 46 (Speech); UOre summer 62. 6: Fr. 7: Tchr High Sch, Alexis Ill 39-44; Tchr-libn High Sch, Sandwich Ill 44-48; Asst libn Monmouth Col (Ill) 48-51; Libn Proviso High Schs, Maywood & Hillside Ill 51-65; Asst Prof West Mich U 65-. 8: Visting Prof UIll, UKy& UOre, summers 53, 59-60, 65. 9: ALA; NEA; AALS; IllLA; IllASchL (sec 63-64); MichASchL; MichLA. 10: PEO; Beta Phi Mu. 14: Catlg, sch libnship. 15: 1301 Greenwood ave, Kalamazoo Mi 49007.

GILLHAM, MARY (MEWBORN). b Atlanta 12 Jl 1899. 4: Richard E Gillham DDS. 5: UToledo 19-27 (Eng Lit) BA, 27-31 (Eng Lit) MA; UMich 41 BA in LS. 6: Sp, Portu, Fr. 7: Libn U Toledo 21-, Prof 50-, Chm Dept of Lib Sci 53-. 9: ALA (Friends of Libs Com); OhioLA (v-pres 37-38, Exec Bd 55-56, chm elect Col & U Round Table 57-59). 10: Friends of the U Lib (Exec sec 38-); UToledo Annual Endowment drives (Exec sec 43-47); Lib Bldg Com (chm 48-53); Adv Bd WPA Projs City of Toledo 38-41; Ohio Sesquicentennial Commsn 51-53; Toledo Municipal League (Treas, Bd Dir 56-59); UMich Lib Sci Alumni (pres 43-45); Org for Study of Peace (Bibliog Com 43-45); AAUW; U Toledo Alumni Assn; UMich Alumnae Assn; Phi Theta Psi; Alpha Omicron Pi; Delta Kappa Gamma; Phi Kappa Phi; Zonta Club; Samagama Club of Toledo; Ohio Col Amer; Beta Phi Mu; Toledo Dental Soc Auxiliary. 11: Outstanding Woman of the Toledo Area, Chi Omega 67. 14: Bibliog, rare bks, ref. 15: UToledo Lib, Toledo Oh 43606.

GILLHAM, OTHA (WADE). b Adamville Tenn 20 S 19. 4: Phil M Gillham. 5: Freed-Hardeman Col 37-39 (Elem Educ); Memphis State U 43 (Elem Educ); Union U (Jackson Tenn) 4 8-49 (Secondary Educ) BS; UTenn summers 52-54 (Supv, Admin, LS MS. 7: Hardin Co Schs (Elem Tchr) Shiloh Tenn 40-44, Elem Tchr Crum Tenn 46-48, Elem Tchr Savannah Tenn 49-50, Elem Tchr, Cerro Gordo Tenn 50-55; Libn Central High Sch, Savannah Tenn 57-. 9: NEA (life mem); ALA; SELA; TennLA; TennEA; West Tenn EA; Hardin Co TA. 10: Hardin Co (Tenn) Pub Lib; AAUW; Friends of the Lib; Bus & Profess Women; Delta Kappa Gamma. 15: Crump Tn 38327.

GILLIAM, AGNES (HARRELL). b Lumber Bridge NC 3 Ja 09. 4: Paul Denny Gilliam. 5: Chowan Col 27-29 (Eng) AB; UNC 33-34 AB in LS. 7: Eng tchr High Sch, Red Oak NC 31-33; Libn High Sch, Mooresville NC 34-35; Child libn Pub Lib, Columbia SC 35-36; Asst libn Pub Lib, Charlotte NC 38-41; Sch libn Charlotte- Meck Schs, Charlotte NC 47-. 9: NEA; NCLA; NCEA. 10: Libn First Baptist Church, Charlotte (about 5000 vols) 46-. 14: Elem sch libs. 15: 515 Toddville rd, Charlotte NC 28214.

GILLIAM, DOROTHY JANE. b Charlotte NC 24 Mr 40. 5: Mars Hill Jr Col 58-60 AA; Wake Forest Col 60-62 (Religion) BA; Japan Internat Christian U 62-63 (Asian Studies); SP Baptist Theol Sem 63-64; UNC 64-65 (LS) MA. 6: Fr. 7: Asst catlgr Princeton Theol Sem Lib 65-68; Hd catlgr Union Theol Sem Lib, Richmond Va 68-. 9: ALA; ATheolLA; VaLA. 10: Beta Phi Mu. 14: Catlg, ref. 15: 1012 Melrose ave, Richmond Va 23227.

GILLIAM, J J. b S Pittsburg Tenn 27 S 25. 4: Phyllis Jean Fike Gilliam. 5: Kent STATE 47-52 (Biol) BS Ed, 52-54 MALS. 7: Gen ref sci & tech Akron Pub Lib, Akron Ohio; Head bus & tech Canton Pub Lib, Canton Ohio; Head research lib Firestone Tire & Rubber Co; Head research lib Babcock & Wilcox Co Research Center; Head admin serv, Thiokol Chem Corp Space Booster Div; Head Libn Brevard Jr Col. 9: FlaLA. 14: Admin. 15: 1020 Seminole dr, Rockledge Fla.

GILLIES, ELLEN (JOHNSON). b Worcester Mass 7 Ap 18. 4: Kenneth Gillies. 5: Simmons 35-39 (LS) BS. 7: Asst libn Med Col Lib UVt 65-. 15: Dana Med Col Lib Univ of Vt, Burlington Vt 05401.

GILLIES, THOMAS D. b South Bend Wash 18 O 20. 5: UMich 42 (Eng) AB; Cornell U 47 (Amer Lit) MA; Columbia 48 BS in LS. 6: Fr, Russian. 7: US Army 42-46; Asst libn & Instr in Eng Willamette U 48-49, Act libn & Instr in Eng 49-50; Ref libn UKan City, Kan City Mo 50-52; Acquis libn Jackson County (Mo) Lib, Independence Mo 52-53; Ser & documents libn Linda Hall Lib, Kansas City Mo 53-63; Asst Visiting Prof Sch of Libnship UWash 63-64; Asst dir Linda Hall Lib, Kansas City Mo 64-. 9: ALA;-ACRL (chm Subj Spec Sect 68-69); PNLA. 14: Acquis, ref, ser. 15: 606 W 49th Terrace, Kansas City Mo 64112.

GILLILAND, (WILLIAM) MELVIN. b Grand Junction Col 19 N 25. 4: Freda Eastin. 5: Union Col 45-49, summer 51-58 (Relig) BA; So Missionary Col summer 54; UDenver summers 62-65 (Libnship) MA. 7: Tchr Seventh-day Adventist Ch, Duluth Minn 49-51, Covington Ky 51-55, Greeley Colo 58-60; Salesman Grolier Soc, Lincoln Neb 55-56; High sch libn Sch dist #1, Powell Wyo 61-66; Asst & assoc libn Walla Walla Col 66-. 9: ALA; PNLA. 14: Catlg. 15: 441 So E 5th, College Place Wa 99324.

GILLILAND, PAUL MICHAEL. b Brewer Me 10 D 32. 4: Lorraine (Amidei). 5: Purdue 49-51, 55-58 (Chem) BS, 58-59, 62-64 (Eng) MA; Ind U summers 64, 65-66 (LS) MA; UChicago 68-69 (LS). 6: Ger. 7: Lab asst Gilliland Enterprises Inc, Lafayette Ind 51-52; Personnel specialist US Army 52-55; Chem Desoto Chem Coatings Inc, Chicago 61-62; Jr prof Purdue U Libs (Lafayette) 63-66, Asst hd card prep 66-68; Asst prof McGill U Lib sch 69-. 9: ACS; ALA. 10: Jr C of C; AAAS. 11: Beta Phi Mu. 14: Lib hist, automation. 15: Grad School of Lib Sci McGill Univ, Montreal Can.

GILLINGHAM, MELBA JEAN. b Many La 22 My 39. 4: Robert G Gillingham. 5: La Polytech Inst57-61 (Soc Sci) BA; LSU summer 61-64 MSLS. 6: Fr. 7: High sch libn, DeQuincy La 61; Jr high sch libn, Bossier City La 61-64; Instr of Lib Sci La Tech 65-. 8: Wkshop Consul Child Bks, Lincoln Parish summer 68. 9: ALA; LaLA; LaASchL (Memb Chm 66), treas 66-68); LaTA. 10: AAUW. 14: Ya & child bks. 15: Sch of Educ, La Tech, Ruston La.

GILLIS, F (FLORENCE) ELIZABETH. b Derby Conn 9 Mr 26. 5: Bethany Col (W Va) 44-47 (Eng); Northeastern U 49-50 (Eng) BA; Simmons 64-66 (LS) MS. 7: Gen asst Medford Pub Lib, Medford Mass 51-53, Br libn Wellington br 53-55; Asst child libn E br Watertown Free Pub Lib, Watertown Mass 55-63, Child libn 64-. 9: ALA; MassLA (Intel Freedom Com 61-68); NERT of child libns. 10: East Mass Bk Rev Com; Child Sci Bk Rev Com. 12: Appraisal ed bd (67-). 14: Child lit. 15: 6 Bower rd, Madison Ct 06443.

GILLIS, FRANK J. b Toronto Can 22 Ag 14. 4: Ruth Kathan Gillis. 5: Wayne State U 48-53 (Humanities) BA; Columbia 53-55 (Musicology); UMinn 56-58 (LS) MA. 6: Fr, Sp. 7: US Army Spec Serv & Supply Sgt (S/Sgt) 42-45; Stud & practicing musician, NY & Detroit 45-55; Archivist, Ref libn UMich 58-59, Head Map Lib 59-61, Asst curator James Ford Bell Collection 61-64; Assoc dir Archives of Traditional Music Ind U 64-. 9: Amer Musicological Soc; Amer Folklore Soc; Internat Folk Music Coun; Soc for Ethnomusicology (chm Archives Com); Asia Soc; MusLA. 10: AAUW. 12: Ed "Ethnomusicology" (66-). 14: Housing music materials (sound recordings). 15: Arch of Tradit Music, 013 Maxwell Hall Ind Univ, Bloomington In 47405.

GILLIS, HILDA (WINIFRED). b PEI 28 D 10. 5: St Fx (Antigonish NS) 28 (Eng) BA; UMontreal 36 B Paed; UBC, UAlta 48, 49 B Educ; Syracuse summer 64, 65, 66 (LS), summer 67, 68 (Film Tech). 6: Fr, Latin. 7: Inspector of schs PEI Educ 28-36; Libn visual educ PEI Libs 37-41; Supv NAT Film Bd, PEI 41-46; Tchr, Fernie BC 46-47; Lib-tchr, Alberta 47-58; Libn, sec lib council, Campbell Riber BC 57-58; Tchr, Ata 58-62; Tchr Picton Collegiate, Commercial Ont 62-63; Libn St Francis High Sch, Calgary Alta 62-69. 8: Tchr summer sch: UBC 60-61, Syracuse U 64-68. 9: CanLA; ALA; Alta Sch Lib Coun; AltaTA; Media Assn. 10: Univ Club. 13: Yes. 14: Catlg, rare bks, canadiana. 15: 877 Northmount dr, Calgary 48 Alta Can.

GILLIS, JULIA HALL (GRISWOLD). b Macon Ga 10 Jl 18. 4: John Evans Gillis. 5: UCLA 45-49 (Sociol, Psych) AB; Barry Col 56-59 (LS); UMiami(Fla) 57-62 (Educ, LS); Fla State U summer 65 (LS), summer 66, 67 (LS). 6: Fr. 7: Elem tchr Screven Co Schs, Sylvania Ga 39-40; Elem tchr Chatham Co Schs, Savannah Ga 52-54; Elem tchr Dade Co Schs, Miami Fla 56-59; Libn Miami Edison Sr High Sch, Miami Fla 59-65; Libn Mattie Lively Elem Sch, Statesboro Ga 65-67; Asst dir Screven-Jenkins Reg Lib, Sylvania Ga 67-. 9: ALA; NEA; GaEA; GaLA; SELA. 10: AAUW. 14: Child & yp serv, ext serv. 15: 327 Savannah ave, Statesboro Ga 30458.

GILLIS, RUTH JEANETTE (KATHAN). b Tulsa Okla 26 Jl 21. 4: Frank J Gillis. 5: Wayne State 48-53 (Eng); Barnard 53-54 (Eng); UMinn 56-60 (Eng) BA, 60-64 (LS) MA. 6: Fr. 7: Tech sgt WAC, US 43-45; Cashier-switchboard Harmonie Club, Detroit 47-50; Salesperson J L Hudson Co, Detroit 55; Sec Amer Motors Corp, NYC 54-55; Sec UMinn (Minneapolis) 56-60, Libn Lab Sch 61-64; Libn Univ Elem Sch IndU (Bloomington) 64-. 8: Tchg fac, Inst for Train in Libnship for Elem Sch Libns, Title II B, Higher Educ Act, Ind U 68. 9: NCTE (Com on Learning Materials in the Elem Sch); ALA; -AASchL; IndSchLA; IndLA (sec-treas, Child & YP RT). 10: Pi Lambda Theta; Beta Phi Mu. 13: Yes. 14: Child bks, illusrs. 15: 3508 Morningside dr, Bloomington In 47401.

GILLON, ELIZABETH (HOLLAND). b Butler Penn 21 Ag 11. 5: Thiel Col 29-33 (Fr) AB (cum laude); West Res (LS); Kent State 55-59 (LS) MA; Temple 64 (West Civiliz); Kent State 65 (LS); U Pittsburgh 67-68. 6: Fr, Ital, Lat. 7: Instr Thiel Col 42; Tchr Delphos-Jefferson High Sch, Delphos Ohio 54-55; Tchr-libn N Royalton Bd of Educ, N Royalton Ohio 55-65; Libn Slippery Rock State Col 65-. 9: ALA; PennLA; Penn State EA. 10: AAUP. 13: Yes. 14: Ya, ref, curric materials. 15: 129 E High, Slippery Rock Penn 16057.

GILLOTTI, ESTELLA M. b New Fairfield Conn 31 My 33. 5: Danbury State Col 50-52 (Gen Educ) AS; UTex 53-55 (Eng) BA, 67-68 MLS. 7: Sec Off Publ Off U Tex 55-58; Clerk UTex Lib catlg dept 59; Libn elem sch Austin Pub Schs, Austin Tex 59-62; Elem Libn Los Alamos Pub Schs, Los Alamos NM 62-63; Tchr New Fairfield Elem Sch, New Fairfield Conn 63-64; Coord of Elem Sch Libs Danbury Pub Schs, Conn 64-67; Libn Elem Sch Austin Pub Schs, Austin Tex 68-. 9: ALA; TexLA; NEA; Tex State TA; AustinEA; Assn Childhood Educ. 11: Phi Beta Kappa. 14: Elem sch libs. 15: 50 Gillotti rd, New Fairfield Ct 06810.

GILLROY, MARY MARGARET. b Stamford Conn 25 Mr 42. 5: Tex Womans U 60-62, 63-64 (LS) BS; University Col (Dublin) 62-63 (Arts); Drexel 64 (LS). 6: Ital, Fr. 7: Desk asst Ferguson Lib, Stamford Conn summers 58-60; Sec St Josephs Hosp, Stamford Conn summer 61, Med libn summer 62; Child libn Perrot Mem Lib, Old Greenwich Conn 65-66; Recr spec Amer Red Cross, Republic of S Vietnam 66-67; Catlgr Ferguson Lib, Stamford Conn 68; Ya libn Arlington pub lib syst, Arlington Va 68-. 9: ALA-YASD. 10: Cath Alumni Club; Overseas Serv League. 14: Ref, pub rel, publ. 15: 2000 S Eads st, Arlington Va 22202.

GILLUM, SANDRA (STRUWE). b Cairo Ill 25 Je 44. 4: David Eugene Gillum. 5: SEMo State Col 62-65 (Hist) BA; UKy 66-67 MSLS. 6: Ger. 7: Jr high libn Charleston R-1 Sch Dist, Charleston Mo 65-66; Ref libn UKy Med Ctr Lib (Lexington) 67-. 9: MedLA; KyLA. 14: Ref. 15: Univ of Ky Med Center Lib, Lexington Ky 40506.

GILMAN, CHARLES FRANCIS. b Johnstown Penn 5 My 24. 5: George Washington U 46-48 (Chem, Fr) AB; UIll 49-50 (Chem) MS, 50-51 (r) MA; UParis 51-52 (Fr) Certif dAssiduite; Harvard 55-56 (Romance Ling MA; Columbia 56-58 (LS) MS. 6: Fr, Ger, Sp, Ital, Russian. 7: Personnel off US Army (S/Sgt) 43-46; Instr of Fr Washington-Lee High Sch, Arlington Va 52-55; Assoc in Fr Geroge Washington U 53-55; Ctlg libn Brooklyn Col Lib, Brooklyn NY 56-, Act deputy chief catlg libn 65-66, Deputy chief catlg libn 66-, Asst Prof. 9: NY Tech Serv Libns; Lib Assn City Univ NY (sec 62-64). 10: Phi Beta Kappa. 11: Fulbright Fellow to France. 14: Catlg, ref. 15: 270 Jay st, Brooklyn NY 11201.

GILMAN, NELSON JAY. b Los Angeles 30 Mr 38. 4: Virginia Ford. 5: USoCal 55-59 (Educ) BS in Ed 60; UCal 63-64 MLS. 7: Math tchr Pasadena High Sch, Pasadena Cal 60-61; Correspondence Clerk US Army, Ft Ord Cal 61; Math tchr Tamalpais High Sch, Mill Valley Cal 62-63; Lib admin Intern UCLA Lib 64-65, Asst to U Libn in chg of lib bldg & development 65-66, Asst to biomedical libn 66-67, Asst biomedical libn 67-69, Assoc dir Pacific Southwest Reg Med Lib Serv 69-. 8: UCal Statewide Com on Lib Space Standards 65-67. 9: ALA; MedLA. 10: USoCal Alumni Assn; UCal(Berkeley) Lib Schs Alumni Assn; San Diego Zool Assn;B BLDG ; PLANNING, ADMIN. 14: Lib bldg & planning. 15: 3014-A Colordoave, Santa Monica Ca 90404.

GILMARTIN, SYLVIA (COOPER). b Malden Mass 11 Ap 11. 4: Thomas Gilmartin. 5: Radcliffe 27-31 (Econ) AB; Tex Womans U 58-59 MLS. 6: Fr. 7: Ref asst Bus Br Boston Pub Lib 31-39; Circ libn UTulsa Lib 56-57; Catlgr Tex Christian U 59-66; Libn NIMH Clinical Research Ctr, Fort Worth 66-. 9: ALA; TexLA; SWLA; MedLA. 10: Radcliffe Alumnae Assn; Seven Colleges Group; CL 14: Pub serv. 15: 5837 Waltham ave, Ft Worth Tex 76133.

GILROY, RUPERT EDWARD. b Natick mass 17 S 31. 5: UNH 54-58 (Econ) BA; Simmons 60-62 MSLS. 7: Cpl US Army 52-54; Ref asst Kirstein Bus Br Bost Pub Lib 58-62; Libn Res Bk Program Yale U Lib 62-66; Asst to the dir Fordham U 67, Asst dir 68-. 8: White House Lib Proj 63; Consul Old Dominion Found 65-66; Consul CathU of Puerto Rico 68-. 9: NY Metro Ref & Res Lib Agency (sec Personnel Com). 14: Lib admin. 15: 2431 Webb ave, Bronx NY 10468.

GILSON, ANN (MARGARET). b Angleton Tex 12 Ja 27. 4: Earl A Gilson. 5: Tex Womans U 43-45 (Speech); Central Mo State Col 60-62 (Eng) BA; UOkla 63 MLS. 7: Circ libn Colo State U Lib 63-. 9: ColoLA. 10: Beta Phi Mu. 14: Circ. 15: 615 W Lake, Ft Collins Co 80521.

GILSTRAP, MAX M. b Chickamauga Ga 2 N 35. 5: Young Harris Col 54-55, 55-56; UGa 56-57, 57-58 (Fr) AB; Emory 60-64 (LS) MA. 6: Fr, Sp. 7: Tchr Monroe High Sch, Monroe Ga 58-59; Lib asst UGa Libs 59-60; Ser asst Emory U Lib 60-63; Asst acquis libn UGa Libs 64-67, Hd acquis div 67-. 9: SELA; GaLA (chm Res & Tech Serv Sect 67-69). 10: Sigma Delta Pi. 14: Acquis, periods, ref. 15: 441 Milledge Circle, Athens Ga 30601.

GIMMI, ROBERT D(AVID). b Philadelphia Penn 20 My 42. 4: Carol Kooken. 5: Shippensburg State Col 60-64 (Bio) BS Ed; Drexel 64-66 MSLS. 7: Penn Military Col: Circ l ref asst 64-65, Asst catlgr 66; Circ & ref asst UPenn Biddle Law Lib 64-66; Elem sch libn S Huntingdon Co Schs, Orbisonia Penn 66-68; Asst catlgr Juniata col 67; Sci libn Shippensburg State Col 68-. 9: AAAS; PennLA; CumberlandValleyLA. 10: AAAS. 14: Ref serv & catlg in pure scis. 15: RD 3, Shippensburg Pa 17257.

GINADER, GEORGE HALL. b Buffalo NY 5 Ap 33. 5: Allegheny Col 51-55 (Hist) BA; Drexel 63-64 MSLS. 6: Ger. 7: Asst buyer Lord & Taylor, NYC 57-59; Job analyst InsuranceCo of N Amer, Phila 59-60; Asst buyer John Wanamaker, Phila 60-61; Act curator Thomas McKean Automobile Ref Collection, Free Lib of Phila 61-63; Libn Chamber of Commerce of the State of NY, NYC 64-66; Chief libn NY Stock Exchange, NYC 66-67; Exec dir SLA 67-. 9: SLA; Coun Nat Lib Assns. 10: C of C; Nat Assn Exhibit Mgrs; Amer Soc of Assn Execs. 14: Ref, NY City hist (espec early Dutch). 15: 351 Broad st, Newark NJ 07104.

GINGERICH, MELVIN. b Kalona Iowa 29 Ja 02. 4: Verna (Roth) Gingerich. 5: Goshen Col 24-26 (Hist) BA; UIowa 38 (Amer Hist) PhD. 6: Ger, Fr. 7: Soc studies tchr high sch & jr col, Washington Iowa 27-41; Hist tchr Bethel Col (No Newton Kan) 41-47; Hist tchr Goshen Col 49-61; Lecturer Mennonite Central Com serving in Tokyo 55-57; Exec sec Mennonite Research Found, Goshen Ind 47-55; Exec sec Mennonite Hist & Research Com 59-; Archivist Archives of the Mennonite Church, Goshen Ind 58-. 8: Managing ed "Mennonite Encyclopedia 48-59; Managing ed "Mennonite Quarterly Review 49-55, 58-. 9: Relig Res Assn; SAA(Church Records Com 59-). 12: "The Mennonites in Iowa" (39); "Service for Peace" (49); Ed "Mennonite Historical Bulletin"; "The Christian and Revolution" (68). 13: Yes. 14: Archives. 15: 1700 So Main st, Goshen Ind 46526.

GINGHERICK, MILDRED E. b Grand Island Neb 20 Mr 10. 5: Chadron State Tchrs Col summers 30-37, & 36-37 (Eng) AB; Grand Island Col summers 28, 29; UDenver summers 38-40, 56 BS in LS; UMich summers 47, 49 AMLS. 6: Lat, Sp. 7: Rural sch tchr, Sheridan Co Neb 28-36; Eng, hist tchr High Sch, Pagosa Springs Colo 37-39; Libn High Sch, Delta Colo 39-42; Libn High Sch Rock Springs Wyo 42-44; Temp libn Ariz State Col 44-45; Catlg libn & Asst Prof of Lib Sci Central Mich U 45-. 8: Periods libn East Mich U, summer 65. 9: NEA; MichLA; MichEA. 10: AAUW; Faculty Womens Club, Central Mich U. 14: Catlg, tchg. 15: 1001 S University, Mt Pleasant Mich 48858.

GINN, MARJORIE JANE. b St Paul 21 O 39. 5: Hamline U 57-61 (Eng) BA; UMinn 63-64 (LS) MA. 7: Sec West Publishing Co, St Paul 61-63; Instr & ref libn Iowa State U 65-68; Circ libn Mayo Clinic, Rochester Minn 68-. 9: ALA; MedLA. 10: AAUW. 14: Ref. 15: Mayo Clinic Lib, Rochester Mn 55901.

GINSBERG, MARJORIE (KANEF). b Brooklyn NY 12 Je 45. 4: Barry Ginsberg. 5: Harpur Col 62-66 (Phil) BA; Pratt Inst 66-67 MLS. 6: Fr. 7: Tchr of lib NYC Bd of Educ Jr High scg 135, Bronx 67-. 9: ALA; NYCSchLA. 10: Beta Phi Mu. 11: Wilson scholar at Pratt Inst. 14: Child lit. 15: 1580 Pelham Pkwy, Bronx NY 10461.

GINTHER, CAROLYN KATHRYN. b Phila Pa 11 D 42. 5: Kutztown State Col 60-63 (LS) BS in Ed; Syracuse summers 64-67 MS in LS; Temple 65; Villanova 66. 7: Libn Lower Merion High sch, Ardmore Penn 63-67; Libn Ellen Cushing Jr Col 66-67; Libn Main Line Project learning, Ardmore Penn 65-66, 67-68; Hd libn Conestoga Sr High Sch, Berwyn Penn 67-. 9: ALA; NEA; PennLA (Recr Com v-chm); Chester-MontgomeryCoSchLA (sec); PennStateEA. 10: Beta Phi Mu. 14: Sch lib serv, educl media. 15: Conestoga Senior High School, Conestoga & Irish rds, Berwyn Pa 19312.

GINZLER, HELEN BELL. b Detroit Mich 4 My 20. 4: Emanuel M Ginzler. 5: Wayne State 64 (LS) BA, 67 MSLS. 6: Ger. 7: Hd libn N Farmington High Sch, Farmington Mich 65-67; Hd libn & a-v dir Brother Rice High Sch, Birmingham Mich 67-. 9: ALA; MichASchL. 10: ORT; Pioneer Women; LZOA. 14: A-V serv. 15: 2197 Avon, Oak Park Mi 48237.

GIOIA, CAROLEIGH (KEMP). b Worcester Mass 13 N 34. 5: Bucknell 52-56 (Eng) AB; Columbia 56-59 (LS) MS. 6: Sp. 7: Eng tchr & libn Ridgefield Jr High Sch, Ridgefield NJ 56-57; Child libn Long Beach Pub Lib, Long Beach NY 57-58; Child libn Plainview Pub Lib, Plainview NY 58-60; Bkmob libn Albertson Pub Lib, Orlando Fla 60-61; Ref libn Plainview Pub Lib, Plainview NY 61-64; Child libn Plainedge Pub Lib, Plainedge NY 64-65; Child libn Freeport Pub Lib, Freeport NY 65-68; Child libn & Act dir Eau Gallie Pub Lib, Eau Gallie Fla 68-69. 9: NYLA; FlaLA. 10: Tobay Players (Plainview NY). 14: Child wk. 15: Ocean Villa apts #4, 2625 S Atlantic ave, Cocoa Beach Fl 32931.

GIORDANO, FREDERICK (SALVATORE). b Newton Mass 24 Mr 38. 4: Joan Palmera Giordano. 5: UMich 56-60 (Sp) BA; Boston State Col 63-64 (Eng, Amer Lit); Rutgers 65-67 MLS. 6: Sp, Fr. 7: Personnel Specialist E-5 US Army 1st Missile Brigade, Ft Sill Okla 60-62; Eng tchr Mass Pub Schs 64; Libn trainee NYC Pub Lib 65-66, Libn Central circ br 67, Sr libn Manhattan Borough off 67-68, Sr asst br libn Seward Park br 68, Act supv asst br libn 69-. 9: ALA. 10: Beta Phi Mu. 14: Adult serv, lib admin. 15: 39 Duncan ave, Jersey City NJ 07304.

GIPSON, JUDITH (KATHRYN) A(NDREWS). b Los Angeles Cal 15 S 39. 4: Martin T Gipson. 5: Chico State Col 57-61 (Philos) BA; Drexel 61-62 MS in LS. 7: Asst ref libn & lib sch libn Peabody Col 62-65; Ref & circ libn Stanislaus State Col 65-66; Asst ref libn UPacific Lib 66-. 9: CalLA (Memb Chm San Joaquin Co). 10: LWV; Beta Phi Mu. 14: Ref. 15: 2217 Crafton way, Stockton Ca 95024.

GIRAUD, LISE (KURZMANN). b Vienna 27 Mr 24. 4: Raymond Giraud. 5: Simmons 41-45 (LS) BS. 6: Ger, Fr, Lat. 7: Nursing sch libn Hartford Hosp, Hartford Conn 45-47; Med libn Michael Reese Hosp, Chicago 47-50; Catlgr Yale U Lib 50-51; Catlgr Stanford U Lib 58-. 14: Catlg. 15: 1981 Middlefield rd, Palo Alto Cal.

GIROIR, DORIS MARIE (PERTUIT). b Raceland La 5 N 40. 4: Curtis Joseph Giroir. 5: Francis T Nichols State Col 58-61 (Elem Educ) BA; LSU summers 62-66 (LS) MA. 6: Fr. 7: Tchr: Holy Saviour High Sch, Lockport La 61-62, Raceland Elem Sch, Raceland La 62-67; Libn Raceland Upper Elem Sch, Raceland La 67-. 9: ALA; IRA; LaLA; LaASchL; LaTA; Lafourche Parish TA; Lafourche Libns Org (chm 67-70). 10: Alpha Beta Alpha; Lafourche Assn for Retarded Child; Nicholls Alumni Fed; LSU Alumni Fed. 14: Elem libs, a-v materials. 15: Rte Box 225-A, Schriever La 70395.

GIRVIN, GERALD THOMAS. b Rochester NY 2 Ap 29. 5: LeMoyne Col 47-50 (Fr); St Bernards Sem 50-54 (Philos); St John Fisher Col 55-56 (Eng) BA; URochester 56-57 (Educ); State U Col (Geneseo NY) 57-60 (LS) MS. 6: Lat, Fr. 7: Eng tchr Rochester (NY) Bd of Educ, Edison Tech & Ind High Sch 56-57; Libn McQuaid Jesuit High Sch, Rochester NY 57-68; Libn Fred Douglass Jr High Sch, Rochester NY 68-69. 8: Middle States Assn Accredit Com 62. 9: ALA; CathLA; NYLA. 10: Great Lakes Hist Soc; Steamship Hist Soc Amer; Great Lakes Maritime Inst. 13: Yes. 14: Tech serv, instrl materials ctrs. 15: 108 Delmar st, Rochester NY 14606.

GITLER, ROBERT L(AURENCE). b NYC 1 My 09. 5: UCal(Berkeley) 25-30 (Pol Sci, Hist) BA, 30-31 Grad Certif

Libnship, 36-37 (LS); Columbia 38-39 (LS) MS. 6: Japanese, Sp. 7: Asst UCal Lib (Berkeley) 27-30; Tchg asst Dept Pub Speaking UCal(Berkeley) 30-31; Circ libn San Jose State Col 31-36, Sr libn, Instr 36-42; Lt(jg), Lt, Lt Cmdr) US Navy, Hawaiian Sea Frontier, Pacific 42-45; Visiting Faculty Columbia Sch of Lib Serv summers 46, 47; Dir, Assoc Prof UWash Sch of Libnship 46-53; Founding Dir, Prof Japan Lib Sch Keio U (Tokyo) 51-56; Exec Sec Lib Educ Div, Sec Com on Accreditation ALA, Chicago 56-60; Visiting Prof, Consul Japan Lib Sch Keio U (Tokyo) 61; Dir, Div Lib Educ SUNY(Geneseo) 62-63; Dir, Prof Peabody Lib Sch Geo Peabody Col 64-; U libn & Prof Gleeson Lib, USan Francisco. 8: Consul: UHawaii, East-West Center 61; USan Francisco, 61-62; Kan State Tchrs Col 62 & 65; UWash 62. 9: ALA (Com on Accred 56-60);-ACRL;-RSD;-LAD;-LED (Standards Com 54-56); AALS (Exec Bd 47-49); JapanLA; Japan SchLA; CalLA; TennLA; NYLA; SELA; Amer Assn of Col Tchr Educ (Coord Com 56-60); Chicago Lib Club; ALA Staff Assn (pres 60); Nashville Lib Club; CalLA (Golden Gate Dist; v-pres 68, pres 69). 10: Japan Amer Soc; Amer-Japan Soc; AAUP; Prometheus; Beta Phi Mu; Roxburghe Club (SF). 11: Deans Scholarship Award, Sch of Lib Serv, Columbia U 38-39; PhD (Hon) Keio U, Tokyo Japan 56; Japan LA 70th Anniv Citation "Distinguished Serv to Lib World of Japan 61; Japan Govt Emperors Decoration "Fourth Order of Merit with Cordon of Rising Sun 61; ALA-LED Beta Phi Mu Award "Distinguished Serv to Educ for Libnship. 12: Lib report "Education for Librarianship at the University of Hawaii (61). 13: Yes. 14: Lib educ, admin (personnel), recr, libnship & internat scene. 15: 222 Willard N apt 102, San Francisco Ca 94118.

GITOMER, IRENE (STROLLER). b Edinburgh Scotland 14 Je 24. 4: Irving Gitomer. 5: Rutgers 50-61 (Pol Sci, Soc) BA; Drexel 61-62 MSLS. 7: Admin asst to dean Drexel Grad Sch Lib Sci 60, Dir of pub rel 60-61; Dir Cherry Hill Free Pub Lib, Cherry Hill NJ 62-. 8: Instr Drexel Grad Sch of Lib Sci, 65; Commun Col of Phila 69; Glassboro State Col, Glassboro NJ 69. 9: ALA (NJ Coord Recr Netwk 64-, Loc Arr Com 69);-LAD (Staff Devel Com 65-);-ASD (Publs Liaison Com 65-); Jr mem Round Table (chm 64-65);-ALTA (Publs Com 65); SLA; JLA; LPRC; NJLA (chm Recr Com 64-68, chm Scholarship Com 69, Personnel Com 65-68, Legis Com 67-68, 2nd v-pres 6768); NJ Lib TNCam CoLA (pres 67). 10: Camden-Burlington Ref Group; Phila Bksellers Assn; PTA; LWV; ACLU; WILPF; Zonta; Phi Kappa Phi; Beta Phi Mu; Libraries Unlimited; Drexel Inst Alumni Assn. 13: Yes. 14: Admin, lib educ. 15: Cherry Hill Free Pub Lib, Cherry Hill NJ 08034.

GITTELSOHN, MARC. b San Francisco 7 Mr 29. 4: Mai Lon Wong. 5: UCal(Berkeley) 46-50 (Hist) BA; UWis(Madison) 50-51 (Hist); UCal(Berkeley) 55-56 MLS. 6: Fr, Ger. 7: (Spec-3) US Army 53-55; Research asst Sch of Libnship UCal(Berkeley) 55-56; Intern in Admin Gen Lib UCal(Berkeley) 56-58, Head Morrison Lib 58-62, Head Agric Libs 62-64, Asst in Admin 64-65, Head Agric Sci Libs 65-68, Br lib coord 68-69, Hd Moffit Undergrad Lib, Libn V 69-. 9: ALA; SLA; Internat Assn Agric Libns & Documentalists; CalLA (chm Com on Acad Status 67-68, Intel Freedom Com). 10: Agric Hist Soc; Phi Beta Kappa. 12: Ed "CU News" 60-62. 13: Yes. 14: Ref, acad research libs, serv to undergrad. 15: 1136 Fresno ave, Berkeley Cal 94720.

GIVENS, J(OSEPHINE) ELOISE. b Newport Va 30 Ja 18. 5: Randolph Macon Womans Col 35-39 (Eng) AB; UIll 39-40 BS in LS. 6: Ger, Fr, Ital, Sp, Russian. 7: Tech asst ext div & Washington Co, Va State Lib 40-46; Spec serv libn US Navy 41-46; Asst libn Tech Lib, Ft Detrick Md 46-48; Libn Tech Lib Knoll Atomic Power Lab GE, Schenectady NY 48-51; Libn Sterling Winthrop Research Inst, Sterling Drug Inc, Rensselaer NY 51-66; Ref libn IBM Inc Fed Systs Ctr, Gaithersburg Md 66-. 8: ASAZ39 Sub-com on Period Abbrevs. 9: SLA. 10: AAUW. 14: Admin, biomed lit, data proc. 15: PO Box 454, Gaithersburg Md 20760.

GIVENS, MISS JOHNNIE E. b Pleasant View Tenn 7 S 25. 5: Austin Peay State Col 42-46 (Eng) BS; Peabody summers 47-49 BS in LS; Chicago 54-57 (LS) AM. 7: Asst libn Austin Peay State Col 46-57; Order libn Peabody Col summer 47; Head Libn Austin Peay State Col 58-. 8: Assignment to Eval & Study Coms by So Assn of Cols; ACRL Consul to architect for 2 bldg programs. 9: ALA (Var com assignments in ALA-ACRL & -LAD); NEA; SELA (Exec Bd 63-64, var coms, treas 67-68); TennLA (treas 58-59); Col Sect: chm 56-57, sec 55-56); TennEA. 10: AAUP; Beta Phi Mu; Kappa Delta Pi; Delta Kappa Gamma; Commun Ambassador Assn; Commun Concert Assn. 13: Yes. 14: Admin, bldgs. 15: Austin Peay State Univ, Clarksville Tn 37040.

GLACKIN, PAULINE (CHOWN). b Peoria Ill 29 Jl 11. 4: Glenn A Glackin. 5: Bradley U 29-33 (Langs, Lit) BA; West Res 41-42 BS in LS. 6: Fr. 7: Br child asst Peoria Pub Lib, Peoria Ill 34-37, Br child head 37-41; 1st asst main child Toledo Pub Lib, Toledo Ohio 42-45; Br child head Peoria Pub Lib, Peoria Ill 45-48, Br head 48-50; Nursing sch libn Methodist Hosp of Central Ill, Peoria Ill 57-, Med libn 64-67; Br head Peoria Pub Lib 67-. 9: IllLA. 14: Child wk, readers' asst. 15: 6221 W Van Deusen, Peoria Ill 61604.

GLADDING, AURILLA (HURD). b Andover Vt 8 D 10. 4: Royal H Gladding. 5: Simmons 31-35 (LS) BS. 6: Fr, Ger, Sp. 7: Circ asst Providence Pub Lib 35-37; Catlgr Middlebury Col Lib, Middlebury Vt 37-39; Ser catlgr Brown U Lib 39-45; Libn Fletcher Mem Lib, Ludlow Vt 45-52; Libn St Johnsbury Athenaeum, St Johnsbury Vt 52-. 8: Ref Instr Lib Inst, Montpelier Vt 47; Nat Lib Week chm 58; Adv Coun, Title III LSCd 68-69. 9: ALA; VtLA (pres 57, program chm 59; pres Pub Lib Sect 69-70). 10: Audubon Soc; PTA. 14: Admin, catlg. 15: RFD 2, St Johnsbury Vt 05819.

GLADE, CATHARINE ADELAIDE. b Grand Island Neb 26 Ja 07. 5: UNeb 36 (Hist) AB; Columbia summers 30, 31, 37; West Res 41 BLS. 7: Libn Barr Jr High Sch, Grand Island Neb 31-48; Libn Grand Island Army Air Base, Grand Island Neb 45; Libn Sr High Sch, Grand Island Neb 48-. 9: ALA (Memb Chm for Neb 52-54);-AASchL; NEA; Neb State EA; NebLA; Grand IslaEA. 15: Sr High Sch Lib 2124 N Lafayette ave, Grand Island Neb 68801.

GLADECK, ALBERTA A. b Phila. 5: Beaver Col (Hist) BA; Drexel MS in LS. 7: Registrar The Franklin Inst, Phila; Libn Machine & Tool Designing Co, Phi la; Tchr & libn Cheltenham Elem Sch, Cheltenham Penn; Libn Thomas Williams Jr High Sch, Wyncote Penn. 9: NEA; ALA; PennLA; PennEA (Supv & Curric Div); PennSchLA (sec-treas 68-70); Chester-Montgomery Co LA (pres 65-70). 10: Alpha Delta Kappa. 14: Sch lib wk. 15: Thomas Williams Jr High, Wyncote Pa 19095.

GLADISH, MARY LOUISE. b Prospect Tenn 15 My 20. 5: UTenn 37-42 (Home Econ) BS; UNC 43-44 (Pub Health Educ) MSPH; Chicago 47-48, 51-52, 56-58 (Adult Educ) MA; Harvard 48-49 (Pub Health); Peabody 66 MLS; Emory summer 64 (Med Libnship). 6: Fr. 7: Home econ tchr Hornbeak High Sch, Hornbeak Tenn 41-43; Pub health educator Camp Forrest Dist Health Dept, Shelbyville Tenn 44-45; Pub health educator Lee Co Health Dept, Tupelo Miss 45-47; Assoc Prof Health Educ E Tenn State U 58-63; Med research libn Vanderbilt Med Lib 64-. 9: Soc of Pub Health Educs (Charter Fellow, chm &/or mem var coms); Amer Pub Health Assn (Fellow); MedLA; TennLA; Nashville Lib Club; AAUW; WNBA. 10: Pilot Club Internat; Amer Red Cross; Wesleyan Serv Guild; Pi Lambda Theta; Delta Kappa Gamma; Beta Phi Mu; Kappa Delta Pi; Goodwill Ind Aux; Vanderbilt Hosp Aux; Univ Club; Vanderbilt Woman's Club; ESU. 12: Co-auth "Cunningham Classification of Medical Literature (rev ed 66). 13: Yes. 14: Med research. 15: Orleans Apts apt 2 3210 Orleans dr, Nashville Tn 37212.

GLANZ, LENORE. b Chicago 16 S 33. 5: UIll 51-58 (Hist) BA, MA, 58-60 MS in LS; De Paul U 60-62 (Russian); Loyola 62- (Hist). 6: Fr, Ital, Russ, Ger, Sp, Lat. 7: Clerk "American Encyclopedia, Chicago summer 51) Clerk Local Loan Co Exec Off Accting Div, Chicago summers 52-59; Coun UIll Dormitories (Urbana) 55-59; Bibliog researcher UIll Lib (Urbana) 59-60; Ref libn Chicago Pub Lib 60-61; Ed research libn Field Enterprises Educ Corp, Chicago 61-65, Asst ed 65-67, Ed research libn 67-. 8: Jr Mems Round Table of ALA for Ill Membership Rep 65-; Asst ed Ill Chap Bulletin, SLA 65-. 9: ALA; SLA (several coms); AHA. 14: Ref, hist. 15: 6151 W Roscoe st, Chicago Il 60634.

GLARUM, MARIAN R (OCONNOR). b New Haven Conn. 4: Sivert Herth Glarum. 5: Vassar 49-53 (Fr) AB; Brown 58 AM; Simmons 60 MS in LS. 6: Fr, Ger. 7: Child libn Morristown Lib, Morristown NJ 60-. 10: AAUW. 14: Ref, child wk, sch lib wk. 15: 7 Vanderpool dr, Morristown NJ 07960.

GLASBY, DOROTHY KATHRYN (JOENS). b Blue Island Ill 3 Je 27. 4: Jonathan P Glasby III. 5: Thornton Jr Col 46-48 (Biol); Elmhurst Col 48-50 (Biol) BS; Northwestern 50-53 (Eng) MA; UIll 57-59 (LS) MS. 6: Fr, Ger. 7: Bkkeeper Amer Boarding & Supply Co, Blue Island Ill 45-51; Lib asst, jr catlgr Northwestern U Lib 51-54; Tchr Kamehameha Sch for Girls, Honolulu 54-55; Field dir Chicago Area Coun of Camp Fire Girls 55-57; Ser catlgr UIll Lib (Urbana) 57-59; Spec recruit LC 59-60, Ser catlgr 60-62: Catlgr Toledo Pub Lib, Toledo

Ohio 62-63; Ser catlgr & reviser LC 63-68; Hd ser catlg LC 68-. 9: ALA; DCLA. 10: Beta Phi Mu. 13: Yes. 14: Ser catlg. 15: 3612 Thornapple st, Chevy Chase Md 20015.

GLASBY, JONATHAN PERRINE 3d. b Newark NJ 13 My 21. 4: Dorothy Kathryn Joens. 5: Marlboro Col 51-55 (Sci) BA. 7: B-25 Flight Engnr US Army Air Corps (Cpl) 42-46; Salesman J P Glasby Manufacturing Co, Belleville NJ 46-51; Deck attendant, asst at central desk searcher-loan division LC 56-62; Lib asst Toledo Pub Lib, Toledo Ohio 62-63; Ref libn US Geological Survey, Wash DC 63-. 9: ALA; DCLA. 14: Ref. 15: 312 Thornapple st, Chevy Chase Md 20015.

GLASCOFF, ELISABETH ANN (DIETER). b Milwaukee Wis 23 S 43. 4: Walter George Glascoff III. 5: Wells Col 61-63 (Hist); SUNY (Albany) 63 (Hist); Edgewood Col 63-64 (Hist); UWis (Madison) 64-66 (Hist) BA, (LS) MA. 7: Asst ed Air Univ Lib, Maxwell AFB Ala 66-. 9: SLA (sec-treas Ala Chap 68-69). 14: Indexing, editing. 15: 3783 MacLanar rd, Montgomery Al 36111.

GLASGOW, (BONNIE) JEAN (LOYD). b Chicago Ill 28 Je 42. 4: Charles Wayne Glasgow. 5: N Tex State U 60-62, 63-64 (Govt) BA; LSU 62-63, 65-67 (LS) MS. 7: Asst Tech Serv Libn NC State Lib, Raleigh 67-68; Interlib loan & docs libn Tex Woman's U 68-. 9: ALA. 10: Phi Kappa Phi; Beta Phi Mu. 14: Govt docs, acquis, interlib loan. 15: 2716 Nottingham, Denton Tx 76201.

GLASS, DEWEY LEE. b Graceville Fla 13 D 22. 4: Ruth Edith (Purdy) Glass. 5: Fla State U 50-53 (LS) BS, 53-54 (Av Educ & LS) MA. 7: Clerk in lib Tactics Div ATS Tyndall AFB Fla 47-49; Chief Documents clerk ATS Lib Tyndall AFB Fla 49-50; Lib intern Bay County Materials Center & Schs, Panama City Fla 53; Classroom asst Lib Sch AV Center, Fla State U 53-54; Adm asst AV Center Air U Lib (Maxwell AFB Ala) 54-55, Supv libn chief film lib 55-62, Educ Spec AV Aids 62-. 9: NEA-DAVI. 10: Montgomery Area Square Dance Assn. 13: Yes. 14: A-v materials & equip. 15: 1051 Druid Hills dr, Montgomery Ala 36111.

GLASS, GERALD. 5: London Sch of Econ (Econ & Sociol); McGill 62 BLS. 6: Fr, Ger, Sp, Ital. 7: Tchr Buckingham, Que; Libn UMontreal; Dir Academic Bk Shop, Montreal. 8: Consul on setting up libs. 9: CanLA (Life Mem). 10: Can Econ Assn (Life Mem); Can Pol Sci Assn (Life Mem). 14: Ref, catlg. 15: Acad Bk Shop, 1026 Sherbrooke st W, Montreal 110 Can.

GLASS, KATHERINE FAVER. b Newnan Ga 18 My 12. 5: LaGrange Col 29-33 (Eng, Fr) AB; Emory 33-34 AB in LS, summers 33, 37, 40 (Eng). 6: Fr, Sp, Ger. 7: Libn Wayne Co High Sch, Jesup Ga 34-35; Libn Carrollton High Sch, Carrollton Ga 35-38; Asst libn Ga State Col for Women 38-43; Libn Callaway Inst Inc, LaGrange Ga 43-47; libn Callaway Mills Co Research & Devel Div, LaGrange Ga 47-61; Assoc libn LaGrange Col 61-. 9: ALA; SLA (Ga Chap: Charter mem, dir 54-56, consul off 60-62); SELA; GaLA. 10: Poetry Soc of Ga; Ga Writers Assn. 12: Ed "Callaway Textile Abstracts (51-61). 13: Yes. 14: Spec lib wk, col lib wk, catlg. 15: 105 Harwell ave, LaGrange Ga 30240.

GLASS, NELLIE L(EOTA). b New Philadelphia Ohio 14 Mr 03. 5: Heidelberg Col 20-22 (Lang); Ohio U 22-24 (Modern Lang) AB; Northwestern summers 24, 25 (Speech); West Res 28-29 (LS) BS. 6: Fr. 7: Tchr High Sch Jewett Pub Schs, Jewett Ohio 24-25; Tchr High Sch Goshen Twp Schs, Midvale Ohio 25-26; Asst Cleveland Pub Lib Schs Div, Hawthorne Sch, Cleveland 27-28; Libn Stowe Pub Lib, Stowe Ohio 29-32; Supv Lib Proj WPA in Ohio, Perry Co, later Dist 3 38-40; State supv WPA WVa Lib Proj 40-41; Consul WPA Nationwide Lib Proj 40-42; Recreation wker Amer Nat Red Cross, European Theatre 42-45; Pub libn Pomeroy Ohio & Gallipolis Ohio 46-47; Libn Montgomery Pub Lib, Montgomery Ala 47-54; Br libn Cleveland Heights Pub Lib, Cleveland Heights Ohio 54-60; Libn Salem Pub Lib, Salem Ohio 60-. 9: ALA; OhioLA; Ohio Adult Educ Assn. 10: AAUW; Delta Kappa Gamma; Little Theatre. 14: Admin, ref, recr. 15: 1484 Cleveland st, Salem Ohio 44460.

GLASS, PHYLLIS FRANCES (METZ). b Battle Creek Twp Mich 14 Mr 25. 4: Charles D Glass. 5: Siena Heights Col 43-47 (Eng) BP; Aquinas Col summer 48 (Soc Sci); Mich State U fall 48 (Soc Sci); West Mich 64-65 (LS) MA. 7: Clerical Ralston Purina Co, Battle Creek Mich summers 45-47; Tchr Holy NAME Catholic Sch, Grand Rapids Mich 47-48; Traffic control asst Ralston Purina Co, Battle Creek Mich 48-50; Asst libn Highland Park Pub Lib, Dallas 51; Tchr St Joseph Catholic Sch, St Joseph Mich 63-64; Circ libn Lake Michigan Col 65-. 8: Acad "Hot Line" Libn. 9: ALA; Berrien Co Coop Libs Assn (sec 65-68). 14: Circ, ref. 15: Lake Michigan Col 711 E Britain ave, Benton Harbor Mich 9022.

GLASSER, SYLVIA BLANCHE. b Brooklyn NY 21 Ap 24. 4: Isidore Glasser. 5: Brooklyn Col 40-45 (Psych) BA; Pratt Inst 63-67 MLS. 6: Fr. 7: Libn trainee Brooklyn Pub Lib 65-67, Libn 67-68, Sr libn 68-. 9: ALA; NY Lib Club. 10: Beta Phi Mu. 14: Child serv. 15: 2507 E 23 st, Brooklyn NY 11235.

GLASSMAN, JANET. b NYC 5 Ja 29. 5: Hunter Col 45-47, 63-64 (Hebrew) AB; Columbia 64-65 (LS) MS. 6: Hebrew. 7: Agric wker Kibbutz Barkai, Israel 49-55; Asst libn Givat Chaviva Seminar, Israel 55-56; Sec Jewish Agency, Israel 56-62; Lib asst Hunter Col 63-64; Lib asst Albert Einstein Col of Med 64-65; Ref libn Esso Research & Engnr, Linden NJ 65-66; Hd libn Negev Inst Arid Zone Res, Beer-Sheva Israel 66-, Instr Cat Inst Higher Learning, Beer-Sheva 68 9: SLA; ASIS. 14: Ref. 15: 105 E 177 st, New York NY 10453.

GLASSON, BETTY. b Wash DC 14 F 12. 5: Asbury Col 30-34 (Eng) AB; Scarrett Col 37-38 (Religious Educ) MA; LSU 55-56 MSLS; Wash State U 66 (Map reading). 7: Exec dir Stud YWCA U Cincinnati 45-50; Club dir Commun YWCA, Lexington 51; Lib asst Ft Richardson, Alaska 51-54; Adult serv libn Brooklyn Pub Lib 56; Libn educ dept & child libn Cincinnati Pub Lib 57-61; Ya libn San Diego Pub Lib 62-65, 66; Libn hist Seattle Pub Lib 65-66. 8: Instr LSU 55; Adv sr citizens activities 56; Speakers for Cincinnati & Seattle Pub Libs 62-66 9: CalLA. 10: Beta Phi Mu; Photographic Soc Amer; San Diego Zool Soc. 14: Catlg, ref, child lit. 15: 3570 First ave, San Diego Ca 92103.

GLASTRAS, THOMAS. b Collinsville Ill 25 D 24. 5: Oberlin 46-50 (Music, piano) BM; Ind U 50-53 (Musicology) MM, 58-61 (LS) MA. 7: Army (Cpl), US 43-46; Instr of music Knox Col 53-58; Asst ref libn Ind U Lib 61-64, Asst documents libn 64-68, Assoc docs libn 68-. 14: Docs, ref. 15: RR1, Box 69 B, Bloomington In 47401.

GLAU, HELEN LUCILLE. b Aberdeen SD 13 N 06. 5: No State Tchrs Col 25-29 (Educ) BS; UMinn 52 BSLS. 7: Asst libn Alexander Mitchell Lib, Aberdeen SD 33-44, Head Libn 44-. 9: ALA; MPLA; SDLA (past pres). 10: Zonta Internat; Bus & Prof Womens Club; Delta Kappa Gamma; AAUW. 14: Admin, SD bks. 15: 413 9th ave, Aberdeen SD 57401.

GLAZER, FREDERIC JAY. b Portsmouth Va 20 F 37. 4: Sylia Lerner. 5: Columbia 54-58 (Econ) BA, 63-64 MSLS. 6: Fr. 7: US Army Infantry (Pvt), Ft Dix NJ 60; US Army spec serv (Pfc), Ft Lee Va 61-62; Lib asst spec serv lib, Ft Lee Va 62-63; Libn I Bus Tech Soc Sci Norfolk Pub Lib, Norfolk Va 64-67; Dir Chesapeake Pub Lib Syst, Chesapeake Va 67-. 8: Creator of "Library Six Pack" 69; Producer "The World of Books," weekly radio prog, Chesapeake 68-. 9: ALA; VaLA; SELA. 10: ACLU; Metro Sear 14: Adult serv, admin. 15: 525 Redwood dr, Chesapeake Va 23320.

GLAZER, MILDRED RUTH (LASSER). b Houston 7 F 09. 4: Samuel Glazer. 5: UMich 27-29, 30-32 (Fr) BA in Ed; Simmons summers 41-43 BS in LS. 7: Bk selling & spec order J L Hudson Co, Detroit 29-30, 32-33; Survey taker US Pub Health Serv, Boston 35-36; Math Stud Survey Boston U 36-37; Ref asst Sci & Tech Dept Boston Pub Lib 37-44; Head of Bus & Tech Room Ferguson Lib, Stamford Conn 44-46; Br head Enoch Pratt Free Lib, Baltimore 46-49; Head bus & tech dept Bridgeport Pub Lib, Bridgeport Conn 49-. 9: ALA; SLA; ConnLA. 10: LWV; Phi Kappa Phi. 14: Ref. 15: 97 Geneva ter, Fairfield Ct 06430.

GLAZER, SUZANNE M. b NYC. 5: Hunter Col 53-57 (Pol Sci) BA; Columbia 57-58 MLS. 7: Child libn Brooklyn Pub Lib 58-62, Asst coordinator child serv 62-; Currently Dir lib serv Atheneum Publrs. 9: ALA; NYLA; NY Lib Club. 10: Bksellers League. 14: Child wk. 15: Atheneum Publishers, 122 E 42nd st, New York NY 10017.

GLAZIER, KENNETH MacLEAN. b Canada 21 S 12. 4: Teresa Ferster. 5: Toronto 33-36 (Hist) BA; Union Theol Sem 36-39 (Theol) BD; Yale 41-44 (Religion & Educ) PhD; UCal 61-62 MLS. 7: Minister Glenview Presbyterian Church, Toronto 46-59; Supt of Schs Can Mission, British Guiana 60-61; Deputy curator Hoover Inst, Stanford U 62-65, Libn 65-. 9: ALA-ACRL; African Studes Assn (Fellow); SAA. 10: Can-Amer assn (dir).' 11: Fellow, Yale U 43-44. 12:"Checklist of Serials for African Studies, with Peter Duignan (63); "Africa South of the Sahara: a Select and Annotated Bibliography, 1958-1963 (64). 13: Yes. 14: U lib admin. 15: Hoover Inst Stanford U, Stanford Cal 94305.

GLEASON, DOROTHY (MANN). b St Louis 3 Ap 12. 4: Henry B Gleason. 5: Central State Col (Edmond Okla) 29-32 (Langs) BA; Peabody 33-34 BS in LS; UOkla 60-61 MS in LS. 6: Fr, Sp. 7: Tchr Marland High Sch, Marland Okla 32-33; Libn Pub Lib, Tonkawa Okla 34-36; Sch br libn Carnegie Lib, Okla City Okla 36-41; Curriculum libn Bd of Educ, Okla City Okla 47-48; Law Libn Okla City U 53-54; Ref libn Pub Lib, Okla City Okla 54-56; Asst libn Central State Col (Edmond Okla) 57-60, Prof & Coordinator of Lib Educ 61-. 9: ALA; -AASchL; NEA-DAVI; OklaLA; SWLA; OklaEA. 10: AAUP; AAUW; NCTE; ACEI; Internat Reading Assn; ASCD PEO. 13: Yes. 14: Lib educ, pub sch libs, instrl material centers. 15: Rt 5, Guthrie Okla 73044.

GLEASON, MARGARET. b Madison Wis. 5: UWis 29-33 (Eng) BA, Lib Sci Diploma, 33-34 (Educ) Tchrs Certif; Columbia summers 38, 39 (LS); UWis 48 (Hist). 7: Asst Pub Lib, Davenport Iowa 34-37; Sch libn Hawthorn Sch, Davenport Iowa 37-39; Libn George Rogers Clark Sch, Hammond Ind 39-41; Libn Pub Lib, Whitewater Wis 42; Libn Co Lib, Cleveland Ohio 43; Libn Longfellow Jr High Sch, Wauwatosa Wis 44-46; Asst libn State Hist Soc of Wis, Madison Wis 46-47; Ref libn Beloit Col 47-49; Ref libn State Hist Soc of Wis, Madison Wis 48-. 9: Org Amer Histns; State Hist Soc Wis; Wis State Geneal Soc; Lincol Fellowship of Wis; WisLA; Amer Assn State & Loc Hist. 10: Zonta Internat; Phi Delta Gamma; Univ of Wis League; DAR; OES. 12: "Printe Resources for Genealogical Searching in Wisconsin: a Selective Bibliography (64). 14: Ref. 15: 4728 Regent st, Madison Wi 53705.

GLEASON, VIRGINIA LEE. b Buckhannon W Va 7 S 23. 4: George Donald Gleason. 5: WVa Wesleyan Col 45 BA; Columbia 46 BL; Northwestern 49 MA. 7: Circ dept Northwestern U; Child wk br San Diego Pub Lib; Libn Central High Sch, Superior Wis; Ref wk UIowa Lib; Catlgr, child libn Pub Libs of Springfield & Green Co, Springfield Mo 58-68; Child coord 68-. 9: ALA; MoLA. 10: PTA. 14: Child lit. 15: Springfield & Green Co Pub Lib, Springfield Mo 65804.

GLEAVES, EDWIN SHEFFIELD JR. b Nashville 28 F 36. 4: Georgia Montandon Gleaves. 5: David Lipscomb Col 54-58 (Eng) BA; Emory 58-60 (LS) MA; Escuela Normal de Profesores (Saltillo Mex) summer 62 (Span) Certif; Emory 60-64 (Eng) PhD. 6: Sp, Fr. 7: Ser & bind asst Emory U Lib 59-60, Grad tchg asst Eng 60-61; Ref libn Atlanta Pub Lib summer 61; Eng tchr Pace Acad, Atlanta 63; Libn & Asst Prof Eng David Lipscomb Col 64-65; Asst Prof Eng Peabody Col 66-67; Dir & Assoc Prof Peabody Lib Sch 8: Visiting Prof Peabody Lib Sch, summer 65Visiting Asst Prof Libnship UWash summer 66; Lib & Media Ctr Consul, Country Mus Hall of Fame, Nashville 68-. 9: ALA; -LED (com on Legisl 69-71); SELA (chm Lib Educ Com 68-); Mid-StateLA (Exec Coun 69-); TennLA. 10: AAUP; The Wilderness Soc; Ga Appalachian Trail Club; Tenn Folklore Soc; Tenn Citizens for Wilderness Planning; So Atl Mod Lang Assn. 12: "Characteristics of the Research Materials Used by Scholars Who Write in Journals in the Field of American Literature, ACRL Microcard series no 130 (61); "The Spanish Influence on Ernest Hemingways Concepts of Death, Nada, and Immortality, PhD diss "Dissertation Abstracts, 64-11,215 (64); Ed "Library Information Bulletin, Quarterly, David Lipscomb Col (64-). 13: Yes. 14: Lib educ, admin, ref. 15: 4518 Granny White Pike, Nashville Tn 37204.

GLEDICK, CECELIA. b Tallahasse Fla 15 Je 45. 5: So Conn State Col 63-67 (LS) BS. 7: Libn Granby High Sch, Granby Conn 67-. 9: ALA. 14: YA lit. 15: 34 Robert st, Windsor Locks Ct 06096.

GLENN, CLARA CELESTINE. b Beaver Falls Minn 11 O 1898. 5: Col of St Catherine 16-20 (Classical langs) BA; UMinn 20-34 (Eng Lit) MA, 41-46 BS in LS. 7: Instr Col of St Catherine 20-22; Tchr Pub High Sch, Nevis Minn 24-25; Tchr St Josephs Acad, St Paul 25-38, Libn 29-38; Tchr Sr High Sch, Chisholm Minn 39-43; Asst libn & Instr Col of St Scholastica 43-44; Libn St Thomas Acad, St Paul 44-. 8: Libn US VA, Gulfport Miss summer 40, Sheridan Wyo summer 43; Instr Dept of Lib Sci Cath U, summers 50-51; Consul "Standard Catalog for High School Libraries 62-65. 9: ALA; CathLA (chm Com on Cath Supp to "Standard Catalog for High School Libraries 61-65; chm Minn-Dak Unit 56-57); MinnASchL; Minn Hist Soc. 10: AAUW; Minn Coun on Civil & Human Rights; Cath Interracial Coun of the Twin Cities; Phi Beta Kappa. 12: Ed "Catholic Suppement to Standard Catalog for High School Libraries (62-65). 13: Yes. 14: Sch libnship. 15: St Thomas Acad 949 Mendota Heights rd, St Paul Mn 55118.

GLENN, JAMES ROBERT. b Butler Tenn 6 D 21. 5: E Tenn State U 45-49 (Hist)BS; Peabody 50-51 MA in LS. 7: Tchr-libn Boones Creek High Sch, Boones Creek Tenn 49-50; Libn Staunton Mil Acad, Staunton Va 51-52; Asst ref libn WVa U 53-57; Asst ref phys sci Va Polytech Inst 57-59, Head biol sci ref dept 60-62, Head res bk Dept 62-, Hd res bk & spec servs 68-. 9: VaLA; SELA. 14: Ref, circ, a-v. 15: Lib Va Polytech Inst, Blacksburg Va 24061.

GLENN, RACHEL (MADDOCKS). b Augusta Me 26 Ag 13. 4: J Gaylord Glenn. 5: Simmons 31-35 (LS) BS. 7: Asst child libn Utica Pub Lib, Utica NY 35-40; Order libn Carlson Lib Clarion State Col 65-. 9: ALA; PennLA. 14: Acquis. 15: 402 Liberty st, Clarion Pa 16214.

GLENS, RONALD V. b Des Moines Iowa 15 N 29. 5: Kan State U 48-52 (Ind Journalism) BS; Breadlof Sch of Eng Middlebury Col 55 (Eng); Kan State Tchrs Col (Emporia) 56-57 (LS) MS. 7: US Army Info Spec (Sgt) (T) 52-55; Salesman Col Bk Store, Manhattan Kan 55-56; Grad asst Kan State Tchrs Col (Emporia)56-57; Gen libn UIda Lib 57-60; Ex sec ref serv div ALA, Chicago 60-63; Dir of Libs Elmira Col 63-67; Dir of Libs Brandeis U 67-. 9: ALA; ASIS; BSA. 12: Publn Off "College & Resarch Libraries; "Idaho Annual Bibliography, PNLA quarterly (58-59). 13: Yes. 14: Ref, rare bks, admin. 15: 182 Beacon st, Boston Ma 02116.

GLICK, EDGAR A. b Pittsburgh Penn 16 Ag 23. 4: Bernice Shapiro. 5: UWis 46-48 (Eng) BA, 48-50 (Comparative Lit) MA, 50-51 (LS) MA. 7: S/Sgt US Army Air Corps 42-45; Jr libn pub lib, Brooklyn NY 51-53; Asst to dir pub lib, Des Moines Iowa 53-56; Personnel off pub lib, Queens NY 56-59; Asst dir pub lib, New Rochelle NY 59-61; Sr libn United Nuclear Corp, White Plains NY 61-62; Libn Hudson Inst, Croton-on-Hudson NY 62-67, Admin off 67-. 9: SLA; Amer Soc Indus Sec; In-Plant Printing Mgt Assn; WestchesterLA. 10: Archons of Colophon; Melvil Dui Chowder and Marching Soc. 11: WWII: Distinguished Unit Citation - ETO ribbon with 9 battle stars. 14: Admin of pub & spec libs. 15: The Croft Hunter Brook rd, Yorktown Heights NY 10598.

GLINKA, JOHN L. b Kan City Kan 24 My 20. 4: Charlotte Rabb. 5: Kansas City (Kan) Jr Col 38-40 Hist) Diploma; Kansas State Tchrs Col (Emporia) 46-48 BS Ed Lib Certif; UIll 57-62 MSLS. 6: Polish, Fr. 7: Clerk A&P Tea Co 40-41; Asst manager A&P Tea Co, Kan City Mo 41-42, 45-46; (Cpl) USArmy Signal Corps 42-45; UKan Lib: Exch libn 48-49, Head accessions dept 49-53, Head prep dept 53-60, Asst dir 60-65, Assoc dir 65-. 9: ALA; -ACRL; KanLA. 10: AAUP; Nat Assn for Retarded Child; Kan Assn for Retarded Child; Douglas Co Assn for Retarded Child. 14: Catlg, bind, admin, phys plant, personnel. 15: 909 Maine st, Lawrence Kan 66044.

GLOCKNER, HAROLD ANTHONY JR. b Bogalusa La 21 Mr 30. 4: Sylvia Lea Wilson. 5: SEast La Col 55-58 (Liberal Arts) BA, 61-64 (Educ) BA; LSU 65-67 MSLS. 7: Stud asst SEast La Col 55-58; Libn St Paul's Sch, Covington La 61-65; Grad asst LSU Lib 9baton Rouge) 65-67; Catlgr LC 67-69; Ref Naval Ship Syst Command, Wash DC 69-. 9: Potomac Tech Proc Libns. 14: Catlg, bibliog, ref, acquis, info retr. 15: 6710 Wakefield dr apt B-2, Alexandria Va 22307.

GLOVER, MRS MARY HETHERINGTON. b LI City NY 30 Ap 09. 4: John Stiven Barrie Glover. 5: Centenary Jr Col 29-31 AA; Boston U 33-35 (Soc Wk) BS in SW; Pratt 38-39 BS in LS. 7: Child libn Queensboro Pub Lib 39-42; Br libn Medford Pub Li, Medford Mass 42-43, 58-59; Sch libn Robbins Mem Lib, Arlington Mass 59-. 14: Child wk. 15: 37 Judkins rd, Medford Mass 02155.

GLOVER, PEGGY (NEAL). b Vancouver Wash 5 O 31. 4: Richard Glover. 5: Pomona Col 51-53 (Eng) BA; Carnegie 53-54 (LS) MS; Drexel 62-64 (Info Sci). 7: Gen asst Enoch Pratt Free Lib, Baltimore 54-56; Base libn USAF in Europe, Germany, Eng 56-60; Libn Free Lib of Phila 60-61; Libn Defense Ind Supply Center, Phila 61-65; Hd commun servs off of wk with adults & ya Free Lib of Phila 65-. 9: PennLA. 10: Phi Kappa Phi; Beta Phi Mu. 14: Admin, bk sel, adult serv, ya serv. 15: 5931 Carpenter st, Phila Pa 19143.

GLOYD, KATHRYN (JOHNS). b Rockfork Ill 20 Jl 18. 4: Howard K Gloyd. 5: UIll 36-39 (Chem) BS; UMd 39-40 (Plant Physiol) MS; UIll 40-42, 47-48 BSLS. 7: Libn Chicago Acad of Sci 42-47; Asst libn chem UIll(Urbana) 47-48; Libn & recorder Chicago Acad of Sci 48-55, Exec sec & libn 55-58; Catlg libn Sci UAriz 59, Ref libn Sci 59-63, Sr sci libn 63-64, Sr Ref libn 64-67; Asst ref libn Col of Med 67-. 9: MedLA; SLA; Ariz State LA; SWLA. 10: UIll Lib Sch Assn. 14: Ref, report lit, hist of med. 15: 4244 E 4th st, Tucson Az 85711.

GLYMPH, ESTHER NELL (KNUCKLES). b Gaffney SC 25 N 16. 5: Johnson C Smith 45 (Elem Educ) AB; West Res 55 MS in LS; Peabody summer 65 (LS); USoCar summer 67 (LS); Case West Res summer 68 (LS). 7: Tchr Camp Hgh Sch, Cleveland Co NC 36-46; Tchr-libn Academy St Sch, Blacksburg SC 46-52; Libn Granard High Sch, Gaffney SC 52-66; Supv elem sch libs 66-. 9: ALA; NEA; Amer Tchrs Assn; SELA; SCLA. 10: Womans Soc of Christian Serv; Delta Sigma Theta. 14: Child, ya. 15: 359 E Smith st, Gaffney SC 29340.

GNAT, RAYMOND EARL. b Milwaukee 15 Ja 32. 4: Jean Monday. 5: UWis 50-54 (Bus Admin) BBA; UIll 565 (LS) MS; UWis(Milwaukee) 59- (Pub Admin). 7: Page Milwaukee Pub Lib 50-53, Jr libn 54; US Army Adjutant Gen Corp (2d Lt) USAR 54-56; Circ asst UIll(Urbana) 56-57, Ser catlgr 57-58; Libn II Milwaukee Pub Lib 58-63; Asst dir Indianapolis Pub (Marion Co) Lib 63-. 8: Exec dir Ind Nat Lib Week, 65; Pub Lib Com Survey & Bldg Consul. 9: ALA (Life mem); BSA; IndLA. 10: Waygoose Soc; Greater Indianapolis Info Inc; Indianapolis Adult Educ Coun; Literary Club. 13: Yes. 14: Bibliog, admin, systems analysis. 15: 40 E St Clair st, Indianapolis Ind 46204.

GNOZA, EDMOND. b Milwaukee 25 My 18. 5: UWis 36-40 (Eng) BA; Columbia 46-47 BSLS; Chicago 49-51 (LS). 6: Fr, Polish, Russian. 7: (2d Lt to Maj) Infantry US Army, US & W Pacific 40-46; (Maj to Lt Col) Infantry US Army, US Japan & Korea 51-54; Fellow ref dept City Col Lib (NY) 46-47; Admin asst to libn UOre 47-49; Asst libn readers serv UIda 54-58; Admin asst & humanities libn Portland State Col 58-62; Humanities libn Portland State Col Lib 62-. 8: Consul, Survey of Circ Dept, Deering Lib, Northwestern U, 51. 10: AAUP. 14: Ref, humanities. 15: 1431 SW Park ave, Portland Or 97201.

GNUDI, MARTHA (TEACH). b Sycamore Ill 26 O 08. 4: Dante Gnudi. 5: UCLA 25-26 (Eng); UOre 26-27 (Gk); USoCal 27-29 (Classics) BA, 29-30 (Hist); UBologna (Italy) 30-31 (Ital Lit) Dott in lett; USoCal 35-36 Ital Lit); Columbia 62-63 MLS. 6: Fr, Ger, Ital, Lat. 7: Research in hist of plastic surgery Dr Jerome P Webster Columbia U 30-42; Libn Webster Lib of Plastic Surgery Columbia U 42-63; Admin Army Courses in Plastic Surgery Columbia U 42-46; Head hist & spec collections Dept Biomed Lib UCLA 64-. 9: Amer Assn Hist Med; BSA; Hist of Sci Soc; MedLA; Societa di storia delle scienze mediche e naturali (Hon); Renaiss Soc Amer; Soc Hist Med Sci, Los Angeles (sec-treas 64-). 10: AAAS; Amer Assn Tchrs Ital; Beta Phi Mu; Phi Kappa Phi; Sigma Alpha Iota; Phi Beta Kappa; UCLA Assn of Faculty Women. 11: Fellowship Inst of Internat Educ to Italy; Silver medal of merit from UBologna for the bk "The Life and Times of Gaspare Tagliacozz; William H Welch Medal from Amer Assn Hist Med "for particular contributions of outstanding merit in the field of med hist (with Dr Jerome P Webster). 12: "Of Typecasting in the Sixteenth Century with C S Smith (41); "The Pirotechnia of Vannoccio Biringuccio, tr from Ital with C S Smith (42); "The Life and Times of Gaspare Tagliacozzi, Surgeon of Bologna, 1545-1599., with Jerome P Webster (50). 13: Yes. 14: Rare bks. 15: 8400 Reading ave, Los Angeles Ca 90045.

GOAN, FAVA E. b Millville Wis 9 Ap 1898. 5: UWis(Platteville) 19-21 (Eng); Lawrence U 24 (Eng) BA Simmons 28 BLS; Garrette Theol Sem 44 (Rel Educ) Prof Certif. 6: Ger, Fr. 7: Tchr-libn Cuba City High Sch, Cuba City Wis 22-23; Libn Sioux Falls Pub Sch, Sioux Falls SD 25; Libn Marinette High Sch, Marinette Wis 26-27; Asst ref libn Ind U 2843; Dir of child wk Halsted St Institutional Church, Chicago 45-53; Reserve bk room libn Deering Lib Northwestern U 54-. 9: ALA; IndLA. 10: AAUW. 12: Comp "Union List of Serials in Indiana Libraries (40). 14: Ref. 15: 1940 Sherman ave, Evanston Ill 60201.

GOBBLE, RICHARD LEE. b Albia Iowa 11 Ja 22. 4: Martha Goetz. 5: UUtah 43-44; UDenver 46-48 (Bus Admin) BSBA, 48-49 (Hist), 49-50 (LS) MA; Colo State Col 52-53 Hist). 6: Sp, Ger. 7: Recording engnr Rocky Mountain Radio Coun, Denver 41-42; T/4 radio announcer US Army Armed Forces Radio 43-46; Radio writer Radio Station KMYR, Denver 46; Documents libn Denver Pub Lib 50-51; Ref libn Colo State Col 51-52, Head Libn 53-54; Chief catlg div USAF Acad 55-66; Catlgr LC 66-67; Hd Union catlg project HEW Lib 67; Dir Ft Lewis Col 67-. 9: ColoLA. 10: Sons Amer Rev; Phi Alpha Theta. 14: Col libs. 15: 180 Riverview dr, Durango Co 81301.

GOBOLOS, MARJORIE (CRAW). b Springfield Ill 8 D 38. 4: Joseph Gobolos. 5: Wis State Col (Whitewater) 56-60 (Eng) BE; Peabody 60 MALS. 7: Young adult libn NY Pub Lib 60-64; Young adult consul Ramapo Catskill Lib System, Middletown NY 64-68; Ref coord Rampo Catskill Lib Syst 68-. 9: ALA; NYLA. 15: 107 Cupsaw dr, Ringwood NJ 07456.

GOCEK, MATILDA A(RKENBOUT). b Hoboken NJ 18 F 23. 4: John A Gocek. 5: Orange Co Commun Col 59-62 (Eng) AAS; SUNY (New Paltz) 62-64 (Eng) BA; SUNY (Albany) 67 MLS. 6: Russian. 7: Libn Monroe Free Lib, Monroe NY 58-62; Processor New Paltz Col Lib 62-63; Dir Tuxedo Park Lib, Tuxedo Park NY 63-. 8: Lib consul Tuxedo Unio Free Sch, Tuxedo NY 67-; Co-chm Spec Com to Study Lib Resources Available to Commuting Students in Eight SE cos of NY, NYLRC. 9: ALA; NYLA; Orange-Sullivan Pub Lib Assn (Pres); OrangeCoSchLA; SEast NY Lib Resource Coun. 12: "Tuxedo Park Library: Social Aspects of Growth, 1901-1940 (69). 13: Yes. 14: Lib research. 15: Dunderberg rd, Monroe NY 10950.

GODBEY, MARYBELLE (UMBERGER). b Cabarrus Co NC. 4: Stanley Taylor Godbey. 5: Randolph Macon Womans Col 26 (Sci) AB; Radford Tchrs Col 49 Lib Certif. 6: Fr. 7: Christiansburg High Sch, Christiansburg Va 49-52; Libn Christiansburg Elem Sch, Christiansburg Va 52-. 9: NEA; ALA; VaEA; VaLA. 10: Va Fed of Womens Clubs; Christiansburg Bk Club; Alpha Delta Kappa. 15: 865 W Main st, Christiansburg Va 24073.

GODDARD, BURTON L(ESLIE). b Dodge Center Minn 4 Jl 10. 4: Esther Anna Hempel. 5: UMinn 28-30 (Hist); UCLA 30-33 (Hist) AB; Westminster Theol Sem 34-37 ThB; Harvard Divinity Sch 37-43 (Old Testament) STM, ThD; Simmons 56-57 (LS) MS. 6: Lat, Gk, Hebrew, Aramaic (Biblical), Syriac, Assyrian, Arabic, Fr. Ger. 7: Pastor Carlisle Congregational Church, Carlisle Mass 37-41; Asst in Semitic Langs Harvard U 38-39, 40-41; Instr in Bible & Christian Educ Gordon Col & Divinity Sch 41-44, Prof of Old Testament & Dean 44-51, Prof of old testament & Dean, Gordon Divinity Sch 51-61, Prof Biblical langs & exegesis & Dir of lib 61-. 9: ATheolLA; Soc of Bibl Lit & Exegesis; Evangelical Theol Soc (ed 49-54, pres 64). 10: Deerwander Bible Conf Assn (treas, past pres); Phi Beta Kappa; Pi Gamma Mu. 12: "Animals of the Bible (63); Ed "The Encyclopedia of Modern Christian Missions (67). 13: Yes. 15: Gordon Div Sch, Wenham Mass 01984.

GODDARD, SUSANNE (SANDBORN). b Wausau Wis 1 Je 33. 4: Joe Dean Goddard. 5: Hendrix Col 52-54; N Tex State U 54-56 (Eng) BA, 56-57 BS in LS. 6: Sp, Fr. 7: Assoc libn Pasadena Pub Lib, Pasadena tex 57-58; Asst catlgr Ft Worth Pub Lib, Ft Worth Tex 58-59; Asst catlgr Tex A&M U 60-62; Asst catlgr Tex Tech Col 63-. 9: TexLA; TexClrTA. 14: Catlg, ref. 15: 2208 Elgin ave, Lubbock Tx 79410.

GODFREY, JEAN (ORTH). b NYC 8 Mr 15. 4: George Godfrey. 5: St Lawrence 36 AB; Columbia 37 BS. 6: Fr. 7: NY Pub Lib: Gen asst ext div 37-40, 1st asst Morrisania Br Lib 40, 1st asst Webster Br Lib 40-41, 1st asst Hunts Point Br Lib 42, Asst supt ext div 42-43; Libn Welch Convalesent Hosp US Army 44; NY Pub Lib: Asst supt ext div 45-52, Supt ext div 52-54, Coordinator Manhattan br libs 54-57, Asst chief circ dept 57-63, Chief br libs 63-. 8: Trustee Emma S Clark Mem Lib, Setauket NY; Bd of Dilarge pub libs; mem of Lincoln Ctr Educl Coun. 9: ALA; Amer Assn of Museums; NYLA; NY Lib Club; Assn NY Libs Tech Serv (v-pres Bd Trustees). 10: Trustee, Emma S Clark Mem Lib, Setauket NY. 12: Ed "Library Trends (July 65). 14: Admin, personnel. 15: 8 East 40th st, New York NY 10016.

GODFREY, LOIS(EWIN). b Cambridge Mass 26 Mr 28. 4: Thomas N K Godfrey. 5: UMich 45-46; Simmons 47-50 (LS) BS. 7: Ref libn Johns-Manville Research Center, Manville NJ 50-54; Los Alamos Sci Lab, Los Alamos NM: Main lib sect leader 54-55, Tech lit searcher 56-59, Asst br libn 59-63, Asst head libn 63-. 9: SLA; (Consul Serv Com 68-; pres Rio Grande Chap 59-60); NMLA.;(chm Legisl & Intel Freedom Com 67-70). 10: LWV. 11: Co-recipient SLA Sci-Tech Div Publication Award, 63. 12: Co-ed "Dictionary of Report eries Codes (62); Ed, Rio Grande Chap SLA "Bulletin (64-66). 14: Admin. 15: 156 Tunyo, Los Alamos NM 87544.

GODFREY, MAUD E C. b Toronto Can. 5: Toronto 36-40 BA, 40 BLS. 6: Fr. 7: Ref asst Hamilton Pub Lib, Hamilton Can 41-54, Head Kenilworth br 55-67; Hd ref servs NS Province Lib, Halifax Can 67-. 9: ALA; CanLA; APLA; OntLA; Inst Prof Libns Ont; HalifaxLA. 13: Yes. 14: Ref. 15: 1253 Edward st Apt 43, Halifax NS Can.

GODOY, ALICIA F. b Matanzas Cuba 27 F 17. 4: Jose A Godoy. 5: UHavana 38-41 (Doctorate Philos & Letters), 59-60

(LS) BS; UMiami 66 (LS). 6: Sp, Eng, Fr. 7: Libn Nat Lib, Havana Cuba 59-60; Foreign Lang Libn Miami Pub Lib, Miami Fla 61-. 14: Ref, catlg. 15: 324 SW 23rd st, Miami Fl 33135.

GODWIN, FRANCES LOUISE (ELLIOTT). b Colorado City Tex 13 My 20. 4: Charles Marion Godwin. 5: Tex Womans U 37-41 (LS) BA; Hardin-Simmons U 47-48, 65-6 7: Libn Pecos High Sch, Pecos Tex 41-42; Libn Colorado High Sch, Colorado City Tex 42-43; Purchasing dept United Air Lines, Cheyenne Wyo 43; Clerk Ore State Lib 43; File clerk San Bernardino AFB, San Bernardino Cal 43; Libn Colorado High Sch, Colorado City Tex 45-49; Sec Elliott-Godwin Insurance, Colorado City Tex 58-62; Libn Colorado High Sch, Colorado City Tex 62-. 9: ALA-AASchL;-YASD; NEA; TexLA; Tex State Tchrs Assn; TexASchL (Ya RT). 10 Jaycee-ettes; Womans Soc of Christian Serv. 14: igh sch lib, ref, ya lit. 15: 735 E 16th st, Colorado City Tex 79512.

GOEBEL, ELIZABETH (RITTS). b Apollo Penn 7 Ap 12. 4: George Jordan Goebel. 5: Wooster 30-31; Allegheny 31-32; Carnegie 32-34 BS in LS. 7: Headbind proj SERB, Titusville Penn 34-35; Head circ desk Allegheny Col Lib summer 35; Manager bk shop & lend lib Walden Book Co, Wilkes Barre Penn 35-38; Br libn Osterhaut Free Lib, Wilkes Barre Penn 38-41; Child libn Aurora Hills Arlington Co Lib, Arlington Va 50-59, Head child dept Central Lib 59-. 8: Consul, Wash DC Dept of Recreation 52-55; Visiting lecturer, George Washington U, 52 Consul, Nat Instr Television-program "Cover to Cover 68-70; & "Matter of Fiction 69-70. 9: ALA; VaLA. 10: Arlington (Va) Hist Soc; Washington (DC) Bksellers Assn. 13: Yes. 14: Child wk. 15: 2801 S Grant st, Arlington Va 22202.

GOEBEL, OTTIE BREITHER. b New Britain Conn. 4: Gregory Goebel. 5: Caldwell Col for women (Even 64-. 7: Saleslady & buyer The Silhouette Shoppe, Bridgeport Conn 36-41; Payroll clerk The Bridgeport Thermostat Co, Bridgeport Conn 41-42; Receptionist The Singer Co, Bridgeport Conn 42-, Cost clerk libn The Singer Co, Denville NJ. 9: ALA. 14: Tech bks, ref bks. 15: 16 Medford rd, Morris Plains NJ 07950.

GOEDICKE, LUCY PHYLLIS. b Baltimore 27 Jl 27. 4: Hans Goedicke. 05: St Joseph Col(Emmitsburg Md) 45-49 (Fr) BA. 6: Fr, Sp. 7: Sec Emery Advertising Corp, Baltimore 50-56; Tchr Garrison Jr High Sch, Baltimore 56-57; Catlgr Johns Hopkins U Lib 57-. 9: MdLA (sec Col & Res Div). 14: Catlg. 15: 3959 Cloverhill rd, Baltimore Md 21218.

GOEHRING, ELEANOR ELIZABETH. b Norfolk Va 5 D 04. 5: Randolph Macon Womans Col 25 (Eng Lit) AB; Columbia 27 S in LS; UTenn (Pol Sci, Econ). 7: Lib asst Randolph-Macon Womans Col 25-26; Head circ dept UTenn 27-46, Ref libn 46-. 8: Libn, Tenn Civil Defense Survival Plan Study, Knoxville 56. 9: ALA; SELA; TennLA. 10: Phi Beta Kappa. 14: Ref. 15: Univ of Tenn Lib, Knoxville Tenn 37916.

GOEHRING, LOUISE G. b Phila 24 Jl 17. 5: UPenn 35-39 (Econ) BA; Temple 60 (ElEduc) M Ed; Drexel 63 MS in LS. 6: Ger. 7: Sec to pres of two corps, Phila 44-60; Sch libn Cooke Jr High sch, Phila 64-65; Sch libn Roxborough High Sch, Phila 65-. 14: Child & ya lib materials. 15: Lamplighter lane, Gwynedd Pa 19436.

GOEKE, SISTER MARY LILLIAN OSB. b Newport Ky 2 Ap 03. 5: Xavier U (Cincinnati) BA; Catholic U55-60 (LS) MS; Life certif as sch libn Ky Dept of Educ. 7: Tchr Villa Madonna Acad, Covengton Ky 30-47; Film libn Villa Madonna Col 47-50; High schtchr St Henry High Sch, Erlanger Ky 53-55; Asst libn Villa Madonna Col 55-60; Libn St Henry High Sch, Erlanger Ky 60-65; Libn Holy Cross High Sch, Covington Ky 65-, Acquis libn Thomas More Col Summer 68. 8: Admins St John Orphanage, Ft Mitchell Ky 50-53. 9: CathLA(sec Greater Cincinnati Unit); ALA; KyLA. 13: Yes. 14: Sch lit. 15: Holy Cross High Sch 3617 Church st, Covington Ky 41015.

GOEL, KRISHAN S. b Adda-Kotbi Panjab 26 Mr 40. 5: Govt Panbir Col (Panjah) 58-62 9liberal Arts) BA; SUNY (Geneseo) 65-67 (LS) MA. 6: Hindi, Panjabi. 7: Catlgr SUNY (Buffalo) 67-. 9: ALA. 14: Catlg. 15: 53 Englewood ave, Buffalo NY 14214.

GOERDT, BROTHER ARTHUR L SM. b Dyersville Iowa 13 Ja 12. 5: Maryhurst Normal Kirkwood Mo 31-34 (Eng); UDayton 34-35 (Eng) BS in Ed; Our Lady of the Lake Col 37-42 BS in LS; St Louis U 45-50 (Eng) M Ed. 6: Ger. 7: Libn-Eng Cathedral High Sch, Belleville Ill 35-38; Libn-Eng Central Catholic, San Antonio Tex 38-40; Libn-Eng St Marys High Sch, St Louis 40; Libn-Eng Holy Redeemer High Sch, Detroit 41-44; Libn-Eng Don Bosco, Milwaukee 44-47; Libn-Eng Wm Cullen McBridge High Sch, St Louis 47-57; Dir Scholasticate St Marys U (SAN Antonio Tex) 57-63, Assoc Prof 57-. 8: Kaltenborn Foun Grant summer, 68, 69. 9: CathLA (Life mem, past pres); at Coun Tchrs Eng. NCTE. 10: San Antonio Eng Tchrs Club. 12: "A Unit Manual. 13: Yes. 14: Admin, Shakespeare. 15: 2700 Cincinnati ave, San Antonio Tex 78228.

GOETTEL, HAROLD M. b Sumneytown Penn. 4: Dorothy Aronsson Goettel. 5: UPenn (Hist, Eng) AB UCal(Berkeley) Certif of Libnship; Columbia (LS). 6: Ger. 7: Med libn Newark Pub Lib, Newark NJ 45-, Org Newark City Hosp Med Staff Lib 65-. 8: Org loc hosp med staff libs in NJ; Lib consul to serveral loc hosp sch of nurs libs. 9: ALA; MedLA; NJLA. 14: Ref. 15: 42 Ethan dr, Murray Hill NJ 07974.

GOETZ, DOROTHY (ELLEN COOPER). b Indianapolis Ind 13 S 12. 4: Byron E Goetz. 5: Ind Central Col 29-30, 31-34 (Eng, Hist) AB (cum laude); NoIllU 66; Rosary 66-69 ma in LS. 7: Tchr, FERA Adult Educ, Wabash Ind 34-35; Exec sec Clay Co Chap Amer Red Cross, Brazil Ind 42-44; Libn Cook Co Dist #113, Lemont Ill 67-. 8: Discussion Leader, World Politics, Downers Grove, LaGrange Ill 53-54. 10: Alpha Psi Omega; LWV; Bd of Dirs, Downers Grove Ill, Bay Village Ohio. 14: Ref. 15: 1300 Maple ave, Downers Grove Il 60515.

GOFF, CAROL M(ELISSA). b Blissfield Mich 23 D 09. 5: Lenawee Co Normal Sch 28-29 Tchg Certif; East Mich U summers 30-38, & 38-40 (Eng, Geog, Hist) BS. 7: Silberhorn Sch, Riga Mich 29-30; Scholzen Sch, Raisin Mich 30-32; Culbertson Sch, Tecumseh Mich 32-36, 37-38; eaton Rapids Pub Schs, Eaton Rapids Mich 40-42; Schultz-Holmes Mem Lib, Blissfield Br Lenawee Co Lib, Blissfield Mich 45-. 9: ALA; MichLA (sec Dist 2 65). 10: Pi Gamma Mu; Kappa Delta Pi. 14: Ref, ya, child bks. 15: 421 S Lane st, Blissfield Mich 49228.

GOFF, FREDERICK RICHMOND. b Newport RI 23 Ap 16. 5: Brown 33-39 (Hist) AB, AM, 65 Litt D. 6: Fr. 7: Asst to curator Annmary Brown Mem, Providence 37-40; Asst to curator Rare Bk Collection LC 40-42, Asst chief 42-45, Chief Rare bbk Div 45-. 8: Com of Mgt Annmary Brown Mem Providence; Visting Com Hunt Lib Carnegie Inst. 9: BSA(v-pres); ALA-ACRL(past chm Rare Bks Sect). 10: Grolier Club; AAS; Baltimore Bibliophiles; Bibliog Soc (London); Bibliog Soc UVa; Phi Beta Kappa; Literary Soc (Wash). 12: "The Dates in Certain German Incunabula (40): "Fifteenth-Century Books in the Library of Congress (50-0;"The Rare Book Division: A Guide to itsCollections and Services (50, rev ed 65); "The Rosenwald Collection (54); Ed "Essays Honoring Lawrence C Wroth (51); "Catalog of the Jean Hersholt Collection of Hans Christian Andersen (54); Ed "Bishop White Kennett and his Bibliothecae Americanae Primordia (59); "Joseph Sabin (64); Ed & comp "Incunabula in American Libraries: a hird Census (64). 13: Yes. 14: Rare bks (spec Incunabula). 15: 5034 Sherrier pl NW, Wash DC 20016.

GOFF, WILLIAM JAMES. b Kansas City Kan 31 My 34. 4: Janet Guthrie. 5: Kan City Kan Jr Col 52-53; UMo (Kan City) 57-60 (Geol) BS; UWash 60-66 (Geol) MS, MLibnship. 6: Fr, Sp, Russian. 7: Draftsman 2 & surveyor 2 USN 53-57; Grad resident asst UWash 61-62; Engring aide Boeing Co, Seattle 62; Asst libn Scripps Inst of Oceanography, La Jolla Cal 66-67, Libn 67-. 9: ALA. 14: Admin, lib automation, info stor & retr. 15: 1743 Legaye dr, Cardiff Ca 92007.

GOGGIN, MARGARET (ENID) (KNOX). b Nyack NY 24 F 19. 5: Maryville Col 40 (Eng) AB; Peabody 42 BS in LS; UIll 48 MS in LS, 57 PhD. 6: Fr, Sp, Ger, Gk. 7: Tchr-libn Flintville High Sch, Flintville Tenn 40-42; Ref asst Joint U Lib, Nashville 42-43, Act ref libn 43-45; Visiting Instr Peabody Lib Sch 43-45, summer 48 Readers adv Youngstown(Ohio) Pub Lib 45-46; Bibliogr & ref libn Off of Tech Serv Dept of Com, Wash DC 46-47; Ref asst UIll 48-49; Asst to the dir UFla Libs & Asst Prof of Lib Sci 49-50; Head Dept of Ref & Bibliog UFla Libs & Assoc Prof of Lib Sci 50-62; Asst dir for readers serv UFla Libs & Assoc Prof of Lib Sci 62-. 66, Prof of Lib Sci 66-68, Act dir UFla Libs 67-68; Dean grad sch of libnship UDenver 68-. 8: Visiting Lecturer, Emory Univ Sch of Libnship 65; Visiting lecturer, UOkla Lib Sch, summer 59; Mem, So Assn Eval Com, 3 Jacksonville (Fla) high schs; Trip to Haiti to negotiate for microfilming of newspapers & docs, sponsored by Rockefeller Foun, 58; Research in Paris to select and arrange for microfilming of docs relating to hit of Haiti, sponsored by Rockefeller Foun, 61-62. 9: ALA-RSD (sec 52-54, Publ Com 58-60, v-pres & pres-elect 68-69); -ACRL (Col Libs Sect: sec 58-59, Exec Bd 58-61, chm Nomin Com 60;

Univ Libs Sect: sec 56-57); ALA Jt Com to Study the Content of Ref Courses 62-63; SELA (com mem 61-62); FlaLA; ASIS. 10: Beta Phi Mu; Nat League of Amer Pen Women; Delta Kappa Gamma. 12: Ed Bibliographie Series UFla Libs (53-); Ed University of Florida Publications and Theses (54-62); Ed "Library Trends (Jan 64). 13: Yes. 14: Ref, lib ed. 15: 6658 South Gallup st, Littleton Co 80120.

GOGO, JEAN L(OUISE MAY). b Cornwall Ont Can. 5: Toronto 20-24 (Modern Langs) BA; McGill 46-47 BLS. 7: Fashion copywriter T Eaton Co, Montreal 25-36; Fashion copywriter Gussow-Kahn Advertising Agency, NYC 39-41; Fashion copywriter Ronalds Advertising, Montreal 41-43; Fashion ed "Fashion Magazine, Montreal 44-46; McGill U Sch of Soc wk, Montreal 47-56; Ref & catlg Cornwall Pub Lib, Cornwall Ont 56-64. 9: OntLA. 10: Univ Womens Club. 12: "Lights on the St Lawrence (58), "History of Cornwall General Hospital" (67). 14: Ref, rare bks, local hist. 15: 7 Adolphus st, Cornwall Ont Can.

GOGUEN, FERNANDE (BOUDREAU). b Moncton NB 28 Jl 43. 4: Francis Goguen. 5: U of moncton 60-64 BA; U d'Ottawa 64-65 BLS. 6: Fr. 7: Asst libn & catlgr Econ Coun of Can 65-. 9: CanLA; SLA; Assn canadienne des bibliothecaines de langue francaise. 14: Catlg. 15: 305 Laurier ave E, Ottawa 2 Ont Can.

GOIN, SANFORD W JR. b Gainesville Fla 8 Mr 37. 5: UFla 59-63 (Eng) BA; UMinn 64-65 (LS) MA. 7: YN2 USN 55-59; Libn (staff) NYC Pub Lib 65; Libn Holt Rinehart & Winston Inc, NY 66-. 9: ALA; SLA. 10: NY Libna RT on Soc Respons. 14: Ref, bibliog. 15: 320 W 105th st, New York NY 10025.

GOJDICS, MARY ANNE. b NYC 4 My 44. 5: Notre Dame Col of (SI) 61-65 (Eng) AB; Columbia 66-67 (LS) MS. 6: Fr. 7: Page NY Pub Lib, Staten Is NY 60-61, Clk 61-65; Libn trainee Hempstead Pub Lib, Hempstead NY 66-67; Libn Kenyon & Eckhardt Inc, NYC 67-. 9: SLA (Advertising & Marketing Div). 14: Ref. 15: 116 Pinehurst ave apt 5, New York NY 10033.

GOLD, (SOLOVIOFF) ETHEL. b NYC 22 My 24. 4: Harry Gold. 5: Hunter Col 40-44 (Econ) AB; LIU 63-66 (LS) MS. 7: Libn Old Bethpage Sch, Old Bethpage NY 65-66; Libn W Babylon High Sch, W Babylon NY 66-68; Libn NY Inst of Tech Lib 68-. 10: AAUP. 14: Ref. 15: 24 Jayson ave, Great Neck NY 11021.

GOLD, GERALD. b Milwaukee 4 Je 27. 5: UWis(Milwaukee) 47-49; UCal(Berkeley) 49-51 (Psych) BA; Columbia 51-52 MLS. 7: (Pvt 1/c) US Army, US & Germany 45-47; Page Milwaukee Pub Lib 47-49; Gen Libn & br libn NY Pub Lib 51-55, Admin asst & methods analyst 55-60; Lib consul Coun of Lib Resources, Chicago 60-61; Asst borough coordinator NY Pub Lib 61-62, Bronx borough coordinator 62-. 8: Consul Coun of Lib Resources 60-61 with the George Fry Mgt Consul Firm, Chicago, on "Study of Circulation Control Systems, Lib Tech Proj of ALA, 1961. 9: ALA-LAD(chm Pub Lib Statistics Com). 14: Admin. 15: 60 E 8th st apt 30B, New York NY 10003.

GOLD, SANDRA (ABRAMSON). b Shreveport La 9 Jl 35. 4: Joseph Gold. 5: Newcomb Col Tulane 52-54; UBirmingham (England) 54-55 (Eng); UWis (Madison) 55-56 (Eng) BA, 56-57 (LS) MA. 7: Libn I Madison Pub Lib, Madison Wis 57-59; Libn UManitoba Lib, Winnipeg man Can 60-66, Libn-ref 68-. 14: Ref. 15: 237 Oak sr, Winnipeg 9 Man Can.

GOLDBERG, DOROTHY (LENZNER). b Buffalo NY 25 Mr 11. 5: UBuffalo 29-32 (Hist) BA, 29-33 Lib Sci Certif. 7: Asst libn brs Buffalo & Erie Co Pub Lib 5361; Head Libn br Town of Tonawanda Libs, Tonawanda NY 61-65; Coordinator pub lib & sch Nioga Lib System, Niagara Falls NY 65-69, Adult servs consul 69. 9: ALA; NYLA (Memb Chm 64-) (62-65). 10: NY State Commsn on Human Rights. 13: Yes. 14: Pub serv. 15: 800 W Ferry st, Buffalo NY 14222.

GOLDBERG, ROSE (CUTLER). b New Haven Conn 2 Mr 17. 4: Adolph D Goldberg. 5: Tchrs Col of Conn 33-37 Elem Educ) B Ed; LIU Grad Lib Sch 59-64 (LS) MS. 6: Fr, Yiddish. 7: Eng tchr Elem Sch, Hamden Conn 37-39; Eng tchr Jr High Sch, NYC 55-59; Sch libn Elem Sch, Deer Park NY 59-. 9: ALA; NY State SchLA; NY State Tchrs Assn; Nassau-Suffolk SchLA Deer Park Sch Lib (Chm 64-67). 10: LIU Lib Sch Alumni Assn. 14: Child lit. 15: 467 Charles lane, Wantagh NY 11793.

GOLDBERG, SHIRLEY (COHEN). b Brooklyn NY 17 S 24. 4: Murray Goldberg. 5: Brooklyn col 41-46 (Econ) BA; Pratt Inst 61-65 MLS. 7: Libn (staff) Brooklyn Pub Lib, Brooklyn NY 65-67, Sr libn 67-. 9: ALA. 10: Beta Phi Mu. 14: Ref. 15: 2143 E 24th st, Brooklyn NY 11229.

GOLDEN, JAMES M. b New Haven Conn 27 Mr 11. 4: Mary E ODay. 7: 188th Gen Hosp Tech Sgt Admin NCO, ETO 43-46; Clerk Municipal Court, Hamden Conn 49-41, 55-60; Circ libn Yale Law Lib 27-. 9: AALL. 14: Readers serv. 15: 127 Wall st, New Haven CT 06511.

GOLDEN, JUNE (BAKER). b Schuylkill Haven Penn 4 Je 07. 5: Hood Col 25-27; UWis 28-30 (Biol) BA, 35-38 (Endocrinology) MA; UMich 64-65 AMLS. 6: Fr, Ger. 7: Research asst UWis(Madison) 36-38; Tech asst West Res U 38-40; Lib asst (volunteer) UMich 65-;Lib asst Ann Arbor High Sch 67-68. 14: Ref, reading guidance. 15: 1133 Michigan, Ann Arbor Mich 48104.

GOLDENBERG, MICHAEL. b Cairo Egypt 6 Ag 36. 5: City Col(NY) 53-57 (Lit & Linguistic Studies) BA; Queens Col 58 (LS); Pratt summer 58 (LS); Rutgers 58-59 MLS; New Sch for Soc Research 67-68 (Psych). 6: Fr, Yiddish, Sp. 7: Sr libn child wk Stone Ave Br Brooklyn Pub Lib 59-62, Young teens spec 62-64; Child libn 64-66; Adult Serv & Asst libn 66-; Sec-stenog SP5 Army Nat Guard-HQ & Hq Co 42d Inf Div G2, 60-65. 8: Chm, Young Teens Bk Sel Policy, Brooklyn Pub Lib 63-64. 9: Ala (Soc Respons RT), Sociedad Bibliotecarios de Puerto Rico; NYLA; NY Lib Club. 11: Friends of the Brooklyn Pub Lib Award, 64. 14: Child & yp (disadvantaged), commun improvement. 15: 40 Clinton st, Brooklyn NY 11201.

GOLDMAN, MARCENE (SALSBURG). b Cleveland Heights Ohio 24 Je 28. 4: Alan B Goldman. 5: Ohio State U 45-48 (Bacteriology) BS. 6: Sp, Hebrew. 7: Bacteriologist Strong Cobb & C, Cleveland 48-52; Chem Texaco Inc, Bellaire Tex 52-62, Tech libn 62-. 9: ACS; SLA;Geosci Info Soc. 15: 3510 Norris, Houston Tx 77025.

GOLDMAN, MAURICE S. b NYC 4 My 33. 4: Jyce Levy. 5: C C NY 51-56 (Psych, Speech) BA; Temple 56-58 (Speech Path) MA; UPittsburgh 58-60 (Speech Path); Carnegie 60-61 MLS. 7: Libn Queensborough Pub Lib, Jamaica NY 61-64; Dir Willingboro Pub Lb, Willingboro NJ 64-. 8: Co-Author of NJ State Library incentive aid grant applications-on behalf of libs, UNL. 9: ALA-Jr Mem Round Table (chm 67); NJLA(Recrchm 68-); Libs, Unlimited; Pub Rel Assn Greater Phila. 10: Rotary. 11: Runner-up. 14: Adult serv recr. 15: 36 Hollis lane, Willingboro NJ 08046.

GOLDMAN, NANCY JANE. b Orange Cal 11 S 45. 5: Skidmore 63-67 (Amer Studies) AB; UMich 67-68 AMLS. 6: Fr. 7: Ref libn Young & Rubicam, NYC 68-. 9: SLA (Advertising & Marketing Div). 14: Ref. 15: Young & Rubicam 285 Madison ave, New York NY 10017.

GOLDSMITH, ARTHUR A JR. b Portland Ore 24 Ag 27: 05: Cornell U 49-51 (Floriculture) BS, 51-52 (Bus Admin) MBA; UWash 58-59 (LS) ML. 4: Martha Dykes Goldsmith. 5: Cornell 51 (Floriculture) BS in Agr, 52 (Business) MBA; UWash 58-59 M of Libnship. 7: (Pvt) US Army 45-47; Owner-manager of a retail store, Corvallis Ore 53-57; Libn Queens Borough Pub Lib, Queens NY 59-64; A-v consul Mid-Hudson Libs, Poughkeepsie NY 64-65; Spec collections catlgr Ariz State U 65-67, Spec collections libn 67-69, Circ libn 69-. 8: Libn Typographic Ref Lib, NYC 62-65; Consul on Spec Collections, 69. 9: ALA (Life mem); BSA; Private Libs Assn; Bibliog Soc Va; ArizLA (Exeb Chm 69); Bibliog Soc (London). 10: Bk Club of Cal; The Typophiles; Caxton Club; Kiwanis; West Hist Assn; Phoenix Corral Westerners. 12: "How to Catalogue the Private Library (61). 13: Yes. 14: Rare bks, fine & private pres printing. 15: 42 Hudson lane, Tempe Az 85281.

GOLDSMITH, DOROTHY ANN (ROBERTSON). b SC 30 Ja 31. 5: Harbison Jr Col 47-49; Barber-Scotia Col 49-51 (Soc Sci) BS; NC Col summer 53 (LS); SCar Col summer 57 (LS); NC Col summer 60 (LS); UCincinnati 66 (Media). 6: Fr. 7: Tchr-libn Florence Chapel High Sch, Wellford SC 51-56; Libn Colleton High Sch, Walterboro SC 56-61; Asst libn Johnson C Smith U 61-62; Libn Shaw High Sch, Laurinburg NC 62-63; Child libn Cincinnati Pub Lib 63-64; Lib Cincinnati Bd of Educ 64-68; Sch libn Kent State U 68-.08. Consul lib planning, at the Cincinnati Sci Ctr 67; Adv Amer Studies Team Kent State U Sch on Black Hist 68-69. 9: ALA; OhioLA; Ohio Assn Sch Libns. 10: AAUP; AAUW; Kent State U Women; Delta Sigma Theta. 13: Yes. 14: Ref. 15: 260 Spaulding dr apt 201, Kent Oh 44240.

GOLDSTEIN, ALLAN. b NYC 26 S 27. 4: . 5: Brooklyn Col 47-51 (Hist) BA; Columbia 51-53 MLS, 56-59 (Educ) MA; UCal 62-. 7: Asst br libn NY Pub Lib 53-57; Libn Rhodes Sch, NYC 57-60; Libn Hayward Unified Sch Dist, Mt Eden High Sch, Hayward Cal 60-63; Coordinator lib serv Berkeley Unified Sch Dist, Berkeley Cal 63-. 8: Adv Coun on Educ for Libnship, UCal 64-67. 9: Cal ASchL. 14: Adult educ. 15: 1707 Russell st, Berkeley Cal 94703.

GOLDSTEIN, ANITA (TANNEN). b Wilmington Del 23 F 17. 4: Jacob Goldstein. 5: UPenn 34-38 (Lat) AB; Drexel 38-39 BLS. 6: Ger. 7: Jr lib asst Mt Vernon Pub Lib (Mt Vernon NY) 39-40; Jr lib asst Social Security Bd Lib, Wash DC 41-42; Libn OASI Br Soc Security Admin Lib, Baltimore 42-58; Chief libn Bur of Old Age & Survivors Insurance, Baltimore 58-63; Chief libn Soc Security Admin Lib, Baltimore 63-. 9: SLA (Baltimore Chap: Nomin Com 64-65). 14: Admin, ref. 15: 3055 Essex rd, Baltimore Md 21207.

GOLDSTEIN, DAIDEE ELIZABETH (SPRINGER). b England 16 O 39. 4: Melvin Leon Goldstein. 5: UWis (Milwaukee) 57-61 (Eng) BA; UIll 61-62 (LS) MS; UWis (Madison) 64-65 9comparative Lit). 6: Fr, Ger. 7: Clk & jr libn Milwaukee Pub Lib 56-61; Jr libn buffalo & Erie Co Pub Lib, Buffalo NY 62-63; Libn I & II Madison Pub Lib, Madison Wis 65-65; Hd adult serv & asst dir Kokomo Pub Lib, Kokomo Ind 65-. 9: IndLA (memb Com). 10: LWV; Ind U Kokomo Fac Wives. 13: Yes. 14: Ref, admin. 15: 2513 Sherman dr, Kokomo In 46901.

GOLDSTEIN, ELISBETH ANNE. b Pittsburgh Penn 24 S 44. 5: DenisonU 62-66 (Speech) BA; UPittsburgh 68-69 MLS. 6: Fr, Sp. 7: Stud asst DenisonU 63-66; Lib asst US Steel Corp, Pittsburgh Penn 66-68; Grad asst UPittsburgh Grad Sch Lib & Info Sci 68; Libn Dravo Corp, Pittsburgh Penn 69; Asst ref libn & instr lib admin Wright StateU 69-. 9: SLA. 14: Ref, spec ind libs. 15: 425 Dayton Towers dr apt 7B, Dayton Oh 45410.

GOLDSTEIN, ESTELLE LORAINE (GOLDSTAUB). b NYC. 4: Mac Goldstein. 5: NYU 34 (Eng) BA; Columbia (Philos); Rutgers 58 (LS); Pratt 59 MLS. 7: Pub rel "New York Times, NYC 36; Br libn Queens Borough Pub Lib, Jamaica NY 62, Asst reg libn 63, Ext serv dept asst 64; Coordinator child serv Smithtown Lib System, Smithtown LI NY 64-; Asst Dir Adult servs Elmont Lib Sys, Elmont LI 68-. 8: Amer Womens Volunteer Serv NYC Research Dept 42. 9: ALA; NYLA; NY Lib Club. 10: NYU Wash Sq Col Alumni Assn; Grad Sch of Lib Sci (Pratt Inst) Alumni; Pratt Inst Alumni Assn; Arthritis Found; Beta Phi Mu; Tau Alpha Beta. 13: Yes. 14: Programs & serv, admin, pesonnel. 15: 83-15 Lefferts blvd, Kew Gardens LI NY 11415.

GOLDSTEIN, GAIL. b Englewood NJ 25 Ja 43. 5: Wheaton Col 64 (Eng Lit) AB; ColumbiaU 65 MS. 6: Fr. 7: Stud asst Wheaton Col Lib 63-64; Libn Nat Soc for Prevention of Blindness, NYC 65-66; Hd libn Kenyon & Eckhardt Inc, NYC 66-. 9: SLA (NY Chap Advertising & Marketing Div: sec-treas 68-69, chm 69-70). 10: ColumbiaU Sch Lib Sci Alumni Assn. 14: Ref, admin. 15: 18 Norfolk st, Bergenfield NJ 07621.

GOLDSTEIN, GITELLE (BARBARA). b NY 14 S 46. 5: Hunter Col 63-67 (Sociol) BA; Columbia 67-68 MS. 6: Fr, Sp. 7: Asst libn Dewey, Ballantine, Bushby, Palmer & Wood, NYC 68-. 9: AALL; SLA. 10: Phi Beta Kappa; Beta Phi Mu. 14: Ref wk, legal research. 15: 499 E 8th st, Brooklyn NY 11218.

GOLDSTEIN, HAROLD. b Norfolk Va 3 O 17. 4: Julia S Deutsch. 5: UMd 38-42 (Educ) BS; Columbia 46-47 BSLS; Columbia 48-49 (Educ) MA, Ed D. 6: Yiddish, Fr, Ger. 7: Br asst Enoch Pratt Free Lib, Baltimore 38-42; Army Air Corps Electronics Off (1st Lt) 42-46; Asst Prof UMinn(Duluth) 49-51; Dir Lib Serv USTS, Colombo Ceylon 51-53; Visiting assoc prof of lib sci UIll(Urbana) 54-55; Dir Davenport Pub Lib, Davenport Iowa 55-59; Prof Grad Sch of Lib Sci UIll(Urbana) 59-67; Dean Sch of Lib Sci FSU, Tallahassee Fl 67-. 8: Consul: Neb Lib Survey 61; Miss Lib Survey 62; Elmhurst Pub Lib 62; Edina Minn 63; Columbia, Howard County, Md 65; Penn State Lib A-V Survey 65; ALA A-V Com 65; NY State A-V Survey 63; etc. 9: ALA; NEA-DAVI; FlaLA; SELA. 10: Phi Gamma Delta. 12: Ed "Implications of the New Media for the Teaching of Library Science, (63); "Library Trends (61). "Library School Teaching Methods (67). 13: Yes. 14: Pub lib admin, a-v serv, adult educ. 15: Sch of Lib Sci Fla State U, Tallahassee Fl 32306.

GOLDSTEIN, SAMUEL. b Malden Mass 15 D 29. 4: Joan (Grady). 5: Boston U 48-52 (Govt) BA, 57-58 (Govt) MA, Simmons 60-62 MSLS. 6: Russian, Sp, Ger. 7: Analytic aide Dept of Defense, Wash DC 52-53; PFC Army Security Agcy, Germany 53-55; Lib asst Boston Pub lib 55-59; Hd libn Computer Control Co, Framaingham Mass 59-65; Sci libn Brandeis U 65-67; Assoc dir reader serv UMass 68; Project dir New England Lib & Info Network, Wellesley Mass 68-. 9: SLA; MassLA. 10: Phi Beta Kappa. 12: Ed "Directory of New England College and University Libraries," (69). 13: Yes. 14: Admin, reader serv, tech processing, sci libnship. 15: 35 Whittemore rd, Framingham Ma 01701.

GOLDTHORPE, MARY JANE. b Duluth Minn 29 Je 45. 5: UPittsburgh 63 (Math); E Stroudsburg state Col 64-67 (Math) BS in Ed; Rutgers 67-68 MLS. 6: Sp. 7: Math & astronomy libn northwesternU 68-. 9: ASIS. 10: Sigma Zeta. 14: SPI & other info retr serv. 15: 36 Lilac lane, Levittown Pa 19054.

GOLDWYN, A(LVIN) J. b Cleveland 27 S 21. 5: West Res 39-42 (Eng, Biol) BA; UCLA 47-50 (Eng) MA. 6: Fr, Ger. 7: US Army (Staff Sgt) US Port of Embarkation, Seattle 42-46; Train off US VA, Canton Ohio 46-47; Tchg asst Dept of Eng, UCLA 48-52; Instr Dept of Eng west Res U 54-58; Lexicographer World Publ Co, Cleveland 58-61; Asst dir CDCR & Instr, Asst Prof of Lib Sci, West Res U 61-63; Exec Dir Center for Documentation & Communication Research, Sch of Lib Sci West Res U & Assoc Prof of Lib Sci 63-; Prof of Lib Sci 66-, Assoc Dean Sch of Lib Sci 67-. 8: Consul to NLM & NIH on med info problems; Invited lecturer, NATO Advanced Study Inst, The Hague, 65. 9: ASIS (past pres Cleveland Chap) ALA;-ISAD (Spec Insts Subcom); -LED; AALS. 10: Exec Com, Commun Research Conf, Cleveland; Phi Beta Kappa; AAAS. 12: Ed "Education of Science Information Personnel, with A Rees (65); Mem Ed Bd "Journal of Library Automation 13: Yes. 14: Documentation, info retrieval, & lib automation. 15: Case West Res Univ, Cleveland Oh 44106.

GOLTER, ROBERT. b Chicago 13 D 28. 4: Joanna Weber. 5: Wheaton Col 50-54 (Hist) BA; USoCal 54-57 MSLS. 7: (Pfc) USAAF, US & Alaska 46-49; Ref libn Pasadena Pub Lib, Pasadena Cal 55-57; Libn Wheaton Col (Wheaton Ill) 57-68; Libn Meyer Mem Lib & Asst dir Univ Libs Stanford U 68-. 8: Consul to indus for res info 58-68; Adv coun on lib devel, Ill State Lib 66-68. 9: ALA ACRL; IllLA (chm-elect Col & Res Libs Sect). 10: Friends of the Wheaton (Ill) Pub Lib. 13: Yes. 14: Admin, ref, rare bks. 15: J Henry Meyer Mem Lib, Stanford Univ, Stanford Ca 94306.

GOLTON, PATRICIA LOUISE. b Jackson Cal 24 Ap 18. 5: UCal (Berkeley) 35-39 (Pol Sci) AB, 39-40 Certif in Libnship. 6: Fr, Sp, Ger, Ital. 7: Asst libn econ Lib UCal (Berkeley) 40-51; USNR Lt 42-46; Libn Cal Dept of Fish & Game, San Francisco 52; Docs libn UCal (Davis) 52-55, Ser order libn 55-56, Acquis libn 56-58; Bk selection libn stockton & San Joaquin Co Lib, Stockton Cal 58-. 9: ALA; CalLA. 10: AAUW; Bus & Profess Women's Club. 12: "Economics of Water Resources Development in the Eleven western States: an Inventory of Research," (51). 14: Ref, acquis, docs. 15: 1523 Telegraph ave, Stockton Ca 95204.

GOLUB, FRANCES M. b Brooklyn NY 14 Mr 18. 5: Brooklyn Col 33-37 (Chem BA; Pratt 60-63 MLS. 6: Yiddish, Hebrew, Fr. 7: Lib trainee Shelter Rock Pub Lib, Albertson NY 63, Ref libn 63-65, Dir 65-. 9: ALA; NYLA; NCLA (Chm pub rel com; Nat Lib Week Com). 10: Phi Beta Mu. 11: John Cotton Dana Publicity Award 67. 14: Ref, admin, pub rel, automation. 15: 2 Corncrib lane, Roslyn Heights NY 11577.

GOLUMB, BERNARD M. b San Francisco 20 O 26. 4: Barbara Scammell. 5: Mont State U 44; Stanford 45; San Francisco State Col 47-49 (Internat Rel) AB; UCal 49-51 BLS. 6: Sp. 7: (Pfc) US Army Air Corps, US 44-46; Libn I & II San Francisco Pub Lib 51-53; Libn I Dearborn Pub Lib, Dearborn Mich 54-55; Libn III Hayward Pub Lib, Hayward Cal 56-. 9: CalLA. 10: Pub Lib Execs Central Cal; San Francisco Bay Area Ref Coun. 14: Ref, admin, bk sel. 15: 22737 Mission blvd, Hayward Ca 94521.

GOMEZ, OSBORNE L. b Charleston SC 25 Mr 21. 4: Marianne Snyder. 5: USoCar 46-49 (Eng, Sp) AB; UFla 55-57 (Eng) MA; Fla StateU 67-69 MLS. 6: Sp. 7: Tchr SC Opportunity Sch, Columbia 49-51; Ed asst USC Press (Columbia) 51-53; Hd research & surveys gen ext div, Gainesville Fla 53-58, Hd lib 58-63; Dir ext lib FICUS & U So Fla 64-. 8: Instr of rapid reading classes, Columbia SC 53; Instr of creative writing classes, Gainesville Fla 56; Consul church libs in Fla 62. 9: FlaLA; SELA. 10: Phi beta Kappa; Phi Kappa Phi; Omicron Delta Kappa; Blue Key. 12: Ed "Blue Key" (nat frat quarterly, 55-62), soc sci bulletins (Gainesville Fla 58-64). 14: Admin. 15: 4801 Ninth st S, St Petersburg Fl 33705.

GONCAR, JOHN J. b Bridgeport Conn 4 Je 30. 4: Mary Batcha. 5: UConn 50-52; UAriz 52-54 (Geol) BS; Pratt 59-60 MSLS. 6: Sp. 7: Regimental Mail Supv US Army 54-56; Sales correspondent Manning Maxwell & Moore, Stratford Conn 56-57; Metallographer Amer Chain & Cable, Bridgeport Conn 57-59; Br libn Pratt & Whitney Aircraft, N Haven Conn 61-65; Head of ref dept United Aircraft, E Hartford Conn 65-66, Hd ref & circ sect 66-68, Supv main lib 68-. 9: SLA. 10: Jr C of C. 14: Ref, admin. 15: 23 Tall Timbers rd, Glastonbury Ct 06033.

GONCE, NANCY (CUMMINGS). b Birmingham Ala 21 My 39. 4: Robert Lowery Gonce. 5: UAla 57-61 (LS) BS; Peabody 61 (LS) MA. 7: Lib asst Friedman Lib, Tuscaloosa Ala 60; Ala Pub Lib Serv: Area libn, Tuscaloosa Ala 61-62; Area libn, Florence Ala 62-65, Field rep, Florence Ala 65-68, Lib Consul 68-. 9: ALA; SELA; AlaLA (chm Friends & Trustees Div 68-69). 10: Alpha Beta Alpha; AAUW; Ala Hist Soc. 13: Yes. 14: Reg lib serv, serv to child & ya. 15: 213 Colonial dr, Florence Al 35632.

GONZALEZ, ARMANDO EUGENIO. b Havana Cuba 24 Ap 21. 4: Virginia Medina. 5: UHavana 39-43 Doctor of Law; Columbia 64-65 MLS. 6: Sp. 7: Attorney Zaldivars Law Off, Havana 43-54; Attorney Saladrigas-Aquino- Diagos Law Off, Havana 54-60; V-sec & legal coun Godoy-Sayan SA, Havana 56-60; Serv engnr R E Foote Inc, Belmar NJ 60-64; Asst circ libn Columbia U 65-66; Sr leg spec Hispanic law div LC 67-. 9: AALL; SLA. 10: Havana Bar Assn. 14: Circ, ref, Hispanic law. 15: 3308 Curtis dr, Hillcrest Heights Md 20023.

GONZALEZ, EFREN W. b NYC 16 Je 29. 4: Rita Ciliotta. 5: Iona Col 47-51 (Phil) BA; Columbia 51-52 (LS) MS. 7: Libn Military Sea Transportation Serv, Atlantic Area, NY 54-54; Asst libn Material Lab NY Naval Shipyard 54-56; Tech libn Nepera Chem Co, Yonkers NY 56-57; Dir tech communications Grove Labs, St Louis 57-68; Mgr tech communications Bristol-Myers Prods, Hillside NJ 68-. 9: SLA (Dir 67-70); MedLA; Amer Med Writers' Assn. 14: Mgt communications, info stor & ret. 15: 1350 Liberty ave, Hillside NJ 07207.

GONZALEZ, ONDINA (SANTOS). b Cardenas Cuba 11 F 33. 4: Jorge Augusto Gonzalez. 5: Ins Pre-Universitario del Vedado (Letters) BL; Union Theol Sem (Matanzas Cuba) (Christian Educ) ICB; Emory MLn. 6: Sp, Fr, Portu. 7: Act libn Union Theol Sem (Matanzas Cuba) 60-61; Asst libn catlgr Mem Lib Berry Col 62-. 9: ALA; SELA. 10: AAUP; Women Soc of Christian Serv. 12: . 14: Catlg, Col libs. 15: P O Box 153, Mt Berry Ga 30149.

GOOCH, DONALD WILLIS. b Wash DC 30 Ap 06.04: Elizabeth Brubaker Gooch. 5: George Washington U 25-31 (Fr) AB; Harvard 31-32 (Bus Admin); George Washington U 32-35 (Fr) MA; US Dept Agric Grad Sch 48-49 (Econ). 6: Fr, Ger, Sp, Ital. 7: Jr ref asst, sr ref asst, assoc libn LC 22-42; Assoc in Fr George Washington U (Wash DC) 38-39; Lt(jg), Lt, LCDR USNR 42-46; Mgt analyst PMA US Dept Agric Wash DC 46-47; Libn div of bibliog US Dept Agric, Wash DC 47-52; Head gen ref br Sci Lib US Patent Off, Wash DC 52-. 9: . 10: Patent Off Soc; Patent Off Profess Assn. 12: Bibliographies: "Land Ownership (53); "Marketing of Dairy Products (48); "Marketin of Livestock, Meat and Meat Products (51); "Packaging and Prepackaging of Fresh Fruits and Vegetables(49); "Snow (48); "World Land Reform (51). 14: Admin. 15: 2832 Cleave dr, Falls Church Va 22042.

GOOCH, JANIE (MERRITT). b Malvern Ark 22 S 16. 4: Elmer Gooch. 5: SEast State (Okla) 33-37 (Eng, Hist, Lat) AB, summer 42; UKy summer 50-53 MSLS; Miami U Ext (Ohio) 57. 7: Tchr Choctaw Co, Hugo Okla 37-40; Dist supv WPA Lib Serv Bk Repair Okla 40-42; Tchr & libn Goodland Indian Acad, Hugo Okla 42-43; Clk Air Material Command, Dayton Ohio 45; Tchr & libn Madison Twp Schs, Trotwood Ohio 45-49; Asst libn Roosevelt High Sch, Dayton Ohio 49-53; Libn Dayton Ohio Colonel White High Sch 53-56, Belmont High Sch 56-. 9: ALA; -AASchL (Dir Reg III 68-70; chm State Assembly Planning Com 64-68; reg rep to State Assembly 63-64); NEA; OhioASchL (Pres 60-61, v-pres 59-60, district rep 56-58); OhioEA; Dayton Clr Tchrs. 10: AAUW; Dayton Eng Club. 14: Sch libs. 15: 1460 Allenwood lane, Dayton Oh 45432.

GOOD, CAROL (MONICH). b Bristol Conn 24 Ap 41. 4: Robert Morrison Good. 5: WVa wesleyan 59-62; UBridgeport 62-63 (Psych) BS; Fla StateU 65-67 (LS) MS. 7: Hd libn briarwood High Sch, E Point Ga 67-68; Catlgr Orlando Jr Col 68-. 14: Tech proc. 15: 546 Eastbrook blvd, Winter Park Fl 32789.

GOODALE, GRACE ELIZABETH (PEARCE). b Ashland Ohio 24 O 07. 5: Hiram Col 25-29 (Span) AB; National YWCA Sch (NY) summer 29 Diploma; West Res 48-51 MS in LS. 6: Sp. 7: Girls sec YWCA, Pottstown Penn 29-32; Asst bkmob libn Portage Co Lib, Hiram Ohio 42-45; Asst Col libn Hiram Col 45-47; Head libn Portage Co Lib, Hiram Ohio 52-. 9: ALA; OhioLA. 10: Garden Club; Pomona Grange (Portage Co); Hiram Grange; Delta Kappa Gamma. 14: Ext serv. 15: Box 51, Hiram Ohio 44234.

GOODALL, SARA FRANCES. b Valley Mills Tex 18 S 16. 5: Daniel Baker Col 35-37; Tex Womans U 37-38, 39-40 (LS) BA; UColo summer 41; Peabody summers 48-50 (LS) MA. 6: Sp. 7: High sch libn Seminole Pub Schs, Seminole Tex 40-43; Ector County Schs, Odessa Tex 43-; Ref libn Stephen F Austin State Col summer 47; Ref libn Ector County Lib, Odessa Tex summer 50; Prof of Lib Sci Murray State Col summers 53 & 60; Prof of Lib Sci Tex Womans U summer 54. 9: TexLA; Tex State Tchrs Assn. 10: DAR; Permian Playhouse; Odessa Symphony; Delta Kappa Gamma, Civic Mu Ass. 15: 1200 N Lee apt 10, Odessa Tx 79760.

GOODART, CATHERINE (MITCHELL). b Council Bluffs Iowa 16 N 06. 4: James M Goodart. 5: UColo 25-27 (Eng); UWyo 27-29 (Eng) BA; Columbia 29-30 BS in LS. 6: Fr, Ger, Lat. 7: Prof lib asst Laramie Co Pub Lib, Cheyenne Wyo 30-33; Prof lib asst Seattle Pub Lib 37-38; Lib asst King Co Med Soc Lib, Seattle 40-42; Prof lib asst Laramie Co Pub Lib, Cheyenne Wyo 43-45; Lib clerk Hillsborough Sch Dist, Hillsborough Cal 56; Bkmob libn San Mateo Co Lib, Redwood City Cal 56-60; Libn Millbrae Lib San Mateo Co Lib, Millbrae Cal 60-. 9: ALA; CalLA; PeninLA (pres 63-64). 10: Soroptimist Club; Soroptimist Fed of Americs Inc; Alpha Delta Pi. 15: 919 Cloud ave, Menlo Park Cal 94026.

GOODE, PAUL K. b Boston 4 My 28. 4: Patricia Welsh Goode. 5: Boston Col 52 (Eng) AB; Catholic U 61 MSLS. 6: Fr. 7: Research analyst US Dept of Defense, Wash DC 52-54; Lib asst Georgetown U 54-55; Lib asst US ODM 56-57; Asst ref libn Notre Dame U (So Bend Ind) 57-59; Asst ref libn NH State Lib 60-63; Asst coordinator adult serv Baltimore County Pub Lib, Towson Md 63-65; Undergrad Libn Ohio State U 65-67; Hd libn Tex A&I U 67-. 8: Exec Dir, State of NH, Nat Lib Week 62; Instr Md State Dept of Educ Train Program for Lib Aides. 9: ALA; TexLA; Coastal Bend LA; TACT. 14: Ref, bk sel. 15: 723 Santa Anita, Kingsville Tx 78363.

GOODE, STEPHEN H. b Charlotte NC 25 D 24. 4: Jean Advena. 5: UMd 46-49 (Eng) BA; UPenn 52-58 (Eng) MA PhD. 7: (1st Lt) Inf 44-46, 49-51; Asst prof Eng Rensselaer Polytech Inst 58-59; Asst prof Eng Fairleigh Dickinson U 60-65; Dir of libs & assoc prof Eng Russell Sage Col 65-. 8: Adv Johnson Reprint Corp; Dir Whitson Publish Corp. 10: Bibliog Soc UVa; BSA, Bibliog Soc (London); Soc of Indexers. 12: "Index to Little Magazines, 1940-42, 1943-48" (2v 65); Ed "Connotation, Magazine of the Arts"; Ed "Studies in the 20th Century 13: Yes. 14: Bibliog, 20th century lit. 15: Hudson dr, Troy NY 12180.

GOODEMOTE, RITA L(aTOUR). b Jersey City NJ. 5: Col St Elizabeth 3741 (Chem Biol) AB; Columbia 5253 MS in LS. 6: Fr, Ger. 7: Analytic chem Mallinckrodt, Jersey City NJ 4142; Analytic chem HoffmannLa Roche Inc, Nutley NJ 4249; Mgr, Lib Schering Corp, Bloomfield NJ 53. 9: SLA (Tellers Com; Pharmaceut Sect; chm & sec, Bus mgr Co PNIP; NJ Chap; chm Nomin Com, Planning Com); ASIS; MedLA; ACS (Chem Lit Div). 10: AAAS; AMWA; DIA; Kappa Gamma Pi. 14: Ref, admin. 15: Schering Corp 60 Orange st, Bloomfield NJ 08540.

GOODEN, GERALD L. b Los Angeles 19 Ag 25. 4: Inez Hunt. 5: Marshall U 56-60 (LS) BA; UCLA 63-65 MLS. 6: Fr, Ger, Gk. 7: Asst libn Biola Col 62, Ref libn 62-69, Col libn 69-. 9: ALA; AtheolLA; West TheolLA; ChristianLA (pres 68-70); CalLA. 10: Internat Soc of Bible Collectors; Beta Phi Mu; Christ Lib Fellowship; Mission Lit Foun. 14: Ref, admin. 15: 11716 Ronald dr, La Mirada Cal 90638.

GOODENOUGH, ANNA RUTH. b Bandera Tex 16 My 15. 5: Southwest Tex State Tchrs Col 32-33 & summers 34-36 (Educ); Scarritt Col for Christan Wkers 38-40 (Religious Educ) AB; Peabody 40-41 BS in LS; UTex summers 42, 48, 50 (Educ); Tex West Col (Educ) MA. 7: Tchr Turtle Creek Sch, Kerr Co Tex 33-34; Tchr Indian Creek Sch, Bandera Co Tex 35-36; Tchr Vanderpool Sch, Vanderpool Tex 36-38; Tchr-libn Council High Sch, Council Va 41-43; Libn Eagle Pass High Sch, Eagle Pass Tex 43-48; Libn Jasper High Sch, Jasper Tex 48-49; Libn El Paso Pub Schs, El Paso Tex 49-. 9: ALA; NEA; Tex State Tchrs Assn; TexLA; Tex ClrTA; El Paso Border

RegLA. 10: Delta Kappa Gamma; Altrusa Club; Wesleyan Serv. 14: Sch lib. 15: 3332 Porter ave, El Paso Tex 79930.

GOODFELLOW, MARJORIE (ELIZABETH). b Sherbrooke Que Can 12 Je 38. 5: Bishops U 55-59 (Hist) BA; McGill 59-60 BLS, 67 MLS. 6: Fr. 7: Asst libn Can Dept of Cit & Immig, Ottawa Ont 60-61; Catlgr Bell Telephone Co of Can, Montreal 61-62; Asst libn 62-63; Co libn United Aircraft of Can Ltd, Longueil 63-67; Hd pub servs Sir George Williams U Lib 68-. 8: Mem Comite pour la formation de la corporation des bibliothecaires professionnels du Quebec 65-. 9: ALA; CanLA (chm Com on the Use of Profess Staff 66-67); QueLA; Inst Profess Libns Ont; SLA (Deputy Conf chm 1969 Conf 67-69; Montreal chap; Memb Chm 63-64, pres 66-67). 15: 1520 McGregor st, Montreal 109 Que Can.

GOODGER-HILL, JEAN CAROL (FAUSETT). b Peterborough Ont Can 18 S 37. 4: Gareth goodger-Hill. 5: Univ Col UToronto 54-58 (Eng) BA; Ontario Col of Educ 58-59 (Educ) Certif; McGill 62-63 BLS; UToronto summer 66 (Med Lit). 6: Fr, Ital. 7: Secondary sch tchr: Collingwood Collegiate Inst, Collingwood Ont Can 58-59, Ridgeway Collegiate inst, Ridgeway Ont Can 62; Asst libn Canadian Med Assn Lib, Toronto Ont Can 64-66; Asst libn Acad of Med, Toronto Ont Can 66-67; Libn II UCal (Santa Barbara) Lib. 14: Med ref. 15: W Anapamu st, Santa Barbara Ca 93104.

GOODHART, LILLIAN B(LANCHE). b NYC 16 Mr 07. 5: Goucher 24-28 (Eng) AB; Johns Hopkins summer 30 (Eng); Columbia 28-29 BS in LS, 41-42 (Eng) MA. 6: Fr, Ger, Lat, Sp, Ital, Dutch, Scandinavan. 7: Tchr-libn Eastern High Sch, Baltimore 29-31; Documents asst & ref asst civics & social dept,Enoch Pratt Free Lib, Baltimore 34-43, Sr catlgr 42-44; Sr catlgr Pub Lib, Worcester Mass 44-46; Sr catlgr Yale Law Sch Lib 46-47; Chief catlg dept Douglass Col 47-56; Instr in Govt Pubs NJC Lib Sch (New Brunswick NJ) 51-52; Head period dept Rutgers U Lib 56-67; Instr in catlg Rutgers U Grad Sch of Lib Serv 62; Admin asst to U libn Rutgers U Lib 68-. 9: NJLA (chm Pub Rel & Publ Com 1 yr, other com assignments). 10: AAUP; YWCA; Eng Speak Union. 12: "NJLA Newsletter (ed one year); "Guide to the University Libraries, Ed Rutgers U; (68); Ed Rutgers U, bib "Newsletter 14: Catlg, ser, admin, personnel. 15: 715-A Donaldson st, Highland Park NJ 08904.

GOODMAN, DELENA ELLA. b Mt Olive Ill 16 Ag 18. 5: Anderson Col 41-42, 44-45 (Religious Educ) BS; Oberlin Sch of Theol 47-48 & summer 50 (Religious Educ) MA; UIll summers 53-56 MS in LS; Union & Columbiasummer 60 (Religion & LS); Pacific Sch of Religion summer 62 (Religion). 7: Dir of religious educ Church of God, Decatur Ill 45-47; Dir of religious educ 10th & Shartel Church of God, Okla City Okla 48-50; Libn Sch of Theol Anderson Col 52-. 9: ATheolLA; IndLA. 10: . 14: Catlg. 15: 502-1/2 College dr, Anderson Ind 46012.

GOODMAN, DOROTHY (RHODES). b Pueblo Col 21 Ap 21. 4: Hart Tavel Goodman. 5: UCal (Berkeley) 39-43 (Psych) BA, 47 (Child Development), 64-65 MLS. 6: Fr. 7: Nursery sch tchr: Richmond Child Care Ctr, Richmond Cal 46-48, Child Commun Ctr, Berkeley Cal 56-57; Playfround dir Berkeley Sch, Berkeley Cal 61-62; Child libn Beverly Hills Pub lib, Beverly Hills Cal 66-68, Circ & y-a libn 68-. 9: CalLA. 10: PTA. 14: Child lit. 15: 6330 So Highland, Los Angeles Ca 90036.

GOODMAN, HELEN (CRELL). b NYC 14 N 20. 4: Paul W Goodman. 5: Queens Col 43-47 (Econ) BA; Pratt 47-48 BLS. 6: Sp, Ger. 7: Asst libn bus & labor serv Akron Pub Lib, Akron Ohio 48-49; Ref asst El Paso Pub Lib, El Paso Tex 50-52; Head Post Lib William Beaumont Army Hosp, Ft Bliss Tex 52-54; Head order dept El Paso Pub Lib, El Paso Tex 58-63 Catlg asst libn UColo Libs 63-66; Acquis libn El Paso Pub Lib, El Paso Tex 66-. 9: ALA; TexLA; Border Reg LA. 10: Hadassah Bus & Prof Group; AAUP; LWV; Nat Coun Jewish Women. 11: Fourth Army Publ Award, 53. 12: Program Notes for El Paso Symphony (50-52). 13: Yes. 14: Catlg (Span, Portu & Ger), ref, readers adv, publ. 15: 408 Chermont dr, El Paso Tx 79912.

GOODMAN, LAURA (ROSENBLUM). b Brooklyn NY 1 My 21. 4: Roger B Goodman. 5: Brooklyn Col 40-42, 46-48 (Educ) BA; Pratt 59-62 MLS. 7: Elem tchr Bd of Educ, Brooklyn NY 50-62, Tchr of lib 62-. 9: NY Lib Club; NY City Sch Libns Assn (rec sec 65-67). 15: 2005 Pearson st, Brooklyn NY 11234.

GOODMAN, MARCIA BENAY. b NYC 7 Ap 44. 5: Harpur Col SUNY 61-65 (Eng, Gen Lit) BA; Syracuse 65-67 MLS. 6: Ger. 7: Lib intern SUNY (Binghamton) 66, Asst libn (Catlg) 67-. 9: ALA; -ACRL (Internat Rel Com 69); Assn of Libns SUNY, Binghamton (sec, mem Bylaws Com). 10: Ad hoc Com for a Free Univ, SUNY (Binghamton). 11: Beta Phi Mu. 14: Technical Services (mainly cataloging); Computerization. 15: RD 3, Windsor NY 13865.

GOODMAN, MARIE CLECKNER. b Harrisburg Penn 23 F 24. 4: Thomas A Goodman. 5: Notre Dame(Md) 43-45 (Fr, Span) BA; West Res 46-47 BSLS; George Washington U Law Sch 48-50; American U 47-48 (Geog). 6: Fr, Sp. 7: Lib asst US Supt Documents, Wash DC 45-47; Lib asst Case Inst Tech 46-47; LC; Catlgr 47-48, Acquis asst 48-51, Head acquis sect map div 51-56; Chief libn Off of Geog Interior, Wash DC 56-59; Volunteer libn St Pius X Lib, Wash DC 59-; Free lance ed Indexing Research, Wash DC 59-; Libn DC Pub Schs 67-. 9: SLA (Geog & Map Div; var offs in Div & DC Chap); ALA; CathLA; Assn Amer Geogr; DCLA; DCASchL. 10: Chevy Chase Commun Coun; Girl Scout Leader; PTA; Kenwood Country Club; Delta Epsilon Sigma; ACLU. 11: Honors Award, 55, SLA (Geog & Map Div). 12: "Map Collections in US & Canada (54): Ed SLA Geog & Map Div "Bulletin (52-58). 13: Yes. 14: Acquis, admin, ref. 15: 3259 Van Hazen st NW, Wash DC 20015.

GOODPASTURE, ANN W. b Nashville Tenn. 5: Vanderbilt 49-53 (Hist) AB; Peabody Col 64-65 MLS. 7: Tchr Davidson Co Bd of Educ, Nashville 53-61; Tchr US Army Dependents Schs, Germany 61-63; Period libn Peabody Col 65-67; Libn Metro Bd of Educ, Nashville 67-. 9: ALA; NEA; TennLA; TennEA; MTEA. 14: Child lit. 15: 4501 Granny White Pike, Nashville Tn 37204.

GOODRICH, JAMES RALPH. b Toledo Ohio 12 S 27. 4: Helen Kruk. 5: UToledo 47-50 (Biol) BS (cum laude); Rutgers 59-60 MLS. 7: Army Engnrs clerk T/5, Japan 46-47; Asst ref libn Summit Pub Lib, Summit NJ60-61; Adult serv libn Somerville Pub Lib, Somerville NJ 61-63; Bkmob libn Ramapo Catskill Lib System, Middletown NY 63-64; Ref libn State U Col (New Paltz NY) 64-; Assoc libn Reader Servs 67-. 9: NYLA. 10: Phi Kappa Phi; ACLU. 14: Ref. 15: 5 Brewster dr, Middletown NY 10940.

GOODRICH, MARGARET. b Cheyenne Wyo 5 D 09. 5: UWyo 27-31 (Geol) BA; Columbia 31-32 BLS. 7: Libn Carbon Co Pub Lib, Rawlins Wyo 37-41; Spec Serv libn US Army: Ft F E Warren Wyo 41-45, Germany 45-47, Ft Dix NJ 47-51; Libn John D Rockefeller Jr Off, NYC 51-54; Dir W Tex Amer Heritage Proj ALA, Lubbock Tex 54-55; Ref libn Lubbock Pub Lib, Lubbock Tex 55-57; Staff Denver Pub Lib 57-62; Post libn US Army Fitzsimmons Gen Hosp, Denver 62-66; Post libn US Army Ft Sam Houston, San Antonio Tex 66-68; Field dist cr US Army LibsVietnam 68-. 8: Colo Governors Commsn on Status of Women, 65. 9: ALA-AHIL (Coun 65-69); LPRC (treas 49-51); AEA; WyoLA (pres 4041); ColoLA; TexLA. 10: DAR; PEO; Pi Beta Phi; Bus & Prof Womens Club; Zonta Internat. 14: Pub libs, rare bks. 15: 1255 Ash st, Denver Colo 80220.

GOODRUM, CHARLES A. b Pittsburg Kan 21 Jl 23. 4: Donna Mueller. 5: UWichita 41-43, 45-46 (Amer Hist) BA; Princeton 43-44 (Chem); Columbia 48-49 (LS) MA. 7: US Army 43-45; Head circ UWichita 46-48; Ref lbn Legis Ref Serv LC 49-50, Pol sci Bibliog 50-53, Leg ref serv libn 53-62, Asst to deputy dir 62, Coordinator of research 62-. 9: SLA; DCLA. 10: . 11: Joseph Towne Wheeler Award Columbia U 49. 12: "I'll Trade You An Elk" (67). 13: Yes. 14: Ref. 15: Legis Ref Serv LC, Wash DC 20540.

GOODSTEIN, LILLIAN (SCHER). b Chicago 28 S 14. 4: Hyman A Goodstein. 5: Port Huron Jr Col 32-34 AA; UChicago 34-36 (Soc Studies) BA; UDenver 48-49 MALS. 7: Tchr Port Huron (Mich) High Sch 37-42; WAC T/4 Stark Gen Hosp, Charleston SC 42-45; Tchr Port Huron (Mich) High Sch 45-46, Libn 46-47; Lib Instr UDenver summer 49; Libn Colo State Dept of Health, Denver 50-51; Libn Mapleton High Sch, Denver 57-. 8: NDEA Inst Sch Libns 66; Denver NDEA Inst,Multi-media instr, Greeley Colo 69. 9: NEA; Colo EA; Adams Co (Colo) SchLA (chm 60-63); Mapleton EA (pres 64-65). 10: Dolls for Democracy; BNai BRith Women; Writers Club. 14: Sch libs. 15: 1931 Eudora st, Denver Colo 80220.

GOODWELL, NANCY (JOAN). b Indianapolis Ind 4 O 46. 5: Col of Wooster 64-68 (Hist, Sp) BA; Columbia 68-69 MSLS. 6: Sp. 7: Bus libn Northwestern U 69-. 9: ALA. 10: Sigma Delta Pi; Phi Alpha Theta. 14: Ref, bus. 15: 6977 N Ashland "E", Chicago Il 60626.

GOODWELL, ROBERT CHESTER. b Valporaiso Ind 11 Ag 24. 4: Mary Marguerite Vant. 5: IndU 50 (Comparative Lit)

AB; Syracuse 51 MSLS. 7: Cpl Army Air Corps 43-46; Asst div hd NYC Pub Lib 51-55; Asst dir Riverside Pub Lib, Riverside Cal 55-59; Chief libn Alhambra Pub Lib, Alhambra Cal 59-64; Asst co libn Los Angeles Co Pub Lib Syst 64-. 9: CalLA (pres Pub Lib Div; Lib Devel & Standards Com). 10: Rotary Club. 12: Assoc ed "New York Library Association Bulletin" (53-55). 13: Yes. 14: Lib admin, bldgs, data proc, a-v. 15: 1812 Meridian ave, Alhambra Ca 91803.

GOODWIN, DIANE. b Chicago Ill 22 Jl 39. 5: De Paul U 57-58; Thornton Jr Col 58-59; No Ill U 59-61 (Elem Educ) BS in Educ; Immaculate Heart Col 67-68 MLS. 7: Elem tchr bd of Educ, Harvey Ill 61-64; Elem tchr DOD Dependent's Sch: Okinawa 64-65, Germany 65-66; Elem libn El Segundo Unified Sch Dist, El Segundo Cal 68-. 9: ALA; CalASchL; CalTA. 14: Elem sch libs. 15: 409 21st st, Manhattan Beach Ca 90266.

GOODWIN, GEORGE HAMILTON JR. b Ware Mass 30 N 24. 4: Barbara Doore. 5: Iowa State Col 46-48 (Eng); Syracuse 48-51 (Eng, Hist) AB, 51-52 MSLS. 7: (SGT) US Army, US 43-46; Smithsonian Inst, Wash DC: Libn dept 52-54, Catlgr 54-56, Act head catlg sect 56-58; Asst libn tech serv State Col (New Paltz NY) 58-60; Libn Amer Museum of Natural Hist, NYC 60-68; Assoc dir dept & div libs UMass, Amherst Mass 68; Chief libn US Geol Survey Lib, Wash DC 13: Yes. 14: Bibliog. 15: US Geol Survey Lib, Rm 1033 GSA Bldg 18th F st NW, Wash DC 20242.

GOODWIN, GEORGIE JEANNE. b Almyra Ark 12 Ap 28. 5: Ouachita Baptist Col 45-48 (Eng, Phys Educ) BA; Peabody summers 49-51, 53 (LS) MA. 7: Tchr-libn DeWitt High Sch, DeWitt Ark 48-50; Tchr-libn Collinston Sch, Collinston La 50-51; Libn Pensacola High Sch, Pensacola Fla 51-52; Libn Electronics Dept Industrial Manager 9 ND USN, Great Lakes Ill 52-53; Libn Stuttgart High Sch, Stuttgart Ark 53-55; Libn USAF Dependent Schs, Nagoya Japan 55-56; USAF Dependent Schs, Mildenhall Eng 56-57, Libn Wiesbaden Germany 57-59, Libn Clark Air Base, Philippine Islands 59-62; Dir of sch libs & tchg materials State Dept of Pub Instr, Indianapolis 63-66; Dir of ICCRC MSD Perry Twp, Indianapolis Ind 66-. 9: ALA; NEA-DAVI; IndLA; Ind State Tchrs Assn; IndSchLA. 10: AAUW. 13: Yes. 14: Sch libs. 15: Dir ICCRC, MSD Perry Township, 971 Banta rd, Indianapolis In 46227.

GOODWIN, JACK (SPENCER). b Oriental NC 1 O 28. 5: Col of William & Mary 46-50 (Eng) AB; Catholic U 54-56 (LS). 6: Fr. 7: A-v libn Col of William & Mary 50-51; Lib asst USDA Lib, Wash DC 51-52; US Army 52-54; Ref libn USDA Lib, Wash DC 54-58; Libn Museum of Hist & Tech Smithsonian Inst, Wash DC 58-. 8: Consul on bks, Bd of Regents, Gunston Hall (Home of George Mason), 62-. 9: Soc Hist of Tech; (chm bibliog com 64-); Soc Hist of Discoveries; AHA; Internat Coun of Museums; SLA (Wash DC Chap: treas 57-60, Convention treas 62, ch Museum Div 64-65); DCLA. 12: Ed SLA "Museum Division News 63-64; Comp current bibliography of the history oftechnology; pub annually in "Technology and Culture 64-. 13: Yes. 14: Admin, ref, bibliog. 15: 902 Massachusetts ave NE, Wash DC 20002.

GOODWIN, MARION L. b Goffstown NH 26 Ag 09. 5: Boston 27-31 (Lat) AB; Plymouth State Col 32-33 (Educ) Grad Certif; Simmons 39-40 BLS; Boston summers 55-58 (Elem Educ) M Ed; Simmons summer 65 (LS). 7: Sec & bkkeeper Clyde B Foss Insurance Agency, Moultonboro NH 34-39; Bkmob libn NH State Lib, Concord NH 40-43, Reg libn Littleton Br 43-48, Asst catlgr 48-50; Co-Libn Keene Tchrs Col 50-53; Chief Libn Keene State Col 53-; Hd libn Mt Anthony Union High Sch 66-. 9: ALA-ACRL; -AASchL; NEA; NHEA; NHSchLA; NELA; NESchLA (2nd v-pres 61-63); VtEA; VtLA; VtSchLA. 10: AAUW; AAUP; Simmons Col Club of NH. 14: Catlg, ref. 15: 106 Putnam st, Bennington Vt 05201.

GOODWIN, RICHARD BERLEW. b Sunbury Penn 19 Jl 31. 5: Kutztown State Col 49-53 (Art) BSAE; Drexel 64-67 MSLS. 6: Sp. 7: Art instr Johnson Jr High Sch, Stratford Conn 53-56; Lib asst Reading Pub Lib, Reading Penn 56-62, Bkmob libn 62-64; Bkmob libn Chester Co Lib, W Chester Penn 64-66, Hd tech serv 66-. 9: ALA; PennLA. 14: Catlg. 15: 615 Downingtown Pike, W Chester Pa 19380.

GORCHELS, CLARENCE CLIFFORD. b Oshkosh Wis 26 Ag 16. 4: Eugenia Hayes. 5: Wis State U (Oshkosh) 36-40 (Eng) BS; UWis 44-45 BLS; Columbia 51-52 (LS) MS; Wash State U 50-51 (Hist); Columbia 59-60 (LS). 6: Fr, Ger. 7: Various incl act asst dir of libs, Chief Tech Serv, Chief Readers Serv Wash State U 45-58; Visiting prof of libnship UWash 58-59; Assoc in lib serv Columbia U 59-60; Dir of libs Central Wash State Col 60-63; Dir of libs Cal State Col (Palos Verdes 63-66; Dir of libs Ore Col of Ed 66-. 8: Lib bldg adv UWash 59; Lib bldg consul Pacific Luth U 62; Consul for libs on new campuses, Cal State Cols 63; Consul on univ lib devel UTasmania, Hobart Australia 65-. 9: ALA (Coun 56-57, chm Stat Com 52-54 & 56-57, chm Budget Costs & Acctg Com 65-68); CAL Col Libns (sec 64-65); PNLA (v-chm 56); Wash State Higher Educ Libns (chm 62-63); WashLA (Exec Bd 61-63); OreLA (scholarship com). 10: AAUP; Kappa Delta Pi; Phi Alpha Theta; Kiwanis; Wash Governors com for Youth to Brussels 56-57; World Affairs Inst; City Beautifiation Com, Ellensburg Wash; Boy Scout Coun, Palos Verdes Estates Cal; lib bldg com Monmouth Ore; Rhodes Scholarship Trust Oreg Col 66-. 12: Ed "Foreshadow (57-61); Asst to ed "College and Research Liraries (59-62). 13: Yes. 14: Lib planning & devel, lib automation, lib bldgs, acquis of lib resources. 15: 342 Stadium dr S, Monmouth Or 97361.

GORDON, BARBARA (ALICE) B(INGHAM). b Wash Penn 21 O 24. 5: UMich 42-46 (Zool) AB, 62- (LS); 66 MALS. 7: Supv Child Zoo Belle Isle Detroit Zool Park Commsn 47-49; Museum Guide Cranbrook Inst of Sci, Bloomfield Hills Mich 51-52; Tech libn &Staff Biol Space/Defense Corp, Birmingham Mich 64-66; Sci libn Oakland U (Rochester Mich) 66-68; Ref libn Gen Motors Res Labs 68-. 9: SLA (treas; Mich Chap Recruitment chm 66-67; Hospitality Chm 1970 Conf). 10: LWV; Cranbrook Skating Club; Sierra Club; Soc Women Engrs; Marine Tech Soc; Parents Without Partners; Vols for Intl Tech Assistance. 13: Yes. 14: Sci & tech info (bioengring & oceanography). 15: General Motors Res Lab Lib, 12 Mile Mound rds, Warren Mi 48090.

GORDON, ELIZABETH. b London 20 Je 07. 5: Hunter Col 25-29 (Eng) AB; Queens Col (NY) 50-52 (LS). 7: Staff writer "Universal Jewish Encclopedia, NYC 34-39; Indexer "Americana Encyclopedia, NYC 42-44; Researcher, libn Francis S Bushman, NYC 49-53; Libn NY Acad of Med, NYC 55-57; Libn Labs for Pharmaceutical Development, NYC 60-63; Libn Beth Jacob Schs, NYC 63-65; Libn Newark Beth Israel Hosp, Newark NJ 65-. 9: SLA; MedLA; Composers, Authors and Artists of Amer (v-pre). 13: Yes. 14: Admin, ref, catlg, abstracting. 15: 10 Lehigh ave, Newark NJ 07112.

GORDON, GALVY EARL. b Indianapolis 30 Ja 25. 4: . 5: Butler U 41-42 (Chem Engnr); Ind U even 41-43 (Chem Engnr); UMo 43-44 (Mech Engnr); Ohio State U even 55-60 (Journalism). 6: Ger. 7: Jr chemist & bacter Indianapolis Water Co 42-43; US Army 43-45; Ed Mil Govt Report Allied Commsn, Austria Vienna 45-47; Reporter Indianapolis Times 47-50; Camp newspaper ed War Dept, Indiantown Gap Penn 50-52; Pub info Off Defense Dept Ft Haye, Columbus Ohio 52-53; Ed Hartley Newspapers, Columbus Ohio 53-55; PR Dir Columbus Pub Lib, Columbus Ohio 55-. 9: ALA-LAD (chm Pub Rel Sect 65-66); - ALTA (chm 64 St Louis Inst), OhioLA (Memb, Chm 69). 10: Adult Educ Coun of Greater Columbus; Columbus Film Coun; Hilltop Commun Coun, Columbus. 13: Yes. 14: Lib pub rel. 15: 215 S Huron ave, Columbus Ohio 43204.

GORDON, HAROLD DUNBAR. b Patchogue NY 20 N 19. 4: Sara Margaret Jones. 5: Wheaton Col (Wheaton Ill) 38-41, 47-48 (Pol Sci) BS; Duke 48-50 (Pol Sci) MA; Syracuse 52-53 (Pol Sci); Columbia 53-54 (LS) MS. 6: Fr. 7: US Naval Res Mine Warfare (Ensign) 41-44; Amer Airlines Traffic Dept, NYC 44-47; Instr Wheaton Col (Wheaton Ill) 50-52; Asst libn UMiami(Coral Gables Fla) 54-56; Admin asst to Dir Cornell U 56-58; Circ libn Columbia U 58-60; Asst dir UConn 60-65; Assoc dir UKy 65-, Act dir 68-. 8: Lib consul US Army Materials Research Agency Watertown Mass 65; Chm Ky Bd for Certif Libns 68-. 9: ALA; ConnLA; SELA; KyLA (chm Col & Ref Sect 66-68). 14: Circ, admin, mechanization. 15: UKy Lib, Lexington Ky 40506.

GORDON, HARRIET S. 4: David Gordon. 5: Central Mich U 60 (Soc Studies) BA; LIU 69 (LS) MS. 7: Libn Yonkers Pub Lib, Yonkers NY 67-. 9: WestchesterLA. 10: AAUW; Yonkers Staff Assn. 14: Ref, YA serv, admin. 15: 25 Black Birch lane, Scarsdale NY 10583.

GORDON, LUAN ELIZABETH. b Spokane Wa 21 F 32. 5: Immaculate Heart Col 61-65 (Eng) BA, 66 MALS. 7: Gen libn pub lib, Long Beach Cal 66-68, coord y-a serv 67-68, Br libn 68-. 10: Commun Welfare; Bouggess White Scholarship Found; Immaculate Heart Col Alumni. 14: Ya, films, a-v. 15: 3213 Marber, Long Beach Ca 90808.

GORDON, MARY JANE (VINCENT). b Winnipeg Can 2 S 41. 4: Ian A Gordon. 5: UManitoba 59-62 (Eng) BA; McGill 63-64 BLS. 6: Fr. 7: Catlgr UManitoba Libs 66-67, Educ Libn 67-. 9: CanLA; ManitobaLA. 15: Ed Lib Univ of Manitoba, Winnipeg 19 Manitoba Can.

GORDON, MAXWELL. b USSR 13 F 21. 4: Ethel Mayer. 5: Phila Col of Pharm & Sci 37-41 (Chem) BS; Polytech Inst of Brooklyn 41-42 (Organic Chem); UPenn 46-48 (Organic Chem) MS, PhD; EiTechnische Hochschule, Zurich 48-49 (Organic Chem); UCal(Berkeley) 49-50 (Organic Chem); Imperial Col (London) 50-51 (Organic Chem) DIC. 6: Ger, Fr. 7: US Navy 41-45, Capt USNR 69; Research assoc Squibb Inst for Med Research 51-55; Sr sci Smith Kline & French Labs, Phila 55-57; Head phys sci sect Sci Info Dept SK & F Labs, Phila 57-67; Assoc dir research activities Sci Info Dept SK&F 67-. 8: NRC/NAS Com on Modern Methods of Handling Chem Info; Subcom on Drug Info Program of Dept of HEW & NLM; Subcom on Compatibility of Chem Typewriters; Chm, Subcom on Economics and Planning. 9: ACS (chm loc sect com on abstracting & indexing 59-64, Alternate Coun); Mem Investment Bd of Trustees. 10: AID; ADI; Amer Pharmaceut So; Swiss Chem Soc; Chem Soc of London; Austrian Chem Soc; German Chem Soc; Pharmaceut Soc of Japan; External PhD Examiner UBombay. 12: Ed "Psychopharmacological Agents (64)67).1 13: Yes. 14: Chem documentation, computers in documentation, medicinal research. 15: 1500 Spring Garden st, Phila Pa 19117.

GORDON, NORMA S. b NYC 15 Ap 20. 4: Donald C Gordon. 5: Vassar 37-39; UNC 39-41 (Sociol) BA; Cath U 58-62 MS in LS. 6: Fr. 7: Soc Wkr Dept of Pub Welfare, Norfolk Va 41-42; Jr econ War Labor Bd, NYC 43-44; Assoc libn UMd 62-. 9: ALA-RSD; MdLA. 10: Phi Beta Kappa; Beta Phi Mu. 12: Co-ed "Fossil Finds in Maryland; a Retrospective Bibliography (67). 14: Ref. 15: 4201 Woodberry st, University Park Mo 20782.

GORDON, ROBERT S. b Tokyo 18 Ap 23. 4: Frances Marion Jacqueline Wilson. 5: McGill 48-52 (Hist) BA. 7: Archivist Public Archives of Can, Ottawa Ont 56-63, Sect head 63-65, Chief of mss div 65-. 9: Can Hist Assn (treas). 12: Ed "Union List of Manuscripts in Canadian Repositories. 13: Yes. 15: 244 Clemow ave, Ottawa 1 Ont Can.

GORDON, RUTH. b Hartford Conn 1 S 07. 5: Simmons 31 BSLS; Boston U Sch of Educ summer 43. 7: Child libn Pub Lib, Brooklyn NY 31-43; Ya libn Free Lib, Wilkes Barre Penn 43-44; Child libn Providence Pub Lib 44-45; Ya libn Free Lib, Wilkes Barre Penn 45-53; Lib Dir Farmington Free Lib, Farmington NY 53-56; Child libn Pub Lib, Phoenix 56-62, Br libn 62-. 9: ALA-YP & CD (Bd Dirs 49-51); NYLA; PennLA; ArizLA; Salt River LA (v-pres); ArizLA (sec 66-67). 10: Nat Bus & Prof Assn; Puppetry Guild of Phoenix. 13: Yes. 14: Child & ya serv, pub lib br operations. 15: 1915 E Campbell ave, Phoenix Az 85016.

GORDON, RUTH. b NY 12 O 31. 4: Jerome J Gordon. 5: CUNY (Queens Col) 49-53 (Anthrop, Sociol) BA; Immaculate Heart Col 65-68 MLS. 6: Sp. 7: Libn Mental Health Development Ctr, LA 68-. 9: SLA. 15: 3551 Meier st, Los Angeles Ca 90066.

GORDON, THOMAS FREDERICK JR. b Wilmington NC 7 Ag 45. 5: Duke 62-67 (Hist) AB; UNC (Chapel Hill) 67-69 MS in LS. 6: Lat. 7: Stud asst William R Perkins Lib DukeU 63-66, Stud asst Woman's Col Lib 66-67; Staff mem Louis R Wilson Lib UNC (Chapel Hill) 67-. 8: Pres lib sci club UNC (Chapel Hill) 68-69. 9: ALA. 10: Eta Sigma Phi. 14: Readers serv, ref. 15: 813 Burke st, Raleigh NC 27609.

GORDON, WILLIAM B. b Liberty Miss. 4: Eloise Bowlan Gordon. 5: Tulane U 48-50 (Eng) BA, 51 (Eng); LSU 51-52 BSLS. 6: Fr, Ger, Sp. 7: Sr transcriber Fed Communications Commsn, Wash DC 41-42; (Sgt) US Army Hq 10th Armored Div & Hq US Berlin Dist 42-45; Adjudication clerk Va, New Orleans 46-48; Ser catlgr Fla State U Lib 52-56; Head catlgr Col of William & Mary 56-57; Head ser dept UMo Lib 57-60; Head ser dept Johns Hopkins U 60-65; Hd tech serv Catonsville Commun Col (Md) 66-67; Hd sers dept Trenton State Col (NJ) 67-68; Hd sers dept USC (Columbia) 68-. 9: ALA.14. Ser, catlg. 10: Phi Kappa Phi; Beta Phi Mu. 14: Tech serv. 15: 1817 Senate st, Columbia SC 29201.

GORDON, WILLIAM BILL ROBERT. b Pratt Kan 24 S 36. 4: Joyce Gudenburg. 5: Baker U 54-55; Hutchinson Jr Col 55; Baker U 55-57, 59-60 (Sociol) BA; UKan 60-61 (Sociol); UDenver 61-62 (LS) MA; Ida State U 64-65 (Eng). 7: Asst libn Renton Pub Lib, Renton Wash 62-63; Head Libn Pocatello Pub Lib, Pocatello Ida 63-66; Dir SE Idaho Lib Agency Inc, Pocatello Ida 64-; Dir Arrowhead Lib Sys, Virginia Minn 66-. 9: ALA; PNLA; IdaLA (chm Pub Libs Div 65-66); MinnLA. 14: Admin. 15: 445 S 8th, Pocatello Ida 83201.

GORE, DANIEL JACK JR. b Wilmington NC 20 F 30. 5: UNC 47-51 (Eng) AB, 55-56 (Eng) MA, 58-59 (LS) MS. 6: Fr, Sp. 7: Lt jg US Coast Guard, New Orleans 52-54; Cost analyst Electrical Equipment Co, Raleigh NC 54-55; Eng instr UNC(Chapel Hill) 56-58; Catlgr Duke U 59-61; Catlgr NY Pub Lib 61-62; Asst libn Asheville-Biltmore Col 63-67; Lib dir McMurry Col 67-68; Coord of Pub Servs & Faculty senator West Mich U Libs 68-. 10: AAUP; Phi Beta Kappa Beta Phi Mu. 12: "Bibliography for Beginners, (68). 13: Yes. 14: Admin, catlg, tchg bibliog, lib censorship. 15: Asheville-Biltmore Col, Asheville NC 28801.

GOREN, MORTON S. b Chicago Ill 6 My 37. 4: Roberta Saferstein. 5: UColo 54-58 (Pol Sci) BA; UDenver 59 (Educ) 64-68 MALS; AmericanU 68- (Pub Admin). 7: Clk US Army, Germany 60-63; Grad lib asst UDenver 64-66; Spec recruit LC 66-67, Subject catlgr 67-. 8: Spec lib recr LC 66-67. 9: ASIS; DCLA. 14: Info sci. 15: 304 No Carolina ave SE, Washington DC 20003.

GOREN, SIMON L. b Gencs Hungary 9 N 13. 4: Hilda Feuerstein. 5: Law Classes of the British Mandatory Govt (Jerusalem Palestine) 41-48 Diploma of Law; Columbia 59-60 MS in LS. 6: Ger, Fr, Hungarian, Hebrew, Arabic. 7: Private law practice, Haifa Israel 51-59; Law Libn Cleary Gottlieb et al, NYC 60-64; Acquis 7 ref libn Cornell Law Lib 64-67; Law libn Member of the faculty of law Case West Res U Sch of Law 67-. 9: AALL; ALA; Law Libns Assn Greater NY Internat Assn of Law Libs. 10: Order of the Coif. 13: Yes. 14: Bk sel, ref, admin. 15: 507 Warren rd, Ithaca NY 14850.

GORLIN, CLAIRE (GAIDEMAK). b Newark NJ 30 Ja 25. 4: Jerome W Gorlin. 5: Montclair State Col 42-45 (Soc Studies) AB; Trenton State Col 59-62 Tchr-Libn Certif. 7: Libn Atlantic Highlands High Sch, Atlantic Highlands NJ 59-62; Libn Middletown Twp High Sch, Middletown NJ 62-. 9: ALA-AASchL; NEA; NJ SchLA; NJEA. 10: LWV; Kappa Delta Pi; Monmouth Co (NJ) Mental Health Assn; Rumson Co (NJ) Bd of Recreation Com; Shore Aquatic Club. 14: Bk sel, catlg. 15: 59 Bingham ave, Rumson NJ 07760.

GORMAN, EDITH. b Wentworth Mo. 5: Kan State Col (Pittsburg) 29-33 (Music) BS; Peabody 46-48 MALS, 55-56 MS in LS, 6th year degree. 6: Fr. 7: Asst libn Joplin Pub Lib, Joplin Mo 34-38; Libn Joplin Jr Col 38-38; Ref libn & Assc Prof Northwestern State Col (Alva Okla) 48-. 8: Visiting Instr Lib Sch Peabody 59; Okla Educ Assn Adv Coun; Chm & publicity chm, Sequoyah Childs Bk Award. 9: NEA; OklaLA (v-pres 58-59, chm Col Sect 58-60). 10: Delta Kappa Gamma; Sigma Alpha Iota; PEO; Kappa Delta P; Pi Sigma Mu. 12: "A Teaching Guide for School Library Administration" (57); Co-auth "A Check-Sheet for School-Home Encyclopedias". 14: Ref, admin, non-bk materials, govt docs. 15: 1141 8th st, Alva Ok 73717.

GORMAN, EVELYN (STEVENS). b Olean NY 31 Mr 22. 4: Warren E Gorman. 5: AlfredU 39-43 (Classical Lang) BA; Syracuse 58-66 (LS) MS. 6: Fr, classical Lat. 7: Libn Mfrs Assn of Syracuse, Syracuse NY 59-66; Subject analyst SUNY Biomed Communications network (Syracuse) 66-67; Acquis libn SUNY Upstate Med Ctr Lib (Syracuse) 67-. 9: MedLA; ALA. 10: AlfredU Alumni Assn; Beta Phi Mu. 14: Acquis. 15: 107 Albernaty st, Liverpool NY 13088.

GORMAN, SISTER MARY JOSEPH DC (MARY JANE). b Lynchburg Va 14 Ap 33. 5: St Joseph Emmitsburg Md 51-60 (Soc Studies) AB; St John'sU Jamaica NY 61-66 MLS; Va State Col 68. 7: Elem sch tchr Dioceses of Syracuse 54-66, Wash, Raleigh, Richmond; Tchr Diocese of Richmond, Petersburg Va 66-; Libn Gibbons High Sch, Petersburg Va 66-. 9: ALA; SELA; CathLA (co-chm Elem Sect Wash-Baltimore Unit 61-63, Richmond area rep Richmond Unit 67-69). 10: Nat Coun Tchrs Soc Studies; Human Rel Coun Va. 14: High sch lib, instr materials ctr. 15: 123 Franklin st Box 326, Petersburg Va 23803.

GORMLEY, MARK McGUIRE. b Superior Wis 4 N 24. 4: Margaret Joyce Dunn. 5: Wis State Col (Superior) 51 (Hist) BS; UDenver 54 MALS. 7: US Maritime Serv 42-43; US Navy Qtrmstr 2/c 43-46; Tchr-libn High Sch, Milltown Wis 51-53; Sr high sch libn, Janesville Wis 53-56; Asst to dir of libs Colo State U 56-58, Assr dir of libs, Assoc Prof of Lib Sci 58-61; Exec Sec ALA-ACRL 61-62; Prof, Dir, U Archivist UWis Lib (Milwaukee) 62-. 8: Visiting Prof Grad Sch of Libnship UDenver, summers 62, 65; Grad Sch Lib SciState U Col (Geneseo) summer 68; Grad Sch Lib & Info Sci UWis (Milwaukee) 68, 69;Acad Lib Survey Activities; 4 confs 62-65; 4 lib surveys 61-69; Lib bldg consul;8 cols & univs 65-68. 9: ALA (Life mem Publ Bd 67); -ACRL (Life mem, mem &/or

chm Com on Grants 62-65, Publ Com 63-69, Com on Standards 66-68, Urban Univs Lib Com 66-67); ColoLA(pres 59-60; Exec Bd 58-61); NMA; WisStateLA. 10: Denver U Sch Libnship Alum Assn; Lib Associates UWis (Milwaukee). 12: "The Sioux Falls College Library: A Survey, with Ralph H Hopp (61). 13: Yes. 14: Acquis, catlg, automated techniques in tech serv. 15: 4764 N Ardmore ave, Milwaukee 53217.

GORMLEY, MARY THERESA. b Oak Park Ill. 5: Mundelein Col 49 (Chem) BS; Rosary Col 66-69 MALS. 7: Amer Can Co; Chemist Maywood Ill, Tech libn Barrington Ill 65-. 9: ACS; SLA. 10: Beta Phi Mu. 15: American Can Co Research Center, 433 N Northwest pkwy, Barrington Il 60010.

GORNELL, CLAIRE. b NYC 2 S 13. 5: Hunter Col 30-36 (Fr) BA; CatholicU 47 (LS). 7: Correspondence clk Macfadden Publ, NYC 32-42; Statistics War Prod Bd, Wash DC 42-45; Catlgr LC 45-67, Supv libn (catlg) 67-. 14: Catlg. 15: 1650 Harvard st NW, Washington DC 20009.

GOROKHOFF, BORIS I(VANOVITCH). b NYC 2 Jl 17. 5: Yale 35-39 (Eng) BA; Drexel 41-42 BSLS. 6: Russ, Polish, Bulgarian, Fr, Ger. Ital. 7: Ed asst "Scientific Monthly, Wash DC 39-41; Contract negotiator US War Dept, Springfield Mass 42-45; Catlgr Yale U Lib 46-50; Catlgr Slavic Langs Sect Descr Catlg Div LC 50-51, Slavic ref libn 51-52, Head Slavic Langs Sect 52-57, Area Spec (USSR) Ref Dept 57-60; Lib fellow in Soviet Lit MIT 60-67; Hd Slavic Langs Sect Shared Catlg Div LC 67-. 8: Research grants from Nat Research Coun (52); Coun on Lib Resources (57); Nat Sci Found (60); Dept of Health Educ & Welfare (62). 9: ALA; SLA; ADI. 12: "Materials for the Study of Soviet Specialized Education (52); "Publishing in the USSR (59); "Proposals for the Transliteration of Church Slavic (60); "Technical Information in the USSR, transl from the Russian (61); "List of Russian Scientific Journals Available in English (61); "Providing US Scientists with Soviet Scientific Information (62); "Languag Development in the Soviet Union (63); "Transliteration of Non-Slavic Languages Written in the Russian Alphabet (65). 13: Yes. 14: Soviet info retrieval, libs, publ catlg. 15: Box 8841, Wash DC 20003.

GORSKI, LORRAINE K M. b Irvington NJ 6 Ja 21. 5: NJ Col for Women 48 (LS) BA; Columbia 51 (LS) MS. 7: Page to sr lib asst Irvington (NJ) Pub Lib 39-43; USMC (Sgt) 43-46; Reg libn Vt Free Pub Lib Commsn, Rutland Vt 48-50; Prin libn to asst lib dir serv to child & schs E Orange (NJ) Pub Lib 51-. 9: NJLA; NJSchLA. 12: "ABC Classification for Children Using School and Public Libraries (58). 13: Yes. 14: Child serv, catlg, ref. 15: 188 Glenwood ave, East Orange NJ 07017.

GOSHKIN, IDA. b Russia 3 Jl 02. 5: UWis 24 (Eng) BA; Columbia 40 (LS). 6: Russ. 7: Catlgr Racine Pub Lib, Racine Wis 27-29; Catlgr Akron Pub Lib, Akron Ohio 30-41, Adult educ 41-43, Coordinator of Group Serv 43-67; Tchg West Res Lib (Cleveland) 63; Tchg Kent State Lib Sch 64-; Tchg UIll 68; Tchg Cornell U Ext 68-. 8: Dir of Train, Amer Heritage Proj, ALA 51-53. 9: ALA-ASD (pres 57-58); OhioL (chm Intel Freedom Com). 11: Brotherhood Award 59. 13: Yes. 14: Adult educ. 15: 185 West End ave apt 3S, New York NY 10023.

GOSLING, WILLIAM ARTHUR. b Newport RI 13 Ja 43. 5: Bates Col 61-65 (Hist) BA; UPittsburgh 65-66 MLS. 6: Fr. 7: Page Barrington Pub Lib, Barrington RI 57-64; Stud asst Bates Col Coram Lib 63-65; Asst art & mus Providence Pub Lib, Providence RI 65; Recruit trainee LC 66-67, Catlgr mss sect descr catlg 69-; Supply clk (Sp/5) US Army, Vietnam 67-68. 10: Beta Phi Mu. 14: Acad, ref, admin. 15: Apt 3 408 New Jersey ave SE, Washington DC 20003.

GOSNELL, CHARLES F(RANCIS). b Rochester NY 7 Jl 09. 4: Helen Kuhlman. 5: URochester 26-30 (Gk) AB; Columbia 31-32 (LS) BS, 32-37 (LS) MS; NYU 37-43 (Statistics) PhD. 6: Sp, Portu, Ger, Fr. 7: Asst URochester Lib 27-31; Spec correspondent "Rochester Democrat Chonicle, Rochester NY 28-31; Ref asst NY Pub Lib 32-37; Libn & Assoc Prof Queens Col (NY) 37-45; Assoc Columbia U Sch of Lib Serv 43-47; State Libn & asst commsnr of educ NY State Lib SUNY (Albany) 45-62; Dir of Libs & Prof of Lib Admin NYU 62-. 8: Consul on libs, UMadrid Spain 34; Hd, US Del to UNESCO Conf on Lib Serv, Sao Paulo Brasil 51; Hd, Survey of UNESCO Pilot Pub Lib, Medellin Colombia 59; Consul to Ford Found on lib educ in Brasil, & Chm of Adv Comm to UBrasilia 63-; Consul, Interamer Devel Bank 66. 9: ALA (Coun, Exec Bd); -LAD (past pres); -AAStateL (past pres); CNLA (past chm); Nat Fire Prot Assn (Com on Lib & Museum); Illum Engrg Soc (Com on Lib Lighting); NYLA (pres). 10: Grolier Club NY; Trustee, Skidmore Sec, Pub Affairs Info Serv Inc. 11: SAR Good Citizenship Gold Medal; Royal Soc of Arts, Benjamin Franklin Fellow. 12: "Spanish Personal Names (38); "Obsolescence of Books in College Libraries (44); "New York State Freedom Train (50). 13: Yes. 14: Rare bks, lib bldgs, copyright. 15: 11 Orchard circle, Suffern NY 10901.

GOSNELL, JAMES HAMILTON. b Lansdowne Penn 10 Ag 30. 4: Lois Gemmer. 5: St Lawrence U 48-50 (liberal Arts); Fla State U 55-58 (Ind Arts) BS, 55-58 (AV Educ) MS; Millersville State Col summers 59-62 (LS). 7: Instr-Instrument Flying USAF (Staff Sg) 50-54; Asst libn & dir a-v serv The Hill Sch, Pottstown Penn 58-67, Dir lib & a-v serv 67-. 9: NEA-DAVI PennLA. 10: Boy Scouts, YMCA. 14: A-v instr & materials, admin. 15: Hill School, Pottstown Pa 19464.

GOSS, DOROTHY (KNAPP). b Canton Ohio 2 D 19. 4: Jonathan Carver Goss. 5: AlfredU 38-39 (Liberal Arts); McMasterU 39-40 (Liberal Arts); UToronto 40-41 (Fine Arts); Masters Sch 41-42 (Fine Arts). 7: Supv tech info serv Ramo Woodbridge Corp, Los Angeles 54-61; Sr lit analyst & libn Aerospace Corp, Los Angeles 61-64; Admin libn NASA West Support Off, Santa Monica Cal 64-68; Sr libn Lockheed Co, Los Angeles 68; Libn Rand Corp, Santa Monica Cal 68-. 8: Lectr State Tech Serv Act Program 67. 9: SLA. 12: "DCAS Science Abstracts" (61-63). 14: Catlg, ref. 15: 12421 Rochedale lane, Los Angeles Ca 90049.

GOSS, JO ANN (FLATTERY). b Cleveland 28 Mr 29. 4: Robert Jackson. 5: Otterbein 48-50 (Sociol, Speech) GA; SUNY(Geneseo) 64 MLS. 7: Libn Spencerport Central Sch, Spencerport NY 65-67; Libn World of Inquiry Sch, Rochester NY 67-. 15: 164 Augustine st, Rochester NY 14613.

GOSSAGE, WAYNE. b Bellingham Wash 13 Je 26. 4: Grace Villella. 5: UWash 43-47 (Psych) BS; Columbia 50-51 MLS; Columbia U Tchrs Col 64-69, (Higher Educ Admin) MA. 6: Fr, Ger. 7: Asst head of adult serv E Orange Pub Lib, E Orange NJ 51-54; Head of adult serv Levittown Pub Lib, Levittown NY 54-55; Dir Warner Lib, Tarrytown NY 56-63; Dir Finkelstein Mem Lib, Spring Valley NY 63-64; Asst to libn Tchrs Col Lib Columbia U 64-67; Dir Bank St Col of Educ Lib, NYC 67-. 14: Lib admin, ref. 15: 382 W Clinton ave, Irvington NY 10533.

GOSSELIN, JEAN-LOUIS. b Masson Que Can 1 Ja 35. 5: Petit Sem DOttawa 50-57 BA; Grand Sem DOttawa 57-61 BTheol; UDOttawa 63-64 BLS High sch asst 68. 6: Fr, Eng. 7: Prof High Sch, Petit Seminaire, Ottawa 61-65 Pretre spiritual guidance 61-65; Asst libn high sch & col libs, Ottawa 61-63, Chief libn 63-68; Asst libn Pavillon Des 13 annees, Ottawa 69-. 9: CanLA; Association canadienne des bibliothecaires de langue francaise. 14: Catlg, clsf. 15: 1245 ave Kilborn, Ottawa 8 Ont Can.

GOTHBERG, HELEN M (BURKE). b Casper Wyo 5 Ap 30. 5: UColo 48-51, 54, 56 (Eng Lit)BA; UCal(Berkeley) summer 59-62 MLS. 6: Sp, Portu. 7: Catlgr Natrona Co Pub Lib, Casper Wyo 56-62; Libn C Y Jr High Sch, Casper Wyo 62-68; Hd libn Central Wyo Col, Riverton 68-. 9: ALA; ClrTA; WyoLA (pres 69-70, chm Intel Freedom Com 65-66); WyoASchL(v-pres 64-66); WyoEA; MPLA. 10: Phi Beta Mu. 13: Yes. 14: Catlg, wk with yp, organ of new libs. 15: 302 Antelope dr, Riverton Wy 82501.

GOTHE, ARTHUR G. b Eugene Ore 18 Mr 41. 5: Ventura Col 59-61 (Psych) AA; UCal (Santa Barbara) 61-63 (Psych) BA; UCal (Berkeley) 64 MLS. 7: Ref libn Fresno State Col 65-. 14: Ref. 15: 1311 Pollasky apt G, Clovis Ca 93612.

GOTHIE, DANIEL LLOYD. b Lewisburg Penn 3 O 36. 4: Katya Shoemaker. 5: Princeton 54-58 (Eng) BA; UVa 62-64 (Marketing) MBA; Columbia 68-69 (LS) MS. 6: Sp, Fr. 7: Lt US Army USNAB, Little Creek Va 59-62; Account exec Compton Advertising Inc, NYC 64-66; V-pres Peterson's Guides Inc, Princeton NJ 66-67; Libn Grad Sch of Bus Admin UVa (Charlottesville) 69-. 9: ALA; SLA; VaLA. 10: Omicron Delta Kappa. 13: Yes. 14: Lib admin, info retr. 15: 105 Bennington ct, Charlottesville Va 22901.

GOTLIEB, HOWARD BERNARD. b Bangor Me 24 O 26. 5: George Washington U 44-46, 47-49 (Hist) BA; Columbia 49-50 (Hist) MA; Georgetown U 50 (Hist); London Sch of Econ 51 (ist); Oxford U 51-53 (Hist) PhD. 6: Fr, Sp. 7: US Army (Signal Corps) 45-47; Lib asst Worcester Pub Lib, Worcester Mass 55; Ref asst Yale U Lib 55-56, Libn of Hist Mss 56-63, Libn of Edward M House Collection 56-63, U Archivist 62-63; Chief of ref & spec collections Boston U Libs 63-66, Chief of spec collections 66-, Adjunct Prof of Hist 69-. 9: SAA; AHA. 12: "William Beckford (60). 13: Yes. 14: Ref, spec collections, mss, rare bks. 15: 322 Beacon st, Boston Ma 02116.

GOTLOBE, JACK LAWRENCE. b York Penn 27 N 21. 5: Temple 41-43, 46-49 (Secondary Educ) BS; Boston Col 43 (Lang Area) Certif; UBiarritz (AUC) 46 (Lang) Certif; UMexico 48 Lang) Certif;Drexel 53-54 (LS) MS. 6: Sp, Ital, Fr. 7: US Army Infantry (Cpl) 43-46; Head libn Curtis Inst of Music (Phila) 54-61; Documents libn UPenn Biddle Law Lib 61-65; Libn Community Col of Phila 65-. 9: MusLA (pres Phila Chap); ALA; PennLA (Com mem Jr Col Sect; Col & Ref Div; chm Prog Com East Div). 14: Admin, ref, lib educ, info sci, govt docs. 15: Commun Col of Phila, Phila Pa 19107.

GOTT, JOHN KENNETH. b Alexandria Va 12 Je 29. 5: Bridgewater Col 46-50 (Hist) AB; Madison Col summer 50, 51 (LS); Catholic U 52-53 MS in LS. 6: Sp. 7: Libn Luray High Sch, Luray Page Co Va 50-52; Archivist Va State Lib 55-56; (Cpl) clerk Chem Corps Sch US Army, Ft McClellan Ala 53-55; Asst libn Falls Church High Sch, Falls Church Va 56-58, Libn 58-59; Libn JEB Stuart High Sch, Falls Church Va 59-62; Asst supv sch libs, Fairfax Co (Va) Schs 62-68; Libn Langley High Sch, McLean Va 68-. 9: NEA; VaLA (v-pres); VaEA (Lib Sect); ASchL, Fairfax Co (Va); FairfaxEA (Bd Dirs). 10: Va Baptist Hist Soc; Fauquier Co (Va) Hist Foun, Fairfax Co Hist Preserv Comsn. 12: "The Lake Family of Virginia (53); "A History of Marshall (Formerly Salem) Fauquier County Va(59); "Fauquier County, Virginia (1759-1959) (59); "The Years of Anguish, Fauquier County, Va 1861-1865 (65); "Fauquier County, Va Marriage Bonds, 1759-1854 (65) "History of Long Branch Baptist Church, Fauquier County Va, 1787-1967(67). 13: Yes. 14: Ref, sel, bibliog, rare bks. 15: P O Box 107, Marshall Va 22115.

GOTTESMAN, MURIEL (SCHIFRIN). b Brooklyn NY 18 F 23. 4: Elihu Gottesman. 5: CUNY (Hunter Col) 39-43 (Pre-med) BA; C W Post Col LIU 62-68 MLS. 7: Chem Endo Labs Inc, Garden City NY 43-51; Ed asst Chancery House Publ NYC 49-52; Libn Union Free Sch Dist #5, Levittown NY 65-. 9: ALA. 15: 148 Mead ct, Wantagh NY 11793.

GOTTSCHALK, CHARLES M. b Germany 2 F 28. 4: Marianne Besser. 5: Fenn Col 48-50 (Physics, Eng) BES; Penn State U 50-51 (Germanic Lang, Lit) MA; George Washington U 54-56 (Engnr Mgt); Catholic U 60-66 MS in LS. 6: Ger, Fr, Dutch. 7: US Army T/5, Korea 46-47; US Marine Corps Res (Cpt) 47-49; Research analyst LC 51-54; Physicist Nat Bur of Standards, Wash DC 54-56; LC: Head Ref Sect Sci-Tech Div 56-61, Chief Stack & Reader Div 61-62, Head Systems Analysis Sect 62-63; Off asst dir for systems development USAEC, Wash DC 63-66, Dir libs 66-68; Sr off Intl Atomic Energy Assn, Vienna 69-. 8: Consul, Arctic Bibl of N Amer, 56-61; Research assoc Ohio State U, 58-60; Exec sec Cosati Operating Com, 64; Exec sec Cosati Panel on Educ & Train, 65-66; Mem Nuclear Cross Sections Adv Com to AEC, 64-; Chm Fed Lib Com Task Force on Role of Libs in Lib Syst 67-69. 9: SLA (chm Nucl Sci Sect); ASIS; ACM; AmerPhysSoc; ANS. 10: AAAS; N Amer Mensa; Phi Beta Kappa; ASM; NY Acad of Sci; Phi Beta Mu. 12: Ed "SIPRE Bibliography" (52-54); Contrib Amer Inst of Phys "Handbook" (63); Contrib "Arctic Bibliography" (56-61). 13: Yes. 14: Computer storage & retrieval, physics, nuclear sci, ref, intl info sci, syst design & analysis. 15: Intl Atomic Energy Agcy, Vienna Austria.

GOUDY, FRANCES L. b Risingsun Ohio 3 Ag 21. 5: Findlay Col 40-42 (Hist); UMich 42-45 (Hist) AB & MA, 53 MALS; NorthwesternU 46-48 (Hist). 6: Fr. 7: Ref libn Grosvenor Lib, buffalo NY 54-56; Ref libn Ohio Hist Soc, Columbus 56-59; Libn Grove City Col 59-62; Acquis libn Lafayette Col 62-63; Ref libn Ga State Col 63-65; Spec collections libn Vassar Col 65-. 9: AHA. 14: Rare bks, mss, archives, ref. 15: 142 College ave, Poughkeepsie NY 12603.

GOUGH, CAROLYN (HARLEY). b Paterson NJ 23 S 22. 4: George Harrison Gough. 5: William & Mary 39-43 (Hist) BA; Drexel 63-66 MS in LS. 6: Fr. 7: Research asst Young & Rubicam, NY 43-44; Serv rep NJ Bell Tel, Ridgewood NJ 46-47; Lib dir Cabrini Col 66-. 9: ALA-ACRL; CathLA. 10: Beta Phi Mu; Questers Inc; Freedoms Found Com. 14: Admin, catlg. 15: 532 Timber lane, Devon Pa 19333.

GOULD, ANNA MARIE (BOSELY). b Sutton WVa 9 mr 40. 4: Allan Robert Gould. 5: Alderson Broaddus Col 58-59; WVaU 59-62 (LS, Eng) BA; UIll 62-63 MLS. 6: Fr. 7: Lib intern WVa State Lib summers 61-62; Br coord Douglas Co Lib,Roseburg Ore 63-66, 67-; Eugene Pub Lib, Eugene Ore 66-67. 9: ALA; PNLA; OreLA. 10: Phi Beta Kppa. 14: Larger units of serv, ref, bkmble. 15: 303 SE Oak st apt 16, Roseburg Or 97470.

GOULD, DANA G. b Mobile Ala 31 Jl 36. 4: Betty Neese. 5: Spring Hill Col 56-60 (Hist) BS; LSU 64-66 (LS) MS. 7: 1st Lt USA Transportation Corps 60; Br mgr 1st Fed Savings & Loan, Mobile Ala 61-62; Job interviewer Ala State Employment Serv, Mobile 62-64; Libn Patrick Henry Jr Col 66-67; Acquis libn U S Ala 67-. 9: ALA; AlaLA. 10: Beta Phi Mu. 14: Acquis. 15: 1018 W Woodside dr, Mobile Al 36608.

GOULD, THEODORE F(REDERICK). b Alameda Cal 11 Ag 27. 4: Marilyn Curryer. 5: UCal(Berkeley) 45, 46-50 (Eng) AB, 50-51 (Eng), 51-52 BLS. 7: Storekeeper 3/c US Navy 45-46; Libn I circ dept Pasadena Pub Lib, Pasadena Cal 52-53, Libn I ref dept 53-54; Libn I ya libn in a br lib Free Lib of Phila 54-55, Libn II head br lib 55-56; UCal Lib (Berkeley): Asst in admin 56-57, Bibliog acquis dept 57, Head gift div, acquis dept 57-59; Head loan dept 59-63; Asst libn pub serv UCal Lib (Davis) 63-68, Ref libn 68-. 9: ALA; PennLA 54-5; CalLA (chm No Div of Col Univ & Res Libs Sect 61-62; pres Golden Empire Dit 65-66). 13: Yes. 14: Ref serv, collection devel. 15: 826 Linden lane, Davis Cal 95616.

GOULT, VIRGINIA B(OYD). b Decorah Iowa. 4: Philip S Goult. 5: Clarke Col 26-30 (Eng) AB; De Paul U 36-41 (Eng) AM; Chicago 48 BLS. 6: Fr. 7: Libn De Paul U 31-67-; Dir of the Lib. 9: ALA; CathLA; IllLA. 10: Chicago Park Dist Jr Achievement Com. 12: "Catalog of the Napoleon Library of De Paul University". 14: Ref, admin. 15: 25 E Jackson blvd, Chicago Il 60604.

GOURLEY, JANET (WILHELMINA) (HELLER). b Lowell Mass 16 O 31. 4: Hugh James Gourley III. 5: Pembroke 49-53 (Fr) BA; Simmons 56-57 (LS) MS. 6: Fr. 7: Messenger Wm H Hall Free Lib, Edgewood RI 43-53; Merchandise trainee Gladdings Inc, Providence 53-54; Lib trainee & gen asst Providence Pub Lib 54-56; Catlgr Yale U Lib 57-59; Child libn Providence Pub Lib 59-61, Asst br libn 62; Child libn Elmwood Pub Lib, Providence 63- Libn Albert Church Brown Lib, China Me 66-. 9: ALA; RILA (chm Recruiting Com 63-64, corr sec 64-65); MeLA; NELA (By-Laws Com 67-68). 10: AAUW; Colby Col; Friends of Art; Child Prog; Thayer Hosp Auxil. 14: Child wk. 15: Box 33, China Me 04926.

GOVAN, JAMES F. b Chattanooga Tenn 9 My 26. 4: Ann Bright. 5: U of the South 44-48 (Hist) BA; Emory 52-53, 55 (LS) MA; Johns Hopkins 48-51, 60 (Hist) PhD; Inst of Hist Research ULondon 51-52 (Hist. 6: Fr, Ger. 7: US Navy 44-46; US Army 53-55; Asst prof U of the South summer 49; Pub serv libn UAla 55-61; Libn & Prof Hist Trinity U (San Antonio Tex) 61-65; Libn Swarthmore Col 65-, Lectr hist 69-. 9: ALA (chm AASchL/ACRL Com on Instr & Use of Libs 68-, chm Liaison Com with Educ &Profess Orgs 68-); Delaware Valley ACRL (dir 66-69); PennLA (chm Intel Freedom Com68-69). 10: Phi Beta Kappa; Beta Phi Mu. Philobiblon Club (Phila); Bd dirs Penn Union Lib Catlg; Archons ofColophon. 13: Yes. 14: Rare bks, admin. 15: Swarthmore Col, Swarthmore Penn 19081.

GOWDY, LAURA E(LLEN). b Joy Ill 28 N 27. 5: Monmouth Col (Ill) 45-49 (Eng) AB; UColo summers 51-55, 59 (Eng) MA; UIll summers 62, 65-67 (LS) MS. 7: Tchr-libn: Kirkwood (Ill) High Sch 49-52, Princeville (Ill) High Sch 52-56; Fulbright tchr H B S voor Meisjes, Leiden Netherlands 56-57; Tchr-libn Princeville (Ill) High Sch 57-64; Tchr Mendota (Ill) High Sch 64-67; Catlgr Milner Lib Ill StateU 67-. 9: ALA; IllLA; IllEA. 10: Delta Kappa Gamma. 15: 613 N School st, Normal Il 61761.

GOWER, LESLIE M. b Clarksville Tenn 5 F 27. 4: RoNetta Davis. 5: Austin Peay State Col 47-50 (Hist, En) BA; Vanderbilt 50, 57 (Hist) MA; Peabody 56-57 (LS) MA. 6: Sp. 7: USAAF 45-47; Libn Tenn DEPT OF Pub Health, Nashville Tenn 57; Base libn Clarksville Navy Base, Ft Cambell Ky 58; Asst libn UTenn Martin Br, Martin Tenn 58-60; Asst Prof of Lib Sci Northwestern State Col (Natchitoches La) 60-63; Libn Pan Amer Col 63-. 9: ALA; TennLA; aLA; TexLA; SWLA. 10: Pi Gamma Mu. 14: Ref, acquis, admin. 15: 1500 N Sugar rd, Pharr Tx 78577.

GOY, A PETER. b Ukraine 12 Jl 25. 4: Olena Stanchak. 5: Tchrs Sem 41-44 Diploma; Ukrainian Free U 45-49, 54-55 (Hist); Laski Inst of Tech 53-54; Ill Inst of Tech 54 (Econ); Columbia 55-58 (LS) MS. 6: Slavic Langs, Ger. 7: Period reading room asst Columbia U 55-57, Ser catlgr 58-61; Slavic libn City Col City U(NY) 61-. 9: ALA-ACRL (Slavic & E Europ Subsect); Amer Assn Adv Slavic Studies; Assn of Ukr Libns in USA (v-pres 63-64); Shevchenko Sci Soc Inc (sec Terminol Sect 62-66); NYLibCub. 12: Comp "Bibliography of Reference Materials for Russian Area Studies (62); "Russian Area Studies at City College Library (64); Co-auth "Technical

Dictionary of Librarianship, English-Spanish (64); Comp 2 ed "Directory of Librarians in the Field of Slavic and East European Studies in USA and Canada (65). 13: Yes. 14: Bibliographer, acquis, catlg. 15: 101 Second ave, New York NY 10003.

GOYETTE, MAURICE W. b Hemmingford Que Can 24 F 24. 4: Gertrude J Farrell Goyette. 5: St Bernadine of Siena 46-50 (Biol) BS, 50-51 (Educ) MS in Ed; SUNY (Albany) 60-65 MS in LS. 7: Engnr Gunner USAF (T/Sgt) US, Europe 42-46; Elem tchr Porter Cor Sch, Porter Cor NY 51-52; Jr high sci tchr Scotia Jr High Sch, Scotia NY 52-57; High sch biol tchr Scotia Glenville Central, Scotia NY 57-59; Jr high sch libn Scotia Jr High Sch, Scotia NY 60-67; A-V libn Van Antwerp Jr High Niskayana Schs, Schenectady NY 68-. 9: NY State Tchrs Assn. 10: Lions Club; Boy Scouts. 14: Info storage & retrieval, documentation. 15: 413 Reynolds st, Scotia NY 12303.

GOYETTE, SISTER LUMINA CECELIA FCSCJ. b Malone NY 6 O 08. 5: Mt St Joseph Tchrs Col summers 47-54 (Eng, Educ) BS in Ed; Marywood Col summers 61-65 MSLS; Salve Regina Col summer 67; Col of St Rose summer 68. 6: Fr. 7: Tchr St Marys Acad, Champlain NY 33-53; Tchr Our Lady of Grace Acad, Colebrook NH 54-58; Tchr-libn St Marys Acad, Champlain NY 58-60; Libn Acad of Our Lady of Grace, Colebrook NH 60-69; in-chg Soc Studies 67-69. 9: ALA; -AASchL; -YASD; CathLA; NHSchLA; White Mountain Reg SchLA (sec 65-) NESchLA; NECathLA. 14: Catlg, ref (ya). 15: 166 Main st, Colebrook NH 03576.

GRABB, MIGNON STRICLAND. b Chickasha Okla 6 N 41. 4: Laurence W Grabb. 5: East Ill U 58-62 (Eng) BS in Ed; UIll 63-64 MSLS. 6: Fr. 7: Eng tchr Mattoon High Sch, Mattoon Ill 62; Tchr-libn Oakland High Sch, Oakland Ill 62-63; Libn Unity High Sch, Tolono Ill 63-66; Libn Lab Sch E Ill U, Charleston Ill 66-67; Dir lib serv Lake Land Col 67-. 9: ALA; -ACRL; NEA; IllLA. 10: Beta Phi Mu. 14: Lib admin. 15: 3312 Prairie, Mattoon Il 61938.

GRABLE, ALICE ELIZABETH. b Auburn Neb 10 Ja 14. 5: Col of Idaho 32-36 (Lat) BA; UIda summer 48 (LS); UOre summer 50 (LS); UWash summers 54, 56, 57-59 (LS) ML. 6: Fr. 7: Sr Lat asst Col of Idaho 35-36; Tchr-libn Middleton High Sch, Middleton Ida 37-38; Libn Farm Labor Camp, Caldwell Ida 40-42; Lib asst Col of Idaho 42-44; Tchr-libn Cambridge High Sch, Cambridge Ida 4749; Tchr-libn Fruitland High Sch, Fruitland Ida 49-. 8: Mem of com that revised sch lib standards in Ida. 9: NEA; IdaEA; IdaLA. 10: Ida For Lang Assn; DAR; Delta Kappa Gamma. 14: High sch lib. 15: Rt 1, Fruitland Ida 83619.

GRACE, MARGUERITE NICHOLS. b Mentone Ind. 4: H Ted Grace. 5: Central State Col (Okla) 32-39 (Eng) BS; UArk 55-57 (LS); UGuam 63-64 (LS); UOkla 64 (LS). 7: Libn Govt of Guam, agana 62-64, Lib consul 66-68; Libn Berryville Pub Sch, Berryville Ark 64-66; Pub serv libn Julia Tutwiler Lib, Livingston Ala 69-. 9: ALA; NEA; GaLA (sec). 14: Ref. 15: PO Box 5, Livingston Al 36606.

GRACE, SISTER MELANIA (FLORENCE GRACE). b Erie Penn 3 Ja 1898. 5: Seton Hill Col 25-29 (Eng) AB; Carnegie 28-29 (LS) Certif; Chicago 39-42 (LS) MA. 6: Ger, Fr. 7: Chief Libn Seton Hill Col 29-. 8: Mem Bd of Corporators, Seton Hill Col 51-. 9: SLA (sec Col & Univ Group 42-43); CathLA (chm var sects; chm West Penn Unit 43-45). 12: Ed "Books for Catholic Colleges (48-); Ed "Bibliography Section of "Catholic Booklist(42-). 13: Yes. 14: Bk sel, catlg. 15: Seton Hill Col, Greensburg Pa 15601.

GRADY, DORIS (LOCKE). b Paulsboro NJ 2 Ja 19. 4: William Grady. 5: William & Mary 36-40 BSLS. 7: Libn Tazewell Sch Syst, Tazewell Va 40-41; Libn Taylor Sch, Columbia SC 41-42; Sr asst Elizabwth Pub Lib, Elizabeth NJ 42-43; Link trainer operator Sp (T) 2/c USNR (W-R) 43-45; Coord East Air Lines, NYC 45-47; Libn Ebasco Serv Inc, NYC 47-57; Child libn Caldwell Pub Lib, Caldwell NJ 57-65; Dir Cape May Co Lib, Cape May court House NJ 66-. 9: ALA; NJLA (chm Insts Com 67-68, rec sec 68-70); NJ Co Libns Conf (chm 69-70, sec 67-68). 10: Soroptimist Club. 15: 111B Seaview ct, N Wildwood NJ 08260.

GRADY, DOROTHY (McCORMACK). b N Andover Mass 2 Jl 6. 4: Allan B Grady. 5: Cornell U 33-37 (Eng Lit) BA; Columbia 37-38 (Tchg of Eng) MA; Rutgers 59-61 MLS. 7: Eng tchr Whitcomb High Sch, Bethel Vt 38-39; Eng tchr Peapack-Gladstone Sch, Peapack NJ 55-57; Asst lbn W Morris Reg High Sch, Chester NJ 60-61; Libn Bedminster Twp Sch, Bedminster NJ 61-. 9: ALA; NJLA; NJ Sch Libns Assn; NJEA. 10: Beta Phi Mu; PTA; AAUW Kappa Delta Epsilon; Nat & NJ Audubon Societies; Sierra Club; Bedminster - Far HillsPub Lib Bd Trustees. 12: Ed "New Jersey in the Classroom, a bibliog (65). 14: Child reading, lib recruiting conserv. 15: Box 156, Bedminster NJ 07921.

GRADY, EILEEN. b Great Neck NY 21 Ag 24. 5: CornellU 41-43, 49-51 (Journalism) BS; UMich (Ann Arbor) 51-52 MALS. 6: Ger. 7: Space buyer Young & Rubicam Advertising, NYC 43-49; Field libn US Army, Munich Germany 52-55; Ref libn ColumbiaU 55-56; Ref libn UCal (Santa Barbara) 56-57; Ref libn YaleU 57-63; USAF: Asst libn, Frankfurt Germany 63-69, Base libn, Wethersfield England 69-. 14: Ref (univ libs). 15: Box 1482, APO NY 09120.

GRADY, SISTER MARY PAULINE. b Farmer City Ill 12 D 17. 5: St Louis U 38-41 (Eng) AB (Summa cu laude), 41-43 (Eng) AM; UIll 40, 60 (LS); Marquette U 52 (Journalism); Notre Dame summer 60 (Eng, Theol). Univ per Stranieri (Perugia Italy) 66 Ital. 6: Lat, Ital. 7: Libn St Teresa Acad E St Louis Ill 68- 41-64, Lib supv 64-; Tchr St Teresa Acad & St Louis U 43-64; Tchr Ruma Center (Sister Formation Col) of St Lois U (Ruma Ill) 64-66; Sec Intl Commsn for Rev Const Ad PPS, Rome Italy 66-68. 8: Research on foundress & early hist of Congregation of Sisters Adorers of the Most Precious Blood, Italy 62, 66-68. 9: ALA; CathLA(2 coms); IllLA; IllASchL. 10: Nat Coun Tchrs Eng Ill Assn Tchrs Eng. 12: "Girl in a Hurry: The Story of Blessed Maria de Mattias Foundress, Sisters Adorers of the Most Precious Blood, 1805-1866 (64); Ed "The Precious Blood Sister. (64-66); Ed "Internat Bulletin Ad PPS (66-68). 14: Adv serv, bibliotherapy on high sch level. 15: St Teresa Acad 2501 Ridge ave, E St Louis Il 62205.

GRAF, JOHN A. b Providence 12 S 17. 5: UMinn 38-40 (Educ) BS, 40-41 (Eng); NYU 48-49 9educ); NJ State Tchrs Col (LS) summer 49; Columbia 49-53 (LS) MS, 53-56 (Eng, Comparative Lit). 6: Fr. 7: Tchr Pub High Sch, Ellsworth Mich 41-42; Production machinist Everede Tool Co, Chicago 42-43; Tchr Kern Road Pub Sch, Roseville Mich 43-44; Tchr Flint Pub Sch, Flint Mich 44-45; Tchr Freehold (NJ) Mil Sch 45-46; Newark (NJ) Pub Lib: Sr lib asst 48-51, Jr libn 51-54, Sr libn 54-. 8: Sr libn, Newark (NJ) Bus Lib 58-62. 9: ALA; NJLA (Pub Rel Com 51). 14: Catlg, ref, bus bks. 15: 761 Mt Prospect ave, Neward NJ 07104.

GRAFF, MARY ELLEN (WALTERS). b Ill 3 Jl 15. 4: A K Graff. 5: West Ill U 33-39 (Educ) B Ed; UIll 61-62 BSLS; IndU summer 65. 6: Fr. 7: Elem tchr Ill 35-60; Sch libn Springfield Ill 61-62; Elem libn West Ill U 62-. 9: ALA; IllEA; IllLA; IllASchL. 10: Kappa Delta Pi; Delta Kappa Gamma; Bus & Prof Womens Club LWV. 13: Yes. 14: Child lib. 15: 1362 Parkview dr, Macomb Ill 61455.

GRAFF, RUTH. b Pittsburgh 5 O 12. 5: Chatham 31-35 (Eng) AB; West Res 61-63 MS in LS. 7: Tchr Stowe Twp, Penn 35-39; Asst in secs off Oberlin Col 52-61; Oberlin (Ohio) Pub Lib & Elyria (Ohio) Pub Lib 61-63; Acquis libn Oberlin Col Lib 63-, Hd acquis libn 68-. 9: ALA-ALTA; -RTSD (sec Acquis Sect 68-71). 10: Beta Phi Mu. 14: Acquis. 15: 238 Morgan st, Oberlin Oh 44074.

GRAFTON, (CONNIE) ERNESTINE. b Hubbard Tex 17 Ja 13. 5: Trinity U (San Antonio Tex) 33 AB; UOkla 34 AB in LS; Chicago 40 MA. 7: Stud asst Lib Trinity U 30-33; Ref asst circ dept Cincinnati Pub Lib 36-41; Tri-County Libn Orange County Libs, NC 41-45; Head ext div Va State Lib, Richmond 45-56; Dir State Travel Lib, Des Moines Iowa 56-. 8: Bldg consul for pub libs (ALA Lib Arch & Bldg Planning Com state consul 45-48). 9: AEA(Iowa Mem Coordin 60-, chm Nom & ElecCom 63-64); ALA (Coun mem at large 64-68); ASL(Planning Com 64-); IowaLA(Exec Com 56-); IowaEA(pres 59-60, Exec Com 60-); Mo Valley EA. 10: Iowa Coun for Com Improvement (pres 65-). 11: Va Woman of the Year 51; Mo Valley EA Achievement Award 63. 12: Ed "North Carolina Libraries (42-44); Ed "Virginia Library Bulletin (45-56); Ed "Iowa Library Quarterly (56-). 13: Yes. 14: Admin, ext, pub rel, State level serv. 15: State Traveling Lib Hist Bldg, Des Moines Iowa 50319.

GRAHAM, CLARENCE R. b Louisville Ky 28 F 07. 4: Esther Lothman. 5: UNC 24-27 (Eng); ULouisville 34 (Eng) AB; West Res 35 BS in LS; Northwestern U 37-38 (Educ). 7: Libn Parkland Jr High Sch, Louisville Ky 30-34; Asst to libn Louisville Free Pub Lib, Louisville Ky 35-36; Dir Nat Col of Educ Lib 36-42; Dir Louisville Free Pub Lib, Louisville Ky 42-. 8: Lib consul: Milwaukee Pub Lib Renovation, 52; Macon (Ga) Pub Lib, 56; Madison (Ind) Pub Lib, 64; Bartholomew County (Ind) Pub Lib, 65; Visiting Assoc Prof Dept of Lib Sci UKy 63. 9: ALA(pres 50-51, Life Coun mem); SELA (pres

48-50); KyLA(pres 46-47). 10: Ky Libs Certif Bd 43-50; Filson Hist Club; Arts Club; Rotary; Co-founder & consul to free "Neighborhood Colleges in br libs, sponsored by ULouisville & Louisville Free Pub Lib 47; Beta Phi Mu; Louisville Theatrical Assn (Bd Dir 65-); Childrens Theatre (Bd Dir 64-); Jr Art Gallery (treas 50-). 11: Citizen Laurate, Younger Womans Club of Louisville 62. 12: "First Book of Public Libraries (59). 13: Yes. 15: Louisville Free Pub Lib 4th & York sts, Louisville Ky 40203.

GRAHAM, DOROTHY H. b Milford Ohio 22 Ja 10. 5: Lib Train Class Pub Lib of Cincinnati 29-30; UCincinnati (Eng Lit) 40 AB; Columbia 42 BS in LS. 6: Fr, Ger, Sp, Lat. 7: Pub Lib of Cincinnati & Hamilton Co: Child libn 30-41, Catlgr 42, Head wk with schs dept 42-56, Head order dept 56-60, Head tech processes 60-; Instr in Lib Sci Col of Mt St Joseph on the Oh 67-. 9: ALA; OhioLA (sec Tech Prc Round Table 61-62); Ohio Valley Group Tech Serv Libns (sec 60-61); OhioanaLA. 10: Delta Kappa Gamma; Columbia Club of Greater Cincinnati. 14: Tech serv. 15: 3529 Shaw ave, Cincinnati Oh 45208.

GRAHAM, DOROTHY MARIE. b Oakland Cal 1 D 40. 5: Compton Col 58-60 AA; UCLA 60-62 (Pre-libnship) BA, 62-63 MLS. 6: Sp. 7: Ref libn Kern Co Lib, Bakersfield Cal 63-65; Ser catlgr UCLA Res Lib 65-Peace Corps Libn, Tchg Lib Sci 67-68, Asuncion Paraguay 67-68; Hd libnAsuncion BiNat Ctr 69. 9: CalLA. 10: Amer Assn for UN; UCal Lib Schs Alumni Assn. 14: Catlg, univ libs, libs in Latin Amer. 15: 350 S Fuller ave apt 5-H, Los Angeles Ca 90036.

GRAHAM, EARL C. b New Plymouth Ohio 24 N 11. 5: Simpson Col 29-33 (Eng Lit) AB; Ohio State U 33-36 (Educ, Lit) BS in Ed; UCal(Berkeley) 39-40 Lib Certif. 6: Fr. 7: Editorial wker on dictionaries, encyclopedias & textbks Consolidated Bk Publs & Follett Publ Co, Chicago 36-39; Sr ed asst ALA, Chicago 41; Asst libn Know Col 42-43; US Army libn in Troop Sch Lib, clerk in publ sect Adj Gen DEPT, PERSONNEL CLERK IN AA train unit, Camp Stewart Ga 43-44; US Army spec agent Counter-Intelligence Corps, European Theater 44-45; Asst libn then Chief Libn & Ed of "Rehabilitation Literature Nat Easter Seal Soc for Crippled Child & Adults, Chicago 47-. 8: Mem of Lib Com of Presidents Com on Employment of the Handicapped. 9: Var com assignments & offs on nat & reg levels in: MedLA, SLA, & ALA-AHIL. 12: Asst Bus Mgr & Bus Mgr "Bulletin of the Medcal Library Association (56-60); Comp (with Marjorie M Mullen) "Rehabilitation Literature, 1950-1955 (56); Ed "Rehabilitation Literature, monthly journal (59-). 13: Yes. 14: Admin, editing & writing, bk rev. 15: Nat Easter Seal Soc for Crippled Child & Adults 2023 W Ogden ave,Chicago Il 60612.

GRAHAM, ELIZABETH (CARLSON). b Chicago Ill 9 Ag 19. 4: Jarlath J Graham. 5: Valparaiso 37-41 (Eng) BA; Peabody Col 42-43 BLS. 7: Law libn Valparaiso U 41-42; Asst libn S Bend Pub Lib Bus Lib, S Bend Ind 43-44; Libn Advertising Publ Inc, Chicago 44-. 9: SLA (Ill Chap: pres 2 terms). 14: Ref. 15: Adv Pub Inc 740 N Rush st, Chicago Il 60611.

GRAHAM, ELIZABETH (MacFADYEN). b Randleman NC 30 D 08. 5: Duke 26-32 (Hist) AB, MA; Cornell U 32-34 (Hist) PhD; UDenver 62-63 (LS) MA. 6: Fr. 7: J Franklin Jameson Fellow, Mss Div LC 34-35; Research asst "Dictionary of American Biography Wash DC 35-36; Research asst Dept of Rural Govt Cornell U 36-37; Research asst Colo State Archives, Denver 61; Mss west hit div Denver Pub Lib 62; Ref libn Charlotte Col 63-65; Asst docuents libn Duke U 65-. 8: Visit Prof, Sch of Lib Sci UNC, summer 68. 9: NCLA; SELA; DurhamCoLA. 10: Delta Kappa Gamma; Phi Kappa Phi; Trinity Col Hist Soc; Duke Univ Faculty Club; Duke Univ Campus Club; Kappa Alpha Theata; Duke Univ Alumnae Coun. 14: Ref, pub docs. 15: 13 Alastair ct, 300 Swift ave, Durham NC 27706.

GRAHAM, GARTH (THOMAS). b Ottawa Ont Can 27 F 42. 4: Anne Gillies. 5: UWest Ont 61-64 (Eng, Hist) BA; UBC 66-67 BLS. 7: Lib asst Hamilton Pub Lib, Hamilton Ont Can 64-66; Dir lib serv Govt of the Yukon Territory, Whitehause Can 67-. 9: CanLA; ALA; AlaskaLA. 10: Yukon Film Soc; White Horse Drama Club; Yukon Fish & Game Assn; Whitehorse Hist Soc; Yukon Voyageur Canoe Club. 13: Yes. 14: Lib mgt & admin. 15: Yukon Regional Lib Box 2703, Whitehorse Yukon Can.

GRAHAM, JANET. b Olean NY 18 N 06. 5: Syracuse 24-28 (Romance Langs) AB, 37-43 BS in LS. 6: Fr. 7: Ref & interlib loan Syracuse U 47-49, Leisure reading room head 49-59, Acquis bibliog 59-62, Asst libn citizenship lib 62-66, Libn Lib Sci Lib 66-67, Catlg info 67-68, Humanities bibliogr & ref libn 68-. 14: Circ, ref, bibliog. 15: 319 Euclid ave, Syracuse NY 13210.

GRAHAM, KATHRYN M. b Tampico Ill. 5: UIll 31-35 AB, 46-47 BLS. 6: Fr. 7: Sec to mgr America Fore Insurance Cos, Chcago 3642; Accoutant Interstate Aircraft & Eng Corp, DeKalb Ill 43-45; Asst registrar No Ill State Tchrs Col 46; Catlg libn UIll(Galesburg) 47-49; Libn Insurance Lib of Chicago 49-60; Admission sec Newberry Lib, Chicago 60-63; Ser catlgr No Ill U 63-. 9: ALA; SLA (sec-treas Insur Div 59); IllLA; IllEA. 10: AAUW; AAUP; Alpha Omicron Pi; Dames Club of No Ill Univ; Faculty Club of No Ill Univ; UIll Lib Sch Assn; Phi Beta Kappa; Phi Kappa Phi; Beta Phi Mu; Alpha Lambda Delta. 12: Comp "Bibliography of Insurance Books, 1950-60. 13: Yes. 14: Catlg. 15: 324 N First st, DeKalb Il 60115.

GRAHAM, MAE. b Florence SC 29 S 04. 5: Womans Col UNC 25 (Eng) AB; UIll 34 BS in LS; Johns Hopkins 65 MLA. 7: Tchr NC secondary schs 25-27; Libn Sr High Sch, High Point NC 28-33, 35-36; Libn Sr High Sch, Kingsport Tenn 34-35; Asst Prof Lib Sci DEPT Col of William & Mary 36-42, Assoc Prof & dept head 42-62; Dir summer sessions of sch libns Fisk U 36-41; Chief Placement Off, ALA 46-48; Supv Sch Libs Md State Dept of Educ 48-66, Asst dir 66-. 8: Sch lib adv, CI&E, SCAP, Tokyo Japan 47. 9: ALA (Coun, Exec Bd);-YASD (pres, Exec Bd); MdLA (pres). 13: Yes. 15: State Dept of Educ, 600 Wyndhurst ave, Baltimore Md 21210.

GRAHAM, (MARJORIE) RUTH (KILLEBREW). b Kan City Mo 25 S 15. 4: Carl F Graham. 5: Okmulgee Jr Col 32-34 AA; UOkla 34-36 (LS, Fr) BLS; UMich (Grand Rapids) 68-69 LS. 6: Fr. 7: Ref libn Kan City (Kan) Pub Lib 36-39; Libn Jr Col, Kan City Kan 39-40; WPA lib supv Kan WPA, 11 counties NE Kan 40-41; Asst circ dept Detroit Pub Lib 41-44; Interviewer Mich Emloyment Serv, Wyandotte Mich 44-45; Instr, pub rel dir John Robert Powers Sch, Detroit 50-55; Libn LaQuinta High Sch, Garden Grove Unified Sch Dist, Westminster Cal 63-67; Libn Central High Sch, Grand Rapids Mich 67-. 8: Lecturer, John Robert Powers Sch, Detroit 50-57. 9: NEA; Cal Tchrs Assn; CalASchL; MichTA; MichASchL. 10: Phi Bea Kappa; Gamma Phi Beta; PTA. 13: Yes. 14: Ref, pub rel. 15: 2648 Berwyck rd SE, E Grand Rapids Mi 49506.

GRAHAM, MERCEDES DOYLE. b Buffalo NY 30 D 06. 5: SUNY(Geneseo) 24-27 (LS) Diploma; Roosevelt U 49-51 BA, 57-58 MA. 7: Libn Elem Sch Lew Wallace Sch, Gary Ind 37-61, Jr High libn 61-63, Sr high sch libn 63-. 8: Instr of Lib Sci Purdue U (Calumet). 9: ALA(Life mem); IndSchLA; A-v Instr Dirs (Ind). 10: Delta Kappa Gamma; College Club. 12: "How to Use Your School Library (45). 13: Yes. 14: Sch libs. 15: 3572 Harrison st, Gary In 46408.

GRAHAM, PAULINE (CAIN). b Pittsburgh 7 Je 23. 5: UPittsburgh 40-43 Secondary Educ) BA, 62-63 MLS. 7: Head Libn Bethel Park Pub Lib, Bethel Park Penn 63-. 9: ALA; PennLA; (chm SW Chap). 10: Delta Zeta; South Hills Col Club. 14: Book sel, clsf, admin. 15: 11141 Logan rd, Bethel Park Pa 15102.

GRAHAM, RUSSELL (MONROE). b Walla Walla Wash 21 S 37. 4: Yvonne Bannister. 5: East Ore Col 59-61 (Sci) BS; UOre 61-62 (Educ); UDenver 62-63 (LS) MA;UWash summer 66 Lib Mechanization; Simon Fraser U 68 MBA. 7: (Cpl) USMC, Cal 56-58; Lib asst Soc Sci Found, Denver 62-63; Ref spec Gen Electric Co, Richland Wash 63-65; Supv ref Pacific Northwest Lab, Richland Wash 65-66; Libn MacMillan Bloedel Ltd 66-68, Mgr admin serv div 68-. 8: Part-time lecturer in libnship, UWash Grad Sch of Libnship, 64-. 14: Ref, info, sci, bus mgt, admin. 15: 7356 Punnett close, Burnaby 1 British Columbia Can.

GRAHAM, RUTH(CURTIS). b McComb Miss 20 N 10. 4: W J Graham. 5: Miss State Col for Women 28-32 (Eng) AB; Peabody 54-55 (LS) MA. 7: Libn II Detroit Pub Lib 55-57; asst libn Pan American Col Lib 62-. 9: TexLA; Rio Grande Valley LA (se); Tex Assn Col Tchrs. 14: Circ, ref, govt docs, acquis. 15: 1111 Vine, McAllen Tx 78501.

GRAHAM, SANDRA DALE. b Colorado Springs Col 24 D 41. 5: Colo State Col 59-60; West State Col 61-64 (Hist) BA; UDenver 62, 64, 66, 67 (LS) MA. 7: Clk Handy Store, Aurora Colo summers 56-59; Stud libn Aurora Pub Schs, Aurora Colo summer 59; Student lib asst West State Col 63; Lib asst Aurora Pub Lib, Aurora Colo 64-66, Ref libn II 67-. 9: ColoLA. 10. Beta Sigma Phi. 14: Ref. 15: 1664 Jamaica st, Aurora Co 80010.

GRAHEK, MARILYN G. b Virginia Minn 11 N 41. 5: Creighton U 59-64 (Eng, Hist) AB; Rosary Col 64-65 MALS. 7: Asst libn UNeb 65-67; Ref libn Park Col 67-. 9: ALA (Jr Mems RT). 10: AAUP. 14: Ref, pub serv. 15: 6004 NE Bircain pl apt 1A, Kansas City Mo 64118.

GRAINGER, WILLIAM KEITH. b Pasó Robles Cal 17 D 22. 4: Loa Louise Starrh. 5: UCal(Berkeley) 42-43 BA, 46-47 BLS; USoCal 57-58 MSLS. 7: Lt jg US Naval Reserve Pacific Area 44-46; Asst libn Compton Col 47-53; Libn Compton Sr High Sch 53-54; Asst libn Bakersfield Col 54-59; Libn Pasadena City Col 59-. 9: ALA; NEA; CalLA; Cal Tchrs Assn. 10: Beta Phi Mu; Phi Delta Kappa; Christ Businessmens Com of Pasadena. 11: HEA Fellowship (SoCal) 67-68. 14: Admin, lib educ. 15: 9231 E Wedgewood st, Temple City Ca 91780.

GRALAPP, MARCELEE GAYL. b Winfield Kan 2 N 31. 5: Southwestern Col (Winfield Kan) 49-50; Kan State Tchrs Col (Emporia) 50-52 (LS) BA; UDenver 60-63 (LS) MA. 7: Child libn Pub Lib, Hutchinson Kan 52-57; Child libn Pub Lib, Lawrence Kan 57-59; Assoc libn Pub Lib, Boulder Colo 59-, Lib dir 66. 8: Tchr of child lit, UDenver, Kan State Tchrs Col, & Colo U Ext 65-. 9: ALA; NCTE (Com on Bklist for Elem Grades); Internat Reading Assn; ColoLA; MPLA (chm Child Serv Div 65-67). 10: Soroptimist Club; UN Assn. 14: Child serv, admin. 15: P O Drawer H, Boulder Colo 80301.

GRAMS, THEODORE CARL WILLIAM. b Portland Ore 29 S 18. 5: UWash 45-47 (Econ) BA; Harvard Law Sch 47-48; USoCal 50-51 MSLS. 6: Ger, Fr. 7: Land title asst & capital records acct US Bonneville Power Admin, Portland Ore 39-45, 48-50, Libn 51-52; Head catlgr Lib Portland State U 52-59, Head of tech processes 60-. 8: Mem Bd Dirs, Hub-CAP (inner city community action program) 67-. 9: ALA; PNLA; MedLA; OreLA; Portland Area Spec Libns Soc (past pres). 10: AAUP; Beta Phi Mu. 12: "Allocation of Joint Costs of Multiple Purpose Projects (52); "Textbook Classification Schedule, Class LT (60, rev ed 68); "Selected Readings in Elementary Education (61). 13: Yes. 14: Tech proc. 15: 1000 SW Vista ave, Portland Ore 97205.

GRAMSE, ERNA L. b Holyoke Mass 31 My 11. 5: Mt Holyoke 28-32 (Chem) BA; Cornell U 32-33 (Chem) MA, 34-35 (Chem). 6: Ger. 7: Asst on chem Wheaton Col 33-34; Asst libn Texaco Inc, NYC 35-46; Hd central info serv FMC Corp, NYC 46-. 9: ACS; SLA (dir NY Chap 50-52); ASIS; Amer Inst of Chemists (sec 68, NY Chap 62-). 13: Yes. 15: FMC Corp 633 Third ave, New York NY 10017.

GRANAT, BRUCE (A). b Chicago 21 Jl 39. 4: Jacqueline Kraft. 5: Roosevelt U 59-61 (Psych) BS; UChicago 61-64 (LS) MA. 6: Fr. 7: Libn trainee tech dept Chicago Pub Lib 61-62; Ref libn John Crerar Lib, Chicago 62-64; Head libn bus info serv Abbott Labs, N Chicago 64-65; Manager, Head Libn, Lib Continental Ill Nat Bank & Trust C, Chicago 65-. 8: Lib consul & adv work, var organization 67-69. 9: ALA; SLA; ASIS; Assn Comp Mach. 10: UChicago Alumni Assn; Beta Phi Mu; Gov bd mem Lib of Internat Relations, Amer Inst of Banking; Bank Pub Rel & MarketingAssn; Chicago Assn of Commerce & Industry. 12: Ed "Bibliography on Future Trends in Bank Automation (Checkless Society) 67-69. 13: Yes. 14: Admin, ref, info sci. 15: 1617 Ridge ave Apt 3-G, Evanston Ill 60201.

GRANDBOIS, MILDRED. b Minneapolis 26 My 06. 5: Andrews U 25-29 (Romance Langs) AB; UMich summers 30-33 (Romance Langs) MA; Sorbonne summer 31 (Fr); USoCal 52-53 MS in LS. 6: Fr, Sp. 7: Instr & Dean of girls Adelphian Acad, Holly Mich 29-30; Instr in Fr Oshawa Missionary Col (Oshawa Ont) 30-31; Instr in Sp & Fr Andrews U 31-35; Instr & Dean of girls Auburn Acad, Auburn Wash 35-37; Instr in Sp & libn Lynwood Acad, Lynwood Cal 37-43; Exec Sec & Libn Voice of Prophecy, Glendale Cal 43-56; Libn Glendale Adventist Hosp, Gendale Cal 56-. 8: Consul; sch of Nursing Lib Cal Hosp, Los Angeles 54-55; Lib of Kettering Mem Hosp,Kettering Ohio 66. 9: ALA; SLA; MedLA; CalLA; Med Lib Group of SoCal. 12: Ed "Cumulative Index to Nursing Literature. 13: Yes. 14: Admin, ed wk. 15: 1570 E Chevy Chase dr, Glendale Cal 91206.

GRANDE, MARILYN A. b Cleveland Ohio 19 Jl 42. 5: Cleveland StateU 60-65 (Eng) BA; Case west Res 66-67 MSLS. 6: Fr, Sp. 7: Tchr S Euclid-Lyndhurst Ohio Schs 65-66; Asst libn Sch of Lib Sci Case West Res 67-69, Libn 69-. 9: ALA. 10: AAUP; ACLU. 14: Ref. 15: 1848 Grantham rd, Cleveland Oh 44112.

GRANESE, MARY ALICE. b Wakefield Mass 28 Ap 14. 5: Radcliffe Col 32-36 (Chem) AB. 6: Fr, Ital, Ger. 7: Asst libn US Rubber Co, Passaic NJ 36-37; Lit searcher Gen Chem Co, LI City NY 37-40; Libn Burroughs- Wellcome Co, Tuckahoe NY 41-43; Chem The Melrose Labs, Melrose Mass 43-51; Asst libn Lincoln Lab MIT, Lexington Mass 51-. 9: SLA (chm Sci-Tech Div, Boston Chap); ASIS. 10: Radcliffe Club of Boston; MIT Matrons. 14: A system has been developed using the IBM 360/67 Computer to catlg and circreports issued by DOD, NASA, AEC, etc for a collection of 100,000 reports. 15: 26 Franklin st, Wakefield Mass 01880.

GRANGER, JANE (HAFFNER). b Toledo Ohio 18 S 31. 4: William S Granger. 5: Miami U (Oxford Ohio) 49-52 (Geol) AB, fall 52 (Geol); UToledo summer 54, 56; UMich 57-61 MALS. 7: Tchr Escambia Co, Fla 54-55; Tchr, Madison Heights Mich 57; Catlgr & asst to libn Madison Heights Pub Lib, Madison Heights Mich 58-63; Main floor libn Lucas Co Lib, Maumee Ohio 64-66, Hd (Ore br) 67-. 9: ALA; OhioLA. 10: Beta Phi Mu; Garden Club. 14: Catlg, circ, ref. 15: 1993 Cherrylawn, Toledo Ohio 43614.

GRANNIS, FLORENCE VIRGINIA (SPRAGUE). b Yakima Wash 9 O 19. 5: UWash 43-50 (Sociol) BA, 51 (LS) BA; USoCal 56-61 (LS) MS. 7: Lib asst Seattle Pub Lib 51-62, Head Lib for the Blind 52-60; Asst Dir in Chge of lib & soc serv Iowa Commsn for Blind, Des Moines Iowa 60-. 9: ALA; SLA. 10: Phi Beta Kappa; Beta Phi Mu; Toastmistress Club; Quota Club. 15: Box 48, Des Moines Iowa 50309.

GRANNIS, MABEL (VIOLA). b USA. 5: UMich 46-52 AB (Hist), AMLS. 7: Clerk Grand Rapids (Mich) Pub Lib 42-44; Clerk Womens Army Corps Air Force, US 44-45; Catlgr Mich Hist Commsn, Lansing Mich 52-53; Catlgr Mich State Lib 53-59, Ref 59-61; Hd catlg unit 66-67; Catlgr West Mich U 61-66; Hd catlg processing ser & bind unitMich Dept of Educ bur of lib serv 67-. 8: Tchr of lib sci courses, West Mich U 62-64. 9: ALA; MichLA. 14: Catlg, ref. 15: 3729 Oakland dr, Kalamazoo Mi 49001.

GRANSTAFF, HAZEL (KEMP). b Smith Co Tenn 25 Ap 19. 4: (Birchard) LaDon Granstaff. 5: Tenn Tech U 37-39, 56-58 (Educ) BS; Middle Tenn State U 62- (Educ). 7: Intermediate tchr Smith Co, Defeated Tenn 39-42, Elem tchr 49-63; High sch libn Smith Co, Carthage Tenn 63-. 9: NEA; ALA; TennEA; TennLA. 10: 4-H Club Leader. 14: Ref, circ. 15: Upper Ferry rd, Carthage Tn 37030.

GRANSTEIN, MARK. b Westfield Mass 10 Jl 45. 4: Gale Nussbaum Granstein. 5: William & Mary 63-67 (Hist) BA; EmoryU 67-68 MLn. 6: Fr, Ger, Sp. 7: Ref asst libn Hartford Pub lib, Hartford Conn 68-. 9: ALA; ConnLA. 14: Ref, bk selection. 15: 88 Montclair dr, W Hartford Ct 06107.

GRANT, BELLE (MARY). b Strathclair Man Can. 5: Columbia 35 (Educ) BS; UWis 49 BLS; UMich 58 MLS. 7: Libn admin Prov Normal Sch, Calgary Alta 41-45; Libn admin UAlta 45-57; Libn ref Toronto Pub Lib 57-63; Libn ref head UWaterloo (Waterloo Ont) 63-. 9: ALA; BSCan; CanLA; OntLA; Inst Prof Libns Ont. 10: Fed of Univ Women. 14: Ref. 15: 112 Roslin ave, Waterloo Ont Can.

GRANT, DOROTHY (ESTES). b Mexico Mo 12 D 42. 4: James E Grant. 5: UMo (Columbia) 60-64 (Soc Studies) BS in Ed. 7: Asst ref libn State Hist Soc of Mo, Columbia 64-66, acquis libn 66-. 14: Map catlg, ref, rare bks. 15: Rte 2 Sunrise Estates, Columbia Mo 65201.

GRANT, GEORGE CALVIN. b Memphis (Shelby County) Tenn 22 O 39. 4: Alice Morgan Grant. 5: Owen Jr Col 57-59 (Gen Educ) AA; Morehouse Col 59-61 (Pol Sci) BS; Atlana U 61-62 MSLS. 6: Fr. 7: Head Libn Henderson Bus Col, Memphis Tenn 62-65; Head Libn Owen Jr Col 62-65; Head Libn E St Louis (Ill) Br SoIll U 65-67, Circ libn 67-69, Asst dir for pub serv Lovejoy Lib. 8: Lib evaluation com So Assn Col & Schs, Memphis 63-64. 9: ALA; TennLA; SELA;IllLA; Midwest Acad LA. 10: Northeas Memphis Bk Club; Memphis Area Lib Com for the establishment of a Union List of Ser. 12: Contrib "Bibliographic Survey - The Negro in Print. 14: Col lib admin, catlg. 15: Lovejoy Lib So Illinois Univ, Edwardsville Il 62025.

GRANT, GEORGE ELLIS. b Portsmouth Va 17 S 41. 4: Shirley Conant. 5: Rensselaer 60-61 9electrical Engring); Wagner Col 62-66 (Eng) BA; Rutgers 66-67 MLS. 6: Fr, Ger. 7: Ref libn Bell Tel Labs, Greensboro NC 67-. 9: SLA. 14: Spec libs. 15: 2549 Hyde st, Burlington NC 27215.

GRANT, JACQULYN E. b Montgomery Ala 7 Ap 44. 5: SouthernU 61-65 (Eng) BS; Spring Hill Coll summer 63; West MichU 66-67 MSLS. 7: Pre-libn Mobile Pub Lib, Mobile Ala

65-66, child libn 67-68, Br libn 68-. 9: ALA; NEA; SELA; AlaStateTA. 10: NAACP. 14: Child serv. 15: 468 Stanton st, Mobile Al 36617.

GRANT, JUANITA G. b Princeton WVa 25 Jl 28. 5: Concord Col 50-53 (Eng) BS; UNC summers 53-56 BS in LS, summers 63, 64 (LS); Johns Hopkins summers 65, 66, 68, 69 (Hist). 6: Fr, Sp. 7: Libn Roanoke Rapids High Sch, Roanoke Rapids NC 53-56; Libn US Army Spec Serv, Germany & France 56-58; Asst libn Nicholls State Col 58-59; Asst libn Carson Newman Col 60-63; Libn Judson Col 64-67; Dir Avenett Col Lib 67-. 9: ALA; SELA; VaLA. 10: AAUP; Wednesday Club. 14: Ctlg, admin. 15: 203 Troupe st, Marion Ala 36756.

GRANT, (FLORENCE) MADELINE. b Grenada W Indies 12 S 38. 5: UToronto 57-60 (Geog) BA, 60-61 BLS; Univ Col of Rhodesia 65 (Educ) PCE (London). 6: Afrikaans. 7: Catlgr UToronto Law Lib 61-63; Catlgr Legis Lib Toronto Ont Can 64; Tchr Mumbwa Secondary Sch, zambia 66-67; Libn Canadian Inst of Intl Affairs, Toronto Ont Can 67-. 14: Ref, catlg. 15: 31 Wellesley st E, Toronto 5 Ont Can.

GRANT, MARY A. b Montello Wis. 5: UWis 51 (Russan) BA, 54 (LS) MA. 6: Fr, Russian, Sp. 7: Catlgr-tr LC 52-53; Catlgr UWis(Milwaukee) 54-. 9: ALA. 14: Catlg. 15: 3059 N Maryland ave, Milwaukee Wi 53211.

GRANT, PATRICIA J. b Pontiac Ill. 4: Lewis O Grant. 5: UWis 37-41 (Dance) BA; Ill State Normal U summer 40; UDenver 55-65 (LS) MA. 7: Cal Inst Tech 46-49; Cache La Poudre Jr High Sch, La Porte Colo 64-68. 9: ColoASchL. 14: Humanities, adolescent lit, ref, child lit, lit & social protest. 15: 908 Pitkin, Ft Collins Co 80521.

GRANT, VIRGINIA. b Manchester Iowa 22 Ap 43. 5: Sterling Col 61-65 (Eng) BA; UWis 67-68 (LS) MA. 7: Stud asst V A Hosp Libs, Downey Ill 60; Prof trainee Cedar Rapids Pub Lib, Cedar Rapids Iowa 65-67, Libn I 68-. 9: IowaLA. 14: Ref, interlib loan. 15: PO Box 925, Cedar Rapids Ia 52406.

GRANTIER, JOHN ROBERT. b Utica NY 30 Jl 37. 5: Col of William & Mary 55-59 (Hist) AB; West Res 61-62 MSLS. 7: A-v asst Col of William & Mary Lib 59-61; Catlgr URochester Lib 62-64; Acquis libn Washington U Libs (St Louis) 64-65, Asst chief acquis dept 65-66; Hd acquis dept York U (Toronto) 66-69, Hd acquis & ser 69-. 9: ALA; CanLA. 10: ACLU. 14: Tech serv, acquis, collections devel. 15: 55 Oakmount rd apt 1112, Toronto 9 Ont Can.

GRASBERG, GABRIEL. b Warsaw Poland 17 N 23. 4: Virginia Deschenes. 5: McGill 48-51 (Sociol) BA; Harvard 51-53 (Reg Studies, Soviet Union) MA; Simmons 58-62 MS in LS. 6: Russ, Polish, Czech, Fr, Ger, Ital, Lat. 7: Accountant, Poland 41-47; Factory wk, Sweden 47-48; Research asst research projs connected with Soviet Union 52-58; Slavic catlgr Harvard Col Lib 58-. 9: ALA. 11: Grad Fellowship Harvard U 51-52. 14: Catlg. 15: 80 Marlboro st, Boston Ma 02116.

GRASS, SISTER MARY WINIFRED. b Beckley WVa 16 Je 13. 5: St Josephs Col for Women 35-39 (Hist) AB; Columbia 39-40 (LS) BS, 43-47 (LS) MS. 6: Fr, Ger, Sp. 7: Clerk Metropolitan Life Insurance, NYC 32-33; Tchr St Anthonys Elem Sch, Brooklyn NY 34-35; Asst libn St Josephs Col for Women (Brooklyn NY) 40-43, Chief Libn 43-. 8: Instr St Johns U Lib Sch (NY), summers 54-59; Mem Middle States Assns eval teams. 9:CathLA ATheolLA Chm, chm Catlg & Clsf Sect, past chm Metro Cath Col Libns Unit); ALA; ALA (Nat Memb Chm 67-69); NYLA. 12: Ed "Tracings, CathLA Catlg & Clsf Sect Newsletter. 13: Yes. 14: Catlg, ref, admin. 15: 222 Clinton ave, Brooklyn NY 11205.

GRASSAU, BRENDA A (TAYLOR). b Montreal Can 30 Jl 34. 4: Peter Grassau. 5: MacDonald Col 53-54 Tchg Certif; Sir George Williams 54-59 BA; McGill 60-61 BLS. 7: Libn Ont Veterinary Col 61-62; Catlgr Queen's U Lib 62-65; Libn Faculty of Pharmacy UToronto 65-67; Libn Listowel Dist Secondary Sch, Listowel Ont Can 68-. 9: CanLA. 15: PO Box 965, Listowel Ont Can.

GRATION, SELBY U. b Summit NJ 17 Mr 30. 4: Dorothy Hoffmeyer. 5: Barrington Col 48-52 (Bible) BA; Gordon Divinity Sch 52-55 (Theol) BD; Simmons 58-59 (LS) MS. 6: Gk. 7: Minister N Leverett Baptist Chuch, N LeverettMass 55-58; Libn Barrington Col 58-61; Asst libn RI Col 61-62, Dir of Lib 62-68; Dir of libs SUNY (Cortland) 68-. 8: Lib consul: Millman & Sturges, Architects, Providence RI 63-67; RI Jr Col 64-65; Instr Div of U Ext URI Lib Techniques Program 62-67; Lecturer Grad Sch of Lib Sci URI 65-68; RI State Bd of Lib Commissioners 65-68; Lecturer Syracuse University,School of Lib Sci 68-; Consul Lib Educ Exper Proj, Syracuse U 69-. 9: ALA(Coun 64-65); RILA(pres 65-66). 10: AAUP; SUNYLA. 14: Admin. 15: State Univ Col, Cortland NY 13045.

GRATKE, PAUL. b Strawberry Point Iowa. 4: Conice Alba DeVol. 5: Wartbury Col 30-32; Upper Iowa U 32-33 (Educ) AB; UDenver 35-36 BS of LS; Chicago 36; Northwestern 38-42. 7: Catlgr Meadville Theol Sch (Chicago) 36-38; Catlgr Northwestern U 38-42; Milwaukee Pub Li: Head educ dept 42, 43, 45-56, Chief bk sel 43-45, Coordinator serv to adults 56-. 8: Consul LC "D D Clsf 16th ed. 9: ALA (chm Relig Bks Round Table 48, chm Notable Bks Coun 61); Adult Educ Assn; WisLA (pres 53-55); Milwaukee Coun for Adult Learning (pres 65-66). 10: YMCA; Bus & Prof Mens Club; PTA; World Affairs Coun. 13: Yes. 14: Adult educ. 15: 2122 So Mound st, Milwaukee Wis 53207.

GRATZ, DELBERT L. b Allen Co Ohio 5 Mr 20. 4: Thelma Dailey. 5: Bluffton Col 38-42 (Hist) AB; Ohio State U 42, 45 (Hist) MA; UBern 48-50 (Hist) Dr Phil; UMich 51-52 AMLS. 6: Ger, Fr. 7: Research asst Mennonite Central Com, Akron Penn 45-46; Relief wker MCC, Germany 46-48; Libn Bluffton Col 50-. 9: Church Hist Soc; Soc for Reformation Research; ALA. 10: Beta Phi Mu. 12: "The Bernese Anabaptists (53). 13: Yes. 14: Mennonite & Anabaptist materials. 15: Musselman Lib Bluffton Col, Bluffton Ohio 45817.

GRAUER, FRIDA (ESKIN). b Harbin Manchuria 26 D 19. 4: Alvin Grauer. 5: NYU 38; UWis 38-40 (Comparative Lit); UCal 40-41 (Slavic Langs) BA; Pratt 49-50 BLS; Columbia 44 (Russian Lit); Pratt 53 MLS. 6: Russian, Fr. 7: Research & catlg, Russian Sect LC Descript Catlg Div 45-46; Ref libn GHQ SCAP, Tokyo Japan 6-47; Ref libn Time Inc (Morgue), NYC 50-51; Libn NY Pub Lib 51-53, 55-56; Bibliog Pacific Book & Supply Corp, NYC 53-54; Libn Barnett Patients Lib NYU Bellevue Med Center 59-60; Asst to libn Hunter Col 63-64; Libn The Emerson Sch, NYC 65; Asst libn The Dalton Schs Inc, NYC 65-66; Libn Downtown Commun Sch NYC 67-. 8: Escort guide & interpreter US Dept of State (accompanied 4 Soviet Libns on official visit to US during their entire tour), 61. 9: SLA. 14: Ref, child wk, Slavic langs, Russian lit, interpreting transl. 15: 220 E 67th st, New York NY 10021.

GRAVE, ELIZABETH (FRANCE). b Baltimore 25 O 07. 4: Thomas B Grave. 5: Hunter Col 35-38 (Educ) BS (cum laude); Columbia 38-40 MLS; NYU 60-(Educ). 6: Fr. 7: Brooklyn Friends Sch, Brooklyn NY 31-40; Libn Rye Neck Elem Schs, Mamaroneck NY 54-64; Libn Rye Neck High Sch, Mamaroneck NY 64-; Visiting Prof of Lib Sci SUNY(Geneseo) 66. 9: NEA: NY State Tchrs Assn; Westchester Co LA. 10: Beta Phi Mu; Delta Kappa Gamma. 13: Yes. 14: Wk with child & YP, tchg lib sci. 15: 94 Forest ave, Rye NY 10580.

GRAVES, ANN R. b Orange Tex. 5: UTex 41-45 (Eng) BA; LSU 63-64 (LS) MS. 7: Ref asst Tulane U Lib (New Orleans) 61-63, Gifts & exch lign 64; Dir of ref div Tex State Lib 64-. 9: ALA; TexLA; SWLA. 14: Ref. 15: 407 W 18th st, Austin Tex 78701.

GRAVES, CAROLYN A. b Buena Vista Va 9 Jl 26. 5: Richmond Prof Inst of William & Mary 44-48 (Drama) BFA; Whittier Col 51-52 (Drama) MA; Peabody Col 62-63 MLS. 7: Lib asst Dept of Army, Ft Lee Va 52-55; Entertainment dir Dept of Arm y Yokohama Japan 54-57; Lib asst State Lib, Hartford Conn 58; Command entertainment dir Dept of Army, Berlin 58-61; Libn Fla State U 62; Asst post libn Dept of Army, Ft Richardson Alaska 63-65; Asst base libn Dept of Navy, Great Lakes Ill 65-66; Main post libn Dept of Army, Ft Braggs NC 66-. 9: ALA (Armed Forces Lib Sect: Sect Devel Com, Subcom on Booth Arrangements. 10: AAUW; Fayetteville Little Theatre. 14: Ref, pub serv. 15: Box 2, Fort Bragg NC 28307.

GRAVES, DAN W(ESLEY). b Mt Hope Kan 12 Mr 20. 5: UDenver 40-44 (LS) AB; UMich 54-58 (Amer Hist) MA, 65-(LS). 6: Fr, Ger. 7: Head Libn Willamette U 44-49; Photoreprod & acquisUIll(Urbana) 49-51; Catlgr UKan 51-53; Head circ dept UWichita 53-54; Head exch & gift UMich(Ann Arbor) 54-61; Chief order libn UMich LAW Sch (Ann Arbor) 61-62; Assoc Libn Franklin & Marshall Col 62-65; Head Libn Clarion State Col 65-. 9: ALA-ACRL (Phila Chap Chm 65-67; Tri-State Chap; v-pres 68-69, pres 69-70); Ore LA (Legis&Stand Coms 46-47, Cert Com 47-48, Mem-Large 49-50); NW Col Librns (chm 47-48); PennLA (chm NW Chap 66-68, Lib Dev com 68-69, Educ&Scholarship Com 68-69); Penn State Col Librns (chm 67-69). 10: AAUP. 13: Yes. 14: Admin, tech serv. 15: 171 So 6th ave, Clarion Pa 16214.

GRAVES, ELIZABETH (JOHNSON). b Harrogate Tenn 5 Jl 20. 4: Marshall LaVerne Graves. 5: Lincoln Mem U 39-42, 43-44 (Fr) AB; Peabody summers 46-50 BS in LS. 7: Tchr Clairfield Sch, Cairfield Tenn 42-43; Tchr libn Forge Rdge High Sch, Harrogate Tenn 44-46; Tchr libn Claiborne County High Sch, Tazewell Tenn 46-48; Elem libn Oak Ridge Pub Sch, Oak Ridge Tenn 49-50; Assoc libn Lincoln Mem U 50-51, Libn 51-52, Asst libn 53-. 10: . 14: Catlg, ref. 15: P O Box 132, Harrogate Tenn 37752.

GRAVES, ELIZABETH ANN. b Stamfor Conn 1 Jl 29. 5: Wells Col 47-51 (Music) BA; Katherine Gibbs 51-52 (Sec) Diploma; Boston U 56-58 (Music) MM; Simmons 60-63 MLS. 6: Ital, Fr, Ger. 7: Sec Amer Bible Soc, NYC 51-52; ec Amer Bible Soc, NYC 51-52; Sec Allyn & Bacon Publ, Boston 54-56; Libn to Head Libn Gen Educ Fine & Applied Arts Lib Boston U 59-66, Hd circ Mugar Lib 67-68, Hd audio dept 68-. 9: Amer Musicological Soc; MusLA. 10: Perkins Inst for the Blind; Internat Inst of Boston. 14: Admin, ref, music. 15: 9 Claflin rd, Brooklinr Ma 02146.

GRAVES, FRANCES M. b Sacramento Cal 7 S 19. 5: Sacramento City Col 37-39 (Math); St Mary-of-the-Wasatch 39-40 (Eng); Sacramento State Col 50-51, 51-53, 58 (Eng) AB; USan Francisco 49, 53, 59, 54-55 MA in LS; San Jose State Col summer 60 (LS)UCal 63,67. 6: Ger, Lat. 7: Tchr Holy Rosary Acad, Woodland Cal 47-49; Tchr-libn Holy Angels Sch, Sacramento Cal 49-55; Catlgr St Marys Col (Notre Dame Ind) 56, summer 58; Libn Chicago Jewish Acad 55-56; Libn Kit Carson JrHigh Sch, Sacramento Cal 56-. 8: Libn (volunteer) Newman Center, Sacramento Cal; Asst to Mothers Clubs org libs in parochial schs, Sacramento Cal 61-69 Libn (volunteer) org Jesuit High Sch Lib, Sacramento Cal 3-65. 9: Ala; CathLA (No Cal Unit past treas, mech Chm); NEA; CalLA; CalASchL (part chm Scholarship Loan Fd); Cal Tchrs Assn; SacramentoaschL (past pres); second Sch Lib (sec); Sacramento Area Lib Organ. 10: Libn Lit Com, Diocesean Coun; Jr Museum. 14: Catlg ya lit. 15: 901 36th st, Sacramento Cal 95816.

GRAVES, HARRIETTE (STEWART). b Waterville Mr 16 My 18. 4: Bryon Irwin Graves. 5: UMe 35-39 (Psych) BA. 6: Fr. 7: Research asst New England Bd of Higher Educ, winchester Mass 60-62; Profess lib asst Winchester Pub Lib, Winchester Mass 64-. 9: ALA; MassLA; NELA; RT of Child Libns. 14: Catlg, ref, circ, child lib. 15: 3 Parker rd, Winchester Ma 01890.

GRAVES, LESSIE LOUISE H. b Halls Hill Va 8 N 08. 5: WVa State Col 27-30 (Eng, Fr) AB; McGill 32 Certif in Lib Sci; UIll 33-34 BS in LS, summers 50-53 MS in LS; West Res 59, 61 (L). , U Ill 69 CAS. 6: Sp, Fr, Ger. 7: Ref libn Fla A&M U; Libn Shaw U 39-41; Libn Campbell Street High Sch, Daytona Beach Fla 49-56; Asst libn, tchr Fla A&M U summer 55, 56; Period reading room asst, asst head of Hough Br, Cleveland Pub Lib 56-63; Libn Central Jr High Sch, Cleveland 64-. 9: ALA; SLA (Biol Scis Div); OhioASchL; NE Ohio Tchrs Assn. 10: Amer Guild of Organists; Delta Sigma Theta; Kappa Mu Epsilon. 12: Jt auth "Bibliography of the Biological Sciences (61). 14: Ref, lib educ, documentation, applications of new tech to sch libs. 15: 10307 Marlowe ave, Cleveland Oh 44108.

GRAY, ALMA (LONG). b Tyler Tex. 4: Walter E Gray. 5: Spelman Col 27-31 (Eng, Fr) AB; Atlanta 41-42 BLS, 31-32 (Eng). 6: Fr. 7: Music & Eng tchr Ocala High Sch, Ocala Fla 32-33; Eng tchr-libn Jessup High Sch, Jessup Ga 33-35; Libn-Eng & Fr tchr LaGrange High Sch, LaGrange Ga 35-38; Eng-Fr tchr-libn Bainbridge High Sch, Bainbridge Ga 38-41; Army libn US Army, Camp Stewart Ga 42-44; Br libn Enoch Pratt Free Lib, Baltimore 44-57; Sch libn Douglass High Sch, Baltimore 57-. 8: Com mem Enoch Pratt Free Lib-New brs 50; Program The Patron Takes Over-Enoch Pratt Free Lib 46; Chm Adv Com Sch Libns, Baltimore 65-. 9: ALA-YASD (Mag Eval Com 62-64); MdLA (treas 54-56); MdASchL (treas 63-65). 12: Co-comp "Bibliography of Materials by and about Negro Americans for Young People" (67-68). 13: Yes. 14: Ref, reviewing, ya in ghetto schs. 15: 1 D Hamill rd, Baltimore Md 21210.

GRAY, ANNIE RAE. b Calico Rock Ark 16 Ja 22. 5: Ark State Col 47 (Soc Sci) BSE; Peabody 51 (LS) MA. 7: Tchr Ark Pub Schs 41-50; Asst libn Ark State Col 50-51; Dir Cherokee Re g Lib, Lafayette Ga 51-59; Pub lib consul Tex State Lib 59-61; Pub lib consul Mo State Lib 61-64; Libn Jefferson Co 64-. 9: ALA. 10: B us & Profess Women's Club; Delta Kappa Gamma; Phi Theta Kappa; Great Bks Gps. 13: Yes. 14: Devel lib serv. 15: Hillsb oro Mo 63050.

GRAY, ARLENE ELIZABETH. b Niagara Falls NY 27 S 09. 5: State U Col (Fredonia NY) 27-30 (Music Educ) State Diploma; Eastman Sch of Music (Rochester) summers 31-33 (Music Educ) BM, summers 34-41 (Music Educ) MM; SUNY (Buffal) 40-41 (LS), ext 43-44 (Span & Latin Amer Hist); Niagara U 46-48 (Educ); Syracuse 48-50 Bs in Ls; NY State U Col (Geneseo) summer 51 (LS);Eastman Sch of Mus 63 (Mus). 7: Music K-12 vocal & inst Groveand High Sch, Groveland NY 30-31; Vocal inst music LaSalle High Sch, Niagara Falls NY 32-47; Vocal music K-12 Lewison- Porter, Lewiston NY 47-48; Vocal music K-12 Blodgett Voc High Sch, Edw Smith Jr High Sch, Syracuse NY 48-50; Libn K-12 Griffith Inst, Springville NY 50-51; Libn 7-12 Central schs, Port Byron NY 51-53; Vocal music K-8 Fairmount Sch, Camillus NY 53-56; Libn 7-9 N Tonawanda Jr High Sch, N Tonawanda NY 56-67; Libn DYonville Col (NY) 68-. 9: NEA; MusLA; ALA; Amer Educl Res Assn; NY State Tchrs Assn; NYLA. 10: Red Cross; YWCA; Womens Relief Corps; Grand Army of the Republic; Pi Lambda Theta; Alpha Delta Kappa. 14: Sch lib admin, stud lib assts, rare music bks. 15: Box 134, 117 Ridgeway rd, Crystal Beach Ont Can.

GRAY, BARBARA (VASSAR). b St Paul Minn 2 S 32. 4: Wilfred J Gray Jr. 5: UMinn 49-53 (Hist) BS; Col St Catherine 54 BSLS. 7: Lib asst St Paul Pub Lib 51-53; Libn II Detroit Pub Lib 54-65; Hd lib for the blind & physically handicapped Wayne Co Federated Lib Syst, Wayne Mich 65-. 8: Adv Coun Recording for the Blind, Detroit Unit; Bd mem Mich Chap of Amer Assn of Wkrs for the Blind; Mem Adv Coun, Title IV-B, Mich State Lib. 9: ALA; Amer Assn of Wkrs for the Blind; Mich Assn of Child with Learning Disabilities; Detroit Assn for Retarded Child. 14: Lib serv to blind, visually and physically impaired. 15: 19192 Pennington dr, Detroit Mi 48221.

GRAY, DOROTHY L. b Eminence Ind 19 Ja 16. 5: Butler U 33-37 (Eng, Lat) AB; West Res 39-40 BS in LS. 7: Jr Asst schs div Indianapolis Pub Lib 38-39, 40-42, Head schs div 43-52; Libn Park Sch for Boys Indianapolis 57-60; Child libn Broad Ripple Br Indianapolis Pub Lib 60-. 8: Tchr lib sci, Butler U and Ind U Ext, 40s, 50s & 68. 9: ALA; IndLA. 14: Child serv. 15: 5934 Gladden dr, Indianapolis In 46220.

GRAY, DOROTHY (VILLMOW). b Milwaukee 11 N 26. 4: Richard A Gray. 5: UWis 44-48 (Zool) BA, 48-49 BLS. 6: Ger, Fr. 7: Child libn Pub Lib, Milwaukee 49-50, Br head 50-51; Jr catlgr Wellesley Col Lib 53-56; Ref libn Ohio State U Libs61, 63-. 13: Yes. 14: Ref. 15: 3019 St Johns ct apt 1, Columbus Oh 43202.

GRAY, GORDON W(ELSHONS). b Marine on St Croix Minn 5 Ag 05. 5: Macalester Col 24-28 (Soc, Pol Sci) AB; Ill U 28-29 BS in LS; Columbia 34-42 (Eng) MA, 49 (Eng) Prof Diploma, 52 (Eng) Ed D. 7: Page & clerk StPaul Pub Lib 24-28, Ref libn summer 29; Asst loan desk UIll 28-29; Asst ref libn UMo 29-32; Asst ref libn City Col (NY) 32-47, In chg of res & materials 54, Asst libn 52-, In chg of Sch of Educ Lib 54, Educ & Psych 64, Assoc Prof 68. 8: Elected to Sch of Educ Faculty, City Col; Bd of Dir acalester Col Alumni NY area;Com on Com and Bylaws, Sch Educ, City Col NY. 10: Kappa Delta Pi. 13: Yes. 14: Educ, Eng lit. 15: 417 Riverside dr, Apt E New York NY 10025.

GRAY, HELEN (RODD). b Windsor Ont 4 Ag 20. 4: Ian Gray. 5: Toronto 43 (Eng) BA; Fletcher Sch Tufts 45 (Internat Law & Diplomac) MA; UBCCC 62 BLS. 6: Fr. 7: Catlgr New Westminster Pub Lib, New Westminster BC 63-66; Soc Sc Libn Simon Frasen U, Burnaby BC 66-. 9: CanLA; BCLA. 14: Catlg. 15: Simon Fraser Univ, Burnaby BC Can.

GRAY, JOHN (COLIN FRAMPTON). b Hindhead End 25 Ap 13. 4: Margaretha Klazina de Boer Gray. 5: Cambridge U 31-34 (Lat, Fr, Geog) BA, 62 MA; Sorbonne U 32 & 33 (Cours D'Etrangers) Certificat; Ecole Hoteliere (Lausanne) 34-36 Diplome; UBC 63-64 BLS. 6: Fr, Ger, Dutch, Sp, Lat. 7: Catlgr UBC 64-. 14: Catlg. 15: 3180 W 43rd ave, Vancouver 13 BC Can.

GRAY, JUDITH ANN (ONDICH). b Pittsburgh 30 N 42. 4: N Gordon Gray. 5: Ind State Col(Penn) 60-63 (Educ, Eng) BS in Ed; UPittsburgh 63-64 MLS. 6: Fr, Swahili. 7: Stud asst Ind State Col Lib(Penn) 60-63; Stud asst ref div Carnegie Lib of Pittsburgh 63-64; Asst libn Tanganyika Lib Serv, Tanzania E Africa 65-67; Sch Libn H W Smith Jr High, Syracuse NY 68-. 8: Consul under Peace Corps; to NUTA (National Labor Union), Tanzania, on Lib for NUTA; to interested prim sch on a practical prog for operating a sch lib. 9: ALA; East AfricanLA; Onondago-Oswego Sch LA. 10: Kappa Delta Pi. 12: Handbook for Primary School Libraries (in Swahili &

English (67); "Handbook for "Book-Box Librarians (in Eng & Swahili) memco (66), DSaloam. 14: Child & sch wk, ref (esp local hist), EAfrican libnship. 15: 140 Clarencedale, Youngstown Oh 44512.

GRAY, JUDY ANN. b Sewickley Penn 29 Ap 42. 5: Carnegie Inst 60-64 (Bus Studies) BS; UPittsburgh 65-66 MLS. 7: Ref libn Carnegie Lib of Pittsburgh 66-. 9: ALA. 10: Phi kappa Phi; Beta Phi Mu. 14: Ref, catlg. 15: Box 98 RD 1, Sewickley Pa 15143.

GRAY, LAURIE W(ILLIAMS). b Tunica Co Miss. 4: James Everett Gray. 5: Miss State Col for Women 29-33 (Hist) AB; Murray State Col 54-55 (Educ) MA, 56-58 (LS); Peabody 58, 62-63 (LS) MA. 7: Libn Heath High Sch, W Paducah Ky 55-58; Instr Lib Sci Murray State Col 58-, Asst libn 58-. 9: Nat Coun Soc Studies; SELA; KyLA; KyEA; NEA; Amer Assn Higher Educ. 10: Pi Gamma Mu; Kappa Delta Pi; Nat Geog Soc. 14: Catlg, acquis, ref. 15: Rte 1 Martin Chapel rd, Murray Ky 42071.

GRAY, LEONA STEWART. b Barksdale Tex 5 F 05. 4: Zac B Gray. 5: Abilene Christian Col 27 (Span) BA; Southwest Tex State Col 31 (Home Econ) BS; UTex 36 (Sci) MS; E Tex State U 61 MS in LS. 6: Sp. 7: Dietician San Marco Acad 38-42; Tchr Eng & span, Instru home econ Uvalde Tex 42-50; Libn Southwest Tex Jr Col 59-. 9: Tex Jr Col Tchrs Assn. 10: Delta Kappa Gamma; AAUW. 14: Ref, rare bks, ser. 15: Rocksprings rd, Uvalde Tex.

GRAY, MALCOLM E. b Albany NY 19 F 21. 5: Kutztown State Col 41-43, 46-47 (Eng, Soc Studies, LS) BS; Ed; Syracuse summers 47-50 MS LS; Columbia 49-50 (LS), summer 51; UBridgeport 62; UConn summer 69. 7: US Army (T/Sgt) Greenland 42-45; Libn Central Sch, Jeffersonville NY 47-49; Libn Panzer Col of Phys Educ & Hygiene 49-50; Libn Norwalk High Sch, Norwalk Conn 50-. 8: Conn Com Presidents White House Conf on Child & Youth 60. 9: NEA Life mem); ALA (Institutional mem); ConnSchLA (pres 58-60, chm 2 coms); NESchLA; ConnEA (Life mem); NorwalkTA (chm &/or mem several coms). 10: Pi Lambda Sigma; Beta Phi Mu. 14: Sch libnship. 15: Norwalk High Sch, 125 E ave, Norwalk Ct 06851.

GRAY, MARGARET CARROLL. b Lane Ohio 9 Mr 12. 5: West Res 29-32 (Eng) BA, 35-36 (LS) BS. 6: Ger. 7: Child libn Cleveland Pub Lib 36-44, 45-5; Navy libn US Naval Train Center, Bainbridge Md 44-45; Child libn Hawaii County Lib, Hilo Hawaii 53-58; Bkmob libn of Hawaii, Honolulu 58-60, Child libn 60-. 8: Staff "Library 21", Seattle World's Fair 62. 9: ALA; HawaiiLA (past chm Child Sect). 10: Womens Com of Honolulu Commun Theatre; Friends of the Lib; Alum Ass FS Mather Col Honolulu Acad of Arts; UN Assoc of US. 13: Yes. 14: Child wk. 15: 573 Kaimake Loop, Kailua Oahu Hawaii 96734.

GRAY, MARY E. b Durand Mich 29 Ap 44. 5: Albion Col 62-66 (Physics) BA; UMich 66-67 AMLS. 6: Ger. 7: Tech libn Westinghouse Electric Corp Nuclear Energy Syst, Pittsburgh Penn 67-. 9: SLA (Pittsburgh Chap sec). 10: Sigma Pi Sigma. 14: Ref. 15: 3-935 Hamlet ct, Monroeville Pa 15146.

GRAY, RICHARD A. b St Paul Minn 6 O 27. 4: Dorothy Woelfl. 5: UMinn 45-50 (Anthrop, Eng) BA, 51-52 MSLS, 54-55 (Amer Studies). 6: Fr, Ger. 7: Acquis libn Minn Hist Soc, St Paul 52-54; Bibliogr acquis dept UMinn Lib (Minneapolis) 54-55; 1st asst ref dept Gary Pub Lib, Gary Ind 55-62; Ref libn Monsanto Chem Co, St Louis 62-63; Sr ref libn Ohio StateU Lib (Colubus) 63-. 9: ALA; -RSD. 12: "Guide to Book Review citations: a Bibliography of Sources" (68). "Serial Bibliographies in the Social Sciences and Humanities" (69). 13: Yes. 14: Ref, bibliog, publ bibliog. 15: 676 Riverview dr apt A-3, Columbus Oh 43202.

GRAY, SARAH VIRGINIA. b Durham NC. 1 O 34. 5: Duke 52-56 (Hist) AB; UNC 59-64 MS in LS. 6: Fr. 7: Asst to curator of mss Duke U Lib 56-58; Asst res reading room UNC Lib (Chapel Hill) 58-60, Res libn 60-64, Stud asst ref dept summer 64; Clerk typist for Treasurer NCLA summer 64; Period libn Col of William & Mary Lib 64-. 8: Exch libn 1968 UExeter, England. 9: VaLA. 10: Sigma Kappa. 12: Ed "Selected List of Periodicals (65), 69). 14: Ref, rare bks, mss, documents. 15: Building 900 apt 204 Conway Garden apts, Williamsburg Va 23185.

GRAY, SUZANNE (KALDECK). b Vienna Austria 30 D 24. 4: Ira C Gray Jr. 5: Simmons 41-45 (Chem) BS, 66-68 (LS) MS. 6: Fr, Ger. 7: Research chem Bird & Son, E Walpole Mass 45-49; Spec projects Countway Lib of Med, Boston 65-66, Dir ser acquis project 66; Research asst spec project on data elements Subcommittee on Data Elements, needham Mass 66-67; Sci ref libn Boston Pub Lib 68, Curator of sci 69-. 9: ALA; SLA. 14: Ref, bk sel, lib automation. 15: Boston Pub Lib Copley Sq, Boston Ma 02117.

GRAZIANO, EUGENE EDWARD. b Pittsburgh 10 Ag 27. 4: Freida E Mullen. 5: UOkla 48-51, 54-56 (Philos) BA, MA; Carnegie 53-54 (LS); Kan State Tchrs Col (Emporia) 58 (LS); San Jose State Col 63-65 (Educ) Libnship Credential; UCal (Santa Barbara) 67-69 (Philos). 6: Ital, Sp, Ger, Fr. 7: Aviation machinist Mate 3/c US Navy, PR 45-48; (1st Lt) Quartermaster, Civil Affairs & Sales Off US Army, Germany 51-53; Head Libn Duncan Okla) Pub Lib 56; Head Libn Parsons (Kan) Pub Lib 56-57; Head ibn Emporia (Kan) Pub Lib 57-58; Asst sci libn So Ill U 58-59, Chief sci libn 59-61; Research Info Spec Lockheed Missiles & Space Co Labs, Palo Alto Cal 61-65; Asst libn-serv UCal(Santa Barbara) 65-. 8: Associate; R&D Consultants Co Los Altos Cal 67-. 9: SLA; CalLA; EDUCOM; Cal Sch Facil Coun. 10: Great Books Discussion Groups. 11: Distinguished Military Graduate. 12: Numerous Sci & Tech Bibliog in Aerospace Scis, Linguistics, Logic, Optics, Computer Scis, Engnr, Med, Mgt, Marketing. 13: Yes. 14: Univ lib admin tchg-research, sci libnship, automation, bldg planning, info sci. 15: 6815 Pasado rd, Goleta Cal 93017.

GRAZIER, MARGARET HAYES. b Denver Col 19 D 16. 4: Robert T Grazier. 5: Colorado state Col 34-37 (Educ) BA, 38-41 (Educ) MA; UDenver 37-38 Diploma in LS; UChicago 52-54 (LS). 6: Fr. 7: Libn & supv libs pub schs, Greeley Colo 39-42; Libn Lake forest High Sch, Lake Forest Ill 42-45; Sch lib consul W K Kellogg Foundation, Battle Creek Mich 45-46; Chief ref libn pub serv div UDenver Libs 46-48; Asst prof UDenver Sch of Libnship 48-52; Visiting lecturer & asst prof Grad Lib Sch UChicago 54-56; Secondary sch libn Birmingham Bd of Educ, Birmingham Mich 56-65; Tchr UMich Dept of Lib Sci summers 58-65; Assoc Prof Wayne State U Dept of Lib Sci 65-. 8: Consul US Off of Educ, Libr Serv Div, Ed Prof Pers Dev 64-68. 9: ALA (Com chm Sect Sch Libs, Dutton-Macrae Fellowship Com, Adult Bks for Slow Readers Com, Magaz Evalu Com); ASCD; Dept of A-V Instr; MichLA; MichASchL; Mich A-V Assn. 10: AAUP. 13: Yes. 14: Sch libnship, sel & eval materials, lib educ. 15: 17565 Pennington dr, Detroit Mi 48221.

GRAZIER, ROBERT T. b Altoona Penn 14 Jl 17. 4: Margaret Hayes. 5: Oberlin Col 35-39 (Hist) AB (cum laude); West Res 39-40 BSLS; Penn State U 41-47 (Hist) MA; Chicago 50-54 (LS).07: Circ libn Penn State U 42-44; Circ libn Wayne State U 44-45; Ser libn Penn State U 45-48; Libn Penn State Tchrs Col 48-50; Asst to dir UFla Libs 50-52, Asst dir 52-55; Assoc dir Wayne State U Libs 55-. 9: ALA (Life mem); MichLA. 10: AAUP. 13: Yes 14: Admin. 15: 17565 Pennington, Detroit Mi 48221.

GRAZIER, VIRGINIA (ORBETON). b Boston 16 My 16. 5: Bates Col 34-36; Simmons 36-38 (LS) BS. 7: Lib asst Trinity Col (Hartfor Conn) 38-40; Catlgr Penn State Col 40-44; Bkmobile asst Detroit Pub Lib 44-45 Catlgr Penn State Col 45-47; Head Libn Santa Fe Reg Lib, Gaiesville Fla 53-61; Head Libn Hudson Lib & Hist Soc, Hudson Ohio 61-. 8: Consul; Sarasota (Fla) Pub Lib 59, Venice (Fla) Pub Lib 62. 9: ALA; FlaLA (chm Pub Lib Div 59); SELA; OhioLA. 10: LWV; Bus & Prof Womens Club. 14: Ref, bk sel. 15: 49 E Main st, Hudson Ohio 44236.

GREANEY, W(ILLIAM) J. b NYC 3 My 28. 5: Villanova 48-52 (Econ) BS; LIU 65-67 (LS) MS. 6: Sp. 7: Eng instr: high sch, Hauppauge NY 55-57, jr high sch, Levittown NY 57-58, high sch, N Vancouver BC Can 61-62; Jr libn jr high sch, Brentwood NY 58-61; Libn-media specialist high sch, Brentwood NY 62-. 8: Adv Brentwood Pub Sch Libs 62-. 9: ALA; NEA-DAVI; NYStateTA; BrentwoodTA. 10: Adv local chap Nat Honor Soc; Mem Suffolk Museum. 14: Instr materials. 15: Spring Hollow rd, St James LI NY 11780.

GRECH, ANTHONY PAUL. b NYC 16 Jl 30. 5: Manhattan Col 48-52 BBA; Columbia 59-61 MS in LS. 6: Fr, Sp, Maltese. 7: Assn of the Bar of the City of NY, NYC: Ref asst 52-55, House asst 55-58, Asst ref libn 58-65, Ref libn 65-67, Libn 67-. 9: Internat Assn of Law Libs; AALL (chm Com on Microfacsimiles, rep to ASA PH5); ALA; Bibliog Soc UVa; CathLA; Nat Microfilm Assn; SLA; Law Lib Assn of Greater NY (treas 61-62); Assn of Law Libs of Upstate NY; NY Lib Club. 10: Beta Phi Mu. 12: Co-comp, Bibliog on internat Financing in McDaniels "International Financing and Investment (63); Co-comp, Bibliogs in Surrey & Shaw "Lawyers Guide to International Business Transactions (63); Ed "Current

Publications of "Law Library Journal (62-65). 13: Yes. 14: Ref (legal), microfacsimiles. 15: Assn of the Bar of City of NY Lib, 42 W 44 st, New York NY 10036.

GRECO, ANTHONY. b Cucamonga Cal 8 Ap 25. 5: Chaffey Col 42-43; Pomona Col 46-49 (Latin-Amer Studies) BA; Claremont Grad Sch 49-50 (Span); USoCal 52-53 MA in LS. 6: Sp. 7: Pharmacists mate 2/c US Navy 43-46; Sr lib asst ref dept UCLA Lib 51-52, Sr lib asst circ dept 52-53, Asst catlgr biomed lib 53-54, Head acquis sect Biomed Lib 54-57, Head periods reading room 58-60, Head ref dept UCal(Santa Barbara) 60-62, Chief of pub serv San Fernando Valley State Col 63-66; Asst Univ libn for personnel Harvard U Lib 67-68, Assoc univ libn 68; Asst univ libn for personnel UCLA 69-. 9: ALA; CalLA. 10: Beta Phi Mu. 14: Admin. 15: 234 Amalfi dr, Santa Monica Ca 90402.

GREDINGER, HAZEL JANE (PENNINGTON). b Vernon Ala 24 Ag 15. 5: UAla 31-35 (Eng) AB; Columbia 41-42 BLS. 7: Ref libn Norwich U 42-43; Period libn Miss State Col for Women 57-62; Ref libn Air U Lib, Maxwell AFB Ala 63-. 9: SLA; AlaLA. 10: Kappa Delta Pi; Psi Chi; Alpha Beta Alpha. 14: Ref. 15: Apt 205, 395 Felder ave, Montgomery Ala 36104.

GREDLER, CHARLES ROGERS. b Brockton Mass 15 O 23. 4: Eloise Electa Proper. 5: Cornell U 41-42, 46-49 (Russ Lang & Hist, Lit); AB; Simmons 49-50 (LS) MS. 6: Slavic langs, Fr. 7: Staff sgt 456th Fighter Squadron Air Corps AUS 43-46; Russian catlgr Cornell U Lib 49; Harvard Col Lib:Russian catlgr 49-51, Slavic catlgr 51-54, Asst in chg Slavic Collection 54-56, Chief of the Slavic Div 56-61, Asst libn in chg Slavic Collections 61-, Archibald Cary Coolidge bibliog(r) 68-. 8: Study of the Cyrillic Union Catlg at LC with Eleanor Buist at request of COCOSEERS which led to Reader edition of the catlg. 13: Yes. 14: Catlg, bk sel. 15: 119 Burlington st, Lexington Mass 02173.

GREEAR, YVONNE ETNYRE. b Austin Tex 19 Je 22. 5: UTex 44-48 (Radio, Speech) BFA, 55-62 MLS. 6: Fr, Sp, Ger. 7: Continuity writer Gilbert Co, Austin Tex 48-50; Pub rel asst El Paso Nat Bank, El Paso Tex 50; Sec & admin asst to libn Tex West Col 50-56; Tech libn El Paso Natural Gas Co, El Paso Tex 57-61; Ref libn Ft Bliss ADC Lib, El Paso Tex 62-63; Ref libn UTex (El Paso) 64-. 8: Instr UTex (El Paso) 59-60; Lib consul 63-; lectr Grad Sch Lib Sci, Tex U summers 68-. 9: ALA; SLA(Tex Chap var offs 58-64); TexLA(chm Spec Lib Div 60-61); SWLA; Border Reg LA (var offs). 10: Zeta Tau Alpha; Soroptimist. 11: Libn of the Year, 1968; Border Regl LA. 13: Yes. 14: Ref, catlg. 15: 3449 Greenock, El Paso Tex 79925.

GREELEY, ELIZABETH M (DENNIS). b Boston Mass 16 O 17. 4: John H Greeley. 5: Simmons 35-39 (LS) BS. 6: Ger, Fr. 7: Asst in child room Fordham Br NY Pub Lib 39-41; Child libn Watertown Free Pub Lib N Br, Watertown Mass 41-43; Patient's libn Naval Hosp, Newport RI 43-44; Asst to sta libn Naval Hosp, Chelsea Mass 44-46, Med libn 47-. 9: MedLA; SLA; NELA. 14: Med & nursing bks. 15: Med Lib Naval Hospital, Chelsea Ma 02150.

GREELEY, MABEL (FORWARD). b Medford Mass 23 My 17. 4: William Hancock Greeley. 5: Tufts 35-39 (Hist) AB; Simmons 39-41 (LS) BS. 6: Fr, Ger. 7: Asst ref libn Medford Pub Lib, Medford Mass 39-41; Col Libn Farmington State Tchrs Col 41-42; Lib asst Needham Pub Lib, Needham Mass 50-56; Col Libn Newton Jr Col 57-. 9: ALA; MassLA; NE Jr Col Coun Libns. 10: Simmons Col Sch of Lib Sci Aumni Assn. 14: Admin, lib educ. 15: 73 Parker rd, Needham Heights Mass 02194.

GREELY, GEORGIANA (MATHEWS). b Worcester Mass 13 My 33. 4: John M Greely. 5: Wheaton Col 51-55 (Fr) AB; Middlebury Col Grad Sch of Fr in France 55-56 (Fr) AM; Middlebury Col summers 55, 57, 59; Assumption Col summer 60; CatholicU 64-66 MSLS. 6: Fr, Sp, ital, Portu, Ger. 7: Apprentice libn Worcester Free Pub Lib, Worcester Mass 56-57; Instr in Fr Wheaton Col 57-60; Instr in Fr Abbot Acad, Andover Mass 61-62; Subj catlgr LC 66-. 10: Phi Beta Kappa; Beta Phi Mu. 14: Catlg. 15: 1600 So Eads st apt 513, So Arlington Va 22202.

GREEN, (EMMA) ALICE. b Coffey Co Kan 20 S 16. 5 Amarillo Col 34-36; W Tex State U 36-37 (Liberal Arts); UOkla 37-38 BS in LS; LSU 68-69 (Lib Sci); N Tex State U 69- (Lib Ser). 7: Libn Tex Mil Col 38-39; Gen asst Tex State Lib 39-41; amarillo Pub Lib, Amarillo Tex: Gen asst 41-42, Asst libn 42-46, Act libn 46-47; City Libn Mary E Bivins Mem Lib, Amarillo Tex 47-. 9: ALA; TexLA (chm Pub Libs Div, Head Lib Devel Com, var minor assignments); SWLA. 10: Altrusa Club; Delta Kappa Gamma; AAUW; C of C, Womens Div. 13: Yes. 14: Pub lib admin. 15: 403 Virginia, Amarillo Tex 79106.

GREEN, ARTHUR L. b Bentonville Ark 16 F 28. 4: Janice Baxter. 5: Tex A&M 5 (Engnr); So Methodist U 47-50 (Eng) B; Sam Houston State 55-57 (Educ) MEd; N Tex State U 57-62 (Educ); LSU 68-69 (Lib Sci); N Tex State U 69- (Lib Ser). 6: Fr, Ger, Sp. 7: Army Transportation Corps Tec4 Admin NCO 46-47; Traffic clerk Int Harvester Co, Dallas 51-52; Tchr-libn Liberty Jr High Sch, Liberty Tex 52-57; Libn C O Wilson Jr High Sch, Nederland Tex 57-. 9: Tex State Tchrs Assn. 10: Phi Delta Kappa. 15: 211 S 2-1/2 st, Nederland Tx 77627.

GREEN, BERTHA (MARIASHA). b Cleveland 8 Mr 16. 4: James Ernest Green. 5: Penn State U 33-37 (Econ) BA; UMich 39-40 ABLS, 58-63 AMLS. 6: Ger, Fr. 7: Adult serv libn Pub Lib, Lakewood Ohio 40-42; UMich: Libn circ dept 46-47, Libn East Engnr 47-48, Libn Col of Arch & Design 48-57; Jr high libn Plymouth Schs, Plymouth Mich 57-61, Dir of Libs 61-. 9: ALA; MichASchL (Exec Bd, chm Recr Com 62-64, chm Supvrs Sect 69-70). 14: Sch libs. 15: 1103 Kingwood, Ypsilanti Mich 48197.

GREEN, DOUGLAS A. b Gilmer Tex 17 F 25. 4: Clovis Elwell. 5: N Tex StateU 51 (LS) BA; E Tex StateU 51 (Hist) MA; LSU 68 MS in LS. 6: Sp. 7: Bkkeeper Croley Hardware Co, Gilmer Tex 42-43; SKD 1/c USN (Seabees), US & SW Pacifix 43-46; Libn Crystal City High, Crystal City Tex 51-52; Tchr Ozona So Elem, Ozona Tex 53-56; Libn Woodsboro High Sch, Woodsboro Tex 56-63; Chief bibliogr UArk 63-67; Hd libn Bee Co Col 68-. 9: ALA; ArkLA; TexLA; TexJrColTA. 14: Acquis. 15: Bee County Col, Beeville Tx 78102.

GREEN, ELIZABETH (PACKER). b Rockport Mass 7 Ag 15. 4: Burges Green. 5: Jackson Col 33-37 (Hist) AB; Simmons 37-38 (LS) BS 07: Ref & circ Elmwood Lib, Providence 38-40; Ref & br Great Neck Lib, Great Neck NY 40-42; Libn colored & white libs, New Bern NC 43; Personnel mgr Ideal Toth Inc, Cambridge Mass 44-46; Catlg asst John Carter Brown Lib, Providence 60-. 8: Bd of Trustees Providence Country Day Sch (sec 58-63). 10: RI Planned Parenthood; Bk Com Providence Athenaeum. 14: Catlg, rare bks, ref. 15: 29 Benefit st, Providence RI 02904.

GREEN, GLORIA ANN. b Dothan Ala 20 My 33. 5: Gallaudet Col 56-60 (LS) BS; CatholicU 62-68 MSLS. 6: Fr. 7: Libn (catlg) Dept of Health, Educ & Welfare, Wash DC 60-68; Libn (catlg) AirU Lib, Maxwell AFB Montgomery Ala 68-. 9: SLA. 14: Catlg. 15: 3441 Audubon rd apt C-8, Montgomery Al 36111.

GREEN, JEAN (MITCHELL). b Columbus Ohio 12 Ap 23. 4: Emerson P Green. 5: Denison U 40-44 (Hist) BA; West Res 44-45 BS in LS. 7: Asst libn Licking Co Lib, Newark Ohio 45-46; Lib asst Newark Pub Lib, Newark Ohio 46-47; Lib asst acquis dept UPenn Lib 47-69, Acquis lib 69-. 9: ALA-ACRL (treas Phila Chap 63-65). 15: 112 W Richardson ave, Langhorne Penn 19047.

GREEN, JEANNINE ANN (SHIVERS). b Baton Rouge La 11 Jl 39. 5: UConn (Storrs) 57-61 (Fr lit) BA; UWis (Madison) 62-63 MLS. 6: Fr, Sp. 7: Acquis & govt docs asst UConn 61-62; Catlgr romance langs UWis (Madison) 63-65; Info specialist & catlgr Nat Ind Conf Bd, NY 66-67, Chief libn 67-68, Dir div of info serv 68-. 9: ASIS; SLA (NY Chap: sec-treas Bus & Fin Gp 68; mem Documentation Div 67-). 10: UWis Lib Sch Alum Assn. 14: Admin, consulting. 15: 200 Wyckoff st, Brooklyn NY 11217.

GREEN, JOAN C(ATHERINE). b Providence RI 22 O 42. 5: URI 60-62, 63-64 (Home Econ) BS, 65-67 MLS; Skiringssal Foukehoy Skole (Norway) 62-63 (Crafts); Boston U 64-65 (Hist of Art). 6: Fr, Norwegian. 7: Lib asst (circ) RI Col 65-67; Asst Collections libn Dalhousie U 67-. 9: CanLA; ALA; APLA; HalifaxLA. 14: Collections develop, ref. 15: Dalhousie Univ Lib, Halifax Nova Scotia Can.

GREEN, RENEE (SALAMON). b Pittsburgh Penn 23 Jl 44. 4: Norman Allen Green. 5: UPittsburgh 62-66 (Eng Lit) BA, 66-67 MLS; Penn StateU 63; UWis 66 (LS). 6: Fr. 7: Lib oage Carnegie Lib of Pittsburgh Penn 59-62; Lab asst Child Hosp, Pittsburgh Penn 62-63; Lib aide UPittsburgh 64-65; Research aide Amer Inst of Research, Pittsburgh Penn 66-67; Libn Penn StateU (Pittsburgh) 67-. 9: ALA; PennLA. 10: Org for rehab Train; Beta Phi Mu. 14: Med ref. 15: 5816 Elmer st, Pittsburgh Pa 15232.

GREEN, ROSA F. b Carlisle Ky 16 F 10. 5: Ky Wesleyan 28-29; UKy 29-32, 33-36 (Eng) AB; UWis 37; Catherine Spalding Col 55-57 MS in LS; 67,68; East State Col summer 65; West State U 67. 6: Fr. 7: Libn Louisville Pub Schs, Louisville Ky 34-43; Libn Jefferson County Pub Schs, Louisville Ky 54-; Lecturer in Lib Sci Catherine Spalding Col 60-; Ref U louisville Lib 67, 68. 8: Chm various coms for bds of educ; chm revision of handbk for lib serv State Dept of Educ. 9: ALA; NEA; KyLA; KyASchL; KyEA; Jr Col EA. 14: Sch lib wk, wk with yp. 15: 827 Melford ave, Louisville Ky 40217.

GREEN, SUE (BAILEY). b Camilla Ga. 4: Marvin Wilson Green. 5: Asbury Col (Eng Lit) BA; Emory (Eng Lit) MA; Columbia (LS) MS; Newark State Col (Educ). 6: Fr, Anglo-Saxon. 7: Stud asst Asbury Col & Emory U; High sch libn, Tallapoosa Ga; Ref & res Drew U; Child libn Free Pub Lib, E Orange NJ; Sch libn, Montclair NJ; Sch libn, Newark NJ currently. 8: Consultant, Dover Free Public Library. 9: ALA; ; -YASD; ISAD; NEA; NJEA; NJSchLA; NJ A-V Educ Assn. 10: Newark Sch Libns Assn; Newark Tchrs Assn; Col Club of Dover (NJ). 14: Sch lib serv, child lit, ref. 15: 15 Lawrence st, Dover NJ 07801.

GREEN, SUSAN. b Buffalo NY 27 Jl 39. 5: Buffalo State Tchrs Col 57-60 (Educ); UBuffalo 60-62 (Hist) BA, 61-66 (Educ) EdM; Syracuse 64-65 MSLS; Fresno State Col 66-68 (Hist). 6: Sp. 7: Tchr Attica Central Sch, Attica NY 62-63; Libn Kern Co High sch Syst, Bakersfield Cal 65-68; Child libn Fair Lawn Pub Lib, Fairlawn NJ 68-69; Base libn USAF, Kunsan Korea 69-. 9: CalASchL; Bergen-PassaicLA. 10: Red Cross. 14: Ref, reader's adv, sch lib. 15: Box 515 354th Combat Support Group, Apo san Francisco Ca 96264.

GREEN, WALTER H JR. b New Orleans 30 My 32. 4: Kathleen Byars. 5: LSU 55-59 (Music, Voice) B Mus, 59-61 M Mus, 61-62 (LS) MS. 7: tock clerk Mine Safety Appliances, New Orleans summers 49, 50; Copy boy Times-Picayune Publ Co, New Orleans 51; Charge clerk Shushan Bros Dry Goods Co, New Orleans 51; Office manager Delta Fire & Safety Equip Co, New Orleans 51-54; Seaman (SN) US Coast Guard Reserve 51-54; Insurance clerk Time Finance Co, New Orleans 54; Office manager Walter Kidde Sales & Serv, New Orleans 54-55; Chauffeur Toye Bros Cab Co, New Orleans 55; LSU: Clerk, Dean of Men 57, Clerk, page Dept of Archives 58, Bldg proctor Sch of Music 58-62, Lib clerk records Sch of Music 58-60, Lib clerk circ & photoreprod lib 61, Counselor, phys ed Instr, asst Choral Dir, Tenor Soloist, Brevard Music Center & Transylvania Music Camp, Brevard NC summer 61; Grad asst, trainee LSU Lib (circ, ser, govt documents) 61-62; Head of period div & Asst Prof of Lib Sci Southwest Mo State Col Lib 62-. 9: ALA; MOLA (1968 Publ Chm, State Conv 10: AAUP; Phi Mu Alpha Sinfonia; (pres 61-62). 14: Admin, pub serv, period, tech serv. 15: 2103 Luster st, Springfield Mo 65804.

GREENAWAY, EMERSON. b Springfield Mass 25 My 06. 4: Helen Kidder. 5: U Mass 23-27 BS; UNC 34-35 (LS) AB. 7: Ref asst Springfield City Lib, Springfield Mass 28-30; Asst libn & supv of brs Hartford Pub Lib, Hartford Conn 30-34; ,36; Spec asst Enoch Pratt Free Lib, Baltimore 35; Libn Pub Lib, Fitchburg Mass 37-40; Libn Pub Lib, Worcester Mass 40-45; Dir Enoch Pratt Free Lib, Baltimore 45-51; Dir Free Lib of Phila 51-69. 8: Consul in pub libs for Unesco, 47; Mem Governors Commsn on Pub Lib Devel of Penn, 57-61; Penn Adv Cou on Lib Devel, 61-68 Adv Bd "Grolier Encyclopedia; Surveys: Pub Lib, San Francisco, Santa Clara Co Cal, Bucks Co Penn, New Haven Conn, Durham NC, Princeton NJ, Richmond Va; Mem Adv Bd "Wilson Library Bulletin"; Mem, Visiting Com, Wheaton Col, 1968-; Mem Govt Adv Com on Internat Bk & Lib Progs, US Dept of State 68-; US Deleg of Librns to the USSR 61; Union Lib of Penn; Mem Library Com, Franklin Inst; Mem Phila Reg Med Lib Com. 9: BSA; ALA (Lie mem, Coun, pres 58-59, chm Com on Legis 60-66); PennLA; Lib Coun of Metro Phila (chm 64-); MassLA (Lfe mem); MdLA (Life mem); chm Int Rel Com 68-; Executive Com, IFLA section on Public libraries; mem, Presidents National Advisory Com on Libraries. 10: Grolier Club; Philobiblon Club; Nat Bk Com; Phila Art Allince; Amer Philos Soc; Mus Coun of Phila; Amer Inst of Arch, Phila Chap (Hon). 11: Litt D (Hon) West Md Col, 50; LHD (Hon) UMass, 52; Citation & Good Government Award, Phila Jr C of C & US Jr C of C, 55, 54; Lippincott AWARD ALA, 55; LLD (Hon) Temple U, 58; Litt D (Hon) Drexel, 59; Distinguished Serv Award, PenLA 60; Distinguished Achievement Award, Alumni, Grad Sch of Lib Sci Drexel, 65. 13: Yes. 15: 97 E Bells Mill rd, Phila Pa 19118.

GREENBAUM, HARRIET. b Brooklyn NY 23 Ap 37. 5: Brooklyn Col 55-58 (Fine Arts) BA; NU 58 (Fine Arts); Pratt 61-62 MLS. 6: Hebrew. 7: Tchr Bd of Educ, NYC 59-63; Tchr of Lib at PS 207, Brooklyn NY 63-66; Tchr of lib at Alex Hamilton Voc & Tech High Sch 66-. 9: ALA-CSD; NYC Sch Libns Assn. 15: 135 Eastern Parkway, Brooklyn 38 NY 11238.

GREENBERG, BETTE R. b Chicago Ill 22 Jl 37. 5: UMo 56-57; UPittsburgh 58-59 (Psych, Comparative Lit) BA, 64-65 MLS. 6: Fr, Ger. 7: Catlgr Yale Med Lib 65-67, Sr ref libn 67-. 9: MedLA. 14: Ref, bibliog. 15: 111 Park sr 11-0, New Haven Ct 06511.

GREENBERG, CELIA K. b Kiev Russia 8 N 10. 5: Crane Jr Col 28-30 (Eng); Roosevelt U (Anthrop); Columbia 49-50 (Eng, Hist). 6: Fr, Yiddish. 7: Asst to dept hd (1st Lt Army) LA Signal Depot 43-44; Sr libn NY Pub Lib 49-50; Libn II Chicago Pub Lib 30-. 9: ALA; Chicago Lib Club. 10: Chicago Pub Lib Staff Assn. 14: Ref, hist collection. 15: 4100 Marine dr, Chicago Il 60613.

GREENBERG, EDITH (SCHULER). b Cleveland 21 S 12. 4: Marcel. 5: Cleveland Col West Res 30-40 (Psych) BA; West Res 59-62 MSLS. 6: Fr. 7: Desk asst Cleveland Pub Lib Sterling Br 30-31, Desk asst E 131st st Br 31-39, Head of desk Nottingham Br 39-40, 1st asst Woodhill Sta 40-41; Secondary sch libn Mayfield (Ohio) City Schs, Mayfield Jr & Sr High Sch 61-62; Head Libn Mayfield High Sch 63-. 8: Consul for org & catlg of Med Lib of Doctors Hosp, Cleveland Heights Ohio, summer 60. ; Co-proj dir ESEA Title III Planning Grant for an innovative prog in Art 66-68. 9: ALA-AASchL; NEA-DAVI; OhioASchL; OhioLA (mem & chm Intel Freedom 68-69); OhioEA. 10: Hadassah. 14: Ya wk, adult ref. 15: 1489 Middleton rd, Cleveland Heights Ohio 44121.

GREENBERG, ESTHER (SIEGEL). b NYC 25 My 23. 4: Arthur Greenberg. 5: NYU 40-44 (Home Econ) BS; West Res 61-63 (LS) MS. 7: Lib asst Cleveland Heights Pub Lib, Cleveland Heights Ohio 61-63; Libn Temple Brith Emeth, Cleveland 62-63; Catlgr Case Inst of Tech 63-68; Chief Catlgr Case West Res U 68-. 9: ALA, ASIS; NEOhio Tech Serv Libns. 10: Beta Phi Mu. 14: Catlg. 15: 3562 Bendemeer rd, Cleveland Heights Oh 44118.

GREENBERG, FANNIE. b Newark NJ. 5: Barnard 30 (Statistics) BA; Columbia 35 BSLS; NYU 51 (Educ, Voc Guidance) MA. 7: Libn Bd of Educ, Newark NJ 33-; Libn Central even High Sch, Newark NJ 38-41, 46-. 9: NJEA; NJ A-V Assn; Newark TA; Newark SchLA; Essex Co EA. 10: Commun volunteer. 14: Sch libs. 15: 60 So Munn ave, East Orange NJ 07019.

GREENBERG, GERTRUDE T. b NYC 29 S 15. 4: Martin Greenberg. 5: Brooklyn Col 31-35 (Fine Arts) BA; American U 37 (ECON); UGeneva(Switzerland) 58-59(Fr); Rutgers 61-62 MLS. 6: Fr, Ger. 7: Research & statistics Bur of Labor Statistics US Dept of Labor, Wash DC 36-37; Research assoc Womens Bur US Dept of Labor, Wash DC 38-39; Research assoc NY State Dept of Labor, NYC 39-42, Asst to depty Comm 42-43; Ref libn S Orange Pub Lib, S Orange NJ 61-62; libn Harry A Sprague Lib Montclair State Col 62-. 9: NJLA. 10: LWV. 15: 170 Mayhew dr, S Orange NJ 07079.

GREENBERG, HERMAN. b Philadelphia Penn 19 Mr 30. 4: Helen Katz Greenberg. 5: Penn state U 48-52 (Soc Sci) BS; Drexel 63 (Bus Admin) MBA. 7: Intelligence analyst (Cpl) USA, Wash DC 52-55; Personnel asst Phila Dept of Pub Health 56-58, Act personnel off 59-60, Asst personnel off Free Lib of Phila 60-64; Personnel off Phila Dept of Pub Health 64-65; Personnel off Free Lib of Phila 65-. 9: ALA; Pub Per Assn. 14: Personnel admin. 15: Free Lib of Phila Personnel Office, Logan Square, Phila Pa 19103.

GREENBERG, RAYMA RITA (WURTZ). b New Haven Conn 1 Je 31. 4: Murray Greenberg. 5: UConn 49-51; UMich 51-53 (Psych) AB; UCLA 62-63 MLS. 7: Libn USoCal summer 63; Libn Garnett Corp, Torrance Cal 63-. 9: SLA; So Cal Tech Proc Gp. 10: UCal Lib Schs Alum. Assn. 12: Co-comp "Directory of Special Libraries of Southern California," (3rd ed 68). 14: Admin, ref. 15: 13225 Admiral ave, Marina del Rey Ca 90291.

GREENBERG, STANLEY. b NYC 24 Ag 24. 4: Bernice Colodny. 5: NY State Col of Agric 45-46; Cornell 46-50 (Eng) BS; Columbia 5051 (Educ) MA; Simmons Col 53-61 (LS) MA. 6: Russ. 7: (Pfc) US Army Med Det 11th Inf, N Ireland, Fr, Eng 43-45; Inspector Springfield Armory, Springfield Mass 51-53; Store manager Hampshire Furniture Co, Northampton Mass 53-57; Lib asst Springfield Pub Lib, Springfield Mass 53; Ref libn Holyoke Pub Lib, Holyoke Mass 57-62; Asst libn Forbes Lib, Northampton Mass 62-. 9: MassLA; West Mass

LA; NELA. 10: Mass Archaelog Soc; Sch Com (Town of Westhampton Mass); Dir Civil Defense (Town of Westhampton Mass). ; Trustee, Westhampton Mem Lib; Northampton Hist Soc. 14: Ref. 15: RFD 1 Southampton rd, Easthampton Ma 01027.

GREENBIE, VLASTA KORAN. b Prague Czechoslavokia. 4: Barrie B Greenbie. 5: Hunter Col 54-58 (Econ, Statistics) AB; RutgersU 58-59 MLS. 6: Czech, Ger, Fr, Russian. 7: Statistician Nat Foundation for Infantile Paralysis, NYC 53-58; Ref libn econ div NYC Pub Lib 58-59; Research libn Fed Res Bank, Richmond Va 59-61; Chief ref libn US Bur census, Wash DC 61-62; Consul libn 1st Boston Corp, NYC 62-65; Libn Grad Sch Bus UWis (Madison) 66; Instr UWis Lib Sch (Madison) 66-. 9: SLA; ASIS; AALS; WisLA. 10: AAUW. 14: Admin & mgt, ref, consul. 15: Lib School Univ of Wis 425 Henry mall, Madison Wis 53711.

GREENBLATT, RUTH. b Phila Pa 25 My 25. 4: Newton Greenblatt. 5: Penn State U 43-47 (LS) BA; Drexel 64-67 (LS) MLS. 7: Ref libn Atlantic Co Lib, Mays Landing NJ 67-. 8: Dir (volunteer) Beth Israel Cong Lib. 15: 40 Northwood dr, Vineland NJ 08360.

GREENE, ANN (McVEIGH). b Rochetser NY 30 Ag 43. 4: Charles Stuart Greene. 5: Syracuse 61-65 (Eng) AB, Syracuse 65-66 MSLS, 66 NY State Sch Libn Certif. 6: Sp. 7: Lib clk syracuse U catlg dept 65; Libn Commun-Gen Hosp Sch of Nursing, Syracuse NY 66; Libn Fabius Central Sch, Fabius NY 66-. 8: Summer Libn: Jamesville-DeWitt - Tecumseh Elem 67, 68; Genesee Hills Elem 67, 68. 9: NEA; ALA; NYLA; OOSLA. 15: 704 Scott ave, Syracuse NY 13224.

GREENE, B P. b Blue Mountain Ark 5 Jl 23. 5: Ark State Tchrs Col 41-43, 62-65 (Hist) BSE; Ark A&M 43; Peabody Col 65-68 MLS. 7: Lt jg USN 44-46, Lt 51-53; Cattle buyer Cudahy Packing Co, Kan City Mo 47-51; Libn Conway Co Lib, Morrilton Ark 63-. 15: 703 N Moose, Morrilton Ar 72110.

GREENE, CLAIRE (HARGIS). b Natchitoches La 30 N 20. 4: Glenn B Greene. 5: NWest State col 36-40 (Phys Educ, Bio) BS; LSU 56-62 (LS) MS. 6: Fr. 7: Tchr (elem) La: McDonnell French Mission, Houma 40-41, Marthaville High Sch, Marthaville 41-42, Lake Charles City Schs, Lake Charles 42-43, VA, Natchitoches Parish 48-49; Tchr & libn Cloutierville High sch, Cloutierville La 49-59; Libn Natchitoches High Sch, Natchitoches La 59-63; Libn (asst catlg) NWest State Col 63-. 9: ALA; LaLA; LaTA. 10: Delta Kappa Gamma; Beta Phi Mu. 14: Catlg. 15: 225 S Williams, Natchitoches La 71457.

GREENE, DORIS (DANZIG). b Newark NJ 2 D 45. 4: Mark H Greene. 5: Skidmore 63-67 (Amer Studies) BA; Simmons 67-68 MLS. 6: Fr. 7: Summer intern (catlgr) Newark Pub Lib, Newark NJ summer 67; Catlgr TuftsU Med-Dental Lib 68-. 14: Catlg, ref. 15: 125 Forest Hills st #3, Jamaica Plain Ma 02130.

GREENE, FAY (LIVESAY). b Hancock County-Sneedville Tenn 23 N 24. 4: Rector Greene. 5: UTenn 42-56 (Home Econ) BS; Peabody 60-65 MLS. 7: Tchr Hancock County High Sch, Sneedville Tenn 44-46, Tchr-libn 46-51, Libn 51-. 9: NEA; ALA; TennEA; TennLA. 14: Ref. 15: Sneedville, Tenn 37869.

GREENE, GWENDOLYN M (CHICK). b Los Angeles Cal 5 Ag 26. 4: Robert Edwin Greene. 5: Oceanside-Carlsbad Col 48-49 (Hist) AA; San Diego State Col 49-51 (Hist) BA; USoCal 52-57 (LS) MS; UCal (San Diego) 68- (Hist). 6: Fr, Sp. 7: Stenographer-clk San Diego State Col 51-56, Catlgr 56-57; Asst libn a-v dir Mary Baldwin Col 64-65; Evening div libn Mira Costa Col 68-. 9: ALA. 10: Assn Preserv Va Antiquities; PTA. 14: Catlg, clsf, ref, acquis. 15: 819 Neptune ave, Encinitas Ca 92024.

GREENE, IRMA (THERESA BROWN). b Charleston SC 4 D 28. 4: Calvin R Greene Sr. 5: SC State Col 45-50 (LS) BA; UWis summer 52; Ind U 54-55 (Educ) MS; Drexel summer 65. 6: Fr. 7: Tchr libn Laing High Sch, Charleston SC 50-52; Libn Avery Inst, Charleston SC 52-54; Libn Burke High Sch, Charleston SC 54-62; Head Libn Charles A Brown High Sch, Charleston SC 62-. 9: ALA; SELA; SCLA; Charleston Co TA; Central Coun of Tchrs. 10: Women in Community Serv. ; Delta Sigma Theta; Jack & Jill of Amer; WICS; YWCA; Ouettes; Les Mesdames. 14: Wk with ya. 15: 1729 Heritage Park rd, Charleston SC 29407.

GREENE, K RICHARD. b Akron Ohio 10 Ja 33. 4: Ellin Peterson. 5: Gettysburg Col 50-54 (Sp) BA; Rutgers 58-59 MLS. 7: US Army-Inf 54-56; Y-a libn Buffalo & Erie Co Pub Lib 59-62; Y-a libn NYC Pub Lib 62-65, Asst br libn 65-67; Coord adult serv Free Pub Lib, Woodbridge NJ 67-. 9: ALA; FLIC; NYLA (Exec Bd, Child & Ya Serv Sect); NJLA (v-pres A-V Sect; pres Adult Serv Sect). 14: Adult & ya serv, a-v serv. 15: 113 Chatham lane, Point Pleasant NJ 08742.

GREENE, L(AURENT) RICHARD. b Bonnaventure Que Can 28 S 42. 4: Marcelle Lamothe. 5: Sem de St-Jean 65 (Phil) BA; U de Montreal 66 (LS) B Bbibl. 6: Fr. 7: Asst libn Assn of Univs and Cols of Can, Ottawa 66-67, Chief libn 67-. 12: Comp "Select Bibliography on Higher Education," quarterly (67-). 14: Ref. 15: 114 McClellan rd, Ottawa 6 Ont Can.

GREENE, MRS LUCY R(UFFIN). b Norfolk Va 13 Ap 19. 4: Preston A Greene. 5: William & Mary 35-39 (LS) AB. 7: Asst libn High Point High Sch, High Point NC 39-40; Tchr-libn Kempsville High Sch, Princess Anne Va 40-43; Libn NC State Sch for theBlind, Raleigh NC 46-48; Libn Spec Schs Br, QMRTC Ft Lee Va 51-53; Libn Quartermaster Bd, Ft Lee Va 53-54; Supv of stations Richmond Pub Lib, Richmond Va 56; Catlgr US Army Quartermaster Sch Lib, Ft Lee Va 58-. 9: SLA; VaLA. 14: Catlg, admin, ref. 15: Rt 2 Box 21, Charles City Va 23030.

GREENE, MICHAEL WILLIAM. b NYC 3 Jl 43. 5: City Col of NY 61-66 (Eng) BA; LIU 66-69 (LS) MS. 6: Fr. 7: Jr high sch tchr NYC Bd of Educ 66-67; US Coast Guard, Cape May NJ 67; Libn Bronx High Sch of Sci, Bronx NY 68-. 9: SLA. 11: Grand Street Boys Assn Award. 14: A-v wk. 15: 549 W 123 st, New York NY 10027.

GREENE, ROBERT JOHN. b Wellsville NY 2 Mr 33. 4: Elesta Dilmore. 5: Bowling Green State U 50-54 (Sci) BS; Fla State U 58-59 MSLS. 7: (Pfc) 71 Qmstr US Army, Alaska 54-56; Sci tchr Swanton Loc Sch, Swanton Ohio 56-57; Asst sci-tech libn Ga Inst of Tech 59-61, Tech reports libn 61-66; Libn Kennesaw Jr Col 66-. 9: SELA; Atlanta Lib Club. 10: Beta Phi Mu. 13: Yes. 14: Ref, tech reports, admin. 15: 359 W Wieuca rd, Atlanta Ga 30305.

GREENE, TOM (THOMAS ROBERT). b Liberal Kan 7 Je 44. 4: Shirley Brown. 5: San Angelo 62-63; Ga State 63-67 (Geog) AB; Emory 67-68 MLS. 6: Fr. 7: Catlgr US Army Inf Sch lib, Ft Benning Ga 68-69. Hd tech processes & asst libn 69-. 9: ALA. 14: Acquis, admin. 15: PO Box 6312, Columbus Ga 31907.

GREENE, VICTORIA (WEBER). b Bridgeton NJ 8 Mr 43. 4: Benjamin B Greene Jr. 5: West maryland Col 61-65 (Psych) BA; Rutgers 65-68 MLS. 6: Fr. 7: Ref libn WashDC Pub Lib 66; Circ asst Newton Col of the Sacred Heart 67-68; Supv field serv Commonwelath of Mass Dept of Educ Bur of Lib Ext, Boston 68-. 9: MassLA. 14: Ref. 15: 253 N Beacon st, Boston Ma 02135.

GREENER, BARBARA R (BURCKY). b Brooklyn NY 31 My 27. 4: Robert A Greener. 5: Brooklyn Col 45-49 (Romance Langs) BA; Pratt 49-50 BLS. 6: Sp, Portu, Ital. 7: Pre-prof libn Brooklyn Pub Lib 46-49, Libn grade 1 49-50; Music libn Queens Col (NY) 50-. 9: MusLA; NY Lib Club.10: CUNY Lib Staff Assn. 13: Yes. 14: Music libnship. 15: Rolling Hill rd, Old Westbury NY 11568.

GREENFIELD, MARJORIE. b Phila 13 Mr 37. 5: Brandeis U 54-58 (Sociol) BA; Drexel 63-64 MS in LS. 6: Fr, Sp. 7: Asst Paperbk Gallery, Wilmington Del 61-63; Libn Frankford Hosp Sch of Nursing, Phila 64-66; Dir UPenn Hosp Lib 66-. 9: Med LA (treas local unit 68-); SLA. 10: . 13: Yes. 14: Admin. 15: 110 S 19 st, Phila Pa 19103.

GREENGRASS, ALAN RICHARD. b NYC 6 D 42. 5: Columbia 59-63 (Govt) AB, 63-65 (Govt) MA, 66-68 (LS) MS. 6: Fr. 7: Staff asst for info serv, NY Times 67-. 9: ALA; ASIS; Amer Soc of Indexers (pres pro-tem 68-); Soc of Indexers (Gt Brit). 11. Tauber-Begner Award. 14: Indexing, info ret, lib automation. 15: 915 W End ave, New York NY 10025.

GREENHILL, BARBARA C(HRISTEN). b Lakewood Ohio 17 N 17. 4: . 5: Flora Stone Mather Col 35-39 (Hist) AB; West Res 43-44 BSLS. 6: Ger. 7: Tchr Roosevelt Elem Sch, Willoughby Ohio 39-42; Ref libn hist dept Cleveland Pub Lib 44-53; Libn Lewis Sands Elem Sch, Chagrin Falls Ohio 60-. 9: OhioLA; OhioEA; OhiaASchL; NE Ohio TA. 10: Flora Stone Mather Col Alumnae Assn; Eng Speak Union. 14: Hist ref, elem sch lib wk. 15: 34 W Summit st, Chagrin Falls, Oh 44022.

GREENHORN, EDNA (WETTON). b Akron Ohio 17 My 28. 4: Richard J Greenhorn. 5: UAkron 46-50 (Eng) BA; West Res 50-51 MS in LS. 6: Fr, Ger. 7: Non-prof positions Akron Pub Lib Firestone Park Br 46-50; Stud asst libn Cleveland Pub Lib 50-51; Catlg & bus ref libn Akron Pub Lib, Akron Ohio

51-55; Catlg & ref libn Stow Pub Lib, Stow Ohio 64-. 10: PTA; Stow Commun Club; Girl Scout troop leader. 14: Catlg, ref. 15: 2341 Lynnwood dr, Stow Ohio 44224.

GREENISEN, LORETTA J. b Salem Ohio 16 F 19. 5: Kent State 38-42 (Eng) BS in Ed, 52 (Eng) MA; UDenver 57-60 (LS) MA. 7: Tchr Fairfield Tp High Sch, Columbiana Ohio 42-56; Eng tchr Boardman High Sc, Youngstown Ohio 56-57, Libn 57-. 8: NDEA Lib Inst, Kent State U, 65; Taught Basic Catlg Kansas State Teachers' Col, summer sessions 66-67. 9: NEA; ALA-YASD (Magazine Sel Com 63-67; NE Ohio ta; OhioASchL; MahoningCoSchLA (pres 68-70). 10: Delta Kappa Gamma; AAUW. 14: Catlg, ref, instr in use of lib for studs. 15: 3934 Lemoyne, Youngstown Ohio 44514.

GREENLAW, LENA G (FISHER). b Des Moines Iowa 12 Jl 08. 4: James P Greenlaw. 5: Iowa State Col 26-28 (Home Econ); Southwest Mo State Col 55-6 (LS); UMo 56-60 (LS) AB. 7: Jr Catlg asst Iowa State Col Lib 38-39; Control desk Southwest Mo State Col Lib 55-56; Lib clerk UMo 56-57, Lib asst 58-60, Journalism libn 60-. 9: ALA; MoLA. 10: LWV; Womens Internat League for Peace & Freedom. 14: Ref. 15: Journalism Lib UMo, Columbia Mo 65202.

GREENLEY, BESS (OELBERG). b Fayette Co Iowa 6 Ja 06. 5: Upper Iowa Col 23-27 (Eng, speech, Drama) BA; State U Iowa (summers) 45-50 (Eng) MA; UNo Iowa (summers) 57, 58, 65 (LS) certif libn. 7: Hogh sch tchr: Tripoli Iowa 27-29, Oelwein Iowa 29-31, 47-56, Elkport Iowa 41-43, Monticello Iowa 43-47; Tchr Upper Iowa Col summers 30, 31; High sch libn, Oelwein Iowa 57-66; Dir lib serv Dubuque Commun Schs, Dubuque Iowa 66-. 9: NEA; ALA; -AASchL; NCTE; IowaStateEA; IowaASchL; NEDistASchL (sec 55-59). 10: Sigma Tau Delta; Delta Kappa Gamma. 13: Yes. 14: Supv, & admin coord. 15: Dubuque Ia 52001.

GREENMAN, BETTY F (YELLIN). b Boston 16 F 21. 4: Leon Greenman. 5: Smith 38-39; Simmons 3-42 (LS) BS, 68 (Urban & State PoL); Boston Col Grad Sch of Arts & Scis 65-66. 6: Fr. 7: Child libn Attleboro Pub Lib, Attleboro Mass 42-43; Child libn Quincy Pub Lib, Quincy Mass 63-64; Libn Mignon Rubenovitz Lib Temple Mishkan Tefila Chestnut Hill, Newton Mass 60-; Catgr Pine Manor Jr Col, Brookline Mass 69-. 8: Bibliog Peter Bent Brigham Hosp Nursing Lib "Alumnae Who Published since First Graduating Clss 1913, (63). 9: NELA. 14: Catlg, admin. 15: 267 Hartman rd, Newton Centre Ma 02159.

GREENWAY, ADELE (JOAN). b ChathamOnt Can 25 F 41. 5: UWest Ont 59-63 (Eng) BA; Toronto 62 ARCT, 63-64 BLS. 7: Libn UWest Ont 64-66; Libn U Windsor Lib 66-. 14: Ref. 15: 1515 Dufferin pl, Windsor 14, Ont Can.

GREENWOOD, ANNA (STARBUCK). b Glendale Cal 13 My 23. 4: David Charles Greenwood. 5: USoCal 53 (Eng) AB, 61 (LS); CatholicU 62-66 MSLS. 7: Clerk Security-First Nat Bank, Los Angeles 42; Clerk typist So Cal Telephone Co, Los Angeles 43-45; Clerk to sr clerk-steno Los Angeles City Health Dept 45-52; Tchr Torrance Sch Dist, Torrance Cal 53-56; Tchr Wiseburn Sch Dist, Hawthorne Cal 56-61; Tchr Montgomery Co Schs, Rockville Md 61-62, Libn 62-. 9: ALA; NEA; Assn for Childhood Educ Internat (Sch chm); Md State Tchrs Assn; Md Media Assn; MdLA; DCLA; Montgomery Co SchLA. 10: Epsilon Phi. 14: Child lit, sch libs. 15: 4748 East ave NE, Wash DC 20017.

GREENWOOD, MARY (MARGARET). b Hamilton Ont Can 4 Ag 33. 5: Queens U 52-54 (Eng) BA; Toronto 59 BLS. 7: Lib asst Hamilton Pub Lib, Hamilton Ont 54; Libn Polymer Corp Ltd, Sarnia Ont 55-. 9: CanLA (Coun Res & Spec Libs Sect 68-69); SLA. 14: Admin. 15: Polymer Corp Ltd, Sarnia Ont Can.

GREENWOOD, R(OBERT) W(ALLACE). b Boston 3 J 24. 5: Col of St Thomas 46-48 (Classical Langs); Tulane 48-50 (Classical Langs) BA; UMich 50-51 AMLS. 6: Lat, Fr. 7: US Signal Corps Cryptographer Cryptanalyst West Europe, US 43-45; Attendant Harvard Col Lib 46, summers 47-50; Attendant Col of St Thomas Lib 46-48; Attendant Tulane U Lib 48-50; Attendant Ann Arbor Pub Lib 51; Head circ dept Tulane U Lib 51-60, Head acquis dept 60-. 9: Private Libs Assn; BSA; LaLA. 10: New Orleans Lib Club; Oxford Bibliog Soc; Nat Trust; La Hist Soc; Phi Beta Kappa; La Landmarks Soc; AAUP. 12: "Major Microform Holdings of ASERL Members (65). 14: Acquis, rare bks, private presses. 15: 707 Saint Peter st, New Orleans La 70116.

GREER, ELIZABETH (STONE). b Newbern Tenn 5 Jl 18. 4: Junius S Greer. 5: Georgetown Col 35-39 (Econ) BA; Peabody 39-41 BS in LS. 6: Fr, Lat. 7: Dist supv WPA Lib Serv Program, Nashville 40-41; Soc studies libn Stephens Col 41-42; Catlgr East State Tchrs Col 43-46; Ref libn Peabody Col 46-47; Catlgr Joint U Libs, Nashville 47-49, Analytics catlgr 55-61, Head catlg libn61-. 9: ALA-RTSD (Coun Reg Groups, Ser Sect Com on Policy & Research); SELA (sec-treas SE Reg Group, Res & Tech Serv Libns); TennLA (chm Tech Serv Libns). 14: Catlg. 15: 208 Heady dr, Nashville Tenn 37205.

GREER, GLYNDON FLYNT. b Fayetteville Tenn. 4: Conright Greer. 5: Tenn A & I U 39 9agirc) BS; Pratt Inst 46 BLS; Columbia 56 (Educ) MA, 58 (Reading & Supv) Prof diploma. 7: Elem sch tchr & supv, Redford, Marshall & Lincoln Cos Tenn; Child libn NYC Pub Lib 44-54; Elem sch tchr Englewood Bd of Educ, Englewood NJ 54-61, Jr high sch libn 61-. 9: ALA; NEA; NJEA; NJLA; BergenCoLA; EnglewoodTA. 10: PTA; AAUW; NAACP. 13: Yes. 14: Child & yp wk. 15: 326 Decatur ave, Englewood NJ 07631.

GREER, JAMES NEAL. b Crystal City Tex 16 N 25. 5: UTex 43-52 (Span) BA, MA; Columbia 53-63 (LS) MS. 6: Sp, Fr, Ger. 7: Asst Prof Ibaraki Christian Col (Hitachi Japan) 54-60; Catlgr NY Mercantile Lib, NY 60-63; Catlgr Southwest Mo State Col 63-. 9: MoLA. 10: AAUP. 12: Ed "Lope de Vegas el Piadoso Aragones (51); Comp "Spanish Language and Literature in Publications of American Universities and Colleges (53). 14: Catlg. 15: Rt 1 Box 1-8, Pleasant Hope Mo 65725.

GREER, NATALIA (MARKULIS). b Orchard Park NY 13 Je 25. 4: Roger Clement Greer. 5: Fredonia State Tchrs Col 46 (Educ) E ED; McGill 50 BLS. 6: Polish. 7: Y libn Brooklyn Pub Lib 50-51; Army Libn US Army (Overseas), Germany 51-53; Ext wk yp libn Brooklyn Pub Lib 54-55; Lib consul Piscataway Twp Lib, Piscataway NJ 62-64; Libn Potsdam Pub Lib, Potsdam NY 64-68; Libn Onondaga Hill Free Lib, Syracuse NY 68; Lib Consul Potsdam Pub Lib Potsdam NY 68, Instr Lib Skills St Cecilias Jr high sch, Syracuse NY Spring 9: ALA; CathLA; NYLA; No Country (NY) Ref, Research & Resources Coun. 14: Lib recr, adult serv, ya, illiteracy. 15: 5011 Skyline ter, Syracuse NY 13215.

GREER, PEARL (HAYES). b Charley Ky 3 D 16. 4: Truman Winthrope Greer. 5: East Ky State Col 38 (Hist, Eng) AB; Peabody 41 BS in LS. 7: Tchr-libn Gatliff High Sch, Gatliff Ky 38; Tchr Louisa High Sch, Louisa Ky 3940; Proj tech WPA Ky Lib Proj, Louisville Ky 40-42; Jr libn Oakland Pub Lib, Oakland Cal 43; Travel libs libn Ky Dept of Libs, Frankfort Ky 45; Libn Louisa High Sch, Louisa Ky 47-48; Tchr Lawrence County Schs, Louisa Ky 62-64; Reg libn Ky Dept of Libs, Louisa Ky 64-. 9: ALA; KyLA (V-chm Pub Lib Sect). 10: Ky Farm Bureau; Big Sandy Riding Club; Louisa Womans Club. 14: Lib consul. 15: Rt 1 Box 80, Louisa Ky 41230.

GREER, ROGER CLEMENT. b Chatfield Minn 29 Ap 28. 4: Natalia Markulis. 5: UMinn 47-48 (Hist); St Johns U (Minn) 48-50 (Hist) BA; Columbia 54-55 (Hist); Rutgers 55-56, 60-64 (LS) MLS PhD. 6: Fr, Ger. 7: US Navy Amphibians Seaman 1/c 45-46; US Army Intelligence (28th Div Hdqtrs) Sgt 51-53; Pre-prof trainee Brooklyn Pub Lib 54-55; Bus libn Linden Pub Lib, Linden NJ 55-57; Head Card Prep Unit, Asst Prof Purdue U 57-60; Instr Rutgers U 60-64; Assoc Prof UHawaii summer 65 & 66; Dir of Libs State U Col (Potsdam NY) 64-67; Asst Dean, Assoc Prof Sch of Lib Sci Syracuse U 67-68, Dean 68-. 8: Consul; Gaylord Library Supplies, Syracuse NY 68-; System Development Corp, Santa Monica Cal 67-68; US Off Educ 68-; NY State Dept of Educ, Registr Div 69-; Mem Adv Bd, Mater Dei Col, Ogdensburg NY 66-. 9: ALA-ACRL (chm Nomin Com Col Lib Sect);-RTSD;-RSD; SLA (West NY Chap); No Country (NY) Ref Research & Resources Coun (pres 64-67, pres Bd Trustees 67); ASIS; NYLA-CULS (pres 68-69). 10: Aircraft Owners & Pilots Assn; Onondaga Hill Volunteer Fire Dept. 11: Hon Trustee N Country Ref, Research & Resources Coun 67-. 13: Yes. 14: Col & univ lib admin, ref, lib educ, documentation, bibliog, acad libnship. 15: 5011 Skyline ter, Syracuse NY 13215.

GREEY, KATHLEEN MARGARET. b Princeton NJ 8 My 37. 5: Ore State Col 54-56, 57-59 (Educ) BA; UParis 56-57; UDenver 59-60 (LS) MA. 7: Ref libn Wethersfield Pub Lib, Wethersfield Conn 60-63; Jr libn San Francisco Pub Lib 63-67; Act educ libn Portland State U (Ore) 68-. 9: ALA; OreLA. 10: Phi Kappa Phi. 14: Ref. 15: 1717 SW Park ave apt 1005, Portland Or 97201.

GREGG, ETHEL (HARROD). b Morris Ill9 Je 08. 4: Gordon G Gregg. 5: Northwestern U 26-30 (Eng) BA; UIll summers 34-37 BS in LS. 7: Period asst Northwestern U (EvANSTON) 30-34, Circ asst 35-37, Catlgr 38-45; Catlgr Nat Col Educ

45-46; Libn Morris Pub Lib, Morris Ill 57-. 9: ALA; IllLA; LACONI. 10: Bus & Prof Womens Club. 14: Admin, catlg, ref. 15: 604 Liberty st, Morris Ill 60450.

GREGG, JOSEPH PAUL. b Kan City Mo 7 My 37. 5: UKan City (Mo) 55-59 (Art Hist) BA; Chicago 59-61, 64 (LS) MA. 6: Ger. 7: Page Kan City (Mo) Pub Lib 52-55; Stud asst UKan City (Mo) Lib 55-59; UChicago Lib: Asst ser records 59-61, Asst ref libn ref dept 61-65, Art libn Art Lib 65-. 8: Lib consul, Witco Chemical Co, 60-61; Libn Graham Foun for Advanced Studies in Fine Arts, 64-. 10: Art Inst of Chicago; State Hist Soc of Mo; Grey Towers (UChicago Lib Staff org); Omicron Delta Kappa. 14: Art libnship, ref. 15: 5301 S Kimbark 3-G, Chicago Il 60615.

GREGG, MARIE (PARKER). b Bridgeville Del 9 Ja 04. 4: Willett A Gregg. 5: Udel 23-27 (Biol) BA; UPenn summer 28 (Educ); Johns Hopkins summer 32 (Educ); UColo summer 55 (LS); UDenver 58-60 MA in LS. 7: Tchr of sci & math Cecil Co Bd of Educ, Elkton Md 28-36; Production clerk Triumph Explosive Inc, Elkton Md 41-45; Tchr of sci Cecil Co Bd of Educ, Elkton Md 45-52; Manager-designer Elkton Florist, Elkton Md 52- 54; Tchr of sci, libn Cecil Co Bd of Educ, Elkton Md 54-57, Libn 57-. 9: NEA; Md State Tchrs Assn; MdLA; MdASchL. 10: PTA: Friends of the Cecil Co (Md) Lib; Calvert Grange; Cecil Co (Md) HistSoc; Wilderness Soc; Phi Kappa Phi. 14: High sch libs. 15: Rt 3, Elkton Md 21921.

GREGG, NAN VESTA. b Welsford NB 11 O 14. 5: Mt Allison U 31-35 BA; McGill 35-36 BLS. 6: Fr. 7: Catlgr Montreal Neurological Inst 36-37; Libn Engrg Inst of Can, Montreal 37-40; Gen libn McGill Med Sch 40-43; Med records libn Royal Can Navy (Lt) 43-46; Catlgr circ libn UNB Lib 46-52, Ref libn 52-. 9: CanLA; APLA. 10: Can Fed Univ Women. 14: Ref. 15: 106 Grey st, Fredericton NB Can.

GREGGS, DONALD H. b Meadville Penn 23 S 29. 4: Annette Davidson. 5: Clarion State Col 55-59 (LS) BS; Westmnster Col 61 (Pb Sch Admin). 7: Pipe fitter helper Amer Viscose, Meadville Penn 48-51; (Sgt) 47th Div US Army Infantry, Ft Rucker Ala 51-53; Pipe fitter helper Amer Viscose, Meadville Penn 53-55; Libn Jamestown Area High Sch, Jamestown Penn 60-. 9: Penn State EA (Mercer Co sec 62-63). 14: Ref, clsf, catlg. 15 Rt 2, Jamestown Penn 16134.

GREGGS, ELIZABETH M. b Delta Colo 7 N 25. 4: Raymond J Greggs. 5: Colo Col 43-44 (Eng); UDenver 46-48 (LS) AB with Lib Certif. 6: Sp. 7: Child libn Grand Junction Pub Lib, Grand Junction Colo 44-46; Child libn Wenatchee Pub Lib, Wenatchee Wash 48-52; Child libn Seattle Pub Lib 52-53; Child libn & br libn Renton Pub Lib, Renton Wash 57-67; Arca child supv King Co Lib Syst, Seattle Wash 68-. 9: PNLA; WashLA. 10: PTA; Boy Scouts; Cub Scouts; Allied Arts of Renton. 14: Child wk, ref. 15: 800 Lynnwood ave NE, Renton Wa 98055.

GREGO, NOEL (RUSSELL). b Chicago Ill 21 D 27. 4: Frank M Grego. 5: Rosary Col 44-48 9lat) BA, 48-49 BA in LS, 60-61 MA in LS. 6: Fr, Lat, Greek. 7: Catlgr Chicago Pub Lib 49-52, Hd br catlg unit 52-59; Catlgr Alfred Whital Stern Priv Abraham Lincoln collection, Chicago 51-52; Asst prof & hd catlg dept Chicago State & Wilson Cols 59-; Lecturer Lib Tech Program Wilson Col 68-. 8: Adv bd Felician Col 69-; Visitation com n central Assn, Chicago: Good Counsel High Sch 68, Flower Voc High Sch 69. 9: ALA (Com on Instr & Use, Jr Col Sect 61-63, -ACRL; Coun on Lib Tech (chm Nomin Com 68-69; Exec Bd 68-69); CatgLA (Adv Coun 69-; No Ill Unit: Col & Univ Sect: v-chm 65-66, chm 66-67, Exh Chm 69, v-chm & chm-elect 68-69, Exec Bd 65-67 & 68); Chicago Reg Gp of libns in Tech Serv; Chicago Lib Club. 10: Chicago Urban League; Sigma Gamma Rho. 14: Catlg, tchg. 15: 8722 Calumet ave, Chicago Il 60619.

GREGOR, DOROTHY DEBORAH. b Dobbs Ferry NY 15 Ag 39. 4: A James Gregor. 5: Occidental 57-61 (Phil) BA; UHawaii 61-63 (Phil) MA; UTex 66-68 MLS; UCLA Internship in Biomed Libnship. 6: Ger, Japanese. 7: Lib intern Biomed lib UCLA 68; Ref libn UCal Med Ctr, San Francisco 68-. 9: SLA; MedLA. 14: Ref, computer applic in the lib. 15: 1483 Olympus ave, Berkeley Ca 94708.

GREGOR, MARTIN. b Czechoslovakia 30 Ag 19. 4: Fernande Gregor-Delbecque. 5: Charles U (Prague Czechoslovakia) 45-48 (Humanities) BS; Columbia 59-61 (Slavic Studies); SUNY 60-61 (Russian Lang); Rutgers 61-63 MLS Equivalent. 6: Russ, Polish, Romanian, Bulgarian, Yugoslav, Slovak, Fr, Ital, Sp, Ger, Hungarian, Czech, Portu. 7: NCO British Czech Army WWII Tank Brigade, Africa Italy France Great Britain Germany Czechoslovakia 40-45; Prep Div Searching Sec Cat NY Pub Lib 60-62; Research-archivist Archives of Amer Art, Detroit 63; Chief med libn Montefiore-Morrisania Affiliation NYC 64; Tech libn GSA, NYC 65; Libn admin HQ 1st US Army Camp Drum, Watertown NY 65-; Lib Dir The Ft Lee Free Pub Lib, Ft Lee NJ 63-. 66; Hosp, NYC 67-; A-V spec, Catlgr, Reg libn & Modern lang lab dir The Dalton Schs Inc, NYC 66-67; Libn-in-charge, A-V spec Professional Child Sch, NYS 67-68; Libn-tchr Dept of Educ in NYC 68-. 8: Albert Einstein Col of Med Lang spec; Spec Proj Cornell U Med Lib reorg period dept; estab V/Index Yeshiva U Grad Sch; org tech serv vertical file & estab tech lib Arch & Engnr, Fed Govt. 9: SLA(NY Chap); NY Tech Serv Libns. 10: Small Pub Libs Assn NJ. 14: Admin, acquis, rare research. 15: Ft Lee Pub Lib, Ft Lee NJ 07024.

GREGOROVICH, ANDREW. b Saskatoon Sask Can 18 Jl 35. 4: Jennie Harmansky. 5: McMaster U (Hamilton Ont) 59-62 (Hist) BA; Toronto 62-63 BLS. 6: Russian, Fr, Ukrainian. 7: Cost accounting clerk Tuckett Tobacco, Hamilton Ont 56-59; Slavic libn clerical The Lib UMan 62; Original & reclsf catlgr UToronto 63-64, Catlgr, Sect Head, Automated Bk Catlg 65-67; Hd tech serv Scarborough & Erindale Col Libs UToronto 67-. 9: Can Bibliog Soc; OntLA. 10: Ont Hist Soc; Canadian Hist Assn; Ukrainian-Can Res Foun; Shevchenko Sci Soc; Inter-Univ Com on Can Slavs (sec-treas 67-). 12: "Books on Ukraine and the Ukrainians" (64); Ed "Taras Bulba, by N Gogol" (62). 14: Catlg, automation, bibliog. 15: 239 Chaplin crescent, Toronto 199 Can.

GREGORY, AGNES LEE. b Chase City Va 3 Je 04. 5: Randolph-Macon Womans Col 22-26 (Eng) AB; Col of William & Mary summers 37-41 ABLS UMich 47-48 MALS. 7: NCO British Czech Army WW11 Tank Brigade, Africa Italy France Great Britain Germany Czechoslovakia 40-45; Prep div searching sec cat NY Pub Lib 60-62; Research-archivist Archives of Amer Art, Detroit 63; Chief med libn Montefiore-Morrisania Affiliation NYC 64; Tech libn GSA, NYC 65; Libn admin Hq 1st US Army Camp Drum, Watertown NY 65-; Lib dir the Ft Lee Free Pub Lib, Ft Lee NJ 63-66; Med libn Knickerbocker Hosp, NYC 67-; A-V spec catlgr, Ref libn & Modern lang lab dir The Dalton Schs Inc, NYC 66-67; Libn in charge, A-V spec Professional Child Sch NYS 67-68; Libn-tchr Dept of Educ in NYC 68-. 8: Mem, Survey Com: Four Arts Lib, Palm Beach Fla 56; Fla Devel Commsn Lib 61; Landon High Sch, Jacksonvile Fla; Consul Wkshop, Roddenberry Lib, Cairo Ga. 9: ALA (var coms); AALS (Bd Dirs 3 yrs); SELA (sec Sect for Wk with Child); FlaLA (sec, me sev coms). 10: AAUP; AAUW; Delta Kappa Gamma; Beta Phi Mu; Pi Lambda Theta; Delta Delta Delta. 13: Yes. 14: Admin, acquis, rare bks, archives, research. 15: 1162 Seminole dr, Tallahassee Fla 32301.

GREGORY, ESTHER M (JOHNSTON). b Spokane Wash 26 Mr 09. 5: UWash 28-31 (Math) BS in Educ; USoCal BS in LS. 7: Clerical Seattle Pub Lib 31-39; Libn US Govt Demonstration, Seattle 40; Libn US Govt Demonstration, Raymond Wash 41; Sub libn Seattle Pub Lib 58-59; Sub libn Seattle U 59-64, Ref libn 64-67; Ref libn Bellevue Commun Col 68-. 9: CathLA (chm Seattle Unit 62-63; chm Parish Sect f Pacific NW Reg 63-64). 14: Ref. 15: 14612 SE 16th pl, Bellevue Wa 98004.

GREGORY, JAMES. b Hendersonville NC 24 D 23. 5: East Ky State U 41-45 (Hist) AB; UNC 45-46 (Hist) MA; UKy 46-48 (Hist); Columbia 53-54 MS in LS. 7: Instr UKy 46-48; Instr Tulane U 48-51; Hea of tech serv Pub Lib, Aurora Ill 54-55; Gen asst Brooklyn Pub Lib 55-56; Head catlg dept NY Hist Soc, NYC 56-64, Asst libn 65-66, Libn 66-. 9: ALA; BSA; NYLA; NY Tech Serv Libns (pres 66-67). 10: Grolier Club. 13: Yes. 14: Catlg, rare bks. 15: NY Hist Soc, 170 Central Park W, New York NY 10024.

GREGORY, LOIS (VIRGINIA) (SULLENGER). b Crittenden Co Ky 29 Mr 12. 4: James Lee Gregory. 5: UKy 33 (Eng) AB; Murray State Col 60 (Hist, Educ) MA; Peabody Col 68 (LS) MA. 6: Fr. 7: Libn Crittenden Co Bd of Educ, Marion Ky 55-68; Ref libn Murray SateU 68-. 8: Mem State Adv Com on Title II 67; Mem State Adv Com on Tchr Educ & Certif 67-68. 9: ALA (Memb Com; Recr Com); -AASchL (Ky rep); KyASchL; (pres); KyLA (Exec Bd; Scholarship Com, Nomin Com); Ky ApV Assn (Nomin Com); FDEA Libns (pres); SELA; KyEA; NEA; NCTE. 10: Ky Hist Soc; Kappa Delta Pi& Beta Phi Mu. 13: Yes. 14: Ref. 15: 108 Broach ave S, Murray Ky 42071.

GREGORY, MARGERY (BERFIELD). b Lafayette Ill 19 D 05. 5: Grinnell Col 23-24; Ellsworth Col 24-26; State U Iowa

26-27 (Math) BA; UDenver 57-58 (LS) MA. 7: Asst libn Wartburg Col Lib 58-. 9: ALA; IowaLA. 10: Wa-Tan-Ye. 14: Catlg. 15: 1122 First ave NW, Waverly Ia 50677.

GREGORY, MARY LOU (SHUPE). b Seattle Wash 9 F 41. 4: Dennis Riley Gregory. 5: Seattle Pacific Col 59-63 (Math) BS; UWash summer 64, 65 (Libnship); UIll 66-67 MS in LS. 7: Clk Seattle Pub Lib, Seattle 58-63; Tchr Hoquiam High Sch, Hoquiam Wash 63-64, libn 64-66, 67-69. 9: NEA; WashEA; WashStateASchL; WashLA; HoquiamEA. 14: Sch libnship (high sch level). 15: 402 Chenault ave, Hoquiam Wa 98550.

GREGORY, MELISSA (AUGUSTA) RITTER. b Streator Ill 11 F 33. 4: James Arnold Gregory Jr. 5: Ill State U 51-55 (Soc Sci) BS in Educ; UIll(Urbana) 57-59 MS in LS. 7: Libn Ela-Vernon Twp High Sch, Lake Zurich Ill 55-57; Libn Lyons Twp High Sch & Jr Col, La Grange Ill 57-58; Engnr libn Internat Harvester Inc, Hinsdale Ill 59-62; Tech libn Motorola Inc, Chicago 62-68; Tech libn Argonne Nat Lab, Argonne Ill 68-. 9: SLA. 10: Kappa Delta Pi; Pi Gamma Mu; Alpha Beta Alpha; Beta Phi Mu. 14: Serv. 15: 550 Ridgemoor dr, Hinsdale Il 60521.

GREGORY, ROMA (SANTELLA). b Hibbing Minn 6 Je 21. 5: Wis State U (Eau Claire) 40-42 (Hist); Macalester Col 42-43 (Hist) BA; UWis 43-44 BLS; West Res 64-65 MSLS. 6: Fr, Sp. 7: Army Lib Serv: Asst to exec libn, Hawaii 44-46, Post libn, Kyoto Japan 46-4, Chief post lib system, Ft Sill Okla 51-53; Asst chief acquis dept Washington U Libs (St Louis) 55-59, Chief acquis dept 59-63; Asst libn Mo Botancal Garden, St Louis 63-64; Head order dept Bowling Green State U Lib 65-68; Asst dir CaseWest Res U Libs 68-. 9: ALA; RTSD (chm Com to Revise List of Internat Subscription Agents); OhioLA. 10: AAUW, AAUP. 14: Tech serv, acquis. 15: 2501 Kemper rd 103, Shaker Heights Oh 44120.

GREGORY, RUTH W. b West Point Neb 20 F 10. 5: UNeb 29-33 (Art, Hist) AB; UWis 37-38 (LS). 6: Fr. 7: Gen lib asst Lincoln City Lib, Lincoln Neb 34-36; Libn ed dept Rotarian Magazine, Chicago 37; Act libn Stevens Point Pub Lib, Stevens Point Wis 38-39; Head Libn Waukegan Pub Lib, Waukegan Ill 39-. 8: Assoc serv, ALA Survey of Austin (Minn) Pub Lib 46, Instr; drexel Lib Sch summer 62, UWis Lib Sch 66; Mem Ill State Lib Adv Coun on Lib Devel 9: ALA (Coun 51-54, chm Jury on Citation of Trustees 52-53, Exec Bd 56-60; -PLD (pres 54-55); IllLA (pres 47-48. 10: AAUW Waukegan Planning Commsn. 12: Ed; "Public Libraries" 47-48; "ASD Newsletter" 67. 13: Yes. 14: Admin, adult educ. 15: Waukegan Pub Lib, 128 N County, Waukegan Il 60085.

GREGORY, SARA McDOWELL. b Conyers Ga 30 Ap 17. 4: John Willis Gregory. 5: Womans Col of Ga 34-37, 38-39 (Chem) BS; UVa summer 43 (Chem); Peabody summers 61-64 (LS) MA. 7: Tchr Ola High Sch Henry County, McDonough Ga; Tchr Douglas High Sch, Douglas Ga; Tchr LaGrange High Sch, LaGrange Ga; Tchr Ga Mil Col; Jr chemist Davison Chem Corp, Baltimore; Tchr OKeefe High Sch, Atlanta; Libn Oxford Col of Emory U (Oxford Ga) 58-, chem tchr 47-49; Tchr Peabody Lib Sch summers 66,67. 9: GaLA; SELA. 10: Beta Phi Mu; Delta Kappa Gamma; Womans Soc of Christian Serv Allen Mem Church; Dir Methodist Youth Fellowship Allen Mem Church; Phoenix Hon Soc (Ga Col). 14: Ref, tchg lib sci, lib orientation. 15: 501 N Emory st, Oxford Ga 30267.

GREIWE, HERMINA HOPPE. b Cincinnati 15 Ja 1899. 4: Raymond E Greiwe. 5: UCincinnati 18-21 (Eng, Hist) AB; UKy 54-57 (LS) MA. 6: Ger. 7: Coun Wright Aeronautical, Evendale Ohio 42-45; Sr asst in educ & religion dept Cincinnati & Hamilton County Pub Lib, Cincinnati 45-60, Home lib adv 68-. 8: Coun mem Cincin nati Alcoholism Assn 55-; Adv mem, Marquis Biog Lib Soc 69-. 9: ALA; CathLA; OhioLA. 10: Theta Phi Alpha; Cincinnati Group for Study of Parapsychology; Internat Platform Assn; Cincinnati Hist Soc; Nat Coun Cath Men; Cincinnatus Soc; Friends of the Lib; Cincinnati Art M useum; Nat Wildlife Fed. 14: Ref. 15: Box 43652, Cincinnati Oh 45243.

GRELLINGER, SISTER M JOHN LOUIS SSND. b Milwaukee Wis 27 Ag 23. 5: Mt Mary Col (Milwaukee) 53 (Sec Sci) BA; Col of St Catherine 59 (LS) MA. 7: Tchr St Alphonsus com, Chicago 45-53, Sacred Heart High Sch, Laurium Mich 53-55, Central Cath High Sch, Ft Wayne Ind 55-59; Tchr & libn Marinette Cath Central High Sch, Marinette Wis 59-. 9: CathLA (chm Wis Unit). 14: Sch libs. 15: 1200 Main st, Marinette Wi 54143.

GREMLING, RICHARD C. b Toledo Ohio 24 My 17. 5: UToledo 34-38 (Biol, chem) BS; West Res 40 BSLS. 7: Asst Toledo Pub Lib, Toledo Ohio 40-42; T/5 US Army Signal Corps, ETO 42-46; Asst chief libn Linda Hall Lib, Kansas City Mo 46-53; Chief Libn Bell Telephone Labs, NYC 53-58; Gen manager Del-Mar, Montgomery Penn 58-60; Chief Libn Lockheed Electronics Co, Plainfield NJ 60-64; Chief Libn ITT Fed Labs, Nutley NJ 64-66; Chief libn Ortho Res Found, Raritan NJ 66-. 8: Pres, Lit Serv Associates; V-pres, Publishers Intermediary Bk Serv 65-66. 9: SLA (div chm); ASIS; OhioLA; MoLA. 12: Ed 6 union lists covering 9 states. 13: Yes. 14: Ser. 15: Rt 1 Box 234B, Bound Brook NJ 08805.

GRENFELL, ADRIENNE CAMERON. b Scotland. 4: K Pascoe Grenfell. 5: McGill 40 (Zoology) BS; SUNY (Albany) 66 MLS. 7: Documentalist VITA, Schenectady NY 67-68; Sci libn RPI 69-. 9: ALA; SLA; NYLA. 10: Schenectady Civic Playhouse. 13: Yes. 14: Ref, info ret, bibliog. 15: 1168 Lowell rd, Schenectady NY 12308.

GRENFELL, ROBERT WALLIS. b Colusa Cal 31 Mr 26. 5: Stanford 43-44, 45-49 (Sociol) AB; UCal(Berkeley) 49-51 (Sociol), 55-56 MLS. 6: Ger, Fr. 7: Lib, ed UCal(Berkeley) 56-63; Research libn Wilsey Ham & Blair, San Mateo Cal 64-. 9: ALA; SLA; Amer Sociol Assn; CalLA. 10: Stanford Club of San Francisco; Cal Alumni Club of the Peninsula; Press Club of San Francisco; Mechanics Inst (San Francisco); Cal Hist Soc; Eng-Speaking Union; Beta Phi Mu. 12: Ed "International Relations Digest of Periodical Literature 58-63. 14: Editorial wk, research, ref. 15: 32 Elgin park, San Francisco Pa 94103.

GREVE, MARILYN RAE (SHEPARD). b Chariton Iowa 3 Ap 34. 4: Clyde L Greve. 5: UNoIowa 52-56 (Eng, LS) BA; UIowa 63-64; UDenver 65-66 (Libnship) MA. 7: Eng tchr Ramey AF Base, PR 56-57; Receptionist Oscar Mayer Co, Davenport Iowa 57-63; High sch libn Iowa City Commun Schs 63-65; Asst dir Iowa City Pub Lib 66-68; Catlg libn UNoIowa 68-. 8: Hd Tech Proc Dept, Seven Rivers Lib Syst, Iowa City 66-68. 9: ALA; IowaLA. 11: Purple and gold award for outstanding scholarship in lib sci UNI 56. 14: Catlg, tech processing. 15: 315 Washington st apt 6-A, Cedar Falls Ia 50613.

GRIB, HENRY WALTER. b Homestead Penn 9 My 28. 5: Alliance Col 49-53 (Eng) BA; Kent State 53-54 (LS) MA. 6: Polish, Russian. 7: US Army Signal Corps (Pc) 47-48; Ref libn in tech Pub Lib of Ft Wayne & Allen Co Ft Wayne Ind 54-56; Ref libn UMd Math & Phys Sci Lib 56-58; Armed Serv Tech Info Agency, Tech Lib of Clsfd Documents, Arlington Va & NYC 58-59; Queens Borough Pub Lib, Jamaica NY 60-63; Ref libn Rockville Centre Pub Lib, Rockville Centre LI NY 63-65; Ref libn Nassau Commun Col 65-; Hicksville Sch Dist 17 59-. 9: ALA; NYLA; Nassau-Suffolk LA. 14: Ref. 15: 18 Milldam rd, Smithtown NY 11787.

GRIBBIN, JOHN HAWKINS. b Charleston SC 22 S 20. 4: Lenore Sipes Gribbin. 5: UNC 38-42 (Chem) AB; UCal(Berkeley) 46-47 BLS, 49-50 MLS; Chicago 51-58 (LS) PhD. 7: Chem warfare US Army, Aleutian Islands 42-46; Documents libn UMo 47-49; Geol libn & Instr Lib Sch UTex 50-51; Assoc libn Rice U 53-54; Libn NAS-NRC, Wash DC 55-61; Assoc Libn UNC(Chapel Hill) 61-66; Lib dir Tulane U 66-. 8: Lib consul evaluation com of So Assn of Col & Schs 63-. 9: ALA; LaLA. 10: AAUP. 12: Ed "Industrial Research Laboratories of the United States (11th ed 60); Ed "Scientific and Techncal Societies of the United States and Canada (7th ed 61); Ed "The Southeastern Librarian (64-)66. 13: Yes. 14: Admin. 15: Tulane Univ Lib, New Orleans La 70118.

GRIBBIN, LENORE (SIPES). b Columbia Mo 31 Ag 22. 4: John H Gribbin. 5: UWis 40-44 (Fr & Eng) BS(Educ), 43-44 BLS; Chicago 45-54 (LS) MA. 6: Fr. 7: Libn Central High Sch Lib, Sheboygan Wis 44-46; Libn US Army Spec Serv, Japan Germany 46-48; Catlgr UTex(Austin) 49-51; Catlgr UChicago 53; Catlgr NLM 54-58; Catlgr US Dept of Interior, Wash DC 58-60; Descr catlgr LC 60-61; Asst libn Internat House, New Orleans 68-. 8: Bibliog consul & curator detective story collection UNC Lib 63-. 9: ALA. 10: AAUW. 12: "The Case of the Missing Detective Stories" (66); "Who's Whodunit" (68). 13: Yes. 14: Catlg. 15: 3915 St Charles ave, New Orleans La 70115.

GRIDER, MARCELLA HERMINE. b Clearmont Mo 27 Je 11. 5: Northeastern State Col 29-32 (Music, Educ) BA; Okla State U 36, 37, 38 (Educ) MS; Peabody 44 BS in LS. 6: Fr. 7: Tchr Wyandotte High Sch, Wyandotte Okla 32-37; Tchr Skiatook High Sch, Skiatook Okla 37; Tchr Westville High Sch, Westville Okla 38-40; Tchr-libn Ramona High Sch, Ramona Okla 40-42; Libn Wagoner High Sch, Wagoner Okla 42-47; Assoc prof of educ UArk 47-. 9: ALA; NEA; ArkLA; ArkEA. 10: Delta Kappa Gamma; Kappa Delta Pi. 14: Lib educ. 15: 421 Adams, Fayetteville Ar 72701.

GRIEDER, ELMER (MOERY). b Dubuque Iowa 14 Ag 09. 4: Dorothy Underhill Grieder. 5: UDubuque 26-30 (Hist) BA; Columbia 35-36 (LS) BA; Harvard 39-47 (Hist) AM. 6: Fr, Ger. 7: Tchr La Porte City High Sch, La Porte City Opes 30-35; Jr asst Detroit Pub Lib 36-38; Asst libn Grad Sch of Pub Admin Harvard 38-46; Military intelligence specialist us army Corps of Engs 43-45; Gen asst Harvard U Lib 46-47; Libn W Va U 47-49; Asst dir of libs Stanford U 49-51; Assoc dir of libs 51-. 8: Dir & Prof Inst of Libnship, UAnkara Turkey 55-57; Act dir Stanford U Libs, 59-61, 62-64. 9: ALA; CalLA. 13: Yes. 14: Bldg of research collections. 15: 401 Gerona rd, Stanford Ca 94305.

GRIEDER, JOHN ROBERT. b Hawthorne NJ 21 Ap 27. 4: Suzanne Jeanne Ferrand. 5: Columbia Col Columbia U 47-50 (Hist) AB; Columbia U 50-51 (LS) MS. 6: Sp. 7: Asst libn Fairleigh Dickinson U 51-52; Ind engnr Curtiss-Wright Corp, Woodridge NJ 52-57; Ind engnr IT&T, Clifton NJ 57; Dir Hawthorne Pub Lib, Hawthorne NJ 57-61; Ref libn Long Beach Pub Lib, Long Beach Cal 61-62; Head tech serv div Orange Co Lib, Orange Cal 62-. 9: CalLA. 14: Tech serv. 15: 6853 Espanita st, Long Beach Cal 90815.

GRIER, CONSTANCE HAMILTON. b St Louis 16 N 10. 5: Washington U (St Louis) 27-31 (Eng) AB; St Louis Lib Sch St Louis Mo 32 Certif; Washington U (St Louis) 47 AM in Educ; UIll 65 MS in LS. 7: Resource file clerk & libn St Louis Relief Admin, St Louis 33-36; Libn Nat Bible Inst, NYC 39; Asst circ dept St Louis Pub Lib 40-43; Head libn University City Pub Lib, University City Mo 43-59; Asst state libn Ore State Lib 59-62; Supv of elem sch libs Corvallis Pub Schs, Corvallis Ore 62-64; Circ libn Lovejoy Lib So Ill U, Edwardsville Ill 65-67, Catlg & ref libn Lovejoy Lib 68-. 9: ALA; IllLA. 10: Womans C of C of University City Mo (Life mem); Kappa Delta Pi. 14: Admin, pub serv, circ, ref 15: 135 E Washington ave apt #3, Kirkwood Mo 63122.

GRIER, ELEANOR (MEACHAM). b Acton Ind 22 Mr 20. 4: Paul Livingston Grier. 5: IndU 38-39, 42-44 (Eng) AB; UMich 45-47 ABLS. 7: Catlg typist IndianaU Lib (Bloomington) 43-44; Stenographer AF, Indianapolis 44-45; Caltg typist & circ asst UMich Lib (Ann arbor) 45-47; Sec to pres Hampden-Sydney Col 47-53; Lib asst Hampden-Sydney Col Lib 61-65, Asst catlgr 65-68, Acquis libn 68-. 10: Assn for Preserv of Va Antiq; Phi Beta Kappa; Phi Kappa Phi. 14: Acquis, catlg. 15: Hampden-Sydney Va 23943.

GRIER, PAUL L(IVINGSTON). b Clover SC 26 My 14. 4: Eleanor Jane Meacham. 5: Erskine Col 32-36 (Hist) AB; UNC 37-38 BA in LS; UMich 46-47 MA in LS. 7: Lib asst Pub Lib, Wash DC 36-37, Tech asst 38-40; Libn Hampden-Sydney Col 40-42; Communications Off US Naval Reserve (Ensign to Lt) 42-46; Libn Hampden-Sydney Col 47-. 8: Mem evaluating coms So Assn of Col & Schs. 9: ALA; SELA; VaLA. 10: Assn for Preserv of Va Antiquities, Amer Assn of Museums; Eng Speak Union. 14: Ref, rare bks, admin. 15: Hampden-Sydney Col, Hampden-Sydney Va u3943.

GRIERSON, M RUTH. b Ottawa Kan 24 D 02. 5: Alma Col 20-24 (Eng) AB; UMich 33-34 ABLS; Columbia summers 40-46 (LS) MS. 7: Libn Presbyterian Church USA, NYC 35-40; Libn Maryville Col (Tenn) 40-52; Catlgr Vassar Col 53-55; Libn Lycoming Col 55-65; Asst libn NY State Lib 65-. 9: ALA (Coun); TennLA (past pres). 10: AAUW; Soroptimist Fed. 14: Admin, catlg. 15: 175 S Swan st, apt 10E, Albany NY 12202.

GRIFFEL, EUGENE B. b Brooklyn NY 23 Jl 31. 4: Rhina Holtz. 5: Brooklyn Col 50-54 (Pol Sci & Econ) BA; West Res 60-61MSLS. 7: US Army Engnrs (Spec 4th Class) 54-56; Lib asst Cuyahoga Co Pub Lib, Cleveland 60-61; Ref libn Willoughby-East Lake Pub Lib, Willoughby Ohio 61-62, Br libn 62-63; Assoc libn 63; Head Libn Elmwood Park Pub Lib, Elmwood Park Ill 63-66; Exec dir Mideast Mich Lib Coop, Flint Mich 68-. 9: ALA (life mem); IllLA (chm Exh Com 65); Lib Adminrs Conf No Ill; MichLA (chm Legis Com 68-69). 10: Citizens Adv Com of the Leyden Twp Youth Commsn; Toastmasters Internat; Genesee Co Health & Rehab Fair Com. 14: Admin. 15: 2106 Pierce st, Flint Mi 48503.

GRIFFIN, ALVA (JACO). b Snowball Ark 29 Ja 09. 5: Ark State Tchrs Col 26-29 (Eng) LI Certif; Fla State U 53-54 (Eng) BS, summers 54-59 (LS) MS. 6: Fr. 7: Tchr High Sch Eng Princeton High Sch, Princeton Ark 29-30; Tchr Sarasota Jr High Sch, Sarasota Fla 54-55; Libn Brookside Jr High Sch, Sarasota Fla 55-. 8: Chief Traffic Clerk Defense Plant, Jacksonville Ark WW II. 9: NEA; FlaEA; FlaLA; FlaASchL. 10: Sarasta Co Educ Media Coun (sec). Beta Phi Mu. 14: Child bks, catlg. 15: 3641 Jacinto pl, Sarasota Fla 53579.

GRIFFIN, REV BARRY JAMES (SDS). b Boston 4 Ja 35. 5: Jordan Col 55-57 (Philos); Catholic U 57-59 (Philos) BA, 59-64 MS in LS. 6: Lat, Fr. 7: Libn Mackin High Sch, Wash DC 59-60; Head Libn DIVINE Savior Sem 60-64; Head Libn Mt St Paul Col 64-. 8: Prefect of scholastics for the Salvatorian Order at Mt St Paul Col. 9: ALA; CathLA(Nat chm Sem Sect 64-66); WisLA. 10: Beta Phi Mu. 12: Ed ""Indicator (61-63); Ed "Newsletter, Sem Sect, CathLA. 14: Admin. 15: 500 Prospect ave East, Waukesha Wis 53186.

GRIFFIN, DOROTHY W. b Kirkwood Mo 8 S 15. 4: Charles Griffin. 5: WashingtonU (St Louis) 34-37; Hunter 42-44 BA; Columbia 48-50 MS in LS; UCLA 57-64. 7: Catlg libn govt docs Hanover Bank Lib, NYC 45-48; Subject analyst "Industrial Arts Index" H W Wilson, NYC 48-50; Ref, tech proc Army Lib Serv (Pacific Area) 50-53; Hd period div UCal (Berkeley) 53-56; Catlg libn, order libn proc Los Angeles Valley Cal 61-64; Catlg libn tech processes Los Angeles City Cal 64-67, Coord systems analyst in charge of automation prog 68-. 13: Yes. 14: Tech proc, automation, computer application to lib prob, info stor & retr, admin. 15: 17262 Dearborn st, Northridge Ca 91324.

GRIFFIN, GERALD THOMAS. b Lawrence Mass 22 Ap 26. 4: Olga Flietel. 5: Mass Div of univ Ext 59-60, UMd 61-63 (Pol Sci); UOmaha 63-64 (Pol Sci) BGenEd; Simmons 66-67 (LS) MS. 6: Ger. 7: Catlgr UMe (Portland) 67-. 8: Instr Lib Serv UMe 68-. 9: MeLA. 10: Phi Alpha Theta; Org Amer Histns, Kiwanis. 14: Catlg. 15: Woodsmere ave Rte 2, South Windham Me 04082.

GRIFFIN, HILLIS L. b Tacoma Wash 16 D 30. 4: Kathryn Kenney. 5: Col of Puget Sound 48-50 (Chem); UWash 54-57 (Sociol) AB, 57-58 MLS. 7: (S/Sgt) US Air Force Judge Advocate Gen Dept 51-54; Asst libn Nat Reactor Testing Station Tech Lib Phillips Petroleum Co Atomic Energy Div, Idaho Falls Ida 58-62; Info systems libn Argonne Nat Lab, Argonne Ill 62-65, Info systems libn & Head tech processing 65-. 8: Instr in computer applications in libs; UIll summer 64-; U Wash summer 65, Rosary Col 67-, UWis 68. 9: ASIS; Assn for Computing Machinery; Com on Lib Automation; PNLA (sec 60-61); IdaLA (sec 61-62). 10: Beta Phi Mu. 13: Yes. 14: Computer applications to present areas of libnship and extension of serv through new applications. 15: Argonne National Laboratory Lib Serv Dept Bldg 203-CE 120 9700 S Cass ave, Argonne Il 60439.

GRIFFIN, JO ANN. b Hopkins Co Tex 10 Ja 35. 5: E Tex State 51-54 (Eng) BA, 57 (LS); Tex Woman's U 56, 65-67 (LS). 7: Tchr Alba High Sch, Alba Tex 54; Clk typist, Sheppard AFB Tex 55-56, Lib asst 56-58, Libn 58-60, Base libn 60-65; Libn SW Reg FAA, Ft Worth Tex 65-. 9: SLA; TexLA. 15: Fed Aviation Admin, Lib Sect, SW-461, PO Box 1689, Fort Worth Tx 76101.

GRIFFIN, LLOYD W. b Haverhill Mass 27 N 19. 4: Rachel Reed. 5: UMe 37-41 (Eng) BA, 46-47 (Eng) MA; Harvard 47-49 (Eng) AM; Simmons 49-50 MS in LS. 6: Ger, Fr. 7: (T/Sgt) Operations US AAF, Eng France Belgium 42-45; Grad asst Eng UMe 46, Instr in Eng 46-47; Catlgr ref & research div Boston Pub Lib 50; Ref libn Peabody Inst Lib, Baltimore 51-53; Catlgr Md Hist Soc, Baltimore 52-53; Asst libn in chg of humanities UWis(Madison) 53-63, Chief div of ref serv 63-. 10: Phi Beta Kappa; Phi Kappa Phi. 12: Ed "Farmington Plan Newsletter. 13: Yes. 14: Ref, admin. 15: 1910 Rowley ave, Madison Wis 53705.

GRIFFIN, MARGARET. b New Castle Ind 18 Je 05. 5: Earlham Col 23-27 (Eng, Biol) AB; Peabody summers 35-37 BS in LS; Ind U even 54-56 (Educ) MS in Ed. 6: Sp. 7: Eng tchr High Sch, Aurora Ind; Eng tchr Lincoln High Sch, Cambridge City Ind; Libn High Sch, Shelbyville Ind; Libn Anderson High Sch, Anderson Ind; Libn Mishawaka High Sch, Mishawaka Ind; Libn University Sch, Bloomington Ind; Lib tech Ind U Educ Contract, Bangkok Thailand; Asst Prof of Lib Sci Grad Lib Sch, Ind U; Libn Grad Lib Sch. 9: ALA-AASchL; AALS; IndSchLA; IndLA. 10: Delta Kappa Gamma; Phi Lambda Theta. 14: Sch libnship, lib sch lib. 15: 1009 Greenwood ave, Bloomington In 47403.

GRIFFIN, MARJORIE. b Vancouver BC Can 30 Je 14. 5: UBC 36 (Lit) BA; USoCal 48 MSLS. 7: Libn Victoria Col 43-47; Asst libn Jr Col Modesto Cal 48-50; Libn US Army, Germany 50-52; Libn IBM, San Jose Cal 52-63; Lib mgr IBM-ASDD, LDS Gatos Cal 64-. 9: ALA; SLA (Documentation Div: past chm; Bay Area Chap: chm Consul Serv); CalLA. 10: USA/UNA. 13: Yes. 14: Automation in libs, ref. 15: 20 E Main st, Los Gatos Ca 95030.

GRIFFIN, MARY FRANCES. b Cross Hill SC 24 Ag 25. 5: Benedict Col 43-47 (Eng) BA; SC State Col summers 48, 51 (LS); Atlanta U summer 53 (LS); Ind U 54-57 (LS) MS. 7: Tchr Edgefield Co Train Sch, Johnston SC 47-51; Libn Dennis High Sch, Bishopville SC 51-52; Tchr & libn Fountain Inn Sch, Fountain Inn SC 52-54; Libn Bryson High Sch, fountain Inn SC 54-65; Asst projects supv State Dept of Educ, Columbia 66-68; Lib supv State Dept of Educ, Columbia SC 68-. 9: ALA; NEA; ASCD; SELA; SCLA; SCEA. 14: Sch libs. 15: 2228 Taylor st, Columbia SC 29204.

GRIFFIN, PAMELA B. b Victoria BC Can 11 O 21. 5: Victoria Col 40-41; Sec & Bus Col 41-42; UToronto 46-48 (Soc Sci) BA, 48-49 BLS. 6: Fr. 7: Admin (Flight sgt) RCAF (WD), Toronto, Dafoe, Scotland, London 42-46; Vancouver Pub Lib, Vancouver BC: Sci dept 48-53, Bus div 53-59, Soc sic hd 59-65; Hd ref & dir of train UCalgary 65-68, hd soc sci div 68-. 8: Sub-Profess Courses Adv Com, UCalgary 67-. 9: CanLA; ALA; AtlaLA. 14: Ref. 15: 1202-835 6th ave SW, Calgary 1 Alberta Can.

GRIFFIN, WILLIAM HUGH. b Okla City Okla 18 O 46. 5: UOkla 63-65 (Fr) BA, 67-68 MLS. 6: Fr. 7: Lib fellow UOkla 67-68; Extramural loan libn UTex (Austin) 68-. 9: ALA; TexLA. 10: French Club (UTex). 14: Acquis. 15: 2400 Longview, Austin Tx 78705.

GRIFFIS, (BARBARA) MARJORIE. b Johnson City NY 26 O 19. 5: UCincinnati 38-42 BS in Ed; Union Theol Sem 47-50 Bd, 51, 59 STM, 59-61 UNCL; Columbia 63-65 (LS) MS; New Sch for Soc Research 66-69 MA Soc. 6: Fr, Ger, Lat, Biblical Gr, Hebrew. 7: Pub sch tchr, Staatsburg NY & Clinton Conn 42-44; Indexer of Govt Documents Fed Register, Wash DC 45-47; Parish Minister First Congregational Church, Portland NY 51-54; Assoc Missionary Tchr, V-Prin, Libn Amer Bd of Commsnrs for For Missions, Aleppo Col (Aleppo Syria) 54-58; Circ asst Missionary Research Lib, NYC 59-61; Asst in catlg dept Union Theol Sem, NYC 63-65, Ref libn 65-. 9: ATheolLA. 10: Ministerial mem West Assn of NY Conf of United Church of Christ, Americans for Justice in the Middle East. 14: Acad libs. 15: 400 W 119th st, apt 5-B, New York NY 10027.

GRIFFIS, BARBARA A(NN). b Lake Forest Ill 12 D 29. 5: Beloit Col 48-52 (Govt) BA. 7: Tchr pub schs, Rockford Ill 52; Asst in catlg dept Union Theol Sem Lib (NY) 53-55, libs William Adams Brown Ecumenical Lib 55-. 8: Asst docs ref room World Coun of Churches 4th Assembly, Uppsala Sweden 68. 15: 80 LaSalle st, New York NY 10027.

GRIFFITH, CONNIE GARZA. b Rio Grande City Tex 18 Ag 04. 5: UTex 19-22 (Span) BA, 27 (Span & Fr) MA; Sorbonne summer 34 (Fr). 6: Sp, FR. 7: Instr of Span UTex 22-24; Asst Prof Span & Fr Tex Christian U 28-32; Asst Prof Span & educ UTex 33-43; Asst dir, then Dir Div of Educ OIAA, Wash DC 43-45; Dir reg serv Bur for Central Amer, Guatemala CA 46-47; Assoc Prof Span & educ UTex 47-48; Assoc Prof Span Newcomb Col 51; Head Head Mss div Tulane U 53-59, Head mss & rare bk room 59-67, Dir spec Collections div 68-. 9: SAA; LaLA; La Hist Assn La Hist Soc; LA Geneal & Hist Soc. 10: La Landmarks Soc; Friends of the Cabildo; Soc Welfare Planning Coun; YWCA; Phi Beta Kappa; Mortar Board, Sigma Delta Pi; Delta Kappa Gamma; Pi Lambda Thta. 12: "Course of Study for Spanish, Grades 3-5. State of Texas (43);"Transcriptions of Manuscript Collections of La. The Favrot Papers, v 8, 10-12 (61-63). 13: Yes. 14: Mss. 15: 360 Audubon st, New Orleans La 70118.

GRIFFITH, DOROTHY (ANN). b Phoenixville Penn 1 S 32. 5: Ursinus Col 50-54 (Eng) BA; Drexel 65-66 MSLS. 7: Sec Amer Baptist Publ Soc, Phila 55-56; Claim asst Travelers ins Co, Phila 56-65; Asst ref libn Norristown Pub Lib, Norristown Penn 67; Hd ref Montgomery Co Norristown Pub Lib, Norristown Penn 67-. 9: ALA; PennLA. 10: Bus and Profess Women. 14: Ref, adult serv. 15: 117 Walnut st, Mont Clare Pa 19453.

GRIFFITH, JERRY (LYNN). b George West Tex 29 Ag 38. 5: Wharton Co Jr Col 56-58 AA; N Tex State U 58-60 (LS) BA; LSU summer 62; E Tex State U summer 63-65. 7: High sch libn Ganado High Sch, Ganado Tex 60-66; Admin lib 2nd Infantry Div 8th Army, Seoul Korea 67-68; Ft Polk (La) Spec Serv Lib; br lib N Fort Lib 66-67, 68, Libn lib serv ctr 68-. 9: ALA; LaLA; SWLA. 10: Jr C of C. 14: Catlg, ref. 15: 208 Fifth st, DeRidder La 70634.

GRIFFITH, MRS MARY BETH (TERRY). b Prescott Ark 15 O 05. 5: Galloway Col 22 (Eng); Ark Col 23-25, 53 (Eng) BA; Tex Womans U 45-46 (LS). 7: Speech Instr Walnut Ridge High Sch, Ark; Speech Instr Conway High Sch, Ark; Speech Instr Huntsville High Sch, Huntsville Ala; Chief clerk Civilian Personnel ff, Newport Air Base, Newport Ark; Head Libn White River Reg Lib, Batesville Ark 45-. 8: Exec dir, Nat Lib Week, Ark, 61. 9: ALA; ArkLA (treas 59, pres 66; chm Pub Lib Sect 47); SWLA. 10: Pi Beta Phi; UDC; DARD Ark Arts Center. 14: Ref, readers adv. 15: 658 Boswell st, Batesville Ark 72501.

GRIFFITH, WINIFRED (FREDRICKSON). b Great Falls Mont 30 Jl 14. 4: John F Griffith. 5: West Mont Col of Educ 37-39, summers 40, 42, 43 (Eng) B Ed; UWash summers 41, 64, 65 (LS), 66 M Lib. 6: Sp. 7: Jr clerk Great Falls Pub Lib, Great Falls Mont 33-3; Elem tchr Goodman Siding Mont 39-40; Elem tchr Stanford Pub Sch, Stanford Mont 40-42; Elem tchr Billings Sch System, Billings, Mont 42-43; Libn Sr High Sch, Billings Mont 43-46; Catlg libn Parmly Billings Mem Lib, Billings Mont 46-66; Catlg libn East Mont Col 66-. 9: ALA; MontLA; PNLA. 14: Catlg. 15: 1847 Alderson, Billings Mt 59102.

GRIFFITHS, NAOMI PINA. b NYC 23 Je 28. 4: Robert G Griffiths. 5: Queens Col 45-50 (Psych) BA; NYU 49 (Sociol); City Col(NY) 47 (Psych); Pratt 5-51 MLS; Queens Col 55-56 (LS). 6: Fr, Ital. 7: Child libn Queensborough Pub Lib, Queens NY 51-55; Sch libn Main St Sch, Port Washington NY 55-58; Elem tchr Garden St Sch, Brewster NY 60; Tchr San Salvador, Bahamas 64; Sub tchr Garden St Sch, Brewster NY 63-64; Lib consul Green Chimneys Sch, Brewster NY 64-; Hd sch libn Media spec 68-. 9: NEA; ALA; NY State Tchrs Assn. 10: AAUW. 14: Child bks & storytelling, a-v & multi-media materials. 15: Easthill RFD #3, Brewster NY.

GRIFFITHS, SUZANNE (NICHOLS). b Syracuse NY 4 Jl 25. 4: Albert Owen Griffiths. 5: Syracuse 43-45, 46-47 (Eng) AB; Queens U(Ont) 45-46 (Eng); Birmingham U(Eng) summer 47 (Eng); UCol ULondon 47-48 (Eng); Syracuse 48-49 (Eng, Educ) MA Ed; UIll 59-60 MSLS. 7: Asst rate bk room UIll Lib (Urbana) 60-66, Classics libn 66-. 9: IllLA. 10: AAUP; Irish Terrier Club of Amer. 14: Rare bks. 15: RR #1, Urbana Il 61801.

GRIGAR, SAM WAYNE. b Rosenberg Tex 15 N 38. 5: Baylor 57-61 (Eng) BA; Sam Houston State Col summers 64, 67-68 (Eng) MA & Libn's Certif. 6: Lat, Sp. 7: Tchr: Sam Houston High Sch, Houston Tex 61-62, Brezosport High Sch, Freeport Tex 62-64; Asst libn & Lat tchr Angleton High Sch, Angleton Tex 64-67; Libn Brazoria Elem & Intermed schsm Brazoria Tex 67-68; Libn Levi Fry Jr High Sch, Tex City Tex 68-. 9: Amer Class League; TexStateTA; TexLA. 10: Alpha Chi; Sigma Tau Delta; Pi Gamma Mu. 15: 1814 W 11th, Freeport Tx 77541.

GRIGG, DOROTHY CLAIRE. b Shelby NC 9 Jl 24. 5: Womans Col of UNC 41-45 (Eng) BA; UNC 46 (LS) BS. 6: Fr, Sp. 7: Asst libn Rockingham County Lib, Leaksville NC 46-47; Libn Shelby Pub Lib, Shelby NC 47-49; Order libn Greensboro Pub Lib, Greensboro NC 50-51; Asst libn ref & order depts Womans Col UNC (Greensboro) 51-52, Jr asst catlg libn 52-54; Order libn Winthrop Col Lib 54-59; Catlgr NCState Lib 59-62, Head catlgr 62-. 9: ALA; SELA; NCLA. 14: Catlg, acquis. 15: Shelton Apt H-3 Myo st, Raleigh NC 27603.

GRIGG, VIRGINIA C(AFFEE). b Baltimore 5 Mr 24. 4: Dr Charles Meade Grigg. 5: Randolph-Macon Womans Col 41-45 (Eng) AB; UNC 48-49 BSLS. 7: Instr-libn UNC (Chapel Hill) 49-50; Libn Sociol City & Reg Planning Lib UNC (Chapel Hill) 50-51; Br libn Providence Pub Lib, Tochwotten Br 53-55; Ast libn Leon Co Pub Lib, Tallahassee Fla 56-59; Instr Fla State U Lib Sch 60-63; Pub lib consul Fla State Lib 63-. 8 Exec dir Fla Nat Lib Week 69.09: ALA (SE Reg Rep 67-,-Lad (Equipment Com) 68-); SELA (Legis Com 67-); FlaLA (Pub Rel Com; sec 64-65, chm 66-67); Pub Lib Sect; v-chm 65-66, chm 6667). 9: ALA; SELA; FlaLA (sec Pub Rel Com 64-65, v-chm Pub Libs Sect 65-). 10: PTA; Tallahassee Womans Club; Easter Shore (Va) Hist Soc; LaMoyne Art Foun; Tallahassee Little Theatre; Pi Beta Phi. 12: Ed Fla State Lib "Newsletter (63-65); Ed Florida Library Directory & Public Library Statistics (63-65). 13: Yes. 14: Ext, pub rel. 15: 1559 Cristobal dr, Tallahassee Fla 32302.

GRIGGS, BEATRICE ESTHER. b Seneca Falls NY 16 S 33. 5: State U Col (Geneseo NY) 50-54 (LS) BS; State U Col (Oswego NY) 59-63 (Elem Educ) MS; Syracuse -69 MSLS. 7: Elem libn a-v dir Moravia Elem Sch, Moravia NY 54-58; Elem libn Lakeshore road Eem Sch, Syracuse NY 58-66; Colonie Central Schs, Albany NY 66-69; Lib spec Reg Instrl Materials Ctr, Schenectady NY 69-. 9: NEA; ALA-AASchL;-CSD;

NYLA; Sch Lib Sect "Newsletter" (ed 69-70). NY State Tchrs Assn; Onondaga-Oswego Co Sch Libns (pres 60-61, Pub Chm 64-65); Cayuga Co Libns Assn (pres 57-58); NY Central Zone Tchrs Conf (chm Lib Sect 59); EastNYSchLA (pres 68-70). 10: Delta Kappa Gamma. 14: Sch libs. 15: Rt 1 Box 84, Seneca Falls NY 1318.

GRILIKHES, SANDRA B. b NYC 1 D 32. 5: Queens Col (NYC) 50-52, 56-58 (Hist of Art) BA; Columbia U 58-60 (LS) MS; Grad Sch Bryn Mawr Col 60-61 (Hist of Art). 6: Fr, Ger. 7: Page stacks ref div NY Pub Lib 50, Lib tech asst 50-58, Asst head Film Lib circ dept 58-60; Head Temple U Ambler Campus Lib 61-65; Head ground floor lib Paley Lib of Temple U 65-67, Hd audio, exhibits & spec activities 67-. 8: Ambler Campus Temple U Faculty Lectures Com 63-64 (chm 64-65); creative writing (poetry), Co-chm, Experiments in Art & Technology, Phila Pa member Dance Committee Arts Council YM-YWHA (Phila). 9: ALA; MusLA. 10: Col Art Assn; Amer Oriental Soc; Archaeol Inst of Amer; AAUP. 11: Winner John Golden Award, Creative Writing Queens Col 54. 13: Yes. 14: Bk sel, readers adv, pub programming, phonodisc libs. 15: 630 W Sedgwick st, Phila Pa 19119.

GRILL, MRS EMOGENE (OLER). b Greenville Tex 17 My 11. 5: Tex Womans U 41 (LS) AB. 7: High sch libn, Harlingen Tex 31-46; Base libn US Air Force, Harlingen AF Base Tex 52-61; Base libn US Air Force, Randolph AF Base Tex 61-. 9: ALA; TexLA; BexarLA. 10: New Braunfels Conserv Soc; Commun Actors Theatre. 14: Superv, catlg, ref. 15: 667 Rosemary, New Braunfels Tx 78130.

GRILLO, ANTHONY L. b Philadelphia Penn 20 Je 41. 4: Carolee Messick. 5: Penn State 58-62 (Sci) BS, 62-64 (Gen Studies), 64 (Educ); TempleU summer 65 & spring 66 (Educ); St Joseph's Col fall 65 (Educ); UPenn NSF 66-67 (Chem) Certif; Villanova 67-68 MSLS. 6: Ital. 7: Supv chem preparation rooms Penn StateU (Univ Park Pa) 62-64; Tchr Phila Sch Dist 65-67; Ser libn Bloomsburg State Col 68-69; Asst libn pub serv Lycoming Col 69-. 9: ALA; PennLA. 10: AAUP. 14: Ser, ref. 15: 50 Grampian blvd, Williamsport Pa 17701.

GRIMES, GRETCHEN. b Nashville Tenn 25 D 40. 5: 238 S Colonial Homes dr NW, Atlanta Ga 30309. 6: Fr. 7: Readers' serv libn Georgia Inst of Tech 68-. 9: SELA. 14: Ref. 15: 238 S Colonial Homes dr NW, Atlanta Ga 30309.

GRIMES, MAXYNE (MADDEN). b Raymond Miss 21 My 25. 4: George Lindsay Grimes. 5: Millsaps Col 42-45 (Hist) BA; La State U 46-47 BS in LS; American U 61 Certif in Archival Mgt. 7: Catlgr Dept of Archives & Hist, Jackson Miss 47-48; Assoc Libn Millsaps Col 48-49; Catlgr Jackson Pub Lib, Jackson Miss 49-50; Libn Dept of Archives & History, Jackson Miss 51-53; Head tech processes Jackson Mun Lib, Jackson Miss 54-57; Archivist Dept of Archives & History, Jackson Miss 60-63; Sr libn in chg of tech processing Rowland Med Lib UMiss Med Center (Jackson)63-. 9: MissLA (pres 65, v-pres 64, chm Spec Libs Sect 63); MedLA (So Reg Group); SAA. 10: Miss Hist Soc; AAUP. 14: Catlg. 15: Rowland Med Lib UMiss Med Center 2600 N State st, Jackson Miss 39216.

GRIMLEY, ARLENE (MARKS). b San Jose Cal 23 N 14. 4: Vann Grimley. 5: Emmanuel Missionary Col 32-36 (Elem Educ) BA; UIll summers 39-42 BS in LS; UMich 45-47 MA in LS. 7: Elem tchr Broadview church sch, La Grange Ill 36-40; Tchr-libn Broadview Acad, La Grange Ill 40-43; Emmanuel Missionary Col: Asst libn 43-44, Act libn 44-45, Libn 45-56; Gen lib staff Central Mich U 57-61, Circ libn 61-. 9: ALA; Mich Assn Higher Educ; MichLA. 10: AAUW; Pi Lambda Theta. 15: Central Mich Univ, Mt Pleasant Mich 48858.

GRIMM, BEN EMMET. b Jersey City NJ 27 S 24. 4: Jean Bohrer. 5: Washington & Lee 46-49 (Eng) BA; Columbia 49-50 (LS) MS. 7: Radio-operator-mechanic-gunner & gunnery instr US Army Air Force T/Sgt, Europe (UK) & US 42-45; Libn I Detroit Pub Lib 50-52; Sr libn Fair Lawn Pub Lib, Fair Lawn NJ 52-54; Ref & lending libn Montclair Pub Lib, Montclair NJ 55-56, Asst dir 56-61; Dir Belleville Pub Lib, Belleville NJ 61-. 8: Lib bldg consul: Sayreville NJ 66-, Perth Amboy NJ 67, West Paterson NJ 68, Oakland NJ 68, Passaic Twp NJ 69-. 9: ALA; NJLA (pres 68-69). 10: Belleville Commun Coun; Belleville Hist Soc; Rotary. 11: Better Belleville Award 68. 13: Yes. 14: Pub lib serv & bldgs. 15: 76 Sherman ave, Glen Ridge NJ 07028.

GRIMM, DOROTHY JEAN (BURGESS). b Milwaukee Wis 12 Jl 17. 5: Milwaukee Downer Col 34-36; Milwaukee State Tchrs Col 36-38; Marquette U 38-39 (Hist) PhB; West Res summers 41-44 BS in LS. 6: Fr. 7: Libn clerk South Div High Sch, Milwaukee 39-42; Libn Milwaukee Pub Lib 42-45; Libn San Diego Pub Lib 54-. 9: ALA, CalLA. 10: Bus & Prof Womans Club. 14: Ref. 15: 1675 Law st, San Diego Ca 92109.

GRIMM, L(UCY) EMILY. b Carlisle Penn 2 Mr 39. 5: Dickinson Col 57-61 (Fr) BA; UIll 61-63 MS in LS. 6: Fr, Sp. 7: Asst catlgr Lafayette Col Lib 63-67; Research resources libn Bowling Green U 67-. 9: ALA. 10: AAUP. 14: Catlg, ref. 15: 311 S Enterprise st, Bowling Green Oh 43402.

GRIMM, RUTH FAHR (CURTIS). b Pittsburgh 10 My 09. 4: William Carey Grimm. 5: UPittsburgh 27-31 (Eng, LS) AB; Carnegie 30-31 (Child Lib Wk) Certif; U Pittsburgh 32-37 (Bot) MS. 7: Tchr & libn Glassport High Sch, Glassport Penn 35-41; Tchr & libn Linesville High Sch, Linesville Penn 42-45; Libn Winyah High Sch, Georgetown SC 51-55; Tchr Pickens High Sch, Pickens SC 55-56; Libn Sans Souci Jr High Sch, Greenville SC 56-64; Catlg asst Furman U Lib summer 63-65; Libn Monaview Jr High Sch, Greenville SC 64-. 8: Eval Com of So Assn of Secon Schs & Cols, 54. 9: ALA; NEA; SCEA; SCLA. 10: Carolina Bird Club. 14: Sch lib wk. 15: 15 Strawberry dr, Rt 9, Greenville SC 29609.

GRIMM, RUTH. b Cincinnati 9 O 08. 5: UCincinnati 27-30 (Eng Lit) AB; Columbia 35-36 (LS) BS. 7: Cincinnati Pub Lib: Asst in circ dept 31-39, Adult asst-Norwood Br 39-41, Libn-Evanston Br 41-43, Asst in ref dept 43-52, Head lending dept 52-55, Head info desk 55-60, Head order dept 60-67, Hd Lending dept 67-. 9: ALA; OhioLA. 10: LWV. 14: Ref 15: 2136 Madison rd, Cincinnati 45208.

GRIMSLEY, CAROLYN. b Springfield Mo 25 Jl 33. 5: Los Angeles State Col 53-55 (Educ) BA; USoCal 57-58 MSLS. 6: Fr. 7: Libn mun ref dept water & power div Los Angeles Pub Lib 58-62, Sr libn police div 62-. 9: ALA; SLA; CalLA. 10: Beta Phi Mu. 15: 150 N Los Angeles st, Los Angeles Ca 90012.

GRIPPE, BARBARA ANN HARCHUCK. b Wilkinsburg Penn 29 Mr 40. 4: Frank Grippe Jr. 5: Clarion State Col 58-62 (LS, Eng) BS in Educ; UPittsburgh 62-64 MLS, 68-69. 6: Fr. 7: Libn & Educ Media spec Hamilton Lib Edinboro State Col 62-. 9: PennLA (pres) Northwest Chap 64-65. 10: Edinboro State Col Faculty Assn; Sigma Sigma Sigma. 14Non-bk instr materials, closed circuit TV. 15: Box 501, Edinboro Pa 16412.

GRIPPER, CLAUDINE (WINSTON). b Winter Park Fla 16 Ag 22. 4: Rudolph V Gripper. 5: Fla A&M U 43 (Soc Studies) AB; NC Col 58 (LS) Certif. 6: Fr. 7: Jones High Sch, Orlando Fla: Soc studies tchr 43-58, Asst libn 58-64, Chm of lib dept 64-; Asst libn William Boone High Sch. 9: ALA; NEA; FlaASchL; FlaStateTA. 10: C of C; Zeta Phi Beta. 14: Ref. 15: 804 Bethune dr, Orlando Fla 32805.

GRISHAM, EDITH P (MOLES). b Pinch W Va 27 Mr 26. 5: San Antonio Col 53-57 AA; St mary'sU 57-61 (Marketing) BBA, 61-62 (Mgt); Our Lady of the Lake Col 62-64 (LS). 7: Clk (Sgt) USA Spec Serv, US & Europe 44-48; Cryptographer (Sgt) USAF, US 48-53; Sales serv Azrock Floor Prods, San Antonio Tex 53-62, 65-66; Off mgr Data Processing Ctr, San Antonio Tex 62-64; Ser libn Houston Pub Lib, Houston Tex 64-65, Hd lit & biography 66-68, Libn bus tech dept 68-. 9: TexLA. 10: Alpha Beta Alpha; Kappa Pi Sigma. 14: Ref. 15: 3219 Rice blvd, Houston Tx 77005.

GRISHAM, FRANK (PHILLIPS). b Birmingham Ala 28 Ag 28. 4: Louise Fly Grisham. 5: Birmingham-So Col 49 (Hist) AB; Vanderbilt U Divinity Sch 52 BD; Peabody 58 (LS) MA. 7: Libn Divinity Lib Joint U Libs, Nashville 52-54; Dir of religious life Birmingham-So Col 54-56; Assoc Prof Vanderbilt Divinity Sch 56-64; Libn Divinity Lib Joint U Libs, Nashville 56-64; Assoc Prof Bibliog Vanderbilt U 65-; Asst Dir Joint U Libs Nashville 65-67; Assoc dir 67-68, Dir 68-. 8: Nashville Metropolitan Sch Bd (v-chm 64); Nashville Metropolitan Action Com (64-66). 9: ALA; SELA; TennLA; Amer Sch Bds Assn; Tenn Sch Bds Assn. 10: Civic Com on Pub Educ; Tenn Congress of Parents & Tchrs (Life mem). 13: Yes. 14: Univ lib admin. 15: CO Joint U Libs, 419 21st ave S, Nashville Tn 37203.

GRISHAM, MADELINE A. b Osborne Co Kan 30 Je 13. 4: Roy A Grisham. 5: Okla State U 55-56, 59-61 (Educ) BS; Central State Col 62-65, (LS, Soc Sci) MT; UOkla 68 (LS). 7: Tchr Okla City Schs 61-64; Libn Bur of Indian Affairs, Tes Nos Pos Ariz 65-66; Libn Sand Springs High Sch, Sand Springs Okla 66; Libn Bur of Indian Affairs Chilocco indian Sch 66-67; Patient's libn VA Hosp, Okla City 67-. 9: ALA; OklaLA. 15: 1744 SW 18th, Oklahoma City Ok 73108.

GRISSO, KARL M. b Sidney Ind 22 My 37. 4: Dorothy L Novosel. 5: Manchester Col 55-59 (Hist) BS; Ind U 60-62 (Hist) MA, 65-66 (LS) MA. 7: Documents libn Ft Wayne Pub Lib, Ft Wayne Ind 62-67; Asst libn Hanover Col (Ind) 67-69; Ref libn E Ill U (Charleston) 69-. 9: ALA; BSA. 10: AHA; AAUP; Amer Acad Polit on Soc Scis; Beta Phi Mu. 14: Soc sci ref wk, govt documents, bk sel, rare bks, admin. 15: 2424 Village rd, Charleston Il 61920.

GRISWOLD, (ALICE) JEAN. b Ind 3 D 28. 4: William R Griswold. 5: Ind U 46-50 (Educ) BS; UPittsburgh 62-64 MLS. 7: Advertising copywriter RCA Record Div, Camden NJ 50-52; Homebound tutor Morris Twp Sch Dist, Morristown NJ 58-62; Elem libn Peters Twp Sch Dist, McMurray Penn 63-. 9: ALA; NEA; Penn State EA; Penn Tchrs Assn; PennLA. 10: Womans Club; Girl Scouts; PTA. 14: Elem sch libs. 15: 128 Oakwood rd, McMurray Pa 15317.

GRISWOLD, ARDYCE MARION. b Clinton Mass 14 Ap 36. 5: Atlantic Union Col 54-58 (Elem Educ) AB; Catholic U 61-64 MS in LS. 7: Eng & math tchr asst dean of girls Forest Lake Academy, Orlando Fla 58-59; Tchr Culver Jr Academy, Rochester NY 59-60; Asst libn olumbia Union Cl 60-64; Libn Sligo Elem Sch, Takoma Park Md 60-. 9: ALA; MdLA. 14: Catlg, elem sch libnship. 15: 8315 Flower ave, Takoma Park Md 20012.

GRITTEN, MARY LOUISE. b Republic Kan 1 Mr 04. 5: Ft Hays State Col summers 27-38 (Eng) BS in Educ; UColo; UDenver summers 53-56 MA in Libnship. 7: Elem grades Republic Co Rural, Republic Kan 25-31; Elem tchr & prin Republic Grade Sch, Republic Kan 31-38; Soc sci & Eng Republic High Sch, Republic Kan 38-42; Soc sci Esk ridge High Sch, Eskridge Kan 42-45; Eng & libn Bird City High Sch, Bird City Kan 45-57; Libn Grant Co High Sch, Ulysses Kan 57-58; Eng & libn Bird City High Sch, Bird City Kan 58-67, Elem & High sch libn, 68-. 9: NEA; NCTE; Kan Assn Tchrs Eng (Ed of Bull); KanASchL (Dist dir); Kan State Tchrs Assn (chm Round Tables). 10: Study Club; Pub Lib Bd; Womens Federated Club; Delta Kappa Gamma. 11: Kan Master Tchr Award, 60. 13: Yes. 14: Ref. 15: Bird City Ks 67731.

GRITZMACHER, GLENN SYLVAN. b Wausau Wis 31 Ja 30. 4: Arlene May Andrus. 5: UWis 48-51, 53-54 (Recreation) Admin) BS, 62 (LS) MS, 62 (Educ) MS, UIll 66,67-. 7: US Army Infantry (Sgt), Korea 51-53; Exec Boy Scouts of Amer, Janesville Wis 54-58; Exec Boy Scouts of Amer, Eau Claire Wis 58-60; Tchr John Muir Jr High Sch, Milwaukee 61; Period libn Ill State U 62-. 9: ALA; IllLA; IllEA. 10: Beta Phi Mu; Alpha Beta Alpha; Wis Lib Sch Alumni Assn. 12: "Library Materials for Recreation (62). 14: Periods; pub serv tchg. 15: 1312 S Madison st, Normal Ill 61761.

GROBEL, OLIVE M(AURINE). b Malden Wash 14 D 09. 5: Yankton Col 28-29; UMont 29-30; Wash State U 36-38, 39 BA (summa cum laude), B Ed; UWash 42-43 BS in LS; Columbia 51-52. 6: Lat, Gk, Fr, Sp, Ger. 7: Music supv, Valley Wash 38-39; High sch tchr, Wilson Creek Wash 39-42; Libn City Lib, Colfax Wash 43-47; Elem sch libn, Evanston Ill 47-48; Libn Pub Lib, Mitchell SD 48-50; Libn Sacred Heart Sch Nursing, Spokane Wash 50-51; Head catlg dept Gen Theol Sem (NY) 51-62; Head catlgr Finch Col 62-. 9: ATheolLA (past chm Catlg & Clst Com); NY Tech Serv Libns; NY Lib Club. 10: Phi Kappa Phi; Mu Phi Epsilon. 13: Yes. 14: Catlg. 15: 425 Riverside dr apt 4-K, New York NY 10025.

GROBEN, MARTHA (ZIMMERMAN). b Buffalo NY 15 S 16. 4: Elmer S Groben. 5: UBuffalo 34-38 (Hist, Educ) BA, 39 BS in LS. 7: Hosp libn Buffalo Pub Lib 40-41; High sch libn Columbus Commun Schs 50-. 8: Adv Com; Title III, Area IX, State of Iowa 65, 67, 68. 9: ALA. 14: Ya & hosp libnship. 15: 808 Main st, Columbus Junction Ia 52738.

GROESBECK, JOSEPH. b Detroit 30 D 11. 5: Wayne State 29-33 (Eng Lit) AB, 35-36 (Eng) MA; UMich 37-39 ABLS, 39-41 (LS). 6: Fr, Sp, Ger. 7: Newspaper libn Detroit Pub Lib 36-37; Ref libn UMich(Ann Arbor) 40-42; Liaison Off US Army Mil Police, Eng & France 42-45; Deputy chief LC Mission to Germany, Frankfort Germany 46; Chief bk sel Detroit Pub Lib 46-48; Assoc libn for acquis NLM 48-51; Deputy Dir UN Lib 51-. 8: Lecturer in lib sci UMich 61,62; Columbia U 64-68. 9: SLA; AALL; Internat Assn Law Libs; AIL. 10: Phi Kappa Phi. 13: Yes. 15: UN Box 20, Grand Central Sta, New York NY 10017.

GRONDIN, GILLES (JOSEPH JEAN-GUY). b Shawinigan-Sud Que Can 3 F 43. 4: Monique Bacon Grondin. 5: Sem Ste-Marie 55-63 BA; UMontreal 64-65 BLS. 6: Eng, Fr. 7: Asst libn Sem Ste-Marie (Shawinigan Que) 63-64, Head Libn 65-. 68; Hd libn GEGEP de Shawinigan 68-. 8: Pres Commsn of Dirs, Bibliotheque de CADRE; Mem Adv Com of the Serv of Tchg Libs, Ministry of Educ Can. 9: CanLA; Association Canadienne des Bibliothecaires de Langue Francaise. 14: Admin, ref. 15: 565 111th rue, Shawinigan-Sud Que Can.

GROPP, DOROTHY MURIEL (GEDDES). b Wellington Kan 27 My 07. 4: Arthur E Gropp. 5: Kan State Tchrs Col (Emporia) 25-29 (LS) BS in Educ. 6: Sp, Portu, Fr. 7: Asst Kan State Tchrs Col Lib (Emporia) 25-29; Lib consul Mackenzie Col (Sao Paulo Brazil) 29-31, Dir Lib Sci Course 29-31; Lib asst Middle Amer Research Inst Tulane U 32-33; Catlgr Tulane U Lib-Howard Mem Lib merger, New Orleans 38-39; Prof Sch of Lib Sci, Montevideo Uruguay 43-44; Prof Eng Tchg Program Artigas-Washington Lib, Montevideo 47-48; Chief catlgr "Meteorological and Geoastrophysical Abstracts, Wash DC 51-. 8: Volunteer lib consul Delgado Mus of Art, New Orleans, 35-36 & 40-41; Field sec Lib & Archives Survey, Central Amer & W Indies under Rockefeller Foun grant 37-38. 9: DCLA. 10: AAUW; Frendship Citizens Assn (Wash DC); Xi Phi; Kappa Delta Pi. 14: Catlg, bibliog, indexing. 15: 5113 Western ave NW, Wash DC 20016.

GROSCH, AUDREY (NOISKE). b Minneapolis 10 Ja 34. 4: Charles B Grosch. 5: UMinn 52-55 (Fr) BA, 55-56 (LS) MA. 6: Fr. 7: Asst libn Gen Mills Inc Electronics Div, Minneapolis 57-63, Consul libn Gen Off Minneapolis 64-65; Instr & libn Systems Coordinator UMinn Lib (Minneapolis) 65-. 8: Consul Augustana Col Sioux Falls SD 68. 9: SLA (treas Docs Div; Minn Chap Consul Off); DPMA; ASIS (Minn Chap Chm). 10: Nat Rifle Assn of Amer Sigma Kappa; Amateur Trapshooting Assn. 13: Yes. 14: Lib systems & Procedures, data processing, info retrieval, indexing, On-line systems design,terminal & communications hardware. 15: 3314 Kyle ave N, Minneapolis Mn 55422.

GROSE, WILMA. b Ogden Utah 13 D 11. 5: Weber Col 31-32 (Elem Educ) Assoc BS; UUtah 35 (Elem Educ) BS; UDenver summers 39-41 BS in LS; USoCal summers 50-52 (Secondary Educ) MS in Ed. 6: Fr. 7: Sch libn Salt Lake City Schs 35-39; Weber State Col: Ref libn 39-55, Head Libn 55-61, Head catlgr 61-. 9: UtahLA; UtahEA. 10: Soroptimist Club; College Womens Club of Ogden; Weber State Col Faculty Assn; AAUP. 14: Catlg. 15: 1422 Lake st, Ogden Utah 84401.

GROSS, DEAN COCHRAN. b Waterville Ohio 21 F 22. 4: Gertrude Sharpe Gross. 5: Miami U (Ohio) 41-42, 4547 (US Hist) AB; UAriz 47-48 (Muic); USoCal 48-49 (Music); Drexel 51-52 MS in LS. 6: Fr. 7: US Army Hq 88th Inf Div, US, Italy 43-45; Lib asst UPenn 50-52: Asst libn Drexel Inst of Tech 52-53; Libn asst Great Neck Lib, Great Neck NY 53-58; Asst libn New Rochelle Pub Lib, New Rochelle NY 58-59; Head circ dept Ferguson Lib, Stamford Conn 59-62; Lib Dir Cambria Pub Lib, Johnstown Penn 62-66; Lib dir Harrisburg Pub Lib 66-. 8: Survey of libs of Altoona & Blair Cos, Penn, 64. 9: ALA; PennLA. 10: Rotary Club; Harrisburg Arts Coun; Adult Educ Coun of the Harrisburg Area-Capital Area Chap; Internat Reading Ass. 13: Yes. 14: Pub lib admin. 15: 845 Luzerne st, Johnstown Penn 15905.

GROSS, IVA HELEN. b Colorado City Tex 28 D 39. 5: Tex Womans U 57-61, & 63 (LS) BA & BS; Sul Ross State Col 65; UWis 67-68. 7: Elem libn Andrews Ind Sch Dist, Andrews Tex 61-66; Elem IMC Consul Madison Pub Schs, Madison Wis 66-. 9: NEA-DAVI; ALA; WisLA; Madison Tchrs; WisEA; So Wis EA. 10: PTA. 14: Curric planning, media coord, reading guidance. 15: 5424 Monona dr '6, Madison Wi 53716.

GROSS, JOHN. b Hungary 18 Ag 22. 4: Mary E Shippen. 5: UMich 48-51 (Econ) BA, 51-52 MALS. 6: Hungarian, Ger. 7: Libn I, II, III Detroit Pub Lib 52-62; Head Central Lib Fresno County, Fresno Cal 62-64; Lib Dir Salinas Pub Lib, Salinas Cal 64-. 8: Adult educ programs Lib Week; chm Yosemite Valley Libs; Lib Execs of Monterey Bay Area Libs (pres). 9: ALA; CalLA. 10: Kiwanis. 12: "Survey of City of Sanger Calif" (63). 15: Salinas Pub Lib 110 W San Luis, Salinas Ca 93901.

GROSS, MARY DELL. b Lutcher La 9 F 39. 4: Bernard Melvin Gross. 5: Southern U 57-61 (Eng) BS; Atlanta 61-62 MSLS; LSU 67-68. 06: Fr. 7: Ya libn Free Lib of Phila 62-63; Supv tech serv Southern U (New Orleans) 63-68 ; Catlgr Temple U 68-. 9: ALA; LaLA. 10: Kappa Delta Pi; Beta Phi Mu; Alpha Kappa Alpha; Women's Auxiliary, Flint Goodridge Hosp; YMCA. 14: Catlg. 15: 6201 Crittenden st, Phila Pa 19138.

GROSS, SALLY LUCILLE (SEKERAK). b Cleveland Ohio 17 F 43. 4: Douglas Hale Gross. 5: Baldwin-Wallace 61-65 (Hist, Pol Sci) BA; West Res 66-67 MSLS. 6: Sp. 7: Lib asst cuyahoga Co Pub Lib, Berea Ohio 65-67; Libn I Denver Pub Lib 67-68, Libn II 68-. 9: ALA; OhioLA. 10: Beta Phi Mu. 14: Ref, docs. 15: 3220 W 14th ave apt 361, Denver Co 80204.

GROSS, SHARON. b Los Angeles Cal 15 Mr 38. 5: Los Angeles City Col 55-56 (Hist); URedlands 56-59 (Hist) BA; USoCal 59-60 MSLS; UHawaii 60-62 (Hist). 7: Asst govt doc libn UHawaii 60-62; Ref libn Batton, Barton, Durstine & Osborne NY 63-65; Ref libn fash fashion Inst of Tech 65; Ref libn Spray, Gould & Bowers, Los Angeles 66; Med libn Los Angeles Co Gen Hosp 67-. 9: MedLA. 14: Ref. 15: Medical Lib Unit I, LA County Gen Hospital, 1200 N State st, Los Angeles Ca 90033.

GROSSMANN, MARIA (SCHWEINBURG). b Vienna 12 Je 19. 4: Walter Grossmann. 5: UVienna 37-38 (Law); Smith 40-42 (Hist) BA; Radcliffe 42-43 (Hist) MA; Simmons 54-56 (LS) MS; Harvard 60 (Hist) PhD. 6: Ger, Fr, Dutch, Lat, Danish, Norwegian, Ital. 7: Order libn Harvard Divinity Sch Lib 56-60, Asst libn 60-65, Libn 65-. 9: ATheolLA; Renaissance Soc of Amer; Luther Gesellschaft (Hamburg Germany); Amer Soc of Church Hist. 11: Fellow of the Amer Philos Soc; Coun of Learned Socs fellowship 64-65. 13: Yes. 15: Andover- Harvard Theol Lib 45 Francis ave, Cambridge Mass 02138.

GROSSMANN, WALTER. b Vienna Austria 5 Je 18. 4: Maria Schweinburg. 5: Yankton Col 4041 AB; Harvard 42-51 (Hist) PhD; Simmons 60-61 (LS) MS. 6: Ger, Fr. 7: Assoc Prof Simmons Col 48-51; Asst libn Harvard Col Lib 52-65; Asst libn for bksell Harvard U Lib 65-, Archibald B Coolidge bibliogr 65-66, Lecturer in inst 60-66; Assoc Prof UMass (Boston) 60-68, Dir lib, Prof of Insr 68-. 8: Lectr sch of Lib Sci; mcGill U summer 67-, Simmon Col summer 67-. 9: ALA; AHA; MassLA. 10: Mod Lang Assn. 11: Guggenheim Fellow, 64-65. 12: Ed Johann Christian Edelmann, "Gesammelte Werke. 13: Yes. 14: Bk sel. 15: 97 Waverley st, Belmont Ms 02178.

GROSSO, NICHOLAS DANIEL. b Trenton NJ 30 O 20. 4: Mary Lansing Grosso. 5: Trenton State Tchrs Col 38-42 (Gen Secondar) BS Ed; NYU 45-48 (Soc Studies) MA Ed; Rutgers 54-55 MALS. 6: Ital, Fr. 7: Tchr-libn Jr High Sch No 2, Trenton NJ 43-46; Libn Jr High Sch No 5, Trenton NJ 46-57; Catlgr & ref libn NJ State Lib; Libn Westlake High Sch, Thornwood NY 57-67; Dist coord sch lib & A-v Mt Pleasant Central #1, Thornwood NY 67-. 8: Mem, Middle States Evaluation Team; Consul Praeger Publ Co, NY Univ Press. 9: NEA-DAVI; ALA; NY State Tchrs Assn; NYLA; Westchester LA; NY A-V A; Westchester A-V Assn; Amer Film Inst; Lincoln Ctr Film Soc; Assn Film Socs; Channel 13; Mus of Modern Art. 10: Amer Field Serv. 12: Ed "NJ School Libraran. 14: Sch libs. 15: 250 Garth rd, Scarsdale NY 10583.

GROTHEER, RUTH DOROTHY. b Brooklyn NY 13 Ap 09. 5: Hunter Col 27-31 (Hist) BA; Columbia 31-32 (Hist) MA, 36-37 BLS. 7: Queens Borough Pub Lib, Jamaica NY: Head bus sci & tech div 47-56, Asst chief of ext serv 56-58, Asst libn Central Lib 58-6, Libn Central Lib 64-67; Assoc curator NYU Grad Sch of Bus Admin 67-. 8: Mem Wilson Index Com, 55-. 9: ALA; SLA; NY Lib Club. 14: Ref. 15: 120-10 85th ave, Kew Gardens NY 11415.

GROTZINGER, LAUREL ANN. b Truman Minn 15 Ap 35. 5: Carleton Col 53-57 (Eng) AB; UIll(Urbana) 57-58 (LS) MS, 62-64 PhD. 6: Fr, Ger. 7: Instr asst libn Ill State U 58-62; Tchg fellow UIll(Urbana) 62-63, Grad fellow 63-64; Ast Prof West Mich U 64-66; Assoc Prof 66-68; Prof 68-. 9: ALA-ACRL; AALS; IllLA; MichLA. 10: AAUP; Phi Beta Kappa; Bta Phi Mu. 12: "The Power and the Dignity: Librarianship and Katharine Sharp (66). 13: Yes. 14: research methods, ref & bibliog (sci), info sci. 15: Dept of Libnship West Mich U, Kalamazoo Mi 49001.

GROVE, LOUISE. b Sharpsburg Wash Co Md 13 F 02. 5: Carnegie 20-24 BS in LS; Carnegie 23-24 (LS). 7: Child libn Lakewood Pub Lib, Lakewood Ohio 24-28, Schs libn 28-36; Asst libn Punahou Sch, Honolulu 36-37; Schs libn Lakewood Pub Lib, Lakewood Ohio 37-44; Libn Spec Serv US Army, Hawaiian Command 44-49; Hosp libn head order dept, asst command libn, Dir SCAP Civil Info & Educ Program, Japan 49-52; Libn Sch of Nursing Washington Co Hosp, Hagerstown Md 53-. 8: ALA rep to 3rd Word Health Conf Citizens Groups, 63. 9: ALA-AHIL (Bd 60-61; Com on Standards 63); MedLA; Nat League for Nursing; MdLA; Md League for Nursing (Hist Source Materials Com 59-60); Cumberland Valley LA; Baltimore Hosp LA. 10: AAUW; LWV; Washington Co (Md) Hist Soc; Washington Co (Md) Mus of Fine Arts; DAR. 12: "Discover a New World, Lib man for nurs stud (rev 64). 13: Yes. 14: Admin, ref, publ. 15: 640 Oak Hill ave, Hagerstown Md 21740.

GROVE, PEARCE SEYMOUR. b Augusta Ga 21 S 30. 4: Elaine Adams Grove. 5: UTampa 5253 (Soc Sci); UFla 5356 (Soc Studies) BAE, 5657; Found of Educ (Med); UIll 5758 MS in LS; E N Mex U 67 (Ed Admin). 6: Sp. 7: US Navy 4852; Reserve US Coast Guard 5259; Commissioned US Navy 59; Currently Lt in USN Reserve, Educ Lib Stud asst UFla 5356; Grad asst 5657; Grad asst UIll Lib Sch 5758; Asst Educ Psych & Phil Depts Libn UIll Urbana 5860; Head acquis & ser Dept UIll Chicago 61; Head libn Colo Womans Col 6165; Asst dir of libs Kan State U (Manhattan) 6567; Lib dir & hd dept of LS East New Mex U 67. 8: Mem Instit Study Com, Colo Womans Col 6165; Chm Denver Dist Libns 63; Chm Reorg Com for Cold Lib Assn 64; Guest ed & contrib Illinois Libraries--. 9: ALA (Coun, life mem); ACRL (AV Com 66); RTSD (Ref Stat Com 68); ColoLA; KanLA; NMLA (Exec Bd 68); SWLA (Com Chm 68). 10: AAUP; Phi Delta Kappa; US Naval Reserve; NMAVA; NEADAVI. 12: Ed Colorado Academic Library--, 3 Issues 6365; The Three Bears--, 20Min Film (57). 13: Yes. 14: Col & univ admin, lib educ, bldg & planning, media. 15: 1331 S ave I, Portales NM 88130.

GROVE, R GENEVIEVE (RUTH WOODRUFF AULT). b Spokane Wash 2 Ap 12. 4: John P Grove. 5: UWash 33-37 BA, 51-53 (LS) MA. 6: Fr, Ger. 7: Catlg libn UWash Lib 53-56; Catlg libn UWash Law Lib 56-62, Asst libn tech serv 62-65; Br libn Seattle Pub Lib 66-67; Doc libn UWash Law Lib 68-. 9: ALA; AALL (Memb Com, Recr Com). 11: West Scholarship AALL (64). 14: Catlg, tech serv, docs, info sci. 15: 6309 Evanston N, Seattle Wa 98103.

GROVE, ROBERT C. b Mt Pleasant Mich 17 Jl 32. 4: Wilda M Wiley. 5: Central MichU 67-69 (Sp) 58-61 (Geog) BS (cum laude); UMich 63-64 AMLS; Mich StateU 61-62 (Geog). 6: Sp. 7: Machinery repairman 2nd class USN 52-56; High sch libn Howell Pub Schs, howell Mich 62-63; Original catlgr Mich StateU Lib (E Lansing) 64-66, Hd reclsf sect 66-67; Bibliogr in tech serv Central MichU Lib 68-. 9: ALA. 14: Maps, acquis, catlg. 15: 611 N Washington, Mt Pleasant Mi 48858.

GROVER, ARLENE H. b Ithaca NY 25 My 09. 4: Roscoe A Grover. 5: Brigham Young 25-29 (Home Econ) BA, 32-34 (Eng) MA; Columbia 31-32 (Eng); UUtah 60-62 (LS). 6: Sp, Fr. 7: Tchr Juarez State Acad, Colonia Juarez Chih Mexico 29-31; Instr Col of So Utah 47-49; Libn VA Hosp, Salt Lake City 60-62; Dir tech serv Utah State Lib 62-. 9: ALA; MPLA; UtahLA (v-pres 67-68). 14: Catlg. 15: Suite 16 2150 S 2nd W, Salt Lake City Ut 84115.

GROVER, IVA SUE. b Eau Claire Wis 21 Je 41. 5: UPuget Sound 60-64 (Econ) BA; UWash 64-66 MLib; East Wash State Col summers 67 & 68 Educ Certif. 7: Jr high libn Granger Pub Schs, Granger Wash 66-. 8: Establ & operate ESEA-TITLE I Lib Resource Ctr for Granger (Wash) Jr High Sch 66-69. 9: ALA; Wash State ASchL (chm Profess Train Com 68-69); Wash Dept of A-V Instr; WashLA; WashEA. 10: Beta Phi Mu; Granger Lib Club. 14: ya serv. 15: Rte 1 Granger Wa 98932.

GROVER, THELMA I. b Rowley Iowa 18 D 05. 5: State U of Iowa 34-38 BA; LSU summer 40; West Res 41-4 BLS. 7: Elem & high Sch libn, Davenport Iowa 39-42; Highsch libn, Waukegan Ill - Wauwatosa Wis 43-48; 1st asst circ dept Pub Lib, Indianapolis 48-50; Dir Pub Lib, Ft Dodge Iowa 50-51; Head of adult dept Pub Lib, Cedar Rapids Iowa 51-56, Asst dir56-. 8: Act dir 64-65 Cedar Rapids Pub Lib, Cedar Rapids Iowa. 9: ALA (Life mem); IowLA. 14: Adult wk. 15: 1400 2nd ave SE, Cedar Rapids Iowa 52403.

GROVER, WAYNE C (LAYTON). b Garland Utah 16 S 06. 4: Esther Thomas. 5: UUtah 30 (Eng) AB; American U 37 (Pol Sci) MA, 46 (Pol Sci & Pub Admin) PhD. 7: Archivist War Records Div Nat Archives 35-41; Tech asst to Bd of Analysts Off of Strategic Serv, Wash DC 41-43; Chief Records Mgt Br AGO War Dept, Wash DC 46-47; Asst Archivist of the US Nat Archive 47-48, Archivist of the US 48-65; Chm Nat Hist Pub Commsn NARS GSA 48-. 65; Consul on archives 66-. 8: Consul US Com on Org of the Exec Br of Govt 49-; Can Royal Com on Govt Org 61; Coun Mem & West Hemis v-pres of Internat Coun on Archives 50-53, 60-64; Mem of US Nat Com for UNESCO 61-65. 9: SAA(Fellow, pres 54); AHA; Amer Pol Sci Assn; Amer Soc for Pub Admin; Mass Hist Soc. 10: Cosmos Club Wash DC. 11: LLD Brown U 56; Bucknell U 60; Belmont Abbey Col 64; Leg of Merit 46; Dist Serv Award of GSA 59; Career Serv Award Nat Civ Serv League 61. 13: Yes. 14: Archival admin, records mgt. 15: 2303 Linden lane, Silver Spring Md 20910.

GRUBB, ANNETTE (HERMAN). b Mosinee Wis 9 N 38. 4: Earl S Grubb. 5: Wis State U 56-59, 60-61 (Eng) BS; Rutgers 61-63 MLS; Shippensburg State Col summer 65, 66. 7: Child libn Coyle Free Lib, Chambersburg Penn 63-65; Sch libn Carlisle Area Sch System, Carlise Penn 65-. 9: PennLA; Penn State EA; Carlisle Area EA. 10: AAUW; LWV. 14: Ya, ref. 15: Rt 3, Newville Penn 17241.

GRUEN, SONIA L. b Roumania 28 D 14. 4: Kurt H Gruen. 5: UPittsburgh 41 (Hist) BA (Magna cum laude); Carnegie 42 BS in LS; Columbia 62-63 (LS); Med LA Med Lib Certif 58. 6: Rus,Ger,Yiddish. 7: Catlgr Carnegie Lib of Pittsburgh 32-43; Ref & Yp work NY Pub Lib 43-53; Ref libn & head catlgr Cornell Med Lib, NYC 53-55; Chief Libn Asst Prof of ed Bibliog Albert Einstein Col of Med 55-. 8: Consul to libns of dept libs Albert Einstein Col of Med. 9: MedLA (Adv Com on Med Prob, chm 66-); NY Lib Club. 10: AAAS; Delta Phi Alpha. 12: . 13: Yes. 14: Ref, med bk sel & bibliog. 15: Albert Einstein Col of Med, Eastchester rd & Morris Park ave, Bronx NY 10461.

GRUHLER, ALINE HELEN. b Gretna La 16 Ag 18. 5: Tulane 38-42 BA; LSU 60-62 (LS) MS. 7: Classroom tchr Orleans Parish Schs, New Orleans 36-60; Libn Behrman Hgh Sch, New Orleans 60-. 10: Phi Kappa Phi. 14: Catlg. 15: 517 Huey P Long ave, Gretna La 70053.

GRUNAWALT, JACQUELINE L (JOHNSON). b Michigan 6 Je 36. 4: Richard J Grunawalt. 5: UMich 54-58 (Sociol) AB; URI 66-68 MLS. 7: Tchr Saline Pub Sch, Saline Mich 58-60; Libn Portsmouth Schs, Portsmouth RI 68-. 9: ALA; NEA; RISchLA; RIEA. 14: Sch libs, child bks. 15: 155 Lexington, Middletown RI 02840.

GRUNDT, LEONARD. b Brooklyn NY 5 S 36. 4: Barbara Schwartz. 5: Brooklyn Col 54-58 (Econ) BA; Columbia 58-60 (LS) MS; Rutgers 61-65 (LS) PhD. 6: Fr, Ger. 7: Clerk Brooklyn Pub Lib 55-57; Acquis asst Brooklyn Col Lib 58-60, Soc sci libn 60-61; Sr libn Free Pub Lib, Linden NJ 61-62; Research asst Boston Pub Lib 62-63; Asst research spec Grad Sch of Lib Sci(Rutgers U) 64-65; Asst Prof Lib Dept Nassau Community Col 65-, Deputy dir of lib 66-67, Dir lib 67-. 8: Ref libn Library/USA NY Worlds Fair 65; Visiting Prof Lib Educ SUNY (Geneseo) 66. 9: ALA; NEA-DAVI; NY State LA; Nassau CoLA; LI Educ Communications Coun. 10: Phi Beta Kappa; Beta Phi Mu; AAUP. 12: "Efficient Patterns for Adequate Library Service in a Large City" (68); Co-ed "Research on Library Service in Metropolitan Areas" (67). 13: Yes. 14: Reader serv, admin, tchg, automation, a-v serv. 15: 12 Commander Vic lane, Nesconset NY 11767.

GRUNDY, CAROLYN (RUTH). b Mercer Penn 28 O 41. 5: Grove City Col 59-63 (Eng) BA; UIll(Urbana) 63-64 MLS; Indiana U of Pa 67-. 6: Ger. 7: Acquis libn Slippery Rock State Col 64-66; Asst libn Indiana U of Pa 66-. 9: ALA(Internat Rel Round Table). 14: Ref. 15: Apt 4, 931 Lilac st, Indiana Pa 15701.

GRUNDY, DIANE (HELENE). b Mercer Penn 19 Jl 43. 5: Grove City Col 61-65 (Eng) BA; Case-West Res 65-66 MSLS. 6: Fr. 7: Sr high libn Grove City Area Sch Dist, Grove City Penn 66-69; Hd libn Grove City Col 69-. 9: ALA; NEA; PennStateEA. 10: Lambda Iota Tau. 15: RD 6, Mercer Pa 16137.

GRUTCHFIELD, WALTER R. b Lynchburg Va 18 F 36. 4: Martha Welday. 5: URichmond 54-57 (Chem); NYU 58-59 (Fr); City Col 61-62 (Eng) BA 67- (Eng); Pratt Inst 63-66 MLS. 6: Fr. 7: Catlgr City Col of NY 66-69; Programmer trainee NYC Pub Lib 69-. 9: ALA. 10: Phi Beta Kappa; Internat Assn for the Study of Dada and Surrealism. 14: Catlg, lib automation. 15: 612 W 144th st, New York NY 10031.

GUALTIERI, BERNADETTE (GAMBLE). b Toledo Ohio. 4: Carlo Gualtieri. 5: UWash 33-38 (Mus, Eng) BA, Secondary tchg certif, 59 MLS. 7: Libn Sunnyside High Sch, Sunnyside Wash 38-39; Lib asst Seattle Pub Lib 39-62; Hd humanities ref UWash 62-. 9: ALA; PNLA (chm Ref Div, chm Hospitality Com 69); WashLA (Scholarship & Loan Com, Col Contacts Com 62), 10: Beta Phi Mu. 14: Ref. 15: Univ of Washington Lib, Seattle Wa 98105.

GUASCO, JEAN A. b Lancaster Ohio. 4: Dante V Guasco. 5: Capital U 39-40; Ohio State U 41-43 (Lat, Eng) BS in Educ, 43-45 MA in Educ; Columbia 51-53 (LS) MS. 7: Tchr Mifflin HighSch, Columbus Ohio 42-46; Libn Rogers Jr High Sch, Stamford Conn 46-48; Lib asst US Navy Underwater Sound Lib, New London Conn 48-49; Circ libn UConn 49-51; Asst libn Ft Jay Post & 1st Army Ref Lib, Governors Island NY 51-53; Ref libn & catlgr McGraw-Hill Inc, NYC 53-55, Assoc libn 55-60, Chief Libn 60-. 9: SLA (NY Chap; dir 64-66, chm Publ Gp 66-67, chm Awards Com 66-68, chm Publ Div 68-69); ALA; ASIS; Nat Microfilm Assn; NY Lib Club; NY Tech Serv Libns. 10: Beta Phi Mu. 14: Admin, lib automation. 15: 5425 Fieldston rd, Bronx NY 10471.

GUAY, BERNARD. b Saint-Bernard Cte Dorchester 26 Jl 35. 4: Gloria Hodgson. 5: Sem St-Alphonse, Ste-Anne de Beaupre 48-54 Baccalaureat en Rhetorique; U Laval 57-59 Baccalaureat en pedagogie, 61-63, 65-67 Licence es lettres; UMontreal 68 Baccalaureat en bibliotheconomie. 6: Fr, Sp, Ital. 7: Prof Ecoles secondaires et colleges, Quebec Can 59-61, 63-65; Bibliothecaire U Laval 65-. 9: Assn canadienne des bibliothecaires de langue francaise. 10: Choeur Symphonique de Quebec; Archiviste et musicothecaire. 14: Catlg, rare bks. 15: 3450 Chemin St-Louis apt 102, Ste-Foy Quebec 10 Prov Que Can.

GUBERT, BETTY (KAPLAN). b NYC 20 Ja 34. 4: Erminio Gubert. 5: City Col (NY) 51-56 (Eng) BA; Middlebury Col summer 56 (Ital); Columbia 57-61 (LS) MS. 6: Ital, Fr. 7: Libn trainee Brooklyn Pub Lib 56-58; Libn Columbia U Bus Lib 62-63; Libn NY Pub Lib 63-, catlgr Unicef Info Ctr for Child Cultures summer 67; Libn NY Pub Lib 68-. 14: Rare bks, ref. 15: 150 W 96th st apt 3D, New York NY 10025.

GUDATH, ANN (LYLES). b Tampa Fla 1 S 37. 4: Ernest Andrew Gudath. 5: Wesleyan Col 55-57; UTampa 57-58; Fla State U 58-59 (LS) BA, 60-61 (LS) MS. 7: Stud asst Fla State u 59; Br libn Tampa Pub Lib, Tampa Fla 59-60; Grad asst Fla State U 60; Docs libn UDel 61-62; Libn Sidney Lanier Sch, Tampa Fla 63-64; Libn Watson Clinic, Lakeland Fla 66-. 9: ALA; -ACRL. 10: Jr League of Tampa. 14: Ref, catlg. 15: 413 So Bryan cir, Brandon Fl 33511.

GUDELIUS, ELFRIEDE. b Germany 15 N 08. 5: UWash 27-31 BS in LS. 6: Ger. 7: Pub Lib, Tacoma Wash; Ref asst 31-38, 1st asst Ref Dept 38-52, Head Hist Div 52-54, 1st asst Gen Serv Dept 54-61, Head Gen Serv Dept 61-. 9: ALA; PNLA; WashLA. 10: Wash State Hist Assn; Phi Beta Kappa. 14: Ref, adult serv. 15: 506 N 2nd ave apt 405, Tacoma Wa 98403.

GUENTHER, CHARLES (JOHN). b St Louis 29 Ap 20. 4: Esther Klund. 5: Jefferson Col 37-38 (Bus Admin); Harris Tchrs Col 38-40 (Modern Langs) AA; St Louis U 52-54 (Geog); Agen (Lot-et-Garonne) France 57 Litt M (Hon). 6: Fr, Sp, Ital, Portu. 7: Ed asst "St Louis Star-Times 38; Clerk Soc Security Commsn of Mo, St Louis 41; Claims clerk Dept of Labor US Employment Serv, St Louis 41-42; Clerk War Dept Corps of Engnrs, St Louis 42-43; Lib asst head archives unit AAF Aero Chart Serv, St Louis 43-45, Sr clerk head research unit 45-47; USAF Aero Chart & Info Center, St Louis: Chief lib sect 47-48, Tr-histn asst chief lib 48-49, Libn-histn asst chief lib 49-51, Geographer-histn asst chief lib 51-56, Supv cartographer asst chief lib 56-59, Chief tech li 57-, Libn admin 59-. 8: Detailed to Proj Crossroads USAF 46 (civilian lib spec); Instr creative writing Peoples Art Center, St Louis 53-56; Lecturer & poetry wkshop leader McKendree Writers Confs McKendree Col 55-; Visiting Lecturer & consul Grad Sch of Libnship UDenver 65. 9: ALA; SLA. 10: Greater St Louis Lib Club; St Louis WritersGuild; McKendree Writers Assn; Poetry Center of St Louis; St Louis Camera Club. 11: Agen (Lot-et-Garonne) France 57 Litt M (hon); Decorated Commander Order of St George of Carinthia 58; Diplome honneur Academie D Alsace, Strasbourg 57 (cor mem); Les Violetti Picards et Normands, Paris 57 (hon mem); Academia de Ciencias Humanisticas y Relaciones, Mexico, DF 57 (hon mem); Academie Chablaisienne, Thonon-les-Bains France 58 (hon mem); International American Institute 58 (assoc mem); Biblioteca Partenopea, Naples 59 (hon mem). 12: "Modern Italian Poets (61); co-transl "Selected Pems of Alain Bosquet (63); Contrib to "Anthology of Spanish Poetry (61); "The French in the Mississippi Valley (65); "From the Hungarian Revolution (65); & other bks. 13: Yes. 14: Historical cartography, European & Latin-Amer poetry, mss collections, French Canadiana. 15: 2935 Russell blvd, St Louis Mo 63104.

GUENTHER, ELEANOR RUTH (KUHL). b Clarksburg W Va 5 Mr 40. 4: Detlef Gustave Guenther. 5: W Va U 57-61 (Eng) BA; Divinity Sch Duke 61-63 (Relig Educ) MRE; Syracuse 66-67 9relig Educ), 67 MS in LS. 6: Sp. 7: Dir Christian educ 1st Methodist Ch, Ocala Fla 64-65; Dir Christian educ 1st Methodist Ch, Syracuse NY 65-67; Asst circ libn Duke U 67-68, Ref libn 68; Ref libn Inter amer U 68-69, Campus sch libn 69-. 9: ReligEA; ALA; Sociedad de Bibliotecarios de Puerto Rico. 10: AAUP; AAUW; LWV. 14: Ref. 15: Box 332 Inter American Univ, San German Puerto Rico 00753.

GUENTHER, MARTHA MARIE. b Burlington Iowa 22 D 1900. 05 UIowa 19-23 (Fr) BA; UIll 30-31 BS in LS; UMich 35, 38 MA in LS. 5: UIowa 19-23 (Fr) BA; UIll 30-31 (LS) BS in LS; UMich summer 35, 38 (LS) MA in LS. 6: Ger, Fr. 7: Tchr High Sch, Millersburg Iowa 23-24; Tchr-libn A Lincoln High Sch, Council Bluffs Iowa 24-26; Gen asst Free Pub Lib, Burlington Iowa 26-30; Libn Iowa Wesleyan Col 31-36; Asst catlg & ref depts Deering Lib Northwestern U 36-40; Catlgr & tchr of Lib Sci E Carolina Tchrs Col 41; Ref libn Grinnell Col Lib 41-44; Asst libn & head catlg dept Lib Ida State U 44-59; Catlg libn Ore State U 59-62; Catlgr Free Pub Lib, Burlington Iowa 62-. 9: ALA; IdahoLA (pres 55-56, mem var coms); IowaLA (chm Resources & Tech Serv Sect 66-67). 10: Bus & Prof Womens Club; Phi Beta Kappa. 13: Yes. 14: Catlg, ref. 15: 903-1/2 N 4th st, Burlington Iowa 52601.

GUERNSEY, MARJORIE (EMPIE). b Seward NY 26 Jl 16. 4: Charles Guernsey. 5: Hartwick Col 34-38 (Eng) AB; State U (Albany NY) 40-41 BS in LS; Syracuse summer 42 (Soc Sci); Hobart Col even 57-58 (Guidance). 6: Fr, Ger. 7: Tchr-libn Central Sch, Hartford NY 41-43; Asst libn High Sch, Baldwin LI NY 43-44; Libn Munsey Park Sch, Manhasset LI NY 44-47; Asst circ libn USCar 47-48; Eng tchr High Sch, Cobleskill NY 54-55; Libn High Sch, Waterloo NY 55-. 9: NY State Tchrs Assn; NYLA. 10: Waterloo (NY) Research Club. ; Phi Beta Psi. 14: Yp. 15: 142 Virginia st, Waterloo NY 13165.

GUEST, FRANCES (WILLARD). b Wellston Ohio 22 Mr 12. 5: Denison U 30-32 Ohio State U 32-33 (Eng Lit) BA; UWash 51-52 BA in LS. 7: Asst to libn Chula Vista Pub Lib, Chula Vista Cal 48-51; Br libn Spokane Pub Lib, Spokane Wash 52-53; Libn Ft Belvoir Post Sch, Ft Belvoir Va 53-55; Bkmob libn San Diego Pub Lib, San Diego Cal 55-56; Young adult libn Chula Vista Pub Lib, Chula Vista Cal 56; Sub libn San Diego Pub Lib, San Diego Cal 59-61; Child libn Valencia Park br, San Diego Cal 61-63; Head Central Child Room San Diego Pub Lib, San Diego Cal 63-, Asst coord child serv San Diego Pub Lib UCA SD Extension Instructor Book Selection for Pre-School 69. 8: Instr Bk Sel for PreSch, UCal (San Diego) Ext 69. 9: ALA; CalLA. 15: 711 Madison, Chula Vista Ca 92010.

GUEST, SISTER M ROSE MARGARET SNJM. b Birkenhead Eng. 5: Marylhurst Col 45 (Eng) BA; UPortland 53 MLS. 6: Lat, Fr. 7: Libn tchr Sisters of Holy Names of Jesus & Mary Prov of Ore & Wash 35-. 9: CathLA (Reg rep 39th Ann Conv 63; sec Seattle Unit 60-62); Cath Poetry Soc Amer, ALA; OreLA. 13: Yes. 14: Catlg, ref. 15: Holy Names Acad, 728-21 St ave E, Seattle Wa 98102.

GUGLIOTTA, ANTOINETTE FRANCES. b Atlantic City NJ 19 O 06. 5: UPenn 24-28 (Lat) BS in Ed; Drexel 53, 56-58 MS in LS. 6: Sp. 7: Elem tchr Bd of Edu, Hammonton NJ 28-32, Tchr-libn High Sch 32-43; Off-gen duty (Lt) USNR Waves NATTC, Memphis, NAS Quonset Pt43-45: High sch libn Bd of Educ, Hammonton NJ 46-63; Tech libn Owens-Illinois Glass Co, Berlin NJ 47-49; Med libn NJ State Hosp, Ancora nj 55; Co Libn Wilmington Inst Free Lib 7 New Casle Co Free Lib, Wilmington Del 63-, Asst dir. 9: NEA; ALA; NJEA; DelLA. 10: Delta Kappa Gamma: Quota Club. 14: High sch libs, pub lib admin. 15: 208 Claymont Garden Apts, Claymont De 19703.

GUIDER, GENEVA. b Lenoir City Tenn. 5: Tenn Tech 37 (Hist) BS; Peabody Col 41 BS in LS; UTex (El Paso) 56 (Educ) MA. 6: Fr. 7: Tchr-Prin Martel Sch, Martel Tenn 38-41; Libn Gibbs High Sch, Corryton Tenn 41-44; Libn Beardon High Sch, Beardon Tenn 44-47; Libn Professional Lib, El Paso Tex 47-49; Libn El Paso High, El Paso Tex 49-. 8: Eval Com Lib Chm 49. 9: NEA; ALA: TexEA; TexLA; Trans Pecos Border Reg LA (v-chm Lib Sect). 10: Kappa Delta Pi. 14: Sch libs. 15: 2312 Arizona, El Paso Tx 79930.

GUIDO, JOHN (FOOTE). b Tarrytown NY 31 Mr 29. 4: Jane Cary. 5: Hofstra 51-55 (Hist) BA; Columbia 55-57 (Hist) MA; Rutgers 59-60 MSLS; NYU 64-67 (Amer Studies). 6: Fer, Ger. 7: Export clk Binney & Smith Intl Inc, NYC 48-51; Lib asst Hofstra Col Lib 57-59; Asst libn rare bks Cornell U Lib 60-63; Spec collections libn 63-. 9: ALA; BSA; SAA; Nassau Co Hist Soc. 10: Phi Alpha Theta; Hofstra Lib Assocs. 13: Yes. 14: Rare bks, mss, lib resources. 15: Hofstra Univ Lib, Hempstead NY 11550.

GUIDRY, EDITH (MARY WINTERROWD). b Tallulah La 23 D 18. 4: Francis Guidry. 5: La Col 57-61 (Elem Educ) BA; LSU 66 (LS). 7: Libn Menard High Sch, Alexandria La 61-62; Tchr Prompt Succor Sch, Alexandria La 62-63; Libn N Bayou Rapides Sch, Alexandria La 63-. 9: LaLA; LaTA; La Dept Clr Tchrs; Rapides Parish Clr Tchrs; Rapides TA. 10: Alpha Chi; Kappa Delta Pi; Phi Kappa Phi. 14: Child serv. 15: 3407 Elliott st, Alexandria La 71301.

GUIDRY, GEORGE JOSEPH JR. b Plaquemine La 13 N 22. 4: Ida Helen Dupont. 5: LSU (Baton Rouge) 40-47 (Math) BS, 47-48 (Educ) MA, 48-50 BSLS. 7: Lib asst LSU Lib circ dept 46-48, Sr libn photoduplication dept 49-52, Asst libn photoduplication dept 52-62, Asst dir special serv 62-64, Assoc dir public serv 64-. 9: ALA; SWLA; LaLA. 10: Jr C of C; Plaquemine City Coun. 13: Yes. 14: Admin. 15: 918 Robertson st, Plaquemine La 70764.

GUIGNARD, ALICE M. b Ottawa Can 11 Jl 31. 5: UToronto 49-52 (Gen Arts) BA; Ottawa Tchrs Col 58-59 Elem Sch Tchrs Certif; Columbia summers 64-67 MS in LS. 6: Fr. 7: Sec Moore Bus Forms Ltd, Ottawa Can 52-58; Tchr Ottawa Pub Sch Bd Ottawa Can 59-66; Tchr & libn Etobocoke Bd of Educ Toronto 67-68, 68-. 9: CanLA; OntLA. 10: Ont Tchrs Fed. 14: Sch libs, child lit, educ libs. 15: apt 204 235 E Mall, Islington Ont Can.

GUILBAULT, OSCAR R. b Woonsocket RI 14 D 31. 5: Providence Col 55-59 Eng AB; URI 66-68 MLS. 6: Fr. 7: USAF 51-55; Copy ed "The Woonsocket Call," Woonsocket RI 59-66; Libn Burrillville Jr-Sr High Sch, Burrillville RI 66-67; Coord No Interrelated Lib syst, Pawtucket RI 67-68; Readers serv libn Providence Col Lib 68-. 8: Co-consultant on a feasibility study for a proposed Blackstone Valley Area Lib to serve three communities in Northern RI. 9: ALA; RILA. 10: Amer Newspaper Guild. 14: Admin, readers serv. 15: 22 Edgewater dr, Blackstone Ma 01504.

GUILES, KAY DEAN. b North Platte Neb 25 S 31. 5: UNeb 50-53 (Educ) BSc E, 53-55 (Hist) MA; UMich 57-58 MSLS. 6: Fr, Sp. 7: Tchg asst Hist Dept UNeb 54-55; Clerk typist US Army Transportation Corps Sp 4 55-57; Searcher order div Gen Lib UMich 57-58; Catlgr LC 58-65 Lib syst analyst Info Syst Off, LC 66; Hd Fr Lang Sect shared Catlg Div 67, Lib syst analyst Info Syst Off 68-. 8: Mem Subcom SC2 (Machine input records) of Z39 com of USASI. 9: ALA; DCLA. 12: Co-auth "A Proposed Format for a Standardized Machine-Readable Catalog Record"; A Preliminary Draft (65). 14: Catlg. 15: Apt 818, 1301 Delaware ave SW, Wash DC 20024.

GUITE, PAUL VILBON. b Waterville Me 2 D 33. 5: UNotre Dame 53-57 BA; Georgetown U 57-60 (Amer Hist) MA; Simmons 63-64 (LS) MS. 6: Fr. 7: Libn I UNotre Dame (Notre Dame Ind) 64-65; Asst libn Windham Col 65-67; Catlgr UMe (Portland) 67-68; Catlgr Nat Archives Lib 69-. 8: Instr Hist Widham Col; Instr Lib Sci UMe (Portland) 68. 9: ALA; CathLA. 14: Ref, catlg, archival sci. 15: 2116 Bancroft pl NW, Wash DC 20008.

GUIVER, MELVA LILLIAN. b Salt LAKE City 7 Ja 08. 5: UUtah 26-28, 30-39 (Elem Educ) BS; UDenver 44-47 BSLS; UUtah 52-54 (LS) MS, Secondary Educ Certif, Secondary Lib Certif. 7: ELEM TCHR Farmington Sch, Davis Co Utah 28-29; Elem tchr ountiful Sc, Davis Co Utah 29-30; Salt Lake City: Elem tch Oquirrh Sch 30-31, Elem tchr Franklin Sch 31-41, Elem libn Wasatch Sch 41-47, Libn Irving Jr High Sch 47-54, Libn East High Sch 54-. 8: Visiting instr lib sci UUtah, summers 60-62. 9: NEA; UtahLA; UtahEA. 10: Delta Kappa Gamma; Womans Soc for Christian Serv; Humane Soc. 14: Wk with studs, catlg, rare bks (Utah hist). 15: 1917 S 23rd E, Salt Lake City Ut 84108.

GULICK, ISABEL. b Maplewood NJ 13 Mr 13. 5: Wellesley 30-34 (Span) A; Columbia 48-50 (LS) MS. 6: Sp, Fr. 7: Receptionist & cashier W & J Sloane & Co, NYC 3638; Stenographer Fidelity Union Trust Co, Newark NJ 39-40; Welder Orange creen Co, Maplewood NJ 4345; Sec Mistaire Lab, Millburn NJ 4546; Asst Maplewood Pub Lib, MaplewoodNJ47-48, Ref libn 48-52; Asst dir Maplewood Mem Lib, Maplewood NJ 52-. 8: Orgr Great Bks Discussion Group, 58-. 9: ALA-RSD; NJLA (pres Ctlgr Sect 60-61). 10: LWV; Nat Audubon Soc; NJ Audobon Soc; Nat Wildlife Assn; Bd mem South Orange-Maplewood Adult Sch. 12: Edl coun Whos Who in Lib Serv (3rd ed 55). 14: Catlg, ref. 15: 138 Maplewood ave, Maplewood NJ 17040.

GULLETT, SHARON (BLACKWELL). b Longview Tex 2 Jl 44. 4: Ray Gullett. 5: N Tex State U 62-65 (LS) BA. ; LSU 67-69 MLS. 6: Sp. 7: Asst libn Irving pub schs, Irving Tex 65-67; Lib asst LSU, Baton Rouge La 67-68; Libn Bellingrath Hills Elem Sch, East Baton Rouge Parish, Baton Rouge La 68-69. 9: Tex State Tchrs Assn, LaTA. 14: Sch libs. 15: 10243 San Lorenzo ave, Dallas Tx 75228.

GULLETTE, MRS IRENE (DAUGHTREY). b Marion Ky 25 F 06. 5: UKy 59 MS in LS. 7: Ed Young People's Books "The Booklist" ALA, Chicago 49-53; Dir Ky Bkmob Proj Lib Ext, Frankfort Ky 53-54; State supv sch libs Dept of Educ, Frankfort Ky 54-56; Head child wk Gary Pub Lib, Gary Ind 57-59, Head popular lib dept 59-62; Elem sch libn Pompano Beach Fla 62-65; Elem lib consul Broward County S chs, Ft Lauderdale Fla 65-. 9: ALA (var coms & chm AASchL Adv Com E B Awards 68-69);-YASD (Bd); NEA; FlaLA (chm Sch & Child Div 68-69); FlaASchL (chm 69-70, var coms); FlaEA. 10: Beta Phi Mu; Zonta Internat; Bus & Prof Womens Club; AAUW. 13: Yes. 14: Young adult & sch lib wk. 15: 3200 NE 7th ct, Pompano Beach Fl 33062.

GULLION, SUSAN LYNN. b Pittsburgh 30 O 40. 5: Carnegie 58-62 (Tech Writing & Ed) BS; UPittsburgh 2-64 MLS. 6: Ger, Fr. 7: Lib asst Grad Sch of Pub & Internat Affairs UPittsburgh 62-64; Intern Biomed Lib UCLA 64-65, Catlgr 65-65, Hd catlg-bindery div 68-. 9: MedLA. 10; beta Phi Mu. 14: Catlg, ref. 15: Biomedical Lib Center for the Health Sciences UCal, Los Angeles Ca 90024.

GUNDERSON, RACHEL (SORENSEN). b Ueling Neb 27 Mr 18. 4: Milo M Gunderson. 5: Wayne State Tchrs Col 35-39 (Eng, Hist) BA; Dana Col 57-59 (Elem Educ); Omaha U 61-65 (LS). 7: Off manager Oakland Bd of Educ Central Catlg Dept 41-43; Tchr Blair (Neb) Elem Schs, West Sch 57-61; Libn Blair High Sch, Blair Neb 61-. 9: NEA; ALA; NebStateEA; NebLA; Neb Educ Media Assn. 14: Ref. 15: 1553 Grant st, Blair Neb 68008.

GUNDRUM, EMMA T. b York Penn 26 d 09. 4: Paul C Gundrum. 7: Sec York Corp, York Penn 43-49; Libn York Div Borg-Warner, York Penn 50-. 9: SLA. 10: York Hiking Club. 14: Ref. 15: York Div, Borg-Warner Corp, York Pa 17405.

GUNN, THEODUS LAFAYETTE. b Burlington NC 22 Ja 03. 4: Floretta D Gunn. 5: Johnson C Smith U 27 AB; Hampton Inst 30 BLS; Columbia summers (LS). 7: Libn Johnson C Smith U 30-. 9: ALA; NCLA; SELA; Mecklenburg LA. 10: Bd of dirs, Mecklenburg Investment Corp; Bd of dirs Grier Development Corp; Omega Psi Phi; Notaries Assn of NC. 11: Service Award from Johnson C Smith Alumni. 12: "History of the Johnson C Smith University Library. 14: Catlg. 15: Johnson C Smith U, Charlotte NC 28208.

GUNTER, JEAN. b New Philadelphia Ohio 28 Jl 24. 5: David Lipsvomb Col 43-45 (Eng) JC Diploma; Harding Col 45-47 (LS) BA; Peabody Col 49-50 (LS) MA. 6: Sp. 7: Welfare libn Miss State Dept of Pub Welfare, Jackson Miss 51-. 9: SLA; MissLA. 10: Miss Conf on Soc Welfare. 14: Social work literature. 15: 827 N State st, Jackson Ms 39201.

GUNTHER, BARBARA. b Danzig 29 Ap 41. 5: Toronto 59-63 (Art Hist) BA, 64-65 BL, 68-69 (Art Hist). 6: Ger, Fr. 7: Sub-prof libn NY Pub Lib, Willowdale Ont 63-64, Libn 65-69; Libn Dept Fine Arts UToronto 69-. 9: CanLA. 14: Yp, fine arts. 15: 419 Roselawn ave, Toronto 12 Ont Can.

GUNTHER, ELLEN P. b Berlin Germany 19 Mr 25. 4: William C Gunther. 5: Chemotechnische Schule (Berlin) 41-46 (Chem) BS; Rosary Col 66- (LS). 6: Ger. 7: Chem Armour & Co, Chicago 48-60; Chem & libn Julian LABS, Franklin Park Ill 60-63; Libn Alberto-Culver Co, Melrose Park Ill 63-. 9: ACS; SLA; Soc Cosm Chemists (Memb com Midwest Chap). 13: Yes. 14: Ref. 15: Alberto-Culver Co Res Lib, 2525 Armitage ave, melrose Park Il 60160.

GUNZENHAUSER, DOROTHY (GREENE). b NYC 28 F 21. 4: Hans Gunzenhauser. 5: Ethical Culture Tchr Train Sch 37-40 (Early Childhood Educ) Certif; Columbia 40-42 (Early Childhood Educ) BS; Queens Col 62-65 MLS. 7: Child libn Franklin Sq Pub Lib, Franklin Sq, NY 65-. 10: Certified Braille trnscriber. 13: Yes. 14: Child lit. 15: 715 Carlyle ave, Franklin Square NY 11010.

GUPTILL, BARBARA (WILLIAMS). b Bonners Ferry Ida 30 MY #'. 4: Fred Elray Guptill. 5: Col of Ida 49-53 (Hist) BA; UWash 53-55 (LS) ML. 6: FR. 7: Clerical Col of Ida 49-53; Clerical gen reading UWash 53-55; Seattle Pub Lib: Asst gen reading 55-60, Asst lit dept 60-63, 1st Asst lit dept 63-. 9: PNLA. 13: Yes. 14: Ref. 15: 210 NE 82nd, Seattle Wa 98115.

GUPTILL, FRED ELRAY. b Seattle 14 Jl 30. 4: Barbary Williams Guptill. 5: Linfield Col 48-49; UWash 49-50, 53-55 (Hist) BA, 55-56 Tchg Certif, 63-64 (LS) ML. 6: Ger. 7: Seaman tech libn US Navy; Clerical gen reading UWash 53-55; Tchr Renton Pub Schs, Renton Wash 56-62; Tchr Seattle Pub Schs 62-64; Libn Boren Jr High Sch, Seattle 64-. 9: Wash SchLA; WashLA. 14: Sch libn. 15: 210 NE 82nd, Seattle Wa 98115.

GUREGHIAN, LUCY CHILD. b Phila 19 Jl 26. 5: Temple 44-45, 45-46. 6: Armenian. 7: Lib asst Womens Med Col 46-47; Lib asst Phila Bar Assn 48-63, Act libn 63-68, Asst dir 69-. 9: AALL. 15: 600 City Hall, Phila Pa 19107.

GUREWICH, JERRY J. b NYC 1 Ap 24. 5: Temple 46 (Psych) AB; Temple Sch Theol 49 (Theol) STB; Columbia 52 MSLS; Bank St Col of Educ 62-68 (Elem Educ). 6: Fr, Ger, Ital, Sp. 7: Asst catlgr Lehigh U 52-53; Asst libn Divinity Sch of Phila 60-62; Gen asst Temple U Sch of Law Lib 60-62; Asst libn Bank St Col of Educ, NY 62-68; Libn lib sch Pratt Inst summer 68; Asst catlgr 68-. 8: Mem Fac Coun, Bank Street Col of Educ 67-68. 9: SLA. 14: Catlg, ref. 15: 421 W 24 st, New York NY 10011.

GURNEE, RITA MAE (FRATI). b Allentown Penn 6 S 22. 4: Robert Townsend Gurnee. 5: Maryville Col 40; USoCal 48-52 (Eng) BA, 52 MLS. 7: Advertising make-up "Business Week", NYC 40-42, 45-48; Yeoman 1/C WAVES, Wash DC 42-45; Ref libn Pasadena Pub Lib, Pasadena Cal 52-57; Asst libn Electrodata Div Burroughs, Pasadena Cal 57-59; Ref libn sci tech Mt San Antonio Col 59-. 8: Staff, "Library 21" Exhibit, Seattle World's Fair (stationed at "Encyclopedia Britannica" Ready Reference Desk 62). 9: SLA (So Cal Chap: past Recr Chm, Pub rel Chm Profess Devel Chm Hospitality Chm); CalLA (past chm Doc Libns' RT, Recr Chm Ref Libns' RT, presently mem Profess Educ Com). 10: AAUW; USoCal Lib Sch Alum Assn; Beta Phi Mu; Libraria Sodalitas. 14: Ref, docs, vocat info. 15: 927 So Shasta, West Covina Ca 91790.

GURR, GENEIVRA M(IRIAM)(SMART). b Dayton Ohio 29 Je 07. 5: West Col for Women 25-29 (Lat, Gk, Educ) AB; UCincinnati 29-30 (Educ) B of Ed; West Res 55-56 (Child Lit) MS LS; UWash summer 62; West Mich summer 65 (NDEA Scholarship). 7: Tchr Dayton Pub Schs, Dayton Ohio 30-31; Tchr Wooster City Schs, Wooster Ohio 53-55, Libn 56-65, Circuit libn K-12 65-. 9: ALA-AASchL; NEA (Life mem); Nat A-V Assn; OhioEA; OhioASchLA; NCTE; WoosterEA. 10: AAUW; PTA; Fireside Study Club; Wooster Commun Hosp Aux. 14: Sch lib, child lit. 15: 1644 Beall ave, Wooster Oh 44691.

GURRERI, LORENZO ANTHONY. b Baltimore Md 16 Mr 37. 4: Linda Grisanti. 5: Canisius Col 55-60 (Eng) BS; Sy col 55-60 (Eng) BS; Syracuse 61-62 MSLS. 7: Jr libn Buffalo & Erie Co Pub Lib, buffalo NY 62-63; Catlgr SUNY (Binghamton) 63-66; Catlgr St BonaventureU 66-. 9: CathLA. 14: Catlg. 15: 125 N First st, Allegany NY 14706.

GURVIN, ANNE (JEANNE). b Rochester Minn. 5: UMinn 53 (Eng, Span) BS, 57 (LS, Span) MA; Universites de Nancy, Poitiers, Paris 59-61; UMadrid 62. 6: Fr, Sp. 7: Eng tchr-libn Olivia High Sch, Olivia Minn 53-55; Circ libn UMinn(Minneapolis) 55-57; US Army libn (GS-9) Spec Serv Div, France 57-61; Ref libn II UCal(Berkeley) 62-66; Asst cultural affairs off & reg libn (Uruguay, Paraguay, Bolivia) 66-. 9: ALA; Mod Lang Assn; AHA. 13: Yes. 14: Ref, readers adv, bibliog. 15: Dir Biblioteca Artigas-Washington, Montivideo Uruguay, New York APO 09879,.

GUSE, MARTHA. b Kalamazoo Mich 3 Jl 16. 5: Kalamazoo Col 33-37 (Hist) AB; Drexel 40-41 BSLS. 6: Ger. 7: Admin asst educ dept Enoch Pratt Free Lib, Baltimore 42-45, Br libn 45-48; Dir of Lib Serv USIS, Madras India 49-51; Foreign Affairs Off Dep of State, Wash DC 51-53; Dir of Lib Serv USIS, Tehran Iran 54-56; Dir of Lib Serv USIS, TOKYO 56-61; Dir of Lib Serv USIS, Bonn Germany 61-64; Internat Info Program Spec USIA, Wash DC 65-. 9: ALA. 10: Amer Foreign Serv Assn. 15: 5209 Nebraska ave NW, Wash DC 20015.

GUSTAFSON, ALICE CATHRYN. b Maynard Minn. 5: Bethel Col (St Paul) 32-33; UMinn 33-37 (Eng) BS, 39-40 (LS); Columbia summers 46-51 (LS) MS (6th yr). 7: Eng tchr Browns Valley High Sch, Browns Valley Minn 37-38; Eng tchr New London High Sch, New London Minn 38-39; Eng tchr 7 libn N St Paul Pub Schs, N St Paul Minn 41-43; Libn Union High ch, Grand Rapids Mich 43-45; Libn Peoria Pub Schs, Peoria Ill 45-52 Libn Proviso Twp High Schs, Maywood Ill 52-. 9: ALA; NEA; IllLA; IllEA; IllASchL. 15: 918 Roosevelt rd, Broadview Il 60153.

GUSTAFSON, ELAINE SHANNER. b Ventnor City NJ 8 S 23. 4: Philip C Gustafson. 5: Columbia 4345 (LS); Temple U 58 (Educ); George Washington U 5960 (Educ); Foothill Col 6869 (Lib Arts); UIowa 5556 (Lib Arts). 6: Fr. 7: Libn Thomas

M England Gen Hosp, Atlantic City NJ 4247; Libn US Navy Pub Works, Norfolk Va 4749; Libn Tripler Hosp, Honolulu 5556; Med libn ReesStealy Med Group, San Diego 5859; Lib Sc Illus US Geolog Survey, Silver Spring Md 5961; Med libn Atlantic City Hosp, Atlantic City NJ 64. 9: Consul Kaiser Hosp, Redwood City Cal 68. 10: Gen Fed of Womens- Clubs; NJ Hist Soc; Cal Art Club. 13: Yes. 14: Med research. 15: 108 Meadow View ave, Linwood NJ 08221.

GUSTAFSON, MARJORIE (JONES). b Butte Montana 17 Ja 24. 4: Harry L Gustafson Jr. 5: Duke 41-45 (Zoology) BA; Simmons 63-66 MLS. 6: Ger. 7: Tchr George W Miller sch, Nanuet NY 61-63; Elem lib consul Newton Pub Sch, Newton Mass 64-67; Libn East Sch, New Canaan Conn 67-68; Libn E Ridge Jr High Sch, Ridgefield Conn 68-. 9: ALA; NEA. 14: Sch libs, ref, bibliog, media ctrs. 15: Box 246, Mill River Ma 01244.

GUSTAFSON, VIOLA. b Burlington Iowa 19 Ja 08. 5: Iowa Wesleyan Col 25-29 (Fr) AB. 6: Fr,Ger. 7: CLERICAL ASST, CATLG UChicago Lib 30-32, Catlgr 32-47; John Crerar Lib, Chicago: Asst chief catlgr 47-49, Chief catlgr 49-50, Chief of tech serv 50-52, Asst libn for acquis & catlg 52-59; Head catlgr UChicago Lib 59-. 9: ALA; Chicago Reg Goup of Libns in Tech Serv; Chicago Lib Club. 14: Catl. 15: 5550 Dorchester ave, Chicago Il 60637.

GUSTASON, BERENICE BOYLE. b Beresford SD 12 Ag 19. 4: Robert S Gustason. 5: Yankton Col 37-41 (Eng, Speech) BA; UDenver 42-43 BS in LS. 7: Eng tchr High Sch, Ponca Neb 41-42; Cleveland Pub Lib: Ref libn W Tech High h 43-44, 1st asst libn Lincoln High Sch 44-45, 1st asst libn W High Sch 45-47; Libn Conneaut High Sch, Conneaut Ohio 49. 9: OhioASchL (Reg dir). 14: Ref, admin. 15: 232 West st, Conneaut Ohio 44030.

GUSTON, (GUSTAF) DAVID. b Brockton Mass25 Je 07. 4: Helen Rlou Lundeen. 5: UNH 26-30 (Arch) BS; Bethel Theol Sem 32-36 (Theol) B; UMinn 49-62 MA i LS. 7: Pastor Henning Baptist Church, Henning Minn 36-37; Pastor Goodwin Baptist Church, Bristol Conn 37-40; Pastor Bethany Baptist Church, Schenectady NY 40-43; Pastor Trinity Baptist Chruch, NYC 43-49; Assoc libn Bethel Col & Sem (St Paul) 49-56, Libn 56-64; Libn Bethel Theol Sem (St Paul) 64-. 8: Archivist, Baptist Gen Con 60-. 9: ATheolL(chm Com on Bldgs & Equipt); MinnLA, AtheolLA (treas 67-). 14: Catlg, admin. 15: Bethel Theological Seminary Lib, 3949 Bethel dr, St Paul Mn 55112.

GUSTOW, HAZEL (MENKIN). b Phila 24 S 17. 4: Herbert Gustow. 5: Temple 3538 (Eng) BS in Sec Ed; Drexel 63-64 LS. 6: Fr. 7: Asst ed Holiday Magazine, Phila 46-57; Free-lance ed, Phila 57-64; Head Libn Phila Col of Art 65-. 9: ALA; SLA; PennLA. 10: ACLU; SANE; AAUP. 14: Admin, ref, communication. 15: 524 Westview st, Phila Pa 19119.

GUTH, DORIS JUNE (PURDY). b Kennewuck Wash 11 Je 17. 4: Dean Guth. 5: UWash 41 (Eng) BA, 69 MLS. 6: Fr. 7: Br libn Sno-Isle Reg Lib, Lynnwood Wash 69-. 10: Soroptimist Club. 14: Ref. 15: 18606 64th ave W, Lynnwood Wa 98036.

GUTH, REBECCA (PRASOW). b Phila 3 S 10. 4: Nathan Guth. 5: UPenn 29-33 (Lat, Gk) BA; Drexel 41-42 (LS) BSLS. 6: Lat, Fr, Ger. 7: Head Meyers Lib Reform CONGREGATION Keneseth Israel, Elkins Park Penn 48; Temple U Lib: Head Lib Freshman Unit Cedarbrook Campus 48-51, Head res bk room & educ materials Lib 52-65, Dir instr materials center Col of Educ 65- Instr Lib Techniques in Educl Media 68-69. 8: Consul & lectr; Summer Inst Jr Cols, TempleU 67-68, Eng Lang Tchg 68. 9: ALA; -ACRL; Penn Learning Resources Assn. 10: West Mt Airy Neighbors Assn; Allens Lane Art Assn; Cheltenham Art Assn. 14: Admin, instr materials. 15: 709 W Carpenter lane, Phila Pa 19119.

GUTHRIE, MARY (FOSTER). b Lynchburg Va 2 N 23. 4: William Bell Guthrie. 5: Randolph-Macon Womans Col 40-44 (Eng) BA; Emory 44-45 BA in LS. 7: Asst libn Va Mil Inst 45-51; Period libn UVa 51-55; Indexer Va State Lib 55-56, Catlgr 57-58; Catlgr URichmond 62-63, 64-68; Res asst Va State Lib 68-. 9: VaLA. 14: Catlg, ref. 15: 7704 Dartmoor rd, Richmond Va 23229.

GUTIERREZ, MANFREDO. b Orocovis PR 27 Mr 39. 5: LSU (New Orleans) 58-63 (Govt) BA; LSU (Baton Rouge) 63-65 (LS) MS. 6: Sp. 7: File clerk US Fidelity & Guaranty Insurance Co, New Orleans 58; Period desk attendant New Orleans Pub Lib 60-63; (Cpl) NCO Head of Operations Sect Marine Corps Reserves, Belle Chasse La 56-64; Newspaper room attendant LSU Lib 64-65; Ref libn San Diego Pub Lib 65-. 14: Ref, bldgs, equipt. 15: 3899 Haines st Bldg 8 #106, San Diego Ca 92109.

GUTTMAN, (ANNETTE) SARAH. b Toronto Can 19 Ag 43. 4: Joseph Guttman. 5: UToronto 61-64 (Sci) BS, 64-65 BLS. 7: Catlgr UToronto Lib 65-67; Libn Centennial Centre for Sci & Tech, Toronto Can 67-68; Libn Ontario Dept of Pub Recs & Archives, Toronto Can 67-. 9: SLA; Inst Prof Libns Ont. 15: 80 Forest Manor rd apt 1507, Willowdale Ont Can.

GUTZ, ROBERT R(ICHARD). b Buffalo NY 19 Ap 38. 5: Diocesan Prep Sem (Buffalo NY) 57-59 (Certif); St Mary's Col (Orchard Lake Mich) 59-61 (Philos) AB; Pontificial Urban U (Vatican City) 61-63 (Theol); SUC (Geneseo) 64-65 MLS. 06: Polish, Ital, Sp. 7: Lib work study USVA Hosp, Buffalo NY 64-65; Ser catlg (asst lib) SUNY (Buffalo) 65-67, Acquis lib 9assoc lib) Law Lib 67-. 8: Participant Intl Assn Law Lib Seminar, Cambridge Eng 68. 9: ALA (var positions); AALL; SUNY LA; Assn Law Libns Upstate NY. 10: AAUP; ACLU; SUNY (Buffalo) LA. 14: Admin, tech serv, ref. 15: 139 Detroit st, Buffalo NY 14206.

GUY, ELIZABETH BARBARA. b Manly Iowa 29 Je 18. 5: UCal (Berkeley) 40-41, 46-49 (Anthrop) BA; UHawaii 49-50, 50-51 (Anthrop); USoCal 51-52 MS in LS; UNM summer 47 (Anthrop); Mexico City Col summer 51 (Anthrop). 7: 1st Lt US Army Nurse Corps 42-46; USAF Lib Program, Korea, Japan, Morocco, Turkey, Formosa, France, Germany 52-65; Ref & circ San Luis Obispo City Lib 66; Org & catlgr bk collection Santa Barbara Hist Mus 68; Act hd libn UHawaii Hilo Campus Lib 68-. 12: PACAF Bibliog "Pacific Area" (63). 14: Admin, ref. 15: 657 Park st, San Luis Obispo Ca 93401.

GUYOT, DON(ALD) A(LBERT). b Pocatello Ida 4 Jl 44. 4: Karen Grant. 5: Ida StateU 62-66 (Hist) BA; UWis (Madison) 67 (LS); UNC (Chapel Hill) 67-68 MS in LS. 6: Lat, Fr. 7: Coord Title III LSCA Ida State Lib 68-. 14: Rare bks, automation. 15: 1110 W State, Boise Id 83702.

GUZMAN, ISIDRO JR. b Beeville Tex 20 Jl 45. 5: Del Mar Jr Col 62-64 (Math) AA; UTex 9austin) 64-66 (Math) BA, 66-68 MLS. 6: Sp, Portu. 7: Ser catlgr UTex (Austin) 68-. 14: Catlg, ser. 15: 2613 Terrace st, Corpus Christi Tx 78404.

GWYN, ANN STEWART (MacDOUGALL). b Hong Kong China 15 F 35. 4: William Bretn Gwyn. 5: USt Andrews (Scotland) 53-56 (British Hist) MA; ULondon 67-68 (LS) Academic Post- grad diploma. 6: Fr, Ger. 7: Asst libn BucknellU Lib 57-58; Libn TulaneU Lib 68-. 9: LaLA. 15: 8011 Jeannette st, New Orleans La 70118.

GYI, THANT (MYA MYA) (MRS). b Pakokku Burma 16 F 17. 4: U Thant Gyi. 5: RangoonU 34-39 (Pali) BA, 39-41 (Educ) BEd; CatholicU 56-59 MSLS. 6: Burmese, Fr, Pali, Sanskrit. 7: Tchr Methodist High, Syriam Burma 41-42; Prin Jr High, Hlegu Burma 43-46; Lecturer State Train Col for Tchrs, Rangoon Burma 47-52; Dir USIS Jr Lib, Rangoon Burma 52-54; Asst dy dir USIS Lib, Rangoon Burma 60-65; Fescr catlgr S Asian & Eng lang sects LC 65-. 8: Adv for lib ext wk in Burma; Set up libs & given profess help in bldg collection & tech servs for pub & govt libs, Burma 60-65. 9: BurmaLA. 14: Catlg Pali & Sanskrit bks, ref wk. 15: 5245 Oakcrest dr, Oxon Hill Md 20021.

GYDESEN, SHIRLEY (PATT). b St Joseph Mo 22 F 27. 4: Carl H Gydesen. 5: St Joseph Jr Col 45-47 (Chem) AS; Colo Col 47-49 (Chem) BS. 7: Chem Quaker Oats Co, St Joseph Mo 49-51; Tech Lit Specialist GE Co, Richland Wash 52-56, Supv ref publ 56-59, Ref specialist 64; Ref specialist Battelle Northwest, Richland Wash 65-66; Chief libn Donald W Douglas Labs McDonnell-Douglas Corp, Richland Wash 66-. 9: SLA; Nat Sec Indus Assn (Tech Info Adv Com). 10: LWV; Kappa Kappa Gamma; Delta Epsilon. 14: Organ & mgt of spec tech lib tech ref, aerospace & nucl tech. 15: Donald W Douglas Labs, 2955 Geo Washington Way, Ruchland Wa 99352.

GYLLENSKOG, MARIE. b Lander Wyo 15 Jl 43. 5: Utah State U 61-65 (Elem Educ) BS; UWash 66-67 MLib. 7: Tchr Edwards Elem Sch, Edwards Cal 65-66; Ref libn Seattle U 66-67; Libn Renton Sch Dist, Renton Wash 67-. 9: NEA; ALA; WashEA; RentonEA. 10: Phi Kappa Phi. 14: Child lit. 15: 5602 12th ave NE, Seattle Wa 98105.

GYORGYEY, FERENC A(LADAR). b Budapest 14 Mr 27. 4: Clara Takacs. 5: UBudapest 43-48 (Hist of Art) Absolutorium (BA); So Conn State Col 59-61 (LS) MS; Yale 63-67 (Hist of Sci & Med); MA. 6: Hungarian, Ger. 7: Asst in circ Yale U Lib 8-61; Sr catlgr Yale U Med Lib Hist Lib 61-,

Asst libn of historical collections 67-68, Historical libn 68-. 9: MedLA. 15: 42 Derby ave, Orange Conn 06477.

H

HAABALA, SYLVIA H. b Me Twp Minn 12 p 18. 5: UMinn 39-43 (LS) BS. 6: Finnish. 7: Catlgr LCrosse Pub Lib, Lcrosse Wis 43-4; Psychometrist Stud Coun Bur UMinn 45-47; Period libn Mayo Clinic Lib, Rochester Minn 47-, Period & circ libn 51-67, Ref libn 67-. 9: MedLA; (sec 69-); Amer Assn Hist Med; MinnLA. 10: AUW; Min Hist Soc. 14: Period, circ, ref. 15: 206 Third st SE apt 16, Rochester Mn 55901.

HAAG, MARY(VIRGINIA ANDERSON). b Los Angeles Cal 29 Ap 31. 4: (Charles) Robert Haag. 5: Bakersfield Col 49-51 AA; UCal(Berkeley) 51-53 AB; UCLA 60-61 MLS. 6: Ger, Sp. 7: Tchr El Segundo Unified Sch ist, El Segundo Cal 53-63, Elem libn 63-66, Tchr 66-. 9: ALA-CSD; -AASchL; CalASchL; CalTA. 10: PTA; AAUW; So Cal Symphony Assn; El Camino Col Faculty Wives; Beta Phi Mu (Patron); S Bay Chamber Music Soc; Mu Phi Epsilon (Patron); Chm El Segundo Negotiating Coun. 14: Sch libs. 15: 2653 233rd st, Torrance Ca 90505.

HAAK,JOHN R. b Oakland Cal 10 My 38. 4: Camela Corallo. 5: UCal(Berkeley) 56-61 (Hist) BA, 61-62 MLS, 66-67 (Admin). 6: Sp, Ger. 7: Asst soc ci libn UNev 62-64, Mines libn64-66; Undergrad Libn UCal (San Diego) 67-. 9: Geosci Info Soc; ALA; CalLA. 10: Human Rel Coun; Univ Bach Aria Group; Reno Musicians Union. 14: Documentation, undergrad libs, admin, automation. 15: 621 Glencrest pl, Solana Beach Ca 92075.

HAAKER, NANCY VIRGINIA (BROSIUS) (WEISIGER). b Cleveland 1 Ap 3. 4: Herbert Haaker. 5: Knox Col 38-39 (Liberal Arts); UMiami (Fla) summer 41 (Liberal Arts); UIll 39-42 (Educ) BS in Ed, 60-61 MLS. 6: Fr, Ge. 7: Tchr Enos Sch, Springfield Ill 56-60; Libn Thomas Jefferson Jr High Sch, Springfield Ill 61-63; Libn Springfield High Sch, Springfield Ill 63-. 9: ALA; PNLA. 10: ; AAUW; Central Wash State Col Lib Staff Assn. 14: ;, child lit, pub sch curr. 15: Springfield High Sch, SPRINGFIELD Ill.

HAAN, BEATRICE (BAKER). b Cuba Ky 10 Je 02. 5: Central Wash State Col 53 (Educ) BA in Edu; UDenver 54 MA in LS. 7: Circ libn Central Wash State Col 51-53, Circ libn 54-62, Ref libn 62-66, Curriculum libn 66-. 9: ALA; PNLA. 10: AAUP; UN Assn; AAUW; Central Wash State Col Lib Staff Assn. 14: Ref, child lit, pub sch curr. 15: Central Wash State Col Victor J Bouillon Lib, Elensburg Wash 98926.

HAAS, ANN S (KLEIN. b Cleveland 24 N 23. 4: Caser G Has. 5: Wellesley 41-45 (Chem) AB; West Res summers 59-61 MLS; UTenn 65 (Programming). 7: Systems development libn Oak Ridge Nat Lb, Oak Ridge Tenn 57-. 8: Abstractor for "Chem Abstracts 50-. 9: SLA. 13: Yes. 14: Lib mechanization, info retrieval, programming. 15: 402 Wesley rd, Knoxville Tenn 37019.

HAAS, DOROTHY (ELIZET) (BREHM). b Redlands Cal 5 My 03. 5: UWis 21-25 (Eng) BA; UWis(Milwaukee) 57-58 (LS), 60-61 (LS) MA. 6: Fr. 7: Eng, speech tchr Baraboo High ch, Baraboo Wis 25-26; irc asst Racine Pb Lib, Racine Wis 26-27, Bkmob libn 58-60; Research asst Ext Lib UWis(Madison) 60-61; Head alt dept Beloit Pub Lib, Belit Wis 6-162; Libn for the blind Milwaukee Pub Lib 62-. 9: ALA; WisLA (Round Table chmb). 10: AAUW. 13: Yes. 14: Readers serv, ref. 15: 1504 N Prospect apt 312, Milwaukee Wi 53203.

HAAS, ELAINE (SYLVIA HALPERN). b Brooklyn NY 27 Jl 18. 4: Herbert Haas. 5: Hunter Col 35-39 (Chem) AB; City Col even 40-48 (Electrical Engnr); Columbia 62-63 (LS) MS. 7: Sec to pres Rado Navig Instr Corp, NYC 40-44; Purchasing agent Munston Mfg & Serv Inc, NYC 45; Data analyst Avien Inc, Woodside NY 59-62; Gen asst Columbia U Lib 62-63; Asst to libn Queens Col (Flushing NY) 64; Consul libn Amer Power Jet Co, Ridgefield NJ 64; Asst Prof Borough of Manhattan Community Col 65-66; Dir Tech Lib Serv NYC Indexer for ERIC-IRCD 67-68. 8: Consul: General Foods Corp, White Plains NY 64-65; Soc for Advancement of Judaism, NYC 64; Explorers Club, NYC 65; J C Penney Co Inc, NYC 64-; Private research 62-. 9: SLA (sec NY Docs Gp 67-69); ASIS; ALA; Amer Soc Indexers. 10: Amer Jewish Congress; Hunter Col Alumni Assn; Alumni Fed of Columbia U, Guild of Bk Wkers; Int Inst Conserv, NAVA. 14: Computer applications to li procedures, rare bks, ref(engnr & phys sci), lib bldgs. 15: 35-20 Leverich st, Jackson Heights NY 11372.

HAAS, JANE BARKER. b Eau Claire Wis 22 Ag 44. 4: Robert A Haas. 5: UWis(Madison) 62-67 (Eng) BA, 67-69 (LS) MA. 7: Stud asst UWis Memorial Lib (Madison) 67-68; Jr ref serv libn Marquette U Memorial Lib 69-. 14: Ref. 15: 1485 N Farwell ave, Milwaukee Wi 53202.

HAAS, MARILYN (LOOMIS). b Columbus Ohio 19 N 31. 4: Roger C Haas. 5: UMo 48-51 (Sociol) BA; SUNY (Geneseo) 65-67 MLS. 7: Ref libn SUNY (Buffalo) 67-. 14: Ref. 15: 4725 Ransom rd, Clarence NY 14031.

HAAS, WARREN JAMES. b Racine Wis 22 Mr 24. 4: Peggy Tinker. 5: Wabash Col 42-48 (Hist) AB; Washington U 43; UWis 48-50 (Hist, LS) BLS. 7: USAF 43-46; Head ext serv Racine (Wis) Pub Lib 50-52; Acquis libn J Hopkins U 52-54, Asst libn 54-59; Consul Coun of Higher Educ Inst, NYC 59-60; Assoc dir Columbia U Lib 60-66; Dir of Libs UPenn 66-69; Dir of libs Columbia U 69-. 8: Commner's Com on Ref and Res Lib (NY) 60-62; Inst for Higher Educ (Columbia) Study of Predominantly Negro Cols 64; Consul col and univ on lib bldgs (12 assignments in last 4 yrs; Adv Com Rutgers Grad Lib Sch; Lehigh Lib Vis Com13272 9: ALA, ARL (Board 67-, pres 69-70). 10: Grolier Club (NY); Philobiblon. 13: Yes. 14: Admin, mgt. 15: Univ of Penn Libs, 3520 Walnut st, Phila Pa 19104.

HAASE, ALICE M (RUNNING). b Eau Claire Wis 23 N 20. 4: Lawrence P Haase. 5: Wis State U (Eau Claire) 38-45 (Eng, Soc Studies) BS; UWis(Madison) summers 61-64 MS in LS; UMinn (NDEA Inst) 67 (LS). 6: F. 7: Tchr State Graded Sch, Eau Claire County Wis 40-45; Tchr Eau Claire Jr High Sch, Eau Claire Wis 46-48; Tchr-libn Eleva Strum High Sch, Eleva Wis 54-57; Libn Cornell High Sch, Cornell Wis 57-62; Libn E C Mem High Sch, Eau Claire Wis 62-; Instr Lib Sci Wis State U (Eau Claire) summer 69. 9: ALA;-AASchL (State Rep 69-71); WisEA; WisLA (2 coms 65-66). 10: Grace Lutheran Reading Lib; Chippewa Valley Hist Soc; Exec dir & camp dir Girl Scouts 46-50; People-to-People. 13: Yes. 14: Sch libs, non-print materials in sch libs. 15: 2004 W Mead st, Eau Claire Wi 54701.

HABAN, MARY F. b Columbus O 6 Ja 35. 5: Col of Mt St Joseph (Ohio) 52-56 (Eng) BA; Carnegie 58-59 MLS; UPittsburgh 64- (Educ). 7: Tchr Our Lady of Angels High Sch, Cincinnati Ohio 56-58; Libn Carnegie Lib of Pittsburgh 60-62; Libn Cetral Dist Catholic High Sch, Pittsburgh 62-66; Asst Prof & dir of Lib Sci Educ Sch of Duquesne 66-68. 8: Pittsburgh Diocesan Sch Lib Com. 9: ALA; CathLA; PennLA. 10: Beta Phi Mu; AAUP. 14: Yp lit, higher educ, lib educ, tchr-training, Instr Maters Research. 15: 1116 Peermont ave, Pittsburgh Pa 15216.

HABER, WALTER HERBERT. b NYC 19 Je 28. 4: Barbara Angle. 5: NYU 49-52 (Bus Admin)BS; Pratt 63-64 MLS. 6: .-7 7: Electronic Tech US Navy 46-48; Tech Sperry Rand, NYC 52-53; Field engnr to marketing manager Avien Inc, Woodside NY 53-63; Asst libn Great Neck NY 64-65; Dir New Milford (NJ) Pub Lib 65-. 8: Instr in basic lib operation NJ State Lib spring 69. 9: ALA; NJLA (com wk); NY Lib Club; LPRC; Bergen & Passaic Cos LA. 10: Beta Phi Mu; New Milford Profess Adv Com on Drug Abuse; Mid-Bergen Fed Pub Lib. 14: Admin, ref. 15: 235 Madison Ave, River Edge NJ 07661.

HABERFIELD, MAMIE. b NYC 12 Ja 40. 4: Paul Haberfield. 5: Columbia 57-59, 60-61 (Comparative Lit) BS; HebrewU (Jerusalem) 59-60; Jewish Theol Sem 57-59, 60-61 (Hebrew Lit) BRE; Columbia 63-64 MLS. 6: Hebrew. 7: Research asst Jewish Theol Sem (NYC) 61-63; Sci libn Brooklyn col 64-66; Libn JHS 223 66-67. 9: ALA; NY Lib Club. 14: Ref. 15: 1675-52 st, Brooklyn NY 11204.

HABERLAND, JODY JEAN. b Phila 8 Ag 29. 5: Converse Col 52 (Liberal Arts) BA; George Washington U 54-55 (Educ); American U 56-57 (Lit); Catholic U 63 MS in LS. 6: Sp, Fr, Ital. 7: Ed asst Human Resources Res Of George Washington U 54-5; Pub ed Producers Coun, Wash DC 57-58; Pub ed Nat Paint Varnish & Lacquer Assn Wash DC 58-59; Educ tech USAF, Taranto Italy 60-61; Head Bkmob div Prince Georges County MEM Lib Hyattesville Md 63-65; Ref libn Montgomery County Dept Pub Libs, Md 65-68; Reg Libn adult serv E Mass Reg Lib Syst Boston Pub Lib 68-. 8: Spec asst to Dir US Com for the UN, Wash DC 55-57. 9: ALA MdLA, (Memb Com 67); DCLA (chm Bk Review Com 66); Montgomery Co (Md) Lib Staff Assn (pres 67); Prince Georges Lib Staff Assn. 10: LWV, Beta Phi Mu; Theta Sigma Phi. 14: Bk sel, readers adv, ref, admin, adult serv. 15: 50-D Allerton pl, Glover Landing,Marblehead Ma 01945.

HACKER, HAROLD S. b Buffalo NY 9 Jl 16. 5: Canisius Col 37 (Philos) AB; UFuffalo 41 BLS. 7: Page Buffalo Pub Lib, Buffalo NY 34-37; Asst Grosvenor Lib mus dept, Buffalo NY 41-42, Dir of pub rel 41-44; Dir of pub rel Grosvenor & Buffalo Pub Libs, Buffalo NY 4546; Admin asst Grosvenor Lib, Buffalo NY 46-47; 1st deputy dir Erie Co Pub Lib, Buffalo NY 48-52; Dir Grosvenor Lib, Buffalo NY 52-53; Dir Rochester Pub Lib & Monroe Co Lib System, Rochester NY 54-. 8: Chm commner of Educ's Com on Lib Devel 67-69; mem Bd of Regents; Adv Coun on Libs 62-; chm Adv Com on Librns, Rochester Reg Res Lib coun 66-; Governor's Com on Library AVD 49, Comm Com on Pub Lib Serv 56-57; Commner's Com on Libs 65-66. 9: ALA (Coun 66-69); (chm Com on State Legis 56-57, chm Recr Adv Com 65-);-LAD (Bd Dirs 62-64; chm Sect on Lib Org & Mgt 62-64); NYLA (pres 47; chm Legis & Standars Com 51-53, chm Recr Adv Com 65-). 10: Rochester Area Educl TV Assn Cath Family Centr (R ochester); Coun of Soc Agencies (Rochester & Monroe Co); Bd of Regent, St John Fisher Col (Rocheste) 60-. 11: Velma K Moore Mem Award from Lib Trustees Foun of NY State for State Service, 63, Citation for Educl Leadership, Rochester Civic Commun Coun. 13: Yes. 14: Admin, state-wide lib planning. 15: 115 South ave, Rochester NY 14604.

HACKER, RAY KENNETH. b Quakertown Penn 7 Ag 30. 4: Agnes Rosenfeld. 5: Kutztown State Col 48-52 LS BS in Ed; UMich 54-55 MALS; Columbia 64. 6: Ger. 7: Libn Pennsbury High Sch, Yardley 55-57; Circ libn State Col (West Chester PENN) 57-62; Libn Mennonite Biblical Sem, Elkhard Elkhart 62-65; Readers serv libn Rider Col 65-66, Ref libn Millersville State Col (Millersville Pa) 66-. 9: ALA; ATheolLA; NJLA; PennLA; Lancaster Co LA (treas 69-). 10: AAUP; Penn-German Soc, Lancaster Co Commun Hists; East Penn Mennonite Hist Lib (sec-treas of Bd). 14: Circ, ref, archives. 15: 5323 Lake dr, E Petersburg Pa 17520.

HACKETT, ALICE ELIZABETH. b Boston 17 Jl 05. 5: Emmanuel Col 23-27 (Hist, Soc Sci) AB; Simmons 46-47 (LS) BS 06: Fr. 7: Boston Pub Lib: Asst catlgr 28-44, Catlgr 45-50, Admin asst 50-56, Chief catlgr & clsf HRCS 56-65, Coordinator catlg & clsf 65-, Coord of Processing 66-. 9: ALA; MassLA. 10: Eire Soc of Boston. 14: Catlg. 15: 83 Prince st, Jamaica Plain Mass 02130.

HACKETT, NANCY JUNE. b Sunbury Penn 13 N 38. 5: Wilson Col 56-60 (Eng) BA; Drexel 61-62 MLS. 6: Sp. 7: Page J R Kauffman Pub Lib, Sunbury Penn 53-56; Clerk-typist Squehanna Valley Bank & Trust Co, Sunbury Penn summer 58; Clerk-typist Penn Dept of Highways, Highspire Penn summer 59; Child libn Enoch Pratt Free Lib, Baltimore 60-61, 62-. 9: ALA; MdLA. 10: Beta Phi Mu. 14: Child Wk. 15: 6668-B Collinsdale rd, Baltimore Md 21234.

HADLOCK, ROBERT LEWIS. b Detroit 27 N 27. 5: Kan State Tchrs Col (Pittsburg) 45-46; George Washington U 48-50 (Foreign Affairs) AB; Universite de Paris summer 50 (Fr lang); UCal(Berkeley) 57-58 MLS. 6: Fr, Ital, Sp. 7: US Army Med Corps T/5 rating, Korea 46-48; Lib clerk FAO, Rome 51-55; Manifest clerk Cunard Steamship Co Ltd, San Francisco 56-57; Bibliog UCal Lib (Berkeley) 58-63; Hd Tech Serv State U Col (New Paltz NY) 63-66; Hd acquis dept MIT Libs 66-. 9: ALA; NY State LA; Southease NY Lib Res Coun. 14: Tech serv, acquis, bibliog, automation. 15: 19 Union Park, Boston Ma 02118.

HAERTLE, ROBERT J. b Milwaukee 26 My 29. 4: Dolores Werner. 5: St Lawrence Sem (Mt Calvary Wis) 47-49 AA; St Francis Sem 49-51 (Philos0; Marquette U 53-56 (Philos) BA, MA; UIll 58-59 (LS) MS. 7: Marquette U Lib: Lib clerk 56-58, Reader serv staff 59-63, Admin asst 63- Hd Acquis Dept 66-. 9: ALA; CathLA (chm Wis Unit 65-67; chm Col & Univ Sect 68-); WisLA. 10: Beta Phi Mu; AAUP. 13 Yes. 14: Ref, admin. 15: 520 E Homer st, Milwaukee Wi 53207.

HAFER, JAMES. b Canton Oio 25 D 27. 4: Nancy Kennell. 5: Heidelberg Col 45-49 (Sociol) AB; Carnegie 49-50 MLS. 7: Ref asst Akron Pub Lib, Akron Ohio50-52; 50-52 Kate Love Simpson Lib, Mconnelsville Ohio 52-54; Libn Libn Salem Lib, Salem Ohio 55-59; Libn Newark Pub Lib, Newark Ohio 6-. 8: State Lib Review Com for construction grants under LSCA 64-67; Bldg Consul; Wellston Pub Lib Wellston Ohio 66-68; Richwood Pub Lib Richwood Ohio 67-; Portsmouth Pub Lib Portsmouth Ohio 6 67-. 9: Pres Bd of Dirs Lib Serv Ctr East Ohio 65-66; Pres, Central Ohio Film Circuit 67-. 14: Admin. 15: 88 W Church st, Newark Oh 43055.

HAFFNER, BARBARA (HEWES). b Oak Park Ill 5 N 25. 4: Richard Glenn Haffner. 5: Beloit Col 43-47 (Eng Lit) BA; Rosary Col 62-67 MLS. 7: Good Teeth Council puppeteer, Tex 47-48; Field Rep Camp Fire Girls, Chicago 48-49; Libn Suburban Lib System, Western Springs 67-. 9: ALA. 12: Ed "Suburban Library System Newsletter". 14: Admin. 15: 125 Spring lake, Hinsdale Il 60521.

HAGAN, HELEN. b Sylvania Ga 15 Mr 09. 5: Ga State Col or Women 26-30 (Eng) AB; Peabody summers 3-33 BS in LS; Columbia summers 35-41 MS in LS. 7: Asst libn in chg of ref & circ Ga State Col for Women 30-36; Libn Judson Col 3640; Libn & Asst Prof of Lb Sci Coker Col 41-54; Asst Prof & asst dir Div of Libnship Eory U 54-64; Libn Wilmington Col 64-. 8: Visiting tchr Dept of Lib Sch Appalac ian State Tchrs Col ummers 49-50. 9: ALA; SELA; GaLA; NCLA. 10: AAUP; AAUW. 14: Admin, ref, lib educ. 15: APT C-3 Oleander ct, Wilmington NC 2403.

HAGE, ELIZABETH B. b Madelia Minn 12 My 11. 5: La Crosse State Tchrs Col 29-30; Carleton Col 30-3 (Hist) AB; UWis 36-37 Certif. 7: Libn Pub Lib, Wahpeton ND 37-39; 1st Asst circ dept Pub Li, Davenport Iowa 39-40; SUPV State WPA Lib Proj, Des Moines Iowa 40-42; Co Libn Pub Lib,Virginia Minn 42-45; Libn Lyon Co Lib, Lyon Co Marshall Minn 45-48; Ref ln Pub Lib, Appleton Wis 48-49;libn Scott Co Lib, Scott Co Eldridge Iwa 50-57; Dir Prince Georges Co Mem Lib, Hyattesville Md 57- . 9: ALA (var coms); PLA (chm Legisl Com 68-69); MdLA (pres 63, var coms); DCLA (Exec Bd 61-64); Md Assn Pub Lib Admin (pres 62). 13: Yes. 14: Admin, lib bldgs. 15: 6532 Adelphi rd, Hyattsville Md 20782.

HAGEDORN, DOROTHY. b McKeesport Penn 4 S 29. 7: Research asst in Genetics Columbia U 52-54; Asst ref & circ libn Barnard Col 54-56; Supv libn US Army, Germany 56-58; Physics libn Columbia U 58-60; Tech info spec Lawrence Radiation Lab, Berkeley Cal 60-63; Head bus & sci dept Pub Lib, New Orleans 64-67, Hd adult serv 67-. 9: SLA; LaLA; ALA. 10: AAAS. 14: Ref, admin. 15: 5033 Danneel st, New Orleans La 70115.

HAGELIN, DANIEL WARN. b Jamestown NY 11 S 16. 4: Virginia Morgan. 5: Fenn Col 36-41 (Hist) BA; West Res 45-46 BLS, 48-52 (Eng Hist) MA. 7: Page Cleveland Pub Lib 37-41; (Sgt T-4) Radio US Army 41-45; Prof asst hist div Cleveland Pub Lib 46-52; 1st asst in ref dept Lakewod Pub Lib, Lakewook Ohio 53-56, Head of ref dept 56. 9: ALA(past mem & chm 2 coms); OhioLA(past chm &sec of Round Tables); Ref RT; v-chm & chm-elect 69-70. 10: West Res U Lib Sch Alumni Ass. 14: Ref. 15: 4818 W 19th st, Cleveland Oh 44109.

HAGEMANN, DOROTHY (HAMBLETON). b Louisville Ky. 5: ULouisville (Eng) AB; Rosary Col (LS) MA. 7: Tchr Park Ridge Pub Schs, Park Ridge Ill 52-60; Head ref libn Park Ridge Pu Lib, Park Ridge Ill 60-62; Libn Augusta Military Acad, Ft Defiance Va 62-64; Catlgr Ky So Col 64-67 Libn Jefferson Commun Col (Louisville Ky) 67-. 9: ALA. 10: PEO; Soroptimist. 15: 2211 Tyler lane, Louisville Ky 40205.

HAGEN, ELAYNE (PALMER). b Rockingham Vt 31 Mr 44. 4: Walter John Hagen. 5: Syracuse 62-66 (Eng) BA, 66-67 MSLS. 7: Ref asst Crandall Lib, Glens Falls NY 67-. 9: ALA; NYLA. 14: Ref, catlg. 15: 30 Sherman ave, Glens Falls NY 12801.

HAGER, DOROTHY ELIZABETH (JACKSON). b Davidson Co NC 27 F 28. 5: Cecil Bus Col 45-46. 7: Corr Mecklenburg Gazette, Davidson NC 56-; Br libn Pub Lib of Charlotte & Mecklenburg Co, Charlotte NC 56-. 8: Staff org Pub Lib of Charlotte & Mecklenburg Co. 9: ALA. 10: Staff Organization, Public Library of Charlotte & Mecklenburg County. 14: Ya. 15: PO Box 476, Cornelius NC 28031.

HAGER, H LUCILLE. b Cape Girardeau Mo 26 Ap 2. 5: SE Mo State Col 41-45 (Bus Educ) BS in Ed; UIll 47-48 BS in LS. 7: Asst SE Mo State Col 45-47, 48-52; Asst dir tech serv Concordia Sem em (St Louis) 52-, Dir 68-. 9: ALA; ATheolLA; MoLA. 14: Ctlg, Ref. 15: 7203 Sarah apt 8, St Louis Mo 63143.

HAGER, MARILYN. b Nashville. 5: Vanderbilt U 36-37; Randolph-Macon Womans Col 37-40 (Soc Sci) AB; Peabody 40-41 BS in LS, 61-62 MA in LS. 7: Circ supv Horace Mann Lib, Antioch Col 41-42; Lib asst Randolph-Macon Womans Col 42-44; Tech adv Church Lib Dept Sundy Sch Bd of the SO Baptist Conv, Nshville 54-. 9: ALA; SLA; SELA. 10: Red Cross; Phi Beta Kappa; Pi Gamma Mu. 13: Yes 14: Clsf & catlg. 15: 127 Ninth ave, Nashville Tn 37205.

HAGERTY, MARTHA M. b Burlington Vt 10 Ap 03. 4: Thomas L Hagerty. 5: Wellesley 21-25 (Eng Lit) AB; Columbia

26 (Eng Lit) MA; So Conn State Col 51-53 (LS) MS. 7: Res libn Conn Col 48-50, Asst circ libn 51-53; Circ libn 5357; Reg pub lib consul Conn ept Educ 57-59; Libn Groton Conn Pub Lib 60-. 8: Governors Com for libs (chm rural libs com) 63-65. 9: ALA; NELA(sec 64-65); ConnL(mem-at-large 65-66). 10: LWV; Soroptimist Club. 13: Yes. 14: Bk sel, ref, lib devel. 15: Brook st, Noank Ct 06340.

HAGGERTY, THOMAS M. b NYC 21 p 36. 4: Mary Esther McHugh. 5: St Johns U (NY) 54-58 (Soc Sci) BA, 60-62 MLS. 7: Asst ed McGraw-Hill Publ Co, NYC 58-60 Libn trainee & libn II Queens Borough Pub Lib 61-62; Ser & DOCUMENTS LIBN St Johns U (NY) 62-65; Chief ref Asst Southampton Col of LI U 65-66; Sr libn Exec Dept State of NY 66-. 9: SLA; NYLA; Coun of Planning Libns (chm Lib Adv Com). 10: US Power Squadron; Adirondack Mt Club. 11: Murray Medal St Johns U 58. 12: Ed "Planning Library Notes". 13: Yes. 14: Data processing, planning, tech processing. 15: 9 River Hill apts, Menands NY 12204.

HAGLE, ALFRED DARIUS. b Jonesboro Ark 2 p 21. 4: Nina Story. 5: Central State Col (Okla) 47 (Hist) BA in Ed; George Washington U 51 (Educ) MA in Ed; Catholic U 58 MS in LS. 7: US Army Radiology Tech Med Corps 42-46; LC: File clerk & messenger Ref Dept Off 51-52, Facsimile transmitter operator Loan Div 52-53, Searcher Loan Div 53-55, Sr searcher Loan Div 55-57, Asst head Local Loan Sect Loan Div 57-58, Ref libn div for the Blind 59-68, Project off Div for the blind & physically handicapped 68-. 9: ALA (chm Awards Com Round Table on Lib Serv for the Blind 65-66); AHIL. 13: Yes. 14: Ref, admin. 15: 2608 Ridge rd dr, Alexandria Va 22302.

HAHN, ARLENE CLARA. b Frackville Penn 26 N 28. 5: Kutztown State Col 46-50 (LS) BS in ED; Penn State U summer 50 (Lit); Peabody summer 51, 54 MA in LS. 7: Sch libn Columbia High Sch, Columbia Penn 50-51 Br libn Bainbridge Naval Train Station Md 51-52; Bkmob libn Indiantown Gap Mill Reservation, Penn 52-53; Bkmob libn Ft Meade Md 53-54; Catlgr Camp Kilmer NJ 54-55; Asst post libn, Ft Monmouth NJ 55-67; Hd libn USAF, Korea 67-68; Ref libn, Ft Monmouth NJ 68-. 8: Army libn Library/USA Worlds Fair NY 64. 9: ALA. 10: Ft Monmouth Choral Soc; AAUW. 11: 1st place John Cotton Dana Pub Award for Scrapbook 67-. 14: Catlg, ref. 15: 99 S Main st, Mahanoy City Pa 17948.

HAHN, BOKSOON (HA). b Korea 15 F 31. 4: Kyu Young Hahn. 5: Ewha Womans U (Seoul Korea) 50-54 (Eng Lit) BA; So Conn State Col 63-65 (LS) MA. 6: Korean, Japanese, Eng, Fr, Chinese. 7: Secretariat to press off ROK Govt, Seoul Korea 55-58; Secretariat Korean Embassy in Paris 58-60; Clerical asst catlg dept Yale U Lib 61-62, catlgr 65-68, Sr catlgr 68-. 14: Catlg. 15: 91 Clark st, New Haven Ct 06511.

HAHN, JAMES M. b Grey Eagle Minn 2 Je 36. 4: Sherryll Freeberg. 5: UMinn 55-60 (Eng Lit) BA, 61-62 MA MLS. 6: Lat. 7: Staff libn Minn Dept of Corrections, St Paul 61-62, Supv of libs& info center 62-65; Chief Libn (GS-9) 7375th Combat Support Group, Sculthorpe Eng 63; Chief Libn (GS-11) 48th Combat Support Group, Lakenheath Eng 63-68; Asst chief lib br USAF-Europe, Wiesbaden Ger 68-. 9: ALA; The Lib Assn (Brit); AFLS. 14: Admin. 15: HQUSAFE (DPSRL), APO NY 09633.

HAHN, MARJORIE WHITE. b Almira Wash 7 D 14. 4: Gerald L Hahn. 5: Whitworth Col 57 (Educ) BA; UWash 64 (Libnship) M of L. 6: Fr. 07: Credit manager Sears Roebuck & Co, Wenatchee Wash 35-40; Cashier Sears Roebuck &Co, Portland Ore 40-43; Order office manager Sears Roebuck & Co, Coulee Dam Wash 49-51; Printing dept Whitworth Col 52-57; Tchr & libn Mead Jr High Sch, Spokane ash 58-. 9: NEA; Wash State ASchL (Reg 7 pres 63); WashEA. 10: AAUW. 14: Sch libs. 15: R2 Box 293B, Spokane Wa 99207.

HAINES, HELEN DORMAN. b Princess Anne Co Va 23 O 09. 5: Randolph-Macon Woman's Col 27-31 (Lat) BA; Fla State U 49-50 (LS) MA. 6: Fr, Lat. 7: High sch tchr Norfolk Co Pub Sch System, Va 31-39; Tchr Woodrow Wilson High Sch, Portsmouth Va 39-46; Tchr Manatee Co High Sch, Bradenton Fla 46-49; Fla State U Lib: Asst in acquis 50-52, Asst in ref 52-56, Asst in humanities div 56-57, Head humanities div Robert Manning Strozier Lib 57-. 9: ALA; SELA; FlaLA. 10: Beta Phi Mu. 14: Ref. 15: 416 Beard st, Tallahasse Fl 32303.

HAINES, HELENA C. b Dover NJ. 5: Guilford Col (Sp) AB; CatholicU 59- (LS). 6: Sp. 7: Catlgr & acquis asst John I Thompson & Co, Wash DC 64-67; Asst to chief Tech Serv Br Lib US Dept of Com, Wash DC 67-. 9: DCLA; Potomac Tech Proc Libns. 14: Catlg. 15: 511 Thayer ave, Silver Spring Md 20910.

HAINES, NANCY STUTLER. b Akron Ohio 25 Ag 34. 4: Clifford F Haines. 5: Akron U 52-54; Kent State 54-56 (Hist) BA, 56-58 (LS). 6: . 7: Jr asst Akron Pub Lib, Akron Ohio 56-59; Libn VA, Northampton Mass 59-61; Med libn VA, Brecksville Ohio 61-62, Libn admin 62-64, Chief libn 64-. 9: ALA-AHIL; No Ohio Med Libns Assn. 14: Readers adv, ref. 15: 7035 Carriage Hill dr Suite 104, Brecksville Ohio 44141.

HAIR, MARY JANE (STEWART). b Salt Lake City Utah. 5: UUtah 36-40 (Speech, Eng) BA, 46-47 (Secondary Educ, LS) MA; UWash 57-59 (Libnship) MA; UHawaii summer 60. 6: Fr, Russian, Hebrew, Ger. 7: Tchr Drama Speech Eng Weber High Sch, Ogden Utah 40-41; Eng & speech tchr libn South High Sch, Salt Lake City 41-46; Utah Lib: Order dept 46-47, Period libn 47-48, Circ libn 48-57, Instr of Lib Sci 57-58, Asst Prof of Lib Sci 58-, Educ libn 62-67 Behavioral scis libn 68-. 8: Faculty Coun UUtah 59-62, 63-66; Panel Mem First Intermountain Child Lit Conf 61; in charge bk exhibits for Second and Third Confs 63, 65; Assoc dir First & Second Confs of YA Lit 66, 68. 9: ALA (Utah rep Recruitment Com 55-61); MPLA; UtahLA(v-pres 60-61, mem 2 coms). 10: AAUP; AAUW; Faculty Womens Club; Phi Kappa Phi; Beta Phi Mu; Theta Alpha Phi; Beehive Hon Soc. 12: "Index of Colored Reproductions in the U Utah Lib, with Carol Selby (55); "Selected Bibliography of the Tillmn D Johnson Collection, (57); "Handbook to the George D Thomas Lib, (59). 14: Ref, educ, behav scis. 15: 31 East 1 North, Salt Lake City Ut 84103.

HAIRE, MARY LOU (FIELDS). b Lampasses Tex 12 Ag 33. 4: Gerald Hamilton Haire. 5: Kilgore Jr Col 50-52 (Liberal Arts) AA; N Tex State U 52-53 (Liberal Arts) BA; USoCal 60-63 MLS. 6: Sp. 7: Libn Dallas Independent Sch Dist, Dallas Tex 53-56; Acquis specialist Stanford Research Inst, Menlo Park Cal 57-58; Libn Ampex Corp, Redwood City Cal 58-59; Asst libn Sylvania Electric Prods, Mt View Cal 59-60; Libn I Highes Aircraft Co, Fullerton Cal 60-63; Asst lib dir Anaheim Pub Lib, Anaheim Cal 63-. 9: ALA; Amer Soc Pub Admin; CalLA; OrangeCoLA (Memb Chm 64-66). 10: C of C (Women's Div); Hist Com Chm. 14: Admin. 15: 104 E Villa Rita dr, La Habra Ca 90631.

HAISFIELD, STELLA L. b NYC. 4: Rudolph M Haisfield. 5: Hunter Col 27-30 (Latin) AB; AmericanU 40-45 (Pol Sci); UMd 66-68 MLS. 7: Bus econ US For Econ Adm, Wash DC 42-45; Libn (staff) US Dept of Com, Wash DC 69-. 9: DCLA. 10: Beta Phi Mu. 14: Law, clsf. 15: 9808 Cherry Tree lane, Silver Spring Md 20901.

HALADUS, REV VICTORIAN (JAMES) OFM. b Cleveland 25 O 33. 5: St Josephs Col (Westmont Ill) 52-54; Our Lady of Angels Sem 55-58 (Philos) BA; St Joseph Sem (Teutopolis Ill) 58-62 (Theol) SB; Rosary Col summers 63-68 (LS), 68 MA in LS. 7: 7 yrs in Sem Libs; Libn Padua Franciscan High Sch, Parma Ohio 63-. 9: CathLA (No Ohio Unit; chm High Sch Sect 65-66, "Newsletter" ed 66-68);OhioLA; OhioASchL. 14: High sch wk. 15: 6750 Riester st, Parma Ohio 44134.

HALAMAY, STEPHEN. b Ukraine 13 N 13. 4: Maria Pawlyk. 5: King Kasimir U (Lviv) 34-37 (Law) Master; Ukrainian Free U (Prague) 39-41 (Pol Sci, Law) PhD; Seton Hall U 55-58 (Econ) MA; Rutgers 60-62 MLS. 6: Ukrainian, Russian, Ger Polish, Slovak, Lat, Gk. 7: Asst Prof of admin law Ukranian Free U (Munich Germany) 49-50; Cost-acct Wm Dixon Ind, Newark NJ 55-60; Catlgr MacLaughlin Lib Seton Hall U 60-62, Ref libn 62-66, Dir of libs & Prof of econ WVa Inst of Tech 66-. 8: Econ tchr, Sch of Bus Admin, Seton Hall U. 9: ALA; NJLA; NEA; WVaEA.' 10: Ukrainian Congress Com of Amer; Schevczenko Sci Soc; Org for Defense of Four Freedoms for Ukraine; Assn of Ukrainian Culture; AAUP AAAS. 13: Yes. 14: Ref, admin. 15: Box 137, Montgomery WV 25136.

HALBERG, LILLIAN LUCILE (EKBLAD). b Topeka Kan 10 Jl 13. 4: Charles L Halberg. 5: UNeb 31-35 (Eng, Sp) BA, 35-37 (Eng) MA; UIll 39-40 BSLS. 6: Sp. 7: Circ dept asst Lincoln City Lib, Lincoln Neb 37-38; NE Br asst Lincoln Neb 38-39; NE Br asst & Belmont br libn, Lincoln Neb 40-41; Info desk libn Lincoln City Libs, Lincoln Neb 41-45, Hd catlg dept 45-56, Hd tech processes dept 56-63, Coord tech processes div 63-. 9: ALA; MPLA (sec-treas Catlg Sect 2 yrs); NebLA (treas 2 yrs); LincolnLA (past pres). 10: Bus & Profess Women's Club; Women's Div C of C. 14: Catlg. 15: 6010 Meadowbrook lane, Lincoln Nb 68510.

HALCLI, ALBERT. b Saginaw Mich 1 O 26. 4: Marie Ellen Szkudlarek Halcli. 5: UDetroit 47-51 (Educ) BSED, 52-55 (Educ) M Ed; UMich 57-59 MLS; UDetroit 60-62 (Hist). 6: Fr. 7: Instr St Therese High Sch, Royal Oak Mich 52-58; Ref libn UDetroit 58-60, Head of ref 60-62; Head of ref dept Mich State Lib, Lansing Mich 62-63; Dir Upper Peninsula Br Mich State Lib, Escanaba Mich 63-65; Research assoc Upper Peninsula Com on Area Progress (temp pos), Escanaba Mich 65-. 9: ALA; Mich Hist Soc. 14: Ref. 15: 1203 Delta ave, Gladstone Mich 49837.

HALDA, DIANA (COFFEY). b Wellman Iowa 22 Mr 18. 4: Francis A Halda. 5: Coe 41 (Mus) BA; Virginia Commonwealth 61-64 (LS); Rosary Col 65-68 (LS) MA. 6: Fr. 7: Tchr Ainsworth Consolidated Sch, Ainsworth Iowa 41-43; Libn Richmond Memorial Hosp, Richmond Va 60-63; Libn Highland Park Elem Sch, Richmond Va 63-64; Libn Marine Twp High Sch S, Park Rodge Ill 64-. 9: ALA; IllLA; IllEA. 10: AAUW; Friends of the Lib; Beta Phi Mu. 11: Delta Delta Delta. 14: Catlg, ref, child lit, hist of the bk. 15: 1131 S Seminary ave, Park Ridge Il 60068.

HALDERMAN, MARJORIE. b Astoria Ore 11 Ja 11. 5: UOr 29-33 (Eng) BA; USoCal 49-50 MS in LS. 6: Fr. 7: Libn Astoria High Sch, Astoria Ore 35-. 8: Coord Pub Sch Libs,Astoria Ore 47-. 9: ALA; OreASchL (past pres); PNLA; OreLA. 10: AAUW; Beta Phi Mu; Phi Beta Kappa. 13: Yes. 14: Ya lit. 15: 469 Bond st, Astoria Ore 97103.

HALE, ALLISON. b NJ. 5: UMich 46-48 (Hist) AB; West Res 48-50 (Soc Wk) MS SA; UMich 54-55 AMLS. 7: Nurse US Army Nurse Corps, US & N African & European Theater 41-46; Med soc wker Benjamin Rose Inst, Cleveland 48-53; Med soc wker UMich Hosps 53-54; Catlgr, acquis libn & subj catlgr UMich 55-68, Chief order libn Law Lib 68-. 10: Beta Phi Mu. 14: Tech serv, med & sci libnship. 15: 1807 Orchard st, Ann Arbor Mich 48103.

HALE, BETTY LOUISE. b Park Ridge Il 9 My 16. 5: Northwestern U 34-38 (Eng) BS; UIll 38-39 BS in LS. 7: Period libn UKan 40; Asst catlgr Securities & Exchange Commsn, Wash DC 41; Ref libn War Dept Off of Quartermaster Genl, Wash DC 42-44; Asst libn-libn gen Foods Corp Central Labs, Hoboken NJ 45-46; Chief index dept "Brooklyn Eagle", Brooklyn NY 46-51; Info researcher Mobil Oil Corp pub rel dept, NYC 51-. 9: SLA (Picture Div: v-chm 54-56, chm 56-58, NY Chap: sec 47-48, Newspaper Gp chm 48-50, Dir Com chm 52-53, Picture Gp chm 53-54, Nomin Com chm 53-54, 1st v-pres 59-60, 60-61). 10: UIll Lib Sch Assn. 12: Ed "Special Libraries Directory of Greater New York" (53); Co-ed "Picture Sources" (60 & 64 eds). 13: Yes. 14: Ref, archives. 15: 305 E 86th st, New York NY 10028.

HALE, FRANCES. b Brockton Mass 8 Je 12. 5: Simmons 30-34 (LS) BS; Boston U 36-37; Hofstra Col 53-58 (Eng Lit) MA. 7: Head catlgr Brockton (Mass) Pub Lib 35-41; Head catlg div Schenectady (NY) Pub Lib 41-45; Professorial Lecturer Pratt Inst Lib Sch 52-55; Dir Floral Park (NY) Pub Lib 45-59; Dir arden City (NY) Pub Lib 59-. 8: Mem, Pub Libns Exam Com, NY State Bd of Regents, 57-59. 9: ALA; LPRC; NYLA; Nassau Co LA (pres 50-52); NELA; MassLA. 10: AAUW; NE Hist Geneal Soc; Soroptimist Sooptimist; Commun Club of Garden City; Soc Mayflower Descendants. 14: Admin. 15: 70 Tulip ave, Floral Park NY 11001.

HALE, MARGARET. b Modesto Cal 17 N 09. 4: Harold R Hale. 5: San Jose State Col 30-33 (LS, Educ) BA. 7: Br lib supv Stanislaus Co Lib, Modesto Cal 33-. 8: Act Libn, Stanislaus Co Lib May-Dec 51, Aug-Nov 52, Dec 66-Sept 67. 9: ALA; CalLA. 14: Ext, bk sel. 15: Stanislaus County Lib 1402 Eye st, Modesto Ca 95354.

HALE, MARJORIE JEAN. b Strathroy Ont Can 7 D 40. 4: Michael Hale. 5: Toronto 60-64 (Music) BA, 64-65 BLS. 6: Fr, Ger. 7: Tourist receptionist dept of tourism & info, Sarnia Bureau summers 61-63; Clerical music lib Toronto Pub Libs summer 64, Libn I and II 65-68, Hd libn Mus Lib 68-. 9: CanLA; Can MusLA; OntLA; Internat MusLA. 10: Jr Womens Comtoronto Symphony; UToronto Sch Lib Sci Alum Assn. 14: Music libs. 15: Metropolitan Toronto Music Lib, 559 Avenue rd, Toronto 7 Ont Can.

HALE, RUTH CARLTON. b Griffin Ga 16 F 34. 5: Newcomb Col 51-53; UArk 53-55 (Eng) BSE; Columbia 55-56 MS in LS. 6: Fr. 7: Ref libn UTex 56-64; Gen studies libn Ga Inst of Tech 65, Interlib serv libn 66-. 9: ALA; SELA. 14: Ref. 15: 70 Biscayne dr NW, Apt 16, Atlanta Ga 30309.

HALEVY, BALFOUR J. b Brighton Eng 3 Mr 33. 5: ULondon Kings Col 53-56 LL B; Sch of Law Tulane 57-58 (Law) MCL; Columbia 61-63 MS in LS. 6: Fr, Hebrew. 7: Asst lecturer in law Faculty of Laws U Col of Wales (Aberystwyth) 58-61; Ref libn Columbia U Sch of Law Lib 61-63; Act libn & Lecturer SUNY (Buffalo) Sch of Law 63-64, Libn & Asst Prof of law 64-67; Libn & Prof of law Osgoode Hall Law Sch York U (Ontario Can) 67-. 9: AALL; Assn Law Libs Upstate NY; Law Lib Assn Greater NY; CanALL. 12: "Selective Bibliography on State Constitutional Revision, New York (63). 14: Law libnship. 15: York Univ Law Lib, 4700 Keele st, Downsview Ont Can.

HALES, DOROTHY G (HENKEL). b Baltimore 24 S 12. 5: Johns Hovkins U 33 (Ger, Fr) BS, 36 (Ger) MA; Peabody 64 (LS) MA; UBerlin 34; UMunich 35. 6: Ger, Fr. 7: Tchr UTenn 47-50; Tchr Wesleyan Col (Macon Ga) 50-55; Ref libn Washington Mem Lib, Macon Ga 55-64; Coordinator: ref & a-v materials Middle Ga Reg Lib, Macon Ga 64-66, Assoc dir 67-. 9: ALA; SELA; GaLA. 10: Beta Phi Mu. 14: Ref, a-v materials, admin. 15: Middle Georgia Reg Lib 911 First st, Macon Ga 31201.

HALEY, FRANK H. b Tacoma Wash 18 Je 11. 4: Nellie LaBelle Zink. 5: Willamette U 30-35 (Phil, Psych) AB (Summa cum laude); Drew U 37, 44-48 BD; UZurich 47; UCambridge 47; UWash 49-50 ABLS. 6: Gk, Fr, Ger. 7: Clergy Methodist Church Pacific Northwest Conf 38-44; Ref asst Seattle Pub Lib 50-51; Catlgr Pacific Lutheran U 51-52, Act libn 52-55, Libn 55-. 8: Adv Com Wash State Lib Commsn, 67-; Founding chm NW Assn of Private Col& Univ Libs. 10: Pacific Northwest Asn of Church Libns (founder & pres). 15: 513 102nd st, Court South, Tacoma Wash 98444.

HALEY, MARGARET (PHILLIPS). b Nashville 20 Je 18. 4: Charles Young Haley. 5: Carson-Newman Col 35-39 (Eng) AB; Peabody 39-40 BS in LS. 7: Libn Smith Co High Sch, Carthage Tenn 41-43; Elem tchr Providence Elem Sch, Hartsville Tenn 53-55; Libn Trousdale Co High Sch, Hartsville Tenn 55-. 8: Sec Bd of Trustees Trousdale Co Pub Lib 61-. 10: Providence Commun Club; 4-H Club Wk. 14: Ref. 15: Rt 2, Lebanon Tn 37087.

HALEY, MRS MARY T. b Memphis Tenn 20 My 05. 5: Memphis State Col 34-37 (Eng) BS; UIll 41 BS in LS. 6: Fr, Sp. 7: Memphis (Tenn) Pub Lib: Br lbn 30-36, Supv of brs 37-41, Head circ & Supv of Brs 41-60, Coordinator ault serv 60-. 9: ALA; TennLA; SELA. 10: Beethoven Club; Amer Recorder Soc. 13: Yes. 14: Adult educ. 15: Memphis Pub Lib 258 S McLean, Memphis Tenn 38104.

HALGREN, JOANNE VIRGINIA (RHODES). b Goldendale Wash 16 O 44. 4: John Gunnar Halgren. 5: George Fox Col 62-66 (Lang Arts) BA; UWash 66-67 (Libnship) ML; UOre 69- (Educ). 6: Sp. 7: Sci libn UOre Sci Div Lib 67-. 14: Ref, univ & commun cols. 15: 2457 N 17th, Springfield Or 97477.

HALL, AGNEZ. b Tracadie NB Can 26 N 33. 4: Doria Noel. 5: U du Sacre-Coeur 50-57 ba& u de Montreal 62-63 BLS. 6: Fr. 7: Clk accountant Civil Serv Fed Govt Treasury Off, Montreal 58-5q; Catlgr LauentianU 63-64; Hd Fr sect Tchr Col (Fredericton NB) 64-66; Hd tech serv U de Moncton 66-67, Chief libn 67-. 9: ALA; CanLA; APLA; Assn canadienne des bibliothecaires de langue francaise. 10: Cercle Universitaire 9moncton). 12: "Compte rendu du 22e Congres annuel de l'ACBLF du 14-17 aout 1966, moncton NB Canada"; 'Developpement dès bibliotheques scolaires au Nouveau-Brunswick'. 13: Yes. 14: Admin, acquis. 15: 86 Walsh st, Moncton NB Can.

HALL, ALICE MARION. b NYC2 O 18. 5: NY State Tchrs Col (Fredonia) 36-39 (Educ); NY State Tchrs Col (Geneseo) 39-40 (LS) BS in Educ; UMich 44-46 AMLS. 6: Fr. 7: Gen asst Darwin R Barker Pub Lib, Fredonia NY 40-42; Libn Canton Twp High Sch, Canton Ohio 42-43; Asst catlg dept Canton Pub Lib, Canton Ohio 43-44; Asst catlgr Fla State U 46-51; Catlgr Baldwin-Wallace Col Lib 51-59; Head catlgr Lafayette Col Lib 59-. 9: OhioLA; North Ohio Catlgrs Assn(treas 53-54); ALA-ACRL (Phila Area). 10: Great Books Group; Foreign Policy Assn; AAUP. 14: Catlg. 15: 3777 Fleetwood dr, Easton Pa 18042.

HALL, ANN ELIZABETH. b Berkeley Cal 14 Ag 33. 5: UCal (Berkeley) 51-55 (Hist) AB; Carnegie Inst 55-56 MLS; Columbia 65- (LS). 6: Fr. 7: Catlgr UCal (Davis) 56-57; Ref libn Berkeley Pub Lib, Berkeley Cal 57-60; Assoc libn US Steel Corp, NYC 60-62; Elem schs libn Piedmont Unified Sch Dist, Cal 62-65; Catlgr ColumbiaU Libs 65-66; Asst Prof Grad Sch Lib & Info Sci Pratt Inst 69-. 9: ALA. 14: Sch libs, catlg. 15: 142 E 16th st apt 8A, New York NY 10003.

HALL, ANNA (COBB). b Malvern Ark 4 Mr 17. 4: John Oliver Hall. 5: Okla Col for Women 34-48 (Home Econ) BS; UPittsburgh 62-63 MLS, 63- (LS), 69 (Lib & Info Sci) PhD. 6: Sp, Fr. 7: Proj dir Nat Youth Admin, El Reno Okla 39-41; Typist Dept of Agric, Wash DC 41-42; Manager Embassy Commissary, Montevideo Uruguay 55-56; Prin Karachi American High Sch, Karachi Pakistan 57-59; Manager Off Campus Center American U, Hunter Air Force Base Savannah Ga 62; Info Off Center for Lib & Educ Media Studies UPittsburgh Grad Lib Sch 63-64; Tchg Fellow Grad Sch of Lib & Info Sci UPittsburgh 64-; Asst to dir Carnegie Lib, Pittsburgh 66-, Assoc dir for admin serv 69-. 9: ALA; AALS; PennLA. 10: Beta Phi Mu; Carnegie U Lib Sch Alum Assn. 13: Yes. 14: Admin, lib educ. 15: 4210 Centre ave, Pittsburgh Pa 15213.

HALL, ANTHONY. b London Eng 26 S 28. 5: Colby Col 48-52 (Psych) BA; NYU 56-57 (Math); Columbia 58-59 MLS. 7: Tech writer Bell Aircraft Corp, Niagara Falls NY 52-53; Engnr staff rep Sperry Gyroscope Div of Sperry Rand, Great Neck LI NY 53-58; Dir of lib systems devel UCLA Lib 59-. 8: Consul, Planning Research Corp, Los Angeles 65-; UCal Lib Research Inst Operations Task Force, 65-; Brasenose Conf on Lib Automation 66. 9: ALA; ASIS; COLA; Systems & Procedures Assn. 14: Lib automation, lib systems analysis, admin, info sci. 15: Univ Research Lib UCLA, 405 Hilgard ave, Los Angeles Ca 90024.

HALL, BEVERLY A. b Wheeling W Va 29 D 35. 5: UCincinnati 53-57 (Hist, Educ) BA, BS in ed; Carnegie Lib Sch 57-59 (Wk with child) MLS. 6: Lat, Fr. 7: Carnegie Lib of Pittsburgh 57-59; Sr high libn Penn Hills Sch Dist, Pittsburgh Penn 59-61; Elem libn Commun Consolidated Sch Dist #65, Evanston Ill 61-64; Elem libn Upper Merion Area Sch dist, King of Prussia Penn 64-67; Coord child serv Baltimore Co Pub Lib, Towson Md 67-. 9: ALA (Chm CSD ADV Com to the US Jaycees GRFY Prog); MdLA (sec of CYASD). 10: Kappa Delta Pi; Phi Beta Kappa. 13: Yes. 14: Wk with child. 15: 4 Straw Hat rd apt 2-B, Owings Mills Md 21117.

HALL, BEVERLY ANN. b Charleston W Va 14 D 42. 5: St Xavier Col 60-62; Ohio U 62-64 (Eng) AB; West Res 64-65 MSLS. 6: Fr. 7: Libn I Gen Sci Dept Memorial Lib U of Notre Dame 65-68; Sci ref libn Boston Pub Lib 68-. 9: ALA. 10: Notre Dame Lib Staff Assn. 14: Ref. 15: 71 Nonantum st, Brighton Ma 02135.

HALL, BRYAN. b Pocahontas, Ark 1 Ag 26. 4: Mary Lois Flippin. 5: Ark StateU 44-47, 58-59 (Eng) BSE; UIll 62-66 MLS. 7: Jr high libn Consolidated Sch Dist #6, Arnold Mo 65; Catlgr St Louis Co Lib, St Louis 67-. 11: Mo State Lib scholarship. 14: Sch libs, tech processing. 15: Box 557 Rte 2, Arnold Mo 63010.

HALL, CATHERINE (JONES). b Tacoma Wash 6 Ap 10. 4: Stanley R Hall. 5: Ariz State Col (Flagstaff) 24-27 (Eng) Tchrs Diploma; UWash 27-28, 29-30 BS in LS; UIda 38-39 (Homemaking); USoCal summers 62-65 (LS). 7: Tchr pub sch, Cibecue Ariz 28-29; Libn UIda 30-37; High sch libn Los Angeles Pub Schs 49-. 9: ALA AASchL; CalASchL; Los Angeles SchLA; CalLA. 10: Associated Tchrs of Los Angeles. 14: Sch lib wk. 15: Cleveland High Sch Lib, 8140 Van Alden ave, Reseda Ca 91335.

HALL, CLEM M. b Charlottesville Va 22 Jl 43. 5: Duke 61-65 BA; UDenver 65-66 (LS) MA. 6: Sp. 7: Circ libn UTex Law Sch Lib (Austin) 66-67; Ya libn Montgomery Co Pub Lib, Bethesda Md 67-68; Asst dir ALA, Wash DC 68-. 9:ALA; DCLA. 10: Adult Educ Assn of Grtr Wash. 14: Wk with disadvantaged, lib educ. 15: 522 21st st NW, Washington DC 20006.

HALL, CYNTHIA S. b NJ 19 Je 38. 5: Pembroke Col 56-57; UMich 58-62 (Eng) BA; NYU 59; USoCal 66-67 MSLS. 6: Fr, Russian. 7: Asst to motion picture producer Francis Lee studios/Ring 3 Productions, NYC 57-58; Sales Doubleday and Co, NYC 62-63; Asst Joseph rubinstein Antiquarian Bks, Tucson Ariz 64; Lib asst UAriz Lib (Tucson) 64-66; Asst sci & tech libn San Francisco State Col 67-. 9: ALA; ASIS. 14: Sci & med ref. 15: San Francisco State Col Lib Sci Lib 1630 Holloway ave, San Francisco Ca 94132.

HALL, EDNA MAY (WELLS). b Adams Mass 8 O 18. 4: Donald Elery Hall. 5: Wheaton (Ill) 36-38; Simmons 38-40 BLS. 6: Fr. 7: Asst child libn Berkshire Athenaeum, Pittsfield Mass 40-43, Asst ref libn 61-62, Readers asst Libn 62-66, Libn 66-. 9: WestMassLA. 14: Catlg. 15: 15 Deerfield st, Pittsfield Ma 01201.

HALL, EDWARD BYRON. b Mt Sterling Ky 10 N 28. 4: Elizabeth Kinard. 5: UKy 47-51 (Hist) AB, 53-54 MSLS. 7: Page & circ asst Lexington Pub Lib, Lexington Ky 43-51; (Capt) USAF, US, Eng, France 51-53; Circ head Lexington Pub Lib, Lexington Ky 53-54; Libn I ya Free Lib of Phila 54-56, Libn II libn-in-chg of br lib 56-59; Dir So Md Reg Lib Assn, La Plata Md 59-62; Dir Washington Co Free Lib, Hagerstown Md 62-. 8: Consul: Law Lib, Washington Co Md, 63; Mercersburg Acad Lib, 65. 9: ALA; MdLA. 10: Phi Alpha Theta; Beta Phi Mu; Kiwanis Club; Torch Club. 13 Yes. 14 Admin, bldgs. 15: 102 Paramount ter, Hagerstown Md 21740.

HALL, EDWARD TESSON. b St Louis 30 Ja 17. 5: Washington U 33-38 (Eng, Psych) AB; Chicago 42 (Psych); UIll 47-48 BSLS. 7: Instr voc guidance US Army, US, Europe 42-45; Voc coun Vet Serv Center, St Louis 46-47; UMiai(Fla): Catlgr 48-49, Documents libn 49-51, Asst acquis libn 51-52, Ser lbn 52-. 9: FlaLA; SELA. 10: Beta Phi Mu; Friends of the UMiami Lib. 14: Periods, govt docs. 15: 1520 San Ignacio, Coral Gables Fl 33146.

HALL, EILEEN. b Three Rivers Mich 16 Ap 08. 4: James C Hall. 5: Ga State Col 57-61; Fla Inst of Tech 61-66; Rollins Col 67-. 7: Writer "Daily News, Ft Lauderdale Fla 28-30; Writer "Atlana Journal & "Constitution Magazine, Atlanta 44-51; Libn St Johns Parish Lib, Hapeville Ga 59-60; Lib asst Ga State Col Lib 60-61; Libn Brevard Engnr Col 61-. 12: Ed, Bk Review Sect "Atlanta Bulletin (44-60). 13: Yes. 14: US govt docs. 15: Fla Inst of Tech Lib, PO Box 1150, Melbourne Fl 32901.

HALL, ELVAJEAN. b Hamilton Ill 30 My 10. 5: Oberlin Col 26-30 (Speech, Sociol) BA; UWis 31-32 (LS) Diploma; Lake Forest Col 33-34 (Educ); Columbia 37-41 (LS) MS. 6: Fr. 7: Libn Elgin (Ill) High Sch 34-37; Libn Milwaukee U Sch, Milwaukee 37-42; Supv sch libs Jackson Pub Schs, Jackson Mich 42-44; Libn Stephens Col 44-46; Supv of lib serv Newton (Mass) Pub Schs 46-. 8: Spec assignment, sch libs US Off of Educ, spring 60; Lib consul, Chung Chi, Chinese Univ of HongKong, 62-63; Guest lectr Univ Col, Dublin (Ireland) Lib Sch summers 67-69. 9: NEA; ALA-AASchL (Recr Chm); SLA (pres Mass Unit); NESchLA; MassSchLA; ASCD. 10: Womans Nat Bk Assn; Delta Kappa Gamma; NE Women's Bk Assn; Nat League Amer Pen Women; Boston Authors' Club;Authors Guild; Kappa Delta. 12: "Land & People of Argentina (60); "Land & People of Norway (63);"Pilgrim Stories (62); "Land & People of Czechoslovakia (66); "Pilgrim Neighbors (64); "Volga; lifeline of Russia" (65); "Hong Kong" (67); "The Psalms" (68);"Picture Map Geography of Eastern Europe" (68); "Proverbs" (69). 13: Yes. 14: Child bks. 15: Div of Instruction, 88 Chestnut st, W Newton Ma 02165.

HALL, FRANCES HUNT. b Panama City Panama 14 Jl 19. 5: Womans Col of UNC 36-40 (Hist) BA; UNC 54-59 (Hist) MA, MSLS, JD. 7: US Naval Reserve 42-54 LCDR; Asst law libn UNC 59-63; Ref libn UChicago Law Lib 63-65, Asst law libn 65-66; Docs libn & asst ref libn UNC (Greensboro) 66-68; Asst Prof Sch ofLib Sci, UNC (Chapel Hill) 68-. 9: AALL; ALA; SELA; AALS; SLA; NCLA (Fed Rel Coord 68-). 10: NC State Bar; NC Bar Assn; Amer Bar Assn. ; AAUP. 13: Yes. 14: Ref law, docs. 15: Sch of Lib Sci, Univ of NC, Chapel Hill NC 27514.

HALL, HALBERT WELDON. b Waco Tex 29 O 41. 4: Betty Gloff. 5: UTex (Austin) 60-64 (Bio) BA; N Tex State U 67-68 MLS. 7: Bio tchr W Independent Sch Dist, West Tex 64-66; Ser libn Sam Houston State Col 68-. 9: ALA; TexLA. 10: Beta Phi Mu; Alpha Lambda Sigma. 15: PO Box 2284 SHSC, Huntsville Tx 77340.

HALL, HELEN V (ERICKSON). b Minneapolis 29 Ap 18. 4: Harry Raymond Hall. 5: Gustavus Adolphus Col 35-39 (Chem & Eng) BA; UMinn 37; USDA Grad Sch 42-43; Immaculate Heart Col 54. 7: High sch tchr Holt Consolidated, Holt Minn 39-40; High sch tchr Silver Lake Sch, Silver Lake Minn 40-42; Chem Food & Drug Admin, Wash DC 42-44, 45; Chem Twin City Testing & Engnr Lab, St Paul 52-56; Chem & prod manager XZIT Chem Co, Los Angeles 56-58; Libn Carnation Co Research Labs, Van Nuys Cal 58-. 9: SLA; ASIS. 10: Veterans of Foreign Wars Aux. 14: Abstracting Carnation Co research reports. 15: Carnation Co Res Labs 8015 Van Nuys blvd, Van Nuys Cal 91412.

HALL, JOHN B. 5: Bowling Green 61-65 (Eng, Bus Admin) BA; West Mich U 65-66 MS in LS; UMich 68. 6: Fr. 7: Circ libn Albion Col 66-68, Catlg libn 67-. 8: Consul libn, Starr Commonwealth for Boys, Albion Mich 68-. 9: ALA; ASIS. 15: 306 Linden ave, Albion Mi 49224.

HALL, JOHN GREGORY. b Sherman Tex 28 Jl 36. 5: So Methodist U 54-58 (Eng) BA& UTex 58-60 MLS. 6: Fr. 7: 1st asst lit & hist dept Dallas Pub Lib 60; Clerk US Army Sp-4 61-62; Ref libn Austin Coll 62-67; Ref asst Barnett Pub Libs, London England 67-68; Col libn Austin Col 68-. 9: Texla; ALA. 14: Ref, acquis. 15: Rt 2, Ravenna Tx 75476.

HALL, LOUISE McG. b Scotland Neck NC 4 Ja 20. 5: St Marys Sch & Jr Col 36-38; UNC 38-40 (Hist) AB, 40-41 BS in LS; UIll 41-44 MA. 6: Fr, Gk. 7: Asst union browsing room UIll Lib (Urbana) 41-44; Bibliog ref libn US Army Map Serv Lib bk sect, Wash DC 4447; Asst ref libn UNC(Chapel Hill) 47-, Head humanities div 57-; Act libn, Amer Sch of Classical Studies, Athens 66. 9: ALA; SELA; NCLA. 12: "The Graduate School: Dissertations and Theses 1st sup (60); Chief comp, "Medieval and Renaissance Studies; a Location Guide to Selected Reference Works.in the Libraries of the UNC & Duke U (65, rev ed 67). 14: Ref. 15: Univ of NC Lib, Chapel Hill NC 27515.

HALL, MARY A. b Great Bend Kan 18 Je 30. 5: Kan Wesleyan U 48-50 (Gen Sci); Kan State U (Manhattan) 50-52 (Eng) BS; UIll 52-54 (LS) MS. 7: Dir of Ext, Asst libn Jackson Co Lib, Independence Mo 54-58; Head libn Manhattan Pub Lib, Manhattan Kan 58-59; Ext consul Kan State Lib 59-60; Head of Ext Topeka Pub Lib, Topeka Kan 60-62, Head adult serv 63-66, Admin-coord Kan Info Circuit 67-69; Asst dir Prince George's Co Mem Lib, Hyattsville Md 69-. 8: Mem State Adv Coun, LSCA, Title IVB 68; consul for lib materials, Cul Herit & Arts Ctr (an ESEA, Title II proj) 68; Dir NW Kan Lib System Lib Clinic Ag 68. 9: ALA (Coun 68-70);-PLA (Publ Com 65-69); KanLA (treas 59-61, pres 65-66, Exec Coun 59-); MPLA. 10: Kan State Hist Soc; Mo Hist Soc; Shawnee Co Hist Soc; Topeka Friends of the Zoo. 12: Landmarks and Pioneers in Early Kansas History; A List of Suggested Readings-- (60); Comp A County That Grows; A Library With Wings-- (60); Coed A Report on Seven Regional Meetings of the Kansas Library Association-- (64). 13: Yes. 14: Ref, interlib coop. 15: Prince George Co Mem Lib 6532 Adelphi rd, Hyattsville Md 20782.

HALL, MARY ELLIS. b Orrville Ala 18 Ap 04. 5: Va Intermont Col 21-22; Judson Col 22-25 (Eng) AB; Emory U 26-27 Certif in LS; UMich summers 50, 51, 53, 54 AMLS. 6: Fr, Sp. 7: Circ ref libn Greensboro Pub Lib, Greensboro NC 27-36; Asst libn Ark A&M Col 38-43; Catlgr Ala Col 43-44; Asst catlgr UVa Law Lib 44-45; Catlgr Randolph-Macon Woman's Col 46-48; Catlgr UTenn (Martin) 48-60, Libn 60-. 9: ALA; SELA; TennLA. 15: Hannings lane, Martin Tn 38237.

HALL, MARY JOAN. b Peking China 31 Jl 32. 5: Barnard 50-54 (Eng) BA; Pratt Lib Sch 61-63 MLS; Hunter Col 69- (Art Hist) MA. 6: Fr. 7: Libn Solomon R Guggenheim Mus 63-. 15: Solomon R Guggenheim Museum, 1071 Fifth ave, New York NY 10028.

HALL, MARYELLEN TRAUTMAN. b Milwaukee Wis 13 Ag 43. 7: Child libn Okla Co Lib, Okla City 66-67; Legislative ref libn Okla Dept of Lib 67-68, Docs libn 68-. 9: ALA; SLA; OklaLA; SWLA. 10: Alpha Chi; Kappa Delta Pi. 14: Docs, ref. 15: 2933 NW Eleventh st, Oklahoma City Ok 73107.

HALL, MONA MARIE. b St James Ark 15 Jl 17. 5: Ark Col 41-47 (Eng) BA; Peabody 50, 54-57 MA LS; UNC summer 66 LS; UArk 67(Econ); UOkla summer 67 LS. 6: Sp. 7: Elem tchr Stone Co Dist, Mountain View Ark 42-47; High Sch tchr Pleasant Plains, Pleasant Plains Ark 47-48; Jr High Sch tchr Stone Co Dist, Mountain View Ark 48-50; Jr High Sch tchr DeWitt, DeWitt Ark 50-51; High Sch tchr Stone Co Dist, Mountain View Ark 51-55; Tch-lbn 55-56; High Sch tchr, Desha Ark 56-57; High Sch tchr Jacksonville Ark 57-58; Libn So Baptist Col 58-62; Asst libn Ark State Tchrs Col 62-66; High Sch libn Pulaski Co Spec Dist, Scott Ark 66-. 9: ALA; ArkEA; ArkLA (v-chm Col Sect 61-62). 10: AAUW; Women's Nat Bk Assn. 14: Catlg, period. 15: 150 Roosevelt rd, Jacksonville Ar 72076.

HALL, RUTH GERALDINE. b Thomasville NC 22 Mr 36. 5: Towson State Col 54-58 (Elem Educ) BS; Rutgers 62-63 MLS. 7: Elem tchr Baltimore Co Bd of Educ 58-60; Child libn Enoch Pratt Free Lib, Baltimore 61-62, 63-67; Libn High John Proj, Prince George's Co Md 67-69; Hd in-serv train & commun serv Off Wk with Child Free Lib Phila 69-. 9: ALA; PennLA. 14: Child lit & lib activities, pub lib in urban ctrs. 14: Child lit & lib activities, pub lib in urban ctrs. 15: Office of Work with Children Free Lib of Phila Logan Square, Phila Pa 19103.

HALL, RUTH LOUISE (MRS). b Wash DC 23 Ag 07. 5: Howard U 27-29, 48-49 (Educ) BA; Catholic U 52-54, 60-63 MSLS. 6: Fr. 7: Clerk typist Legis Ref Serv FSA, Wash DC 45-50, Asst libn acquis div FSA 50-53; Catlgr US Dept Health Educ Welfare, Wash DC 53-65; Ref libn Educ Br 66-. 9: SLA; DCLA; Potomac Tech Processing Libns. 10: Brookland Civic Assn. 14: Catlg, ref. 15: 1319 Shepherd st NE, Wash DC 20017.

HALL, SHIRLEY E (BADGER). b New Castle Penn 28 Mr 42. 4: Donald Elliott Hall. 5: Clarion State Col 60-63 (LS) BS; UPittsburgh 63 (LS). 6: Sp. 7: Elem libn Mohawk Area schs, Bessemer Penn 63-; Period libn Ohio U Lib (Athens) 68-. 9: NEA; Penn State EA; ALA; OhioLA. 10: Beta Phi Mu. 14: Sch libnship, periods. 15: Box 149, The Plains Oh 45780.

HALL, VIRGINIA (BARRICK). b Cleveland 12 Ag 13. 4: Richard L Hall. 5: Baldwin-Wallace Col 30-32; Oberlin 32-34 (Bot) BA; Mt Holyoke 34-36 (Bot) MA; West Res 36-37 BS in LS. 6: Fr. 7: Grad asst Mt Holyoke Col 34-36; Lib asst Cleveland Pub Lib 37-42, 43-45; Ref libn Ohio State U EducLib 65-; Hd Pharmacy-Micro Lib 66-67, Hd Pharmacy Lib 67-, Hd Microbiol Lib67-68, Hd Home Econ Lib 68-. 9: SLA; Amer Assn of Cols of Pharmacy (co-chm Pharmacy Libns Sect Meeting,Cincinnati 69). 14: Ref. 15: 5573 Ashford rd, Dublin Oh 43017.

HALLAHAN, JOHN J. b Boston Mass 12 Ag 27. 4: Julie E Sarjeant. 5: Boston Col 47-51 (Eng) BA; Simmons 51-52 MSLS. 7: Lib clk Boston Pub Lib 44-45; B Yeoman 3/C USN 45-47; Various sub-prof Boston Pub Lib 48-52, Prof asst 52-55; Chief libn Norwalk Pub Lib, norwalk Conn 55-66; City lib dir Manchester Pub Lib, Manchester NH 66-. 8: Chm Adv Coun Lib Com Norwalk Commun Col 62-65. 9: ALA; ConnLA (v-pres). 10: American Red Cross; United Fund Committee. 11: Jaycees' Man of the Year 63. 15: 84 Healion st, Manchester NH 03103.

HALLAM, NORMAN (EDWIN). b Bremerton Wash 30 Je 33. 4: Shirley Hallam. 5: Seattle Pacific Col 51-54, 57-58 (Educ) BA i Ed; UWash 60-61 M of Libr. 6: Ger, Fr. 7: Tr US Army ASA, Frankfurt A/M Germany 55-57; Elem tchr Raymond Sch Dist, Raymond Wash 58-59; Elem tchr Washougal Sch Dist, Washougal Wash 59-60; Br libn Renton Pub Lib, Renton Wash 61; Head bkmob dept King Co Lib System, Seattle 62-67; Adult serv libn Yolo Co Lib, Cal 67-69, Act Co libn 69-. 9: ALA; CalLA. 14: Catlg, ref, adult serv, admin. 15: 604 McKinley ave apt 3, Woodland Ca 95695.

HALLBORG, DOROTHY (FRANTZEN). b Dunkirk NY 25 My 17. 4: Robert Hallborg. 5: Allegheny Col 36-37, 38-39 (Lit); Simmons 39-40 BLS. 7: Catlgr Baker Lib Harvard Grad ch of Bus Admin 40-41; Catlgr Lib of Consolidated Edison, NYC 41-43; Child libn Fairfax Co Pub Lib, Fairfax Va 61-62; Educ libn Hofstra U 62-. 15: 289 Crowell st, Hempstead NY 11550.

HALLENBERGER, LORENE (WHERRY). b Tribbey Okla 18 Je 11. 4: John H Hallenberger. 5: W Tex State U 28-30, 31-32 (Eng) AB; UMich 35-36, summer 37 (Eng) MA; UArk summer 50; Peabody Col summers 51-54 MALS. 7: Tchr: Liberty Sch, Near Muleshoe Tex 30-31, Miami High Sch, Miami Tex 32-35, Sam Houston Jr High, Amarillo Tex 36-39, Gentry High Sch, Gentry Ark 47-50; Tchr & libn Gentry High Sch 50-55; Libn sr high sch, Portales NM 55-65; Asst Prof in lib sci East NM U 65-. 9: ALA; NEA; NMLA (chm Lib A-V Educ RT); NMEA; SWLA. 10: AAUP; AAUW; C of C. 14: Lib educ, sch libs. 15: 223 South ave J, Portales NM 88130.

HALLIDAY, MARGARET EMILY. b Newport News Va 12 O 46. 5: UNC (Greensboro) 64-68 (Eng) BA; UNC (Chapel Hill) 68-69 MSLS. 6: Ger. 7: Catlgr Charles H Taylor Pub Lib, Hampton Va 69-. 10: Phi Beta Kappa. 14: Ref, adult serv, catlg. 15: 4027 Monitor dr, Hampton Va 23369.

HALLIGAN, JOHN THOMAS. b Lynn Mass 1 Ag 33. 4: Joan M Auerbach. 5: Northeastern U 52-54 (Liberal Art): Boston U 54-56 (Journalism) BS: Boston State Col 58-59 (Educ) M Ed; C W Post Col of LIU 60-63 (LS) MS. MLS. 6: Sp, Ger. 7: US Army 53; Newspaper reporter & ed 56-58; Tchr Farmingdale Jr High Sch, Farmingdale NY 59-61; Libn Carlsbad High Sch, Carlsbad Cal 61-64; Ref libn Philipps Andover Acad, Andover Mass summer 64; LibnCambridge High Schs, Cambridge Mass 64-65; Libn Fallbrook High Sch, FallbrookCal 65-68; Ref & bkmob libn Oceanside Pub Lib, Oceanside Cal summers 67, 68; Ref& periods libn Sacramento City Col 68-. 9: Cal Assn Sch Libns Legis Com); CalLA; CalTA; Los Rios TA. 10: Cal Jr Col Fac Assn; Amateur Ath Union. 13: Yes. 14: Ref. 15: 3177 Lincoln st, Carlsbad Cal 92008.

HALLIWELL, DEAN WRIGHT. b Estevan Sask Can 26 Jl 24. 4: Marjory Robertson. 5: USask 39-43 (Eng) BA, 45-48 (Eng) MA; Toronto 48-49 BLS. 7: RCAF Navigator, Flight Lt 43-45; Bkmob libn Cuyahoga Co Pub Lib, Cleveland 49-52, Coordinator of ref serv 52-55; Canadiana libn USask 55-57, Asst libn 57-60; U Libn UVictoria (BC) 60-. 9: ALA; CanLA (Coun 64-67); BCLA (pres 65-66); Can Assn Col & Univ Libs (pres 67-68). 12: Ed "Saskatchewan Lib Assn Bulletin" 58-60. 13: Yes. 14: Ref. 15: 1828 St Ann st, Victoria BC Can.

HALLOCK, MARGARET B. b Rochester NY 27 Mr 07. 4: Charles B Hallock. 5: URochester 25-29 (Eng) BA; Syracuse 37-38 BLS. 7: Sr asst Rochester Pub Lib, Rochester NY 36-38, Head bus div 44-64; Libn Nixon Hargrave Devans & Doyle, Rochester NY 64-. 9: AALL; Assn Law Libns of Upstate NY. 15: 56 Brighton st, Rochester NY 14607.

HALLORAN, HELEN (KENNEDY). b Eagle Pass Tex 24 Ag 19. 4: John K Halloran. 5: Tex Womans U 37-41 (LS) BA, 52, 66; No Tex State U summer 47; UTex ext48-49; Tex A & I Col ext 50. 6: Sp. 7: Asst libn Austin High Sch, Austin Tex 45-46; Libn Webster High Sch, Webster Tex 46-47; Supv libs Clear Creek Consolidated, Webster Tex 47-50; Asst libn R Miller High Sch, Corpus Christi Tex 50-53, Libn 53-57; Libn M Carroll High Sch, Corpus Christi Tex 57-59; Ref libn La Retania Pub, Corpus Christi Tex 60-62, Ext libn 62-; Coord libn for ref referral syst 69-. 8: Consul & Eval Com; several Tex sch systems; Lib spec for Nat Lib, Develop Sem, Caracas Venezuela 69. 9: ALA (State Memb Com 66-69, Recr Com 66-); Tex State TA (past chm Lib Sect);TexLA (chm Dist IV 65, chm Ref RT 67, chm Pub Libs Dir 68); Coastal Bend LA(past chm). 10: AAUW; Kiwanis; Wesleyan Serv Guild; Tex Women's Univ Alum Corpus Christi Br;State Com Nat Lib Week 69. 14: Ref, admin. 15: 105 Glendale dr, Corpus Christi Tex 78404.

HALLORAN, JOSEPH G. b Richmond Hil NY 10 Je 20. 4: Georgette Swink. 5: Brooklyn Col 50 (Fr) AB Columbia 55 (LS) MS. 6: Fr, Ital. 7: Ref libn Queensborough Pub Lib, Jamaica NY 50-55; Br asst Detroit Pub Lib 55-58; Dir Mentor Pub Lib, Mentor Ohio 58-61; Br libn Yonkers Pub Lib, Yonkers NY 61-63; Dir Syosset Pub Lib, Syosset NY 63-. 8: Bldg consul Mentor Ohio 59-60, Syosset NY 65-69. 9: NYLA; NCLA (pres 67-68). 13: Yes. 14: Ref, admin, tech serv. 15: 29 Jackson ave, Syosset NY 11790.

HALLS, GWENDOLYN (FIELDS). b Atlanta 6 Ap 29. 4: Lee Halls. 5: Spelman Col 45-49 (Eng) AB; Atlanta 59-62 MSLS. 6: Fr. 7: Tchr Barnesville High Sch, Barnesville Ga 50-51; Soc wker Fulter Co Dept Welfare, Atlanta 57-60; Libn Lynwood Park High Sch, Atlanta 60-62; Libn Hubert Jr High Sch, Atlanta 62-. 10: YWCA; Girl Scout Leader; Beta Kappa Mu. 14: Rare bks, Negro life & lit. 15: 268 Spellman, Atlanta Ga 30314.

HALMAN, RUTH BARNETTE. b NYC 8 Je 41. 5: Wheeling Col 59-63 (Hist) BA; USoCal 66-67 MSLS. 7: Asst ref libn UCal (Riverside) 67-. 9: ALA; CalLA. 10. Libns Assn UCal. 14: Ref, acquis. 15: 3662 Monroe st, Riverside Ca 92504.

HALPERN, BARBARA JEAN. b Albany NY 10 Je 41. 4: Michael Steven Halpern. 5: Barnard 59-63 (Zool) AB; Columbia 62-64 (LS) MS. 6: Ger. 7: Pub serv libn circ & ref Albert Einstein Col of Med Lib 64-66; Asst sci libn MIT 66; Libn I Pub Health Lib UCal(Berkeley) 66-67; Asst libn Alameda-Contra Costa Med Assoc Lib 67-. 15: 2552 Le Conte ave apt 3, Berkeley Ca 94709.

HALPERN, GERTRUDE E. b Boston 31 Mr 12. 4 Dr Ben Halpern. 5: Radcliffe 29-33 (Biochem) A; Columbia 40-43 BS in LS. 6: Fr. 7: Lib asst NY Pub Lib 39-42; Ref libn Columbia Lib Sch 53-54; Asst libn Biol Lib Harvard U 56-61; Sr catlgr Harvard Med Lib (Boston) 61-. 9: MedLA. 14: Catlg, ref. 15: 187 Mason ter, Brookline Ma 02146.

HALPIN, JOAN ELIZABETH (WU). b London 7 F 34. 4: Peter Halpin. 5: Mt Mercy Col 52-56 (Chem) BA; Catholic U 58-60 BS in LS. 6: Chinese. 7: Bibliog & sci libn LC, Wash DC 59-67, Supv libn & asst catlg ed 67-. 9: SLA. 12: Comp "Chinese Scientific and Technical Serial Publications in the Collectionsof the Library of Congress" (rev ed 61). 13: Yes. 14: Bibliog (phys scis), scientific transl. 15: 6611 Glassell Ct, Alexandria Va 22310.

HALPIN, KEUM CHU (PAK). b Seoul Korea 08 Mr 31. 4: James Halpin. 5: UWash 63 (Russian) BA, 65 MLib, 65- (Far East). 6: Korean, Japanese. 7: Ref & catlg libn olympic Col 65-66; Ref libn Seattle Commun Col 66-. 8: Part time teaching of the Far Eastern History at junior colleges; (Seattle Community College, Bellevue Community college). 9: NEA; WashEA; Assn Asia Studies. 14: Ref. 15: 7736 30th NE, Seattle Wa 98115.

HALPORN, BARBARA (CRAWFORD). b Amsterdam Mo 14 D 38. 4: James Halporn. 5: UMo 56-60 (Eng) AB; IndU 60-66 (LS) MA. 6: Fr, Ital. 7: Gifts libn IndU (Bloomington) 66-68, catlgr 68, Libn (philos, classics, hist & philos of sci) 69-. 9: ALA. 15: Ind Univ Lib, Bloomington In 47401.

HALSELL, WILLIE D. b Itta Bena MIss 9 N 05. 5: Miss State Col for Women 21-25 (Hist) BA; Vanderbilt 25-26 (Hist) MA; Johns Hopkins 31-32, 36-37 (Hist); LSU 50-51 BS in LS. 6: Fr. 7: Prin of High Sch dept Averett Jr Col 26-27; Libn hist tchr Humphreys High Sch, Itta Bena Miss 27-28, 41-50; Head of hist dept Chowan Col 28-31; Head Libn Lee Co Lib, Tupelo Miss 51-53; Ref libn Mitchell Mem Lib Miss State U 53-59, Head of ref dept 59-66, Hd of spec collections dept 66-. 9: Amer Assn State & Loc Hist; SELA; So Hist Assn; MissLA; Miss Hist Soc; Miss Folklore Soc. 10: Phi Alpha Theta. 11: John Cotton dana Award for Excellence in public relations 53. 12: Bibliog ed "Journal of Mississippi History" (57-). 13: Yes. 14: Mississipiana, rare bks, mss, univ archives. 15: Box 1062, State College Ms 39762.

HALSEY, REBECCA. b Oxford Ohio 12 Ja 43. 5: MiamiU 61-65 (Eng) BA; UMich 66-67 MLS. 7: Lib asst Lane Pub Lib, Oxford Ohio 65-66; Libn Cleveland Pub Lib, Cleveland Ohio 67-. 9: OhioLA; Young Libns Assn. 14: Ref. 15: 1330 W blvd #304C, Cleveland Oh 44102.

HALSEY, RICHARD SWEENEY. b Los Angeles 8 Ap 29. 4: Patricia Siver. 5: New Eng Conservatory of Music 48-52 (Music Composition) B Mus, 52-54 (Music Educ) M Mus; Simmons 59-62 (LS) MS. 6: Fr, Ger. 7: Instr of gen milit subjects US Army, Ft Ord Cal (SP-4) 56; Interlib-loan asst Col of Liberal Arts Lib Boston U 59-60; Circ asst Harvard Med Sch Lib (Boston) 59-60; Grad asst in Lib Simmons Col Lib 60-62; Chief A-V dept Washington U Lib 9st Louis) 62-65; Lecturer in Libnship U Col Wash U (St Louis) 63-; Dir of learning resources & Secondary schls-pub libs Microform Coop Planning Proj of St LouisArea Sch Dist of University City, University City Mo 65-68; Info sci & dir of educ materials ctrs, Central Midwest Reg EducLa, St Ann Mo 68-. 8: Composer of music; performances of works at Boston Arts Festival, Tanglewook Eastman Sch of Music, Jordan Hall (Boston), radio & television 54-60; Library & a-v consultant for St Louis Job Corps Center for Women, 67-68. 9: ALA; Nat Microfilm Assn; NEA-DAVI; ASIS. 10: AAUP; Pi Kappa Lambda. 13: Yes. 14: Sch lib devel, lib admin, clsf theory. 15: 1000 Emerald lane, Carbondale Il 62901.

HALTER, REV ROBERT OSB. b St Joseph Mo 28 N 33. 5: Conception Col 51-55 (Philos) AB, Conception Sem 55-60 (Theol) STB MA; Creighton U 60-61 (Eng); UDenver 61-64 (LS) MA. 6: Sp, Lat. 7: ng Prof & Libn St Johns Sem (Elkhorn Neb) 60-. 9: ALA; CathLA; NCTE; NebCathLA. 15: Mt Michael Abbey, Elkhorn Nb 68022.

HALVERSON, EMILY (BENEDICT). b Troy NY 12 Ja 13. 4: Alfred W Halverson. 5: Conn Col for Women 30-34 (Fine Arts) AB; SUNY(Albany) 58-60 MSLS. 6: Fr. 07: Ref libn & asst catlgr So Adirondack (NY) Lib Sys 60-62, A-v libn & asst catlgr 62-. 9: NYLA. 14: Catlg, a-v, ref. 15: RD 3, Amsterdam NY 12010.

HALVERSON, ROLF T. b Seattle Wash 20 Ag 31. 5: UCal (Berkeley) 49-53 (Eng) BA, 55-56 MLS. 6: Ger, Fr. 7: Troop info & educ spec, Eng instr USA camp, Tortuguero PR 53-55; Jr libn soc sci & sci LA of Portland (Ore) 56-58, Sr libn catlg dept 58-60; Sr asst gen ref Enoch Pratt Free Lib, Baltimore 60-61, Admin asst to asst dir 61-63, Exec asst to dir 63-. 9: ALA (memb chm Staff Orgs RT 66-68); -RSD/RTSD (Pub Docs Interdiv Com 66-68); MdLA (Fed Rel Com 63-65; chm 63-64). 13: Yes. 14: Ref, admin. 15: 304 Charter Oak ave, Baltimore Md 21212.

HAM, F GERALD. b Toms River NJ 13 Ap 30. 4: Elsie Magill. 5: Wheaton Col (Ill) 47-52 (Hist) AB; UKy 52, 56-58 (Hist) MA, PhD. 7: Asst curator WVa U 58-64, Asst Prof of hist 63-64; State Archivist & Head div of archives & mss State Hist Soc of Wis (Madison Wis) 64-; Lectr in Archives Admin, UWis Lib Sch 67-. 8: 1st consul to Shakertown at Pleasant Hill Inc, Lexington Ky; Lectr in Archives Admin, UWis Lib Sch 67-; Archival consul Ind State Lib 68-69, Ohio Hist Soc 69. 9: SAA (Exec sec; Col & U Archives Com). 11: Fellow, SAA 68. 12: "Guide to MANUSCRIPTS IN THE West Virginia Collection, Number II, 1958-1963 (65); Co-auth "Pleasant Hill and Its Shakers" (69). 13: Yes. 14: Amer rel & soc hist, admin of archives. 15: State Hist Soc of Wis, 816 State st, Madison Wi 53706.

HAM, JESSIE GILCHRIST. b Florence SC 3 F 13. 5: Randolph-Macon 30-34 (Fr) AB; Peabody 34-35 BS in LS. 6: Fr, Ger. 7: Tchr-libn Williston-Elko High Sch, Williston SC 35-36; Supv SC Lib Catlg Proj WPA, Columbia SC 36-38; Asst catlgr McKissick Mem Lib UScar 38-48, Head catlg dept 48-. 9: ALA(mem var coms); SELA (var coms); SCLA(sec, pres). 10: Columbia (SC) Lib Club; SC State Employees Assn. 13: Yes. 14: Catlg. 15: 3515 Wilmot st, Columbia SC 29205.

HAMANN, EDMUND G. b NYC 25 Ap 33. 4: Barbara S. 5: Hamilton Col 5155 (Hist) BA; UMich 5556 MALS, 5659 MA. 6: Fr. 7: Jr catlgr UMich Law Lib 5658; catlgr/ref UAuckland NZ 5961; Serials libn UNH (Durham) 6166; Order libn Albert R Mann Lib, Ithaca NY 6667; Libn Central Ser Record Dept, Cornell U Libs 68. 9: ALA. 13: Yes. 14: Acquis, admin. 15: Box 111, Jacksonville NY 14854.

HAMBRICK, THERA(OLLIS). b Lowndes County Ga 4 Ja 17. 5: Ga State Womans Col 34-42 (Eng) BA; LSU 44-47 BS in LS; Fla State U 60-61 (LS). 6: Fr, Sp. 7: Tchr Charlton Co Sch System, St George ga 36-39; Tchr-libn Echols Co Sch SYSTEM, Statenville Ga 39-42; Libn Pasco Co Sch System, New Port Richey Fla 42-43; Libn The Bolles Sch, Jackoville Fla 43-46; Asst libn Ga State Womans Col, Valdosta Ga 46-61; Libn Valdosta State Col, Valdosta Ga 61-. 9: ALA; SELA; GaLA; GaEA; Ga Academic Libns (chm). 10: Ga Mental Health Assn; Womans Club; Beta Phi Mu. 14: Admin. 15: Rt 1 Box 120, Hahira Ga 31632.

HAMDY, MOHAMED (NABIL). b Cairo Egypt 12 Ap 36. 4: Amira Hafez M Ismail. 5: Cairo U 53-57 (LS) BA; UMinn 63-65 (LS) MA; UPittsburgh 65- (LS) PhD. 6: Arabic, Fr. 7: Ref lib Nat Lib of UAR, Cairo 57-58, Asst legal deposit lib 58-60, Hd of purchasing 60-62, Hd of purchasing & legal deposit 62-63; Stud trainee UMinn 64-65; Searcher UPittsburgh 65-66, Catlgr 66-68, Coord catlg 68-. 8: Planning & organ of the Pub Lib Admin, Cairo Egypt 6-. 9: EgyptLA; ALA. 12: Ed "The Egyptian Publications Bulletin" 58-62. 13: Yes. 14: Catlg, tech serv. 15: 5841 Beacon st, Pittsburgh Pa 15217.

HAMEL, DOROTHY MAE (FORSBERG). b Marquette Mich 14 O 30. 4: John Christian Hamel Jr. 5: Henry Ford Col 53-56; East MichU 56-65 (Hist, LS) AB; UTenn 66; UMich 66-67 AMLS. 6: Ital. 7: Sch libn Garden City Sch Bd, Garden City Mich 66-67; Tech libn USAEC-DTIE, Oak Ridge Tenn 67-68; Acquis libn UNev (Las Vegas) 68-69, Tech libn (for AEC) 69-. 9: SLA; AAUW; NevLA. 10: Kappa Delta Pi. 14: Tech libnship. 15: 5213 Churchill, las Vegas Nv 89107.

HAMELBERG, EILEEN (THEA). b Cincinnati 19 O 40. 5: UMinn 58-61 (Ger) BA, 61-63 (LS) MA; UFlorence Center of Culture for Foreigners 65-66. 6: Ger, Ital, Fr. 7: Asst ref libn Bellingham Pub Lib, Bellingham Wash 63-65; Libn II hist dept Seattle Pub Lib, Seattle 67-. 9: PNLA. 14: Ref. 15: 1938 Yale ave E #26, Seattle Wa 98102.

HAMER, ELIZABETH EDWARDS. b Copperhill Tenn 4 Ja 12. 4: Philip May Hamer. 5: UTenn 29-33 (Hist) AB, 33-34, 35; Chicago 34-35; American U 39-42. 7: Res asst, adm asst & ed-in-chief "Inventory of Federal Archives in the States, 36-40; Nat Archives: Ed-writer 42, Asst chief div info & publ 42-43, Asst admin sec 43-46; Exhibits & info off 47-50, Chief exhibits & Publ sect 50-51; LC: Info & publ off 51-60, Asst libn for pub affairs 60-63, Asst libn 63-. 8: Alternate for the Libn of Congress on Lincoln Sesquicentennial Commsn, 58-60; Sec Lib Com Theodore Roosevelt Centennial Commsn, 58-59; Mem Exh Com Civil War Centennial Commsn, 59-65; Mem DC Com on Nat Lib Week 58-; Mem Govt Com Educ & Train for Internat Coop Year, 65; Del to White House Conf on Internat Coop, 65; Program Com Third World Congress of Agric Libns & documentalists; Govt Liaison Group on Staffing Internat Orgs; Del to InternatCongress on Archives, Florenc, Florence, Brussels, 64; 64, Wash DC, 66, Madrid, 68; ICA Conf, Wash 66; Alternate for libn of Congress on Nat Hist Publs Commsn 68-; Del Intl Fed Lib Assns 66. 9: ALA (Internat Rels Round Table, Round Table for the Blind; Ms Soc; Amer Hist Assn; SAA (Hon Fellow); DCLA; Intl Coun on Archives. 10: Hon Trustee, Greater Wash Educ TV Assn; Phi Kappa Phi; SC Hist Soc; NYU Coun Grad Sch Arts & Sci. 12: Auth of govt publs & brochures; Contrib "Dictionary of American History & Wonderful World of Books; Ed: "Inventory of Federal Archives in the States (37-40). 13: Yes. 14: Admin, legis, hist bibliog, pub rel. 15: Library of Congress, Wash DC 20540.

HAMILL, HAROLD LOUIS. b Wash 23 Mr 08. 4: Frances Collins. 5: George Washington U 27-34 (Eng) AB; Columbia 34-35 BS in LS. 7: Circ asst Pub Lib, Wash DC 24-29, Order asst 30-34; Sr asst Pub Lib, Mt Vernon NY 35-38; Asst libn Pub Lib, Yonkers NY 9; Libn Pub Lib, Schenectady NY 40-41; Asst libn Enoch Pratt Free Lib, Baltimore 41-43; Libn Pub Lib, Kansas City ity Mo 43-47; City Libn Lib Li, Los Angeles 47-. 9: ALA (chm 3 coms 42-66);-PLA (pres 61-62); CalLA (pres Pub Lib Sect 55, chm 2 coms 56-62); Pub Lib Exec Assn of So Cal (pres49). 10: Lakeside Golf Club; Town Hall, Libraria Sodalitas. 12: Surveys of pub libs: Houston (53); Beverly Hills Cal (61); Hanford-Kings Co Cal (63); Whittier Cal (64): Memphis 66; Chap 4 in Bowler R ed "Local Public Library Administration (64); Chap in Coplan K & Castagna E "The Library Reaches Out (65). 13: Yes. 14: Pub lib admin. 15: Los Angeles Pub Lib, 630 W 5 st, Los Angeles Ca 90017.

HAMILTON, CARL W. b Wash DC 25 O 17. 4: Ramona Dixon. 5: Miami U (Ohio) 42 (Eng) AB; UCal(erkeley) 47 BLS. 7: Jr libn UDenver 47-50; Asst city libn Richmond (Cal) Pub Lib 50-52; County & City Libn Stanislaus County, Modesto Cal 5264; City Libn Alameda (Cal) Free Lib (E Bay Coop Lib Syst) 64-; Off Exec Com E Bay Coop Lib Syst 66-. 8:Cal Cal Pub Lib Standards Wkshop 53; Working Com for cooperative (computer) activity in Bay Area (4 counties & 20 cities) 65. 9: ALA; MPLA; ColoLA CalLA (pres Yosemite Dist & Mun Sect); CalLA (Coun). 10: Kiwanis; Torch Club. 14: Admin, cooperative systems, computers & machines, bk catlgs, films. 15: Alameda Free Lib Santa Clara & Oak, Alameda Ca 94501.

HAMILTON, CHARLES E(VERETT). b Minn 17 D 26. 5: Visalia Jr Col 40-42; UCal(Berkeley)42, 46-48 (Oriental Lang) BA, BLS. 6: Fr, Japanese. 7: Chief catlgr EAsiatic Lib UCal(Berkeley) 48-. 9: ALA-RTSD (chm CCS Far Eastern Materials Com 58-68). 14: Catlg. 15: E Asiatic Lib UCal, Berkeley Cal 94720.

HAMILTON, DAVID. b Grand Rapids Mich 16 Ag 27. 4: Christine Pearson. 5: No Ill U 57-60 (Eng) BS in Ed, 60-64 (LS) MA in LS. 6: Fr. 7: Deckhand various tankers, freighters, Great Lakes 45-50; (Cpl) S Army Engineer Corps (Air compressor Operator Tex 50-52; Accountant No Ill Corp, DeKalb Ill 52-53; Claims manager No nsurance Agency, DeKalb Ill 53-59; Eng tchr Waterman High Sch, Waterman Ill 60-62; Libn Simmons Jr High Sch, Aurora Ill 62-64; Bind libn Swen Parson Lib No Ill U 64-65, Period libn 65-. 9: IllLA. 14: Periods. 15: 425 Dresser rd, DKalb Ill 60115.

HAMILTON, DENNIS CLARK. b Los Angeles Cal 20 Ja 40. 4: Sylvia Courtney Sloat. 5: UCLA 59-63 (Fr) AB; USoCal 65-66 MSLS. 6: Fr, Sp. 7: Ref libn UCal (Santa Barbara) summer 67; Evening sch libn Santa Barbara City Col 67-69; Libn La Colina Jr High Sch, Santa Barbara Cal 66-69; Ref libn Riverside City Col 69-. 9: ALA; NEA; CalASchL; CalLA; CalTA. 14: Ref, child lit. 15: Lib Riverside City Col, 3650 Fairfax ave, Riverside Ca 92506.

HAMILTON, ELEONORE FRIEDA (FROESE). b Winnipeg Can 6 Ja 45. 4: David Hamilton. 5: United Col 62-65 (Eng & Fr) BA; UMan 65-68 (summers) Certif in Educ; UToronto 68-69 BLS. 6: Fr, Ger. 7: Tchr Westwood Collegiate, Winnipeg 65-67; Libn Winnipeg Pub Lib, Winnipeg Can 67-68; Libn Edmonton Pub Lib, Edmonton Can 68-. 14: Ref. 15: 9 Rowand ave S, Winnipeg 12 Man Can.

HAMILTON, (ELLA) LUDOVINE. b Jacksonville Ala 21 My 09. 5: Radcliffe 27-31 (Math) AB; MIT 31 (MATH; Simmons40-41 Simmons 40-41 BS. 7: Br libn & gen asst Pub Lib, Belmont Mass 32-40; Pub Lib, Lynn Mass: Libn 41-49, Ref libn 49-62, Catlgr63-. 8: Correspondence INSTR Mass Dept of Educ, Catlg & Clsf, Lib Ref Serv. 9: ALA; MassLA; NELA. 10: Lynn Hist Assn. 14: Catlg, ref. 15: 77 Edgehill rd, Lynn Ma 01904.

HAMILTON, IGERNA (MEARS). b Bowling Green Ohio 21 Ja 1894. 4: Harry B Hamilton. 5: Cleveland Pub Lib 10 (Apprentice Course); West Res 11 (LS) Certif, West Res 48. 7: Cleveland Pub Lib: Page 08-0, Clerical wk catlg dept 10, Desk asst Main Lib 12-13, Libn Clark Br 13-15; Ref libn Shaker Heights Pub Lib, Shaker Heights Ohio 38-55; Volunteer work org ready ref pamphlet file Winter Park Pub Lib, Winter Park Fla 58-. 8: Research Div Curtis Publg Co, Phila 35-38; Volunteer wk, reorg lib Federated Church, Chagrin Falls Ohio 69. 10: West Res Lib Sch Alumni Assn; Bd, Hannibal Square Negro Lib, Winter Park Fla; Friends of the Lib, Winter Park Pub Lib; Garden Club; Womans Club; Coun Human Rel. 14: Ref. 15: 6000 Nob Hill dr apt 308, Chagrin Falls Oh 44022.

HAMILTON, JUDITH MAE. b Plymouth Ind 18 Je 41. 5: MacMurray Col 59-61 (Hist); Ind U 61-64 (Educ) BS, 64-67

MLS. 7: Elem libn: Crown Point Ind 64, Metropolitan Sch Dist of Martinsville Ind 65-67, Wayne Twp, Indianapolis 67-68; High Sch Libn Univ Sch, Bloomington Ind summer 67; Libn UWis (Racine) 68-. 9: WisLA. 10: Pi Lambda Theta. 14: Ref. 15: Univ of Wis Parkside, 1001 S Main, Racine Wi 53403.

HAMILTON, LEO FRANKLIN. 4: Hamilton Elizabeth (Corley). 5: Simpson Col 47-49, 57-59 (Hist) BA; UIll 58-59 MSLS. 7: (S/Sgt) Personnel clk USAF 50-54; Lib asst Simpson Col Lib 57-59; Acquis asst Lib UTex (Austin) 59-69. 9: TexLA. 14: Lib acquis. 15: 1314 Yorkshire dr, Austin Tx 78723.

HAMILTON, MALCOLM C. b Bath Me 29 Ja 38. 5: UMe 57-61 (Eng) BA; Simmons 67-68 MLS. 6: Fr. 7: High sch tchr, Chelmsford Mass 61-67; Ref libn Harvard Grad Sch of Educ 67-. 9: ALA. 10: Harvard Lib Club. 14: Ref, ser. 15: Harvard Grad School of Educ Lib 13 Appian way, Cambridge Ma 02138.

HAMILTON, MARTHA E. b Grove City Penn 28 Je 24. 5: Geneva Col 46 (Eng) BA; Carnegie 47 BS in LS. 6: Fr. 7: Libn NW Brighton (Penn) Area Schs 47-. 9: ALA; PennLA. 10: AAUW. 14: Young adults activities. 15: 559 10th ave, New Brighton Penn 15066.

HAMILTON, PHILIP TOURQIS. b Gary Ind 28 Jl 24. 4: Thelma Cornelius. 5: Miami U 44-50 (Eng) BA; Pratt Inst 52 MA in LS. 7: Y-a libn Evansville Pub Lib, Evansville Ind 52-54; Dir Seymour Pub Lib, Seymour Ind 54-57; Dir Kokomo Pub Lib, Kokomo Ind 57-. 9: ALA; IndLA (mem Bd). 10: Elks; Moose; YMCA; Men's Club; Rotary. 14: Lib admin, ref, ya. 15: Kokomo Pub Lib 220 N Union, Kokomo In 46901.

HAMILTON, PHYLLIS I (LEVCHUK). b Peabody Mass 9 Je 26. 4: Willard E Hamilton. 5: Simmons 43-47 (Chem) BS. 6: Fr, Ger, Russian. 7: Lib chem Shell Development Co, Emeryville Cal 47-57; Libn Chem Lib Serv, San Francisco 60-. 9: ACS; SLA; Amer Transl Assn. 14: Ref, searching. 15: 1850 Funston ave, San Francisco Ca 94116.

HAMILTON, RAPHAEL NOTEWARE. b Omaha 5 N 1892. 5: Creighton U 13 (Philos) AB; St Louis U 19 (Hist) M, 32 (Hist) PhD. 6: Lat, Fr. 7: Hist tchr Campion Col 20-23; Hist instr St Louis U 28-29; Hist Prof Marquette U 30-62, U Archivist 61-. 9: SAA; AHA; State Hist Soc of Wis; Org of Amer Histns; Amer Cath Hist Assn. 10: Dean of Grad Sch, Marquette Univ 40-44. 12: Ed Bd, Mid-America (35-); "The Story of Marquette University (53). 13: Yes. 14: Archives. 15: 1131 W Wisconsin ave, Milwaukee Wi 53233.

HAMILTON, ROBERT E(UGENE). b Akron Ohio 22 Je 20. 4: Marjorie Clayton. 5: Ohio U 3841, 46-47 (Accounting) BS in Com; West Res 46-47 BS in LS. 7: Gen asst Lorain Pub Lib, Lorain Ohio 48-49; Head of catlg & order dept Racine Pub Lib, Racine Wis 49-51; Ext libn Cnton Ohio 51-53; Head Libn Hayner Pub Lib, Alton Ill 53-57; Head Libn Martin Co Pub Lib, Stuart Fla 57-62; Head Libn Grand Junction Pub Lib, Grand Junction Colo 62-64; Chief of tech serv Providence Pub Lib 64-66; Chief lib operation Ill State Lib 66-68; Hd techprocesses Ill U Libs 68-. 8: Temp admin Bk Processing Center, Orlando Fla March 62; Lectr Clinic on Lib Data Processing 68. 9: ALA(Bk of Month Club Com 62); WisLA; OhioLA; IllL(Legis IllLA FlaLA(Legis Com); ColoLA(Legis Com); RILA. 10: Kiwanis; Data Processing Mgt Assn. 12: Ed rila bulletin 13: Yes. 14: Catlg, data processing in libs, automation, centralized bk ordering & processing centers. 15: Lincolnshire West Apts, Apt 9106, DeKalb Il 60115.

HAMILTON, ROBERT MORRIS. b Lachine Que Can 25 Mr 12. 4: Anne Harrington. 5: McGill 30-34 (Eng) BA, 34-35 BLS; Columbia 36-37 Carnegie Fellow. 6: Fr. 7: Circ & ref Lib of Parliament, Ottawa 37-44; Ref asst NY Pub Lib 44-46; Asst lbn Lib of Parliament, Ottawa 46-61; Assoc Prof of Sch of Libnship, Vancouver BC 61-64; Asst libn UBC Lib 64-. 9: CanLApres 61-62). 12: "Canadian Quotations & Phrases (52); "Canadian Book-Prices Current, 3 vols (50-62); "Orchid Flower Index" (67). 13: Yes. 14: Ref, collections. 15: 921 Beckwith rd, Richmond BC Can.

HAMILTON, RUTH (HEWITT). b Yakima Wash 19 Ja 09. 4: Edwin EwellHamilton. 5: UWash 26-30 BS in LS; Columbia 55-57 MLS. 7: Libn Walla Walla High Sch, Walla Walla Wash 31-33; City libn Puyallup Pub Lib, Puyallup Wash 33-37; Bkmob libn Hawaii Co Lib, Hilo Hawaii 38-39; Reg br libn Lib Assn of Portland, Portland Ore 39-46; Head child serv & asst libn Seattle Pub Lib 46-56; Asst & Assoc Prof Grad Lib Sch Pratt Inst 56-65; Assoc Prof Grad Lib Sch URI 65-69; Lib spec, Wash State Lib 69-. 12: Gen chm Consul Wkshop; NE State Lib Ext Agencies, U RI 69. 14: Admin, personnel, child serv, pub libs. 15: Wash State Lib, Olympic Wa 9501.

HAMLIN, ARTHUR TENNEY. b Haverill Mass 8 F 13. 4: Pauline Randolph. 5: Harvard 30-34 (Lat, Ital Lit) AB, 36-37 (Govt); Columbia 38-39 BS in LS. 6: Fr, Ital, Lat. 7: Order asst Harvard Col Lib 34-36, Curator of Poetry 36-38; Ref asst NY Pub Lib 39-40; Asst-at-Large UPenn Lib 40-42; Research analyst Off of Naval Intelligence, Wash DC 42-45; Asst libn UPenn 45-49; Exec sec Assn of Col & Ref Libns, Chicago 49-56; U Libn & Prof of Bibliog UCincinnati 56-68; Dir of libs & Prof Temple U 68-. 8: Conducted lib surveys for Army War Col (52), Park College (56) Nebraska Wesleyan (58); Fullbright ecturer to U of Pavia (Italy) 962); Consul on lib problems to various institutions; Fulbright Research Scholar Birmingham (England) 66-67; ALA Rep to floodedItalian libs 66. 9: ALA (Coun 58-62, 64-68; chm Lippincott Award Com 63-64);-ACRL (chm Grants Com 56-58, 64-66; chm Com on Coms 58-59);-ASD (chm Spec Projs Com 59-60);-LAD (chm Bldg & Equip Sect 57-58, chm Personnel Sect Res Com 63-66); OhioLA (Exec Bd 63-67, chm Developments Com 64-65, v-pres & pres-elect 65-66); Ohio Col Assn (pres Libs Sect 60-61); BSA; PennLA. 10: Grolier Club (NY); Philobiblion (Phila); Queen City Assn; Harvard Clubs ofChicago & Philadelphia; AAUP. 11: Citation from Ital Govt for serv to flooded libs. 12: "Harvard in Cincinnati, a Century of Civic Service" (69). 13: Yes. 14: European libnship, role of libs in independent study, pub serv. 15: 2612 St Davids lane, Ardmore Pa 19002.

HAMLIN, OMER JR. b Tollesboro Ky 16 Jl 30. 4: Evon Thompson. 5: Milligan Col 52-56 (Religion) AB; Col of the Bible 57-58; Morehead State Col summer 58; UKy 58-60 MS in LS. 6: Gk, Ger. 7: Head Libn Milligan Col 59-62; UKy Med Lib: Ser libn 62, Ref cir libn 62, Asst med libn 63, Act med libn 63, Med libn 63-69, Dir of Med Ctr Lib & Communication Systs 69-. 8: Act Dir of U Libs UKy 65; Act dir Communications & Serv UKy 68-69; Governor's Planning Com on Libs67-; Chm Exec Com LSCA Title III 67-; v-chm Exec Com KOM Regl Med Prog 68-. 9: MedLA (Gift & Exch Com, pres So Reg Gp 65-66; chm Dental Lib Gp); KYLA (chmSpec Lib Sect 65; v-pres & pres-elect 67, pres 68); SELA; Lexington LA; ALA. 10: Coun Med TV. 11: KyLA Outstanding Spec Libn 65. 13: Yes. 14: Admin. 15: 3405 Westridge Circle, Lexington Ky 40502.

HAMM, G PAUL. b Fort Smith Ark 11 F 30. 4: Joyce Ann Hopper. 5: Westark Jr Col 48-49; Ouachita BaptistU 53-56 (Psych) BA; Golden Gate Baptist Theol Sem 56-60 BD, 61-63 (Old Testament) ThM; UCal 68-69 MLS. 6: Fr, Ger. 7: Mailer Fort Smith Times-Record & Arkansas Gazette, Ft Smith & Little Rock Ark 44-53; Pastor; Acorn Baptist Church, Acorn Ark 54-56, First Baptist Church, Galt Cal 57-59, Burlingame Southern Baptist Church, Burlingame Cal 59-61, First Baptist Church, Vacaville Cal 61-67, First Baptist Church, Rancho Cordova Cal 67-68; Libn Golden Gate Baptist Theol Sem, Mill Valley Cal 68-. 9: ATheolLA. 14: Info sci. 15: Golden Gate Baptist Theol Sem Seminary dr, Mill Valley Ca 94941.

HAMMAN, FRANCES. b Hartford Kan 6 D 12. 5: Col of Emporia 29-33 (Eng) AB; Kan State Tchrs Col 33-34 (Eng) MS; UMich(Ann Arbor) 37-38 (LS) ABLS. 7: Instr Eng & Lat Clifton High Sch, Clifton Kan 36-37; Jr catlg libn UMich Arbor) 38-40; Head catlg dept Kan State Thrs Tchrs (Emporia) 40-44; Catlgr Microfilm Mss Proj UMich(Ann Arbor) 44-48; Catlg libn UMich Lib (Ann Arbor) 48-57, Head searching & printed card sect 57-63, Head ser& documents sec acquis dept 63-68, Asst hd descr catlg 68-. 9: ALA; MichLA. 10: AAUW. 13. Yes. 14: Catlg & acquis. 15: 1211 Gardmer, Ann Arbor Mich 48104.

HAMMARGREN, BETTY LOU CECELIA. b Minn 17 D 26. 5: Col of St Catherine 44-48 (LS) BS; UNotre Dame (Notre Dame nd) 51-52 (Russian). 6: Fr. 7: Catlgr USanta Clara 48-50; Catlgr UNotre Dame (Notre Dame Ind) 50-53; Catlgr Ramsey Co Lib, St Paul 53; Exec Sec Golden Rule Dept Store, St Paul 54; Ref dept asst Minneapolis Pub Lib 54-55, Asst in brs 55-58, Catlgr 58-. 8: Active in parish lib wk 57-; set up lib at Cathedral in St Paul & 10-15 other parish libs. 9: CathLA (chm Parish Lib Sect Minn-Dakota Unit 58-62), Parish & Lending Lib Sect; v-chm 66-67, chm 67-68); ALA; MinnLA; Church &SynagLA. 13: Yes. 14: Catlg. 15: 231 Dayton ave, St Paul Mn 55102.

HAMMEL, LANA RAE (SCHAAL). b Lancaster Wis 20 S 41. 4: Lawrence A Hammel. 5: Wis State u 9platteville) 59-63 (Secondary Educ) BS; UWis summers 63-66 (LS) MA. 6: Sp. 7: Libn & tchr: Waupun Sr High Sch, Waupun Wis 63-65, Darlington High Sch, Darlington Wis 65-66, East Allamakee Commun Sch, Lansing Iowa 66-. 9: ALA; AASchL; IowaStateEA; IowaASchL. 14: Sch libs, jr col libs. 15: Box 322, Lansing Ia 52151.

HAMMELL, DOROTHY B(ARNES). b Brooklyn NY 17 Je 05. 5: Adelphi Col 30 (Eng Lit) BA; Columbia 34 (LS) BS; NYU 45 (Higher Educ) MA. 6: Gk, Lat, Fr, Ger. 7: Ref & circ libn NY Pu Lib 30-36; Asst libn & catlgr Adelphi Col 36-37; Ref & circ libn Brooklyn Col 38-46; Head Educ Lib USoCal 47-48; Ref & bibliog research US Dept of State, Wash DC 48-49; Ref libn Smith Col 49-52; Chief ref libn Providence Pub Lib 52-56; Asst libn Scarsdale Pub Lib, Scarsdale NY 56-60; Dir Mt Kisco Pub Lib, Mount Kisco ny 60-. 8: Train class instr ref course, Providence Pub Lib 52-56. 9: ALA; NY State LA; Westchester LA. 10: Bedford Hills Woman's Club. 13: Yes. 14: Ref, catlg, admin. 15: 16 Dakin ave, Mount Kisco NY 10549.

HAMMER, CAROLYN READING. b Versailles Ky 19 Jl 11. 5: Transylvania Col 28-32 (Hist, Eng) AB; Columbia 32-33 (LS) BS. 6: Fr, Ger. 7: Catlgr LC 33-34; Libn & tchr Stuart Robinson Sch, Back K 34-37; Ref libn Lib Ext Div Ky State Lib, Frankfort Ky 37-40; Acquisdept asst UKY Lib (Lexington) 40-43, Acquis dept head 43-65, Bibliogr 65-68, Curator rare bks, 68-; Lecturer UKy Sch of Lib Sci 67-. 8: Conduct sem for UKy Lib Spec Colls, Dept in calligraphy & hand-press printing, 10: Owner (Publisher & Printer 12: "Two Color Initial Letters" (66). 14: Rare bks, cartography, typography. 15: U Ky Lib, Lexington Ky 40506.

HAMMER, DONALD P. b Pottsville Penn 16 D 21. 4: Louise K Hammer. 5: Kutztown State Col 44-48 (LS, Hist) BS in Ed; Peabody Col 55 MLS. 6: Ger. 7: USAF 42-44; Asst libn & catlgr Gettysburg Col Lib 48-50; Gifts & exchange libn Penn State Lib, Harrisburg 50-55, Law libn 55; Bkstack libn UIll Lib (Urbana) 55-58; Hd ser unit PurdueU Libs (Lafayette) 59-65,ST DEVEL #'. 8: Amer Soc for Testing & Materials spec com on numerical ref data CODEN subcom 67-; USA Standards Inst com Z39 on standardization in field of lib wk, documentation & related publishing practices 68-; Ind Adv Coun, Lib Serv & Construction Ac Title III 68-; Com on Inst Coop, Lib System Analysts Subcom 69-. 9: ALA-RTSD (Bk Catlgs Com 64-71; Ser Sect; Policy & Research Com 64-69, chm 6 &67; Exec Com 68-71); -ISAD (Lib Syst Standards Com 69-71); ASIS (Com on Lib Automation); Ohio Valley Gp Tech Serv Libns. 10: Beta Phi Mu. 13: Yes. 14: Lib automation, mechanized info retr n 47906. 15: RR9, W Lafayette In 47906.

HAMMOND, CHARLES ROBERT. b Table Grove Ill 7 N 15. 4: Jean J. 5: UCLA 38 (Astronomy) AB. 6: Ger, Sp. 7: Asst libn Lockheed Aircraft Corp, Burbank Cal 40; Chief libn Vega Aircraft Corp, Burbank Cal 40-42; Chief of Lib Div Naval Ordnance Lab, WASH DC 42-46; 47- & mgr off serv Emhart Corp, Bloomfield Conn 46-;Faculty mem UHartford 52-. 8: Central Navy Indexing Panel 45; Spec Lecturer of Astron St Joseph Col (West Hartford Conn) 62, 64. 9: SLA; Brit Astron Soc; Royal Astron Soc Meteoritical Soc; Greater Hartford Astron Soc; Central ConnAmateur Astron Soc; Astron Soc of Pacific; Astron Soc Can. others. 10: Torch Club; Bd trustees Child Mus of Hartford; Talcott Mt Sci Ctr. 13: Yes. 14: Ref, sci & tech. 15: 17 Greystone rd, West Hartford Conn 06107.

HAMMOND, ELIZABETH LOUISE. b Somerville Mass. 5: Millesville 49 BS in Ed; UPenn 53 MS in Ed; Columbia summer 49 (Educ),summer 60 (LS). 6: Fr. 7: (1st Lt) ANC, Middle East, West Pacific 41-46; Asst libn Beaver Col 49-60, Head libn 60-66; Catlgr in charge reclsf Mt Holyoke Col Lib 66-. 9: ALA. 10: Alpha Beta Alpha; AAUW; AAUP. 15: 110 Amherst rd, S Hadley Ma 01075.

HAMMOND, GEORGE P. b Hutchison Minn 19 S 1896. 4: Carrie Nelson. 5: UCal 20 (Hist) BA, 21 (Hist) MA, 24 (Hist) PhD. 6: Sp, Danish, Ger. 7: Instr UND 23-25; Asst Prof UAriz 25-27; Assoc Prof USoCal 27-35; Dean of Grad Sch & Prof of hist UNM 35-46; Dir of the Bancroft Lib & Prof of hist UCal(Berkeley) 46-65. 8: Fulbright Prof, UMadrid Spain, 61-67. 9: AHA; Cal Hist Soc; SoCal Hist Soc; West Hist Assn; etc. 11: LLD UN, 54; LLD UCal (Berkeley) 66. 12: Numerous pblications. 13: Yes. 15: 810 Contra Costa ave, Berkeley Cal 94707.

HAMMOND, HAROLD A. b Boston 8 My 27. 5: Harvard 45-49 (Hist) AB; Simmons 49-50 (LS) MS. 6: Sp. 7: Sr asst Rochester Pub Lib, Rochester NY 50-56; Clsfr Boston Pub Lib 57-63; Sr subj catlgr Yale U Lib 63-67; Catlgr U Bridgeport Lib 67-. 14: Clsf, ref. 15: Taunton Hill rd, Newtown Ct 06470.

HAMMOND, HARRIETE (CHAPMAN). b Macon Ga 29 Ja 19. 4: Allen Williams Hammond. 5: UAla 36-37; Randolph Macon 37-38; Mercer U 38-40 (Eng) AB; Emory 40-41 AB in Lib Sc. 6: Fr, Sp. 7: Child libn Washington Mem Lib, Macon Ga 41-44; Asst child libn Birmingham Pub Lib, Birmingham ALA 44-45; Asst circ libn Washington Mem Lib, Macon Ga 45-46; -v libn & interlib loan libn Brunswik Pub Lib, Brunswick Ga 61-. 9: ALA; SELA; GaLA; GaEA. 15: 104 Asbury st, St Simons Island Ga 31522.

HAMMOND, HARVEY. b Holden Mass 31 Ja 32. 5: Boston U 50-51 (Hist); Ohio State U 55-59 Philos) BA; USoCal 59-60 MSLS. 7: USAF (Airman 1st class) Armament tech 51-55; Ref libn Long Beach Pub Lib, Long Beach Cal 60-64; Ref libn The Rand Corp, Santa Monica Cal 64-66; Br Lib Hughes Aircraft space syst div, El Segundo Cal 66-68; Hd PhysicsLib UCLA 68-. 8: Lib consul, Phys Scis, UWyo. 9: ALA; SLA; CalLA; LARC; ASIS. 10: AAUP. 14: Admin, scis. 15: 21924 Badeau ave, Torrance Cal.

HAMMOND, JANE L. b Nashua Iowa. 5: UDubuque 45-50 (Eng) BA; Columbia 50-52 (LS) MS; Villanova U 58-64 JD. 7: Libn I NY Pub Lib 50-52; Catlgr Harvard Law Lib 52-54; Asst libn Law Lib Villanova U 54-62, Libn 62-. 8: Admitted to practice of Law in Penn. 9: ALA; SLA; AALL (sec 65-; chm Com on Exch of Dups 61-64); Phila Area Tech Serv Libns (pres 60-61). 10: PEO. 13: Yes. 14: Law libs (admin, acquis, catlg). 15: Law Lib Garey Hall, Villanova U, Villanova Penn 19085.

HAMMOND, KATHERINE ANN. b W Palm Beach Fla 1 Ag 36. 5: Rollins Col 54-58 (Eng) AB; Fla State U 58-60 (LS) MA. 6: Ger. 7: Circ asst UFla Libs 60-61; Head libn Maitland Pub Lib, Maitland Fla 61-65; Ref & a-v libn Polk Jr Col 65-68, Hd libn 68-. 9: SELA; FlaLA. 12: "Basic Materials for Florida Junior College Libraries (62). 14: Ref. 15: 448 Seymour ave, Winter Park Fla 32789.

HAMMOND, MARY (WARD). b Peoria Ill 28 My 44. 4: Robert Kempson Hammond. 5: Earlham col 62-64; UMich 64-66 (Elem Educ) BA, 66-67 AMLS. 7: Libn III-A lib ext serv UMich 67; Libn Adrian Pub Schs, Adrian Mich 68; Dir Lenawee Co Lib, Adrian Mich 68-. 9: ALA; MichLA. 10: AAUW; Pi Lambda Theta; Phi Kappa Phi. 13: Yes. 14: Admin of small pub libs. 15: 128 S Charles apt 18, Adrian Mi 49221.

HAMMOND, RICHARD ROLFE. b Spokane Wash 11 My 28. 4: Marjory K Mason. 5: U of Puget Sound 47-51 Music Educ) Mus B, BE; UWash 53-55 (LS) ML. 7: (Pfc) clerical USMC 46-47; 2d Lt) Supply off USMC 51-53; Catlg typist UWash Lib 53-55; Libn Madison Jr High Sch, Seattle 55-60; Libn Chief Sealth High Sch, Seattle 60-. 8: Visiting lecturer UWash Lib Sch summers 55-; Lecturer Seattle Pacific Col Dept of Libnship, Seattle 65; State Reading List Com 66-68. 9: ALA; NEA; AALS; WashLA; Wash State Sch Lib Assn; Wash EA; Amer Fed Tchrs; Wash Fed Tchrs. 10: Mens Garden Club of Seattle; Seattle Begonia Soc; Seattle Saint Paulia Soc. 14: Sch libnship, catlg, lib educ. 15: Rte 1 Box 241, Burton Wa 98013.

HAMOR, W CLARK. b Kalispell Mont 6 N 35. 4: Mary Lou Pitt. 5: UMont 53-58 (Music, Educ) BA in Educ; East Mich U 65 (Speech; UMich 60-66 MALS. 6: Fr. 7: Music tchr Corvallis (Mont) Pub Schs 57; Catlg asst Lib Mont State U 58-60; Elem sch libn Livonia Pub Schs, Livonia Mich 60-66; USAR (supply sgt) 58-64; Catlgr Salem Pub Schs, Salem Ore 66-67; LibnBend Ore; Kenwood Elem Sch 67-68, Cascade Jr High Sch 68-. 8: Visiting consul Child Catlg 65-; Taught ext courses UOre Sch Libnship 66-. 9: NEA; ALA-AASchL (Prof Status & Growth Com 65-); OreEA; OreASchL; Ore InstrMaterials Assn. 10: Friends of Livonia Pub Lib. 14: Story-telling, child lit, sch libs. 15: 723 Innes lane, Bend Or 97701.

HAMPTON, CLARA (HECK). b Charlettesville Va 10 Jl 12. 4: James William Hampton. 5: Vassar 29-33 (Zool) AB; UCal 33-34 (LS) Certif. 6: Ger. 7: Lib asst UCal Med Lib (San Francisco) 39-43; WAVE (Ensign) Med Lib Nat Naval Med Center, Bethesda Md 44-46; Ref asst Army Med Lib, Wash DC 46-48; Circ & ref libn UCal Med Lib (San Francisco) 48-51; Army libn US Army (European Command), Germany 51-53; Bkmob libn Kanawha County Pub Lib, Charleston WVa 61-63, Br libn St Albans Br, St Albans WVa 63-. 9: ALA; WVaLA. 10: AAUW. 14: Circ, wk with child. 15: Seneca Circle Shawnee Estates, Winfield WV 25213.

HAMPTON, JANET (COREY). b Providence RI 17 Ja 21. 4: Morton W Hampton. 5: Conn Col 39-43 (Econ) AB; URI 64-66 MLS. 7: Merchandise asst Gladdings Inc, Providence RI 44-46, Copywriter 46-51; Lib sci libn URI (Providence) 65-68; Supv processing ctr Dept of State Lib Serv, Providence RI 69-. 9: RILA (corr sec 68-69). 14: Lib educ, tech processes. 15: 49 Pleasant st, Rumford RI 02916.

HAMPTON, ROBERT LEE. b Ft Scott Kan 3 S 37. 5: Iola Jr Col 55-57; UKan 57-58; Kan State Tchrs Col (Emporia) 58-59 (Eng) BA; UDenver 59-60 (LS) MA; Chicago 64-65 (LS). 6: Ger. 7: Asst catlgr William Allen White Lib Kan State Tchrs Col (Emporia) 60-62, Head Acquis dept 63-64, Head acquis dept & asst libn 65-66, Act dir 66-67, Dir 67-. 8: Assoc Prof Dept of Libnship Kan State Tchrs Col (Emporia) 60-. 9: ALA; NEA; Amer Assn Higher Educ; KanLA (sec 64-66, Pub Bd chm 66-, chmW A White Child Bk Award 66-). 12: "Higher Education, a Bibliography" (67); "India; an Analytical Subject Bibliography" (68). 14: Tech processes, admin. 15: 1219 Merchant apt 3-D Emporia Kan 66801.

HAMRICK, DEANE ROBERSON. b Candler NC 18 N 17. 4: William Holmes Hamrick. 5: West carU 36-40 (Eng) BS; Appalachian StateU 62-64 (LS) Certif; UNC summer 67 (Av) Certif. 7: Tchr-Buncombe Co Bd of Educ, Asheville NC;Tchr-Dade Co Bd of Educ, Miami Fla; Tchr-libn Buncombe Co Bd of Ed, Asheville NC 60- tchr-libn Buncombe Co Bd of Ed, Asheville NC 60-67; Av specialist Charlotte Mecklenburg bd of Educ, Charlotte NC 67-68, Instr Media Coord 68-. 8: UChicago (Child Welfare: Scholarship League) Reading Wkshop 56; NDEA Media Inst. 9: NEA; ALA; AAUW; SELA; So Libns; CTA; NCHSLA; SEast Libns; NC Libns; NC Dept of A-V Educ. 10: AAUW; Bus & Prof Womens Club; Democratic Women; BuncombeLA; Alpha Delta Kappa; Alpha Phi Sigma. 14: Resource & research in media secondary sch & jr col levels. 15: 1210 F Green Oaks lane, Charlotte NC 28205.

HAMRICK, LILLIAN (ALINE). b Birmingham Ala 21 S 10. 5: UChattanooga 29-35 (Eng) BA; Peabody 38-43 (LS) BS; George Washington U 45-55 (Modern Langs, Sci). 6: Sp, Fr. 7: Tchr elem & high sch Dade & Walker Cos, Ga 28-33; Tchr Chattanooga & Hamilton Co, Tenn 36-41; High sch libn, Chattanooga Tenn 41-43; Catlgr UPittsburgh Lib 43-44; Asst libn West State Psychiatric Hosp, Pittsburgh 44-45; Lib asst Union Catalog LC 45; LC: Ref libn 45-48, Ed 48-50, Ref libn Tech Info DIV 50-52, Head Ref Sect Tech Info Div 52-56, Asst Chief Tech Info Div 56-57, Chief Tech Info Div 57-58; Chief Tech Info Div Off of Tech Serv US Dept of Com, Wash DC 58-64; Chief Document Analysis & Ref Br Clearinghouse for Fed Sci & Tech Info, Springfield Va 64-66, Chief Atmospheric Scis Lib Environment SciServs Admin US Dept of Com 67-. 8: Consul, Wash DC Chap SLA 60-. 9: SLA (Chm Biol Scis Div 57-58; pres Wash DC Chap 64-65). 10: AAAS; Wash Hist of Sci Club; Bus & Profess Women's Club. 12: Ed, "A Guide to the Microfilm Collection of Early State Records". 13: Yes. 14: Org, admin, info center, ref. 15: 3119 Quesada st NW, Wash DC 20015.

HANAFI, BETTY (WINFRED ELIZABETH). b N Rhodesia 14 Ap 36. 5: UBC (Eng, Relig); QueensU (Eng, Relig) BA; CarletonU (Ottawa) (Eng, Relig); UToronto BLS. 6: Fr, Ger, Sp. 7: Acad Spec & Govt Libs, Ottawa Can 56-61; Admin asst to com sec Embassy of UAR, Ottawa Can 61-65; Tech off ref & union catlg div Nat Lib of Can, Ottawa 65-67; Libn Sch of Bus Algonqion Col 67-69; Dir of lib resources St Lawrence Col 69-. 9: ALA; CanLA; OntLA. 10: Can Fed of Univ Women. 14: Admin. 15: St Lawrence Col, Kingston Ont Can.

HANBURY, PAUL (J E). b Can 24 My 43. 5: UOttawa 60-65 (Chem) BSc, 65-67 (Chem) MSc; UBC 68-69 BLS. 6: Fr. 7: Chem Food & Drug Directorate, Ottawa Can 67-68. 13: Yes. 14: Sci ref. 15: 220 Nelson st, Ottawa Ont Can.

HANCE, (MARY) ELIZABETH. b Pasadena Cal 1 My 06. 5: Olivet Col 24-28 (Eng) AB; UMich summer 40, 41, 44 ABLS. 6: Fr, Ger. 7: Catlg, period, order, ref Mich State Lib 36-48; Asst libn SD State Col 48-52; Act libn & Assoc libn Albion Col 52-. 9: ALA; MichLA. 10: Bus & Prof Womens Club; AAUW; Pi Beta Phi; Delta Kappa Gamma. 14: Acquis, ref. 15: 711 1/2 E Michigan, Albion Mi 40224.

HANCHEY, MARGUERITE M. b Merryville La. 4: Richard Howard Hanchey. 5: Northwestern State Col 32 (Eng, Lat) BA; LSU 40 BS in LS, 61 (Geog, Anthropology) MA. 7: LSU(Baton Rouge): Art Libn 40, Geol libn 41-43, Order libn 44, Ref libn, then head of ser 45-46, Agric-biol libn 48-58, Assoc libn & head of sci div 58-. 9: Assn Amer Geog; ALA; Geosci Info Soc; LaLA; SLA. 10: Phi Kappa Phi; Phi Lambda Pi. 14: Sci, ref, bibliog, info retrieval, acquis. 15: 911 Magnolia Woods dr, Baton Rouge La 70808.

HANCOCK, EVA W. b Leland La. 4: Elve A Hancock. 5: Dunbar Jr Col 31-33 LI; Howard U 47-53 (Hist) BA; Catholic U 53-60 MS in LS. 6: Fr, P. 7: Lib asst US Nat Lib of Agric, Wash DC 46-51; Lib asst US Dept of Health Educ & Welfare Lib Wash DC 51-58, Ref libn 58-59, Head of circ interlib loan & stack maintenance unit 59-62, Ref libn 62-65; Ref libn DC Tchrs Col Lib 65-. 8: Law Libn detailed to Health Educ & Welfare Law Lib & performed ref serv in the field of law & legis ref. 9: Law Libns Soc Wash DC. 10: Howard U Womens Club; Howard U Alumni Assn; Cath U Alumni Assn. 12: Comp "Legislative History, P L 89-791 (H R 16958) DC Pub Educ Act 1966" (66);"Legislative History, P L 90-354 (S 1999) To Amend the DC Pub Educ Act1968" (69). 14: Ref (gen & legal). 15: 429 Kenyon st NW, Wash DC 20010.

HANCOCK, MILDRED (REED). b Houston Tex 16 Ag 26. 5: UHouston summer 44; Sam Houston state Col 44-45, 45-46, 58-60 (LS) BS; E Tex StateU summers 66, 67, 68 MS in LS. 7: Libn-reading tchr Dayton Ind Sch Distr, Dayton Tex 60-61; Libn Levelland Ind Sch Dist, Levelland Tex 61-67; Libn (gifts & exchange) Stephen F Austin State Col, Nacogdoches Tex 67-. 9: TexLA. 10: Wesleyan Serv Guild. 14: Bk selection. 15: 224 King, Macogdoches Tx 75961.

HANCOCK, MRS MARGARET (ANN). b Houston 25 Ja 14. 5: UArk 31-33 (Eng); Lamar State Col 56-57 (Eng) BA; Tex Womans U 57-58 MLS. 6: Sp. 7: Ref libn Southwest Tex State Col 58-60; Ref libn & Asst Prof of Lib Sci Okla Col for Women 60-64; Ref libn Tex Col of Arts & Ind 64-. 9: ALA; TexLA; SWLA; Tex Assn of Col Tchrs. 10: AAUW; Chi Omega; Womans Club; DAR. 14: Ref. 15: 728 Santa Anita, Kingsville Tx 78363.

HANCOCK, PHYLLIS (LINES). b Pima Ariz 27 O 08. 5: Gila Jr Col 25-27; UAriz 27-29 (Eng) BA; Los Angeles State Col 55-59; Brigham Young U 63-64 (LS); Ariz State U 64-67. 7: Tchr Pima Jr High Sch, Pima Ariz 29-30; Sub tchr Glendale Jr High Schs, Glendale Cal 55-60; Dist libn Deer Valley Sch Dist No 97, Phoenix 64-. 9: ALA; AEA; Ariz State LA. 10: Alpha Beta Alpha. 12: Co-auth "Out of the Years". 15: 1547 W Mission lane, Phoenix Az 85021.

HAND, CATHERINE ELSIE F(AUST). b Reading Penn 5 Je 27. 4: Thomas Spencer Hand. 5: Ursinus Col 45-49 (Hist, Soc Sci) AB; Penn State U summer 50; Drexel 52-53 MS in LS. 6: Ger. 7: Tchr Upper Dublin Jr High Sch, Ft Washington Penn 49-52; Libn Upper Darby Jr High Sch, Upper Darby Penn 53-57; Libn Upper Merion Sr High Sch, King of Prussia Penn 58-. 9: ALA-AASchL-DLCYP; NEA; PennEA; PennLA; PennSchLA; Sch Libns Phila & Vicin (pres); Chester-Montgomery Co SchLA (past pres). 10: Drexel Lib Sch Alumni Assn; Plays & Players; Lib Assocs of Haverford Col; Friends of Haverford Twp Lib. 13: Yes. 14: Sch libs. 15: 2836 Haverford rd, Ardmore Pa 19003.

HAND, JANE FOLEY. b Syracuse NY 8 Ja 16. 4: Dudley S Hand. 5: Syracuse 33-37 (Fr) AB; Middlebury Col summer 38 (Fr); Syracuse 62-65 MSLS. 6: Fr. 7: Sec admissions Wells Col 43-46; Libn So Cayuga Central Sch, Aurora NY 62-. 9: NYLA; NY State Tchrs Assn; NEA. 10: Beta Phi Mu; Amer Field Serv. 14: Ref, read adv. 15: 938 Indian Field rd, Genoa NY 13071.

HAND, MARY ELIZABETH. b Great Falls Mont 22 F 15. 5: State Col (Lock Haven Penn) 34-38 (Secondary Educ) BS in Ed; Carnegie 49-50 MLS. 6: Fr. 7: Asst libn Ross Lib, Lock Haven Penn 42-43; Columbus Pub Lib, Columbus Ohio; Asst libn 43-49, Br libn 50-55, Vice libn circ 55-. 9: ALA; Franklin Co (Ohio) LA (pres 56). 10: German Village Soc; Pilot Club. 14: Adult educ. 15: 205 E Berger, Columbus Ohio 43206.

HAND, T(HOMAS) SPENCER. b Phila 10 Ap 27. 4: Catherine Elsie Faust. 5: Haverford Col 45-49 (Pol Sci) AB; UPenn 50-51 (Pol Sci) MA; Drexel 52-53 MS in LS; UPenn 65- (Internat Rel). 6: Sp, Fr, Ital. 7: Researcher Friends Com on Nat Legis, Wash DC 51-52; Asst libn Ursinus Col 53-59; Libn-in-chg of tech processes Penn Mil Col 59-67; Liberal arts libn PMC Cols 67-. 9: ALA-ACRL (Phila Area Chap). 10: AAUP; Drexel Lib Sch Alumni Assn; Haverford Club; Penn Pol Sci & Pub Admin Assn; Plays & Players; Lib Assocs of Haverford Col; Friends of Haverford Twp Lib. 12: Ed of Penn Mil Col "Faculty Bulletin (62-64);Ed Drexel Sch of Lib Sci Alum "Newsletter (68-). 13: Yes. 14: Catlg, rare bks, soc sci, hist, lit. 15: 2836 Haverford rd, Ardmore Penn 19003.

HANDELMAN, ADELAINE (SACHAR). b NYC 6 O 18. 4: Fred Jay Handelman. 5: Hunter Col 35-39 (Biol) BA; Columbia 39-40 (Educ) MA, 62-63 MLS. 6: Fr, Ger, Lat. 7: Statistician Bur of the Census, Wash DC 40-42; Biol Food Research Labs, NYC 42-43; Interior decorator self-employed, NYC 45-61; Libn Bd of Educ, Yonkers NY 63-. 9: NYLA; WestchesterLA. 10: Beta Phi Mu. 14: Data processing for sch libs. 15: 30 Hickory Hill rd, Eastchester NY 10709.

HANDELSMAN, WENDY (HAMMER). b NYC 15 F 45. 4: Lawrence Haldelsman. 5: URochester 62-66 (Psych) BA; Simmons 66-67 (LS) MS. 6: Fr, Sp. 7: Ser catlgr SyracuseU Lib 67-. 14: Ser. 15: 5860 Thompson rd, Syracuse NY 13214.

HANDLEY, LAURA (COATS). b Albion Ind 28 Ja 07. 4: Claude O Handley. 5: Earlham Col 33 (Hist, Eng) AB; UMich 48 ABLS. 7: Clerical & bkkeeper Richmond Fireproof Door Co, Richmond Ind 36-46; Morrison-Reeves Lib, Richmond Ind Clerical asst 46-48, Catlgr 48-. 9: ALA; IndLA; Ohio Valley Reg Group of Tech Serv Libns. 10: AAUW. 14: Catlg. 15: 408 SW 3rd st, Richmond In 47374.

HANDY, MRS CATHERINE (HICKEY). b Holyoke Mass 10 My 32. 5: UMass 49-53 (Foreign Lang) BA; Springfield Col summer 54 (Guidance, Psych); Central Conn State Col summer 62 (Hist), So Conn State Col 62-65 MS in LS. 6: Fr. 7: Tchr New Salem Acad, New Salem Mass 53-54; Tchr Longmeadow Jr High Sch, Longmeadow Mass 54-56; Sch libn Wilson Jr High Sch, Windsor Conn; Sch libn Sage Park Jr High Sch, Windsor Conn 69-. 9: ALA; ConnEA; ConnSchLA; WindsorEA. 10: Windsor Sch-Lib Coun. 14: Sch libs, materials ctrs. 15: 63 Preston st, Windsor Conn 06095.

HANDZO, DORIS CAROLYN (KREUCHAUFF). b North Bergen NJ 4 F 19. 4: George Handzo. 5: Montclair State Col 35-39 (Eng) BA; Rutgers 63-65 MLS. 6: Ger. 7: Serv rep NJ Bell, Union City NJ 40-46; Libn Colts Neck Bd of Educ, Colts Neck NJ 63-65; Libn Monmouth Co Lib, Freehold NJ 65-. 9: ALA; NJLA; MonmouthLA. 10: Colts Neck Hist assn; NJ Hist Assn; Amer Assn State & Loc Hist, geneal. 15: Box 36 RR 1, Colts Neck NJ 07722.

HANEL, NAJWA L (NABTI). b Lebanon 1 Ap 40. 4: Robert J Hanel. 5: Middle East Col (Beirut Leb) 54-59 (Educ) BA; Pacific Union Col 61-62 (Sec Sci & Bus) BS; USoCal 62-64 msls. 6: Arabic, Fr. 7: Sec & asst libn Middle E Col (Beirut Lebanon) 59-61; Admin asst to Dean Sch Dentistry Loma LindaU 62-63; Hd libn (Dir of Lib Serv) USoCal Sch dentistry 64-. 8: Consul Hollywood Presby Hosp Lib, Los Angeles 67; Dir seminar on Lib Serv for Dentists, San Diego 69. 9: MedLA; Med Lib Group So Cal (chm Memb Com; Program Com); Amer Assn Dental Schs. 10: Sch of Dentistry Lib Com (USoCal); Phi delta Gamma. 13: Yes. 14: Ref, pub serv in med lib, admin & supv in med lib. 15: USC School of Dentistry 925 W 34th st, Los Angeles Ca 90007.

HANES, FRED WILLIAM. b Vandlia Ill 21 Ag 20. 4: Betty Louise Haines. 5: Earlham Col 38-42 (Eng) AB; Wittenberg Col 46-47 (Eng); Ind U 49-51 (LS) MA. 7: Army Air Force US, European Theater 43-45; Eng tchr Nevis High Sch, Nevis Minn 47-49; Asst ref libn & asst circ libn Ind U Lib 51-58; Bibliog Modern Lang Assn 57-58; (On leave from Ind U to serve MLA in preparation of publication, "American Literary Manuscripts"); Dir of libs & chm dept of lib sci Ind State U 58-67; Col libn Humboldt State Col 67-68; Dir of libs & Prof of Lib Sci Ind State U (Terre Haute) 68-. 8: Served with Agency for Internat Development 61-63; Developed Lib Facilities & Serv for Inst of Educ & Research Lahore W Pakistan; Prof of Lib Sci U of the Punjab, Lahore W Pakistan. 9: ALA; IndLA. 10: AAUP. 13: Yes. 14: Admin, ref. 15: 1212 Elizabeth lane, Terre Haute In 47802.

HANEY, PATRICIA DEE. b Miami Beach Fla 22 S 39. 5: No Ill U 57-61 (En) BA; UIll 61-62 MSLS; Northwestern U summer 64 (Eng). 7: Grad asst Grad Sch of Lib Sci Ill(Urbana) summer 62; Asst libn E Leyden High Sch, Franklin Park Ill 62-. 9: ALA; Amer Fed of Tchrs; IllLA; High Sch Libns of Chicagoland(Rec sec 68-69). 10: Beta Phi Mu. 14: High sch libnship. 15: 2824 Rose st, Franklin Park Ill 60131.

HANKINS, FRANK (DALE). b Harlingen Tex 1 Mr 22. 4: Margaret Bragg. 5: UTex 49 (Journalism) BJ, 51 MLS. 6: Sp, Ital. 7: US Army (S/Sgt) Med Corps 42-46; Libn Montavilla Br Lib Assn of Portland Ore 51-52; Libn Parsons Pub Lib, Parsons Kan 52-55; Asst libn Wichita Pub Lib, Wichita Kan 55-58; Libn Del Mar Col 58-. 9: ALA; MPLA; SWLA; KanLA(chm Intel Freedom Com); TexLA(pres-elect 65-66, Pres 66-67; Freedom Com);Jr Col -ACRL (Stand & Bibliog Coms). 10: Tex Jr Col Tchrs Assn (chm Libs Sect); Tex State Tchrs Assn; Tex A-V EA. 13: Yes. 14: Ref, bk sel (intel Freedom, admin. 15: 721 Crestview, Corpus Christi Tex 78412.

HANKINSON, FRANCES. b Brooklyn NY 29 Mr 06. 5: Cornell U 23-27 (Eng) BA; Columbia 33-34 BS in LS; NYU summer 34; Middlebury Col summer 39; Tchrs Col summer 45; Inst Allende Mexico 57. 6: Fr. 7: Inf & ref asst Newark Pub Lib, Newark NJ 27-33; Sch wk asst NY Pub Lib St George Br, SI NY 34-36; Lib asst NYC Bd of Educ McKee Voc & Tech High Sch 36-49, Tchr of Lib 49-. 8: Voc High Sch Standing Com on Libs (chm) 43-46; Lib Com SI Tchrs Assn (chm) 41-43. 9: ALA(Life mem); NYLA; NY Sch LA(sec 41-42, v-pres 60-61, Prof & Nom coms). 10: Delta Kappa Gamma; Womens Nat Bk Assn; NY Lib Club; SI Hist Soc; SI Inst; St Cecilia (Music); SI Museum; Cornell Club of SI. 13: Yes. 14: Ref, wk with yp. 15: 101 Daniel Low terrace apt 4-J, SI NY 10301.

HANKS, (DOROTHY MOSS) MRS JOHN BLAKE. b Texarkana Tex 12 Ja 13. 4: John Blake Hanks. 5: Centenary Col 30-33 (Relig Educ) BA; UNC 33-34 BS in LS; UChicago 44 (LS); LSU 63 (LS); Northwestern State Col 64- (Eng, Educ). 6: Lat, Fr, Ger. 7: Libn Centenary Col (La) 34-36; Dir of Lib Shreve Mem Lib, Shreveport La 36-38; Period UChicago (Chicago La) 44; Med libn VA Hosp, Shreveport La 50-51; Sch libn Byrd High Sch, shreveport La 54-65; Asst Prof Lib Sci Northwestern State Col (Natchitoches La) 65-. 8: Consul elem sch lib program, Caddo Parish La summer 66-67; Instr Pub Lib Training-Proj, Rapides Parish La spring 69. 9: ALA; LaLA; LaEA. 10: Delta Kappa Gamma; Alpha Xi Delta; Alpha Beta Alpha. 13: Yes. 14: Sch libnship. 15: PO Box 4292 450 Albany ave, Shreveport La 71104.

HANLEY, MS JEAN KURTYKA. b Fleetwood Penn 10 My 32. 4: James Hanley. 5: Kutztown State Col 50-54 (LS) BS in Ed. 6: Polish. 7: Asst libn Central Bucks Joint Schs, Doylestown Penn 54-55; Libn & tchr Fleetwood Joint Schs, Fleetwood Penn 56-58; Sub tchr Oley Valley Area Schs 58-64; Asst libn Kutztown State Col 64-66; Libn Exeter Tmp Jr High Sch 66-. 9: PennLA; Berk Co Sch Libns (pres 68-69); Sch dir Oley Valley Area Schs, Oley Penn. 10: AAUW. 14: Sch lib, order wk, instr materias center in col lib. 15: RD 3, Fleetwood Pa 19522.

HANLEY, MARY (CAROLYN) DUKE. b HENRY Ill 8 Ja 22. 4: John Thomas Hanley. 5: Kalamazoo Col 40-44 (Eng) AB; UIll 58-62 MS LS. 6: Fr, Sp, Ital. 7: Non-Prof lib asst child dept Kalamazoo Pub Lib 44-45; UIll Lib(Urbana); Clerk circ dept 58-59, Info spec div Engnr Dept 62-63, Ser asst 59-63; Libn catlg dept UMinn(Minneapolis) 63-65, Hd sci catlg dept 65-. 9: ALA; SLA (Minn Chap: Memb & Recr Chm 65-66); ASIS; MinnLA; Twin Cities Catlgrs Round Table. 13: Yes. 14: Catlg, lib mechanization, interlib coop. 15: 5705 Lawndale lane, Hamel Mn 55340.

HANLEY, MARY L. b Concord Mass 23 Ap 18. 5: Simmons 36-39, 46-47 (LS) BS. 7: Ser catlgr Harvard U 47-68, Chief ser catlgr 68-. 9: . 14: Catlg. 15: Harvard Col Lib, Cambridge Mass 02138.

HANLIN, SARA LOUISE. b Birmingham Ala 30 Ag 12. 5: Birmingham-Southern Col 30-33 (Romance Lang) AB (cum laude); UNC 33-34 AB in LS. 7: Birmingham Pub Lib, Birmingham Ala; Asst br libn 33, 34-35, Br libn 35-40; Dist supv of lib projs WPA, Mobile Ala 40; Asst proj tech WPA, Montgomery Ala 40-41; Libn Naval Air Station, Pensacola Fla 41-42; Libn Naval Air Tech Train Center, Memphis Tenn 42-45; Catlgr & ref libn Pub Lib, Mishawaka Ind 45-46; Head libn Woodsfield Pub Lib, Woodsfield Ohio 46-47; Reg libn U T Jr Col, Martin Tenn 47-49; Main post libn Ft Benning Ga 49; Tech libn Charleston Naval Shipyard, Charleston SC 49-50; Libn Memphis Acad of Arts, Memphis Tenn 50-51; Med libn Methodist Hosp, Memphis Tenn 51-53; Med libn VA Center, Dayton Ohio 53-55; Libn gen & med units US Naval Hosp, Memphis Tenn 55-. 9: ALA; MedLA. 10: Phi Sigma Iota. 14: Admin. 15: 6951 Eighth rd, Memphis Tenn 38128.

HANLIN, FRANK SAMUEL. b Fonda Iowa 24 Mr 24. 4: Eunice Fritz. 5: Cornell Col 42-43, 46-49 (Eng) BA; UIowa 49-50 (Eng) MA; UMich 52-53 (Eng Lang), 53 AMLS. 7: Admin supv US Army 43-46; Research asst Linguistic Atlas of Upper Midwest, Iowa 50; Personnel supv US Army 50-51; Tchg fellow Dept of Eng U Mich 52-53; Asst circ libn UNC Lib (Chapel Hill) 53-55; Asst acquis libn UIowa Lib 55-57, Head acquis dept 57-. 66, Bibliog 66-. 9: ALA-ACRL;-RTSD; BSA; IowaLA(chm Tech Serv Sect 61). 12: Asst ed "Books at Iowa. 13: Yes. 14: Acquis, rare bks. 15: 1425 Laurel st, Iowa City Iowa 52240.

HANNA, ALFREDA (CHRISTINE) HUHNKE. b New Rockford ND 28 Ap 32. 4: Gordon L Hanna. 5: Bethany Nazarene Col 50-52, 54-55 (Eng) BA; UOkla 59-60 (LS) MA. 6: Ger. 7: Tchr Putnam City Pub Schs, Okla City Okla 55-59; Ref circ libn Bethany Nazarene Col 60; Catlg libn Post Lib, White Sands Missile Range NM 61; Admin libn Post Lib Wm Beaumont Gen Hosp, El Paso Tex 61-64; Asst libn CARI Lib Fed Aviation Agency, Okla City Okla 64, Med admin libn 65-66; Sers & Sc ref libn Bethany Nazarene Col 66-. 8: Period indexer subj heading comp Nazarene Publishing House 60-61. 9: ALA; SLA; ColoLA. 10: Beta Phi Mu. 11: Grace E Herrick Award in Lib Sci. 14: Acquis, admin. 15: 6509 NW 31, Bethany Okla 73101.

HANNA, ALICE M. b Maryville Mo 19 S 16. 5: Northwest Mo State Col 34-38 (Educ & Eng) bs in Ed; UIll 40-41 BS in LS. 6: Fr. 7: Head circ Pub Lib, Quincy Ill 41-43; Ref libn Mo State Lib 43-46; Head sch dept Kern County, Bakersfield Cal 46-49; County Libn Siskiyou County, Yreka Cal 49-53; High sch libn Klamath County, Klamath Falls Ore 53-54; County Libn Kings County, Hanford Cal 55-. 9: ALA; IllLA; MoLA; OreLA; CalLA(pres Yosemite Dist 60-61). 10: Bus & Prof Womens Club; AAUW; Soroptimist Club. 14: Bk sel, ref. 15: 1508 N Green, Hanford Ca 93230.

HANNA, ARCHIBALD Jr. b Worcester Mass 24 S 16. 4: Edith Sue Mensch. 5: Clark U 34-39 (Eng) AB; Yale 41-42, 46-48, 51 (Hist) MA, PhD; Columbia 48-49 (LS) MS. 6: Fr, Ger, Sp. 7: Lang Off USMC Reserve (now Col) 42-; Sr catlgr Yale U Lib 49-52, Curator Yale Collection of Western Americana 52-. 9: BSA; West Hist Assn; Amer Antiquar Soc. 10: Grolier Club (NYC). 12: John Buchan: a Bibliography (54). 13: Yes. 14: Rare bks. 15: Yale U Lib, New Haven Ct 06520.

HANNA, MARY ANN (JONES). b Greencastle Ind 8 Ag 20. 4: Albert KENNETH Hanna. 5: DePauw U 38-42 (Eng Lit) AB; UIll 43-44 BS in LS; West Mich U 63-69 MLS. 7: Ref asst John Adams High Sch, Cleveland 44-45; Asst libn Lincoln High Sch, Cleveland 45-46; Libn Clarkston High Sch, Clarkston Ga 51-54; Ref libn Birmingham Pub Lib, Birmingham Ala 54; Libn Trussville High Sch, Trussville Ala 55-57; Asst libn West End High Sch, Birmingham Ala 57-58; Libn UAla Ext Center (Birmingham) 58-60; Sch lib consul Mich State Lib 60-.08: Lib 21 Seattle Worlds Fair 62; Staff mem NDEA Media Inst Mich State U 65; Hd sch Lib Consul Mich Dept of Educ Bur Lib Serv 66-. 9: ALA; AASchL; MichLA MichASchL; Mich A-V Assn; ich Assn Supv & Curric Development; NEA-DAVI. 10: PEO; Kappa Alpha Theta. 13: Yes. 14: Sch libs, media spec. 15: 323 N Walnut, Lansing Mi 48933.

HANNA, MRS EDNA FRANCES (HARTMANN). b Springfield Ill 6 Jl 08. 5: UIll 30-31, 50-51, 53 (Eng Lit) BA, 60-61 MLS. 6: Fr. 7: Ill State Lib:, Libn I child 46-48, Libn II ref 48-55, Libn III head phono record unit 55-60; Libn IV libn No Ill Reg Lib, DeKalb Ill 61-63; Dir N Bay Cooperative Lib System, Santa Rosa Cal 63-. 9: ALA; AEAUSA; CalLA (v-pres & pres-elect, Pub Libs Div 69-70); ALECC. 10: AAUW; Zonta Internat; Pi Beta Phi Alumnae Club; Beta Phi Mu. 13: Yes. 14: Lib systems, ref. 15: 1600 Yulupa ave apt 32, Santa Rosa Ca 95405.

HANNA, RUTH E. b N Vernon Ind 20 O 13. 5: Hanover Col 36-39 (Lat, Fr, Eng) AB; Ball State Tchrs Col summer 40 (Eng, LS); McCoy Col Johns-Hopkins U even 42 (Writing); Catholic U 60-61 MSLS. 6: Fr. 7: Tchr of En, Lat, Fr Scipio Hgh Sch, Scipio Ind 39-41; Change order writerPProd Dept Martin Aircraft, Baltimore 42-43; Tchr of Lat, Eng, Hist Girls Latin Sch, Baltimore 44-46; Prod planner make-up planner Waverly ress, Baltimore 46-59; Asst acquis libn Health Sci Lib UMd 60-67, Ref libn Health Sci Lib 68-. 8: Pub rel for health sci 68-. 9: ALA-RSD(Md Chap) SLA(Baltimore Chap treas 66); MedLA. 10: Wilderness Soc; Bus & Prof Womens Group (Church); AAUW; Mountain Club of Md; Appalachian Trail Conf; Choir Roland Park Presbyt Church (18 yrs); Church libn; Deacon 64-67. 12: A History of The Williams & Wilkins Company, Publishers of Books and Periodicals in Medicine and the Allied Sciences, published in installments in "The Kalends House Organ of the W & W Co 61-64. 14: Acquis, ref, catlg, soc wk collection. 15: Health Science Lib U Md 111 South Greene st, Baltimore Md 21201.

HANNAH, HELEN (KATHLEEN). b Camrose 30 S 16. 4: M Russell Hannah. 5: U Alberta 34-37 (Fr) BA; Toronto 37-38 BLS. 6: Fr. 7: Circ asst UAlta 3843; Supv Bank of Can, Ottawa 43-44; Lib asst Nat Museum of Can, Ottawa 45; Lib asst elec engnr dept MIT 46; Catlgr C W Post Col, Brookville LI NY 54-, Hd Union Catlg 68-. 14: Catlg. 15: The Glen, Locust Valley NY 11560.

HANNAH, MONA M(ARIE) (HERZIGER). b Appleton Wis 29 D 22. 4: David Hardgrave Hannah. 5: Marquette 44 (Eng) BA; UWis (Milwaukee) 47 (LS); UTex (Austin) 60 MLS. 6: Lat. 7: Advertising copywriter Pharmaceutical Co, Milwaukee 46-47; Libn Milwaukee Pub Schs 47-58; Organized lib Texas State Dept Health, Austin Tex 58-59; Recatalogued Durango pub Lib, Duranco Colo 61; Libn Harpers Ferry Job Corps NPS, Harpers Ferry W Va 66; Libn Middletown Elem Sch, Middletown Md 66-. 9: ALA; NEA; MdLA; MdEA. 10: AAUW. 14: Sch media ctrs. 15: 916 Hollywood, Dallas Tex 75208.

HANNAH, NORMA (RATHBUN). b Reedsburge Wis 29 My 09. 4: Leslie J Hannah. 5: UWis 28-32 (LS) BA; West Res 34-36 MA; Columbia 39 (Educ). 6: Fr. 7: Child libn, Rochester NY 36-37; HeadLibn Wheaton Pub Lib, Wheaton Ill 37-41; Libn Willimantic Tchrs Col (Conn) 41-43; Head of child wk New Rochelle Pub Lib, New Rochelle NY 43-47; Coordinator of wk with youth Milwaukee Pub Lib 47-61; Dist Libn Kentfield Sch Dist, Kentfield Cal 61-. 8: Follett Award Consul 55-58; Consul: Our Wonderful World 58-59 (Spencer Press); Childrens Hour 58-59 (Spencer Press); Dir of child radio & TV progams for pub libs, Milwaukee 50-61; Lecturer in chld lit, Marquette U 49-60. 9: ALA(Radio Com 50)-CSD; WiLA; CalSchLA. 10: Zonta; Delta Kappa Gamma. 11: Awards for radio & TV Programs 58, 59, 60, 61. 13: Yes. 14: Wk with child in pub libs & schs. 15: 105 Pixhey ave, Corte Madera Ca 94925.

HANNIBALL, AUGUST. b Jersey City NJ 24 S 22. 4: Alice Marilyn Bolinder. 5: Rutgers 40-42 (Geol); UMd 58-61 (night) (educ); UDenver 65 (Soc Sci) BA, 65-66 (Libnship) MA. 6: Ger. 7: Air Force pilot 44-54; War Plans off 54-62; Field Maint off 68th FMS, Lake Charles La 62-63; Intelligence off 98th Bomb Wg, Lincoln Neb 63-65; Ref libn Cadet Lib, USAF Acad 67-. 9: ALA; MtPlainsLA; ColoLA. 10: Bd of Govrs Eng-Speaking Union, Colo Springs; Air Acad Jr High Sch PTO; Retired Offs Assn; Colo Mt Club; Egypt exploration Soc. 11: Air Medal, WWII. 14: Admin, ref. 15: 904 Shrider rd, Colorado Springs Co 80907.

HANNIGAN, MARGARET C(ATHERINE). b Austin Minn 27 Ja 08. 5: St Catherine Col 25-29 (Math) BA, 45-46 BS in LS. 7: Tchr-libn Pub Sch, Foley Minn 29-41; Supv WPA Co Lib Dem, New Ulm Minn 41-43; (Maj) USMC Womens Res, Camp Lejune NC 43-46; Asst chief UVA Br Off, Ft Snelling Minn 46-49; Assoc Prof St Catherine Col 47-49; Chief Libn VA Hosp, Northport NY 49-53; Asst Prof Marywood Col 53-53; Libn Patients Lib NIH, Bethesda Md 54-62; Sr lib supv adult serv, lib ext div NY State Lib 62-67; Coord LSCA-IV DivLib Prog, USOE67-. 9: ALA (past off 57-59, Coun 62-66);-AHIL (pres 56-57);-ASD (chm Spec Proj Com 62-64; Bd 62-66); AEAUSA; Amer Corr Assn. 10: Adirondack Mountain Club. 13: Yes. 14: Adult serv, hosp & instn libs. 15: 527 Delaware ave, Delmar NY 12054.

HANNON, MRS (E) KATHRYN McCALL. b Green County Ohio 10 Mr 18. 5: Ohio State U 56 (Bus Educ) BS; Peabody 64 (LS) MA. 6: Sp. 7: Tchr Hamden High Sch, Hamden Ohio 44-47; Tch-libn Zaleski Sc, Zaleski Ohio 47-65; Libn admin Grove City Pub Lib, Grove City Ohio 65-68; Lib admin Grandview Heights Pub Lib, Grandview Heights Ohio 68-. 9: ALA; OhioLA; FranklinCoLA. 10: Franklin Co (Ohio) Libns Coun; Quota Club. 14: Ref, admin. 15 3250 Tamara dr, Grove City Oio 43123.

HANSARD, JAMES WILLIAM. b Charleston Ark 2 My 36. 4: Ruth Bishop. 5: Ft Smith Jr Col 54-56; State Col of Ark 56-58 (Hsit) BSE; LSU 65-66 (LS) MS. 7: Tchr & libn Corning high Sch, Corning Ark 58-60; Libn Memphis U Sch 60-64; Acquis libn Ark State U 64-65, Asst lib dir & chm of lib sci div 64-. 9: ALA; ArkLA (v-pres); NEArkLA. 14: Acquis, admin. 15: Box 273, State Univ Ar 72467.

HANSBERRY, VERDA R(OMAYNE) (GUENZI). b Sterling Colo 19 Ag 19. 4: Orvus L Hansberry. 5: UDenver 35-38 (LS) AB. 7: Br asst Denver Pub Lib 38-42; Co Libn Big Horn Co Lib, Basin Wyo 42-44; Hosp libn Denver Pub Lib 45; Ext libn King Co Publ Lib, Seattle 46-47; Libn Seattle Pub Lib 55-57, bkmob Libn 58-65, Hd Circ Servs 66-. 9: ALA; ColoLA; WyoLA; WashLA; PNLA. 10: Bus & Prof Womens Club. 14: Lib ext, circ. 15: 5603 30th ave SW, Seattle Wa 98126.

HANSELL, RUTH ERIE. b Avon Park Fla 22 F 21. 5: Mercer U 44-47 (Soc Sci) AB; Fla State U 63-64 (LS) MS. 7: Legal sec, Hollywood Fla 38-42; Sec Port Everglades, Ft Lauderdale Fla 42-44; Tchr Baxley High Sch, Baxley Ga 47-48; Tchr Douglas High Sch, Douglasville Ga 48-49; Sec Clearview Window Corp, Ft Lauderdale Fla 49-51; Church sec First Baptist Church, Delray Beach Fla 51-63; Asst libn Indian River Jr Col 64-. 9: ALA; FlaEA; FlaLA (sec Tech Serv RT 69-70); SELA. 10: AAUW; Beta Phi Mu; AAUP. 14: Catlg, ref, acquis. 15: 112 1/2B N 12th st, Ft Pierce Fl 33450.

HANSEN, ALBERTA (PYMM). b Suffern NY 2 O 31. 4: Donald Otto Hansen. 5: NY State Col for Tchrs (Albany) 49-53 SL; Syracuse summers 56-58, 63, 64 MSLS. 7: Child libn

Enoch Pratt Free Lib, Baltimore 53-55; Org elem libs Bedford Central Sch Dist, Mount Kisco NY 55-57; Org elem libs Ramapo Central Sch Dist, Spring Valley NY 57-59; Catlgr Missionary Orientation Center, Stony Point NY 61-62; Prof libn of Inst Resource Center, Spring Valley NY 63-; Elem sch libn Ramapo Central Sch Dist, Spring Valley NY 64-. 9: ALA; NEA; NYStateLA; NY State Tchrs Asn. 10: Church Orgs; Beta Phi Mu. 14: Catlg, child, spec libs. 15: West Maint st, Stony Point NY 10980.

HANSEN, ALICE ELIZABETH (McBRIDE). b Pittsburgh 6 Je 1898. 5: Vassar 15-19 (Hist, Psych) AB; Columbia 19-20 (LS); Harvard 31 (Educ, Hist) Ed M. 6: Ger, Fr. 7: Catlgr Columbia U 20-22; Period asst NY Pub Lib 22-24; Tchr-libn Norwin Union High Sch, Irwin Penn 25-27; Libn Munhall High Sch, Munhall Penn 27-28; Libn Slippery Rock State Tchrs Col 28-42; Libn Chatham Col 42-51; Order libn Rollins Col 51-52, Head Libn52-. 9: ALA; SLA; PennLA(sec 44); FlaLA; SELA. 10: Pi Gamma Mu; Sigma Tau Delta; Central Fla Vassar Club; Harvard Club of Central Fla; Zonta Club. 15: 1531 Lasbury ave, Winter Park Fla 32789.

HANSEN, ANDREW M. b Storm Lake Iowa 25 Mr 29. 4: Rina Rennie Smith. 5: UOmaha 4751 (Math) BA; UMd (overseas) 55; UMinn 5556, 62 (LS) MA; UIowa 68. 7: S/Sgt USAF 5155; Tchg asst Lib Sch UMinn 5556; Libn Pub Lib, Bismarck N Dak 5763; Libn Pub Lib, Sioux City Iowa 6367; Visiting Asst Prof Ind State U summer 66; Instr Sch of Lib Sci UIowa 67. 8: Consul Charles City (Iowa) Pub Lib 6869. 9: ALA; Adult Educ Assn; NDakLA (pres 59; sectreas 6263); IowaLA (pres 6768). 10: ACLU; AAUP. 14: Pub lib admin, ref, adult serv, educ for libnship. 15: 3310 Shamrock dr, Iowa City Ia 52240.

HANSEN, DOROTHY (ELIZABETH) (HAYS). b Danville Ill 2 Je 28. 4: Robert C Hansen. 5: UIll 46-50 (Eng) AB; 51-54 MLS. 7: Tchr & libn Morrisonville High Sch, Morrisonville Ill 50-51; Dist libn Arcola Commun Unit Sch Dist, Arcole Ill 51-53; Libn Urbana Jr High Sch, Urbana Ill 53-55; Title I project libn Manhattan Beach (Cal) Schs Grandview & Ladera Schs 66-67; Ann Arbor (Mich) Pub Sch elem libn: Allen & Mack Schs 67-68, Allen & Dixboro Schs 68-. 8: Elem sch lib consul Manhattan Beach (Cal) Sch Dist 66-67. 9: NEA; ALA; MichEA; MichASchL; Ann Arbor EA. 10: Phi Beta Kappa; Phi Kappa Phi; Beta Phi Mu. 14: Sch libs. 15: 2040 Welch ct, Ann Arbor Mi 48103.

HANSEN, IRENE M. b Upland Neb 30 S 07. 5: UDenver 38-39 (LS) BA; Colo State Col 39-42 (Educ) MA; UMich 55-56 MALS. 6: Fr, Ger. 7: Grad lib intern Colo State Col 39-42; Asst libn New Trier High Sch, Winnetka Ill 42-47; Libn Wyandotte High Sch, Kan City Kan 48-49; Dept of Libnship Kan State Tchrs Col (Emporia): Asst Prof 47-57, Assoc Prof 57-65, Prof 65-, Prof of Lib Servs & Assoc libn 69-. 8: Visiting instr UDenver Lib Sch, summers 60, 63. 9: ALA; KanLA; MPLA. 10: AAUW; Beta Phi Mu; Kappa Delta Pi; Pi Lambda Theta; PEO. 14: Catlg, ref, lit (soc sci). 15: 1738 Old Manor rd, Emporia Ks 66801.

HANSEN, JOANNE. b Arcadia Mich 13 Mr 33. 5: East Mich U 51-55 (Music Educ) B Mus Ed; West Res 59, 62, MSLS; East Mich U 58-63 (Geog) MA; UMich 61 (Music). 7: Tch-libn Huron Valley Schs, Milford Mich 5759, Tchr 60-62; Tchr Centro Colombo Americano, Cucuta Columbia 64-65; Sci & Tech libn East Mich U 65-. 9: SLA; Assn of Amer Geog; Mu Phi Epsilon. 10: Washtenaw Lib Club. 14: Maps, geog. 15: 714 Atlantic, Milford Mich 48042.

HANSEN, LOIS N. b Boise Ida 24 D 20. 5: UIdaho 38-42; USoCal 44-45 BS; ULondon (England) summer 59. 7: Supv US Army Libs in Cal, Utah, Phillippines, Okinawa, Korea 45-48; Libn Boise (Idaho) High Sch 48-50; Supv US Army Libs in Germany & France 51-54; Asst libn & catlgr Boise Jr Col 54-62; Instr lib sci Col of Idaho summers 55-60; Libn USAF Hosp & Air Base, Wiesbaden Germany 62-65; Adult serv coord Phoenix Pub Lib 65-68; Acquis libn Glendale Commun Col (Maricopa Co Jr Col Dist) 68-. 9: ALA; ArizStateLA. 10: AAUP. 14: Acquis. 15: 3026 N 40th st apt 8, Phoenix Az 85018.

HANSEN, MARY JEANNE KEIGER. b Hobart Okla 6 K 22. 5: Willam & Mary 41-45 (LS) AB; UOla 62 MLS. 6: Sp, Fr, Ger. 7: Asst order libn Mich State Col (East Lansing) 45-46; Army libn Camp Hakata Japan 46-47; Asst ref libn Okla City Libs, Okla City Okla48; Asst libn Fairmont State Col, Fairmont WVa 48-50; Libn Okla Hist Soc, Okla City Okla 50-51; Documents libn Okla City Lis, Okla City Okla 53-62; Head tech serv div Okla City Libs, Okla City Okla 62-66; Libn AFLC Maintenance Tech Off, Tinker AFB 66-. 9: ALA; Sec Staff Orgs Round Table 60-65; SAA; SLA (treas Okla Chap 69-). 10: Okla Hist Soc; Okla Geneal Soc; Lincoln Co Hist Soc; Nat Hall of Fame for Famous Amer Indians; Nat Geneal Soc; Nat Cowboy Hall of Fame; Civil War Round TABLE OF Okla City; Womens Dinner Club. 14: Tech servs, ref, loc hist & geneal. 15: 2315 NW 22nd st Oklahoma City Ok 73107.

HANSEN, MARY LOUISE (COX). b Arcadia Tex 2 My 32. 5: UHouston 50-54, 59- (Hist, Pol Sci, Educ) BS; Claremont Grad 54 (Hist); UTex 60-61 (LS); Sam Houston State 61-62 (LS). 6: Fr. 7: Clk-cashier-asst bkkeeper 3 Sisters Clothing Store, Houston Tex 51-54; Sec Dept Phila & Relig UHouston 53-54, Grader Pol Sci Dept 51-54; Sr ref clerk UHouston Lib 56-59; Tchr-libn St Peter's Parochial Sch, Houston Tex 59-61; Itinerant libn Houston Independent Sch dist 61-. 8: Adv St Benedicts Jr High Sch Lib 68-. 9: ALA; NEA; TexStateTA; TexClrTA; TexLA; HoustonTA (fac rep 61-63, 64-65, 67-68; del to state convention 65, de& to NEA convention 68). 10: Houston Lib Club; Houston ASchL; PTA; St Benedicts Womens Club; Kappa Delta Pi; Phi Kappa Pi. 14: Child lit, elem sch. 15: 15311 Vandalia way, Houston Tx 77045.

HANSEN, ODA (BALI). b Hurley SD 30 My 21. 4: Ralph John Hansen Jr. 5: UOre 41-44 (Eng) AB; UMich 44-46 ABLS, 47-51 AMLS. 6: Fr, Ger. 7: Lib asst UOre 41-44; Jr libn UMich 44-46; Libn I Enoch Pratt Free Lib, Baltimore; Libn I UMich 47-51; Libn I Wash State Col 51-55; Libn I to asst libn Lawrence Radiation Lab, Berkeley Cal 57-67; Lecturer Sch of Libnship UCal spring & summer 68; Libn Amer Express Investment Mgt Co, San Francisco Calif 68-. 9: SLA. 14: Catlg, rare bks, spec libs. 15: 1582 Euclid ave, Berkeley Ca 94708.

HANSEN, ORVAL J. b Delta Utah 16 S 20. 4: Ruth Gummersall. 5: Idaho State Col 46-51 (Hist) BA; UOre 51-53 (Hist, Eng) MS; UWash 64-68 MLS. 7: US Coast Guard 42-45; Union Pacific RR 46-51; Tchr & libn Port Orford High Sch, Ore 53-55; Libn Redmond Union High Sch, Ore 55-56; Hd high Sch, Ore 55-56; Hd libn Central Ore Col 56-64; Hd libn Green River Col 64-. 8: Pacific NW v-pres Col Assn for Pub Events & Serv. 9: NEA; AAUP; WashLA; PNLA; WashEA. 15: 32409 46th pl S, Auburn Wa 98002.

HANSEN, PHYLLIS JEAN. b Ames Iowa 28 N 34. 5: UIll 56-60 (Hist) AB, 61 (LS) MS. 6: Fr, Sp. 7: Stud asst UIll(Urbana) 59-61; Libn Queens Borough Pub Lib, NYC 61; Libn ref San Leandro Commun Lib Center, San Leandro Cal 62-63; Libn II ref Cal State Polytech Col (San Luis Obispo) 63-66, Libn II Catlg 66-. 9: ALA; CalLA. 10: AAUW; Altrusa Internat. 14: Ref, catlg. 15: 1241 Fredericks st, San Luis Obispo Ca 93401.

HANSEN, RALPH W. b NYC 14 My 27. 4: Lillian Strong Hansen. 5: Brigham Young U 47-51 (Hist)AB, 51-52, summer 53 (Hist) Hist, 54 Harvard-Radcliffe Archival Inst summer 56; UOre 59-60; UCal (Berkeley) Sch of Libnship summer 67, 68. 6: Ger. 7: US Army Med Corp 45-47; Tchr Alpine Sch Dist, Orem Utah 52-53; Asst ref libn Brigham Young U 53-56, U archivist & mss libn 56-62; Research assoc Ore Collection UOre 59-60; Curator Stanford Collection & Mss libn Stanford U 62-65, U Archivist & Mss Libn 65-67, Chief libn Acquis Div Univ Archivist 67-. 8: Palo Alto City Historian 63-67; Cal Heritage Preservation Commsn 63-. 9: ASA; West Hist Assn. 11: Summer scholar, Harvard Grad Sh of Bus 62. 13: Yes. 14: Acquis, archives, mss. 15: 975 Wing place, Stanford Ca 94305.

HANSON, AGNES O(LIN). b Northfield Minn 1 Mr 05. 5: St Olaf Col 23-27 (Hist) BA; UWis 27-28 9ls0 certif; Columbia summer 33 (LS); UMich 36-38, summer 40 MA in LS, Case-West Res U (Internatl Bus Development Program) 68. 6: Fr, Ger, Sp, Scandinavian, Ital. 7: Catlgr E Chicago (Ind) Pub Lib 28-29; Sr Rev asst Lib Sch UWis(Madison) 29-30; Recatlgr Peter WHITE Pub Lib, Marquette Mich 30-32, Act libn 32-33; Asst Gen Motors Corp Research Lib, Detroit 34-38; Ref & research asst bus info div Cleveland Pub Lib 38-56, Head libn bus info div 56 Dept 56-. 8: Overseas visitor in com libs, Great BRITAIN 54 Rep SLA at ASLIB Conf, London 54. 9: SLA(sec 53-54, chm var coms; Cleveland Chap pres & chm var coms); ALA; Amer Marktg Assn; Amer Statist Assn; Womens Nat Bk Assn; OhioLA. 10: Cleveland Museum of Art; Friends of the Cleveland Symphony Orchestra; AAUW; Friends of the Cleveland Play House. 12: Contrib to prof & trade pub; compof Bus Info Sources; Ed "Round Table in Print (Bulletin of Bus Div SLA) (50-51). 13: Yes. 14: Admin, ref & research, biblig in bus field. 15: Bus Info Dept Cleveland Pub Lib, Cleveland Oh 44114.

HANSON, EUGENE R. b Bertrand Neb 4 S 26. 4: Wilma Jean Bunsen. 5: Chadron State Col 49-53 (Hist, Eng) BA; UDenver 57 (LS) MA; UPittsburgh 66-69 (Lib & Info Sci). 7: Libn & Eng Instr Madison Pub Sch, Madison Neb 53-57; Head Libn Southern State Col 57-61; Catlgr Wayne State Col 61-63; Head Libn Minot State Col 64-; Tchg fellow & Grad asst, UPittsburgh 67-68. 9: ALA; MPLA; NDLA; NDEA. ;AALS. 10: AAUP; Nat Rife Assn; Dakota Gun Collectors Assn;Ohio Gun Collectors Assn. 14: Admin (col libs), catlg, tech serv, lib sci educ. 15: Minot State Col Memorial Lib, Minot ND 58701.

HANSON, GEORGE STEINGRIMUR. b Chicago 19 Ap 34. 5: UIll 52-54; Northwestern 54-56 (Eng) BA; Chicago 60-63 LS) MA. 6: Icelandic. 7: Tchr Chicago Bd of Educ 57-61; Tchr US Navy, Iceland 61-62; Staff UChicago Lib 63; Asst lib Chicago City Jr Col Amundsen-Mayfair Br 64-. 9: ALA-ACRL. 10: Icelandic Nat League (Winnipeg); Amer-Scand Found. 13: Yes. 14: Catlg, ref. 15: Amundsen-Mayfair City Col 4626 N Knox, Chicago Il 60630.

HANSON, IRENE. b Milwaukee Wis 15 N 11. 4: Kenneth K Hanson. 5: Marquette 29-30 (Chem) 41-42; UWis (Milwaukee) 30-31. 7: Lib page Milwaukee Pub Lib 31-33, Asst libn 33-43, Hd libn 43-57, Ref libn 57-60; Mus libn Milwaukee Pub Mus 60-. 9: ALA; WisLA; State Hist Soc Wis. 12: Co-comp "Supplement to Bibliography of Museums and Museum Work" (61); Asst ed, "Lore," museum quarterly (63-). 14: Ref. 15: 800 W Wells st, Milwaukee Wi 53233.

HANSON, JANET (AILEEN) LEWIS. b Ft Edward NY 25 Je 28. 4: Herbert F Hanson Jr. 5: SUNY 45-49 (Eng) BA; SUNY (Albany) 49-50 S in LS. 7: Libn Johnsburg Central Sch, N Creek NY 50-53; Libn Hudson Falls Central Sch, Hudson Falls NY 54-. 9: NYLA; NYStateTA; East NY Sch LA. 10: AAUW; PTA. 15: 30 Kelly ave, Hudson Falls NY 12839.

HANSON, JEAN (WARE). b Oak Park Ill 9 N 43. 4: Thomas B Hanson. 5: Denison 61-65 9eng) BA; UWis 66-67 MA in LS. 6: Sp. 7: Sec Knapp Sch libs project Oak Park-River Forest High Sch, Oak Park Ill 65-66; Catlgr Franklin & Marshall Col Lib 67-. 9: ALA; Area Col Lib Coop Prog. 14: Catlg, ref. 15: 807 N President ave, Lancaster Pa 17603.

HANSON, JOHANNA DOWNEY. b Menominee Mich. 4: Harold S Hanson. 5: St Joseph Col Emmitsburg Md) 42-46 (Eng) AB; Catholic U 46-48 BS in LS. 6: Fr. 7: Spec serv libn US Army, Germany 48-49; Libn Amer Lib, Paris 49-50; Young adultasst coordinator Enoch Pratt Free Lib, Baltimore 50-53; Sch libn Baltimore City Md 54-58; Libn Catonsville Jr High Sch, Baltimore County Md 62-65; Asst coordinator child serv Baltimore County Pub Lib 65-, ya spec 68-. 9: ALA; CathLA; MdLA. 12: Ed "Top of the News (69-). 15: Baltimore County Pub Lib Admin Offices 25 W Chesapeake ave,Baltimore Md 21204.

HANSON, MARTHA MASON. b Williamson NY 2 S 27. 4: James Francis Hanson. 5: NY State Col For Tchrs (Albany) 49 (Eng) BA, summers 50-53 (Guidance); SUNY(Genese0 summers & even 58-63 MLS. 6: Sp. 7: Eng tchr Macedon High Sch, Macedon NY 49-51; Eng tchr Palmyra-Macedon Central, Palmyra NY 51-54; Eng tchr Pa-Mac Central Sch Hyde Park Bldg, Palmyra NY 54-60, Libn Jr-Sr High Sch 60-. 8: Summer sch tchr: Eng 4 Monroe High Sch, Rochester NY 56, & libn R L Thomas Jr-Sr High Sch, Webster NY 62. 9: NYLA; NY State Thrs Assn. 10: Adv to: Dramatic Club; Press Club; Stud Coun: Lib Club; Nat Honor Soc; Pub chm for Williamson Coop Nursery 65-66. 14: Child bks, young adults. 15: 123 W Main st, Williamson NY 14589.

HANSON, MARY (COATES). b Hasty Ark 13 D 20. 4: William A Hanson. 5: WashU 37-41 (Liberal Arts) AB; UMich 63-66 MALS. 6: Fr, Sp. 7: Tchr Poplar Bluff High Sch, Poplar Bluff Mo 41-42; Deputy asst censor, translator US Bureau of Censorship, Miami Fla 42-45; Lay reader Ferndale Pub Schs, Ferndale Mich 62; Lib aide child libn Oak Park Pub Lib, Oak Park Mich 63-. 10: Phi Beta Kappa. 14: Ref wk, child wk. 15: 2820 Crooks rd, Royal Oak Mi 48073.

HANSON, MAXINE C (ANDERSON). b Black Hawk Co Iowa 2 Jl 20. 5: Iowa State Tchrs Col 38-40 Elem Educ Tchg Certif; UNo Iowa 60-63 BLS. 7: Elem tchr Alexander (Iowa) Consolidated Schs 40-42; Clk-typist State Col of Iowa 59-60; Child lib hd Pub Lib, Waterloo Iowa 62-68; Catlgr Command & Gen Staff Col Lib, Ft Leavenworth Kan 68-. 10: Altrusa Club. 14: Catlg, ser, child wk. 15: Box 6, Cedar Falls Ia 50613.

HANSON, PAUL STEPHEN. b Pittsburgh Cal 25 Je 43. 5: UCLA 61-67 (Botany) BA, 67-68 MLS. 6: Ger, Lat, Swedish. 7: Intern Biomed Lib UCLA 68-. 14: Ref. 15: 1450 S Barrington apt 3, Los Angeles Ca 90025.

HANSON, PETER P. b Jersey City NJ 11 Ap 33. 4: Elizabeth Bownan. 5: Seton Hall 58-60 (Classical Lang) BA; Rutgers 64-66 MSLS. 6: Ger, Fr, Ital. 7: Lit scientist Colgate-Palmolive Co, Piscataway NJ 62-66; Libn E I Du Pont de Nenours & Co, Parlin NJ 66-. 9: SLA. 10: Beta Phi Mu. 13: Yes. 15: E I DuPont sw Nemours & Co Photo Products Dept, Parlin NJ 08859.

HANSON, ROGER K. b Aneta N Dak 24 N 32. 4: Gretchen Mary Leupp. 5: Mayville State Col 57-61 (Math) BS in Ed; UDenver MALS. 6: Norwegian. 7: Aircraft Mechanic: USN 52-56, NDak Air Nat Guard, Fargo N Dak 56-57; Tchr & libn: Pembina High Sch, Pembina N Dak 61-62, Johnson Co High Sch, Buffalo Wyo 62-63; Order libn UN Dak 63-66, Asst libn 66-67; Asst to dir libs & chief of ref serv UMinn (Minneapolis) 67-69; Dir of libs U N Dak 69-. 8: Lib moving consul for Ray Hamilton Comp on moving Akron Pub Lib March 69. 9: ALA; MinnLA. 14: Tech serv. 15: Chester Fritz Lib Univ of NDak, Grand Forks ND 58201.

HANSSEL, ELIZABETH B (BUCHHOLTZ). b Buffalo NY 5 S 18. 4: John E Hanssel. 5: UBuffalo 35-39 (Hist) BA; SUNY Col (Geneseo) 65-67 (LS) MS. 6: Fr. 7: Exec sec to pres Coop GLF Mills, Buffalo NY 40-41; Libn Benjamin Franklin Jr High, Kenmore NY 67-. 9: ALA; NYStateTA. 14: Wk with students. 15: 65 E Girard blvd, Kenmore NY 14217.

HANSSEN, NANCY E. b NYC 14 F 39. 5: Bry Maw 55-56; Barnard 56-59 (Anthrop) BA; Pratt Inst 62-65 MLS. 6: Fr. 7: Asst catlgr Pratt Inst 65-67, Asst art ref libn 67-. 9: ALA; SLA; NY Lib Club. 10: AAUP; Beta Phi Mu. 14: ref, student orientation. 15: 275 Clinton ave, Brooklyn NY 11205.

HARBESON, ELOISE LINTON. b Lloyd Fla 11 N 24. 4: Kelly Richard Harbeson Jr. 5: Fla State U 41-43, 46-47,56-57 (LS) BS, 57-60 (LS) MS, 67-68. 7: Asst chief clerk US Army Med Supply, Camp Gordon Johnston 43-44; Asst libnSci & Tech Fla State U Lib 57-68; Asst Prof Sch of Lib Sci 68-. 9: FlaLA; ALA; SELA. 10: Fla State U Alumni Assn; AAUP; Beta Phi Mu. 14: Ref, catlg. 15: 2002 W Randolph circle, Tallahassee Fl 32303.

HARBORD, HEATHER (ANNE). b Liverpool England 26 Je 39. 5: Edinburgh U 57-60 (Soc, anthrop, Geog) MA Lib Assoc (of GB) 60-64 ALA; UBC 66-67 BLS. 6: Fr. 7: Geol libn Imperial Col, London Eng 60-63; Br libn Fraser Valley Reg Lib, Chilliwack BC 63-66; Asst libn N Central Sask Reg Lib, Prince Albert Sask 67-68; Chief libn Wheatland Reg Lib, Saskatoon Sask 68-. 9: CanLA (Coun 68-71); SaskLA (v-chm). 10: Univ Womens' Club. 13: Yes. 14: Reg libs. 15: 54 301 3rd ave N, Saskatoon Sak Can.

HARCLERODE, VERONA (LESKO). b Richeyville Penn 8 D 23. 4: Donald Mason Harclerode. 5: State Col (Cal Penn) 42-45 (Biol, Sci, Eng) BS in Ed; UPittsburgh 62-63 MLS;Frostburg State Col 64. 7: Tchr Meyersville High Sch, Meyersdale Penn 45-46; Tchr-libn Hyndman-Londonderry High Sch, Hyndman Penn 46-, Libn 66-. 8: Bedford County Eng Com on Curriculum Revision 63-. 9: NEA (life mem); NCTE; PennStateEA; PennLA (Dept Supv & Curr). 10: Delta Kappa Gamma; United Church of Christ Sunday Sch; Beta Phi Mu, Easter Seal Soc; VFW Aux. 14: Ref, young adult serv. 15: Box 258, Hyndman Penn 15545.

HARD, ELEANOR (KNIGHT). b Milan Mo 13 Je 06. 4: Harry D Hard. 5: La Grange Jr Col 24-26 AA; Northeast Mo State Tchrs Col 30-37 (Eng) BS; Peabody 40 BSLS. 7: Rural elem tchr Sullivan County Mo 22-39; Libn Ft Lewis Col 3944; Asst libn Minot State Tchrs Col 44-45; Ref libn UWYO 45-46 Circ libn Colo State U 46-53, Live Life libn 53-59, Asst ref libn 62-. 9: ALA; MPLA; ColoLA. 10: Delta Kappa Gamma; Bus & Prof Womens Club; Archaeol Club; Rock Club. 14: Ref. 15: Rt 4 Box 160, Ft Collins Colo 80521.

HARD, LYNN R. b Henderson Tex16.Ap 38. 5: Compton Col 55-58 (Eng) AA; Long Beach State Col 58-60 (Eng) BA; USoCal 60-61 (LS) MS. 6: Fr. 7: Ref libn Los Angeles Pub Lib 61-62; (Sp-4) US Army Engnr, Ft Leonard Wood Mo 62; Humanities ref libn Ariz State U62-63; Asst tech libn Burroughs Corp, Pasadena Cal 63-65, Lib manager 65-66; Data proc consul NY State div of lib dev 66-67; Asst dir for reader servs,Brandeis U 67-68, Asst dir for tech servs 68-. 8: Consul to NY State Lib Div of Lib Devel 67-. 9: ACM; ADI; SLA; ALA (mem Telo-Facsimile Com -71). 12: Ed "Abstracts of Computer Literature 65-66. 14: Admin, data proc, telo-facsimile. 15: 130 Bowdoin st apt 1506, Boston Ma 02108.

HARDAWAY, ELLIOTT. b Nashville 1 Ja 13. 4: Sylvia Shaver. 5: Vanderbilt 35, 36 (Math) BA, MA; UIll 38, 40 BS in LS, MS in LS. 7: Assoc dir LSU 53-55; Asst dir UFla 55-57; Dir USFla 57-64, Dean of Instr Serv 65-67, v-pres admin affairs 67-. 9: ALA(Coun 62-66); FlaLA(pres 60-61); SELA. 14: Col & U lib admin. 15: 11337 Oakleaf ave, Tampa Fla 33612.

HARDEE, MRS HELEN (READDICK). b High Point NC 6 Ap 12. 5: High Point Col 34-3; Elon Col 48-50 (Eng) AB; UNC (Chapel Hill) summers summers 53, 54, 56, 57, 59 59 BSLS; ;UNC (Greensboro)summers night 66-67. 7: Tchr Alexander-Wilson Sch, Graham NC 47-48; TchrGibsonville Sch, Gibsonville NC 48-51; Tchr Liberty Drive Sch, Thomasville NC 52-53; Supv of sch libs, Mebane NC 53-55; Libn Chapel Hill Schs, Chapel Hill NC 55-60; Ref libn Elon Col 61-62; Libn Rankin Sch, Greensboro NC 62-65; Ragsdale High Sch, Jamestown Sch, Guiford Tech Inst, Jamestown NC f5-66. 8: Co-ord Lib Sci Prog, Bennett Col, Greensboro NC 68-69; Tchr lib sci (mostly part-time)Guilford Tech Inst 63-69. 14: Pub serv, child, tchg lib sci. 15: 1410 Chestnut dr, High Point NC 27260.

HARDESTY, MRS (EARLE R). b Morgantown WVa 8 D 07. 5: UAkron 26-31 (Sociol) AB; West Res 48 MS in LS. 6: Fr. 7: Asst br libn Akron (Ohio) Pub Lib 33-45; Ref libn & Asst libn Roanoke (Va) Pub Lib 49-53; Ref asst Cleveland Pub Lib Bus Info 53-58; 1st asst Bus & Labor Div Akron (Ohio) Pub Lib 58-64, Head of Bus & Govt Labor Serv 64-. 9: SLA (Bulletin ed Bus & Fin Div 64-65, Div Chm 65-66, Cleveland Chap; pres 56); OhioLA; Amer Marketing Assn; Nat Assn Accountants. 10: College Club of Akron; Soroptimist Club. 14: Ref in field of bus. 15: 901 Cordova ave, Akron Ohio 44320.

HARDIE, BETTY. b Port Credit Ont Can 5 O 16. 5: Victoria Col UToronto 3438 (Hist, Eng) BA; Toronto 38-39 BLS. 7: Libn adult dept Orillia Pub Lib, Orillia Ont 39-42; Libn adult dept Chatham Pub Lib, Chatham Ont 42-44; Libn Kent Co Lib, Chatham Ont 42-44; Br libn Windsor Pub Lib, Windsor Ont 44-46; Libn Essex Co Lib, Windsor Ont 44-46, Chief Libn 46-50; Chief Libn Etobicoke Pub Lib, Etobicoke Ont 50-. 8: Spec Lecturer Sch of Lib Sci UToronto 54-64;Consul lib bldgs, Chatham & Wallaceburg, Ont. 9: ALA; CANLA (mem and/or chm var coms); OntLA (past pres, mem and/or chm var coms); Inst Prof of Ontario. 10: University Womens Club, Zonta Internat, Alumni Rep UToronto Senate 64-68. 13: Yes. 14: Admin. 15: Box 501, Etobicoke Ont Can.

HARDIE, FRANCES H (ISLEY). b Gary Ind 14 Je 26. 4: Robert H Hardie. 5: Rockford Col 44-48 (International Rel) BA; Mt Holyoke Col 48-50 (Russian hist) MA; Vanderbilt 61- (Russian lang & lit); Peabody Lib Sch 66-68 MLS. 6: Russian, Chinese, Fr, Sp. 7: Ed & tr Mapping & Charting Serv Ohio StateU 51-52; Lecturer Russ lang & hist UTenn Nashville Center 58-; Slavic catlgr & bibliogr Jr Univ Lib, Nash utenn Nashville Center 58-; Slavic catlgr & bibliogr Jt Univ Lib, Nashville Tenn 66-. 9: ALA; Tenn Tech Serv Libns. 10: Beta Phi Mu. 11: A Stan Rescoe Award for Catlg 68. 15: Joint Univ Lib, 21st ave S, Nashville Tn 37203.

HARDIN, CLARENCE A JR. b Leesburg Fla 28 Ja 33. 5: Mercer U 51-55 (Hist) AB; Rutgers60-63 MLS. 7: US Army 1st Lt) 55-57): Tchr Griffin High Sch, Griffin Ga 57-61; Libn N Plainfield High Sch, N Plainfield NJ 61-62; Libn Roosevelt Jr High Sch, Westfield NJ 62-66; US Army Libn, Erlangen Germany 66-67; Libn NATO/SHAPE, SHAPE Belgium 67-. 9: ALA; NEA; NJEA; NJSchLA (treas). 10: Westfield Opera Theatre. 14: Sch libs. 15: SHAPE Special Services Recreational Lib, APO NY 09055.

HARDIN, MARY (ALAGOOD). b Gainesville Tex 19 Ja 43. 4: Neal C Hardin. 5: Okla StateU 61-64 (Soc Sci) BA; UOkla 64-66 MLS. 7: Lib consul Okla Dept of Lib, Oklahoma City 66-67, Interlib loan libn 67-. 9: ALA; OklaLA; SWLA. 10: AAUW. 14: Interlib loan. 15: 1707 Charles, Norman Ok 73069.

HARDIN, MINERVA ELIZABETH (KIVETT). b Speedwell Tenn 19 Je 21. 4: David O Hardin. 5: Berea Col 38-42 (Sociol) AB; Peabody 46-47 (Hist) MA, 48-49 BS in LS;Emory summer 53 Med Lib Certification. 7: Tchr Miller Co High Sch, Colquitt Ga 42-43; WAAC and WAC 43-45; Tchr Jefferson Jr High Sch, Oak Ridge Tenn 47-48; Libn E Tenn State Col Train Sch (Johnson City Tenn) 49-53; Libn VA Hosp Mountain Home Tenn 53-66; Catlg asst E Tenn State U Lib 66-. 15: Baileyton rd, Rte 6, Greenville Tn 37743.

HARDIN, NANCY ELIZABETH. b San Antonio Tex 7 Mr 44. 5: UIll (Urbana) 62-66 (Botany) BS, 66-67 (LS) MS. 7: Ref libn Div of Tech Info Ext AEC, Oak Ridge Tenn 69-. 14: Ref. 15: US Atomic Energy Commission PO Box 62 Attn: Ref Serv Section, Oak Ridge Tn 37830.

HARDING, FLORENCE MARIE. b Staunton Ill 1 My 02. 5: UIll 20-24 (Romance Langs) AB, 28-29 (LS) MA. 6: Fr, Sp, Portu. 7: Catlgr UIll(Urbana) 24-26, Libn Modern Lang Lib 27-. 9: ALA; Mod Lang Assn Amer; Inst Internacional de Literatura Iberoamericana. 10: Phi Beta Kappa; Sigma Delta Pi; Pi Delta Phi; Nat Audubon Soc & loc Audubon Club; Mod Lang Assn; Delta Zeta Alumnae Club. 14: Catlg, ref. 15: 425 U Lub UIll, Champaign Il 61820.

HARDING, NELSON FRANK. b Springfield Mass 19 S 24. 4: Lucille Place. 5: American Internat Col 46-50 (Hist) BA; UWis 51-52 (Educ) MS, summers 55-59 (LS) MS; Columbia 67 (Lib Media); UBridgeport 68-69 (A-V). 07: (GM 2/c) US Navy 43-46; Tchr-coach Verona High Sch, Verona Wis 52-56; Sch libn Two Rivers Bd of Educ, Two Rivers Wis 56-59; Sch libn Greenwich Conn 59-65; Head of Lib Serv Norwalk Sch System, Norwalk Conn 65-; Catlgr Perrott Mem Lib, Old Greenwich Conn 60-65; Dir instr sources Norwalk Bd of Educ 67-. 8: State of Conn Title II consul 66-68; NDEA Inst Columbia U 67; New Dimensions in Lib NDEA Media inst Bridgeport U 68-69; Tchr EPDA Inst UBridgeport 69. 9: NEA-DAVI; ConnSchLA; Conn A-V Educ Assn; NESLA; NTA; ALA. 12: Media Happenings editor (Norwalk city publication). 13: Yes. 14: Catlg. 15: 49 Maher dr, Norwalk Ct 06850.

HARDING, THOMAS S(PENCER). b Gaines NY 24 F 10. 5: UBuffalo 29-33 (Hist) BA, 33-36 bsls& uchicago 36-39 (Libnship) MA, 51-53 (Hist) PhD. 6: Fr, Sp. 7: Asst UBuffalo Libs 30-36; Libn Univ Col NorthwesternU 37-42; Yeoman US Naval Res, Stateside & Pacific 42-45; Libn Mo Valley Col 46-48; Libn Evansville Col 48-66; College libn WashburnU of Topeka 66-. 9: ALA; IndLA (chm Col & Univ Libs RT 51); KanLA; Tri-State Libns. 10: AAUP. 13: Yes. 14: Acad lib admin, hist libs, interlib coop. 15: Washburn Univ of Topeka, Topeka Ks 66621.

HARDISTY, A(LICE) PAMELA. b Winnipeg Man Can 1 N 19. 5: UMan 3841 (Eng, Fr) BA; Toronto 46-47, 54 BLS, MLS. 6: Fr. 7: Ref libn Toronto Pub Lib 47-53; Asst to dir ref serv Nat Lib of Can, Ottawa 53-62; Asst libn Lib of Parliament, Ottawa 62-. 9: CanLA (past mem Research Sect, Govt Ref Libns Com, & var others); Inst ofProf Libns (Ont) pres, 65-66. 10: Prof Inst of the Pub Serv of Can; Beta Phi Mu; Zonta Club; Golf Club. 13: Yes. 14: Ref, admin. 15: Lib of Parliament, Ottawa Ont Can.

HARDKOPF, JEWEL C. b Chicago. 5: UWis 35 (LS) AB; Columbia 49 (LS) MS. 7: Asst to chief of memb org ALA 34-37; Libn NY Pub Lib 37-41; Ref libn Cleveland Heights Pub Lib41-45; Asst supt of bk ordering NY Pub Lib 45-49, Supt of bk ordering 49-51; Mgt analyst Brooklyn Pub Lib 51-58; Libn-Mgt consul (free lancing) 58-. 8: Instr at Lib Schs summers in Lib Methods Analysis. 9: ALA; SLA. 10: Soc for the Advancement of Mgt (sec 55-56); Soc of Women Engnrs; Municipal Assn of Management Analysts, NY Processing Centers Operated by Libs. 13: Yes. 14: Mgmt of libs. 15: 4010 Lowell ct, Midland Mi 48640.

HARDY, ANN ABBOTT. b Orange NJ 18 Ap 17. 5: Wooster Col 34-35 (Eng); Simmons 35-38 (Eng, Publishing) BS; URI 66 summer (LS). 6: Fr. 7: Mfg estimator Macmillan Co, NYC 38-44; Sec-bkkeeper Bd of Educ, Summit NJ 44-49; Sec & publicity Monadnock Reg Assn, Peterborough NH 51; Sec-bkkeeper Bd of Educ, Peterborough NH 52-54; Sec to dir Museum of Sci, Boston 54-55; Lib asst & clerk Naval War Col Logistics Lib, Newport RI 55-56, Libn 56-58, Ref libn & Ed (Mahan) 58-. 10: Point Assn of Newport. 12: Ed "Naval War College Library Bulletins and Evaluations". 14: Ref. 15: 4 Training Sta rd, Newport RI 02840.

HARDY, FLOYD. b Pleasant Hill NC 27 Ag 33. 4: Peggy Slaughter. 5: NCar Col 52-56 (Hist) BA; UMich 59-61 MALS. 7: Asst ref libn NY State Lib 61-63; Catlgr Nat Agric Lib, Wash DC 63-66; Sci libn NYU 66-68; Sci bibliogr Rut gers (New Brunswick) 68-. 9: NY Lib Club. 10: Urban League. 14: Sci bibliog & ref. 15: 100 Memorial pkwy, New Brunswick NJ 08901.

HARDY, MRS FRANCES WILLIAMS. b Helena Ark 23 D 26. 5: Millsaps Col 44-47 (Eng) BA; Tex Womans U 56-57 MLS 07: Child libn Dallas Pub Lib, Oak Cliff Br 57-58; Libn Meridan Jr Col 58-. 7: Child libn Dallas Pub Lib, Oak Cliff Br 57-58; Libn Meridan Jr Col 58-, Dir learning resources 68-. 9: MissLA (sec 63-65, pres Sch Lib Sect 61-62); MissLA (pres 69). 10: Delta Kappa Gamma. 15: 5500 Highway 19 N, Meridan Miss 39304.

HARDY, JUDITH (IRENE). b Ottawa Ont Can 21 F 31. 5: Queens U 50-53 (Eng) BA; UToronto 54 BLS. 6: Fr. 7: Soc sci bibliogr YorkU, Toronto 67-. 15: 131 Bloor st W apt 917, Toronto 5 Ont Can.

HARDY, LAURENCE A OFM. b NYC 8 Ja 17. 5: St Bonaventure 39-43 (Phil) BA; Catholic U 43-48 BSLS. 6: Fr. 7: Libn Holy Name Col, Wash DC 46-48; Libn St Joseph's Sem, callicoon NY 48-51; Assoc libn St Bonaventure U 51-63; Libn Siena Col 63-. 9: ALA; -ACRL; CathLA (past chm West NY Unit, past chm Albany Unit); NYLA. 14: Admin, catlg, interlib coop. 15: Siena Col Lib, Loudonville NY 12211.

HARDY, MARGARET (CROOKER). b Hamilton Onr Can22 Mr 26. 4: C DeWitt Hardy. 5: West Res 45-49 (Hist) BA, 58-61 MS in LS. 7: Sec Hist Dept Cleveland Col of West Res 50-52; Research analyst Reg Planning Commsn, Cleveland52; Office asst Glatte & Co, Cleveland 52-53; Sec Minister Old Stone Church (Presbyterian), Cleveland 53-57; Asst to dir Huron Road Hsp Sch of Nursing, Cleveland 57-61; Asst ref libn Worthington Pub Lib Worthington Ohio 62-63; Libn Miam Valley Hosp Mem Med Lib, Dayton Ohio 64-. 8: Member Task Force on Med Libs, Ohio Valley Regl Med Prog; Consul St Elizabeth HospMed Lib (Dayton) 68-; Mem Ed Bd "Union List of Serials in the Libraries in the MiamiValley 68-. 9: SLA (chm Educ Com, Dayton-Columbus Chap 68-69). 10: Univ Women of Wright State Campus. 15: Mem Med Lib Miami Valley Hospital 1 Wyoming st, Dayton Oh 45409.

HARDY, NANCY F. b San Antonio Tex 30 O 41. 5: UMich 62 (Sp & Lat Amer Studies) BA; UMich 66 (LS) MA; MedLA Certif GradeI 68. 6: Sp, Ger. 7: Catlg dept UMich 62-63; Catlg dept UMich Med Lib 63-65; Libn Mercy Sch of Nursing of Detroit 66-67; Asst libn UUtah Med Sci Lib (Salt Lake City) 67-. 9: ALA; MedLA; AAUP; UtahLA (pres-elect 69). 10: Beta Phi Mu; Phi Sigma Iota. 14: Tech serv admin, info retrieval, data proc (electronic). 15: Univ of Utah Med Sci Lib, Salt Lake City Ut 84112.

HARGRAVE, VICTORIA E(LIZABETH). b Ripon Wis 22 Ag 13. 5: Ripon Col 30-34 (Ger, Lat) AB; UWis 37-38 Lib diploma; Chicago 46-47 (LS) MA. 7: Tchr Brandon High Sch, Brandon Wis 34-37; Ext libn Iowa State Col 37-44; Libn Ripon Col 44-46; Libn MacMurray Col 47-. 8: UIll Grad Sch of Lib Sci Adv Coun 62-64. 2-64. 9: ALA (Coun 51-53)-ACRL (sec Col Lib Sect 59-60, Steering Com 60-62); IllLA (chm 2 coms 57-61); Midwest Acad Libna. 10: NEA; Assn for Higher Educ; AAUW; LWV; Morgan Co Hist Soc; Jacksonville Art Assn. 13: Yes. 14: Ref, ext, admin. 15: Hery Pfeiffer Lib MacMurray Col, Jacksonville Ill 62650.

HARKER, LOIS (ANNE). b Iowa City Iowa 23 Ja 39. 5: UNo Iowa 57-61 (Soc Sci) BA; UIowa 62-65 (Lib Educ) MA. 7: Libn Sigourney Independent Schs, Sigourney Iowa 62-64; Libn Clinton Commun Sch Dist, Clinton Iowa 64-67; Lib consul Muscatine-Scott Co, Davenport Iowa 67-. 9: ALA; IowaASchL. 10: Pi Lambda Theta. 14: Catlg, establ elem sch libs. 15: 2605 Jefferson, Davenport Ia 52803.

HARKINS, ANNA (WUJNOVICH. b Pittsburgh 20 Ag 26. 4: Robert G Harkins. 5: Penn State U 48-52 (Elem educ) BS; UPittsburgh 53-55 (Educ) M Ed, 63-64 BSLS. 6: Serbian, Fr, Sp. 7: Clerk Carnegie Lib of Pittsburgh 43-48; Tchr-libn Bd of Pub Educ Phillips Sch, Pittsburgh 52-66, Supv Sch Libs Bd of Pub Educ 66-. 9: ALA; -AASchL (Newberry-Caldecott Award Com 70-71); NEA; PennLA;PennStateEA. 10: Pi Lambda Theta; Pi Gamma Mu; Beta Phi Bu;Nat Lib Week Com 69; Admin Women. 14: Child. 15: 1150 Bower Hill rd, Pittsburgh Pa 15243.

HARKNESS, MARGERY (HELLEM). b Waterloo Iowa. 7: Catlgr Waterloo (Iowa) Pub Lib 51-58; Catlgr Asst Prof Lib Sci Fort Hays n State Col 59-. 9: KanLA. 14: Tech processes. 15: Forsyth Lib Fort Hays Kan State Col, Hays Ks 67601.

HARKNESS, MARY LOU (BARKER). b Denby SD 19 Ag 25. 5: Neb Wesleyan U 43-47 (Eng) BA; UMich 47-48 ABLS; Columbia 57-58 (LS) MS. 7: Jr catlgr UMich Law Lib 48-50; Asst catlgr Cal State Poly Col Lib 50-52; Catlg libn Ga Inst of Tech Lib 52-57; Catlg libn USoFla Lib 58-67; Acting dir 67-68; Dir 68-. 8: Consul in catlg Nat Lib of Nigeria 62-63. 9: ALA (life mem); FlaLA (chm Catalogers Round Table 61-62; SELA (chm Reg Group of Tech Serv Libns 60-64). 10: AAUW. 14: Catlg. 15: 2338 Lake dr, Tampa Fl 33612.

HARLAMERT, RUTH EVELYN. b Lincoln Neb 16 My 11. 5: UNeb 25-29 (Eng) BA; UMich summer 29 (LS); UWash 43-48 (LS) BA. 6: Fr, Sp. 7: Clerical page, sub UNeb(Lincoln) 25-29; Catlgr UNeb Col of Med (Omaha) 30-37; Libn King County Med Soc, Seattle 37-51; Asst libn Tulane U Sch ofMed 51-52; Libn King County Med Soc, Seattle 51-. 9: MedLA(Bd 65-67, chm var coms); SLA. 14: Ref, admin. 15: 105 Cobb Medical Centre, Seattle 98101.

HARLAN, DONNA (BELAT). b Columbus Ohio 19 D 26. 5: Stephens Col 44-46 (Liberal Arts) AA; Morris Harvey Col 47-48 (Pol Sci) BA; Columbia 48-50 MLS. 7: Field wker WVa Lib Commsn, Morgantown WVa 50-52; Ref & br libn Racine Pub Lib, Racine Wis 52; Catlgr Fed Res Bank, Chicago 53-54; Consul for readers serv WVa Lib Commsn, Charleston WVa 62-65; Staff & train off UPittsburgh Libs 65-66; Libn IndU (S Bend) 66-. 8: Consul for Wkshops, Mich State Lib 54 & 56; Consul WVa State Lib Commsn 54. 9: ALA; Reg VI Memb Chm; IndLA. 15: 1411 Northside Bend, South Bend In 46615.

HARLAN, IRMA (RUTH). b Columbia Tenn 17 Ap 31. 5: Middle Tenn State Col 49-53 (Elem Educ) BS; Peabody 55-62 MA LS.07: Tchr Water Valley Elem Sch, Santa Fe Tenn 51-52; Tchr Hay Long High Sch, Mt Pleasant Tenn 53-55; Libn Blue Gass Reg Lib, Columbia Tenn 55-64, Reg Libn 64-. 9: ALA; SELA; TennLA (Dir Nat Lib Week 69). 10: AAUW. 11: AAUW. 14: Pub lib admin, child serv. 15: 104 W Fifth st, Columbia Tenn 38401.

HARLAN, RONALD J. b Long Beach Cal 23F 29. 5: Fresno State Col 45-50, 54-55 (Musi) BA; UCal(Berkeley) 55-56 MLS. 6: Sp, Fr, Ger. 7: Musician 2d class US Navy, Pensacola Fla 50-54; Jr order libn Fresno State Col Lib56-60, Head Music lib 61-. 9: CalLA. 10: UCal Lib Schs Alumni Assn; Musical Director, Col & Commun Theater. 14: Music libnship, catlg phonorecords & tapes. 15: 1726 No Wishon ave, Fresno Cal 93704.

HARLAND, SIDNEY. b Cleckheaton England 21 Je 23. 5: Leeds U 41-42, 46-48 (Eng, Fr) BA, 48-49 (Eng Lit) MA; (British) Lib Assn 52 ALA, 57 FLA. 6: Fr. 7: Asst libn Devon Co Lib, Devon England 49-53; Sub & br libn Sheffield City Libs, Sheffield England 53-58; Dept hd Okanagan Reg Lib, Kelowna BC Can 58-59; Exec asst UAlta Lib 59-60, Asst libn 60-67; Chief libn USask Regina Campus 67-. 9: ALA; CanLA (chm Com on Univ Lib Standards 60-63); LA .(London); AltaLA; SaskLA. 13: Yes. 14: Lib admin, lib bldg, planning, collections devel. 15: Lib U of Sask Regina Campus, Regina Saskatchewan Can.

HARLESTON, REBEKAH (MAINORD). b Jackson Tenn 18 N 16. 5: Lambuth Col 34-38 (Fr) BA; So Methodist U 40-41 (Eng) MA; Peabody 57-58 (LS) MA. 7: Tchr St Andrews Parish High Sch, Charleston SC 42-44; Tchr Huntington High Sch, Huntington Tenn 44-46; Tchr N Side High Sch, Jackson Tenn 46-50; Tchr Jackson High Sch, Jackson Tenn 50-57; Staff UKy 58-. 9: KyLA. 10: Bus & Prof Womens Club. 14: Govt publs. 15: Ref Dept UKy Lexington Ky 40506.

HARLOW, ANN KATHARINE. b Statesville NC 3 Ap 28. 5: Duke 46-50 (Pol Sci) AB; UNC 50-51 BS in LS. 7: Post Libn US Army Spec Serv, Japan 51-56; Post Libn US Army Spec Serv First US Army, Ft Jay NY 57-63; Chief readers serv USMil Acad 63-. 13: Yes. 14: Ref. 15: Wilson pl, Cornwall NY 12518.

HARLOW, ETHELYN. b Digby Nova Scotia 23 D 26. 5: McMaster Divinity Col 55-57 (Relig, Educ) Certif in Leadership Training; McMaster U 57-60 (Eng & Phil) BA (Honors); UMich 61-65 AMLS. 7: Private sec Whittaker & Daniels, St John NB 44-45; Personal asst to v-pres Brooke Bond Can Ltd, Montreal 45-55; Student asst Canadian Bapt Hist Collection, Hamilton Ont 55-60, Libn 60-65; Ref libn UToronto Lib, Toronto Ont 65-66, Univ archivist 66-. 9: CanLA; Can Assn Col & Univ Libs; Can Hist Assn; SAA; ALA; OntLA. 14: Ref (humanities), ms collections, archival materials. 15: 25 St Mary st apt 1706, Toronto 5 Ont Can.

HARLOW, MARY HALE. b Nubia ex 15 Jl 06. 4: Forrest W Harlow. 5: Hardin-Simmons U 23-27 (Eng) BA, 47, summer 50 (Eng) MA; Abilene Christian Col 28 Diploma in Speech; Theodora Irvine Studio for the Theatre (NYC) summer 28; Northwestern summer 30; UGa summers 31, 32; 33 summers 52, 54, 56 (LS); Tex Womans U summer 65 (LS). 7: Tchr Elem sch, Taylor Co Tex 26-27; Tchr High sch, Hamby Tex 27-28; Tchr Abilene Christian Col 28-32; Libn David-Lipscomb Col 32-33; Tchr Abilene Christian Col 33-34; Tchr Hardin-Simmons U 47-48; Asst libn in chg of ref Abilene CHRISTIAN Col 48-. 9: ALA; TexLA. 10: AAUW; Delta Kappa Gamma; UDC. 14: Ref, interlib loans. 15: 1733 Cedar Crest dr, Abilene Tex 79601.

HARLOW, NEAL. b Columbus Ind 11 Je 08. 4: Marian Gardner. 5: Fresno State Col 25-26 (Eng); Santa Ana Jr Col

27-29 (Hist); UCLA 29-32 (Fine Arts) Ed B; UCal(Berkeley) 32-33 Certif in Libnship, 49 (LS) MA. 7: Jr libn UCal Bancroft Lib (Berkeley) 34-38; Sr libn Cal State Lib Cal Sect 38-45; UCLA: Gifts & exch libn 45-47, Head dept spec collections 47-50, Asst libn 50-51; U Libn UBC 51-61; Dean Grad Sch of Lib Serv Rutgers 61-. 8: Mem NIH Biomedical Com Study Sect 66-; Bd Dirs US Bk Exch 62-68; Consul onLib Educ Progs & Spec Probl of Acad Libs. 9: ALA(Coun 52-61, Exec Bd 59-63; mem and/or chm Com on Accred 59-64);-ACRL(Bd, pres 63-64); CanLA (Coun 53-56, pres 60-61); NJLA(Exec Bd 61-). 10: Bd of Managers Pacific Northwest Bibliog Center (chm 54-57); BC Bd of Examiners Prof Libns (59-61); Leon & Thea Koerner Found (sec Proj Com, Vancouver BC 56-61); Vancouver BC Comun Arts Coun (Bd 54-61); Rounce & Coffin Club (Los Angeles); AAUP; Can Bibliog Soc. 11: LHD, Hon Degree, Moravian Col Penn 67. 12: "The Maps of San Francisco Bay from the Spanish Discovery to the American Occupation" (50); Ed "Cal Lib Bulletin," (57-59). 13: Yes. 14: Acad & res libs, admin, bldgs, educ. 15: 896 River d, Piscataway NJ 08854.

HARMAN, ANNE (LOUISE). b LaGrange Ga 11 O 38. 5: LaGrange Col 57-60 (Hist) BA; Fla State U 60-62 (LS) MS. 7: Libn Forest Park High Sch, Forest Park Ga 62-63; Br libn spec serv, Ft Benning Ga 64; Asst libn Abraham Baldwin Col 64-. 9: GaLA; SELA. 10: Pi Gamma Mu. 14: Ref, catlg. 15: Greenville Ga 30222.

HARMAN, ELEANORA (PATTERSON). b Hickory NC 1 Jl 16. 5: Duke 33-37 (Lit) BA; Union Theol Sem 37-39 (Ch Mus) MSM; Rutgers 60-62 MLS. 7: Organist Berea Col 44-47; Acting libn Foundation Sch Berea Col 44-46; Organist Choir Dir Universalist Ch, Barre Vt 53-58; Lib Clk Sch Br Elizabeth Pub Lib, Elizabeth NJ 58-59, Act hd art dept 59-61; Ref libn Free Pub Lib Serv, Montpelier Vt 61-66; Sch Lib Consul Dept of Educ, Montpelier Vt 66-. 9: ALA; -AASchL; NEA; VtLA (chm Nat Lib Week Com 65-67; pres 68-69); NELA; NESchLA. 10: AAUW. 11: Hon Mention, Grolier Award NLW 67. 13: Yes. 14: Sch libs, ref. 15: 30 Terr st, Montpelier Vt 05602.

HARMAN, JOSEPH C. b Czechoslovaki 25 F 28. 4: Laura Elkins. 5: St Mary's Sem 49-51 (Philos) BA, 51-55 (Theol) BD; St LouisU 55-57 (Lat) MA; UMich 66-67 MALS. 6: Lat, Gk, Slovak. 7: Asst dir Holy Ghost Prep, Cornwells Hts Pa 57-59; Asst dir The Novitiate, Ridgefield Conn 59-62, Dir 63-65; Lib asst OaklandU (Rochester Mich) 65-66; Libn Oakland Commun Col (Auburn Hts Mich) 67-. 10: Bd of Dir CONTACT Inc; Faculty Assn at Auburn Hills Campus, Oakland Commun Col; Acad Senate at Auburn Hills Campus. 11: Fulbright scholarship 62, Rome. 14: Ref. 15: Box 4232, Auburn Hts Mi 48057.

HARMER, DOROTHY (LOUISE). b Brighton Ala 30 S 07. 5: Birmingham-Southern Col 25-28 (Hist) AB; Emory 28-29 BA in LS; Chicago summer 33 (LS); UMich 32, 34, 35 AMLS. 7: Assoc libn Birmingham- Southern Col 29-41; Catlgr Johns Hopkins U 44-45; Catlgr Emory U 45-47; Catlgr UGa 47-59; Catlgr ser sect Penn State U 59-63; Catlgr reclsf serv sect UMich 42-44, 63-65; Catlgr reclsf proj UNC(Chapel Hill) 65-. 67, Sers 67-. 9: NCLA. 14: Catlg. 15: Univ of NC Lib, Chapel Hill NC 27514.

HARMON, ELVA (LEE ANDERSON). b Colorado Springs Colo 2 Jl 27. 4: Ralph Einer Harmon. 5: Southwest Mo State Col 45-48 (Hist) AB (magna cum laude); UIll summers 49-52 MSLS. 7: Tchr Springfield (Mo) Pub Schs 48-49; Libn Harry P Study Sch, Springfield Mo 49-53; Post Libn US Army Spec Serv, Korea 53-54; Libn Kan City (Mo) Pub Lib 54-55; Base Libn Richards-Gebauer AFB, Grandview Mo 55-57; Staff libn Hq Central Air Defense Force, Grandview Mo 57; Asst libn Field Enterprises Educ Corp, Chicago 57-61; Libn Cheltenham High Sch, Wyncote Penn 61-63; Coordinator of child & ya serv Tulsa (Okla) City-Co Lib System 63-67; Hd libn Kistler Lib Holland Hall Sch, Tulsa Okla 68-. 9: ALA (Good Reading for Youth Adv Com); NEA; MoLA (Const Com); MoASchL; OklaLA (chm Child & YP Div 65-66, chm Sequoyah Award Com 64-65). 10: Beta Phi Mu; AAUW. 13: Yes. 14: Child serv, ya serv, sch libs, ref. 15: 1316 E 26th pl, Tulsa Okla 74114.

HARMON, ROBERT BARTLETT. b Helper Carbon Utah 29 N 32. 4: Merlynn Swens. 5: Brigham Young U 54-58, 58-60 (Pol Sci) BA, MA; Rutgers 61-62 MLS. 6: Fr, Ger. 7: Libn II San Jose State Col 62-. 9: ALA. 12: "A Preliminary Checklist of Harmon-Harmon Genealogy" (64); "The Cole Family; A Brief Bibliography" (64); "A Bibliography of Bibliographies in Political Science" (64); "Political Science; Bibliographical Guide to the Literature" (65); "Sources of Bibliography in Political Science" (66); "Basic Source Materials in Pol Sci" (69); "A Selected and Annotated Guide to the Art and Practice of Diplomacy" (69). 14: So sci ref, acquis. 15: 2570 Sue ave, San Jose Ca 95111.

HARMON, THELMA JEAN. b Chicago 19 O 32. 5: Harding Col 50-54 (Soc Studies) BA; UArk 54-57 (Educ) MEd; Wayne State U 55-57 (LS); UIll 61-64 (LS) MS. 6: Fr. 7: Libn Lakeview High Sch, St Clair Shores Mich 55-59; Asst libn Hinsdale Twp High Sch, Hinsdale Ill 59-62, Head Libn 62-. 8: Mem Lib Tech Asst Adv Com for Col of Dupage. 9: IllLA; IllEA. 14: Admin, ref. 15: 1639 Forest rd, LaGrange Park Il 60525.

HARMSEN, TYRUS G. b Pomòna Cal 24 Jl 24. 4: Lois Spaulding. 5: Stanford 41-43, 46-47 (Hist) BA; UMich 47-48 ABLS; Stanford 49-50 (Hist) MA. 7: Catlgr dept of mss Henry E Huntington Lib, San Marino Cal 48-49, 50-59; Col Libn Occidental Col 59-. 8: Visiting Lecturer Sch of Lib sci USoCal, summer 58. , 68. 9: CalLA. 10: Zamorano Club (Los Angeles); Rounce & Coffin Club; Book Club of Cal. 12: "The Plantin Press of Saul and Lillian Marks (60); Ed "Hoja Volante (54-64). 13: Yes. 14: Col libs, rare bks. 15: Occidental Col Lib 1600 Campus rd, Los Angeles 90041.

HARNAU, FLORENCE A(UGUSTA). b Muskegon Mich 25 Ag 04. 5: UMich 22-26 (Math, Eng, Educ) AB, Mich Life Tchg Certif; West Res 31-32 BS in LS, Life Tchg Certif in Ohio & Ill. 7: Libn Moon Sch, Hackley Pub Lib, Muskegon Mich 26-3, Libn Bunker Sch 30-31; Libn East High Sch Akron Pub Schs, Akron Ohio 32-36; Libn Horace Mann Jr High Sch Lakewood Pub Schs & Pub Lib, Lakewood Ohio 36-37; Libn Nichols Intermediate Sch Evanston Pub Schs, Evanston Ill 37-45; Asst ref libn Hackley Pub Lib, Muskegon Mich 45-48, Head ref dept 48-. 9: ALA; MichLA (Memb Com 49-50, chm Ref Sect 51); West Shore LA; NEA; MichEA; Greater Mich Adult Educ Assn. 10: Greater Muskegon Serv League; Delta Zeta; Port CITY Play House; Muskegon Country Club; Friends of Art, Hackley Art Gallery. 14: Ref. 15: 154 Campus ave, Muskegon Mi 49441.

HARNED, ROBERT LAURENCE. b Des Moines Iowa 4 My 44. 5: UHawaii 62-66 (Bus) BBA, 66-67 MLS. 6: Fr. 7: Catlgr Shared Catlg Div LC 67-68; Hd res rm UPenn Lib (Phila) 68-. 9: ALA. 14: Catlg, tech serv. 15: 2101 Chestnut st apt 914, Philadelphia Pa 19103.

HARNETT, AGNES H. b Cleveland 20 S 03. 5: West Res 27 (LS) Certif; Denison U 28-30; West Res 31 (En) AB. 7: Asst libn Cleveland Pub Lib 27-41, Br libn 42-. 9: OhioLA. 10: Bus & Prof Womens Club; Libn Garfield Trinity Baptist Church. 14: Adult educ. 15: 4156 E 123 st, Cleveland Oh 44105.

HARNSBERGER, THERESE (COSCARELLI). b Muskegon Mich. 4: Frederick Owen Harnsberger. 5: Pasadena City Col 49 (Eng, Educ) AA; Marymount Col 50-52 (Eng) BA; USoCal 52-53 (LS, Educ) MSLS; UCLA 61. 6: Ital, Fr, Lat,Sp. 7: Libn San Marino High Sch, San Marino Cal 53-56; Consul, catlgr San Marino Hall,So Pasadena Cal 56-61; Ref, educ, curriculum, fine arts libn Los Angeles State Col 56-59; Jr high, high sch libn Covina-Valley Unified Sch Dist, Covina Cal 59-64, Dist Libn 64-, Pasadena Pub Lib 68-; Freelance writer 66-. 9: NEA; ALA; Cal Tchrs Assn; CalASchL (chm Legis Newsletter, mem Adv Coun); So Cal Coun on Lt for Child & YP. 10: AAUW; Pi Lambda Theta; Covina Coord Coun; Commun Values Com; Covina Unified Educl Assn; Amer Nutrition Soc; Nat Health Fed. 11: Fellowship for grad wk, Villa Schifanoia, Florence ITALY. 13: Yes. 14: Child lit, music libnship, sch libs, spec libs, bibliog. 15: Covina-Valley Unified Sch Dist, Box 269, Covina Cal 91724.

HARO, ROBERT PETER. b Sacramento Cal 9 S 36. 4: Pauline Johanna Kessemeier. 5: Sacramento City Col 54-56 (Hist) AA; UCal 56-58, 58-59 (Hist) BA, MA 61-62 MLS. 6: Sp, Fr, Ger. 7: Tchg asst UCal(Berkeley) 59-60; (Pfc) Weapons expert US Army Spec Forces, Ft Ord Cal 60-61; Lib asst UCal Documents Lib (Berkeley) 61-62; Catlgr Cal State Col (Hayward Cal) 62-63; Subj spec SUNY(Buffalo) 63-65; Soc sci bibliog(r) UCal(Davis) 65-67, Prin libn of Govt Affairs 67-. 9: ALA; SLA; CalLA. 10: Nat Geog Soc; Nat Rifle Assn. ; West Government Research Assoc. 12: "A Directory of Governmental, Public and Urban Affairs Research Centers at AmericanColleges and Universities (68); "Latin American Research Centers and Library Collectionsin the United STATES AND Canada (69). 13 Yes. 14: Automation, acquis, admin, bk selection, ref. 15: 1007 Alice st, Davis Cal 95616.

HARPER, ELIZABETH ALICE. b MGregor Tex 25 Ja 11. 5: UTex 28-32 (Hist) BA; Columbia 34-37 BLS. 6: Sp. 7: Elem tchr Crystal City Tex 32-35; Libn Schreiner Inst Jr Col 35-41;

Libn grade 3 Brooklyn Pub Lib 41-47; Sr libn field wk Morris County Free Lib, Morristown NJ 63-67; Consul Pub libs NJ State Lib 67-. 14: Adult educ, lectg, tchg. 15: Box 656, Mendham NJ 07945.

HARPER, MRS FLORENCE (LAWRENCE). b Paris Tex 31 O 03. 5: Southwest Tex State Col 45-50 (Soc Sci) BS, 50-55 (Coun, Guidance) MA; UTex 53-54 (LS);Peabody 63 MA(LS). 6: Lat. 7: Chief clerk War Price & Rationing Bd, Raymondville Tex 41-45; High sch tchr Hunt Independence Sch Dist, Hunt Tex 45-50; Libn Southwest Tex State Col 50-64; Peabody Col Catlg Instr 63, summers 64-65; 67. 9: ALA; AALS; TexLA; Tex Reg Group Catlgrs & Clsfrs. 10: Friends of Libraries, San Marcos Tex; AAUW; Fac-sponsor Baptist Stud Union 64. 12: "Role of the School Library in the High School Guidance Program (55). 14: Catlg, acquis, subject analysis. 15: 715 N Comanche, San Marcus Tex 78666.

HARPER, LEO G(ORDON). b St Marys Penn 8 My 24. 4: Alice Hacherl. 5: Penn State Col 40-42, 48-50 (Physics) BS; UPittsburgh 61-62 (LS) MS. 6: Ger. 7: Engnr Stackpole Carbon Co, St Marys Penn 42; Platoon Leader 363 Inf, 47th Inf (2nd Lt Inf) 43-48; Co commander Heavy Mortar Co 224th Inf (1st Lt Inf) 50-52; Engnr Stackpole Carbon Co, St Marys Penn 53-61; Supv lib & tech info, Westinghouse Research & Development Lab, Pittsburgh 63-. 8: Visiting Lecturer in Lib Sci UPittsburgh 63-. 9: SLA(treas Pittsburgh Chap 65); Tri-State Assn of Col & Res Libs. 10: Nat Rifle Assn (Life mem); Sr Mem Inst of Electrical & Electronic Engnrs; Murrysville Dist Sportsmens Assn. 14: Admin, microfilm, microfiche. 15: 965 Garden city dr, Monroeville Penn 15146.

HARPER, MARGARET COREY. b Bridgeport Conn 11 Ag 38. 5: Oberlin 5660 (Hist) AB; Rutgers 6061 MLS. 6: Fr. 7: Ser catlgr Boston U Libs 6164, Asst chief catlg div 6566; Sr catlg libn UOre Lib 6667, Asst hd catlg libn 6768; Asst chief catlg div Stanford U Libs 68. 9: ALARTSD (CCS Com on Subj Analysis 67); CalLA. 10: Sierra Club; LWV; AAUW. 14: Catlg, ser. 15: 131 Hawthorne ave, Palo Alto Ca 94301.

HARPER, PEGGY. b Pioneer La 26 D 18. 5: Northeast Jr Col (LSU 35-36, 37-39); LSU 39-41 (Prim Educ) BA, 41-43 BS in LS. 6: Fr, Ger, Ital. 7: Jr catlgr LSU 43; Catlgr Law Sch LSU 44-. 9: AALL; SLA; ALA; LaLA (pres 68-69). 10: Baton Rouge Lib Club. 14: Catlg, rel. 15: 260 Maxine dr, Baton Rouge La 70808.

HARPER, THELMA G. b Springfield Mo. 4: Wilbur M Harper. 5: Wilberforce U 21-23 (Elem Educ) Diploma; Hampton Inst 31-32 BSLS; Wilberforce U 41-42 (Educ) BS; UMich summers 43-47 MALS. 6: Sp, Fr, Ger. 7: Elem tchr Hillside Sch, Durham NC 23-26, Sch libn 26-31; Lib asst Hampton Ist 32-37; Res asst Wilberforce U 37-39, Circ & ref asst 39-47; Circ & ref asst Central State Col (Wilberforce Ohio) 47-59, Assoc libn 59-. 8: Ohio Governors Commsn for Sr Citizens, 59-61;Bd dir United Christian Fellowship Central State U 62-. 9: ALA; OhioLA. 10: Delta Sigma Theta AAUP; AAUW; Greene-Montgomery Co Heart Assn; Miami Valley Consortium; Mgr Civil Defense shelter; Moles. 12: "Index to Selected Periodicals, Hallie Q Brown Librar. 14: Ref, circ, ephemeral materals. 14: Ref, docs, ephemeral materials, interlib loan. 15: Box 62, Xenia Ohio 45385.

HARPER, VIOLA (WHITE). b Mt Vernon Ala 19 Ag 25. 4: Willard Ray Harper. 5: E Miss Jr Col 48-50; Miss State Col 51-53 (Eng) BS; LSU 63-67 MLS. 6: Fr. 7: Tchr Lynville High Sch, Preston Miss 53-57; Tchr Eng & soc sci Meridian Jr Col 57-62; Libn child lib Mobile Pub Lib, Mobile Ala 62-63; Libn Satsuma High Sch, Satsuma Ala 63-67; Ref libn U S Ala 67-, Tchr lib sci 67-. 8: Coe Foun Fellow in Amer Studies, Miss Col 62. 9: NEA; ALA; AlaLA; AlaEA; MobileCoSchLA (chm 66-67). 13: Yes. 14: Ref, bldg collections, storytelling, research. 15: 401 Thornton pl, Mobile Al 36609.

HARPER, V(IRGINIA) CAROLYNA. b Pensacola NC 10 Ja 19. 5: Lander Col 39-43 (Eng, Sociol) AB; Peabody summers 45-47 MA in LS; USCar 54; UNC summer 60; Fla State U 67-68 (LS) Post-Master's Certif. 6: Fr. 7: Tchr-libn Pickens Hgh Sch, Pickens SC 43-46; Libn Cheraw Pub Schs, Cheraw SC 46-50; Libn Newberry Col 50-52; Libn Opportunity Sch, W Columbia SC summers 53, 56, 57; Spec asst Aiken Pub Lib, Aiken SC summer 58; Visiting Instr USCar summer 62, 64, 65; Field instr Div of Gen Studies U SCar 60; Libn Columbia High Sch, Columbia SC 52-68; Asst Prof Ill State U (Normal) 68-. 9: ALA; AASL; NEA; SCLA(sec 64, chm Sch Sect 61); SCEA(pres Sch Libns Div 60-61); SELA; IllLA; IHEA. 10: AAUW; SC Coun for the Common Good;AAUP. 13: Yes. 14: Sch libs, ref, lib educ. 15: 705 S University apt 212, Normal Il 61761.

HARPOLE, MRS PATRICIA CHAYNE (ANDERSON). 03Two Harbors Minn 14 N 33. 5: UMinn(Minneapolis) 51-55 (Fine Arts) BA; UDenver 61-62 (LS) MA. 7: Lib asst St Paul Pub Lib 55-60; Lib asst UDenver Lib 61-62 Asst ref libn Minn Hist Soc, St Paul 63-. 9: Minn Geneal Soc (chm 69). 14: Ref, govt documents, art hist. 15: Minn Hist Soc, St Paul Mn 55101.

HARPOOL, RUTH LEE (CLAWSON). b Best Water Ark 22 S 18. 4: William Roscoe Harpool. 5: UArk 37-40, 43 (Soc Sci, Math) BSE: PEABODY 57- (LS) MA. 6: Lat. 7: Elem tchr Central Grade Sch, Garfield Ark 40-42; Math tchr High Sch, Rogers Ark 43; Payroll dept Pine Bluff Arsenal, Pine Bluff Ark 44; Math tchr Parkin High Sch, Parkin Ark 45-47; Math tchr Gentry High Sch, Gentry Ark 48-49; Libn Rogers High Sch, Rogers Ark 49-59; Libn Sr High Sch, Rogers Ark 60-. 9: ALA; ArkLA (past treas); ArkEA; NW Ark Libns Assn (sec-treas 65), pres 66); ArkEA. 10: AAUW; Altrusa Club; PTA; Brightwater Home Demon Club. 14: Circ, rare bks. 15: Rt 4, Rogers Ark 72756.

HARRAR, ELIZABETH (LAURA). b Wilmington Del 10 N 09. 5: UDel 28-32 (Hist) BA; UPenn 32-33 (Hist) MA; Drxel 48-49 BS in LS. 6: Fr. 7: Tchr Commodore MacDonough Sch, St Georges Del 34-48; Continuations catlgr Swarthmore Col Lib 49-63, 65-, 68, 69-, Act tech serv libn 63-65, Act hd catlg dept 68-69. 9: ALA-ACRL; Phila Area Tech Serv Libns. 10: Phi Kappa PHI. 14: Catlg. 15: 325 Dartmouth ave apt J-1, Swarthmore Pa 19081.

HARRAH, H ELEN JOANNE. b Bastrop La 5 O 31. 4: John Frederick Harrell Sr. 5: Northeast Jr Col 48-50 Certif; LSU 50-52 (Educ, Eng) BS, 53-55 (LS) MS. 7: Asst libn Iberville Parish Lib, Plaquemine La 52-55; Asst libn University High Sch 55; Libn Evangeline Parish Lib, Ville Platte La 55-59; Libn Oak Hill High Sch, Elmer La 59-. 9: ALA (Mem Com Chm SC 65-69);-ACRL (A-V Com 65-67, Col Sect Nomin Com 65-66);-LED (Research Com 67-70); SCLA (chm Com Lib Rel & Res 65-69); SELA (Schlp Com 64-68, chm 66-68, Mem chm for SC 65-69). 14: Bkmob, sch lib wk. 15: 4508 Hargis st, Alexandria La 71303.

HARRELL, ARTHUR E. b Elwood Ind 14 Ap 08. 4: Ruth Jones. 5: IndU 27-33 (Govt) AB, 60-62 (Govt) MA, 65-67 MLS. 6: Fr. 7: Colonel (ret) US Army 33-60; LSCA funds Ind State Lib 67-68; Libn Franklin Pub Lib, Franklin Ind 68-. 9: ALA; IndLA. 10: Indianapolis Civil War RT. 13: Yes. 14: Pub lib. 15: Box 219 RR3, Franklin In 46131.

HARRELL, BARBARA JOY (SPIER). b Bastrop La 5 O 31. 4: John Frederick Harrell Sr. 5: Northeast Jr Col 48-50 Certif; LSU 50-52 (Educ, Eng) BS, 53-55 (LS) MS. 7: Asst libn Iberville Parish Lib, Plaquemine La 52-55; Asst libn University High Sch 55; Libn Evangeline Parish Lib, Ville Platte La 55-59; Libn Oak Hill High Sch, Elmer La 59-. 9: LaLA; La Tchrs Assn; La Assn Clr Tchrs. 14: Bkmob, sch lib wk. 15: 4508 Hargis st, Alexandria La 71303.

HARRELL, CHARLES BAYNE. b Decatur Tex 27 Ag 40. 4: Marilyn Smith. 5: UTex (Arlington) 60-67 (Eng) BA; LSU 67-68 MSLS. 6: Ger. 7: Stud asst UTex(Arlington) 65-67; Grad asst LSU 67-68; Asst ref libn UTex(Arlington) 68-. 9: ALA; TexLA. 10: Alpha Phi Omega. 14: Ref, govt docs, admin. 15: Box 115 UTA, Arlington Tx 76010.

HARRELL, GEORGE FIELDS. b Taylor Tex 31 Ag 23. 5: Rice U 40-43 (Eng Lit); Southwestern U 46-48 (Eng Lit) BA; NYU 48-50 (Eng Lit); Pratt 50- BLS. 7: US Navy Yeoman, Pacific 43-46; Libn Brooklyn Pub Lib 50-51; Libn NYU 51-54; Libn Great Neck Lib, Great Neck NY 54-57; Dir Field Lib, Peekskill NY 57-59; Dir Floral Park Pub Lib, Floral Park NY 59-. 9: ALA; NYLA; Nassau Co LA. 10: Rotary. 14: Admin. 15: 82 Cambridge ave, Garden City LI NY 11530.

HARRER, GUSTAVE A(DOLPHUS). b Durham NC 30 D 24. 4: Elizabeth Varnado. 5: UNC 48 (Ger) AB, 50 (Ger) MA, 53 (Germanic Langs) PhD; UIll 54 (LS) MS. 6: Ger, Fr. 7: German inter US Army 43-45; Asst prof Ger & Lat Millsaps Col 49-51; Assoc order libn UTenn 54-57; Chief acquis div Stanford U 58-59, Asst dir Central Serv 59-60; Dir of libs & museums Boston U 60-68; Dir of libs & Chm Dept of lib sci UFla 68-. 8: Maj Intel USAR Ret; Consul lib bldg Lasell Jr Col 66, Salem State Col 67-, Colby Jr Col 67-. 9: ALA-ACRL. 10: Rotary. 13: Yes. 14: Lib bldg design, hist of bks & printing. 15: 2815 NW 29th st, Gainesville Fl 32601.

HARRICK, ROSEMARY (DERR). b Kent Ohio 2 Je 29. 5: Kent State 47-52 (Geog) BS in Ed, 57 MA in LS. 7: Kent Free Lib, Kent Ohio: Clerk-page 47-51, Asst libn 51-57, Act libn 58,

Asst libn 59-60; Soc Studies libn Kent State U Lib 60-68, Hd ref dept 68-. 8: Chm Kent State U Lib Bldg Com 66-. 9: ALA-Tri-State ACRL; OhioLA. 14: Subject bibliog. 15: 644 Marilyn st, Kent Oh 44240.

HARRIGAN, JOAN (BURNSIDE). b Syracuse Kan 12 O 27. 4: John J Harrigan. 5: Colo State Col 45-49 (Eng) AB; UDenver 58-61 (LS) MA. 7: Tchr Galeton Schs, Galeton Colo 50-51; Tchr Sugar City Schs, Sugar City Colo 52-54; Tchr-libn Hayden Pub Schs, Hayden Colo 54-59; Libn J K Mullen High Sch, Ft Logan Colo 59-64; Sch lib consul Colo State Dept of Educ Div. of State Lib, Denver 65-69; Consul Interlib Cooperation, Title III LSCA 69-. 9: ALA; NEA (life mem); ColoEA; ColoLA; ColoASchL; Colo A-V Assn. 10: Sigma Kappa Alumnae;PTA; SW Denver Human Rel Coun; Lat Amer Research & Serv Agency. 12: "Tesoro de Oro, bks for Span-speaking students (66); "Materiales Tocante LosLatinos (67); "Directory of Colorado Libraries and Librarians (67). 13: Yes. 14: Interlib cooperation, human rel, state agency role, responsibility & programs. 15: 2640 So Lowell blvd, Denver Co 80219.

HARRINGTON, CHARLES W. b Miami Fla 29 Jl 23. 5: William & Mary 41-43 (Govt); UNC 43-44 (Pol Sci) BA; UNM 51-53 (Inter-Amer Affairs) MA; Tulane 53-60 (Hist); LSU 60-61 (LS) MS. 6: Sp. 7: Lt(jg) Supply Corps US Navy 43-46; Dir of activities US Cultural Center, Guatemal City 47-49; Dir US Cultural Center, Ciudad Trujillo 49-51; Gen asst Queens BOROUGH Pub Lib, NYC 61-62; Head Libn Centenary Col (Shreveport La) 62-, Lib Consul U de Concepcion, Concepcion Chile 67-69. 9: ALA; LaLA. 11: Buenos Aires Convention Scholarship, Guatemala 56. 14: Admin, ref, col & pub libs. 15: Centenary Col Lib, Shreveport La 71104.

HARRINGTON, ELAINE RAE. b Stratford Ont Can 18 S36. 5: U West Ont 58 (Econ) BA; McGill 59 BLS. 7: Asst libn Bank of Montreal 59-60, Libn 60-65; Libn Ind Acceptance Corp, Montreal 65-68, Can Dept of Consumer & Corporate Affairs 68-. 9: SLA; CanLA. 15: Industrial Acceptance Corp 1320 Graham blvd, Montreal 16 Que Can.

HARRINGTON, RT REV JOHN H. b NYC 13 Jl 16. 5: Fordham U 33-34 (Bus Admin); Fordham Col 34-35 (Liberal Arts); Cathedral Col 35-36; St Josephs Sem 36-42 (Theol) AB; Columbia 42-56 BLS, MLS, DLS. 6: Lat, Fr, Ger, Ital. 7: Asst Parish of St Elizabeth, NYC 42-46; Libn & Faculty St Josephs Sem(Yonkers NY) 44-65; Dir Princeton U Index of Christian Art Vatican Copy 51-52; Pastor Church of St Theresa, Briarcliff Manor NY. 9: Cath Theol Soc Amer; US Cath Hist Soc (Bd Dirs 48-, Sec 65-). 12: Ed-in-Chief "Catholic Encyclopedia for School and Home (60-); Ed Cath Theol Soc Amer "Proceedings (47-60). 13: Yes. 14: Ref, bk arts. 15: Church of St Theresa, 1394 Pleasantville rd, Briarcliff Manor NY 10510.

HARRINGTON, MARY GRACE. b Akron Ohio. 5: UAkron 29-33 (Hist) AB; UMich 37-39 BALS. 7: Circ asst UAkron 33-38, Circ libn 38-44; Asst libn Fed Reserve Bank, Clevelnd 44-59; Bus & labor serv sr libn Akron Pub Lib, Akron Ohio 59-60; Asst Prof of Bibliog & bus admin libn UAkron 60-. 9: ALA-ACRL (Tri-State Chap); SLA. 10: AAUP; Friends of the Univ (of Akron) Lib; Akron Art Inst; Akron Col lub; Delta Gamma. 14: Ref, econ & bus admin. 15: Univ of Akron, 302 E Buchtel ave, Akron Ohio 44304.

HARRINGTON, PATRICIA ADDISON. b Columbus Ohio. 5: Wells Col 44-48 (Aesthetics) BA; UCal(Berkeley) 62 MLS. 6: Fr. 7: Asst, ed Dun & Bradstreet Inc, NYC 48-50; Libn, ed USALHRU Geo Washington U, Monterey Cal 58-60; Humanities ref libn Humboldt State Col 62-65; Hd readers servs Rockford Col 65-. 9: ALA; IllLA. 10: AAUP; Rockford Art Assn; LWV. 14: Ref, pub serv. 15: 732 Garfield ave, Rockford Ill 61103.

HARRINGTON, RICHARD BUCK. b Worcester Mass 9 F 26. 5: Harvard 44-48 (Fine Arts) AB; Simmons 50-51 MLS. 6: Fr, Ger, Sp, Ital. 7: Asst Redwood Lb & Athenaeum, Newport RI 49-50; Curator Anne S K Brown Mil Collection, Providence 51-. 10: Soc Arch Hist; Nat Trust Hist Preservation; Providence Preservation Soc; Providence Art Club. 14: Catlg, rare bks, prints & drawings, research, exhibitions. 15: 23 James st, Providence RI 02903.

HARRINGTON, WALTER ELLIOTT. b Oakland Cal 25 N 15. 4: Margaret Pirt. 5: San Diego State Col 34-39 (Econ) AB; Canadian Army Staff Col 53 PSC; UToronto 64-65 BLS. 6: Fr. 7: Bkkeeper Bank of Amer, Nat City Cal 39-40; Major Canadian Army 40-65; UBC Lib: Ser libn 65-66, Hd gifts & exchange 66-69, Hd reading rooms div 69-. 9: CanLA (Tech Serv Sect: sec-treas 68-69); BCLA. 11: Military Cross; Canadian Decoration. 15: 7250 Killarney st, Vancouver 16 BC Can.

HARRIS, (ALAN) PAUL. b Toronto 18 Ja 35. 5: UCLA 52-56 (Eng) BA; UCal (Berkeley) 56-57 MSL. 7: Libn Brooklyn Pub Lib 57-59; Libn I Alameda Co Lib, Alameda Co Cal 60; Libn II UCLA Sch of Law Lib 60-. 9: AALL; SoCal ALL. 14: Catlg. 15: 8522 Walnut dr, Los Angeles Ca 90046.

HARRIS, ALICE (DIMON). b Brooklyn NY 10 Jl 30. 4: Ira Whitney Harris. 5: Russell Sage 47-51 (Amer Civilization) BA; UPenn 52-53 (Amer Civilization); Drexel 53-56 (LS) MS. 6: Sp, Russian, Fr. 7: Libn I Free Lib of Phila 53-56; Sr bus libn Newark Pub Lib, Newark NJ 56-57; Catlgr, ref libn & asst dir Paramus Pub Lib, Paramus NJ 60-62; Br libn for Rutgers U Lib (New Brunswick) Eagleton Inst & Govt Research Lib 63-65; Catlgr E-W Ctr Lib, Honolulu 65-. 9: ALA; NJLA; HawaiiLA. 10: Phi Kappa Phi; Girl Scout leader. 13: Yes. 14: Catlg, ref, spec libs. 15: 3030 Felix st, Honolulu Hi 96816.

HARRIS, CAROL HOWARD. b Morgantown WVa 19 N 27. 5: UFla 45-46, 49-53 (Educ) BAE, 53-54 (Secondary Educ) M Ed; Mexico City Col 59 (Span); UWis 60 (Span); Fla Presbyterian Col 61, 62 (Russian); UCal(Berkley) 63-64 MLS. 6: Sp. 7: Stock clerk Great A&P Store, Sebring Fla 43-45; Clarinetist (Cpl) US Army, Ft Brooke PR 46-49; Clerk Webbs City Inc, St Petersburg Fla 51, 53; Stock clerk Mound Park Hosp, St Petersburg Fla 52; Tchr Andrew Jackson High Sch, Jacksonville Fla 54-63; Libn Jacksonville Pub Lib, Jacksonville Fla 64-. 8: Mem com prep curriculum guide tchg Sp in secondary schs, Duval Co Jacksonville Fla 63. 9: Duval Co (Fla) LA; Duval Co CLR Tchrs Assn; ALA; FlaLA. 10: Phi Beta Kappa; Sima Delta Pi; Duval Co Lang Tchrs Coun; Jacksonville Pub Lib Staff Assn; UN Assn Coun Orgs. 14: Ref. 15: apt 1 1613 Flagler ave, Jacksonville Fl 32207.

HARRIS, DOROTHY G. b Richmond Ind 13 D 02. 5: Wellesley 22-25 Bot) BA; Drexel 36-37 BS in LS; Woodbroke Col (Eng) (Soc & Religious Studies) Certif; American U summer 51 (Admin of Archives) Certif; UPenn 55-56 (Amer Civilization) MA. 7: Free lance illustrator UCal & Harvard U -37; Asst i ref & circ depts Swarthmore Col Lib 37-40; Asst in Friends Hist Lib Swarthmore Col 40-, Asst libn, act dir. currently assoc dir. 8: Exch libn, Friends House Lib, London 47. 9: SAA (past mem Comon Col Archives, & Com on Church Archives); Friends Hist Assn (Bd, past sec). 10: Bd, Pendle Hill Sch, Wallingford Penn; Appalachian Mountain Club; Phila Trail Club. 13: Yes. 14: Catlg, ref, archives admin, lib admin. 15: 219 N Swarthmore ave, Swarthmore Pa 19081.

HARRIS, DOROTHY. b Montgomery Ala 15 Jl 27. 5: Vassar 45-46; UAla 46-49 (Eng) BA; UNC 49-50 BS in LS. 6: Sp, Fr. 7: Juvenile lib, sr br libn, supv libn, bkmob libn Brooklyn Pub 50-65, Princ libn Kings Highway Br 65-; Asst Supt of Brs 67-. 9: ALA; NYLA. 10: Brooklyn Heights Assn; south Brooklyn Neighborhood House. 14: Adult serv, admin, personnel. 15: 87 Columbia Heights Apt 56, Brooklyn NY 11201.

HARRIS, ELEANOR BARNHART. b Bellefonte Penn 30 N 10. 4: Howard G Harris. 5: Lake Erie Col 27-28; Syracuse 28-32 (LS) BS. 6: Fr, Lat. 7: Asst libn Van Antwerp Sch, schenectady NY 34-36; Libn: Concord Sr High Sch, Concord NH 36-37, E Hampton High Sch, E Hampton LI NY 37-38, William Penn Charter Sch, Phila 47-49, Egg Harbor Twp Jr High Sch, Atlantic Co NJ 57-58, Chelsea Jr High Sch Lib, Atlantic City NJ 58-. 9: ALA; NEA; NJEA; NJSchLA. 10: Delta Delta Delta; Orpheus Soc of Atlantic City; AAUW. 14: Ref, child serv. 15: 2500 Bayshore ave, Brigantine NJ 08203.

HARRIS, ELISABETH (BROWN). b Greenville Ala. 4: Phillip A W Harris. 5: Fisk 31-35 9hist) BA; Hampton Inst 37 BLS. 7: Asst libn Carnegie Pub Lib, Atlanta 38-40; Libn us army Serv, Ft Benning Ga 41-; Catlg libn Howard U; Libn Howard U Freedmen's Hosp Sch of Nursing Lib 47-. 8: Consul Fed City Col Sch of Nursing 69. 9: SLA (Biol Scis Div). 14: Catlg, ref, reader's adv. 15: 3809 17th pl NE, Washington DC 20018.

HARRIS, EMMA (CORTEZ). b New Orleans La 23 O 1878. 5: Columbia 23; State U of Iowa 27; Spring Hill Col 39 (Eng Lit) BA. 06: Sp. 7: Hd libn Mobile Pub Lib, Mobile Ala 28-45, hd local hist div 45-61, Lib dir emeritus 61-. 10: Mobile BPW; DAR; UDC; Colonial Dames; Ala Hist Soc; Hist Mobile Preservation Soc. 11: Mobile's First Lady of the Year 60; 63 Spec Citation from AlaLA; 23 Oct 68 proclaimed Miss Emma Day by Mayor of Mobile Ala. 14: Local hist, ref. 15: 701 Government st, Mobile Al 36602.

HARRIS, EVELYN J. 5: UAriz 34-38 (Eng) BA, 61-64 (LS) MEd; UDenver summer 65-67 (LS) MA. 7: Clerical asst Ind Psych Inc, Tucson 54-57; Off mgr harris Custom Kitchens, Tucson 57-61; Grad asst Col of Educ UAriz 62-63, Grad asst Instr Materials Lib 63-65, Asst 65-66, Libn 66-68; Libn Educ & Curriculum Lib San Diego State Col 68-. 9: ALA; CalLA; ArizStateLA; CalASchL. 12: "Instructional Materials Cataloging Guide". 14: Curr & instr materials (non-book materials), educ ref. 15: Ed & Curriculum Lib San Diego State Col, San Diego Ca 92115,

HARRIS, HARRIET SAFFORD. b C umming Ga 6 N 10. 5: Wesleyan Col (Ga) 27-31 (Biol) AB; Emory 31-32 (Biol) MA, 41-42 AB in LS. 7: Tchr Crisp Co Ga Bd of Educ 33-34; Case aid Fera & Gera Crisp Co & Pulaski Co Ga 34-35; Tchr Wheeler Co Bd of Educ, Alamo Ga 35-36; Tchr Crawford Co Bd of Educ, Roberta Ga 36-38; Tchr Evans Co Bd of Educ, Claxton Ga 38-41; Circ asst VA Polytech Inst 42-45, Govt Documents asst 45-46; Documents asst Ga Inst of Tech 46-53; Spec collections libn Ga Inst of Tech 53-. 9: ALA; SLA(Adv Coun 56-8, v-chm Geog & Map Div 59-60, Ga Chap pres 56-58, Exec Bd 58-60); GaEA; GaLA (chmSpec Libs Sect 63-65); SELA; Metro Atlanta LA. 10: Atlanta Lib Club; DeKalb Hist Soc; AAUW; Nat Audubon Soc. 14: MAPS, PATENTS. 15: 125 Greenwood pl, Decatur Ga 30030.

HARRIS, MRS HELEN (MATHEWS). b Ft Myer Va 10 N 14. 4: Lt Col Arthur C Harris Jr. 5: Rosary Col 32-33 (Fr); UOkla 33-36 (LS) AB, 38-39 (Fr) AB; UNC 60-61 (LS), 66 MS in LS. 6: Fr. 7: Libn Gretna High Sch, Gretna La 36-38; Tchr-libn Ft McKinley Elem Sch, Ft McKinly Pl 40-41; High Sch libn Amer Sch in Japan, Tokyo 52-53; Catlgr Spec Serv Libs, Ft Dix NJ 56-57; High sch m7 Jr col libn The Marion Int, Inst, Ala 57-60; Asst catlgr Mary Washington Col 62-67; Libn Burrows Elem Sch Quantico Marine CorpsBase 67-. 9: VaLA; VaEA; QuanticoEO. 10: Beta Phi Mu, Mortar Board. 14: Elem sch lib. 15: 105 Goodloe dr, Fredericksberg Va 22401.

HARRIS, HILDA FRAME. b Haverhill Mass 8 Ja 10. 5: Wheaton Col 28-31 (Eng) BA; Simmons 31-32 (LS) BS. 6: Fr. 7: Libn Farlow Ref Lib of Cryptogamic Bot Harvard U 33-46; Asst libn Lib Sch of Med & Pub Health Harvard U 46-51; Ref libn Phillips Acad, Andover Mass 51-52; Publicity dir Haverhill Pub Lib, Haverhill Mass 52-57; Ref libn Tufts U Lib 58-61; Libn Wheaton Col Lib (Norton Mass) 61-. 9: ALA; NELA; MassLA. 12: Ed "Farlowia" (43-46). 14: Admin, ref. 15: P O Box 991, Norton Ma 02766.

HARRIS, HILDA G. b Danville Va 21 Ap 14. 4: Norman Harris. 5: Westhampton Col 31-32; Averett Col 32-33; Randolph-Macon 33-35 (Eng) BA; UNC summers 37-39 BSLS. 7: Libn-tchr Toano High Sch, Toano Va Randolph-Macon Libn Berkeley Elem Sch, Danville Va 40-43; Libn Woodrow Wlson Jr High Sch, Danville Va 43-44; Libn George Washington High Sch, Danville Va 44-47; Libn Stratford Col 50-55; Ref & asst libn UAla Med Center Lib 56-. 9: MedLA; SLA; AlaLA; Birmingham Lib Club. 14: Ref, policies, pub serv. 15: 2511 Gerald Way, Birmingham Ala 35223.

HARRIS, IRA W(HITNEY). b Ossining NY 14 Ap 24. 4: Alice Dimon. 5: UDetroit 42-43 (Engnr); UPenn 47-49 (Fine Arts); Pratt 49-52 (Indus Design) BID; Rutgers 55-57 MLS, 62-66 PhD in LS. 6: Fr, Ger. 7: Orientation & Info US Army 43-46; Libn trainee Newark Bus Lib, Newark NJ 55-56; Libn lending & ref dept Newark Pub Lib, Newark NJ 56-58; Asst libn Newark Col of Engnr 58-62; Instr Rutgers U Grad Sch of Lib Sci 62-65; Research assoc UHawaii 65-66, Dir undergrad lib & assoc prof Grad Sch Lib Studies 66-69, Asst Dean Grad Sch Lib Studies 69-. 9: ALA-ACRL;-LED; AALS; NJLA(sec-treas Col & U Lib Sect 60-61); HawaiiLA (chm Intel Freedom Com 66-68, v-pres & pres-elect 69-). 13: Yes. 14: Reader serv. 15: Sinclair Lib U of Hawaii 2425 Campus rd, Honolulu Hi 96822.

HARRIS, JEAN ELIZABETH ROANE. b Portsmouth Va23 S 37. 4: Robert Leon Harris Sr. 5: Va State Col 55-59 (LS) BS; Drexel 61-65 (LS). 6: Sp. 7: Libn Carver-Price High Sch, Appomattox Va 59-60; Asst child libn Moorestown Free Lib, Moorestown NJ 60-61; Libn Cathedral High Sch, Trenton NJ 61-63; Sch lib consul NJ State Dept of Educ, Trenton NJ 68. 8: Mem of eval teams, Middle States Asn of Secon Schs & Col, 62, 65. 9: ALA; CathLA; NJLA; NJSchLA; NJ Secon Sch Tchrs Assn; NJEA; NEA-DAVI. 10: AAUW; Metro Civic League; NAACP; NJ Fed of Colored Womens Clubs; Nat Fed of Colored Womens Clubs; Ewing Commun Club; Ana Louise White Circle; Counts and Countesses; Zeta Phi Beta; Nat Assn of Col Women; Va State Col Alum Assn; Bd of Christ Educ; YWCA; YMCA. 14: Secon sch libnship. 15: 179 Woodland ave, Trenton NJ 08638.

HARRIS, JESSICA L(EE) MILSTEAD. b Bryans Road Md 4 Je 39. 4: Robert L Harris. 5: East Nazarene Col 56-60 (Soc Sci) AB; Columbia 64-65 MSLS, 66-69 DLS. 6: Fr. 7: Lib asst East Nazarene Col Lib, Quincy Mass 57-60; Lib asst Shorewood High Sch Lib, Shorewood Wis 60-61; Ed & tr Midwest Translation Bur, Milwaukee 61-62; Tr self-employed 62-63; Lib asst Bethel Pub Lib, Bethel Conn 63-64; Research assoc Rothines Assocs, NYC 65-; Asst Prof of Lib Sci Columbia U 69-. 9: ALA; ASIS; Soc of Indexers; Amer Soc of Indexers (sec 68-69); ACM; NY Tech ServLibns; SLA. 10: Beta Phi Mu; Phi Delta Lambda. 12: Co-auth "Computer Filing of Index, Bibliographic, and Catalog Entries (66). 13: Yes. 14: Documentation, indexing, tech serv. 15: 43 Wilson pl, Freeport NY 11520.

HARRIS, JUDITH ANNE. b Chicago 16 D 36. 5: Mich State U 54-59 Hist TE) BA & MA; UMich 59-62 MALS. 7: Tchr Albion Pub Schs, Albion Mich 59-61; Circ libn Iowa State U Lib 62-63; Asst Flint Pub Lib, Flint Mich 63-. 9: Adult Educ Assn; Adult Educ Assn Mich; MichLA (sec-treas Dist 5). 15: 1151 Clearview dr, Flushing Mich 48433.

HARRIS, KENNETH. b Long Island NY Je 32. 5: UIll 51-55 (Rhetoric, Comp) BA, 55-56 (Eng) MA; Columbia 58-59 (LS) MS. 6: Fr. 7: Catlgr State U Iowa 59-61; Catlgr ref Lib of Hawai, Honolulu 61-62; Ref Chicago Pub Lib 62-64; Ref, asst ref, libn West Mich U 64-. 9: ALA. 14: Ref. 15: c/o Philip Harris 5417 N Kenmore st, Chicago Il 60640.

HARRIS, MARGARET (LEACH). b Brooklyn NY. 4: Travis E Harris. 5: Middlebury Col 32-36 (Music) AB; Columbia 59-63 LS) MS. 7: Asst in circ dept Ferguson Lib, Stamford Conn 56-57; Child libn Manhasset Pub Lib, Manhasset NY 59-. 15: Manhasset Pub Lib 30 Onderdonk, Manhasset NY 11030.

HARRIS, MARGARET (PHILLIPS). b Linden Va 23 Je 15. 4: Quinton P Harris. 5: William & Mary 34-38 (GER) BA; UWis 38-39 BLS; UAlaska 56 (Creat Writing), 65 (Comp Relig). 6: Ger. 7: County Libn Warren County Pub Lib, Monmouth Ill 3941; Asst libn Kern County Pub Lib, Bakersfield Cal 41-42; Ensign USNR US Naval Reserve, Wash DC 42-43; Interviewer Alaska Employment Serv, Fairbanks Alaska 56-58; UAlaska Lib: Head readers serv 58-60, Head ctlg 60-63, Head documents dept 63-. 8: Lib consul Nordale Sch, Fairbanks Alaska 62-63; Chm Reading & Lib Serv for State PTA, Fairbanks Alaska 62-64; Comp of Directoryof Libs & Libns in Alaska; Lib consul Fairbanks Evang -ASD (Com on Rel with State & Regl Lib Assns);Luth Church 66-. 9: ALA (Recruit Com Alaska);-ACRL; Alaska State LA (pres-elect); PNLA(Recruit Pres 66-67 Alaska). 10: AAUP; Alaska State Hist Soc; Tanana Yukon Hist Soc. 12: Ed "Directory of Libraries and Library Personnel in Alaska (63-). 13: Yes. 14: Ref, govt publ, bibliog. 15: PO Box 3102, Fairbanks Alaska 99701.

HARRIS, MARGARET J. b Mansfield Penn 15 S 30. 5: The Col of Wooster 48-52 (Fr) BA; West Res 63-64 MS in L. 6: Fr. 7: Serv rep Mich Bell Telephone Co, Grand Rapids Mich 52-55; Sec Unit Plan Div United Appeal of Greater Cleveland, Cleveland Ohio 56-63; Ya libn Cuyahoga Co Pub Lib, Cleveland 64-66, Br libn 66-. 9: ALA; OhioLA. 10: AAUW. 14: Adult, ya. 15: 3960 Elmwood rd, Cleveland Oh 44121.

HARRIS, MARY ELIZABETH (THOMAS). b Houston Tex 11 F 41. 4: James Lynn Harris. 5: Sam houston Col 59-62 (LS) BS. 6: Ger. 7: Asst med libn M D Anderson Hosp, Houston Tex 62-63; Ref libn Humble Oil & Ref Co, Houston 63-64; Asst br supv Houston Pub Lib, Houston 64-67; Libn World Bk Sci Serv, Houston 67-. 9: ALA; TexLA (Scholarship Party Com for 69 State Convention); SWLA. 10: Girl Scouts. 14: Ref, West hist of US, child wk, sci (med & space), sociol, acquis. 15: 1963 Campbell rd, Houston Tx 77055.

HARRIS, MRS MARY ELIZABETH (BROWNE). b Colo Springs Colo 10 O 28. 4: Howell Harris. 5: San Diego State Col 47-50 (Zool) BS; UOkla 51-52 BA in LS; USoCal 56-57 MSLS; Emory summer 52 (Med Libnship) Grade 1 Certif. 6: Ger, Fr. 7: Asst libn Southwestern Med Sch UTex 52-55; Sci libn USoCal 55-57; Sch libn Dept Educ Group US Army, Baumholder Germany 57-58; Head catlgr dept Educ Group US Army, Karlsruhe, Germany 58-59; Ser catlgr San Diego State Col 59-64; Catlgr Cal West U 64-65; Ser libn Lafayette Col 65-68; Ser libn Wis State U (Whitewater) 68-. 9: ALA. : Grace E Herrick Award UOkla 52. 10: Alpha Gamma Delta. 11: Grace E Herrick Award UOkla, 52. 14: Ser, catlg. 15: P O Box 351, Whitewater Wi 53190.

HARRIS, PATRICIA MACAULAY. b Chicago Ill 11 N 16. 5: Principia Col 34-38 (Sociol) BA; UMd 65-67 MLS. 7: Staff Dean of Girls Principia High Sch, St Louis 38-40; Tchr NIKI Sch, Honolulu 40-41; Soc wkr Amer Red Cross, San Diego 42p45; Lib aide Anne Arundel Co, Annapolis Md 63-64; Br libn pub lib, Annapolis Md 64-68, Br coord 68-. 10: AAUW; Nat Capital Girl Scouts Bd. 14: Admin. 15: PO Box 566, Severna Park Md 21146.

HARRIS, PHOEBE M. b Seattle 16 Ag 18. 5: UWash 36-40 Fr) BA, 41-42 BA in LS. 6: Fr. 7: Seattle Pub Lib: Asst circ dept 42-44, Asst ref dept 44-45, 1st asst ref dept 55-57, Head ref dept 57-60, Head hist dept 60-. 8: Visit lectr UWash Sch of Libnship 66-67; Consul on bio "The Readers Adviser11th ed (68). 9: ALA; PNLA; WashLA. 10: Phi Beta Kappa; Wash Hist Soc. 12: Ed "Whos Who Among Pacific Northwest Authors, First Supplement (61). 13: Yes. 14: Northwest hist, ref. 15: Seattle Pub Lib 4th & Madison, Seattle Wa 98104.

HARRIS, RENA ELLA (SAFFORD). b Kingfield Me 2 Je 06. 5: Farmington State Tchrs Col 23-25 (Educ, Eng) 2-yr tchg diploma; Southeast Mo State Col47-48 (Ed, Eng, Art, Soc Studies, Sp) BS Ed; Washington U (St Louis) 52-59 (Eng, Speech); Peabody 61-66 MA (LS) 64, MA in EdS 66. 6: Fr, Sp. 7: Dept Eng Rogers Jr High Sch, Fairhaven Mass 27-31; Dept Eng Riverbend Jr High Sch, Athol Mass 31-43; (Cpl) WAC med tch libn Cushing Neuropsychiatric Hosp, Framingham Mass 43-45; Dept Eng, sp, deb, art Richland Reorg Dist High Sch, Gray Ridge Mo 53-59; Dept Eng, art Ste Genevieve Sr High Sch, Ste Genevieve Mo 61-63; Libn, art, devel, read Clopton High Sch, Clarksville Mo 63-64; Libn Herculaneum High Sch, Herculaneum Mo 64-65; Libn Grand Haven Sr High Sch, Grand Haven Mich 65-66, Libn Zeeland Sr High Sch, Zeeland Mich 66-68, Libn Solivet Sr High Sch,Olivet Mich 68-69. 8: Gave Speech Correction Therapy for Crippled Child Serv at Sikeston Mo, 52-53. 9: NEA; NCTE; ALA; MichEA; Lake Mich Libns Assn. 10: AAUW; Bus & Prof Women. 15: 104 Selma st, Sikeson Mo 63801.

HARRIS, RICHARD W. b LaPorte Ind 22 Ja 19. 4: Carolyn Simmons. 5: N Central Col 36-40 (Eng, Soc Studies) BA; E Carolina Col 63 (Lit); UNC 64 (LS) MS. 7: Meteorologist Major USAF 40-64; Acquis ser Duke U Med Ctr Lib 66-67; Sci & tech libn Tex A&M U Lib 67-69; Dir James Connally Tech Inst Lib, Waco Tex 69-. 9: ALA. 10: Beta Phi Mu; Air Force Assn. 14: Admin. 15: 4116 Mockingbird lane, Waco Tx 76708.

HARRIS, ROBERT. b Glasgow Scotland 21 Ag 36. 5: UBC 55-59 (Physics) BA, 61-62 BLS. 7: Circ libn UBC 62-67, Chief libn BC Inst of Tech 67-. 9: CanLA; ALA; BCLA; ABCL. 14: Info systems. 15: Lib UBC, Vancouver 8 BC Can.

HARRIS, SARAH LUCILLE. b Evanston Wyo 27 O 15. 5: Westminster Col 34-36 AA; UUtah 36-38 (Eng) BA; UDenver 45-47 BS in LS. 6: Fr, Sp. 7: Libn Judge Mem High Sch, Salt Lake City 39-43; Asst circ dept Salt Lake City Pub Lib 43-49, Hd circ dept 49-52, Asst libn 52-. 9: ALA; MPLA (treas 55-56); UtahLA (sec-treas 51-52, v-pres 56-57, pres 57-58, past chm var coms). 10: Zonta Club; Delta Kappa Gamma; YWCA. 14: Adult serv. 15: 136 Lincoln st, Salt Lake City Ut 84102.

HARRIS, SELMA S. b Carteret NJ 2 Je 15. 5: Woodbury Col 46-48 (Journalism) BBA; U of the Americas 49-50 (Eng Lit) BA; Rutgers 58-63 MLS. 7: Bkkeeer Newark NJ 35-42; (1st) Lt Info & Educ Off WAC 42-46; Editorial "Rosemead Review & "Westlake Post Cal 48-49; Bkkeeer Newark NJ 50-57; Montclair State Col: Jr lib asst 57-59, Sr libn 59-63, Asst Prof II ref libn 63-. 9: NJLA (Recruit Com 63-65); NJEA. 10: LWV; AAUW; Montclair State Col Fac Assn. 14: Ref. 15: 188 Bellevue ave, Upper Montclair NJ 07043.

HARRIS, SUSAN McMILLAN. b Gainesville Ga 24 Ap 11. 5: UGa 27-29 (Fr); Piedmont Col 35-37 (Fr) AB; Peabody 44-45, 47-50 BS in LS, MS in LS. 6: Fr. 7: Tchr lbn Ga State sch Systems 32-44; Libn N Ga Col 45-. 8: Mem Ga Univ System Regents Com on Lib 68-. 9: ALA; SELA; GaLA(chm Col & U Div 57-59); GaEA. 10: Kappa Delta Pi; Dahlonega Womans Club; Dahlonega Baptist Womens Missionary Union (pres). 13: Yes. 14: Admin, ref. 15: Box 146, Dahlonega Ga 30533.

HARRIS, VALERIE (DECIMA). b Scotland 1 F 42. 5: Hamilton Tchrs Col 60-61 Elem Tchrs Certif; McMasterU -66 (Eng, Hist) BA; UToronto 68-69 BLS. 7: Elem sch tchr Bd of Educ, Hamilton Ont Can 61-65; Asst libn Hamilton Pub Lib, Ont 66-68, Child libn 69. 14: Child wk. 15: 256 Edgemont st S, Hamilton Ont Can.

HARRIS, VIRGINIA. b Jennings La 18 D 15. 5: McPherson Col 35-39 Hist) AB; LSU summers 41-44, 45 BLS, summers 52-55 MLS. 7: Tchr-libn Jefferson Davis Parish Sch Bd, Fenton La 39-40; Tchr-libn Jefferon Davis Parish Sch Bd, Hathaway La 4-44; Libn McPherson Col 44-. 9: ALA; KanLA; MPLA. 10: AAUW; Beta Phi Mu; Kan Ornithological Soc; AAUP. 14: Catlg, ref. 15: McPherson Col Lib, McPherson Ks 67460.

HARRIS, VIRGINIA (TODD BIERBRIER). 5: Syracuse 47-51 (Eng) AB; Columbia 51-54 (Eng drama); UCal (Berkeley) 67-68 MLS. 6: Fr, Ital. 7: Clk-typist Silver Burdett Co, NYC 52-54; Sec Houghton Mifflin Co, San Francisco 54-55; Sec Friends Com on Legis, San Francisco 55-57; Ed Friends Bulletin (Quaker), San Francisco 62-66; Sec Consumers Coop, Berkeley Ca 66-67; Libn Ctr for Study of Law & Soc, Berkeley Ca 68-69; Ref libn Oberlin Col 69-. 9: ALA; AAUW. 10: ACLU. 14: Ref, inter-lib loan. 15: Oberlin College Lib, Oberlin Oh 44074.

HARRISON, (ROBERT) BRUCE. b Cicago 20 Ap 14. 5: Catawba Col 41 AB; Northeastern State Col (Elem Educ) 61 MAT UOla 63 MLS; Universidad Inter-americana (Latin Amer studies) 65 PhD. 6: Lat, Sp, Ital, Fr. , Portu. 7: Vice pres Carlin Inc, NJ 41-49; Naval ff active 42-46) USNR (Lt Cmdr) 42-: Commercial flight instr (FAA No 32976) USA 42; Pres The Bruce Harrison Corp, NJ 46-51; Mgt consul 46-60; Sch prin pub schs, Kirkland Ariz 51-52; Independent lib consul Rocky Mount Va 63-, Prof of Lib Sci & Dir Learning Materials Resource Ctr Col of S Ida 66-. 8: Travelled in 65 countries, observing lib & educ conditions; Guest lectr, NDEA Grad Inst, E Carolina U summer 68; Dir EPDA Lib Technicians Prog, Col of So Idaho summer 69. 9: ALA; NEA; AAHE. 10: AAAS; Amer Akad Registered Criminologists; AAUP; Amer Vocational Assn. 11: John Marshall U 61 LLD (Hon). 12: "Reading by Sightation (61); "Juvenile Delinquency (55); "The First Profession. 13: Yes. 14: Lib sci educ, comparative libnship. 15: Rt No 1, Rocky Mount Va 24151.

HARRISON, ANNIE (WILLIS). b Powhatan Va 27 S 28. 4: Moses Harrison. 5: Va State Col 45-49 (LS) BS; Syracuse summers 58-63 MS in LS. 6: Sp. 7: Tchr-libn Pocahontas High Sch, Powhatan Va 49-55; Libn Luther H Foster High Sch, Nottoway Va 55-56; Asst libn St Pauls Lawrenceville (Lawreneville Va) 5-. 9: ALA; VaLA. 10: Beta Phi Mu. 14: Catlg, ref. 15: Rte 1 Box 259, Lawrenceville Va 23868.

HARRISON, ANNIE S. b Hopkinsville Ky 13 Ag 33. 4: Damon Wilson Harrison. 5: Bethel col (Hopkinsville Ky) 51-53 AA; Georgetown Col 53-55 (Eng) AB (summa cum laude); Vanderbilt 56-57 (Eng) MA; Peabody Col 63-64 MA in LS. 7: Ref libn Ky Dept of Libs frankfort 64-. 9: ALA; SELA; KyLA. 10: AAUW; Bus & Profess Women's Club. 14: Kentuckiana collection. 15: 216 Briarcliff apt 12, Frankfort Ky 40601.

HARRISON, CYNTHIA ELLEN. b Brooklyn NY 29 O 46. 5: Brooklyn Col 63-66 (Eng) BA; Columbia 66-67 MS in LS; City Col (CUNY) 68-69 (Eng). 6: Fr. 7: Libn Rugby br brooklyn Pub Lib 67-68; Libn Tele Ref Brooklyn Pub Lib 68-. 8: Volunteer adv for church lib, Fed of Prot Welfare Agencies, NY 69; Founder & pres Soc for Future Libns, Brooklyn Col 65-66. 9: ALA. 14: Ref. 15: 985 E 77 st, Brooklyn NY 11236.

HARRISON, DOROTHY M (McDONALD). b Highland Park Mich 21 Jl 14. 4: Edward Woodberry Harrison. 5: Albion Col 32-34 (Hist); UMich 34-37 (Hist) BA, BALS; UCal 39-40, 41 (Libnship) MA; ULouisville 64-65 Tchr's Certif. 7: Asst libn Detroit Pub Lib 37-42; Asst ref libn UCal Lib (Berkeley) 41; Aeroclub dir Amer Red Cross European Theatre Operations 42-45; AV libn Durrett High Sch Jefferson City Bd of Educ, Louisville Ky 65-68, Coord of lib serv 68-. 8: Asst field dir Amer Red Cross, Kelly Field San Antonio Tex 45-46; Lectr Catherine Spalding Col Dept of Lib Sci 66-68. 9: KyEA; JCEA; KyLA; KASL. 14: A-V. 15: 817 Huntington rd, Louisville Ky 40207.

HARRISON, ELIZABETH (COTHRAN). b Charleston SC 12 F 16. 5: Winthrop Col 33-37 (Art, Fr, Eng) AB; UMich 46 (LS); Duke 52-59; UNC 57-60 MS in LS. 6: Fr. 7: Off manager Hugh Grey Hosiery C, Concord NC 38-42;Kindergarten tchr Twaddell Sc, Durham NC 47-55; Duke U Lib: sst in mss 55-56, Under grad libn 56-57, Subj catlgr 57-65, 1st asst in subj catlg 65-; Hd libn Frank L Boyden Lib Durham Acad, Deerfield Mass 68-. 8: Adv Heritage Foundation Lib, Deerfield Mass 68-69. 9: ALA; Nat Assn Independent Schs; NELA. 10: Beta Phi Mu; Deerfield Womans Club. 12: "Current Reference Practices in Four Universty Librares in North Carolina, ACRL microcard ser 140 (62). 13: Yes. 14: Catlg, admin, ref. 15: P O Box 166, Old Deerfield Ma 01342.

HARRISON, EVELYN (JENNINGS). b Williamston NC 29 O 08. 5: Louisburg Col 26-28 Certif; Duke 28-30 (Eng) AB; UIll 32-3 BS in LS. 7: Womans Col Lib Duke U: Asst in order dept 30-31, Head of order dept 31-32, Asst in catlg dept 33-37, Head of catlg dept & asst libn 37-49, Libn 49-. 9: ALA; SELA; NCLA. 10: Altrusa Internat; Womans Club. 14: Col lib admin, tch proc. 15: Womans Col Lib Duke Univ, Durham NC 27708.

HARRISON, FLOREL (ANN) (FACIANE). b Slidell La 2 My 40. 4: Solomon Leslie Harrison. 5: So U 57-61 (Eng) BS, summers 61 & 62 Certif in Soc Studies; LSU Baton Rouge 65-69 (LS) MS, 68-69. 6: Fr. 7: Libn St Tammany High Sch, Slidell La 61-. 9: ALA; CathLA; LaLA; LaEA; LaASchL. 10: Girl Scout Leader. 14: Ref, ya serv. 15: PO Box 625, Slidell La 70458.

HARRISON, FRANCES (ERWIN). b Wellston Okla 11 Jl 13. 4: Arthur Harrison. 5; okla City U 32-35 (Eng) AB; UOkla summers 59 & 60 (EDUC); UIda corres 62-63 (LS). 7: Asst Prof of Speech Okla City U 35-6; Receptionist & acting NBC, Wash DC 36-38; Speech, Eng, drama tchr El Reno High Sch, El Reno Okla 57-61, Libn 62-. 9: NEA; Clr Tchrs Assn (pres); OklaEA; OklaLA. 10: PEO; CWF; Bus & Profess Women of Year Award 62. 11: Woman of the Year Award 1962 (B&PW). 15: 1329 S Reno, El Reno Okla 73036.

HARRISON, JOHN CLEMENT. b Liverpool Eng 27 F 13. 4: Alice Willis. 5: Liverpool Col of Tech 31-34 (LS) FLA; Liverpool U 38-40 (Admin) DPA; UIll 60-62 (LS) MS, 62-(LS). 6: Fr. 7: Various Liverpool Pub Libs, Liverpool Eng 31-40; Royal Air Force Operational Flying Duties (Bomber Command) (Flight Lt) 40-46; Dir Sch of Libnship, Manchester Eng 46-60; Instr Grad Sch of Lib Sci, UIll 60-62; Grad Sch of Lib & Info Sci, UPittsburgh: Asst Prof 62-64, Asst Dean 64-65, Assoc Dean 65-. 8: Mem of Brit del, Congress of Libns & Documentalists, Brussels 55; Adv to Govt of Ghana on lib educ, 60. 9: ALA; AALS; Lib Assn, Brit (Fellow; Coun mem 48-60); chm Register & Exams Exec Com 56-60); Internat Rel Round Table; PennLA; Pittsburgh Lib Club. 10: AAUP; Pittsburgh Bibliophiles; Gaelic Arts Soc of Pittsburgh; UIll Lib Sch Assn; Beta Phi Mu. 11: Distinguished Flying Cross (Brit). 12: "Five Hundred Years of the Printed Bible" (64). 13: Yes. 14: Admin, hist of the bk, hist of printing, lib coop, lib educ, personnel mgt, rare bks, comparative libnship. 15: 226 Lytton ave, Pittsburgh Pa 15213.

HARRISON, JOHN PHILIP. b Everett Mass 2 N 41. 5: Tufts U 59-63 (Eng) AB; Simmons 63-65 (LS) MS. 6: Fr. 7: Res collection libn Northeastern U 63-64, Libn suburban campus 64-65, Catlgr 65-66, Sr catlgr 66-68; Hd catlgr Boston Athenaeum 68-. 9: ALA; NELA. 14: Catlg, acquis. 15: 247 Park ave, Arlington Ma 02174.

HARRISON, MRS KEITH F. 03Salisbury NC 7 S 08. 5: Womans Col of UNC 25-29 (Fr) AB; UNC(Chapel Hill) summers 57-61, 63, 65 (LS). 7: Tchr Badin Pub Sch, Badin NC 29-32, Tchr-libn 57-59 Libn Albemarle Sr High, Albermarle NC 59-. 9: NEA; NCLA; NCEA. 10: Badin Br Lib Com; Badin Friends of the Lib. 14: Ref, pub sch lib. 15: PO Box 805 Tallassee st, adin NC 28009.

HARRISON, MARCIA TAPLEY STEPHENSON. b Salem Mass 12 F 28. 4: Raymond G Harrison. 5: Smith 45-47, 49 (Hist) BA; UGeneva 47-48; Grad Inst Geneva 47-48; Simmons 50-51 MS in LS. 6: Fr. 7: Aide Swampscott Pub Lib, Swampscott Mass 49; Asst Lamont Lib Harvard U 49-5; Asst circ libn Widener Lib Harvard U 55-56; Catlgr Lowell State Lib, Lowell Mass 63-. 68; Catlgr Bradford Jr Col 68-. 9: MassLA. 10: Open Gate Garden Club; LWV. 12: "Survey of Chelmsford Pub Lib. 14: Catlg. 15: RFD 1A Killam Hill rd, Boxford Ma 01921.

HARRISON, NANCY (ELLEN) CAPPS. b Indian Head Md 14 Je 42. 4: William Lovette Harrison. 5: Duke 60-64 (Eng) BA; UNC 64-65 MS in LS. 6: Fr. 7: Asst catlgr-order libn Randolph-Macon Woman's Col Lib 65-66; Hd searching unit acquis dept DukeU Lib 66-. 9: RowanCoLA. 10: Beta Phi Mu; Rowan Citizens for Better Libs. 14: Acquis, ref, rare bks. 15: 831 N Jackson st, Salisbury NC 28144.

HARRISON, THOMAS DEMETRIUS JR. b Brunswick Ga 25 My 2. 5: Emory 46-48 (Eng, Philos) AB, AM; Villanova U 59-60 (LS) MS, Rutgers 69 MLS. 6: Fr, Ger, Lat. 7: US ARMY Qtrmstr Corps, USA, ETO 42-45; Grad fellow Emory 48; Grad asst Eng Dept Ohio State U 49-50; Asst prod manager Crucible Steel Casting Co, Lansdowne Penn 51-60; Asst libn Elizabethtown Col 60-61; Head Libn Helen Kate Furness Free Lib, Wallingford Penn 61-64; Dir of sch libs Haverford Sch, Haverford Penn 64-. 9: ALA; PennLA. 10: Phi Beta Kappa; Mod Lang Assn. 12: Contrib work Simplification in Small Public Libraries (65). 14: Sch lib, catlg, ref. 15: 311 Owen ave, Lansdowne Pa 19050.

HARRISON, VIRGINIA (HOUGHTON). b Mass 31 Ja 09. 5: Carleton Col 25-29 (Fr) BA; ULyon(s) (France) 30-31 (Fr lit) Certif d'Etudes; Middlebury French Sch summer 32 (Fr lang & lit); Bryn Mawr Col 33-34 (Fr) MA. 6: Fr, Ital, Ger, Russian, Lat, Grk (ancient), Sp. 7: Stud asst Carleton Col Lib, Northfield minn 27-29; Tchr Emma Willard Sch, Troy NY 31-33; Tchr Fermata Sch, Aiken SC 34-38; Tchr eng to Russians Soviet Purchasing Com, Wash DC 45-47; Tchr Babson Inst, Babson Park Mass 53-56, Lang tutor 59-, Curator of Sir Isaac Newton Collection 59-. 9: ALA (Rare Bk Sect); BSA. 10: Phi Beta Kappa. 11: Inst of Intl Educ exchange fellowship 30-31. 14: Rare bks, hist of sci (esp Newton). 15: Babson Inst Lib, Babson Park Ma 02157.

HARRISON, WILLIAM FLETCHER. b Tuskegee Ala 26 Mr 28. 4: Marjorie Menefee. 5: Auburn U 47 (Chem); Emory 48-50 (Eng) AB; UMunich 55 (Ger); Oxford U 55 (Lit); Peabody 56-57 (LS) MA. 6: Ger, Fr, Lat, Sp. 7: Owner Clothing Shop, Tuskegee Ala 50-55; Asst libn ORINS, Oak Ridge Tenn 57-58; Print catlgr Va State Lib 58; Catlgr & libn Fla Presbyterian C, St Petersburg Fla 59-63; Asst catlgr U U of So Fla 64-. 8: Mem f a Special Libraries team, helped comile Oak Ridge Union List of Ser; Org print & photograph collection of Va State Lib; Participated in feasibilty study on a union list of ser in five priv cols in Fla; 57-58, 58, 62 resp. 9: FlaLA. 14: Catlg, acquis. 15: 730-60th ave So, St Petersurg Fla 33705.

HARRISON, WILLIAM LOVETTE. b Williamston NC 14 My 42. 4: Nancy Capps. 5: UNC 61-64 (Hist) BA, 65-68 (Hist) MA, 68-69 MSLS. 6: Fr. 7: Libn Rowan Tech Inst 69-. 9: ALA; NCLA; NC Commun ColLA. 10: Beta Phi Mu. 14: Admin, ref. 15: 831 N Jackson st, Salisbury NC 28144.

HARROP, MARGARET (SIMMS). b Muskogee Okla 16 Jl 12. 4: Allen Edward Harrop. 5: UOkla 32-33 BALS; Depauw U 29-31; Tulsa U 31-32, 34-35 (Hist) BA; Columbia summers 37-40, 42 (LS) MS. 7: Stud lib asst UTulsa 33-34; Catlgr elem Sch Bd of Educ, Okla Cty Okla 35-40; High sch libn Foster High Sch, Okla City Okla 40-42; Catlgr Carnegie Lib, Okla City, Okla 43; Detroit Pub Lib: Child libn 44-47, Catlgr 48-51, Child libn 51-53, Supv catlg home Reading Serv 53-. 66; Libn Pinellas Park Pub Lib, Pinellas Park Fla 67-. 9: ALA; MichLA; FlaLA. 10: Detroit Hearing Center; Quota Club. 11: Staff Award, Detroit Pub Lib, 61. 14: Catlg, child lib wk, admin. 15: 12866 Hubbell, Detroit Mi 48227.

HARRSCH, REID R(ALPH). b Niobrara Neb 20 Ja 25. 4: Patricia Goldin. 5: UNeb 46-50 (Hist, Pol Sci) AB, 50-51 (Hist) MA; UWis 52-53 (Hist), 53-54 MA in LS. 6: Fr. 7: US Army (active Duty 43-46; US Army Reserve 48-64 (Major Ret) Mil Pers O; Tchg asst hist UNeb 50-51; Research asst hist UWis (Madison) 52-53; Asst ref libn UKan 54-57; Asst order libn Syracuse U 57-60, Order libn 60-63; Ref libn Ind State U 63-65; Chief of acquis UWis(Madison) 65-68; Bibliog serv libn (State) Ref & Loan Lib,Madison 69-. 9: WisLA. 10: Beta Phi Mu; Phi Alpha Theta; Phi Beta Kappa. 14: Acquis. 15: 434 Virginia ter, Madison Wi 53705.

HARRY, RUTH. b Reading Penn 27 My 15. 5: Hood Col 32-36 (Eng) AB; Drexel 37-38 BS in LS. 7: Circ asst Drexel Inst 38-42; Asst libn Coast Artillery Sch,Ft Monroe Va 42-43; Ref asst Pub Lib, White Plains NY 43-46; Child libn Warner Lib, Tarrytown NY 46-47; Circ head Ferguson Lib, Stamford Conn 47-53; Dir Rye Free Reading Room, Rye NY 53-. 9: NYLA; Westchester LA (chm Union Catlg Com, chm Pub Rel, chm Circ Sect). 10: Rye Golf Club; Manursing Island Club. 15: 60 Beverly dr, Rye NY 10580.

HARRY, RUTH. b Petersburg Ill 4 S 19. 5: Western Col for Women 37-41 (Lit)AB; Carnegie 43-44 BS in LS. 7: Lib asst in br Indianapolis Pub Lib 41-43, Sr libn ext dept 44-46; Washington U Lib (St Louis): Res libn 46-47, 1st asst circ dept 47-52, Act head circ dept 52-53, Head Order dept 53-55; Br asst Indianapolis-Marion Co Pub Lib 55-58, Head arts div 58-. 9: ALA; IndLA. 10: Nat Soc of Arts & Letters; Art Assn of Indianapolis. 14: Ref, bk sel. 15: 4807 Round Lake rd apt C, Indianapolis In 46205.

HARSAGHY, FRED J JR. 7: Lib asst ref dept NY Pub Lib 3037; Newspaper libn & ed asst Newsweek Magazine--, NYC 3744; Supv ref sect US State Dept IBD, NYC 4547; Asst tech libn Yonkers (NY) Pub Lib 4748; Libn Central Lib NY QMPO Army, NYC 4849; Dir Amer Info Ctr (Hakodate,

Kanazowa, Nagoya) GHQ, SCAP, CIE, Japan 4952; Reviews ed Inst Aeronautical Sci, NYC 5256; Chief field libn Arabian Amer Oil Co, Dhahran Saudi Arabia 5660; Tchr soc studies Danbury High Sch, Danbury Conn 6165; Asst Prof Danbury State Col 6265; Dir lib serv Col Petroleum & Minerals, Dhahran Saudi Arabia 6569; Area dir libs InterAmer U of PR, San German 64. 15: Vivoni Nuevo apt 1, San German PR 00753.

HARSCH, LOUISE (CLARKE). b Richmond Va. 5: UCal (Santa Barbara) 54 (Hist) BA; UCal (Berkeley) 56 MLS. 6: Fr. 7: Gen clerk The Christian Sci Monitor, Boston 36-42; US Navy WAVES US Naval Station, Anacostia DC 43-45; Ref libn Principia Col 57-62; Govt docs libn UCal Lib (Santa Barbara) 63-67; Soc sci libn UHawaii 67-68; Libn San Francisco State Col (Downtown Ctr) 68-. 14: Ref, govt publ. 15: 2500 Chestnut st apt 4, San Francisco Ca 94123.

HARSHE, FLORENCE E. b Lima Ohio 16 O 17. 5: Ohio State U 35-39 (Educ, Eng & Soc Sci) BS in Ed; Wes Res 40-41 BS in LS. 7: Libn North Br Lima Pub Lib, Lima Ohio 41-43, Head of circ dept 43-47; Head of circ dept Lib of Hawaii, Honolulu 47-49, Head of order dept & bind 49-51; Chief of adv serv & asst dir NY State Reg Lib Serv Center, Watertown NY 51-57; Dir North Country Lib System, Watertown NY 57-59; Dir So Adirondack Lib System, Saratoga Springs NY 59-. 9: ALA (past treas Lib Ext Sect); NYLA (Coun 57-60 & 62 res Adult Serv Sect 62); Capital Dist Lib Coun (trustee 66-); NY State Pub Libns Prof CertifExam Com (68-). 10: AAUW; Bus & Prof Womens Club. 13: Yes. 14: Lib devel, admin. 15: 22 Whitney pl, Saratoga Springs NY 12866.

HART, ALICE (SCHMITT). b New Haven Conn 8 Ag 18. 4: John Augustine Hart. 5: Albertus Magnus 35-39 (Eng) BA; UPittsburgh 64-65 MLS. 6: Fr, Ital, Lat. 7: Catlgr YaleU Lib 40-43; Catlgr US Govt Off of Price Admin, Wash DC 44-45; Catlgr Hillman Lib UPittsburgh. 9: ALA. 14: Catlg. 15: 2811 Shady ave, Pittsburgh Pa 15217.

HART, DOROTHY EDWARDS. b Peabody Mass 13 Je 14. 5: BostonU 32-36 (Eng Lit) BA, 36-37 (Eng Lit) MA. 6: Fr, Ger, Russian. 7: Asst libn BostonU Sch Med 40-42; Asst libn Arthur D Little Inc 42, Libn 42-. 8: Instr NortheasternU Spec Libs Course; Instr URI Spec Libs Serv Summer Course. 9: SLA (pres Boston Chap; founding mem & chm Boston Sci-Tech Group; chm Educ Com; Consul Off). 14: Admin, lib educ, train of lib tech. 15: Arthur D Little Inc 15 Acorn park, Cambridge Ma 02140.

HART, EARL DURWOOD. b Durham NC 14 Je 39. 5: E Carolina Col 58-61 (Soc Studies & LS) BS, 62-64 (LS) MA in Ed; Peabody 66-67 (LS) MLS; LSU 67-68 (LS). 6: Fr. 7: Libn Tarboro Pub Sch, Tarboro Pub Schs, Tarboro High Sch 61-63; Co-libn Raleigh Pub Schs, N Broughton High Sch 63-64; Asst order libn E Carolina Col 64-66; Bibliog searcher Joint U Libs, Nashville 66-67;Asst Prof of Lib Sci LSU 68-. 8: Adv to Acquis & Automation Depts LSUNO Lib summer 68. 9: ALA; LaLA; SWLA; SELA. 10: Alpha Chi Omega. 14: Acquis, ref, tchg. 15: 301 S Harding st, Greenville NC 27834.

HART, EUGENE D. b Bryant Ind 2 S 08. 4: Loleta Williams. 5: Iowa State Col 28-33 (Forestry) BS; UMich 33-34 (Soc Sci) AB, 34-36 ABLS; American U 53-58 (Pub Admin) MA, PhD. 6: Ger, Fr, Russian. 7: Tech ref libn Los Angeles Co Pub Lib, Los Angeles 38-40; Asst libn Tulsa Pub Lib, Tulsa Okla 40-41; Libn Pacific Aero Lib, Hollywood Cal 41-42; (Lt Col) US Army Intelligence 42-46, (Col) 48-57; Head Libn Glendale (Cal) Pub Lib 46-48; State Libn Idaho State Lib 57-59; Assoc Prof Sch of Lib Sci USoCal 59-. 8: Consul in pub libs: Commerce (Cal) Pub Lib (60); Black Gold Cooperative Lib System, Ventura Cal 63-64; San Bernardino (Cal) County libs 65-. 9: ALA; SLA; CalLA; IdaLA. 14: Tchg in lib schs, pub libs, admin. 15: 516 E Grace ave apt 3, Hayward Ca 90301.

HART, HAZEL CATHARINE (HEINTZ). b Chicago 23 Ag 16. 5: UWis 34 BA, BLS; No Ill U 65 MA in LS. 6: Fr. 7: Child libn Pub Libs, New PhiladelphiaOhio 38-39; Child libn Pub Lib, Jacksonville Ill 3941; Libn Elem Sh Dist 2 Blackhwk Jr High Sch, Bensenville Ill 59-. 8: Consul-org Itsca Pub Lib 55-5; Bensenville Pub Lib 58-59. 9: NEA; IllEA; IllLA. 14: Materials centers. 15: 312 N Rush st, Itasca Ill 60143.

HART, MR JEAN FRANCIS. b New Britain Conn 4 Ap 26. 5: UConn 46-49; St Marys Sem Col 54-56 (Philos) BA; Central Conn State Col summers 57-59 (Educ); So Conn State Col 61-(LS)68 MSLS. 6: Lat. 7: Mailman 2/c US Navy, S, Okinawa 44-46; Elem tchr Sch Dept, Berlin Conn 57-60; Libn, manager Catholic Lending Lib & Bkstore, Hartford Conn 60-61; Curriculum libn Central Conn State Col 61-64, Circ libn 64-; Readers servs libn 64-67; Dir of lib servs Greater Hartford Commun Col 67-. 9: CathLA; ConnLA; So Conn State Col LA. 10: Conn St Emp Assn; Admin Coun Conn Commun Cols. 14: Admin, acquis. 15: 75 West End ave, New Britain Conn 06052.

HART, JOSEPH THOMAS. b NYC 8 S 16. 4: Ruth Ellen Grady. 5: Fordham Col 34-37 (Hist) AB; Columbia 40-41 BLS; Fordham U 48-58 (Law & Govt) MA, PhD. 6: Fr, Ger, Lat. 7: Libn Regis High Sch, NYC 39-41; Libn Seton Hall Prep, S Orange NJ 41-42; (T/Sgt) AAC Engnrs US ARMY, US, ETO 42-46; Col Libn Fordham U 46-49, Head of readers serv 49-51, U Libn 51-66, Hd of tech serv 66-68; Libn Gould Mem Lib NYU 68-. 15: 636 Washington ave, Pleasantville NY 10570.

HART, LYN (LINTHICUM). b Baltimore 28 D 22. 4: Richard Hart. 5: Goucher 40-44 (Eng) AB; Catholic U 50-55 MSLS; Johns Hopkins 55-60 (Aesthetics of Lit) MA. 6: Fr. 7: Asst Popular Lib Enoch Pratt Free Lib, Baltimore; Asst to asst coordinator 58-59, Asst to coordinator 59-64, Sch liaison libn 64-65, Asst coord adult serv 65-. 9: ALA-RSD; MDLA; PLA (chm Com on Starter List for New Br Collections 67-); Md Assn Adult Educ. 10: Citizens Planning & Housing Assn; POE (sec) Hopkins Faculty Club. 13: Yes. 14: Bk sel, adult educ. 15: 42 E 26th st, Baltimore Md 21218.

HART, MARGUERITE L (KNAPP). b Westerville Ohio 6 S 08. 5: Otterbein Col 26-30 (Eng, Educ) BA; Ohio U summer 36-37; West Res summer 59-61 (LS) MS. 6: Fr, Sp. 7: Tchr-libn Neale Jr High Sch Wood Co Sch Dist, Vienna WVa 45-55; Libn Westminster Jr High Sch Millcreek Twp Sch Dist, Erie Penn 55-67; Libn James S Wilson Jr High Sch, Millcreek Twp, Erie Pa 67-69. 9: ALA; Penn State EA. 14: Ref, child libs. 15: 403 Clifton dr, Erie Pa 16505.

HART, NANCY MERLE. b Albany Ga 28 O 39. 5: Mills Col 57-59; UKy 61-63 (Fr) BA; Fla state U 63-64 MLS. 6: Fr. 7: Ref libn NY Pub Lib Allerton br & Bronx Ref 64-65; Br hd San Mateo Pub Lib, San Mateo Cal 65-68: Lecturer Emory U 68-69; Coord of outside serv & resources Atlanta Pub Lib 68-69; Libn III br hd 69-. 9: ALA; GaLA; SELA. 14: Ref. 15: 181 N Colonial Homes cir NW, Atlanta Ga 30309.

HART, PATRICIA WARBURTON (FOWLER). b St John NB Can 26 Ja 11. 4: James Gilbert Hart. 5: UCLA 29-32 (Hist); UCal(Berkeley) 32-33 (Hist) BA, 34-35 Certif. 7: Asst Santa Monica (Cal) Pub Lib 29-36; Chief Libn St John (NB) Pub Lib 48-53; Catlgr Aluminum Co of Can, Montreal 54; Order dept asst UToronto 55; Ref libn N York Pub Lib, Willowdale Ont 56-58, Head adult serv 58-69; Chief libn Richmond Hill Pub Lib 69-. 9: Can LA; OntLA; Inst Prof Libns Ont. 10: No York Hist Soc. 11: Can Centennial Medal; N York (Can) Civic Award 67. 12: "Pioneering in North York (68). 13: Yes. 14: Loc hist, admin, Canadiana. 15: 5 Norlington dr, Willowdale Ont Can.

HART, RICHARD. b Baltimore 5 Ja 08. 4: Evelyn Linthicum. 5: Pratt 31 (LS) Certif. 6: Fr, Ital, Ger, Lat. 7: Asst Enoch Pratt Free Lib, Baltimore 29-30; Asst NY Pub Lib 30-31; Asst, then head lit dept Enoch Pratt Free Lib, Baltimore 31-65, Chm humanities dept 65-. 8: US War Dept Hist Serv Bd, 42-46; Md Governors Commsn on Outdoor Drama; Md Governors Commission of Educational Television. 9: ALA; Adult Educ Assn (Bd); Adult Educ Assn of Md (past pres); MdLA. 10: Robert Lindner Foun; Johns Hopkins Theatre; Amer Nat Theatre & Acad; Amer Educ Theatre Assn; Soc for Theatre Research; Delta Kai Sigma; Johns Hopkins Faculty Club; E A Poe Soc; Hist of Ideas Club; Tudor & Stuart Club; Founder, Baltimore Writers Forum 46-. 12: "Enoch Pratt, the Story of a Plain Ma (35); "Edgar Allan Poe, Letters and Documents (41); "A Winters Journey (45); "What Shall Be Done About Japan (45); "Eclpse of the Rising Sun (46); "Papers of Identity (63); Opera libretti and one act plays. 13: Yes. 14: Lib adult educ serv to readers in the humanities, educ TV series;Counselling creative writers & theatre groups. 15: Enoch Pratt Free Lib, Baltimore Md 21201.

HART, SHEILA KIRWAN. b Yorkshire Eng 25 Mr 30. 4: Wilbur Dyre Hart III. 5: University Col (Galway Ireland) 47-50 (Soc & Pol Sci) BA; Simmons 60-62 (LS) MS. 7: Lib asst Harvard U Lib 58-60, Lib interne 60-62; 62-, In chg Theodore ROOSEVELT Collection 62-66; Asst lib ref Harvard U Grad Sch Educ 66-68; Ref lib Harvard Col Lib 62-66, 68-. 14: Ref. 15: Widener Lib Harvard U, Cambridge Mass 02138.

HART, THOMAS L. b Auburn Ind 7 Mr 38. 4: Sherry Lynne (Diekman). 5: Ball State U 56-60 (Elem Educ) BS; West Res 61-64 (LS) MS; Ball State U 60-62 (Elem Admin) MA; Ind U 62; Case West Res 66-67. 6: Fr. 7: Materials Center Dir

Kokomo-Center Twp Schs, Kokomo Ind 60-65; Prof of Educ Media Purdue U 65-66; Prof of Lib Sci Ball State U (Graduate Prog). 8: State Media Center Consul from Purdue U, State Adv to the Hoosier Stud Libns Assn; chm ISLA Conf, chm ILA Lib Ed Comm, Dir Sch Lib Academic Yr Institute. 9: NEA-DAVI; Ind State Tchrs Assn; IndSchLA; EIndLA; ALA. 10: AAUP; Phi Delta Kappa. 11: ISLA Media Man of the Month. 13: Yes. 14: MCC, sch media ctrs, lib educ, fed dev progs, lib & media research. 15: 100 S McKinley ave, Muncie In 47303.

HARTENSTEIN, JEANNE (LEWIS). b Pittsburgh 24 Jl 25. 4: Fred V Hartenstein. 5: UPittsburgh 43-47 (Bus Admin) BS; West Mich U 60-61 (LS) MA. 7: Asst libn Bronson Methodist Hosp, Kalamazoo Mich 61-63, Dir of Libs 63-. 8: Spec lectr West Mich U Lib. 9: ALA; Med LA(sec Midwest Reg Group); MichLA(chm Hosp & Inst Sect). 10: Trustee Portage Lib. 14: Ref. 15: 3704 Wedgwood dr, Portage Mi 49081.

HARTGEN, FRANCES CAROLINE (LUBANDA). b Reading Penn 4 O 13. 4: Vincent A Hartgen. 5: Syracuse 32-36 (Hist) AB; UMe 53 (Counseling) MEd, 69 MS. 7: Playground dir Reading (Penn) Dept of Recreation 32-37; Tchr Washingtonville Jr High Sch, Washingtonville NY 37-42; Personnel Strawbridge & Clothier, Phila 42; Meteorol ogist US Govt Weather Bureau, Phila 42-43; Lending libn Remington's Bkstore, Baltimore 43-44; Tchr Old Town-Orono Jr High Sch, Me 50-67; Ref libn UMe 67-68, Hd Special Collections 68-. 8: Leave of absence to study & visit schs & libs for ya, Great britain & Europe 69-70. 9: MeLA. 14: Tchg, ref, child & ya lit. 15: 109 Forest ave, Orono Me 04473.

HARTIN, J(OHN) S(YKES). b Columbus Miss 26 O 16. 4: Rita Miller. 5: UMiss 35-39 (Eng, Fr, Psych) BA; UMich 39-40, 40-42 ABLS, AMLS, 52-53 (Eng Lang, Lit) AM, 53-56 (LS) PhD. 6: Fr, Ger, Sp. 7: Stud asst UMiss Lib 35-39; Gen asst UMich Lib (Ann Arbor) 40-42; Libn Sch of Music Lib 42-45; Chief pub serv Swarthmore Col Lib 45-47; Dir of Libs UMiss 47-. 8: Miss Lib Survey 49-51; Subscription Bks Com 50-54. 9: ALA(Coun 60-63); BSA; SELA; MissLA. 10: Beta Phi Mu; Phi Kappa Phi; UMich Assn of Lib Sci Alumni (pres 45-46). 11: General Educ Bd Fellowship 52-53. 13: Yes. 14: Rare bks, hist of printing, local bibliog. 15: Box 25, Univ Ms 38677.

HARTJE, GEOGE N(ICHOLAS). b St Louis 27 S 24. 4: Virginia Hohlt. 5: Harris Jr Col 41-43 (Pre Engnr) AA; Washington U (St Louis) 45-47 (Eng) AB; UIll 49-50 (LS) MS. 7: Shelver St Louis Pub Lib 41-44; Asst to plant engnr Laclade Steel Co, Madison Ill 44-45; Ref asst St Louis Pub Lib 45-48; Acquis asst UIll(Urbana) 48-50; Washington U (St Louis); Asst chief Acquis Dept 50, Catlgr in chg of reclsf 50-53; St Louis Pub Lib; Catlgr 53-55, Asst chief catlg & order dept 55-56, Chief catlg & order dept 56-60, Supv tech processes 60-63; Dir of Libs & Head Div of Lib Sci NE Mo State Col 64-. 8: Lecturer in libnship Washington U 62-64; Served on survey team, RB Downs, Resources of Mo Libs 66. 9: BSA; ALA(Ins Com 50-52)-LAD(2 coms 59-0;-RTSC (8 coms 56-); MoLA(Col & U Lib Survey Com 64-); MoAssn Col & Res Libs (sec 65-); Greater St Louis Lib Club (pres 57); Mo State TA. 10: Westerners; Independent Order of Oddfellows; St Charles Co Hist Soc; Mo Hist Soc; Elder Presbyterian Churc. ; Kiwanis; AAUP. 12: "Centralized Serial Records in University Libraries (51); "Serial Practices in Public Libraries (56). 13: Yes. 14: Admin, tchg, bibliog. 15: RR 3, Kirksville Mo 63501.

HARTLEY, NANCY JANE. b Darby Penn 18 My 41. 5: UPenn Col for Women 59-63 (Chem) AB; Columbia 63-64 (LS) MS. 6: Fr. 7: Ref libn Atlas Chem Ind Inc, Wilmington Del 64-66; Ref libn Hofstra U 66-68; Tech libn Foster D Snell Inc, NYC 68; Asst libn Amer Metal Climax Inc, NYC 68-. 9: SLA; ALA; ACS. 10: Phi Beta Kappa. 14: Ref, ser, bus & tech lit. 15: 7 W 14 st apt 11-B, New York NY 10011.

HARTMAN, DOLORES (ANN). b Pigeon Mich 14 My 35. 5: East Mich U 53-57 (Chem) BA; UMich 57-59 MALS. 7: Tech libn The Dow Chem Co, Midland Mich 59-62, ;Mgr Chem Lib 62-. 9: SLA; ACS. 10: ACS. 15: Rt 4, Midland Mi 48640.

HARTMAN, ELIZABETH R(OSE). b East Lansdowne Penn 13 Ap 10. 5: Penn State U 27-31 9journalism) BA; Union Theol Sem 39-43 (Sacred Mus) SMM; Drexel 44-48 BS in LS. 6: Fr. 7: Investigator Dept Pub Assistance, Phila 33-36; Organist & piano tchr, Phila & NYC 35-50; Desk asst Drexel 43-46; Libn Curtis Inst Mus, Phila 46-53; Asst hd mus dept Free Lib of Phila 53-65, Hd mus dept 65-. 9: ALA; MusLA (Phila Chap: chm, treas); Assn for Recorded Sound Collections (Memb Chm 67-); PennLA (Memb Com 65, Conv Local Arrang Com 68). 10: AAUW; Drexel Lib Sch Alum Assn. 14: Ref. 15: The Chatham Walnut sts, Phila Pa 19103.

HARTMAN, HELEN (SHULER). b Manning SC 28 My 09. 5: Converse Col 26-30 (Lat) AB; U S Car 60-67 (LS) Certif. 6: Fr. 7: Tchr high sch: Jefferson SC 30-36, Latta SC 36-37; Kershaw SC 47-58; Libn high sch, Kershaw SC 58-. 9: ALA; -AASchL; NEA; SCEA (Legisl Com); SCLA. 10: SC State Garden Club; Local Garden Club; Chesterfield Co Bd of Educ; Nat Assn Sch Trustees. 14: Sch lib serv. 15: 97 Miller, Jefferson SC 29718.

HARTMAN, MAXINE (BROWN). b 9 Mr 36. 4: Roy L Hartman. 5: Panhandle A & M Col 54-56; W Tex State U 60-61 (Elem Educ) BS; Okla State U 63, 64 (Secondary Educ, LS), 68 MS. 7: Sec Hereford State Bank, Hereford Tex 56-58, Teller 59-60; Libn Stanton Jr High, Hereford Tex 61-65, La Plata Jr High 66-. 8: Consul St Anthonys Elem Sch 68-69. 9: ALA; NEA; Tex State Tchrs Assn; TexASchL; Tex Assn Educl Tech. 14: Sch lib wk. 15: 412 Sunset dr, Hereford Tx 79045.

HARTMAN, SISTER MARY CLARE OSF. b Cedar Rapids Iowa 3 Jl 09. 5: Marquette U 27-28; Chicago Normal Sch summer 29; Loyola U 30-41 (Hist) BA; DePaul U summers 42, 43; Mont State U summers 52-55 (Educ) ME; NY Sch of Filing summer 44 Certif of Filing. 6: Bohemian, Lat, Sp, Ger. 7: Tchr St Joseph Sch, Wilmette Ill 28-33; Tchr St Clara Sch, Chicago 34-38; Tchr Holy Rosary Sch, Medford Wis 38-39; Tchr libn St Paul Mission, Hays Mont 39-. 8: Sch Club Moderator 43-. 9: ALA; NSTA; MontLA; MontEA; MFTA; UBA. 10: PTO. 11: Adopted into Gros Ventres Indians as "Speaks Holy". 13: Yes. 15: St Paul Indian Mission Box 85, Hays Mt 59527.

HARTMANN, DALE WALTER. b Corunna Ind 12 My 32. 4: June Duesterhoft. 5: Concordia Tchrs Col 50-54 (Geog) BS in Ed; UDenver 54-57 (LS) MA. 7: Elem tchr Immanuel Lutheran Sch, Kan City Mo 54-55; Libn Luther High Sch North, Chicago 55-65; Assoc Dir of Libs Concordia Theol Sem (Springfield Ill) 65-. 14: Catlg, tech serv. 15: 2621 Manor ave, Springfield Ill 62703.

HARTUP, HELEN (WERT). b Roseville Ohio 12 N 1898. 4: Paul C Hartup. 5: Adrian Col 19-22 (Fr) AB; Kent State 56-61 (LS) MA. 6: Fr, Ger. 7: High sch tchr Sandusky County Schs, Burgoon & Woodville 22-27; High sch tchr Wapakoneta City Schs, Wapakoneta Ohio 46-56, High sch libn 56-. 9: NEA; OhioLA; OhioSchLA; OhioEA. 15: 408 Defiance st, Wapakoneta Oh 45895.

HARTWEG, MARGARET W. b Warren Penn 29 My 07. 4: Dr Norman Hartweg. 5: East Mich U 29 (Elem Educ) Life Certif; UMich 31 (Zool) AB, 59 MLS. 7: Elem sch libn Plymouth Commun Schs, Plymouth Mich 59-. 9: MichASchL; MichEA. 10: Pi Lambda Theta; Beta Phi Mu; Ann Arbor Lib Club; Phi Beta Kappa. 14: Child libnship. 15: 2506 Geddes ave, Ann Arbor Mich 48104.

HARTWELL, (JAMES) GLENN. b Chehalis Wash 29 Jl 33. 4: Claribel Louise Nobbe. 5: Walla Walla Col 51-54 (Relig); Andrews U 55-57 (Relig) BA; West Mich U 62-66 MSL. 6: Ger. 7: Summer recruiting & elem tchr Mich Conf of SDA, Lansing Mich 60-61; Elem tchr Berrien Co Intermediate Sch Dist, St Joseph Mich 61-64, 58-60; Grad asst period dept West Much U Lib 64-66, Period libn 66-67, Hd phys processing 67-68, Circ libn ERC 68-69; Consul inst lib serv State Lib of Ohio, Columbus 69-. 9: ALA. 10: Beta Phi Mu. 14: Tech processing, machine use in libs & lib automation, consul serv. 15: 2401 Towne House lane, Kalamazoo Mi 49001.

HARTWELL, WAYNE MAITLAND. b Flint Mich 17 Ag 16. 5: UMich 38 (Eng) AB, 40 BS in LS. 7: Gen serv asst UMich Lib (Ann Arbor) 36-40; Ref asst Swarthmore Col Lib 40-41; Exec asst ALA Com on Aid to Libs in War Areas URochester 41-42; Tech asst (Staff Sgt) USAF Lib, Wash DC 43-45; Research asst (Master Sgt) Off of Strategic Serv, New Delhi India 45-46; Dir US Info Serv Lib, Bombay India 46-48; Cultural affairs off US Info Serv, Bombay India 48-51; 1st asst acuis div ref dept NY Pub Lib 51-52; Libn ed dept F E Compton Co, Chicago 52-65; Libn Encyclopaedia Britannica, Chicago 65-. 9: ALA(chm 2 coms 53-57)-RSD(pres 65-66); SLA; IllLA; Chicago Lib Club (pres 55-56). 13: Yes. 14: Ref. 15: 1435 Astor st, Chicago 60610.

HARTY, ROSE MARIE BABBINI. b Eveleth Minn 8 Ag 31. 5: Va Jr Col (Virginia Minn) 49-51 (LS) AA; Col of St Catherine 51-53 BS in LS. 6: Fr. 7: Child libn Owatonna Pub Lib, Owatonna Minn 53-54. Catlg & ref libn 54-57; Libn Albert Lea Pub Lib, Albert Lea Minn 59-. 9: ALA; MinnLA (pres) Pub Lib Sec 61-62). 10: Civic Music Assn; Letter Carriers Auxiliary of Albert Lea(Minn). ; Amer Leg Aux. 14: Catlg, ref. 15: 1606 Frank Hall ave, Albert Lea Minn 56007.

HARTZ, FREDERIC R. b Annville Penn 31 Mr 33. 5: Kutztown State Col 50-54 (Hist, LS) BS; Syracuse 57-63 MSLS; Drexel 65-67 (LS), Temple U 68- (Ed Media). 6: Ger. 7: Sch libn Pennsbury Schs, Fallsington Penn 54-58; Mil ed US Army Adj Gen Corps, Heidelberg Germany (Sp 4th class) 58-60; Sr libn nj state Lib 60; Circ libn Rider Col 60-64; Dir Pub Lib of Levittown, NJ 60-64; Asst Prof Lib Dept Program Trenton State Col 64-. 8: Lib consul State Prison, Trenton nj 62-63. 9: ALA; NJLA; NJEA; Penn Learning Resources Assn. 10: AAUP; Beta Phi Mu. 13: Yes. 14: Child lit, ref, sel of bk & non-bk materials. 15: Trenton State Col, Trenton NJ 08625.

HARVEY, ALMA (LILLY MARGOT). b Lithuania 6 D 24. 4: Roland Harvey. 5: Carleton U (Ottawa) 62 (Bio, Chem) BA; Ottawa U 65 BLS. 6: Lithuanian, Ger, Russian, Fr. 7: Med tech Ottawa Civic Hosp, Ottawa Ont Can 49-53; Tech off (research) Nat Research Coun of Can, Ottawa Ont Can 53-64; Libn hd of interlib loan Nat Sci Lib of Can Nat Research Coun, Ottawa Ont Can 65-67, Libn asst hd catlgr 68-. 9: Profess Inst Pub Serv Canada 9sec-treas Libn's Gp 67-); OttawaLA (Coun 67-68). 10: Civil Serv Recreat Assn, Ottawa. 13: Yes. 14: Catlg, ref, staff training, systems analysis. 15: 635 Carson rd apt 4, Ottawa Ont Can.

HARVEY, HELEN. b Leon Iowa 5 N 10. 5: Northwestern 27-31 BS; Columbia 41-42 MLS. 7: Clerical Des Moines Pub Lib, Des Moines Iowa 36-40; Libn NY Pub Lib 41-53; Libn US Navy, Norfolk Va, Honolulu, Oakland Cal 42-45; Libn Berkeley Pub Lib, Berkeley Cal 46-47; Order libn UWash 48-53; Ref libn Fed Reserve Bank of NY, NYC 54-56; Acquis libn Pasadena Pub Lib, Pasadena Cal 56-, Hd tech servs 65-. 9: ALA; CalLA. 15: 1183 Romney dr, Pasadena Cal 91105.

HARVEY, JOHN F(REDERICK). b Maryville Mo 24 Ag 21. 5: Dartmouth 3943 (Eng Lit) BA; UIll 4344 BS in LS; UChicago 4549 (LS) PhD. 7: Priv US Army 4243; Asst catlgr John Crevar Lib, Chicago 4445, Asst med ref libn 4547; Admin asst UChicago Lib 4950; Libn & Prof Parsons Col 5053; Hd libn, chm dept lib sci & prof State Col (Pittsburg Kan) 5358; Dean & Prof Grad Sch Lib Sci Drexel Inst 5867, Dir libs 5862, Dir Drexel Press 6467, Prof lib sci (on leave) 67; Chm dept lib sci Col of Educ UTehran, Iran 6768; Dir Iranian Documentation Ctr & Tehran Bk Proc Ctr, Iran 6871. 8: Dir & ed, Drexel Press--; Consul; Publishers Agency, Phila 6567, Lib Col Conf, Jamestown Col 65; Founder Drexel Library Quarterly-- (65). 9: ALA (Coun 5761 & 6667; chm Resol Com 6263; chm Jt Com on Libnship as a Career 5558; chm Lib Periods RT 5556; Wilson Lib Recr Award Jury 6667); LAD (Compar Org Com 6568; Lib Educ Statist Com 6668); LED (chm Recr Com 6162; chm Res Com 6567); ACRL (Bd Dirs 5761; chm Constit Com 5961; Nomin Com 6567; Univ Libs Sect; Res Com 5862; Jr Col Lib Sect; Standards Com 6769); ASIS (Exec Coun 6264; chm Adv Bd 6264; chm Stud Memb Com 6567; Founder, Del Valley Chap 60); Church & Synagogue LA (Founder 67); IranianLA (4 coms 67); Lib Pub Rel Assn of Phila (Founder 66); Melvil Dui Chowder & Marching Assn; Archons of Colophon. 10: AAUP; French Club, Tehran Iran; Iran Amer Soc; Phi Kappa Phi; Amer Bus & Profess Club, Tehran. 12: Iran ed Eastern Librarian--, E PakistanLA (68); Coed LibraryCollege Newsletter-- (6667); Ed Drexel Information Science Series-- (6467); Ed Drexel Library School Series-- (6067); Ed ALA Lib Periods RT Newsletter-- (5456); Ed John Crerar Lib Quarterly-- (4547); Coed Data Processing in Public and University Libraries-- (66); The LibraryCollege-- (66). 13: Yes. 14: Info sci, lib educ, admin, research libs. 15: P O Box 1286, Tehran Iran.

HARVEY, JUDY BURNSIDE. b Owensboro Ky 27 O 42. 5: Scripps Col 60-64 (European Studies) BA; UWash summer 62 (European Studies), 64-66 MLibr, 64-65 MLIBR; ULondon summer 64 (English Lit). 6: Fr. 7: Waitress Scripps Col 61-64; Ref libn LC 65-67; Research libn Bur of Ed Ref Time Inc 67; Ref libn LC 67-. 10: Scripps Col Alum Organ. 14: Ref. 15: 12424 Rebecca Dr SW, Tacoma Wash 98499.

HARVEY, MARY E. b Orviston Penn 4 O 11. 5: Lock Haven State Col 30-34 (Educ, Eng, Fr) BS in Ed; Drexel 38-39 BS in LS; Penn State U summer 37 (LS). 7: Ast Huntingdon Co Lib, Huntingdon Penn 35-40; Schs asst Harrisburg Pub Lib, Harrisburg Penn 40-41; Libn E J Gray Lib Dickinson Jr Col 41-46; Spec asst J V Brown Lib, Williamsport Penn 46-48; Catlgr Lib Wilkes Col 48-50; Libn Pottsville Pub Lib, Pottsville Penn 50-63; Catlgr Ocean Co Lib, Toms River NJ 63-. 9: ALA; NJL; PennLA. 10: Soroptimist Club. 14: CATLG. 15: Magnolia Manor, Maiden lane, Toms River NJ 08753.

HARVEY, MARY FRANCES. b Osceola Neb 5 D 19. 7: Tech processing dir Lompoc Pub Lib, Lompoc Cal 60-65; Elem sch libn Lompoc Unified Sch Dist, Lompoc Cal 66-67; Tech processing dir azusa Pub Lib, Azusa Cal 67-68; Reg consul Neb Pub Lib Commsn, Lincoln Neb 69-. 9: ALA; MtPlainsLA; NebLA. 15: Nebraska Pub Lib Commission, Lincoln Nb 68509.

HARVEY, OPAL A. b Buda Tex 27 D 05. 5: Mary Hardin-Baylor Col 44 (Eng) BA; Tex Womans U 61 MLS. 7: Tchr Bishop Ind Sch Dist, Bishop Tex 23-25; Tchr Kingsville Ind Sch Dist, Kingsville Tex 26-27; Tchr Mirando City Ind Sch Dist, Mirando City Tex 43-58; Jr High & elem libn Bishop Pub Schs, Bishop Tex 58-64; Circ libn Tex A&I U 64-. 8: Elem sch prin, Mirando City 43-48; High sch prin, Mirando CITY 48-58. 9: ALA; TexLA; (chm Dist IV 66-67); Coastal BendLA (chm 64-65). 10: PTA; Delta Kappa Gamma. 14: Cir, ref, tchg. 15: P O Box 305, Bishop Tx 78343.

HARVEY, ORLANE (HUFF). b Rankin County Miss 6 Mr 40. 4: Robert Curtis Harvey. 5: Hinds Jr Col 58-60 Diploma; USoMiss 60-62 (LS) BS. 7: Summer intern Miss Lib Commsn, Jacson Miss summer 61; Waterways Exp Station Research Lib, Vicksgurg Miss summer 62; Jr high libn Franklin Attendance Center, Meadville Miss 62-63; Catlgr Waterways Exp Station Research Lib, Vicksburg Miss 63-64; Circ head Miss Lib Commsn, Jackson Miss 64-, Chief tech proc 65-. 9: Miss LA. 14: Circ, catlg; tech proc. 15: Rt 5 Box 119, Jackson Ms 39212.

HARVEY, ROBERT DUNCAN. b Brooklyn NY 9 F 19. 4: Mary Jane Hatfield. 5: Wesleyan U 37-41 (Govt) BA; Columbia 49-50 (LS) MS. 6: Fr. 7: Priorities & traffic US Army Air Force, India 42-45; Air freight agent Amer Airlines, NYC 45-49; Asst dir pub serv UVt Lib 50-56; Chief of ref & spec serv Northwestern U 56-59; Head Libn & Head Dept of Lib Sci Southwest Mo State Col 59-. 9: AL; MoLA; Mo State TA; ;Mo Assn Col & Res Libs (chm 68-69). 10: AAUP. 13: Yes. 14: Ref, admin. 15: 821 E Delmar st, Springfield Mo 65804.

HARVIN, MARIE (JANICE). b Alto Tex 5 My 24. 5: Stephen F Austin State Col 40-43 (Eng) BA; Peabody 43-45 BS in LS; McCoy Col Johns Hopkins U 53-54; Little Rock U 63-66. 6: Fr. 7: Catlg asst Harvard Law Lib 45-46; Asst libn catlgr Vanderbilt Med Lib 46-49; Catgr UMd Med Lib 49-55; Asst libn ref UNeb Med Lib 55-56; Asst libn ref Vanderbilt Med Lib 56-57; Ref libn NLM 57-60; Head Libn UArk Med Center 60-66; Head libn UTex M D Anderson Hosp (Houston) 66-. 9: ALA; SL; MedLA(chm Com Standards 63-64, So Reg Group); Amer Assn hist Med; ArkLA. 10: Altrusa Club; AAAS. 12: Asoc ed "Bulletin of the Medical Library Assn (49-50). 13: Yes. 14: Ref, interlib loans, train hosp libns. 15: 3515 Deal st, Houston Tx 77025.

HARWELL, LINDA JEAN (RENFROE). b Moss Point Miss 17 Ja 43. 4: John Wayne Harwell. 5: Miss State Col for Women 61-65 (Eng) BA; Fla State U 65-66 (LS) MS. 7: Lib consul Miss Library Commsn, Jackson 66-68; Catlgr Randolph-Macon Woman's Col 68-. 9: ALA; SELA; VaLA. 14: Acquis, ref, child lit. 15: 1815 Rivermont ave apt 32, Lynchburg Va 24503.

HARWELL, RICHARD BARKSDALE. b Washington Ga 6 Je 15. 5: Emory 33-37 (Eng) AB, 37-38 ABLS. 6: Fr. 7: Asst to dir Flowers Collection Duke U Lib 38-40; Catlgr spec collections, Asst libn spec collections Lib Emory U Lib 40-43, 46-55 (Lt) US Navy, Pacific 43-46; Dir Southeastern Interlib Research Facility SREB, Atlanta 54-56; Dir of publ Va State Lib 56-57; Exec sec ACRL, Assoc Exec Dir ALA, Chicago 57-61; Libn Bowdoin Col 61-68; Col libn Smith 68-. 8: Surveys: Alma Col, Ariz State U, Franklin S Marshall Col, Mary Baldwin Col, Norwich U; Consul in southern bibliog UVa Lib (53); Bibliog consul, Boston Athenaeum (53); Consul on archival problems; The Coca-Cola Co (53-); Consul lib UJordan & other libsin Middle East fall 66. 9: ALA (Coun 62, var coms)-ACRL; AAS; ABS; Bibliog Soc UVa; MeLA(Bd 62-); NELA; SWLA(Exec sec 52-54). 10: Amer Civil War Round Table (London); Atlanta Civil War Round Table (founder 59); US Civil War Centennial Commsn (adv mem); Confederate Mem Lit Soc (Richmond); Me Hist Soc (Bd 63-); Alpha Beta Alpha; Beta Phi Mu; Phi Beta Kappa; Sigma Alpha Epsilon; Caxton Club (Chicago); Grolier Club (NY); Cumberland Club (Portland); Atlanta Hist Soc (Bd 54-56); Ga Hist Soc; Freedom Hall (Oak Park Ill). 11: Grant recipient from Henry E Huntington Lib 51; Carnegie Foundation 51; 12: Author or compiler: "Confederate Belles-Lettres (41); "Confderate Music (50); "Songs of the Confederacy (51); "Cornerstones of Confederate Collecting (52, 2d ed 53); "A Union List of Serial Holdings in Chemistry and Allied Fields (55); "Research Resources in the Georgia-Florida Libraries of SIRF (55); "Virginia State Publications, 1955 (56); "More Confederate Imprints, 2 vols (57); "The Confederate Reader

(57); "The Union Reader (58); "The War of 1861-1865 As Depicted in the Prints of Currier & Ives (60); "The War They Fought (60); "The Confederate Hundred (64); "A Confederate Marine (64); "Confederate Imprints in the University of Georgia Libraries (64); Editor of numerous books, espec Civil War and Reconstruction perods, and contrib to many more. 13: Yes. 15: Smith College Lib, Northampton Ma 01060.

HARWOOD ELIZABETH M. b Nashville Tenn 22 Ag 42. 5: Randolph-Macon Womans Col 59-63 (Music) AB; UWis 63-64 (LS) MS. 6: Fr, Ital. 7: Libn Marquette U Mem Lib 64-66; Ref asst Boston Pub Lib 66-. 9: ALA. 14: Ref, interlib loans. 15: 3953 N Maryland ave Apt 40, Milwaukee Wi 53211.

HARWOOD, ELEANOR (CASH). b Buckfield Me 29 My 21. 5: Amer Internat Col 40-43 (Eng) BA; USNR Midshipman Sch Smith Col 43-44 Ensign (W) USNR; New Haven State Tchrs Col 54-55 (LS) BS. 6: Fr. 7: Math tchr Pratt High Sch, Essex Conn 43; Operations off Air Pilot Hdqrs East Sea Frontier, NYC 44-45, Custodian of registered publs 45-46; Libn Rathbun Mem Lib, E Haddam Conn 55-56; Asst libn Kent Boys Sch, Kent Conn 56-63; Consul Chester Pub Lib, Chester Conn 65-. 8: Consul: Rosemary Hall, Greenwich Conn 58; St Marks Sch, Dallas 58; Chester Pub Lib, Chester Conn 6. 9: ALA; ConnLA; So Conn State Col LA. 13: Yes. 14: Ref, rare bks, catlg. 15: Maple st, Chester Conn 06412.

HARY, NICOLETTA CAROLINA (MATTIOLI). b Turin Italy 2 S 27. 4: Laszlo B Hary. 5: Istituto Universitario Orientale 47-51 (Langs) LittD; Scuola Vaticana di Biblioteconomia 51-52 (LS) Diploma. 6: Ital, Ger, Fr, Lat, Sp, Hungarian. 7: Ser asst UNotre Dame Lib 53, Catlgr 53-56, Catlg specialist 56-59; Consul & catlgr US Info Serv Lib, Rome 60-63; Catlgr UDayton Lib 64-65; Hd catlgr 65-. 12: "Menschengestalten in Ernst Wiechert's Werke" Doctoral diss (51); "Libri tedeschi nelle biblioteche di Roma" Lib sci thesis (52). 14: Catlg, rare bks. 15: 913 Twin Oaks dr, Dayton Oh 45431.

HASCHKE, SISTER MARY REGA OSF. b Humphrey Neb 23 Ja 07. 5 St Francis Normal Sch & Col (Lafayette Ind) summers 27-34; Creighton U summers 37-46 (Educ) BS; Col of St Joseph on the Rio Grande summers 48, 49, 54; Notre Dame U (Notre Dame Ind) summer 60; Rosary Col summers 56-62 (LS) MA. 6: Ger, Lat. 7: Prin St Boniface Sch, W Point Neb 47-50; Prin St Bonaventure Sch, Columbus Neb 52-56; Prin St Bernard Sch, Lindsay Neb 59-61; Asst libn Col of St Joseph on the Rio Grande 61-62; Libn St Joseph Convent High Sch & Col (Colo Springs Colo) 62-68; Libn St Francis Central High Sch, Humphrey Nebr 68-. 8: Tchr in elem schs Ind, Ill, Neb & Kan 23-61; Instr in Lib Sci at Col of St Joseph on the Rio Grande 61-62; Instr in Typewriting I at St Joseph Convent High Sch, Colo Springs Colo 62-. 68; Instr in Typewriting I St Francis Central High Sch 68-. 9: CathLA; Colo Assn SchL. 13: Yes. 14: Ref. 15: St Francis Central High Sch Box 277, Humphrey Nb 68642.

HASELDEN, CLYDE L(EROY). b Latta SC 26 Ag 14. 4: Erva Lee Buchanan. 5: Furman U 34-38 (Hist) BA; Columbia 38-39 BS in LS; Chicago 46-47 (LS) MA. 7: Stud asst Furman U 34-38; Grad Fellow City Col NY 38-39; Ref asst & supv Govt Documents UArk 39-43; Libn Parsons Col, Fairfield Iowa 47-50; Libn Baldwin-Wallace Col 50-59; Libn Lafayette Col 59-. 8: Col lib bldg consul. 9: ALA-ACRL (Delaware Valley Chap; pres 65-67);-LAD (Col Sect, chm Bldg Com for Col & Univ Libs 65-67); PennLA; Ohio Col LA (pres 54-56). 10: AAUP; Phi Kappa Phi. 13: Yes. 14: Lib bldgs, admin, bldgs & equip. 15: 1018 Cattell st, Easton Pa 18042.

HASELHUHN, RONALD PAUL. b Dalls Iowa 10 Jl 33. 4: Janice Elaine Salvatori. 5: Concordia Tchrs Col 50-52; Omaha U 52, 56-58 (Fine Arts) BFA; UDenver 58-59 (LS) MA; UMinn Educ, (Edu, AV). 7: US Army Med Corps (Cpl) 53-56; Pub serv libn USAF Acad Lib 59-61; Documents & ser St Cloud State Col 61-. 9: MinnLA. 14: Docs, ref, tchg ref. 15: 821 14th ave S, St Cloud Minn 56301.

HASELMAYER, LOUIS A. b Newark NJ 4 Je 11. 5: Williams 29-33 (Eng) BA; Yale 33-36 (Eng) PhD; Gen Theol Sem 38-41 (Church Hist) STB. 6: Fr, Lat. 7: Inst eng UMinn (Minneapolis) 36-38; Inst gk Gen Theol Sem, NYC 38-41, Church wk 41-49; Dean Cathedral Sch, Dallas 49-50; Dean Daniel Baker Col 50-52; Prof eng Iowa Wesleyan Col 52-, Dir of Archives of Col & Iowa Methodism 63-. 9: MLA; CEA; NTCE; Ch Hist Soc; Iowa Col Conf on Eng (pres 57-60); Iowa Poetry Assn (pres 60-65). 10: Phi Beta Kappa; Sigma Tau Delta; Alpha Psi Omega; AAUP; Rotary; Mt Pleasant Commun Concert Assn. 12: Assoc ed "Anglican Theological Review" (48-); Assoc ed "Lyrical Iowa" (59-); Assoc ed "Iowa English Yearbook" (57-65); "Medieval English Episcopal Registers" (38); "Lambeth and Unity" (48); "The Church of South India" (48); "Beauty for Ashes" Poems (56); "Fatal Grandeur" Poems (57); "Structure of English Poetry (60); "The 125th Anniversary History of Iowa Wesleyan College" (67); "The Presidents of Iowa Wesleyan College" (68). 13: Yes. 14: Org of archives of Iowa Wesleyan Col, Iowa United methodism. 15: Iowa Wesleyan Col, Mt Pleasant Ia 52641.

HASELWOOD, (ELDON) LaVERNE. b Barnard Mo 19 Jl 33. 4: Joan McQuiddy. 5: Com Ext Sch of Com 51 (Sec) Diploma; UOmaha 57-60 (Eng) BS Sec Educ; UDenver summers 61-63 (LS) MA; UNeb (Lincoln) 69. 7: Steno-clerk Diesel record clerk Union Pacific RR, Omaha 51-57; Chief clerk Criminal Investigation Detachment US Army, Ft Leonard Wood Mo 53-57; Libn Omaha Pub Schs 60-61; Libn Lewis Central Commun Schs, Council Bluffs Iowa 61-63; Govt document libn UOmaha 63-66; Chm dept of Lib Sci UNeb (Omaha) 67-. 8: Exec dir Nat Lib Week, Neb 67. 9: ALA-LED (Mount Plains Regl Rep); Neb Educ Media Assn; SW IowaLA (sec-treas 62); NebLA. 14: US govt docs, ref, lib educ. 15: 6843 N 65th st, Omaha Neb 68152.

HASEMEIER, ALFRED C. b St Elmo Ill 6 O 28. 4: Mary Jane Hessel. 5: St Louis U 46-50 (Hist) BS; Syracuse 50-51 MS in LS. 7: Lib asst St Louis Co Lib, Normandy Mo 51-52; Dir Platte Co Lib, Platte City Mo 52-62; Dir Mid-York Lib Syst, Utica NY 62-. 8: Mgt & bldg consul Utica Pub Lib 67-; Trustee Central NY Ref & Resource Coun 67-. 9: ALA; NYLA. 10: Rotary Club; Oneida Co Hist Soc. 14: Admin. 15: 2215 Douglas Crescent, Utica NY 13501.

HASEMEIER, FRANCES ELLEN. b Richmond Ind 14 Jl 41. 5: MiamiU 59-62 (Fr); IndU 62-63 (Fr) AB, 65-66 (LS) MA. 6: Fr. 7: Child libn Indianapolis Pub Lib 63-65; Lib assoc Nat'l Lib of Med, Bethesda Md 66-67, Asst to the construction program off 67-. 9: MedLA. 13: Yes. 14: Ref. 15: 5480 Wisconsin ave apt 1012, Chevy Chase Md 20015.

HASHIMOTO, MONICA F. b San Mateo Col 16 S 41. 5: UCal(Berkeley) 59-62; U of the Americas (Mexico City) 62-63 (Latin American Studies) BA; UWash 63-65 M Libr. 6: Sp. 7: Ref libn Los Angeles Pub Lib 65-, Adult ref libn Canoga Park Br 68-. 9: ALA; CalLA. 10: So Cal Hist Soc.; Alpha Mu Gamma. 14: Ref. 15: 7231 Alabama ave apt H-1, Canoga Park Ca 91303.

HASHISAKA, KENNETH K. b Japan 25 Mr 31. 4: Chiyoko Hashisaka. 5: Doshisha U 52-56 (Pol Sci) BA, 56-58 (LS) BL. 6: Eng, Japanese. 7: Tech libn Applied Research Div, Chicago 61-. 9: ALA.12: "My Life in Education. 14: Catlg. 15: 6422 N Paulina st, Chicago Il 60626.

HASKELL, DONNA M(ARIE). b Marngo Ill 20 Mr 15. 5: Kan State Col (Emporia) 33-35, 39-40 (LS) BS in Educ; UMich 43-45 AMLS. 6: Fr, Ger. 7: High sch libn Atchison Kan 40; Jr col libn Kan City (Kan) Jr Col 41-43; Sr catlgr UMich (Ann Arbor) 43-45; Catlg libn West Wash Col of Educ 45-47; Libn II catlg dept UCal (Berkeley) 47-50, 51-63; Catlg libn Los Angeles County Law Lib, Los Angeles 50-51; Head catlg dept Ariz State U Lib, Tempe Ariz 53-. 9: ALA(dir Div of Catlg & Clsf); Ariz State LA. 10: Soroptimist. 14: Catlg. 15: Matthews Lib Ariz State U, Tempe Ariz 85281.

HASKELL, INEZ KATHERINE. b Portland Ore 19 Je 22. 5: Multnomah Col 40-42 (Hist); Reed Col 42-44 (Hist) BA; UWash 45 BSin LS. 7: Accessions libn, Libn Ore Hist Soc Lib, Portland Ore 46-53; Catlgr Lib Assn of Portland, Portland Ore 53, Head order dept 58-. 9: ALA; OreLA (chm Regist Com 63); PNLA; Portland Area Spec Libns(pres 66-67). 10: Staff Assn, Lib Assn of Portland. 14: Acquis, catlg, hist libs. 15: 6725 NE Cleveland ave, Portland Ore 97211.

HASKELL, JOHN DUNCAN JR. b Providence 3 Ja 41. 4: Mary Binkowski. 5: URI 58-62 (Eng) AB; Rutgers summer 62, 63-64 MLS; George Washington U 69- (Amer Civilization). 7: Stud asst URI 60-62; Documents asst RI State Lib 62-63; US Army (Pvt) Ft Dix NJ 6465; 64-65. libn UMd 65-; Libn UMd Baltimore Co Campus 65-69. 9: ALA (Jr Mem RT); BSA; MdLA; Potomac Tech Proc Libns Assn; Amer Studies Assn. 10: Sigma Pi. 13: Yes. 14: Rare bks. 15: 5314 Carriage ct, Baltimore Md 21229.

HASKELL, MARY (BINKOWSKI). b Chelsea Mass. 4: John D Haskell Jr. 5: Vassar 59-63 (Pol Sci) AB; CatholicU 64-65 MS in LS. 7: Gifts & Exchange libn UMd 65-66; Catlgr Health Sci Lib UMd 66-67; Catlgr Enoch Pratt Free Lib, Baltimore 68-. 9: Potomac Tech Proc Libns. 10: Beta Phi Mu. 14: Catlg, indexing. 15: 5314 Carriage ct, Baltimore Md 21229.

HASKELL, PETER C. b Providence RI 9 F 39. 4: June H Daulton. 5: Bowdoin 57-61 (Govt) BA; Gothe Inst (Berlin) 66-67 (Ger); Rutgers 67-68 MLS. 6: Ger, Ital. 7: Liaison off 1st Lt US Army Inteligence, Weiden Ger 62-66; Asst ref catlg libn CornellU Lib 68-. 9: ALA. 14: Ref. 15: Albert R Mann Lib Cornell Univ, Ithaca NY 14850.

HASKINS, NORMA W. b Warsaw NY 16 D 21. 4: Joh Albert Haskins. 5: State Tchrs Col (Geneseo NY) 39-43 (LS) BS in Educ; Cornell U summer 47; Alfred U Ext 47-48 (Logic, Philos, Speech); State Tchrs Col (Geneseo NY) 64-65. 7: Libn WAVE US Navy SK/2c Sampson Naval Base, Geneva NY 44-45; Libn Thomas A Edison High Sch Bd of Educ, Elmira Heights NY 46-49; Libn Corning Northside High Sch Bd of Educ, CorningNY NY Hosp libn VA, Bath NY 61-. 10: Bus & Prof Women. 15: 6 Rumsey st, Bath NY 1810.

HASKINS, SUSAN M(cCALLUM). b N Adams Mass 8 Ap 07. 5: Mt Holyoke 29 AB; UMich 37 AB LS. 6: Ger, Lat. 7: Catlgr & clsfr Harvard Col Lib 29-36, Supv union catlg 37-42; Act chief catlg unit UN 49-50; Harvard Col Lib Head catlgr 42-55, Assoc libn for catlg 56-65, Assoc u libn for catlg 65-; Mem of the faculty of Arts and Scis Harvard U 65-. 9: ALA(Catlg & Clsf Sect); NE Tech Serv Lbns. 11: UMich Lib Sci Fac & Alum scholarship for 1968, made in my honor. 13: Yes. 14: Catlg. 15: Harvard ULib, Cambridge Mass 02138.

HASSAN, HAZEL (NICE). b Morrison Ill 31 Ag 25. 4: W Richard Hassan. 5: Goshen Col 46-47 Sec Certif, 50-52 (Elem Educ) BS Educ; UIll 58-60 MSLS. 6: Fr. 7: Gen off Goshen Ind, Chicago 47-50; Elem tchr Whiteside Co Ill, Albuquerque NM 52-57; Lincoln Lib of Essential Info The Frontir Press, Whiteside Co Ill & Albuquerque NM 57-58; Instr in Lib Sci & asst lbn Ball State U 60-62; Instr in Lib Sci & asst libn Milner Lib Ill State U 62-65. ; Elem libn Huntington Ind 66-67; Asst libn Rock Valley Col 67-69. 9: ALA; IllLA. 10: Beta Phi Mu. 12: "The Nice Family History (65); Jt auth "The Hassan Family (68). 14: Catlg. 15: 5307 East dr apt 1, Rockford Il 61111.

HASSLER, BEATRICE GOEDHART. b Cogswell ND 18 N 09. 5: All Saints Jr Col 26-27 (Fr); USD 27-30 (Fr) BA; UColo 30-31 (Romance Langs); Pasadena Jr Col 31-32 Sec Certif; UCal (Berkeley) 57-58 MLS. 6: Fr, Sp. 7: Accountant & Jr Partner Cedar Rapids Grain Co, Cedar Rapids Iowa 32-38; FHA & Loan Dept Investigator Bank of America (Long Beach Cal) 39-42; Br lib asst San Diego County Lib, Mesa Cal 48-57, Br Sr libn 58-. 9: ALA; CalLA. 10: AAUW. 14: Ref, br libn admi. 15: P O Box 573, La Mesa Ca 92043.

HASTINGS, HENRY C. b Albany NY 23 Ja 22. 4: Katherine Jantzen. 5: Brown 44 (Eng) AB; Columbia 48 BSLS: State Tchrs Col (Albany NY) 52 (Eng) MA. 7: (Cpl) USAF, European Theater 43-45; Ref asst Brown U Lib 48-49; Ref libn Kenyon Col 50-51; Asst head ref UKan 53-56; Head ref Gary Pub Lib, Gary Ind 56-. 8: Lib/USA, NY Worlds Fair, 65. 9: ALA; IndLA(Subscrip Bks Com 64-69). 10: Civitan Club of Gary. 12: "Spoken Poetry on Reords & Tapes, ACRL Monograph 18 (57). 13: Yes. 14: Ref. 15: Gary Pub Lib 220 W Fifth ave, Gary In 46402.

HASTINGS, RICHARD S(TAUNTON). b Wash DC 25 Je 37. 4: Eileen Ditman. 5: West Md Col 56-60 (Hist, Educ) AB; UMich 62-63 AMLS. 7: (Pvt) US Army Reserve program, Ft Knox Ky 60-61; Gen prof asst Baltimore Co Pub Lib Arbutus Br 63, Catonsville Area Br 63-64; Br libn Baltimore Co Pub Lib PERRY Hall Br 64-65, Essex Br 65-69; Asst co libn Marin Co 69-. 9: MdLA; CalLA. 14: Admin, bk sel. 15: 119 nova Albion way apt 316, San Rafael Ca 94903.

HATCH, BENTON LeROY. b Kittery Me 12 Ja 13. 5: Yale 31-32, 34-35 (Gk) BA. 7: Circ asst catlgr Yale U Lib 35-43; Woods accountant Me Seaboard St Regis, Bucksport Me 43-47; Catlgr head catlgr Colby Col Lib 48-54; UMass Lib: Asst libn acquis 54-60, Assoc libn & chief acquis 60-65, Assoc libn spec Collections 65-68; Assoc dir spec collections 68-. 10: Royal Geog Soc (Fellow); Amer Geog Soc (Fellow); Me Hist Soc; NE Hist Geneal Soc; Appalachian Mountain Club. 12: "Appalachia; index to Vols XI-XXV (52); "Preliminary Check List of Waterville, Maine, Imprints to 1850 (52); "Check List of the Publications of Thomas Bird Mosher (66); Ed Com "Appalachia 39-58. 13: Yes. 14: Catlg, acquis, spec collections. 15: PO Box 757, Amherst Mass 01002.

HATCH, MARY C. b Richmond Utah. 4: Edgun V Wulff. 5: UUtah 37 (Eng) BA; Columbia 38 (LS) MA, 40 (Eng) MA. 6: Fr, Ger. 7: Libn NY Pub Lib 37-39 Libn Columbia U 39-41; Libn NY Pub Lib 41-43; Br libn 44-55, Readers adv 56-61, Princ libn 62-66; Coord Mid-Manhattan Lib 67-. 8: Instr Fla State U Sch of Libnship summer 58, 60. 9: ALA; AEA; TLA; CNLA (sec-treas); NYLA; SLA. 10: NY Lib Club; Columbia U Grad Faculties Alumni Assn; UUtah Alumni Assn; Colmbia U Lib Sch Alumni Assn. 12: Childrens Books: "osamunda-Warne (46); Thirteen Danish Tales (47); "More Danish Tales (9). 14: Adult serv, admin, ref. 15: NY Pub Lib 5th ave & 42nd st, NYC 10018.

HATCHER, JEAN (BUCKNER). b Owensboro Ky 27 S 20. 4: Earl C Hatcher. 5: Bethel Womans Col 38-39; West Ky State Col 39-42 (Eng) AB; Catherine Spalding 61-65 MSLS. 6: Fr, Lat. 7: Eng - lib Shippensburg High Sch, Fordsville Ky 42-43; Eng- lib Stearns High Sch, Stearns Ky 43-45; Eng-lib Bloomfield High Sch, Bloomfield Ky 48-49; Eng-lib Hodgenville High Sch, Hodgenville Ky 49-58; Libn La Rue County High Sch, Hodgenville Ky 58-; Coord child serv Corpus Christi Pub Libs, Corpus Christi Tex 68-69; Libn Big Spring Jr High, Newville Penn 69-. 9:NEA; NEA; KyASchl; KyEA. 10: Fourth Dist (Ky Libns Assn (treas)61-62, pres 66-67.13716 14: Catlg. 15: Rt 2, Hodgenville Ky 42748.

HATFIELD, FRANCES S. b Tennille Ga 2 F 22. 5: Fla State Col for Women 39-43 (Sci Educ) BS; Fla State U 48-49 (LS) MA. 7: Tchr Ft Lauderdale High Sch, Ft Lauderdale Fla 43-47; Supv of instr materials Broward County Schs, Ft Lauderdale Fla47-. 8: Instr UMd summer 64; consul several NDEA Insts for Sch Libns; Consul ESEA Title III Wkshop in SC summer 68; Consul for US Off of Educ on sch projs. 9: ALA; (Coun, A-V Com 66-69, Memb Com 64-66); AASch(Legis Com); NEA-DAVI; ASCD; FlaEA; Fla A-V Assn (pres 57-58, Bd 58-65); FlaASchL (Bd60-65, Legis chm 65, chm-elect 65-66); SELA. 10: Delta Kappa Gamma; Beta Phi Mu; Soroptimist Club. 12: Several Fla State Dept of Educ BULLETINS IN AREA OF MATERIALS. 13: Yes. 14: Sch lib serv, dist level materials ctrs. 15: Broward Co Bd of Pub Instr 1320 SW 4th st, Ft Lauderdale Fl 33312.

HATFIELD, PATRICIA ANN. b Chambersburg Penn 8 Mr 43. 5: Millersville State Col 61-63 (LS); Shippensburg State Col 63-65 (LS) BS in Educ 69- LS; Temple U 65. 7: Stud lib asst Shippinsburg Pub Lib, Shippensburg Penn 58-65; Libn Northeastern Jr High Sch, Manchester Penn 65-; Coord child serv Corpus Christi Pub Libs, Corpus Christi Tex 68-69; Libn Big Spring Jr High, Newville Penn 69-. 9: ALA; PennLA; TexLA; PennStateEA. 14: Rare bks, ref, yp serv. 15: 325 Walnut st, Shippensburg Pa 17257.

HATHAWAY, BERTHA (LOGAN). b Woonsocket RI 18 S 03. 4: Leonard B Hathaway. 5: Pratt 25 (LS). 7: Br libn Providence Pub Lib 25-27; Sr asst Evanston Pub Lib, Evanston Ill 27-29; Sr asst Detroit Pub Lib 29-33; Child libn Rocky River Pub Lib, Rocky River Ohio 46-55; Child libn Hennepin County, Edina Minn 55-58; Child libn Rocky River Pub Lib, Rocky River Ohio 58-. 9: ALA; OhioLA. 14: Catlg. 15: 1975 Hampton rd, Rocky River Ohio 44116.

HATHAWAY, CHRISTINE (RUSSELL) DROWNE. b Providence 13 O 05. 4: Robert Winfield Hathaway Jr. 5: AM (hon) Brown U 67. 7: Brown U Lib: Cpyist 24-25, Asst catlgr 25-28, Sec to libn 28-44, Admin asst 44-63, Spec collections libn 63-. 9: RILA; Mss Soc; SAA. 10: Abraham Lincoln Assn. 14: Spec collections, rare bks, archives. 15: 58 Chapin rd, Barrington RI 02806.

HATHAWAY, EDITH L. b Kokomo Ind 22 D 43. 5: Wheaton Col (Norton Mass) 61-65 (Eng) AB; Simmons 66-67 MS. 6: Fr, Sp, Portu. 7: Actress-apprentice Cleveland Playhouse, cleveland Ohio 65-66; Asst to registrar Radcliffe 66; Bkmob libn Boston Pub Lib summer 66; Hd libn Chamberlayne Jr Col, Boston 67-68; Catlgr Harvard Law Sch 68-. 12: Case study in Kister's "Social issues and library problems: Case studies in the social sciences' (68). 14: Acquis, catlg. 15: 383 Harvard st #8, Cambridge Ma 02138.

HATHAWAY, JUDITH ANNE. b Sedalia Mo 3 Ag 46. 5: Whittier Col 64-68 (Sociol) BA; UCLA 68-69 MLS. 6: Sp, Fr. 7: Catlgr UAriz 69-. 9: ALA; CalLA. 10: Alpha Kappa Delta. 15: 416 Dorothy dr, Fullerton Ca 92631.

HATHAWAY, LULU (BAILEY). b Leamington Spa Eng 24 Ja 03. 4: Rev Behrends Bailey Hathaway. 5: Leeds U (Eng) 21-24 (Bot) BSc; URochester 24-26 (Educ) AM; Hartford Theol Found (Conn) 30-32 (African Educ); Syracuse 61 MS BS in LS. 6: Fr, Lingala. 7: Chm child wk NY State Coun of Curches, Syracuse NY 50-60; V-pres Nat Coun Amer Baptist Women, NYC 52-57; Libn Edmeston Central Sch, Edmeston NY 57-59; Dir of lib serv Fabius Central Sch, Fabius NY 59-64; Head Libn Edison Jr Col, Ft Myers FLA 69-. 10: United Church Women Phi Beta Mu. 12: Child bks in the religious field;

"Westward the Church (62); "The BOY Who Could Not Talk (63); "They Lived Their Love (64); "Especially Rotia (68). 15: 23 E 47th st, Cape Coral Fla 33904.

HATHAWAY, RICHARD F. b Limestone Me 27 Je 34. 4: Betty Ann (Abs). 5: Lincoln Christian Col 58-63 (Ministerial Sci) AB; UIll 64-66 (LS) MS. 7: Grad asst supv circ desk UIll Lib 65-66; Asst libn Lincoln Christian Col Lib 66-. 9: ALA; ATheolLA; IllLA. 10: Phi Beta Mu. 14: Ser, catlg, ref, acquis, admin. 15: 11 Singleton dr, Lincoln Il 62656.

HATHAWAY, RICHARD J. b Pontiac Mich 12 Mr 40. 4: Sharon Briggs. 5: Albion Col 58-62 9hist) BA; UMich 62-63 (Hist) MA, 63-65 (LS) MA. 6/ fr. 7: Reg libn Burton Hist Collection, Detroit Pub Lib 64-66; Hd Mich Unit State of Mich Bureau of Lib Serv 66-. 9: AHA; MichLA; Hist Soc of Mich. 10: Phi Alpha Theta. 13: Yes. 14: Hist collections, rare bks, ref. 15: Mich Unit Bureau of Lib Sci 735 E Mich ave, Lansing Mi 48913.

HATTASCH, MAUREEN BARBARA (BARTLETT). b London Eng 11F 38. 4: Claus E Hattasch. 5: N Western Polytech Lib Sch (London) 55-59 ; Assoc of Lib Assn. 7: Asst libn Hornsey Pub Lib, London 55-58; Asst libn Westminster Pub Lib, London 58-60; Libn Research Services LTD, London 61-62; Asst libn US Brewers Assn NYC 62-65; Indexer H W Wilson Co, Bronx NY 65-67; Asst catlgr Greenwich (Conn) Lib 67-. 9: SLA; ALA; ConnLA. 15: 923 New Norwalk rd, New Canaan Ct 06840.

HATTON, JOHN (FREDERIC). b Buffalo NY 25 Mr 21. 4: Margaret Elizabeth Phillpotts-Brown. 5: UToronto Victoria Col 44-47 (Philos, Eng) BA, 47-48 (Philos) MA, 52-53 BLS. 6: Fr. 7: Reader Dept of Eng Victoria Col UToronto 47-48, 51-52; Reader Dept of Philos UToronto 47-48; Jr Master Upper Can Col (Toronto) 48-49; Instr Dept of Eng UKan 49-51; Libn Defence Research Establishment Toronto Lib, Downsview Ont 53-. 9: SLA (Toronto Chap; sec 64-66, programme chm 66-68; pres 68-69); Prof Inst Pub Serv Can; OntLA; Inst Prof Libns Ont. 10: Japanese Garden Club. 14: Bk sel. 15: Lib Defence Res Est Toronto P O Box 2000, Downsview Ont Can.

HAUCK, HELEN (GIFFIN). b Spingfield Ohio 6 Mr 11. 5: Wittenberg Col 29-32 (Hist) AB; West Res 32-33 BS in LS; UMich summers 39, 40, 42, 43 (LS) MA. 6: Fr, Ger. 7: Catlgr Wittenberg Col 33-35; Period libn UCincinnati 35-37; Libn Blackburn Col 37-41; Libn Westminster Col (New Wilmington Penn) 41-43; Pt Libn Air Force Ga, Tex 44-46; Ref libn Rensselaer Polytechnic Inst 47-49; Ref libn Westinghouse Res Labs, Pittsburgh 50-52; Libn Pittsburgh Ordnance Dist 52-54; Ref libn NASA Lewis Research Center, CLEVELAND 54-60; Head Sc-tech Dept Cleveland Pub Lib 60-. 9: ALA; SLA; OhioLA. 13: Yes. 14: Ref (sci & engnr). 15: 11820 Lake ave apt 104, Lakewood Ohio 44107.

HAUER, MARY (GARRETT). b Calhoun La 26 Ag 15. 4: Nelson A Hauer. 5: LSU 31-35 (Fr & Eng) BA; LSU 63-66 MS in LS; UTex 42-43 (Sp); Universidad Nacional de Mex 43 (Sp); UMadrid 68 (Sp). 6: Sp, Fr. 7: Tchr Radford Sch for Girls, El Paso Tex 43-44; Tchr ithaca High Sch, Ithaca NY 47-48; Instr and acting chm Dept Books & Libraries, LSU 65-. 9: ALA; LaLA. 10: Beta Phi Mu; Phi Sigma Iota; Sigma Delta Pi. 14: Ref. 15: 305 Cornell ave, Baton Rouge La 70808.

HAUGAARD, ANNE. b Luverne N Dak 19 Ag 14. 5: Mayville State Col 43 (Eng) BS; UMinn 50 BSLS; UWash 68 MLS. 6: Danish. 7: Tchr rural sch, Luvwrne N Dak 33-35; Tchr pub sch, Osnabrock N Dak 39-43; Prin & tchr pub sch: Clyde N Dak 43-46, McClusky N Dak 46-52, Harvey N Dak 52-58; Tchr & libn pub sch, Valley City N Dak 58-67, Asst libn Valley City State Col 67-. 8: Field repres State Lib Commsn, Bismarck ND 5 summers. 9: NEA; ALA (Jt Com 58-63); NDEA (pres 65); NDEA (Bd 63-66). 10: PEO; Delta Kappa Gamma. 14: Ref, tchg lib sci. 15: 252 2nd ave SW, Valley City ND 58072.

HAUGE, HARRIS R. b Clarkfield Minn 17 Ag 25. 4: Donna Shapira Hauge. 5: St Olaf Col 46-49 (Econ, Hist) BA; UMinn 50-51 (LS) MA. 6: Ger, Norwegian. 7: (Radioman 3/) US Navy 43-45; High sch tchr Canton High Sch, Canton SD 49-50; Catlgr Gustavus Adoiphus Col 51-63; Libn Monmouth Col (Monmouth Ill) 63-. 9: ALA; IllLA; 10: AAUP. 14: Admin. 15: Monmouth Col, Monmouth Ill 61462.

HAUGHT, ALBERTA YVONNE. b Uniontown Penn 27 O 44. 5: Juniata Col 62-66 (Eng) BA; UPittsburgh 66-67 MLS. 7: Asst libn Huntingdon Co Lib, Huntingdon Penn 67-. 9: ALA; PennLA. 10: Beta Phi Mu. 14: Child serv, circ. 15: 328 Miffin st, Huntingdon Pa 16652.

HAUGHTON, CLARIBEL (LOUISE)(DAWE). b Milwaukee 2 D 28. 4: George Thomas Haughton. 5: Mt Holyoke 47-51 (Eng Comp) BA; UWis summer 51; Rosary Col ; 63-67 (LS) MA. 6: Ger, Fr. 7: Sales corresponent Bostrom Mfg Corp, Milwaukee 51-52; Statistical clerk Neilsen Corp, Chicago 54-57; Clerk Nat Merit Scholarship, Evanston 59; Math asst Glencoe Pub Schs, Glencoe Ill 61-; Clerk 62-65; Ya libn Glencoe Pub 62-65; Ya libn 65-; Catlgr 67-. GLENCOE Ill 61-. 9: ALA; IllLA. 10: LWV. 14: Ya wk, catlg. 15; 601 Greenwood ave, Glencoe Ill 6022.

HAURY, GERTRUDE. b Claflin Kan 30 Je 07. 5: Phillips U 25-28 (Eng) AB; UKan 35 (Educ) ms in Ed; UIll 47 BSLS; UDenver summer 55; Kan State Tchrs Col (Emporia) summer 62. 7: Eng tchr Claflin (Kan) High Sch 28-30; Eng tchr Hutchinson (Kan) High Sch 30-45; Libn Hutchinson Jr Col 45-61; Libn Hutchinson (Kan) High Sch 64-66; Acquis libn Hutchinson Pub Lib 66-68; Tchr-Lib Sci Kan State Tchrs Col Emporia) summers 62-67. 8: KanStateTA (Sch Lib Com 59-65). 9: ALA-YASD; -AASchL; NEA; KanLA; KanStateTA; KanASchL; MoStateTA. 10: Beta Phi Mu; Pi Lambda Theta; PEO; UIll Lib Sch Assn. 13: Yes. 14: Bk sel. 15: Baxter Area, Lampe Mo 65681.

HAUSE, AARON (HAROLD). b Brooklyn NY 4 My 36. 5: NYU 54-57 (Amer Hist & Govt) BA, 58-62 (Intl Rel) 63 (Educ); Georgetown U 57-58 (Law); Pratt Inst 65-66 MLS. 7: Soc investigator NYC Dept of Welfare 60-62; Researcher NYC Bd of Ethics 62-64; Sr ref libn Queens Borough Pub Lib, Jamaica NY 66-68; Docs libn Hofstra U 68-. 9: ALA; SLA; Amer pol Sci Assn; NYLA; NY Lib Club. 14: Govt docs, law, ref. 15: 217 E Mount Eden pky, Bronx NY 10457.

HAUSER, JOHN NORMAN. b NYC 19 Ap 37. 4: Susan Elizabeth Burger. 5: NY City Community Col 54-56 (Dental Tech) A of Applied Sci; Moravian Col 56-60 (Hist) BA; Kutztown State Col 61-63 Certif in LS & equivalent MS; Syracuse summers 65, 66, 67, MSLS. 7: Hosp Corpsman (3rd class Petty ff) USNR 54-62; Lib clerk NY Pub Lib 60-61; Head Libn Central Bucks High Sch, doylestown Penn 63-. 9: ALA; NEA; PennLA; Penn SchLA; Penn State EA (Dept of Supv & Curr). 10: Nat Railway Hist Soc; Electric Railroaders Assn. 14: High sch libs, period. 15: P O Box 8, Fountainville Pa 18923.

HAUSER, NANCY ANN (SUCHENSKI). b Yonkers NY 4 O 42. 4: Paul Edward Hauser. 5: Col of Mt St Vincent 60-64 (Eng) BA; Columbia 64-65 (LS) MS. 6: Fr, Polish. 7: Tech serv libn Columbia Engineering Lib 65-67; Ref libn for mss Columbia Special Collections 67-. 10: Friends of Columbia Libs. 14: Rare bks, mss. 15: 332 W 88th st apt C-1, New York NY 10024.

HAUSER, RUTH (MARGUERITE). b Oklaunion Tex 8 My 14. 5: Chaffey Jr Col 31-33 (Liberal Arts) AA; URedlands 33-36 (Romance Lang) AB; UCal (Berkeley) 38-39 Certif in Libnship. 6: Sp, Fr. 7: Prof asst Glendale Pub Lib, Glendale Cal 39-48; Home reading serv asst Detroit Pub Lib 48-60; Catlgr La Verne Col Lib 60-65; Spec collections libn Honnold Lib for Claremont Cols 65-. 9: ALA; CalLA (sec So Dist 69). 10: Zonta Internat; Bus & Profess Women; AAUW. 14: Spec collections, rare bks, mss, archives. 15: 152 Ford ave, Pomona Ca 91767.

HAUSMANN, ALBERT FRANCIS. b Litchfield Conn 6 F 21. 4: Marilyn Cade. 5: Brown 39-43 9eng) BA, 47 (Eng) MA; Post Col of Com (Bus Admin) Certif; So Conn State Col (LS) MS. 6: Fr. 7: Aviation gunnery instr specialist G USN 44-46; Life ins salesman F N Clark Ins Agy, Litchfield Conn 47-53; Asst mgr group accounts Conn Med Serv, New Haven 53-55; Sr correspondent Olin Mathieson Chem Corp, New Haven Conn 55-64; Asst dir Godfrey Memorial Lib, Middletown Conn 64-65; Libn Glastonbury High Sch, Glastonbury Conn 65-66; Asst libn processing & serv New Haven Col 66-. 9: ALA; ConnLA. 10: Phi Beta Kappa; AAUP; YMCA. 13: Yes. 14: Catlg, ref, circ. 15: 38 Laurel dr, Wallingford Ct 06492.

HAUSRATH, DONALD CRAIG. b Ames Iowa 19 F 34. 4: Sydney Clar. 5: State U Iowa 59-61 (Eng) AB; Army Lang Sch 56 (Russian) Grad Tr; UCal(Berkeley) 63-64 MLS. 6: Fr. 7: Russian interpreter US Army Intelligence, US, Vietnam 56-59; Eng tchr Khai Mihn High Sch, Saigon Vietnam 58-59; Supv of circ help UIowa Lib 59-61; Supv in res room UCal Lib (Berkeley) 63-64; Libn Vanden High Sch, Travis AFB Cal 64-. 8: Supv movement of UIowa Lib collection int new bldg 61; Established lib at Vanden High Sch 64; Curriculum Coordinating Com Travis Unified Sch Dist 65-; Asst libn for pub serv Hartnell Col 66-68; Dir of learning resources Kalamazoo ValleyCommun Col 68-. 9: ALA; CalL; CalASchL;

Cal Tchrs Assn. 14: Collection & program development, sel & learning resources for jr cols. 15: 919 Edward Circle, Vallejo Cal 94593.

HAUSRATH, LILLIAN D. b Cleveland Ohio 4 My 04. 5: Hiram Col 22-23; Wayne U 44 (LS); UMich Ext (Detroit) 50 (LS); West Res 55-59 (LS). 6: Ger, Fr. 7: Libn GE Co metallurgical, Detroit 44-51; Ref libn Cleveland Electric Illuminating Co 53-64; Period libn sci & tech dept Cleveland Pub Lib, Ohio 65-. 9: SLA; ASIS (No Ohio Chap: sec-treas 68-69). 14: Periods. 15: 4316 Norma dr, Cleveland Oh 44121.

HAVASY, JUDITH ESTHER (CAIN). b Washington Penn 2 D 42. 4: Richard Alexander Havasy. 5: Clarion State Col 60-64 (LS) BS; Drexel (LS). 7: Bkkeeer Webers Clothing Store, Vandegrift Penn 59-60; Sec biol dept Clarion State Col 60-62, Sec Lib sci dept 62-64; Libn Abington (Penn) Sch Dist 64-66; A-v adv & libn Beaver Sr High Sch, Beaver Penn 66-. 9: NEA; ALA; PennStateEA. 10: PTA; Zeta Tau Alpha. 11: Outstanding Citizenship Award. 14: Ref, child lit, a-v materials. 15: 5G st Van Burns Hms, Beaver Pa 15009.

HAVENS, RUTH WOOD. b Troy NY 20 Ag 16. 4: Thomas E(dward) Havens. 5: Russell Sage 34-38 (Eng) BA; SUNY 38-39 BS in LS, 44-49 (Eng) MA. 6: Fr. 7: Tchr libn Tivoli High Sch, Madalin NY 39-40; Libn Center Moriches High Sch, Center Moriches NY 34, 40-46; Libn Mt Kisco High Sch, Mt Kisco NY 46-48; Libn Second Supv Dist Suffolk, Patchogue NY 59-60; Libn Nathaniel Woodhull Elem Sch, Shirley NY 60-. 8: Bd of Trustees Center Moriches Free Pub Lib, Center Moriches NY (pres) 50-58. 9: NEA; NYLA; NY State Tchrs Assn. ; SuffolkSchLA; William FloydTA. 14: Tchg use of lib, ref, story telling. 15: P O Box 611, E Moriches NY 11940.

HAVENS, SHIRLEY ELISE. b NYC 19 N 25. 5: Hunter Col 43-47 (Eng) BA (cum laude); Columbia 47-52 (Eng). 6: Sp. 7: Asst to the bursar Tchrs Col, Columbia U Sec Sect to exec sec Mental Health Film Bd, NY 52-54; Asst to the libn Carnegie Endowment of Intrnat Peace, NY 54-57; Ed asst & Asst ed, Assoc ed managing ed "Library Journal 57-. 8: Lib Com, Presidents Com on Employment of the Handicapped. 9: NY Lib Club (Bul Ed), 65-67. 10: Phi Beta KAPPA. 12: Ed of annual "Architectural Issue of "Library Journal. 13: Yes. 14: Arch. 15: 43-71 164th st, Flushing NY 11358.

HAVERSTOCK, WILLIAM WESLEY. b Minneapolis 27 Jl 18. 4: Myrtle Moberg. 5: Macalester Col 37-41 (Hist) BA; Stanford 47-48 (Educ) MA; UCal 51-52 BLS. 7: Tchr soc studies High Sch, Upsala Minn 41; US Army MAC(1st Lt) 42-46; Tchr soc studies Jr High-High Sch, Santa Cruz Cal 48-52; Catlgr Humboldt State Col 52-60, Order libn, head tech serv 60-64; Catlgr Chico State Col 64-. 9: ALA; CalLA. 14: Catlg. 15: 315 W Lincoln ave, Chico Cal 95926.

HAVILAND, LEONA. b Stamford Conn 10 N 16. 5: UAla 34-35, 37-40 (LS) BS in Educ; USDA Grad Sch 46-48 (Ger); UIll 50-51 MS in LS; Columbia 43, 58-60 (Educ). 6: Fr. 7: Jr asst Ferguson Lib, Stamford Conn 36-37, summers 38, 39; Stud asst UAla Lib 37-40; Sr asst ref det Ferguson Lib, Stamford Conn 40-43, Sr asst child dept 43-44; Asst to catlgr US Nat Museum, Smithsonian Inst, Wash DC 44-48; Libn of the arts & ind Museum Smithsonian Inst, Wash DC 48-50; Ref libn US Merchant Marine Acad 52-. 9: ALA; SLA. 10: Alpha Beta Alpha; LI Hist Soc; NY Geneal & Biog Soc. 14: Ref. 15: 10 Welwyn rd apt 2G, Great Neck LI NY 11021.

HAVILAND, MORRISON CHANDLER. b Glens Falls NY 7 Ap 15. 4: Mary Elizabeth Mooney. 5: Harvard 33-37 (Eng Lit) AB; Columbia 37-38 (LS) BS; UCal 46-47 (LS) MA. 6: Fr, Ger. 7: Catlgr Adams House Lib Harvard Col 35-37; Stack supv & attendant in Amer hist room & theatre collection ref dept, NY Pub Lib summers 36-38; Circ ref& exch asst Harvard Col Lib 38-42; (Lt) USNR 42-46; Act head res bk room UCal Lib Berkeley 47; Asst to libn & ref in Lamont Lib Harvard Col Lib 47-50; Libn Wabash Col 50-55; Dir UVt Lib 55-61; Chief reader serv div Air U Lib, Maxwell AFB Ala 61-64; Asst dir Tulane U Lib 64-65; Assoc libn Admin UMass Lib 65-67; Dir readers serv div SUNY at Albany U Lib 67-. 9: SLA (Met/Mat Div: Bibliog Com); ALA (Bldgs & Equip Sect: Bldgs Com for Col & Univ Libs);-ACRL (chm Col Sect59-60); BSA; Bibliog Soc (London); Assn Spec Libs & Info Bur; Internat Fed of Documentation; LaLA; MassLA; NELA; SELA; VtLA (Fed Rel Coord); NYLA. 10: AAUP. 13: Yes. 14: Admin, reader serv, ref. 15: 1092 Van Antwerp rd, Schenectady NY 12309.

HAVILAND, VIRGINIA (ALICE). b Rochester NY 21 My 11. 5: Cornell U 29-33 (Econ) BA. 6: Fr. 7: Boston Pub Lib: Asst 34-63, Child libn 41-48, Br libn 48-52, Readers adv for child 52-63; Head Child Bk Sect LC 63-. 8: Bk reviewer "Horn Book Magazine 52-; Tchr child lit Simmons Col 57-63; ALA-(SDI) Adv Com ALA Library/USA, Worlds Fair 63-65; Juror Nat Bk Award for child lit (69). 9: ALA(chm and/or mem 4 coms & panel 58-); - Child Lib Assn(pres 54-55, com chm 53-54); -CSD (chm and/or mem 4 coms 59-66); DCLA (rogram Com 65-66). 10: Washington Childrens Book Guild; DC Coun of Exec Women in Educ; Pi Lmbda Theta. 11: Caroline M Newins Lecturer 50. 12: "Travelogue Story Bok of the Nineteenth Century (51); "Ruth Sawyer (65); "Childrens Literature, A Guide to Reference Sources (66); "William Penn, Founder and Friend (52); "Favorite Fairy Tales Series 10 vols to date. 13: Yes. 14: Bk sel, ref, child bks. 15: 520 N st SW, Wash DC 20024.

HAVLICE, PATRICIA (PATE). b Cleveland Ohio 2 F 43. 6: Sp, Fr. 7: Adult serv libn Cuyahoga Co Pub Lib, Cleveland Ohio 66-67; Ref libn Ohio StateU (Columbus) 67-68; Ref libn In 67-68; Ref libn IndU (Gary) 69-. 9: ALA. 14: Ref, bibliog. 15: 1422 N Glenwood ave #1G, Griffith In 46319.

HAVLIK, ROBERT JAMES. b Chicago 13 O 25. 4: Dorothy Naujoks. 5: Ill Inst of Tech 43-49 (Chem Engnr) BSChE; UIll 50-51 MSLS. 6: Ger, Russian. 7: Pilot plant oper Corn Prods Refining Co, Argo Ill 46-47; Research asst in oranic chem Armour Res Found, Chicago 47-50; Staff mem John Crrar Lib, Chicago 50; Exch libn Inst Iowa State Col 51-53; Asst ref libn Instr Purdue U 53-55; Tech libn Linde Div Union Carbide Corp, Tonawanda NY 55-63; Research lib spec US Off of Educ Lib Serv Br, Wash DC 63-67; Dir libs Nova U 67-. 8: Dir Study of Spec Libs, Probs and Coop Potentials for the Nat Adv Com on Libs 67. 9: SLA(mem 4 coms 60-; Wash DC Chap chm 2 groups 64-66), ALA (life mem); -ACRL; ASIS; FlaLA; DCLA. 10: The Lincoln Group of Wash DC; Buffalo Civil War Round Table. 13: Yes. 14: Spec libs in the US, spec lib statist, sci & tech lit, info retrieval, hist of sci, col lib admin. 15: Nova Univ, Ft Lauderdale Fl 33314.

HAWES, LILLA (KENNERLY). b Camden SC 1 F 08. 4: Foreman McConnell Hawes. 5: Converse Col 24-2; Agnes Scott 26-28 (Math) AB; Peabody 37-39 (LS) BS; American U summer 48 Certif in preservation & admin of archives. 6: Fr. 7: Sec Chem dept Ga Inst of Tech 30-36; Savannah Pub Lib: Asst 37-40, Ref asst 40-43, Br libn 43-48; Dir Ga Hist Soc, Savannah 48-. 9: SAA; Amer Assn State & Loc Hist; GaLA; SELA. 10: Savannah Hist Res Assn; Ga Hist Soc; Telfair Acad Arts & Sci; So Hist Assn; Hist Savannah Found Inc; Savannah-Chatham Co Hist Site & Monument Commsn Youth Museum of Savannah; Friends of the Lib; LWV; AAUW; ASCD; Pi Gamma M; Mu; Kappa Gamma; Nat Trust for Hist Preserv. 11: Award of Merit, Lachlan McIntosh Chap DAR 56. 12: Ed "Collections of the Ga Hist Soc vols 10-14 (52-64); "Lachlan McIntosh Papers in the University of Georgia Libraries (68). 13: Yes. 14: Ref, nat & loc hist. 15: 501 Whitaker st, Savannah Ga 31401.

HAWK, AUDREY (GRAFF). b Fallon Mont 6 D 15. 5: Mont State U 33-37 (Eng) BA; UMinn 40-41 BSLS; UWash 67 MSLS. (LS). 6: Fr, Ger. 7: Head Libn State Normal & Ind Sch, Ellendale ND 41-42; Engnr aide Boeing Airplane Co, Seattle 44-48; High sch libn Seattle City Sch System 50; Engnr aide Boeing Airplane Co, Seattle 53-56, Head Libn Engnr Lib Ind Prod Div 57-60; SUPV SCI & tech libn John F Kennedy Mem Lib Cal State Col (Los Angeles) 60-. 9: SLA (Adv Coun 66-67; (sec Puget Sound Chap 59-60); CalLA(Rec Com 64-65; chm Recr Com So Cal Chap 63-64). 10: Sierra Club; Fac Womens Assn. 12: "New Patterns in the Lives of Women (63). 13: Yes. 14: Ref (sci &tech). 15: 125 S Granada ave apt 1, Alhambra Ca 91801.

HAWK, W(ILLARD) G(EORGE). b Allentown Penn 16 Ja 16. 4: Evelyn A Brong 5: Moravian Col 34-38 (Eng) BA; Kutztown State Col 46-47 (LS); Carnegie & Columbia 51-52 (LS). 7: Newspaper corres Allentown (Penn) Call-Chronicle, Northampton Penn 39-41; Chainman Penn Dept of Highways, Allentown Penn 41-42; (T/5) Med Corps US Army 42-43; Ordnance-Inspector Bethlehem Steel Co, Bethlehem Penn 43-44, Subclerk-carrier US Post Off, Allentown Penn 44-45; High Sch Libn Charleroi Sr High Sch, Charleroi Penn 47-51; Libn Naval Supply Corps Sch US Navy, Bayonne NJ 51-53; Documents 54; Naval Train Device Center Propulsion Sands Ctr LI NY 53-54; Tech libn Naval Air Turbine Test Sta (USN), (West) Trenton NJ 55-. 9: SLA (Princeton Trenton Chap; dir/ed "Newsletter, 68-69, treas/memb chm 69-70). 0: Pi Delta Epsilon. 14: Bibliog. 15: US Naval Air Propulsion Test Center Att Tech Lib, Trenton NJ 08628.

HAWKE, LAURA B(IDDLE). b Ann Arbor Mich 21 O 11. 5: UMich 29-33 (Lit Sci & Arts) AB, 34 ABLS, 37-40 AMLS. 7:

Asst catlg dept UMich 34-35, Asst Phil UMich 35-37, Asst Med Lib 37-39, Libn Hosp Lib 39-40; Asst & libn Henry Ford Hosp, Detroit 40-45; Libn UMich League Lib, Ann Arbor 47-49; Jr med libn UMich Med Ctr Lib 49-55, Sr med libn 55-69, Hd ref libn 69-. 9: MedLA; ALA. 10: Ann Arbor Lib Club. AAUW. 12: Comp "Medical Incunabula in the United States with Special Reference to the University of michigan Collection," University Microfilms (59). 14: Ref, sel, rare bks. 15: U of Mich Med Ctr Lib, 4400 Kresge Med Res Bldg, Ann Arbor Mi 48104.

HAWKES, JULIA ANN. b Torquay Gt Britain 22 Ag 43. 5: Westfield Col (LondonU) 62-65 (Hist) BA (Honors); NW Polytechnic (London) 67 (LS) Diploma LS. 6: Fr, Ital, Lat. 7: Grad trainee EdinburghU Lib, Edinburgh UK 65-66; Asst (ref) Westminster Pub Libs, London 66; Catlg ref libn Biomed Lib UCLA 68-. 8: BritishALA. 14: Catlg, rare bks, med libnship. 15: 938 11th st #D, Santa Monica Ca 90403.

HAWKINS, (B) ELIZABETH (LAMB). b Vancouver BC 2 F 42. 4: Hubert E. Hawkins. 5: Carleton U 60-63 (Psych) BA; UToronto 63-64 BLS. 6: Fr. 7: Circ libn UToronto 64-65; Catlgr Nat Lib, Ottawa Can 65-66; Hd Canadiana acquis sect 66-. 15: National Lib of Canada, Ottawa Ont Can.

HAWKINS, BETTY (PIERATT). b West Liberty Ky 28 Mr 07. 5: Ga State Col for Women 24-27 (Eng, Hist) BA; Peabody Col summers 31, 32, 35 BS in LS. 6: Fr. 7: Tchr: Zebulon Ga 27-29, Forest City NC 29-30, Covington Ga 30-32; Sch libn, Covington Ga 33-53; Pub libn Newton Co, Covington Ga 47-53; Fine arts libn Rockdale, Newton, DeKalb Reg Lib, Decatur Ga 53-57; Dir Polk-Floyd Reg Lib, Rome Ga 57-64; Adm asst DeKalb Reg Lib, Decatur Ga 64-. 9: ALA (Conf Planning Com 63; State Recruit Com 68-69); SELA; GaLA. 10: Metro Atlanta Lib Club; Alpha Delta Kappa; Bus & Profess Women. 13: Yes. 14: Admin, bk sel. 15: 632 Clairmont cir, Decatur Ga 30033.

HAWKINS, (OLA) FRANK E(LROD). b Russell County Ala 11 My 16. 4: Chad B Hawkins. 5: Athens Col 33-35; UAla 37-38 (Hist) BS, summers 54-57 (LS) MS, (Certif in Libnship 56). 7: Secondary tchr DeKalb Co, Winston Co Ala 38-41; Tchr Clay County High Sch, Ashland Ala 41-48; Tchr Camden High Sch, Camden Ala 48-53; Libn Valley Head High Sch, Valley Head Ala 53-62; Tchr Collinsville High Sch, Collinsville Ala 62-66; Asst libn Gadsden State Jr Col, Gadsden Ala 66-68, Libn 68-. 8: Mem Ala State Text Bk Com 64; State delegate to NEA 60. 9: NEA; SELA; AlaJrColLA; AlaLA; AlaEA. 10: AAUW; PTA; Delta Kappa Gamma. 14: Catlg. 15: 109 Bridlewood dr, Gadsden Al 35901.

HAWKINS, DAVID (ROBERT). b Toronto Ont Can 11 Mr 39. 4: Patricia Ann Stammers. 5: UAlberta 56-60 (Eng) BA; UToronto 63-64 BLS. 7: Ref libn Dartmouth Reg Lib 64-65, chief libn 65-. 9: CanLA (Sub-com on Lib Technic Training); APLA; HalifaxLA (Prog Chm). 14: Ref. 15: 4 Roblea dr, Dartmouth Nova Scotia Can.

HAWKINS, ELINOR (DIXON). b Masontown WVa 25 S 27. 4: Carroll Woodard Hawkins. 5: Fairmont State Col 45-49 (Eng) AB; UNC 49-50 (LS) BS. 7: Child libn Enoch Pratt Free Lib, Baltimore 50-51; Head of circ dept Greensboro Pub Lib, Greensboro NC 51-56; Libn Craven-Pamlico Lib Serv, New Bern NC 58-62; Dir Craven-Pamlico-Carteret Reg Lib, New Bern NC 62-. 8: Storyteller, child television program"Tele-Story Time WFMY-TV Greensboro NC 52-58, WNBE-TV New Bern NC 63-.09: NCLA. 10: NCA Ret Child Inc; Pilot Club; International (res 57-58, v-pres 62-63). 14: Reg lib serv, child dept & pub rel. 15: New Bern-Craven Co Pub Lib 400 Johnson st, New Bern NC 28560.

HAWKINS,JANE. b NewCastle Penn 5 Mr 13. 5: Allegheny Col 31-35 (Eng Lit) AB; Ohio State U 35-36(Eng Lit) AM; West Res 44-47 BS in LS. 6: Fr, Sp. 7: Tchr George Washington Jr-Sr High Sch, New Castle Penn 37-41; Asst Prof, catlgr Westminster Col Lib (New Wilmington Penn) 44-; Assoc libn 69-. 9: ALA-ACRL (Tri-State Chap); PennLA. 10: AAUW; Delta Kappa Gam; College Club. 14: Catlg, rare bks. 15: McGill Lib Westminster Col, New Wilmington Penn 16142.

HAWKINS, JEAN V. b Waukesha Wis 13 Ag 18. 4: James O Hawkins. 5: Carroll Col (Waukesha Wis) 36-40 (Bus Admin) BA; UWis(Madison) 40-41 BLS. 7: Mead Pub Lib, Sheboygan Wis 41-42; Libn Med Staff Lib, Waukesha (Wis) Mem Hosp 60-. 8: Hosp lib consul, De Paul Rehab Hosp, Milwaukee 68-69. 9: MedLA; Mem Exec Com Midwest Reg Gp 69-71). 10: Great Books; Milwaukee Peace Corps Serv Org. 14: Catlg & ref in the med & nurs field. 15: Waukesha Mem Hosp Med Staff Lib 725 American ave, Waukesha Wis 53187.

HAWKINS, JESSIE NELL (HAMILTON). b Decatur Ala 28 D 39. 4: Don Paul Hawkins. 5: UAla 58-61 (Elem Educ) BA; Peabody Col 61-62 (LS) MS. 7: Sch libn Howey Acad, Howey in the Hills 63; Asst child libn Coral Gables (Fla) Pub Lib 66; Asst acquis libn UMiami 66-. 9: SELA. 14: Acquis. 15: 9381 SW 110 ter, Miami Fl 33156.

HAWKINS, JO ANNE (WALKER). b El Paso Tex 28 N 38. 4: Daniel Fleming Hawkins. 5: Tex A & M U (summer) 57 & 58; UTex (Austin) 57-60 (Art) BSA, 63-66 MLS. 6: Sp. 7: Artist Texas A&M Info Off (summers) 58 & 59; Graphic Designer, Publication Advisor's Off, UTex 62-65; Ref libn II Interlibrary Borrowing, UTex Lib, Austin 68-. 14: Ref. 15: 824 E 30th, Austin Tx 78705.

HAWKINS, JOHN JAMES. b Somerville Mass 16 Jl 32. 4: Margaret McCarthy. 5: St John's Se, 49-55 (Phil) AB; Simmons 57-59 (LS) MS; State Col Boston 64-67 (Educ) MEd. 6: Fr, lat. 7: A-v asst Simmons Col 57-59; Asst dir Bentley Col Lib 59-63, Asst prof of Eng 63-69, Dir of stud activities 66-69, Dir Baker Vanguard Lib 69-. 9: ALA; NCTE; NE Assn Tchrs Eng; MassLA. 10: NAACP. 14: Ref, admin. 15: 87 Fair Oaks ave, Newtonville Ma 02160.

HAWKINS, KATHERINE. b Phila 22 O 05. 5: Goucher Col 23-25 (Chem); Penn State U 27-29 (Chem) BS; Drexel 31-32 BS inLS. 7: Asst Phila Free Lib 30-31; Libn Collingdale High Sch, Collingdale Penn 33-34; Libn Royersford High Sch & Pub Libs, Royersford Penn 34-54; Libn Unionville High Sch, Unionville Penn 54-. 9: ALA; NEA; Penn State EA; Delaware-Chester Co (Penn) LA. 10: Bus & Prof Women. 15: 127 E State st, Kennett Square Penn 19348.

HAWKINS, KATHLEEN (ANNE). b Port Jefferson NY 9 F 42. 5: Molloy Cath Col for Women 59-63 (Eng) BA; LIU (C W Post) 63-67 MLS. 7: Asst libn Bd of Coop Educ Serv Hauppage High Sch, Hauppage NY 63-64; Suffolk Coop Lib Syst: Lib trainee, Patchogue NY 65-66, jr catlgr, Patchogue NY 66, Bkmob supv, Bellport NY 66-. 9: ALA; NYLA (Bkmob Com); SuffolkCoLA. 14: Reader's serv. 15: Montauk highway, Moriches NY 11955.

HAWKINS, LOUISE J (JENNINGS). b Greensboro NC 19 S 10. 4: Rainey T Hawkins. 5: High Point Col 27-31 (Eng) AB; UNC 31-32 BA in LS. 6: Sp. 7: Asst libn Pub Lib, High Point NC 32; Libn High Point Col 32-35; Libn Pub Lib, Kinston NC 35; Libn Pub Lib, burlington NC 36-39; Training supervisor WPA Lib Project, Raleigh NC 39-42; Bk order consul NC Lib Commsn, Raleigh NC 42; Libn Fairchild Aircraft Corp, Burlington NC 43; Catlgr Lib Commsn, Raleigh NC 43-46; Catlgr State Lib, Raleigh NC 46-47; Catlgr (ser) UNC Lib (Chapel Hill) 57-58, Libn (docs) 58-. 9: NCLA. 14: Ref. 15: Rte 1 Box 72, Mebane NC 27302.

HAWKINS, NORMA JEAN (BECK). b Yorkton Sask Can 2 My 23. 4: Rev David G Hawkins. 5: USask 46-49 (Eng) BA; Toronto 55-56 BLS. 7: Br libn Saskatoon Pub Lib, Saskatoon Sask 56-59; Lib asst NCentral Sask Reg Lib, Prince Albert Sask 61-62; Child libn Kitsiland br Vancouver Pub Lib, Vancouver BC 62-. 13: Yes. 14: Child & yp wk. 15: Suite 7 920 Bidwell st, Vancouver 5 BC Can.

HAWKINS, SANDRA JEAN. b Wash DC 14 Je 44. SH DC 14 Je 44. 6: Fr, Ger. 7: Descr catlgr LC 68-. 9: MusLA. 10: Gamma Sigma Sigma. 14: Catlg, mus, ref. 15: 5529 Marlboro pike #14, District Hts Md 20028.

HAWKS, HELEN (WORTHINGTON). b Knoxville Tenn 10 Jl 19. 4: Ned A Hawks. 5: Asheville teachers Col 36-40 (Elem Educ) BS; Appalachian State U 68-69 MLS. 6: Fr. 7: Elem tchg, NC 40-47, 50-58, 61-63; High sch libn, NC 63-68; Catlgr West Car U summer 68. 8: Lib Inst participant, Appalachian State U 68-69. 9: ALA (Recr Com NC 63-65); NCLA; JacksonCoLA. 10: Halcyon Woman's Club; Wesleyan Serv Guild. 11: Clubwoman of the Year 64. 13: Yes. 14: Catlg. 15: Hidden Valley Farm Fairview rd, Sylva NÇ 28779.

HAWLEY, HELEN JEANNE (WELLS). b Oswego Labette County Kan 3 Je 04. 5: Union Col (Lincoln Neb) 25-29 (Eng) BA; USOCAL 53-55 MA in LS. 6: Sp. 7: Dir of food serv Oak Park Acad, Nevada Iowa 29-30; Head of Eng Dept Laurelwood Acad, Gaston Ore 35-38, 45-48; Libn Montefiore Hosp, Pittsburgh 49-51; ; Periods libn Loma Linda U 55-56, Catlgr 66-69. 9: ALA; MedLA (treas So Cal Group 62-64); Christ Libns Assn. ssn; Med Lib Gp So Cal. 10: Beta Phi Mu. 14: Ser, hist med. 15: 25039 Starr st, Loma Linda Ca 92354.

HAWLEY, MARY BARBARA. b Ludlow Mass 25 Ag 25. 5: Park Col 43-47 (Eng Lit) BA; Syracuse 48-49 (Eng Lit) MA;

Columbia 59-60 (LS) MS 06: Fr, Sp. 7: Eng tchr Madison Pub Schs, Madison Kan 47-48; Upper grades tchr Bd of Nat Missions United Presbyt Church USA, Holman NM 49-51, Sec, sub tchr Santa Fe NM 52-55, Off manager, sec, NYC 55-59; Asst catlgr Hartford Sem Found, Hartford Conn 60-62; Ref libn Coe Col 62-. 9: ALA; IowaLA. 14: Ref, catlg. 15: 1305 1/2 B ave NE, Cedar Rapids Iowa 52402.

HAWTHORNE, GLADYS (SCROGGS). b Rogers Ark 14 Jl 1889. 5: UOkla 0610 (Liberal Arts) BA; UDenver 3840 (Psych) MA. 6: Fr, Ger, Sp. 7: Sec USAF, Denver 4446; Libn US Geol Survey, Denver 4659; Libn Mental Health Ctr, Chicago 6264; Libn Charles F Read Zone Ctr 64. 9: ALA; MedLA; SLA; IllLA. 10: AAAS; Psi Chi; Amer Guild of Organists; Nat League of Pen Women; Colo Sci Soc. 12: Verse; An Angel Touched My Hand--; Subj Guide vs 120, Mental Health Book Review Index--. 13: Yes. 14: Catlg, ref, indexing. 15: 4329 W Shakespeare, Chicago Il 60639.

HAWTHORNE, RUTH ANN (MARTIN). b Franklin Penn 25 Ap 14. 4: Frank Sylvester Hawthone. 5: Mercyhurst Col 30-32 (Lat); Cornell U 33-35 (Lat) BA; Hofstra Col 51-54 (Hist); St Johns U (Jamaica NY) 55-57 (LS); Albany State (NY) 59-60 (LS), Sch Lib Certif. 6: Lat. 7: High sch tchr Summit Twp Schs, Harmonsburg Pa 35-41; Info desk Met Mus of Art, NYC 45; Sub tchr Uniondale Free Sch Dist 2, Uniondale NY 50-53, Elem sch libn 55-58; Elem sch libn Beth Central Schools, Delmar NY 59-. 8: Consul NY State Educ Dept, Albany NY 58-59. 9: ALA; NEA; NYLA; NY State Tchrs Assn. 10: Cornell Womens Club; Phi Alpha Theta. 14: Elem sch libs. 15: 5 Van Dyke rd, Delmar NY 12054.

HAY, BETTY LEE (STEWART). b Columbus Ohio 4 Je 21. 4: Roy D Hay. 5: Ohio State 47 (Elem Educ) BS in Ed; UGuam 60-65 Lib Sci Certif; UHawaii summers 67, 68 (LS). 7: Tchr: Hyatts Twp Elem & High, Ohio 47-48, Madison Twp Elem Sch, Licking Co Ohio 48-54, Hazlewood Elem Sch, Newark Ohio 54-58, Adelupe Elem Jr High, Guam 58-60, Wettengel Elem Sch, Guam 60-63; Tchr & libn Andersen Elem Sch, Guam 63-66; Libn Andersen Elem Sch, Guam 66-68; Libn Yigo Intermediate Sch, Guam 68-. 9: NEA; ALA; OhioEA; GuamEA; GuamLA. 10: AAUW. 14: Sch lib, a-v media. 15: Box 2438, Agana Guam 96910.

HAY, GEORGE W. b McGrew Neb 5 O 26. 4: Deborah Marcionette. 5: UCLA 48 (GEN Studies) BA; Fuller Theol Sem 51 BD; USoCAL 53 (Eng, LS). 7: US Navy 44-46; Group insurance analyst Occidental Life Insurance Co, Los Angeles 55-58; Supv personnel records Hughes Aircraft Co, Los Angeles 58-59; Supv indus rel data processing Space Tech Labs, Los Angeles 59-61; Lib asst Aerospace Corp, Los Angeles 61-62; Teh reports libn Jet Prop Lab, Pasadena Cal 62; Asst libn MMRBM Div Hughes Aircraft Co, Los Angeles 62-63; Supv tech report center Bell Telephone Labs, Whippany NJ 63-65; Supv NC Bell Tel Labs-WECO Jt Lib, Greensboro NC 65-. 9: ASIS. 14: Computer applications, documentation, indexing, admin. 15: 2120 Pinecroft rd, Greensboro NC 27407.

HAYCRAFT, HOWARD. b Madelia Minn 24 Jl 05. 4: Molly Costain. 5: UMinn 23-28 AB. 7: Staff UMinn Press, Minneapolis 28; Staff H Wilson Co, NYC 29, Dir 34-; Capt & Maj US Army Serv Forces 42-46; V-pres H Wilson Co, NYC 40-52, Pres & treas 53-67, Chm of Bd 67; Dir Forest Press 51-68, Pres 61-62. 8: Spec consul, War Dept, 42; Mem Presidents Com on Employment of the Handicapped, 63-; V-chm, Library Com, 64-. 9: ALA (chm RT Lib Serv to Blind 68-69); SLA; NYLA. 10: Mystery Writers of Amer. 11: UMinn Outstanding Achievement Award, 54; F J Campbell Medal & Citation Award RTL 56, 66; SLA Spec Cit 68. 12: Auth, ed, or jt-ed "Authors Today & Yesterday" (33); "Junior Book of Authors" (34); "Boys Sherlock Holmes" (36); "British Authors of the 19th Century" (36); "Boys Book of Great Detective Stories" (38); "American Authors 1600-1900" (40); "Murder for Pleasure; The Life & Times of the Detective Story" (41); "Crime Club Encore" (42); "Twentieth Century Authors" (42); "Art of the Mystery Story" (46); "Fourteen Great Detective Stories" (49); "British Authors Before 1800" (52); "Treasury of Great Mysteries" (59); "Five Spy Novels" (62); "Three Times Three" (64); "Books for the Blind & Phys Handicapped" A Postscript 3rd ed rev 68; "Sherlock Holmes Greatest Cases" (Large Print) 67. 13: Yes. 15: 950 University ave, Bronx NY 10452.

HAYDEN, ELIZABETH LUCRETIA. b Cecilia Ky 29 N 24. 5: UKy 43-47 (Eng, LS) AB, BS in LS; UMich 59-61 MA in LS. 7: Br asst pub lib, S Bend Ind 47-49, Br libn 49-54; Supv child wk & ext serv, Pub Lib Muncie (Ind) 54-56; Hd libn pub lib, Albion Mich 56-61; Supv ext sect pub lib, Lansing Mich 61-. 9: ALA; NEA; MichLA (treas); MichEA; LansingEA. 10: Beta Phi Mu; AAUW; Bus & Profess Women's Club; Delta Kappa Gamma; Pilot Club. 13: Yes. 14: Branch libs, hosp lib serv, bk sel. 15: 521 N Walnut, Lansing Mi 48933.

HAYDEN, HAROLD WALTER. b Creson Iowa 26 D 05. 4: Margaret Murray Hayden. 5: Neb State Col (Kearney) 23-27 (Bus Admin) AB; UIll 28-29 BS in LS; UMich 37-38 AM in LS. 6: Fr, Sp, Ger. 7: Lib asst Neb State Col (Kearney) 26-28; Sr asst UND 29-31; Supt of ser & exch State U Iowa 31-34, Supv of dept libs 34-37; Head Libn Bucknell U 38-65; Head Libn Lycoming Col 65-. 8: Mem Gov Com on Pub Lib Development in Penn 58-60; Consul Lycoming Col Lib 62. 9: ALA-ACRL; PennLA (pres 57-58). 13: Yes. 14: Admin. 15: 550 Harding ave, Williamsport Pa 17701.

HAYDUK, SARAH HUMPHREY (HOBBS). b Neton Mass 13 S 35. 4: Duke Arnold Hayduk. 5: Lake Erie Col 53-57 (Biol) BA; UWsh 64-65 MLibnship. 6: Fr. 7: Mus Instr Amer Mus Natural Hist, NYC 57-59; Recreation dir US Army Spec Serv, Germany 59-60; Res Parasitologist US Fish Wildlife Serv, Seattle 60-64; Sci catlgr UCal (San Diego) 66-68; Assoc libn Salk Inst, La Jolla Cal 68-. 13: Yes. 14: Catlg. 15: 2211 Ocean Front, Del Mar Ca 92014.

HAYES, ANNIE LAURIE (GREEN). b Guin Ala 26 Mr 03. 4: William Elbert Hayes. 5: Livingston State 47 (Eng) BS; UAla 58 (LS) MA . 6: Sp. 7: Tchr, prin, libn, Ala 23-65; Libn Walker Col 61-. 9: NEA; ALA; AlaEA; AlaLA; Jr Col LA. 10: PTA; Bus & Prof Women; ADK; AAUW; Toastmistress Club. 15: Rt 5 Box 344, Jasper Al 35501.

HAYES, DENNIS JOSEH. b Jersey City NJ 17 Ja 34. 5: St Peters Col 52-56 (Hist) BS; Rutgers 56-58 MLS; Jersey City State Tchrs Col 59. 7: Jersey City (NJ) Free Pub Lib: Lib clerk 51, Jr lib asst, Libn trainee 56, Sr libn 58, Prin libn 60-. 9: NJLA; HudsonCoLA (v-pres 69-70). 10: Rutgers Univ Grad Sch of Lib Serv Alumni Assn. 14: Br wk, catlg, readers adv. 15: 50 Stuyvesant ave, Jersey City NJ 07306.

HAYES, DOROTHY (MIRIAM). b New Castle Ind 19 O 11. 5: Miss State Col for Women 30-34 (Educ, Eng) BA; Duke summer 39 (Prim Educ); UIll summer 51 (LS) 06: Lat. 7: Tchr Leflore Co Sch, Swiftown Miss 34-38; Tchr Inverness City Sch, Inverness Miss 38-39; Tchr Vicksburg City Sch, Vicksburg Miss 39-42; Asst libn Greenwood-Leflore Pub Lib, Greenwood Miss 42-44; Hd libn 44-. 8: Mem, Com on Basic Ref Bks, 58; Survey Com, Columbus Lib (Miss) 59. 9: ALA (Recr Netwk 59-);-PLA; Miss LA (chm Awards Com 63). 10: AAUW; Delta Kappa Gamma; Altrusa; Leflore Co (Miss) Hist Soc; Greenwood Art Assn; Greenwood Commun Concert Assn; Mental Health Assn; Leflore Co Com on Aging; Greenwood Recr Com; Greenwood Educ Comm. 14 Pub lib admin, geneal research, music, art. 15: 613 W Market st, Greenwood Miss 38930.

HAYES, GENEVIEVE. b Greenfield Ill 8 My 09. 5: Illinois Col 26-30 (Lat, Eng) AB; UIll summer 44-48 (LS) BS. 7 Tchr of Lat & Eng Ashland Comm High Sch, Ashland Ill 31-38; Tchr of Lat & Eng Waterloo High Sch, Waterloo Ill 38-44; Libn Salem Commun High Sch, Salem Ill 44-. 9: NEA; ALA; IllEA; IllLA. 10: Delta Kappa Gamma; Beta Phi Mu. 15: Salem Commun High Sch, Salem Ill 62881.

HAYES, HAZEL (HEW). b Clinton Ind 13 Mr 896. 4: Curtis Howard Hayes. 5: Ind State Normal 14-16 (Hist, Eng); Ind State Tchrs Col 46-52 (Eng, Hist, LS) AB; UIll 52-53 MSLS. 6: Ger. 7: Tchr Clinton Pub Sch, Clinton Ind 1417; Tutor, Clinton Ind 18-29; Tutor & dramatic tchr., Terre Haute In d 36-40; Owner Tea Room, Indianapolis 40-41; Acct clerk Insurance Co, Indianapolis 41-44; Libn Clinton Pub Lib, Clinton Ind 46-53; Dir Herrick Pub Lib, Holand Mich 53-66; Med libn Ingalls Mem Hosp 68. 8: Adv on lib bldgs; Consul St Joseph Mich 66, Allegan Mich 67-68. 9: ALA; MichLA (treas 59-61). 10: Womans Literary Club; AAUW. 11: Woman of the Year, Holland Mich, 60; Mich Libn of the Year 67-68. 13: Yes. 14: Admin, consul or adv serv. 15: 161 Shabbona dr, Park Forest Il 60466.

HAYES, JOHN THOMAS. b Yonkers NY 22 F 19. 4: Sylvia Channel. 5: LSU 38-42 (Hist) BS; Rutgers 63-66 MLS. 6: Fr. 7: US Army Lt Col Infantry 42-64; Libn Westfield Sr High, Westfield NJ 64-66; Ref libn Miami Dade Jr Col, Miami Fla 66-. 9: FlaLA; Dade CoLA. 10: Fla Assn Pub Jr Cols. 14: Ref. 15: 12501 NW 27th ave, Miami Fl 33167.

HAYES, SISTER MARY ALMA PBVM. b Oakland Cal. 5: San Francisco Col for Women 47 (Eng) BA; Rosary Col 52 MA in LS; USan Francisco 51- Secondary Tchg Credential. 6: Sp. : Cost accountant, chief of payroll dept Packwell Cop,

Oakland Cal 30-36; Tchr-libn St Annes Elem Sch, San Francisco 38-47; Tchr-libn Presentation High Sch, San Francisco 47-58; Coordinator of wkshops & insts, San Fancisco 54-, Dir Lib Sci Prog 58-. 8: Sch lib consul, Archdiocese of San Francisco, 54-; Mem Cal State Task Force, Title II ESEA, rep all private schs, 65. 9: CathLA (High Sch Adv Bd 59-62; High Sch Bk Sel Com for Cath Sup of High Sch Catlg 61-63; No Cal Unit: chm 56-60); CalASchL (Program Chm 64-65); Cal Central Coun Tchrs of Eng (Exec Bd 64-66); Cal Assn Tchrs Eng (Exec Bd 68-). 11: Silvr Book Award, Lib Binding Inst 61. 12: Ed "Basic Reference Books for Catholic High Schools (59); "Master Order List for Catholic Elementary School Libraries (64); Auth "Teacher-Librarian Handbook for School Libraries (4th ed 65). 13: Yes. 14: Lib educ. 15: Univ of San Francisco, San Francisco Ca 94117.

HAYES, PHOEBE F(RANK). b Cleveland 12 Ag 15. 5: UWis 33-37 (Amer Hist) BA, 36-37 (LS) Diploma; Chicago 38-39, 41-42 (Pol Sci); UWis 45-46 (Pol Sci); UDenver 61-65 (LS) MA. 6: Fr. 7: Lib asst Joint Ref Lib Pub Admin ClearingHouse, Chicago 38-39; Ref asst US Bureau of the Budget, Wash DC 41-44; Libn Amer Fed of State County & Mun Employees AFL Madison Wis 44-50; Libn Nat Farmers Union, Denver 50-61; Dir Bibliog Center for Research Rocky Mountain Region Inc, Denver 61-. 9: SLA (Nat Exec Bd 65-68; sec of Bd 65-66, Convention chm 63; pres Colo Chap 53-54; "Bulletin ed 48-52; com chm 56-59, div chm 54-55); ALA 63-68; 63-)-RSD (com chm 64-); ColoLA (Exec Bd 61-, Legis Com 59-65); MPLA. 10: Colo Coun for Lib Development; ACLU. 11: MPLA Award for outstanding serv. 12: "A Communications System for Wyoming Libraries (68). 13: Yes 14: Bibliog, admin, ref, info retrieval. 14: Bibliog, admin, ref, coop lib programs. 15: 4955 S Inca dr, Englewood Co 80110.

HAYES, ROBERT M. b NYC 3 D 25. 4: Alice Peters . 5: UCLA 43-45; UColo 4546; UCLA 46-52 (Math) BA, MA, PhD. 7: US Nay 4546; US Air Force 49; Mathematician at Nat Bureau of Standards, Wash DC & Los Angeles 49-52; TECH STAFF OF Hughes Aircraft Co, Culver City Cal 52-53; Visiting Lecturer UCal(Los Angeles) Phys Sci Ext Div 52-; Head of Applications Group Nat Cas h Register 53-55; Head of Bus Systems Dept Research Rsearch 55-59; (: V-pres-sci dir & pres of the Advanced Info Systems Co (Div of The Electrada Corp) 59-64; Prof I UCLA Sch of Lib Serv 64-. 8: Consul: US Navy; NLM; Off of Educ (Mem of Adv Com); NSF; State Lib of the State of Wash; Civil Serv Commsn; Heliodyne, Los Angeles; Planning Research Corp, Los Angeles; John Wiley Inc, NY; Harvey Mudd Col; Off of Si & Tech (Off of the President) Wash DC; Amer Med Assn Adv Com on Info Needs of the Practicing Physician. 9: ASIS; ALA; SLA. 10: Amer Math Soc; Sima Xi; Phi Beta Kappa; Soc for Ind & Applied Math; Assn for Computing Machinery. 12: "Iterative Method of Solving Linear Problems on Hilbert Space (53); "Operational Characteristics of the NCR 102D (54); "Mathematical Models for Information System Design and A Calculus of Operations (61); "Organizaton of Large Fies with Self-Organizing Capability (61); "Economics of Book Catalog Production: AStudy Prepared for Stanford University libraries and the Council on Library Reources, with Ralph M Shoffner (64). (This is only a partial list.) 13: Yes. 14 Lib system analysis, data processing, inf retrieval. 15: Sch of Lib Serv, UCal (Los Angeles), Los Angeles90024.

HAYGOOD, WILLIAM CONVERSE. b Atlanta 11 Mr 10. 4: Kathleen Taylor 5: Emory 27-31 (Fr) BPH, (Rosenwald Fellow) 32 AB in LS; Chicago Grad Lib Sch Fellow 34-39, 47-48. 6: Sp. 7: Asst ref lbn Emory U 32-34; Ast readers adv NY Pub Lib 35; Field agent Amer Ass n for Adult Educ 37-38; Libn & reorganizer Lib Ga Tchrs Col 38-39; Exec Dir ALA Com on Lib Co-operation with Latin-America 39-40; Sec Julius Rosenwald Fund, Chicago 40; Dir for Fellowships Julius Rosenwald Fund 41-47; (Sgt) US Infantry 43-45; Instr Army AEIS Lib Courses, Paris, Oberammergau 45; Dir US Inf Libs, Madrid Spain 49-51; Free-lance writer, Mallorca Spain 51-53, Madison Wis 54-57; Ed "Wisconsin Magazine of History; & dir ed div State Hist Soc of Wis 57-. 8: Consul PR Govt on lib programs, San Juan PR, 55; Visiting lecturer UWis Lib Sch, 57, 58. 10: Voyageurs Madison Wis). 12: "Who Uses the Public Library (36); "The Ides of August: a Novel (56); Co-ed "The Soviet View of the American Past (64). 13: Yes. 14: Lib hist. 15: State Hist Soc of Wis, 816 State st, Madison Wis 53706.

HAYMES, MARY F. b Tipp City Ohio 10 My 22. 5: Longwood Col 39-43 (Chem) BS; Carnegie 50-51 (LS) MS. 07: Chem E I duPont de Nemours & Co, Richmond Va 43-47, Asst libn 47-50; Libn E I duPont de Nemours & Co, Phila 51-. 9: SLA; ASIS; ACS. 10: . 14: Tech lib admin, lit searching, info retrieval. 15: E I duPont de Nemours & Co 3500 Grays Ferry ave, Phila 19146.

HAYNE, FRANCES SWAIN (MRS). b bay City Mich 27 Ja 02. 5: UMich 19-22-, 23-24 Eng) AB, 24-25 (Eng), MA, summer 55, & 60 (LS). 6: Fr. 7: Stud asst, "rhetoric libn UMich 24-25; Eng tchr West State Tchrs Col (Kalamazoo) 25-30; Checker DAB, Wash DC 34-35; Prof-reader in ed off UMich 36-37; Clerk then asst Mich State U Lib 53-55; Nursing libn Edward W Sparrow Hosp Sch of Nursing, Lansing Mich 56-59; Libn Edward W Sparrow Hosp, Lansing Mich 59-. 9: ALA; MedLA. 11: Avery Hopwood award in creative writing, UMich, 33. 13: Yes. 14: Ref, catlg. 15: 832 E Grand River, Williamston Mich 48895.

HAYNE, REBECCA RAE (BOND). b Lansing Mich 7 O 40. 4: Robert Tenbrook Hayne. 5: Kalamazoo Col 58-62 (Sociol) AB; UMich 62-63 AMLS. 7: Descr catlgr UMich (Ann Arbor) 63-66; Catlgr UGa (Athens) 66-67; Catlgr UCal (La Jolla) 67-. 14: Catlg. 15: 6366 Bonnie View dr, San Diego Ca 92119.

HAYNER, C(HARLOTTE) IRENE. b Brunswick NY 14 Ja 1896. 5: Cornell U 13-17 (Eng,Hist) BA; NY State Lib Sch 22-24 BLS; UMich (Educ) MA. 7: Tchr secondary schs NY, NJ 17-21; Libn U High Sch UMich (Ann Arbor) 24-45; Visiting Instr UIll (Urbana) 38-39; Instr Lib Sci NY Lib sch (Albany, Syracuse NY) 26, 27, 28-38; Asst Prof Lib Sch UMinn(Minneapolis) 45-47, Assoc Prof Lib Sci 47-54; Assoc Prof Lib Sch UMich (Ann Arbor) 55-63. 8: Consul for Mich State Lib, Lansing summers 39-41; Survey of sch-pub libs for Mich State Lib summer 45. 9: ALA(chm Ed Com & Subscrip Bks Bull Com; chm Sch Libs Sect); AALS (past pres); MichLA(past pres); MichASchL (past pres). 10: Mich Schoolmasters Club (Lib Sect); Phi Beta Kappa; Pi Lambda Theta; Delta Kappa Gamma. 13: Yes. 14: Child & young peoples wk, sch libs. 15: 1310 Granger ave, Ann Arbor Mich 48104.

HAYNES, MARY RUTH (PETEFISH). b Scott City Kan 6 N 38. 4: Herbert R Haynes. 5: Central Col (Kan) 56-58; Bethany Nazarene Col 59-61 (Eng) AB; Kan State Tchrs Col 63-64 (Lib Educ) MS. 6: Sp. 7: Asst libn (catlgr) Olivet Nazarene Col (Kankakee Ill) 64-65; Prof asst Main Boys & Girls Room, Omaha Pub Lib Neb 65-66; Bkmobile libn omaha Pub Lib, Neb 66-. 9: ALA-CSD; NebLA. 10: Omaha-Council Bluffs Libns' Club. 14: Juv wk. 15: 4212 Nebraska ave, Omaha Nb 68111.

HAYNES, SARAH (WYNDER). b Pensacola Fla 5 O 31. 4: Charles Haynes. 5: Ala State 48-52 (Eng) BS; Fla A&M U 54; Ind U 58-61 (LS) MAT; UWis (NDEA Inst) 66. 6: Fr. 7: Tchr Darden High Sch, Opelika Ala 52-54; Tchr Washington Jr High Sch, Pensacola Fla 54-56; Tchr Washington Adult High Sch, P ensacola Fla 57-60; Libn Ransom High Sch, Pensacola Fla 60-61; Libn Goulding Elem Sch, Pensacola Fla 62-. 9: NEA; ALA; Fla State Tchrs Assn; W Fla LA; FlaASchL. 10: Alpha Kappa Alpha; Jack & Jill, Inc. 14: Catlg. 15: 1916 W Gonzalez st, Pensacola Fl 32501.

HAYS, ANNIE LORIECE (THOMAS). b Little Elm Tex 24 S 24. 4: Nea l C Hays. 5: N Tex State U 42-44 (LS) BS; Tex Womans U 59-63 MLS. 7: Multi-sch libn Pub Sch, Sanger Tex, Krum Tex 58-66; Lib specialist Educl Resources Coop Assn, Sherman Tex 66-68; Libn curr materials ctr Col of Educ Tex Womans U 68-. 9: Tex State Tchrs Assn; TexLA. 15: Rt 2 Box 497B, Denton Tex76201.

HAYS, CARL H. b Des Moines Iowa 11 Ap 38. 4: Christie A Swanson. 5: State Col Iowa 55-61 (Elem Educ) BA; UDenver 63-64 (LS) MA; UWis 68-69 (LS). 7: Elem sch tchr, Algona Iowa 57-59, 60-61; Elem sch tchr, Waverly Iowa 61-62; Elem sch tchr, Sioux City Iowa 62-63; Ref libn Wayne State Col 64-68. 9: ALA; (Exec Com Jr Mem RT); NebEA MPLA; NebLA (Col &Univ Sect: chm 6-66). 10: AAUP. 14: Ref, info serv for undergrad educ. 15: 1117 Catalpa circlr, Madison Wi 53713.

HAYS, EVA M (TILTON). b Stark County Ohio 12 N 13. 4: Raymond A Hays. 5: Flora Stone Mather Col West Res 36 (Eng) BA; Kent State 57 (LS) MA. 7: Various stenographer-sec positions, Cleveland & Massillon Ohio 36-46; Off mgr-bkkeeper Canton Jewish Commun Ctr, Canton Ohio 46-56; Asst catlgr Kent State U 57-60; Asst catlg ref Montana State U 60-. 12: "A Union List of Publications in Opaque Microform" (59); suppl (61); (2d ed 64). 14: Catlg, ref. 15: MSU Lib, Bozeman Mt 59715.

HAYS, PATRICIA LOUISE. b Karns City Penn 28 Mr 28. 5: Westminster Col 46-50 (Eng) BA; Carnegie 50-51 MLS. 7: Libn Schs Dept Carnegie Lib, Pittsburgh Penn 51-55, Ya libn Wright Lib, Oakwood Ohio 55-57; Br libn Carnegie Lib, Pittsburgh Penn 57-63; Hd libn Monroeville Pub Lib,

Monroeville Penn 63-69. 9: ALA; PennLA (chm SE Chap 67-68). 10: AAUW; LWV. 14: Admin, pub libs. 15: 2520B King Lear dr, Monroeville Pa 15146.

HAYUM, RENATE. b Tuebingen Germany 29 Ja 30. 5: Reed 48-50; UWash 50-52 (Bus Admin) BA, 67-68 M of Lib. 6: Ger. 7: Auditor Army & Air Force Exchange Serv, San Francisco 53-54; Off mgr Inst of Judaeo-Christian Studies Seton Hall U 56-66; Libn Seattle Pub Lib 67-. 8: Instr in Lib Clsf & Filing, evening class, lib technic prog, Highline Commun Col Midway Wash spring 69. 9: SLA; ALA; PNLA; WashLA. 14: Ref. 15: 220 13th ave E, Seattle Wa 98102.

HAYWARD, EDWARD BEARDSLEY. b Rutland V 21 Ja 16. 5: Middlebury Col 34-38 (Eng Lit) BA, 39 (Amer Lit) MA; UIll 47 BLS. 6: Fr. 7: Instr New Hampton Sch, New Hampton NH 39-41; Ed asst W W Norton & Co, NYC 40-42; US Army CIC 42-46; Bkmob libn Akron (Ohio) Pub Lib 47-48; Racine (Wis) Pub Lib; Br supv 48-50, Head Adult Dept 50-52, Asst libn 52-55; Instr UWis (Madison) summer 50; Chief libn Hammond (Ind) Pub Lib 55-. 8: Tchr of Lib Sci UWis 50. 9: ALA (Coun 62-65); NEA; IndLA (pres-elect 65-66. 10: Kiwanis; YMCA; C of C; Hammond Hist Soc; Mayors Commun on Educ & Recreation. 13: Yes. 14: Ref, admin. 15: Hammond Pub Lib 5011 Hohman ave, Hammond Ind.

HAYWARD, NANCY N. b Framingham Mass 23 M 34. 4: Robert O Hayward. 5: Mich State U 52-54 (Psych); UMass 54-56 (Psych) BA. 7: SERV REP New Eng Tel & Tel, Milford Mass 56-57; Jr lib asst Medfield State Hosp, Medfield Mass 57-. 9: MedLA; MassLA. 15: Medfield State Hosp Box A, Harding Ma 02042.

HAYWARD, OLGA (HINES). b Alexandria La. 4: Samuel E Hayward. 5: Dillard U 41 (Soc Sci) AB; Atlanta 44 BS in LS; UMich 59 (LS) MA. 6: Ger. 7: Tchr High Sch, Marksville La 41-42; Head Libn Grambling Col 44-46; Br libn New Orleans Pub Lib Nora Narva Br 47-48; ; Hd ref libn & Assoc Prof Southern U 48-. 8: Consul Libns Wkshop Southern U summer 64. 9: ALA; LaLA. 10: YWCA; Girl Scouts of Amer; Nat Assn Col Women; AAUP. 12: Lib Handbk for Southern University Students, 10th ed 68. 13: Yes. 14: Ref. 15: 1632 Harding blvd, Baton Rouge La 70807.

HAYWARD, SISTER STEPHEN MARIE OP. b Ft Riley Kan 5 Ap 41. 5: Madison Col (Va) 59-63 (Lib Sci & Educ) BA; Peabody Col 64-65 MLS. 6: Fr. 7: Sales clk Ft Belvoir Va Post Exchange Summer 57 & 58; Clk typist Engr Sch Lib, Ft Belvoir Va 61 & 62; Descr catlgr LC 63-64; Libn & Fr tchr St Cecilia Acad, Nashville 66-. 9: ALA; CatholicLA; TennEA. 14: Catlg, ref wk in high sch & col. 15: 4210 Harding rd, Nashville Tn 37205.

HAYWOOD, LUCILLE (GERTRUDE). b Louisville Ky 10 Ja 18. 5: Ursuline Col (Louisville) 35-36; Nazareth Col (Louisville) 39-40; Loretto Jr Col 36-40; Webster Col (St Louis) 40-51 (Hist) BA; UDetroit 54-60 (Elem Educ) Masters; UKy 68-69 (LS) Masters. 7: Elem tchr: Co Pub Sch Syst, Springfield Ky 38-44, Parochial Syst, Sterling Ill 44-52, Co Pub Sch Syst, Loretto Ky 52-58, Parochial Syst, Louisville Ky 58-65; Clk US Post Off, Nerinx Ky 65-66; Lib Tech I Dept of Libs, Frankfort Ky 68-69; Ext Libn II Reg Lib, Elizabethtown Ky 69-. 14: Ref, circ. 15: Loretto Motherhouse, Nerinx Ky 40049.

HAZARD, THERESA MARY (MAURICE). b Italy 9 Ap 09. 4: Orvis R Hazard. 5: SUNY (Albany) 27-31 AB, 31-32 BS in LS; Drexel summer 66, 67. 6: Ital. 7: Libn Fort Ann High Sch, Fort Ann NY 36-37; Engnr libn Gen Electric, Syracuse NY 3-45; Libn Blasdell High Sch, Blasdell NY 46-48; Tchr W Haverstraw Sch, W Haverstraw NY 52-62; Libn James A Farley Sch N Rockland Central Sch, Stony Point NY 62-. 9: NYLA; NY State Tchrs Assn; Rockland Co (NY) SchLA; NEA; Sch Libns SE Zone. 10: AAUW. 14: Child. 15: 105 Jay st, Stony Point NY 10980.

HAZEKAMP, PHYLLIS ALBERTS. b Chicago Ill. 4: Berdette Hazekamp. 5: De Paul U 43-47 (Eng) AB; LSU 58-59 MSLS; Santa Clara U 63- (Law). 7: Libn De Paul Acad Chicago 47-48; Libn De La Salle Prep Sch Chicago 48-54; Asst libn Vet Hosp Tucson 55-58; Docu libn & catlgr LSU 58-60; Circ libn Pub Lib Phoenix 60-62; Tech libn catlgr Tech Lib Lockheed Missiles (Cal) 62-63, Libn Computer Lib Dept; Asst libn catlgr Law Lib santa ClaraU 63-. 14: Law, ref, catlg. 15: 1375 Civic Center dr No 15, Santa Clara Ca 95050.

HAZEL, JESSAMINE (CELESTE) (BROTT). b Louisville Ky 6 F0 F 09. 4: Donald Prnce Hazel. 5: Oberlin 26-30 (Fr) AB; West Res 37-38 MSLS. 6: Fr. 7: Asst libn Cleveland Pub Lib 31-39; Asst lib Colliwood High Sch, Cleveland 39-40; Asst libn James Ford Rhodes High Sch, Cleveland 40-42; Asst libn Bedford Lib, Bedford Ohio 52-53; Asst libn Mem Br Lib, Cleveland 60-61; Asst ibn Collinwood Br Lib, Cleveland 61-63; Head Libn Euclid Sr Hgh Sch, Euclid Ohio 63-. 8: Head Libn Adult Educ John Hay Even Sch, Cleveland 35-38. 9: ALA; OhioSchLA; OhioLA; OhioEA. 10: Oberlin Alumni Club; West Res Alumni Assn; Euclid Tchrs Assn; N E Ohio Tchrs Assn; PTA Board. 13: Yes. 14: Admin, ref, lib planning. 15: 319 Bonniewood dr, Cleveland 44110.

HAZELGROVE, A RONALD. b Ottawa Ont Can 5 My 12. 4: Alice Axford. 5: Queen U (Kingston Can) 35-39 (Chem Engnr) BS. 6: Fr. 7: Instr Queens U (Ontario Can) 39; Five assayist Can Ind Ltd, Toronto Ont 40; Lab supv Defence Ind Ltd, Nobel Ont 40-44; Research engr Can Ind Ltd, McMasterville, Que 45-54; Serv engr Du Pont of Can Ltd, Kingston Ont 54-46, Trades & Lib Group Leader 66-. 9: Chem Inst Can; Soc Chem Ind; Assn Prof Engnrs Prov of Ont; SLA. 10: Kingston Hist Soc; Kingston Gallery Assn; Domino Theatre Inc (sec). 15: 211 Victoria st, Kingston Ont Can.

HAZELTINE, ROBERT E(ARL). b Fremont Ohio 30 My 16. 4: Anna Theis Hazeltine. 5: UAkron 46-49 (Eng) AB: West Res 49-50 MSLS. 6: Ger. 7: US Army 8th Air Force, Eng 42-45; Operated Used Bk Store, Akron Ohio 35-42; Asst catlgr Bowling Green State U 50-54, Catlgr 54-55; Head of tech processes Canton Pub Lib, Canton O 55-60; Dir Portsmouth Pub Lib, Portsmouth Ohio 60-66; Dir Ashtabula Co District Lib, Ashtabula Ohio 66-. 9: ALA-LAD Recr Rep); OhioLA (chm Recr Com); No Ohio Catlgrs (chm 54-55). 10: PTA; Kiwanis Club; Ashtabula C of C; Ashtabula Area Devel Assn. 13: Yes. 14: Rare bks, pub rel. 15: Portsmouth Pub Lib 1220 Gallia st, Portsmouth Ohio 45662.

HAZELTON, LOUISE (CLEMENT). b Boston 3 Jl 11. 4: Philip A Hazelton. 5: UMe 33 (Eng) BA; Simmons 38 BS in LS. 6: Fr. 7: Asst Rochester Pub Lib, Rochester NY 39-42; Proj dir Pub Lib Serv "Standards Revision" ALA 65-66. 9: NHLA. 11: H W Wilson-ALA Lib Period Award for North Country Libraries 62. 12: Ed "North Country Libraries" 58-; Comp "Directory, Special Subject Resources in Maine" (67). 15: Hebron NH 03241.

HAZELTON, PHILIP ARTHUR. b Milo Me 5 My 08. 4: Louise Clement. 5: Bates Col 25-27;Antioch Col 28-31 (Educ) AB; Columbia 32-33 (LS) BS. 6: Fr. 7: Asst Bowdoin Col Lib 33-34; Libn BirdsEye Labs, Boston 34-36; Head soc sci div Rochester Pub Lib, Rochester NY 36-42; Weather observer & forecaster USAAF 42-45; Act chief acquis US Off of Tech Serv, Wash DC 46-47; Libn Nat LABOR Rel Bd, Wash DC 47-52; Self-employed bk business, Hebron NH 52-53; Libn Grenier AFB, Manchester NH 53-54; Law & legis ref libn NH State Lib 54-. 9: AALL; NELA; NHLA. 10: State Employees Assn of NH; NH Hist Soc. 12: Coauth "History of State Employees t Assn of NH, 1940-1965. 14: Legal & legis ref. 15: NH State Lib, Concord NH 03301.

HAZELTON, RUTH ARDELLE. b Oakland Me 7 O 12. 5: Simmons 30-34 (L) BS. 7: Circ asst Curtis Mem Lib, Meriden Conn 35-37; Catlgr Yale Law Lib 37-42; Child libn Waterville Pub Lib, Waterville Me42-45; Br libn Newton Free Lib, Newton Mass 45-50; Libn Belmont Pub Lib, Belmont Mass 50-58; State Libn Me State Lib 58-. 9: ALA; NELA (dir 59-60); MeLA (pres 59-60). 10: AAUW; Zonta Club. 15: 20 Sewell st, Augusta Me 04330.

HAZEN, ALLEN T(RACY). b Portland Conn 4 N 04. 4: Edith Patterson. 5: Yale 23-27 (Eng) AB; Harvard 31-32 (Eng) AM; Yale 32-35 (Eng) PhD. 6: Fr, Lat. 7: Instr in Eng Yale 36-40; Catlgr & research asst Yale Lib 40-42; Instr in Eng Hunter Col 42-45; Assoc Prof of Eng & Bibliog, Lib UChicao 45-47, Prof of Eng & Dir of U Lib 47-48; Prof of Eng Sch of Lib Serv, Columbia U 48-. 8: Consul in bibliog LC summer 42. 9: ALA; BSA; Bibl Socs of London, Oxford & Cambridge; NY Lib Club. 10: Mod Lang Assn; AAUP. 11: Guggenheim Fellow 52-53. 12: "Johnsons Prefaces & Dedications (37); "Bibliog of Strawberry Hill Press (42); "Bibliog of Horace Walpole (48); Gen ed Yale Ed of Johnson (58-)66; "Catalogue of Walpoles Library (69). 13: Yes. 14: Rare bks, resources, univ & res libs, 18th cent lit, descriptive bibliog. 15: Sch of Lib Serv Columbia U, NY 10027.

HAZLETT, FLORENCE ELLEN. b Tarentum Penn 28 My 10. 5: UPittsburgh 26-30 (Math) AB; carnegie Lib Sch, summer 30; Drexel summer 31 (LS); West Res 36-40 BS in LS, 55-57 (LS) MS; UMinn summer 44. 7: Tchr libn McKeesport Jr High Sch, McKeesport Penn 30-35; Tchr libn Ingram Jr High Sch, Ingram Penn 35-40; Libn Sr High Sch, Midland Mich 40-46;

Libn Spec Serv Div US Army of Occupation, Japan 46-47; Libn Sr High Sch, Midland Mich 47-; Instr Central Mich U 55; Instr Mich State U summer 56. 9: ALA; NEA; MichLA; MichEA; MichASchL. 10: Delta Kappa Gamma; Bus & Prof Womens Club; Kappa Delta. 14: Young adults, sch libs. 15: 3903 Concord st, Midland Mi 48640.

HAZLETT, GWENDOLYN (CHARLOTTE). b Montreal Can 1 Ja 23. 5: McGill 44 BA, 45 BLS, 65 MLS. 7: Asst libn Sun Life Assurance Co of Can, Montreal 45-53; Libn prof serv div Warnock Hersey Intl Ltd, Montreal 54-. 9: SLA (past sec & pres Montreal Chap; Printing Chm 69 Conf). 15: 302 Addington ave, Montreal 28 Can.

HAZLEWOOD, AUDREY CLAIRE (BLACKBOURNE). b Vancouver BC 5 O 17. 4: Richard Hazlewood. 5: UBC 35-38 (Eng Lit) BA, 68-69 BLS. 7: Sec British Air Comsn, Wash DC 42-47, Sec, London England; Libn Port Coquitlam High Sch, Port Coquitlam BC 63-68. 9: CanLA; ALA; BCSchLA. 14: High sch libs. 15: 301 Seaview dr, Port Moody BC Can.

HAZLEWOOD, JUDITH (EVANS). b McKenzie Tenn 30 Mr 30. 4: Bob J Hazlewood. 5: Memphis State U 48-52 (Eng) BS; Vanderbuilt 53-54 (Eng) MA; Peabody 58-59 MA (LS). 7: Eng tchr Pub Sch Syst Memphis Tenn 54-57; Sec UFla 57-58; Eng tchr Pub Sch Sys, Nashville 58-59; Catlgr Pub Lib, Nashville 62-63; Asst libn Lambuth Col 64-. 9: TennLA. 10: Sigma Kappa; AAUW; Delta Kappa Gamma. 15: 404 Roland, Jackson Tn 38303.

HEACOCK, ELLEN LUCILLE. b Emporia Kan 8 Ap 40. 5: Central Col (Pella Iowa) 58-62 (Chem) BA; UDenver 62-65 (LS) MA. 7: Libn Denver Pub Lib 63-67; Consul West Slope br Colo State Lib 67; Dir Learning Resource Ctr Colo Mt Col 67-. 9: ACS; ALA; ColoLA; ColoASchL. 15: 810 Harrison ave #1, Leadville Co 80461.

HEADLEY, CAROLINE (NEEF). b Hanover NH 29 S 17. 4: Robert Leigh Headley Jr. 5: Conn Col for Women 35-39 (Eng Lit) BA; Columbia 40 (Col & Univ Ref) BS. 6: Fr. 7: Asst Howe Lib, Hanover NH summer 39; Asst ref dept Providence Pub Lib 40-42; Asst circ dept dartmouth Col Lib 42-43, Acting libn ref dept 43-44, Chief ref dept 45-47; Asst ref dept UPenn Lib 47-50, 52-53; Asst ref dept Dolly Madison Br Fairfax Co Lib, McLean Va 67-. 8: Summer replacement, Arabian Affairs Research Lib, Arabian Amer Oil Co, Dhahran Saudi Arabi 62. 14: Ref, bibliog, govt docs. 15: 1118 Guilford ct, McLean Va 22101.

HEADLEY, DORIS (MUTCH). b Rugby Colo 12 Mr 21. 4: Frank A Headley. 5: Linfield Col 39-41 (Eng); Drew U 58-60 (Eng) BA; Rutgers 60-61 MLS. 7: Nursery sch tchr Central NY Sch for Deaf, Rome NY44-45; Nursery sch tchr Denville Community Nursery, Denville JN 50-5; Libn W Morris Reg High Sch, Chester NJ 61-64; Libn Ironia Elem Sch, Randolph Twp NJ 64-67; Libn Fernbrook Elem Sch Randolph Twp NJ 67-. 9: ALA; NEA; NJSchLA (sec 68-69); NJEA; NJL Trust Assn. 10: Bd of Trust Denville Pub Lib; Denville Juv Conf Com; Morris Co Family Serv. 14: Elem sch libs, developing curric materials center. 15: Box 601 Rt 1, Dover NJ.

HEADY, PATRICIA (HARROLD). b Rushville Ind 26 Mr 26. 5: Stephens Col 43-45 (Speech) AA; IndU 45-47 (Speech) AB; USoCal 67-68 MSLS. 7: Sec C J LaRoche & Co Inc, Los Angeles 59; Sec KTTV, Los Angeles 60; Sec Show Mgt, Los Angeles 61; Sec Larwin Co, Beverly Hills Cal 61-64; Real Estate Sales Wm Justice Co, Beverly Hills Cal 64-67; Libn Getty Oil Co, Los Angeles 68-. 9: SLA. 15: 11409 Waterford st, Los Angeles Ca 90049.

HEAFNER, BARBARA (EAKER). b Bessemer City NC 14 Jl 11. 4: B F Heafner. 5: UNC(Greensboro) 27-31 (Hist) LS BA. 6: Fr. 7: Tchr-libn Stanley Schs, Stanley NC 31-35; Libn New 33-52; Circ libn Tex Wilmington NC 36-37; Co Libn Gaston Co Pub Lib, Fla 53-61 coordinator Dade Dir Gaston-Lincoln Reg Lib, Gastonia NC 6-. 9: ALA; NEA-DAVI; SELA; NCLA (Bd Dirs 63-65); NCEA. 10: Altrusa; Gaston Co (NC) Hist Assn; C of C; Mental Health Assn; Nat Foun ; Met Opera Guild; Little Theater Guild. 15: Cherryville rd Rt 2, Bessemer City NC 28016.

HEALD, DOROTHY WOODWARD. b Rockford Ill 27 My 10. 5: Fla State Col for Women 28-32 (Educ) AB; Peabody 47, 49-50 (LS) MA. 7: Libn tchr Dade Co Elem Schs, Miami Fla 33-52; Circ libn Tex Christian U 52-53; Libn Dade Co Elem Schs, Miami Fla 53-61; Coordinator Dade Co Pub Schs, Miami Fla 61-. 8: Prof child lit UMiami 64. 9: FlaSchLA (chm 65-66); Dade Co Child EA (pres 62-63); DadeCoSchLA (pres 58-59). 10: Delta Kappa Gamma. 14: Elem libnship, child lit. 15: P O Box 1074, Tallahassee Fl 32302.

HEALEY, GEORGE HARRIS. b Wellsville NY 10 My 08. 4: Rita Slaughter. 5: WVa U 27-32 (Philos) AB, 32-35 (Eng) MA; Cornell U 40-42, 46-47 (Eng) PhD. 6: Fr, Ger. 7: Asst Prof of Eng Judson Col 38-40; Instr in Eng Cornell U 40-42; Intelligence Off (Lt to Capt) AAF 42-46; Cornell U; Martin Sampson Fellow in Eng 46-47, Asst Prof of Eng 47-53, Assoc Prof of Eng & bibliog 53-57, Prof of Eng & curator of rare bks 57-. 9: Mod Lang Ass; BSA; Bibliog Soc (London). 10: Phi Beta Kappa; Grolier Club (NY). 11: Legion of Merit (Army). 12: "Wordsworths Pocket Notebook (42); "The Meditations of Daniel Defoe (46); "The Letters of Daniel Defoe (55); "The Cornell Wordsworth Collection: a Catalogue (57); "The Dublin of f Stanislaus Joyce (62) (Fr, Ger & Ital tr); Ed "Cornell Library Journal (66). 13: Yes. 14: Rare bks. 15: 106 Olin Lib Cornell U, Ithaca NY 14850.

HEALEY, JAMES S. b Chicago 14 Jl 31. 4: Evelyn J Murphy. 5: Stonehill Col 50-55(Eng 0 ab; Simmons 55-58 (LS) MS; URI 67 MBA. 7: Ref circ asst Harvard U Lib 55; Ref asst Boston Pub Lib 55-56; Libn Stoneham Pub Lib, Stoneham Mass 56-61; Libn Free Pub Lib, New Bedford Mass 61-67; Chief div of lib ext RI Dept State Lib Serv 67-68; Asst Prof Lib Sci URI (Kingston) 68-. 8: Org of Melville Whaling Room, New Bedford Mass 62; Chm Lib Com, Bristol Co (Mass) House of Correction 63-; Bldg consul Somerset (Mass) Pub Lib 65; Lib consul Swain Sch of Design, New Bedford Mass 65; Lecturer on pub libs Grad Sch of Lib Sci URI 65-66; Consul; somerset Mass 68, Cumberland & Woonsocket RI 66; Feasibility study of area lib for No RI 68; Exec dir statewide NLW, RI 68. 9: ALA (Subscription Bk Com 62-65, 67-); -ASD (chm NLW Com 68-); -AHIL (Jt NLW Com, Survey Com 67-69); RILA; NELA. 10: Old Dartmouth Lib Club; Mass Reg Lib Adv Coun; Waterfront Hist Area League New Beford; John F Kennedy Mem Com; Old Dartmough Hist Soc; Amer Mus Assn: Adult Educ Assn; New Bedford Port Soc. 13: Yes. 14: Admin, autmation, libnship educ. 15: 30 Carriage Hill rd, N Kingstown RI 02852.

HEALY, SISTER FRANCES. b Martinsburg W Va 3 N 18. 5: Catholic U 41-44 (Nursing) BS, 44-45 (Nursing Educ) MS, 65-66 MS in LS. 7: Dir of nursing St Vincent's Hosp, Bridgeport Conn 46-55; Dir of nursing St Mary's Hosp, Rochester NY 55-60; Asst dir nuring serv Providence Hosp, Detroit 60-64; Dir of nursing Sacred Heart Hosp, Cumberland Md 64-65; Asst libn St Joseph Col (Emmitsburg Md) 66-. 9: ALA; MdLA. 12: "A Study of the Cost of Educating a Student in a Basic Professional Degree Curriculum in Nursing" (46). 13: Yes. 14: Catlg. 15: St Joseph Col, Emmitsburg Md 21727.

HEANEY, HOWELL J(OHNSON). b Beacon NY 7 Jl 17. 4: Harriet Benedict. 5: Cornell U 35-39 (Govt) AB; Law Sch Cornell U 38-40 (Law); Cornell U 40-41 Comparative Lit (MA); Columbia 41-42 BS (LS). 7: Order libn UNH 42; (Pvt-2nd Lt) Med Admin Corps US Army Ref libn UNH 46-47; Libn Priv Lib of Thomas W Streeter, Morristown NJ 47-55; Bibliog rare bk dept The Free Lib of Phila 55-. 8: Adjunct instr, Grad Sch of Lib Sci, Drexel Inst of Tech, 62-68; Adj Asst Prof 68-. 9: ALA; Bibliog Soc (London); BSA; Bibliog Soc UVa; PennLA. 10: Grolier Club (NY); Philobiblon (Phila); Pittsburgh Bibliophiles; Phi Beta Kappa. 12: Asst to Thomas W Streeter in prep of his Americana-Beginnings (52) & his "Bibliography of Texas, 1795-1845 (55-60). 13: Yes. 14: Rare bks. 15: 341 W Mt Airy ave, Phila 19119.

HEARD, JOSEPH NORMAN. b Austin Tex 29 O 22. 4: Joyce Boudreaux. 5: Tex Col of Arts & Ind 39-41 (Bus Admin); UTex 45-51 (Journalism & LS) BJ, MJ, MLS; LSU 64-69 (Hist). 7: (Aer M 1/c) US Navy, Cal NJ Nicaragua Panama Galapagos 42-45; Orders asst UTex Lib 49-51; Order libn Tex Tech Col 51-53; Asst libn Tex Col of Arts & Ind 53-55; DIR OF Libs Pan Amer Col 55-62; Order libn Northwestern State Col (Natchitoches La) 62-63; Chief acquis libn LSU 63-65; Dir of Lib Southeastern La Col 65-. 8: Helped org Tex State Lib Demonstration Proj, Lower Rio Grande Valley 57. 9: ALA; LaLA (chm Col Sect 69); SWLA; TexLA. 10: Rio Grande Assn for the Mentally Retarded; Valley Botanical Garden Assn; Tex Assn for Retarded Child; La Assn for Retarded Child. ; Civitan; Phi Kappa Phi. 11: First place Child Welfare Essay Contest, Found for Voluntary Welfare 56. 12: "Handbook of Texas, (contr 20 articles) (52); "Bookmans Guide to Americana (3rd ed 64); "Hope Theough Doing" (68). 13: Yes. 14: Acquis, bibliog. 15: 901 W Colorado ave, Hammond La.

HEARD, RUTH (RAMSTAD). b Austin Tex 10 D 42. 4: George E Heard. 5: Frank Phillips Col 60-62 (Speech) AA; UTex 62-64 (Eng) BA, summers 65 & 66 (LS) Tex Lib Cert; UIll summers of 67 & 68, fall semester 68-69 MS in LS. 7: Pasadena Pub Lib, Pasadena Tex 64-65; Jr high libn Deer Pk

Independent Sch Dist, Deer Park Tex 66; Dir Clinton Job Corps Ctr, Clinton Iowa 66-67; Jr high libn Clinton Commun Sch Dist, Clinton Iowa 67-68; Asst dir Clinton Pub Lib, Clinton Iowa 69. 9: ALA. 10: Beta Phi Mu. 14: Ref, child wk. 15: R3 Box 97, Clinton Ia 52732.

HEARN, CAROLYN B. b RI 7 F 23. 4: John H Hearn Jr. 5: URI 44 (Econ) BS, 62 (Hist & Educ) Teach Certif, 68 (LS) MS. 7: Gen accounting Gen Electric Corp, Bridgeport Conn 44-46; Soc wkr R I Dept Soc Welfare 46-49; Hist tchr Stonington Conn High Sch, Stonington Conn 62; Sub tchr Reg Sch, Chariho Woodriver Jct RI 62-64; High sch libn S Kingston High Sch, Wakefield RI 65-67; Libn for handicapped RI Dept State Lib Serv 67-. 9: ALA; Amer Assn Wkers for the Blind; NELA; RILA; RISchLibnsAssn. 10: League of Women Voters; Westerly RI Col Club; URI Alumni Assn. 14: Ya, materials for handicapped, ref. 15: Post rd, Charlestown RI 02813.

HEARSEY, HERBERT (ROSSBOROUGH). b Somerville Mass 27 N 10. 4: Laura Beth Davis. 5: Tufts Col 30-34 (Eng) BS, 35 (Educ) Ed M; UIll 37 BS in LS, 40 MA in LS. 6: Fr, Ger. 7: Ser-catlgr Harvard 34-37; Acquis UIll(Urbana) 38-40; Ref West Wash State Col 41-63, Pub serv libn 64-67, Assoc dir 68-. 8: Assoc Prof of lib sci, West Wash State Col, 4-; Lib eval consul, Nat Assn Col of Tchr Educ, 50-51. 9 ALA; NEA; WashLA; PNLA; WashEA. 10: AAUP; Nat Assn Intercol Athletics; Nat Eligibility Com). 14: Ref, pub serv,admin.;13822 15: West Wash State Col, Bellingham Wash.

HEARTBERG, CECILIA (DARRY). b Ashand Wis 1 Ag 11. 4: Joseph H Heartberg. 05: Nrthland Col 28-32 (Hist) AB; UMinn 33 (Hist); NJ Dept of Educ Prof Libns Perm Certif 58. 6: Ger. 7: Tchr-libn High Sch, Woodville Wis 32-35; Asst dir Pub Lib, Englewook NJ 56-63; Libn ext serv Pub Lib, E Orange NJ 63-. 9: NJLA. 14: Ext serv to shutins. 15: Apt 912B Troy Towers, Bloomfield NJ 07003.

HEATH, ELINOR (JEANNE). b Buffalo Minn 31 O 10. 5: UMinn 28-32 (Lat) BS, 50-51 (LS) BS. 7: Army hosp lib US Army Spec Serv, West Germany 51-54; Br libn Hennepin Co Lib, Edina Minn 55-67; Adult bk selector Hennepin Co Lib, Minneapolis 67-. 9: ALA: MinnLA. 10: AAUW. 14: Adult bk sel. 15: 4539 France ave S, Minneapolis Mn 55410.

HEATH, FLORENCE MARSH. b Detroit Mich 11 F 19. 5: Wayne State 49-54 (Educ) BS; UMich 55-59 MALS. 6: Fr. 7: Eng tchr Lakeshore Sch, St Clair Shores Mich 54; Lib asst wayne State U Gen Lib 54-59; Child libn Detroit Pub Lib 59-. 9: ALA. 10: AAUW. 14: Child serv. 15: 2163 E Eight Mile rd, Grosse Pointe Woods Mi 48236.

HEATH, (HENIETTA) WINIFRED FOLSE. b Oak Ridge La 17 S 10. 4: CharlesMaples Heath Sr. 5: Sophie Newcomb 28-32 (ART) B DES; Mary Hardin Balor 34-37 (Humanities) BA; Peabody summers 60-65 MLS. 6: Sp, Fr, 07: Art tchr Mary Hardin Baylor Col 34-37; Art tchr Elem Pub Schs, Birmingham Ala 37-40; Free Lance Art, Birmingham Ala 38-41; Custodian Morehouse Pub Lib, Bastrop La 43-44; Owner, Mgr Textile Mil, Sottsboro Ala 49-55; Libn Scottsboro High SchLib, Scottsboro Ala 59-. 8: So Assn Evaluating Com 64. 9: AlaSchLA (chm Dist 8, Organ chm Dist 9 65-67); Scottsboro TA (pre s). 10: Jackson Co Park Bd; Scottsboro Pub Lib Bd; AAUW; DAR. 14: Catlgr, ref, wk with stud. 15: PO Box 518, Scottsboro Ala 35768.

HEATHCOTE, LESLEY M(URIEL). b Edmonton ALTA Can 12 My 04. 5: UAlta 21-24 (Modern Langs) BA, 24-28 (Philol) MA; UWash 28-29 BS in LS, 39-52 (Hist). 6: Fr. 7: Asst registrar UAlta 24-28; Ser libn UWash 29-44; Research asst Internat Labor Off, Montreal 45-46; Mont State Col: Gen asst 46-47, Libn & Assoc Prof 47-52, Libn & Prof 52-65; Dir of Libs & Prof Mont State U 65-69. 9: ALA(chm Ser Sect 39-41); PNLA(pres 51-52, chm Constitution Com var times, chm Rorg Com 64-66); MontLA(pres 53-54, chm and/or mem r coms). 10: AAUP; Agric Hist Soc; Phi Alpha Theta; Alpine Club of Can; Bozeman Symphony Soc. 11: Silver Medal in Italian 30; Gold medal in French UAlta 24. 12: Ed "Montana Library Quarterly" 55-63; Comp Indexes to "PNLA Quarterly & Montana Library Quarterly". 13: Yes. 14: Admin, tech proc. 15: 421 South Black, Bozeman Mt 59715.

HEBALKAR, VIJAYA GURUNATH. b Poona India 24 Ap 43. 5: UPoona (India) 58-62 (Eng) BA, 62-64 (Eng) MA, 66-67 BLS; Simmons 68-69 (LS) MS. 6: Fr, Hindi, Marathi. 7: Lectr in Eng Shahu Col (Poona India) 64-66; Libn Col of Nursing (Bombay) 67-68. 9: ALA. 11: Parkhi Prize for clsf (India 67). 14: Info retrieval, ref. 15: 231 Park dr, Boston Ma 02215.

HECHT, BETTY (HOWARD). b Columbus Ohio 25 Mr 26. 4: James A Hecht. 5: Ohio State 47 (Hist of Fine Arts) BFA, 48 (Hist of Fine Arts) MA. 7: Br libn Warder Pub Lib, springfield Ohio 56-58; Sch libn Shawnee High Sch, Springfield Ohio 58-66; Acquis libn wittenbergU 66-, Asst Prof child lit 68-. 9: OhioLA. 10: AAUP; Alpha Chi Omega. 14: Yp lit, art collections. 15: 302 Rosewood ave, Springfield Oh 45506.

HECHT, RACHEL (REBEKAH). b Brooklyn NY 21 S 36. 5: Cornell U 53-57 (Econ) BA; Fletcher Sch of Law & Diplomacy 57-58 (Internat Affairs) AM; Columbia 60-61 (LS) MS. 6: Fr. 7: Sch libn Pub Schs, NYC 60-61; Foreign serv off USIA, Wash Paris 61-63; Sch libn Pub Schs, Wash DC 63-67; Lecturer DC Tchrs Col 65-66; Law libn Covington & Burling 67-. 9: DCLA; SLA; AALL. 13: Yes. 14: Law libnship. 15: 800 4th st SW, Wash DC 20024.

HECKEL, FLORENCE. b NJ 19 F 26. 5: Trenton State Tchrs Col 43-47 (Bus Educ) BS. 7: Dir Little Ferry Free Pub Lib, Little Ferry NJ 49-63; Dir River Edge Free Pub Lib, River Edge NJ 63-. 15: River Edge Free Pub Lib Elm & Tenney ave, River Edge NJ 07661.

HECKEL, JOHN WILLIAM. b Los Angeles 31 Mr 19. 4: Catherine 05: UCal(Berkeley) 37-42 (Hist) AB, 42-43 Certif in Libnship. 7: Ref libn UCal Sch of Law (Berkeley) 42-52; Head ref libn Los Angeles Co Law Lib, Los Angeles 52-64; Chief libn US Court of Appeals for the Ninth Circuit, San Francisco 64-69; Law libn Santa Clara Co Law Lib, San Jose Cal 69-. 9: AALL. 10: Sierra Club. 13: Yes. 14: Ref. 15: 190 N Market st, San Jose Ca 95113.

HECKMAN, FLORENCE ELIZABETH. b W Reading Penn 28 Ap 38. 5: Gettysburg Col 56-60 (Span) BA; Catholic U 63-64 MS in LS. 6: Sp, Fr. 7: LC: Searcher Card Div 60, Searcher catlgr Preliminary Catlg Sect 60-62, Sr searcher catlgr 62-63, Descr catlgr Descr Catlg Div 64, Libn Nat Referral Center for Sci & Tech 64-66; Ref libn Nat Sci Foundation, Wash DC 66-. 9: SLA. 10: Beta Phi Mu; Phi Sigma Iota. 14: Catlg, ref, interlib loan. 15: 11 Second st NE apt 403, Wash DC 20002.

HEDDERICK, ALICE MARIE. b Waterloo Ont Can 13 Je 22. 5: Waterloo Col U West Ont 39-44 (Eng) BA; Toronto 62-63 BLS 06: Fr. 7: Proof-reader Maclean-Hunter Pub Co, Toronto 44-48; Sch sec & libn Swansea Pub Sch, Swansea Toronto 48-62; Catlgr UToronto Lib 63-64; Libn Anglican Church of Can, Toronto 65-. 9: CanLA; OntLA; Can Assn Adult Educ; Fed Ont Naturalists. 14: Ref. 15: 600 Jarvis st, Toronto 5 Ont Can.

HEDE, AGNES ANN. b Downey Cal. 5: UWash (Eng) BA; Immaculate Heart Col 60-61 MALS; USoCal 63- (Eng). 6: Fr. 7: Admin asst UCLA 53-59; Acquis libn Immaculate Heart Col 61-62; Hd catlgr 62-68; Ref libn Los Angeles City Pub Lib 68-. 9: ALA. 14: Acquis, lib educ, ref. 15: 17457 Stagg st, Northridge Ca 91324.

HEDENBERG, ELISABETH MANN. b Milton Penn 28 Jl 07. 5: Simmons 24-26, 27-28 BS; UColo 26-27, summers 31 & 37; Bucknell U summer 34. 7: Child libn Hillside Center Lib, Endicott NY 28-30; Asst in child dept Detroit Pub Lib 31-39; Child libn Pub Lib, Sewickley Penn 39-40; Co sch libn Coshocton Co Dist Lib, Coshocton Ohio 41-47; Bkmob libn Greene Co Dist Lib, Xenia Ohio 47-52; Child libn Washington Co Free Lib, Hagerstown Md 52-57; Spec in child wk New Castle Co Free Lib, Wilmington Del 58-64; Coordinator of child wk Wilmington Inst & New Castle Co (Del) Free Libs 64-. 9: ALA-CSD; -Sch Libns Div; DelLA. 10: ACLU; Quota Club; Storytellers' Club. 14: Wk with child , storytelling. 15: 38 Eastview lane, Clifton Park, Wilmington Del 19802.

HEDERMAN, SARA (SMITH). b Jackson Miss 11 My 11. 4: Robert Michael Hederman Jr. 5: Millsaps Col 28-31 (Eng) BA; Carnegie 31-32 BS in LS. 7: Libn U High Sch, Oxford Miss 32-35; Staff Cossitt Lib, Memphis Tenn 35-37. 8: Bd mem Miss Lib Commsn. 9: ALA. 10: Girl Scouts; Nat Fed Press Women; Kappa Delta Pi. 14: Child lit. 15: 1320 Belvior circle, Jackson Ms 39202.

HEDGCOCK, NANCY LOU. b Frankfort Ind 11 Mr 38. 5: Stephens Col 55-57 (Liberal Arts) AA; Tex Woman's U 58-60 (LS) BA. 7: Asst libn Frankfort Pub Lib, Frankfort Ind 60-62; Child libn Indianapolis Pub Lib 62-68; Catlg libn Indianapolis-Marion Co Pub Lib 68-. 9: ALA; IndLA. 10: Indianapolis Pub Lib Staff Assn. 14: Catlg, ref, child bks. 15: 3373 Tara lane, Indianapolis In 46224.

HEDLUND, BETTA (ESKELI). b Oneonta NY 17 My 40. 4: James H Hedlund. 5: Cornell U 58-62 BS; SUNY (Geneseo) 62-63 MLS. 7: Libn Orchard Park Central Sch, Orchard Park NY 63-64; Libn Novi (Mich) Pub Schs 64-66; Ref libn Ann Arbor Pub Lib, Ann Arbor Mich 66-68; Ref libn Jones Lib, Amherst Mass 68-. 9: ALA. 14: Ref, ya & adult serv. 15: North rd RFD 2, Amherst Ma 01002.

HEDRICK, MILDRED (KATHRYN SPEIRS). b Highmore SD 26 O 22. 4: Gerald Eugene Hedrick. 5: SD State U 40-44 (Hist) BS; UIll 46 BSLS. 6: Sp. 7: Aer 2/c (Aerographers Mate 2d class) US Navy WAVES, Wash DC Norfolk Va 44-46; Lib asst catlg UIll Lib (Urbana) 46-48; Lib asst ref Kalamazoo Pub Lib 48-50; Lib asst circ West Mich U summer 53; Libn First Methodist Church Lib, Kalamazoo 61-64; Lecturer in Dept of Libnship West Mich U 64-. 9: ALA; MichLA. 10: Bta Phi Mu; AAUW; Nat Cong Parents & Tchrs; UN Assn USA. 14: Catlg, ref. 15: 2135 Frederick ave, Kalamazoo Mi 49001.

HEER, PHILIPP RICHARD. b Billings Mont 22 My 39. 4: Judith Lawrence. 5: Eastern Montana Col 60-61; Brigham Young U 64-67 (Hist) BA, 67-68 MLS. 6: Ger, Navajo. 7: Command Maintenance inspector (electronics) USA 57-60; Missionary Latter Day Sts Ch, Navajo Indian Res & reg 62-64; Grad asst bibliog & ref Brigham Young U 67; Bibliog sect hd 68, Asst aquis libn & act hd collection & standing order sect 69-. 9: ALA; UTahLA. 10: Phi Alpha Theta; Repub Party: Voting Dist Chairman, Co Del, State Del. 14: Admin, lib educ, automation, acquis. 15: 1083 So 545 E, Orem Ut 84057.

HEETER, BESS (DRAKE). b Elmwood Place Ohio. 4: Eldon Heeter. 5: Miami U (Eng) BA; UKy 64 MS in LS. 07: Br libn Dayton & Montgomery Co (Ohio) Pub Lib, West Carrollton Br 65-, Hills br, Dales br 68-. 9: ALA; OhioLA. 10: Beta Phi Mu; Phi Beta Kappa. 14: Adult serv. 15: 45 E Pease ave, West Carrollton Oh 45449.

HEFFERNAN, JOSEPH F. b Phila 6 F 10. 4: Catherine Martin. 5: Girard Col 18-28; Biarritz (Amer U) 45. 7: Investigator with Mil Police US Army (Cpl) 43-45; Asst libn Phila Bar Assn 28-; Ref libn Theodore F Jenkins Mem Law Lib 66-. 9: AALL. 10: Amer Legion; Amvets; Jt Veteran's Coun. 15: 600 City Hall, Phila Pa 19107.

HEFFLER, DAN L. b NYC 11 Ap 12. 4: Simmie Match. 5: NYU 51 (Educ) BS Ed; Pratt '63 MLS. 6: Sp, Yiddish, Hebrew, Mod Gk. 7: Pub speaking Instr Masters Inst, NYC 37-43; Clerk US Post Off, NYC 44-46; Clerk Labor Dept, NYC 47-50; Sr clerk motion picture iv NYC Educ Dept 50-59; Libn trainee Queensboro Pub Lib, Queens NY 60-61; Libn trainee Brooklyn Pub Lib 61-63; Libn NY Pub Lib 63-66; Queensboro Pub Lib Soc Sci div, Queens NY 66-67, Lang & lit div 67-68, Sr libn art & mus div 68-. 9: SLA. 11: Bossom Award (Spanish); NY Times Oratorical Contest. 14: Ref, research, bk eval. 15: 2200 Morris ave, Bronx NY 10453.

HEFLEY, BERYL F. b Prescott Kan 10 F 23. 4: Jo S Hefley. 5: UMo(Kan City) 46-50 (Geog, Geol) BA; West Res 50-51 MSLS. 6: Fr, Sp. 7: Kansas City (Mo) Pub Lib: Ref libn 51-53, Asst head acquis 53-54, Head acquis 54-62; Ref libn Sandia Corp, Livermore Cal 62-63, Libn 63-. 8: Spec consul for reorg of Acquis Dept, Okla City Pub Lib, 55. 9: SLA; ASIS. 13: Yes. 14: Ref. 15: Sandia Corp, Livermore Ca 94550.

HEFNER, CECIL G JR. b Atlanta 28 Ja 33. 4: Melanie Martin. 5: Emory 51-53 (Liberal Arts); Auburn U 56-58 (Math) BS; UDenver 61-63 (LS) MA. 7: Communications US Army 53-56; Lib asst Denver Pub Lib 61-63, Libn I 63-64; Chief tech processing Tech Lib US Army Electronic Proving Ground, Ft Huachuca Ariz 64-65; Science & Ind head Phoenix Pub Lib 65-68, Coord of adult serv 68-. 8: Lib consul West Bible Inst, Denver 63; Mgt Info Systems user coord Rep for Phoenix Lib. 9: SLA; Ariz State LA (Spec Lib Div: v-pres 68-69, pres 69-70); ALA-ISAD. 10: Pi Mu epsilon; Radio Amateur License. 14: Ref, develop, prog, automation, systems analysis, operations research, mgt. 15: 1808 E Marshall, Phoenix Az 85016.

HEFNER, DOROTHY A. b Forestburg Tex 12 Ja 09. 4: H A Hefner. 5: N Tex State U 26-30 (Home Econ) BS, 52 (Sch Admin) M Ed, 63 Lib Certif. 7: Elem tchr Pub Sch, Garden Valley Tex 28-29; Home econ pub sch, Batson Tex 30-34; Elem tchr pub sch, Batson Tex 41-42; Elem tchr pub sch, Graham Tex 43-54, Jr high sch libn 54-. 9: Graham TA. 10: Delta Kappa Gamma; Woman's Club, Wesleyan Serv Guild. 14: Child bks. 15: 1431 Scenic dr, Graham Tx 76046.

HEGARTY, MARY SUZANNE (LOHR). b Kearny NJ 19 D 41. 4: Kevin Hegarty. 5: Douglass Col 60-64 (Hist) BA; Rutgers 64-65 MLS. 7: Jr libn Free Pub Lib of Woodbridge NJ 65-66, sr libn 67-68, Sr libn-br libn Port Reading Br 68-. 9: NJLA; MiddlesexCoLA (treas). 14: Ref, child wk. 15: 2 Primrose lane apt 2N, Fords NJ 08863.

HEGARTY, KATHLEEN B. b Watertown Mass 4 N 30. 5: Radcliffe 48-52 (Hist, Lit) AB; Simmons 54-58 MLS. 6: Fr. 7: Extra asst & unclsf asst 46-53; Boston Pub Lib: Pre-prof asst supv off, admin wk 53-57, Ref asst gen ref dept 57-59, Adults libn group wk 59-62, Coordinator of adult serv 62-. 8: Instr YWCA Course on intro to libnship, 62-. 9: ALA-ASD (chm Com on Lib Serv to an Aging Population 64-65, mem Reading Improve for Adults Com 65-68, chm Ad hoc Com on Goals 68-69); AEAUSA (sec Sect on Educ for Aging 64-66); MassLA (chm adult Educ Com 62-64); Adult Educ Assn Mass (chm Basic Adult Educ Proj 65-). 10: Brighton Hist Soc; LWV; mem NCCJ Awards Com, Boston. 14: Adult educ, commun wk, prof train. 15: 95 Arlington st, Brighton Ma 02135.

HEGARTY, KEVIN. b Ennis County Clare Ireland 20 F 36. 4: Mary Suzanne Lohr. 5: Queen of Peace Col & Sem 55-60 (Philos) BA; Catholic U summers 56-59 (LS); Rutgers 62-64 MLS. 6: Fr, Gk, Lat. 7: Asst libn Queen of Peace Col & Sem 56-60; Lib trainee Bloomfield Pub Lib, Bloomfield NJ 61-64, Sr libn circ 64-66; Prin libn Passaic Pub Lib, Passaic NJ 66-67; Br libn Woodbridge Pub Lib, Woodbridge NJ 68, Chief libn main lib 68-. 9: NJLA(chm Human Rel Com). 10: Beta Phi Mu; Rotary. 14: Readers adv wk, ref, bibliog, bk catlgs. 15: 2 Primrose la apt 2n, Fords NJ 08863.

HEGENWALD, SHIRLEY (BETHARD). b Coushatta La 4 S 27. 5: Brenau Col 44-45; LSU 45-48 (Eng) BA, 48-49 BS in LS. 7: Libn Metairie Br Jefferson Parish Lib, Metairie La 49-52; Ref libn Jefferson Parish Lib, Gretna La 54; Child libn Bossier-Red River Parish Libs, Benton La summer 65; Asst libn Bossier Parish Lib, Bossier City La 65-67; Chief libn VA Hosp, Shreveport La 67-. 9: LaLA. 10: St Paul's Day Sch Bd, Shreveport La (chm 64-65); PTA. 14: Ref. 15: 445 Pennsylvania ave, Shreveport La 71105.

HEGGIE, GRACE F. b Toronto Can. 5: UToronto 55-59 BA, 60-61 MA, 61-62 BLS. 6: Fr. 7: Soc sci bibliogr YorkU 66-. 9: IPLS. 15: 19 Allangrove Crescent, Toronto Ont Can.

HEGLAND, MAXINE LILLIAN. b Greenbush Minn 9 My 08. 5: UND 26-30 (Eng) BA; UIll 30-31 BS in LS; San Jose State Col 47-60 (Educ) MA. 6: Fr. 7: Catlgr St Mary Col (Kan) 31; Sr libn UND 31-33; Sr libn UMinn(Minneapolis) 34-36; Asst to Dir Stanford U 37-42; (Lt) USNR WAVES Operation Off 42-45; Chief Libn US Cadet Sch, San Mateo Cal 45-46; Sr Libn State Hosp, Agnew Cal 46-52; Chief Libn Menlo-Atherton High Sch, Atherton Cal 52-; Libn US Dependent Sch Rochfort France 55-56. 9: NEA; ALA (Life mem); CalLA; Cal Tchrs Assn; CalASchL. 10: ACLU; KQED (Educ TV). 13: Yes. 14: Lib develop, admin. 15: 111 Chester, Menlo Park Ca 94025.

HEHR, RUSSELL ALLON. b Cleveland 27 F 19. 5: Cleveland Col of West Res 38-41, 46-47 (Art, Music) AB; West Res U 47-48 BSLS; Inst of Fine Art NYC 48-50 (Art Hist); UMinn 60 (Art Hist). 6: Fr. 7: Taught classes in art & music, POW Camp, Germany 42-45; Head of musical activity Stalag III B, Fu2rstenburg A/o POW Camp, Germany 42-45; US Army, Europe 41-45; Libn in fine arts Cleveland Pub Lib 50-59, Libn in chg of the picture collection 59-; Asst hd fine arts dept 68-. 10: Ludlow Assn; Asst organist & choirmaster, Trinity Cathedral, Cleveland, 37-41 & 45-48; Dir of Music, Church of the Master, Cleveland Hts, Ohio 50-. 14: Picture collection clsf, art hist. 15: 3079 Albion rd, Cleveland Oh 44120.

HEIBEL, MARY CLARE. b Butler Penn 12 F 10. 5: Grove City Col 29-32 (Eng) & (LS) AB; Columbia summer 49 (Med Lib Sci). 6: Fr. 7: Child libn Butler Pub Lib, Butler Penn 34-47; Med libn VA Hosp, Butler Penn 47-51; Chief Libn VA Hosp, Btler Penn 51-. 9: ALA; PennLA. 10: AAUW; Beta Sigma Phi; Nat Coun Cath Women. 14: Med ref. 15: 10 Butler Towers, Butler Pa 16001.

HEIBERG, SISTER RUTH. b Seattle Wash 24 My 15. 5: Marylhurst Col (Eng) BA; Rosary Col BALS; UMich AMLS. 7: Libn high sch Pacific NW 43-58; Libn Ft Wright Col, Spokane Wash 58-. 9: ALA; CathLA (past chm Pacific NW Unit); PNLA. 14: Acquis, catlg. 15: Ft Wright College, Spokane Wa 99204.

HEICHELBECH, MARY LOUISE. b Indianapolis Ind. 5: Ind Central Col 59-63 (Eng) AB; UIll 65-66 (LS) MS. 6: Sp, Ger. 7: Tchr Center Grove Sch Corp, Greenwood Ind 63-64; Asst loan libn Ind State Lib, Indianapolis 64-65; Asst hd ref dept Ind State U (Terre Haute) 66-. 9: ALA. 10: Beta Phi Mu; AAUP. 14: Ref. 15: 2232 N 12th, Terre Haute In 47804.

HEIDENREICH, RALPH (LEE). b Yakima Wash 12 My 35. 5: UWash 53-54, 56-57 (Clothing Design) BA; UDenver 60-61 (LS) MA. 7: Libn I Lib of Hawaii, 61-66, Libn III 66-68, Libn IV 68-. 9: HawaiiLA. 14: Fine arts, a-v educ. 15: 1143 Hassinger st, apt 108, Honolulu Hi 96822.

HEIDERSTADT, DOROTHY. b Geneva Neb 8 O 07. 5: UKan 36 (Eng) AB; Simmons 37 BS in LS. 6: Fr. 7: Dir of child wk Pub Lib, Bethlehem Penn 37-42; Libn Louis George Br Kan City (Mo) Pub Lib 42-68, Libn Prospect Br 68-. 9: ALA. 10: Round the World Club; Okla Hist Soc; Phi Beta Kappa. 12: "Book of Heroes" (54); "A Bow for Turtle" (60); "Frontier Leaders & Pioneers" (62); "Indian Friends and Foes" (58); "Knights and Champions" (60); "Lois Says Aloha" (63); "Marie Tanglehair" (65); "More Indian Friends and Foes" (63); "Ten Torchbearers" (61); "To All Nations" (59); "Stolen by the Indians" (68). 14: Child wk, pub lib wk. 15: P O Box 396, Independence Mo 64050.

HEIDORN, PATRICIA ANN (ELLIS). b Granite City Ill 11 Mr 37. 4: Robert Don Heidorn. 5: Ill State U 55-58 Soc Sci BS; UIll 59-60 MSLS. 6: Fr. 7: Libn-tchr Alton Pub Sch Dist #11, Alton Ill 58-59; Circ & ref asst (Fine Arts Lib) UIll(Urbana) 60-63; Ref asst Fogler Lib UMe (Orono) 66-67, Asst Prof of Lib Serv (tchg catlg & clsf) 67-68; Instr elem educ dept (tchg child lit) Wis State U(Whitewater) 69-. 9: ALA (Intl Rel RT);-RTSD;-ACRL. 10: Beta Phi Mu; Pi Gamma Mu; Kappa Delta Pi; Alpha Beta Alpha. 14: Ref, tchg (catlg & clsf, child lit). 15: 1237 Yoder lane, Whitewater Wi 53190.

HEIDT, DONALD PETER. b Columbus Wis 20 My 31. 4: Mabel Danner. 5: Catholic U 58 (Philos) BA; Ga So col 63-64 (Educ); UGa Ext 63-64 (LS) UGa 65-69 (Educ). 7: Libn M Mary Mission High Sch, Phoenix City Ala 61-62; Libn St John Sem, Savannah Ga 62-68; Libn Benedictine Mil Sch 68-. 9: CathLA; GaLA. 10: RC Gallon Club. 15: 50 Dolan dr, Savannah Ga 31406.

HEIDT, ELIZABETH. b Regina Sask Can 29 Mr 19. 5: Sacred Heart Col 37-39 (Philos) BA; Tchrs Col (Regina Sask) 39-40; UMan summers 44-45 B Ed; McGill 47 BLS; Columbia 59; UWash 64, 65, 66 (ML). 6: Fr. 7: Tchr Collegiate, Indian Head Sask 42-46; Libn catlg asst Regina (Sask) Pub Lib 48; Ref libn Sask Legis Lib 49-56; Libn Sheldon-Williams Collegiate, Regina Sask 56-68; Educ libn USaskatchewan (Regina Can) 68-. 9: CanLA; ALA; SaskASchL (co-chm Standards Com, past pres); ReginaLA. 10: Can Univ Women; Sask Tchrs Fed. 14: Catlg, sch libnship. 15: 905 Tower Gardens, Regina Sask Can.

HEIL, GRANT WALLACE. b Glen Ullin N Dak 6 Mr 10. 4: Marion R E Youngborg Heil. 5: UPacific 28 (Hist); Sacramento Jr Col 29-30 (Hist); UCLA 30-32, 33-35 (Hist) AB & MA; UCal (Berkeley) 32-33, 35-36 (Educ, Lib) GS, BLS. 6: Lat, Medieval Lat, Fr, Ger. 7: Asst libn Modesto Jr Col 36-39, Instr 39-43; Libn Visalia Union High Sch, Visalia Cal 43-46; Col libn Ventura Col 46-. 8: Lectr Univ Ext Santa Barbara Cal 47-48; Instr Ventura Evening Col Ventura Cal 47-. 9: ALA. 10: St Paul's Episcopal Parish, lay reader & Sunday school superint; Alum Assn UCal Lib Schs; Ventura Co Hist soc. 12: "Mission San Buena Ventura" (57); Ed "Ventura County Historical Society quarterly" (65-); Ed "The CALibrariab," 58-. 14: Admin, a-v. 15: 221 N Katherine dr, Ventura Ca 93003.

HEILIGER, EDWARD (MARTIN). b Rockford Ill 14 D 09. 4: Beatrice Kelley. 5: U of the Pacific 28-33 (Hist) AB; UDenver 34-35 BS in LS, 40-41 (Hist) MA. 6: Sp. 7: Jr asst Detroit Pub Lib 35-37; Asst libn Wayne U Lib 37-43; Dir Amer Lib of Nicaragua (ALA), Managua Nicaragua 44-46; Dir adv Universidad de Chile (RF), Santiago Chile 46-48; Head Program Mgt Overseas Libs, US Dept of State, Wash DC 49; Dir Benjamin Franklin Lib US State Dept, Mexico D F 50-53; Assoc dir NY State Lib 53-55; Dir UIll Lib, Chicago 55-63; Dir Lib & info retrieval serv Fla Atlantic U 63-67; Sr scientist United Aircraft Corp Systs div 67-68; Prof Lib Sci & dir ctr for lib studies Sch of Lib Sci Kent State U 68-. 8: Official US Delegate Internat Conf on Sci Documentation, Lima Peru 62; Pres Pan Amer League of Detroit 43; Nat Scholarship Commsn of Chile 46-48; Bd mem Chilean N Amer Cultural Inst 46-48; Prof of Lib Sci UChile 46-48; Mexican Amer Cultural Commsn 51-53; Visiting Prof Syracuse U Lib Sch summer 55; Chm Sears Found Proj ALA 58; Delegate US Nat Commsn for UNESCO 7th Nat Conf 59 & 8th Nat Conf 61; Bd mem Adult Educ Coun of Greater Chicago 58-63; Chm Mayor's Com Pan Amer Bk Fair Chicago 59; Bd of Dir Nat Educ Assn for Research & Development Inc 65-; Consul to Bd of Regents State of Fla 65; Consul to var libs; Adv Com Info Systems Proj LC 60-63. 9: ALA-RSD (chm Info Retrieval Com 63-67;-ACRL (chm A-V Com 64, chm Com Coop Educ & Prof Orgs 65); SLA (chm Document Reprod Com 63-64); ASIS; FlaLA; SELA; IllLA (pres-elect 62-63, treas 61-62); Chicago Lib Club (pres 58-59); OhioLA. 12: Co-author "Advanced Data Processing in the University Library" (62); Transl "Codigo para Clasificadons" (55); Co-author "Catalogacion clasificacion" (49); Ed "Illinois Libraries" (58-63). 13: Yes. 14: Info retrieval, data processing, admin. 15: 1571 Stratford dr, Kent Oh 44240.

HEILMAN, ALICE (MARY) S(YLVESTER). b Baltimore Md 22 Mr 25. 4: Carl Ernest Heilman. 5: Towson State 42-45 (Educ) BS; Columbia 47-48 BLS; TempleU 53-54 (Psychol). 6: Fr. 7: Tchr Washington Co Schs, Williamsport Md 45-47; Libn Elizabethtown Col, elizabethtown Penn 48-59; Libn Elizabethtown Pub Lib, Elizabethtown Penn 60-63; Lib asst Franklin and Marshall Col, Lancaster Penn 61-62; Co libn Lancaster Free Pub Lib, Lancaster Penn 62-63, Asst dir 63-68; Asst dir Martin Mem Lib, York Penn 68-. 8: Catlgr Klein Chocolate Co spec research lib 57-58; Tchr child lit Elizabethtown Col 48-58; Tch col 48-58; Tchr catlg Sci Press, Ephrata summer 66; Tchr elem catlg Penn State Off- campus Div (Harrisburg) 67. 9: ALA; PennLA (Memb Com; Lib Development Com; Nominating com 68; chm Ad Hoc Com to Study Com Expenses; v-chm & chm S Central Chap; program chm s central Chap); LancasterCoLA (sec, treas, v-pres, pres). 14: Admin, org, planning & consul, new bldg plans, ext. 15: 592 W Main st, Mt Joy Pa 17552.

HEILMAN, MARY (ELIZABETH) (MITCHELL). b NYC 27 D 22. 4: Kenneth A Heilman. 5: Douglass Col 40-44 (Chem) BS; Drexel 51-54 MS in LS. 7: Chem DuPont, Parlin NJ 44-47, Tech file supv 47-50; Asst libn DuPont, phila 50-54; Libn DuPont, Parlin NJ 54-66; Supv research libn, Wilmington Del 66-. 9: SLA; ASIS; ACS; DelLA. 10: Phi Beta Kappa; Beta Phi Mu. 15: E I duPont de Nemours & Co, Tech Lib, Wilmington De 19898.

HEILMANN, MARGARET (AYERS). b Athens Ill 25 Jl 14. 4: John E Heilmann. 5: State Tchrs Col (Geneseo NY) 33-36 (Educ) Life Tchg Certif; State U Col (Geneseo NY) 36-37 (LS) BS in Ed; NYU 45 (Educ) MS; Queens Col (NY) 54-55 (Educ); C W Post Col of LIU 61 (LS). 7: Libn, tchr Pub Sch, Shelter Island NY 37-38; Tchr Pub Sch, Schoharie NY 39-42; Tchr Park Ave Sch, Williston Park NY 42-43; Libn Herricks Pub Schs, New Hyde Park LI NY 43-58; Libn NY Pub Lib summers 46-50; Dir of Libs Herricks Pub Schs, New Hyde Park LI NY 58-. 8: Adj Asst Prof Grad Lib Sch LIU, Greenvale LI NY 62-. 9: NEA-DAVI;ALA-SLS; ASCD; NYLA (chm Publns Com 65-66);-SLS (Bd 64-66; Adv Standards Com 59-60); NY State Tchrs Assn; NY State SchLA (pres). 10: PTA; DAR. 13: Yes. 14: Sch libs. 15: 214-08 Hillside ave, Queens Village NY 11427.

HEILNER, IRWIN (JOHN). b NYC 14 My 08. 4: Florence Kronhaus. 5: Columbia 52, 53 (Music Educ) BS, MA; Columbia 59 (LS) MS. 6: Fr. 7: Priv piano tchr & composer NYC; Music tchr Bd of Educ, Passaic NJ 54-56; Music tchr Bd of Educ, Wayne Twp NJ 56-57; Desk asst Physics Lib Columbia U 57-59; Sr libn Passaic Pub Lib, Passaic NJ 59-65, Prin libn 65-. 9: NJLA. 10: Amer Composers Alliance. 11: Numerous performances & broadcasts of music. 12: "Chinese Songs" recorded by Composers Recordings Inc CRI 143; Compositions published by Assd Music Publ; New Music, etc. 14: Catlg, ref. 15: 101 Dawson ave, Clifton NJ 07012.

HEILPRIN, LAURENCE BEDFORD. b NYC 26 My 06. 4: Marilyn Heyman. 5: UPenn 24-28 (Econ) BS, 29-31 (Physics) MA; Harvard 32-35, 40-41 (Physics) PhD. 6: Fr. 7: Instr Northeastern U 35-40; Asst in thermodynamics Harvard U 40-41; Physicist var grades Nat Bur of Standards, Wash DC 41-51; Physicist Taub Engnr Co, Wash DC 52-54; Analyst MIT-OEG, Wash DC 54-56; Physicist Documentation Inc, Wash DC 56-57; Staff physicist CLR, Wash DC 58-67; Prof of infor sci, UMd 67-. 8: Professorial lecturer, American U, George Washington U, Nat Bur of Standards, UMd, etc; Prof Lecturer on Info Retrieval, American U, 65-66; Dir & v-pres, Com to Investigate copyright Problems 58-; Chm Study Group, CICP. 9: ASIS (pres 65); Assn Computing Machinery; Amer Physical Soc; Amer Optical Soc; Operations Res Soc Amer; Amer Math Soc; Inst Electric & Electronics Engnrs; Philos Soc Wash. 10: Fed of Amer Scis; Harvard Club of Wash. 12: Co-ed "Education for Information Science" (65). 13: Yes. 14: Info sci. 15: 6402 Tone dr, Bethesda Md 20034.

HEIM, FERN VIOLA (BLOOM). b Stamford Neb 10 Ja 16. 4: Richard A Heim. 5: UNeb 33-37 (Math) BS; Columbia summers 40-43, 49 BLS. 7: Libn Chem Dept UNeb 40-42, Circ dept 42-44, Hd period dept 44-46; Research libn B F Goodrich Research Div, Akron Ohio 46-59; Ref dept Nebr Lib Comsn, Lincoln Neb 61-. 9: SLA (chm Chem Sect). 10: AAUW; Women's Soc of World Serv; Soroptimist Club. 14: Spec libs, ref. 15: 3245 Starr, Lincoln Nb 68503.

HEIM, HELEN R. b Lisbon Ohio 19 D 06. 4: Herbert W Heim. 5: Mt Union Col 23-24; Genera Col 54-59 (Educ) BS Ed; Kent State 60-65 MLS. 7: Tchr Bearer Local Schs, RD Elkton Ohio 54-56; Libn Leetonia Schs, Leetonia Ohio 56-60; Libn Lepper Lib, Lisbon Ohio 60-61; Libn Salem Sr High Sch, Salem Ohio 61-. 9: ALA; NEA; OhioEA; OhioASchL. 10: AAUW; DAR. 14: Ref. 15: RD 5, Lisbon Oh 44432.

HEINECKE, MARGARET T. (BRAND). b NYC 13 S 23. 4: Heinrich Heinecke. 5: Col of St Elizabeth 41-45 (Hist) BA; Columbia 49 (Pol Sci) MA, 54 (LS) MS. 7: Libn & instr of hist Panzer Col of Phys Educ & Hyg 53-57; Libn Watchung Hills Reg High Sch, Warren Twp NJ 57-60; Supv libn GS 9 USAF, Hahn AB Germany 60-61; Libn (admin) GS-11 USAF, Ramstein Germany 61-65; Libn III San Diego Co Lib 67-69, Supv libn 69-. 9: ALA; CalLA. 15: 3338 S Bonita, Spring Valley Ca 92077.

HEINEKE, CHARLES (DAVID). b Galveston Tex 30 Sp 43. 4: Sharon Halstead. 5: UCorpus christi 61-65 (Relig) BA; UTex (Austin) (LS); N Tex State U 66-67 MLS. 7: Stud asst UCorpus Christi Lib 64-65; Stud asst UTex (Austin) Lib 65-66, Grad asst 66; Grad asst n tex State U 67; Pub serv libn Midwestern U Lib 67-68, Asst dir 68-. 9: ALA; TexLA; SWLA; Tex Assn Col Tchrs. 13: Yes. 14: Public serv (esp ref & lib instr), automation. 15: 3400 Taft blvd, Wichita Falls Tx 76308.

HEINMILLER, VIRGINIA (WINE). b Kansas City Mo 17 Ja 10. 4: Adelbert J Heinmiller. 5: Kan City Jr Col 27-29 AA; UWis 29-31 (Ger) AB, 30-31 (LS) Certif. 6: Fr, Ger. 7: Head gen asst Sci Dept Milwaukee Pub Lib 31-34; Br asst Kan City Pub Lib 34-39; Asst libn Portland Cement Assn Res & Devel Labs, Skokie Ill 57-. 9: SLA. 10: Girl Scouts; PTA; Univ Women's Club. 14: Ref. 15: 608 Echo lane, Glenview Il 60025.

HEINRITZ , FRED JOHN. b Piqua Ohio 1 Mr 31. 5: UCincinnati 48-52 (Eng) BA, 55-56 (Educ) BS; Rutgers 57-58 MLS, 61-63 (LS) PhD. 6: Ger. 7: Field scout exec Boy Scouts of America, Cleveland Area Coun 52-53; US Army (Pfc) Spec Serv, Alaska 53-55; Math tchr Hughes High Sch, Cincinnati Oh 56-57; Sci catlgr UCalLA 58-59, Geol-geophysics libn 59-60; Elem sch libn Santa Monica (Cal) Pub Sch Sys 60-61; Asst Prof of Lib Sci UNC(Chapel Hill) 63-67; Prof of Lib Sci So Conn State Col 67-. 9: ALA; ConnLA. 10: Sierra Club. 12: Co-auth "Scientific Management of Library Operations" (66). 13: Yes. 14: Lib sch educ, sci mgt, documentation, sci lit, govt publ. 15: Div of Lib Sci, Southern Conn State Col, New Haven Ct 06515.

HEINS, ETHEL L. b NYC 9 Ap 18. 4: Paul Heins. 5: Montclair State Col 34-35 (Educ); Douglass Col 35-39 (LS) BA; Columbia U 39 (LS); Harvard U Sch of Educ 64. 6: Fr. 7: Child libn NY Pub Lib 38-43; Child libn Louisville Free Pub Lib, Louisville Ky 44-45; Child libn Boston Pub Lib 55-62; Elem sch libn Lexington (Mass) Pub Schs 62-. 8: Instr child lit, Boston Col 68. 9: ALA; NESchLA; MassSchLA; Round Table of Child Libns NE; Mass Tchrs Assn. 13: Yes. 14: Child bks, sch libs. 15: 18 Warwick rd, W Newton Ma 02165.

HEINTZ, EDWARD C. b Attleboro Mass 2 Jl 15. 5: Brown 34-38 (Econ) AB (cum laude); UMich 40-42 ABLS. 7: Ref asst Springfield City Lib, Springfield Mass 38-40; Circ asst UMich Lib (Ann Arbor) 40-42; Supv Dept Libs, UIowa (Iowa City) 42-43; Instr machine sch Pratt & Whitney Aircraft, E Hartford Conn 43, Supv gp leader train 44-45; Hd order dept Brown U Lib 45-46; Asst libn Bowdoin Col Lib 46-52; Libn Kenyon Col Lib 52-. 8: Consul for moving, Harvard Med Lib & Boston Med Lib 64. 9: ALA (Coun 54-57); -ACRL; MeLA (pres 50-51); NELA (dir 51-52); OhioLA (Exec Bd 54-55). 10: AAUP; ACLU; Elks. 13: Yes. 14: Admin, bk sel, rare bks. 15: Box 41, Gambier Oh 43022.

HEINTZ, SISTER M CANDIDA OSF. b Chicago 7 Mr 01. 5: Col of St Francis 19-21; De Paul U 21-24 (Lat, Gk) AB, 28-35 (Eng) MA; UMich 37-38 ABLS. 06: Lat, Sp, Ital, Fr, Ger. 7: High sch tchr St Francis Acad, Joliet Ill 23-27, 33-37; Tchr St Mary High Sch, Columbus Ohio 27-33; Asst libn Col of St Francis (Joliet Ill) 38-40; Libn St Francis Acad, Joliet Ill 40-44; Libn Sacred Heart High Sch, Chicago 44-47; Libn St Clement High Sch, Chicago 47-48, 54-58; Prin St Mary High Sch, Columbus Ohio 48-54; Libn St Peter High Sch, Mansfield Ohio 58-67; Libn Our Lady of Angels Retirement Home, Joliet Ill 67-. 09: CathLA. 14: Catlg, ref, bk sel, circ (high sch). 15: St Francis Convent 520 Plainfield ave, Joliet Il 60435.

HEINTZ, SISTER MARY ST LAMBERT BVM. b Milwaukee 18 Ag 13. 5: Clarke Col (Dubuque) 42-44; Mundelein Col 52 (Eng) BA; Catholic U summers 58-62 MS in LS; State U Iowa summer 57; UIll summer 68 (Sch Libnship) (NDEA Inst). 6: Fr. 7: Res libn Mundelein Col Lib 44-60; Asst libn clarke Col Lib 60-65; Libn Our Lady of Peace High Sch, St Paul 65-. 9: ALA; CathLA (Scholarship Com; v-chm Minn-Dak Unit); MinnASchL; NCTE. 12: "Bibliography of the Writings of the Sisters of Charity, BVM" (62). 13: Yes. 14: Ref, sch libnship. 15: Our Lady of peace Convent, 40 N Milton, St Paul Mn 55104.

HEINTZ, ROBERT LeROY. b Pipestone Minn 22 My 42. 5: State Col of Iowa 60-65 (LS) BA; Central Mo State Col 68 (LS). 7: Libn Holmes Jr High Sch, Cedar Falls Iowa 64-66; Libn Spencer High Sch, Spencer Iowa 66-. 9: ALA; NEA; Iowa State EA; IowaASchL. 14: Catlg, ya. 15: 905 E 8th st, Spencer Ia 50701.

HEINTZEN, ANNE IRENE (BARSUN). b Greenville Tex 14 N 08. 4: Frank Walter Heintzen. 5: UTex 25-27; Our Lady of the Lake Col 32-34 (Eng) BA; St Mary's U summer 40; Trinity U (Tex) summers 50, 54, 57; Our Lady of the Lake Col 60-64 (Ed) M Ed, Lib Certif. 6: Ger, Sp, Fr. 7: Grade sch tchr (Briscoe, Collins Garden), San Antonio Tex 27-50; Eng tchr Sam Houston High Sch, San Antonio Tex 50-58; Eng tchr Highlands High Sch, San Antonio Tex 58-60; Libn Jefferson Davis Jr High Sch, San Antonio Tex 61-. 8: Chm, High Sch Eng Dept, Sam Houston High Sch, San Antonio 50-58; Supvg tchr in Trinity U tchr train program, 59-60. 9: NEA; Tex State Tchrs Assn; TexLA; San Antonio Coun of Sch Libns (pres 64-66). 10: San Antonio Hist Assn; San Antonio Eng Club. 14: Ya. 15: 1136 Avant ave, San Antonio Tx 78210.

HEINZ, CATHARINE FRANCES. b Anaheim Cal 21 Mr 20. 5: Rosary Col 37-41 BA in LS; Columbia 46-47, 52 (LS) MS. 6: Fr. 7: Libn-tchr St Vincent's Col & Acad (Shreveport La) 41-42; Sch dept libn Orange Co Free Lib, Santa Ana Cal 42-43; Communications Off US Navy, San Francisco 43-46; Newspaper clsf Columbia U Journalism Lib 46-47; Crew & med libn US Naval Hosp, Brooklyn NY 47; Asst dir Hosp Lib Bur United Hosp Fund, NYC 47-48, Dir 48-56; Research libn Mutual of NY (Mutual Life Insur Co), NYC 56-59; Libn Television Info Off, NYC 59-. 8: Mem NY Adv Com, Amer Merchant Marine LA 48-; Consul "Encyclopedia Americana" 55. 9: ALA (pres Hosp Libs Div 50-51);-LAD-PRS-PRSL (chm Radio/Television/Film Festival 66-67, PRSL Com 65-68); Amer Women in Radio & TV (chm Ind Info Com 64-66, Memb Chm NY Chap 68-69); SLA (chm Com on Standards for Hosp Libs 49-52, chm Pub Rel Com 59-61; NY Chap: sec 62-63; chm Hosp Group 47-48); LPRC; NY Lib Club. 10: Columbia U Sch Lib Serv Alum Assn. 12: Co-ed "Objectives & Standards for Hospital Libraries" (53); Exec ed "Spec Libraries of Greater NY Directory" (63). 13: Yes. 14: Spec libnship, pub rel, ref, bibliog. 15: 100 W 57th st, New York NY 10019.

HEINZ, SARAH LOUISE. b Flandreau S Dak 19 Jl 34. 5: BakerU 52-56 (Elem Educ) BA; West Res 58-59 MLS. 7: Lib asst Wichita Pub Lib, Wichita Kan 57-58; Child libn Kan City Pub Lib, Kan City Mo 59-. 10: AAUW. 14: Child lit & serv to child. 15: 4144 Warwick blvd, Kansas City Mo 64111.

HEINZKILL, JOHN RICHARD. b Appleton Wis My 33. 4: Theda Lange. 5: St John's U (Collegeville Minn) 51-55 (Eng) BA; UMich 63-64 AMLS. 7: Advertising staff The Liturgical Press, Collegeville Minn 56-59; Mgr College Store Wis State U (Oshkosh) 59-62; Ref staff John M Olin Lib Washington U (St Louis) 64-67; Humanities libn UOre (Eugene) 67-. 14: Ref. 15: 514 S Wilson, Little Chute Wi 54140.

HEISE, GEORGE FRANKLIN. b Murphysboro Ill 30 Jl 34. 4: Barbara Ann Mosby. 5: So Ill U 52-57 (Govt) BA, 59-61 (Local Govt) MA; Peabody 61-62 MA in LS. 7: (Sp 4) US Army 1st Div 1st Ba Combat Eng 57-59; Bkmob libn & head of bkmob serv So Ill Reg Lib, Carbondale Ill 59-61; Asst city mgr, Centralia Ill 60; Consul Dir Ill State Lib & West Ill Reg Lib, Macomb Ill 62-63; Head educ & train Ill State Lib 64; Documents libn West Ill U 64-65, Acquis libn 65-67; Admin asst, Asst dir indexing serv H W Wilson Co, Bronx NY 67-. 8: Library USA/NY World's Fair 64. 9: ALA-ACRL; -RTSD; -LAD; -RSD; -ISAD; SLA; ASIS; Internat City Managers Assn; NY Lib Club. 10: Beta Phi Mu; Melvil Dewey Chowder and Marching Soc. 12: Ed "Western Illinois Library News". 13: Yes. 14: Admin, catlg, ref, acquis. 15: 110 Vreeland ave, Bergenfield NJ 07621.

HEISER, REV W CHARLES S J. b Milwaukee 16 Mr 22. 5: St Louis U 40-47 (Lat) MA, (Philos) PhL, 50-54 (Theol) STL; Catholic U 55-58 MS in LS. 6: Lat, Fr, Ger, Sp, Ital. 7: Libn Divinity Sch of St Louis u 55-, Asst Prof of theol 66-. 9: ALA; CathLA; ATheolLA; MPLA; KanLA. 12: Ed "Theology Digest Book List." 13: Yes. 15: Sch of Divinity, Saint Louis Univ, 3655 W Pine blvd, St Louis Mo 63108.

HEISLER, OLGA KARLOVNA. b Moscow Russia. 4: Michael A Heisler. 5: USask 48-52 (Biol) BA; Toronto 57-58 BLS. 6: Fr, Ger. 7: Sci libn McMaster U 58-61; Asst libn-sci Queens Col (Queens NY) 61-64; Asst libn NYU Col of Dentistry 64-68, Libn 68-. 9: SLA; ALA. 10: YWCA; AAUP. 14: Ref, rare bks. 15: NYU Col of Dentistry Lib, 421 First ave, New York NY 10010.

HEITGER, ABBIE (DEAN). b Bedford Ind 15 Je 19. 5: St Mary-of-the-Woods Col 37-41 (Soc Sci) BA; Ind U 64-66 (LS) MA. 6: Fr. 7: Sec Crane Naval Ammunition Depot, Crane Ind 41-45; Sec UChicago 48-52; Woman's program dir Radio Station WBIW, Bedford Ind 54-58; Field consul Ind State Lib, Indianapolis 66-67, Hd ext div 68-. 9: ALA; IndLA; IndASchL. 10: Beta Phi Mu. 12: Ed, "Extension Division Bulletin". 14: Admin, consul, pub sch, acad, spec lib serv & coop. 15: 3710 N Meridian apt 607, Indianapolis In 46208.

HEITMAN, ELLEN A. b Spring Valley NY 26 Ag 09. 5: Donovan Bus Col 31; NY State Lib Train Courses. 6: Fr. 7: Libn in chg Finkelstein Mem Lib, Spring Valley NY 46-62, Child libn 62-69, Libn local hist div 69. 9: ALA; NYLA. 10: Bus & Prof Women's Club; Friends of Lib; Red Cross; Nat Wildlife Fed; Rockland Co Conservation; Valley Garden Club. 14: Child serv, pub rel, loc hist, educ. 15: 6 S Myrtle ave, Spring Valley NY 10977.

HEITMANN, MARGUERITE MICHEL. b Dayton Ohio 12 My 13. 4: William Arthur Heitmann. 5: Miami U (Oxford Ohio) 31-35 (Hist) AB; Emory 35-36 BLS; Ursuline Col 50-55 (Educ); Ind U Ext (Jeffersonville) 55-56 (Educ); George Washington U 60-65 (Guidance & Adult Educ) MA. 6: Fr. 7: Libn Pub Lib Cincinnati & Hamilton Co, Cincinnati Ohio 36-37; Libn Pub Lib, Dayton Ohio 37-39; Elem tchr Masonic Home Sch, Louisville Ky 52; Tchr Louisville Country Day Sch, Louisville Ky 53-55; Elem tchr & remed reading Eastlawn Elem & Port Fulton Elem Schs, Jeffersonville Ind 55-56; Elem sch libn Arlington Co Pub Sch, Arlington Va 56-60; High sch libn Fairfax Co Pub Sch, Fairfax Va 60-62; Head high sch libn George C Marshall High Sch 62-67; Learning ctr coun & ref libn Marymount Col (Arlington) 67-. 10: NE Area Two-Year Col Reading Assn; AAUP; Bellevue Forest Citizens Assn; Country Club. 14: Instructing col students in use of lib as learning ctr, ref. 15: 3607 N Piedmont st, Arlington Va 22207.

HEITZEBERG, VIRGINIA (WELDON). b Kansas City Mo 8 D 14. 5: Sullins Jr Col 32-33; UMo (Columbia) 33-36 (Design) BFA; Kan State Tchrs Col (Emporia) 68-69 MLS. 7: Bkmob libn Johnson Co Lib, Merriam Kan 56-58, Br supv 62-68, Ref coord, 69-. 9: ALA; KanLA. 14: Ref. 15: 6101 Woodson rd, Shawnee Mission Ks 66202.

HEITZMAN, HALINA (KONOPCZNSKA). b Warsaw 17 S 12. 4: Marian Heitzman. 5: Jagiellonian U (Cracow) 31-36 (Hist) MA; UMinn 50-51 BS in LS. 6: Polish, Fr, Ital. 7: Lib asst old bks sect Cracow U (Poland) 36-37; Co-ed Poradnik Swietlicowy, Polish YMCA in Great Britain 41-43; Chief libn Polish Research Centre, London 43-49; Libn Biochem Lib UMinn(St Paul) 51-54; Lib Sch of Arch UMinn(Minneapolis) 54-55; Catlgr St Paul Pub Lib 56-60; Prof asst hist dept Minneapolis Pub Lib 60-; Asst libn MIT Sch of Arch, Cambridge Mass 65-67; Asst chief catlg dept, Bapst Lib Boston Col 67-. 08: Exec Sec Polish Hist Soc in Great Britain 47-49. 13: Yes. 14: Ref, catlg. 15: Catalog Dept Bapst Lib, Boston College, Chestnut Hill 02167.

HEIZER, DOROTHY (ELEANOR LAWSON). b Avalon Penn. 5: West Col for Women 23-27 (Eng, Soc Sci) BA; West Res 27-28 BS in LS. 7: Asst br libn Lima Pub Lib, Lima Ohio 28-30; Legis sec Cal Congress of Parents & tchrs, Los Angeles 46-55; Catlg dept Sch of Law Lib UCLA 57, Head acquis dept 58-61; Order libn Los Angeles Co Law Lib, Los Angeles 61-. 9: AALL (chm Com on Lib Exhibits 64-66); So Cal ALL (pres 62-63). 14: Acquis, govt documents. 15: 11400 Cashmere st, Los Angeles Ca 90049.

HELD, CHARLES H. b Detroit 26 Ja 29. 5: Albion Col 46-50 (Hist) AB; UMich 50-52 AMLS; UEdinburgh 57 (Hist) Certif; Albion Col 61-62 (Hist) MA; Wayne State 63- (LS). 7: USMC 52-54; US Army Reserves (Capt) MOS 2420 Archivist 55-; Libn Fordson High Sch, Dearborn Mich 54-58, Tchr 58-63; Instr in Lib Sci Wayne State U 63-65; Head Libn Albion Col 65-. 8: Com for Lib Development State Lib, Lansing Mich 64-65; Consul Albion Col Lib 65. 9: ALA; CanLA; MichASchL. 10: Mich Hist Soc; Ont Hist Soc; Can Hist Soc; Medieval Acad of Amer; Phi Delta Kappa. 14: Sch lib educ, col lib admin. 15: Albion Col Lib, Albion Mi 49224.

HELD, RAY E(LDRED). b Portsmouth Ohio 29 Mr 18. 4: Naomi Edwards. 5: Fla So Col 37-40 (Soc Studies) BS in Educ; Ohio State U 40-41 (Hist); Emory 46-48 BA in LS, 47-48 (Hist) MA; UFla 48-55 (Hist) PhD; UMich summer 50 (LS). 7: (S/Sgt) US Army 41-45; Tchr Sarasota High Sch, Sarasota Fla 46-47; UFla: Soc sci libn 48-49, Instr in Lib Sci 49-50, Soc sci libn 50-52, Asst libn ref & bibliog 52-53; Visiting Lecturer in Lib Sci UTex summers 52, 53; Visiting Asst Prof of Libnship Emory U 53-54; Asst Prof & Asst dir Sch of Lib Sch UOkla 55-57; Asst Prof Sch of Libnship UCal(Berkeley) 57-64, Assoc Prof 64-, Assoc dean 66-. 9: ALA; AALS; CalLA. 10: Cal Hist Soc. 12: "Public Libraries in California, 1849-1878" (63). 13: Yes. 14: Ref, bibliog, hist of libs. 15: Sch of Libnship Univ of Cal, Berkeley Ca.

HELENE, SISTER MARIE OP. b Milwaukee 10 Ag 17. 5: Edgewood Col 37-49 (Educ) BS in Ed; Rosary Col 50-51 MA in LS; UWis(Madison) summer 55; American U summer 56 (Archives) Certif; UWis(Madison) summer 62 (A-v). 7: Tchr-libn Sacred Heart High Sch, Omaha 51-54; Visiting Instr Dept of Lib Sci Rosary Col summers 52-54, 58, 59-61; Libn Heelan High Sch, Sioux City Iowa 54-64; Acquis libn Rosary Col 64-65; Asst dir Dept of Lib Sci, Rosary Col 65-66; Libn Central Catholic High Sch, Bloomington Ill 66-69. 9: ALA; CathLA; IllLA; McLeanCoLA. 14: Sch libs, a-v methods & materials. 13: Yes. 15: 106 W Chestnut st, Bloomington Il 61701.

HELFMAN, RICHARD. b NYC 2 Jl 23. 5: Brooklyn Col 53-57 (Psych) BA; Rutgers 57-58 MLS. 7: S/sgt US Army Air Force 43-45; Adult serv Brooklyn Pub Lib 58-60; Asst ref libn E Meadow Pub Lib, E Meadow NY 60-61; Hd ref Engring Soc Lib, NYC 60-. 9: SLA. 15: Eng Societies Lib, 345 E 47 st, New York NY 10017.

HELFRICK, MARGARET (JANE). b Elkhart Ind 25 Mr 10. 5: Rockford Col 27-28; Goshen Col 33-34, 50-51 (Psych) BA; Ind U (South Bend); Columbia summers 35, 43, 44. 6: Ger. 7: Elkhart Pub Lib, Elkhart Ind: Gen asst 29-33, Ref & yp libn 33-43, Ref libn 44-48, Org bkmob serv 48-50, Asst libn 50-62; Ref libn Miles Labs Inc, Elkhart Ind 62-65; Sci libn 65-. 9: ALA; MedLA; IndLA (treas 46-49, mem chm Pub Rel Com, etc). 10: AAUW; PEO. 14: Ref. 15: 603 Gladstone, Elkhart In 46514.

HELGESEN, MARTIN WESTLYE. b Brooklyn NY 11 N 38. 5: St Francis Col (Brooklyn NY) 57-61 (Math) BS; Pratt 64-65 MLS. 6: Russian. 7: Pvt E-2 Mil Police Corps US Army 56; Actuarial research clerk Equitable Life assurance Co, NYC 61; Sgt (E-5) Mil Pol Corps US Army 61-62; Actuarial research clerk Equitable Life Assurance Soc, NYC 62-64; Instr Cohen Lib City Col (NY) 65-. 9: ALA; CathLA. 10: Beta Phi Mu; Cath Interracial Coun of LI; Cath Evidence Guild of NY. 14: Catlg, ref. 15: 11 Lawrence ave, Malverne NY 11565.

HELGESON, ESTELLA HANSINE (ANDERSEN). b Perham Minn 20 Ag 06. 4: Andrew Helgeson. 5: Neb State Tchrs Col (Chadron) 24-25, 26-27 (Educ) 2 yr Certif; UMinn 28-30 (Eng) BS, 50-53 BS in LS; USoCal 67-68 MS in LS. 6: Sp. 7: Rural sch tchr, Custer Co SD 33-35; High sch instr Span Eng, Lusk Wyo 35-37; High sch instr Sp Math, Custer SD 43-48; High sch Eng instr, Lemmon SD 48-49; Tchr libn Flandreau High Sch, Flandreau SD 49-50; Asst libn SD Sch of Mines & Tech (Rapid City) 53-67, Assoc libn 68-. 09: ALA; MPLA; SDLA (treas 60-62). 10: Delta Kappa Gamma; Women's Club; Fine Arts Study Group; AAUW. 14: Catlg, ref, State docs. 15: 418 E Madison, Rapid City SD 57703.

HELLENE, DOROTHY (LORRAINE) INGALLS. b Crosby N Dak 15 Je 16. 4: Sigurd A Hellene. 5: Wash State U 34-39 (Eng, Hist) BA; UWash 45-49 (Amer Lit) MA, 67 (Educ); UDenver 50-54 (Libnship) MA. 6: Norwegian. 7: Tchr & libn: Creston Pub Schs, Creston Wash 39-40, Quillaxute Union High Sch, Forks Wash 40-42; Libn Shumway Jr High, Vancouver Wash 42-43; Link trainer operator (Sgt) USMC, El Toro Cal 43-45; Dist libn Issaquah Pub Schs, Issaquah Wash 49-51; Libn Seattle Pub Schs 51-67. 9: ALA; -AASchL; NEA; WashStateASchL (pres 66-67); Wash Dept A-V Instr. 10: Pi Lambda Theta. 14: Devel of integrated media-library prog for schs. 15: 9529-244th SW, Edmonds Wa 98020.

HELLER, MARY (MacGRUER). b Ogdensburg NY 24 Jl 13. 4: John D Heller. 5: St Lawrence U 30-34 (Lat) BA; NY State Tchrs Col (Albany) summer 56; Syracuse summer 56; C W Post Col of LIU 59-62 (LS) MS. 6: Lat, Fr. 7: Lat tchr Adams High Sch, Adams NY 34-39; Libn & Lat Southampton High Sch, Southampton NY 53-58; Libn Plainedge High Sch, Bethpage NY summer 61; Ref asst LIU summer 63; Head Libn Friends Acad, Locust Valley NY 58-; Adj asst Prof Grad Lib Sch LIU 65-. 8: Middle States Assn of Cols & Secon Schs eval com, 65, 67. 9: ALA; NYLA; Nassau-Suffolk SchLA (treas 61-62); Hudson Valley LA (Ind Schs); Nassau Co LA; LI Educ Communications Coun. 10: LIU Grad Lib Sch Alumni Assn; Delta Kappa Gamma; Beta Pi Theta. 14: High sch libs, ref. 15: 15 Todd dr, Glen Head NY 11545.

HELLERICH, JANET L. b Nome Alaska 21 Je 33. 5: Fresno State Col 51-55 (Soc Sci) BA; UCal(Berkeley) 55-56 MLS. 7: Stud page Fresno State Col Lib 52-55; Child libn Coalinga Dist Lib, Coalinga Cal 56-59; Br libn Fresno Co Free Lib, Reedley & Clovis Cal 59-61; Asst child libn Santa Rosa Pub Lib, Santa Rosa Cal 61-62; Prin libn, child & yp Santa Rosa-Sonoma Co Lib, Santa Rosa Cal 62-; Child coord Kauai Pub Lib Hawaii State Lib Syst. 9: ALA; CalLA (sec Yosemite Dist 57-58); Assn of Child Libns of No Cal (sec 65-66). 10: Santa Rosa Boys Club; AAUW. 14: Child & ya wk, br wk. 15: PO Box 824, Lihue Kauai Hi 96766.

HELLERMANN, ELISABETH B (WOOD). b Atlanta 31 D 08. 5: UWis 30 BA, 49 BLS. 7: Libn adult serv Wauwatosa (Wis) Pub Lib 49-52; Libn III sci Milwaukee Pub Lib 52-. 9: SLA. 10: Beta Phi Mu. 15: 4043 N 69th st, Milwaukee Wi 53216.

HELLMAN, MRS MARY (HALPERIN). b NYC 16 F 13. 5: Brooklyn Col 33 (Music) BA; Rutgers 58 MLS. 6: Ger, Fr. 7: Sec & music libn Brooklyn Col 36-42; Journalist Morristown Record, Morristown NJ 53-55; Libn W Morris Reg High Sch, Chester NJ 58-61; Hd Ref libn Harry A Sprague Lib Montclair State Col 61-. 8: Lib consul, Eval Com of Middle States Assn, 61-62; Lib consul & coord, Ctr for Urban Educ, to evaluate Title II Prog of Demonstration & Tchr Train Prog of NYC Bd of Educ 65. 9: ALA; NJLA; AAUP; MusLA. 10: NJ State Col Faculty Assn; Montclair State Col Fac Coun & Coord Coun. 12: Asst ed "Musical Mercury" (39-40). 14: Ref, bk sel, freshman orientation, govt docs. 15: 60 W 13 st, New York NY 10011.

HELLMANN, REV GEORGE. b Cincinnati 6 S 20. 5: Duns Scotus Col 40-44 (Philos) BA; Catholic U 49-50 MS in LS; Holy Family Friary (Oldenburg Ind) 44-48 (Theol). 6: Lat, Fr, Ger, Ital, Sp. 7: Libn Roger Bacon High Sch, Cincinnati 48-49; Libn Holy Family Sem (Oldenburg Ind) 50-52; Libn Duns Scotus Col 52-60; Libn Roger Bacon High Sch, Cincinnati 60-65; Libn St Leonard Col 65-. 8: Prov Libn Franciscan Fathers Prov of St John Baptist, Cincinnati 65. 9: ALA-ACRL;-RTSD;-LAD;-RSD;-ISAD; CathLA; MALC. 10: Liturgical Arts Soc. 12: Bk review ed "St Anthony Messenger. 14: Clsf, rare bks, catlg. 15: 8100 Clyo rd, Dayton Oh 45459.

HELLUM, MRS BERTHA (DUBINSKI). b El Paso Tex 2 N 11. 5: UTex Col of Mines & Metallurgy 28-30 (Educ) Elem Tchg Certif; UCal(Berkeley) 30-33 (Hist, Pol Sci) BA, 33-34 (LS) Certif & Certif in Sch Libnship. 6: Sp, Fr, Ger. 7: Chief of brs Sacramento City Lib, Sacramento Cal 34-37; City libn Monterey Pub Lib, Monterey Cal 37-46; County Lib El Dorado Co Lib, Placerville Cal 47-49; Demonstration libn La State Lib, Baton Rouge & Gretna 49-50; Parish libn Jefferson Parish Lib, Gretna La 50-52; Lib consul Cal State Lib 52-54; County libn Contra Costa Co Lib, Pleasant Hill Cal 54-; County libn Alameda Co Lib, Hayward Cal 64-. 8: Lecturer 58-68 UCal Sch of Libnship in Pub Lib Admin; Univ libn of New John F Kennedy U (Martinez Cal) 65-67; Consul Walnut Creek Cal 50-; Lecturer UCal(Berkeley) 58-. 9: CalLA (past chm Legis & var other coms, past pres 63). 10: Contra Costa Co Hist Soc; Dir CCC Park & Recreation Coun; 32nd Dist (Cal) PTA Adv Com; Honorary Life mem PTA; Cal Cong of Parent & Tchr Adv Com. 13: Yes. 14: Admin, friends of libs, lib bldgs. 15: 1917 Golden Rain rd #6, Walnut Creek Ca 94595.

HELM, SALLIE (HARPER). b Crowville La 7 Ag 31. 4: E Eugene Helm. 5: Northwestern (La) Sate Col 48-52 (Eng, LS) BA; LSU 52-55 (LS) MA. 6: Ger. 7: Tchr-libn La Pub Schs 52-55; Br libn, staff consul, head gen ref dept Dallas Pub Lib 55-58; Catlgr Neb State Tchrs Col 58-59; Catlgr ser libn UIowa 60-64; Head Libn Iowa City Pub Lib, Iowa City Iowa 64-68; Supv of adult bk sel, Fairfax Co Pub Lib, Fairfax Va 68-. 9: ALA; IowaLA (chm Adult Serv Div 66); Mo Valley Adult Educ Assn; VaLA. 10: UN Assn; LWV; Beta Phi Mu. 14: Adult serv, catlg. 15: 5238 Nebraska ave NW, Washington DC 20015.

HELM, WILLIAM. b Brooklyn NY 29 N 32. 4: Elizabeth Thomas. 5: Brooklyn Col 53-56 (Eng Educ) BA; Columbia 60 (LS) MS. 6: Fr. 7: NY Pub Lib: Clerk 52-56, Tech asst I searching sect 57-58, Tech asst II procurement sect 58-60, Libn Francis Martin Br 60-61, Act 1st asst Wakefield Br 61-62, Sr libn Wakefield Br 62-63, Br libn Melcourt Br 64-68, Supv br libn Mosholu br 68-. 10: Classical Guitar Club. 14: Admin. 15: 1055 E 228th st, Bronx NY 10466.

HELMBOLD, F WILBUR. b Fowlerville Penn 13 My 17. 4: Neola Wood Helmbold. 5: Howard Col 46-49 (Hist) AB; Duke 50-54 (Relig) MA; Cumberland Sch Law 63-64 (Law). 6: Fr, Greek. 7: Newspaperman various, Penn 34-42; Musician 559th Air Force Band 42-46; Pastor Baptist chs, Ala, NC 47-54; Catlgr Birmingham Pub Lib, Birmingham Ala 49-50; Catlgr DukeU 50-51; Chief libn Barrington Col 54-57; Chief libn SamfordU 57-. 8: Lib consul Birmingham Baptist Hosps 58-68; Curator Ala Baptist Hist Soc 57-; Var consul assignments in educ & libnship 58-; Gen ed Banner Press, Birmingham Ala 61-. 9: SELA; AlaLA (var offs; pres 63-64); AlaEA. 10: Ala Writers Conclave; So Baptist Hist Soc; Ala Hist Soc. 12: Ed "Alabama Baptist Historian" (67-). 14: Rare bks, spec collections. 15: 2305 Harmony lane, Birmingham Ala 35226.

HELMRICH, HAROLD ERNST. b Seattle 15 Jl 11. 4: Virginia F Luther. 5: UWash 30-34 (Hist) AB, 34-35 AB in Libnship; Columbia 37-39 (LS) MS. 6: Ger. 7: Col Libn Seattle Pacific Col 36-37; Prof asst Columbia U Libs 37-39; Libn I Brooklyn Pub Lib 39-41; Immigrant inspector US Immigration Serv, NYC 41-43; US Army Infantry tech 3rd grade, Mediterranean Theatre 43-45; Chief lib div br off 11 US VA 46-49; City Libn Yakima Pub Lib, Yakima Wash 49-51; City Libn Pub Lib, Santa Monica Cal 51-52; Libn in chg acquis group tech lib Hughes Aircraft Co, Culver City Cal 52-59; Lib supv Boeing Sci Research Labs, Seattle 59-60; Asst libn tech dept Tacoma Pub Lib, Tacoma Wash 61; Head tech serv Denison U Lib 63-65; Chief Libn Slippery Rock State Col 65-. 8: Adv Bd ERIC/CCM Info Scis 69. 9: ALA; PNLA (Ed Com 36-37); PennLA. 10: AAUP; Pi Sigma Alpha; Lambda Chi Alpha. 11: Summer internship Nat Inst Pub Affairs 35. 13: Yes. 14: Col & univ lib admin, tech serv. 15: Rt 1, Slippery Rock Pa 16057.

HELMS, FRANK QUIGG. b Wilmington Del 28 Je 37. 4: Judith Shaw. 5: UDel 55-59 (Biol) BA; Rutgers 60-61, 64-MLS. 6: Fr, Ger. 7: Ref asst Wilmington Inst Free Lib, Wilmington Del 59-60; Ref asst Rutgers The State Univ Lib 60-61; Agric libn UDel 61-63, Sci libn 63-64; Research fellow Rutgers Sch of Lib Serv 64-66; Dir of lib serv West Chester State Col (Pa) 66-. 9: ALA; SLA; ASIS; PennLA (sec-treas Col & Res Lib Sect 68-69). 10: Del Air Nat Guard, AAUP. 14: Admin, ref. 15: Irwin Place RD #3, Coatesville Pa 19320.

HELMS, HARRIET MARY. b Hastings Neb 1 Ja 08. 5: UNeb 26-30 (Elem Educ) BS in Educ; West Res 40-41 BS in LS. 7: Asst to head child wk Lincoln City Lib, Lincoln Neb 41-43, Head child wk 43-50; Br child libn Detroit Pub Lib 51-52; Child libn Central Lib Grosse Pointe Pub Lib, Grosse Point Mich 52-53; Head child wk Lincoln City Lib, Lincoln Neb 54-56; Child libn Br & Central Grosse Pointe Pub Lib, Grosse Pointe Mich 57-62, Chief child serv 62-. 9: ALA-CSD (chm Memb Com 56; Jaycees Good Reading Adv Com 65-68); MichASchL (co-chm Jt Spring Inst withMichLA); MichLA. 10: Soroptimist Club; AAUW. 14: Child serv. 15: Grosse Pointe Pub Lib, 10 Kercheval ave, Grosse Pointe Mi 48236.

HELPS, MARY (WERTMAN). b Phila 27 Jl 11. 5: Temple 28-32 (Eng) BS in Educ; Drexel 62-65 MSLS; Brigham Young summer 68 (Instr Media). 7: Tchr libn (sub) Penn-Treaty Jr High Sch, Phila 34; Tchr libn (sub) Fitzsimmons Jr High Sch, Phila 34; Tchr libn Springfield High Sch, Springfield Penn 34-36; Tchr asst to headmaster St Peters Choir Sch, Phila 49-58; Libn Marple-Newtown Jr High Sch, Newtown Square Penn 58-61; Libn Paxon Hollow Jr High Sch (M-N dist), Broomall Penn 61-66; Sch lib development adv div of sch libs Dept of Pub Instr, Harrisburg Pa 66-67; Elem lib-coord West Chester Area Sch Dist, West Chester Pa 67-. 09: ALA; NEA-DAVI; PennSchLA; Penn State EA; Delaware Co SchLA; Chester-Montgomery SchLA; PennLA (chm child, YP & Sch Libns Div). 10: Bksellers Assn of Phila; Lib Pub Rel Assn Greater Phila. 14: Sch libnship, lit for child & ya, pub rel. 15: 504C Philmar ct, Springfield Pa 19064.

HELSABECK, WYAT. b Troy NC 26 Je 21. 5: Pfeiffer Col 39 42 Diploma; UNC (Chapel Hill) 46-56 (Eng) AB, 58-62 (LS); Fla State U 63- (LS). 6: Fr, Ger. 7: (Cpl)

Communications 86th Fighter Wing 5th AF, SW Pacific 43-46; Stud manager U Stores UNC(Chapel Hill) 51-57, Desk clerk The Carolina Inn 57-58, Clerk-typist Wilson Lib, 58-63; Ref asst Charlotte-Mecklenburg Pub Lib, Charlotte NC 64-. 9: NCLA; ALA; SELA. 10: Phi Beta Kappa. 14: Ref, catlg, for langs. 15: Apt B-5-56 Myrtle apts, 1121 Myrtle ave, Charlotte NC 28203.

HELVERSON, LOUIS G. JR. b Phila 1 S 35. 4: Elva Marie Metzger. 5: Temple 55-59 (Elem Educ) BS in Elem Ed; Drexel 63-65 MS in LS. 7: Lib page Free Lib of Phila 52-57, Page supv 57-59; Tchr, Levittown NJ 59-60; Tchr Neshaming Sch Dist, Langhorne Penn 60-61; Lib trainee Free Lib of Phila 61-65, Libn 65-. 14: Ref, ya serv. 15: 1337 Herschel pl, Phila Pa 19116.

HELYAR, L E JAMES. b London England 18 Ag 31. 4: Thelma Winchester. 7: Accessions dept Nat Central Lib, London England 47-55; Acquis dept UKan Libs 55-57; Info off Engineering Ltd, London England 57-61; Hd acquis UKan Libs 61-66, Asst dir 66-. 9: Lib Assn (Gt Brit); ALA; -ACRL. 10: AAUP; Soc Army Hist Research; Samuel Johnson Soc of Kan. 12: Ed "Univ of Kansas Library Series". 13: Yes. 14: Acquis, ed, design & publ. 15: 933 Ohio st, Lawrence Ks 66044.

HEMINGSON, ELIZABETH JANE (EDGERLY). b Cashmere Wash 10 Je 17. 4: Ernest C Hemingson. 5: UWash 35-39 (Eng) BA, 39-40 (Eng) Tchg Certif; 55-56 (Eng) Renewal of Certif, 58-63 (LS) ML. 6: Fr. 7: Eng tchr Montesano High Sch, Montesano Wash 40-42; Eng tchr Bellevue Jr High Sch, Bellevue Wash 43-44; Eng tchr Kirkland Jr High Sch, Kirkland Wash 56-57; Libn Lake Washington High Sch, Kirkland Wash 57-. 9: NEA; WashEA; Wash State ASchL. 15: 4302 LW blvd NE, Kirkland Wa 98033.

HEMINGWAY, CAROL JO. b Benton Harbor Mich. 5: West Mich U BA. 7: Bkmob libn Jefferson City & Cole Co Libs, Jefferson City Mo; Child libn River Forest Pub Lib, River Forest Ill; Child libn Detroit Pub Lib; Sch libn St Joseph Catholic Sch, St Joseph Mich. 9: ALA; CathLA. 15: 1412 Langley ave, St Joseph Mich 49085.

HEMMING, RICHARD THOMAS. b St Paul 18 D 38. 4: Janice Helen McIntosh. 5: UMinn 56-60 (Philos) BA, 60-63 (LS) MA. 6: Lat, Gk, Danish. 7: Ref asst J J Hill Ref Lib, St Paul 61-63; Instr UMinn Lib Sch (Minneapolis) 63-64; Instr libn ref dept UMinn Lib (Minneapolis) 64-67; Asst Prof UDenver 67-68; Libn St Paul Pub Lib 68-. 10: Phi Beta Kappa; Beta Phi Mu. 12: "A Study of Faculty Members in Library Schools in the US Not Accredited by the American Library Association," ACRL Microcard Serv (63). 14: Ref, lib educ, admin. 15: 1596 Race st, St Paul Mn 55102.

HEMMINGS, MARIAN. b Lee County Iowa 7 Jl 02. 5: Stephens Jr Col 20-22 (Math) AA; State uiowa 23-25 (Math) BA, 28-29 (Math) MS; UIll 31-32 BS in LS. 7: Tchr: Hillsboro Iowa 22-23, Calamus Consolidated Sch, Calamus Iowa 25-27, Bonanza Ky 27-28; Math tchr Earlham Jr Col 29-30; Governess Pythian Child Home, Springfield Ohio 36-37; Dining room matron Monett Sch for Girls, Rensselaer Ind 37-41; Libn & tchr Dorland Sch for Girls, Hot Springs NC 41-42; Libn & math tchr Wilson Memorial High Sch, Halifax Va 42-44; Libn Haysi High Sch, Haysi Va 44-45; Libn Jamestown Col 45-48; Libn Iowa Wesleyan Col 48-65, Ref libn 65-. 9: ALA; IowaLA. 14: Ref. 15: 410 N Adams st, Mt Pleasant Ia 52641.

HEMPHILL, B FRANKLIN. b Lincoln Neb 21 Ja 36. 4: Marilyn Miller. 5: UNeb 54-59 (Eng, Anthropology) BA; Rutgers 59-60 MSLS. 7: Lib asst Neb Pub Lib Comm, Lincoln Neb 54-59; Baltimore Co Pub Lib, Baltimore Co Md: Bkmob libn 60-61, Admin asst 61-62, Admin serv off 62-63, Asst co libn 63-. 8: Consul Neb Pub lib Comm, Lincoln Neb 63, 64, 68, 69, Henrico Co Pub Lib 69-70. 9: ALA; MdLA (chm 2 coms 63-64); Potomac Tech Process Lib (Coun 64-66). 13: Yes. 14: Lib arch procedure analysis. 15: 1809 Landrake rd, Baltimore Md 21204.

HEMPHILL, FAITH (NEAL). b Greensboro Ga 8 F 40. 4: G William Hemphill Jr. 5: Spelman Col 57-61 (Eng) BA; Atlanta 61-62 MSLS. 6: Fr. 7: Elem sch libn Atlanta Pub Schs 62-. 8: Training of Headstart tchrs. 9: NEA; Ga Tchrs & Educ Assn (Libns Div). 10: YWCA; YMCA; NAACP. 14: Child wk, esp storytelling. 15: 414 Haldane dr SW, Atlanta Ga 30311.

HEMPHILL, FRANK A JR. b Lafayette La 19 Ag 39. 5: UTex 57-60 (Pol Sci); USWestLa 58 (Pol Sci); West Mich U 53-64 (Soc Sci) BA 64-66 MLS. 6: Ger. 7: Radar repairman USAF, Battle Creek Mich 60-64; Dir Pub Lib, Allegan Mich 65-66, City Libn Portage Pub Lib, Portage Mich 66-. 9: ALA; MichLA (Memb Com). 10: Kappa Sigma; Assn West Mich U Dept of Libnship Alum; Optimist Internat; Portage Teen Ctr Bd mem; Assn of West Mich Pub Adminrs; Kennel Club. 14: Admin, ref. 15: 3228 Coy ave, Kalamazoo Mi 49001.

HEMPHILL, JEANETTE MARIE (FRANKE). b Amana Iowa 17 S 32. 4: William Edward Hemphill. 5: UIowa 49-53 (Ger) BA; Denver U 55-56 (LS) MA. 6: Ger. 7: Tchg asst Ger UIowa 51-53; Lib asst ref Denver Pub Lib 54-55; Sr libn & instr in bibliog UColo(Denver) 56-. 8: Delfi, Inc.-Study/Travel Adv, Denver Colo 68 & Schwandorf, Germany 69. 9: MPLA; ColoLA. 10: Delta Phi Alpha; Edelweiss soc; AAUP; Internat Platform Assn. 11: DIB Certif of Merit 68. 14: Admin. 15: Denver Center Lib 1100 Fourteenth st, Denver Co 80202.

HEMPHILL, MABEL G HUNT. b Vicksburg Miss 31 Mr 17. 4: Edgar Nathaniel Hemphill. 5: Northeast La State Col 33-35, 60-63 (Eng, Educ) BA; LSU (Baton Rouge) 63-64, 67-68 (LS) MS, Post Master Fellow in Lib Sci. 6: Fr. 7: Libn Neville High Sch Monroe City Sch Syst, Monroe La 64-67; Asst Prof & catlg libn La Polytech Inst 68-. 8: NDEA Inst summer 67. 10: Jr Charity League Inc of Monroe; Beta Phi Mu; Phi Lamdo Pi; AAUW; AAUP. 13: Yes. 14: Catlg, sch libs & media ctrs. 15: 1035 Park ave, Monroe La 71201.

HEMPHILL, RUTH R. b NC. 4: T Marl Hemphill. 5: Scripps Col 37-41 (Fr, Eng Lit) BA; Catholic U 62-64 MSLS. 6: Fr. 7: Asst libn Amer Sch, Tehran Iran 60-61, Libn 67-68; Ref libn Hillcrest Hills br Prince George's Co (Md) Lib 64-67, Readers' serv libn 68-69, Hd readers' serv 69-. 9: ALA; MdLA. 14: Pub lib, readers' serv, ref. 15: 315 Ottawa, Forest Hts Md 20021.

HEMPHILL, W(ILLIAM) EDWIN. b Wake Co NC 28 Je 12. 4: Susan Moffett. 5: Hampden-Sydney Col 28-32 (Hist) BA; Emory 32-33 (Hist) MA; UVa 33-34, 35-37 (Hist) PhD. 7: Act Prof of hist & govt Hampden-Sydney Col 34-35; Act archivist UVa Lib summers 35, 36; Act dir Hist Records Survey in Va summers 36, 37; Act Asst Prof of hist Davidson Col 37-38; Act Asst Prof of hist & act archivist of the Lib UVa 38-39; Instr of hist & Archivist Mary Washington Col 39-40; Act Asst Prof of hist Emory U 40-41; Asst Prof of hist Mary Washington Col 41-44; Asst dir Va World War II Hist Commsn, Charlottesville Va 44-45, Dir 46-50; Dir hist div Va State Lib 50-59; Ed SC Archives Dept, Columbia SC 59-. 8: Ed Adv Bd, Colonial Records Proj, NC Dept of Archives & Hist, 65-. 9: SAA (Fellow); AHA; Amer Assn State & Loc Hist; Org Amer Histns; So Hist Assn; Va Hist Soc; SC Hist Soc; SC Hist Assn. 10: Toastmasters Club; Kiwanis Club. 12: Ed: "Papers of the Albemarle County Historical Society" (46-48), "Gold Star Honor Roll of Virginians in the Second World War" (47), "Extracts from the Journals of the Provincial Congresses of South Carolina, 1775-1776" (60), "The Papers of John C Calhoun, v 2, 1817-1818" (63); Ed & co-auth: "Pursuits of War" (48), "Virginia Cavalcade" (51-59); Co-auth "Cavalier Commonwealth: History and Government of Virginia" (57, rev ed 63). 13: Yes. 14: Univ archives, govt archives, priv & personal mss collections. 15: 846 Camellia st, Columbia SC 29205.

HEMPSTEAD, JOHN ORSON. b La Crosse Wis 27 My 38. 4: Marilyn Zahl. 5: Winona State Col 56-57; UMinn(St Paul) 57-60 (Ag Econ) BS; UMinn(Minneapolis) 60-61 (Ger Educ) BS; UWis(Madison) 63-65 (LS) MA. 6: Ger. 7: USMCR 55-61; Tchr St John's Mil Acad, Delafield Wis 61-65; Libn Giese Elem Sch, Racine Wis 65-67, Hd libn Case High School 67-68; Elem lib consul Racine Unified Sch Dist 68-. 9: NEA; WisEA. 10: PDK. 14: Child bks & serv, sch libs. 15: 1505 Roosevelt ave, Racine Wi 53406.

HENDERSON, ADAMAE PARTIN. b Meridian Miss 8 N 12. 5: Miss State Col for Women 29-31 (Eng); Millsaps Col 31-33 (Eng) BA; Fla State U 64-65 (LS) MS. 6: Fr. 7: Eng tchr pub schs, Meridian Miss 33-37; Play supv Child Aid Soc, NYC 38-39; Tchr USMC Camp Lejeune Sch, Camp Lejeune NC 44-45; Dir Kendalwood Playschool, Meridian Miss 50-51; Act child libn Meridian Pub Lib, Meridian Miss 57-58; Eng tchr pub schs, lauderdale Co Miss 62-64; Deputy dir Meridian-Neshoba Co Pub Lib Serv, Miss 65-68; Child libn Meridian Pub Lib, Meridian Miss 65-68; Sr child libn NY Pub Lib 68-. 9: ALA; NYLA. 10: LWV; Com for the UN; Mental Health Assn. 12: Ed "Guide for Mississippi Voters" (62). 14: Child & yp serv, pub rel, research. 15: 126 E 79 st, New York NY 10021.

HENDERSON, BEATRICE (HAWLEY). b Lacona NY 6 Jl 08. 4: Millard L Henderson. 5: Sy 05: Syracuse City Normal 28-29 (Educ); SUNY (Oswego) 33-34, 43 (Educ) BE; SyracuseU 45-46 BS in LS. 7: Tchr & chm jr high dept Parish High Sch,

Parish NY 37-45; Law libn Court of Appeals Lib, Syracuse NY 54-66; Ref libn Syracuse U Lib 46-47, 48-54, 66-. 10: Syracuse Lib Staff Assn; Alpha Delta; Epsilon Omega; Beta Phi Mu. 14: Law libn, ref libn. 15: 220 Dorchester ave, Syracuse NY 13203.

HENDERSON, CAROL C. b Columbus Ohio 25 O 38. 4: Eric D Henderson. 5: Col of St Mary of the Springs 56-59 (Eng); Ohio State (Columbus) 59-60 (Eng) BA; CatholicU 67-68 MSLS. 6: Fr. 7: Copywriter Blum & Bruce Advertising Agcy, Columbus Ohio 58; Research asst CatholicU Lib Sci Dept 68-69; Ref libn George Mason Col 69-. 9: ALA. 14: Ref. 15: 11456 Orchard lane, Reston Va 22070.

HENDERSON, DIANE (SHIRLEY) (STOTT). b Regina Sask Can 25 Ag 35. 4: L S Henderson. 5: Toronto 60-63 9hist) BA, 63-64 BLS, 65-67 MLS. 7: Lib asst U Toronto Lib 60-63, Catlgr 64-65, Indexer ref dept 65-66, Tchg asst Sch of Lib Sci 66-68, Lect Sch of Lib Sci 68-. 9: CanLA; ALA. 14: Catlg, ref, lib hist, documentation. 15: 17 Foxwarren dr, Willowdale 432, Ont Can.

HENDERSON, FLOYD (LEE). b Muskogee Okla 18 May 32. 4: Susan Smith. 5: Valparaiso U 51-53, 55-57 (Bus Admin) BA; UMinn 59-61 (LS) MA. 6: Sp. 7: Co clerk US Army (Cpl) 53-55; Forestry libn UMinn Libs (St Paul) 59-61; Libn UMinn Libs (Minneapolis) 61-65; Asst libn Cargill Inc, Minneapolis 65-69; Corp libn Control Data Corp 69-. 9: SLA; (pres Minn Chap); MinnLA; ASIS; NMA (chm Non Ser Publ Com). 14: Ref, catlg, admin. 15: 1706 Newton ave N, Minneapolis Mn 55411.

HENDERSON, FRANCES (O'NEAL). b Paris Tex 29 Mr 19. 4: George Robert Henderson. 5: UTex 37-41 (Voc Home Econ) BS; Iowa State Col 42-43 (Child Devel); N Tex State U 44-45 (LS) BS. 7: Fellow in child devel Iowa State Col 42-43; Clerk-typist MRTC Lib, Camp Barkley Tex 43; Clerk-libn Post Lib, Ft Dix NJ 44; Asst catlgr N Tex State Col 44-45; Asst in brs NY Pub Lib 47-48, Catlgr Ref div 48; Catlgr DC Pub Lib 48-50; Decimal clsf LC 50-53; Libn Tex Electric Serv Co, Ft Worth Tex 53-55; Libn Tex Instruments Inc apparatus div, Dallas 55-62; Libn Maple Lawn Sch Dallas Ind Sch Dist 62-. 9: TexLA (chm child RT 66-67); Dallas Sch Libns Club (v-pres & pres elect 68-69). 14: Child libs, organiz of materials, lib admin. 15: 45 Livingston, Dallas Tx 75205.

HENDERSON, GEORGE (ROBERT). b Ft Worth Tex 7 My 18. 4: Frances O'Neal. 5: Tex Wesleyan Col 37-40 (Music) B Mus; N Tex State U 40-41, 46 (Music) M Mus; Pratt 47-48 BLS. 6: Fr, Ger, Sp. 7: Music tchr Pub Schs, Farmersville Tex 41-42; US Army Med Corps (Sgt) 42-45; Music catlgr NY Pub Lib 47-48; 1st asst music div DC Pub Lib 48-49, Chief music div 49-53; Fine arts libn Tex Christian U 53-54; Head fine arts dept Dallas Pub Lib 54-; Instr Mus Dept SoMethU 67-68. 8: Bibliog researcher for proj of Music Ed Assn, Wash DC 50-51; Dir & consul Fine Arts Inst, Dallas 66; Guest lectr HEA Inst for Mus Libns, Denton, Tex 69. 9: MusLA (sec 50-53); IFLA; TexLA (chm Fine Arts Round Table 65-66). 10: Dallas Print & Drawing Soc (pres 66-68). 12: Ed "Supplement to Notes," MusLA (50-53). 13: Yes. 14: Music & fine arts. 15: Dallas Pub Lib, Dallas Tx 75201.

HENDERSON, JAMES WOOD. b Carthage Mo 6 Je 17. 4: Sourya Pisano. 5: UOkla 36-39 (Letters) BA, 39-41 (Eng) MA; Columbia 47-48 (LS) BS; NYU 51-58 (Pub Admin) MPA. 6: Fr, Ger, Ital. 7: Asst libn Bartlesville (Okla) Pub Lib 41-42; Asst to Dean & Instr U Col UOkla 43-44; US Army Signal Corps (Sgt) 44-46; Lib asst NY Pub Lib NYC 47-48, Head searching sect 48-50; Head catlg sect NY State Lib 50-52; NY Pub Lib: Head entry investigation sect 52-53, Chief acquis br 53-59, Asst to the dir 59-63, Chief research libs 63-. 8: Lecturer in Libnship Pratt Inst Lib Sch 55-63; Consul WVa Lib Commsn 58-59; Adv Com on Conversion of Retrospective Bibliog, Data (LC) 68-69. 9: ALA; BSA; Amer Assn Museums; NYLA; NY Lib Club; Ms Soc. 10: Columbia Club; Grolier Club; Columbia Lib Sch Alumni Assn; Phi Beta Kappa. 12: Ed "NY Lib Assn Bulletin" 60-63; Ed "Library Catalogs" (68). 13: Yes. 15: 175 W 12th st, New York NY 10011.

HENDERSON, JESTINA T(UTT). b Birmingham Ala 6 Jl 14. 4: Dr Romeo C Henderson. 5: Shaw U 31-33 (Biol) BS; Catholic U 51-52 MSLS. 6: Ger. 7: Tchr pub schs of NC 33-45; Tchr & asst libn Swift Mem Jr Col 47-49; Tchr Douglass High Sch, Upper Marlboro Md 49-50; Catlgr State Tchrs Col (Elizabeth City NC) 50-52; Ref libn SCar State Col 52-56, Head Libn 56-60; Assoc libn Del State Col 60-64, Head Libn 64-67; Dist libn Marshallton Sch Dist, Wilmington Del 67-. 9: ALA; DelLA (sec 65); NEA; Del State EA. 13: Yes. 14: Ref. 15: Del State Col, Dover De 19901.

HENDERSON, JOHN DALE. b Oakland Cal 21 Mr 03. 4: Ethel McGough. 5: UCal(Berkeley) 21-25 (Eng) AB, 28-30 Certif of Libnship. 6: Ger, Fr. 7: Ref libn Kern Co Free Lib, Bakersfield Cal 30-33, Co Libn 33-37; Field rep Cal State Lib 37-43; Lecturer UCal Sch of Libnship (Berkeley) 38-43; Asst Co libn Los Angeles Co Pub Lib 44-46, Co Libn 47-63; Visiting Prof: UCLA Sch Libnship summer 62, USoCal Lib Sci summers 63, 65, 66, UIll Grad Sch Lib Sci spring-summer 64; Lecturer UCal (Berkeley) Sch of Libnship 66-68. 8: Lib bldg consul: Fresno Co Free Lib Fresno Cal 58, Santa Monica (Cal) Pub Lib 62, Hanford City & Kings Co Lib 65; CONSUL: Siskiyou Co Cal 58, Santa Monica (Cal) Pub Lib 62, Hanford City & Kings Co Lib 65; Siskiyou Co (Cal) Free Lib 65, Santa Cruz (Cal) Lib 63-67, Astoria (Ore) Pub Lib 65, Salem Ore Pub Lib 69; Lib consul serv & org Alameda Co Free Lib, Oakland Cal 63-67; Guest coordinator Pub Lib Bldgs Inst Coos Bay Ore 65; Consul: Minneapolis Pub Lib & Hennepin Co Lib Minn 66, Mechanics Inst Lib San Francisco 67-68, Solano Co Cal Free Lib 68 & 69. 9: ALA(chm Intel Freedom Com 55; chm Lippincott Award Com 60; chm Nom Com 51; pres Ext Div 52; Coun 52-56); Pub Lib Execs Assn So Cal (pres 45); CalLA (pres 40-41, pres So Dist 48, var chmships). 10: Los Angeles Town Hall; Zamorano Club; Speakers' Club; Death Valley 49ers; Hist Landmarks Com, Los Angeles Co (chm 58-63). 12: "Alameda County Library: a Report with Recommendations" (64). 13: Yes. 14: Admin, bldg planning, bk sel, co & reg lib serv. 15: 27 Westminster ave, Berkeley Ca 94708.

HENDERSON, KATHRYN (LUTHER). b Champaign Ill 12 Jl 23. 4: William T Henderson. 5: UIll 40-44 (Hist) AB, 46-48 BS in LS, 48-51 MS in LS. 6: Ger, Fr, Gk. 7: Clerical asst catlg dept UIll Lib (Urbana) 44-47; Asst Lib Sch UIll 47-50; Ser catlgr UIll Lib 50-53; Circ libn McCormick Theol Sem (Chicago) 53-56, head catlgr 56-65; Instr Grad Sch of Lib Sci UIll Lib Sch 65-67, Asst Prof 67-. 8: Visiting instr, Grad Sch of Lib Sci, UIll 64-65. 9: ALA (Cat Code Rev Com 62-65);-RTSD (chm Elections Com 60-62; Subject Headings Com 66-67; mem var coms); ATheolLA (chm Catlg & Clsf Com 59-62, consul to Catlg Code Rev Com 62-65; mem Sub-com on Rel Headings); AALS; IllLA (chm Catlg & Clsf Com 56-57); Chicago Reg Group Libns in Tech Serv. 10: AAUP; Kappa Delta Pi; Beta Phi Mu. 12: "Trends in American Publishing" (68). 13: Yes. 14: Catlg, lib educ. 15: 1107 E Silver st, Urbana Il 61801.

HENDERSON, LOIS (ENGLAND). b Florence Ala 17 D 15. 4: Ellis W Henderson. 5: Florence State Col 39-47 (Elem Educ) BS; Peabody 49-51 (Secondary Educ) MA; Florence State Col 55-57 (LS); LSU 59-64 MA in LS. 07: Tchr of Eng & Soc Studies Lauderdale Co Bd of Educ, Florence Ala 42-57; Elem sch libn Dade Co Bd of Educ, Miami Fla 58-62; Supv of Libs Florence City Bd of Educ, Florence Ala 63-. 8: Tchr, Alabama A & M Col Lib Div, Normal Ala (part time) 68-69. 9: NEA (Life mem); ALA; AASchL; SELA; AlaLA; AlaEA; Florence TA. 10: AAUW; Bus & Prof Women's Club; Federated Garden Club; Delta Kappa Gamma. 14: Child libn. 15: Florence City Bd of Educ, Florence Al 35630.

HENDERSON, MARIAN (KERR). b El Dorado Ark 27 F 38. 5: Randolph-Macon Woman's Col 56-58; UArk 58-60 (Eng) BA; UCLA 65-66 MLS. 6: Sp, Fr. 7: Ref libn El Camino Col Lib 66-. 9: CalLA. 10: El Camino Col Faculty Assn. 14: Ref. 15: 1900 Rockefeller lane, Redondo Beach Ca 90278.

HENDERSON, MARY L. b Caledonia Ill 27 My 1900. 5: Rockford Col 18-22 (Eng) BA; UWis 24-25 (LS) Certif. 7: Asst libn Free Pub Lib, Burlington Iowa 25-27; Catlgr Rockford Pub Lib, Rockford Ill 27-44, Asst libn 44-66; Libn Westminster Presb Church, Rockford Ill 68-. 8: Personnel off 44-66. 9: ALA; IllLA; Church & Synagogue LA. 10: Winnebago Co Hist Soc. 13: Yes. 14: Bk sel, ref, catlg, personnel. 15: 4156 Eastridge dr, Rockford Il 61107.

HENDERSON, MARY LIMA. b Syracuse NY. 5: Syracuse 42 BLS. 7: Asst libn Rochester Pub Lib, Rochester NY 42-45; Asst libn Educ Lib Syracuse U 45-48; Br libn Maxwell Sch of Citizenship Syracuse U 48-66, Libn soc scis Carnegie Lib 67-. 9: ALA. 10: AAUW. 14: Ref. 15: 203 Wellesley rd, Syracuse NY 13207.

HENDERSON, PATRICIA ANN WILLIS. b Dallas 8 Je 42. 4: Joe Charles Henderson. 5: Tex Woman's U 60-64 (LS) BA. 6: Sp, Fr. 7: Lab asst Tex Child Hosp, Dallas 57-58; Lab tech Bio-Assay Lab, Dallas 58-63; Asst libn VA Hosp Lib, McKinney Tex 64; Asst libn Collins Radio Corp Lib of Engnr, Dallas 64; Asst libn Ft Worth Pub Lib, Ft Worth Tex 64-65; Hd of acquis Wyoming State Lib, Cheyenne Wyo 65-67. 9: TexLA. 10: Officer's Wives Club; Family Serv. 14: Sci & tech, state & Govt docs, acquis, ref. 15: 722 N Oak Cliff blvd, Dallas Tx 75208.

HENDERSON, RALPH LEONARD. b Wash DC 6 Jl 11. 4: Eileen Simmons. 5: George Washington U 37 (Hist) AB; Catholic U summer 64 (Lib Mgt). 7: LC: Messenger (page) 28, Deck attendant & searcher 29-38, Head Record Sect Loan Div 39-61, Asst chief Loan Div 62-. 9: SLA(DC Chap chm Soc Sci Group 61, treas 62-64); DCLA. 10: Pres Bd Dir LC Fed Credit Union 62-69. 15: 4440 Wells Parkway, Hyattsville Md 20782.

HENDERSON, ROSEMARY (NEALE). b Coffeyville Kan 15 Jl 36. 5: Stephens 54-56 (Humanities) AA; UKan 56-57 (Educ); Tex Wesleyan Col 57-59 (Soc Sci) BS; Texas Christian U 62-63 (Educ); Kan State Tchrs Col 66-67 MLib. 6: Ger. 7: Asst Prof lib sci U N Dak 67-68; Dir lib serv Coffeyville Commun Jr Col 68-. 9: ALA; NEA; NFA; KanLA; KanStateTA; KanSchLA. 10: AAUP. 14: Admin, commun Jr Cols, tech processing, non-bk materials. 15: 1311 W 5th, Coffeyville Ks 67337.

HENDERSON, SHANNON J. b Wayton Ark 27 D 29. 4: Ruby J Henderson. 5: Ark Polytech Col 49-52 (Educ); UArk 54 (Educ) BSE, 61 (Educ) MEd; Peabody 65 MLS. 7: Prin libn Deer High Sch, Deer Ark 50-61; Asst libn Ark Polytech Col 61-66, Assoc libn 66-. 9: ALA; ArkLA; SWLA; ArkEA. 10: Kappa Delta Pi. 14: Ref, circ. 15: 237 East L st, Russellville Ar 72801.

HENDERSON, WILLIAM T. b Ridge Farm Ill 5 O 29. 4: Kathryn Luther. 5: UIll 47-51 (Floriculture) BS; McCormick Theol Sem 53-57 (Theol) BD; Chicago 57-60 MA in LS. 6: Ger. 7: US Army Qtrmstr Corps (1st Lt), US & Korea 51-53; Stud asst McCormick Theol Sem Lib (Chicago) 53-57, Acquis asst 57-65; Asst bind libn UIll Lib (Urbana) 65, Act bind libn 65-, Bind libn 66-. 8: Minister, United Presbyt Church in the USA. 9: ALA-RTSD (chm Elect Com 63-64); ATheolLA (chm Aud Com 60); IllLA (chm Aud Com 64-6 5, chm Resources & Tech Serv Sect 65); Chicago Reg Group Libns in Tech Serv (chm 64). 10: Beta Phi Mu . 14: Acquis, preservation. 15: 1107 E Silver st, Urbana Il 61801.

HENDERSON, WILLIAM THOMAS. b Mobile Ala 12 D 16. 4: Laura Mae Winston. 5: Livingstone Col 37-41 (Rel Bio) AB; Hartford Sem Found 41 (Rel Educ) MA; SUNY(Geneseo) (Lib Educ) MS; Syracuse (Chattauqua) summer 60. 7: Minister Zion Methodist Church, Providence 41-42, New Britain Conn 43-45, Ansonia Conn, Jamestown NY, Washington DC, Pittsburgh 45-59; Circ dept Jamestown (NY) Lib 51-56, Head ref dept 56-60; Readers adv N Country Lib System, Watertown NY 60-61; Asst libn NY State Lib 61-63; Instit lib consul Mich State Lib 63-68, Head Instit Unit 68-. 9: ALA; NYLA; MichLA. 10: NAACP; Ministerial Assn; Assn of Crippled Child & Adults; Exec Bd Westside Activity Ctr (Lansing Mich). 12: Co-auth "Narcotic Addicts Take up Reading" (63); "Bookmobile Service to Correctional Institutions," AHIL (69); "Bookmobile Service to State Institutions," PLA (68). 14: Ref, bk sel, consul. 15: 735 E Michigan ave, Lansing Mi 48913.

HENDRICKS, DONALD (DUANE). b Flint Mich 3 N 31. 4: Mary Elrich. 5: Flint Jr Col 51-53; UMich 53-54 9pol Sci) AB; UMich 54-55 AMLS; UIll 63-66 (LS) PhD. 6: Fr, Ger. 7: Young adult libn Detroit Pub Lib 55-57; Head Libn Owosso (Mich) Pub Lib 57-60; U Libn Millikin U 60-63; Research assoc Doctoral Candidate Lib Research Center Grad Lib Sch UIll 63-66; Dir of Libs, Sam Houston State Col 66-. 8: Grant from the Coord Bd, state of Tex, for study of Resources of Tex Libs 67-68; Grant from the US Off of Educ for study of Comparative Costs of centralized vs. Indiv Lib Proc 65-66. 9: ALA (chm Centralized Proc Com 68-69); BSA; Bibliog Soc (London); TexLA; Bibliog Soc Va. 10: Kiwanis Club; C of C. 12: "Comparative Costs of Book Processing in a Processing Center and in Five Individual Libraries" (66); "Resources of Texas Libraries" (68). 13: Yes. 14: Admin, tech serv, resources, rare bks, univ libnship. 15: 2117 Roundabout rd, Huntsville Tx 77340.

HENDRICKS, MARY E. b Dayton Ohio 1 S 08. 5: Denison U 26-30 (Math) BA; Columbia 38 (LS) BS. 7: Lib asst Dayton Pub Lib, Dayton Ohio 30-38; Br asst Westwood br 39-48; Br libn E C Doren br 48-66; Br libn Trotwood br 66-. 9: ALA; OhioLA. 15: 5818 Seven Gables ave, Dayton Oh 45426.

HENDRICKS, EPSY JANE (YEARBY). b Olla La 15 N 33. 4: John Ira Hendricks Jr. 5: So U 52-56 (Soc Studies) BA; UColo summer 57; UWis 59-60 MS in LS; UIll 65-66 Certif in Libnship. 6: Fr. 7: Libn Utica Jr Col 56-59; Libn Alcorn A & M Col 60-. 8: Mem eval teams for the accred of second schs in Miss, So Assn of Schs & Cols. 9: ALA; SELA; MissLA. 10: Alpha Kappa Alpha; Parni Nous. 14: Admin, ref. 15: Alcorn A & M Col PO Box 677, Lorman Ms 39096.

HENDRICKSON, KENT HERMAN. b Radcliffe Iowa 4 Mr 39. 4: Rosemary Bergeson. 5: Ellsworth Jr Col 57-59 AA; Ariz State U 59-60 (Hist); Iowa State U 60-61 (Hist) BS, 61-63 (Hist); UMich 63-64 MALS. 6: Fr. 7: Asst libn soc studies div Love Lib UNeb 64-66, Sr Asst tech serv div UNeb Libs 66-68, Asst dir for tech serv 68-. 9: ALA-ACRL; NebLA; ASIS. 10: AAUP. 13: Yes. 14: Bibliog, bk sel, acquis, systems analysis, admin. 15: 1610 Atlas, Lincoln Nb 68521.

HENDRICKSON, RUTH M (MARIA). b Bridgeport Conn 6 S 14. 5: Oberlin 33-37 (Lat) BA; Columbia summer 40 (LS); UTex 59-60 MLS. 6: Fr, Ger. 7: Lib asst tech dept Bridgeport Pub Lib, Bridgeport Conn 38-40; Libn Conn Agric Expt Sta, New Haven Conn 40-57; Asst libn Los Alamos Sci Lab Lib, Los Alamos NM 57-59; Reg Libn NM State Lib, Aztec NM 60-62; Field consul NM State Lib 62-63, Coordinator LSCA Proj & ext serv 63-67; Ext libn Arizona Dept Lib & Archives 68-. 9: ALA (Friends of Libs Com, Pub Rel Com);-LAD;-LED (Subcom to study Undergrad Lib Courses); SWLA; ArizLA. 10: Altrusa Club; AAUW; Southwestern Assn Indian affairs; Archaeol Soc of NM; Heard Museum, Phoenix. 13: Yes. 14: Admin. spec libs, state libs. 15: 4560 N 15th ave, Phoenix Az 85015.

HENDRIX, (THOMAS) CAL. b Johnson City Tenn 28 Jl 25. 4: Violet Hendricks. 5: E Tenn State U 46-50 (Eng) BS; Emory 53-54 (LS) ML. 7: Bkmob libn Ft Loudoun Reg Lib, Lenoir City Tenn 50-51; Asst dir 52-53; (Cpl) US Army, Augusta Ga 51-52; Ext libn Brunswick Reg Lib, Brunswick Ga 54-56; Dir Sequoyah Reg Lib, Canton Ga 56-62; Dir Kingsport Pub Lib, Kingsport Tenn 62-. 9: ALA; GaLA (sec 54-56); TennLA (chm Pub Lib Sect 67). 10: Sertoma Club. 14: Admin. 15: Kingsport Pub Lib, Broad & New sts, Kingsport Tn 37660.

HENDRON, GINNY (STIRLING). b Salem Ohio 14 O 41. 4: Jerome H Hendron. 5: Heidelberg col 59-62 (Chem) BS; Case-West Res 65-66 MSLS. 6: Russian. 7: Research chem Sherwin-Williams Co, Cleveland Ohio 62-65; Tech libn Union Carbide Corp, Niagara Falls NY 66-. 9: SLA (Memb Chm Upstate NY Chap); West NY Lib Resources Coun. 11: Amer Assn of Chemists Award 62. 14: Mgt of tech libs, info ret. 15: 176 So Union rd H-4, Williamsville NY 14221.

HENDRY, BARBARA L(OUISE). b W Palm Beach Fla 4 S 30. 5: Fla State U 51 (Eng) AB, 58 (LS) MA. 7: Eng tchr Pahokee High Sch, Pahokee Fla 51-52; Lib asst Fla Geol Survey, Tallahassee Fla 53; Catlgr, Instr (Monographic Serials) UGa 53-56; Ser catlgr, Instr, Admin asst Fla State U 57-59; Catlgr to ser libn Los Alamos Sci Lab, Los Alamos NM 59-68; Indexer Air U Lib Maxwell AFB , ALA. 9: SLA. 10: Adv wk with YMCA; Sigma Tau Delta. 12: "Selected Bibliography of Publications of LASL Research, 1957-1962," with Marjorie Johnson (63, supp 65); Comp "Selected Contributions to High Pressure Research from the Los Alamos Scientific Laboratory" (64); "Published Works of Stanislaw M Ulam" (68). 14: Ser, machine records, computers in libs, bibliog, indexing. 15: 414 Villa Court, Montgomery Al 36014.

HENEBRY, AGNES C. b Macon Co Ill. 5: Millikin U 36-(Psych); UMich (Ann Arbor) 62 (Lib); Ext courses at: UIll (LS), UWis (LS), Columbia (recs control). 7: Libn "Decatur Daily Review", Decatur Ill 29-31; Asst libn "Decatur Herald & Review" 31-45, Libn 45-. 8: Instr Communications Wkshop, Syracuse U 60-63; Mem Adv Com UIll Grad Sch of Lib Sci 62-64. 9: SLA (Non-ser Publ Com 55-59); Newspaper Div: chm 48-49, Bd mem 51-53, Bull ed 51, Archivist 54-63, v-pres 47). 10: Zonta; St James Credit Union Bd; Cath Daughters Amer. 11: Nat Off Mgrs Assn key award 63. 13: Yes. 14: Loc hist. 15: Herald and Review 365 N Main PO Box 311, Decatur Il 62525.

HENEGHAN, MARY A (ANN). b Somerville Mass 12 D 26. 5: Boston Col 45-48; Simmons 49-52 (LS)·BS; CatholicU 52-55 MS in LS. 7: Asst Somerville Pub Lib, Somerville Mass 44-50; Inst asst Simmons Col Sch Lib Sci 50-52; Libn GeorgetownU Sch Nursing 52-54; Providence Pub Lib: Asst ref dept 54-63, Hd ref dept 63, Hd ref-period dept 64-67; Consul Arthur D Little Inc, Cambridge Mass 67-. 8: Survey of Providence Interrelated Lib Syst 67; Participant in Amer Mgt Assn Course, "Fundamentals of Co Lib Mgt" 68 & 69; Visiting lectr SyracuseU Sch Lib Sci summers 66, 67. 9: ALA; CathLA; SLA; RILA; NYLA. 10: Simmons Col Alum Assn; Women's Educ & Ind Union. 14: Ref, admin, netwks. 15: 1558 Massachusetts ave apt 21, Cambridge Ma 02138.

HENES, ELIZABETH MARY. b Liverpool NY 18 Ja 20. 5: Syracuse 38-42 (Eng Educ) MA, 42-43 (Eng Educ) MS in Ed, 51 MS in LS. 6: Fr. 7: Eng tchr-libn Truxton Central Sch, Truxton NY 43-46; Syracuse U Lib: Asst order libn 47-57, Asst ser libn 58-63, Act ser libn 64-65, Back sets libn acquis unit 65-66, Periods libn 66-67, Ref libn & Hd of micromedia div 67-. 9: ALA; NYLA. 10: Syracuse Univ Lib Staff Assn; Phi Beta Kappa; Syracuse Gem & Mineral Club; Nat Audubon Soc; Nat Wildlife Fed; Beta Phi Mu; Phi Kappa Phi; Pi Lambda Theta; Tabard (Eng hon); Profess Libns Assn of Syracuse U; Liverpool Citizens Com for a New Lib 68-69. 14: Acquis of ser & period, back sets, microforms, ref. 15: 208 Tamarack st, Liverpool NY 13088.

HENINGER, IRENE CALLEN (SUGG). b Jerome Ida 20 F 23. 5: Whitman Col 41-44 (Eng); Barnard 44-46 (Eng) AB; Columbia 54-55 MLS. 7: Asst child libn NY Pub Lib 55-57; Libn & asst libn & child libn Twin Falls Pub Lib, Twin Falls Ida 65-68; Act asst prof Sch of Libnship UWash (Seattle) 68-. 8: Mem Adv Coun State of Idaho, Lib Serv & Construction Act, Title III Lib Coop. 9: ALA; -CSD; PNLA; IdahoLA (sec 65-66); WashLA. 14: Child libnship, tchg libnship. 15: 6830-48th NE, Seattle Wa 98115.

HENINGTON, DAVID MEAD. b El Dorado Ark 16 Ag 29. 4: Barbara Gibson. 5: UHouston 47-51 (Hist) BA; Columbia 55-56 MSLS. 7: Personnel spec USAF (S/Sgt) 51-55; Libn Brooklyn Pub Lib 56-58; Head lit & hist dept Dallas Pub Lib 58; Dir Waco Pub Lib, Waco Tex 58-62; Asst dir Dallas Pub Lib 62-67; Dir Houston Pub Lib, Houston Tex 67-. 8: Consul: Richardson Tex Pub Lib 64, Garland Tex Pub Lib 65, Fredericksburg Tex Pub Lib (66), Liberty Tex Pub Lib (68). 9: ALA (chm LAD-PRS Publ Com 67); TexLA (v-pres 61-62, chm Constit Com 63-65, chm Lib Develop Com 65-66, pres 67-68); SWLA. 10: Rotary. 13: Yes. 14: Admin. 15: Dallas Pub Lib, Dallas Tx 75201.

HENKE, DAN. b San Antonio Tex 18 F 24. 4: Shirley Lynn. 5: Georgetown U Sch of For Serv 40-43 (For Rel) BS; Georgetown U Sch of Law 47-51 JD; UWash 55-56 (Law Libnship) MLL. 6: Sp, Ger. 7: US Army Communications Sgt 85th Mountain Infantry, US & Italy 43-46; Info spec US War Assets Admin, San Antonio Tex 46-47; Asst pub distribution US Dept of State Off of Pub Affairs 47-48; Econ info spec US Dept of Commerce Off of Bus Econ 48-51; Attorney at law, San Antonio Tex 51-55; Asst to law libn Sch of Law UWash 55-56; Head bureau of law & legis ref NJ State Lib 56-59; Prof of Law & Law Libn UCal(Berkeley) 59-. 8: Consul: State Bar of Cal 63, San Joaquin Co (Cal) 63, Amer Bar Found 65, Bancroft, Avery & McAlister, San Francisco 68-; Dir summer Inst in Law Libnship, UCal (Berkeley) US DHEW OE 68-69; Prof Sch of Libnship UCal(Berkeley) 65-. 9: AALL (chm 2 coms 64-65); ALA; SLA; ASIS; CalLA. 10: Amer Bar Assn; DC Bar; State Bar of Tex; State Bar of Cal; US Supreme Court Bar; Beta Phi Mu; Order of the Coif. 12: Legal Research Guide for Cal & Fed Law 63; Contr 6th ed How to Find the Law; Chm Com on the Law Lib Journal; Mem Com on Index to Legal Periodicals. 13: Yes. 14: Law lib admin, legal res & bibliog tchg. 15: 230 Sch of Law UCal, Berkeley Ca 94720.

HENKE, ESTHER MAE. b Orlando Okla 4 Ap 25. 5: St Johns Jr Col 43-44; UOkla 44-47 BSLS, 52-53 (Hist) MA. 07: Bkmob libn Ray Co Lib, Richmond Mo 47-48, Co Libn 48-51; Field libn Okla State Lib 53-56, Ext libn 56-68; Okla Dept of Libs, assoc dir 68-. 7: Bkmob libn Ray Co Lib, Richmond Mo 47-48, Co Libn 48-51; Field libn Okla State Lib 53-56, Ext libn 56-68; Okla Dept of Libs, assoc dir 68-. 9: ALA-LED (sec); -ALTA (Coun, v-pres); AEAUSA; OklaLA (sec Fed Rel Coord); SWLA. 10: Soroptimist Club. 11: Theta Sigma Phi Award 66. 12: Ed "Lib Ext Div Newsletter"; Pub Lib Serv Newsletter. 13: Yes. 14: Ext, lib devel. Okla 73105. 15: 4316 Woodland dr, Oklahoma City Ok 73105.

HENKLE, HERMAN H(ENRY). b Colo Springs Colo 26 Mr 1900. 4: Ann Walker Davis. 5: Whittier Col 24-28 (Zool Chem) AB; UCal(Berkeley) 29-31 Lib Sci Certif; 31-33 (LS) MA; Chicago 35-36 (LS) Research Fellow. 7: Jr libn UCal Biol Lib (Berkeley) 30-35; Associate UIll Lib Sch 36-37; Prof of Lib Sci & Dir Sch of Lib Sci Simmons Col 37-42; Dir Processing Dept LC 42-47; Libn The John Crerar Lib, Chicago 47-65; Lecturer UChicago Grad Lib Sch 50-; Exec Dir The John Crerar Lib 63-69; Dir planning J J Hill Ref Lib, St Paul 69-. 8: Consul: Pub Admin Serv survey of Brookline Mass 40, survey of Ind U libs 40, Detroit Pub Lib & Ford Motor Co lib survey 46, lib planning UWis Med Sch 63, Deere & Co 63, Elmhurst Col 64; Mem Spec Com on Tech Info, Research & Development Bd Nat Mil Establishment 48-50; Unesco Seminar on Sci Documentation for S E Asia, New Delhi 61; Treas Joint Com on Union List of Serials 58-68; Consul Nat Sci Libs, Pakistan, UNESCO 66. 09: AALS (pres 41-42); SLA (Exec Bd 41-47, pres 45-46); ALA (Bd Educ Libnship 42-44); ASIS(pres 57-58). 10: Dir Center for Research Libs (48-69) (chm 61-63); Caxton Club (Chicago); Amer Soc Metals; AAAS (Fellow). 11: Hon D Litt, Whittier Col 61. 12: Assoc ed "American Documentation" & "Library Quarterly. 13: Yes. 14: Admin, lib arch, sci info serv, rare bks. 15: 325 Third st North, Naples Fl 33940.

HENLEY, ATHA LOUISE. b Marshall Mo 17 My 27. 5: Mo Valley Col 45-49 (Hist) AB; UCal(Berkeley) 55-56 MLS. 6: Sp, Ger. 7: Clerical asst, ref St Louis Pub Lib 49-50; Asst libn St Louis Col of Pharmacy 50-51, Libn 51-53; Asst libn N Kan City (Mo) Pub Lib 53-54; Pharmacy-bacteriol libn Ohio State U 55-60; Sci libn UFla Libs 60-66; Libn div plant ind Fla State Dept Agric 66-. 8: Instr in lib sci UFla, 63-65. 9: ALA; FlaLA; SLA. 10: AAUW; Alpha XI Delta. 15: Div of Plant Industry Florida State Dept of Agriculture, Box 1269, Gainesville Fl 32601.

HENN, BARBARA J. b Beech Grove Ind 2 Ag 36. 5: Concordia Tchrs Col 54-58 (Educ) BS; IndU 66-67 MLS. 6: Sp, Fr. 7: Sec-teller Ind Nat Bank, Indianapolis 58-60; Sr acct clk Inland Container Corp, Indianapolis 60-62; Audit clk Economy Finance Corp, Indianapolis 62-66; Ref lib Purdue U (Lafayette) 67-68; Acquis lib Ind U (Bloomington Off) Reg Campuses 68-. 9: ALA. 10: Beta Phi Mu. 14: Acquis. 15: 2635 E 2nd st apt 9, Bloomington In 47401.

HENN, SHIRLEY EMILY. b Cleveland Ohio 26 My 19. 5: Hollins Col 37-41 (Phil' AB; UNC 64-65 MS in LS. 6: Fr. 7: Asst in lib Collinwood High Sch, Cleveland Ohio 41-43; Circ libn Hollins Col 43-44; Advertising mgr R M Kellogg Co, Three Rivers Mich 46-47; Fund dir & exec sec Alumnae Assoc, Hollins Col 47-55; Real estate saleswoman Fowlkes & Kefauver, Roanoke Va 55-61; Asst in lib Hollins Col 61-65, Ref libn 65-. 8: Dir Women's Activities, Amer Alum Coun 52-54; Moderator Ref Session, Col & Univ Conf VaLA 69. 9: ALA; VaLA. 10: Quota Club Internat; Amer Alum Coun; Roanoke Valley Soc Prev of Cruelty to Animals; Hollins Col Triangle Club. 12: Ed "Hollins Alumnae Magazine," 47-55; Auth child bk "Adventures of Hooty Owl and His Friends" (55). 14: Ref, rare bks, exhibits. 15: 6915 Tinkerdale rd, Hollins Va 24019.

HENNESSEY, REGINALD (GEORGE). b Nottingham Eng 15 F 22. 4: Helen Lamberta. 5: UBC 47-51 (Eng, Psych) BA; McGill 51-52 BLS. 6: Fr. 7: Acquis libn UBC 52-55; Rare bk libn UKan Lib 55-57; Assoc order libn UMich Lib (Ann Arbor) 58-60; Head acquis dept USoCal Lib 60-64; Lib consul acquis 65-. 8: Lib adv AID Grad Sch of Bus Admin Lib UKarachi (Karachi Pakistan) 61. 9: ALA; CalLA. 10: BSA; Bibliog Soc UVa. 12: "Southern California Booksellers: a Directory" (64); "L'Analyse of Francoise Andre Danican Philidor; an Analytic Bibliography" (65). 13: Yes. 14: Acquis, rare bks. 15: 8325 Campion dr, Los Angeles Ca 90045.

HENNESSY, MILDRED LORINE. b NYC 15 Ag 11. 5: Brooklyn Col 29-33 (Econ) BA; Columbia 33-34 BLS. 7: Queens Borough Pub Lib: Sub libn 34-35, Child libn 35-45, Br libn 45-51, Ed 51-56, Dir pub rel 56-64, deputy dir 64-. 9: ALA (chm Dana Awards Com, chm Nomin Com Pub Rel Sect); NYLA (Memb Chm, Conf Publ Chm); LPRC (pres); NY Lib Club (Coun); St John's Congress of Libns (Adv Com). 12: Ed, ALA Lib Periods Round Table "Newsletter." 13: Yes. 15: Queens Borough Pub Lib, Jamaica NY 11432.

HENNIG, WINIFRED (ST JOHN). b Hamilton NY 10 S 1895. 4: Herman Carl Hennig. 5: Simmons 20 (LS) BS. 7: Ref asst & Instr in lib methods Kan State Agric Col 20-23; Br asst in ref & circ Detroit Pub lib 23-26; Libn of Ed Lib Ginn & Co, Boston Mass 26-31; Various sub positions 31-43; Libn Raytheon Mfg Co, Waltham Mass 43-45; Asst order libn Wellesley Col 45-46, Catlgr 46-61; Catlgr & asst libn Wheelock Col 61-. 9: ALA; NE Tech Serv Libns. 10: Alumnae Assn Simmons Col Sch Lib Sci; Wellesley-Needham Simmons Club; Natl Retired Tchrs Assn. 14: Catlg, ref. 15: 1839 Washington st, Auburndale Ma 02166.

HENNIGAN, MILLICENT (MERRITT). b Baton Rouge La 10 Je 18. 04: Wilson P Hennigan. 5: LSU 35-39 (Eng, Hist) BA, 39-41 BS in LS. 7: Libn Istrouma High Sch, Baton Rouge La 41-46; Asst East Baton Rouge Parish Lib, Baton Rouge La summer 42, summer 43; Ser catlgr LSU 46-. 9: ALA; LaLA; Baton Rouge Lib Club; SWLA (sec 67-68). 10: Baton Rouge Foun for HistLA Inc; Kappa Delta. 14: Catlg (ser). 15: Box 18157 Univ sta, Baton Rouge La 70803.

HENNING, JANE (CONROW). b Connersville Ind 30 N 44. 4: Richard L Henning. 5: IndU 62-66 (Anthrop) BA, 66-68

MLS. 6: Fr. 7: Ref libn Monroe Co Lib Bloomington Ind 65-66, Hd circ 66-67, Br libn 68; Arch libn Ariz StateU 68-. 9: ArizStateLA. 10: Soc of Arch Histns; AAUW. 14: Pub serv, slide libnship. 15: Apt 2 1915 E Osborn rd, Phoenix Az 85016.

HENNING, MARY ELIZABETH (HAUSE). b Louisville Ky 28 Mr 09. 4: Eugene Somers Henning. 5: ULouisville 30 (Eng Lit) AB; UIll 32 BS in LS; Va State Certif Libn 55. 7: Catlgr U Louisville Lib 32-36; Asst catlgr UFla 36-37; Catlg asst US Nat Archives Lib, Wash DC 37-39; Lib asst Fairfax Co Pub Lib, Fairfax Va 54-57; Libn Huntsville High sch Lib, Huntsville Ala 62-64; Libn Huntsville Jr High Sch, Huntsville Ala 66-. 9: ALA; NEA; AlaEA; AlaASchL. 10: Woodcock Soc ULouisville; AAUW; Wanderbird Hiking Club, Wash DC. 14: Catlg, circ, ref (high sch libs). 15: 604 Randolph ave SE, Huntsville Ala 35801.

HENNINGS, LeROY JR. b Mt Kisco NY 17 Ag 36. 5: UMiami 55-60 (Hist) AB; Fla StateU 63-64, 68 (LS) MS. 7: Sch libn & tchr Glades Co Sch System, Moore Haven Fla 61-62; Departmental libn Engring & Phys Lib UMiami 62-63; Libn acquis & ref depts Miami Dade jr Col 64-65; Libn bus sci & tech dept Miami Pub Lib, Fla 66-67; Ref libn interlib loan Fla StateU 68; Dir Martin Co Pub Lib, Stuart Fla 68-. 9: ALA; FlaLA. 14: Admin, ref. 15: 6 Gardner lane, Jensen Beach Fl 33457.

HENRICH, MARGARET MARY. b Phila 19 D 08. 5: Trinity Col (Wash DC) 26-30 (Fr, Lat) AB; Drexel 30-31 BS in LS. 6: Fr. 7: Asst libn Fels Inst of Local & State Govt UPenn 38-41; Asst libn Villanova U 42-55; Libn Fels Inst of Local & State Govt UPenn 55-58; Asst libn St Leo Col 58-65; Asst libn Biscayne Col 65-. 9: ALA; CathLA (Exec Bd 61-67); FlaLA. 13: Yes. 14: Catlg. 15: Biscayne Col Lib, 16400 NW 32nd ave, Miami Fla 33054.

HENRIKSEN, FINN. b Copenhagen Denmark 2 S 15. 4: Alice H C Gramann. 5: UCopenhagen 41-43 (Philos) Filosofikum, 43-50 (Law) Cand Juris; UWash 58-60 MLS; St LouisU 61-65 (Law) Juris Doctor. 6: Scandinavian langs, Ger. 7: Asst law libn & asst prof of law St LouisU Sch of Law 61-65; Acquis libn & ref libn Harvard Law Sch Lib 65-67; Law libn UKan Law Lib 67-. 9: AALL; Intl Assn Law Libns. 10: AAUP. 13: Yes. 14: Admin, law libnship. 15: Univ of Kan Law Lib Green Hall, Lawrence Ks 66044.

HENRY, BARBARA (DEARBORN). b Bangor Me 28 S 34. 4: Otto W Henry. 5: Boston U 52-56 (Music Educ) Mus b, 56-58, 62 (Music Hist) MM; UPittsburgh 63-64 MLS. 6: Ger, Fr. 7: Lib asst New Eng Conservatory of Music Lib, Boston 58-61; Ref libn Citizens Lib, Washington Penn 63-65; Head catlgr Loyola U Lib (New Orleans) 65-66; First asst art & mus div New Orleans Pub Lib 66-68, Hd info ref div 68; Catlgr & ref libn E Carolina U Lib 68-. 9: ALA; MusLA; Internat Assn of Mus Libs (US Br); Amer Musicological Soc. 10: Beta Phi Mu; Mu Phi Epsilon. 13: Yes. 14: Catlg, music libnship. 15: 407 S Student st, Greenville NC 27834.

HENRY, BETTY (McSHANE). b San Antonio Tex 3 Je 26. 5: Incarnate Word Col 43-44 (Eng, Span); UAla 44-45. (Eng, Span); Fla State Col for Women (LS) summer 46; Catholic U (LS) summer 63; IBM Research Inst summer 65. 6: Sp. 7: Circ-ref asst UAla Col Med 45; Head Med Libn Robert B Green Hosp, San Antonio Tex 54-55; Br med libn Emory U 55; Bkkeeper USAF Off Club, Stewart AF Base 56; Circ-interlib loan libn UMiami Med Lib 56-62; Ref libn NLM 62-. 8: Library/USA NY World's Fair rep NLM summer 65. 9: MedLA (chm Subcom on Scholarship); ALA. 10: PTA; Kappa Kappa Gamma. 14: Ref. 15: 8600 Rockville Pike, Bethesda Md 20014.

HENRY, C HELEN. b Milton Mass 27 S 11. 5: UNH 30-34 (Educ) BS; Case-West Res 51-52 MSLS; UDenver 62-64 (LS). 7: Libn: Ins Lib Assn of Boston 42-44, Nat Fire Protection Assn, Boston 45-51, Bridgewater High Sch, Bridgewater Mass 52-55, Brookline High Sch, Brookline Mass 55-57, Foxborough High Sch, Foxborough Mass 57-66, Quincy High Sch, Quincy Mass 66-68; Coord Mass Bur of Lib Ext, Boston 68-. 9: NESchLA (sec). 15: 648 Beacon st, Boston Ma 02515.

HENRY, HELENA (FROST). b winston-Salem NC 6 F 38. 4: William Henry. 5: UNC(Greensboro) 55-59 (Music) B Mus; Columbia 60-62 MSLS. 6: Fr, Ital, Sp. 7: Trainee libn NY Pub Lib 59-62, Libn 62-65; Ref libn NY Inst of Tech 65-67; Hd libn NY Assn for the Blind 67-. 9: ALA. 10: Caccilian Soc Inc; Cape May Playhouse Theater Orchestra; Bob Brown Marionettes; Helena Henry Marionettes; AAUP; Amer Assn Women Bus; NY Assn Women Bus. 14: Ref, catlg, tchg lib materials organ & use to blind pre-college students. 15: 117 E 10 st, New York NY 10023.

HENRY, JANET ELIZABETH. b Youngsville Penn 10 S 06. 5: Wilson Col 24-28 (Lat) AB; Columbia 30-31 (Lat) MA; West Res summers 49-52 MS in LS. 6: Sp, Ger. 7: Tchr: jr high schm Corry Penn 28-30, Verona High Sch, Verona Penn 31-32, Somerville High Sch, somerville NJ 32-40, Youngsville Jr-Sr High Sch, Youngsville Penn 47-48; Libn Youngsville Jr-Sr High Sch 48-66; Hd libn Youngsville High Sch 67-. 9: NEA; ALA; -AASchL; PennStateEA; WarrenCoEA. 10: Delta Kappa Gamma; Beta Phi Mu; Youngsville Pub Lib Assn; Episcopal Church Vestry mem 64-67. 14: Ya wk, catlg. 15: 220 N Main st, Youngsville Pa 16371.

HENRY, LOUISE (SARAH). b Magazine Ark. 5: USt Mary's 39 (Hist) BA; Our Lady of the Lake Col 48 BS in LS; Tex Woman's U 59 MLS (6th Yr). 6: Sp. 7: Tchr san Antonio Pub Sch, San Antonio Tex 23-43; Hosp Recreation Amer Red Cross US Military, Europe 44-47; Order libn Baylor U 48-49; Ref & research hd Tex State Col 49-51; Libn Highland Park Independent Sch Dist, Dallas Tex 51-61; Field Consul Ore State Lib 61; Research & abstractor Standard Oil of Cal, San Francisco 62; Libn Highland Park Jr High Sch, dallas Tex 62-. 8: Principal, Amer Sch, Pachuca Mexico 31-33. 9: ALA; TexLA; SWLA. 10: Epis Church Profess Women; AAUW. 15: 3637 Rosedale, Dallas Tx 75205.

HENRY, SELMA RAE. b Ranger Tex 21 My 18. 5: Abilene Christian Col 42-47 (Span); N Tex State Tchrs Col 47-48 (LS) BA. 6: Sp. 7: Libn Ward Co Lib, Monahans Tex 49-51; Head of child dept Ector Co Lib, Odessa Tex 51-58; Libn Ward Co Lib, Monahans Tex 58-69; Hd of ext serv of Lubbock City Co Libs 69-. 9: ALA; SWLA; TexLA (sec Pub Libs Div 52, chm Child Div 57). 10: Bus & Prof Women's Club; Beta Sigma Phi; Amer Bus Women's Assn; C of C. 11: Citation for meritorious wk from President's Com on Handicapped; Award for outstanding citizen's serv (Monahans C of C). 14: Catlg, child bk sel, ref, Friends of the Lib. 15: 805 E Third, Monahans Tx 79756.

HENRY, SHARON L. b St Cloud Minn 29 S 43. 5: Col of St Catherine 61-65 (LS) BA. 7: Libn I St Paul Pub Lib 65-. 9: ALA; MinnLA. 14: Ref. 15: 2010 Marshall ave apt 4B, St Paul Mn 55104.

HENRY, SYLVIA (GOLDSMITH). b Merano Italy 3 My 38. 4: Ivan Henry. 5: Ciudad Universitaria summer 56; Simmons 56-60 (LS) BS; Columbia 61-65 (LS) MS. 6: Ger, Sp. 7: Clerk-sec Columbia U Libs 59; NY Pub Lib 60-63; Libn LI collection E Hampton (NY) Free Lib. 9: ALA; SLA. 10: Great Bks Leader. 14: Adult circ, child wk, spec collections (rare bks). 15: 22 McGuirk st, E Hampton NY 11937.

HENRY, ZOMA (HARPER). b Ringgold La 14 Ag 13. 5: NWestern State Col 32-38 (Eng) BA; LSU summers 39-42 BS in LS. 6: Fr. 7: Tchr La Sch Syst, Red River Parish 34-40; Libn La Sch Syst: Jefferson Davis Parish 41-42, Morehouse Parish 42-43; Libn morehouse Parish Lib, Bastrop La 43-44; Libn LSU (Baton Rouge) 44-45; Libn 51st fighter Wing, Naha Okinawa 48-49; Libn Far E AF, Nagoya Japan 55-57; Libn Riverside Pub Lib, Riverside Cal 65-. 9: ALA; CalLA. 14: Ref. 15: 3362 10th st, Riverside Ca 92501.

HENRYSON, HILDA JEANNETTE (RYLANDER). b Le Grand Iowa 26 O 17. 4: Albert S Henryson. 5: Iowa State U 36-40 (Home Econ) BS; U No Iowa summers 60-62 (LS) Iowa Certif. 7: Voc home econ instr Earlham Consol Sch, Earlham Iowa 40-41; Home econ tchr Randall Consol Sch, Randall Iowa 44-45; Libn Story City Commun Sch, Story City Iowa 60-69; High Sch libn Roland-Story Commun Sch, Story City Iowa 69-. 9: NEA; ALA; -AASchL; -YASD; Iowa State EA; IowaASchL (treas 65-67, chm Dist 5 64-66, chm Standards Implementation Com 68-69). 10: Delta Kappa Gamma. 14: Secon sch libs, catlg. 15: Rt 1, Story City Iowa 50248.

HENSEL, JANET (WAGNER). b Cleveland 14 D 23. 4: Robert E Hensel. 5: Allegheny Col 41-45 (Eng Lit) BA; Syracuse 45-46 MS in LS; NY State Permanent Certif; NJ State Sch Libn Certif. 6: Fr, Sp, Ger, Ital, Scandinavian, Russian, Portu. 7: Asst libn Triple Cities Col of Syracuse U (Endicott NY) 46-47; Asst libn Little Falls Pub Lib, Little Falls NY 47-48; Asst libn Hartwick Col 48-51; Order & ser libn, Jr libn Champlain Col 51-52; Libn & m useum asst Sch enectady Museum, Schenectady NY 52-54; Saratoga Springs Pub Lib summer 55; Catlg libn Skidmore Col 55-59; Art libn Yaddo Corp, Saratoga Springs NY 55-59; Catlgr & ref libn Engnr Lib IBM Corp, Kingston NY 59-62; Catlg libn Mohawk Valley Community Col 62-65; Catlg libn Utica Col of Syracuse U (Utica NY) 65-66; Libn Claude O Markoe Sch, Frederickssted St Croix US VI 66; Catlg libn Rose Mem Lib Drew U 66-. 8: Bd of Trust, Town of Ulster Pub Lib, Kingston

NY 60-62; Wk with Schenectady Museum. 9: ALA (Person-to-Person netwk 64-65); NYLA; Central NYLA. 10: AAUP; AAUW; Schenectady Museum Assn; Munson Williams Proctor Inst; Woodstock Guild of Craftsmen; Oneida Co Hist Soc. 14: Catlg. 15: 851 Springfield ave, apt 145, Summit NJ 07901.

HENSELMAN, FRANCES (LORAINE) WOOD. b Emmett Ida 2 S 16. 4: Edward Roddy Henselman. 5: UCal(Los Angeles) 39 (Pol Sci) BA; USoCal 42 BS in LS; Chicago summer 46 (LS); UCal (Los Angeles) 66 (Pub Admin MPA. 7: Jr asst Boise Lib, Boise Ida 35-36; Long Beach Pub Lib, Long Beach Cal: Page 37-38, Clerical aide 38-42, gen libn 43-48, Dept head pub rel 49-51, Dept head admin 51-53, Asst libn admin 53-69, City libn 69-. 9: ALA-PRD (Chm); -LAD (Act chm Pub Rel 65-66; Personnel admin com 67; Memb chm Reg II 68-70); AEAUSA; CalLA (var coms 55-65 (pres So Dist 69, sec pub lib, dir 69). 10: USoCal Sch Lib Sci Alumni Assn; Libraria Sodalitas; Pi Sigma Alpha; LWV; City Employees Assn; Long Beach Civic Light Opera Assn; Museum Assn; C of C Aux; NAACP; Amer Museum Natural Hist; UNAssnUSA; Nat wildlife Fed. 12: Ed Long Beach Pub Lib "Eye" (39); Ed Long Beach "Municipal Employee" (40-41). 13: Yes. 14: Lib admin, serv to adults. 15: Long Beach Pub Lib Ocean & Pacific, Long Beach Ca 90802.

HENSHAW, FRANCIS HAROLD. b New Castle Ind 8 F 03. 4: Marie Molnar. 5: Occidental Col 27 AB; Columbia 32 MS. 7: Order asst Pub Lib, Los Angeles 29; Exec asst Pub Lib, Queens Borough NY 32; Libn Berkshire Athenaeum, Pittsfield Mass 34; State libn Tex State Lib 46; LC: Asst chief Card Div 50, Admin off Processing Dept 51, Chief Order Div 52-. 13: Yes. 15: 4802 R st SE, Wash DC 20027.

HENSHAW, MARIE (MOLNAR). b Budapest Hungary 2 F 05. 4: Francis H Henshaw. 5: URochester 22-26 (Chem) BA; Los Angeles Pub Lib Sch 28-29 (LS) Certif; Columbia 33-34 (Psych) MA; UCLA 65 (Computers) Certif. 6: Ger, Fr. 7: Taylor Instrument Cos, Rochester NY 26-28; Tulane Med Sch 29-30; E I duPont de Nemours & Co, Wilmington Del 30-33; Hogg Found UTex 49-50; LC: Card prep & filing sect 50-51, SIPRE Proj 51-54, Decimal clsf off 54-66; Free-lance consul & Lecturer on clsf 67-. 8: ASAZ39 Subcom on Clsf, 63-; Lecturer DDC, Grad Sch Dept of Agric, Wash DC, spring 65. 13: Yes. 14: Clsf, bibliog. 15: 4802 R st SE, Wash DC 20027.

HENSILL, BETTY. b Alberta Can 23 O 21. 4: John Hensill. 5: Ill State Normal U 39-43 (Eng) BEd; UIll 44-46 BS in LS, 47-50 (LS) MS. 7: Illini Union Browsing Room Lib UIll (Urbana) 46-50; Catlgr Chase Nat Bank Lib, NYC 51-52; Readers ref serv asst Collier's Encyclopedia, NYC 52; Bus educ lib asst City Col of NYC 53; Asst educ libn San Francisco State Col 53-54, Natural sci libn 54-66, Asst libn for pub serv 66-. 9: SLA; ASIS; CalLA. 14: Biol lit, sci bibliog. 15: 2 W Summit dr, Redwood City Ca 94062.

HENSLER, MRS HELEN PHARES. b Fairhaven Ohio 29 Ag 02. 5: West Col for Women (Eng) BA; UCincinnati (Eng) MA; W Res MS in LS. 6: Fr, Lat, Gr. 7: Eng & speech tchr High Sch, Middletown Ohio; Libn & speech tchr High Sch, Gunnison Colo; Eng tchr & libn High Sch, Grand Junction Colo; Dir of Libs Mesa Co Valley Schs, Grand Junction Colo 62-68; Lib volunteer wk & wk in Pub Lib & sub libn & tchr. 9: ALA; NEA; ColoASchL (past off); ColoEA. 10: Altrusa; Knife & Fork Club. 14: Catlg, reading, guidance, centralized catlg, sch lib supv. 15: 528-1/2 Elm dr, Grand Junction Co 81501.

HENSLEY, CHARLOTTA COOK. b East Liverpool Ohio 7 O 42. 4: Herbert Bruce Hensley. 5: Maryville Col 60-64 (Eng Lit) BA; UNC 67-68 MSLS. 6: Fr. 7: Peace Corps Vol Chude Girls Grammar Sch, Sapele Nigeria 65-66; Catlgr Mars Hill Col Lib 68-. 9: ALA. 14: Ref, catlg. 15: Box 1021 Warren Wilson Col, Swannanoa NC 28778.

HENSLEY, DOROTHY (THOMPSON). b NYC 16 O 10. 4: Edward M Hensley. 5: Adelphi Col 27-31 (Eng, Chem) BA; LSU 65-66 MLS. 6: Fr. 7: Supv adjustment dept R H Macy & Co, NYC 33-53; Catlgr Tucson Pub Lib 66-67, Order libn 67-. 9: ALA (Jr Mem RT); SWLA; ArizStateLA (Jr Mem). 10: Beta Phi Mu; Friends of the Tucson Pub Lib; Tucson Art Ctr; Desert Museum. 12: Ed, ArizStateLA "Newsletter"; Asst ed "The Arizona Librarian". 14: Bk sel. 15: 128 S 5th ave apt 37, Tucson Az 85701.

HENSLEY, MADELINE. b Ulysses Neb. 5: UNeb 23-27 (Math) AB; USoCal 47 (LS) BS. 7: Asst to catlgr Lincoln City Lib, Lincoln Neb 27-37; Asst So Pasadena Pub Lib, So Pasadena cal 43-47, Asst city libn 47-67, City libn 67-. 9: ALA; CalLA; Pub Lib Exec's Assn So Cal. 13: Yes. 15: 705 No Marguerita ave, Alhambra Ca 91801.

HENTSCHEL, THELMA E. b Cincinnati Ohio 3 Ap 11. 5: Ohio Wesleyan U 28-30 (Lat); Carnegie Inst 30-32 BS in LS; UPenn 33-34 (Educ) MS in Ed. 7: Libn & tchr Nether Providence High Sch, Wallingford Penn 34-36; Libn Temple U High Sch, Phila 36-38; Elem lib supv Mt Lebanon Pub Sch, Pittsburgh 38-46; Libn Radnor High Sch, Wayne Penn 46-. 9: ALA; NEA; -DAVI; PennLA (chm Nomin Com Adv Bd); PennStateEA; Radnor Twp EA; DelawareCoSchLA (pres 52; var coms). 10: Pi Lambda Theta; DPI Lib Ctr Upper Darby. 14: Sec sch resource ctrs. 15: 113 Hillside rd, Strafford Wayne Pa 19087.

HENZE, RONALD A. b Evansville Ind 21 Ap 43. 5: Wabash Col 61-65 (Psych) BA; UKy 67-69 MSLS. 6: Ger. 9: ALA; -ACRL. 10: Sigma Xi. 14: Catlg. 15: 7410 N Harmony rd, Evansville In 47712.

HEPFER, WILLIAM EDWARD. b Duncannon Penn 16 My 44. 4: Nan Reeder. 5: Juniata Col 62-66 (Eng) BA; UPittsburgh 66-67 MLS. 6: Fr. 7: Asst libn for continuing educ Penn StateU (Univ Park) 67-68, Period libn 68-. 14: Ser, tech processes, ref, admin. 15: 156 Hillview ave, State College Pa 16801.

HEPLER, JUANITA (MIDGETTE). b Portsmouth Va 30 Ja 46. 4: Arthur Clinton Hepler. 5: Radford 63-64 (LS); VPI 65-66 (Eng); MdU 66-68 (LS) BA. 7: Sec Amer Red Cross, Alexandria Va 64-65; Libn Prince Georges Co Schs, Upper Marlboro Md 68-. 9: ALA; NEA; MdStateTA; Prince Georges Co EA. 10: Phi Kappa Phi; Kappa Delta Pi. 14: Sch libs. 15: 6405 Livingston rd apt 402, Oxon Hill Md 20022.

HEPLER, RUTH (MERRYMAN). b Wellington Kan 22 Ja 08. 4: George Ernest Hepler. 5: Kan State Tchrs Col (Emporia) (Educ, LS); Southwestern Col 62, 63 (Educ, LS); FriendsU 64, 65 (Educ) BS. 7: Co libn Tuscarawas Co, New Phila Ohio 43-61; Lib off US Info Serv, Brazil 62-68; Reg libn Lat Amer US Info Agcy, Wash DC 69-. 9: ALA; KanLA (sec 50-54; archivist 42-52; Exec bd 40-42); KanASchL. 10: AAUW; Bus & Prof Women; Wichita Lib. 14: Ref, sch libs. 15: 501 W Lincoln, Wellington Ks 67152.

HEPP, THOMAS A. b Chicago 6 Jl 23. 4: Naomi Herndon. 5: Ariz State U 43-44, 48-51 (Educ) BA Ed; UCal(Berkeley) 54-56 MLS. 7: Passenger agent TWA Inc, Phoenix Ariz 43-49; Jr & sr libn Oakland (Cal) Free Lib 54-56; Asst libn Diablo Valley Col 56-61; Col Libn Grossmont Col 61-. 8: Member Accred Team 66, 68. 9: ALA; CalLA (pres, Commun Col Div 68); Cal Tchrs Assn. 10: Cal Jr Col Fac Assn. 14: Admin. 15: Grossmont Col, El Cajon Ca 92020.

HEPPELL, SHIRLEY (GAUKER). b Reading Penn 8 Mr 24. 4: Roger C Heppell. 5: Penn State U 42-45, 47-49 (Hist) BA, MA; UMich 53-54 MALS. 6: Sp, Ger. 7: Instr Penn State U Ext Serv 48-50; Subprof asst Penn State U Lib 50-53; Catlgr Sarah Lawrence Col 54-56; Pub Serv libn Cortland Free Lib, Cortland NY 56-58; Asst col libn tech serv State U Col (Cortland NY) 58-64, Assoc col libn 65; Libn Cortland Co (NY) Hist Soc 66-. 9: SAA. 10: NY State Hist Assn. 13: Yes. 14: Acquis, catlg, ser, mss, preserv. 15: 33 Lincoln ave, Cortland NY 13045.

HERALD, ALTHEA CONLEY. b Rutherford NJ 29 Mr 04. 4: Alvin Louis Herald. 5: Syracuse 22-26 BLS. 6: Fr. 7: Catlgr & ref libn Amer Tel & Tel Develop & Res Lib 26-28; Trustee, Rutherford Free Pub Lib 37-43; Libn Fairleigh Dickinson Jr Col 42-44; Dir Narberth Commun Lib, Narberth Penn 50-54; Trustee, new Milford (NJ) Free Pub Lib 54-62; Chief Libn Fairleigh Dickinson U (Teaneck) 54-60; Dir Teaneck Campus Libs Fairleigh Dickinson U 60-69, Dir emeritus 69-, Lib consul. 8: Consul on lib floor plans. 9: ALA (Col & Unif Sect); MedLA; NJLA (past treas & sec Col & Univ Sect). 10: Nat Button Soc; Bergen Co Hist Soc; Betsy Ross Club of Phila; Twentieth Century Club (Lansdowne Penn); Kappa Delta; DAR; Canal Soc NY. 11: Kappa Delta Citation, 26; Fairleigh Dickinson Citation, 53; Circle K Citation, 65; Dentistry Citation, 64, 65. 12: "Processing Manual: A Pictorial

Workbook of Catalog Cards" (61, 63). 14: Catlg. 15: 228 Woodland rd, New Milford NJ 07646.

HERBERT, ADDIE LEE (HIBLER). b Eufaula Okla 19 My 21. 5: Langston U 38-42 (Home Econ) BS; Wichita U summer 47; USoCal summer 48, 50, 65; Okla State U summer 50, 51 (Home Econ, Educ) MS; Atlanta U 60-61; NEast State Col summers 65, 66; Okla State Dept of Educ certif in LS 66. 7: Libn Morton High Sch, Taft Okla 46-47; Sec & registrar Manual Train High, Muskogee Okla 47-53, Libn 64-66; Libn & coun Sadler Jr High, Muskogee Okla 53-64; Libn Muskogee Schs Media Ctr, Muskogee Okla 66-. 8: Conducted an In-Service training Program for 17 elem tchr-libns 67; Adv Com for Consultative Ctr for Sch Desegregation; Mem Ctr of Cont Educ, Norman Okla 66-68; Mem Okla Lib Devel Com 68-69; Okla Nat Lib Week Com 69; Muskogee Nat Lib Week Com 69; Okla State Health Planning Coun 68; Mayor's Coun for Youth Opportunities, Muskogee 69-; Organized Muskogee Schs materials Media Ctr 66. 9: NEA; ALA; -AASchL; OklaLA; OklaEA; MuskogeeEA; Muskogee Clr Tchrs. 10: Delta Sigma Theta; Lit Phy So Club; Coterie Club; Urban League; NAACP. 13: Yes. 14: Catlg, bks by & about minority gps. 15: 710 Fondulac, Muskogee Ok 74401.

HERCEG, JOYCE D. b Buffalo NY 3 D 35. 5: SUNY (Geneseo) 68-69 MLS; SUNY (Buffalo) 60-66 (Psych) BA; UBuffalo 56-60 AA. 7: Libn trainee Buffalo & Erie Co Pub Lib, Buffalo NY 66-68. 9: ALA. 10: Phi Beta Kappa. 14: Ref. 15: 224 Crowley ave, Buffalo NY 14207.

HERCHE, MADELINE MAY. b Jersey City NJ 12 D 15. 5: Douglass Col 32-36 (Eng) BA; Trenton State Col summers 38, 39, 47, 48 BLS. 7: Libn Jamesburg High Sch, Jamesburg NJ 37-. 8: Adv to pres NJ Sch Lib Councils Assn 56-57. 9: ALA; NEA-DAVI; NJEA; NJStateLA; NJLA; NJ A-V Coun. 10: Exec Bd Library-at-Jamesburg (sec 56-). 12: Ed "New Jersey School Librarian" 49-53; Ed NJStateLA "Newsletter" 61-64. 13: Yes. 14: Yp. 15: 16 Half Acre rd, Jamesburg NJ 08831.

HERING, MILLICENT BLAND. b Springfield Col 28 N 21. 4: Donald M Hering. 5: Colo State Col 40-46 (Secondary Educ) AB; UAlaska 64-65; UDenver summers 62-65 (Libnship) MA. 7: Tchr: Tintic High Sch, Eureka Utah 46-48, Jackson-Wilson High, Jackson Hole wyo 48-50, Union High Sch, Carbondale Colo 50-52, Middle Park High Sch, Granby Colo 52-54, Fruitdale Sch, Grants Pass Ore 54-56; Tchr & libn Lathrop High Sch, Fairbanks Alaska 56-66; Hd reader serv dept UAlaska Lib 66-. 9: ALA; AlaskaLA (chm No Chap 66-67); Alaska Eng Coun. 10: Pioneers of Alaska Aux; ACLU. 12: Ed AlaskaLA "Newsletter" (65-65); Delta Kappa Gamma State Newsletter "Nugget" 65-67. 14: Ref, reader serv. 15: 1041 Pedro st, Fairbanks Ak 99701.

HERIOT, CAROLINE (CHANDLER). b Dalzell SC 29 Jl 18. 5: Montreat Jr Col 35-36; Lander Col 36-39 (Hist) BA; UNC 53-54 BS in LS, 56-60 LLB. 7: Tchr New Zion High Sch, New Zion SC 39-41; Tchr Ninety Six High Sch, Ninety Six SC 41-44; Research analyst foreign affairs Nat Security Agency, Wash DC 44-52; Ref asst Bur Ord Navy Dept, Wash DC 54-56; Asst law libn UNC(Chapel Hill) 56-59; Asst law libn UIowa 60-61, Law Libn 61-65; Law Libn Supreme Court of NM, Santa Fe NM 65-67; Law libn Loyola U (New Orleans) 67-. 8: Consul Law Lib USD Law Sch 65. 9: AALL; SLA; LaLA; New Orleans Lib Club. 10: AAUW. 14: Admin, ref. 15: Loyola Univ Law Lib, 6363 St Charles ave, New Orleans La 70118.

HERK HELEN RUTH (WITHERSPOON). b Webster Penn 6 Jl 12. 4: Michael J Herk. 5: Geneva col 29-33 (Lat, Fr) AB, 29-33 (Speech) BO; UPittsburgh 35-40 (Soc Studies) ML; DuquesneU 63-65 (LS). 6: Fr, Lat. 7: Tchr Jr High Donora Pub Sch 34-40, Tchr Sr High 41-43, Libn Jr & Sr 60-63; Libn Ringgold Sch Dist Donota Sr High 64-. 8: Chm Ringgold Sch Dist Lib Com; Mem Bd of Trustees Donora Public Library; Consul State of Penn for summer Lib Program at Clarion State Col 69. 9: PennLA; PennStateEA; PittsburghSuburbanLA. 10: Donora Woman's Club; DAR; RinggoldEA. 14: Ref. 15: 301 Allen ave, Donora Pa 15033.

HERLING, ELEANOR (BRINKMANN). b NYC. 4: John P Herling. 5: Barnard 32-36 (Fr) AB; Inst d'Art et d'Arche3ologie (Paris) 36; Columbia 36-38 (Romance Philol), 39-42 (LS) BS. 6: Fr, Ger, Sp, Ital, Dutch, Portu. 7: Ref asst Bus Br Newark Pub Lib, Newark NJ 38; Filer, searcher in authority slip sect, prep div, catlgr Berg collection, ref libn econ div, ref dept NY Pub Lib 38-42; Head Libn New Sch for Soc Research 43-44; Ref libn econ div & info desk, head filing & transferring sect prep div, supv main reading room, ref dept NY Pub Lib 45-50; Indexer "Library Literature" & "International Index" The H W Wilson Co 48-61; Child libn, ref libn S Orange Pub Lib, S Orange NJ 61-63, Act dir 63; Catlgr, Head catlg dept, Assoc libn readers serv E H Butler Lib State U Col (Buffalo NY) 64-68; Chief, sel dept Case-West Res U Libs, 68-. 8: Bibliogr "The Engineering Index" (59-60). 9: ALA; SLA; OhioLA. 10: Beta Phi Mu; AAUP; Ling Soc Amer; Women's Nat Bk Assn. 11: Paris Fellowship Societe Francaise of Barnard Col, 36. 14: Catlg, ref, admin. 15: 2853 Berkshire rd, Cleveland Heights Oh 44118.

HERLING, JOHN P. b Madison Wis 7 Jl 17. 4: Eleanor Brinkmann. 5: UWis 34-38 (Eng) BA, Lib Sci Diploma; UMich 42-43 (LS); UWis 50-51 (Eng) MA; Columbia 52-53 (Eng). 6: Fr, Ger, Ital. 7: Gen asst Wis State Col (Stevens Point) 38-41; Engnr lib asst UMich(Ann Arbor) 41, Gen serv asst 42, 1st asst circ dept 43; Ref libn ref desk NY Pub Lib 46-50; Eng libn Engnr Socs Lib, NYC 53-61; Head Libn Lummus Co, Newark NJ 61-63; Asst dir for readers serv SUNY(Buffalo) 63-67, Asst dir 67-68; Dir of libs Cleveland State U 68-. 9: ALA; SLA; ASIS; OhioLA. 10: AAUP. 13: Yes. 14: Ref, admin. 15: 2853 Berkshire rd, Cleveland Heights Oh 44118.

HERLINGER, MARGARET ELLEN (RUDDELL). b Brooklyn NY 22 Mr 39. 4: Daniel Herlinger. 5: Rutgers 56-60 (Eng) BA; Ind U 60-62 (Eng), 62-63 (LS) MA. 6: Fr. 7: Asst documents libn Ind U Lib(Bloomington) 62-65; Ser records libn Linda Hall Lib, Kanss Kansas Mo 65-67; Ref libn Lippincott Lib UPenn 67-68; Sr catlgr Paley Lib Temple U 68-. 9: ALA. 10: Phi Beta Kappa; Beta Phi Mu. 14: Documents, serials, ref, acquis, catlg. 15: Duval Manor apt 820, Phila Pa 19144.

HERMAN, ELIZABETH STEWART (CARBEE). b Los Angeles 22 Jl 22. 4: Gunter Fredrick Herman. 5: UCal(Los Angeles) 39-43 (Psych) BA; USoCal 62-64 MSLS. 7: Asst libn University Elem Sch at UCLA 65-67; Catlg dept URL-UCLA 67-. 9: ALA- rtsd&-AASchL;-CSD;-ISAD; CalLA; So Cal Tech Proc Gp. 10: Beta Phi Mu; The Palm Soc. 14: Catlg, child serv. 15: 701 Tigertail rd, Los Angeles Ca 90049.

HERMAN, GERTRUDE (BECKER). b Fond du Lac Wis 20 Je 15. 4: Henry B Herman. 5: UWis 36 (Eng) BS in ED; Columbia 42 BS in LS; UWis 68 MSLS, Spec in Libnship. 07: Eng tchr High Sch, Marshfield Wis 36-38; Asst in child wk NY Pub Lib 38-41; Libn Fieldston Sch NYC 41-42; Libn & tchr Fieldston Lower Sch, NYC 45-65; Libn Madison Pub Schs, Madison Wis 65-67; Asst Prof Lib Sch UWis 68-. 8: Wk Camp Co-director Internat Stud Serv New Milford Conn summer 42; Fieldston Sch Highland Farm Wk Camp Co-dir, Highland NY summer 43; Asst Dir, University Settlement House Camp, Beacon NY summer 44; Fieldston Sch N Country Group, Potsdam NY summer 58. 9: ALA; WisLA (Film Com 68-, Child & YP Sect); Coop Child Bk Ctr (Exec Bd). 10: Soc for Ethical Culture. 12: "Golden Stamp Book of Dogs" (53); Co-auth "Golden Stamp Book of Flags" (53); Co-ed "Golden Book of Indian Crafts & Lore" (54); Co-comp "Harper's Magazine Holiday Book list for Children" (58). 13: Yes. 14: Story-telling, sch libs, child lit, child serv. 15: 1425 W Skyline dr, Madison Wi 53705.

HERMAN, LINDA ERMINE. b Los Angeles 21 My 36. 5: Cal State Col (Los Angeles) 56-59 (Eng) BA; UCal(Los Angeles) 61-62 MLS. 6: Fr. 7: Lib asst Occidental Col 60-62; Harry A Levinson Rare Bks, Beverly Hills Cal 62-64; Catlgr Cal State Col (Fullerton) 65-67, Spec Collections libn 67-. 9: CalLA. 10: CSCF Faculty Women; UCal Schs Alumni Assn; Belle Aire Trio; Bit & Bridle Club. 14: Rare bks. 15: 424 So Fonda st, LaHabra Ca 90631.

HERMAN, STEVEN J. b NYC 23 O 41. 5: City Col (NY) 59-63 (Psych) BS; Rutgers 63-64 MLS. 6: Fr. 7: Processing dept Brooklyn Pub Lib 57; Clerk & tech asst NY Pub Lib 58-63; Libn Free Lib of Phila 64; Dir Highland Park Pub Lib, Highland Park NJ 65-69; Institutional serv libn NJ State Lib 69-. 8: Co-chm com to compile Union List of Ser for Middlesex Co. 9: ALA; ASIS; NJLA (Educ for Libnship Com; past chm Registration); Middlesex Co (NJ) LA (past treas). 10: Rutgers Grad Sch Lib Serv Alumni Assn (Exec Bd). 14: Readers serv, admin, wk with spec gps, ref. 15: 3 Redcliffe ave, Highland Park NJ 08904.

HERMENS, DOROTHY MARIE. b Forest Grove Ore 9 My 25. 5: Mt Angel Col 43-46 (Educ) Tchg Certif; Marylhurst summer 47-48, & 49 (Soc Sci) BS in Ed; Portland Ext of Ore Syst of Higher Educ 47-48; Seattle U summers 51-54 (Educ Psych) M Ed; UPortland 54; UHawaii summer 55; Stanford summer 56; UWash summers 60, 62, 64, 65 M Libr; Portland U summer 68. 6: Fr. 7: Elem tchr, Garden Home Ore 46-48; Dist 48, Beaverton Ore: Elem tchr 49-59, Elem libn 59-63, Jr high libn 63-. 9: NEA (Life mem); ALA; OreEA; OreLA. 10:

AAUW. 14: Catlg, wk with child. 15: 711 S E Allen ave #17, Beaverton Or 97005.

HERMES, MARGARET A. b Arapahoe Neb 6 Ag 11. 5: Concordia Tchrs Col (Seward) 33-35 (Educ); Concordia Tchrs Col (River Forest) 42-43 (Educ); Rosary Col 49-52 (LS) BA; West Mich U 61-65 (Eng) MA. 6: Ger, Sp. 7: Asst libn Concordia Tchrs Col River Forest 49-52, libn 52-55; Asst libn (Assoc Prof) Concordia Sr Col (Ft Wayne Ind) 56-. 14: Catlg, reader guidance. 15: Concordia Sr Col, Ft Wayne In 46805.

HERN, JEAN (HARTLEY). b Indianapolis 14 Jl 21. 5: Pensacola Jr Col 55-60; Fla State U 60-62 (Eng) BA, 63-64 (LS) MS. 7: Personnel clerk US Civil Serv, Pensacola Fla 53-60; Eng tchr & asst libn Tate High Sch, Pensacola Fla 62-63, Libn 64-65; Libn Pensacola Jr Col 65-. 9: ALA; NEA; FlaEA; FlaASchL; EscambiaEA. 10: Beta Phi Mu, Sigma Tau Delta; AAUW. 14: Readers serv, ref. 15: 100 E Adkinson dr, Pensacola Fl 32506.

HERNANDEZ, CAROLEENA. b Lexington Ky 16 N 40. 5: UKy 57-62 (Hist) AB; Emory 63-64 (LS) MS; UGa 65-67 (Bot). 6: Sp. 7: Asst ref libn rare bks USCar 64-65; Readers adv libn Nat Communicable Disease Ctr, Atlanta Ga 68-. 11: NSF Research grant, 59. 14: Rare bks. 15: Box 15245, Emory Univ Branch, Atlanta Ga 30333.

HERNANDEZ, MARJORIE (RAY). b Hemingway SC 6 Mr 27. 4: Harley Holt Hernandez. 5: USCar 47-49 (Eng, Hist); UCal 59-62 (Eng) AB, 62-65 MLS; No Ill U 65 (Educ); UIll 65-67 (Educ) Tchg Certif. 6: Fr, Sp. 7: Transportation clerk US Army Transportation Corps, Charleston SC 43-47; Sec USCar Alumni Assn 47-49; Catlg clerk Pub Lib, Birmingham Ala 49-50; Admin sec Cutter Labs, Berkeley Cal 51-56; Legal sec Contra Costa Court Reporters, El Cerrito Cal 59-65; Libn Westmont Pub Schs Dist 57 DuPage Co, Westmont Ill 65-67; Lecturer: Nat Col of Ed 66-67, George Williams Col 66; Coord child serv Pub Lib, Tampa Fla 68; Dir prof serv A-V Studio, Weston Woods Conn 68-69; Asst dir Pub Lib, Danbury Conn 69-. 8: Consul Weston Woods Studio, Weston Conn 69-. 9: ALA-CSD;-YASD;ConnLA. 10: PTA; Beta Phi Mu; Hinsdale (Ill) Tennis Club. 13: Yes. 14: Lib admin, tchg child lit, child libnship, ya. 15: High Ridge rd, Brookfield Center, Ct 06805.

HERNDON, MILDRED E (DENNY). b Ind 28 O 09. 5: West Wash State Col 27-38 (Educ) BA in Ed; UWash 33 (Educ); Riverside Lib Sch 34-35 Lib Sci Certif. 7: Child libn Bellingham Pub Lib, Bellingham Wash 48-50; Bkmob libn Stanislaus Co Free Lib, Modesto Cal 52-53, Co Child Libn 53-58; Los Angeles Co Pub Lib, Los Angeles: Child libn 58-60, Reg Child libn 60-62, Reg Libn 61-62; Br supv Stanislaus Co Free Lib, Modesto Cal 62-66; Br libn Santa Clara City Lib 66-67; Ref libn Gavilan Col 67-68; Br supv Sacramento City-Co Lib 68-. 9: ALA; CalLA. 10: AAUW; Audubon Club. 14: Wk with child, adult serv. 15: 2319 T st Apt b, Sacramento Ca 95816.

HERNER, SAUL. b Brooklyn NY 29 Ja 23. 4: Mary Alexander. 5: UWis 40-45 (Agric) BS. 6: Fr, Ger. 7: Research chem US Army Air Corps, Madison Wis 45-46; Chem ref asst NY Pub Lib 46-48; Engnr libn NYU 48-50; Chief Libn Johns Hopkins U 50-53; Head Lib Plan Gr Atlantic Research Co, Alexandria Va 53-56; Pres Herner & Co, Wash DC 56-. 9: ACS; ASIS; ALA-ACRL; SLA; AFCEA. 10: AAAS. 13: Yes. 14: Lib planning, info system design & eval. 15: Herner & Co, 2431 K st NW, Wash DC 20037.

HEROLD, JEAN. b Jennings Mo 30 Jl 24. 5: WashU 41-43; UTex (Austin) 55-58 (Eng) BA, 61-62 MLS. 7: Elem tchr Austin Independent Sch Dist 58-61, Asst libn Lamar Jr High Sch 62-64; Ref libn UTex (Austin) Undergrad Lib 64-65, Ref libn & interlib loan Main Lib 65-69, Ref libn soc scis 69-. 9: TexLA. 10: Phi Beta Kappa. 14: Ref. 15: Box 7048 Univ Sta, Austin Tx 78712.

HERON, DAVID WINSTON. b Los Angeles 20 Mr 20. 4: Winifred Wright. 5: Pomona Col 38-42 (Eng) BA; UCal (Berkeley) 46-48 BLS; UCal(Los Angeles) 49-51 (Pol Sci) MA. 6: Fr. 7: US Army Armored Infantry (1st Lt) 42-46; Research asst UCal Lib (Berkeley) 46-48; Libn I-II UCal Lib (Los Angeles) 48-52; Libn Amer Embassy, Tokyo 52-53; Libn II UCal Lib (Los Angeles) 53-55; Asst to the dir Stanford U Lib 55-57; Asst libn Hoover Inst, Stanford Cal 57-59; Asst dir Stanford U Lib 59-61; Dir of Libs UNev 61-68, Dir of libs UKan 68-. 8: Lib Adv U of the Ryukyus, Naha (Okinawa) 60-61. 9: ALA (Coun);-ACRL (chm &/or mem 3 coms); NevLA (pres 63-65); -RTSD (chm Films Telefacsimile Com 67-70); KanLA. 10: UCal Lib Sch Alumni Assn; Rotary Club; AAUP; Internat House of Japan; Johnson Soc. 12: Ed "ACRL Monographs" (66-69). 13: Yes. 14: Univ libs, internat rels, interlib serv. 15: 802 Tennessee st, Lawrence Ks 66044.

HEROY, INGRID CARLSON. b Baltimore 22 O 41. 4: James H Heroy III. 5: Mary Baldwin Col 59-60, 62-63 (Philos) BA; Columbia 63-64 MLS. 6: Fr. 7: Alexander Brown Investment firm, Baltimore summer 60; Baltimore Co Lib summer 62; Columbia U Sch of Lib Serv Lib 64-66; Assoc Libn Spec Lib Cleveland Electric Illuminating Co, Cleveland Ohio 66-68; Libn US Navy Weather Research Facility, Norfolk Va 68-. 9: ALA. 10: Jr League. 14: Ref, admin. 15: 1351 Andes ct, Norfolk Va 23502.

HERR, MARY ELIZABETH (ROGERS). b Waterloo Iowa 25 My 33. 4: Herbert H Herr. 5: Marycrest Col 51-55 (LS) BA; UWis (Madison) summers 57, 58, 59, 60 (LS) MS. 6: Sp. 7: Lib sec & circ ref asst Davenport (Iowa) Pub Lib 55-56, Asst in child dept 56-60, Asst in circ & ref dept 60, Asst ref libn 61-. 9: IowaLA. 14: Ref. 15: 321 Main st, Davenport Ia 52801.

HERRICK, (MARY) ELIZABETH. b Manchester NY 6 Je 06. 5: Keuka Col 24-28 (Math) AB; Columbia 34-35 (LS) BS Columbia 47-50 (Found of Educ, Soc Found) MA. 6: Fr, Sp, Ger. 7: Math tchr Horseheads High Sch,Horseheads NY 28-29; Priv sec to Wayne Co Attorney, Newark NY 30-34; Asst to assoc dean Sch Lib Serv Columbia U 35-42; Sr asst Rochester Pub Lib, Rochester NY 42-46; Asst libn catlg dept Tchrs Col Lib, Columbia U 46-57, Supv libn acquis dept 57-. 9: ALA; NY Tech Serv Libns; NY Lib Club. 10: Volunteer wk Riverside Church Lib NYC. 15: 90 LaSalle st apt 5-F, New York NY 10027.

HERRICK, CHARLES C. b Montello Wis 7 Mr 32. 5: Wis State Col (Oshkosh) 50-52; UWis 52-54 BA, 58-59 (LS) MA. 6: Sp, Fr. 7: US Army 54-56; Jr libn Milwaukke Pub Lib 56-58, Libn I 59-60; Tech educ rep McGraw-Hill Bk Co, NY 60; Ref & asst libn Winnetka ill 61-63; Dir Helen M Plum Mem Lib, Lombard Ill 63-. 8: Lib Adminrs Conf of No Ill, mem 63-, v-chm 67-68, chm 68-69; Adv Com, Col of DuPage Lib Tech Asst Prog (chm 68-69); Exec Dir Nat Lib Week 68. 9: ALA; IllLA (Recr Netwk 64-; Pub Lib Sect v-chm 67-69, chm 68-69); Central DuPage Libns Assn. 11: Citation, Exec Dir Nat Lib Week, Ill 68. 13: Yes. 14: Ref, adult serv, pub rel, sch-pub lib coop. 15: 123 W Willow, Lombard Il 60148.

HERRICK, MARY DARRAH. b Waterville Me 23 N 08. 4: Reginald O'Halloran. 5: Simmons 25-29 (LS) BS; UMe 31-32 (Eng) AB; Columbia 47-48 (LS) MS. 7: Catlgr Jones Lib, Amherst Mass 29-32; Assoc libn Pub Lib, Waterville Me 34-39; Catlgr Colby Col 39-45; Libn Nasson Col 45-47; Asst Prof Pratt Lib Sch 47-48; Asst dir for bibliog org & Asst Prof Col of Liberal Arts Boston U 48-. 9: ALA (Coun twice); -RTSD (chm var coms); NELA (Dir 46-47); MeLA (pres 44-46). 10: AAUW; AAUP. 12: Ed "Boston University Catalog of African Documents" (2d ed 65); Ed "Boston University Index to the Classed Catalog" (2d ed 65). 13: Yes. 14: Clsf, rare bks, modern mss. 15: Boston U Libs, Boston Ma 02115.

HERRICK, SALLY CAROL (WARNOCK). b Columbus Ohio 16 My 40. 5: Graceland Col 58-60 (Liberal Arts) AA; Central Mo State Col 60-62 (Span) BA; UWash 64-65 M of Libnship. 6: Sp, Fr. 7: Clerk III wk with child Seattle Pub Lib 63-65; Libn & Instr Central Mo State Col 65-68; Asst child libn Peoria Pub Lib, Peoria Ill 68-69; Prof asst (grade 2) child lib Kansas City Pub Lib, Mo 69-. 9: ALA (Jr Mem RT); MoLA; Mo State Tchrs Assn. 14: Wk with child. 15: Children's Lib, Kansas City Pub Lib, Kansas City Mo 64106.

HERRING, BILLIE GRACE (UNGERER). b Flatonia Tex 16 N 32. 4: James Craig Herring. 5: Utex 49-53 (Elem Educ) BS; Austin Presbyt Theol Sem 56-57; UTex (Austin) 61-67 9ls0 mls, 67-68 (LS) 6th yr special. 7: Parish wkr 1st Lutheran Ch, Austin Tex 53-56; Dir of educ Westminster Presbyt Ch, Austin 56-57; Tchr/libn Fly Jr High Sch, Crystal City Tex 61-62; Libn Harris Elem Sch, Austin 62-67; Asst prof UTex Grad Sch of Lib Sci (Austin) 68-. 9: ALA; DAVI; NEA; TexStateTA; Tex Assn for Educ Tech; TexLA; SWLA. 10: AAUW; City Coun; PTA; Pi Lambda Theta; Mortar Bd. 13: Yes. 14: Sch libs, catlg, educ for libnship. 15: 1510 Glencrest dr, Austin Tx 78723.

HERRING, MILDRED C(ATHERINE). b Clinton NC 26 F 07. 5: E Car U 24-28 (Eng, Fr) AB; UNC (Chapel Hill) 37-39 BLS. 6: Fr. 7: Tchr: Angier High Sch, Angier NC 28-30, Dunn high Sch, Dunn NC 30-35; Personnel resettlement admin (govt), Raleigh NC 35-36; Libn: Hugh Morson High Sch, Raleigh NC 36-44, Grimsley Sr High Sch, Greensboro NC 44-; Prof lib serv NC Col summer 40; Instr lib sci Appalachian State Tchrs Col summers 41-56; Instr lib sci Fla State U summer 46; Instr lib sci West Car Col summers 58-62. 8: Member Jt Com NC Eng Tchrs and NCLA; Mem Adv Com NC Communication Study Commsn 51-53; One of organizers of NC High Sch LA 48. 9: NEA; ALA; NCEA; SELA; NCLA (v-pres 51-53, dir 68-69). 10: Delta Kappa Gamma; Beta Phi Mu; Garden Club; Wesleyan Serv Guild. 14: Ref, admin. 15: 618 1/2 Scott ave, Greensboro NC 27403.

HERRINGTON, PATRICIA ANNE. b Lansing Mich 29 D 34. 5: Flint Jr Col 53-55 (Liberal Arts) AA; West Mich U 55-58 (Eng) AB Elem Provisional; UMich 58-61 AMLS. 7: Elem tchr Dryden Community Schs, Dryden Mich 58-60; Asst child libn Flint Pub Lib, Flint Mich 61-64; Child libn Albion Pub Lib, Albion Mich 64-68; Hd child dept Bloomfield Twp Pub Lib, Bloomfield Hills Mich. 9: MichLA. 10: Girl Scouts of America; Big Sisters. 14: Child wk, elem libs, pub libs. 15: 46 Canary Hill, Pontiac Mi 48055.

HERRMANN, EDITH (MARIE LOUISE). b Berlin 30 Ap 20. 5: Pembroke Col 38-42 (Ger Lit) AB; Columbia 42-43 BS, MS equivalency; Rutgers 61-62 (LS). 6: Fr, Ger. 7: Volunteer catlg dept Brown U summer 41; Asst circ dept NY Pub Lib 43-44; Gen asst catlg dept Providence Pub Lib 44-45; 2nd asst catlg dept Conn Col Lib 45-47; Circ-ref asst Elmwood Pub Lib, Providence 48; Asst catlgr Smith Col Lib 49-50; Circ-ref asst Free Pub Lib, Westfield NJ 50-51; Br libn Elmwood Br W Hartford (Conn) Pub Lib 51-52; Sr libn head of tech serv Hillside (NJ) Pub Lib 52-. 8: Adv Marquis Biog Lib Soc. 9: ALA-RTSD;-PLA;NJLA (Bd; pres Catlgrs Sect, mem Tech Serv & Ref Sects, pres 59-60); NY Tech Servs Libns. 10: Columbia U Grad Lib Sch Alumni Assn; NJ Pembroke Col Club; Bus & Prof Women's Club; Internat Platform Assn. 14: Catlg, ref, pub lib admin, automation, info retrieval. 15: 204 Westfield ave apt 2f, Elizabeth NJ 07208.

HERRON, ANN. b Trezevant Tenn. 5: Columbia Col of Drama (Chicago) summer 33; Northwestern U summer 39; UColo summer 40; Murray State U 33-37 (Eng, Speech) BS; UIll 43-44 BS in LS; UMich 51-52 (LS, Theatre) AMLS. 6: Fr, Sp. 7: Act libn Murray state U 44-45, Catlg libn 46-51, Asst libn in chg of ref 52-69, Assoc dir of libs 69-. 8: Tchr, lib sci summer courses: UKy 54; LSU 55, 56; UCal(Berkeley) 57; UDenver 58, 63-65, 67,68; UWash 59; UOkla 60; Drexel 62. 9: ALA (Exec Bd exhibits Round Table 63-66, Memb Com 63-69);-ACRL (Memb Com 65-67); TheatreLA; SELA (Nomin Com 62-64, Memb Com 63-69); KyLA (chm Col & Ref Sect 57-59; Exhibits Chm 59-, Bd Dirs 57-). 10: AALS; AAUP; AAUW; Delta Kappa Gamma; PEO; Alpha Beta Alpha; Kappa Delta Pi; Alpha Psi Omega. 12: "Guide to the Use of murray State College Library" (53). 13: Yes. 14: Humanities, theatre libnship, ref, catlg, admin. 15: Box 142 Univ Station, Murray Ky 42071.

HERRON, MARGIE (ELEANOR). b Aiken SC 26 Ja 41. 5: Winthrop Col 59-63 (Hist) BA (magna cum laude); Rutgers 63-64 MLS. 6: Fr. 7: Ext libn ABBE Reg Lib, Aiken SC 64-66; Field serv libn SC State Lib Bd 66-. 8: SC State Lib Bd Recr Caravan, 65. 9: ALA; SCLA (Recr Com 65-68; chm Pub Libs Sec 67-68; SCLA (sec 69-70). 10: Book & Key (Winthrop Col); Phi Alpha Theta; Kappa Delta Pi; Phi Kappa Phi. 14: Ref, lib admin, lib ext, adult serv. 15: Senate Plaza apt 6C, 1520 Senate st, Columbia SC 29201.

HERRON, THOMAS JAMES. b Boone Iowa 21 Mr 28. 4: Yvonne Jacobson. 5: St Joseph's Col 46-48; Muskegon Jr Col 49-50; Rockhurst Col 50-52 (Educ) AB; UKan City 53; UMich 54-58 (Eng) MA; UIowa 61; UMich 61-64 MALS. 6: Lat. 7: Tchr Norway High Sch, Norway Mich 52-55; Tchr Beecher High Sch, Flint Mich 55-58; Tchr-libn Northern High Sch, Flint Mich 58-64; Libn Northwestern High Sch, Flint Mich 64-65; Dean of Instr Southwestern High Sch, Flint Mich 65-, Ref libn Flint Pub Lib, Flint Mich summers 65-69. 09: ASCD; MichASchL (Publicity Chm 65-66, mem Planning Com for Stud & Child Sect Meeting 65); Flint (Mich) Assn Sch Adminrs. 10: Delta Epsilon Sigma; Urban League. 12: Co-auth "The Teacher and the Newspaper." 14: Sch libs, instrl materials centers. 15: 1409 Lillian dr, Flint Mi 48505.

HERRON, YVONNE (JACOBSON). b Flint Mich 28 My 35. 4: Thomas Herron. 5: Flint Jr Col 53-55 AA; UMich 55-57 (Hist) BA, 58-61 (Educ) MA, 62-64 MA LS. 7: Tchr Beecher High Sch, Flint Mich 57-63; Libn Southwestern High Sch, Flint Mich 63-66; Libn Doyle Elem Sch (Instr Materials Ctr) 67-. 8: Survey of encyclopedias on two major entries for "World Book." 09: MichASchL (com duties). 10: AAUW; Pi Lambda Theta; Phi Kappa Phi; UMich Lib Sci Alum Assn. 14: Instrl materials centers (secon schs). 15: 3208 N Stevenson st, Flint Mi 48504.

HERSCHER, EUGENE. b Bronx NY 27 Jl 23. 4: Patricia Kreger. 5: Col of the City of NY 40-43, 46-47 (Sociol) BSS; Columbia 47-49 (Sociol); Columbia 50-51 (LS) MS. 6: Fr, Ger. 7: (Cpl) US Army Air Force 43-46; Libn Neurological Inst, NYC 50-51; Head gifts & exch Deering Lib Northwestern U 51-52; Asst acquis libn UWis(Madison) 52-59; Assoc dir SoIll U 59-. 9: ALA; IllLA. 10: St Louis Lib Club. 14: Tech serv. 15: 476 Buena Vista, Edwardsville Ill 62025.

HERSCHER, REV IRENAEUS (JOSEPH) OFM. b Guebwiller Haute-Alsace France 11 Mr 02. 5: St Bonaventure U 25-29 BA, 30 MA; Catholic U 31 STB; Columbia 33-34 MS in LS. 6: Ger, Lat, Fr, Hebrew, Gk. 7: Master of Clerics St Stephen Friary, Croghan NY 32-33; Asst Pastor St Stephen Parish, Croghan NY 32-33; Asst libn St Bonaventure U 34-37, Libn 37-, Prof of Educ & ancient langs 34-39. 8: Prof of courses in High Sch Lib Mgt, 35-39; Mem Bd of Operations, St Bonaventure U (2 terms); Bd of Discretes, Friary (2 terms); Chaplain St Joseph Manor, Olean NY. 9: CathLA; ALA; Franciscan Educ Conf (treas 47-); Inter-Amer B & LA; NYLA; West NY Cath Lib Conf (Charter mem); NY State Hist Soc. 10: O-Pa-Hi Hist Soc; Gallery of Living Cath Authors. 11: Citation from Canisius Col, Buffalo NY 58; Hon degree from St Bonaventure U. 12: Comp: "Preliminary Checklist of Franciscan literature" (52); "Franciscana: Bibliography of Works on St Francis in English (53);" "Checklist of Franciscan Literature (58). 13: Yes. 14: Rare bks, Franciscana, microfilm, microprint. 15: Friedsam Mem Lib, St Bonaventure NY 14778.

HERSCHMAN, JUDITH (SHAPIRO). b Brooklyn NY 6 Ap 39. 4: Arthur Herschman. 5: Goucher 56-58; Clark U 58-60 (Eng) BA; Columbia 66-68 MSLS. 6: Fr. 7: Asst to fine arts prof Clark U 60-61; Tchr North Jr High Sch, Brentwood NY 61-62; Asst libn Col Lib Columbia U 68-. 8: Mem Research Com, Columbia U Sch of Lib Serv. 9: ALA. 10: Phi Beta Kappa; Beta Phi Mu; ACLU; NAACP. 15: 215 W 88th st, New York NY 10024.

HERSE, DORIS LOUISE (WILDMAN). b Portland Ore 17 Ja 02. 4: Corvallis David Herse. 5: Portland Art Mus Sch 19-21 (Art); UOre Ext 22 (Art, Music); Northwestern Sch of Com 58-59 (Bus); Portland State Col Ext 60-62 (Russian). 7: Clerical Lib Assn of Portland, Ore 20-39; Window display designer First Nat Bank of Portland, Ore 30-59; Flutist Portland Symphony Orchestra 34-38; Flutist Radio Sta KWJJ 44-45, various other -60; Window displays Ore Mutual Savings Bank 45, 46; Artist free lance 30-60; Lib asst II UOre Med Sch 60-. 9: Portland Area Spec Libns. 10: Beaux Arts Soc. 14: Exhibits. 15: 5151 SW Cameron rd, Portland Ore 97221.

HERSHEY, FRANCES (BROOKS). b Baltimore Md 24 Ag 46. 4: Leon S Hershey Jr. 5: Kutztown State Col 64-66 (LS); Millersville State Col 66-68 (Lib Educ) BS in Ed. 7: Libn Warwick Sch Dist, Brunnerville 68-. 9: ALA; PennStateEA; WarwickEA. 14: Elem libnship. 15: RD 1, Gordonville Pa 17529.

HERSHEY, MARY SPENCER (ELIZABETH). b Detroit Mich 26 O 12. 5: UMich 32-35 (Fr, Hist of art) BA; UWis 31-32; Wayne State U 65-68 LSMS. 6: Fr. 7: Inter designer Jacob Co, Detroit Mich 35-39; Ref libn Marygrove Col, 67-. 9: UMich Alumnae; Village Women's Club; Otsego Ski Club; Wayne State U Lib Sci Alum Assn. 14: Ref. 15: 559 Half Moon rd, Birmingham Mi 48010.

HERSTEIN, SHEILA R. b Brooklyn NY 22 S 42. 5: Brooklyn Col 56-63 (Eng) BA; Columbia 63-64 (LS) MS; Brooklyn Col 66 (Hist). 6: Fr, Ger. 7: Soc sci & Acquis libn City Col Lib (NYC) 64-. 9: ALA; SLA; NY Lib Club; NY Tech Serv Libns; LACUNY. 10: AHA; AAUP; Victorian Soc Amer. 14: Ref, acquis. 15: 8001 Bay Parkway, Brooklyn NY 11214.

HERVI, WILLIAM M. b Rockport Mass 30 Mr 06. 5: Suomi Col 25-26; Eveleth Jr Col 26-27; UMinn(Minneapolis) 27-29 (Soc Sci) BS, 40 (Pub Sch Admin) MA, 55 (LS). 6: Finnish. 7: Prin & tchr St Louis Co, Duluth Minn 29-42; 3rd Armoured Div Code Clerk T-5 42-45; Tchr Soc Sci Morris Minn Pub Schs 46-47; Supt of Schs Hanska Pub Schs, Hanska Minn 47-54; Libn LLW High Sch & Gogebic Community Col 55-. 9: ALA; MichEA; Mich Assn of Higher Educ. 14: Ref, acquis. 15: 211 Hibbert st, Ironwood Mich 49938.

HERVIEUX, JANICE LEE. b Auburn NY 10 Ja 32. 5: SUNY (Plattsburgh) 49-53 (Home Econ, Educ) BS in Ed; SUNY (Cortland) 54-57 (Elem Educ) MS in Ed; URI 65-67 MLS. 6: Fr. 7: Tchr: Herkimer Sch Dist, Herkimer NY 53-55, Skaneateles Central Sch, Skaneatles NY 55-57, Dept of

Defense Schs, France, Japan, Philippines, Turkey, Libya 57-65; Libn N Smithfield Sch Dept, N Smithfield RI 65-67; Elem libn Wm T Sampson Sch, Guantanamo Bay Cuba 67-68; Educ specialist Dept of the Navy Atlantic Area Overseas Schs 68-. 8: Traveling interviewer Dept of Defense Overseas Schs 69. 9: ALA; NEA; -DAVI; OverseasEA; DCLA. 14: Sch libs. 15: Brookside apts 601 Four Mile rd, Alexandria Va 22305.

HERX, MARYBETH. b Chicago 31 D 28. 5: Rosary Col 46-50 (LS) BA; Washington U 52-53; Ill Inst of Tech 57-58; UWis 62-63 MALS. 6: Fr, Ger. 7: Asst libn St Louis U Lib 50-51; Asst libn Washington U Libs (St Louis) 51-53; Army libn US Army Europe Spec Serv, Frankfurt Germany 54-56; Asst libn World Book Encyclopedia Ref Lib, Chicago 56-62; Ref libn Wright Jr Col Lib 63-. 9: ALA. 10: Chicago Lib Club; AAUP; Beta Phi Mu; Coun Lib Tech. 14: Ref, chem lit. 15: 3130 N Menard ave, Chicago Il 60634.

HERZINGER, SANDRA SUE (OTT). b Lincoln Neb 14 Ag 39. 4: Morelle H Herzinger. 5: Neb Wesleyan U 57-60 (Educ, Hist) BA; UIll 62-63 (LS) MS. 7: Tchr Pawnee City Pub Schs, Pawnee City Neb 60-61; Jr libn UNeb Libs 61-62; Asst libn Rantoul Twp High Sch, Rantoul Ill 63-65; Assoc catlgr UNeb Libs 65-66, Abel libn 67-69, Pre-catlg libn 69-. 9: NebLA. 10: Beta Phi Mu;Kappa Delta Phi; Pi Gamma Mu; Phi Kappa Phi. 14: Catlg. 15: 611 Leavitt lane, Lincoln Neb 68510.

HESELMEYER, CAROLYN LOUISE. b St Louis 19 Ap 40. 5: Peabody 58-60 (Home Econ); Catawba Col 61-63 (Soc Sci) AB; Peabody 64-65 MLS. 7: Tchr Bradley Co Bd of Educ, Cleveland Tenn 63-64; Asst ref libn USoFla 65-67; Hd pub serv Birmingham So Col 67-68; Hd ref dept Chattanooga Pub Lib, Chattanooga Tenn 68-. 9: SELA; TennLA; Chattanooga Area LA. 14: Ref. 15: 3501 Dayton blvd apt B26, Chattanooga Tn 37415.

HESKETH, LILLIAN E (SEMPLE). b West Middlesex Pa 11 Jl 22. 4: Thomas H Hesketh. 5: Westminster Col 40-44 (Fr) AB; UWis 45 (Educ, Lang); UOhio summer 54 (Journalism); Kan State Equiv MLS; UUtah Equiv MLS; Allegheny Col 68-69 (Educ) MA. 6: Fr, Sp. 7: Tchg: W Middlesex High Sch 44-46, Mercer Joint High Sch 46-51, New Brighton High Sch 51-52, Sharon High Sch 52-55; Sub tchr Randolph-E Mead Schs 55-59, Hd Eng dept & libn 59-66, Lib supv 66-67; Ser libn Hamilton Lib Edinboro State Col 67, Asst prof Lib Sci Dept 67-. 8: Mem Middle State Eval Com 67. 9: ALA; NCTE; NEA; PennLA (Pub Rel Com 68); PennStateEA. 10: Alpha Beta Alpha; Phi Sigma Phi; Kappa Delta Phi; Culbertson Hills Country Club; Heather Club; AAUP; AAHE. 13: Yes. 14: Tchg lib sci & ref. 15: Valley View dr RD 1, Edinboro Pa 16412.

HESLAM, BARBARA MARSHALL. b Fitchburg Mass 19 S 16. 5: Jackson Col 39 (Hist) BA; Columbia 47 (LS) BS. 7: Libn Dean Acad & Jr Col, Franklin Mass 42-45; Br libn Morrill Mem Lib, Norwood Mass 45-48; Libn Levi Heywood Mem Lib, Gardner Mass 48-61; Asst libn Wellesley Free Lib, Wellesley Mass 61-62; Reg libn Central Mass Reg Lib System, Fitchburg Mass 62-. 9: ALA; NELA; MassLA. 10: Quota Internat; Bay Path Lib Club. 15: 108 Prichard st, Fitchburg Mass 01420.

HESLIN, JAMES J. b Cambridge Mass 25 Je 16. 4: Phyllis Stacy Brissette. 5: Boston Col 49 (Hist); Boston U 49 (Hist) MA, 52 (Hist) PhD; Columbia 54 (LS) MS. 6: Fr. 7: US Army 43-46; Ref dept NY Pub Lib 52-54; 1st asst Amer hist div NY Pub Lib 53-54; Asst dir U libs UBuffalo 55-56; NY Hist Soc: Asst dir, libn 56-58, Assoc dir, libn 58-60, Dir, libn 60-. 8: Middle States Accredit Program (Lib) 56; Mem, NY State Educ Dept (var projs rel to hist observances); Analysis of state histns off; Consul on NY State Mus; Lecturer in hist, Columbia U 59-; Consul, NY State Coun on the Arts. 9: Amer Antiq Soc; AHA; Amer Assn State & Loc Hist (Coun); BSA (2nd v-pres); Colonial Soc of Mass; Mass Hist Soc. 10: Trustee, Sleepy Hollow Restorations Inc; Trustee, Soc for Preserv of LI Antiquities; Grolier Club (NY); Century Assn (NY); Coffee House (NY). 12: Co-auth: "Keepers of the Past," (65); "Museum and Education" (68); chm Publns Com, Soc Preserv of LI Antiquities. 13: Yes. 14: Admin, ref. 15: 170 Central Park W, New York NY 10024.

HESS, ADELINE (LAYAOU). b Dorranceton Penn 6 N 15. 4: Charles Frederick Hess Jr. 5: Bloomsburg State Tchrs Col 32-34 (Elem Educ) Certif; Mansfield State Tchrs Col 50-52 (Elem Educ) BS; Clarion State Col 58 (LS); Penn State U 56-57 (Secondary Eng, SS, Guidance); Marywood Col 59-62 MSLS. 6: Fr, Lat. 7: Elem tchr Kingston Twp Schs, Trucksville Penn 34-35; Tchr Language Arts 52-55; Eng, Soc Studies, Guidance tchr Jr High Sch, Wellsboro Penn 55-58; Libn Jr High Sch, Wellsboro Penn 58-63; Spec reading Sr High Sch, Manheim Penn 63-64; Libn Lower Paxton Jr High Sch, Harrisburg Penn 64-65; Asst Prof Mansfield State Col 65-66; Sch lib development adv Pa Dept Pub Instr 66-. 8: Cooperating tchr with Mansfield State Col Dept of Lib Educ 62-63. 9: ALA; NEA; PennLA; Penn State EA. 10: AAUP; Certified Lay Speaker Methodist Church Central Penn Conf; Delta Kappa Gamma; Kappa Delta Pi. 14: Sch lib admin. 15: Rt 3 Box 586, Harrisburg Penn 17112.

HESS, ANNE (ELIZABETH). b Lake Charles La 1 O 40. 5: Tex Lutheran Col 58-62 (Soc Sci) BA; Southwest BusU summer 59, 60; UTex 62-63 MLS. 7: Lib intern Cal State Col (Los Angeles) 63-64; Ref libn Douglas Aircraft Co, Huntington Beach Cal 64-65, Lib supv 65-68; Admin asst (lib) Cal State Col (Los Angeles) 68-. 9: ALA; CalLA; OrangeCoLA (dir 66-67; rec sec 67-68). 14: Admin, ref. 15: 4600 E Broadway, Long Beach Ca 90803.

HESS, DOROTHY JEAN (COBLE). b Uniontown Penn 7 Ap 30. 5: Bethany Col 49-53 (Eng lit) BA; USoCal 56-57 MS in LS. 7: Libn San Diego Pub Lib 57-62; Hd libn Uniontown Pub Lib, Uniontown Penn 67-. 9: ALA; PennLA. 10: Art Club; DAR. 14: Catlg. 15: 70 Virginia ave, Uniontown Pa 15401.

HESS, EDWARD FREDERICK JR. b Chicago 15 Ja 19. 4: Betty Jane Stone. 5: Northwestern 37-41 (Zool, chem) BS; UIll Col of Law 45-47 JD; UIll 62-63 (LS) MS. 6: Ger. 7: (Lt) USNR 41-45; Attorney Stone Stone & Hess, Bloomington Ill 48-52; Sr property adjuster State Farm Insur Co, Bloomington Ill 52-53; Asst reporter of decisions Ill Supreme Court, Bloomington Ill 53-62; Libn US Court of Appeals 9th Circuit, San Francisco 63-64; Ref asst UIll Col of Law Lib 64-65; Assoc law libn UIll Col of Law Lib (Champaign) 65-. 9: AALL (Automation & Scientific Devel Com); ChicagoALL; IllLibA; Ill State Bar Assn. 14: Automation in Law Libraries. 15: Lib, Univ of Ill Col of Law, Champaign Ill 61822.

HESS, EDWARD J. b Hamburg Iowa 18 F 25. 5: Iowa State U 42-43 (Electrical Engnr); Peru Neb State Col 46-49 (Secondary Educ-Soc Sci) BA; USoCal 49-50 (Pol Sci) MA, 56-57 MSLS, 63-65 (LS). 6: Fr, Ger. 7: Combat engnr soldier US Army, US & Europe 43-46; Tchr High Sch & Jr High Sch, Mo & Cal 50-56; San Diego State Col Lib: Catlgr 57-58, Ser libn 58-59, Supv of pub serv 59-61, Tech serv libn 61-63; Lib Dir Lompoc Pub Lib, Lompoc Cal 65-66; Asst col libn San Fernando Valley State Col 66-. 8: Lect & Asst Prof Sch of Lib Sci, USoCal 67-68; Bldg consul to Lompoc Pub Lib, Lompoc Cal 67-68. 9: ASIS; ALA; SLA (Mem chm San Diego Chap 61-62); AALS; CalLA (chm Bylaws Com 68-); So Cal Tech Proc Gp. 10: Beta Phi Mu; Kappa Delta Pi; Libraria Sodalitas. 12: Ed "California Librarian" (69). 13: Yes. 14: Admin, lib automation, info sci. 15: 517 N Vista Bonita ave, Glendora Ca 91740.

HESS, JOYCE. b Shreveport La 4 F 18. 4: George A Hess. 5: Tex ChristianU 51-66 (Art & Eng) BA; UTex 66-69 MLS. 6: Fr. 7: Clerical Shreve Mem Lib, Shreveport La 35-42; Reservations Chicago & So Air Lines, Shreveport La 42-45; Ticket agt Nat Air Lines, Miami Fla 45-48; Art libn UTex (Austin) 67-. 9: ALA; TexLA. 10: Laguna Gloria Art Mus. 15: 908 Red Bud trail, Austin Tx 78703.

HESS, MARION (GALLUP). b Homer NY 5 Ap 08. 4: Orion E Hess. 5: Syracuse 26-29, 30-31 (Hist) AB, summers 31-34 BS in LS, summer 35 (Fr, Lat). 6: Fr. 7: Hist tchr & high sch libn Weedsport Central Sch, Weedsport NY 31-37; Libn Lyman Hall High Sch, Wallingford Conn 37-39; Assoc libn State U Col (Potsdam NY) 48-. 9: NYLA; NY State Tchrs Assn. 10: No Zone, NY State Tchrs Col Faculties; Civil Serv Employees Assn; Fac Assn SUNY; St Lawrence Co Hist Assn; Pi Gamma Mu; N Country 3R Coun. 14: Ref, interlib loan, personnel. 15: 97 Main st, Potsdam NY 13676.

HESS, SUE IRENE (THOMSON) HYDE. b Emporia Kan 10 N 21. 4: Will D Hess. 5: Col of Emporia 39-43 (Home Econ) BA; Kan State Tchrs Col (Emporia) 59-60, 61 (LS) MS. 6: Sp, Portu. 7: Sch libn Lawrence Pub Schs, Lawrence Kan 60-62; Catlgr UKan Watson Lib 62-; Libn curriculum materials resources ctr Lawrence Pub Schs 68-. 9: KanLA. 12: Comp "An Annotated Bibliography of Education Periodicals in William Allen White Library, Kansas State Teachers College, Emporia," with R S Thurman (60). 14: Catlg. 15: 1531 Davis rd, Lawrence Kan 66044.

HESSER, ELIZABETH. b Wash DC 23 D 09. 5: Mary Baldwin Col 26-30 (Eng) BA; Johns Hopkins summer 30 (LS), summer 31 (Liberal Arts); Columbia 31-32 BS in LS. 7: Asst circ dept Enoch Pratt Free Lib, Baltimore 30-31; Prof asst

Queens Borough Pub Lib, Jamaica NY 32-33, Sch libn 33-35; 2nd asst circ dept Enoch Pratt Free Lib, Baltimore 35-41, Br libn 41-45; Dir Lockport Pub Lib, Lockport NY 45-49; Supv of brs Indianapolis Pub Lib 49-57; Libn Osterhout Free Lib, Wilkes-Barre Penn 57-. 9: ALA (chm Personnel Admin Sect 62-63); Penn LA (sec 59-60). 10: Soroptimist Club; Adver Club of Wilkes-Barre; UN Assn; C of C; Luzerne Co Mental Health Assn; Citizens Assembly of Welfare Planning Coun. 14: Admin, adult serv, personnel, pub rel. 15: Osterhout Free Lib, 71 S Franklin st, Wilkes-Barre Pa 18701.

HESSLEIN, SHIRLEY (BOB). b NYC 2 S 18. 4: Milton Hesslein. 5: Barnard 40 (Chem) AB; Columbia 41 (High Sch Sci Tchg) MA; Rutgers 64-67 MLS. 7: Asst lib Fed Water Pollution Control Admin, Edison NJ 66-67; Libn Nassau Co Dept of Health, Mineola NY 67-69; Asst lib SUNY at Buffalo 69-. 9: ALA; MedLA; SLA. 10: Beta Phi Mu. 14: Med, ref. 15: 94 Lexington ave, Buffalo NY 14222.

HESTER, BERNICE (JOHNSON). b Middlesex Co Va 27 N 23. 4: Gandhi G Hester. 5: Virginia State Col 41-43 (Soc Studies) AB; Columbia 49 (LS); Hampton Inst 61. 6: Fr. 7: Libn w side High Sch, Smithfield Va 43-65; Ref libn J C Breckinridge Lib, Marine Corps Base Quantico Va 65-. 8: Mem Performance Rating Bd, Marine Corps Base Quantico Va 66-69. 9: VaLA. 14: Ref, circ, interlib loan. 15: 324 McKinney st, Fredericksburg Va 22401.

HESTER, GOLDIA (ANN). b Graham Tex 5 Je 33. 5: Austin Col 50-54 (Eng) BA; UTex 55-56 (Eng) MA, 61-65 MLS. 7: Tchr Colo High Sch, Colorado City Tex 54-55; Asst libn Austin Col 55-61; Catlgr Austin Presbyterian Sem 61-65, Act libn 64; Ref libn UTex 65-. 9: ALA; TexLA. 14: Ref. 15: 703C W 25th st, Austin Tx 78705.

HESTER, HELEN WILSON. b Rustburg Va 5 Ja 28. 5: Randolph-Macon 46-50 (Lat) AB; Rutgers 65 MLS. 7: Lab tech Merck & Co, Rahway NJ 51-65, Libn 65-. 15: 831-21 Academy Terr, Linden NJ 07085.

HESTER, IRENE. b Winston-Salem NC 28 S 08. 5: UNC(Greensboro) 26-30 AB in LS. 7: Libn Burlington Pub Lib, Burlington NC 30-36; Libn Kinston Pub Lib, Kinston NC 36-40; Dist train supv WPA Lib Proj, Williamston NC 40-43; Libn Sheppard Mem Lib, Greenville NC 43-50; Head ref dept Greensboro Pub Lib, Greensboro NC 51-. 9: ALA; NCLA; SELA; Greensboro Lib Club, 10: Bus & Prof Women's Club. 14: Ref, NC & loc hist. 15: 533 Audubon dr, Greensboro NC 27410.

HESTER, WILDA M (MULLINS). b Clinton Mo 29 Je 13. 4: Daniel LeRoy Hester. 5: State U Iowa 31-35 (Sociol) BA, 35-36 (Sociol & Lib Educ) MA. 7: Visiting tchr Des Moines Schs, Des Moines Iowa 37-40; Bkkeeping machine operator Fed Housing Agency, Wash DC 42-43; US Army Hostess-libn US Army, Ft Des Moines Iowa 43-44; Dir spec facilities Fed Housing Agency, Wash DC 44-45; Catlg clerk State U Iowa Libs 52-53; Sec VA Hosp, Iowa City Iowa 53-59, Libn 59-. 9: ALA; IowaLA. 10: LWV; Alpha Kappa Alpha. 14: Admin, hosp & inst libs. 15: VA Hosp, Iowa City Ia 52241.

HETLER, ELIESE (FELSENTHAL). b Germany 20 Ag 20. 4: Louis Hetler. 5: UOkla 39-43 (Soc Wk) BA, 42-43 BALS; State U Col (Brockport NY) 60-. 6: Ger. 7: Ref libn NY Pub Lib 45-46; Head of govt documents & period UDenver 51-52; Asst br libn Denver Pub Lib 56-57; Asst col libn State U Col (Brockport NY) 58-60; Elem sch libn Hilton Central Sch, Hilton NY 60-63; Lib Dir Chili Pub Lib, Chili NY 64-65; Asst col libn State U Col (Brockport NY) 65-. 8: Steering com for reg Union List of Ser. 9: ALA; NYLA. 10: AAUW; SUC(Brockport) Fac Senate 14: Ref, ser, tchg, bk sel, govt docs. 15: 29 Carolin dr, Brockport NY 14420.

HETRICK, CATHERINE R(ICKERT) Q(UINN). b Phila 24 Ap 15. 5: UIll 33-37 (Hist) BA; USDA Grad Sch 56-57 (Russian) Certif; US Civil Serv Courses 62, 64, 65 (Info Storage & Retrieval) Certifs. 6: Ger, Russian. 7: Jr lib asst USDA NE Br, Upper Darby Penn 42-43; Lib asst USDA Beltsville Br, Md 43-44; Lib asst ser div LC 44-45; Asst libn & Libn US Naval Station Libs, Norfolk Va & Cal 45-46; Catlgr Pub Roads Admin Lib, Wash DC 47-49; Catlgr ser The Army Lib Pentagon, Wash DC 49-56; Chief Libn Air Force Off of Sci Research, Wash DC 56-. 8: Consul on Cataloging to US Army War Col Lib, Carlisle Penn. 9: ALA; SLA (Wash DC Chap: pres, other minor offs; Mil Libns Group: var offs); DCLA; Potomac Valley Proc Libns; Bus & Profess Women's Club. 11: Outstanding Performance & Sustained Superior Performance Awards (USAF), 59 & 61. 12: Chm of ed Com, "Union List of Military Periodicals" (60). 14: Catlg, admin. 15: 3506 15th st N, Arlington Va 22201.

HETZNER, BERNICE M(ARTIN). b Omaha Neb 15 Ap 09. 4: Ralph W Hetzner. 5: Creighton U 30-33 (Biol Sci); UDenver 33-34 BALS; Colo State Col (Greeley) 34-35 (Educ) MA. 7: Supv sch libs Omaha pub schs 35-38; Libn II Los Angeles Co Lib, Los Angeles 38-43; Asst Amsterdam Br NY Pub Lib, NYC 43; Catlgr St Elizabeth Hosp Sch Nursing, Lincoln Neb 44; Admin asst Lincoln City Lib, Lincoln Neb 44-46; Catlgr UNeb Col of Med 47-48, Libn 48-. 8: Consul VA Hosp Libs, Omaha & Lincoln Neb 56; Assn Amer Med Col-Med LA joint Com on Guidelines for Med Sch Libs 63-64. 9: MedLA (Bd Dir 59-62, chm coms on Standards, Finance, Central Off & Gifts & Grants; Adv Com on Med Lib Problems); ALA; SLA; MPLA; NebLA; Central States Reg Med Lib Gp (v-chm, sec-treas, Exec Com). 11: MedLA Murray Gottlieb Prize Essay Award 58. 13: Yes. 14: Med lib admin. 15: UNeb Col of Med, Omaha Nb 68105.

HEUMANN, KARL F(REDRICH). b Chicago 3 Mr 21. 4: Doris Wilkinson. 5: Iowa State U 38-42 (Chem) BS, 43 (Chem) MS; UIll 51 (Organic Chem) PhD; Catholic U 53-54 (LS). 6: Ger, Span. 7: USNR (Lt jg) 44-46; Tech aide Chem-Biol Coord Center NAS-NRC, Wash DC 46-47; Chem Tech Info 3M Co, St Paul 50-52; Dir Chem-Biol Coord Center NAS-NRC, Wash DC 52-55; Dir of Research Chem Abstracts, Columbus Ohio 55-59; Dir Off of Documentation Nat Acad of Sci, Wash DC 59-66; Exec ed Fed of Amer Socs for Expt Biol 66-, Dir off of editing info serv 68-. 8: Dir USBE; Trustee, "Engnr Index"; Adv Com, "American Men of Science"; Chm Gordon Research Conf, 62; chm Jt Com "Union List of Serials" 68-; Sec Coun Biol Eds 69-; Adv Com Nat Translations Ctr 69-; Dir Council Biol Sci Info 68-; Consul Consejo de Rectores Chilean Univs 68. 10: Pacific Sci Assn (Com on Sci Info 64-); ASIS (pres 59); ACS (chm Div Chem Lit 60); ASA Z39; Internat Fed for Documentation (v-pres 61-64); SLA (Sci-Tech Chm Wash DC Chap). 12: Exec ed: Federation Proceedings; Journal of Nutrition; Am J Clinical Nutrition. 13: Yes. 14: Sci info, machine documentation, internat rel. 15: 6410 Earlham dr, Bethesda Md 20034.

HEURTLEY, JASNA. b Split Yugoslavia 24 S 14. 4: Richard W Heurtley. 5: UZagreb(Yugoslavia) 39 (Law) Dr Jur; Columbia 55 MLS; NYU 58-63 (Art Hist). 6: Fr, Sp, Ital, Ger, Serbo-Croatin, Lat, Portu, Czech, Bulgarian. 7: Chief of Transl Sect Internat Refugee Org, Rome 45-49; Humanities libn Hunter Col 55-56; Ref libn Metropolitan Museum of Art, NYC 56-63; Libn Parapsychology Found, NYC 65-66; Lang tchr Tutoring Sch of NYC 63-65; Spec Serv Grant Project NY Acad of Med, NYC 67-. 9: SLA. 10: Westchester Sport Club; Association des Professeurs de Francais; Eng-Speaking Union; Volunteers of the Shelter; United European Amer Club; Harvard Club; Appalachian Mountain Club. 13: Yes. 14: Ref, rare bks. 15: 16 E 98th st, New York NY 10029.

HEUSER, PHYLLIS ELAINE. b Louisville Ky 18 My 32. 5: UKy 50-54 (LS, Hist) AB in Ed, 60-63 MSLS; Simmons summer 66. 07: Assoc supv of lib serv Edgewood Ind Sch Dist, San Antonio Tex 54-55; Libn Boone Co High Sch, Florence Ky 55-60; Libn Waggener High Sch, Louisville Ky 60-. 9: ALA; AASchL; NEA; KyASchL; KyLA; KyEA; SELA. 10: AAUW; Kappa Delta Pi; Delta Kappa Gamma; Ky Hist Soc; Filson Club; UKy Dept Lib Sci Alum. 14: Catlg. 15: 2905 Arlington rd, Louisville Ky 40220.

HEUSSMAN, JOHN WILLIAM. b Atwood Kan 24 Ag 28. 4: Johanna Schoenberg. 5: Concordia Col (Seward Neb) 46-50 (Educ) BS; UDenver 50-53 (LS) MA; UIll 62- (LS). 6: Ger. 7: Asst libn Concordia Tchrs Col (Seward Neb) 50-52; Libn Concordia Tchrs Col High Sch, Seward Neb 52-54; Concordia Theol Sem (Springfield Ill): Dir of the Lib 54-67, Registrar 58-60, Act acad dean 63-64; Tchg asst Grad Lib Sch UIll summer 63, Lib admin asst U Ill (Urbana-Champaign) 67-. 8: Dist archivist Lutheran Church Mo Synod 54-67. 9: ALA; Lutheran Educ Assn; IllLA. 10: Phi Kappa Phi. 12: Ed Bd "Concordia Hist Inst Quarterly." 14: Admin, tech serv, collections, surveys. 15: 1005 Hollycrest, Champaign Il 61820.

HEWITT, CHARLES H(ENRY). b Charles City Iowa 30 Mr 22. 4: Betty Jane Everett. 5: UAriz 40-44 (Anthropology) BA; Chicago 44-46, 49 (Soc Anthropology) MA; UIll 51-52 MLS. 6: Fr, Sp. 7: Soc anthropologist Gen Educ Bd UChicago 47-48; Depth interviewer Social Research Inc, Chicago 50; Driver bkmob Ext Dept Gary (Ind) Pub Lib 50-51; Stud libn Nat Hist Lib UIll(Urbana) 51-52; Libn I-III Detroit Pub Lib 52-59; Head br dept Flint Pub Lib, Flint Mich 59-. 8: Commissioned (57-58) by Off for Adult Educ ALA to prep report of all projects financed through the Fund for Adult Educ & admin by the ALA 51-58. 9: ALA (mem Notable Bks Coun); MichLA (chm Adult Educ Sect; Exh Com, Recr Com). 10: Beta Phi Mu; Bd of Deacons Woodside Church (Flint Mich); Greater

Flint (Mich) Coun of Churches (Church in Soc Com). 12: "Grant Evaluation Study" (58). 14: Br lib admin, adult educ. 15: 1913 Forest Hill ave, Flint Mi 48504.

HEWITT, IRENE MARIE (TROTTIER). b Belle River Ont Can 14 F 10. 4: Robert D Hewitt. 5: UWest Ont 27-30 (Romance Langs) BA; UToronto Col of Educ 30-31 High Sch Specialist's Certif; UMich 61-63 AMLS. 6: Fr, Sp, Ital. 7: Tchr Smooth Rock Falls High Sch, Smooth Rock Falls Ont 31-32; Payroll clerk Studebaker Corp, Walkerville Ont 33-38; Lib asst Windsor Pub Lib, Windsor Ont 56-62; Libn Windsor Tchrs Col (Windsor Ont) 62-. 8: Staff Summer Sch for Elem Sch Libns, Toronto Ont Dept of Educ. 9: OntLA. 10: Univ Women's Club of Windsor. 14: Child lit, rare bks (child). 15: 224 Prado pl, Windsor Ont Can.

HEWITT, JOHN HOLLIS. b Boston 4 D 15. 4: Barbara Burleigh. 5: Harvard 34-38 (Ger) BA; Cornell U 38-39 (Ger) MA; Syracuse 40-41 BLS. 6: Ger, Fr. 7: Br libn Buffalo (NY) Pub Lib 41-42; Sr design engnr Raytheon Co, Newton Mass 43-46; Head document room Res Lab of Electronics MIT 46-. 8: Lib Bd, Episcopal Diocese of Mass 65-70. 9: SLA (Exhib Chm 57 meeting, Bul Distrib Mgr 59-60, 67-; Boston Chap: Placement Chm 52-54, Adv Chm 60-63). 14: Documentation, lib automation. 15: 1371 Walnut st, Newton Highlands Ma 02161.

HEWITT, JULIA FRANCES. b Schuylerville NY 4 O 29. 5: SUNY (Albany) 47-51 (Com) BS, 61-64 (LS) MS. 7: Accountant Gen Electric Co, Schenectady NY 51-61, Lib trainee 61-62, Lib catlgr 62-65, Ref libn 65-. 9: SLA (Upstate NY Chap: asst bulletin ed 65-66; bulletin ed 66-67; sec 67-68); Hudson MohawkLA; Capital Dist Ref & Research Resources. 10: Chi Sigma Theta; Pi Omega Pi. 13: Yes. 14: Ref. 15: General Electric Co Main Library Bldg 2 1 River rd, Schenectady NY 12305.

HEWITT, MARYLOUISE (MANN). b Reading Penn 27 F 35. 4: Robert George Hewitt. 5: State Tchrs Col (Kutztown Penn) 52-56 (LS) BS Ed; State U Col (Geneseo NY) summers 57-58 (LS). 7: High sch libn Liberty Central Sch, Liberty NY 56-58; Dir Pub Lib, Port Jervis NY 58; Asst libn Compton Adv Agency, NYC 59; Ref libn Equitable Life Assurance Soc, NYC 60-61; Indexer "Education Index" H W Wilson Co, Bronx NY 61-. 9: ALA; NY Lib Club. 14: Catlg, indexing. 15: 1309 University ave, Bronx NY 10452.

HEWITT, VIVIAN (ANN) D(AVIDSON). b New Castle Penn. 4: John H Hewitt. 5: Geneva Col 43 (Fr, Psych) AB; Carnegie 44 BS in LS; UPittsburgh 47-48. 6: Fr. 7: Sr asst libn Homewood br Carnegie Lib, Pittsburgh 44-49; Instr-Libn Sch of Lib Serv Atlanta U 49-51; Researcher & asst to Dir Readers' Ref Serv, NYC 53-55; Libn Rockefeller Found, NYC 55-63; Libn Carnegie Endowment for Internat Peace, NYC 63-. 8: Consul to Ed of "Library Literature" regarding changes in subj headings 49; Lib of the Rockefeller Found's Mexican Agric Program, Mexico City summer 58; UN Nongovernmental Orgs observer for SLA 64-; SLA Rep to Pacem In Terris Convocation 65; SLA Rep to White House Conf on Internat Coop Year 65. 9: ALA; SLA (Non-Govtal Observer to UN 64-; NY Chap chm Med-Biol Dir 61-63); MedLA (chm Hospitality, NY Chap 64-65; Asst sec 66-67; Prog chm 67-68 & 68-69; Deputy Conv chm 67; 1st v-pres & pres-elect NY Chap 69-70). 10: Alpha Kappa Alpha; Marriage Inst St Philips P E Church, NYC (chm); Jack & Jill of Amer Inc (pres). 11: Creative Writing Award, Geneva Col. 12: Contr Article on Foundations & Funds "Collier's Yearbook" (56-); Consul to ed of "Catalogue of Publications," Carnegie Found for Internat Peace 68. 14: Ref, acquis, ser, UN docts, recr, tchg. 15: Carnegie Endowment for Internat Peace, 345 E 46th st, New York NY 10017.

HEWLETT, LEROY. b Salem Ore 26 O 29. 4: Alyce Kay Whitesell. 5: UOre 48-51 (Hist) BA; West Res 51-52 MSLS; UMich(Ann Arbor) 56-57 (Hist) MA, 56-58 (LS) PhD. 6: Fr, Ger. 7: Asst libn Boise Jr Col 52-54; 1st Asst tech serv Ore State Lib 58-64, Fine & Applied arts consul 64-. 8: Research asst Sch of Lib Sci UMich 57-58, Travel fellowship 57-58. 9: ALA; PNLA; OreLA. 10: Phi Beta Mu. 12: 'James Rivington' in "Books in America" (66). 14: Americana (espec Revolutionary period), catlg, ref. 15: 680 Thompson ave NE, Salem Or 97301.

HEWLETT, RUTH VARICK. b Buffalo NY 30 My 06. 5: UBuffalo 27-30 (LS, Sociol, Ethn) BA & Certif in Lib Sci; UAriz 33-38 (Archaeol); UMich summer 38, 39 MA in LS. 6: Fr, Sp. 7: Asst open shelf dept Buffalo Pub Lib, Buffalo NY 30-32; Asst in circ ref & catlg UAriz 33-38; Catlgr child bks Akron Pub Lib, Akron Ohio 39-40; Catlgr UMd 41-44; Jr libn USDA Bur Animal Ind Zool Div, Beltsville Md 44-47; Supv Art Lib Syracuse U 47-61; Ref libn Tufts U Lib 61-. 9: SLA. 10: AAUW. 13: Yes. 14: Ref, spec collections. 15: 49 Dover st, Somerville Ma 02144.

HEYER, ANITA (LIDEN). b Norrkoping Sweden 5 N 39. 5: ULund (Sweden) 59-52, 64-65 MA; Augustana Col (Rock Island Ill) 62-63 BA; UIll (Urbana) 63-64 MSLS. 6: Swedish, Norwegian, Danish, Ger, Fr, Sp. 7: Libn Bibliotekstjanst The Lib Serv Inc, Lund sweden 61-62, 65; Dir of lib and ref serv The Swedish Info Serv, NYC 65-. 9: SLA. 10: Beta Phi Mu. 12: "20 ars basta barnbocker" (65). 13: Yes. 14: Ref. 15: 2 Tudor City pl, New York NY 10017.

HEYER, ANNA HARRIET. b Little Rock Ark 30 Ag 09. 5: Tex Christian U 26-30 (Math) BA, 26-30 (Piano) B Music; UIll 32-33 BS in LS; Columbia 38-39 MS in LS; UMich 42-43 (Musicology) M Music. 6: Fr, Ger. 7: Elem music tchr Ft Worth Pub Schs, Ft Worth Tex 31-32, High sch libn 34-38; Catlgr UTex 39-40; Music libn & Asst Prof of Lib Serv N Tex State U 40-65; Consul on music lib materials Tex Christian U 65-. 9: ALA; MusLA; Amer Musicological Soc; Tex LA; Tex Musicological Soc. 10: AAUP; AAUW; Delta Kappa Gamma; Pi Kappa Lambda; Alpha Chi; Sigma Alpha Iota; Alpha Beta Alpha; Woman's Club of Ft Worth; Fine Arts Dept of Woman's Shakespeare Club, Denton Tex; Altrusa; Univ Place Bk Dept of Univ Place Study Club, Fort Worth, Tex. 12: "A Check-List of Publications of Music" (44); "A Bibliography of Contemporary Music in the Music Library, No Tex State Col" (55); "Historical Sets, Collected Editions, and Monuments of Music; a Guide to Their Contents" (ALA 57, 2nd ed 69). 13: Yes. 14: Music libnship. 15: 2538 Greene ave, Ft Worth Tex 76109.

HEYER, MILDRED (ALMINA) J. b Sawyer ND 2 Ja 08. 5: State Tchrs Col (Minot ND) 23-25, summers 26-28 (Educ); UND summer 29; UMinn summer 31; State Tchrs Col (Minot ND) summer 32 BA; UDenver summers 57-59 (LS) MA. 7: Tchr pub schs, ND 25-42; Tchr pub schs, Nev 42-57; Libn Rancho High Sch, Las Vegas Nev 57-59; Sch lib supv Clark Co Schs, Las Vegas Nev 59-61; State Libn State of Nev, Carson City Nev 62-. 8: Chm, Sch Lib Devel Proj, NevLA 61-62; V-chm & sec Nev Coun on Libs 65-. 9: ALA; MPLA; NevLA (pres 59-60). 10: Delta Kappa Gamma; Soroptimist Club; Bus & Prof Women; Toastmistress Club. 14: Admin. 15: 205 Corbett st, Carson City Nev 89701.

HEYMAN, JULIANE M. b Free City of Danzig 25 Mr 25. 5: Barnard 42-46 (Intl Studies) BA; UCal 46-48 (Intl Rel) MA, 48-49 MLS. 6: Ger, Fr, Sp. 7: Libn USAF, Japan 50-52; Libn San Francisco State Col 53-55; Research pol scientist UCal (Berkley) 55-56; Research off Asia Foundation, San Francisco 56-58; Libn Adv Mich State U, Vietnam 57-59; Train off Peace Corps, Wash DC 62-65; Deputy dir George Washington U 65-66; Project off Intl Rel Off ALA, Wash DC 67-. 8: Lib consul: Ford Found, Pakistan 61; Asia Found (Vietnam & Cambodia). 9: ALA. 10: Asian Studies Assn; Amer Pol Sci Assn; Com on SE Asian Research Materials. 12: Ed "Libraries in International Relations"; Co-auth "Survey of Nepal Society," HRAF; Co-auth "Pakistan Politics," HRAF. 13: Yes. 14: Intl devel, ref. 15: 2828 Connecticut ave, Washington DC 20008.

HEYNEMAN, ALAN LIONEL. b San Francisco 14 Mr 24. 4: Martha Tarpey. 5: Pomona Col 41-42 (Eng, Econ); UCal(Berkeley) 46-48 (Eng, Econ) AB, 48-49 BLS. 7: US Army, US, N Africa, Europe 43-45; LC: Spec recr, Wash DC 49, Admin asst, Wash DC 50-51, NYC rep, 51-52, Documents expediter, Wash DC 53-55; Chief of the Personnel Off NY Pub Lib 55-64; U Dir of Personnel URochester 64-. 8: Consul: Amer-Korean Found 54, Royal Govt of Afghanistan 55, var libs, corps, assns & govt agencies 55-; Instr in lib serv, Rutgers U summer 60. 9: ALA (Subs Bk Com 54-55, Pub Docs Com 55-57);-LAD (chm Nomin Com 58-59; mem Exec Com personnel Admin Sect 61-63; chm Recr Com NY-NJ 59-61); -LED (mem & chm Awards Com 64-67; -PLA (chm Nomin Com 62-63); NYLA (chm var coms 55-). 10: Overseas Press Club; Amer Soc for Personnel Admin; Amer Mgt Assn; Archons of Colophon; C of C; Urban League. 12: Books for Korea" (54); "Library Development Plan for Afghanistan" (55). 13: Yes. 14: Admin, org, personnel. 15: Admin Bldg, Univ of Rochester, Rochester NY 14627.

HEYSER, MARJORIE (ERWIN). b Austin Tex 7 S 14. 4: Robert Edward Heyser. 5: UTex (El Paso) 31-34 (Eng) BA; Pratt Inst 34-35 (LS) BA. 6: Fr, Sp. 7: Asst libn UTex (El Paso) Library 36-43; Coord tech serv El Paso Pub Lib, El Paso Tex 59-. 9: ALA; TexLA; Border Reg LA. 14: Tech serv (esp catlg). 15: 3259 Lebanon ave, El Paso 79930.

HIATT, LINDA RAE (SMITH). b Chicago Ill 15 F 44. 4: Peter Hiatt. 5: IndU 62-66 (Slavic Studies) AB, 66-67 (LS) MA. 6: Russian, Fr, Polish, Ger. 7: Catlg libn Ind StateU (Terre Haute) 67-68; Admin asst to dir IndU Lib (Bloomington) 68-. 8: Ind U's project libn for the Ind Libs Ser Data Bank 68-. 9: ALA; IndLA. 10: Beta Phi Mu. 13: Yes. 14: Slavic catlg, ser, writing & ed wk, tech serv. 15: 703 Gourley pike #199, Bloomington In 47401.

HIATT, PETER. b NYC 19 O 30. 4: Linda Rae Smith. 5: Colgate 48-52 (Hist) BA; Rutgers 55-57 MLS, 60-63 PhD. 7: (Cpl) US Army Ordnance, Aberdeen Md 52-54; Trainee Elizabeth (NJ) Pub Lib 54-57, Br libn 57-60; Research asst grad Lib Sch Rutgers U 60-61, Instr 61-62; Asst Prof Div of Lib Sci Ind U 63-65, Assoc Prof 66-; Consul Ind State Lib 66-; Dir Ind Lib Studies, Bloomington Ind 68-. 08: Consul & performer TV Ser "Legacy of the Library" 64; Dir adult serv Wkshop Wyo U State lib 65; Pub Lib consul & wkshop dir Ind 63-; Consul WICHE Coop Educ Devel Prog for Lib Personnel 68-69. 9: ALA (Jt ASL/LED Com on Educ of State Lib Personnel; Com on Organ);-RTSD (chm Reg Processing Com); SLA; AALS; ASIS; NJLA (sec, chm &/or mem 3 coms); IndLA (pres Ref Div); IndSchLA. 10: AAUP; Adult Educ Assn; Ind Adult Educ Assn. 12: "Public Library Branch Services for Adults of Low Education" (64); Monroe County Public Library: Planning for the Future (66); Co-auth & Public Library Services for the Functionally Illiterate: a Survey of Practice (67). 13: Yes. 14: Adult serv, pub lib lib educ, contin educ for libns. 15: 703 Gourley Pike 199, Bloomington Ind 47401.

HIBBERT, G JOYCE. b Tillsonburg Ont Can 16 S 32. 7: Reporter "Tillsonburg News" Tillsonburg Ont Can 51-54; Libn Ontario Paper Co Ltd, Thorold Ont Can 54-59; Libn Lond Free Press, Lond Ont Can 59-. 9: SLA. 10: Lecturer, Sch of Journalism, U West Ont, London Ont. 13: Yes. 14: Newspaper lib. 15: Libn London Free Press PO Box 2280 Terminal A, London Ont Can.

HIBBS, AGNES (RUTH). b Osborne Kan 27 F 10. 5: Kan State Tchrs Col 28-32, summer 38 9ls, bio Sci) BS in Ef; UMich 47-51 (Educ) AM. 7: Tchr & libn Osborne High Sch, Osborne Kan 33-38; Libn Franklin Jr-Sr High Sch, Cedar Rapids Iowa 38-47; Asst libn No Mich U 47-49; Catlg libn Coe Col 49-55; Hd tech serv dept pub lib, Cedar Rapids Iowa 55-. 9: ALA; IowaLA (chm Resources & Tech Processes Sect 52 & 61). 10: College Club. 14: Catlg. 15: 822 16th st SE, Cedar Rapids Ia 52403.

HIBBS, JACK EUGENE. b Toledo Ohio 14 Ja 33. 4: Janet Manley. 5: Kent State 51-53; UToledo 58-60 (Soc Sci) BEd, 65-69 MALS. 7: Cost clk Doehler-Jarvis Div, Toledo Ohio 54-58; Libn & tchr Woodville High Sch, Woodville Ohio 60-64; Instr in hist Whitmer High Sch, Toledo Ohio 64-65; Libn Northwood High Sch, Toledo Ohio 65-. 9: ALA; OhioASchL; OhioEA. 14: Sch libs, ref. 15: 210 Windsor rd apt 1, Walbridge Oh 43466.

HICKERSON, JOSEPH C(HARLES). b Highland Park Ill 20 O 35. 4: Lynn Russell. 5: Oberlin Col 53-57 (Physics) AB; Ind U 57-63 (Folklore) MA. 7: Folklore archivist Ind U Folklore Archive 60-63; Ref libn Archive of Folk Song LC 63-. 9: MusLA; Amer Folklore Soc; Soc for Ethnomusicology; Amer Inthrop Assn; Folklore Soc of Greater Wash (Memb Chm). 12: Bk review ed Bibliogr "Ethnomusicology: Journal of the Society for Ethnomusicology," "Newsletter of the Folklore Society of Greater Washington," (Ed). 13: Yes. 14: Ref, bibliog, archives (folk music & ethnomusicology). 15: Rt 1 Box 706-A, Accokeek Md 20607.

HICKEY, ANNE-THERESE (PISANI). b NYC 28 Mr 28. 4: Herbert Augustine Hickey. 5: Georgian Court Col 45-48 (Eng) BA; Simmons 49-50 MS in LS; Bridgewater State 61-62; Harvard ext 62-63; Suffolk U 63-64 Tchrs Certif. 7: Apprentice libn Mt Vernon (NY) Pub Lib 48-49, Child libn 50-51; Br libn Wildermere Br, Milford Conn 51-52; Sr asst Thomas Crane Pub Lib, Quincy Mass 57, 58-59; Child libn Hingham Pub Lib, Hingham Mass 59-61; Br libn Thomas Crane Pub Lib, Quincy Mass 64-65; Chief Libn Ventress Mem Lib, Marshfield Mass 65-67; Elem sch lib coord Hingham Pub Sch 67-. 9: ALA; NESchLA; MassSchLA; So Shore SchLA. 10: Mus of Sci; Citizen's Comm for Hingham Pub Schs. 14: Ref, child lit, catlg, admin. 15: 606 Main st, Hingham Mass.

HICKEY, DORALYN JOANNE. b Houston 5 O 29. 5: Rice U 47-51 (Math) BA; Presbyterian Sch of Christian Educ 51-53 (Eng Bible) MA; Rutgers 56-57 MLS; Duke 53-54, 60-62 (Religion) PhD. 6: Sp, Fr, Ger. 7: Stud asst 48-51; Asst catlg Rice U Lib 48-51, summer 52; Stud libn Presbyterian Sch of Christian Educ 51-53; Asst descr catlg Duke U Lib 53-54; Asst libn Duke Divinity Sch 54-56; Asst research spec Rutgers U Sch Lib Serv 57-58; Ser catlgr Rice U Lib 58-60; Asst Prof of Lib Sci Sch of Lib Sci UNC(Chapel Hill) 62-68, Assoc Prof 68-. 8: Spec asst Ser Duke U summers 62-64,67; Visiting Lecturer in Lib Sci UWis summer 64; Spec asst Mss McCormick Theol Sem summer 65; Visitor to Phila Lutheran Sem for Lib Development Program ATheolLA 64; Lib consul Operations Research Lib Research Triangle Inst, Durham NC 63; Instr for Peace Corps trainees UNC 62; Visiting asst prof, Lib Sch UMinn summer 66; Consul Atlanta U Wkshop on Tech Serv 68. 9: ALA-RTSD (Acquis Sect Exec Com 67-70); ATheolLA (chm Catlg & Clsf Com 64-65); AALS; SELA; NCLA (chm Res & Tech Serv Sect 65-67); SE Reg Group Res & Tech Serv Libns (chm 65-68); American Society of Indexers. 10: AAUW; AAUP; Phi Beta Kappa; Beta Phi Mu; Assoc Sigma Xi; Delta Kappa Gamma. 12: 'Coding in Yes-No Form' in "The State of the Library Art" vol 4 pt 5 (61); Managing ed "Library Resources and Technical Services" (65-). 13: Yes. 14: Tech serv, theol libnship 15: Sch Lib Sci UNC, Chapel Hill NC 27514.

HICKEY, MARY ELIZABETH (SCHOLFIELD). b Wausau Wis 24 N 16. 5: Principia Col 34-38 (Eng & Aesthetics) BA; IndU 58-59 (LS) MA; ULausanne (Switzerland) 66-67 (Fr). 6: Fr. 7: Sec Principia Upper Sch, St Louis Mo 39-40; Sec Jam Handy Org, Detroit 40-43; Recreation wker American Red Cross, Ark & Tex 44-45; Club dir US Army Sp Serv, Germany 47-49; Catlgr Skidmore Col 59-61; Hd acquis No IllU (De Kalb) 61-. 9: IllLA. 10: League of Women Voters. 15: 325 Knollwood dr, DeKalb Il 60115.

HICKEY, (MARY) KATHLEEN (IRISH). b Colchester Ill 7 Ag 14. 4: Joseph LeRoy Hickey. 5: West Ill State Tchrs Col 33-38 (Hist) B Ed; UIll 40-41 BS in LS, 41-43 (LS). 7: Lib asst West Ill State Tchrs Col Lib 38-40; Lib asst Map Lib, Army Map Serv, Wash DC 43-44; Chief bk & period br Lib Div Army Map Serv, Wash DC 44-68; Asst chief analysis br info res div US Army Topographic Command 68-. 9: ALA; SLA; ASIS; DCLA. 14: Admin, ref, catlg, automation. 15: 9927 Edward ave, Bethesda Md 20014.

HICKMAN, MARGARET GABRIEL. b Red Wing Minn 25 S 1888. 5: Pratt 12-13 (LS) Certif. 6: Fr, Sp, Ital, Ger. 7: Act libn Hearst Free Lib, Lead SD 12; Head Libn: Carnegie-Lawther Lib, Red Wing Minn 13-14, Pub Lib, Eveleth Minn 14-23, Pub Lib, Rochester Minn 23-28, Frances Clarke Col 28, Foreign Dept Los Angeles Pub Lib 28-58; Free lance research serv 58-. 8: Consul libn: Cathedral Films, Engnr Dept UCLA, Inst of Traffic & Transport. 9: ALA; Pasadena Lib Club. 10: All-City Employees Assn, Los Angeles; Retirement bd, Los Angeles City Schs Dist; Soroptimist Club; Women in Govt. 12: Comp Fr-Eng sect of Lanz' "Aviation Dictionary." 14: For lit, ref. 15: 386 S Burnside ave, Los Angeles Ca 90036.

HICKMAN, THOMAS E. b Burrville Tenn 13 Ag 41. 5: OaklandU 59-63 (Hist) BA; UMich 63-64 AMLS. 6: Fr, Sp. 7: Personnel specialist (Spec 4) US Army; Asst libn catlg dept Rush Rhees Lib URochester 64-. 14: Catlg. 15: Rush Rhees Lib Univ of Rochester, Rochester NY 14627.

HICKMAN, VIVIAN ELAINE (TUTTLE). b Peterson Iowa 22 Mr 20. 4: Forrest F Hickman. 5: Buena Vista Col 37-41 (Eng) BA; State Col Iowa summers 59-62 (LS); UDenver summers 63-65 (LS) MA. 7: Eng, math Maurice High Sch, Maurice Iowa 41-42; Math Battle Creek High Sch, Battle Creek Iowa 42-44; Eng, math Highview Cons Sch, Linn Grove Iowa 46-47; Tchr-libn Geneseo Cons Sch, Buckingham Iowa 59-64; Libn Bunger Jr High Sch, Evansdale Iowa 64-65; Catlg libn UIowa 65-. 9: ALA; IowaLA. 10: Amer Legion Aux; Iowa Geneal Soc. 14: Catlg, reader guidance. 15: Univ of Iowa Libs, Iowa City Iowa 52240.

HICKOK, BEVERLY. b San Francisco 31 O 19. 5: UCal(Berkeley) 38-41 (Hist) AB; UCLA 41-42 Gen Secondary Credential; UCal (Berkeley) 46-47 BLS. 06: Fr. 7: Tchr Bell Gardens Jr High Sch, Bell Gardens Cal 43-44; Spec Q US Navy, Wash DC 44-46; Libn I documents dept UCal Lib(Berkeley) 47-48; Libn Inst of Transportation & Traffic Engnr Lib UCal(Berkeley) 48-. 9: SLA (chm Transp Div 56-57, chm Non-Ser Publns Com 65-66, 68-69; Pres San Francisco Chap 57-58); CalLA. 13: Yes. 14: Admin, ref. 15: 1066 Creston rd, Berkeley Ca 94708.

HICKOK, FLORENCE (NELSON FLANDERS). b Winnipeg Man Can. 22 N 17. 4: Benjamin B Hickok. 5: Vassar 35-39 (Astronomy) AB; Columbia 41-42 BS in LS. 6: Fr, Sp, Ital, Ger. 7: Catlgr UNH Lib 42-43; Libn Lib Presque Isle Army

Air Force, Me 43-44; Libn USDA Reg Poultry Research Lab, E Lansing Mich 50-51; Lecturer Central U(Quito Ecuador) 58-59; Instr Centro Ecuatoriano-Norteamericano, Quito Ecuador 58-59; Libn humanities reading room Lib Mich State U 63-67; Catlgr UIceland, Reykjavik Iceland 67-68; Hd Ref Lib Mich State U 68-. 9: ALA; MichLA. 14: Ref. 15: 622 MAC ave, E Lansing Mich 48823.

HICKS, CAROLINE B(LAIR). b Quebec City Can 25 Jl 14. 5: McGill 34-37 (Eng, Hist) BA, 37-38 BLS. 6: Fr. 7: Catlgr Fraser Inst, Montreal 38-39; Gen br head Ottawa Pub Lib 38-51; Catlgr & chief catlgr UAlta 51-57; Chief catlgr Sarnia Pub Lib, Sarnia Ont 57-61; Head tech serv Toronto Bd of Educ 61-62; Head of reclsf Ottawa Pub Lib 63-. 9: CanLA (chm Catlg Sect 56-57); ALA; OntLA; Inst Prof Libns Ont. 14: Catlg, ref. 15: 153 Nepean st No 311, Ottawa Ont Can.

HICKS, CARROLL ANN. b Raleigh NC 4 D 41. 5: Meredith Col 59-63 (Hist) AB; UNC (Chapel Hill) 65-66 MS in LS. 6: Sp. 7: Lib asst NC State U 63-65; Hd catlgr UNC (Charlotte) 66-68; Libn Delholm Ceramics Inst, Charlotte NC 67-68; Catlgr H W Wilson Co, NYC 68-. 8: Mem Ed Bd "North Carolina Libraries" 67-68. 9: ALA; NCLA; SELA; NYLA; NY Lib Club. 10: AAUP. 13: Yes. 14: Catlg. 15: 736 Tyvola rd, Charlotte NC 28210.

HICKS, CHARLES LEWIS. b Boston Mass. 4: Patricia Richards. 5: UMiami 51-54 (Elem Educ) B Educ; Fla StateU 65-67 MSLS. 6: Fr. 7: Elem sch tchr US Dependents Schs, Overseas 59-65; Sch libn US Dependents Schs, Turkey 66-67; Sch libn Dade Co Pub Schs, Miami Fla 67-68; Act hd acquis UMiami Lib 68-. 9: ALA; FlaLA; DadeCoLA. 10: Kappa Delta Pi; Phi Beta Mu. 14: Acquis. 15: 10161 SW 99th ave, Miami Fl 33156.

HICKS, ENOLA (WOOSTER). b New Britain Conn 26 O 13. 4: Edward Hicks. 5: Oberlin 30-35 (Hist of Art) BA; Columbia 44-45 (LS) BS; UCal 50-54 (Ger). 6: Ger, Fr, Ital. 7: Sec UChicago, Sch of Soc Serv Admin 36; Stenographer-sec GE Co, Bridgeport Conn 36-40; Stenographer US Govt Fed Pub Housing Authority, Conn 41-42; Stenographer-sec Bullard Co, Bridgeport Conn 42-44; Catlgr UCal (Berkeley) 45-. 9: ALA; CalLA. 14: Catlg. 15: 61 Rio Vista ave, Oakland Ca 94611.

HICKS, FRANCES YVONNE. b Jacksonville Fla 8 Ag 44. 5: Fla A&M U 61-65 (LS) BS; Syracuse 68 MS in LS. 6: Sp. 7: Asst libn in chg of a-v Raines Sr High Sch, Jacksonville Fla 65-. 9: Duval Co(Fla) Libns Assn; Duval Tchrs Assn. 10: Alpha Beta Alpha; YWCA; Las Mujeres Elegantes. 14: Reading guidance, ref, a-v. 15: 1021 W Monroe st, Jacksonville Fla 32204.

HICKS, FREDERICK MARTIN. b Saginaw Mich 10 Ja 44. 5: Delta Col 62-64 Assoc Certif; Valparaiso 64-66 BS (Bus Admin); UMich (Ann Arbor) 66-68 MALS. 6: Ger. 7: Ref asst Saginaw Pub Libs, Saginaw Mich 68-. 9: ALA. 14: Ref. 15: 3514 Adams st, Saginaw Mi 48602.

HICKS, JOAN (THOMPSON). b Worcester Mass. 4: Bruce Lathan Hicks. 5: Col of William & Mary (Chem) BS; UIll 62-65 (LS) MS; MLA Certif. 6: Fr. 7: Jr chemist Nat Adv Com of Aeronautics, Cleveland 43-44; Catlg asst UIll Lib (Urbana) 63-65; Lib asst ILL Natural Hist Survey, Urbana Ill summer 65; Catlgr UIll Lib (Urbana) 65-; Ref libn U Alta Med Sci Lib 68-69. 9: ALA; IllLA; UIllLA. 10: Beta Phi Mu; AAUP; UN Assn USA; LWV. 15: Univ of Ill Lib, Urbana Il 61803.

HICKS, JUNE (ISCHY). b Austin Tex 13 D 21. 4: James R Hicks. 5: UTex 38-42 (Home Econ) BS, 55-58 MLS. 7: Ref asst Northwestern U 56-59; Asst libn Internat Minerals & Chem Corp, Skokie Ill 59-61; Ref asst Dartmouth Col 61-62, Biomed libn Dana Biomed Lib 62-. 9: MedLA; SLA; NHLA. 10: AAUW. 14: Ref, admin. 15: 80 E Wheelock, Hanover NH 03755.

HICKS, MARY ELLEN (NUNES). b Syracuse NY 1 Je 38. 4: Robert B Hicks. 5: Syracuse 56-60 (Eng, LS) BA, 60-62 MSLS. 7: Asst to dir Educ Film Lib, Syracuse NY 59-61; Church libn Trinity Methodist Church, Huntsville Ala 63-65; Volunteer catlgr Merritt Island Pub Lib, Merritt Island Fla 65-66; Church libn U Methodist Church, Syracuse NY 67-. 8: Consul to the Church Libs, Syracuse District, Central NY Conf of Methodist Church 67-. 9: ALA; Syracuse U Lib Sch Assn. 14: Admin, a-v, info retrieval. 15: 311 Cooper la, Dewitt NY 13214.

HICKS, WARREN B. b Denver Colo 25 Jl 21. 4: Wilhelmina Kuster. 5: UDenver 46-48 (Bus Admin) BBA, 49-50 MBA in LS; West State Col of Colo 50-53 (Educ) Lib Cred; U of the Pacific 54-60 (Educ) Tchg Cred; U of San Francisco 61-63 (Educ) Admin Cred. 7: Lib asst UDenver 46-48, Ref libn Bus Admin Col 48-49; Head Libn West State Col 49-53; Head Libn Lodi Union High Sch Dist, Lodi Cal 53-61; Lecturer in Lib Sci U San Francisco 58-; Supv of sch libs Berkeley Unified Sch Dist, Berkeley Cal 61-63; Dir of lib serv Chabot Col 63-. 8: Bldg planning consul UDenver Bus Admin Lib 50; Lib consul St Joseph's Col (Mt View Cal) 63, 65, 67-69; Australia, 2 cols, 1 Boys Ctr 67-69. 9: ALA-ACRL;-AASchL (Standards Com 63-66); NEA; Cal Tchrs Assn; CalASchL (off & chm or mem 6 coms, v-pres & pres-elect 69, pres 70. 11: Kirkbride Award for most orig res in Cal hist, 54. 12: "Preparation and Cataloging Time for School Libraries" (55); "History of Lodi, Cal to 1906" (53); "The Organization of Nonbook Materials in School Libraries" (67). 13: Yes. 14: Ref, lib admin. 15: 1672 Orchard way, Pleasanton Ca 94566.

HIDEY, MARGARET JEAN. b Baltimore Co Md 30 S 21. 5: Towson State Col 38-42 (Educ) BS; Rutgers 62-64 MLS. 7: Elem tchr Bd of Educ of Baltimore Co, Md 42-49; Elem tchr McDonogh Sch, McDonogh Md 49-61; Child libn pre-prof Enoch Pratt Free Lib, Baltimore 61-62; Libn Lower Sch McDonogh Sch, McDonogh Md 63-. 9: ALA; MdLA; Assn of Indep Md Schs. 10: Beta Phi Mu. 14: Child lit. 15: 6700 Dogwood rd, Baltimore Md 21207.

HIEBER, DOUGLAS MARTIN. b Waterloo Iowa 25 Ap 33. 4: Wanda Rosdail. 5: Cornell Col 51-55 (Art) BA; UIll 58-59 (LS) MSLS. 7: IBM billing dept Rath Packing Co, Waterloo Iowa 55-56; US Navy radarman 3rd class USS Eldorado (AGC 11) 56-57; Sales promotion rep Rath Packing Co, Waterloo Iowa 57-58; Art libn UIowa Libs 59-62, Head circ dept 62-67; Hd circ UNo Iowa Lib 67-. 8: Curator, Herbert Hoover Presidential Lib, W Branch Iowa 64-; Advisor, Spirit Lake Massacre Mus, Okoboji Iowa; Bd Dirs, Norweg-Amer Mus, Decorah Iowa. 9: ALA. 10: Univ of No Iowa Credit Union; Phi Beta Kappa. 14: Circ, admin, exhib. 15: 33 Timberledge pl, Cedar Falls Ia 50613.

HIEBERT, HARVEY C. b Mountain Lake Minn 16 N 32. 4: Alison Deckert. 5: Bethel Col (Kan) 50-54, 57-58 (Music) BA; Ind U 60-62 MALS. 7: Offset printer Mennonite Central Com 54-57; Bib checker acquis dept UKan Lib 62-63, Asst head acquis dept 63-65; Assoc libn Musselman Lib Bluffton Col 65-. 9: ALA; MusLA. 10: Nat Audubon Soc; Wilderness Soc. 14: Acquis. 15: Musselman Lib Bluffton Col, Bluffton Ohio 45817.

HIEBING, DOROTHEA R (HOFER). b Oak Park Ill 16 Mr 44. 4: Roman G Hiebing. 5: UIowa 62-65 (Elem Educ); UWis (Madison) 65-66 (Elem Educ) BS; Rosary Col 68 MLS. 6: Fr. 7: Tchr Pub Sch, Middleton Wis 66-67; Ya libn Pub Lib, Skokie Ill 69-. 10: Beta Phi Mu. 14: Ref, ya serv. 15: 1224 Harvard ter, Evanston Il 60202.

HIELKEMA, ARTHUR. b Pease Minn 18 O 32. 4: Joan Carol Roos. 7: Pfc US Army Helicopter div 53-55; Tchr & elem libn Holland Area Pub Schs, Holland Mich 60-65; Hd catlgr Grand Haven Pub Schs, Grand Haven Mich 65-66; Hd tech serv Hope Col 66-. 9: MichLA; Midwest Acad Libns. 14: Tech serv. 15: 420 5th st SW, Orange City Ia 51041.

HIER, HELEN MADISON. b Cincinnati. 5: UTenn 46-50 (Sociol) BA; Fla State U 58-59 (LS) MA. 6: Fr. 7: Circ asst UTenn Lib 51-52, Ref asst 52-58; Gen studies asst Gen Studies Lib, Ga Inst of Tech 59-61, Chief gen studies libn 61-64; Undergrad ref libn UTenn Lib 64-67, Interlib loan libn 67-. 9: ALA; TennLA; SELA. 10: Beta Phi Mu. 14: Ref. 15: 2809 Kingston Pike, Knoxville Tenn 37919.

HIESTAND, JOHN PAUL. b Hillsboro Ohio 29 Mr 43. 5: Ohio State 61-65 (Hist) BA; UTex 65-68 MLS. 7: Asst hd pub serv UCincinnati 68, Asst to univ libn 69-. 9: OhioLA. 15: 1966 Westwood Northern apt 4, Cincinnati Oh 45225.

HIETALA, "CARL" ARTHUR. b Hancock Mich 25 Jl 40. 6: Sp. 7: Tchr Farmington Pub Schs, Farmington Mich 62-65; Libn Oakland Commun Col Highland LAKES Campus (Union Lake) 65-67, Libn Orchard Ridge Campus 9farmington) 67-. 9: ALA. 10: Beta Phi Mu; Kappa Delta Pi. 14: Ref, acquis. 15: 29076 Lancaster, Livonia Mi 48154.

HIGDON, THOMAS DAVID. b Walters Okla 7 Mr 30. 5: UOkla 48-50, 55-57 (Hist) BA; Columbia 57-58 MSLS. 6: Fr, Sp. 7: Train instr USAF 51-55; Jr libn to hd tech serv LA Co Med Assn Lib, LA 58-60; Ref libn Biomed Lib UCal LA 60-61, Asst hd catlg div 61-64; Hd ser sect San Fernando Valley State Col Lib 65; Hd catlg div UAriz Col of Med Lib 65-. 9: MedLA; ArizStateLA. 13: Yes. 14: Catlg, med bibliog. 15: Col of Med Lib Univ of Ariz, Tucson Az 85721.

HIGGASON, ELIZABETH (MARGARET). b Knoxville Ill 25 Jl 13. 5: Mac Murray Col for women 31-32, 33-36 (Eng) AB; Knox Col 32-33. 6: Ger, Fr, Lat, Sp. 7: Tchr Towanda Twp High Sch, Towanda Ill 36-37; Tchr Lostant Commun High Sch, Lostant Ill 37-45; Research asst Paramount Pictures Corp, LA 45-67, Hd libn 67-. 9: SLA. 14: Ref. 15: 526 N Van Ness ave, Los Angeles Ca 90004.

HIGGINS, BERTHA GERALDINE. b NS Can 19 Jl 35. 5: Mt Allison U 54-57 (Hist, Pol Sci) BA; McGill 60-61 BLS. 7: Catlgr NS Prov Lib, Halifax NS 61-64, Chief catlgr 64-. 9: CanLA; APLA; HalifaxLA. 14: Catlg. 15: 6085 Shirley st, Halifax NS Can.

HIGGINS, CHARLES L. b Boston 9 N 11. 4: Celeste M LeVangie. 5: Boston Col 30-34 AB, 47-48 (Sociol) AM; Simmons 46-47 BS in LS. 7: Ref libn Boston Pub Lib 34-50, Chief gen ref dept 50-57; Asst state libn Mich State Lib 57-61, Act state libn 61-62; Prof NY State U Col(Geneseo) 62-64; Libn Nazareth Col (Rochester NY) 64-. 8: Lecturer, Simmons Col Sch of Lib Sci, 49-57; Lecturer, UMich Dept of Lib Sci, 57-62. 9: ALA (Coun 60-64, 66-69; var coms); BSA; CathLA (chm Subs Bks Com 63-64); NYLA. 10: AAUP. 12: "Bibliography of Philosophy" (65). 13: Yes. 14: Admin, ref, research, lib educ. 15: 3E Jefferson circle, Pittsford NY 14534.

HIGGINS, JAMES EDWARD. b NYC 1 Ap 26. 4: Emily Annette. 5: St Bonaventure U 45-49 (Eng) BA; Columbia 49-50 (Eng) MA; St John's U 50-52 BLS; Columbia 59-65 (Curriculum, Elem) Ed D. 7: (Pvt) USAAF, US 43-44; Libn-Eng Brooklyn Prep, Brooklyn NY 50-53; Libn-Eng UFSD 5, Levittown NY 53-65; Assoc Prof of educ SUNY(Stony Brook) 65-. 9: ALA; NEA; NCTE; ASCD; ACEI; NYLA. 12: Contrib "Using Literature with Young Children," ed by L B Jacobs (65); "Beyond Words: Books for the Inner Child" (69). 13: Yes. 14: Child bks, sch libnship. 15: 8 Shetland lane, Stony Brook NY 11790.

HIGGINS, JUDITH (HOLDEN). b White Plains NY 9 My 30. 5: Simmons 47-51 (Publishing) BS; Columbia 64-67 (LS) MS. 6: Ital. 7: Reporter Life Magazine, NYC 51-61; Storyteller White Plains Pub Lib, White Plains NY 66-67; Y-A libn Mamaroneck Free Lib, Mamaroneck NY 67-. 9: ALA; -PLA (Publ Com); NYLA; WestchesterLA (v-chm Prog Com, YA & Child Div), 10: Beta Phi Mu; Westchester Co Simmons Col Club; White Plains Woman's Club. 13: Yes. 14: YA & child wk, ref, film. 15: 90 Maple ave, White Plains NY 10601.

HIGGINS, LUCY (McKENNEY). b Mt Chase Me 7 Ap 13. 5: Bridgewater State Col (Educ) BS in Educ; UHawaii 68-69 MLS. 6: Fr. 7: Tchr, Patten Me 33-35; Elem sch tchr, Harwich Mass 54-68. 9: NEA; BarnstableCoTA. 10: Delta Kappa Gamma; HarwichTA. 14: Child wk. 15: North rd, W Harwich Ma 02671.

HIGGINS, NANCY GUSTAFSON. b E Orange NJ 24 S 39. 4: John Rowland Higgins. 5: UMinn 57-61 (Humanities) BA, 61-63 (LS) MA. 6: Fr. 7: Jr libn Walter Lib ref dept UMinn (Minneapolis) 63-64, Libn 64-68, Instr-libn Wilson Lib Ref Dept 68-. 9: ALA. 14: Ref. 15: 1000 University ave SE, Minneapolis Mn 55414.

HIGGINS, THOMAS C. b Pittsburgh 29 N 27. 4: Millicent Guptill. 5: UMe 46-50 (Hist, Govt) BA; Bridgewater State Col 60 (Educ) M Ed; Simmons 64 MS in LS. 7: BM 3rd class US Navy; Tchr Washington Acad, East Machias Me; Tchr Northfield High Sch, Northfield Mass; Tchr Hasbrouck Heights High Sch, Hasbrouck Heights NJ; Tchr Weymouth High Sch, Weymouth Mass; Libn Lexington High Sch, Lexington Mass; Libn Weston High Sch, Weston Mass. 8: Vis lectr, Bridgewater State Col 67-69; Assoc Prof Northeastern Univ 67-69; Fac, Boston U Media Inst 69. 9: NEA; ALA-AASchL; MassLA; MassSch Libns; NELA (Asst dir Stud Leadership Conf 68). 10: South Shore Umpires Assn; East Mass Bd of Approved Basketball Officials. 13: Yes. 15: 351 Weston rd, Wellesley Ma 02181.

HIGGINSON, JEAN (MURIEL). b New Liskeard Ont Can 17 S 37. 5: McMaster U (Hamilton Ont) 55-59 (Nursing Sci) BScN; Toronto 62-63 BLS. 7: Staff nurse Halton Co Health Unit, Oakville Ont 59-62; Libn Nat Lib of Can, Ottawa 63-65, Head gen acquis 65-. 9: ALA; CanLA; OntLA; Inst Prof Libns Ont; LA Ottawa. 10: Prof Inst Publ Serv Can (Libns Group); Bd Dirs Inst Gen Mgt (Fed Inst Mgt). 14: Bk sel. 15: 185 Clearview ave apt 1007, Ottawa 3 Ont Can.

HIGH, LILLIAN EVA (HELLYER). b Bristol Penn 10 Ja 30. 4: Russell E D High. 5: Alma White Col 47-53 (Eng, Hist) BA; Rutgers 55-57 MLS. 6: Lat. 7: Libn Alma White Col Lib 55-59; Tchr Belleview Prep Sch, Westminster Colo 59-60; Col tchr Alma White Col 60-, Libn 60-. 8: Consul, Alma White Col Lib. 10: Minister in Pillar of Fire Church org. 14: Ref, bk sel. 15: Box 65, Zarephath NJ 08890.

HIGHFIELD, BETTY JANE. b Chicago 24 Je 17. 5: Rockford Col 33-37 (Hist) AB; UIll 38-39 BS in LS, summers 42-47 MS in LS. 6: Fr, Ger, Swedish, Span. 7: Asst libn N Park Col 39-44; Libn Col Acad & Sem, N Park Col 44-61, Libn Col & Acad 61-. 9: ALA (Coun); ATheolLA (Exec Bd); IllLA (var coms). 10: Beta Phi Mu; Chicago Lib Club; Rockford Col Club of Chicago Metro Area. 14: Admin, ref. 15: 811 Hinman ave, Evanston Ill 60202.

HIGHFILL, WILLIAM C. b Heavener Okla. 4: Claudia Thompson. 5: Okla Baptist U 53-57 (Eng) AB; Kan State Tchrs Col 61 (LS) MS; UIll 65-69 (LS) PhD. 6: Fr, Ger. 7: Tchr-libn Isabel High Sch, Isabel Kan 57-59; Tchr-libn Chase Co Community High Sch, Cottonwood Falls Kan 59-62; Asst libn William Allen White Lib Kan State Tchrs Col (Emporia) 62-65, Visiting instr dept of libnship 66, 68; Dir lib East Tex State U 69-. 9: ALA; KanLA. 10: Phi Delta Kappa; Kan Friends of Libs; Phi Kappa Phi; Beta Phi Mu. 14: Admin, acquis (acad libs), lib educ, catlg (Subject readings). 15: 1736 Valley rd, Champaign Il 61820.

HIGHTOWER, DOLORIES (HODDE). b Brenham Tex 5 Ag 32. 4: Johnny P Hightower. 5: Blinn Col 51-53 (LS) AA; Tex Women's U 53-55 (LS) BA. 6: Ger. 7: Libn Cameron Elem Sch, Odessa Tex 55-61; Ya libn Abilene Pub Lib, Abilene Tex 62-63; Elem lib coordinator Abilene pub schs, Abilene Tex 63-65; Elem tchr Brenham pub schs, Brenham Tex 65-66, Lib coord 66-. 9: TexLA; Tex State TA. 10: PTA. 11: Tchr of the Year, 58. 14: Child libn. 15: 904 Geney st, Brenham Tex 77833.

HIGHTOWER, (MARY) GRACE. b Brundidge Ala 27 S 18. 5: Ga State Col for Women 37-41 (Elem Educ) BS; Peabody 41-43 BS in LS, 64-65 MLS. 7: Decatur Co Schs, Bainbridge Ga: Elem tchr-libn 38-41, Elem tchr 41-42, High sch libn 42-43; Child libn Nashville Pub Lib 43-46; Libn demon sch & inst dept of educ Ga State Col for Women 46-48; Lib consul Ga State Dept of Educ, Atlanta 48-68, Coord 68-. 8: Instr in Lib Sci Ga State Col for Women summers 47, 48; Consul prins wkshop So Methodist U summer 48; Instr Lib Sch Peabody Col summers 64, 66. 9: ALA;-AASchL;-LAD; GaLA; SELA; GaEA; NEA; Ga Dept of Instr Supv. 12: Ed "Ga Libraries News Bulletin" (48-63); Ed "Ga Librarian" (64-). 13: Yes. 14: Sch lib supv. 15: State Dept of Educ, Atlanta Ga 30334.

HIGHTOWER, ELIZABETH GERALDINE. b Wash DC 27 Ag 25. 5: UAriz 42-44; Boston U 44-46 (Romance Langs) BA; Catholic U 46-47 BS in LS. 6: Fr, Sp. 7: Asst libn Aquinas Col 47-48; LC: Searcher-filer 48-53, Prelim catlgr 53-58, Sr catlgr Descr Catlg Div 58-. 9: DCLA. 10: Delta Sigma Theta. 14: Catlg. 15: 946 T st NW, Wash DC 20001.

HIGLEY, LUELLA (BALDRIDGE). b Chico Tex. 4: John A Higley Sr. 5: McMurray Col 29 (Eng) BA; Tex Woman's U 54 MS LS. 7: Tchr High Sch, Chico Tex 30-33; Tchr High Sch, Fabens Tex 33-34; Elem tchr, El Paso Tex 34-44; Libn Arlington Heights High Sch, Ft Worth Tex 45-57; Consul in lib serv Ft Worth Ind Sch dist, Ft Worth Tex 57-, Asst coord instr materials & lib serv 67-68, Coord instr materials & lib serv 68-. 9: NEA-DAVI; ALA; AASchL (Com for Implementation Fed Programs);-RTSD (Jt Com with Amer Bk Publ Coun); Tex Assembly (mem 55-56); Assn for Supv & Curr Devel; Nat Elem Principals Coun of Admin Women; TexLA (Exec Bd 61-62); SWLA (Tex Rep to Bd 62-64); Tex State Tchrs Assn; Tex Assn for Supv & Curr Devel; Tex Elem Principals & Supvs Assn; TexASchL (pres 55-56); Tex Assn Educ Tech. 10: AAUW; Delta Kappa Gamma; Coun of Admin Women. 15: 4321 El Campo Ft Worth Tex 76107.

HIGLEY, LUTIE LEE. b Knoxville Tenn 28 Ja 17. 4: Thomas S Higley. 5: Phoenix Jr Col 34-36 (Liberal Arts) AA; USoCal 36-38 (Comparative Lit) BA; UCal 38-39 (LS) Certif. 7: Jr libn Oakland Pub Lib, Oakland Cal 39-45; UAriz Lib: Asst ref libn 47-49, Asst catlgr 50-51, Sr ref libn 51-63, Chief soc sci libn 63-65, Chief Pub Serv libn 65-. 9: ALA; ArizLA. 10: Phi Beta Kappa; Phi Kappa Phi. 14: Ref, lib instr. 15: 3126 E Towner ave, Tucson Az 85716.

HILAND, LEAH F. b Lebanon Ind 30 D 32. 5: IndU 51-55 (Soc Studies) BS, 59-60 MALS, 66-69 (LS). 6: Fr, Ger. 7: Libn Merrillville High Sch, Crown Point Ind 55-59; Libn U High Sch, Ind U summer 60; Libn Nurnberg Amer High Sch, Nurnberg Germany 60-62; Libn Homewood-Flossmoor High Sch, Flossmoor Ill 62-66; Asst Prof UIowa Sch of Lib Sci 69-.

8: Visiting Asst Prof Dept of Libnship, West Mich U summer 65. 9: ALA; AASchL; NEA; IllLA; ASIS; AALS; IndASchL. 10: Pi Lambda Theta; Beta Phi Mu. 14: Sch libs, a-v, admin, lib educ, info storage & retr. 15: 612 S Knightridge rd, Bloomington In 47401.

HILD, ALICE PATRICIA. b Wash DC 24 D 40. 5: Roanoke Col 58-62 (Eng) AB; George Washington U 61; UDenver 62-63 (LS) MA; Richmond Prof Inst 64; UWyo 67; NDEA Media Inst UColo 68. 7: Libn A Va State Lib 63-66; State sch lib supv Wyo State Dept of Educ 66-. 9: ALA; VaLA; WyoLA; Wyo Instr Media Assn (sec-treas 67-68); MPLA; DAVI. 10: AAUW; LWV. 13: Yes. 14: Bk sel, juvenile lit, consul wk for sch libs. 15: 704 W 31st st, Cheyenne Wy 82001.

HILGERT, ELVIRE ROTH. b Geneva Switzerland 29 Mr 25. 4: Earle Hilgert. 5: Pacific Union Col 42-45 (Langs) AB; Mills Col summer 44; U of the Philippines 48-50 (Eng); Catholic U 53-56 MS in LS; U of Basel (Switzerland) 57-58. 6: Fr. 7: Instr of Fr & Eng Philippine Union Col 47-51; Lib asst Seventh-day Adventist Theol Sem 52-53, Catlgr 53-56; Act libn Potomac U 59-60; Head catlgr Andrews U 60-65; Head catlgr McCormick Theol Sem Lib 65-68, Asst libn 68-. 9: ALA; ATheolLA; IllLA; Berrien Co Coop Libns Assn (sec 63-65). 10: Beta Phi Mu. 14: Catlg. 15: McCormick Theol Sem 800 W Belden, Chicago Il 60614.

HILKER, EMERSON WALLACE. b Racine Wis 20 Mr 31. 4: Vivian Chun. 5: UWis 49-51 (Liberal Arts); UIll 51-55 (Hist) BA, 58 (LS) MS. 7: Lt(jg) US Navy 55-58; Catlgr Northwestern U Tech Lib 58-60; Chief of tech serv Franklin Inst Lib, Phila 60-66, Libn 66-. 9: ALA; SLA; Phila Area Tech Serv Libns (pres 62-63); ASIS. 14: Catlg, acquis, ref, rare bks, archives (Sci & Tech). 15: 431 Pine lane, King of Prussia Pa 19406.

HILKER, HELEN-ANNE. b Springfield Ohio 5 Jl 20. 5: Allegheny Col 37-41 (Hist, Pol Sci) AB; State UIowa 41-42 (Journalism) MA. 6: Ital, Fr. 7: Reporter "Meadville Tribune", Meadville Penn 37-41; Reporter "Dayton Journal-Herald", Dayton Ohio 42-45; News writer amer Nat Red Cross, Alexandria Va 45-46; Asst info off LC 46-51; Ed research Scripps-Howard Newspaper Alliance, Wash DC 51-54; Press off LC 54-60, Info off 60-69, Interpretive projects off 69-. 9: Women's Nat Press Club (2d v-pres 61-62, chm Memb Com 63-65); AHA; Renaiss Soc Amer; ALA; DCLA. 10: Phi Beta Kappa; Kappa Tau Alpha; Kappa Delta Epsilon; Ohio Newspaper Women's Assn; 1945 Award for best series on general subject; LC; Outstanding Serv Citation 51. 13: Yes. 14: Pub rel. 15: 4201 Cathedral ave NW, Washington DC 20016.

HILL, ALMA (DUTSCHKE). b Cecilia Ky. 5: West Ky State Col (Eng) AB (summa cum laude); UIll BS in LS cum laude; Uky (Admin, supv, guidance) MA cum laude. 6: Fr, Lat. 7: Elem tchr Hardin Co Bd of Educ, Hardin Co Ky 30-34; Elizabethtown Bd of Educ, Elizabethtown Ky: Elem tchr 34-37, Eng tchr & Libn Dean of Girls Elizabethtown High Sch 37-45, Eng tchr, libn, coun Elizabethtown High Sch 45-60, Libn Elizabethtown High Sch 60-, Supv commsn for Stud Tchrs 63-. 8: Mem, 10 eval teams, So Assn. 9: ALA (var offs);-AASchL (Reg 5 Standards Com); KyLA (v-pres); KyASchL (pres, chm Scholarship Com); NEA; KEA; Ky A-V Assn. 10: Beta Phi Mu; Kappa Delta Pi; Woman's Club. 11: KyLA Award for being outstanding school librarian, S of Ky, 65. 13: Yes. 14: Reading guidance, wk with yp. 15: 411 N Main st, Elizabethtown Ky 42701.

HILL, BARBARA MAE. b Keene NH 19 S 24. 5: Keene Tchrs Col 42-46 (Sci) BE; Simmons 49-52 (LS) MS. 7: Tchr Thayer High Sch, Winchester NH 46-47; Asst in lib Keene Tchrs Col summer 47; Child libn Keene Pub Lib, Keene NH 47-52; Asst libn Mass Col of Pharmacy 52-58, Assoc libn 58-69, Libn 69-. 9: MedLA (chm Pharm Group 65-66); SLA (Boston Chap sec 54-56, sec or chm 3 sects 54-61); NE Tech Serv Libns; Drug Info Assn; ASIS. 12: Mem Editorial & adv bd of "Unlisted Drugs." 13: Yes. 14: Ref, catlg, drug info serv. 15: Sheppard Lib Mass Col of Pharmacy 179 Longwood ave, Boston Mass 02115.

HILL, BRUCE ALANDER SR. b Faison NC 11 D 09. 4: Willie Blanche Baker. 5: UNC(Durham) 27-30 (Sci) BS, 40-43 (Educ) MA, 54-57 MLS. 6: Fr. 7: Tchr Duplin Co High Sch, Faison NC 30-37; Prin Cedar Grove Sch, Hillsborough NC 37-54; Tchr Caswell Co High Sch, Yanceyville NC 54-57; Libn Apex Consolidated High Sch, Apex NC 57-. 9: ALA (Recr Netwk); NEA; NCTA. 10: Assn of NC High Sch Lib Clubs; NC Assn of Stud Couns. 12: "A Study of Certain Hillsborough High School Students ." 14: Catlg. 15: 1609 Fayetteville st, Durham NC 27707.

HILL, CHARLES EDWARD. b Norman Okla 5 O 29. 5: UNev 47-51 (Bus Admin) BS in Bus Admin; UOkla 53-55 MLS; UColo 58-59 (Personnel). 7: Squadron adj USAF (Lt), Korea 51-53, & presently Maj USAF Reserve; Catlgr Okla State U Lib 55-58; Community development libn Mich State U 59-62; Personnel & circ libn Central State Col (Edmond Okla) 63-. 9: OklaLA; SWLA; OklaEA. 15: 403 College Circle, Edmond Okla 73034.

HILL, DONNA MARIE. b Salt Lake City. 5: Phillips Gallery Art Sch 40-43 (Drawing, painting, design); George Washington U 43-48 (Sociol) AB; Columbia 51-52 (LS) MS. 6: Fr. 7: Code clerk US State Dept, Wash DC 44-49; Code clerk US Embassy, Paris 49-51; NY Pub Lib 52-59; Various part-time lib wk & free lance writing & illustrating 60-62; Asst to libn City Col (NYC) 62-63; Asst to libn Hunter Col 64-. 10: The Amer Recorder Soc; Phi Beta Kappa; Pi Gamma Mu. 11: Maurice Fromkes painting scholarship to Segovia Spain 53; Weekly Reader Fellowship to SI Writers Conf 57. 12: "Not One More Day," juvenile (57); "Catch A Brass Canary," novel (65); Ed-in-chief "The American Recorder" (62-63). 14: Art, ref, educ. 15: 315 Avenue C, New York NY 10009.

HILL, DORIS (NAOMI) TAYLOR. b Walterboro SC 9 N 39. 4: Diggs Olanda Hill. 5: So Car State Col 58-62 LS BS; No Car Col (Durham) 64; USoCar 68-69. 7: Libn SC Area Trade Sch 62-65; Libn Brockington Elem Sch 65-67; Libn McClenaghan High Sch 67-. 9: NEA; ALA; SCEA; FCEA; SCLA. 15: 900 W Marion st, Florence SC 29501.

HILL, ELIZABETH JANE (QUINSEY). b Ridgeway Ont Can 21 N 25. 4: Raymond Charles Hill. 5: McMaster U 42-46 (Eng) BA; UToronto 47 BLS. 6: Fr. 7: Libn Pub Lib Commsn of BC Peace River br 48-51; Libn Vancouver Pub Lib, Vancouver BC Can 53-58; Dist libn Sch Dist #64, Gulf Islands BC Can 66-. 9: ALA; BCLA. 15: Churchill rd, Ganges BC Can.

HILL, HELEN (HEARN). b Madill Okla 25 Ag 21. 4: Walter M Hill. 5: Bethany Nazarene Col 38-42 (Speech, Eng) AB; Okla U summers 53, 54; Central State Col 62-64 (LS) MT. 7: Tchr Bethany Schs, Bethany Okla 42-43, 49-56; Aircraft inspector Douglas, Okla City 43-44; Lib clk Ashburn Gen Hosp, McKinney Tex 44-46; Libn West Hts Sch, Okla City 60-. 9: ALA; NEA; OklaLA; ClrTA. 14: Catlg. 15: 4309 N Wheeler, Bethany Ok 73008.

HILL, HOWARD CLINTON. b Toppenish Wash 16 F 20. 5: UWash 50 (Hist) BA, 58 (LS) MA. 6: Fr. 7: Sgt Radio- tech Army Air Corps, Australia, New Guinea 42-45; High sch libn Pasco Sch Dist, Pasco Wash 51-52; High sch libn Moses Lake Sch Dist, Moses Lake Wash 53-62; Catlg libn Ore Col of Educ 62-. 9: PNLA; OreLA; Ore Sch Libns. 10: AAUP; ACLU; Ore Hist Soc; Sierra Club; Wilderness Soc. 14: Catlg, sel, lib educ. 15: 403 N Echols, Monmouth Ore 97361.

HILL, LAURENCE G. b New Bedford Mass 4 My 14. 4: Madia E Brooking. 5: Bowdoin 32-36 (Philos) AB; Columbia 38-39 BLS. 6: Fr. 7: Libn Reg Lib Center, Greenfield Mass 39-42; Welder Bethlehem Steel Co, Quincy Mass 42-44, Libn 44-48; Dir Free Pub Lib, New Bedford Mass 48-60; Dir Nioga Lib Syst, Niagara Falls NY 60-67; Dir Westchester Lib Syst, Mt Vernon NY 68-. 8: Consul: Dartmouth Mass 58, Yarmouth Mass 59, So Tier Lib System 65; Asst Prof Grad Program Lib Sci SUNY (Geneseo) 65-66; NY State Adv Com on Libs 66-; NY State Commsners Com on Lib Devel 67-. 9: ALA; MassLA (Exec Com); NYLA (pres Adult Serv Sect). 13: Yes. 14: Admin, bldgs, interlib coop. 15: Westchester Lib Sys, 28 S First ave, Mt Vernon NY 10550.

HILL, REV LAWRENCE HENRY OSB. b Tarentum Penn 4 My 37. 5: St Vincent Col 56-61 (Phil) AB; St Vincent Sem 61-65 (Theol); UPittsburgh 65-67 MLS. 6: Fr. 7: Acquis & ref asst st Vincent Col Lib 65-68, 69-, Act dir libs 68-69. 9: ALA; ATheolLA; CathLA; ABA; Amer Soc of Indexers; PennLA. 14: Ref, periods. 15: St Vincent Col, Latrobe Pa 15650.

HILL, LEONARD E. b Minneapolis 28 F 13. 4: Dorothy Kraner. 5: Andrews U 43-44 (Hist) BA; Mich State U 46-47 (Hist) MA; UMich 60-61 MALS. 6: Fr. 7: Elem tchr Seventh Day Adventists, Ill 32-37; Secondary tchr Seventh Day Adventists, Mich 37-61; Libn Andrews U 61-, Chm lib sci dept 62-. 8: Consul and mem of eval teams for sda second schs, Wis, Ill, Ind, Mich 61-. 9: ALA; MichLA (Recr & Scholarship Coms). 13: Yes. 14: Periods, tchg lib sci. 15: 144 George, Berrien Springs Mi 49104.

HILL, MARJORIE (DERBY). b Birmingham Ala 30 Je 13. 4: Edward B Hill. 5: Howard Col 32-36 (Fr, Sociol) BA; Drexel

40-41 BS in LS. 6: Fr. 7: Staff NY Pub Lib 41; Ref staff Birmingham Pub Lib, Birmingham 42-43; US Army libn, Europe, Alaska, US 43-64; Base libn, MacDill AFB, Fla 64-. 9: ALA; FlaLA. 15: Base Lib, MacDill AFB Fla 33608.

HILL, MARNESBA (DAVIS). b La Crosse Wis. 5: Langston U 39-40 (Elem Educ) BS; Atlanta 46-47 BSLS; Columbia 59-62 (Guidance & Personnel) MA; ULondon 52-53 (Archives Admin). 6: Fr. 7: Spec serv libn Atlanta U 47-58; Educ & sci libn Hunter Col 58-62, Asst Prof (Exec Off) 62-67; Assoc Prof & Assoc libn Herbert H Lehman Col 67-. 8: Assisted in setting up the lib at the Univ of Nigeria, Nsukka Nigeria (Headed catlg sect) 61-62. 9: LACUNY. 10: Delta Kappa Gamma. 14: Ref. 15: 110 Bleecker st, New York NY 10012.

HILL, MILDRED M. b Farmland Ind 24 Je 07. 5: Colorado Col 24-25; Colo State Col of Educ 29-33 (Educ) AB; UDenver 39-41 BS in LS. 6: Sp. 7: Sch libn pub schs, Pueblo Colo 40-42; Ref sci & tech Pub Lib, Grand Rapids Mich 42-44; Ref libn Pub Lib, San Bernardino Cal 44-45; Br libn Pub Lib, San Diego 45-46; Wash State Lib: Documents libn 46-49, Ref libn 49-59, Chief of reader serv 59-67. 8: Spec consul: Ore State Lib Serv to State Govt, Cal State Lib State Tech Serv Act program 68. 9: ALA; PNLA; WashLA. 10: AAUW; LWV; ACLU. 12: Article on Washington State in Colliers Encyclopedia; "Library Services for State Government, a Study of the Oregon State Library and its collection." 14: Pol sci, ref. 15: Rt 10, Box 670, Olympia Wash 98501.

HILL, PENNY (COLLIER). b Dallas 23 Mr 39. 4: Joseph M Hill Jr. 5: Bradford Jr Col 56-58; UTex 58-60 (Eng) BA, 60-(LS), 66 MLS. 6: Sp. 7: Catlg asst UTex 61-62; Dallas Pub Lib: Lib intern 62-63, Dept head 63-64, Br head 64-. 9: TexLA. 14: Adult serv (pub lib). 15: 6331 Chesley lane, Dallas Tx 75214.

HILL, PHYLLIS MALIE (SITES). b Indian Springs Md 30 N 23. 5: Asst libn W Frederick Jr High Sch 63; Libn Boonsboro (Md) Sr High Sch 63-66; Libn Resource Ctr Lib Wash Co Bd of Educ 67-, Coord sch libs 69-. 7: Frostburg State Tchrs Col 41-43 (Secondary Educ) BA; Shepherd Col 63; UMd 63; Shippensberg State 65-69. 9: NEA; ALA; Cumberland Valley LA; MdStateTASchL. 14: Sch libs. 15: R #2, Boonsboro Md 21713.

HILL, RICHARD L. b Temple Tex 19 Ag 41. 5: Temple Jr Col 59-60; St Edward's U 60-63 (Eng) BA; UTex 63-64 MLS. 6: Fr, Sp. 7: Intern Yale U Libs 64-65; Ref asst econ dov NYC Pub Lib research libs 65-68, 1st asst annex div 68-. 8: NYPL Res Libs Adv Coun Com on Training 68-69. 9: ALA; SLA; NY Lib Club. 14: Ref. 15: 301 E 38th st, New York NY 10016.

HILL, RUTH (DEANE) WHITE. b Ingraham Ill 11 O 21. 4: John B Hill. 5: UIll 39-43 (Eng) BA, 48-50 (LS) MS. 7: UIll Lib(Urbana): Acquis asst 49-50, Catlg asst 50-52, Acquis asst 52-53, Bibliogr 53-58; Head Libn Champaign Sr High Sch, Champaign Ill 58-64; Coord high sch libs Champaign Commun Schs Unit Dist #4, Champaign Ill 64-67, Coord libs 67-68; Chm Lib Serv Lincoln Land Commun Col 68-. 8: Faculty mem NDEA Inst for Sch Libns UIll Grad Sch of Lib Sci summer 65. 9: ALA-AASchL (mem Ill Com, Sch Lib Devel Proj 62); -ACRL; IllASchL (chm Implem of Standards Com 64-; Exec Bd 68-70; Program Chm IASL-IAVA-IASCD Jt Conf 70; chm Election Com 66-67); Ill A-V Assn. 10: Friends of the Urbana Free Pub Lib; Delta Kappa Gamma. 13: Yes. 14: High sch libs, bk selection, admin. 15: Lincoln Land Comm Col, 3865 S Sixth st Frontage rd, Springfield Il 62703.

HILL, SARA INGER. b Wichita Kan 21 D 40. 5: Okla U 58-59, summer 64; Okla State U 59-62 (Hist) AB; Wichita U summers 58-60, 62-63; Simmons 63-64 MSLS. 7: Filing dept Inst of Logopedics, Wichita Kan summers 57-61, 1st grade aphasoid tchr 62-63; Stud lib asst Simmons Col 63-64; Asst law libn UKan 64-68; Res assoc Kan Reg Med Program UKan Med Ctr 68-. 9: KanLA (chm Spec Lib Sect; SLA (Heart of Amer Chap Bulletin ed). 10: Pi Beta Phi. 14: Law, ref, med. 15: 207 N Pinecrest, Wichita Ks 67208.

HILL, SYLVERINE (MARTIN). b Linden Tex 19 Ap 32. 4: William Earl Hill. 5: "rairie View A&M Col 48-52 (Elem Educ) BS; UTex summer 58; Tex Woman's U 65-67 MLS. 6: Fr. 7: Libn M F Nichols High Sch, Biloxi Miss 56-59; Libn Richardson Independent Sch Dist Hamilton Park High Sch 61-. 9: ALA; TexStateTA; TexLA; DallasCoLA; RichardsonEA. 10: Jr High Y Teen adv. 14: Ref. 15: 8412 Glen Regal dr, Dallas Tx 75231.

HILL, VESTA (FIELDS). b Jeffersonville Ind 24 Ag 09. 4: Joseph Weldon Hill. 5: Rice Inst 27-31 BA; UTex 56 (Provisional), 60 Sch Libn Certif. 7: Stud asst Houston Pub Lib Heights Br 27-31, Asst 31-34; Libn-sec Clear Creek Schs (Kemah Elem Sch) LaVace Stewart Elem Sch, Kemah Tex 49-58, Libn 59-. 8: Sec, Galveston Co(Tex) Lib Study Com. 9: ALA; NEA; TexLA; Tex State Tchrs Assn. 10: PTA (Life mem). 14: Child lit. 15: Rt 1, Box 481, Dickinson Tx 77539.

HILL, WILLIAM JAMES JR. b Richlands NC 19 Ja 36. 4: Carole L Reuther. 5: East IllU 55-57, 60-62 (Hist) BS Educ, summer 63, 64 (Hist); Ill StateU 62 (LS); UKy NDEA Lib inst summer 65; UIll 65-68 MS in LS. 6: Fr. 7: Libn-tchr Roanoke Pub Schs, Roanoke Ill 62-63; Libn-tchr Richwoods High Schs, Peoria Hts Ill 63-64; Libn Urbana Pub Schs, Urbana Ill 64-68; Asst libn Learning Materials Ctr Univ Lib Wis StateU (Whitewater) 68-. 9: Assn Wis StateU Faculties; Wis Dept A-V Instr; WisLA; State Hist Soc of Wis. 10: Aircraft Owners & Pilots Assn; Amer Radio Relay League; Flying Hawks of Wis StateU; Whitewater, Palmyra Flying Club; Flying Hams Club. 14: Educ media, catlg, sch libs. 15: 248 S Woodland dr, Whitewater Wi 53190.

HILL, WILLIAM W. b Huntington NY 30 Mr 37. 4: Elizabeth Anne (Rocco) Hill. 5: St michael's Col (Winooski Vt) 55-59 (Eng Lit) BA; LIU (Brookville) 66-68 (LS) MS. 7: Intelligence analyst US Army, US & Germany 59-62; Media specialist, Hauppauge Sr High Sch, Hauppauge NY 68-69; Catlgr spec collections Colby Col 69-. 9: ALA; -ACRL; -AASchL; NEA; NYLA; Nassau-Suffolk Sch Libns; Hauppauge Clr TA. 14: Rare bks, films, a-v. 15: 142 Sandy Hollow rd, Northport NY 11768.

HILL, WILLIE (BAKER). b Vaughan NC 30 N 20. 4: Bruce A Hill. 5: Shaw U 38-42 (Eng) AB; Atlanta 46-47 BLS; NC(Durham) 53-55 MLS. 7: Libn Shaw U 47-49; Libn Hillside High Sch, Durham NC 49-. 9: NEA; SELA; NCLA (rec sec); NCTA; Assn of NC Lib Clubs (exec sec 59-). 10: Delta Sigma Theta; YWCA. 14: Ref. 15: 1609 Fayetteville st, Durham NC 27707.

HILLARD, JAMES MILTON. b Nortonville Ky 27 S 20. 4: (E) Louise Winzenried. 5: Ohio U 40-42, 46-47 (Hist) BA; UIll 47-48 MLS. 6: Fr, Ger. 7: US Army 42-46; Asst libn Free Pub Lib, Summit NJ 48-50; Dir Carnegie City Lib, Ft Smith Ark 50-52; Dir Curtis Mem Lib, Meriden Conn 52-55; Assoc libn US Mil Acad 55-57; Libn The Citadel 57-. 9: ALA; NJLA (chm Jr Mems 50); ArkLA; ConnLA (sec 55); SCLA (sec 59-60, treas 66-). 10: AAUP; Optimist Club. 13: Yes. 14: Admin. 15: The Citadel, Charleston SC 29409.

HILLER, CAROL LOUISE (SISTER) OP. b Detroit 11 O 21. 5: Siena Heights Col 41-43 (Eng) PhB; De Paul U 45-51 (Eng) AM; UMich (Ann Arbor) 59-63 AMLS. 7: Catholic Sch Bd of Educ: Tchr, Chicago 43-51, Tchr-libn, Buffalo NY 51-58, Tchr, Upper Mich 58-60, Tchr-libn, Chicago 60-62, High sch libn, Chicago 62-66; High sch libn, W Palm Beach Fla 66-67; High sch libn, Ft Lauderdale Fla 67-. 9: ALA; CathLA (No Ill Unit; chm Nat Memb Com; Mem Exec Bd 64-66; Fla Unit; chm Adv Com Newsletter High Sch Sect 67-69; v-chm & chm-elect High Sch Sec 69-); IllLA; High Sch Libns of Chicagoland; FlaLA; FlaASchL. 15: Dominican Motherhouse, Adrian Mi 49221.

HILLER, MARGARET (CRANE). b S Orange NJ 18 Ag 07. 4: Eldredge Hiller. 5: Wells Col 24-27 (Classics); Simmons 27-28 BLS. 7: Catlgr NJ Col for Women 28-30; Child libn Brooklyn Pub Lib 30-35; Jr libn Scarsdale pub Lib, Scarsdale NY 57-61, Child libn 61-. 9: WestchesterLA. 10: LWV; Visiting Nurse Assn. 14: Child wk. 15: 65 Rockledge rd N, Bronxville NY 10708.

HILLERY, SISTER NORA, CSJ. b Brooklyn NY 27 S 20. 5: Manhattan Col 52 (Fr) BA; St Johns U 55 MLS; Columbia 63. 6: Sp, Fr. 7: Tchr elem schs, Brooklyn & Queens NY; Libn St Brendans High Sch, Brooklyn NY; Tchr & libn, San Conrado, Ponce PR; Catholic U (Ponce PR): Circ libn, Ref libn, Dir of Lib. 8: Univ Senate, Catholic U PR; Supv he lib in The Ctr. 9: ALA; CathLA; Brooklyn LI Unit (Exec Coun 57-58); Sociedad de Bibliotecarios de PR. 14: Ref. 15: Catholic Univ of PR, Ponce PR 00731.

HILLMAN, STEPHANIE. b Los Angeles Cal 19 S 35. 5: Mt San Antonio Col 53-55 AA; UCLA 55-57 (Pre-libnship) BA; UCal (Berkeley) 57-58 MLS. 7: Jr ref libn Fresno State Col 58-60, Sr ref libn 60-61, Hd period dept 61-66, Hd acquis dept 66-68, Asst col libn 68-. 9: ALA; CalLA. 10: Assn Cal State Col Profs. 14: Admin, acquis, ref. 15: 742 East Carmen ave, Fresno Ca 93728.

HILLMAN, THOMAS ALECK. b Kingston Ont Can 31 My 43. 5: Sir George Williams 63-67 (Canadian Hist) BA; McGill 67-69 MLS. 6: Fr. 7: Ser & govt docs libn Pub Archives of Can, Ottawa Ont 69-. 9: SLA. 14: Ser, govt docs, microforms. 15: 395 Wellington st, Public Archives of Canada, Ottawa Ont Can.

HILLS, NELDA (MILLER). b Rumsey Ky 7 D 41. 4: Larry Kenneth Hills. 5: West Ky State Col 59-63 (LS, Eng) AB. 6: Fr. 7: Catlgr Bowling Green Pub Lib, Bowling Green Ky 63; Sch libn Foust Jr High Sch, Owensboro Ky 63-64; Acquis libn Margie Helm Lib West Ky State Col 64-. 9: NEA; KyLA; KyEA; SELA. 10: Sigma Kappa; Jr Womans Club. 14: Acquis, catlg, o-p bks. 15: 170 Virginia ave, Bowling Green Ky 42101.

HILLS, THEODORE S. b Bournemouth Eng 15 O 07. 4: Esther Mazer. 5: Cleveland Col West Res 27-36 (Accounting) BBA. 7: Accountant Shaker Heights Bd of Educ, Shaker Heights Ohio 26-36; Accountant Rayon Machinery, Cleveland 36-41; Pub accountant Card Palmer & Sibbison (Accts), Cleveland 41-42; Clerk-treas, bus manager Cuyahoga Co Lib, Cleveland 42-. 8: Surveyor, Lorain Co (Ohio) Lib Survey, 63. 9: ALA; OhioLA (chm Clerk-Treas RT); Lib Admin of Greater Cleveland. 10: Kiwanis Club. 14: Admin, fin & fiscal control, purchasing. 15: 4510 Memphis ave, Cleveland Oh 44144.

HILLS, VIRGINIA CARTER. b Essexville Mich 23 Ap 20. 4: Benjamin O Hills Jr. 5: Radford Col 38-42 (Sci, Eng) BS; Catholic U 45-51 BS in LS. 7: Nat Geog Soc, Wash DC: Period asst 43-50, Catlgr & ref asst 51-56, Asst libn 57-65, Libn 65-. 9: SLA; DCLA (Bd Dir 68-69 & 69-70); ASIS; AAG; AAUW; Zonta Internat (Bd Dir 69-71, sec 68-69). 14: Admin, catlg, ref. 15: Nat Geog Soc, 16th & M sts NW, Wash DC 20036.

HILSINGER, ANNA (DAUM). b Livingston NJ 22 Ap 07. 4: Ralph F Hilsinger. 5: Montclair Normal Sch 23-25 (Elem Educ) Certif; Ballard Sch 52 (Ref); Rutgers 58 (LS). 7: Tchr Bd of Educ, Livingston NJ 25-30, 31-50; Sr libn Pub Lib, Livingston NJ 50-66, hd adult serv & lending 66-. 9: ALA-LAS; LPRC; NJLA. 10: Daughters of Amer; Bus & Prof Woman's Club; Livingston Hist Soc; Friends of the Livingston Lib. 14: Ref (loc hist & New Jerseyana), adult serv. 15: 43 Virginia ave, Livingston NJ 07039.

HILTON, ROBERT CHADWICK. b Boston 28 Ag 35. 4: Margaret Lewis. 5: Boston U 56-58 (Classics) AB; Simmons 58-60 (LS) MS. 6: Gk, Lat, Fr. 7: Stud asst Creagh Research Lib, Brighton Mass 55-56; (Spec 4) US Army & Natl Guard 57-63; Grad asst Simmons Col Lib 58-60; Asst libn Waltham Pub Lib, Waltham Mass 60-62; Asst libn & coordinator of adult serv Fitchburg Pub Lib, Fitchburg Mass 62-67; Dir Cary Mem Lib, Lexington Mass 67-. 9: ALA; NELA; MassLA; Mass Pub Lib Adminrs (pres 67-68). 10: Simmons Col Lib Sci Alum; Jr C of C; Rotary; Lexington Hist Soc; Lexington Arts & Crafts Soc. 13: Yes. 14: Adult serv, admin. 15: Cary Memorial Lib, Lexington Ma 02173.

HILTON, SYLVIA CAROLINE. b Yarmouth NS Can 21 S 08. 5: Cornell 26-30 (Hist, Govt) BA; Pratt 30-31 BLS. 6: Fr. 7: Head of circ Larchmont Pub Lib, Larchmont NY 31-33; Head of bkmob Mt Vernon Pub Lib, Mt Vernon NY 33-39; Asst libn Scarsdale Pub Lib, Scarsdale NY 39-48, Libn 48-53; Asst libn NY Soc Lib, NYC 53-54, Libn 54-. 9: ALA; SLA; NYLA. 10: NY Lib Club; AAUW; Zonta Club. 14: Admin, rare bks, serv to shut-ins. 15: 53 E 79th st, New York NY 10021.

HILTS, DAVID GLENN. b Breakabeen NY 24 D 1894. 4: Margarete L Ambs. 5: Union Col 18-22 (Eng) MA; UNeb 30-31 (Eng) MA; UIll 36-38 BS in LS; Chicago summers 33, 42-44 (LS). 6: Ger, Fr. 7: Tchr Spencer (Neb) High Sch 22-23; Instr Union Col (Lincoln Neb) 24-33, Libn 27-41; Libn Atlantic Union Col 41-48; Libn La Sierra Col 48-68; Assoc dir of libs Loma Linda U 68-. 10: Beta Phi Mu. 14: Col lib admin, catlg. 15: 11636 Richmond st, Riverside Ca 92505.

HILTY, MARGARET. b Decatur Ind 22 Je 07. 5: Lakeland Col 25-27; UWis 27-29 (Eng) BA; Oshkosh State Col summer 29; UWis 60 MA in LS. 7: Tchr libn High Sch, Lake Mills Wis 29-30; Tchr in Phillipines High Sch, Catbalogan Samar, 31-32, Lingayen Pangasinan 32-33; Tchr libn High Sch, Sheboygan Falls Wis 42-47; Farragut Col 47-49; Wash State U Lib 49-. 8: Consul, Wash State Sch LA State Reading List Com, 65-66. 10: AAUW; Beta Phi Mu. 13: Yes. 14: Ref, educ libn, childs lit consul. 15: 612 Michigan st, Pullman Wash 99163.

HILTZHEIMER, SARA KEESEE. b Sycamore Va 24 D 18. 4: Fitzhugh Lee Hiltzheimer Jr. 5: Longwood Col 37-40 (Fr) BS in Ed; UVa 56-. 6: Fr. 7: Tchr Pulaski (Va) Schs 40-41, 51-53; Clk US War Dept New River Ordnance Plant, Dublin Va 41-42; Libn Danville Pub Schs, Danville Va 67-. 9: NEA; ALA; VaEA (Sch Libns Dept pres 67-69). 10: Commun Concert Assn; Wednesday Club; Lady Astor Garden Club; Delta Kappa Gamma. 15: 200 Robertson ave, Danville Va 24541.

HIME, GARY D. b Wellington Kan 7 N 39. 5: Georgetown U 57-58 (Intl Rel); U of the Americas (Mexico City) 58-60 (Intl Rel) BA; UOkla 64-65 MLS. 6: Sp. 7: Personnel recs specialist (Sp/5) US Army 61-64; Libn Queensborough Pub Lib, NYC 65-66; Asst libn Wichita Pub Lib, Eichita Kan 66-. 9: SLA; MPLA. 10: Kiwanis; Pan-American Club. 14: Admin. 15: 223 S Main st, Wichita Ks 67202.

HIMENO, EMMA (KIMOTO). b Modesto Cal 9 Ag 13. 4: M Hilo Himeno. 5: Pasadena Col 34-35, 36-38 (Phil) AB; Modesto Jr Col 35-36; Drew U 38-40 (Theol & Philos of Relig) MA; UHawaii 65-66 MLS. 6: Japanese. 7: Instr in conversational Japanese Harvard U 44-45; Program asst USO Monterey Calif 47-49; Sub tchr, Hawaii 53-63; Publ asst Hawaii Sugar Planter's Assn Experiment Station, Honolulu 63-64; Libn Hawaii State Lib 66-. 10: PTA; Women's Soc Christ Serv; Windward Music Club. 12: Wrote articles for social Process (publication of Soc Dept U of Hawaii). 13: Yes. 14: Ref. 15: 554 Kaha st, Kailua Hi 96734.

HIMES, MARGIE ERLENE (TROUTMAN). b Cabarrus County NC 2 Ja 41. 4: Bobby Russell Himes. 5: Appalachian StateU 59-61 (Elem Educ); Campbellsville Col 61-62 (Elem Educ) BS; West KyU 67-69 (Elem Educ LS) MA. 6: Fr. 7: Tchr Taylor Co Bd of Educ 62-64; Tchr Metropolitan Bd of Ed, Nashville 64-65; Educ media specialist Campbellsville Col lib 67-. 9: ALA. 10: AAUW. 14: Ref, a-v. 15: 721 Lebanon ave, Campbellsville Ky 42718.

HIMES, NANCY E(LLEN). b Roanoke Va 9 Jl 13. 5: Radford Col 30-34 (Eng) BS; Peabody 35-36 BS in LS; Columbia 53-54 (LS) MS. 6: Fr, Sp. 7: Tchr-libn Callands High Sch, Callands Va 36-38; Asst libn Ouachita Parish High Sch, Monroe La 38-39; Libn T Jefferson Jr High Sch, Arlington Va 39-41; Libn Va High Sch, Bristol Va 42-45; Supv of Libs Dept of Mental Hygiene & Hosps, Richmond Va 45-52;Circ libn C Burr Artz Lib, Frederick Md 54-55; Ref asst Dir Roanoke Pub Lib, Roanoke Va 55-66, Dir 66-. 9: ALA; SELA; VaLA. 10: Quota International; Roanoke Hist Soc; Va Hist Soc. 14: Ref, adult serv, admin. 15: Roanoke Pub Lib 706 S Jefferson st, Roanoke Va 24015.

HIMMELSBACH, CARL J. b Buffalo NY 25. 5: Carnegie 44 (Eng); Kenyon Col 47-50 (Hist) AB; UCal(Tokyo Ext) 52 (Sociol). 6: Fr, Sp. 7: US Army, US, Europe, Japan 43-46; Adv US, Korean, Thailand AF, Asia 50-54; Instr St John's U (Minn) 54-55; Gen Electric Co, NY State 56-57; Libn Special Metals Inc, New Hartford NY 59-62; Chief Libn Kennecott Copper Corp, Lexington Mass 62-. 8: Adv on the re-equipping of war- ravaged libs in Korea. 9: SLA (Transls Activities Com, Bul Ed Boston Chap); Amer Soc Metals. 10: AAAS. 12: "A Selected and Annotated Bibliography of Three Superalloys" (61); "A Guide to Scientific and Technical Journals in Translation" (68). 13: Yes. 14: Tech journals, transl, automation. 15: Ledgemont Lab Kennecott Copper Corp, 128 Spring st, Lexington Mass 02173.

HIMMELSTEIN, DOROTHY (STONES). b Wayne Co Penn 23 Je 33. 4: Lawrence Himmelstein. 5: Penn State U 50-54 (Fr) BA; Drexel 55-56 BSLS. 7: Asst catlgr Franklin Inst, Phila 55; Tech info spec Gen Electric Co, Phila 56-60; Libn acquis Frankford Arsenal, Phila 61. 9: ALA; SLA (Phila Unit: sec 57-58; Memb Chm 58-59). 14: Acquis, catlg, ref, research. 15: 100 Kingfield rd, Phila Pa 19115.

HINCHLIFF, WILLIAM EMERSON. b Rockford Ill 7 O 18. 5: Harvard 36-40 (Econ) AB, 40-41 (Bus); UCLA 60-61 MLS. 6: Fr. 7: Salary admin Dept of Defense, Los Angeles, Boston.

& Wash DC 41-44; Supply off US Naval Res USS Rudyerd Bay 44-46; Salary admin VA, Los Angeles 46-48; Salary admin Occidental Life Insurance Co, Los Angeles 48-49; Sales & advertising manager Korth-Jefferson Inc, Jefferson Wis 49-50; Rep Western Oil & Gas Assn, Los Angeles 50-60; Chief Libn Santa Barbara Pub Lib, Santa Barbara Cal 61-63; Chief train & personnel Milwaukee Pub Lib 63-67; Dir Lib-IMC Ill Central Col 67-68; Assoc dir Media Serv Fed City Col 68-. 8: Founded Pacific Palisades LA; engaged in pub lib devel 53-60; Consul: Boston Pub Schs Secondary Educ Complex 68, Fed City Col Media Serv Conf 68. 9: ALA; CalLA (v-chm Legis Com 62); WisLA (chm Memb Com 65, chm recruitment Com 65-66). 11: Citizen of the Year, Pacific Palisades, 60; CofC "Golden Service Award. 12: "IN: The Library College" (66). 13: Yes. 14: Admin, pub rel, recr, staff devel, lib arch, ya serv. 15: apt V-128, 201 Eye st SW, Washington DC 20024.

HINCKLEY, ANN T. b Ogden Utah 25 My 33. 4: Paul R Hinckley. 5: Stanford 51-55 (Eng) BA; UCLA 63-64 MLS. 6: Fr, Ital. 7: Libn interlib loans ref dept UCLA 64-, Ref & bibliog sect ref dept 68-. 10: AAUP. 14: Ref. 15: 22719 Napa st, Canoga Park Cal 91304.

HINCKLEY, EVELINE M(ARY). b Normanton Yorks Eng 6 Ja 09. 5: U Col U of London 28-31 Diploma in Libnship; Ariz State Col summer 60 (Span lang). 6: Fr, Ger, Ital Sp. 7: Br libn Shipley Pub Lib, Yorks Eng 34-35; Sr asst Coulsdon & Purley Pub Lib, Purley Surrey Eng 35-37; Linguist examiner Postal Censorship, Liverpool Eng 40-43; Asst libn British Launderers' Res Assn, Hendon Eng 44-47; Asst libn Pocatello Pub Lib, Pocatello Ida 47-49; Asst libn Umatilla Co Lib, Pendleton Ore 49-52; Asst soc div Cleveland Pub Lib 53; Sr catlgr IndU Lib 53-55; Head catlgr El Paso Pub Lib, El Paso Tex 56-58; Catlg libn Ariz State U 58-60; Head of tech serv Santa Ana Pub Lib, Santa Ana Cal 60-61, Catlgr Prof Lib Serv 61-63; Asst libn in chg of tech serv Strahorn Lib Col of Ida 63-68; Tech libn Douglas United Nuclear Inc, Richland Wash 68-. 9: Lib Assn (Eng) (Fellow); ALA; IdaLA (sec 64-65); PNLA. 10: Ida Hist Soc; OES. 14: Tech serv. 15: 37 Log lane, Richland Wa 99352.

HINDE, THOMAS ROBERT. b Independence Mo 6 Ja 19. 4: Elizabeth Breese Jones. 5: Park Col 37-41 (Eng) AB; Columbia summers 45, 46 (Eng); UKan summers 48-51 (Educ Admin) MA; UColo 57, 58 (Educ); UDenver summers 62-64 (LS) MA. 7: (1st Lt) Inf, US Army 41-44; Eng tchr Topeka(Kan) Pub Schs 44-56; Eng tchr, Head of Eng Dept S Denver High Sch Denver Pub Schs 56-65; Libn Denver Pub Schs 64-69. 8: Visiting lect UND (Grand Forks) summers 67,68. 9: NEA; ColoEA; Denver Clr Tchrs Assn; ColoASchL. 14: Circ & selection of bks. 15: 3295 S Newton, Denver Co 80236.

HINDMAN, DOROTHY EPPLER. b Oak Park Ill 28 Ja 37. 4: William Murphy Hindman. 5: Wright Jr Col 53-54; UChicago 54-56; Macmurray Col 56-57; Rosary Col 57-60 (Ger) BA, MALS. 6: Ger. 7: Lib asst Rosary Col Lib, River Forest Ill 58-60; Lib asst geyer Morey Madden & Ballard, NYC 60-61; Libn-sr libn NY Pub Lib 61-65; Lib asst UMiami (Fla) 65; Libn II Miami Pub Lib, Miami Fla 67; Med libn Baptist Hosp, Miami Fla 68-. 9: Fla Med Libns. 14: Med libnship, EDP applications. 15: 4150 SW 106th ave, miami Fl 33165.

HINDMAN, JANE (FERGUSON). b Phila 22 Je 05. 5: Drexel 23-24 (LS) Certif; Temple 24-29 (Eng) BS in Ed. 7: South Phila High Sch for Girls, Phila 24-30; Libn Theo Roosevelt Jr High Sch, Phila 30-40; Libn Benj Franklin High Sch, Phila 40-50; Libn A Lincoln High Sch, Phila 50-60; Asst libn Holy Family Col (Phila) 60-63; Asst to exec dir Catholic LA & Ed "Catholic Library World," Haverford Penn 63-. 9: CathLA; ALA; PennLA; Pub Rel Assn Greater Phila. 12: "Mathew Carey; Pamphleteer for Freedom" (60); Ed "Catholic Library World," Phila Area Unit (CathLA) Newsletter. 13: Yes. 14: High sch, adult church libs. 15: The Mermont (207), Bryn Mawr Penn 19010.

HINDS, CHARLES FRANKLIN. b Henderson Ky 31 O 23. 4: Doris May Rooney. 5: UKy 46-50 (Hist) AB; ULouisville 50-52, 53-56 (Eng); American U 61 Certif in Archival Admin; UKy 52-53 (Hist) MA, 59-68 (Hist, LS) MS in LS. 6: Fr, Ger, Sp. 7: Accounting & rates L & N RR, Louisville Ky 41-53; Communications Sgt Reconnaissance Platoon 2nd Arm'd Div 41-45; Mil Instr & admin ROTC Male High Sch, Louisville Ky 53-56; Dir Ky Hist Soc, Frankfort Ky 56-59; Field rep UKy Libs 59-60; Dir Ky Archives & Records Serv, Frankfort Ky 60-67; Dir of libs Murray State U (Murray) 67-. 8: Ky Highway Markers Program (sec) 56-62; State Records Control Bd (chm) 56-58. 9: SAA (chm State & Loc Records Com 65); Amer Records Mgt Assn (Bd); Ky Microfilm Assn; Ky Soc Pub Admins. 10: Toastmasters Club; Ky State Tennis Assn; YMCA (Bd); SAR; Ky Soc War of 1812; Phi Beta Kappa; Phi Alpha Theta; Frankfort Little Theater. 12: Ed "Register," State Hist J (56-59); "Frankfort During the Civil War" (61); Checklist of Ky State Publ (62-). 13: Yes. 14: Archives, mss, rare bks. 15: 809 S 18th st, Murray Ky 42071.

HINDS, DOROTHY F. b Crowell Tex 11 N 11. 5: TWC (Ft Worth Tex) 28-30; Sul Ross State Col 32-34 (Span) BA; Wis State Col (Whitewater) summers 53, 56, 57; UWis summers 61-64 (LS) MA. 6: Sp, Fr. 7: Elem & high sch tchr in Tex schs 30-44; Sec & libn McDonald Astronomical Observatory, Ft Davis Tex 44-51; Receptionist radiology Billings Hosp, Chicago 51-52; Tchr & libn Williams Bay High Sch, Williams Bay Wis 52-. 9: ALA; WisEA; WisLA. 10: "Music-by-the-Lake," summer concert ser (pres 61-65); Deaconess United Church of Christ, Congregational; Williams Bay Study Club (past pres); Alpha Chi. 13: Yes. 14: Sch libs, spec libs. 15: 270 Park st, Williams Bay Wis 53191.

HINES, DAVID (LOWELL). b Chehalis Wash 22 Jl 39. 5: Centralia Col 57-58; Wash State U 58-59 (Ger); UWash 59-61 (Ger) BA, 61-62 MLS; UCal 64- (LS); UCal 64-67 (LS). 6: Sp. 7: Asst libn West High Sch, Bremerton Wash 62-63; Asst libn Olympic Col 63-64; Tchg asst Sch of Libnship UCal (Berkeley) 64-66, Research asst 66-67; Libn IBM Lab, Rochester Minn 67-. 10: Delta Phi Alpha; Phi Delta Kappa; Beta Phi Mu. 14: Ref. 15: 210 16th st NE apt 301, Rochester Mn 55901.

HINES, RUTH (HARRINGTON). b Bartlett Neb 2 O 04. 4: Theodore C Hines. 5: UNeb 22-27 (Lat) BS Ed; Rutgers 57-60 MLS. 6: Fr. 7: Tchr & prin Nelson High Sch, Nelson Neb 27-30; Tchr Lincoln Pub Schs, Lincoln Neb 30-31; Libn Linden Pub Lib, Linden NJ 57-61; Indexer Grolier Inc, NYC 61-. 9: ALA; Soc Indexers (British); Amer Soc Indexers. 14: Indexing. 15: 54 North dr, East Brunswick NJ 08816.

HINES, THEODORE CHRISTIAN. b Wash DC 9 S 26. 4: Ruth (Harrington). 5: George Washington U 47-50 (Eng) AA, AB; American U 50-56 (Bus Admin); Rutgers 57-58, 58-61 (LS) MLS, PhD. 6: Fr, Ger. 7: Miscellaneous clerical Dept of Agric White House, Wash DC 42-44; (Pvt) Rifleman signalman US Army, US Italy Germany 44-47; Messenger to chief Ext Dept DC Pub Lib, Wash DC 47-57; Stud research asst Instr Asst Prof Rutgers U 57-63; Spec asst to dean Asst Prof Sch of Lib Serv Columbia U 63-65; Visiting Prof UCLA summer 65; Assoc Prof Sch of Lib Serv Columbia U 65-. 8: Consul, bibliogs & indexes: McGraw-Hill, Van Nostrand, R R Bowker; Indexer, prentice-Hall, "Chemical Abstracts," Lib surveys: John Wiley 65; Internat Pipe & Ceramic 63; E Providence RI 64; Matawan NJ 65, "Engineering Index"; Md Pub Libs 68, Mid-Hudson 68; Designer of computer filing code, research sponsored by Bro-Dart Found 65; consul on var lib mechanization projs, sci info systems, systems design, and programming info, index systems 65-. 9: ALA (var divs); ASIS (Coun 67-68, chm NY Metro Chap 65); BSA; SLA (Catlg Code Rev Com); Lib Assn (British); Assn Spec Libs & Info Bureaux; Association Internationale des Documentalistes; etc; (Mem Bd East Brunswick Pub Lib). 10: NY Lib Club; AAAS; ACM (Natl Coun). 12: Transl "L-N Malcles Bibliography" (62); Rev ed "American Documentation (64-); "Machine Arrangement of Bibliographic, Catalog, and Index Entries," with J Harris (65); McGraw-Hill Basic Bibliography of Science-Technology (67). 13: Yes. 14: Documentation, indexing, catlg, bibliogs, tech serv, computer applications, string langs. 15: 54 No dr, East Brunswick NJ 08816.

HINK, LORNA LOU (ROYALL). b Seattle Wash 7 F 39. 4: Gary Richard Hink. 5: UPuget sound 57-61 (Educ) BA in Ed; UWash summer 62. 7: Tchr Highline Sch Dist, Seattle 61-62; Research Specialist tech research group Airplane Div Lib Boeing Co 62-. 9: SLA. 14: Lit search, bibliog. 15: 5938 Scenic dr NE, Tacoma Wa 98422.

HINKLE, ELIZABETH (TORP). b Aberdeen SD 23 D 20. 4: Robert J Hinkle. 5: No State Tchrs Col 39-43 (Biol) BS; Presentation Sch of Nursing 40-43 (Nursing) RN; Centenary Col (La) 58; UTex 58-60 MLS; UTenn (Memphis) 66-67 (Med Libnship) Certif; Memphis State U 66-67. 6: Sp. 7: Priv duty nursing, Camp Nursing, SD Minn 43; (1st Lt) anesthesia Army Nurse Corps, US 43-45; Catlgr ref libn Tex Med Assn Lib, Austin Tex 60-62; Ref libn Sect head Manned Spacecraft Center, Houston 62-64; Assoc libn M D Anderson Hosp Lib, Houston 64-65; Ref libn Tex Med Assn Lib, Austin Tex 65-66; Head ref dept UAriz Col of Med Lib 67-. 9: MedLA; SLA (sec Tex Chap); Med Lib Gp Ariz (pres); ArizStateLA; Border RegLA; Assn West Hosp (Lib Sect). 10: Amer Nat Red Cross Nurse; AAAS; AAUP; DAR; Amer Legion; Austin Lib Club; UTex Grad Sch Lib Sci Alumni Assn. 14: Med ref. 15: 5000 E Grant rd 203, Tucson Az 85716.

HINKLE, JOHN E. b Ponca City Okla 23 S 34. 4: Karen Johnson. 5: PhillipsU 53-57 (Instrumental Mus) Bachelor Mus; George WashingtonU 57-58 (Art); UOkla 67-68 (LS). 7: Bandsman USAF Acad Band 62; Instr of instrumental mus Pub Schs, Boise City Okla 66; Asst OklahomaU Lib automation div 67; Lib dir Choctaw Nation Multi-Co Lib, McAlester Okla 69-. 9: ALA; OklaLA. 15: 701 North C, McAlester Ok 74501.

HINKLE, JOSEPHINE (KERCHER). b Reading Penn. 4: James O Hinkle. 5: Kutztown State Col 36-40 (LS) BS, 68 MA in Lib Ed; NYU 44. 7: Libn St Joseph Hosp Sch of Nursing, Reading Penn 40-41; Libn Pine Grove High Sch, Pine Grove Penn 41-45; Br libn Allentown Pub Lib, Allentown Penn 47-48; Libn Emmaus High Sch, Emmaus Penn 48-65; Libn Emmaus Jr High Sch, Emmaus Penn 65-. 9: NEA; Penn State EA. 10: Woman's Club of Emmaus; Kappa Delta Pi. 14: Ref, sch libs. 15: 123 Spruce st, Emmaus Penn 18049.

HINKLE, SARAH ROPES. b Boston 15 O 40. 4: Joseph D Hinkle. 5: Vassar 58-62 (Eng) AB; Simmons 62-64 (LS) MS. 6: Fr. 7: Circ asst RADCLIFFE Col Lib 62-64; Asst ref libn Columbia U Libs 64-68; Libn Winsor Sch Boston 68-. 9: ALA. 12: Co-ed "Index to Little Magazines (65-66). 14: Ref. 15: 69 Revere st, Boston Ma 02114.

HINKLE, SISTER MARY MARTIN RSM. b Fairview Penn 18 Ap 27. 5: Erie Com Col 45-46 (Sec Sci); Mercyhurst Col 47-51 (Biol) BA; Rosary Col summers 58-63 MA in LS. 6: Lat, Ger. 7: Tchr St Justin Grade Sch, Pittsburgh 51-52; Tchr St Walburga Grade Sch, Titusville Penn 53-54; Tchr St Catherine High Sch, Du Bois Penn 54-55; Tchr Mercyhurst Prep Sch, Erie Penn 55-63; Asst libn Mercyhurst Col Lib 63-65; Asst libn Mercyhurst Prep Sch, Erie Penn 63-; Dir of lib Mercyhurst Col 66-69. 8: Lib consul, 1 high sch & 1 sem lib, 63-65; Dean of Resident Studs, Mercyhurst Col. 9: ALA; CathLA; PennLA. 12: Assoc ed, YA Sect "Best Sellers," UScranton (63-65); Ed "Catholic School Journal" (Feb 63). 13: Yes. 14: Catlg, bk sel, admin. 15: Mercyhurst Col Lib, 501 E 38 st, Erie Penn 16501.

HINKLEY, MARY ELIZABETH. b Springfield Mo 2 S 10. 5: Drury Col 28-32 (Eng Lit) AB; UIll 33-34 BS in LS; Columbia summers 45, 46, 48, 50, 51 MS in LS. 7: Ref libn Pub Lib, Springfield Mo 34-47; Dir of the Lib Drury Col 47-66; Catlgr SWest Mo State Col Lib 66-67, Asst ref libn 67-. 9: ALA; MoLA (treas 48-49, v-pres 49-50, pres 50-51). 10: Beta Phi Mu; AAUP; AAUW. 14: Ref. 15: 1539 N Jefferson ave, Springfield Mo 65803.

HINN, ALFREDA (PENCE). b Sidney Ohio 27 S 08. 4: Rev H Theodore Hinn. 5: Wheaton Col 26-30 (Eng, Soc Sci) BA; Princeton Sem 49-50 (Christian Educ); Washington U (St Louis) 61-65 (LS); E Mich U 67-69 LS. 06: Portu, Sp, Fr, Lat. 7: Tchr pub schs, Blumenau Santa Caterina Brasil 39-43; Co-Dir Col Dois de Julho (Bahia Brasil) 43-46; Tchr Presbyterian Sem, Recife Pernambuco Brasil 46-53; Tchr Agnes Erskine Presbyterian Col (Recife Pernambuco Brasil) 46-53; Amer Colony Lib, Recife Pernambuco Brasil 46-53; Tchr Bayless Sch Dist, St Louis 60-61; Barnes Hosp & Wash U schs of nursing Lib (St Louis) 61-66; Libn E Jackson Middle Sch 66-69. 8: Presbyterian Youth work & women's work in USA & Brasil. 9: SLA; ALA; NEA; MissASchL; MissEA; E Jackson TA. 14: Nursing. 15: 1704 Plateau dr, Jackson Mi 49203.

HINRICHS, FRIEDA ALBERTA. b Kalamazoo 28 F 04. 5: Kalamazoo Col 22-26 (Fr) BA; Simmons 27-28 (LS) BS; UMich summers 45, 47, 48 (LS) MA. 6: Fr, Ger. 7: Br asst Kalamazoo Pub Lib 26-27; Catlgr Iowa State U 28-43; Ser catlgr Mich State U 43-46, Head catlgr 46-68, Spec catlgr 68-69. 9: ALA; MichLA (past chm Cat Sect). 14: Catlg. 15: Mich State Univ Lib, E Lansing Mich 48823.

HINSCH, MRS FRANCES (FITZGERALD). b Waterville Kan 3 S 06. 5: Lindenwood Col 23-25 AA; UNeb 25-27 (Eng, Span) AB; Columbia 33-34 (LS) BS. 7: Tchr high schs, Kan, Neb 27-33; Libn Ft Lee Jr Sr High Sch, Ft Lee NJ 34-37; Libn Jr Sr High Sch, E Orange NJ 37-38; Libn Garden City Lib, Garden City NY 52-56; Sr libn Floral Park Pub Lib, Floral Park NY 56-59; Sr libn Garden City Pub Lib, Garden City NY 59-. 9: Nassau Co(NY)LA. 10: Commun Club of Garden City-Hempstead; Nassau Hosp Auxiliary; LWV. 14: Catlg. 15: 164 Wickham rd, Garden City NY 11530.

HINSETH, LOIS. b St Louis Mo 14 O 23. 5: UMinn 47-50 (Pub Health Nursing) BS; UDenver 63-65 MALS. 7: Asst co libn Jefferson Co Pub Lib, Golden Colo 65-66; Ref libn UDenver 66, Hd ref 66-67; Med lib USoDak 67-69; Libn No State Hosp, Sedro Woolley Wash 69-. 9: MtStateLA; SDakLA. 14: Med libnship, bibliotherapy. 15: 720 N University, Vermillion SD 57069.

HINSON, ANN (JONES). b Shady Grove Ala 13 Mr 37. 4: Prince Hinson Jr. 5: Fla A&M U 61 (LS) BS; Atlanta U 69 MSLS. 6: Fr. 7: Lib asst Coleman Mem Lib Fla A&M U 61-. 10: Alpha Beta Alpha. 14: Ref. 15: 3028 Parkridge dr, Tallahassee Fl 32304.

HINTON, BARBARA (JOAN ETTINGER). b Kingston Ont Can 31 D 27. 4: John Hinton. 5: Queen's U (Kingston Ont) 44-49 (Eng, Fr) BA; Toronto 50-51 BLS. 6: Fr. 7: Cashier Bell Telephone Co, Ottawa 49-50; Asst child libn Peterboro Pub Lib, Peterboro Ont 51-53; Child & ref libn St Catharines Pub Lib, St Catharines Ont 53-54; Child libn Toronto Pub Libs 54-55; Libn Scarborough Pub Lib, Scarborough Ont 59, Child libn 64-. 14: Child wk. 15: 31 Halkin Cresc, Toronto 16 Ont Can.

HINTON, BETTY JEAN (GRAHAM). b Amarillo Tex 15 F 40. 4: David Wayne Hinton. 5: W Tex State Col 58-62 (Educ) BS; W Tex StateU 62-64 (Hist) MA; UDenver 65-66 (Libnship) MA. 7: Tchr Amarillo Independent Sch Dist, Amarillo Tex 63-64; Clk W Tex StateU Lib 64-65; Libn Gallaudet Col 66-67; Libn Fairfax Co Pub Lib, Fairfax City Va 67-. 9: VaLA. 10: Delta Zeta. 14: Pub lib. 15: 4850 Kenmore ave apt 103, Alexandria Va 22310.

HINTON, ELIZABETH (GORE). b Coventry Colo 10 Jl 05. 4: Everett Vachel Hinton. 5: UWis 24-28 (Eng) BA with Lib Sci Certif. 6: Fr. 7: Asst ref & catlg libn Gary Pub Lib, Gary Ind 28-32; Dist lib supv wpa, sc 35-42; Libn Limestone Col 55-. 9: ALA; SELA; SCLA (chm Col Sect, chm Trustee Sect; Planning Com). 10: Trustee Cherokee Co(SC) Pub Lib; Delta Kappa Gamma; AAUW; Salvation Army Adv Bd. 14: Ref, admin, circ. 15: 717 S Limestone st, Gaffney SC 29340.

HINTZ, CARL W(ILLIAM EDMUND). b London Eng 14 O 07. 4: Frances Julia Bryant. 5: DePauw U 28-32 (Pol Sci) AB; UMich 32-33 ABLS, 34-35 AMLS; Chicago 52 (LS) PhD. 6: Ger. 7: Jr clerk British Passport Control Off, Berlin Germany 22-24; Clerk Studebaker Corp, S Bend Ind 24-27; Asst libn DePauw U 33-37; Libn UMd 37-46; Libn Chicago Natural Hist Museum, Chicago 46-48; Libn UOre 48-; Dean of libs Ore State Syst of Higher Educ 65-. 8: Md State Planning Commsn, Statewide Lib Survey Com 41-45; lect, Catholic u dept of Lib Sci, 41-45; Consul: Mt Angel Abbey Lib bldg 66-68,evelad (Ore) High Sch Curr Study 59; Chm Title II LSCA Adv Com, Ore State Lib 67-. 9: ALA (Bd on Resources of Amer Libs 46-51, Pac NW Subcom 51-52; mem &/ora Career 58-59; Commsn on Nat Planning for Lib Educ 63-67);-ACRL (Com on a-v wk 52-53, Adv Com on Coop with Educ & Profess Orgs 65-67, State Rep (Wash & Ore) 54-60; Univ ibSeg& Mgt Sect: Stat Com for Col & Univ Libs 64-66);-LED (pres 62-63, chm 2 coms 52-55, 62-64); MdLA (pres 41-43); Middle East LA (v-pres 38-39); OreLA (v-pres 54-55, pres 55-56); PLA (v-pres 56-57, pres 57-58). 10: AAUP; Beta Phi Mu; Rotary Internat. 11: Fulbright Award, Univ of Rajasthan, India, 61. 13: Yes. 14: Admin, bldgs. 15: 2460 Pioneer pike, Eugene Ore 97403.

HINZ, NELDA (SALVNER). b Saginaw Mich 10 Ap 14. 5: Valparaiso U 31-35 (Hist, Eng Lit) BA; UMich 56 AMLS. 6: Ger, Fr. 7: Saginaw Pub Lib, Saginaw Mich: Asst circ dept 35-39, Asst ext dept 53-60, Asst ref libn 60-62, Asst dir 62-. 9: ALA; MichLA. 10: AAUW; Zonta. 14: Ref. 15: 1727 Fairfield st, Saginaw Mich 48602.

HINZE, ADRIEN C. b Djocjacarta 17 My 19. 4: Elody Kolster. 5: UUtrecht 43 LLM; ULeyden 50 LLM; West Res 63 MSLS. 6: Dutch, Ger, Fr. 7: Info off NIDER, The Hague 43-45; Asst dist attorney, Dutch E Indies 46-49; Legal off & coun, City of The Hague, 51-60; Adult serv libn Cuyahoga Co Pub Lib, Ohio 61-64; For law libn UPenn 64-66; Libn & asst prof Emory U Law Sch 66-. 9: AALL; SLA; Internat Assn of Law Libs. 10: Beta Phi Mu. 14: Legal research, foreign & comp law. 15: 2772 Briarcliff rd NE, Atlanta Ga 30329.

HIPPS, DONNA M. b Waterloo Iowa 18 My 25. 4: Robert O Hipps. 5: Iowa State U 42-46 (Home Econ) BS; UMinn 61-63 (LS) MA. 7: Asst libn U High Sch UMinn 61-63; Libn Lincoln High Sch, Bloomington (Minn) 63-. 9: ALA; MinnEA. 10: LWV; Beta Phi Mu. 15: 6604 Dakota Trail, Edina Mn 55424.

HIRATO, ASTHA A. b Honolulu Hawaii 5 Ap 43. 5: UHawaii 61-67 (Educ, LS) BEd, 5th yr diploma, MLS. 7: Libn Highline Sch Dist, Seattle 67-. 9: NEA; WashEA; WashStateASchL. 10: PTA. 13: Yes. 14: School libs, ref. 15: 18225 1st ave So #218, Seattle Wa 98148.

HIRSCH, FELIX EDWARD. b Berlin 7 F 02. 4: Elisabeth Feist. 5: UBerlin summers 20, 23 (Hist); UHeidelberg 20-23 (Hist) PhD; Columbia 35-40 BS in LS. 6: Ger, Fr, Lat, Classic

Greek. 7: Pol ed Acht Uhr-Abendblatt (National Zeitung) & Berliner Tageblatt, Berlin 24-34; Libn Bard Col 36-54, Lecturer 37-42, Asst Prof 42-45, Assoc Prof 45-46, Prof of Hist 46-54; Chm Area Program ASTP Unit Bard Col 43-44; Libn & Prof of hist Trenton State Col 55-; Visiting Lecturer of hist Technical U (Karlsruhe Germany) 62; Adjunct Prof Grad Sch of Lib Sci Drexel Inst of Tech 63-68; Visiting Prof of hist U of Heidelberg (Germany) 65. 8: Lecture tours through West Germany for US Mil Govt in 49 and 54-55; lecture tour through Can for Can Inst of Internat Affairs 51. 9: ALA (Coun 53-57);-ACRL (chm Com Stand 57-63); NY Bd of Regents Com Col & Univ Lib Resources 52-54; NJLA (Exec Bd 58-61, 2nd v-pres 62-63, pres Col & Univ Sec 59-60). 10: Amer Coun on Germany; AHA; AAUP. 11: Grant for Research Abroad, Amer Philos Soc 54-55; Bard Medal for distinguished service, Bard Col 61. 12: "Germany Ten Years After Defeat" (55); "Biography of Gustav Stresemann" (64); Contr "Studies in Diplomatic History and Historiography in Honor of G P Gooch" (61); "Bibliotheca docet: Essays in Honor of Carl Wehmer" (63); "Memorial to President Theodor Heuss" (64); Ed "NJ Libs" (61-65). 13: Yes. 14: Admin, bibliog. 15: 14 Pershing ave, Trenton NJ 08618.

HIRSCH, JANE (KLEIN). b Chicago Ill 14 Je 26. 4: Philip Hirsch. 5: Northwestern U 44-48 (Eng Lit) BA; Catholic U 62-66 MLS. 7: Child libn Montgomery Co Dept of Pub Libs, Bethesda Md 63-64, Ref libn 64-65, 66-67, Asst reg libn 67-68, Asst coord Adult serv 68-. 15: 9805 Singleton dr, Bethesda Md 20034.

HIRSCH, RUDOLF. b Munich Germany 5 S 06. 4: Mildred Norgaard. 5: UMunich & Vienna 25-30 (Hist of Art) cand hist art; Chicago 34-35 (LS) MA; UPenn 49-54 (Hist) PhD. 6: Lat, Fr, Ger. 7: Catlg subj head NY Pub Lib 35-40; Dir Union Lib Catlg, Phila 40-44; Asst libn assoc dir UPenn 45-. 8: Exec com Union Lib Catlg 48-67, Bd Dirs 68-; Chm Middle Atlantic Renaiss Conf, 63-69. 9: BSA; Renaissance Soc. 12: Comp "Union List of Microfilms" (41-44); "Catalog of Manuscripts in the University of Pennsylvania" (65); "Printing, Selling and Reading, 1450-1550" (67); Ed "Changing Patterns of Scholarship and the Future of Research Libraries" (51). 13: Yes. 15: 204 Benjamin West ave, Swarthmore Penn 19081.

HIRSCHFIELD, (ETTA) CLAIRE. b Minneapolis Minn 14 Je 03. 5: UMinn 20-24 (Eng) BS, 29-30 (LS) BS. 6: Fr. 7: Tchr grantsburg & Superior Wis 24-28; Lib asst & instr in lib methods UMinn (Minneapolis) 30-36; Lib asst & libn US Dept Agirc, Wash DC & Phila 36-41; Libn Off of Civilian Defense, Wash DC 41-45; Chief libn Jacobi Lib Mt Sinai, NYC 46-49. 8: Chm adv group of libns Med Lib Ctr of NY 66-67. 9: MedLA; SLA; ALA. 12: Ed "Faculty Bibliography" (Mt Sinai Med Sch 67-68); "Monthly Newsletter" (Mt Sinai Med Sch). 13: Yes. 14: Ref. 15: 150 W 21 st, New York NY 10011.

HIRST, (ROBERT) KENT. b Liberal Kan 8 Mr 39. 5: UKan 57-62 (Music Hist); UIll 62-64 (LS) MS. 7: Mus catlgr Ohio State U 64-68; Mus libn UColo 68-. 9: ALA; MusLA; Amer Musicological Soc; Internat Musicological Soc; Assn for Recorded Sound Collections. 14: Audio Archives. 15: 4927 Thunderbird circle #18, Boulder Co 80302.

HIRST, ROBERT ILLINGWORTH. b Grove City Penn 11 Ag 24. 5: Kenyon Col 42-43, 46-47 (Math); Toronto 47-49 BA, 49-50 BLS. 6: Fr. 7: US Army Corps of Engnrs (Tech/5) 43-45; Act dir Group Serv Dept Akron Pub Lib, Akron Ohio 50-52; Sr libn Brooklyn Pub Lib 52-61; Head circ dept Yonkers Pub Lib, Sprain Brook Br, Yonkers NY 62-63; Lib Dir N Bellmore Pub Lib, N Bellmore NY 63-65; Chief Libn Mills Col of Educ 65-. 9: ALA; SLA; CanLA; NYLA. 13: Yes. 14: Admin. 15: 66 Fifth ave, NYC 10011.

HISER, WANDA JEAN (LEACH). b Carlinville Ill. 4: Homer W Hiser. 5: Blackburn Col 43-45 (Sp) AA; Associate of Arts; UIll 46-48 (Fr) BS, 53 (LS) MS. 6: Sp, Fr. 7: Libn Champaign High Sch, Champaign Ill 53-55; Libn S Miami Jr High Sch, Miami Fla 55- 67; Ins clsf & catlgr UMiami 58-; Libn Glades Jr High Sch, Miami Fl 67-. 9: DadeCoASchL (pres 59-60). 10: UMiami Women's Club; Delta Kappa Gamma; AAUW. 13: Yes. 14: Catlg. 15: 4705 University dr, Coral Gables Fl 33146.

HISZ, EVELYN. b Brooklyn NY 1 D 22. 5: NYU 40-44 (Sociol) BA, 47-49 (Govt) MA; Long Island U 66-69 (LS) MS. 7: Research Chase Manhattan Bk NYC 50; Research Metro-Goldwyn-Mayer NYC 51; Sub libn Oceanside Free Lib, Oceanside NY 69-. 9: Nat Film Coun; SLA. 10: NYU Alumnae Club; Mem, NYU Soc for the Libs. 14: Research. 15: Metro Goldwyn Mayer Inc, 1350 ave of Americas, New York NY 10019.

HITCHCOCK, JENNETTE E(LIZA). b Woodbury Conn 1 Je 10. 5: Smith 27-31 (Pre-med) BA; Columbia summer 35 (LS); Chicago 35-36, 38 (LS) MA. 7: Catlgr Yale U Lib 31-52, Head subj catlg div 52-58; Chief libn catlg div Stanford U Libs 58-. 9: ALA (Coun 66-;-Div Catlg & Clsf (Nomin Com 52-53); -RTSD (Catlg & Clsf Sect: mem & chm Catlg Policy & Research Com 57-61, mem Nomin Com 61-62, chm Award of the Margaret Mann Citation com 62-63, Tech Serv Costs Com 67-; Sect chm 64-65); NY Reg Catlg Group (chm Program Com 50-51); CalLA (Sec CURLS 61); NoCalTech Serv Group 10: Friends of the Palo Alto Pub Lib). 13: Yes. 14: Catlg. 15: 203 Heather lane, Palo Alto Cal 94303.

HITCHCOCK, NANCY LEE (GOWER). b Newton Mass 26 Ag 27. 4: Robert N Hitchcock. 5: Simmons 45-49 (LS) BS. 7: Asst Newton Free Lib, Newton Mass 43-48; Asst ref libn 48-54; Libn Claypit Hill Sch, Wayland Mass 63-. 15: 11 Waltham rd, Wayland Mass 01778.

HITCHINGS, PATRICIA (BURNS). b Pittsburgh Penn 3 O 41. 4: C Gordon Hitchings. 5: Edinboro State 59-63 (Educ) BS; Kent State 64-67 MLS; SUNY Col (Buffalo) 66; UPittsburgh 67-; Allegheny 68. 7: Tchr Belknap Sch, Lockport NY 63-65; Libn Newfane Central Sch, Newfane NY 65-66; Circ libn Edinboro State Col 66-68; Asst Prof lib sci 66-; Ref libn 68-. 8: Part-time libn Lockport Pub Lib, Lockport NY 63-66; Coord NLW, Edinboro Penn 67; Asst dir Inst in Libnship 68. 9: ALA; PennStateEA; Edinboro Faculty Assn, 10: AAUW; Alpha Beta Alpha. 13: Yes. 14: Ref, educ for libnship. 15: Box 469, Edinboro Pa 16412.

HITT, GAIL. b NY 27 D 35. 5: URochester 57 (Eng) BA; Rutgers U 65 MS in LS. 7: Asst ref libn ref dept NY Pub Lib 65; Acquis libn SUNY Maritime Col Lib(Ft Schuyler) 65-67; Asst chief libn AIAA Tech Info Serv, NY 67-. 9: SLA. 10: Phi Beta Kappa; ACLU; Friends of Freedom Libs. 13: Yes. 14: Acquis, ref, bibliog. 15: AIAA Tech Inf Ser, 750 Third ave, New York NY 10017.

HITT, SAM W. b Prescott Ark 13 N 21. 4: Harriette Thompson. 5: Little Rock Jr Col 39-41 (Eng) AA; UMo 46-48 (Eng) BA; USoCal 48-49; Emory 50-51 (LS) MA. 6: Fr. 7: US Naval Res 42-46; UMo Bibliogr Order Dept 51-52, Head Ser Dept 52-58, Dir of Tech Processing 58-65; Health Center libn UConn(Farmington) 65-. 9: ALA; MoLA; MedLA; ConnLA. 13: Yes. 14: Admin. 15: 95 Everett ave, W Hartford Ct 06107.

HITT, VALERIA JEAN (NICHOLS). b Hammond Ind 15 F 24. 4: Robert George Hitt. 5: Purdue 43-48 (Soc Sci, Educ) BS; Atlanta U 67-68 (LS) MA. 7: Libn Madison Pub Schs, Madison Wis 42-43, DeKalb Co Schs, Atlanta 65-67, Fairfax Co Schs, Alexandria Va 68-. 10: Beta Phi Mu. 15: 5601 Viceroy ct, N Springfield Va 22151.

HIVALE, KUNJAVIHARI R. b Kolhapur India 2 F 36. 4: Jasmin Malini. 5: Hislop Col Nagpur U 53-57 (Lit, Soc Sci) BA; Nagpur U 57-58 Diploma in LS; Syracuse 59-61 MS in LS. 6: Eng, Marathi, Hindi, Sanskrit. 7: Asst libn Hislop Col (Nagpur India) 58-59; Grad asst Syracuse U Lib 59-61; Libn Laubach Literacy Fund, Syracuse NY 60-61; Adult serv libn Brooklyn Pub Lib 61-63; Spec bibliog UToronto Lib 63-64; Catlgr Co-operative Bk Centre, Toronto 64-65; Catlgr York U Lib (Toronto) 65-66, Hd sers dept 66-69; Asst libn Humber Col, Toronto 69-. 08: Org for Laubach Literacy Fund Lib in Syracuse NY 60-61; Spec Bibliog for E Asiatic Studies UToronto. 9: IPLO. 14: Ref, catlg, a-v materials, admin, automation, syst & procedures. 15: 281 Sheppard ave E Bldg 9 Apt 1, Willowdale 441 Ont Can.

HIVELY, RUTH ANN. b Felton Penn 13 O 44. 5: Juniata Col 62-63 (Liberal Arts); Lebanon Valley Col 63-66 (Eng) BA; West Res 66-67 MSLS. 6: Fr. 7: Docs & ref libn W Chester State Col Lib 67-68; Asst ref libn Penn State U Lib 68-. 9: ALA. 14: Ref, govt docs. 15: Hamilton Court Bldg apt 37 210 E Hamilton ave, State College Pa 16801.

HIXSON, IMOGENE. b Paris Ark 15 O 14. 5: Ark State Col 31-33; Northeastern State Col 34-36 (Eng, Home Econ, Educ) BS; LSU 48-49 BS in LS; UFla 49-54. 6: Portug, Sp. 7: Tchr: pub sch, Hanna Okla 36-38, pub sch, Okmulgee Okla 38-43, WAVE USN, NY, Atlanta Fla 43-45; Escola Tecnica de Aviacao, Sao Paulo Brazil 45-47, pub sch, Tahlequah Okla 47-48; Catlgr UFla Libs 49-62, Chm catlg dept 62-. 8: Acquis participant: Rockefeller Grant to UFla West Indies 56; Creole Found Grant to UFla, Colombia, Ecuador, Peru 60; Ford Found consul to Univ Nacional Biblioteca, Bogota 67. 9: ALA; FlaLA (chm Tech Serv RT); (RTSL Chm-Elect); SELA (chm-elect RT Sch libns). 12: Rapporteur Gen (56); Ed "Caribbean Acquisitions" (59, 60); "Seminar on acquisitions of

Latin American Library Materials Final Report & Papers". 13: Yes. 14: Catlg, Latin Amer (Brazil). 15: 730 NE 5th ave, Gainesville Fl 32601.

HJERMSTAD, NORVALD REIDAR. b New Lisbon Wis 1 My 08. 4: Edith Munson. 5: Luther Col 26-30 (Classical langs) AB; Luther Theol Sem(St Paul) 31-34 (Theol) BTh; UWis 63-64 MALS. 6: Norwegian, Ger. 7: Lutheran ministry Amer Luth Church, Wis 37-63; Asst libn Wartburg Col 64-. 15: 117 Iowa st, Waverly Ia 50677.

HJORT, ILLAH D. b Wis 19 Ap 38. 5: UWis (Milwaukee) 56-60 (Eng, Secondary Educ) BS; UIll 62-63 MLS, 65-66 (Educ Admin & Supv). 7: Jr libn Milwaukee Pub Lib 60-62; Libn Ridgewood High Sch Norridge Ill 63-65; Instr UIll Grad Sch of Lib Sci 65-66; Lecturer UIowa Col of Educ 66; Reg supv Instr Materials Ill State Dept of Educ 66-67; Dist libn monterey Peninsula Unified Sch Dist 67-. 8: Consul "Junior High School Library Catalog" 69-70. 9: ALA; -AASchL (Profess Status & Growth Com); NEA-DAVI; CalTA; CASL; CalASchL (chm Curr Libns No Sect 68-69); IllASchL (chm Recr Com 66-67). 14: Sch libs, wk with child & yp. 15: 86 Mar Vista, Monterey Ca 93940.

HLUHANY, SISTER MARY PATRICIA VSC. b Canonsburg Penn 20 Jl 21. 5: Duquesne U 40-52 B Ed; St Joseph's (Ind) summers 46-49; Duquesne U 54-56 Lib Sci Certif; West Res (NDEA Inst), summer 66; Rosary Col summer 67-. 7: Tchr Catholic schs, Pittsburgh Diocese 41-58; Tchr Catholic schs, Greensburg (Penn) Diocese 52-54; Tchr-libn Catholic schs, Mobile-Birmingham (Ala) Diocese 56-62; Tchr-libn Catholic schs, Youngstown (Ohio) Diocese 62-63; Libn Vincentian Acad, Pittsburgh 63-64; Libn Bishop Boyle High Sch, Homestead Penn 64-. 8: Adv wk in org & recatlg elem sch libs: St Denis, Versailles Penn; St Robert Bellarmine, E McKeesport; St Anne, Homestead Penn; St Michael (Parish lib), Munhall Penn; St Teresa, Munhall Penn; Practical Nursing at Vincentian Home & Villa de Marillac- summers 42-55; Consul, Vincentian Sisters, Pittsburgh & Greensburg Dioceses. 9: CathLA; ALA; PennLA; Mid South Reg Conf (chm Elem Sect 60-62; Penn State LA; WPCLA (Ed of Newsletter 68-). 10: Nat Cath Stud Lib Assts Assn; Pittsburgh Lib Club. 13: Yes. 14: Catlg, consul wk. 15: Boyle High Sch Lib 120 E Ninth st, Homestead Penn 15120.

HO, DON T. b Shanghai China 4 S 22. 4: May Yu. 5: Nat Tsing Hua U 45-49 (Chem) BS; Drexel 50-51 (LS) MS. 6: Fr, Ger, Chinese. 7: Night libn Moore Sch of Electrical Engnr UPenn 50-51; Abstractor Jefferson Chem Co, NYC 51-52, Tech libn 52-55; Asst libn W R Grace & Co, Clarksville Md 55-59; Head Libn 3M Co, st Paul 59-63; Lib Supv Bell Telephone Labs, Holmdel NJ 63-69, Supv Tech Info Lib Bell Tel Labs, Murray Hill NJ 69-. 9: ACS; SLA (Abstractor for "Documentation Digest" 60-63, sec-treas Chem Sect 62-63, Spec Rep to ALA's Lib Tech Prog 66-, spec Rep to USASI Sect Com on Lib Equipt & Suppl (Z-85) 66-; Minn Chap: chm Employment Com 60-61, Chap dir 61-62, mem H W Wilson Award Com 61-62, Chap Consul 61-63; NJ Chap: mem & chm Educ-Recrt Com 63-66, Program Com 64-65, sci-Tech Liaison Off 64-65); Chap Dir 66; 1st v-pres & pres-elect 66-67, pres 67-68, chm Planning Com 66-67. 13: Yes. 14: Tech lib admin & planning. 15: 403 Quantuck lane, Westfield NJ 07090.

HOADLEY, MARY ANNE (MISEL). b Lansingburgh NY 5 N 43. 4: David E Hoadley. 5: SUNY (Albany) 61-63 (Math); SUC (Geneseo) 63-66 (LS) BS; Col of St Rose 67- (Elem Educ). 7: Sr clk So Adirondack Lib Syst, Saratoga Springs NY 66; Elem sch libn Forest Park sch Colonie Central Sch Dist #1, Albany NY 66-. 9: ALA; NYLA; EastNYLA; NY State Teachers Assoc; Nat Wildlife Fed; Forest Park TA. 14: Child lit. 15: 54 Bayberry dr, RD 1, Waterford NY 12188.

HOAG, ROBERT E(DWARD). b Joliet Ill 14 Je 13. 5: UMinn 34 (Journalism) BA, 39 (LS) BS. 7: US AAF 42-46; Head music room St Paul Pub Lib 40-53, Head ref room 53-. 9: ALA; MinnLA. 10: Minn Hist Soc; Ramsey Co Hist Soc. 13: Yes. 14: Ref. 15: 11 Summit ct apt 10, St Paul Mn 55102.

HOAGLAND, ROBERT E. b Trenton NJ 6 Mr 27. 5: UPenn 50-62 (Socio) BA; Drexel 63-64 MLS. 6: Fr. 7: Pharm Mate 3/c US Navy 45-46; Free Lib of Phila: Lib asst I 54-55, Lib asst II 55-61, Lib trainee 62-63; Libn nj state Depts of Health & Agric, Trenton NJ 65-. 8: Mem Lib Planning Com of Reg Med Prog of NJ. 9: SLA; MedLA (Act chm Trenton Gps). 14: Lib netwks, bibliog control. 15: 333 W State st apt 5D, Trenton NJ 08618.

HOARE, JANE ELIZABETH. b S Bend Ind 13 My 21. 5: Ind U 39-44 (Educ) BS in Ed, 50-52 (Guidance) MS in Ed. 7: Tchr-libn Lakeville High Sch, Lakeville Ind 44-49; Libn Chesterton High Sch, Chesterton Ind 49-50; Libn James Monroe Sch, S Bend Ind 51-. 9: NEA; ALA-AASchL; Ind State Tchrs Assn; IndLA; IndSchLA; South Bend Commun EA. 10: Alpha Delta Pi; AAUW; Ind Univ Club of St Joseph Co. 14: Sch libnship. 15: 242 Rue Flambeau apt 715, S Bend In 46615.

HOBBIE, JANET (ELIZABETH) (HAMILTON). b Brooklyn NY 28 My 19. 4: John Remington Hobbie. 5: Stephen's Col 30-33 AA; Smith 33-35 (Psych) AB; Columbia 39-40, summers 42-48 BS, MS equivalent; NYU 40-42 (Secondary Educ) MA. 6: Fr, Ger. 7: Lib asst Newark Pub Lib, Newark NJ 36-39; Libn Quantico Post Sch, Marine Barracks Quantico Va 41-42; Libn McKinley Jr High Sch, Newark NJ 42-43; Libn Franklin High Sch, Hasbrouck Heights NJ 43-45; Head libn Monmouth Jr Col 45-56; Head Libn Monmouth Col 56-. 9: ALA; NEA; NJLA; Monmouth Libns Assn. 10: AAUW; LWV; Forest Hill Lit Soc. 14: Admin, book sel, lib arch. 15: 31 Hendrickson pl, West Long Branch NJ 07764.

HOBBS, CECIL. b Martins Ferry Ohio 22 Ap 07. 4: Cecile Mae Jackson Hobbs. 5: UIll 25-29 (Hist) BA, 29-30 (Tch 25-29 (Hist) BA, 29-30 (Tching, Hist); Colgate-Rochester Div Sch 30-33 (Educ) BD, 41-42 (Educ) ThM. 6: Burmese. 7: Tchg eng & european hist UIll 29-30; Field admin Burma Baptist Mission 35-40; Prof Pierce Div Col, Burma 40-41; Specialist on SE Asia LC 43-58, Hd so asia sect 58-. 8: Exec sec Conf on Amer Lib Resources on So Asia 57-58, sec 57-60, chm 60-68; Consul Philippine Project Sub-Com ALA; Survey of SE Asia Collections at ColumbiaU 67; Mem P L 480 team to Indonesia. 9: ALA; Assn for Asian Studies; Wash Oriental Club (pres 50); Burma Research Soc; Bibliog Soc of Philippines. 11: LC Award for Meritorious Serv 67. 12: "Southeast Asia, 1935-45: a Selected List of Reference Books" (46); "Report on a Field Trip in Southeast Asia" (48); "Indochina: A Bibliography of the Land and People" (50); "An Account of an Acquisition Trip in the countries of Southeast Asia" (52); "The Burmese Family: An Inquiry Into Its History, Customs and Traditions" (52); "Southeast Asia: An Annotated Bibliography of Selected reference Sources" (52); "Account of a Trip to the Countries of Southeast Asia for the Library of Congress, 1952-1953" (53); "Channels for Procurement of Publications in Southeast Asia" (57); "Southeast Asia Publication Sources: An Account of a Field Trip, 1958-59" (60); "Southeast Asia: an Annotated Bibliography of Selected Reference Sources in Western Languages" (64); "Understanding the Peoples of Southern Asia" (67); "Account of a Trip to the Countries of Southeast Asia for the Library of Congress, August- December, 1965" (67); Bibliog ed "American Historical Review" (55-); Ed "Southern Asia Accessions List" (51-60); Assoc ed "Far Eastern Quarterly" (46-48), Mem adv ed bd (48-50). 13: Yes. 14: Bibliog, SE Asia. 15: 5100 Backlick rd, Annandale Va 22003.

HOBBS, MARYLOU. b Rochester NY 22 Ja 45. 5: Bridgewater Col 61-65 Sp BA; UIll 65-66 MLS. 6: Sp, Fr. 7: Ref aide Bridgewater Col Lib 64-65; Lib aide Fairfax Co Pub Lib summers 62-64, Child libn 66-. 9: ALA; VaLA. 10: Proj Headstart. 14: Child serv. 15: 7005 Skyles way, Springfield Va 22151.

HOBBS, NOLA ANN. b McKenzie Tenn 5 N 37. 5: Bethel Col 55-59 (Biol, Eng) BA; Peabody 59-60 (LS) MA. 6: Fr. 7: Lib asst Memphis Pub Lib, Memphis Tenn 60; Med libn St Jude Hosp, Memphis Tenn 61-63; Catlgr Va Polytech Inst 63-64; Catlgr UArk Med Center Lib 64-66; Catlgr UTenn (Martin) 66-. 9: ALA-RTSD (Tenn Chap: sec-treas 69-70); TennLA. 10: Pi Sigma Phi. 15: 1000 Stonewall, McKenzie Tenn 38201.

HOBERT, COLLIN BRUCE. b Slayton Minn 19 Mr 45. 5: UMinn 63-67 (Eng) BA, 67-68 (LS) MA. 6: Fr, Ger. 7: Order libn-instr Iowa StateU (Ames) 69-. 9: ALA. 14: Ref, bibliog, acquis. 15: 2707 Luther dr apt 3, Ames Ia 50010.

HOBGOOD, BETSY (BOWEN). b Cincinnati Ohio 5 Je 29. 4: Ben Clay Hobgood. 5: William Woods 45-46; Transylvania Col 46-50 (Eng) AB; UKy 50-51 (Educ) MA, 68-69 MLS. 6: Lonkundo, Lingala, Fr. 7: Libn Amer Sch of Kinshasa, Kinshasa Congo 64-66; Asst libn Univ Libre du Congo, Kisangani Congo 66-68. 14: Sch libnship. 15: Univ Libre du Congo BP 2012, Kisangani Rep of Congo.

HOBSON, BARBARA DIANTHA. b Springfield Mass 1 Ap 27. 5: Conn Col 44-48 (Hist) BA; Smith 48-50 (Hist) MA; Simmons 59-61 (LS) MS. 7: Tchg Fellow Smith 48-50; Mass State Lib: Jr lib asst 51-52, Sr lib asst 52-57, Lib ref asst in leg ref div 57-59; Asst spec collections libn Brown U Lib 61-. 9:

ALA; MassLA; RILA; NE Tech Serv Libns. 10: Friends of Old Sturbridge Village; RI Simmons Col Club; RI Hist Soc. 14: Spec collections, mss, ref, catlg. 15: 11 Brown st, Palmer Ma 01069.

HOBSON, JANE BAKER. b Franklin Vt 1 Ap 03. 5: Mt Holyoke 23-27 (Psych) AB; Columbia 27-28 BSLS, 31-35 (Sch Lib). 7: Libn Danbury State Col 31-36; Libn Brattleboro Pub Lib, Brattleboro Vt 41-45; Hd of loan dept UMd (College Park) 45-47; Sch lib consul E Orange Pub Lib, E Orange NJ 47-49; Sch lib consul Pub & Sch Lib Serv Bur, Trenton NJ 49-57; Exec sec Free Pub Lib Serv, Montpelier Vt 57-64; Libn Bellows Falls High Sch, Bellows Falls Vt 64-. 8: Pres State Sch Lib Consuls 53. 9: NELA (pres). 10: AAUW. 11: Montpelier Vt BPW Woman of the Year 62. 12: "New Vermont Guide" (64); "Enrichment aids" (Random House) (68-). 14: Sch libs. 15: 28 Green st, Bellows Falls Vt 05101.

HOBSON, JANE. b Monroe NC 11 F 37. 5: Greensboro Col 55-58; UNC 58-59 (Art Educ) AB; Emory 65-66 MLibn. 7: Tchr Greensboro City Schs, Greensboro NC 59-60; Ed asst Gen Bd of Educ of Methodist Ch, Nashville 60-65; Ref libn Ga State Col Lib 66-. 9: SELA; GaLA. 14: Ref, interlib loans. 15: 843 St Charles ave NE, Atlanta Ga 30306.

HOBSON, JANICE M. b Marshalltown Iowa 7 O 39. 5: UDenver 58-61 (Elem Educ), 61-62 (LS) MA; UHawaii summer 67; Portland State Col summer 68. 7: Elem sch lib Sch Dist #1, Great Falls Mont 62-67; Elem sch libn Sch Dist #37, Vancouver Wash 67-; Instr Clark Col (Vancouver Wash) 69. 9: NEA; ALA; MontEA; MontLA; PNLA; WashEA; VancouverEA; Wash State ASchL (recording sec 69-70). 14: Elem sch lib (wk with child). 15: 5505 E Evergreen blvd 316, Vancouver Wa 98661.

HOCAMP, DIANNE (SAMPLE). b Charlotte NC 31 O 41. 4: Marvin Leroy Hocamp. 5: Mary Washington Col & UFla 59-61; Fla StateU 61-63 (Eng & Libnship) BA, 64-65 (LS) MS. 6: Sp. 7: Ref libn Cadet Lib USAF Acad 65-. 8: Participated in med lib wk USAF Acad Hosp. 9: AreaLA (Pikes Peak Colo). 14: Ref, med & patients' lib wk, ya. 15: 3128 N Arcadia st, Colorado Springs Co 80907.

HOCH, EILEEN (ANDERSON). b Oregon Ill 28 S 30. 4: Wendel Hoch. 5: UMinn 48-52 (Soc studies) BS (tch's certif), summer 68 (LS). 6: Sp. 7: Libn Farmington Pub Schs, farmington Minn 52-56; Libn Dist 833 Pub Schs, St Paul Park Minn 56-63; Libn Park Sr high Dist 833 Schs, Cottage Grove Minn 66-. 8: Adv Bd Farmington Pub Lib 53-56. 9: ALA; -AASchL; NEA; MinnASchL (panel wk 52, 66, 67); MinnEA. 10: Settlement House; PTA. 14: Wk with yp, reading guidance, ref. 15: Rte 1 Upland dr, Cottage Grove Mn 55071.

HOCH, MARION H. b Phila 21 Ap 09. 5: Wilson Col 26-30 (Eng) BA; Drexel 31-32 BS in LS; Columbia 42-44 (LS) MS. 6: Ger. 7: Libn Media High Sch, Media Penn 32-42; Asst libn Tchrs Col Columbia U 42-44; Asst libn & tchr Millersville State Tchrs Col 44-46; Theatre libn Dependents Sch Serv, Germany 46-47; Ref libn Berlin OMCUS Lib, Germany 47-50; Libn Manhasset Pub Schs, Manhasset NY 50-. 8: Consul in co & loc lib activities; summer tchg at Columbia Lib Sch, Geneseo State Tchrs Col, C W Post Col; Wrote & produced film on sch lib serv "The Carpet Under Every Classroom." 09: NEA; ALA; NYLA; NY State Tchrs Assn. 14: High sch libnship. 15: 275 Nassau ave, Manhasset NY 11030.

HOCH, MINNIE (BELLE). b Pittsburgh 30 S 13. 4: Myron L Hoch. 5: UPittsburgh 32-34 (Hist) BA; Carnegie 34-35 BS in LS; Columbia 40-41 MS in LS. 6: Fr, Ger. 7: Ref asst Carnegie Lib of Pittsburgh 35-40; Asst libn US Off of Emergency Mgt, Wash DC 42-43; Info off Australian War Procurement Off, Wash DC 43-45; Research assoc US Senate Small Business Com, Wash DC 45; Chief catlg sect US Off of Tech Serv, Wash DC 45-47; Research libn Standard Brands Corp, NY 47-48; Sch libn, Baltimore 54-61; Catlg libn & Asst hd libn Baltimore Jr Col 61-. 9: ALA-Col & Res Libs Div; MdLA; Md Assn of Jr Cols (Learning Resources Div). 10: AAUP. 12: Co-auth "Australia, the New Customer" (46). 13: Yes. 14: Ref, catlg, admin, bibliog, tchg lib tech. 15: 3740 Oak ave, Baltimore Md 21207.

HOCHSTETTLER, PHYLLIS. b Aurora Neb 2 Jl 15. 5: Hastings Col 33-37 (Mus) BA; UDenver 51-55 (LS) MA. 7: Tchr pub schs, 39-45; Libn pub sch, North Platte Neb 46-59; Libn State Tchrs Col (Kearney Neb) summers 57,58, (Chadron Neb) 59; Consul on sch libs Dept of Educ, Salem Ore 59-67; Assoc Prof Portland State U 67-. 8: Summers in Kearney State Tchrs Col & Chadron State Tchrs Col libs 57-59. 9: ALA (Coun 61-65);-AASchL (pres 68-69, Publ Com); NEA-DAVI;-ASCD; OreLA; PNLA; OreASchL; Ore A-V Media Assn; OreEA; Chm Knapp Sch Proj 65-68. 10: Delta Kappa Gamma; AAUP. 13: Yes. 14: Sch libnship. 15: 255 SW Harrison 7c, Portland Or 97201.

HOCHWALD, ILSE EVA (WOLFSBERG). b Plauen i V Germany 22 Mr 11. 5: Studienan stalt (Plauen) 27-30 (Ger, Hist, Geog) Abitur; UJena, Munich, Leipzig 30-34 (Ger, Hist) Tchg Certif; UMinn 39-42 (Ger, Hist) MA; Columbia 45-48 (LS) BS, 52-57 (Ger). 6: Ger, Fr, Dutch, Lat. 7: Research wkr & tutor UMinn (Minneapolis) 39-42, Asst (orientation) 40-42; Tchr Hudson High Sch, Hudson Wis 42-44; Lib asst NYC Pub Lib 44-51; Sr catlgr Columbia U 52-58; Catlg libn Sarah Lawrence Col 58-59; Asst catlg libn American U 68-69. 9: ALA. 10: AAUW; Columbia U Alum Club; Volunteer wk DC schs. 13: Yes. 14: Catlg, ref, tchg. 15: 6311 33rd st NW, Washington DC 20015.

HOCKER, MARGARET (LOUISE). b S Carrollton Ky. 5: West Ky State Col 41 (Eng) AB; UKy 46 BS in LS; UMich 50 MALS, summer 61. 7: Tchr-libn Bremen High Sch, Bremen Ky 41-43; High sch libn High Sch, Central City Ky 43-47; Head ref libn UCincinnati 47-49; Head ref libn & tchr of Lib Sci Wis State U (La Crosse) 50-67, chm Lib Sci Dept 67-. 8: Tchr Lib Sci UOre summer 58; Tchr Lib Sci UWis(Madison) summer 65, 66, 67. 9: ALA-ACRL; WisLA (Lib Educ Com 61-67, 68-); WisEA. 10: Delta Kappa Gamma; Beta Phi Mu; WisEA; AAUW; AAUP. 14: Ref, lib educ, lib sci tchg, sch libs. 15: 420 S 15th st, LaCrosse Wis 54601.

HODAPP, GLADYS MURIEL. b NYC 11 O 21. 5: Hunter Col 39-43 (Eng) BA; Pratt Inst 64-66 MLS. 6: Fr. 7: Continental Ins Co, NYC: Fidelity bond examiner 43-63, Asst libn 63-65, Chief libn 65-67; Chief libn Continental Research Inst, NYC 67-. 9: SLA. 10: Beta Phi Mu; Hunter Col Alum Assn. 14: Bibliog, ref, catlg. 15: Continental Res Inst, 25 Cedar st, New York NY 10038.

HODAPP, PATRICIA CONOR. b Kalamazoo Mich 10 My 44. 4: Paul F Hodapp. 5: West Mich U 62-65 (Eng) BA, Secondary tchg certif, 66-67 MSLS; Washington U (St Louis) 66 (Eng). 6: Fr. 7: Catlgr Mona Shores Pub Sch, Muskegon Mich 65; Lib specialist Muskegon Pub Schs Curriculum Enrichment Program, Muskegon Mich summer 65; Child libn St Louis Pub Lib 66-67, Chief child dept 67-. 9: ALA; MoLA (Jr Mem RT Publ Chm; mem Child Serv Div). 10: Volunteer Improvement Prog; Mortar Bd; Alpha Beta Alpha. 13: Yes. 14: Child libn, ref. 15: 6340 Northwood, Clayton Mo 63105.

HODGE, CAROL ANN (KOHL). b Grand Island Neb 10 S 43. 4: Larry Gene Hodge. 5: Hastings Col 61-65 (Eng) BA; Kan State Tchrs Col 66-67 ML. 6: Ger. 7: Child lib asst Hastings Pub Lib, Hastings Neb 63-66; Child libn Emporia Pub Libm Emporia Kan 66-. 9: KanLA; EmporiaLA. 10: AAUW; Amer Legion Aux. 14: Child lit. 15: 1507 Prairie, Emporia Ks 66801.

HODGE, ELIZABETH (MARGARET). b Savannah Ga 20 S 10. 5: Col of Wooster 28-32 (Fr) AB; Emory 32-33 AB in LS. 7: Savannah Pub Lib, Savannah Ga: Jr asst 35-36, Sr asst 36-40, Ref libn 40-51, Asst libn 51-. 9: ALA; GaLA; SELA. 10: AAUW; LWV; Altrusa. 14: Ref. 15: 1113 E 49th st, Savannah Ga 31404.

HODGE, H(ARRIET) MURIEL. b Geneva NY 6 D 09. 5: William Smith Col 31 (Hist) BA; Cornell U 45 (Hist) MA; Syracuse 46 (LS) BS. 7: Tchr of soc studies High sch: Fillmore NY 31-35, Mahopac NY 35-43, Port Jervis, NY 43-45; Catlgr & clsf Wharton Sch UPenn 46-51; Catlgr & clsf Col of Physicians, Phila 51-54, Asst libn 54-62; Ref-Ser libn Hobart & Wm Smith Cols(Geneva NY) 62-. 9: MedLA (Placement adv 59-61); ALA; NYLA. 10: Beta Phi Mu. 14: Ref, catlg. 15: 11 Goodelle ter, Geneva NY 14456.

HODGE, JONATHAN R(OBERT). b Bridgeport Conn 5 My 45. 5: UBridgeport 63-67 (Eng) BA; NYU 67-68 (Eng) MA; Columbia 68-69 MS. 6: Fr. 7: Stock Smith-Comstock Inc, Bridgeport Conn summers 61-63; Salesman-cashier E J Korvette Co Inc, Trumbull Conn 65; Letter carrier-clk US Govt Post Off, Birdgeport Conn 65-66. 9: ALA. 14: Ref. 15: 92 Evelyn st, Trumbull Ct 06611.

HODGE, STANLEY PHILIP. b Baltimore Md 22 S 39. 4: Sallye Wallis. 5: AmerU 57-61 9sociol) BA; Case West ResU 66-67 MSLS. 6: Fr. 7: Stud asst AmericanU Lib 58-59; Lib asst US Post Off Dept Lib, Wash DC summer 59, 60; Lib asst DC Pun Lib 60-61; USAF Aircraft Controller TAC PACAF 62-66; Ser asst Case Inst Tech Lib 66-67; Asst acquis libn Ind State U Lib (Terre Haute) 68, Asst hd acquis 68-. 9: ALA. 10: Beta Phi

Mu. 14: Acquis, ser, automation. 15: 1609 S 4th st, Terre Haute In 47802.

HODGES, A HOPE. b Vernon BC Can. 5: Victoria Col 24-26; Toronto 26-28 BA; UWash 30-31 BS in LS. 7: Catlgr Okanagan Valley Reg Lib, Kelowna BC 36-38; Ext libn Pub Lib Commsn, Victoria BC 38-42; Asst Inspection Bd of UK & Can, Ottawa 42-45; Asst libn Fraser Valley Reg Lib, Abbotsford BC 46-58; Co Libn Clallam Co Lib, Port Angeles Wash 58-. 15: 2210 Peabody st, Port Angeles Wa 98362.

HODGES, GERALD GARANT. b Sewanee Tenn 20 Ja 44. 5: UNC 61-65 (Hist, Sp) AB; UFla 65-67 (Lat Amer Hist) MA; Rutgers 67-68 MLS. 6: Sp, Fr, Portu. 7: Lib asst UFla Lib 64, Lib clerk 66-67; Libn Sp tchr Fla Central Acad, Sorrento Fla 68-. 9: ALA; -AASchL; FlaLA. 10: Phi Alpha Teta. 11: Hon Woodrow Wilson Scholar. 12: CO-comp "A Selected New Jersey Bibliography" (68). 14: Ref, Lat Amer bibliog (nat). 15: Fla Central Academy, Sorrento Fl 32776.

HODGES, JUDITH (ROSENBLOOM). b Montreal Que Can 10 Jl 39. 6: Fr. 7: Adult serv libn Brooklyn Pub Lib, Brooklyn NY 61-62, Tele ref 63; Ref libn Brookline Pub Lib, Brookline Mass 66; Libn Abbie E Dunks Mem Lib Mass Hosp Assoc, Boston 67-. 8: Selection of recreational reading materials for Aesculapian Rm Countway Lib Harvard Med Sch 65. 9: NELA (Hosp Lib Sect program chm 68-69). 14: Ref. 15: 146 Thorndike st, Brookline Ma 02146.

HODGES, MARCIA J. b Brinson Ga 3 O 36. 5: Ga State Col for Women 54-57 (Hist) AB; Fla State U 59-60 (LS) MS. 7: Ref libn San Diego Pub Lib, San Diego Cal 60-63; Army libn US Army Spec Serv, Karlsruhe Germany 63-65; Ref libn Wilmington Inst Free Lib, Wilmington Del 66-67; Br libn Annapolis Area Lib, Annapolis Md 67-. 9: ALA. 14: Ref. 15: Box 635, Brinson Ga 31725.

HODGES, (MARTHA) FRANCES (WEISSER). b Maxwell Tex 20 F 36. 4: Tom Hodges. 5: Tex lutheran Col 54-55 (Liberal Arts); N Tex State U 55-58 (LS) BA; Tex Woman's U 61-67 MLS. 7: Libn New Braunfels Sr High Sch, New Braunfels Sr High Sch, New Braunfels Tex 58; Libn Canyon High Sch, New Braunfels Tex 59-62; Catlgr Faust Pub Lib, New Braunfels Tex 60; Libn Wheat Ridge Sr High Sch, Wheat Ridge Colo 62-67; Libn Carmody Jr High Sch, denver 67-. 9: ALA; ColoASchL; ColoEA; JeffersonCoEA. 10: Friends of Mountain Libs. 15: 9533 Alpine Village, Indian Hills Co 80454.

HODGES, (SARAH) MARGARET (MOORE). b Indianapolis 26 Jl 11. 4: Fletcher Hodges Jr. 5: Vassar 29-32 (Eng) AB; Carnegie 58 MLS. 6: Fr. 7: Radio & TV storyteller Carnegie Lib of Pittsburgh 53-64, Child libn 58-64; Story spec Pittsburgh Pub Schs 64-68; TV storyteller Schs Serv Dept WQED 65-; Visiting Lecturer Grad Sch Lib & Info Sci UPittsburgh 64-68, Asst Prof 68-. 12: "One Little Drum" (58); "What's for Lunch, Charley" (61); "A Club Against Keats" (62); "Tell It Again" (63); "The Secret in the Woods" (63); "The Wave" (64); Ed of 4 titles in "The Young Traveler" ser (53-55); "Tell Me a Story" (66); "The Hatching of Joshua Cobb" (67); "Constellation" (68); "Sing Out, Charley" (68); "Lady Queen Anne" (69). 13: Yes. 14: Story-telling, child lit. 15: GSLIS Univ Pittsburgh, Pittsburgh Pa 15213.

HODGES, T GENE. b Clinton Okla 30 Ja 13. 4: Claire Surbeck. 5: UOkla 30-34 (Bus Admin) BS; McCormick Sem 37-39 (Theol) BD; UOkla 55 MLS. 6: Ger, Gk. 7: Pastor First Presbyterian Church, Pawhuska Okla 39-43; Pastor First Presbyterian Church, Lawton Okla 44-47; Acquis libn UOkla 55-58; Dir of the Lib Central State Col(Edmond Okla) 58-. 9: NEA; OklaLA (pres 65-66); SWLA; OklaEA. 14: Acquis. 15: Central State Col Lib, Edmond Okla 73034.

HODGES, T(ERENCE) MARK. b Sheffield Eng 18 Je 33. 4: Judith Rosenbloom. 5: Leeds Sch of Libnship (Eng) 55-56; Assoc of the Brit LA. 6: Fr. 7: Libn (Brit) Army Educ Centre, Suez CZ 52-53; Lib asst sci & com div Sheffield (Eng) Pub Lib 53-55; Br libn Woodhouse Br Sheffield (Eng) Pub Lib 56-57; Ref libn Hamilton Col Lib 57-60; Circ libn Swarthmore Col Lib 60-61; Sr libn lang & lit div Brooklyn Pub Lib 61-63; Circ libn Francis A Countway Lib of Med in Harvard Med Sch (Boston) 64-67; Dir NE Reg Med Lib Serv, Boston Mass 67-70; Assoc libn SE Reg Med Lib Serv, Emory U Atlanta Ga 70-. 9: Lib Assn (Brit); ALA; MedLA. 10: Harvard Lib Club. 13: Yes. 14: Pub serv, admin, interlib coop. 15: 146 Thorndike st, Brookline Ma 02146. 15: 146 Thorndike st, Brookline Ma 02146.

HODGIN, ALLIE AUSTIN. b Union Co NC 31 Jl 08. 4: David Reid Hodgin. 5: Appalachian State Tchrs Col 26-27, 32-34 (Educ) BS; Peabody 40 BS in LS; Columbia 46 (LS); Peabody 65 MLS. 7: Tchg elem schs, Marshville NC 28-32; Circ libn Appalachian State U 34-39, Ref libn 39-. 8: Mem Fac Senate Appalachian State U 67-, sec 68-69, Lib & Instr Serv Com 69-72. 9: ALA; SELA; NCLA (chm Lib Resources Com 68-70). 10: Delta Kappa Gamma; AAUW; Bus & Prof Women's Club; AAUP. 14: Ref. 15: Rt 1 Box 120, Boone NC 28607.

HODGINS, GORDON WILLIAM. b Toronto Ont 29 Mr 43. 5: UToronto 61-65 (Eng) BA, 65-66 BLS, 67-69 (Eng) MA. 6: Fr, Ger, Chinese. 7: Catlgr UToronto Lib 66-67; Catlgr N York Pub Lib, Willowdale Ont Can 69-. 10: Nat Audubon Soc. 14: Catlg. 15: 73 Glenaden ave E, Toronto 18 Ont Can.

HODGMAN, SHIRLEY G. b Brennen SD 19 My 22. 5: Black Hills Tchrs Col 55 (Elem Educ) BS of Ed; UWash 62 MS of Lib. 6: Sp. 7: Elec tchr Rapid Valley Rural Sch, Rapid City SD 42-43; Elem tchr New Underwood Sch Dist, New Underwood SD 43-46; Elem tchr Sturgis Sch Dist, Sturgis SD 46-49; Elem tchr Port Angeles Sch Dist, Port Angeles Wash 49-60; Jr high libn Port Angeles Sch Dist, Port Angeles Wash 60-61; Asst to supv of instr materials Salem Sch Dist, Salem Ore 61-64; Supv of Libs W Linn Sch Dist, W Linn Ore 64-. 9: NEA; ALA-AASchL (chm Standards Implem Com); OreEA; OreASchL (chm Regs 11,12,13); ASCD. 10: Delta Kappa Gamma. 14: Sch libnship, tchg lib skills, sch media serv, Standards implem. 15: 1355 Hallinan st, Lake Oswego Or 97034.

HODGMAN, SUZANNE. b Chicago 16 Jl 25. 5: No Ill State Tchrs Col 43-45 (Soc Sci); UNM 45-47 (Inter- Amer Affairs) BA; Nat U of Mexico summer 46 (Span); Tulane 48-50 (Latin Amer Studies) MA; UTex 58-60 MLS. 6: Sp, Portu, Fr. 7: Grad tchg fellow Tulane U 48-50; Bi-lingual sec Inter-Amer Orange-Crush Co, Chicago 52-54; Sec-treas Hodgman Bus Trans Co, Oak Forest Ill 54-58; Ref libn San Antonio Pub Lib, San Antonio Tex 59-60; Lat Amer Spec in acquis UFla 60-65; Bibliog to Ibero-Amer Studies UWis(Madison) 65-. 08: Seminars on the acquis of Latin-Amer Lib Materials. 9: ALA; SWLA; TexLA; FlaLA. 10: SE Conf on Lat Amer Studies; Amer Assn Tchrs Spanish; Phi Sigma Iota. 12: Ed "Microfilming Projects Newsletter" (64-). 13: Yes. 14: Latin-Amer Area Studies, acquis, bibliog. 15: 495 N Wythe st, Pentwater Mich 49449.

HODINA, ALFRED. b Linz Austria 26 N 23. 4: Loree Closson. 5: SUNY(Albany) 56-60, 61-62 (Physics) BS, MS; UWash 62 (Oceanography); SUNY(Albany) 63-64 MLS. 6: Ger. 7: Marine engnr Atlantic Refining Co, Phila 52-55; High sch sci tchr Colonie Central High Sch, Albany NY 60-61; Tchg asst Physics Dept SUNY (Albany) 61-62; Research asst UWash Dept of Oceanography 62; Ser & ref asst Rensselaer Polytech Inst 63-64, Sci libn 64-65; Lib systems analyst UHouston 65-67; Dir admissions & stud affairs UMd Sch of Lib & Info Serv (Col Pk) 67-. 9: ASIS; ALA; Systems & Procedures Assn; TexLA; AALS. 10: Sigma Pi Sigma; AAAS; Wilderness Soc. 14: Lib systems analysis & data processing, sci ref & info retrieval, admin. 15: 155 Westway rd apt 203, Greenbelt Md 20770.

HODKINSON, CATHERINE B(AILEY). b Pittsburgh 28 Mr 1900. 5: Carnegie 19-23 (Sec) BS; Pratt 31-32 (LS) Certif. 7: Sec Armstrong Cork Co, Pittsburgh 23-24; Ref libn Morristown Pub Lib, Morristown NJ 32-43; E Orange Pub Lib, E Orange NJ: Ref libn 43-45, Head of order dept 45-48, Prin libn order & catlg dept 48-63, Supv libn catlg & order depts 63-. 9: ALA; NJLA (Catlg Sect). 14: Catlg, acquis. 15: 60 Park End pl, E Orange NJ 07018.

HODNETTE, MILTON G(ARDNER) JR. b Denver 23 Ag 18. 4: Emilie S(yrova). 05: Colorado Col 38-42 (Span) BA; Stanford 44-45 (Russian); UCal 45-46 (Russian); UColo summer 49 (Spanish); UDenver summers 42, 43, 50-51 (LS) MA. 6: Sp, Portu, Fr, Lat, Ger. 7: Tchr of Lat, Span & Fr Colo Mil Sch, Denver 47-48; Tchr of Lat & Span Webb Sch, Bell Buckle Tenn 48-50; Libn documents dept Denver Pub Lib 51-54, Mun ref libn 52-54; Documents libn Cal State Polytech Col Lib 54-58; Catlgr Chico State Col Lib 58-60, Head catlgr 60-68; Dir Nevada Ctr for Coop Lib Serv 68-69; Hd catlgr Ohio U Lib (Athens) 69-. 9: CalLA; ALA; NevLA. 14: Catlg, tech serv, lib coop. 15: Ohio Univ Lib, Athens Oh 45701.

HODOWANEC, GEORGE V. b Peremyshl Ukraine 5 N 35. 4: Oksana Stasiuk Hodowanec. 5: Temple 54-58 (Music) BS in Ed, 58-59 (Math, Physics); Drexel 59-60 MS in LS; Temple 61-64 Equiv to a BS (Math, Physics); Perm prof libn certifs in

Penn & NJ; UPittsburgh 68- (Libnship). 06: Russian, Polish, Ukrainian. 7: US Army Res Interrogator MI Unit (Sp 4) 61-; Ref libn Free Lib of Phila 60-62; Catlg libn Temple U Lib 62-63; Math tchr Plymouth- Whitemarsh Jt High Sch, Plymouth Meeting Penn 63-65; Lib Dir Cartaret Free Pub Lib, Cartaret NJ 65-67; Lib admin Cambria-Somerset Lib Syst, Johnstown Penn 67-69. 8: Tchr Lib Sci UVt summer 68. 9: ALA; PennLA (sec-treas Co Pub Lib Div); NJLA (past chm Human Rel Com). 10: Johnstown Kiwanis; Bd Dirs Johnstown Area Arts Coun. 11: Meritorious Tchr Award. 14: Admin, lib educ. 15: 5021 Bayard st, Pittsburgh Pa 15213.

HODSON, KAY E(THEL). b Ithaca 19 Je 40. 5: So Ill U 58-62 (Elem Educ) BS; UIll 64-65 (LS) MS. 7: Elem tchr Alton Sch Dist, Alton Ill 62; Elem tchr Harmony-Emge Sch Dist, Belleville Ill 62-64; Ref libn Dayton & Montgomery Co Pub Lib 65-. 9: ALA; OhioLA. 14: Ref. 15: 425 Dayton Towers Ct, B 3, Dayton Ohio 45410.

HODUSKI, BERNADINE ESTHER (ABBOTT). b New Deal Mont 27 Ja 38. 4: Ronald Frank Hoduski. 5: Avila Col 55-59 (Hist) BA; UDenver 64-65 (Libnship) MA. 6: Sp. 7: Lib asst Kan city (Mo) Pub Lib 59-60; Hd govt docs Central Mo State, Warrensburg Mo 65-. 9: ALA; MoLA; MoStateTA. 10: AAUP. 14: Govt docs. 15: 315 Anderson, Warrensburg Mo 64093.

HOEFER, MARGARET J. b Brooklyn NY 28 Jl 09. 5: Kans State Col (Pittsburg) 28-32 (Eng) BS in Ed (cum laude); Colo State Col 38-39 (Eng) MA; UDenver 41-43 BS in LS; John Hopkins 62. 6: Sp, Fr. 7: Chief asst circ & ref Greeley Pub lib, Greeley Colo 38-39; Hd circ Topeka Free Pub Lib, Topeka Kan 43-44; Libn Pueblo Jr Col, Pueblo Colo 44-46; Army libn nurnberg Military Post Hq, Nurnberg Germany 46-48; Lib dir SCAP C I & E Information Ctr, Osaka Japan 48-50; Command libn USAF, Clark AF Base Manila 50-51; Staff libn Central Air Defense Force Hq, Kans City Mo 51-53; Co libn Carroll Co Pub Lib, Westminster Md 58-62; Head libn Woodlawn Jr High Sch Baltimore Co Md 62-63; Hd ref serv Smithtown Lib, Smithtown NY 63-65; Dir Emma S Clark Memorial Lib Setauket NY 65-67; Hd ref serv Nassau Commun Col Lib, Garden City NY 67-. 8: High sch Eng tchg: Smith Ctr, Kans 34-38, Iola Kan 39-43, Army Educ Ctr, Nurnberg Germany 47-48, SCAP C I & E Info Ctr Osaka Japan 49-50. 9: ALA; NYLA; NassauCo(NY)LA. 10: Suffolk Symphonic Society; LWV. 14: Ref, admin, adult serv. 15: PO Box 847, Setauket NY 11733.

HOEFFGEN, HELEN ELIZABETH (HERBST). b Flint Mich 10 Je 15. 4: Kurt Hoeffgen. 5: Flint Col UMich 58-60 (Eng) BA; UMich 60-62 MALS. 6: Ger. 7: Trainee Flint Pub Lib, Flint Mich 60-61; Libn Civic Park Br Lib, Flint Mich 61-. 9: MichLA. 11: Loleta D Fyan Award 64. 13: Yes. 14: Adult educ, ref. 15: 1829 Greenbriar lane, Flint Mich 48507.

HOEGBERG, ERICK I(NGVAR). b Minneapolis 31 Jl 16. 4: Ruth Grotz. 5: Trinity Col (Conn) 34-38, 38-40 (Chem) BS, MS; Columbia 52-53 (LS). 6: Swedish, Ger, Fr. 7: Amer Cyanamid Co, Stamford Conn: Research chem 40-51, Libn 51-55, Group leader coding & indexing 55; Head tech info group Amer Viscose Corp, Marcus Hook Penn 56-63; Head tech info group FMC Corp Amer Viscose Div, Marcus Hook Penn 63-. 8: Chm USNCFID Subcom on the universal DC 65-67. 9: ACS (chm Del Valley Chem Lit Group 65); ASIS (chm US Com Univ Dec Clsf 65-67); SLA. 13: Yes. 14: Admin of info serv, internat sci communication, marketing lit, clsf. 15: FMC Corp Amer Viscose Div R & D, Marcus Hook Penn 19061.

HOEY, EVELYN (LEVINE). b Estill SC 28 Ag 19. 4: Reid A Hoey. 5: Meredith Col 35-39 (Gen Sci) BS; Simmons 39-40 BSLS. 6: Fr, Ger. 7: Catlgr Charlotte Pub Lib, Charlotte NC 40-43; Br libn Savannah Pub Lib, Savannah Ga 43; Libn US Off of Postal Censorship, Chicago 43-44; Libn US QM Subsistence Research & Development Lab, Chicago 44-46; Libn US Army Spec Serv, European Theater 46-49; Plant Libn Union Carbide Oak Ridge Gaseous Diffusion Plant, Oak Ridge Tenn 49-60; Chief documents lib Rome Air Development Center, Griffiss AFB NY 60-62; Spec lit acquis & research Gen Electric Co Electronics Lab, Syracuse NY 62-66, Admin Libn, Asst Prof admin med lib serv 66-. 8: Lib subcom assignments for AEC tech info panel 57-60; Vis Fac Syracuse U Sch of Lib Sci 67. 9: SLA (pres Oak Ridge 54-55), dir Upstate ny chap 65-66); MedLA (Exec Bd mem-at-large 68-69). 10: Profess Woman's League. 12: Ed chm Union List of Serials in the Tech Libs of the Oak Ridge-Knoxville Area (3rd ed 57). 13: Yes. 14: Ref, admin. 15: 215 Wedgewood Terrace, Dewitt NY 13214.

HOEY, REID A. b Syracuse NY 12 Jl 20. 4: Evelyn Levine Hoey. 5: Syracuse 45-49 (Eng Lit) BA, 50 MS in LS. 7: Enoch Pratt Free Lib, Baltimore: Jr libn popular lib 50-52, Sr libn hist biog travel 52-53, Admin asst popular lib & circ 53-57; Dir Oak Ridge Pub Lib, Oak Ridge Tenn 57-59; City Libn Santa Fe Springs Lib, Santa Fe Springs Cal 59-60; Dir Mid-York Lib System, Rome NY 60-62; Dir Onondaga Lib System, Syracuse NY 62-. 8: Lib consul to Granger & Gillespie Architects Inc 64-; Guest lecturer: Syracuse U Lib Sch, Marina Reg Col. 9: ALA (chm Com for Coordinating Matls); NYLA (mem com area rep 62-, Recr Com area rep 62-); TennLA (pres Publ Lib Div 57-58). 10: Rotary; Syracuse U Lib Sch Alumni Assn (pres 64-66); Bd Trustees NY Ref & Resources Coun; Bd Trustees Lit Volunteers. 12: Bk reviewer "Baltimore (Sunday) Sun" (54-61). 13: Yes. 14: Admin, bldgs, circ, bk sel. 15: Onondaga Lib System 419 W Onondaga st, Syracuse NY 13202.

HOFFBERG, JUDITH A. b Hartford Conn 19 My 34. 5: Brandeis U 51-52 (Pol Sci); UCLA 53-56 (Pol Sci) BA (cum laude), 58-60 (Ital Lang & Lit) MA, 63-64 MLS. 6: Ital, Fr, Hebrew, Lat, Sp. 07: Hebrew tchr Temple Beth Am, Los Angeles 53-56; Ital instr UCLA 58-60; Lib asst Grad Bus Lib UCLA 63-64; Acquis libn Johns Hopkins U Bologna Center (Bologna Italy) 64-65; Libn (recruit) LC 65-, Catlgr prints & photographs 66-67; Fine Arts libn UPenn 67-. 8: Delegate to IFLA, Rome Italy 64. 9: ALA-ACRL (Art Subsect); SLA; Spec Libs Coun Phila; Coun Planning Libns. 10: Phi Beta Kappa; Pi Sigma Alpha; Renaissance Soc Amer; UCal Lib Schs Alumni Assn; Col Art Assn; Soc of Arch Histns; Washington Print Club; Print Club of Phila; Amer Fed of the Arts; Touring Club Italiano; ACLU. 11: Italian Nat Govt pre-doctoral grant 60-61: Study of Leonardo da Vinci in Florence Italy. 13: Yes. 14: Ref, catlg, rare bks, admin. 15: Fine Arts Lib Furness Bldg, Univ of Penn, Philadelphia Pa 19104.

HOFFELD, SHEILA KATHERINE (WAKEFIELD). b Erie Penn 11 F 10. 5: West Res 28-31 (Eng) BS, 31-32 BS in LS. 7: Asst child room Erie Pub Lib, Erie Penn 27-28; Child libn JVL Pruyn Br Albany Pub Lib, Albany NY 32-42; Child libn Pensacola Lib, Pensacola Fla 65; Child libn Albany Pub Lib, Albany NY 68-. 9: ALA. 14: Child wk. 15: 1044 Washington ave, Albany NY 12203.

HOFFMAN, BETTY S. b Harrisburg Penn 7 N 17. 4: William M Hoffman. 5: Hood Col 35-39 (Fr) AB; Syracuse 39-40 BSLS. 6: Fr. 7: Asst libn pub lib, Sunbury Penn 54-55; Libn Shikellamy High Sch, Sunbyry Penn 57-. 9: ALA; NEA; NCTE; PennStateEA; SunburyEA. 10: Bus & Profes Women. 14: Ref. 15: 1132 N Front st, Sunbury Pa 17801.

HOFFMAN, DAVID R. b Brownwood Tex 28 S 34. 5: Daniel Baker Col 51-52; Davis & Elkins Col 52-54 (Eng) BA; West Res 54-55 MSLS. 7: Ref asst Dayton Pub Lib, Dayton Ohio 55-57; US Army 57-59; Admin asst Wis Free Lib Commsn, Madison Wis 59-63; Head info serv Lib Tech Proj ALA, Chicago 63-66, Asst dir Intl Rel Off ALA 66-68; Coord lib development Mont State Lib 68-. 8: Exec Dir Nat Lib Week in Wis 63. 9: ALA-LAD; AASL; WisLA (past Memb Chm; past treas; past NLW exec dir); MontLA; PNLA. 12: Ed "Wis Lib Bulletin" (59-63). 13: Yes. 14: Admin, equipment. 15: 716 Harrison ave, Helena Mt 59601.

HOFFMAN, ELIZABETH (PARKINSON). b Pittsburgh Penn 23 Mr 21. 4: James W Hoffman. 5: Dickinson Col 42 AB; Drexel 61 MSLS. 6: Fr. 7: Tchr libn Womelsdorf Sch Dist, Womelsdorf Penn 42-45; Libn (sub) New Hope-Solebury Sch Dist, New Hope Penn 45-48; Ed-child page & bk reviewer "Presbyterian Life", Phila 48-57; Libn, chm of elem lib Haverford Twp Sch Dist, Havertown Penn 58-66; Sch lib specialist Div of Sch Lib E Area Br Dept of Pub Instr Comm of Pa, Upper Darby Penn 66; Dir div of sch lib & coord of esea title II Bureau of Gen & Acad Educ Dept of Pub Instr Comm of Pa, Harrisburg Penn 66-. 8: Consul sch dists in Phila area 60-65; consul New Hope area 45-48; Schoolmen's Week Proceedings; Temple Reading Clinic. 9: NEA; ALA; AASL; State Sch Lib Supvs; PennStateEA; PennLA; HTEA; DELCO Sch Libns (pres). 10: Beta Phi Mu. 13: Yes. 14: Sch lib dev. 15: 805 Beechwood rd, Havertown Pa 19083.

HOFFMAN, LA VINIA JEAN. b Grove City Penn 23 Ag 20. 5: Cleveland Sch of Art 42-46 (Illustration) Certif; Flora Stone Mather Col 45-46 (Art) BS; West Res 46-47 BSLS. 7: E Cleveland(Ohio) Pub Lib: Child libn 47-48, Br child libn 48-60, Br libn 60-63, Head of child dept 63-. 9: ALA; OhioLA. 10: Womens Nat Bk Assn; West Res Sch of Lib Sci Alumna Assn; Flora Stone Mather Alum Assn. 14: Child serv. 15: 927 Aintree Park dr, Mayfield Village Oh 44143.

HOFFMAN, LYDIA (MAYER). b NYC 5 Ap 28. 4: Frank Anton Hoffman. 5: IndU 61-66 (Eng) BA; Syracuse 67-68 MSLS. 6: Fr. 7: Lib research asst Inst for Sex Research, bloomington Ind 62-66; Lib trainee Buffalo & Erie Co Pub Lib Crane Br 66-67, Asst libn N Jefferson Br 68-. 9: ALA; NYLA. 10: Beta Phi Mu. 14: Inner City wk. 15: 197 Ridgewood dr, Snyder Amherst NY 14226.

HOFFMAN, MARILYN LEE. b Wichita Kan 24 O 46. 5: Central State Col (Edmon Okla) 63-67 (Hist) BA; UDenver 67-68 (Libnship) MA. 6: Ger. 7: Ref libn Tucson Pub Lib 68-. 9: ALA; AirzStateLA. 10: Beta Phi Mu; Alpha Chi. 14: Ref, archival docs, a-v materials. 15: PO Box 1461, Tucson Az 85702.

HOFFMAN, MORRIS. b St Paul 24 Ap 23. 4: Joan Kniberg. 5: Sorbonne 45; UMinn 46-49 (LS) BS, 50 (Educ) Masters Certif. 6: Ger, Sp. 7: Army 101st Airborne Div (Cpl), European Area 43-46; UMinn(Minneapolis): Lib page 46-49, Tchg asst & Instr Lib Sch 50, Engnr libn Sch of Engnr 50-51; Libn St Anthony Falls Hyd Lab, Minneapolis 51-52; Head tech serv, Assoc Prof & assoc libn US Naval Postgrad Sch, Monterey Cal 52-59; Lib researcher No Natural Gas Co, Omaha 59-. 8: Tchr of "Efficient Reading" 60-, "Technical Writing" 63-. 9: SLA (v-chm Pub Utilities Sect); NebLA. 10: B'nai B'rith. 12: Comp "Union List of Serials for Public Utility Libraries" (65). 13: Yes. 14: Spec lib admin. 15: 6940 Cuming st, Omaha Nb 68132.

HOFFMAN, WILLIAM B. b NYC 16 Ap 08. 4: Regina M Meyer. 5: Cornell 30-33; Brooklyn Law Sch 33-36 LLB. 7: Clerk Connolly & Frey, Brooklyn NY 36-37; Manager attorney James W Andrews, Mineola NY 38-39; Priv practice, Mineola NY 40-51; Legal aid attorney Nassau Co Bar Assn, Mineola NY 48-51; Libn Nassau Co Law Lib, Mineola NY 51-; Libn Nassau Co Supreme Court Lib 68. 8: Adv consul to Appellate Div of Supreme Court Second Dept concerning scope org & arrangement of their law lib 64. 9: Amer Bar Assn; NY State Bar Assn; Nassau Co Bar Assn. 13: Yes. 14: Rare bks, catlg, ref. 15: 67 Ships Point lane, Oyster Bay NY 11771.

HOFFMAN, WILLIAM JOHN. b Glidden Wis 2 S 22. 4: Edythe Buelke. 5: Lakeland Col 46-50 (Eng, Hist) BS; UWis 50-51 (Eng) MS; UDenver 61-63 (LS) MS. 7: Bombardier (1st Lt) US Army Air Corps 41-45; Statistician Salt River Proj, Phoenix 52-53; Eng tchr North High Sch, Phoenix Ariz 53-60, Libn 61-62; Head Libn maryvale High Sch, Phoenix 62-67; Program off US Off of Educ, King City Mo 67-68; Libn Johnson Co Commun Col 69-. 09: ALA; NEA-DAVI; Ariz State LA (pres-elect 67-68, pres Sch Libs Div 65-66); MoLA; MoSchLA. 14: Jr col & sch libnship, data proc. 15: 401 Lincolnwood dr, Lee's Summit Mo 64063.

HOFFMANN, MAURINE. b St Paul Minn 3 O 12. 5: Hamline U 30-34 (Eng Lit) BA; UMinn 35-39 (LS) BS. 7: Lib page pub lib, St Paul 34-40, Lib asst 40-43, Br libn 43-59, Supv ext serv 59-. 9: ALA (Coun 54-59); MinnLA (pres 52-53). 10: UMinn Lib Sch Alum Assn; City of St Paul Profess Employees Assn; Quota; Inter-Club Coun of St Paul. 14: Ext, commun rel. 15: 1452 Hewitt ave, St Paul Mn 55104.

HOFFMANN, PAUL E. b Vienna 2 F 15. 4: Eva G. 5: U Sch of World Trade (Vienna) 33-37 (Bus Admin) BS (Econ); Columbia 51-54 MS(LS). 6: Ger, Fr. 7: Brooklyn Pub Lib: Bind asst 54, Gifts & exch libn 54-58, Asst coordinator of bk order & supv of bind 58-. 9: ALA-RTSD (Bkbinding Com 62-64; Adv Com for Develop of Perf Stands for Lib Bind 64-65); BSA. 14: Conserv of lib materials, acquis, ref. 15: 523 W 112th st, New York NY 10025.

HOFFMEISTER, DONALD CHARLES. b Troy NY 28 N 31. 5: Siena Col (Loudonville NY) 49-51 9classical Lang); Boston Col 56-58 (Hist) BA; SUNY (Albany) 61-62 (Educ) MA, 64-66 MLS. 6: Ger, Lat. 7: Tchr Tri-Valley Sch, Grahamsville NY 62-64; Lib intern circ SUNY (Albany) 64-66, Asst catlgr 66, Hd current period unit 66-68; Circ libn SUNY (Geneseo) 68-69, Ser libn 69-. 9: ALA; NYLA. 14: Ser, circ systems. 15: 12 E South st, Geneseo NY 14454.

HOFFPAUER, DORISLEE RILEY. b Portland Ore 27 My 24. 4: Rieves M Hoffpauer. 5: UOre 42-44; UCal (Berkeley) 46-47, 48-51 AB; Tex Woman's U 63-67 MALS. 7: Sp 9t0 2c USNR (WAVES) 44-46; Libn Northwood Jr High Sch, Richardson Tex 67-. 15: 609 Arapaho rd, Richardson Tx 75080.

HOFLAND, FREDA (MAE) B(UNDY). b Athens Ohio 2 Ap 42. 4: John A Hofland. 5: Syracuse 60-64 (Eng) AB; Case West ResU 67-68 MS in LS. 6: Fr. 7: Circ desk clerk SyracuseU 64, Circ desk supv 64; Lib asst in charge period Robert Col, Istanbul Tirkey 65-67; Ref libn LawrenceU 68-. 8: Delegate to state & dist Democratic Party Convention. 9: ALA. 10: League of Women Voters; ACLU; A Better Chance; Sierra Club; Wilderness Soc; Audubon Soc; Beta Phi Mu. 14: Ref, pub serv, automation of proc. 15: 2300 Woodlark rd, Appleton Wi 54911.

HOFSTAD, RICHARD (JOSEPH). b Minneapolis 27 S 26. 5: UMinn 44-49 (Eng, Educ) BS, 50-51 BS in LS; UNotre Dame 49; Georgetown U 52-53. 07: Pharm Mate 3/c US Navy 45-46; High sch tchr, Delavan Minn 49-50; Acquis dept head Georgetown U 51-54; Soc sci libn UNotre Dame (S Bend Ind) 54-55; Libn LC US Dept of Agric Lib, Wash DC 55-56; Minneapolis Pub Lib: Prof Asst II 56-59, Asst head lit dept 59-62, Head order dept 62-. 9: ALA; MinnLA (chm Conv Exhibits 61-65). 14: Tech processing, acquis. 15: 4047 Dupont ave N, Minneapolis Mn 55412.

HOFSTETTER, ELEANORE O. b Camden NJ 16 My 39. 5: Marywood Col 57-61 (Hist) BS; Drexel 62-63 MSLS; UDel 63-66 (Hist) MA. 6: Ger. 7: Instr Trinity Col (Burlington Vt) 61-62; Ref libn UDel 63-66; Chief of ref lib Towson State Col 66-68, Chief of pub serv 68-. 9: ALA; Del Valley Col & Res Assn; MdLA (chm Col & Univ Sect 69-70). 10: Beta Phi Mu. 13: Yes. 14: Ref. 15: 11 Debonair ct apt 3, Baltimore Md 21234.

HOGAN, ALAN D. b Cleveland 5 D 38. 4: Barbara J Smallbrook. 5: John Carroll U 57-61 (Lat) AB; West Res 61-63 MS in LS. 7: Lib trainee Cleveland Pub Lib 62-63; Asst libn SUNY(Binghamton) 63-65, Assoc libn 65-66; Systs automation libn & instr Wright State U 66-69, Asst Prof 69-. 10: AAUP. 14: Tech serv, data processing, automation, microforms. 15: 4561 Penhurst pl, Dayton Oh 45424.

HOGAN, DANIEL EDWARD. b Brownville Jct Me 30 Ag 31. 5: St Jerome's Col 49-50; Farmington State Col 50-52 (Educ); Boston U 56-57 (Soc Studies) BS Ed. 7: QM US Armed Forces, US, Germany 52-55; Tchr Brownville Me 56-57, 58-60; Sch libn Bath Me 60-61; Tchr & sch libn Medfield Mass 61-, Supv sch libs 69-. 9: NEA; ALA; NESchLA; MassTA. 10: Internat Assn Free-Lance Photographers. 11: National Honor Society. 13: Yes. 14: YA. 15: 76 Pleasant st, Medfield Ma 02052.

HOGAN, JAMES WILLIAM. b London Eng 13 Ag 38. 4: Gillian Collins. 5: Kings Col (LondonU) 56-69 (Geog) BA (honours); Univ Col (LondonU) 62-63 (Libnship) Postgrad Diploma; BritishLA. 6: Fr. 7: Chinese linguist RAF, England & Hong Kong 59-61; Lib asst Westminster City Coun, London England 61-62, Ref libn 63-64; Libn Hong Kong Govt, London England 64-67; Circ & ser libn BrockU 67-68, Act univ libn 68-. 8: Consul to Dir Com Niagara Reg Lib Syst -69; Adv Com on Lib Tech Programme Niagara Col of Applied Arts & Tech -69. 9: Inst Prof Libns Ont. 14: Tech serv. 15: 34 Kings Grant rd, St Catharines Ont Can.

HOGAN, MARVIN P. b Chapel Hill NC 17 F 23. 4: Frances Thompson. 5: UNC 40-42, 46-47 (Philos) AB, 47-48 BSLS, 49-52 LLB. 7: USAAF Gunner (Sgt) 42-46; Asst circ libn UNC 48-49; Asst libn US Tax Court, Wash DC 52-55, Libn 55-56; Asst libn US Dept of Justice, Wash DC 56-57, Libn 57-. 8: Perm mem of Fed Lib Com; Panel mem of Bd of US Civil Serv Examiners at US Civil Serv Commsn Wash DC; Adv on several lib problems & projs, DC area. 9: AALL (mem var coms); Wash DC Law Libns Soc (v-pres, treas, Exec Bd, chm var coms). 13: Yes. 14: Admin. 15: US Dept of Justice, Wash DC 20530.

HOGAN, MARY JOANNE (OSTROWSKI). b Corner Brook Newfoundland Can 28 S 43. 4: Michael Hogan. 5: UToronto 61-64 (Eng) BA, 64-65 Ont Tchg Certif, 67-68 BLS. 7: TC"LBN Niagara FALLS COL Niagara Falls Ont 65-67; Tchr-libn Montcalm Secondary Sch, London ont 69-. 9: ALA; CanLA. 14: Sch libs. 15: 767 Dufferin ave, London Ont Can.

HOGAN, MILDRED E(LINOR). b Pine Bluff Ark 30 Jl 11. 5: Centenary Col 26-30 (Eng) BA; LSU 33-34 BS in LS; Columbia summer 41 (LS). 6: Lat, Fr, Sp. 7: Tchr-libn High Sch, Mooringsport La 30-33; Sec to state supv of libs State Dept Educ, Baton Rouge La 34-41; Research libn State Dept of Educ, Baton Rouge La 41-44; Asst to dir of libs LSU 44-45; Research libn State Dept of Com & Ind, Baton Rouge La 45-51; Libn Transcontinental Gas Pipe Line Corp, Houston 51-. 8: Spec lecturer UTex Grad Sch of Lib Sci summers 60, 61. 9: SLA. 13: Yes. 14: Spec lib admin. 15: P O Box 1396, Houston Tx 77001.

HOGAN, REBECCA J (ADAMS). b Dallas 6 My 32. 4: Frank M Hogan. 5: Tex Womans' U 49, 52-55 (LS) BA. 7: Catlgr UTex(Austin) 55-56; Catlgr Arlington State Col 56-57; Catlgr & acquis Texas Instruments Inc, Dallas 57-66; Supv tech processing Richardson Pub Lib 67-68; Libn Richardson Jr High Sch, Richardson Tex 68-. 9: SLA (Bus Mgr Tex Chap Bulletin 65-66); ALA; TexLA (chm Bk Selection Policy Com 68-69). 10: Alpha Beta Alpha. 14: Catlg, acquis. 15: 1017 Pacific dr, Richardson Tx 75080.

HOGAN, (MARGARET) ROSE. b Little Rock Ark 23 Ja 32. 5: St LouisU 50-54 (Biol) BS; Woodshole Marine Biol Lab summer 54; UArk 57-59 (Biochem) MS; Little RockU 61-62; Emory summer 62. 6: Ger. 7: Research asst VA Hosp, Little Rock Ark 60-62; Research asst UArk Med Ctr 57-60, Ref libn 62-66, Hd libn 66-. 8: Lib USA NY World's Fair 64. 9: ALA; SLA; MedLA (Continuing Educ Staff 63-68); ArkLA (2nd v-pres 68; 1st v-pres & pres-elect 69). 13: Yes. 14: Ref, admin, educ. 15: 212 Vernon W, Little Rock Ar 72205.

HOGAN, SARAH (TURNER). b Creston Iowa 7 Ap 27. 4: Bernard J Hogan. 5: Smith 45-49 (Hist) BA; Katharine Gibbs 49-50 (Sec) Certif; UDenver 57-58 (LS) MA. 7: Catlg libn soc studies USAF Acad Lib 58-62; Asst catlgr N Tex State U 63-64, Act catlg libn 65, catlg libn 66-. 9: ALA; TexLA. 14: Catlg. 15: 130 W Scotland, Irving Tex 75060.

HOGDEN, ALLEN JOHN. b Ettrick Wis 17 Ag 14. 5: UMich 36-41 (Music) B Mus, 46-48 (Pol Sci) MA; Konservatorium (Heidelberg) 49-51 (Music); London Sch Econ & Pol Sci 51-52 (Pol Sci); Columbia 55-56 MLS. 6: Ger. 7: Admin asst (v-consul) US High Commsn for Germany, Heidelberg 48-52; Jr catlgr LC 52-53; Sect hd acquis br NY Pub Lib 54-56, Sr catlgr 56-63; Hd catlgr Suffolk Coop Lib Syst, Patchogue NY 63-65; Hd catlgr UIll (Chicago) 65-69; Chief proc div research libs NY Pub Lib 69-. 8: Morris Raphael Cohen Lib, CCNY 61. 9: ALA-ACRL. 14: Catlg, econ, pol sci, music. 15: 480 Halstead ave apt 1E, Harrison NY 10528.

HOGENSON, ALEITA ALLEN. b Newburyport Mass 25 Je 02. 5: Widener Lib, Harvard train course in LS 20-24; Bradley U 34-38 (Lang, Lit, Art) BA. 6: Fr, Sp, Ger, Russian. 7: Lib & research asst Nat Educ Assn, Wash DC 38-39; Home serv correspondent Nat Hdqrs ARC & Peoria Cy Chap, Wash DC 42-45, 53-58; Asst & act libn Republican Nat Committee, Wash DC 45-47; Libn Webber Col 53-54; Asst libn Freer Gallery of Art, wash DC 54-66; Ref libn Nat Col Fine Arts/Nat "ortrait Gallery Smithsonian Inst 66-. 9: ALA; DCLA. 10: Eng Speaking Union. 14: Ref. 15: 5034 Eskridge terr NW, Wash DC 20016.

HOGUE, HELEN MARIE. b Oshkosh Wis 6 D 18. 5: Wis State U (Oshkosh) 37-41 (Eng) BS; Tchr-libn License. 6: Lat, Fr. 7: High Sch: Tchr Norway Mich 41-42, Rosholt Wis 42-44; Lib staff Oshkosh Pub Lib, Oshkosh Wis 44; Libn S Side Br Lib, Oshkosh Wis 57. 9: ALA; WisLA; Fox River Valley LA (sec 55). 10: Wis State U; Oshkosh Found; Alpha Xi Delta; Wis State Hist Soc; Oshkosh Commun Concert Assn; Town & Gown of Performing Arts; Oshkosh Women's Symphony. 14: Admin. 15: 1115 Winnebago ave, Oshkosh Wis 54901.

HOGUE, MRS MABEL (WHITE). b Antioch Ga 22 N 01. 5: LaGrange Col 18-22 (Eng) AB; Peabody summers 37-41 BS in LS. 6: Lat. 7: Tchr of Eng & Lat Meriwether Co High Sch, Woodbury Ga 22-23; Tchr of Eng & Lat Abbeville High Sch, Abbeville Ga 23-24; Tchr of Eng & Lat Adel High Sch, Adel Ga 24-27; Lat tchr Newnan High Sch, Newnan Ga 27-29; Eng tchr Albany High Sch, Albany Ga 29-39, Libn 39-64; Dir of Sch Libs Dougherty Co, Albany Ga 64-. 8: Prof Lib Com of Ga for sel of bks to be included on Ga Lib List 58-64; Visiting Com to help evaluate Ga schs for accred. 9: ALA; NEA; GaEA; GaLA (chm Stud Lib Assts Com 63-65). 10: Delta Kappa Gamma; Commun Concert Org. 13: Yes. 14: Sch lib supv. 15: 628 Third ave, Albany Ga 31701.

HOGYE, IDA (MOLNAR). b Budapest Hungary 19 S 16. 4: Michael Hogye. 5: Tchrs Col(Hungary) 34-36 (Educ) BA; Soc Wkers Sch(Hungary) 36-37 Soc Wker Certif; ULille(France) 37-38 (Fr Lit); Pazmany Peter U(Budapest) 41-43 (Fr Lit); Business Sch(Budapest) 43-44 (Sec); Catholic U 60-63 MSLS. 6: Hungarian, Fr, Ger. 7: Soc wker Socie3te3 Centrale Evange3lique, Roubaix Lille France 37-41; Tchr Grade Sch, Hungary 41-42; Sec to Mayor of Budapest, City of Budapest Hungary 42-46; Fairfax Co Pub Lib, Falls Church Va: Lib aide 57-63, Ref libn 63-65, Br libn 65-. 9: VaLA. 10: Beta Phi Mu. 14: Ref. 15: 6006 Lebanon dr, Falls Church Va 22041.

HOHMANN, MARY ALICE. b Holland Mich 27 N 33. 5: Trinity Col 51-52; MarquetteU 52-55 9hist & Sp) BS, 56-59 (Law) LLB; UWis (Milwaukee) 69- (LS). 6: Sp, Lat. 7: Lawyer Morrisey, Doyle & Hohmann, Shorewood Wis 59-62; Law libn & Assoc Prof of law marquetteU 62-. 9: Amer Bar Assn; AALL; Amer Judicature Soc; Wis Bar Assn; Chicago Law Lib Assn. 10: Milwaukee Bar Assn; Gamma Pi Epsilon. 12: Assoc ed "Marquette Law Review". 13: Yes. 14: Law lib admin. 15: 1103 W Wisconsin ave, Milwaukee Wi 53233.

HOIT, OERTEL (AADNESEN RILEY). b Ogden Utah 4 O 13. 4: Warren Sturdevant Hoit. 5: UUtah 31-32 (Educ); Weber State Col 32-33 (Educ) Standard; Utah State U 33-35 (Educ) BS; UIdaho summer 35; Idaho State U 63-69 (LS). 7: Doc distribution Adj Gen Depot Govt, Ogden Utah 42-43; Tchr: Ogen Utah 35-37, 43-44, Provo Uy depot Govt, Ogden Utah 42-43; Tchr; Ogden Utah 35-37, 43-44, Provo Utah 51-52, Pocatello Idaho 63-. 9: IdaLA (var offs & coms). 10: Trustee Pocatello Pub Lib; Pocatello Music Club; Amer Leg Aux; State Fed Music Clubs; Beta Sigma Phi; 8 et 40. 12: Mem Publ Com "The Idaho Librarian". 13: Yes. 15: 119 S 14th, Pocatello Id 83201.

HOKE, MRS ELIZABETH (GLASS). b Hartford Conn 24 O 17. 5: Smith 35-39 (Eng) AB; UMinn 63-64 (LS) MA. 6: Fr. 7: Libn Wadsworth Athenaeum, Hartford Conn 64-. 9: ALA-ACRL (Nom Com Art Subsect 65); SLA; ConnLA. 12: "Minnesota Libraries" (64). 14: Art ref. 15: Auerbach Art Lib, Wadsworth Athenaeum, Hartford Ct 06103.

HOKE, SHEILA WILDER. b Greensboro NC 15 Jl 28. 5: UKan 50 (Hist) AB, 51 (Educ) BS; UWis 55 (LS) MS. 7: Tchr Fredonia High Sch, Fredonia Kan 52-54; Br child libn Enoch Pratt Free Lib, Baltimore 55-58; Libn Army Spec Serv, Straubing Germany 58-59; Catlgr SWest State Col Lib 63-. 8: Lib consul on Concho Proj 58. 14: Catlg, ref, child wk. 15: 817 N Kansas, Weatherford Ok 73096.

HOLBROOK, (BEULAH) BEATRICE. b Sparta NC 1 O 02. 8: Ed Bk Reviewing Proj Sch Lib Sect NCLA 57; Ed "Reference Books for School Libraries" Dept of Pub Instr summer 58; Consul "Junior High School Library Catalog " (H W Wilson Co) 65-68. 13: Yes. 15: 18 Horne st apt 3, Raleigh NC 27607.

HOLBROOK, FRANCES KARR. b Memphis Tenn. 5: Mt Holyoke (Eng) AB; Columbia 39-40 MS. 6: Fr, Sp. 7: Catlgr Sch of Law Lib Columbia U 35-43; Libn Chadbourne, Wallace, Parke & Whiteside, NY 43; Libn Scarborough Sch, Scarborough NY 50-52; Head catlg dept Sch of Law Lib UCLA 52-68, Asst law libn Law Lib 68-. 8: Instr in catlg 1st AALL Inst, 53; Dir AALL Rotating Inst (Catlg), 66. 9: ALA; AALL (chm Com on Catlg & Classification 55-56, 64-66; chm Com on Chaps 56-57); CalLA; So Cal assn Law Libs (pres 54-56). 12: Ed staff "Law Library Journal" (56-68. 13: Yes. 14: Catlg. 15: 328 N Bowling Green wy, Los Angeles Ca 90049.

HOLCOMB, ALICE TALBOT. b Plymouth Ill 16 Je 11. 4: Edward A Holcomb. 5: UIll 29-33 (Com) BS; West Ill U 33-34 (Educ) BE; No Ill U 67 MALS. 7: Period libn No Ill U 62, Asst soc sci libn 63-66, Asst humanities libn 67, Art dept slide curator 68-. 9: ALA; Col Arts Assn; IllLA. 10: AAUW. 14: Art ref & research. 15: 417 E High st, Sycamore Il 60178.

HOLCOMB, JEANNE (SCHLEIS). b Waupaca Wis 9 Ag 27. 5: Marquette U 45-49 (Eng) B Ph; Columbia 50-51 (LS) MS. 7: Ref libn Pub Lib, Ft Worth Tex 51-54; USAF Germany: Libn 54-56, Libn Richards-Gebaur AFB Mo 57-60; Libn Milwaukee Wis 60-63; Med Libn VA Center, Wood Wis 63-. 9: MedLA; SLA. 15: Med Lib VA Center Wood Wis 53193.

HOLCOMB, LAUREL (ERNESTINE). b Wessington Springs S Dak. 5: UCLA 41-43 (Hist) BA, (Berkeley) 43-44 (Libnship) BS; UIll (Urbana) 47-48 (LS) MS; West Washington State Col 67-68 (Hist) MA. 6: Sp. 7: Hd libn NW Nazarene Col 44-45; Ref libn Ore State U 45-47; Asst libn Neb State Col (Kearney) 50-60; Ref libn Bellingham Pub Lib (Bellingham) Wash 61-67. 9: ALA; -ACRL; NebLA (chm Col Sect 55-57). 14: Ref, Latin Amer collections. 15: 2739 Cedarwood ave, Bellingham Wa 98225.

HOLDEN, HARLEY PEIRCE. b Shirl ey Mass 18 Ag 37. 5: Boston U 56- 60 62-65 (Hist) AB, AM; Simmons 65-67 MS; AmericanU Nat Archives 67 Certif in Archives Admin. 6: Fr, Sp. 7: Asst archivist Harvard U 66-. 9: SAA. 10: Phi Alpha Theta; Cambridge, Groton & Count Rumford Hist Soc; Bay Statr Hist League; Soc for Preservation of NE Antiquities; Appalachian Mt Club; Sierra Club; Wilderness Soc; Mass Forest & Pk Assn; Middlesex Canal Assn; Mass Archeol Soc;

Thor eau Soc; Thoreau Lyceum. 14: Archives, rare bks, maps. 15: Horse Pond rd, Shirley C enter Ma 01465.

HOLDEN, JEANNE (POULSEN). b San Francisco 7 My 14. 4: William D Holden. 5: UCal(Berkeley) 33-36 (Eng) AB, 38 (LS) Certif. 6: Fr. 7: Catlgr-clsf H E Huntington Lib, San Marino Cal 38-43; Libn Muroc Army Air Field Cal 43-45; Army libn Dijon & Rheims, France 45-46; Sr catlgr Harvard Col Lib 47-. 14: Catlg, rare bks. 15: 24 Henry st, Winchester Mass 01890.

HOLDEN, KATHARINE M(acDOWELL). b Yonkers NY 2 D 12. 5: Cornell U 29-33 (Gen Sci, Educ) BS; Columbia 35-43 (LS) BS, MS. 6: Fr. 07: Pub Lib, Yonkers NY; Bkmob libn 36-37, 1st asst circ 37-40, Head ext dept 40, 41-42, Head circ dept 42-44; Libn Jr high sch, Yonkers NY 40-41; Asst libn Nat Assn of Manufacturers, NYC 44-46; Bibliog US Internat Bk Assn, NYC 46; Libn Schenley Research Labs, Larchmont NY 47; Ed H W Wilson Co, NYC 47-49; Asst dir Pub Lib, Mt Vernon NY 49-56, Dir 56-60; Dir Westchester Lib System, Mt Vernon NY 59-67; Pub lib consul 68-. 8: Assoc in lib serv, Columbia Sch of Lib Serv, 50. 9: ALA (Coun 55-59)-LAD (sec Pub Rel Sect 60-62, chm Constit & Bylaws Com 60-61, chm Jr Mem Sect 43-44); NYLA (pres 60, chm var coms); Westchester LA (pres 54-56); NY Lib Club. 10: Columbia Sch Lib Serv Alumni Assn; Zonta Club; YWCA. 12: "Educ Film Guide" (47-49); "Filmstrip Guide" (48-49). 13: Yes. 14: Pub lib admin. 15: Flanders rd RFD #1, Box 128A, Bethlehem Ct 06751.

HOLDER, ELIZABETH (JEROME). b Winston-Salem NC 1 Jl 14. 5: Duke 31-33; Salem Col 33-35 (Eng, Hist) AB; UNC 52-55 MS in LS. 6: Fr, Ger, Lat, Gk, Russian. 7: Asst lib Salem Col 35-37; Asst in child wk NY Pub Lib 37-40; Asst circ libn Walter Clinton Jackson Lib UNC(Greensboro) 47-58, Asst to libn & Asst ref libn 58; Libn James Addison Jones Lib, Brevard Col 58-63; Head ref dept Walter Clinton Jackson Lib UNC (Greensboro) 63-. 9: ALA (sec Col & Univ Sect 66-68); SELA; NCLA (Sec Col & Univ Sect, Ed Bd NC Libs). 10: Beta Phi Mu; Alumni Assn; UNC Sch Lib Sci; Greensboro Lib Club; Trustee Salem Col; AAUP; AAUW; NC Lit & Hist Soc; Wachovia Hist Soc; Greensboro Jr League. 12: Illus: "Tell Me s Story" by K B Rondthaler (48); "North Carolina & Old Salem Cookery," by E H Sparks (55). 14: Ref. 15: Walter Clinton jackson Lib UNC, Greensboro NC 27412.

HOLICKY, BERNARD H. b Cleveland 1 S 37. 5: Ohio U 55-59 (Govt) AB; West Res 59-61 MSLS. 7: Page Cleveland Pub Lib, 53-55; Stud asst Ohio U Lib 56-57; Ref asst Bus Info Div Cleveland Pub Lib 59-61; Acquis libn Cornell U Law Lib 61-63; Asst ref libn Purdue U Libs 63-64, Soc sci libn 64-66, Libn (Calumet Campus). 9: ALA; Assn Law Libs Upstate NY (sec 62-63); IndLA. 10: AAUP. 13: Yes. 14: Ref, admin. 15: 7218 Ontario ave, Hammond In 46323.

HOLIFIELD, BETTY LOU. b Forest Miss 15 Mr 39. 5: Fla A&M 58-62 BS in LS; UMich 64-65 MA in LS. 6: Fr. 7: Stud lib asst Fla A&M U 59-61; Head Libn Utica Jr Col 62-63; Law Libn Genesee Co Law Lib, Flint Mich 63-67; Gen Motors Inst Tech serv libn 67-. 8: Consul to Genesee Mem Hosp Med Lib, Flint Mich 64-. 9: ALA; SLA; MichLA (Newcomer's Com 65). 10: Flint Lib Club; Bus & Prof Women's Club. 12: Contrib "Basic Books for Junior College Libraries; 20,000 Vital Titles" ed by Charles Trinkner. 13: Yes. 14: Ref, spec lib wk. 15: 905 Edmund st, Flint Mich 48505.

HOLLAND, CARL BYRON. b Weatherly Penn 26 Je 38. 4: Susan Del Terrill. 5: Mich StateU 56-60 (Soc Sci) BA; Lutheran Sch of Theol (Chicago) 60-64 (Theol) BD; UIll 66-67 (LS) MA. 7: Pastor Lutheran Ch in Amer, Chadwick Ill 64-66; Supv lib serv Nursing Homes pierce Co Pub Lib, Tacoma Wash 67-. 10: Nat Audubon; Nat Wildlife; Farmhouse Fraternity. 15: 222 S 58th st, Tacoma Wa 98408.

HOLLAND, CAROLYN (MARTIN). b Durham NC 23 Mr 38. 4: Robert Edward Holland MD. 05: Bennett Col 55-59 (Fr) BA; UNC 59-61 MSLS. 07: Searcher LC summer 61, Ref libn 61-64; Catlgr Dept of Labor Lib, Wash DC 65; Libn, Woodson Jr High Sch Wash DC Pub Schs 66-. 9: DCASchL. 14: Catlg. 15: 99 Webster st NE, #104, Wash DC 20011.

HOLLAND, EDNA (WU). b Antigo Wis 15 D 21. 4: Arthur Holland. 5: Northland Col 39-44 (Eng) BA; West Res summers 47-50 BS in LS. 7: Child libn Antigo Pub Lib, Antigo Wis 44-47, Act libn 47-51, Head Libn 51-60; Field libn Wis Free Lib Commsn, Madison Wis 60-62; Head Libn Gail Borden Pub Lib, Elgin Ill 62-. 9: ALA; IllLA (sec 66-67); WisLA (chm Co Sect 58-59); AEAUSA. 10: Zonta Club; AAUW. 11: John Cotton Dana Award 65. 14: Pub lib admin. 15: Gail Borden Pub Lib 50 N Spring st, Elgin Ill 60120.

HOLLAND, HAROLD EDWARD. b Nashville 16 Jl 24. 4: Geraldine Young. 5: David Lipscomb Col 41-43 J C Diploma; Harding Col 43-45, 54-55 (Eng, Religion) BA, MA; Vanderbilt 46-47 (Sci); Columbia 55-57, 64 (LS) MS; USoCal 61-63 (LS). 6: Fr. 7: Minister & missionary Church of Christ, Tenn, Ark, NY, Cal, Japan, NC 43-67; Instr physics David Lipscomb Col 46-47; Assoc Prof Eng & Bible, act dean Ibaraki Christian Col (Omika Japan) 50-54; Tchr-libn Franklin Jr High Sch, Yonkers NY 56-57; Lib asst Chemists Club, NYC summer 57; Asst tech libn Linde Co (Union Carbide), Tonawanda NY 57-58; Libn Pepperdine Col (Los Angeles) 58-61; Visiting lecturer Lib Sci USoCal summer 61; Supv tech serv Aerospace Corp Lib, El Segundo Cal 61-63; Asst Prof Lib Sci UOkla 63-64; Tchg asst Columbia 64-65; Chm Lib Sci Appalachian State 65-67; Visiting lecturer Lib Sci Peabody summer 68; Asst Prof Lib Sci UMo (Columbia) 67-. 9: ALA; SLA (Dir Okla Chap 63-64, Dir NC Chap 65-67); MoLA. 10: AAUP; Hymn Soc of Amer; Disciples of Christ Hist Soc. 14: Ref, sci bibliog, relig publ, govt pubs. 15: 213 Longfellow lane, Columbia Mo 65201.

HOLLAND, LAWRENCE. b Providence RI 22 Jl 28. 4: Susan Siusing Cheng. 5: Columbia 59-62 (Sociol) BS; Pratt 62-63 MLS. 6: Sp. 7: MP US Army US, Tokyo 51-53; Ref libn Hunter Col, Manhattan & Bronx Campuses 63-67; Hd of res room Jersey City State Col 68-. 9: CUNYLA. 10: Assn of NJ State Col Faculties; Japan Soc; Amer Legion. 14: Ref. 15: Gregory Park I 280 Henderson st, Jersey City NJ 07302.

HOLLAND, SARAH (BOWLING). b Brunswick Co Va 17 Ap 12. 4: Wiley M Holland. 5: Judson Col 28-31 (Eng) AB; UNC summers 35-38 AB in LS. 7: Dist supv Pub Libs WPA, Mobile Ala 40-41; Order libn Woman's Col of UNC (Greensboro) 38-40, 41-44; Catlgr Pub Lib Serv Div State of Ala, Montgomery Ala 45; Head of acquis Howard-Tilton Mem Lib Tulane U 47-57; Dir Coosa Valley Reg Lib, Pell City Ala 57-59; Libn & Instr in Lib Sci Judson Col 59-63; Admin St Clair Co Lib, Pell City Ala 63-66; Asst acquis libn in charge of ser UTenn Lib 66-. 9: ALA; SELA; TennLA. 10: Delta Kappa Gamma; DAR. 12: Assoc ed "North Carolina Libraries" (vols 1-2). 14: Acquis, ser, in-serv train prog. 15: 340 Live Oak lane, Knoxville Tn 37920.

HOLLEMAN, MARIAN PATTERSON (ARNOTT ISABEL). b Toronto 23 Jl 23. 4: Willard Roy Holleman. 5: Victoria U (U of Toronto) 41-45 (Hist) BA; Toronto 45-46 BLS, 46-48 (Hist) MA. 6: Fr. 7: Asst libn Acad of Med, Toronto 47-51, Chief Libn 52-61; Libn ref dept Doheney Lib USoCal 61-62; Visiting lecturer Grad Sch of Lib Sci USoCal summer 62; Libn UCLA Biomed Lib 62-63; Libn Bishop's Sch, La Jolla Cal 64-66; Libn Asst Prof USan Diego Col for Women 66-. 08: Supv libn & spec lecturer UToronto Lib Sch, 52-61; Libn ALA Lib 21, Seattle World's Fair, 62. 9: SLA (dir 58-60; chm Biol Scis Div 56-57; pres San Diego Chap); MedLA (Convention Chm 59); CalLA. 10: Univ Women's Club, Toronto; Zonta Club; Pi Delta Phi; Delta Epsilon Sigma. 12: Ed, SLA, "Scientific Meetings" (62-). 13: Yes. 14: Ref, rare bks, catlg. 15: 2069 Sea View ave, Del Mar Cal 92014.

HOLLEMAN, W ROY. b Alderson Okla 18 N 09. 4: Marian Patterson. 5: Okla State U 25-29 (Biol Sci) BS; UIll 37 MLS; Okla State U 42-43 (Physics) MS. 06: Ger, Fr, Russian. 7: Sci tchr McAlester High Sch, McAlester Okla 30-37; Ref libn Okla State U 38-42; Physics instr Army Air Forces Okla State U 42-44; Chief Libn Boeing Airplane Co, Wichita Kan 44-48; Chief Libn Mead Corp, Chillicothe Ohio 48-49; Libn Balboa U San Diego 49-50; Libn Scripps Inst of Oceanography UCal(LaJolla) 50-61; Assoc Prof USoCal Grad Sch Lib Sci 61-63; Libn & Assoc Prof Lib Sci USan Diego Col for Women 63-. 8: Libn ALA Lib 21, Seattle World's Fair, 62; Ed Adv Bd, Inst for Sci Info, 60-. 9: ALA (Lib Bldgs Inst Com 60-61; Coun); -LED (treas 48-51; Nomin Com 52, 57, 61); SLA (National: Scholarship Awards Com 62-65, ALA Spec Com 63-64, dir Engring sec 59-62, Prof Consul (life), Prof Standards Com 65-68, chm Sci-Tech Div 63-64; Nominating Com; SoCal Chap: Consul Com 62-63, pres 57-58, adv 63-64; San Diego Chap: Adv 62, pres 60-61, Sci-Tech Chm 63); ACS; Amer Geophys Union; AALS; CalLA (coun & pres Palomar Dist). 10: Kappa Delt Pi; Phi Kappa Phi; Scabbard and Blade; Phi Beta Kappa; Rotary Club; San Diego Sci & Tech Lib Resources Com; La Jolla Lib Assn; San Diego Sci Libs; West Soc of Naturalists; Zool Soc of San Diego; Oceanographers Credit Union; AAUP; Phi Delta Kappa; H W Wilson Awards Com. 13: Yes. 14: Sci bibliog, ref, rare bks, tchg. 15: 2069 Sea View ave, Del Mar Ca 92014.

HOLLEY, BARBARA ANN. b York Penn 21 Je 32. 5: Gettysburg Col 50-54 (Hist) BA; Drexel 55-58 MSLS. 7: Ser asst Lippincott Lib UPenn 54-59, Acquis libn 59-. 9: SLA; Phila Area Tech Serv Libns (sec-treas 63-65). 14: Acquis, ser. 15: 3717 Chestnut st, Phila Pa 19104.

HOLLEY, EDWARD GAILON. b Pulaski Tenn 26 N 27. 4: Robbie Lee Gault. 5: David Lipscomb Col 46-49 (Eng) BA; Peabody 49-50, 51 (LS) MA; UIll 51-52, 56-61 (LS) PhD. 6: Fr. 7: Asst libn David Lipscomb Col 49-51; Libn photographic reprod lab UIll(Urbana) 51-52; US Naval Res active serv (Lt sg) 53-56; Asst Lib Sci Lib UIll(Urbana) 56-57, Libn Educ Philos & Psych Lib 57-62; Dir of Libs U Houston 62-. 8: Lectr, UWis Lib Sch summer 68; Adv Coun on Col Lib Resources, USO Educ 68-; Chm Lib Formula Study Com, Tex Coord Bd, 69-; Adv Com LSCA Title III, Tex State Lib 67-; So Assn Visit Teams; Chm Tex Coun State Col Libns 65-67; Adv Com Regl Info & Communications Exch 68-; Ed ACRL "Monographs" 69-. 9: ALA-ACRL (Pub Com 68-70, Urban Univ Libns Com 65-67, Com on Coop Educ & Profess Organ 66-70); TexLA (Adv Com Regl Info Com Exch 68-); SWLA; Tex Assn Col Tchrs. 10: Beta Phi Mu; Kappa Delta Pi; Phi Kappa Phi; Tex Gulf Coast Hist Assn; Tex Coun State Col Libns. 11: Scarecrow Press Award 64. 12: "Charles Evans, American Bibliographer" (63); "Raking the Historic Coals" (67); Co-auth "Resources of Texas Libraries" (68); Ed of ACRL Monographs, (69). 13: Yes. 14: Univ lib admin, Amer lib hist. 15: 4837 Briarbend, Houston 77035.

HOLLIS, CATHERINE O'DAY. b Racine Wis 8 Ap 07. 4: George H Hollis. 5: UWis Lib Certif; Marquette U 44 (Eng, Hist) PhB; Columbia 52 Med Lib Certif. 7: Lib asst Racine Pub Lib, Racine Wis -44; Asst libn Aquinas Col 44-47; Libn Mercy Central Sch of Nursing, Grand Rapids Mich 47-; Med libn St Mary's Hosp, Grand Rapids Mich 66-. 9: CathLA (chm Hosp Sect; sec-treas Mich Unit 44-47); MedLA; MichLA (chm Hosp Sect); Grand Rapids Libns Club; Member Com for Libns in Health Facilities C.H.A. 12: Ed 'Hospital Section Newsletter' in "Catholic Library World" (52-57). 13: Yes. 14: Nurs sch, integrated med, nurs libs. 15: St Mary's Hosp Med Nursing Lib, 201 Lafayette ave SE, Grand Rapids Mi 49503.

HOLLIS, JEANNE. b Phenix City Ala 13 D 15. 5: Ga State Col for Women 33-37 (Eng) AB in LS; Peabody 45 BS in LS, 58 MA; Ala Polytech Inst 38, 43; UGa summer 62. 7: Eng tchr Central High Sch, Phenix City Ala 38-40; Libn Central High Sch, Phenix City Ala 40-45; Libn Jordan High Sch, Columbus Ga 45-48; Ref libn W C Bradley Mem Lib, Columbus Ga 48-. 9: GaLA; SELA. 10: AAUW. 14: Ref. 15: W C Bradley Mem Lib, Columbus Ga 31906.

HOLLISTER, KATHLEEN (MILLIS). b Rensselaer. 5: SUNY (Albany) 29-33 BLS, 37 (Eng) AB. 7: Libn Rensselaer Pub Lib 33-47; Libn Albany Pub Lib 47-51; High sch libn e greenbush Cent Sch 51-62, Dir libs 62-. 9: NEA; ALA; NYLA; NYStateTA; EastGreenbushEA; ENYSchLA (past pres). 10: Red Cross. 14: Wk with stud. 15: Troy rd, E Greenbush NY 12061.

HOLLMAN, EDWARD GEORGE. b Joplin Mo 29 O 22. 4: Margaret L Healy. 5: Mo Sch of Mines 41-43 (Civil Engnr); UMo 46-47 (Bus, Econ) BS in BA, 47-51 (Eng) BA, MA; UIll 54-55 MS in LS. 7: US Naval Res Aviation Radioman's Mate 3rd Class Combat Air Crew 43-46; UMo Lib: Bibliogr, ref asst 55-56, Head order dept 56-58, Catlgr catlg dept 58-60; Soc sci libn UOre Lib 60-61; Bibliogr, ref asst East Wash State Col 61-63; Soc sci libn UOre Lib 63-64, 66-67, Asst ser catlgr 64-65; Hd Bus Admin Lib URochester 67-68, Personnel Off URochester Lib 68-. 14: Ref, acquis, admin. 15: 50 Blackwell lane, Henrietta NY 14467.

HOLLORAN, SISTER MARY MARTINEZ RSM. b Waverly Tenn 23 O 19. 5: Athenaeum of Ohio(Cincinnati) summers 40-43; Siena Col summers 44-54 (Eng) BA; Peabody summers 59-62 MA(LS); Mundelein Col (Rel Educ Program). 07: Elem tchr for -5 yrs grades 1-8 var schs in Tenn; Prin in elem schs for 3 yrs; Libn Father Ryan High Sch for Boys, Nashville 59-64; Libn Immaculate Conception High Sch for Girls, Memphis Tenn 64-. 9: CathLA (Bk Fairs Com; chm Memphis (Tenn) Unit); TennLA; NCTE. 14: High sch wk, ref. 15: St Bernard High Sch, Bernard ave at 24th, Nashville Tn 37212.

HOLLOWAY, DONALD PHILLIP. b Akron Ohio 18 F 28. 5: Ohio U 46-50 (Bus Admin) BS in Com; Akron Law Sch 50-55 LLB; Kent State 61-62 MALS. 7: Abstracter Bankers G T & T Co, Akron Ohio 50-54; Accountant Robinson Clay Product Co, Akron Ohio 55-60; Libn Akron Pub Lib, Akron Ohio 62-66, Sr libn 67-69, Hd fine arts 69-. 8: Admitted to Ohio Bar, 55. 9: Amer Bar Assn; ALA; Ohio Bar Assn; OhioLA. 10: Nat Trust for Hist Preserv; Soc of Arch Histns; Nat Lawyer's Club, Wash DC; Akron Bar Assn. 14: Rare bks, music, arch. 15: 601 Nome ave, Akron Ohio 44320.

HOLLOWAY, ELIZABETH MANDELL. b Lake Charles La 12 O 08. 4: James Madison Holloway. 5: USouthwestern La 23-28 (Educ) BA. 6: Sp. 7: Libn-tchr St Martin Parish Sch Bd, Cecilia La 28-33; Tchr Lake Charles Sch Bd, Lake Charles La 33-34; Libn Iberville Parish Sch Bd, Maringouin La 43-46; Libn Pointe Coupee Parish Sch Bd, Livonia La 46-48; Head Libn Pointe Coupee Parish Lib, New Roads La 52-. 9: LaLA (past sec, past chm Pub Lib Sect & Legis Com). 10: Delta Kappa Gamma; La Geneal & Hist Assn; Pointe Coupee Parish Welfare Bd; Pointe Coupee Parish Econ Adv, Inc; Tuberc & Respir Diseases Assn. 11: Pointe Coupee Parish Lib received the Modisette award LaLA, 62. 14: Loc hist & research, ref. 15: Kenmore Plantation, Maringouin La 70757.

HOLLOWAY, GEORGE MARTIN. b Hickory NC 28 N 23. 4: Lisabeth M Feind. 5: UNC 42, 46-48 (Radio Production) BA; Drexel 49-50 MSLS. 7: US Army Infantry (Pfc) 43-45; Asst Libn The Hill Sch, Pottstown Penn 50-53; Libn II ref, educ, philos, religion dept Free Lib of Phila 53-58, Head educ films dept 58-65, Hd Reg Film Ctr 66-. 08: Chm Penn State Lib Com to plan a state-wide films serv for pub libs, 64. 9: ALA (A-v Com "Booklist"Film Preview subcom 60-67); PennLA (chm A-v Com 63-65, 67-68). 13: Yes. 14: Films. 15: Free Lib of Phila, Regional Film Ctr, 114 N 19th st, Phila Pa 19103.

HOLLOWAY, LISABETH MARIE (FEIND). b Mitchell S$ 5My 26. 4: George Martin Holloway. 5: Bryn Mawr 41-43; Col for Women UPenn 44-45 (Eng Lit) BA; Drexel 49-50 BS in LS. 6: Ger, Fr, Lat. 7: Enrollment off Harcum Jr Col 45-47; Typist-proofreader Amer Friends Serv Com, Phila 47-50; Catlgr UPenn Lib 50-52; Med libn VALLEY Forge Army Hosp, Phoenixville Penn 52-53; catlgr catlg dept Free Lib of Phila 53-54; Ed asst "Journal of Pediatrics," Phila 60-68; Assoc curator & catlgr Lib hist collection Col of physicians(Phila) 64-. 9: MedLA; Amer Assn Hist Med. 12: Ed "Directory of Libraries and Information Sources in the Philadelphia Area" (12th ed 68). 14: Catlg. 15: 58 W Tulpehocken st, Phila Pa 19144.

HOLLOWAY, O WILLARD. b Trenton NJ 25 Mr 15. 4: Mary Frances Ray. 5: Buffalo State Tchrs Col 32-35 (Educ); George Washington U 35-39 BA in LS; UBuffalo summer 38; George Washington U 39-41 (Law); Columbus 45-46 (Educ); George Washington U 35-39 BA in LS; UBuffalo summer 38; George Washington U 39-41 (Law); Columbus 45-46 (Law). 6: Fr. 7: Legis ref libn Soc Security Bd, Wash DC 41; Attorney VA, Winston-Salem NC 47; Libn Off of Tech Serv, Wash DC 45-46, 48-49; Asst libn Air U, Maxwell AFB Ala 49-51; Libn USIS, Paris 51-53; Libn Artillery Sch, Ft Sill Okla 54-62; Libn Defense Supply Agency, Wash DC 62-66; Libn Defense Intelligence Agency, Wash DC 66-67; Dir Army Lib, Wash DC 67-. 9: ALA; SLA (chm Mil Libn Div 60-61); DCLA; AALL. 10: Jr C of C; Kiwanis; Toastmasters Internat. 13: Yes. 14: Mil hist, admin. 15: 4301 Starr Jordan dr, Annondale Va 22003.

HOLLOWAY, RALPH (TIDWELL). b Salt Lake City Utah 2 Je 41. 4: Darlene Nunn. 5: Amarillo Col 60-62 (Hist) AA; Hardin SimmonsU 62-64 (Hist) BA; N Tex StateU 65-68 MLS. 6: Ger. 7: Libn-tchr Springtown Independent Sch Dist, Springtown Tex 65-68; Asst campus libn Tarrant Co Jr Col NE Campus (Ft Worth) 68-. 9: ALA; TexLA; TexJr ColTA. 14: Admin. 15: 345 James lane, Bedford Tx 76021.

HOLLREIGH, (MARGUERITE) MOLLIE HELEN. b Big Sandy Mont 19 Ap 18. 5: Wash State Col (Pullman) 37-41 (Eng) BA; UWash (Seattle) 41-42 (Libnship) BA. 6: Sp, Ger. 7: Mech Boeing Aircraft Co, Seattle 42-43; Post libn Douglas Army Air Field, Douglas Ariz 43-45; Libn UCLA circ & acquis div 46-49; Dir Pacific NW Bibliog Ctr UWash Lib (Seattle) 49-. 9: ALA; PNLA; WashLA. 10: Phi Beta Kappa. 13: Yes. 14: Catlg, bibliog, ref. 15: 1239 NE 91st, Seattle Wa 98115.

HOLLY, JAMES F. b Pittsburgh 9 Je 15. 4: Margaret Beckwith. 5: Penn State Col 35-39 (Eng Lit) BA, 39-40, 50 (Amer Lit) MA; Carnegie 40-41 BS in LS. 6: Sp, Fr. 7: Staff libn Carnegie Lib of Pittsburgh 41-42; Army (pvt to maj) Infantry, US, Europe, Asia 42-57; Assoc libn & Asst Prof Gene Eppley Lib UOmaha 57-59; Libn & Assoc Prof Weyerhaeuser Lib Macalester Col 59-69; Dean of Lib Serv, The Evergreen State Col 69-. 8: Lib serv eval, 2 cols, 65; Visiting Prof Div of Lib Educ State U Col(Geneseo) summer 65. 9: ALA-ACRL; ASIS; Midwest Acad Libns Conf (chm 9th & 10th confs); MinnLA. 10: AAUP; Torch Club; ACLU; Twin Cities Ms Soc; Res Offs Assn. 12: Managing d "Army Information Digest" (50-52); Cartographic ed Off of the Chief of Mil Hist Dept of the Army (53-57). 13: Yes. 14: Undergrad acad libnship. 15: The Evergreen State Col, Olumpia Wa 98501.

HOLMAN, (MARY) KATE. b Celeste Tex 27 Ja 05. 5: Kidd-Key Col & Conservatory 25-27 (Eng); N Tex U 56 (LS, Eng) BA. 7: Libn Corsicana Pub Lib, Corsicana Tex 29-57; Libn Kilgore Pub Lib, Kilgore Tex 57-60; Child libn Amarillo Pub Lib, Amarillo Tex 60-. 9: ALA; TexLA Alpha Lambda Sigma, NTSU. (Library) 10: AAUW; Delta Kappa Gamma; DAR. Nat Soc Magna Charta Dames. 14: Child, ref. 15: 1607 S Tyler st, Amarillo Tx 79102.

HOLMAN, ANNA (LUELLA ARMSTRONG). b Kinburn Ont Can 1 Ap 27. 5: Carleton U 47-49 (Eng) BA; McGill 49-50 BLS. 6: Fr. 7: Libn Nat Gallery of Can, Ottawa 50-51; Asst libn Acadia U(Wolfville NS) 51-52; Asst libn Pub Lib, Leamington Ont 53-61; Chief of pub serv Carleton U(Ottawa) 61-65; Supv of Libs Pub Sch Bd, Ottawa 65-. 9: ALA; CanLA; OntLA; LAOttawa; Inst Profess Lib Ont. 14: Ref, sch libs. 15: Apt 517, 315 Holmwood ave, Ottawa 1 Can.

HOLMAN, WILLIAM R. b Okla City Okla 7 S 27. 4: Barbara Louise Switzer. 5: UOkla 46-49 (Hist) BA; UIll 49-50 MS in LS. 6: Lat, Sp. 7: Ref asst ref dept UIll Lib (Champaign-Urbana) 49-50; Circ libn UKan Lib 50; Head Libn Pan Amer Col Lib 51-54; Dir: Rosenberg Lib, Galveston Tex, 54-56, San Antonio Pub Lib, San Antonio Tex 56-60, San Francisco Pub Lib 60-67; Prof Humanities Research Ctr UTex 67-. 9: ALA (Coun 62-66; chm Friends of Libs Com; mem Pub Rel Com); TexLA (chm Leg Com); SWLA (chm Pub Libs Sect). 10: Bk Club of Cal; Roxburghe Club, San Francisco; Cal Hist Soc. 12: "Library Publications" (65). 13: Yes. 14: Admin, bk design, typography, bkbinding, spec collections. 15: San Francisco Pub Lib, Civic Center, San Francisco Ca 94102.

HOLMES, CORNELIA ELIZABETH (CALLISON). b Palco Kan 27 O 04. 5: Northwest Nazarene Col 30-33 (Hist, Educ) AB (summa cum laude); UWash 37; Northwestern U summers 44, 47-49 (Educ) MA (magna cum laude). 6: Lat, Gk. 7: Elem tchr Graham Co Schs, Kan 23-30; Secondary tchr Greenleaf Acad, Greenleaf Ida 35-39; Elem tchr Canyon Co, Ida 39-43; Secondary-hist, speech & lib tchr, Wilder Ida 43-58; Secondary tchr & libn Sr High Sch, Caldwell Ida 58-. 9: NEA; IdaEA; Ida Speech Assn. 10: Delta Kappa Gamma; Pi Lambda Theta; Phi Delta Lambda; AAUW. 14: Stud guidance. 15: Rt 2, Caldwell Ida 83605.

HOLMES, EDITH (REYNOLDS). b Calhoun Falls SC 4 F 24. 4: Dr J Arthur Holmes. 5: Allen U 39-44 (Fr) AB; NC Col 47-48 BLS; UIll 56-57 MLS. 6: Fr. 7: Libn Brockington High Sch, Timmonsville SC 45-48; Libn Carver High Sch, Spartanburg SC 48-50; Asst libn Allen U 50-64, Head Lib Sci Dept 64-67, Admin libn & hd Lib Sci Dept Allen U 67-. 9: ALA; SCLA. 10: Alpha Kappa Alpha; State Ministers Wive's Alliance; YWCA; Interdenom Minister's Wives' Alliance. 14: Child lit, catlg. 15: 2507 Waites rd, Columbia SC 29204.

HOLMES, ELIZABETH (ANTHONY). b Decatur Ga 18 Ja 31. 5: Fla StateU 49-52 BA, 54 MA; Mex City Col 54 (Mex Hist & Anthrop). 6: Sp. 7: Asst law libn UFla 52-53; Ref & ser libn Mexico City Col 54; Asst ref libn UTex (Austin) 55-56; Dir Materials Ctr & Film Lib McNeese Col 60-61; Libn UAla (Birmingham Ctr) 63-65; Acquis libn St Andrews Col 66-. 9: SELA; NCLA. 10: Beta Phi Mu; AAUP. 14: Acquis, ref. 15: Rte 4 Box 129, Laurinburg NC 28352.

HOLMES, JEANNE M(AIDEN). b Dayton Ohio 10 F 22. 4: Robert Reynolds Holmes. 5: George Washington U 43 (Eng Lit) BA; Columbia 52 MS in LS. 7: Visa ed asst USDA, Wash DC 43-47; Tchr Arlington Co Pub Schs, Arlington Va 42, 45-46, 47; In chg Internat Serv Columbia U Press 47-49; Supv period reading room Columbia U Libs 49-52; Nat Agric Lib, Wash DC: Ref libn 52-53, Catlgr 53-54, Catlg review 54-56, Asst chief 56-62, Chief div of catlg & records 62-. 08: Act coord Agric Vocabulary Project Nat Agric Lib 65-68; Mem var gps Nat Libs task Force 67-; Mem subpanel on descr catlg Com on Sci & Tech Info 65-67. 9: IAALD; ALA; SLA; ASIS; DCLA; Potomac Tech Proc Libns. 10: Beta Phi Mu. 11: USDA Spec Merit Award for Outstanding Cost Reduction; USDA Award for Superior Serv. 14: Catlg, ser, admin, catlg devel. 15: Apt 723, 4501 Connecticut ave NW, Wash DC 20008.

HOLMES, JILL (MARIAN). b Tulsa Okla 30 N 40. 5: Hendrix Col 58-59; So Methodist U summers 58-60; N Tex State U 59-61 (Elem Educ) BS in Elem Ed; Tex Women's U 61-63 MLS; Okla State U 68-. 6: Sp, Ger. 7: Jr libn Okla State U 63-65; Army spec serv libn Ulm Sub Dist 65-66, Munich 66-67; Jr libn Okla State U 67-68, Educ libn & Asst Prof 68-. 9: ALA; NEA (life mem); SWLA; OreEA; OklaLA (Recr Com 64-65). 14: Ref, educ, bus, econ. 15: Spec Serv Lib Wiley Brks Ulm Sub Dist, APO US Forces 09035.

HOLMES, JOHN LIVINGSTONE. b Windsor Ont Can 24 D 23. 4: Joan Apol. 5: U West Ont 46-50 (Econ, Pol Sci) BA; Toronto 56-57 BLS. 6: Fr. 7: Royal Can Artillery 41-45; Banking bus, London Ont & Detroit 50-53; Wholesale hardware bus, London Ont 53-56; Readers adv & Head bus & tech dept, Grand Rapids (Mich) Pub Lib 57-59; Head bus & tech dept, Peoria (Ill) Pub Lib 59-61; Libn Sturgis (Mich) Pub Lib 61-62; Head central lib div Riverside (Cal) Pub lib 63-65; Dir Mich City Pub Lib, Mich City Ind 65-68; Dir Auburn Pub Lib, Auburn Wash 68-. 09: ALA (Life mem); MichLA; IllLA; CalLA (Fin Com, chm Bus & Tech Libns Round Table); PNLA; WashLA; IndLA (Pub Lib Devel Com). 10: Rotary Club; White River Valley Hist Soc. 13: Yes. 14: Ref, admin, chg systems, bk sel. 15: 12630 SE 27th st, Bellevue Wa 98004.

HOLMES, MARY HELEN. b Northville Mich 18 F 1896. 5: UMich 20 (Eng); UWis 33-34 (LS); UCal summer 45; Claremont Grad summer 46. 6: Ger, Sp. 7: Tchr & lib supv Bd of Educ, Highland Park Mich 20-24; Sr asst Detroit Pub Lib 25-31; Libn Flint Bd of Educ, Flint Mich 37-44; Libn Coalinga Jr High-Jr Col, Coalinga Cal 44-46; Libn Fullerton Jr Col 46-48; Libn Berkley Schs, Berkley Mich 48-58; Dir Madison Heights Pub Lib, Madison Heights Mich 58-66. 8: Consul to Fullerton Cal High Sch 46-48; Adv wk to Berkley Schs Berkley Mich 56-58; Floor plan consul Cranbrook Found Bloomfield Hills Mich 58; Bldg consul City of Madison Heights for new lib bldg 62-63; Adv Marquis Biog Lib Soc. 9: ALA (Plan Com 61-63); MichLA. 10: UMich Alumni Club; UWis Alumni Club; Gamma Phi Beta; Altrusa Club; LWV; Woman's Nat Farm & Garden Assn; Birmingham Beautification Com. 14: Admin, ref. 15: 875 S Bates st, Birmingham Mich 48024.

HOLMES, MURRAY KENT. b Tulsa Okla 11 Ag 25. 4: Frieda Lou Fine. 5: UTulsa 47-50 (Speech, Drama) BA, Lifetime Tchg Credential in Secondary Educ for State of Okla; Cal State Col 56 (Elem Educ) Jr High Sch Credential for State of Cal; USoCal 63-65 (LS). 6: Lat. 7: Radio operator-aerial gunner (Sgt) USAF, US Europe Africa 43-46; Manager Tulsa Downtown Theaters, Tulsa Okla 50-51; Assembly dir Tulsa Pub Schs, Tulsa Okla 52; Planning coordinator Douglas Aircraft Corp, Tulsa Okla 52-55; Proj coordinator Douglas Aircraft Corp, Long Beach Cal 55-60; Drama dir Marywood High Sch, Anaheim Cal 61-62; Ref libn Buena Park Lib Dist, Buena Park Cal 62-63; Head circ dept Buena Park Lib Dist, 63-64, Asst lib dir, personnel dir 64-. 8: Consul Buena Park Silverado Days 63; Buena Park Sister City Proj lib consul 64; Buena Park Women's Club lib consul 64; Buena Park Friends of the Lib 64-65; Consul Buena Park Commun Playhouse 65. 9: ALA; NEA; CalLA; OklaEA. 10: Theta Alpha Phi; PTA; Buena Park Boys Club; Fullerton Footlighters (Commun Theater); Theater-As-You-Like-It (Commun Theater). 14: Admin, ref, drama collection. 15: 6660 San Haroldo Way, Buena Park Cal 90620.

HOLMES, PEGGY RUTH. b Summittville Tenn 10 Ja 28. 5: UTenn 45-47, 49-51 (Educ) BS; USoCal 56-57 MSLS. 7: Tchr libn Maynardville High Sch, Maynardville Tenn 47-48, 50; Child libn Bkmob libn Pub Lib, Oak Ridge Tenn 51-53; US Navy Aviation Ground Off 52-56, released as LTJG present reserve CDR; 1st asst child dept Mt Vernon Pub Lib, Mt Vernon NY 57-59, 1st asst circ dept 57-61; Chief of child serv Jacksonville Free Pub Lib, Jacksonville Fla 61-63; Br libn Long Beach Pub Lib, Long Beach Cal 63-. 9: ALA; CalLA. 10: Res Off Assn; Navy League; Beta Phi Mu. 14: Adv & ref in pub lib. 15: 1134 E Second st, Long Beach Cal 90802.

HOLMES, ROBERT REYNOLDS. b Camden NJ 31 My 22. 4: Jeanne Maiden. 5: George Washington U 40-47 (Eng Lit) AB; Columbia 47-48 (Eng Lit) MA, 48-49 (Eng Lit), 1-52 MS in LS. 6: Fr, Ger. 7: Staff Sgt US Army Air Force, CBI Theater 42-45; Tutor Eng City Col(NY) 49-51; LC: Spec recruit 52-53, Asst documents expediter 53-54, Head Amer & British Exchange Sect 54-56; Head European Exch Sect 56-58, Head E European Accessions Index 58-61, Asst chief Subj Catlg Div 61-67, Chief subj catlg div 67-. 9: ALA; ASIS; DCLA; Potomac Tech Proc Libns; AALL. 10: Beta Phi Mu. 13: Yes. 14: Catlg, admin. 15: 4501 Connecticut ave NW, Wash DC 20008.

HOLMES, ROSALIE. b Savannah Ga 15 Ag 43. 5: Savannah State Col 60-64 (Educ) BS; Atlanta U 64-65 MSLS. 7: Asst catlgr Morgan State Col 65-. 9: ALA; MdLA; Potomac Proc Libns Assn. 10: NAACP. 14: Catlg. 15: 817 Radnor ave, Baltimore Md 21212.

HOLMES, SARAH (ELIZABETH ARNY). b Cleveland 11 N 06. 4: Harold A Holmes. 5: Mt Holyoke 24-28 (Bot) AB; Tulane 28-30 (Bot) MS; Rutgers 60-62 MLS. 7: Lab asst Tulane U 29-30; Lab asst Barringer High Sch, Newark NJ

30-31; Research asst Columbia U 31-37; Lib trainee N Plainfield Lib, N Plainfield NJ 60-62; Tech reports libn Lockheed Electronics, Plainfield NJ 62-64, Sr tech lib 64-. 9: SLA. 10: Mt Holyoke club of Raritan Valley; Plainfield Col Club; AAUW; Woman's Auxiliary of Muhlenberg Hosp. 14: Ref, indexing. 15: 3 Ivy pl, North Plainfield NJ 07062.

HOLMGREN, EDWIN SURL. b Rock Springs Wyo 13 Je 34. 4: Priscilla Talbot. 5: NM A&M 51-52; Stanford 52-55 (Eng) AB; UIll 55-56 MS in LS. 7: Ref asst Gary Pub Lib, Gary Ind 56-57; Asst dir Summit Free Pub Lib, Summit NJ 57-60, Act dir 60; Consul libn Chas M Upham Assoc Inc for Royal Thai Highway Dept, Bangkok Thailand 60-62; Asst libn New Orleans Pub Lib, 62-65; Asst dir Gen Admin & Tech Serv rochester (NY) Pub Lib 65-. 8: Asst Prof Lib Sch, LSU summer 64. 9: ALA; Thai LA; NYLA; Assn of NY Libs Tech Serv (pres 67-69). 10: Beta Phi Mu; Phi Beta Kappa; Amer Soc Pub, admin. 14: Admin, bldgs & equipt, personnel, tech serv. 15: Rochester Pub Lib 115 South ave, Rochester NY 14604.

HOLSINGER, EDYTHE (REDDING). b Middletown Ind 21 S 05. 4: Frank Holsinger. 5: Ball State U 23-36 (Elem, Soc Sci, Art) BS; UIll 37-41 BLS. 6: Lat, Fr. 7: Elem tchr Henry Co, Devon & Mt Summit Ind 25-27; Elem tchr, Richmond Ind 28-42; Elem tchr & libn, Richmond Ind 42-. 9: NEA; IndSchLA; Ind State Tchrs Assn. 10: Bus & Prof Women's Club; AAUW; Ind Sch Women's Club. 14: Child, ya. 15: 701 South 20th, Richmond In 43734.

HOLT, DAVID EARL. b Magna Utah 17 My 28. 4: Mary Elizabeth Black. 5: UUtah 47-48, 50-54, 58-59; Brigham Young U 56-57 (Music) BA, 57-58 (Music) MA; Emory 62-63 MLibnship. 7: Travel musician with var Orchestras including Tex Beneke, Billy May and Ray Anthony 48-52; Trombonist for the Tommy Dorsey Orch 54-55; Lib asst Salt Lake Co Lib, Midvale Utah 58-59; Area Dir Reading Dynamics, Atlanta 59-62; Head Libn Hayner Pub Lib, Alton Ill 63-65; Dir of Libs Waco Pub Lib, Waco Tex; Dir of libs Austin Pub Lib, Austin Tex 67-. 8: Ref libn Lib/USA, NY World's Fair, 65. 9: ALA; TexLA. 10: Rotary Club. 12: Bk ed "American-Statesman" 67-68. 14: Admin, bk sel. 15: 1802 Forest Trail, Austin Tx 78703.

HOLT, GRACE FRANCES. b New Haven Conn 23 N 07. 5: Keuka Col 26-30 (Classics) BA; Pratt 31-32 BLS. 6: Fr. 7: Gen asst Conn Col, New London Conn 32-34; Asst in catlg dept Yale U Lib 34; Asst in catlg dept New Haven Pub Lib, New Haven Conn 34-36; Asst in circ dept Smith Col Lib 37-42, Head ser dept 42-. 9: ALA. 10: Holt Assn of Amer (genealogical); Miles Merwin Assn Inc (genealogical). 14: Catlg. 15: 20 Belmont ave, Northampton Mass 01060.

HOLT, MABEL H(ANCOCK). b Martinsville Va 13 D 23. 5: Stephens Col 41-43 AA; Madison Col 43-46 (Bio) BS; UNC 53-54 (Relig) BA; Presbyterian Sch of Christian Educ 55-57 9bible) MA; Drexel 64-65 (LS) MA. 7: Chem Lab Tech Osborne Zoological Lab Yale U 47-49; Dir of Religious Life YWCA Randolph-Macon Woman's Col 57-59; Circ libn Union Theol & Sem (Richmond Va) 59-63; Ref libn Richmond Pub Lib, Richmond Va 66-. 9: ALA; VaLA. 10: Sierra Club; Va Soc of Ornith; Richmond Natur Hist Soc. 14: Bk sel, ref, bibliog. 15: 3706 Patterson ave, Richmond Va 23221.

HOLT, OLIVE (SMITH). b Harrisville Ohio 19 N 10. 4: Clifford B Holt Jr. 5: Earlham Col 28-32 (Eng, Hist) AB; Drexel 32-33 BS in LS. 6: Ger, Fr. 7: Asst catlgr Penn State U Lib 34-43, Ser catlg libn 65-, Ser libn 66-. 14: Ser. 15: 221 S Barnard st, State Col Penn 16801.

HOLT, RAYMOND MILTON. b San Bernardino Cal 3 Je 21. 4: Sadie Campi Holt. 5: URedlands 42 (Hist) AB; USoCal 46 BS in LS. 7: Ref libn Fullerton Pub Lib, Fullerton Cal 47-50; Chief libn Pomona Pub Lib, Pomona Cal 50-. 8: Lib consul 4 Cal & 1 Ida pub lib 64-69; Adv studies 2 lib systems & 1 pub lib 64-68. 9: ALA (chm Lib Period RT 59); CalLA (chm Bylaws Com 65-68, chm Lib Devel & Standards Com 66-, parliamentarian 55-68; pres Si Dist 64); Pub Lib Execs So Cal (pres 64). 10: Kiwanis Club; Pomona Valley Hist Soc; Pomona Valley Art Assn; Pomona Civic Music Assn; So Cal Loc Hist Coun. 12: Ed "California Librarian" (54-60); "San Gabriel Valley Study", report (65); "East Los Angeles County Study", report (66). 14: Administration; Library Buildings; Library System Development; Local History. 15: 1841 Westwood pl, Pomona Ca 91767.

HOLT, SANDRA (ANDERSON). b Lynchburg Va 17 Ja 43. 4: Yuille Holt III. 5: Madison Col 61-65 (LS) BS. 7: Summer asst Lynchburg Col Lib 64; Libn Sheffield Elem Sch, Lynchburg Pub Schs, Lynchburg Va 65-68; Libn Malibu Elem Sch, Va Beach Pub Schs, Va Beach Va 68-69; Libn Children's Dept Enfield Central Lib, Hazardville Ct 69-. 9: NEA; VaEA; VaLA. 10: PTA; Kappa Delta Pi. 13: Yes. 14: Child lit, reading guidance, pre-school & elem lib programs. 15: 131 Old County rd, apt B9, Windsor Locks Ct 06096.

HOLTER (SIGRID GADDA). b Ashland Wis 4 F 05. 4: Cap Holter. 5: Northland Col 25-26, 57-59 (Elem Educ) BA; UWis 60-61 MSLS. 6: Swedish. 7: Head Libn Tomah Pub Lib, Tomah Wis 57-61; 4 co bkmob libn 61-62; Head Libn Ashland High Sch Lib, Ashland Wis 62-64; Head Libn & LS Asst Prof Northland Col Lib 64-. 9: WisLA. 10: AAUW; LWV. 15: Box 304, Ashland Wi 54806.

HOLTON, MARGARET (LAWRENCE). b Glenwood Wash 27 S 14. 4: John Wolcott Holton. 5: UCLA 32-33, 34-35 (Eng); Whittier Col 35-37 (Educ) AB; Syracuse 37-38 BS in LS; UHawaii 49-. 7: Catlgr Cornell U Law Sch Lib 38; Asst libn Kent State U 39-41; Catlgr Elyria Pub Lib, Elyria Ohio 41-43; Asst libn & catlgr Whitman Col 43-47; Catlgr UHawaii 47-48; Catlgr Punahou Sch Lib, Honolulu 48-49; Libn Kapaa High & Elem sch, Kapaa Hawaii 49-50; Libn Kahuka High & Elem Sch, Kahuka Hawaii 50-51; Libn Wash Intermed Sch, Honolulu 51-. 9: ALA; NEA; HawaiiLA (treas 53-54; Bd of Dir 47, 59-60; chm Program Com 60-61; chm Constitution Revision Com 61-62); HSLA; HawaiiEA; HAVA. 10: Zonta Club of Honolulu; Phi Kappa Phi; Pi Lambda Sigma. 15: 2415 Ala Wai blvd apt 1508, Honolulu Hi 96815.

HOLUM, KATHARINE (MARIE). b LaCrosse Wis 13 Jl 25. 5: Luther Col 43-46 (Music) BA; UMinn 48-50 (LS) BS, 46-48, 55-57 (Music) MA. 7: Music libn UMinn 50-. 9: MusLA (chm Com Lib Train & Recr 58-61). 10: Sigma Alpha Iota; Lutheran Soc for Worship Music & the Arts. 12: Ed Bulletin ser of Lutheran Soc for Worship Music & Arts (58-). 13: Yes. 14: Ref, acquis. 15: 103 Walter Lib U Minn, Minneapolis Mn 55455.

HOLZBAUER, HERBERT. b Linz Austria 5 Je 27. 4: Molly Miranker. 5: Brooklyn Col 47-50 (Sociol-Econ) BA; Columbia 50-51 (LS) MS; Ohio State U 60 (Psych). 6: Fr, Ger. 7: Film serv dir Lib of Hawaii, Honolulu 51-53; Chief Libn US Navy Quality Evaluation Lab, Hawaii 54-57; Chief Lib Br USAF Foreign Tech Lab, Wright-Patterson AFB Ohio 57-61; Lib research spec US Off of Educ, Wash DC 62; Asst libn US Dept of the Interior, Wash DC 63-67; Agency libn US Dept of Defense, Wash DC 68-. 08: Fed Lib Com Task Force on Automation 65-; Exec dir nlw, wash DC 66-68. 9: ASIS (rep to USBE 67-69); ALA; SLA (Adv Com, chm Documentation Div 65-68; Wash DC Chap pres elect 66, chm Sci-Tech Group 65); DCLA. 10: AAAS; Amer Philatelic Soc; Soc of Philatelic Amers. 12: Ed "Chapter Notes," SLA-Wash DC Chap (64-66). 13: Yes. 14: Mgt, info communication & automation applications. 15: 8585 Brae Brook dr, Lanham Md 20801.

HOLZBAUR, FREDERICK WILLIAM. b Phila 4 D 32. 4: Johanna Emilie Von Koppenfels. 5: Rutgers 51-56 (Soc Sci) BA; Drexel 58-59 MS in LS. 6: Ger. 7: Stud lib asst Rutgers U 51-56; Electronics tech US Army Air Defense Bd, Ft Bliss Tex 56-58; Grad Stud asst Drexel Sch of Lib Sci 59-61; IBM: Assoc libn systs & acquis 61, Lab lib manager 62-64, Document processing manager Tech Info Ctr 64, Lib processing serv manager Systs Development Div 64-66, Terminal info systs coord Systs Development Div Corporate Hdqrs Info Ctr, Armonk NY 69-. Development Div 64-66, Terminal info systs coord Systs Development Div 66-68, Coord Corporate Hdqrs Terminal-Oriented info Systs 68-69, Corporate Hdqrs Info Ctr, Armonk NY 69-. 09: SLA (Sci-Tech Div NY Chap Mem chm 63-64; Documentation Div NY Org Com sec 64-65); SE(NY) Lib Res Coun (Trustee 63-65); ASIS; Dutchess Co LA. 10: Nat Rifle Assn; Grinnell Pub Lib Bd Trustees. 13: Yes. 14: Terminal-oriented computer info proc & retrieval syst, on-line mgt info & control syst, lib syst design, lib application of digital computers. 15: McNair dr rd #2, Mahopac NY 10541.

HOM, KIMIYO (TAMURA). b Los Angeles 13 D 28. 4: S W Hom. 5: Brooklyn Col 46-58 (Soc Anthropology) BA; Columbia 58-60 (LS) MS. 6: Japanese, Sp. 7: Lib asst SUNY Downstate Med Center(Brooklyn) 50-55, Jr libn 55-57, Ref asst & libn 58-61; Lib assoc NYU 61-62; Libn I Astronomy-Math-Stat Lib UCal Gen Lib (Berkeley) 63-64, Libn II 64-68, Libn III 68-. 9: MedLA; SLA; CalLA. 10: AAAS; Alpha Kappa Delta. 14: Ref, admin, lib planning. 15: 1137 Bush st, San Francisco Ca 94109.

HOME, PAULINE MARY ADELA. b Toronto Can 2 Ag 28. 5: Trinity Col UToronto 45-49 (Modern Hist) BA; Toronto 52-53 BLS, 60 MLS. 6: Fr, Ger. 7: Fr tchr Edgehill Sch, Windsor NS 50-52; Young moderns libn Halifax Mem Lib,

Halifax NS 53-57; Circ & ref libn UToronto Lib 57-59; Chief circ libn Halifax City Reg Lib, Halifax NS 59-. 9: CanLA (Coun Adult Serv Sect 55-56, sec-treas 60-61); Halifax LA (sec-treas 55-56, programme Chm 62-63); APLA (sec-treas 64-68). 10: Bd Trustees Heritage Trust of Nova Scotia 65-68; Can Fed UW; UToronto Alumni; Beta Phi Mu. 11: Ruby E. Wallace Travel Fellowship Awarded By CalLA 67. 13: Yes. 14: Bk sel, br & bkmob admin. 15: Apt 4 952 McLean st, Halifax NS Can.

HOMES, NELLIE M. b Warren Co Iowa 24 Jl 1898. 5: West Res 18-19 (LS); Flora Stone Mather Col 25 (LS) BS; West Res 47 (Hist) MA. 6: Ger, Fr. 7: Asst Waterloo Pub Lib, Waterloo Iowa 19-20; 2nd asst Jefferson Br Cleveland Pub Lib 20-22, 2nd asst Glenville Br 22-24; Asst in lib Flora Stone Mather Col West Res U 24-25, 26-39; 1st asst Superior Br Cleveland Pub Lib 25-26; Ref libn Beloit Col Lib 39-45; Libn Cottey Col 45-66, Asst libn UMo Lib (Columbia) 66-68; Act hd, hist div Kan City Pub Lib, Kan City Mo 68-. 8: Consul: Col of Sch of Ozarks 56; Kemper Jr Col 58. 9: ALA-ACRL (sec Col Sect 42-46, chm Jr Col Sect 54-55); MoLA (chm Col & Univ Div 52-53, pres 55-56, Adv Bd "Quarterly" 62-67). 10: Altrusa Club; AAUW. 14: Admin, ref. 15: 1213 Wyandotte st, Kansas City Mo 64105.

HOMESTEAD, MAGNUS MACK C. b Stavanger Norway 20 My 21. 4: Iris Barker. 5: Bard Col 47-49 (Hist); Kenyon Col 49-51 (Philos) BA; U Col(London) 51-52 (Philos); UVa 53-55 (Philos); UWash 56-58 (LS) ML. 6: Fr. 7: Documents & ref Nev State Lib 58-59; Asst ref libn UNev 59-61; Asst libn Hartwick Col 61-62; Catlg libn Trenton State Col 62-65; Soc sci libn UNM 65-. 10: Carson City Commun Theatre; Campus Players of UNev; Oneonta Commun Players; Princeton Commun Theatre; Corrales Theatre (NM). 14: Ref. 15: 1108 Bryn Mawr dr NE, Albuquerque NM 87106.

HONEA, ANN BURLESON. b Dallas Texas 27 N 26. So Methodist U 45-47 (Eng) BA; UTex 61-62 MLS; ULond summer 48; UOslo (Norway) summer 50; Netherlands Inst for Art Hist summer 53. 6: Fr, Sp, Ger. 7: Pub affairs asst USIA, Bern Switzerland & Brussels 57-60; Hd adult serv Santa Fe Pub Lib, Santa Fe NM 63-65; Adult libn Dallas Pub Lib, Dallas Tex 66-69; Lib dir Farmers Branch Pub Lib, Farmers Branch Tex 69-. 9: ALA; NMLA; TexLA. 11: Theta Sigma Phi; Kappa Alpha Theta. 14: Ref. 15: 4614 Munger ave, Dallas Tx 75204.

HONEY, HELEN ELEANOR. b Seymour Conn 12 Ja 06. 5: Mt Holyoke Col 23-27 (Gk) BA; Yale 27-29 (Amer Hist) MA; Columbia 31-32 (LS) BS. 6: Fr, Ger. 7: Tchr St Mary's Female Sem (St Mary's Md) 30-31; Temp catlgr Albany Pub Lib, Albany NY 32; Libn Seymour Pub Lib, Seymour Conn 33-40; Head catlgr UConn 40-43; Catlgr Harvard U Widener Lib 44-45; Head of catlg dept Baker Lib Harvard Sch of Bus Admin (Boston) 45-. 9: ALA; NE Tech Serv Libns; Harvard Lib Club. 10: Appalachian Mountain Club. 14: Catlg. 15: 84 Prescott st, Cambridge Mass 02138.

HONEYCUTT, LOUISE THURBER. b Washington C H Ohio 23 Mr 10. 5: Guilford Col 27-29 (Lang); Asheville Normal Sch summer 29 (Educ Psych); UNC 29-30 (Sociol) Tchr Certif, 30-31 (LS); UFLa (Ficus) 64 (Voc Educ). 07: Tchr-Libn Pub Schs, High Point NC 29-30, 52-54; Tech Libn Martin Co, Orlando Fla 56-58; Hd Libn Radiation Inc, Orlando/Melbourne Fla 58-63; Tech Libn Mid-Fla Tech Inst, Orlando Fla 63-65; Libn ya Winter Park Pub Lib, Winter Park Fla 65-. 8: Adv serv various inds during employment with Radiation Incorp 60-63. 9: SLA; SELA; FlaLA; 13: Yes. 14: Tech research, documentation. 15: 3308 Raeford rd, Orlando Fla 32806.

HONKE, MARY WOFFORD. b Gainesville Ga 10 Jl 21. 4: Martin T Honke Jr. 5: Los Angeles City Col 38-41 AA; UCLA 41-43 BA; Peabody 61-63 MA (LS). 7: Tchr Pub Schs; Hawthorne Cal 43-44, Monroe La 44, Lakewood Colo 47-48, Flat River Mo 50-51, Benton Ark 52-55; Asst in circ Ark State Lib 58-59; Libn Ark Sch for the Deaf, Little Rock Ark 61-62; Asst acquis libn Georgetown U 64-66; Asst libn & catlgr Nat Gallery of Art, Wash DC 66-. 10: Beta Phi Mu; Alpha Gamma Delta. 14: Acquis. 15: 3253 Arcadia Pl NW, Wash DC 20015.

HONOUR, FRANCES M (MRS). b The Rock Ga 9 O 11. 5: Auburn U 51-54; Tenn Polytech Inst 55 (Hist) BA; USoCal 59 (LS) MS; Auburn U 62 (Hist) MA. 7: Ref libn Auburn U Lib 55-60, Gift & Exch libn 65-. 11: "Journal of Library History" Award for excellence in hist writing 68. 13: Yes. 14: Ref, rare bks. 15: 414 E Magnolia, Auburn Al 36830.

HONTZ, (MARTHA) GLADYS (SMITH). b Scotland County NC 5 Ag 17. 4: Lloyd Harold Hontz. 5: Flora Macdonald Col 34-38 (Eng. Hist) BA; E Car U 63-64 (LS); Appalachian State U summer 65 Certif in LS. 7: Tchr Wayne Co Schs Mt Olive High Sch, Mt Olive NC 38-40; Tchr & libn: Sampson Co Sch, Pine Grove Sch, Faison NC 53-54, Duplin Co Sch, Calypso high, Calypso NC 54-55, Duplin Cp Sch, N Duplin High Sch 55-60, Wayne Co Sch, Rosewood Sch, Goldsboro NC 63-65; Sales mgr Field Enterprises Educ Corp, Wayne & Johnson Co 60-63; Libn Wayne Co Schs, Mt Olive Schs, Mt Olive NC 65-. 9: NEA; ALA; NCLA (chm NCASchL 67-69); SELA; NCEA. 10: PTA. 14: Child, ya. 15: 307 N Southerland st, Mt Olive NC 28365.

HOOD, BESS (BEASLEY). b Hazlehurst Miss 4 O 14. 5: Copiah-Lincoln Jr Col 32-33; UOkla 62-65 (Eng, Hist, LS) BA, 65-66 (LS) MA. 6: Fr, Ger, Lat. 7: Sec 34-39; Lib asst fellowship UOkla Lib 65-66, Catlgr 66-. 9: ALA; OklaLA; SWLA. 10: AAUP; Med Aux Cleveland-McClain Co; Norman Munic Hosp Aux; Univ Women's Club. 14: Catlg. 15: 420 E Keith, Norman Ok 73069.

HOOD, MARJORIE JANE. b Winston-Salem NC 13 Ap 05. 5: Woman's Col of UNC (Greensboro) 22-26 (Eng) BA; Emory 35-36 BA in LS. 7: Asst in catlg dept Woman's Col of UNC(Greensboro) 29-35, Head of circ dept 36-; NY Pub Lib summers 44, 45. 9: ALA; SELA; NCLA (treas 55-61). 10: Beta Phi Mu. 12: "Circulation Work in Administration of College Library" (3d ed 61). 13: Yes. 14: Circ, ref, archives. 15: 428 Forest st, Greensboro NC 27403.

HOOGENBOOM, DENNIS RICHARD. b Goshen Ind 1 N 41. 4: Rita Bongw. 5: Calvin Col 59-66 (Eng) AB; UMich 67-68 AMLS. 7: Clk typist Grand Rapids Pub Lib, Grand Rapids Mich 67; Asst catlg libn Robt L Pierce Stout StateU, Menomonie Wis 69-. 9: AWSUF. 10: UMich Assn of Lib Sci Alumni. 14: Catlg. 15: 1401 Stout rd, Menomonie Wi 54751.

HOOK, ALICE (PALO). b Superior Wis 4 F 09. 5: UMinn 26-30 (LS) BS. 7: Asst in order dept UMinn Lib (Minneapolis) 30; Taft order asst UCincinnati Lib 31-37; Head order dept Temple U 37-43; Head acquis dept UCincinnati 43-46; Libn Hist & Philos Soc of Ohio, Cincinnati 47-63; Libn Cincinnati Art Museum 64-. 9: SLA (chm Pub Rel Com 58, chm Scholarship & Stud Loan Com 63-64; chm Picture Div 58-60; chm Mus Div 65-66); ALA; OhioLA. 10: Altrusa Internat; YWCA; Alpha Xi Delta; Col Club of Cincinnati; Cincinnati Woman's Club. 13: Yes. 14: Pictures, ms catlg. 15: 359 Resor ave, Cincinnati Oh 45220.

HOOK, HELEN (KONDRAT). b Rochester NY 22 0 14. 4: Clarence Hook. 5: URochester 32-36 (Eng) AB; State U Col (Geneseo NY) summers 35-38 (LS) BS; Columbia 40, 41, 43 (LS); UMich 46-48 MALS. 6: Fr, Sp, Lithuanian. 7: Eng-lib Holley Central Sch, Holley NY 36-41; Libn Vestal Central Sch, Vestal NY 41-43; Libn Brockport Central Sch, Brockport NY 43-48; Asst libn State U Col 62-66; Libn Merton Williams Sch, Hilton NY 66-. 14: Bk sel, tech processes. 15: 1207 Spencerport rd, Rochester NY 14606.

HOOKER, BILLIE J (SHAIFER). b Port Gibson Miss 29 N 38. 4: William Edward Hooker. 5: Albany State Col (Ga) 54-57 (Eng) AB; Atlanta U 66-67 MLS. 6: Sp. 7: Tchr & libn Carver High Sch, Dawson Ga 57-60; Tchr: Addison High Sch, Port Gibson Miss 60-62; Raleigh Pub Schs, Raleigh NC 62-66, 67-68; Asst libn Sch of Lib Serv Lib Atlanta U summers 67, 68; Act hd libn St Augustine's Col, Raleigh NC 68-. 9: ALA; NEA. 10: Beta Phi Mu; Silhouettes of Raleigh. 11: Delta Sigma Theta; Alpha Kappa Mu. 14: Ref, child serv. 15: PO Box 84, Method NC 27554.

HOOKER, MILDRED D (BEEMAN). b Cass Co Mich 30 O 09. 4: Joe Hooker. 5: West Mich U 28-31 (Art, Soc Studies), 58-59 (Art, Soc Studies) BS, 59-61 (LS) MA. 6: Sp, Fr. 7: Art Tchr Wyandotte Pub Schs, Wyandotte Mich 31-32; Curriculum libn Kalamazoo City schs, Kalamazoo Mich 61-. 8: Sel Com for "Recommended Materials for a Professional Libn in the School", MichASchL 2nd ed. 9: NEA; ALA; MichEA; Kalamazoo City EA. 10: Beta Phi Mu; Prose and Poetry; PEO. 14: Ref, research. 15: 1578 Spruce dr, Kalamazoo Mi 49001.

HOOKS, JAMES DARWIN. b Kittanning Penn 14 S 42. 5: Ind State Col (Penn) 60; Clarion State Col 60-64 (LS) BS Ed; UPittsburgh 64-66 (MLS), 67-. 7: Asst libn Sr High Sch, Fox Chapel Penn 64; Libn Hampton Twp Jr-Sr High Sch, Allison Park Penn 64-. 9: NEA; ALA; PennStateEA; PennLA. 10: Suburban Coun Sch Libns; Hampton TwpEA. 14: Catlg, ya serv. 15: RD 1, Adrian Penn 16210.

HOOLE, W(ILLIAM) STANLEY. b Darlington SC 16 My 03. 5: Wofford Col 20-24, 31 AB, AM; Duke 31-34 PhD; N Tex U 43 BSLS; Wofford Col 54 Litt D. 7: Dean of libs UALA 44-. 9: Assn SEast Res Libs (chm). 12: Ed "The Alabama Review" (48-67); Ed "Confederate Cente nmial Studies" 56-65. 13: Yes. 14: Admin, rare b kks. 15: UAla, University Al 35486.

HOON, NANCY LOU. b Minneapolis 25 Ja 36. 5: Winona State Col 54-57, 59-60 (Elem) BS; Mankato State Col 60-61 (LS minor). 7: Tchr Blue Earth Elem Schs 57-59; Elem libn Columbia Heights Minn 61-62; Elem libn Bloomington Minn 62-. 9: ALA; MinnSchLA; MinnEA. 14: Elem sch lib wk. 15: 4000 W 88th, Minneapolis Mn 55431.

HOOVER, CLARA JEANNE (GUNDERSON). b Waterloo Iowa 9 Jl 42. 5: Colo Woman's Col 60-61; Iowa StateU 61-64 (Eng, Speech) BS; West Res 64-65 (LS) MS. 7: Lib asst DASA Doc Lib Pentagon summer 63; Asst libn Cleveland Inst of Mus 65; Libn Ames High Sch, Ames Iowa 65-68; Circ libn Iowa StateU (Ames) 68-. 9: ALA; NEA; AASL; IowaLA; IowaASchL (sec 66-68); IowaEA. 14: Yp wk, ref. 15: 921 Burnett, Ames Ia 50010.

HOOVER, DOLLY B (DAVIS). b Wash DC. 4: Dewey A Hoover. 5: Miner Tchrs Col 40-44 9fr, Eng) BS; CatholicU 44-45 BS in LS; UChicago 47-48 (LS) MS, 67-68 (Info Sci). 6: Fr, Ger. 7: Catlgr Lib Tuskegee Inst 45-49; Libn St Philip's Col 49-54; Sr catlgr lib Ind StateU (Terre Haute) 58-67, Asst hd catlg dept 68-. 9: ALA-RTSD; -ISAD; IndLA; Ohio Valley Group Tech Serv Libns. 10: NAACP; YWCA; AAUP. 14: Catlg, info sci. 15: 2146 8th ave, Terre Haute In 47804.

HOOVER, GENEVA KAY (REED). b Murfreesboro Tenn 16 S 40. 4: John Robert Hoover. 5: Middle Tenn State U 59-63 (Elem Educ) BS; Peabody 64-65 MLS. 7: Tchr-libn Middle Tenn Christian Col 62-64; Libn & Asst Prof Lib Sci Okla Christian Col 65-. 9: NEA; ALA; TennEA; OklaLA. 10: Kappa Delta Pi; Ladies Assn for Christian Educ; PTA. 12: Auth "A Road to Faith (grades 1 & 2). 13: Yes. 14: Catlg, child serv. 15: Rte 1 Box 141, Oklahoma City Ok 73111.

HOOVER, HESTER ELIZABETH. 5: Beaver Col 59-61; Cornell NY Hosp Sch Nu sch Nursing 61-62; Penn StateU 63-64; UPittsburgh 66-67 MLS. 7: Tchr Lorain City Bd of Educ, Lorain Ohio 65-66; Catlgr Falk Lib of Health Professions, UPittsburgh 67-. 9: SLA. 10: Beta Phi Mu. 14: Original catlg. 15: 4716 Ellsworth ave apt 811, Pittsburgh Pa 15213.

HOOVER, MELBA (BECK). b Lincolnton NC 22 S 32. 4: Richard Lindsay Hoover. 5: Woman's Col UNC 50-53 (Eng); UNC 53-54 (Eng) BA; UDenver 63-64 (LS) MA. 7: Libn Fulton High Sch, Atlanta 54-55; Libn Hampton High Sch, Hampton Va 55-56; Base libn Spangdahlem Air Base, Germany 60-62; Libn Jermantown Elem Sch, Fairfax Va 65-68; Libn-Media Coord Beech Tree Elem Sch, Falls Church Va 68-. 9: ALA. 10: Phi Beta Kappa; Sigma Delta Pi. 14: Child & yp wk, sch libnship. 15: 4208 Nutwood Way, Fairfax Va 22030.

HOPE, ARLENE. b Lowell Mass 12 Ap 13. 5: Simmons 39 (LS) BS; Boston U 44 (Hist) MA; UMich 54 MSLS. 6: Fr. 7: Art catlgr Harvard U Fogg Art Museum 39-43; Ref asst Brookline Pub Lib, Brookline Mass 43-49; Ref asst MIT 49-50; Libn Col of Gen Educ Boston U 51-53; Ref head Flint Pub Lib, Flint Mich 55-56; Consul Cal State Lib 56-62; Dir Reg Central Mass Reg Lib, Worcester Mass 63-64; Spec Lib Serv Br Off of Educ, Wash DC 64-68; Lib, serv program off reg US Off of Educ, Boston Mass 68-. 9: ALA; SLA; NELA. 10: Beta Phi Mu; Appalachian Mountain Cub; Women s' Nat Bk Assoc. 14: Ref, consul wk. 15: 255 Beacon st apt 61, Boston Ma 02116.

HOPE, NELSON W. b Maysville Okla 17 O 16. 4: Vera Ellen Vanderpool. 5: UOkla 36-41 (Engnr, LS) BA; Ariz State U 66-. 6: Lat, Fr, Ger. 7: Stud asst UOkla Lib 36-41; Foreman Remington Arms Co, Kan City Mo 41-43; Engnr UChicago 43-44; Engnr E I DuPont Co, Richland Wash 44-46; Shift supv Gen Electric Co, Richland Wash 46-56, Ref libn 56-61; Head document center Gen Atomic, San Diego Cal 61-63, Asst libn 63-66; Hd libn AiResearch Mfg Co, Phoenix Ariz 66-. 8: Lib Adv Bd Palomar Col 65-. 9: SLA; ArizLA. 10: Bi-County T B Assn; Scoutmaster & Troop Committeeman; Toast masters Internat. 13: Yes. 14: Catlg, ref, docs. 15: 1104 E Broadmor dr, Tempe Az 85281.

HOPEWELL, HELEN JEANENE. b Birmingham Ala 18 Ap 25. 5: UAla 42-46 (Sociol) BA; Fla State U 52-53 (LS) MA. 06: Fr. 7: Asst circ dept Gorgas Lib UAla 48-52; Air University Lib, Maxwell AFB Ala: Chief bks circ 53-58, Ref libn 58-60, Sr ref libn 60-. 9: SLA; AlaLA. 12: Jt ed "Union List of Foreign Military Periodicals" (57); Comp "Union List of Military Periodicals" (60). 14: Period, ref. 15: 34-D The Prado Montgomery Al 36105.

HOPKINS, ISABELLA LOUGHBOROUGH (GIBSON). b Birmingham Ala 1 S 39. 4: Carmon Hopkins Jr. 5: Tex Woman's U 57-60 (LS, Educ) BA, 60-61 MLS. 6: Sp. 7: Bkmob demonstration lib Ser Act Tex State Lib, Abeline Tex 60; Asst libn & act libn US Naval Propellant Plant, Indian Head Md 61-63; Acquis libn US Naval Weapons Lab, Dahlgren Va 63-64; Asst ref libn M E Bivins Mem Lib, Amarillo Tex 64-65; Assoc ref libn Texas Tech Col 66-67; Army libn Spec Serv Lib, Kleber Kaserne (Kaiserslautern Germany) 68-. 9: SL A; ALA;-AFLS (Pub chm Europ Subsect); TexLA; East Coast Coun Naval Lab Libns. 10: AAUW. 14: Acquis, ref, machine retrieval, ext serv recr. 15: Hq Sq 26th csg, Box 6019, APO NY 09012.

HOPKINS, JOSEPH S. b Brookline Mass 19 Ag 25. 4: Mary A McKenney. 5: Boston U 48-5, AA, 50-52 (Econ) BA; Simmons 54-56 MLS. 7: (Pfc) US Army Air Force, USA, Europe 43-46; Investigator Dun & Bradstreet Inc, Boston 52-54; Grad asst Simmons Col 54-56; Lib asst Providence Pub Lib 56-57; Dir Meadville Pub Lib, Meadville Penn 58-63; Dir Watertown Pub Lib, Watertown Mass 63-. 9: ALA; MassLA (pres Pub Lib Adminrs Div 65-66). 15: 24 Channing st, Newton Ma.

HOPKINS, JUDITH. b Wilkes-Barre Penn 15 Jl 34. 5: Wilkes Col 51-55 (Hist) BA; UIll 55-57 MS(LS), 67-. 6: Fr. 7: Ser asst UIll Lib (Urbana) 55-57; Catlgr Mt Holyoke Col Lib 57-65; Asst hd in catlg dept Yale Law Lib 65-67. 8: Visiting instr Sch Lib Sci SUNY (General) summer 69. 09: ALA; LibAssn of Greater NY; Law Libns of NE. 9: ALA. 10: Beta Phi Mu. 14: Catlg, lib educ. 15: 309 South State st Apt 8,Champagn Il 61820.

HOPKINS, LODA MAY. b Danbury Conn 14 F 06. 04Iving Cooper. 05: Vassar 23-27 (Lat) AB; Colum bia 28-30 BS. 6: Fr. 7: Grade I asst NY Pub Lib 27-30; Asst libn Warner Lib, Tarrytown NY 30-31; NY Pub Lib: Asst br libn 31-44, Br libn 44-53, Adult group spec 53-55, Asst coordinator of adult serv 55-58, Asst coordinator of Donnell Lib Center 58-60, Coordinator of Donnell Lib Center 61-64; Asst dir of Lib & Lecturer in Sch of Lib Sci Simmons Col 64-66, Dir of lib & lecturer in sch of lib sci 66-. 9: ALA (Amer Heritage Proj); NY State LA (Bd Adult Sect); MassLA. 10: NY Lib Club; Co Sch of Lib Sci Alumni Assn; Past Bd mem & off in many civic orgs in NYC; AAUP. 13: Yes. 14: Serv to adult readers. 15: 118 The Riverway, Boston Ma 02215.

HOPKINS, MARY (CUTLER). b Evansville Ind 19 My 07. 5: West Col for Women 24-28 (Eng) AB; West Res 28-29 BLS. 6: Fr. 7: 1st asst & child libn pub lib (br), Lakewood Ohio 32-32; Libn of Burlington & Alamance Co, Burlington NC 42-45; Staff UNC Lib (Chapel Hill) 58-, Libn Math-Physics Lib & Chem Lib 65-. 9: NCLA. 14: Admin. 15: 24 Village apts, Chapel Hill NC 27514.

HOPKINS, NETTIE MAE (NEFF). b Jonesville Va 5 Ja 10. 4: J Elmer Hopkins. 5: Lincoln Memorial U 52-55 (Educ, Eng) BS; Radford State Tchrs Col summers 57-58; E Tenn U summers 60-61 (LS). 7: Tchr Lee Co Schs 28-32, 40-50; Tchr Keokee High Sch, Keokee V a; Tchr Sunshine, Harlan Ky 53-54; Tchr-libn Blackwater High Sch, Blackwater Va 54-58; libn Pennington High Sch, Pennington Gap Va 58-. 8: Review lib bks for State Aid Lists State Bd of Educ, Richmond Va. 9: NEA; VaEA; VaLA; (Lee Co TA). 10: Lee Players; Asst clerk Pwriver Baptist Assn; Flatwoods Commun Club. 14: Ref. 15: Jonesville Va 24263.

HOPKINS, PEGGY JO. b Central SC 23 Je 40. 5: N Greenville Jr Col 58-60 AA; Blue Mountain Col 60-62 (Math) BA; UIll 64-65 (LS) MS. 6: Fr. 7: Libn Easley Jr High Sch, Easley SC 62-63; Math tchr Lockhart High Sch, Lockhart SC 63-64; Asst Chem Lib UIll (Urbana) 64-65; Ref libn sci tech div Clemson U Lib 65-68, Hd Sci Tech Div 68-. 9: SLA; SCLA. 10: AAUW. 14: Ref. 15: Clemson Univ Lib, Clemson SC 29631.

HOPKINS, RICHARD LEONARD. b Vancouver BC Can 28 Ag 40. 5: UBC 59-67 (Libnship) BEd, 68-69 BLS. 7: Tchr Coquitlam (BC) Sch Bd 65-66; Tchr-libn Burnaby (BC) Sch Bd 67-68; Ref libn UBC 69-. 9: BC Tchrs Fed. 10: Beta Phi Mu. 14/ Ref, lib educ. 15: 5257 Portland st, South Burnaby BC Can.

HOPKINS, SISTER VIVIAN MARY OSF. b Lake Geneva Wis 26 My 14. 4: Ref, reader's adv. 5: Cardinal Stritch Col 47 (Eng, Educ) PhB; Rosary Col 47, 48 (LS); UWis (Milwaukee) 63-65 (LS); UWis (Madison) 65-69 MS in LS. 07; Elem sch tchr Cath Sch, Mid-west US 33-55; Asst lib cardinal Stritch Col 55-63; Libn St Mary's Acad, Milwaukee 63-. 8: Midwest chm Nat Catholic Stud Lib Assts Assn 67-; Moderator Wis Catholic Stud Lib Assts Guild 65-66; Archdiocesan dir Milwaukee Archdiocese 67-69. 9: ALA; CatholicLA; WisLA (Child & Ya Serv 63-); WisCathLA. 13: Yes. 15: 3195 S Superior st, Milwaukee Wi 53207.

HOPKINS, (WALTER) MONROE. b Houston Tex 4 Ap 26. 4: Evelyn Mae Drake. 5: Hannibal-LaGrange Col 51-52 (Religion) AA; UMo 53-55 (LS) BA, Summer 67; Emory summer 57 (LS); Peabody 57-58 MA(LS). 7: Baptist minister Ill, Ga, Mo 47-; Libn Brewton-Parker Col 56-57; Asst libn Belmont Col 57-58; Libn Hannibal-LaGrange Col 58-67; Libn William Woods Col 68-, Instr UMo Sch Lib & Inf Sci summer 67. 8: Mo Ste Nat Lib Week Com 64-65. 9: ALA-ACRL (Nat Lib Week Com 65-67); MoLA (Lib Devel Com 63-67; (chm Col & Res libs Dir 61-62) ; 14: Ref. 15: William Woods Col Lib, Fulton Mo 65251.

HOPKINS, WILLIAM STEPHEN. b Troy NY 30 Je 24. 4: Margery Anne Stroud. 5: Russell Sage Col 46-50 (Sociol) BA; Oneonta State Tchrs Col 54-57 (Educ) MS; Syracuse 57-58 MS in LS. 7: Cir clk NYU Main Lib 55-56; Lib trainee Rochester Pub Lib, Rochester NY 56-57; Catlgr Penn StateU (Univ Park) 58-59; Lib Penn StateU (McKeesport) 59-60; Ext libn NH State Lib, Conco rd 60-62, Ref ass 62-64, Catlgr 64-66; Ref coord So Adirondack Lib Syst, Saratoga Springs NY 66-. 9: ALA; NYLA; Hudson-MohawkLA. 10: Beta Phi Mu. 13: Yes. 14: Catlg, ref, info retrieval. 15: 4 Spa dr, Saratoga Springs NY 12866.

HOPKINSON, MRS MARGARET L. b Sioux City Iowa 20 O 14. 5: Morningside Col 32-36 (Romance Langs) AB; UIll summers 37-39 BS in LS; Columbia summers 43-45 (LS). 6: Fr, Ger. 7: Various capacities from page to chief catlgr Pub Lib, Sioux City Iowa 31-47; Ref libn Pub Lib, W Allis Wis 47-51; Staff libn VA Hosp, Wood Wis 52-54; Chief Libn VA Hosp, Waukesha Wis 54-57; Med libn VA Hosp, Westside, Chicago 57; Chief Lib Serv VA Hosp-Research, Chicago 57-. 9: MedLA. 14: Med libs. 15: 401 E 32nd st, Apt 1505 , Chicago Il 60616.

HOPKINSON, SHIRLEY LOIS. b Boone Iowa 25 Ag 24. 5: Coe Col 42-43 (Hist); UColo 43-45 (Hist) BA (cum laude); Claremont Grad Sch 45-46, 52 (Hist, Asian studies) MA; UCal(Berkeley) 48-49, 52-53 BLS; UOkla summers 46-57 (Educ) EdM, EdD. 6: Fr, Sp, Ital. 7: Tchr Stigler High Sch, Stigler Okla 46-47; Tchr Palo Verde High Sch-Jr Col, Blythe Cal 47-48; Asst libn Modesto Jr Col 49-51; Libn Fresno High Sch, Fresno Cal 51-52; Tchr-libn La Mesa Jr High Sch, La Mesa Cal 53-55; Libn a-v dir Chaffey Col 55-58; Assoc Prof Libnship San Jose State Col 58-. 8: Spec consul Sch Lib Proj Cal Dept of Educ 65. 9: CalASchL (Br dir 61-64). 10: Phi Beta Kappa; Phi Kappa Phi; Alpha Lambda Delta; Kappa Delta Pi; Alpha Beta Alpha; AAUW; Bus & Prof Women's Club; LWV. 12: "Descriptive Cataloging of Library Materials" (63); "Instructional Materials for Teaching the Use of the Library" (65); Ed "California School Libraries" (61-64). 13: Yes. 14: Tchg lib sci, catlg, govt publ, instr materials. 15: San Jose State Col, San Jose Ca 95114.

HOPP, RALPH H(ARVEY). b Cook Neb 24 O 15. 4: Dorothy Gade. 5: Peru State Col 34-38 (Educ) ; UNeb 38-43 (Chem Engnr) BS; UIll 49-51, 56 (LS) MS, PhD. 6: Ger. 7: Tchr, Otoe Co Neb 35-37; Asst in tech dept Carnegie Lib of Pittsburgh 39-40; Res libn asst in circ dept & engnr libn UNeb 41-43; Process chem Martin-Nebraska Co, Omaha 43; Research fellow Mellon Inst of Ind Research, Pittsburgh 43-44; Research fellow Bituminous Coal Research Inc, Pittsburgh 44-45; Libn Battelle Mem Inst, Columbus Ohio 46-49; Agric libn & div libn sci & tech UNeb 51-53; UMinn(Minneapolis): Asst dir of libs 53-57, Assoc dir of libs 57-65, U Libn 65-. 8: Survey of Sioux Falls Col Lib 61; Visiting lecturer UDenver Sch of Libnship, summer 58. 9: ALA; MinnLA. 10: Beta Phi Mu; AAUP. 11: Fulbright Award & Ford Foun Grant, Univ of Ankara, Turkey, 62-63. 12: "A Study of the Problem of Complete Documentation in Science and Technology," PhD diss (56); "Survey of Sioux Falls College Library," with M M Gormley (61); "Survey of Faculty of Letters Libraries, University of Ankara, Turkey," Ankara (63). 13: Yes. 14: Lib admin, pers, lib bldgs, sci & tech lit. 15: 1341 Keston st, St Paul Mn 55108.

HOPPER, JEAN (GOLDMAN). b NYC 13 S 11. 5: Hunter Col 29-32 (Math) BA; Columbia 49-51 (LS) MA. 7: Traffic mgt aide statistician S-M News Co, NYC 33-43; Engnr inspection supv US Signal Corps, Ft Monmouth 43-45; Off manager Royal Dist Inc, Long Island City NY 46-49; Libn grade 3 Brooklyn Pub Lib 49-53; Head bus sci & ind dept Free Lib of Phila 53-. 9: ALA (Jt Com on Lib Serv to Labor Bus Ref Serv Com); SLA; PennLA; ASIS. 10: AAAS. 12: Ed "Library Service to Labor Newsletter". 14: Ref, adult serv. 15: 2101 Walnut st, Apt 1111, Phila Pa 19103.

HOPPER, MILDRY (SLUTH). b Tacoma Wash 22 Jl 08. 4: H Pearson Hopper. 5: U of Puget Sound 26-29 (Fr) AB; UWash 30-31 (Fr) MA, 37-38 BALS. 6: Sp, Norwegian, Fr, Ger, Swedish. 7: Sec O B Gufler Brokerage, Seattle 34-37; Catlgr UWash Lib 38-40; Tr US Navy Dept, Wash DC 40-42; Catlg asst DC Pub Lib 50-54; Catlgr NLM 54-60; Tr-analyst Maritime Admin, Wash DC 60-. 9: ALA. 10: Girl Scouts. 11: Head Scandinavian Exchange for US Girl Scouts 59. 13: Yes. 14: Catlg, for materials. 15: 3713-35th st NW, Wash DC 20016.

HOPPER, TERRELL W. b Anchorage Alaska 9 My 16. 5: UWash 34-39 (Philos) BA; Harvard 39-40, 42 (Philos) AM; UCal 40-41 Certif Lib; Course in Lib Sci for prof libns in US Army, London & Birmingham Eng summer 45. 6: Fr, Ger. 7: US Army, US and Europe 42-46; Ref asst NY Pub Lib 46-47; Ref asst Seattle Pub Lib 47-49; Asst Business Info Bur Cleveland Pub Lib 49; Libn II Brooklyn Pub Lib 49-53; Libn II Free Lib of Phila 53-60, Libn III 60-. 10: Phi Beta Kappa. 14: Ref. 15: Free Lib of Philadelphia, Phila Pa 19103.

HOPPING, ANN. b Hollywood Cal 2 D 31. 5: Fresno State Col 58-62 (Sociol, Anthropology) BA; UCal(Los Angeles) 62-63 MLS. 6: Sp. 7: Real estate salesman Mark Lee Realty, Visalia Cal 61-62; Asst to libn Visalia Pub Lib, Visalia Cal 53-62; Libn II Fresno State Col 63-. 9: CalLA (Dist pres 69). 13: Yes. 14: Ref. 15: Fresno State Col Lib, Fresno Ca 93726.

HOPSON, REX (CARROLL). b Mound Tex 12 Je 33. 5: Baylor 50-54 (Eng) BA; Southwestern Sch of Relig Educ 54-56 (Relig Educ) MRE; Peabody Col 59-60 (Eng) MA; UDenver 65-68 (Libnship) MA. 6: Ger, Sp. 7: Tchr Albuquerque Pub Schs 60-61; Tchr Colegio Bolivar, Cali Colombia 61-62; Eng instr U de los Andes, Bogota Colombia 62-63; Eng & journalism tchr Canal Zone Schs, Coco Solo 63-64, Libn 65-66; Libn Albuquerque Pub Schs 66-67; Soc sci libn UNM 67-. 8: Asst Prof lib sci UNM 69. 9: ALA (SSS Educ & Behavioral Sci Subsect Sec 69-); SLA; NMLA; Greater Albuquerque LA; Asociacion de Bibliotecarios Graduados del Istmo de Panama. 10: Zimmerman Lib Staff Assn. 14: Ref. 15: 1301 Coal ave SW, Albuquerque NM 87106.

HORAK, JANICE (JOHNSON). b Mason City Iowa 28 Ap 45. 4: Richard Horak. 5: Hanover Col 63-65 (Mus); UIowa 65-67 (Fr) BA; Alliance Francaise (Paris) 67 (Fr); UIowa 68-69 (LS) MA. 6: Fr, Sp, Ital. 7: Adult serv libn Cedar Rapids Pub Lib, Cedar Rapids iowa 69-. 9: ALA; IowaLA. 10: Alpha Lambda Delta; Phi Beta Kappa. 14: Ref, for lang collections. 15: 1520 8th ave SE, Cedar Rapids Ia 52403.

HORAL, FRANCES STEPHANIE (HANBY). b Monterey Pk Cal 11 N 42. 4: Donald Claude Horal. 5: Occidental Col 62-64 (Hist) BA; USoCal 66-67 (LS) MS. 6: Fr, Sp. 7: Lib asst Anaheim Pub Lib, Anaheim Cal 65-67; Docs libn Orange Co Pub Lib Adult Ref Ctr 68-. 9: CalLA; Orange CoLA. 10: Beta Phi Mu. 14: Docs, ref. 15: 11385 La Vereda, Santa Ana Ca 92705.

HORDE, MARIBESS (JACKSON). b Nashville 20 Jl 30. 5: Madison Col 48-52 (LS) BS Ed; UTenn 68-69 MS in LS. 07: Elem sch libn Arlington Co Sch Bd, Arlington Va 52-53; Elem sch libn Norfolk City Sch Bd, Norfolk Va 53-54; Jr high sch libn Tuscaloosa City Sch Bd, Tuscaloosa Ala 54-57; Ref libn Birmingham So Col 59-60; Elem sch libn Rockingham Co Sch Bd, Harrisonburg Va 62-68. 15: 75 Grattan st, Harrisonburg Va 22801.

HORDUSKY, CLYDE WALTER. b Union City Pa 23 Ja 37. 5: Grove City Col 54-58 (Eng) BA; West Res 60-63 MSLS. 6: Fr. 7: Med corpsman US Army, Heidelberg Germany 58-60; Lib asst Case Inst 60-63, Ref libn 63-64, Acquis libn 64-68, Sci & tech selection off Case West Res U 68-. 9: SLA; ALA. 12: Ed, SLA Cleveland Chapter Bulletin (67-68). 14: Acquis, ref. 15: 27651 Tungsten rd, Euclid Oh 44132.

HORECKY, PAUL LOUIS. b Trutnov Czechoslovakia 8 S 13. 4: Emily Ivey. 5: Prague U 31-36 (Law, Pol Sci) Dr Jur; Sorbonne Paris 34 (Law, Pol Sci); Harvard 49-51 (Russian Studies) MA. 6: Fr, Ger, Russian, Czech & other Slavic &

East European langs, Lat. 7: Gen law practice, Prague 36-37; Trial attorney US Off of Chief of Counsel, Nuremberg War Crimes Trials 47-49; Researcher Harvard U Russian Research Center 49-51; Slavic & Central European Div LC: Slavic research analyst 51-56, E European spec 56-58, Asst chief & E European spec 58-. 8: US Off of Educ eval of grad scholarships pursuant to NDEA, 64; Field Reader for projects supported by US Off of Educ 66-; Mem of Subcom on E Central and SE Europ Studies & Adv Comm on Lib Needs in E Central & SE Europ Studies (ACLS & SSRC), 68-; US Contr Ed to "Bibliographie d'Etudes Balkaniques", publ by Bulgarian Acad of Sci. 09: ALA (sec Slavic & E European Subsect 64-66); DCLA. 10: Harvard Club Wash DC; Amer Pol Sci Assn; Amer Assn Advance Slavic Studies Czechoslovak Soc Arts & Scis in Amer (Publ Com). 11: Charles Smith Scholarship Harvard U 50-51. 12: Ed & cont "Southeastern Europe: A Guide to Basic Publications" (69); Ed & Contr "East Central Europe: A Guide to Basic publications" (69); Ed & contrib "Russia & the Soviet Union. A Bibliographic Guide to Western-Language Publications" (65); Comp "The USSR and Eastern Europe: Periodicals in Western Languages," with R G Carlton (3rd ed 68); Ed & contrib "Basic Russian Publications: A Selected and Annotated Bibliography on Russia and the Soviet Union" (62); Comp "Newspapers of the Soviet Union in the Library of Congress" (62); "Libraries and Bibliographic Centers in the Soviet Union" (59); Comp "East and East Central Europe: Periodicals in English and other West European Languages" (58); Comp "Czech and Slovak Abbreviations" (56); Comp "Russian, Ukrainian and Belorussian Newspapers 1917-1953: A Union List" (53); Comp "Preliminary Checklist of Russian, Ukrainian, and Belorussian Newspapers published since January 1, 1917" (52); Co-ed "Trials of War Criminals before the Nuernberg Military Tribunals" (vol X, XI 50-51); Contrib & articles: "Encyclopedia Americana" (Libs in East Europe); "The Language of the Foreign Book Trade" (62); "Soviet Libraries and Librarianship" (62). 13: Yes. 14: Bibliog, ref, E European & USSR cultural & Polit affairs. 15: 2207 Paul Spring rd, Alexandria Va 22307.

HORGAN, JOHN D. b NYC 29 Jl 32. 4: Myrtie L Sawyer. 5: UUtah 55-56 (Stratigraphic Geol); UDenver 56-58 (Humanities) BA; UMich 58-59 (LS) MA; UNev 59-. 7: Sr aircraft instrument repairman & tech photographer USAF 50-54; Asst circ libn UNev (Reno) 59-60; Docs-ref libn Nev State Lib 60-62; Libn Carson Sr High Sch, Carson City Nev 62-. 9: NevLA; Nev Educ Media Assn. 14: Ref, a-v, tech libnship, ya wk. 15: 2210 Utah st, Carson City Nv 89701.

HORN, ANDREW H(ARLIS). b Ogden Utah 22 Jl 14. 4: Mary Baier. 5: Santa Monica City Col 32-35 (Pre-med) AA; UCal(Los Angeles) 35-43 (Hist) BA, MA, PhD; UCal(Berkeley) 47-48 BLS. 6: Sp, Ger, Fr, Lat. 7: Lab asst in zool Santa Monica City Col 33-35; Teach asst in hist UCLA 37-42, Research asst hist 40-41; Lecturer in hist UCLA Ext Div 41-42; Tech writer & ed Douglas Aircraft Co, Santa Monica Cal 42-43; Staff Sgt US Army Med Dept 43-46; Asst Prof hist Johns Hopkins U 46-47; UCLA Lib: Sr lib asst 47, Asst head dept spec collections 48-50, Head dept spec collections 50-51, U Archivist 50-54, Asst U libn 51-52, Assoc U libn 52-54; U Libn & Prof of Libnship UNC(Chapel Hill) 54-57; College Libn Occidental Col 57-59; UCLA Sch of Lib Serv: Lecturer 59-60, Act dean 60-63, Assoc Prof 60-63, Asst Dean 60-65, Prof 63-, Dean 66-. 8: Inst on Archives & Mss Amer U Nat Archives LC Md Hall of Records 51; Los Angeles Civil Serv Examining Bd for Libns 51; NC State Lib Bd of Trustees 55-57; "Know Your Library" educ TV UNC 55-57; Adv Bd of the Bureau of Pub Records Collection and Research UNC 57-60; Adv Bd of America: History and Life; Consul to UCLA Lib on bldg plans 57-58; Consul to Cal State Lib on map collection 49-50; Survey of UNev Libs 61; Survey of Lib of the Las Vegas Campus of UNev 64; Survey of Honnold Lib of the Assoc Claremont Cols Cal 65; other consulting & surveying; Adv Bd Dir Med Lib Scholarship Found (Med Lib Gp So Cal). 09: ALA (Coun 57-58, 69-72, chm Jt Com ALA & CanLA 56-57, num other coms);-ACRL (Exec Bd 69-72), (var coms Rare Bks Sect);-RTSD (var coms);-LED;ADI;BSA;SAA (var coms);SLA;CalLA (Coun 68, Exec Bd 68-89); (pres Col, Univ & Res Libs Sect 59; chm &/or mem num coms). Former member of other regional & state assns; AALS 10: Medieval Acad Amer; AAUP; Bibliog Soc (London); Printing Hist Soc (London); Soc for the Hist of Med Sci (UCLA); Center for Medieval & Renaissance Studies (UCLA); Rounce & Coffin Club (Los Angeles); Friends of the Lib orgs UNC, UCLA & Occidental Col; Phi Eta Sigma; Phi Beta Kappa; Pi Gamma Mu; Phi Delta Kappa; Bibliog Soc UVa. 11: Hattie Hellar Scholar in History UCLA 41. 12: "Great American Historical Documents & Books," with E H Carpenter (49); "Southern California Union List of Microtext Editions" (59); Ed Cal State Centennial issue of "California Library Bulletin" (June 50); Ed "Library Trends," vol 4 no 2 (Oct 55). 13: Yes. 14: Bibliog, hist of bks & libs, ref, col & univ lib admin, lib educ, rare bks. 15: Sch of Lib Serv UCLA, Los Angeles Ca 90024.

HORN, ANNA ELIZABETH. b Wilmington Del 4 Ag 36. 5: Goucher Col 54-58 (Hist) AB; UMich 58-59 AMLS, 64-65 (Hist) AM. 6: Fr, Ger. 7: Ya libn Cleveland Pub Lib 59-61, Asst br libn 62-64; Catlgr LC 65, Catlg ref libn 65-67; Br libn Enoch Pratt Free Lib, Baltimore 67-68, Asst to coord adult serv 68-. 9: ALA; DCLA; MdLA. 10: Phi Beta Kappa; Beta Phi Mu. 14: Ref, pub libs, adult serv. 15: 222 S t Paul pl, Baltimore Md 21202.

HORN, JANICE HELENE (ANDERSON). b Eau Claire Wis 16 Jl 35. 4: Roger G Horn. 5: Luther Col 53-57 (Eng) BA; UMich 59-61 AMLS. 7: Libn Mayville Pub Schs, Mayville Wis 57-59; Wk-Study Scholar UMich Libs 59-61; Catlgr Ohio State U 61-62, Ser catlgr 62-65; Catlgr Wright State U (Dayton) 65-66; Hd catlgr Clarion State Col 66-. 9: ALA -ACRL 09: ALA-ACRL-RTSD;PLA; Tri-State ACRL. 10: AAUP; LWV. 14: Cat lg, ser, acquis; govt docs. 15: 32 Barber st, Clarion Pa 16214.

HORN, ROGER GARLAND. b Brooklyn NY 8 Je 32. 4: Janice Helene Anderson. 5: LSU 54-59 (Music) BME; UMich 59-61 AMLS. 7: Tuba player US Army 5th Armored Div Band, Arkansas 50-52; Wk-study scholar UMich Music lib 59-61; Ref libn Ohio State U 61-65; Acquis libn Wright State Campus(Dayton) 65-66; Ref libn & bibliogr Clarion State Col 66-. 09: ALA; PennLA (v-pres NW Chap); Tri-State ACRL. 10: AAUP; Bd Clarion Free Lib. 13: Yes. 14: Ref, lib organ, personnel. 15: 32 Barber st, Clarion Pa 16214.

HORN, ZOIA (POLISAR). b Odessa Russia 14 Mr 18. 5: Brooklyn Col 35-39 (Eng) BA; Pratt Inst 41-42 BLS, Equiv MLS. 6: Fr. 7: Ref lib (br) NYC Pub Lib 42-43; Catlgr Rutgers U Lib (New Brunswick) 47-48; Asst ref libn Montclair Pub Lib, Montclair NJ 52-54; Asst ref libn Summit Pub Lib, Summit NJ 55-59; Hd libn Watchung Hills Reg High Sch, Warren twp NJ 60-65; Asst ref libn col lib UCLA 65-68; Hd ref dept Bertrand Lib Bucknell U 68-. 9: ALA; PennLA; CalLA. 10: LWV; AAUP. 11: John Hay Fellowship in the Humanities 64. 13: Yes. 14: Ref. 15: RD 1, Lewisburg Pa 17837.

HORNAK, ANNA (FRANCES). b College Station Tex 3 Je 22. 5: UTex 40-44 (Eng) BA; UIll 44-45 BS in LS; UHouston 52-56 (Admin Educ) M Ed. 6: Czech. 7: Child libn Schenectady Pub Lib, Schenectady NY 45-47; Child libn Pasadena Pub Lib, Pasadena Cal 47-49; Supv juvenile div Houston Pub Lib 49-57, Asst dir 57-. 9: ALA (Coun 67-70); SWLA (chm &/or mem 3 divs & coms); TexLA (chm Pub Libs Com). 10: Kappa Delta Pi; Alpha Gamma Delta Alumnae Club; C of C; Houston Lib Club. 13: Yes. 14: Child wk, admin, loc hist. 15: 1831 W Main apt 5, Houston Tex 77006.

HORNBROOK, CECELIA. b Pleasantville NJ 15 S 15. 5: Marshall U 36-43 (Educ) AB, MA; Catholic U 48-53 BS in LS. 6: Fr. 7: Tchr elem schs, Wood Co WVa 40-45; Statist clerk USDA, Wash DC 45-47; Lib asst nat Agric Lib, Wash DC 47-50; US Dept of Housing & Urban Development, Wash DC: Lib asst 50-51, Ref libn 51-56, Ref supv libn 56-58, Libn chief of ref, asst to dir 58-66, Chief readers serv 66-. 9: SLA (Wash DC Chap Exec Coun, sec Soc Sci Group). 10: Internat Toastmistress Club; Kappa Delta Pi. 12: "60 Books in Housing and Community Development" (62); "Films, Filmstrips and Slides in Housing and Community Development: a Selected Bibliography" (65); "Housing and Planning References," bi-monthly (48-). 14: Ref, bibliog, law, circ, readers serv. 15: 8421-11th st, Silver Spring Md 20903.

HORNBURG, MARTINE AUGUSTA. b Laredo Tex 9 Je 32. 5: Tex Women's U 49-53 (LS) BA; USoCal 57-67 MSLS. 7: Br libn El Paso Pub Lib, El Paso Tex 53-57, Asst Ref Libn Orange Co Pub Lib, Orange Cal 57-59, Bkmob Libn 60-62, Child Coord 62-63, Br Coord 63-67, Dir Spec Serv 67-. 9: ALA; CalLA (Intell Freedom Com Educ Com); OrangeCoLA. 10: Amer Mensa Soc. 14: Admin, adult & juv bk & record eval, pub rel. 15: 1485A N Glassell, Orange Ca 92667.

HORNE, ERNEST LINCOLN. b Boston 9 Ag 26. 5: Harvard 44-48 (Hist) AB; Simmons 52-54 (LS) MS. 6: Fr. 7: US Navy 45-46; Ref asst MIT Engnr Lib 52-54; Ref asst tech dept Detroit Pub Lib 54-57, Catlgr dept 57-61; Catlg libn Gen Motors Research Lib, Warren Mich 61-. 9: SLA (Mich Chap: treas 58-61, pres 62-63, dir 65-66; Transp Div: sec-treas 68-69). 10: Algonquin Club; Sierra Club. 14: Catlg, indexing, info retrieval. 15: GM Res Lib GM Tech Center, 12 Mile & Mound rds, Warren Mich 48090.

HORNE, NORMAN P(HILIP). b Rochester NH 18 Mr 14. 4: Elizabeth Raley. 5: UNH 32-34, 37-39 (Bus) BS in Liberal Arts; Catholic U 58-61 MSLS; Certified for Co Libn State of Cal 63. 6: Fr. 7: (Lt Col) Adjutant Gen Corps US Army Ret 58; Asst libn Mil Assistance Inst, Arlington Va 58-59; Admin asst ref dept LC 60-61; Head ext div Riverside Pub Lib, Riverside Cal 61-63, Asst lib dir 63-67; Dir pub libs br Hawaii State Lib Syst 67-. 9: ALA; CalLA; Pub Lib Execs Assn So Cal; HawaiiLA. 10: World Affairs Coun, So Cal; Retired Officers Assn; Rotary Club. 13: Yes. 14: Admin. 15: 1515 Ward ave 1505, Honolulu Hawaii 96822.

HORNE, PHYLLIS G. b Somerville Mass 10 F 17. 5: RI State Col 35-39 (Home Econ) BS; Simmons 43-44 BS in LS; Trinity Col (Hartford Conn) 47-50 (Lit) MA; Hillyer Col 53-55. 6: Fr. 7: Home econ tchr pub schs, Norwich Conn 39-43; Libn John Fitch High Sch, Windsor Conn 44-46; Asst libn Bulkeley High Sch, Hartford Conn 46-55, Libn 55-. 8: Prof wk at Bureau of Libs Hartford Conn; Lib Serv Center Middletown Conn 2 yrs; Catlg & org Central Processing Center for elem sch libs W Hartford Conn pub schs 65. 9: ALA; NEA; ConnSchLA; ConnEA. 14: Catlg, ref. 15: 18 Elm, Wethersfield Conn 06109.

HORNER, JOHN WESLEY. b Beaver Falls Penn 17 Je 28. 4: Janet Dick Horner. 5: Geneva Col 48-52 (Eng) AB; Boston U Sch of Theol 52-55 (Theol) STB; USoCal 64-66 MSLS. 7: Assoc minister Hayes Mem Methodist Ch, Fremont Ohio 55-56; Tchr: Ross High Sch, Fremont Ohio 56-60, Ventura High Sch, Ventura Cal 60-65; Hd catlg libn Riverside City Col 65-. 8: Newspaper Fund Fellowship to UCal (Berkeley) summer 62. 9: ALA; CalTA; CalLA. 10: Phi Delta Kappa. 14: Admin, catlg, ref. 15: 3644 Castle Reagh pl, Riverside Ca 92506.

HORNER, MARGARET L. b Shawville Que Can 23 Ag 28. 5: Houghton Col 45-49 (Eng, Fr) BA; Carnegie 53-54 MLS. 7: Child libn Brooklyn Pub Lib 54-59, Dist libn 59-60; Head child wk Gary Pub Lib, Gary Ind 60-63; Child consul Onondaga Lib System, Syracuse NY 63-65, Asst dir 65-. 9: ALA (Subcom on Standards for Pub Libs); NYLA (sec Child & YA Serv Sect, mem Com on Standards for Child Serv). 10: Women's Nat Bk Assn; Amer Bus Women's Assn; Zonta Internat; Profess Women's League. 13: Yes. 14: Child serv. 15: 111 Lincoln Park dr, Syracuse NY 13203.

HORNER, WILLIAM CONWAY. b Pittsburgh Penn 2 Ap 29. 4: Helene Goodrich. 5: Carnegie Inst 47-50 (Engring); UPittsburgh 50-52 (Bus) BBA, 63-64 (Info Sci) MSLS. 7: Sales Correspondent Harbison-Walker Refractories Co, Pittsburgh Penn 52-54; Off Mgr Gates Rubber Co, Pittsburgh Penn 54; Sales Mgr Admiral Homes Inc, W Newton Penn 55-58; V-pres & treas Horner Bros Inc, Irwin Penn 58-63; Instr Educ Inst of Pittsburgh, Pittsburgh Penn 63-65; Sci & Eng Libn Tufts U 65-. 9: Amer Soc Engrg Educ (Prog chm NE Sect, Lib Div 66, 67); SLA; Assn for Computing Machinery. 10: AAUP. 14: Systems, automation, info ret. 15: 16 Dearborn rd, Medford Ma 02155.

HORNEY, MARGARET (KENDRICK). b NYC 21 F 12. 4: William Johnston Horney Jr. 5: Woman's Col of UNC 28-32 (Hist) AB; Columbia 32-33 BSLS. 7: Ref libn Greensboro Pub Lib, Greensboro NC 44-46; Asst libn Guilford Col Lib 46-48; Head catlgr Greensboro City Sch Libs, Greensboro NC 57-61; Catlgr UNC Lib (Greensboro) 61-. 9: ALA; SELA; NCLA. 10: Guilford Col Art Appreciation Club; Dolly Madison Garden Club. 15: 1402 Fleming rd, Greensboro NC 27410.

HORNY, KAREN LOUISE. b Highland Park Ill 22 Ap 43. 5: Pembroke Col (Providence) 61-65 (Fr Lit) AB; UMich 65-66 MALS. 6: Fr, Ger. 7: Asst core libn Northwestern U Lib 66-67, Act hd 67-68, Hd 68, Hd poetry collection 69-. 9: ALA. 10: Pembroke Col Club f Chicago; Phi Beta Kappa; Beya Phi Mu; Phi Kappa Phi. 14: Acquis (Bk sel). 15: 816 Simpson st apt 3B, Evanston Il 60201.

HORODECKA, OXANA. b Sianik Ukraine 26 My 44. 5: Syracuse 62-66 (Hist) BA, 66-68 MSLS. 6: Ukrainian, Fr, Sp, Russian, Lat. 7: Grad asst Grad Sch of Lib Sci Syracuse 66-68; Catlgr LC 68-. 9: ALA; ASIS; DCLA; Potomac Tech Proc Libns. 10: Phi Beta Kappa; Beta phi Mu. 15: 2844 Wisconsin ave NW apt 901, Washington DC 20007.

HORODECKYJ, ILLIA. 4: Maria Klisz. 5: Polish & UkrainianU (Lvov) 32-37 (Law, Philos & Divinity) BA; AustrianU (Innsbruck) 37-38 (Philos & Divinity) MA; Ukrainian FreeU (Munich) 47-48 (Hist of Civ); Columbia 56-57 MLS. 6: Ukrainian, Polish, Ger, Classical Grk & Lat, Russian, Slovak, Czech, Bulgarian. 7: Tchr & prin high Sch, Ukraine 39-41; Imprisoned by Gestapo, Lvov & Krakow 41-42; Soc wkr Ukranian Relief Committee, Stryj Ukraine 42-44; Soc wkr D P Camp, Regensburg Germany 45-49; Manual wker YaleU 49-56; Slavic libn SyracuseU Lib 57-. 8: Adv to col students 9ukrainian), Germany 45-49; Adv to univ students in Slavic Studies 57-. 9: Ukrainian Libns' Assn of N Amer; Libns' Assn of StracuseU. 10: Ukrainian Sch (Ridna Shkola); PLAST-Ukrainian Youth Organization; Ukrainian Congress Com of Amer. 13: Yes. 14: Catlg, ref, rare bks. 15: 207 Roosevelt ave, Syracuse NY 13210.

HOROWITZ, BESS G. b Brooklyn NY 18 N 16. 4: William Horowitz. 5: Brooklyn Col 32-37 (Hist) BA; Yeshiva 63-64 (Educ); Pratt Inst 64-66 MLS. 7: Asst libn Good Counsel Col 67-. 9: ALA; WestchesterLA. 10: Beta Phi Mu. 14: Ref, readers adv, "Listening Rm libn". 15: 96 Garden rd, Scarsdale NY 10583.

HOROWITZ, MARJORIE (BRAILOVE). b Philadelphia Pa 7 O 27. 4: Irvin M Horowitz. 5: Wellesley 45-49 (Eng) BA; Columbia 62-64, 66-67 MLS; Montclair State Col 68. 6: Fr. 7: Publicity Asst Save the Children Federation, NYC 49-51; Libn Watchung Sch, montclair NJ 66-. 9: ALA; NEA; NJSchLA; EssexCoSchLA; NJEA; MontclairEA. 10: Beta Phi Mu; PTA; Wellesley Club of NJ. 14: Sch libnship. 15: 10 Prospect ave, Montclair NJ 07042.

HORROCKS, NORMAN. b Manchester Eng 18 O 27. 5: Sch of Libnship Manchester Eng 48-50 FLA; U of West Australia 56-60 (Hist) BA; UPittsburgh 63-64 MLS; 63 Assoc of LA of Australia. 7: Various Manchester Pub Libs, eng 43-45, 50-54; (Sgt) Intelligence Corps British Army 45-48; Libn British Coun, Cyprus 54-56; Tech libn State Lib West Australia 56-63; Instr Grad Sch of Lib & Info Sci UPittsburgh 63-68, Asst Prof 69-. 9: ALA; The Lib Assn (Brit); Lib Assn Australia; AALS; Penn LA. 10: Beta Phi Mu; Nat Bk League (Eng); AAUP; Pittsburgh Lib Club. 12: Ed "North Western Newsletter," Eng (52-53). 13: Yes. 14: Ref, lib resources, educ for libnship. 15: Grad Sch of Lib & Info Scis UPittsburgh, Pittsburgh Pa 15213.

HORSEMAN, JEAN MARY. b Baltimore 31 Jl 32. 5: Towson State Tchrs Col 49-53 (Educ) BS; Johns Hopkins 55-58 (Educ) MEd; Catholic U 60-64 MS in LS. 7: Baltimore City Dept of Educ: Tchr Sch 83 53-54, Tchr Sch 44 54-58, Tchr-libn Sch 235 58-65, Tchr-libn Sch 233 65-68, Tchr-Libn Sch 77 68-. 9: ASchLMd. 10: Phi Delta Gamma; Pi Lambda Theta; Beta Phi Mu. 14: Sch libs. 15: 7915 Roseland ave, Baltimore Md 21237.

HORSLEY, LUCILE (HAMILTON). b Franktown Va 13 Jl 14. 5: Marshall Col 32-37 (Art) BS; Peabody 50 BS in LS. 7: Libn: Eastville High Sch, Eastville Va 37-38, Forest Hills Sch, Danville Va 38-42, Manassas High Sch, Manassas Va 42-43, Wicomico High Sch, Salisbury Md 47-49; Catlgr Wicomico Co Lib, Salisbury Md 49-50, Admin 50-; Admin Eastern Shore Bk Processing Center, Salisbury Md 61-. 9: ALA; MdLA. 13: Yes. 14: Admin, catlg. 15: P O Box 950, 122-126 S Division st, Salisbury Md 21801.

HORSMAN, JOYCE (DICKERSON). b Mineville NY 7 Ag 27. 4: Robert E Horsman. 5: SUNY(Albany) 45-49 (Eng, Soc Studies) AB, 50-54 MS in LS, 63 (Educ Curriculum). 7: High sch Eng-libn Lake George Central Sch, Lake George NY 49-51; Elem libn N Colonie Central Sch, Nwtonville NY 51-56, Chm lib dept K-12 58-, Dir of lib-AV Serv. 8: Lib consu r Family & Child Serv of Albany; Exec dir Nat Lib Week, NY State. 09H East Zone Lib Sect 62); NY State ASCD; NY State ECA. 10: Girl Scout Leader; Pi Gamma Mu. 13: Yes. 14: Supv, curriculum, pub rel, innovations in li serv. 15: 925 Mohegan rd, Schenectady NY 12309.

HORSMAN, PHYLLIS A. b Brockton Mass 20 Je 10. 5: Simmons 04(LS) BS; Bridgewater State Col 36-37 (Educ) BS in Ed. 7: WPA Supv of Catlg for Mass Div of Pub Libs, Boston 39-43; Catlgr Boston U Col (Bus Admin) 43; Sr asst Medford Pub Lib, Medford Mass 43-46, Yp libn 46-48, Asst catlgr 48-50, Br libn 50-. 8: Org & Catlg Bk Collection for Bouve-Boston Sch of Phys Educ of Tufts U 61-62. 9: MassLA. 10: Charles River Lib Club; Simmons Col Lib Sch Alumni Assn; Bridgewater Alumni 29 Royall st, Medford Mass 02155.

HORST, STANLEY EUGENE. 4: Phyllis Ann McNatt. 5: Penn State U 51-55 (Arts & Letters, Relig) BA; Episcopal Theol Sch 57-59; UWis Law Sch 64-65; UWis Lib Sch 65-67 MLS. 6: Sp. 7: Specialist 4th class US Army 55-57; Sales mgr UWis Press 60-61; Holt, Rinehart & Winston col dept 62-64; Circ & res libn UWis Law Lib 67; Acquis libn UIowa Law Lib 67-69; Asst law libn O'Melveny & Myers, LA 69-. 9: ALA; AALL (Educ Com). 14: Acquis, info sci. 15: O'Melveny & Myers, 611 W Sixth st, Los Angeles Ca 90017.

HORTON, ELENA DOROTHY (EVERETT). b Manila PI 14 My 17. 5: Smith 34-38 (Hist) BA; Columbia 47 BLS, 51-58 (LS). 6: Sp. 7: Trainee NY Pub Lib 38-43; Asst dir Thrall Lib, Middletown NY 50-51; Dir Orange Co Community Col 51-60; Dir Ramapo Catskill Lib System 60-65; Exec sec Free Pub Lib Serv, Vt 65-68; Exec dir N Country Ref & Research Resources Coun 68-. 8: Instr Lib Tech Program Orange Co Community Col; Interstate Compact Coordinator So Vt Lib. 9: ALA (Coun 66-68); VtLA (Exec Bd 65-68); NELA (chm Ext Div 66-67); NYLA; SLA. 10: Bus & Prof Women's Club; AAUW; Alumnae Assn of Smith Col & Columbia U. 14: Admin. 15: Box 161, Colton NY 13625.

HORTON, GRACE (BISCHOFF). b Summerville SC 19 My 06. 5: El Paso Jr Col 25-27; Pratt 28-29 (LS). 7: Jr libn El Paso Pub Lib, El Paso Tex 25-28; Jr libn Passaic Pub Lib, Passaic NJ 29-39, Br libn & Jr High Sch libn 40-47; NY State Sch of Ind & Labor Rel Cornell U; Asst catlg libn 48-55; Catlg libn 55-56, Catlg libn & bibliog 65-68; Docs libn Labor Mgt Documentation Ctr. 9: SLA; Ind Rel Res Assn (Subj Heading Subcom); CUIRL (chm Subj Hdings Subcom 69-). 12: Comp "Recent Publications Sect of Industrial and Labor Relations Review"; Comp Annual Index of Same Publ; Comp Bibl Sec of "Key Issues in Industrial Society". 14: Catlg, ref, bibliog, labor mss. 15: 108 Eddy st, Ithaca NY 14850.

HORTON, RITA (ISOBEL) (MADEL). b Barss Corner NS Can 10 My 17. 4: Sydney Rowland Horton. 5: Acadia U 32-36 (Psych) BA; McGill 36- BLS. 6: Fr, Ger. 7: Gen libn Acadia U(NS) 38-41, 54-55, Head catlgr 55-. 9: CanLA; APLA. :N FED OF Univ Women; NS Craftsmen's Guild. 14: Catlg. 15: Box 588, Wolfville NS Can.

HORVATH, GEORGE. b Trenton NJ 5 My 24. 4: Kerttu Pietilainen. 5: Tulane 47-50 (Mus) BA; East Mich U 57-60 (Eng) MA in Ed; Wayne State 64 (Educ). 6: Russian. 7: Cpl US Army 43; Tchr Melvindale High Sch, Melvindale Mich 55-66; Ref libn Dearborn Pub Lib, Dearborn Mich 64-66; Lib dir Fiske Free Lib, Claremont NH 66-67; Lib dir McArthur Pub lib, Biddeford Me 67-. 8: Fulbright Exch Tchr to Norway 58-59. 9: ALA; MeLA; NELA. 14: Pub lib serv, bk sel. 15: 50 Foley ave, Saco Me 04072.

HORVATH, HELEN (SCRUGGS). b St Louis 1 S 31. 5: Washington U (St Louis) 49-53 (Art Hist) BA; UIll(Urbana) 55-57 (Art Hist) MA, 61-63 (LS) MS. 7: Catlgr Corvallis Pub Lib, Corvallis Ore 64; Asst catlg libn Ore State U 65-. 9: ALA; PNLA. 10: AAUP; Ore State Employees Assn. 14: Catlg. 15: 4060 Houston pl, Corvallis Or 97330.

HORVATH, MICHAEL JOSEPH. b Zagreb Hungary 30 Je 15. 5: UBudapest (Pazmany Peter) 33-37 (Maw) LLD; Western MichU 63-64 MLS. 6: Ger, Fr, Hungarian. 7: Sales mgr Ont Tobacco Co Ltd, Toronto Ont Can 54-63; Catlgr CatholicU 64-65; Asst loan libn UMd (Col Park) 45-. 8: Com mem on automation at UMd (Col Pk) 67-. 10: Amer Hungarian Fed. 15: 4021 8th st NE, Washington DC 20017.

HORVATH, PAUL J. b Cleveland 24 5Fenn Col 46-51 (Chem Engnr) BChE. 7: B F Goodrich Chem Co Development Center, Avon Lake Ohio: Engnr 51-55, Assoc dev sci 56-60, Info sci 60-. 9: ASIS; Amer Inst Chem Engnrs; Info Systems Com. 13: Yes. 14: Automatic processing of info. 15: 4487 Camellia lane, N Olmsted Oh 44070.

HORWITZ, MARSHA VICTORIA. b Detroit 16 Ja 42. 5: Wayne State U 59-63 (German) BA; Middlebury Col summer 63; Columbia 63-66 (German) MA, 67-68 MS. 6: Ger, Fr, Dutch. 7: Tchg asst Columbia U 64-67; Ref libn Columbia U (Social Work) 67-68; Catlgr CCNY 68-. 9: NY Tech Serv Libns; LACUNY. 10: AAUP; Phi Beta Kappa. 14: Catlg. 15: 316 W 105th st apt A, New York NY 10025.

HOSKIN, BERYL MARGARET. b Schreiber Ont Can 23 S 11. 5: San Jose State Col 30-34 (Eng Lit) BA, 34-35 (LS) Spec credential; USoCal summer 49; San Jose State Col 57-61 (LS) MA. 6: Fr. 7: Asst libn Santa Clara Pub Lib, Santa Cara c6-39; Ref libn USanta Clara 40-. 9: CalLA; CathLA. 10: AAUP; Hibernians; Canisius Bk Club. 12: "History of the Santa Clara Mission Library" (61); "California Fine Printing in the University of Santa Clara Library." 13: Yes. 14: Ref, miniat bks. 15: 2266 Cherrystone dr, San Jose Cal 95128.

HOSKING, RICHARD LOUIS. b Augustana Col (Rock Island Ill) 53-57 (Bus Admin) AB; Mich StateU 57-63 (Secondary Educ) MA. 7: Tchr Centreville High Sch, Centreville Mich 58-63; Libn Lake Fenton High Sch, Fenton Mich 63-68; Libn Waverly Sr High, Lansing Mich 68-. 8: Tchr & coun, Wkshop for Stud Lib Assts, West MichU. 9: NEA; MichEA; MichASchL; Mich A-v Assn. 14: Wk with stud libn assts. 15: 5525 W St Joseph apt A2, Lansing Mi 48917.

HOSLER, DORIS KELLER. b Berwick Penn 2 Jl 21. 4: Robert Clark Hosler. 5: Bloomsburg State Col 39-48 (Bus Educ) BS; Millersville State Col 57-59 (LS); Franklin & Marhsall 59-60 (Fr); Drexel 66-67 MSLS. 6: Fr. 7: Bus educ tchr Penn Manor High Sch, 07: Bus educ tchr Penn Manor High Sch, Millersville Penn 47 -58, Libn 58-68; Libn Millersville State Col 68-. 8: Middle States Eval Team 58-68. 9: NEA; ALA; PennStateEA; PennLA; LancasterCo(Penn)LA; Penn State Col &Univ FacAssn. 10: NAACP; Alpha Beta Alpha; AAUP; Millersville State FacAssn. 14: Circ, ref. 15: RD2, LancasterPa 17603.

HOSTETTER, DORIS RIVETT (LOCKWOOD). b Hull Mass 18 Ag 13. 5: Radcliffe 30-34 (Romance Langs) AB; Columbia 34-36 (Religious Educ) MA, Columbia 61-64 (LS) MS. 6: Fr, Sp. 7: Lib trainee NY Pub Lib Intrr loan 60-63; Catlgr NY Pub Lib 63-64; Libn Grolier Info Serv, NYC 64-. 8: Employed in rels educ & rels soc wk, 34-40. 9: SLA (NY Chap: Museum & Publ Groups). 14: Ref, catlg. 15: 165 West End av, New York NY 10023.

HOSTETTER, JOHN D. b Corning NY 2 O 38. 6: Fr, Sp. 7: Asst ser libn USoFla 66-. 9: SELA; FlaLA. 14: Acquis. 15: 625 Belmont ave, Temple Terrace Fl 33617.

HOTALING, DONALD O(LIVER). b Schenectady NY 25 Ja 16. 5: Union Col (Schenectady NY) 34-38 (Eng) BA; SUNY(Albany) 37-42 Bnl& columbia 44-45 MS in LS. 7: Eng tchr Corinth High Sch, Corinth NY 38-44; Acquis asst Columbia U Libs 44-45; Ref asst NY Pub Lib 45-47; Chief Libn Newsweek, NYC 47-65; Astmr internatl pblns Serv, NYC 66-. 9: SLA (var positions Chap y state Lib Assn; NY Lib Club. 13: Yes. 15: 448 W 22 st, New York NY 10011.

HOTCH, THEODOSIA. b Brunswick Ga 4 F 12. 5: Ga State Col for Women 29-32 (Hist) AB; Peabody 33-34 BS in LS; UIll 45-46 MS in LS. 7: Libn Cox Col 34hlin Winona High Sch, Winona Miss 34-35; Libn McComb High Sch, McComb Miss 35-36; Libn Glynn Acad, Brunswick Ga 36-42; Catlg libn Ga State Col for Women 42-49; Reviser in catlg Fla State U 49-51; Dir Satilla Reg Lib, Douglas Ga 51-62; Dir Brunswick Pub Lib, Brunswick Ga 62-. 9: ALA; SELA (sec Catlg Div 49-50); GaLA (v-pres 56-57). 10: Pi Gamma Mu; Beta Phi Mu; Delta Kappa Gamma. 14: Admin, ref. 15 loucester st, Brunswick Ga 31520. 15: 208 Gloucester st, Brunswick Ga 31520.

HOTIMSKY, CONSTANTINE MICHAEL. b Tomsk Russia 6 F 15. 4: Stella Repin. 6: Russian, Fr, Bulgarian, Belorussian. 7: Accountant: RCA Victor of China Shanghai 34-39, Commercial Factors Corp Ltd Brisbane Australia 39-41, Repins Pty Ltd, Sydney 46-61; 2d AIF Australian Army Ordinance Corps 41-45; Asst libn USydney Lib 61-64; Research lib UMelbourne 65-67; Lecturer UWest Ont Sch Lib & Info Sci 67-. 9: ALA. 10: AAAS. 12: "Melbourne Slavonic Studies"; "Canadian Slavic Studies". 13: Yes. 14: Slavic collections, Slavic lib sci. 15: 488 Lawson rd, London 72 Ont Can.

HOUCK, CATHERINE M(AGILL). b Wash O 07. 4: William C Huck. 5: George Washington U 24-30 (Eng) BA; Columbia summers 36-39 BS in LS. 7: DC Pub Lib: Asst circ & fiction 30-37, Circ asst Mt Pleasant Br 37-38, Asst catlg dept 38, Asst personnel off 38-42, Personnel off 42-54, Admin asst & budget off 54-57, Assoc dir 57-. 9: ALA. 10: Zonta Internat; Delta Zeta. 11: Sustained Superior Performance Rating, 57; Outstanding Performance Ratings, 62 & 64. 12: Jt auth (with H N Peterson): "Access to the DC Public Library" (63); "Distribution and Characteristics of DC Public Library Agencies" (64). 14: Admin, lib bldgs. 15: 2732 Rittenhouse st NW, Wash DC 20015.

HOUCK, PAULINE (ASHLEY). b N Vernon Ind 5 O 09. 4: Walter E Houck. 5: IndU 27-31 (Fr) AB; UIll 31-32 BLS; Butler U 56; NDEA Inst for Sch Libns Ind U 65. 6: Fr. 7: Child libn Pub Lib, Indianapolis Ind 34-37; Sch libn MSD Wayne Twp, Indianapolis 51-. 9: ALA; NEA; Ind State Tchrs Assn; IndSchLA; IndLA; Wayne Twp ClrTA. 10: Delta Kappa Gamma; Beta Sigma Omicron; Amer Red Cross; Women's Symphony Soc (Indianapolis). 13: Yes. 14: Elem sch libs & child & yp lib wk. 15: 6160 Gregory dr, Indianapolis In 46241.

HOUGH, CAROLYN ADELE (SMITH). b Providence 5 Jl 40. 4: Raymond L Hough. 5: UNH 58-62 (Eng Lit) BA; Simmons 62-63 (LS) MS; Wayn U 65-66 (Eng Lit). 6: Sp. 7: Clerk Educ Dept UNH 60-62; A-v libn Northeastern U 63; Libn I gen info dept Detroit Pub Lib 63-64, Libn II lang & lit dept 64-68; Indexer, Bk review digest h w Wilson Co, NYC 68-. 9: ALA; NY Lib Club. 10: Phi Beta Kappa; Phi Kappa Phi. 13: Yes. 14: Ref, bk reviewing. 15: 15 Kenyon rd, Cranston RI 02910.

HOUGH, CORINNE H. b Shamokin Penn 3 N 18. 5: Hood Col 36-40 (Hist, Biol Sci) BA; Columbia 47 (Hist) MA; Rutgers 55-58 MLS. 7: Tchr Bd of Educ Baltimore Co, Towson Md 41-55, Libn 55-. 9: Baltimore Co LA (sec, v-pres, pres). 14: Catlg, ref. 15: 8213 Loch Raven blvd, Baltimore Md 21204.

HOUGH, EMMA (SMITH). b Murphysboro Ill 10 F 1900. 4: Robert E Hough. 5: UIll (Urbana) 20-24 (Eng) AB; SoIll U 44-48 (Eng) MS in Ed; UIll 44-48 BS in LS. 07: Eng tchr High Sch, Princeville Ill 24-27; Eng tchr High Sch, Murphysboro Ill 27-30; Tchr of handicapped Daelby Sch, Pittsburgh 30-42; Libn High Sch, Murphysboro Ill 43-63; Libn Sallie Logan Pub Lib, Murphysboro Ill 63-. 9: ALA; IllEA; IllLA. 10: Bus & Prof Women's Club; MURPHYSBORO Women'S Club. 15: 222 N 14th st, Murphysboro Il 62966.

HOUGH, JEAN (DOROTHY) (MILLER). b Eugene Ore 2 D 13. 4: Louis Hough. 5: Ball State U 32-37 (Eng, Hist) AB, summer 38 (LS); UMich 61-65 MALS. 6: Fr. 7: Lib page Muncie (Ind) Pub Lib 28-32, Asst libn child 32-37; Asst libn period rec UChicago Libs 39-40; Ed Soc for Visual Educ, Chicago 40-42; Survey research (own bus), Pittsburgh Penn 51-54; Survey research UMich Survey Research Ctr, Pittsburgh Penn 50-54; Tchr Adams Twp, Ohio 55-59; Elem libn & a-v chm Farmington (Mich) Schs 60-69. 8: Radio wk Muncie Lib; Coun for Study League, France & Switzerland summer 68. 9: ALA; MichASchL; Mich A-V Assn; NEA; MichEA. 10: FarmingtonEA; Pi Gamma Mu. 13: Yes. 14: Child wk, elem lib curriculum. 15: 6847 Alden dr, Union Lake Mi 48085.

HOUGH, MARIANNE (HELMKE). b Toledo Ohio 21 F 22. 4: Macon Moore Hough. 5: Oberlin 39-43 (Eng) BA; West Res 43-44 BS in LS. 7: Br child libn Toledo Pub Lib, Toledo Ohio 44-45; Asst child libn NY Pub Lib 45-46; Child libn Miami Pub Lib, Miami Fla 47-48; Toledo Pub Lib, Toledo Ohio Br child libn 48-56, Coordinator wk with child 63-65, Coordinator wk with child & young teens 65-66; Coord youth serv Orlando Pub Lib, Orlando Fl 66-. 8: Instr, Storytelling, Creative Arts Wkshop, U So Fla summer 68. 9: ALA; OhioLA; FlaLA. 10: Fla Profess Serv League; Orange Co Com for Child & Youth. 13: Yes. 14: Wk with child & yp, inst libs. 15: Orlando Pub Lib Serving Orange A and Osceola Counties, 10 N Rosalind, Orlando Fl 32801.

HOUGH, SUZANNE (NINOMIYA). b NYC 8 Jl 21. 5: Smith 38-42 (Ger) AB; UDenver 63-66 (LS) MA; UColo 65. 6: Ger, Fr. 7: Ed asst "Natural History" Magazine, NYC 42-46; Asst & child room pub lib, Kalamazoo 47-48; Searcher card div LC 48-51; Tech info off NBS Corona Lab, Corona Ca 51-52; Hd tech serv dept pub lib, Boulder Colo 61-. 9: ColoLA. 10: LWV; YWCA. 14: Catlg, ref. 15: 60 S 31st st, Boulder Co 80302.

HOUGH, WILLIAM E III. b Cincinnati 20 D 30. 4: Valeria Deroner. 5: King's Col (NY) 52-55 (Math) BA; Dallas Theol Sem 55-59 ThM; Columbia 59-61, 64-65 MS in LS. 7: King's Col (NY): Asst libn 59-64, Act libn 64-65, Libn 65-66; Libn U Dubuque 66-. 9: ALA; Christian Libns Fellowship; IowaLA. 14: Tech proc, admin. 15: London Bridge Acres, RD #3, Mahopac NY 10541.

HOUGHTON, RODNEY M. b Portland Ore 24. 4: Brbara Gantz. 5: Reed Col 42-43, 46-48 (Econ); UDenver 48-50 BA (Econ) MA(LS Uan Francisco 57-60 jd. 07: Aviation cadet Flight Official (Navigator) USAAC 43-46; Asst libn US Bureau of Reclamation, Billings Mont 50-51; Valuation dept asst Pacific Gas & Electric, San Francisco 52-57; Asst law libn Cal Supreme Court, San Francisco 57-59; Law Libn, Asst Prof UMont 60-66; Dir Maricopa Co Law Lib, Phoenix Ariz 66-. 8: Consul for evaluating law lib collection. 9: AALL. 13: Yes. 14: Law lib admin. 15: Maricopa Co Law Lib, Superior Court Bldg, 101 W Jefferson, Phoenix Az 85003.

HOUK, JUDITH ANN. b Muncie Ind 2 F 35. 5: West Col for Women 53-54; Ball State Tchrs Col 54-56; Ind U 56-58 (Hist) BA, 58-59 (LS) MA. 7: Ref asst Dayton & Montgomery Co Pub Lib, Dayton Ohio 59-63; Ref libn USAF Inst of Tech, Wright-Patterson AFB Ohio 63-64; Libn Westminster Pub Lib, Westminster Colo 64-67; Reg libn Denver Reg Coun of Govts 67-68; Syst libn Central Colo Pub Lib Syst 68-. 9: ALA; ColoLA (pres 67-68, Exec Bd 66-69); MPLA. 10: Beta Phi Mu; Phi Beta Kappa. 12: "Classification System for Ohio State Documents" (62); "Public Libraries in the Denver Metropolitan Area; A Plan and Program for Public Library Development to 1985" (68). 14: Ref, admin. 15: 4140 W 80th pl, Westminster Colo 80030.

HOUK, WALLACE EUGENE. b S Bend Ind 18 Ag 25. 4: Sally Ann Sell. 5: Purdue U 45-49 (Entomology) BS in Agric; Mich State U 49-50, 51-54 (Entomology) MS, PhD; UMich summers 55-57 MALS. 6: Ger, Fr. 7: (Pfc) US Army 314th Reg 79th Inf Div, Europe 43-45; Instr nat sci dept Mich State U 54-55, Biol sci libn 56; Agric libn Amer Cyanamid Co, Princeton NJ 57-58; Info sci Lederle Labs Amer Cyanamid Co, Pearl River NY 59; Manager of Lib Serv Phillips Petroleum Co, Bartlesville Okla 60-61; Ref libn Gen Motors Research Lib, Warren Mich 62-64; Assoc Prof Dept of Libnship Kan State Tchrs Col 65-. 9: SLA. 10: Sigma Xi. 14: Ref, lit searching in biol & phys sci. 15: Kan State Tchrs Col Dept of Libnship, Emporia Ks 66802.

HOUKES, JOHN (MARTIN). b Rotterdam Netherlands 7 Jl 22. 4: Maxence Daniel. 5: Grand Seminaire(France) 43-47 (Philos) License; Ind U 60-61 (LS) MA. 6: Fr, Ger, Dutch, Sp, Russian. 7: Export manager Compagnie Meissonnier, Paris 48-54; Head freight dept Ruys & Co, Paris 54-59; Purdue U Libs: Order accountant 59-60, Asst order libn 61-63, Libn Krannert Lib 63-. 9: SLA; CUIRL; IndLA (Univ Bus Libs Com). 10: Beta Phi Mu; AAUP. 12: Ed "Management Information Systems and the Information SAS"(6. Yes. 14: Rare bks, bus ref, econ, hist. 15: 1700 Summit dr, W Lafayette Ind 47907.

HOULAHAN, PAT KATHERINE. b Chicago 4 S 38. 5: Our Lady of the Lake Col 56-60 BA in LS, 68- (LS). 6: Sp. 7: San Antonio Pub Lib, San Antonio Tex: Lib asst 56-60, Ya libn 60-61, Act head child & yp dept 61; Head Libn St Anthony's Sem (San Antonio Tex) 61-. 8: Lib consul, Oblate Col of the Southwest 60, 68. 9: ALA; CathLA (Steering Com for 1966 Nat Conv; San Antonio Unit: treas, mem Nomin Com, Exh Chm); TexLA; Bexar (Co) LA (Recrt Com, Prof Res Com). 10: Alpha Beta Alpha; Alpha Chi; Lambda Chi. 12: Ed "Bexar (Co, Tex) Library Directory"; Mem Ed Com "Catholic Supplement to Senior High School Library Catalog," (9th ed 67). 14: Ya wk. 15: 408 Ira apt 3, San Antonio Tx 78209.

HOULE, GEORGES J. b Troy NY. 5: USoCal 65 (Hist, Sociol) BA; West Mich U 67 (LS) MS. 6: Fr, Lat. 7: Asst mgr 42nd st Bk Store, LA 62-65; Intake Interviewer San Bernardino Co Welfare Dept, San Bernardino Cal 65-66; Hd Tech Serv Corona Pub Lib, Corona Cal 67-68; Asst Acquis Libn Cal State Col (Pomona) 68-69; A-v Coord Beverly Hills Pub Lib, Beberly Hils Cal 69-. 8: Catlgr, Bk Auction Catlg, Newman Galleries, Los Angeles 69. 9: ALA; CalLA; Book Club of Cal (Pub Com). 10: Beta Phi Mu; Riverside stamp & Coin Club; Inland Empire Bk Collectors Club. 14: A-v, tech serv. 15: PO Box 255, Riverside Ca 92502.

HOULE, REV GERARD SJ. b Montreal Can 16 Ag 08. 5: St Mary Col 22-28; Immaculate-Conception (Montreal) 32-35 (Philos) BA, 38-42 (Theol); Ecole de Bibliothecaires UMontreal 41 Certif. 6: Fr, Eng. 7: Tchr Sacred-Heart Col (Sudbury Ont) 35-38; Li bn Facutes de Philosophie et de Theologie Immaculee- Conception (Montreal) 43-56, 60-63, Archivist 64-68; Libn & Archivist Maison Daniel, Montreal 68-. 8: Scouts Chaplain since 1945 ; Montreal Association for Retarded Childred Chaplain since 60; Prof Ecole des Bibliothecaires Universite Montreal 50-56. 9: Association canadienne des bibliothecaires de langue francaise (life mem) CanLA (life mem). 12: "Inventaire chronologique des livres, brochures, journeaux et revues ... 1764-1820" (42). 13: Yes. 14: Ref, archives. 15: 1287 rue du Parc Lafontaine, Montreal 177 PQ Can.

HOULROYD, MAGDALENA H. b Trenton NJ 28 Ap 17. 5: Trenton State Col 35-39 (Elem Educ) BS; Temple 43-46 (Educ Admin) EdM; Drexel 47-52 MSLS. 6: Fr, Sp. 7: Elem tchr Montgomery Twp Bd of Educ, Somerset Co NJ 39-42; Elem tchr Hamilton Twp Bd of Educ, Mercer Co NJ 42-45; Libn Hamilton High Sch Hamilton Twp Bd of Educ, Mercer Co NJ 45-59; Libn Bridgewater-Raritan High Sch, Somerset Co NJ 59-62; Spec collections libn & Asst Prof of Lib Sci Glassboro State Col 62-. 8: Tech proc lib Duke U summer 54-60; Instr of Lib Sci at Trenton State Col 60-64, 67-69. 9: ALA-AASchLA; NJLA; NJSchLA. 10: Phi Delta Gamma AAUW; AAUP. 12: Ed "Bibliographer," NJLA (63); Mem Edl Com of "Negro Bibliography," NJLA (67-68). 14: Catlg, rare bks, hist. 15: 15 Fairmount dr, Glassboro NJ 08028.

HOUSE, DAVID LaVALLE JR. b Greenville Miss 7 N 20. 5: USNA 38-41 (Naval Sci) BS; Delta State Col 59-63 (Hist) BA; LSU 64-66 (LS) MS. 7: USN 41-59; UTenn Med Units:

Postgrad trainee program for sic libns 66-67, Research bibliogr Mooney Mem Lib 67-. 9: ALA; MedLA. 11: Beta Phi Mu; Pi Gamma Mu. 14: Ref. 15: 1733 Union apt 710, Memphis Tn 38104.

HOUSEL, JAMES ROBERT. b Cripple Creek Col 16 F 17. 4: Virginia Ebert. 5: UWyo 37-41 (Pol Sci) BA; UCal (Berkeley) 47-48 BS in LS. 7: (1st Lt) USA Engrs, European Theater 41-46; Machinist Bercut Richards Food Cannery, Sacramento Cal 46-47; Jr libn Richmond Pub Lib, Richmond Cal 48-50; Hd libn Ellensburg Pub Lib, Ellensb Richmond Pub Lib, Richmond Cal 48-50; Hd libn Ellensburg Pub Lib, Ellensburg Wash 50-52; Dir First Reg Lib of Miss, Hernando Miss 52-56; Hd libn Monterey Pk Pub Lib, Monterey Pk Cal 56-59; Lib dir Ontario City Lib, Ontario Cal 59-. 9: ALA; CalLA; Pub Libs Exec Assn So Cal; Inland Lib System Coun. 10: Chaffey Communs Cultural Ctr; Fine Arts Coord Coun; West End Symphony Assn; Amer Legion. 14: Parapsychology, writing & reading poetry. 15: 1253 College Way, Ontario Ca 91762.

HOUSER, FLORENCE. b Worcester Mass 6 N 23. 4: Abraham Houser. 5: Brooklyn Col 40-44 (Sociol) BA; Columbia 44-46 BLS; Brooklyn Col 49-53 (Sociol), NYC Bd of Educ (Child Lit) Certif. 06: Fr, Hebrew, Ger. 7: Catlg asst Columbia U 44-45; Asst libn Schenley Distillers, NYC 45-47; Catlgr & ref asst Equitable Life Assur Soc, NYC 47-48; Circ & ref libn LIU 48-55; Tchr of lib Lafayette High Sch, Brooklyn 57-58; Even libn NYC Commun Col(Brooklyn) 60-64; Asst libn Kingsborough Commun Col(Brooklyn) 64-, Hd tech serv 67-. 8: ALA; Lib Assn U City of NY. 14: Ref, catlg, acquis. 15: 2223 E 8th, Brooklyn NY 11223.

HOUSER, LLOYD J. b Ashland Il 25 Ap 22. 5: WashU (St Louis) 46-49 AB; UIll 55-57 (LS) MS; Rutgers 64-68 (LS) PhD. 7: Catlgr Ill State Lib, Springfield 52-55; Circ asst uill Lib (Urbana) 55-57; Bibliog UCal Lib (Berkeley) 58-60; Order libn Amer U of beirut Lib 60-63; Order libn UMass 63-64; Instr Rutgers Grad Sch Lib Serv (New Brunswick) 66-67, Asst prof 67-. 9: ALA; NJLA. 10: AAUP. 12: "New Jersey Area libraries: a Pilot Project Toward the Evaluation of the Reference Collection" (68). 14: Bibliog organ & control of lib & info sci lit. 15: Grad School of Lib Serv Rutgers State Univ, New Brunswick NJ 08903.

HOUSTON, EVELYN (DORSEY). b Atlanta 3 My 25. 4: James Daniel Houston Jr. 5: Spelman Col 42-46 (Home Econ) BS; Atlanta U summers 53-59 MSLS. 6: Fr. 7: Home econ lab asst Spelman Col 47-50; Tchr-libn Westside High Sch, Talladega Ala 53-59; Tchr-libn Ea stside Elem Sch, Talladega Ala 61-67; Libn Talladega High Sch, Talladega Ala 67-. 9: Nat Sci Tchrs Assn; NEA; NCTE; Ala State Tchrs Assn. 10: YWCA; PTA; Girl Scouts; Beta Phi Mu. 14: Child libn. 15: 208 S 25th st, Talladega Al 35160.

HOUSTON, GUYLA ANN (BOND). b Wash DC 27 F 38. 4: Donald Eugene Houston. 5: St Petersburg Jr Col 56-58 (Liberal Arts) AA; Fla StateU 58-60 (LS) BA; LSU 61-63 (LS) MS. 7: Stud asst St Petersburg Jr Col 57-58; Dept mgr W T Grant Co, New Orleans, Tallahasse Fla 58-60; Lib stud asst LSU (Baton Rouge) 61-62; Lib trainee 62-63; Asst acquis libn Okla StateU (Stillwater) 63-. 9: ALA; OKLA; SWLA. 10: US Naval Inst; Beta Phi Mu; AAUP. 12: "Nuclear-Powered Submarines: 1950-1965" (66); "Voyage to the Bottom: 1955-1965" (66); "Thomas Edward Lawrence: 1915-1965: A Checklist of Lawrences" (67). 14: Acquis, ser, rare bks. 15: PO Box 564, Stillwater Ok 74074.

HOUSTON, MARIAN TREVORROW. b Salisbury Penn 22 Je 17. 4: Edward Curry Houston. 5: Otterbein Col 33-37 (Eng) BA; Carnegie 40-41 BLS; UPittsburgh 53-54. 6: Fr. 7: High sch tchr pub schs, Lee Co Va 37-40; Asst libn sr high & yp room Cleveland Heights Pub Lib, Cleveland Heights Ohio 41-43; Readers asst Carnegie Lib Allegheny Reg Br, Pittsburgh summers 61-64; Libn Allegheny Valley Schs, Springdale Penn 51-. 9: NEA; ALA; PennEA (Supv & Curr Com); PennLA; Coun of Sch Libns Suburban Pittsburgh (chm 60-61). 10: AAUW; Amer For Policy Assn; Bd of Springdale Free Pub Lib. 14: Bk sel, yp. 15: 340 Washington st, Springdale Pa 15144.

HOUSTON, MARTHA (PETERSON). b Kan City Mo 17 O 24. 4: Max S Houston. 5: MacMurray Women's Col 41-42 (Dietetics); Kan State U 42-45 (Med Tech) BS; Wichita State U 58-63 (Educ, LS); Kan State Tchrs Col 67-68 ML. 06: Fr. 7: Lab asst Kan State U 45-46; Research libn Midwest Med Research Found, Wichita Kan 62-64; Med libn St Francis Hosp, Wichita Kan 64-68; Ref & catlg libn Wichita State U 68-. 9: ALA; MedLA; KanLA (Spec Lib Div); SLA. 14: Ref, catlg, acquis (all in biomed). 15: 403 N Fountain, Wichita Kan 67208.

HOUSTON, NADINE CHRISTENA (BANISTER). b Kan City Kan 29 O 20. 40: Chester Warren Houston. 5: Kan City (Kan) Jr Col 38-40 (Eng) AA; UKan 40-42 (Eng) AB; UIll 42-43 BSLS, 43-46 (Bacteriology) MS; RI Col 51; URI 51-54. 6: Fr. 7: Asst libn Natural Hist Lib UIll(Urbana) 43-46; Ref libn Abbott Labs, N Chicago Ill 46-48; Libn Westerly Pub Schs, Westerly RI 50-55; Libn S Kingstown High Sch, Wakefield RI 55-65; Coordinator lib serv S Kingstown Pub Schs, Wakefield RI 65-, Instr URI summers 55-59; Instr UWash (Seattle) summer 66. 8: NDEA Summer Inst for Sch Lib Supvrs, UWash 65; Dir ESEA Title I Prog, S Kingstown Sch Dept 67. 9: ALA; RILA; RISchLA; RIEA; NESchLA; S Kingstown TA. 10: Trustee, Kingston Free Lib & Reading Room; S Kingstown Lib Coun; S Kingstown Tchrs Assn; S Kingstown Interrelated Lib System. 14: Sch libs. 15: 16 Diane dr, Kingston RI 02881.

HOUZE, ROBERT ALVIN. b Buffalo NY 10 Ap 18. 4: Mary Payne. 5: UDenver 36-40 (Zool, Educ) AB, 40-41 BS in LS; Tex A&M U 58-69 (Educ) MS. 06: Sp. 7: Order libn UDenver Lib 41-42; Veterinary libn Colo State U 42; US Army (1st Lt) Field Artillery, Overseas-Mediterranean T 42-45; Libn Longmont Pub Lib, Longmont Colo 45-46; Acquis libn UTex Lib 46-49; Libn & Lib Dir Tex A&M U Lib 49-65; Head Libn Trinity U Lib(San Antonio Tex) 65-. 8: Adv to Coordg Com on Water Research & Info Center Tex A&M U 52-53; V-chm Lib Subcom of Adv Com to Tex Commsn on Higher Educ 61-65. 9: TexLA (treas 52-54, chm Col Div 59-60, chm legis Com 61-63); SWchm Col & Univ Dir); Coun of Tex State Col Libns (chm 61-65); Bexar LA (pres 67-68); Coun of Res & Acad Libs, San Antonio (pres 68-69). 10: Rotary Club. 11: Special Citation from the Coun of State Col Libns, 65. 14: Admin, lib planning. 15: George Stroch Mem Lib, Trinity Univ, San Antonio Tex 78212.

HOVDA, MARY LOU. b Tyler Minn 8 Ag 27. 4: Wilford M Hovda. 5: Northwestern Col (Minneapolis) 48-53 (Bible) BA; Macalester Col 59-62 (Eng) BA; UMinn 62-65 (LS) MA. 6: Fr, Gk. 7: Minnesota Supply Co, Minneapolis 50-53; Sec Northwestern Col (Minneapolis) 53-54; Lib asst 54-59; Stud asst Macalester Col Lib 60-6, Acquis asst 6263, Asst circ libn 63-64; Asst libn Northwestern Col Lib (Minneapolis) 64-67; Admin libn Metropolitan State Jr Col 67-. 9: ALA; Christian Libns Fellowship; Midwest Acad Libns; MinnLA (chm Ref Sect 65-66). 10: Minn Jr Col Faculty Assn. 14: Acquis, ref. , admin. 15: 50 Willow st, Minneapolis Mn 55403.

HOVDE, OIVIND M. b Stanley ND 10 S 11. 4: Harriet Knutson. 5: Luther Col 28-32 (Lat) BA; UMich 37-41 MALS. 6: Norwegian, Danish. 7: Lib asst Luther Col 35-38; Asst in circ & clsf depts UMich(Ann Arbor) 38-40, Catlgr Law Lib 40-41; Libn Concordia Col 41-44; Assoc libn Luther Col 44-49, Libn 49-. 8: Area Com on Lib Serv Dept of Pub Instr State of Iowa 57-; Mem NCATE visitation teams 67-. 9: ALA (chm Mem Com 56-62);-ACRL; IowaLA (pres 56, mem several coms). 10: City Planning Commsn; Norwegian-Amer Hist Assn. 12: "The Research Paper" (46). 13: Yes. 14: Admin, catlg. 15: Luther Col Lib, Decorah Iowa 52101.

HOVDEN, NORMA LOIS. b Minneapolis 7 Mr 22. 5: UMinn 39-43 BS in LS. 7: UMinn(Minneapolis): Jr libn ref dept 43-45, Libn ref dept 45-49, Sr libn ref dept 49-51, Prin libn ref dept 51-52, Asst Prof & chief circ libn 52-61, Asst Prof & chief ref libn 61-. 9: ALA; MinnLA (Acad Libs Sect & Ref Sect). 10: AAUP; LWV; Minn Hist Soc; UMinn Fac Womens Club. 14: Ref. 15: 4608 Coffey lane, Minneapolis Mn 55406.

HOVEN, EARL E. b Milwaukee 29 Ap 13. 4: Isabel Szczys. 5: UWis 42-43, 46-47 (Biol Sci) BA, 47-48 (LS) BLS. 6: Lat, Ger, Sp. 7: Page Milwaukee Pub Lib 32-34, Sub prof libn 35-42; US Navy Seabees (Y 2/c) 43-46; Prof libn USDA, Wash DC 48-49; Asst libn USDA, Madison Wis 49-50; Libn US Fish & Wildlife Serv, Honolulu 50-51, 53-58; Ref libn USAF Acad 58-. 8: Ref libn Library/USA NY World's Fair 65. 10: Air Force Assn; Beta Phi Mu. 12: "Tunas and Tuna Fisheries of the World, 1930-1953: an annotated bibliography," US Fish & Wildlife Serv Fisheries Bull 111. 13: Yes. 14: Ref, application of computers to lib problems. 15: 434 Valley Hi Circle D23, Cold Springs Co 80910.

HOVERTER, CLARICE (M) DIKEMAN. b Woodside LI NY 22 Ja 15. 4: Terence J M Hoverter. 5: Hunter Col 32-37 (Hist) AB; Columbia 41-43 (LS); Syracuse 63-68 MLS: 06: Fr, Ger. 7: Sec to libn Queens Col (NY) 38-46; Tchr St Frances de Chantal Sch, Bronx NY 58-60; Tchr Holy Family Elem Sch, Syracuse NY 60-61; Sub tchr Solvay Sch Dist, Solvay NY 61-65; Libn Tecumseh Elem Sch, Jamesville NY 65-67; Libn Solvay Elem Schs, Solvay NY 67-. 8: NY State perm certif as tchr of common br subjs 61; NY State perm certif as sch libn

67. 9: NYLA; NYStateTA; SolvayTA. 10: Beta Phi Mu. 14: A-v serv, acquis. 15: 402 E Kimberly dr, Syracuse NY 13219.

HOVERTER, TERENCE J(OSEPH) (MICHAEL). b NYC 3 My 16. 4: Clarice Dikeman. 5: Fordham 34-37 (Hist) BA; Columbia 38-39 BS in LS, 48-50 (LS); Fordham 51-54 (Hist) MA, 54-59 (Hist). 6: Ger. 7: Circ libn Catholic U 39-41; Ser libn Queens Col (Flushing NY) 41-46; US Army Med Corps, Pers (Tech/Sgt) 42-45; Libn SUNY Maritime Col (Ft Schuyler NY) 46-60; Libn & Prof SUNY Col of Forestry (Syracuse NY) 60-. 8: Survey of Amer Merchant Marine LA for ALA, NYC 48-52; Chm SUNY Libns' Conf 54-55; Chm SUNY com on Lib Development 54-63; Lib Com of Coun of Higher Educ Insts in NYC Inc 58-60; Pres Metropolitan Inter-Col LA NYC 58-60; Ad Hoc Com on 3 R Program, Syracuse NY 64-; INTRACOM Task Force on Shared Lib Facilities, Albany NY 65-. 9: SLA (chm Forestry Libns Wk Shop); NYLA (Dir Col & Univ Sect). 10: Archons of Colophon; Melvil Dui Chowder & Marching Assn. 14: Ser, acquis, lib bldgs, data processing. 15: 402 E Kimberly dr, Syracuse NY 13219.

HOWARD, AILEEN DELL (WIL SON). b Muncie Ind 17 My 44. 4: William J Howard. 5: Hanover Col 62-63; Ball State 63-66 (Eng) BS in Educ; UMich 66-67 MA in LS. 7: Child libn W Lafayette Pub Lib, W Lafayette Ind 67-. 8: Visiting asst prof PurdueU Educ Dept summer 69. 9: ALA; IndLA. 10: Pi Lambda Theta; Sigma Tau Delta; Story Art League; Beta Phi Mu. 11: LSCA scholarship. 13: Yes. 14: Child wk. 15: 103 E Columbia st, W Lafayette In 47906.

HOWARD, ANNA LILA. b Ashland Ky 15 S 18. 5: UMinn 42-43 (LS) BS; Columbia 47-48 MS in LS. 6: Fr, Ger. 7: Chief libn USVA, Lexington Ky 43-44; Supv inst libs Dept of Welfare Commonwealth of Ky, Frankfort Ky 44-47; Libn Mead Corp, Chillicothe Ohio 48-64; Asst sci libn So Ill U 64-69, Act med libn 69-. 9: SLA; ALA; MedLA. 10: Altrusa internat. 13: Yes. 14: Med, sci & tech libs. 15: RR 2, Carbondale Il 62901.

HOWARD, ARTHUR LINCOLN. b Boston 31 O 23. 5: Trinity Col 46-49 (Hist) BA; Boston U summers 51-58 (Educ) M Ed; USoCal summer 60. 6: Fr. 7: Volunteer Amer Field Serv, Syria & Italy 43-45; Hist tchr Hoosac Sch, Hoosick NY 50-57; Lat tchr Harvard Sch, N Hollywood Cal 58-59, Libn 60-. 9: ALA; CalASchL. 14: Sch libnship. 15: 3700 Coldwater Canyon rd, N Hollywood Cal 91604.

HOWARD, DONALD HUGH. b Nampa Ida 20 Mr 41. 4: Jocelyn Kingdon. 5: UIda 59-63 (Hist) BA; UCal(Berkeley) 63-64 MLS. 7: Asst circ libn Brigham Young U 64-65, Documents & maps libn 65-67; Catgr Wesleyan U (Middletown Conn) 67-69; Hist & relig libn Brigham Young U 69-. 14: Pub serv. 15: 130 S 400 East, Provo Ut 84601.

HOWARD, EDWARD ALLEN. b Erlanger Ky 10 My 31. 4: Phyllis Vincent. 5: ULouisville 49-53 (Eng) AB; UIll 54-56 (LS) MS. 6: Fr. 7: (Staff/Sgt) US Army Reserve 51-60; Film libn Free Pub Lib, Louisville Ky 53-54; Research asst Lib Sch UIll(Urbana) 54-56; Head fine arts div Pub Lib, Topeka Kan 56-58; Head Libn Free Pub Lib, Lawrence Kan 58-62; Dir EPL-VCPL Pub Lib, Evansville Ind 62-. 8: Consul Kan State Lib Travel Libs Commsn 59; Exec sec Nat Lib Week in Kan 59. 9: ALA; KanLA (pres 61). 10: Kiwanis; Chamber of Commerce; Phi Delta Epsilon; Pi Kappa Phi; PTA. 12: Ed "Focus on Indiana Libraries" (65). 13: Yes. 14: Pub lib admin, personnel mgt. 15: 22 SE Fifth st, Evansville In 47708.

HOWARD, EDWARD NEAL. b Carlisle Ind 22 Ja 20. 4: Rolandia Wolfe Rotramel. 5: IndU 61-65 (Eng) BA, 66-67 (LS) MA. 6: Japanese. 7: Warrant off USN 37-57; Prisoner of war Japan 41-45; Power plant engr Westinghouse Electric Corp, Bloomington Ind 57-60; Asst dir Monroe Co Pub Lib, Bloomington Ind 64-66; Asst dir Bureau of Pub Discussion IndU 66-67; Dir Vigo Co Pub Lib, Terre Haute Ind 68-. 9: ALA; SLA; IndLA. 10: Phi Eta Sigma; City of Terre Haute Mayor's Citizens Adv Com; Phi Beta Kappa; Family Serv Assn in Terre Haute; Wabash Valley Coun of Navy League; Ret Offs Assn; Amer Legion. 12: Ed "Focus on Indiana Libraries" (67-). 13: Yes. 14: Pub lib serv. 15: 7001 Dixie Bee rd, Terre Haute In 47802.

HOWARD, ELIZABETH BRADY. b Charlotte NC 18 S 22. 5: UGa 40-43 (Eng) BA; West Res 58-59 MLS. 7: Stud trainee Atlanta Pub Lib Inman Br summers 41, 42; Off asst Ft Monmouth Signal Corps Labs, Ft Monmouth NJ 44; Off asst US Treasury Dept Atlanta Br 45; Asst catlgr Oak Ridge Pub Lib, Oak Ridge Tenn 45-47; Head Libn Fairchild Engine and Airplane Corp NEPA Project, Oak Ridge Tenn 47-51; Libn document collection sect Oak Ridge Nat Lab, Oak Ridge Tenn 51-. 9: SLA (treas Sci-Tech Div 66-68; pres So Appalachian Chap 65-66, 68-69). 10: Beta Phi Mu. 14: Rept lit. 15: Oak Ridge Nat Lab, PO Box X, Oak Ridge Tn 37831.

HOWARD, ELIZABETH M. b Brookline Mass 25 Ag 15. 5: Radcliffe 33-37 (Classics) AB; Simmons 41 (LS) BS, 53 (LS) MS. 7: Chief ser div Harvard Business Sch 39-41; Chief Hosp Lib US Army, Camp Edwards 41-45; Chief Hosp Libs VA: Cushing Hosp 45-52, Jamaica Plain 52-53, Brockton Mass 53-. 9: ALA; MedLA; MassLA; Mass Hosp Lib Group. 14: Bibliotherapy, med libnship. 15: 681 Hammond st, Chestnut Hill Ma 02167.

HOWARD, HELEN (ARLENE) (CREIGHTON). b Kingston Ont Can 7 S 27. 4: George Marshall Howard. 5: Queen's U (Kingston Ont) 45-48 (Fr, Ger) BA; McGill 55-56 BLS, 64-67 MLS. 6: Fr. 7: Lib asst Aluminium Labs Ltd, Kingston Ont 48-51; Tech off Defence Research Bd, Kingston & Ottawa 51-53; Lib asst Nat Research Coun, Ottawa 53-55; Ref libn McGill U 56-57; Libn in chge Newsprint Assn of Can, Montreal 57-58; Libn in chg Montreal Engnr Co Ltd, Montreal 58-64; Head pub serv Sir George Williams U Lib (Montreal) 64-67, U libn 67-. 9: ALA; CanLA; SLA; QueLA; ASIS; Inst Professl Libns Ont. 10: Can Inst for Internat Affairs. 15: Sir George Williams Lib 1435 Drummond st, Montreal Que Can.

HOWARD, JANE (ELIZABETH HUGHSON). b San Francisco 21 N 19. 5: UCal (Berkeley) 37-41 BA; USoCal 63-64 MSLS. 6: Sp, Fr. 7: Asst catlg libn UNev Lib 64-65; Adult serv libn III Washoe Co Lib, Reno Nev 65-68; Mines libn UNev 69-. 9: ALA; NevLA (Com on Certif 65-68). 10: Sierra Club. 14: Pub serv. 15: 680 Winston dr, Reno Nv 89502.

HOWARD, JOSEPH HARVEY. b Olustee Okla 15 Ja 31. 5: UOkla 48-52 (Music Educ) BME, 56-57 MLS. 6: Malay. 7: (Cpl) US Army, Ft Riley Kan 52-54; Vocal music instr Kiowa Pub Schs, Kiowa Kan 54-56; Music libn UColo 57-58, Circ libn 58-59, Assoc dir pub serv 59-63; Peace corps volunteer UMalaya Lib & Malayan Tchrs Col(Kuala Lumpur Malaysia) 63-65; Chief catlg dept Washington U(St Louis) 65-67; Lc; Asst chief descr catlg div 67-68; Chief descr catlg div 68-. 9: ALA. 12: "Malay Manuscripts: a Bibliographic Guide," UMalaya Lib (66). 14: Catlg, tech se rv. 15: 336 M st SW, Washington Dc 20024.

HOWARD, JOSEPH WILLIAM. b Washington Ind 6 F 17. 4: Shirley Ann (Conard). 5: Spring Hill Col 39-44 (Hist) BS; LSU summers 48-51 BS in LS; La & Miss Life certif as tchr or libn; Va Collegiate prof as tchr or libn. 6: Fr. 7: Tchr of US hist, Fr, chem, typing La 37-51; Libn Menard High Sch, Alexandria La 51-56; Libn Jefferson Jr High Sch, Alexandria Va 58-65; Libn T C Williams High Sch, Alexandria Va 65-, Dir of secondary libs 65-66, Dir of all sch libs 66-. Asst Supv of Sch Libs, Dir of Processing Ctr. 8: Instr of Lib Sci UVa(Arlington) 64-65; evaluating com for W T Woodson High Sch in Fairfax Co for So Assn conducted by Va State Dept of Educ. 9: ALA; AASchL; VaEA; Sch Libns NVa. 14: Admin, ref. 15: 6014 Amherst ave, Springfield Va 22150.

HOWARD, KAREN R (GREENAWALT). b Allentown Penn 14 N 43. 4: William P Howard. 5: Kutztown State Col 61-65 (Lib Educ) BS. 7: Elem libn Allentown Sch Dist, Allentown Penn 65-. 9: NEA; PennEA. 14: Child lit. 15: 341 E Main st, Kutztown Pa 19530.

HOWARD, LORE. b Germany 26 Ag 28. 4: James E Howard. 5: Hunter Col 46-48 (Soc Sci); SUNY(Albany) 58-60 (Soc Sci) BA, 60-62 MLS. 6: Ger. 7: Libn Schalmont Schs , Schenectady NY 60-66; Sch lib supv NY State Educ Dept 66-. 09: ALA; NYLA; NY State Tchrs Assn; ASCD; NEA-DAVI69; Chief, Bur of Sch Libs, NY State 69-. 10: Pub Lib Trustee, Baytown Tex; Kerrville Garden Club Beauceant; 11: Commun Serv Award, 60, Baytown Tex. 14: Child bks, sch libs. 15: State Ed Dept, Albany NY 12224.

HOWARD, MATTIE (NELSON). b Denton Co Tex 30 Ja 12. 4: R G Howard. 5: UTex 33-37 (Sociol) BA; Tex State Col for Women 47-48 BS in LS. 6: Sp. 7: Tchr Baytown Tex 36-43; Prof Girl Scout Dir, Gulf Coast Are a 46-47; Libn Tivy High Sch, Kerrville Tex 48-49; Libn Robert E Lee High Sch, Baytown Tex 49-55, Libn Lee Col Lib 55-67; Libn Butt-Holdsworth Mem Lib, Kerrville Tex 67-. 9: ALA-ACRL (Com on structure & function of Jr Col Libs 61-62); TexLA (Exec Bd 63-66; chm Dist 5 58); SWLA (sec Col & Univs Sect 63-67); Tex State Jr Col Tchrs Assn (Lib Standards Com 59-60). 10: Pub Lib Trustee, Baytown Tex; Kerrville Garden Club Beauceant. 11: Commun Serv Award, 60, Baytown Tex. 14: Ref, (pub libs). 15: 1214 Oriole lane, Kerrville Tx 78028.

HOWARD, PAUL. b Ft Worth Tex 4 F 05. 4: Lois Watson. 5: UOkla 23-27 (Hist) BA; UIll 29-30 Library Science BS in LS; UChicago 38-39 MALS. 7: Libn Panhandle A & M Col 27-29; Asst libn Mo Sch of Mines 30-32, Libn 32-39; Hd ind & sci dept Enoch Pratt Free Lib, Baltimore 39-41; Libn Gary Pub Lib, Gary Ind 41-45; Dir Wash DC Off ALA 45-49; Libn US Dept of the Interior, Wash DC 49-65; Exec sec Fed Lib Com, Wash DC 66-. 8: Hd Lib Serv Div, Off of War Info, Wash DC 43; Consul Asst Sec of War, Wash DC 44. 9: ALA (chm Jr Mem RT, chm Fed Rel Com, chm Bkbinding Com); MoLA (v-pres); MdLA (v-pres); IndLA (pres); DCLA. 11: Distinguished Serv Award, US Dept of the Interior. 13: Yes. 15: 2755 N Wyoming st, Arlington Va 22213.

HOWARD, RUTH SHEAHAN (LATCHAW). b Defiance Ohio 22 S 12. 4: Arthur Melvine Howard. 5: Defiance Col 30-31, 40-41 (Educ) BSEd; UMich (Ann Arbor) 31-34 (Soc Sci, Eng) AB; Peabody Col 42-43 BSLS; CatholicU 65 (Info Storage & Retrieval). 6: Fr. 7: Asst libn Co Pub Lib, Defiance Ohio 39-42; Libn Sandusky Co, Fremont Ohio 43-44; Libn Deshon Gen Hosp, Butler Penn 44-46; Libn 3d Serv Command, Baltimore 46; Staff libn: Hdqrs Second USA, Ft George Meade Md 46-66, Hdqrs First USA, Ft George Meade Md 66-68; Deputy dir Army lib prog Off of the Ad Gen Dept of the Army, Wash DC 68-. 8: Consul to Mil Hist Research Lib, Army War Col, Carlisle Barracks Penn 69. 9: ALA (Awards Com 60-, chm 64-; chm Grolier Award Jury 62-63; Clarence Day Award Jury 63-64); -ASD (Nomin Com 57, 61, chm 60-61; Standards Com 60-65); PLA (Armed Forces Sect: Proj Chm 51, 55, sec 53-55; chm Const & Bylaws Com 58; Mil Commun Lib Study Com 65-67); SLA; MdLA (chm ASD Const & Bylaws Com 57, Prog Chm 58-59, 63-64; ASD Pres 59-60; NLW State Bd 61-62; chm Recr Com 61-63). 10: AAUW; DAR; Delta Delta delta. 11: Achievement Award, Geo Peabody Col 43; Outstanding Perform Award & Qual increase, Dept of Army 64; Armed Forces Achievement Award, ALA 67. 13: Yes. 14: Admin, rare bks, legisl. 15: 4606 Harvard rd, College Park Md 20740.

HOWARD, SHARON LYNN. b Columbus Ohio 3 N 42. 5: Ariz State U 60-63 (Hist) BS; UGeneva 64 (Fr Culture); UCLA 65-66 MLS. 6: Fr, Sp. 7: Lib trainee LA Pub Lib, San Pedro 65; Libn Tempe High Sch, Tempe Ariz 66-67, Hd libn 67-68; Law libn Bancroft, Avery & McAlister, San Francisco 68-. 8: Ariz Exec dir Nat Lib Week 68. 9: ALA; -AASchL; SLA; AALL; ASIS; ArizStateLA; ArizEA; West Pacific Law Libns; Bay Area Spec Libns; ArizStateSchLA. 10: World Affairs Organ of No Cal; Nat Aerospace Educ Coun. 13: Yes. 14: Ref, ya wk. 15: 449 - 15th ave #104, San Francisco Ca 94118.

HOWDER, MURRAY LOUIS. b Wash DC 10 Ag 32. 5: George Washington U 50-54 (For Affairs) BA; Edinburgh U 54 (European Hist) Certif; Middlebury Col 58-60 (Russian) MA; Catholic U 61-68 MSLS. 6: Russian, Fr, Sp. 7: Sp-3 NATO Unassigned US Army 55-57; Research analyst LC (DRD) 58-60, Catlgr & tr (MIRA) 61-63; Asst prof lecturer (Slavic) George Washington U 65; Sr tech ed (ATD) 63-67; Brigade libn USNA Lib 67-68; Acquis libn Gallaudet Col Lib 68-. 9: Soc of Federal Linguists (pres); SLA; DCLA. 10: Nat Hon Soc; Nat Slavic Honor Soc; Internat Visitors Info Serv. 11: DAR Medal; NDEA Fellowships. 13: Yes. 14: Acquis, translations, ref. 15: 3711 Livingston st NW, Washington DC 20015.

HOWE, LUKE T. b Santa Monica Cal 25 Ag 40. 4: Linda Koonce. 5: UMd 61-62 (Mod Langs); UCal (Berkeley) 63-66 (Slavic Langs) BA, MLS. 6: Russian. 7: Page Whittier Pub Lib, Whittier Cal 59; Russian linguist Spec 5 US Army, Turkey 60-62; Lib asst Rare bks Morrison Lib, UCal (Berkeley) 63-66; Jr specialist Inst of Lib Research UCal (Berkeley) 67-. 9: ALA; ASIS. 10: Polish Univ Club; Cal Sailing Club. 11: NDFL Fellowship 66-67. 13: Yes. 14: Info sci. 15: 1540 Hearst, Berkeley Ca 94703.

HOWE, MARIAN (DECKER). b Malden Mass 27 D 02. 5: Simmons 20-24 (LS) BS. 6: Fr. 7: Hd libn Paul Pratt Mem Lib, Cohasset Mass 24-26; Ref libn Free Pub Lib, Livingston NJ 65-. 9: ALA; NJLA. 10: YM-YWCA. 14: Ref, bus. 15: 108 Fellswood dr, Livingston NJ 07039.

HOWE, MARLYS CAROL. b St Paul 10 D 37. 5: UMinn 55-58 (Elem & Spec Educ), 58-60 (Scandinavian Lang & Lit) BA, 60-63 (LS) MA; UOslo Internat summer sch 58 Certif. 6: Norwegian, Sp. 7: Lib asst St Paul Pub Lib 60-63; Pub lib consul lib div Dept of Educ State of Minn, St Paul 63-65; Dir Cass Co Lib System, Pine River Minn 65-. 9: ALA; MinnLA (sec Co & Reg Sect 64-65, chm Child & YP Sect 66-67). 10: Amer Scand Foun; Amer Motorcycle Assn; YWCA. 11: Scholarship, Sons of Norway, to Summer Sch, Univ of Oslo, Norway; Certif of M erit, Minn LA 67. 14: Pub lib serv, org & admin. 15: Pine River Mn 56474.

HOWE, MARY TAYLOR (SWARTZ). b Urbana Ill 6 Mr 11. 5: UIll 28-32 (Journalism) BS, 33-34 (Educ) MS in Ed; Columbia 39 BS in LS; Columbia U Tchrs Col 49-51. 7: Stud asst period dept Com RR UIll (Urbana) 28-34; Asst in bus & tech Peoria Pub Lib, Peoria Ill 35-36; Libn Peoria Heights Pub Lib, Peoria Heights Ill 36; Stud asst Columbia U 36-37, Asst engnr libn 38-40; Asst in br NY Pub Lib 40-42; Head circ dept UAriz 42-44; Br libn NY Pub Lib 44-53; Asst libn Evansville Pub Lib, Evansville Ind 53-54; Asst libn Decatur Pub Lib, Decatur Ill 54-57, City Libn 57-66; Dir Lewis & Clark Lib Syst, Edwardsville Ill 66-. 9: ALA (chm Bibliog Com 51-52; chm LAD-LOMS Statist Com for Pub Libs 66-69); IllLA; Piasa LA. 10: AAUW; Bus & Profess Women. 12: "Professional Librarian's Salary Survey" (60-65); Ed "In Progress Reports" (57-66). 13: Yes. 14: Admin, bibliog, data proc. 15: 678 W Harrison, Decatur Il 62526.

HOWELL, ALIBETH (McCARTNEY). b Ithaca NY 23 Ja 26. 5: Cornell Col (Mt Vernon Iowa) 44-45; Barnard 45-48 (Eng Lit) AB; Columbia 49-50 MSLS. 7: Field libn Spec Serv US Army, Stuttgart Germany 50-52; Child libn Mt Vernon Pub Lib, Mt Vernon NY 53-54; Child libn New Rochelle Pub Lib, New Rochelle NY 54-58; Youth libn E Orange Pub Lib, E Orange NJ 58-, Franklin Br 58-61, Ampere Br 61-65, Br libn 65-. 9: ALA; NJLA. 10: Little Theatre. 15: 676 Park ave, East Orange NJ 07017.

HOWELL, CHARLENE (WILSON). b Lake City Fla 20 F 44. 4: D Warren Howell. 5: Col of charleston 62-66 (Hist, Eng) BS; N Tex StateU 68-69 MLS. 6: Fr. 7: Vol Farmers Br Lib, Dallas Tex 69-. 9: ALA. 10: Alpha Lambda Sigma; Chi Omega. 14: Child serv. 15: 2877 Meadow Port, Dallas Tx 75234.

HOWELL, DAVID BUFORD. b Aberdeen Miss 21 Ag 34. 4: Emma Jean Tallett. 5: Tex Christian U 52-54 (Liberal Arts); Mexico City Col 53 (Liberal Arts); UMiss 54-55 (Hist) BA, 59-60 MLS; LSU 63-64 (LS); Miss State U 64-66 (Educ Admin) M Ed. 7: Stud asst UMiss 54-55; US Army Mil Police, Ft Hood Tex (sp-4) 57-59; Page spec serv, Ft Hood Tex 58-59; Catlg La Col 59-60, Dir Libs 60-64; Catlg head Miss State U 64-67; Head Libn Delta State Col 67-. 9: LaLA; MissLA (treas 69); SELA. 10: Tex Christian Alumni; La Col Alumni; UMiss Alumni; Kappa Delta Pi; Phi Delta Kappa; Lions Intl. 13: Yes. 14: Catlg, tech processing admin. 15: 1507 College st, Cleveland Ms 38732.

HOWELL, EULA (CARPENTER). b Gaston Co NC 10 My 04. 5: UNC (Greensboro) 24-28 (Eng) AB; Emory 39 (LS). 7: Libn high sch, Roanoke Rapids NC 28-29; Lib asst Charlotte Pub Lib, Charlotte NC 29-34, Ser libn 39; Tchr Cornelius High Sch, Cornelius NC 34-39; Area supv Ga Lib Commsn, Atlanta 39-40; Ser libn & hd info bur Pub Lib of Charlotte & Mecklenburg Co, Charlotte NC 40-44, Proc asst 55-56, Br libn 56-57, Ser libn 67-. 9: ALA; NCLA; MecklenburgLA. 10: YWCA. 13: Yes. 14: Ser, ref. 15: 214 Circle ave, Charlotte NC 28207.

HOWELL, EVERETT LESTER. b Ute Iowa 28 Jl 29. 5: Joan Huston. 6: Fr. 7: High sch libn Chariton Pub Schs, Chariton Iowa 51-53; Sch libn Iowa Falls Pub Schs, Iowa Falls Iowa 53-56; State Col Iowa: Asst ref libn 56-57, Circ libn 57-65, Asst dir of lib serv 65-67; Hd libn Coe Col 67-. 9: ALA; IowaLA. 10: AAUP. 14: Pub serv, admin, lib educ. 15: 2730 2nd ave SE, Cedar Rapids Ia 52403.

HOWELL, FRANK J. b Red Bluff Cal 6 F 38. 5: Shasta Jr Col 56-57 (Psych); Chico State Col 57-61 (Psych) BA; San Jose State Col 63-68 (Libnship) MA. 9: CalLA. 14: Ref, censorship. 15: Hayward Pub Lib 22737 Mission blvd, Hayward Ca 94541.

HOWELL, HANNAH JOHNSON. b Oskaloosa Iowa 22 Je 05. 4: Henry Wilson Howell Jr. 5: Penn Col 24-25; Chicago 27 PhB; Columbia 28 BLS. 6: Fr. 7: Reviser Summer lib sch UIowa 28; Frick Art Ref Lib, NYC: Research asst 28-34, Head ref dept 35-47, Asst libn 42-47, Chief Libn 47-. 9: ALA (Art Subsect); SLA (Picture Div). 15: 10 E 71st st, New York Ny 10021.

HOWELL, ISABEL. b Nashville 31 Ag 1900. 5: Vanderbilt 18-22 (Eng Lit) BA; Columbia 26-27 (LS) MS; Peabody 40 (Amer Hist) MA. 7: Asst in catlg Columbia U 22; Ref libn Vanderbilt U 23-26; Asst in catlg NY City Col 26-27; Ref libn Vanderbilt U 27-29; Exec asst & ref libn Peabody Col 29-31; Act libn Vander bilt U 31-35; Asst libn head of tech processes Joint U Libs, Nashville 35-45; Libn Methodist Publ House, nashville 45-50; Dir state lib div Tenn State Lib & Archives 50-65 ret; Archivist & Spec Collections libn Jesse Ball duPont Lib U of the South 65-. 8: Tchr lib sci courses, Peabody Lib Sch, 29-65. 9: ALA-RSD (rep on Catlg Code Revn Com; Hist Sect: chm 65; chm Org Com); SELA (chm Ref Serv Div 64, chm Program Com 62); TennLA (actg pres 42). 10: Phi Beta Kappa. 11: Award of merit from Amer Assn State & Loc Hist, 44. 13: Yes. 14: Catlg, ref, mss, archives, rare bks. 15: Univ of the South, Sewanee Tn 37375.

HOWELL, JOHN B. b Greer SC 25 O 25. 5: Furman U 42-45 (Eng) BA; Emory 45-46 BA in LS; UIll 52-53 (LS) MS. 7: Acquis libn Emory U 46-51; Asst libn Furman U 51-52; Ref libn Va Polytech Inst 53-54; Asst libn Clemson U 54-58; Circ libn UGa 58-60; Libn Mississippi Col 60-. 8: Bus manager & col reporter "Mississippi Library News," 62-. 9: ALA; SELA; MissLA (treas 66, V-pres & pres-ellect 69). 12: Ed "The South Carolina Librarian" (56-58). 13: Yes. 15: 118 Fairmont st, Clinton Ms 39056.

HOWELL, JOHN BRUCE. b Greensburg Penn 17 Je 41. 4: Barbara Anson. 5: Columbia 59-65 (Mus) BA; UMich 65-66 AMLS; UWis 66 (African Lang). 6: Swahili, Ger. 7: Sr ref libn & bibliog LC, African Sect 69-. 9: African Studies Assn; ALA. 11: Ford Fellow; NDFL Title VI Fellow 67-69. 14: Ref (East Africa). 15: PO Box 58, Ardara Pa 15615.

HOWELL, KATHERINE ELIZABETH. b Rome Ga 28 Jl 20. 5: Converse Col 37-41 (Sociol) AB; Emory 46 (LS) AB. 7: Sec-bkkeeper First National Bank, Rome Ga 42-45; Ref libn Long Beach Pub Lib, Long Beach Cal 47-48; Catlgr Carnegie Lib, Rome Ga 50-52; Catlgr Rome Br UGa 53; Catlgr Polk-Floyd Reg Lib, Rome Ga 53; Asst libn Wilmington Pub Lib, Wilmington Pub Lib, Wilmington NC 54-56, Libn 56-. 9: ALA; NCLA (Dir 66-67; chm Personnel Com Pub Libs Sect 68-69); SELA. 10: Lower Cape Fear Hist Soc; AAUW; Carolina Yacht Club; Nat Trust Hist Preserv; Ne lit & Hist Soc. 14: Rare bks admin. 15: 12 S 5th ave, Wilmington NC 28401.

HOWELL, MABLE (SMITH). b Beaufort County 21 S 42. 4: Bruce Inman Howell. 5: E Car U 60-64 (Eng, LS) BS, 64-67 (LS) M of Ed. 7: Dir lib-learning ctr Lenoir Co Commun Col 64-. 9: ALA; SELA; NCLA; NC Commun Col LA (dir East Reg 67-68, treas 68-69). 10: AAUW; Jaycettes. 14: Ref, rare bks, admin. 15: 1311 McAdoo st, Kinston NC 28501.

HOWELL, MARGARET (ANDERSON). b Penrose Colo 16 Ja 36. 4: Herbert Howell. 5: SW Mo State 53-57 (Sociol, Educ) BS in Ed; UIll 58-59 MS in LS. 6: Sp. 7: Ext libn Daniel Boone Reg Lib, Columbia Mo 59-61; Lib sci libn UMo (Columbia) 68-. 9: ALA; MoLA. 10: AAUW. 14: Bk selection, ext serv, lit of libnship. 15: 17 E Craig st, Columbia Mo 65201.

HOWELL, MARGARET (COCKLEY). b York Penn 4 Ja 39. 4: John Edward Howell. 5: Radcliffe 56-60 (Govt) BA; Catholic U 61-68 (LS). 6: Fr. 7: Asst libn Military Asst Inst, Arlington Va 61-65; Child libn Prince George's Co Memorial Lib 65-67; Asst hd Nat Collections for the Blind & Physically Handicapped LC 67-68, Hd 68-. 9: ALA; Amer assn of Wkers for the Blind; RT on Lib Serv to the Blind (chm Memb Com); DCLA (chm Dir Com). 10: DC Health & Welfare Coun; Rehab Conf. 13: Yes. 14: Reader serv, admin. 15: 5628 Old Temple Hills rd, Temple Hills Md 20031.

HOWELL, MARJORIE (JEAN). b Victoria BC 14 O 42. 5: UVictoria 60-64 (Sociol, Hist) BA; UBC 65-66 BLS. 7: Lib asst UBC 64-65; Ref libn UAlberta 66-68, Catlgr 68-. 9: CanLA. 14: Catlg, ref. 15: 2666 Topp ave, Victoria BC Can.

HOWELLS, JAMES MORRISON. b Union Utah 9 N 31. 6: Sp. 7: Tchr Granite Sch Dist, Sale Lake City 58-59; Tchr Jordan Sch Dist, Salt Lake Co 60-63; Instr Com art Salt Lake City Trade Tech 64-66; Tchr Salt Lake City 66-67; Bkmob consul Utah State Lib Commsn 67-. 8: Lib commsn rep Nat Lib Week Com (permanent); Publicity mgr UtahLA Convention 69. 09 UtahLA. 12: Art ed "Utah Libraries". 13: Yes. 14: Syst analysis, admin of pub libs. 15: 5674 Spacerama dr, Murray Ut 84107.

HOWEY, JOSEPH IRWIN. b Pontiac Mich 1 Ag 45. 5: OaklandU (Rochester Mich) 63-67 (Soc Sci) BA; UMich 67-68 AMLS. 7: Dir Troy Pub Lib, Troy Mich 68-. 9: ALA; MichLA (chm-elect Jr Mem RT 69); Detroit Suburban Libns RT. 13: Yes. 14: Pub lib. 15: 1030 Adams rd S, Rochester Mi 48063.

HOWEY, MARION L (DRESSER). b Leavenworth Kan 5 Jl 16. 4: Richard S Howey. 5: St mary Col (Leavenworth Kan) 34-36 (Eng); UKan 36-38 (Bus) BS; Columbia 64-67 MLS. 6: Fr. 7: Ref libn Grad Sch of Bus & Econ Columbia U 66-67; Docs libn UKan 67-. 9: ALA. 14: Govt docs. 15: 943 Avalon rd, Lawrence Ks 66044.

HOWISON, BEULAH (CLARK). b Tomahawk Wis 14 F 10. 4: William K Howison. 5: Northland Col 26-30 (Math) UMich summer 37 (LS); Northland Col 26-30 (Maths) BA. 07: Libn Jr-Sr high sch, Marinette Wis 30-31; Libn Sr High Sch, Wausau Wis 31-40; Ref libn Stout StateU 42-. 9: ALA; WisLA. 10: Dunn Co Hist Soc. 14: Ref. 15: 714 3d st, Menomonie Wi 54751.

HOWLAND, CECIL (MORRILL). b Hinton Okla 7 Ja 15. 4: Marguerite Smith. 5: Ark City Jr Col 33-34; Northeastern Okla State Col 34-35, 36-37 (Hist); Okla State U 46, 49-50 (Ag Ed) BS; UOkla 52-53 (LS) BA. 7: Clerk USDA, Collinsville Okla 38-40; Combat Engnr (Pfc) US Army, US Europe 41-45; Biol sci libn Okla State U 53-. 9: ALA; Internat Assn Agric Libns & Documentalists; OklaLA; SWLA. 10: Phi Sigma, Pi Gamma Mu. 14: Ref, biol sci. 15: 2216 University ave, Stillwater Ok 74074.

HOWLAND, MARGUERITE (SMITH). b Wellington Kan 26 Mr 15. 4: Cecil M Howland. 5: No Okla Jr Col 31-33; Okla State U 33-35 (Educ) BS in Educ; Columbia summer 36 (LS); UIll 41-42 BS in LS. 7: Eng tchr Foss High Sch, Foss Okla 35-36; Eng tchr Tonkawa High Sch, Tonkawa Okla 36-37, 40-41; Jr acquis libn UIll (Urbana) 42-43; Asst libn Parks Air Col, E St Louis Ill 43; Libn Nat Gas & Gasoline Dept Phillips Petroleum Co, Bartlesville Okla 44-46; Head documents libn Okla State U 46-, Coord Soc Sci, humanities & does areas 57-. 9: ALA; SWLA; OklaLA; OklaEA. 10: Beta Phi Mu; Pi Gamma Mu; Phi Alpha Theta; Kappa Delta Pi; Bus & Profess Women's Club; Okla State U Fac Club. 14: Govt documents, soc scis. 15: 2216 University ave, Stillwater Ok 74074.

HOWLETT, (CHRISTINA) ANNE (LOUISE). b Delaware Ont Can 1 Ap 33. 5: UWest Ontario 51-55 (Hist) BA; McGill 58-59 BLS; Ontario Col of Educ 66-67 Specialist certif in sch libnship. 7: Sarnia Pub Lib, Sarnia Ont Can 55-64; Br libn Edmonton Pub Lib, Alberta can 62-64; Ref libn Eccles Lanes, England 65; Sch libn N York Bd of Educ, Willowdale Ont Can 66-. 14: Ref. 15: 52 Leacrest rd apt 7, Toronto 17 Ont Can.

HOWLEY, EDITH (CADWALLADER). b Philadelphia 14 Je 10. 4: Frank L Howley. 5: UPenn 30 (Eng) BS in Ed; Rutgers 62 MLS. 7: Tchr Springfield Twp High Sch, Montgomery Co Penn 30-35; Ref libn Berkeley Heights pub Lib, Berkeley Heights NJ 62-63; Ref libn Fairleigh Dickinson U 64-67; Adult serv E O range Pub Lib, NJ 67-. 9: ALA; NJLA. 15: 44 Crescent rd, Madison NJ 07940.

HOWSE, LOUISE LeBARON. b El Paso Tex. 4: S Eric Howse. 5: UCal(Los Angeles) 31-35 (Hist) BA; Immaculate Heart Col 64 (LS) MS. 6: Fr. 7: Child libn Glendale Pub Lib, Glendale Cal 63-. 9: Young Adult Libns Cal; CalLA. 10: AAUW; Hollywood Lit Club. 14: Child, young adult, bk reviewing. 15: 2000 W Mountain st, Glendale Ca 91201.

HOWSER, RAY E. b Urbana Ill 3 Je 23. 5: UNotre Dame 43 (Navy V-12 Engnr); Drake U 46-47 (Liberal Arts); UIll 47-49 (Pol Sci) BS, 49-51 MS in LS. 6: Fr. 7: Asst US Navy Lib Depository, Guam 45; Page Des Moines Pub Lib, Des Moines Iowa 46-47; Instr UIll Lib Sch 51; Head a-v dept Peoria Pub Lib, Peoria Ill 52-55; Coordinator of group serv Peoria Pub Lib, Peoria Ill 55-59, Asst dir 59-, Asst dir Ill Valley Lib Syst, Peoria Ill 67-. 8: Chm Subcom Ill State Adv Coun, LSCA Title I & II 67-. 9: ALA Recr Netwk for Ill, var com duties, conf assignments, etc); IllLA (chm Recr Com, Mem a-v com). 10: Peoria Jr C of C; Friendship House; Cosmopolitan Internat; UN Assn; Peoria Child Commun Theatre; Co-chm Peoria Co Stud Sci Fair. 13: Yes. 14: Lib admin, personnel, pub rel, adult serv. 15: Box 204, Groveland Il 61535.

HOYER, DOROTHY LOUISE. b Penn 19 Ja 30. 5: Dickinson Col 47-49 (Pol Sci); Kutztown State Col 50-53 (LS, Soc Sci) BS in Ed; UWis summer 56 (Pol Sci); Rutgers summers 57, 58 & 61 MLS. 7: Libn Plymouth-Whitemarsh High Sch, Plymouth Meeting Penn 53-56; Asst libn Susquehanna U 56-61; Asst libn Hq Lib Air force Systems Command, Wash DC 62-63; Libn Libs Sect Hq USAF, Wash DC 63; Libn Communications Studies Group Off of Info, Off of the Sec of the Air Force, Wash DC 63-68; Libn Gov Mifflin Jr High Sch, Shillington Pa 69-. 8: Unofficial tour of the USSR to study its lib & bibliog systems 59. 10: Zeta Tau Alpha; Kappa Delta Pi. 15: 326 Amy Court, Shillington Pa 19607.

HOYER, MRS MINA (TRICK). b Anderson Ind 23 My 28. 5: Anderson Col 46-50 BS; Ball State U summer 51 Grad Sch; Ind U Ext (Indianapolis) 59-61 LS; IndU(Bloomington) 62-(LS) MA in LS; UMo 65- (Langs); No Ill U 69 (Bus Admin). 6: Lat, Sp, Japanese, Ger. 7: Gen lib asst Pub Lib, Anderson Ind 57-58; Asst libn US Army Post Lib, Ft Benjamin Harrison Ind 58-62; Undergrad libn UMo 62-65; Head Libn Miami U (Ohio) 66-; Hd Undergrad lib serv No Ill U 68-. 8: USAF Serv Clubs, Honshu Japan 54-55; Pres Faculty Women UMo 64-65; Exec Dir Nat Lib Week in Mo 64-65; Mo Commsn on the Status of Women. Consul, World Publishing Co. & National Cash Register Co, PCMI Proj, 67; Part-time instr, Miami Uv 68. 9: ALA-ACRL (Nat Lib Week Com 65-67); OhioLA; IllLA; IllSchLA. 10: UMo Faculty Women; AAUW; University Club; Fortnightly Club; Single Faculty Club; Beta Phi Mu; Dames Club; De Kalb m, No Ill U. 11: Nat Lib Week Award 65. 12: Edc Bd "Choice" 67-. 13: Yes. 14: Bk sel, ref, col & univ wk, med libnship, tchg, planning & devel for new acad lib facilities, and instrl materials ctrs. 15: Swen Parson Lib, Nort hern Illinois Univ, DeKalb Il 60115.

HOYLE, NANCY (ELIZABETH). b Richmond Va 2 Jl 13. 5: William & Mary 30-33 (LS) AB; URichmond summer 37; Columbia 37-38 MS in LS; LU 67-68. 7: Tchr-libn Andrew Lewis High Sch, Salem Va 33-34; Asst supv sch libs Va State Dept of Educ, Richmond Va 34-45; Instr in Lib Sch Col of William & Mary summers 35-36; Field rep So Assn of Cols & Secondary Schs 45-46; Chm Dept of Lib Sci Col of William & Mary 46-47; Assoc dir lib serv F E Compton Co, Chicago 47-63, Assoc dir Encyclopedia Britannica Educl Corp 63-68; Bibliogr Grad Sch of Lib Serv Rutgers 68-. 9: ALA-AASchL; NJLA; VaLA. 10: AAUW. 14: lib schs child & yp libs, pub, ref. 15: Century Apts 3c, 85 Easton ave New Brunswick Nj 08901.

HOYLE, RUTH ALICE. b Woodstock Ont Ont Can 13 S 43. 5: UWest Ont 61-64 (Fr, Hist) BA; McGill 64-65 BLS. 06: Fr. 7: Ref libn UWest Ont 65-66; catlgr Bell Telephone Mtl 66-68; Hd libn Fanshawe Col, London Ont 68-. 9: SLA (Mtl Programme 66-68). 10: Caat Coun of Libns. 12: "U West Ont Libraries: Peridocials Currently Received" 66. 14: Ref. 15: 18 Becher st, London Ont Can.

HOYLER, MARJORIE (JACKMAN). b Arlington NJ 21 Ap 18. 4: Hermann F Hoyler. 5: Douglass Col 34-38 (LS) AB; Columbia U Ext 39-41 (Spec Libs). 7: Lib clerk Pub Serv Elec & Gas Co, Newark NJ summers 36, 37; Circ asst Paterson Free Pub Lib, Paterson NJ 38-39; Asst libn & libn Nopco Chem Co, Harrison NJ 39-45; Libn S-F-D Labs Inc, Union NJ 63-. 9: SLA. 10: Boy Scout Com Church & Col Activities; Douglas Alum Club; Rutgers Grad Sch Lib Serv Alum Club. 14: Ref, Govt documents, small spec libs, admin. 15: 334 Old Grove rd, Mountainside Nj 07092.

HOYT, ANNE (KELLEY). b Muskogee Okla 31 Mr 19. 4: Don L Hoyt. 5: UArk 38-42 (Eng) BA, summers 58-61 (Secondary Educ) M Ed; LSU 64-65 (LS) MS. 6: Fr. 7: Tchr High Sch, Winslow Ark 42; Br libn Pub Lib, Muskogee Okla 42-43; Libn Bacone Col 43-45; Libn Washington Co Lib, Fayetteville Ark 47; Libn Okla State Tech 48-50; Libn Jr High Sch, Springdale Ark 57-64; Educ div libn NM State U 65-66; Asst libn Northeast ern State Col, Okla 66-69; Asst Prof Lib Educ Okla State U, Stillwater 70-. 9: ALA; NEA; ArkLA; OklaLA. 10: AAUP. 12: Co-auth "Oklahoma Fact & Fancy, a Selected, graded Annot ated Bibliography for Schools" (68); Auth "Bibliography of the Cherokees" (69). 14: Sch libs, child lit. 15: Okla State U Lib, Stillwater Ok 74074.

HOYT, BERYL E. b Scranton Iowa. 5: Simpson Col (Eng) BA; UIll BS in LS; Northwestern 42 (Hist & Lit of Religions) MA; UCal(Berkeley) summer 47; UNev summer 49. 7: Libn Ind Central Col; Libn Dakota Wesleyan U 43-44; Libn Simpson Col 44-53; Asst to chief publ dept ALA, Chicago 53-56; Publ libn Racine Pub Lib, Racine Wis 56-65; Ed & train libn Div for Lib Serv State Dept of Pub Instr, Madison Wis 66-, Visiting lecturer dept of lib sci UMich summer 68. 8: Spec assignment to design promotional materials, ALA Hdq, 53. 9: ALA (Coun 49-53 Iowa Memb Chm 52); -ASD (Com on Coord Materials 62-65, Publns Adv Com 65-); IowaLA (Coun 49-53; chm Col Sect 48-49); WisLA (pres 64-65, Exec Bd 63-66, mem & chm Pub Rel Com 59- 63), Memb Directory chm 66-68; chm Credo for Libns Com 66); Wis AdultEA. 10: Racine Adult Educ Round Table; AAUW; Racine Art Guild; Phi Kappa Phi; Delta Kappa Gamma; Wis Fellowship of Poets; Wis Regl Writers Assn; Madison Area Writers Wkshop. 12: Ed & contrib "Lyrics from the Three River Land" (46,52); "Books Around the Globe" (60); Contrib "Iowa Centennial Poetry Anthology" (46); "Lyrical Iowa" (46-53); "Sea to Sea in Song" (47-64); "Wisconsin History in Poetry" (69); Ed "Wisconsin Library Bulletin" (66-); "Channel DLS" (66); ALA-ASD "Guides to the Literature of A dult Services" (67-); "Public Library Management I Institute Proceedings" (67). 14: Pub rel, ed wk. 15: Div for Lib Serv Box 1437, Madison Wis 53701.

HOYT, DOLORES J (CHAPO). b Tonawanda NY 21 Je 43. 4: Giles R Hoy. 5: SUNY (Binghamton) 61-65 (Gen Lit, Russian) BA; UIll 67-69 (LS) MS. 6: Russian, Ger. 7: Lib internship SUNY (Binghamton) 65-67; Spec lang asst UIll (Champaign-Urbana) 67-69; Spec lang catlgr 69-. 9: ALA. 14: Tech serv, info sci. 15: 62 Evans st, Binghamton NY 13903.

HOYT, SISTER JOAN MARIE. b Endicott NY 17 N 25. 5: St Joseph Col(Emmitsburg Md) 62 (Soc Sci) AB; Catholic U summers 52, 53 Certif as Tchr of Blind; St John's U(NY) 62-63 MLS; Loyola Col(Baltimore) 64-65 State Certif. 6: Fr. 7: Tchr St John Evang Sch, Baltimore 45-52; Tchr-libn St Michael Archangel Sch, Overlea Md 52-58; Tchr Holy Childhood Sch, Boston 58-61; Libn Seton High Sch, Baltimore 63- 68; Libn Cardinal McCloskey High Sch, Albany NY 68-. 9: ALA-AASchL; CathLA (High Sch Sect); NYLA; ENYSLA. 14: Bk sel, ya. 15: Cardinal McCloskey High School 99 Slingerland st, Albany Ny 12202.

HOYT, WILLIAM D(ANA) JR. b New Brunswick NJ 20 O 11. 5: Washington & Lee U 28-32 (Hist, Eng) BA, 32-33 (Hist, Eng) MA; Johns Hopkins 33-40 (Hist) PhD. 6: Fr. 7: Sr asst Alderman Lib UVa 41-42; Faculty Governor Governor Dummer Acad, S Byfield Mass 42-43; Asst dir Md Hist Soc, Baltimore 43-47; Loyola Col (Baltimore): Asst Prof hist 47-50, Assoc Prof hist & pol sci 50-58, Adv libn 53-56; Lecturer in hist Catholic U 59-61; Curator Sandy Bay Hist Soc 68-; Coord Inst Reg Hist N Essex Commun Col 68. 8: Chm Com on John Carroll Papers, 56-6 9; Curator Sandy Bay Hist Soc, 63-; Chm of Lib, Ipswich Hist Soc, 64-; Consul on Mss & Lib, Haverhill Hist Soc, 65-. 9: ALA; AHA; BSA; SAA; Org of Amer Histns; Amer Geog Soc; Amer Assn State & Local Hist (ed 43-49); MdLA (sec 44-46, ed 46-47); NELA. 10: Phi Beta Kappa; Friends of Lib (Rockport); Essex Co Hist Assn; So Hist Assn; West Hist Assn. 12: "Col William Fleming on the Virginia Frontier, 1755-83" (42); Ed "State & Local Hist News" 43-49; Ed "Maryland Historical Notes" 43-47; Ed "Between Librarians" 46-47. 13: Yes. 14: Mss, rare bks (Amer soc hist, state & loc hist). 15: Box 179, Rockport Ma 01966.

HRIBIK, LOUIS J. b Ford City Penn 17 My 33. 4: Rosemond Di Gregorio. 5: Clarion State Col 59-63 (LS) BS; UPittsburgh 64-65 MSLS, 69 (A-V). 6: Slovak. 7: Glass checker Pittsburgh Plate Glass Co, Ford City Penn 51-53; Staff Sgt US Air Force Radar Repairman 53-57; Lib asst Pittsburgh Plate Glass Co Research Center, Pittsburgh summer 65; Libn Penn Hills Sch Dist, Pittsburgh 63-. 8: Bk Purchasing Consul , Allegheny Commun Col. 09: Penn State EA; PennLA. 10: Ford City Sportsmen Assn; Slovak Cath Union; Beta Phi Mu. 14: Catlg, ref, a-v. 15: 2071 Holiday Pk dr, Pittsburgh Pa 15239.

HRUBY, GEORGE J. b Prague Czechoslovakia 26 O 25. 4: Malenka Horava. 5: Charles U(Prague) 45-49 (Arts, Philos) MLit-Philos; UGeneva 50-51 (Philos) L es Sc Morales; UMontreal 51-54 (Slavic Studies) PhD, 55-56 BLS; McGill 59 (LS). 6: Fr, Ger, Czech, Slovak, Polish, Russian Ital. 7: Asst libn Col Brebeuf (Montreal) 51-59; Catlgr Nat Lib, Ottawa 59-68; Catlgr UVictoria BC 68-. 9: CanLA. 14: Catlg. 15: Univ of Victoria Lib, Victoria BC Can.

HSI, CECILIA (MH). b Szechman China. 5: Nat TaiwanU 57-61 (Eng Lit) BA; UWash 62-63 9eng); Rosary Col 63-65 MALS. 6: Chinese, Ger. 7: Tr Ministry of Nat Defence Rep of China, Taipei Taiwan 61-62; Catlgr of child books Oak Park Pub Lib, Oak Park Ill 64; Catlgr NorthwesternU Lib 64-65; Catlgr Skokie Pub Lib, Skokie Ill 66; Gen libn Bavarian State Lib, Munich Germany 66-68. 9: ALA; CanLA. 14: Catlg, ref. 15: 28 Winter ave. St John's, Newfoundland Can.

HSIA, GLORIA (WANG). b Shanghai China 17 S 26. 4: Tao-tai Hsia. 5: Aurora U 44-48 (Eng Lit) BA; Columbia 48-50 (Educ) MA, 57-58 (LS) MS. 6: Chinese, Fr. 7: Instr Yale U 55-57, Ser catlgr 58-60; Catlg ed Union List of Ser 3rd Ed LC 60-62, Asst ed 62-63, Sr catlg ed Union Catlg Div 63-64, Asst hd Post 51 Imprints Sect Catlg M & P Div 64-66, Hd 66-67, Asst chief catlg M & P Div 67-. 8: Internship UN 52. 9: ALA; DCLA; Potomac Tech Proc Libns. 11: President's Scholar, Columbia U 51-52. 14: Catlg, admin. 15: 7522 Sweetbriar dr, College Park Md 20740.

HSIA, TAO-TAI. b Kiangsu China 1 Jl 21. 4: Gloria H Wang. 5: Yale Law Sch 48-52, 58-60 JSD; Columbia 57-58, 63 MS in LS. 6: Chinese. 7: Lecturer Nat Provisional U of Shanghai

46-47; Intern UN 50; Instr Inst of Far East Langs Yale U 52-59; Chief Far East Law Div LC 60-; Professorial lect in law George Washington U 66-. 8: Orientalia Processing Com LC 60-; Consul Chinese Law Proj UMich Law Sch 62-. 9: AALL (Com For Law Indexing). 10: Yale Club of Wash DC. 12: "China's Language Reforms" (56); "Guide to Selected Legal Sources of Mainland China" (67). 13: Yes. 14: Communist Chinese law. 15: 7522 Sweetbriar dr, College Park Md 20740.

HSING, HENRY CHIH-CHENG. b China 26 My 26. 4: Anna (Tao) Hsing. 5: Nat Taiwan U 47-51 (Eng Lit) BA; UOttawa 56-60 (Econ) MA ; Toronto 60-61 BLS, 63-66 MLS. 06: Chinese, Fr, Japanese. 7: Catlgr UToronto Lib 61-64, Head reclsf sect catlg dept 64-67, Head E Asian Sect 67-. 09: ALA; CanLA; OntLA; Inst Prof Libns Ont. 10: Assn for Asian Studies. 11: Can Coun Fellowship 59-60. 14: Catlg. 15: 70 Runnymede rd, Toronto 2B Ont Can.

HSU, CHARLES C T. b Shanghai China 28 Ap 35. 4: Maria Deng Hsu. 5: Taiwan Normal U 55-59 (Hist, Geog) BA; SUNY(Geneseo) 62-63 MLS; Columbia 64-65 (Hist, LS). 6: Chinese. 7: Tchr Taipei High Sch, Taiwan 59-61; Asst br libn Queens Borough Pub Lib, NYC 63-65, Sr libn bkmob 66-. 9: ALA. 13: Yes. 14: Admin, ref. 15: 32-50 70th st apt 3-C, Jackson Heights NY 11371.

HSU, CHIA-PI. b Shasi Hupeh China 27 Jl 07. 4: Winifred Ts'ao. 5: Hua Chung (Central China) U 26-30 BA in Ed; Boone Lib Sch(Wuchang Hupeh China) 28-30 Diploma in Libnship; Columbia U 47-49 MS in LS; Columbia 49-50 MA (Adult Educ). 6: Chinese. 7: Catlgr br libn & head div of documents Nat Lib of Peiping, Peiping China 30-38; Head ser sect Nat Southwest Associated U Lib, Kunming Yunnan China 38-39; Assoc ed Quarterly Bulletin of Chinese Bibliography, English ed, Kunming Yunnan China 39-40; Act libn Assoc ed Quarterly Bulletin of Chinese Bibliography, English ed, Kunming Yunnan China 39-40; Act libn Hua Chung U Lib, Hsichow Yunnan China 40-42; Libn Engnr Lib Yunnan-Burma Railway Admin Ministry of Communications, Mitu Yunnan China 42-43; Admin asst in chg of microfilm serv in World War II Internat Cultural Serv of China Ministry of Educ, Chungking China 43-45; Asst Prof of Lib Sci Boone Lib Sch (Chunking China) 43-45; Sr catlgr in chg of the Chinese Collection E Asian Lib Columbia U 46-62; Chinese bibliogr & research asst E Asian Collection Yale U Lib 62-68, Assoc curator in chg of Chinese & Korean materials 68-69; Libn for E Asian studies E Asian Collection Ind U Lib 69-. 8: Visiting Libn to the United Kingdom, under a grant from the Brit Coun, London, 45-46. 9: Lib Assn of China (Life mem; mem Supv Bd 45-50); Assn for Asian Studies. 13: Yes. 14: Tech serv, E Asian acquis, ref. 15: 412 E 19th st, Bloomington In 47401.

HSU, JANE YC (SWEN, YEN-CHENG). b Kiangsu China 8 O 17. 4: Philip CY Hsu. 5: Boone Lib Sch(Wuchang China) 38-40 (LS) Certif; Ginling Girls' Col(Nanking China) 41-46 (Sociol) BA. 6: Chinese. 7: Libn Ginling Girls' Col(Chengtu China) 40-46; Catlg libn Cheeloo U Lib(Tsinan Shangtung) 46-47; Catlg libn US Info Serv Lib, Hongkong 51-56; Catlg libn UOre Lib 56. 14: Catlg. 15: 1360 E 21st ave, Eugene Or 97403.

HSU, JEN-JEN. b Taiwan 31 My 35. 4: Evelyn M Guiher. 5: Nat TaiwanU 55-59 (Anthrop) BA; UPittsburgh 66-69 MLS. 6: Japanese, Chinese, Taiwanese. 7: 2nd Lt Chinese Army inf, Taiwan 59-61; Research asst Academia Sinica, Taiwan 61-64; Japanese instr UPittsburgh 64-65, Japanese catlgr E Asian Lib 66-67, Asst libn 68-. 9: CEAL. 14: Catlg, ref. 15: E Asian Lib Univ of Pittsburgh, Pittsburgh Pa 15213.

HSU, MARIAN M. b Taiwan Rep of China 30 Ja 41. 5: SoochowU 59-63 (Lit) BA; CatholicU 65-67 MS in LS. 6: Chinese, Fr. 7: Asst libn Quincy Col Lib 67-. 9: ALA. 14: Catlg. 15: Quincy Col Lib, Quincy Il 62301.

HSU, MARILYN (Ho). b Shanghai China 4 Ag 33. 4: Joseph C Hsu. 5: Nat Taiwan U 52-56 (Law) BA; Immaculate Heart Col 59-61 (LS) MA. 6: Chinese, Japanese, Fr. 7: Court clerk Taipei Dist Court, Taipei 56-57; Catlgr Los Angeles Co Law Lib, Los Angeles 61-66; Catlgr LC 67; Libn II Fresno State Col Lib 68-. 9: AALL; CalLA. 14: Catlg. 15: Fresno State Coll Lib, Fresno Ca 93726.

HSU, MARTHA (RUSSELL). b Wheeling W Va 6 S 41. 4: John T Hsu. 5: Col of Wooster 59-63 (Ger) BA; UBonn (Germany) 63-64 (Ger); CornellU 64-66 (Ger) MA; UMich 66-67 AMLS. 6: Ger, Fr. 7: Microform asst UMich (Ann Arbor) 66-67; Asst libn Phys Sci Lib CornellU 67-68, Asst libn ref dept Olin Lib 68-. 14: Ref. 15: 713 Hanshaw rd, Ithaca NY 14850.

HSU, RAYMOND CHEN-HUAN. b China 3 Je 23. 4: Tsing-yang Hsu. 5: Nat Tsing-hua U(China) 44-48 (Econ) BA; SoIll U 60-62 (Econ) MA; Peabody 62-63 (LS) MA (MS). 6: Chinese, Japanese. 7: Clerk to asst manager of br bank Land Bank of Taiwan(China) 48-59; Catlgr Pope Pius XII Lib, St Joseph Col(Hartford Conn) 63-67; Catlgr UMiami 67-. 8: Instr of Econ, St Joseph Col, W Hartford 65-. 14: Catlg, ref. 15: 1520 Delgado ave, Coral Gables Fl 33146.

HSU, SHERLY LYN (SHERYL LYN SHU-HSUN KU). b China 4 Ja 40. 4: John Yu-Sheng Hsu. 5: Chun ShengU 57-61 (Econ) BA; Brigham YoungU 62-64 (Bus Tech); USoCal 64-66 (LS) MS. 6: Chinese, Ger. 7: Tchr Kai-Ping Priv High Sch, Taipei Taiwan 61-62; Asst libn USoCal Educ Dept 66; Hd libn Cal Concordia Col 68-. 9: ALA; CalLA. 14: Catlg. 15: 861 Riley dr, Albany Ca 94706.

HSU, VERONICA (SUN). b Nanking China 25 F 29. 4: Marshall M P Hsu. 5: Holy Names Col 51-52 (Eng Lit) BA; Columbia 57-59 (LS) MS. 6: Chinese, Fr. 7: Asst libn Amer Nurses Assn, NYC 59-60; Catlgr MIT 61-62; Chief catlgr Avco Corp, Wilmington Mass 62-64; Tech libn RCA Aerospace Syst Div, Burlington Mass 64-. 9: SLA. 13: Yes. 15: 8 Jennie Dugan rd, Concord Ma 01742.

HU, SHU CHAO. b Kiangsi China 4 S 34. 4: Tsu Shan Hu. 5: Nat Taiwan U 53-57 (Law) BA; Nat Chengchi 57-60 (Pol Sci) LLM; Columbia 63-65 (Govt) MA; Villanova 66 MSLS. 6: Chinese. 7: Research assoc Ministry of Defense, Taipei China 57-60; Chief info & compilation sec Secretariat of the Nat Assembly, Taipei China 60-63; Asst catlgr E Asian Lib Columbia U 66-67; Catlgr St Francis Col Lib, Loretto Penn 67, Instr in lib sci 67-. 8: Contrib ed "Encyclopedia of Social Sciences", Taipei China 68-. 9: ALA; CathLA; Assn Asian Studies; Assn of Chinese Culture; PennLA. 12: "A Study of the Treating-Making Power of the American Senate" (69); "The Parliamentary System of Switzerland" (62); "Woodrow Wilson" (63). 13: Yes. 14: Catlg, ref, lib admin. 15: 312 E Lloyd st, Ebensburg Pa 15931.

HUANG, ANN MARIE (SUNG). b Kiangsu China 14 Ag 37. 4: Dr Bernand Huang. 5: Burlington Col 54-56 AA; Coe Col 56-58 (Fr) BA; UMich 58-60 ABLS. 6: Chinese. 7: Asst libn John Hancock Mutual Life Insurance Co, Boston 60-65; Libn Corn Prods Food Tech Inst, Waltham Mass 65-66; High Voltage Engrg Corp 66-. 9: SLA. 14: Ref. 15: 8 Tricorne rd, Lexington Ma 02173.

HUANG, ANSON. b China 14 Jl 34. 5: Nat TaiwanU (Taipei Taiwan) 53-57 (Eng lit) BA; Col of Insurance (NYC) 64-65 (Bus Admin) Certif; Columbia 66-67 MLS. 6: Chinese. 7: Catlgr Ladycliff Col 67-68; Asst dir Missionary Research Lib, NYC 68-. 14: Ref, catlg. 15: Missionary Research Lib 3041 Broadway, New York NY 10027.

HUANG, CHUNG-KAI. b China 29 D 27. 4: Janie Lai. 5: Mil Acad (China) 46 (Mil Sci) BS; Far East U (Manila) 60 (Econ) BA; St Tomas U (Manila) 61 (Econ); UMich 63 MALS. 6: Chinese. 7: Libn Mil Acad Lib, China 47-49; Chief liasion & tr off with MAAG, Taiwan 54-58; Hd E Asian Stud MND, Taiwan 61-63; Mil attache Chinese Embassy, Philippines 58-61; Hd E Asian Lib URochester 65-68; Libn E Asian Lub UKan 68-. 9: Assn for Asian Studies (com on E Asian Libs). 11: Distinguished Serv Med al from Pres of the Republic of China. 14: E Asian collection. 15: 2213 Naismith dr, Lawrence Ks 66044.

HUANG, GEORGE WENHONG. b Miao Li Taiwan 20 Ap 36. 4: Linda Hsu. 5: Taiwan NormalU 55-59 (Educ, LS) BA; Peabody Col 62-63 MALS; NM HighlandsU 65-67 (Educ) MEd; UIda 67-69 (Educ) PhD. 6: Chinese, Japanese, Ger. 7: Acquis libn Nat Central Lib, Taiwan 59-60; Libn Prov Hsin Chu High Sch, Taiwan 61-62; Libn Taipei Amer Sch, Taiwan 62; Libn NM HighlandsU 63-67. 9: ChinaLA; ALA. 10: Phi Delta Kappa. 14: Lib educ for sch libns. 15: Div of Educ Chico State Col, Chico Ca 95926.

HUANG, JENN C. b Chengkiang Kiangsu China 21 Je 37. 4: Chau-Lin. 5: Taiwan Prov Col of Law & Com 55-59 (Econ) BA; Rutgers 61-63 MLS. 7: Trainee Linden Pub Lib, Linden NJ 62-63; Catlgr Econ Lib YaleU summer 63; Catlgr Brooklyn Col Lib 63-. 9: CUNYLA; NY Tech Serv Libns Assn. 14: Catlg. 15: 624 E 38th st, Brooklyn NY 11203.

HUANG, SAMUEL TZENG-SAN. MOY Fukein Republic of China 23 Je 39. 5: Tamkang Col of arts & Sci 58 (For Lang & Lit) BA; NoIllU 64 MALS. 6: Chinese, Fr. 7: Asst humanities ref NoIllU 67-. 9: IllLA. 15: 911 Greenbrier apt 5, DeKalb Il 60115.

HUANG, THEODORE S. b Shanghai China 25 Mr 28. 05: Nat Fuh Tan U 43-47 (Sociol) BA; Rutgers 59-61 MLS. 5: Nat Fuh Tan U 43-47 (Sociol) BA; Rutgers 59-61 MLS, 64-67 (LS) PhD. 6: Chinese. 7: Employment consul Shanghai Soc Serv, Shanghai China 47-48; Tchr & sch libn Hsinchu Middle Sch, Hsinchu Taiwan China 48-50; Ed Commercial Press, Taipei Taiwan China 50-53; Lecturer Tamkang English Col (Tamsui Taiwan) 53-54; Acquis libn Nat Central Lib, Taipei Taiwan China 54-59; Catlg asst NY Pub Lib 59-60; Ref libn, Asst br libn, Br libn Queens Borough Pub Lib, Queens NY 61-64; Research assoc, Research fellow Grad Sch of Lib Serv, Rutgers U 64-68; Dir Tri-State Col Lib 68; Dir lib Tri-State Col, Angola Ind 68-69; Dir libs Fairleigh Dickinson U, Teaneck NJ 69-. 9: ALA; Lib Assn of China (exec sec & mem Bd Dirs 58); NY Lib Club; ASIS. 10: Beta Phi Mu. 11: English Prize, Nat Fuh Tan Univ, 47; Mod Poetry Prize, 55. 12: "Return to Nanking" (48); "Economic Concepts" (53); "Time, Poems" (53); "Night, Poems" (55); "Book of Hours, tr of Rilke's Poems" (58); "Harp and Flute, Poems" (58); "Shelf Work in Libraries, Tr of Jesse's Bk" (58); Chief ed, "Rainbow-Bridge Literary Series"; Ed, "Bulletin of the Library ASSOCIATION OF China" (Taipei 58-). 13: Yes. 14: Tech serv, documentation, admin, info sci, research. 15: 18 Lincoln ave, Cliffside Park, NJ 07010.

HUANG, THERESA C. b Nanking China. 5: Nat Taiwan U 51-55 (Foreign Langs & Lit) BA; Syracuse 56-58 MSLS. 06: Chinese. 7: Catlgr Chinese-Japanese Lib Harvard U 58-60; Child libn Brooklyn Pub Lib 60-65; Libn Lib USA World's Fair, NYC Dist child serv specialist Brooklyn Pub Lib 65-. 9: ALA-CSD (Com on Child Bks on Asia 65-66; Com on Eval of Lib Tools 68-71); NYLA. 12: Co-comp "Asia: a Guide to Books for Children" (66). 14: Child serv, admin, folkore, ref, research. 15: 18 Lincoln ave, Cliffside Park NJ 07010.

HUBBARD, (FRANCES) JOYCE. b E Orange NJ 21 Sp 18. 4: Edwin S Hubbard. 5: Oberlin Conservatory 35-37 (Voice); Radcliffe 37-40 (Mus) BA; Simmons 66-68 (LS) MS. 7: Asst curator Robt Hull Fleming Mus, Burlington Vt 41-42; Supv elem sch libs Summit Pub Schs, Summit NJ 42-43; Research libn & asst Croft Educ Serv, New London Conn 64-65; Spec libn Harbridge House, Boston 66-67; Child libn Dedham Pub Lib, Dedham Mass 67-68; Dir child serv Nashua Pub Lib, Nashua NH 68-. 8: Instructor of Creative/ Modern Dance, 4 institution 53-63. 9: ALA; NELA; NERT Child Libna; NESchLA; NHLA. 14: Child serv. 15: 13 High Rock rd, Wayland Ma 01778.

HUBBARD, BARBARA. b Providence 13 Ap 15. 5: Pembroke Col 32-36 (Math, Psych) AB; Columbia 40-41 (LS) BS. 7: Gen asst Providence Athenaeum 37-40; Ref asst NY Pub Lib 41-42; Ref libn Middlebury Col 42-45; Libn Col of Arch Cornell U 45-47; Head of readers' serv Mt Holyoke Col 47-50, Asst libn 50-56; Libn Kellogg- Hubbard Lib, Montpelier Vt 56-64; Adult serv consul Vt Free Pub Lib Serv, Montpelier Vt 65-68; Ref libn New Britian Pub Lib, New Britian Conn 69-. 9: ALA; VtLA (pres 59-60); NELA (dir 64-65) CTLA. 10: AAUW; Various Art Assns Vt Hist Soc ; Various art assns; Vt Hist Soc. 11: Layman's Award Montpelier Tchrs Assn. 14: Pub lib serv to adults & yp. 15: New Britian Pub Li b, New Britian Ct 06050.

HUBBARD, JEAN (LOUISE). b Wash DC 23 Ap 34. 5: Oberlin 52-54; Amer U summer 53; Miami U (Oxford Ohio) 54-57 (Art) BA; UMich 66-68 AMLS. 7: Clk-typist Miami U Lib (Oxford Ohio) summer 55; Clk-steno Personnel off Nat Gallery of Art, Wash DC 58, Sec to asst treasurer 60, Clk-steno chief curator off 60-61, Mus aid (Lib) 61-66; Asst ref libn Va Commonwealth U 68-. 9: ALA; VaLA. 10: Interlochen Alum Assn; Miami U Alum Assn; UMich Assn of Lib Sci Alum. 14: Art ref. 15: 104 W Franklin st, Richmond Va 23220.

HUBBARD, LEE (LUICK). b San Diego Cal 15 My 31. 4: Shirley Lane. 5: UChicago 49-50, 51-53 (Anthrop); UCal (Berkeley) 50-51, 55-58 (Gen Studies) AB, MLS; CambridgeU spring 53 (Archaeol); UAriz Archaeol Field Sch summers 52 & 55. 6: Fr, Sp. 7: Pfc (radio repair) US Army 53-55; Arch libn UTex (Austin) 58-62; Art, archaeology, mus libn UMo (Columbia) 62-66; City libn Hardley Lib, Winchester Va 66-. 9: VaLA. 10: Va Archeological Soc. 12: "Old Buildings & Battlefields of Southeast England: a Tourist atlas" (61). 13: Yes. 14: Reader-interest arrangement, lib bldg planning, a-v materials. 15: Box 58, Winchester Va 22601.

HUBBARD, MARGUERITE (BERTHIAUME). b Holyoke Mass 6 Jl 20. 4: E Stuart Hubbard Jr. 5: UMass 38-42 (Eng) AB; Columbia 59-63 MS. 6: Fr. 7: US War Dept, Wash DC 42-43; Ref libn Vassar Col Lib 61-. 9: SE NY Lib Resources Coun; Dutchess Co(NY)LA. 10: Jr League of Poughkeepsie; 4-H Group Leader. 14: Ref. 15: "Heartsease," Overlook rd, Poughkeepsie NY 12603.

HUBBARD, MARTHA J. b Baltimore 3 S 13. 5: Pratt 36-37 (LS) Certif. 7: Johns Hopkins U Lib: Asst in order dept 30-36, Asst in main reading room 37-39, Libn in chg main reading room 39-64, Libn in chg bibliog center 64-. 14: Ref, bibliog wk. 15: 5607 Roland ave, Baltimore Md 21210.

HUBBARD, WILLIS M(cCRACKEN). b Monmouth Ill 18 S 40. 4: Marilyn S Kessinger. 5: Monmouth Col (Monmouth Ill) 58-62 (Lit) BA; American U 61; UIll 62-63 (LS) MS; So Ill U 67-68 (Pol Sci) MA. 7: Asst sci libn SoIll U 63-68; Hd libn Eureka Col 68-. 9: ALA;-ACRL; IllLA. 10: AAUP; Pi Alpha Sigma. 14: Ref, admin, tchg. 15: Box 58 RR2, Edgewood rd, Eureka Il 61530.

HUBBLE, GERALD BLAINE. b Eubank Ky 21 Ap 34. 5: Berea Col 53-56, 60-61 (Econ) BA; UKy 61-63 MS in LS. 06: Ger. 7: Personnel Man 2d/c (E-5) US Navy 56-60; Berea Col: Period libn 61-64, Asst libn 64-67, Asst Prof of Lib Sci 65-67; Dir of Lib Stephens Col 67-. 8: Lecturer Catherine Spalding Col Dept of Lib Sci summer 65; Lib moving consul Ray Hamilton Co, Cincinnati 68-. 9: ALA (chm JMRT 70); Ohio Valley Group Tch SERV Libns; KyLA (chm Col & Ref Sect 66); Mol a 9bus mgr "MLA Quarterly" 68-69). 14: Tchg, admin, ref. 15: Stephens Coll Lib, Columbia Mo 65201.

HUBER, BERTHA MAY (BASLER). b Cobden Ill 4 My 18. 4: William F Huber Jr. 5: So Ill U 37-42 (Sociol) B Ed; UIll 50-53 MS in LS. 7: Tchr Elem Sch, Cobden Ill 42-45; Tchr-libn High Sch, Dongola Ill 46-48; Tchr-libn High Sch, Alto Pass Ill 48-50; Tchr-libn High Sch, Nashville Ill 50-51; Acquis libn U Lib UIll(Urbana) 53-55; Libn US Army Spec Serv, Japan 55-58; Libn US Army Med Field Serv Sch Ft Sam Houston, San Antonio Tex 60-64; Libn Air Force Inst of Tech, Wright-Patterson AFB Ohio 64-65; Libn US Army Med Field Serv Sch Ft Sam Houston, San Antonio Tex 65-. 9: ALA; Bexar Co LA. 14: Ref, docs, catl. 15: 615 Sumner dr, San Antonio Tx 78209.

HUBER, LAWRENCE R. b Tallmadge Ohio 6 Jl 14. 4: Mary Kendall. 5: Kent State 32-36 (Math) AB; West Res 48-50 MSLS. 7: Co Libn Wooster Pub Lib, Wooster Ohio 50-52; Order libn Canton Pub Lib, Canton Ohio 52-56; Head Libn Gallia Co Dixt Lib, Gallipolis Ohio 57-66; Admin Meig Co Lib Ext Serv, Pomeroy Ohio 65-66; Asst libn Jeanette Albiez Davis Lib 66-67; Dir 67-. 9: OhioLA. 10: Amer Red Cross. 15: PO Box 145, Gallipolis Oh 45631.

HUBER, MARY SUMNER. b Ludlow Vt 24 Jl 21. 4: Alfred L Huber. 5: UVt 39-43 (Chem) AB; Rutgers 62-65 MLS. 6: Fr, Ger. 7: Lab tech Gen Chem Co, Edgewater NJ 43-44; Abstractor Amer Smelting & Refining, Plainfield NJ 63-64; Catlgr Col of St Elizabeth 64-68, Asst libn 68-. 9: ALA; ASIS. 14: Catlg, spec libs. 15: 139 Summit rd, Florham Park NJ 07932.

HUCKABEE, GLORIA (COMSTOCK). b Shirley Mass 24 Ag 21. 4: Harlow M Huckabee. 5: Boston U 46-49 (Educ) BS in Ed; Catholic U 60-63 MS in LS. 7: Libn Flint Hill Priv Sch, Fairfax Va 63-64; Libn McLean High Sch, McLean Va 64-67; Libn Joyce Kilmer Intermed Sch, Vienna Va. 9: NEA; VaEA; NVALA. 10: Phi Delta Theta. 14: Ref. 15: 5000 25th rd N, Arlington Va 22207.

HUCKS, HERBERT JR. b Conway SC 2 Je 13. 4: Sarah Jones. 5: Wofford Col 34 (Fr, Ger, Educ) AB; Emory 35 (Fr) MA; Sorbonne US Army Training-with-Civilian-Agencies Program summer 45 (Advanced Fr Lang & Civilization) Certif; Emory 46 AB LS; Ga Dept of Archives & Hist, Emory U archives Inst 67 Certif. 6: Fr, Ger, Russian. 7: Fr tchr Sr High Sch, Greensboro NC 35-42; (1st Lt & Capt) US Army 42-46, Asst Prof Mil Sci & Tactics UKan, Mil Intelligence Serv in N Africa, Italy & France, now Lt Col ret Mil Intelligence; Assoc libn Wofford Col 47-53, Libn 53-66, Archivist 66-. 8: So Assn of Cols & Secondary Schs Visiting Accreditation Teams: Mars Hill Col, Georgetown Col, Greensboro Col. 9: ALA;NEA;SCLA (treas 50, pres 52); SELA (Exec Bd 56-60, treas Col & Univ Sect 54-56) ; SAA. 10: Foreman Spartanburg Co Grand Jury 65-66; Phi Beta Kappa; SAR. 12: Ed "Civitan Builder" (48 -); Ed "South Carolina Librarian" (59-). 13: Yes. 14: Archives, loc hist (SC). 15: PO Box 5193, Spartanburg Sc 29301.

HUDDLE, ANNETTE (WATLER). b Kingston Jamaica WI 28 Ag 43. 4: Jesse William Huddle Jr. 5: William Carey Col 61-64 (Hist) BA; LSU 64-66 (LS) MS. 7: Ref asst Mobile Pub Lib, Mobile Ala 66-68, Hd Bus & Sci Div 68-. 9: ALA;

AlaLA. 10: Beta Phi Mu. 14: Ref. 15: 15 So Hathaway rd, Mobile Al 36608.

HUDNUT, SOPHIE (KWAITKOWSKI). b Detroit 30 N 38. 4: F Vernon Hudnut. 5: Ariz State U 56-59 (Chem) BS; UCal (Los Angeles & Berkeley) summers 57, 58; Ariz StateU 59-61, 62 (Chem) MS; UCal (Los Angeles) 63-64 MLS. 6: Polish. 7: Ref asst UCal (Los Angeles) 63-64; Lit research analyst Aerospace Corp, El Segundo Cal 64-65, Subj ed 65-. 8: Panelist; Project Lex Wash DC 66, SLA wkshop Lib Asst, Los Angeles 67. 9: ACS; ASIS; SLA (2 coms); CalLA. 10: Kosciuszko Found; Polish Univ Club; Friends of the UCLA Lib; Beta Phi Mu; Poland's Millenium Lib Los Angeles; UCLA Sch Lib Serv Alum Assn. 14: Catlg, ref. 15: 13320 S Doty apt 264, Hawthorne Ca 90250.

HUDON, MARCEL. b Montauban Que Can 23 Jl 25. 4: Candide Tessier. 5: Se3minaire de Que3bec 38-45 BA; Catholic U 60-61 MS in LS. 6: Fr. 7: Catlgr Laval U Lib(Quebec) 47-56, Head of tech serv 57-60, Head of Sci Lib 63-66, Hd of Bus Lib 66-. 8: Mayor of Notre-Dame-de-Lorette, Que, 63-68. 9: CanLA; Association canadienne des bibliothe3caires de langue franc6aise. 10: Beta Phi Mu; C of C. 12: Co-auth "Analyse des postes de travail a5 la Bibliothe5que de l'Universite3 Laval" (63). 13: Yes. 14: Admin, lib sci tchg. 15: 1373 ave Rochette, Ancienne-Lorette Que Can.

HUDON, SISTER MARY OLIVER. b Rochester NY 22 S 32. 5: Col of Notre Dame (Educ) BA; UMd MLS. 7: Tchr Notre Dame Prep Sch, Baltimore 53-65; Tchr-libn St Mark Sch, Catonsville Md 65-67; Lib supv Dept of Catholic Educ, Baltimore 67-. 9: ALA; CathLA (Bd 67-69; sec Supv Sect 69-71; Md-Wash Unit: chm Elem Sch Sect 61-63 & 65-67); MdLA; Educ Media Assn of Md. 13: Yes. 14: Sch libs. 15: 29 Melvin ave, Catonsville Md 21228.

HUDSON, EARLINE H (HUNDLEY). b Huntsville Ala 2 My 19. 4: Robert Jackson Hudson. 5: Flora Stone Mather Col 37-41 (Hist, Sociol) AB; West Res 41, 42-44 BS in LS; 58 MS in LS, Peabody 68-. 7: Sub tchr Cleveland Pub Schs 41-42, Lib-aide 42-44; 1st asst libn Central Sr High Sch, Cleveland 44-45; Head Libn Fairmount Jr High Sch, Cleveland 45-46; Head Libn Kennard Jr High Sch, Cleveland 47-57; Head Libn Patrick Henry Jr High Cleveland 57-58; Order libn & Asst Prof Tenn A&I State U 58-. 8: Sub-com at Cleveland Pub Lib for inclusions in the Standard Catalog for High Sch Libs, 57 ed; Cleveland Pub Lib Com for the revised ed of Reading Ladders for Human Relations 53-54; Spec wk with the lib sect of the Tenn Educ Congress 59, 63, 64. 9: ALA; TennLA. 10: Child Welfare Com (Nashville); Beta Phi Mu. 13: Yes. 14: Acquis, child & yp. 15: Tenn Agric & Ind State U, Nashville Tn 37203.

HUDSON, GEORGE EDWARD. b Lynn Mass 10 Je 15. 4: Mary Rita (Kavanaugh) . 05: Boston Col 35-39 (Educ) BS, 40-41 (Eng) MA; Post Col (LI NY) 60-61 MSLS. 6: Fr. 7: US Army Combat Intel Off, Pacific Theatre Joint Assault Co (1st Lt) 42-46; Chief spec train & rehabilitation VA Boston Reg Off 46-50; Prof writer, Boston 50-54; Eng tchr Central Islip High Sch, Riverhead High Sch, NY 54-57; Libn Southampton High Sch 58-60; Libn Parkside Jr High Sch, Massapequa NY 60-61; Head libn Alfred G Berner Jr-Sr High Sch, Massapequa NY 62-. 9: ALA; NEA; NY State Tchrs Assn. 13: Yes. 14: Ref. 15: 4 Tenth ave, So Farmingdale Ny 11737.

HUDSON, IVAN LEROY. b Graettinger Iowa 23 D 37. 4: Jane Ferguson. 5: City Col of San Francisco 61-63; UCal (Berkeley) 63-66 (Eng) MLS. 7: Ref libn Econ Div NY Pub Lib 66-68; Ref & docs libn USan Francisco 68-. 9: ALA; CalLA. 10: ACLU; AAUP; Beta Phi Mu. 14: Govt docs, ref, bk sel. 15: 2375 O'Farrell st, San Francisco Ca 94115.

HUDSON, JEAN R. b Montclair NJ 8 Ap 25. 5: Seton Hall 42-49 (Chem) BS; Rutgers 56-58 MLS. 7: Libn Merck Sharp & Dohme, Rahway NJ 47-59; Lib supv Thiokol/Reaction Motors Div, Denville NJ 59-61; Tech libn Union Carbide Corp/Linde Div, Newark NJ 61-. 8: Lib consul St Voncent's Hosp Sch of Pract Nursing. 9: SLA (treas & chm var coms in NJ Chap 54-). 10: Mt Carmel Guild for the Visually Handicapped. 15: 14 Munn st, Montclair NJ 07042.

HUDSON, JOHN ALLEN. b Beaumont Tex 14 My 27. 4: Genevieve Lynch. 5: UTex 47-51 (Eng) BA, 52-54 (Comparative Lit) MA; West Res 56-57 MSLS. 6: Fr, Gk, Hungarian. 07: Libn I journalism UTex 51-53, Libn II journalism 53-54; Dir of ext Tex State Lib 55-56; Col libn Arlington State Col 57-63; U Libn UTex (Arlington) 63-. 8: Consul on Lib Ext Texas State Lib 57; Bd of Trust Arlington Pub Lib, Arlington Tex. 9: ALA; SLA; TexLA; SWLA. 10: AAUP; AHA; Beta Phi Mu; SW Soc Sci Assn. 12: Ed "Texas Libraries" (55-56); Ed "Texas Library Journal" (54); Co-authr "All But the People; The Critics of Franklin Roosevelt, 1933-1939". (69). 13: Yes. 14: Admin, rare bks. 15: Lib Arlington State Col, Arlington Tx 76010.

HUDSON, JOHNNIE (BERNICE) STEWART. b Baldwyn Miss. 4: Harold Hudson. 5: M I Col 48-51 (Sci Educ) AB; Atlanta 54 (LS); Syracuse summers 58-63 MSLS. 7: Sci tchr Dunbar High Sch, Earle Ark 51-53; Sci tchr Louisville Pub High Sch, Louisville Miss 53, Libn 55-. 9: ALA; Amer Tchrs Assn; Miss Tchrs Assn. 14: Ya serv. 15: 611 Anderson ave, Louisville Ms 39339.

HUDSON, JOSEPHINE ANN. b Albany NY 17 S 32. 5: Simmons 51-55 (Soc Sci) BS; Carnegie 57-58 MLS. 7: Sr lib asst Albany Pub Lib Harmanus Bleecker Lib, Albany NY 56-57; Libn I Free Lib of Phila 58; Ref libn Mitre Corp, Burlington Mass 59-60; Sr lib asst Div of Lib Ext, Boston 60-61; Child libn Albany Pub Lib, albany NY 62-. 9: NYLA. 10: Delta Sigma Theta; NAACP. 14: Child wk. 15: 29 N Lark st, Albany NY 12210.

HUDSON, JULIE. 5: Barnard 30 (Eng) AB; Columbia 31 (LS) BS. 6: Fr. 7: Princeton U Lib: Circ dept 31-43, Curator rare bks & spec collections 43-. 9: ALA; SLA; BSA. 10: Princeton Hist soc; Bd, Monhegan (Me) Mem Lib. 13. Yes. 14: Rare bks. 15: 49 Palmer Square, Princeton NJ 08540.

HUDSON, LYNN (EVALYN SCOTT). b Omaha Neb 6 O 42. 4: Boyce A Hudson. 5: Roanoke Col 60-64 (Hist) BA; UNC 64-65 MSLS. 6: Fr. 7: Child libn Fairfax Co Pub Lib, Alexandria Va 65-67; Circ libn Undergrad Lib UNC (Chapel Hill) 67-. 9: VaLA. 14: Ref, child wk, circ. 15: Rte 3 Box 125, Chapel Hill NC 27514.

HUDSON, SUSAN FRANCES. b Warren Co Bow ling Green Ky 25 Ap 12. 5: Randolph-Macon Woman's Col 29-33 (Eng, Math) AB; West Ky State Col 34, 45-47 (Educ) MA, 56, 57 Lib Certif. 7: Elem tchr Warren Co Sch System, Ky 44-54; Eng tchr Richardsville High Sch, Warren Co Ky 54-55; Libn Warren Co High Sch, Warren Co Ky 55-56; Libn Bristow High Sch, Warren Co Ky 56-. 9: NEA; KyEA; KyASchL; KyLA. 10: Phi Beta Kappa ; Delta Kappa Gamma. 14: Second sch libnship. 15: Rt 3, Old Scottsville rd, Bowling Green Ky 42101.

HUDZINSKI, JOSEPHINE. b Toledo Ohio. 5: UToledo 30 (Lit) BA; West Res 32 BSLS. 7: Toledo Pub Lib, Toledo Ohio: Asst in catlg dept 24-47, Film serv head 47-53, Catlg dept head 54-. 9: ALA; OhioLA; No Ohio Tech Serv Libns. 14: Catlg, a-v libnship. 15: Toledo Pub Lib, 325 Michigan st, Toledo Oh 43624.

HUDZINSKI, ROBERT G. b Blossburg Penn 25 Ag 43. 4: Barbara Ann Morgan. 5: Mansfield State Col 61-65 (LS, Soc Studies) BS Ed; Drexel (LS). 7: Libn Corning-Painted Post Area Sch Dist, Corning NY 65-. 8: Chm of Second y Libns, Corning-Painted Post Area Sch Dist. 9: ALA; NY State LA; So Tier Libns. 14: Ref, reading guidance. 15: Rte 352 Birchland Acres rd 1 , Corning Ny 14830.

HUEBSCHER, RALPH H. b St Paul Minn 27 O 10. 5: UMinn 30-34 (Statistics) BA, 49-51 bs in LS. 7: Lib clk St Paul Pub Lib 37-42; Rifleman (Pfc) USA; Lib asst St Paul pub Lib 46-52, Libn I 52-. 9: SLA (treas Minn Chap 64). 14: US docs. 15: 916 W Iowa ave, St Paul Mn 55117.

HUETER, EIKE. b Berlin Germany 31 Jl 38. 5: UAla 57-61 (Eng) AB, 61-65 (Secondary Educ) MA; LSU 67-68 (LS) MS. 6: Ger. 7: Lib asst UNC (Chapel Hill) 65-66; Circ ref libn Sweet Briar Col 66-67; Ref libn Radford Col 68-. 9: ALA; SELA; VaLA. 10: Beta Phi Mu. 14: Ref. 15: Box 728 Radford College, Radford Va 24141.

HUEY, CHARLES F. b Sanger Tex 9 S 20. 5: N Tex State Tchr Col 41-44 (Hist) BS; N Tex State U 57-58 BS in LS. 7: Sanitarian Tex State Health Dept, Sherman, Gainsville Tex 44; CAF-3 Civilian Personnel Camp Howze, Gainesville Tex 44-45; Photogr-manager Huey's Studio, Paris Tex 46-51; Photo-reproduction tech Consolidated Vultee Aircraft Corp, Ft Worth Tex 51-57; Assoc ref libn Tex Tech Col Lib 58-63; Asst order libn 63-. 9: ALA; TexLA. 14: Ref, microfilm photography, accessions. 15: PO Box 4525, # Tech Br, Lubbock Tx 79409.

HUFF, MARGARET JOAN (FARRIS). b Danville Ky 23 O 25. 4: Frank Rouse Huff. 5: Mary Baldwin Col 43-45; UNC 45-47 (Hist) AB, 47-48 BS in LS. 7: Asst Libn VA Hosp, Columbia SC 48-49; Tchr Cameron High Sch, Cameron SC

62-65. Asst libn Calhoun Co Pub Lib 67-68; Libn Orangeburg-Calhoun TEC 68-. 9: ALA; SCLA; SELA. 14: Admin. 15: Dantzler st, St Matthews SC 29135.

HUFF, SISTER JAMES ELLEN. b Harrodsburg Ky 23 F 04. 5: Nazareth Col 38 (Eng) BA; Col of St Catherine 38 BS in LS. 6: Fr, Lat, Sp. 7: Elem tchr Co System, Bardstown Ky 23-25; High Sch tchr St Catherines Acad, Lexington Ky 25-26; Catlg dept Okla City Pub Lib, Okla City Okla 26-30; High Sch tch r, Memphis Tenn 32-33; Elem & high sch tchr Sisters of Charity, Helena Ark 33-36; Tchr & Libn St Andrew High Sch, Roanoke Va 38-45; Instr Nazareth Col (Louisville Ky) 45-46; Head Libn & Instr Catherine Spalding Col 46-. 8: Served on Eval Com for So Assn, 3 high schs, 63-64; Governor's Commn on Planning for Libs 67-. 09: ALA-ACRL (a-v Com); CathLA (Leader Col Eval Group Study 65; chm of sloc Arrangements 56 Conf); SELA; KyLA (sec Ref Sect; Col & Univ Sect: panel mem Ref Sect); (V-Chm & chm-elect Cola Ref Sect). 10: AAUP; AAUW; Adv Com, Recording for the Blind Inc, Louisville Ky; Ky Hist Soc. 12: Scripture bibliog in "Worship" (Je-Jl 61); Current Cath Scripture Bks "Worship" (Je-Jl 62). 14: Col lib admin, bldg & collections. 15: Catherine Spalding Col, 851 S Fourth, Louisville Ky 40203.

HUFF, WILLIAM HOWARD. b Detroit 29 My 22. 4: Mary Josefowich. 5: East Mich U 46 (Eng Lit); UMich 47-50 (Eng Lit) AB, 50 AMLS. 7: Stationary engnr Ford Motor Co, Detroit Mich 40-41, 42-43; Cable Splicer Mich Bell Telephone Co, Detroit 41-42; US Army Air Corp, Infantry, US, France, Germany, Belgium 43-45; Ref asst Northwestern U 50-54; Adv libn & sers-acquis libn UIll (Chicago Navy Pier) 54-57; Ser libn UIll (Urbana) 57-. 9: ALA-RTSD (chm Ser Sect Policy & Research Com 62-64, Chm Ser Sect 67-68); IllLA. 10: AAUP. 12: Auth of the Bibliog in "Poetry of Dylan Thomas," by Elder Olson (54); Ed for ser "Library Resources and Technical Services" (65-67). 13: Yes. 14: Sers, ref. 15: 805 S Coler, Urbana Il 61801.

HUFFER, MARY-A (HANAGAN). b NYC 7 S 30. 4: John W Huffer. 5: Trinity Col (Wash DC) 48-52 (Pol Sci) AB; Georgetown U Sch of Law 52-55; Catholic U 55- (LS). 6: Fr. 7: Stud lib asst Trinity Col(Wash DC) 48-52; Lib asst ref & catlg Fed Power Commsn, Wash DC 52-54; Smithsonian Inst, Wash DC: Loan desk libn 54-56, Ref libn natural hist 58-60, Ref libn in chg 60-62, Chief ref & circ 62-64, Act libn 64-67, Asst dir of libs 67-. 9: ALA; SLA; ASIS; DCLA. 10: Kappa Beta Pi. 14: Admin, ref, lib equip, lib stat, lib, automation, info systems. 15: 6327 Hardwood dr, Lanham Md 20801.

HUFFMAN, ANN (MARIE). 5: Miss Col 59-62 (Math) BS; Fla stateU 62-65 (LS) MS. 7: Libn E Jr High Sch, Gulfport Miss 62-64; Child libn gulfport-Harrison Co Lib, Gulfport Miss 65-66; Acquis libn Hume Lib UFla 66-. 8: Libn Gainesville Little Theatre. 9: FlaLA. 14: Acquis, ref. 15: 1122 SW Sixth ave, Gainesville Fl 32601.

HUFFSTUTTER, MARY IMOGENE (SMITH). b Nebo Tenn 26 N 14. 4: W E Huffstutter. 5: Union U 29-32 (Eng) AB; Peabody summers 33-36 (Eng) MA, summers 39-41 BS in LS. 7: Elem tchr Reagan, Dyersburg Tenn 32-34; Elem tchr Jennie Bell Grammar Sch, Dyersburg Tenn 34-37; Elem tchr Fowlkes Grammar Sch, Fowlkes Tenn 37-39; Child libn Springfield Pub Lib, Springfield Ohio 44; Tchr-libn Newbern Grammar Sch, Newbern Tenn 39-46; Libn Newbern City Schs, Newbern Tenn 46-49, 55-56; Libn Dyersburg High Sch, Dyersburg Tenn 59-. 9: NEA; ALA; TennEA. 10: Pi Gamma Mu; Alpha Delta Kappa. 13: Yes. 14: Wk with child & yp. 14: Wk with child & yp 15: 5015 Ditmore rd, Newbern Tn 38059.

HUGGINS, ELIZABETH (OVERSTREET). b Hasty NC 13 F 14. 5: Flora MacDonald Col 31-35 (Hist, Educ) AB; UNC 36, (summers) 52, 61, 62, 63 Certif in LS; Appalachian StateU NDEA Inst 67 (summer). 7: Elem tchr: Mecklenburg Co, Charlotte NC 37-42, 43-44, Durham City Schs, Durham NC 51-58; Lib asst UNC (Chapel Hill) 44-49, Lib asst Health Affairs Lib 62-63; Lib supv Laurinburg-Scotland Co Schs, Laurinburg NC 63-. 8: Mem visitation team So Assn Ft Bragg Schs 66; Mem Com on Tools and Materials of the Governor's Study Comsn 68. 9: NEA; NCEA; NCLA. 10: Wesleyan Serv Guild; Laurinburg Wed Afternoon Bk Club. 14: Supv sch libs, ref. 15: 803 W Church st, Laurinburg NC 28352.

HUGGINS, BETTIE ANN (ADEN). b Paris Tex 25 D 27. 4: Dow Huggins. 5: Paris Jr Col(Tex) 45-47; N Tex State U 47-49 (LS) BA. 7: Libn Lamar Co Schs, Paris Tex 49-57; Asst acquis libn N Tex State U 63-. 9: TexLA. 10: Alpha Lambda Sigma. 14: Acquis, periods. 15: 2806 Glenwood lane, Denton Tx 76201.

HUGHES, (LANAH) GERALDINE. b Burgessville Ont Can 31 Mr 18. 5: UWest Ont 51 (Phil, Psych) BA; UMich 68 AMLS; Lond Tchrs' Col (Ont) 39 First Class Tchr's Certif. 6: Fr. 7: Tchr, Can 39-65; Catlgr Mackinac Col 65-68, Readers' serv libn 68-. 10: Beta Phi Mu. 14: Ref, catlg. 15: Mackinac College, Mackinac Island Mi 49757.

HUGHES, ANNE MARIE (CIERI). b Reading Penn 26 Jl 11. 4: Robert James Hughes. 5: Elmira Col 29-33 (Eng, Fr) AB; SUNY(Albany) 34-35 BLS; Cornell U summer 37; UMich(Ann Arbor) summers 40, 41 (LS); George town U 51 (Russian). 6: Fr, Ital. 7: Libn Col Misericordia 35-36; Head Libn Col of New Rochelle 36-40; Instr in Lib Sci Catholic U 40-42; Head Libn Fed Pub Housing Auth, Wash DC 42-44; Libn Central Intel Agency, Wash DC 51-53; Catlgr Alexandria Pub Lib, Alexandria Va 56-59; Libn So Railway Co Test Dept, Alexandria Va 60-62; Act libn George Mason Col of UVa 62-63, Asst libn 63-67. 8: Consul in org lib at Corcoran Sch of Art, Wash DC 63; Initial comp on a Catholic Supplement to the Shaw "List of Books for College Libraries" under direction of Charles Shaw & ALA 40-42. 9: "Very many in past." 10: Strawberry Hill Community Assn. 13: Yes. 14: Admin, catlg. 15: 119 N Floyd st, Alexandria Va 22304.

HUGHES, CATHERINE (WERNER). b NYC 12 Ap 20. 4: Thomas P Hughes. 5: Fordham 37-41 (Math, Physics) BS in Ed; Simmons 67 MSLS. 6: Fr. 7: Libn Carrington Electronics, Needham Mass 60; Catlg libn Raytheon Wayland, Wayland Mass 61-64; Libn Framingham Union Hosp, Framingham Mass 67-. 9: SLA. 14: Ref. 15: 87 Glen rd, Wellesley Hills Ma 02181.

HUGHES, CHARLES Z. b Ft Payne Ala 18 Ja 18. 5: Jacksonville (Ala) State Tchrs Col 34-38 (Educ) BS; Emory 50-51 (LS) ML. 7: Tchr DeKalb Co Ala Bd of Educ, Ft Payne Ala 39-41; Army Field Artillery S/Sgt 42-46; Order libn Auburn U 51-53; Ser libn Drake U 53-57, Head tech serv 57-58; Ser libn UIll Med Lib (Chicago) 58-. 9: ALA; MedLA; IllLA. 14: Ser, acquis. 15: P O Box 7509, Chicago Il 60680.

HUGHES, CORA L (BARNETT). b Trenton Gibson Co Tenn 29 D 32. 4: Earl W Hughes. 5: Lane Col 51-55 (Phys Educ) BS; Tenn State U summers 64-67 (LS). 7: Tchr Lake Co Bd of Educ, Mooring Tenn 55-63, Tchr & libn Lincoln Sch 63-68, Libn Lake Co High 68-. 9: NEA; ALA; TennEA; W Tenn EA; LakeCoEA. 14: Ref. 15: 316 College st, Tiptonville Tn 38079.

HUGHES, EDWIN J. b Adrian Wash 30 N 22. 4: Edith Carter. 5: East Wash Col of Educ 48-49 (Bus); UMinn 49-52 (Sociol) BA, 52-54 (LS) MA; Mankato State Col 61-62 (Educ) BS. 7: Clerk US Post Off, Ephrata Wash 42-43, 46-48; (2nd Lt) (Reserve) Army US, Europe 43-46; Page UMinn(Minneapolis) 54; Head Libn Martin Co Lib, Fairmont Minn 54-69; Hd libn Oxnard Pub lib, O xnard Col 6 9-. 9: ALA; MinnLA (past chm Co Libs Sect, v-chm Adult Serv Sect); Minn Libs Film Circuit Corp (pres); State C oun on Interlib coop. 10: United Fund; Boy Scouts; Red Cross; Off Bd Fairmont Methodist Church; PTA. 14: Admin. 15: Oxnard Pub Lib, 214 S "C" st, Oxnard Ca 93030.

HUGHES, EDWIN (NORRIS). b Erie Penn 15 N 10. 4: Ruth Gearing. 5: Ohio State U 28-32 (Fr) BS Educ, 32-33 (Fr) MA; UMich 38-39 ABLS. 6: Fr, Sp. 7: Circ asst Gen Lib Ohio State U 32-38; Circ asst Gen Lib UMich(Ann Arbor) 39-41; Act libn Chicago Tchrs Col 41-43; Asst ref libn John Crerar Lib, Chicago 45-47; Ref asst Los Angeles Co Pub Lib, Los Angeles 47-51; Libn Pacific Colony State Hosp, Spadra Cal 51-52; Catlgr Col of Osteopath Physicians & Surgeons, Los Angeles 58-61; Libn Kaiser Found Hosp, Los Angeles 61-. 9: MedLA (pres So Cal Group 65-66); SLA (past pres So Cal Chap). 13: Yes. 14: Ref. 15: 933 S Kingsley dr, Los Angeles Ca 90006.

HUGHES, EVELYN (HILL). b Morgantown W Va 9 S 20. 4: Robert Tucker Hughes Jr. 5: WVaU 38-42 (Home Econ) BS, 52-59 (Home Econ Educ) MS, 63- (LS); UPittsburgh 68 (LS). 7: Vocational tchr Wayne Co WVa Bd of Educ 42-43; Foods research Purity bakeries, Chicago 44-45; Catlg-typist WVaU Med Ctr Lib 59-65, Jr catlgr 65-66, Catlgr 66-67; Libn Sewickley Valley Hosp Sch of Nursing, Sewickley Penn 68-. 9: ALA; Nat League for Nursing. 10: Alpha Xi Delta; Kappa Delta Pi. 14: Catlg. 15: 542 Pat Haven dr, Pittsburgh Pa 15243.

HUGHES, EVELYN M. b Utica NY 7 Ag 20. 4: John T Hughes. 5: SUNY(Albany) 38-42 (Eng, SS) BA, summers 41-45 BS in LS. 7: Eng-lib Constableville Central Sch, Constableville NY 42-45; Libn S Kortright Central Sch, S Kortright NY 45-46; Libn So Lewis Central Sch, Turin NY 54-. 9: NY State Tchrs Assn (delegate); NYLA; Central NYLA (past pres). 10:

Amer Field Serv . 14: Sch lib wk. 15: R D Box 14, Port Leyden NY 13433.

HUGHES, FRANK M (LEAH STAPLES). b Roopville Ga 28 F 11. 4: Frank M Hughes. 5: W Ga Col 26-29 (Eng, Hist) AB; Emory 59-62 (LS) ML. 6: Fr. 7: Soc Studies, Fr tchr Hiram High Sch, Hiram Ga 30-34; Head social studies dept Cook High Sch, Adel Ga 55-59; Asst libn Campbell High Sch, Fairburn Ga 59-60; Libn Lakeshore High Sch, College Park Ga 60-. 9: NEA; ALA; SELA; GaEA; GaLA. 10: Delta Kappa Gamma; Youth Missionary Orgs. 14: Reading programs for gifted studs. 15: 2619 Colonial dr, College Park Ga 30337.

HUGHES, GORDON PHILLIP SSJ. b Green Bay Wis 14 D 22. 5: St Francis Sem 42-46 (Sociol) BA; Loyola U of South 50-51 (Educ) BS; LSU 60-61 (LS) MS. 6: Fr, Ger. 7: Libn & Eng Instr St Augustine's High Sch, New Orleans 52-63; PhD program LSU 63-65; Libn & Eng Instr Epiphany Col 65-. 8: Com on lib legis CathLA; Catholic Bk Week Sel Com CathLA. 9: ALA; CathLA (past chm New Orleans Unit); LaLA. 10: Eng Speaking Union; NCTE; Phi Kappa Phi. 11: Bishops Medal, Mid-South CathLA 65; Study Grant Oxford Eng 63. 12: "Basic Reference Books for Catholic High School Libraries" (63); Ed New Orleans Unit CathLA "Newsletter" (60-63). 13: Yes. 14: Sem libs. 15: PO Box 390, Newburg Ny 12553.

HUGHES, GWYNNETH EIRALYS. b Montreal 18 Mr 41. 5: McGill 58-62 (Hist) BA, 62-63 BLS. 7: Asst libn Colchester-E Hants Reg Lib, Truro NS 63-. 9: CanLA; APLA. 10: Univ Women's Club. 14: Bkmob, ref. 15: Colchester-E Hants Reg Lib, 754 Prince st, Truro NS Can.

HUGHES, J MARSHAL II. b Concord NC 2 Ap 45. 4: Ann T Hughes. 5: Campbell Col 63-67 (Eng) BS; William & Mary 67-68 (LS); Peabody Col 68-69 MLS. 7: Libn NASA, Hampton Va 67-. 8: Consul York Co Vol Assn Lib 68-69. 9: ASIS; SLA; ALA; Hampton Rds Spec lib Club. 13: Yes. 14: Computer applications to info retrieval. 15: Box 207 Rte 2 Grafton Branch, Yorktown Va 23490.

HUGHES, M VIRGINIA. b Baltimore 31 Jl 20. 5: Goucher Col 36-40 (European Hist) BA; Columbia summers 40-44 MS of LS. 6: Ger. 7: Tchr libn Baltimore City Schs 40-44; Jr col libn Monmouth Jr Col 44-45; US Army libn, Baltimore, Hawaii, Germany 45-51; Dependents sch libn for France & Germany US Army, Karlsruhe Germany 51-52; Br libn Enoch Pratt Free Lib, Baltimore 52-53; Bkmob libn Long Beach Pub Lib, Long Beach Cal 53; Consul in wk with schs Enoch Pratt Free Lib, Baltimore 53-57; Lib consul Cal State Lib 57-. 8: Proj dir for 3 Lib Serv Act demonstration programs in Cal, 58-64. 9: ALA; CalLA. 10: AAUW. 13: Yes. 14: Consul, child & yp serv. 15: Cal State Lib PO Box 2037, Sacramento Ca 95809.

HUGHES, MARGARET (HARVEY). b Cleveland 12 D 05. 5: Oberlin 24-27 (Math) BA; Carnegie 27-28 Lib Sci Certif, 32 BS in LS; Columbia summers 44-46, 49 (LS) MS. 7: Ref libn John A Howe Br Albany Pub Lib, Albany NY 28-30; Circ Pittsburgh Pub Lib 35-37; Circ Birmingham-So Col 40-43; Ref Tulane U 45-48; Birmingham-So Col: Ref 48-50, Catlgr 50-51, Dir 51-65; Chief Catlgr Shepherd Col 65-. 8: So Assn of Cols evaluations: Our Lady of the Lake Col 62; Union Col (Barbourville Ky) 62; Berea Col 63; David Lipscomb Col 64, Fla So Col 66. 9: ALA; SELA; AlaLA (chm scholarship Com 56-65). 13: Yes. 14: Catlg, ref. 15: Lib Shepherd Col, Shepherdstown WV 25443.

HUGHES, MARGARET E(LIZABETH). b Grimsby Ont Can 22 Je 11. 5: UMinn 32-35 (LS) BS. 7: UOre Med Sch: Circ libn 37-41, Circ libn Instr 41-51, Asst Prof circ libn 51-65, Prof Libn 65-. 9: MedLA (chm &/or mem 4 coms); SLA (dir PNW Chap, chm &/or mem 3 coms); ALA; PNLA; OreLA. 10: AAUW. 14: Ref, admin. 15: 3181 SW Sam Jackson Park rd, Portland Or 97201.

HUGHES, MARGARET. b Wallaceburg Ont Can 17 Ag 10. 5: U West Ont 32 (Gen Arts) BA; Toronto 34 (LS) Diploma, 38 BLS. 7: Gen libn Sarnia Pub Lib, Sarnia Can 34-36; Gen libn U West Ont 36-43; Libn (Lt) WRCNS 43-46; Asst to dir Prov Lib Serv, Toronto 46-59; Deputy chief libn Etobicoke Pub Lib (Metro) Toronto 60-. 9: CanLA (Coun 60-63); Inst Prof Libns Ont (past pres). 10: UWC of Etobicoke; WRCN Assn of Toronto. 12: Ed "Ontario Library Review" (46-59). 13: Yes. 14: Admin. 15: Box 501, Etobicoke Ont Can.

HUGHES, (MARY) RUTH (BROWNE). b Detroit Mich 15 S 18. 4: George A Hughes. 5: Wayne U 36-40 (Hist, Geog) AB; Simmons 42-43 (LS) BS. 7: Clk Detroit Pub Lib 37-42; Asst libn Chrysler Corp, Highland Park 43-47; Libn Fisher Body Engring, Detroit 47-48; Libn Ross Roy Advertising, Detroit 48-49; Libn DetroitInst of Arts 50-51; Libn UMich (Detroit) 51-. 8: Loaned by UMich to New Detroit (local urban coalition) 68; Bibliog Research for H A Montgomery Co 52-; Chm Lib Citizens Action Com (organ due to finan crisis facing the Detroit Pub Lib). 9: SLA (Memb Chm) ALA. 10: Friends of the detroit Pub Lib; LWV; Detroit Area Coun on World Affairs; Mayor's Register & Vote Com; Mayor's Task Forceon Coty Financ; Mich Assembly for Ombudsman; Coord Coun on Human Rel; Citizens Action Com for Sch Financ. 11: Nmed one of Top Ten Working Women in Detroit Metro Area 68. 14: Ref. 15: 60 Farnsworth, Detroit Mi 48202.

HUGHES, MRS MERLIE C(OONEY). b Butte Mont 13 F 06. 5: UMont 24-28 (Eng) BA, 29-30 (Lib Admin). 7: Child libn asst NY Pub Lib 30; Child libn Boise Pub Lib, Boise Idaho 31-32; Child libn Missoula Pub Lib, Missoula Mont 32-33; City Libn Twin Falls Pub Lib, Twin Falls Idaho 52-53; Asst City Libn, Anchorage Alaska 54-59; Libn Arctic Health Research Center PHS, Collefe Alaska 59-. 9: SLA; Alaska State LA (pres 63, chm Leg Com 65). 14: Arctic hist & research. 15: US Pub Health Serv, College Ak 99701.

HUGHES, NELLIE DONELAN. b Springfield Ill 5 O 02. 5: UIll 22-23; Lib Sch UWis 23-24; Lib Sch West Res 24-25; Springfield Col (Ill) 30-32. 6: Ger. 7: Tchr storytelling Springfield recreation com, Springfield Ill 25-26; Libn Lincoln Lib North Br, Springfield Ill 26-. 9: ALA. 10: De Mariallic Guild; Woman's Club. 14: Ref. 15: 417 E Canedy, Springfield Il 62703.

HUGHES, PAUL JOHN. b Akron Ohio 30 Ja 24. 4: Eileen Wilderman. 5: UAkron 46-50 (Sp) BA; West Res 50-51 MS in LS. 6: Sp. 7: Med corpsman (Cpl) USA 43-45; Asst catlgr Lincoln Pub Lib, Springfield Ill 51-55; Hd acquis dept UNotre Dame Lib, Notre Dame Ind 55-57; Catlgr Lockheed Aircraft Co Engring Lib, Burbank Cal 57; Chief catlg & processing sect Gen Dynamics Corp Astronautics Lib, San Diego 57-62; Assoc libn Tech Reports Ctr IBM Space Guidance Ctr, Owego NY 62; Asst libn Gen Atomic Div Gen Dynamics Corp, San Diego 62-63; Chief tech serv sect Nat Inst for Health (DRS) Lib Br, Bethesda Md 63-65; Tech libn Aerojet-Gen Corp, Sacramento Cal 65-67; Dir tech serv div State Lib of Ore, Salem 67-. 9: SLA; ALA; PNLA; OreLA. 14: Catlg, acquis, ser, info stor & ret. 15: 960 Parrish st NE, Salem Or 97301.

HUGHEY, ELIZABETH (HOUSE). b Robersonville NC 2 F 16. 4: A Miles Hughey. 5: Atlantic Christian Col 32-36 (Eng) AB; Peabody 37-38 BS in LS. 7: Libn High Sch, Simpsonville SC 38-39; Libn Cool Springs High Sch, Forest City NC 39-41; Libn BHM Reg Lib, Wash DC 41-46; Field libn NC Lib Commsn, Raleigh NC 46-50, Sec & dir 50-56; State Libn NC State Lib 56-65; Lib ext spec Lib Serv Br, Off of Educ, Wash DC 65-68, Chief lib programs & facilities br 68-. 9: ALA; AEAUSA; Nat Coun on Aging; SELA; NCLA. 10: Bus & Prof Women; Delta Kappa Gamma. 11: Hon degree of DLit, Atlantic Christian Col. 13: Yes. 14: Pub lib devel. 15: 8013 Greeley blvd, Springfield Va 22152.

HUGHEY, ELIZABETH. b Smyrna Tenn 7 Je 15. 5: Middle Tenn State U 33-37 (Math) BS; Peabody 38-39 BS in LS, 60 (LS) MA. 7: Libn Central High Sch, Murfreesboro Tenn 39-42; Libn Stewart Air Base, Smyrna Tenn 42-46; Field libn NC Lib Commsn, Raleigh NC 47; Libn The Methodist Pub House, Nashville Tenn 48-. 8: Methodist Libns Fellowship (v-chm 60, 61, chm 61-62); Southeastern Jurisdictional Hist Soc Honorary Mem 61-; Assn of Methodist Hist Socs Exec Com 64-68; Joint Com for Union Card Catlg of Methodist Materials 64-; Com to Frame an Archival Policy The Methodist Church (sec 65-68); Mem Commsn on Archives and Hist, Unit Meth Church 68-. 9: SLA; SAA; SELA; TennLA. 10: Woman's Nat Bk Assn; Beta Phi Mu; Tau Omicron. 12: Ed "Methodist Periodical Index" (60-69); Ed "United Methodist Periodical Index" (69-). 15: 201 Eighth ave S, Nashville Tn 37203.

HUH, MARGARET P(ALMER). b Chicago Ill 5 Je 39. 4: Hubert C Huh. 5: Augustana Col (Rock Island Ill) 57-59 (Hist); WashU 59-61 (Hist) AB; UIll 61-63 (LS) MS. 6: Fr, swedish. 7: Catlgr UMo Lib (Columbia) 63-66; Asst catlgr TuftsU Lib 66-. 9: ALA. 14: Catlg, automation, ch libs. 15: 287 Harvard st, Cambridge Ma 02139.

HUISH, LOIS R(UTH) (HUFFMAN) (MRS). b Redlands Cal 4 Ja 28. 5: UCal (Berk eley) 47-49 (Ger) BA, 50 (Ger) MA, 60-61 MLS. UCal (Berkeley) 47-50 (Ger) BA, MA, 60-61 06: Ger, Sp. 7: Br libn Contra Costa Co Lib, Cal 61-67, Reg libn Walnut Creek Cal 68; Libn College Preparatory High Sch, Oakland Cal 68-. 9: ALA; CalLA (past chm Echange Com).

10: UCal Lib Schools Alumni Assn ; Soc for Gen Semantics; ACLU; UCal Alumni Assn. 13: Yes. 14: Pub lib, ref & reader's adv. 15: 1631 Grant st, Berkeley Ca 94703.

HUISMAN, GARY BRANT. b Grand Haven Mich 8 Ap 40. 4: Julie Linda (Webb). 5: Calvin Col 59-63 (Mus) AB; UMich summer 63 (Mus); West Mich U 64-66 MSL. 7: Libn trainee VA Hosp, Battle Creek Mich 65-66; Libn Covenant Col 66-. 9: ALA. 10: Chattanooga Area Libn's Assn; Assn Advanc Christ Scholarship. 14: Admin, ref. 15: 216 Hardy rd, Lookout Mountain Tn 37350.

HULBERT, JEANETTE A. b Abbeville La. 4: James H Hulburt. 5: Col of Sacred Heart (La) 46-47; Seattle U 47-50 (Sociol) BS; MLibnship. 47-50 (Sociol) BS; UWash 63-64 MLibnship. 06: Fr. 7: Asst catlg libn Seattle U Lib 64-66; Chief catlg libn 66-. 9: ALA; PNLA. 10: AAUP. 14: Catlg, rare bks. 15: 1703 NW Greenbrier Way, Seattle Wa 98177.

HULBERT, KENNETH LEAMANN. b Somervil e Mass 19 Je 14. 5: Clark 36 AB; Boston 40 Ed M; Simmons 48 BS. 07: LCDR, US Navy 40-46; Tchr Westboro Mass 46-47; Asst NYC 48-49; Asst libn Post lib Ft Devens Mass 49-51; Catlgr Sch of Theol Boston U 51-52; Asst catlgr UMass 52-53; Ref libn & archivist 54-55; Ref libn Mass State Lib 56-68; Asst Libn Framingham State Col (Mass) 68-. 10: Trustee Westboro Pub Lib; Lambda Chi Alpha; Kappa Delta Phi; Mass Soc of Colonial Wars; Mass Chap Mayflower Descendants. 12: "Hulbert Genealogy"; "My Royal Descent"; "Bartlett Genealogy. 14: Ref, geneal research. 15: 33 Ruggles st, Westboro Ma 01581.

HULBERT, LOUISE HULBERT (CONKLE). b Bucyrus Ohio 10 O 14. 4: Kenneth Hudson Hulbert. 5: AkronU 33 (Home Econ); Kent StateU 35-39 (Home Econ) BS, 51-54 MALS; MiamiU 68. 7: Dietitian Robinson Mem Hosp, Ravenna Ohio 38-40; Libn Ravenna High Sch, Ravenna Ohio 51-68; Tchr Kent StateU 65-67; Asst supv sch lib Cleveland Pub Schsm Cleveland Ohio 68-. 9: ALA; Womens Nat Bk Assn; OhioLA; OhioASchL (reporter; reg dir). 10: AAUW; Alpha Sigma Alpha. 15: 7566 st Rte 43, Kent Oh 44240.

HULBUSH, MRS DOROTHY L. b Forest Grove Ore 1 F 18. 5: UWash 36-40 (Bot) BS; UWash 53-54 (LS). 6: Ger, Fr. 7: Jr libn bkmob Pierce Co Lib, Tacoma Wash 55-58; McChord Air Force Base Libn US Air Force, McChord AFB Wash 58-. 14: Readers adv wk. 15: Base Lib, McChord AFB Wa 98438.

HULEATT, RICHARD S. b Boston 13 Ag 31. 4: Irene Meymaris. 5: Boston U 49-51 (Gen Educ). 7: Control tech USAF US, Far East 51-54; Publ supv Comm of Mass Civil Defense, Natick Mass 55-57; Data coordinator Raytheon Co, Sudbury Mass 57-60; Mgr LFE Tech Info Center, Lab for Electronics Inc, Boston 60-67; Chief Libn Tech Info Ctr Gen Dynam Electric Boat Div Groton Conn 67-68; Tech info mgr Tech Lib Stone & Webster Engrg Corp, Boston 68-. 9: SLA (ed Boston Chap Bulletin 69-). 14: Tech info admin & mgt. 15: 22 Savoy rd, Framingham Ma 01701.

HULING, MARGARET J (FARKAS). b Coraopolis 30 Je 38. 4: Gene Paul Huling. 5: Clarion State Col 56-60 (LS) BS Ed; UPittsburgh summers 61, 62 , 66-68 MLS. 6: Hungarian. 7: Sch libn Northeastern Beaver Co Sch Dist, Ellwood City Penn 60-67; Sch libn Bellevue Jr-Sr High Sch, Bellevue Penn 67-68. 8: Mem of Evalg Com: Youngsville High Sch, Youngsville Penn, 65, Punxsutawney A rea High Sch, Punxsutawney, Penn. 09: NEA; ALA; Penn State EA; PennLA. 10: Zeta Tau Alpha; Beta Phi Mu. 14: Ref, sch lib wk. 15: 626 Westland dr, Gibsonia Pa 15044.

HULL, BARBARA A. b NY 30 Jl 32. 5: SUNY (Geneseo) 65 (Lib) BS; West Mich U 68 MSL. 7: Elem sch libn Clarence Central Schs, Clarence NY 65-67; Elem sch libn W Seneca Central Schs, Buffalo NY 68-. 8: Sec to dir, NDEA Inst Geneseo 65. 9: ALA; NEA; NYLA; ErieCoTA; W SenecaTA; Suburban Libns Assn. 10: Chm Camp Fire Girls; Kappa Delta Pi. 14: Child wk, tech proc. 15: 72 Harvard pl, Orchard Oark NY 14427.

HULME, MRS MILDRED (KUMER). b Detroit 19 Jl 11. 5: Wayne State U 29-36 (Sch lib sci) AB in Educ; West Res 42-43 BS in LS. 6: Fr. 7: Lib asst "Detroit News" 37-42; Ref asst Royal Oak Pub Lib, Royal Oak Mich 43-44; Libn I US Naval Train Station, Farragut Ida 44-45; Libn I US Naval Air Station, Santa Ana Cal 45; Asst libn Ford Motor Co Train Dept Lib, Dearborn Mich 46-48; Act ref libn Dearborn Pub Lib, Dearborn Mich 48-49, Head of ref 50-67; Ref consul SC State Lib Bd 68-. 9: ALA; SLA (Mich Chap: treas 47-49, pres 63-64, dir 64-65, 67; mem SAtlantic Chap); MichLA (chm Ref Sect 50-51); SELA; SCLA. 14: Ref, adult educ. 15: South Carolina State Lib Bd, 1001 Main st, Columbia SC 29201.

HULSART, DOROTHY N. b Gunnison Colo. 4: Edward Pittman Hulsart. 5: Ohio State U 32-35 (Eng) BA; Carnegie 35-36 BS in LS. 7: Staff asst circ dept Carnegie Lib of Pittsburgh 36-39; Circ head Rose Mem Lib Drew U 64-. 9: NJLA. 15: Drew Univ Rose Mem Lib, Madison NJ 07940.

HULSE, ZELMA ROBERTA (FERGUSON). b Winnsboro Tex 18 F 18. 5: N Tex State U 40-42 (Eng) BA; Midwestern U 51-52 (Educ) MEd. 7: Tchr Hackberry Ind Sch, Cottle Co Tex 42-43; Tchr Crowell Ind Sch, Crowell High Sch, Crowell Tex 43-45, 48-50; Tchr-libn Crowell Ind Sch, Crowell Tex 50-55; Tchr-libn Hamlin Ind Sch, Hamlin High Sch, Hamlin Tex 55-60; Libn Sweetwater High Sch, Sweetwater Tex 60-. 9: NEA; Tex State Tchrs Assn (chm Lib Sect, Dist 7 64-65, 67-68); TexLA (sec-treas 68-69). 10: Bus & Prof Women's Club. 14: Sch libn. 15: 1617 Woodruff lane, Sweetwater Tx 79556.

HULT, ELIZABETH J (JARMAN). b Baltimore Md 5 N 17. 4: Robert Hult. 5: Goucher 35-39 (Eng) BA; Rosary Col 64-66 MALS. 6: Fr. 7: Receptionist Goucher Col 39-40; Tchr Southern High School, Baltimore 40-42; Tchr Calvert Sch, Baltimore 42-44; Sec USAF, Tonopah Nev 44-45; Tchr orchard Hill, Midlothian Ill 54-58; Tchr Forest Ridge Sch, Midlothian Ill 58-64; Head libn Hillcrest High Sch, Country Club Hills 66-. 8: North central Evaluation Com 69. 9: ALA; NEA; IllASchL; IllEA. 10: Phi Beta Kappa. 13: Yes. 14: High sch libs, jr col libs. 15: 17235 - 69th ave, Tinley Park Il 60477.

HULTON, CLARA (ADAMS). b Sharon Penn 10 Ap 19. 4: John G Hulton Jr. 5: Lake Erie Col 36-38; Mt Holyoke 38-40 (Eng) AB; Carnegie Lib Sch 43 BS in LS. 7: Asst child rooms NY Pub Lib 41-42, Child libn 43-45; Ref asst Dun & Bradstreet Lib, NYC 45-46; Child libn NY Pub Lib (Manhasset) 46-49; Y-a libn NY Pub Lib 49-52, Child lobn 63-65, Br libn 65-67, Asst coord child serv (storytelling & group wk specialist) 67-. 9: ALA; -CSD (chm Bk Re-Eval Com 68-); NYLA (Child & YA Serv Div): chm Recordings for Child Com 68-); NY Lib Club. 10: LWV. 13: Yes. 14: Child lit, storytelling. 15: 186 Emerson pl, Brooklyn NY 11205.

HULTON, JOHN G JR. b Latrobe Penn 25 O 22. 4: Clara Adams. 5: Washington & Jefferson Col 40-43 (Econ) BA; Harvard 46-48 (Hist) MA; Columbia 50-51 (LS) MS. 6: Fr. 7: USAAF 43-45; Circ dept NY Pub Lib 49-61, Coordinator Richmond Borough 61-63; Assoc Prof Lib Sci Pratt Inst 63-. 8: Surveys of 5 libs for Ramapo Catskill Lib System 67-68. 9: ALA; NY Lib Club. 10: Phi Beta Kappa; SI Commun Chest & Coun. 13: Yes. 14: Pub libs, bibliog, ref, hist of bks & libs. 15: Pratt Inst Lib Sch, Brooklyn NY 11205.

HULZENGA, WILLIAM. b Nykerk Holland 3 Ag 42. 5: Orange Co Commun Col 62-64 (Hist) AA; SUNY (New Paltz) 64-66 (Hist) BS; SUNY (Geneseo) 67-68 MLS. 6: Fr, Dutch. 7: Circ libn Essex Co Col 68-. 14: Ref. 15: Apt 202 1304 Springfield ave, Irvington NJ 07111.

HUMBERTSON, JANE VINTON. b Richmond Va 14 F 31. 5: Washington Col 49-53 (Hist) AB; Carnegie 53-54 MLS. 7: Catlgr West Md Col 54-62; Libn Hagerstown Jr Col 62-. 9: ALA; NEA; MdLA; Md State Tchrs Assn. 10: Bus & Prof Women's Club. 15: 2325 Marsh Pike, Hagerstown Md 21740.

HUMES, DIANE CAROL. b Los Angeles 16 Jl 42. 5: San Fernando Valley State Col 60-64 (Eng) BA; UCLA 64-65 MLS. 7: LC: Descr catlgr 65-68; Asst hd Eng sect shared catlg div 68-. 14: Catlg. 15: 2430 Penna ave NW apt 708, Was hington Dc 20037.

HUMES, DOROTHY TRUESDALE. b Rochester NY 11 Mr 12. 5: URochester 29-35 (Hist) BA, MA; Columbia 42-43 (LS) BS. 06: Fr. 7: Sec-res asst sociol URochester 35-37; Sec-res asst City Histn Rochester Pub Lib, Rochester NY 37-43; Admin asst hist travel biog Enoch Pratt Free Lib, Baltimore 43-47; Chief ref dept Pub Lib, White Plains NY 47-54; Rochester Pub Lib, Rochester NY: Sr libn bus div 54-56, Head hist travel div 56-57, Asst libn Main Lib 57-60, Consul info serv 60-. 9: ALA (pres Pub Libs Ref Sect 55-56)-Subs Bks Com; NYLA (pres Adult Serv Sect 58-59). 10: AAUW; Phi Beta Kappa; Amer Soc Pub Admin. 13: Yes. 14: Ref, & info serv. 15: 115 S ave, Rochester NY 14604.

HUMESTON, EDWARD JUDSON JR. b Oak Lane Phila 12 D 10. 4: Mary Leiphart. 5: Hamilton Col 28-32 (Eng) AB; Princeton 32-34 (Modern Langs) AM, 42 (Modern Langs) PhD; Peabody 46 BS in LS. 6: Fr, Sp, Ital. 7: Master Fr Taft

Sch, Watertown Conn 34-36; Instr Fr, Span Hollins Col 37-42; Non-com off Army Airways Communication System, US 42-45; Libn Kan State Tchrs Col(Pittsburgh) 46-48; Assoc Prof UTex 48-53; Head of Dept of Lib Sci UKy 53-59; Dir of Studs Drexel Lib Sch 59-64; Dean Grad Lib Sch URI 64-. 9: ALA (Subs Bks Com 50-53);-ACRL (Ed Bd Microcard Ser 62-68); KyLA (pres 57-58); RILA (Exec Bd 64-67); NELA (By-laws Com 69-70). 10: Lansdowne Symphony Orchestra, Lansdowne Penn 62-64; Alpha Delta Phi. 12: Ed "Texas Library Journal" (52-53); Ed AALS "Newsletter" (56-58). 13: Yes. 14: Lib educ, lib in soc. 15: Univ of RI Grad Lib Sch, Kingston Ri 02881.

HUMMEL, FRANCES (COPE). b Ann Arbor Mich 13 My 11. 4: Ralph D Hummel. 5: Wayne State U 26-28 (Gen Lit); UMich 28-31 (Chem) BS, MS; UCal(Berkeley) 56-57 (Chem); Columbia 60-62 MS in LS. 6: Fr, Ger. 7: Assoc nutrition research Child Fund of Mich, Detroit 31-40; Microanalyst Parke Davis & Co, Detroit 41-42; Lib trainee, libn I NY Pub Lib 61-63; Catlgr Expt Sta Hawaiian Sugar Planters Assn, Honolulu 63-64; Info asst fibers div Allied Chem, Petersburg Va 65-. 9: ACS; SLA; ASIS; VaLA. 10: Sigma Kappa; Phi Beta Kappa; Phi Kappa Phi; Iota Sigma Pi; Va Federated Women's Club; Richmond Spec Lib Club. 13: Yes. 14: Lit searching, indexing, abstracting, mechanization. 15: 11 Beechwood ave, Colonial Heights Va 23834.

HUMMEL, RAY O(RVIN) JR. b Lincoln Neb 22 O 09. 4: Roberta Harrison. 5: UNeb 26-32 (Amer Hist) AB, AM; UIowa 32-33 (Amer Hist); UNeb 33-34 (Amer Hist) PhD; UMich 35-36 ABLS. 7: Asst hist dept UNeb 30-32; Educ adv Civilian Conservation Corps, Hamburg Ark 34-35; Catlgr Folger Shakespeare Lib, Wash DC 36-42, 45-46; Libn Wash Cathedral Lib, Wash DC 40-42; Instr Catholic U 38-42; LCDR US Navy 42-45; Chief catlg libn & Asst Prof UMinn(Minneapolis) 46-48; Asst state libn Va State Lib 48-. 9: ALA (Coun 50-59); Bibliog Soc (London); BSA; SELA; VaLA (pres 57-58). 12: "List of Places Included in 19th Century Virginia Directories" (60); Managing ed "Library Resources & Technical Services" (60-65). 13: Yes. 14: Bibliog, tech serv, rare bks. 15: 11th & Capitol, Richmond Va 23219.

HUMPHREY, GRAHAM H JR. b Escondido Cal 6 Ap 31. 5: Antioch Col 50-54 (Art) AB; UCLA 54-55 (Art) USoCal 62-63 MS in LS. 6: Sp. 7: Off manager Richfield Oil Corp, Los Angeles 57-62; Ref Libn Los Angeles Pub Lib 63-64; Libn Escondido Pub Lib, Escondido Cal 64-. Libn 65-. 9: ALA; CalLA. 14: Adult ref. 15: 1006 S Ontario, Escondido Ca 92025.

HUMPHREY, HELEN (CHAMBERLIN). b Harrison Co Ky 12 Jl 17. 4: Edgar F Humphrey. 5: Ky Wesleyan Col 35-39 (Eng) AB; UKy 64-65 MS in LS. 7: Eng tchr Harrison Co Ky, Connersville Ky 39-42; Program chm Girl Scouts, St Petersburg Fla 42-44; Eng tchr Cynthiana Ky, Cynthiana High Sch 45-46, 52-62; Eng tchr Harrison Co High Sch 62-64; Libn Harrison Co Ky Westside Elem Sch 65-. 09: NEA; ALA-AASchL; KyEA; KyLA; KyASchL; SELA; Ky AV Assn. 10: Beta Phi Mu. 14: Child serv. 15: RR 6, Cynthiana Ky 41031.

HUMPHRY, JAMES III. b Springfield Mass 21 Jl 16. 4: Priscilla Eaton. 5: Harvard 35-39 (Econ) AB; Columbia 39-41 BS in LS. 6: Fr. 7: Lib asst NY Pub Lib 39-41; Major ARTY US Army 42-46; Chief map div NY Pub Lib 46-47; Libn Prof Bibliog Colby Col 47-57; Lt Col ARTY US Army 51-54; Chief Libn The Metropolitan Museum of Art, NYC 57-68; V-president The HW Wilson Co, Bronx NY 68-. 8: Bus manager Colby Col Press 47-57; Conducted survey of Norwich Univ Lib at request of ALA-ACRL, 57; Lib consul, Coun for the Advnt of Small Cols, 56-57; Consul to Lib Bds of Trustees of Greater NY Communs on lib bldgs, 62-; Lib surveys conducted: Boy Scouts of Amer 64, Art Inst of Chicago 64-65, State of Del 65, Greenwich(Conn) Lib 65-66, RI Sch of Design 65-66; New London Co nn Pub Lib 66; Wadsworth Atheneum, Hartford 67; Winterthur Museum, Wilmington Del 67; State of La 68; Hammond Museum, No Salem NY 68; Art Ctr Lib , WesleyanU 68; Del, Regl Lib, Georgetown 69. 9: Internat Coun of Museums, Paris (corr memb Com on Documentation); Amer Assn of Museums (chm Lib Group 65; ALA (Coun 59-63; 67-69; Coord MeLA for ALA sponsored Lib Serv Bill 48-49 & 55-57; Bldgs Com for Col & Univ Libs 59-63, Subs Bk Com 63-66; Com on Accredit 68-); -RSD (Com on Wilson Indexes 61-65, Com on Art Index 57-58); -ACRL (Bd Dirs 59-63, 66-69, Subj Spec Sect: v-chm & chm 64-66; chm Art Subsect 61-62 & 64-65; mem Planning & Action Com 62-65), (67-69); -LAD (Com on Org 63-65); SLA (Com on Copyright Law Rev 61-64, Convention Chm 1967 Conv; NY Chap: chm Mus Group 62-64; chm Nomin Mus Div 69); Me LA (pres 55-56; chm Exhib Com 55-56); NELA (Nomin Com 56-57, Hospitality Com 56-57); NYLib Club (Coun 59-67, pres 65-66; chm Arts Com 58-60); NyLA. 10: Grolier Club; Metro Mus of Art Employees Assn; Archons of Colophon; St John's Univ Congress; Dir H W Wilson Com 65-; Lib of Presidential Papaers, Nat Bd 67-; NY State Coun on the Arts; Metro Ref and Res Lib Agency; Archives of Amer Art; Lectr Sch of Lib Ser, Colu mbia U 67-68; Consul: Amer Heritage Publ Co. 65-68; John Wiley & Sons, 66-; Dir Huguenot YMCA, New Rochelle NY 68-; Mem Harvard U Fine Arts Vis Com 67-. 12: "Early Printers and Printing in Europe and the United States; the Library of Edwin Arlington Robinson" (59); Co-auth "Fitzgerald's Rubaiyat," Centennial Ed (59); Ed "Bulletin" MeLA (53-56). 13: Yes. 14: Admin, ref, rare bks. 15: The H W Wilson Co, 950 University ave, Bronx Ny 10452.

HUMPHRY, JOHN AMES. b Springfield Mass 21 Jl 16. 4: Elizabeth Daniell Humphr y. 5: Harvard 35-39 (Econ) AB 42-43; Columbia 40-41 BSLS. 07: Gen asst Harvard Col Lib 39-40, 41-44; Gen asst ref dept NY Pub Lib 40-41; Field serv consul Off of Chief of Naval Operations, Operations Res Gp, Off of Sci Res & Devel, Wash DC 44-46; Dir of bk proc Enoch Pratt Free Lib, Baltimore 46-48; Dir Springfield Lib & Museums Assn, Springfield Mass 48-64, Exec Dir 60-64; Dir Brooklyn Pub Lib 64-67 ; Asst commsner for libs NY St Educ Dept, Albany 67-. 8: Dir, Forest Press, Lake Placid NY 65-; Adv com Div of Lib Sci SoConn State Col 63-; Spec consul to the Operations Eval Group, Off of the Chief of Naval Operations, DOD 51-53; Vis lectr in lib sci Amer Internat Col 59-61; Assoc in Pub Lib Admin Simmons Col 52-54; Adv com "Who's Who in Library Service," 4th ed, 65-66; Consul for sch, col, pub, & state libs; Fed Elem & Second Educ Act 65: Adv com NY State Educ Dept, Title II, 65; Adv com NY City Bd of Educ, Title I, II, III, 65; Steering Com Nat Lib Week, 66; Adv Coun, Off Urban Lib Res, Wayne StateU 68 -. 9: ALA (Coun 60-64, chm Memb Com for NE 58-64; Com on NY Conf 66); -RTSD (Bd Dirs 60-64); -AASchL (pres 68-69); CLR (Bd Dirs 68-); NELA (Bd Dirs 53-54); Mass Bd of Lib Commsnrs 57-64; MassLA (pres 57-64); Mass Reg Pub Lib System (chm Exec & Coord Coms 60-64); NYLA (Legis Com 64-); NY Metro Ref & Res Lib Agency (Bd of Trustees 64-); NY Lib Club. 10: Melvil Dui Chowder & Marching Assn; Archons of Colophon; W Mass Lib Club. 12: "Library Cooperation; The Brown University Study of University-School-Community Library Coordination in the State of Rhode Island" (63); "Library Service in Louisiana" (68). 13: Yes. 14: Admin, research. 15: NY State Educ Dept, Albany NY 12224.

HUNENKO, MARIA (PSHENICHNY). b Ukraine 1 S 36. 4: Alexander Hunenko. 5: UMinn 56-60 (Fr) BA, 61-62 (LS) MA. 6: Ukrainian, Russian, Fr, Sp, Ger, Ital. 7: Descr catlgr Yale U Lib 62-63; Catlgr UMinn Lib (Minneapolis) 64-66; Subjt catlgr Yale U Lib 69-. 9: ALA. 14: Catlg. 15: 544 Whitney ave, New Haven Ct 06511.

HUNG, RUTH LI-YU. b Taipei Taiwan China 13 Mr 38. 5: Taiwan NormalU 56 (Eng) BA; SUNY (Albany) 67 MLS. 6: Chinese. 7: Tchr High Sch of Taiwan NormalU 60-66; Med lib asst Episcopal Hosp, Phila 67; Libn Coppin State Col 69-. 14: Catlg. 15: 1098 Cameron rd, Baltimore Md 21212.

HUNGERFORD, ANTHOS (FARAH). b Flint Mich 13 O 21. 4: Leonard R Hungerford Jr. 5: UMich 41-43 (Eng Lit) AB, 44-45 ABLS. 6: Fr, Ger. 7: Circ asst Northwestern U Deering Lib 45-46; Circ asst Flint(Mich) Pub Lib 46-48; Engnr Lib asst UMich 48-49; Catlgr UMich Flint Col Lib 58-60; Ref libn Chas Stewart Mott Lib, Flint Mich 61-68; Med Libn Hurley Hosp, Flint Mich 68-. 9: SLA. 15: Hurley Hospital Med Lib, Flint Mi 48502.

HUNSBERGER, LOUISE. b S Bend Ind 5 My 26. 5: Ind U 43-48 (Soc Studies) BS, summers 50-53 (LS) MA. 7: Various S Bend Pub Lib, S Bend Ind 43-45, summers 46-48; Asst Educ Lib UIll(Urbana) summer 49; Ref libn Syracuse U summers 54, 56; Libn Washington High Sch, S Bend Ind 48-. 9: NEA; Ind State Tchrs Assn; Ind State Libns Assn. 10: Pi Lambda Theta; YWCA; AAUW. 15: 846 S 26th st, South Bend Ind 46615.

HUNSBERGER, WILLARD D(ETWEILER). b Souderton Penn 19 Jl 26. 4: Ann Raber. 5: Goshen Col 46-50 (Soc Sci) BA; Temple 53-55 (Educ) M Ed; Fla State U 57-59 (LS) MA. 7: Tchr Deep Run Valley Pub Schs, Blooming Glen Penn 51-55; Tchr Geo Washington High Sch, Agana Guam 55-57; Ref libn UFla Lib 58-59; Head Libn Geo Washington High Sch, Agana Guam 59-63; Instr Lib Sci Col of Guam 62-63; Asst Prof Lib Sci Tex Woman's U 63-64; Dir of Lib Ind Inst of Tech 64-68; Hd libn Indiana-Purdue Reg Campus Lib, Ft Wayne In d 68-. 09: Guam Educ Assn (v-pres 62-63). 12: "Franconia Mennonites and War" (51). 14: Ref, admin. 15: 1833 Embassy dr, Ft Wayne In 46806.

HUNSUCKER, DAVID LEE. b Kannapolis NC 20 Ag 26. 5: Lenoir Rhyne Col 46-50 (Bus Admin) AB; Appalachian State Tchrs Col summers 54-58 (Educ) MA; UNC summers 59-62 (MSLS). 06: Sp. 7: Tchr Mt Holly Pub Schs, Mt Holly NC 54-55; Tchr Gastonia City Schs, Gastonia NC 55-58; Libn Gastonia City Schs, Gastonia NC 58-62; Assoc Sch lib supv State Dept of Pub Instr, Raleigh NC 62-64, Instrl materials supv 64-; Sch lib supv 65-68, libn Gaston Col, Dallas NC 68-. 9: ALA; (Standards Com); NEA-DAVI; SELA; NCLA (Lib Resources Com); NCEA . 10: Beta Phi Mu; Phi Delta Kappa; Alpha Psi Omega. 14: Ref. 15: Gaston Col, Dallas Nc 28034.

HUNT, ANNICE (ELIZABETH). b Palmette F&a 30 Mr 34. 5: Fla State U 52-54, 62-63 (LS); Abilene Christian Col 58-61 (Educ, Soc Studies) BS; Jones Col 68 (Computer Tech). 7: Bkkeeper Bank of Palmetto Fla 54-58; Tchr Fla Col Acad, Temple Terrace Fla 61-62; Period dept libn Nat Bur of Standards, Wash DC 63-65; Catlg dept libn Defense Documentation Ctr, Alexandria Va 65-67; Catlg dept libn Fla State Bd of Health, Jacksonville Fla 67-. 9: ALA; MedLA. 10: Duval Co (Fla) Mental Health Assn; Soc for programmed Instr. 14: Catlg, period. 15: 2741 Stardust ct, Jacksonville Fl 32211.

HUNT, DONALD HAROLD. b Detroit 14 Ja 20. 5: Mich State 40-41 (Eng); Wayne State U 46-50 (Eng) BA & MA; UMich 51-52 MALS; U of the Americas (Mexico) 49 (Span). 6: Sp, Fr. 7: (1st Lt) Adjutant & Personnel Off US Army 41-45; Instr Wayne State U 50-51; Stack curator UMich Gen Lib (Ann Arbor) 52-53; Br libn Brooklyn Pub Lib 53-55, Admin asst 55-57; Dir Franklin Sq Pub Lib, Franklin Sq NY 57-59; Deputy dir Nassau Lib System, Hempstead NY 59-62; Lib career consul Grad Sch Lib Sci Drexel Inst of Tech 62-69; Deputy dir Free Lib of Phila 69-. 8: Asst Prof in Lib Sci Drexel Inst ; Cou sul Statewide Recr Prog, Wis, Ill, Mich, NE. 9: ALA; -LAD (chm Off for Recr); -ALTA (v-chm Prog Com); Amer Personnel & Guidance Assn; CathLA (chm Pub Rel Com); Coun Nat Lib Assns (chm Recr Com); LPRC; PennLA (pres 68-69). 10: Melvil Dui Marching & Chowder Soc; Philobiblon Club; Booksellers League; Jt Com on Lib Careers. 12: Ed "Drexel Library Quarterly"; past ed "Odds & Book Ends" (Nassau Co NY). 13: Yes. 14: Recruitment, admin, pub rels, lib educ. 15: 1530 Locust st, Phila Pa 19102.

HUNT, DONALD R. b Richmond Ind 5 N 21. 4: Virginia Clark . 5: UCincinnati 40-42 (Engnr); UColo 46-51 (European Hist) BA, MA; Stanford 51-53 (European Hist); UMich 53-54 MALS. 6: Fr. 7: US Naval Air Corps 43-46; Lib asst Hoover Lib Stanford U 51-53; Grad asst dept of hist Stanford U 52-53; Lib asst Natural Resources & Sci Lib 53-54; Asst libn Soc Sci Div Wash State U 54-55; Ore State U: Asst ref lib Asst Prof 55-57, Head ref dept 57-62, Asst Prof 57-61, Assoc Prof 61-, Head of pub serv Assoc Prof asst libn 62-65; Assoc libn Prof 65-. 9: ALA; OreLA; PNLA. 10: AAUP; Phi Kappa Phi. 13: Yes. 14: Admin, ref, pub serv. 15: Oregon State U Lib, Corvallis Or 97331.

HUNT, FLORINE ELIZABETH. b Richmond Va 11 Ag 28. 5: Richmond Prof Inst of the Col of William & Mary 45-49 (Soc Sci) BS; West Res 49-50 (Soc Case Wk); Rutgers 54-55 (LS) MS. 6: Fr. 7: Lib aide Richmond Pub Lib, Richmond Va summers 45-49; Child welfare casewker Soc Serv Bureau, Norfolk Va 50-52; Jr libn Free Pub Lib, Trenton NJ 52-55; Pub Serv Electric & Gas Co, Newark NJ: Jr asst libn 55-59, Sr asst libn 59, Libn 59-. 9: ALA; SLA (chm Nom Com, Pub Utilities Sect 60-61);-NJ Chap : Several offs & Comm chmnships 58- NJLA. 10: Trinity Cathedral (Trenton): Women of Trinity (Altar Guild); Rutgers Grad Sch Lib Serv Alumni Assn; NAACP; Trenton Coun on Human Rels. 12: "Public Utilities Information Sources" (65). 14: Admin, spec libs. 15: Room 8236 80 Park pl, N

HUNT, FRANCES K(ATHARINE). b Paoli Penn 21 Ja 06. 5: Drexel 24-25 (LS) Certif. 6: Fr, Lat, Ger. 7: Catlgr Free Lib, Phila 25-26; Catlgr Presbyterian Hist Soc, Phila 28-34; Supv Union Lib Catlg, Phila 36; Catlgr Villanova U 37-44; Catlgr Temple U 44-. 9: ALA; Phila Reg Catlgrs Assn. 14: Catlg. 15: 216 Wayne ave, Narberth Pa 19072.

HUNT, GERTRUDE COUSENS. b Portland Me 13 D 16. 4: Thomas Chapman Hunt. 5: Wellesley 33-37 (Hist of Art) BA; Columbia 37-38 BS in LS; USoCal MS in LS. 6: Ger, Fr, Sp. 7: Libn NY Pub Lib 37-39; Libn Princeton U Lib 39-40; Child libn Oakland Pub Lib, Oakland Pub Lib, Oakland Cal 44-46; Relief admin Amer Friends Serv Com, Germany 46-47; Pasadena Pub Lib Child libn, Pasadena Cal 49-50, Br libn 50-56; Libn Arcadia high Sch, Arcadia Cal 56-67; Lib supv Colegio Americano de Guatemala 68-. 8: Consul for libs Colegio Americano de Guatemala Fall 68. 9: CalLA (chm Childrens & YP Sect). 10: Sierra Club. 14: Bk selection. 15: Colegio Americano de Guatemala Apartado postal 83, Guatemala Central America.

HUNT, HANNAH. b Chicago 27 F 03. 5: Earlham Col 27 BA; West Res 31 BS in LS, 55 MS in LS. 7: Storyteller Cleveland Pub Lib 21-23; Elem sch libn Dist 76 schs, Evanston Ill 31-34; Asst to dir wk with schs, child libn sch lib Lakewood Pub Lib, Lakewood Ohio 34-44; Young adult libn Lib of Hawaii, Honolulu 44-48; Young adult libn Rockford Pub Lib, Rockford Ill 49-51; Visiting Prof Japan Lib Sch, Keio U (Tokyo) 51-52; Young adult spec ALA Amer Heritage Proj, Chicago 52-54; Asst Prof Sch of Lib Sci West Res U 54-60, Assoc Prof 61-67, Assoc Prof Emeritus 67-. 8: Amer Friends Serv Com in France 27-28; Instr Parents Course in Child Lit Los Angeles Pub Lib 48; Visiting Prof Dept of Libnship West Mich U summers 50, 51. 9: ALA- YASD (pres 61); OhioLA; OhioASchL. 10: AAUP. 13: Yes. 14: Pub lib wk with child & ya. 15: 1293 French ave, Lakewood Oh 44107.

HUNT, JAMES ROBERT. b Brownsville Penn 5 My 25. 4: Gloria Beth Solli. 5: UDetroit 46-51 (Philos) PhB, 51-55 (Pol Sci) MA; UMich 55-59 MALS. 6: Fr. 7: USAF Radar Spec (S/Sgt) 43-46; Co-manager Madonna Bkshop, Detroit 51-56; Wayne Co Lib, Wayne Mich: Bkmob libn 56-57, Admin asst 57-59, Hd central serv 59-62; Asst state libn Mich State Lib , Lansing 62-64; State Libn Hawaii State Lib 64-. 8: Mem Lib Tech Com Lansing Commun Col, Lansing Mich; Chm Governor's Com on State Lib Resources, Hawaii 64 -; Mem , Adv Bd Sch of Lib Studies UHawaii, 68- ; Mem, Accred Team, West Assn of Schs n Cols, Wake Island Sch 68; Adv Com, Lib Technicians ROG, Leonard Commun Col, Oahu 68-. 09: ALA (life mem, Coun 64-68); -RTSD (Reg Proc Com 63-67; Tech Serv Cost Com 66-); MichLA (chm &/or mem5coms 61-67); HawaiiLA. 10: Cath Soc Serv Adv Bd, Honolulu; Nat Multiple Sclerosis Soc Bd of Dirs, Honolulu Chap; Amer Soc Pub Admin. 11: Pud Admin of The Year, Amer Soc Pub Admin 67; Commendation by Hawaii House of Rep 67; Commendation By Pacific & Asian Affairs Coun 67. 13: Yes. 14: Admin, P pub serv. 15: Office of Lib Serv, P O Box 23 60 Honolulu Hi 96804.

HUNT, MARY ALICE. b Lima Ohio 14 Ap 28. 5: Fla State U 46-50 (Journalism) AB, 52-53 (LS) MA. 6: Sp. 7: Photographer engraver "Tallahassee Democrat" Tallahassee Fla 51-52; Lib Sch Fla State U; Grad asst 52-53, Exec sec 53-55, Libn & Instr materials center 55-58, Instr 57-59; Fla State U; Asst Prof A-v educ Sch of Educ 59-62, Asst Prof Art Educ & Constructive Design 62-, Asst libn USch 62-66; Asst Prof Sch of Lib Sci Fla StateU 66-. 8: Co nsul Escambia Co Sch System on visual aids prod, pre-sch wkshops 65; Consul Gadsden Co Sch System wkshops 61; state adv com on Title III NDEA rep the Fla State U Sch of Educ 63, 64; Asst Prof ext courses through the state for Fla Inst for Continuing U Studies yearly Consul No Fla Jr Col Proj; T aylor Co Schs 68, 69; Consul Pre-sch Wkshop, Okaloosa Co Sch System 68. 9: NEA; SELA; FlaLA (Exec Bd, Publ Com); FlaEA; FlaASchL; Fla A-V Assn. 10: Kappa Delta Pi; Beta Phi Mu. 12: Ed "Florida Libraries" (61-67); f Fla state rep "Southeastern Librarian" (63-). 13: Yes. 14: A-v educ, sch libs, instr materials, publ rels. 15: 1603 Kolopakin Nene, Tallahassee Fl 32301.

HUNT, MARY C. b Arlington Minn 15 Ag 04. 5: Col of St Catherine 22-26 (Lat, LS) AB; Creighton U 32-34. 06: Lat, Fr, Ger, Sp. 7: Tchr & libn Stratford High Sch, Stratford SD 26-27; Libn Creighton Prep Sch, Omaha 28-38; Libn Creighton U 38-. 9: CathLA; NebLA. 10: Phi Delta Gamma. 13: Yes. 14: Ref. 15: 507 N 28th ave, Omaha Nb 68131.

HUNT, MARY JANE (O'DONNELL). b Bronx NY 6 Ja 43. 4: John Patrick Hunt. 5: Molloy Catholic Col 60-64 (Eng) BA; St John's U 65-67 MLS. 7: Trainee Oceanside Free Lib, oceanside NY 64-67, Jr libn 67-69, Y-a libn 69-. 9: ALA. 10: St John's U & Lib Alum Assn. 14: Ya, ref. 15: 93-03 - 214 pl, Queens Village NY 11428.

HUNT, MARY. b Kirksville Mo 15 Ap 12. 4: Lee Hunt. 5: UWichita 32 (Fr) BA; State U Iowa 35 (Speech) MA; Columbia 46 (LS) BS. 6: Fr. 7: Ref asst DesMoines (Iowa) Pub Lib 41-42; Ref asst Wichita City Lib, Kan 43-44; Asst spec collections Columbia U Libs 44-45; Asst Rye(NY) Free Reading Room 46-47; Libn NY- Phoenix Sch of Design, NYC 47-49; Asst libn circ dept Columbia U Libs 49-51, Catlgr catlg div 58-66, Asst hd gen catlg 66-69, hd gen catlg sect 69-. 9: ALA, NY Lib Club NY Tech, Serv, Libns. 14: Catlg, ref. 15: 245 W 107th s t, New York Ny 10025.

HUNT, RICHARD G(ABRIEL). b Baltimore 21 S 09. 4: Katherine Reed. 5: Johns Hopkins 27-30 AB, 30-33, 34 (Eng)

MA; Drexel 38-39 (LS) BS. 6: Fr. 7: Stack attendant LC 39-40; Libn Naval Gun Factory, Wash DC 40-45; DC Pub Lib: 1st asst acquis 45-47, Asst curator Washingtoniana 47-49, Asst bus div 49, Act br libn 49-50, 1st asst sociol div 50-56, Chief lit div 56-67, Asst coord adult serv 67-. 9: ALA; DCLA. 15: 327 Paddington rd, Baltimore Md 21212.

HUNT, ROGER W. b Fennville Mich 12 Jl 19. 4: June Marsh. 5: AndrewsU 47-51 (Relig) BA; Peabody Col 47 MLS. 7: US Army 41-46; Sales rep Home Health Educ Serv 52-57; Catlg libn AndrewsU Liv 65-. 14: Catlg. 15: Box 140 Andrews Station, Berrien Springs Mi 49104.

HUNT, SUELLYN (MARY). b Rockville Center NY 9 My 42. 5: SUC (Geneseo) 60-64 (LS) BS; Syracuse 67-69 MSLS. 6: Ger. 7: Lib clk Massapequa Pub Lib, Massapequa NY summers 61-62, 64, Jr libn 63; Y-a & asst br libn Cleveland Pub Lib, Cleveland Ohio 64-66, Asst br libn 66-67; Libn trainee VA Hosp, Syracuse NY 68; Bkmob libn Suffolk Co Pub Lib Syst, bellport NY 68; Grad asst Syracuse U Sch of Lib Sci 68-69. 8: Com Pleasurable Reading of the 1960's for Young Adults, Cleveland Pub Lib 65; Chm Com on Significant Bks 64-65, Cleveland Pub Lib (66); Chm Res Team on Curriculum for Grad Study in Info Transfer (68); Res Team on Career Recognition & Recruiting for Info Sci (69); Res Team on Computers & Pattern Recognition (69). 9: A;A CathLA; NYLA. 14: Pub serv, ref, readers adv, commun serv, admin. 15: 47 McKinley st, Massapequa Park NY 11762.

HUNTER, CAROLYN PAUL. b Raleigh NC 30 My 34. 5: Mars Hill 52-54 AA; Wake Forest 54-56 (Eng, Fr) BA; UNC 57-59 MSLS. 6: Fr. 7: Ref asst Pub Lib of Charlotte & Mecklenburg co, Charlotte NC 64-. 9: ALA; SELA; NCLA; MecklenburgLA. 14: Ref. 15: Pub Lib of Charlotte & Mecklenburg County, Charlotte NC 28202.

HUNTER, DAVID A. b Honolulu 26 Jl 26. 5: Pasadena City Col 46-48 (Span, Fr) AA; UCal(Berkeley) 48-50 (Hist) AB; Fresno State Col 54-55 (Soc Sci, Educ); UWash 55-56 MLS; State of California Tchg Credentials: Jr Col, Libnship. 6: Sp, Fr, Ital. 7: US Marine Corps Personnel Admin (Pfc) 51-53; Asst educ libn San Jose State Col 56-57, Asst ref libn 57-60; Chief Libn Cal Maritime Acad, Vallejo Cal 60-68; Libn Jr High San Francisco Unified Sch Dist, San Francisco 68; Ref Libn Cal Sect Cal State Lib 69-. 10: Cal State Employees' Assn; Pi Gamma Mu; Beta Phi Mu. 14: Ref. 15: 1500 7th st apt 3-0, Sacramento Ca 95814.

HUNTER, DORIS A. b Hartford Conn 24 Ag 20. 5: UPenn 38-42 (Eng) AB; Trinity Col Hartford Conn 42-43 (Educ) Certif; Columbia 54-55 MSLS, 56 (Short Story Writing) Certif. 6: Fr. 7: Info asst US Info Serv, Calcutta, India & Tangier, Morocco 50-53; Libn Brooklyn Pub Lib 55-56; US Army Spec Serv; Field libn France & Germany 56-60, Depot libn Orleans France 61, Ref libn Heidelberg Germany 62-64, Staff libn, Hawaii 64-68; Staff libn Korea 68-. 8: Libn Career Prog Coord; Hawaii 67-68, Korea 68-; Panel mem Civil Serv Examrs, Hawaii 67-68. 9: ALA; HawaiiLA. 14: Ref. 15: 14 W Hill dr, W Hartford Conn 06119.

HUNTER, ELAINE (HOWE). b Worcester Mass 20 Mr 12. 4: John F Hunter. 5: State Tchrs Col(Bridgewater Mass) 29-33 (Educ) BS in Educ; USoCal 46-48 BS in LS. 6: Fr, Sp. 7: Libn Pub Lib, Weston Mass 39-44; Club dir Amer Red Cross, New Caledonia & Japan 44-48; Br libn Niles Br Lib, Niles Cal 48-50; Libn Mather Air Force Base, Cal 50-53; Sr libn USoCal Med Sch Lib 53-55; Libn 7546th Support Sq, Molesworth Eng 55-57; Libn 81st Tac Ftr Wg, Bentwaters Eng 57-64; Chief Libn US Army Aviation Center, Ft Rucker Ala 64-66; Base libn USAF: Luke AFB, Ariz 66-68, Seville Spain 68-. 9: ALA; CalLA; MassLA. 14: Serv to mil commun. 15: 2945 NW 32d st, Oklahoma City Ok 73112.

HUNTER, FRANCES LEE GWALTNEY. b Smith Co Tenn 18 F 23. 4: William M Hunter. 5: Tenn TechU 41-43 (Bus Educ); Peabody Col 46-47 (Bus Educ, Hist) BS; Middle Tenn StateU 64-65 (Educ) MA; Peabody Col summer 66, 67 (LS). 07: Sec US Pub Health Serv, Wash DC 44-46; Bus tchr: Sumner Co, Portland Tenn 47-58, Maury Co, Columbia Tenn 58-64; Libn Middle Tenn StateU 65-. 9: NEA; SELA; TennLA; TennEA; Middle TennEA. 10: Delta Kappa gamma; AAUW; Dames Club of Middle TennU; Delta Zeta; Woman's Club of Murfreesboro. 14: Ref, circ. 15: 1106 Whitehall rd, Murfreesboro Tn 37130.

HUNTER, GEORGE (H). b Coeur d'Alene Ida 9 F 21. 4: Joan Mary Pinhorn. 5: West Wash Col of Educ 39-41 (Arts & Sci); UWash 41-42, 46-48 (Far East) BA, 49-50 BALS, 60-62 (Russian Hist) MA. 7: US Marine Corps Radar tech (Cpl) 42-46; Ref libn Cal State Polytech 50-51, Asst catlgr 51-53; Catlg libn UOtago Med Lib (Dunedin New Zealand) 54-57; Documents libn Ore State Col 57-58; Sci libn Ida State Col 58-60; Med libn UVt 62-. 9: MedLA (Program com 66; Reg chm NEgp 68-69); SLA. 14: Med lib admin, catlg, acquis. 15: Coon Hill rd, Colchester Vt 05401.

HUNTER, JAMES H. b Lamar Col 30 D 24. 4: Wilma Bruns. 5: Lamar Jr Col 42-43; UDenver 46-48 (Sociol) BA, 49-58 (Educ) MA, 63-65 (LS) MA. 7: Tchr Denver Pub Schs, Smedly 48-55, Libn 56-58; Libn Sabin Sch, Denver 58-68; Libn Kennedy High Sch, Denver 68-. 9: NEA; CalEA; DCTA. 14: Sch libs, child bks. 15: 10300 W Montgomery ave, Littleton Co 80120.

HUNTER, LORA C. b Little Rock Ark 28 Jl 26. 4: Robert A Hunter. 5: Little Rock Jr Col 42-44; Ouachita Col 44-46 BA; Fla State U 52 (LS) MA. 7: Asst libn Ouachita Col 46-47; Bus tchr Altha High Sch, Altha Fla 47-49; Asst libn-bus tchr Mainland High Sch, Daytona Beach Fla 49-52; Asst libn Mainland Jr-Sr High Sch, Daytona Beach Fla 52-55; Libn Mainland High Sch, Daytona Beach Fla 55-61; Libn Corbin Ave Elem Sch, Ormond Beach Fla 61-62; Lib Sch Instr UFla summers 60-62; Consul Lib Serv State Dept of Educ, Tallahassee Fla 62-63; Libn Bear Creek & Blanton Elem Schs, St Petersburg Fla 63-64; Libn Boca Ciega High Sch, St Petersburg Fla 64-65; Libn St Petersburg Col, Clearwater Campus 65-. 8: Exec dir Fla Nat Lib Week 66-67. 9: FlaLA (sec 62-63); FlaEA (Dist dir Classroom Tchrs Dept 61-62); FlaASchL (pres 59-60, Legis chm 60-61). 13: Yes. 14: A-v, catlg. 15: 4500 Ninth ave N, St Petersburg Fl 33713.

HUNTER, M EDWARD. b Ft Wayne Ind 25 O 30. 4: Melva Joyce Doxtater. 5: Ind U 49-53 (Ger) AB; Chicago 53-59 (Lit, Theol) BD, MA; Simmons summers 61-64 MS. 6: Ger, Gk, Hebrew. 7: Asst libn UChicago Divinity Sch 59-60; Asst libn Methodist Theol Sch (Delaware Ohio) 60-63; Libn Bexley Hall Kenyon Col 63-6 8; Libn Methodist Theol Sch, Delaware Ohio 68-. 09: ATheolLA. 14: Rare bks, catlg. 15: 24 Darlington rd, Delaware Oh 43015.

HUNTER, MARGARET ELIZABETH (UPJOHN). b Salem Ore 19 Ag 18. 4: Lloyd L Hunter. 5/ willamette U 36-39 (Fr) BA; UCal 40-41 Certif of Libnship. 6: Fr, Sp. 7: Stud helper Willamette U 37-39; Asst ref libn Ore State Lib 41-43; Asst libn US Tech Train Lib Navy Pier US Navy, Chicago 43-45; Asst libn US Naval Hosp, Brooklyn NY 45-46; Head of circ Willamette U 60; Ore State Lib; Legis ref libn 60-61, Soc sci libn 61-63, Head of ref & asst head of readers servs & govtl res libn 63-; Libn Ore State Dept of Educ 65-66; Sch libn NSalem High Sch 66-. 9: OreSchL; Ore Instr Materials Assn. 14: Ref; sch lib wk; educ. 15: 715 McGil christ SE, Salem Or 97302.

HUNTER, MARY CECELIA. b Detroit 24 Ja 08. 5: Col of the City of Detroit 25-29 (Eng) AB; Columbia 38-42 AB in LS. 7: Detroit Pub Lib 29-, Chief of dept of Jessie Chase Br 52-. 9: ALA; AEAUSA; MichLA ; CathLA. 10: Delta Kappa Gamma; Soroptimist Club. 15: 18444 Glastonbury rd, Detroit Mi 48219.

HUNTER, (MARY) DARLENE. b Scioto Co Ohio 8 Mr 39. 5: Ohio State U 56-60 (Eng) BS in Ed; Ohio U 61-62; West Res 62-64 MS in LS. 7: Eng tchr Clay Twp High Sch, Scioto Co Ohio 60-63; Eng tchr W Portsmouth High Sch, Scioto Co Ohio 63; Asst libn Linden-McKinley High Sch, Columbus Ohio 64-65; Head Libn Walnut-Ridge Jr-Sr High Sch, Columbus Ohio 65-; Lib Sci tchr Marshall U summer 67. 9: NEA; OhioEA; OhioASchL. 10: LWV; Beta Phi Mu; Delta Kappa Gamma. 15: 1150 Sunset st, Portsmouth Oh 45662.

HUNTER, SUZANNE. b Salt Lake City 5 F 43. 5: UUtah 61-64 (Eng) BA; UCal (Berkeley) 64-65 MLS. 6: Ger, Fr. 7: Asst ref libn UUtah 6 5-66; SFPL hist & soc sci 66-67; San Mateo Pub Lib 68-. 14: Ref, rare bks. 15: P O Box 5493, San Mateo Ca 94402.

HUNTLEY, WILLIAM ROBERT. b Spindale NC 7 Ap 28. 4: Louise Self. 5: Brevard Col 47-49 9lang) AA; UNC 49-52 (Lang) AB; CatholicU 58-64 (LS). 6: Sp, Fr, Ital, Portu, Ger. 7: Stud lab mgr Lang Lab UNC 49-52; Soldier US Army 52-54; Stock clk Guy Curran & Co, Wash DC 54-55; Stock clk DC Air Nat Guard 55-57; Ed asst Nat Union Catlg Div LC 59-60; Preliminary catlgr Desc Catlg Div LC 57-59, Ser catlgr 60-61, Supv of searching 61-62, Asst hd preliminary 62-63, Hd preliminary catlg sect 63-. 14: Catlg, tech processes. 15: 5411 Border dr, Oxon Hill Md 20022.

HURD, HELLEN (JOHNS). b Union Co Ky 2 My 32. 4: James D Hurd. 5: West Ky State Col 50-54 (LS) AB. 7: Catlgr Ky Lib Ext Div, Frankfort Ky 54-58; Catlgr Owensboro Pub Lib, Owensboro Ky 58-59; Catlgr & circ libn Ky Wesleyan Col 59-60; Assoc reg libn Audubon Region, Owensboro Ky 60-. 9: KyLA (sec-treas Pub Lib Sect 64-65); SELA. 10: Friends of Ky Libs. 14: Tech proc, ref. 15: 1220 Woodmere lane, Owensboro Ky 42301.

HURKETT, JACK W. 5: Alice Lee Marston. 7: Armorer (Cpl) USAAF 8th Air Force 43-45; Head Libn The Henry Carter Hull Lib Inc, Clinton Conn 59-62; Dir Westerly Pub Lib, Westerly RI 62-67; Dir S C Interrelated Lib Syst, Westerly RI 62-67; Dir Nioga Lib Syst, Niagara Falls NY 68-. 8: Exec dir, Nat Lib Week, RI, 64. 9: ALA (Memb Chm for RI 64-67); ConnLA (Exec Com 62; chm Adult Serv Div 62); RILA (Com on Govt Rel 62-65, chm 65); NELA (Exhib Com 64). 10: Riverdale Gardens Assn. 14: Lib admin. 15: Nioga Lib System, 2510 Seneca ave, Niagara Falls NY 14305.

HURLBUTT, HELEN (MARIE). b Beaman Iowa 8 O 07. 5: Grinnell Col 25-27; State U of Iowa 28-30 (Eng) BA; Columbia 31-32 (LS) BS, 41-42 (LS) MS. 7: Clerical asst State U Iowa Libs (Iowa City) 29-31; Ser catlgr Iowa State U Lib (Ames) 32-48; Libn pub lib, Marshalltown Iowa 48-64; Catlgr pub lib, Cedar Rapids Iowa 64-. 9: ALA; IowaLA. 15: Cedar Rapids Pub Lib, Cedar Rapids Ia 52401.

HURLEY, FRANCES (KEMP). b Decatur Co Iowa 28 F 09. 4: Frank H Hurley. 5: Drake U 26-29 (Fr) BA; Columbia 31-32 (LS) BS, 41 (LS) MS. 6: Fr. 7: Tchr Eng & Lat Jr High Sch, Manning Iowa 29-31; Asst libn Sarah Lawrence Col 32-41; Libn Lake Erie Col 41-44; Libn Reed Col 44-51; Lib consul Tchrs Col Columbia U 51-54; Libn Douglass Rutgers State U 54-61; Lecturer West Res U Sch of Lib Sci 61-66; Lecturer Rutgers U Grad Sch of Lib Serv summers 67-69. 9: ALA. 10: LWV; Friends of Lib, Cleveland Heights, Bd mem music orgs; Phi Beta Kappa. 13: Yes. 14: Admin, ref, readers adv, tchg. 15: 2472 Overlook rd, Cleveland Heights Oh 44106.

HURLEY, MARIE V. b Elmira NY 25 D 10. 5: Elmira Col 28-32 (Hist, Fr) BS; Columbia 32-33 BSLS. 7: Sch & ref libn NY Pub Lib 33-40, Asst br libn 40-42; Libn The Riverdale Neighborhood & Lib Assn 42-46; Asst libn US Info Lib, Sydney Australia 46-47; Libn The So Euclid-Lyndhurst (Ohio) Pub Lib 48-52; Br libn The S Euclid Reg Br, Cuyahoga Co Ohio 52-54; Asst dir The Ferguson Lib, Stamford Conn 54-65, Dir 65-. 8: Consul Pub Lib of New S Wales Australia 47. 9: ALA; NELA; ConnLA (pres 67-68); LPRC. 10: Women's Nat Bk Assn; Stamford Forum for World Affairs; Stamford-Darien Mental Health Assn; Columbia U Lib Sch Alum Assn . 15: 96 Broad st, Stamford Ct 06901.

HURLEY, RICHARD JAMES. b Little Falls NY 21 Jl 06. 4: Cecile E Reusch. 5: NY State Lib Sch summer 26 Certif; UMich 28-32 BA; Columbia 33-34 BSLS; Columbia Tchrs Col 34-36 AM; UMich 39-41 AMLS. 7: Asst libn Little Falls Pub Lib, Little Falls NY 25-28; Sch libn pub schs, Roslyn LI NY 34-39; Visiting Prof State Tchrs Col (Statesboro Ga) summer 38; Libn State Tchrs Col (Kutztown Penn) 39; Asst Prof Dept of Lib Sci Catholic U 39-45; Div libn in ed UNeb 45-47; Asst Prof Dept of Lib Sci UMich 47-50; Visiting Prof Lib Sch Peabody Col summer 50; Asst Prof Dept of Lib Sci Catholic U 51-57; Supv of Lib Fairfax Co Bd of Educ 57-6 8; Dir of media Hayfield High Sch Fairfax Va, 68-. 8: Ed Sch Catlgs, Doubleday & Co, 30-; Sel Com, Teen Age Book Club, Arrow Book Club, Scholastic Co, 55-; Research Asst Lib Serv Br, US Off of Educ, 54; Lect in lib sci, Catholic U, 62-68; Le ctr Ext Div UVa 68-. 9: ALA (Legis Chm, Va); NEA; CathLA (past pres); VaLA; VaEA; Child Bk Guild, Wash DC (past pres). 10: Phi Delta Kappa; Beta Phi Mu. 12: "Key to Out-of-Doors" (38); "Campfire Tonight" (40); "Your Library" (56); "Trends and Issues in Catholic Education" Sas (68). 13: Yes. 14: Sch libnship. 15: Fairfax Co Sch Bd, Fairfax Va 22030.

HURSON, FRANCES (GORHAM). b Knoxville Tenn 25 S 12. 4: Frank Joseph Hurson. 5: Georgetown Visitation Jr Col 30-32; Col of St Elizabeth (Convent NJ) 32-34 (Eng) AB; Indiana U (LS). 7: Lab tech Killian Research Labs, NYC 35-41; Libn (hd) Carnegie Pub Lib, Wash Ind 65-. 8: Trustee, Carnegie Pub Lib, Wash Ind 49-64. 9: ALA; IndLA (Legisl Com 67-; chm District V ann mting 66). 10: Amer Red Cross. 13: Yes. 14: Bk sel, admin. 15: 300 W Main st, Washington In 47501.

HURST, ELEANOR ANNE. b Albany Ga 14 Jl 26. 5: Ga Southwestern Col 43-44 (Educ) Normal Diploma; Ga State Col for Women summers 45-50 (Eng) BS in Ed; Emory 51-52 (LS) ML. 6: Sp. 7: Elem sch tchr Richland High Sch, Richland Ga 44-48; Elem sch tchr Schley Co High Sch, Ellaville Ga 48-49; High sch Eng tchr Butler High Sch, Butler Ga 50-51; Circ libn Stetson U 52-. 9: ALA; SELA; FlaLA. 10: AAUP; AAUW; UDC; Friends of the DeLand Pub Lib; Stetson U Women's Club. 14: Bibliog, adv wk, ref, interlib coop. 15: 202-1/2 N Woodland blvd, DeLand Fla 32720.

HURST, FRANCES (WEEKLEY). b Birmingham Ala. 5: UAla 37-41 (Eng) AB in Ed; Emory 44-45 AB in LS. 6: Fr. 7: Tchr Pub schs of Ala 41-44; Asst libn Tenn Valley Authority Wilson Dam 45-46; Circ libn & catlgr UAla 46-50; Tchr Talladega Co Pub Schs, Talladega Ala 50-52; Case wker Talladega Co Dept Pensions & Securities, Talladega Ala 52-54; Tchr Talladega & Talladega Co Schs, Talladega Ala 58-62; Catlgr UAla 62-69; Catlgr Jefferson State Jr Col 69-. 9: ALA; AlaLA; SELA. 10: Kap pa Delta Pi; Pi Tau Chi; Triangle. 14: Catlg, ref. 15: 2601 Carson rd, Birmingham Al 35215.

HURST, GENEVA (SNIPES). b 26 D 21. 4: Baxter Hurst. 5: Ark State Tchrs Col 40-42, 57-61 (Elem Educ) BSE; Peabody 62-65 MLS. 6: Sp. 7: Elem tchr Marion Co Ark 40-44; Elem tchr Cotter Akr 57-60; Libn, Flippin Ark 60-. 9: NEA; ArkLA. 14: Sch libs. 15: Rt B, Flippin Ak 72634.

HURST, JEAN McEWEN. b Decker Man Can 17 Jl 21. 5: Regina Col 39-40; USask 40-42 (Econ, Pol Sci) BA; Toronto 43-44 BLS, 53-56 MLS. 6: Fr, Ger. 7: Circ asst USask 42-43; Circ libn McMaster U(Ont) 44-45, Catlgr 45-. 9: CanLA; Ont LA. 14: Catlg. 15: Mills Mem Lib, McMaster Univ, Hamilton Ont Can.

HURST, PATRICIA (WITWER). b Danville Ill 18 S 23. 4: Robert Hurst. 5: UIll 41-45 (Chem) BS; USoCal 63-66 MSLS. 7: Chem Edwal Labs, Chicago 45-47; Patent dept asst corn Prods Refining Co, Chicago 47-49; Branch lib asst Ventura Co Lib, Ventura Cal 63-66, Sr libn 66-. 9: ALA; CalLA. 10: Beta Phi Mu; Ventura Co Employees Assn. 14: Ref. 15: 3550 Willlwick dr, Ventura Ca 93003.

HURST, VIRGINIA (FLENER). b Morgantown Ky 6 O 12. 5: Bethel Woman's Col 29-31 (Eng); West Ky Col 31-33 (Music) AB; Peabody 61-64 (LS) MA. 7: Tchr Butler Co Schs, Morgantown Ky 33-50; Libn Butler Co High Sch, Morgantown Ky 50-. 9: Ky Third Dist LA (past pres); Butler Co(Ky) EA (pres-elect). 10: Lioness Club. 15: Morgantown Ky 42261.

HUSBAND, BRYAN (ERIC). b Vancouver NC Can 10 Ag 35. 5: UBC 64 BLS, 69 Master of Bus admin. 7: Libn Coquitlam Sch Bd, Vancouver BC Can 64-65; Ref libn Vancouver Is Ref Lib, Nanaimo BC 65-66; Asst Col libn Canadian Serv Col 66-67; Col libn College of New Caledonia 69-. 9: CanLA; BCLA. 15: Coll of New Caledonia 2001 Central st, Prince George BC Can.

HUSBAND, JANET (GRAY). b Pittsburgh Penn 4 Jl 42. 4: Jonathan F Husband. 5: UPittsburgh 62-66 (Eng) BA; Rutgers 66-67 MLS. 6: Fr. 7: Asst libn bk sel Free lib of Phila 67-. 9: ALA; PennLA. 13: Yes. 14: Bk sel. 15: Apt F-4 415 S Van Pelt st, Phila Pa 19103.

HUSBAND, JONATHAN FENTON. b Springfield Mass 8 S 38. 4: J anet Gray. 5: Boston U 55-59 (Eng) BA; UPenn 62-63 (Eng) MA; Drexel 63-64, 65 MS in LS. 6: Ger, Fr. 7: Spec 5th Class US Army Security Agency 59-62; Libn I roving asst central pub depts Free Lib of Phila 64-65, Libn II lit dept 65-67, Libn III -hd ser sect 67-. 9: ALA; PennLA. 14: Ref. 15: 415 S Van Felt st, Phila Pa 19146.

HUSBANDS, CHARLES WILLIAM. b Beatrice Neb 10 S 39. 4: Nancy West. 5: Amherst 57-61 (Mus) BA; Simmons 65-67 (LS) MS. 7: Asst mgr DeWolf & Fiske Co, Boston 63-65; Lib intern Harvard Col Lib 65-67, Syst libn 67-. 9: ALA; ASIS. 13: Yes. 14: Systems anal. 15: 135 Charles st, Boston Ma 02114.

HUSKETH, ALMA (ORMOND). b Dover NC 17 Ag 18. 4: Edward Thomas Husketh Jr. 5: Woman's Col UNC 35-39 (Eng) AB; UNC (Chapel Hill) 63-66 (LS) MS. 6: Fr. 7: Tchr Granville Co Schs, Wilton NC 39-44; Tchr Lenoir Co Schs, Contentnea NC 44-46; Tchr Granville Co Schs, W ilton NC 46-51, 57-61; Libn Granville Co Schs, Creedmoor NC 61-62; Libn Granville Co Schs, S Granville NC 62-. 9: NEA; ALA (Recr Prog); NCEA (Dist sec); ClrTA (sec pres); NCLA; SELA. 10: Alpha Delta Kappa; Jr Woman's Club; PTA; Den mother for Boy Scouts. 14: Young adult lit, ref. 15: Box 198 Brassfield rd, Creedmoor NC 27522.

HUSSELBEE, MARGARET VANYS (KATHLEEN STONE). b London Eng 1 N 18. 5: Tex State Col for Women 48-49, 50-51 (Secondary Educ) BS; Barry Col 49-50; UNC summers 59-62 MS in LS. 7: Tchr Dade Co Bd of Pub Instr, Miami Fla 53-59, Libn 59-; Instr UMiami (Coral Gables). 8: Libn, George T Baker Aviation Sch, 61-65. 10: Pi Lambda Theta; Phi Alpha Theta. 14: Ref, acquis. 15: 12727 NW 27th ave, Apt 106, Miami Fl 33167.

HUSSEY, BARBARA M. b Berkeley Cal 25 Mr 21. 5: UCal 39-43 (Psych) AB, 53-54 BLS. 7: Hosp recreation Amer Red Cross, Cal, Japan, Korea 43-46, 50-53; Camp dir or dist dir Seattle King Co Girl Scouts Coun, Seattle 46-49; Libn UCal (Berkeley) 54-58; Libn-tchr Amer Sch of Tangier, Tangier Morocco 58-59; Libn Cal State Col(Hayward) 60; Libn Antioch Unified Sch Dist, Antioch Cal 61-. 8: Volunteer lib wk in Tangier, Morocco. 9: Cal Tchrs Assn; CalASchL; Antioch Clr Tchrs Assn (sec 2 yrs). 10: AAUW; Amer Overseas Assn. 14: Tchg lib skills, ref. 15: 225 Matsqui rd, Antioch Ca 94509.

HUSTON, (HAZEL MAY) DOROTHY. b Danville Ill 9 Mr 05. 5: Intermountain Union Col 22-26 (Modern Langs) BA; UWash summer 30; NoMont Col 30-31; Pratt 34-35 BLS. 6: Fr. 7: Tchr country sch Hill Co Schs, Near Havre Mont 26-27; Tchr Custer High Sch, Custer Mont 27-30; Tchr Chester High Sch, Chester Mont 30-33; Libn Fordham Br NY Pub Lib summer 35; Ref libn Parmly Billings Mem Lib, Billings Mont 35-44; Madison Pub Lib, Madison Wis: Asst libn ref div 44-45, Act ref libn 45-46, Supv ref div 46-65, Supv bus & sci div 65-70. 9: ALA; WisLA (chm Ref Sect 60-61). 10: YWCA; Madison Civic Mus Assn. 13: Yes. 14: Ref. 15: 1433 E Johnson st, Madison Wi 53703.

HUSTON, ESTHER LORRAINE. b Chicago 10 Jl 34. 5: Manchester Col 52-56 (Elem Educ) BS; UIll 63-64 (LS) MS. 6: Ger. 7: Elem tchr commun schs, Nappanee Ind 56-58; Volunteer Brethren Serv Comm, Germany 58-60; Elem tchr pub schs, Elgin Ill 61; Elem tchr city schs, Modesto Cal 61-63; Ref-documents libn Colorado Col 64-67; Asst libn Ewha Womans U, Seoul Korea 68-. 9: ALA. 10: KAUW Ill Lib Sch Alumni Assn. 14: Catlg, ref, interlib loans. 15: Methodist Mission P O Box 1182, Seoul Korea.

HUSTON, EVELYN ELEANOR. b Pomona Cal 13 O 11. 5: UCal(Berkeley) 31-33 (Pol Sci) BA, 33-34 (LS) Certif, 39-40 (LS) MA. 7: Jr libn Educ Lib USoCal 34-37; Libn Bur of Govt Research UCLA 37-42; Documents libn Cal State Lib 42-55; Head pub serv Los ngeles State Col 55-56; Assoc dir of libs Cal Inst of Tech 56-63; Head govt publ dept UCal(Riverside) 64-66; Hd pub serv div UCAL(Irvine) 66-. 09: ALA; SLA (pres SoCal Chap 38-39); CalLA (chm Documents Com 46-47 & 66, Legisl Com 68-, treas 51-52, pres Col Univ & Research Libs Sect 62). 10: LWV; West Govtl Res Assn; Phi Beta Kappa; Pi Lambda Theta; Pi Sigma Alpha; Sacramento Bk Collectors Club. 13: Yes. 14: Govt publs. 15: 465-1/2 Seaward rd, Corona Del Mar Ca 92625.

HUSTON, ISABELLE B. b Carlisle Penn 22 S 22. 5: Millersville State Col 40-44 (LS) BS in Ed; West Res 51-52 MS in LS; Rutgers 58 (LS). 7: Libn Sr High Sch, Steelton Penn 44-48; Libn Beirut Col for Women (Beirut Lebanon) 48-51; Head Libn Hoyt Pub Lib, Kingston Penn 52-57; Libn Huntingdon Jr High Sch, Abington Penn 57-58; Clsf & Asst Prof Millersville State Col 58-. 8: Helped to organize several sch libs in the Middle East, 48-51. 9: ALA; PennLA; PennStateEA. 10: LWV; AAUP; Delta Kappa Gamma; Lancaster Co(Penn) Hist Soc. 13: Yes. 14: Tchg lib educ courses. 15: 2030 Temple ave, Lancaster Pa 17603.

HUSTON, SISTER WILHELMINA (CATHERINE C). b Brooklyn NY 15 Mr05. 5: Hunter Col 24-26 (Math, Phys Sci); Manhattan Col 37-41 (Educ) BA; Fordham 41-44 (Educ, Phsics) MS in Ed; St Johns U 55-56 MS in LS. 6: Lat, Fr, Sp, Ger. 7: Instr secondary sch 28-47; Instr & Libn St Dominics Normal 47-52; 37-52; Libn Dominican Jr Col 52-56; Instr Dominican Jr Col & Dominican Col 52-64; Libn Dominican Col (Blauvelt NY) 56-. 9: ALA; NEA; Nat Coun Tchr Educ & Prof Standards; NYL; SENY Coun on Lib Resources; CathLA (Metro Div). 10: AAUW; Rockland Co LA; Rockland Co Hist Soc; Pro Deo Assn Cath Cols. 14: Admin. 15: Dominican Col, Blauvelt NY.

HUTCHINS, ELIZABETH MARIE (SMITH). b E Brunswick NJ 22 O 17. 5: Drake's Bus Col(New Brunswick NJ) 35-36 Bus Certif; Duke 37-41 (Lit) BA, magna cum laude; UMich 55-56 MA in LS. 7: Exec sec Johnson & Johnson, New Brunswick NJ 41-46; Exec sec Kelley & Ryan, Houston 46-51; Asst libn Young & Rubicam Inc, NYC 56-64; Lib dir Fremont Pub Lib, Fremont Mich 64-67; Dir of lib serv Young & Rubicam, NYC 67-. 9: SLA (chm-elect Adv Coun 63-64; Adv Div: chm 61-62, Bd Dirs 67-, chm Nomin Com NY Chap 69; Hdqtrs operations Com 68-); MichLA (chm Dist 4 66-67); Newaygo CoLA (chm 64-66). 10: Phi Beta Kappa Beta Phi Mu; Phi Kap pa Phi; LPRC. 11: Fremont Pub Lib received John Cotton Dana Pub Award, 65. 14: Admin, pub rel. 15: 122 Summerhill rd, E Brunswick Nj 08816.

HUTCHINS, JOY ELLEN. b Flint Mich 15 Mr 43. 5: Flint Commun Jr Col 61-63 (Chem) AS; UMich 63-65 (Chem) BS, 65-67 MALS. 7: Lib trainee US VA Hosp, Ann Arbor Mich 66-67; Asst ed Chem Abstracts Serv, Columbus Ohio 67-. 8: Sec US Study Group for Universal decimal Clsf Chem & Chemical Tech (UDC 54 & 66). 9: ACS; ASIS. 14: Chem nomenclature, chem documentation, chem clsf. 15: Chemical Abstracts Serv, Columbus Oh 43202.

HUTCHINS, RICHARD GILBERT. b Flint Mich 1 S 32. 4: Mary Louise Janssen. 5: Flint Commun Col 50-52 AA; Central Mich U 52-54 (Soc Sci) AB; UMich 56-57 (Hist) AN, 61-64 9law) JD, 65-66 AMLS. 7: Purchasing Agt VA Hosp, Ann Arbor Mich 57-60, Chief of purchasing 60-61; Attorney-At-Law Flint Mich 64-66; Asst Prof of Law & Dir Law Lib uiowa (Iowa City) 66-. 9: ALA; Amer Bar Assn; AALL (chm Lib Exh Com 68-69); IowaLA; Mich State Bar Assn; Chicago Area Law Lib Assn; Iowa City LA. 10: AAUP; UMich Lib Sci Alum. 14: Admin, acquis, ref, govt docs. 15: 1218 Oakcrest, Iowa City Ia 52240.

HUTCHINS, RONALD D. b La 10 My 41. 4: Bobbie Killingworth. 5: La Polytech Inst 60-63 (Zool); Fla StateU 63-64 (Biol) BS, 64-66 (LS) MS. 7: Lit search specialist Francis A Countway Lib of Med, Boston 66-69, Program dir Vision Info Ctr 69-. 8: Consul Grad Lib Sch UChicago 68. 9: ASIS (chm Memb Com New England Reg Chap). 13: Yes. 14: Automated info storage & retrieval syst, SDI, personal indexes, educ for info sci. 15: 10 Shattuck st, Boston Ma 02115.

HUTCHINS, THELMA J. b Roanoke Va 14 Ag 40. 5: Mars Hill Col 58-60 AA; Wake Forest 60-62 (Hist) BA; SEast Baptist Theol Sem 62-65 (Relig Educ) BD; UNC 66-68 MSLS. 6: Fr, Grk (classical). 7: Soc casewker Warren Co Welfare Dept, Front Royal Va 65-66; Ref libn Campbell Col, Buies Creek NC 66-67; Asst tech serv libn S Ga Col 68-. 9: ALA; AAUP; SELA; GaLA. 14: Catlg, clsf. 15: Rte 2 Town & Country Mobile Hm Pk, Douglas Ga 31533.

HUTCHINS, VIVIEN ANNE. b Rochester NY 10 Ag 43. 5: State U Col (Geneseo) 61-65 (LS, Elem Educ) BS. 7: Salesclerk Sibley Lindsay & Curr, Rochester NY summer & Christmas 62-65; Libn Greece Central Sch Dist, Barnard Sch, Rochester NY 65-68, Kirk Rd Sch 68-. 9: NYLA; NY StateTA. 14: Elem lib wk. 15: 1709 Stone rd apt 1, Rochester NY 14615.

HUTCHINSON, ANN (PICKETT) MRS. b Orange NJ 26 N 27. 5: Radcliffe 46-50 (Eng Lit) AB; Carnegie 50-51 MLS; Certified by NY State 55; Columbia summer 64 (Med Lit) Certif by MLA 65 Syracuse summer 65 (Info systems). 6: Fr, Sp. 7: Libn Gr I and II NY Pub Lib 51-53, Pub rel rep I 52-53; Jr libn, Sr libn I Lockport Pub Lib, Lockport NY 53-55; Med asst to Dr Victor D Dembrow, Miami Fla 57-58; Sec to the manager of the Miami Br Conn Gen Life Insurance Co, Miami Fla 58-59; Med libn Deaconess Hosp, Buffalo NY 62-64; Ref libn Health Sci Lib SUNY(Buffalo) 64-67; Assoc libn, med NY State Med Lib, Albany 67-69; Dir Reg Med Lib Program NY Acad of Med Lib 69-. 9: MedLA; chm Upsta te NY Regl Group 68-69, Mem Com 68-69; SLA (Placement Chm West NY Chap 65). 10: Girl Scout leader. 13: Yes. 14: Pub rel, ref. 15: 235 87th st, New York Ny 10028.

HUTCHINSON, BARBARA (GRIFFIN). b Paterson NJ 2 O 19. 4: John L Hutchinson. 5: Vassar 37-41 Psych AB; CatholicU 61-64 MS in LS. 6: Fr. 7: Child libn Pub Lib, Va Beach Va 64-65; Libn USAF, Honolulu 66; Catlgr & ref Pub Lib, So San Francisco 66-. 9: ALA; CalLA; PLA. 10: AAUW; VCAA; Beta Phi Mu. 14: Catlg. 15: 2700 Sunset ter, San Mateo Ca 94403.

HUTCHINSON, BARBARA JANE. b Neptune NJ 17 D 40. 5: Drew 58-62 (Pol Sci) BA; Rutgers 64-66 MLS. 6: Sp. 7: Lib asst Monmouth Co Lib, Freehold NJ 65-66; Asst libn Monmouth Col, W Long Branch NJ 66-68; Assoc libn Fla Atlantic U 68-. 9: ALA; SELA; FlaLA. 10: Beta Phi Mu. 14: Ref, lib automation. 15: 201 SW 7th st, Boca Raton Fl 33432.

HUTCHINSON, WILLIAM LEGRAND. b Leon Iowa 24 Ja 17. 4: Helen D Thomas. 5: Northwest Mo State 35-39 (Eng-Speech) BS; UIll 48 BSLS. 7: Lib asst Northwest Mo State 39-42; Eng tchr High Sch, Leon Iowa 42-44; Libn Labette Co Community High Sch, Altamont Kan 44-49; Libn Ottawa U (Ottawa Kan) 49-57; Libn Linfield Col 57-60; Libn Pacific Power & Light Co, Portland Ore 60-. 8: Consul Pacific Power

& Light Co 59. 9: SLA. 14: Ref. 15: Public Service Bldg, Portland Or 97204.

HUTCHISON (VESTA) VERN. b Newtonia Mo. 5: Ark Polytech Col 32-34; UOkla 39-41 BA in LS. 6: Fr, Russian. 7: Ref libn Muskogee Pub Lib, Muskogee Okla 41-43; Chief Libn VA Hosp, Muskogee Okla 43-46; Asst libn Muskogee Pub Lib, Muskogee Okla 47; Libn admin phys sci & engnr US Bureau of Mines, Bartlesville Okla 47-. 9: ALA; SLA (past pres & dir Okla Chap); ASIS OklaLA; SWLA. 10: Okla Acad Scis; Okla Ornithological Assn; Great Bks sponsor. 11: Superior Performance Award (US Dept Interior) 58. 12: "Review of Well Stimulation & Techniques to Prevent Formation Damage in Oil & Gas Production," with 2 others (65); "Selected List of Bureau of Mines Publications on Petroleum & Natural Gas, 1910-62" (64); "Bibliography of Thermal Methods of Oil Recovery" (65); "Bibliography on Secondary Recovery, 1950-June 30, 1957 Suppl," with 3 others (57). 13: Yes. 14: Info scis. 15: 132 NE Meadowlark, Bartlesville Ok 74003.

HUTCHISON, DOROTHY (DRURY). b Paradise Kan. 4: Willis A Hutchison. 5: Emporia State Tchrs Col 37-39 (Eng, LS) BS in Ed, Lib Certif; USC 68 MLS. 6: S p, Ger. 7: Libn Sterling Col 39-45; Libn No Baptist Theo Sem(Chicago) 45-47; Catlgr Pub Lib, Salina Kan 47-49; Ser documents asst State Col(Pittsburg Kan) 57-61; Assoc libn Cal Baptist Theol Sem 61-. 9: ALA; ATheolLA; Christian Libns Assn; CalLA (CURLS); SoCal Tech Proc Group (sec-treas 65-66); WestTheolLA. 14: Tech proc. 15: 1300 E Covina Ca 91722.

HUTCHISON, ELIZABETH (BREWER). b Muncir Ind 23 Je 12. 4: James D Hutchison. 5: Whittier Col 30-34 (Chem) BA; USoCal summers 49-54 MSLS. 7: Soc wkr State Emergency Relief Assn, Whittier Cal 34-36; Lab tech Child Hosp, LA 37-40; Lab tech Pacific Mutual Life Ins Co, LA 40-43; Asst dir Ventura Co & City Lib, Ventura Cal 49-. 9: CalLA (pres, Black Gold Dist 66). 10: Bus & Profess Women's Club; AAUW. 13: Yes. 14: Admin, tech serv. 15: 1119 Via Cielito, Ventura Ca 93003.

HUTSON, DOROTHEA (SIEGEL). b NYC 14 Jl 21. 4: Oliver Hutson. 5: Hunter Col 38-42 (Chem) BA; Rutgers 43-44 (Plastics Chem); USDA Grad Sch 47-48 (Phys Chem), 50-51 (Russian). 6: Fr, Ger, Ital. 7: JPA, later Eng Aid GS5, Ft Monmouth Signal Lab, Ft Monmouth NJ 42-45; Lib asst US Patent Off GS3 47-48; Lib asst GS6 Armed Forces Med Lib, Wash DC 48-53; Research assoc NAS, CVLP, Wash DC 60-61, Libn Inst Advanced Med Comm CVLP, Wash DC 61-64; Research assoc American U CVLP 64-69. 09: MedLA; ASIS; ADI; ACS; S Advanced Med Comm CVLP, Wash DC 61-64; Research assoc American U CVLP 64-69. 9: MedLA; ASIS; ACS; SLA (Biol Scis Div). 10: Arlington Fairfax Jewish Center. 14: Documentation, med transl, pharmac, indexing. 15: 1834 N Quesada st, Arlington Va 22205.

HUTTNER, MARIAN ALICE. b Minneapolis 10 Ap 20. 5: Macalester Col 37-41 (Hist) BA (summa cum laude); UMinn 41-42 BS in LS. 7: UMinn(Minneapolis): Jr libn 42-43, Staff 43, Prin libn ser 43-46, Prin libn archives 46-53; Minneapolis Pub Lib: Prof asst II 56-60, Research asst to the libn 61-64, Adult group consul 64-67, hd, Sociol dept 67-. 9: ALA (Life mem); MinnLA (sec 62-68); Minn Adult Educ Assn. 14: Archives, bibliog, adult serv. 15: 3144 30th ave S, Minneapolis Mn 55406.

HUTTO, JESSIE LEE (WILLIAMS). b Aiken SC 25 S 16. 4: Elijah Marion Hutto. 5: Furman U 33-37 (Eng, Speech) BA; US Car 42, 50, 55 (LS), NDEA Inst summer 66 (LS); Clemson 47, 54-55 (Educ). 6: Fr, Sp, Lat. 7: Aiken Co (SC) Schs: Tchr, New Holland 37-42, 48-50, Tchr Warrenville 46-47, Elem prin 48-49, Tchr & libn Wagener 51-56, Libn, Aiken 56-; Libn & tchr Lexington Co, Fairview SC 42-44. 9: NEA; ALA; SCEA; AikenCoEA. 10: Garden Club of South Carolina; Wagener Garden Club. 14: Ref, rare bks. 15: Rte 2, Wagener SC 29164.

HUTTON, EUNICE. b Green River Wyo 10 N 06. 5: UWyo 33-35 (Elem Educ) Normal Diploma, 36-39 (Elem Educ) BA; USoCal 43-44 BS in LS. 7: Asst libn Co Lib, Laramie Wyo 36-43; Asst libn City Lib, Santa Paula Cal 44-47; High sch libn sch dist No 2, Green River Wyo 48-51, 57-. 8: Asst dorm dir Merica Hall UWyo 39-43. 9: ALA; NEA; WyoLA; WyoEA. 10: PTA; Classroom Tchrs Assn; Wyo State Hist Soc. 14: Ref. 15: P O Box 283, Green River Wy 82935.

HUTTON, JANICE JEANNERO. b Canton Ohio 13 Je 36. 4: Malcolm M Hutton. 5: Northwestern U 54-58 (Eng) BA; Kent State 58-61 (Secondary Educ) BS, 60-62 (LS) MA. 6: Fr, Sp. 7: Tchr Bd of Educ, Canton Ohio 58-60, Libn 61-. 8: Head of Libns Canton Ohio 64-65; Libn Canton Pub Even Sch 62-. 9: NEA; OhioEA; OhioSchLA. 10: Canton Col Club; Alpha Chi Omega. 14: Bk sel. 15: 2216 Mt Vernon blvd NW, Canton Oh 44709.

HUTTON, RODNEY JOE. b Durant Okla 18 Ag 38. 4: Patsy Driver. 5: SEast State Col (Durant Okla) 56-60 (Bus Educ) BS in Ed; N Tex StateU summers 63-65, 66-67 MLS. 6: Sp. 7: Tchr Albuquerque Pub Sch 60-66; Ser catlgr UNM 67-68; Ser catlgr LC 68-. 9: ALA. 10: Tau Kappa Epsilon; Pi Omega Pi; Alpha Lambda Sigma. 14: Ser catlg. 15: 6129 Leesburg pike apt 1106. Falls Church Va 22041.

HUTTON, SUZANNE THOMAS. b Morea Penn 18 D 18. 4: Charles Wetherill Hutton. 5: Col of Wooster 36-40 (Hist, Eng) BA; Drexel 40-41 BS in LS. 7: Child libn Brooklyn Pub Lib 41-43; Child libn Providence Pub Lib 43-45; Libn Oakwood Sch, Poughkeepsie NY 58-62; Catlgr Winterthur Museum, Wilmington Del 64-. 10: Child Guidance Center, Wilmington; Phi Beta Kappa; Com on George Sch, Bucks Co Penn. 14: Catlg, Americana, child lit. 15: 101 Alapocas dr, Wilmington De 19803.

HUTZLER, HELEN (CURRIER). b Pittsfield Mass 7 S 16. 4: Leroy Hutzler III. 5: Antioch Col 34-35; Col of Our Lady of the Elms 35-38 (Eng) AB; Columbia summer 41 (LS); N Adams State 50-51, summers 55-57 (Eng, Educ); Catholic U 60-63 MSLS; RI Col 68-69. 6: Lat, Fr. 7: Lib asst Berkshire Athenaeum, Pittsfield Mass 39-42, Morningside Br libn 42-45; Even libn Carnegie Lib, Rome Ga 53-56; Tchr-reading spec St Mary's Sch, Rome Ga 57-59; Ref libn Carnegie Lib, Rome Ga 59-65; Ref asst Providence Pub Lib 65-66; Libn Central High Sch, Providence RI 66-. 8: Diocesan chm, Lib Com, Savannah-Atlanta, of Nat Cath Women's Coun, 58-62. 9: ALA; CathLA; SELA; RILA; RIsch (v-pres 69-70). 10: AAUW; LWV; Cath Interracial Coun; Cath Liturgical Conf; Beta Phi Mu. 13: Yes. 14: Ref, loc hist, readers adv, multi-media. 15: 183 Brown st, Providence Ri 02906.

HUXSTER, ELEANOR L (MOORE). b Boston 10 O 02. 4: Walter J Huxster. 5: Simmons 20-24 (LS) BS. 7: Asst Harvard Landscape Arch Lib 24-26; Asst libn Free Pub Lib, Watertown Mass 26-46; Catlgr Mass Div of Pub Libs, Boston 46-47; Head Libn Pub Lib, Belmont Mass 48-50; Supv ser sect Princeton U 50-52; Sr lib asst Pub Lib, Plainfield NJ 52-. 9: NJLA. 14: Ref. 15: 93 Rockview ave, N Plainfield NJ 07060.

HUYCK, SISTER MARGARET CSJ. b Baton Rouge La 4 Ap 18. 5: Tchrs Col (Cincinnati) 42-46 (Math) BS Ed; Xavier U (Cincinnati) 48-53 (Admin) M Ed; LSU 51-58 MSLS. 7: Tchr-libn Guardian Angels Sch, Cincinnati 46-48; Tchr-libn McNicholas High Sch, Cincinnati 48-56, 62-64; Tchr-libn St Joseph Jr Col (New Orleans) 56-62; Tchr-libn Catholic High of Pointe Coupee, New Roads La 64-66; Libn St Joseph Acad , New Orleans 66-. 9: CathLA (chm High Sch Sect); ALA; -AASchL; -YPD; LaLA; LaSchL. 14: Catlg, yp libn. 15: 1453 Crescent st, New orleans La 70122.

HWANG, LUCY (JU-HSUN). b China 24 O 42. 5: Taiwan NormalU 60-65 (Adult Educ) (LS) BEduc; Appalachian StateU 66-67 (LS) MA. 6: Chinese. 7: Asst ed "The United Daily News", Taipei Taiwan 64-65; Sch libn Teays Valley High Sch, Ashville Ohio 67-68; Child libn E Orange Pub Lib, E Orange NJ 68-. 9: NJLA. 14: Child wk, catlg. 15: 449 Main st, Orange NJ 07050.

HYATT, HANNAH. b Pittsburgh 29 S 08. 5: Wheaton Col (Norton Mass) 25-29 (Eng) BA; Wellesley Col 29-31 (Eng Lit) MA; UMich summer 37 (Eng Lit, Educ), Wayne U summer 49 (Lib Film Serv). 06: Fr. 7: Eng Instr Wheaton Col (Norton Mass) 31-33; Sec educ dept YWCA, Hartford Conn 33-37; Sec & admin asst UConn 38-43; Asst dir USO Clubs, Port Clinton Ohio & Fayetteville NC 43-45; Admin asst u ext UCal(Westwood) 45-47; Film libn Fitchburg Pub Lib, Fitchburg Mass 47-62; Film libn Central Mass Reg Lib, Fitchburg & Worcester Mass 62-67; A-V consul Mid-Hudson Libs, Poughkeepsie NY 67-. 8: Org and/or leader of adult discussion groups at Fitchburg Pub Lib: World Politics, Great Decisions, Great Books 50-60; Conducted wkshop for child li bns on film programming, Com 66. 09: ALA ("Films for Libs" publ 61-62); NEA; Ed Film LA (film reviewer & festival juror); NELA; MassLA (chm Adult Educ Com 64-); Mass Libs Film Coop (chm 56-59, 65-); NYLA; Mass A-V Assn; REAUSA; NY State A-V Assn. 10: LWV; Bus & Profess Women's Club; Dramatic Wkshop; World Politics Discussion groups. 13: Yes. 14: Films, recordings, all other info media. 15: Mid-Hudson Libs, 103 Market st, Poughkeepsie Ny 10601.

HYATT, RUTH. b Pittsburgh 16 D 06. 5: Wheaton Col(Norton Mass) 24-26 (Hist); Pratt 35 (LS) Certif; Boston

41-43 (Educ) BS. 7: Asst circ dept Pub Lib, Somerville Mass 27-28; 1st asst Pub Lib, Belmont Mass 28-29; Br libn Pub Lib, Hartford Conn 30-34; Sub NY Pub Lib 35; Br libn Pub Lib, Greenwich Conn 35-37; Circ libn Pub Lib, Fitchburg Mass 37-43, Head Libn 43-61; Head Libn Pub Lib, Farmington Conn 61-. 8: Coord Clark U Eve Col Lib Techniques 54-57; Mem Adv Bd "New Standard Encyclopedia" 55-; Mem Adv Coun on Regl Lib Serv 65-68; Mem Capitol Reg Lib Coun 68-69. 9: ALA; NELA; (Sch Com 63-65); ConnLA; (Com on Training Non-Professls 68-); MassLA. 10: LWV. 12: Ed, "Directory of Health & Welfare Resources for the Fitchburg Community Council". 13: Yes. 15: 200 Garden, Farmington Ct 06032.

HYATT, VIRGINIA (LANGLEY). b Huntsville Tex 25 D 22. 4: Cecil M Hyatt. 5: Sam houston State Col 40-43 (LS) BS; SWest Baptist Theol Sem 44-46 (Relig Educ) MRE. 6: Sp, Fr. 7: Libn Cypress Fairbanks Independent Sch Dist, Houston Tex 43-44; Stud asst SWest Sem Lib, Ft Worth Tex 44-45; Ref libn Cal Baptist Col 64-. 9: CalLA. 14: Ref, period. 15: 8432 Magnolia ave, Riverside Ca 92504.

HYDE, ANN (LOUISE). b NYC 31 Ag 30. 5: Wheaton Col (Norton Mass) 50-52 (Eng); UKan 58-60 (Eng) BA; UEdinburgh 61-62 Postgrad Diploma in Palaeography & Ms Studies; UMinn 65-66 (LS) MA. 6: Lat, Fr, Sp, Greek, Ital. 7: Lib asst Dept of Special Collections UKan 63-65, Libn I 66-68, Assoc spec collections libn (rank II) Kenneth Spencer Research Lib 68-. 9: ALA (Rare Bks Sect; Ms Collections Subsect). 10: Medieval Acad of Amer; AAUP; Beta Phi Mu. 13: Yes. 14: Catlg mss & rare bks, assisting pub. 15: 737 Lawrence ave, Lawrence Ks 66044.

HYDE, EDWARD CLARENDON. b Columbia Mo 8 Je 15. 4: Mary Ruth Rogers. 5: UMo 33-37 (Ger) AB; Union Theol Sem 37-40 (Church Hist) STB; UPenn 47-50 (Classical Studies); Phila Divinity Sch 47-50; UMinn (LS) MA. 6: Ger, Lat, Gk. 7: Priest in chg All Saints' Mission, W Plains Mo 40-42; Priest in chg Transfiguration Mission, Mountain Grove Mo 40-42; Jr curate Trinity Church, Tulsa Okla 42-45; Priest in chg Trinity Church, Guthrie Okla 45-46; Priest in chg St Mary's Church, Edmond Okla 45-46; Asst to dean St Paul's Cathedral, Okla City Okla 46-47; Curate St Mark's, Frankford Penn 47-49; Vicar St John's Church, Concord, Ward Penn 49-51; Vicar Grace Church, Hulmeville Penn 51-53; Vicar All Saints' Church, Fallsington Penn 51-53; Research asst UMinn(Minneapolis) 54-55; Libn I catlg dept UColo 55-57; Jr libn catlg dept UMo 57-59, Asst libn catlg dept 59-. 8: Priest of the Protestant Episcopal Church in the USA 40-. 9: ALA; MoLA. 10: Eta Sigma Phi; Phi Beta Kappa; Beta Phi Mu; NAACP; Columbia (Mo) Coun on Religion & Race; AAUP. 13: Yes. 14: Catlg. 15: 509 Thilly ave, Columbia Mo 65201.

HYDE, ELIZABETH (MONROE WANAMAKER). b Greenwich Conn 24 Je 03. 4: John Worthington Hyde. 5: Smith 21-25 (Eng) AB, Conn Perm Secondary Certif; UMich 60, 61; East Mich U 59-62 (LS, Educ) MA in Ed. 6: Fr. 7: Circ asst NY Pub Lib summer 24; Internship with libn Greenwich Pub Lib, Greenwich Conn summer 25; Tchr of Eng & Libn Greenwich(Conn) High Sch 25-31; Elem sch libs & ext Greenwich(Conn) Pub Lib 35-37; Org elem sch libs Ann Arbor (Mich) Pub Schs 58-; Lecturer Eng lang & lit dept E MichU 67-. 9: NEA; ALA-AASchL; MichEA; MichASchL; MichLA. 10: AAUW; Smith College Club; Phi Kappa Psi; Delta Kappa Gamma. 14: Child lit, org of elem sch programs in sch libs. 15: 1721 Wells st, Ann Arbor Mi 48104.

HYDE, SAMUEL ROWE. b Houston 8 D 37. 5: UHouston 56-62 (Art, Drama) BFA, MA; UTex summer 63 (LS); LSU 64-65 (LS) MS. 7: UHouston Libs: Sr ref clerk 61-62, Ref asst 62-63, Instr & arch libn 63-65, Instr & asst catlg libn 65-. 9: ALA; TexLA; Tex Assn Clr Tchrs. 10: Beta Phi Mu; A AUP. 14: Catlg. 14: Catlg. 15: U Houston Libs 3801 Cullen blvd, Houston Tx 77004.

HYDE, WILLIAM HUMPHREY JR. b Cleveland 12 N 03. 5: Oberlin Col 21-25 (Hist) BA; Columbia 28-29 BLS, 36-37 MLS; UChicago 46-47 (LS). 6: Sp. 7: Asst libn University Club, NYC 28-36; Engring libn CornellU 38-45; Libn & Prof Ill Inst of Tech 45-. 9: ALA-ACRL (Bd); Amer Soc Electrical Engrs (Engring Sch Libns). 12: Ed "Recommended List of Basic Periodicals in Engineering and the Engineering Sciences". 13: Yes. 14: Engrng & sci lit. 15: 55 E Oak st, Chicago Il 60611.

HYLE, DOROTHEA FRANCES. b Oklahoma City Okla. 5: Ward-Belmont Col 20 (Eng); UMo 21-22 (Eng); UKan 22-24 (Eng) AB; Columbia summers 38-40 (LS). 6: Ger, Fr, Sp. 7: Gen asst Kan City (Mo) Pub Lib 26-44, First asst circ dept 44-45, Chief of circ & pub rel 45-47; Cass Co Lib Dir, Harrisonville Mo 47-51; Libn (USIS), Barcelona Spain 51-53; NY Pub Lib, Staten Is 53-54; Dir Smithtown Lib, Smithtown NY 54-. 8: Pub Rel Dir, Kansas City pub Lib 44-47; Tchr Eng in USIS Lib Barcelona Spain 51-53. 9: ALA; NYLA; SuffolkCoLA (pres). 10: Altrusa Club; Women's Club of Smithtown Twp. 11: John Cotton Dana Publicity Award (Twice). 13: Yes. 14: Pub rel, child wk, adult serv, admin. 15: 52 Roundabout rd, Smithtown NY 11787.

HYMAN, FERNE B. b Pittsburgh Penn 17 Ag 26. 4: Harold M Hyman. 5: UCLA 41-46, 48 (Pol Sci) BA; LoyolaU (Los Angeles) 60- (Hist); UIll 67-69 (LS) MS. 7: Statistician lever Bros, NYC 48-52; Acquis asst UIll Lib (Urbana) 67-68; Gifts & exchange libn Fondren Lib, RiceU 68-. 9: ALA; TexLA. 14: Tech serv, acad libs. 15: 4910 Braesvalley, Houston Tx 77035.

HYMAN, RICHARD JOSEPH. b Malden Mass 11 F 21. 5: Harvard 39-42 (Hist, Lit) AB; Boston Hebrew Tchrs Col 39-42 (Hebrew Lang & Lit) BJL; Harvard Bus Sch 47-48 (Bus Admin) MBA; Columbia 61-62 (LS) MS. 6: Fr, Sp, Ital, Ger, Hebrew. 7: Lt (Intell) USNR 42-46; Admin asst to vice pres Venus Corp, NYC 51-62; Asst to libn Queens Col (NY) 62-63; Lib assoc NYU, 63-68; Asst Prof lib sci Queens Col, NY 68-. 63-. 8: Consul to Survey of Med Lib Resources of Greater NY, Inc 64-65; Research asst Columbia U Lib Sch 65-66. 09: NY Tech Serv Libns; NY Lib Club. 10: Phi Beta Kappa; Mod Lang Assn. 13: Yes. 14: Ref, tech serv. 15: 300 W 109, New York Ny 10025.

HYMAN, SYLVIA (SCHUTZ). b Hungary. 4: Malcolm A Hyman MD. 5: Hunter Col 36 (Biol, Zool) BA; Columbia 36 (Chem); Cornell U Med Col 36-38 (Microbiol) MA; Pratt 57-58 MLS. 6: Ger, Fr, Yiddish. 7: Tchr-in- train biol Julia Richman High Sch, NYC 38-39; Research asst pathology Cornell U Med Col (NYC) 39-41, Research asst cancer & leukemia 41-43; Med sec Pathology Lab 45-50; Tchr of Lib Sci Tilden High Sch, NYC 58-. 9: NYC Sch Libns Assn. 10: Phi Beta Kappa; Beta Phi Mu; Cornell Women's Club. 14: Catlg, ref, art, med & sci bks. 15: 55 Lenox rd, Brooklyn NY 11226.

HYMES, JUDITH IRVIN. b Blossburg Penn 20 S 41. 5: Mansfield State Col 59-63 (LS) BS; Penn State U 66 (Psych); Drexel 64-67 MSLS. 7: Elem libn Manheim Central Sch Dist, Manheim Penn 63-67; Acquis libn Inter Amer Univ of PR 67-. 9: ALA; Sociedad de Bibliotecarios de PR. 14: Bk sel, child lit, ref. 15: Box 363 Inter American U of PR, San German PR 00753.

HYMON, MARY (WATSON). b Hagerstown Md 19 Je 18. 4: George J Hymon. 5: Ky State Col 36-40 (Eng) AB; UDenver 40-41 BS in LS, 53 (Educ) MA; Ind U 60 (Adult Educ) EdD. 6: Fr. 7: Libn Bishop Col(Marshall Tex) 43-47; ACT LIBN Ky State, Frankfort Ky 43; Libn Grambling Col 47-. 8: Dir Media Inst for Col Tchrs of academically deprived col studs, co-sponsored US, Off of Educ and Grambling Col. 10: AAUP; Delta Sigma Theta; Pi Lambda Theta. 14: Col lib admin, educ for libnship. 15: PO Box 3, Grambling La 71245.

HYNEMAN, BETTY JO (CALENDER). b Greensburg Ind 18 Ap 30. 4: Franklin Keese Hyneman. 5: Purdue 48-52 (Home Econ) BS; Drexel 62-63 (LS); IndU 64-69 MLS. 6: Fr. 7: Tchr jr-Sr High Sch, Plymouth Ind 52-53; Tchr High Sch, Morristown NJ 53; Libn Univ Sch, Bloomington Ind 65-. 9: ALA; IndSchLA. 10: Pi Lambda Theta. 14: Sch libs. 15: RR 5, Columbus In 47201.

HYRAK, WASYL. b Czerczyk Ukraine 20 Je 14. 4: Maria Liebl. 5: Pedagogium (Krakow Poland) 34-36 (Math); Universitas Jagiellonica (Krakow) 37-39 (Law); Ukrainian Free U (Munich Germany) 46-50 (Law) Dr iur. 6: Ukrainian, Po.ish, Ger. 7: Catlgr UAlta 62-64, docs libn 64-. 9: CanLA. 10: Can Assn of Univ Tchrs; Assn Profess Libns UAlta& assn acad Staff UAlta. 14: Catlg, ref. 15: Univ of Alberta Rutherford Lib, Edmonton 7 Alberta Can.

HYRE, CHARLOTTE V. b Grand Junction Colo 19 Mr 11. 5: Mesa Jr Col 30-32 (Educ); Colo State Col 42 (Soc Sci) BA; UDenver 45-46 BLS. 7: Tchr rural schs, Garfield & Measa Cos Colo 32-39; Elem tchr, Rifle Colo 39-41; Elem tchr Grand Junction Colo 42-45; Bkmob libn Yakima Co, Yakima Wash 46-55; Bkmob libn Douglas Co, Roseburg Ore 55-. 9: ALA; PNLA; OreLA (sec). 10: Bus & Prof Women; Altrusa Club. 14: Bkmob libn, child serv. 15: 3064 NE Porter, Roseburg Or 97470.

HYSLOP, MARION (FRANCES). b Fredericton nb can 6 Ap 45. 7: Libn I UAlberta 68-. 8: Search editor for CAN/SDI Project. 9: AltaLA. 14: Ref, current awareness. 15: 211 10405 Saskatchewan dr, Edmonton 60 Alberta Can.

HYSLOP, MARJORIE R. b Cleveland 24 Mr 08. 4: John A Hyslop. 5: Ohio State U 30 (Metallurgy) AB. 6: Fr. 7: Amer Soc for Metals: Ed asst Metal Progress 30-52, Managing ed Metal Progress 53-59, Ed Metals Review 34-57, Manager of documentation 60-63, Ed ASM Review of Metal Lit 44-, Assoc dir documentation serv 63-67, Dir Metals Info 67-, Joint ed Metals Abstracts 68-. 9: SLA (past chm Clsf Com); ASIS; (sec 66-67); Nat Fed of Sci Abstracting & Indexing Serv (past sec & treas, mem Bd Dirs 59-) ; Amer Soc for Metals (Sec Documentation Com 55-). 10: AAAS; ASLIB; ACS (Chem Lit Div). 12: Managing ed "Metal Progress" (53-59); Ed "Metals Review" 934-57); "Review of Metal Literature" (44-67); , Ed "Metals abstracts" 68 13: Yes. 14: Documentation, info retrieval, abstracting & indexing. 15: Amer Soc for Metals, Metals Park Oh 44073.

HYSLOP, MARTHA CONSTANCE. b Phila 5 Je 07. 5: Mt Holyoke 24-28 (Philos, Fr) BA; Sorbonne 26-27 (Fr, Fr Civilization) Diploma; UPenn 31-33 (Fr) MA; Bryn Mawr 34-36 (Fr). 6: Fr, Sp. 7: Tchr Fr, Span, Psych Arlington Hall, Arlington Va 36-42; Clerical wker Soc Security Bd, Baltimore summer 42; Cryptanalyst Signal Corps Mil Intelligence Div, Arlington Va 42-44; Tchr-Fr, Span, Latin America St Mary's Hall, Burlington NJ 44-47; Tchr-Fr, Span, Lat Storer Col 47-52; Catlgr documents libn Haverford Col Lib 52-. 09: ALA-ACRL. 10: Phi Beta Kappa; Beta Phi Mu; United World Federalists; Women Strike for Peace; Fair Housing Coun; Fellowship of Reconciliation; Drexel Lib Sch Alum Assn. 14: Govt docs, internat docs. 15: 516 Panmure rd, Haverford Pa 19041.

HYZAK, SISTER MARY CASILDA. b Granger Tex 5 Je 20. 5: Our Lady of the Lake Col 39-47 (Eng) BA, 48-55 (LS) MS; Kan State Tchrs Col summer 65 (NDEA Inst in Secondary Sch Libn). 06: Czech. 7: Tchr Lindsay (Tex) Pub Sch 42-46; Tchr-Libn: St Anthony Sch, Okmulgee Okla 46-52, Moye Mil Sch, Castroville Tex 52-56; Asst libn Our Lady of the Lake Col summers 55-63; Tchr-libn St John Sch, Ennis Tex 56-59; Tchr-libn St Augustine High Sch, Laredo Tex 59-64; Libn Bishop Kelley High Sch, Tulsa Okla 64-. 8: Ref libn Our Lady of the Lake Col summers 56, 64, 66, 68 . 9: ALA; CathLA; (Midwest Unit chm Catholic Bk Week); OklaLA; NCTE. 10: Tulsa Eng Club. 14: Ref. 15: Bishop Kelley High School, 3905 S Hudson ave Tulsa Ol 74135.

I

IACONO, PAULINE J. b Minneapolis 26 D 38. 5: Col of St Catherine 56-60 (LS) BA; UIowa 68-69 (LS). 06: Fr. 7: Catlgr UNotre Dame Law Lib (Notre Dame Ind) 60; Catlgr St Mary's Col (Notre Dame Ind) 61-64; Catlgr Stout State U 64; Asst catlg libn Macalester Col 64-66, Catlg libn 66-. 8: Consul to the catlg dept Bemediji State Col 68. 9: ALA; MinnLA (chm tech serv sect 67-68). 12: Co-ed: "Weyerhauser Library Periodical List" (Macalester Col) (66), "Periodical List" (SLA-Twin Cities Chap 3rd ed 68). 13: Yes. 14: Catlg. 15: 2834 Brighton ave NE, Minneapolis Mn 55418.

IAMS, ROBERT ELTON. b Wood River Neb 24 N 25. 4: Shirley Ann Branton. 5: UWash 47-49 (Eng) BA, 49-50 BA in Libnship. 7: HM1C US Navy 50-51; Asst circ dept talibTacoma Wash 50-52, Asst human relations dept 52-54, YA libn 54-55; Libn Camas Pub Lib, Camas Wash 55-60; Br libn Seattle Pub Lib 60-. 9: ALA; WashLA (Bd 55-57, treas 57-59). 14: Open depts, 4 9NE, Seattle Wa 98115. 14: Open depts, pub libs. 15: 7294 29 NE, Seattle Wa 98115.

IAMS, SHIRLEY A (BRANTON). b Goldendale Wash 4 Jl 27. 4: Robert E Iams. 5: Central wash Col of Educ 45-49 (Educ) BA in Ed; UWash 49-50 (LS) BA. 7: Asst br dept Tacoma Pub Lib, Tacoma Wash 50-52, Asst lit dept 52-53; Tchr Camas Pub Schs, Camas Wash 58-60; Asst educ dept Seattle Pub Lib 60-67, Asst Henry br 67-. 14: Open depts, pub libs. 15: 7294 29th NE, Seattle Wa 98115.

ICE, DOROTHY (STEINER). b Canton Ohio 23 My 16. 4: Lewis M Ice. 5: Oberlin 34-38 (Hist of Art) AB; UMich summers 39, 40, 41 ABLS. 7: Asst libn McKinley High Sch, Canton Ohio 38-42; Libn Lincoln High Sch, Canton Ohio 42-43; Ref & sch wk asst NYC Pub Lib 43-45; Libn Leonia High Sch, Leonia NJ 45-46; Libn Wooster Jr High Sch, Stratford Conn 54-. 9: ConnSchLA (pres 66-68). 10: AAUW. 14: Sch libs. 15: 490 Hilltop dr, Stratford Ct 06497.

ICE, LEWIS M. b Greencastle Ind 16 O 07. 4: Dorothy Steiner. 5: DePauw U 24-28 (US Hist) AB; Columbia 29-33 (Secondary Sch Supv) MA, 34-37 BS in LS.Libn The Morristown Sch, Morristown NJ 37-39; Asst in chg of bk car serv Ferguson Lib, Stamford Conn 39-41; Armed forces 41-42; Asst econ div NY Pub Lib 43-44; Asst in chg of hist reading room C Teaneck High Sch, Teaneck NJ 44-46; Libn Sampson Col 46-49; Libn UBridgeport 49-. 8: Eval Com for Conn State accred of Hillyer Col, 53; Spec Com to eval the Norwalk lr exam Bd for applicants for Conn State Lib positions, 64. 9: ALA (Memb Com Chm); ConnLA (past chm Col & Univ Sect). 10: YMCA; Torch Internat. 13: Yes. 14: Ref. 15: 303 Univ ave, Bridgeport Conn 06602.

IDDINS, MILDRED LUCILLE. b Fountain City Tenn 14 S 15. 5: Carson-Newman Col 36 (Eng) BA; Peabody 41 BS in LS. 6: Fr. 7: Tchr city schs, Knoxville Tenn 36-37; Tchr-libn Roane Co High Sch, Kingston Tenn 37-41; Tchr-libn Maury High Sch, Dandridge Tenn 41-43; Libn US Army Lib, Ft Oglethorpe Ga 43-44; Libn Carson-Newman Col 44-. 9: ALA; SELA; TennLA. 10: AAUW; Monday Lit CUd Lit Club. 14: Admin. 15: 403 Russell st, Jefferson City Tenn 37760.

IDEMA, CELENE ELEANOR. b Grand Rapids Mich 22 S 25. 5: Grand Rapids Jr Col 43-45 (Art) AA; Mary Washington Cl5-47 (Art) BA; UMich 58-62 MALS. 6: Sp, Fr. 7: Free lance art, Chicago 47-49; Cost accounting Amer Med Assn, Chicago 49-51; Tchr Shenandoah Co Schs, New Market Va 51-55; Off wk Joppes Dary,RAPDSMich 55-56; Map wk Fideler Publishers, Grand Rapids Mich 56-57; Lib asst & libn Grand Rapids Pub Lib, Grand Rapids Mich 57-. 9: ALA; MichLA. 10: Beta Phi Mu; Grand Rapids Libns Cub; WN.'Loleta D Fyan Award 65. 14: Child serv. 15: 2501 W Leonard st, Grand Rapids Mich 49504.

IDEN, (CARROLL) SAM. b Delaplane Va 21 F 18. 4: Mina Rosenfeld. 5: UVa 35-39 (Chem) BS; Columbia 484 (LS) MS. 7: Tchr Fairfax High Sch, Fairfax Va 39-41; Signal Off US Army Signal Corps (Capt) 41-45; Salesman Phipps & Bird Co, Richmond Va 46-47; Lib asst DC Pub Lib 48; Lib asst LC, Wash DC 49-50; Lib asst UIll Lib (Urbana) 50-52; Libn Internat Harvester Co, Chicago 54-59; Research reports libn GM Research Lib, Warren Mich 59-63; Tech libn Delco Radio Div-GMC, Kokomo Ind 63-. 9: SLA (sec-treas Metals Div 62-63; Ind chap; dir 67-68, consul off 68-69, v-chm 69-70; GM Com on tech lit chm 62-63 & 66-67); IndLA (Educ for libnship com 69-70). 10: Lions; ACLU; Amer Friends Serv Com. 14: Spec libnship. 15: 3211 S Reed rd, Kokomo Ind 46902.

IDLER, BASIL TERRANCE. Lamar Colo 7 O 21. 4: Edith Blauvelt. 5: Jr Col of SE Colo 39-41 (Engring); Tex Col of Arts & Inds 59-60 (Bus Admin) BBA; UHawaii 65-67 MLS. 6: Sp. 7: Off US Marine Corps Naval Aviator (Lt Col) 42-66; Asst ref libn (sci & tech) & map libn Hamilton Lib UHawaii 67-. 9: ALA; HawaiiLA. 10: Beta Phi Mu; Marine Corps Assn. 14: Ref, maps, admin. 15: 1054 Mokapu blvd, Kailua Hi 96734.

IGLAR, JOHN L. b Pittsburgh Penn 27 Ja 27. 5: St Francis Col 53 (Phil) AB; St Francis Sem 53-56 (Theol); Rosary Col 62-64 AMLS; UIll 67 (LS). 6: Slovak. 7: Catlg asst Northwestern U Law Lib 62-63; Circ libn UChicago Law & Harper Libs 63-65; Libn St Joseph's Col (E Chicago Ind) 65-. 9: ALA; CathLA. 10: Beta Phi Mu. 15: St Joseph's Coll, E Chicago In 46312.

IGNATIA, SISTER M (BAGNELL) OP. b Joliet Ill 13 D 11. 5: Siena Heights Col 38 (Eng, Philos) PhB; Rosary Col 44-49 BA in LS. 6: Fr, Ger. 7: Child lib Joliet Pub Lib, Joliet Ill 32-38; Libn Holy Name High Sch, Escanaba Mich 57-60; Libn Muldoon High Sch, Rockford Ill 60-62; Libn Barry Col 62-. 9: ALA; CathLA; FlaLA; SELA; CathLA (Fla U: chm Col & univ sect); Dade CoLA (v-pres, pres-elect). 14: Admin, ref, child wk. 15: 11300 NE Second ave, Miami Fla 33161.

IGNATIEFF, ANATOLY. b Vladivostok Russia 27 D 19. 4: Wanda Zbiec. 5: Harbin Sch of Music (Manchuria) 27-35 (Musicology) MMus; Aurora U (Shanghai China) 35-36 (Langs); Internat Inst of Machine Engnr 36-38 (Heavy Mach Engnr) Diploma; Inst of Com Sci (Manchuria) 38-40 (Accounting) Diploma; UColo 45-46 (Foreign Affairs); UMd 58 (Space Tech); American U 64-65 (Math). 6: Russian, Ukrainian, Polish, Fr. 7: Tchr- violin, viola, piano, Harbin Manchuria 37-40; 1st violinist Harbin Symphony Orch, Harbin Manchuria 37-40; Tr-analyst Army Map Serv, Wash DC 48-50; Head iccountant Giant Food Stores, Wash DC 50-51; Mil intelligence spec LC 51-58, Staff 58-63; Info spec 63-65; Phys sci Defense Documentation Ctr, Alexandria Va 65-. 8: Spec assignment to Tokyo Symphony Orchestra for command performance before Emperor 39. 9: SLA. 10: Amer Ordnance Assn; CSOOM. 11: Spec Certif of Merit for performance with

Harbin Symphony Orchestra. 14: Bibliog, indexing, ref, catlg, transl. 15: 2207 Iverson st, Hillcrest Heights Md 20031.

IGNATIEFF, WANDA Z(BIEC). b Latrobe Penn 26 Ja 14. 4: Anatoly Ignatieff. 5: Bethany Col (WVa) 32-36 (Math, Physics) AB; Penn State Col Ext (Latrobe) 43-44 (Engnr Dwg) Certif; Geo Washington U 46-48 (Psych); UMd(College Park) 58 (Space Tech); American U 64-65 (Math); UNIVAC Sch of Programming 63, 68 9computer Programming) Certif. 6: Polish, Russian, Fr. 7: Tchr Penn sch syst 36-45; Instr Bethany Col (Bethany WVa) 45-46; Ed, tr, research analyst LC 51-57; Libn ASTIA, Arlington Va 57-58; Ref libn Dept of Com, Wash DC 58-63; Ed, phys sci Defense Documentation Center, Alexandria Va 63-. 8: Consul to ASTIA Thesaurus Proj while libn with Dept of Com 61; wked on proj for mechanization of info serv at Off of Tech Serv with staff from Nat Bureau of Standards; Served on study of Man-Machine Compatability, Directorate rep for Quality Assurance Suggestion Awards, Zero Defects, Equal Employment Opportunity, Grievance Com. 9: SLA; Amer Math Soc; ASIS; Fed Linguists. 10: CSOOM. 14: Ref, indexing, lexicog, mgt, bibliog. 15: 2207 Iverson st, Hillcrest Hts Md 20031.

IGOE, JAMES GERARD. b Lackawanna NY 20 Ag 31. 4: Joan Marie Davis. 5: Fordham U 49-56 (Classical Langs, Philos) AB, PhL; Army Language Sch 57-58 Russian Certif; Simmons 60-61 (LS) MS. 6: Lat, Ger. 7: (Sgt) US Security Agency, Cal, Berlin 57-60; Detroit Pub Lib: Ref libn philos, religion & educ 61-63, Head serv bur 63-64, Br 1st asst 64-65; Head ref sect Mich State Lib 65, Head reader serv div 65-68; Program off reg lib serv US Off of Educ, Chicago 68-69; Vt State Libn 69-. 8: Tchr, Lib Admin, West MichU summer 66. 9: ALA (life mem, Memb Com 64-65, Newcomers Com 65-67, Personnel Practices Com 67-68); -RSD (sec-treas 67-68); MichLA (Legis Com 62-64). 14: Lib admin, interlib coop, state lib serv & statewide lib devel, research, ADP applications. 15: 693 Easy st, Glendale Hts Il 60137.

IHNDRIS, RAY W(ILL). b Sterling Ind 1 Ap 20. 4: Violet E Parrish. 5: Rollins Col 50-55 (Chem) BS; UMd (College Park) 57-59 (Chem); American U 60-61 (Documentation). 7: Staff Sgt USAF Personnel Off 41-45; Chem Entomology Research Div US Orlando Fla 46-56; Chem Pesticide Chem Research US DA, Beltsville Md 56-60; Head Sci Records Sect CCNSC Nat Cancer Inst, NIH 60-67; Toxicology Info Program, NLM 67-. 8: Chem Abstracts Organic Chem Nomenclature for Naming Compounds, Chem Structure Fragmentation Info, Storage & Retrieval for Cancer Agents "Synonyms of Cancer Chemotherapy Agents. 9: ACS (Div of Chem Lit); ASIS; Internat Fed Documentation. 11: Unit Award for Superior Service. 13: Yes. 14: Chem structure storage & retrieval, chem-biol ac tivity, Wiswesser line-formula chem notation. 15: 128 Whitmoor ter, Silver Springs Md 20901.

IHRIG, ALICE BENNETT. b St Paul 19 Ag 21. 4: Robert S Ihrig. 5: UMinn 43 (Educ) BS. 7: Reporter & columnist: "Minneapolis Tribune," "Chicago Daily News," "Chicago Sun-Times"; Pub rel Wheat Flour Inst, Chicago; Pub rel dir Evergreen Park Shopping Center, Evergreen Park Ill; Ed "Oak Lawn Independent," Oak Lawn Ill; Ed "Suburbanite," Oak Lawn Ill; Freelance writing & tchg. 9: ALA-ATLA (Bd; Publ Com); Ill Lib Trustees Assn (Bd Dirs); ALA (Com on organization); -ALTA (Act exec sec 68-69, program com). 10: Chm, Oak Lawn Planning & Devel Commsn; Pres, Oak Lawn Pub Lib Bd; LWV; Adv Com, Southwest Area Welfare Coun of Metro Chicago; Red Cross; YMCA; Suburban Lib Syst (memb Bd); Urban Action Commsn; Dir Ill Hist Soc; Mem Constit Study Commsn State of Ill. 12: Ed "Public Library Trustee", "Reporter" (ILA). 14: Trustee. 15: 4944 Paxton rd, Oak Lawn Ill 60453.

ILEY, GERALDINE (STRATTON). b Warrensburg Mo 10 O 09. 5: Central Mo State Col 27-30 (Foreign Lang, Eng) BS in Ed; Boston U 35-36 (Eng) MA; Catholic U 53-58 MSLS; UMd summer 64. 7: Asst libn Central Mo State Col 30-37; Tchr Eng & math Calvin Coolidge Sch, Melrose Mass 37-39; Eng tchr Harpers Ferry High Sch, Bolivar WVa 42; Libn George Fox Jr High Sch, Anne Arundel Co Md 49-58, 61-63; Libn Rolling Knolls Elem Sch, Anne Arundel Co Md 63-. 9: NEA; MdASchL; Md State Tchrs Assn; TA of Anne Arundel Co (Faculty rep from Rolling Knolls Sch Faculty to Rep Coun 4 yrs; Legis com 63-65; Calendar com 65-66; Leadership Training Inst 66-67; Pub Rel Com 67-68; Nom Com; del to Md Sch Tchrs Assn (Legislative Assembly) 67,68; del to NEA Conv 69). 10: AAUW; Col Women's Club; Garden Club. 14: Child serv. 15: Epping Forest Rt 1 Box 504, Annapolis Md 21401.

ILVES, ENDEL (IRENE REBANE). b St Petersburg Russia 6 Ja 27. 4: Endel Ilves. 5: StockholmU (Sweden) 48-52, 54-56 (Slavic Lan 05: StockholmU (Sweden) 48-52, 54-56 (Slavic Lang) Fil.kand (MA); Columbia 67-69 MS in LS. 6: Estonian, Russian, Swedish, Ger. 7: Br libn Stockholm Pub Lib 53-56; Tr- correspondent Rand Development Corp, NYC 58-59; Lib asst Radio Liberty Research Lib, NYC 66-67; Asst libn Leonia Pub Lib, Leonia NJ 67-69, Ref libn 69-. 8: Free-lance tr (Russian & Estonian) US Govt Joint Publ Serv, NYC 60-61. 9: ALA. 14: Ref. 15: 481 Grand ave, Leonia NJ 07605.

IMBERMAN, MILTON. b NYC 23 S 23. 4: Hennie Berkowitz. 5: City Col of NY 40-47 (Econ) BS in Soc Sci; Columbia 48-49 MS in LS, 49-51 (Pol Sci). 6: Ger. 7: Research libn Time Inc, NYC 49-. 8: Library/USA NY World's Fair 64. 9: SLA. 14: Ref. 15: 106 W 69th st, New York NY 10023.

IMBRIE, AGNES (ELIZABETH). b NYC 10 Ag 19. 5: Grove City Col 37-41 (Lat, Ger) 41; USoCal 42-43 BS in LS. 6: Ger. 7: Lib asst Santa Paula Pub Lib, Santa Paula Cal 43-45; Libn I catlg Los Angeles Co Lib, Los Angeles 45-46; Hosp libn Los Angeles Co Hosp, Los Angeles 46-51; Pub health libn Los Angeles Co Pub Health Dept, Los Angeles 52-61, Libn 62-. 9: ALA; MedLA; SLA; CalLA. 10: AAUW. 14: Ref, catlg, med libnship. 15: 220 N Broadway Room 300P, Los Angeles Ca 90012.

IMELDINE, SISTER MARY (MARIE STREFF). b Stayton Ore 22 Jl 09. 5: Marylhurst Col 27-33 (Eng) BA; UWash summers 34, 35 Tchr-Libn Certif; Seattle U 40-41 (Educ) Wash Tchg Certif; UWash summers 52-55 MLS. 6: Fr, Ger. 7: Lib asst Holy Names Acad, Seattle 33-36; Lib asst Marylhurst Col 36-38; Libn Marylhurst Normal Sch (Ore) 38-42; Libn Holy Names Acad, Spokane Wash 42-44; Asst libn Marylhurst Col 44-51, Libn 51-. 9: ALA; CathLA; PNLA; NW Col Libns. 10: Beta Phi Mu. 12: Jt auth "Library Manual" (60); jt auth "Joy in Books" (61). 13: Yes. 14: Ref, catlg. 15: Marylhurst Col, Marylhurst Ore 97036.

IMMROTH, BARBARA (FROLING). b NJ 21 F 42. 4: John Phillip Immroth. 5: Brown 60-64 (Span) AB; UDenver 64-65 (LS) MA. 6: Sp. 7: Stud asst John Hay Lib Brown U 63-64; Grad asst Mary Reed Lib UDenver 64-65, Educ Inst libn 65; Sub boys & Girls room libn Carnegie Pub Lib, Pittsburgh Penn. 15: 519 Bigelow st, Pittsburgh Pa 15207.

IMMROTH, JOHN PHILLIP. b La Junta Colo 30 S 36. 4: Barbara Froling. 5: Pueblo Jr Col 54-56 (Arts & Sci) AA; UColo 56-59 (Speech & Dramatics) BA, 59-62 (Eng Lit) MA; UDenver 64-65 (LS) MA; UPittsburgh 68-. 06: Ger, Fr. 7: Jr lib clerk McClelland Pub Lib, Pueblo Colo 61-62; Instr of speech Tarleton State Col 62-64; Sr lib clerk McClelland Pub Lib, Pueblo Colo summers 63-64; UDenver: Verifier 65, Catlgr 65, Instr of Libnship Grad Sch of Libnship 65-66; Asst Prof of Lib Sci SUNY (Geneseo) Sch of Lib Sci 66-68; Instr in Lib & Info Sci GSLIS UPittsburgh 68-. 9: ColoLA; ALA; ASIS; Bliss Clsfn Assn. 10: AAUP. 12: "A Guide to Library of Congress Classification" (68). 13: Yes. 14: Catlg, clsf & subject analysis, analytical & critical bibliog. 15: 519 Bigelow st, Pittsburgh Pa 15207.

INAGAWA, KAORU (KAWAMURA) (MRS). b Tokyo Japan 2 Ja 33. 4: Masaaki Inagawa. 5: Tsuda Col 51-55 (Eng Lit) BA; Keio U Japan Lib Sch 55-57 (LS) BA; UWash 57-58 M in Libnship. 6: Japanese, Eng, Fr. 7: Libn queens Borough Pub Lib, Jamaica NY 59; Ref libn Amer Cultural Center (USIS) Lib, Tokyo 60-. 9: JapanLA; Tokyo Metro LA. 13: Yes. 14: Ref. 15: 27-7 2-chome Kamiochiai, Shinjuku-ku, Tokyo 161 Japan.

INEZ, SISTER MARIE (JOHNSON). b Mitchell SD 2 Je 09. 5: Col of St Catherine 25-29 (Eng) BA, 38-39 BS in LS; Columbia 39-40 (LS) MS; UDenver (Folklore); USoCal (Bibliog). 6: Fr, Ger. 7: Tchg elem schs, St Paul 30-38; Libn ref Col of St Catherine 40, Head Libn 42-. 8: Lib Consul, Survey of Mt Mercy Col, 63-64; Bldg Consul to Fontbonne Col, 64-66. 9: ALA (past com mem, sect chm); CathLA (sec, Program Chm, mem Com on Eval 55; chm Minn-Dak Unit; Exec Bd 69-75); MinnLA (chm Col Sect). 11: Butler Scholarship for Foreign Study, 58; Minnesota Libn of Year 67. 12: "Development of Separate Service for Young People in Public Libraries" (40); "Library Manual for Parish Librarians" (55); "The Catherine McAuley Library; A Survey Report" (64). 13: Yes. 14: Admin, acquis, child lit. 15: Col of St Catherine, 2004 Randolph ave, St Paul Mn 55116.

INGRAM, ADA (ARMSTRONG). b Gage Okla 17 S 14. 4: Ray P Ingram. 5: Tex Wesleyan Col 43-44 (Religious Educ) BA; UOkla 53-57 MLS; Southwestern Baptist Theol Sem 41-44 (Religious Educ) MRE. 7: Asst dir for tech serv Max Chambers Lib, Edmond Okla 57-. 9: OklaLA (Tech Serv Div).

10: Beta Phi Mu. 12: Ed "Oklahoma Librarian" (63-66). 13: Yes. 14: Catlg. 15: Box 216, Edmond Okla 73034.

INGRAM, BARBARA JEAN. b London England 6 Jl 37. 5: Pasadena City Col 63-67 (Eng) AA; Cal State (Los Angeles) 67-68 (Eng) BA; UCLA 68-69 MLS. 6: Fr, Ger. 7: Serv orders rep Pacific Tel & Tel, Alhambra Cal 55-60; Tech proofreader Jet Propulsion Lab, Pasadena Cal 60-66; Copy ed Hixson & Jorgensen Advertising Agcy, Los Angeles 66-67. 9: SLA; ALA; CalLA. 10: Alpha Gamma Sigma. 11: SLA scholarship; HEW grad fellowship for lib sci. 14: Ref. 15: 325 1/2 N Atlantic blvd, Alhambra Ca 91801.

INGRAM, CHARLES DEAN. b Lawton Okla 29 D 28. 5: Okla City U 46-49; UOkla 49-51 (Art) BFA in Art, 60-63 MLS. 6: Sp. 7: Lib asst Okla City Libs, Okla City Okla 48-53, Chief prod asst 54-59; Asst acquis libn UOkla, Norman Okla 62-63; Asst libn for pub serv UOkla Med Center 63-65; Docs libn Okla City U Lib 65-68, Acquis libn 68-. 9: OklaLA; ALA. 10: Beta Phi Mu; Midwest City Art Guild. 14: Tech serv, ref. 15: 225 Leonard lane, Midwest City Okla 73110.

INGRAM, HELEN Y. b Chester WVa 11 Ap 08. 5: Ohio U 25-29 (Fr, Eng) AB; Cornell U 37; UAriz 58; Duquesne U 59-62 (LS) MA. 6: Fr. 7: Lit tchr Hancock Co Pub Schs, Chester WVa 31-39; Commsnr of accounts for the State of WVa, Hancock Co 51-58; Libn & Instr materials Beaver Co (Penn) Sch System 59-63; Lib consul Jamestown (NY) Pub Sch System 63-66, Libn 66. 8: Memb Bd of Trustees Lakewood Mem Lib, Lakewood NY. 09: NEA; ALA; NY State Tchrs Assn; NYLA. 10: Chautauqua Lit & Sci Circle; AAUW; PTA. 14: Instr materials. 15: P O Box 316, Lakewood NY 14750.

INGRAM, VIRGINIA H. b Gibson County Tenn 7 Je 12. 4: William T Ingram Jr. 5: Bethel Col 30-33, 35-36 (Mathm Eng) BA; Peabody Col 53-56 (LS) MA. 7: Libn: McKenzie High Sch, McKenzie Tenn 52-65, Fraser High Sch, Memphis Tenn 65-66; Asst catlg libn Memphis State U 66-. 9: ALA; TennLA; W TennEA (pres, Lib Sect 57-58); McKenzieEA (pres 61-62). 10: YWCA. 11: Delta Kappa Gamma; Pi Gamma Mu. 14: Catlg. 15: 210 N Avalon, Memphis Tn 38112.

INMAN, JUNE FRANCIS. b Birmingham Ala 31 Ja 22. 5: Fla State U 42 (Educ) AB, 48 (LS) MA; Syracuse 47 (A-V Wkshop); Emory 55 Med Lib Certif; UMiami 68-69. 7: US Off of Censorship US Govt, Miami Fla 43; Libn UMiami (Miami Fla) 46; Ref libn Miami (Fla) Pub Lib 49, Br libn Riverside Br 52; Libn Sch Bd Ponce Jr High Sch 53; Libn Sch Bd, W Miami Fla 59-62; Libn Sch Bd Miami Jackson High Sch 65-. 9: ALA; FlaLA. 10: Alpha Delta Kappa; Woman's Club; Women's Panhellenic Assn. 12: Co-comp "Florida Bibliography" (60); Co-comp: "Guidance Bulletin," "Occasional Papers" (69). 14: Ref. 15: 200 SW 23 rd, Miami Fla 33129.

INMAN, ROBERT ANTHONY. b San Francisco 13 Je 31. 4: Joan Marshall Inman. 5: Stanford 48-52 (Eng) BA (magna cum laude); UGraz(Austria) 52-53 (Ger); UVienna 53-54 (Ger); Free U of Berlin 56-57 (Ger); UWash 57-59 (Ger) MA. 6: Ger, Fr. 7: Linguist & battalion clerk US Army (Cp l) Hq 522nd Mil Intelligence Bn, Frankfurt/M ain Germany 55-56; Instr Dept Germanics UWash 57-59, Ed & admin asst Off Pub Serv & U Rel 60-62; Pub rel Nat Jewish Hosp, Denver 63; Libn & Head libn "The Denver Post," Denver 64-. 8: Lecturer on Amer Lit (for US Educ Commsn & Austrian Fed Ministry of Educ) in Austria, 53-54; Co-auth of play "Die Stadt und das Herz," scenes performed in Austria, 54. 9: SLA. 10: ACLU; YMCA; Denver Art Museum; Phi Beta Kappa. 11: Fulbright Scholarships, Graz & Vienna, 52-54. 12: "The Torturer's Horse," novel (65); Ed "Washington Alumnus & University Record" (60-62). 15: Lib The Denver Post, 650 15th st, Denver Co 80202.

INNIS, HELEN (GREENING). b South Bend Ind 20 Ja 01. 5: Ind U 18-21 (Hist) BA; St mary's Col 47; Ind U 48-50 Ohio & Ind Certif in LS. 6: Ger, Sp. 7: Dir Bryan Pub Lib, Bryan Ohio 45-66; Reg consul State Lib of Ohio, Columbus 66-. 9: ALA; OhioLA. 10: Fortnightly Study Club; Bus & Profess Women; Internat Platform Assn. 14: Adult & adv serv. 15: 209 Ave B, Bryan Oh 43506.

INOUYE, JUDY. b Kelowna BC Can 11 Mr 43. 5: UBC 61-66 (Eng & Fine Arts) BA, 68-69 BLS. 6: Fr, Japanese. 7: Hostess Expo 67, Montreal 67; Lib asst UBC, Vancouver NC 66-. 15: 4595 Brentlawn dr, N Burnaby BC Can.

INSEL, LILLIAN R (SOLOMON). b NYC 29 Ag 17. 4: Ralph D Insel. 5: Washington Sq Col, NYU 33-37 (Eng) BA; Carnegie 55-56 MLS. 6: Fr. 7: Asst libn catlgr Carnegie Lib of Pittsburgh 56-59; Libn Temple Beth Emeth, Albany NY 60-; Libn Govt Affairs Found, Albany NY 59-60; Asst libn Albany Med Col 60-63; Libn Albany Col of Pharmacy 63-. 9: Hudson-Mohawk LA. 10: Beta Phi Mu; Phi Kappa Phi. 14: Catlg, lib admin. 15: Hays rd, Rensselaer NY 12144.

INSKIP, ANITA LOUISE. b Hanover Penn 18 D 35. 5: Millersville State Col 53-57 (LS) BS; Syracuse summers 58-61 MSLS; Rutgers 60-61; Drexel summer 64; Rutgers summer 66; Temple 68-. 7: Libn Biglerville High Sch, Biglerville Penn 57-60; Libn Coun Rock High Sch, Newtown Penn 60-64; Libn Coun Rock Intermediate Sch, Richboro Penn 64-67; Curriculum assoc Educ Media Coun Rock Sch Dist, Richboto Penn 67-. 9: ALA; NEA; PennLA; Penn State EA; Bucks Co (Penn) Sch LA (pres 65-68). 10: Beta Phi Mu. 14: Coord of a-v program with lib program, sch lib supv. 15: 77 Bustleton Pike, Churchville Penn 18966.

INWOOD, JEANNE (DOROTHY J). b Long Beach Cal 11 Ap 26. 5: U of Pacific 44-48 (Liberal Arts) AB; UCal 59-60 MLS. 6: Fr. 7: Lib asst British Info Serv, San Francisco 48-54; Lib asst USAF Lib, London 54-55; Lib asst US Army Lib, Ft Ord Cal 56-57; Documents clerk Off of Naval Research, London 57-59; Asst libn Monterey Peninsula Col 60-65, Head Libn 65-. 9: CalLA; ALA. 10: ACLU; Sierra Club; Bk Club of Cal. 14: Rare bks, private presses. 15: Rt 1 Box 165, Carmel-by-the-Sea Cal 93921.

IPPOLITO, ANDREW VINCENT. b NYC 6 Mr 30. 4: Constance Mary DiMitrio. 5: Queens Col 48-50 (Hist); Georgetown 53-55 (Foreign Serv) BS FS; St Johns Law Sch 55-57 (Law); Pratt MLS. 7: Hosp corpsman US Navy, USA 50-52; Law clerk Berg Mezansky & Mendes, NYC 58; Dir Lindenhurst Pub Lib, Lindenhurst NY 59-60; Dir N Babylon Pub Lib, N Babylon NY 60-62; Dir Merrick Lib, Merrick NY 62-65; Dir of Lib & Research Newsday, Garden City NY 65-. 8: Lib consul to Avicon Assocs. 9: Admin Mgt Soc; ALA (reg Memb Chm); NYLA; Nassau Co LA (chm Stat Com); NY Lib Club; SLA (chm NY chap newspapers news group; chm newspaper div, chm com). 10: Sunnyside Progressive Sch; Bayside Nursery Coop; Adult Educ Adv Bd; Beta Phi Mu; PTA. 13: Yes. 14: Info retrieval, admin. 15: 42-46 209 st, Bayside NY 11530.

IRBY, ANGELA G(IRAL). b Madrid (Spain) 11 Ag 35. 4: James E Irby. 5: Nat U of Mexico 53-56 (Sp Lit); UMich 56-59 MLS. 6: Sp, Portug, Fr, Ital. 7: Ref libn Nat Univ of Mexico 56; Sr catlgr Princeton U Lib 62-67; Libn Amer High Sch, Rio de Janeiro 64-65; Libn Urban & Environmental Studies Lib Princeton U 67-. 8: Spec "book-scout" for the princeton U Lib while in Brazil 64-65. 9: ALA; SLA (Princeton-Trenton Chap: chm Recr Com 68-69; v-pres 69-70); Coun Planning Libns; NJLA. 14: Catlg, ref. 15: 67 Olden st, Princeton NJ 08540.

IRBY, GERALDINE A. b Mobile Ala 7 S 29. 5: NC Col (Durham) 47-51 (Biol, Educ) BS; Columbia 58-60 MSLS. 7: Lib asst US Info Agency, Wash DC 54-57; Jr prof libn Columbia U Libs 57-60; Asst to libn ref dept Lederle Labs, Pearl River NY 60-64; Lib assoc NYU 64-65; Hd bus-sci div Mobile Pub Lib, Mobile Ala 65-68; Govt docs libn USo Ala 68-. 9: ALA; SELA; AlaLA. 10: Nat Coun of Negro Women; Delta Sigma Theta; LWV; NAACP. 13: Yes. 14: Govt docs, ref. 15: 2945 Cedar Crescent dr, Mobile Al 36605.

IRELAND, ROSE M (BANNISTER). b Kansas City Kan 5 S 14. 4: Millard K Ireland. 5: Kan State Tchrs Col (Emporia) 33-35 (Educ) BS in Ed; UWash 57-65 (LS) Tchg Certif & ML. 7: Tchr Protection (Kan) Schs 35-37; Tchr Kansas City (Kan) Schs 37-40; Tchr Seattle Pub Schs 55-60, Tchr-libn 60-. 9: ALA; NEA; WashLA; WashEA; Wash State ASchL (chm Reg 6). 10: Delta Kappa Gamma. 14: Child serv. 15: 8709 Forest Hill pl NW, Seattle Wa 98107.

IRONSIDE, DIANA JOAN. b Campbellford Ont Can 19 N 25. 5: Toronto 45-49 (Eng) BA, 49-50 BLS; Syracuse 67-69 MA. 06: Fr. 7: Bibliog UToronto Lib 50-51& film catlgr British Film Inst, London 51-52; Educ therapist St Crispin (Mental) Hosp, Northlands Eng 53-55; Info off Can Assn for Adult Educ, Toronto 55-63, Program off 63-64; Assoc dir The Lib of Continuing Educ, Syracuse NY 64-68; Project dir dept of adult educ Ont Inst for Studies in Educ, Toronto Can 68-. 9: CanLA; Assn Spec Libs & Info Bureaux; SLA (Program chm Toronto Chap); Ont Inst Prof Libns (Educ chm); ASIS (chm program upstate NY Chap). 10: Can Assn Adult Educ; Adult Educ Assn USA; Nat Inst Adult Educ, Eng. 12: Comp "Bibliography of Canadian Writings in Adult Education," with M Thomson (56); "Seminar on Residential Adult Education: Camp Laquemac, 1958" (58); "The Literature of Adult Education: a Selected List ." (61); "Adult Education

Information Services . A Prototype System" with R Decrow, R Miller (67). 13: Yes. 14: Info retrieval, clsf theory. 15: Lib of Continuing Educ 107 Roney lane, Syracuse NY 13210.

IRONSIDE, EUGENIA E. b Oakland Cal 2 Ja 15/ 05: San Jose State Col 33-37 Special credential in libnship. 6: Fr. 7: Libn circ dept San Jose Pub Lib, San Jose Cal 37-43; Sr grade lt USN Waves 43-46; Asst libn Shell Oil Co, San Francisco 46-48; Tech libn Shell Development Co, Emeryville Cal 49-. 9: ALA; SLA; CalLA. 14: Catlg. 15: 1945 Broadway, San Francisco Ca 94109.

IRSHAY, PHYLLIS CAROLINE. b Danville Ill 29 Jl 24. 5: Maryville Col 41-44 (Home Econ); Wayne State 44-45 (Home Econ) BS, 48-53 MLS. 7: Sch libn Detroit Bd of Educ 48-61; Prin libn Anaheim Pub Lib, Snaheim Cal 61-62, Asst dir 62-67; Lib dir A K Smiley Pub Lib, Redlands Cal 67-. 8: Ed asst: Ginn & Co, Boston, 59-60; Detroit Bd of Educ 60. 9: ALA; CalLA. 10: AAUW; C of C Woman's Div. 12: Contr Junior High School Library" (61); Ed "Biblio Cal Notes" 68-. 13: Yes. 14: Admin. 15: A K Smiley Pub Lib PO Box 751, Redland Ca 92373.

IRVINE, JAMES SHEPPARD. b Altoona Penn 21 D 27. 5: Washington & Jefferson Col 45-49 (Eng Lit) BA; West Theol Sem 49-52 (New Testament) BD; Johns Hopkins 53-58 (Oriental Langs) PhD; Carnegie 58-61 MLS. 6: Ger, Fr, Hebrew, Gk, Aramaic. 7: Libn Pittsburgh Theol Sem 58-66; Asst to the libn Princeton Theol Sem 66-. 9: Soc Bibl Lit; ATheolLA; Tri-State ACRL. 10: Beta Phi Mu; Presby Hist Soc Upper Ohio Valley; Phi Beta Kappa. 13: Yes. 14: Ref, admin. 15: Speer Lib, Princeton Theol Sem, Princeton NJ 08540.

IRVINE, JOYCE (JOHNSTON). b Winnipeg Can 18 My 23. 4: G Norman Irvine. 5: UMan 40-45 (Eng & Hist) BA; McGill 46-47 BLS. 6: Fr. 7: Lib asst Jr Lib UMan 45-46; Child libn Winnipeg Pub Lib, Winnipeg Can 47-48, 49-51; Ref libn McGillU Lib 48-49; Writer & broadcaster CBC, Winnipeg 56-64; Ref libn UMan Main Lib 64-. 9: ManLA. 10: Canadian Inst of Intl Affairs. 14: Ref, govt docs. 15: 215 Elm st, Winnipeg 9 Manitoba Can.

IRVINE, KATE TIPTON. b Winchester Ky 20 O 10. 5: Transylvania Col 27-29; Georgetown Col 29-31 (Eng, Fr) AB (summa cum laude); UKy 31-32 (Eng, Fr) MA, 33-34 (LS) Certif, 46-47 BS in LS. 6: Fr, Sp. 7: Instr in Fr & Eng Georgetown Col (Georgetown Ky) 32-33; Libn & Instr in Fr Campbellsville Col 34-36; Libn Picadome High Sch, Lexington Ky 36-39; Libn Lafayette High Sch, Lexington Ky 39-43; UKy: Asst ref libn 43-47; Instr in Lib Sci 47-48, Head circ dept 47-64, Head ref dept 64-. 8: Instr in Lib Sci UKy 47-48. 9: ALA; SELA; KyLA (past sec-treas, past chm col & ref sect). 10: AAUP; AAUW; UKy Woman's Club; Sigma Tau Delta; Beta Phi Mu; Central Ky Mental Health Assn; Ky Hist Soc. 14: Pub serv. 15: 345 Winchester st, Paris Ky 40361.

IRVINE, SHARON LOUISE (SMITH). b St Paul Minn 2 My 41. 4: Stanley Gray Irvine. 5: UChicago 59-63 (Intl Rel) AB, 63- (LS). 6: Ger, Swedish, Sp. 7: Circ asst UChicago 60-62, Inter-lib loan asst 62-64, Asst res libn 64-65, Res libn 65-67, Asst circ libn 68, Hd circ-res libn 68-. 10: Art Inst of Chicago. 14: Admin, reader's serv. 15: Univ of Chicago Lib 1116 E 59th st, Chicago Il 60637.

IRVINE, STANLEY GRAY. b San Diego Cal 12 Mr 41. 4: Sharon Smith. 5: UChicago 58-62 (Liberal Arts) AB, 61-65 (Law) JD, 65- (LS). 6: Ger, Swedish. 7: Circ asst UChicago Law Lib 62-65, Catlgr 65-66, Sr catlgr 66-67, Hd tech serv 67-. 9: AALL; ChicagoALL. 10: Art Inst of Chicago; Nat Rifle Assn; Delta Upsilon. 13: Yes. 14: Admin, tech serv, law libs. 15: Univ of Chicago Law Lib 1121 E 60th st, Chicago Il 60637.

IRVING, DOROTHY (WHYTE). b NYC 13 Ag 15. 4: William Joseph Irving. 5: NY State Col for Tchrs 32-37 (Eng, Fr) BA; NY Sch of Soc Wk 39-41 (Casewk); SUNY(Albany) 57-62 MSLS. 6: Fr. 7: Housemother Hawley Home for Child, Saratoga NY 37-39; Casewker Child Aid Soc, NYC 40-41; Child wkr Dept of Pub Welfare, Essex Co NY 41-43; Libn Hudson Area Lib, Hudson NY summers 62-65; Libn Germantown Central Sch, Germantown NY 57-. 8: Legis Coun 2nd Supv Dist, Columbia Co Tchrs Assn; Ed Adv Com High Sch Lib Bk Club, columbus Ohio; Lib consul ESEAI & II to Horicon Central Sch, Brant Lake NY; Adhoc Adv Com on preliminary guide for integration of performing arts for Bur of Secondary Curriculum Development, State Educ Dept, Albany NY. 9: NY State Tchrs Assn; NYLA; East Dist (Penn) Sch Libns. 10: PTA; Drama Workshop (Dir of plays); Student Exchange Project. 14: Reading guidance, curriculum correlation, planning. 15: Star rt, Livingston NY 12523.

IRVING, OPHELIA (McALPIN). b Gadsden Ala 4 Ap 29. 4: Charles Garfield Irving Jr. 5: Clark Col 47-51 (Soc Sci) AB; Atlanta summer 52; Syracuse summers 54-58 MLS; Drexel summer 64 (LS). 7: Libn Center High Sch, Waycross Ga 51-54; Libn Spencer Jr High Sch, Columbus Ga 54-55; Catlgr St Augustine's Col 55-61, Head Libn 61-68; Gen ref serv libn NC State Lib 68-. 9: ALA; NCLA; SELA. 10: Alpha Kappa Alpha; YWCA; Jack & Jill of Amer. 14: Catlg, acquis, ref. 15: 533 E Lenoir st, Raleigh NC 27601.

IRWIN, EDITH (ALICE). b San Francisco. 5: Stanford 36-40 (Eng) BA; Columbia 40-41 MLS. 6: Fr. 7: Jr libn catlg sect Lib of Hawaii, Honolulu 41-49; Cal State Lib; Jr libn order sect 50-51, Jr libn catlg sect 51-52, Period libn 52-66, Supv acquis libns 66-. 9: ALA; CalLA. 10: Stanford Alumni Assn. 12: Ed "Hawaii Library Association Journal" (47-48). 14: Ser, tech serv, acquis. 15: 2325 "T" st apt "D", Sacramento Ca 95816.

IRWIN, VIRGINIA (PULLIAM). b Clarkson Ky 13 F 13. 4: Ross Irwin. 5: Hamilton Col 29-31 Jr Col Certif; UKy 31-33 (Eng) BA; Columbia summers 35-38 BS in LS; Chicago 39-40 (LS). 7: Tchr-libn Leitchfield High Sch, Leitchfield Ky 34-38; Asst libn Lake Forest Pub Schs, Lake Forest Ill 38-39; Lib Fellowship Ref Lib Quarrie Corp, Chicago 39-40; Libn Ground Sch Lib Brooks AFB, San Antonio Tex 41-42; Sub libn Alamo Heights High Sch, San Antonio Tex 57-63; Ref libn Our Lady of the Lake Col 63-. 9: ALA; TexLA; Bexar CoLA. 10: LWV. 14: Ref. 15: 114 Rosemary, San Antonio Tex 78209.

IRWIN, ZOLA ALICE (BURNAP). b Touchet Wash 12 D 69. 4: Arthur H Irwin. 5: Wash State U 26-27 (Music); Central Wash State Col 27-28 (Educ) Tchg Certif; East Wash State Col 59-61 (Educ) BA; UDenver 64 (Summer Wkshop Lib). 7: Elem tchr Medical Lake Sch, Medical Lake Wash 53-56; Elem tchr Sch Dist 81, Spokane Wash 56-59, Elem libn 59-. 9: ALA; NEA; WashEA; Wash State Assn Sch Libns (pres-elect). 10: SpokaneEA; Intl Reading Assn; Political Unity of Leaders in State EA; Delta Kappa Gamma. 13: Yes. 14: Child bk collections. 15: W 3902 Longfellow ave, Spokane Wa 99205.

ISAACS, BOBBY D(EAN). b Lowgap NC 16 My 37. 4: Phyllis McGee. 5: Syracuse U 60 (LS) Wkshop certif. 7: Teletypist, photo asst Piedmont Pub Co, Winston-Salem NC 55-56; Journal & Sentinel, Winston-Salem NC: Radio-TV ed Lib 56-57, Radio-TV ed, head of wire copy, receiving room, Libn 57-60, Day libn 60-61, Head Libn 61-. 9: SLA. 14: Newspaper retention files. 15: 418 N Marshall, Winston-Salem NC 27102.

ISAACSON, LANAE. b Salt Lake City Utah 13 Je 45. 5: WillametteU 63-67 (Fr) BA; UCLA 68-69 MLS. 6: Fr. 7: Tchg asst Brigham YoungU 67-68; Claims sec Security Ins Group, San Jose Cal 68; Lib clerk UCLA 69; Libn I USanta Clara 69. 8: Tchg asst in Fr Brigham YoungU 67-68. 9: ALA. 10: AAUW; Cal Scholarship Fed; Phi Sigma Iota& Pi Delta Phi. 14: Catlg. 15: 1001 Malott dr, San Jose Ca 95121.

ISABELLA, SANTINA MARIA. b Phila 18 D 37. 5: UPenn 55-59 (Chem) BA; Drexel 63-64 (Info Sci) MS. 6: Ital. 7: Research chem Purex Corp, Phila 59-62; Dir of Info Serv & Systems Penn State U Center Air Env Studies 64-66; Off Sci & Tech Relations, Pharm Manufacturers Assoc, Wash DC 66-68; Sr mem of tech staff Computer Sci Corp, Silver Springs Md 68-. 8: Consul to pharmaceutical ind on drug info problems. 9: ACS; ADI; SLA. 10: Amer Mgt Assn; Amer Indust Hygiene Assn; Phi Beta Kappa. 13: Yes. 14: Info storage & retrieval; design & development of computer based drug/biomedical systs. 15: Computer Sci Corp, Silver Springs Md.

ISBELL, (DOLLIE) EVELYN (WILLIAMS). b Bowie Tex. 4: Victor B Isbell. 5: Westminster Jr Col 38-39; Arlington Jr Col 56-58 (Elem Educ); N Tex State U 57-62 (Elem Educ, LS) BS in Ed, BS in LS. 6: Fr. 7: Tchr Elem Sch, Dallas 60-62, Libn Elem Sch of Dallas Ind Sch Dist 62-. 9: NEA; Tex State Tchrs Assn; Dallas Clr Tchrs Assn; Dallas Sch Libns Club. 10: Alpha Lambda Sigma; oy Scouts; Den Mother; Amer Bus Women's Assn; PTA; BSA. 11: Tall Texan Chapter's "Woman of the Year" for 65-66, Irving Tex. 15: 1723 W Shady Grove rd, Irving Tex 75060.

ISBELL, MARY CHARLOTTE. b Visalia Cal 12 Ag 28. 5: UCal(Santa Barbara) 48-50 (Sociol) AB; USoCal 59-60 MSLS. 7: Clerk-typist Los Angeles Co Med Assn, Los Angeles 51-53; Quotations clerk Merrill Lynch, Los Angeles 54-56; Clerk Simpson Thacher Bartlett Law Firm, NYC 56-57; Clerk Amer Inst of Mgt, NYC 57; Lib asst USoCal Lib 57; Catlgr Rutland Free Lib, Rutland Vt 60-65; Catlgr Rochester Pub Lib, Rochester Minn 65-67; Jr catlgr Tucson Pub Lib 67-68; Catlgr Coronado Pub Lib, Coronado Cal 68-. 9: ALA. 10: Beta Phi Mu. 14: Catlg, ref. 15: 23 7th ave SW, Rochester Mn 55901.

ISCHE', JOHN P. b Brooklyn NY 2 N 19. 4: Bernice Horne. 5: Taylor U 50 AB; Pratt 51 MLS. 7: Med Soc Co Kings, Brooklyn NY 38-47; J Hillis Miller Health Center UFla 47-49; LSU Med Center 49-. 8: Consul Med Lib UCosta Rica 61,63. 9: Assn Amer Med Cols; MedLA; LaLA. 13: Yes. 15: 1542 Tulane ave, New Orleans La 70112.

ISEMAN, JEANNE (KAPLAN). b NYC 18 Je 22. 4: Abraham Iseman. 5: LIU 39-43 (Econ) BA; Pratt 43-44 BLS; NYU 47-48 (Bus Admin). 7: Asst libn Sch of Bus ColumbiaU 44-46; Libn blue Ridge Corp, NYC 46-49; Libn Princeton Surveys PrincetonU 49-52; Libn Com Investment Trust, NYC 52-55; Assoc libn Newark Pub Lib, Newark NJ 55-57; Hd ref dept Br Yonkers Pub Lib, Yonkers NY 63-66; Hd gen ref UMd (College Park) 67-. 14: Ref. 15: 1220 East West highway, Silver Spring Md 20910.

ISENSEE, ROSEMARY. b Pittsburgh 25 S 06. 5: UColo 24-27; UDenver 33-35 (Eng Lit, LS) AB, 35 Lib Certif. 7: Carnegie Lib of Pittsburgh: Jr asst 28-33, Sr asst 35-43, Br libn 43-58, Head central lending dept 58-. 9: ALA; PennLA. 10: Pittsburgh Lib Club. 14: Bk sel. 15: 226 Hastings st, Pittsburgh Pa 15206.

ISENSTEIN, ELLEN (SUSAN). b Cambridge Mass 24 Jl 43. 5: UPenn 61-65 (Educ) BS; Simmons 66-68 (LS) SM. 6: Fr. 7: Intern gift & exchange sect Harvard Lib 65-67, Intern docs receipts sect 67-68; Prof asst govt doc dept Boston Pub Lib 68-. 9: ALA. 14: Ref, acquis. 15: 26 Plymouth ave, Belmont Ma 02178.

ISERMAN, MYRA L (SCHNEIDER). b St Charles Mo 4 Ja 33. 4: Carl L Iserman. 5: St louisU 52-55 (Sociol) BS; Colu louisU 52-55 (Sociol) BS; Columbia 56-57 (LS) MS. 7: Clerical asst St Louis Pub Lib 52-53, 55-56; Asst to readers' adv NY Pub Lib 57-60; Asst acquis libn Pius XII Mem Lib, St Louis 60-61; Child libn San Diego Pub Lib 62-63, Br libn 63-68; Br libn San Diego Co Lib 68-. 9: ALA; CalLA. 10: Sierra Club. 14: Ref. 15: 4611 Landis st, San Diego Ca 92105.

ISHAQ, MARY ANN (RUSH). b Minneapolis Minn 17 S 38. 4: Khalid S Ishaq. 5: UMinn 58-67 (Intl Rel) BA, (LS) MA. 6: Sp, Fr. 7: Libn Intl Rel UMinn (Minneapolis) 62-64, Libn Asian Lib 64-68; Libn Humanities UNC (Chapel Hill) 69-. 9: ALA; MinnLA. 14: Asian libs & resources, ref. 15: B2 Northampton plaza, Chapel Hill NC 27514.

ISHII, FRANCES AIKO. b Long Beach Cal 18 Jl 32. 5: Col of Wooster 50-54 (Sociol) BA; USoCal 58-60 (LS) MS. 7: Mem Hosp of Long Beach, Cal: Clerk 48-54, Admin asst 54-59, Med Libn 59-. 9: MedLA (pres So Cal Group 63-64). 10: Soroptimist Club; Japanese Amer Citizens League. 13: Yes. 14: Ref. 15: 6487 Rendina st, Long Beach Cal 90815.

ISHIMOTO, CAROL FUMIYE. b San Jose Cal 6 F 26. 5: Simmons 44-48 (LS) BS. 6: Japanese, Sp, Fr. 7: Asst Lib Sci Simmons Col 48-49; Harvard Col Lib: Catlgr Widener Lib 49-51, Gen asst catlg dept 51-55, Ref libn Lamont Lib 55-57; Catlgr UPenn 58-60; Catlgr reviser Widener Lib Harvard Col 60-. 9: ALA; Boston Reg Catlg Group (sec-treas 51-52). 14: Catlg. 15: 12 Fernald dr, Cambridge Mass 02138.

ISKENDERIAN, YERCHANIK. b Istanbul Turkey 27 Jl 01. 5: Constantinople Woman's Col (Istanbul) 16-19 (Hist) BA; UMich (Ann Arbor) 26-27 (Sociol) BA; NY Sch Soc Wk 28-29; Columbia 30-31 BLS; Columbia 38-42 MLS. 7: Asst catlgr Detroit Pub Lib 22-23; Catlgr CCNY Lib 31-42, Chief catlgr 43-45, Hd catlgr 45-53; Assoc libn 53-61, Act libn 61-62, Asst chief libn tech serv 62-. 9: ALA; BSA; NY Lib Club. 10: Bd of Dirs Armenian Educ Coun; AAUP; NSF. 14: Catlg, rare bks. 15: 45 Wadsworth terrace, New York NY 10040.

ISLEY, (DORIS) NATELLE. b Jacksonville Fla 18 O 29. 5: Fla State U 47-51 (Hist) BA, 51-52 (LS) MA. 6: Fr, Sp. 7: Asst br libn Atlanta Pub Lib 52-53; Sch of Arch Libn Ga Inst of Tech 53-57; Tech Expert UNESCO, Ankara Turkey 58-59; Ga Inst of Tech; Sch of Arch Libn 59-, Asst Prof of City Planning 64-, Research asst 65-66; Mgr info serv div Miss Research & Development Ctr, Jackson Miss 67-. 8: Lib consul; Del State Planning Off 62; E Central Fla Reg Planning Coun 65; Atlanta Planning Dept 65; Atlanta Region Metropolitan Planning Commsn 65. 9: Coun Planning Libns (past v-pres, mem ed bd); GaLA; SELA; MoLA (Nat Lib Week Com, chm Scholarship com). 12: Comp "Civic & Cultural Centers; a Planning Bibliography," with L J Zuber (53); "Bibliography on the Control of Roadside Development" (55, supplement 56); "A Manual for Small Planning Agency Libraries" (66). 13: Yes. 14: Ref, admin, catlg. 15: Mgr Info Serv Div, Miss Research and Development Ctr, PO Drawer 2470, Jackson Ms 39205.

ISOM, BILL V. b Dongola Ill 25 Jl 26. 4: Regina Ulrich. 5: So Ill U 45-49 (Hist) BS in Ed; UIll 53-55 MS(LS); So Ill U 58-61 (Secondary Educ) MS in Ed. 7: Tchr Eng & hist Thebes High Sch, Thebes Ill 49-50; Army Artillery, Korea & Japan 50-52; Tchr Eng & hist Thebes High Sch, Thebes Ill 52-53; Grad asst in ser UIll (Urbana) 53-55; Asst circ libn Pub Lib, Ft Wayne Ind 55-56; Asst mail ref libn Ill State Lib 56-57; Asst educ libn SoIllU Lib 57-64; Asst circ libn East Ill U Lib 64-67, Circ libn 67-. 10: Phi Delta Kappa; Kappa Delta Pi; Phi Kappa Tau; AAUP. 14: Circ, ref. 15: 806 Kenton dr, Charleston Ill 61920.

ISOM, DOROTHY PORTER. b Seattle 18 F 03. 5: UWash 22-26 (Eng Hist) AB; UOre 28 (Soc Wk); Chicago 42-43 (Soc Wk); Columbia 43-45 (Personnel) MA & Prof Diploma; Immaculate Heart Col 57- (LS) Credential. 7: Five yrs of high sch tchg in Wash State; Five yrs of soc wk in Wash State, Chicago & Orange NJ; Coun for women UHawaii 45-46; Educ adv US Army USAFI Prog, Honolulu & Tokyo Japan 46-48; Dir Student Houses City Col (NY) 48-51; High sch libn Inglewood, San Dieguito, Compton & Downey Cal 52-; Ref libn Cal West U summer 65; Sub libn Pasadena City Lib & Los Angeles Pub Lib 60-. 9: ALA; CalLA; CalSchLA. 10: AAUW; Nat Assn of Women Deans & Counselors; Pi Mu Gamma; Delta Kappa Gamma. 14: Ref, sch libs. 15: 294 Marguerita lane, Pasadena Cal 91106.

ISON, SHIRLEY (COLWELL). b Kodak Ky 9 Ap 37. 4: Clarence Edward Ison. 5: Lees Jr Col 57 (Elem Educ); East Ky U 59-64 (LS, Elem Educ) BS. 7: Tchr Perry Co Bd of Educ, Hazard Ky 60-65, Elem libn 65-67; Elem libn Collier Co Bd of Pub Instr, Naples Fla 67-. 9: NEA; ALA; KyEA; FlaEA (State Delegate); KyASchL; FlaLA. 10: Bus & Profess Women's Club. 11: Kappa Delta Phi. 14: Child bks, catlg. 15: 2895 10th st N, Naples Fl 33940.

ITKIN, STANLEY LAWRENCE. b Brooklyn NY 23 Mr 32. 5: NY City Commun Col 50-52 (Hotel Admin) AAS; Columbia 54-57 (Hist) BA, 57-58 MSLS; Fla State U 59-60 (Hist) MA. 6: Fr, Ital, Sp. 7: Catlgr NY Psychoanalytical Soc, NYC 56-58; Ref libn Queensboro Pub Lib, NYC 58-59; Bkmob libn Leon Co Pub Lib, Tallahassee Fla 59-60; Asst dir Westbury Pub Lib, Westbury NY 60-61; Dir E Paterson Pub Lib, E Paterson NJ 61-66; Dir Hillside Pub Lib, New Hyde Park NJ 66-; Vol Dir Nassau Co Prison Lib 68-. 8: Literacy volunteer Nassau Co. 9: ALA; NYLA. 10: NY Lib Club; Phi Alpha; Internat Reading Assn; Prison Ed Assn. 12: "Operations of the East Gulf Blockade Squadron in the Blockade of Florida in 1862-5" (62). 13: Yes. 14: Admin, ref. 15: 25-11 Union st, Flushing NY 11352.

IVANOFF, EVELYN IRENE. b Aberdeen SD 31 Mr 20. 5: No State Col 38-42 (Educ) BS; Peabody 50-51 (LS) MA. 6: Ger. 7: High sch tchr pub schs, Barnard SD 42-43; High sch tchr pub schs, Selby SD 43-50; Asst libn No State Col (Aberdeen SD) 51-53; Sch libn pub schs, Mountain Lake Minn 53-57; Sch libn pub schs, Ortonville Minn 57-66; Asst libn, Asst Prof of Lib Sci Augustana Col (SD) 66-68; Asst Libn, Asst Prof of Lib Sci NM Highlands U 68-. 9: ALA; NEA; NMEA; NMLA. 10: Amer Bus Women's Assn; AAUP. 14: Lib educ. 15: 704 Lori lane, Las Vegas Nm 87701.

IVANTCHO, BARBARA (PORTEOUS). b Newton Mass 23 F 15. 4: John B Ivantcho. 5: Springfield Jr Col 31-32; Wellesley 32-35 (Ger) BA; Columbia 40-41 BS in LS. 6: Fr, Ger. 7: Lib asst Enoch Pratt Free Lib, Baltimore 37-42; Libn Spec Serv USAF 42-46; Libn McGraw-Hill Publ Co, NYC 47-48; Libn US Info Serv Lib, Istanbul Turkey 49-53; Libn US Info Serv Lib, Karachi Pakistan 54-56; Head tech processes Stanford Research Inst Lib, Menlo Park Cal 57-61, Asst manager Lib Serv 62-. 9: SLA (pres San Francisco Bay Reg Chap 68-69); CalLA. 14: Ref, admin. 15: 783 27th st, San Francisco Ca 94131.

IVERS, FRANCIS XAVIER SJ. b Yonkers NY 17 Ag 12. 5: Woodstock Col 36 BA, 37 MA, 44 STL; Columbia 46 BS in LS. 6: Fr, Ger, Lat. 7: Libn Woodstock Col 46-60; Dir of Libs St Peter's Col 60-. 8: Prof of Philos, LeMoyne Col 50-51. 9: ALA; CathLA; Cath Theol Soc Amer; NJLA. 12: Bk rev ed "Theological Studies" (51-60). 14: Col lib admin, tech proc. 15: St Peter's Col, Jersey City NJ 07306.

IVES, CORNELIA MERRIMAN. b Baltimore Md 20 My 43. 5: Mt Holyoke 61-65 (Amer Studies) BA; Columbia 65-66 MLS. 7: Prof asst Baltimore Co Pub Lib 66-68, Sr prof asst 68-. 9: MdLA (Prog Chm; RS/Md Affiliate ALA). 14: Ref. 15: 10 Dunkirk rd, Baltimore Md 21212.

IVES, HELEN ELIZABETH (HEITMANN). b Louisville Ky 31 Jl 40. 4: Robert Loyal Ives. 5: Swarthmore 58-63 (Hist) BA; Rutgers 63-64 MLS; UPittsburgh 67-69 (Hist). 6: Fr. 7: Stud asst Rutgers U Lib 63-64; Ref libn Fed Res Bank of NYC 64-67; Info libn (Ref) UPittsburgh Lib 67-. 9: SLA; ASIS; PennLA. 14: Ref. 15: 240 Melwood ave, Pittsburgh Pa 15213.

IVEY, BARBARA M. b Ottawa Kan 17 D 28. 5: Ottawa U (Kan) 46-48 ; Park Col 48-49; Kan State Tchrs Col 55-57 (Eng, BA; 66-67 MLibnship. 6: Fr. 7: Libn Spec Serv Dept of Army, Japan, France, Italy, Germany 50-52, 57-66; Libn Ft Vancouver Reg Lib Vancouver Wash 67-69; Asst command libn Hq Strategic Air Command, Offu tt AFB Neb 69-. 8: Lib/USA, NY World's Fair, 64. 9: ALA; WashLA; PNLA. 10: AAUW; Soroptomist. 14: Pub Lib Admin, Armed Forces Libs. 15: 1915 S 44th st #308, Omaha Nb 68105.

IVEY, FANNIE MARY (SPOTTS). b Georgetown Ky 21 F 18. 5: Ky State Col 35-39 (Hist, govt Sociol, Econ) AB; Fisk 41-43 (LS) Certif, summer 58 (soc studies); UChicago 45-46 MLS; UHawaii 66. 6: Fr. 7: Tchr & asst libn David High Sch, Georgetown Ky 39-43; Libn morris Col 43-45; Libn AllenU 46-48; Tchr & chm of dept soc studies Lincoln High Sch, Sumter SC 48-. 8: Tchr adult eve classes Lincoln High Sch, Sumter SC; Wk with voter registration; Helped set up lib at Morris Col; Wked correcting catlg at AllenU; Libn, morris Col summer 54-; Vis prof of Lib Sci Morris Col. 9: NEA; Nat Coun of Soc Studies 9adv Com); SCEA (Soc Studies Div: co-chm 67, sec-treas 69); SEast Reg Textbk Com. 10: UChicago Grad (Lib Sch Alumni); Coun on Hu 10: UChicago Grad (Lib Sch Alumni); Coun on Human Rel; LWV; SumterCoTA; PalmettoEA; Girl Scouts; YMCA; PTA; Assn of Fed Women's Clubs; Nat Assn of Colored Women's Clubs; Frank Madison Reed Club; Sigma Gamma Rho. 11: Plaque from Tchrs Col ColumbiaU for study on improving school attendance 53; Woman of the Year SEast Dist of Nat Coun of Negro Women 56; Woman of the Year Pee Dee Dist of Fed Clubs 57; Citation for outstanding commun & youth serv, Elks 57; Recognition from Okla Sch of the Air for wk on Truancy 57; Citation for commun, state, & nat serv, Sacred Heart, Elks 64. 13: Yes. 14: Selection of bks for high sch students. 15: 106 S Washington st, Sumter SC 29150.

IVEY, VIVIAN (HARRIS). b NC 19 Je 33. 4: Van Francis Ivey. 5: Va State Col 52-56 (LS) BS; Mass U Ext at Boston State Col 63 (LS); Boston U 64 (LS). 6: Fr, Sp. 7: Libn Sch Bd, Williamsburg Va 56-57; Libn Johnston Co Sch Bd, Smithfield NC, Richard B Harrison Sch, Selma NC 58-59; Post libn Dept of the Army, Ft Devens Mass 63; Med libn VA, Bedford Mass 63-64; Libn Pitt Co Bd of Educ, Greenville NC, Bethel Union Sch, Bethel NC 64-65; Lib supv Rocky Mt Schs, Rocky Mt NC 65-69; Libn Prince William Co Sch Bd, Manassas Va 69. 9: NEA; NCTchrs Assn. 10: Delta Sigma Theta. 14: Ref. 15: 14824 Danville rd, Dale City, Woodbridge Va 22191.

IYENGAR, SRINIVASA (T K). b Mysore India 12 Ja 33. 4: Sudha Ranganayaki. 5: Mysore U (India0 48-52 (Physics) BS; Banaras U Lib Sch 54-55 DLS; Simmons 61-63 MSLS; Chicago 64- (LS), Fellow of the Grad Lib sch 64-65. 6: Ger, Fr, Hindi, Kan, Sanskrit. 7: Asst libn Food Research Inst, Mysore India 53-54; Asst libn Tech Research Lab (Min F & Ag), Calcutta 55-56; Ed tech asst Sahitya Akademi Bibliog, Calcutta 56-57; Sr tech asst Nat Lib of India, Calcutta 57-60; Sr documentalist Nat Sci Doc Center, New Delhi 60-61; Order libn Boston U Libs 62-64; Sci libn John Crerar Lib, Chicago 64-66; Chief Libn Chicago Med Sch 66-68; Hd Sci Lib UWaterloo (Ont) 68-69, Dir Ind Inst of Sci Lib 69-. 8: Participated in the compilation of "Indic Material" for UNESCO's "Index Translationum," Calcutta 59; occasional consul & adv serv towards Indic material received under PL480 program while at Boston U 62-64; Memb Adv Bd Reg Med Lib Planning, Chicago 66-67; Consul Med Lib Mt Sinai Hosp 68; Observer IFLA meeting 67; Visiting Prof, lib sci Rosary Col 66, 67, sum mer 69. 9: Amer Oriental Soc; Indian Assn Spec Libs & Info Centers; SLA; MedLA; AAAS; AAUP; AALS. 12: "Bibliography of India Botany" (61); "Documentation and Facets" (63) ; "Education for Librarianship" (67). 13: Yes. 14: Sci info serv, research & acad libnship, admin. 15: Dir Ind Inst of Science Lib, Bangalou India.

IYER, THANGAM R. b Nabha India 22 4 23. 5: Banaras Hindu U 43-44 (Math) MA; UChicago 59-60 (LS) MA. 6: Malayalam, Tamil, Hindi. 7: Libn USIA, Madras 52-66; Catlgr LC 66-. 9: ALA; SLA (India). 14: Catlg. 15: 6402 Leyte dr, Oxon Hill Md 20021.

IZANT, HAROLD ALFRED. b London 18 Je 13. 4: Veronica Nora. 5: Kings Col ULondon BA; University Col ULondon Diploma in Libnship. 6: Fr. 7: Asst libn & deputy libn London Sch of Hygiene & Tropical Med 35-46; Med Libn British Coun, London 46-47; Ed World Health Org, Geneva 47-52, Chief Libn 52-. 8: Survey of Med Libs in Middle East 62-63; World Health Org lecturer on med libnship American U of Beirut 64-65. 9: Assn Internat Libns; (Brit) LA (Fellow). 10: III Internat Congress of Med Libnship. 12: "Bibliography of WHO Publications." 13: Yes. 14: Med bibliog. 15: 178 route de Grand Lancy 1213 Onex, Geneve Switzerland.

IZARD, ANNE REBECCA. b Henderson NC 22 Ap 16. 5: Duke 33-37 (Eng) AB; Simmons 39-40 (LS). 6: Fr, Sp. 7: Asst in catlg dept Duke Lib 37-39; Jr asst NY Pub Lib 40-41, Child libn 40-45; Head wk with child Greenwich Conn 45-46; 1st asst wk with child, Mt Vernon NY 46-48, Head of wk with child 49-55; Admin asst to chief of circ dept NY Pub Lib 55-58; Asst br libn & chief br child libn NY Pub Lib 58-59; Child consul Westchester (NY) Lib System 59-. 8: Nat Ed Bd, Scholastic Bk Serv , See-Saw Bk Program 67; Vista Training Program 68; Lecturer WMich U Inst 69; Lecturer Kutztown Annual Conference for Stud Assn 67, 69; Memb Doubleday 69 Bks for Young Readers Adv Com 69. 09: ALA (mem & chm CBC Com 62-65, chm Dutton McRae Award Com 60-61, Subs Bks Bul Com 61-63);-CSD (treas 51-52 & 64-67, mem 5 coms 47-67); NYLA (Memb Com 53-56, mem & chm Publs Com 59-65; Child & YA Serv Sect: sec- treas 52-53, pres 54-55, Bd 55-56 & 63-65); WestchesterLA (org Westchester Sch & Child Libns Com) (past pres) now Westchester YA & Child Serv Sect Westche ster LA. 10: Nat Audubon Soc; Zonta Inter nat. 12: Bk Column in "Grade Teacher" magazine (52-66). 13: Yes. 14: Wk with child in pub libs. 15: 151 Clarence rd, Scarsdale Ny 10585.

J

JAANSCO-JOE, TIIU MAI. b Estonia 28 D 40. 5: Sir George Williams U 59-63 (Sociol) BA; McGill 63-64 BLS. 6: Eng, Fr, Estonian, Swedish. 7: Circ clerk Sir George Williams U (Montreal) summers 62, 63; Asst libn Aluminum Co of Can, Montreal 65-68; Nat Gallery of Can Lib, Ottawa Ont Can 68-. 9: CanLA. 14: Catlg. 15: National Gallery of Canada Lib, Ottawa 4 Ont Can.

JABLONOWSKI, CHRISTINA (WASYNCZUK). b Warsaw Poland 22 N 22. 4: Thaddeus Jablonowski. 5: Gymnasiun in Lvov Poland 32-39 (Math) Maturity Certif; Johann Wolfgang Goethe U (Frankfurt Ger) 46-48 (Mod Lang) Certif. 6: Ger, Polish, Russian, Fr, Ukrainian. 7: Nurse (med sec) 1077 Lab Supply Co Det B Hosp US Army 46-48; Libn Chandler Evans Inc, W Hartford Conn 59-. 9: SLA. 14: Ref, transl. 15: 211 Portman st, Windsor Ct 06095.

JACCAUD, ROBERT (DALE). b Powell Ohio 21 S 40. 4: Sylvia Ann Weiss. 5: Ohio Wesleyan U 58-62 (Hist) BA; IndU 62-63 (LS) MA. 6: Fr. 7: Lib asst Delaware Co Dist Lib, Delaware Ohio 58-62; Ref asst IndU 63; Lima Pub Lib, Lima Ohio: Bkmob libn 63-64, Ref asst 63-64, Asst head ext dept 64-65; Hd ref dept 65-66; US Army 66-69; Dartmouth Col Lib ref asst 69-. 9: ALA. 10: Beta Phi Mu; Alpha Tau Omega; Amer Polit Items Collectors. 11: $2000 Scholarship from State Lib of Ohio 63. 14: Ref, ext. 15: 6 Fletcher cir, Hanover NH 03755.

JACKETT, MRS LYNN HARRIS. b Cleveland 21 O 13. 5: Bowling Green State U 31-33 (Educ) 2 yr Ed Certif; West Res 58-60 (Educ) BS, 60-63 MSLS. 7: Tchg Cleveland Day Nursery Assn, Cleveland 33-35; Asst child libn Cleveland Pub Lib 36-40; Sch libn S Euclid-Lyndhurst Bd of Educ, Lyndhurst Ohio 60-. 9: ALA- AASchL; OhioEA; OhioLA; OhioASchL ; Women's Nat Bk Assn; Educl Media Coun of Ohio. 10: Beta Phi Mu. 14: Ya, ref, child serv. 15: 1675 Richmond rd, Cleveland Oh 44124.

JACKMAN, MABEL E(MILY). b Sanborn ND 3 Ja 03. 5: State Tchrs Col (Duluth Minn) 18-20; UMinn 23-25 (Hist) BS, summers 27-32 (LS); Chicago summers 34-40 (LS) MA. 7: Tchr-libn High sch, Bingham Lake Minn 25-27; Tchr, libn High sch, Wells Minn 27-30; Libn High Sch & Jr Col, Coleraine Minn 30-37; Libn U High Sch UMinn(Minneapolis) 37-42; Libn Milne Sch SUNY(Albany) 42-, Instr of catlg & clsf Dept of Lib Sci 42-60. 9: ALA; NYLA (past Coun mem & Sect Bd). 10: Delta Kappa Gamma. 12: Co-auth "Fare for the Reluctant Reader" (52); Co-auth "Fare for the Reluctant Reader" (64). 14: Sch lib. 15: 11 So Lake ave, Albany Ny 12203.

JACKSON, ADELE BERNICE (MARTIN). b North Garden Va 15 O 18. 4: Hezekiah Jackson. 5: Va State Col 34-38 (Fr) AB; UMich 45-46 ABLS. 6: Fr. 7: Tchr Buckingham Co Train Sch, Dillwyn Va 38-41, 42-43; Tchr & libn; Greenville Co Train Sch, Emporia Va 41-42, Albemarle Co Train Sch, Charlottesville Va 43-45; Catlg libn Southern U 46-48, 53-; Negro serv libn LSU (Baton Rouge) 48-51; Lib asst Mich State U Lib (E Lansing) 51-52. 8: Freshman adv Southern U 57-59. 9: ALA; LaLA; SWLA. 10: Baton Rouge Chapter links Inc; YWCA; Audubon Coun Girl Scouts. 11: Alpha Kappa Alpha. 14: Catlg, ref. 15: 2066 - 79th ave, Baton Rouge La 70807.

JACKSON, ALICE A(TWATER). b Petersburg Va 16 Mr 07. 5: Va State Col 23-27 (Chem) BS; Hampton Inst 29-30 (LS) BS; Columbia 37-38 (LS) MS. 7: Catlgr Va State Col 30-44; Catlgr Morgan State Col 44-45; Supv acquis Howard U 45-47; Catlgr Manhattanville Col of the Sacred Heart 47-57; Libn Fayetteville State Col 57-60; Libn Del State Col 60-62; Educ libn Va State Col 62-. 8: Coord Negro Collection-Schomburg Collection (then 135th St Br) Countee Cullen Br NY Pub Lib 36; Dir Recatlg Proj, Ala State Tchrs Col, 43; Mem Middle States Assn Rating Team, 50; Survey tech serv Morgan State Col, 53. 9: ALA-Col & Res Libs & Tech Serv; Va LA. 10: Alpha Kappa Alpha. 14: Catlg. 15: 123 New st, Petersburg Va 23803.

JACKSON, ALTHEA HALL (MRS). b Taunton Mass 27 Je 22. 5: Middlebury Col 40-44 (Span) AB; Simmons summers 61-65 (LS) MS. 6: Sp. 7: Preliminary catlgr Widener Lib Harvard U summers 42, 43; Lab tech Gen Radio Co, Cambridge Mass 44; Sr admitting clerk Mass Eye & Ear Infirmary, Boston 51; Asst to the catlgr Littauer Lib Harvard U 52; Asst libn & Sp tchr Howard Sch, W Bridgewater Mass 59-60; Libn Whitman-Hanson Reg High Sch, Whitman Mass 60-64; Libn St Anne's Sch, Arlington Mass 64; Asst ref libn Medford Pub Lib, Medford Mass 65; Hd Libn Mt Ida Jr Col 65-66; Elem Sch Libn Pub Schs, Braintree Mass 66-67; Sch Libn Pub Schs, Weymouth Mass 67-69; Tech Libn Microwave & Tube Operation Lib Raytheon Co, Waltham Mass 69-. 9: ALA; NELA; South Shore Sch Libns (chm 63-64 permanent pres); MassSchLA (Bd 63-64). 14: Col libnship, tech libs & sch libs. 15: 40 Jones ave, Randolph Ma 02368.

JACKSON, ANN (ROGERS). b Birmingham Ala 15 Je 32. 5: Memphis State U 60 (Eng) BS; Tex Woman's U 61 MLS; Simmons (NDEA Inst) 66; Boston U (A-V). 06: Ger, Fr. 7: Head Libn Stoughton Pub Lib, Stoughton Mass 61-62; Libn Needham Pub Schs, Needham Mass 62-67; Libn Northeastern U Instr Media Info Ctr, Boston 67-69; A-V Libn Boston Pub Lib 69-. 10: Great Books groups. 12: Ed "Educational Innovations". 14: Ya serv, admin, a-v. 15: 3 Gould st, Needham Heights Ma 02194.

JACKSON, ANNE (L STINGLEY). b Blevins Ark. 5: Henderson State Tchrs Col (Eng) AB; Tex Womans U MLS. 6: Fr, Ger. 7: Tchr-libn pub sch, Washington 40-46; Head Libn Arkadelphia City & Clark Co Lib, Arkadelphia Ark 46-53; Consul high sch & pub libs Ark Lib Commsn, Little Rock Ark 53-65; Coord ESEA Title II fed Programs div State Dept of Educ Little Rock Ark 65-. 8: Adv Ark Stud Libns Assn 54- (State Sponsor); Consul for local & state wkshops; Guest Lecturer Tex Woman's U summer 65; Bk talks for television; United Nations. 9: ALA; NEA; ArkLA; SWLA (publ chm); ArkEA. 10: AAUW; Amer Assn for UN; Altrusa Internat; Ark Hist Assn; Ark Arts Center; Delta Kappa Gamma; Kappa Delta Pi; Alpha Chi; Adv memb Marquis Biographical Lib Soc. 11: Certif of Merit 56 by Ark Jr C of C . 12: Ed Com (ALA) "Basic Book Collection for High Schools" (57); Comp "Arkansiana for High Schools" (55, rev ed 64). 13: Yes. 14: Consul, supv rare bks, state hist. 15: 321 E Seventh st, Little Rock Ar 72202.

JACKSON, AUDREY (LEE) NABOR. b New Orleans 10 Jl 26. 4: Freddie Jackson Sr. 5: Southern U 44-46, 47-51 (Soc Sci) BS; LSU 54 (LS); Chicago Tchrs Col 60 (LS); Southern U 63-66 (Admin & S upv) MA; LSU 68-69 (LS). 7: Libn J S Dawson High Sch, St Francisville La 51-54; Libn Southdown High Sch, Houma La 54-55; Libn Chaneyville High Sch, Zachary La 55-. 8: Consul: State meeting 60,62, wkshop Southern U summer 61; Chm Prof Group E Baton Rouge Parish 64-. 9: ALA-AASchL;-CSD; LaEA (pres Lib Dept 51-); LaLA. 10: YWCA; La Club De Charmette; Futurama Soc Club; Jr League of Amer; E Baton RougeEA. 13: Yes. 14: Ref, publ. 15: Rt 2 Box 62 F, Zachary La 70791.

JACKSON, BARBARA (BRIDGES). b Richmond Va 9 N 42. 4: Ronald L Jackson. 5: William & Mary 60-64 (Eng) BA; CatholicU 66-67 NS in LS; UMd 69 (LS). 6: Fr, Ger. 7: Elem sch libn, Anne Arundel Co Md 64-66; Bkmob libn Prince George's Co Memorial Lib, Md 66; Lib asst Walter Reed Med Ctr Lib 66-67; Assoc ref libn tech & sci div McKeldin Lib UMd (Col Park)67-. 9: DCLA. 10: Beta Phi Mu. 14: Ref, sci & med libs. 15: McKeldin Lib Univ of Md, College Park Md 20742.

JACKSON, BERNADINE (ROACH). b Addison NY 18 Jl 21. 4: William A Jackson. 5: State U Col (Geneseo NY) 39-43 (LS) BS; State U Col (Buffalo NY) 55, 57; State U Col (Geneseo NY) summers 57-60 MLS. 7: Libn High Sch, Phelps NY 43-44; Tchr Elem sch, Gowanda NY 46-48; Libn High Sch, Cattaraugus NY 55-. 9: NY State Tchrs Assn; NYLA. 10: Monday Evening Lit Club. 15: 83 Erie ave, Gowanda Ny 14070.

JACKSON, BETTY HARVEY (MARY ELIZABETH). b El Paso Tex 14 Je 20. 4: Earl Armstrong Jackson. 5: UAriz 37-41 (Home Econ); Ariz State U 59-61 (Home Econ) BA, 61-63 (LS) MA in Ed. 6: Sp. 7: Libn Mesa (Ariz) Sch Dist, Westwood High Sch 63-. 9: ALA; NEA; ArizSchL; ArizEA. 10: Phi Kappa Phi. 14: Wk with teen-agers. 15: 819 E 9th pl, Mesa Az 85201.

JACKSON, BETTY SOUTHGATE (HARRIET). b Geneva NY 23 Ap 21. 4: Jasper A Jackson. 5: Swarthmore 40-42; UMich 42-44 (Zool, Chem) BS. 7: Med tech Maloney Clinic UPenn 46-48; Med tech Nutrition Clinic Penn Hosp, Phila 48-49; Los Alamos Sci Lab, Los Alamos NM: Biomed tech 50-55, Biomed research asst 55-58, Asst libn Main Lib 58-65, Report libn Report Lib 65-66, Ref libn 66-. 9: SLA. 13: Yes. 14: Ref, admin. 15: 120 Sherwood W R, Los Alamos Nm 87544.

JACKSON, BRYANT HARVEY. b Los Angeles 2 Ag 23. 4: Donette Davis Jackson. 5: U of Redlands 41-45 (Hist) BA; UCal(Los Angeles) 45-46 (Educ); USoCal 49-50 MSLA; UIll 62- (LS). 7: Tchr Bishop High Sch, Bishop Cal 46-49; Libn Kan Wesleyan U 50-51; Head tech serv Kan State Col (Pittsburg) 51-60; Ser catlgr Ill State U 60-65, Assoc dir 65-. 9: ALA; IllLA. 10: AAUP; Phi Delta Kappa; Alpha Beta Alpha. 15: 303 Oakdale ave, Normal Il 61761.

JACKSON, CAROLYN (JANE). b Paris Tex 2 My 37. 5: Tex Woman's U 55-59, 59-60 (LS) BA, MLS. 6: Sp, Fr. 07: Lib asst Midwestern U 60-62, Acquis libn 62-67, Bibliogr 67-68; Asst Libn Sul Ross State Col 68-. 9: ALA; TexLA; SWLA; Tex Assn Col Tchrs. 10: Bus & Prof Women's Guild; AAUW; Alpha Beta Alpha; Faculty Dames MidwesternU. 14: Acquis, catlg, ref. 15: Claridge apts 107, Alpine Tx 79830.

JACKSON, CLARA (OSTROWSKY). b NYC 5 Jl 15. 4: Dr Sidney L Jackson. 5: UMinn 32-37 (LS) BS; Columbia 56-58 (Early Childhood Educ) MS, 39, 59 (LS) MA. 6: Fr, Ger. 7: Asst Educ Seminars UMinn(Minneapolis) 37-39; Ser catlgr Columbia U Butler Lib 39-44; Libn Agnes Russell Center Tchrs Col (NY) 58-59; Temp Asst Prof Kent State U Dept of Lib Sci 63-. 8: Child Study Assn Bk Sel Com 45-53; Ohio Liaison Encyclopaedia Britannica Sch Lib Awards Program 66 -; Dir sch lib workshop Kent StateU 66-. 9: NEA; NCTE; ACEI; IRA; OhioLA (chm Lib Serv To Schs Rdt 67-69); ALA; EMCO; Ohio A Schl (sec 68-69). 10: AAUW; LWV; Phi Beta Kappa. 13: Yes. 14: Catlg, child wk, bk sel, ref, sch libs. 15: 424 E Summit st, Kent Oh 44240.

JACKSON, DOROTHY GAIL. b Cherokee County Chesnee SC 16 Ja 39. 5: Gardner-Webb Col 57-59 AA; Appalachian State U 59-61 (Eng) BS, 62-66 (LS) MA. 6: Fr. 7: Hd libn Gaffney Sr High Sch, Gaffney SC 61-63; Instr lib sci USCar ext 67-69; Lib dir Anderson Col (Anderson SC) 63-. 8: State Coord of Jr Cols of SC for ALA 68-. 9: ALA; SELA; SCLA. 10: Altrusa Club. 14: Admin, ref. 15: 4-A-3 Bailey ct, anderson SC 29621.

JACKSON, EDITH MATILDA (KLOR, SEIDEL). b NY 13 Je 26. 4: Frank Lester Jackson. 5: Hunter Col 45-49 (Eng) BA; Columbia 49-52 (LS) MS; Hofstra Col 57 (Educ); St John's U 57-59 (LS, Educ); Fordham 60 (Educ). 6: Ger. 7: Asst to catlgr NYU catlg dept, Wash Sq NY 51-52; Libn US Army & Air Force Mitchel Air Force Base, Germany, Japan, Camp Kilmer NJ 52-56; Elem sch libn Gallow Sch, Island Trees Levittown NY 56-59; Elem sch libn Central Sch Dist 4, Plainview NY 59-61; Catlgr Long Beach Pub Lib, Long Beach NY 61-62; Dir W Hempstead Pub Lib, W Hempstead NY 62-64; Dir Amityville Free Lib, Amityville NY 64- 65; Jr high sch libn Lindenhurst Pub Schs, Lindenhurst NY 65-67; Asst dir North Bellmore Pub Lib, N Bellmore NY 68-. 14: Ref, catlg. 15: 23 Oakley pl, West Islip LI Ny 11795.

JACKSON, EDWARD SARGENT. b Seattle 5 My 26. 5: Ore State Col 44-46, 47-49 (Gen Sci); UOre 47-50 (Educ) BS, 54-55 (Gen Studies) MS; UWis 61-62 (LS) MS. 7: Supply clerk Army Air Force (Pfc) 46-47; Computer E F Hutten Co, San Francisco 50-51; R & D Off USAF, Sacramento Cal 51-55; Tchr-libn high sch, Elmira Ore 55-56; Tchr-libn Jr High Sch, La Grande Ore 56-58; Tchr-libn USAF Dependent Schs, Turkey, Libya, France 58-61; Ref libn UIda 62-66; Asst libn Central Ore Commun Col 66-. 9: PNLA; ALA; OreLA. 14: Ref. 15: 209 Po rtland ave, Bend Or 97701.

JACKSON, EDWIN G(EORGE). b Detroit 28 F 11. 4: Archer Sims Jackson. 5: UMich 29-33 (Lit, Sci, Arts) AB; Columbia 36-38 (LS) BS. 7: Br libn NY Pub Lib 38-42; Corp trust administrator & chief job analyst Bank of Manhattan, NYC 42-50; Asst libn Akron Pub Lib, Akron Ohio 51-57; Dir Free Pub Lib, Trenton NJ 57-61; Libn Hartford Pub Lib, Hartford Conn 61-. 8: Mem & chm Conn Governor's Com on Libs, 61-65. 9: ALA (Coun at large 67-71); Intel freedom com, 64-69; Circ control com, memb H W Wilson Lib Recruitment Award Jury 65-66; Spec Com on interrelated lib serv to studs);-LAD (Bd Memb 67-71); NELA; ConnLA (past-pres); Capitol Reg LA. 10: Hartford Rotary Club; Torch Club of the Conn Valley Hartford Club. 13: Yes. 14: Pub lib admin. 15: 500 Main st, Hartford Ct 06103.

JACKSON, ELIZABETH (CARTER CHRISTIAN). b Baltimore 17 F 34. 4: William Rudolph Jackson. 5: Ala Col 51-53; Oglethorpe Col 53-55 (Soc Sci) BA; Emory 55-56 (LS) MLn; Roanoke Col summer 59; Emory summers 60, 63. 7: Child libn Decatur-DeKalb Reg Lib, Decatur Ga 56-58; Libn Briarcliff High Sch, DeKalb Co Ga 58-60; Pub serv asst Allentown Free Lib, Allentown Penn 60; Ref libn Ga State Col 61-63; Libn So Sch of Pharmacy Mercer U 63-. 9: ALA; SLA (v-pres Ga Chap 65-66); SELA; GaLA (chm spec lib); MedLA. 13: Yes. 14: Ref. 15: 1715 Ridgewood dr NE, Atlanta Ga 30307.

JACKSON, EUGENE B(ERNARD). b Frankfort Ind 18 Je 15. 4: Ruth Whitlock. 5: Purdue 33-37 (Sci) BS; UIll (Urbana) 37-38 BS in LS, 38-42 (LS) MA; Tex Tech Col 43-44 (Mech engrg); US Army Lib Sch (Paris) 45. 6: Ger, Fr. 7: Jr Prof Asst Engnr Lib UIll(Urbana) 38-40, Asst in chg Newspaper Room 40-41; Documents libn UAla 41-42; Prof asst tech dept Detroit Pub Lib 42-46; (Sgt) US Army 43-46, Lib tech Spec Serv Depot US Army, Ruisbruck Belgium 45; Libn Wright Field Ref Lib & Chief Lib Sect Central Air Docs, Off Army-Navy-AF, Wright Patterson AFB Ohio 46-49; Chief res info sect R&D Command OQMG, Wash DC 49-50; Chief res info div Nat Adv Com for Aero, Wash DC 50-56; Head lib dept Gen Motors Research Labs, Warren Mich 56-65; Dir of info retrieval & lib serv Corporate Hdqrs IBM, Armonk NY 65-. 8: US mem Documentation Com Adv Group for Aeronautical Research & Development (NATO) 53-61; McBee Lecturer Simmons Col 56; J C Dana Lecturer UMich 64; J C Dana Lecturer Simmons Col 65; Trustee Kresge-Hooker Sci Lib Assn Wayne State U 58-65 (pres 64); Visiting Lect Lib Sci UMich summer 64; Org & Chm GM Com on Tech Lit 59-65; Prof consul SLA 62-; Info Systems Steering Com, Engineers Jt Coun 62-67; Lincoln Series Lecturer on Tech Problems Col of Bus Admin Ariz State U(Tempe) 69; Assoc Fellow Amer Inst of Aero nautics & Astronautics Concul Sci Lib Project, METRO 67. 9: SLA (pres Exec Bd 61-62, Div chm, Chap pres 48-50 (Prof consul 63-); ALA; Nat Commsn Lib Educ; Adv Com Lib Tech Proj (chm 65-); ASIS (US Nat Com to Internat Documentation Fed, del to Internat Documentation Fed Gen Assemblies: Tokyo 67, The Hague 68). 10: Tech Adv Com Macomb Co (Mich) Planning Commsn; Mich State Lib Com on Research Needs; Amer Inst Aeron & Astron; Engnr Soc of Detroit; Amer Standards Assn Com Z39; Amer Mgt Assn; Engineering Index, Inc , Tripartite Com of The Engnr Profession EI-EJC-UEI. 12: "Books and Publishing" (56) (Boston, Simmons Col); Co-ed "Library Trends," Jan 66 issue: "Library Service to Industry." 13: Yes. 14: Aero engnr lit, automotive lit, info retrieval, ref, mechanization , abstracting engnr lit, admin of ind libs. 15: IBM Corp Rt 22, Armonk NY 10504.

JACKSON, HARRIETT (DAVIS). b Ripley Miss 21 O 28. 5: Miss State Col for Women 45-49 (Elem Educ) BSE; UMiss summer 60-62 MLS. 7: Tchr: Corinth Elem Sch, Corinth Miss 49-52, Ripley Elem Sch, Ripley Miss 52-60; Libn: South Tippah High Sch, Ripley Miss 60-63, Oakhaven High Sch, Memphis Tenn 63-65, Winchester Elem Sch, Memphis Tenn 65-66; Libn Whitehaven Pub Lib, Memphis Tenn 66-. 14: Ref, reader adv, child wk. 15: 4974 Haleville, Memphis Tn 38116.

JACKSON, JACQUELINE ADAMS. b Hatonia Tex 19 Jl 13. 5: Baylor 30-34 (Eng, Fr) BA; UColo 35; Barnard 38; Our Lady of the Lake Col 66-68 (LS) MS; EmoryU 68 Med Lib Certif. 6: Fr, Ger. 7: Tchr Hondo High Sch, Hondo Tex 35-38; Tchr Northside Jr High, corpus Christi Tex 38-39; Tchr Robert Driscoll Jr High, Corpus Christi Tex 39-41& jr libn San Antonio Col Lib 68-. 9: ALA; TexLA; BexarLA. 14: Ref. 15: 1530 W Gramercy pl, San Antonio Tx 78201.

JACKSON, JAMES EMMITT JR. b Passaic NJ 18 S 35. 5: Wilberforce U 54-57 (Chem, Math) BS; Rutgers 64-66 MLS. 6: Ital, Ger. 7: Navigator (1st Lt) USAF, Minot AFB N Dak 58-63; A-v libn E Orange Pub Lib, E Orange NJ 63-. 8: Instr A-V Wkshop NJLA; Pre-Screening Com EFLA Film Festival 68-69. 9: ALA; EFLA; FLIC; NJLA. 14: Films, slides, filmstrips, recordings. 15: 275 Springdale ave, E Orange NJ 07017.

JACKSON, JOSEPH ABRAM. b Brewton Ala 17 O 33. 5: Howard Col 54 (Soc Sci, Eng, Music) AB; Peabody 55 MA(LS). 06: Sp. 7: Catlgr UAla 55-63, Head sci lib 63-67 , Asst univ libn 67-. 8: Tchr Ethiopia Africa 56-57; UAla Faculty Coun , 67, 68-. 09: SELA; AlaLA (sec 64-65). 14: Admin, spec sci libs, catlg. 15: Box S, University Al 35486.

JACKSON, JUANITA (CHEATHAM). b Burning Springs W Va 19 D 17. 5: Peabody Col 50-54 (Eng) BA, 54 MALS. 7: Asst ref libn UKy Lib 54-62, Hd ref dept 62-64; Dir of pub serv & chief ref Towson State Col Lib 64-66; Hd ref dept New Britain Pub Lib, New Britain Conn 67-. 9: ALA; ConnLA; KyLA (Recr Chm; ALA recr rep); LexingtonLA (var coms, v-pres & pres-elect). 12: Co-ed "List of Faculty and Staff Publications of the University of Kentucky" (55-61). 13: Yes. 14: Ref, bibliog, govt docs, interlib loan. 15: 67 Cold Spring dr, Vernon Ct 06086.

JACKSON, LILLIE RUTH (McINTYRE). b Decatur County Ga 14 Ja 35. 4: Charles Lee Jackson. 5: Albany State Col 50-54 (Elem Educ) BS; UOkla summer 62; Fla A & M U 56-58 (LS) Certif, 63-66 (Secondary Educ, Eng) MEd. 7: Tchr elem educ, Gadsen Co Fla 54-56; Libn, Gadsen Co Fla: Elem sch 56-59, Jr & sr high 59-. 9: ALA; NEA; FlaLA; FlaEA. 10: PTA; Amer Leg Aux; Fla A & M U Assn. 14: Ref, circ. 15: 433 Cone st, Quincy Fl 32351.

JACKSON, LOUISE LOVEJOY. b New Orleans 19 S 06. 4: James Holland Jackson . 05: Agnes Scott 23-27 (Biol) AB; Emory 56-58 (LS) MLn. 6: Fr. 7: Research tech Emory U 27-30; Asst in lib Gordon Mil Col 56-59, Libn 59-. 9: ALA; NEA; GaEA; Ga Assn Jr Cols (Lib Div); GaLA. 10: Women's League ; AAUP. 14: Acquis, ref. 15: Gordon Mil Col, Barnesville Ga 30204.

JACKSON, MARY (BYRNE). b Windsor Locks Conn 15 Ap 07. 4: Robert F Jackson. 5: Smith 25-29 (Fr) BA; UParis 27-28 Diplo4me d'E3tudes Supe3rieures; Smith 30-34 (Fr) MA, 35-37 (Ger). 6: Fr, Sp, Ital, Ger. 7: Lib asst Smith Col Lib 30-37; Med Libn Inst of Living, Hartford Conn 37-; Assoc ed Digest of Neurology & Psychiatry 52-; Generoso Pope Ed Inst of Living, Hartford Conn 62-. 9: ALA; SLA; NELA. 10: Smith Col Alumnae Assn. 12: Bk reviews "Digest of Neurology & Psychiatry" (42). 13: Yes. 14: Catlg, ref. 15: 71 N Main st, Windsor Locks Ct 06096.

JACKSON, SISTER MARY MERCITA SCL. b Helena Mont 21 S 17. 5: St Mary Col (Kan) 36-40 (Fr) AB; Catholic U 46-47 BS in LS; St Mary Col (Kan) summers 55-59 (Educ) MS, UDenver summer 63. 6: Fr, Sp. 7: Tchr elem grades Sisters of Charity, Mont & Kan 41-50; St Mary Col (Kan): Period libn 50, Circ libn 51, Head catlgr 51-, Assoc libn 60-. 9: ALA; CathLA; Nat Soc Study Educ; KanLA. 14: Catlg, ref. 15: St Mary Col, Xavier Ka 66098.

JACKSON, MARY (TYLER). b San Antonio Tex 18 N 21. 4: Sargent Prentiss Jackson. 5: NorthwesternU 43-45 (Eng); Ill Tchrs 60-65 (LS) MEd; Amer Conservatory of Mus 59-62 (Mus Ed). 6: Fr, Ital. 7: Tchr & libn Chicago Pub Schs 58-68; Period libn DePaulU 68-. 8: Annual vol Miracle of Bks Fair sponsored by Chicago Tribune; Radio appearances lecturing on music; Subcom preparing Tchg Guide for Mus for Chicago Pub Schs 65; Founder & mgr Opera Profiles Inc non-profit org presenting opera to yp. 9: ALA; IllASchL. 10: Chicago Tchr-Libns Club. 13: Yes. 14: Ref. 15: 9441 S Union, Chicago Il 60620.

JACKSON, MARY ALICE (FOLK). b Columbia SC 29 Je 30. 5: Winthrop Col 47-48; USCar 47-51 (Eng) BA; Columbia 52-53 MSLS. 7: Libn ref Armed Forces Med Lib, Wash DC 53; Asst libn St Louis U Sch Med 54-55; Libn ref Armed Forces Med Lib, Wash DC 55; Chief Libn Off of The Surgeon Gen (Army), Wash DC 56-61; Chief Libn Walter Reed Army

Inst of Research, Wash DC 61-66; Chief libn Nat Communicable Disease Ctr, Atlanta 66-. 9: MedLA (Ed Com; chm Research Gp); SLAIS Atlantic Chap bulletin ed). 10: Phi Beta Kappa. 11: Dept Army Certif Achievement. 12: "Union List of Biomedical Periodicals in the Libraries of Walter Reed Army Institute of Research, Walter Reed Army Hospital, Armed Forces Institute of Pathology" (64). 14: Admin, ref. 15: 1652 N Gatewood rd NE 6-D, Atlanta Ga 30329.

JACKSON, MARY LOUISE. b Clover SC 29 Je 36. 5: N Greenville Jr Col 54-56; Winthrop Col 56-58 (Hist) AB; Emory summers 61-64 MLS. 7: Tchr St Paul High Sch, St Paul Va 58-61; Circ libn Winthrop 61-67; Ref libn Wilmington Col (NC) 67-. 9: ALA; NCLA; SELA. 10: Beta Phi Mu; Delta Kappa Gamma. 11: Listed 65 Outstanding Young Women of America. 14: Documents, sers, ref. 15: Oleander Court c-8, Wilmington Nc 28401.

JACKSON, MILES MERRILL (JR). b Richmond Va 28 Ap 29. 4: Bernice Jackson. 5: Va Union U 51-55 (Eng) BA; Drexel 55-56 MSLS; IndU 60, 62 (Adult Educ & LS). 6: Fr. 07: Adult br libn Free Lib of Phila 56-58; Act libn Hampton Inst 58-59, Asst Prof & Head Libn 59-62; Territorial libn Govt of Eastern Samoa, Pago Pago Samoa 62-64; Chief Libn Trevor Arnett Lib Atlanta U 64- , Fulbright lecturer UTehran (Iran) 68-69. 8: ACRL Concul Nat Found for The Humanities; Consul: Paine Col 66, Amer Assn of Univ Presses. 9: ALA; GaLA; SELA. 10: AAUP. 11: Fellow Amer Philos Soc 66. 13: Yes. 12: Auth "A Bibliography of Negro History and Culture for Young Readers" (68); auth "Readings in Comparative and International Librarianship" (70); Ed column 'Libraries Abroad' in "Journal of Library History" (66-). 14: Ref, internat libnship, admin, comparative libnship. 15: Trevor Arnett Lib Atlanta U 273 Chestnut st SW, Atlanta Ga 30314.

JACKSON, NANCY GERTRUDE. b Ft Wayne Ind 23 Ap 43. 5: Concord Col 61-65 (Eng) BA; UNC 65-67 MSLS. 7: Grad asst UNC (Chapel Hill) 65-67; Descr catlgr LC 67-. 9: ALA. 10: Beta Phi Mu. 14: Ref, bibliog, catlg. 15: 2100 Connecticut ave NW apt 610, Washington DC 20008.

JACKSON, PATIENCE KENNEY (ENDSLEY). b Pittsburgh 9 Mr 43. 4: Thad Alwill Jackson. 5: Middlebury Col 60-64 (Ger) BA, 61, 63 (Ger); UPittsburgh 64-65 MLS. 6: Ger, Fr, Russian, Lat. 7: Lib trainee GSPIA Lib UPittsburgh 64-65; Lib asst Spec Serv Lib US Army,P Pirmasens Germany 65-66, Army libn 66-67; Hd Libn Peters Twp Lib, McMurray Pa 67-68; Research libn E I du Pont de Nemours & Co, Wilmington Del 69-. 9: ALA; PennLA. 14: Ref, acquis (for lang wks). 15: 211 South rd, Lindamere Wilmington De 19809.

JACKSON, PAUL TRESCOTT. b Traverse City Mich 21 N 35. 4: Violette Nada (Krstich) Jackson. 5: East Mich U 54-58 (Music) BS; Colgate Rochester Divinity Sch 58-59 (Philos); UMich 64-65 AMLS. 7: Music libn East Mich U Music Dept 54-58; Stage manager Nat Music Camp, Interlochen Mich 56-58; Bandsman 214th Army Band, Anchorage Alaska 59-62; Coun Interlochen Arts Acad, Interlochen Mich 62-63; Pre-prof libn Detroit Pub Lib Music Dept 63-64; Music asst WUOM-FM Music Lib UMich(Ann Arbor) 64-65; Libn NY Pub Lib Rodgers & Hammerstein Recordings Archive at Lincoln Center 65-67; Info-Materials Control mgr The Richmond Org NYC 67-68; Performing arto libn Oakland U(Mich) 68-. 09: ALA; MucLA; SLA; Assn for Recorded Sound Collections (corves sec). 10: Phi Mu Alpha (Life mem). 12: "Music Awards for String Players" (64). 13: Yes. 14: Music ref & archival sound recordings. 15: 510 Wilcox st, Rochester Mi 48063.

JACKSON, REBA JUNE (COMBS). b Allais Ky 15 Ja 35. 4: David Lee Jackson. 5: Cumberland Col 54-55 (Elem Educ) summers 60, 61 (Elem Educ) BS; UKy summers 56, 58, 59 (Elem Educ), summer 66 Certif for sch libn; East Ky U summers 67, 68 Certif for sch libn. 7: Tchr Perry Co Schs, Hazard Ky 55-66; Elem sch libn Big Creek Elem Sch, Perry Co 66-. 9: NEA; ALA; KyLA; KyEA; KyASchL. 14: Sch libs. 15: PO Box 171, Hazard Ky 41701.

JACKSON, REBECCA JANE. b Erie Penn 29 Jl 33. 5: Penn State U 51-53, 55-57 (Hist) BA; Syracuse summer 58 (LS); UDenver 64- (LS), 64-67 MA. 07: Jr-Sr high libn Lewistown Sch Dist, Lewistown Penn 57-59; Libn Erie Re sistor Corp, Erie Penn 59-60; Libn Lord Mfg Co, Erie Penn 61-63; Med Libn & Sch of Nursing libn Mercy Hosp, Denver 63-68; Supv of tech serv & Catlgr Met State Col Lib, Denver 68-. 8: Adv Bd, Colo Acad Lib Bk Processing Ctr, Boulder Colo 68-. 9: SLA; Colo Coun Med Libns; ALA. 14: Bibliog, info retrieval, catlg, Tech Serv. 15: 1426 High st, Apt 2, Denver Co 80218.

JACKSON, RUTH LILLIAN (WHITLOCK). b Indianapolis 9 Mr 16. 4: Eugene B Jackson. 5: UIll(Urbana) 33-37 (Ger) BA, 37-38 BS in LS, 38-41 (LS) MA. 6: Ger, Fr. 7: Jr prof asst Ricker Lib Arch UIll(Urbana) 37-41; Med libn Air docs div Wright AFB, Dayton Ohio 46-48; Catlgr Army Med Lib US Army, Wash DC 49-50; Catlgr Lib Bur of Ships US Navy, Wash DC 50-52; Libn Engnr Staff Gen Motors Corp, Warren Mich 59-64; Asst libn Central Off Lib Ford Motor Co, Dearborn Mich 64-65; Bibliog(R) Engrg Socs Lib, NY 66-68. 9: SLA (Consul Serv Com 63-65); ALA. 12: "Author Headings for the Official Publications of the State of Wis" (54); "Author Index to NACA Publications, 1915-1949," with co-author. 14: Engnr lit, catlg, ref. 15: 85 Round Hill dr, Briarcliff Manor NY 10510.

JACKSON, SARA J. b Centerville Miss 22 O 37. 5: Southwestern (Memphis) 55-59 (Bio) BA; MSU 64-66 MSLS. 6: Fr. 7: Lab tech Ochsner Clinic, New Orleans La 60-62; Lab tech Lady of the Lake Hosp, Baton Rouge La 62-64; MEDLARS searcher UAla Med Ctr, Birmingham 67-. 9: MedLA; SLA; AlaLA. 14: Ref. 15: 1245 38th st So #1A, Birmingham Al 35222.

JACKSON, SARAH WHITE. b Collinsville Ala 8 Ag 07. 4: George Stuyvesant Jackson. 5: Agnes Scott Col 24-28 (Fr) AB (cum laude); Emory 29-30 BLS; UMe 63-64 (Eng) MA. 6: Fr. 7: Lib asst Emory U 28; Lib asst Carnegie Lib of Atlanta 29; Asst libn Washington & Lee U 30-37; Asst libn Va Mil Inst 37-43; Libn Falls Church High Sch, Falls Church Va 50-57; Libn Westbrook Jr Col 58-, Tchr of Eng UMe (Portland) summers 67, 68, 69. 8: Act libn, So Portland Pub Lib, So Portland Me, summer 65. 9: ALA; MeLA; NE Libns of Amer Assn Jr Cols; NELA. 12: Asst ed "Virginia Library Handbook." 13: Yes. 14: Reader serv, tchg, research, poetry, drama. 15: Surf rd Cape Cottage, So Portland Me 04106.

JACKSON, SIDNEY L. b NYC 13 S 14. 4: Clara Ostrowsky Jackson. 5: Columbia 31-35 (Hist) AB; Tchrs Col 35-36 (Tchg of Hist) MA; Columbia 36-41 (Amer Hist) PhD, 49-50 MSLS. 6: Fr, Ger. 7: (Capt) US Army Signal Corps 44-46; Free lance research writer 46-48; Assoc histn Amer Nat Red Cross, Wash DC 48-49; Catlgr Brooklyn Pub Lib 50-58, Br serv 58; Assoc Prof of Lib Sci Kent State U 58-65, Prof of Lib Sci 65-. 8: Kent State U Grad Sch Evaluation of Grad Faculty 65-66, chm of one team ; Org Kent State U Mission to Commun on UnivImage (for AAUP). 9: ALA; OhioLA (chm Intel Freedom Com 64-65); No Ohio Tech Serv Libns (v-pres 65-66). 10: NAACP; Interfaith & Commun Coun; AAUP. 12: "America's Struggle for Free Schools' (41); "Catalog Use Study" (58); Ed 'Review of Current Research' in "J Educ for Libnship." (-68), Ed "Book Review" (68-). 13: Yes. 14: Hist of libs & libnship, catlg, research methodology. 15: Sch of Lib Sci Kent State U, Kent Oh 44240.

JACKSON, STEWART PHILLIP. b Canton Ohio 8 Jl 21. 4: Anna Palish Jackson. 5: Kent State U 46 (Eng); Rutgers 59 (Eng) BA, 61 MLS. 7: Catlgr-clsf US Army MIS GHQ-FEC, Tokyo 47-50; Readers adv Canton Pub Lib, Canton Ohio 50-51; Expeditor Allen B DuMont Labs, Clifton NJ 51-52; Dir a-v aids Morris Co Free Lib, Morristown NJ 52-55; Salesman DoAll New Jersey Co, Nutley NJ 55-60; U Col Libn McKeldin Lib, UMd 61-65, Asst to dir UCol 65 , Asst dir UCol 66-. 9: ALA; UMd Senate Com on Libs UCol Lib Liaison. 10: Rutgers Alumni Coun; Adult Educ Coun of Prince George's Co (Md); Prince George's Co Civil Defense. 14: Adult educ, automation, info storage & retrieval, recr for libnship, admin of col & univ libs. 15: Adult Educ Center Univ of Md, College Park Md 20742.

JACKSON, SUSAN LUCILE. b Los Angeles 30 Je 41. 5: Wellesley 59-63 (Eng) BA; UPittsburgh 66 (Info Sci) MLS. 6: Fr. 7: Libn Harvard U Off of Programmed Instr 64-65; Instr materials libn Home for Crippled Child, Pittsburgh Penn 66; Libn Learning Research & Development Ctr UPittsburgh; Educ ref libn Ariz State U 67; Staff info scientist & managing ed PCD Galton Inst, Beverly Hills Cal 67-. 9: ASIS (sec Spec Int Gp on Behavioral/Soc Scis 69-71); Prog Chm Los Angeles Chap 68); ALA; SLA. 10: Beta Phi Mu; Sierra Club; Synsnon Found. 12: Mng ed "Perceptual-Cognitive development". 14: Info sci (behav & soc scis). 15: 319 S Robertson blvd, Beverly Hills Ca 90211.

JACKSON, VIOLETTE NADA (KRSTICH). b Chicago 1 Jl 37. 4: Paul Trescott Jackson. 5: Wayne State U 55-56 (Music Educ); UMich 56-58 (Music Lit) BM, 58-59 (Music Lit) MM, 59-61 AMLS. 6: Ger. 7: Stud asst UMich Mus Lib 57-59; Pre-prof libn Detroit Pub Lib gen info dept 59-60; Record catlgr Radio Station WUOM UMich 60-61; Libn II ref Detroit Pub Lib music & performing arts dept 61-64, Libn II music catlgr 64-65; Catlg libn II music UMich 65; Libn music catlgr NY Pub Lib Ref Div 65-66; Catlgr of private lib 66-67; Ref libn Finkelstein Mem Lib, Spring Valley NY 67; Tech serv libn Pace Col 67. 9: MusLA; ALA; Amer Musicological Soc; Mich LA; Assn for Recorded Sound Collections (Recording sec). 10: Amer Fed of Musicians; Chamber Music Wkshop, Detroit; Phi Kappa Lambda; Sigma Alpha Iota. 14: Mus catlg, mus ref, tech ser. 15: 510 Wilcox st, Rochester Mi 48063.

JACKSON, W(ILLIS) CARL. b Beverly Mass 20 My 23. 4: Elisabeth Lett Jackson. 5: Fla State U 48-51 (Hist) BA, 51-52 (LS) MA. 6: Fr. 7: Rifleman (Pfc) US Army Paratroops, Europe 42-45; Asst order libn UTenn, Knoxville 52-54; Head Order Dept State U of Iowa 54-55, Head acquis dept 55-57; Chief acquis libn UMinn (Minneapolis) 57-63; Assoc dir of libs UColo 63-65; Dir of Libs Penn State U (University Park) 65-. 8: Consul: SUNY (Buffalo) on Tech Processes 63-64, Col Center of Finger Lakes on automation & cooperative process center 64-65; Chm of Colo Academic Libs Com to establish a cooperative processing center 63-65; Consul: UNeb 66, Uga 68, Mansfield State Col 69. 9: ALA (chm Bkdealer-Lib Rel Com 62-, Coun 65-69, Appts com 66-67; program planning com 66-67); -ACRL (Coun 65-, var coms);-RTSD (chm &/or mem var coms); ColoLA; MinnLA; TennLA; PNLA; Bd of dirs Penn Reg Resource Ctrs; Bd of dirs Penn Union Catlg. 10: OX-5 Club; Amer Aviation Hist Soc; Soc of World War I Aero Histns; Air Power Hist Soc; AAUP; Beta Phi Mu. 13: Yes. 14: Acquis, admin, tech processes, automation. 15: Pattee Lib Penn State U, State College Pa 16802.

JACKSON, WILLIAM VERNON. b Chicago 26 My 26. 5: Northwestern 43-45, 46 (Span) BA (summa cum laude); UCal(Berkeley) 45 (Span); Harvard 46, 47-50 (Romance Langs & Lits) AM, PhD; UIll 50-51 MS in LS. 6: Sp, Fr, Portu. 7: Tchg asst UCal(Berkeley) 45; Tchr York Commun High Sch, Elmhurst Ill 46-47; Tchg Fellow Harvard U 48-50; Spec recruit LC 50-51; Libn Undergrad Lib & Asst Prof UIll(Urbana) 52-58, Assoc Prof Grad Sch of Lib Sci 58-62; Assoc Prof Span & Portu UWis 63-65; Consul ref dept NY Pub Lib 65-; Prof of Lib Sci & Dir Intl Lib Info Ctr UPittsburgh 66-. 8: Visiting lecturer or Prof of lib sci summer courses: UMinn 54-56, Columbia 60, Syracuse 62; Consul to Dept of State on Libs in Argentina, 56; Brazil & Ecuador, 59; Latin Amer, 61; Latin Amer & Europe, 62; Visiting Prof 60,68, Adv Internat Exec Coun 61-63; Consul Peace Corps Train Program for Brazil, UWis(Milwaukee) 64; Consul on Bibliog, Hispanic Foun LC 64-65; Consul Reg Off for Central Amer & Panama, Agency for Internat Devel 67-; Del US Nat Commsn for Unesco 59, 61. 9: ALA (chm Internat Rel Round Table 65-66); TheatreLA; AALS; ACRL; Mod Lang Assn; Amer Assn Tchrs Span & Portu; BSA; Asociacio3n Pacen7a de Bibliotecarios, La Paz Bolivia (Hon mem); IllLA. 10: Harvard Club (Chicago); Phi Beta Kappa; Beta Phi Mu; Phi Sigma Iota. 11: Fulbright Research Scholar, France, 56-57; Fulbright Lecturer UCo3rdoba Argentina, 58; Faculty Research Fellowship UWis, summers 63, 64; Honorary diploma Escuela de Biblioteconomia y Archives, Universidad Central de Venezuela. 12: "Basic Library Techniques" (55); "A Handbook of American Library Resources" (55 2d ed 62); "Studies in Library Resources" (58); "The Foundation Grants Program" (59); "The Libraries of the Associated Colleges of the Midwest" (60); "Aspects of Librarianship in Latin America" (62); "Library Guide for Brazilian Studies" (64); Ed ALA-"ACRL Monographs" (61-66); Edl staff "Library Trends" (58-62); "National Textbook Program and libraries in Brazil" (67); "Resources of Research Libraries" (69). 13: Yes. 14: Resources of Amer & for libs, comp libnship, Latin-Amer bibliog, ref, mod Span drama. 15: 196 W Kathleen dr, Park Ridge Ill 60068.

JACOB, ALICE KATHERINE. b Montgomery Ala 11 N 36. 5: AuburnU 55-61 (Mus) BA; Columbia 62-65 (LS) MS. 6: Fr, Ger. 7: Desk asst Columbia Mus Lib 61-64; Libn NY Pub Lib (Donnell Br) 65; Instr-catlgr Hunter Col Lib 65-68; Catlg libn & instr AuburnU Lib 68-. 9: MusLA. 14: Catlg, mus. 15: Ralph Brown Draughon Lib AuburnU, Auburn Al 36830.

JACOB, EMERSON D. b Canton Ohio 17 Mr 17. 4: Doris (Geiger) Jacob. 5: Mt Union Col 35-39 (Eng) AB; West Res 41-42 BSLS; Columbia 49-51 (Hist) MA; West Res 59-61 (Hist) PhD. 6: Ger, Fr, Lat. 7: Asst libn Mt Union Col 43-45; Order libn UMd(College Park) 45-48; Acquis libn Mich State U 48-58; Libn Baldwin Wallace Col 59-64; Libn Cal State Polytech Col 64-65; Libn State U Col (Fredonia) 65-68; Libn Rutgers U 68-. 8: Host libn ALA Col Sect Meeting, Baldwin Wallace Col 61; Lib consul Lake Erie Col 63; Libns Com Cleveland Commsn on Higher Educ 60-64; Trustee West NY Lib Resources Coun 66-68; NJ Pub Lib Coun 69; Consul NY Times lib serv div 68-69. 9: ALA; AHA; MichLA; DCLA; MdLA; OhioLA; NYLA. 12: "Disraeli's Social Reforms, 1874-1880," PhD Diss (61). 13: Yes. 14: Acquis, admin. 15: 3 Winthrop pl, Maplewood NJ 07040.

JACOB, HELEN. b Chicago 29 N 15. 5: DePaul U 39 (Eng) AB; UIll 42 (LS) BS. 6: Ger. 7: Lib asst Pub Lib, Chicago 39-41; Child libn Pub Lib, Park Ridge 42; Child libn Pub Lib, Chicago 43; Child libn Pub Lib, Elmhurst 44-45; Child libn Pub Lib Glencoe Ill 46-. 9: ALA; IllLA. 10: UIll Lib Sch Assn; No Shore Lib Assn. 13: Yes. 14: Wk with child. 15: 2713 Central st, Evanston Ill 60201.

JACOB, JEROME F. b Buffalo NY 18 S 13. 4: Anna Viele Jacob. 5: UBuffalo 44-48 (Eng) BA; Columbia 48-49 MSLS. 7: (Sgt) US Army Signal Corps, US, Europe 43-46; Buffalo & Erie Co Pub Lib, Buffalo NY: Jr libn 49-51, Sr libn I 52-59, Sr libn II 59-63, Sr libn III, Head Lang lit & fine arts dept 63-. 14: Ref. 15: 308 Highland ave, Buffalo NY 14222.

JACOBIUS, ARNOLD J. b Augsburg Germany 2 Ag 16. 4: Emmy Schoeffel. 5: U's of Milan & Pavia (Italy) 34-38 (Chem) BS; Columbia 41-42 (Chem); NYU 47-51, 55 (Ger Lit) MA, PhD; Columbia 50-51 (LS) MS. 6: Ger, Ital, Sp, Fr. 7: Educ off US Army Mil Govt, Germany 45-46; Instr of Ger NYU 47-51; Bibliog LC 52-57, Project supv 57-66, Assoc field dir LC Off Wiesbaden 66-. 8: Spec recr LC, 51-52. 9: Internat Astronaut Fed (chm Sub-com on Bioastronautics Info Exch 62-65); SLA (Com on Engnr & Abstr Serv 54-55); Aerospace Med Assn (Sci Communications Com 63-;) Armed Forces (NRC Bioastronautics Com, Panel on Info 60-61); Mod Lang Assn (Bibliog Com 55); Inst of Aeronaut & Astronaut. 10: Fairfax Commun Theatre: AAAS. 11: NYU Founders Day Achievement Award. 12: Ed Bd "Aerospace Medicine" (63-66); Ed-in-chief "Aerospace Medicine & Biology. An Annotated Bibliography," 11 v, Wash (54-65); Ed 'Abstracts of Current Literature' in "Aerospace Medicine" (57-66); Assoc ed "APCA Abstracts" (58-60), Air Pollution Control Assn (58-59). 13: Yes. 14: Bibliog, info serv. 15: 4036 Poplar st, Fairfax Va 22030.

JACOBS, ALMA (SMITH). b Lewistown Mont 21 N 16. 4: Marcus Jacobs. 5: Talladega Col 34-38 (Sociol) BA; Columbia 42 BS & LS; Mont State Col 62 LittD; Mt Holyoke 68 Dr of Humane Letters. 7: Asst libn Talladega Col 38-46; Catlg libn Great Falls Pub Lib, Great Falls Mont 46-54, Libn 54-. 9: ALA (Bd 64-68); MontLA (pres 60); PNLA (pres 57). 10: Commun Chest Bd; Exec Bd YWCA; Adv Com to US Civil Rights Commsn; Delta Kappa Gamma; AAUW. 13: Yes. 14: Lib ext, pub libs. 15: 616 Eighth ave So, Great Falls Mont 59401.

JACOBS, ARLENE MARY. b Milwaukee 14 Ap 39. 5: Marquette U 56-57; Alverno Col 57-58; Marquette U 58-61; (Eng) AB; UWis(Milwaukee) 62-63 (LS); UWis 63-64 MSLS. 7: Clerk Amer Off Serv, Milwaukee 62; Machine operator Con ental Can Co, Milwaukee summers 57-62; Jr libn Milwaukee Pub Lib summer 63; Jr adult assn gen ref dept Enoch Pratt Free Lib, Baltimore 64-65, Sr adult asst 65-68; Sr prof asst Baltimore Co Pub Lib 68-. 9: ALA (memb Ref & Subscription Bks Review Com 69-70); MdLA. 10: ACLU; Amer Friends Serv Com; Women's Internat League for Peace and Freedom. 14: Ref, adult serv. 15: 4712 Wakefield rd, Baltimore Md 21216.

JACOBS, IRENE (OSTREICHER). b Budapest Hungary 2 F 21. 4: Walter W Jacobs. 5: Hunter Col 36-40 (Biol) BA; Catholic U 51-56 MS in LS. 6: Fr, Hungarian. 7: Libn NEA, Wash DC 51-59; Ref libn Dept of Agric Lib, Wash DC 59-61; Head ref circ depts Patent Off Lib, Wash DC 61-62; Sr ref libn Nat Inst of Health, Bethesda Md 62-63; Asst libn Princeton U Lib Dept of Aero Engnr, Forrestal Research Center 63-64; Ref libn Health Scis Spec Dept of Health Educ & Welfare, Wash DC 64-. 9: MedLA; SLA; DCLA. 12: Contrib "Mental Health Book Review Index." 14: Ref. 15: 1812 Metzerott rd apt 31, Adelphi Md 20783.

JACOBS, ROGER E. b Detroit 1 Ja 37. 4: Alice Reekstin. 5: UDetroit 60-62 (Hist) AB; UMich 62-64 MALS; UDetroit Sch of Law 64-. 7: Page Cleveland Pub Lib 53-54; US Navy Electronics Tech 2/c 54-59; UDetroit Lib: Page 60-61, Desk asst 61-62, Pre-prof staff 62; UDetroit Sch of Law Lib: Act law libn 62-63, Law Libn 63-67; UWindsor Fac of Law Lib: Law libn & Asst Prof 67-69, Law libn & Assoc Prof 69-. 9: AALL; Ohio ALL; ALA; CanLA. 10: Phi Alpha Theta. 14: Law lib admin. 15: 15410 Fielding, Detroit Mi 48223.

JACOBSEN, EDWARD T. b Chicago Ill 22 Jl 22. 4: Marjorie H (Graham) Jacobsen. 5: Ripon Col 40-43, 46 (Hist) AB; UOkla 47-49 (Hist) MA; UWis 49-51 (LS) MA; UChicago 60-61 (LS). 7: Infantryman (Sgt) US Army, US & ETO (35th Div) 43-45; ref libn S Dak State Col 51-53; Dir col libs

Winona State Col 53-. 9: ALA; MinnLA (Exec Bd 68-); MinnSchLA; UpperMississippiLA. 10: AAUP; Exchange Club; Junto Club. 14: Ref, lib educ. 15: 1767 W Mark, Winona Mn 55987.

JACOBSEN, ERLAND LYDIK. b San Francisco 10 Ap 34. 4: Marian Rose Digioia. 5: Stanford U 51-55 (Hist) BA; UCopenhagen 53-54 (Hist); UCal 58-59 (LS) MLS. 6: Sp, Danish, Ger. 7: Stud asst Stanford U Lib 51-52; (Pfc) US Army 55-57; Lib asst Staford U Lib 57-58; Libn ref Fresno State Col Lib 59-64, Head govt publ dept 64-. 9: CalLA. 10: Phi Beta Kappa. 12: Index to vols 24 & 25 of "Cal Libn." 14: Govt publ, ref, sers, catlg. 15: 4538 N Hayston, Fresno Cal 93726.

JACOBSON, ANGELINE. b Milwaukee 5 N 10. 5: St Olaf Col 31 (Hist) BA; UMich 50 BALS, 61 MALS. 6: Ger, Norse. 7: High sch tchr-libn, Finlayson Minn 42-43; High sch tchr-libn, Cottonwood Minn 43-45; High sch tchr-libn, Marengo Ill 45-47; High sch sec-libn, Hartland Wis 47-50; High sch libn, Beaver Dam Wis 50-51& ref libn & Asst Prof of Lib Sci Luther Col 51-61, Ref libn & Assoc Prof of Lib Sci 61-. 9: ALA ACRL; IowaLA (Recr Com). 10: AAUW; AAUP; Amer Scand Foun. 14: Ref. 15: Luther Col Lib, Decorah Iowa 52101.

JACOBSON, DONALD JOSEPH. b Cleveland Ohio 21 Mr 38. 4: Nancy Holdam. 5: Adelbert Col 61-65 (Russian) BS; Case-West Res 65-67 (LS). 7: Ref libn Wright State U 67-. 9: ALA. 14: Ref. 15: 240A Dayton-Yellow Springs rd, Fairborn Oh 45324.

JACOBSON, JEANETTE HELEN (KEES). b Wausau Wis 21 Je 41. 4: Franklin Paul Jacobson. 5: Wis StateU (Stevens Point) 59-63 (Mus) BS; UWis (Madison) summers 64-69 (LS) MS. 7: Catlgr Eastman Sch of Mus Lib 63-67; Asst libn Westminster Choir Col 67-. 9: MusLA. 14: Catlg, ref. 15: 10 Grove st, Rocky Hill NJ 08553.

JACOBSON, JOSEPHINE (HECK). b Barry Minn 19 Ap 07. 4: Ingemar Jacobson. 5: Moorhead state Col 27-60 (Elem Educ) BS, summers 61-63 (LS). 6: Ger. 7: Tchr, Minn: Stephen 27-29, Marietta 32-35, Browns Valley 35-39, 42-44, Wheaton 47-51, 52-60; Tchr, Corona S Dak 30-32; Elem libn, Wheaton Minn 60-. 9: WheatonEA (pres). 14: Catlg. 15: 1103 4th ave N, Wheaton Mn 56296.

JACOBSON, LILLIAN (LANGEMO). b Fingal N Dak 23 Ag 19. 4: John Jacobson. 5: Valley city State Col 36-40 (Eng) BA in Ed; UDenver (summers) 45-47 BS in LS; UMinnesota summer 65 (LS). 7: High sch, N Dak: Libn Valley City 40-44; Bismarck 44-46; Lib asst Pacific Lutheran U 46-49; High sch, Libn Moorhead Minn 49-50; Asst libn Moorhead State Col 50-51; Circ libn No Ill State U 51-56; Col sch libn State Col, Valley City N Dak 56-65, Hd libn 65-. 9: ALA; NEA; NDEA. 11: Delta Kappa Gamma. 14: Ref. 15: 252 Second ave SW, Valley City ND 58072.

JACOBSON, SOLOMON. b Bronx NY 18 S 33. 4: Barbara Wolff. 5: City Col (NY) 52-56 (Soc Studies) BA; Columbia 59-60 (LS) MS. 7: Stud asst City Col Lib (NY) 52-56; Claims rep trainee Soc Security, NYC 57-58; Various NY Pub Lib 58-61, Sr ref libn 61-; US Army Res Infantry (Capt). 12: "Functional Directory," annual. 13: Yes. 14: Ref (govt, law, legis). 15: 59 Arlo rd, SI NY 10301.

JACOBSTEIN, J MYRON. b Detroit 27 Ja 20. 4: Belle Lottman. 5: Wayne State 38-46 (Hist) BA; Columbia 49-50 MSLS; Chicago-Kent Col of Law 50-53 LLB. 6: Sp. 7: UChicago Law Lib 50-53; UIll Law Lib (Urbana) 53-55; Columbia U Law Lib 55-59; UColo Law Lib 59-63; Prof of Law & Law Libn Stanford U 63-. 8: Adv com Project Lawsearch CLR 60-65; Adv com Lib Studies Project Assn of Amer Law Schs 65-; Consul to various law libs. 9: AALL; ASIS; CalLA; Amer Soc Internat Law; Internat ALL. 12: Ed "Law Books in Print," 2 vol (66); Ed "Index to Periodical Articles Related to Law." 13: Yes. 14: Admin, ref, documentation. 15: Law Lib Stanford U, Stanford Cal 94305.

JACOBSTEIN, PEARL (SCHNEIDER). b Detroit 13 N 04. 4: S Raymond Jacobstein. 5: Wayne State 59-62 (Educ, LS) BS; UMich 62-64 MASL. 7: Med sec, Detroit 53-58; Med sec, NYC 58-59; Libn Detroit Bd of Educ, Detroit mich 62-64; Libn Bloomfield Hills Bd of Educ, Bloomfield Hills Mich 64-. 8: Ed Bd and column in "Forward" magazine publ by Mich Assn of Sch libns, Detroit 63-. 9: ALA; MichEA; MichASchL (treas Oakland Co Chap); NEA. 10: Pi Lambda Theta. 11: Tchrs Grant Fund 67. 12: Column in "Forward" (Mich SLA). 13: Yes. 14: Ref, catlg. 15: 21643 Stratford ct, Oak Park Mich 48237.

JAECH, CAROL RITA (SEITZ). b Chicago Ill 23 S 42. 4: Ronald Bruce Jaech. 5: Glendale Jr Col 60-62 AA; UCal (Berkeley) 62-65 (Sociol) BA, MLS. 7: Child libn Glendale Pub Lib, Glendale Cal 65-66; Child libn San Bernardino Co Lib, San Bernardino Cal 66-68; Br libn Morgan Hill Br Santa Clara Co Lib, Morgan Hill Cal 68-. 9: CalLA; Assn Child Libn of No Cal. 14: Child wk, ref, adult bk selection. 15: 353 Springpark cir, San Jose Ca 95136.

JAEGER, LUCJA (ADLER). b Kozlow Poland 14 S 10. 5: UJoannis Casimiri (Lwow Poland) 28-32 (Law, Pol Sci) Master, 33-34 (Consular & Diplomatic Studies); Royal U of Uppsala (Uppsala Sweden) 48-49 (Swedish, Econ, Hist); Columbia 59-61 (LS) MS. 6: Polish, Fr, Ger, Swedish. 7: Recorder District Courts, Lwow Poland 32-34; Law apprentice, Jr Partner Law Offs, Lwow Poland 35-39; Barrister M Bar Assn of Warsaw, Poland 45-46; Lib trainee NY Pub Lib 59-61; Prof ref asst Boston Pub Lib 61-65, Ref libn 65-. 9: ALA; MassLA. 10: Columbia Sch of Lib Serv Alumni Assn; Boston Mus of Fine Arts. 14: Ref & bk sel in soc scis, govt docs, rare bks, area interest - East Europe, Africa. 15: 80 Fenway, Boston Ma 02115.

JAFFARIAN, SARA. b Haverhill Mass 7 S 15. 5: Bates Col 33-37 (Hist, Govt) AB; Simmons summers 43-47 (LS) BS; Boston U summers 53-57 (Educ, A-V) M Ed; Harvard 65 (Elem Educ); U So Cal 69 (Info Sci). 07: Lib asst Haverhill Pub Lib, Haverhill Mass 37-42; Tchr-libn High Sch, Ossipee NH 42-43; Libn Jr High Sch, Quincy Mass 43-53; Dir of Libs Greensboro Pub Schs, Greensboro NC 53-60; Supv of sch libs Seattle Pub Schs 60-61; Coordinator instr materials & serv Lexington Pub Schs, Lexington Mass 61-. 8: Instr in lib sci summer courses: UOre 57; Queens Col LI 59; UNH 64, 68; Consul on lib serv to var NE pub sch systems & to Va Bd of Educ; Dir of Sch Lib Inst UHawaii 68. 09: ALA (var offs & mem several coms);-AASchL (var offs, chm Sch Lib Supvrs, & chm var coms);-CSD (Newbery- Caldecott Com); NE Sch Devel Coun (chm Lib Com); NELA (Bd Dirs); NESchLA (v-pres); MassSchLA (pres); Mass Tchrs Assn; Assn Supv & Curr Devel; NEA-DAVI. 10: Delta Kappa Gamma; Pi Lambda Theta; Simmons Lib Sch Alumni Assn. 11: Britannica Sch Lib Award, Lexington Pub Schs, 64. 12: Ed "Junior Libraries" (Feb 15, 57); "Every School Needs a Library" (52); 'The Library-Centered School' in "Teaching in a World of Change" (66). 13: Yes. 14: Sch libs (supv). 15: 58 Bateman st, Haverhill Mass 01830.

JAFFE, KATHARINE W(EISMAN). b Boston 27 Ap 27. 4: Myron I Jaffe. 5: Colby Col 48 (Amer Civilization) AB; Simmons 52 MLS; Boston U 51-52 (Amer Lit); Brandeis U 61-62 (Intellectual Hist & Amer Poetry). 6: Ger, Lat, Hebrew. 7: Asst child libn Mem Br, Boston Pub Lib 48-51; Libn Temple Emanuel, Newton Mass 54-56; Libn Temple Mishkan Tefila, Newton Mass 58-60; Lib asst Brandeis U Lib 60-62; Asst ref libn Boston Col Lib 63-. 9: NE Col Libs Assn (Reg Interlib Loan Com). 10: Commsn on Commun-Interrels; Amer Jewish Congress (Regl Governing Coun). 13: Yes. 14: Ref, readers serv, bibliog. 15: 45 Old Colony rd, Chestnut Hill Mass 02167.

JAFFE, STEVEN. b NYC 7 S 28. 4: Louise Neuwirth. 5: Yeshiva Col 48-52 (Hist) BA; Columbia 52-53 (Hist) MA, 56-58 (LS) MS. 6: Ger, Hebrew. 7: Ref & circ libn Pollack Lib Yeshiva U 52-60; Ref libn US Naval Applied Sci Lab, Brooklyn NY 60-65, Chief Libn 65-. 9: ALA; SLA (Soc Sci Div, Sci Tech Div, Mil Libns Div sec-treas 68-69); E Coast Coun of Naval Libns (sec 67-68, chm 69). 10: Amer Hist Assn; Exec com of Yeshiva Col Alumni Assn. 14: Ref, admin. 15: 2411 E 3rd st, Brooklyn NY 11223.

JAFFEE, DIANA BARTNIKAS (DANGUOLE). b Lithuania 15 Mr 25. 4: Oscar C Jaffee. 5: UVilnius 43-44 (Pharmacy); UMunich 45-46 (Pharmacy); NYU 51-53 (Biol, Ger) BA; Columbia 55-57 (LS) MS. 6: Lithuanian, Ger, Fr. 7: Tech asst NY Pub Lib 52-57; Abstractor Nopco Lib, Harrison NJ 57-60; Libn Newark Pub Lib, Newark NJ 60-61; Libn Buffalo & Erie Co Pub Lib, Buffalo NY 61; Libn Dayton & Montgomery Co Pub Lib 68-. 9: SLA. 14: Ref, (sci & tech). 15: 1823 Harvard blvd, Dayton Oh 45406.

JAHANGIR, MOHAMMED. b India 5 Jl 36. 5: UAllahabad (India) 54-56 (Econ) BA; UKarachi (Pakistan) 60-62 (Sociol) MA; IndU 62-63 (LS) MA. 7: Asst libn Inst Bus Admin, Karachi 59-62; Libn UKarachi Dept of Lib Sci 63-66; Prof libn Enoch Pratt Free Lib, Baltimore 66-67; Asst circ libn UAlta Lib 67-. 9: EdmontonLA; AltaLA; Assn of Prof Libns of UAlta. 14: Ref, a-v, selection of materials. 15: 9520 63 ave, Edmonton 81 Alta Can.

JAHNS, JANET M (HALLE). b Fond du Lac Wis 3 Je 35. 4: Dennis Don Jahns. 5: Wis State Col (Oshkosh) 53-57 (LS) BA; UWis 58-59 (LS) MA. 7: Jr libn Milwaukee Pub Lib 57-58; Head (libn II State) Southwest Wis Lib Serv Center, Fennimore Wis 59-61; Sch consul Kent Co Lib, Grand Rapids Mich 62-64, Asst dir 65-. 9: ALA; MichLA (sec-treas Pub Lib Div 69). 10: Women's Nat Bk Assn. 14: Tech proc, admin. 15: 9930 10 Mile rd NE, Rockford Mi 49341.

JAHNS, ROBERT WILLIAM. b Burlington Wis 3 Ja 25. 5: UIowa 46-49 (Psych) BA; Yale 49-53 (Parish Ministry) BD; UCal 59-61 MLS. 7: Chaplain's asst (T/5) US Army (226th Gen Hosp) 43-46; Resident Chaplain Norwich State Hosp, Norwich Conn 53-54; Pastor Congregational Church, Tonganoxie Kan 54-57; Youth Minister Kensington Com Church, San Diego 57-58; Asst to libn Cal West U 58-60; Catlgr San Francisco Theol Sem 60-63; Acquis libn Central Wash State Col 63-64; Acquis libn West Wash State Col 64-67; Ref & doc libn West Wash State Col 68-69. 8: Ordained United Church of Christ in 53. 9: ALA; ATheolLA. 10: AAUP; ACLU. 14: Acquis. 15: Woodstock Farm, Bellingham Wash 98225.

JAHODA, GERALD. b Vienna 22 O 25. 4: Gloria Love. 5: NYU 45-47 (Chem) AB; Columbia 51-52 (LS) MS, 55-60 DL. 6: Fr, Ger. 7: Asst sci & tech div NY Pub Lib 51-52; Chem libn UWis(Madison) 52-53; Head tech info group Colgate-Palmolive Co, Jersey City, NJ 53-57; Head systems research & lib tech info div Esso Res & Eng Co, Linden NJ 57-63; Prof Lib Sch Fla State U 63-. 8: Consul: Esso Res Engnr Co, Clemson U, Fla Jr Cols, US Army Corps of Engnrs. 9: ASIS (Coun 64-65, chm Educ Com 68-); ALA; ACS; SLA; InstnfoNTISTS Fla: AAAS. 12: Ed bd "Amer Documentation" (64-); Ed bd "J Chem Documentation." 13: Yes. 14: Educ, indexing, systems studies, info gathering. 15: Lib Sch Fla State U, Tallahassee Fla 32406.

JAIN, NIRMAL. b Kalka (Simla Hills) 1 Je 36. 5: PanjabU 52-56 (Eng, Math, Phys) BA; BanarasU 58-59 (LS) Dip LS; UDelhi 61-63 (Philos) MA; UToronto 65-67 MLS. 6: Hindi, Urdu, Panjabi. 7: Libn Civil Aviation Dept (Govt of India), New Delhi 59-63; Libn pub serv Lond Pub Lib & Art Mus, Lond Ont Can 63-. 8: Sec BHU Lib Sci Assn, Banaras 58-59; Sec Cultural Assn Govt Col, Chandigarh 54-56. 9: CanLA; OntLA; IPLO. 10: Intl House; Army, Navy & Airforce Veterans in Can; Fr Assn; India Can Assn. 13: Yes. 14: Ref, bk selection, automation, govt publ, case hist procedure of admin. 15: 200 St James st 14, London Ont Can.

JAIN, SUSHIL KUMAR. b Faridkot India 9 S 42. 4: Christine Horswell. 5: Panjab U (Chandigarh India) -57 (Eng Lit) BA; Aligarh Muslim U (Aligarh India) 57-59 (Eng Lit) MA; Govt Central Train Col (Faridkot India) 59-60 (Educ) B Ed; Panjab U (Chandigarh India) 60-61 Dip Lib Sci; Aligarh Muslim U (Aligarh India) 61-62 (Pol Sci) MA; London Sch of Libnship ULondon 63-64 (LS) Dip Lib. 6: Hindi, Urdu, Pajabi, Fr. 7: Asst libn Ravensbourne Col of Art & Design (Bromley Kent Eng) 62-63; Catlgr USask 64-65; Work-study-scholar S Asia Unit catlg dept UMich 65-66; Ref libn USask 66-67; Ref libn UWindsor 67-; Visiting lecturer USask summer 68. 8: Bibliogr div soc sci USask 66-67; Research assoc Dept Asian Studies UWindsor 68-. 9: SLA; CanLA; Lib Assn (Gt Brit); Linguistic Soc of Ind (Life mem); Col & Res Libs, London; IndianLA; Bibliog Soc of Can; BSA. 10: Red Cross, YMCA; Youth Hostels Assn; Kipling Soc; Mod Lang Assn; Fellow Royal Commonwealth Soc; Assn for Asian Studies; Royal Anthrop Inst; Assn for Commonwealth Langs & Lit; Canadian Hist Soc. 12: Comp "Indian Literature in English: A Bibliography" (64); Comp "A Bibliography of Indian Autobiographies and Biographies" (65); Comp "Folklore of India & Pakistan" (65); Comp "A Preliminary Draft Towards the Compilation of A Bibliography of Indian Bibliographies in European Languages" (65); Comp "Louis 'David' Riel & the North-West Rebellion: A List of References" (65); Comp "Poetry in Saskatchewan: A Bibliography" (65); "The Negro in Canada" (67); "Twenty Years of Flying Saucers" (68); "French-Canadian Literature in English" (66). 13: Yes. 14: Bibliog, research. 15: 377 Rosedale ave, Windsor 10 Ont Can.

JALSO, ALEXANDER. b Budapest Hungary 18 F 30. 4: Irene Sabo. 5: Reformed Theol Acad (Budapest) 49-54 (Theol) BD; Lancaster Theol Sem (Lancaster Penn) 57-58 (Theol) BD; West MichU 62-64 MALS. 6: Hungarian, Ger. 7: Asst libn (catlgr) SUNY (Buffalo) 66-. 8: Minister United Ch of Christ: Morgantown W Va 58-60, Kalamazoo Mich 60-66, Buffalo NY 66-. 14: Catlg. 15: 1940 Clinton st, Buffalo NY 14206.

JAMBREK, WILLIAM LLOYD. b Kenosha Wis 14 Ag 37. 5: Milton Col 56-60 (Hist) BA; UWis 60-61 MS in LS. 7: Libn I Milwaukee Pub Lib 60; Libn asst Lib US Navy Train Center, San Diego Cal 61; Yeoman 2/c US Navy 61-65; Assoc libn Milton Col Lib 65-66, Hd libn 66-68; Coord SEast Wis Reg Lib Planning Program 68-70. 9: ALA; WisLA. 14: Catlg, admin. 15: 944 Aurora st, apt 4, Waukesha Wi 53186.

JAMERSON, DOROTHY (BREAUX). b Birmingham Ala 6 O 15. 4: J W Jamerson Jr DDS. 5: Fisk U 34-39 (Biol) AB; Atlanta 41-42 BS in LS; Peabody 62-63 EdS. 6: Fr. 7: Act libn Carnegie Pub Lib, Savannah Ga 49-50; Libn Beach Adult Educ Center, Savannah Ga 51-54; olJohnson Sch, Savannah Ga 58-61; Ref libn Fisk U 61-63; Curriculum materials lib Savannah State Col 64-. 9: ALA; GaLA. 10: Beta Phi Mu;Alpha Kappa Alpha; NAACP. 14: Lib educ, lib tech. 15: 525 E Henry st, Savannah Ga 31401.

JAMES, ALICE PEARSON. b Chicago 23 Jl 11. 4: Virgil E James. 5: Carroll Col 28-32 (Eng) BA; Rosary Col 60-63 (LS) MA. 6: Ger, Fr. 7: Libn Lyons Twp High Sch, LaGrange Ill 61-. 9: ALA; IllLA; NEA; IllEA. 10: AAUW; Mental Health Assn; Commun Park Dist Commsnr; Girl Scouts; Family Serv; Village Zoning Bd. 14: Ya serv. 15: 808 N Stone ave, LaGrange Park Ill 60528.

JAMES, BEATRICE M. b Union City NJ 26 S 08. 5: Savage Col 25-27 (Phys Educ): NJ Lib Commsn 28-30 (LS); NJ State Dept of Educ 49 Permanent Libns Certif. 7: Asst libn Public Lib, Bergenfield NJ 25-55, Lib dir 55-. 8: Bergen Co Lib Study Com 67-; Exec sec Mid-Bergen Fed of Free Pub Libs 63, 69; Library Development Committee; New Jersey Library Association. 9: CNLA (sec-treas, pres); LPRC (Memb Chm, v-pres, pres); ALA; -LAD (Pub Rel & Recr); NJLA (2d v-pres, pres 69; Lib Devel Com); Bergen-PassaicLA many coms, pres); Small Libs Gp many coms, pres. 10: Jr Woman's Club; Contemp Woman's Club; Zonta Internat; Bergen Co Hist Assn; C of C; etc. 11: Brotherhood Award, Outstanding Citizenship, Bnai B'rith 58; First Woman of the Year Citizen Award 65. 14: Admin. 15: Bergenfield Free Pub Lib, 50 W Clinton ave, Bergenfield NJ 07621.

JAMES, FLORENCE FITZGERALD. b Minneapolis 16 Ja 21. 4: Bernard B James. 5: Col of St Catherine 39-43 (LS) BS. 6: Sp. 7: Dental libn Marquette U 43-46; Ed asst ALA 46-47; Med ref libn VA Reg Off, Chicago 48-49; Med ref libn VA Hosp, Ann Arbor Mich 53-54; Sr serv libn UMich(Ann Arbor) 50; Catlgr Hughes Aircraft Co, Fullerton Cal 62; Libn-catlgr Fullerton Pub Lib, Fullerton Cal 65-. 15: 15349 San Bruno dr, Lamirada Cal 90638.

JAMES, GERTRUDE R. b Chandler Ariz 30 Jl 16. 5: Phoenix Col 34-36; Ariz State U 36-38 (Educ) BA; UDenver summers 39, 40, 41 BSLS; UChicago summers 46, 47, 49-52 MALS. 7: Libn Chandler Pub Schs, Chandler Ariz 38-42; Ref libn Phoenix Pub Lib 42-44; Libn Emerson Sch, Phoenix Elem Schs 44-45; Lib consul Phoenix Elem Schs 45-. 8: Instr Lib Sci UAriz summers 54, 55 & Night ext courses in Phoenix 57-. 9: ALA (Coun 51-54); -ASCD;-AASchL (dir 53-54); NEA (Life mem); Ariz State lares). 10: Delta Kappa Gamma. 11: Ariz Libn of the Year 62. 14: Sch libs. 15: 5530 N Marion Way, Phoenix Az 85018.

JAMES, HENRY. b NYC 16 Ag 16. 5: Yale U 36-40 (Eng, Hist) BA; Stanford 40-42 (Eng) MA; Columbia 50-52 (LS) MS. 6: Fr, Sp. 7: Research-writer Life Magazine, NYC 42-43; Ed Doubleday & Prentice-Hall, NYC 43-48; Writer Voice of America, NYC 48-50; Libn pub rel Brooklyn Pub Lib 52-55; Chief adult serv Stamford Conn Pub Lib 55-59; Libn LaMont Lib Harvard U 60-65; Libn Briarcliff Col 66-. 8: Exch libn to Gloucester City Lib, Eng 54-55. 9: ALA (Life mem); NCTE; ConnLA; NELA. 10: Elizabethan Club, Yale U Signet Soc, Harvard U. 13: Yes. 14: Bk sel. 15: Lib Briarcliff Col, Briarcliff Manor NY.

JAMES, JOHN E. b Phila 30 My 37. 4: Kathleen M James. 5: Villanova U 55-59 BS, 59-60 MSLS. 6: Fr, Ger. 7: Period libn Villanova U 60-61; Chief Libn Philco Corp, Blue Bell Penn 61-67; Managing ed "Sci Citation Index Inst for Sci Info" 67-. 9: SLA; ALA; ASIS; CathLA. 13: Yes. 14: Info retrieval. 15: 111 Garth rd, Oreland, Pa 19075.

JAMES, LUCIA (MARIAN). b Camden SC 28 My 25. 5: NC Col 41-45 (Eng, LS) AB; UIll 47-49 MS in LS; UConn 59-63 (Curriculum, Supv) PhD. 6: Sp, Fr. 7: Libn B T Washington High Sch, Columbia SC 45-47; Asst Prof of Lib Sci Atlanta U 49-53; Asst Prof of Lib Sci Fla A&M U 53-56, Asst Prof of Lib Sci & Dir of Curriculum Lab 56-59; Grad asst curriculum lab UConn 60-62; Dir curriculum lab & Assoc Prof Educ Fla A&M U 63-65; Assoc Prof of Lib Sci Educ, Dir of Curriculum Lab UMd 65-. 8: Consul for sch systems of Fla, 53-65, on reading & org of sch libs; Rep of So Assn of Cols & Secon Schs on visint coms for sch accredit, 54-59, 63-65; Consul Faculty Inst, Claflin Col, on col lib usage 59; Libn/USA, NY World's Fair, 64; Ordained Elder, United Presbyt Church, USA; Consul sch lib programs Anne Arundel & Charles Co Md 66-68; Consul Tchr Educ Inst Media Inst Allen U 68, 69; Chm Study & Job-A-Like Groups ASCD 65, 68, 69. 09: ALA; MdLA; Md State Tchrs Assn; ASCD (chm Study & Job-A-Like Gps 65, 68, 69); MdASCD; Educ Media Assn Md (chm Scholarship Com); AASL (Com on Treatment of Minorities in Textbks). 10: Kappa Delta Pi; AAUP; AAUW; Pi Gamma Mu; YWCA; Den Mother; Delta Sigma Theta; Phi Delta Gamma; Beta Phi Mu. 11: Carnegie Research Grant 51; John Hay Whitney Fellow 59-60. 12: "Curriculum Laboratories in Teacher Education Institutions," PhD diss (63); Ed "Journal & Newsletter" (66-68). 13: Yes. 14: Sch lib admin, bks & related materials for child, ref. 15: Col of Educ Univ of Md, College Park Md 20742.

JAMES, MARTHA W. b Belton Tex. 5: Mary Hardin-Baylor Col 35-36, 38-39 (Eng) BA; UTex 39-40 (Eng) MA; UMich 41-42 BS in LS. 6: Fr, Ger. 7: Sr libn ref Detroit Pub Lib 42-48; Libn III catlg Cal State Lib 48-55; Libn III catlg Free Lib of Phila 55-60; Libn III 1st asst ser UPenn Lib 60-. 9: ALA; PennLA. 14: Catlg, ser, ref. 15: 2201 Benj Franklin pky, apt 1011, Phila Pa 19130.

JAMES, SISTER MARY RDC. b NYC 23 O 18. 5: Good Counsel Col 35-39 (Eng) BA; Columbia 46-49 BS in LS; St John's U 52-56 (Eng) MA. 6: Fr. 7: Tchr St Frances de Chantal, NYC 43-50; Tchr & libn Preston High Sch, NYC 50-67; Libn John F Kennedy High Sch, Somers NY 67-. 8: Consul for Sch Librs NYC Diocesan Schs 64-; Coordinator Title II, NYC Diocesan schs 65-; Series of Instructions and Wkshop for Lib Aides, ITV, NY Diocese 65-67. 9: ALA; CathLA (Nat treas supvrs Sect); NYLA. 14: Readers adv, catlg. 15: John F Kennedy High School Rte 138, Somers NY 10589.

JAMES, VIOLA LOUISE. b Eskridge Kan 28 7. 5:Greenville Col 38-40 (Lat) BA; UIll 44-45 BS in LS; Chicago 50-51 (LS) AM. 7: Tchr Crossville Commun High Sch, Crossville Ill 40-42, Tchr-libn 42-44; Libn Leyden Commun High Sch, Franklin Park Ill 45-48; Ext Instr UIll 48-57; Visiting Lecturer in Instr Materials SoIllU 57-58; Dir Dept of Lib & A-V Serv Des Moines Pub Schs, Des Moines Iowa 58-67; Coord instrl materials Deerfield-Highland Park High Sch Dist, Highland Park Ill 67-. 8: Tchr, summer courses: Syracuse, 57; Purdue, 60; Participant 6 lib sch insts, 62-66; Ed adv bd, Standard Educ Corp 65-. 9: ALA-AASchL; NEA-DAVI; IllLA; IllASchL (pres 54-56); Ill A-V Assn; IllEA. 10: ACLU; Assn of UN; Beta Phi Mu; Delta Kappa Gamma; AAUW; Iowa Soc for the Preservation of Hist Landmarks; Highland Park Hist Soc; High Sch Libns of chicagoland; Chicago Suburban Av RT. 13: Yes. 14: Centralized proc instrl materials centers for elem & secondary schs. 15: 1040 Park ave W, Highland Park Il 60035.

JAMES, WENDELL E. b Des Moines Iowa 28 Je 35. 4: Andrea Bakken. 5: State Col Iowa 53-57 (Educ) BA; Oxford U Oriel Col summer 58 (Soc Sci); UIowa 57-59; UWis 63-64 (LS) MS. 7: Tchr 58-63; Sch libn Kitzingen American Sch, Kitzingen Germany 64-65; Libn Mannheim High Sch, Mannheim Germany 65-66; Sch libn Overseas Dependent Schs, Germany & Japan 64-67; Ref libn UIowa 67-68; Sch libn Overseas Dependent Schs, Germany 68-. 9: ALA. 10: PTA; Phi Delta Kappa. 14: Stud wk, instr materials ctrs. 15: Rte 4 Box 220, Boone Ia 50036.

JAMESON, ELIZABETH. b Marmaduke Ark 5 O 26. 4: Norman L Jameson. 5: Bob JonesU 51 (Eng Bible) BA; Ark StateU 53-65; UMich 65-68 MALS. 7: Tchr Annapolis High Sch, Annapolis Mo 53-54; Sub tchr pub sch, Farmington Mo 54-55; Tchr Caruthersville Jr High, Caruthersville Mo 56-1; Tch caruthersville Mo 56-61; Tchr Chaffee High Sch, Chaffee Mo 61-62; Tchr-libn Southland High Sch, Arbyrd Mo 62-65; Tchr Northwestern High Sch, Flint Mich 65-68; Libn Carter Middle Sch, Clio Mich 68-. 9: NEA; MichLA; MichASchL. 15: 208 S Mill Box 38, Clio Mi 48420.

JAMESON, HARRIET C(LARA). b Kalamazoo Mich 2 D 09. 5: Wheaton Col (Wheaton Ill) 27-31 (Lat, Gk, Bot) AB; UIll(Urbana) 31-32 (Classics) MA, 32-34,cs) PhD; UMich 44-45, 45-48 ABLS, AMLS. 6: Lat, Gk, Fr. 7: Asst Prof of Gk & Lat Wheaton Col (Wheaton Ill) 34-36, Assoc Prof of Gk & Lat 36-44; Asst curator of rare bks UMich(Ann Arbor) 46-47, Sr catlg libn 47-49; Head catlg sect Army Med Lib, Cleveland 50-54; Chief hist of med div Armed Forces, Cleveland 54-59; Head dept of rare bks & spec collections UMich(Ann Arbor) 59-. 9: ALA; BSA; Med Acad Amer; BS (London); Amer Philol Assn, Cambridge (Eng) Bibliog Soc; MssSoc; Bibliog Soc UVa. 10: Women's Research Club, UMich; AAUW; Women of Univ Faculty UMich. 12: "Studies in the Text Tradition of St Jerome's Vitae Patrum," with others (43). 13: Yes. 14: Bibliog, rare bks, rare bk catlg. 15: UMich Lib, Ann Arbor Mich 48104.

JAMESON, V LLOYD. b Putnam Conn 14 Ap 38. 5: UNH 52-56 (Sociol) BA; Simmons 62-65 (LS) MA. 7: Soc casewker US Army 5B Lib: Pre-prof lib asst 59-64, Prof lib asst 64, Ref libn 64-65, Off- in-chg of reader serv 65-68, Curator of Govt Doc 68. 9: ALA. 10: Alpha Kappa Delta. 12: Contrib & illus, "Camp Magic," Ed by M S Desmond (55). 14: Govt documents, admin. 15: 36 Dwight st, Boston Ma 02118.

JAMIESON, ALEXIS (JEAN). b Montreal Can. 5: McGill 43-46 (Hist) BA, 48-49 (LS) BLS; McMaster U 62 (Hist) MA. 6: Fr. 7: Child libn Brooklyn Pub Lib, Brooklyn NY 49-51; Child libn Kensington Pub Lib, London Eng 51-53; Asst circ libn McMaster U 53-54; Asst ref libn 54-56; Circ libn 56-60; Hd of ref & circ 60-67; Asst libn 64-67; Asst libn in charge of Lib Tech Training Programme Seneca Col of Appl Arts & Tech 67-69; Assoc Prof Lib & Info Sci UWest Ont 69-. 9: CanLA; ALA; SLA; Coun Lib Tech; OntLA (chm Ref Wkshop 65-66); Inst Profess Libns Ont. 10: Hamilton Association. 14: Ref. 15: 196 Cline ave N, Hamilton Ont Can.

JAMIESON, EDNA MARY. b Camborne Ont Can. 5: Peterborough Normal Sch 38 1st Class Interim Elem-Sch Tchg Certif; UWest Ont 53 BA; Toronto 65 BLS. 6: Fr. 7: Elem-sch tchr Sch Sect 14 Hamilton Twp, Northumber land Co Ont 38-42; Elem-sch tchr Sch Sect 5 Hamilton Twp, Northumberland Co Ont 42-46; Elem-sch tchr Bd of Educ, St Catharines Ont 46-64; Youth dept head Pub Lib, Oshawa Ont 65-. 14: Ref. 15: 614 Lansdowne dr, Oshawa Ont Can.

JAMIESON, ROSEMARY. b Santa Monica Cal 20 Ap 20. 5: UCal(Los Angeles) 37-42 (Mus) BA; USoCalb. 7: Bank teller Sec 1st Natl Bank, Santa Monica Cal 42-44; Petty off US Navy 44-46; Libn I Long Beach Pub Lib, Long Beach Cal 47-48; Santa Monica Pub Lib, Santa Monica Cal: Libn I 48-51, Libn II 51-58, Br libn 58-. 9: ALA; CalLA. 10: AAUW. 14: Br libn. 15: 921 19th st, Santa Monica Cal 90403.

JAMISON, LELIA B (MRS RICHEY JAMISON). b Kansas City Mo 3 S 21. 5: Pasadena City Col 37-40 AA; UCLA 41-42 (Psych) BA; USoCal 62-63 MSLS; Cal State Col (LA) 65-67. 6: Sp. 7: Owner machine shop Millipart, Glendona Cal 54-63; Asst libn Citrus Col 63-67; Pub serv libn Col of the Redwoods 67-. 8: Tchr Advanced Lib Practices, Col of the Redwoods. 9: ALA; CalEA; CalLA; CalASchL. 10: Humboldt Aets Coun. 14: Instr in use of the lib, ref. 15: 1860 Longview rd, Eureka Ca 95501.

JAMSEN, EDITH CAROL (DARLING). b Grand Rapids Mich 15 O 37. 4: G Charles Jamsen. 5: N Mich Col 57-59 (Hist) BA; UWash 61-62 MLS. 7: Lib asst Boeing Co Lib, Seattle 60-61; Mich State Lib: Ref libn Mich sect 62-64, Asst head ref sect 65, Act head Mich sect 65-66; Asst libn Haslett Br Ingham Co Lib 69-. 14: Ref, especially concerning Mich. 15LETT Branch Ingham Co Lib, 5681 Shaw, Haslett Mi 48840. 14: Ref, especially concerning Mich. 15: Haslett Branch Ingham Co Lib, 5681 Shaw, Haslett Mi 48840.

JANASKE, PAUL C. b Shamokin Penn 28 Jl 20. 4: Virginia Lightner. 5: Dickinson Col 38-42 (Biol) BS; Columbia 49 (LS) MS. 7: Communications off US Nvy, Pacific 42-48; Head serv div Kent State U Lib 49-51; Libn US Govt, Wash DC 51-61; Info spec Amer Inst Biol Sci, Wash DC 61-63; Exec Dir Amer Documentation Inst, Wash DC 63-64; Asst br chief Clearinghouse for Fed Sci & Tech Info, Springfield Va 64-67; Chief Lib & Info Sci Br Div Lib Programs US Off of Educ. 8: Chm COSATI Task Group on Vocabulary Compatibility 64-65; Mem COSATI Panel on Operational Techniques & Systems 65-67; Mem COSATI Panel on Educ & Training 67-. 11: US Dept of Com Sci & Tech Fellow 65-66. 12: Ed "Information

Handling and Science Information" (62); Ed "Automation & Scientific Communication" part III (63). 13: Yes. 14: Info handling. 15: 4508 N Dittmar rd, Arlington Va 22207.

JANE, SISTER MARY CSFN. b Worcester Mass 20 F 14. 5: Marywood Col 35-38 (Math) AB; St John's U (NY) 44-46 BS in LS; Drexel 55-58 MS in LS. 6: Polish, Fr. 7: Elem tchr Holy Cross Sch, Maspeth LI NY 33-34; Secondary sch tchr Nazareth Acad, Torresdale Phila 38-39; Secondary sch tchr Little Flower C G Hig Sch, Phila 39-43; Elem tchr St Stanislaus Kostka, Brooklyn NY 43-46; High sch tchr-libn Nazareth Acad, Torresdale Phila 46-55; Libn Holy Family Tchr Train Sch, Torresdale Phila 46-55; Lin : Mem middle States Evaluation team Central High Sch, Lancaster Penn 53; Consul col schs hosp libs; leader wkshop on small col libs, Phila 65. 9: ALA;-ACRL;-RTSD; CathLA (Local arrangements com, Nat Conv 54, 65; sec Phila Unit High Sch Sect 48-49); PennLA. 10: Beta Phi Mu; Moderator Our Lady of Letters Club 47-55; Treas Friends of Holy Family Col Lib 58-; Com chm Tri-state Col Lib Coop 67-. 11: ACRL - US Steel grant 60, 66. 13: Yes. 14: Admin, consul. 15: Holy Family Col, Torresdale, Phila Pa 19114.

JANECEK, KILBOURN L. b Richland Co Wis 8 O 21. 4: Coila Mae Schoenmann Janecek. 5: UDenver 46-48 (BS, 49-51(LS) MA. 7: Tchr Woodstock Sch, Gillingham Wis 41-42; USAF Radio Mech Sch (S/Sgt) 42-46; Com tchr Denver Pub Schs 48-49; Gen serv libn Mary Reed Lib Denver U 50-51; Assoc libn Omaha U 51-57& assoc libn SD State U 57-61; Admin asst Modesto Jr Col 61-62; Assoc libn SD State U 62-67; Dir of libs ND State U 67-. 9: MPLA; NDLA. 14: Admin, personnel. 15: N Dak State Univ Lib, Fargo ND 58102.

JANES, IRENE. b Montreal Can 15 My 06. 5: UNC 41 BA, 41 (LS) Certif; Montclair State Col 59 MA. 7: Pub Lib, Paterson NJ: Br asst 24-35, Circ asst 35-38, Ref asst 38-42, Ref libn 42-57; Sch libn Central High Sch, Paterson NJ 57-65; Sch libn Kennedy High Sch, Paterson NJ 65-. 9: ALA; NJLA; NJEA; NJSchLA. 10: LWV. 12: "Early History of Libraries in Paterson" (49); "Government of Paterson" (52). 14: Ref, sch libs. 15: 771 E 22nd st, Paterson NJ 07513.

JANEWAY, RAY CURTIS. b Siloam Springs Ark 14 Mr 16. 4: Bonnie Ethel Fenstemaker. 5: UKan 33-38 (Philos) BA; UIll 40-44 (LS) BS in LS, MS. 7: Libn Bradley U 44-46; Asst dir UKan 46-49; Libn Tex Tech Col 49-. 9: TexLA (pres); SWLA (sec). 10: AAUP; Rotary; Tex Assn of Col Tchrs. 11: TexLA Libn of the Year, 63. 13: Yes. 14: Admin, bldgs, collection bldg. 15: Tex Tech Col Lib PO Box 4079, Lubbock Tx 79409.

JANITZ, JOHN. b Brooklyn NY 30 S 34. 5: Providence Col 52-56 (Pol Sci) BA; Boston Col 64-65 (Hist) MA. 6: Fr. 7: Capt US Army, US & Europe 57-62; Instr Annhurst Col 66-68; Mss libn Me Hist Soc, Portland 68; Mss processor SyracuseU Lib mss div 68-. 9: OAH; AHA. 10: AAUP; ACLU; Conf on Peace Research in Hist; Inst for Computer Research in Humanities. 14: Mss & spec collections related to hist research. 15: 113 Fordham rd 3C, Syracuse NY 13203.

JANKE, LESLIE H. b Wis 24 N 18. 5: Wis State Col (Platteville) 37-41 (Soc Sci, Educ) BA; UWyo 49-50 (Hist) MA; Fla State U 53-54 MLS. 6: Fr. 7: Pein jr high, Benton Wis 41-42; Radar research USAF 42-46; High sch tchr pub schs, Morrison Ill 46-48; Libn commun schs Morrison Ill 48-50, Dir curriculum materials 50-56; Dir adult educ Whiteside Co Schs, Morrison Ill 55-56; Prof a-v & lib Ida State Col summer 64; Chm dept libnship & prof of educ San Jose State Col 56-. 8: Consul: Cal State Dept of Educ 60-63, US Off of Educ 60, 64; State Chm Adv Com ESEA for Cal 66-69; State Col rep to Cal Coun on educ for Tchrs 65-69. 9: ALA (Reg dir AASchL 66-68; chm Adv Com Sch Lib Manpower Proj 68-71); -LAD Nat Chm; -LED (Nat Chm 68-71); NEA-DAVI; CalLA (Profess Educ Com 59-64); CalASchL (Pres 63-64); A-VEA Cal. 13: Yes. 14: Lib educ, lib admin. 15: 107 Kim Louise dr #3, Campbell Ca 95008.

JANKEL, ADELAIDE (CUTTER). b Bisbee Ariz 21 O 09. 5: USoCal 29-31 (Fr) AB; Columbia 32-34 BSLS, 37-41 (LS); UWash 47-48 (Hist). 6: Fr. 7: Asst NY Pub Lib 31-42; Admin asst US Off Strategic Serv, NYC 42-43; Asst libn The Cooper Union Museum, NYC 43-44; Aircraft communicator US Civil Aeronautics Admin, Kodiak Alaska 44-47; Libn The French Inst, NYC 53-57; Asst Ferris Inst, Big Rapids Mich 57-59; Libn Dean Jr Col 59-. 9: SLA; NELA. 13: Yes. 14: Ref, acquis. 15: PO Box 328, Franklin Ma 02038.

JANKOWSKI, DOROTHY A. b Cleveland 13 Je 42. 5: West Res 59-62 (Chem) BA, 62-63 MSLS. 6: Fr. 7: IBER, Akron Ohio 63-64; Market research libn Standard Oil Co (Ohio), Cleveland 64-69, Supv info serv 69-. 9: ACS; SLA (chm Employment Com Cleveland Chap). 10: Iota Sigma Pi (chm Fluorine Chap). 14: Spec libs (chem), bus & tech info retrieval. 15: 5280 Case ave, Lyndhurst Ohio 44124.

JANN, EDMUND CARL. b Portland Ore 1 F 15. 4: Helen Rae Davis. 5: Law Sch (Berne Switzerland) 35-37 (Law); CatholicU 38-39 (Law); Nat U Law Sch 40-42 (Law) LLB (JD). 6: Ger, Fr. 7: Capt US Army Inf 42-45; Lib asst Law Lib LC 39-42, 46-49, Ref libn 49-50, Research asst 50-56, Assr chief European Law Div 56-62, Chief 62-. 9: AALL; Law Libns' Soc of Wash DC. 13: Yes. 14: Research in European law. 15: 802 S Royal st, Alexandria Va 22314.

JANOWSKI, BRONISLAW (MIKE). b Poland 23 N 13. 4: Mary-Ellen Tilley. 5: Tchrs Col (Poland) 30-35 (Educ) Tchg Diploma; Southwestern U 49-52 (Secondary Educ) BS in Ed; LSU 58-59 MLS. 6: Polish, Ukrainian, Russian, Ger, Ital. 7: Tchr, Poland 37-39; (Sgt) Cadet Off Infantry & Transport Polish Free Army under British Command, Middle East, Ialy & Eng 41-48; Computer Geotechnical Corp, Dallas 52-55; Clerk Pure Oil Co, Morgan City La 55-57; Asst libn Allen Parish Lib, Oberlin La 59-62; Libn Evangeline Parish Lib, Ville Platte La 62-. 9: ALA-ALTA (chm Wkshop Regis Com 63-65); -RSD (New Reg Tools Com 69-71); LaLA (chm Pub Lib Sect 63, mem Legis Com), -PLS (chm Study Com 68-69). 10: Rotary; KC. 14: Admin, catlg, ref. 15: P O Box 491, Ville Platte La 70586.

JANS, LUCILLE (DOROTHY). b White River S Dak 2 S 21. 5: UCal (Berkeley) 47-50 (Eng) AB, 59-60 MLS. 6: Fr, Sp, Ger. 7: Clk US Treasury, Wash DC & Chicago 41-43; Chief yeoman USN 43-46; Prin clk Registrar's Off UCal (Berkeley) 51-53; Sec For Serv State Dept wash DC, Mexico & Germany 54-59; Asst hd loan dept UCal (Berkeley) 60-66; Gift & exchange, ser libn acquis dept UCal (Davis) 66-69; Acquis libn UCal (Santa Cruz) 69-. 9: ALA; CalLA. 10: Sierra Club. 14: Acquis. 15: 372 Searidge rd apt 4, Aptos Ca 95003.

JANSEN, GUENTER (ALFRED). b Phila 19 S 30. 4: Herge Meykranz. 5: Muhlenberg Col 48-50; UPenn 51-55 (Eng) AB; Drexel 55-56 MS in LS. 6: Ger. 7: Libn I Lit Dept Free Lib of Phila 56; Interne spec recruit LC 56-57, Ser catlgr 57-58; Head of Ext Cedar Rapids Pub Lib, Cedar Rapids Iowa 58-60; Asst dir Mobile Pub Lib, Mobile Ala 60-61, Dir 61-65; City libn New Orleans Pub Lib 65-67; Dir Suffolk Coop Lib Syst, Bellport NY 67-. 8: Spec Guest Lecturer in ten cities in Germany 65. 9: ALA (numerous coms 57-); SLA; NYLA; NY Lib Club; Suffolk Co LA; LPRC. 10: Bd of Trustees Assn of NY Libs for Tech servs; Lib Futures; Pub Libs of NY (Radio-Television Project). 12: "Univac Electronic Data Processing in the Public Library Systems of Long Island" (68). 13: Yes. 14: Admin, electronic data processing, centralized tech serv, bldgs & equipment, pub rel. 15: PO Box 187, Bellport NY 11713.

JANSENS, GERTRUDE (MILLARD). b San Jose Cal 29 D 13. 4: John A Jansens. 5: Stanford 30-32 (Eng); San Jose State Col 38-42 (LS) AB. 6: Fr. 7: San Jose Pub Lib, San Jose Cal: Lib asst 30-32, Jr libn 37-43; Supv libn child div 43-53, Supv libn catlg div 53-. 9: ALA; CalLA (past chm Sect for Wk with Boys & Girls); Assn Child Libns No Cal (chm); No Cal Group Tech Processes. 10: Bus & Prof Women's Club; Quota Club. 14: Child wk, catlg. 15: 555 N 2nd st, San Jose Cal 95112.

JANSMA, RUTH VIRGINIA (GEZON). b Holland Mich 26 O 11. 4: Rev Theodore J Jansma. 5: Calvin Col 28-32 (Eng, Hist) AB; Rutgers 62 (LS); Paterson State Col 59-63 NJ Certif; Columbia 60-63 (LS) MS. 6: Fr, Dutch. 7: Sec US Govt Dept Labor-Wage-Hr, Grand Rapids Mich 52-53; Sec US Govt VA, Grand Rapids Mich 53-56; Sec US Govt Air Force Procurement, Grand Rapids Mich 56-57; Sec to dean of admissions Paterson State Col 57-58; Prof lib circ Paterson (NJ) Pub Lib 58-59; Elem tchr Wyckoff Chr Sch, Wyckoff NJ 59-60; Sch libn Manchester Reg High Sch, Paterson NJ 60-. 9: NJEA; Nat Assn Sec Sch Tchrs. 14: Ref. 15: 638 Goffle Hill rd, Hawthorne NJ 07506.

JANSSEN, LILLIAN (TERHUNE). b NYC 6 Ag 06. 4: Robert H Janssen. 5: Columbia 25-28 (Health Educ) BS; Rutgers 55-58 MLS. 6: Fr. 7: Tchr health educ NYC Bd of Educ Jane Addams High Sch 38-45; Libn Ft Lee (NJ) Bd of Educ 54-. 9: NJEA; Bergen Co SchLA (past v-pres in chg of memb); Bergen Co EA; Ft Lee TA. 10: Audubon Soc; Palisades Nature Assn; Mus of Nat Hist (NYC). 14: Elem sch lerv. 15: 218 Vanorden ave, Leonia NJ 07605.

JANUSKIS, LOLA. b Siauliai Lithuania 12 Ap 24. 5: Boston U 56-60 (Psych) AB, AM; Simmons 61-63 MLS; Emmanuel Col 64-65 (Russian Lang & Lit) AM. 6: Sp Russian, Ger, Lithuanian. 7: Research asst in psych VA Hosp & Boston Mass Mental Health Serv 60-61; Lib intern Widener Lib Harvard U 61-63, Slavic catlgr 63-64; Catlgr Garland Jr Col Lib 64-65; Catlgr Temple U Sullivan Lib 65-. 9: Amer As Tchrs Slavic & E European Langs. 10: Phi Beta Kappa. 12: Ed Women's Page of "Keleivis," Lithuanian Weekly (51-56). 14: Catlg, bibliog. 15: 4039 Chestnut st apt 116, Phila Pa 19104.

JAQUES, (CHRISTINE) MARION. b New Orleans 9 Mr 15. 5: Newcomb Col 32-33 (Chem); Loyola U (New Orleans) 33-36 (Chem) BS; Catholic U 38-39 BS in LS. 6: Fr. 7: Catlgr New Orleans Pub Lib 39-40; Head catlgr Loyola U 40-44; Catlgr Catholic U 44-46; Head bk div of lib US Naval Ordnance Lab, Silver Spring Md 46-48; Head Libn Vitro Labs Silver Spring Lab, Silver Spring Md 48-. 8: Library/USA NY World's Fair 64. 9: SLA; IntfElectricaronic Engnrs; Amer Inst of Aeronautics & Astronautics. 14: Admin, catlg. 15: 2800 Quebec st NW , Wash DC 20008.

JAQUITH, F LUREE. b Chicago 31 My 36. 5: Ill State U 62-63 (Educ) BS; West Mich U 63-65 (LS) MA. 7: Tchr Willow Springs Pub Sch, Willow Springs Ill 56-60; Tchr Chicago Ridge Pub Sch, Chicago Ridge Ill 60-62; Libn Lexington Pub Sch, Lexington Mass 65-. 9: ALA; MassSchLA; NEA; NEA-DAVI; Mass A-v Assn. 14: Elem sch lib. 15: 52 Jacqueline rd apt 16, Waltham Ma 02154.

JARBOE, JENNIE (KELLY). b Lebanon Ky 12 Ap 10. 4: Joseph B Jarboe Jr. 5: East Ky State Col 27-31 (Foreign Lang) AB; West Ky State Col summer 33; Nazareth Col (Louisville Ky) 54-56 (Minor in LS). 6: Lat, Fr. 7: Tchr-libn Lebanon High Sch, Lebanon Ky 33-35; Libn St Augustine High Sch, Lebanon Ky 48-55; Libn St charles High Sch, Lebanon Ky 55-66; Libn Lebanon High Sch, Lebanon Ky 66-. 9: ALA; NEA; KyEA; KyLA; KyASchL; SELA. 14: Ref. 15: 245 Koet ave, anon Ky 40033.

JARCHO, SAUL. b NYC 25 O 06. 4: Irma Seijo. 5: Harvard 21-25 (Eng Lit) AB (magna cum laude); Columbia 25-26 (Lat Lit) MA, 26-30 (Med) MD. 6: Fr, Ger, Sp, Ital. 7: Consul to Med Lib French Hosp, NYC 65-; Ed Bulletin NY Acad of Med 67-. 8: Lib Com NY Acad Med, NYC 46-; Armed Forces Med Lib Adv Group, Wash DC 54-56; Lib Com Albert Einstein med Col 55-58; Bd of Regents NLM, Bethesda Md 61-65. 9: AMA; Med LA; Amer Assn Hist Med (v-pres 66-68, pres 68-); AHS; NY Hist Soc; Hist Sci Soc; NY Acad Med; NY Acad Sci; Amer Assn Path & Bact; Harvey Soc; Amer Anthropol Assn. 10: AAAS (Fellow); Amer Geog Soc; Soc Med Consuls to Armed Forces; NIH (Hist of Life Sci Study Sect chm 60-63, memb 68-); Amer Pub Health Assn; Amer Soc Parasitol. 11: Fielding Garrison Lecturer, Amer Assn Hist Med, 63; Welch Medal, Amer Assn Hist Med, 63. 13: Yes. 14: Hist of med, Americana, lib arch, admin. 15: 35 E 85, New York NY 10028.

JARDINE, VIRGINIA (LEE). b Portland Ore 5 Ja 42. 5: Portland State Col 59-60 (Pol Sci); Reed 60-63 (Hist) BA; UCLA 65-66 MLS. 7: Stud asst Reed Col Lib 61-63; Clerical Norcrest China Co, Portland Ore 63-64; Lib asst UOre Med Sch Lib (Portland) 64-65; Stud asst UCLA Research Lib 65-66; Catlgr LC 66-. 9: ALA. 10: Potomac Appalachian Trail Club. 14: Catlg, mss, child bks. 15: 101 G St SW A-805, Washington DC 20024.

JARMAN, LYNNE (WALTER). b Toronto Ont 11 J 32. 4: Bryan Jarman. 5: UBC 61-65 (Mus hist) B Mus, 66-67 BLS. 7: Clerical -61; Coach-accompanist UBC opera wkshop 62-66; Stud asst UBC recordings collection summer 65; Stud asst UBC Lib summer 66; Catlgr Nat Lib of Can, Ottawa Ont 67-. 8: Music director, Marat/Sade, Frederick Wood Theatre, Nov 66. 9: CanLA; ALA; CanMusLA (Coun 66-67). 10: Amer Fed Musicians; Mayor's Com on Youth (Ottawa); Civil Swrv Recreation Assn; Theatre Soc. 14: Catlg (esp music). 15: Apt 907 201 Bell st, Ottawa 4 Ont Can.

JARMON, JEANNE S (SCHOONMAKER). b Boston 12 Ag 15. 4: Oscar F Jarmon. 5: Vassar 33-37 (Eng) AB; Simmons 55-56 MSLS. 6: Fr. 7: Child Room NY Pub Lib 38-40; Correspondent Book-of-the-Month Club, NYC 40-42; Ed asst "Psychosomatic Medicine" NYC 42; WAVE Off US Navy 42-44; Asst libn Norview Sr High Sch, Norfolk Va 57-58; Child libn Leominster Pub Lib, Leominster Mass 59-60; Libn Mt Wachusett Commun Col 64-65; Libn Oakmont Reg High Sch, S Ashburham Mass 65-. 8: Reviewer "Round Table of Young Adult Librarians" 65; Mass Sch Lib Steering Com 60-64; Mass State Adv Com for Title II of PL 89-10 (66-69); Demonstration Ctr Lib Title II 67-69. 9: NEA; MassSchLA; NESchLA. 12: "Planning Your School Library." 14: Child young adult & sch libs. 15: High st, Ashburnham Mass 01430.

JARNAGIN, NORA (OWEN). b Collinsville Tex 28 My 19. 4: Bayless N Jarnagin. 5: Tex Woman's U 35-37, 38-40 (LS) BA, 64, 65, 67 (LS). 7: Libn High Sch, Elgin Tex 42; Libn Jesuit High Sch, Dallas 42-44, 45-48; Ref libn Ext Lib UTex (Austin) 44; Materials requirements analyst Temco Inc, Grand Prairie Tex 52-59; Cost acct clerk Moore Bus Forms Inc, Denton Tex 60-64; Libn Sr High Sch, Grapevine Tex 64-67; Libn Middle Sch Lewisville Tex 67-. 9: ALA; Tex State Tchrs Assn; TexASchL; TexLA (sec-treas YA 69-70). 10: Tex Woman's Univ Alumnae Assn (past-pres). 15: 1208 Linden dr, Denton Tx 76201.

JARRELL, JUDITH MAY (BATES). b Oak Park Ill 8 My 43. 4: Lawrence E Jarrell. 5: Coe Col 61-62; Fla State U 62-64 (Hist) BA, 65 (LS) MS. 7: Ref & Petroleum Libn, Shreve Mem Lib 66-68. 9: ALA; LaLA. 10: Phi Alpha Theta. 14: Ref. 15: 375 Sandefur dr, Shreveport La 71105.

JARRETT, EULA MAE (CARTER). b Ohio Co Ky 25 Ag 31. 4: Dallas Ralph Jarrett. 5: UKy 49-53 (LS) AB; Peabody 55; UNC(Greensboro) 65 (Educ, LS) M Ed. 6: Sp. 7: Libn U Elem Sch levels K-6 UNC (Greensboro 53-. 9: ALA; NCLA; NCEA; SELA. 14: Elem multi-media lib. 15: 621 Scott ave, Greensboro NC 27403.

JARRETT, GLADYS JANET (WYNNE). b Barnesville Ga 6 F 16. 4: Hobart Sidney Jarrett. 5: Hunter 32-36 (Span) BA; Columbia 36-37 (Span) MA; UNC summer 60 (LS); Pratt 62-63 MLS. 6: Sp, Ger, Fr, Ital. 7: Instr Span & Eng Langston U 37-41, 46-47; Tech asst NY Pub Lib 48-51; Pub serv clerk Syracuse U Lib 53-54; Head catlgr & supv F D Bluford Lib A&T Col (Greensboro NC) 57-61; Searcher in catlg dept Brooklyn Pub Lib 61-62; Acquis ref libn Pace Col 64-67; Hd catlg dept York Col of CUNY 67-. 9: NY Lib Club; NYLA; NYLA; LACUNY; sec Lib Com of Univ Senate of CUNY. 10: Beta Phi Mu; Pratt Inst Lib Sch Alumni Assn; Brooklyn Col Faculty Wives Club; Assn for Study of Negro Life & Hist; United Negro Col Fund. 12: Bk reviews in "Greensboro Daily News" (54-55). 14: Ref, acquis, catlg. 15: 175 Willoughby st apt 16L, Brooklyn NY 11201.

JARRETTE, MARGARET UVAUGHN (MOORE). b Waynesboro Ga 21 Mr 35. 4: George Eddie jarrette Jr. 5: Paine Col 62 (Biol) BS; Atlanta U 66 MSLS; Columbia summer 66. 6: Fr, Ger. 7: Asst in lib Paine Col 62-65, Catlg libn 66-. 9: ALA; SELA; GaLA. 14: Catlg. 15: 197 Augusta Homes apts, Augusta Ga 30901.

JARVI, EDITH (TYYNE). b Toronto Ont Can 12 My 21. 5: Toronto L S Diploma Course 43; Toronto 46-48 (Eng) BA, 54 BLS, 64 MLS. 7: Gen asst Windsor Pub Lib, Windsor Ont 41-42, 43-45; Dist libn Can Army, Calgary 45-46; Windsor Pub Lib, Windsor Ont: Br libn 49, Ref libn 50-54, Head of ref dept 55-63; Asst Prof UToronto Lib Sch 64-. 9: CanLA (past dir Ref Sect); ALA-Subs Bks Com; OntLA (Ref Wkshop); Inst Prof Libns Ont (past sec & dir); SLA. 10: Delta Kappa Gamma; Beta Phi Mu; Windsor Coun of Women; Windsor UN Branch; Univ Women's Club. 13: Yes. 14: Ref. 15: 77 St Clair E #1101, Toronto 7 Can.

JARVIS, DALE O. b Martinez Cal 27 My 30. 5: Neb Wesleyan 48-52 (Speech) BA; La State U 58-60 MS in LS. 7: Owner & partnership Travelers Motel, Boulder Colo 52-57; LSU: Head music & speech lib 57-58, Head listening rooms 58-60, Sr catlgr 60-63, Asst ser libn 63-64, Head prep dept 64-65; Head circ dept USoCal 65-68, Asst libn pub serv 68-. 9: ALA. 14: Tech serv, circ, ref, admin. 15: 11983 Laurelwood dr apt 2, Studio City Cal 91604.

JASENAS, MICHAEL. b Velziai Lithuania 1 Je 12. 4: Eliane Passeroni. 5: Gymnasium for Men (Panevezys Lithuania) 27-31 (Lang & Lit) Baccalaureate; UKaunas (Lithuania) 31-35 (Philos) MA; Sorbonne 37-39 9diplomat Hist & Internat Law) Diploma; Columbia 51-53 (LS) MS, 67 DLS. 06: Fr, Ger, Lat, Lithuanian, Russian. 7: Admin asst, then Head admin serv UNRRA/IRO Hdqrs, Neuenbuerg Germany 47-49; Searcher, then catlgr NY Pub Lib 51-54; Ref libn Rutgers U Lib 54-59; Rare bk libn Cornell U Libs 59-60; Ser libn UNev Libs 60; Rare bk libn Cornell U Libs 60-64; Summer session Faculty Sch of Lib Sci Syracuse U summers 61, 62, 64; Bibliog in the humanities & Assoc Prof SUNY(Binghamton) 64-. 8: Visiting faculty Syracuse U Sch of Lib Sci summers 59, 61, 62, 64; Surveys of resources of Ithaca Col & SUNY (Oneonta) 69. 9: Mod Lang Assn; S Central Research Lib Coun NY (Acad Resources Com 68-). 12: "History of the Development of the

Bibliography of Philosophy" (67); "Cataloging Small Manuscript Collections" (readings in nonbook libnship, 68). 13: Yes. 14: Ref, bibliog, rare bks, bk sel in acad libs, lib educ, catlg. 15: Lib State Univ of NY, Binghamton NY 13901.

JASON, NORA H. b Schenectady NY 15 Ja 36. 5: SUNY (Albany) 60-64 (Soc Studies) AB, 65-66 MLS. 7: Elem libn Clinton Elem Sch, Clinton NY 64-65; Catlgr Sacramento State col 66-67; Arm libn Spec Serv Lib, Nellingen Germany 67-. 9: ALA; NYStateLA; Cal Tech Serv No Cal; Armed Forces LA. 14: Ref, admin. 15: RD 4 Washout rd, Scotia NY 12302.

JASPER, GERTRUDE R(ATHBONE). b NYC 7 Jl 07. 5: Wells Col 25-29 (Romance Langs) BA summa cum laude; Columbia 30-31 (Fr) MA, 32-47 (Fr) PhD; Pratt 49-50 MLS. 6: Fr, Sp, Ital. 7: Tchg fellow to Asst Prof of Romance Langs Hunter Col 32-50; Asst Prof to Prof of Lib Sci Pratt Inst Lib Sch 50-55; Sec-treas Toby Coppock Inc, NYC 56-62; Asst libn catlgr foreign lang materials Tchrs Col Lib Columbia U 62-. 9: ALA; Mod Lang Assn; Amer Assn Tchrs of Fr; NY Tech Serv Libns Assn. 10: Phi Beta Kappa; The Fashion Group; The Brooklyn Museum. 12: "Adventure in the Theatre, Lugne-Poe and the Theatre de l'Oeuvre" (47); Co-ed "Bibliography of Critical and Biographical References for the Study of Contemporary French Literature". 13: Yes. 14: Catlg. 15: 250 E 39 st, New York NY 10016.

JASPER, JAMES M. b Kingman Kan 20 Ag 29. 5: Kan U 47-50 (Fine Arts); Mo Valley Col 54-56 (Bus Admin) BS; Kansas State Tchrs Col 59-60 (LS) MS. 7: Naval accounts clerk USMC 51-54; Asst field dir Amer Nat Red Cross, Randolph AFB Tex 57; Admin asst Nat HQ Telecommunication Amer Nat Red Cross, Richmond Va 57-58; Head circ dept Kan State U Lib 60-61; Head adult serv asst libn Pub Lib, Salina Kan 61-64; Coordinator of serv Johnson Co Pub Lib, Shawnee Mission Kan 64-66, Hd tech serv Saskatoon Pub Lib 66; Hd catlg & acquis Upper Iowa Col 67-68; Catlg libn Baker U 68-69; Libn Newton Free Lib, Newton Kan 69-. 9: ALA; KanLA; MPLA. 10: AAUP; Optimists Internat. 14: Catlg. 15: Public Library, Newton Ks 67114.

JAVID, RUHA. b Iran 14 Jl 15. 5: Tehran U 39-42 (Fr Lang) BA; NYU 51-53 (Fr Lit) MA; McGill 58-60 BLS. 6: Persian, Turkish, Arabic, Urdu, Tajik, Kurdish, Fr, Eng, Ger. 7: Tr Mines Dept, Tehran Iran 39-42; Interpreter & sec US Army, Tehran Iran 42-45; Tchr Persian Govt, Tehran Iran 45-51; Announcer Voice of Amer, NYC 52-54; Sec Mission of Iran to UN, NYC 52-58; Catlgr Islamic Inst McGill U 58-61; Catlgr Columbia U 61-. 9: SLA. 14: Catlg. 15: 1353 River rd, Edgewater NJ 07020.

JAX, JOHN JOSEPH. b Cazenovia Wis 17 Je 35. 4: Judith Annette Weiss. 5: Wis State U (LaCrosse) 54-58 (Hist) BA; UWis 58-59 MSLS; UMinn summer 65; UIll 67-68. 6: Sp. 7: (Staff/Sgt) Wis Nat Guard communications spec 52-61; Asst libn Stout State U 59-. 8: N Central Assn of Second Schs & Cols Evaluation Com, Chetek Wis 64, Bloomer Wis 65, Mondovi Wis 66; Asst basketball coach, Stout State U, Menomonie Wis 65-69. 9: ALA; WisLA; WisEA (local treas 65-66); Assn Wis State Univ Faculties; Univ Faculty Senate (v-chm 67-68, chm 68-69). 10: Lions Club. 14: Circ, admin, personnel. 15: 401 12th ave W, Menomonie Wis 54751.

JAY, DONALD FREDERICK. b Ainsworth Neb 13 Je 27. 5: UNeb 44-45, 46-47; Northwestern U 47-49, 50, 52-53 BS (Eng) MA (Fr); ULausanne 51-52 (Fr) Diplome; UCal(Berkeley) 53-55 (Fr, LS) MLS. 6: Fr. 7: LC; Spec Recruit 55-56, Asst head European Exch Sect 56, Head Orientalia Exch Sect 56-58, Head European Exch Sect 58-59; Libn US Coast Guard Acad 59-61; Dir PL-480 Proj Middle East LC, Cairo UAR 61-64; Coordinator PL-480 Programs LC, Wash DC 64-66; Coord Overseas Programs 66-67, Chief Overseas Operations Div 67-. 9: ALA; DCLA. 10: Beta Phi Mu. 15: 521 South Lee st, Alexandria Va 22314.

JAYATILLEKE, RAJASINGHE ATTANAYAKAGE. b Gampaha Ceylon 6 Ja 32. 4: Elizabeth Dabare. 5: St Joseph's Col (Colombo Ceylon) 44-52 (Gen Sci) LONDON GCE; UCeylon 53-57 (Zool) BS; Columbia 62-63 MS in LS. 6: Sinhalase, Tamil, Fr, Ger. 7: UCeylon: Demonstrator in zool 57-58, Asst lecturer in zool 58-59, Asst libn (sci) 60-67, Act libn 67-68; Research off in nematology Tea Research Inst of Ceylon 59-60; Tchg asst ColumbiaU 68-. 8: UNESCO Fellow from Ceylon, Reg Sem in Sci Document, org by UNESCO S Asia Sci Coop Off, INSDOC Nat Phys Lab, New Delhi India Oct 63. 9: CeylonLA (secy 64-65, v-pres 67-68); ALA; -RTSD; -CRL. 10: Ceylon Assn Advanc of Sci; Automobile Assn Ceylon. 12: Jt comp: "Union List of Scientific Periodicals in the Libraries in Ceylon" (in press); Ed Bio Sci Sect of Sinhalese Sci Magazine "Vidya" (67-68). 13: Yes. 14: Lib admin, catlg, acquis, proc, documentation. 15: School of Lib Serv 516 Butler Lib Columbia Univ, New York NY 10025.

JAYNES, PHYLLIS EDITH. b Flint Mich 11 Ja 38. 5: Southwest Mo State 55-58 (Bus) BS; Rutgers 58-59 MLS. 6: Sp, Ger. 7: Asst ref libn Genesee Co Lib, Flint Mich 59-60; Ref libn Gen Motors Inst, Flint Mich 60-64, Supv of lib operations 64-68; Libn Sci & Engnrg Lib Haile Sellassie I U, Addis Ababa Ethiopia 68-. 9: ALA (chm Jr Mem Round Table); SLA; MichLA (sec-treas Dist V, chm Dist V, Newcomers Com chm). 10:Flint Lib Club (pres). 14: Ref, admin. 15: Science Lib, Haile Sellassie I U, PO Box 399, Addis Ababa Ethiopia.

JEBB, MARCIA G. b Manchester NH 11 O 34. 5: Colby Col 51-55 (Fr) AB; ULyons(France) 55-56 Diplo4me; George Washington U 57-60 (Fr) MA; Simmons 61-62 MLS. 6: Fr, Sp, Ger, Russian. 7: Ed asst US Govt, Wash DC 56-59; Asst child libn br DC Pub Lib 59-60, Asst libn gen ref & info div 60-61; Ref asst fine arts dept Boston Pub Lib 61-62; Asst ref libn Cornell U Lib 62-65; Asst ref libn Temple U 65-66, Asst hd ref div 67-68; Assoc libn ref Cornell U Lib 68-. 9: ALA; Mod Lang Assn; NYLA. 10: Phi Beta Kappa; Phi Sigma Iota. 11: Fulbright grant, 55-56. 14: Ref. 15: 329 Spruce, Phila Pa 19106.

JEFFERSON, MARY EVELYN. b Danville Va 9 My 21. 5: Stratford Col 39-41; UNC (Chapel Hill) 55-57 (Eng) AB, 66-68 MSLS; UVa 59-61 (Eng) MA. 6: Fr. 7: Sec: 1st National Bank, Danville Va 41-50, 1st Nat Exchange Bank, Roanoke Va 50-51, Dan River Mills, Danville Va 51-52, City Mgr, Danville Va 52-55; Teacher Stratford Col 57-64, Asst Prof of Eng 64-66, Asst Prof of Eng & Asst Libn 66-68, Assoc Libn 68-. 9: ALA; VaLA. 10: Phi Beta Kappa; YWCA, Wednesday Club; Mod Lang Assn. 13: Yes. 14: Tech proc. 15: 160 Gray st, Danville Va 24541.

JEFFERY, KATHERINE (PLUMMER). b Boston 6 Ag 06. 4: Clifton Adams Jeffery. 5: West Res 28-29 (LS) Certif. 7: Child libn Roslindale Br Boston Pub Lib 24-28; Stud asst child dept Cleveland Pub Lib 28-29; Child libn Mattapan Br Boston Pub Lib 30-33; Yp libn Brockton (Mass) Pub Lib 45-50; Child & young adult libn Milton (Mass) Pub Lib 50-58, Young adults libn 58-. 9: ALA-PLA;-YASD; MassLA; Mass Round Table Libns Young Adults (co-founder & first pres, pres 68-69); Old Colony Lib Club (pres 64-66). 13: Yes. 14: Young adults. 15: 558 Ash st, Brockton Ma 02401.

JEFFRESS, IRIS (POWELL). b Hattiesburg Miss 24 Jl 19. 4: Victor Conley Jeffress. 5: Phillips U 37-38; Tex A & I U 61-63 (Eng) BA; UTex 63-65 MLS. 7: Asst libn seguin-Guadalupe Co Pub Lib, Seguin Tex 65-66; Lib consul Gen Tel Co SW, San Angelo Tex 66-68; Hd catlg dept Angelo State Col 68-. 9: ALA; SLA; TexLA. 10: AAUW. 14: Tech proc. 15: 2320 W ave J, San Angelo Tx 76901.

JEFFRESS, VICTOR CONLEY. b Eufaula Okla 21 N 17. 4: Iris Powell. 5: Okmulgee Jr Col 36-38 AA; Okla State U 38-39; Tex A & I U 58-60 BBA; UTex (Austin) 63-65 MLS. 7: Libn Seguin-Guadalupe Co Pub Lib, Seguin Tex 65-66; Lib dir Tom Green Co Pub Lib, San Angelo Tex 66-. 9: ALA; TexLA (chm District II); SWLA. 10: Rotary. 14: Admin. 15: 2320 W ave J, San Angelo Tx 76901.

JEFFREY, PENELOPE (STIFFLER). b Buffalo NY 6 Mr 44. 4: David Harold Jeffrey. 5: Rosary Hill Col 61-65 (Eng) BA; Pratt 65-66 MLS. 6: Fr. 7: Asst br libn Woodstock Br NY Pub Lib, Bronx NY 68-. 8: Juror EFLA Film Festival 68 & 69. 9: ALA (YASD com evaluating ya mags); NYLA (Rec Com Child & YA Div). 13: Yes. 14: Ya serv. 15: 2025 Continental ave apt 7e, Bronx NY 10461.

JEFFREY, WILLIAM (BUCKLEY) JR. b Sioux City Iowa 8 Ag 21. 4: Margaret L Mitchell. 5: UChicago 38-42 AB, Grad Lib Sch 46-47 BLS; Drake U 49-50 LLB. 7: Circ asst UChicago 40-42; US Army 33d Infantry Div PTO 43-45; Circ asst UChicago Law Lib 46-48; Law Libn Drake U 49-50; Circ asst Harvard Law Lib 50-51; Asst law libn Yale Law Lib 51-56; Law Libn & Prof UCincinnati Law Lib 56-. 13: Yes. 14: Legal hist. 15: UCincinnati, Cincinnati Oh 45221.

JEFFRIES, B(EATRICE) RUTH. b Sherbrooke Que Can 22 Je 09. 5: UWash 27-35 (European Hist, Pol Sci) BA & BS in LS; Harvard U summer 40. 6: Fr. 7: Lib asst catlg div UWash Lib 28-36; Legis ref asst NH State Lib 36-38; Catlgr Colby Jr Col for Women 38-42; Libn Watertown Arsenal Metallurgical Lib, Watertown Mass 42-44; Catlgr UWash Lib 44-45, Libn Pol Sci Lib 45-. 9: SLA; PNLA. 10: Pi Sigma Alpha. 12: "New

Hampshire Constitutional Conventions" (37, rev ed 56 by P A Hazelton); Ed "Social Science Bulletin," SLA (54-55); Ed "Puget Sound Specialist," SLA (61-64). 14: Ref. 15: 12225 Evanston ave N, Seattle Wa 98133.

JEFFRIES, MARY (WAIT). b Greenville Ill 24 Mr 22. 4: Theodore W Jeffries. 5: Greenville Col 40-44 (Langs, Math) BA; UIll 44-45 BS in LS. 7: Catlgr Purdue U Lib 45-52; Catlgr UWash Lib 52-53; Libn Elma Pub Lib, Elma Wash 54-55; Catlgr Grays Harbor Co Rural Lib, Montesano Wash 55; Catlgr Longview Pub Lib, Longview Wash 60-61; Br Libn Wayne Co Lib, Plymouth Mich 61-62, Belleville Mich 62-63; Inkster Mich 63; Tech libn Alpena Community Col 63-65; Catlgr Lorain Co Community Col 65-. 9: ALA; OhioLA; No Ohio Tech Serv Libns (Exec Bd 68-). 10: AAUW. 14: Catlg. 15: 310 Furnace st, Elyria Oh 44035.

JEFFRIES, OLEN CHARLES. b Jenks Okla 25 Ja 14. 4: Reba Hallum Jeffries. 5: UOkla 34-38 (Eng) BA, 38-39 (Eng), 39-40 BA in LS; UDenver 57-60 MA in LS; Highlands U summer 61 (Educ); East NMU summers 58-63 (Educ); Corr courses from var cols 58-61 (Educ); Colo State Col summer 65; East NMU summer 68, 69 (Educ). 06: Ger, Lat. 7: Stud ref asst UOkla 39-40; Jr prof ref asst US Dept of State, Wash DC 40-41; Yeoman 1/c USNR 41-45; Admin libn (GS-1410-9) US Artillery & Guided Missile Sch, Ft Sill Okla 46-57; Tchr-libn Ft Sumner Mun Schs, Ft Sumner NM 57-60; Libn Zia Jr High Sch, Artesia NM 60-62; Tchr Grand Heights Elem Sch, Artesia NM 62-67; Asst libn & Eng Prof ENMU (Roswell 67-68; Tchr NE Elem Sch, Farmington NM 68-69, Eng Prof NM State U (San Juan) 68-69. 9: NEA; NMLA; NMEA. 10: Phi Delta Kappa. 13: Yes. 14: Admin, ref, catlg, clsf. 15: 1216 Camina Vega, Farmington NM 87401.

JEFFRIES, VIRGINIA (McDANIEL) MURRILL. b Lewisburg WVa 30 D 11. 5: Morris Harvey Col 31-33; UKy 33-35 (LS) AB. 7: Libn Floyd Co High Sch, Prestonsburg Ky 35-41; Libn ULouisville 55; Tchr Franklin Co High Sch, Winchester Tenn 58-59; Libn Duncan U Fletcher High Sch, Jacksonville Beach Fla 59-63; Libn Meller Jr High Sch, Pico Rivers Cal 63-. 9: Cal Tchrs Assn; CalASchL. 10: Chi Delta Phi. 12: "Calling for Isabel" (51); "Keys for Tori" (61). 14: Sch libn. 15: 8702 E Fifth st apt 9, Downey Ca 90241.

JEFFS, JOSEPH E. b Phila 1 Jl 24. 4: Jeannine Rouillard. 6: Fr. 7: Asst libn Dumbarton Oaks Lib 53-54; Georgetown U: Ref libn 54, Chief of tech serv 55-56, Assoc libn 56-59, Libn 60-. 15: Georgetown U Lib, 37 & O sts NW, Wash DC 20007.

JEN, NEIL T H. b Fukien China 17 Ag 36. 4: Lilly P L Lin Jen. 5: Off Lang Sch 55-57 (Eng) Certif; Nat TaiwanU 59-63 (Lit) BA; AtlantaU 66-68 (LS) MS. 6: Fr, Chinese. 7: Tr & interpreter Hqs of Chinese Marine Corps, Taiwan 57-59; Eng tchr Cheng Kung High Sch, Taipei Taiwan 63-65; Tech serv libn Ga Col (Milledgeville) 68-. 14: Catlg. 15: 302 N Wayne st, Milledgeville Ga 31061.

JENCKS, LOUISE A(DCOOK). b Rio Ill 28 N 08. 5: Knox Col 27-30 (Romance lang) BA; UIll 30-31 BS in LS. 6: Fr, Sp, Ger. 7: Acquis dept State U Iowa (Iowa City) 32-35; Libn Buena Vista Col 35-36; Catlgr (hd) State Lib of Ohio, Columbus 36-38; Acquis dept Queens Col (NY) 38-40; Catlgr Columbia U 40-42; Ser catlgr Ohio State U)(Columbus) 60-65; Catlgr (hd) Knox Col 65-. 9: ALA; OhioLA; Miami Valley Reg Tech Serv; IllLA. 10: Phi Beta Kappa. 14: Catlg. 15: Rte 1, Wataga Il 61488.

JENDRACH, REV GEORGE GREGORY CR. b Chicago 1 Ap 23. 5: St Louis U 44 (Philos) AB, 49 (Hist) MA; Catholic U 50 MSLS; De Paul U 59 (Educ); Loyola U (Chicago) 60 (Educ). 7: Libn St John Cantius Sem 42-49; Libn Weber High Sch, Chicago 50-60, A-v dir 55-60, Chm Ill Catholic Lib Assn Second Schs, Chicago 58-59; Prin Weber High Sch, Chicago 60-66; Lib Sci Instr De Paul U 65-. 9: NEA; ALA; Ill Assn Sec Sch Prins; IllASchL; CathLA. 13: Yes. 14: Ref. 15: 5252 W Palmer st, Chicago Il 60639.

JENEWEIN, LELA MARY (BURNS). b Danvers Ill 7 O 04. 5: Bradley U 26-29 (Hist) BA; UWis 29-30 BLS. 7: Clerk Peoria Pub Lib, Peoria Ill 25-29, 30-31, Asst adult circ & asst ref dept adult serv 31-39; Catlg asst & documents libn UAriz 39-40; Head catlgr Tucson Pub Lib 40-62, Head tech serv div 62-. 9: ALA (var coms incl Memb Com for Ariz); Ariz StateLA (off & chm var coms). 10: Soroptimist Club; Toastmistress Club; Inter-Club Coun of Tucson. 14: Catlg, ref. 15: 1739 E Silver st, Tucson Az 85719.

JENIK, FRANTISEK. b Vienna 10 S 18. 4: Jana Sajicova. 5: KarlovaU (CharlesU) 39, 45-50 PhD. 6: Czech, Polish, Russian, Ger. 7: Clk KOVO np, Prague 50; Clk, catlgr of old printed bks KMHA np, Prague 50-53; Catlgr of old printed bks Univ Lib, Czechoslavokia 53-58; Hd acquis dept Slavic Lib, Czechoslavokia 58-68; Clk Kubon & sagmer, Munich W Germany 68-69; Slavic catlgr UNC Lib (Chapel Hill) 69-. 8: Mem com for reorg of acquis wk in State Lib of Czechoslavokia during reform year 68. 9: ROH (trade unions, enforced memb). 12: Co-auth of bibliog "Soupis del J A Komenskeho Ceskoslovenskych Kniohvnach" (Prague 58). 13: Yes. 14: Slavic catlg, bibliog wk, rare bks. 15: 508 Northampton plaza, Chapel Hill NC 27514.

JENKINS, (E) VALERIE. b Amherst Ohio 7 S 13. 5: Baldwin-Wallace Col 33-36 (Speech, Eng) BA; West Res 36, 50, 66 (Theatre, LS); State UIowa 38-39 (Theatre); Ohio State U 60 (Theatre); Kent State 61-63 (Theatre, LS) MA, 67-69 (LS). 6: Fr. 7: Tchr: St Elmo High Sch, St Elmo Ill 40-42, Clearview High Sch, Lorain Ohio 42-49, Libn & tchr Clearview high Sch, 49-56; Libn Amherst High Sch, Amherst Ohio 56-66; Sch lib coord Amherst Schs, Amherst Ohio 66-. 8: Speech instr: Kent State U (evenings) 63-66, cleveland State U (evenings) 66; Lect Kent State U Lib NDEA Inst 65; Lectr on theatre subjects and sch lib/pub lib organiz. 9: ALA (life mem); NEA (life mem); Amer Educ & Theatre Assn; OhioEA; OhioASchL (Legisl Com); N East Ohio Tchrs Assn (Liaison Com & Conf Planning); Ohio Lib Trustee Assn; AmherstTA (pres 63-65). 10: Amherst Pub Lib Trustee; Delta Kappa Gamma. 13: Yes. 14: Sch lib organiz planning; non-bk coord, catlg. 15: 439 Shupe ave, Amherst Oh 44001.

JENKINS, BEVERLY WAGGONER. b Cleveland 10 My 36. 4: Edgar William Jenkins. 5: Wellesley 54-58 (Hist) BA; Chicago 58-59 (LS) MA; UAriz 67 (Educ). 06: Ger. 7: Ref asst Harper Lib UChicago 58-59; Bd of Cooperative Educ Serv high sch libn, Eastport NY 60; Catlgr Suffolk Co Lib Assn, Patchogue NY 59-60; Ref libn Patchogue Lib, Patchogue NY 62-64; Bk reviewer Virginia Kirkus Serv, NYC 63-64; Catlgr Law Lib UAriz 67-. 9: ALA; Suffolk Co LA. 10: Beta Phi mu; Tucson Wellesley Club; Whitmore Family Fac Assn. 13: Yes. 14: Ya & child bk reviewing, ref, catlg. 15: 4938 E Glenn st, Tucson Az 85716.

JENKINS, ELIZABETH. b Richmond Ind. 5: Ohio Wesleyan U 32 (Eng) BA; UIll 36-37 BLS. 7: Reserve room libn Ohio Wesleyan U 37-38, Circ libn 38-41; Asst libn Earlham Col 41-43; Systems & procedures analyst Belden Mfg Co, Richmond Ind 43-54; Systems engnr Gardner Board & Carton Co, Middletown Ohio 54-58; Libn Sch of Sco Wk Ohio State U 58-59, Asst head circ dept 59-, Hd circ dept 68-. 9: ALA; OhioLA; Franklin Co LA. 10: Faculty Women's Club Ohio State U; AAUW. 14: Pub serv. 15: 1858 Neil ave, Columbus Ohio 43210.

JENKINS, FRANCES BRIGGS. b San Diego Cal 15 O 05. 5: UIll 22-26 (Chem) BS; Tulane 27-28 (Biochem) MS; UUIll 29-37 (Biochem) PhD; UCal 46-47 BLS; Columbia summer 51 (LS). 07: Asst biochem Agric Experiment Sta UTenn 28-29; Instr Dept of Biochem UIll Col of Med 29-41; Supv correction sect Communications Div 11th Naval Dist, San Diego Cal 42-44; (Lt) USNR 44-46; Head of br libs UCal 47-51; Prof of Lib Sci UIll 51-. 8: Adv com for Manpower & Training NLM 66-68. 09: ALA (Coun 54-57, 62-; Exec Bd 65-; Ed Com 60-65, Publn Bd 68-69); -ACRL;-RSD (pres 62-63; reg chm Memship Com 55-59); Commsn Nat Plan Lib Educ 62; ASIS; AAAS; ACS; AALS; MedLA; IllLA. 10: Beta Phi Mu; Sigma Delta Epsilon; Sigma Xi. 11: Isadore Gilbert Mudge Citation (66). 12: Ed staff ACRL "Monographs" (52-60); Publ bd "Library Trends" (55-); Ed "Collecting Science Literature for General Reading" (60); Auth "Science Reference Sources" (5th ed 69); Co-ed: "Bibliography: Current State and Future Trends" (67). 13: Yes. 14: Sci lit & ref serv, info storage & retrieval, lib admin. 15: Grad Sch of Lib Sci UIll, Urbana Ill 61803.

JENKINS, HAROLD RICHARD. b Pottstown Penn 23 Ag 18. 4: Margaret Houston Leech. 5: Ursinus Col 53 (Bus Admin) BA; UMich 56 (LS) MA. 7: Catlg libn Washington & Lee U 56-58; Dir Kingsport Pub Lib, Kingsport Tenn 58-59; Dir Wise Co Pub Lib, Wise Va 59-61; Dir Pottstown Pub Lib, Pottstown Penn 61-63; Dir Lancaster Free Pub Lib, Lancaster Penn 63-. 9: VaLA (pres Pub Lib Sect); PennLA (pres Pub Lib Sect; 2nd v-pres 67-68). 10: Beta Phi Mu; Phi Gamma Mu; Rotary Internat. 14: Admin. 15: Lancaster Free Pub Lib 125 N Duke st, Lancaster Pa 17602.

JENKINS, JUDITH (GRIPTON). b Greeley Colo 28 Je 42. 4: Thomas L Jenkins. 5: UKan 60-64 (Mus Hist & Lit) BM; Kan StateU 64; UDenver 64-65 (LS) MA. 6: Fr, Ger. 7: Ser catlgr UIowa 65-67; Ser catlgr UIll (Chicago Circle) 67-. 9: ALA; IllLA. 12: "Dr Malcolm Glenn Wyer; a bio-bibliography" (66).

13: Yes. 14: Ser, ser catlg. 15: 6335 N Magnolia, Chicago Il 60626.

JENKINS, NORMA (PACKARD HEINRICH). b Elmira NY 29 Ap 28. 4: Weston H Jenkins. 5: Syracuse 45-49 (Chem) AB. 7: Asst libn Corning Glass Works, Corning NY 49-57; Assoc libn Corning Museum of Glass, Corning NY 66-. 10: AAUW; Phi Beta Kappa. 14: Catlg. 15: Corning Museum of Glass Lib Centerway, Corning NY 14830.

JENKS, GEORGE MERRITT. b Purcell Okla 1 Ag 29. 4: Zoya Hochstein Jenks. 5: UOkla 46-49 (Sp) BA, 49-51 (Sp) MA, 58-59 MLS; UCLA 54-56 (Sp). 6: Sp, Fr, Portug. 7: Infantryman (Pfc) USMC 51-53; Prim lib asst UCLA 56; Reports off CIA, Wash DC 56-57; For lang instr NMA&M Col 57-58; Libn I Queens Borough Pub Lib, Jamaica NY 59-60; Catlg libn San Fernando Valley State Col 60, Hd acquis 60-63; Asst libn utasmania Hobart, Tasmania Australia 63, Act libn 64-66; Chief tech serv Bucknell U 66-68, Asst libn 68, Univ libn 69-. 8: Mem Australian Adv Coun on Bibliog Serv 64-66. 9: ALA; Lib Assn Australia (Coun 66; pres Tasmanian Br 65-66). 10: ACLU; UTasmania Staff Assn. 11: Grace E Herrick Award. 12: Ed "Library Opinion," (64-65). 13: Yes. 14: Tech serv, admin. 15: 202 N 2nd st, Lewisburg Pa 17837.

JENNINGS, GERTRUDE ANN. b Petroleum Ind 28 S 05. 5: Hanover Col 29 (Fr, Soc Studies) AB; UKy 49 BS in LS. 6: Fr. 7: Tchr-libn Pulaski Co, Shopville & Mt Victory Ky 30-41; Tchr of Eng & Fr Greenbrier Co, Quinwood WVa 41-42; Eng tchr Champion Jr High Sch, Painesville City Ohio 42-47; Libn Harvey High Sch, Painesville City Ohio 47-53; Libn High Sch, Ashland Ohio 53-54; Libn Lemon Monroe High Sch, Middletown City Ohio 54-. 9: NEA; OhioEA; OhioASchL; MTA. 10: Delta Kappa Gamma; Middletown Civic Assn. 14: Ref. 15: Apt 4 131 Ohio ave, Monroe Oh 45050.

JENNINGS, JANET S(URDAM). b Candor NY 21 S 07. 5: Cornell U 24-26, 27-30 (Eng) BA; Drexel 31-32 BS in LS. 07: Asst catlg dept Binghamton Pub Lib, Binghamton NY 32, Head catlg dept 32-59; Head of processing Binghamton Pub Lib, Binghamton NY & Four Co Lib System 59-65, Coord Tech Processes 65-. 9: ALA; NYLA. 10: Women's Nat Bk Assn; AAUW; LWV; Amer Civic Assn; Phi Beta Kappa; Phi Kappa Phi; Broome Co Hist Soc; Broome Co Mental Health Assn; Interracial Assn of Binghamton. 14: Tech proc, catlg. 15: 99 Oak st, Binghamton NY 13905.

JENNINGS, JOHN MELVILLE. b James City Co Va 22 O 16. 5: William & Mary 34-38 (Hist, Pol Sci) BA; American U 47-48 (Hist, Archival Admin) MA; William & Mary 68 LLD. 7: Curator of rare bks William & Mary Col 39-43, Curator of mss 46-47; Libn Va Hist Soc, Richmond Va 48-53, Dir & Libn 53-. 9: AAS; BSA; SAA (Fellow); AHA; Bibliog Soc UVa; etc; Mass Hist Soc; VaLA; etc. 12: "The Library of The College of William and Mary, 1693-1793" (68); "Virginia Historical Society Occasional Bulletin". 13: Yes. 14: Va bibliog & mss. 15: 204 N Granby st, Richmond Va 23220.

JENNINGS, LAURA L. b Watertown NY 16 Ap 12. 5: Cornell U 29-33 (Ger) BA; Columbia 33-34 BS. 7: Catlgr Cornell U Lib 34-54, Catlg libn 54-. 9: ALA. 14: Catlg. 15: 1200 Hanshaw rd, Ithaca NY 14850.

JENNINGS, MARIE (DAPOLONIA). b Des Moines Iowa 19 Ap 20. 5: UMd 60-64 (G&P) BA; Peabody Lib Sch 67-68 MLS. 6: Ital. 7: Recreation supv USAF: Eng 54-58, Japan 58-60, libya 60-64, Ankara 64-66, Sewart AFB Tenn 66-69; Libn, UBON Thailand 69-. 14: Ref. 15: 8th CSG Box 3085, APO San Francisco Ca 96304.

JENNINGS, PAULINE (WHITLOCK). b SD 17 F 07. 4: Charles H Jennings. 5: U of Tulsa 22-23; Huron Col 23-26 (Foreign Langs) BA; UIowa summers 28-31 (Fr) MA; UWash summer 33; Columbia 42-43 BS in LS. 06: Fr. 7: High sch tchr, SD & Wash 26-36; Catlgr Nat Agric Lib, Wash DC 43, Bibliog-indexer 43-44; Br libn Nat Agric Lib, St Louis 44-46; Ref libn Nat Agric Lib, Wash DC 46-48; Libn US Econ Cooperation Admin, Wash dc 48-49, Asst chief div lending 49-61, Chief Div Lending 61-. 9: SLA (Nat Memb Com 52; DC Chap: 2d v-pres 51-52, Memb Com Chm 48-50); Internat Assn of Agric Libns & Documentalists; Nat Microfilm Assn; Internat Micrographic Congress; DCLA (membership com NAL rep); ALA-ACRL (Agric & Biol Sci Sub Sect: sec 65-66, v-chm 66-67, chm 67-68). 13: Yes. 14: Ref, circ, photoreproduction. 15: 4116 Blackthorn st, Chevy Chase Md 20015.

JENNINGS, RITA JOYCE. b Jacksonville Tex 22 Mr 44. 5: Greenville Col 62-64 (Eng & 9psych) AB, 66-68 (Educ); UIll 68-69. 6: Sp. 7: Lib staff mem Greenville Col 62-64, 66-67; Jr high sch libn Hillsboro Sch Syst, Hillsboro Ill 69-. 9: NEA; ALA; IllEA; IllLA. 10: Beta Phi Mu. 14: Child wk, catlg. 15: 324 N Prairie, Greenville Il 62246.

JENNISON, PETER SAXE. b Swanton Vt 2 Jl 22. 4: Jane Lowe. 5: Middlebury Col 47 (Amer Lit) BA. 7: (Tech Sgt) US Army Off of Strategic Serv, Europe 43-46; Asst Ed "Publishers Weekly," NYC 47-52; Info off ECA Spec Mission to Sweden 48-49; Asst managing dir Amer Book Publ Coun 56-59, 63-64; Asst dir Grad Inst of Bk Publ NYU 59-62; Exec Dir Nat Bk Com, NYC 64-; Dir Nat Lib Week Program, NYC 64-. 8: Consul Franklin Bk Programs 62-64; Consul Bur of Educ & Cultural Affairs Dept of State 61; Lect Sch Lib Serv Columbia U 64-. 9: ALA; ALTA (program chm 67-68); Authors Guild; PEN. 10: Friends of the Weston (Conn) Pub Lib; Exec Com Pequot Lib Southport Conn. 12: "The Mimosa Smokers" (59); "Books in the Americas," with W Kurth (60); "The Governor" (63); "Freedom to Read" (64). 13: Yes. 14: Pub rel, trusteeship. 15: Nat Bk Com One Park ave, New York NY 10016.

JENSEN, ALLENE (ANNA). b Garland Utah 11 Ag 07. 5: UUtah 26-30 (Hist) BA, 57 (LS) MS. 6: Fr. 7: Tchr- libn Nebo Sch Dist, Spanish Fork Utah 30-57; Libn Granite Sch Dist, Salt Lake City 57-61; Libn Brigham Young U 61-. 9: ALA; MPLA; UtahLA. 10: Utah Valley Opera Assn; Commun Concert Assn; AAUP; Altrusa Internat; Delta Kappa Gamma; Utah Acad of Sci Arts & Letters; BYU Women; Utah Hist Soc; Folklore Soc of Utah. 12: "Utah Writers of the Twentieth Century: A Reference Tool" (57). 14: Cur, educ. 15: 454 E Center st, Provo Utah 84601.

JENSEN, BARBARA CAROL (HOLLOWELL). b Santa Monica Cal 24 Mr 46. 4: John Wayne Jensen. 5: Fla State U 64-67 (Eng) BA, 67-68 (LS) MS. 6: Fr, Ital. 7: Asst catlgr Fla State Lib 68-69; Sch libn Griffin Jr-Sr High Sch, Tallahassee Fla 69-. 9: ALA. 14: Ref. 15: 418 E Glenview, Tallahassee Fl 32303.

JENSEN, BETTY (HARRIS). b LaPorte Ind 30 My 22. 4: Kenneth G Jensen. 5: Ind U 40-44 (LS) BS in Ed; UIll summers 47-50 BS in LS. 6: Fr. 7: Asst high sch libn LaPorte High Sch, LaPorte Ind 45-46; High sch-pub libn, Bellaire Ohio 46-47; Bkmob libn Jackson Co Lib, Jackson Mich 47-48; Child libn Escanaba Pub Lib, Escanaba Mich 48-. 9: ALA (Child & Sch Lib Sect); MichLA (Recr Com 53). 10: NAACP. 14: Child lit, readers adv. 15: 504 S 7th st, Escanaba Mich 49829.

JENSEN, IDA-MARIE (CLARK). b Logan Utah. 4: Lyman Jensen. 5: Utah State U 56 (Eng) MS; UDenver 60 (LS) MA. 6: Fr. 7: Research asst Agric Econ Dept Cornell U 41-44; Utah State U: Instr Eng Dept 47-49, Head ref libn 47-63, Head sci & engnr div 64-68, Assoc libn 69-. 9: MPLA (pres Univ Sect 63-65); UtahLA (pres Col & Univ Sect 62-63). 10: Dir, No Utah Safety Coun; Phi Kappa Phi; Delta Kappa Gamma; Alpha Lambda Delta; AAAS; AAUW; Pi Gamma Mu; Logan Lit Club; Utah Acad Sci Arts & Letters. 11: Jasper Award, by Bibliog Center for Res, Denver. 12: "A Bibliography of Theses and Dissertations Concerning Utah or the Mormons Written Outside the State of Utah"; "A Statistical Method for Evaluating Serial Holdings." 13: Yes. 14: Bibliog, IBM data proc, info retrieval. 15: 130 E Center st, Logan Utah 84321.

JENSEN, JAMES H. b Cleveland 27 Je 03. 4: Helen E Graf. 5: Johns Hopkins 22-26 (Bus Admin) BS; UKy 60 (College Bus Mgt). 7: Infantry US Army (Capt) 40-44; Real estate salesman Allan Rutherford Realtor, Baltimore 45-51; Examiner Administrator of Loan Laws, Baltimore 51-55; Asst state auditor State of Md, Baltimore 55-59; Bus manager Md Inst of Art, Baltimore 59-61; Bus manager Enoch Pratt Free Lib, Baltimore 61-. 9: ALA; Amer Soc for Pub Admin. 10: Optimist Club; Johns Hopkins Club; University Club; MdSoc Train Dirs Inc. 14: Methods improvement & work simplification, program budgeting. 15: 427 Wingate rd, Baltimore Md 21210.

JENSEN, JOAN W (BUTLER). LASGOW Scotland 31 Ja 33. 4: Reginald Jensen. 5: BristolU 51-54 BA; Columbia 68 MSLS. 7: Libn I (ref) UConn Lib (Storrs) 68-. 9: ConnLA. 10: Beta Phi Mu. 14: Ref. 15: Box 272 RFD #2 Flood rd, Marlborough Ct 06424.

JENSEN, KENNETH OTTO. b Milwaukee 23 Je 39. 4: Margaret (Hapke) Jensen. 5: St Olaf Col 58-60 (Eng); UWis 60-62 (Eng) BS, 63-64 (LS) MA. 6: Fr. 7: (A/3c) USAF 57-58; Lib asst UWis Mem Lib (Madison) 62-64; Circ libn Harvard Col Lib 64-67, Asst libn for acquis 67-. 9: ALA. 14: Univ libs, pub serv, acquis. 15: Harvard Col Lib, Cambridge Ma 02138.

JENSEN, MYRIL JOAN. b Minneapolis Minn 21 Ag 27. 4: Wilbur F Jensen. 5: UMinn 45-49 (LS) BS, 53-56 (Art, Hist). 7: Libn I Cambridge State Sch & Hosp, Cambridge Minn 51-52; Jr libn UMinn (Minneapolis) 52-55, Libn Arch Libn 55-56, Lib asst Law Lib 60-68; Libn Santa Monica Pub Lib, Santa Monica Cal 55; Sub libn Minneapolis Pub Lib 67-69; Libn minneapolis Pub Schs 68-. 10: PTA; UMinn Lib Staff Assn. 14: Univ wk, art & arch, child wk. 15: 248 Bedford st SE, Minneapolis Mn 55414.

JENSEN, PATRICIA (E). 5: Colby Col 46-50 (Psych, Sociol) AB; UNH 57-61 (Educ) MEd; So Conn State Col 63-69 (LS) MS. 7: Elem tchr: Moses Brown Sch, Providence 50-58, New Canaan Bd of Educ, New Canaan Conn 58-63; Sch libn New Canaan Bd of Educ 63-66, Coord media ctr 66-68; Asst Prof lib sci So Conn State Col 68-. 8: Consultant: Great Neck LI NY 68, Helene Grant Sch, New Haven Conn 68-, Ansonia Conn 68-. 9: ALA (chm Reg State Assembly); ConnSchLA (sec, v-pres). 10: Pi Gamma Mu. 13: Yes. 14: Sch libnship, media ctrs. 15: 75 Kaye-Vue dr, Hamden Ct 06514.

JENSEN, THORKEL H. b Denmark 19 F 19. 4: Jane White. 5: State Tchrs Col (Kutztown Penn) 38-42 (Educ) BS in Ed; Syracuse 46-47 BS in LS; UMich 48-49 AMLS; Chicago 51-54 LS. 6: Danish, Ger. 7: US Army (Pfc) 42-46; Circ libn East Ill State Col 47-48; Asst circ libn Ore State Col 49-51; Assoc libn & sci libn Rice U 54-59; Head tech libn US Naval Ordnance Test Sta, Pasadena Cal 59-; Hd Lib Div Naval Undersea Research & Development Ctr, Pasadena Cal 69-, Hd Publns Div 69-. 9: SLA-SoCal Chap (Pub Rel Dir 62-63, treas 63-64); CalLA. 10: AAAS. 14: Ref (sci & tech), admin, info retrieval. 15: 3202 E Foothill blvd, Pasadena Ca 91104.

JENSEN, WILMA W(ESTBURG). b Hopkins Minn 11 Je 16. 4: E T Jensen. 5: Gustavus Adolphus Col 34-38 (Math, Eng) BA; UMinn 39-40 BSLS; UCal (Berkeley) 44; Pacific Sch of Religion 45. 6: Fr. 7: Asst ref dept UMinn Lib (Minneapolis) 40-43; Coun UCal Nat Lutheran Coun, Berkeley Cal 43-47; Coun Iowa SU Nat Lutheran Coun, Ames Iowa 47-48; Sec Donovan-Lovering- Boyle, Pickstown SD 51-56; Off sec Lutheran World Fed, Minneapolis 57; Off sec Augustana Lutheran Church Bd of Amer Missions, Minneapolis 58-63; Exec Sec Lutheran Church Lib Assn, Minneapolis 63-. 9: ALA; Lutheran Church LA (Bd Dirs 62-63, pres); MinnLA; Ch & Synagogue LA (Bd Dirs 67-69). 10: Minnetonka Music Assn; Nat adv, Lutheran Student Assn of Amer; Lutheran Ch in America (nat del 66). 13: Yes. 14: Church libs. 15: 3620 Fairlawn dr, Minnetonka Minn 55345.

JENSON, FLORENCE L. b Mayville N Dak 23 Ap 20. 5: Roosevelt Col 46-51 (Hist) BA; Columbia 53-55 MSLS. 7: Lib (pub lib': Brooklyn NY 54-57, la 57-59; Libn USAF, Germany 59-65; Pub lib consul NJ State Lib, Trenton 65; Field libn USAF, Osan AB Korea 66; USAF, Tan Son Nhut Vietnam: Base libn 67-68, 7AF staff libn 68-. 14: Ref, admin. 15: CMR 1 Box 8458, APO San Francisco Ca 96201.

JENSON, GLORIA (DAWN). b Provo Utah 6 Jl 28. 5: Brigham Young U 46-50 (Educ) BS; Columbia 53-54 (LS) MS. 06: Fr. 7: Libn Dixie Jr Col 50-53; Libn Brigham Young U 54-. 9: ALA; UtahLA. 14: Catlg. 15: Lib Brigham Young U, Provo Ut 34601.

JENSON, JANET. b Athens Ga 10 Ap 37. 5: Brigham Young 55-58 (Eng) BA, 58-60 (Phil, Relig) MA; Columbia 65-66 (LS) MS. 6: Fr, Sp, Ital. 7: Chief catlgr Latter Day Saints Ch Hist's Lib, Salt Lake City 63-. 9: ALA; UtahLA. 14: Catlg, West Americana. 15: 1082 4th ave, Salt Lake City Ut 84103.

JENSON, JOHN RICHARD. b Red Wing Minn 7 O 33. 5: Augsburg Col 51-55 (Eng) BA; UMinn 55-57 (LS) MA. 6: Sp. 7: Catlgr (ref) Augsburg Col 55-57, 61-66; Personnelman 2nd class 57-61; Rare bks libn UMinnesota Dept of Spec Collections 67-. 9: ALA; BSA; MinnLA. 10: James Ford Bell Lib Assocs. 14: Bibliog, rare bks, catlg. 15: 3404 32nd ave S, Minneapolis Mn 55406.

JERABEK, ESTHER. b Silver Lake Minn 15 O 1897. 5: Macalester Col 15-18 BA; UMinn 9minneapolis) 24 MA, 29 Certif in LS. 6: Czech, Fr, Sp. 7: Lang tchr, Minn & Wyo 19-23, 25-28; Asst UMinn Lib (Minneapolis) 24-25, 29; Hd acquis Minn Hist Soc (St Paul) 29-52, Hd tech serv 52-63, Research fellow 63-. 8: Tchr of catlg UMinn Lib Sch 54. 9: ALA; MinnLA; Twin City Catlgrs RT (pres & sec). 10: Upper Midwest Hist Conf. 12: Comp "Bibliography of Minnesota Territorial Documents" (36); "Check List of Minnesota Public Documents 29-40" (52). 13: Yes. 14: Catlg, bibliog, hist. 15: 842 - 21st ave SE, Minneapolis Mn 55414.

JERNIGAN, ELIZABETH T(HORNE). b Chester Ill 26 My 09. 4: Claude H Jernigan. 5: Western Col 26-28; UWis 28-30 (Eng) BA, 29-30 (LS) Certif; Fla State U 65-66 (MS). 06: Fr. 7: Asst catlg dept UFla Lib 30-34, Head catlg dept 34-42; Catlgr Fla State Lib 45-53; Asst bkmob libn Leon Co Pub Lib, Tallahassee Fla 57-; Curriculum libn Fla State Dept of Educ 66-. 9: SLA; ALA; SELA; FlaLA (sec, treas, var coms); Assn for Educ Data Systems. 10: Beta Phi Mu; Zeta Tau Alpha; AAUW; Pilot Club; PTA; Fla Heritage Assn; Tallahassee Hist Soc. 13: Yes. 14: Catlg, ref, info serv, documentation. 15: 630 E College ave, Tallahassee Fl 32301.

JERNIGAN, MARTHA MacKENZIE. b Portsmouth Va 29 O 46. 5: Mary Bladwin Col 64-68 (Eng) BA; UNC 68-69 (LS) MS. 6: Fr. 7: Stud asst UNC Lib (Chapel Hill) 68-69. 9: ALA. 14: Ref, spec libs. 15: 1702 Park ave, Richmond Va 23220.

JERNIGAN, WILLIAM WADE. b Savannah Ga 4 Mr 35. 4: Juanita Darlene Orndoff. 5: Trevecca Nazarene Col 53-57 (Theol) BA; Nazarene Sem 57-60 (Church Hist) BD; Peabody 60-61 MALS. 7: Asst libn Trevecca Nazarene Col 60-65; Dir of Libs Oral Roberts U 65-67, Dir Learning Resources 67-. 8: Consul Okla Col of Liberal Arts Learning Resources & Lib Ctr; Consul Com for lib development OklaU. 9: ALA; TennLA (sec Col & Univ Div); SELA; SLA; NEA-DAVI. 10: Nashville Lib Club; Nashville Catlgrs; Tulsa Friends of The Lib. 14: Admin. 15: Oral Roberts U 7777 S Lewis st, Tulsa Okla 74105.

JEROME, SISTER MARY OP. b Chicago 15 D 14. 5: Rosary Col 37 BA; UIll 47 (LS) MS. 6: Lat, Fr, Ger. 7: Tchr-libn Trinity High Sch, Bloomington Ill 39; Tchr-libn Cathedral High Sch, Sioux Falls SD 39-40; Libn Visitation High Sch, Chicago 40-50; Libn Catholic High Sch, Okla City Okla 50-53; Libn Edgewood Col of the Sacred Heart 53-. 8: Consul for new lib at the Sinsinawa Dominican Educ Center, Sinsinawa Wis, 64-65. 9: ALA; WisLA (Col & Univ Sect: sec-treas 62-63, chm Nomin Com 56, sec 67-68, dir Exec Bd 67-70); CathLA (Wis Unit: chm Col Sect 58-59; chm Diocese of Madison 54-62). 10: Mem Adv Bd for Coop of Madison Libs 68-69. 13: Yes. 14: Ref, admin. 15: Edgewood Col of the Sacred Heart, Madison Wi 53711.

JEROMITA (BROWN) SISTER M(ARY) CSC. b San Francisco 7 O 05. 5: St Mary-of-the-Wasatch 32-36 (Eng) BA; UWash 36-37 BA in LS; Chicago summer 53 (LS); USan Francisco summers 62, 64, 68 (Theol). 7: Libn St Mary-of-the-Wasatch 37-57; Libn San Joaquin Mem High Sch, Fresno Cal 57-. 9: ALA; CalASchL; CathLA; Nat Cath Stud Assts Assn (chm West Reg). 14: Child & young adults. 15: 1402 N Fresno st, Fresno Cal 93703.

JERWICK, VERA (IVANCEVIC). b Dubrovnik Yugoslavia 23 Mr 35. 4: Eugene Jerwick. 5: BelgradeU 53-59 (Yugoslav lit) Diploma; Columbia 66-68 MLS. 6: Serbocroatian, polish, Russian. 7: Ref libn Nassau Commun Col, Garden City NY 68-. 9: ALA; NYLA; NassauCoLA (sec Col & Univ Div). 14: Ref. 15: 145 Carpenter ave, Sea Cliff NY 11579.

JESSE, ELIZABETH FRANCES. b Versailles Ky 17 D 06. 5: Transylvania U 30 (Econ) AB; UKy 38 (LS) BS, 42 (Hist) MA. 6: Sp, Fr, Ital, Ger. 7: Tchr High Sch, Wayland Ky 30; Tchr-libn High Sch, Johnson Co Ky 30-33; Asst libn Jessamine Co Lib, Nicholasville Ky 33-34; Libn Dry Ridge High Sch, Dry Ridge Ky 34-37; Libn Versailles High Sch, Versailles Ky 37-42; Asst ref libn Cincinnati Pub Lib 42-43; (Capt) WAC 43-46; Lib consul US Govt, Wash DC 46-58; Ref libn Norfolk Pub Lib, Norfolk Va 58-61; Libn Armed Forces Staff Col (Norfolk Va) 61-. 9: ALA; SELA; VaLA. 14: Admin, ref. 15: 414 Mowbray Arch, Norfolk Va 23507.

JESSE, FRANK H JR. b Waddy Ky 11 Ja 27. 4: Peggy Arnold. 5: Georgetown Col 47-50 (Hist, Eng) BA; Columbia 51-52 (LS); UKy summer 52 (Pol Sci); Columbia summer 56 (LS) MS. 6: Fr. 7: Libn USAAF, Okinawa & Far East 46-47; Asst ch libn VA Hosp, Marion Ind 53; Ch libn VA Hosp, Dawson Springs Ky 53-62; Libn VA Hosp, Louisville Ky 62-. 9: ALA; KyLA (sec-treas 63-64). 10: Louisville Lib Club; Filson Club (Hist). 14: Hosp bibliotherapy. 15: 2815 Woodward dr, Louisville Ky 40220.

JESSE, WILLIAM H(ERMAN). b Versailles Ky 16 S 08. 4: Edith Miller. 5: Transylvania Col 29-31; UKy 31-33 (Eng) AB; Columbia 37-38 (LS) BS; Brown 45 (Bibliog) MA. 6: Fr. 7: Tchr-libn Johnson Co Schs, Johnson Co Ky 33-35, Dir of Libs 35-36; Salesman Nat Life & Accident Insurance Co, Lexington Ky 36-37; Readers div chief Brown U Lib 38-42; Asst dir UNeb Lib 42; Readers & ref libn USDA Lib, Wash DC 43; Dir of Libs UTenn 43-. 8: Visiting lecturer lib schs at Fla State U, UIll, Columbia U, various summer sessions 46-; Lib surveys, lib bldg consul serv 45-; Adv Com to Keyes D Metcalf in prep of bk on planning & constructing lib bldgs 60-65. 9: ALA-ARL (chm &/or mem var coms); SELA (pres 46, var coms); TennLA. 10: AAUP; Commsn on Higher Educ So Assn of Col & Schs (chm Lib Com). 12: "Statements of Program for Library Building Construction." 13: Yes. 14: Admin, bldg planning. 15: Lib UTenn, Knoxville Tenn 37916.

JESTES, EDWARD C. b Nairobi Kenya 19 O 29. 4: Toshiko Takahashi. 5: UCLA 48-50, 52-54 9geol) AB, 54-58 (Geol) MA, 62-63 (Geol) PhD; UCal (Berkeley) 65-66 MLS. 7: Sect chief photo interpretation (Sgt 1st class) 40th Inf Div, Japan & Korea 50-52; UCLA: Geol tchg asst 54-56, Post grad research geologist 63-64, Geol lecturer 63-64; Asst Prof geol UHawaii 60-62; Asst Prof geol Wash State U 64-65; Rwf & map libn UCal (Davis) 66-. 9: Geol Soc of Amer; SLA; GeoSci Info Soc; West Assn of Map Libs. 10: Sigma Xi; Sierra club. 13: Yes. 14: Ref, maps. 15: 1314 Alice st, Davis Ca 95616.

JETT, DON W(ILLIAM). b Knoxville Tenn 10 Ag 36. 4: Barbara Breeden. 5: UTenn 55-59 (Transportation) BS; Fla State U 60-63 (LS) MS. 7: Air operations spec (S/Sgt) on active duty at Ramstein AFB, Germany 61-62, Tenn Air Nat Guard, Knoxville Tenn 59-67; Ref asst UTenn 60, Grad asst Fla State U 60-61; Ref asst UTenn 61-63, Sci libn 63-. 8: Lib devel consul UAgric Sci, Mysore Bangalore India 68. 9: SLA (treas Oak Ridge Chap 65-66); TennLA (bus mgr "Tennessee Librarian" 65-67; chm Spec Lib Sect 67-69); SELA. 14: Ref, spec libs, sci, admin. 15: 3801 Seeber dr, Knoxville Tenn 37918.

JEWELL, RUTH (MOORE) MRS. b El Dorado Ark 17 Jl 14. 5: El Dorado Jr Col 33-35 (Educ); So State Col summer 62 (LS). 7: Sec Murphy Oil Corp, El Dorado Ark 53-55, Libn 55-. 8: Libn El Dorado Art League 68-69. 9: SLA; ArkLA (chm Spec Libs Div 68). 10: Desk & Derrick Club (for women employed in the oil ind). 15: Murphy Oil Corp, 200 Jefferson ave, El Dorado Ark 71730.

JINNETTE, ISABELLA. b Wayne Co NC 12 My 08. 5: Guilford Col 27-31 (Eng) AB; UNC 37 AB in LS; Columbia summer 42. 7: Asst in Lib & Eng Dept Guilford Col 31-32; Tchr Rosewood Elem Sch, Goldsboro NC 33-36; Libn Central Elem Sch, Winston-Salem NC 36-39; Enoch Pratt Free Lib, Baltimore: Child libn 40-42, Head central child dept 43-45, Asst coordinator wk with child 48-56, Coordinator wk with child 56-. 8: Org child libs for State Lib of Tasmania Australia, 46-47. 9: ALA (Coun 55-57); CSD (numerous coms, v-pres & pres-elect 68-69); MdLA (2nd v-pres 53-54); ASchL, Md. 13: Yes. 14: Wk with child. 15: Enoch Pratt Free Lib, 400 Cathedral st, Baltimore Md 21201.

JIRA, JAROSLAV. b Chvalkovice Czechoslovakia 6 S 06. 4: Angela Koza3kova3. 5: Doctor of Laws & Pol Sci UPrague(Czechoslovakia) 33; Master of Comp Law in the Amer Practice, George Washington U 53; Catholic U 56 MS in LS. 6: Fr, Czech, Ger. 7: Legal analyst & sr spec Law Lib LC 51-61; Libn Nat Press Club, Wash DC 61-62; Head Libn DC Govt Health Dept Glenn Dale Hosp 62-. 9: MedLA; Law Libns Assn, Wash DC; DCLA. 14: Admin, ref, catlg. 15: 2129 Suitlan terrace SE, Wash DC 20020.

JIRAN, JOAN C. b Hollis NY 26 Ag 25. 5: Syracuse 43-47 (Psych) BA; Pratt 57-60 MLS; C W Post Col of LIU 60-65. 6: Fr. 7: Jr libn Levittown Pub Lib, Levittown NY 57-60; High sch libn Massapequa High Sch, Massapequa NY 60-. 9: ALA; AFT; NYLA; Nassau-Suffolk Sch Lib Assn. 10: Beta Phi Mu. 14: Catlg, ref. 15: 161 Saddle lane, Levittown NY 11756.

JOANNA, SISTER MARY GSIC. b Los Angeles 3 F 26. 5: Ottawa U 44-47 (Eng) BA, 59 (Eng Lit) MA, 57-61 BLS. 06: Fr. 7: Tchr-libn Immaculata High Sch, Ottawa 57-; Libn for Grey Sisters of the Immaculate Conception 57-. 8: Head of Eng Dept Immaculata High Sch 65. 9: ALA; CathLA (Ont Unit: sec 62-65, treas 65-67; chm High Sch Sect 65-67); CanLA. 14: Sch libs, ya, religious bks. 15: Immaculata High Sch, 211 Bronson ave, Ottawa 4 Can.

JOAQUIN, FREDERICK C. b Boston 8 Ja 08. 4: Edna Blanchard. 5: Harvard 25-27 (Classics); Nashotah House 36-39 (Theol) BD; UOkla 45-50 (Psych) MS, 50-51 (LS) AB. 7: Documents libn E T S T C 51-53; Libn Nashotah House, Nashotah Wis 53-. 9: ATheolLA. 15: Nashotah House, Nashotah Wis 53058.

JOB, AMY G SEGEAR. b Orange NJ 8 Mr 42. 5: Montclair State 60-64 (Soc Studies) BA; Rutgers 64-65 MLS. 6: Sp. 7: Sr clerk Livingston Pub Lib, Livingston NJ 58-64; Asst coun Douglass Col 64-65; Asst libn I State U Col (Potsdam NY) 65-67; Asst libn Paterson State Col 68-. 9: Nat Coun Soc Studies; NYLA; NJ Coun Geog Educ. 10: Gamma Theta Upsilon. 14: Catlg. 15: RD 3 Box 588, Butler NJ 07405.

JOB, ROSE ANNE (CUNNINGHAM). b Des Moines Iowa 10 S 40. 4: John Job. 5: Jamestown Col 58-61 (Eng) BA; Tex Woman'sU 67 (LS); N Tex StateU 67-68, 69 MLS. 6: Fr. 7: Circ desk asst UNeb Love Lib (Lincoln) 62; Clerical Union Col Lib (Lincoln) 62-63; Catlg asst Lincoln City Libs, Lincoln Neb 64-66; Lib asst III Ft Worth Pub Lib 68-69. 9: ALA. 14: Catlg, admin, child bks. 15: Hinsdale Il 60521.

JOCHIMSEN, ELIZABETH (ELLIOTT). b Cal 22 Ap 17. 4: Robert Jochimsen. 5: Whittier Col 39 (Hist) AB; UCal 40 (LS) Certif. 7: McHenry Pub Lib, Modesto Cal 40-42; Los Angeles Co Lib, Los Angeles 42-44; Aerographer's Mate 1/c US Navy 44-46; Los Angeles Co Lib, Los Angeles 46-47; Sub Pomona Pub Lib, Pomona Cal 47-50; Circ libn Sch of Theol (Claremont Cal) 64-. 15: Sch of Theol, Claremont Cal 91711.

JOERG, OSWALD HEATON. b Brooklyn NY 12 Mr 14. 4: Fay Lucas. 5: NYU 34-43, 46-49 (Pub Admin) AB; Columbia 49-50 (LS) MS; NYU, IndU, & Columbia 51-57. 6: Fr. 7: Page & clerical asst NYU Lib 36-41; Off manager NY State Off of Price Admin, NYC 41-43; (Tech/Sgt) US Army Signal Corps Cryptography 43-46; Ref libn Sch of Com Finance & Accts NYU Lib 46-50; Asst personnel off DC Pub Lib 50-52; Admin asst NY Pub Lib 52- 53; Catlgr Va Polytech Inst 54-55; Asst chief libn Evansville Pub Lib, Evansville Ind 55-57; Asst libn Youngstown Pub Lib, Youngstown Ohio 57-59; Dir Davenport Pub Lib, Davenport Iowa 59-. 8: Exec dir, Nat Lib Week, Iowa, 63. 9: ALA (mem & chm Notable Bks Coun 62-64); -LAD (Circ Serv Sect: v-chm 66-67, chm 67-68; Arch Com for Pub Libs 66-69); IowaLA (v-pres 63-64, pres 64-65). 10: Rotary Club; Con temporary Club; Beta Phi Mu. 13: Yes. 14: Admin, data proc, ref, lib bldgs & arch. 15: Davenport Pub Lib 4th & Main sts, Davenport Iowa 52801.

JOHNS, CLAUDE J JR. b Jacksonville Fla 28 Ag 30. 4: Rachel Ann Sutton. 5: Fla StateU 48-52 (Pub Admin) BS, 52-53 (Pub Admin) MS; UNC 62-64 (Pol Sci) PhD. 7: Instr Lt USAF acad 61-62, Assoc Prof (Capt USAF) 62-66, Tenure Assoc Prof (Maj USAF) 66-69, Dir Lib (Maj USAF) 69-. 8: USAF Intern with Policy Planning Coun, Dept of state 65; Consul, Dir of Intel, Hqs 7th AF, Saigon, South Vietnam 66. 9: Amer Polit Sci Assn; West Polit Sci Assn. 10: Colorado Springs Fine Arts Ctr. 12: Auth: "The USAF ICBM Program" (65); "The Air Intelligence Officer's Guide to Combat Units in Southeast Asia" (66); Co-ed "American Defense Policy, 2d ed" (68). 13: Yes. 14: Lib admin. 15: 1604 Wood ave, Colorado Springs Co 80907.

JOHNS, FRANCIS ASHLEY TREMENHEERE. b Ringwood Eng 5 My 23. 4: Beatrice Dewson. 5: Brighton Tech Col 50 (LS) ALA; Rutgers 55-57 (Fr) AB (summa cum laude), 57-58 MLS, 65 (Fr) MA. 6: Fr, Sp, Ital, Lat, Gk. 7: Royal Air Force 40-48; Lib asst Holborn Pub Lib, London Eng 48-54; Asst libn St John Pub Lib, New Brunswick Can 54-55; U bibliog Rutgers U Lib 58-. 9: BSA; ALA; Lib Assn Gt Brit (Fellow); NJLA. 10: Oriental Ceramic Soc (London); Molesworth Inst; Phi Beta Kappa. 12: "Bibliography of Arthur Waley" (66). 13: Yes. 14: Bibliog, Oriental art, archaeology. 15: Box 406a Rt 3, Somerset NJ 08873.

JOHNS, JEAN (BROWNE LORD). b Manchester NH 16 Je 31. 4: John E Johns. 5: Bates Col 49-51 (Psych); UNH 52-54 (Psych) BA; Emory 61-62 (LS) ML. 7: Lib asst UTenn 54-57; Lib asst Pack Mem Lib, Asheville NC 59; Lib asst UTenn 59-61; Bus admin libn UCincinnati 63-. 9: Beta Phi Mu. 15: 539 Lowell ave, apt 6, Cincinnati Oh 45220.

JOHNS, JOHN EDWARD. b New Richmond Ohio 19 N 32. 4: Jean Browne Johns. 5: Wilmington Col 50-55 (Eng, Soc Studies) AB; Peabody 58-61 (LS) MA. 7: Tchr Clarksburg Sch, Clarksburg Ohio 55-57; Tchr Goshen High Sch, Goshen Ohio 57-58; High sch libn New Richmond (Ohio) High Sch 58-62; Educ & psych libn UCincinnati 62-64; Libn Cincinnati Pub Lib 64-. 9: SLA; OhioLA. 14: Ref in sci, films, recordings, a-v materials. 15: Apt 6 539 Lowell ave, Cincinnati Oh 45220.

JOHNS, LOETA LOIS. b Charter Oak Iowa 4 D 04. 5: UWash 24-28 (Econ, LS) BS in LS (cum laude), 30 (Econ) MA. 6: Fr, Ger. 7: Asst acquis div UWash Lib 28-30; Asst to ed Decimal Clsf, Wash DC 30-32; Asst catlg dept Yale U Lib 32-37; Libn Inst for Consumer Educ Stephens Col 37-47; Dir Pacific NW Bibliog Center, Seattle 47-49; Head of order dept Seattle Pub Lib 49-. 9: ALA; PNLA (chm PNBC Exec Com 58-64); WashLA (chm Lib Devel Com & Lib Serv Act Com); Wash State SchLA. 10: Zonta; Phi Beta Kappa. 13: Yes. 14:

Acquis, catlg, automation. 15: 1000-8th ave, apt A413, Seattle Wa 98104.

JOHNS, LOUISE (GRACE) KERR. b Aspinwall Penn 26 Je 13. 4: Henry Johns. 5: UPittsburgh 29-30 (Eng); Margaret Morrison Carnegie Col 30-32 (Eng) BS; Carnegie 33-34 (LS) Certif. 7: Asst child libn Carnegie Lib, Pittsburgh 34-36, Admin asst to head of boys & girls dept 36-44; Child libn Enoch Pratt Free Lib, Baltimore summer 44, Br libn 44-45; Reporter & staff writer "The Parkersburg News," Parkersburg WVa 46; Asst child libn Carnegie Lib, Pittsburgh 56-63, Br child libn 64-65, Interlib loan libn dist, serv 65-. 9: ALA; PennLA; SW PennLA. 10: DAR; Pittsburgh Lib Club. 14: Wk with child, interlib loan. 15: 115 Mitchell dr, Pittsburgh Pa 15228.

JOHNSEN, URSULA E. b Kansas City Mo 22 Je 15. 5: Hiram Col 33-34; CapitalU 34-35; West Res 48-49 (Chem) AB, 49-50 (Organic Chem) MS. 6: Ger. 7: Chemist Knoll pharmaceutical Co, Orange NJ 50-64; Research libn S B Penick & Co, Orange NJ 64-. 9: ACS; ASIS; SLA. 10: Iota Sigma Phi. 14: Lit search, sci. 15: S B Penick & Co research 215 Watchung ave, Orange NJ 07050.

JOHNSON, ADELLE (ELNA) A(RNOLD). b Tenn 29 My 14. 4: Robert Lee Johnson. 5: Lambuth 33-35 (Elem Educ) Certif; Union U 37, 52; Bethel Col 56-58 (Hist, Educ) BS; Memphis State U 62-63 (Admin, Secondary Educ) MA, 65 (LS) Certif. 7: Tchr New Friendship Elem Sch, Pinson Tenn 53-61; Libn Chester Co High Sch, Hend erson Tenn 62-67; Beech Bluff High Sch Beech Bluff Tenn 67-. 9: NEA; TennEA; TennLA. 10: OES; Red Cross vol Chester Co; Bpts WMS. 14: Acquis. 15: Rte 2 Box 53, Pinson Tn 38366.

JOHNSON, ALBERT McDILL. b Covington Tenn 31 Ag 08. 5: Southwestern at Memphis 26-30 (Eng) AB; Emory 31-32 AB in LS. 6: Fr, Sp. 7: Asst circ & ref depts Memphis Pub Lib, Memphis Tenn 32-34, Head ref dept 34-42, 45-46; US Army Air Force 42-45 (S/Sgt, celestial navigation training instr); Chief libn US VA Med Tchg Group Hosp, Memphis Tenn 46-57; Libn Southwestern at Memphis 57-. 9: ALA; SELA (sec-treas 36-38); TennLA (chm Col & Univ Libs Sect 63-64). 10: Alpha Tau Omega; Omicron Delta Kappa; Amer Guild of Organists; Memphis Libns Com. 14: Ref, admin. 15: 2000 N Parkway, Memphis Tenn 38112.

JOHNSON, ALICE K. b East Pt Ga 28 Mr 13. 4: Carl G Johnson. 5: Central Wash State Col 49-55 (Fr) BA; UWash 58 MSLS. 6: Swedish, Fr. 7: Child libn Seattle Pub Lib 55-57; Res libn UWash 58-61; Ref music & art, child Everett Pub Lib, Everett Wash 63-65; Asst circ USoCal summer 64; Ref & documents West Wash State Col 65-. 9: ALA; Wash State LA. 10: ACLU. 14: Ref. 15: 854 NW 190th st, Seattle Wa 98177.

JOHNSON, ALICE M. b Minneapolis 12 Ap 15. 4: Norris Johnson. 5: UMinn 32-35 (Fr) BA, 35-36 BSLS. 6: Fr. 7: Minneapolis Pub Lib: Br asst 36-38, Asst clippings 39, Asst child room 40-42, Asst ref dept 43; Period libn Hamline U 53-54; Libn Bethesda Hosp, St Paul 54-64; Libn Brown & Bigelow, St Paul 64-67; Libn Ramsey Co Pub Lib, White Bear Lake Mn 67-. 9: SLA; ALA; MinnLA. 14: Ref. 15: 1300 Galtier, St Paul Mn 55117.

JOHNSON, ALLIE MAYBELLE (VISE). b Decatur Co Tenn 30 N 03. 4: James Hobart Johnson. 5: Blackstone Col 19-22; Wesleyan Col (Macon Ga) 22-24 (Eng) AB; Peabody summers 24-50 BS in LS. 6: Fr. 7: Tchr Decatur Co High Sch, Decaturville Tenn 24-26; Tchr Parsons High Sch, Parsons Tenn 26-30; Tchr Decatur Co High Sch, Decaturville Tenn 32-44; Clerk Army Finance Off, Camp Blanding Ga 44-45; Saleslady, Columbus Ga; Sales lady, Decaturville Tenn; Libn Central High Sch, Bolivar Tenn 47-48; Libn Decatur Co High Sch, Decaturville Tenn 48-65; Libn Riverside High Sch, Parsons Tenn 65-. 8: Sponsor of Beta Club; Sponsor Future Teachers Chap. 9: NEA; ALA; SELA; TennEA; TennLA. 10: Delta Kappa Gamma; Home Demonstration Club; Womans Soc of Christian Serv; Bd of Stewards (Meth Church); Chm on Commsn on Missions (Meth Church); Bus & Prof Women's Club. 14: Sch libs. 15: Box 206, Decaturville Tenn 38329.

JOHNSON, ALYS M (OMODT). b Houston Minn 17 Jl 09. 4: Clare A Johnson. 5: St Olaf Col 27-29; UMinn 29-31 (LS) BS; Minneapolis Sch of Bus 31-32. 7: Sub tchr Houston High Sch, Houston Minn 43-50, Tchr 47-48, Tele operator 54-56; Child libn Rochester pub Lib, Rochester Minn 56-. 9: MinnLA (sec-treas Child & YP Sect). 10: Sons of Norway; Civic League; YWCA; Band Mothers; PTA. 14: Child wk. 15: 428 6th st SW #104. Rochester Mn 55901.

JOHNSON, ANAMARIE. b Holly Bluff Miss 29 Jl 25. 5: UArk 43-47 (Art) BA; UIll 47-52 (LS) MS. 7: High sch libn blytheville Pub Schs, Blytheville Ark 47-49; Libn Conway Perry Reg Lib, Morrilton Ark 49-51; Libn I on bkmobs Erie Co Pub Lib, Buffalo NY 52-53; Ocean View Br libn Norfolk Pub Lib, Norfolk Va 53-56, Head of bkmob serv 56-. 9: ALA; SELA; VaLA. 10: Quota Club. 14: Admin, lib ext, pub lib. 15: 6444 Crafford ave, Norfolk Va 23518.

JOHNSON, ANN TELFAIR. b Wilmington Ohio 16 N 08. 5: Ohio State U 31-33 (Pol Sci, Psych) AB; Drexel 48-49 BS in LS; UIll 49-52 (Soc Sci Educ) LSMS; UMe (Bethel) summer 60 (Human Rel Lab); Ohio U 65 (Fine Arts). 6: Fr, Ger. 7: Soc case-wk adjustor Phila Dept Pub Assist 33-40; Circ & catlg UIll Lib (Urbana) 49-52; Admin commun sch lib Roxana Commun & High Sch Lib, Roxana Ill 52-54; Ref & catlg Wittenberg U & Warder pub Lib, Springfield Ohio 54-58; Admin High Sch Lib Beavercreek Pub Schs, Xenia Ohio 58-60; Catlg & ref Antioch Col Lib 60-64; Instr in ref & bibliog Lib Sch UNC summer 63; Educ libn Ohio U Lib 64-. 8: Lecturer & adv in lib resources for "Introduction to Research," grad level course at Ohio U. 9: NEA; OhioLA; ALA; AEAUSA. 10: AAUW; LWV. 13: Yes. 14: Col lib admin, ref, bibliog. 15: PO Box 514 , Athens Ohio 45701.

JOHNSON, ANNA (BOOTHE). b Victoria Va 25 Ag 13. 4: Ernest Lewis Johnson Jr. 5: Longwood Col 50-56 (LS) BS; Harvard summer 61 (Law Libnship). 7: Tchr Lunenburg Co Sch Bd, Victoria Va 50-52, Libn 53-59; Law Libn Col of William & Mary 59-68, Law Lib dir 68-. 8: Evaluation Com for Va State Bd of Educ on High Sch Libs at: Park View High Sch, South Hill Va 57, Deep Creek High Sch, chesapeake Va 59. 9: ALA; AALL (Com on Microfacsimiles; SEast chap: Local arrangement chm 61, Nominating Com 66); VaLA. 10: Delta Kappa Gamma; Col Faculty Women's Club. 14: Acquis, catlg. 15: 116 Oak rd, Williamsburg Va 23185.

JOHNSON, ANNE BEASLEY (MRS J DOBSON). 5: David Lipscomb Col 24-26; Peabody 26-28 (Phys Educ) BS; Middle Tenn State 56 (LS); Peabody 59 (LS). 7: Assoc libn Florence State Normal 28-30; Tchr Williamson Co, Triune Tenn 31-33; High sch tchr Williamson Co, Franklin Tenn 56-58, Libn 58-66; Eng instr David Sipscomb Col 66-67, Periods libn DLC 67-. 9: ALA; NEA; TennEA; TennLA. 10: Church of Christ libn; Assn for Preservation of Tenn Antiquities; Delta Kappa Gamma; Cheekwood (The Tenn Bot Gardens & Fine Arts Ctr); Williamson Co Hist Assn. 14: Ref. 15: 308 Battle ave, Franklin Tn 37064.

JOHNSON, ANNITA (MELVILLE) KER. b Mexico City 29 My 08. 4: George Duncan Johnson. 5: George Washington U 25-26, 35; Wellesley 26-30 (Span, Eng) BA; UNC 68 MS in LS. 6: Sp, Portu. 7: Catlgr LC 31-40, Asst Hispanic Found 40-41; Span tchr Pikeville Col 59-61; Catlgr Wesleyan Col (Macon Ga) 61-62; Catlgr & asst libn Tift Col 62-. 8: Recipient ALA Fellowship 36-37; Tech Adv to Dir of Nat Lib, Venezuela 39-40. 9: ALA (Com on Lib Rel with Latin Amer 35-40); Inter-Amer Bibliog & Lib Assn; SELA; GaLA. 10: Soc of Woman Geographers; LWV; Macon (Ga) Com on Human Rel; Phi Beta Kappa. 12: "Survey of Mexican Scientific Periodicals" (31); "Mexican Government Publications" (41); Contrib ed "Handbook of Latin American Studies" (39-41). 13: Yes. 14: Catlg. 15: 3850 The Prado, Macon Ga 31204.

JOHNSON, BARBARA (ANN) COE. b Detroit 19 Ja 23. 5: Bryn Mawr 40-44 (Classical Archaeol) AB; Columbia 44-45 (Gk, Archaeol); UCal(Berkeley) 50-51 BLS. 6: Fr, Ger, Sp. 7: Patients' Libn VA Hosp, Palo Alto Cal 51-52, Med libn 52-56; Dir of Libs Harper Hosp, Detroit 56-. 8: Consul: SLA 60-; Certification MedLA 59; Indexing to Amer Journal of Nursing Co 63; Standards to: Jt Commsn Accreditation Hosp 68, AHIL-ALA 65-. 9: SLA; Amer Med Writers' Assn (var offs & chmships in nat & reg groups); MedLA (mem Bd of Dirs 68-). 13: Yes . 14: Med & nursing subjects, admin. 15: Harper Hosp Dept of Libs 3825 Brush st, Detroit Mi 48201.

JOHNSON, BARBARA G(AYLE). b Holdrege Neb 1 Mr 31. 5: UNeb 49-51, 61-64 (Philos) BA; UDenver 64, 65, 67-68 (LS) MA. 7: Libn Holdrege Carnegie-Phelps Co-S Central Reg Lib, holdrege Neb 64-67; Title IV consultant Neb Pub Lib Commsn, Lincoln 68-. 9: ALA; NebLA; MtPlainsLA. 14: Ref, serv to inst. 15: 1201 J st apt 703, Lincoln Nb 68508.

JOHNSON, BERNICE W. b Raleigh Miss 29 Ag 16. 5: Jones Jr Col 33-35; Belhaven Col 35-37 (Hist) BS; Emory U summers 49-53 MLS). 7: Tchr Miss high schs: Taylorsville 44-48, Brookhaven 48-53; Ser & bibliog libn UMiss (Univ) 53-. 9: SELA; MissLA. 14: Ser, ref. 15: Box 371, University Ms 38677.

JOHNSON, BETTY JO (DREES). b Sidney Ohio 1 D 37. 4: Evans Combs Johnson. 5: Stetson U 55-59 (Hist) AB, 59-61 (Hist) MA; Columbia 61-64 (LS) MS. 6: Sp. 7: Acquis libn Stetson U 61-63, Catlg libn 63-. 9: ALA; FlaLA; SELA. 10: Phi Alpha Theta; Kappa Delta Pi; Sigma Delta Pi; Beta Phi Mu. 12: Abstract: "Historical Abstracts", "America - History and Life". 14: Catlg, acquis. 15: 307 Cumberland rd, DeLand Fl 32720.

JOHNSON, BEVERLY M (BAYNES). b Beloit Wis 8 O 26. 4: Albert W Johnson. 5: UColo 51-53; UAlaska 56-58 (Eng) BA; UCLA 61-62 MLS; San Diego State Col 66-68. 6: Norwegian, Danish, Fr. 7: Acquis libn Systems Development Corp, Santa Monica Cal 62-63; Asst to Latin Amer Bibliog UCLA Main Lib 63; Ser libn San Diego State Col 64-. 9: CalLA (State Col Div v-pres 69, pres 70; chm Accreditation & Certif Com 69). 13: Yes. 14: Ser procedures (manual & automatic), acad status for libns. 15: 4680 Monroe ave, San Diego Ca 92115.

JOHNSON, C(AROLYN) ELIZABETH MRS. b Jellico Tenn 19 Je 04.05UMinn 29 (His BA lui BS. 7: Instr Albany State Col (Ga) 29-31; Libn Central High Sch, Louisville Ky 31-52; Instr Ala State Col 52-63; Ya libn Rochester Pub Lib, Rochester NY 63-66, Calg 66-. 09: ALA-PLA;-ATA;NYLA ;NEA. 14: Yp, ref, catlg. 15: 202B Chatham Gardens, Rochester NY 14605.

JOHNSON, CAROLE (LOUISE ALLVINE). b NYC 2 O 39. 5: UKan 57-61 (Hist) AB; Simmons 64-67 (LS) MS. 6: Fr. 7: Hd libn Allied Research Assocs, Concord Mass 62-64; Hd libn Mass Gen Hosp Sch of Nursing, Boston 64-66; Hd libn Raytheon SISD, Sudbury Mass 66-. 9: SLA (Boston Chap Coms). 15: 61 Garfield, Cambridge Ma 02138.

JOHNSON, CAROLYN (HASSLER). b Oakland Cal 29 My 21. 4: Benjamin Alfred Johnson. 5: UCl9erey39-46 (Journalism) BA; Immaculate Heart Col 54-58 (LS) Pub Lib Certif; Cal State Col (Fullerton) 66 (E duc) Cal State Sch Lib Credential; Immacula ro6 M NPUBLib, Fullerton Cal 46-57, Supv of child serv 58-; Coord, gen ist 58-. 8: Coordinator, gen adv to Fullerton Elem Sch Dist libs 58-. 9: CalLA (Se hlect 66); OrangeCo LA (v-pres 65); So Cal Coun on Lit for Child & Young People. 10: Natural Sci for Yout Found; PTA Coun; Theta Sigma Phi; Phi Beta Kappa; PTA. 14: CHID sev, YASe. 01 N Pomona ave, Fullerton Ca 92632. 14: Child serv, ya serv. 15: 301 N Pomona ave, Fullerton Ca 92632.

JOHNSON, CAROLYN MILLS. b Spartanburg Co SC 23 F 21. 4: Alderman Bonham Johnson. 5: Mars Hill Col 39-41 (Liberal ArtOrop Col 4-4 in LS. 6: Fr. 7: Libn & tchr Jordon High Sch, Greenville Co SC 43-45NKLIN NC; Libn Midway High Sch, Dunn NC 59-64; Libn Union High Sch & Turkey Elem Union High Sch, Clinton NC 65-. 8: V-pres Southeastern Dist of NCEA for Libns 61-62; Adv exeexec Bd of Southeastern Lib Dis Org; Chm Com in publ "Lirgide" for Sampson Co Schs; Chm Sampson Co Libns & Tchrs 65. 9: ALA; NCEA; NC High Sch LA; SELA (adv to pres 68-70); Clrm TA. 10: Home Demonstration Club; Womans Missionary Union; Nat Congress of Parents & Tchrs; Alpha Delta Kappa. 15: Rt 1, Magnolia Nc 28453.

JOHNSON, CHARLES (HOSMEN). b Carlisle Penn 12 Ja 16. 5: Park Col 54-56 (Eng) Col of Wooster 56-58 (Eng) BA; Columbia 58-60 MLS. 6: Fr. 7: Ser libn asst Queens Col Lib, NY 59; Pre-prof Music Lib City Col (NY) 60; Prof, asst hist & popular lib depts Enoch Pratt Free Lib, Baltimore 60-. 9: ALA -ACRL (fine arts sect)& MDLA; MusLA; Theatre LA. 10: Columbia Sch of Lib Serv Alumni Club. 14: Ref, readers adv, rare bks, bk arts, fine arts, theatre libwk. 15: 1002 N Calvert st, Baltimore Md 21202.

JOHNSON, CLEOPATRA (WHITTINGTON). b Montgomery Ala 9 Je 29. 4: Leroy R Johnson. 5: Spelman Col 46-48, 51-53 (Eng) BA; Atlanta U 53-54 (LS); UGa 66-68 Supv Dir of Libs Certificate; Atlanta U 68-69 (LS) 6th Year Certif. 7: Libn VA Hosp, Tuskegee Ala 54-57; Libn Atlanta Pub Schs 57-66, Lib supv 66-. 8: Instr, Title I, Instr Materials Ctr Wkshop 67; Leader, conf sponsored by Atlanta U Sch of lib Serv on the Ga child's Access to Materials Pertaining to Amer Negroes 67. 9: ALA; ASCD; NEA; SELA; GaLA; Ga Div Instr Supv; Ga Assn for Supvrs & Curr Devel; GaTchrsEA (Libns Sect); MetroLA. 10: Beta Phi mu; Alpha Kappa Alpha; Metro Grils Club Guild; Girls Club of Amer; YWCA. 14: Lib automation, lib supvn & admin, materials by and about Negroes. 15: 372 Larchmont dr NW, Atlanta Ga 30318.

JOHNSON, CLIFFORD R(OBERT). b Rock Island Ill 1 Jl 24. 5: Augustana Col (Ill) 42-45 (Gk) BA; Claremont Grad Sch (Cal) 48-53 (Amer Hist); USoCal summer 52 (LS); Columbia summer 54-57 (LS) MS. 6: Swedish, Ger. 7: (Cpl) Weather forecaster Train Command USAAF 45-47; Clerk materials scheduling dept Internat Harvester Co, E Moline Ill 47-48; Period libn Claremont Col Lib 49-50, Circ ref libn 51-52; Ref libn Honnold Lib Assoc Cols (Claremont Cal) 52-53; Libn pre-prof Brooklyn Pub Lib 53-55; Asst libn Ford Found, NYC 55-57, Libn 57-66; Catlg lit analyst project URBAN DOC Research Foundncy 66-68; Ref Libn Richmond Col CUNY 68-. 8: Mem of Task Force & Catlg Consul to URBANDOC, NYC 64. 9: ALA -ACRL; SLA (var positions local & nat); NY Lib Club. 10: Archons of Colophon; Amer-Scand Found; Episcopal Churchmen for S Africa; Episcopal Soc for Racial & Cultural Unity; Phi Alpha Theta; Pi Kappa Delta; Columbia Sch of Lib Serv Alumni Assn (pres 68-69). 12: Assoc ed "Social Science Serials in Special Libraries in the New York Area" (61); Assoc ed "Serials: Advertising, Business, Finance, Marketing, Social Science, in Libraries in the New York Area" (65). 13: Yes. 14: Ref, catlg, acquis. 15: 245 E 87th st, New York Ny 10028.

JOHNSON, D COLLEEN. b Wichita Kan 30 D 25. 5: Lindenwood Col 43-47 (Mus) BM; Oberlin 47-49 (Mud) MM; IndU 66-68 MLS. 6: Ger. 7: Mus tchr: Westtown Sch, Westtown Penn 49-51, Tchr William Penn Charter Sch, Phila Penn 51-52; Hd piano dept Peace Col 52-61; Asst Prof of mus Ind Central Col 61-66; Catlgr Ind State Lib, Indianapolis 68-. 9: ALA; IndLA. 15: 4252 S State, Indianapolis In 46227.

JOHNSON, DAVID L. b Galesburg, Ill 10 My 40. 4: Patricia Ann (Dallas). 5: East Ill U 58-62(Soc Sci) BS; UIll 62-66 (LS) MS. 6: Fr. 7: Libn & a-v dir Champaign Sr High sch, Champaign Ill 62-66; Supv instr materials Off of Supt of Pub Instr, Springfield ill 66; Dir learning resource ctr Robert Morris Col 66-. 8: Consul: Off of Supt of pub Instr 66, Hancock Co ESEA Title III Proj; Ext Instr West Ill U. 9: ALA; NEA-DAVI; Ill A-V Assn; IllLA (treas IllASchL Div). 10: District Comssnr Boy Scouts of Amer. 14: Admin, jr col libs. 15: 723 Questover dr, Carthage Il 62321.

JOHNSON, DIANA (JORJORIAN). b Worcester Mass 16 S 32. 4: Richard G Johnson. 5: Radcliffe 50-54 (Biochem Sci) AB; Simmons 56-57 (LS) MS. 7: Research tech Commonwealth of Mass, Worcester 54-56; Earth sci libn MIT 58-59; Art & mus libn Providence Pub Lib 59-60; Ref/interlib loan Worcester Polytech Inst 61-. 14: Ref. 15: 9 Wetherell st, Worcester Ma 01602.

JOHNSON, DIANNE B. b Harrisburg Penn 7 N 42. 5: Millersville State Col 60-64 (LS, Eng) BS in Ed; Kutztown State Col summer 66 (Lib Educ); upittsburgh 69- (LS). 6: Ger. 7: Jr high sch libn Palmyra Area Schs, Palmyra Penn 64-67; Libn Norwin Jr High Sch W, Irwin Penn 67-. 9: ALA; PennLA; PennStateEA. 14: Yp, child serv. 15: 509 Fairview dr, Greensburg Pa 15601.

JOHNSON, DONALD CLAY. b Clintonville Wis 19 Ag 40. 5: UWis 58-62 (Asian Studies) BA; Chicago 63-67 (LS) MS. 6: Fr, Ger, Hindi, Thai, Urdu. 7: Lib asst UWis Law Lib (Madison) 62-63; Asst to the South Asia bibliog spec UChicago 63-64; Southeast Asia libn No Ill U 64-67; Curator Southeast Asia Col YaleU 67-. 9: Assn Asian Studies (Com on Amer Lib Resources in SEast Asia 65-68; Com on Research Materials of SEast Asia 69-); ALA (chm SEast Asia Sect, Internat Rel Round Ta ble 68-). 10: YaleU Lib Staf f Assn. 12: Ed "C ORMOSEA (Com on Research Materials of SEast sia 67-) Newsletter". 14: Ref, catlg, area studies libnship. 15: 142 E Marquette st, Berlin Wi 54923.

JOHNSON, DONALD WILLIAM. b Chicago 26 Ag 26. 4: Maralou Rose Beckerich. 5: Wright Jr Col 44-45 (Pre- law); UNotre Dame 45-46 (Pre-law); Chicago 49-52 (LS) MA; UPortland 57-58 (Ger). 6: Ger, Sp. 7: Asst cost accountant Vassar Co, Chicago 46-48; Bkkeeper Dean Co 48-49; Ms ed Amer Med Assn 52; Asst order libn UKan 52-53; UNotre Dame (Notre Dame Ind): Asst acquis libn 53-54, Act acquis libn 54-55, Asst acquis libn 55-56; Catlg & processing libn UPortland 56-59; Law Libn Creighton U 59-61; Libn Chicago Bd of Health 61-65; Dir tech processes & cooperative processing center Nev State Lib 65-67; Asst univ libn Ariz State U 67-. 8: Cnul; Scottsdale riz) Pub Lib opaco Jr Col Dist 68, Prof computer Inst, Mesa Ariz 68; Chm Nevada Lib Planning Systs 67. 9: Ariz State LA (PROCT DIR Ariz Union List of Serials 67-69, chm Ad Hoc Com on Intermountain Union List of Serials 69-); SWLA (mem Ad Hoc Com on Feasability of SWest Union List of Serials 69-); ALA-ACRL. 10: US Chess Fed; Phoenix Chess Club. 12: "Intermountain (69). 13: Yes. 15: 1101 E Del Rio dr, Tempe Az 85281.

JOHNSON, DOROTHEA (MARTIN). b Tampa Fla 16 Je 31. 4: Andrs W Johnson. 5: UHawaii 63 (Art Hist) BA; Fla State U 63-64 (LS) MA. 6: Ger, Sp, Japanese, Fr. 7: (1st Lt) WAC Personnel, US 48-52; Libn, Naha Okinawa 57-59; Libn St Petersburg Jr Col 64-65; Act libn Fla Presbyterian Col 65-66, Ref Libn 66-68; FPC Bergen Commun Col acquis libn 69-. 9: SLA; FlaLA; NJLA. 14: Ref. 15: 258 Hillside ave, Palisades Park Nj 07650.

JOHNSON, DOROTHY (EADIE). b Newark NJ 2 Jl 29. 4: David A Johnson. 5: Douglass Col 47-51 (LS) BA; Rutgers 55-58 MLS; NJ State Bd of Educ 58 Prof Libns Permanent Certif. 6: Fr, Lat. 7: Lib asst Douglass Col 51-52; Ref libn Bloomfield Pub Lib, Bloomfield NJ 52-. 08: Instr wkshop on ref serv & tools NJ Bur of Pub & Sch Lib Serv 68. 9: ALA (chm Essex Co (NJ) Ref Serv Div 58-60); NJLA (chm Ref Sect 60-62; chm Scholarship Com 64-65); mem: Publns Com, NJ Bibliog Com Com ro Consider Adult Serv Functions inNJLA, Educ for Libnship 10: Citizens Com for Educ; Hist Sites Inventory Com; Inter-Agency Coun of Bloomfield (NJ) ; AAUW; Bloomfield Citizen 's Com for Col Opportunity Staff Assn of Bloomfield Pub Lib. 12: "Free Public Library, Bloomfield NJ Jarvic Foundation" (57). 14: Ref. 15: 20 Wagner st, Bloomfield NJ 07003.

JOHNSON, DUANE (WILBUR). b Ottumwa Iowa 9 O 30. 5: Augustana Col (Rock Island Ill) 48-52 (Hist) AB; UIll 58-59 MSLS; UDenver summer 63; Ind U 67-. 7: Tchr Knoxville Commun Schs, Knoxville Ill 52-55; Libn Knoxville Jr-Sr High Sch, Knoxville Ill 55-57; Sch libn Ottumwa High Sch, Ottumwa Iowa 57-58; A-v libn Oak Park- River Forest High Sch, Oak Park Ill 59-60; Sch libn Ottumwa High Sch, Ottumwa Iowa 60-64; Sch lib consul Mich State Lib 64-65; Head libn N Central High Sch, Indianapolis 65-67. 8: OE Doctoral Fellow Ind U (Bloomington) 67-. 9: ALA; NEA-DAVI; ASCD; IowaASchL (pres 62-63); AASL (chm Pub Rel Com Recording Sec 69-70). 10: Kiwanis Club; Beta Phi Mu; Guild of Amer Organists. 12: Ed "Hoosier School Libraries" (66-67). 13: Yes. 15: Indiana Univ Grad Lib Sch, Bloomington In 47401.

JOHNSON, EDWARD ROY. b Denver Col 29 N 40. 4: Benita Hulbert. 5: UColo 61-64 (Hist) BA; UWis 65-66 MALS. 6: Fr. 7: Lib asst UColo 64-65; Ref libn UIowa 66-67; Bus libn 67-. 9: SLA. 10: Phi Alpha Theta; Beta Phi Mu. 14: Ref, bibliog. 15: 708 Eastmoor dr, Iowa City Ia 52240.

JOHNSON, EDWIN A. b Schenectady NY 24 S 16. 4: Jean Allet Johnson. 5: Valparaiso U 34-38 (Music) AB; Northwestern 38-39 (Music, piano) M Mus; West Mich U 63-64 (LS) MA; UMo 68 (Info Systems). 6: Ger. 7: Priv music studio, Scottsbluff Neb 39-42; Choir dir-organist First Methodist Church, Scottsbluff Neb 39-42; Automatic machine operator McGill Mfg Co, Valparaiso Ind 42-46; Priv music studio, Valparaiso Ind 46-; Libn Valparaiso U 46-64; Ref libn Valparaiso U 64-; Organist Immanuel Lutheran Church, Valparaiso Ind 46-. 9: ALA; Mus Tchrs Nat Assn; Ind Mus Tchrs Assn (Exec sec-treas 59-61, chm Certif Bd 59-61, State Piano Chm 62, Student Activities Chm 63). 10: Valparaiso Commun Concert Assn; Rotary Club; PTA; Beta Phi Mu; Pi Kappa Lambda. 14: Ref, lib educ. 15: 201 Harmel dr, Valparaiso In 46383.

JOHNSON, EDWINA (DAVID) (MRS). b Bennettsville SC 13 D 08. 5: Winthrop 26-30 (Music) BS; UNC 53-54 BS in LS. 6: Fr. 7: Libn Biol-Forestry Lib Duke U 50-. 9: SLA (treas & v-pres NC Chap); NCLA. 10: AAUW; Durham Woman's Club. 14: Ref, admin. 15: 1606 Peace st, Durham NC 27701.

JOHNSON, ELIZABETH (LAMKIN). b Augusta Ga 11 Ap 19. 4: Joseph Robert Johnson. 5: Wesleyan Col 40 AB; UGa 40, 65-69 MEd, 68 Instr supv Certif, 69 6th yr Certif (Lib Ed). 6: Fr. 7: Tchr & sch libn Columbia Co Bd of Educ, Evans Ga 40-43; Tchr Fulton Co Bd of Educ, Atlanta 43-46; Tchr Richmond Co Bd of Educ, Augusta Ga 56-65, Lib coord 65-. 9: NEA; ALA; GaEA (chm 10th Dist Lib Dept); RichmondCoEA (pres); CSRALA (pres); GaLA; SELA; ASDC; GaASDC; Ga Dept Instr Supv. 10: Phi Kappa Phi; Kappa Delta Pi; Alpha Delta Kappa. 14: Bks, lit serv. 15: 1014 Magnolia dr, Augusta Ga 30904.

JOHNSON, ELIZABETH (NELSON). b St Paul 6 N 34. 4: David Paul Johnson. 5: St Olaf Col 51-55 (Hist) BA; UMinn 58-59 MA in LS. 7: Asst libn Alpena Bd of Educ, Alpena Mich 55-56; Asst libn Edina-Morningside Bd of Educ, Edina Minn 56-57; Child lib Kitsap Reg Lib, Bremerton Wash 57-58; Field consul Iowa State Travel Lib, Avoca Iowa 62-64; Ref lib Cedar Falls Pub Lib, Cedar Falls Iowa 63; Asst libn Waverly Pub Lib, Waverly Iowa 66-68; Elem libn Waverly Shell Rock Commun Sch Dist, Waverly Iowa. 8: Child Bk Adv Com Augsburg Publ House 64-66. 9: ALA; Lutheran Church LA; IowaLA; Iowa ASchL. 13: Yes. 14: Elem sch libs, church libs. 15: Box 372, Denver Ia 50622.

JOHNSON, ELIZABETH (SHEPHERD). b Lawrence Kan 22 My 1900. 5: UKan 20-24 (Eng) BA; Northwestern 36 (Speech); Tex Woman'sU 53-54 MLS. 7: Tchr sr high sch, Kan 24-37; Libn Dallas Pub Lib, Tex 54-55; Libn Ft Worth Pub Lib 55-63; Libn Tex Women's U Demonstration Sch 63-67, Instr Lib Sci 67-. 9: TexLA. 14: Child serv. 15: 3209 Merida, Fort Worth Tx 76109.

JOHNSON, ELIZABETH ANNE. b Seattle 27 Ja 17. 5: UWash 34-38 (Lit) BA, 38-39 BA in LS. 7: Gen asst Greene Co Lib, Xenia Ohio 40-42; Lib Assn of Portland, Portland Ore: Gen asst ref 42, 1st asst ref 55, So sci 56, Head lit & hist 60-. 8: Subscription Bks Com 54-55; Consul "Essay & General Literature Index" 60-; Ore State Great Decisions Com 61-63. 9: ALA; PNLA; OreLA. 14: Ref. 15: 2260 NW Everett, Portland Or 97210.

JOHNSON, ELIZABETH ELLEN. b Peoria Ill 7 Jl 18. 5: Bradley U 36-40 (Soc Sci) AB; UIll 55-56 MLS. 6: Ger, Fr. 7: Asst libn Peoria Pub Lib, Peoria Ill 41-43; Soc casewker Amer Red Cross, Peoria & Ft Worth 43-47; Asst research lib Caterpillar Tractor Co, Peoria Ill 48-58, Libn bus lib 58-. 9: SLA. 10: AAUW; Beta Phi Mu; Chi Omega. 14: Ref in bus. 15: 2115 N Linn st, Peoria Il 61604.

JOHNSON, ELLEN M (SCHULTZ). b Beatrice Neb 4 N 18. 4: Dale M Johnson. 5: Friends U 35-39 (Eng) AB; UIll 40-41 BS in LS. 7: Asst libn Roosevent Jr High Sch, Wichita Kan 39-40; Ref libn Wichita City Lib, Wichita Kan 41-43; Documents libn UColo 43-44; Asst child libn Wichita City Lib, Wichita Kan 59-60; Circ & ref libn Wichita State U 60-67; Asst P rof West Kentucky U 68-. 09: ALA; KanLA (chm Col & Ref Sect 61-62); KyLA. 10: AAUP; Coun of Univ Women; Girl Scout Leader. 12: "A Study of Student Use of Study Facilities" (62); "Western Kentucky University Audio Library Catalog" (69). 13: Yes. 14: Ref, circ, personnel, tech serv, computers. 15: 631 Cottonwood dr, Bowling Green Ky 42101.

JOHNSON, ELLEN MARIE. b Onida S Dak 4 Je 41. 5: No State Col (Aberdeen S Dak) 59-62 (Bus educ) BS; UDenver 63-64 (Libnship) MA. 7: Libn Fed Res Bank of Kansas City Mo 64-. 9: SLA (Admiss Com 69-72; pres, Heart of Amer Chap 68.69). 10: Amer Inst Banking. 15: Fed Res Bank of Kansas City, Kansas City Mo 64198.

JOHNSON, ETHEL (EMMA). b Akron Ohio 31 Ag 13. 5: IndU 33-37 (Eng) AB; UIll 38-39 BS in LS. 7: Adult circ asst pub lib of Ft Wayne & Allen Co, Ft Wayne Ind 37-38, Catlg bks 39-40, phonograph records catlgr 40-45, Child lib asst 45-50, Head of child lib 50-; Art bk catlgr 58-68. 9: ALA; IndLA. 14: Child wk, catlg. 15: 3717 Shady ct, Fort Wayne In 46807.

JOHNSON, ETHEL M(ARIE). b Powers Mich. 5: Hibbing Jr Col 30-32; Cleveland Col of West Res U 32-33 (LS) Certif, UMinn 50. 7: Chisholm Pub Lib: Clerk 26-32, prof catlgr 33-43, catlgr & asst libn 41-43; Off wk Los Angeles & Dayton Ohio 43-45; Libn Gen Mills Inc 46-. 9: SLA. 11: SLA Nat Lib Week Publ Award, 2nd place 64. 14: Catlg, ref. 15: Gen Mills Inc 9200 Wayzata blvd, Minneapolis Mn 55440.

JOHNSON, EUGENE M. b Milwaukee 10 My 19. 4: Ruth (M Johnson) Mewaldt. 5: Lawrence Col 41-42, 46-48 (Fine Arts) BA; UWis summer 46; UMich 48-49 AMLS; UNeb 51-52 (Philos). 06: Ger. 7: US Army (Cpl) bandsman 42-46; UNeb Libs: Asst humanities div 49-52, Sr catlgr 52-54, Acquis libn 54-63, Chm bd on Lib Resources 59-, Asst dir for soc studies 63-64, Assoc dir for publ serv 64-. 8: Neb Lib Development Com 63-; Notable Bks Coun (ALA) 64-. 9: ALA; MusicLA; NebLA (chm Col & Univ Sect 52-53). 10: AAUP. 12: Contrib ed "Faulkner Studies " (52-54). 13: Yes. 14: Acquis, catlg, collections, admin. 15: 3550 Normal blvd, Lincoln Nb 68506.

JOHNSON, EVELYN L. b Dagus Mines Penn 14 J& 23. 5: Cleveland Col 45-46; Augustana Col 50-53 (Mus) AB; UIll 62-63 MSLS. 07. Sylvania Electronic Prods Corp, Emporium Penn 41-42; Stackpole Carbon Co, St Mary's Penn 42-45; Sex: Conkey Co, Cleveland Ohio 46-48, baker, Hostetler & Patterson Law Firm, Cleveland Ohio 48-50, Augustana Col (Admissions Dean) 53-62; Pub serv & libn grad lib sci sch UDI (Urbana) 63-67; Hd ref & period libn wis State U Lib (Eau Claire) 68-. 9: ALA; WisLA. 10: Beta Phi Mu; AAUP. 14: Ref. 15: 2805 Stein blvd, Eau Claire Wi 54701.

JOHNSON, FERNE (ROLLINS). b Dover NH 30 Ja 20. 4: George L Johnson. 5: UNH 37-41 (Eng) BA; Pratt 41-42 BLS; St John's U (NY) 45 (LS) 6 cr for Sch Certif; U Nacionale de Mex summer 45 (Educ); NYU 45-47 (Elem Educ) MA. 6: Fr. 7: Child libn Great Neck Pub Lib, Great Neck NY; Sch libn Edgemont Rand and Geo Washington Schs, Montclair NJ; Ref libn Pratt Inst Lib; Sch libn Kensington Sch, Great Neck NY; Supv of child wk Great Neck Pub Lib, Great Neck NY; Sub tchr Overseas Sch, Abadan Iran 56-59; Dir Delaware Twp Free Pub Lib, Delaware Twp NJ; Sch libn Heritage Jr High Sch, Cherry Hill NJ; Sch libn Roberts Baker No 7 Schs, Mooristown NJ; Sch Libn Garfield E E Sch, Willingboro NJ. 09: NEA; NJEA; NJLA; NJSchLA; Burlington Co Sch Libns (pres 68-70). 10: Pratt Inst Lib Alumni Group; Jr Women's Club; Brownie Scout Leader, Abadan Iran; Girl Scout Leader; Cub Scout Leader; first woman elected to Church Bd, Abadan Iran. 14: Child wk. 15: 134 Chestnut st, Mooristown Nj 08057.

JOHNSON, FLORENCE EVELYN. b Toronto Can 1 Je 17. 4: George Henry Johnson. 5: UToronto Victoria Col 36-39 (Liberal Arts) BA; Ontario Col of Educ 39-40 (Public & High Sch) 2 certifs; Toronto 47-52 (Geog) MA; Chicago 60-64 (LS) AM. 6: Fr. 7: Tchg fellow UToronto Dept of Geog 47-49; Research analyst Dept of City Planning, Chicago 52-53; Libn DeLeuw Cather & Co Consul Engnrs, Chicago 53-60; Lib clerk Lib Internat Rel, Chicago 60; Asst ref libn Mun Ref Lib, Chicago 61-64, Head tech processes dept 64-65; Libn Chicago Col of Osteopathy 65-. 8: V-chm & chm SLA Soc Sci Div, Planning Bldg & Housing Sect 63-65; Planned nat convention programs 64-65; SLA Consul to ALA Catlg Code Revision Com 64-. 9: ADI; ALA-ACRL; MedLA; SLA (Biol Sci Div); Chicago Reg Group of Libns in Tech Serv. 10: Art Inst of Chicago (Life mem); Amer Youth Hostel. 11: Prince of Wales Silver Medal (with BA degree 39); SLA Eleanor S Cavanaugh Scholarship 61. 13: Yes. 14: New Lib bldg planning, multimedia in med educ. 15: 5476 So Harper ave, Chicago Il 60615.

JOHNSON, FLORENCE (FRAZER). b Little Rock Ark 30 O 13. 4: Howard Heisler Johnson. 5: Ouachita Col 30-31; Wichita Falls Jr Col 31-32; Tex State Col for Women 32-33 (LS) BS, 34-35 (Eng, Educ) MA; Columbia 52 (LS). 6: Sp. 7: Prim tchr, Irene Tex 35-37; Sch libn, Gladewater Tex 37-39; Sch libn, Conroe Tex 39-42; Post libn Blackland Army Air Field, Waco Tex 42-44; Libn high sch, Bentonville Ark 50-51; Libn & Eng tchr high sch, Alexander Kan 51-52; Asst head acquis UKan Lib 52-55; Head period dept Dallas Pub Lib, Dallas Tex 55-57, Hd child dept Oak Cliff br 57; Head period sect UKan Lib 57-65, Head ser dept 65-. 9: ALA; KanLA; MPLA. 10: Bus & Prof Women's Club; AAUW; AAUP; Lawrence Adult Educ Adv Bd; Nat Assn of Parliamentarians; Kan Univ Senate; Kan U Lib Staff Assn. 14: Ser, period, ref, pub serv. 15: 1633 Illinois st, Lawrence Ks 66045.

JOHNSON, FLORENCE HAZELL. b Cleveland Ohio 29 F 24. 5: Cleveland StateU 41-43, 48-52 (Psych) BA; UWash 55-57 (Nursing Educ) MA; EmoryU 67-68 (LS) MLn. 7: Staff nurse Metro Gen Hosp, Cleveland Ohio 46-47, 48-51; Staff nurse VA Hosp, Tucson 47-48; Instr St Luke's Hosp, Cleveland Ohio 51-55; Dir of nursing educ Mem Hosp, Lima Ohio 57-61; Research assoc in nursing Highland View Hosp, Cleveland Ohio 61-67; MEDLARS search analyst MEDLARS Ctr UAla, Birmingham 68-. 9: Amer Nurses Assn; ALA; AlaLA. 14: Ref. 15: 1919 7th ave S, Birmingham Al 35233.

JOHNSON, FRANCES (BEULAH). b Keokee Va. 5: Radford Col 48 (Educ) BS; Peabody 53 (LS) MA. 7: Elem tchr, Lee Co Va 31-49; Libn High Sch, Lee Co Va 49-51; Libn Radford Col 51-. 9: SELA; VaLA; VaEA. 10: AAUW; Delta Kappa Gamma. 14: Catlg. 15: 1030 Calhoun, Radford Va 24141.

JOHNSON, FRANCES R. b Denver Colo 3 Jl 29. 5: DenverU 47-51 (Phys Educ) BA; UWis 52-54 9veterinary Sci) MS; DenverU 65-66 (LS) MA. 7: Instr Evergreen High Sch, Evergreen Colo 51-52; Instr phys ed St Petersburg Fla Jr Col 56-60; Hd womans phys educ Ariz West Col 63-65; Circ libn Mesa Community Col 67-69; Dir Maricopa Tech Col Lib 69-. 9: ALA; ArizStateLA (Educ Com mem 68-, chm 69-). 10: Amer Assn Health, Phys Educ & Recreation. 14: Circ, lib tech educ, curriculum, devel of tech col libs. 15: 7717 E Pasadena ave, Scottsdale Az 85251.

JOHNSON, GEORGE LAWRENCE. b SI NY 24 My 23. 4: Lorraine Hagen Johnson. 5: Syracuse 46-52 AB (Ger), MA (Ger), MS (LS). 6: Ger, Sp. 7: USAAF (Sgt) Troop Carrier, US & Europe 43-45, Maj USAAFR 48-; Tech libn Panelyte Div SI Regis Paper Co, Trenton NJ 52-53; Ref libn Johns-Manville Corp, Manville NJ 54-. 9: SLA. 14: Indexing, abstracting, sci-tech. 15: 11 N Cadillac dr, Somerville NJ 08876.

JOHNSON, (MYRA) GENEVA (DRUM). b Newton NC 31 Mr 21. 4: Moody S Johnson. 5: Emmanuel col (Franklin Springs Ga) 38-40 Diploma; Hight Point Col 40-41; E Car Tchrs Col 41-43 9eng, Soc Studies) AB; UNC (Chapel Hill) (LS); UMich (Ann Arbor) 65-66 MALS. 6: Fr. 7: Clk War Dept Chief of Staff, Wash DC 43-45; Libn Emmanuel Col (Franklin Springs Ga) 45-47; Br libn Kan City (Kan) Pub Lib 47-49; Tchr & libn Geneva Pub Schs, Geneva Ind 50-51; Tchr: Point Place Sch, Toledo Ohio 53-54, Flat Rock (Mich) Elem Sch 57-58, Lincoln Park (Mich) Schs 58-62, Reese (Mich) Pub Schs 63-64; Libn Reese (Mich) Pub schs 65-66; Asst libn & Asst Prof Lib Sci Olivef Nazarene Col 66-. 9: NEA; ALA; MichASchL. 14: Catlg, sch lib wk. 15: 175 Spencer ct, Bourbonnais Il 60914.

JOHNSON, GERTRUDE (SHANKS). b Danville Ill 30 D 10. 4: James I Johnson. 5: Flora Stone Mather Col 29-33 (Pol Sci) BA; West Res Law Sch 32-35 LLB; Kent State 62-65 MLS. 7: Asst Dept of Pol Sci West Res U 33-34; Law ed Banks Baldwin Law Publ Co, Cleveland 35-36; Clerk, Twinsburg Twp Ohio 55-65; Deputy clerk Municipal Court of Cuyohoga Falls 59-65; Private practice of law, Cleveland 36-41, Twinsburg Ohio 55-65; Law Libn UAkron Col of Law 64-. 9: AALL (Exch of Dups Com); Akron Bar Assn; Ohio Assn of Law Libs (treas). 10: Citizens Adv Com to Juvenile Court, Summit Co; Citizens Com for Improvement of Correctional & Law Enforcement Facilities; Phi Beta Kappa; Order of Coif. 14: Ref, acquis. 15: 9372 Liberty rd, Twinsburg Oh 44087.

JOHNSON, GERTRUDE (WIENCKE). b Grand Island Neb 24 My 18. 4: Charles Wilford Johnson. 5: Midland Col 37-40 (Ger) BA; UWis summer 39; UChicago 40-41, 44-45 (Relig, Educ) MA; UUtah 59; UWash 60, summers 58 & 59 MLS. 7: Research sec Soils Dept UWis (Madison) 46-48; Assoc libn Westminster Col Lib (Salt Lake City) 58-60; Ser libn & gifts & exchange UUtah Lib 60-61; Ref libn Ore Col of Educ Lib 61-63; Hd ref dept Willamette U Lib 63-. 9: ALA; PNLA; OreLA (chm Ore Authors Com); Willamette Christ Col Libns Assn. 10: Delta Kappa Gamma; Lib Com St Mark's Luth Church; League of Baylor Parents; Beta Phi Mu. 13: Yes. 14: Ref. 15: R 1 Box 943, Salem Or 97304.

JOHNSON, H THAYNE. b Rupert Ida 12 Ja 22. 4: Iris Helen Schlerf. 5: Brigham Young U 48-52 (Archaeol) BA, (Hist) MA; USoCal 57-59 MS in LS. 7: Asst libn Brigham Young U 52-55; Engnr Douglas Aircraft Co 53-59; Manager tech lib serv Ramo Wooldridge 59-61; Head Electronic Properties Info Center Hughes Air craft 61-65; Head tech lib serv Hughes Aircraft Co 61-65; Dir Grad Dept of Lib & Info Serv Brigham Young U 65-. 8: Consul ed, Plenum Press Ind, 65-. 9: ALA; UtahLA. 10: Beta Phi Mu; Phi Alpha Theta. 12: Ed "Electronic Properties of Materials; A Guide to the Literature" (65). 13: Yes. 14: Admin, tchg, info sci. 15: Jrc Lib Brigham Young Univ, Provo Ut 84601.

JOHNSON, HARLAN R. 4: Sharon Erickson. 5: Dickinson State Col 57-61 (Eng) BS; Peabody 66-67 MLS. 7: Eng tchr: Steele High Sch, Steele N Dak 61-64, Mandan High Sch, Mandan N Dak 64-66; Libn Westside High Sch, Omaha Neb 67-68; Lib sci instr & coord curriculum materials No ArizonaU 68-. 9: ALA; ArizLA. 14: Ref, tchg of catlg & lib admin. 15: Box 5774 No Arizona Univ, Flagstaff Az 86001.

JOHNSON, HAZEL (MARIE). b Sylvania Ohio. 5: UMich 38-42 (Lat) AB, 43 AB in LS, 50 AM in LS. 7: Circ libn UNM 43-44; Forestry libn Colo State U 44-47; Catlgr UDenver 47-50; UMich Bur of Govt Lib 51-54; Assoc ref libn Ohio State U 55-60; Head ref & info serv UPittsburgh 60- 68, Consul collections development 68-. 8: Lecturer UPittsburgh Grad Sch of Lib & Info Serv, 62-. 9: ALA-ACRL (Tri-State Chap); PennLA; AALS. 10: AAUP; Beta Phi Mu; Phi Delta Gamma. 14: Ref, lib instr, bibliog. 15: Univ of Pittsburgh, G49 Hillman Lib, Pittsburgh Pa 15213.

JOHNSON, HELEN (LEAHY). b St Louis 25 O 05. 4: John Sevier Johnson. 5: Maryville Col Sacred Heart (St louis) 23-27 (Eng) AB; UWis summer 29 (Eng). 6: Fr. 7: Map libn Aeronautical Chart Plant, St Louis 43-45; Research libn Lambert Pharmacal Co, St Louis 49-55; Med libn St Louis Med Soc 56-58; Catlgr Aeronautical Chart & Info Center, St Louis 58-. 9: SLA (chm Program Com Greater St Louis Chap 53, chm Mem Com 54). 14: Catlg, ref. 15: 4610 Westminster pl, St Louis Mo 63108.

JOHNSON, HELEN S. b Hudson Mass 10 Ap 16. 4: Don Cooper Johnson. 5: Simmons 33-37 (LS) BS. 7: Ref asst Brookline Pub Lib, Brookline Mass 37-41; Child libn Wooster Pub Lib, Wooster Ohio 41-43; Libn Wayne Co Pub Lib, Wooster Ohio 41-45; Child wk coordinator Hawaii Co Lib,

Hilo Hawaii 45-48; Supv libn lit & langs San Diego Pub Lib 58-. 9: ALA; OhioLA (sec-treas 45). 13: Yes. 14: Admin, ref. 15: 1020 Devonshire dr, San Diego Ca 92107.

JOHNSON, HERBERT FREDERICK. b St Paul 1 Ag 34. 4: Delores Madson. 5: UMinn 52-57 (Pol Sci) BA, 58-59 (LS) MA. 6: Chinese. 7: (2nd Lt) US Army 58; Libn US Govt, Wash DC 59-61; Asst libn Bus Lib Columbia U 61-64; Head Libn Assoc Prof Hamline U 64-; Visiting lecturer UMinn Lib Sch 67. 8: Consul Minn Republican State Central Com in establishing a research dept 58; Prin investigator of NSF sponsored research study 67-; Consul Hope Col Lib 69. 9: ALA; ASIS; AAUP. 10: Capt US Army Reserves; Com on Internat Programs Nat Stud Coun of YMCA's (NYC); PTA; Beta Phi Mu; Minn Republican Task Force on Educ 66, 68; Minn Republican Research Adv Com. 11: Recipient 3M Co Research Grant 68-. 13: Yes. 14: Ref, admin, research, tech serv. 15: 2895 N Pascal ave, St Paul Mn 55223.

JOHNSON, IRMA (YARBROUGH). b Loretto Tenn 18 D 23. 5: UNM 45 BA, 48 (Sociol) MA; Simmons 51 BSLS. 6: Sp, Russian. 7: Lib asst Albuquerque Pub Lib, Albuquerque NM 44-45 Lib asst UNM Lib 46-47; MIT Lib: Gen asst 47-48, Econ libn 49-53, Asst ref libn 54-55, Ref libn 56-65, Sci libn 66-. 8: Exch libn U Edinburgh (Edinburgh Scotland) 55-56; Guide US Tech Bk Exhibit, USSR 63; US-USSR Exch of Spec Libns, 66; Lib Consul Kanpur Indo Amer Program, Indian Inst of Tec h, Kanpur India 68-70. 09: SLA (chm Transl Activities Com 64-67); ASIS. 13: Ye s. 15: Sci Lib, Mass Inst of Tech Cambridge Ma 02139.

JOHNSON, J LaRUE. b Sedalia Mo 3 D 08. 5: Stephens Col 26-28 (Piano) AMus; So Methodist U 29-31 (Piano, Organ) BMus; Columbia 46, 47 Certif of LS; So Methodist U 47, 48 (Piano) MM (Piano, Organ) Bmus; Columbia 46, 47 Certif of LS; So Methodist U 47, 48 (Piano) M Mus. 7: Piano instr So Methodist U 31-37; Libn Dallas Independent Sch Dist 36-; (Lt) Women's Reserve US Navy, Alcoa Tenn, Wash DC 43-46; Asst libn Pretoria Pub Lib, Pretoria S Africa, 66-67. 09: ALA; NEA; TexLA. 10: Pro Musica; Dallas Chamber Music Soc; AAUW ; Dallas Sch Libns Club; Mu Phi Epsilon. 13: Yes. 14: Brit publ for child & yp. 15: 4524 Belclaire ave, Dallas Tx 75205.

JOHNSON, J PETER. b Ithaca NY 22 Mr 39. 4: M Teresa Lopez de Castro. 5: HofstraU 61-65 (Psych, Sociol) BA; LI Grad Lib Sch 67-68 (LS) MS; SUNY (Stony Brook) 69-9liberal Studies). 6: Sp. 7: Communications specialist USAF, Spain & Morocco 57-61; Hd circ dept C W Post Col Lib 66-67; Hd reader's serv SUNY (Farmingdale) 67-; Coord & instr Lib Wlshops SUNY (Farmingdale) Eve Div 68-. 9: Coun on Lib Tech (treas); NassauCoLA (finance off Exec Bd; finance chm Col & Univ Div). 14: Read serv, lib tech. 15: 51 Engelke ave, Huntington Sta NY 11746.

JOHNSON, JAMES (LEONARD). b Roswell NM 28 Je 17. 4: Leah Johnson. 5: East NM Col 41 (Eng) BA; UDenver 47 BS in LS. 6: Sp. 7: Tchr NM Pub Sch 36-47; Asst libn Southwestern Col 47-48; Asst libn NW Mo State Col 48-49, Libn 49-. 9: ALA; MoLA; MoTA; MoACRL. 10: Kiwanis; Alpha Beta Alpha; Danforth Assn. 14: Admin, ref. 15: Wells Lib NW Mo State Col, Maryville Mo 64468.

JOHNSON, JAMES P. b Flint Mich 3 O 29. 4: Hazel Long. 5: Ohio StateU 54-58 (Hist & Lit) BA 58; Rutgers 65-68 (LS) MA 68. 6: Fr, Ger. 7: Pfc USA-Personnel Serv Specialist 51-53; Lib asst Ohio StateU (Columbus) 54-58; Libn asst Dept of Agric Lib, Wash DC 60-61; Circ libn HowardU 61-65; Libn-trainee Brooklyn Pub Lib, NYC 65-67; Catlgr HowardU 67, Ref libn 68-. 10: HowardU Lib Staff Assn. 14: Ref. 15: 2821 Brentwood rd NE, Washington DC 20018.

JOHNSON, JANE (GAULT). b Union SC 28 S 35. 4: J Delane Johnson. 5: Mary Wash Col UVa 53-54; USoCar 54-56, 62-63, 65-66, 66-67, 68; Converse Col 56-57 (Mod Langs, Eng) AB; Wofford Col summer 54, 55; Queens Col (NY) summer 65; LSU summer 63-68 (LS) MS. 6: Sp, Fr. 7: Sp instr Spartanburg High Sch, Spartanburg SC 60-61; Asst libn Greenville Sr high Sch, Spartanburg SC 61-62; Libn Spartanburg Day Sch, Spartanburg SC 62-63; Libn fremont Elem Sch, Spartanburg SC 63-68; Sr libn Spartanburg Reg Campus USoCar 68-. 9: ALA; SELA; SCLA. 10: Delta Kappa Gamma; AAUW; Univ Woman's Club. 14: Tech serv. 15: 438 Mills ave, Spartanburg SC 29302.

JOHNSON, JOHN MILTON. b Rowland NC 9 Mr 34. 5: UNC 52-53, 55-58 (Hist) AB, 58-59 9educ) Certif, 59-67 MSLS. 07: Sgt (personnel specialist) USA, US 53-55; Asst ref libn UNC Lib (Chapel Hill) 59-63; Ref-doc libn NC StateU 63-67; Dir & libn Durham Tech Inst 67-. 9: SLA; NCLA (chm Recruiting); NC Commun ColLA (pres). 14: Ref, acquis. 15: Rte 7 Box 217, Durham NC 27707.

JOHNSON, JOSEPHINE (STURTEVANT). b Buckfield Me 23 Ap 09. 4: Alvin Johnson. 5: Simmons 27-31 (LS) BS. 6: Fr. 7: Ser catlgr Harvard Grad Sch of Bus 31-40; Libn Hamilton-Wenhom Reg Sch, Hamilton Mass 62-64; Catlgr Salem State Col Lib (Salem mass) 64-. 9: ALA; NELA; N Shore Lib Club. 10: Beverly Col Club. 14: Catlg. 15: 67 Canterbury rd, Waltham Ma 02154.

JOHNSON, JOSEPHINE ANN (ROACH). b Chicago. 4: Norman L Johnson. 5: St Mary's Col (Notre Dame Ind) 31-35 (Eng, Journalism) AB; Nazareth Col 56-58 MSLS. 7: Libn asst Virginia M Tutt Br Lib, S Bend Ind 38-40; Ref asst Louisville Free Pub Lib, Louisville Ky 44-57, Head of ref dept 57-63; Head Libn "Courier- Journal" & "Louisville Times," Louisville Ky 63-. 9: SLA (Newspaper Div chm 67-68, dir 68-69); SELA; KyLA (pres 61-62). 10: Louisville Lib Club. 14: Ref, info serv, admin. 15: Courier Journal Louisville Times Lib, Louisville Ky 40202.

JOHNSON, JOYCE (GRUHLER). b Gretna La 16 N 21. 4: Charles Davis Johnson. 5: LSU 38-41 (Eng Lit) BA, 41-42 BS in LS. 6: Lat, Sp, Fr, Ger. 7: Fellowship La Room LSU Lib 38-40; Fellowship Eng Dept LSU 41; Libn Sch of Engnr UTex 42-43; Ref libn UTulsa 43-44; Catlgr Fondren Lib So Methodist U 56-59; Libn Shadow Oaks Elem Sch 59-61; Reviser of Series catlg Rice U 62-. 10: Mu Sigma Rho; Pi Gamma Mu; Phi Kappa Pi. 14: Catlg. 15: 1615 Imperial Crown dr, Houston Tx 77043.

JOHNSON, JUDITH M. b Tacoma Wash 13 Mr 35. 5: UWash 61-65 (Hist). 7: News ed: "Tacoma Star", Tacoma Wash 51-54, "Times-Journal" Parkland Wash 54-55; Credit interviewer Lincoln Electric Co, Tacoma Wash 55-56; Tech libn Boeing Co Aerospace Div, Seattle 57-59; Mss specialist UWash Spec Collections 59-64; Acquis libn Boeing Co Com Airplane Group, Renton Wash 66-. 8: Del Discussion Gp Recorder, Wash State governor's Conf on Libs, Olympia Wash 67. 9: SLA. 12: Ed "Interface" Bull of SLA Pacific NW Chap. 13: Yes. 14: Lib systems, info dissem/retr systems. 15: 815 E Howe st, Seattle Wa 98102.

JOHNSON, JUDY LENORE. b Marshalltown Iowa 16 O 44. 5: Ft Hays Kan State Col 62-66 9eng) BA; Kan State Tchrs Col 66-67, summer 68 MLib. 7: Stud asst Forsyth Lib Ft Hays Kan State Col 62-66; Libn Summer Lab Sch, Hays Kan summers 65, 66, 67; Grad asst Kan State Tchrs Col Dept Libnship 66-67; Libn Hays High Sch, Hays Kan 67-. 9: ALA; KanLA; KanASchL; KanStateTA. 10: Phi Kappa Phi. 14: Sch libs, ref. 15: Box 82, Hays Ks 67601.

JOHNSON, JUNE BEVERLY (LOMBARD). b Galesburg Ill 10 O 30. 5: Pueblo Jr Col 48-50 (Educ) AA; Colo State Col 50-52 (Educ) BA; UDenver 55-60 (LS) MS. 6: Sp. 7: Tchr Portland Pub Schs, Portland Ore 52-54; Libn Iliff Sch of Theol 55-57; Tchr Aurora Pub Schs, Aurora Colo 57-59; Libn Lamar Jr Col 60-62; Libn Pueblo Pub Schs, Pueblo Colo 62-. 9: NEA; ColoEA; ColoASchL ; Pueblo EA. 14: Ref. 15: 1506 Horseshoe dr, Pueblo Co 81001.

JOHNSON, KARL BERNARD. b Marinette Wis 25 Mr 42. 4: Bette Boyd. 5: UAriz 60-64 (Educ) BA; Ariz State U 64-65; UDenver 65-67 (LS) MA. 7: Tchr Coolidge Elem Schs, coolidge Ariz 64, Libn 64-66; Libn W High Sch, Denver Colo 66-67, Dir IMC 67-68; Libn educ ref, Hayden Lib Ariz State U 68, Libn Ariz Collection 68-. 9: ALA; ArizStateLA. 10: Phi Delta Kappa; Comp of Mil Histns; Orders and Medals Soc of Amer; Orders and Medals Res Soc of Gt Brit. 14: Ariz & the West. 15: Arizona Collection Hayden Lib, Arizona State Univ, Tempe Az 85281.

JOHNSON, KATHRINE ELISABETH. b Duluth Minn 2 N 18. 5: Wayne U 37-42 (Geog, Geol) AB; UDenver 43-44 BSLS; Conn Col for Women 44 (Aero Engnr); UOslo 52 (Norway Orientation); UCal 60-62 (Engnr, LS); Foothill Jr Col 62 (Computer Tech) MIT 68 (Info Tech). 6: Norwegian, Fr, Ital. 7: Draftsman Willow Run Bomber Plant, Ypsilanti Mich 43; Libn United Aircraft Corp, E Hartford Conn 44-45; Head Libn sci & engnr div Stanford U Libs 45-52; Stud, consul, Scandinavia 52-53; Supv lib serv Sylvania Electronic Defense Lab, Mt View Cal 53-60; Supv lib serv Varian Associates, Palo Alto Cal 61-. 8: Lib consul (Marshall Plan) SNI, Oslo Norway, 52-53. 9: SLA (San Francisco Bay Reg Chap; Lib consul Com 60-, treas 61-62); ASIS; Fed for Internat Documentation. 10: AAAS; Sierra Club; Amer-Scand Foun; Wildenness Soc. 11: Marshall Fund Award for SNI proj in Norway, 52-53. 14: Lib admin, automation, lit searching. 15: Varian Assoc, 611 Hansen way, Palo Alto Ca 94303.

JOHNSON, KATHRYN ANN. b Twin Valley Minn 28 S 23. 5: UMinn(Duluth) 42-46 (Hist) BS. 7: Asst St Louis Co Hist Soc, Duluth Minn 44-46; Tchr of hist & soc studies Deer Creek High Sch, Deer Creek Minn 46-47; Tchr of hist & soc studies Ogilvie High Sch, Ogilvie Minn 47-48; Asst curator of mss Minn Hist Soc, St Paul 48-. 10: Minn Democratic-Farmer-Labor Party (var positions); Minn Hist Soc (Com to Study the Role of the Negro in Minn). 12: Comp with L M Kane "Manuscripts Collections in the Minnesota Historical Society" (55). 14: Catlg, political collections. 15: 23 So St Albans st, St Paul Mn 55105.

JOHNSON, KORDILLIA C(HRISTEEN). b Valley Springs SD Ap 12. 5: Augustana Col (Sioux Falls SD) 30-34 (Eng) BA; UWis 46-47 BLS; UIll 59-60 (LS) MS; UWis 67-68; UCLA 68 (Oral Hist Libnship). 6: Ger, Lat. 7: Tchr rural sch, Willow Lake SD 34-35; Tchr high sch Eng Sand Creek Cons Sch, Wessington SD 35-37; Tchr high sch Eng Glenham High Sch, Glenham SD 37-39; Tchr high sch Eng Ashton High Sch, Ashton SD 39-42; Tchr Code & Procedure Army Air Force Tech T C, Sioux Falls SD 42-45; Libn Augustana Col (Sioux Falls SD) 47-68; Div libn Soc Scis & Humanities, Spec collections libn Wis State U 68-. 9: ALA; SDLA (sec-treas 50-52, v-pres 52-54, pres 62-64); MPLA; WisLA; Wis Lib Sch Assn. 10: AAUW; SD Women's TV Coun; Soroptimist Club; SD Ornithological Union; Sioux Falls Audubon Group; Minnehaha Co (SD) Hist Soc; SW Wis Audubon Club; Oran Hist Assn. 13: Yes. 14: Rare bks, West Americana, catlg. 15: 885 Stonebridge #22, Platteville Wi 53818.

JOHNSON, LAVINIA (LOWERY). b Sterling Kan 28 F 18. 4: Keith V Johnson. 5: Sterling Col 36-38 Tchrs Certif; Knoxville Col 40-42 (Eng) BA; UWis 46-47 BLS. 6: Fr. 7: Lib asst US Army Spec Serv, Ft Leonard Wood Mo 43-45; Asst br libn Akron Pub Lib, Akron Ohio 47-48; Br libn Wayne Co Lib, River Rouge Mich 48-59; Libn II Detroit Pub Lib 62-63; Med libn VA Hosp, Allen Pk Mich 63-. 9: MichLA; Detroit Med Libns; ALA. 10: Alpha Kappa Mu; Knoxville Col Alumni Assn. 14: Ref, church libs. 15: 1890 S Electric, Detroit Mi 48217.

JOHNSON, LEE ZEUNERT. b Great Falls Mont 1 Jl 30. 4: Marlene Fuchs. 5: Mont State U 48-52 (Eng) BA; Syracuse 54-55 (Journalism) MS, 5-57, 63 (Communications) PhD. 6: Ger. 7: Admin & pub rel USAF (1st Lt) 52-54; (Capt) USAF Res currently; Asst ed sect Com on Publ, The First Church of Christ Scientist, Boston 57-62; Archivist, The First Church of Christ Scientist, Boston 62-. 9: Soc of Amer Arch; ARMA. 10: Appalachian Mountain Club; Wilderness Soc. 13: Yes. 14: Research, ref, archival. 15: 107 Falmouth st, Boston Ma 02115.

JOHNSON, LEONARD LEE. b Forsyth Co NC 5 Jl 31. 4: Mary Frances Kennon Johnson. 5: Appalachian State Tchrs Col 50-54 (Soc Studies) BS, 54-55 (LS) MA; UIll 56; Duke 61. 7: Grad asst Appalachian State Tchrs Col 54-55; Coordinator of libs High Point Pub Schs, High Point NC 55-57, 58-59; (Pfc) US Army 4th Armored Div 57-58; Lib supv NC Dept Pub Instr, Raleigh NC 59-61; Dir of Libs Greensboro Pub Schs, Greensboro NC 61-. 8: Consul Sch Lib Wk Conf at LSU summer 64; Consul NC Advancement Sch Lib, Winston- Salem NC 64-65; NDEA Lib Educ Consul US Off of Educ 65; Consul NDEA Insts; Appalachian U 66, East Car U 65, LSU 66, 68, USoCar 68; Tchr Lib Sci UNC (Greensboro) 62, 64, 65. 9: NEA; ALA-AASchL (Instr Materials Com chm 68-69); SELA; NCLA (Chm Membship Com 62, Sch Lib sect, exhib chm 63, treas 65-67); NCASchL (chm Standards Com 65-67); NCEA. 10: Nat Conf of Christians & Jews, Educ chm; Greensboro Lib Club; YMCA; Treas BenL Smith Mem Fund, Inc 64-69. 12: Guest ed "North Carolina Libraries ;" Bibliog : "B ooks for Greensboro Students" (63); "Centralized Processing and Cataloging: An Outlined, Greensboro Public Schools" (67). 13: Yes. 14: Sch lib supv. 15: 712 N Eugene st, Greensboro NC 27401.

JOHNSON, LEONARD R(OBERT). b Los Angeles Cal 2 Ja 25. 4: Eleanor Riley. 5: USoCal 46-49 (Journalism) AB; Rutgers 55-57 MLS. 6: Fr. 7: Acquis libn Wesleyan U (Middletown Conn) 57-60; Assoc libn State U Col (New Paltz NY) 60-63; Libn Suffolk Co Commun Col 63-. 9: ALA. 10: AAUP. 15: P O Box 181, Shoreham NY 11786.

JOHNSON, LINDA (LEE). b Kansas City Mo 9 F 40. 4: John Eric Johnson. 5: Kan StateU 58-61 (Eng) BA, 61-63 (Eng) MA; UMinn 66-67 (LS) MA. 7: Grad asst Kan StateU 61-63; Tchr Army Educ Ctr, Maine, Germany 63-64; Tchr Shawnee Mission High Sch, Prairie Village Kan 64-66; Tchr Title V Program, Minneapolis 66-67; Libn S F Parson Lib noIllU 67-. 14: Juv lit, educ media, Afro-Amer bibliog. 15: 303 Bush, DeKalb Il 60115.

JOHNSON, LOUISE M (SKUTEZKY). b Vienna Austria 9 Ag 23. 4: Gerald M Johnson. 5: McGill 41-43 (Fr) BA (Honors), 43-44 BLS. 6: Fr, Ger. 7: Asst libn Toronto Pub Lib bus tech ref dept, Toronto Can 44-46; Libn Aluminium Labs Ltd Hd off, Montreal 46-47, Chief libn 47-48; Ref dept hd McGill (Ste Anne de Bellevue) 68-. 9: SLA. 10: African Video Society of Amer; Saintpaulia Intl; African Violet Society of Can; McGillU Lib Staff Amer; Pointe Claire Aquatic Club; Alpha Omicron Pi. 14: Admin, ref in spec subj field, govt docs, pamphlet materials. 15: PO Box 107, Hudson Heights Que Can.

JOHNSON, LUCY C (TRENT). b Hinton WVa 11 S 07. 5: Frelinghuysen U 32-33 (Embalming) Diploma; Howard U 31, 43-45 (Hist) AB; Catholic U 45-49 BSLS; NYU 50-52 (Ed & Voc Guidance) AM; Columbia spring 62, summer 63 (LS). 6: Lat, Fr, Sp. 7: Circ asst Howard U 45-49, 50-52, Asst supv 49-50; Catlgr LC 52; Ref libn Brooklyn Pub Lib 52; Br libn Norfolk (Va) Pub Lib 53-54; Libn in chg Cardoza High Sch, Wash DC 54-55; Ref asst Amer U Grad Sch Lib 55-56; Catlgr in chg Dunbarton Col 56-57; Asst libn Sch of Soc Wk Catholic U 56-57; Ya libn Queens Borough Pub Lib, Jamaica NY 57-58; Ya ref libn Mt Vernon (NY) Pub Lib 58; Catlgr NY State Downstate Med Center (Brooklyn) 58-59; Catlgr Hunter Col 59-60; Libn in chg Brentwood High Sch, Brentwood NY 60-62; Libn in chg Hofstra Col Brentwood Ext even 60-62; Libn in chg Central Islip Sum High Sch, Central Islip NY 62; Ref libn E Orange (NJ) Pub Lib 62-63; Catlgr, archivist, & bibliog Columbia U Union Theol Sem Missionary Research Lib 63-64; Catlgr summer 62; Libn St Clare's Hosp Nursing Sch, NYC even 62-65; Wash DC pub schs 65-67; Catlgr Dominican Col Catholic U 68. 8: Lincensed in NY & NJ as Prof Libn, Sch Libn & Guid ance Coun, in Wash DC as an embalmer & tchr-libn. 9: ALA; DCLA (Memship Com 67-69, Recruitment Task Force 66-69); NEA; DCEA. 10: Women's Nat Bk Assn; Red Cross; YWCA ; NAACP; Amer Legion Aux; Assn for Study of Negro Life & Hist; Bus & Prof Women's Club. 13: Yes. 14: Ref, catlg, spec libs; personnel admin. 15: PO Box 3274, Wash DC 20010.

JOHNSON, M JEANINE. b Flint Mich 29 Ap 37. 5: UMich 57-59 (Sociol) BA, 59-60 MALS. 7: Libn Chicago Pub Lib 60-63; Libn Flint Pub Lib, Flint Mich 63-67; Libn UMich Law Lib (Ann Arbor) 67-. 14: Ref, govt docs. 15: 400 Maynard st #203, Ann Arbor Mi 48108.

JOHNSON, MADELEINE CLARK. b Brooklyn NY 26 D 24. 4: William V Johnson. 5: Smith 41-45 (Eng) BA; Rutgers 60-63 MLS. 6: Fr. 7: Sec ed asst Odyssey Press, NYC 46-47; Clerical Columbia U 48-49; Sec fund-raiser Manhattanville Neighborhood Center, NYC 49-51; Libn Westfield Pub Lib, Westfield NJ 60-62; Libn Vail-Deane Sch, Elizabeth NJ 63-65; Libn Campus Sch Newark State Col. 8: Trustee, Mountainside Free Pub Lib, Mountainside NJ 65-. 9: NJSchLA; NJ Assn Indep Schs (pres Lib Div 64-65); NJLA; ALA. 14: Child libs. 15: 32 Bayberry lane, Mountainside Nj 07092.

JOHNSON, MAE S (SHIVERS). b Birmingham Ala 2 Ja 09. 4: Walter E Johnson. 5: Leland col 30-39 (Eng) AB; AtlantaU 42-43 BSLS; UMich summers 57-59 MALS. 6: Fr. 7: Libn Leland Col 30-42; Circ libn Talladega Col 44-45; Chief libn Benedict Col (SC) 45-. 08. Consul for Tchr-Libnship courses Allen-Benedict 50; Chm Bk Review Com; Mem bldg com for new lib Benedict Col 68-. 9: NEA; ALA; SCLA; SELA. 10: YWCA; Delta Sigma Theta. 14: Spec collections. 15: 5117 Farrow rd, Columbia SC 29203.

JOHNSON, MARILYN K. b Rutland Vt 18 F 28. 5: Wellesley 45-49 (Chem) BA. 7: Tchr Greenwood Sch, Ruxton Md 49-50; Supv info serv Shell Development Co, Emeryville Cal 50-. 9: SLA (var nat & loc activities); ASIS; ACS; CalLA. 14: Sci ref. 15: 740 Oakland ave, Oakland Ca 94611.

JOHNSON, MARION (MIDDLETON). b Greensboro NC 30 O 22. 4: Junius Edgar Johnson Jr. 5: Woman's Col of UNC 39-43 (Hist) BA; UNC 43-44 BSLS. 7: Ref asst NY Pub Lib 44; Libn Lee Co Lib, Sanford NC 45-47; Libn Stanly Co Pub Lib, Albemarle NC 48-54; Dir NC State Lib Processing Center, Raleigh NC 60-. 9: NCLA (v-pres 54-55). 10: PTA. 12: "NC State Library Processing Center Manual of Procedures" (61). 14: Tech serv. 15: 1303 Lorimer rd, Raleigh NC 27606.

JOHNSON, MARION EILEEN (SEARLE). b Vancouver BC Can. 4: Stephen Johnson. 5: UBC 44-48 (Eng, Ger) BA; Toronto 57-58 BLS. 6: Ger, Fr. 7: Can Broadcasting Corp,

Vancouver BC 49-57; Libn I gen ref UBC Lib 58-60, Libn II sci div 60-62; Libn Forest Products Lab Can Dept of Fisherics & Forestry, Vancouver BC 63-. 9: CanLA; SLA; PNLA. 10: Univ Women's Club; Beta Phi Mu. 14: Ref. 15: 4571 W Third ave, Vancouver 8 BC Can.

JOHNSON, MARJORIE (J). b Pittsburgh 12 Mr 27. 4: Ross H Johnson. 5: UPittsburgh 45-49 (Bus Admin) BS; Catholic U 59-60 MS in LS; George Washington U 60-61 (Lang); Goucher 63-64 (Educ); U Ill 69- (Communications). 06: Ger. 7: Ref libn DC Lib 60-61; Music ref libn Carnegie Lib of Pittsburgh 61-62; Ref libn Baltimore Jr Col 62-63; Head Libn Md State Health Dept, Baltimore 63-64; Libn-in-chg Lower Merion Lib Assn Processing Center, Bryn Mawr Penn 65-66; Hd libn Cabrini Col 66-68. 9: ALA; IllLA. 10: Beta Phi Mu, LWV, Jr League, AAUW. 14: Admin. 15: 7 Regent ct, Champaign Il 61820.

JOHNSON, MARJORIE JANE. b New Lisbon Ind 23 O 24. 5: Ball State U 52-59 (Eng) BA; UIll 59-62 MLS. 6: Fr. 7: Chief operator New Lisbon Telephone Co, New Lisbon Ind 42-48; Gen asst New Castle Pub Lib 48-56; Ref catlgr New Castle Pub Lib, New Castle Ind 56-63, Dir 63-. 9: ALA; IndLA (chm 62-63, sec 65- 66; Program Chm Ref Sect 61-62); Ohio Valley Tech Serv Libns (treas 64-65). 10: Altrusa Intl Bus & Prof Women's Club; First Nighter's; Henry Co Sch for Retarded Child. 14: Pub lib admin. 15: 1313 Haue, New Castle In 47362.

JOHNSON, MARY ELIZABETH. b Warsaw Ind 3 My 16. 5: Butler U 33-34, 35-37 (Math) AB; Franklin Col 34-35; Purdue summers 39-41, 44, 45 (Educ) MS; IndU summers 52, 53; Columbia 59-60 MSLS. 7: Math & Eng tchr & libn Batesville High Sch, Batesville Ind 37-39; High sch libn & math tchr Marion High Sch, Marion Ind 39-49; Ref dept Denver Pub Lib summer 46; Sch libn & Asst Prof Burris Lab Sch Ball State U 49-. 8: Consul elem libs -67. 9: NEA; ALA; IndLA; IndSchLA (Sec, chm &/or mem 2 coms 50-63); Ind State TA; EISLA. 10: Kappa Delta Pi. 13: Yes. 14: Elem & high sch libs, child lit, lib educ. 15: 224-1/2 N Talley, Muncie In 47303.

JOHNSON, MARY FRANCES (KENNON). b Columbia SC 1 N 28. 4: Leonard Lee Johnson. 5: Wesleyan Col (Macon Ga) 45-46; USoCar 46-49 (Eng) ABEd (magna cum laude); UNC (Chapel Hill) summers 50-54 MSL. 6: Sp, Fr. 7: Tch-libn Forsyth Co Pub Schs, Winston-Salem NC 49-50; Elem sch libn Charlotte Pub Schs, Charlotte NC 50-54; Sch lib specialist (asst supv) Baltimore City Schs 54-56; Assoc supv Sch Lib Serv State Dept Pub Instr Raleigh NC 56-61; Dir Sch Lib Devel Project ALA, Chicago 61-62; Instr (Lib Educ) UNC (Greensboro) 62-66, Asst Prof 66-. 8: US Off of Educ, Wash DC: Consul conf on evaluating sch lib development programs ESEA Title II 68, Evaluator applications for NDEA grants 65; Mem Exec Adv Coun for Educ Media Selection Ctrs Project Nat Book Com Inc, 68-; NC Governor's Study Commsn on NC Pub Sch Syst; mem adv com on Materials & Tools of Instr, Chm subcom on Educ Media Serv; Consul wk conf on revision of secondary sch lib standards SoAssn Cols & Schs, Atlanta 65; Consul & speaker Knapp Sch Libs Project, Austin Tex 66; Consul & speaker Ga State Dept of Educ, Atlanta 66. 9: ALA (Ed Com: mem 63-69, chm 65-69; Publ Bd 66-69); -AASchL (Bd Dir 66-68; Adv Coun for Knapp Sch Libs Project 62-64; chm Publ Com 63-64; Nominating Com; chm 63, mem 66); -CSD; -LAD; -LED (Nominating Com 64; Tchrs Sect Nominating Com 69); NEA (DAVI); ASCD; SELA (Lib Educ Com 66-; Nomin educ Com 66-; Nominating Com 64); NCLA; NCEA; NCASchL. 10: AAUP; Phi Beta Kappa. 12: Co-auth "Planning School Library Development" (62); Ed "School Libraries" (column in "Wilson Library Bulletin" 60-63); Mem ed bd "North Carolina Libraries" (63-). 13: Yes. 14: Sch libs & libnship, reading interests & guidance, child lit & materials, ya lit & materials, a-v materials, sch lib supv. 15: 109 Falkener dr, Greensboro NC 27410.

JOHNSON, MARYELISABETH (SIMS). b Columbus Ohio. 4: Edward A Johnson. 5: Ohio wesleyanU 52-53; Ohio StateU 53-55 (Eng) BA; Mexico City Col 53; UMadrid (Spain) 51; UCal (Berkeley) 59 MLS; San Francisco State Col 60 MLS. 7: Asst libn Columbus Pub Lib, Columbus Ohio 55-58; Asst libn San Francisco Pub Lib 59; Libn I-II San Francisco State Col 60-. 9: CalLA; CalTA; Amer Fed Tchrs. 14: Catlg, art, other creative arts publ. 15: 765 San Luis rd, Berkeley Ca 94707.

JOHNSON, (MARY) MALINDA. b Chattanooga Tenn 11 F 44. 5: UChattanooga 62-66 (Soc Sci) BS; Emory 66-68 (LS) MLn. 6: Sp, Fr. 7: Circ asst EmoryU 66-68, Asst catlgr Law Lib 68; Asst catlgr Ga Inst of Tech 68-. 8: Law Libnship Inst UCal (Berkeley) 68. 9: ALA; SLA; GaEA; SELA. 14: Catlg. 15: 12 28 Woodland ave NE apt 5, Atlanta Ga 30324.

JOHNSON, MATA-MARIE HENRIETTA (EGAN). b Kankakee Ill 29 Ja 33. 4: Robert A Johnson. 5: Ill State U 50-53 (Eng) BS; Olivet Nazarene Col 55; UIll summers 57-60, correspondence 61-62 MS in LS; Rockford Col summer 63; UNev 65, 66, summer 67. 6: Fr, Sp. 7: Tchr & libn Central High Sch, Clifton Ill 53-54; Tchr, Ill; Kankakee Co 54-55, Momence 55-59; Elem sch libn, Rockford Ill 59-61, Elem sch libn & libn of prof curriculum 62-64; Asst libn Reno High Sch, Reno Nev 64-65; Libn Bishop Manogue High Sch, Reno Nev 66-67; Asst libn & lib sci instr Zimmerman Lib Metcalf Sch Ill State U 67-. 9: ALA; NEA; IllLA; MPLA; IllASchL; McLeanCoLA; IllEA. 10: PTA; Beta Phi Mu; UIll Lib Sch Assn. 14: Sch libs. 15: 1105 Clinton blvd, Bloomington Il 61701.

JOHNSON, MAURINE A. b Bluffton Ohio. 4: John J Johnson. 5: Miami U (Oxford Ohio) 32 AB; West Res 33 BS in LS, 33-35 MA. 7: Asst pub serv dept West Res U 35-37, Head pub serv dept 37-39; Act libn Central Wash Col 39-40, Asst libn 40-42; Asst ref dept UCal Lib (Berkeley) 42-46, Head ref dept 46; Libn Wilbur Jr High Sch, Palo Alto Cal 55-. 9: NEA; Cal Tchrs Assn; Sch Lib Assn Cal. 10: Fair Play Coun, Palo Alto Cal. 14: Sch & univ libs. 15: Wilbur Jr High Sch 480 E Meadow dr, Palo Alto Ca 94306.

JOHNSON, MERLIE (DAMERAU). b Fair Water Wis. 4: Earl G Johnson. 5: Lawrence U 22-26 (Eng) AB (cum laude); UIll 30-31 MS in LS. 6: Ger. 7: Tchr-libn Sturgeon Bay High Sch, Sturgeon Bay Wis 26-28; Libn Boyd Jr High Sch, Knoxville Tenn 28-30; Libn Hibbing High Sch & Jr Col, Hibbing Minn 31-32; Libn Narimasu High Sch & Jr High Sch, Tokyo 59, 60; Libn New Canaan High Sch, New Canaan Conn 55-56; Libn Norwalk State Tech Col, Norwalk Conn 62-. 14: Catlg, bk sel, ref. 15: 196 Mariomi rd, New Canaan Ct 06840.

JOHNSON, MILDRED FONTAINE. b Madison Ind 17 F 05. 5: Randolph-Macon 23-27 (Lat) AB; ULouisville 27-28; UMich 34-35 ABLS. 6: Lat, Ger. 7: Stud in train class Louisville Free Pub Lib, Louisville Ky 28, Temp asst ref dept 28; Ref libn Randolph-Macon Woman's Col 29-. 9: ALA-ACRL; SELA; Bibliog Soc UVa; VaLA (Var offs & chm 2 coms). 10: Woman's Club; LWV; Alumnae Assn of Randolph-Macon Woman's Col; AAUW; Colonial Dames; Phi Beta Kappa. 14: Ref, period. 15: Lipscomb Lib Randolph-Macon Woman's Col, Lynchburg Va 24504.

JOHNSON, MILDRED YOUNG. b Ala 24 S 12. 4: Malcolm Johnson. 05: Huntingdon Col 29-33 (Biol, Eng) AB; UNC 37-39 AB in LS. 7: Pub sch libn, NC 37-41; Various positions Army Lib Serv, US Army 41-47; Chief Army Lib Serv US Army, Wash DC 47-51; Exec asst Brooklyn Pub Lib 51-53, Asst chief libn 53-56; Asst dean & Assoc Prof Grad Sch Lib Serv Rutgers U 56-61; Asst chief libn Queens Borough Pub Lib, Jamaica NY 61-64; Asst dean Grad Sch Lib Serv Rutgers U 64-. 8: Bk sel consul, Franklin Bk Program, NYC 52-56. 9: ALA (Coun; mem var coms; chm Armed Serv Sect); AALS; NJLA (var coms); NYLA (var coms). 13: Yes. 14: Admin, Systs analysis. 15: 10 Landing Lane, New Brunswick Nj 08901.

JOHNSON, MINNIE (REDMOND) BOWLES. b Clarksville Tenn 27 F 11. 4: E Milton Johnson. 5: Fisk U 28-32 (LS) BA; Atlanta 43-44 BLS; Chicago 44-45 (LS) MA. 7: Tchr Memphis City Schs, Memphis Tenn 33-37; Libn Manual Train Sch, Bordentown NJ 37-43; Instr Sch of Lib Serv Atlanta U 45-46; Asst libn Fisk U 46-49, 50-52, Act libn 49-50; Head Libn Hampton Inst 52-58; Libn (Crane Br Ill Tchrs Col South) WCte Chicago State Col 58-. 8: Dir Hampton Book Fair 56-58. 9: ALA-ACRL (Com on Standards for Col Libs); IllLA. 10: AAUP; Ch icago Lib Club. 13: Yes. 14: Ref, col lib admin. 15: 501 E 32nd st, apt 1915, Chicago Il 60616.

JOHNSON, NAN. b West Point Ga 31 My 43. 5: Huntingdon Col 61-65 (Hist) BA; Simmons 65-66 (LS) MS. 6: Fr, Sp. 7: Lib asst Huntingdon Col 63-65; Lib asst Fed Res Bank of boston 65-66; Catlgr Fletcher Sch of Law & Diplomacy Tufts U 66-. 9: SLA. 14: Catlg. 15: 186 Gardner st apt 21-. Arlington Ma 02174.

JOHNSON, NANCY L(EE). b Punxsutawney Penn 26 Ja 38. 5: Clarion State Col 56-60 (LS) BS Ed; Drexel 61-66 MSLS. 7: Libn: Red Lion Schs, Red Lion Penn 60-61, Scotland Sch for Veterans Child, Sctoand Penn 61-66, Glenrock Schs, Glenrock Wyo 66-. 9: ALA; NEA; WyoEA; WyoLA. 14: Sch libs. 15: Box 395, Glenrock Wy 82637.

JOHNSON, NOEL WILLIAM. b Reno Nev 23 N 25. 5: UNev 46-49 (Econ) BA, 50-51 (Hist); UCal 53-54 BLS. 7: Yeoman 2/c US Navy, 44-46; Research analytic spec Dept of Defense, Arlington Va 51-53; Ref libn Cal State Lib 54-55,

Catlgr 55-60; Catlgr UWash Lib 60-61; Air U Lib: Catlgr 61-63, Asst chief tech serv 63-65, Chief tech serv 65-69; Chief systems libn UCalgary Lib 69-67; Coord systs planning & development UAlta Lib 67-69. 9: ALA-ACRL; -ISAD; -LAD; -RTSD. 10: US Naval Inst; Phi Kappa Phi; Phi Alpha Theta. 13: Yes. 14: Catlg, admin, systs automation. 15: Univ of Calgary Lib, Calgary 44 Alta Can.

JOHNSON, NORMA J(OSEPHINE). b Laurel Neb 15 Mr 10. 5: Hamline U 28-32 (Chem) BS; UMinn summers 36-42 (LS) BS. 7: Sci & math tchr pub high sch, Balaton Minn 32-39; Sci & Eng tchr pub high sch, Staples Minn 39-42; Sch libn pub schs, Jackson Minn 42-43; Chem libn Ind U 43-44; Asst libn Gen Mills Inc, Minneapolis 44-48; Tech libn The Pillsbury Co, Minneapolis 48-. 9: SLA (pres Minn Chap 54-55). 14: Ref. 15: 623 Aldine st, St Paul Mn 55104.

JOHNSON, NORMA W. b Frankfort Ky 4 S 34. 4: Charles Martin Johnson. 5: Murray State Col 52. 7: Dir of Volunteer Serv, ColumbiaU; Dir of Volunteer Servs-Mental Health , Ky Dept of Mental Health, Frankfort Ky 67-69, Dir of Med & Patient Libs 69. 8: Coun rep Nat Found March of Dimes 66-67. 9: ALA,-ALTA (chm Exhibits com 66-67, coun admin 66-67, bd dirs 66-69, Reg dir, reg 3); Ky Lib Trustee Assn (pres 63-65, Bd dirs 65-67); SEast Lib Trustee Assn (Sec 6 4-66, chm 68-70); Friends of Ky Libs (Bd of Dirs 62-67). 10: United Fund Bd of Dirs; Jr League; Girl Scout Leader; PTA; Mayfield- Graves Co Lib Bd; Adv Coun Urban Renewal and Housing Development; PTA Prof Adv Bd. 11: Outstanding Ky Lib Trustee 65, United Fund Appreciation Award 66. 14: Trustees. 15: 507 Central ave, Mayfield Ky 42066.

JOHNSON, (JANET) PAMELA (ROGERS). b Cleburne Tex 25 My 43. 4: William Charles Johnson. 5: NTex StateU 61-65 (LS) BA, 67-69 MLS; Baylor 66-67. 7: Govt docs libn Ft Worth Pub Lib 65; Asst ser libn Baylor (Waco) 65-67; Lib clerk Temple High Sch, Temple Tex 68; Tchr-libn Troy High Sch, Troy Tex 68-. 9: TexLA; TexStateTA (corr sec). 15: 3701 Arthur lane, Temple Tx 76501.

JOHNSON, PETER ALBERT. b Astoria Ore 5 Jl 29. 4: Virginia Curtis. 5: Deep Springs col 46-48; StanfordU 48-50 (Pol Sci) BA; UMinn 50-52 (Scandinavian Area Studies) MA; UOslo (Norway) 52-53 (Sociol); UOre 55-58 (Sociol), 59-60; UCal 64-66 MLS. 6: Norwegian, Danish, Swedish, Fr. 7: Sociol instr AmericanU 59; Asst Prof of sociol Linfield Col 60-65; Asst Prof of sociol Luther Col 65-66; Ref libn StanfordU 66-67, Asst libn 67-. 9: CalLA. 13: Yes. 14: Admin, ref. 15: 3363 Kipling st, Palo Alto Ca 94306.

JOHNSON, RALPH WALTER. b Covina Cal 17 N 28. 5: UCLA 46-50 (Hist) BA; Cal 50-52 (Hist) MA; Rutgers 57-58 MLS. 7: Clerk (Sp-3) Chief of Staff Hq 8th Army, Seoul Korea 56-57; Spec collections libn UCLA Lib 58-64, Spec collections catlgr 64-67; Catlgr shared catlg div 67-68; Asst Head catlg sept UCLA Lib 68-. 9:ALA; CalLA; SoCal Tech Processes Gp. 10: New Eng Hist Genealogical Soc; So Cal Genealogical Soc. 14: Catlg. 15: 4546 W 16th pl, Los Angeles Ca 90019.

JOHNSON, RICHARD COLLES. b Petoskey Mich 7 S 39. 5: Yale 57-61 (Eng) BA; UMich 62-63 (LS) MA; Northwestern 63-66 (Eng) MA. 7: Asst to curator Collection of Amer Lit Yale U Lib 61-62; Bibliog of Amer Lit Newberry Lib, Chicago 63-68, Edward E Ayer Bibliog of Amer history & lit 68-. 8: Assoc bibliog, Melville ed proj, Chicago 65-. 10: Caxton Club (Chicago); Yale Club of Chicago; Phi Kappa Phi. 14: Acquis & ref in Amer lit & hist, rare bks. 15: Newberry Lib 60 W Walton st, Chicago Il 60610.

JOHNSON, RICHARD DAVID. b Cleveland Ohio 10 Je 27. 4: Harriett Herzog. 5: Yale 46-49 (Amer Studies) BA; U Chicago 49-50 (Internat Rel) MA, 55-57 (LS) MA. 6: Fr, Ger, Sp. 7: (Sgt) AG Sect Hq 3d Inf Div US Army, Korea 52-54; Research asst market research dept Griswold-Eshelman Co, Cleveland 54-55; Libn Nat Opinion Research Center UChicago 56-57; Stanford U Libs: Soc sci libn Stanford U Libs 57-59, Sr libn catlg div 59-60, 61-62, Admin asst to dir 60-61, Chief libn acquis div 62-64, Chief libn Undergrad Lib Proj 64-67, Chief tech serv libn 67-68; Libn Honnold Lib, Claremont Col 68-. 8: Mem Adv Coun on Educ for Libnship, UCal 68-; Reviewer in Amer hist "Choice". 9: ALA; SLA; ASIS; CalLA (chm No Div Col, Univ & Research Libs Sect 64). 10: Beta Phi Mu. 11: H W Wilson Co Lib Period Award 68. 12: Ed "Stanford Library Bulletin" (59-61); Ed "California Librarian" (66-68). 13: Yes. 14: Tech serv, lib automation. 15: 571 Northwestern dr, Claremont Ca 91711.

JOHNSON, RICHARD LINCOLN. b Alhambra Cal 11 Jl 35. 4: Jaqualyn Schneider. 5: Fullerton Jr Col 53-54 (Art); Pasadena City Col 55-56 (Art) AA; UCLA 56-58, 59-60 (Art) AB; USoCal 65-66 MSLS. 7: Tank Driver USA, Ft Ord, Ft Knox 58-59; Art tchr Montebello Unified Sch Dist, Montebello Cal 60-65; Asst libn Grossmont Col 66-. 9: ALA; CalTA; CalLA. 10: War Resisters League; ACLU; Ctr for the Study of Democ Institutions; Fac Adv, Open Forum Club; Fac Adv, Focus Newspaper. 14: Catlg, acquis. 15: 5750 Amaya dr apt 18, La Mesa Ca 52041.

JOHNSON, RICHARD WILLIAM. b Burlington Iowa 18 Ag 24. 5: State U Iowa 45-48 (Eng) BA, 50-51 (Eng); Columbia 51-52 MS in LS. 6: Fr. 7: Tchr Monticello High Sch, Monticello Iowa 48-50; Circ libn Iowa State Col 52-55; Asst circ libn Washington U (St Louis) 55-59; Asst circ libn Columbia U 59-61; Acquis libn Brooklyn Col 61-. 9: NY Tech Serv Libns; Lib Assn City U NY; NY Lib Club. 10: Phi Beta Kappa. 11: Roberts Fellowship, Columbia U. 14: Acquis, ref. 15: 16 D 333 E 14th st, New York, Ny 10003.

JOHNSON, ROBERT KELLOGG. b Grand Rapids Mich 27 Jl 13. 4: Loretta Franks Johnson. 5: UMich 32, 34; N Mont Col 32-34; UMont 35-37 (Modern Langs) AB; UWash 37-38 (LS) BAL; UIll summers 40, 41 & 46 (LS) MS; UIll 48-52 (LS) PhD. 6: Fr. 7: Ref asst Lib Assn of Portland, Portland Ore summer 38; Asst libn & Instr in Fr Pacific U 38-39, Act libn & Instr in Lib Sci 39-40; Head Libn & Instr in Lib Sci Central Col (Fayette Mo) 40-42; Payroll auditor Gen Motors Corp, Detroit 42-43; Pharmacist's Mate 2/c & Med Lab Tech US Navy, US 43-44; Communications off (Ltjg) US Navy, Pacific Theatre 42-43; Head Libn & Assoc Prof of Lib Sci Pacific U 46-48; Bibliog acquis dept UIll 48-50; Catlgr UIll(Urbana) 50-52; Chief catlg br Air U Lib 52-53, Chief tech serv div 53-57, Chief acquis br 57-59, Chief circ br 59; Asst Dir of Libs & Prof of Lib Sci Drexel Inst of Tech 59-62; Dir of Libs & Prof of Lib Sci 62-64, Univ Libn & Prof of Lib Sci UAriz 64-. 8: Lib consul Penn-NJ-Del Metrop Projs Inc (Penjerdel), Phila 61-64; Lib Coun of Metrop Phila 63-64; Consul: Harcum Jr Col 61-63, Nat Assn on Standard Med Vocabulary 61-, Media Free Pub Lib Media Penn 59-60, Macalester Col 57, Tucson Pub Lib 65; Com on Careers in Soc Wk Delaware Co Penn 62-64; Com on Jr Cols in Phila Metrop Area 62-63; Lib Bd Media (Penn) Free Lib 59-60; Mem Ad Hoc Com on Bibliog & Info Serv on Latin Amer 68; Mem, Ariz Bd Lib Examiners 64. 09: ALA (Bd Dir Exhibits Round Table 62-65);9com XXX Latin Amer 68; Mem, Ariz Bd Lib Examiners 64. 9: ALA (Bd dir exhibits Round Table 62-65);-LED (Com on Revision of Study Grants 60-61);-RTSD (chm &/or mem 2 coms 62-65);-ACRL (chm &/or mem 2 coms 58-64);-LAD (chm & mem LOMS 64-65); Northwest Col Libs (chm 41-42); OreLA (chm mem Com & Exec Bd 48-49); PennLA (Asst chm & chm Exhibits 61-64, Exec Bd 62-64); Ariz State LA (chm &/or mem 3 coms 64-66, Exec Bd 65-66, v-pres 67-68, pres 68-69); Sem Acquis of Latin Amer Lib Materials (Constit & Bylaws Com 68-). 10: Melvil Dui Marching & Chowder Assn (NY); Philobiblon Club (Phila); Ariz Hist Conf Ann Conf Com 64-. 12: Ed Bd "MOLA Quarterly" (42-43); "Air University Library Study in Selected Military Educational Institutions" (56); "Publicity for the University Library" (57); "Characteristics of Libraries in Selected Higher Military Educational Institutions in the US," PhD diss (57). 13: Yes. 14: Admin, personnel, budget, spec collections, rare bks. 15: Univ of Arizona Lib, Tucson Az 85716.

JOHNSON, ROBERT O'NEILL. b Hutchinson Kan 17 Mr 35. 4: Nina Sackett. 5: UKan 53-57, 62-63 (Composition) BMus; UIll 63-65 (LS) MS. 6: Fr, Ger. 7: Personnel specialist (Sp/4) US Army; Grad asst circ dept UIll Lib (Urbana) 64-65; Mus libn SyracuseU 65-68; Mus libn Col Conservatory of Mus UCincinnati 68-. 9: MusLA (chm NY State Chap 66-68). 10: Phi Mu Alpha Sinfonia. 13: Yes. 14: Mus bibliog, mus lib admin. 15: Music Lib 101 Emery Hall Univ of Cincinnati, Cincinnati Oh 45221.

JOHNSON, ROGER MAE. b Birmingham Ala 29 Je 20. 5: Clark Col 50-54 (Sociol); West res 55-57 MSLS. 7: Lib page Central High Sch, Cleveland Ohio 37-39; Asst tchr mod dance Karamu House, Cleveland Ohio 40-43; Dancer: Carmen Jones Co (road co), NY 43-47, Inside USA Co (road co) 49-50; Dance instr Clark Col 51-53; Child libn Cleveland Pub Lib, Cleveland Ohio 54-68; Lib consul (serv to the handicapped) State Lib of Ohio 68-. 9: ALA; OhioLA. 12: Introduction to "Black on Black" (68). 14: Pub lib wk with disadvantaged handicapped. 15: State Lib of Ohio Columbus Oh 43215.

JOHNSON, ROSS S. b Ashtabula Ohio 21 N 17. 4: Elizabeth Blackmore. 5: OhioU 37-41 9hist) AB; Ohio State U 47-49 (Hist) MA; Case-West Res 49-50 (LS) MS. 7: Capt Army Air Corps Supply 41-46; Tchr Lorain Pub Sch, Lorain Ohio 46-47; Catlgr circ Ohio State U (Columbus) 50-54; Libn Heidelberg

Col 54-58; Loan serv libn & asst libn for reader serv Ball State U 58-. 9: ALA; IndLA. 10: AAUP. 15: 607 Shellbark rd, Muncie In 47304.

JOHNSON, ROY S C. b Guyana 26 Ja 26. 4: Brenda S Guerra. 5: LIU 50-54 (Biol) BS; Tuskegee Inst Sch Vet Med 56-59 (Vet Med); Pratt 62-64 MLS. 6: Fr. 7: Telephone asst ref dept NY ACAD Med Lib 50-56; NYU Med Center: Circ asst 59-63, Psychiatric libn 63, Staff libn ref dept 64-66; Supv libn Goldwater Mem Hosp 66-. 9: MedLA-NY Reg Group. 10: Pratt Inst Lib Alumni Assn. 14: Ref, bibliog. 15: 35 Lefferts ave, Brooklyn Ny 11225.

JOHNSON, RUDOLPH. b Kirkenes Norway 7 Mr 16. 4: Solveig Arneng. 5: Hamline U 33-37 (Liberal Arts) BA; Columbia 46-47 (Hist) MA; UOslo 48-49; UMinn 50-51 BS in LS. 6: Norwegian. 7: Ref UMinn(Minneapolis) 51-52; Acquis UMinn (St Paul) 52-59; Dir UMinn(Duluth) 59-. 8: Act libn Universidad de Concepcion , Concepcion Chile 67. 9: ALA; MinnLA. 10: AAUP; ACLU. 14: Col lib admin. 15: 709 N 17th ave E, Duluth Mn 55812.

JOHNSON, RUTH ELAINE. b Cleveland Ohio 30 Ja 35. 5: West Res 58 (Hist) AB (cum laude), 59 MS in LS. 6: Sp. 7: Y-a libn Cleveland Pub Lib, Cleveland Ohio 59-61, 1st asst br libn 61-62; Period libn West Res U 62-63; Hd libn US Small Bus Admin, Cleveland Ohio 63-64; Ref libn Columbus Pub Lib, Columbus Ohio 64-65; Hd libn anchorage Com Col, Anchorage Alaska 65-. 9: ALA; AlaskaLA (sec 68-69, Anchorage Chap Sec 66-68). 10: Beta Phi Mu; Mensa. 14: Commun cols. 15: 2207 Culver pl, Anchorage Ak 99503.

JOHNSON, SARA G (Graham). b Columbia SC 23 Mr 12. 4: W Talbert Johnson. 5: Columbia Col 33-35 (Piano & Mus Educ) BS Mus; USoCar 30-34 (Lat) AB; summer 37, 38, 40, 58, 66, 68 (LS) Certif LS. 7: Tchr Indiantown High Sch, Cades SC 35-36; Tchr Prin Antioch elem Sch, Gal Ferry SC 47-49; Tchr Prin Joyner Swamp Elem Sch, Gal Ferry SC 49-50; Tchr Aynor Elem Sch, Aynor SC 51-56; Libn Aynor High Sch, Aynor SC 36-42, Libn 56-. 9: ALA; SCLA; SCEA; HarryCoTA. 10: Chm Aynor Meth Woman's Soc of Christ Serv. 14: Develop a high sch material ctr. 15: Box 254, Aynor SC 29511.

JOHNSON, SHARON (ERICKSON). b Forsyth Mont 29 O 42. 4: Harlan R Johnson. 5: Bismarck Jr Col 60-61; UND 61-62; Dickinson State Col 62-63 (Eng) BS; Peabody 63-64 (LS) MA. 6: SP. 7: Catlg libn St ate Lib Commsn, Bismarck ND 64-66, libn Stratford High Sch, Nashville Tenn 66-67; Libn Burke High Sch, Omaha Neb 67-68. 8: Consul State Lib Commsn, ND. 9: ALA; MPLA; NDLA; ArizLA. 14: Tech serv, consul serv. 15: 3122 Monte Vista dr #8, Flagstaff Az 86001.

JOHNSON, SHIRLEY E. b Ayr ND 3 Ag 26. 5: Jamestown Col 44-48 (Eng) BA; UDenver 59-60 (LS) MA. 6: Fr. 7: Tchr of Eng, soc sci 48-56; tchr-libn Minot Pub Schs, Minot ND 53-56; Tchr Denver Pub Schs 57-59; Stud asst ref UDenver Lib 59-60; Asst govt documents UIowa Libs 62-66; Ref libn soc sci U Ariz Lib 66-67; Asst lib Ill Col 67-. 9: ALA. 10: AAUW; LWV. 14: Ref. 15: 702 W Beecher, Jacksonville Il 62650.

JOHNSON, SIDDIE JOE. b Dallas 20 Ag 05. 5: Tex Christian U 28-32 (Eng) BA; LSU 37-38 BS in LS. 6: Sp. 7: Tchr pub schs, Refugio Tex 33-34; Libn La Retama Pub Lib, Corpus Christi Tex 34-37; Head of child wk Dallas Pub Lib 38-54, Coordinator of child serv 54-65, ret. 8: Tchr child lit: SMU, UTex, Tex Woman's U, UAriz. 9: ALA; TexLA. 10: Tex Inst of Letters; Poetry Soc of Tex. 11: Tex Inst of Letters Juvenila Award, 52; Grolier Award through ALA, 54; Tex Libn of The Year 64. 12:"Agarita Berry" (33); "Debby" (40); "New Town in Texas" (42); "Texas, the Land of the Tejas" (43); "Cathy" (45); "Gallant the Hour" (45); "Month of Christmases" (52); "Cat Hotel" (55); "Feather in My Hand" (67); Child Bk Reviewer in Dallas News" (38-69). 13: Yes. 14: Child wk, child bks, creative writing for child, storytelling. 15: 1816 Summit ave, Dallas Tx 75206.

JOHNSON, STEPHEN. b Hungary. 5: Windsor Ont Can 53-54 BA; UBC 54-55; UMontreal 55-56 BLS. 6: Ger, Ital, Fr. 7: Undergrad libn McGill U 56-57; Gifts & exchange libn UBC 57-60, Ser libn 61-. 9: CanLA; ALA. 14: Tech serv. 15: 4571 W 3rd ave, Vancouver BC Can.

JOHNSON, THEODORA LUCIA. b Wash DC 27 Ap 18. 5: Long Beach Jr Col 35-36; Compton Jr Col 36-37 (Liberal Arts) AA Certif; San Diego State Col 37-38 (Eng Lit); George Washington U 38-41 (Eng Lit) AB; San Jose State Col 52-53 Certif in Lib Sci; USoCal 64- (LS). 7: Reporter "Bethesda Journal," Bethesda Md 39-41; Clerk-typist US Naval Air Sta, Pensacola Fla 41-42; Priorities advisor/contract clerk US Naval Air Sta, Moffett Field Cal 42-43; Photolith typist Stanford U Press 43-44; Reporter "Sunnyvale Standard," Sunnyvale Cal 44-45; Reporter "San Jose Mercury-News," San Jose Cal 45-46; Ed Campbell Press, Campbell Cal 46-51; Palo Alto Pub Lib, Palo Alto Cal: Lib asst 51-52, Asst catlgr, asst ref libn 53-54, Order libn 54-59, Adult serv coordinator 59-60; City Libn Lompoc Pub Lib, Lompoc Cal 60-62; City Libn Azusa Pub Lib, Azusa Cal 62-. 9: ALA; CalLA; Pub Lib Execs Assn So Cal (sec-treas 65-66, v-pres 68-69); Pub Lib Film Circuit Comsn (pres 69); Metropolitan Coop Lib Syst (sec 68, v-chm 69). 10: Azusa Women's Club; Soroptimist Club; Azusa Hist Soc; Girl Scouts (leader, coun); Amer Red Cross Motor Corps. 14: Ref, bk sel, Californiana. 15: 1309 N San Gabriel ave, Azusa Ca 91702.

JOHNSON, WANDA MAE. b Hastings Okla. 5: Okla State U 25-29 (Lit) BS; UOkla 29-30 (LS) BA; Okla State U 31-32 (Lit) MA; Columbia 34, 37 (LS). 7: Stud asst Okla StateU Lib 28-29; Summer asst Carnegie Lib, Okla City Okla 29; Head Libn Pub Lib, Stillwater Okla 30-36; Lib asst US Dept of Com Lib, Wash DC 36-37; Loan asst Nat Agric Lib, Wash DC 37-39; Loan asst US Bur Agric Econ Lib, Wash DC 39-41; Asst libn US Treasury Dept Lib, Wash DC 41-43; Chief Libn US Off of Price Admin, Wash DC 43-47; Dir US Dept of Com Lib, Wash DC 47-. 8: Off of Price Admin (dir OPA ration currency hist proj for libs & hist socs 46); Economic Stabilization Agency (org ESA Lib 50); Dept of Com rep on Fed Lib Com 65-. 9: SLA (President's Conf on Tech & Distrib Res 57); DCLA; Law Libns Soc of Wash DC. 10: Nat League of Amer Pen Women; Okla State Soc; Washington Club; Assn Preservation of Va Antiquities; DAR; Bus & Prof Women's Guild; Adv mem Marq uis Biographical Lib Soc. 12: "Department of Commerce Publications, Catalog & Index, 1790-1950" & "Supplements 1951-1953"; "Business Service Checklist," weekly (49-54). 13: Yes. 14: Admin, ref, bibliog. 15: US Dept of Com Lib, Wash DC 20230.

JOHNSON, WILLIAM GUSTAVE. b Phila 28 My 22. 4: Marian Lucille Johnson. 5: Purdue 40-41 (Chem); Anderson Col & Theol Sem 46-50 (Fine Arts) AB; UTex 50-51 (LS); Kent State 61-65 MLS. 7: Radar tech SSgt USMCR 42-46; YNC USNR 56-65; Routine chem Delco Remy Div Gen Motors, Anderson Ind 46-48; Jr asst Carnegie Pub Lib, Anderson Ind 48-50; Electronics lib USMC, San Francisco 51-52; Asst ref libn Dallas Pub Lib 52; Ref libn Carnegie Pub Lib, Anderson Ind 53-59; Ext libn Kokomo Pub Lib, Kokomo Ind 59-60; Ref lib bus & labor Akron Pub Lib, Akron Ohio 60-. 9: Ohio LA. 10: Commun Theater, Wadsworth Ohio. 14: Ref, art, rare bks. 15: 137 W Prospect st, Wadsworth Oh 44281.

JOHNSON, WILLIAM R. b Vivian La 31 Ag 25. 5: Tex Col Arts Ind 45-49 (Music) AB; Columbia 51-53 MSLS. 6: Ger. 7: US Navy PhM2/c, Asian Theatre 42-45; Bandmaster Rio Hondo Schs, Tex 49-51; Libn brs NY Pub Lib 53-57; Brooklyn Pub Lib: Asst chief hist Central Serv 58-60, Bkmob libn 60-62, Asst personnel dir admin 62-64, Br libn Flatlands Agency 64-, Chief art & music central serv 66-. 9: ALA; NYLA; MusLA. 10: NY Lib Club. 14: Re f. 15: 31 Jane st, apt 18-A, New York Ny 10014.

JOHNSON, WILLIAM R. b Bloomington Ill 20 My 26. 5: UIll 47-50 (Hist) AB; Catholic U 55-60 (LS). 7: (Cpl) Army Air Corps, US, Aleution Islands 44-46; Lib asst DC Pub Lib 52-57; Readers adv, br libn, ref, supv libn US AEC, Wash DC 57-61; Libn in chg NASA Ames Research Center, Moffett Field Cal 61-64, Chief tech info div 64-. 9: SLA. 14: Ref, info retrieval, documentation. 15: 999 Helena dr, Sunnyvale Ca 94087.

JOHNSON, WILLIAM STANLEY. b Effingham Ill 3 Jl 40. 4: Keren Ami Jacobson. 5: Tulane U 57-63 (Eng) BA; UMich 64-65 (LS) MA. 7: Clerk in govt documents dept Howard Tilton Mem Lib Tulane U 63-64; Asst circ libn Widener Lib Harvard U 65-67; Reader serv libn for fine arts Harvard Col Lib 67-. 8: Consul to The Spec Collection for The Carpenter Ctr for Visual Stud 66-68. 10: New Eng Film Educators Soc. 14: Spec materials. 15: 24 Fletcher st, Winchester Ma 01890.

JOHNSRUD, THOMAS EDWARD. b Montevideo Minn 7 F 29. 5: UMinn 47-51 (Psych) BA, 60-67 9ls, amer Studies) MA; UChicago 51-56 (Theol) BD. 6: Ger. 7: Freshman adv UMinn (Minneapolis) 61-65, Instr Communication Program 65-68; Ref lib Central Wash State col 68-. 10: NCTE; Conf on Col Composition & Communication; Amer Studies Assn. 14: Ref, bibliog, acquis. 15: 700 E 5th ave, Ellensburg Wa 98926.

JOHNSSON, GIL R. b Mason City Iowa 15 S 33. 4: Lillian Starkenburg. 5: UMinn(Duluth) 52-56 (Eng) BS; UMinn 58-59 (LS) MA. 6: Ger. 7: Dir Blue Earth Co Lib, Mankato Minn 59-65; Dir Nobles Co Lib, Worthington Minn 65-. 9: ALA; MinnLA ; M inn Lib Film Circuit (sec/treas); Wis Lib Admin RT. 14: Admin, adult serv. 15: Nobles Co Lib, Worthington Mn 56187.

JOHNSTON, ALETHEA (MARGARET). b Kitchener Ont Can 21 Ag 13. 5: UWest Ont Waterloo Col 31-34 BA; Toronto 34-35 BLS. 6: Fr. 7: Libn Hespeler Pub Lib, Hespeler Ont 36-38; Asst chief libn & child libn Kitchener Pub Lib, Kitchener Ont 38-. 8: Instr in Lib Sci Waterloo Col (Can) 47-49. 9: Can Assn of Child Libns; OntLA (past chm Childs Lib Sect). 13: Yes. 14: Child libs. 15: 130 Lancaster st East, Kitchener Ont Can.

JOHNSTON, ELLEN A. b Newcastle NB Can 9 Ap 22. 4: R R Johnston. 5: McGill 40-44 BA, 60-61 BLS. 7: Catlgr Sun Life Assurance Co of Can, Montreal 61-65, Chief libn 65-67; Chief libn Alcan Aluminum Ltd, Montreal 67-69. 9: SLA; CanLA; QueLA. 10: Royal Montreal Tennis Club; Montreal Badminton & Squash Club. 14: Admin. 15: PO Box 6090, Montreal 101 Que Can.

JOHNSTON, EZELYN (STARSTEAD). b Superior Wis 22 Ag 08. 4: Frank M Johnston. 5: UWis 26-30 (Eng, Lat) BA, 32-33 (LS) Certif; Chicago 37-39. 6: Fr, Swedish, Sp. 7: Br libn Superior (Wis) Br 33-34; Br libn, Clintonville Wis 34-36; Catlgr & br libn E Chicago Ind. Br 36-. 9: ALA; IndLA. 10: Ind Harbor Women's Club. 14: Ref, circ. 15: 1702 E 136th st, E Chicago In 46313.

JOHNSTON, FRANCES (RUMPF). b Belle Plaine Kan 10 Mr 29. 4: James P Johnston. 5: Wichita StateU 46-50 (Hist) AB; UMich 52-53 AMLS. 6: Fr, Sp. 7: Libn's sec & order clk Wichita StateU Lib 50-52, Catlgr 54-; Docs libn Kan State Col Lib 53-54. 14: Catlg. 15: 1557 Matlock dr, Wichita Ks 67208.

JOHNSTON, HAROLD G. b Ellston Iowa 12 Ag 20. 4: Nina Lyman. 5: State U Iowa 37-38; St Ambrose 39-42 (Amer Hist) BA; Yale 46-48 (Drama); UMich 49-51 MALS. 7: Lt (jg) USN 42-46; Lib asst Davenport Pub Lib, Davenport Iowa 48-49; Hd ref dept Lansing Pub Lib, Lansing Mich 51-54; Libn Owosso Pub Lib, Owosso Mich 55-57; Hd ref dept & asst dir Flint Pub Lib, Flint Mich 57-66; Dir Detroit Metropolitan Lib Research & Demonstration 67-68; Dir Bloomfield Twp Lib, Bloomfield Hills Mich 68-69; Jt dir Bloomfield Twp Lib & Baldwin Pub Lib, Bloomfield Hills & Birmingham Mich 69-. 9: ALA; SLA; MichLA. 10: Betha Phi Mu. 15: 2465 W Wattles rd, Troy Mi 48084.

JOHNSTON, JEANNE (ALTA) (SHEETZ). b Burlington Iowa 27 Ja 19. 4: Howard Wright Johnston. 5: Burlington Jr Col 36-37; Coe Col 38-41 (Eng) BA; Columbia 41-42 BS in LS, 44-46 (Musicology) MA. 6: Fr, Ger, Gk. 7: Asst dir order dept UIowa Lib 42-44; Asst dir Hosp Lib Bur, NYC 46-47; Volunteer libn Silver Spring (Md) Intermediate Sch 58; Libn Anatolia Col (Thessaloniki Greece) 59-64; Spec adv for lib serv Iowa Wesleyan Col 64-65; Act dir of lib serv Iowa Wesleyan Col Lib 65-69, Spec asst to pres for lib serv 69-. 9: ALA; LARC Assn. 10: LWV; Phi Kappa Phi; AAUW. 14: Admin, acquis, mus catlg, planning new libs. 15: 305 W State st, Mt Pleasant Ia 52641.

JOHNSTON, JOAN L. b Montreal Can. 5: Toronto BA (Hist), BLS. 7: Ref & circ libn North York Pub Lib, Toronto; Soc sci libn Guelph Lib, Guelph Ont. 9: CanLA; Inst Prof Libns Ont. 14: Ref. 15: Univ of Guelph Lib, Guelph Ont Can.

JOHNSTON, LINDA (MANGHAM) (MRS). b Atlanta. 5: Ga Southwestern 32-34; LaGrange Col 34-36 (Eng-Hist) AB; Peabody 41, 42, 43 BS in LS. 7: Tchr Muscogee Co Schs, Columbus Ga 36-42; Libn Gillespie Park Jr High Sch, Greensboro NC 42-43; Libn Atlanta Pub Lib 43-48; Libn Fed Reserve Bank, Atlanta 48-. 9: SLA (pres S Atlantic chap) 63-64); SELA; GALA. 10: Bus & Prof Women's Club; Metropolitan Opera Guild; Amer Inst of Banking; Metro Atlanta Lib Assn. 14: Ref. 15: 100 Biscayne dr NW apt B-6, Atlanta Ga 30309.

JOHNSTON, LYNWOOD (SPEED). b Springfield Mass 2 S 33. 4: Anna Kottis. 5: Boston U 53-55 (Amer Lit) AB, 56-58 (Educ) Ed M; UDenver 59-60 (LS) MA. 7: Catlgr & ref libn San Jose State Col 60-65; Gifts & exch & ref libn UVt 65-. 15: Univ of Vt Lib, Burlington Vt 05401.

JOHNSTON, MARGARET Y. b Buffalo NY 17 F 09. 5: UBuffalo 27-28 (Biol) BA, LS Certif; Chicago summer 63 (LS). 6: Ger, Fr, Lat, Sp, Ital. 7: Catlg libn Lockwood Mem Lib now SUNY(Buffalo) 31-. 8: Com mem 5 Associated Univ Lib s. 9: ALA; NYLA. 10: AAUP; University Women's Club; Lake Placid Club Educ Foun. 14: Catlg. 15: 1531 Wehrle dr, Williamsville Ny 14221.

JOHNSTON, MAXINE. b Gillham Ark 21 D 28. 5: Sam Houston State Tchrs Col 50-53 (Eng, LS) BS; UTex 54-58 MLS; UIll summer 66 (LS). 6: Fr, Ger. 7: Admin off asst Tyrrell Pub Lib, Beaumont Tex 47-53; Asst libn S Park High Sch, Beaumont Tex 53-55; Ref libn Lamar State Col of Tech 55-. 8: Visiting lecturer UTex Grad Sch Lib Sci summer 69. 9: ALA; TexLA (off, chm &/or mem 4 coms 60-66; Chm Ref RT 68-69). 10: Tex Assn Col Tchrs; AAUP; LWV; Alpha Chi; Big Thicket Assn. 12: "Public and College Library Personnel in Texas, 1955," ACRL microcard series No 110 (59). 14: Ref. 15: Box 154, Batson Tx 77519.

JOHNSTON, NORMA VIVIAN. b Coshocton Ohio 18 O 05. 5: Ohio State U 23-27 (Lat) BS in Educ; UWis summers 32-34, 36, 38 (Lat) MA; West Res summers 45-48 BS in LS. 7: Tchr of Lat & Eng E Palestine High Sch, E Palestine Ohio 27-29; Tchr of Lat & Eng Gallia Acad High Sch, Gallipolis Ohio 29-45; Libn & reading Donnell Jr High Sch, Findlay Ohio 45-49; Head Libn Alpena Pub & High Sch Lib, Alpena Mich 49-66, High Sch libn 66-. 9: NEA; MichEA. 10: Women's Civic League. 15: 414 W Mirre st, Alpena Mi 49707.

JOHNSTON, SALLY READ (SARAH LOUISE). b N Vernon Ind 28 D 09. 4: Vilas C Johnston. 5: UWash 27-31 (LS) BS. 6: Lat, Fr. 7: Circ dept UWash Lib 31-36; Ed dept UWash Press 57-63; Br asst Seattle Pub Lib 63-64; Catlg libn UWash Law Lib 64-68; Ref, libn 68-. 9: AALL; WashLA. 10: Phi Beta Kappa; Amer Rock Garden Soc. 15: 6214-24th NE, Seattle Wa 98115.

JOHNSTON, THOMAS WILLIAM. b Ogden Utah 12 N 28. 4: Irmgard Degner. 5: Brigham Young 52 (Chem) BS; Ricks 53 (Educ) BA; UChicago 53 (Sci Educ); Carnegie Sch of Lib Sci 58 MLS. 7: Analytical chemist Simplot Fertilizer Co, Pocatello Ida 53-54; Chem spectroscopist phillips Petroleum Co, Ida Falls Ida 54-56; Lit chem Callery Chem Co, Callery Penn 56-58; Tech libn MSA Research Corp, Callery Penn 58-60; Tech lib & patents mgr Sybron Corp, Rochetser NY 60-66; Dir tech info ctr URochester 66-. 8: Sec Res & Devel Planning Com, The Pfaudler Div, Sybron Corp 65-66; Bus mgr "Directory of Special Libraries . . . Upstate NY, SLA chap pub 65-68. 9: SLA (treas Upstate NY Chap 66-68); ACS. 10: C of C; Monroe Co Lib Club; Society for Early Hist Archaeol; Amer Mus Natural Hist; National Honor Soc. 11: Bausch & Lomb Sci Award. 12: Comp Proprietary book on "Boron Compounds", (58); Ed "Liquid Metals Technology Abstract Bulletin", (58-60). 13: Yes. 14: Admin of libs & info serv, sci & tech info serv, automated stor & retr of info. 15: 2 Pine Tree Trail, Rush NY 14543.

JOHNSTON, WALTER (THOMAS). b Americus Ga 2 S 23. 4: Ida Lee (Mosley) Johnston. 5: Ga Southern Col 41-42, 47 (Eng) BS; Peabody 47 (Eng) MA, 48 BS in LS. 7: (1st Sgt) US Army Artillery, US & Europe 42-46; Libn Lee Col 48-50; Libn Armstrong Col 50; (M/Sgt) US Army Logistics, US 50-51; Ref libn Mercer U 52; Libn Abraham Baldwin Col 52-67; Adult serv coord Coastal Plain & Colquitt Thomas Reg Lib Systs 67-68; Dir Coastal Plain Reg Lib 68-. 09: GaLA (pres 63-65); SELA. 13: Yes. 14: Catlg, admin. 15: Box 236 Abac Sta, Tifton Ga 31794.

JOHNSTON, WARREN R. b Brooklyn NY 29 O 13. 4: Eunice Carpen. 5: Columbia Col (NYC) 33-36 (Pol, Soc Sci) AB; UColo (Navy Jap Lang Sch) 43-44 (Japanese lang) Diploma; Columbia summer 44 (Intl Admin) Certif; Army War Col (Carlisle Pa) 54-55 (US For Policy) Diploma. 6: Japanese, Fr, Gk. 7: Int erviewer & statistician Gallup Poll, NYC 36; Remedial tutor & casewkr, NYC 37, 40-42; Sales promotion rep Copeland & Thompson Inc, NYC 38-39; Lt USN Res, Tinian Marianas 43- 46; For affairs analyst ed US Govt Exec Br, Wash DC 46-59, 64-67; Ed & admin US Mission to Greece, Athens 59-64; Asst chief foreign affairs div Legis ref serv LC 67-. 8: Mayor, Garrett Park Md 66-. 9: Amer Pol Sci Assn; Intl Studies Assn; Amer Soc Pub Admin; Amer Soc Planning Offs. 10: Soc for Intl Dev elopment; Army War Col Alumni Assn; Md Mun League. 12: Ed first US report to US on Trust Territory of Pacific (48). 14: Mgt for affairs, nat defense research. 15: Foreign Affairs Div Legislative Ref Ser Lib of Congress, Washington DC 20540.

JOHNSTON, WILLIAM WINFRED. b Cleburne Tex 15 S 16. 5: Hardin Col 46-49 (Eng, Span) BA; N Tex State U 50-52 BS in LS, 52-53 (Eng) MA, 54, 63, 64 , 65-67 (MLS); Tex

Educ Agency Lib Certif 51. 6: Fr, Sp. 7: Clerk US Dept of Agric, Archer City Tex 38-42; USAAF 42-45; Clerk Guaranty Abstract Co, Archer City Tex 45-46; Eng tchr Holliday High Sch, Holliday Tex 49-50, Tchr-libn 50-52; Libn Milam Elem Sch, Odessa Tex 53; Libn Bowie Jr High Sch, Odessa Tex 53-55; Libn Bonham Jr High Sch, Odessa Tex 55-66; Libn Nimitz Jr High Sch Odessa Tex 66-. 8: Asst Prof N Tex State U NDEA Inst for Sch Libns, summer 65, Lib serv dept summer 66-67. 9: NEA; Tex State Tchrs Assn; Tex Clr Tchrs Assn; TexLA; TexASchL (Exec Bd 63-64) ; SWLA. 10: Alpha Chi; Phi Theta Kappa; Phi Delta Kappa; Alpha Lambda Sigma; Sigma Tau Delta ; Beta Phi Mu. 14: Catlg, sch libs. 15: Box 1005, Archer City Tx 76351.

JOHNSTONE, ELIZABETH (STEVENS). b Selbyville Del 3 Jl 15. 4: MacDonald Johnstone. 5: UNC 35-37 (Hist) AB; Simmons 37-38 BSLS. 7: Child libn Brooklyn Pub Lib 38-42; Sch libn St Johns Pub Sch System Ketterlinus Jr High Sch, St Augustine Fla 61-. 9: FlaASchL ; FlaLA. 10: Altrusa Internat; NCTE; Alpha Delta Kap pa. 14: Child bks. 15: 9 Avista Cir, St Augustine Fl 32084.

JOHNSTONE, JOAN MARGARET (WARREN PRICE). b Montreal 14 Jl 19. 4: Alan Timothy Johnstone. 5: McGill 36-40 (Eng, Fr) BA. 6: Fr, Ger. 7: Asst libn, Connaught Med Research Labs, Toronto Can 55-56; Libn Sch Hygiene UToronto 57-58; Chief libn Acad Med, Toronto Can 60-64; Libn McIntyre-Falconbridge Lib, Toronto Can 68-. 14: Admin, ref. 15: 94 Crescent rd apt 207, Toronto 5 Ont Can.

JONAH, DAVID ALONZO. b Sackville NB Can 19 Mr 09. 4: Elizabeth Wright. 5: Mt Allison U 29 (Math) BS; Brown 31 (Math) MS; Mt Allison U 60 LLD. 7: Instr Math Dept Brown U 32-34, 43-44; Brown U Lib: Gen asst 35-38, In chg phys sci lib 38-46, Act libn 46-48, Assoc libn 48-49, Libn 49-60, Libn & Dir of Libs 60-. 8: Lib Bldg Commsn, Warwick RI 63-65; Consul Newport Pub Lib, Newport RI 67. 9: ALA; BSA; RILA (pres 56-58). 10: East Greenwich Free Lib Assn; Medieval Acad of Amer; Sigma Xi; Caxton Club; Grolier Club; Club of Odd Volumes; University Club. 13: Yes. 15: Brown U Lib, Providence Ri 02912.

JONAS, ROBERT. b Brooklyn NY 25 Je 12. 4: Betty Lewis. 5: Williams Col 31-33 (Fr); Stanford 33-35 (Fr) BA; Columbia 50-51 MLS. 6: Fr, Sp, Ger, Brazilian, Portu, Romanian, Turkish, Norwegian. 7: Manager H G Knoll & Co Inc, NYC 36-44; Warehouseman US Army Depot, Belle Mead NJ 44-46; Claims examiner US RR Retirement Bd, NYC 46-51; Br lib dir Brooklyn Pub Lib 51-54; Br lib dir Elizabeth Pub Lib, Elizabeth NJ 54-58; Lib dir W Orange Pub Lib, W Orange NJ 58-. 10: Lions Club. 12: "Ingle3s de Jona3s" (45) . 15: 200 Mt Pleasant ave, Apt D6 W Orange Nj 07052.

JONES, ALICE RATCLIFFE GURNETT (MRS CATESBY T). b Chicago 5 Ja 11. 5: Radcliffe 28-31, 32-33 (Soc Psych) AB; U's of Perugia & Rome 31-32 (Ital Studies); Columbia 38-39 BSLS, later certif MSLS. 6: Sp, Ital, Fr. 7: Ms Div LC 36-38; Spec libn 39-41; Econ analyst, Asst chief Doc Security Sect War Agencies, Wash DC 41-45; Adv on Libs Overseas Documentation Spec US State Dept, Wash DC 45-47; Tchr of Geog UDel 48; Newspaper reporter "Island Times," San Juan PR; Eng tchr jr high sch, Mayagu2ez PR 48-63; Head ref catlgr Inter-Amer U (PR) 63-66; Dir of lib serv, Santa Fe Jr Col, Gainesville Fla 66-67; Asst dir tech serv Westchester Lib Syst 67-68; Head libn Boston Museum of Fine Arts 68-. 08: Co-founder Hazen Lib, Mayagu2ez PR 54; Founder Jr Readers, 56; Founder & Hon Libn New Readers' Lib, 59-; Founder & pres, More Books Inc, 61-; Consul to libn, Mayagu2ez Vocat High Sch 58-61, other libs in commun. 9: ALA; Sociedad de Bibliotecarios de PR; SLA. 10: Sociedad Mayagu2ezana Pro Bellas Artes; Coop de Consumo de Mayagu2ez; Assoc Padres y Maestros de la Escuela Libre Musica de Mayagu2ez; Radcliffe Club of Boston; WILP; SANE. 14: Bk sel, catlg, admin, acquis ; materials in var for langs). 15: Apt 1455 Commonwealth ave Brog (Brighton) Boston Ma 02135.

JONES, ANDREA L. b Pittsburgh 28 Jl 38. 5: UPittsburgh 56-60 (Span) BA; Carnegie 61-62 MLA. 6: Fr, Sp, Ital. 7: Residence manage Albany State Col (Ga) 60; Child libn Carnegie Lib of Pittsburgh 62-. 10: Alpha Kappa Alpha; Sigma Kappa Phi. 14: Child wk. 15: 505 N Euclid ave, Pittsburgh Pa 15206.

JONES, ANNA E. b Burlington NJ 7 Ja 28. 5: Trenton State Col 44-48 (Eng, Hist, Secondary Educ) BS, summers 50-53 BLS. 7: Tchr Bordentown City Bd of Educ 48-49; Sr lib asst Burlington Co Lib, Mt Holly NJ 51-55, Sr libn 55-60, Supv libn 60-63, Asst lib dir 63-. 9: ALA; NJLA; NJSchLA. 10: Bd dirs Lib Comp of Burlington. 14: Child & yp bks & serv, sch serv. 15: 444 Washington ave, Burlington NJ 08016.

JONES, ANNE FIELD. b Columbus Ohio 10 F 09. 5: Hollins Col 27-31, 33 (Sociol) BA; West Res 41-42 BA in LS. 7: Y-p libn (br) Cleveland (Ohio) Pub Lib 40-43, 1st asst (br) 43-45, Asst br libn 45-48; 7th div libn Armed Forces Libs, Seoul Korea 48-49; Far E field supv Armed Forces Libs, Tokyo Japan 49-50; Libn Robert Col, Istanbul Turkey 52-59; Asst supt Dade Co Bkmobs Miami Pub Lib, Miami Fla 66-. 9: ALA; SELA; FlaLA; DadeCoLA. 10: Pi Beta Phi. 13: Yes. 14: Adult serv. 15: 101 SW 60th ct, Miami Fl 33144.

JONES, ARTHUR EDWIN JR. b Orange NJ 20 Mr 18. 4: Rachel Mumbulo Jones. 5: URochester 35-39 (Eng) AB; Syracuse 39-41 & 46-49 (Eng & Amer Lit) MA & PhD; Rutgers 63-64 MLS. 6: Fr. 7: Grad asst Eng Dept Syracuse U 39-41; (1st Lt) AAA US Army 41-43; (1st Sgt) Infantry US Army 43-46; Instr Eng Dept Syracuse U 46-49; Eng Dept Drew U: Instr 49-51, Asst Prof Eng 51-54, Dir of Libs & Prof of Eng 55-. 8: Middle States Visitation Team Assignments 54-. 9: ALA; NATE; ATheolLA; (pres 67-68); NJLA. 10: Modern Lang Assn; Trustee Madison Pub Lib, Madison NJ; Phi Beta Kappa. 12: "Darwinism and Realism in American Fiction" (51); 'Years of Conflict' in "History of American Methodism" (63). 13: Yes. 14: Admin. 15: Drew U Lib, Madison NJ 07940.

JONES, BARBARA (OGLESBY). b Atlnta 23 Ap 37. 5: Agnes Scott Col 55-59 (Hist, Pol Sci) BA; Emory 64 (LS) MLn. 6: Fr, Lat. 7: Agnes Scott Col Lib: Asst to libn 59-61, Asst catlgr 61-63, Catlgr 63-. 9: ALA; GaLA; SELA. 10: Atlanta Lib Club. 14: Catlg, yp serv, ref, adv serv. 15: 1037 North Valley dr, Decatur Ga 30033.

JONES, BARBARA J. b Junction City Kan 26 Ja 36. 5: Kan State U 54-58 (Eng) BS; Denver U 59-60 (LS) MA. 6: Sp. 7: Tchr Alma High Sch, Alma Kan 58-59; Libn ref dept UKan Libs 60-. 9: ALA; KanLA. 10: Phi Kappa Phi; AAUP. 14: Ref. 15: 1203 Oread apt 9, Lawrence Ks 66044.

JONES, BETTY M (LOMBARD). b Grand Rapids Mich 25 D 19. 4: Robert Edward Jones. 5: Albion Col 37-38; UMich 38-41 (Soc Studies) AB, 60 MALS. 6: Lat, Fr, Sp, Ger. 7: Head bus & tech dept Grand Rapids Pub Lib, Grand Rapids Mich 59-60; Libn Ridgeview Jr High Sch, Grand Rapids Mich 60-65; Coordinator of lib serv Grand Rapids Bd of Educ 65-68; Ref libn Grand Valley State Col 68-. 9: ALA; MichLA. 10: Grand Rapids Libns Club; Women's City Club; Mortar Board; Phi Kappa Phi; Pi Lambda Theta; Beta Phi Mu; Women's Nat Bk Assn. 14: Ref. 15: 2056 Francis ave SE, Grand Rapids Mi 49507.

JONES, C(LAUD) LEE. b Anderson Ind 22 S 36. 4: Patricia Turner. 5: Carleton Col 54-55, 56-59 (Sociol) BA; UTex 63-64, 65 MLS. 6: Sp, Fr. 7: US Marine Corps Sgt 55-56; Ind engnr Procter & Gamble, Green Bay Wis 54-63; Lifeguard & soc wk spec US Army, San Antonio Tex (Sgt) 59-62; Lib intern Dartmouth Col 64-65; Ref libn Trinity U (San Antonio Tex) 65-66; Dir of tech serv 66-67: Dir UTex Med Br Lib 67-. 9: TexLA; SLA; MedLA; SWLA; AAUP; Tex Coun of Health Sci Libs (v-pres). 10: Rotary; Bd of Dirs of William Temple Found . 12: Edl Bd of "Texas Reports on Biology and Medicine"; "Evaluation of The Serial Holdin gs of 24 Biomedical Libraries in Texas (68). 13: Yes. 14: Ref, admin, sers. 15: 2902 Beluche, Galveston Tx 77550.

JONES, CAROLYN (NANCY). b Jackson Miss 21 F 36. 5: Mississippi State Col for Women 54-57 (LS) BS; Peabody Col 58-59 (LS) MA. 6: Russian, Dactology. 7: Libn Cove Elem Sch, Panama City Fla 57-58; Catlgr New Orleans Baptist Theol Sem 59-63; Catlgr Eastern Kentucky StateU 63-65; Special collections libn Gallaudet Col 65-. 8: Interpreter for the deaf So Baptist Ch. 9: Convention of Amer Instr of the Deaf. 14: Catlg, materials relating to deafness. 15: 920 Palmer rd apt 13, Oxon Hill Md 20022.

JONES, CATHERINE ANN (DELANTY). b Conneaut Ohio 30 Ap 36. 4: Thomas M J ones. 5: DuquesneU 53-55 (Educ); St Mary's (Leavenworth Kan) 63-64 (Eng); UAla (Tuscaloosa) 64-65 (Eng) BA; CatholicU 66-69 MSLS. 7: Recreation sec Amer Red Cross US Army Hosp, Ft Campb ell Ky 58-60; Ed speciali st European Exchange System, Nuernberg Germany 60-63; Ref libn US Bur of Budget Lib, Wash DC 67-. 9: ALA; SLA; DCLA. 10: YWCA; Old Town Walled Garden Club; Old Town Civic Assn. 12: Ed "DCLA Newsletter" (67-68). 14: Ref. 15: 326 South Pitt st, Alexandria Va 22314.

JONES, CHARLES (ALVIS). b Alexander City Ala 7 Ag 26. 4: Hazel Smith. 5: Howard Col 48-51 (Rel Educ) AB;

Southwestern Baptist Theol Sem 57-58, 61-62, 63-64 (Theol) BD; Emory 64-65 MLn. 6: Fr, Gk. 7: Drug clerk Thagard Drug Co, Andalusia Ala 45-48, 51-52; Baptist minister Baptist churches, Ala, Tex, Okla, Ga 50-; Elem sch prin & tchr, Covington Co Ala 55-57, 58-59; Jr high sch tchr, Covington Co Ala 59-60; Ser asst Fleming Lib Southwestern Baptist Theol Sem 61-62; High sch tchr Hawaii Baptist Acad, Honolulu 62-63; Catlg dept clerk Fleming Lib Southwestern Baptist Theol Sem 63-64; Asst Emory Div of Libnship Emory Theol Lib, & Atlanta Pub Lib 64-65; Libn Reinhardt Col 65-69; Libn Truett-McConnell Col 69-. 8: Vis iting instr div of libnship EmonyU 66; Instr for UGa Ext, Canton Ga 67. 9: GaLA; SELA; GaEA. 10: Trident; Beta Pi Theta. 14: Ref, catlg, admin. 15: Truett-McConnell Col, Cleveland Ga 30528.

JONES, CHARLES (EDWIN). b Kansas City Mo 1 Je 32. 4: Beverly Anne Lundy. 5: Central High Sch 47-50; Bethany-Peniel Col 50-54 BA; UOkla summer 54; UMich 54-55 MALS; UWis 59-68 MS, PhD. 7: Ref & circ libn Bethany Nazarene Col 55-56; Head Libn Nazarene Theol Sem (Kan City) 58-59; Asst in tech processes St Paul Sch of Theol (Mo) 61-63; Tchg asst Hist UWis(Madison) 60-64; Libn Park Col 61-63; Ms curator Mich Hist Collections UMich 65-; Visiting instr in hist Tuskegee Inst spring & summer 68-69. 9: Amer Hist Assn; Organ of Amer Hist; Southern Hist Assn. 13: Yes. 14: Ms catlg. 15: 1407 Broadway, Ann Arbor Mi 48105.

JONES, CHARLOTTE (WOODRUFF). b Kendallville Ind 11 Ap 27. 4: Paul F Jones. 5: Jackson Jr Col (Jackson Mich) 45-47 (Phys Sci) AS; UMich 47-49 (Journalism) BA; IGa 52-53; UPittsburgh 66-67 MLS. 6: Ger. 7: Lib asst Jackson Pub Lib, Jackson Mich 49-50; Asst libn Tokyo Army Hosp 50-53; Asst libn Post Lib, Ft Gordon Ga 53-55; Adm & Tech Libn McCormick Selph Assoc, Hollister Cal 60-64; Br libn Douglas Co Libs, Roseburg Ore 65-66; Br libn Spokane Pub Lib, Spokane Wash 67-68; Ser libn East Wash State Col 68-. 9: ALA; SLA; PNLA; WashLA. 10: AAUW; Beta Phi Mu. 14: Ser acquis. 15: PO Box 189, Cheney Wa 99004.

JONES, CHRISTINE (SPIVEY). b Gallatin Tenn 23 Jl 24. 4: Roger Gaw Jones. 5: Tenn Tech U 47 (Bus Admin) BS; Peabody 48 BS in LS. 7: Elem tchr Putnam Co, Cookeville Tenn 43-44, Elem prin 45-46; Head circ sect Army War Col (Carlisle Barracks Penn) 51-53; Circ libn & Asst Prof of Lib Sci Tenn Tech U 48-51, 53-. 9: ALA; TennLA; TennEA. 10: Tenn Hist Soc; Bus & Prof Women's Club. 12: Comp "Draper Families in America," with others (64). 14: Circ, ref, rare bks. 15: 1489 Barnes st, Cookeville Tn 38501.

JONES, DAISY EMERYETTA. b Clinton Ind 19 D 18. 5: Valparaiso U 46-47; American U 47-50 (Eng) BS; UWash 50-51 BS in LS. 7: Yeoman 1st US Navy Res, Wash DC 43-46; Post libn US Army, Wash DC 51-53; Post libn US Army, Japan 53-56; Libn Chicago Pub Lib 59; Libn Los Angeles Pub Lib 60-66, Sr libn 66- . 9: ALA; CalLA. 10: Naval Air Station, Los Alamitos Cal (Chief Yeoman). 14: Adult serv; Social responsibility of libs. 15: 5923 S Western ave, Los Angeles Ca 90047.

JONES, DAVID GLYNN. b Nanaimo BC Can 13 N 44. 5: UVictoria 63-67 (Eng, Hist) BA; UBC 67-68 BLS. 7: Temp libn Vancouver Pub Lib, Vancouver BC Can 68; Y-p libn Toronto Pub Lib, Toronto Ont Can 68-. 9: ALA; CanLA; OntLA. 11: Marion Harlow Prize UBC. 15: 601-33 Eastmount ave, Toronto Ont Can.

JONES, DIANA L (BRETT). b Ardmore Okla 11 Ag 28. 5: UOkla 46-50 BA in LS. 7: Catlgr UOkla Lib 50-52; Lib asst UCLA Law Lib 53-54; Humanities ref libn Sacramento State Col 64-. 9: CalLA. 10: Kappa Kappa Gamma Alumnae Assn. 14: Ref. 15: 7828 Olive st, Fair Oaks Ca 95628.

JONES, DOROTHY (EVE) SCOTT. b Phila 20 Mr 26. 4: Joseph Samuel Jones Sr. 5: NJ State Tchrs Col (Jersey City) 42-44 (Eng); Howard U 44-45 (Eng); Upsala Col 48-49 (Eng) BA; Pratt 50-51 MLS. 7: Ya libn Nathan Straus Br NY Pub Lib 51-52, Sch & ref libn Tompkins Sq Br 52-53; E Orange Pub Lib, E Orange NJ: Sr libn youth 54-58, Br libn Ampere Br 58-59, 1st asst to coordinator youth serv 60-67, Coord youth serv 68-. 9: ALA; NJLA (Recr Com, chm Scholarship Com 65-66; Mem 66-69); Local affairs chm ALA-YASD conf 69. 10: Beta Phi Mu; E Orange Lib Staff Assn; LWV; Boy Scouts Coun; Amer Contract Bridge League; E Orange Youth Guidance Com. 12: Asst for column "Adult Books for Young Adults" in "School Lib rary Journal" (64-68). 13: Yes. 14: Ya, ref. 15: 22 Webster pl, E Orange NJ 07018.

JONES, DOROTHY CAHOON. b Scranton Penn 9 Jl 25. 5: Douglass 43-47 (Eng Lit, LS) AB; Rutgers 59-60 MLS. 7: Somerset Co Lib, Somerville 47-51; Penn State U (State Col) 51-56; Penn State U (Pottsville) 57-59; Wallace Labs, Cranberry NJ 60-61; Plainfield Pub Lib 61-64; Plainfield High Sch, Plainfield 64-. 9: ALA; NJLA; NJEA. 14: Ref, high sch libs. 15: 82 Harrison ave, Highland Park NJ 08904.

JONES, DOROTHY (KIRBY). b Charlotte NC 30 N 17. 5: Columbia Col 34-38 (Fr) BA; USCar 56-58 (Educ) MA; Columbia Col 60-62 BALS. 6: Fr. 7: High Sch tchr pub schs of SC & NC 38-44, 47-59; Libn US Army, Ft Jackson SC 60-61; Libn VA Hosp, Columbia SC 61-63; Med libn VA Hosp, Augusta Ga 63-64, Chief Libn 65-. 9: SCLA; SELA. 14: Med ref. 15: 681 Lorraine dr, N Augusta SC 29841.

JONES, DOROTHY MOUNCE. b Cheyenne Wyo 22 S 08. 5: Ward-Belmont 26-28 (Eng) Certif; H Sophie Newcomb Col 28-30 (Eng) BA; St Louis Lib Sch 31-32 (LS) Certif; George Washington U Law Sch 41-42. 6: Fr, Ger. 7: Clerk US Treasury Dept, Wash DC 36-39; Lib asst US Soc Security Bd, Wash DC 39-41, Law Libn 41-42; Chief ref & period US Soc Security Admin, Wash DC 42-50; Chief ref & loan US Fed Security Agency Lib, Wash DC 50-54; Head ref libn US Dept Health Educ & Welfare, Wash DC 54-60, Soc Welfare spec Lib 60-, Hd ref & bibliog sect 68-. 9: SLA. 10: Brooke Manor Country Club; Kappa Alpha Theta. 12: "Aging in the Modern World." Auth "Children Who Need Protection" (66); Auth "Coummunity Planning for Health, Education, and Welfare" (67); Auth "Words on Aging" (60). 14: Ref, bibliog. 15: 105 E Hamilton ave, Silver Spring Md 20901.

JONES, E(DWIN) PAUL. b Phila 31 D 12. 4: Myra Wilson. 5: Swarthmore 30-32 (Chem); Temple 32-34 (Chem) AB; Drexel 35-36 BS in LS; Columbia summers 37-39, 43 (LS) MS. 6: Ger, Fr. 7: Ref asst Free Lib of Phila Main Lib summer 36; Ref asst Temple U 36-41; Mineral industries libn Penn State U 41-42; Ref libn Allied Chem Corp, Morristown NJ 42-. 9: SLA. 10: United Church of Christ Supt of Ch School. 12: Contrib "Encyclopedia of Chemical Reactions." 13: Yes. 14: Lit searching, ref. 15: 73 W Cedar st, Livingston NJ 07039.

JONES, EDNA LOUISE. b Milton Mass 2 Ap 10. 5: Simmons 28-32 (LS) BS. 6: Fr, Ger. 7: Asst libn Dept of Arch Lib Harvard U 34-57; Libn Superv of Shipbuilding USN, Groton Conn 57-61; Catlgr US Coast Guard Acad Lib 61-. 9: SLA (Com Valley chap corres sec). 10: New London Co Hist Soc; Bus & Prof Women's Soc. 11: Outstanding performance USN, USCG. 14: Catlg, ref. 15: 23 Litton ave, Groton Ct 06340.

JONES, ELIZABETH (HAYS). b Pensacola Fla 17 Je 16. 5: Pensacola Jr Col 51-58 (Liberal Arts) AA; Fla State U 61-63 (Eng, LS) BA, 63-64 (LS) MS. 7: Admin asst to pres Pensacola Jr Col, Pensacola Fla 55-57, 60-61, Acquis libn 64-65; Map libn UGa 65-68; Catlgr Okaloosa-Walton Jr Col 68-. 9: SLA; FlaLA; SELA. 10: AAUW; AAUP. 14: Catlg. 15: 430 Sherry Cir, Ft Walton Beach Fl 32548.

JONES, (EMMA) FRANCES. b Parkersburg W Va 21 Ap 17. 5: Randolph Macon Woman's Col 35-37; Ohio State U 37-39 (Eng) BS in Ed; West Res 39-40 BS in LS; Columbia 52-53 (Ling). 6: Fr. 7: Br libn Euclid Pub Lib, Euclid Ohio 40-42; 1st Lt USAF (WAC) Air transport Command 42-46; Hd libn Carnegie Pub Lib, Steubenville Ohio 46-52; Ref libn ny pub Lib 52-53; Ref libn Cleveland Pub Lib, Cleveland Ohio 53-54; Ext libn Wash Co lib, Marietta Ohio 54-56; Hd libn Carnegie Pub Lib, E Liverpool 56-63; Field consul (chief) W Va Lib Com, Charleston 63-. 9: ALA; OhioLA; WVaLA. 10: Delta Kappa Gamma; AAUW; Nat Assn Bus & Profess Women. 14: Pub Lib Devel, Serv in Instns & to the Handicapped. 15: 4305 Washington ave SE, Charleston W Va 25304.

JONES, FAIRLYE (COSTLEY). b Meadville Miss 25 F 02. 4: L Leroy Jones. 5: USoMiss 58 (LS) BS. 7: Tchr Franklin Co Miss 19-23; Libn Franklin High Sch, Meadville Miss 45-. 8: Sponsor of High Sch Lib Club 59-. 9: MissLA; SELA; MissEA. 14: Ref. 15: Box 393, Meadville Ms 39653.

JONES, FAUSTINA (WILLIAMS). b Miller's Ferry Ala 27 Je 22. 4: John H Jones. 5: Knoxville Col 38-42 (Eng) AB; Atlanta U 45-46 BLS. 7: Tchr Wilcox Co Train Sch, miller's Ferry Ala 45; Catlg libn Langston U 46-48; Catlg libn Ala State Col 48-. 9: ALA; AlaLA. 14: Catlg. 15: PO Box 242, Tuskegee Institute Al 36088.

JONES, FLORENCE (CRANMER). b Darby Penn 8 Jl 26. 4: Robert Jones. 5: Asbury Col 45-49 (Christian Educ) AB; Drexel 54-55 MS in LS. 7: Home missionary Methodist Church

WSCS, Phila 49-54; A-v libn Asbury Col 55-62; Ser libn UKy Med Center Lib 62-. 9: MedLA-So Reg Group; KyLA. 10: Girl Scouts. 14: Ser, a-v. 15: 817 Arrowhead dr, Lexington Ky 40503.

JONES, FRANCES M (NACHTSHEIM). b Little Rock Ark 27 D 42. 4: Ronald B Jones. 5: Col of St Catherine 60-64 (LS) BA. 6: Portu. 7: Libn Peace Corps Vol UBrasilia, Brasilia Brazil 67; Libn Mt Senario Col 66-67; Libn St Paul Pub Lib, St Paul 67-. 8: Inst Faculty on Pub Lib Serv to Disadvantaged Col of St Catherine 69. 9: ALA (ALA-AFL-CIO Jt Com on Lib Serv to Labor). 14: Pub & commun rel, inner city lib serv, serv to labor. 15: 1080 University ave, St Paul Mn 55104.

JONES, FRANK (JOHN). b Lebanon Tenn 21 D 13. 5: Middle Tenn State Tchrs 32-36 (Eng) BS; UMich 43 (Speech) MA; Peabody 49-50 BS in LS. 7: Tchr Mountainburg Ark 36-37; Tchr St Andrew's Sch, Sewanee Tenn 37-43; Tchr Menlo Sch & Jr Col 43-44; Dir of Pepper Tree Playhouse (theatre) 44-49; Ref dept Stockton Pub Lib, Stockton Cal 50-66. 8: Head of ref dept Stockton Pub Lib 58-60; Dir of Commun Rel 55-66; Ref dept U Pacific 66-. 9: ALA; CalLA. 10: Stockton Civic Theatre. 11: John Cotton Dana Award for publicity 62; Annual Award of Merit (for furtherance of dramatic arts) City of Stockton 65. 12: Consul ed "Pacific Historian" (68 -). 13: Yes. 14: Ref, publ rel. 15: 605 N El Dorado st, Stockton Ca 95203.

JONES, FRANK NICHOLAS. b Reading Penn 19 N 06. 4: Leona Wise Felsted. 5: Harvard 26-30 (Bibliog, Lit) AB, 32-33, 41 (Elizabethan Lit & Bibliog) MA; Columbia 40-41 BS in LS. 6: Fr, Ger, Ital. 7: Asst Queensborough Pub Lib, Jamaica NY summer 30; Asst libn Assn of the Bar Lib, NYC 30-31; Asst in office of dir Boston Pub Lib 33-34; Libn Newburyport Pub Lib, Newburyport Mass 34-36; Deputy supv & chief Sci & Tech Boston Pub Lib 36-40; Asst in ref dept NY Pub Lib 40-41; Gen asst & asst to dir Columbia U Libs 41-42; Admin asst Harvard Col Lib 46-49; Libn & Asst Prof Lib Sci Ohio U 49-57; Dir Peabody Inst Lib 57-66; Chief libn SEast Mass Tech Inst, North Dartmouth Mass 66-; Lecturer Grad Lib Sch URI 68-. 8: Survey of Collections : Towson State Col 63, Wilmington Col (Ohio) 53; Consul collection & plans for new quarters Swain Sch, New Bedford Mass 67; Visiting consul Boston Col 68. 9: ALA (Coun 62-66; Memb Com; Mass State Chm 36-40; Ohio State Chm 51-53; Reg VII 55-57; Com on Bds & Coms 55-57);-ACRL (sec Spec Subj Sect 58-61);-RTSD (sec Copying Methods Sect 61-64);-RSD (Bd 65-68); MassLA (v-pres 69-); OhioLA (pres 53-54); MdLA (pres 61-62); NELA (sec Reg Planning Com 68-). 10: Fellow Amer Geog Soc NY; Baltimore Bibliophiles; Assoc John Carter Brown Lib; Map Collectors' Circle London; 14 West Hamilton Street Club (B altimore); Cartophiles, Cambridge Mass; Old Dartmouth Lib Club. 12: "Atlases on Parade" (64); "George Peabody and the Peabody Institute" (65); "Roads Through History" (66). 13: Yes. 14: Ref, res, admin, exhibs, map collections, cartography, rare bks, lib educ. 15: 635 Elm st, South Dartmouth Ma 02748.

JONES, II FREDERICK S. b Chicago 8 F 30. 4: Sona Mary Tatoian. 5: Yale 48-52 (Soc Sci) AB; Simmons 68-69 MLS. 7: Communications USN 52-55; Chief credit analyst: IrvingTrust Co, NYC 55-59, 3d Nat Bank of Hampden Co, Springfield Mass 59-61; Off serv mgr Star Market Co, Cambridge Mass 61-68; Hd admin serv MIT Libs 69-. 9: ALA; SLA; ASIS. 15: 52 Wildwood dr, Westwood Ma 02090.

JONES, GEORGE HENRY GABRIEL. b Mt Vernon Ohio 25 O 09. 4: Elizabeth Clisby. 5: Oberlin 27-31 (Fine Arts) AB; Kent State 56-57 MLS; Harvard 66 Phd. 6: Fr, Ger. 7: Art dealer, Oberlin Ohio 32-41; Instr URochester 42-43; US Navy LSM 37, Pacific 43-45; Asst Prof & Assoc Prof Lawrence Col 46-53; Libn Community Lib, Northfield Ohio 55-57; Libn Youngstown U 57-. 10: Bd of Trustees, Youngstown Mental Health Assn; Bd of Trustees, Arms Hist Mus. 15: 417 Main st, Poland Oh 44514.

JONES, GERDA ANNEMARIE (HAASE). b Gera Germany 7 Jl 23. 4: Elmer David Jones. 5: Long Beach City Col 53-55 (Hist, Geog) AA; UCal 60-62 (Soc Sci) BA; USoCal 65-66 (LS) MS. 6: Ger. 7: Stud asst UCal (Riverside) 62; Lib asst Rhein-Main AFB Lib 62-65; Catlgr (libn II) ICal (Riverside) 66-. 9: ALA; CalLA; So Cal Tech Proc Gp (SCTPG). 10: Libraria Sodalitas; UCal Alum Assn; USoCal Alum Assn; UCal (Riverside) Fac Club. 11: Alpha Mu Gamma. 14: Catlg, lib admin. 15: 484 Glenhill dr, Riverside Ca 92507.

JONES, GRANT. b Portland Ore 6 O 44. 5: Stanislaus State Col 67 (Hist) BS; USoCal 68 mls. 7: Ref libn Modesto Pub Lib, Modesto Cal 69-. 15: 1200 Marshall, Turlock Ca 95380.

JONES, GWENDOLYN. b Wash DC. 5: CornellU (Sociol) AB; Columbia MLS. 7: Libn St Regis paper Co, NYC 56-. 9: SLA. 12: "Packaging Information Sources" (67). 15: St Regis Paper Co 150 E 42nd st, New York NY 10017.

JONES, H(OUSTON) G(WYNNE). b Yanceyville NC 7 Ja 24. 5: Appalachian State Col 46-49 (Hist) BS; Peabody-Vanderbilt U 49-50 (Hist) MA; Duke 53-55, 65 (Hist) PhD. 6: Fr. 7: US Navy Yeoman 42-46; Prof of hist Oak Ridge Mil Inst (Oak Ridge NC) 50-53; Chm Div of Soc Sci W Ga Col 55-56; State Archivist State of NC, Raleigh NC 56-68; Dir NC Dept of Archives & Hist 68-. 8: Consul: Survey of Lib Functions of the States (AAStateL) 61-65; Governor's Commsn on Lib Resources NC 64-65; Lecturer Radcliffe Col Inst on Hist Admin 60. 9: Fellow, SAA (treas 61-67, v-pres 67-68, pres 68-69, chm State Records Com 61). 10: Various nat & reg hist assns. 11: R D W Connor Hstorical Award 56; Waldo G Leland Prize 67. 12: Union List of North Carolina Newspapers" (63); "The County Records Manual" (62); "The M unicipal Records Manual" (61); "Bedford Brown; State Rights Unionist" (56); "Records o Nation" (69); "For History's Sake" (65). 14: Archival & records admin. 15: P O Box 1881, Raleigh NC 27602.

JONES, HAROLD D. b Phila 26 Je 11. 4: Ferrell Taylor Jones. 5: Swarthmore 29-33 (Econ) BA; Drexel 34-35 BS in LS; UPenn 36-40 (Econ) MA; Temple 41; Columbia 41, summer 47-51, 57-61 (LS). 7: Libn Haverford Penn 35-41; Libn William Penn Charter Sch 41-42; AUS Info Educ Spec (Sgt) 42-45; Libn Admiral Farragut Acad 46; Head libn & Chm Lib Sci Dept Fairmont State Col 47-52; Asst libn Brooklyn Col of City U 61-65, Asst to libn 52-61, Asst Prof 65-, Visiting asst Prof to Conn State Col Sch of Lib Sci summer 66; Visiting asst prof Sch of Sci UOkla (Norman) summers 67-69; Lecturer Pratt Inst 68-69. 8: Lib Bldg Planning consul; Consul Mitchel Col LIU 63 (collection bldg) Tech Serv Dept 64. 9: ALA; BSA; Gutenberg Gesellschaft; WVaLA (pres Col Sect 50-51); Sec Educ Bd Lib Commsn (sec 38-42); NY Lib Club; LACUNY (pres 64-66); NYLA (mem bldg com). 10: AAUP; St David's Soc in State of NY; Brooklyn Col Faculty Club; LI Hist S oc. 12: "The Development of Reference Services in Colleges for Teacher Education, 1929-1958," ACRL Microcard Series No 139 (63). 13: Yes. 14: Admin, ref, bibliog, acad lib bldg planning; tchg lib sci tchg classes in subject bibliog & in effective use of lib. 15: Brooklyn Col Lib, Brooklyn NY 11210.

JONES, HAROLD JOSEPH. b Abington Penn 18 O 36. 5: West Chester SC 54-58 (Secondary Educ) BS; UPenn 58-59 (Amer Civilization) MA; Drexel 63-65 (LS) MS. 7: Tchr Upper Darby Sch Dist, Upper Darby Penn 59-64; Libn Marple-Newtown Joint Schs, Newtown Square Penn 64-66; Lib supv sch dist Phila Penn 66-. 9: ALA; NEA; Penn State EA; PennLA. 14: Sch libnship. 15: 205-1/2 Benezet st, Phila Pa 19118.

JONES, HAZEL S (JOHNSON). b Port Gibson Miss 20 O 17. 5: Alcorn Col 30-42 (Eng, Educ) BS; Atlanta 47-50 BS in LS; UMich 62 MA in LS. 6: Fr. 7: Tchr-libn Addison High Sch, Port Gibson Miss 37-42; Tchr-libn Valena C Jones Bay, St Louis Miss 42-45; Tchr libn Magnolia High Sch, Magnolia Miss 45-49; Asst libn Grambling Col 49-. 9: ALA; LaEA; LaLA. 10: Beta Phi Mu; Delta Sigma Theta; Oral Hist Assn. 14: Ref, archives. 15: P O Box 472, Grambling La 71245.

JONES, HELEN (IRENE). b Vaiden Miss 12 Jl 21. 5: Miss State Col for Women 42 (Eng) BA; Emory 45-46 BALS. 7: Libn VA, Memphis Tenn 46-47; Libn VA, Bay Pines Fla 47-48; Libn VA, Memphis Tenn 48-51, Chief Libn 51-. 9: MedLA (So Reg Group). 14: Ref. 15: 1030 Jefferson ave, Memphis Tn 38104.

JONES, HOLWAY ROY. b New Orleans 11 O 22. 4: Frances Doreen Lockstone. 5: Santa Ana Jr Col 41-42 (Hist); USoCal summers 45, 47; UCal(Berkeley) 45-48 (Hist) AB, 49-51 BLS, 48-55 (Hist) MA. 6: Fr, Sp. 7: Tool planner & designer Douglas Aircraft Co, Long Beach Cal 42-45; UCal(Berkeley): Documents libn 51-54, City & reg plan libn 55-62, Jr research city planner 58-62, City & reg plan libn 62-63; Head soc sci libn UOre 63-. 8: Consul & instr, Dept of Urban & Reg Planning UWis, Ap & My 65; Assoc Prof of Libnship UOre 66-. 9: Coun of Planning Libns (treas 63-, chm By-Laws Com 60, chm Com on Index & Abstr 63-64, chm Com on Exch Bibliog 60-); SLA; PNLA; West Hist Assn; AHA; Cal Hist Soc (Hon). 10: Sierra Club; Friends of the Three Sisters Wilderness; Phi Alpha Theta; Wilderness Soc; Nat Parks Assn; Oregon Environmental Coun; North Cascades Conservation Coun; Fed of West Outdoor Clubs. 12: "City Planning: A Basic Bibliography of Sources and Trends," with G C Bestor (62);

"John Muir and the Sierra Club: The Battle for Yosemite" (65); "Urban an Regional Planning Resources of the University of Wisconsin and of the Community of Madison" (65); "Selected Bibliography of Books and Reports on the Forest Product Industries," with S U Rich (63); "Exchange Bibliographies" (57-)67; Co-auth "French Pete Creek Intermediate Recreation Area; A Prototype" (68). 13: Yes. 14: Ref, spec collections, research & tchg. 15: Univ of Ore lib, Eugene Ore 97403.

JONES, HUGO WILLIAM. b Long Beach Cal 12 Ja 20. 4: Nancy Old. 5: UAriz 37-39 (Bus admin); USoCal 39-41 (Bus Admin) BS in BA, 61-66 MSLS. 7: Lt Aviator US Navy, USA 41-45; Advertising production Andrews- Johnson Adv, Los Angeles 46-47; Publ production Crow Publishing Co, Los Angeles 47-49; Advertising prod mgt Kay-Christopher Adv, Los Angeles 49-51; Northrop Norair, Hawthorne Cal: Tech publs prod 51-55, Tech reports admin 55-58, Tech info lib admin 58-. 8: Chm Adv Com Pacific Tech Info Lib 67-68. 9: ASIS (LA chap & treas 62-65, chm elect 69; Treas Nat Conv (ADI) 66); SLA (So Cal Chap; Publns Chm 67, treas 68-69). 10: Manhattan Beach Badminton Club; Toastmasters Club; Northrop Mgt Club (sec 63-64, parliamentarian 64-66). 12: "Index of Northrop Reports on the Snark Missile Project" (58); "Index of Northrop Engineering Reports," for years 54, 55, 56, 57. 14: Admin, info retrieval, machine applications to lib operations. 15: 432 30th st, Manhattan Beach Cal 90266.

JONES, J ELIAS. b Cleveland 18 O 16. 4: Bonnee May Koger. 5: West Res 37-41 (Pre-med, Chem) AB, 41-42 BS in LS, 49-51 (Romance Lang, Fr) AM, 58-64 (Romance Lang, Fr) PhD. 6: Fr, Ger, Russian, Welsh. 7: Asst libn bus info bur Cleveland Pub Lib, Cleveland Ohio 42; US Army 42-45; Libn Morale Serv Br, Guadalcanal (US Army) 43-45; Asst sci & tech div Cleveland Pub Lib 45-47; Research libn Ferro Corp, Cleveland Ohio 47-49; Asst head sci & tech div Cleveland Pub Lib 49-52, Chief catlg div 52-57; Dir of Libs Drake U 57-, Assoc Prof Romance Langs 64-, Assoc dir & bibliog 68-. 8: Visiting Instr: Rutgers Grad Sch of Lib Sci summer 56, UDenver Grad Sch of Lib Sci summer 57, UMinn Lib Sch summer 63; Instr in Russian UCollege Drake U 59-65; Visiting instr UIll Grad Lib Sch summer 67. 9: ALA (Coun 56-58, chm Clsf Com 54-58); BSA; IowaLA (chm Mem Com 58-59). 10: Lib Club of Cleveland; Lib Club of Des Moines; Hist of Sci Soc; Mod Lang Assn; Phi Sigma Iota; Torch Club of Des Moines. 12: Managing ed "Enamelist," magazine Ferro Corp (47-50). 13: Yes. 14: Documentation, bibliog control of lib materials, ref methodology, subj bibliog, lit of scis. 15: Cowles Lib 28th & University ave, Des Moines Iowa 50311.

JONES, JAMES L. b Mauston Wis 7 D 18. 4: Jeanne M Erickson. 5: UWis 39-4 9 (Agric) BS; UIll 49-51 (LS) MS. 6: Fr, Ital, Sp. 7: Pharmacy libn UWis(Madison) 51-56; Head br libs Colo State U 56-57; Tech libn Armour Pharmaceutical Co, Kankakee Ill 57-58; Med libn VA Hosp, Tomah Wis 58-61; Optometric libn Ill Col Optometry 62-65; Acquis libn Bemidji State Col, Bemidji Minn 65-; Ref libn Bowling Green State U 68-. 9: Amer Assn Col of Pharm (chm Lib Com); Assn Schs & Cols of Optometry (chm Lib Com). 13: Yes. 14: Ref (sci & tech). 15: 1104 East Wooster, Bowling Green Oh 43402.

JONES, JANE (SADLER). b Phila 26 O 19. 4: Donald W Jones. 5: Temple 36-40 (Fr) BS in Ed; Drexel 40-41 (LS) Masters Equivalent; Sorbonne & UMex summers Certifs. 6: Fr, Sp. 7: Ref dept Free Lib of Phila 41-42; Libn Sch Dist of Phila: Bartlett Jr High Sch 42-54, Fels Jr High Sch 53-. 8: Amateur ham radio operator. 9: ALA; Sch Libns Assn of Phila & Vicinity (sec 64-66). 10: Amer Fed of Tchrs. 14: Sch lib wk. 15: Fels Jr High Sch, Devereaux & Langdon Phila 19111.

JONES, JEAN CLARK (MRS). b Youngstown Ohio 6 D 13. 5: Wells 33-34; West Res 34-37 (Eng) BA; Carnegie 38-39 BS in LS.; Fairmont State Col 53-55 (Educ) Tchrs Certif. 6: Fr. 7: Catlgr Fairmont State Col 55-58; Libn Linmoor Jr High Sch, Columbus Ohio 58-61; Libn Ross Labs, Columbus Ohio 61-63; Libn Amer Psychiatric Assn, Wash DC 63-. 8: Active in promoting libnship in psychiatric insts. 9: ALA; MedLA; SLA (Soc Sci Div, Biol Scis Div; Sec Biol Scis Div DC Chap); SAA; ADI. 10: SANE; LWV; Amer Assn for the Hist of Med; Hist of Med Soc of Wash DC; Oral Hist Assn. 14: Hist of Amer psychiatry & psychiatry in general. 15: Amer Psychiatric Assn 1700 18th st NW, Wash DC 20009.

JONES, JEWEL E (SCHOCK). b Allentown Penn 7 N 30. 4: Stanley L Jones Jr. 5: Kutztown State Col 48-52 (LS) BS in Ed. 7: E Penn Union Sch Dist, Emmaus Penn: Sr high sch libn 52-54, Eng tchr 54-55, Jr high sch libn 55-60, Eng tchr 60-61; Elem libn Allentown Sch Dist, Allentown Penn 61-64, Supv of libs 64-. 9: NEA; ALA; ASSchL; Penn State EA; PennLA. 10: Bus & Prof Women's Club; AAUW. 14: Child wk. 15: Rt 3, Allentown Pa 18104.

JONES, KOHAR (KANTZIAN). b Pine Hill NY 28 S 23. 4: Theodore Jones. 5: George Washington U 40-41; Queens Col 58-59, 60-61 (Christian Educ) BS; UNC 64-65 MSLS. 6: Fr, Sp, Armenian. 7: Claims rep Dept Health Educ & Welfare, Va, WVa, NC 61-62; Lib trainee Pub Lib of Charlotte & Mecklenburg Co, NC 63-64; Ref libn Pub Lib of Charlotte & Mecklenburg Co, NC 65-. 14: Ref. 15: 434 Poindexter dr, Charlotte NC 28209.

JONES, LAURIE (ANNIE). b Americus Ga 25 D 14. 5: Ga State Col for Women 32-36 (Eng, Sp) AB; UNC 44-45 BS in LS. 6: Sp, Fr. 7: Tchr-libn Pub high schs, Ga 37-44; Libn High Sch, Gainesville Ga 44-45; Br libn GS5-7 Spec Serv, Ft Benning Ga 45-47; Libn Pub Lib, LaGrange Ga 47-48; Ref & circ libn GS7 & GS9 US Army Infantry Sch Lib, Ft Benning Ga 48-. 14: Ref. 15: 1105 Lockwood ave, Columbus Ga 31906.

JONES, LOIS MARIAN. b Puyallup Wash 20 Ag 16. 5: Linfield Col 34-36 (Lit); UWash 36-39 BA (Lit), BS in LS. 7: Libn Aberdeen Pub Lib, Aberdeen Wash 39-41; Ref libn UWash 41-46; Ref libn Lib of Hawaii, Honolulu 46-48; Ref libn Los Angeles Pub Lib 48-53, Dept libn Lit & Philol 53-. 9: ALA; CalLA (Ed Com 64-). 14: Ref. 15: Los Angeles Pub Lib 630 W 5th st, Los Angeles Ca 90017.

JONES, LOWELL (JACK). b Glennsferry Ida 28 Ja 23. 4: Winifred Guss Jones. 5: Wash State U 46 (Pre-med); East Wash State Col 47-48 (Educ) BA in Ed; Colo State U 53-54 (Admin) MA; UWash 64-65 M in Libnship; UOre 68-69 (Lib Mech). 6: Fr. 7: Aviation electronics instr US Navy, US 43-45; Tchr & admin pub educ, Wash State 48-50; Tchr pub educ, Ariz State 51-52; Tchr pub educ, Colo State 53-54; Tchr pub educ, Ore State 54-57; Tchr pub educ, Wash State 57-61; Libn ref Pierce Co Pub Lib, Tacoma Wash 65-. Supv brs & ref Boeing Co Commun Div, Seattle -Renton Wash 66-67; Dir Renton Pub Lib, Renton Wash 67-. 8: Ind engnr Boeing Co, Renton Wash 62-64. 9: ALA; SLA; Wash State LA; PNLA. 10: Civitan Rotary. 14: Ref, admin. 15: 8025 NE 124th, Kirkland Wa 98033.

JONES, MABEL (BARRETT). b Ponce PR 25 F 11. 4: Clifford Foy Jones. 5: Elon Col 28-29, 31-32, summer 42 (Eng) BA; UNC 45-46 BS in LS. 6: Sp, Portu, Ital. 7: Supv of Lib Proj WPA, Caldwell-Wilkes Cos NC 37-41; Jr high sch tchr Caldwell Co Sch System, Hudson NC 42-43; Asst libn Caldwell Co Lib, Lenoir NC 43-45; Catlgr UNC Lib (Chapel Hill) 46-. 9: NCLA; SELA. 10: Faculty Club. 14: Catlg. 15: P O Box 302, Chapel Hill NC 27514.

JONES, MARGARET (BOWER). b Kingston Mo 29 O 25. 4: Forrest L Jones. 5: Central Col 43-45; UKan 45-47 (Educ) BS; UIll 51-52 (LS) MS. 7: Child libn Kan City (Mo) Pub Lib 52-57; Tchr Army Dependent Sch, Boeblingen Germany 58-61; Tchr Pub Sch, Rapid City SD 62-64; Yp libn Pub Lib, Sioux Falls SD 65-. 14: Child & yp wk. 15: 2909 E 13th st, Sioux Falls Sd 57103.

JONES, MARGARET F. b E Lynn WVa 24 Mr 30. 5: Berea Col 47-51 (Biol) BA; Bryn Mawr 51-53 (Biol) MA; Simmons 63-65 (LS) MS. 6: Fr. 7: Research asst UIll(Chicago) 53-54; Research asst Northwestern U 54-57; Research asst UChicago 57-59; Research asst UIll(Chicago) 59-60; Research asst MIT 61-62; Ref libn Harvard U Med Lib 62-65; Senior ref libn Countway Lib Med Sch, Boston 65-66; Senior ref libn Calhoun Med Lib Emory U 66-67; Chief reader's serv Med Ctr Lib Duke U 66-. 9: SLA; MedLA. 10: Mensa. 15: 4427 Erwin rd, Durham Nc 27705.

JONES, MARION (GRAY). b Sharon Hill Penn 9 Ap 12. 4: Wm Lane Jones Jr. 5: Wilson Col 30-34 (Eng) BA; Columbia 42 (LS) BS. 6: Fr. 7: Sec Charles E Ellis Sch, Newtown Sq Penn 35-36, Libn 37-42; Libn Wm Penn Charter Sch, Phila 43-47; Ed wk Scott Foresman & Co Publ, Chicago summers 43, 44; Church libn Methodist Church, Lansdowne Penn 54-62; Libn No Home for Child, Phila 55; Bkmobile libn Upper Darby Pub Lib, Upper Darby Penn 61-. 14: Child libs, sch libs; bkmobs. 15: 246 Congress ave, Lansdowne Pa 19050.

JONES, MARION ADELL (ROWLEY). b Lonoke Ark 8 N 17. 4: Haskell Lee Jones. 5: Central Baptist Col 35- 37 (Dramatics) AA & Dramatics; UArk 52 (Speech, Eng, Soc Studies) BSE; UKy 54, summers 55-57, & 58 MS in LS; USoCal summer 64 (LS); Uill summer 67. 07: Jr high tchr Carlisle Pub Schs, Hamilton Ark 37-39; Elem tchr Lead Hill Pub Schs, Lead Hill Ark 40-41; Elem tchr Western Grove Pub Schs, Western Grove Ark 42-48; Elem tchr Valley Springs Pub Schs, Bellefonte & Valley Springs 49-52; Libn N Ark Reg Lib, Harrison Ark 53-58; Libn Arkadelphia Pub Schs, Arkadelphia Ark 58-63; Libn Walnut Ridge Jr Sr High Sch, Columbus Ohio

63-65; Asst libn Henderson State Col 65-. 9: ALA; NEA; ArkLA (Life mem); ArkEA. 13: Yes. 14: Catlg. 15: Rt 3 Box 227, Arkadelphia Ar 71923.

JONES, MARY (MARGARET) CHAMBERS. b Aberdeen SD 22 Jl 28. 5: Duchesne Col of the Sacred Heart 46-50 (Eng Lit) BA; UMinn summers 51, 52 (Educ); UPortland summer 58 (LS); Portland State Col ext 55-61 (Educ, LS); UCLA 62-63 MLS. 7: Eng tchr Leon High Sch, Leon Iowa 50-52; Tchr-libn Belk Plaine High Sch, Belk Plaine Iowa 53-54; Libn Lake Oswego Jr High Sch, Lake Oswego Ore 56-60; Stud prof libn Neuro-Psychiatric Inst UCLA 63; Lecturer UOre summer 64; Libn Henry D Sheldon High Sch, Eugene Ore 63-65; Catlg lib Multnomah Co Lib, Portland Ore 65-66; Libn John Marshall High Sch, Portland Ore 66-. 8: Sch lib consul Proj Eng UOre summer 64. 9: NEA; ALA-AASchL (Improvement & Extension of Sch Lib Programs Com); OreASchL (sec-treas 58-59, Conf chm 59 & 64); OreEA; OreLA; AASL (Quotable Quotes Com). 14: Sch libs, catlg. 15: 1719 SW 16th apt 13, Portland Or 97201.

JONES, MAUDE IRENE. b Dowagiac Mich 3 D 02. 5: UWis 21-25 (Eng) BA, 24-25 (LS) Certif; UInd 28 (Eng). 6: Fr, Sp. 7: Jr catlgr Utica Pub Lib, Utica NY 25-27; Catlgr Ind U Lib 27-28; Catlgr med sci dept Detroit Pub Lib 28-41, Catlgr Burton Hist Collection 41-45; Asst to chief catlg div US Army Med Lib, Wash DC 45-47, Head of subj catlg sect 45-49; Assoc libn Tenn U Med Units Mooney Mem Lib 49-59, Libn 59-. 8: Consul US VA Med Lib Evaluation Program 58; Mem of coun on postgrad training for sci libns UTenn Med Units 66-. 09: ALA; MedLA (Bd Dirs 60-63, Pub Rel Off 48-50, chm &/or mem 5 coms 43-58); Tenn State LA; Memphis Libns Com (chm 66-68). 10: AAUW; UWis Alumni Assn; YWCA; Alpha Omicron Pi; Delta Kappa Gamma. 12: 'Classification,' in Handbook of Medical Library Practice" (1st ed 43, 2d ed 56). 13: Yes. 14: Admin. 15: 1467 Tutwiler ave, Memphis Tn 38107.

JONES, MILBREY L. b Macon Ga 22 N 28. 5: Woman's Col of Ga 49 (Eng) AB; Emory 53 MLibnship; Rutgers 63 PhD. 7: Sch libn Eatonton High Sch, Eatonton Ga 49-50; Sch libn Cairo High Sch, Cairo Ga 50-53; Sch libn High Point City Schs, High Point NC 53-55; Child libn Coleman Lib, LaGrange Ga 56; Asst Prof Lib Sci Madison Col (Harrisonburg Va) 56-63, Assoc Prof Lib Sci 63-65; Sch lib spec instr resources sect Div of Plans & Supplementary Centers Off of Educ, Wash DC 6568, Program off northeast program operations br div or State Agency Coop 68-. of Plans & Supplementary Centers Off of Educ, Wash DC 65-68, Program off northeast program operations br Div of State Agency Coop 68-. 9: ALA-RTSD (chm Sch Lib Tech Serv Com 65-67). 13: Yes. 14: Sch libs. 15: Office of Educ, Wash DC 20202.

JONES, MYRTIS. b Prescott Ark 16 My 08. 5: Little Rock Jr Col 50-52 (Liberal Arts) Diploma; Ark State Tchrs Col 50-58 (Educ) BSE; Peabody 62-65 MLS. 7: Lib asst Little Rock Jr Col 51-52; Libn Holly Grove High Sch, Holly Grove Ark 55; Libn Vanndale High Sch, Vanndale Ark 55-56; Libn Stuttgart Sr High Sch, Stuttgart Ark 56-59; Suov sch libs Pub Schs, Stuttgart Ark 56-59; Libn Ark Sch for the Blind, Little Rock Ark 59-. 8: Lib Com Commsn on Standards & Accreditation of Servs for the Blind; Chm Lib Sci Wkshop of Amer Assn of Instr of the Blind; Sponsor ASLA Exec Coun; Sponsor Exec Coun Dist XIX ASLA; Awards Com Joseph Campbell Citation, Round Table for the Blind ALA. 9: NEA; ALA; CEC; Amer Assn Instr Blind; ArkLA; SWLA; ArkEA. 10: Libn Harrison Mem Lib Geyer Springs Method Church. 11: John Cotton Dana Publicity Award 57; AAIB Citation for Outstanding Service 62; Outstanding Achievement Award Commsn on Standards and Accreditation of Serv for the Blind 66. 13: Yes. 14: Org visually handicapped. 15: 5608 Geyer Springs rd, Little Rock Ar 72004.

JONES, MYRTLE C (EMERSON). b Conway Ark 17 Mr 09. 4: Rufus Jones. 5: Northeastern State Col 24-27 (Eng) AB; Peabody 31 (LS) Certif. 7: Head libn State Tchrs Col (Florence Ala) 28-46; Ref libn Nurnberg Mil Post, APO NY 46-48; Command libn 13th Air Force, APO San Francisco 48-50; Post libn Ft Polk, La 50-54; Catlgr AFPTRC Lib, Lackland AFB Tex 54-55; Post libn Ft Hood, Tex 55-56; Base libn Edwards AFB, Cal 56-58; Chief libn Tech Lib, Edwards AFB Cal 58-. 9: ALA; CalLA. 13: Yes. 14: Catlg, ref. 15: 43626 N Fig ave, Lancaster Ca 93534.

JONES, NANON HILBUN. b Malad Ida 6 Ja 29. 4: Robert M Jones. 5: UWash 47-52 (Sociol) BA, 63 (LS) ML. 7: Clerk documents sect UWash Lib 50-52; Libn US Army Lib, Ft Ord Cal 52-54; Br libn King Co Pub Lib, Bellevue Wash 56-. 9: ALA; PNLA; Wash State LA. 10: Soroptimist Fed. 14: Ref, admin. 15: 12833 SE 45th pl, Bellevue Wa 98004.

JONES, NORMA LOUISE. b Poplar Wis. 5: Wis State U (Superior) (Eng) BE; UMinn 52 (LS, Eng) MA; UIll 57 (LS); UMich 58-65 (LS, Eng) PhD. 7: Tchr-libn pub schs, ND, Wis, Mich; Libn pub schs, Grand Rapids Mich; Instr Central MichU 54-55; Lect UMich (Grand Rapids) 61; Libn pub schs, Benton Harbor Mich 62-63; Lectr UMich 63-65; Asst Prof 66-68; Asst Prof Wis StateU (Oshkosh) 68-. 8: Consul to Libs at Huron Valley (Mich) Schs, 66-67. 9: ALA (mem of all divisions & sections); WisLA (Lib Educ Com). 10: Phi Beta Kappa; Phi Kappa Phi; Sigma Pi Epsilon; Pi Lamba Theta; Beta Phi Mu. 12: "A Study of the Book Collections in the Biological Sciences in Fifty-Four Michigan High Schools" (65); "Survey and Analysis of the Extent to Which Junior and Senior High School Pupils Read the Same Material" (52); "A Survey of the Huron Valley Michigan School Libraries, with Eugenia Schmitz (67). 15: Dept of Lib Sci, Wisconsin State Univ, Oshkosh Wi 53807.

JONES, PATRICIA ANN (IWAN). b Pierre SD 24 Jl 41. 4: Gary A Jones. 5: Huron Col 59-63 (Eng, Lit) BA; UDenver 63-64 (LS) MA. 6: Sp. 7: Stud asst Huron Col Lib 59-63; Asst libn Ella McIntire Lib Huron Col 65; Period libn Lincoln Mem Lib SD State U 66-; Circ libn 66-67. 9: ALA; SDLA. 10: AAUW. 14: Catlg, period, circ. 15: 1217-1/2 8th st, Brookings SD 57006.

JONES, REBA W. b Wilkes Co Ga 21 Je 09. 5: Appalachian State Tchrs Col 52 (Soc Sci, LS) BS, 56 (Educ) MA. 7: Elem libn supv Statesville City Schs, Statesville NC 54-57; Libn Decatur High Sch, Decatur Ga 57-60; Sch lib supv USAF, Japan 60-62; Libn DeKalb Co, Decatur Ga 62-63; Libn US Army, Europe, Germany 63-64; Libn Decatur High Sch, Decatur Ga 64-. 14: Ya bks. 15: 820 Stratford rd, Avondale Estates Ga 30002.

JONES, ROBERT ALLEN. b Strasburg Ohio 19 O 38. 4: Christine Coolidge. 5: Col of Wooster 56-60 (Hist) BA; UIll 60-62 (LS) MS; West Res 63- (Amer Culture) MA, 69- (Amer Culture). 07: Circ asst UIll Lib (Urbana) 61-62, Acquis asst 62-63; Asst catlgr Col of Wooster Lib 63-64, Head catlgr 64-68, Asst libn & head tech serv 68-. 9: ALA; OhioLA; No Ohio Tech Serv Libns (v-chm 68-69; chm 69-70). 10: Amer Studies Assn; Faculty Club, College of Wooster; Phi Alpha Theta; Beta Phi Mu. 13: Yes. 14: Tech serv, lib arch, admin. 15: 418 Bloomington ave, Wooster Oh 44691.

JONES, ROGER GAW. b Gainesboro Tenn 29 Ja 29. 4: Christine Spivey Jones. 5: Tenn Tech U 47-50 (Soc Sci) BS; Peabody 56 MA(LS). 6: Fr. 7: Elem prin Jackson Co, Gainesboro Tenn 50-51; US Army, Army War Col (Carlisle Barracks Penn) 51-53; Second sch libn Monterey High Sch, Monterey Tenn 53-55; Catlg libn Tenn tech U 55-. 9: ALA; TennLA; TennEA. 11: Louis Shores Lib Medal, George Peabody Lib Sch 56. 14: Catlg. 15: 1489 Barnes st, Cookeville Tenn 38501.

JONES, ROSA ELLEN (HALLARD). b Pecos Tex 15 Ag 39. 4: Robert Elbert Jones. 5: Odessa Col 58-60 (Educ) AA; Tex Woman's U 62-63 (LS) BS. 7: Clerk Ector Co Lib, Odessa Tex 58-62; Stud asst Tex Woman's U Lib 62-63;Lbn Hudler Jr High, Monahans Tex 63-. 9: Tex State Tchrs Assn; TexLA. 10: Amer Bus Women's Assn; Beta Sigma Phi; Ward Co Friends of the Lib. 1child & yp bks. 14: Child & yp bks . 15: 1204 South Bruce P O BO 734, Monahans Tx 79756.

JONES, RUBY (BROUGHTON). 5: Sue Bennett Jr Col 36-38 (Educ) Certif; East State Tchrs Col 39 (Educ); Catherine Spalding Col 54-55 (Educ) BS, 5 MSLS. 7: Elem tchr Charleston Mo 48-50; Elem tchr Jefferson Co Pub Schs, Ky 54-60; Libn Jefferson Co Pub Schs, Kerrick Ky 60-69. 8: Libn Rockford Lane Baptist Church. 9: NEA; KyLA; KySchLA; KyEA; Jefferson Co TA. 15: 4809 Ranchland dr, Louisville Ky 40216.

JONES, RUTH NAOMI. b Buffalo NY 12 Ja 38. 5: NY State Col for Tchrs (Buffalo) 55-57 (Elem Educ); UWash 57 -59 (Eng, Educ) BA, 59-64 M of Libnship. 7: Jr hi gh sch tchr Highline Sch Dist, Seattle 59-62, Jr high sch libn 62-67; Asst Prof of Lib Sci & Educ East Wash State Col 67-69. 9: ALA; NEA; Wash State ASchL; WashEA. 14: Young adults, sch lib admin. 15: W 2007 Grace, Spokane Wa 99205.

JONES, SARAH DOWLIN. b Media Penn 20 S 16. 5: UPenn 33-37 (Eng) AB, 37-39 (Eng) AM, 54 (Eng) PhD; Pratt 43-44 BLS. 6: Fr, Ger. 7: Order asst Lippincott Lib UPenn 39-43lerk NY Pub Lib 43; Ref asst Pratt Inst Lib 43-44; Ref libn Amer Lib, London 45-47; Libn Math-Physics Lib UPenn 47-49, Head ref libn 49-52; Libn Goucher Col 52-. 8: Visiting Coms Middle StatesAssn; Consul on Md State Col Libs, Bd of Trustees of the State Cols 65. 9: ALA (Coun 68-71); ACRL; MDLA. 10: Mod Lang Assn; Women's Internat League for Peace & Freo& pi Beta Kappa; Mortar Board. 13: Yes. 14: Admin, acquis, ref. 15: 24 Aylesbury rd, Timonium Md 21093.

JONES, SHIRLEY ANN (TIPPETT). b Oxford NC 3 F 42. 4: John Tucker Jones. 5: E Car U 64 (Bus Educ, Eng) BS, 66 (LS) MA. 7: Asst periods libn E Car U 66-67; Dir Learning Resources Ctr Craven Tech Inst 67-. 9: NCLA (sec-treas JMRT); NCEA (chm local Legis Com). 10: Alpha Beta Alpha; New Bern-Craven Co Friends of Pub Lib; Pilot Club. 15: 501 Metcalf st, New Bern NC.

JONES, SHIRLEY (LEONE). b Moncton NB Can 8 N 29. 5: Mt Allison U 47-51 (Hit) BA; Toronto 51-52 BLS. 6: Fr. 7: Gen libn Pub Lib, St Catharines Ont 52-56, Ref libn 56-60; Chief Libn Pub Lib, Welland Ont 60-. bns Com Nigara Reg Lib Syst St Catharines Ont 63-, Adv com lib techn course Niagara Col of Applied Arts & Tech 67-. 9: CanLA; Inst Prof Libns Ontario; OntLA (Exec ADUT Serv6165). 10: Bus & Prof Women's Club; Can Fed Univ Women. 13: Yes. 14: Ref, loc hist. 15: 211 Willson rd, Welland Ont Can.

JONES, SHIRLI (O'BRIEN). b Tacoma Wash 7 D 25. 4: . 5: UCal (Los Angeles) 47-49 (Psych); San Jose State Col 46-47 (Radio Engnr). 6: Sp. 7: Engnr libn Douglas Aircraft Co, Santa Monica Cal 55-61, Engnr admin libn 61-64, Corporate libn 64-67, 69-, Chief libn 67-69. 9: SLA; ASIS. 13: Yes. 14: Admin, mechanized systems. 15: McDonnell Douglas Corp, St Louis Mo 63166.

JONES, STELLA MARGUERITE. b Waukon Iowa 11 Ap 06. 5: Upper Iowa U 33 (Hist, Eng, Educ) BA; State U Iowa summer 3, 57; State U Colo summer 39, 41; Northwestern summer 53; UDenver 62 (LS) MA. 7: Normal train supv Shell Rock High Sch, Shell Rock Iowa 35-44; Eng tchr Decorah High Sch, Decorah Iowa 44-47; Hist tchr Jr High Sch, Arlington Heights Ill 47-49; Eng tchr DeWitt Commun High Sch, DeWitt Iowa 53-60; Libn DeWitt Commun High Sch, DeWitt Iowa 60-61; Libn Camanche High Sch Lib, Camanche Iowa 61-69. 9: ALA; NEA; Iowa State EA; IowaLA; IowaCTE. 10: AAUW; Wa Tan Ye (Nat Serv Club); Delta Kappa Gamma; Daughters of Amer Colonists; YWCA; DAR; Pi Kappa Delta; Sigma Tau Delta; PTO. 14: Catlg, ref (hist & geneal). 15: 2385 Chancy st, Clinton Ia 52732.

JONES, THELMA (HICKS). b Clearview Okla 9 Mr 28. 4: Joe Jones. 5: Langston U 44-48 (Sociol) BA; UOkla 57 MLS. 6: Sp. 7: Tchr High Sch, Hugo Okla 48-52; Tchr-libn Dunjee High Sch, Choctaw Okla 52-54; Libn Dunbar Elem Sch, Okla City Okla 54-57; Elem sch lib consul, Okla City Okla 57-67, Coord sch media ctrs 67-. 8: Instr lib sci OklaU; Asst dir HEW Inst for pub & acad libns OklaU 68. 9: NEA; ALA; OklaEA; O klaLA (chm Recruitment Com). 10: Alpha Kappa Alpha; Urban League Vista Club Delta Kappa Gamma. 14: Child wk, ya, sch libnship. 15: 1233 NE 47th st, Okla City Ok 73111.

JONES, VANCE HARPER. b Washington NC 2 Mr 38. 5: UMiami 56-61 (Organ) BMus, 61-63 (Organ) MMus; Emory 63-64 MLibnship. 7: Art & music libn Miami Beach Pub Lib, Miami Beach Fla 64-; AUP; Pi Kappa Lambda. 63-64 MLibn7:USILIBN Miami BeachPub Lib, Miami Beach Fla 6466; Organist Bryan Memorial Methodist Church, Miami Fl 64-66; Astref libn Caldosta State Col 66-68; Organist Christ Espiscopal Church, VadostGa 68; Organist St Timothy's Episcopal Church, Raleigh NC 69; Ref libn St Augustine's Col 68-. 9: SELA; FlaLA; ALA; NEA. 10: Omicron Delta Kappa; Phi Mu Alpha Sinfonia; Amer Guild of Organists; Organist Bryan Mem Method Church, Miami Fla 64-; AAUP; Pi Kappa Lambda. 14: Ref, pub serv. 15: P O Box 319, Washington Nc 27889.

JONES, VESTA KATHARINE. b Brooklyn NY 21 Ap 10. 5: Hunter Col 27-31 (Hist) BA; Columbia 31-32 (Pol Sci, hist) MA; Pratt 39-40 BLS. 7: Queens Borough Pub Lib, Jamaica NY: Asst br libn & child libn Seaside Br 40-45, Child libn Jackson Heights Br 45-51, Asst head tchrs collection 51-55, Br libn 55-57, Reg libn 57-, Dir "Operation Head Start" & reg libn 65-. 9: ALA; NYLA; NY Lib Club. 10: Pratt Lib Sch Alumni Assn; Beta Phi Mu. 14: Ref, child serv, admin. 15: 120-10 85 ave, Kew Gardens NY 11415.

JONES, VIRGIL LEROY. b Leedey Okla 24 My 36. 5: SWest State Col (Weatherford Okla) (summer) 55; UOkla (Norman) 55-71 (Bus Admin) BBA, 61-68 (Lib Sci) MLS. 7: Lib stud asst UOkla (Norman) 55-62; Lib asst Presbyterian Hosp Lib (Okla City) 62-66; Research libn UOkla Med Ctr (Okla City) 66-. 8: MedLA certif grade I. 9: MedLA; OklaLA. 14: Med libnship, ref. 15: 1344 Dorchester dr, Norman Ok 73069.

JONES, VIRGINIA (CHURCHILL). b Madisonville Ky 23 O 11. 5: Hamilton Jr Col 28-30 (Eng) Diploma; Southwestern at Memphis 35-36 (Eng) AB; UIll 44-45 BS in LS. 6: Fr, Sp. 7: Math tchr Franklin Jr High Sch, Paducah Ky 42-44; Head of ABS dept for yp Carnegie Pub Lib, Paducah Ky 45-60, Dir of Lib Serv 60-. 68; Child consul Mid-York Lib Syst, Utica NY 68-. 9: ALA; SELA; KyLA (past pres); Central NY LA. 10: Assn Amer Pen Women; Puppeteers of Amer; Assn for Childhood Educ Internat; Chi Delta Phi; Phi Kappa Psi; Beta Phi Mu; Paducah Woman's Club; Delphic Club. 13: Yes. 14: Yp wk, puppetry, story-telling, bk reviewing. 15: Children's Consultant Mid-York Library System, 1602 Lincoln ave, Utica NY 13502.

JONES, VIRGINIA (LACY). b Cincinnati 25 Je 12. 4: Edward Allen Jones. 5: Hampton Inst 29-32, 35-36 (Soc Studies) BS, 32-33 BLS; UIll 37-38 MS in LS; Chicago 43-45 PhD. 7: Libn Louisville Mun Col 33-39; Instr Prairie View A&M Col summers 36-39; Catlg libn Atlanta U 39-41; Instr Atlanta U Sch of Lib Serv 41-43, Dean & Prof 45-. 8: Ed consul "Library Journal" 62-63; Ed Bd "Phylon" The Atlanta University Review of Race and Culture 47-; Consul on lib develop & reg accreditation of schs & cols in the Southeast. 9: ALA (Coun 46-50, 55-59 3 coms);-LED (Bd Dirs 61-63); AALS (sec-treas 48-54, Bd dir 60-64, chm &/or mem 2 coms 57-62); SELA (Com on lib educ, Com on lib serv as a career). 10: AAUW; NAACP; YWCA; Ga Coun on Human Rel; Beta Phi Mu. 11: Two fellowships from the Gen Educ Bd. 13: Yes. 14: Acad libs, res in lib serv. 15: Sch of Lib Serv Atlanta U, Atlanta Ga 30314.

JONES, VIRGINIA M (SWANSON). b Springfield Ill 21 Ap 09. 4: Vincent Jones. 5: Ill State Normal U 27-31 (Hist, Educ) BEd; UIll summers 39-41, 45, 47 BS in LS. 6: Fr. 7: Tchr & libn Hennepin High Sch, Hennepin Ill 31-34; Tchr Nash Sch, Hennepin Ill 35-38; Post Off asst, Hennepin Ill 38-39; Co libn Putnam Co, Hennepin Ill 39-43; Sub tchr Joliet High Sch, Jr Col, Joliet Ill 45-47; Asst libn Blue Island High Sch, Blue Island Ill 47-59; Head libn Downers Grove High Sch, Downers Grove Ill 59-. 9: NEA; IllEA; IllSchLA; Chicagoland High Sch Libns Assn. 13: Yes. 14: Admin, a-v educ materials, lib sci instr. 15: 1116 Grove st, Downers Grove Il 60515.

JONES, WARREN WILLIAM. b Seattle 2 Je 30. 4: Gayle M(yers) Jones. 5: UWash 48-52 (Music) BA, 56-57 (Elem Educ) BA, summers 62-65 (LS) ML. 7: Musician & clerk USAF, US, Panama 52-56; Tchr Hillcrest Elem Sch, Renton Wash 57-62; Libn Nelsen Jr High Sch, Renton Wash 63-. 9: NEA; WashEA; WashASchL; NEA-DAVI. 14: Sch libnship. 15: 12914 74th ave S, Seattle 98178.

JONES, WYMAN H. b St Louis 29 D 29. 4: Janet Grigsby. 5: So Ill U 47-50 (Lit); Adams Col 55-56 (Lit) BA; UIowa 56-57 (Lit); UTex 57-58 MLS. 7: Head sci & ind dept Dallas Pub Lib 58-60, Chief of br serv 60-64; Dir Ft Worth Pub Lib, Ft Worth Tex 65-. 8: Bldg consul on more than 20 lib bldg projects. 9: ALA; TexLA (chm Dist VII 61-62, chm Legis Com 63-65, chm-elect Pub Libs Div 65-66); SWLA. 10: Toastmasters; Youth Orchestra Bd; Rotary Club. 11: Pentagon commendation for writing USAF radio series 53-54. 12: Columnist, 'On the Grindstone' for "Library Journal" (64). 13: Yes. 14: Admin, ref, bldg planning. 15: Ft Worth Pub Lib 9th & Throckmorton, Ft Worth Tex 76102.

JOOST, LAURA (REED). b Concord NC 26 My 17. 4: Nicholas T Joost. 5: Woman's Col of UNC(Greensboro) 33-37 (Eng) AB; UNC(Chapel Hill) 37-38 BS in LS. 6: Fr, Dutch, Ger. 7: Reviser-libn UNC Sch of Lib Sci 38-40; Asst libn Ga State Woman's Col 40-46; Gen asst High Bridge Br NY Pub Lib summer 45; Documents libn UNC(Chapel Hill) 46-47; Ref asst Charles Deering Lib Northwestern U 47-49; Ref asst So Ill U 64-. 67, Ref libn Alton Ctr 67-. 8: Pres Alton-Marquette Chap Amer Field Serv 69-70. 10: LWV. 12: "Bibliography on Marriage and Family Relations" (48). 14: Ref, documents. 15: 1703 Liberty st, Alton Ill 62003.

JORAMO, ARDEN D. b New Ulm Minn 23 D 33. 4: Marjorie Froland Joramo. 5: Mankato State Col 52-54, 56-58 (Eng) BS, summers 58-60 (LS minor); Peabody summers 64-66 (LS) MLS. 6: Norwegian. 7: US Army (Pfc) Artillery, Schwabach Germany 54-56; Jr High Eng & Soc Studies Kasson-Mantorville Sch, Kasson Minn 58-59; Tchr-libn Cosmos Consolidated Sch, Cosmos Minn 59-60; Tchr-libn Milford Comm Sch, Milford Iowa 60-62; Sch libn LaPorte City Comm Sch, LaPorte City, Iowa 62-68; Sch libn Brooklyn Jr High, Minneapolis 68-. 9: NEA; ALA; Iowa State EA; IowaSchLA. 10: PTA. 14: Sch libnship. 15: 806 Madison, LaPorte City, Iowa 50651.

JORDAN, ALMA THEODORA (WARNER). b Tunapuna Trinidad 29 D 29. 4: Lennox Jordan. 5: London U (Sp) BA; Columbia 58-59, 64 (LS) MS, DLS. 6: Sp, Fr. 7: Jr asst libn Central Lib, Trinidad & Tobago 49-51, Sr asst libn 52-54; Reg libn & libn in charge Carnegie Free Lib, Trinidad & Tobago 55-56; Brooklyn Pub Lib summer 57; NY Pub Lib summer 58; Libn Ind Development Corp, Trinidad & Tobago 59-60; Deputy libn in charge UWest Indies, St Augustine 61-. 8: Consul Trinidad & Tobago Govt Com on Integration of lib serv in Trinidad & Tobago 67. 9: Lib Assn of Trinidad & Tobago (chm 61, 62); ALA; Chm Organiz Com for proposed Lib Assn of Caribbean Univ & Res Insts 68-69. 10: Assoc of the Lib Assn (Gt Brit); Assoc of the Royal Col of Music (London). 13: Yes. 14: Ref, admin. 15: 28 Gilwell rd, Valsayn Park Curepe Trinidad.

JORDAN, BARBARA ALDRICH. b Boston 1 O 08. 5: Wheaton Col (Norton Mass) 26-30 (Eng Lit) AB; Simmons 45 BS in LS; Mass Gen Hosp Course in Inst Lib Org 41. 6: Fr, Ger. 7: Publicity & records Morrill Mem Lib, Norwood Mass 34-42, Adult dept libn & hosp libn 42-45; Head Libn James Prendergast Free Lib, Jamestown NY 45-47; Head Libn Plymouth Pub Lib, Plymouth Mass 47-48; Asst libn & catlgr Penn Col for Women 48-50; Interim Instr Carnegie Lib Sch 51; Readers asst Carnegie Lib of Pittsburgh 51-68; Dir Morrill Memorial Lib, Norwood Mass 68-. 8: Consul & bk sel for initial collection, Michael Benedum Lib Bridgeport WVa 56; Pres Henry Clay Frick Educ Commsn Wilson Col summer 57. 9: ALA (chm Staff Org Round Table); MassLA. 10: AAUW; Pittsburgh Coun Intercultural Educ; Carnegie Lib Pittsburgh Staff Assn; Old Colony Lib Club; Greater Boston Lib Admins. 12: Ed semi-weekly bk review column 'Footnotes from the Morrill Memorial Library' in "Norwood Messenger" (37-45). 13: Yes. 14: Adult educ, catlg, admin, bk reviews & annotations. 15: 99 Day st, Norwood Ma 02062.

JORDAN, CASPER LeROY. b Cleveland 5 Mr 24. 5: West Res 43-47 (Hist) AB; Atlanta 50-51 MS in LS. 6: Fr. 7: Tchr Cleveland Bd of Educ 47-48; Asst Cleveland House of Correction 48-50; Chief Libn Wilberforce U 51-61; Supv tech serv Nioga Lib System Niagara Falls NY 61-67, Asst dir 67-68; Asst Prof Sch Lib Serv Atlanta U 68-; Visiting Prof SUNY(Buffalo) 63, 65 & Atlanta U 67; Coord Ford Foundation Projects Sch Lib Serv, Atlanta U 68-. 8: Adv com Nelson Study NY State centralized processing; Adv com NY Assn Libs Tech Serv; Consul Penn on state wide centralized processing. 9: ALA-ACRL;-RTSD;-LED;-ISAD; ATheolLA; OhioLA; NYLA (pres Resources & Tech Serv); SAA; AALS; Ohio Col Assn. 12: Ed "Free Lance, a Magazine of Poetry and Prose" (50-); Bk review ed "AME Church Review" (55-); Co-auth "Centralized Processing for Six Colleges in Alabama and Mississippi" (68). 13: Yes. 14: Catlg, info sci, bibliog of the Negro. 15: 22 Whitehouse dr SW, Atlanta Ga 30314.

JORDAN, CHARLES MILLARD. b Dow City Iowa 25 F 25. 4: Noreen Gress. 5: Iowa State tchrs Col 47-49; Buena Vista Col 60-62 (Soc Sci) BS; UWis 62-66 MALS. 7: Radioman 2/c USN 43-46; Jr-high tchr (Pub sch) Iowa: Arcadia 53-54, Havelock 54-58, Wesley 58-61; Catlgr Buena Vista Col 61-63; Libn pub sch, Britt Iowa 63-68; Coord lib serv Pub Sch Dist, Waterloo Iowa 68-. 9: NEA; ALA; IowaASchL (sec, v-pres, pres 68-69); BrittEA (v-pres, pres); WaterlooEA. 14: Sch libs. 15: 2566 Saratoga dr, Waterloo Ia 50702.

JORDAN, LOIS (BREEDLOVE). b Decatur Tex 2 My 12. 4: Howard J Jordan. 5: Decatur Baptist Col 28-30 (Mus) Diploma; N Tex State U 30 (Mus); Arlington State Col 43 (Math, Blueprint Reading) Certif; Tex Woman's U 60-63, 65-66 (LS) BS & MLS. 6: Sp. 7: Bkkeeper: Tex Marine Distributors, Ft Worth Tex 55-60, Mobile Homes Inc, Decatur Tex 60-61; Libn Bridgeport High Sch, Bridgeport Tex 63-66; Libn Sch of Lib Sci Tex woman's U 66-. 9: ALA; TexLA; Tex Assn Col Tchrs. 10: Alpha Beta Alpha; Civic Club; Woman's Forum; Lib Bd, Bridgeport Tex. 14: Ref. 15: 1716 Lanice ave, Bridgeport Tx 76026.

JORDAN, MEL. 5: Lee Col 59-60; Arlington State Col 60-61; UTex 61-63 (Geog) BA, 63-66 MLS. 6: Sp. 7: Radioman 2/C US Navy, Pacific Theater 43-45; Ch 43-45; Chem plant employee Union Carbide Corp, Tex City Tex 48-59; Clerical asst utex Archives (Austin) 62-64; Catlgr TrinityU 65-66; Libn Laredo Jr Col 66-67; Asst to libn SW Tex State Col 67-68, Assoc libn 68-. 9: ALA; TexLA (chm Constitution Com 68-69). 10: AAUP. 14: Admin, bldg planning. 15: 1025 Haynes, San Marcos Tx 78666.

JORDAN, MORTON PHILLIP. b Calgary Alberta Can 25 S 19. 4: Margaret Susan Lynn. 5: UToronto 46-48 (Eng Lit) BA; McGill 48-49 BLS; UBC -54 (Eng Lit) MA. 6: Fr. 7: Bkkeeper Nat Fruit Co, Calgary Alta Can 38-40; Pilot (Flight Lt) RCAF, Europe 41-45; Aquis libn Vancouver Pub Lib, Vancouver BC Can 49-50, Br libn 50-51, Br hd libn 51-54, Acquis hd 54-58, Asst dir 58-. 9: CanLA; BCLA; Assn BC Libns. 12: Ed staff "BC Library Quarterly" (57-66). 14: Admin. 15: 750 Burrard st, Vancouver BC Can.

JORDAN, PETER ALEC. b London 30 O 29. 4: Frances Wolverton. 5: McMaster U 52-55 (Geog) BA; UBC 59-60 9agric), 60-61 (Educ) Tchg Certif, 63-64 BLS. 7: Tchr & libn Revelstoke Secondary Sch, Revelstoke BC 61-63; Head period, circ libn, catlgr UCalgary 64-67; Spec libn Can Dept Fisheries & Forestry, Calgary Can 67-. 9: CanLA; ALA; SLA; AltaLA. 14: Spec libnship, educ libs. 15: 4407 Valiant dr, Calgary 49 Alta Can.

JORDAN, ROBERT THAYER. b Chicago 3 Ag 22. 4: Bessie Rogers. 5: Antioch Col 39-43, 46-47 (Soc Sci, Accounting) AB; Scandinavian Seminar 50-51 (Scandinavian adult educ & culture); UDenver 52-53 (Anthropology); UCal 55-57 MLS. 6: Danish. 7: Petty off Merchant Marine 43-45; Auditor Consumer's coop Assn, Denver 47-48; Accountant Luxurest Furniture, Denver 48-50; Cost accountant Cutter Labs, Berkeley Cal 53-56; Deputy auditor Co of Alameda, Oakland Cal 55-56; Libn Taft Col Sr staff mem lib spec Coun on Lib Resources Inc, Wash DC 60-68; Dir of media serv Fed City Col 68-. 8: Consul: US Off of Educ, Higher Educ Act 65-; CEIR Inc, 65-; Nat Assn Better Radio & TV (Bd of Dirs 66-). 9: NEA-DAVI; ALA; NEA; SLA; Illum Engnr Soc (Lib Lighting Com 63-); DCLA (Bd of Dirs 67-69); Lib-Col J Edl Bd 67-. 10: Amer- scand Foun; Wash Internat Center; Fund for the Republic; Sierra Club; AAUP. 12: "750 Desirable Books for the Lower Division College Library" 58-60; "The Libraries of the State-Assisted Institutions of Higher Education in Ohio," with V W Clapp (64); "Library College Newsletter" (63-67); "The Library-College" (66); "Tomorrow's Library; Direct Access 2nd Delivery" (59); "Media power" (69). 13: Yes. 14: Lib educl role, readers serv. 15: Federal City College, Media Services Div, Wash DC 20001.

JORGENSEN, WILLIAM E(RNEST). b Heber Utah 13 O 13. 4: Margaret Boyle. 5: UIda 33-38 (Ger) BA; UCal 39-40 (LS) Certif; Ore State U 41-42 (Gen Studies) MA. 6: Ger, Fr. 7: Engnr libn Ore State U 40-42; Commander US Naval Reserve, Wash DC 42-45; Chief Libn US Navy Electronics Lab, San Diego Cal 46-. 8: Bd of dir San Diego Sci Lib 52-54; Interlib Task Group San Diego Commun Educ Resources Proj 60-69; Pres UCal Schs of Libnship Alumni Assn 63; John Cotton Dana lecturer at UCLA, Oct 64; Adv coun on Educ for Libnship UCal 65-68; Lib com San Diego Fine Arts Soc 65-67; Chm Mil Libns Workshop 66; Navy Research Lib Coun 67-69. 9: SLA (Recr Com 60-61, chm Engnrg Sect Sci-Tech Div 50; Consul Off San Diego Chap 63-64); CalLA (chm Recr Com 64, pres Palomar Dist 63, Reg Resources Com 53-54, Legis Com 67, coun 69-70). 10: Phi Beta Kappa; Phi Kappa Phi. 12: "NEL Reliability Bibliography," PB No 121838 & suppls (56-58). 13: Yes. 14: Admin. 15: 4139 Atascadero dr, San Diego Cal 92107.

JORN, DELMAR J. b Hillsboro Ill 6 O 37. 5: Bradley U 55-57 (Geog); St Mary's U (Tex) 57-60 (Hist) BA; Catholic U 61-66 MS in LS; SUNY (Geneseo) summer 65 (LS); SUNY (Potsdam) summer 67 (Educ Media). 7: Libn & a-v coord McBride High Sch, St Louis 61-. 9: CathLA (Mem Bd, High Sch Sect; pres St Louis Unit); ALA; NEA-DAVI. 12: Ed, Greater St Louis Unitm CathLA Newsletter (65-68). 14: Sch lib admin. 15: 1909 N Kingshighway, St Louis Mo 63113.

JORSTAD, DOROTHY (PHINNEY). b Dooley Mont 18 Ap 14. 4: Melvin E Jorstad. 5: UMinn 35-39 (Hist) BA, 39-40 BS in LS. 6: Ger. 7: Jr libn entymology UMinn (St Paul) 41, Jr libn forestry 42, 43-45; Asst libn Pub Lib, So St Paul, Minn 50-51, Head Libn 51-62; Consul Ill State Lib, No DeKalb Ill 63; Circ asst No Ill U Lib 63-65, Soc studies 65-. 9: ALA; IllLA. 10: Bus & Prof Women's Club; AAUP; AAUW. 13: Yes. 14: Circ, ref, pub lib admin. 15: 219 Phyllis ave, Rochelle Ill 61068.

JOSACK, RUTHE (BELL). b Philadelphia Penn 11 N 19. 4: Joseph Josack. 5: TempleU 37-39 (Eng); Rutgers 67-68 (Eng). 7: Libn Boy Scouts of Amer, New Brunswick NJ 61-68; Libn Easton Area Sch, Easton Penn 69-. 9: ALA. 10: YWCA. 14: Ref, children's libs. 15: 360 Taylor ave, Easton Pa 18042.

JOSE, JEAN. b Indianapolis 28 Mr 35. 5: ButlerU 52-56 (Eng) AB; IndU 65-67 MLS. 7: Sr legsl sec Eli Lilly & Co, Indianapolis 58-67; Libn Granville Pub Lib, Granville Ohio 67-68; Field consul Ind State Lib, Indianapolis 68-. 10: Beta Phi Mu. 15: 6114 N Ewing st, Indianapolis In 46220.

JOSEL, NATHAN A. b New Orleans 28 S 41. 4: Clair Solomon. 5: Tulane 59-63 (Hist) BA; LSU 63-65 (LS) MS. 6: Ger, Sp. 7: Room asst browsing room Tulane U 61-63; Room asst govt documents LSU Lib 63-65; Various positions Enoch Pratt Free Lib, Baltimore 65-69; Hd hist dept Memphis Pub Lib , Memphis Tenn 69-. 14: Ref, admin. 15: Memphis Public Lib, 33 S Front st, Memphis Tn 38103.

JOSEPH, ELEANOR (COHEN). b Waco Tex 10 Jl 19. 4: Percy T Joseph. 5: Newcomb 36-40 (Eng) BA; LSU 40-41 BS in LS. 6: Fr. 7: Libn adult dept New Orleans Pub Lib 41-43; Asst libn Rapides Parish Lib, Alexandria La 47-48; Hd ref dept E Baton Rouge Parish Lib, Baton Rouge La 53-. 9: LaLA (chm Pub Lib Sect 65-66; chm La Lit Award Com 62-63). 10: United Cerebral Palsy Assn. 11: Baton Rouge Jaycees Outstanding Pub Servant Award 62-63. 13: Yes. 14: Ref. 15: 4948 Woodside dr, Baton Rouge La 70808.

JOSEY, E(LONNIE) J(UNIUS). b Norfolk Va 20 Ja 24. 5: Howard U 46-49 (Hist) AB; Columbia 49-50 (Hist) MA, 52 (Hist); SUNY(Albany) 52-53 MSLS. 6: Fr. 7: Desk asst Journalism Lib Columbia U 50-52; Tech asst I NY Pub Lib Central Br 52; Clerical asst NY State Lib 52-53; Libn I Free Lib of Phila 53-54; Instr of Soc Sci Savannah State Col 54-55; Libn & Asst Prof Del State Col 55-59; Libn & Assoc Prof Savannah State Col 59-. 66, Assoc in acad & research libs 66-68; Chief Bureau of Acad & Research Libs Div of Lib Development State Educ Dept, Albany NY 68-. 8: Certification Revision Study Com for Sch Libs, Del State Dept of Pub Instr 58-59; Inaugurated Tchr-Libn Curriculum, Savannah State Col 60; Lib consul So Assn of Cols & Secondary Schs for accreditation of Risley High Sch, Brunswick Ga 61; Lib bldg consul Boggs Acad, Keysville Ga 65; Survey of Tex So U Lib (Houston) 67. 9: ALA-ACRL (chm Ad Hoc Com on Commun Use of Acad Libs);-ASD (mem Standards Development Com); GaLA; GaEA (chm Libns Sect); NYLA. 10: Bd of Mgrs Savannah Pub Lib; NAACP (Exec Bd of Albany NY br); Kappa Phi Kappa; AAUP; Amer Acad of Polit & Soc Scis. 11: NAACP Nat Off Youth Adv Award 65; Savannah State Col Award for serv to libnship 67. 12: Ed "Del Lib Assn Bulletin" (59); Ed "A Directory of College and University Libraries in New York State" (67), "A Directory of Reference and Research Systems in New York State" (67, 68). 13: Yes. 14: Admin, ref, lib educ. 15: Bur of Acad and Re search Libs, Div of Lib Development, State Educ Dept, Albany NY 12224.

JOSIEK, JULIANNE. b Chicago Ill 4 O 42. 5: Miami-Dade Jr Col 61-63 (Liberal Arts) AA; Fla StateU 63-65 (Hist) BA, 63-65 (LS) BA. 6: Sp. 7: Lib asst Brockway Mem Pub Lib, Miami Fla 65-66; Catlgr De PaulU Campus Lib 66-. 9: ALA; IllCatholicLA. 14: Descr catlg bks & period. 15: 2054 N Cicero ave, Chicago Il 60639.

JOSLYN, JEAN L. b Woodstock Ill 2 F 27. 5: West Col 45-49 (Hist) BA; Simmons 51-52 (LS) MS. 6: Sp. 7: Sec McHenry Co TB Assn, Woodstock Ill 49-51; Catlgr Penn State U Lib (University Park) 52-55; Order libn Lincoln Lib, Springfield Ill 55-56, Hd tech processes 56-. 9: ALA; IllLA (sec Catlg & Clsf Div 61-62). 14: Catlg. 15: 201 W Lawrence ave, Springfield Il 62704.

JOURDAN, ANNE CATHERINE. b Frankfurt Germany 2 My 21. 5: Brooklyn Col 37-41 (Eng) BA; Pratt 41-42 BLS. 6: Ger, Fr. 7: Child libn Brooklyn Pub Lib 42-55, Head of br lib 55-. 9: NY Lib Club. 10: Soc for the Exchange of Ethnical & Cultural Affairs. 14: Child wk, pub lib serv. 15: 1401 Eva ct, Baldwin NY.

JOW, GRACE. b Macau 21 D 33. 4: Frank Jow. 5: Chu Hai Col (Hong Kong) 51-55 (Educ) BS; Peabody Col 61-62 MALS. 6: Chinese. 7: Catlgr Monmouth (Ill) Col 62-63; Catlgr mt St Mary's Col, Newburgh NY 63-66; Catlgr White Plains Pub Lib, White Plains NY 66-. 9: ALA; WestchesterLA. 10: YWCA. 14: Catlg. 15: 10 Old Mamaroneck rd, White Plains NY 10605.

JOYCE, SISTER M THERESE OSF. b Co Galway Ireland 10 Ag 19. 5: Nazareth Col (Rochester NY) 48-63 (Eng) BS Ed; Marywood Col 65-67 MSLS. 7: Tchr Christ the King Sch, Haddonfield NJ• 42-59; Prin Assumption Sch, Pomona NJ 59-65; Libn St Mary of the Angels Acad, Haddonfield NJ 67-. 9: CathLA; ALA; NJLA. 10: Haddonfield Friends of the Lib Org; Sch Lib Assn (Camden Co NJ). 15: St Mary of the Angels Academy, Haddonfield NJ 08033.

JOYCE, CHARLES (RAYMOND JR). b Tremont Me 3 Ja 29. 4: Ingrid Thale. 5: Tufts U 47-51 (Econ) BA; Simmons 54-55 (LS) SM. 6: Ger. 7: (2d Lt) US Army Anti-aircraft & Guided Missiles, Ft Bliss Tex 51-53; Credit reported Dun & Bradstreet, Boston 54; Films & youth libn Detroit Pub Lib 55-57; Libn Blackstone Mem Lib, Branford Conn 57-59; Asst libn Wellesley Free Lib, Wellesley Mass 59-61; Asst libn Winchester Pub Lib, Winchester Mass 61-62; Dir Morrill Mem Lib, Norwood Mass 62-68; Assoc state libn Conn State Lib, Hartford 68-. 9: ALA; MassLA (chm Pub Rel Com 67-68); Greater Boston Pub Lib Adminrs; NELA. 13: Yes. 14: Mgt, bldg, catlg. 15: 27 Deer Park rd, Weatogue Ct 06089.

JOYCE, MRS LORA A (HASENBANK). b Alma Kan 10 S 14. 4: Frank D Joyce Sr. 5: Kan State Tchrs (Emporia) 34-40 (LS) BS in ED, Lib Sci Certif; MoU (Kan City) summers 58-63 (Secondary Educ, LS) MA. 6: Ger. 7: Rural tchr Dist No 75, Wamego Kan 33-34; Prim tchr, Wabaunsee Kan 34-36; Rural tchr Dist No 22, Alma Kan 36-37; Libn Sr High Sch, Nevada Mo 40-42; Libn Sr High Sch, N Platte Neb 42-44; Libn Kan City (Mo) Pub Lib 44-45; Sub tchr Kan City (Mo) schs 55-57; Eng tchr Central Jr Kan City (Mo) Schs 57-58; Libn Bingham Jr Kan City (Mo) Schs 58-68; Askew & Stark Elem Schs, Kan City Mo 68-. 14: Wk with teenagers. 15: 6303 Goodman dr, Shawnee Mission Kan 66202.

JOYCE, PHYLLIS (BRAY). b Buckland Mass 16 Ap 25. 5: North Adams State Tchrs Col 43-44; Simmons 44-47 (LS) BS. 6: Fr, Sp, Ger. 7: Asst circ & ref libn URI Lib 47-59, Ref libn 59-63; Assoc ref libn UMass Lib 63-69; Ref libn Mt Holyoke Col Lib 69-. 9: ALA; RILA; NELA; West Mass Lib Club. 14: Ref. 15: 21 Hartman rd, Amherst Mass 01002.

JOYCE, WILLIAM D. b New Bedford Mass 21 Je 18. 4: Aida A Rizzo. 5: Devens Col 46-48; Harvard 48-50 (Soc Rel) AB; Simmons 50-51 (LS) MS. 7: (S/Sgt) US Army Aviation Engnr, CBI 43-46; Ref libn Devens Col 48; Ref asst Baker Lib Harvard U 49-51; Asst to dept head Milwaukee Pub Lib 51-53; Head Libn State Col Lib (Lowell Mass) 53-58; Dir Reg Pub Lib, Levittown Penn 58-61; Head Libn State Col Lib (Worcester Mass) 61-. 8: Pres State Col at Worcester Bkstore Corp 65-; Chm Staff Standards Com, Coun of State Col Libns (Mass) 56-58, 65-, & their Com on Undergrad Lib Sci Curriculum 61-63; Worcester State Col Inst Rep to MIT Computation Center 65. 9: ALA (chm Religious Bk Sel Com 52-54); MassLA (Planning Com; past pres Coun State Col Libns); PennLA (pres-elect Phila Dist, chm Worcester Area Coop Libs 68-69; Mass Conf Chief Libns Pub Higher Educ Inst). 10: Commun Sailing Club (Worcester); Milwaukee Co Mental Health Soc (51-53). 11: Jewish War Veterans Commun Serv Award 61; Bristol Twp (Pa) Citizenship Award 61. 13: Yes. 14: Ref, admin, tchg. 15: 45 So Flagg st, Worcester Mass 01602.

JU, WILLIAM CHIA-CHIUN. b Shanghai China 11 Ja 25. 4: Judith Yu-Ying Liu. 5: Nat Wu-han U 41-44; Soochow U Law Sch 44-47 LLB; John Marshall U Law Sch 58-61 LLM & JD; Peabody 61-62 MA in LS. 6: Chinese, Japanese. 7: Judicial clerk Shanghai Dist Court 47-49; Judicial clerk Ministry of Justice, Taipei Taiwan 49-50; Judge advocate (Maj) Ministry of Nat Defense, Taipei Taiwan 50-51; US Dept of Army civilian (GS-7) CIE, UNC, Tokyo & Korea 51-54; Navy Prosecutor (Lt Comd) Navy GHQ, Taipei Taiwan 54-58; Bibliog & libn of Asian studies IndU 62-69; Hd E Asian Lib URochester (NY). 12: "Law of Coporation sic" in Chinese (Taipei 58). 13: Yes. 14: Ref, Chinese publns. 15: East Asian Lib, Univ of Rochester, Rochester NY 14627.

JUDAH, JAY STILLSON. b Leavenworth Wash 7 Jl 11. 4: Lucile Baker. 5: UWash 29-35 (Philos, Oriental Studies) AB; UCal 37-41 (Semitics, Ger, LS) Certif in Lib Sci; UColo Navy Lang Sch 44-45 (Japanese Lang); UCal 46-50 (Sanskrit & other Indic Langs & Phil). 6: Ger, Jap, Fr, Sanskrit, Pali, Maharashtri, Prakrit, Hebrew, Arabic, Gothic, Gk. 7: Tchg asst UWash 34-35; Supv of man-hour dept Richmond shipyards 43-44; (Lt) Navy, Boulder Colo & Japan 44-46; Libn & Prof of Hist of Religion Pacific Sch of Religion 41-; Dir Bibliog Ctr

Grad Theol Union 66-. 8: Dir for org Internat Assn of Theol Libns under World Coun of Churches, 52-55; Dir for estab libs in Japanese WRA camps during World War II under Fed Coun of Churches, 41-43; Dir of survey of Berkeley Baptist Theol Sem Lib, 54. 9: ATheolLA (treas 48-49, pres 64-65, chm var coms); Internat Assn of Theol Libs (sec-treas 55-60; chm var coms); West Theol LA (pres 54-55). 10: El Cerrito Tennis Club; Cal Soc for Psychic Research; Soc for Sci Stud y of Religion. 11: Guggenheim Fellowship, 34; Sealantic Fund Fellowship grant, 57; Lit D hon degree Chapman Col, 55; Elected Fellow of Internat Inst of Arts & Lit. 12: Comp & ed "Index to Religious Periodical Literature, 1949-1952"; "Jehovah's Witnesses" (65); "The History and Philosophy of the Metaphysical Movements in America (67). 13: Yes. 14: Admin, bk sel. 15: Pacific Sch of Religion 1798 Scenic ave, Berkeley Cal 94709.

JUDD, J VAN DER VEER. b Phila 4 Je 39. 4: Janet Miller. 5: Bates Col 58-62 (Hist) AB; Columbia 63-65 MS in LS; T's Col (Winona) 66-68 (Phys Sci); Winona State Col 67 (Chem). 06: Fr. 7: (Sgt) US Army Reserve Med 62-68; Trainee Westchester Lib System, Mt Vernon NY 63-65; Columbia U 65; Libn IBM, Rochester Minn 65-66; Data Processing libn St Mary's Col (Winona) 66-68; EDP Consul NY State Educ Dept Div of Lib Development 68. 9: SLA; ASIS; ALA; NYLA. 10: US Army Nat Guard. 12: Ed Winona College Serials Directory (67). 14: Automation, info retrieval. 15: 27th st NE, Rochester Minn 55901.

JUDD, JANET (MILLER). b Phila 9 N 40. 4: J Van der Veer Judd. 5: Bates Col 58-62 (Eng) AB; Columbia 63-65 MS in LS; Winona State Col 67 (Educ). 06: Fr. 7: Libn trainee Westchester Lib System, Mt Vernon NY 63-65; Circ libn Winona State Col 65-67, Instr & head readers' serv 67-68; Catlgr Rensselear 68; Libn Linton High Sch, Schenectady NY 69; Libn Burnt Hills-Ballston Lake High Sch, Burnt Hills NY 69-. 9: Westchester LA; NYLA; Hudson-MohawkLA; ALA. 10: AAUW. 14: Sch libs, reader's serv. 15: 5 Latham Village lane apt 2, Latham NY 12110.

JUDD, SARAH LARGE. b Denver Colo 10 D 06. 4: James Weston Judd. 5: UDenver 24-28 (Hist, Pol Sci) AB; Columbia 28-29 BS in LS. 6: Fr, Ger. 7: Ref libn: Little Rock Pub Lib, Little Rock Ark 29-47, Bronx Ref Ctr NY Pub Lib 47-48; Hd bus div Denver Pub Lib 48-53, Hd ref unit gen serv dept 53-55; Docs libn & ref libn Colo State Lib 55-. 9: ALA; ColoLA; ColoASchL. 15: 3047 Raleigh, Denver Co 80212.

JUDGE, SISTER GAIL RSM. b Trenton NJ 8 Je 35. 5: Georgian Court Col 53-56, Bus Admin (BS); Rutgers 61-63 (MLS), Fordham 64-66, (Philos), USan Francisco 67- (Theol). 7: Legal sec Johnson & Johnson, New Brunswick NJ 57-58; Tchr Notre Dame High Sch, Trenton NJ 60-61; Libn Georgian Court Col 61-66; Tchr Mt St Mary Acad, N Plainfield NJ 66-68; Tchr Cathedral High Sch, Trenton NJ 68-. 8: Mem ESSA Title II Adv Com in NJ 65-. 9: ALA; CathLA; NJLA. 10: Beta Phi Mu. 14: Admin, ref, lib instr. 15: Cathedral High School Bank st & Chancery lane, Trenton NJ 08618.

JUDICE, CECILE MARIE. b St Martinville La 15 My 09. 5: USWestLA 29 (Educ) BA in Ed; LSU summer 37 (Fr, Educ), 42 BS in LS; UTex summer 51 (LS). 6: Fr, Sp. 7: High sch tchr & libn Lafayette Parish Schs, Scott La 28-42; Grad sch libn La State Bd of Educ lsu 42-44; Hd acquis libn La State Bd of Educ USWestLa 44-. 9: ALA; -ACRL; NEA; SWLA. 10: Delta Kappa Gamma; AAUW; LSU Alum Assn; USWestL Alum Assn. 13: Yes. 14: Acquis. 15: 207 Stephens st, Lafayette La 70501.

JUDITH, SISTER MARY CSJ. b NY 2 Ap 09. 5: Col of St Rose 42 (Hist) BA; St John's U (NY) 57 MLS. 6: Fr. 7: Tchr Diocesan-Commun Schs, Albany & Syracuse NY 31-55; Tchr-libn Diocesan-Commun Schs, Syracuse NY 55-69; Libn St Bernard's Summer High Sch, Cohoes NY summers 60-. 8: Asst in processing, accessioning & catlg The College of St Rose Lib Summers 57-59; Asst Commun Diocesan Sch libs & trained Lib Aides in St Bernard's Summer High Sch, Cohoes NY 65-. 9: CathLA (also Syracuse Chap). 14: Clsf, processing, catlg. 15: 3131 James st, Syracuse NY 13206.

JUGOVIC, MARIA (BALENOVIC). b Croatia Yugoslavia 28 F 22. 4: Zvonimir T Jugovic. 5: Tchrs Col (Gospic Croatia) 37-41 (Elem Educ); Higher Sch of Pedagogy (Zagreb Croatia) 51-53 (Biol); Chicago 62-67 (LS) MA. 06: Croatian, Serbian. 7: Tchr elem sch, Croatia Yugoslavia 41-51; Ref libn E Chicago Pub Lib, EChicago Ind 64, Supv of child wk 65-. 9: ALA; IndLA. 14: Wk with child. 15: 1324 Beatrice lane, Munster In 46321.

JUHLIN, ALTON P. b Lakeland Fla 17 My 19. 4: Myrtle White. 5: Bradley U 36-40 (Lang & Lt) AB; UMich 42-43 ABLS, 45-46 AMLS. 07: Asst educ dept Peoria Pub Lib, Peoria Ill 40-42; Ref period & document libn Wheaton Col Lib (Wheaton Ill) 43-45; Tchg Fellow UMich(Ann Arbor) 45-46; Head ref dept Okla State U Lib 46-50; Chm Dept Lib Sci UMo 50-51; Head ref dept Okla State U Lib 51-55, Head spec serv dept 55-60; Asst Prof Dept Lib Sci Tex Woman's U 60-61; Order libn So Ill U Lib 61-66, Asst soc studies libn 66-67, asst catlg libn 67-. 9: ALA; IllLA; OklaLA (off). 10: Phi Kappa Phi; Beta Phi Mu; Pi Gamma Mu; Phi Alpha Theta; Kappa Delta Pi. 14: Ref, maps, tchg lib sci, catlg. 15: 205 Glenview dr, Carbondale Ill 62901.

JULIAN, MARGARET (ODETTE) ELLER. b Gold Hill NC 31 Jl 11. 4: Wilbur Craft Julian. 5: Catawba Col 27-31 (Eng) AB; Peabody summers 38-39, 43 BSLS. 7: Grammar Grade A Tchrs Certif, Salisbury NC City Schs 31-38; Libn Thomasville Pub Lib, Thomasville NC 39-43; Circ asst Peabody Col Lib 43; Chief circ Nashville Pub Lib 43-46; Asst head ref Forsyth Co Pub Lib, Winston-Salem NC 60-. 14: Ref, readers adv, rare bks. 15: 2215 Westfield ave SW, Winston-Salem NC 27103.

JUNG, NORMAN OLIVER. b Harvey Cook Co Ill 27 My 34. 4: Barbro Christenson. 5: Oberlin Col 52-56 (Govt) AB; Chicago 56-59 (Hist) AM; Ind U 62-63 (LS) MA. 6: Ger. 7: Claims rep Bur of Old Age & Supv Insurance Dept of Health, Educ, & Welfare, Columbus Ind 59-61, Field rep, Madison Wis 61-62; Asst ref libn Cornell U Libs 63-66; Circ libn SUNY (Stony Brook) 66-68, Ref libn 68-. 9: ALA. 14: Ref, acquis, rare bks, circ. 15: 1 Cedar Hill rd, Stony Brook NY 11790.

JUNKIN, RUTH (MARTINDALE). b Austin Tex 16 Ap 10. 5: UTex 27-31 (Eng) BA, 49-53 (Admin & Supv) MEduc; Columbia summers 33, 37 (LS) BS. 7: Elem tchr Austin (Tex) Pub Schs 31-32, Elem libn 33, Jr high libn 33-44; Navy libn Civil Serv: Atlantic City NJ 44-45, New London Conn 45-46; High Sch libn, Austin Tex 46-47; Austin (Tex) Pub Lib summers 413; Lib coord Austin (Tex) Independent Sch Dist 47-. 8: Lect Lib Sci; UTex summer 52. 9: ALA; -CSD (Bd, mem several coms); NEA; ASCD; TexLA (past pres, sec & chm several coms; chm Sch Lib Div); Tex As' Supv & Curr Devel; TexStateTA; TexEPSA. 10: Delta Kappa Gamma. 14: Sch libs. 15: 3307 Liberty st, Austin Tx 78705.

JUNKINS, IMA MAE (VAN HOOK). b Burnside Ky 28 Mr 14. 4: Howard Junkins. 5: Ohio State U 31-35 (Psych) AB; UKy 45 BS in LS; Columbia 37-38, 46 (Eng Lit) MA. 7: Tchr of high sch Eng & Fr, Eubank Ky 35-37; High sch & pub libn, Somerset Ky 39-46; Libn reviser dept sec Lib Sci Dept UKy 46-47; Elem libn, Oak Ridge Tenn 47-50, 56-. 9: NEA; TennEA; TennLA. 10: PTA; AAUW. 15: 396 East dr, Oak Ridge Tenn.

JUPITER, MARK M. b Austria. 5: UVienna 21-26 (Classics) PhD, 32-34 (Med); Columbia 44-46 BSLS, 48-51 (Psych) MA. 6: Ger, Fr, Sp, Lat, Gk, Polish, Dutch, Czech, Russian, Hebrew. 7: Tchr of Lat, Gk, Ger & philos in various schs in Vienna 25-39; Eng tchr Lord Kitchener Camp, Richborough Eng 39-40; Catlg asst NY Pub Lib 44-46; Catlg Columbia U 46-. 10: Amer Philol Assn. 13: Yes. 14: Catlg, ref (psychol), rare bks. 15: 606 W 114th st apt 8, New York NY 10025.

JURKANIN, LEELA S(MITH). b Rochester Ind 3 Je 06. 4: John P Jurkanin. 5: Ball State Tchrs Col 24-28 (Fr, Music) AB; UIll 30-31 BS in LS. 6: Fr. 7: Catlgr Ball State Tchrs Col 31-37; Catlgr Queensborough Pub Lib, Jamaica NY 38-40; Instr Lib Sci Ball State Tchrs Col summers 40-41; Asst gen ref div Cleveland Pub Lib 42-50; Elem tchr pub schs, Strongsville Ohio 53-54; Sch libn Cuyahoga Co Pub Lib, Cleveland 56-57; Libn Pleasant Valley Jr High Sch, Parma Ohio 59-. 9: ALA; NEA; OhioASchL; OhioLA; OhioEA. 10: PTA; NEOhio Tchrs Assn. 14: Catlg, young adults. 15: 18016 Boston rd, Strongsville Ohio 44136.

JUROW, LUCIE (SCHUMER). b NY 27 F 08. 5: Adelphi Col 25-28 (Econ) BA; Brooklyn Law Sch 27-30 LLB, 30-31 JD. 6: Fr, Sp. 7: Asst dir Practice Court Brooklyn Law Sch 30-35, Sec to faculty 35-42, Law Libn 50-. 9: Amer Bar Assn; AALL. 10: Brooklyn Bar Assn; Law Lib Assn Greater NY; Pi Gamma Mu. 15: Brooklyn Law Sch Lib 375 Pearl st, Brooklyn NY 11201.

JUSTICE, ILA TAYLOR. b Crestmont NC 22 S 16. 4: John Mitchell Justice. 5: Berea 36 AB; George Peabody Col 41 BS in LS, 47 MS in LS. 06: Fr, Ger. 7: Libn Pleasant Hill Acad, Pleasant Hill Tenn 41-43; Asst Prof Ill State U 43-47; Assoc Prof of Lib Sci Appalachian State U 47-, Chm Dept Lib Sci 47-65. 8: Various consultships, NC; Southern Assn Evaluations.

09: ALA; NCLA (v-chm Sch Lib Sect 66-67); SELA; NCEA. 10: AAUW; Beta Phi Mu; Phi Theta Kappa; Pi Gamma Mu. 13: Yes. 14: Graphic arts, lib hist, child lit. 15: 109 Blanwood dr, Boone NC 28608.

JUSTICE, LaDONNA (HENRY). b Montgomery City Mo 29 O 39. 4: Gary E Justice. 5: Central Methodist Col 57-61 (Educ) BS; UMo 67-68 (LS) MA. 6: Sp. 7: Ref libn Daniel Boone Reg Lib, Columbia Mo 68-. 9: ALA; MoLA. 14: Ref, child serv. 15: 908 N Garth, Columbia Mo 65201.

JUSTIN, LAURA DELL. b Vernon Tex 3 Jl 11. 5: N Tex State U 37 BS, 41 (LS) BS. 7: Libn A C Jones High Sch, Beeville Tex 37-40; Libn Corpus Christi High Sch, Beeville Tex 40-50; Libn W B Ray High Sch, Corpus Christi Tex 50-. 9: NEA; ALA; TexLA (pres & rec sec); TexASchL; SWLA. 10: Corpus Christi Clr Tchrs Assn. 14: Sch libnship. 15: 1201 16th st NW, Wash DC 20036.

JWAIDEH, ZUHAIR ELIAS. b Baghdad Iraq 3 Je 20. 4: Kathleen McManus. 5: Iraq Col 44 9law) Licentiate; George WashingtonU 52 (Law) Master of Comp Law, 56 (Law) Doctorate of Juridical Sci. 6: Arabic, Fr. 7: Lawyer Own Firm, Baghdad Iraq 44-48; Tchr Sch of Advanced Intl Studies Johns HopkinsU (Wash advanced Intl Studies Johns HopkinsU (Wash DC) 49-59; Ref libn Orientalia Div LC 56-59; Chief Near East & African Law Div LC 59-. 8: Acquis trip to Middle East & N Africa for LC 61 & 64; Org PL480 Ctr for LC, Cairo Egypt 61, Act div 61 & 64; Conducted seminar on Middle East for Army offs, Ft Meade Md 66. 9: Intl Assn Law Libs; AALL (Com on For Law Indexing); Fed Bar Assn; Wash For Law Soc; Law Libn's Soc (Wash DC). 10: African Studies Assn; Middle East Studies Assn. 13: Yes. 14: Ref. 15: 2828 Connecticut ave NW, Washington DC 20008.

K

KABAKERIS, DOROTHY. b Poland 7 Ja 45. 5: UPittsburgh 63-67 (Elem Educ) BS, 68-69 MLS. 7: Salesgirl Sun Drug Store, Pittsburgh Penn 63; Salesgirl Kaufmann's Bk Dept, Pittsburgh Penn 67; Stud asst to lib UPittsburgh Med Lib 69. 14: Ref. 15: 6119 Jackson st, Pittsburgh Pa 15206.

KABELAC, KARL SANFORD. b Ithaca NY 30 Je 42. 5: Auburn Commun Col 59-61 (Math) AA; Syracuse 61-63 (Hist) AB, 63-64 MSLS; Cooperstown Grad Program NYState Hist Assn SUNY (Oneonta) 66-67 MA. 07: Asst catlgr State U Col (Brockport NY) 64-66; Asst libn dept of spec collections URochester 68-. 9: ALA. 10: NY State Hist Assn; Beta Phi Mu. 14: Catlg, bibliog, spec collections. 15: Aurora NY 13026.

KABLER, WALTON EVANS. b Richmond Va 2 My 39. 4: Elizabeth Morales. 5: UCLA 57-59; San Fernando Valley State Col 60-65 (Eng) BA, MA; USoCal 65-66 MS in LS. 7: S/Sgt USAF 60; Asst Ser Libn San Fernando Valley State Col 66-68, Humanities Bibliogr 68-. 8: Concurrent appt as Asst Prof of Eng San Fernando Valley State Col 68-. 9: ALA; CalLA; So Cal Tech Proc Gp. 10: AAUP; Mod Lang Assn. 13: Yes. 15: 18300 Nappa st, Northridge Ca 91324.

KACENA, CAROLYN (ANN). b St Louis Mo 25 Ja 44. 5: U No Iowa 62-66 (LS, Math) BA with tchg; Case West Res 66-67 MS in LS. 6: Ger. 7: Catlg libn Deere & Co, Moline Ill 67-69; Catlg libn UAriz 69-. 9: ALA; ASIS. 10: Augustana Symphony Orchestra; Tomahawk. 11: Beta Phi Mu; Kappa Delta Pi. 14: Catlg, info ret, tchg. 15: Univ of Ariz lib, Tucson Az 85721.

KACZMARSKYJ, MARTHA SAWICKI. b Ternopol Ukraine 28 Jl 43. 4: Lt Orest Kaczmarskyj. 5: Queens Col 61-65 (Mod European Hist) BA; Pratt 65-67 MLS. 6: Ukrainian, Russian. 7: Summer helper Radio Liberty Research Lib, NYC summer 64; Lib trainee Queens Borough Pub Lib, Jamaica NY 65-67; Asst libn JFK Special Warfare Ctr Lib, Ft Bragg NC 67-68; Hd libn US Naval Sta Lib, Brooklyn NY 68-. 14: Mil libs. 15: 170-11 83 ave, Jamaica NY 11432.

KACZOROWSKI, JOSEPH P(AUL). b Weehawken NJ 3 S 44. 5: Manhattan Col 62-66 (Eng Lit) BA; Columbia 66-67 MLS. 6: Ger, Sp. 7: Desc catlg in Germ langs LC 67-. 14: Catlg, a-v materials (non-print media). 15: 219 3rd st NE, Washington DC 20002.

KADELA, IRMA (ELLEN WANSBROUGH). b Dufferin Co Ont Can 18 Jl 30. 4: Stanislaw Kadela. 5: UWestOnt 47-50 (Gen Arts) BA; Toronto 50-51 BLS. 7: Asst child dept Pub Lib London Ont 51-52; Child libn Pub Lib, St Thomas Ont 53-54; Head child dept Pub Lib, NYork Ont 55-57; Chief libn Pub Lib, Richmond Hill Ont 58; Chief libn Pub Lib, Port Credit Ont 59-66; Libn Conrad Grebel Mennonite Col 67-; Lib coord Waterloo Pub Schs 67-. 9: CanLA; Inst Prof Libns; OntLA; OntEA. 10: Univ women's Club; United Church Women. 14: Child serv, yp, univ libs. 15: 660 Avondale ave, Kitchener Ont Can.

KADILIS, JANIS JOHN. b Latvia 16 Ja 03. 4: Alexandra Tomson. 5: ULatvia(Riga) 26-33 (Econ) MS; Columbia 54-56 MS in LS. 6: Latvian, Russian, Ger, Fr. 7: Tchr French Lyceum, Riga Latvia 23-37, 40-41; Dir Valters & Rapa Pub Co, Riga Latvia 37-40; Instr Russian lang, Syracuse U 51-52; Searcher Columbia U Lib 54-56; Libn catlgr US Info Lib, Wash DC 56-59; Libn sr catlgr US Dept of State Lib, Wash DC 59-68; Libn prin catlgr US Dept of State Lib, Wash DC 68-. 9: DCLA. 12: Ed-in-chief, monthly mag of lit & art "Daugava," Riga Latvia (37-40). 15: 3620 16th st NW, Wash DC 20010.

KADIN, ELINOR (M). b Paterson NJ 24 N 24. 4: Harold Kadin. 5: Columbia 50-51 (Sociol); Paterson State Col 59-61 (Elem Ed) BS; Rutgers 64-68 MLS. 7: Sub tchg, Franklyn Twp NJ 60-67, Tchr & libn 67-68; Sch libn, Madison Twp NJ 68-. 9: NJLA. 10: LWU. 14: Sch lib. 15: 30 Shelly dr, Somerset NJ 08873.

KADIS, AVERIL JORDAN. b Lucknow India 28 F 34. 4: Phillip Michael Kadis. 5: Isabella Thorburn Col 49-53 (Philos) BA; LucknowU 53-54 (Eng Lit); West Res 54-55 MLS; Syracuse 55-56 (Eng Lit); Oxford summer 61 (Eng Lit). 6: Urdu. 7: Lib asst Cleveland Pub Lib, Ohio 56-57; Libn Emassy of India, Wash DC 57-58; Libn (ya) Cleveland Pub Lib 58-61; Hd libn Isabella Thoburn Col, Lucknow India 61-62; Libn ya Enoch Pratt Free Lib, Baltimore 62-63, Ref libn 63-64, Admin asst films dept 64-65, Asst to coord of adult serv 65-68, Asst chief pub rel div 68-. 9: ALA; MdLA. 13: Yes. 14: Films, lib publ, ref. 15: 1613 Harvard st NW, Washington DC 20009.

KAFES, FREDERICK WILSON. b Trenton NJ 20 D 39. 5: Grinnekk Col 57-61 (Hist) BA; Drexel 66-69 MLS. 7: Mgt trainee Mutual of NY, NYC 61-62; Trainee USA Res Ft Dix, Ft Gordon Ga 62; Passport reviewer US Dept of State, Wash DC 63; Scheduler US Steel Corp Fairless Wks, Morrisville Penn 64; Lib trainee Free Lib of Phila 66-68; Libn Info Ctr NW Ayer & Son Inc, Phila 69-. 9: SLA. 10: Philobiblon (Phila). 14: Info, ret sp (soc sci, hist, law, bus). 15: 330 S Junifer st, Phila Pa 19107.

KAGANICH, DOROTHY M. b Mt Olive Ill 4 S 33. 5: UIll 51-55 (Hist) BA; Rutgers 65-66 mls. 6: Fr, Sp, Russian. 7: Sec UN, NYC 57-63; Sec Senie & Stock, Attys,Westport Conn 63-65; Ref libn Greenwich Pub Lib, Greenwich Conn 66-68; Reader serv libn FairfieldU Lib 68-. 9: ALA; ConnLA. 10: Alpha Lambda Delta; Phi Alpha Theta. 14: Ref. 15: 81 S Compo rd, Westport Ct 06880.

KAGEE, MARGARET (YEAKLEY). b Pittsburgh 18 Je 10. 5: Wittenberg U 27-30 (Eng); Simmons 31 (LS) BS; UTampa 36 (Educ). 6: Fr, Ger, Sp. 7: NY Pub Lib 31-36; Libn Arlington Co High Sch, Arlington Va; Reg Libn Tidewater Reg Lib; State supv WPA Lib Proj of Va, Richmond Va; Dist libn 8th Naval Dist US Navy Hq, New Orleans; Circ dept head Tampa Pub Lib; Base libn MacDill AFB, Tampa Fla 57-64; Private research 64-. 9: FlaLA. 14: Admin, train, research. 15: 14601 Lake Magdalene Circle, Tampa Fla 33612.

KAGER, JOHN JAMES. b Buffalo 27 My 22. 4: Marguerite Stevens. 5: Canisius Col 40-47 (Hist) BA, 48-51 (Hist) MA; Columbia 53-58 (Guidance), 60-63 (LS) MS. 6: Ger, Lat, Gk. 7: Tchr Canisius High Sch, Buffalo 48-56, Instructor Canisius Col even sess 49; Sales rep Walden Bk Co, Buffalo 52-53; Inspec in Nematude Control US Dept of Agric, Hicksville NY summer 53; Tchr Massapequa High Sch, LINY 56-60; Lib asst Bedford Pub Sch 61-62, Head of circ & a-v coordinator Ryan Lib Iona Col 60-67; Hd libn Westchester Commun Col 67-. 8: Instr Wkshop for Police Instrs Iona Col 65; Planning Com NYS a-v coun conf 64-65. 9: CathLA (Chm Recr Com 65-66; WestchesterLA (pres 68-, (Recr Com); NYLA; NY State a-v Assn (Chm Mem Com). 10: AAUP. 13: Yes. 14: Electronic retrieval systems, a-v communications. 15: 65 Prospect st apt 8H, Stamford Conn 06902.

KAGER, MARGUERITE M (STEVENS). b Ridgewood Queens NY 6 N 25. 4: John James Kager. 5: D'youville Col 43-47 (Eng) BA; Columbia 56-59 (LS) MS, 60-65 (Instr Matls). 6: Ger. 7: Lib asst Canisius Col Lib 47-50; Sales Walden Bk Co, Buffalo NY 51-52; Libn Canisius High Sch, Buffalo NY 52-56; Libn Massapequa High Sch, LINY 56-60; Libn a-v coordinator Pound Ridge Elem Sch Instr Matls Center, Pound Ridge NY 60-; Instr lib sci dept Queens Col CUNY summer 66. 8: Instr Westchester A-V Coun Wkshop 63-64; Adv coun Iona Col 1st Writers Conf 64; Consul: Bailey Films 68; Mgt & Econ Research Inc, Palo Alto Cal 69; Vis lect Queens Col Lib Sch, NDEA Inst 65, NDEA Title VI B Fac Devel Inst in Col Media - Tchrs Col, Columbia. 09: NEA-DAVI; ALA; AASchL; NY State Tchrs Assn; NY State A-v Assn (Mem Chm); NYStateLA; WestchesterLA; NCTE; Westchester Co A-V Assn (pres 67-68). 10: Nat Wildlife Fed. 11: Congressional Delegate to President's White House Conf on Child & Youth 60; NDEA Media Inst Award 65. 12: Ed NY State Educ Dept "Proceedings of 1965 Communications Convocation." 14: Media resources centers, Instr matls centers. 15: 65 Prospect st apt 8H, Stamford Ct 06901.

KAHAO, MARY JANE (FLY). b Shanghai China 17 Jl 24. 4: Kenneth Hanson Kahao. 5: Newcomb Col 41-45 (Music) BA; LSU 51-63 (Vocal Music) tchr certif, 60-63 (LS) MS. 6: Fr. 7: Music supv Holy Family Sch, Port Allen La 51-52; Music supv W Baton Rouge Parish Elem Sch, Port Allen LA 52-53; Music supv Devall Elem Sch, Chamberlin La 54-55; Stud clerk LSU Lib Sch Lib 63, Ref libn LSU Lib 63-. 8: LSU Lib Lecturers Com 64 (chm 65-69; Soc & Program Com LSU Lib Staff Assn (chm 64); Lib Art Exhibits Com (chm 64), (v-chm 65); Handbk Revision Com 65; Hospitality chm LA Conf 65-66. 9: ALA; LaLA (Modisette Awards chm 67-69). 10: Baton Rouge Lib Club; Pi Beta Phi Alumnae Club; Newcomb Alumnae Club; Tulane Alumni Club; Baton Rouge Civic Symphony Auxiliary, Music Club of Baton Rouge; Jr League of Baton Rouge; Baton Rouge Arts & Science Center; Friends of the LSU Lib; Beta Phi Mu. 14: Ref sch lib, rare bks. 15: Rt 1 box 48, Port Allen La 70767.

KAHLER, BETTY JUNE (WHEELER). b Ft Worth Tex 21 Ja 37. 4: Edwin D Kahler. 5: Lamar State Col of Tech 55-56; N Tex State U 56-58, 65- (LS) BA; Tex Tech Col 65; N Tex State U 65-68 MLS. 7: Libn Ector Co Pub Schs, Odessa Tex 58-61; Tchr Ft Worth Pub Schs, Ft Worth Tex 61-62, Libn 62-. 10: Delta Kappa Gamma. 14: Elem sch libs. 15: Rt 1 Box 510, Azle Tx 76020.

KAHLER, GEORGE WALTER. b Philadelphia 11 Je 20. 4: Mary Ellis. 5: Temple 37-39, 45-46 (Educ) BS; Drexel 48-49 BLS; George Washington U 51-53 (Hist) MA; AmericanU 56-60 (Hist). 6: Fr. 7: Communications US Army (Sgt) 41-45; Ref asst US Dept of Agric Lib, Wash DC 49-53, Bibliogr 53-54, Catlgr 54-55, Catlgr rev 55-58; Asst libn US Coast & Geodetic Survey, Wash DC 58-65; Asst libn Geophysical Scis Lib, Rockville Md 65-68; Asst chief Libs Br US Environmental Sci Serv Admin, Rockville Md 68-. 9: ALA; SLA; SAA; DCLA (treas 61-62); Potomac Tech Processing Libns (treas 60-61). 10: AHA. 14: Admin. 15: 6395 Lakeview dr, Falls Church Va 22041.

KAHLER, MARY (ELLIS). b Santiago Chile 2 Ag 19. 4: George W Kahler. 5: Swarthmore 36-40 (Hist) AB (Magna cum laude); Drexel 48-49 BLS; George Washington U 51-53 (Hist) MA; AmericanU 56-68 (Latin Amer & US Hist) PhD. 7: Lib asst Post Lib, Fort Dix NJ 44-48; LC spec recr 49; Bibliogr Order Div 49-50, Head Bibliog Unit Order Div 50-51, Position clsf Personnel Off 51-52; Ed of Publ Union Catlg Div 52-53, Asst chief Ser Record Div 53-57, Chief Ser Record Div 57-66; Asst chief union catlg div 66-. 9: ALA (DCLA rep Coun 68-72; DC rep Recruiting Netwk 66-68); -RTSD (chm Ser Sect 59-60; var coms 61-68; Bd Dir 67-70); SLA (Soc Sci Div Nominating Com 66; Wash Chap: corresponding sec 63-64); DCLA (sec 64-65; var coms 63-65); Potomac Tech Proc Libns; SAA. 10: AAUW; Phi Beta Kappa; Phi Alpha Theta; AHA Conf on Lat Amer Hist; Lat Amer Studies Assn. 13: Yes. 14: Ser, ref, resources, subj bibliog. 15: 6395 Lakeview dr, Falls Church Va 22041.

KAHLER, SARAH (HEWLETT). b Brooklyn NY 16 Je 33. 4: Carl H Kahler. 5: Adelphi Col 51-55 (Educ) BSE; Columbia 56-59 (LS) MS. 6: Fr. 7: Prim tchr Lawrence Cedarhurst schs, Dist 15, #6 Sch, Woodmere NY 55-60; Jr libn NY Pub Lib, Bronx 60-61; Sr libn, head of child dept Elmont Pub Lib, Elmont NY 61-65; Asst dir Sayville Lib, Sayville NY 65-. 9: ALA; SLA; NYLA. 14: Programs for child. 15: 288 McConnell ave, Bayport NY 11705.

KAHN, HERMAN. b Rochester NY 13 Ag 07. 4: Anne E Suess. 5: UMinn 24-28 (Hist) BA, 28-31 (Hist) MA; Harvard 33-34 (Hist). 7: Tchg asst Hist UMinn (Minneapolis) 29-31; Asst prof Hist Neb State Tchrs Col 31-33; Hist Nat Park Serv, Wash DC 34-36; Archivist Nat Archives 36-48; Dir Franklin D Roosevelt Libs, Hyde Park NY 48-61; Asst archivist for Civil Archives Nat Archives 62-64; Asst archivist for Presidential Lib 64-68; Assoc libn for mss & archives Yale U 68-. 9: AHA; SAA (past mem coun, v-pres 68-69); Miss Valley HA. 11: Distinguished Service Award GSA. 13: Yes. 14: Research matls on the presidency in the 20th cent. 15: 98 Everit st, New Haven Ct 06511.

KAHN, MARGARET ELLEN. b Vladivostok Russia 14 S 13. 5: UCal(Berkeley) 30-34 (Eng) AB, 48 (Eng) MA, 52-53 BLS. 6: Fr. 7: Libn I ref dept UCal(Berkeley) 53-54, Libn II ref dept 54-61; Instr East Ill U 61-62; Sr ref libn Ohio State U 62-66; Libn III, Hd Ref Serv UCal (Irvine) 66-69, Libn IV 69-. 9: ALA. 14: Ref. 15: 434 San Bernardino ave, newport Beach Ca 92660.

KAHNE, GERTRUDE M. b Ashtabula Ohio. 5: Conn Col for Women 26-28 (Eng); Flora Stone Mather Col 28-29 (Eng) BA; West Res U 29-30 (LS) Certif; Columbia U 40-41 (LS) MS. 6: Fr, Ger. 7: Asst order & catlg dept Akron Pub Lib, Akron Ohio 30-32, Br libn 32-40; Asst sociol dept Cleveland Pub Lib 42-47, Asst br libn 47-54, Br libn 54-. 9: ALA; OhioLA; LPRC (sec Cleveland Chap). 10: Cleveland Pub Lib Staff Assn; West Side Commun Coun; Bus & Prof Chap, Cleveland Hadassah; West Res Sch Lib Sci Alumni; Lib Club Greater Cleveland; Cleveland Ostomy Assn. 13: Yes. 14: Br lib, adult educ. 15: 2880 S Moreland blvd, Cleveland Oh 44120.

KAIGE, ALICE TUBB. b Obion Tenn 27 Ja 22. 4: Richard H Kaige. 5: Vanderbilt 40-44 (Eng) BA; Peabody Col 46-47 BS in LS. 7: Libn Martin High Sch, Martin Tenn 46-47; Elem libn Jt Univ Lib, Nashville 46-52; Acquis libn Lincoln Lib, Springfield Ill 67-. 9: ALA; IllLA. 10: WILPF. 15: 701 S State st, Springfield Il 62704.

KAIGE, RICHARD HENRY. b Milwaukee 9 My 23. 4: Alice Tubb. 5: UWis 45-48 (Hist) BS in Ed; Peabody 50-51 MA in LS. 7: Ref asst Milwaukee Pub Lib 51-53; Ref asst Ill State Lib 53-61; Asst libn Educ Lib Ohio State U Libs 61-63; Ill State Lib: Ref asst 63-64, Head publ unit 64-65, Head consul off 65-66, Hd collection development unit 66-68, Consol lib development division 68-. 9: ALA; IllLA. 12: Ed "Illinois Libraries" (64-65). 14: Lib devel, ref, acquis. 15: 701 S State st, Springfield Ill 62704.

KAIHARA, YASUTO. b Kealia, Kauai Hawaii 29 Mr 32. 5: UHawaii 50-54 (Psych) BA; UIll 56-58 (LS) MS. 6: Sp, Fr, Ger, Russian, Hawaiian. 7: Stud asst UHawaii Lib 51-54; Personnel spec (Sp4) US Army, Honolulu 54-56; Catlg asst UIll Lib (Urbana) 57-59; Catlg libn UHawaii Lib 59-60, Foreign lang catlg libn 60-63, Hawaiian & Pacific libn 63-. 9: ALA; Hawaii LA. 10: Hawaiian Hist Soc; Bishop Museum Assn; Friends of Ulu Mau Village (a restored Hawaiian village complex); Beta Phi Mu. 12: Co-auth "A Selective Reading List of Hawaiian Books, 1968" (68); Assoc ed "Current Hawaiiana," quarterly (66-). 14: Ref, bibliog, catlg (Hawaii & Pacific). 15: 2553 Peter st, Honolulu Hi 96816.

KAISER, FRANCES (ELKAN). b Atlanta Ga 13 S 22. 5: Agnes Scott Col 39-43 (Eng) BA; Emory 48-49, (LS) MA. 6: Fr, Ger. 7: Act law libn Emory U Law Sch 43-46, Sec to dean 43-48; Interlib loan libn Ga Tech 50-64; Reader's serv libn 65-. 9: SLA (Transl Activs Com 59-65; v-chm & chm Paper & Textile Sect 64-66; pres S Atlantic Chap 68-69); SELA (Ref Serv Div); GaLA. 10: Phi Beta Kappa; Mortar Board; Beta Phi Mu; LWV. 11: Dogwood Award, SLA, Ga Chap, 56 & 59. 12: Ed "Translators and Translations: Services and Sources," SLA (59); "Translators and Translations: Services and Sources in Science and Technology," SLA (65). 14: Ref, tr, archives. 15: Slaton Manor apt 402, 2965 Pharr Ct So NW, Atlanta Ga 30305.

KAISER, JOHN BOYNTON. b Cleveland 1 Ja 1887. 5: West Res 04-08 (Liberal Arts & Law) AB; NY State Lib Sch (Albany) 08-10 BLS; UIll 12 (Internat Law); NYSLS 17 MLS. 7: Asst state libn Tex State Lib 10-11; Lecturer UIll Lib Sch & Econ & Sociol libn, Champaign 11-14; Libn pub Lib, Tacoma Wash 14-24; Dir UIowa Lib & Dir Lib summer Sch 24-27; Dir pub libs, Pub Museums, Pub Art Gallery, Oakland Cal 27-43; Dir Pub Lib, Newark NJ 43-58; Exec Dir ADI, Wash DC 60-63; ret. 8: Adv Bds: Wash State Lib 16-19, UWash Lib Sch 17-22; Columbia Sch Lib Serv 53-, Rutgers 50-57; Lecturer: Columbia Sch Lib Serv summers 45, 58; UWash, UIll, UCal, Rutgers, Chicago. 9: ALA (v-pres 49-50, chm var coms); PNLA (pres 17-18); CalLA (pres 32-33); NJLA (pres 48-49); NYSLSA Inc (pres 47-). 10: Phi Beta Kappa Alumni; ALA Delegate to NGO Group at UN 59-62; Camp libn Ft Knox Ky 18-19; Camp Upton NY 19; Collectors Club, NY; UCal Fac Club; Cal Writers Club. 11: Hon LHD Rutgers 60. 12: Ed "Legal Aspects of Library Administration" (58). 13: Yes. 14: Admin, finance, bibliog, personnel. 15: 4201 Massachusetts ave NW, Wash DC 20016.

KAISER, JOHN ROBERT. b Everett Penn 29 F 32. 5: Penn State U 52-54, 58-60 (Eng, Fr) BA, 60-62 (Fr) MA; Columbia 63-64 (LS) MS. 6: Fr, Sp. 7: Personnel spec USAF, US, Germany, France 54-58; Bibliog searcher Penn State U 62-63, Asst acquis libn 64-66, Order libn 67-, Deputy chief acquis libn 68-69, Chief 69-. 9: ALA; Amer Mss Soc. 14: Acquis, rare bks, bibliog. 15: 1136 S Atherton st, State College Penn 16801.

KAISER, WALTER HERBERT. b Cape Girardeau Mo 27 F 10. 4: Virginia Conover. 5: Southeast Mo State Col 27-31 (Educ) BS in ED; St Louis Lib Sch 32-33 certif; Chicago 39-40 MA in LS. 6: Sp, Fr. 7: Tchr Birch Tree (Mo) High Sch 31-32; Lib asst St Louis Pub Lib 32-34; Ref asst & br libn Tenn Valley Authority, Knoxville Tenn 34-36, Chattanooga Tenn 36-39; City Libn Muncie (Ind) Pub Lib 40-45; Co Libn Wayne Co Lib, Wayne Mich 45-. 8: Pub lib surveyor & bldg consul: Okla City Okla, Mt Lebanon Penn, Oak Park, Warren, Albion, Tecumseh, Berkley Mich Libs; Inventor of var mechanized lib processes. 9: ALA (coun nom com & other assignments); MichLA; TennLA; IndLA (pres-elect). 10: Torch Club. 11: Melvil Dewey Award for eminent achievements in libs & libnship 67; Libn of the Year 66. 13: Yes. 14: Admin. 15: 33030 Van Born rd, Wayne Mich 48184.

KAJUTI, LAURA S. b Fitchburg Mass 18 Ja 12. 4: Eino W Kajuti. 5: Stevens Bus Col 36 (Bkkeeping); So Conn State Col 58 (LS). 6: Fin, wk with all langs except Asiatic. 7: Sec Fitchburgh Chamber Com, Fitchburg Mass 48; Catlg asst Yale U 49-52; Asst libn in chg clsf & catlg & all govt sponsored research documents Olin Mathieson Chem Corp, New Haven Conn 52-. 9: SLA. 10: Little Colony Assn; Coop Consumers of New Haven Credit Union. 14: Catlg, IBM computer programming, Dept of Defense Res Documents (indexing & storage), retrieval, bibliog , lit surveys. 15: 60 Sheldon terr, New Haven Conn 06511.

KALAMARAS, CAROL J (MRS PETER A). b Muskegon Mich 27 Ag 38. 5: UMich 56-60 (Eng) BA & Mich Tchr Certif; UCal 62-63 MLS & Cal State Sch Lib Credential. 6: Sp, Fr. 7: Eng tchr Southfield Schs, Southfield Mich 60-62; Child libn Oak Park Pub Lib, Oak Park Mich 63-64; Secondary sch libn, Las Lomas High Sch, Walnut Creek Cal 64-66; Libn Berkeley High Sch, Berkeley Cal 66-. 8: Curriculum consul on Acalanes Union High Sch Eng Wkshop summer 65; Cal State Dept of Educ Curriculum Seminar April 7, 1965 on the Elem & Second Educ Act, Representative from a Secondary Sch lib Program; Survey Com Alameda Sec Sch Lib 67; Review Com Adult Bks for Young Adults, SLJ 67-. 9: CalASchL; CalLA. 12: "Meaning & Function of Language (65). 13: Yes. 14: Curr & sch lib wk (Eng & soc studies). 15: 72 Paseo Arboles, Suisun Ca 94585.

KALANGIS, GEORGE P. b Georgitsion Sparta Greece 16 My 35. 4: Helen E Kalangis. 5: Corinth Theol Sem (Greece) 49-56 (Theol, Liberal Arts) BTh; "Holy Cross" Greek Orthodox Theol Sch (Brookline Mass) 56-60 (Theol) BA; Andover Newton Theol School 62-64 (Psych) STM; URI 65-66 MLS. 6: Gr, Lat, Fr, Hebrew. 7: Asst dean Greek Orthodox Cathedral of New England, Boston 60-63; Greek Orthodox priest Greek Orthodox Ch, Ft Lauderdale Fla 63-64; Libn Marlboro High Sch, Marlboro Mass 65-66; Asst libn Assumption Col (Worcester Mass) 66-67; Gifts & exchange libn Brandeis U 67; Greek Orthodox priest Greek Orthodox Ch, Marlboro Mass 64-. 13: Yes. 14: Lib automation. 15: 199 Prospect st, Marlboro Ma 01752.

KALDOR, IVAN L. b 31 D 20. 4: Sheena Maysel Brown. 5: U London 57-58 (Russian Lang& Lit) BA (Hons), Hungarian Lang & Lit BA 59-60 (LS) DL; UChicago 63-66 (LS) PhD. 6: Hungarian, Russian, Ger, Fr. 7: CPA Hungarian Ministry of Educ, Budapest 39-42; Mil serv Signal Corps 42-45; UNESCO rep Hungarian Ministry of Educ, Budapest & Paris 46-48; Freelance tr State Publ Houses, Budapest 49-50; Dean Army Sch for Interpreters, Budapest 50-52; Res libn Ikarusz Works, Budapest 53-56; Asst libn ULondon 57-59; Asst ser libn Purude U 60-62, Aeronauics astronautics & engnr sci libn 62-65; Assoc Prof Dept of Lib Sci Kent Prof Sch of Lib Sci SUNY (Genesco) 68-. 9: LA (Gt Brit); ALA-ACRL;-ISA;-LED; AALS; SLA; ASIS; NYLA. 10: AAUP. 12: "Russian Language Manual for Military Personnel (I-III)" (50-52); "Guide to Research Reports in the Fields of Aeronautics, Astronautics and the Engineering Sciences" (76); Ed "Aspects of Librarianship" (65-69). 13: Yes. 14: Paleography, hist of printing, data processing, sci ref, info storage's retr. 15: Sch of Lib Sci State Univ Col, Geneseo NY 14454.

KALE, SHIRLEY W (KLEIN). b Brooklyn NY 24 S 24. 4: Gary S Kale. 5: Brooklyn Col 41-45 (Art, Classics) BA; Queens Col 64-68 MLS. 6: Lat, Fr, Sp. 7: Sch sec Bd of Educ, NYC 49-52; Libn (staff) Mus of Mod Art, NYC 68-. 9: SLA. 11: The Norma Loewenstein Drabkin Award for excell in Class Langs and Lit (Brooklyn Col 45). 14: Catlg, ref. 15: 134-25 Franklin ave, Flushing NY 11355.

KALINA, MARGIT (RAAB). b Karvina Czechoslovakia 23 S 22. 4: Kalina Ladislav. 5: KomenskyU (Bratislava Czechoslovakia) 56-61 (LS) Prom Phil. 6: Czech, Slovak, Ger, Russian. 7: Libn Slovak Acad of Sci Central Lib, Bratislava 55-65; Libn Lib of Islamic Arts, Jerusalem 65-66; Libn (staff) BrownU Rockefeller Lib 66-. 8: Hd catlg, circ & spec collection dept Slovak Acad of Sci Central Lib, Bratislava Czechoslovakia 64-65. 14: Catlg. 15: 343 Lloyd ave, Providence RI 02906.

KALKHOFF, ANN LYNN. b Chicago Hts Ill 20 D 44. 5: UIll 62-66 (Hist) BA, 66-67 (LS) MS. 7: Page & circ desk hd Arlington Hts (Ill) Pub Lib summers 60-65; Ch libn & reading club hd McKinley Foundation, Champaign Ill 66-67; Asstship UIll Lib Sch (Urbana) summer 67; Child libn Brooklyn Pub Lib, Brooklyn NY 67-. 9: ALA (Jr Mem RT). 10: UIll Lib Sch Assn; UIll Alum Assn. 14: Child wk (esp serv to the disadvantaged). 15: 220 Berkeley pl #1d, Brooklyn NY 11217.

KALKUS, STANLEY (STANISLAV). b Prague Czechoslovakia 27 Ap 31. 4: Marta J Pokorna. 5: Classical Gymnasium (Prague) 42-50 (hu) matura; UChicago 55-56 (Slavic linguistics), 56-59 (LS) MA, 59-60 (Slavic linguistics); Joh Gutenberg U (Mainz, Germany) 66-68 (Philos); Charles U (Prague, Czech) summer 68 (Slavic Stud). 6: Czech, Slovak, Ger, Russian, Polish, Lat. 7: Clerk Radio Free Europe, Munich Ger 51-52; (Cpl) US Army, 525 MI Grp, Ft Bragg NC 53-55; Searcher UChicago Lib 55-57; Libn Nat Opinion Research Center, Chicago 57-59; Hq libn Hq 5th US Army, Chicago 59-60; Libn Southeast Jr Col 60-62; Base libn Sidi Slimane AF Base, Sidi Simane Morocco 62-63; Base libn Hahn AFB (USAFE), Hahn AF Base Ger 63-68; Slavic bibliogr & lecturer in Slavic ling UNC (Chapel Hill) 68-. 8: Lib/USA NY World's Fair 65. 9: ALA; Assn Adv of Slavic Studies. 10: Czechoslovak Nat Coun in amer; UChicago Alum Assn; Grad Lib Sch Alum Assn; Soc for Arts & Scis (NY). 13: Yes. 14: Admin & ref; a-v. 15: 601 Park pl, Chapel Hill NC 27514.

KALLAM, MINNIE SPENCER. 5: North Carolina 29 AB; UNC 35 AB in LS. 7: Libn Granville Sch, Winston-Salem NC 35-40; James A Gray High Sch 40-44; Readers adv & bk consul Wills Bk & Stationery Co, Greensboro NC 45-48; Asst catlg libn, Wake Forest Col 48; Circ div NY Pub Lib summers 37-41; Asst acquis libn Tchrs Col Columbia U summers 42; Asst to post libn US Army Air Corps, Greensboro NC summer 43; Asst circ libn Wake Forest Col 49-56, ref libn 56-67; Ref libn Wake Forest U 67-. 9: ALA; SELA; NCLA (treas 43-47). 15: 1956 Faculty dr, Winston-Salem NC 27106.

KALLENBACH, JESSAMINE (SHIVELY). b Laconia NH 22 O 15. 4: Joseph E Kallenbach. 5: Mt Holyoke 32-36 (Hist) AB; UMich 60-62 AMLS. 6: Fr. 7: Eng tchr Brewster Acad, Wolfeboro NH 36-39; House dir in men's residence UMich 39-43; Lib asst Grad Lib UMich 60-62; Asst catlg libn East Mich U 62-, Asst humanities libn 65-. 9: ALA; MichLA. 10: Beta Phi Mu; Phi Kappa Phi; Pi Lambda Theta. 15: 1745 Glenwood rd, Ann Arbor Mi 48104.

KALLENBERG, RUTH ANN (BARRETT). b Honolulu 19 Jl 42. 4: John Kenneth Kallenberg. 5: Whitman Col 60-64 (Eng Lit) AB; Ind U 64-65 (LS) MA. 6: Fr. 7: Catlgr Fresno State Col 65-66, Head reclassification project 66-. 9: ALA; CalLA. 10: Beta Phi Mu. 14: Rare bks, catlg. 15: 3878 E Swift ave, Fresno Ca 93726.

KALLMANN, HELMUT. b Berlin Ger 7 Ag 22. 4: Ruth Singer. 5: Toronto 46-49 (Music) Mus Bac. 6: Ger, Eng, Fr. 7: Music clerk Can Broadcasting Corp, Toronto 50-51, Music libn 51-61, Sr music libn 61-62, Supv of Music Lib 62-. 8: Ed Bd Can Music Journal 56-62; Mem of Music Com, Can Govt Participation in 1967 Exposition. 9: CanLA; CanMusLA (chm 57-58 & 67-68); BSCan; Can Music Coun; Internat Assn of Mus Libs (Can Delegate). 10: UToronto Faculty of Music Alumni Assn. 12: "Catalogue of Canadian Composers" (rev ed 52); "A History of Music in Canada 1534-1914" (60). 13: Yes. 14: Documentation & bibliog of Can musical hist. 15: 53 Gwendolen ave, Willowdale Ont Canada.

KALLUS, EUGENE L. b Czechoslovakia 18 D 05. 4: Elizabeth Lukacs. 5: Gymnasium 17-25; Charles' U (Prague) Law Sch 26-30, JU Dr; Rutgers 59-61 (LS) DJ. 6: Czech, Ger, Hungarian, Slovakian, Ukranian. 07: Attorney Czechoslovakia 39; US Army infantry Mil Govt (Sgt) 42-45; Queens Borough Pub Lib, NY 59-. 9: ALA; NYLA; NY Lib Club. 14: Pub lib serv. 15: 39-38 47 st, Long Island City NY 11104.

KALLWEIT, VIOLA ESTHER (BASE). b Murdock Kan 26 N 19. 4: William Frederic Kallweit. 5: Pomona Jr Col 37-39 AA; Tufts 39-42 (Relig Educ) AB; USoCal 59-63 MSLS; Cal State col (Los Angeles) 63-67 (Educ). 6: Ger, Sp. 7: Soc wker All Nations Foundation, Los Angeles 44-46; Admin asst Pomona Pub Lib, Pomona Cal 57-60; Pub rel libn 60-63; Libn Chaffey Union High Sch Dist, Ontario Cal 63-. 8: Consul Chaffey High Sch Lib Enrichment Program ESEA Title I Chaffey Union High Sch Dist, Ontario Cal 65-68. 9: CalLA; CalASchL. 10: San Antonio Lib Club; Pi Lambda Theta; Kappa Kappa Iota; Ontario-Upland Altrusa Club; Ontario-Upland AAUQ; Pomona Valley Art Assn; Pomona Commun Art Assn. 13: Yes. 14: Lib admin, ref. 15: 1245 N Euclid ave, Ontario Ca 91762.

KALP, MARGARET ELLEN. b Middletown NY 17 Ap 15. 5: NJ Col for Women 32-36 (LS) AB; UMich summers 39-42 ma in LS; UChicago 56, summers 52, 53 (LS). 6: Fr, Sp. 7: Reviser Lib Sch NJ Col for Women 36-37; Instr sec Lib Sch Hampton Inst 37-39; Asst Hunterdon Co Lib, Flemington NJ 39-40; Asst libn Central High Sch, Ypsilanti Mich 40-43; Libn Rumson High Sch, Rumson NJ 43-46; Visiting instr Lib Sch Peabody Col summer 45, 46, Libn Demonstration Sch Libs & Lecturer in Lib Sci 46-47; Asst prof Sch Lib Sci UNC 47-55, Associate prof 55-, Act dean 64-67. 8: Various consultantships & accreditation visits for State Dept of Pub Instr in NC; NDEA sch lib insts evaluation panel Wash DC 65; consul to Dept of Pub Instr on revision of Guidelines for Title III, NDEA Raleigh 62; Consul Grad Dept Lib Sci, Our Lady of the Lake Col, San Antonio Tex 68. 9: ALA (Coun 63-67, chm Dutton-Macrae Award Jury 63); -AASchL (Bd Dirs 63-67); AALS; NEA; SELA; NCLA (pres 63-65). 10: AAUP; Delta Kappa Gamma; Beta Phi Mu; Pi Gamma Mu; Altrusa. 13: Yes. 14: Sch libnship, wk with child & yp, lib educ. 15: POBox 973, Chapel Hill NC 27514.

KALT, ADOLPH LOUIS SM. b Detroit 23 N 1884. 5: UDayton 08-12 (Eng) BA; UDetroit 26-29 (Eng) MA; Catholic U summers 33-36 (LS); West Res U summers 37-39 BS in LS. 6: Ger. 7: Elem & high sch tchr San Francisco, Baltimore, Wash, Cincinnati, Dayton Ohio, Cleveland, Detroit, Mineola, Sioux City, Phila 08-32; Elem prin 21-22; Instr Trinity Col, Sioux City Iowa 35-36; Instr UDayton summer 22; Libn Trinity Col, Iowa 33-38; Libn Chaminade High Sch, Dayton 39; Libn Cathedral Latin, Cleveland 42-59; Libn St James High Sch, Penn 35-59; Libn Chester Penn 59-. 8: CathLA No Ohio (pres 45-52); Cath Bk Week Cleveland (chm 44-59); Prin St Anthony Sch, Cincinnati 21-22; V-prin Catholic High Sch, Hamilton 24-26; Life tchrs certif Diocese of Cleveland; Life tchrs certif State of Ohio. 9: CathLA (Nomin Com); ALA. 11: Honorary certif for serv CathLA. 14: Catlg, bk reviews. 15: 2001 Providence ave, Chester Penn 19103.

KALVONJIAN, ARAXIE. b Kenosha Wis 31 Jl 21. 5: UWis 40-43 (Bacteriology) BA 69; Rosary Col 61-63 MALS; Carthage Col 65- (Educ) Tchrs Certif. 6: Fr, Armenian. 7: Bacteriologist US Standard Prods, Woodworth Wis 43-44; Research asst Amer Cyanamid Co Lederle Labs Div, Pearl River NY 44-45; Ext libn Marietta Pub Lib, Marietta Ohio 54-60; Lab tech Pinellas Co Health Dept, St Petersburg Fla 60-61; Head br libn GM Simmons Pub Lib, Kenosha Wis 61-66; Hd libn Kenosha Tech Inst 66-. 8: Wkd with D B M Duggar, founder of drug mold "aureomycin," antibiotic Jan 45 at Lederle Labs & was his research asst at time of discovery. 9: ALA; WisLA; Amer Vocatl Assn; Wis Assn Vocat & Adult Educ. 10: Kenosha Lib Assn; Civic Theatre (Kenosha); Ninety-Nines (Women's Pilot Assn). 14: Ext, ref, ya. 15: 6740 14th ave, Kenosha Wis 53140.

KAMENOFF, LOVISA. b Huntington NY 28 N 41. 5: Syracuse 59-60 (Nursing), 60-63 (Amer Lit) BA; Simmons 65-66 MLS. 6: Fr. 7: Nurses' aide Huntington Hosp, Huntington NY 58-59; Lab tech Syracuse U 60-63; Med sec Peter Bent Brigham Hosp, Boston 63-64; Med & nursing sch libn Brockton Hosp Brockton Mass 66-. 9: ALA; MedLA; Nat League for Nursing; NELA; NE Hosp Lib Gp. 14: Med ref & bibliog wk. 15: 12 Watson st apt 2, Brockton Ma 02401.

KAMENS, HARRY H. b Cambridge Md 15 Mr 45. 5: UDel 63-67 (Accounting) BS; UPittsburgh 67-68 MLS. 7: Asst acquis UDel Lib (Newark) 65-. 9: ALA. 10: Beta Phi Mu; Omicron Delta Kappa. 14: Acquis, ser. 15: 644 Lehigh rd apt K-6, Newark De 19711.

KAMINSKI, GAIL PATRICIA. b Buffalo NY 18 Jl 46. 5: URochester 64-68 (Econ) BA; Simmons 68-69 (LS) MS. 9: ALA. 14: Bus & financial libs. 15: 295 Depew ave, Buffalo NY 14214.

KAMMER, FERDINAND. b Baltimore Md 7 O 38. 5: Loyola 64 (Psych, Math) BA; UPittsburgh 66 (Info Syst) MLS. 6: Fr, Sp. 7: Instr of math Baltimore Co Bd of Educ, Towson Md 62-65; Ref libn Enoch Pratt Free Lib, Baltimore 68-69; Lib syst analyst UMd (College Park) 66-. 9: ASIS (Assoc pres Pittsburgh Stud Chap 65-66). 10: Staff Alliance Assn of the UMd Libs. 14: Lib automation, systems design & devel. 15: 2505 Chesterfield ave, Baltimore Md 21213.

KAMMERMEYER, JANET CATHERINE (DAY). b Joplin Mo 1 Ap 45. 4: John Arthur Kammermeyer. 5: UMo 63-64; Laredo Jr Col 65; UWash 66-67 (Fr) BA, 68-69 MLibnship. 6: Fr, Ger. 7: Libn I Santa Clara Co Lib, San Jose Cal 69-. 9: ALA; WLA. 14: Inst libs. 15: 124 Carriage way, Hinsdale Il 60521.

KAMPER, ALBERT F. b Pittsburgh 23 F 42. 4: Julie M Mangold. 5: Duquesne U 60-64 (Math, Physics) BA; UPittsburgh 64-65 MLS, 65-66 (LS). 6: Ger. 7: Libn page Carnegie Lib of Pittsburgh 59-60; Clerical asst 60-64, Lib trainee 64-65, Libn I 65-66, Head bk order off 67-. 9: SLA; PennLA (chm Tech Serv Sect). 10: Beta Phi Mu. 12: Ed "Technical Book Review Index" (SLA). 14: Sci & tech info retrieval, tech serv. 15: 373 Huntington ave, Pittsburgh Pa 15202.

KAMRA, ARDIS DAPHNE (STEWART). b Edmonton Can 25 My 30. 4: Krishan Kamra. 5: UAlta 49-52 (Eng, Hist) BA; Toronto 52-53 BLS; UAlta 65- (Educ), 67-69 MEd; UWash 69-. 07: Child libn Edmonton Pub Lib, Edmonton Can 53-57, Br libn 59-61; Asst circ libn UAlta 63-65; Sch libn St Albert Protestant Separate Sch Bd, St Albert Alta 65-66. 14: Child & sch serv. 15: 4170 42 ave NE, Seattle Wa 98105.

KANALY, MARION ELIZABETH. b Malden Mass 10 D 23. 5: St Mary-of-the-Woods Col 41-45 (Eng Lit) BA; Columbia 47-48 (LS) BS; Boston Col 63 (Hist) MA. 6: Fr, Lat, Sp, Ger. 7: Claims analyst US VA, Boston 45-47; Wellesley Col: Circ libn 48-52, Documents libn 52-64, Assoc libn for readers serv 64-. 8: Guest lecturer Simmons Sch of Lib Sci 64, 65; Part time lecturer lit of soc sci Simmons Col 65-67. 9: AHA; HistAssn(London); ALA-RSD (Hist Sect: Program Com, Communications Com, v-chm 68-69, chm 69-70); MassLA; NETechServLibns. 14: Bibliog, ref serv, hist of libs, govt docs. 15: Wellesley Col Lib, Wellesley Mass 02181.

KANASKY, WILLIAM FRANK. b Shamokin Penn 30 D 18. 4: Mary L (Sekscienski). 5: State Col (Bloomsburg Penn) 36-40 (Soc Studies) BS; Bucknell U 46-47 (Hist) MS; Drexel 64-67 msls. 7: (1st Lt) Platoon leader, Heavy Weapons 89th Mortrar Bn, ETO 41-46; Tchr Shamokin High Sch, Shamokin Penn 46-50; 1st Lt G-2 Research and Analysis GHQ FECOM Tokyo 50-52; Libn No Burlington Co Regional High Sch, Columbus NJ 60-63; Libn Tyrone Jr High Sch, St Petersburg Fla 63-64; Libn Haddon Twp High Sch, Westmont NJ 64-66; Assoc prof Kutztown State Col 66-. 9: NEA; ALA; PennStateEA; PennLA; PennSchLA. 10: Beta Phi Mu; Alpha Beta Alpha; Phi Delta Kappa. 13: Yes. 14: Tchr of lib educ. 15: 335 E Walnut, Kutztown Pa 19530.

KANASY, JAMES EMERY. b Hungary 13 Mr 27. 4: Elizabeth Czinczoll. 5: UWindsor 52-56 (Biol) BS, 63-67 (Hist) BA; UMich 56-58 AMLS; UPittsburgh 67-68 Certif in LS. 6: Hungarian, Ger, Fr. 7: Sci libn UWindsor 58-62, Hd sci div 63-64, Hd sci div & Act hd tech serv 64-66, Deputy univ libn 66-. 9: ALA; CanLA; Can Assn Col & Univ Lib 9com on Lib Automation 65-67); OntLA (chm Catlg Cost Study Com 65-66). 10: Hist of Sci Soc; Soc Hist Tech. 11: Nat Res Coun Can Scholarship 67-68. 13: Yes. 14: Sci ref, lib automation, lib admin, lib educ. 15: 515 Bartlet dr, Windsor 22 Ont Can.

KANCHENIAN, LUCIA. b Timisoara Romania 21 Je 27. 4: Dikran Kanchenian. 5: C I ParhonU Col of Philos (Bucharest Romania) 45-49 (Romanian lang & lit) BA; URI 65-67 MLS. 6: Romanian, Fr, Ital, Armenian. 7: Ed Broadcasting Com, Bucharest Romania 49; Asst Prof C I ParhonU, Bucharest Romania 49-52; Researcher Romanian Acad, Bucharest Romania 51-61; Fr tchr, Beirut Lebanon 62-64; Asst catlgr BrownU Lib 64-67, Catlgr 67-. 9: RILA. 10: Intl Inst of RI. 12: Ed "Transylvanian Stories" (57); Ed "Stories from Old Times" (58). 13: Yes. 14: Catlg, rare bks. 15: 100 Lydia st, Providence RI 02908.

KANE, ADA (PETTINGILL). b Chicago Heights Ill 5 N 16. 4: William Edward Kane. 5: Mich U 34-38 (Hist) BA; Suny (Geneseo) 38-39 BLS; URochester 40-46 (Guidance) G Certif; UMich (LS) BLS. 7: Libn Skaneateles High Sch, Skaneateles NY 30-41; Brighton Elem Lib 41-42; Libn & eng Harley Sch, Rochester NY 43-55; Libn Gillette Sch, Henrietta NY 55-61;

Libn Pittsford Jr High Sch, Pittsford NY 62-. 9: ALA; Nat Reading Assn; NY State Tchrs Assn. 11: John Cotton Dana Award 46. 13: Yes. 14: Child. 15: 85 S Main st, Pittsford NY 14534.

KANE, FLORENCE SIMPSON. b NYC. 4: Walter T. 5: Good Coun Col 43 (Hist) AB; Columbia 45 BLS; NY State Certif. 7: Semi-prof clerk & graded prof NY Pub Lib 39-46; Libn Regis High Sch, NYC 46-51; Staff Fordham U 52-53; Libn Mary Immaculate Sch, Ossining NY 63-67; St Vincent's Sch, Tarrytown NY 67-. 9: ALA; NYStateLA; CathLA. 14: Org libs. 15: 253 Hunter ave, N Tarrytown NY 105692.

KANE, JOSEPH P. b Herkimer NY 17 Mr 37. 4: Ida Lucille (Johnson). 5: State U Tchrs Col (Geneseo) NY 54-58 (Elem Educ & LS) BS; Syracuse 62-63 (LS) MS, 69-70 (Higher Ed, Admin). 07: Elem Sch libn Cooperative Bd, Attica NY 58-59; Elem sch libn Cooperative Bd, Alexander NY 58-60; Elem sch libn Cooperative Bd, Pavilion NY 59-60; Elem sch libn Dunkirk Pub Sch, Dunkirk NY 60-62; Head libn CZ Col 63-. 8: Middle States Assn evaluation team on Balboa High Sch lib 65; State Chm for Jr Col Libns. 9: ALA. 10: AAUP; Beta Phi Mu; Amer Fed Tchrs; Nat Coun Cath Men; Confraternity of Christ Doctrine. 14: Admin, catlg, acquis. 15: Libn, Canal Zone Col Box 3009, Balboa Canal Zone.

KANE, LOIS A. b McKeesport Penn. 5: Manhattanville Col of the Sacred Heart 60 (Sacred Music) BSM; Rutgers 63-65 MLS. 6: Fr. 7: Priv piano tchr, church organist 50; Eng tchr, choral dir Pittsburgh Schs; Supv of music 20 Catholic schs, Pittsburgh; Music instr Mt Mercy Col; Newark Pub Lib, Newark NJ: Trainee child dept 63-65, Jr libn ref dept 65, Sr libn ref dept 66-; Supv A-V serv Arlington Co Pub Lib, Arlington Va 67-. 9: VaLA; Film Lib Info Coun); Amer Film Inst; MusLA; DCLA; Wash Film Coun. 10: Beta Phi Mu; Women's Com for Arlington Symphony; Quota Internat; Rutgers Alum Assn. 13: Yes. 14: Rev, a-v. 15: 4204 Muir place, Alexandria Va 22312.

KANE, LUCILE M(ARIE). b Maiden Rock Wis 17 Mr 20. 5: River Falls State Col 38-42 (Eng) BS; UMinn 43-46 (Hist) MA. 6: Fr. 7: Tchr Osceola High Sch, Osceola Wis 42-44; Publicity UMinn Pres, Minneapolis 44-46; Research & Editing Forest Hist Found, St Paul 46-48; Mss curator Minn Hist Soc, St Paul 48-. 9: SAA (Fellow Coun, Com on mss); Amer Mss Soc. 12: "Military Life in Dakota" (51); "Guide to the Care & Administration of Manuscripts" (60); The Manuscripts Collection of the Minn Hist Soc with A Johnson (55); "The Waterfall that Build a City" (66); "The Public Affairs Collection of the Minnesota Historical Society," (68). 13: Yes. 14: Catlg & collecting, admin of mss. 15: 1298 Fairmount ave, St Paul Mn 55105.

KANE, SISTER MARY RUTH OP. b New Haven Conn 10 Ap 1898. 5: Col of New Rochelle 15-19 (er) BA; Columbia summers 35-39 BS in LS. 6: Ger, Fr. 7: Sec to asst libn in ser Yale U Lib 20-22; Tchr West Haven High Sch, West Haven Conn 22-25; Tchr various schs, Ohio, Penn; Libn & Head of Lib Sci Dept Col of St Mary of the Spring 41-55; Libn St Marys High Sch, New Haven Conn 55-. 9: CathLA (Cath Period Index Conn 53-54, Book Fair Com 60-, Memb Com 63; Columbus Unit: chm 49-55; Conn Unit: chm 52-53, 67-69; Memb Chm 64-); ConnSchLA; ConnLA; ALA. 10: Columbus Libns Coun. 14: Sch lib mgt, ref. 15: 444 Orange, New Haven Conn 06511.

KANE, RITA (BECHT). b Erie Penn 29 Ap 31. 5: St Mary-of-the-Woods Col 49-50 (Biol); Boston U 50-53 BS; UHawaii 66-67 MLS. 6: Lat, Fr. 7: Ref libn UHawaii 67-68, Hd sci-tech ref 68-. 8: Instr Grad Sch of Lib Studies, UHawaii fall 68; Instr Fulbright Orientation Prog summer 68. 9: ALA; ASIS; HawaiiLA. 10: Fac Senate UHawaii; Hawaiian Acad of Sci; Beta Phi Mu. 13: Yes. 14: Ref, indexing theory, info ret, user educ. 15: 2502 Pacific Heights rd, Honolulu Hi 96813.

KANEN, RONALD ARTHUR. b Brooklyn NY 15 Mr 33. 5: NY State Col for Tchrs (Albany) 50-54 (Span) AB; Emory U 56-57 (LS) ML. 6: Sp. 7: US Army Radio operator (Sp3) 54-56; Catlgr Miami Pub Lib, Miami Fla 58, ser libn 58-59, Br libn 59-63, Head ext div 63-65, Hd adult serv 66-. 9: ALA-ASD (mem Notable Bks Coun 69-); FlaLA; Dade Co LA (pres 68-69). 13: Yes. 15: 3903 W Flagler st apt 3, Miami Fl 33134.

KANGRO, AIME. b Tartu Estonia. 5: TartuU(Tartu Estonia) 33 (Ger, Eng Philol); Chicago 51-57 (LS) MA. 6: Ger, Fr, Russian, Finnish, Estonian. 7: Libn Baptist Missionary Train Sch, Chicago 50-52; Asst head acquis dept UChicago Lib 52-. 9: ALA; Chicago Reg Group for Libns in Tech Serv; ChicagoLibClub. 10: Beta Phi Mu; Chicago Estonian Soc. 14: Acquis, bk sel. 15: 5710 S Kimbark ave, Chicago Il 60637.

KANJI, ZAINAB JENNY. b Kampala Uganda 22 Mr 45. 4: Amir Kanji. 5: AmericanU 61-65 n01291 kanji, zainab jenny. 6: Fr, Gujerati, Arabic, Swahihi. 7: Lib asst Tanganyika Pub Lib, Daressalaam 65-66; Lib asst Kensington Pub Lib, London 66-67; Lib asst Burnaby Pub Lib, Vancouver Can 67-68. 9: CanLA; ALA. 14: Child wk. 15: Suite 1002-1250 Lomox st, Vancouver British Columbia Can.

KANN, PAUL J(AMES). b Binghamton NY 23 F 16. 4: Barbara Hewitt. 5: Yale 33-37 (Fr) BA, 37-42 (Romance Langs, Fr) MA, 49 (Romance Langs, Fr) PhD; West Res 54-55 MS in LS. 6: Fr, Sp, Ger, Ital. 7: Instr Fr & Span Simmons Col 47-51; Master Fr & Span St Paul's Sch, Concord NH 52-54; Libn modern langs Grad Lib Ohio State U 55-63; Libn spec romance langs Stanford U Libs 63-65, Curator romance langs 65-. 9: ALA- CRLA; Mod Lang Assn; Mod Humanities Res Assn; CalLA. 10: AAUP; Univ Club of Palo Alto; Yale Club of NYC; Yale Club of Palo Alto. 13: Yes. 14: Bk sel, ref, rare bks. 15: Stanford Univ Lib, Stanford Cal 94305.

KANNER, ELLIOTT E(LISHA). b NYC 14 S 29. 5: Col of the City of NY even 46-50 (Liberal Arts); Columbia 51-54 (Sociol) BS, 54-55 (LS) MS; 6th yr UWis 68; UWis 68-. 06: Ital, Fr. 7: Jr lib asst Cooper Union Lib, NYC 46-51; Law catlg asst ColumbiaU 51-55; Prof interne LC 55-56; Ref libn Mich State Lib 56-58; Chief ref & adult serv Columbia River Reg Lib Demonstration, Wenatchee Wash 58-60; Asst dir NCentral Reg Lib, Wenatchee Wash 61-63; Liaison libn Wash State Lib 63-65; Asst libn Great Falls Pub Lib, Great Falls Mont 65-67; Fellow UWis Lib Sch 67-. 8: Spec consul Conn State Lib summer 67. 9: ALA-ACRL; -Subs bks com 62-63; MichLA (chm Recr Com 57-58); WashLA; MontLA; PNLA (chm Adult Educ Com 63-64); WisLA. 10: Beta Phi Mu. 13: Yes. 14: Ref, adult serv. 15: Univ of Wisconsin Lib Sch, Madison Wi 53706.

KANNO, IRENE (SACHIE). b Hilo Hawaii 9 S 36. 5: UHawaii 54-58 (Elem Educ) BEd, 59-60 (Elem Educ) 5th Yr Certif; Rutgers 62-63 MLS. 7: Libn aid Lib of Hawaii, Honolulu 60-62; Libn Queens Borough Pub Lib, Queens NY 63-64; Asst lib spec UHawaii (Hilo) 64-66; Catlgr US Army Garrison Command, Japan 66-. 9: ALA; HawaiiLA. 10: AAUP. 14: Ref, catlg, automation in libs. 15: 144 Mauna Loa st, Hilo Hawaii 96720.

KANSAS, (RAY) HAROLD. b New Orleans La 8 Mr 37. 5: Tulane 54-59 (Geol) BSc; LSU 66-68 9ls0 msc. 7: Air weather observer A/3C Air Nat Guard, Cal 59-60; Combat engr (Sp4) USA, Hawaii 60-62; Oil well logger Monarch Logging Co Inc, San Antonio Tex 62-63; Real estate salesman Kan Real Estate, New Orleans 63-65; Asst curator LSU Sch of Geol (Baton Rouge) 66-68; Summer participant (geog & map div) LC 68; Asst libn Orleans Parish Sch Bd New Orleans 69-. 9: ALA; SLA; Geosci Info Soc. 14: Documentation, electronic data proc. 15: 751 W Roosevelt st, Baton Rouge La 70802.

KANTAUTAS, ADAM. b Daskoniai Lithuania 19 Ja 10. 4: Filomena Augyte. 5: Sch of Econ & Bus Admin (Copenhagen Denmark) 31-34 (For Trade) B Com; UWash 59-60 MLS. 6: Lithianian, Polish, Russian, Ger, Danish. 7: Prin Sch of Com, Lithuania 34-36; Gen mgr "Maiastas" Ltd, Lithuania 37-40; Numerous jobs Edmonton Can 48-59; Order libn UAlta 60-63, Asst hd order dept 64-. 9: ALA; CanLA; AltaLA; EdmontonLA (Coun 61-62); UAlta Profess Libns Gp (pres 63-65). 10: Philos Soc of Alta; Wash Sch of Libnship Alum Assn; Assn Aca Staff UAlta; Can Assn Univ Tchrs. 13: Yes. 14: Bibliog, acquis, bk trade. 15: 12010-87 ave, Edmonton 61 Alberta Can.

KANTOR, DAVID. b Atlanta 2 N 15. 4: Lee Finberg. 5: UFla 34-38 (Biol) BS; Universite3 Libre de Bruxelles 38-39 (Microbiol) Licenciate; Drexel 40-41 BSLS. 6: Fr, Sp, Ger. 7: Catlgr UFla 41-42; Chem-pharmacy libn 42-43; Tech libn US Army Signal Corps, Ft Monmouth NJ 43-44; Libn Wash State Reformatory, Monroe Wash 44-46, 47-49; Libn Farragut Col, Idaho 46-47; Libn Cal Dept of Corrections, Folsom Prison 49-62; Dir of ext Volusia Co Pub Libs, Daytona Beach Fla 62-63, Dir of Libs 63-. 8: Lecturer on rehabilitation & correctional problems of criminals at UWash 47; Lib bldg consul 4 Fla libs 67-68; Institl libs consul, Fla State Lib (67-68). 9: ALA (Reg mem com 55, hosp & Inst coms 56); CalLA (pres Golden Empire Dept 58, Bd Dirs 58, pres Hosp & Inst com 53); FlaLA 62-. 11: Bysse-Rolin music scholarship Brussels 39. 12: "Survey of Public Library Service in Volusia County" (64); "Survey of Libraries and Library Services in the State Institutions of Florida" (67). 13: Yes. 14: Pub serv. 15: Volusia Co Pub Libs, City Island, Daytona Beach Fla 32014.

KANTOR, J(AMES) R(OLAND) K(RISTOFER). b NYC 7 Ap 28. 5: Cornell U 45-49 (Eng) AB; UCal 55-60 MA(Eng), MLS. 6: Fr, Ger. 7: Inquiry correspondent Brentano's Inc, NYC 49-52; Claims manager The Viking Press Inc, NYC 52-53; Personnel (sgt maj) US Army Infantry, Ft Benning Ga 53-55; Stud asst Bancroft Lib, UCal 55-60; Rare bks libn Ohio State U Lib 60-61; Ref libn Bancroft Lib UCal 61-63, U Archivist Bancroft Lib 64-. 9: BSA; SAA (chm Col & Univ Archives Comm 67-). 10: Willa Cather Pioneer Mem, Red Cloud Neb; Andrew Dickson White Art Mus Assocs Cornell Univ. 12: Ed "Grimshaw's Narrative" (64). 13: Yes. 14: Rare bks, mss, Cal hist. 15: 425 Panoramic wy, Berkeley Cal 94704.

KANWISCHER, DOROTHY E. b Rochester NY 24 N 11. 4: Ewald A Kanwischer. 5: URochester 28-32 (Hist) BA (cum laude); Syracuse 41, 45 BSLS. 6: Ger, Fr. 7: Clerical asst URochester Lib 32-41; Jr libn US Govt Civil Serv, W Point NY 41-43; Asst to libn URochester Med Lib 43-45; Jr prof libn Rochester Pub Lib 45-48; Color tech libn eastman Kodak Co, Rochester NY 48-50; Libn Kemp Research Org, Rochester NY 53-56; Libn Acad of Med Lib, Rochester NY 58-60; Circ libn Rochester Inst of Tech 60-65; Asst catlgr U of the Pacific 66-. 9: SLA (past memb chm); CalLA. 10: Mental Health Assn. 13: Yes. 14: Catlg, clsf. 15: Univ of the Pacific Lib, Stockton Ca 95207.

KAO, BERNICE (TZE-WEI CHOW). b Soochow China 19 D 34. 4: George C Kao. 5: Nat Taiwai U 53-57 (Eng) BA; UCincinnati 57-58 (Eng); Case West Res U 58-60 (LS) MA. 6: Chinese, Fr, Eng. 7: Catlgr Cuyahoga Co Libs, Cleveland 60-62; Catlgr UFla Libs 62-65. 9: ALA; Amer Studies Assn. 14: Catlg, ref. 15: 6502 Janice st NW, Huntsville Al 35806.

KAO, MARY MEI-LI (LIU). b Yun-Nan China 5 S 42. 5: Nat TaiwanU 59-63 LLB; Tex Woman'sU 63-65 MLS. 6: Chinese, Ger, Sp. 7: Circ libn DenisonU 65-67; Tech serv libn Sacred HeartU (Bridgeport Conn) 67-. 9: ALA. 10: Chinese Inst of Libns. 14: Catlg, ref. 15: 17 Abner ct, Bridgeport Ct 06606.

KAO, YASUKO (WATANABE). b Urawa-shi, Saitama-ken Japan 30 Mr 30. 4: Shih-Kung Kao. 5: Tsuda Col 47-50 (Eng) Teaching Certif; Waseda U 53-55 (Lit) BA, 55-57 (Lit); UCLA 57-59 (Educ); USoCal 59-60 (LS) MS. 6: Japanese, Chinese, Ger. 7: Tchr Saitama Jr High Sch, Urawa-shi Japan 50-52; Tchr Takinogawa Sr High Sch, Tokyo 53-57; Catlgr UUtah 60-. 9: ALA; UtahLA. 10: Beta Phi Mu. 14: Catlg. 15: 2567 Blaine ave, Salt Lake City Ut 84108.

KAPENSTEIN, HENRY MARK. b NYC 20 Ap 30. 4: Dorothy Goldstein. 5: NYU 47-51 (Hist) AB; UPenn 58-62 (Pub Admin) AM; Pratt 51-52 MLS; UPenn 58-68 (Pub Admin) AM. 06: Ger. 7: Clerical & preprof ref dept NY Pub Lib 44-51; Info spec US Army (Cpl) Japan 53-54; Young adults libn Free Lib of Phila Brs 54-55, Head, central young adults dept 55-57, Bkmob libn 57-59, Br lib head 60-63, Northeast area administrator 63-; Instr in Lib Sci Drexel Inst 64-. 9: ALA; Amer Soc Pub Admin; PennLA (chm Recr Com 64-65); AALS; FLIC. 10: Exec Bd, Northeast Phila Area Health & Welfare Coun Permanent sec, Northeast Week (Phila) 63-; NE Phila Jewish Commun Rel Coun. 11: Award, Fels Inst of Local & State Govt (Phila) 61. 13: Yes. 14: Urban pub lib ser, recr for libnship. 15: 7215 Rupert st, Phila Pa 19149.

KAPLAN, DORIS (FLAX). b Staunton Va 14 Jl 26. 4: Arthur M Kaplan. 5: Pratt 38-42 (Food& Nutrition) BS; Columbia 43-45 (Food & Nutrition) MA; UMe 65-67 MLS. 6: Fr. 7: Pub health nutritionist Me State Dept of Health & Welfare, Augusta 55-; Instr clinical nutrition UMe Sch of Nursing 60-; Ref libn UMe (Orono) 67-. 9: MeLA. 10: AAUW; LWV. 14: Ref, sci. 15: 117 Forest ave, Orono Me 04473.

KAPLAN, EDWARD H. b NYC 27 Mr 21. 5: Juilliard Inst of Music 41-42 (Tuba); Rutgers 46-49 (Soc Sci) BA; NYU 49-50 (Hist) MA, 50-60 (Hist) PhD; Rutgers 58-62 MLS. 7: Instr in hist NYU, Rutgers U, Newark State Tchrs Col 50-57; Lib trainee E Orange Pub Lib, E Orange NJ 58; Lib assoc Lib Grad Sch Bus Admin NYU 58-59; Asst scis & ref libn Barnard Col Lib 59-60; Instr in hist Hamilton Col 60-61; Instr in hist Rutgers U 61-62; Bibliog in the soc scis & asst prof of hist SUNY (Binghamton) 62-65; Bibliog in the soc scis & assoc prof of hist 65-. 9: ALA; AHA. 14: Bibliog, bk sel. 15: RD3 Crocker Hill rd, Binghamton NY 13904.

KAPLAN, GEORGE R. b Brooklyn NY 31 Ag 26. 5: Brooklyn Col 43-48 (Econ) BA; Rutgers 63-65 MLS. 7: Case wker NYC Dept of Welfare 49-57, 58-61; Interviewer Mem Home & Hosp, Brooklyn NY 57; Tax collector NY State 61-62; Housing asst NYC Housing Authority 64-65; Tchr of lib Jr High Sch NYC Bd of Educ 65-. 9: NYCSchLA. 14: Sch lib. 15: 3020 Surf ave, Brooklyn NY 11224.

KAPLAN, JANET GAIL. b Poughkeepsie NY 31 O 46. 5: UMich 64-68 (Geog) BA, 68-69 AMLS. 6: Fr. 7: Br libn Va Beach Pub Lib, Va Beach Va 69-. 9: ALA; VaLA. 10: Beta Phi Mu. 14: Map libnship. 15: 1376 Stephens rd, Virginia Beach Va 23454.

KAPLAN, LOUIS. b NYC 27 Ja 09. 4: Esther Alk. 5: UChattanooga 26-31 (Chem) BS; UIll 36-37 BS-LS; Ohio State U 32-35, 39 (Hist) PhD. 6: Ger, Fr. 7: Chief ref dept UWis (Madison) 37-43; Lt Sr Grade US Navy Europe 43-46; Soc dir pub serv UWis Libs, Madison 46-47, Act dir 57-58). 9: Assn Res Libs (Bd Dirs 64-66, chm Farmington Plan Com; Foreign Newspapers Microfilming Com 57-58, 68-); ALA-ACRL (chm Research Planning Com 51-53). 12: "Research Materials in the Social Sciences" (39); "History of Reference Work in the US" (52); Comp "Bibliography of American Autobiographies" (62). 13: Yes. 14: Admin, bibliog. 15: 5725 Elder pl, Madison Wi 53705.

KAPLAN, SYLVIA Y. b Chicago 23 My 21. 4: Milton I Kaplan. 5: NorthwesternU 49-56 PhB; Rosary Col 58-61 MA in LS, 61 (LS); UIll 64-(LS); (CAS) Advanced certif in Libnship); 68 Certif I from MLA; 67 Ind Secondary Tchrs Life Certif in Eng, Sch libnship, AV Materials. 06: Fr, Ger, Yiddish. 7: Lib clerk Argonne Nat Lab UChicago 45-53; Med libn Mun Tuberculosis Sanitarium, Chicago 53-57; Sch libn Tolleston High Sch, Gary Ind 57-59; Assoc libn Lab for Applied Sci UChicago 59-60; Chief libn & instr of Lib Sci Chicago Med Sch 60-63; Assoc libn Prospect High Sch, Mt Prospect Ill 63-64; Libn Sch of Nursing Michael Reese Hosp, Chicago 64-66; Libn II for Dept of Mental Health State of Ill 67-. 08: Consul Methodist Hosp, Gary Ind 63-. 9: SLA; Recr com for spec libs; NEA; SLA; MedLA; ALA. 10: AAUW; Christopher House, Chicago (welfare wk); Hadassah Womens' Zionist Org. 14: Libn as educ. 15: 5541 S Everett apt 815, Chicago Il 60637.

KAPLAR, LORETTA CAROLYN (GAIL). b Cleveland Ohio 7 N 42. 4: James E Kaplar. 5: Hiram Col 61-65 (Eng) AB; Case West Res 65-66 (LS) MS. 7: Libn Cleveland Pub Lib 66-67; Ya libn Cuyahoga Co Pub Lib, Maple Heights Ohio 67-. 9: OhioLA. 14: Ref. 15: 13005 Beachwood ave, Cleveland Oh 44105.

KAPOSI, THOMAS. b Budapest 19 My 31. 5: UBudapest 49-53 (Hist & Archival Sci) Certified Archivist; Columbia 59 (LS); USoCal 59-60 (LS) MS. 6: Hungarian, Ger. 7: Archival asst Hungarian Nat Archives, Budapest 53-55; Deputy head archivist Co Archives, Debrecen Hungary 55-56; Clerk Stechert-Hafner Inc, NYC 57-59; USoCal Lib: Libn I 60-62, Libn II 62-65, Head of Acquis dept 65-. 9: CalLA. 10: Beta Phi Mu. 14: Acquis, bibliog. 15: 11509 Killion st, North Hollywood Cal 91601.

KAPOTSY, BELA ARMAND. b Budapest Hungary. 04: Ilona Fabiny. 5: U of Econ(Budapest Hungary) 43-48 (Econ) PhD; U of Econ (Budapest Hungary) 48-49 (Museology); Columbia 58-60 (LS) MS. 6: Hungarian, Ger. 7: Sec Hungarian-Amer Soc, Budapest Hungary 45-49; Non prof libn USIS Lib, Budapest Hungary 49-51; Clerk USIS, Amer Legation, Budapest Hungary 49-55 & 56; Non prof lib asst Columbia U Libs 57-60; Clerk Proj on Nat Income of E Central Europe at Columbia U 58-; Instr Hunter Col CUNY 60-. 9: NY Tech Serv Libns. 10: Cath Assn for Internat Peace. 13: Yes. 14: Catlg, acquis, ref. 15: 395 Riverside dr, Apt 14-C, New York NY 10025.

KAPP, DAVID (LEE). b Elmira NY 14 Jl 39. 4: Billie M Buchko. 5: Nyack Col 57-61 (Theol) BS; Wheaton Col 61-63 (Biblical Lit) MA; BrandeisU 63-66 (Near East & Judaic Studies) MA; Simmons 66-68 MLS. 6: Fr, Ger. 7: Ref asst

BrandeisU Goldfarb Lib summer 66; Lib intern Baker Lib Harvard Bus Sch 66-68, Hd of circ 68-. 9: ALA. 14: Lib admin. 15: 25 Falmouth st, Belmont Ma 02178.

KAPPLER, SALLY JEANNE ELIZABETH. b Cincinnati Ohio 3 D 43. 5: Centre Col of Ky 61-65 9hist) BA; Columbia 65-66 (LS) MS. 7: Camp dir Swift Water Girl Scout Council Inc, NH summer 65; Asst libn Plymouth State Col 65-67; Lib supv Supv Union No 32, Lebanon NH 67-. 8: Couns, Leadership Conf NESchLA, Durham NH 68; State adv, NH Arts for Instrl Media. 9: ALA; -AASchL; NEA-DAVI; MESchLA (Stud Leadership Conf Com 67-); NHSchLA (Educ Com 68-, Standards Com 69-); NH A-V Assn. 10: Girl Scout Council. 13: Yes. 14: Sch media progs (esp supv). 15: 145 Hanover st, Lebanon NH 03766.

KAPSNER, OLIVER LEONARD OSB. b [illegible]kman Minn 26 Jl 02. 5: St John's U 20-22; St Vincent Sem [illegible]25 (Philos) BA, PhL; St John's Sem 25-29 (Theol)STB; Col di S.Anselmo (Rome) 30-32 (Philos). 6: Lat, Ger, Fr, Ital. 7: St John's U (Collegeville Minn): Asst libn 25-30, 32-34, Libn 34-39, Catlgr 39-43; Chaplain US Army 43-46; Catlgr St John's U (Collegeville Minn) 46-50; Research catlgr Catholic U 51-58; Research catlgr St Vincent Col (Latrobe Penn) 58-64; Dir Monastic Ms Microfilm Proj St John's U (Collegeville Minn) 64-. 9: ALA; CathLA; Amer Benedictine Acad. 11: LD, St Vincent Col, 58; Hon PhD in Lib Sci, St Bernard Col, 63 LD, St John's U, 66. 12: Comp "Catholic Subject Headings" (42, 5th ed 63); "Catholic Religious Orders" (48, 2d ed 57); Comp "Benedictine Bibliography," 2 v (49-50, 2d ed 62); "Manual of Cataloging Practice for Catholic Author and Title Entries" (53); Comp "Catalog of the Foster Stearns Collection on the Sovereign Military Order of St John of Jerusalem, called, of Malta" (55). 13: Yes. 14: Catlg, ref, mss. 15: St John's Univ Lib, Collegeville Minn 56321.

KAPST, MARY IRETON. b California Ky 30 Ap 12. 4: Michael R Kapst. 5: Wilmington Col 29-33 (Educ) BS in Ed; UCincinnati summers 36-37 (Eng); UIll summers 38-42 BS in LS. 6: Sp. 07: Tchr-libn New Richmond High Sch, New Richmond Ohio 33-46; Libn Delphos Pub Lib, Delphos Ohio 46-49; Libn US Pub Health Serv, Cincinnati 49-51; Libn US Info Serv, Manila Philippines 51-57; Libn US Navy Dependents Sch, Sangley Point Philippines 58-62; Libn Amer Chamber of Com, Manila Philippines 63-66; Libn Honokoa High & Elem Sch Honokoa Hawaii 67-68; Adult serv libn Hawaii Pub Lib, Hilo 69-. 9: ALA; PhilippineLA; Assn of Spec Libs in the Philippines; Amer Assn of the Philippines; HawaiiLA. 14: Admin, ref, adult serv. 15: 342 Twalani st, Hilo Hi 96720.

KARALLES, DOROTHY (AILEEN HEFNER). b Hickory NC 7 Ag 29. 5: Lenoir Rhyne Col 47-51 (Eng) AB; UNC 51-52 BS in LS. 7: Asst libn Elbert Ivey Mem Lib, Hickory NC 52-54; Libn Lawson AFB, Ft Benning Ga 54; GS-5 Ft Benning Ga 54-55; Catlgr UCalif (Riverside) 55-56; Libn III San Bernardino Co Lib, San Bernardino Cal 58-67, Supv libn 67-. 9: CalLA. 15: 9697 Date st, Fontana Cal 92335.

KARCIC, MARIA HEYA. b Budapest Hungary. 4: Milivoj H Karcic. 5: Villa Maria Col 51 (Langs) BA; Catholic U 52 MSLS. 6: Ger, Hungarian, Fr, Lat, Ital. 7: Period libn, asst libn Gannon Col 53-. 9: ALA; CathLA; PennLA. 10: Zonta Club; Erie(Penn) Hist Soc. 14: Periods, a-v materials. 15: 223 W Seventh st, Erie Penn 16501.

KARCZAG, EDNA ROSE (MANROSE). b Chicago 12 Jl 16. 4: Dr Leo Karczag. 5: Maryville Col(Tenn) 37-41 (Ger) AB; UMich 41-42 ABLS. 6: Ger. 7: Catlgr Marygrove Col Lib 42-44; Catlgr Royal Oak Pub Lib, Royal Oak Mich 44-47; Catlgr Wayne Co Pub Lib, Detroit 49-50; Bkmob libn Grand Traverse Area Lib Proj, Traverse City Mich 54-55; Asst libn Traverse City Pub Lib, Traverse City Mich 55-57; Br libn Kauai Co Lib, Kapaa Hawaii 57-58; Catlg libn Kauai Co Lib, Lihue Hawaii 58-63; Co libn Klamath Co Lib, Klamath Falls Ore 63-. 9: ALA; OreLA; PNLA. 10: AAUW. 14: Catlg. 15: 126 S Third st, Klamath Falls Ore 97601.

KARELL, SVEN OLOV. b Roslagsbro Sweden 4 Mr 14. 4: Colleen K Wyckoff. 5: UCal(Berkeley) 36-37, 46-48 (Ger) BA; UStockholm 48-50 (Scandinavian); UPenn 53-56 (Oriental Lang); UMich 60-61 MALS. 6: Swedish, Ger, Fr, Danish, Norwegian, Icelandic, Old Norse, Sanskrit, Hindi. 7: Head of visa sec Allied High Commission for Germany, Stockholm 50-51; Catlg asst UPenn Lib 53-56; Catlgr UVt Lib 56-59; Libn III UMich Lib (Ann Arbor) 59-60; Sr catlgr Or State U 61-62; Sr catlgr Portland State Col 62-66; Assoc curator lib NY Botanical Garden 66-. 9: ALA. 10: Amer Scand Found. 12: Tr "Scandal in Troy" by Eva Hemmer Hansen (56). 14: Catlg, bk sel. 15: 663 Britton st, Bronx NY 10467.

KARKHANIS, SHARAD. b Khopoli India 8 Mr 35. 4: Lieselotte Karkhanis. 5: U Bombay 54-58 (Econ) BA (Spl); Bombay Lib Assn 55-56 Diploma in libnship; Rutgers 59-62 MLS; Brooklyn Col of CUNY 65-67 (Pol) MA; NYU 67- (Pol). 06: Eng, Hindi, Marathi, Gujarathi. 7: Lib asst USIS Lib, Bombay India 55-58; Lib asst Leyton Pub Libs, London 58-59; Lib trainee Montclair Pub Lib, Montclair NJ 59-60; Lib trainee E Orange Pub Lib, E Orange NJ 60-63; Asst to libn Brooklyn Col Lib 63-64; Asst Prof & Libn-in-charge Kingsborough Commun Col 64-. 9: ALA (Subscription & Ref Bks Bull Com 68-); LACUNY (pres 67-69). 10: Lib Student Org, rutgers; Asia Soc. 14: Admin, ref. 15: 2138 Brigham st, Brooklyn NY 11229.

KARLAK, STELLA. b Buffalo NY 27 N 13. 5: SUNY(Buffalo) 32-36 (Eng) BS in Ed; UBuffalo 37-40 (Fr, Ger); Columbia 38-41 BS in LS, 58-60 (LS) MS, 61- (Russian). 6: Russian, Fr, Ger. 7: Catlgr Lockport Pub Lib, Lockport NY 36-44; Br libn Dearborn Pub Lib, Dearborn Mich 44-57; Sch libn Edgemont High Sch Lib, Scarsdale NY 57-. 9: ALA; NEA; NYStateEA; NYStateLA. 14: Catlg, ya, sch libs, ref. 15: 12 Cleveland pl #3, Yonkers NY 10710.

KARLIN, ESTELLE R (WENOCUR). b Boston Mass 8 Ap 28. 7: Lab asst Dept Pub Safety State of Mass, Boston 48-50; Chemist Polaroid Corp, Cambridge Mass 50-54; Libn Solar Satellite Project Harvard Observatory 66-. 14: Spec libs. 15: 40 Bound Brook rd, Newton Ma 02161.

KARLS, KAREN HELEN. b Saginaw Mich 15 Ja 43. 5: Marion Col (Marion Ind) 61-65 (Hist) AB; IndU 65-67 MLS. 6: Ger. 7: Lib intern IndU Libs (Bloomington) 65-67; Ref libn george Mason Col UVa (Fairfax) 67-69; Ref libn Sch of the Ozarks, Pt Lookout Mo 69-. 9: VaLA. 10: Beta Phi Mu. 14: Col ref. 15: School of the Ozarks, Pt Lookout Mo 65726.

KARLSON, MARJORIE (ELIZABETH). b Taunton Mass 15 Ap 25. 5: Col of William & Mary 42-43; Agnes Scott Col 43-46 (Eng) BA; Emory 46-47 BALS; Yale 48-49 (Eng) MA. 7: Catlgr Agnes Scott Col Lib 47-48; Ref asst rare bk room Yale U 49-52; Sr ref libn LSU 52-55; Asst chief ref dept Washington U(St Louis) 55-56, Chief ref dept 56-68, Asst dir readers serv 69-. 8: Lecturer in Libnship, Univ Col Washington U(St Louis), 56-62. 9: ALA (Coun 63-65; Subs Bk Com 61-65); -RSD (Interlib Loan Com: 61-69, chm 66-69); -ACRL (Lib Serv Com 65-67; chm Nomin Com of Univ Libs Sect 65); BSA; Amer Assn Adv of Slavic Studies. 10: Phi Beta Kappa. 14: Ref, bibliog, interlib loan, collection dev. 15: 6615 University dr, University City Mo 63130.

KARNES, RUTHE ELLEN. b Galletin Co Ill 11 My 03. 5: UCal (Los Angeles) 24, Santa Barbara 24-26 (Educ); SoIllU 26-32 (Eng, Music) BS; UDayton 61-63. 6: Russian. 7: Tchr rural sch, Blue Mound Ill 24-25; Tchr rural sch, DuQuoin Ill 25-26; Tchr Sandoval High Sch, Sandoval Ill 32-33; Adult educ tchr Carbondale Ill 34-39; Eng tchr High Sch, Ludlow Ill 39-41; Clerk & libn US Govt, Chanute Field & Dayton Ohio 41-61; Libn Foreign Tech Lib, Dayton Ohio 61-. 9: SLA. 10: Bus & Prof Women's Club; Athenian Toastmistress Club. 14: Catlg, ref. 15: 541 Hayden ave, Dayton Ohio 45431.

KAROLYI, ALEXANDER F. b Budapest 23 Je 07. 4: Margaret Matyas. 5: UBudapest 30 (Law) SJD; UMich 57 MLS. 6: Fr, Ger, Hungarian, Sp. 7: Info spec Budapest Hungary 32-35; Info spec Hungarian State, NYC 36-38; Bus, London 38-41, 41-56; Asst acquis libn Ore State Col 57-59; Asst libn Colo Col 59-62; Acquis libn Sonoma State Col 62-. 11: Pasquitch-Senger Prize, UBudapest 30; Fellowship Harvard Law Sch 31-32. 12: "Hungarian Pageant," (38). 13: Yes. 14: Acquis. 15: Sonoma State Col Lib, Rohnert Park Ca 94928.

KARON, BERNARD LOUIS. b St Paul Minn 19 Ag 42. 4: Jaylene Abramovitz. 5: UMinn 60-64 (Botany) BS, MLS. 6: Fr, Ger, Hebrew. 7: Libn UMinn (Minneapolis) 65-67; Instr libn 67-. 8: Consul on the establishment of a synagogue lib (Temple of Aaron, St Paul Minn). 9: ALA; SLA; ASIS; Church & Synagogue Lib Assn. 14: Catlg, bibliog, ref. 15: 1370 S Cleveland ave, St Paul Mn 55116.

KARPEL, LEON. 5: NYU (Sociol) BA; Columbia (LS) MS; US Army Capitol Radio Engnr Inst, Teletype Maintenance Sch, Sigaba Maintenance Sch, Brisbane Australia. 7: NYPub Lib 38-41; US Army 41-45; Bus 46-47; NY Pub Lib 48-52; Asst col libn New Paltz State Tchrs Col 52-59; Admin libn in chg of Alanar Bk Processing Corp 59-61; Dir Mid-Hudson Libs 62-. 8: Catalogued collection of NY Jockey Club; Catalogued spec collection of materials on Worker's Educ under Ford Found grant prog. 9: ALA; NYLA; Bd Dirs of SE(NY) Lib Resources Coun (pres). 10: AAUP; Bd Dir Lib Trustees

Found, NY State; Bd Trustees Mid-Hudson Regl Suppl Educl Ctr. 13: Yes. 14: Admin, tech serv, ref. 15: 55 Grand ave, Poughkeepsie NY 12603.

KARPEVYCH, CHRISTINE M. b Lvov 27 D 36. 5: Hunter Col 52-56 (Mus) BS; Columbia 57-60 MLS. 6: Ukrainian, Ital, Fr, Ger. 7: Sr libn Queens Pub Lib, Queens NY 60-63; Asst libn Compton Advertising, NYC 63-65; Asst libn Equitable Life Assurance Soc NYC 65-67; Hd libn Harcourt, Brace & World, NYC 67-. 9: SLA. 14: Ref, admin. 15: Harcourt Brace & World Lib, 757 Third ave, New York NY 10017.

KARPINSKI, LESZEK M. b Lwow Poland 11 S 37. 6: Polish, Russian, Danish, Fr, Ger. 7: Res asst Nat Mus, Cracow Poland 62-65; Catlgr Royal Danish Lib, Copenhagen 65-66; Slavic libn State and Univ Lib, Aarhus Denmark 67-68; Lib asst Simon FraserU 68-. 9: CanLA. 10: Dansk magistrenes forening. 12: "Wazy greckie w Krakowie", The Greek Vases at cracow (64); "Egyptian Ancient Art" (65). 13: Yes. 14: Oriental paleog, archaeol. 15: 6070 Cartier st, Vancouver 13 BC Can.

KASER, DAVID. b Mishawaka Ind 12 Mr 24. 4: Jane Jewell. 5: Houghton Col 47-49 (Eng) AB; UNotre Dame 49-50 (Eng) MA; UMich 50-52 AMLS, 54-56 (LS) PhD. 6: Fr, Ger. 7: USArmy (Armored Force) Alaskan, European Theaters 43-47; Ser libn Ball State U 52-54; Exch asst UMich,(Ann Arbor) 54-56; Chief of acquis Washington U, St Louis 56-59; Asst dir of libs 59-60; Dir Joint U Libs, Nashville 60-68; Dir Cornell U Libs 68-. 9: ALA (Coun 65-69, chm U Libs Sect 61-62, chm Acquis Sect 60-61); -ACRL (pres 68-69); BSA (Reg Adv Bd 58-62); Amer Studies Assn;TennLA; Tenn Hist Soc; SELA (chm Col & U Sect 64-66); ARL (Exec Bd 68-); Assn SE Research Libs (chm 66-68). 10: Rotary Club; AAUP; Amer Antiquarian Soc; Phi Beta Kappa. 11: Research grants 57, 60; Amer Philos Soc; Guggenheim Fellowship 67. 12: Auth "Messrs Carey & Lea of Philadelphia" (57); "Joseph Charless, Printer in the Western Country" (63); Comp "Directory of the St Louis Book and Printing Trades to 1850" (61); Ed "The Cost Book of Carey & Lea, 1824-1838" (63); "Books in America's Past" (66); "Mo LA Quarterly" (58-60); Asst ed "Lib Resources & Tech Services" (58-62); Ed "College & Research Libs," (63-69); auth "Book Pirating in Taiwan" (69); Jt auth "Library Development in Eight Asian Countries" (69); Comp "Directory of the Book and Printing Trades in Antebellum Nashville " (64). 13: Yes. 14: Univ lib admin. 15: Cornell Univ Libs, Ithaca NY 14850.

KASIAN, LOUISE (WELLS). b Lake Forest Ill 20 Je 30. 4: Edward S Kasian. 5: Lake Forest Col 48-51, 55-57 (Romance Lang) BA; Rosary Col 64-67 (LS) MA. 6: Fr, Sp. 7: Page Lake Forest Lib, Lake Forest Ill 47-50, Lib asst 50-60, Catlgr asst 60-67, Catlgr 67-68, Hd libn 68-. 9: ALA; IllLA. 10: Alpha Zi Delta; Phi Sigma Iota. 14: Lib admin. 15: 764 Northmoor rd, Lake Forest Il 60045.

KASKELA, ELAINE DIANE. b Utica NY 7 S 42. 5: Syracuse 60-64 (Eng lit) AB; Rutgers 64-65 MLS. 6: Fr. 7: Tech doc indexer Nat Security Agcy, Ft Meade Md 65-68; Info scientist Johns HopkinsU Applied Physics Lab, Silver Spring Md 68-. 9: ASIS (sec protem); SIG/SDI; Potomac Valley Proc Libns. 10: Mensa. 14: Selective dissemination of info, indexing, thesaurus revision. 15: 8314 Sunset dr, Ellicott City Md 21043.

KASPAREK-OBST, CHRISTOPHER. b Edinburgh Scotland 9 My 45. 5: Monterey Peninsula Col 62-65 (pre-med) AA; UCal (Berkeley) 65-66 (Slavic Langs & Lits) AB; Monterey Inst of For Studies 66 (Fr); UCal (Berkeley) 66-67 MLS. 6: Bulgarian, Czech, Fr, Ger, Latin, Polish, Russian, Serbo-Croatian, Ukrainian. 7: Libn Naval Postgrad Sch, Monterey Cal 67-. 9: ALA. 10: Phi Beta Kappa. 14: Computerized bibliog retrieval. 15: 95 Wellings pl, Monterey Ca 93940.

KASSOVER, JUDITH M (USDAN). b NYC 9 S 29. 4: Bernard Kassover. 5: Washington Sq Col NYU 46-49 (Eng) BA; Pratt 57-59 MLS; Hofstra U 61-64 MS in Secondary Ed. 7: Ya libn & ref asst Hewlett-Woodmere Pub Lib, Hewlett NY 58-59; Libn-tchr CHSD #3 Merrick Ave Jr High Sch, Merrick NY 60-69. 9: NEA; ALA; NY State Tchrs Assn; NYLA; NY State SchLA. 10: Trustee N Merrick Pub Lib; Beta Phi Mu. 14: Ya, ref. 15: 1363 Millwood lane, Merrick NY 11566.

KASTEN, PATRICIA JOAN (HOWELL). b San Diego 3 F 27. 4: George William Kasten. 5: UCal 43-46 BA; Columbia 46-47 BSLS; Diablo Valley Col 61; St Mary's Col 62-64 (Pub Admin); Col of the Sequoias 69. 06: Fr, Ger. 7: Stud asst UCal(Berkeley) 45, 46; Libn II NY Pub Lib 47-48; Jr libn NJ Col for Women 48; Jr libn Newark Pub Lib, Newark NJ 49; Libn I UCal(Berkeley) 49-52; Sch libn Berkwood Sch, Berkeley Cal 57-58; Libn I child libn Orinda Contra Costa Co(Cal) Lib 61-62, Libn II Orinda Br libn 62-65, Concord Br Libn 66-68; Co libn Tulare Co Cal 68-. 9: ALA; CalLA. 14: Pub lib adult serv & admin. 15: 1510 W Beverly dr, Visalia Ca 93277.

KATELEY, MARGARET ANNE. b Mt Vernon NY 15 Ap 14. 5: Temple 32-33; UPenn 33-36 (Eng Lit) AB; Drexel 37-38 (LS) BS. 6: Fr. 7: Br asst Rochester Pub Lib, Rochester NY 38-43, Ref asst art div 43-45; Head Libn Upper Darby Free Pub Lib, Upper Darby Penn 45-53; Dir Scarsdale Pub Lib, Scarsdale NY 53-. 9: ALA; LPRC (Exec Bd 60-64); NYLA; WestchesterLA (pres 62-64); NYLibClub. 10: Scarsdale Adult Sch Adv Bd; Scarsdale Woman's Club; Phi Beta Kappa. 13: Yes. 14: Admin, bk sel, ref, bldgs & equip. 15: Scarsdale Pub Lib, Post & Olmsted rds, Scarsdale NY 10583.

KATHAM, MICHAEL DENNIS. b Quincy Ill 12 D 43. 5: St Procopius Cp& 62-66 (Eng Lit) BA; UMich 66-67 MALS, 67-69 (Amer Studies) MA. 7: Ref & period libn Monroe Co Commun col, Monroe Mich 68-. 9: ALA; Amer Studies Assn; MichLA. 14: Lib automation, periods. 15: 829 Tappan ave, Ann Arbor Mi 48104.

KATO, AYAKO (MARGARET MARY AGNES). b Tokyo Japan 28 Mr 22. 5: Maryville Col of the Sacred Heart (St Louis) 57 (Philos) BA; Catholic U 59 MS in LS. 6: Japanese, Fr, Eng. 7: Tchr Obayashi Seishin Joshi Gakuin, Takarazuka 52-55; Tchr Sankocho Seishin Joshi Gakuin, Tokyo 55-56; Libn & Lecturer U of the Sacred Heart (Tokyo) 60-, Asst Prof 68-. 9: JapanLA; Private Daigaku (Universities) LA. 10: Soc of the Sacred Heart. 14: Bk sel, ref, lib admin. 15: Univ of the Sacred Heart, Hiroo 4 chome 3-1, Shibuya-ku, Tokyo Japan.

KATO, SADAKO (SEKI). b Seattle Wash 17 Jl 08. 5: UWash 28-32 (Sociol) BA. 6: Japanese. KATO, SADAKO (SEKI). 7: Casewkr Fed Emergency Relief Admin, Seattle 33-34; Supv/organizer Tchrs Wk Progress Admin, Seattle 35-36; Off & field casewk supv Hyogo Mil Govt, Kobe Japan 47-49; Sec SCAP CIE Info Br, Kobe & Tokyo Japan 50-52; Property & stock clerk USA Spec Serv Lib Br, Tokyo Area 52-54, Lib asst 55-58, Libn 58-. 8: Advisor Eng & etiq ette Bank of Kobe, Japan 46. 9: ALA. 10: UWash Alumni Japan. 14: Admin, ref. 15: US Army Garrison Command Japan Spec Serv Lib Cp Drake, APO San Francisco Ca 96267.

KATONA, FLORENCE C (CIHLAR). b Cleveland Ohio 10 My 19. 7: Personnel off May Co, Cleveland Ohio 38-40; Clk Selective Serv Local Bd, Bedford Ohio 41-43; Tchr Maple Htd Bd of Educ Granger Sch, Maple Hts Ohio 66, Libn Raymond Sch 56-67; Child asst Cuyahoga Co Pub Lib, Maple Hts Ohio 57-68; Child libn Cuyahoga Co Pub Lib, Warrensville Hts Ohio 67-68. 9: ALA; OhioLA. 10: Kappa Delta Pi; Maple Hts Chap Amer Field Serv. 14: Child serv. 15: 5258 Joseph st, Maple Heights Oh 44137.

KATTERJOHN, CATHERINE LYNN. b Paducah Ky 21 D 08. 5: UKy 27-31 (Eng) AB; UIll 31-32 BS in LS. 7: Libn Paducah Jr Col 33-34; Asst catlgr UKy Lib 34-48, Ser catlgr 48-62; Head ser sect catlg dept 62-. 9: ALA; KyLA; Ohio Valley Reg Group Tech Serv Libns. 14: Catlg, ser. 15: UKy Lib, Lexington Ky 40506.

KATZ, BEATRICE. b Pittsburgh 13 O 18. 4: Boris Katz. 5: Wayne State U 36-40 (Educ) BS, 53-57 (LS) MA. 7: Tchr Roseville Mich Bd of Educ 40-42; Soc studies tchr Bd of Educ, Detroit 42-44; Housing Aid City of Detroit 44-46; Libn Park Mich Bd of Educ 54-57; Dir sch lib serv, Oak Park Mich 57-67; Resource spec info serv Wayne Co Schs, Detroit Mich 67-. 8: Instr, Wayne State U 63-; Consult, Oakland Co Schs 64-67. 9: ALA (Com on Sch Lib Facilities); MichLA (chm Sch & Child Sect). 13: Yes. 14: Sch serv, a-v materials , ref. 15: 25881 Greenfield, Southfield Mi 48075.

KATZ, BERNARD (MELVIN LORNE). b Toronto Can 4 Ja 40. 4: Gilda Mitchell. 5: UToronto 58-60, 62-64 (Eng) BA, 68-69 BLS; Johns HopkinsU 64-65 (Mod Lit & Creative Writing) MA. 6: Fr, Yiddish. 7: Lib asst UToronto Lib 60-61; Programmer Mfrs Life Ins Co, Toronto Can 64; Casewker Protective Serv, Baltimore Dept of Welfare 65-66; Instr ryerson Polytech Inst (Toronto) 66-68; Catlgr McLaughlin Lib UGuelph 69-. 8: Pres Stud Assn UToronto Sch of Lib Sci 68-69. 9: CanLA; ALA; ASIS; OntLA. 10: CORE. 11: E J Pratt Medal & Prize in Poetry 64. 13: Yes. 14: Catlg, documentation, info retrieval. 15: 353 Victoria rd apt 7, Guelph Ont Can.

KATZ, CHARLES LEONARD. b Philadelphia Pa 16 Ag 04. 4: Esther V Kircheis. 5: Temple U 24-28 (Secondary Educ) BS in Ed, 30-33 MEd; Drexel 29-30 (Lib Admin) BLS; Columbia summers 33-36 (Lib Admin). 7: Asst libn & chief ref libn Temple U 29-43; Tech ed US Ordnance Dept, Phila 43-46; Research engr Franklin Inst Labs for Research & Development, Phila 46-48; Chief libn Lincoln U 49-51; Chief libn Frankford Arsenal (US Army), Phila 51-60; Assoc libn (sci & tech) New York State Lib, Albany 60-. 8: Dir Temple U summer Lib Sch 40-43; Planned: Sullivan Mem Lib Temple U; remodeling of Vail Mem Lib, Lincoln U; Lectr Drexel Lib Sch. 9: SLA (pres Phila Chap 38); NYStateLA. 10: Kappa Phi Kappa; Phi Delta Kappa. 13: Yes. 14: Ref, admin. 15: 14 Wellington rd, Delmar NY 12054.

KATZ, EDWARD B. b NYC 13 Mr 28. 5: City Col of NY 45-49 (Soc Sci & Educ) BSS; Columbia 50-52 MSLS. 7: Tchr of soc studies NY Bd of Educ, NYC 49-50; Tchr of lib NYC Bd of Educ Haaren High Sch, NYC 50-55; Libn Amer Inst of Banking NYC Chap, NYC 52-59; Tchr of lib NYC Bd of Educ Brooklyn Tech High Sch 55-, Libn-in-charge 63-. 10: Phi Beta Kappa; Kappa Delta Pi-CCNY. 12: Co-auth "Advanced Placement Bibliography in Physics" (65). 13: Yes. 14: Sch lib serv, tchg. 15: 150 W 96th st, New York Ny 10025.

KATZ, LORRAINE FRANCES (KATZ). b Brooklyn NY 13 N 19. 4: Benjamin Katz. 5: Brooklyn Col 35-39 (Eng) BA; LIU 62-67 (LS) MS. 6: Fr. 7: Salesgirl Oppenheim Collins, Brooklyn NY 35-39; Secretary: Odette Martin Facial Expert, NYC 39-40, Otto Buschke photographer, NYC 40-46, Sterling Corrugated Inc, NYC 46-47; Trainee Shelter Rock Pub Lib, Albertson NY 65-67, Jr libn 67-68, Ref libn adult serv 68-. 14: Ref. 15: 8 Round Hill rd, Lake Success NY 11020.

KATZ, MINERVA (ANN). b Brooklyn NY 20 Mr 21. 5: Brooklyn Col even 39-43 (Eng); NYU Washington Sq Col 43-44 (Eng) BA; Columbia 44-45 BS in LS. 7: Child libn Brooklyn Pub Lib Brs 45-46; Child libn Los Angeles Pub Lib Br 46-47; Asst libn Vassar Col Music Lib, Poughkeepsie NY 48-49; Asst libn Popular Sci Publ Co, NYC 49-50; Yp libn & ref libn NY Pub Lib Brs 47-48, 50-54; Libn Ramaz Schs, NYC 57-58; Asst libn Yeshiva U Grad Sch of Educ 58-59; Asst libn Nat Health Lib, NYC 54-57, 59-61; Ser acquis libn Brooklyn Col Lib 61-68, Ref libn humanities div 68-. 9: LACUNY. 10: Hadassah; Hillel Faculty Assocs of Brooklyn Col; Jewish Publ Soc of Amer; Libns Chap of United Fed of Col Tchrs(NYC). 14: Ref. 15: 1755 E 24th st, Brooklyn Ny 11229.

KATZ, MINNA T(RENK). b Antwerp Belgium 4 D 12. 4: Sidney Katz. 5: Hunter Col 28-32 (Fr) AB; NYU 35; Hunter Col 35-39 (Fr, Educ); Queens Col 60-65 MLS. 6: Fr, Ger. 7: Sch sec NYC Sch System 37-55; Sch libn Lawrence (LI) Sch System #3 Sch 62-65; Sch libn E Brunswick (NJ) Sch System, Hammarskjold Sch 65-. 9: NJEA; NJSchLA; E BrunswickEA. 14: Tchg lib skills. 15: 22 Sullivan Way, E Brunswick NJ 08816.

KATZ, RUTH M. b Bridgeport Conn 11 Jl 37. 5: Clark U 55-59 (Chem) AB; Rutgers 62-65 MLS. 7: Radiochemist URochester Atomic Energy Proj, Rochester NY 59-60; Chem Amer Cyanamid Co, Princeton NJ 60-63; Libn Rutgers U Center for Info Processing, New Brunswick, NJ 63-65; Index ed doumentation Inc Biomed Div, Bethesda Md 65-66; Sci red specialist LC 66-67; Senior systems analyst Systems Development Corp, Falls Churc Va 67-. 9: ACS (Chem Lit Div); SLA; ASIS. 12: Index to vol 3 "Annual Review of Information Science & Technology," cumulative index to vols 1-3. 14: Lib & infor syst analysis & design. 15: 11330 Links dr, Reston Va 22070.

KATZ, SOLOMON BERNARD. b Hamilton Ont Can 24 O 30. 4: Carol Goldenberg. 5: McMaster U 50-53 (Econ) BA; UToronto 57-58 BLS. 6: Fr, Ger, Russian, Hebrew. 7: Ref libn UBC 58-59; Gen catlgr UManitoba 59-63; Hd Recatlg unit Sir George Williams U 63-. 9: CanLA; QueLA. 14: Catlg. 15: Catalogue Dept Sir George Williams Univ Lib, 1435 Drummond st, Montreal 107 Can.

KATZ, WILLIAM. b Seattle Wash 6 Jl 24. 4: Stephanie Welden. 5: UWash 41-47 (Journalism) BA, 54-56 (LS) MA; UChicago 65 (LS) PhD. 6: Fr. 7: Pvt US Army Inf, Europe 42-45; Reporter; "Vancouver Columbian," Vancouver Wash 48-49, "Oakland Post Inquirer", Oakland Cal 49-50, "San Francisco News" 50-51, "Seattle Times" adv dept 54-57, Ed "The Record", Daly City Cal 50-54; Area libn King Co Lib, King Co Wash 57-60; Asst to dir Publ Dept ALA 60-63; ASSOC PROF Dept Lib Sci UKy 63-66; Prof Sch Lib Sci SUNY(Albany) 66-. 9: ALA. 12: Ed "Journal of Education for Librarianship," "RQ" (ALA-RSD); "Introduction to Reference Work" (2 vols 69); "Magazines for Libraries" (69). 13: Yes. 14: Ref, film, hist bks, period. 15: School of Lib Sci, State Univ of NY, Albany NY 14904.

KAUER, ERMINIA (UBALDI). b Waterbury Conn 22 S 27. 4: Donald T Kauer. 5: Mary Washington Col 45-49 (Chem) BS; Columbia 51-52 (LS) MS. 6: Ital. 7: Chem Naugatuck Chem Co, Naugatuck Conn 50-51; Tech libn EIDU Pont De Nemours & Co, Aiken SC 52-. 9: ACS; SLA. 14: Ref, circ, interlib loan. 15: Rt #5 Box 23, Aiken SC 29801.

KAUFFMAN, ALICE FISHER. b NYC 27 S 08. 4: Abraham J Kauffman. 5: State U (Albany NY) 28 (Hist, Eng) BA, 32 (Pol Sci) MA, 34 BS in LS. 6: Fr. 7: Tchr Elem Sch, Albany NY 28-31; Researcher Legis Ref Lib State Lib, Albany NY 34; Civil serv examiner Civil Serv Commsn State Office Bldg, Albany NY 35; Eng tchr & sch libn High Sch, N Lawrence NY 35-39; Asst libn Lib Ext Div State Lib, Albany NY 41; Catlgr Agric Tech Inst Lib, Canton NY 61 ; Assoc libn govt documents spec collections State U Col Lib(Potsdam NY) 61-. 8: V-pres, Exec Com of NY State Ext Serv, St Lawrence Co, Home Demonstration Dept, 52-59; SUNY at Potsdam - Fac Admin Comm on International Programs. 9: ALA; NYLA (Com on Pub Docs). 10: AAUW; AAUP. 12: Book Review in ALA Library Resources and Technical Services, spring 65. 14: Docs, ref, maps, archives. 15: Morris st, Norfolk NY 13667.

KAUFFMAN, BERNICE. b Lincoln Neb 21 F 13. 5: UNeb 31-36 (Eng, Hist) BS in Ed, 36-37 (Eng) MA; Columbia 39-40 BS in LS. 6: Fr. 7: Lincoln City Libs, Lincoln Neb: Apprentice 37-39, Asst circ dept 40-41, Br libn 41-42, Act head ref dept 42-44, Hd ref dept 44-60, Coord ref serv 60-65; Ref consult Mid-York Lib Sys, Utica NY 67-68; Hd ref dept Utica Pub Lib, Utica NY 68-. 9: ALA. 13: Yes. 14: Ref, biblio. 15: 1619 Sunset ave, Utica Ny 13502.

KAUFFMAN, BRUCE R(OBERT). b Dowagiac Mich 7 Ap 29. 4: Nancy White. 5: Col of Wooster 47-51 (Pol Sci) BA; UPittsburgh 63-64 MLS. 6: Ger. 7: Gunnery Off & First Lt, amphibious ships USNR 52-55; Supv Open Hearth Dept Pittsburgh Wks, J & L Steel Corp 56-63; Grad asst Grad Lib Sch UPittsburgh 63; Ref asst Hunt Lib Carnegie Inst Tech 63-64, Asst ref libn 64-65; Head libn Anthony Wayne Lib, Defiance Col 65-68; Asst dir U Cincinnati Libs 68-, Act dir 68-70, Dir 70-. 9: ALA; ASIS; OhioLA (v-chm CURT 68-69). 10: Pi Sigma Alpha; Beta Phi Mu; US Naval Inst. 14: Admin, lib, automation. 15: 683 Glensprings dr, Cincinnati Oh 45246.

KAUFFMAN, INGE (SALOMON). b Berlin Germany 20 Ap 28. 5: UTampa 48-50 (Langs) BA; Fla StateU 50-51 (LS) MA. 6: Ger, Sp. 7: Catlgr UFla Lib 51-55; Catlgr UTex 55-56; Asst adult serv libn Fresno Co Free Lib, Fresno Cal 56-57, Catlgr 65-. 9: ALA. 10: Phi Kappa Phi. 14: Catlg . 15: 546 E San Ramon ave, Fresno Ca 93726.

KAUFFMAN, WILHELMINA. b Bellefountaine Ohio 2 N 16. 5: UDI 43-44 ()ccupational Therapy); UMich 39 (Eng) AB, 53 (Eng) MA, 53 AMLS. 7: Occup ational therapist Percy Jones Gen Hosp, Battle Creek Mid 45-46; Lib asst Mich Eng Lib (Ann Arbor) 47-52, Catlg ub Gen Lib (Ann Arbor) 53-57; Ref libn (asst) AnnArbor Lib , Ann Arbor Mich 57-66; Hd libn Instr Materials Ctr Ann Arbor Pub Schs 66-. 9: NEA; MichEA; MichLA; MichASchl; Mich A-V Assn; AAEA. 14: Instr materials, ref readers adv. 15: 401 N Divis ion st, Ann Arbor Mi 48104.

KAUFHOLD, O G. b Miami Fla 1 Ag 31. 5: Hofstra Col 49-53 (Eng, Drama) BA; Rutgers 61-62 MLS. 6: Ger. 7: US Army Spec Serv (Sp/3) 55-57; Lib trainee Queens Borough Pub Lib, Queens NY 60-62; Asst libn Hillside Pub Lib, New Hyde Park NY 62-64; Dir Bellmore Mem Lib, Bellmore NY 65-. 9: ALA; NYLA; NYLibClub;Nassau Co LA (chm Fin Com, mem Intel Freedom Com, Exec Com, v-pres 67-68, pres 69-70). 14: Lib bldgs, lib admin & pub rel. 15: Bellmore Mem Lib, 2288 Bedford ave, Bellmore NY 11710.

KAUFLIN, ANTHONY CHARLES. b Dayton 21 My 33. 5: UDayton 52-55 (Phil) BA; St John's U 60-65 MLS. 6: Fr. 7: Tchr & libn: Chaminade High Sch, Mineola NY 55-61, Chaminade High Sch, Dayton Ohio 61-62, St Joseph High Sch, Cleveland Ohio 62-65; Dir of media ctr Cathedral Latin, Cleveland Ohio 65-. 8: Com on bks for ya, Cleveland Pub Lib 66-; Cath Suppl of Sr High Sch Lib Catlg Com 66; Chm Cath Lib World Ed Com 69-71. 9: ALA; CathLA (No Ohio Unit: chm 69-71, chm High Sch Sect 65-67); OhioASchL; Cleveland East suburban Sch Libns. 11: Certif of Merit, High Sch Sect CathLA 68. 12: Ed High Sch Sect newsletter (65-71). 14: A-v, machines & materials. 15: 2056 E 107th, Cleveland Oh 44106.

KAUFMAN, DAVID. b Johnstown Penn 8 Je 34. 5: UPittsburgh 52-56 (Eng) AB; Carnegie 58-59 MLS; UPittsburgh 62-64 (Eng) MA, 65 -66 (Eng). 6: Fr, Ger. 7: Lib aide Cambria Free Lib, Johnstown Penn 51-53; Reporter

"Johnstown Tribune-Democrat," Johnstown Penn 56; Asst purchasing dept Bethlehem Steel Co, Johnstown Penn 57-58; Readers' asst circ Carnegie Lib of Pittsburgh 59-61, Ref libn 61-65; Teaching fellow Eng Dept UPittsburgh 65-67; Head circ dept Rhodes R Stabley Lib Ind U (Penn) 67-. 9: ALA; PennLA. 10: US Chess Fed; Brashear Assn, Pittsburgh; Phi Theta Kappa; AAUP. 13: Yes. 14: Ref, rare bks, circ, lib automation. 15: 897 R 119 S, Indiana Pa 15701.

KAUFMAN, DOROTHY W(ILLARD). b Clarion Penn 17 Mr 18. 5: Clarion State Col 34-38 (Educ) BS, 40-41 (LS); George Washington U 47-49 (Psych); Catholic U 54-64 (LS). 7: Tchr Strattanville High Sch, Strattanville Penn 38-41; Tchr-libn Penn Soldiers' Orphans Sch, Scotland Penn 41-42; Lib asst to asst libn Mun Ref Serv US Bur of the Census, Wash DC 42-52; Asst libn US Bur of the Census Lib, Wash DC 52-64, Libn 64-. 8: Chm, Task Force Pub Rer, Fed Lib Com 66-68. 9: SLA; ASIS; ALA. 10: LWVS. 11: Dept of Com Meritorious Service Award. 12: "Elections Data in State Docs" (44). 14: Admin, ref. 15: 8611 Vistula dr, Oxon Hill Md 20022.

KAUFMAN, MARGUERITE SARA. b Woodstock Ill 14 Ag 13. 5: Carthage Col 31-35 (Modern Langs) BA; UColorado summers 37, 38 (Eng Lit); UIll summers 41-44 BS in LS, 51-54 (LS) MS, summer 56 (LS). 6: Ger, Fr. 7: Tchr & tchr-libn Woodstock High Sch, Woodstock Ill 37-44; Tchr-libn Iowa State Sch for the Blind, Vinton Iowa 44-48; Libn Midland Col 48-50; Libn Carthage Col 50-51; Asst in Arch Lib UIll(Urbana) 51-54; Libn Elmhurst Col 54-57; Ref Libn Grad Sch of Design, Harvard U 57-63; Asst libn Arch Lib UIll 63-64, Libn Arch Lib(Urbana) 64-. 8: Harvard U Lib Club (sec) 61-63. 9: ALA. 10: Soc Arch Histns; The Shelter House Soc. 14: Ref, acquis. 15: Apt 1 115 W Washington st, Urbana Il 61801.

KAUFMAN, MILDRED. b Boston. 5: Tchrs Col 31-35 (Amer Hist) BS in Ed; Boston U 37-45 (Soc Sci) MEd; Simmons 52 (LS) Certif. 6: Fr, Ger. 7: Tchr Boston Pub Schs, E Boston Mass 37-38; Child room asst Boston Pub Lib 35-41; Child libn Mt Bowdoin Br 41-49, Child libn Mattapan Br 49-53, Br libn Mem Br 53-64, Br libn Mattapan Br 64-. 8: Consul Intercultural Educ Wkshops, Boston U & Boston Chap of the Nat Conf of Christians and Jews 49-53; Mem of Com to Prepare Buying List of Bks for Fed Job Training Corps Program 64; Consul Boston U Folk Arts Center; Consul Ethnic Dances, chm Stage Program Internat Ball 63-69; Mgr stage prog First Internat Spring Festival, Boston Mus of Fine Arts. 9: ALA; MassLA. 10: Internat Inst of Boston; Sunnyside Day Nursery, Roxbury Mass; Krakowiak Polish Dancers, Boston; Italian Hist Soc, Boston; Pi Lambda Theta; Boston Pub Lib Staff Assn; Dorchester Interagency Coun. 13: Yes. 14: Intergroup rel. 15: Mattapan Br Lib 10 Hazleton st, Mattapan Ma 02126.

KAUFMAN, OXANNA S. b Rochester NY. 5: UToledo 51-55 (Secondary Educ) BEd; UMich 55 (LS); UMich 56 (LS); Carnegie 58-59 MLS; UPittsburgh 67 (LS) Advanced Certif. 6: Russian, Ukrainian, Sp. 7: Circ clerk Toledo Pub Lib, Toledo Ohio 50-55, Ref dept lib aide 55-56; Co-ordinating libn Dundee Commun Schs, Dundee Mich 55-58; Ref dept-stud asst Carnegie Lib of Pittsburgh 59; Libn Bus br 59-62; Libn Grad Sch of Soc Wk, Pittsburgh 63-, Libn & instr in Soc Wk Bibliog 65-. 8: Consul: UHouston Sch Soc Wk, UTex Sch of Soc Wk, Index proj Case West Res. 9: SLA; ALA-Tri-State ACRL. 10: Nat Conf Soc Welfare; Beta Phi Mu; Coun Soc Wk, Educ; AAUP. 14: Ref, bibliog, lib educ. 15: 5645 Hobart st #6, Pittsburgh Pa 15217.

KAUFMANN, HELEN SUSANNA. b Chicago. 5: Simmons (LS) BS. 6: Sp, Fr. 7: Asst in chg of period room Kirstein Bus Br of Boston Pub Lib; Period acquis & indexing asst Pan American Union Lib, Wash DC 45-58, Chief tech processes sect 58-. 8: Act libn Inter-Amer Inst of Agrl Scis, Turriala Costa Rica, 56-57. 9: ALA; DCLA. 10: AAUW. 14: Tech proc. 15: 1020 19th st NW, Apt 510, Wash DC 20036.

KAUFMANN, LOIS ANNE (BROWN). b Mullica Hill NJ. 5: Rutgers 52-56 (Natural Sci) BA. 6: Fr. 7: Chem Merck, Sharpe, Dohme, Phila 56-59; Chem Dupont, Gibbstown 59-62; Tech libn Shell Chem, Woodbury 62-63; Tech libn Pittsburgh Corning, Pittsburgh 64-65; Tech libn Firestone Tire & Rubber 65-67; Ref libn Union Carbide Corp, Bound Brook NJ 67-. 9: SLA. 15: 264 King George rd, Warren Nj 07060.

KAUSKAY, ROBERTA BORK. b Buffalo NY 14 Jl 16. 4: Stanley Stuart Kauskay. 5: Elmhurst Col 33-35; Washington U(St Louis) 35-37 (Eng) BA; UBuffalo 38-40; Syracuse 63-64 (LS); UOkla 64-65 MLS. 6: Ger, Lat, Gk. 7: Case wker Erie Co Dept of Soc Welfare, Buffalo NY 39-42; Admin asst Army Air Forces, Buffalo NY 42-47; Sub tchr Rome Bd of Educ, Rome NY 57-63; High sch Eng tchr Rome Free Acad, Rome NY 63-64; Libn soc sci UOkla 65-66, Dir lib ctr Research Inst 66-. 9: ALA; OklaLA (Memb Com 67-68); SWLA. 10: AAUW; Nat Coun of Parents & Tchrs. 14: Ref (soc scis), educ for libnship, sch col libs. 15: 1621 Chestnut Lane-Forest Hills, Norman Ok 73069.

KAVANAGH, NANCY (W). b Orange NJ 7 Jl 30. 4: Paul M Kavanagh. 5: Bryn Mawr 48-52 (Geol) AB; UColo summer 51 (Field Geol); UToronto 66-67 BLS. 6: Fr. 7: Asst Geol-Biol Lib Princeton U Lib 52-54; Bk selector in sci UToronto Lib 67-. 9: ALA; -ACRL; CanLA; Can Assn Col & Univ Libs; Inst Profess Libns Ont. 10: Beta Phi Mu; Univ Women's Clubs, N York & Toronto. 14: Acquis (sci); ref. 15: 463 Lytton blvd, Toronto 12 Ont Can.

KAVANAGH, RUTH (WEBER). b Pittsburgh. 5: West Res 24-28 (Eng Lit) 28-29 (LS) Certif. 6: Fr. 7: Desk asst Cleveland Pub Lib 27-28; Readers asst Carnegie Lib, Pittsburgh 29-30, 1st asst Brookline & Carrick Brs 30-36; 1st asst Sch Libs Cleveland Pub Lib 49-51; Catlgr Shaker Heights Pub Lib, Shaker Heights Ohio 51-58, Hd ctlg dept 58-69. 9: ALA; OhioLA; NoOhio Tech Serv Libns. 14: Catlg, ref tech proc. 15: 12700 Shaker blvd, Cleveland Oh 44120.

KAVANAUGH, IRENE M. b Millers Falls Mass 20 Ja 26. 5: UMass 43-47 (Hist) BA; Simmons 48-50 (LS) MS. 6: Lat, Ger, Sp. 7: Asst instr catlg & clsf Sch of Lib Sci Simmons 49-50; Catlgr Wellesley Col Lib 50-51, Ser catlgr 51-57; Catlg asst UMass Lib 47-48, Hd catlg dept 57-64, Hd ser catlg dept 64-. 9: ALA. 14: Ser catlg. 15: 34 Memorial dr, Amherst Ma 01002.

KAVASCH, DOROTHY (RAPALJE) B(ONNEY). b Youngstown Ohio 23 Jl 14. 4: John Arthur Kavasch. 5: Cornell U 31-35 (Fr) AB; LIU MLS. 6: Fr. 7: Tchr & clk, Verona Pub Schs, Verona NJ 36-41, Tchr (secondary) 46-56; Sub tchr Central Sch Dist #6, Greenlawn NY 56-63, Tchr (secondary) 63-64; Asst libn SUNY A & T Col (Farmingdale) 64-67, Assoc libn 67-69, Chief libn 69-. 9: ALA; NassauCoLA; SuffolkCoLA; NY Lib Club. 14: Lib admin, ref. 15: 24 Prospect dr S, Huntington Sta NY 11746.

KAVIN, ROBERT L W KAVIN. b Boston Mass 20 S 46. 5: Northeastern U 65-66 (Pol Sci). 6: Fr. 7: Shelf asst Boston Pub Lib 62-63, Asst fine arts 63-64, Asst stack serv 64-65, Supv stack serv 65-67, Ser acquis asst 67-; Acquis libn Suffolk Co Jail, boston 68-. 8: Lib & Educ Coms for the Suffolk Co Jail. 9: ALA; MassLA. 10: Men libns Club; Boston Pub Lib Staff Assn; Boston Pub Lib Employees; Contracts Negotiations Com; Fairmount Hill Civic Assn; Boston Com on ABM; Amer for Democ Action; Citizens for Partic Polit; NAACP. 12: Mg ed, "Agora" (liter magazine). 14: Ser, acquis. 15: Boston Pub Lib, Boston Ma 02117.

KAWAGUCHI, AI (MARIA KATHARINA). b Tokyo Japan 11 Je 20. 5: Seishin Joshi Gakuin(Tokyo) 37-41 (Eng) Tchrs Diploma; Inst for the Train of Libns of the Ministry of Educ 48-50; Meiji U(Tokyo) 52-54 (Eng) BA; UDenver 54-55 (LS) MA. 6: Japanese, Fr, Ger, Chinese. 7: Interpreter & ref asst GHQ, SCAP, CIE, Tokyo Info Center 47-50; Tchg asst & libn Japan Lib Sch, Keio8 U(Tokyo) 51-54; Catlg supv Hoover Inst Stanford U 55-56; Catlgr & ref asst Japanese Sect Orientalia LC 56-57; Catlgr Far East Lang Sect, Descr Catlg Div, Processing Dept 58-61, Asst head, of the Sect, 61-67, Hd Japanese Lang sect shared cat div Processing Dept 68-. 08: Lib adv, Tokyo Lang Sch collections, 57. 9: ALA-RTSD (Catlg & Clsf Sect: Far East Materials Com 62-); JapanLA; DCLA; Potomac Tech Proc Libns; Assoc Asian Studies. 13: Yes. 14: Catlg, proc of Japanese materials. 15: 4101 Cathedral ave NW, Wash DC 20016.

KAWAKAMI, TOYO (SUYEMOTO). b Oroville Cal 14 Ja 16. 5: Sacramento Jr Col 33-35 (Eng, Lat) AA; UCal 35-37 (Eng, Lat) BA, 39-41 (Eng); UCincinnati Even Col 57-59 (LS); UMich 63-64 (LS) MA. 7: High Sch tchr Eng & Lat, Topaz Utah 42-45; Libn Topaz Pub Lib (War Relocation Authority), Topaz Utah 43-45; Libn Col of Nursing & Health UCincinnati 46-57; Period rm libn UCincinnati 59; Asst libn Cincinnati Art Museum 59-63; Asst head Educ Lib Ohio State U 64-. 9: ALA; Nomin Com Educ & Behavioral Sci Sub sect); OhioLA, (ed Col & Univ RT Newsletter); ASIS. 10: Ohio State U Fac Women's Club. 14: Ref, catlg. 15: 295 E 18th ave, Columbus Oh 43201.

KAY, MARJORIE (KENNELLEY). b E Orange NJ 16 S 30. 4: Archie Kay. 5: Newark Col of Rutgers 48-52 (Psych) AB; Rutgers 57-59 MLS. 7: Asst buyer Bamberger's Dept Store, Newark NJ 52-57; Lib trainee Newark Pub Lib, Newark NJ 57-59; Child libn E Orange Pub Lib, E Orange NJ 63-67, Prin libn 67-. 9: ALA; NJLA. 10: Beta Phi Mu. 14: Child lit, adult serv. 15: 32 N Willow st, Montclair Nj 07042.

KAY, OLGA (MATTA). b Newton Mass 4 N 08. 4: Nathan Kay. 5: BostonU 25-27 (Pre-Law); BostonU Law Sch 27-30 LLB; Simmons 58-60 MS in LS. 6: Fr. 7: Legal clerk Law Off AL Meckleburg, Boston 30-33; Revision supv Boston Pub Lib Reclass proj (WPA) 34-39; Assessing clerk Legal research dept Mass Div Employment Security, Boston 39-45; Libn asst Newton Free Lib Newton Mass 57-59; Asst Simmons Col Lib 59-60; Catlgr HarvardU Law Lib 60-66; Asst c hief catlg div, Boston U Lib 66-. 9: ALA; NE Tech Serv Libns. 14: Law libnship, catlg. 15: 78 Bentempo rd, Newton Center Ma 02159.

KAYASTHA, VED P. b Kangra Punjab India 12 O 34. 5: Benares Hindu 53-55 (Psy, Geog, Econ) BA, 55-58 MA in Geog, 60 Diploma in Lib Sci; Syracuse U 63 MS in LS. 6: Hindi, Panjabi, Urdu, Sanskrit, Gujarati, Marathi, Arabic, Parsian, Dogri, Napali. 7: Catlgr Panjab U Lib, Chandigarh 60-61; Asst John G White dept Cleveland Pub Lib 63-65, Asst libn 63-65; Asst libn Cornell U Lib 66-68, Sr asst libn 68-. 9: ALA. 10: Cleveland Coun of World Affairs (Inter-Nation Students Group); World Federalist; CornellULA. 13: Yes. 14: Rare bks, ref, catlg, documentation. 15: 134 College ave, Ithaca Ny 14850.

KAYE, EDWIN HENRY. b San Francisco 25 Ag 22. 4: Lois. 5: Black Mountain Col 41-43 (Hist); Reed Col 43-45 (Hist); UCLA 45-46 (Hist) BA; UCal(Berkeley) 46-53 MA (Latin Amer Hist), BLS. 6: Sp, Fr. 7: UCLA: Asst br libn Inst of Ind Rel Lib 53-59, Ind rel Libn 59-64, Head soc sci materials serv U Research Lib 64-66, Soc scis bibliogr 66-. 9: Com of Univ Indl Rel Libns; SLA; CalLA; UCLA LAssn (chm Com on Appointment, Promotion). 12: Co-ed "Industrial Relations Theses and Dissertations Accepted at Thirty Six Universities" (56-57 & 59-60, annual). 14: Ref, bibliog. 15: 217 N Bowling Green Way, Los Angeles Ca 90049.

KAYLOR, ALLIEGORDON (PARK). b Richmond Ky 11 Ag 10. 4: Noel H Kaylor. 5: East State Col(Richmond Ky) 27-31 (Lat) AB; Peabody 31-32 BS in LS. 6: Fr. 7: Asst libn East State Col(Richmond Ky) summer 32 & 33; Libn Benham High Sch, Benham Ky 33-44, 46-62, Ser libn Berea Col 44-46; Libn Danville High Sch, Danville Ky 62-65; Libn Cumberland High Sch, Cumberland Ky 65-; Assoc Prof LS Union Col (Barbourville Ky) summer 67, 68. 9: NEA; KyEA; KyLA; KyASchL. 10: Womens Soc Christian Serv. 13: Yes. 14: High sch serv, col catlg, periods, ref. 15: PO Box 385, Benham Ky 40807.

KAYLOR, MARY (FENLON). b Tully NY 16 F 17. 4: Thomas Kaylor. 5: UMich 34-38 (Eng & Soc Studies) BA in Ed; SUNY (Geneseo) 38-39 (LS) MS; Columbia 51-54 (LS); New Sch for Soc Research 57-58 (Pub Rel). 7: Sch libn S Haven Pub Schs S Haven Mich 39-43; Communications USNR (WR) Norfolk Va 43-46; VA Hosp Patients' & Med Lib, Bronx & Brooklyn NY 46-51; Prin libn NYC Dept of Health 51-. 8: Consul: Pub Health Research Inst 51-; Bulova Research & Development Corp 55-56; Adj Lib Assoc NYU 68-. 9: MedLA (Bd of Dirs 65-68, Chm Nom Com 57-58; Placement Dir 61-62; Mem com 54-55; Recr & Train 59-60); NY Reg Group (Exec Com 58-60, 61-63; chm 60-). 11: Citation for Meritorious Service, Amer Legion 60. 12: Ed "Laboratory Newsletter," NYC Dept of Health (60-). 13: Yes. 14: Admin. 15: 287 Avenue "C", NYC 10009.

KAYSER, ELFRIEDE M. b Forest Park Ill 3 Je 25. 5: Illinois Col 43-47 (Psych) AB; UIll 60-62 (LS) MS. 6: Ger. 7: Ser libn Francis A Countway Lib of Med Harvard Med Sch 62-. 9: MedLA; SLA. 14: Ser mechanization. 15: 93 Marion st, Brookline Ma 02146.

KAZLAUSKAS, EDWARD JOHN. b Cleveland 4 Ja 42. 5: John Carroll U 59-63 (Eng) AB; UIll 63-64 (LS) MS. 6: Ger. 7: Grad asst Undergrad Lib UIll 63-64; Asst acquis libn FlaAtlantic U 64-65, Acquis libn 65-67; Lib Systs analyst San Fernando Valley State Col 67-. 9: ALA; SLA; CalLA; SoCal Tech Proc Gp (Prog Com). 14: Acquis, ser, computer applications, tech serv. 15: Library Office, San Fernando Valley College, North ridge Ca 91324.

KAZUNAS, ELEANOR (DOUGLAS). b Kashing China 24 N 22. 5: Flora McDonald 39-40; UAla 40-43 (LS) BS. 7: Yeoman 2nd class US Navy, Pensacola Fla 43-46; Lib asst & libn (Law) Fed Communications Commsn, Wash DC 48-54; Libn Industrial Col of the Armed Forces 54-64; Libn (Law) Dept of Commerce, Wash DC 64-67; Chief libn Securities & Exchange Commsn, Wash DC 67-. 9: SLA (Soc Sci Div); Law Libn Soc of Wash. 10: Bus & Prof Women; Pol Study Club. 14: Ref (Law). 15: 4111 Emery pl NW, Wash DC 20016.

KEARLEY, DAVID ARTHUR. b Mobile Ala 23 F 29. 4: Marion Bourgeois. 5: UAla 46-51 (Hist) BA, 54-56 (Hist) MA; Gen Theol Sem 55-58 (Theol) STB; Peabody 68-69 MLS. 7: Lt jg USNR 51-53; Parish Ministry of Episcopal Church 58-68. 9: ALA. 13: Yes. 14: Ref, admin. 15: c/o Main Lib University of Ala, University Al 35486.

KEARNEY, EILEEN. b Phila Pa 1 Ja 29. 4: Edward J Kearney. 5: Immaculata Col 46-50 (Eng) AB; Villanova 64-67 MSLS. 7: Libn St Margaret Elem Sch, Narbeth Penn 66-; Hd catlgr Ryan Memorial Lib St Charles Sem 67. 9: ALA; CathLA. 14: Catlg, rare bks. 15: 519 S Narberth ave, Marion Sta Pa 19066.

KEARNS, REV ROBERT JOHN. b Detroit 9 Ag 19. 5: Loyola U(Chicago) 44 (Eng) BA, 46 (Eng) MA; UMich 54-58 (Eng) PhD. 7: Asst Prof Eng UDetroit 58-62, Dir of Libs 60-. 9: ModLangAssn; NCTE; CathLA. 10: Mem of the Soc of Jesus (Jesuit Order). 14: Admin. 15: Univ of Detroit, 4001 W McNichols rd, Detroit Mi 48221.

KEASBEY, SAMUEL (THOMAS). b Dunkirk Ind 1 Jl 30. 6: Fr, Ger, Sp. 7: Rate clerk Fed Express, Muncie Ind 50-58; Tchr Columbus High Sch, Columbus Ind 58-59; Proofreader W C Jones Intertype, Los Angeles 59-61; Writer/ed Aerospace Corp, El Segundo Cal 61-66; Ref libn UCal (Santa Cruz) 68-. 14: Ref, bibliog. 15: 300 Charles st, Los Gatos Ca 95030.

KEASLER, SALLY (O'KEEFE). b Buffalo NY 29 Jl 41. 4: Andrew J Keasler. 5: SUNY (Buffalo) 59-64 (Home Econ) BS Ed; Emory 68-69 MLibnship. 6: Fr. 7: Asst libn Deerfield Beach Pub Lib, Deerfield Beach Fla 64-67; Asst libn Emory U Sch of Dentistry 69-. 10: Beta Sigma Phi. 14: Ref. 15: 4735 Roswell rd NE apt 32A, Atlanta Ga 30305.

KEATE, (MARY) HEATHER (McRITCHIE). b Cranbrook BC Can 28 F 45. 4: Richard Stuart Keate. 5: UBC 62-66 (Microbiol) BSc, 66-67 BLS. 7: Sci libn UOre (Eugene) 67-. 9: PNLA. 14: Ref. 15: 1601 Olive st #703, Eugene Or 97401.

KEATING, LUCILLE (TATE). b Minneapolis Minn 23 Je 15. 4: L Clark Keating. 5: UMinn 32-36 (Hist) BS; UParis 49-50 (Cours de Civilization) Certif; Bi-Nat Ctr (Lima Peru) 60-61 (Sp) Certif; UKy 64-66 MSLS. 6: Fr, Sp. 7: Acquis asst M I King Lib UKy, (Lexington) 64-66; Ship's libn Chapman Col Univ of the Seven Seas 67; Law period libn UKy Law Lib 67-69. 9: ALA; KyLA. 15: 608 Raintree rd, Lexington Ky 40502.

KEATING, MARY FULTON. b Erwin Tenn 11 Ap 15. 4: B Joseph Keating. 5: Salem Col 28-32 (Fr) AB; UMass summer 38 (Eng); Drexel 45-47 (LS) BS, 64-65 Certif as Med Libn. 06: Sp. 7: Asst libn Temple Law Lib 47; Asst catlgr Villanova U 56-57; Asst libn Baldwin Sch, Bryn Mawr Penn 57-58; Head Libn Penn Wynne Pub Lib, Penn Wynne Penn 60; Head Libn Presbyterian - U Penn Med Ctr 61-. 9: ALA; MedLA. 14: Ref, catlg. 15: 135 Fairfax rd, Rosemont Pa 19010.

KEATTS, ROWENA (WEATHERLY). b Gatesville Tex 18 N 15. 4: Robert Sidney Keatts Sr. 5: Paul Quinn Col 34-35 (Eng) AA; Prairie View A & M Col 36-40 (Eng) BA, 49 (Eng) MA; N Tex StateU 63 BS in LS. 6: Sp. 07: Tchr Pub Rural Sch, Gatesville Tex 35-39; Tchr Mexia Pub Schs, Mexia Tex 39-64; Libn & Tchr libn Dunbar High Sch, Mexia Tex 64-66; Libn John F Kennedy Sch, Dallas Tex 66-67; Catlg libn Paul Quinn Col 67-. 8: Instr: Prairie View Ext Sch, Mexia Tex 49-50, Eng & Elem Educ Paul Quinn Col 50-54. 9: NEA; ALA; Tex State Assn of Tchrs; TexLA. 10: Delta Sigma Theta; LWV; YWCA; Friends of the Lib. 14: Circ, ref, catlg. 15: 310 W Milan, Mexia Tx 76667.

KEBABIAN,ELEANOR (LOGAN). b Bowling Green Ky 23 D 16. 4: John S Kebabian. 5: Antioch Col 34-39 (Eng) AB; Queens Col 60-65 MLS. 7: Asst curator NY Hist Soc NYC 41-44; Lib tchr New Rochelle (NY) Pub Schs 62-65; Lib tchr Scarsdale(NY) Pub Schs 65-. 9: ALA; NEA; NYStateLA; NYSchLA; Westchester LA; NY State Tchrs Assn; Scarsdale TA. 13: Yes. 14: Sch libs. 15: 2 Winding lane, Scarsdale Ny 10583.

KEBABIAN, PAUL BLAKESLEE. b Watch Hill RI 24 Jl 17. 4: Justine Richardson. 5: Yale 34-38 (Econ) BA; Columbia 47-48 BS in LS. 6: Fr. 7: Ser catlgr Yale U Lib 39-42; Cryptographic security off Army Air Force (1st Lt) 42-46; Supv of exchs Yale U Lib 46-47; Ser catlgr Columbia U Libs 47-48; NY Pub Lib Prep Div: Asst to chief 48-50, chief catlgr & 1st asst 51-63, act chief 63; Assoc dir & Assoc prof Dept of Lib Sci UFla Libs 63-66; Dir of libs UVt (Burkington) 66-. 8: Off of Instr Columbia U Sch of Lib Sci summer 60; Ford Found

Program Spec in Lib Development Central Lib U Baghdad Iraq 61-62; State of Vt adv to Nat Union Catlg. 9: ALA (var coms catlg & clsf sect); -ACRL-RTSD; ASIS; NELA; VELA; group (pres 51-52). FlaLA; NY Reg Catlg Group (pres 51-52). 10: AAUP; Early Amer Industries Assn; Internat Wood Collectors Soc; Chittendeu Co Hist Soc. 13: Yes. 14: Catlg, tech serv. 15: 11 Scotsdale rd, S Burlington Vt 0540 1.

KECK, LUCILE L(IEBERMANN). b Watertown Wis 3 Ja 1898. 4: George Fred Keck. 5: UWis 15-20 (Eng) BA, 19-20 (LS) Certif. 6: Ger, Fr. 7: Asst circ NY Pub Lib 20; Indexer, ed asst H W Wilson Co, NY 21; Research libn bk sect Marshall Field & Co, Chicago 22-23; Libn Inst for Research in Land Econ & Pub Utilities, Chicago 28-31; Libn Joint Ref, Chicago 32-63; Volunteer Ryerson Lib, Art Inst, Chicago 64-; Midwest Off Inst of Intntl Educ 66-. 8: Surv of var libs, incl Bacon Lib, Amer Hosp Assn; ALA Hdqtrs Lib & Bur of Pub Admin, UAla. 9: SLA (pres 53-54, dir var terms; pres Ill Chap 35-37); ALA (Bd of Educ for Libnship 44-48); Amer Soc for Pub Admin; Hyde Park-Kenwood Commun Conf. 10: Phi Beta Kappa. 11: SLA Hall of Fame. 12: "Public Administration Libraries; a Manual of Practice," with Ione Dority. 13: Yes. 14: Admin, bk sel. 15: 5551 University ave, Chicago Il 60637.

KEDDY, MARJORIE. b Edmonton Alta Can 30 Je 26. 7: Vancouver libn Law Soc of BC, Vancouver BC 54-. 9: AALL; CanALL. 15: Law Soc of BC Lib, Court House, Vancouver 112 ' BC Canada.

KEE, S(ARAH) JANICE. b Young County Tex 23 F 08. 5: Tex Wesleyan 35 (Eng, Educ) BS; Tex Womans U 51 MLS. 07: Pub Sch tchr Anson Tex 27-28, 29-30; Pub sch tchr DeLeon Tex 30-35; Tchr-libn Sabine High Sch, Gladewater Tex 35-37, Libn 37-40; High sch libn So Park, Beaumont Tex 40-41; Co Libn Jefferson County, Beaumont Tex 41-43; Post libn US Army Air Force, Independence Kan 43-44; Command libn US Army Air Force, Randolph Field 44-46; Instr Lib Sci UMo summer 49; Ext libn Mo State Lib 47-48; Act state libn Mo State Lib 48-49, Asst state libn 49-50; Instr Lib Sci UWis (Madison) summer 51; Instr Lib Sci UWis Ext Div (Madison) 50-52; Exec Sec ALA Pub Lib Div 52-56; Sec, Wis Free Lib Commsn, Madison Wis 56-65; Lecturer Dept Libnship Kan State Tchrs Col (Emporia) 65-67; Lib serv program off US Off of Educ, Dallas Tex 67-. 8: Adv; Facing the '60's; The Pub Lib in Wis, Bur of Govt, UWis Ext Div 61; A Statewide Ref Network for Wis Libs, UIll Lib Research Center 64; Pub Lib Facilities in Wis, Div of Planning, State Dept Resource Development 65; Nat Adv Coms; ALA-LAD; Internat City Manager's Proj Com to Adv on the prep of "Local Public Library Administration" 60-64; ALA-LAD Conf on the lib statistics coordinating proj 64; ALA-LAD Evaluation Inst on the Small Libs Proj, Little Rock Ark 64; Adv to Nelson Associates on Pub Lib Systems in the US 68. 9: ALA (var offs & coms 49-66);-PLA (chm Operation Lib Com 56-57, Com to Study the Basis of Finan Support of Pub Libs 59-63);-LAD (Bd dirs lib org & mgt sect 61-63);-LED (Com chm 65-66); KanLA; WisLA (Exec Bd 57-65); Wis Lib Trustees Assn. 10: Friends of Wis Libs; Wis Acad Sci Arts & Letters; Wis Arts Found & Coun Inc; Wis Jt Com on Educ; Wis Commun Org Com; Interdepartmental Com on Aging, Wis Lib Film Circuit Inc; Governor's Task Force on Economic Opportunity Act; Wis Cooperative Childs Bk Center; AAUW; Midwest Reg Conf of State Lib Ext Agencies. 11: Spec Serv Award, WisLA 65; Citation, Wis Commsn on Aging 65; Citation, Wis Mental Health Assn 60; Life Patron Award, Okla City Libns 54. 12: 'Public Libraries' 52-56; Ed Wisconsin Library Bulletin (56-59 & 63-65); Ed 'Library Trends' (July 60) State Aid to Pub Libs. 13: Yes. 14: Statewide Library planning & continuing educ for pub & state libns , lib laws. 15: 4014 Hawthorne ave, Dallas Tx 75219.

KEE, WALTER A. b Philadelphia 12 Jl 14. 4: Genevieve O'Hair. 5: Purdue U 46-49 (Sci) BS; Columbia 49-50 MSLS. 7: Inspector Beaunit Mills Inc, Beverly NJ 32-36; Instrument maker Brown Instrument Div Minneapolis Honeywell, Phila 36-42; Aviation instrument spec Petty Off 1/c US Navy 42-45; Engnr & phys sci libn NYU 50-51; Libn E I Dupont de Nemours & Col, Savannah River Lab, Aiken SC 51-55; Chief lib & documents sect The Martin Co, Baltimore 55-59; Libn US AEC, Wash DC 59-66, Tech utilization off 66-69, Chief libn main lib, Germantown Md & branch lib Bethesda 69-. 8: SLA Prof Consul, 61-. 9: SLA (Documentation Div: chm 57-58, Program Chm 58-60; Sci-Tech Div: chm Engnr Sect 64-65, mem Consul Com 56-59; Nuclear Sci Div: chm Bylaws Com 68-69; Bus mgr "Sch/Tech News" 62-66 Baltimore Chap: pres 58-59; Wash DC Chap; chm Documentation Group 63-64); ASIS; Augusta(Ga) Lib Club (pres 53-54). 13: Yes. 14: Admin, ref, computer systems for libs. 15: 5832 Conway rd, Bethesda Md 20034.

KEEFE, MARAGRET (JOHNSON). b New Britain Conn 10 D 41. 4: Thomas J Keefe Jr. 5: Albertus Magnus Col 59-63 (Eng) BA; Rutgers 63-64 MLS. 6: Fr, Lat. 7: Asst ref libn URI 64-68, Ref libn 68-. 9: ALA; RILA. 14: Ref. 15: PO Box 283, Kingston Ri 02881.

KEEFE, MARGARET (JANE). b Kalamazoo 5 F 19. 5: Northwestern 37-38; Kalamazoo Col 38-41 (Eng Lit) BA; Chicago 43-44 BLS. 7: Ref asst Pub Lib, Kalamazoo 44-48; Head gen ref Pub Lib, Grand Rapids Mich 48-50; Ref loan libn Carleton Col 50-53; Ref libn II State Lib, Lansing Mich 53-57; Supv of adult serv Pub Lib, Midland Mich 57-61; Head bus & ind dept Pub Lib, Flint Mich 61-. 9: ALA-RSD (2nd v-pres 68-69, (chm Com on Ref Serv to Bus 64-68); SLA; MichLA (chm Ref Sect 63-64); FlintLibClub. 10: Genesse Co Hist, Soc. 14: Ref. 15: Flint Pub Lib, 1026 E Kearsley, Flint Mi 48502.

KEEGAN, JANE CLAUDIA. T Lyon Colo 30 Jl 22. 5: St Mary Col, Xavier Kan 54 grad (Eng, Philos) BS; UPortland 62, 64, 65 MLS. 7: Staff St Mary Col Lib, Xavier Kan summers 47-61; Libn St Pius X High Sch N Kan City Mo 58-59; Faculty St Mary Col Lib, Xavier Kan 59-60, 63-; Libn Immaculate High Sch, Leavenworth Kan 60-61; Libn Bishop Hogan High Sch, Kan City Mo 61-63; Libn Lewis-Clark Normal Sch, Lewiston Ida 66-. 8: 5 state chm Catholic Bk Week Midwest Unit CathLA 62-63, 64-66; Mem of Worldbook evaluation com of Ralph A Ulveling 64; Volunteer consul for elem & secondary sch lib 58-; UPortland Residents Adv Coun (sec 65); Reg med lib serv task force 68; Title III Coun LSCA 68-69. 9: ALA; (Fed Rel Coord ALA/IdaLA); CathLA; PNLA; Ida LA (chm Col & Univ Spec Lib Div 6 9-70); Ida Coun State Acad Libs. 10: Soroptimist Intl. 13: Yes. 14: Lib educ, sch lib admin, rare bks. 15: 403 Fifth ave, Lewiston Id 83501.

KEEL, ROBERT LEE. b Gurley Ala. 5: Peabody 37-40 (Soc Studies) BS, 46 (Secondary Educ) MA, 49 BSLS, 61 MALS. 6: Sp. 7: Tchr Magnolia Miss 41-42; Staff Sgt USAF 42-45; Tchr W Huntsville High Sch, Huntsville Ala 45-49; Asst libn Southeastern State Col 49-51; Asst prin S R Butler High Sch, Huntsville Ala 51-61; Circ libn Geo Peabody Col 61-62; Circ libn SoIllU 62-. 9: ALA; IllLA. 10: Kiwanis Internat. 14: Circ, ref. 15: RR#6 Dunn's apt #9, Carbondale Il 62903.

KEELER, LOIS HELEN (MANSFIELD). b Waltham Mass 11 My 10. 4: Elisha Crofut Keeler. 5: Wheaton 27-31 (Eng Lit) AB; So Conn State Col 63-64 (LS); Pratt Inst 64-66 (LS). 6/ fr. 7: Admissions coun Mary Byers Sch, NYC 60-61; Libn S Salem Lib, S Salem NY 61-64; Circ asst Darien Lib, Darien Conn 64-65, Ref libn 65-. 9: ConnLA. 10: Wheaton Col Alumnae Assn Coun. 14: Ref. 15: Main st, South Salem NY 10590.

KEELER, RUTH HUDSON (MRS KENNETH). b Salt Lake City 12 Jl 06. 5: UCLA 29-33 (Hist) AB; Pratt 33-34 (LS) Certif. 7: Clerical Los Angeles City Lib 26-29; Staff Los Angeles City Lib 35-40, 44-48; Catlgr Covina Lib, Covina Cal 54-58; Sr libn Los Angeles Co Pub Lib, Los Angeles 58-. 9: CalLA. 10: AAUW; Soroptimist Club; Women's Club of West Covina; LWV; Bus & Prof Women's Club. 14: Ref, catlg, research. 15: 2137 Alaska st, West Covina Ca 91791.

KEELEY, EMILY A. b Toronto. 5: UToronto 30-34 (Lang, Hist) BA, 35 BLS. 6: Fr, Ger. 7: Libn Royal Can Inst, Toronto 35-37; Lib asst orders U Toronto Victoria Col 38-45; Chief libn Oakville Pub Lib, Oakville Ont 46-49; Chief libn Engnr Inst of Can, Montreal 50-54; Chief libn Ind Cellulose Research, Hawkesbury Ont 55-61; Head lib serv Can Dept Forestry, Ottawa 62-. 8: Spec lecturer McGill U Lib Sch 52-62. 9: SLA (pres Montreal Chap 57-58, chm Paper & Textiles Sect, Sci-Tech Div 68-69); CanLA (Memb Com 68-69); Inst Profess Libns Ont (chm Ottawa Valley Gp 67-68). 13: Yes. 14: Catlg, admin. 15: 335 Cooper st #75, Ottawa 4 Canada.

KEEN, EUNICE (ELIZABETH). b Lakeland Fla 20 Ja 1899. 5: Fla State Col for Women 29 (Educ) AB; Emory 30 AB in LS; Chicago summers 44, 49 (LS); West Res summer 54 (LS). 6: Fr, Sp. 7: Tchr Lakeland pub schs, Lakeland Fla 21-28; Catlgr Duke U Lib 31-38; Catlgr UFla Lib 38-43, catlgr Chem Pharmacy Lib 40-42; Libn Lakeland High Sch, Lakeland Fla 43-64; Libn Ft Meade High Sch, Ft Meade Fla 64-65. 8: Var activities for Fla State Dept of Educ; Organiz & catlgr 3 churches & 1 pub lib collection 66-69. 9: ALA-AASchL; -RTSD (Catlgrs & Clsf Sect; chm Spec Com for Bibliog Control of A-V Materials 54-56); FlaLA (sec 58-59; Sch & Child Sect: treas 51-53, chm 60-61; Catlgrs Round Table: chm 58-59); SELA; FlaSchL. 10: AAUW; Lakeland Concert Assn; Kappa Delta Pi. 12: "Manual for Student Library Assistants"

(61); "Second Year Student Library Assistants' Handbook" (61); "Manual for Use in the Cataloging and Classification of A-V Materials for a High School Library" (55). 13: Yes. 14: Catlg, ref. 15: 625 W Park st, Lakeland Fla 33803.

KEEN, MARGARET E. b Waynesboro Penn 31 D 03. 5: Goucher Col 21-25 (Eng) AB; Columbia U 30-31 BS in LS, 51 MS in LS. 7: Tchr Town Schs Jacob Tome Inst, Port Deposit Md 25-26; Libn Hannah Penn Jr High Sch, York Penn 26-30; Libn Nyack High Sch, Nyack NY 31-60; Libn St Mary's Col(Md) 60-. 9: ALA; MdLA. 10: AAUW; AAUP; St Mary's Co Art Assn; St Mary's Co Hist Soc. 14: Admin, bibliog, acquis, catlg. 15: St Mary's Col of Md, St Mary's City Md 20686.

KEENAN, ALICE ANGELA. b Providence 23 Ag 27. 5: Albertus Magnus Col 45-49 (Biol) BA; So Conn Tchrs Col 55-56 (LS) MS. 6: Fr. 7: Medical tech RI Hosp, Providence 49-50; Med tech St Raphael's Hosp, New Haven Conn 50-52; Sec to dean Albertus Magnus Col 52-53; Sci tchr Fair Haven Jr High Sch, New Haven Conn 54-55; Lib tchr Bassett Jr High Sch, New Haven Conn 56-60; Lib tchr N Haven Jr High Sch N Haven Conn 60-. 8: Volunteer adv wk for Catholic elem libs. 9: CathLA (past mem chm Com Unit); NEA; NESchLA; ALA; ConnEA; ConnSchLA (treas 63-68, 1st v-pres 68-69, pres 69-70). 15: 28 Wakefield st, Hamden Ct 06514.

KEENAN, ELEANOR (MACRAE). b Huntington WVa 20 F 16. 4: John Tracy Keenan. 5: Fenn Col 33-34; Rio Grande Col 34-35 AA; Muskingum Col 35-37 (Eng) BA; UWash 43-44 BA in Libnship. 7: Apprentice Cleveland Pub Lib 37-41; Asst in circ dept Kanawha Co Pub Lib, Charleston WVa 62-. 9: ALA; WVaLA. 14: Circ. 15: 740 Holley st, St Albans WVa 25144.

KEENAN, SHIRLEY J. b Rochester NY 24 Ap 36. 5: SUNY 54-58 (Educ) BS; UGrenoble (Grenoble Fr) 61-62 (Fr); UGranada (Granada Sp) 62-63 (Sp); UMinn 66-68 (LS) MA. 7: Tchr w irondequoit Schs, Rochester NY 58-59; Tchr Fairport Central Sch, Fairport NY 59-61; Tchr Rochester Pub Sch, Rochester NY 63-65; Tchr N St Paul Pub Sch, N St Paul Minn 65-66; Evening supv HamlineU Lib St Paul 67-68, Hd pub serv 68-. 10: Minn Civil Liberties Union; AAUP. 14: Ref, faculty-stud lib rel. 15: 415 N Finn st, St Paul Mn 55104.

KEENAN, SISTER MARY MEDARD RSM. b Dixon Ill 10 Ap 1898. 5: St Xavier Col 32-35 (Eng) BA; Our Lady of the Lake summer 36, 37 (LS); Rosary Col 45 BS in LS; Loyola U 44 (Educ), 49-50 (A-V Tech). 6: Fr, Ger. 7: Asst Libn St Xavier Col (Chicago) 36-42; Libn Mercy High Sch, Chicago 42-50; Libn St Xavier Acad Lib 50-51; Libn St Xavier Col Sch of Nursing (Chicago) 52-65; Libn St Patrick's Acad, Des Plaines Ill 65-68. 9: MedLA-Ill Unit (chm Hosp Sect); CathLA; Midwest Reg Med LA. 10: Several grden & art clubs. 14: Ref. 15: 1400 E Touhy ave, Des Plaines Ill 60016.

KEENAN, STELLA. b Barrow-in-Furness GB 4 Jl 33. 5: Liverpool Col of Com 50-54 Registration Exam of Brit Lib Assn. 6: Fr, Lat. 7: Asst Liverpool Ref Lib, Liverpool 50-53; Asst Liverpool U Sci Libs, Liverpool 53-55; Libn Zinc Development Assn, London 55-58; Indexer H W Wilson Co, NYC 59-63; Libn Amer Inst of Physics NYC 63-64; Res assoc Documentation Research Proj Amer Inst of Physics 65-66, Info specialist info div 66-68; Exec sec Nat Fed Sci Abstracting & Indexing Serv Phila 68-69, Exec dir 69-. 8: Mem USASI Z39, Subcom on Journal Title Abbrev; METRO Personnel Com 68; Proj Supvr SLA Info Sci Lit display 67; Consul Amer Inst Physics 68-. 9: Lib Assn (Gt Brit); SLA (NY Chap Documentation Gp: sec 65-66, chm 66-67); ASIS (Conv Sec 67); AsLib. 10: AAAS. 12: Co-auth: "The Journal Literature of Physics" (64), "Current Awareness Methods Used by Physicists prior to Publication of Current Papers in Physics" (67), "Current Papers in Physics User Study" (68), "Use Made of Current Papers in Physics" (68), "Journal Literature Covered by Physics Abstracts in 1965" (68). 14: Spec sci libs, abstracting & indexing, mechanized systems, info retrieval. 15: 1926-1/2 Lombard st, Phila Pa 19146.

KEENER, MARY KATHERINE (LIVELY). b Ardmore Okla 11 Ag 24. 5: William Woods Col 42-43 9arts, Sci); Tex Christian U 63-64; UOkla 42, 43-45, 64-65 (Math, Geol) BA, 66-67 MSLS. 6: Ger. 7: Earth sci libn Ft Worth Pub Lib, Ft Worth Tex 63-64, 65-66; Geol libn asst Okla Geol Survey UOkla 66-67; Tech info specialist & libn NASA-Manned Spacecraft Ctr Houston Tex 67-. 9: ALA; SLA; GSI; MedLA; TexLA; Fort Worth Geol Geophys Soc. 10: Beta Phi Mu. 14: Ref, info ret systems. 15: 16524 Diana lane, Houston Tx 77058.

KEENEY, BRUCE I. b Warsaw NY 24 My 36. 5: CornellU 54-59 (Agric) BS; Syracuse 62-63 mls. 6: Sp. 7: Ya libn Rochester Pub Lib, Rochester NY 61-62, Asst art libn 63-64, Asst sci libn 64-66; Coord of orders serv Lib SUNY (Brockport) 66-. 8: IFYE exchange to Dominican Republic 59-60. 10: Beta Phi Mu. 12: Ed "ESIS Bulletin" (67). 13: Yes. 14: Tech serv, mus ref, sci ref. 15: 7791 Swamp rd, Bergen NY 14416.

KEERDOJA, LIINA. b Tartu Estonia 26 My 42. 5: NorthwesternU 60-61; IndU 61-64 (Fr) BA, 64-66 (Uralic Studies) MA; Columbia 66-67 MSLS. 6: Estonian, Finnish, Fr, Ger. 7: Catlgr LC 67-; Instr US Dept of Agric Grad Sch, Wash DC 68-. 9: ALA. 10: Phi Beta Kappa. 12: Tr "A Grammar of the Votic Language" (68). 14: Catlg. 15: 110 D st SE apt 305, Washington DC 20003.

KEES, STEPHEN JOHN. b London 25 Mr 19. 4: Edith Thomas. 5: ULondon Sch of Libnship 37-39 & 46-48 Lib Assn Fellowship. 6: Fr. 7: Stud asst Royal Entomological Soc, London 37-40; Royal Army Serv Corp, British Army (Sgt) 40-46; Asst libn "The Economist" London 47-49; Libn British Employer's Confederation, London 49-53; Deputy libn "The Financial Times" London 53-57; Libn I Toronto Pub Lib 57-58; Libn The Ontario Paper Co Ltd, Thorold Ont 58-67; Chief libn Niagara Col of Applied Arts & Tech, Welland Ont 67-. 8: Consul Niagara Reg Lib Syst, St Catherine's Ont Can 67-. 9: SLA (pres Upstate NY chap 65-66, chm Paper & Textiles Sect 66-67; chm Statistics Com 67-68); Aslib; Lib Assn (Brit). 10: Eng Club of St Catherines. 14: Ref. 15: Niagara Col of Applied Arts & Tech, Woodlawn rd, Welland Ont Can.

KEETH, JOHN EARL. b Shreveport La 29 Je 45. 5: LSU 63-67 (Eng) BA, 67-68 MSLS. 7: Asst libn acquis dept USoFla Lib (Tampa) 68-. 9: FlaLA. 14: Acquis. 15: Acquis Dept USF Lib, Tampa Fl 33612.

KEETON, KATHERINE (BURKHISER). b Seymour Iowa 15 Je 08. 4: Donovan Thomas Field Keeton. 5: State Col of Iowa 25-26 (Eng); UColo 27-28 (Eng); Drake U 48-49 (Educ) BS Ed, 51-52 (Guidance & Counseling) MS Ed; UIowa (LS); UChicago (LS). 06: Sp, Russian. 7: Lib asst Carnegie Pub Lib, Sanborn Iowa 19-28; Price control clerk Off Price Admin, Lincoln Neb 42; Clerk Iowa State Bd of Soc Welfare, Des Moines Iowa 45; Circ Des Moines City Lib, Des Moines 46-47; Eng & soc studies tchr Des Moines High Sch, Des Moines 46-49; Sr Eng tchr, guidance & libn Johnston High Sch, Johnston Iowa 49-59; Sch libn, high, jr high & elem libs to supv Johnston Commun Sch, Johnston Iowa 59-. 8: Polk Co Soc for Crippled Child (dir) 51-56; Iowa State Sch Lib Development Proj Com 62; Iowa Stud Lib Asst's Exec Bd 61-67 (chm 63). 9: NEA (Life mem); ALA; AASchL; IowaStateEA; IowaASchL (chm Exec Bd 5 yrs); IowaLA; Iowa State LA; APGA (Life mem); ASCA; NVGA. 10: Des Moines Lib Club; DAR; Raymond Blank Hosp Guild; AAUW; OES. 13: Yes. 14: Yp, ref, reading guidance. 15: 9230 Willard circle, Des Moines Ia 50322.

KEHLMANN, (HEINRICH J) HEINZ. b Czernowitz Austro-Hungary 14 Ja 09. 4: Lilly. 5: Law Sch U Czernowitz 27-30 LLM; Law Sch Paris U Inst of Criminology 31 Diploma, Penitentiary Sci 32, 30-34 LLD; Rutgers 61-62 MLS. 6: Fr, Ger, Roumanian, Ital, Lat, Gk, Russian. 7: Asst prof Law Sch U Czernowitz 36-37; Trial & corporation lawyer Czernowitz & Bucharest 34-48; Bkkeeper & sec, Paris 49-53; Asst prod manager Toy Farm Inc, NY 54; Asst financial analyst Vanden Broeck Lieber & Co, NYC 55-60; Libn Queens Borough Pub Lib, Jamaica NY 62-64, Head Soc sci div 65-. 8: Labor relations consul Resita Iron & Coal Wks, Bucharest 46-48. 9: ALA. 12: "La Transaction en droit romain," Paris (34); Ed "Bucovina," legal monthly (Czernowitz 37-38). 13: Yes. 14: Ref. 15: 88-05 Merrick blvd, Jamaica NY 11432.

KEHOE, JANE (MURDOCH). b Pittsburgh 7 O 21. 4: John L Kehoe. 5: Grove City Col 43 AB; UPittsburgh 63 MLS. 6: Fr. 7: Soc Serv Wkr Amer Red Cross, Pittsburgh 43-46; Sub tchr N Allegheny Sch District, Pittsburgh 58-63; Libn Mt Lebanon Sr High Sch, Mt Lebanon Penn 63-. 8: V-pres Bd of Trustees, Northland Pub Lib 67-. 9: NEA; Penn State EA; ALA; Penn PACE. 10: Beta Phi Mu; Gen Fed of Women's Clubs; New Century Club of Ingomar; Ingomar Swim Club. 15: 1532 W Ingomar rd, Pittsburgh Pa 15237.

KEHOE, PATRICK EMMETT. b Olympia Wash 12 N 41. 4: Carole J Fitzgerald. 5: SeattleU 59-63 (Finance) BCS; UWash 63-66 (Law) JD, 66-68 MLL. 6: Fr. 7: Circ libn UWash Law Lib (Seattle) 66, Ref libn 67-68; Asst law libn UHouston 68-. 9: AALL; SWAALL; Wash State Bar Assn. 13: Yes. 14: Law lib admin & ref. 15: Law Lib Univ of Houston 3801 Cullen blvd, Houston Tx 77004.

KEIL, ALICE HASKELL (MUNSON). b Brooklyn NY 25 S 06. 4: M Theodore Keil. 5: Adelphi 28 (Eng) BA; Pratt 34 BLS. 6: Fr. 7: Tchr & libn Boys High Sch, Brooklyn NY 29-33; ref libn Pratt Inst 34-38; Libn Queens Borough Pub Lib, Jamaica NY 58-66; Libn Kew-Forest Sch, Queens NY 67-. 9: ALA; Nat Writers Assn; NYLA. 10: East Meadow Bd of Educ; Dir Merry Whistle Nursery Sch, E Meadow; Forest Hills Women's Club. 13: Yes. 14: Pub sch, child. 15: 38 Slocum Crescent, Forest Hills NY 11375.

KEIM, (MARY) CATHARINE K(AMMERER). b Gettysburg Penn 12 O 44. 4: Brian T Keim. 5: Millersville State Col 62-65 (Lib Ed) BS; Drexel 65-66 MS in LS. 6: Sp. 7: Employee Millersville State Col Lib, Millersville Penn summer 66; Libn Hillcrest Jr High Sch, Sch Dist of Springfield Twp Mont Co Pa 66-68; Child libn Free Lib of Phila summer 67; Libn in the Tech Serv Br Dept of Com Lib, Wash DC 68-. 9: DCLA. 10: Beta Phi Mu. 14: Sch libnship, child wk. 15: 2732 Ordway st NW #3, Washington DC 20008.

KEISLER, MARTHA (LOU). b Lorain Ohio 26 Ap 29. 5: Kent State 46-50 (Eng) BS in Ed, 51-53 (LS) MA; UDenver summer 66. 07: Eng tchr Willard High Sch, Willard Ohio 50-51; Eng tchr Whittier Jr High Sch, Lorain Ohio 51-52; Ref asst BIB in Cleveland Pub Lib 53-55; Libn Hudson High Sch, Hudson Ohio 55-. 9: NEA (Life mem); ALA; OhioEA (Life mem); OhioLA (Co-chm Serv to Schs RT); OhioASchL (Standards Com); Hudson Co EA; Summit Co SchL. 10: Bus & Prof Women's Club; Kent State U Lib Sch Alumni Assn; NEastOhioTA; Summit Co TA. 13: Yes. 14: Sch libnship. 15: 216 Dale dr apt 201, Kent Oh 44240.

KEITH, HOWARD D. b Detroit Mich 6 Jl 33. 5: Mich State U 56-60 (Humanities) BA; UMich 63-64 MALS. 7: Lib asst NYC Pub Lib 64-66; Asst libn for Yale Col 66-. 9: ALA. 14: Pub serv (undergrad & grad libs). 15: 2148 Yale Station, New Haven Ct 06520.

KEITH, NARINDER K. b Phagwara India. 5: Delhi U 39-43 (Econ, Eng) AB; Panjab U 43-45 (Eng) MA, 46-47 Lib Sci Certif; Simmons 50-51 (LS) MS. 6: Hindi, Urdu, Sp, Fr. 7: Libn Govt Girls' Col, Ludhiana India 46; Lib asst Ministry of Educ, New Delhi India 48-50; Ref asst UN Lib 51; Info asst Info Serv of India, NY & Wash DC 52-56; Jt Bank Fund Lib, Wash DC 56-. 9: DCLA. 14: Ref. 15: 19th & H sts NW, Wash DC 20431.

KELEMEN, TIBOR. b Felsovakos, Hungary 6 D 13. 4: Apolonia Bereczky. 5: URegele Ferdinand 1st (Rumania 33-41 (Law) Licentiate; Ferencz Jozsef Todomany (Egyetem Hungary) 41-43 (Law & Pub Admin); Syracuse 61-62 (LS) Master's. 06: Fr, Ger, Hungarian, Romanian. 7: Asst catlg libn Cornell U 62-64, Asst engnr libn 64-66; Hd catlg Southampton Col Lib (NY) 66-67, Dir of Lib 67-. 9: ALA-ACRL; NY State LA; Suffolk Co LA. 10: Kiwanis Club. 14: Admin. 15: 6 Lilliane lane, Southampton NY 11968.

KELLAM, (WILLIAM) PORTER. b McLeansville NC 10 S 05. 4: Mary Umstead. 5: Duke 22-26 (Fr) AB, summers 26-29 (Educ) AM; Emory 30-31 AB in LS; UIll 49-50 (LS). 6: Fr. 7: Tchr Manjum Twp High Sch, Durham Co NC 26-27; Prin & tchr Glenn Elem Sch, Durham Co NC 27-28; Asst circ dept Duke U Lib 28-29; In chg of circ 29-30; Educ libn UNC, Chapel Hill NC 31, Circ libn 32-34; Libn NC State Col 34-39; Libn WVa U 39-46; Libn USCar 46-47; Asst libn UNC, Chapel Hill 47-50; Dir of Libs UGa 50-. 8: Chm WVa Lib Commsn 41-46; Chm & Pres of Bd USBE. 09: ALA (chm: Agric Libs Sect 38-39, Oberly Mem Award Com 44-47, Mem Com 55-59); SELA (v-pres & pres-elect 68-70); Assn SE Res Libs (chm 62-64); WVaLA (pres 43-45); GaLA (pres 55-57 & 69-70). 10: AAUP; WVa Lib Commsn; Rotary Club; Torch Club. 12: Ed "Southeastern Librarian" (52-61). 13: Yes. 14: Admin, rare bks. 15: 399 Parkway dr, Athens Ga 30601.

KELLEHER, LORAINE J. b Albany NY 12 S 28. 5: Marywood Col 47-51 AB in LS. 7: Clerk NY Pub Lib summer 51; Asst libn Duquesne U Lib 51-54; Sch libn South Jr High Sch, Newburgh NY 54-. 9: NYLA; NY State Tchrs Assn. 10: NY State Divers Assn. 13: Yes. 14: Sch libnship, child wk. 15: Box 173A, Smith ave, RD 1, Walden NY 12586.

KELLEHER, SISTER KATHLEEN. b NYC 1 D 32. 5: Marymount Col (Tarrytown NY) 52-56 (Eng) BA; Catholic U 58-62 MSLS. 6: Fr. 7: Eng instr Marymount Col (Arlington Va) 56-62; Eng instr Marymount Col (Boca Raton Fla) 62-67, Libn 62-. 8: Dir Upward Bound Prog 68-69. 9: ALA; CathLA; FlaLA. 15: Marymount College, Boca Raton Fl 33432.

KELLEN, JAMES DALE. b Woodstock Minn 27 Mr 32. 5: Col of St Thomas 51-55 (Eng) BA; UMinn 55 (Educ); Col of St Thomas 55-58 (Educ) M Ed; Col of St Catherine 58-59 BS in LS; UMinn 60-65 (LS) MA; Assumption Sem 68 Certif; UMinn 68-69. 06: Fr, Ger. 7: Reading Instr Col of St Thomas(St Paul) 55-58; Reading Instr St Thomas Acad, St Paul 55-59; Asst catlg libn Col of St Thomas(St Paul) 58-. 8: Mem Adv Coun for Minn, Title IVB Prog. 9: ALA; CathLA (Exhibits Coord Nat Conv 68, Scholarship Com 68-, Convent Prog Coord 69-; Minn-Dak Unit: Exhib Chm 60, sec 66-68, treas 66-, chm Col Sect 61); Twin City Catalogers Round Table (sec-treas 63-64). 10: Serv Club for Handicapped; Minn State Hist Soc. 11: Handicapped St Paulite of the Year 68. 13: Yes. 14: Catlg, maps, bibliog, ref. 15: 2115 Summit ave, St Paul Mn 55101.

KELLER, DEAN HOWARD. b Ashtabula Ohio 20 My 33. 4: Patricia Scheid. 5: Kent State 51-55 (Eng) BA, 57-58 (LS) MA. 6: Ital. 7: SP-2 Radar US Army, Philadelphia 55-57; Asst libn Humanities div Kent State U Lib 58-63, Libn Humanities div 63-66, Assoc libn for readers' serv & spec collections 67-. 9: ALA;-ACRL; Mss Soc; Soc of Ohio Archivists; OhioLA; Tri-State Chap ACRL. 11: Lilly Fellowship in Rare Bk Libnship Ind U 66-67. 12: "An Index to the Albion W Tourgee Papers" 64; Ed "The Serif"; "An Index to The Colophon, New Series, The New Colophon, New Graphic Series, and The New Colophon" (68). 13: Yes. 14: Ref, rare bks. 15: 5887 Roc Marie ave, Kent Ohio 44240.

KELLER, HELEN S(CHMIDT). b Duluth Minn 2 N 07. 5: Buffalo State U 29 (Eng, LS) BA; Rutgers 59 MLS. 6: Fr. 7: Goshen High Sch Lib, Goshen NY 30-31; Babylon High Sch Lib, Babylon NY 32-33; Wilson Jr High Lib, Passaic NJ 49-56; Bloomfield Jr High (South) Bloomfield NJ 56-58; Head child dept Springfield Pub Lib, Springfield NJ 58-69. 9: ALA; NJLA. 10: NJFed Women's Clubs; Florham Park Country Club. 14: Child serv. 15: 39 Short Hills circle, Millburn NJ 07041.

KELLER, HELEN S(TRONG). b Portland Ore 15 N 20. 4: William E Keller. 5: Oberlin Col 38-42 (Biol) AB; Smith 43-45 (Zool) MA. 7: Instr Biol dept Hood Col 42-43; Researcher Science Illustrated McGraw-Hill, NYC 45-47; Ed Los Alamos Sci Lab, NM 50-54; Catlgr Los Alamos Sci Libs 57-59, Head of tech processes 59-61, Assoc libn for the Weapon Data Index 61-. 9: SLA. 10: AAAS; Sigma Xi. 15: PO Box 196, Santa Cruz NM 87567.

KELLER, LOUISE. b Peoria Ill 18 D 15. 5: Bradley U 33-37 (Soc Sci) AB; UIll 40-41 BS in LS. 7: Asst Peoria Pub Lib, Peoria Ill 37-40, 41-42; Asst hist, travel, biog Enoch Pratt Free Lib, Baltimore 42-44; Chief adult serv Gary Pub Lib, Gary Ind 44-51; Libn Ford Found, Pasadena Cal 51-53; Detroit Put Lib: Br asst 53-54, 1st asst bk sel 54-57, Br libn 57-67, Coord bk sel 67-. 9: ALA (chm Notable Bks Coun 59); MichLA. 14: Wk with adults, ref, acquis. 15: Apt 21, 17286 Bentler ave, Detroit Mi 49219.

KELLER, RICHARD LOUIS. b Two Harbors Minn 1 O 21. 5: UMinn, Duluth) 46-50 (Fr) BS; West Res 50-51 MS in LS, NYU 53-55 (Fr); Brooklyn Col 62 (Fr). 6: Fr. 7: US Army (Sgt) US Army Air Force ETO & US 42-46; Div chief Reading improvement Brooklyn Pub Lib 51-. 8: Instr (Reading Improvement & Libs) Pratt Inst Lib Sch. 9: ALA; NYLA. 11: Friends of the Brooklyn Pub Lib First Award 65. 13: Yes. 14: Reading improvement. 15: 195 Willoughby ave, Brooklyn NY 11205.

KELLER, WILLIAM H(EUTIS) 2nd. b Bellefonte Penn 14 Ap 06. 4: Winifred Gridley. 5: Penn State Col 23-27 (Hist, Pol Sci) BA; George Washington U 27-29 (Law); UPittsburgh 29-31 LLB; Columbia 34-35 (LS) BS. 7: Law clerk then attorney Judge Ellis L Orvis, John G Love, Bellefonte Penn 32-34; Br libn Detroit Pub Lib 35-47; Army of the US, Ft Geo G Meade Md 43-45; Lib Dir New Brunswick(NJ) Free Pub Lib, New Brunswick NJ 47-57; Sr libn Newark(NJ) Pub Lib 57; Lib Dir Levittown NY Pub Lib 57-64; Ref libn Suffolk Co-operative Lib System, Huntington(NY) Pub Lib 65-. 9: NJLA (v-pres 54-55). 10: Commun Welfare Coun; Health & Welfare Coun of Nassau Co. 13: Yes. 14: Bk sel, readers adv wk, adult discussion groups, films. 15: 46 Elbow lane, Levittown NY 11756.

KELLEY, CARROLL NEIL. b Atlanta Ga 21 O 36. 5: AuburnU 54-56 (Art); BaylorU 56-58 (Eng) BA; Fla StateU 64-65 (LS) MS. 6: Fr. 7: Serv to the pub asst A W Calhoun Med Lib EmoryU 58-64; Internship Med Lib, EmoryU 66; Asst libn & ref libn UArk Med Ctr Lib 66-. 8: MedLA Certif Grade II. 9: MedLA; SLA. 10: Beta Phi Mu; Sigma Tau Delta;

Chi Omega. 14: Ref. 15: 2100 Rebsamen Park rd apt 404A, Little Rock Ar 72202.

KELLEY, CORNELIA ANN. b Melbourne Fla 1 F 42. 5: Rollins Col 60-64 (Hist & Govt) BA; LSU 64-66 (LS) MS. 7: Temp dir UVa (Ext Wallops Island Va) 66; Alderman Lib UVa 9charlottesville): Catlgr 66, 67, Period libn 67-. 9: VaLA. 14: Catlg, acquis. 15: 4B Jack Jouett apts Univ way, Charlottesville Va 22903.

KELLEY, DAVID OTIS. b Newport Tex 27 S 08. 4: Onetia May Nettles. 5: USoCal 27-32 (Pol Sci) AB, 32-34 (Pol Sci) MA; UCLA summers 36-37 (LS); Chicago summers 39-43 (LS). 7: Non-prof asst USoCal Doheny Lib 33-34; Tchr-libn Burbank Pub Sch, Burbank Cal 34-37; Assoc prof & libn Pepperdine Col 37-45; Div libn soc studies UNeb 45-46, Asst dir & soc studies libn 46-48; Head Dept of Lib Sci UKy 48-49; U Libn UNM 49-. 8: Consul: Lockheed Aircraft, Burbank Cal 38; Los Alamos Sci Lab 50, Sandia Corp, Albuquerque 50; Chm Governor's Adv Com on State Lib Serv NM 60. 9: ALA (Coun); -ACRL (Constitution Com, Exec Bd); CalLA (chm So Sect, Col & U Libs Div 43-45); NMLA (pres 63-64); SWLA (pres 67-68). 10: Elder Church of Christ; Bd Dir Christian Stud Center, UNM; Pi Sigma Alpha; Phi Delta Kappa; Phi Kappa Phi. 12: Ed "SWLA Newsletter" 56-58. 13: Yes. 14: Univ lib admin, soc sci ref. 15: 3417 Groman ct NE, Albuquerque NM 87110.

KELLEY, FERN E. b Topeka Kan 5 N 32. 5: Anderson Col 50-54 (Eng) BS; Ind U 56-57 (LS) MA. 7: Tchr Central High Sch, Traverse City Mich 54-56; Asst libn Anderson Col (Anderson Ind) 57-59; Sr libn Brooklyn Pub Lib, Brooklyn NY 65-67; Assoc Prof in Lib Sci Gallaudet Col 67-. 8: Basic adult educ organiz, Calcutta India 60-65. 9: ALA; Amer Instrs of the Deaf; DCLA. 14: Ref. 15: 3660 - 38th st NW apt C255, Washington DC 20016.

KELLEY, JOHN DENNIS. b Somerville Mass 3 N 1900. 4: Mary A Barry. 5: Boston Col 18-22 (Econ) AB; NYU 23-27 (Bus Admin) MBA. 7: Shoe buyer Nat Cloak & Suit Co, NYC 22-28; Merchandise manager Gilchrist, Boston 28-31; Off manager Carew & McGreenery, Boston 31-37; Libn Somerville Pub Lib, Somerville Mass 37-. 8: Commissioner Bd of Library Commsn Com of Central Cooperative Bank, Somerville Mass Dir 33-, v-pres 40-58, pres 58-. 9: ALA; MassLA (Exec Bd, past pres). 10: Rotary Club; Commun Coun; Red Cross; Trustee Somerville Hosp. 14: Admin. 15: 178 Central st, Somerville Mass 02145.

KELLEY, MARJORIE (EILEEN). b Yarmouth Nova Scotia. 5: Queen's U 63 (Eng) BA, UToronto 66 BLS. 7: Tchr: Yarmouth Sch Bd, Yarmouth N S Can 51-52, Stanstead Col, Stanstead P Q Can 52-53, Macdonald High Sch, Macdonald Col PQ 53-56; Tchr Toronto Bd of Educ, Toronto Ont PQ Can 56-61, Tchr & libn 61-68, Sch lib consul 68-. 14: Sch lib serv. 15: Apt 1 81 Woodlawn ave W, Toronto 7 Ont Can.

KELLEY, MARJORIE (IDELLA). b San Diego 31 My 28. 5: UNev 46-48 (Eng); USan Francisco 50-53 (Philos, Eng); San Francisco State Col 50-53 (Eng) AB; USoCal 57-60 (Music hist, LS) MS in LS; UCal Extension 63-66 (Continuing Educ for Libnship) Certif; Dalhousie U 69 (Computers) Certif. 06: Fr, Sp. 7: Libn San Francisco Pub Lib 49-53, Catlg dept, music 53-57; Lib asst USoCal Music Lib 57-59; Tchr-libn Providence High Sch, Burbank Cal 59-60; Tchr-libn Bishop Le Blond High Sch, St Joseph Mo 60-61; Asst libn & catlg libn Regis Col (Denver) 61-62; Catlg libn Dominican Col (San Rafael Cal) 62-67; Active Univ libn St Mary's U, Halifax NS 67-68; Acting univ libn St Vincent U, Halifax NS 68-69, Univ libn 69-. 9: ALA (chm Reg Gp Resources & Tech Serv Div for NoCal 66-67); CanLA; Can Assn Univ Tchrs; APLA (Nova Scotia rep Archival Com 69); HalifaxLA (Program Chm 69-70). AAUP; Canadian Club. 13: Yes. 14: Catlg, admin, lib educ. 15: Mt St Vincent Univ Lib, Halifax Nova Scotia Can.

KELLIS, MARY L. b Ore. 5: Ore State Col 46-47; USoCal 47-49 (Internat Rel) BA; Catholic U 57-59 (LS) MS; American U 60-65 (Linguistics) MA; Cooper Union 68- (Fine Arts). 06: Sp, Ger, Fr. 07: Sec US HICOG, Bonn Germany 51-53; Pub affairs US Info Serv, Quito Ecuador 53-56; US Info Agency, Wash DC: Foreign affairs off 56-59, Ref libn 59-61, Catlgr 61-68; Lang docs index Lexicog UN Lib, NY 68-. 9: SLA; Ling Soc Amer. 14: Documentation, linguistics, fine arts. 15: 106 E 17 st, New York NY 10003.

KELLISON, DOROTHY D(EALE) (MRS). b Baltimore 6 F 18. 5: DePauw U 35-37 (Eng); So Methodist U 38-40 (Eng) BA; IndU 41-42 (Personnel Educ); Bradley U 44-45 (Watchmaking) Certif; UIll 57-58 MS in LS. 7: Defense wk Chrysler, Briggs, Republic, Evansville Ind 42-43; Asst record clerk IndU 43-44; Watchmaker Koerber's Jewelry, Ft Wayne Ind 46-50; Travel coun Chicago Motor Club (AAA), Ft Wayne Ind 50-57; Head libn Blume Mem Lib, Wapakoneta Ohio 58-60; Young adult libn Muncie Pub Lib, Muncie Ind 62, Supv of child wk 62-. 9: ALA; IndLA (chm child & yp's Round Table 64-65, sec-treas 63-64, Fall Conf Planning com 64-65, Bd 63; chm 65); IndASchL; ACE. 10: Muncie Symphony Assn; Women's League; Matinee Musicale; Nat Wildlife Assn; Women's Symphony League. 14: Serv to child & ya. 15: 303 Tara lane, Muncie Ind 47304.

KELLMAN, AMY (MARKUS). b Pittsburgh 24 D 38. 4: Simon Kellman. 5: Chatham Col 56-60 (Eng, Drama) BA; UCal(Berkeley) 61-62 MLS. 7: Asst revisor catlg course UCal Sch of Libnship(Berkeley) 62-64; Child libn Hayward Pub Lib, Hayward Cal 63-64; Jr libn Westchester Lib System, Mt Vernon NY 66-68, Assoc catlgr Lib journal cards 68-69. 9: Theatre LA; ALA. 10: LWV; Nat Womens Com. 13: Yes. 14: Ref, catlg, child lit. 15: 211 Castlegate rd, Pittsburgh Pa 15221.

KELLMAN, LILLIAN (STRAUSS). b NYC 5 Ag 26. 4: Raymond H Kellman. 5: Brooklyn Col 47 (Eng) BA; Adelphi U 56-58 (Educ); LIU 69 MLS. 7: Sec Fr Div Inst of Intl Educ, NYC 48-51; Libn Locust Valley Elem Sch, Locust valley NY 65-. 9: NEA; ALA; Nassau Suffolk SchLA. 10: Internat Inst for Child & Juvenile Bks (Munich Germany). 15: 23 Ridge Rock lane, E Norwich NY 11732.

KELLNER, THEDA AILEEN (BUTLER). b Farmington Ill 3 Mr 19. 4: Harvey William Kellner. 5: UColo 36-40 (Hist) BA; UDenver summers 55-59 (LS) MA. 7: Tchr Cortez Schs, Cortez Colo 40-42; Tchr Manzanola Schs, Manzanola Colo 46-48; Tchr Holly Jr High Sch, Holly Colo 48-51; Tchr Park Sch, La Junta Colo 51-54; Tchr Herron Jr High Sch; La Junta Colo 54-57; Libn Swink High Sch, Swink Colo 57-59; Libn La Junta High Sch, La Junta Colo 59-67; Consul Colo State Lib 67-. 8: N Central Eval Com (N Central Assn of Cols & Secondary Schs); Joint CLA-CASL Com on Standards for Sch Libs in Colo (ColoLA & ColoASchL). 9: ALA-AHIL (chm A-V Adv Com 69); NEA-DAVI; ColoLA (chm So Dist); ColoASchL (chm Coord Com 68); CAVA. 10: Delta Kappa Gamma; Beta Phi Mu. 13: Yes. 14: Reader guidance, instr materials (including a-v & TV); instit lib serv, lib serv for Handicapped, ETV tapes for in-serv training. 15: 1255 Ogden st #405, Denver Co 80218.

KELLOGG. GEORGE (ALEXIS). b Brooklyn NY 7 Mr 16. 4: Ruth Heningham. 5: Columbia Col 36-40 (Hist) BA (cum laude); Columbia 40-41 BSLS; Yale 46-47 (Eng Lit) MA; Columbia 49-51 (Eng Lit). 6: Fr, Ital, Ger. 7: Attendant physics reading room Columbia U Lib 40-42, 1st asst col study 42-43; US Marine Corps Radio/Radar Technician (Sgt) 43-46; Instr Eng Lafayette Col 47-49; Lib fellow res bk room City Col(NY) 49-51; Instr Eng Queens Col(NY) 51; Head documents, head gift & exch Yale U Lib 51-57; Humanities libn UIda Lib 57-. 9: PNLA (sec Col Div 62; chm Ref Div 68-69); IdaLA (sec 65-66, 68-69). 10: Phi Beta Kappa. 12: "Frederick Manfred: A Bibliography Swallow" (65); Asst ed "The Bookmark" (60-), co-ed (67-). 13: Yes. 14: Ref, humanities, admin, bibliog. 15: Orchard ave, Moscow Id 83843.

KELLOGG. RUTH E. b Davenport Iowa. 5: State U Iowa 29-32 (Music, Eng) BA, 32-33 (Music) MA; UMich summers 40-43 ABLS. 7: Davenport Pub Lib, Davenport Iowa: Gen asst 35-37, Asst circ dept 37-42, Order libn 42-43, Head catlgr 43-50; Dir Elkhart Pub Lib, Elkhart Ind 40-. 9: ALA (Life mem); SLA; Adult Educ Assn; IndLA; Adult Educ Assn Ind (Bd Dirs 64-, Scholarship Com 66-69); No Ind Lib Admins (chm Wkshop Com 63-66). 10: AAUW; Altrusa Club; Exec Breakfast Club; Riverside Club; DAR. 13: Yes. 14: Admin, catlg, a-v materials. 15: 230 W Jackson blvd, Elkhart Ind 46514.

KELLOGG, JEANNETTE H. b Syracuse NY 18 Ap 19. 4: Herbert H Kellogg. 5: Barnard 37-41 (Hist) BA; Columbia 61-65 (LS) MS. 6: Fr. 7: Volunteer libn Palisades Free Lib, Palisades NY 57-61; Asst catlgr Julliard Sch of Music 62-; Ref libn Herbert H Lehman Col CUNY. 8: MusLA; NYLA. 10: PTA; Suburban Symphony Orchestra. 14: Ref, readers adv, music & art. 15: Closter rd, Palisades NY 10964.

KELLOGG, SANDRA LEE. b Alma Mich 17 S 43. 5: UMich 61-65 (Sp) AB; West Mich U 65-66 msls& uutah 67-. 6: Sp. 7: PBX operator UMich (Ann Arbor) 62-65; Gen clk State of Mich, Lansing summer 62-63; Contract employee State Lib, Lansing summer 65; Asst ref libn Upjohn Co, Kalamazoo 66; Catlgr UUtah 67-. 9: ALA; UtahLA; Utah Acad of Scis, Arts & Letters. 10: AAUP; Volunteer, Primary Child Hosp; UUtah

Libs Staff Assn; Faculty Club; Faculty Women's Club. 14: Catlg, re-clsf. 15: 251 S 7th E apt 16, Salt Lake City Ut 84102.

KELLY, ANNE. b St Louis Mo. 5: WashU (St Louis) 47-51 (Hist) AB; ColumbiaU 61-62 (LS) MS, 67- (LS). 6: Sp, Fr, Ger. 7: Ref libn St Louis Pub Lib, St Louis Mo 51-56; Med libn VA Hosp Lib, Jefferson Barracks Mo 58-61; Soc wk libn WashU (St Louis) 63-66, Tchr lib sci 63-66; Sr lib supv NY State Lib Div of Lib Devel 67-68; Asst Prof lib & info sci Pratt Inst 69-. 9: ALA; SLA; ASIS; MoLA. 10: Beta Phi Mu. 14: Readers' serv, ref. 15: 316 W 51 st, New York NY 10019.

KELLY, ARDIE LEE. b Lynchburg Va 19 Ja 32. 4: Martha Midgett. 5: Lynchburg Col 53-57 (Fr) BA; UNC 58-60 MSLS. 6: Fr. 7: Gen asst Jones Mem Lib, Lynchburg Va 52-58; Catlgr Duke U Lib 60-62; Ref circ 62-63; Asst curator Trent Collection in the Hist of Med, Duke Med Center Lib 63-65; Libn Catawba Col 65-67; Libn URichmond 67-. 8: Delegate to the 19th Internat Congress for the Hist of Med, Basel Switzerland 64. 9: NCLA; SELA. 14: Ref, rare bks. 15: Univ of Richmond Lib, Univ of Rich Va 23173.

KELLY, BARBARA FAY (MELLEN). b Rockford Ill 3 N 19. 5: Blackburn Col 38-40 AA; UIll 40-42 BA; UWis 57 MLS. 7: Lib asst Rockford Pub Lib, Rockford Ill 42; Lib asst Highland Park Pub Lib, Highland Park Ill 43-44; Head Burlington Pub Lib, Burlington Wis 47-53; Head Libn Reddick's Lib, Ottawa Ill 53-58; Dir Manitowoc Pub Lib, Manitowoc Wis 58-. 8: Mem Wis Lib Commsn 65; Wis Adv Com for Lib Serv 65-; Exec Dir Nat Lib Week, Wis 68. 9: WISLA (pres 61-62). 10: Bus & Prof Woman's Club. 11: WisLA; Libn of the Year 67. 15: Manitowoc Pub Lib, Manitowoc Wi 54220.

KELLY, CECILIA KINTNER. b McDonald Penn 8 Ap 05. 4: Georde Milo Kelly. 5: Carnegie 26-27 Lib Certif. 6: FR. 7: Libn Mary S Biesecker Pub Lib, Somerset Penn 43-49; Libn Somerset Co Lib, Somerset Penn 45-49; Co Libn Abigdon Free Lib, Jenkintown Penn 49; Bkmob libn Dept of Pub Libs Montgomery Co, Gaithesburg Md 50-55; Libn Washington Co Lib, Russell Co Lib, Abington Va & Lebanon Va 55-61; Libn The Hoyt Lib, KINGSTON Penn 61-. 9: PennLA. 10: Womans Club, Abigdon Va; Wyoming Valley Hist & Geneal Soc; PTA. 14: Admin, pub lib. 15: Hoyt Lib 284 Wyoming ave, Kingston Pa 18704.

KELLY, CLEO B. b Clearwater Neb 20 Ja 14. 5: Neb State Col summers 38-46 (Hist, Pol Sci, Educ); UNeb summers 51-52; UDenver 52-53 (LS). 7: Elem sch tchr, Neb: Spencer 44-45, 46-48, Tilden 48-50, Chambers 50-5, Pilger 51-52, Asst libn Neb State Col 53-57; Ref libn SDStateU 57-60; Catlgr Kan StateU 60-62; Chm tech proc dept Porter Lib Kan State Col (Pittsburg) 62-66; Acquis libn Stephen F Austin State Col 66-69, Bibliogr 69-. 9: ALA-ACRL; -RTSD; MPLA; KANLA (Exec Coun 64-65; Resources & Tech Serv Sect chm 64-65); SWLA; TexLA (chm Dist 6 Col Sect 69). 10: Wayne State Col Alumni Assn; UDenver Grad Sch Libnship Alumni Assn. 14: Ref, bldg lib collection. 15: Lib Stephen F Austin State Col, Nacogdoches Tx 75961.

KELLY, CYNTHIA MARGRET MARIE. b Cheyonne Wyo 22 Jl 44. 5: NW Nazarene Col 63-67 (Philos, Relig) AB; USoCal 67-68 MSLS. 6: Fr, Sp, Ger. 7: Asst sci libn USoCal 68-. 9: CalLA. 14: Lib admin. 15: 1536 W 218 st, Torrance Ca 90501.

KELLY, DONALD V(ICTOR) L(EO). b Utica NY 14 Ja 29. 5: Utica Col of Syracuse U 46-50 (Soc Studies) AB (summa cum laude); UPenn 50-51 (Hist) MA; Syracuse 51-52 MS in LS. 7: Asst in catlg & order dept Champlain Col 52-53; Catlg libn Adelphi U 53-58, Head tech processes 58-65, Asst dir 65-. 9: ALA; NYLA; NY Tech ServLA; NassauCo(NY)LA. 10: Beta Phi Mu; Phi Alpha Theta. 14: Tech processes (catlg, acquis, reclsf), col & univ libs. 15: 286 Dorchester rd, Garden City South LI NY 11530.

KELLY, DORIS KATHERYN (MERRY). b Oswego Kan 11 Ja 20. 4: Guy Warden Kelly. 5: UKan 37-41 (Eng) BA; UWash 61 (LS) ML. 6: Fr. 7: Libn Darrington Schs, Darrington Wash 49-60; Libn West High Sch, Bremerton Wash 60-62; Libn Port Angeles High Sch, Port Angeles, Wash 61-66; Libn West High Sch, Bremerton Wash 66-. 09: ALA-AASchL; NEA-DAVI; WashStateASchL; WashLA; WashEA; WashDAVI. 10: Beta Phi Mu. 14: Sch libs. 15: Rte 2 Box 2112, Port Angeles Wa 98362.

KELLY, (E) ESTHER. b Lawrenceburg Ind 12 F 06. 5: Franklin Col 23-27 (Eng) BA; UIll 30-31 BSLS. 7: Lib asst Dayton & Montgomery Co Pub Lib, Dayton Ohio 28-30; Loan asst Ohio Wesleyan U Lib 32-34, Loan desk libn 34-38; Ref asst Dayton & Montgomery Co Pub Lib, Dayton Ohio 38-39, Br libn E Br 40-47, Head of bkmobile dept 47-58, Coordinator of br & ext serv 58-. 9: ALA; OhioLA (past chm Ext Round Table). 10: Dayton Council on World Affairs; Altrusa Club. 12: Past ed SORT. 13: . 14: Br & ext. 15: 215 East Third st, Dayton Ohio 45402.

KELLY, ELIZABETH C (MONACO). b Chicago. 4: Robert Q Kelly. 5: Rosary Col 38-42 (Eng) BA, 42-44 BLS; De Paul U 47-49 (Educ) M Ed. 6: Fr, Ital. 7: Asst catlgr Wright Jr Col 42-43; Libn Notre Dame High Sch, Chicago 43-46; Catlg libn Wright Jr Col 46-58, 61-62, Acquis libn 63-65, Circ libn 65-, Assoc Prof 68-. 9: ALA; ACRL; IllEA; IllLA. 14: Catlg, ref, acquis. 15: 2208 S Hainsworth, N Riverside Ill 60547.

KELLY, GERALD L. b Baton Rouge La 25 Ag 38. 5: LSU 56-60 (Elem Edu) BS, 67-68 (LS). 7: Elem tchr E Baton Rouge Parish Sch Bd, Baton Rouge La 60-62, 64-66; Clerical US Army, Fort Dix NJ & Texarkana Tex 62-64; Lib asst (circ) TulaneU Lib 66-68, Sci libn 68-. 9: LaLA. 14: Catlg (LC), sci ref. 15: PO Box 5088 Tulane Univ Sta, New Orleans La 70118.

KELLY, HELEN (STIKEMAN). b NJ 31 Ja 17. 4: George H Kelly. 5: RI State Col 34-38 (Econ) BS in Bus admin; Carnegie Lib 40-41 BS in LS. 7: Messenger Providence Pub Lib 31-34; Asst Westerly Pub Lib, Westerly RI 38-40; Asst Newark Pub Lib, Newark NJ 41-44; Asst bus br Providence Pub Lib 44-48, Sub 49-58, Lib asst 58-61; Libn URI Ext Div, Providence 63-. 9: ALA; RILA. 10: PTA; church organizations. 14: Ref (bus & industry). 15: 82 Euclid ave, Riverside RI 02915.

KELLY, JOAN. b NYC 30 Je 31. 5: Marietta Col 48-52 (Eng) AB; Columbia 52-53, 56-60 MSLS. 6: Lat, Fr, Ger, Sanskrit, Ital, Sp, Chinese. 7: Lib asst Gen Theol Sem Lib, NYC 52-53; Head catlgr Brooklyn Museum Lib 59-61; Catlgr Bard Col Lib 63-64; Gen catlgr Brandeis Libs 68-. 9: . 14: Catlg, art ref, bibliog, rare bks. 15: 146 Oxford st apt c, Somerville Ma 02143.

KELLY, JOHN (THEODORE) BROTHER. b Houston Tex 24 Je 27. 5: Col of Santa Fe 46-51 (Soc Sci) BA; USWest La 54-61 (Educ) BA. 7: Tchr Hanson Sch, Franklin La 59-66; Libn St Pauls Sch, Covington La 66-. 14: Sch lib wk. 15: PO Box 928, Covington La 70433.

KELLY, LIAM M. b Donegal Ireland 7 Je 35. 4: Cynthia Dryden. 5: Columban Col (Ireland) 53-57 (Philos) BA; Boston Col 63-65 (Eng) BA; Catholic U 66-67 MSLS. 6: Gaelic, Lat, Fr, Welsh. 7: Com photographer, Ireland 57-62; Catlgr (asst) Boston Col 62-64; Instr Mt St Agnes Col, Baltimore 65; Catlgr Harvard U Widener Lib 67-69; Libn Inforonics Inc, Maynard Mass 69-. 10: Beta Phi Mu. 13: Yes. 14: Lib automation, info netwks. 15: 22 Pine Plain rd, Wellesley Ma 02181.

KELLY, MARIAN (MC MEEKAN). b Hillsboro Ill 17 Jl 17. 4: John H Kelly. 5: MacMurray Col 37-42 (Fr) BA; UNev 54; UWash 57-62 MLS. 6: Fr. 7: Fr tchr Steeleville High Sch, Steeleville Ill 42-43; Jr high libn Elko Sch #1, Elko Nev 44-68; Jr High libn Elko Jr-Sr High Sch, Elko Nev 68-. 8: Instr of Lib Sci UNev Ext Br Tchrs Wkshop summer 63. 9: ALA-AASchL; NEA; NevLA; NevASchL (chm 63-65); Nev StateEA. 10: AAUW; Beta Phi Mu. 14: Sch libnship. 15: PO Box 852, Elko Nev 89801.

KELLY, MARJORIE (MARY) (HINCKLEY). b Needham Mass 16 O 31. 4: Wilbur M Kelly. 5: Simmons 48-52 (LS) BS; Boston U 55-57 (Eng) M Ed; Ind U Summer 58 (Folklore); U Guam summer 68 (LS, AV). 7: Libn Bartow Pub Lib, Bartow Fla 52-54; Lib asst Fitchburg Pub Lib, Fitchburg Mass 54-55; Lib sci instr Alice Lloyd Jr Col Summer 56-57; Eng tchr Wellesley Jr High Sch, Wellesley Mass 57-59; Libn Tumon Jr-Sr High Sch, Guam 59-64; Eng instr Col of Guam 61-64; Libn George Washington High Sch Agana Guam 65-. 9: GuamLA (sec 65; pres 68; Bd 69); ALA. 10: Guam Theatre Guild. 14: Sch libnship. 15: PO Box 2334, Agana Guam 96910.

KELLY, MARY (FLYNN). b Calabogie 21 F 28. 4: Karl Joseph Kelly. 5: UToronto 47-49 BA; Ontario Col summer 58, 60 Secondary Sch Tchg Certif, summer 63, 64, 66 Specialist in Lib Sci. 7: Subscription serv Time Inc, Chicago 50-52; News ed Renfrew Mercury, Renfrew Ont 52-57; Tchr Loretto Abbey, Toronto Ont 57-58; Tchr Perth Collegiate, Perth Ont 59-61; Tchr Deepriver High Sch, Deepriver Ont 65-66; Libn Eastview High Sch, Ottawa Ont 65-66; Libn Oerth Collegiate, Perth Ont 66-. 14: Sch lib wk. 15: 24 Gore, Perth Ont Can.

KELLY, MARY JOHNSON. b Philadelphia 22 N 08. 5: Barnard 26-30 (Fr) BA; Columbia 52-54 (LS) MS. 6: Fr, Ital,

Lat, Sp, Ger. 7: Fr tchr Bedford Hills NY High Sch 31; Off manager Borden Ice Cream Co, Steubenville Ohio 39-43, Manager 43; Order libn Barnard Col 43-45, 51-. 9: ALA-ACRL. 10: Audubon Soc; Greenbrook Sanctuary; Cornell Ornith Soc; Jersey Wild Life Trust (Engl); NY Zool Soc; Nat Wildlife Assn. 14: Acquis, bk sel. 15: 417 Riverside dr, NYC 10025.

KELLY, PATRICK EDWARD. b St Louis. 5: Mexico City Col 47-51 (Econ) BA; UParis 55-57 (Hist, Fr); San Francisco State Col 59-60 (Educ); San Jose State Col 60-62 Lib Certif. 6: Fr. 7: (Cpl) US Army Med Corp 51-54; Jr libn Oakland Pub Lib, Oakland Cal 62-64, Head adult educ div 64-, Hd gen ref div 67-. 9: CalLA. 10: Dolphin Swimming & Boating Club. 14: Ref, adult educ. 15: 949 Columbus ave, San Francisco Ca 94133.

KELLY, REV RAYMOND M. b Providence 31 Ag 23. 5: Our Lady of Providence Sem 42-44 (Humanities); St Mary's Sem (Baltimore) 44-45 (Philos) AB; St Mary's U (Baltimore) 46-49 (Theol) STB; CatholicU 63 MSLS. 7: Tchr Our Lady of Providence Sem, Warwick RI 49-63, libn 55-. 8: Mem of bd NE Church Lib Conference 68. 9: ALA; CathLA (chm RI Unit 67-69); NELA; RILA. 15: 836 Warwick Neck ave, Warwick RI 02889.

KELLY, RAYMOND THOMAS. b Chicago Ill 7 Ja 39. 5: Chicago State Col 66-68 (LS) MS Ed; LoyolaU 56, 60-61 (Sociol) BS; DePaulU 69- (Admin & Supv). 7: Probation off Family Court of Cook Co, Chicago 61; US Army Clerk typist Sp/4 62-64; Probation off Family Court of Cook Co, Chicago 64-65; Tchr-libn Chicago Bd of Educ, Chicago 65-. 9: ALA; IllLA. 14: Sch libn. 15: 9704 So Tripp ave, Oak Lawn Il 60453.

KELLY, RICHARD (JOHN). b Minneapolis Minn 30 S 38. 4: Lois Saba. 5: UMinn 60-66 (Eng) BA, 66-68 (LS) MA. 7: Ref libn UMinn (Minneapolis) 68-. 9: ALA. 14: Ref. 15: 1033 16th ave SE, Minneapolis Mn 55414.

KELLY, ROBERT QUAINE. b Chicago 3 Ap 22. 4: Elizabeth Monaco. 5: St Mary of the Lake Sem 41-45 (Philos) BA; Rosary Col 48-50 MALS; De Paul U Col of Law 50-56 JD. 6: Lat. 7: Law libn De Paul U Col of Law 50-, Asst prof of Law 59-, Assoc Prof of law 67-. 9: AALL (treas 64-66); Amer Bar Assn; BSA; CathLA (chm Constit & Bylaws Com 67-). 10: Caxton Club of Chicago. 13: Yes. 15: 25 E Jackson blvd, Chicago 60604.

KELLY, RUTH (HEMMERLY). b Bethlehem Penn 29 Ja 20. 4: Dale Kelly. 5: Moravian Col 37-41 (Langs) BA; Lehigh 38-47 (Eng) MA; Columbia summers 42-45 BLS; Peabody Lib Sch summer 67; Mercer Col summer 68. 6: Fr, Lat, Ger. 7: Catlgr Bethlehem Pub Lib, Bethlehem Penn 43-45; Libn Moravian Col 45-47; Asst libn catlgr St Mary's U, San Antonio Tex 57-59; Libn New Eng Col 59-62; Ger, Eng, Lat tchr Newport Sch for Girls, Newport RI 62-63; Libn & Lat tchr Portsmouth High Sch, Portsmouth RI 63-65; Libn & Fr tchr Chambliss Child House, Tuskegee Inst Ala 65-; Libn Macon Co Pub Lib, Tuskegee Ala 66-67; Sch libn Auburn City Schs, Auburn Ala 67-. 8: Lib Bd & Bk Sel Com, Portsmouth Free Lib (RI). 9: ALA; NEA; RILA; NELA; Ala Tchrs Assn; AlaLA. 10: AAUW. 14: Catlg, wk with child & yp, lang tchg. 15: Rte 1 Box 167, Auburn Al 36830.

KELNER, LORETTA. b Cazenovia NY 25 D 28. 5: Cazenovia Jr Col 46-48 (Gen Bus); Hartwick Col 48-50 (Eng) BA; Columbia 50-54 (LS) MS. 6: Fr, Ger. 7: Bus libn Eastman Kodak Co, Rochester NY 54-64; Catlgr URochester 64-65, Fine Arts libn 65-68; Ref libn Colgate U 68-. 9: SLA. 14: Spec lib. 15: 7 Burton st, Cazenovia NY 13035.

KELSAY, DOROTHA (BRADFORD). b Strawberry Point Iowa 24 Mr 13. 4: Omar F Kelsay. 5: UWis 39 (Eng) BA, MA; UChicago 44 BLS. 6: Fr. 7: Asst libn Baker U 40-43; Army libn USArmyAF, Roswell NM 44-45; Army libn us 7th Army, Heidelberg Germany 45-46; Ref libn Ore State Lib 62-. 14: Ref. 15: 2660 5th st NE, Salem Ore 97303.

KELSEY, FLORENCE STEWART. b Syracuse NY 11 Ap 09. 5: Syracuse 26-30 BSLS. 7: Circ asst Syracuse U Lib 30-32, Br libn liberal arts lib 32-50, Br libn bus admin lib 50-. 9: ALA; SLA. 10: Bus & Profess Women's Club; Beta Phi Mu; Zeta Phi Eta. 14: Ref. 15: 828 Summer ave, Syracuse NY 13210.

KELSEY, PATTERSON S. b Cleveland 21 N 22. 4: Ruth Luzadder. 5: Yale 40-45 (Philos & Govt) BA; Pratt 62 MLS. 7: Libn Hicksville Pub Lib, Hicksville NY 62-65; Asst dir Huntington Pub Lib, Huntington NY 65-68; Hd circ libn SUNY (Stony Brook) 68-. 9: NYLA. 15: 70 Hollywood pl, Huntington NY 11743.

KELSO, HELEN (CRUMPACKER). b Michigan City Ind 8 O 10. 5: Ind U 27-30 (Psych); Valparaiso U 54-57 (Eng) BA; West Res 61-62 MSLS. 7: Woman's page ed "News-Dispatch," Michigan City Ind 32-33; Feature writer -vidette-Messenger," Valparaiso Ind 53-54; 1st asst Valparaiso Pub Lib, Valparaiso Ind 55-57; Elem tchr Liberty Twp Sch, Porter Count Ind 57-58; Elem tchr Valparaiso City Sch, Valparaiso Ind 58-61; Circ libn Asst Prof Moellering Lib, Valparaiso U 62-. 9: ALA (Recr Com 63-); IndLA. 10: Duneland Hist Assn; Thoreau Soc; Great Books Group; AAUP; Delta Gamma; Kappa Kappa Kappa; Indiana Save-the-Dunes Coun; Beta Phi Mu. 14: Circ, pub rel. 15: 363 McIntyre Ct, Valparaiso Ind 46383.

KELTON, ALLEN. b Leoma Tenn 6 Ap 27. 4: Mai Hogan. 5: Martin Col 44-46; Middle Tenn State Col 46-48 (Eng) BS; Peabody Col 58-59 (LS) MA, 60-61 (LS) Ed S 65- (Educ). 6: Fr, Ger. 7: Personnel admin spec US Army 50-52; Elem tchr, prin Lawrence Co Tenn 53-58; Asst ref libn Nashville Pub Lib 59-60, Head bus info serv 61-68; Bus libn UAla 69-. 10: Beta Phi Mu. 14: Ref, lib serv to bus & ind, lib hist. 15: 13-I Northwood Lake, Northport Al 35476.

KELTON, JON DELVEY. b Norwood Mass 10 Ag 34. 5: Hamilton Col 52-56 (Hist) AB; Rutgers 57-59 MLS. 7: Libn trainee Elizabeth Pub Lib, Elizabeth NJ 57-59; Libn II Pub Lib of Cincinnati 59-62, Br libn 62-65; Dir Wilmington Pub Lib, Wilmington Ohio 66-. 9: OhioLA (v-chm Jr Mems Round Table 65-66, chm 66-67). 14: Ref, bldg collections, state organ, catlg. 15: 207 N South st, Wilmington Oh 45177.

KELTS, LORA (IVES). b Ogden Utah 8 Ag 09. 4: Donald M Kelts. 5: UCLA 38-41 (Bot) BA; UCal(Berkeley) 41-42 (LS) Certif. 7: Circ & ref asst UCal(Davis) 42-43; Asst ref libn Pub Lib, Sacramento Cal 43-44; Ore State U; Ref & ser asst 44-51, Asst ser libn 51-57, Agric-forestry libn 57-. 9: ALA; PNLA; Pac NW Fed of Forestry Libs (chm). 10: AAUP; AAUW; Sierra Club; N Cascades Conserv Coun; Friends of the Oreg StateU Lib; Ore State Employees Assn. 13: Yes. 14: Ref. 15: Ore State Univ Lib, Corvallis Or 97331.

KEMLER, DORIS (McCABE). Pittsburgh 7 D 06. 5: UMinn 51-54 (Educ) BS, 60 (LS) MA. 6: Fr. 7: Asst libn Westover Sch, Middlebury Conn 56-57; Asst libn York Jr Col 57-59; A-V libn Gettysburg Col 59-. 9: ALA; PennLA. 10: AAUW; Pi Lambda Theta; Beta Phi Mu. 14: A-v & microprint matls. 15: 124 Carlisle st, Gettysburg Pa 17325.

KEMP, BETTY (RUTH). b Tishomingo Okla 5 My 30. 5: UOkla 48-52 BA LS; Fla State U 64-65 (LS) MS. 7: Extramural loan libn UTex Lib 52-55; Libn lit & hist dept Dallas Pub Lib 55-56, Head Oaklawn Br 56-60, Head Walnut Hill Br 60-64; Dir Cherokee Reg Lib, LaFayette Ga 65-. 9: ALA; TexLA (sec Pub Lib Div 63-64). ; GaLA; SELA. 10: Bet a Phi Mu. 14: Adult serv. 15: 611 Oliver, Norman Okla 73069.

KEMP, CHARLES H. b Talihina Okla 27 Ja 39. 4: Karen E Monaco. 5: UOkla 61-64 (Sp) BA, 64-65 MLS. 6: Sp. 7: Airman (electronics tech) USAF, Okinawa Colo 57-60; Post libn Spec Serv Lib Br, Korea 65-66; Docs libn NM State U 66-67; Reader's serv libn Pacific U 67-. 9: ALA; OreLA. 10: AAUP. 14: Ref, admin. 15: Box 221, Forest Grove Or 97116.

KEMP, EDWARD C JR. b Boston 3 O 29. 4: Ann M DeVoe. 5: Harvard 51 (Fr) AB; UCal 55 MLS. 6: Fr, Sp. 7: Lib asst Berkeley Pub Lib, Berkeley Cal 51-55; UOre: Ref libn 55-56, Soc sci libn 56-57, Acquis libn 57-. 14: Acquis of ms & bk collections. 15: 320 E 47th ave, Eugene Ore.

KEMP, ERLE PILCHER. b Statesboro Ga 2 S 21. 4: Regina Manson. 5: Ga Tchrs Col 38-42 (Educ) BS; Columbia 46-47 (LS) BS, 48-52 (LS) MS, 53- (LS). 6: Fr. 7: Stud asst Ga Tchrs Col Lib 38-42; (Lt) US Navy (Engnr) 42-46; Lib asst Zool Lib Columbia U 46; City Col(NY): Ref asst 47-48, Ser asst 48-49, Act head ser div 49-50; Ser libn UMiami(Fla) 50-52; Head of acquis div Columbia U 52-. 9: ALA; East Col Libns Conf (chm 60); NY Lib Club; NY Tech Serv Libns. 13: Yes. 14: Acquis. 15: 70 La Salle st, NYC 10027.

KEMPE M(ABLE) ROSALIE. b Chicago. 5: Northwestern U 23-27 (Eng, Fr) BA; Columbia 28 BA in LS. 6: Fr, Sp, Ger. 7: Catlgr Joseph Schaffner Lib Northwestern U 28-31, Head catlg dept 32-54, Asst libn 49-54, Libn 55-. 9: ALA; SLA; Chicago Libns in Tech Serv (pres 49-50). 10: Art Inst of Chicago; Field Mus of Natl Hist; Geog Soc of Chicago; Pan Amer Coun; Chicago Coun on Foreign Rel. 13: Yes. 14: Admin, catlg. 15: 6030 Sheridan rd, Chicago 60626.

KEMPER, SISTER AGATHENA. b Louisville Ky 31 My 1886. 5: Nazareth Col (Ky) 20-34 (Ger, Educ) AB; Xavier Col

(Cincinnati) BSLS. 6: Ger, Sp, Fr. 7: Tchr St Jerome High, Fancy Farm Ky 34-36; Prin St Agnes High Uniontown Ky 36-40; High sch tchr libn, LaSalette Acad, Covington Ky 40-43; Libn & tchr St Vincent High Sch, Mt Vernon Ohio 43-45; Libn Sacred Heart Cathedral High Sch, Richmond Va 45-47; Libn Sacred Heart High Sch, Memphis Tenn 47-60; Libn Holy Family High Sch, Birmingham Ala 60-66; Libn Novitiate Lib, Nazareth Ky 66-. 8: Adv bd Ala Cath Lib Unit; Adv bd Nat Cath Lib Assn; Consul: Holy Family Hosp, Birmingham Ala, Holy Names High Sch Lib, Memphis Tenn; Chm at tchrs insts Lib Sects. 9: CathLA (chm 3 reg & loc chaps). 11: Outstanding Tchr Memphis Tenn- Citation. 12: Ed 3 newsletters for reg & loc chaps of CathLA. 13: Yes. 14: Tech processes. 15: Novitiate Lib, Nazareth Ky 40048.

KEMPER, ANNE. b Reading Penn 31 My 15. 4: Jackson Kemper. 5: Simmons 33-37 (LS) BS; No Ill U summer 66, 67. 7: Child libn Pub Lib, Wyomissing Penn 37-38; Libn Grove Elem Sch, Barrington Ill 66-67; Libn N Barrington Elem Sch, Barrington Ill 67-. 14: Child libn & ref wk. 15: Meadowhill rd Rt 2 Box 75, Barrington Il 60010.

KEMPER, SUZANNE (WHITE). b Pittsburgh 23 Mr 29. 4: Robert F Kemper. 5: Carnegie 47-51 (Music) BFA, 51-54 MLS. 6: Ger, Fr, Ital. 7: Asst music libn Carnegie Lib of Pittsburgh 51-55; Nursing libn Allegheny Gen Hosp, Pittsburgh 58-59; Head libn State Col, N Adams Mass 62-. 8: Part-time instr lib sci N Adams State Col. 9: ALA-ACRL;-RTSD; NELA; MassLA; Mass Coun Chief Libns Pub Higher Educ Insts. 10: Coun Mass State Col Libns; LWV. 14: Admin, acquis, tchg, music libnship. 15: Sand Springs rd, Williamstown Mass 01267.

KEMPTER, PAUL FREDERIC. b Grand Rapids Mich 9 My 17. 4: Sarah Horton Denison. 5: NM Highlands U 53-55 (Eng, Hist) BA; UOre 56-57 (Eng, Eng Hist) MS; USoCal 58-59 (LS); UMich 60 (LS); West Mich U 59-64 MALS. 7: Asst steward Pantlind Hotel, Grand Rapids mich 36-39; Machinist-mech US Army Ordnance, US, Australia 41-45; Real estate, Grand Rapids Mich 46-53; Tchr Quincy High Sch, Wuincy Cal 57-58; Acquisitionist San Bernardino AFB Lib Cal 58-59; Mich hist & geneology lib Grand Rapids Pub Lib 59-62; Libn Kentwood High Sch, Grand Rapids Mich 62-. 8: Consul for libs in Kentwood Sch Dist; Planning new high sch. 9: ALA; NEA; Mich A-V Assn; MichASchL. 10: Alpha Psi Omega; Pi Gamma Mu; Grand Rapids Coun on World Affairs. 14: Ref, instr in use of libs, clsf. 15: 310 Sunset ave NW, Grand Rapids Mi 49504.

KENDRIS, CHRISTOPHER. b Albany NY 5 Ap 23. 4: Yolanda Fenyo. 5: Columbia 44-48 (Fr) BA; UParis 49-50 (Fr) Diploma; Northwestern U 51-55 (Romance Lang) MA, PhD; Columbia 66-67 (LS) MS. 6: Fr, Sp, Ital, Portu, Gr, Lat. 7: Tchg asst in Fr Northwestern U 51-53; Visiting lecturer in Fr UChicago summer 53; Lecturer in French lang and lit Colby Col 56-57; Asst prof of Fr & Sp Rutgers U 57-59; Chm of for lang dept farmingdale High Sch, Farmingdale NY 59-64; Asst Prof of romance lang SUNY (Albany) 64-66, Assoc libn 67-. 8: Foreign lang consul for Barron's Educl Ser Inc, Publishers. 9: ALA; NYStateTA. 12: "Lectures Variees," (59); 8 Titles in Barron's Educl Series inc (63-69); Ed "Biblion," SUNY (Albany) lib journal (68-). 13: Yes. 14: Catlg. 15: 27 Willow st RR 1, Guilderland NY 12084.

KENISTON, MRS ROBERTA (CANNELL). b Rockford Ill 3 Mr 08. 4: Hayward Keniston. 5: UChicago 23-27 (Eng) PhB; UMich 45-47, 49-51 AMLS. 6: Fr, Sp. 7: Head of fiction room Ann Arbor Pub Lib, Ann Arbor Mich 51-52; Head ref dept East Mich U 52-57; Head undergrad lib UMich, Ann Arbor Mich 57-63; Asst libn East Mich U 63-68, Assoc libn 68-. 9: ALA (coun 61-65); MichLA. 10: AAUP. 13: Yes. 14: Ref. 15: 1507 E Park pl, Ann Arbor Mich 48104.

KENN, JOHN MURDOCK. b Port Huron Mich 3 Je 39. 4: Barbara Kay Hagle. 5: Port Huron Jr Col 57-59 (Hist) AA; Central MichU 59-61 (Hist) BA, 62-64 (Hist) MA; West MichU 65-66 MASL. 7: Jr high tchr Shepherd Pub Schs, Shepherd Mich 61-63; Sr high tchr Standish-Sterling Sch, Standish Mich 63-65; Asst libn Lake Superior State Col 67-68; Lib dir Sault Pub Schs, Sault Ste Marie Mich 68-. 8: Histn Sault Ste Marie Tri Centennial celebration. 9: Hist Soc of Mich; Great Lakes Hist Soc. 10: Kiwanis Club of Sault Ste Marie; Chippewa Co Hist Soc. 15: 408 Carrie st, Sault Ste Marie Mi 49783.

KENNEDY, DORIS (AUTREY). b Jonesboro Ark 26 F 24. 4: Lowell E Kennedy. 5: Eureka Col 47-48; PhillipsU 49-51; ButlerU 51-54 (Relig) AB. 7: Libn United Christian Missionary Soc, Indianapolis 54-. 9: SLA. 14: Ref. 15: 222 S Downey ave, Indianapolis In 46219.

KENNEDY, FENTON L. b Newark NJ 20 Ap 10. 4: Virginia Riddleborger. 5: William & Mary 47-50 (Hist) AB; AmericanU 50 (Archives & Rec Mgt) Certif; CatholicU 50-51 (LS). 6: Fr, Ger. 7: Celestial navigator instr US Army AF 43-45; Accounting div Amer Red Cross 45-46; Inspector DC Highway Dept 46-47; Supv libs Johns Hopkins Applied Physics lab, Silver Spring Md 51-65; Chief sci info ctrs br NICHD Nat Inst Bealth, Bethesda Md 65-. 8: Mem Adv Com Montgomery Co (Md) Libs 65-66; Adv Sec's (DHEW) Task Force on Feasibility of a Nat Mental Retardation Info & Resources Ctr. 9: SLA (Wash Chap sci-Tech Div: v-pres, pres, chm). 12: "Application of the IBM 1401 Computer to the APL Storage and Information Retrieval System JHU/APL" (63); "Subject Headings for Cataloging Guided Missile Literature" (59); "Applications of Computers to the APL Storage and Retrieval System" (65); Ed "Sci-Tech News" (SLA 62-64). 14: Admin of libs & sci info ctrs. 15: NICHD National Inst of Health, Bethesda Md 20014.

KENNEDY, FRANCES. b St Louis 2 D 07. 5: Okla City U 24-26; UOkla 26-28 (Eng) BA; UIll 30-31 BS in LS, summers 44-46, 48 MS in LS. 7: Br libn Pub Lib, Muskogee Okla 28-29; Lib asst Pub Lib, Okla City Okla 29-30; Reviser Iowa State U summer 31; Ref libn Pub Lib, Okla City Okla 31-47; Libn Okla City U 47-; Faculty UOkla Lib Sch summers 58-59. 8: Ref cons Okla Dept of Libs 66-. 9: ALA (Coun 56-60 & 68-72 Memb Com);-ACRL (chm mem com); OklaLA (pres 45-47); SWLA (Bd of Dir 55-56). 10: Beta Phi Mu. 11: Distinguished Service Award, OklaLA 65; Distinguished Service Award Variety Health Center 63. 12: Ed "Oklahoma Librarian" (54-57); Ed "SWLA Newsletter" (58-64). 14: Col & Univ libs, ref. 15: Okla City U Gold Star Bldg, Okla City Okla 73106.

KENNEDY, (FRANCES) LA VERNE. b Cleveland Tex 19 S 31. 5: Sam Houston State Col 48-49 9ls0 bs, 49-50 (Prof Elem & Secondary), 53-54 Tchr's Certif, 54-55 Sch Libn's Certif. 7: Tchr Aldine High Sch, Houston Tex 56; Elem tchr Cleveland High School Dist, cleveland Tex 57-59, High sch libn 60-67; Libn "Dallas Morning News", Dallas Tex 67-. 9: SLA (Newspaper Div). 14: Indexing, newspaper clippings, pictures. 15: Dallas Morning News Ref Dept Communications Center, Dallas Tx 75222.

KENNEDY, JAMES (RANDOLPH). b Detroit 28 Ap 28. 4: Laura Bertelson. 5: Cornell 46-50 (Econ) AB; Columbia 53-55 MLS; Lutheran Theol Sem 55-58; Drexel 59-63. 7: Sub-prof NY Pub Lib 53-55; Catlgr & ref asst Lutheran Theol Sem, Philadelphia 55-59; Asst g en ref libn Drexel Inst of Tech 59-63, Soc sci libn 63-64; Ref libn Earlham Col 64-. 9: ALA-RSTD (copying methods sect com chm 63); ATheolLA; Col & ref libns (program chm Phila Sect 61-63); SLA (treas Soc Sci group Phila Chap 55-56). 13: Yes. 14: Ref. 15: 116 SW 7th st, Richmond In 47374.

KENNEDY, JOHN PAYSON. b Atlanta 16 Ja 33. 4: Aurelia Turpin. 5: Erskine Col 50-52; Emory 52-54 (Philos) BA, 56-57 (Sociol) MA; UIll 60-61 (LS) MS. 7: US Army Counter Intelligence Corps 54-56; Instr of Social Hampden-Sydney Col & Longwood Col 57-59; Ref libn Hampden-Sydney Col 59-60; Bkstacks asst UIll(Urbana) 60-61, Com & sociol libn 62-63, Research assoc 63-65; Data processing libn Ga Inst of Tech 65-. 9: ALA; ASIS (Com on Lib Automation). 10: AAUP; Phi Beta Kappa; Ga Canoeing Assn; Boy Scouts Amer. 13: Yes. 14: Data processing, lib automation. 15: 1308 Valley View rd, Dunwoody Ga 30338.

KENNEDY, KATHLEEN A. b Camden NJ 18 N 31. 5: Rutgers 50-54 (Humanities) BA; Villanova 58-62 MS in LS. 7: Pub sch tchr NJ Pub Schs 54-59; Libn Williamstown NJ 59-63; Asst circ libn Swarthmore Col 63-64; Circ libn Glassboro State Col 64-68, Curr lab libn 68-. 9: NEA; NJEA; TheatreLA. 10: AAUP. 14: Circ, ref, sch libs. 15: 281 White Horse, Apt 304, Audubon NJ 08106.

KENNEDY, KATHY (KAY). b New Kensington Penn 21 O 42. 5: Thiel Col 60-64 (Eng) AB; Drexel 64-67 MS in LS. 6: Fr, Ger. 7: Trainee Union Lib Catlg of Penn, Phila 64-67; Ref libn Sci-tech Dept Carnegie Lib of Pittsburgh 67-. 9: ALA; SLA; PennLA. 10: Beta Phi Mu; Bus & Profess Woman's Club. 14: Ref, bibliog. 15: 4716 Ellsworth ave, Pittsburgh Pa 15213.

KENNEDY, LUCILLE. b Hodgenville Ky 19 My 22. 5: Transylvania U 40-41 (Liberal Arts); UKy 41-44 (Educ) AB; InterAmerU summer 47 (Sp); Catherine Spalding Col summers 61-65 MSLS. 6: Sp, Fr. 7: Tchr Hodgenville High Sch, Hodgenville Ky 44-51; Tchr LaRue Co Bd of Educ, Hodgenville Ky 53-65; Libn Ft Knox Dependent Schs, Ft Knox Ky 65-68; Libn Lincoln Trail Elem Sch, Hardin Co Ky

68-69. 9: NEA; KyEA; KyLA (treas 4th dist gp 68-69); KyASchL. 15: 102 College st, Hodgenville Ky 42748.

KENNEDY, SISTER MARIE MARTHA OP. b Chicago Ill 20 S 14. 5: Siena Hts Col summers 38-42 (Eng) BA; DePaul summers 44-48 (Educ) MA; UMich summers 60-64 AMLS; UWis summer 68 grant on non-bk materials. 7: Tchr Adrian Mich Dominican Order: Des Moines Iowa 37-39, Alpena Mich 39-41, St Joseph's Mich 41-49, Elgin Ill 49-50, St Charles Ill 50-58; Libn Adrian Mich Dominican Order. Escanaba Mich 58-65, Harper Woods Mich 65-67, Miami Shores fla 67-. 8: Secondary sch chm Mich CathLA, Harper Woods 65-67. 9: ALA; FlaLA; FlaCathLA (v-chm); DadeCoLA. 13: Yes. 14: Ref, bk selection. 15: 1130 NE Second ave, miami Shores Fl 33161.

KENNEDY, ROBERT ALVIN. b Cumberland Ont Can 17 My 20. 4: Ruth Downie. 5: Toronto 38-42 (Philos) BA; Cornell 42-43 (Philos); Toronto 45-46 BLS. 7: Royal Can AF Electronics Leading Aircraftsman Can & UK 43-45; Indexer & ref asst Aeronautical Lib Nat Res Coun of Can, Ottawa 46-48; Br libn 48-53; Asst chief libn Nat Res Coun of Can, Ottawa 53-58; Head lib systems dept Bell Telephone Labs, Murray Hill NJ 58-. 8: Can rep Documentation Com of NATO Adv Group for Aeronautical Research and Development, 53-58, Chm 56-57. 9: ASIS; SLA; OntLA (pres 52-53). 12: Ed bd "American Documentation" (61-). 13: Yes. 14: Machine systems, lib automation. 15: 33 Holly Glen Lane So, Berkeley Heights NJ 07922.

KENNEDY, SCOTT. b Ft Lewis Wash 14 Jl 19. 4: Margaret Blanche Kelsch. 5: Ore State Col 38-39; San Jose State Col 39-42, 47-49 (Biol Sci) AB; UCal (Berkeley) 49-50 BLS. 7: Acquis libn Biol Lib UCal(Berkeley) 50-52; Catlg Sect Leader UCal Los Alamos Sci Lab, Los Alamos NM 52-54; Physics libn UCLA 54-55; Chief Libn Phillips Petroleum Nat Reactor Testing Station, Idaho Falls Ida 56-57; Catlg libn Gen Electric Co TEMPO, Santa Barbara Cal 57-58, Acquis libn 58-. 9: SLA; ASTIA Com; ASIS. 13: Yes. 14: Acquis, info sci. 15: 879 Via Campobello, Santa Barbara Cal 93105.

KENNELLY, JEAN RUPP. b Elizabeth NJ 27 My 31. 5: UWash 49-53 (Eng) BA & tchg certif, summers 57-61 (LS) ML. 7: Tchr Seattle Sch Dist #101 53-54; Tchr Vista Unified Sch Dist, Vista Cal 58-60; Libn San Jose Pub Lib, San Jose Cal 60-61; Libn Long Beach Unified Sch Dist Hughes Jr High Sch, Long Beach Cal 61-66; Visiting lecturer sch libnship UWash summers 66-69; Dir of libs Yakima Pub Schs, Yakima Wash 66-. 9: NEA; ALA-AASchL; WashEA; WashLA; WashASchL. 10: Alpha Phi; Pi Lambda Theta. 14: Catlg, child lit, standards. 15: 105 N 30th ave, Yakima Wa 98902.

KENNERLY, SARAH LAW. b Winnsboro SC 28 S 10. 5: Winthrop Col 27-31 (Eng) BA; Emory 36-37 BA in LS; UMich 47-56 MA in LS, PhD. 6: Fr, Ger, Sp. 7: Elem sch tchr, Great Falls SC 31-36; High sc libn, Clinton S 37-38; Catlgr A lib 38-41;TO LIBN Fla State Col for Women 41-44; HEAD CATLR LW Ua 44-45; LnMARY Baldwin Cl5-46; Asst Prof Lib Sci Dept inhrp Col 46-51; Assoc Prof Lib Serv Dept N Tex State U 51-57, Prof 57-, Assoc Dir 65-67. 8: Dir NDEA Inst for Sch Libns, No Tex State U, summer 6;Visiting Prof Dept of Lib Sci, UMich, summers 58-59, 61-63; Dir NDEA & HEA insts for sch libns &/or lib personnel US Off Educ summers 65-69. 9: ALA-CSD (chm Melcher Scholarship Com 67-69);-LED (chm Tchrs Sect 68-69); AALS; SWLA (chm Lib Educ Com 68-70); TexLA (chm Dist VII 65; del-at-large 68-71); Tex Coun Lib Educ (chm 64-66); Tex Assn Col Tchrs. 10: Beta Phi Mu; Phi Kappa Phi; Pi Lambda Theta; Ariel Club; AAUW. 11: Silver Bk Award Lib Binding Inst 68. 13: Yes. 14: Lib wk with child & yp, sch libs, non-printed media. 15: 1720 W Mulberry st, Denton Tx 76201.

KENNEWEG, DOROTHY (RODGERS). b Pittsburgh Penn 25 Ja 09. 5: Allegheny Col 29 (Biol) BS; UPittsburgh 32 (Educ) MEd; Carnegie Tech 50 MS in LS. 6: Fr. 7: Asst S Side Br Carnegie Lib of Pittsburgh 49-52, City bkmob libn 52-56, Br libn Brookline Br 56-58, br libn E Liberty Br 58-. 10: Literary Review Club; Tuesday Musical Club; Nature Club of Pittsburgh; Acad of Sci & Art; Archaeol Inst; Salvation Army Hosp Aux. 14: Ref, adult bk sel. 15: 1852 Perrott ave, Pittsburgh Pa 15212.

KENNEY, BRIGITTE (LIDA). b Halberstadt Germany 14 Ag 27. 4: B Higdon Kenney. 5: UGraz (Austria) 45-46 (Eng, Music); UChicago 57-58 (LS) MA. 6: Ger. 7: Lib asst Tombigbee Reg Lib, W Point Miss 52-53; Ref asst Miss Lib Commsn, Jackson Miss 55-57; Prof asst Joint Ref Lib of PAS, Chicago 58; Asst libn Transportation Center at Northwestern U 59-62; Libn Miss Research & Development Center, Jackson Miss 62-65, Head info serv div 65-66; Syst analyst Rowland Med Lib UMiss Med Ctr 66-68, Research assoc Dept Psychiatry 68-. 8: Lib 21 Seattle World's Fair 62; Chm Steering Com Miss Union Catlg 63; Index on Coordinate Indexing, EJC-Battelle Mem Inst Wash DC 63; Consul EDUCOM Biomed Communications Proj 67-68; Consul Ind Lib Studies 68-69. 9: ALA (chm Recr Materials Com 63-64, Cent Processing Com 65-, Com on Automation 66-67, Com on Organ 68-);-RTSD;-LAD;-ISAD; SLA (Consul off La-Miss Chap); ASIS (Memb Com 67-); MissLA (chm &/or mem 6 coms); SELA. 10: Beta Phi Mu; AAUP; Jackson Symphony League; Jackson Music Assn; New Stage. 12: "An Informational Manual to Assist Chambers of Commerce with Research" (65); "A Survey of Interlibrary Communications Systems" (67); "Health Sciences Libraries Today" (67); Ed bd "Mississippi Library News" (64-67). 13: Yes. 14: Info systems, netwks, cent proc, user studies. 15: 1686 Winchester st, Jackson Ms 39211.

KENNEY, CORA (WAYT). b Cincinnati Ohio 17 Jl 18. 5: Ohio State U 37-40 (Journalism); Johns Hopkins 54-59 (Educ) BS; Drexel 66-68 MLS. 7: Tchr Bd of Educ Baltimore Co Md 54-61, Libn 61-66; Lib specialist Bd of Educ Anne Arundel Co Md 66-. 9: ALA; NEA; MdLA (Child & YA Div: Prog Chm 68-69; Div Chm 69-70); MdStateTA; Tchrs Assn of Anne Arundel Co. 14: Sch libs. 15: 7108 Deerfield rd, Baltimore Md 21208.

KENNEY, LOUIS AUGUSTINE. b Dorchester Neb 28 F 17. 4: Josephine Signer. 5: Neb State Tchrs Col (Kearney) 35-39 (Hist) AB; UIll 39-41, 47 BSLA, MSLS; UZurich 49-50 (Hist, Philos); UMd 54-55, 60 (Hist) PhD. 6: Fr, Ger. 7: Asst libn Engnr Lib UIll (Urbana) 40-41, 46, Bibliog acquis dept 47-48; Acquis libn UNotre Dame Lib (Notre Dame Ind) 48-54; Ser catlgr UIll Lib (Urbana) 55-57; Chief of tech serv Ill State Lib 57-59; Chief libn Air Force Inst of Tech, Wright-Patterson AFB Ohio 59-60; Col Libn San Diego State Col 61-. 9: ALA-ACRL; LRTS; AHA; SLA; CalLA (pres Palomar Dist 65). 10: Friends of the Lib, San Diego State Col, Exec Sec; AAUP; Phi Alpha Theta. 12: Ed "Staff News Bulletins" UIll, Ill State Lib & San Diego State Col. 13: Yes. 14: Admin, tech serv, data proc for univ libs. 15: 5026 Yerba Anita way, San Diego Ca 92115.

KENNEY, MARIZETTA (ROBINSON). b LaPorte Ind 13 F 43. 4: Harold Ray Kenney. 5: IndU 62-65 (Ger); Rosary Col 65-67 (Ger) BA, 67-68 MALS. 6: Ger. 7: Clk Taylor's Ben franklin Store, Culver Ind summers 57, 58; Lib asst Culver Pub Lib, Culver Ind summers 59-68; Dining hall server IndU (Bloomington) 62-63, 65, Residence hall libn 63-64, Residence hall hd libn Reed Ctr 65; Wker Rosary Col admissions off 65; Lib asst Rosary Col Lib Sch Lib 67-68; Asst libn Child dept Elkhart Pub Lib, Elkhart Ind 68, 69-. 9: ALA; IndLA. 14: Child wk, pub libs, ya wk, pub libs. 15: 213 Jefferson, Elkhart Ind 46514.

KENNICUTT, HAZELLE (GIER). b Hepler Kan 12 S 19. 4: Walter Charles Kennicutt. 5: Kansas State Col 39-44 (Educ) BS; Central Theol Sem 45-49 (Religious Educ) MRE; UDenver 62-63 (LS) MA. 6: Sp, Fr. 07: Asst libn Kan City Bible Col 54-55; Bkmob clerk Southwest Reg, Bolivar Mo 56-57; Bkmob clerk Northeast Reg, Kahoka Mo 60-61; Bkmob clerk Kinderhook Lib, Lebanon Mo 62-63; Asst libn Sch of the Ozarks, Point Lookout Mo 63-67; Assoc libn Philanders Smith Col 68-. 9: ALA; MoLA; ArkLA; SWLA. 10: Christian Commun Action, Women of the Church, John Calvin Presbytery; AAUW. 12: Ed "Commentator" (54-55). 13: Yes. 14: Catlg, acquis. 15: Ward Ar 72176.

KENT, ALLEN. b NYC 24 O 21. 4: Rosalind Kossoff. 5: City Col of NY 38-42 (Chem) BS; NYU (Metallurg testing) Certif. 6: Ger. 7: USArmyAF 42-45; Chem Essex Chem, Chester Conn 45-46; Assoc ed Intersci Publ, NYC 46-51; Research assoc MIT 51-53; Prin doc engnr Battelle Mem Inst, Columbus Ohio 53-55; Assoc dir & Prof of Lib Sci Center for Doc & Com Res & Sch of Lib Sci West Res U 55-63; Dir Knowledge Availability Systems Center, Prof Grad Sch of Lib & Info Sci Sch of Educ & Dept of Computer Sci, UPittsburgh 63-70, Dir Off of Commun Serv 70-. 8: Consul to dr Stafford Warren; Spec Asst to the Pres White House 63-64; Consul UNeb 62-63; IR Consul Diebold Inc, SCM Inc, Beekley Corp, Goodyear Aerospace Corp; Tech dir, Center for Info Serv UAkron 65-66; Lectured in ussr. spain, Brazil, Italy, Germany, Holland, England; Chm Nat Adv Com on Info Systems, Nat Inst of Neurol Diseases & Stroke 67-. 9: SLA (chm Adv Coun 53-54, chm Com on Spec Clsf 56-58); ACS (past chem Div Chem Lit, Com on Chem Documentation; AAAS (Fellow); AIC (Fellow); ACM; ASIS. 11: Eastman Kodak Award in Info Tech 68. 12: Auth, co-auth, ed & co-ed of 16 bks, mainly on info storage &

retrieval; Co-ed (with H Lancour) of "Encyclopedia of Library and Information on Science (v 1 68; v 2 69) 18 vols planned. 13: Yes. 14: Documentation & info scis. 15: 89 Mayfair dr, Mt Lebanon Pa 15228.

KENT, CHARLES DEANE. b Ottawa 30 Ag 15. 4: Barbara Elaine Russell. 5: McMaster U 35-39 (Eng, Hist) BA; McGill 44-45 BLS; UMich summer 55-56; UMd summer 67. 6: Fr. 7: Wartime Prices & Trade Bd, Ottawa 39-41; Inspection Bd of the UK & Can 41-43; Can Army ADC to Maj-Gen J H Roberts DSO MC 42-44; Asst libn London (Ont) Pub Lib & Art Museum 45; Chief libn Regina Pub Lib 45-48; Asst dir London (Ont) Pub Lib & Art Museum 48-61, Dir 61-; Dir Lake Erie Reg Lib Syst 64-. 8: Dir & sec Lake Erie Reg Lib Co-operative bd 64-; Dir & sec-treas Lake Erie Regl Lib Ststem 67-. 09: ALA (car coms); CanLA (sev coms, pres loc assns); OntLA (pres 59-60, var coms); Inst Prof Libns (pro-chm 58-59); Internat Reading Assn (pres loc coun 63-64); London (Ont) Film Soc (pres 51-52); Ont Assn Curriculum Development (coun 62-64). 10: London (Ont) Coun for Adult Educ; United Appeal; London & Middlesex Hist Soc. 11: Can Coun Fellowship 58-; Four months visit to Libs & Museums Abroad; Brit Coun visitor 63; Can Coun Travel Award 63; Tour of four Ger Libs 64. 13: Yes. 14: Pub libs, reg lib development. 15: 305 Queens ave, London Ont Canada.

KENT, DORIS (MAE KOHLER). b Buffalo NY 12 F 22. 4: Jerol Edward Kent. 5: Geneseo State Tchrs Col 39-43 (LS) BS in Ed; State U Col(Geneseo NY) Buffalo Institutional br 64-67 (LS) MS in LS. 7: Libn Williamsville High Sch, Williamsville NY 43-44; Jr libn State U Col(Buffalo NY) 48-58; Sr libn I Williamsville Pub Lib, Williamsville NY 61-63; Libn Forest Elem Sch, Williamsville NY 63-. 9: NYLA; Assn of Suburban Sch Libns. 10: Ballet Guild of Buffalo. 14: Child bks. 15: 9300 Hunting Valley rd, Clarence NY 14031.

KENT, FREDERICK JAMES. b Miami Fla 21 My 28. 5: DePauw U 46-50 (Music Organ) BM; UIll(Urbana) 50-52 (Music Composition) MM, 54-60 (Musicology),60-61 (LS) MS. 7: Cpl AGC USArmy, Ft Jackson SC 52-54; Libn I Music Dept The Free Lib of Phila 61-65, Libn III Asst head music 65-. 8: Solo organ recitals, both as student & professional. 9: ALA; MusLA (Org & Info Com); PennLA. 10: Trophy Club for Ballroom Dancers; Phila Amer Guild of Organists; Phi Mu Alpha. 11: Rector Scholar DePauw U. 14: Music ref & catlg. 15: Parkway House, 2201 Pennsylvania ave, Philadelphia Pa 19130.

KENT, JOHN W. b Binghamton NY 20 N 11. 4: Elizabeth MacLaren. 5: Washington Sq Col, NYU 46-49 (Econ) AB; Columbia 49-50 (LS) MS. 6: Sp. 7: Sec IBM, Endicott NY 33-41; Code clerk US Embassy, Bogota Columbia 41-42; 1st Lt Infantry, Pacific Area 42-46; Ref asst econ div NY Pub Lib 50-52, Ref asst info div 52-64; Head of ref dept Huntington Pub Lib, Huntington NY 64-. 9: SuffolkCoLA. 10: Phi Beta Kappa. 14: Ref. 15: 21 Old Hills lane, Greenlawn NY 11740.

KENT, KATHARINE MARY (WARD). b Toronto Can 15 F 39. 5: Victoria Col UToronto 57-61 (Eng) BA; UToronto 61-62 MLS. 6: Fr. 7: Catlgr YorkU 62-64; Circ div asst libn UBC Lib 64-67, Hd math lib 67-. 9: CanLA; ALA; Assn BC Libns (Memb Com, Publications Com). 13: Yes. 14: Ref, readers serv, info systems. 15: 201-1855 Balsam st, Vancouver 9 BC Can.

KENT, MARY ANN. b Mt Judea Ark 3 Mr 43. 5: Southwest Mo State Col 60-64 (Art) BS; Ball State U summer 64; E Tex State summer 63; Peabody 65 MLS. 6: Fr. 7: Libn Vitro Corp of Amer, Silver Springs Md 65-66; Libn Booz-Allen Applied Research Inc, Bethesda Md 66-67, Scientist 67-. 8: Wk with Booz-Allen Applied Research Inc as a consul to var govt orgs and large priv comps in Lib Systems Analysis & Lib Automation. 9: ALA; SLA; DCLA. 10: Amer Soc for Cybernetics. 12: "Phase I, Systems Analysis and Design Study for the Nat Agric Lib" (67) & Phase II, Design Study for Automated Documentation Location and Control System Nat Agric Lib" (68). 13: Yes. 14: Lib systems analysis, info systems, lib automation. 15: 4977 Battery lane 718, Bethesda Md 20014.

KENT, MARY CLARA. b Mt Judea Ark 1 Je 15. 4: Howard Kent. 5: Central Col 33; Ark State Tchrs Col Summers 36-47; Ark Tech 48-51 (Educ) BSE; UMo Summer 52; E Texas State Summers 53-55 MS in LS. 7: Tchr Mt Judea High Sch, Mt Judea Ark 34-48; Libn Deer High Sch, Deer Ark 48-51; Libn W Plains High Sch, W Plains Mo 51-55; Circ libn Southwest Mo State Col 55-, Instr in lib sci. 9: ALA; NEA; MoEA; MoLA. 10: Sch & Commun; Delta Kappa Gamma. 15: 827 McCann, Springfield Mo 65804.

KENTON, CHARLOTTE. b NYC 12 Ag 25. 5: Hunter Col 41-46 (Psych) AB; Columbia 47-50 MSLS; New Sch for Soc Research 47; Washington Sch of Psychiatry 50-53; Georgetown U; Drexel 64 (Search); Honeywell 64; American U 68 (Mgt). 6: Fr, Ger, Sp, Ital. 7: Sub-prof asst Columbia U Psych Lib Cooper Union Hunter Col Physiol Lib (NYC) 41-43; Ref libn US Merchant Marine Acad Lib Kings Pt NY 47-49; Libn ref & circ depts NY Pub Lib 42-43, 44-47; Libn Neurological Inst of NY, NYC 49-50; Ref libn Armed Forces Med Lib, Wash DC 50-53; Chief ref sect & asst libn NIH Lib, Bethesda Md 53-64; Chief MEDLARS Search Sect NLM, Bethesda Md 64-. 9: ASIS; MedLA; ACS (Div Chem Lit); Soc of Indexers. 13: Yes. 14: Computer searching, info storage & retrieval, biomed ref, systems analysis. 15: 5480 Wisconsin ave apt 1220, Chevy Chase Md 20015.

KENTON, EGON F. b Nagyszalonta Hungary 22 My 1891. 5: Royal Acad of Music (Budapest) 08-11 (Violin) Diploma; Friedrich Wilhelm U (Berlin) 11-14 (Musicology); NYU 45-47 (Musicology) MA. 6: Fr, Ger, Ital, Hungarian. 7: Concert wk & tchg assoc prof of music 11-61; Libn Mannes Col of Music 61-. 9: MusLA (chm Nomin Com; chm Greater NY Chap 63-65; Internat MusLA (Com on Clsf); Amer Musicological Soc; Internat Musicological Soc; Conn Acad of Arts & Sciences; Renaissance Soc of Amer; Col Art Assn. 12: "The Life and Works of Giovanni Gabrieli" (67). 13: Yes. 14: Clsf of mus lit. 15: 45 Overlook ter, New York NY 10033.

KENYON, CARLETON W. b Lafayette NY 7 O 23. 4: Dora Kallander. 5: Yankton Col 40-43, 46-47 (Soc Sci) BA; USD 47-50 (Hist & Law) MA & LLB; UMich 50-51 AMLS. 6: Fr. 7: Asst UNeb Law Lib 51-52; Head catlgr Los angeles Co Law Lib, Los Angeles 52-60 Law libn Cal State Lib 60-. 8: Consul LC on Class K 63; Consul Cal Co Law Libs; Instr Summer Inst for law libns 68, 69. 9: AASchL; CalLA. 10: State Bar of SD; Bar Assn; Amer Bar Assn. 12: Asst ed "Law Library Journal." 13: Yes. 14: Law lib. 15: 7504 Center parkway, Sacramento Cal 95823.

KEOGH, JEANNE M. b Toledo Ohio 20 S 24. 5: Mary Manse Col 42-46 (Eng) AB; West Res 46-47 BS in LS. 6: Fr. 7: Asst tech dept Toledo Pub Lib 47-54; Libn Libbey-Owens-Ford Glass Co Tech Center 54-. 8: Established Riverside Hosp Sch of Nursing Lib 50-51. 9: SLA (mem &/or chm Scholarship & Loan Com 68-; sec Metals/Materials Div 67-68; Mich Chap: chm Nomin Com 54-, treas 6-63; Memb chm 68-69); Ohio CathLA. 10: Area leader Muscular Dystrophy campaign 61, 62; Quota Internat; Quota Club of Toledo. 14: Tech serv, ref. 15: 1701 E Broadway, Toledo Ohio 43605.

KEOUGH, FRANCIS PAUL. b Brookline Mass 2 Ap 17. 4: Helen Drews. 5: Harvard 36-40 (Hist, Govt, Econ) AdjA; Columbia 46-47 (LS) BS. 7: Gen asst Boston Pub Lib 34-39; Asst Harvard U Archives 39-42; Personnel tech Army of the US (Sgt) 42-45; Archivist Radiation Lab Mass Inst of Tech 45-46; Ref asst Widener Lib, Harvard Col 47-51; Lib Dir Framingham Pub Lib, Framingham Mass 51-64; Lib Dir Springfield City Lib, Springfield Mass 64-. 8: Pub lib consul to Mass communs; Agawam, Amherst, Auburn, Dartmouth, Hampden, Marion, Medfield, Sherborn, S Hadley, Stoughton, Sudbury, Westport, Wilbraham; and to Lewiston Me; Portland Me; Milford Conn; N Kingstown and Warwick RI; sometimes lectr in Ref Methods and Communications, Sch Lib Sci, Simmons Col & Mass Dept of Educ. 9: ALA; NELA; MassLA (past pres, Planning Com, chm Fin Com); West Mass Lib Club. 10: West Mass Reg Pub Lib Serv; Certification Adv Com to State of Mass; Springfield Adult Educ Coun. 13: Yes. 14: Pub lib admin, pub lib bldg planning. 15: Springfield City Lib 220 State st, Springfield Mass 01103.

KEPHART, JOHN EDGAR. b Wilkinsburg Penn 4 Ja 20. 4: Thelma Wilson. 5: Penn State U 45-46; Wheaton Col (Ill) 46-48 (Hist) AB; UIll 48-49 (Hist) MA, 49-51 (LS) MS; UMich 51-60 (LS) PhD. 6: Fr, Ger. 7: Chief spec (Intelligence) USNavy 40-45; Asst libn Wheaton Col (Ill) 49-50, Libn 50-57; Educ Research libn Field Enterprises, Chicago 57-58; Ref libn Pub Lib, Ann Arbor Mich 58-59; Libn Westmont col 59-63; Asst prof Sch of Lib Sci USoCal 63-66; Prof Sch of lib sci SUNY Col at Geneseo 66-. 09: ALA-ACRL; -AASchLS; NYLA. 10: Beta Phi Mu; Phi Alpha Theta; Pi Gamma Mu. 13: Yes. 14: Ref, bibliog, hist of publ, reading of adults, admin of libs. 15: 13 Tuscarora ave, Geneseo NY 14454.

KEPNER, FRANCES (REECE). b Cayuga Ind 20 D 19. 4: Nye D Kepner. 5: Ind State U 37-41 (Eng, Hist, Mus) AB; UMich 41-42 ABLS, 42-44 AMLS. 6: Fr, Ger. 7: Jr asst catlg dept UMich, Ann Arbor 42-43; Asst curator of mss & maps Clements Lib, Ann Arbor Mich 43-46; Asst order libn Ohio State U 47-49; Act libn Thiel col 60-62, Asst libn & catlgr

62-63; Sr catlgr Ind State U 63-67, Hd catlg dept 67-. 9: ALA; BSA; IndLA; Ohio Valley Gp Tech Serv Libns. 14: catlg, rare bks, music libnship. 15: 466 Lea lane, Terre Haute In 47802.

KEPPLE, ROBERT RALPH. b Altoona Penn 26 Jl 25. 4: Beatrice Brazzel. 5: Penn State U 46-49 (Math) BS; Carnegie Inst 50-51 MS in LS. 6: Ger. 7: Scout (T/5) 16th Inf Regiment, Europe 43-45; Staff libn E I duPont de Nemours & Co, Aiken SC 51-56; Hd libn United Aircraft Corp Pratt & Whitney Div, Middletown Conn 56-61; Supv readers' serv argonne Nat Lab, Argonne Ill 61-63; Chief libn Intl Atomic Energy Agcy, Vienna Austria 63-67; Libn Johns Hopkins U Applied Physics Lab, Silver Spring Md 68-. 9: SLA; ALA; Assn Computing Machinery. 10: Phi Eta Sigma; Pi Mu Epsilon. 13: Yes. 15: 14000 Castle blvd apt 601, Silver Spring Md 20904.

KER, ROBERT HAROLD. b San Francisco Cal 6 Ag 20. 5: McGill 37-40, 44-45 (Mus) BA; Sorbonne 46-47 (Fr Lit) DES; UCal (Berkeley) 51-53 (Eng) MA, 54-55 MLS; U de La Laguna (Tenerife) 64 (Sp Lit). 6: Fr, Sp. 7: Lt Royal Navy, England 40-44; Libn (Admin) USAF, Oxford Eng 55-60; Archivist BC Archives, Victoria BC 60-63; Ref libn UVictoria 67-. 8: Research asst UCal (Berkeley) Lib 54-55. 9: CanLA (chm Can Newspaper Index Com 67-68). 14: Ref. 15: 4998 Echo dr, Victoria BC Can.

KERCHNER, DONALD H. b Lenhartsville Penn 15 F 29. 5: Kutztown State Col 49-52 (LS, Eng) BS in Ed; Syracuse 53-55 MS in LS. 6: Ger. 7: Clerk typist US Army Infantry (Tech 4th Grade), Ft Dix NJ 47-48; Libn Lawrence Jr High Sch, Trenton NJ 52-55; Libn Nurnberg Amer High Sch, Nurnberg Germany 55-57; Libn Tokyo Amer High Sch, Tokyo Japan 57-58; Asst libn Slippery Rock State Col 58-59; Asst libn West Chester State Col 59-62; Libn Abraham Levitt Jr Sch, Willingboro NJ 62-. 9: NEA; NJEA. 10: Beta Phi Mu; Pi Lambda Sigma; Alpha Beta Alpha. 14: Sch libs. 15: Lenhartsville Penn 19534.

KERETH, DANIEL D. b Vienna Austria 24 Mr 18. 5: Rockland Commun Col 59-62 (Liberal Arts) AA; SUNY 62-64 (Pol Sci) BA; Pratt Inst 64-65 MLS. 6: Ger, Hebrew. 7: Catlgr Brooklyn Pub Lib, NY 64-66; Adult serv libn Patchogue Lib, Patchogue NY 66-68; Chief libn Leo Baeck Inst, NY 68-. 9: ALA. 14: Rare bks, catlg. 15: Leo Baeck Inst 129 E 73rd st, New York NY 10021.

KERFOOT, JEAN RODGERS. b Picton Ont Can 26 N 16. 5: UToronto 35-38 BA; McGill 46-47 BLS. 7: Lib asst Legis Lib, Toronto 39-46, Sr libn 47-63, Libn 63-. 9: CanLA; SLA; Inst Prof Libns (Ont). 14: Catlg, ref. 15: 511 Spadina rd, Toronto 10 Can.

KERKER, ANN ELIZABETH. b Butte Mont 19 My 12. 5: Purdue U 29-33 (Bacteriology) BS; UIll 57-59 (LS) MS. 6: Sp. 7: Med tech Arnett Clinic, Lafayette Ind 33-45; Med tech & x-ray Tropical Oil Co, El Centro & Barranquilla Colombia SA 45-49; Sr tech Arabian-Amer Oil Co, Dhahran Saudi Arabia 50-52; Med tech Lago Oil & Transport Co, Aruba Netherlands West Indies 52-55; Lib asst Purdue U 56-59, Med libn 59-, Assoc Prof 67-. 9: ALA- ACRL (sec Agr & Biol Sci Subsect 62-65, Internat Round Table 63-, Reading for an Age of Change 64-67; SLA (Adv Coun 68-, Ind Chap Memb Chm 62-63, sec 65-66, v-pres & pres-elect 68-); MedLA (treas 68-; Midwest Reg Group: sec 63-64, chm 64-65); IndLA. 10: Beta Phi Mu; AAUW; Delta Theta Tau; Univ Club(Purdue); Cath Daughters of Amer; Digby Investment Club. 12: Co-auth "The Reference Library in Microbiology" (59); Co-auth "Literature Sources in the Biological Sciences" (61); Co-auth "Biological and Biomedical Resource Literature." (68). 13: Yes. 14: Med ref & bibliog, consul on organiz & planning veter med libs. 15: Sch of Veterinary Medicine, Purdue Univ, Lafayette In 47907.

KERN, BARBARA J. b Berlin Germany 24 F 36. 5: Portland State U 55-59 (Gen Studies) BA; UWash 59-60 MLS. 6: Ger. 7: Libn in lit & hist dept Lib Assn of Portlanf, Ore 60-65, Mus libn 65-. 9: MusLA; PNLA. 10: Ore Hist Soc. 14: Ref. 15: 801 SW 10th ave, portland Or 97205.

KERN, MARILYN JUNE. b Madison Wis 3 Mr 36. 5: UWis (Milwaukee) 54-59 (Geog) BS; UWis 65-66 (LS) MS. 6: Fr. 7: Child libn Maui Pub Lib: Kahului Hawaii 66-67, Wailuku Hawaii 67-. 9: ALA; HawaiiLA. 10: Maui Toastmistress Club; Maui Philharmonic Soc; Maui Arts Coun; AAUW. 14: Wk with child, ref. 15: PO Box 272, Kahului Hi 96732.

KERNAN, MARY ANNE. b Louisville Ky 5 Ap 18. 5: Agnes Scott Col 34-38 (Eng) AB; Emory 38-39 BALS, 47-49 (Eng) MA. 7: Asst in chg sch ext wk & asst boys & girls dept Atlanta Pub Lib 39-42, Reader's adv & circ asst 42-43; Base libn US Army AF 36th st Air Base, Miami Fla 43-44; Post libn US Army AF Gulfport Army Air Field Miss 44-45; Army libn USArmy Germany US Occupation Area 45-46; Law libn Emory U Sch of Law 47-54; Bibliog & ref asst Air U (Maxwell AFB Ala) 54-65; Ref libn U of the South 65-66; Ref libn Joint U Libs, Nashville 66-. 9: ALA; SELA; TennLA. 10: Phi Beta Kappa; Beta Phi Mu. 13: Yes. 14: Ref, bk sel, bibliog, admin. 15: 602 Bowling ave, Nashville Tn 37215.

KERR, AUDREY MARY (CATHERINE). b Winnipeg Man Can 25 D 32. 5: UMan 49-53 BA; UBC 62-63 BLS. 7: Research asst biochem UMan 53-59; Lab tech Food & Drug Directorate Govt of Can, Winnipeg 59-62; Med libn UMan 63-, Asst Prof 63-. 8: Spec com on Lib Resources for the Health Sci in Can 65-. 9: MedLA; CanLA (Med Sci Libs Com); ManLA (pub chm). 10: Winnipeg Art Gallery. 13: Yes. 15: Med Lib 770 Bannatyne ave, Winnipeg 3 Manitoba Can.

KERR, HELEN (FLETCHER). b Trochu Alberta Can 2 Ap 25. 5: Prince of Wales Col 41-45; Mt Allison 46-47 (Math) BA; McGill 48-49 BLS; UAlberta 58-60 BEd, 61-63 (Philos) MA. 6: Fr. 7: Tchr: N Bedeque Sch Bd, N Bedeque PEI Can 45-46, Stellarton Sch Bd, Stellarton NS Can 47-48, Sydney Sch Bd, Sydney Australia 53-54, Durban Sch Bd, Durban S Africa 54, Dept of Educ, Edmonton Alta Can 57-61, Edmonton Pub Sch Bd, Edmonton Alta Can 63-64; Catlgr Provincial Archives, Victoria BC Can 49-53; Libn Montreal Prot sch Bd 55-57; High sch libn Edmonton Pub Sch Bd, Edmonton Alta Can 64-67; Lib supv sturgeon Sch Div, Morinville Alta Can 67-. 8: Evening credit & summer sch lectr in sch Lib Sci UAlta 66-67, 69. 9: CanLA; ALA; AltaTA; AltaLA; Sch Lib Coun. 11: Delta Kappa Gamma. 13: Yes. 14: Sch libs. 15: 607 Stanley Towers 10040 - 114 st, Edmonton 11 Alberta Can.

KERR, HELENA (MATHILDE FOUQUET). b Andale Kan 10 My 07. 4: Gorden Harris Kerr. 5: Adams State Col 26-30, 51-55 (Eng, Educ) BA; UDenver 57-62 (LS) MA. 7: Tchr Alamosa Co Schs, Alamosa Colo 26-28; Tchr Del Norte Consolidated Schs, Del Norte Colo 28-29; Tchr 30-33; Tchr Sargent Sch, Monte Vista Colo 51-55, Libn 55-. 9: ALA; NEA; ColoLA (chm Sch Div 68-69); MPLA; ColoASchL (treas Bd; So Div: dir & bd mem 66-); ColoEA (chm Lib Sect So Div). 10: San Luis ValleyEA; Kappa Kappa Iota; Inter Nos Study Club; Pueblo Coun of Cath Women. 14: Sch libs. 15: RR1, Monte Vista Colo 81144.

KERR, JEANNETTE (AGNES). b Fall River Mass 4 S 19. 4: Doyle John Kerr. 5: Orange Coast Col 58-60 (Eng) AA; Cal State (Long Beach) 62-64 (Eng) AB; UCLA 64-65 MLS. 7: Asst libn Orange Coast Col 65-68; Asst libn ref & instr in lib sci Chapman Col 68-. 9: CalLA; CalSchLA. 14: Ref, bibliog. 15: 850 Governor st, Costa Mesa Cal 92627.

KERR, ROBERT RIGGS. b New Alexandria Penn 15 F 21. 5: Hunter Col 47-50 (Eng Lit) AB; Columbia 50-51 (LS) MS. 6: Fr. 7: Costume designer free-lance, Pittsburgh, NYC 39-42; Personnel tech US Army (Sgt), Ft Dix 42-46; Lib asst City Col(NY) 50-51; Libn The Newark(NJ) Museum 51-67; Supv of catlg Pierpont Morgan Lib, NYC 67-. 9: Amer Assn Museums. 10: Phi Beta Kappa. 13: Yes. 14: Catlg. 15: The Pierpont Morgan Lib, 29 E 36th st, New York NY 10016.

KERR, STEPHEN RENWICK. b Oil City Penn 13 Ja 39. 5: Penn State 56-60 (Pol Sci) BA; Dickinson Sch of Law 63-64 (Law); Case West Res 65-66 MSLS. 7: Admin asst Fed Aviation Ad, Albuquerque 60-62; Field advertising Proctor & Gamble, Cincinnati 62-63; Lib intern Cuyahoga Co Pub Lib Cleveland Ohio 64-66, Adult serv lib 66-68; Interlib loan libn Fla AtlanticU 68-. 9: ALA; FlaLA; SELA. 14: Ref. 15: Florida Atlantic Univ, Boca Raton Fl 33432.

KERRIGAN, HELEN (C). b Dupont Penn 13 Ag 25. 4: Joseph A Kerrigan. 5: Marywood Col 43-47 (LS) AB; Villanova 66- (LS) MS. 6: Polish, Fr. 7: Circ asst Osterhout Free Lib, Wilkes Barre Penn 47-49, Hd circ 49-50; Circ asst Falrey Memorial Lib Villanova U 63-66, Hd circ 66-. 8: Changed the circ system at Villanova U to Electronic Data Proc. 9: ALA; CathLA. 10: Chi Ro Club; Drexel Swim Club. 11: St Pius X Lib Sci Award, Marywood Col 47. 14: Electronic data proc & its pertinence to the lib. 15: 500 s central blvd, Broomall Pa 19008.

KERSEY, BARBARA JUNE. b Enid Okla 11 Jl 33. 5: Okla City U 51-55 (Eng) BA; UOkla 61-63 MLS. 7: Lib asst Okla U Med Center Lib 55-62, Asst libn tech serv 63-. 9: MedLA; OklaLA. 10: Okla Ornithological Assn. 14: Catlg, ref. 15: 4336 NW 44th, Oklahoma City Ok 73112.

KERSEY, LAURA. b Newnan Ga 15 Ag 06. 5: Shorter Col 23-27 (Lat, Hist) AB; UGa summers 27-30 (Hist); Emory 29-30

BA in LS. 6: Sp. 7: Tchr Shorter High Sch, Shorter Ala 27-28; Tchr Minor Sch, Birmingham Ala 28-29; Engnr libn U Tenn 30-41; Speed sch libn ULouisville 41-. 9: ALA; KyLA; Louisville Lib Club. 14: Deptl or tech libn. 15: Speed Sci Sch Univ of Louisville, Louisville Ky 40208.

KERSTING, LUCILLE (ZYNDA). b Buffalo NY 19 Je 42. 4: Richard F Kersting. 5: D'Youville Col 60-64 (Eng) BA; Rutgers 64-66 MLS. 6: Fr. 7: Bibliogr PrincetonU Lib 65; Sr libn Buffalo & Erie Co Pub Lib, Buffalo NY 66-. 10: Libs Assn of Buffalo Pub Lib. 14: Ref (sci & tech). 15: 1617 Kensington ave, Buffalo NY 14215.

KERSTING, RICHARD. b Buffalo NY 30 Ag 37. 4: Lucille Kersting. 5: Buffalo State Tchrs Col 55-60 (Art Educ) BS; Syracuse 61-62 (Educ) MS, 64-65 MSLS. 6: Slavic, Germanic. 7: Art tchr Potsdam Jr High Sch, Potsdam NY 60-61; Libn trainee Buffalo & Erie Co Pub Lib, Buffalo NY 63-64, Libn (jr-sr I) 65-. 10: Libns Assn Buffalo & Erie Co Pub Lib. 14: Ref. 15: 1617 Kensington ave, Buffalo NY 14215.

KERSWILL, DOROTHEA. b Brooklyn NY 10 S 19. 4: Edgar H Kerswill. 5: Brooklyn Col 36-40 (Ger, Fr) BA (cum laude), 50 (Ger, Fr) MA; Queens Col (NY) 64-68 MLS. 6: Ger, Fr. 7: Sec Nat Bd YWCA, NYC 41-44; Translator Fed Govt, NYC 44; Tchr various secondary schs, NYC 51-60; Libn-in-charge Bushwick High Sch, Brooklyn NY 60-. 9: NYC Sch Libns Assn. 14: Sch libnship. 15: 244-23-87 ave, Bellerose NY 11426.

KERTLAND, DIANA CATHERINE. b Montreal 4 Ap 39. 5: Bishop's U 57-61 (Hist) BA; McGill 61-62 BLS. 7: Asst personnel admin off (Flight Cadet) Royal Can Air Force, Comox BC summer 60; Clerk-statistics Nat Research Coun, Ottawa summer 61; Personnel admin off (F/O) RCAF (Aux), Montreal 62-64; Housing off (F/O) RCAF, Trenton Ont summer 62; Asst libn Air Canada, Montreal 62-63; Circ libn Brock U, St Catharines Ont 64-66; Hd acquis Sir George Williams U Lib, Montreal 66-. 08: U seminar leader Brock U 65-66. 9: ALA; CanLA (Subcom on Train Lib Tech); Inst Prof Libns of Ont; QueLA. 10: Royal Canadian Airforce Assn; YWCA; McGill Alumni Assn; Bishop's U Alumni Assn; Canadian Sport Parachuting Assn. 14: Period, circ, acquis. 15: 2500 Benny Crescent apt 704, Montreal 261 Que Can.

KERTZ, A MARGARET (DONOVAN). b Jamestown N Dak 5 N 25. 4: Victor L Kertz. 5: Valley city State Teachers Col 41-43, 48; U N Dak 43-45 (Journalism) BA; UMinn 66 (LS) MA. 6: Sp. 7: News ed Cav Co Republican, Langdon N Dak 45-48; Tchr Langdon Pub Sch Dist, Langdon N Dak 49-52; Tchr High Sch, Osnabrock 53-56, 57-58; Tch & libn LANGDON High Sch, Langdon N Dak 58-. 9: ALA; NEA; NDEA. 10: Phi Beta Kappa; Beta Phi Mu; Theta Sigma Phi. 14: Sch libs. 15: 312 12th ave, Langdon ND 58249.

KESHKEKIAN, MISS SHAKE. b Khartoum Sudan 22 F 34. 5: UKhartoum (Sudan) 50-54 (Liberal Arts) Diploma; Sch of Libnship Northwestern Polytech (London) 57-58 Certif. 6: Armenian, Fr, Arabic, Ger. 7: Asst libn UKhartoum Lib, Khartoum Sudan 54-65; Libn I Stanford U Lib 65-, Libn III 68-. 10: Philos soc of the Sudan. 14: Catlg, ref. 15: 990 College ave, Palo Alto Ca 94306.

KESSEL, (MARGUERITE) BERTA (BALDWIN). b DeLand Fla 10 F 11. 4: Edward L Kessel. 5: UCLA 28-30 (Botany); UCal (Berkeley) 30-35 (Entomology) BS, MS, 39-40 (Educ) Secondary Credentials, 65-67 MLS. 7: Instr & lecturer (botany & zoology): Col of Marin, San Francisco State Col, USan Francisco 37-55; Asst in ornithology & mammalogy cal Acad of Sci, San Francisco 51-54; Asst ref libn Col of Marin 67; Asst catlg libn mills Col 67-. 8: Extensive entomolog field wk with husband in N Amer north of Mexico. 9: ALA; CalLA. 10: Phi Sigma; Beta Phi Mu; UCal Sch of Libnship Alum Assn; Pacific coast Entomolog Soc; Ecologic Soc of Amer; Save-the-Redwoods League; Nature Conserv; Marin Co Recr Com; N Marin Planning Com; Marin Co Com on Racial Discrimination; Marin com for Fair Play in Housing; Marin Coun on Civic Affairs; Wildlife Fed. 12: Circulation Mgr of "Wasmann Journal of Biology". 13: Yes. 14: Catlg. 15: PO Box 265, Novato Ca 94947.

KESSELRING, MARION LOUISE. b Clifton NJ 30 Ag 09. 5: Wheaton Col(Norton Mass) 27-31 (Eng Lit) AB; Columbia 36-38 BS in LS; Brown 39-43 (Eng & Amer Lit) AM. 6: Fr, Ger. 7: Asst catlg, circ, ref Wheaton Col Lib(Norton Mass) 31-38; Catlgr, reviser of catlg Brown U Lib 38-64, Asst chief catlg libn 64-. 8: Instr in lib sci, URI, 63. 9: ALA; BSA; RILA; NETechServLibns (chm 49-50). 10: RI Hist Soc; RI Wheaton Club; Providence Preserv Soc. 12: "Hawthorne's Reading, 1828-1850" (49). 15: 181 Williams st, Providence Ri 02906.

KESSI, MARY. b Hood River Ore 11 Ja 07. 5: UOre 32-36 (Eng Lit) BA, 37-39 (Eng, Romance Langs) MA; UCal (Berkeley) 39-41 (Eng, Romance Langs, Ital); UNC 49-50 BS in LS. 6: Fr, Ital, Ger. 7: Child libn Prince Georges Co Mem Lib, Hyattsville Md 49-52; Child libn Klamath Co Lib, Klamath Falls Ore 52-54; Child libn Shasta Co Lib, Redding Cal 55-62; Asst libn SoCal Col 62-64, Ref libn 64-, Asst prof Lit & Romance Langs 62-66, Hd libn 66-. 9: ALA; Nat Story League; CalLA; Cal Folklore Soc; Shakespeare Soc. 10: AAUW; Nat Assn Internat Rel Clubs; Phi Beta Kappa. 13: Yes. 14: Child lit, Folklore, ref. 15: Southern California Col, Costa Mesa Ca 92627.

KESSLER, LIBBIE. b Bay City Mich 14 O 13. 5: Bay City Jr Col 32-34 (Liberal Arts) AA; UMich 38 (Hist) AB; UIll 42 (LS) MA. 6: Ger, Sp. 7: Asst libn Central High Sch, Bay City Mich 34; Libn Bay City Jr Col 42; Dir of lib Delta Col 61-, Dir of lib Saginaw Valley Col 66-. 8: Org doctor's lib in hosp & nursing lib in Bay City Mich 39, 40; Wkd in directing Church lib 64; Org childs lib and c lass for tchrs in child lit 66-. 9: ALA (Life mem); MichLA; Mich Higher Educ Assn. 10: AAUW; AAUP. 14: Admin, acquis; tchrg. 15: 112 N Grant st, Bay City Mi 48706.

KESSLER, S SIM. b NYC 31 My 26. 4: Geraldine Greenberg. 5: Brooklyn Col 43-50 (Biol) BA; Yale 50-52 (Physiol) MS. 6: Fr, Ger, Sp, Ital, Russian. 07: (Cpl) US Army, US & Pacific 44-46; Asst ed Biological Abstracts, Phila 52-53; Info off Nat Drug Co, Phila 53-58; Dir Medical Literature Inc, Phila 59-; Pres Scientific Literature Consultants Inc, Phila 58-. 9: ASIS; ACS; Amer Translators Assn; MedLA; SLA. 10: AAAS; Phila Physiol Soc; Phil Biochem Club. 13: Yes. 14: Med & other sci info, tr, data-proc. 15: Medical Literature Inc, 37 S 20th st, Phila Pa 19103.

KESSLER, SELMA P (OSTROW). b Atlantic City NJ 31 Ag 22. 4: Alan Kessler. 5: UPenn 39-43 (Pol Sci) BA; Drexel 63-65 MSLS. 6: Fr. 7: Wage rate analyst War Labor Bd & Wage Stabilization Bd, Phila 43-46; Research asst Hosp Assn of Phila 47-48; Ed asst Amer Friends Serv Com, Phila 48-50; Bkkeeper Kessler Bros, Riverton NJ 51-63; Libn Temple Sinai, Cinnaminson NJ 63-; Lib Dir Gloucester City Lib, Gloucester City NJ 65-. 8: Lecturer, Sem in Synagogue Libnship, Drexel, 65; Guest lectr, Drexel Lib Sch 68, 69. 9: ALA; JewishLA; NJLA (chm Trustee Award Com 68, 69). 10: Phi Beta Kappa; Beta Phi Mu; Phi Kappa Phi. 11: John Cotton Dana Award 67. 12: "Bibliography on Industry-Wide Bargaining" (47). 13: Yes. 14: Admin. 15: 10 Oriole WY, Moorestown NJ 08057.

KESSLER, YALE KENNETH. b Peebles Ohio 26 Jl 03. 4: Clara Pol lock. 5: Ohio Wesleyan U 20-21, 22-25 (Pol Sci) BA; Syracuse 25-26 (Pol Sci) MA; Ohio State U 32-35; UIll 38-39 BS in LS. 7: Instr Ohio Wesleyan U 27-30; Asst prof 30-32; Instr Penn State Col 35-36; Asst prof Ohio Wesleyan U 36-38; Asst libn Neb State Tchrs Col, Wayne Neb 39-50, Assoc libn 50-61; Head libn Wayne State Col, Wayne, Neb 61-. 9: ALA; NebEA; NebLA (pres 50-51). 10: Beta Phi Mu; Pi Gamma Mu; Pi Sigma Alpha; Kiwanis Club. 14: Ref. 15: 509 Pearl st, Wayne Nb 68787.

KESTER, DIANE KATHERINE (DAVIES). b Oak Park Ill 21 N 37. 4: Daniel Douglas Kester. 5: Tex Woman's U 55-59 (LS) BA/BS; E Car U 67-69 (LS) MA in Ed. 7: Libn Runnels Jr High Sch, Big Spring Tex 59-60; Asst libn Howard Co Free Lib, Big Spring Tex 63; Libn Protestant Sunday Sch Lib, Webb AFB Tex 64-67; Libn Central High Sch (Grades 1-12), Goldsboro NC 67-. 9: ALA; TexLA; NEA-DAVI; NCLA; NCEA. 10: AAUW; Friends of Howard Co Lib. 14: Sch libs. 15: Rte 4 Box 432a, Goldsboro Nc 27530.

KESTER, ELZIE MARIE (HALL). b Union City Penn 27 Ap 12. 4: Harvey R Kester. 5: Geneseo State Normal Sch 33-34 (Elem Educ) Tchg Certif; UColo Spring 57 (Educ); SUNY (Geneseo) summer 57 (Educ) BS; UDenver summer 59-61 (LS) MA. 7: Tchr NY State 30-40; Elem tchr-libn Denver Pub Schs 55-, Coord of elem educ (wk with libns) Denver Pub Sch 66-. 8: Spec assignment help establish libs for six new elem libs in Denver Pub Schs. 9: NEA; ACEI; ColoEA; Colo State ASchL; (Colo Assn; Admin & Supvrs Assn). 10: Denver Tchrs Club; Admin, Women in Educ. 14: Child lit. 15: 1694 S Knox Court. Denver Co 80219.

KETCHERSID, ARTHUR LLOYD. b Neptune Beach NJ 16 O 32. 4: Betty Tindell. 5: Palm Beach Jr Col 56-57; Fla StateU 57-59 (Hist) BS, 60-61 (LS) MS; UWis 59-60 (Hist). 7: Personnel A-1C USAF 51-55; Catlgr UGa Libs 61-64, 1st asst catlg libn 64-67; Chief tech serv Fla Tech U (Orlando) 67-. 9: ALA; FlaLA. 10: Phi Beta Kappa; Beta Phi Mu; Phi Kappa Phi. 14: Catlg. 15: 1311 Chipola trail, Maitland Fl 32751.

KETOLA, HELEN M. b Lima Ohio 9 Mr 15. 5: Chicago Tchrs Col 38 (Elem Educ) Elem Certif; UNM 49 (Sci in Educ) BS; UDenver 62 (LS) MA. 7: Spec educ tchr Chicago Pub Schs 39-42; WAAC and WAC Non-Comm'd officer Ft Des Moines Train Center & Los Alamos 43-46; US Women's Army Corps Intelligence Spec Staff Sgt Occupied Japan & 4th AF Hdqtrs, Hamilton Field Cal 46-48; Group sec Los Alamos Sci Lab, Los Alamos NM 49-54; Elem tchr Los Alamos Schs, Los Alamos NM 54-59; Libn Pueblo Jr High Sch, Los Alamos NM 59-. 8: Consul Jr High Sch Lib Catlg The H W Wilson Co 65-68. 9: NEA; ALA; NMEA; NMLA (Intel Freedom chm 64-65; t reas 66-67, v-pres 67-68, pres 68-69). 14: Sch libs, ya. 15: 3811 Gold st apt 2, Los Alamos NM 87544.

KETTNER, DOROTHY (HAGEN). b Oakes ND 23 Mr 43. 4: Curtis F Kettner. 5: ND State Sch of Sci 61-63 AAS; St Cloud State Col 63-65 (Eng) BA; UMinn 65-66 MLS. 6: Ger. 7: Tech serv SW Minn State Col 66-. 9: MinnLA. 14: Catlg, admin. 15: 1306 Birch apt 17, Marshall Mn 56258.

KETTNER, IRENE MARY. b Edmonton Alta Can 6 Ag 29. 4: Edgar Kettner. 7: Catlg, asst & gen libn Okanagan Reg Lib Kelowna BC Can 51-52; Asst to libn UAlta (Calgary Br) 52-57; Libn in chg French Petroleum Co Ltd, Calgary Alta 57-59; Libn in chg Sun Oil Co, Calgary Alta 59-. 9: CanLA; SLA; A ltaLA; Geosci Info Soc. 14: Spec libs, ref. 15: Lib Sun Oil Co PO Drawer 38, Calgary Alta Canada.

KETZLE, MARIENNE (RUTH). b Davenport Iowa 30 Je 38. 5: Lawrence Col 56-60 (Hist) BA; Fla State U 61-63 (LS) MS. 7: Tchr-libn St Katharine's Sch for Girls, Davenport Iowa 60-62; Catlg libn Jacksonville Pub Lib, Jacksonville Fla 63-. 9: FlaLA (past chm Catlg RT); Duval CoLA. 10: AAUW. 14: Catlg. 15: 5762 Green Palm lane apt 2, Jacksonville Fl 32211.

KEY, JACK DAYTON. b Enid Okla 24 F 34. 4: Virgie Richardson. 5: PhillipsU 55-58 (Hist) BA; UNM 59-60 (Hist) MA; UIll 60-62 (LS) MS. 6: Sp. 7: YN2 US Navy 52-55; Asst med libn Lovelace Found, Albuquerque NM 59-60; Staff supv circ dept, Urbana 60-62; Pharmacy libn UIowa 62-65; Assoc med libn Lovelace Found, Albuquerque NM 65-66, Libn 66 . 9: MedLA; (Prog Planning Com 68-69, Curr Com 67-70; chm Pharmac Gp 67-68); Amer Inst Hist Pharm; SLA (Statist Com 69-71; Sci -Tech Div: Com on Div & Sec Structure 66-68; Rio Grande Chap: Pres 67-68; chm Awards Com); NMLA (treas 68-69, Adv Coun 67-71). 12: Comp "Cumulative Index to the Proceedings of the Amer Assn of Cols of Pharm Tchr's Seminars, 59-63" (64). 13: Yes. 14: Med & pharm hist, ref. 15: Lovelace Med Found 5200 Gibson blvd SE, Albuquerque NM 87108.

KEYS, THOMAS EDWARD. b Greenville Miss 2 D 08. 4: Elizabeth Schaack. 5: Beloit Col 27-31 (Econ) AB; UChicago 32-34 (LS) MA. 7: Order asst Newberry Lib, Chicago 31-32; Asstship UChicago Grad Lib Sch 33-34; Asst to lib M ayo Clinic, Rochester Minn 34-35, Ref libn 35-42; Lt Col Officer-in-chg Army Med Lib, Cleveland Br 42-46; Libn Mayo Clinic, Rochester Minn 46- 69; Prof hist of med Mayo Grad Sch Med 63-; Sr Lib Consult 69-. 8: Hon consul Army Med Lib 46-50; Mem Bd Regents NLM 59-62. 9: MedLA (pres 57-58); Amer Assn Hist Med; Amer Assn Anesthesiologists (hon mem); Minn Soc of Anesthesiologists (hon); SLA. 10: Mayo Found Soc-Hist Med; Izaak Walton League; Phi Beta Kappa, Beta Phi Mu Sigma Xi, Rotary; Boy Scouts. 11: Distinguished Service Citation Beloit Col 56; MedLA Noyes Award for Distinguished Serv to Med Libnship 66. 12: "Cardiac Classics," with F A Willius (41, reprinted in 2 vol 61); "The Development of Anesthesia" (43); "History of Surgical Anesthesia" (45 Dover ed 62); "Applied Med Lib Practice" (58); "Foundations of Anesthesiology," with A Faulconer 2 vols (65). 13: Yes. 14: Admin, hist of med. 15: Sunny Slopes, Rochester Mn 55901.

KEYSER, BARBARA D(ASKAM). b Burbank Fla 2 Mr 13. 4: Charles H Keyser. 5: West Md Col 29-33 (Educ) AB; San Diego State Col 53-60 (Personnel Supv & Train Govt) MA; USoCal 60-64 Active secondary tching credential MSLS. 7: Soc wkr Baltimore Emergency Relief Commsn & Dept of Pub Welfare, Baltimore & Wash DC 35-37; Typist & jr asst DC Pub Lib 37-38; Clk-steno US Army, Far E Command, SCAP, Tokyo Japan 50-51; Stock control clk USN Naval Supply Ctr, San Diego 57-60; Ref libn Scripps Inst of Oceanography UCal (San Diego) 60-. 8: Resource Spec, Interlib Task Force, San Diego Cal 68-. 9: SLA; CalLA; Marine Tech Assn (San Diego). 14: Ref, ser, tech proc. 15: 7128 Dennison pl, San Diego Ca 92122.

KEYSERLING, POLLY LEA (JACOBSON). b Winston Salem NC 31 Ag 16. 5: UNC 32-35 (Eng) AB, 35-35 AB in LS. 6: Fr, Ger, Yiddish. 7: Lib asst DukeU 36-37; Catlgr UMd Dental Col, Baltimore 37-38; Catlgr Enoch Pratt Free Lib, Baltimore 38-41; Army libn, Va, SC, Fla 39-45; Catlgr UMiami, Miami Fla 47-50; Libn MCAS, Beaufort SC 57-. 9: ALA; (Armed Forces Sect: Memb Com, chm Awards Com); SCLA; SELA. 10: AAUW; PTA; Beth Israel Aux. 11: Superior Performance Civilian Award. 14: Catlg. 15: 113 Elliott st, Beaufort SC 29902.

KHO, JAMES SAYCHOON. b China 15 S 36. 4: Agnes Yewcheng. 5: NanyangU (Singapore) (Hist) BA; UOttawa 65 BLS. 6: Chinese, Malay, Fr. 7: Catlgr Mt AllisonU Lib 65-67; Asst ref libn USingapore 67-68; Catlgr Bishop'sU Lib 68-. 9: ALA; CanLA; CACUL; LA of Singapore & Malaysia. 14: Catlg, ref. 15: 1060 Federal st, Sherbrooke Que Can.

KHOURI, LAURICE (MARGO). b Cranford NJ. 5: Barnard 40-44 (Econ) BA; Pratt 60-62 MLS. 6: Fr, Sp. 7: Serv club dir US Aeermany 56-58 AT ERVS LI Bo Pub Lib 62-63; Catlgr Nassau Commun Col 63-64; Catn m Ref Lib, Brooklyn NY 62-. 9: SLA (Mus Sect); NY Lib Club; Nassau Co LA. 10: Beta Phi M. 14 atlg, at bks. 14: Catlg, art bks. 15: Brooklyn Museum, 188 Eastern pky, Brooklyn NY 11238.

KIBBE, LUCENA J(ULIA). b Sidney NY 16 Ag 17. 5: Hartwick Col 34-38 (Fr) BA; Syracuse 41-42 (LS) BS. 6: Fr. 7: Lib asst Thrall Lib (pub), Middletown 42-50; Catlgr Harpur col 50-60; Hd technical processes Mid-York Lib Syst Rome 60-. 9: ALA; NYLA. 14: Catlg. 15: 912 Shaw st, Utica NY 13502.

KIBBIE, ELOISE (PERKINS). b Sac City Mr 14. 5: Rockford Col 32-34; State U Iowa 34-36 (Journalism) BA; UWis summer 49; UDenver 58-59 (LS) MA. 7: News ed Sac Sun Co, Sac City Iowa 37-40; Libn Sac City Pub Lib, Sac City Iowa 46-58; Ref libn Central Mo State Col 59-. 9: ALA; MoLA. 10: AAUP; AAUW;DR; Northwest Iowa Shuttle Guild; Midwest Weavers; Pi Beta Phi; PEO. 14: Ref, govt docs. 15: 205 Broad st, Warrensburg Mo 64093.

KIBLER, FLOREINE (WHARTON). b DeWitt Mo. 5: Northeast Mo SS Col 31-35 (OME Econ) BS in Educ; Peabody Col 55-56 MA in LS. 7: Home econ instr high sch, Memphis Mo 35-36; Ref libn State Tchrs Col, Kirksville Mo 56-, Asst dir 64-. 9: MoLA; NE Mo State Tchrs Assn; NE Mo aschL (treas). 10: Kappa DETAPi. 14: Ref. 15: 805 S Elson, Kirksville Mo 63501.

KIDD, CAROL ELIZABETH (SCHMOYER). b Allentown Penn 24 D 44. 4: Thomas Charles Kidd. 5: Kutztown State Col 62-65 (Lib Educ), 66-67 (Lib Educ) BS Ed. 7: Research libn kawecki Berylco Ind Inc, Boyertown Penn 67-. 9: ALA; Berks Co Spec Libns. 14: Child and yp libs. 15: Box 246, Zionville Pa 18092.

KIDD, DEBORAH (DOVE). b Wash DC 3 My 41. 4: Lester D Kidd II. 5: Longwood Col (Farmville Va) 59-63 (Eng) BA; CatholicU 65-68 MS in LS. 6: Sp. 7: Tchr Quantico High Sch Marine Corps Sch, Quantico Va 63-65; Grad lib asst CatholicU Lib Sci Lib 65-67; Ref libn Fairfax Co Pub Lib, Fairfax Va 68, Catlgr 68-. 9: VaLA. 14: Catlg. 15: 7408 Tower st, Falls Church Va 22046.

KIDD, JERRY S. b Decatur Ill 29 O 28. 4: Renee A (St John). 5: Ill Wesleyan U 46-50 (Biol) BS; Northwestern U 52-55 (Psych) MA (PhD). 7: Training specialist Rand Corp, Santa Monica Cal 55-56; Assoc dir Lab of Aviation Psychol, Ohio State U 56-61; Research consul (independent) 61-62, 64-65; Prin staff scientist Aircraft Armamets, Baltimore 62-64; Prog dir Off of Sci Info Serv, NSF 65-67; Prof Sch of Lib & Info Serv UMd 67-. 8: Consul, Inst for Defense Analyses. 9: ASIS (treas SIG/BSS); Human Factors Soc; Amer Psychol Assn; ALA; SLA; Amer Soc Planning Libns. 12: Mng ed "Human Factors" (67-69). 14: Systems devel, user needs. 15: 303 Cedarcroft rd, Baltimore Md 21212.

KIDDER, (CHARLES) PETER. b SI NY 30 Ag 25. 4: Harriet Wright. 5: Ripon Col 44-45, 47-48; UWis 48-50 (Econ) BA, 52-53 MA in LS. 6: Fr, Japanese. 7: Japanese student & Jr clerk Off of Defense Transporta tion, Wash DC 43-44; CIC Investigator (Cpl) US Army, US 45-47; Aerial Photo interpreter (Sgt) US Army, Korea 50-52; Libn I youth libn Detroit Pub Lib 53-54; Asst catlgr Colgate U Lib, 54-57; Asst libn Washington Col Lib, Chestertown Md 57-60; Head of tech serv Denison U Lib 60-63; Head catlgr Kenyon Col Lib 63-68; Descr catlgr LC 68-. 9: ALA; DCLA; Potomac Tech Proc Libns. 10: . 12: Programmed learning text on LC card routine for clerks 66. 14: Catlg, ref. 15: 10211 Conn ave, Kensington Md 20795.

KIDDER, CONNIE (HELEN CONLEY). b Augusta Ga 29 S 15 5: Ward Belmont Sch 31-33; Mt Holyoke 33-35 (Eng) AB; UCal 50 BLS. 7: Sec & ed wk Amer Youth Hostels, Northfield Mass 354sec Underwoodelliot-Fisher Co, Hartford Conn 40-41; Sec Aetna Insurance Co, Hartford Conn 41-43; Berkeley Pub Lib, Berkeley Cal: Child libn West Br 50-52, Asst in order dept 52-56, Child libn Claremont Br 56-60, Head boys & girls dept 60-. 9: ALA; CalLA; Assn Child Libns No Cal. 10: Sierra Club; Delta kppa Gamma; UCal Sch of Libnship Alumni Assn. 14: Child serv. 15: 2610-1/2 Benvenue ave, Berkeley Ca 94704.

KIDDER, FREDERICK E(LWYN). b White Bear Minn 22 S 19. 4: Georgina Garrett. 5: UCal(Berkeley) 40 (Internat Rel) AB, 50 BLS, 52 (Pol Sci) MA; UFla 65 (Lat Amer Studies) PhD. 6: Sp. 7: Prin lib asst UCal(Berkeley) 49-50; Ext libn Solano Co Free Lib, Fairfield Cal 50-51; Co Libn Stanislaus Co Free Lib, Modesto Cal 51-52; Asst libn Inter Amer U, San German PR 55; Asst libn UFla 59-60; Libn PR Nuclear Center, Mayaguez PR 61-62; Asst Assoc of soc sci UPR 62-68; Visiting Assoc Prof Lib Sci UIll 68-69; Prof libnship UPR 69-. 8: Asst dir Sch of Inter-Amer Studies, UFla, 56-57; Registrar and Dir of Ext Div Inter Amer U 57-59. 9: ALA; Amer Pol Sci Assn; BSA; Amer Statistical Assn; Sociedad de Bibliotecarios de Puerto Rico (pres 67). 10: Latin Amer Studies Assn; Phi Beta Kappa. 12: "Latin America & UNESCO; The First Five Years" (60); "The Political Concepts of Luis Munoz Rivera (1859-1916) of Puerto Rico" (65). 13: Yes. 14: Tech processes, ref, adult serv, lib educ. 15: Grad Sch of Libnship, Box 21906, Univ Sta, San Juan PR 00931.

KIDMAN, ROY L. b Redondo Beach Cal 25 Jl 25. 4: Marilyn Jensen. 5: UCLA 45-51 (Chem) BS; USoCal 52-53 (LS) MS. 6: Fr. 7: Catlgr UCLA Law Sch 53-54; Sci libn UKan 54-59; Act dir Tulane U Lib 59-60, Asst dir 60-62; Biomed libn UCal(San Diego 63-68; Libn Rutgers U (New Brunswick) 68-. 8: Pub Health Serv Adv Com on Scientific Publs 65-68; Frequent consul for NIH. 9: ALA-ACRL (Publs Com 62-63; Bio Agric Sci Subsect chm 66-67; Univ Sect Steering Com 67-68);-ISAD (Communications Com 67-68). 10: AAUP; Beta Phi Mu. 13: Yes. 14: Admin, ref. 15: Rutgers Univ, New Brunswick NJ.

KIDNEY, SISTER MARY OLIVIA. b Dover NH 4 N 31. 5: Mt St Mary Col (Hooksett NH) 61 (Eng) BA; Simmons 69 (LS) MS. 7: Tchr St Joseph's High, Manchester NH 61-65; Libn Immaculata High, Manchester NH 65-67; Libn Bishop Brady High, Concord NH 67-68; Asst libn Mt St Mary College (Hooksett NH) 68-. 9: Nat Assn Eng Tchrs; ALA; CatholicLA; NELA; NHSchLA; NHLA; NECatholicLA. 14: Catlg. 15: Mt St Mary College, Hooksett NH 03106.

KIEFER, GILBERT (V). b St Louis Mo 19 N 42. 5: St Louis U 60-64 (Geog) BS; LSU 64-66 (LS) MS. 7: Libn Hoech Jr High Sch, St Ann Mo 66-. 9: ALA; NEA. 14: Ref admin. 15: 4003 Brown rd, St Louis Mo 63134.

KIEFER, LAWRENCE L. b Toledo Ohio 28 My 30. 5: UFla 54-58 (Pol Sci) AB; West Res 59-60 MSLS; UMd Law Sch 66 LLB. 6: Sp. 7: (YN 2) US Coast Guard 51-54; Stud asst UFla Lib 54-58; Lib asst Toledo Pub Lib, Toledo Ohio 58-59; Stud asst West Res U 59-60; Lib asst Columbia U 60-62; Assoc libn UMd Law Sch 62-65, Law libn & Asst Prof of Law 66-. 8: Law lib consul UBaltimore Lib 66; Mem Mayor's Comm on the Admin of Justice Under Emergency Conditions (Subcomm on Research & Liaison). 9: ALA; AALL; SLA. 10: Order of the Coif. 12: Index to Proceedings & Reports of the ABA Section on Real Property, Probate and Trust (32-68). 14: Law lib, admin. 15: 929 St Paul st, Baltimore Md 21202.

KIEFER, SHIRLEY E. b Easton Penn 11 Je 33. 5: Beaver Col 51-55 (Relig Educ) BA; McCormick Sem (Chicago) 55-57 (Relig Educ) MA; IndU 66-67 MLS. 6: Fr. 7: Br asst Evanston Pub Lib, Evanston Ill 57-58; Dir of relig educ Hope Ch, Holland Mich 58-61; Eng tchr Amer Col for Girls, Cairo Egypt 61-64; Tchr Weekday Relig Educ, Indianapolis 65-66; Ya libn Hartford Pub Lib, Hartford Conn 67-. 8: Participant British Coun course for tchrs of English as a second lang, Cambridge England summer 63. 9: ALA; State YA Materials Discussion Group (Steering Com). 10: World Affairs Ctr; Urban League; Caucus of Conn Democrats. 13: Yes. 14: Ya serv, adult serv, wking with disadvantaged groups. 15: 57 Imlay st, Hartford Ct 06105.

KIEFFER, LAWRENCE W. b Elba Minn 2 Ja 34. 4: Esther Sasse. 5: Col of St Thomas 51-52, 53-54; UMinn 54-56 (Pol Sci) BA; 59-61 (LS) MA. 6: Ger. 7: Jr libn UMinn, Minneapolis 59-61; Asst soc studies Sacramento State Col 61-63; Soc studies libn UNeb 63-64, Asst dir of libs for soc stud 65-69; Hd of Reader Serv, U North Iowa 69-. 9: ALA. 10: AAUP. 14: Ref, admin. 15: 922 E Seerley blvd, Cedar Falls Ia 50613.

KIEFFER, PAULA. b Hagerstown Md 21 Ja 11. 5: NJState Lib Sch 32-36 Certif; Newark Col of Rutgers U 38-47 (Eng) BA. 6: Fr, Ger. 7: Catlgr S Orange Pub Lib, S Orange NJ 31-42; Catlgr Nat Assn of Manufacturers, NYC 42-43; Sr catlg libn Newark Pub Lib, Newark NJ 43-46; Head catlgr Stevens Inst of Tech 46-49; Head catlg dept Washington Co Free Lib, Hagerstown Md 49-51; Assoc catlgr Peabody Inst Lib, Baltimore 51-53; Head catlgr 53-59; Coordinator tech lib serv Baltimore Co Pub Lib, Towson Md 59-. 9: ALA; MdLA; NJ Catlg Group (chm 47-49); Potomac Tech Processing Libns (chm 61-62). 13: Yes. 14: Tech serv, data processing, bk catlgs. 15: 27 Dunvale rd, apt bt, Towson Md 21204.

KIELY, MARY FRANCES. b Dorchester Mass 19 F 05. 5: RI Col 25 B Ed in LS. 6: Gk, Lat, Fr, Ital, Sp. 7: Child libn Providence Pub Lib 25-37; Ed in chief Pro Parvulis Bk Club, NYC 37-53; Head libn Providence Central Sr High Sch 54-60; Libn of the Col Bryant Col of Bus Admin 60-. 8: Auth "Report on Pulp Literature on Newstands in RI for the Governor's Committee on Pulps and Comics" (53); Com on Shakespeare Tercentennial of Bryant Col 64. 9: ALA; SLA; NELA (pres Col Libns Sect 69-70); NYLA; RISchLA (pres 57-59). 10: AAUW; RI Hist Soc Amer Inst Graphic Arts. 12: "O'Donel of Desting" (39); "New Worlds to Live" (40) (2nd ed 44); "Traffic Lights: Safe Crossways into Children's Literature" (41). 13: Yes. 14: Hist, catlg, ref. 15: 125 Hope, Providence 02906.

KIENHOLZ, MARIAN ELEANOR. b Grand Forks N Dak 10 O 26. 5: Concordia Col 46-48 (mus); UDenver summer 46 (violin); CapitalU 48-49 (mus) BA; Eastman Sch of Mus 51-52 (mus hist); UKy 66-67 MSLS. 7: Premium clk Farm Bureau Ins Co, Columbus Ohio 49-52; Violinist & salesgirl Hormel Girls Caravan, Austin Minn 52-54; Film libn & film ed ohio StateU (Columbus) 51-56; Columbus Symphony Orchestra, Columbus Ohio 51-54; Clk-typist USA Depot, Columbus Ohio 62-63; Asst to prod mgr UCLA Motion Picture Div, los Angeles 64-65; Asst catlgr Hutchins Lib Berea Col 67-68, Spec collections libn 68-. 9: ALA; MLA. 10: Mu Phi Epsilon. 14: Spec libs (mus). 15: Hutchins Lib Berea College, Berea Ky 40403.

KIES, COSETTE NELL. b Platteville Wis 2 S 36. 5: Wis StateU 54-57 (Hist) BS; UWis 59-61 (Art Hist) MA, 61-62 (LS) MA. 6: Fr. 7: Art tchr Grafton Pub Schs, Grafton Wis 57-59; Child libn Fond du lac Pub Lib, Fond du lac Wis 62-63; Asst libn UNeb 63-66, Sr asst libn 66-67; Asst programs coord ALA 68, Prof asst off for recuiment 68-. 9: ALA (Mem Com); NebLA (State Legis Com 65; chm Publicity Com 67; exec dir NLW). 10: JMRT; Col Art Assn; AAUP; Beta Phi Mu. 12: Ed "Love Notes," UNeb Lib Staff Assn (65-67). 14: Ref, fine arts, pub rel. 15: 50 E Huron st, Chicago Il 60611.

KIESER, PORTIA ELIZABETH. b Brookings SD 30 Ap 21. 5: Lasell Jr Col 38-41 (Sec, Journalism) All-Sec Certif; Carnegie 46-47 (Hist, Econ) BS; UToledo 61-64 (LS) MA. 7: Departmental sec Pol Sci Northwestern U; AerM 3/C USNR (WR) Weather Serv 44-46; Standards tech Owens-Corning Fiberglass Corp, Toledo Ohio; Exec sec & libn Employers' Assn of Toledo, Toledo Ohio 52-59; Exec off libn Libbey-Owens-Ford Co, Toledo Ohio 60-. 9: SLA; OhioLA. 10: ZonTA Club. 14: Ref, catlg. 15: 2815 Powhattan pkwy, Toledo Oh 43606.

KIESOW, JOHN HERMAN. b Topeka Kan 9 Jl 28. 5: UKan 52-55 (Lang Arts) BS in Ed; Kan State Tchrs Col (Emporia) 60 MS in LS. 7: US Army Personnel Mgt Supv Sgt First Class 48-52; Libn-tchr Medicine Lodge High Sch, Medicine Lodge Kan 58-64; Libn West High Sch, Shawnee Mission Kan 64-. 9: ALA; KanSchLA (Dist Com Chm 61); KanLA; KanStateTchrsAssn. 14: Acquis, readers ref. 15: Shawnee Mission West High Sch 8800 W 85th, Shawnee Mission Ks 66212.

KIESZ, MRS DOROTHY PURCELL. b E Grand Forks Minn 29 Ag 08. 5: UND 24-28 (Eng) BS in Ed, summers 37, 41 (Eng, LS); UIda summers 39, 49 (Eng, LS); UWash summers 53-57 (LS) ML. 7: High sch tchr: Sharon ND 28-29, Walhalla ND 30-32, Piedmont SD 37-39, Albion Ida 39-41; High sch tchr & libn, Burley Ida 41-48; High sch tchr & libn, Coeur d'Alene Ida 48-53, High sch libn 53-. 9: ALA; NEA; IdaEA; IdaLA (pres 63-64). 10: AAUW; Alpha Delta Kappa. 13: Yes. 14: High sch libn. 15: 810 Indiana ave, Coeur d'Alene Id 83814.

KIEWITT, EVA LORENE. b Crothersville Ind 12 Ag 27. 5: Ball State U 45-49 (Eng, P E, LS) BS in Ed; Chico State Col 55; UCal (Berkeley) 55; IndU 58-60 MA in LS, 68- (LS). 06: Ger, Fr. 07: Tchr Berne-French Unified Sch Dist, Berne Ind 49-54; Jr-sr high sch tchr-libn Paradise Unified Sch Dist, Paradise Cal 54-58; Jr-elem libn E Gary Sch City, E Gary Ind 58-60; Elem-Jr libn Ulm Amer Sch, Ulm Germany 60-62; Jr high sch libn Bloomington Metro System, Bloomington Ind 62-67; Educ libn IndU Sch of Educ 67-. 08: Ind U Wkshop for Stud Libns (summer): coun & tchr 63 & 64; asst dir 65; Asst dir NDEA lib inst IndU (Bloomington) summer 66. 9: NEA; ALA-AASchL; IndState Tssn; IndLA; IndSchLA (Pub Chm 63-; pres 68-69); A-V Instr Dir of Ind. 10: Beta Phi Mu; Delta Kappa Gamma; Pi Lambda Theta. 13: Yes. 14: Col acquis & admin, sch libs. 15: 305 E Vermilya Lot 21, Bloomington In 47401.

KIGHT, MARJORIE A. b St Paul Minn 13 Je 24. 5: Col St Catherine 46-50 (Primary Educ, eng) BA, 54-55 (LS) MA; Col St Thomas Remedial Reading Certif. 7: Storekeeper 1st class USNR(W); Tchr: Cass Lake Elem Sch 44-46, Gaston Elem Sch, Beloit Wis 51-52, US Army Dependent Schs, Bad Nauheim Ger 53-54, Franklin Elem Sch, St Paul 59-64; Libn lansing (Mich) Elem Schs 56-59; Libn Ramsey Jr High Sch, St Paul 64-67; Instr materials specialist St Paul Elem Schs 68-. 9: ALA; -AASchL; MinnASchL. 10: Col of St Catherine Alum Assn; Amer Fed Tchrs; PTA; Delta Kappa Gamma. 14: Elem sch libs as instrl materials ctrs. 15: 1642 Etna st, St Paul Mn 55106.

KILGORE, (ORPHA) CECIL. b Guthrie Center Iowa 7 Ag 1897. 5: Grinnel Col 12-16 (Hist, Ger) BA; UWis summer 24 (Pol Sci); UIll summer 30 (LS); Peabody summers 39-42 BS in LS. 6: Ger, Fr. 7: Soc sci Sr High Sch, Guthrie Center Iowa 22-31; Tchr-libn Sr High Sch, Guthrie Center Iowa 31-; Visiting prof Lib Sci UIowa summers 47-50. 8: Sch lib consul, UIowa wkshop summer 62. 9: ALA (Recr Com, Mem com); IndLA (sec-treas child & yp Sect 65); IndASchL (pres 44-45, Exec Bd 45-46 & 57-60 & 65-68; & coms). 10: Guthrie Center (Iowa) Pub Lib Bd; Beta Phi Mu; Delta Kappa Gamma; PEO; OES. 13: Yes. 14: Catlg, ref. 15: 303 S Fourth, Guthrie Center Ia 50115.

KILGOUR, FREDERICK G. b Springfield Mass 6 Ja 14. 4: Eleanor Beach. 5: Harvard 31-35 AB, 39-42; Columbia summers 39-41 (LS). 6: Fr. 7: Asst Harvard Col Lib 35-42; Off of Strategic Serv, Wash DC 42-46; Deputy dir Off of Intelligences Collection Dept of State, Wash DC 46-48; Libn Yale Med Lib 48-65; Assoc libn for research & development Yale U Lib 65-67; Dir Ohio Col Lib Ctr, Columbus 67-. 8: Adv com on sci publs US Pub Health Serv 62-65; Mem Facilities & resources com Nat Lib Med. 09: MedLA (sec-treas 50-52); Hist Sci Soc (treas 50-52); ALA; Amer Assn Hist Med; Soc Hist Tech; ASIS; Bibliog Soc (London); Bib SA; ACM. 12: Ed Eng Transl Cristobal Mendez "Libro del Exercicio Corporal" (60); "Library of the Medical Institution of Yale College and Its Catalogue of 1865" (60); Managing ed "Yale Journal of Biology and Medicine" (49-65). 13: Yes. 14: Computerization of libs, info retrieval. 15: 1314 Kinnear rd, Columbus Oh 43212.

KILIAN, ANDRE. b Djakarta Indonesia 26 Je 31. 4: Nora Donkersloot. 5: Gemcentelijk H B S Bandung (Indonesia) 48-50 (Liberal Arts) BS; Cor Courses in Lib Sci (Indon) 51-53; Netherlands Inst for Doc (The Hague Holland) 57-59 BSLS. 6: Dutch, Indonesian. 7: Ref libn Pub Lib, City of Bandung Indonesia 53-56; Catlg libn Ministry of Overseas Affairs, The Hague Holland 56-59; Catlg libn Central Bureau of Statistics, The Hague holland 59-60; Ser libn Cal Inst of Tech, Gen Lib 60-61; Catlg libn Research Lib, 20th Century Fox Film Lib 61-62; Hd consul Tech Lib Sales CBC Tech Bk Co 62-67; Hd-libn Hughes Research Newport Beach Div Lib 67-. 9: SLA; Netherlands Assn of Libns; CalLA. 10: Hughes Newport Beach Employees Assn. 15: 16232 Howland lane, Huntington Beach Ca 92647.

KILLEN, JUDITH (MARY GILES). b Salem Mass 21 Mr 42. 4: William Arthur Killen. 5: Emmanuel Col 60-64 (Hist) AB; Simmons Col 64-65 (LS) MS. 6: Fr. 7: Sr ref libn WVaU 65-66; Catlgr Bridgeport Pub Lib, Bridgeport Conn 66; Soc sci catlgr NYC Pub Lib 66-67; Catlgr Hartford Pub Lib, Hartford Conn 67-69; Hd catlgr Fed Res Bank of NY, NYC 69-. 9: SLA; ConnLA. 14: Catlg. 15: 1091 Tompkins ave apt B-19, Staten Island NY 10305.

KILLGORE, FREDERICA E(LIZABETH). b Yoakum Tex 12 S 10. 5: Rice U 28-32 BA; LSU 39-42 BS in LS. 6: Fr. 7: Asst child dept Pub Lib, Houston 32-39; Travel br libn 39-41; Asst Bexar Co Free Lib, San Antonio Tex 41-51, Libn-in-chg 51-53; Head period dept Pub Lib, San Antonio Tex 53-54; Asst dir ext loan lib UTex 54-62; Asst law libn Tarlton Law Lib UTex 62-66; Asst dir tech serv div Tex State Lib, A ustin 66-67, Dir tech serv div 67-. 9: ALA (var coms); AALL (var coms); TexLA (sec 61, chm Dist VIII, chm Publ Com, other com wk); SWLA (chm Publ Com). 10: Libns Coun, San Antonio Tex; Bexar Lib Club, San Antonio Tex; Austin Lib Club, Austin Tex; Phi Kappa Phi; Beta Phi Mu. 12: Ed "Texas Library Journal" (formerly "News Notes") (44-46). 13: Yes. 14: Acquis, tech serv. 15: 3202-1/2 Beanna, Austin Tx 78705.

KILLION, JOHN M. b Davenport Iowa 9 D 25. 4: Rosemary T. 5: St Ambrose Col 46-50 (Biol) BA; Rosary Col 52-53 MALS. 6: Ger, Fr. 7: Libn Lewis Col 53-54; Chem libn Argonne Nat Lab, Lemont Ill 54-56; Libn Dr Salsbury's Labs, Charles City Iowa 56-62; Libn Abbott Labs, NChicago Ill 62-65; Libn St Ambrose Col 65-. 9: ALA; SLA; ASIS. 10: AAAS. 15: 2314 Ripley st, Davenport Ia 52803.

KILMER, RUTH K. b Butler Penn 28 D 10. 5: Slippery Rock State Tchrs Col 29-31 (Elem Educ) Certification; Duquesne U 35-40 (Elem Educ) B of Ed; West Res 45-46 BS in LS. 7: Elem tchr Penn Twp Allegheny Co, Verona Penn 31-45; Br libn Schenectady Pub Lib, Schenectady NY 46-47; Period libn & Asst Prof Bowling Green State U 47-67, Cat lg libn & Assoc Prof 67-. 9: ALA; OhioLA; NOhio Tech Serv Libns. 14: Ser & catlg. 15: 225 Wolfley, Bowling Green Oh 43402.

KILPATRICK, LYNN WESTFALL. b Los Angeles 24 S 39. 4: Gordon Kilpatrick. 5: Los Angeles Valley Col 57-59 (Hist) AA; UCLA 59-61 (Hist) BA, 61-63 (Hist) LS MLS. 7: Asst libn Orange Coast Col 63-65; Hd libn Golden West Col 65-. 9: CalLA; CalTA. 10: Phi Beta Kappa. 11: . 14: Admin, catlg. 15: 7112 McFadden, Huntington Beach Ca 92646.

KILPATRICK, THOMAS LEONARD. b Henry Co Tenn 27 N 37. 5: UTenn(Martin Br) 55-56 (Eng); SoIll U 56-58 (Eng) BS; UIll summers 60-63 (LS) MS. 6: Fr. 7: Libn Herrin Commun Unit High Sch, Herrin Ill 58-64; Asst educ libn SoIll U 64-. 9: ALA; IllLA; IllASchL (Bd mem 64-66). 10: Beta Phi Mu. 14: Sch lib serv. 15: 420 N 10th st, Herrin Il 62948.

KILPELA, RAYMOND EARL OLIVER. b Hancock Mich. 5: Flint Jr Col (Liberal Arts) AA; UMich (Pol Sci) BA, (Pol Sci) MA, MALS, (LS) PhD. 6: Fr. 07: Asst Prof Hillsdale Col; Clerk Chamberlin Co of Amer Group Insurance, Detroit; Asst claims adjustor US Fidelity & Guaranty Co, Detroit; Asst dept manager Mich Hosp Serv, Detroit; Instr UMich (Ann Arbor 60); Head card prep unit Purdue U Libs 60-63; Asst Prof USoCal 63-. 9: ALA; AALS. 10: AAUP; Phi Beta Kappa; Phi Kappa Phi; Beta Phi Mu. 14: Catlg, lib admin, sci bibliog, info retrieval. 15: 2418 Tracey ter, Los Angeles Ca 90027.

KILZER, SISTER MARTHA CLARE OSB. b Richardton ND 15 Ja 20. 5: Col of St Benedict 37-40, 43-44 (Lat) BA; St Alexius Hosp Sch of Nursing 40-42; Dickinson State Tchrs Col summer 46; Marquette U summer 59-61 (Philos); Simmons 61-62 (LS) MS; Villanova U summers 67, 68 (Philos). 06: Ger. 7: Elem sch tchr St Joseph Sch, Dickinson ND 45-53; Elem sch tchr Cathedral Sch, Bismarck ND 53-57; Elem sch tchr St Lawrence Sch, Flasher ND 57-61; Libn Mary Col 62-. 9: ALA; CathLA (chm Bismarck Diocesan Sect Minn-Dak Unit 64-); NDLA. 10: Delta Epsilon Sigma. 14: Ref. 15: RR2 Box 119, Bismarck ND 58501.

KIM, CHOONG HAN. b Seoul Korea 25 S 23. 4: Changjoo Lee Kim. 5: Hong-Ik Col in Seoul Korea 55-59 (Eng Lit) BA; Ind U 59-60 (LS) MA; Rutgers 60-64 (LS) PhD. 6: Korean, Japanese, Chinese, Fr, Ger. 7: Head catlgr European bks The Nat Lib, Seoul Korea 52-54; Head catlgr European bks Yonsei U (Seoul Korea) 54-56; Asst head tech process The Nat Assembly Lib, Seoul Korea 56-58; Catlgr The Korea U (Seoul) 58-59; Br asst Brooklyn Pub Lib 61-62; Catlgr Health Sci Lib UMd 64-65; Asst Prof East Ill U 65- 68; Assoc Prof Ind State U 68-. 8: Com on Tech Matters, Korean Lib Assn 54-59. 9: ALA; KcreanLA; IndLA. 10: AAUP. 12: Korean transl of Aker's "Simple Library Cataloging" (60); "Library in the School (in Korean) KoreanLA (68). 13: Yes. 14: Reader serv, mgt, ref. 15: Dept Lib Sci Indiana State U, Terre Haute In 47809.

KIM, CHUNG HO (CHOI). b Seoul Korea 3 Jl 37. 4: John Y Kim. 5: Ewha Woman's U (Korea) 56-60 (Eng Lit) BA; Ind U 61-62 (LS) MA; NJ Prof Libn Certif. 6: Ger, Korean. 7: Jr libn Brooklyn Pub Lib 62-63; Jr libn Akron Pub Lib, Akron Ohio 63-65; Sr libn Elizabeth Pub Lib, Elizabeth NJ 65-. 14: Ref, catlg. 15: 14 Keen lane, Edison Nj 08817.

KIM, KYUNGSOOK (MISS). b Hamhoong Korea 20 Mr 38. 5: Ewha WomansU (Seoul) 55-59 (Secondary Educ) BA; Crozer Theol Sem 65-67 (Relig Educ); UPittsburgh 67-68 MLS. 6: Korean, Chinese, Japanese. 7: Lang tchr Canadian Mission, Seoul 59-61; Typist Academic Admin Off Ewha WomansU (Seoul) 61-64; Clerical typist Bucknell Lib Crozer Theol Sem 65-67; Catlgr KASC 67-68; Catlgr Ashland Col Lib 68-69; Sr catlgr YaleU Divinity Sch Lib 69-. 8: Joined Students Enlightenment Movement Sponsored by Canadian Mission, Seoul 55-57. 9: ATheolLA. 14: Catlg. 15: 409 Prospect st, New Haven Ct 06510.

KIM, MYUNG DOH. b Korea 20 O 35. 4: Eun Ock Lee. 5: YonseiU 55-59 (Eng) BA. 6: Korean, Japanese, Sp, Ger, Fr, Russian. 7: G2 Opn Sgt (Inf) 6th Republic of Korea 60-63; Tchr Kyung-puk Girl's Com High Sch, Taegu Korea 64-67. 15: PO Box 3008, Eugene Or 97403.

KIM, SANGYOL. b Chinju Korea 6 D 33. 4: Soonja Kim. 5: Keimyong Col (Taegu Korea) 54-58 (Eng Lit) BA; Taegu Col (Taegu, Korea) 59-61 (Eng Lang) 26 credits; SUNY(Albany) 62-63 MLS; Drexel 67- (Info Sci) MSLS. 6: Fr. 7: Asst libn Keimyong Col Taegu Korea 59-60; Interpreter Peabody Col Staff Project in Korea/USOM 61-62; Grad asst SUNY (Albany) 62-63; Catlg libn Bloomfield Col 63-65; Catlg libn Newark State Col, Union NJ 66-69; Hd catlgr Essex Co Col Libs Newark NJ 69-. 9: NJLA; NJEA. 14: Info storage & retrieval syst, mechanization lib tech processing. 15: 13 Willard lane, Towaco NJ 07082.

KIM, SOOK HYUN (CHUNG). b Mokpo Chun-nam Korea 1 N 39. 4: Young Baekim. 5: Ewha Women'sU (Seoul Korea) 57-61 (Eng Lang & Lit) BA; IndU (Bloomington) 63-65 (LS) MA. 6: Korean, Fr. 7: Catlgr UKan Libs 67-. 14: Catlg, ref. 15: 7 Stouffer place 8, Lawrence Ks 66044.

KIM, SOON JA. b Seoul Korea 1 Ja 41. 5: Ewha WomansU (Seoul Korea) 60-63 (LS) BA; Drexel 67-68 MS in LS. 7: Internatl exchange serv libn National Lib, Seoul Korea 64-66; Libn Sch of Nursing Lib The Cooper Hospital, Camden NJ 67-68; Hd catlgr Haverhill Pub Lib, Haverhill Mass 69-. 11: College of Liberal Arts & Sci Scholarships. 14: Catlg, intl docs. 15: 38 Summer st, Haverhill Ma 01830.

KIM, STELLA O (POHNG). b Manchuria 5 O 36. 4: Sun Kee Kim. 5: Nat Taiwan U 55-59 (Foreign Langs) BA; Peabody 61-62 MALS. 6: Korean, Chinese, Japanese. 7: Catlg libn Biola Col Lib 62-69, Acquis libn 69-. 14: Catlg, tech processes. 15: 13800 Biola ave, La Mirada Cal 90638.

KIM, UNG CHANG. b Choon Chun Korea 2 Ap 36. 4: Sue Hi Kim. 5: Pratt Jr Col 56-58 (Soc Sci) AA; Georgetown U 58-61 (Internat Affairs) BSFS; Catholic U 62-64 (Pol Sci, Hist, LS). 6: Korean, Japanese, Fr. 7: Lib clerk typist Pratt Pub Lib, Pratt Kan 58; USBE: Ser asst 61-64, Asst chief ser div 64-65, Chief bks div 65-. 14: Rare bks, docs. 15: L 12603 Brunswick la, Bowie Md 20715.

KIM, YOUNG-JIN. b Soonchun Korea 4 Ja 33. 4: Soon-Kyow (Song). 5: UMinn (Duluth) 59 (Pol Sci) BA; UMinn (Minneapolis) 63 (LS) MA, 63-65. 06: Korean, Fr, Japanese. 7: Jr libn UMinn (Minneapolis) 63-64; Asst Prof & libn Wis State U (River Falls) 64-. 10: AAUP; Wis State Faculty Assn. 14: Acquis. 15: 821 1/2 E Cascade, River Falls Wi 54022.

KIMBALL, RICHARD HAVENS. b Cambridge Mass 10 Ja 27. 5: UNH 47-53 (Geol) BS; Simmons 63-64 (LS) MS. 7: US Air Force Air Force photo-intelligence off (Cpt) 52-63; Staff libn US Army Materials Research Agency Lib, Watertown Mass 64-65; Ref libn Skidmore Col 65-66; Sci bibliog(r) Suny (Albany) 66-. 14: Ref. 15: 108 Front st, Schenectady Ny 12305.

KIMBALL, THOMAS M. b Minneapolis 19 D 16. 4: Ruthalean Peterson. 5: Riverside Jr Col 34-36 (Engnr) AA; UCal(Riverside) 55-57 (Soc Sci) AB; UCal(Berkeley) 57-58 MLS, 68-69. 07: Title searcher Riverside Title Co, Riverside Cal 36-42; Meteorologist Army Air Corps (Pvt to 1st Lt) 42-46; Title off Riverside Title Co, Riverside Cal 46-51; Meteorologist US Air Force (1st Lt) 51-53; Title off Riverside Title Co, Riverside Cal 53-55; Libn Fullerton Jr Col 58-60; Libn Barstow Col 60-. 9: Cal CalTA Tchrs Assn. 10: Cal Jr Col Fac Assn. 14: Admin, acquis, catlg, ref. 15: Barstow Col, 2700 Barstow rd, Barston Ca 92311.

KIMBROUGH, JAMES MARION. b Wales Tenn 27 Ja 26. 5: Martin Col 46-47; Peabody 47-49 (Soc Sci) BA, 49-50 (Hist) MA, summers 59-61 (LS) MA. 7: USNavy 44-46; Eng tchr Giles Co Bd of Educ, Pulaski Tenn 51-61; Libn Cumberland Col 61-64; Asst Prof of Lib Sci LSU (New Orleans) 64-68; Asst libn Martin Col (Tenn) 68-. 9: ALA; SELA; TennLA. 10: Phi Delta Kappa; Beta Pi Mu; Pi Gamma Mu; Kappa Phi Kappa. 14: Catlg, ref. 15: Rte 5, Lawrenceburg Tn 38464.

KIMBROUGH, JOSEPH (W). b Bowling Green Ky 21 Ap 30. 4: Ann C Cornett. 5: West Ky State Col 48-52 (LS) AB; IndU 55-56 (LS) MA. 7: USArmy Infantry 1st Lt 52-54; Desk attendent a-v dept Louisville (Ky) Free Pub Lib 54-55; Ref asst-film consul Grosse Pointe Pub Lib, Grosse Pointe Mich 56-58; Head Libn Sturgis Pub Lib, Sturgis Mich 58-60; Lansing Pub Lib: Supv adult serv 60-63, Dir pub lib 63-65, Act chief libn 65-. 9: ALA-YASD (Com on Sel of Bks & Other Materials;-ALTAC Publ Com); MichLA (treas 63-64, chm Legis Com 59-61 & 62-63, Bus Mgr "The Michigan Librarian" 65-; pres 68). 10: Lansing Exchange Club. 13: Yes. 14: A-v (partic wk with films), admin. 15: 401 S Capitol ave, Lansing Mi 48914.

KIMMICH, ROSALIND. b Cortland NY 6 O 27. 5: Syracuse 47-49 (Econ) BA; Cornell summer 54 (Elem Educ); SUNY (Cortland) 45-47, summer 56, 57, 58 (Elem Educ) MS; Rutgers 63-64 (LS) MLS. 7: Computer Carrier Corp, Syracuse NY 50-53; Computer Cornell U 53-54; Elem educ tchr: Dryden Central Schools Freeville NY 54-58, Curriculum ctr libn SUNY (Cortland) 58-60; Cortland City Schs, Cortland NY 60-61, Alfred I Dupont Schs, Wilmington Del 61-63; Elem sch libn Schenectady (NY) City Schs 64-67; Campus sch libn SUNY (Oswego) 67-. 10: LWV; Zonta Internat. 12: Wk on "Elementary School Library Collection" (65, 66). 14: Sch libs. 15: Sylvan Glen apt F-5, Oswego NY 13126.

KIMSA, TRAN THI. b KienAn Vietnam 27 My 38. 5: UPhilippines 54-56; West Res U 59-60 (LS); IndU 60-62 (Pol Sci) BA, 62-63 (LS & Linguistics) MA. 6: Fr, Vietnamese, Sp, Ger. 7: Hd libn Nat Inst of Admin, Saigon Vn 63-65, Lecturer 63-65; Asst Prof Van haohU, Saigon Vn 64-65; Catlgr YaleU 65-66; Sr ref libn catlgr RooseveltU 66-. 8: Adv Van Hanhu USaigon Lib 64-65; Proj off VietnameseLA 63-64. 9: PLA; IllLA. 10: AAUP; Amer Assn for Asian Studies. 12: "Bibliography on Vietnam" (64); "Index to Vietnamese Periodical Literature" (64). 13: Yes. 14: Catlg, ref, bibliog. 15: 5501 So Cornell, Chicago Il 60637.

KIMZEY, ANN C. b Houston Tex 26 Ag 40. 4: Stephen Lee Kimzey. 5: Rice 58-62 (Romance Lang) BA; UIll 66-67 (LS) MS. 6: Sp, Fr. 7: Ser catlgr Rice U 64-65; Instr Grad Sch of Lib Sci UIll (Urbana) 67-69; Catlgr UIll (Urbana) 67-68. 9: ALA. 10: Beta Phi Mu. 14: Catlg (Latin Amer materials). 15: 18290 Upper Bay rd #105, Houston Tx 77058.

KINCAID, ANNE ELIZABETH. b Detroit 8 Je 35. 5: UMich 53-57 (Eng) BA, 57-59 MALS. 7: Catlgr Gen Motors Tech Center, Warren Mich 57; Lib sci fellow UMich 58-59; Staff UCal (Berkeley) 59-61; Sr libn Detroit Pub Lib 62; Sr libn San Francisco Pub Lib 63-67, Prin libn 67-. 8: Facu Lib Techn Prog, San Francisco City Col 69. 9: ALA; CalLA (pres ya div 69). 14: Pub libs, ya serv. 15: 70 Deming, San Francisco Ca 94114.

KINCHEN, DOROTHY L (SANDFORD). b Dallas 22 Ap 17. 4: J Carlton Kinchen. 5: Southwest Tex State Col 34-35; Tex Woman's U 35-38 (LS) BA, 65 NDEA Inst (LS). 7: Clerk Woolworth, Tyler Tex 36; Packager Frito Co, Dallas 37; Saleslady Avon, Azle Tex 47; Clerk Leonard's Dept Store, Ft Worth Tex 49-50; Libn Lake Worth High Sch Jr High Sch Elem Sch, Ft Worth Tex 50-65; Libn Azle High Sch, Azle, Tex 65-. 9: ALA; TexLA; Tex State Tchrs Assn. 14: Child, young adult wk. 15: 104 Shadow lane, Azle Tx 76020.

KINCHEN, ROBERT PRESTON. b New Orleans 12 Mr 33. 5: Northwestern State of La 56 (Hist) AB; LSU 62-63 (LS) MS. 07: US Army (1st Lt) 56-60; Pre prof libn Enoch Pratt Free Lib, Baltimore 61-62, Libn young adult & adult 63-66; Br admin asst 66-67, Br libn 67-. 8: Radio prog for EPFL on Bal timore FM Station, News of The Lib (interviews). 9: ALA; MdLA. 10: Phi Alpha Theta. 13: Yes. 15: 3511 No Calvert st, Baltimore Md 21218.

KINDER, KATHARINE LOUISE. b Rockford Ohio 21 Mr 12. 5: Miami U 29-35 (Eng Lit) BA; Columia 35-36 BLS; UIll 41-42 bls. 7: Head circ dept Mt Holyoke Col Lib 38-42; (Lt Cdr) US Naval Res 42-46; Chief Libn Johns-Manville Research & Engnr Center, Manville NJ 46-. 9: SLA (pres 56-57, sec 52-53, var com assign ents, pres NJ Chap 51-530. 13: Yes. 14: pec lib admin. 15: 1025 Plainfield ave, Plainfield NJ 07060.

KINDLE, ODIS B MARTIN. b Paris Tex 13 F 26. 5: E Tex State U 48-49 (Music Educ) BMEd, 50-51 (Music, Educ) MEd, 52-54 BSLS; UKy 57-63 MSLS. 7: (S/Sgt) US Army 44-46;

Music tchr Athens(Tex) High Sch 49-54; Libn Greenville(Tex) High Sch 54-56; Libn Navarro Jr Col 56-; Faculty Our Lady of the L ake Col Lib Sch summer 67, 68. 9: TexLA (chm Dist 6 63-64); Tex Jr Col Tchrs Assn (chm Lib Sect 57-58). 14: Acquis, catlg. 15: PO Box 1170, Corsicana Tx 75111.

KINDLE, MARY E THEL. b Aplin Ark. 4: Cecil Haldane Kindle. 5: Little Rock Jr Col 30-32; UArk 34-36 (Eng) BS in Ed; Columbia 39-40 (Child Lit) BS. 6: Sp, Fr. 7: Asst child & adult Little Rock Pub Lib, Little Rock Ark 30-34; Stud asst UArk 34-36; Lib-tchr elem sch Ft Smith Ark 36-39; Stud asst ColumbiaU 39-40; Lib-tchr elem sch Libert St, Nyack NY 40-41; Asst child & adult dept Little Rock Pub Lib, Little Rock Ark summer 36; Org lib Ark Child Home & Hosp, Little Rock Ark summer 37; Libn Little Rock Jr Col summer 38; Yp libn NY Pub Lib 54; Libn Nyack High Sch, Nyack NY 54-57; Libn Hilltop Jr High Sch, Nyack NY 57-68; Libn Rockland Commun Col (NY) Summer 65; Libn Woodlands High Sch, Hartsdale NY summer 66, 67, 68; Libn Valley Cottage Elem Sch, Valley Cottage NY 68. 8: Radio program of stories for child KTHS Ft Smith Ark 38-39; Chm In-Serv Com on Gifted Studs Nyack NY Sch 55-57; Chm In-Serv Com on Study Skills Nyack NY Schs 56-57; Consul Bethlehem (Conn) Pub Lib 58; Tchr of "Books and Libraries" for volunteer pub "libns" Nyack NY Adult Sch 55-63. 9: ALA; NEA (co-chm Rockland Co Memb); Rockland Co (NY) Tchrs Assn (Bd Dir 64-67; NYStateTA; NY StateLA); Roc kland Co SchLA (sec 63). 10: Kappa Delta Pi; Volunteers for Internat Assistance; Lambda Tau. 12: Ed "Authors of Rockland County" (60); Rockland County Materials, "List of Holdings of Libraries on Rockland County" (65). 13: Yes. 14: Org libs, tchg, admin, student-libn relationship. 15: 332 No Midland ave, Upper Nyack NY 10960.

KING, ANNIE (GREENE). b Trenton NC 19 Ja 22. 4: Jay B King. 5: NC Col Durham NC 38-42 (Fr, Hist) AB, summers 44-46 BSLS; UIll 50-51 MSLS; Case West Res summer 68 (LS). 06: Fr. 7: Tchr Jones Co Training Sch, Pollocksville NC 42-43; Tchr-libn Trenton High Sch, Trenton NC 43-46; Libn Jones High Sch, Washington NC 46-47; Libn Fla N & I Col 47-50; Ref libn Tuskegee Inst 51-63, Head pub serv 63-. 9: ALA; SELA; AlaLA. 10: Delta Sigma Theta; Tuskegee Civic Assn; AAUP; AAUW . 14: Ref, acquis, admin. 15: 207 Johnson st, Tuskegee Al 36088.

KING, CLYDE S. b Terre Haute Ind 23 D 19. 4: Ruth Schaffer King. 5: Kan State Tchrs Col (Pittsburgh) 37-40 (Foreign Lang); George Washington U 46-48 (Hist) BA; Kutztown State Tchrs Col 50-51 (LS) Certif; Columbia 58-61 MSLS. 6: Lat, Sp, Ger. 7: A B to 2nd Mate US Merchant Marine 42-45; Tchr Myersville (Md) Elem Sch 49-50; Libn Hunterdon Co Lib, Flemington NJ 51-53; Libn Atlantic Co Lib, Mays Landing NJ 53-57; Libn Horace Mann Sch, NYC 57-. 9: Hudson Valley LA (first chm). 10: N-Y Hist Soc; POAU; Hist Soc York Co (Penn). 12: Comp "Horace Mann, 1796-1859: a Bibliography" (66). 13: Yes. 14: Ref, bibliog. 15: 4670 Tibbett ave, Bronx NY 10471.

KING, CYNTHIA L (WIESE). b Fresno Cal 20 Ag 21. 4: James King. 5: Stephens Col 39-40 (Music); San Jose State Col 40-41 (Home Econ); Fresno State Col 57-59 (Elem Educ) AB; UDenver 59-61 (LS) MA. 6: Fr. 7: Lib asst Fresno Co Boys & Girls Lib 56-60; Br libn Fresno Co, Fresno Cal 60; Ya dept asst Denver Pub Lib 61; Head boys & girls lib Fresno Co Lib, Fresno Cal 61-62, Dir boys & girls serv 62-. 8: Consul in child serv for Tulare Co Cal, 62-64. 9: ALA; CalLA (Yosemite Dist: chm Bk Review Group); Assn Child Libns NoCal. 10: Storyland Bd; People-to-People Sister City Bd for Lahore Pakistan. 14: Wk with boys & girls. 15: 757 W Pico, Fresno Ca 93705.

KING, DAN MADISON. b Muncie Ind 7 N 14. 5: Hanover Col 34-38 (Hist, Eng) AB; McGill summer 37 (Fr) Certif; Ball State Tchrs Col summers 35, 36, 38; Syracuse 39-40 BS in LS; NYU 48-49 (Hist of Arch). 6: Fr. 7: Asst Muncie Pub Lib, Muncie Ind 38-39; Asst ref dept NY Pub Lib summer 40; Dist supv WPA Lib Serv Proj, Indianapolis 40-42; Asst libn in chg of Art Sch Lib, Cooper Union (NY) 42-43; Libn in chg Cooper Union Libs (NY) 43-46; Chief ref dept Grand Rapids Pub Lib, Grand Rapids Mich 46-48; Asst ref dept NY Pub Lib 48-49; Libn Minn Hist Soc, St Paul 49-54; Head Libn Ky Wesleyan Col Lib 54-. 8: Lib consul Tex Gas Transmission Corp, Owensboro Ky 60-61; Spec Coms for Col Visitations, So Assn of Cols & Schs, Atlanta 63-69. 9: ALA; SLA (chm Mus Div 53-54); SELA; KyLA (pres 64-65). 10: Phi Delta Theta; Filson Club, Louisville Ky. 12: Ed NY Lib Club "Bulletin" (44-45). 13: Yes. 14: Ref, catlg. 15: Ky Wesleyan Col Lib, 3000 Frederica st, Owensboro Ky 42301.

KING, DAVID EDGAR. b Waterloo Ind 25 N 36. 5: Ball State 54-58 (Lang Arts) BS; Hofstra 59; Rosary Col 69 (LS). 6: Ger. 7: Libn Sachem Central Schs, Lake Ronkonkoma NY 58-60; Libn (US Army) Nellingen Amer Jr High Sch, Nellingen Germany 61; Volunteer Peace Corps, nabua, Camarines Sur, Philippines 62-63; Col traveler Amer Bk Co, NYC 63-65; Libn R R Donnelley & Sons Co, Chicago 65-. 9: ALA; SLA; (Ill Chap: chm Memb Dir Com, Asst chm Recr Com, Memb Hospitality Com). 14: Fine bks & private presses, ref. 15: 403 Sherman ave, Evanston Il 60202.

KING, DOROTHY A. b Quincy Ill 13 Ag 19. 5: Harris Tchrs Col 37-41 (Soc Sci-Elem Educ) AB; Greenville Col 45-46 (Religion) ThB; Eden Theol Sem 47-48 (Christian Educ) MA; UIll 50-54 MLS; Harvard (Educ) MEd. 6: Fr, Ger. 7: Instr Wessington Springs Jr Col 48-50; Asst libn Greenville Col 50-54; Sem Libn No Park College & Sem 54-55; Catlg libn Olivet Nazarene Col 55-56; Libn East Nazarene Col 56-. 8: Accrediting Com-New Eng Assn of Cols & Second Schs (North Kingston RI, 62; Cranston RI 64). 9: ALA-ACRL; ChristianLA; NELA; NEColLA. 10: Quincy (Mass) Lib Coun. 14: Bk sel, admin, instr in lib use. 15: 121 Elm ave, Wollaston Ma 02170.

KING, DOROTHY BELZ. b Camden NJ 25 F 27. 4: M Donald King. 5: Juniata Col 44-48 (Eng) AB; Rutgers 62-63 MLS. 7: Interim High Sch libn Wall High Sch, Wall NJ 61; Field serv libn Monmouth Co Lib, Freehold NJ 63-67; Wanamessa Sch Lib 68-. 9: ALA; LPRC; NJLA; Monmouth(NJ) Libns Assn; NJEA. 10: Beta Phi Mu. 14: Improvement in small libs. 15: Box 349, RD 1, Wall NJ 07719.

KING, DOROTHY. b Northville Mich 11 Jl 14. 5: UCincinnati 32-36 (Eng) AB, 36-37 (Eng) MA; UMich 40-43 ABLS. 7: Asst in reserve bk rm UCincinnati 38-39, Asst in chg circ 39-41; Asst in catlg dept UMich Lib (Ann Arbor) Mich 41-42, Jr catlgr 42-43, Asst curator rare bk rm 43-44, Asst curator Mich Hist Collections 44-46; Curator of rare bks Smith Col Lib 46-. 9: BSA. 14: Rare bks. 15: 26 Bedford terrace, Northampton Ma 01060.

KING, ELEANOR G. b Elizabethtown Penn 14 My 06. 5: Lebanon Valley Col 41 (Hist) BA; Columbia 52 (LS) MS. 6: Ger. 7: Tchr Milton Hershey Sch, Hershey Penn 30-45; High sch libn 46-; Libn Hershey Archives, Hershey Penn 59-. 8: Research asst Hershey Archives 55-58; Readers adv Elizabethtown Col 64-65. 9: ALA; PennLA. 10: Penn Ger Soc; Pi Gamma Mu. 14: Rare bks. 15: 15 Brandywine, Briarcrest Gardens, Hershey Pa 17033.

KING, ELEANORE WOODWARD. b Wash DC 18 Ag 13. 5: George Washington U 30-34 (Educ) AB, 35-39 (Educ) MA Madison Col summers 54-56 (LS) Lib Sci Certif ; Rutgers summers 57-61 (LS) MLS. 07: Tchr Arlington Co Pub Schs 34-; Sch libn Williamsburg Jr High Sch 56-. 8: Elem sch prin Lee Sch 37-40; Barcroft Sch 40-45; chm Lib Dept 56-. 9: NEA; DAVI; ALA-AASchL (Internat Rel Com); -LED (mem Com); VaLA; VaEA (Sch Libns). 10: Beta Phi Mu; Pi Lambda Theta; Kappa Delta Pi; Phi Delta Gamma; Arlington Symphony Assn. 14: Lib instr, ref, yp wk. 15: 5836 22nd st, Arlington Va 22205.

KING, ELIZABETH VERONICA (CHIU). b Shanghai China 25 Jl 35. 4: Albert Ignatius King. 5: UHong Kong 52-55 (Eng); USan Francisco 56-57 (Eng) BS (magna cum laude); UCal (Berkeley) 58-60 (Eng) MA; UMich 61-66 AMLS. 6: Chinese. 7: Tchr Star of the Sea Sch, San Francisco 57-58; Libn-trainee Hamtramck Pub Lib, Hamtramck Mich 60-61; Pre-prof libn Detroit Pub Lib 64-66, Libn (child) 67; Libn (circ & ser) Henry Ford Commun Col 67-. 10: Hong Kong Govt Scholarship 52-55. 14: Ser, circ, inter-lib loan. 15: 6221 Amboy rd, Dearborn Hts Mi 48128.

KING, EVALENA (CAIRNS) (MRS). b NY State 2 O 05. 5: Pratt 28-29 (LS); NYU 41-45 BS. 7: Asst Jr High Sch Lib, Jamestown NY 26-28; Asst Passaic Pub Lib, Passaic NJ 29-31; Asst Pratt Inst Lib 31-43, Head of circ 43-55; Asst Vassar Col 55-59, Head of readers' serv 59-. 9: ALA. 14: Ref, circ. 15: Vassar Col, Poughkeepsie NY 12601.

KING, GERALDINE B(EATY). b Omaha 23 My 36. 4: Jack B King. 5: Grinnel Col 58 (Eng) BA; UMinn 62 (LS) MA. 6: Lat, Gk. 7: Lib asst UMinn Bio-Med Lib (Minneapolis) 58-62; Tchg asst UMinn Lib Sch 61-62; Ref libn Cedar Rapids Pub Lib, Cedar Rapids Iowa 62-63; Circ & ser libn Iowa U Law Lib 63-64; Ref libn Col of St Thomas Lib 64-67, Assoc libn 65-67; Fellow UMinn Lib Sch 67-68, Lecturer 68-69, Fellow 69-. 9: ALA; MinnLA (Ref, Chm 65, Recr Chm 66-). 10: Beta Phi Mu; AAUP. 14: Admin, ref, lib, educ. 15: 387 Cretin ave s, St Paul Mn 55 105.

KING, GRACE (REENE). b Scottville Mich 19 O 12. 4: Kenneth S King. 5: East Mich U 31-33 (Bus Educ); Wayne State 59 (Bus Educ) BS, 63 MLS. 7: Bus educ Anchor Bay, New Baltimore 60; Bus educ Algonac High Sch, Algonac Mich 61, Libn 61-. 9: ALA; MichASchL; Thumb Area ASchL. 10: Algonac Athena Club; Algonac Music Study Club; Women's Soc of Christ Serv; OES. 15: 448 Willard ave, Algonac Mi 48001.

KING, HELEN (ARNETTE STINSON). b Richmond Va 1 Jl 37. 4: George T King Jr. 5: Madison Col 55-59 (LS) BS in Educ; Fla StateU summers 61-65 (LS) MS; Col of William & Mary 60-66 (Educ) MS. 7: Asst libn Newport News High Sch, Newport News Va 59-61; Libn Christopher Newport Col, Hampton Va 61-62; Libn Deer Pk & S Morrison Elem Schs, NM Va 62-64; Libn Benjamin Syms Jr High, Hampton Va 64-66; Asst supt of sch libs & textbks Va State Dept of Educ 66; Libn John Tyler Sch & asst libn Kecoughtan High Sch, Hampton Va 66-67; Libn Capt John Smith Elem Sch, Jampton Va 67-68; Libn Booker Sch, Hampton Va 68-. 8: Instr lib sci ext Div Col of William & Mary 66-. 9: ALA; VaEA (sec-treasurer Dist B Libns 60-62). 10: Madison Col Alumni Bd of Dirs; Madison Col Alumni Assn. 14: Sch lib supv, acquis. 15: 5 Commander dr, Hampton Va 23366.

KING, JACK B. b Minneapolis 9 S 31. 4: Geraldine Beaty. 5: UIowa 49-50 (Hist); UMinn 50-53 (Hist) BA (magna cum laude); 53-54, 57 (Hist) MA, 61-62 (LS) MA. 6: Fr, Ger, Lat. 7: First Lt US Army Military Intelligence Photo-Interpreter 54-56; Research asst US Army, Ann Arbor 56-57; Tchg asst UMinn (Minneapolis) 58-60; Stud asst UMinn Lib (Minneapolis) 60-61; Lib asst Hennepin Co Law Lib, Minneapolis 61-62; Libn UIowa spec collections 62-64; Ser catlgr UMinn Lib (Minneapolis) 64-65; Catlg libn Hamline U 65-66, Hd Tech Serv 66-. 9: ALA; MinnLA (treas); ASIS. 10: Econ Hist Assn; Soc Econ Hist; Phi Alpha Theta; Beta Phi Mu; AAUP. 13: Yes. 14: Tech serv, mss, rare bks. 15: 387 Cretin ave S, St Paul Mn 55105.

KING, KENNETH E. b NYC 9 Jl 25. 4: Ruth Boulter. 5: Brown U 46-50 (Eng Lit) BA; Simmons 50-51 MSLS. 7: Detroit Pub Lib: Libn I Monteith Br 51-53, Ref asst Simmons Sch of Lib Sch 51, Libn II Monteith Br 53, Lib III Franklin Br 53-55, Br libn Monteith Br 55-56, Coordinator commun & group serv 56-63, Home reading serv dir 63-. 9: ALA-ASD (v-pres 65-, Spec Projs Com 62-, ASD/RSD Com on Common Concerns 67-); MichLA (chm Adult Educ Sect 59, chm 2 coms, 2nd v-pres 67-68); Ad Educ Assn (v-pres Metropolitan Detroit Sect 63-65); Ad Educ Assn Mich (chm Pub Rel Com 60-61). 10: Wayne Co (Mich) Mental Health Soc; Mayor's Dept Coun on Aging; Torch Club; Detroit Model Neighborhood Task Force 67-; Central Budget Com for Spec Serv, United Com Serv of Metro Detroit 68-. 13: Yes. 14: Adult educ, adult reading improvement. 15: Detroit Pub Lib 5201 Woodward ave, Detroit Mi 48202.

KING, LaDONIS JAMES. b Flint Mich 24 D 20. 5: Flint Jr Col 40-42; UMich 46-47 (Hist) AB, 47-48 ABLS, 48-49 (Eng Lang & Lit) MA. 7: Signal Corps Cryptogr Staff Sgt 42-45; Community Libn Willard Lib, Battle Creek Mich 49-50; Detroit Pub Lib: Sr asst lang & lit dept 50-51, Sr asst sociol & econ dept 51-58, Asst chief sociol & econ dept 58-62, Chief gen info dept 63-. 8: Visiting Lecturer UMich Dept of Lib Sci Extension, Detroit, fall 64; Tchr three Ref Wkshops sponsored by Mich State Lib summer 68. 9: ALA; BSA; Bibliographical Soc of UVa; MichLA. 10: Beta Phi Mu. 14: Ref. 15: 1612 Lafayette Towers West , Detroit Mi 48207.

KING, LINDA (ANN) (HENDRICKSON). b NYC 4 Ap 45. 4: Charles M King. 5: Queen's Col (NY) 61-65 (Eng) BA; Columbia 65-66 MS. 7: Sr ref libn NYC Pub Lib 66-. 8: Bk Discussion Leader, Inwood Br Lib 68-. 9: ALA. 10: Phi Beta Kappa; Commun assn for pub affairs; Lib Guild 30. 14: Ref. 15: 321 W 103 st, New York NY 10025.

KING, LOIS (ESTHER SMELTZER). b Elkhart Ind 28 Ag 26. 4: Howard L King. 5: Goshen Col 44-48 (Eng Bible) MA, 49-53 (Elem Educ) BS; West Mich U summers 60-65 (LS) MA. 6: Sp. 7: Tchr Washingtow Twp Schs, Bristol Ind 49-55; Tchr Concord Schs, Elkhart Ind 58-63, Libn 64-65; Libn Jimtown High Sch, Elkhart Ind 65-. 8: Lib Supvr, Bauge Commun Schs, Elkhart, Ind 66. 9: NEA; ALA; Ind State Tchrs Assn; IndSchLA. 14: Sch libnship. 15: RR 3 Box 124, Goshen In 46526.

KING, LOUISA (MURRAY). b Newton NH 20 N 04. 4: Elwyn A King. 5: Tufts U 23-27 (Hist) AB; Simmons 62-68 MS. 7: Eng tchr second sch, Amesbury Mass 27-29; Asst libn Stevens Mem Lib, N Andover Mass 50-63, Head libn 63-. 9: ALA; MassLA (com chm); NELA; Merrimack Valley LA (pres 64-66). 10: N Andover Woman's Club; Jackson Col Assn of Tufts Alumnae; N Andooer Hist Soc. 15: 46 Marblehead st, N Andover Ma 01845.

KING, MAE ELIZABETH. b Roanoke Ind 4 F 08. 5: Earlham Col 27-29 (Eng); Ind U 29-31 (Eng) AB, summers 32, 33, 34, 36 (Hist), (Educ); UIll summers 39, 40, 42, 43, 51 (LS) BLS; Ball State U summers 55, 63 (Art), 65 (Educ). 6: Lat, Sp. 7: Lat, Eng & hist tchr & libn Webster High Sch, Webster Ind 32-36; Lat, Eng & hist tchr & libn Harrison Twp High Sch, Kitchel Ind 36-37; Lat, Eng & hist tchr & libn Driftwood Twp High Sch, Vallonia Ind 37-39; Eng tchr & libn Test Jr High Sch, Richmond Ind 39-49; Head Libn of the secondary schs & libn Richmond Sr High Sch, Richmond Ind 49-57; Period serv libn & Instr of Lib Sci Ball State U Lib, Muncie Ind 57-60, Period serv libn & Asst Prof of Lib Sci 60-. 8: Libn at Burris Lab Sch & Instr of lib sci, Ball State Tchrs Col summer 52. 9: ALA; NEA; IndLA; IndSchLA (treas 51-52); Ind State Tchrs Assn (sec-treas Central Sect of sch libns 49). 10: AAUP; Delta Kappa Gamma; AAUW; Iac Women's Club; libns 2 Wreth churches. 14: Ref wk, period serv, ya. 15: 2107 Linden, Muncie In 47303.

KING, NANCY (NICOL). b Scotland 8 D 16. 4: James Alexander King. 6: Fr. 7: Libn Charles E Frosst, Montreal 37-50, Libn Anatomy McGill U 62-64; Libn Charles E Frosst, Montreal 64-65; Chief libn Merck Frosst Labs, Montreal 66-. 9: MedLA; SLA; CanLA; SLA (Pharmac Sect, Montreal Chap). 10: Pine Beach Citizens Assn; Dorval PO; PTA. 14: Ref (Med & Chem). 15: Lib Frosst & Co, PO Box 1005, Montreal 3 Can.

KING, PATRICIA (JUANITA). b Denver 19 F 23. 5: Kirksville State Tchrs Col 41-44 (Soc Sci) BS; UDenver 52-55 (LS) MA. 7: Off clerk Dun & Bradstreet, Kan City Mo 44-51; Tchr-libn Ferguson Sch Dist, Ferguson, St Louis Co Mo 51-54; Libn Salinas Union High Sch, Salinas Cal 54-57; Libn Coachella Union High Sch, Indio Cal 57-59; Libn Santa Rosa Pub Lib, Santa Rosa Cal 59-60; Sr libn Ventura Co City & Co Lib, Ventura Cal 60-. 9: ALA; CalLA. 10: AAUW. 14: Child serv. 15: 138 N Crimea, Ventura Ca 93001.

KING, PEARL (LAVONNE) TUTTLE. b Wichita Kan 25 N 32. 4: Roy Ray King. 5: UCal (Berkeley) 49-54 (Sp, Fr) BA, 56-58 MLS. 06: Sp, Fr, Portu, Ital, Catalonian, Sp, Rumanian, Russian. 7: Libn II documents catlgr Cal State Lib 59-63; Sr ref libn San Diego Co Lib, San Diego 63-66; Hd ser catlg sect UCal (San Diego) 66-. 10: Phi Beta Kappa. 14: Catlg, ser. 15: 6519 Zena dr, San Diego Ca 92115.

KING, RETA ELIZABETH. b Edgar Neb 3 N 14. 5: Peru State Col 34-37 (Eng) AB; UNeb 47 (Educ); UDenver 52-55 (LS) MA. 7: Instr Rural Sch, Edgar Neb 31-34; Instr High Sch, Crab Orchard Neb 37-40; Instr High Sch, Brodwater Neb 40-41; Instr & prin High Sch, Milford Neb 41-47; Instr High Sch, N Platte Neb 47-52, Libn 52-56; Head Libn Chadron State Col 56-. 8: Consul with Neb Lib Commsn 58-60; Consul for Chadron High Sch 68-69. 09: ALA-ACRL (Mem Com 63-64); NEA; MPLA; NebLA; Neb State EA (past-pres Dist 1). 10: AAUW; Faculty Women's Club; Delta Kappa Gamma. 14: Ref, admin. 15: 828 Bordeaux st, Chadron Nb 69337.

KING, RICHARD LOUIS. b Portland Ore 21 My 37. 5: UCLA 55-58 (Intl Rel); Sacramento State Col 61-63 (Hist) BA; UCLA 64-66 (Hist). 6: Fr. 7: Training & educ monitor USAF, Beale AFB Cal 60-64; Bindery prep U Research Lib UCLA 64-65; Stack supv UCLA 65-66, Hd circ dept Lib Grad Sch of Bus Admin 66-. 8: Chm "Library Staff Handbook" revision com lib Staff Assn UCLA 67-69, Mem Constitution Revision Com 67-68; Speaker Joint Meeting of Bus & Finance Div SLA convention, Los Angeles 68; Act curator Robert E Gross Collection of Rare Bks in the Hist of Bus & Econ Grad Sch of Bus Admin UCLA; Exhibit "The World of Bus," Univ Research Lib UCLA commemorating the SLA convention 68; Mem Lib Work Schedules Advisory Com UCKA 67-68; Mem Lib Asst Clsf & Pay Plan Com UCLA 67-68; Mem Lib Staff Development Com UCLA 66-67. 9: Lib Staff Assn UCLA (Bd of Dir 66-68). 13: Yes. 14: Rare bks. 15: 8308 Clinton #8, Los Angeles Ca 90048.

KING, ROY T. b Sturgeon Mo 26 D 04. 4: Kathleen Fowler. 5: UMo 22-27 (Hist, Pol Sc) AB. 6: Fr, Sp. 7: Newspaper libn State Hist Soc of Mo, Columbia 22-43; Hd ref dept st Louis Post-Dispatch 43-. 8: Newspaper libns API Sem Columbia U 67. 9: SLA (Newspaper Div Chm 66-67). 13: Yes. 14: Ref. 15: 1133 Franklin ave, St Louis Mo 63101.

KING, RUTH (SANBORN). b Loudon NH 20 S 09. 4: Edward D King. 5: Boston U 27-31 (Eng) AB; Columbia 38-39 (LS) BS, Columbia Tchrs Col summers 36-38, 40 MA. 6: Fr. 7: Tchr pub schs, Loudon & Andover NH 31-36; Jr high tchr pub schs, Hampton NH 36-38; Sub libn NH State Tchrs Col 39-40; Circ libn Wheaton Col (Norton Mass) 40-42; Asst libn NY State Tchrs Col (Cortland) 42-44; Curator aviation col Harvard Grad Sch of Bus Admin (Boston) 44-53; Sch libn S River Sch, Marshfield Mass 57-59; Sch libn Broad Meadows Jr High Sch, Quincy Mass 59-. 9: ALA; NEA; NELA; NESchLA; Mass Tchrs Assn. 10: Appalachian Mountain Club. 14: Lib serv for young adults. 15: 37 West st, Braintree Ma 02184.

KING, SANDRA (JEAN). b Antioch Cal 4 My 42. 5: Stanford U 60-64 (Hist) BA; UCal(Berkeley) 64-65 MLS. 7: Libn (staff) Queens Borough Pub Lib NY 65-. 14: Ref, ya. 15: 415 E 82 st, New York NY 10028.

KING, SHELDEN SHEPARD. b Syracuse NY 6 D 31. 5: Cortland Bus Inst 50-51 (Accounting); State U Col (Geneseo NY) 55-59 (LS) BSE. 7: Record clerk Amer Can Co, Geneva NY 51-53, 54-55; Payroll clerk Goulds Pumps Inc, Seneca Falls NY 53-54; Engnr libn Westinghouse Elec Corp Elmira NY 59-66; Admin tech info 66-. 09: SLA (Sci-Tech Div ; ed Engring Sect "Newsletter" & "Sci-Tech News" 65-66; UpstateNY Chap: bulletin ed 61-63, chm Nominating Com 67-68, chm Pub Rel 68-69). 10: Electric Railroaders Assn, NYC; Chemung Co Hist Soc, Elmira NY; Cortland Co Hist Soc, Cortland NY. 13: Yes. 15: 253 Robinwood ave, Elmira Heights Ny 14903.

KING, SUE WYNN. b Jackson Tenn 12 Je 15. 4: Lloyd King. 5: UTenn (Martin) 45-47 (Eng, Soc Sci); UTenn (Knoxville) 48; Peabody Col 48, summers 49, 54 (Eng, LS) BSLS. 6: Lat. 7: Libn Martin High Sch, Martin Tenn 47-50; Supv of buying Milan Military Plant, Milan Tenn 51-54; Asst libn UTenn (Martin) 54-55; Libn Martin High Sch, Martin Tenn 55-. 8: Consul five counties for planning in serv 66; Consul for high sch libs for wkshop 68; Chm Nat Lib Week Com 66. 69. 9: ALA; SELA; NEA, TennLA; W TennLA (pr62). 10: AAUW; Quill & Scroll Library Club. 14: Catlg, ref. 15: 112 South Coll, Martin Tn 38237.

KING, THELMA (RENIFF) MRS. b Kalamazoo 24 S 04. 5: West Mich U 23-28 (Eng) AB; Drexel 30-31 BS in LS. 7: Lib asst Kalamazoo Pub Lib, Kalamazoo Mich 25-30; Head catlg & order dept Warder Pub Lib, Springfield Ohio 31-36, Chief Libn 36-43; Head ref dept Steele Mem Lib, Elmira NY 43-48, Dir 48-; Instr Lib Sch State U Col (Geneseo NY) summers 58-. 8: NYState Governor's Com on Lib Aid 49-50; NYState Pub Libns Examination Com 54-58. 9: ALA (Friends of Libs Com); NYLA (past chm var coms). 10: Zonta Internat; Delta Kappa Gamma; YWCA; Commun Coun; AAUW. 13: Yes. 14: Admin, ext. 15: Steele Mem Lib Lake & E Church st, Elmira Ny 14901.

KING, VIOLA E. b Gardner Mass 12 O 28. 4: Richard I King. 5: Clark U 61 (Eng, Philos) BS; Simmons 63 MA in LS. 6: Sp. 7: Asst libn Worcester Jr Col 60-63, Head Libn 63-. 9: ALA; NELA; Worcester of Coop Libs . 10: Worcester Art Mus. 14: Ref, catlg, adv wk (adults). 15: 45 Montague st, Worcester Ma 01603.

KING, WALTER DARMON. b Griffithville Ark 10 Ag 23. 4: Ruth Virginia Greer. 5: Harding Col 46-48 (Soc Sci) BA; UArk 49-50 (Hist) MA; Ark State Tchrs Col summers 51-53 (LS); Peabody summers 54-56 MA(LS). 7: Aircraft Sheet Metal Mechanic USAF (Sgt) N Africa-Italy Campaign 42-45; Tchr Eng soc sci Gravette High Sch, Gravette Ark 49-51; Eng tchr libn W Point High Sch, W Point Ark 51-52; Eng tchr-libn Osceola High Sch, Osceola Ark 52-53; Eng tchr-libn W Point High Sch, W Point Ark 53-58; W Tex State Col Lib: Catlgr 58-59, Head of catlg dept 59-61, Head of tech serv 61-62; Order libn Southwest Mo State Col Lib 62-. 14: Acquis, tech serv. 15: Route 1 Box 108, Pleasant Hope Mo 65725.

KING, WILLARD (LUCILE) BRINCEFIELD. b Reidsville NC 1 S 11. 5: Fisk U 29-33 (Eng) AB; Atlanta 41-42 BS in LS; Syracuse summer 54-58 MS in LS. 6: Fr, Sp. 7: Libn-tchr John R Hawkins High Sch, Warrenton NC 33-34: Lib asst Fisk U Lib 35-41; Libn Bettis Jr Col 42-43; Libn-tchr William Penn High Sch, High Point NC 43-46; Libn Afro-Amer Newspapers, Baltimore 47; Libn Henryton State Hosp, Henryton Md 48; Libn Sollers Point Jr-Sr High Sch, Dundalk Md 50-66; Libn overlea Sr High Sch, Baltim ore 66-. 9: NEA (Life memb); ALA; Md State Tchrs Assn; MdLA; Assn Sch Libns Md. 10: YWCA; Girl Scouts; Psi Gamma Mu. 14: Catlg, ref, ya serv. 15: 3801 Dolfield ave, Baltimore Md 21215.

KINGERY, PETER (VICTOR) OFM. b Montrose Ill 1 F 24. 5: Our Lady of Angels 42-45 (Phil) AB; St Joseph Sem 45-49 (Theol); West Res summers 52-55 MS in LS, summers 56-59 (Educ) MA. 6: Lat, Ger. 7: Libn Our Lady of Angels Sem 58-60; Libn St Joseph Sem, Oak Brook Ill 60-69; Asst circ libn UChicago Law Lib 69-. 9: CathLA; ALA. 10: Bd, Oak Brook Pub Lib. 15: 3313 Midwest rd, Oak Brook Il 60521.

KINGHORN, CAROL ANN. b Memphis Tenn 9 N 35. 5: SUNY (Albany) 53-58 (Eng, LS) BA, MA; grad wk at various cols with emphasis on psych. 6: Fr, Sp. 7: Tchr, W Islip NY 60-63, Sch libn 63-66; Br libn NY Inst of Tech 66-. 8: Student Affairs Com & Faculty Senate ny inst of Tech. 9: AAUP; Nassau Co Psych Assn. 14: Ref. 15: Box 94, Old Westbury LI NY 11568.

KINGMAN, HOPE. b Bridgeport Conn. 5: Barnard (Modern Langs) BA; Columbia MLS. 6: Ger, Fr, Ital, Sp. 7: Gen libn NY Pub Lib & Ref libn Mun Ref Lib 43-48; Engnr libn Sperry Gyroscope Engnr Div Exploration div Cal Tex Oil Co 52-58; Sch libn Nassau Co & Westchester Co Schs, NY 58-61; Head of high sch lib Lawrence High Sch 62-. 9: NY State Tchrs Assn; Nassau Co SchLA. 10: AAUW; Barnard Col Club; Phi Theta Kappa. 14: Ref (maps & geol regs). 15: 43-16 169th st, Flushing Ny 11358.

KINGSBURY, LAURENCE. b New Haven Conn 15 Ag 38. 4: Katherine Duffield. 5: Washington & Lee U 57-61 (Eng Lit) AB; Washington U 61-63 (Eng Lit) MA; Rutgers 64-65 MLS. 6: Fr. 7: Dir of John Burroughs Sch Lib, St Louis 62-64; Asst in humanities dept Enoch Pratt Free Lib Baltimore Md 65-67, A dmin asst 67-68, Br libn 68-. 8: Chm, Lib Planning Com John Burroughs Sch (64-65). 9: ALA; MdLA. 14: Adult ser in ref & reader's adv wk. 15: 126 Dunkirk rd, Baltimore Md 21212.

KINGSEED, ELIZABETH (ANN). b Sidney Ohio 19 Ja 18. 5: Ohio State U 38-40; Miami U 40-42 (Eng) AB; USoCal 54-55 MSLS. 7: Staff asst Amer Red Cross, Germany 45-46; Jr catlgr Princeton U Lib 49-53; Adult asst Detroit Pub Lib 55-58; Ref asst UMich Lib 58-59; Lib Dir N Castle Pub Lib, Armonk NY 59-62; Br libn New Rochelle Pub Lib, New Rochelle NY 62-64; Asst state Libn NH State Lib 64-. 9: ALA; NHLA; NELA. 10: LWV; Beta Phi Mu; NH Coun on World Affairs. 13: Yes. 14: Admin. 15: NH State Lib, Concord Nh 03302.

KINGSMORE, LOUISE (BURTON). b Ellen Ky 16 F 16. 4: Hugh Kingsmore. 5: Union Col 33-49 (Eng, Soc Sci); UKy 40 (Eng, Soc Sci) AB, summers 50, 51, 56, 57, 58 MS in LS. 7: Rural sch tchr Lawrence Co Ky 34-37; Elem tchr Consolidated Sch, Lawrence Co Ky 37-39; Eng tchr Louisa High, Louisa Ky 40-41; Soc sci tchr Webville High, Lawrence Co Ky 41-42; Sub Man High Sch, Man WVA 42; Soc sci Logan Jr High Sch, Logan WVa 42-43; Machinist & sec Bethlehem Fairfield Shipyard Baltimore 43-44; Inspector Curtiss Wright Airplane Columbus Ohio 44; Libn Louisa High Sch, Louisa Ky 50-. 9: NEA; KyEA. 10: treas Lawrence Co (Ky) Pub Lib. 14: Ref, loc hist. 15: Box 78 Route 1, Louisa Ky 41230.

KINGSTON, BETTY GEORGINA FRANCES. b Toronto 7 O 16. 5: Trinity Col U Toronto 34-38 (Classics) BA; U Toronto 40 BLS. 7: Libn Far East dept Royal Ont Museum, Toronto Can 43-. 9: SLA (Toronto Chap: Prog Chm 61-63, Bulletin Ed 64-69). 10: Com Soc Asian Studies. 15: Royal Ontario Mus 100 Queen's Park, Toronto 5 Canada.

KINGSTON, GAYLE MARIE (UTECHT). b Wakefield Neb 11 O 41. 4: Jerry Kingston. 5: Wayne State Col 59-62 (Home Econ) BA. 7: Hd libn Ft Collins Sr High Sch, Ft Collins Colo 62-65; Asst undergrad libn Penn StateU (Univ Park) 65-. 10: AAUP. 14: Pub serv areas. 15: 720 C W Beaver ave, State College Pa 16801.

KINGSTON, JO ANN (SPRINGGATE). b Fremont Neb 27 O 36. 4: Jack D Kingston. 5: Neb State Tchrs Col (Wayne) 54-58 (Educ, Speech) BA in Ed; UMich 59-62 MALS. 7: Clerk J C Penny Co Fremont Neb 54-55; Tchr Flint Pub Schs, Flint Mich 58-59; Flint Pub Lib, Flint Mich: Trainee br libn 59-62, Sch serv asst 63, Br libn 64-. 9: ALA (Jr Mem RT: chm

Pub/Booth Coun, ed Newsletter 67-); MichLA; (chm pub rel com 65-67, chm recr com 67-69; Jr Mem RT);Flint Area Lib Club (chm Memb Com 68). 10: Trustee Grand Blanc Pub Lib; Grand Oak Assn. 14: Br libs, young adult, culturally deprived. 15: 614 Bedford place, Grand Blanc Mi 48439.

KINGSTON, JOYCE (KAMBARN). b Mineola NY 23 N 31. 4: Ian D Kingston. 5: SUNY (Geneseo) 49-53 (LS) BS; Boston U summer 63; Northeastern U 65-67 (Edux) Master's. 7: Libn Union Free Dist Schls: Valley Stream NY 53-54, Mineola NY 55-56, uniondale NY 56-57, New Hyde Pk NY 57-58; Libn Burlington Pub Schs, Burlington Mass 63-, Hd elem libn 68-. 9: ALA; NEA; Mass A-V Assn; MassSchLA; NESchLA; MassTA. 10: AAUW; Kappa Delta Pi. 14: Tchg lit to elem sch child. 15: 59 Wildwood dr, Bedford Ma 01730.

KINGSTON, SALLY ANN (WEISS). b Hamburg NY 24 Ag 34. 4: Jack R Kingston. 5: State U Col (Geneseo NY) 52-56 (LS) BS; State U Col (Buffalo NY) 62-66 (EE) MS. 07: Libn Peekskill NY Elem Sch, Woodside & Franklin 56-58; Libn Lewisboro Elem Sch, S Salem NY 60-61; Libn Virginia Road Sch, Valhalla NY 61-63; Libn Greenacres Elem Sch, Scarsdale NY 63-65; Tchr-libn Ridgeway & North Street Elem Sch, White Plains, NY 65-. 14: Elem sch libs. 15: 135 S Kensico ave, Valhalla NY 10595.

KINNEY, (MARGARET) RUTH. b Monmouth Ill 10 N 24. 5: Monmouth Col 42-43; West Ill U 43-46 (Eng) BS in Ed; UWis summers 53-57 MS in LS; UIowa summers 48, 50. 7: Tchr-libn Cambridge High Sch, Cambridge Ill 46-47; Tchr-libn Wyoming High Sch, Wyoming Ill 47-52; Tchr-libn Venice High Sch, Venice Ill 52-54; Tchr libn Sandwich High Sch, Sandwich Ill 54-57; Asst libn York Comm High Sch, Elmhurst Ill 57-. 8: Lib 21 Staff, Seattle World's Fair 62. 9: ALA-AASchL (reg chm Sub com on Mem); IllLA; (treas); IllASchL (treas, Conf Prog Chm); High Sch Libns, Chicagoland (sec). 10: Amer Fed Tchrs. 14: Second sch libn. 15: 2N423 Elm, Elmhurst Il 60127.

KINNEY, ALYS MARJORIE (WELSH). b Massilon Ohio 4 D 20. 4: Edward C Kinney. 5: Kent State 37-39 (Elem Educ) Diploma; Ohio State U 40-46 (Amer Hist) BA; (cum laude); Ohio State U Col of Law 46-48; UGa 56; UWVa 61-63 MA in LS. 7: Tchr Massillon City Schs, Massilon Ohio 37-39, 44-45; Libn Stone Inst of Hydrobiology Ohio State U, Put-in-Bay Ohio 48-54; Tchr Oconee Co Schs, Watkinsville Ga 54-56; Tchr Kanawha Co Schs, Charleston WVa 57-62; Libn catlgr Georgetown U 63-66; Libn catlgr George Washington U 66-68, Asst hd catlg dept 68-. 9: ALA; DCLA. 14: Catlg. 15: 5311 Augusta st, Wash DC 20016.

KINNEY, JANIS (POWELL). b Cresson Penn 26 D 35. 4: James L Kinney. 5: Clarion State Col 53-57 (LS) BS; Penn State U 61. 7: Libn N Huntingdon High Sch, Irwin Penn 57-58; Letterer Gwin Larson & Kimbal, Ebensburg Penn 59; Libn Greater Gallitzen Jt Schs, Gallitzen Penn 59-61; Libn Hollidaysburg Com Jt Schs, Hollidaysburg Penn 61-, Lib & a-v research coord. 9: PennLA; PennEA. 10: Soroptimist Club. 14: Young adult. 15: 1900 16th ave, Altoona Pa 16601.

KINNEY, JOHN MARK. b Syracuse NY 4 Je 32. 4: Sue Andrew. 5: UTex (Austin) 51-56 9hist) BS, 67-68 MLS, 67- (Hist); Episcopal Theol Sem of SW 56-58 (Theol) BD; Nashotah Theol Sem summers 64-66 (Hist) STM. 6: Greek, Fr. 7: Asst display mgr Sears Roebuck, austin Tex 54-55; Tank platoon leader USA 1st Lt, Austin Tex 56-57; Missionary priest Episcopal Diocese of Alaska 58-61; Rector Our Lady of Grace Episcopal Ch, Dallas Tex 61-67; Research asst libn Ch Hist Soc, Austin Tex 67-68; Dir Tex State Archives, Austin 68-. 9: SAA; Ch Hist Soc; AHA; ALA; TexLA; Tex State Hist Assn; Assn for State & Local Hist. 10: Lions Club; Bd of Dir League for Educ Advancement; PTA; Catholic Clerical Union. 12: C C Fond du Lac: The Life of Charles Chapman Grafton, Second Bishop of Fond du Lac" (67); "A Guide to the Archives of the General Convention, 1785-1958" (68). 13: Yes. 14: Archives, ref, rare bks, admin. 15: Tex Archives & Lib Bldg Drawer DD Capitol Station, Austin Tx 78711.

KINNEY, MARGARET MARY. b NYC. 5: Hunter Col 30-34 (Math) BA; Columbia 35-37 (LS) BS, 50-52 MS. 7: Ref & sch libn NYPub Lib 35-40; High sch libn James Monroe High Sch, NYC 40-43; WAVE Off admin off US avy, Norfolk Va 43-46; Asst area chief libn US VA Br Off #2, NYC 46-47; Chief Libn USVA Hosp, Bronx NY 47-. 8: WAVE Off, CDR, USNR 52-; Instr Hosp & Med Lib NYG 51; lecturer United Hosp Fund 50, 51, 53, 54-63 ; Consul SLA 68-; ASI Z39 Sub com 62-. 9: ALA (Coun 58-64, Exec Bd 61-64; Adult Educ Bd subcom 55); -DHL (pres 51, Coun 51, Pub Rel Coord 52-55); -AHIL; CNLA (sec-treas 64-68, Trustee 68-69); LPRC (Bd Dirs 51-52, sec 53-54, pres 53-56); SLA (pres Hosp & Nurs Sect 50); MedLA; NY Lib Club (Prog Chm 68-69, v-pres & pres-elect 68-70). 10: US Naval Reserve; NY Lib Club; NY Acad Sci. 12: Co-auth "Objectives & Standards for Hospital Libraries" (53); Co-ed "Mental Health Book Review Index" (64). 13: Yes. 14: Admin, personnel, adult serv, med & sci bibliog data processing, hosp libs, med libs, lib educ. 15: 130 W Kingsbridge rd, Ny 10468.

KINNEY, MARNELLE S. b Folsom City Cal 23 Jl 18. 5: Chico State Col 36-38 (Educ) AA; UCal 38-40 (Educ) BA. 6: Fr. 7: Elem tchr Orland City Schs, Orland Cal 41-42; Elem tchr Lynwood City Schs, Lynwood Cal 43-48; Elem tchr Compton City Schs, Compton Cal 48-50; Bibliog research Autonetics, Downey Cal 60-62; Assoc tech libn Autonetics, Anaheim Cal 62-, Supvr br libs 68-. 9: SLA; Cal Tchrs Assn, Orange Co LA. 14: Ref libn, admin. 15: 1817 E Wilson, apt B, Orange Ca 92667.

KINNEY, MARY R(AMON). b Mt Carroll Ill 14 Je 06. 5: Shimer Col 24-26; UIll 26-28 (Hist) AB, 28-29 BS in LS, 35-37 (LS) MS. 6: Fr, Sp, Ger. 7: Asst catlg dept Cossitt Pub Lib, Memphis Tenn 29-30, Head catlg dept 31-35; Asst libn Sch UIll 35-37, Instr 38-42; Lecturer Sch of Lib Sci Simmons Col 42-43; Asst Prof 43-48, Assoc Prof 48-. 8: Sr asst Ref Dept Detroit Pub Lib, summer 44; Head Gen Ref Dept Enoch Pratt Free Lib, Baltimore summer 46; Lecturer Syracuse U Sch of Lib Sci, summer 57. 9: ALA-ACRL (dir 49-52); SLA; AALS (Subs Bks Com 51-57); MassLA. 10: Beta Phi Mu; AAUP. 12: "Bibliographical Style Manuals" ACRL Monograph no 8 (53); Co-ed "Books and Publishing" (53-56); "The Abreviated Citation," ACRL Monograph no 28 (67). 13: Yes. 14: Ref, bibliog, govt publs, lit of the humanities, research & bibliog methods in subject fields. 15: 101 Monmouth st, apt 307, Brookline Ma 02146.

KINSEY, HELEN E(LOISE). b The Dalles Ore 30 Ja 06. 5: UWash 24-25, 26-30 BS in LS; Columbia 37-38 (LS). 7: Child libn Medford Pub & Jackson Co Lib, Medford Ore 30-37; Child libn Brooklyn Pub Lib 38-41; Ed child bks "The Booklist" ALA 41-. 9: ALA; WNBA; IllLA; Chicago Lib Club; Child Reading Round Table. 15: 1913 Sherman ave, Evanston Il 60201.

KINSMAN, VIOLA (SPIEGEL). b St Louis. 4: Ralph Kinsman. 5: Washington U (Eng, Lat, Span, Gr) AB; UIll BSLS; Washington U (Educ, Eng) MAEd. 6: Lat, Sp, Ger. 7: Libn Jefferson Col 37-44; Lib asst St Louis Pub Lib 44-45; Libn Normandy Sr High St Louis Co Mo 45-. 8: Pres St Louis Suburban Libns 54-55. 9: NEA; ALA; Nat Tchrs Assn; Mo State Tchrs Assn; MoLA; MoASchL (sec 68-69). 10: Alpha Delta Kappa, Delta Kappa Gamma. 13: Yes. 15: 6944 Roberts, St Louis Mo 63130.

KINZER, ROSE (WILLIAMSON). b Hopkinton Iowa 5 Ag 02. 4: Gilbert D Kinzer. 5: UIowa 23-25 (Hist) BA; UIll 30-32 BS in LS, 32-35 (Hist); UDenver summers 61-62 (LS); U Hawaii summer 66 (LS). 07: Head circ Drake U 26-27; Libn Abraham Lincoln High Sch, Des Moines Iowa 27-30; Asst in circ UIll Lib(Urbana) 30-36; Asst in circ Bethesda Br Montgomery Co Lib, Bethesda Md 52-54; Head of tech processing Sul Ross State Col 54-56; Head of tech processing Ector Co Lib, Odessa Tex 56-57; Libn Midland Pub Lib, Midland Tex 57-60; Head of tech processing Odessa Col Lib 60-64, Libn Murry H Fly Lib 64-. 9: TexLA (Legal Com; sec Dist 2 Lib Sect 62); Tex Jr Col Assn (Lib Sect); ALA. 10: Altrusa; Bus & Prof Women; Delta Zeta; AAUW; PEO; LWV. 13: Yes. 14: Catlg, ref. 15: 2606-13 ave, Canyon Tx 790 15.

KINZER, SISTER M FERDINELLE, SDS. b Killam Alta Can 21 Jl 14. 5: Marquette U 34-48 (SS & Reg) (Eng) BA, 58-60 (SS) (Theol); Rosary Col 61-62 MALS. 6: Fr, Lat. 7: Elem tchr Mother of Good Counsel Sch, Milwaukee 37-45; Elem tchr Mater Salvatoris Sch, Abbots Langley Eng 45-47; Jr high Mother of Good Counsel, Milwaukee 48-50, Prin 50-52; Divine Savior High Sch, Milwaukee: Tchr v prin 59-61, Tchr of Eng & Lat & asst libn 60-61, Head Libn 62-. 8: Moderator of Lib Club 62-63. 9: ALA; CathLA (chm Mem Com 63-65); WisLA. 10: Classical Assn Middle West (&South); Classical League; Vergilian Soc. 14: Catlg, ref, reading guidance for young adults. 15: Divine Savior High Sch, 4257 N 100th st, Milwaukee Wi 53222.

KIOK, HILDA. b Poland 6 F 23. 5: Hunter Col 59-61 (Hist) BA; Columbia 63-65 (LS) MS. 7: Lib tchr PS 180, NYC 61-65; PS 73 NYC 66-. 9: ADI; Jewish Tchrs Assn. 14: Child serv. 15: 1576 Parker ave, Ft Lee NJ 07024.

KIP, CHARLES E. b Passaic NJ 28 F 17. 4: Elva Brain. 5: Princeton 34-38 (Chem) BA; MIT 38-40 (Chem Engnr) MS;

West Res 60-61 (LS) MS. 7: Research chem DuPont 40-44; Textile chem Standard Bleachery, Carlton Hill NJ 44-51; Research chem Celanese Research, Summit NJ 51-56; Libn tech writer Gpodyear Atomic, Portsmouth Ohio 56-60; Lit chem Chemstrand Research Center, Durham NC 61-; Visiting lecturer in sci lit UNC (Durham) 68-. 9: ACS; ASIS; SLA (NC Chap past pres, chm Transl Com 68-); NCLA; SELA. 12: Edl avd Bd "Documentation Abstracts" (68-). 13: Yes. 14: Tech lit searching & surveying. 15: 625 Shadylawn rd, Chapel Hill NC 27514.

KIPEL, VITAUT. b Minsk Byelorussia 30 My 27. 4: Zora Savionak. 5: UCatholique de Louvain 49-53 (Geol) MS, 53-55 (Mineralogy) PhD; Rutgers 60-62 MLS. 6: Byelorussian, Russian, Ger, Fr. 7: Consul geol Soc Anon Marche/Dames, Namur Belgium 53-55; Libn NY Pub Lib currently. 8: Abstractor, Chem Abstracts 60-63; Tr in the field of earth scis; Bibliog consul for Eastman Kodak & Gen Motors 62-63. 9: Socie3te3 de Pale3ontologie et d1Hydrologie ; Geol Soc Amer; SLA. 10: White Ruthenian Inst of Arts and Scis, NY. 12: Part-time ed "Engineering Index" (66 -). 13: Yes. 14: Ref. 15: NY Pub Lib, 42 st & 5th ave, Ny 10018.

KIPP, HAROLD STOCKDICK. b Pittsburgh Penn 14 F 34. 4: Pauline Speiglman. 5: UPittsburgh 61 (Educ) BS; 63 MLS. 6: Fr. 7: Bibliog Ohio State U Libs (Columbus) 63-65, Humanities Bibliogr State U Lib (Columbus) 65-66; Acquis libn Oberlin Col Lib 66-68; Acquis libn Ill State U (Normal) 68-. 9: ALA; IllLA. 10: US Chess Fed. 13: No. 14: Acquis, Catlg. 15: 302 HighPoint rd, Normal Il 61761.

KIPP, LAURENCE JAMES. b ND 3 Je 14. 4: Rae Cecelia Kelly. 5: State Col (Valley City ND) 33-37 (Hist) BA; UColo 37-38, 39-40 (Hist) MA; UIll 40-41 BS in LS. 7: Libn Eureka Col 41-42; Pvt-Staff Sgt USAF 42-45; Asst dir & Dir Amer Bk Center for War Devastated Libs, Wash DC 46-47; Asst to dir & Chief of loan serv Harvard Col Lib 48-54; Asst libn assoc libn & Libn Baker Lib Harbard Bus Sch (Boston) 54-. 8: Consul to Interdept Com Wash DC to survey internat exch of publs, 49; Consul to Dept of State to survey libs in India 60-61; Dir three Dept of State-ALA exch programs 54-59; Consul Ford Foundation 66-67. 9: ALA (Adv Com to U Delhi; past mem Coun, past chm Internat Rel Round Table); ASIS; MassLA (past chm Intel Freedom Com); NELA (past treas). 12: "International Exchange of Publications" (50); "Indian Libraries & the India Wheat Loan Educational Exchange Program" (61); Ed "Source Materials for Bus iness and Economic History" (67). 13: Yes. 14: Hist, econ, admin, internat rel. 15: 517 Mass ave, Lexington Ma 02173.

KIPP, RAE CECILIA (KELLY). b Lorain Ohio 20 My 11. 4: Laurence J Kipp. 5: Ursuline Col 32-36 (Hist) AB; West Res 37-39 BLS. 6: Fr. 7: Lib asst Cleveland Pub Lib 37-44; Libn Nat Catholic Sch Soc Serv 44-45; Exec asst Internat Rel Off ALA 44-48; Tchr Grad Lib Sch Simmons Col summers 50,52; Lib spec in India State Dept 60-61; Dir Spec Program for Multinat Libs ALA 61-62 ; Consul Ford Found Program for Delhi U L ib, Delhi India 67-68. 8: Consul, currently, for numerous lib programs ; Vice-chm Bd E duc Mass 66-. 10: LWV. 12: "Indian Libraries and the India Wheat Loan Educational Exchange Program" (US State Dept 61). 14: Ref (hist, philos & psych), devel of pub libs, internat exch programs for libns. 15: 517 Massachusetts ave, Lexington Ma 02173.

KIRALDI, LOUIS. b Hungary 12 O 11. 4: Ilona. 5: Royal Pazmany U(Budapest Hungary) 36 LLD; West Mich U 59 MA in LS. 6: Hungarian, Ger, Fr. 7: Order libn Pontiac City Lib, Mich 59; West Mich U: Asst order libn 60-61, Asst ref libn 62-63, Documents libn 63-, Map libn 68-. 9: MichLA. 13: Yes. 14: Ref, documents, rare bks, maps. 15: 1017 W Kilgore, Kalamazoo Mi 49001.

KIRBY, CAROLYN (SANFORD). b Highland Park Mich 21 Jl 23. 4: Thomas G Kirby. 5: Alma Col 41-45 (Hist) AB; UMich 46-48 ABLS. 7: Catlgr Ford Motor Co Engring & Research Lib, Dearborn Mich 48-. 9: SLA (Mich Chap: treas, chm Memb Com). 14: Catlg. 15: Eng and Research Lib Ford Motor Co, PO Box 2053, Dearborn Mi 48121.

KIRBY, HELEN (ROBINSON). b Morgantown W Va 25 D 22. 4: Eldon W Kirby. 5: WVaU 41-45 9ls0 ab& west Res 48-49 MSLS. 7: Libn: Clay Co High Sch, Clay W Va 45-46, Morgantown High Sch, Morgantown W Va 46-47, Univ High Sch, Morgantown W Va 47-48; Asst Prof of lib sci Ball State U 58-. 8: Field consul Ind Dept Pub Instr 60-64. 9: ALA; IndLA; IndSchLA. 10: AAUW: Bus & Profess Women's Club; Quota Internat; Amer Legion Aux. 14: Lib educ, child & YP. 15: 805 Wayne st apt 101, Muncie In 47303.

KIRBY, HELEN H (MCLENAHAN). b Jamestown Penn 20 Je 01. 5: Westminster Col (Penn) 19-23 (Eng) AB; Columbia 29-31 (Eng) MA; UAriz summers 47-61 (LS); UDenver summer 63 (LS); Brigham Young summers 64, 66 (LS) (Art); West State Cd of Colo summer 67 (Art). 07: Tchr of Eng High Sch, Rainelle WVa 23-28; Tchr of Eng, guidance High Sch, Bessemer Penn 28-30; Tchr of Eng High Sch, Pleasantville NY 31-36; Dean of Girls Frenchburg Mission Sch, Frenchburg Ky 36-42; Tchr of math Ben Franklin Jr High, New Castle Penn 45-46; Tchr of Eng & libn High Sch, Bowie Ariz 48-53; Tchr of Eng & Libn High Sch, Ashfork Ariz 54-56; Tchr of Eng & Libn High Sch, Tombstone Ariz 56-58; Tchr of Eng & Libn High Sch, Salome Ariz 58-61; Libn High Sch, Superior Ariz 61-. 9: NEA; ALA; ArizEA; Ariz StateLA; ClrTA (sec 67-68). 10: PTA. 15: PO Box 70 Superior Az 55273.

KIRBY, MARTHA (JEANNE) Z. b Chicago Hts Ill 6 Ag 42. 4: Edward P Kirby. 5: URochester 60-64 (Chem) BA; West Res 64-65 MS in LS. 7: Asst libn Union Carbide Corp, Parma Ohio 65-68; Ref libn NASA Goddard Space Flight Ctr, Greenbelt Md 68-. 9: SLA. 14: Ref, catlg. 15: 11907 Parklawn dr #302, Rockville Md 20852.

KIRBY, ROBERT J JR. b Wash DC 12 Ag 41. 4: Carolyn Ann Seymour. 5: St Francis Col 60-67 (Eng) BA; CatholicU 67- MLS. 7: Lib asst NASA Goddard Space Flight Ctr, Greenbelt Md 63-66; Lexicographer NAR-Autonetics Div ERIC Project, Wash DC 68-69; Indexer & search analyst Johns HopkinsU Applied Physics Lab, Silver Spring Md 67-68, 69-. 9: SLA. 14: Info storage & retrieval (mechanized), thesaurus construction. 15: 4-D Laurel Hill rd, Greenbelt Md 20770.

KIRCHER, CLARA J. b Newark NJ 8 Ap 08. 5: Seton Hall U 45-49 BS; Columbia 49-51 M in LS. 7: Pub Lib, Newark NJ: Ref asst 40-43, Head of schs div 43-52, Head of child dept 52-63; Assoc Prof of Child Lit UMd 63-64, Child bk spec Prince George's Co Lib, Hyattsville Md 64-69. 8: Adv & bibliog wk in child lit 63-68. 9: CathLA (treas Elem Sch Libs Sect 60-62, Exec Bd NY-NJ Unit 51-57); NJLA (pres & sec Serv to Child & yp 54-55). 10: Child Sect; Brotherhood List; NCCJ; Gustave Weigel Soc. 12: "Character Formation Through Books" (52); "Behavior Patterns in Children's Books" (65); Ed "Children's Section" in "Catholic Booklist" (48-61). 13: Yes. 14: Child lit. 15: 6700 Belcrest rd, Hyattsville Md 20782.

KIRCHER, ROLAND EUGENE. b Stuttgart Germany 3 Je 25. 4: Alberta Lillian Opitz. 5: Eberhard-Ludwig Gymnasium (Stuttgart Germany) Abitur Examen; UErlangen (Germany); Wesley Theol Sem STB; Catholic U MS in LS. 6: Ger, Fr, Lat, Gk. 7: Lecturer Wesley Theol Sem (Westminster Md) 55-57; Catlgr Wesley Theol Sem (Westminster Md & Wash DC) 58-59; Libn Wesley Theol Sem (Wash DC) 59-. 9: ALA; ATheolLA (chm Commsn on Lilly Endowment Scholarships 63-68, Exec Com 64-66; USBE (Bd Dirs 63-69; treas 65-69; Methodist Libns Fellowship pres 68-69). 15: 8009 Beach Tree rd, Bethesda Md 20034.

KIRCHGRABER, NANCY (BRUMFIELD). b Augusta Springs Va 16 F 27. 4: Robert B Kirchgraber. 5: Earlham Col 50 (Hist) BA; UIll 55 MSLS. 7: Ser asst UCincinnati 50-52, Acquis asst 52-53; Grad asst acquis UIll (Urbana) 53-55; Catlgr Clallam Co Lib, Pt Angeles Wash 55-57; Chief tech proc Belleville Pub Lib, Belleville Ill 64-. 8: Inst catlg, UIll Lib Sch Ext 66-67. 14: Catlg. 15: 5 Cathy Ann dr, Belleville Il 62221.

KIRCHGRABER, ROBERT BENJAMIN. b Texarkana Tex 25 Jl 18. 4: Nancy Brumfield. 5: UPortland 37-41 (Eng) AB; UDenver 52-53 (Soc Wk); UIll 53-55 MSLS. 7: Clerk War Dept Army Engnrs Portland Ore 42-46; Group wker Catholic Youth Org, Portland Ore 46-49; Casewker Multnomah Co Pub Welfare, Portland Ore 49-52; Co Libn Clallam Co Lib, Port Angeles Wash 55-57; Consul Colo State Lib 57-60; Co Libn Whitman Co Lib, Colfax Wash 60-62; Asst city libn Decatur Pub Lib, Decatur Ill 62-64; City Libn Belleville Pub Lib, Belleville Ill 64-. 15: 5 Cathy Ann dr, Belleville Il 62221.

KIRCHNER-DEAN, OTTO. b Vienna Austria 2 Je 17. 4: Joan Ellwood. 5: Bard Col 35-37 (Econ); U of the South 37-39 (Econ) BA; Columbia 46-50 (LS) BS, MS. 6: Fr, Ger. 7: City Col (NY) 47-49; DePauw U 49-50; Underwriter Conn Mutual, Bloomington Ind 51-60; Anderson (Ind) Pub Lib 60; Catlgr Air Force Inst Tech, Dayton Ohio 60-61; Info spec Foreign Tech Div, Dayton Ohio 61-63; Head Com Lib Ohio State U 63-64; Bibliog USDA, Wash DC 64-; Catlgr US Post Off Dept Lib 66-68 Libn Amer Podiatry Assoc 69-. 8: Clue Words, Air Force Aerospace Terminology, consul 60-63. 9: ALA; SLA; MedLA; DCLA. 10: Org Prof Employees of US Dept of Agric. 12: "Soybean Processing and Utilization: A Selected List of Ref erences, 1955-1965," NAL List 83. 13: Yes. 15: 7513 Buchanan st, Landover Hills Md 20784.

KIRCHNER, ANDRAS K. b Budapest Hungary 5 Jl 31. 4: Elisabeth Trombitas. 5: UBudapest 50-55 (Lit LS) MA; McGill 60-61 BLS; Columbia 63 (Med Libnship). 6: Fr, Ger, Hungarian. 7: Asst libn Hungarian Sci Doc Center, Budapest 55-56; Asst libn Bibliothe5que des Enfants, Montreal 57-59; Head Libn UMontreal Inst of Microbiol Sch of Hygie5ne 61-63; Head Libn Laval U Med Lib 63-. 9: MedLA; SLA. 14: Ref, admin. 15: Laval U Med Lib, Cite3 Universitaire, Ste Foy Que Can.

KIRCHNER, ELIZABETH. b Budapest Hungary 26 O 29. 4: Andras K Kirchner. 5: "Dobo Katalin" Col(Budapest) 48 BA; Eotvos Lorand U(Budapest) Philol, Lit Div & Lib Sch 54 BLS; Columbia 63 (Med Libnship). 6: Eng, Fr, Hungarian, Ger. 7: Ref Lib of Statistical Off, Budapest Hungary 54-56; Head Libn Nursing Sch, Ste Justin Hosp, Montreal 57-62; Head Libn UMontreal Med Lib 62-64; Head of period dept Laval U Gen Lib Que 64-65; Hd libn Med Lib Christ-Rox Hosp, Que 67-. 9: MedLA. 14: Periods, ref. 15: 84 Ave Louis Francoeur, Box #16, Quebec (Cap-Rouge) Can.

KIRCHNER, MINNA. b NY. 4: Harry Kirchner. 5: Hunter Col (Chem) BA; Queens Col (LS) MEd. 7: Tchr of lib E Meadow Sch Dist, LI NY 59-65; Tchr of Lib Great Neck Sch Dist, LI NY 65-. 15: 147-40 77 ave, Flushing NY 11367.

KIRK, (MARY) VIRGINIA. b Masontown WVa 21 Ap 07. 5: Muskingum Col 25-28, 30-32 (Elem Educ, Eng, Geo) BS in Ed; West Res 46-47 BS in LS, 63 MS in LS. 7: Elem tchr in Ohio schs 28-30, 32-46; Child libn Pub Lib, Dayton Ohio 47-48; Loan libn & Asst Prof Ohio Wesleyan U 48-. 9: ALA; OhioLA. 10: AAUP; Altrusa Internat; LWV; Women's Internat League for Peace & Freedom. 14: Circ, spec collections , training student assts, recruiting. 15: 49 S Liberty st, Delaware Oh 43015.

KIRK, GEORGE. b Providence 27 Mr 11. 4: Winifred Howard. 5: Pomona Col 29-34 (Hist) BA; UCal(Berkeley) 34-35 (Hist) MA, 36-37 Certif in Lib; UMich 38-39 MALS. 6: Fr, Ger. 7: Catlgr Utah State U 37-38; Catlgr Mich State Lib 39-45; Catlgr Ill State Lib 45-46; In chg circ & ref SD State Col 46-47; Catlgr UNeb 47-53; Head catlgr Ohio Hist Soc, Columbus Ohio 53-. 9: ALA; OhioLA. 14: Catlg. 15: 42 E Pacemont rd, Columbus Oh 43202.

KIRK, SHERWOOD. b Kermit W Va 12 Jl 24. 4: Ora (Ward) Kirk. 5: UKy 46-49 (Hist) AB; UIll 49-50 MSLS. 6: Fr. 7: Stud asst UK (Lexington) 46-49; Circ asst UIll (Urbana) 49-51; Circ & ref MarshallU 51-52; Sr asst & libn UNeb (Lincoln) Agric 53-54; Ref asst Nat Agric Lib, Wash DC 54-57; Asst state libn dept libs, Frankf ort Ky 57-69; Dir ept Of State Div Lib Serv, Tallahassee, Fla 69-. 8: Project for USDA Library to compile exchange list publ sent by Nat Agric Lib to foreign libs. 9: ALA-AAStateL; -PLA (Com for Functional Illiteracy); SELA; KyLA (pres 65-66); FlaLA. 10: Optimist Club. 13: Yes. 14: Admin tech serv ref. 15: 1536 Isabel ct apt 1, Tallahassee Fl 32303.

KIRK, STEPHEN SHERRON. b Garvin Okla 5 S 25. 4: Charlotte Wornall. 5: UOkla 44-49 (Eng) BA, MA; LSU 59-60 MLS. 7: US Army Counterintelligence Corps 51-55; Instr of Eng Lamar Col 55-56; Sales rep DC Heath Pub Co, Boston 56-59; Kansas City (Mo) Pub Lib: Head hist dept 61-64, Supv Mo Valley Room 63-, Head acquis dept 65-67, Asst libn 67-69, Hd libn 70-. 9: ALA; MoLA. 10: Jackson Co, Hist, Soc. 15: 5065 Clark dr, Shawnee Mission Ks 66205.

KIRK, SUE ELLEN (GRANNIS). b Maysville Ky 10 Ap 42. 4: Charles L Kirk. 5: UKy 60-64 9eng) AB, 64-65 (LS) MS. 6: Fr. 7: Ext libn Dept of Libs, Frankfort Ky 65-. 8: State Lib repr for Planning for 1970 White House Conf on Child & Youth for Ky. 9: ALA; -AASchL (Discussion Gp of State Lib Consults on Pub Lib Serv to Child); SELA; KyLA (sec). 10: AAUW; Alpha Gamma Delta. 14: Serv to child & ya, admin. 15: Kirk apts, Maysville Ky 41056.

KIRKBY, ARTHUR MARTIN. b Didsbury Alta Can 22 S 11. 4: Carolyn E Pullman. 5: Mt Royal Col (Calgary Alta) 40-42; UBC 42-44 (Hist) AB; Columbia 45-46 BSLS. 7: Asst Calgary Pub Lib, Calgary Alta 31-39, Br libn 40-41; Asst Vancouver Pub Lib, Vancouver BC 42-43; Head instrument reader Boeing Aircraft Co, Vancouver BC 44-45; Admin asst Central Adult Serv Enoch Pratt Free Lib, Baltimore 46-49, Admin asst to asst dir 49-52; City Libn Norfolk Pub Lib, Norfolk Va 52-. 9: ALA (Coun 57-59); SELA; VaLA (pres-67). 10: Rotary; Torch; Norfolk Hist Soc; Boy Scouts. 14: Admin, ALTA. 15: Norfolk Pub Lib 301 E City Hall ave, Norfolk Va 23510.

KIRKLAND, JEAN. b Metter Ga 29 S 29. 5: Brewton-Parker Jr Col 46-48; Ga Tchrs Col 49-52 (Bus Educ, Eng) BS; Emory 64-65 M Libr. 7: High sch bus tchr Emanuel Co Bd of Educ, Adrian Ga 48-50; High sch bus tchr Jeff Davis Co High Sch, Hazelhurst Ga 50-52; Sec Ga Baptist Hosp, Atlanta 52-55; Sec Wieuca rd Baptist Church, Atlanta 55-57; High sch bus tchr The Westminster Schs, Atl anta 58-64; ref libn pri Gilbert Mem Lib, Ga Inst of Tech 65-, Tech reports libn 66-67. 9: ALA; SELA; Metro Atlanta LA. 10: Ga Tech Lib Staff Assn; Beta Phi Mu. 14: Ref. 15: 620 Peachtree st, NE, apt 1902, Atlanta Ga 30308.

KIRKLAND, KENNETH LESTER. b Fort Worth Tex 18 D 38. 5: UHouston 57-61 (Sp) BA; Colby Col summer 59 (Russian); IndU summer 60 (Russian); UCal (Berkeley) 61-65 (Slavic Lang, Lit), 65-67 MLS. 6: Russian, Sp, Ger, Polish. 7: Libn San Francisco Pub Lib 66-67; Ref & circ libn DePaul U 67-. 9: ALA; IllLA. 10: ACLU. 14: Ref, catlg, bibliog, circ, admin. 15: 917 W Waveland ave, Chicago Il 60613.

KIRKPATRICK, ALICE MAY. b Fitchburg Mass 18 F 02. 5: Middlebury Col 18-22 (Biol) BS; NY State Lib Sch Albany 23-24 Certif, 26; UMich Summers 28, 31, 32 AMLS. 7: Libn Mass Sch for the Feebleminded, Waverly Mass 24; Gen asst Lib of New Britain Inst, New Britain Conn 24-26; Asst libn travel lib ext Div NY State Lib 26; Instr NY State Col for Tchrs (Albany) 27, Asst libn 27-47; Libn civil affairs div US Dept of the Army NYC 49; Libn lib serv br US Dept of State, Wash DC 49-52; Catlgr Armed Forces Staff Col (Norfolk Va) 52-53; STATION LIBN US Naval Air Station, Norfolk Va 53-68; Catlgr Pub Lib, Norfolk Va 69-. 9: ALA; VaLA; SELA. 10: Norfolk Mus of Arts & Sci; Metro Opera Guild; NY Philharmonic Symphony Soc; Phi Beta Kappa. 14: Catlg, ref bk sel. 15: 5503 Alson dr apt 171B, Norfolk Va 23508.

KIRKPATRICK, MARY (ELEANOR). b Cleveland Ohio 1 My 38. 5: Oberlin 56-60 (Elem Educ) AB; UMich 65-66 AMLS. 6: Fr, Ger. 7: Tchr Norwood Bd of Educ, Norwood Ohio 60-65; Asst ref libn UCincinnati 66-68, Ref libn 68-. 9: ALA; OhioLA. 10: Sierra Club; Beta Phi Mu. 14: Ref. 15: 2805 Stratford ave, Cincinnati Oh 45220.

KIRKPATRICK, MILDRED ROSETTA (CASTINE). b Ft Worth Tex 29 Ap 14. 5: Wiley Col 28-37 (Educ) AB; N Tex State U 61-65 (Guidance, LS) M Ed. 6: Fr. 7: Sch sec I M Terrell High Sch, Ft Worth Tex 31-36; Tchr Carver Jr High Sch, Ft Worth Tex 37-44, Libn 45-49; Libn Dunbar Jr Sr High Sch, Ft Worth Tex 49-61; Libn Morningside Jr High Sch, Ft Worth Tex 61-. 9: ALA; TexLA; Tex State Tchr Assn. 10: YWCA; Ft Worth Coun of Internat Reading Assn; Alpha Lambda Sigma. 14: Ref. 15: 1500 Evans ave, Ft Worth Tx 76104.

KIRKS, JAMES (HARVEY) JR. b Los Angeles Cal 16 S 37. 4: Barbara Barry. 5: Compton Col 55-57 (Hist) AA; UCLA 57-60 (Hist) BA; USoCal 61-62 MS in LS. 7: Stud asst doheny Lib USoCal 61-62; Libn I City of Inglewood Pub Lib, Cal 62; Communications ctr specialist US Army Signal Corps AFCENT, Fontainebleau France 62-64; Hd ext serv city of Inglewood Pub Lib 64-66; Dir pub serv Arcadia Pub Lib Cal 66-. 9: ALA; CalLA (Legisl Soc Responsibilities Com; So Dist Com). 10: Rotary. 14: Lib admin, pub rel. 15: 2519 W 112th st, Inglewood Ca 90303.

KIRKWOOD, RICHARD EDWIN. b Westbrook Mr 18 S 27. 4: Karin Helander. 5: Dartmouth 47-50 (Eng Lit) AB; Chicago 50-51 (Eng Lit); Columbia 60-63 MS in LS. 6: Fr, Sp, Ital. 7: (Pvt) US Army, US 45-47; Reserva tions agent American Airlines, NYC 52-53; Asst manager group dept Equitable Life, NYC 53-63; Ref libn Bowdoin Col 63-67; Libn Hollins Col 67-. 9: VLA. 10: Phi Beta Kappa. 14: Ref, docs. 15: 816 Dexter rd NW, Roanoke Va 24019.

KIRN, MARJORIE ANN. b Fremont Ind 10 Je 28. 5: Murray State Col 48-52 (LS, Bus) BS; UMich summer 56-62 MALS. 6: Ger. 7: Ref-circ Appleton Pub Lib, Appleton Wis 53-56; High sch libn Kearsley Commun Schs, Flint Mich 56-66, Elem libn & supv 66-. 9: ALA; NEA; MichASchL; MichEA; Flint Area Lib Club. 14: High sch lib. 15: G-4396 Underhill dr, Flint Mi 48506.

KIRSCHNER, BARRY WILLIAM. b St Paul Minn 6 D 44. 4: Charlene Dudovitz. 5: UMinn 62-67 (Art Hist) BA (summa cum laude), 67-68 (LS) MA. 6: Ital, Fr. 7: Art & arch libn UColo 68-. 10: Phi Beta Kappa. 14: Art lib. 15: Univ of Colorado Art and Architecture Lib, Boulder Co 80302.

KIRSCHNER, MADELINE. b Bronx NY 18 Jl 41. 5: Brooklyn Col 58-62 (Eng) BA (cum laude); Columbia 62-63

(LS) MS. 6: Sp, Fr. 7: Libn Brooklyn Pub Lib Kings Highway Br 63-64, Libn Ingersoll Bldg Telephone Ref Div 64-66, Libn Lang & Lit div 67-68, Sr libn for lang spec 68-. 9: ALA; NYLA; NYLibClub. 10: Gamma Sigma Sigma. 13: Yes. 14: Ref, for lang bks. 15: 399 Ocean pky., Brooklyn NY 11218.

KIRWAN, WILLIAM JOSEPH. b Buffalo NY 15 Ap 36. 4: Betty Lynn Kirwan. 5: St Bonaventure U 55-59 (Hist) BA; Drexel 60-61 MS in LS. 7: Jr libn Buffalo & Erie Co Pub Lib, Buffalo NY 61-63; Asst libn Essex Community Col 63-66; Dir of the lib Loyola Col 66-. 9: Lib Coop Prog of Md Indepent Col (treas)XXX 09: CathLA (chm Col & Service Sect Md-DC gp; Lib Coop Prog of Md Indepent Col (treas). 14: Lib bldgs, mergers. 15: 2447 Pickwick rd, Baltimore Md 21207.

KISSNER, ARTHUR J. b NYC 27 Jl 27. 4: Joan Graf. 5: NYU 44-47 (Sci) BA, 47-48 (Sci Educ) MA; Pratt 54-56 MSLS. 6: Fr. 7: Tchr NY City Schs 48-53; Libn Brooklyn Pub Lib 54-58; Asst libn Oak Park Pub Lib, Oak Park Ill 58-61; Chief Libn Fitchburg Pub Lib, Fitchburg Mass 61-. 8: Assoc Dir Central Mass Reg Pub Lib System 62-. 9: ALA; MassLA (chm Planning Com 63-64, pres 67-68); NELA (dir 68-69). 10: Fitchburg Rotary Club; Fitchburg Coun on Aging. 13: Yes. 14: Pub lib admin, lib bldg. 15: Fitchburg Pub Lib 610 Main st, Fitchburg Ma 01420.

KISSNER, JOAN GRAF. b Buffalo NY 9 N 29. 4: Arthur J Kissner. 5: UBuffalo 47-51 (Biol) BS; Columbia 51-53 MS in LS. 6: Ger. 7: Br libn Brooklyn Pub Lib 51-59; Libn Lunenburg High Sch, Lunenburg Mass 62-64; Libn Oakmont Reg High Sch, S Ashburnham Mass 64-65, 67-. 9: ALA; MassSchLA. 10: LWV; 4-H Leader; Girl Scout Leader. 14: Ref, sch lib wk. 15: Corey Hill rd, Ashburnham Ma 01430.

KISTER, KENNETH F. b New Cumberland Penn 3 N 35. 4: Suzon Ott. 5: Shippensburg State Col 53-57 (Eng Lit) BS in Ed; Simmons 61-62 (LS) MS . 7: Tchr Big Spring Joint High Sch, Penn 57-60; Tchr Montpelier(Vt) High Sch 60-61; Grad asst Simmons Col 61-62, Ref libn 62-64; Sr asst Nottingham Pub Lib, Eng 64-65; Asst Prof Simmons Col Sch of Lib Sci 65-. 9: ALA; (Ref & Subscr Bks Rev Com 66-); MassLA; (Recr Com 66-). 10: AAUP; ACLU. 12: "Social Issues and Library Problems: Case St udies in the Social S ciences" (68); Ed, "Bay State Librarian" (68-). 13: Yes. 14: Ref, soc scis, fiction, Censorship & intel freedom. 15: Simmons Col Sch of Lib Sci, 300 The Fenway, Boston Ma 02115.

KISTLER, ELLEN DOWNEY. b Royal Center Ind 10 Ag 1900. 5: Ind U 17-18; UMich summer 19 (LS); UWis 23-24 (LS) Certif, 28-30 (Ger) AB. 6: Ger, Fr. 7: Gen asst Pub Lib, Logansport Ind 18-19; Gen asst Pub Lib, Peru Ind 19-23; Head catlgr Pub Lib, Milwaukee 24-28; Head catlg dept UNotre Dame (Notre Dame Ind) 32-47, Catlgr Dante Collection 30-32; Head local hist dept Pub Lib, S Bend Ind 47-52, Head catlg dept 52-66; Catlgr rare bk rm 2 St Mary's Col (Notre Dame) 66-. 9: ALA; IndLA (sec 46-47; chm Tech Resources Dept 65); Chicago Reg Catlgrs Assn. 10: AAUW; Altrusa Club. 13: Yes. 14: Catlg. 15: 1214 E Madison st, S Bend In 46617.

KITCHEN, PAUL HOWARD. b Toronto 14 N 37. 4: Anne Heaney. 5: Carleton U 60-63 (Eng) BA; UBC 63-64 BLS. 07: Sys Devel Proj Nat Lib of Can, Ottawa 64-. 10: Prof Inst Pub Serv Can. 14: Ref, bibliog. 15: Nat Lib Pub Archives Bldg, Ottawa 2 Can.

KITTEL, DOROTHY (ANN). b Baltimore 30 Mr 23. 5: Md State Tchrs Col 40-44; UChicago 51-53 (LS) MA. 7: Lib asst Enoch Pratt Free Lib, Baltimore 45-51; Asst readers serv Vassar Col Lib 53-55; Head commun living dept Dallas Pub Lib 55-57; Consul Lib-Commun Proj ALA, 57-59; Membership asst ALA 59-61; Adult serv consul NC State Lib 61-63; Adult serv spec US Lib Serv Br Wash DC 63-65, Lib ext spec 65-68, Coord interlib coop 68-. 9: ALA-ASD (Exec Bd 65-68); Ad Educ Assn; DCLA. 13: Yes. 14: Adult serv, pub lib ext. 15: Div Lib Programs, US Off of Educ, Wash Dc 20202.

KITTELSON, DAVID JAMES. b Grand Rapids Minn 28 Ja 31. 4: Marion L Oritz. 5: Itasca Jr Col 49-50; UHawaii 54-57 (Hist) BA; UMinn 57-58 (LS) MA; UHawaii 61-65 (Pacific Hist) MA; UWis 68-69 (Educ). 06: Hawaiian. 7: Storekeeper 2nd Class US Naval Ammunition Depot, Hawaii 50-54; Libn II UHawaii (Honolulu) 58-62; Assoc libn UHawaii (Hilo) 62-64, Head Libn 64-. 8: Mem ALA Recru Netwk Hawaii 66-; Lib Consul Peace Corps Training Ctr, Hilo 67-. 9: NEA; HawaiiLA; HawaiiEA. 10: Omicron Delta Kappa. 13: Yes. 14: Hawaiiana, lib educ. 15: 194 Kuikahi st, Hilo Hi 96720.

KITTILSON, BRUCE JOSEPH. b Ellsworth Wis 20 D 31. 4: Elizabeth Frank. 5: Macalester Col 50-55 (Music- Educ) BA; UMinn 61-62 (LS) MA, 66-69 (Educ). 06: Ger. 7: Music tchr W Concord (Minn) High Sch 55-56; Musician US Army (Sp 3) Frankfurt Ger 56-58; Music tchr Belview (Minn) High Sch 58-60; Libn John H Glenn Jr High Sch, N St Paul Minn 62-66; Grad Fellow UMinn 66-. 8: Participated in the NDEA Inst for Sch Libns UMinn 65. 9: NEA; ALA; MinnEA; MinnASchl (chm Capital Div 67-69). 10: Great Books discussion group; Local educ & lib assns. 14: Sch libs, instr media, catlg. 15: 1428 E Hoyt, St Paul Mn 55106.

KITTLE, ARTHUR THOMAS. b Athena Ga 9 D 20. 5: UGa 37-41 (Journalism) AB; UNC 41-42 BS in LS; Columbia 54-57 DLS. 7: Stud asst UGa 37-41; Ref asst UNC 41-42; Lt commander US Navy 42-46; Acquis libn chief tech processes div asst dir Air U Lib Maxwell AFB Ala 46-53; Libn tchg master Eng Dept St Paul's Sch, Concord NH 53-58; Visiting prof div of libnship Emory U 58-59, summer 60, 64-65; Asst on spec assignment Enoch Pratt Free Lib, Baltimore 59-60; Head, sci-tech lib Ga Inst of Tech 61-65; Prof sch of info sci Atlanta Ga 63-, Assoc dir lib 65-. 9: ALA; SLA; SELA; GaLA; Atlanta Lib Club. 13: Yes. 14: Info sci, tech serv. 15: 4145 Conway Valley rd NW, Atlanta Ga 30327.

KITTNER, SABRA CORBIN (MacDORMAN). b Federalsburg Md 1 N 22. 5: West Md Col 40-44 (Math, Biol, Chem) AB; Johns Hopkins 48, 58; Catholic U 61-62 (LS); West Md Col 64-65 (LS) MEd. 7: Tchr Bd of Educ, Baltimore Co 44-51; Libn N Carroll High Sch, Carroll Co Md 58-66; Supv Bd of Educ, Carroll Co Md 66-. 8: Tchr Lib Sci, West Md Col 68-. 9: NAEB; ALA; -AASchL; NEA-DAVI; Md State TE; MdLA; Assn Sch Libns Md; Md A-V Assn. 10: Phi Delta Gamma. 14: Multi-media approach to learning. 15: 94 Willis st, Westminster Md 21157.

KITTRELL, MRS HELEN (HAND). b Topeka Kan 29 Ap 03. 5: UKan 2024 (Span) BA; Emory 30-31 BA in LS. 7: Reviser Emory U Lib Sch 31-35; Sch libn Norris Sch, Norris Tenn 35-42; Libn Fontana Dam, NC 42-45; Reg libn Fontana Reg Lib, Bryson City NC 45-52; Reg libn Clinch-Powell Reg Lib, Clinton Tenn 52-. 8: Clinton (Tenn) Lib Commun Proj 55-58. 9: ALA; SELA; TennLA. 10: Norris Little Theatre Bd; Great Bks Discussion Gp. 14: Reg wk. 15: Clinch-Powell Reg Lib Box 269, Clinton Tn 37716.

KIVI, (ELSIE) KAREN. b Hibbing Minn 31 Ja 19. 5: Hibbing Jr Col 36-38 (Pre-LS); UMinn (Minneapolis) 39-41 BS in LS; UIll 50-51 MS in LS; UMich (Ann Arbor) 55-56; UIll 64-65 Certif for Advanced Study in LS. 6: Finnish. 7: Sch libn-Eng tchr Deer River Pub Sch, Deer River Minn 41-43; Sch libn Aitkin Pub Schs, Aitkin Minn 43-46; Sch libn Bessemer Pub Schs, Bessemer Mich 46-47; Pub serv libn & Assoc Prof of Lib Sci Moorhead State Col 47-. 8: Consul Detroit Lakes Pub Lib in org child room 58-60; Visiting Prof of Lib Sci Tex Women's U summers 59-61, 63 , 68. 9: ALA; NEA; MinnLA; MinnEA. 10: AAUP; AAUW; LWV; Nat Fed Bus & Prof Women Inc; Inter-Faculty Org (State Cols of Minn); Beta Phi Mu. 14: Ref, tchg lib sci. 15: Moorhead State Col, Moorhead Mn 56560.

KLAHN, LOIS C (PRESTON). b Rochester NY 12 Mr 06. 4: Jordan L Klahn. 5: URochester 30 (Lat) AB; Columbia 34 (LS) BS. 6: Lat, Fr, Gk. 7: Asst libn Rochester Pub Lib, Rochester NY 27-30; Libn Sewanhaka High Sch, Floral Park NY 30-35; Libn Floral Park Pub Lib, Floral Park NY 36-44; Libn Garden City Park Sch, Garden City Park NY 55-67; Libn Hillside Grade Sch, New Hyde Park NY 67-. 09: NYLA; NYSchLA; NY State Tchrs Assn; Nassau Co LA (sec). 10: AAUW; Womans Club. 14: Sch libs, ref. 15: 77 Terrace ave, Floral Park NY 11001.

KLAHRE, ETHEL S(USAN). b Johnstown Penn 28 Jl 05. 5: UAkron 23-27 (Eng) BA; West Res 27-28 BS in LS. 7: Circ libn UAkron 28-38; Asst libn Commonwealth Edison Co, Chicago 39-42; Libn heater engnr dept Stewart-Warner Corp, Chicago 42-43; Libn Fed Reserve Bank of Cleveland 43-65; Asst libn dist lib serv Cuyahoga Commun Col 65-. 9: SLA (pres 62-63; pres Cleveland Chap 59-60). 10: Zonta Club. 14: Spec libs, univ & col libs, tech serv. 15: 3885 Kirkwood rd, Cleveland Heights Oh 44121.

KLAIR, CAROLYN MAE. b Wilmington Del 24 D 42. 5: UDel 60-64 (Elem Educ) BS Ed; West MichU 66-67 MLS. 7: Tchr Christiana Elem Sch, Newark Del 64; E I duPont & Co Inc, Wilmington Del; Patent libn & clk 64-66, Research libn 67-68, Br libn 68-. 9: SLA. 14: Ref. 15: 4312 Miller rd apt 107, Wilmington Del 19802.

KLANIAN, MARY. b Providence 31 O 25. 5: URI 43-47 (Eng) BS; Drexel 51-52 MS in LS. 6: Armenian. 7: Ref libn Providence Pub Lib 47-51; Ref libn Detroit Pub Lib 52-56; Ref libn Ford Motor Co, Dearborn Mich 57-58; Group supv Chrysler Missile Div, Warren Mich 58-61; Lib manager IBM Advanced Systems Development Div, Yorktown Heights NY 61-. 9: SLA (Detroit Chap: Memb Chm 57-58; NY Chap: chm Sci-Tech Group 65-66); ASIS (Spec Libs Com 67-70). 14: Ref, mechanized systems. 15: Cedar Lane Heights, Apt B-8, Ossining NY 10598.

KLASSEN, ROBERT LEONARD. b Patterson Cal 10 N 35. 4: Beverly Isaak. 5: Tabor Col 53-55; Fresno State Col 55-57 (Soc Studies) AB, 58; UCal(Berkeley) 59 MLS. 7: Ref libn Cal Sect Cal State Lib 59-60; Head Libn Pacific Col Fresno Cal 60-62; Asst supv Cal Sect Cal State Lib 62-68; Admin libn div of lib programs US Off of Educ Wash DC 68-. 8: Library/USA, NYWorld's Fair 64. 9: ALA; SLA; ASIS; DCLA. 10: Phi Kappa Phi; Pi Gamma Mu; Beta Phi Mu Sacramento Bk Collectors Club; West Hist Assn. 13: Yes. 14 Ref, lib admin, automation, spec libs. 15: 4513 Nineteenth rd N, Arlington Va 22207.

KLATT, MELVIN JOHN. b Milwaukee 19 My 29. 4: Shirley Ryan. 5: UWis(Milwaukee) 47-49; UWis 54-56 (Hist Econ) BS; UDenver 57-58 (LS) MA. 6: Fr. 7: Combat engnr USArmy (Pfc) Korea 51-53; Truck driver Advance Trucking Milwaukee 53-54; Jr libn Milwaukee Pub Lib 56-57, Libn II ref-catlg 58-62; Acquis libn UIll (Chicago) 62-65; Head of tech serv UDenver 65-67, Act dir 67-69. 8: Chm By-laws Com RockyMt Bibliog Ctr 67-68. 9: Chicago Libns Tech Serv; ColoLA. 10: SW Denver Hu man Rel; AAUP; Chicago Assn Com & Ind; Metropolitan Denver Fair Housing. 12: Co-ed "Colorado Academic Library 1967-68". 13: Yes. 14: Tech serv, admin, publ ind, higher educ philos. 15: 2077 So Newton st, Denver Co 80219.

KLAUSS, DOROTHY M. b Pittsburgh 5 My 10. 5: UPittsburgh 28-31 (Sociol) BA; Carnegie 31-32 (LS) BA. 6: Ger. 7: Carnegie Lib of Pittsburgh: Asst libn W End Br 35-38, Asst libn Brookline Br 38-40, Asst libn Wylie ave Br 40-43, Asst libn SSide Br 43-45, Br libn WEnd Br 45-55, Br libn SSide Br 55-. 9: ALA; PennLA. 10: Pittsburgh Lib Club; C of C. 14: Pub lib. 15: 101 S Grandview ave, Pittsburgh Pa 15203.

KLEIN, AGATHA L (LINDNER). b Sandwich Ill 7 D 13. 4: John A Klein. 5: Aurora Col 32-35 (Hist) BA; UMinn (Minneapolis) Minn 37-38 (LS) BS; UChicago 47 (LS). 7: Lib asst Aurora Pub Lib, Aurora Ill 36-37; Libn pub co & sch libs, Internat Falls Minn 38-42; Supv of pub libs State Lib Div St Paul 42-48; Instr Lib Sch UMinn 48-49; Coordinator adult educ St Paul Pub Lib 52-58, Chief Central Lib 58-. 8: Instr spec lib train classes for in-serv libns to obtain certif UWis (Eau Claire) 52. 9: ALA-ASD (chm 2 coms); MinnLA (pres 48-49, chm var coms & sects) . 10: LWV; Zonta. 14: Adult serv, lib admin. 15: 90 W 4th st, St Paul Mn 55102.

KLEIN, DIANE (BRAND). b Brooklyn NY 13 Je 47. 4: Russell J Klein. 5: UMass 64-68 (Educ) BA; Simmons 68-69 (LS) MS. 6: Sp. 7: Lib asst (NE Merchants Nat Bank), Boston 69-. 9: SLA; ALA. 10: Phi Kappa Phi; Kappa Delta Pi; Alpha Lambda Delta. 13: Yes. 14: Ref. 15: 42 Hickory pl, Livingston NJ 07039.

KLEIN, LEONORE (GLOTZER). b NYC 4 S 16. 4: Joseph M Klein. 5: Barnard 32-36 (Eng) BA; Wellesley 36-37 (Eng) MA; Columbia 64 MS in LS. 6: Fr. 7: Eng tchr LI City High Sch, Queens NY 41, Libn 48-51; Libn Wm Cullen Bryant High Sch, Queens NY 51-53; Libn E T Roux Lib Fla So Col 53-59; Libn Pleasantville Elem Jr High Sch, Pleasantville NY 59-62; Libn Eastview ave Jr High Sch, White Plains NY 62-. 9: Authors' Guild; NYLA; White Plains Tchrs Assn. 12: Auth of child bks publ by Young Scott Books, Grosset & Dunlap, Alfred A Knopf, Scholastic Books, Abelard-Schuman Ltd, Harvey House. 14: Sch libs. 15: 7 Barbara lane, Hartsdale NY 10530.

KLEIN, MARY S. b New Brunswick NJ 15 N 16. 4: Rudolph Klein. 5: Douglass Col 37 BS; Rutgers U (LS). 6: Fr. 7: Libn Squibb Inst Med Research, New Brunswick NJ 42-68, Spec libn 68-. 9: MedLA; Drug Info Assn; SLA (NJ Chap: sec 61-62, numerous coms). 15: Squibb Inst for Med Res, New Brunswick NJ.

KLEIN, MARY MAGDALEN. b Richfield Wis 6 S 29. 5: Cardinal Stritch Col 47-51 (Sociol) AB; Catholic U 53-55 MS in LS. 6: Ger. 7: Ref libn Trinity Col(Wash DC) 53-64; Libn Xaverian Col 64-. 9: CathLA. 10: Beta Phi Mu. 14: Ref. 15: 104 Fort dr NE, Wash DC 20011.

KLEIN, ROBERT F. b Dubuque Iowa 2 Je 37. 5: Loras Col 55-59 (Lat) BA; Catholic U 62-64 MSLS. 6: Ger. 7: Stud asst Loras Col Lib 57-59; Desk attendant LC 60; Adult readers adv DC Pub Lib 60-61; USArmy Personnel Spec 4th Class 61-62; Ref asst Catholic U 62-64; Asst libn Loras Col Lib 64-. 9: ALA; BSA; IowaLA; NE Iowa Acad Lib Assn, (Exec Dir, 69). 10: Iowa State Hist Soc. 14: Rare bks. 15: 3040 Lemon, Dubuque Ia 52001.

KLEIN, SALLY W(RIGHT). b San Francisco 11 S 41. 4: Stanley Allan Klein. 5: Scripps Col 59-63 (Philos) BA; UVienna 62 (Philos) Simmons 64 (LS) MS. 6: Ger, Fr. 7: Catlgr Fletcher Sch of Law & Diplomacy (Medford Mass) 64-66; Readers Adv-Robbins Lib, Arlington Mass 66-67; Readers Adv Pomona Pub Lib, Pomona Ca 67-68. 14: Catlg, ref. 15: 150 Brooks ave, Clare mont Ca 91711.

KLEIN, SHELAGH (ANN CANT). b Surrey Eng 16 Mr 40. 4: Peter Klein. 5: Marygrove Col 57-61 (Hist) BA; UMich 61-63 MALS. 6: Fr. 7: Med records clerk Providence Hosp, Southfield Mich 58; Receptionist Egry Register Co, Detroit 60; Page Marygrove Col Lib 59-60; Ya libn Detroit Pub Lib 61-63; Head Libn Avon Twp Pub Lib, Rochester Mich 63-65; Head child dept Pub Lib, Ann Arbor Mich 65-66; Libn Hawthorn Ctr, Northville Mich 66-. 9: ALA; MichLA. 10: Friends of the Avon Twp Pub Lib. 14: Ref wk with child. 15: Hawthorn Ctr, 18471 Haggerty rd, Northville Mi 48167.

KLEINER, JANE(LLYN) (PICKERING). b Harrisburg Ill 9 D 36. 4: Arthur A Kleiner. 5: LSU 54-58 (Journalism) BA, 63-65 (LS) MS, 67- (Journalism). 06: Sp. 7: Crime & court reporter "Morning Advocate," Baton Rouge La 58-60; Hundemer Pub Relations writer, Baton Rouge La 61-62; Asst circ libn LSU Lib 65-, Hd circ dept 65-66, Asst doc lib 66-67, Info desk libn 67, Hd interlib loan 67-. 9: ALA; LaLA; (Pub Rel Com); SWLA . 10: Theta Sigma Phi; Phi Kappa Phi; Delta Gamma Alumnae Assn; Beta Phi Mu; AAUW; Baton Rouge Press Club; PTA; LSU Lib Staff Assn. 13: Yes. 14: Interl coop, lib pub rel. 15: Bennington ave, Concord Estates, Baton Rouge La 70803.

KLEINER, JOSEPH ROBERT. b Trenton NJ 9 Jl 40. 5: St Joseph's Col 60-63 (Pol Sci) BS; Rutgers 63-65 MLS. 6: Ger, Lat. 7: Free Pub Lib, Trenton NJ: Jr Lib clerk 56-63, Lib trainee 63-64, Sr libn 65, Prin libn 65-66, Supring libn 66-. 9: ALA-RSD (Pub Lib Sect); -ACRL (Rare Bks); NJLA (Ref Div, Pub Lib Sect, Human Rel Com; Hist & Bibliog Sect Bibliog Com). 10: Trenton Hist Soc; YMCA. 13: Yes. 14: Circ procedure, acquis, rare bks (Frankliniana). 15: 138 Boudinot st, Trenton NJ 08618.

KLEINHEINZ, SISTER M LUCILLE, FSPA. b Madison Wis. 5: Viterbo Col (Eng) BA; Rosary Col 52 MALS; UIll (Urbana) NDEA summer 67, HEA Inst 68-69 (New Tech Sch Libs) CAS. 06: Lat. 7: Secondary tchr Mt Carmel Mt Carmel Iowa 41-44; Secondary tchr-libn De Padua High Sch Ashland Wis 44-48; Secondary tchr-libn Cathedral Superior Wis 48-50; Libn Aquinas High Sch La Crosse Wis 50-. 8: Org of libs in the new schs taught by commun Provo Utah & Salem Ore; Direction of high sch lib; Iowa; Consul libn for high schs. 9: CathLA (Adv Bd High sch sect); Natl Cath Stud Lib Aides Assn WisCathLA; WisLA (Scholarship Bd 67-68). 14: Ref, sch libs. 15: 1419 Cass st, La Crosse Wi 54601.

KLEINSCHMIDT, REV ANTHONY A(NDREW). b Sauke Centre Minn 9 N 17. 5: Josephinum Col 39 (Philos) BA; Rosary Col 47 BS in LS; Goethe Inst (Germany) 58 (Ger); St John's U (Collegeville Minn) 65 (Liturgy & Theol). 6: Ger, Lat. 7: Latin instr & Head Libn Josephinum High Sch, Worthington Ohio 43-46; German instr Josephinum High Sch, Worthington Ohio 47-60; Chaplain Ohio State Sch for Deaf, Columbus Ohio 54-60; Chaplain Ohio State Sch for Blind, Columbus Ohio 54-; Prof of Liturgy Josephinum Sem 60-; Head Libn Pont Col Josephinum (Worthington Ohio) 46-. 9: ALA; CathLA (chm Sem Lib Sect 54-55, chm Catlg & clsf sect 58-60); OhioLA (chm Col & Univ Sect 54-55). 10: Liturgical Conf of NA; Josephinum Alumni Assn; Worthington Publ Libr Bd Trustees. 11: Hon Chaplain to the Pope; title Very Rev Msgr. 13: Yes. 14: Catlg, ref. 15: A T Wehrle Mem Lib Pont Col Josephinum, Worthington Oh 43085.

KLEINTOP, CLARA (SMITH). b Eldred Twp Penn 14 D 03. 5: E Stroudsburg State Col summers 21, 22; Hood 22-26 (Eng, Soc Sci) AB; Temple U 42-43, Kutztown State Col 54-55 (LS). 7: Tchr rural sch, Monroe Co Penn 21-22; Stud lib asst Hood Col 22-26; Women's adv wagner Col 33-42; Circ dept Curtis Publ Co 55-56; S Orange (NJ) Pub Lib: Y-a & ref asst 56-65, Co-admin 65-67, Y-a & ref 67-. 9: NJLA. 14: YA, ref, 1st editions. 15: 345 Lincoln ave, Orange NJ 07050.

KLEMM, FLORENCE FREDETTE. b Denver Colo 26 Ap 42. 5: Harding Col 60-64 (Eng) BA; UDenver 66-67 Libnship MA. 6: Ger. 7: Circ libn Pepperdine Col 67-68; Libn intern USAF Acad 68-. 14: Ref, acquis. 15: 1628 E Bijou, Colo Springs Co 80909.

KLEMPNER, IRVING M. b Glowaczow Poland 28 N 24. 4: Miriam S Stern. 5: Brooklyn Col 49-51 (Liberal Arts) BA; Columbia 51-52 MSLS, 59-67 DLS. 6: Fr, Russian, Polish, Ger. 7: Intern libn US Dept State 52-53; Prof libn LC 53-56; Supv libn USNavy Dept Naval Applied Sci Lab NY 56-57; Asst libn USNavy Dept Navy Intelligence Sch Wash DC 57-58; Chief libn United Nuclear Corp (White Plains NY) 58-63; Mgr info serv 63-67; Assoc Prof Sch Lib Sci SUNY(Albany) 67-. 8: Princ invest, Directorate of Info Sci Study, Air Force Off of Sci Res ; Partic, Internat Advanced Study Inst or the Eval of Info Retr Systems, The Hague 65; Consul: Gen Applied Sci Lab, United Nuclear Corp, Pandex Index. 9: SLA (chm Documentation Div 65-66, chm NYSci-Tech Group 63-64); ADI; WestchesterLA. 10: AAUP. 11: Recipient of research grant, US Air Force; Fellowship, NATO Advanced Study Inst. 12: "Diffusion of Abstracting and Indexing Services for Government-Sponsored Research" (68). 13: Yes. 14: Documentation, info retrieval. 15: School of Lib Sci, State Univ of NY at Albany, Albany NY 12203.

KLEMT, REV CALVIN CARL. b Louisville Ky 19 Ag 25. 4: Bette Bartlett. 5: UKy 46-49 (Math); Heidelberg Col 49-50 (Math) BA; Union Theol Sem (NY) 50-53 (Theol) BD; UMich (Ann Arbor) 61-62 AMLS. 7: Radio repairman T/3 Signal Corps USArmy, US, Europe 43-46; Pastor Suffield Evangelical & Reformed Church, Ohio 53-58; Pastor Big Rapids United Church, Big Rapids Mich 58-61; Libn Central Lutheran Theol Sem (Fremont Neb) 62-66; Libn Austin Presbyterian Theol Sem 66-. 9: ATheolLA. 13: Yes. 14: Theol bibliog & acquis, lib admin, interlib coop & planning. 15: Austin Presbyterian Theological Seminary, 106 W 27th, Austin Tx 78705.

KLENE, JOANNE M. b Quincy Ill 30 Ag 26. 5: Mundelein Col 43-45 (Liberal Arts); DePaulU 45-47 (Bus Admin) BSC; Rosary Col 56-58 MLS. 7: Statistician libn Barcus-Kindred Co Chicago 47-50; Insurance broker 51-58; Circ libn DePaulU Lib 58-61; Head of adult dept River Forest Pub Lib River Forest Ill 61-64; Libn Bellwood Pub Lib Bellwood Ill 64-67; Chief consul Suburban Lib Sys, Western Springs Ill 67-. 9: ALA; CathLA (Exec Bd; IllUnit: chm 65-66, Exhib Club 61-62); IllLA; Lib Admins Coop NoIll (chm 67-68). 15: 1321 Balmoral, Westchester Il 60153.

KLENK, RICHARD GEORGE. b Defiance Ohio 9 Ap 07. 4: Lois Wallis. 5: Ohio State U 37 (Biol Sci) BA; Drexel 39 (LS) BS; LSU 58 (Fr) MA. 6: Fr. 7: Asst in brs & music & drama dept Detroit Pub Lib 39-43; Order dept asst IndU Lib 43-46; LSU Lib: Chief acquis libn 46-50, Bibliog 51-53, Act chief tech processes 53-55, Bibliog 55-. 9: ALA-ACRL; LaLA. 10: Phi Kappa Phi; Phi Sigma Iota; ACLU; LCLU; Amer Humanist Assn. 14: Bldg subject collections, acquis. 15: 1761 Cloverdale ave, Baton Rouge La 70808.

KLEVEN, LILLIE M. b Hendrum Minn 17 Ja 11. 5: State Col (Bemidji Minn) 31-33, 35-37 (Educ) BEd; UWash summer 38 (LS) Certif; Peabody Col 40-41 BSLS. 6: Norwegian, Ger. 7: WAVE off (Lt) USN, Northampton Mass, NYC, Honolulu 42-46; Supv libn Info Ctrs Dept of the Army, Tokyo Japan & Korea) Dept of the Army, NY 50-51; Chief Japan & Korea lib unit US Info Agy, Wash DC 51-54, Chief Far E libs 55-67, Lib program adv E Asia & Pacific area 68-. 8: Lib Prog Adv for Far East Area (conferred with staffs of the U S Info Serv Libs in numerous countries) 57. 9: ALA (Internat Rel RT: (treas 66-69, chm East Asia Area 69); DCLA. 10: Pi Gamma Mu; AAUW; Amer Fed of Arts; Amer Foreign Serv Assn; Smithsonian Assocs; Print Club of Wash D C; Pratt Graphic Art Ctr. 14: Lib admin. 15: 3822 Van Ness st NW, Washington DC 20016.

KLEY, ROLAND (GOTTLIEB). b Sheboygan Wis 17 Jl 12. 4: Adeline Hilmes. 5: Lakeland Col 30-35 (Hist) BA; Mission House Theol Sem (Wis) 39-42 BD; UWis (Milwaukee) 57-58 (LS); UWis (Madison) 58-59 MA in LS. 6: Ger. 7: Proofreader Sheboygan (Wis) Press 36, Reporter 37; Railway mail clerk USCivil Serv 38; Minister United Church of Christ: Wausau Wis 42-45, Kohler Wis 45-50, New Holstein Wis 50-57; Libn Mission House Theo Sem (Plymouth Wis) 57-62; Libn United Theol Sem (New Brighton Minn) 62-. 9: ATheolLA. 10: Wis AlumniLA. 12: Co-ed "History of Mission House-Lakeland" (62). 13: Yes. 15: 552 Driftwood rd, New Brighton Mn 55112.

KLIEWER, MARY. b Henderson Neb 9 Jl 1899. 5: Tabor Col 28-30; York Col 37-38 (Eng) BA; UIll 49-50 MS in LS. 6: Ger. 7: Tchr High Sch, Franklin Neb 44-45; Tchr High Sch, Gresham Neb 45-46; Libn Tabor Col 46-. 9: ALA; KanLA. 10: Bus & Prof Womens Club; Mesonite Hist Soc. 14: Catlg, ref. 15: Tabor Col, Hillsboro Kn 67063.

KLIMAS, (JOHN) PERRY. b NYC 8 Je 39. 4: Charlotte Davis. 05: Fla So Col 57-61 (Soc Studies) BA; Middle Tenn State Col 63-64 (Educ Admin & Supv) MA. 7: (2nd Lt) USArmy Ft Jackson SC 61-62; Civics tchr Lakeland Jr High Sch, Lakeland Fla 62-63; Libn Redland Elem Sch, Homestead Fla 64-65; Media spec Driftwood Jr High Sch, Hollywood Fla 65-. 9: NEA; FlaEA; FlaLA; FlaSchL; Fla A-V Assn; Browart Co Assn of Media Specilists. 10: Jr C of C. 14: Stud assts, visual aids, a-v equip. 15: 5640 SW 8th st, Plantation Fl 33314.

KLIMOWICZ, ARTHUR (DOMINICK). b Newark NJ 6 Ag 24. 4: Rose Fortuny. 5: Seton Hall 41-46 (Soc studies) AB; Fordham 45-47 (Sociol); Columbia 49-55 (LS) MS. 6: Polish. 7: Tchr St Patricks High Sch, Elizabeth NJ 46-47; Lib asst Seton HallU 48-65; Sch libn Seton Hall Prep Sch, So Orange NJ 47-. 9: CatholicLA (dir publicity & histn No NJ Unit 62-); NJ Sch Lib Couns Assn. 14: Sch wk, wk with yp, ref, mus. 15: 55 Ward pl, S Orange NJ 07079.

KLIMSTRA, GENE. b Morrison Ill 30 My 30. 4: Theo (Vermeer) Klimstra. 5: Central Col 48-52 (Eng) BA; UIowa 57 (Educ) MA, 67 (LS) MA. 6: Sp. 7: US Army (Sfc) Infantry; Tchr Clinton Pub Schs, Clinton Iowa 57-64; Libn Mankato State Col (Campus Sch) 64-66; Libn Iowa City Pub Schs 67-. 9: ALA; NEA; IowaStateEA; IowaASchL. 14: Sch libn. 15: 2717 Wayne ave, Iowa City Ia 52240.

KLINE, BETTY (FELDMAN). b St Louis Mo 22 My 40. 4: Norman D Kline. 5: WashU 57-61 (Eng Lit) AB; UIll 61-63 MLS. 7: Lib asst St Louis Pub Lib 55-61; Ref asst UIll Lib (Urbana) 61-63; Ref libn Temple U 63-65; Bibliogr US Dept of Labor Lib, Wash DC 66-69; Asst Reg Libn Bethesda Pub Lib, Bethesda Md 68-. 8: Library USA, NY Worlds Fair 65. 10: Beta Phi Mu. 14: Ref, admin. 15: 5802 Madawaska rd, Washington DC 20016.

KLINE, EVA JANE (PETERS). b Duncannon Penn 11 O 42. 4: Glenn Norman Kline. 5: Kutztown State Col 60-63 (LS) BS. 6: Sp, Fr. 7: Libn Greenpark Union High Sch, Elliotsburg Penn 63-64; Sec for Dept Com, Harrisburg Penn 64; Libn Westerly Pwky High Sch, State College Penn 64-65; Central processor College Area Schs, State College Penn 65, Elem libn 65-66; Central processor Susquenita High Sch, Duncannon Penn 66-68; Lib tech Ft Clayton post lib, CZ 68-69. 9: NEA; Penn State EA. 10: Amaranth; Girl Scouts; Alpha Beta Alpha. 14: Lib serv, catlg, ref. 15: PO Box 34, Newport Pa 17074.

KLINE, JOHN M. b Allentown Penn 31 Ja 25. 4: Agnes Frankenfield. 5: Lehigh 46-49 AB; Carnegie 50 MSLS. 6: Ger, Russian. 7: (Pfc) USMC Marshalls 43-46; Catlgr UMoLib 50; Corp (Sqd ldr) USMC, 50-51; Catlgr UMo Lib 51-53; Catlgr Albertson Pub Lib, Orlando Fla 53-55; Catlgr UMo Lib 55-. 9: ALA. 14: Catlg, ref. 15: 1518 St Christopher st, Columbia Mo 65201.

KLINE, LALAH (PAYNE). b Hazard Ky 9 D 43. 4: Roger D Kline. 5: Warren Wilson Col 61-63 (Liberal Arts) AA; Macalester Col 64-66 (Eng) BA; UKy 66-67 MS in LS. 6: Fr. 7: Acquis libn Med Ctr Lib UKy (Lexington) 67-. 9: MedLA; KyLA. 14: Acquis. 15: 109 Desha rd apt 1, Lexington Ky 40506.

KLING, SISTER M EONE. b Kellogg Minn 17 O 05. 5: Col of St Teresa 22-26 (Eng) AB; Columbia 32-33 (LS) BS; UMich 44 AMLS. 6: Fr. 7: Asst libn Internat Falls Pub Lib, International Falls Minn 27-32; Child libn NY Pub Lib 33-35; Child libn Brooklyn Pub Lib 35-36; Libn Col of St Teresa 38-. 9: CathLA (pres 57-59). 13: Yes. 15: Col of St Teresa, Winona Minn.

KLINGER, MARCIA. b NYC 20 N 41. 5: Douglass Col 59-63 (Eng, Vacteriology) BA; UChicago 63-66 (LS) MA, 66-68 (Microbiology) MS. 6: Sp, Fr. 7: Ser catlgr John Crerar Lib, Chicago 64-66; Asst ref libn Mun Ref Lib, Chicago 67-; MEDLARS searcher UCLA Biomed Lib 68-. 9: MedLA; Med Lib Group of SoCal. 14: Info retrieval in biol & med. 15: Biomedical Lib UCLA, Los Angeles Ca 90024.

KLINGERMAN, ETHEL MARIE. b Muncy Penn 4 Mr 29. 5: Wilson Col 46-50 (Math) AB; Drexel 50-51 MS in LS; West Chester State Col 63 (Hist); UPenn 64 (Higher Educ). 6: Fr. 7: Catlgr & clasf Lippincott Lib UPenn 51-54; Catlgr James V Brown Pub Lib Williamsport Penn 54-55; Dist dir Lycoming Co Girl Scout Coun Williamsport Penn 55-56; Libn East

Baptist Col 56-66; Lib dir Moorestown NJ free lib 66-. 9: ALA-ACRL (sec-treas Phila Chap 65-67); NJ LA; Libs Unltd (sec-treas S Jersey 68-69). 10: AAUP. 14: Catlg, admin, bldgs, acquis educ. 15: 505 Camden ave, Moorestown NJ 08057.

KLINGLER, CATHERINE (LAIRD). b Canton China 28 O 11. 4: Lewis A Klingler. 5: Pomona Col 28-32 (Ger) BA; Columbia 32-33 BS in LS. 7: Catlgr Lingnan ULib (Canton China) 33-35; Libn EAsiatic Col Columbia U 35-42; WAVES, Wash DC 42-43; Libn High Sch, Edison Twsp NJ 58-60; Libn Chem Lib Rutgers U 60-. 9: ALA. 15: 26 Runyon S lane, Edison Nj 08817.

KLOK, MARY JANE (AHLSTROM). b Muskegon Mich 29 Ja 21. 4: Lawrence Klok. 5: Muskegon Jr Col 38-40 (Math); UMich 40-41 (Math); West Mich U 41-42 (Math) BS, 42-62 Libn Certif MLS. 7: Tchr Decatur (Mich) Schs 48-52; Libn Milwood Commun Lib, Kalamazoo 53-57; Tchr Plainwell Jr High, Plainwell Mich 57-63; Libn Plainwell Sr High Plainwell Mich 63-. 9: MichEA; MichASchL; MichLA. 10: AAUW; Alpha Beta Epsilon. 14: Reading of young adults. 15: 823 Oak st, Kalamazoo Mi 49001.

KLOSE, ALMA (JULIA SIMMONS). b Leesburg Ohio 4 N 06. 5: Ohio Wesleyan U 26-30 (Eng) AB; Duke summers 35,36,38,42; 38-39 (Eng) MA; Drake U summer 47; UArk summers 58-60; Kan State Tchrs Col (Emporia) summers 64-65 (LS). 6: Ger. 7: Eng tchr Pfeiffer Col 30-38; Eng tchr Whitmell Farm-Life Sch, Whitmell Va 42-43; Eng tchr Baxter Sem 43-46; Tchr of Eng & sociol Mitchell Jr Col 46-47; Eng tchr & sec Buena Vista Col 47-48; Eng tchr Newton High Sch, Newton NJ 48-49; Sec Alfred Politz Research NYC 50; Tchr of Eng & journalism Bentonville High Sch, Bentonville Ark 52-55; Tchr of Eng & journalism The Sch of the Ozarks, Point Lookout Mo 55-57; Eng tchr Alma High Sch, Alma Ark 57-58; Libn & Eng tchr Riverton High Sch, Riverton Kan 58-64; Libn Pittsburg Sr High Sch & Roosevelt Jr High Sch Pittsburg Kan 64-. 9: NEA; ALA; KanASchL (Dist Dir 67-69). 10: Amer Poetry League; Sigma Tau Delta; AAUW; Theosophical Soc of Amer; Tri-State Writers Guild. 13: Yes. 14: Sch lib, bk sel, lib educ. 15: Box 556, Pittsburgh Ks 66762.

KLOSKI, ANELLE (McCARTY). b Tex 4 N 34. 4: Theodore Kloski. 5: UCal (Berkeley) 51-55 (Eng) BA, 67-68 MLS. 7: Libn Water Resources Ctr Archives UCal (Berkeley) 69-. 14: Mss catlg. 15: 712 Sea View dr, El Cerrito Cal 94530.

KLOSTERMANN, HELEN (MARIE). b Hartford Kan 5 N 28. 5: Kan State Tchrs Col (Emporia) 46-50 (Bus) BS, 60-61 (LS) MS. 6: Catlg facility Russian, Sp, & Ger. 7: Program dir Radio Station KTSW, Emporia Kan 50-52; Sr clerk Prudential Insurance Co, Emporia Kan 52-59; Conservation clerk Prudential Insurance Co, Topeka Kan 59-60; Asst catlgr William Allen White Lib Kan State Tchrs Col (Emporia) 61-. 9: ALA; KanLA (treas 67-69). 10: AAUW; Kappa Kappa Iota. 14: Catlg. 15: 1305 Center st, Emporia Ks 66801.

KLOTZ, EDNA M (ROBBINS). b Corry Penn 20 Jl 22. 4: Donald L Klotz. 5: Hiram Col 40-44 (Econ) BA; West Res 44-45 BSLS. 7: Stud asst Hiram Col 41-44; Catlgr Baldwin Wallace Col 45-48; Asst circ libn Ohio State U 48-57; Asst libn Worthington Pub Lib, Worthington Ohio 57-68; Circ libn capital U 68-. 09: OhioLA. 14: Catlg, ref. 15: 1937 Harwitch rd, Columbus Oh 43221.

KLUEVER, GWYN (HUGHES). b Carroll Iowa 26 My 26. 4: Lester L Kluever. 5: UOmaha 62-64 (LS) BS; Purdue Inst in Educ Media summer 67; UIowa 45-47, 69- (LS). 6: Ger. 7: Jr high libn Atlantic Commun Schs, Atlantic Iowa 64-. 9: NEA; ALA; IowaStateEA; IowaASchL. 10: Arthritis Found. 14: Reading guidance for yp. 15: 309 W 14th, Atlantic Ia 50022.

KLUGE, HERBERT CHARLES. b Baltimore 21 Mr 08. 4: Rosa May (Benner). 5: UBaltimore 50-51 (Bus Mgt). 7: Scientific photographer Dept of Embryology Carnegie Inst of Wash, Baltimore 29-44; Clerk (T/Sgt) USArmy Med Dept Wash DC 44-46; Pictorial research supv Armed Forces Inst of Pathology, Washington DC, Chief Illustration Lib Br. 9: SLA (picture div, chm Wash DC Group 53, 69). 11: Off of the Surgeon Gen Superior Performance Award 57. 14: Catlg of Med picture sources. 15: 6304 Everall ave, Baltimore Md 21206.

KLUGMAN, SIMONE (GINZBURG). b Grodno Poland 14 Ja 22. 4: David Klugman. 5: UCal (Berkeley) 58-61 (Slavic) BA, 61-63 MLS. 6: Fr, Russian, Hebrew. 7: Sec, Tel-Aviv & Jerusalem 41-46; Sec UNRRA, Paris 46-48; Lib asst ref Oakland Pub Lib Cal 62; Libn acquis dept UCal Gen Lib (Berkeley) 63-. 10: Phi Beta Kappa. 14: Acquis 9o-p material). 15: 6012 Margarido dr, Oakland Ca 94618.

KLYBERG, ALBERT THOMAS. b Hackensack NJ 8 Ag 40. 4: Beverly Moores. 5: Col of Wooster 58-62 (Econ, Hist) AB; UMich 62- (Hist) MA. 6: Ger, Fr. 7: Asst curator mss Wm L Clements Lib, Ann Arbor Mich 63-68; Libn RI Hist Soc, Providence 68-. 8: Comp & bibliogr "March of America Series" Ann Arbor Univ Microfilms Inc 66; Exec vd 2nd planning com New England Hist Bibliog. 12: Ed "Rhode Island History". 13: Yes. 14: Mss: collecting, catlg, preserving, ed. 15: 121 Hope st, Providence RI 02906.

KNABLE, JOHN P(ARKER), 2nd. b Pittsburgh 22 My 25. 4: Cynthia Boyle. 5: Yale 46-50 (Ind Admin) BS; UPittsburgh 62-63 (LS) MS. 6: Sp, Fr, Ger. 07: T/5 USArmy, US, European Theatre 43-46; Staff asst Bettis Atomic Power Lab, Pittsburgh 51-57, Info analyst 57-59; Admin serv spec RCA-Meadowlands, Meadow Lands Penn 59-64; Acquis libn Gen Motors Research, Warren Mich 64-66; Mgr lib serv Herner & Co, Wash DC 66-68; Subj cat LC 68-. 9: ALA; ASIS; SLA; DCLA. 10: Beta Phi Mu; Yale Engrg Assn; Amer Fern Soc; Birmingham Hist Soc; Longue Vue Country Club (Pittsburgh). 13: Yes. 14: Tech processes. 15: 9117 Cherbourg dr, Potomac Md 20854.

KNAPE, ANNE S(ABRA RAMSEY). b San Angelo Tex 24 Ja 17. 4: Dr Clifford S Knape. 5: UTex 34-38 (Journalism, Educ) BS; Baylor U 51-52 (Child Lit, Educ) MS; Tex Woman's U 53 (LS). 07: Lib asst Austin Pub Lib, Austin Tex 34-38; Lib dept asst Lib Sci Dept UTex 37-38; Libn Austin Ind Sch Dist, Austin Tex 38-44; Libn Manchester Libs, Manchester NH 44-45; Dir Nursery Sch, Waco Tex 48-51; Libn & consul La Vega Ind Sch Dist, Bellmead Tex 53-58; Libn Waco Ind Sch Dist University Jr High Sch, Waco Tex 58-67, Libn Richfield High Sch 67-. 8: Consul Jr High Sch Lib Catlg 69-. 9: NEA (Life mem); ALA; Tex State Tchrs Assn; TexLA; Tex Clr Tchrs Assn. 10: Delta Kappa Gamma; Theta Sigma Phi; Alpha Beta Alpha. 13: Yes. 14: Child lit, yp. 15: 1024 N 18-A st, Waco Tx 76707.

KNAPP, BETSY. b Fayetteville NY 6 Je 10. 5: Smith 28-32 (Hist) AB; Syacuse 33-34 (Pol Sci), 56-57 MSLS. 6: Ger. 7: Municipal finance analyst WPA, Wash DC 35-37; Program sec League of Women Voters of US, Wash DC 37-42; Admin analyst US Bur of Budget, Wash DC 42-48; Commun activities adv US High Commissioner for Germany, Wiesbaden 49-51; Cultural off US Dept of State, Frankfurt/Main Germany 51-52; Circ libn Syracuse U 57-67, Libn 67-. 8: Govt in Action Project of League of Women Voters Educ; staff organizer at Syracuse U 59-60, consul at Ind U & Wash DC 60-61; Survey of women's citizenship wk, Land Hesse Germany 56 - as guest of women's organizations; consul Foreign Policy Assn in Syracuse NY 54-56. 10: Phi Beta Kappa; LWV; Syracuse World Affairs Coun. 12: "The Awkward Age in Civl Service" (40); Pamphlets on personnel, pub fin, civic ed (39-). 13: Yes. 14: Soc sci bibliog & ref. 15: Indian Oven Farm, Fayetteville NY 13066.

KNAPP, CHARLES RICHARD. b Monroe Mich 1 My 13. 4: Elisabeth Shelly. 5: Mich State Normal Col 31-33 (Educ); UToledo 34-36 (Eng) PhB; UIll 39-40 BS in LS, 41-47 MS in LS. 7: Asst UIll Lib Sch summers 40-41; USArmy Air Corps, (Sgt) 42-47; Asst UIll Col of Law Lib (Urbana) 41-47; Lib & Assoc Prof of Lib Sci WVa Wesleyan Col 47-53; Chief Tech Ref Lib Engnr R & D Labs USArmy, Ft Belvoir Va 53-55; Asst chief Lib Br Hq Off Chief of Engnrs USArmy, Wash DC 55-59; Chief lib br Ind Col of the Armed Forces (Ft McNair Wash DC) 59-66; Chief lib div USA Engnr Sch Ft Belvoir Va 66-. 08: Mil libns wkshops 58-68; Mem Fed Lib Com Task Force on Mission 65-68; Hist USArmy Engr Sch 66-. 9: SLA (chm Mil Libns Div 64-65; v-chm 63-64, sec- treas 62-63). 11: Outstanding Performance Rating & Sustained Superior Performance Award (Civil Service) six awards. 14: Admin. 15: 6547 Virginia Hills ave, Alexandria Va 22310.

KNAPP, MRS CLAIRE (BUYS). b Ovid NY 20 D 04. 5: Temple U 25; UKy 29 (Eng) BA; Ind U 60 (LS). 7: Manager Bur of Motor Vehicles State of Ind, Jasper Ind 44-48; Libn Jasper Pub Lib, Jasper Ind 47-51; Adjudicator Army Finance Center, Indianapolis 52; Sec Capitol Distributing Co Ind, Indianapolis 53-57; Libn Marion Co Gen Hosp, Indianapolis 57-61; Libn Indianapolis Pub Lib 61-62; Libn Quantico High Sch, Marine Corps Schs, Quantico Va 62-. 9: ALA; Quantico(Va)EA. 10: Delta Zeta; DAR. 14: Ref, research. 15: 2902-A Marine Corps Schs, Quantico Va 22134.

KNAPP, JOHN FREDERICK. b Sacramento Ca 25 N 35. 4: Suzanne Small. 5: UCal (Berkeley) 54-59 (Eng Lit) BA, 65-66 MLS; UCLA 59-61 (Eng Lit) MA. 7: Personnel specialist (Sp5) USA 24th Inf Div, Korea 55-57; Tchr; West Boys' Scg, Mitcham Surrey England 61-62, Castlemont High Sch, Oakland

Cal 62-63, Coalinga Col 63-65; LC 66-69; Lib syst analyst UCal (Santa Cruz) 69-. 9: ALA. 11: LC Spec Recr Prog 66. 12: "Marc II Forward" (68). 13: Yes. 14: Systems analysis. 15: 827 California st, Santa Cruz Ca 95060.

KNAPP, MARGARET ELIZABETH (BASTERFIELD). b Saskatoon Sask 28 Ag 28. 5: USaskatchewan (Eng) BA; UToronto 52 BLS; Florence (Italy) 56 (Ital Lang & Art); Fla State Lib Sch 59 (A-V Materials & Techniques); UToronto 62 MLS. 6: Fr, Ital. 7: Ref asst London Pub Lib, London Ont 52-53, Art libn 53-55; Chief Libn Nat Film Bd of Can, Montreal 57-61; Sr ref libn Sir George Williams U (Montreal) 62-63, Head of pub serv 63-64; Libn Leslie Frost Lib, York U (Toronto) 64-68; Dir Lib tech program Niagara Col 68. 9: ALA; CanLA; SLA; Inst Prof Libns; Ont. 13: Yes. 14: A-v materials, univ lib admin. 15: Niagara Col, Welland Ont Can.

KNAPP, MARY (ELLIS). b Atlanta Ga. 5: Agnes Scott Col 25-29 (Eng) BA; UVa summer 34 BA in LS; Emory 35-36, summer 67 Certif in Lib Mgt Inst. 7: Tchr & libn N Ave presbyterian Sch, Atlanta 29-51; Libn I Atlanta Pub Lib 51-57, Hd libn Ida Williams Lib 57-. 9: ALA; SELA; GaLA. 10: Eng Speaking Union. 14: Child wk, admin. 15: 4883 Roswell rd NE Apt C7, Atlanta Ga 30322.

KNAPP, MARY E. b Kan City Mo 7 Ap 18. 5: Sacred Heart Col (Wichita Kan) 35-37; Duchesne Col 37-39 (Hist) BA; Rosary Col 39-40 BS in LS. 7: Asst libn UPortland 40-44; Asst catlgr Omaha Pub Lib 45-51, Head catlgr 51-. 14: Catlg. 15: 848 S 93rd st, Omaha Nb 68114.

KNAPP, PATRICIA (BRYAN). b Youngstown Ohio 31 D 14. 4: Robert S Knapp. 5: Chicago 32-35 (Eng) BA, 35-36 (Eng) 39-43 (LS) MA, 53-57 (LS) PhD. 7: Act libn, head tech processes, & catlgr Chicago Tchrs Col 37-43; Army libn USAF, Sarasota & Miami Beach Fla 43-45; Libn George Williams Col 45-55; Asst Prof Lib Sci Dept Rosary Col 55-57; Visiting Lecturer Lib Sci Dept UMich summer 61-64; Asst libn Wayne State U Lib 57-59; Exec Sec & Dir Monteith Lib Proj Monteith Col 59-65; Assoc Prof Dept of Lib Sci Wayne State U 65-. 8: Adv Com Carnegie Pilot Undergrad Study UHawaii. 9: ALA (chm ORD Adv Com 67-69);-ACRL, Adv Com chm 67-69; (chm Lib Serv Com 64-66); -ASD (chm Program Policy Com 65-66); -RSTD; -LED; ALA-APBC Jt Com 62-64; MichLA (chm Planning Com 61- 63); AALS (v-pres & pres-elect 69). 12: "College Teaching and the College Library," ACRL Monograph no 23 (59); "Monteith College Library Experiment" (66). 13: Yes. 14: Col & univ libnship, catlg, research, soc, sci, lit. 15: Lib Sci Dept Col of Educ Wayne State Univ, Detroit Mi 48202.

KNAPP, PAUL (LAVERN). b Kalamazoo Mich 8 O 11. 4: Marian Downs. 5: West Mich U 28-32 (Phys) BS; UNC 35-36 BS in LS; UIll 38-42 AM in LS. 6: Ger. 7: Chem libn UCincinnati 37-38; Chem libn UIll (Urbana) 38-42; Hd tech dept Toledo Pub Lib, Toledo Ohio 42-43; Libn & physics asst Owens Corning Foberglass Corp, Newark Ohio 43-47; Sci Div libn UNeb 47-49; Sci libn Drake U 49-56; Libn Marathan Oil Co, Littleton Volo 56-63; Libn George Williams Col 63-66; Libn Whirlpool Corp, St Joseph Mich 66-67; Sci libn Northern Ill U 67-. 8: Chm Forum on the Abstract and Index of petrol Explor and Product Lit (sponsored by Petrol Sect, SLA). 9: SLA (2nd v-pres & chm Adv Coun 60-61; chm Petrol Sect 59-60; Colo Chap: pres 57-58). 10: World Outlook Y'Men's Internat Del to Centennial Conf of YMCA, Paris 55. 14: Ref & info retr. 15: 438 Normal rd, DeKalb Il 60115.

KNAPP, SARA (DUSINBERRE). b NYC 5 Je 36. 5: Norfolk Div of the Col of William & Mary 55-58 (Sociol) AB; SUNY (Albany) 63-64 MLS. 7: Soc wk aid Albany Hosp Albany NY 58-63; Asst lib supv NY State Lib Ext Div, Albany NY 64-67; Catlgr SUNY (Albany) 67-68, Period libn 68-. 9: ALA; NY State LA; Hudson-Mohawk LA. 10: LWV. 12: Co-auth 'For Your Information' sect in "The Bookmark," monthly publ of NY State Lib. 15: 740 Madison ave, Albany Ny 12208.

KNAUFF, ELISABETH (CHAMBERLAIN) SHEPARD. b Baltimore Md 11 Ap 35. 4: Walter J Knauff. 5: UNC (Greensboro) 53-56 (Hist) AB; Sch of Advanced Intl Studies 56-58 (Interl affairs) MA; Catholic U 61-67 MSLS. 7: Ed asst Amer Auto Assn, Wash DC 58-61; Br libn Prince George's Co Mem Lib, Md 61-64; Ref asst Bur of the Budget Lib, Wash DC 64-66; Ref libn 66-. 9: ALA; DCLA. 10: Phi Beta Kappa; Beta Phi Mu. 14: Ref, govt docs. 15: 2326 - 19th st NW, Washington DC 20009.

KNEEBONE, TED (THEODORE RAMSAY). b Lake Andes SD 21 Ap 34. 4: Jo (Joanne Louise) Dobberpuhl. 5: No State Col (Aberdeen SD) 52-55 (Sec Educ-Eng) BS; UMinn 57-60 (LS) MA. 7: Tchr-libn Wilmot High Sch, Wilmot SD 55-56; Tchr-libn Groton High Sch, Groton SD 56-57; Asst libn No State Col (Aberdeen SD) 57-60; Head Libn Neb Wesleyan U 60-66; Hd Lib & Assoc Prof of Lib Sci Yankton Col 66-. 9: ALA; NEA;-DAVI; SDLA; (chm Legirl Com); SDEA; NebLA (Exhibits Chm 2 yrs, sec & Program chm Col Sect); S Dak Educ Media Assn; Cols of Mid-Amer Consortium (Lib Sect). 10: AAUP; Phi Delta Kappa; Phi Mu Sinfonia; Sigma Tau Delta; Sertoma Club; Yankton Civic Coun; PTA. 12: "Reference Books for Nebraska's School Libraries," & suppl (63, 64). 13: Yes. 14: Admin, acquis, ser, a-v materials, lib coop lib educ. 15: Yankton Col, Yankton Sd 57078.

KNEEDLER, WILLIAM HOWARD. b Chieng Mai Thailand 27 F 39. 4: Margaret Marilyn (Frank). 5: Princeton U 56-60 (Germanic Langs) BA; Rutgers 63-65 MLS; 66- (LS). 06: Ger. 7: Recording Engnr Hagens Recording Studio, Princeton NJ 60-63; Ed asst tech asst The NY Pub Lib 63-65; Asst libn in chg of acquis NYC Commun Col 65-66; Rutgers U Grad Fellow 66-. 9: ALA;-ACRL;-RTSD;-LAD;-ISAD; Lib Research RT; ASIS. 10: Beta Phi Mu; Sierra Club; Adirondak Mt Club; Wilderness Soc; Appalachian Mt Club. 12: Asst ed "Bulletin of the NY Pub Lib," & other lib publs (64-65). 13: Yes. 14: Research; info flow; admin, ref, acquis. 15: 27 Willow rd, Metuchen Nj 08840.

KNEELAND, JANET ELAINE. b Portland Ore 29 S 35. 5: UOre 53-57 (Eng Lit) BA; UWash 63-64 M Lib. 7: Tchr Springfield (Ore) Pub Schs 57-63; Libn Portland (Ore) Pub Schs 64-66; Asst Acquis Libn Portland State U 66-. 9: ALA; PNLA; OreLA. 10: AAUP. 14: Acquis. 15: 3220 SE 66th ave, Portland Or 97206.

KNEIL, GERTRUDE MARGARETTA. b NYC 22 My 24. 5: Bryn Mawr 42-46 (Pol & Hist) AB; Carnegie 46-47 BS in LS. 7: Ref asst UPittsburgh Lib 47-50; Asst libn ULeeds Lib (Leeds Eng) 50-52; Head order dept UPittsburgh Lib 52-59; Asst libn Mellon Nat Bank & Trust Co Lib, Pittsburgh 59-. 8: Sub-warden, Weetwood Hall (girl's hostel), ULeeds (Eng) 51-52. 9: SLA. 10: Bryn Mawr Col Club, West Penn; DAR; Womens City Club; Carnegie Inst Soc; Nat Wildlife Fed; West Penn conservancy. 13: Yes. 14: Catlg, ref, spec libs. 15: 31 Nicholson st, Pittsburgh Pa 15205.

KNEPLEY, B(ERTHA) ADELE. b Phila 14 Ag 12. 5: West Chester State Col 31-35; (Music Educ) BS in Music Educ; UPenn summers 37-43 (Music Educ) MS in Educ; UDel Wkshops in serv wk 46-48; Drexel 55-56 MS in LS. 6: Fr. 7: Music supv Penn Del NJ -55; Art libn Fine Arts Lib UPenn 56-60; Libn Haverford Twp High Sch, Havertown Penn 60-62; Libn Valley Forge Mil Acad & Jr Col (Wayne Penn) 62-64; Libn Settlement Music Sch Phila 64; Asst libn AD Eisenhower High Sch Norristown Penn 65-; Also at present time as "E" - consul libn at Settlement Music Sch; Hd libn art & music dept Free Pub Lib, Trenton NJ 66-. 8: Lib consul Settlement Music Sch, Phila 65-. 9: ALA; (mem & chm Art Sub-Sect 58-60); NJ State LA. 10: AAUW; Drexel Lib Sch Alumni; UPenn Alumni; Alumnae Club of Phila (UPenn); Beta Phi Mu. 13: Yes. 14: Ref, music catlg, admin. 15: 7958 Arlington ave, Upper Darby Pa 19082.

KNEPP, KENNETH BRUCE. b Escalon Cal 8 N 30. 5: UPacific 50-52 (Pre-ministerial) BA; Garrett Theol Sem 52-56 (Theol) BD; UDenver 65-66 (Libnship) MA. 6: Sp. 7: Minister methodist Ch, Byron Cal 56-57, Maxwell 57-62, Chester 62-65; Asst order libn UPacific 66-68; Hd bb 66-68; Hd bibliog serv Lib Ariz StateU 68-69, Catlg libn 69-. 09. ALA; ArizStateLA. 10: ACLU; Phi Kappa Phi. 14: Catlg, acquis, bibliog. 15: 1815 Cutler dr apt H, Tempe Az 85281.

KNEPPER, ROBERT RILEY. b Los Angeles 17 My 26. 4: Freda Eleanor Strickland. 5: Los Angeles City Col 44-47 (Journalism) AA; UCLA 54-56 (Pre-libnship) AB; UCal(Berkeley) 56-57 MLS. 7: Ed "Cal Real Estate News," Los Angeles 47-50; Lib clerk "Los Angeles Examiner" 50-51; Assoc ed "Rocketeer," Naval Ordnance Test Station, China Lake Cal 51-52; US Army (cpl) Signal Corps, libn Pacific Stars & Stripes, Tokyo 53-54; Asst dir Collier's Ref Serv, NY 57-59; Reg ref libn Los Angeles Co Pub Lib, Los Angeles 59-67, Prin libn lib pub servs 67-. 9: CalLA. 14: Ref. 15: 5921 Templeton st, Huntington Park Ca 90255.

KNERR, VALERIE CATHERINE (HIATT). b London England 1 Ag 29. 4: Dietrich H Knerr. 5: IndU 46-50 (Lit) BA, 52-53 (LS) MA. 6: Portu. 7: Libn W Lafayette Pub Lib, w lafayette Ind 50-52; Hd res bk room PurdueU Lib 53-56; Hd ext dept Pack Memorial Pub Lib, Asheville NC 66-. 9: NCLA. 14: Ext wk, catlg, ref. 15: RR 2 Box 156, Arden NC 28704.

KNICKERBOCKER, BURL R. b Waterville Wash 6 F 22. 4: Georgine Caswell. 5: Wash State U 40-42 & 45-47 (Hist, Educ) BA and B Ed; UWash summer 50 (LS); UDenver summers 51-54 MA in Libnship; UWash summer 65 (NDEA Inst for Lib Supv). 6: Sp. 7: Pvt-Sgt US Army 111th Infantry Reg, Hawaii & Palau Islands 42-45; Tchr-libn Pe Ell Schs, Pe Ell Wash 47-50; Libn Peninsula High Sch, Gig Harbor Wash 50-54; Lib supv Peninsula Pub Schs, Gig Harbor Wash 54-. 9: NEA; WashEA; WashStateASchL; WashLA; PeninsulaEA. 14: Centralized proc, supv, planning new lib facilities. 15: PO Box 59B, Wauma Wa 98395.

KNIER, TIMOTHY E. b Sheboygan Wis 23 Ag 45. 4: Janet L Stemper. 5: Divine Word Sem (Duxbury Mass) 63-65 (Liberal Arts); Divine Word Sem (Epworth Iowa) 65-66 (Eng, philos); Lakeland Col 66-67 (Eng) BA; Rosary Col 67-68 MALS. 6: Lat, Grk, Ger, Fr. 7: Lib trainee Chicago Pub Lib 67-68; Asst reader serv MarquetteU Lib 68-. 9: ALA; AAUP. 10: Alpha Psi Omega. 14: Ref, gen pub rel. 15: 907 N 26th st, Milwaukee Wi 53233.

KNIERIEM, ARTHUR CARL. b Brooklyn NY 8 S 43. 4: Barbara Jackson. 5: CCNY 61-65 (Eng) BA; Columbia 65-67 (LS) MS. 6: Ger. 7: Corporal USMCR 62-68; Gen asst Fine Arts Lib Columbia 65-67; Tchg asst Acquis Div City Col Lib 66-67, Instr 67-. 8: Reorganized Dr M Bieber's lib of art & research materials summer 66. 14: Curiosa. 15: 804 Woodward ave, Ridgewood NY 11227.

KNIFFEN, ANNA (TINGLEY). b Montrose Penn 24 O 04. 4: Charles Chester Kniffen. 5: Syracuse 23-24 (Lib) Certif; NebU 24-28 Sci) AB; Columbia 29 (Personnel); CalU 47 (Lib). 6: Fr, Ger. 7: Asst personnal dir Fred Sanders, Detroit 28-38; Child care dir Child Care Ctr, Rodeo Cal 46; Instr Franklin Jr Col Vallejo Cal 46-47; Tchr Detroit Bd of Educ 48-57; Dir of lib Hazel Park Bd of Educ, Hazel Park Mich 61-. 8: Loc, co & state adv SLAAM Club 61-71. 9: NEA; MichEA; MichASchL; MichLA. 10: Kappa Phi; Civil Defense Area Dir; PTA; Hist Comsn Hazel Park Mich; Women Volunteer of Year 52, Detroit Mich. 12: "Credit Library Manual for High School Librarians" (69). 14: Stud libnship. 15: 20100 Cardoni, Detroit Mi 48203.

KNIGHT, CHARLOTTE JEAN. b Campus Douglas Wis 4 Ap 09. 4: R C Knight. 5: UND 26-27; Lawrence Col 29-31 (Hist, Span) BA (cum laude); UColo summer 30 (Ger, Art); UIll 31 (LS); UWis 50-51 MALS. 6: Sp. 7: Circ libn Lawrence Col 28-29; Gen asst Rockford Pub Lib Rockford Ill 31-33; Field rep Ill State Lib 34; Ill State Lib Fed Works Agency 37-41; Hines Hosp, Hines Ill 43-44; Bus & sci libn Rockford Pub Lib, Rockford Ill 45-49; Ext serv libn 49-50; Visiting Lecturer UWis (Madison) 52-55; Dir The Karrmann Lib Wis State U (Platteville) 55-. 8: Org spec libs (eg vocational sch, church libs & hosp libs) as civic contrib; Adv problems in sch libs, pub libs; Org first pub lib in Ill under Pub Lib Dist Law (43). 9: ALA; NEA; IllLA (chm Child Sect); WisLA (life mem, past sec pres; chm Col & Unit Sect); WisEA. 10: AAUW; AAUP; Ill Lib Sch Assn; No Suburban Woman's Club; Red Cross Assn; Wis State Univ Faculty; Beta Phi Mu; LWV. 13: Yes. 14: Admin, rare bks, graphic arts, illus of child books. 15: 1190 No Eastman st, Platteville Wi 53818.

KNIGHT, D(OROTHY) FRANCES. b De Soto Mo 21 Ag 37. 5: Tex Woman's U 55-59 (LS) BS; UMich summer 64 (LS); Tex Woman's U 62-66 LS MLS; Angelo State Col 63-64; U N Dak 66; E Tex State U 68; Tex A&I U 68-69. 06: Sp. 7: Sch libn White Deer Ind Sch Dist, White Deer Tex 59-60; Bkmob libn Tex State Lib 60-61, Field consul 62; Libn San Angelo Col 62-63, Asst libn 63-65; Catlgr Angelo State Col 65-66; Base libn Grand Forks AFB, NDak 66-67; Sch libn Weslaco Ind Sch Dist Weslaco Tex 68-. 9: ALA; SWLA; TexLA; Tex StateTA; ClrTA. 13: Yes. 14: Catlg. 15: Box 194, Pleasanton Tx 78064.

KNIGHT, DOROTHY MARY (LAY). b Cleveland Ohio 5 Mr 19. 4: Kenneth C Knight. 5: Lyons Twp Jr Col 34-36; Ill StateU 36-38 (Soc Sci) BEd; Kan State Tchrs Col 59-61 MSLS; Okla StateU NDEA Sch Lib Inst summer 65. 6: Fr. 7: Hd sec athletic dept Mich StateU (E Lansing) 50-53; Sec to Dean of Sch of Engring, La Polytech Inst 53-55; Libn Haysville Sch Syst, Haysville Kan 56-57; Libn S Riverside Sch, Wichita Kan 57-60; Hd libn Campus High Sch, Wichita Kan 60-65; Libn Wichita High Sch, Wichita Kan 65-66; Hd LC reclsf & instr lib sci Wichita StateU 66-. 8: Lib sci instr Kan State Tchrs Col 66-67. 9: ALA; NEA; KanLA (chm Child & YA Sect 63-64); KanASchL (asst dir & dir Dist 3 62-64; legis chm 66-68). 10: Wichita Lib Club; Kappa Delta Pi; Phi Gamma Mu; Bus & Prof Women's Club; Beta Sigma Phi. 13: Yes. 14: Catlg, lib sci instr. 15: 2055 Porter apt 120. Wichita Ks 67203.

KNIGHT, (THELMA) ERNESTINE (WRIGHT). b Norfolk Va 8 My 34. 5: Madison Col 51-54, 63 (LS) BS in Ed. 7: Libn Va Beach (Va) Sch Bd, Thoroughgood Elem Sch 62-67, Kempsville High Sch 67-. 08: Chm lib bk & materials exhibit Va Beach 68. 9: VBEA; VEA; NEA; ALA; VLA; Chairman-Citizenship Com. 10: Women's Missionary Union; AAUW; PTA; Alpha Delta Kappa. 14: Child bks. 15: 1105 Burlington rd, Virginia Beach Va 23456.

KNIGHT, HATTIE M. b Malad Ida 23 My 08. 5: Brigham Young U 38-41 (Hist) BS; UDenver 41-43 BS in LS; Peabody 49-51 MS in LS; Rutgers 61-62 (LS). 6: Fr. 7: Elem tchr Ida Pub Schs, 26-34, 36-39; Circ libn Brigham Young U 41-49, Ref libn 49-58, Coordinator readers serv 58-60, Chm Dept of Lib Sci 60-66; Instr Peabody Col summer 51; Instr Col Ida summers 62, 63; Asst dir Grad Dept of Lib & info Sci Brigham Young U 66-. 8: Adv Knapp Sch Libs Proj, Provo Utah 65-67; Consul wkshop on instrl materials for Farrer Jr High Sch tchrs in connection with Knapp Proj, summer 65. 9: ALA; MPLA; UtahLA (past pres, com wk, etc). 10: Delta Kappa Gamma; Brigham Young U Women; AAUP; Phi Kappa Phi; Beta Phi Mu. 12: "The 1-2-3 Guide to Libraries" (64); "Family Unity Through Reading: A Selection of Books for the Family" (63); "Better Libraries for Utah Schools-Standards and Goals" (65); Ed Utah Libraries (57-61). 13: Yes. 14: Ref, sch libnship, lib educ. 15: 430 E 5th North, Provo Ut 84601.

KNIGHT, HATTIE RICH (CINDY). b Des Moines Iowa 2 Jl 04. 4: Lee Knight. 5: E CarolinaU 49-51; Campbell Col -65 (Eng) BA; UNC 65-68 MA in LS. 6: Ger. 7: Stud asst ECarU 49-51; Lib asst Campbell Col 60-65; Searcher Wilson Lib, Chapel Hill NC 66-68, Hd NC Union Catlg 68-69, Hd interlib serv ctr 69-. 8: Chm lib com Carrboro Baptist Ch. 9: NCLA; SELA. 14: Pub serv, acquis. 15: Box 231, Carrboro NC 27510.

KNIGHT, HELEN L. b Meadville Penn 14 Mr 07. 5: Allegheny Col 24-27; Skidmore Col 27-28 (Eng Lit) BA; West Res 30-31 BLS; Allegheny Col, Westminster Col, NYU summers Masters Equiv. 7: Cleveland Heights Roxboro Br, Cleveland Heights Ohio 31-32; Child libn & adult libn NY Pub Lib 34-46; Elem sch libn Meadville Area Schs, Meadville Penn 51-57; High & elem schs Highland Suburban, Beaver Falls Penn 59-60; High sch & elem West Forest Area Schs, Tionosta Penn 63-65; Elem sch libn Conneaut Lake Area Elem Schs, Conneaut Lake Penn 65-. 9: ALA; NEA; PennLA; Penn State EA; Friends of Osborne & Lillian H Smith Collections, Toronto, AARP. 10: Mu Phi Epsilon; Kappa Alpha Theta; United Fed of Doll Clubs Inc; Red Cross; Crawford Co Hist Assn. 14: Hist of child bks; foreign libs for child. 15: Box 32A rd 1, Conneaut Lake Pa 16316.

KNIGHT, KATHERINE ANNE. b Sanford NC 15 My 28. 5: Queens Col (Charlotte NC) 45-49 (Fine Arts) AB; Union Theol Sem (NY) 51 (Sacred Music); UNC 59-61 MS in LS. 7: Tchr of piano, Sanford NC 49-56; Admissions coun Queens Col (Charlotte NC) 56-58, Asst Even Col 58-59; Asst art & music sect Hawaii State Lib 61-63, Readers' adv 63-68; Libn Waikiki-Kapahulu Br Lib, Honolulu 68-. 9: ALA; Hawaii LA (Program Chm, Exhibits Chm). 10: Amer Guild of Organists; Libn 1st Presby Church Honolulu. 14: Ref, lit, art, music, current fiction, adult serv, pub lib. 15: 2533 Malama Place, Honolulu Hi 96822.

KNIGHT, KEITH C. b New Holland Ill 24 Je 24. 4: Katherine Good. 5: UTenn 42-45 (Eng) BA; UIll 45-46 BLS, 49-50 MLS. 6: Fr, Sp. 7: Asst ref libn Mich State Col 46-49; Libn Charlottesville-Albemarle Pub Lib, Va 50-51; Bkmob libn Delaware (Ohio) Co Dist Lib 51-54; Ref libn Muncie(Ind) Pub Lib 54-56; Circ asst ref libn Iowa State Tchrs Col 56-58; Ref asst Grand Rapids(Mich) Pub Lib 58-. 9: MichLA. 14: Ref, tech. 15: 6892 Quincy dr SW, Grand Rapids Mi 49508.

KNIGHT, KENNETH C. b Chicago 15 N 08. 4: Dorothy Lay. 5: Knox Col 26-30 (Eng) BS; UIll 46-47 BS in LS, MS(LS). 7: (Capt) AUS, US & Philippines 42-46; Head ext & pub rel Lansing(Mich) Pub Lib 47-48, 50-53; Asst natural hist libn UIll(Urbana) 49; Asst to dir of libs AlaPolytech Inst 53; Assoc libn La Polytech inst 54-55; Libn The Boeing Co, Wichita Kan 55-. 9: SLA. 14: Mechanization of lib admin & tech proc. 15: The Boeing Co Lib, Wichita Div, Wichita Ks 67210.

KNIGHT, NANCY (BABBITT HARSH). b Des Moines Iowa 2 Jl 04. 4: Victor Macaulay Knight. 5: UMich 21-25 (Speech/ Eng) AB, Life Tchr Certif; UToronto 58-60 BLS. 7: Field sec Young People's Religious Union (Unitarian), Boston & NY 25-27; Child libn NY Pub Lib, Willowdale Ont 59-60, Head chi&ld serv 60-. 13: Yes. 14: Child lit. 15: 21 Roxborough st E, Toronto 5 Canada.

KNIGHT, NANCY HOYT (NICHOLS). b Bronx NY 1 S 43. 4: Odon George Knight. 5: Simmons 61-65 (Soc Sci) BS; UChicago 65-67 MA in LS. 6: Fr. 7: Lib asst Fed Res Bank, Boston 63-65; Asst ed "Lib Tech Reports" ALA, Chicago 67-68, Hd info serv LTP 68-. 9: ALA. 10: Beta Phi Mu; UChicago Grad Lib Sch Alumni. 13: Yes. 14: Ref, tech serv, acad. 15: 900 W Belden ave, Chicago Il 60614.

KNIGHTLY, JOHN JOSEPH. b Hutchinson Kan 28 Jl 36. 4: Audrey Valaske. 5: UKan 54-58 (Eng) AB; Kan State Tchrs Col (Emproia) 63-64 (LS) MS. 6: Fr. 7: Armed forces radio serv US Army (E-4), Taipei Taiwam 61-63; Asst instr speech dept UKan 57-58, Lib asst 58-59; Lib asst Kan State Tchrs Col 63-64; Libn I & II UKan 64-67; Libn I & II UNev 67-. 9: ALA; NevLA. 10: AAUP. 14: lib pub rel, pub serv, lib orientation & instr. 15: Univ of Nevada Lib, Reno Nv 85281.

KNIPPENBERG, KATHARIN (LOIS). b Akron Ohio 7 O 41. 5: Kent State 59-62 (Eng, Hist) BS in Ed; Case West Res 64-65 MSLS. 6: Fr. 7: OhioU Lib: Asst ref libn 65-66, interlib loan libn 66-68, Hd ref dept 69-. 9: ALA; OhioLA. 10: Kappa Delta Pi; Pi Alpha Theta; Beta Phi Mu; AAUW. 14: Ref, interlib loan. 15: 8 Patton st, Athens Oh 45701.

KNOBBE, MARY LOUISE (SIEFER). b Cherryvale Kan 26 Ag 18. 4: Ray H Knobbe. 5: Washburn U 36-40 (Hist & Pol Sci) AB; UIll summer 41 (LS); UMd 65-67 (LS). 6: Sp. 7: Stud asst Washburn U 36-40, Lib asst 41-42; Mun ref libn City of Kan City Mo 43-46; Ref libn Carnegie Lib, Steubenville Ohio 50-51; Planning libn Md-Nat Cap Park & Plan Com, Silver Spring Md 61-67; Planning libn Metropolitan Wash Coun of Govts, Wash DC 67-. 9: Coun of Planning Libns; SLA (Nat chm Com to Publish Directory Planning, Bldg & Housing Libs; DC Chap, chm Soc Sci 67-68, dir 68-70). 10: Kan State Soc (Washington DC); Women's Club (Silver Spring); United Church Women (Nat Cap Area). 13: Yes. 14: Ref, research. 15: 2300 Eccleston st, Silver Spring Md 20902.

KNOBLAUCH, CHARLES EDWARD (II). b Bolton Landing NY 21 Jl 19. 4: Helen Seaton. 5: Harvard 37-41 (Govt) AB; Skidmore 50-52 (Philos); SUNY (Albany) 63-65 MLS. 7: (Lt-Maj) US Army 41-46; Sec shop foreman H C Knoblauch & Sons, Inc, Glens Falls NY 46-55; Owner Knobby's Records, Glens Falls NY 55-60; Owner The Knoblauchs' House of Bks, Whitesboro NY 60-; Libn Ballston Spa Pub Lib, Ballston Spa NY 62-65; Asst dir Jervis Lib, Rome NY 65-66; Asst dir MidYork Lib Syst, Utica NY 66-. 10: Lt Col US Air Force reserve, Retired. 14: Admin, rare bks, ref. 15: 112 Main st, Whitesboro NY 13492.

KNOBLER, HERBERT Z. b Brooklyn NY 30 My 28. 4: Shirley Aronofsky. 5: City Col of NY 46-50 (Econ) BBA; NYU even 51-55 (Marketing) MBA; Rutgers 62-63 MLS. 6: Sp. 7: Econ analyst specializing in transporta tion Pub Utilities & Manufacturing Ind 50-58; Econ Commonwealth Serv, NYC 58-61; Staff Brooklyn Pub Lib 62-65; Dir Lib serv Empire Trust Co & Bank of NY (after merger), NYC 65-68; Acquis libn & Asst Prof Queensborough Commun Col 68-. 9: SLA; LACUNY; NY Technical Svces Lb ibrarians. 10: Beta Phi Mu. 13: Yes. 14: Tech serv, admin, ref. 15: 919 E 106 st, Brooklyn NY 11236.

KNOBLER, SHIRLEY (ARONOFSKY). b Brooklyn NY 2 My 31. 4: Herbert Z Knobler. 5: Brooklyn Col 52 BA; Columbia 57 MLS; Tchrs Col Columbia U 63 MA. 6: Sp. 7: Libn Queens Borough Pub Lib, NY 57; Libn NYC Bd of Educ 57-64; Libn Polytechnic Inst of Brooklyn NY 64-65; Libn NYC Bd of Educ 65-. 13: Yes. 14: Juvenile lit. 15: 919 E 106 st, Brooklyn NY 11236.

KNOBLOCH, MURIEL (RUTH). b NYC 1 Ja 34. 5: UMich 55 (Hist) AB; Columbia 55-56 (Hist); Pratt 59-60 MLS. 06: Fr, Norwegian. 7: Sec Revlon Inc NYC 56-59; Circ libn (Hunter Col) Herbert H Lehman Col 60-67, Ref libn 67-. 10: Beta Phi Mu. 14: Rare bks, pub rel, ref. 15: 3081 Villa ave, Brn onx NY 10468.

KNOLL, MARGARET. b Spokane Wash 22 F 10. 4: Kenneth C Knoll. 5: Whitworth Col 27-31 (Hist) BA; UWash summers 33-37 Fifth Yr Tchg Certif, 57-62 MLS. 6: Ger, Fr. 7: Lib clerk Spokane Pub Lib, Spokane Wash 31-33; Tchr & sch libn Coupeville & Prosser Wash 33-37; Lib asst U Br Seattle Pub Lib 44-45; Tchr & asst libn Richland Pub Schs, Richland Wash 52-60; Head Libn Columbia High Sch, Richland Wash 60-. 9: NEA; ALA; WashStateASchL (chm Nomin Com 64-65; chm Reg 5 61-62). 10: Girl Scouts; YWCA; AAUW. 14: Ref, ya. 15: 1807 Hunt, Richland Wa 99352.

KNOOP, GENE HARRISON. b Richmond Va 22 D 25. 4: Alan Richard Knoop. 5: Longwoo Col 43-47 (Eng) BS; UNC 47-48 BS in LS. 6: Fr, Sp, Ital, Lat. 7: Libn, boys & girls libn Richmond (Va) Pub Lib 48-50; Schs libn Pub Sch System, Bethel Park Penn 57; Libn Westover Br Richmond (Va) Pub Lib 60, Sr libn Main Lib 63-66; Asst hd ref Va State Lib, Richmond 66-68; Dir Chesterfield Co Lib System, Chester Va 68-. 9: ALA; VaLA. 10: AAUP. 14: Admin. 15: 2023 Westover hills, Richmond Va 23225.

KNOPF, DORIS M. b Yonkers NY 24 O 29. 5: NYU 47-51 (Eng) BA; Columbia 51-53 (LS) MS, 54-55 Tchr Certif. 6: Ger. 7: Br libn Yonkers Pub Lib, Yonkers NY 53-54; Elem libn Bronxville Pub Sch, Bronxville NY 54-. 8: Chm ACEI Com to Evaluate Ref Bks 62-65. 9: NEA; NYState TchrsAssn; Assn Childhood Educ Internat. 10: Delta Zeta; Delta Kappa Gamma. 14: Child, ext serv. 15: 1122 Midland ave, Bronxville NY 10708.

KNOPP, MARY (FITZGIBBON). b St Paul Mn inn. 4: Keith Knopp. 5: UMinn 30-34 (LS) BS, summer (European Hist); Col of St t Thomas 62 (Gaelic Lang), 65- computer courses). 6: Fr, Lat. 7: Ref & acquis asst Minn Hist Soc 35-40; Catlg libn Col of St Thomas 51-55, Hd catlg libn 55-. 8: Consul Home of Good Shepherd 58; Com on Hospitality for CathLA Nat Convention 67. 10: Minn Hist Soc; Twin City Catlgrs RT. 14: Catlg, rare bks. 15: 1926 Summit ave, St Paul Mn 55105.

KNOTT, MADGE (McCORD). b Albany Ga 11 Ja 29. 4: J Raymond Knott. 5: UGa 45-49 (Sp) BA; Mercer U 64-68; Emory 64-68 M Lib. 7: Tchr GAB Sch of Com, Macon Ga 50-51; Sec: Binswanger & Co, Macon Ga 51-53, Drs Benton, Fry, & Homeyer, Macon Ga 53-55; Libn McEvoy Jr High Sch, Macon Ga 65-. 9: ALA; GaLA; GaEA. 14: Sch libnship. 15: 375 Pio Nono ave, Macon Ga 31204.

KNOTT, MILADA (BEATRICE GESSMAN). b Mlada Boleslav Czechoslovakia 27 S 41. 4: Rudolph Eugene Knott. 5: Talladega Col 58-62 (Linguistics) BA; CatholicU 67-68 MSLS. 6: Czech, Ger, Fr, Russian, Sp. 7: Span & art instr Sessions Sch Talladega Col 59-62; Shelflister sub catlg div LC 62-66, Catlgr descr catlg div 66-67, Dewey decimal clsf specialist 68-. 14: Catlg. 15: 2351 "R" SE, Washington DC 20020.

KNOTT, WILLIAM ALAN. b Muscatine Iowa 4 O 42. 5: UIowa 62-67 (Eng) BA, 67-68 (LS) MA. 7: Nike-Hercules sect chief, Sgt E-5 US Army 65-67; Acquis clerk UIowa (Iowa City) 67-68; Ref lib Ottumwa Pub Lib, Ottumwa Iowa 68-69; Asst admin Prairie Hills Lib System, Ottumwa Iowa 69-. 8: Field consul Iowa State Traveling Lib 69-. 9: ALA; IowaLA. 12: Ed "Iowa State-wide Union List of Serials"; Publ "Arena Magazine" (65). 13: Yes. 14: Adult serv. 15: 129 N Court st, Ottumwa Ia 52501.

KNOTTS, MARY ANN. b Madison Wis 12 Je 35. 5: Huntingdon Col 53-60 (Art) BS; Drexel 66-67 (LS) MS in LS; Cumberland Law Sch 68. 7: Illustrator Chrysler Corp, Huntsville Ala 60-63; Illustrator US Army, Ft Rucker 63-66; A-v coord UAla Med Ctr Lib 67-68, Hd catlgr 68-. 9: SLA; MedLA; Birmingham Lib Club (sec). 10: Kappa Pi; Bus & Profess Women's Club. 14: Catlg rare bks. 15: 1325-A S 34th st, Birmingham Al 35205.

KNOUSE, BERTRAM H. b Sandy Run Penn 6 My 18. 4: Eleanor Schoonover. 5: UPenn 47-50 (Ind Mgt) BS; SUNY(Geneseo) 64-65 MLS. 6: Ger. 7: Period libn SUNY (Geneseo) 65-66; Systems analyst SUNY (Potsdam) 66-67; Acquis libn SUNY (Syracuse) 67-68, Ref & circ libn Col of Forestry 68-. 9: SLA (chm Upstate NY Chap 68). 10: Boy Scouts. 14: Ref, admin. 15: 200 Whitestone dr, Syracuse NY 13215.

KNOWER, BEVERLY M. b Genoa Wis 4 O 26. 5: LaCrosse State Tchrs Col 44-46; UWis 46-49 (Chem) BS, 51-54 (Food Tech) MS; Drexel 55-58 (LS) MS. 6: Fr. 7: Chem Oscar Mayer & Co, Madison Wis 49-51; Research fellow UWis (Madison) 51-54; Sun Oil Co, Marcus Hook Penn: Lit chem 55-60, Tech libn 60-65, Sect chief tech info serv 65-. 9: ACS; ASIS; SLA (chm Petroleum Sect, pres Phila Chap); Amer Petroleum Inst (Adv subcom on Abstracting & Indexing). 13: Yes. 15: Sun Oil Co R & D, Marcus Hook Pa 19061.

KNOWLES, DOROTHY (AILEEN). b Toronto 15 Mr 18. 5: MacDonald Col McGill U 36-40 (Foods & Nutrition) B of Household Sci; McGill U 52-53 BLS. 6: Fr. 7: Dietitian commercial & hosp wk Montreal 40-43; Lab tech (Munitions) Inspection Bd of the UK & Can, St Paul L'Hermite Can 43-44; Lab tech Can Army Nutrition Research Montreal 44-45; Food chem OXO (Can) Ltd Montreal 45-52; Jr libn UBC

53-56; Assoc libn Albert R Mann Lib, Cornell U 56-57; Libn Dept of Fisheries, Ottawa 57-59; Libn-in-chg Nat Energy Bd, Ottawa 59-. 9: SLA (Petrol Div: d sec-treas 64-65, Prog Chm 1969 Conf); CanLA; OttawaLA. 10: Prof Inst Pub Serv Can. 14: Ref. 15: 2060 Palmer ave, Ottawa 8 Canada.

KNOWLES, MARY (GARDNER). b Waltham Mass 14 Jl 10. 5: Bates Col 29-33 (Eng). 7: Child libn Watertown Free Pub Lib, Watertown Mass 33-38; Br libn Morrill Mem Lib, Norwood Mass 47-53; Libn William Jeanes Mem Lib, Plymouth Meeting Penn 53-. 9: ALA; MassLA; PennLA (chm Scholarship Com; chm SE Dist 65-66). 13: Yes. 14: Adult & child wk. 15: 543 N Whitehall rd, Norristown Pa 19401.

KNOWLES, SADIE (ARMITAGE). b Pt Edward Ont Can 27 Mr 1889. 7: Child libn Sarnia (Ont) Pub Lib. 9: ALA; CanLA; OntLA. 10: Indep Order Daughters of Empire; Commun Concert Assn; Can Artists Concerts; Sarnia Little Theatre; Sarnia Art Assn; Hosp Auxiliary. 11: Recipient Can Centennial Medal. 14: Child bks. 15: 332 W Christina st, Sarnia Ont Can.

KNOWLTON, JOHN D. b Greenville Me 25 Jl 34. 4: Carol Nash. 5: UMe 58-61 (Hist) BA, 67 (Hist) MA. 07: US Army QM Corps 55-57; LC Mss Div: Mss asst 61-62, Ref libn 62-64, Head reader serv 64-67, Hd preparation d sect 67-. 9: SAA; Mss Soc. 13: Yes. 14: Mss & archives. 15: 5800 Nevada ave, Wash DC 20015.

KNOX, ALVERA M(OOR). b St Charles SD 16 O 36. 4: Ronald Robert Knox. 5: Yankton Col 54-58 (Eng) BA; UArk 58-60 (Eng) MA; UDenver 63-64 (LS) MA. 6: Ger. 7: Grad asst tchr UArk 58-60; High sch tchr berkeley Unified Sch Dist, Berkeley Cal 60-61; Lib asst I Mary Reed Lib, Denver 63-64; Lib asst UIll Lib (Urbana) 64-65; Elem sch libn Urbana Commun Schs, Urbana Ill 65-66, Hd libn Urbana High Sch 66-68; Libn Southeast Hogh Sch, Springfield Pub Schs 68-. 9: ALA; IllLA; IllASchL. 14: Sch libnship. 15: 2508 Churchill rd, Springfield Il 62702.

KNOX, JO EMILY (GORDON). b Kingstree SC 10 Jl 45. 4: Nathaniel Knox. 5: Benedict Col 62-66 (Elem Ed) BA; Atlanta U 66-67 MSLS. 7: Acquis libn Benedict Col 68-. 9: ALA; SCLA. 10: Alpha Kappa Alpha. 14: Ref. 15: 1905 Willow st, Columbia SC 29204.

KNUDSON, MARY J O'DONNELL. b Dacon Colo 8 Ja 13. 4: Earl G Knudson. 5: Loretto Heights Col 32-36 (Hist, Soc Sci) AB; UDenver 36-37 BS in LS. 6: Sp, Fr. 7: Child libn Co Lib, Amarillo Tex 37-41; Child libn Carnegie Lib, Cheyenne Wyo 41-42; Tech libn US Govt, Lowry AFB, Denver 42-44; Asst libn Warren Base, Cheyenne Wyo 44-46; Asst libn State Lib, Cheyenne Wyo 46-47; Head libn US Govt, F E Warren AFB Wyo 47-52; Asst libn Boise Col Idaho 61-. 14: Child, ref. 15: 4013 Glencoe pl, Boise Id 83705.

KNUTSON, MAURICE CHALMER. b Alamo NDak 31 Ag 26. 4: Lyla Sand. 5: NDak StateU 49-53 (Soc Sci Educ) BS; UDenver 61-62 (Libnship) MA. 6: Norwegian. 7: Ref libn N Dak State U Lib 62-63; Base libn USAF: Grand Forks N Dak 63-64, Portland Ore 64-65; Libn-biol sci Pacific NW Forest & Range Experiment Sta, Portland Ore 65-. 8: In charge lib serv for all Forest Serv personnel in Wash, Ore & Alaska. 9: SLA; OreLA; PNLA; Portland-VancouverAreaLA. 10: Boy Scouts; Gateway Elks. 14: Admin, ref. 15: 12041 NE Siskiyou st, Portpand Or 97220.

KNUTSON, ROBERT LOGAN. b Appleton Minn. 5: USoCal 47 (Bus Admin) BS; UCal(Berkeley) 50 (Hist) MA; Columbia 56 (Hist) PhD; USoCal 59 MLS. 7: Bombardier (Lt) US Army Air Corps 43-45; Tchr Torrance Sch Dist, Torrance Cal 57-59; Ref dept USoCal 59-63, Head dept of spec collections 63-. 9: ALA; SAA; Ms Soc; CalLA; Oral Hist Assn. 10: AAUP; Sierra Club. 14: Spec collections. 15: 10429 Oletha lane, Los Angeles Ca 90024.

KOBASA, JOHN B. b Ukraine 25 S 25. 4: Lidia Pavlenko. 5: Ukrainian Free U 46-49 (Hist); CCNY 54-56 (Educ); Columbia 61-64 (LS) MS, 65- (LS). 6: Bielorussian, Czech, Ger, Polish, Russian, Slovak, Ukrainian. 7: Tchr, Instr E European lang courses G-r Sch, Germany 45-47; (Pfc) 47th Inf Div US Army 52-53; Dir jr dept UAY Assn Inc Hdqrs, NY 54-60; GA, catlg asst, searcher, asst catlgr, catlgr Columbia U Libs, NY 56-; Col assoc CCNY Music Lib 67-. 8: Hd Dept Libnship, Bd Acad Adv of Ukrainian Studies Chair harvard 68-; Bd Dirs Bibliog Ctr Ukrainian Inst Amer Inc, NYC 67-. 9: NY Tech Serv Libns. 12: ED "Youth Path" (55-56, 60-64). 13: Yes. 14: Catlg. 15: 155 E 4th st. Village View New York NY 10009.

KOBYLAK, ROSEMARY H (JUCHEM). b Elyria Ohio 28 O 27. 4: Joe Kobylak. 5: Case West Res 56-61 (Elem Educ) BS in Elem Ed, 63-65 MSLS. 6: Fr, Sp. 7: Lab tech, Cleveland Ohio: BF Goodrich Co 45-61, Union Carbide 47-50, McGean Chem Co 50-61; Tchr St Agela's Elem Sch, Fairview Park Ohio 61-63; Child libn Lakewood Pub Lib, Lakewood Ohio 63-66, Elem sch libn 66-. 8: Planning Com: McKinley Sch Lib Lakewood Ohio 68-70, taft Ohio 69-70. 9: ALA; OhioLA; OhioSchLA; NEast Ohio Tchrs. 10: Women's Nat Bk Assn. 14: Child wk, media ctrs, computer programming. 15: 631 Tampico ct, Berea Oh 44017.

KOCH, CHARLES (WILLIAM). b Sikeston Mo 12 Mr 26. 4: Marilea Paddison. 5: SoIllU 45-49, summer 49 (Hist) BSEd (summa cum laude); WashingtonU summer 54; UIll 57-58, summers 55, 56, 60 MSLS; Columbia summer 64 (Instr Material). 7: Eng & soc studies tchr Martinsburg High Sch, Martinsburg Mo 49-51; Labor rel clerk Wabash RR, St Louis 51-54; Tchr-libn Nashville (Ill) High Sch 54-57; Libn Morton High Sch W, Berwyn Ill 58-61; Head lib serv Hinsdale Twp, Hinsdale Ill 61-62; Consullib serv Pre-S-Col (St Louis) 62-65; Chm Libs Lyons Twp & Jr Col, La Grange Ill 65-67, Dir libs 67-. 8: Consul to Bldg Com John Burroughs Sch, St Louis; Adv Com, KMOX TV Reading Serv; Consul for materials, Riverview Gardens Experimental Schs, St Louis; Adv Com St Louis Metro Lib Survey; Adv Com St Louis Info Needs Survey; Org & Consul Study-Learning Resources Centers, St Louis; Adv com Lyons Twp Multi-Media Instr Ctr. 09: ALA; AASchL; NEA; (Exec Com 1964 Conf); Assn Supv & Curriculum Development; MoLA; IllLA (chm Elections Com 61-62); MoASchL (St Louis Dist Chm 63-64); MoTchrsAssn; IllEA. 10: Kappa Delta Pi; Beta Phi Mu; Lyons Twp EA. 13: Yes. 14: Sch lib serv & facilities. 15: 4241 Sunnyside ave, Brookfield Il 60513.

KOCH, ESTHER. b Brooklyn NY 4 My 14. 5: Brooklyn Col 29-33 (Bio) BA; UOre (Eugene) 63-64 (Eng, Soc Sci) MA, 66-67 MLS; East Wash State Col summer 65 (Soc Sci); Upper Iowa Col 68-69 (Bus). 6: Fr, Ger, Sp. 7: Tchr: Paisely High Sch, Paisley Ore 63-64, Jordan Valley Hogh Sch, Jordan Valley Ore 64-65; Libn & tchr Days Creek Sch Syst, Days Creek Ore 66-67; Co sch libn White Pine Co Schs, E Ely Nev 67-68; Asst libn Upper Iowa Col 68-. 9: NEA; OreLA; NevLA; WhitePineCoLA (sec-treas 67-68). 10: MENSA. 14: Ref, bus, the arts, rare bks, ser. 15: Azalea Or 97410.

KOCH, ESTHER DOROTHY. b Kan City Mo 9 Je 09. 5: UCal(Berkeley) 26-30 (Span) BA, 30-31 (LS) Certif. 6: Sp, Fr. 7: Jr libn Oakland Free Lib, Oakland Cal 35-37; US Dept of Agric Lib, Wash DC; Catlgr 37-43, Chief catlg dept 44-50, Asst chief acquis dept 50-51; Catlgr UCal Lib (Los Angeles) 51-58, Asst head catlg dept 58-67, Hd catlg dept 67-. 8: Reorganizer of Lib of scuela de Agricultura, Chapingo Mex 47. 9: ALA (Div Catlg & Clsf; chm Nomin Com 56-57, chm Bylaws Com 48-49);-RTSD (Catlg & Clsf Sect; chm Bylaws Com 63-65, v-chm & chm-elect 68-69); CalLA (pres Tech Serv Div 68); Los Angeles Reg Group Tech Serv Libns; SoCal Tech Proc Gp. 10: AAUW. 14: Catlg, tech proc. 15: 1510-D California ave, Santa Monica Ca 90403.

KOCH, GARY GROVE. b Mt Vernon Ohio 6 Ja 42. 4: Carolyn Johnson. 5: Ohio StateU 60-62 (Math) BS, 62-63 (Industrial Engring) MS; UNC 63-68 (Statistics) PhD. 6: Fr, ger. 7: Asst Prof Lib Sci (jt with Biostatistics & Sch of Med) UNC (Chapel Hill) 68-. 10: Amer Statistics Assn; Biometrics Soc; AAAS; Amer Pub Health Assn; Sigma Xi. 13: Yes. 14: Info retr, operations research. 15: 703 Longleaf dr, Chapel Hill NC 27514.

KOCH, HENRY CHARLES. b Milwaukee 20 Ap 20. 4: Betty Schumann. 5: Carleton Col 37-41 (Hist) AB; Columbia 41-43 (Hist) MA; Johns Hopkins 48-51 (Medieval Hist); UBasel 51-52 (Medieval Hist); UMich 51-52 MALS. 6: Fr, Ger. 7: Stagg Sgt US Army 222 Inf, Europe 42-46; Instr Mohawk Col 47-49; Asst div head hist-biog div Cleveland Pub Lib 52-55; Head humanities div Mich state U Lib 55-60, Asst dir of libs 60-66, Assoc dir of libs 66-. 09: ALA (com chm 63-64); -RTSD (chm Discussion Gp); MichLA (chm Dist II 57-58, chm Col Sect 62-63). 13: Yes. 14: Tech processes, hist of the bk, admin. 15: Mich State U Lib, East Lansing Mi 48823.

KOCH, MARION M(ARGARET). b St Louis 13 Mr 16. 5: Washington U(St Louis) 33-37 (Geol) AB; UIll 37-38 BS in LS. 7: Libn Washington U Sch of Dentistry(St Louis) 38-41; Asst order libn Penn State Col 41-43; Catlgr UColo Lib 43-46; Chief catlg libn St Louis Pub Lib 46-. 9: ALA; MoLA. 10: Garden Club. 14: Catlg. 15: 8405 Engler Park ct, St Louis Mo 63114.

KOCH, MICHAEL SAMUEL. b Mizocz Poland 15 Mr 05. 4: Rose (Blecher). 5: Washington U (St Louis) 26-30 (Physics-Math, Ger) AB, Tchrs Certif; St Louis Lib Sch 30-31 Lib Certif; Washington & St Louis U 32-38 (Soc Wk); UChicago 39-41 (LS); Columbia 51, 59, 62; LIU Spec Prog Div 62-63 (Electronic Data Processing) Certif. 6: Ger, Fr, Russian. 7: Lib asst St Louis Pub Lib 30-32; Soc wker St Louis Soc Security Commsn 32-38; Order libn & research asst Chicago Tchrs Col 39-41; Libn Olin Corp, E Alton Ill 41-44; Catlgr & revisor USWar Dept Lib, Wash DC 44-47; Subj analyst & bibliog NLM 47-50; Libn US Naval Supply Activities, Brooklyn NY 50-53; Libn Underwood Corp, Electronic Computer Div, LI City, NY 54-55; Sr libn Downstate Med Center SUNY (Brooklyn) 55-. 8: Consul in establishing spec lib 58-60 Nat Psychological Assn for psychoanalysis; Consul in problems of clsfn & subj analysis 62-64, Amer Psychoanalytic Assn. 9: SLA (chm 2 NY groups; organ NY Docs Gp); MedLA; ASIS; NY Lib Club. 10: UChicago Alumni Assn; Washington U Alumni Assn. 12: "Library Classification of U S Military Units" (48); "Gamble-Curran Medical History Collection - A Classified Bibliography" (57). 13: Yes. 14: Documentation, subj analysis, translation, bibliog, consul. 15: 3801 18th ave, Brooklyn NY 11218.

KOCH, PAUL G(ILBERT). b Milwaukee Wis 6 Ag 43. 5: UWis (Madison) 61-65 (Hist) BS; UWis (Milwaukee) 67-69 MSLS. 6: Ger. 7: Specialist UWis Sch of Lib & Info Sci (Milwaukee) 69; Libn Wis State U (Fond du Lac Campus) 69-. 9: ALA. 10: Naval Records Club; US Naval Inst; USN Res. 14: Acquis, govt docs. 15: 1421 E Pinedale ct, Shorewood Wi 53211.

KOCHEN, MANFRED. b Vienna Austria 4 Jl 28. 4: Paula Landerer. 5: MIT 47-50 (Physics) BS; Columbia 50-51 (Math) MA, 51-53, 55 (Applied Math) PhD. 6: Ger, Fr, Ital. 7: Mathemar tician Biot & Arnold, NYC 50-52; Lecturer Columbia U 52-53; Research mathematician Paul Rosenberg Assoc, Mt Vernon NY 53-55; Analyst- programmer Inst for Adv Study, Princeton NJ 53-55; Post-doctoral Fellow Harvard U 55-56; Info theory project IBM Research Center, Yorktown Heights NY 56-60, Manager info retrieval proj 60-64; Assoc Prof depts of lib sci & psychiatry & Research math biologist Mental Health Research Inst UMich 65-. 8: Consul, RCA Labs 65; Survey Team for LC Automation 60-63; United Aircraft Corp Systemd s Ctr 67-68; Study Team on Lang & Computers, RAND, summer 63; Visiting expert (on tech exh), EURATOM, Ispra (Italy) 64; Commun Systems Found. 9: Amer Math Soc; Amer Physical Soc; Assn for Computing Machinery; ASIS; Soc for Ind & Appl Math. 10: Art Students League, NY. 11: ASIS Distinguished Lectr 68; Assn for Comput Mach Nat Lectr 67-68. 12: "Some Problems in Information Science" (65); Assoc ed "Behavioral Science"; "Tg he Growth of Knowledge" (67); "Automation and the Library of Congress" (63). 13: Yes. 14: Math learning and cognitive proc, stability in the growth of knowledge. 15: 1328 Forest ct, Ann Arbor Mi48104.

KOCKINOS, JEAN FREEMAN (LINCOLN). b Okla City Okla 1 Ja 28. 5: Rockford Col 46-50 (Eng) BA; UCal (Berkeley) 50-51 BLS. 6: Sp. 7: Child libn Oakland Pub Lib, Oakland Cal 51-62; Child libn San Diego Pub Lib, San Diego Cal 62-64, YA coord 64-66, Cp oord lib serv to child 66-. 9: ALA; CalLA. 10: San Diego Museum of Man; San Diego Zool Soc; AAUW. 14: Young adult wk. 15: 2689 Cowley way, San Diego Ca 92110.

KOCHER, EVELYN M(AUDE). b Scranton Penn 21 N 25. 5: Meredith Col 43-46 (Fr) BA; UNC 46-47 BS in LS, 57-58 MS in LS. 6: Fr, Sp, Ger. 7: Asst libn Huntingdon Col 47-57; Sr catlg libn WVa U 58-65; Visiting instr Sch of Lib Sci UNC summer 60; Instr WVa U 64-66; Chief catlg libn 65-. Asst Prof 67-. 9: ALA-ACRL (Tri-State Chap); WVaLA. 10: AAUW; Morgantown Women's Music Club; Beta Phi Mu. 14: Catlg, lib educ. 15: 916 Garrison ave, Morgantown WVa 26406.

KODER, SISTER ALMA. b Allentown Penn 13 O 14. 5: Muhlenberg Col 47-50 (Hist) AB; Drexel 50-56 MLS. 6: Ger. 7: Sec Bonney Forge & Tool Co, Allentown Penn; Lutheran Deaconess Artman Home, Ambler Penn; Lutheran Deaconess St John's Church, Easton Penn; Libn Lutheran Deaconess House, Gladwyne Penn; Libn St Paul's Lutheran Church Lib, Ardmore Penn; Libn Lankenau High Sch of Nursing, Phila 53-. 9: ALA; PennLA. 10: Beta Phi Mu; Nat League Nursing; Lutheran Church Women; Women of St Paul's (Ardmore); Drexel Lib Sch Alum Assn. 14: Admin, ref. 15: Lankenau Hosp Sch of Nursing, City ave at 64th st, Phila Pa 19151.

KODREBSKI, JANUSZ I(GNACY). b Kasna-Dolna Poland 4 D 05. 4: Leatrice Hair. 5: Artillery Off Training Sch 24-27 (Math); Nat War Col (Warsaw) 36-38 (Logistics) Diplomat; USoCal 54-55 (LS) MA. 6: Polish, Ger. 7: Major Polish Army 24-47; Printing shop mgr & owner, London England 47-50; Proofreader LaBrea Printing Co, Los Angeles 50-51; Instr US Army Lang Sch, Monterey Cal 51-53; Acquis libn US Naval Ordinance Sta, China Lake Col 55-56; Hd catlgr US Naval Post Grad Sch, Monterey Cal 56-. 14: Catlg. 15: 1027 Bayview ave, Pacific Grove Ca 93950.

KOEHLER, LILLIE B (HESS). b Wash DC 13 N 15. 4: Roy E Koehler. 5: E Stroudsburg State Tchrs Col 31-35 (Secondary Educ) BS in Ed; Drexel 40-41 BS in LS. 7: Tchr Elem Sch, Northampton Co Penn 35-37; Tchr Elem Sch E Bangor Penn 37-40; Tchr-libn Canton Sch & Pub Lib, Canton Penn 41-43; Circ libn Lehigh U 43-49; Tchr Elem Sch, Hellertown Penn 58-64, Libn 64-. 9: NEA; PennStateEA. 10: PTA; High Sch Parents Band Club. 14: Child serv. 15: 1558 Main st, Hellertown Pa 18055.

KOEKER, MARIE L. b St Louis. 5: Denison U PhB; Columbia BS in LS. 6: Fr, Ger, Sp. 7: Lib asst Dayton Pub Lib, Dayton Ohio; Libn & Prog Exec Engnrs Club of Dayton, Dayton Ohio; Libn "Dayton Daily News," Dayton, Ohio; Chief tech info ref br Systems Engnrg Group Research & Tech Div Air Force Systems Command Wright-Patterson AFB ohio, Asst to chief Data Base Mgt Div Deputy for Foreign Tech Aeronautical Syst Div 69-. 10: Col Women's Club. 14: Automation, tech documents & reports. 15: 2445 Fairport ave, F Dayton Oh 45406.

KOEL, AKE ILMAR. b Kuressaare Estonia 20 My 20. 4: Maria Ottilia Nemeth. 5: UToronto 61 (Psych) BA, 62 BLS. 6: Swedish, Estonian, Ger, Fr, Sp, Danish, Dutch, Norwegian, Lat. 7: Documentalist-libn in chg of lib AB Bahco Enkoping Sweden 49-54; Salesman Central Sci Co of Can, Toronto 54-61; Catlgr UToronto Lib 62, Head of ser sect catlg dept 63-65; Head of tech serv Hamilton Col Lib 65-66; Hd Dutch-Scandinavian sect shared catlg div LC 66-. 9: ALA; ASIS; CanLA; Tekniska Litteratursa skapet (Stockholm). 10: Toronto Art Gallery; Munson Williams-Proctor Inst, Utica NY; Kirkland Art Cen ter, Clinton NY. 14: Tech serv. 15: 809 Third st SW, Washington DC 20024.

KOEL, MARIA OTTILIA (NEMETH). b Hungary 3 Ap 23. 4: Ake I Koel. 5: UToronto 60-67 (Philos) BA; Catholic U 67-68 MSLS. 6: Hungarian, Fr, Ger, Ital, Lat. 7: Lib asst utoronto Lib 54-65; Catlgr Georgetown U Lib 68-, Asst hd of catlg dept 69-. 8: Staff super, Hosp of SS John & Elizabeth, London 50-53. 9: ALA; CathLA. 14: Catlg. 15: 809 Third st SW, Washington DC 20024.

KOELBL, DOROTHY JUNE. b Lancaster Penn 7 Je 32. 5: Millersville State Col 58-63 (LS) BS. 6: Sp. 7: Machine operator Central Paper Box Co, Lancaster Penn; Machine operator J L Clark Manuf Co, Lancaster Penn; Clerk Troup Music House, Lancaster Penn; Dept manager W T Grant Co, Lancaster Penn; Elem libn Solanco Sch Dist, Quarryville Penn 63, Jr high sch libn 63-64; Elem libn Lancaster City Sch Dist, Lancaster Penn 64-. 9: NEA; ALA; PennStateEA; Lancaster Co LA. 10: Universalist Serv Com; YWCA; Lancaster Co Philatelic Soc; Lancaster Hiking Club. 14: Sch lib serv. 15: Lafayette Sch Lib, St Joseph & Pearl sts, Lancaster Pa 17603.

KOENIG, ELIZABETH WHITE. b Buffalo NY 22 Jl 16. 4: Norbert C Koenig. 5: Russell Sage Col 38 (Eng) BA; SUNY(Albany) 41 (Eng) MA, 43 (LS) MS. 6: Fr. 7: Asst Albany Pub Lib, Albany NY; Libn E Hartford High Sch, E Hartford Conn; Libn Stewart Sch, Garden City NY; Ref libn Hofstra Col; Libn Locust Sch, Hemlock Sch, Garden City NY 58-. 13: Yes. 14: Creativity in the prim sch learning ctr. 15: 38 Boylston st, Garden City NY 11535.

KOENIG, MICHAEL E D. b Rochester NY. 4: Nancy Packard. 5: Yale 59-63 (Psych) BA; UChicago 66- (LS) AM. 6: Fr, Ger. 7: Communications off USN, USS Shadwell LSD 15 63-65; Asst hd circ dept Sterling Lib YaleU 65-66. 9: ALA; ASIS. 10: ACLU; Beta Phi Mu. 14: Automation, admin, syst analysis, hist of printing. 15: 5107 S Blackstone ave, Chicago Il 60615.

KOENIG, SALLY ANN (McLEOD). b New Orleans 20 D 33. 4: Robert F Koenig. 5: Miss State Col for Women 51-55 (LS) BS. 7: Child libn asst Jackson Municipal Lib, Jackson Miss 55-56; Catlg libn asst Miss State U 57-60; Lib consul Continental Can Co, Clarksburg WVa 65-69; Libn St Mary's Nursing Sch Lib, Clarksburg W Va 68-69. 14: Catlg. 15: 1414 Fairview ave Cherry II, Bowling Green Ky 42101.

KOEPP, DON. b Shell Lake Wis 27 Ap 29. 4: Mary Dale Stewart. 5: Wis State Col 48-52 (Eng) AB; UWis 55-56 MALS; UCal 58-65 DLS. 7: Circ libn Chico State Col 56-57; UCal(Berkeley): Tchg asst 58-60, Libn II Inst of Govt Studies 60-64, Pub admin analyst Inst of Govt Studies 63-64, Act Asst Prof 64-65, Asst U libn 65-68; Col libn Humboldt State Cp u libn 65-68; Col libn Humboldt State Col 68-. 12: Co-auth "California Public Library Commission, Report No 2" (59); "Public Library Government" (68). 14: Pub libs, univ libs. 15: Univ of Cal Lib, Berkeley Ca 94720.

KOERNER, ALBERTA GJERTINE (AURINGER). b Detroit Mich 19 F 42. 4: John Marvin Koerner. 5: UMich 60-64 (Geog) BA, 64-65 MALS. 7: Ref libn Geog & map div LC 65-68; Ref libn umich Libs (Ann Arbor) 68-. 9: SLA; Assn Amer Geographers. 12: "Detroit and Vicinity Before 1900; an Annotated List of Maps (68). 14: Ref, map libs. 15: 1837 Shirley lane apt A-2, Ann Arbor Mi 48105.

KOESTER, ROBERT PETER. b Buffalo NY 2 je 40. 5: St Lawrence U 58-62 (Eng) AB; UToronto 62-63 (Eng); Columbia 64 (African Studies); UMich 66-67 AMLS. 6: Fr, Ger. 7: Secondary sch tchr Peace Corps, West Nigeria 64-66; Ref libn Northwestern U67-. 9: ALA. 10: Com of returned volunteers. 14: African studies, libnship, acquis, ref. 15: 1432 Elmwood ave, Evanston Il 60201.

KOESTERS, SISTER MARY JUSTINA CPPS. b Casella Ohio 2 Mr 04. 5: Xavier U 27-28; Athenaeum of Ohio 28-29 (Educ) Ohio Tchg Certif; UDayton summers 35-40 (Educ) BS in Ed; Catholic U 45, 49-53 MSLS. 6: Ger. 7: Elem tchr & principal parochial & pub schs, Ohio 29-50; Tchr & principal parochial elem schs, Linton ND 50-51; Tchr parochial elem schs, Cincinnati 51-53; Asst libn Mt St Mary's of the West Sem 53-55; Libn Immaculata Lib, Dayton Ohio 55-60; Libn & v-principal St Mary's High Sch, Phoenix 60-63; Libn & tchr Bishop Bennett Lib Central Catholic High Sch, Lafayette Ind 63-68; Immaculata Lib, Dayton Ohio 68-. 9: ALA; CathLA (Com for Cath Sup to "Standard Catlg for High Sch Libs" 61-64); Wabash Valley Educ Materials Cty (Com mem 64-68). 10: Commun Bd Sisters of the Precious Blood (CPPS). 14: Studs reading interests, ref. 15: 4830 Salem ave, Dayton Ohio 45416.

KOHL, THELMA C. b Evansville Ind 15 N 40. 5: UEvansville 61-65 (Ger, Russian) BA; IndU 66-68 MLS. 6: Russian. 7: Acquis libn UEvansville 68-. 10: Phi Kappa Phi. 14: Acquis. 15: RR 3 Box 459, Newburgh In 47630.

KOHLER, BETTY (GRAHAM). b Chicago 6 S 18. 5: UWis (Milwaukee) 35-36; UKan 36-38 (Eng); Marycrest Col 50-51 (Educ) BS; UIll 63-65 (LS) MS. 6: Fr. 7: Eng tchr-libn St Katharine's Sch, Davenport Iowa 53-56; Sch libn Sudlow Jr High Sch, Davenport Iowa 56-58; Head libn Bettendorf Pub Lib, Bettendorf Iowa 58-65; Asst dir Pub Lib, Iowa City Iowa 65-; Area lib consul State Lib 65-66; Dir Warner Lib, Tarrytown NY 66-67; Adult serv coord Cuyahoga Co Lib System, Cleveland Ohio 67-68; Dir Rock Island Pub Lib, Rock Island Ill 68-. 8: Adult serv consul for Iowa State Lib 64-66. 9: ALA; Adult EA; IowaLA (chm Intell Freedom & Memb Com); Mo Valley Adult Educ; NYLA; OhioLA. 10: LWV; AAUW; United World Federalists; PEO; Sigma Kappa; Beta Phi Mu; Beta Sigma Phi. 13: Yes. 14: Admin. adult & ya serv, serv to ghetto. 15: 2920 24th st, Rock Island Il 61201.

KOHLSTEDT, DONALD W. b Milwaukee 16 Ap 09. 4: Ethelyn Dunn. 5: Dakota Wesleyan U 25-28 (Soc Sci); UIll 28-29 (Sociol) AB, 29-30 BS in LS, 34-35 MALS. 6: Fr. 7: Stack supv UIll (Urbana) 29-30; 1st asst Mun Ref Lib, St Louis 30-34; Instr UIll Lib Sch summer 35; Libn Kan City (Kan) Pub Lib 35-41; Lib Dir Grand Rapids Pub Lib, Grand Rapids Mich 41-. 8: Mich State Bd for Libs 49-54; Lecturer, Lib Sci UMich Ext serv 56-57. 9: ALA (chm Lib Radio Bdcasting Com 39-40, Coun 49-52, chm Const & Bylaws Com 54-56, Exec Bd Exhib Round Table 54-56, chm Standards Com 56-59; Lib Exh Consul 69); MichLA (chm Planning Com 44-45, chm Legis Com 45-46, pres 56-57). 10: Torch Club; Rotary; Grand Rapids Hist Soc. 11: Hon life mem, Grand Rapids Furniture Designers Assn; LLD Dak Wesleyan U 53. 13: Yes. 14: Admin. 15: 111 Library st NE, Grand Rapids Mich 59502.

KOHN, MRS CHARLOTTE GOLDFINGER. b Chicago 5 S 10. 5: NWU 40-43; Chicago 53-54 (LS). 6: Ger. 7: Chicago Pub Lib: var 28-60, Libn Chatham Br 61-62, Libn Avalon Br 63-. 9: ALA-ASD IllLA (Rev Com 64-65, chm Info Com 63, chm Regl Com 68); Chicago Lib Club (pres 62-63). 10: Staff Assn, Chicago Pub Lib. 14: Br lib serv (Adult). 15: 5242 Hyde Park blvd apt 512, Chicago Il 60615.

KOHN, SHIRLEY L. b Oak Park Ill 20 Ja 25. 5: Cornell Col 42-43; Northwestern 45-48 (Fr) BS; UIll 49-50 MS in LS. 7: Documents catlgr Wash State U 50; Campus libn De Paul U Lib 51-52; Asst libn ALA Hdqrs, Chicago 52-54; Documents catlgr Wash State U 54-55; Ref libn Oak Park Pub Lib, Oak Park Ill 55-57; Circ libn San Jose State Col 57-63, Humanities libn 63-65, 66-, Acquis libn 65-66. 9: ALA; MusLA; CalLA. 10: Beta Phi Mu; Phi Sigma Iota. 14: Ref, lib instr. 15: 5466 Cribari Green, San Jose Ca 95135.

KOHN, WALTER. b Augsburg Germany 8 F 09. 5: UBerlin 28-31 (Law); UFrankfurt a M 31-33 (Pol Sci); USoCal 54-55 MSLS. 6: Ger, Fr, Lat. 7: Spareparts catlg dept Douglas Aircraft, El Segundo Cal 51-53; Head catlg dept Coalinga Dist Lib, Coalinga Cal 55-61; Ref libn Stanislaus State Col Lib 61-62; Catlg libn Chico State Col Lib 62-. 9: CalLA (Lib Week Com 57). 10: Glendale Lapidary & Gem Soc; Coalinga Rockhound Soc; Golden Empire Gem & Mineral Soc. 11: Hon life mem, Glendale Laxidary & Gem Soc. 12: Numerous articles in Gems & Minerals Magazine (Mentone Cal) since 55; Articles in Lapidary Journal and Westways Magazine (Cal); Newspaper articles, book reviews, and translations of articles from German, French into English. 13: Yes. 14: Catlg, ref, bk reviewing, bk sel. 15: c/o Chico State Col Lib (Catalog Dept), Chico Ca 95926.

KOHRS, LEWIS PAUL. b Burlington Iowa 2 Ap 11. 4: Charlotte Irwin. 5: Santa Barbara State Col 32-33 (Eng); UCal(Berkeley) 33-36 (Philos) AB, 39-42 (Social Institutions) MA, 50-52 (Sociol, Soc Instit) PhD, 53 BLS. 6: Fr, Ger. 7: Libn ref dept Richmond Pub Lib, Richmond Cal 53; Head Libn San Diego Jr Col 54-57; Libn Grossmont High Sch, Grossmont Cal 57-. 14: Ref, bk sel, bldg of collections. 15: 3876 Belmont ave, San Diego Ca 92116.

KOLARIK, RUTH N (NEIMAN). b Bridgeport Penn 24 D 27. 4: P Luther Kolarik. 5: Penn State U 45-49 (Elem Educ) BS; Drexel 66- (LS). 7: Elem Sch Tchr: Arnold Sch Dist, Arnold Penn 49-51, Haverford Sch Dist, Haverford Penn 51-52; Elem Libn: Norristown Area Sch Dist, Norristown Penn 67-68, Upper Dublin Sch Dist, Ft Washington Penn 68-. 9: NEA; ALA; PennStateEA; PennLA. 15: 1314 Hoffman rd, Ambler Pa 19002.

KOLB, AUDREY MAE (PALO). b Astoria Ore 3 O 27. 4: Albert F Kolb. 5: Ore State U 45-49 (Gen Sci) BS, 49-50 (Zool); UWash 60-63 MLibnship. 7: Tissue tech Emanual Hosp, Portland Ore 49; Lab asst Ore State U 49-50; Tissue tech Med Dental Lab, Portland Ore 51; Sec US Army, Alaska 52-53; NCentral Reg Lib, Wenatchee Wash: Child libn 58-60, Bkmob libn 61-63, Hdqrs libn 63-65; Head libn Wenatchee Valley Col 65-. 9: ALA; NEA-DAVI; WashLA; PNLA (chm Circ Div). 10: Beta Sigma Phi. 14: Pub serv, ref. 15: Wenatchee Valley Col 1300 Fifth st, Wenatchee Wa 98801.

KOLB, CLAIRE ELENA. b Hammond Ind 31 My 45. 5: Cal State Polytech Col 63-67 (Soc Sci) BS; UCLA 68-69 (LS) Masters. 7: Libn (bkmob) Santa Barbara Pub Lib, Santa Barbara Cal 69-. 14: Child & sch libs. 15: 6403 Temple City blvd, Temple City Ca 91780.

KOLBET, RICHARD MERLIN. b Spokane Wash 30 N 41. 4: Gale Elaine (Svoboda). 5: Gonzaga U 59-64 (Eng) BA; UWash 64-65 MLibnship. 6: Ger. 7: Journeyman Safeway Stores, Inc, Spokane Wash 55-63; Clerk Bkstore Gonzaga U 63-64; Prepro libn Seattle Pub Lib 65; Map libn spec collections 65-68, H d acquis dept 68-. 9: IowaLA. 10: Friends of the UIowa Lib. 13: Yes. 14: Acquis admin, MSS. 15: Univ of Iowa Lib, Iowa City Ia 52240.

KOLESAR, ANDREW JR. b Homestead Penn 15 Je 33. 4: Margaret Poulos. 5: St Mary's U(San Antonio Tex) 55-59 (Sociol) BA; UPittsburgh 62-63 MLS. 6: Slovak. 7: US Navy Hospital Corpsman (HM2), Europe & Far East 51-55; Casewker Amer Red Cross, Houston 61; Casewker Catholic Soc Serv, Pittsburgh 61-62; Asst acquis libn Ohio U 63-; Catlgr Allianic Col 66-68; Act hd libn 68-. 9: ALA;-PLA. 10: Polish Nat Alliance; AAUP. 14: Acquis, catlg, admin. 15: 236 1/2 Beach ave, Cambridge Springs Pa 16403.

KOLK, MARJORIE (MILLS) S(EELY). b Goshen NY 5 O 17. 4: Nicholas H Kolk. 5: Wells Col 35-39 (Math) BA; Columbia 39-40 BS in LS. 7: Asst ref libn NY Pub Lib, Morrisania Br 40-41; Bkmob libn Ramapo Catskill Lib Serv, Middletown NY 62-63; Libn Moffat Lib, Washingtonville NY 63-68. 10: 4-H Club leader. 14: Sch serv, ref. 15: Maple Knoil Farm, RD #1, Box 140, Goshen NY 10924.

KOLODNY, JOYCE ELAINE. b Montreal 4 Ja 42. 4: Harvey F Kolodny. 5: McGill 58-62 (Eng, Fine Arts) BA, 62-63 BLS, 69 . 7: Catlgr Canadair Ltd, Montreal 63-64; Asst libn Air Canada, Montreal 64-66; Cote St Luc Pub Lib bk sel & catlg, Can 66-67. 9: SLA (treas Montreal Chap 65-66). 14: Catlg, ref. 15: 2092 Place Beaudet, Saint Laurent 378, Quebec Can.

KOMIDAR, JOSEPH STANLEY. b Chisholm Minn 19 Jl 16. 4: Mary Louise Watson. 5: Hibbing (Minn) Jr Col 34-36 (LS) AA; UMinn 36-38 BLS, 38-41 (Hist) BA; Chicago 46-48 (LS) MA. 6: Ger, Slovenian. 7: Ref asst UMinn (Minneapolis) 38-41; Ref & loan libn Carleton Col 41-43; US Army Air Forces personnel & admin Staff Sgt 43-46; Ref libn Northwestern U 48-51, Chief ref & spec serv 51-56; U Libn Tufts U 56-. 8: Visiting Lecturer, U Denver Grad Sch Libnship, summer 55. 9: ALA; ASIS; NELA. 10: AAUP; Beta Pi Mu. 13: Yes. 14: Admin, acquis, ref, coop. 15: 8 Wells rd, Reading Ma 01867.

KOMINEK, IRENE CLAIRE (MERKLER). b Elizabeth NJ 17 Ag 21. 4: Frank J Kominek. 5: Seton Hall U 40 (Fr); Montclair State Col 40-43 (Eng) BA; Trenton State Col summers 44-45 High Sch Lib Certif; Columbia 45-46 (Eng); 46-48 (LS) BS, 62-65 (LS) MS. 6: Fr, Sp. 7: Eng tchr Jefferson Jr High Sch Union NJ 43-44; Eng tchr & Libn Pt Pleasant Beach High Sch, Pt Pleasant Beach NJ 44-46; Asst libn Linden High Sch, Linden NJ 46-47; Jr & sr high sch libn Cranford Jr & Sr High Sch, Cranford NJ 47-48; High sch libn Rhodes Sch, NYC 48-53; Libn Teen Corner, Main Lib Newark NJ 53; Elem tchr Washington Sch, NBergen NJ 59-60; Head high sch libn NBergen High Sch, NBergen NJ 60-. 8: Moderator for Hudson Co Sch Lib Coun Assn, 63-64. 9: ALA; NJLA; NJSchLA (Hosp chm) ; Hudson CoSchLA; NJEA; Hudson CoEA; Secom Sch Dept Assn. 14: Readers adv, ref, pub rel, instr media coord. 15: 9210 Bergenwood ave, N Bergen Nj 07047.

KONA, MARTHA (MISTINOVA). 4: William Kona. 5: USalzburg(Austria) 49-50; Rosary Col 50-53 (Econ, Ger) BA, 57-58 (LS) MA. 6: Slovak, Ger, Russian. 7: Subprof ALA Lib, Chicago 54-56; Asst catlg libn UIll Lib of Med Sci(Chicago) 58-63; Libn Chemurgy Div Research Lib Central Soya Co, Chicago 65-. 9: ALA; MedLA (Midwest Reg Group); Nurs Sch Libns Midwest. 10: AAUP; AAUW; Pi Gamma Mu. 14: Catlg, ref. 15: 2641 N Meade ave, Chicago Il 60639.

KONA, WILLIAM. b Slovakia. 4: Martha Mistina. 5: UBratislava (Law); UCentral (Madrid) (Law); Rosary Col 55-56 (LS) MA; Chicago (LS). 6: Sp, Ital, Slovak, Fr, Russian, Ger, Portu. 7: Dental libn Loyola U(Chicago) 56-57; Head Libn Cook Co Sch of Nursing, Chicago 57-66; Head Libn Rush Med Lib Presbyterian-St Luke's Hosp, Chicago 66-. 8: Staff, Amer Hosp Assn, Inst on Hosp Libnship 61 & 64. 9: ALA-AHIL (Publs Adv Com 62-64, Bibliotherapy Com 64-66); MedLA (chm Memb Com 64-65, chm Nurs Libs Group 63-65, mem Exch Com 63-; Midwest Reg Group: Bd Dirs 64-67, pres 66-67); Tri-State Hosp Assembly, Med Lib Serv (Program Chm 63-64); Nurs Libns Midwest (chm 60-). 13: Yes. 14: Admin, ref. 15: 2641 N Meade ave, Chicago Il 60639.

KONDELIK, JOHN P. b Chicago Ill 28 Ja 42. 5: UFla 61-65 (Hist) BA; Fla State U 65-66 (LS) MS. 6: Fr. 7: Acquis libn Fla Presbyterian Col 66-68, Catlgr 68-. 9: ALA; SELA; FlaLA. 10: Phi Alpha Theta; Beta Phi Mu; AAUP. 14: Catlg, bibliog. 15: 1726 6th st So, St Petersburg Fl 33701.

KONDELIK, MARLENE (ROSENTHAL). b Atlantic City NJ 15 Ap 38. 4: John P Kondelik. 5: UMiami 57-59 (Eng) AB; Fla State U 65-66 MS. 6: Fr. 7: Tchr Nautilus Jr High, Miami Beach Fla 60-65; Ref libn UMiami (Coral Gables Fla) 66-67; Libn Bur of Com Fisheries, St Petersburg Beach Fla 67-. 9: SELA; FlaLA. 10: Phi Kappa Phi; Beta Phi Mu. 14: Catlg, ref. 15: 1726 6th st So, St Petersburg Fl 33701.

KONDY, WALTER KORNEL. b Lynn Mass 25 Jl 25. 5: UCal(Berkeley) 47 (Slavic lang & lit) BA, 48 MLS; UWarsaw (Poland) 48-49 (LS); UPenn 64 (Polish lang & lit); UWarsaw (Poland) 66-68 (Polish lit). 6: Polish, Russian, Czech, Ger, Norwegian. 7: Slavic catlgr Ind U Lib 60-61; Head Libn Assoc Prof Alliance Col Lib 61-64; Acquis dept Free Lib of Phila 65-. 8: Head of Steering Com, Ind U Lib 60-61; Review ed "Polish American Studies" 64-. 9: ALA. 10: Polish Amer Hist Assn; Amer Assn Tchrs of Slavic & E European Langs; Nat Slavic Honor Soc; Alpha Mu Gamma; Sigma Tau Gamma. 12: Ed "Henryk Sienkiewicz; Man and Writer" by M Giergielewicz (66); Slavic reviewer for "Books Abroad" & "Choice". 13: Yes. 14: Admin. 15: 3607 Chestnut st, Phila Pa 19104.

KONECNIK, FRANCES (GEDDES). b Detroit 26 Je 25. 4: Martin Konecnik. 5: Wayne State U 42-51 (Fr) BA; Columbia 51-52 (LS) MS. 6: Fr. 7: Sr clerk Detroit Pub Lib 42-51; Trainee libn NY Pub Lib 51-52; Spec recruit LC 52-54; Asst head var brs Detroit Pub Lib 54-64; Asst ref libn Penn State U 64-65, Period libn 65-68, Ser acquis libn 68-. 9: ALA-RTSD (sec Ser Discussion gp 66-68); PennLA. 10: AAUP; AAUW. 14: Adult educ, ref, aquis, child bks, ser. 15: 482 Westgate dr, State College Pa 16801.

KONECNIK, MARTIN. b Herkimer NY 1 D 27. 4: Frances Geddes. 5: UDetroit 53-55 (Engnr); UColo 55-59 (Ind Mgt) BS Bus; UMich 63-64 AMLS. 6: Slovak. 7: Personnel clerk (Pfc) US Army, US, Korea 50-52; Lab asst Berry Brothers Paints, Detroit 53-55; Engnr aide Nat Bur of Standards, Boulder Colo 56-59; Development engnr US Rubber Co, Detroit 59-63; Data Processing libn Penn State 64-68, Hd lib data processing 68-. 9: ALA; SLA; PennLA; ASIS. 10: AAUP. 14: Automation, tech proc. 15: 482 Westgate dr, State College Pa 16801.

KONIECKO, ALYSON (KISTLER). b E Stroudsburg Penn 24 O 19. 4: Frank Koniecko. 5: Stroudsburg State Col 36-40 (Eng, Soc Studies) BS in Ed; Columbia 41-42 (LS); Drexel 62-63 MS in LS. 7: Tchr Jr High Sch, E Stroudsburg Penn 40-42; Asst libn Kings Point NY 42-43; Asst libn mem lib, Wayne Penn 54-62; Sch libn Ithan Elem Sch, Bryn Mawr Penn 63-; Sch lib adv div of sch lib Dept of Pub Instr, Pa 68. 9: NEA; PennLA; PennStateEA ; Delaware Co LA. 10: Beta Phi Mu; Kappa Delta Pi; Alpha Delta Kappa. 15: 400 Maplewood rd, Wayne Pa 19087.

KOOGLER, JOSEPHINE (CLEMENTS). b Lincoln Co NM 12 Ag 08. 4: C V Koogler. 5: Highlands U 49 (Educ) BA; Adams State 60 (Lib) M Ed. 7: Tchr Pub Schs, Aztec NM 50-; Libn Altrurion Pub Lib, Aztec NM 64-. 8: Lib bd trustee/or chm Altrurian Pub lib, Aztec NM 48-64; Eval of ENMU lib for NCATE 63; Evaluation team of NM State U lib for NCATE 65. 9: ALA; NEA; NW Regl Lib Bd; NMLA; NMSchL; NMEA (pres NW Dist); NM A-V Assn. 10: Delta Kappa Gamma; Kappa Kappa Iota; Amer Legion Aux; Dir of Girls State; Tchr Educ & Profess Standards State Chm; Governor's Commsn on Health 48. 11: "Teacher of the Year," Highlands 59; Freedom's Found Award; Hon MA Highla dsU, Las Vegas plus 59. 12: "Science in the Elementary Grades" (60). 13: Yes. 14: SWest bks & rare bks. 15: PO Box 100, Aztec NM 87410.

KOOLWYK, LOIS (LOWMAN). b Elmira NY 26 D 17. 4: John Koolwyk. 5: UCLA 35-37 (Chem Engnr); Elmira Col 37-40 (Liberal Arts) BA; Syracuse 40-41 BLS. 7: Jr Libn Steele Memorial Lib, Elmira NY 41-43; Act co libn Chemung Co Lib, Elmira NY 43-46; Co ext libn Santa Barbara Lib, Santa Barbara Cal 46-50; Co Libn Monterey Co Lib, Salinas Cal 51-. 9: ALA; CalLA; Pub Lib Exec Central Cal (pres, Bd mem); Lib Exec, Monterey Bay Area (pres & sec). 10: Soroptimist Club; LWV. 13: Yes. 14: Admin, tech proc. 15: Monterey Co Lib 26 Central ave, Court House Annex, Salinas Ca 93901.

KOONCE, DOLORES (CHAPLINE). b Clarendon Ark 5 D 12. 4: Richard Preston Koonce. 5: Monticello Ark A & M 57-60 (Educ & Psych) BSE; Peabody 61 (LS). 7: Tchr libn High Sch, Altheimer Ark 58-60; Libn Wilson Jr High Sch, Pine Bluff Ark 60-68; Libn Trice Jr High , Pine Bluff Ark 68-. 9: NEA; ALA; ArkEA; ArkLA. 10: AAUW. 14: Catlg, ref. 15: 1304 Avondale dr, Pine Bluff Ar 71601.

KOOP, INEZ E (GORSUCH). b Toledo Ohio. 4: Erich S Koop. 5: Bowling Green State U 32-36 (Eng) BS, 40-42 (Eng) MA; C W Post 58-64 Tchr-Libn Certif. 6: Fr. 7: Ref libn Massapequa Pub Lib, Massapequa NY 64; High sch libn Amityville Mem High Sch, Amityville NY 64-; Ref libn W Islip Pub Lib, W Islip NY 68-. 8: Eng Tchr Amityville Mem High Sch, 20 yrs. 9: NY StateLA; Nassau-Suffolk Libns Assn. 14: Ref. 15: 106 Ketcham ave, Amityville NY 11701.

KOPEC, GRACE (BARBARA) (MAZUR). b Poland 14 D 30. 5: UToronto 66 (Psych) BA; UPittsburgh 67 MLS. 6: Polish. 7: Clk UToronto Lib, Toronto Ont Can 62-64; Clk Toronto Pub Lib 64-66; Libn (sci & tech div) Metropolitan Toronto Central Lib, Toronto Ont Can 67-. 8: Mem bk reviewing com at Metropolitan Toronto Central Lib for British bk news 69-. 14: Ref, bk selection. 15: 31 Constance st, Toronto 3 Ont Can.

KOPISCHKE, JOHN L. b Marinette Wis 28 F 28. 4: Nancy Applegate. 5: UWis 46-47, 48-51 (Eng) BA, 51-52 (Eng) Univ Tchg Certif, summers 55, 57, 58 & 59 (LS) MA. 7: Tchr high sch, Wautoma Wis 54-56; Libn St Louis Country Day Sch, St Louis Mo 56-58; Libn USAF Dependent Sch, Azores, Libya, Chateauroux France 58-62; Libn US AFB, Lakenheath england 62-63; Dir NW Neb Reg Lib, Scottsbluff Neb 63-67; Dir Ref

& Loan Lib, Madison wis 67-. 9: NebLA (chm Pub Lib Sect 64, pres 66); WisLA. 15: 4 S Spooner, Madison Wi 53705.

KOPKIN, THEODORE J. b Chattanooga Tenn 6 Ag 24. 4: Ethel Hilowitz. 5: UChattanooga 49 (Hist, Eng) BA; Emory 50 (LS) MA; George Washington U 55-56 (Psychol, Phys); Lockheed-Georgia Co 62-63. 6: Fr. 7: Radio operator US Army Signal Corps 42-46; Bkmob libn Chattanooga Pub Lib, Chattanooga Tenn 50-51; Tech libn Naval Photographic Center, Wash DC 51-54; Tech libn Naval Gun Factory, Wash DC 54-57; Research info spec Lockheed-Georgia Co, Marietta Ga 57-. 8: Tchr course in indexing & abstracting, Atlanta U; Adv wk on technical bks for tech insts; Tchr course in Sci Lit, Emory U. 9: SLA (Ga Chap: past treas & pres; Wash DC Chap: past sec); GaLA. 10: Toastmasters Internat. 12: Ed "Bulletin" SLA Ga Chap; Ed Proceedings of Conference on Organization and Utilization of Technical Information." 13: Yes. 14: Ref, automatic indexing. 15: Lockheed Georgia Co, Dept 72-34/Zone 400, Marietta Ga 30061.

KOPLEIN, BARBARA J. b Coloma Wis 20 O 34. 5: Wis State U 52-56 (LS/Eng) BS in Educ; UWis summer 58; UDenver summers 62-64 (LS) MA. 7: Libn Port Wash High Sch, Port Washington Wis 56-59; Libn Homestead High Sch, Mequon Wis 59-64; Child libn Denver Pub Lib 64-65; Libn Cherry Creek High Sch, Engelwood Colo 65-66; Libn Cherry Creek Et Jr High, Englewood Colo 66-. 8: Consul 1970 ed, "Standard Catalog for Junior High Schools. 9: ALA; AASchL (Nat Lib Week repr for Wis 61); YASD (Slide Proj Com); NEA; WisEA (sec Lib Div); ColoLA; ColoASchL; WisLA; Colo A-V Assn. 13: Yes. 14: Reading guidance, ref. 15: 2085 Buchtel blvd apt 111, Denver Co 80210.

KOPP, ALICE ELEANOR. b Tuscarawas Ohio 24 Ap 16. 5: Syracuse 47-51 (LS). 6: Portu, Sp. 7: Co libn Tuscarawas Co, New Phila Ohio 43-61; Lib off US Info Serv, Brazil 62-68; Reg libn Lat Amer US Info Agcy, Washington DC 69-. 8: Asst cultural affairs off USIS, Brazil 63-69. 9: ALA; OhioLA. 14: Gov lib serv abroad. 15: US Info Agency, Wash DC 20547.

KOPP, EMMA LUE. b Anderson Ind 5 S 24. 5: DePauw U 42-43; Western Col 43-46 (Hist) BA; UIll 46-47 BS in LS; Columbia 66-67 MLS. 7: Asst order libn Purdue U Lib 47-48, Ref asst 49-50; Libn St Johns Hosp, Anderson Ind 50-51; Asst ref libn Amer Med Assn, Chicago 51-52; Catlgr UKan Med Center Lib 52-54; Ref libn Clendening Med Lib UKan Med Center 54-63, Assoc libn 63-. 9: SLA (Heart of A mer Chap: chm Menlo Com 53-54, sec 55-57, v-pres 57-58 & 65-66, treas 64-65); MedLA. 10: Beta Phi Mu. 14: Ref. 15: 6726B W 76 st, Overland Park Ks 66204.

KOPYCINSKI, JOSEPH VALENTINE. b Lowell Mass 14 F 23. 5: Lowell Tech Inst 40-48 (Textile Chem) BS; Va Polytech Inst 43-44 (Civil Engnrg ASTP); Lowell Tech Inst 48-50 (Textile Chem) MS; Simmons 51-60 (LS) MS. 6: Fr, Ger. 7: Lab asst Lowell Tech Inst 41-43; Communications man, US Army-Combat Inf, US, Europe 43-46; Lowell Tech Inst: Stud Instr Chem Dept 46-48, Grad stud Instr 48-50, Even sch Instr 46-50, Libn 50-. 8: Adv to LTI a-v Soc. 9: ALA; Amer Soc Elec Engnrs (v-chm Engnr Sch Libs Com); NETech Serv Libns; NECol Libns; Mens Libn Club (Boston). 10: Varsity Club; Bridge League; Bowling League; TAPPI; Amer Soc Testing Materials. 12: "Textile Industry Information Sources" (64). 13: Yes. 14: Admin, catlg, ref, rare bks, automation. 15: Lowell Technol Inst Alumni Mem Lib, Lowell Ma 08154.

KORAN, ADOLPH ADAM. b Poland 5 D 12. 4: Ann Mulfinger. 5: UMe 33-37 (Ger) BA; UCal (Los Angeles) 38-41 Ger; Syracuse 63-65 MSLS. 6: Ger, Fr. 7: Chief fire control tech USNavy 42-63; Libn USan Diego, Col for Men 65-66; Libn Naval Personnel Research Activity 66-. 9: ALA; SLA. 10: Delta Phi Alpha; Beta Phi Mu. 14: Ref, catlg. 15: 4361 Alder dr, San Diego Ca 92116.

KORAN, ANN (MULFINGER). b Meadville Penn 4 Mr 08. 4: Adolph Adam Koran. 5: UChicago 29 (Eng) PhB, 36 Eng) MA; Columbia U 30 (Journalism) BLit; UVienna 32 (Ger); Stanford 42-45 (Proficiency Certif); USoCal 51-52 MS in LS. 6: Fr, Ger, Russian. 7: Educ of handicapped Columbia U 36-37: Lowell & Holmes Jr High Sch, Oak Park Ill 37-40; Tchg asst Stanford U 45-46; Curriculum Lib San Diego Co Schs, San Diego Cal 47-51; San Diego Pub Lib 52-. 9: ALA; CalLA. 10: Great Books Discussion Group. 14: Ref. 15: 4361 Alder dr, San Diego Ca 92116.

KORDA, MARION (AMELIA). b Portland Me 14 Je 22. 5: Westbrook Jr Col 40-42; UMe 42-43 (Eng, Hist) BA; Columbia 47-53 (LS) MS; ULouisville 48- (Music, Hist): Royal Conservatory of Mus (Copenhagen Denmark) 58-59. 6: Danish, Ger, Fr. 7: Soc Studies tchr Hope Valley High Sch, Hope Valley RI 44; Asst to recorder Boston U 44; Music therapist US Govt Camp Edwards Mass 45; Dir Y-Teen Program YWCA, New Bedford Mass 45-47; Libn ULouisville Sch of Music 47-, Asst Prof of Bibliog. 9: MusLA; KyLA. 10: Louisville (Ky) Orchestra; Sigma Alpha Iota; Louisville Lib Club; Musicians' Union; AAUP. 14: Music libnship. 15: ULouisville Sch of Music Lib, Alta Vista rd, Louisville Ky 40205.

KORIOTH, MARGARET ANN (BAKER). b Wichita Falls Tex 27 O 31. 4: John F Korioth Jr. 5: Kilgore Jr Col 48-50 (Liberal Arts) AA; NTex State U 50-51 (LS) BA, 53-55 (Elem Admin). 6: Ger. 7: Libn Baylor U Col of Dentistry 51; Tchr Pleasant Grove Ind Sch, Dallas 51-54; Libn Dallas Ind Sch 55-56; Libn Sun Oil Research Lab, Richardson Tex 59-60; Asst libn Garland Ind Schs, Garland Tex 61-63; Head Libn Garland High Sch, Garland Tex 63-. 9: TexStateTchrs Assn; Tex Classroom Tchrs Assn. 10: Girl Scout ldr; Alph Lambda Sigma. 14: Catlg. 15: Box 973, Garland Tx 75041.

KORN, BARBARA HENDERSON. b Evanston Ill 16 S 26. 4: Gerald Edward (Jerry) Henderson. 5: Morningside Col 45 (Mus); State U of Iowa 45-48 (Journalism) BA; Our Lady of Good Counsel 61-63 (Humanities); Columbia 63-66 MSLS. 7: Lib clk Larchmont Pub, Larchmont NY 63-65; Child libn St Augustines' Sch, Larchmont NY 66; Libn Mamaroneck High Sch, Mamaroneck NY 66-. 9: ALA; NEA; NYStateTA; MamaroneckTA; WestchesterLA. 10: UN Assn US; Parsonsfield-Porter Hist Soc; LWV; Theta Sigma Phi. 13: Yes. 14: Child & ya serv. 15: 16 Gerlach pl, Larchmont NY 10538.

KORN, GARY M. b Orange Cal 11 Ja 41. 5: UCal (Santa Barbara) 58-62 (Hist) BA; USoCal 66-67 MSLS. 7: Ref libn UCal Lib (Santa Barbara) 67-. 10: Libns Assn UCal; Phi Alpha Theta; Beta Phi Mu. 14: Ref. 15: 1791 W Broadway st, Anaheim Ca 92804.

KORNTHEUER, G(ERHARD) A(RTHUR). b Milwaukee 6 O 12. 4: Alberta Marie (Falke). 5: Concordia Tchrs Col 30-33; Valparaiso U 39 (Ger) BA; UChicago 49 (Eng) MA; IndU 55 MALS. 6: Ger. 7: Elem tchr organist Bethlehem Lutheran Church, Chicago 34-44; Elem tchr, orgnist Holy Cross Lutheran Church, Chicago 44-47; High sch tchr & libn Concordia Lutheran High Sch, Ft Wayne Ind 47-57; Ref libn Ft Wayne (Ind) Pub Lib 55-57; Prof & Libn St John's Col (Winfield Kan) 57-. 9: Nat Soc Study Educ; Lutheran Educ Assn; KanLA; NEA-DAVI. 10: Rotary Club; Winfield Pub Lib Bd. 14: Admin, ref. 15: St John's COL, Winfield Ks 67156.

KORPAL, DEV. b Ludhiana India 15 Ap 35. 4: Urmila Sharma. 5: PunjabU 54-58 (Eng, Pol Sci) BA; LIU (NY) 66-67 (LS) MS. 6: Hindi, Urdu, Punjabi. 7: Off asst UN Child Fund, New Delhi 57-63, Libn 64-67; Libn Queens Borough Pub Lib, NYC 67-68, Asst br libn 68-69, Br libn 69-. 14: Ref, lib org & admin. 15: 144-25 Roosevelt ave, Flushing NY 11354.

KORTENDICK, REV JAMES J, SS. b Pecatonica Ill 19 Mr 07. 5: St Charles Col 26-28; St Mary's Srm (Balti more) 28-34 AB, STB, MA; UWash 34-36; CathU 39-44, 60-62 BS in LS, MA, PhD. 6: Fr, Ger. 7: Sem Prof Seattle 34-36 & Baltimore 36-39; Sem Libn St Mary's Sem (Baltimore) 37-39; Asst & Act libn Catholic U 41-47, Head Dept of Lib Sci 47-. 8: Commsn for Nat Plan on Lib Educ 62-65; Com on Internat Exchange of Persons; Adv Screening Com for Libns 61-64; US Civil Serv Commsn; Chm Test Development Com, Libns Proficiency Test 60-63. 9: ALA (chm &/or mem 4 coms 58-69);-LED (treas 46-47, pres 60-61);-LAD (Exec Com Personnel Admin Sect 63-66, chm Lib Admin Development Com 64-65);-ACRL (Com Liaison with Accred Agencies 67-69); AALS (chm Com on Instr 56-58, chm Research Com 59-60, sec-treas 63-66, pres 69-70); CathLA (Hon life mem, Exec Coun 43-52; chm 2 coms 42-44 & 50-58, rep to 2 orgs 47-56); ATheolLA; SLA (Lib Educ Com 68-; Wash Chap, chm Col & Univs Sect 44-46, first v-pres 47-48, Exec Bd 44-46 & 51-53); CNLA (trustee 69-); DCLA (Exec Bd 42-44, pres 52-55; Jt Com Recr Libnship; chm Clearing House Sub-com 48-50, Ed Clearing House "Bulletin" 49); USBE (sec 48-50, pres 54-55, chm Bd Dirs 48-50). 10: The President's Com on Employment of the Handicapped; Beta Phi Mu; Pi Gamma Mu. 11: Recipient Beta Phi Mu Award for Distinguished Serv to Educ for Libnship 66. 12: Ed "Studies in Library science," CathU (51); Auth "The Library in the Catholic Theological Seminary in the U.S." (65). 13: Yes. 14: Lib educ, admin, research methodology, col & univ libnship, theol libnship. 15: 401 Michigan ave NE, Wash DC 20017.

KOSCIUCH, BARBARA (JUNE) McVEY. b Bellevue Ky 9 Ap 34. 4: William Joseph Kosciuch. 5: Fla State U 58-60 (Eng)

BA, 64-65 (LS) MS. 6: Sp. 7: Mimeograph dept (supv) Central Title & Trust, Orlando Fla 52-56; Sec Orange Co Bd of Pub Instr, Orlando Fla 56-58, Elem tchr 60-63, High sch Eng tchr 63-64, Elem sch libn 65-. 9: ALA; NEA; FlaEA; FlaASchL; FlaLA; Orange CoASchL. 10: AAUW; Phi Beta Kappa; Sigma Tau Delta; Beta Phi Mu; Gamma Alpha Chi. 14: Child lit, sch libs. 15: 2100 Alafaya trail, Orlando Fl 32807.

KOSHALEK, ELIZABETH (BRIAR). b Bemidji Minn 19 N 42. 4: Richard H Koshalek. 5: Bemidji State Col 60-62; UMinn 62-64 (Sp) BA, 66 (LS) MA. 6: Sp. 7: Catlgr Fed Res Bank, Minneapolis 64-65; Catlgr Bus Lib UMinn (Minneapolis) 66, Instr & libn processing dept 66-. 9: ALA; SLA. 15: Univ of Minn Processing Dept 160 OMWL, Univ of Minn, Minneapolis Mn 55455.

KOSKEY, B EUGENE. b Bessemer Mich 25 D 30. 4: Janice E Berg. 5: Augustana Col (Rock is Ill) 48-53 (Mus, Speech) BA; IndU (Bloomington) 62-63 (A-V Communications) MS in Ed, 65- (A-V Communications). 7: Cpl USA Spec Serv, Ft Carsons Colo 53-55; Radio announcer & engr KCAL, Redlands Cal 55-56; Program asst CBS-TV, NYC 56-57; TV studio mgr W-TEN, Albany NY 57-58; Mus tchr elem & secondary pub schs, Berlin, Valley Stream & Bethpage NY 57-62; Asst coord AID Program in Educ Broadcasting IndU 62-63; Dir radio & TV NoIllU 63-66; Asst Prof educ, & lib info sci UWis (Milwaukee) 66-. 8: Media consul: USPHS Grant to UWis (Milwaukee) to develop basic nursing skills materials 66-68, Chas F Kettering Foundation Grant to MarquetteU for study of conceptual reading approach 68, Zeb Billings Music Publishing Co for programming com courses in organ instr (69). 9: NEA (DAVI); Nat Assn Educ Broadcasters; Nat Soc for Study Communication; Wis DAVI; Wis Educ Research Assn; WisLA. 10: Amer Mus Ctr; Phi Delta Kappa. 13: Yes. 14: Instr media, instr materials ctrs. 15: 3321 W Pelican lane, Brown Deer Wi 53209.

KOSKI, LEO GREGORY. b Ashland Wis 21 Ap 21. 4: Karen Anne Thomas. 5: George Wash U 47-49 (Pre-Dental); American U 49-52 (Bus Admin) BS; Catholic U 52-54 MSLS. 7: Libn ref & catlg Aeronautical Chart & Info Center, Wash DC 54-56; Head Libn Admin US Navy Hydrographic Off, Suitland Md 56-59; Libn Catlg US Navy special Proj Off, Wash DC 59-; Catlgr Naval Air Systs Command, Wash DC 69-. 11: Outstanding performance certif, Navy Hydrographic Off. 14: Catlg, ref. 15: 4424 N Henderson rd apt 4, Arlington Va 22203.

KOSLOW, DONALD M. b Boston 14 Mr 24. 4: Mildred A (Mamaty). 5: Harvard 47-50 (Econ) AB; Simmons 52-54 (LS); URI 63-66 (LS) MA. 6: Fr. 7: Tank gunner USArmy Tech 5th Grade 42-45; Test admin Human Engnr Lab, Boston 50; Ref asst Boston Pub Lib 51-56; USNaval War Col Lib: Asst ref lib & bibliog 56-57, Head catlg & ed br 57-58, Head tech process br 58-67; Assoc hd monographic catlg dept UMass (Amherst) 67-68; Hd ref dept 68-. 14: Catlg, ref. 15: 598 Main st, Amherst Ma 01002.

KOSMIN, LINDA JOYCE. b Phila Penn. 5: UPenn 57-61 (Chem) BA; UMd 61-63 (Chem); Drexel 63-66 MSLS. 6: Ger, Lat, Sp. 7: Chem instr UMd (College Park) 61-63; Chem instr Drexel 63-65; Engring libn Scott Paper Co, Lester Penn 65-66; Chief libn USMC Supply Activity, Phila 66-67; Engring libn Drexel 67-, Adjunct instr 67-. 9: Amer Chem Soc; ASIS; SLA (Phila Coun: sec 67-68, v-pres & pres-elect 68-69, pres 69-). 11: Drexel Stud Achievement Award Spec Libnship 1966 Given by Phila Chap of SLA. 14: Documentation, spec libnship, ref. 15: Drexel Inst of Tech 32nd & Chestnut sts, Phila Pa 19104.

KOSTER, (CLAIRE) DESMOND. b Charleston SC 18 N 21. 5: Col of Charleston 39-43 (Eng) AB; UNC 43-44 BLS. 7: Asst libn Hosp #2, Ft Bragg NC 44-45; Libn Serv Club Libs, Ft Bragg NC 45-47; Asst libn Fla State U 47-49; Libn Medical Col of SC 49-68, Health affairs libn 68-. 9: ALA; SLA; MedLA; SELA; SCLA (pres 53; chm Col Sect 65-66). 15: Med Col of SC 80 Barre st, Charleston SC 29401.

KOSTYK, JUNE. b Huntsburg Ohio 26 Ap 21. 5: Youngstown U 44-47 (Bio) AB; Drexel 48-49 BS in LS; UFla 53-58 (Bio, Educ) MEd. 7: Circ libn Mont StateU 49-53; Libn phys educ reading room, catlgr, ref libn UFla 53-58; Asst & ref libn UCLA Engring Lib 58-60; Tech libn Librascope Div of Gen Precision, Glendale Cal 60-62; Asst libn George Washington U 62-66; Tech libn Communications & Syst Inc, Falls Church Va 66-. 9: SLA; Inst Electr & Electro Engrs. 14: Ref, admin, info ret. 15: 6166 Leesburg pike, Falls Church Va 22044.

KOTALA, STANISLAW W. b Boleslawiec Poland 27 S 09. 4: Maria Elizabeth Humburg. 5: Inst of Pedagogy, Poland 33-36 (Pedagogy) BEd; Sch of Design, Poland 36-37 (Art) Diploma; Acad of Fine Arts, Cracov Poland 38-39 (Art); Acad of Fine Arts, Dusseldorf Germany 46-49 (Art) BA; Rutgers 61-65 MLS. 6: Polish, Ger, Russian. 7: Tchr Ministry of Educ, Poland 27-33, Sch Psychologist 37-38 (2nd Lt) Polish Armed Forces, Europe 39-45; 2nd Lt Polish Mil Mission to Hq British Army of Rhine (FNPS Illustrator) 45-46; Artist painter Phila 50-59; Lib trainee The Free Lib of Phila 59-65, Staff 65-. 8: Lecturer Polish People's U, Phila. 9: ALA; PennLA. 10: Rutgers Alumni Assn. 11: Art award 46. 13: Yes. 14: Ref. 15: 8147 Revere st, Phila Pa 19152.

KOTARSKI, ELIZABETH (MATEJA). b Warsaw Poland 20 My 17. 4: Tadeusz Kotarski. 5: McMaster-Hamilton 59-63 BA; Toronto 65 BLS. 6: Polish, Fr. 7: Clerical Hamilton Pub Lib 64; Catlgr Nat Lib, Ottawa 65-. 14: Catlg. 15: 335 MacLaren, Apt 409, Ottawa 4 Can.

KOTEN, BERNARD LOUIS. b NYC 3 N 12. 5: Johns Hopkins U Md 29-32 (Aesthetics); Moscow State Ped Inst of Foreign Lang 33-37 (Foreign Lang) Diploma (BA); Columbia 37-39 (Foreign Lang) BS MA, 50-(Foreign Lang, Linguistics). 06: Russian, Fr, Ger. 7: Instr Moscow State Pedagogic Inst Foreign Lang 35-37; Dir chief proj supv Adult Educ Prog of Bd of Educ NY 37-39; Dir of lib research Amer Russian Inst, NY 41-43; Intelligence Platoon Sgt (S/Sgt) US Army 42-46; Dir of lib & research American Russian Inst Lib, NY 46-65, Admin & supv Lang Sch 41-48; Adj Asst Prof of Russian NYU 58-, Curator Russian Lib NYU Gen Libs NY 65-. 8: Consul & reading Soviet Bks for Pub Recommendations; Consul on Soviet Theater; Ed "Soviet Literary Criticism"; Consul "Time-Life" Cook Bks 68-69; Ed Journal "Studies in Soviet Literature" 64-. 09: ALA-AASchL; SLA; NYLib Club; AATSEEL. 10: 102nd Div Assn; Phi Delta Kappa. 11: Legion of Merit, Bronze Star. 13: Yes. 14: Research in Soviet studies, ling, ref, research, bibliog. 15: 1370 St Nicholas ave, New York NY 10033.

KOTO, ARDIS (ANDERSON). b Glenwood Minn 19 Mr 13. 4: Dean P Koto. 5: Concordia Col (Moorhead Minn 32-36 (Eng) BA; UMinn 41-42 BS in LS. 6: Norwegian, Ger. 7: Eng instr libn Minn high schs 36-41; Jr lib asst UMinn (Minneapolis) 42-43; Ref-circ libn Knox Col Lib 43-44; Libn Waldorf Col 45-58; Head rder libn Cal State Col (Long Beach) 58-61; Asst libn Cal Lutheran Col 61-. 9: ALA-ACRL (chm Jr Col Libs Sect 48-49); IowaLA; CalLA. 10: Altrusa Internat; Women's League of Cal Lutheran Col; Lutheran Church Women. 14: Catlg. 15: 1901 Rutgers dr, Thousand Oaks Cal 91360.

KOTZIN, SHELDON. b Baltimore Md 1 S 43. 4: Loretta Lopata. 5: UMd 60-64 (Hist) BA; E-W Ctr UHawaii summer 67 (LS); IndU 64-68 MLS. 6: Fr, Chinese. 7: Lib intern IndU Chem Lib (Bloomington) 66-68; Lib assoc Nat Lib of Med, Bethesda Md 68-69, Mgt & prod specialist tech serv div 69-. 9: ALA; ASIS. 11: Summer Asian Libnship Fellowship. 14: Tech serv mgt, admin, Asian collections. 15: 12205 Braxfield ct #10, Rockville Md 20852.

KOUDELKA, JANET FARRAND (BROCK). b Spring Lake NJ 16 Mr 21. 4: Karl M Koudelka. 5: Johns Hopkins 55 (Eng Lit) BS; Catholic U 62 MS in LS. 6: Fr. 7: Asst rec libn Johns Hopkins Hosp, Baltimore 39-40, Registrar diag clinic 40-42; Johns Hopkins U: Sec Inst Hist Med 42-49, Asst ed Bulletin Hist Med 49-58, Curator, Welch Med Lib 59-68, Asst libn 68-. 9: MedLA; ALA (Md Chap, Ref Serv Div). 10: Amer Assn Hist Med; Baltimore Bibliophiles. 12: Asst ed "Bulletin of the History of Medicine," (49-58). 13: Yes. 14: Rare bks. 15: 504 Hill Top dr, Lutherville Md 21903.

KOUNTZ, (DIXON) JOHN CHARLES. b San Luis Obispo Cal 28 F 35. 5: The Artillery Sch 53-54 (Electronics) Certif; Fullerton Jr Col 51-53 (Pre-law) AA; Mexico City Col 56-57 (Phil) BA (cum laude); USoCal 58-59 (LS) MS; UCLA 64 (Digital Electronics); Ind Col of Armed Forces 64 (Defense Mgt) Certif; IBM 67 (Syst Analysis) Certif. 6: Portuguese, Ital, Fr, Sp. 7: Enging writer Autonetics, Downey Cal 58; Research analyst Hallamore electronics, Anaheim Cal 59-61; Ind consul 61-63; Engring ed Hughes Aircraft, fullerton Cal 63-64; Program mgr Staff Research Assoc, Orange Cal 64-65; Lib syst analyst Orange Co Pub Lib Orange Cal. 8: Consul on Facility and Product Devel (Afghanistan, Brazil, France, India, Japan, Peru) 61-63; Gp Leader, SCTPG, UCal (Irvine) Conf on Lib Automation 68; Instr UOre Wkshops on Lib Automation 68; Instr ASIS Wkshop on Lib Automation (San Francisco) 69; Adv to Orange Co Lib Assn on Automated Union Serials list Implementation 68-69. 9: ALA; ISAD; -RTSD; ASIS; SCTPG;

CalLA; OrangeCoLA. 10: Adv Coun, Orange Co Employees Assn. 12: Co-auth "Orange County Free Library, 1921- 1965" (66). 13: Yes. 14: Lib data proc hardware & systems, printing tech and its hist, file structure. 15: 1065 Van Dyke dr, Laguna Beach Ca 92651.

KOVAC, L ROBERT. b Royal Oak Mich 13 S 43. 4: Karen Davis. 5: UDetroit 61-65 (Math, Eng) AB (cum laude); Wayne State U 66-68 MSLS. 6: Ger. 7: Catlg asst UDetroit 64-65; Asst libn Oakland Commun Col (Highland Lakes) 65-66; Lib asst II Wayne State U 66-69, Libn I (sci catlgr) 69-. 10: Alpha Sigma Nu. 13: Yes. 14: Sci catlg, application of syst analysis & operations research to lib operations, automation. 15: Catalog Dept Wayne State Univ Univ Libs, Detroit Mi 48202.

KOVACIC, ERIC A. b Ljubljana Yugoslavia 13 Je 21. 4: Nika Pogacar. 5: ULjubljana 40-43 (Slavic studies); UGraz(Austria) 46-48 (Slavic studies); Alliance Col 51-52 (Soc Sci) BA; Catholic U 53-58 MS in LS. 6: Slovenian, Serbo-Croatian, Ger, Ukrainian. 7: Searcher USBE, Wash DC 53-55; LC: Order clerk 55-56, Asst ed "New Serial Titles" 56-62, Subj catlgr 62-. 10: Amer Assn Adv Slavic Studies. 14: Catlg. 15: 235 Hannes st, Silver Spring Md 20901.

KOVACS, GABOR. b Sarkad Hungary 11 Ap 23. 4: Elizabeth Fiala. 5: Air Force Acad (Hungary) 44 (Mil Sci) BA; West Mich U 63 (LS) MA. 6: Hungarian, Ger. 7: (Lt) Hungarian Air Force, Hungary 44-45; Reporter "Hungaria Weekly," Germany 47-51; Reporter-linotype "Detroit Hungarian News" 51-62; Circ libn Colo State Col 63-. 9: ALA; MPLA; ColoLA. 10: AAUP. 14: Automation, info ret. 15: 1945 24th ave, Greeley Co 80631.

KOVALAN, MARY ELLEN. b Mingo Jct Ohio 12 Mr 29. 5: Col of Steubenville 47-51 (Eng) BA; Carnegie 59-61 MLS. 6: Fr, Sp. 7: Ref libn Pub Lib of Steubenville, Steubenville Ohio 51-62, Asst libn 62-. 10: Baconian Soc; Beta Phi Mu; Vincentian Sorority; Jr Women's Club. 14: Ref. 15: 705 St Clair st, Mingo Jct Oh 43938.

KOVAR, HELEN MARGARET (MILLER). b Linlithgo NY 30 N 19. 4: Anton J Kovar. 5: NY State Col for Tchrs (Albany) 37-41 (Fr, Sp) AB (cum laude); Middlebury Col summer 41 9sp); Syracuse 45-46 BS in LS (magna cum laude). 6: Sp, Fr, Portu, Ital. 7: High sch tchr: Central Sch, Mannsville NY 41-42, Central Sch 42-44, Sherrill NY 44-45, Sr High, State Col Penn 60-62; Asst libn NY State Col for Tchrs (Oswego) 46-48; Libn jr high sch, Col Park Penn 62-64; Asst catlg libn Penn StateU (Univ Park) 67-. 9: Soc for Penn Archaeology. 10: Centre Co Hosp Women's Aux; Lat Amer Assn; Beta Phi Mu. 13: Yes. 14: Catlg, rare bks. 15: 437 Glenn rd, State College Pa 16801.

KOVATS, GABOR GYULA. b Szombathely Hungary 24 My 20. 4: Catherine Solti. 5: Peter Pazmany U (Budapest) 38-43 (Law & Pol Sci) Doctor iuris universi; Judges' & Lawyers' Exam (Hungarian Bar Exam) 47 Diploma; IndU (Bloomington) 57-58 MA in LS. 6: Ger, Fr, Hungarian, Lat. 7: Lawyer Ministry of Justice, Budapest Hungary 43-49; Attorney-at-law, Szombathely Hungary 50-56; Libn for Bar Assn, Szombathely Hungary 51-55; Catlgr & instr Miami U (Oxford Ohio) 58-60; WashU (St Louis); Ser libn 60-62, Chief ser dept 62-68; Assoc Prof & lib bibliogr Ball State U 68-. 8: Mem Com for Union List of Ser of Greater St Louis Area 64-67. 9: ALA; ASIS. 10: Faculty Club. 13: Yes. 14: Admin, ref, bibliog. 15: 2540 White River blvd, Muncie In 47303.

KOWAL, JAN STANISLAW. b Rorzyska Poland 1 My 22. 4: Virginia Rodgers. 5: Wayne State 52-62 (Math) BA, 62-65 (Secondary Educ) M Ed, 65-67 MSLS. 6: Russian, Polish, ital. 7: Draftsman Nat Automatic Tool Co, Detroit 51-55; Designer Gen Mtors Co, Detroit 55-58; Tchr East High Sch, Detroit 62-67; Ref libn Mansfield State Col 67-. 9: ALA. 14: Ref. 15: College Manor A-210, Mansfield Pa 16933.

KOWITZ, ALETHA (AMANDA). b Chicago 26 S 25. 5: Wright Jr Col 43-45; UChicago 47-51 (Chem) SB; Rosary Col 55-59 (LS) MA. 6: Ger. 7: Research chem Synthetical Labs, Chicago 45-50; Research chem Glidden Co, Chicago 50-54; Libn 54-59; Circ ref asst UIll Lib of Med Sci (Chicago) 59-67; Periodls libn Archibald Church Med Lib Northwestern U 67-. 9: ACS (Memb Com, Speaker's Bur Com); MedLA; SLA. 10: Iota Sigma Pi, AAUW. 12: Abstractor "Chemical Abstracts". 14: Circ, ref, period (sci). 15: 303 E Chicago ave, Chicago Il 60611.

KOZICKI, RICHARD J(OSEPH). b Chester Penn 5 Ap 27. 4: Annette Miller. 5: Swarthmore 47-49 (Pol Sci, Hist); Allegheny Col 49-51 (Pol Sci) BA; Yale 51-53 (Pol Sci) MA; UPenn 53-59 (Internat Rel) PhD; UIll 64-65 (Lib Admin). 6: Fr, Ger, Hindi, Urdu. 7: US Army Signal Corps 45-47; Instr in hist & pol sci Drexel Inst of Tech 56; Assoc Prof of soc sci Mansfield State Col 59-62; Asst Prof of pol sci Marquette U 62-63; Asian bibliogr UIll Lib(Urbana) 63-64; Lecturer in So Asian hist & politics UHawaii 65-; Lang & area spec So Asia East-West Center ib, Honolulu 64-68; Asst research pol scientist & hd S/SE Asia lib serv Ctr for S & SE Asia Studies UCal (Berkeley) 68-. 64-. 8: Mem, Speakers' Bur World Affairs Coun of Phila 58-59; Visiting Assoc Prof of Pol Sci Asian Inst Bucknell U summer 61; Lecturer in Indian Politics Peace Corps UWis (Milwaukee) summer 63; Vis Assoc Prof of Pol Sci, USan Francisco summer 69. 9: Assn for Asian Studies; Internat Studies Assn, West Polit Ser Assn. 10: AAUP. 11: Res Fellow Foreign Policy Research Inst UPenn 55-56; Ford Found Fellow 56-59 (research in India & Southeast Asia 57-58); ACLS-SSRC Research Grant on Asia 67-68. 12: 'The United Nations and Colonialism,' chap 13 of "The Idea of Colonialism," ed by R Strausz-Hupe & H Hazard (58); Gen ed "Occasional Papers," of the East-West Center Lib 64-68, Genl ed "Occasional Papers of the Center for South & Southeast Asia Studies" UCal 69-. 13: Yes. 14: Acquis, ref (So & SE Asia). 15: Ctr for South and Southeast Asia Studies, Univ of Cal, Berkeley Ca 94720.

KOZLOW, ROBERT DONALD. b Detroit 14 Ap 29. 5: Wayne State U 47-51 (Lit) BA; Columbia 57-59 MSLS. 7: Asst merchandise buyer J L Hudson Co, Detroit 53-57; Asst mss libn NYHist Soc 57-59; Jr catlgr & asst ref libn Detroit Pub Lib 59-61; Mss libn Chicago Hist Soc 61-62; Systems research asst UIll (Chicago) 63-66; Automation libn UIll (Urbana) 66-. 08: Catlgr Dexter M Ferry family archives, Detroit; Albert Kahn arch drawings, Detroit Inst of Arts; Comp of Photographs of Arch Importance for Publ "Detroit Architecture" by W Hawkins Ferry 68. 9: SLA (Hospitality chm Detroit Chap); Detroit Area Libns (pres 60-61). 12: Auth "Report on a Library Automation Project on UIll Chicago Campus" (66); Ed "Com on Lib Automation Newsletter" 66. 13: Yes. 14: Data processing. 15: UIll Urbana Campus, Urbana Il 61801.

KOZOWER, RUTH (LINDENFELD). b Syracuse NY 19 F 44. 4: Michael Kozower. 5: Boston U 61-63 (Phys Therapy); Syracuse 63-65 (Anthrop) BA, 65-67 MSLS. 7: Libn Pub Lib, syracuse 66-67; Asst libn Boston Pub Lib 67. 14: Pub lib serv. 15: 5548 Bear rd apt 17D, No Syracuse NY 13212.

KOZUMPLIK, WILLIAM A. b NYC 5 Ap 14. 4: Mary Ann Mottz. 5: Manhattan Col 31-35 (Philos) AB (summa cum laude); Catholic U 36-38 (Ger) MA; Chicago 38-42 (Ger Linguistics) PhD; Columbia 46-47 MLS. 06: Ger, Fr. 7: Catlg asst LC 38; Descr catlgr Chicago Lib 40-42; USNavy Communications afloat Pacific LCDR 42-45; Acquis checker Columbia Lib 46-47; Assoc dir of libs UNotre Dame (SBend Ind) 47-49; Asst libn Ore State U 49-52; Chief readers serv div Air U (Maxwell AFB, Ala) 52-54; Libn Army Aviation Sch, Ft Rucker Ala 54-55; Chief tech info & intelligence div Rome Air Dev Center, Grifiss AFB NY 55-57; Chief tech info br Air Force Spec Weapons Center Kirtland AFB NM 57-58; Manager tech info Center Lockheed Missiles & Space Co, Palo Alto Cal 58-. 9: SLA (chm Govt Info Serv Com 62); ALA-ACRL (chm Interlib Loan Com 50-52). 10: Confraternity of the Christian Doctrine. 11: 1st prize Chicago Folklore Soc 40. 12: "Phonology of Jacob Ayrer's Language, Based on his Rhymes" (42); Ed "LMSC Published Contributions" (64-68). 13: Yes. 14: Admin. 15: 3181 Mackall way, Palo Alto Cal 94304.

KRAAYENBRINK, JEANETTE (GERTIE) (VENEMAN). b Modesto Cal 30 Ag 19. 4: Ralph Arthur Kraayenbrink. 5: Modesto Jr Col 36-39 (Hist & Eng Lit) AA; UCal 39-42 (Pol Sci) AB, 42-43 (LS) Certif. 7: Libn (hd) Roseville Pub, Roseville Cal 45-49; Child libn stockton-San Joaquin Co Pub Lib, Stockton Cal 49-50; Child libn Roseville Pub, Roseville Cal 53-57; Libn II govt publns Cal State Lib (Sacramento) 58-59, Ed libn 59-60, Consul 60-61; Br libn Stockton-San Joaquin Co Pub Lib Manteca Br 62-68, Br libn & consul for 49/99 lib syst 68-. 9: ALA; CalLA. 10: Nat Congress of Parents & Tchrs. 12: Ed "News Notes of California Libraries". 14: Admin, child wk. 15: 927 S Maple, Manteca Ca 95336.

KRAEMER, RUTH FLORENCE. b Comstock Neb 20 S 05. 5: Doane Col 23-25, 26-27 (Hist) AB; UColo summer 35; UDenver summers 37-39 BS in LS; UIll summer 41, 46-47 (Admin) MS. 7: Tchr-libn High Sch, O'Neill Neb 28-39; Libn Thomas Jefferson High Sch Coun Bluffs Iowa 39-40; Dir of Lib Doane Col 41-54; Dir of Lib Col & Sem Lib Inc, Naperville Ill 54-65; Acquis libn Wis State U (Oshkosh) 65-. 8: Tchr ext cours in Lib Admin UIll 58. 9: ALA; Amer Tech Libns Assn; IllLA; NebLA (past treas). 10: Delta Kappa

Gamma; AAUW; PEO; Beta Phi Mu. 13: Yes. 14: Admin, acquis. 15: 448A Boyd st, Oshkosh Wis 54901.

KRAETSCHMER, DIANA ELIZABETH MALCOLM. b Vancouver BC Can 4 Ja 43. 4: Wilhelm Kraetschmer. 5: UBC 60-64 (Fine Arts) BA, 64-65 BLS. 6: Fr. 7: Lib asst BC Research Coun, UBC 64-65; Libn UBC Lib Fine Arts Div 65-. 8: Art tchr, Orcas Is Found, Orcas Is summers 60-64, Mem of Educ Com 65-. 9: ALA. 10: Theosophical Soc; Faculty Club; Vancouver Art Gallery; Sailing Club; UBC Faculty Wives & Womens Club; Univs Art Assn Can. 13: Yes. 14: Fine arts, ref, art wk & displays, rare bks. 15: 3057 W 44th ave, Vancouver BC Can.

KRAFT, DONALD HOWARD. b Huntington WVa 26 Ap 28. 4: Gloria Zechman. 5: Vanderbilt U 45-49 (Math) BA, 49 (Math) MA; Ohio State U 49-51 (Math). 7: (1st Lt) USAF 51-53; Asst manager Capitol Furniture Co, Huntington WVa 53-57; Applied sci rep IBM, Columbus Ohio 57-58, Sales rep 58-59; Systems engnr dist manager IBM, Cincinnati 59-60; Info retrieval & lib mechanization rep IBM, Chicago 60-66; Sci Research Assocs computer-assisted instr, chicago 66-68; IBM execs computer concepts program, Chicago 69-. 9: ALA. 10: Phi Beta Kappa; Sigma Xi. 13: Yes. 14: Info retrieval, automatic indexing. 15: 618 S Michigin ave, Chicago Il 60605.

KRAFT, GLORIA D (BOWERS). b Seattle Wash 26 Ap 43. 4: James J Kraft. 5: Everett Jr Col 61-63; UWash 63-65 (Botany) BS, 65-66 MSL. 6: Fr. 7: Br libn King Co Lib Syst, Seattle 67-. 9: ALA; PNLA; WashLA. 10: Beta Phi Mu. 14: Ref. 15: 10515 Woodinville dr Space 91, Bothell Wa 98011.

KRAFT, ROSE (COHEN). b Chelsea Mass. 5: UOre (Liberal Arts); UWash BS in LS, (Sociol) AB; Chicago 39-40 (LS) MA; UHawaii 68. 06: Ger. 7: Ref asst Pub Lib, Tacoma Wash, 1st asst ref dept; Ref libn Pub Lib, Boise Ida; Ref asst soc sci Pub Lib, Detroit; Army libn Service Club, Ft Lewis Wash; Army libn European Command, Stuttgart, Bremerhaven Germany; Post libn Naval Ordinance Test Station, China Lake Cal; Post libn Edwards AFB, Cal; Chief Tech Lib Br, Edwards AFB Cal; Chief Libn Tech Info Center Nortronics Div of Northrop Corp, Hawthorne Cal; Ref libn Lawrence Radiation Lab, Livermore Cal 60-63; Biol libn Lawrence Radiation Lab, Livermore Cal 63-64; Head Libn Syntex Research Center Stanford Ind Park, Palo Alto Cal 65-68. 9: SLA (Nat Com on Employment Cal Bay Reg Chap: dir 62-64, Hospitality; Program Chm); ASIS (Com on Info Terminology); MedLA. 10: Phi beta Kappa; Alpha Kappa Delta; Sierra Club; AAUW; Hadassah. 12: Sci bibliogs: "Monte Carlo Methods," 49-63, UCRI 7823 (64); Co-comp "High Pressure Equation of State" 25-62, UCRL 7160 (63). 14: Ref, lit searching, admin. 15: 2680 Bancroft way, Berkeley Ca 94704.

KRAHMER, ALFRED J. b Saugerties NY 22 Ag 07. 4: Rosine Ludwig. 5: Wagner Col 29 (Classics) AB; Columbia 30 (Eng Lit) MA; Lutheran Theol Sem (Phila) 33; Rutgers 60 MLS. 7: Pastor Epiphany Lutheran Church, Laurelton LI 34-42; Pastor Grace Lutheran Church, Forest Hills NY 42-48; Dir of Pub & Alumni Rels Wagner Col 48-56; Dir of Pub Rels Lutheran Welfare Assn Jersey City NJ 56-59; Libn Susquehanna U 60-. 14: Ref. 15: 805 N Ninth st, Selinsgrove Penn 17870.

KRAHN, FREDERIC A. b Milwaukee 8 O 17. 4: Mildred Werner. 5: UWis 47 (Educ) BS; Columbia 48 (LS) BS, 51 (Adult Educ, A-V) MA. 7: Page & sub lib asst Milwaukee Pub Lib 37-41; Jr libn Yonkers Pub Lib, Yonkers NY 47-49; Ed "Educational Film Guide," and "Filmstrip Guide" H W Wilson Co, NYC 49-55; Asst dir E Meadow Pub Lib, E Meadow LI NY 55-. 8: Instr in a-v educ Pratt Inst Grad Lib Sch 63-64; Consul A-V Wkshop Syracuse U Lib Sch summer 57,58; Admin Coop Film Circuit(in Nassau Co) 56-. 9: Educ Film LA (pres 61-63); Amer Fed Film Socs; NYLA (chm Com on Coop Film Serv 56-58); NassauCo(NY)LA; LI Film Coun (pres 63-65). 12: Ed "Educational Film Guide" & "Filmstrip Guide" (49-55). 13: Yes. 14: 16 mm & 8 mm films, lib printing, adult gp discussion leader. 15: 67 Rim lane, Hicksville LI NY 11801.

KRAKAUER, ELIZABETH. b Hanover Germany 2 Ag 11. 5: Munich Germany 31-33 (Chem); SUNY (Buffalo) 59-62 (Psych) BA, 63 (Anthropology) MA; SUNY (Geneseo) 63-65 MLS. 6: Ger, Fr, Ital, Lat. 7: Off manager & lab asst in diagnostic clinic 39-61; Asst in ref dept SUNY (Buffalo) 62-65, Bibliogr Anthropology Human Rel area Files Yale 65-67, Bibliogr of Soc Scis Sterling Lib 67-68; Libn & Assoc Prof of research Prescott Col Lib 68-. 9: NYState Archeol Assn (Publ Com). 14: Ref, subj specialist. 15: Lockwood Lib State U NY, Buffalo NY 14214.

KRALICEK, MARY FERN. b Beloit Kan 16 N 41. 5: Ft Hays State Col 59-63 BS; UIll 63-65 MSLS. 7: Jr asst libn UIowa 65-68; Ref & loan libn MRML at John Crerar Lib, Chicago 68-. 9: SLA; MedLA (chm Pharmacy Gp 69). 14: Ref. 15: 736 W Bueng apt 501, Chicago Il 60613.

KRAMER, CECILE EDITH. b NY 6 Ja 27. 5: City Col(NY) 56 (Educ) BS; Columbi 62, Asst libn 62-. 9: MedLA (Jt Com on Lib Educ: rep to 61-62, mem Exec Bd 62-63, chm Nomin c 3-64r sec 58-60, chm 6566, chm &/or mem ny libCl. 14: Admin, ref. 15: 3184 Grand Concourse, New York NY 10458.

KRAMER, HELEN (TOBABEN). b Walnut Kan. 5: Independence Commun Col 56 (Bus Educ) AA; Kan State Col of Pittsburgh 64 (Educ) BS; Kan State Tchrs Col of Emporia 65 (LS) MS. 7: Consul Roux Distributing Co Inc, NYC 47-55, 58-64; Ref libn Kan State Col of Pittsburgh Porter Lib 65-. 8: Faculty adv Alpha Gamma Delta; Supv Sch of Educ curriculum Lib Kan State Col of Pittsburgh. 9: ALA; AAUP; AAUW; KanLA. 10: Kappa Delta Pi; Pi Omega Pi; Phi Alpha Theta; Phi Theta Kappa. 14: Ref. 15: 1901 S English, Pittsburg Ks 66762.

KRAMER, HELEN AMELIA (THOMPSON). b Meadville Penn 28 D 36. 4: Raymond L Kramer. 5: Clarion State Col 55-59 (LS) BS; Sp Lang Sch (San Jose Costa Rica) 60 (Sp) Certif; Allegheny Col 65 (Liberal Arts); Columbia 65 (Liberal Arts) 66 (LS). 6: Sp, Ger. 7: Libn Conneaut Lake Area High Sch, Conneaut Lake Penn 59-60; Libn Facultad evangelica de Teologia, Buenos Aires 61-64; Libn Population Coun Inc, NYC 65-66; E Deer-Frazier High Sch, Creighton Penn 67-68; Asst catlgr St Vincent Col Lib 68-. 8: Lib consul, Mennonite Sem, Monterideo, Uruguay 63. 9: ALA. 10: Spanish Cultural soc; Allegheny Valley Concert Assn. 12: Ed "Pampa Breezes," Buenos Aires (63-64). 14: Catlg. 15: 2511 Roosevelt st, Natrona Heights Pa 15065.

KRAMER, HELEN AGNES (MILISTEFR). b Bison S Dak 18 Ag 18. 4: Louis J Kramer. 5: Creighton 36-40 (Journalism, Eng) AB; USoCal 61-62 MLS. 7: Los Angeles Co Lib Syst: Libn in charge San Gabriel Lib 62-64, Libn in charge Temple City Lib 64, Asst to reg libn in charge Inst Serv 64-67; Reg ref libn 67-. 9: CalLA; LosAngelesCoStaffLA (pres 66). 10: Los Angeles Co Lib Staff Assn. 15: 5622 Willard ave, San Gabriel Ca 91776.

KRAMPER, S J JAMES P. b Omaha Neb 11 Ap 12. 5: St Louis U 36 (Eng, Latin) AB, 38 (Philos) PhL, 42 (Philos) MA. 6: Lat. 7: Tchr Campion High Sch, Prairie du Chien Wis 38-41, 46-53; Prof Creighton U 53-, Dir of lib 54-. 8: Memb Soc of Jesus, ordained priest 44. 9: ALA; CathLA; Higher Education Assn; NMA; NebLA; MPLA. 14: Admin, automation. 15: 2500 California st, Omaha Nb 68131.

KRARUP, AGNES. b Brooklyn NY 27 J in LS. 7: Eng tchr Pub Schs, Grand Island Neb 26-29; Eng tchr Pub Schs, Iowa City Iowa 29-35; Wk with young adults Lib Assn, Portland Ore 36-8; SV SCH LIBS PBSch prtd ib servub Schs, Pittsburgh Penn 47-. 8: Governor's Commsn on Pub Lib Development 57-60; Rep of ALA Coun to Nat Orgs on Child & Youth 60-61; ALA Dep to White House Conf on Child & Youth 60. 9: NEA; ALA (Coun 60-64, chm Jt Com); ALA-NEA (60-61); PennLA (pres 56-57); Penn State EA. 10: Altrusa Club; Delta Kappa Gamma. 11: PennLA Award of Merit 61; Award of Merit, Alumni Assn Grinnell Col; PennLA Distinguished Serv Award 67. 14: Sch libs. 15: 4716 Ellsworth ave, Pittsburgh Pa 15213.

KRASTINS, JANIS. b Latvia 18 Mr 10. 4: Anna Babiceva. 5: Tchrs Col Riga 24-29 BA; Heidelberg U 45-49 (Hist of Art, Archaeol); Columbia 50-55 (Hist of Art, Archaeol) MA; Pratt 59-62 (LS) MS. 6: Latvian, Ger, Russian. 7: Tchr Latvia 30-42; Art consul NY Graphic Soc, Greenwich Conn 50-61; Catlg libn SUNY; Maritime Col Ft Schuyler 61-. 9: SLA. 10: Faculty Assn SUNY. 13: Yes. 14: Catlg. 15: 3561 DeKalb ave, Bronx NY 10467.

KRATZERT, MONA YVONNE. b Los Angeles 2 D 34. 4: William Kratzert. 5: UCLA 58-60 (Anthropology); SoCal 60-62 (Ger) BA 62-65 (LS) MS. 6: Ger. 7: Nursing libn Los Angeles Co Gen Hosp 63-65; Med libn 65-66; USC 66-. 9: CalLA. 10: Women C of C. 13: Yes. 14: Catlg, acquis. 15: 2200 N Beachwood dr, Los Angeles Ca 90028.

KRAULIS, RUTH L. b Liepa8ja Latvia 21 Je 17. 4: Ernest Kraulis. 5: ULatvia 34-42 (Classics) MA, High Sch Tchrs Certif; Toronto 50-51 BLS, 66-69 MLS. 06: Latvian, Ger. 7: Tchr 1st High Sch in Liepaja, Liepaja Latvia 42-44; Catlgr Etobicoke Pub Lib 51-55; Head catlg dept N York Pub Lib,

Willowdale Ont 55-58, Head tech serv div 58-. 9: CanLA; ALA; OntLA (chm Resources & Tech Serv Group 62-63). 14: Catlg. 15: 42 Elmwood ave, Willowdale Ont Can.

KRAUS, EILEEN FRANCES (SMITH). b Vineyard Haven Mass 23 F 19. 5: UMass 38-42 (Hist) BA; Simmons 43-44 (LS) BS. 7: Asst ref libn USArmy Signal Corp, Ft Monmouth NJ 44-45; Hosp asst (Soc Serv) Amer Red Cross, St Albans Naval Hosp NY 45-46; Hosp libn VA, Hines Ill 46-48; Chief libn VA, Marion Ind 48-51; VA, Montrose NY, Asst chief libn 51-53, Med libn 53-57, Chief libn 57-. 9: ALA-AHIL (Bibliotherapy Com 60-62, Conf Program Com 65-66, chm Nomin Com 68); MedLA; NY State Lib Assn (Insts Libs Com 61-64 & 68-71). 12: "Bibliotherapy in Hospital and Institution Libraries; A Selected List of Articles" (62). 14: Institution libs. 15: 313 Ringgold st, Peekskill NY 10566.

KRAUS, ELIZABETH W(EEKS). b Cornish Me 12 N 18. 4: James P Kraus. 5: Wellesley 36-40 (Chem) BA; Simmons 55-58 MS in LS. 6: Fr, Ger, Sp. 7: Research asst MIT 41-44; Research asst Hosp de la Nutricon, Mex City Mex 46-47; Libn Nat Research Corp, Cambridge Mass 52-58; Head Libn Eastman Kodak Co Research Labs, Rochester NY 58-. 9: SLA (Upstate NY Chap: sec, mem var coms); ACS; Monroe Co (NY) Lib Club (past treas & pres); ASLIB; Nat Microfilm Assn. 10: Rochester Wellesley Club. 11: John Cotton Dana Lectr, Toronto 66. 12: Ed SLA Met Div "Guide to Metallurgical Information. 13: Yes. 14: Ref, info retrieval. 15: 2185 Westfall rd, Rochester ny 14618.

KRAUS, JOE W. b Gorin Mo 31 Ag 17. 4: Betsy Curtright. 5: Culver-Stockton Col 34-38 (Eng) AB; UIll 38-39 BS in LS, 39-41 LS MA, summer 52, 56-57, 60 PhD. 7: Ref asst UIll (Urbana) 39-41, Circ asst 41-42; USArmy & Air Force (Cpt); Instr Ill Lib Sch 46; NWMADISON Col (Harrisonburg Va) 51-61; Dir of Libs Kan StateU 62-66; Dir of libs Ill State U (Normal) 66-. 8: Visiting lecturer, Grad Sch of Lib Sci, UTex summer 58. 9: ALA-ACRL; KanLA; MPLA; Bibliog Center for Research (pres 65-67); VaLA (v-pres 61); IllLA. 10: AAUP. 12: "William Beer and the New Orleans libraries, 1891-1927" (52). 13: Yes. 14: Lib sci tchg, admin, lib hist. 15: 302 Mecherle dr, Bloomington Il 61701.

KRAUS, (MARGARET) ANNE. b St Petersburg Fla 14 O 28. 5: St Petersburg Jr Col 45-47; Fla StateU 47-49 (Eng) AB; UMich 54-55 MALS. 7: Libn Floyd Co Bkmob Serv, Rome Ga 49-52; Bkmob libn Parmly Billings Mem Lib, Billings Mont 52-54; Asst libn Lancaster Pub Lib, Lancaster Ohio 55-56; Libn Kate Love Simpson Mem Lib, McConnelsville Ohio 56-59; Reader's adv DC Pub Lib 59-62; Pub lib consul NH State Lib 62-64, Dir of ext & lib development 64-. 9: ALA (Newbery-Caldecott Com 66-67); NHLA; NELA. 14: Ext, child bks & serv. 15: 194 N Main st Apt 2, Concord NH 03301.

KRAUS, MARY MARGARET. b Vernon Center Minn 15 O 08. 5: Col St Catherine 26-28, 30-31 BSLS; Columbia Summer 38,40 (LS). 6: Ger. 7: Jr high sch libn Pub Schs, Mankato Minn 32-41; Libn Catholic TcrO (Albuquerque NM) 45-46; Jr libn pub asp, Albuquerque NM: Patens' libn 5 ChefLIB Serv 63-. 9: MedLA; NMLA; SLA. 14: Ref (Med). 15: 1748 Richmond dr NE, Albuquerque NM.

KRAUSE, DOROTHEA M. b Antigo Wis. 5: LawrenceU 27-31 (Ger, Eng) BA; UColo 34; UWis 35, 37-38 (LS). 6: Ger. 7: Asst Pub Lib Antigo Wis 34-37; Head catlgr & ref libn Pub Lib Wallis Wis 38-42; Head libn Blue Island (Ill) Pub Lib 42-43; Head libn Wausau Pub Lib, Wausau Wis 43-65; Head acquis & tech serv 65-. 8: Dir Regional Ref System, Wausau Wis 61-65. 9: ALA; WisLA (pres 50-52, Dir 59-62); Wis Valley LA (pres 53-54, 59-60, 64-65). 10: Wausau Wis 61-65. 11: Wis Libn of the yr 57. 13: Yes. 14: Acquis, catlg, lib development, pub rel. 15: 110 1/2 S Third ave, Wausau Wi 54401.

KRAUSE, MARY ANNA (SEARS). b Hutchins Tex 20 N 21. 4: Herbert W Krause. 5: Tex Woman'sU 38-41 (LS) BA. 7: Sec to libn & lib asst Fondren Lib So MethodistU 41-43; Libn US Air Transport Command 5th Ferrying Grp ATC, Dallas Tex 43-45; Bibliog asst Widener Lib HarvardU 45-51; Lib asst (vol) Mt Auburn Hosp, Cambridge Mass 60; Catlgr Law School Lib Harvard 61-65, Acquis asst 66-. 14: Tech processes. 15: 1 Stonehill dr, Stoneham Ma 02180.

KRAUSE, MARY E. b Stratford Ont Can 4 Je 19. 4: Michael H Krause. 5: UWest Ont 37-41 (Liberal Arts) BA; UToronto 42-43 BLS. 6: Fr, Sp. 7: Circ asst pub lib, Lond Ont Can 41-42, 43-45; Lib sci instr Brescia Hall UWest Ont 44; Ref libn Marygrove Col (Detroit) 45-49, Ref wk instr summer 46, Bkstore employee summer 53, Tech serv asst 66-; Libn II Detroit Pub Lib 63-66. 14: Catlg, ref. 15: 15745 Monte Vista, Detroit Mi 48238.

KRAVCHENKO, WALTER. b Belgrade Yugoslavia 1 D 33. 5: UBelgrade 51-55 (Russian Lang & Lit) BA; Acad of Mud (Belgrade) 46-54 (Piano Hist of Mus); Columbia 65-66 MLS. 6: Russian, Serbocroatian, Ger, Fr. 7: Ed in charge Nat Lexicographic Bd, NYC 61-66; First asst R&H Archives NYC Pub Lib 66-68; Libn Rec for Blind Inc, NYC 68-69; Hd circ Fordham Lib 69-. 10: Assn of Recorded Sound Collections. 14: Mus, a-v materials, pub serv, admin. 15: 329 Lexington ave, New York NY10016.

KRAWCHUK, JOAN S. b NY 4 Jl 34. 4: Robert Krawchuk. 5: State U Tchr Col (Geneseo NY) 52-56 (LS) BS; Hofstra Col 61 (Educ); C W Post Col 63, 65-68 (LS). 7: Elem libn Bethpage NY 56-57; Child libn Northport Pub (NY) Lib 57-59; Elem libn UFSD #11, Commack NY 59-61; Elem libn UFSD #7, Deer Park NY 61-67; Elem libn Three Village Central Sch Dist #1, Stony Brook NY 67-. 10: PTA; DPC of Amer; Doberman-Pinscher Club of Conn-NY. 14: Child wk. 15: 37 Woodbury rd, Farmingville NY 11738.

KRAWCZUK, NIKOLAUS. b Kopytiv Ukraine 1 Ja 16. 4: Zenovia Czechut. 5: Ukrainian Free U(Munich Ge4-52, ef Mich59-61 AMLS. 6: Russian, Polish, Ukrainian, Ger, Czech, Slovak. 7: Shipping clerk Globe Parcel Serv, Detroit 58; Sr Slavic catlgr Ind U 61-. 9: ALA-ACRL (Slavic Sub-Seunal (55-61). 12: Ed-in-chief "Feniks, Journal" (55-61). 14: Catlg, bibliog. 15: 1051 Winding wy,bloomington Ind 47401.

KRAWIEC, SEVA J(EANNE KOZITZKY). b Jeannette Penn 15 N 13. 4: Dr Joseph Frederick Krawiec. 5: PeeU 31-35 (Eng) BA, 35-36 (Eng) MA; Simmons 38-39 BS in LS. 6: Russian, Fr, Lat, Sp. 7: Sub tchr (Eng) Ansonia (Conn) High Sch 38; Head Libn NE U Sch of Law 39-42; Searcher indexer catlgr ranking asst in entry investigation NYPubLib 42-59; Searcher Penn StateU Pattee Lib 61-63; Asst acquis libn Penn State U Lib 63-. 14: Bibliog. 15: 241 Homan ave, State Col Penn 16801.

KRCMAR, JANET (ALFARO). b Moorehead Minn 9 Je 31. 4: Ludwig Krcmar. 5: UWash 47-48 (Psych); UCal(Los Angeles) 52-53); Los Angeles State Col 54-55 (Theater) BA; USoCal 61-62 (LS). 06: Fr, Sp. 7: Dir Tanglewood Sch for Girls, Canoga Park Cal 56-58; Lib supv Riker Lab, Northridge C; Libn Bunker-Ramo Corp, Canoga Park Cal 62-. 8: Los Angeles City Schs Career Guidance Bd 67-; Master adv com Los Angeles Trade-Tech Col 67-. 9: ALA; ASIS (ed "OASIS"); SLA (Sci-Tech Chm Los Angeles Chap); Federation Internationale de Documentatione; CalLA; SoCal Ind Educ Coun (proj chm; Eval Com). 10: Natl Womens Bowling Congress; Amer Figure Skatingasn; Knoedeleins Ski Club; Amer Ordinance Assn; ACM; Sierra Club; Adv Bd Berrywood PTA; Adv Com SoCal Auto Club; CalASchL (Adv Bd). 13: Yes. 14: Ref, electronics. 15: 1529 Kane ave, Simi Ca 93065.

KRECKMAN, ELLEN (ELIZABETH). b Fillmore NY 25 N 36. 5: Houghton Col 54-59 (Psych) BA; Syracuse 60-61 MS(LS). 7: Catlgr Houghton Col 61-. 9: ALA. 14: Catlg. 15: 15 York dr, Houghton NY 14744.

KREDEL, STEPHEN FRANCIS. b Frankfurt/Main Germany 28 Je 27. 5: Columbia 47-52 (Ger) BS; Simmons 53-54 (LS) MS. 6: Ger, Russian. 7: Volunteer guide World Assembly of Youth, NYC 51; Volunteer clerical asst Ottendorfer Br, NPBLib 52; Page boy Lib for the Blind, NY Pub Lib 53; Clerical wker order dept Columbia U 53; Catlgr Brown U Lib 55-56; Libn Vet Hosp, Lyons NJ 56; Catlgr Research Lib Rome Air Development Center, Griffiss AFB, Rome NY 56-. 8: Map consul to my father, Fritz Kredel, Illus. 9: ALA; SLA. 10: Rome Commun Theater; Gladiators (Fraternus Gladius); Oneida Co Bird Club. 13: Yes. 14: Catlg, ref. 15: 180 Pinehurst ave, New York NY 10033.

KREIDER, EDITH G (RICE). b Ripley NY 26 S 11. 4: John L Kreider. 5: Lake Erie Col 29-33 (Hist) AB; Carnegie 33-34 BS in LS. 7: Libn High Sch, Westfield NY 34-40; Libn Pub Schs Hamburg NY 40-41; Music libn StateU Col (Fredonia NY) 58-. 14: Mus materials. 15: 426 Swan st, Dunkirk NY 14048.

KREIDER, JANICE (AESCHLIMAN). b Wauseon Ohio 29 D 42. 4: J Evan Kreider. 5: Goshen Col 60-64 (Math) BA; Ohio StateU 64-65 (Math); IndU 65-67 (Math) MAT, MLS. 6: Sp. 7: Physics libn Columbia 68-. 9: ASIS. 14: Sci libnship, info sci. 15: 304-6 W 109th st, New York NY 10025.

KREISSMAN, BERNARD. b NYC 17 Je 19. 4: Shirley Relis. 5: City Col (NY) 48 (Eng Lit) BSS; Columbia 49 (Eng Lit) MA, 54 (LS) MS; UNeb 62 (Eng Lit) PhD. 7: Instr remedial reading NY Bd of Educ NYC 37-38; NY Pub Lib; Acquis searcher 46-48, Main reading room asst 49-50, Supv main reading room 51-54; Asst dir libs & Assoc prof UNeb 54-62; Chief libn & prof City Col (NY) 61-. 8: Coun of Higher Educ Insts (chm Lib Adv Bd 64); Middle States Assn Evaluation Teams; St Josephs Col 64, UPuerto Rico 65; George Wash U 67, Syracuse U 68, Paterson State Co 69; ALA Rep to Nat Coun Tchrs Eng, Nat Commsn on Lit 64-; Mgt surveyor Naval War Col Libs 67; Consul CUNY Tchr Educ Lib 69. 9: BSA; ALA-ACRL (Urban Univ Libs Com 62-69, Com on Lib Surveys 64-);-LAD (Bldgs Com for Col & Univ Libs 64); NY Lib Club (Exec Coun 62-, Scholarships & Awards Com 63-65, pres 66; Metro Spec Proj Com 67-; Coun of Chief Libns CUNY). 10: Archons of Colophon; AAUP; Columbia U Sch Lib Sci Alum. 12: "Pamela-Shamela, A study of the Criticisms, Burlesques, Parodies and Adaptations of Richardson's 'Pamela' " (60); "Sir Walter Scott's Life of John Dryden" (63). 13: Yes. 14: Admin, rare bks. 15: City Col Lib Convent ave & W 135th st, New York NY 10031.

KREITZ, SISTER THERESA (MARY). b Akron Ohio 22 D 08. 5: Marygrove Col 28-44 (Math) BA; Wayne StateU 46-51 (Educ) MEd; UMich 51-52 MALS. 6: Sp. 7: Elem sch tchr in parochial schs of Detroit, Wyandotte & Dearborn Mich 29-50; Libn Immaculata High Schm Detroit 50-51; Elem sch tchr, Flint Mich 51-54; Order libn Marygrove Col (Detroit) 54-59; Div libn Marygrove Col (Monroe) 59-. 9: ALA; CatholicLA; MichLA. 10: Monroe Co Lib Coun. 14: Catlg. 15: 610 W Elm ave, Monroe Mi 48161.

KREK, MIROSLAV. b Ljubljana Jugoslavia 30 Jl 24. 4: Marija Rutar. 5: UVienna 45-47 (Geog, Arabic); USalzburg(Austria) 47-49 (Phlos, Semiticiental Langs & Lits) AM, 56-60 (LS) AM, 60-63 (Oriental Langs & Civ). 6: Slovenian, Ger. 7: UChicago: Bibliog searcher 56-59, Head bibliog searchers 59-63, Asst acquis libn 63; Auis libn UWis(Milwaukee) 63-68; Acquis libn Brandeis U Lib 68-. 9: ALA; Amer Oriental Soc; 10: Amer Philatelic Soc. 11: NDEA (bis), Ford Found 9urbanization) Fellow. 12: "A Catalogue of Arabic Manuscripts in the Oriental Institute of Chicago" (61). 13: Yes. 14: Acquis, hist of the Arabic printed bk, bibliog, rare bks. 15: 15 Temple ter, Bedford Ma 01730.

KREMEN, DOROTHY E(DITH). b Chicago 15 S 24. 5: UChicago 44-46 (Chem) SB; UIll 50-51 (LS) MS. 6: Ger. 7: Libn I Brooklyn Pub Lib 51-52; Libn I Chicago Pub Lib 52-55; Chem libn Instr UWis (Madison) 55-57; Chem libn Asst Prof Purdue U 57-60; Ref libn AMA, Chicago 60-61; Libn I Chicago Pub Lib 61-62, Libn II 62-, 1st asst applied sci & tech 64-. 9: ALA; IllLA. 10: Beta Phi Mu. 14: Ref, phys sci, catlg. 15: 2228 Farwell, Chicago Il 60645.

KREMER, HELEN E. b Fond du Lac Wis 11 F 10. 5: UWis 28-32 (Comparative Lit) BA, 32 (LS) Equiv MA. 6: Fr. 7: Child libn pub lib, Fond du Lac Wis 34-41; Child libn & br libn Akron Pub Lib, Akron Ohio 41-47; 1st asst to hd child serv LA Co Lib 47-48; Consul mich State Lib Commsn 48-51, Consul & dir state aid, Lansing 57-; Consul Wis Lib commsn Madison 51-54; Asst hd child serv Stockton Pub Lib, Stockton Cal 54-56. 8: State aid dir and certif of Libs: Consul to soec proj in Metro libs, Detroit Metro research Demonst proj 66-68. 9: ALA; CathLA; MichLA; Adult Educ Assn Mich. 10: AAUW. 12: "Detroit Metropolitan Library Research and Demonstration Project: Demographic Study" (67). 13: Yes. 14: Systems devel of libs, changing spectrum of serv, spec progs to disadvantaged. 15: 1676 Algoma dr, Okomos Mi 48864.

KRENGEL, JOAN (GILBERT). b NYC 1 My 42. 4: Otto Krengel. 5: George WashingtonU 60-64 (Psych) BA; Drexel 66-67 MLS. 6: Ger. 7: Club dir US Army Spec Serv, N Bavaria & W Germany 64-66; Ref libn Columbia 67-68, Planning libn Avery Arch Lib 68-. 9: Coun of Planning Libns. 14: City planning. 15: 601 W 113th st apt 7-H, New York NY 10027.

KRENITSKY, MICHAEL V. b Duquesne Penn 15 N 15. 4: Jane Rook. 5: Wash & Jefferson Col 34-38 (Econ & Pol Sci) BS; Carnegie 46-47 BS in LS; SoMethodist U 48-54 (Educ) MA; Tex A & M U 54-61 (Agric, Econ). 6: Russian. 7: Staff asst Wash & Jefferson Col 38-41; Libn Penn Ind Sch, Camp Hill Penn 41-43; (S/Sgt) USArmy 43-46; Libn Tex Mil Col 47-49; Circ libn Tex A & M U 49-51, Assoc libn 51-61; Lib Dir Mich Tech U 61-. 8: ICA appointee to Indonesia to survey univ lib problems, 59; Bldg Consul Caudill Rowlett & Scott (architects) Houston 56-58. 9: ALA; MichLA (chm Acad Lib Div 69-70, Ref & Res Resources Adv Com). 10: Kiwanis; Phi Delta Theta. 13: Yes. 14: Admin, automation. 15: 1112 E Sixth ave, Houghton Mich 49931.

KRENTA, NICHOLAS. b Latsko Ukraine 17 Ag 17. 4: Alicia Rozylo. 5: Lakehead Tech Inst 53-55; Queen's U (Kingston Ont) 55-58 (Hist) BA; UToronto 58-59 BLS, 60-63 MLS. 6: Ukranian, Polish, Ger, Russian. 7: Catlgr UToronto Lib 59-65; Head of tech serv Brock U (St Catharine Ont) 65-66; Catlgr Yale U Lib 66-. 9: CanLA (Com on Canadian Subj Hdings); ALA; OntLA; Inst Prof Libns, Ont. 12: Jt ed "A List of Canadian Subject Headings" (66 & 68). 13: Yes. 14: Catlg, bk sel, automation, admin, Canadiana. 15: 111 Park st apt 16F, New Haven Ct 06511.

KREPS, JANET SUZANNE (GRAVES). b Flint Mich 29 Je 44. 4: Robert Wilson Kreps. 05: Central State Col (Edmond Okla) 62-66 (Eng) BA; UDenver 66-67 (LS) MS. 6: Sp, Fr. 7: Ref libn & lib instr Iowa State U Lib (Ames) 67-. 9: ALA. 14: Ref, lib instr. 15: PO Box 1213, Ames Ia 50010.

KRESGE, DORIS (GRIFFITHS). b Taylor Penn 12 Je 16. 5: Marywood Col 32-36 (Eng) BS (cum laude); Leehigh U summer 38 (Journalism); UPittsburgh 59 (Bus); Marywood Col summer 64 (LS); West Md Col 66-68; Drexel Workshop summer 66. 6: Fr. 7: Libn Taylor High Sch, Taylor Penn 36-39; Asst ref&catlg Carnegie Inst of Tech 60; Libn N Potomac Jr High Sch, Hagerstown Md 63-64; Libn N Hagerstown High Sch, Hagerstown Md 64-. 9: NEA; MdSchLA; Md State Tchrs Assn. 10: Kappa Gamma Pi. 14: Ref, acquis. 15: 23 Bittersweet dr, Hagerstown Md 21740.

KRESHKA, EVA (KONRAD). b Prague Czechoslovakia 1 My 24. 4: George Kreshka. 5: Vassar 45-47 (Psych) BA; Charles U (Prague) 47-49 (Comparative Lit); UCal(Berkeley) 58-60 MLS. 6: Czech, Fr, Ger, Russian. 7: Sr lib asst UCal Lib(Berkeley) 53-57; Instr US Foreign Serv Inst (Berkeley Cal) 58-60; Catlgr Mills Col Lib 60-. 9: NoCal Tech Processes Group (chm 64-65); MusLA (sec-treas Bay Area Chap 65-66). 10: Bd Bks Unltd Coop, Berkeley. 14: Catlg, mus libnship. 15: Mills Col Lib, Oakland Ca 94613.

KRETTEK, (JOSEPHINE) GERMAINE. b Council Bluffs Iowa 18 N 07. 5: Col of St Elizabeth 25-29 (Eng) AB; UDenver 40-42 BS in LS. 7: Head publicity dept Supreme Forest Woodmen Circle, Omaha 30-39; Pub Lib, Council Bluffs Iowa: Head circ dept 39-40, Head ref dept 40-45, Chief Libn 45-57; Dir Wash Off ALA 57-; Assoc exec dir ALA 66-. 8: Consul to Commsn on Fed Rel, Amer Coun Educ Official Observer of the Adv Com to the US Commsnr of Educ on Lib Programs. 9: ALA (Coun, Lib Development CO Fdrelpres 52, chm Lib Planning Com 54-55); Omaha-Council Bluffs Libns Club (pres). 10: Women's Jt Congressional Com; Altrusa Internat; Council Bluffs Adult Edud oc bluffs Iowa. 11: Outstanding Alumni Award from Sch of Libnship at the University of Denver's Centennial Celebration 64; Distinguished Achievement Award Drexel Lib Sch Alum Assn 67; Honorary DLL degree, Col of St Elizabeth Convent Sta NJ 69. 12: Regular columns in "ALA Bulletin" & "Wilson Library Bulletin"; Ed "Washington Newsletter" (ALA). 14: Lib legis. 15: The Coronet 200 C st SE, Wash DC 20003.

KRETZSCHMAR, CARL HERBERT. b Villard Minn 3 F 17. 4: Thalia Wittman. 5: UMinn 36-41 BLS, 46 (Chem) AB. 6: Ger. 7: CO Capt Army 387th AAArtillery Br, US, Europe 41-46; IndU: Chem libn 46-47, Sci libn 47-50, Med llibn 50-51; Comd Off Col Army 445th SIRA, Wash DC 51-53; Med libn Ind U 53-57; Head info serv Gen Mills Tech Ctr, Minneapolis 57-. 9: SLA; ACS (Lit Sect). 13: Yes. 14: Admin, systems. 15: RR 4 Box 128, Buffalo Mn 55313.

KREUZ, LORETTA BARBARA. b Menominee Mich 17 F 10. 5: Milwaukee-Downer 28-30; Marquette U 30-32 AB; UMich 35-36 ABLS; UIll 50-51 MS in LS, 54-56, 59-60. 7: Lib asst Detroit Pub Lib 36-47; Libn Army Lib Serv, Japan 47-48; Ref libn Loyola U (Chicago) 48-51; Instr Ill State Normal U 51-54; Asst Prof Tex Woman's U 56-59; Asst Prof So Conn State Col 62-64; Lecturer UMich Ext summer 65-. 9: ALA; AALS; MichLA. 10: Beta Phi Mu; AAUW. 14: Ref, bibliog. 15: 1008 14th ave, Menominee Mi 49858.

KREUZER, SISTER MARY ROSELLA SSND. b Spokane Wash 4 Ja 12. 5: Holy Names Col 40-44 Eng) BA; UPortland summers 61-65 MLS. 6: Ger. 7: Elem tchr & sch libn: Colton Wash 37, Chewelah Wash 54, Clarkston Wash 51, Spokane Wash 62; Ref libn Gonzaga U 64-67; Hd libn Mount Mary Col 67-. 9: CathLA; ALA. 14: Ref. 15: Mankato Campus of Mount Mary College Lib, Good Counsel Hill, Mankato Mn 56001.

KRIBS, ANNA ELIZABETH. b Birmingham Ala 11 Ag 14. 5: La Polytech Inst 54-58 (Sociol) BA; Inst Tech de Monterrey(Mex) summer 54 (Span); LSU 58-59 MS LS. 6: Sp.

7: Clerk US Navy Dept Base Comdt's Off, Newport RI 42-45; Clerk Prudential Insurance Co Mortgage Loan, Birmingham Ala 45-49; Club dir Army Spec Serv, Okinawa Ryukyus Is 49-50; Clerk US Army Signal Corps, Sacramento Cal 50-51; Club dir Army Spec Serv, Germany 51-53; Parish Libn Grant Parish, Colfax La 59-61; Bibliogr & Asst Prof Ralph B Draughon Lib Auburn U 61-. 9: AlaLA. 10: AAUW. 14: Ref. 15: 251 Chewacla dr, Auburn Ala 36830.

KRICHBAUM, MARY. b Canton Ohio 7 Mr 21. 5: Kent State U 39-43 (Educ) BS in Ed; West Res 45-46 BS in LS. 7: Prof asst Canton Pub Lib, Canton Ohio 43-45; Libn Herrick Mem Lib, Wellington Ohio 46-47; Catlgr Hist Med Div US Army Med Lib, Cleveland 47-51; Prof libn Cleveland Pub Lib 51-53; Asst libn Investment Lib Nat City Bank, Cleveland 54-63; Med libn & libn Sch of Nursing Lib Huron Rd Hosp, Cleveland 63-. 9: SLA; MedLA. 14: Ref, bibliog. 15: 1450 Coutant ave, Lakewood Ohio 44107.

KRIEG, CLARICE E(MMA). b Chicago 8 Jl 10. 5: State U Iowa 28-32 (Fr) BA; UIll 33 BS in LS, 35 MA in LS. 6: Fr, Ger. 7: Asst catlgr UIll(Urbana) 33-35; Asst supt catlg dept State U Iowa 35-41; Head catlg libn UOre 41-. 9: ALA; PNLA; OreLA. 10: AAUP; Phi Beta Kappa; Phi Sigma Iota. 13: Yes. 14: Catlg. 15: 3292 Onyx pl, Eugene Or 97405.

KRIEG, LAUREL L. b Burton Ohio 12 Mr 07. 5: Col for Women West Res 24-28 (Eng) AB; West Res 28-29 (LS) BS; UChicago 42 (LS) AM. 7: Child libn Pub Lib, Alliance Ohio 29-37; Dir Co Lib, Ocean Co NJ 37-48; Libn Martins Ferry, Belmont Co Serv, Martins Ferry Ohio 48-. 9: ALA; OhioLA (Bd Dirs, chm Ext Sect). 10: Oglebay Inst; Brooks Bird Club (Wheeling WVa); Bus & Profess Women. 13: Yes. 14: Lib ext, wk with child. 15: Pub Lib Masonic Bldg, Martins Ferry Ohio 43935.

KRIEGER, TILLIE (STEIN). b Detroit. 5: Wayne State -53 (Hist); UCal 59-62 (Hist) BA; USoCal 63-64 MLS; UNev 65. 6: Fr, Sp, Ger, Hebrew. 7: Jr accountant Gilbert L Mayer CPA, Beverly Hills Cal 62-64; Libn UNev 64-66; Catlg & acquis UCal Law Lib (Davis) 67-68; Head acquis Ariz State U Lib 68-. 8: Asst to Dir, Nat Lib Week Nevada 65; Conf on use of KF schedule, Davis Cal 67. 9: ALA; SLA; NevLA (chm Recr Com 65-). 10: Sierra Club. 12: Interim Index to Library of Congress - Class KF - Law of the United States (68). 14: Tech serv, info retrieval. 15: 1233 W 9th st, Tempe Az 85281.

KRIKELAS, JAMES. b Cudahy Wis 17 D 32. 4: Joan Gottfried. 5: UWis (Milwaukee) 50-53 (Engnr); UWis 56-58 (Hist) BS, 58-59 MSLS; UIll 63-67 (LS) PhD. 6: Gk, Fr, Russian. 7: (Pvt-Sgt) US Army, Ft Leonard Wood Mo 53-55; Stud asst UWis (Madison) 58-59; Catlgr Shorewood High Sch, Shorewood Wis summer 59, 61, 62, 63; Head tech serv Milwaukee-Downer Col 59-61, Head Libn 61-63; Visiting Instr UWis (Milwaukee) 62, 63; Spec Instr UIll (Urbana) 65; Research assoc Lib Research Center (UIll) 65-67; Asst Prof Lib Sch UWis 67-. 9: ALA; WisLA; IllLA; ASIS (Lib Research RT); AALS. 10: AAUP; Beta Phi Mu. 13: Yes. 14: Research & educ in libnship, tech serv. 15: Lib School Univ of Wis, Madison Wi 53706.

KRISTELL, L DIANE. b Jersey City NJ 3 S 44. 5: StanfordU 62-66 (fr) AB; UCal 9berkeley) 67-68 MLS. 6: Fr, Ger. 7: Lib asst Stanford Undergrad Lib Projec 66-67; Research asst Inst of Lib Research UCal (Berkeley) 67-68; Ref libn San Jose State Col 68-. 14: Ref. 15: 445 Acalanes dr apt 4, Sunnyvale Ca 94086.

KRITZER, HYMAN WILLIAM. b NYC 9 N 18. 4: Simone Morali. 5: Hiram Col 46, 49-51; American U 51-52 BS; Institut des Etudes Politiques (Paris) 52-53; Catholic U 54-58 MSLS. 6: Fr, Ger, Lat. 7: USArmy 1st Inf Div (Sgt) 41-45; Order clerk American U 54-57; Head acquis dept UNotre Dame Lib (SBend Ind) 57-59; Head acquis dept UMd Lib 59-60; Head acquis dept Ohio StateU 60-62, Asst dir 62-66; Dir Kent State U Lib 66-68, Asst Provost & Dir 69-. 9: ALA (chm Cost of Lib Materials Index Com 63-65; v-pres 66-67); Ohio Col Assn (pres 67-68); OhioLA. 14: Acquis. 15: Kent State Univ Libs, Kent Oh 44240.

KRITZLER, CHARLES A. b Brooklyn NY 13 Ag 32. 4: Carlene Potter. 5: SUNY (Albany) 56-59 (Bus Educ) BS; C W Post Col LIU 60-63 (LS) MS; UConn 65-68; Boston U 68-. 7: (1st Lt) USMC Communications 51-56; Bus educ tchr & a-v dir Central Dist 3, Locust Valley NY 59-62; Catlgr West Americana Collection Yale U Lib 62-63; A-v dir Central Dist 3, Locust Valley NY 63-64; Dir A-v Center So Conn State Col 64-68; Assoc dir U Media Serv, Boston U 68-. 9: NEA-DAVI; Mass A-V Assn. 10: Grad Lib Sch of LIU Alumni Assn. 12: Comp "Catalogue of Western Americana Manuscripts," with J Goddard, ed by A Hanna, Yale U. 14: Catlg, non-bk materials in the lib, libs as instrl materials centers. 15: Burr Hill rd, No Branford Conn 06714.

KRIVATSY, NATI. b Budapest Hungary. 4: Peter Krivatsy. 5: Pazmany U (Budapest) 48 (Art hist) PhD; Catholic U 65 MSLS. 6: Fr, Ger, Lat, Gk, Hungarian. 7: Sr catlgr Folger Shakespeare Lib, Wash DC 57-. 10: Beta Phi Mu. 13: Yes. 14: Rare bks. 15: 5705 McKinley st, Bethesda Md 20034.

KRIVATSY, PETER. b Budapest Hungary 7 Ap 22. 4: Nati Horvath. 5: Pazmany U (Budapest) 45 (Hist) PhD; Catholic U 62 MSLS. 6: Fr, Ger, Lat, Sp, Hungarian. 7: Ed, 17th cent catlg, Hist of Med Div, NLM, Curator of rare bks 67-. 9: MedLA; Amer Assn Hist Med; Wash Soc Hist of Med. 14: Rare bks. 15: 5705 McKinley st, Bethesda Md 20034.

KRIVONAK, PAUL MICHAEL. b Erie Penn 16 F 40. 4: Georganna (Trenner). 5: Edinboro State 61-65 BSLS; Syracuse 68 MSLS. 7: Electrician's mate E5 USN, USS Forrestal 59-61; Libn & a-v dir Watchung Hills High Sch, Warren NJ 65-67; Ref libn Plainfield Pub Lib, Plainfield NJ 66-68; Hd ser dept Oneonta Pub Lib, Oneonta NY 67-68; Ref & readers adv cumberland Co Col 69-. 9: ALA; NJLA. 14: Admin. 15: Rd 3 Box 104C, Millville NJ 08332.

KRIZ, FRANK. b Mor Malkovice Czechoslovakia 7 Je 20. 4: Anna Nosova. 5: Masaryk's U (Brno Czechoslovakia) 39-48 (Med, Clinical Psych) PhD; Zurich U 48-50 (Anthropology); Columbia 60-63, 61 MS. 06: Czech, Ger, Fr, Russian, Polish. 7: Tech libn Zbrojovka Brno Inc, Brno Czechoslovakia 41-45; Consul for UDC Masaryk's U Lib(Brno Czechoslovakia) 45-48; Tech adv for new class system Zurich's U 48-50; Consul for lib Consultant's Bureau Ltd, Sydney Australia 54-59; Columbia U Med Lib: Catlg asst 59-61, Med catlgr 61-62, Head med catlg sect 63-. 12: "Desetinne trideni" (44, 2d ed 45); Plachteni" (47); "Motorove letani" (48); "Abortus criminalis" (48). 13: Yes. 14: Catlg. 15: Columbia Univ Med Lib, 630 W 168th st, New York NY 10032.

KROEHLER, MARJORIE (ENGEL). b Oak Park Ill 23 My 28. 4: Ralph Senf Kroehler. 5: Elmhurst Col 46-50 (Hist, Eng) BA; UChicago 50-51 (LS); West MichU 62 (Hist). 7: Asst Elmhurst Pub Lib, Elmhurst Ill 46-51; Child libn Freeport Pub Lib, Freeport Ill 51, Dir 51-56; Libn Freeport Sr High Sch, Freeport Ill 58-60; Dir Allegan Pub Lib, Allegan Mich 61-63; Tchr-libn Plainwell Jr High Sch, Plainwell Mich 63-. 9: ALA; NEA; MichLA; MichEA. 13: Yes. 14: Admin, pub rel, child. 15: 304 Marshall st, Allegan Mi 49010.

KROEKER, HILDA. b Mt Lake Minn 16 D 24. 5: Tabor Col 50 (Bible) BA; Kan State Tchrs Col 59 (LS) MA. 6: Ger. 7: Tchr Marion Ind Sch, Marion SD 50-52; Tchr & libn Central Christian High Sch, Hutchinson Kan 52-59; Tchr & libn Neb Christian High Sch, Central City Neb 59-62; Tchr & libn Calvary Bible Col 62-. 9: Christian Libns Fellowship (pres 65-66, Mem Exec Com); ALA; MoLA. 10: Kan Bus Tchrs Org. 14: Ref. 15: Calvary Bible Col, 1111 W 39th, Kansas City Mo 64111.

KROENCKE, VERA SOPHIA. b Concordia Mo 7 O 11. 5: Stephens Col 29-31 AA; UMo 31-34 (Span) BS in Ed, 41-47 (Eng) MA; UIll 54-56 MS in LS. 7: Tchr Mayview High Sch, Mayview Mo 37-41; Tchr Cameron High Sch, Cameron Mo 41-45; Instr in Eng UMo 45-51; Tchr William Chrisman High Sch, Independence Mo 51-52; Lib asst UMo Lib 52-54, Catlgr 56-59, Ser catlgr 60-68, Hd records dept 68-. 9: ALA. 10: Beta Phi Mu; AAUW. 14: Catlg. 15: 20 N Greenwood Columbia Mo 65201.

KROHLE, FREDERICK J(ACOB). b Ashland Penn 31 Ag 35. 4: Margaret Burke. 5: Wilkes Col 53-57 (Eng) AB; Drexel 63-64 MSLS. 6: Ger. 7: Clerk (Sp4) US Army, Heidelberg Germany 57-59; Order dept supv Wilkes Col Lib 59-62; Asst ref dept Pub Lib, Allentown Penn 64-65; Ser libn Wilkes Col 65-66, Hd ref dept 66-. 8: Taught basic ref at Allentown Pub in conjunction with Penn State Lib. 14: Catlg, indexing, ref. 15: 131 Academy st, Plymouth Pa 18651.

KROMER, EDITH VIVIAN. b Olivia Minn 30 Je 31. 5: Hamline U 49-53 (Eng) BA; UDenver 55 (LS) UMinn 56-57 (LS) MA, 66 Certif, 69 (Philos). 6: Lat. 7: Tchr of Eng, Hist Willmar Pub Schs, Willmar Minn 53-56; Libn St Anthony Elem Sch, Minneapolis 56-57; Libn Lib Sch Lib UMinn (Minneapolis) 57-58; Ref circ libn & instr of Lib Sci St Cloud State Col 58-59; Libn & Instr University High Sch, UMinn (Minneapolis) 59-65; Instr Lib sci UMinn (Duluth) summer 63; Instr Lib Sch, UMinn (Minneapolis) 60-63, 64-. 8: No Central

Assn consul sch libs 61-68. 9: ALA; MinnASchL. 10: Organ Amer Histns. 11: Grant from Fund for the Advancement of Educ 67-68. 13: Yes. 14: Sch libs, hist of child lit, bibliog. 15: 101 Seymour ave SE, Minneapolis Mn 55414.

KROMPART, JANET ANN (FREEMAN). b Los Angeles 30 Ja 27. 5: USoCal 44-46 (Asiatic Studies); UCal(Berkeley) 46-48 (Pol Sci) AB, 62-64 MLS. 6: Chinese. 7: 1st Lt tr US Army, Ft Lee Va, Tokyo 49-52; Cryptananlyst (foreign lang) Nat Security Agency, Wash DC 52-54; Credentials clerk registrar's off UBuffalo 56; Chief current ser e asiatic Lib UCal(Berkeley) 56-68; Free lance ed for US Dept Com UCal 62-68; Catlgr (spec Oriental bks) Oakland U 69-. 9: CalLA; MichLA. 10: UCal Lib Sch Alum Assn. 14: Oriental libnship. 15: 243 West Tienken rd, Rochester Mi 48063.

KRONICK, DAVID A. b Connelsville Penn 5 O 17. 4: Marilyn Abramson. 5: West Res 36-39 (Amer Lit) BA, 39-40 BLS; UChicago 50-53 (Libnship) PhD. 6: Fr, Ger. 7: Libn West ResU Sch Med 46-50; Lib asst NLM, Wash DC 53-55; Libn med Lib UMich (Ann Arbor) 55-59; Dir Cleveland Med Lib, Cleveland Ohio 59-64; Chief ref div NLM, Bethesda Md 64-65; Prof Med Bibliog, dir med communications (UTex) Med Sch (San Antonio 65-. 8: Lib consul UOkla & UFla 66-67; Consul NLM 66-; Survey med libs in S Amer 65; Survey Tex med libs 67. 9: MedLA (bus mgr; Bd Dirs); Tex Coun Health Sci Libs (pres). 12: "A History of Scientific and Technical Periodicals" (62). 13: Yes. 14: Info serv, hist sci communication. 15: 1223 Mt Riga dr, San Antonio Tx 78213.

KRONISH, SYLVIA (FIEDLER). b Poland 04: Z'er Kronish. 5: Hunter Col 40-44 (Statistics, Math) BA; Columbia 55-60 MLS. 6: Yiddish, Hebrew, Ger, Fr. 7: Bkshop asst Bloch Publ, NYC 45-54; Lib asst Stern Col 54-56; Lib trainee Foreign Collections adult circ br NYPub Lib 56-59; Staff libn picture collection 59-. 09: SLA (Picture Group NYChap, past sec-treas, co chm). 14: Pict wk, judaica. 15: 138-33 Jewel ave, Flushing NY 11367.

KROSCH, PENELOPE (JULIANA STORMS). b Perham Minn 16 F 41. 4: Howard F Krosch. 5: UMinn (Minneapolis) 59-63 (Zool) BA, 63-65 (LS) MA. 7: UMinn Lib (Minneapolis): Libn 65-68, Libn & instr 69-. 9: MinnLA. 14: Catlg. 15: 623 Laurel av, St Paul Mn 55104.

KRUCKO, EUGENE BOHDAN. b Lypovets Ukraine 17 Je 14. 5: Acad for Foreign Trade (Lviv) 35-39; Hochschule fur Welthandel (Vienna) 40-42 B Bus Admin; West Res 58-59 MSLS. 6: Ukrainian, Polish, Ger, Russian, Fr. 7: Catlgr asst Purdue U Lib 59-61; Catlgr asst Kent State U Lib 61-65; Hd catlgr Bemidji State Col 65-69. 9: MinnLA. 14: Catlg, bk sel. 15: Bemidji State Col Lib, Bemidji Mn 56601.

KRUEGER, HANNA ELSA. b Hutchinson Minn 20 Ap 05. 5: UChicago 22-28 (Eng Educ) PhB, 28-29; UIll 37-38 BS in LS; UChicago 39-43 (LS) AM. 6: Ger, Fr. 7: Sec Johnson Publ Co, Chicago 30-33; Sec Wilson & Co, Chicago 33-37; Asst in Lib Sch UIll summer 38; Asst libn & Instr in Lib Sci Carroll Col Lib 38-40; Act Libn Carroll CollLib 40-43; Asst libn & Instr in Lib Sci West Ill State Tchrs Col 43-45; Head catlg dept Wayne Co Lib, Detroit 45-48, Head catlg & order dept 48-49; Wash State U: Head catlg dept 49-50, Chief tech serv div 50-53, Chief Humanities Lib 53-. 9: ALA; CanLA; PNLA; WashLA; Mod Lang Assn. 10: AAUP; AAUW; LWV. 13: Yes. 14: Admin, ref, catlg, acquis, bibliog, tchg lib sci. 15: 1305A Gaines rd, Pullman Wa 99163.

KREUGER, MARY FLORENCE. b Newport RI 4 Mr 11. 5: Pembroke Col 28-32 (Fr) AB; RI Col 32-48 (Educ); Brown 32-50 (Educ); Tampa U 52-53; 2 Life Prof Certifs: Tchr in Secondary Schs 54, Tchr of Lib Sci 59. 6: Fr. 7: Providence Pub Sch Dept: Auditorium tchr Nathanael Greene Jr High Sch 34-40, Soc arts dir Nathanael Greene Jr High Sch 40-48, Libn Oliver H Perry Jr High Sch 48-64, Lib Coordinator 64-. 8: Delegate Alumnae Leadership Conf, Brown U 61; Mem Adv Coun on Interlib Coop, Providence RI 68-. 9: ALA; NESchLA; RISchLA (v-pres, sec, Pub Chm 57-63); RILA (Memb, Prog, Nomin coms 60-68); RIEA (Pub Rel Com 63-66); Providence Tchrs Assn; RI ASCD; RI AV Assn. 10: Girl Scout leader; Pembroke Col Club of Providence; RI Hist Soc; Delta Kappa Gamma; Barker Players of Providence; Pembroke Alum Assn; Our Lady of Fatima Hosp Guild. 14: Child & yp lit. 15: 176 Irving ave, Providence RI 02906.

KRUEGER, NATHALIE SOLOVIEFF. b Bac-Ninh Tonkin Indo China 13 Ag 23. 4: Harold Ervin Krueger. 5: U d'Aix-en-Provence France) 42-45 (Fr, Lat, Ancient Gk, Philol) License-es-Lettres, 45-46 (Fr) Diplome d'Etudes superieures de langues classiques; Catholic U 61-62 MSLS. 6: Fr, Russian, Lat, Classical Gk. 7: Professeur de Lycee de jeunes filles, Nice France 45-47; Sub tchr Glen Burnie High Sch, Glen Burnie Md 54-56; IBM keypunch operator Treasury Dept, Wash DC 57-58; LC: Shelflister 58-60, Preliminary catlgr & searcher 60-61, Descr catlgr 62-65, Subj catlgr 65-09: ALA; DCLA. 10: Beta PhiMu. 13: Yes. 14: Catlg. 15: 4114 N34th st, Arlington Va 22207.

KRUG, ADELE (JENSEN). b Thief River Falls Minn 30 Mr 08. 5: Gallaudet Col 26-30 (Home Econ) BA; Catholic U 56-61 MS in LS. 6: Fr, Norwegian. 7: Tchr Sch for the Deaf, Providence 30-32; Tchr Lab Sch of Gallaudet Col 55-62, Child libn for the lab sch 55-62; Gallaudet Col: Instr in Lib Sci 56-62, libn Instr in Lib Sci 62-64, Preparations libn Asst Prof of LS 64-, Assoc Prof of Lib Sci 67-, Hd catlgr 68-. 08: Taught in Lib Inst for grad stud Gallaudet Col summer 65. 9: ALA; Conv of Amer Instrs of the Deaf; DCLA. 10: AAUP; PTA; Phi Kappa Zeta; Women's Aux; Cafritz Mem Hosp; Women's Aux; Nat Luth Home; Nat Assn of the Deaf. 13: Yes. 14: Catlg. 15: 1915 Gaither st SE, Wash DC 20031.

KRUG, ELSIE E. b Fond du Lac Wis 6 Je 10. 5: Marian Col of Fond du Lac 39-41; UWis 41-43 (Eng) BA, 43-44 BLS. 7: Off clk Reporter Printing Co, Fond du Lac Wis 30-37; Libn in charge Post Lib USAF, Chanute Field Ill 45-46; Libn II G M Simmons Lib, kenosha Wis 46-48, Hd tech serv 48-. 9: ALA; WisLA (sec-treas Catlg Sect 52-53; Bd of dirs Pub Lib Sect 66-68); KenoshaLA. 10: UWis Alum Assn. 14: Catlg. 15: 6516 Fifth ave, Kenosha Wi 53140.

KRUG, JUDITH (FINGERET). b Pittsburgh 15 Mr 40. 4: E Herbert Krug. 5: UPittsburgh 58-61 (Pol Sci) BA; UChicago 61-62 (LS) MA. 6: Fr. 7: Ref libn John Crerar Lib, Chicago 62-63; Head catlgr Northwestern UDental Sch 63-65; Research analyst ALA 65-67, Dir off for Intel Freedom 67-. 9: ALA; IllLA. 10: Phi Beta Kappa; Beta Phi Mu; Delta Sigma Rho; Pi Sigma Alpha. 13: Yes. 14: Research, ref, freedom to read. 15: 1146 W Morse ave, Chicago Il 60626.

KRUG, RICHARD (EUGENE). b Milwaukee 13 Je 05. 4: Lucile Ransom. 5: UWis 23-27 (Pol Sci) BA, 27-29 LLB. 6: Ger. 7: Practicing Attorney, Milwaukee 29-30; City of Milwaukee: Mun ref libn 30-39, Asst city libn 39-41, City Libn 41-. 9: Amer Interprof Inst (pres 58-59, loc pres 64); ALA (Life mem); SLA; WisLA; Wis Marine Hist Soc. 10: ACLU; Milwaukee Area Soc Pub Admin; Milwaukee Coun for Adult Learning (Bd Dirs); Milwaukee Art Center Trustee; State Hist Soc Wis (Life mem); Milwaukee Press Club; Wis Club. 14: Admin. 15: 814 W Wisconsin ave, Milwaukee Wi 53233.

KRUGER, VIVIAN (RAITZ). b Toledo Ohio 13 F 15. 4: Kenneth C Kruger. 5: UToledo 32-33, 35-36 (Fr) BA; West Res 36-37 BS in LS. 6: Fr. 7: Catlgr Toledo Pub Lib, Toledo Ohio 37-46; Libn Whitmer High Sch, Toledo Ohio 47-48; Catlgr Toledo Pub Lib, Toledo Ohio 56-. 9: OhioLA; NOhio Tech Serv Libns. 14: Catlg. 15: 5506 Pageland dr, Toledo Oh 43611.

KRUMM, CAROL (MAE) R(HODEBACK). b Pataskala Ohio 17 Je 23. 4: Delbert R Krumm. 5: CapitalU 41-45 (Eng, Bible) BA; West Res 45-46 BS in LS. 6: Fr, Ger, Lat, Sp. 7: Asst libn Otterbein Col Lib 46-51; Catlgr Ohio State U Libs 52-53; Ser catlgr Cleveland Pub Lib 57-58; Catlgr Ohio State U Libs 59-65, Catlg maintenance libn 65-, Asst Prof of lib admin 68-. 8: Catlg lib of Ohio Legis Serv Commsn, Columbus Ohio 53-54; Indexed The Ohio State University monthly, 09-50, Columbus Ohio 53-57; Libn E Linden Evangelical United Brethren Church Columbus Ohio 65-68. 9: ALA-ACRL; -RTSD; Ohio Valley Group Tech Serv Libns, OhioLA; Franklin Co LA. 10: Fac Women's Club. 14: Catlg, catlg maintenance. 15: 53 S Powell ave, Columbus Oh 43204.

KRUMM, ROGER V(INCENT). b Decorah Iowa 1 F 19. 4: Carmen Rivera y Damia3n. 5: Luther Col 36-40 (Chem) AB; U Denver 50-51 (LS) MA. 6: Ger, Fr, Sp, Ital. 7: Army (Capt) Chem Warfare Serv, S Pacific Fifth AF Group Chem Off 41-46; Chem libn U Fla 51-66, Engnrg & physical scis libn 66-. 8: Centro de Documentacion Cientifica y Tecnica de Mexico, Mexico City June 60; Universidad Nacional Autonoma de Mexico July 30; Taught course in chem lit for Chem Dept U Fla 52-66; trans consul, Coca-Cola Foods Div, Plymouth Fl. 9: SLA (past Mem Chm Ga Chap); ACS. 10: Alpha Chi Sigma; Gamma Sigma Epsilon. 12: Ed "FLACS," off publ of Fla Sect, ACS (58-). 13: Yes. 14: Chem and engng, libnship & lit. 15: 1804 NW 5th ave, Gainesville Fl 32601.

KRUMMEL, DONALD WILLIAM. b Sioux City Iowa 12 Jl 29. 4: Marilyn D Frederick. 5: UMich 47-51 BMus, 51-53 MMus, 52-54 AMLS, 53-58 PhD. 7: Instr in music lit UMich

(Ann Arbor) 52-56; Ref libn music div LC 56-61; Head ref dept Newberry Lib, Chicago 62-64, Assoc libn 64-70; Fac Grad Sch of Lib Sci UIll Urbana-Champaign 70-. 8: US Civil Serv Middle Management Internship 60. 9: ALA (Coun 64-68 Subscr Bk Com 64-69); MusLA (memb at Large 62-64, Coun 68-, chm Amer Mus Bibliog Com 64-67); BSA; Internat Assn Mus Libs (v-pres Commsn on the Dating of Music 68-). 10: Caxton Club (Chicago). 11: H Rackham Grant UMich 54; Grant-in-Aid, Henry E Huntington Lib 65; Scholar-in-Residence, Inst for Humanistic Studies, Aspen Colo 69. 12: Comp 'Quarterly Book List' in "Musical quarterly," (57-60). 13: Yes. 14: History of Amer res libs & bibliog, music printing & bibliog, music libnship. 15: Grad Sch of Lib Sci, UIll Urbana Il 61801.

KRUPP, ROBERT G. b Buffalo NY 12 Je 20. 5: UBuffalo 39-42 (Chem) BS; Columbia 53-55 MSLS. 6: Ger. 7: Research Chem & tech libn Union Carbide Corp, Charleston WVa 42-53; Asst libn Amer Cyanamid Co, NJ 55-59; Libn Bell Telephone Labs, NYC 59-65; NYPub Lib 53-55, Chief sci & tech div 65-. 8: Consul to Chemical Abstracts Serv 67-68. 9: SLA; ACS; ALA; ASIS. 11: John Cotton Dana Award 64 & 67. 12: Ed chm "Special Libraries" (60-65). 13: Yes. 14: Admin, ref. 15: 1 DeWitt rd Apt 103, Elizabeth NJ 07208.

KRUSE, CAROLYN (JOHNSON). b Richfield Ida 23 Ja 16. 4: Howard W Kruse. 5: Ore State Col 35-37 (Chem) BS, 37-39 (Chem) MA; UIll 39-40 BS i LS. 6: Ger. 7: Libn Hall Labs Inc, Pittsburgh 40-41; Research analyst Hist Com Inc, NYC 41-42; Research asst PurdueU Research Found 42-45; Research asst Ohio StateU Research Found 45-47; Libn USNaval Ordnance Test Station, China Lake Cal 47-59, Head lib div 59-68; Hd lib div Naval Weapons Ctr, China Lake Cal 68-. 9: SLA; ASIS. 13: Yes. 14: Admin, ref. 15: 1227 Wayne ave, Ridgecrest Ca 93555.

KRUSE, KATHRYN WARREN. b Pittsburgh 9 D 40. 5: Mt Holyoke 58-62 (Zool) BA; UPittsburgh 62-64 (Anatomy), 64-65 MLS. 6: Fr, Sp. 7: Ref libn Welch Med Lib, Baltimore 65-68; Ref libn Duke U Med Ctr Lib 68-. 9: MEDLA; SLA. 10: Penn Acad Sci; Beta Phi Mu. 14: Ref. 15: 124 Carriage dr, Pittsburgh Pa 15237.

KRUSE, PAUL (ROBERT). b What Cheer Iowa 26 F 12. 5: John Fletcher Col 30-33 (Eng) AB; UIll summers 35, 37,38,40 BS in LS; Chicago 47,48,53 (LS) PhD. 6: Sp, Ger. 7: Libn Bolles Sch, Jacksonville Fla 34-38; Ref libn Pub Lib, Jacksonville Fla 38-42; Ref asst LC 42-45; Bibliogr Encyclopaedia Britannica, Chicago 45-47; Ed asst A N Marquis Co, Chicago 48-49; Libn Rollins Col 51-52; Visiting Prof Lib schs: Peabody, UIll, UDenver 53-55; Libn Golden Gate Col 55-65; Assoc Prof Dept of Lib Serv N Tex State U 65-. 8: Tchr, Even Dept, Lib Sch Cath U 42-45; Establ lib for San Francisco UN Conf 45, and served as Exec Libn; Fulbright Grant: Lib adv UTeheran, Iran 62-64; Lecturer Lib Sch UCeylon 64-65; Lib consul US Aid Panama summer 68; Ed bibliographies for "Ten Eventful Years," 4 v, Encyclopaedia Britannica (48); Ed "Who Knows - And What" (49). 9: ALA; SLA (Conv Chm 61, Sci Meetings Com 67-). 12: "The Story of the Encycloaedia Britannica, 1768-1943," hD diss, microfilm only (58). 13: Yes. 14: Ref, bibliog, admin, hist of printing, lib hist, compar libnship. 15: N Tex State Univ Dept of Lib Serv, Denton Tx 76203.

KRUSE, RHODA E(MMA). b Brooklyn NY 8 Ag 29. 5: Bethany Col 47-51 (Eng) BA (magna cum laude); Pratt 53-54 MLS; Brooklyn Col 51-52; Columbia 55 (LS). 6: Sp, Fr, Ger. 7: Recording clerk Brooklyn Savings Bank, Brooklyn NY 51-53; Clerk NY Pub Lib summer 53; Tchr of lib NYC Bd of Educ Girls' High Sch, Brooklyn 54-57; Staff San Diego Pub Lib summer 56, 57-62, Sr libn 62-. 9: ALA; CalLA. 10: Pacific Beach Woman's Club; acific Beach Town Coun; San Diego Hist Soc; Beta Phi Mu. 13: Yes. 14: Ref, young adult, Californiana, Hispanic materials. 15: 876 Reed ave, San Diego Ca 92109.

KRUSHEL, RUTH L (SMITH). b NYC 13 N 22. 5: Hunter Col 38-42 (Sociol) BA; Queens Col 55-62 (LS) MS. 7: Prof libn Manhasset Pub Sch, Manhasset NY 57-58, Sch libn 58-59; Child libn Bryant Pub Lib, Roslyn NY 60; Sch libn Locust Valley Pub Sch, Locust Valley NY 59-61; Sch libn Syosset Sr High Sch, Syosset NY summer 61; Sch libn Herricks Jr High Sch, New Hyde Park NY 61-65; Sch libn N Shore Jr High Sch, Glen Head LI NY 65-66; Sch libn Jericho Jr High Sch, Jericho NY 66-. 8: Nominating Com, Nassau-Suffolk Lib Assoc 59-60; Libn at Lib/USA NY World's Fair 65. 9: NYStateLA; NYStateTchrsA. 10: Brownies; Audubon; & other conservationist clubs; Nat Trust for Hist Preserv; Soc of Archit Histns. 14: Ref. 15: 460 Round Hill rd, Roslyn Hts NY 11577.

KRUSKO, VILMA M. b Allentown Penn. 5: Kent State 38-41, 43-45; West Res 48 BSLS. 6: Hungarian. 7: Reservations clk Capitol Airlines, Cleveland Ohio 45-46; Cleveland (Ohio) Pub Lib: Jr lib aide 47-48, Y-a asst 48-51, Asst br libn 51-62, Coord wk with y-a 62-. 9: ALA; -YASD (Latin Amer Bklist Com, chm Nomin Com 68); CathLA; OhioLA. 10: Womens Nat Bk Assn; Cleveland Pub Lib Staff Assn. 13: Yes. 14: Ya serv. 15: 389 Kenilworth rd, Bay Village Oh 44140.

KRUUT, EVALD. b Kohtla Estonia 6 D 27. 4: Lilja S Riim. 5: Macalester Col 52-54 (Eng) BA; UMinn 58-60 9ls0 ma. 6: Estonian, Ger, Fr, Russian, Sp, Lat. 7: Libn Dow Corning Tech Lib, Hemlock Mich 60-. 8: Established a Lib & Info Center for Dow-Corning Corp, Electronic Products Div (Hemlock Mich) 60-61; Worked out a system for automatic retrieval of Patent Info (Hemlock Mich) 62-63. 9: SLA (Aerospace Div). 12: Ed "The Silicon Digest: A Monthly Review of Lit on High Purity Silicon" (64-); "Oxygen in Silicon," an annotated bibliog; etc. 14: Info retrieval & systems, ref. 15: 3800 Leonard lane, Midland Mi 48040.

KRUZAS, ANTHONY T(HOMAS). b Brooklyn NY 23 Jl 14. 4: Florence Massulis. 5: Polytech Inst of Brooklyn 31-36 (Chem); City Col (NY) 47-50 (Statistics) BBA (magna cum laude); UMich 50-51 AMLS, 56-60 (LS) PhD. 7: Free lance photographer Brooklyn NY 45-49; USArmyAF (Sgt) 42-45; Assoc libn Med Center UKan 51-52; Asst libn SUNY Col of Ceramics (Alfred NY) 52-56; Dept of Lib Sci UMich: Instr 56-60, Asst Prof 60-64, Assoc Prof 64-68, Prof 68-. 8: Ed consul, Gale Research Co, Detroit Mich 61-. 9: SLA; ALA-ACRL; ASIS. 10: Beta Gamma Sigma. 12: Jt ed "Statistics Sources" (62); Ed "Directory of Special Libraries and Information Centers" 63 2nd ed, 2 v (68-69); Co-ed "Research Centers Directory" (65), "Statistical Survey of Special Libraries" (65), "Business and Industrial Libraries in the United States, 1820-1940" (65). 13: Yes. 14: Spec libs, lit of sci, documentation, info ret. 15: 1810 Longshore dr, Ann Arbor Mi 48105.

KRYSZAK, WAYNE D (DOUGLAS). b Canton Ohio 9 N 36. 4: Sarah J Bauer. 5: Kent State 54-58 (Ind Psych) BS in BA, 58-59 (Clinical Psych), 64-65 MS in LS. 6: Fr. 7: Readers adv DCPub Lib 61-64; Readers adv Akron Pub Lib, Akron Ohio 64-65; Libn bus & tech div DC Pub Lib 65-68, Chief bus div 68-. 9: ALA; DCLA. 10: Sec Com, Town of Cottage City 68-; Police Com, Town of Cottage City 68-; Md Munic League 68-; Munic Police Assn of Prince George Co 68-. 14: Ref. 15: 4117 Cottage ter, Cottage City Md 20722.

KRZYS, RICHARD ANDREW. b Cleveland 30 Ap 34. 5: John Carroll U 52-56 (Span) BSS; NMStateU 56-57 (Span) MA; UDenver 57-58 (LS) MA, Case West Res 58-65 (LS) PhD. 6: Sp, Fr, Portu. 7: Asst in ref Cleveland Pub Lib 58-60; Fulbright Stud Bogota Colombia 60-61; Instr Modern Langs John Carroll U 61-62; Ref libn 62-64; Grad asst West Res Lib Sch 64-65; Asst Prof of LS Fla State U 65; Assoc Prof of LS LIU 67-69; Asst Dir Sch of Lib Serv Dalhousie U 69-. 9: ALA; FlaLA. 11: Fulbright Scholarship Colombia 60-61. 12: "Education for Librarianship in Colombia" Doctoral disser, West Res U (65) ; "A History of Education for Librarianship in Colombia" (69). 13: Yes. 14: Ref, hist of bks & libs, comparative libnship (Latin Amer Area). 15: Sch of Lib Serv Dalhousie Univ, Halifax Nova Scotia Canada.

KRZYZANOWSKI, JAN. b Wilmo Poland 8 Ja 06. 4: Jadwiga Maliszewska. 5: Col J Lelevel (Wilmo Poland) 17-26 (Math Sci); Mil Col (Poland) 26-29 (Mil) BSc in MSc; Mil Lib Course 33 Qualified trained Libn; Gen Staff Col (Warsaw) 36-38 MSc in Mil Sc ; US Com & Gen Staff Col (Ft Leavenworth) 45 06: Polish, Russian, Fr. 7: 2nd Lt-Maj Polish Army, Poland, France, England 29-49, Supv Regimental Lib Poland 33-35 ; Supv microprint lab & lib Polish HQ London 42-44; Clk Toronto 50-59; Asst libn Engnr Lib McGill U 60-62; Instr Exp Med & Surg U Montreal: Codifier & documentalist 62, Asst libn 63, Chief Libn 64-. 9: Internat Fed for Documentation. 10: Royal C on Montreal; Polish Ex Gen-Staff Offrs Assn, London. 11: French Croix de Guerre wit h silver star; Polish Gallantry Cross (4 times). 14: Documentation, lib automation. 15: 2990 Ed-Montpetit blvd, Montreal 250 Que Can.

KU, PETER CHIA-SHAN. b Kwantang China 8 Ap 38. 4: Sophia Shih Chung. 5: Tawain Provincial Chung HsingU 56-60 (Law) BA; UMinn 63-66 (LS) MA; E CarU 66-68 (Educ Admin) MA Ed. 6: Chinese. 7: 2nd Lt Army Force of Republic of China, Taiwan China 60-61; Tchr Provincial Ind & Voc Sch, Taiwan 61-63; Catlgr E CarU Lib 66-68, Asst Prof & hd circ dept 68-. 9: ALA; NCLA (dir Jr Mem RT). 10: Kappa Delta Pi. 14: Admin, automation, catlg. 15: 1311 E 2nd st, Greenville NC 27834.

KUBAL, GENE JOYCE. b Crown Point Ind 26 Jl 28. 5: Ind U 46-50 (Soc Sci) BS; Penn State U summers 51, 53-55 (Educ) M Ed; UDenver 55-56 (LS) MA. 7: Libn Jr High Sch, Muskegon Heights Mich 50-53; Libn Jr-Sr High Sch, Crown Point Ind 53-55; Libn Spec Serv Sect: Augsburg Germany 56-58, Ft Gulick CZ 59-61, 8th US Army, Korea 61-63; Chief maintenance sect Div of Lending Nat Agric Lib, Wash DC 63-65, Libn spec bibliog 65-66, Ref 66-67; Catlgr Agency for Intl Development, Wash DC 67-69; Gen ref libn The Army Lib, Wash DC 69-. 09: ALA; SLL; DCLA. 10: Pi Lambda Theta. 12: "Cooperation in Agriculture 1954-64," an annotated bibliography. 13: Yes. 14: Catlg, ref. 15: 308-1/2 S Fairfax st, Alexandria Va 22314.

KUCERA, LADISLAU (V(LADIMIR). b Prague Czechoslovakia 20 Ja 27. 4: Jeannine Kremenova. 5: Asst hd Dept of Planning PLYNOPROJEKT, Prague 54-64; Asst catlgr YaleU Lib 65-66, Catlgr 67-69, Sr catlgr 69-. 6: Czech, Fr, Ger. 7: Asst hd Dept of Planning PLYNOPROJEKT, Prague 54-64; Asst catlgr Yale U Lib 65-66, Catlgr 67-69, Sr catlgr 69-. 10: Beta Phi Mu. 14: Catlg. 15: 1015 Whalley ave, New Haven Ct 06515.

KUCHAR, ROMAN V(OLODYMYR). b Lviv Ukraine 21 F 20. 4: Adelheid (Nagl) Kuchar. 5: Lviv University (USSR) 39-41 (Slavistics); Heidelberg U (Germany) 46-48 (Russian, Ger) MA; UColo 51-52 (Music) BM; Pratt 57-59 MLS; Ukraine Free U (Munich Germany) -62 (Slavic/studies) PhD. 6: Ger, Russian, Ukrainian, Polish. 7: Lecturer Internat Refugee Org, Amberg Germany 48-49; Emigration off Internat Refugee Org, Frankfurt Munich Germany 49-51; Free lance writer, music performer, Munich Germany, NYC 52-56; Libn Brooklyn Pub Lib 57-59; Asst libn State UCol (Potsdam NY) 59-62; Tchr Potsdam High Sch, Potsdam NY 61-62; Asst Prof Ft Hays Kan State Col 62-, Assoc Prof 66-. 8: Linguistic Specialist (Slavic) for Neb Curriculum Development Center (62-); Ft Hays Dir for Amer Assn Tchrs of German Contest (63-65); Vis Prof, UMunich summer 68; Slavic res in Europe fall 68. 9: NEA. 10: Shevchenko Sci Soc; Amer Assn Tchrs of German; Amer Assn Advancement of Slavic Studies; AAUP; Phi Kappa Phi; Phi Eta Sigma. 12: "Hearts Aflame," book of poetry (64); Co-ed: "Original Works," art, poetry, lit journal (66-); "Svitannia" (The Dawn), Journal of poetry & lit (67-). 13: Yes. 14: Slavic & German lit, Bibliog, bk review, Slavic area study. 15: 2402 Canal blvd, Hays Ka 67601.

KUDRYK, OLEG. b Rohatyn Ukraine 14 D 12. 4: Sophie H Dedynsky. 5: ULvov 33-37 (Law, Pol Sci) LLM, 37-38 (Econ) MA; UVienna 45-46; UMich 59-60 (LS) MA. 6: Ger, Polish, Ukrainian, Czech, Russian, Lat, Gk, Ital, Slovak, Church Slovak, Bulgarian. 07: Manager, Co-op.-Trade & Agric Soc, Chodorov Poland 38-40; Manager Import-Export Corp, Cracov Poland 40-44; Tchr Commercial Sch, ULm Germany 46; Admin UNRRA & IRO Centers, Stuttgart Germany 47-49; Asst treas & manager Self-reliance Fed Credit Union, Detroit 53-60; Rep & consul Prudential Insurance Co, Detroit 53-60; Catlg libn Ind U Libs 60-63, Head order libn 63-. 8: Consul Stillman Col Lib, Tuscaloosa Ala 65. 9: ALA; Amer Econ Assn; Amer Acad Pol & Soc Scis; Midwest Acad LA; Ohio Valley Gp Tech Serv Libns. 14: Bibliog control, acquis, admin, West & Central European Area Studies. 15: 120 N Bryan, Bloomington In 47403.

KUGLER, RUBEN FRED. b Chicago 31 O 14. 4: Lorna Todd. 5: Los Angeles City Col 33-41 (Liberal Arts) AA; UCLA 46-49 (Soc Sci) BA; USoCal 49-50 (Hist) MA, 50-53 (Hist) PhD, 58-59 MSLS. 6: Fr. 7: Clerk & Sgt- Maj US Army, US & Europe 43-46; Tchr Laguna Beach High Sch, Laguna Beach Cal 49-50; Ref libn Cal State Col(Los Angeles) 59-. 9: CalLA; SoCal Hist Guild. 10: Amer Fed Tchrs; ACLU; Cal State Col (Los Angeles) Center for the Study of Armament and Disarmament; Cal Democ Coun. 12: 'U B Phillips' Use of Sources,' in S Fine & G Brown, eds, "The American Past," v 1 (65). 13: Yes. 14: Ref (hist, pol sci, law). 15: 2951 Canal ave, Long Beach Ca 90810.

KUHL, MARY JANE (WARD). b Newark NJ 24 D 24. 4: Norman A Kuhl. 5: Barry Col 42-46 (Eng) AB; UNC 65-66 MSLS. 7: Owner-builder House Construction and Sales, Charlottesville Va 49-61; Sec-receptionist Layne Inc of Fla, Hallandale 61-63; Off mgr fla Mobile Home Parks Inc, Clearwater 63-65; Asst libn U of South Fla Lib 67-. 9: FlaLA. 14: Ref, rare bks, Floridiana. 15: 103 Shore dr, Dunedin Fl 33528.

KUHLMAN, A(UGUSTUS) FREDERICK. b Hubbard Iowa 3 S 1889. 4: Virginia Wood. 5: Northwestern Col 16 BS; UChicago 22 (Sociol) AM, 29 (Sociol) Ph D. 6: Ger. 7: Morale off (Sgt) USA 18-19; Dir of surveys Amer Red Cross 19-20; Asst Prof sociol UMo 20-24, Assoc Prof sociol 24-29; Assoc dir libs UChicago 29-36; Dir Joint Univ Libs, Nashville 36-60; Consul Academic Libs 60-. 8: Consul on 23 new lib bldgs and on remodeling of or additions to 8; Surveys of 31 acad libs (admin, collections, use, & serv, part-time teacher, Peabody Lib Sch. 9: ALA (Coun 32-36, chm Pub Docs Com 32-36 and ed of "Proceedings"; Chm Com Archives and Libs 36-40 and ed of "Proceedings"; Chm Univ & Ref Libns RT 38; chm -ACRL Publications Com 39-41 and ed of "College and Research Libraries); SELA; Assn SEast Research Libs (helped again; chm 56-60); TennLA (pres 54-55); Nashville Lib Club (pres 53-54). 10: Rotarian; member Christ Episcopal Church (Nashville); V U Chapter AAUP. 11: Fellow Amer Lib Inst; Phi Beta Kappa. 12: "A Guide to Material on Crime and Criminal Justice" (29); Auth, 3 chaps survey "University of Chicago Libraries" (32); "Survey of the University of Mississippi Library" (40); "Survey North Texas Regional Libraries" (43); "Cooperation in Library Development in St Pauk (52); "Survey of Six Libraries of the Arkansas Foundation of Associated Colleges" (58); "Some Library Problems and opportunities of the Atlanta University Center" (prelim report) (66); "Consumer Survey of New Serial Titles" for Jt Com Union List of Serials and LC (67); Co-ed "Report on Some Library Problems and Proposed Solutions for the Atlanta University center" (68). 13: Yes. 14: Acad libs, planning bldgs, surveys of admin, collections, use, serv, and tchg. 15: 1908 Blakemore ave, Nashville Tn 37212.

KUHN, ELEANOR ESTHER (WILLIAMS). b Liberty Penn 8 Jl 24. 4: Tracy Miller Kuhn. 5: Lock Haven State Col 42-45 (Eng) BS; William & Mary summer 46 (LS); PennStateU summer 47, 48 (LS); Clarion State Col summer 53, 54 (LS); UPittsburgh summers 63-65 (LS) MA, 69 Advanced Certif, 69-. 06: Sp. 7: Libn Green Free Lib, Canton Penn 45-49, 53- 56; Sch libn Clinton NJ 51-52; Libn USArmy, Okinawa 49-51; Tchr, Kane Penn 52-53; Sch libn, Wingate Penn 56-57; Sch libn, State Col Penn 57-65; Col libn, Lock Haven Penn 65-. 9: NEA; ALA; PennStateEA. 10: Lib of the Month Award (twice in Okinawa). 13: Yes. 14: Acquis, lib instr. 15: RR1 Mill Hall Penn 17751.

KUHN, MARTIN A. b Mannheim Germany 11 Ag 24. 4: Laura Pape. 5: Queens Col 44-48 (Pol Sci) BA; Columbia 48-49 (LS) MS; 53-56 (Pol Sci). 6: Ger, Fr. 7: Finance Corps USArmy Ft Dix NJ 46-47; Libn USNaval Shipyard, Brooklyn NY 48; Chief ref & life sci div City Col of NY 49-62; Libn & assoc prof SI Commun Col 62-67, Asst dean day session 68, Assoc dean day session 68-. 8: Memb, evaluation teams, Middle States Assn 63-. 9: ALA; NYLA; NYState Jr Cols; APSA. 10: AAUP. 12: "Morris R Cohen," Spec Supp of "Journal of the History of Ideas" (56); Co-ed "Debate Index" (64). 13: Yes. 14: Admin, ref. 15: 36 White Beeches dr, Dumont NJ 07628.

KUHN, WARREN BOEHM. b Jersey City NJ 12 F 24. 5: NYU 42-43, 46-48 (Eng, Hist) AB; Columbia 49-50 (LS) MS. 6: Sp, Ger. 7: Ordnance Corps (AUS): Instr Depot Supply Sch, Aberdeen Proving Ground Md 43-45 (2nd Lt), Chief Publs Br Red River Ordnance Depot, Texarkana Tex 45-46 (1st Lt), Asst chief Mil Instrs Sch & Hist Off, Aberdeen Proving Ground Md 46 (1st Lt); Ref Asst NYPub Lib 46-50; Circ libn UNM Lib 50, 52-55; Ordnance Corps (Reserve) Pub Info Off White Sands Proving Grounds NM 50-51 (1st Lt); Ordnance Corps (Reserve) Pub Info Off First Corps Hq (Advance) US 8th Army Korea 51-52 (1st Lt); Asst libn Ariz StateU 55-56; Asst libn for circ Princeton U Lib 56-65; Libn of the Undergrad Lib & asst dir Stanford U Libs 65-67; Dir of libs Iowa State U 67-. 08: Lecturer in Col & Univ Lib Admin, Grad Sch of Lib Sci Drexel 62. 9: ALA (NYWorld's Fair Adv Com 63-64, Com for Circ Serv); -ACRL (Com on Standards 61-63, Jt Com (with Amer Assn Cols) to consider the Problems of Col Libs); -LAD (Lib Costs Com, circ serv sect 68-70); -ASD (sec Rel with State & Loc Assns Com); NJLA (pres Col & Univ Lib Sect 60-61, chm Publ Com 58-60); NMLA (treas 54-55, chm Scholarship Com 54-55); SWLA (chm Recr Com 55-56); CalLA; IowaLA (Chm Rec Com). 10: AAUP; Rotary Internat. 12: Ed "Preliminary List of Titles in the Julian Street Library" (66); Ed "New Jersey Library Association Newsletter" (58-60). 13: Yes. 14: Admin, circ, bldgs , automation, undergrad serv. 15: Lib Iowa State Univ, Am es Ia 50010.

KUHNER, DAVID (ARNOLD). b Columbus Ohio 20 Mr 21. 5: Ohio StateU 39-43 (Phys Sci) BS; UMiami (Fla) 50-51 (Educ) MEd; UCal (Berkeley) 61-62 MLS. 6: Fr, Ger. 7: 1st Lt USAF Texas, Miss 43-46; Tech writer Med Research Found, Miami Fla 49-55; Sci writer Fla Development Commsn, Tallahassee Fla 57-61; Catlgr Stanford U 62-63; Head ref Stanford Grad Sch of Bus Jackson Lib 64-66; Chief ref John Crerar Lib, Chicago 66-. 9: SLA; CalLA; ALA. 12: Ed

"Stanford Library Bulletin" (63); Ed & pub "Map of Florida Industry and Science" (61). 13: Yes. 14: Admin , ref, lib netwks. 15: c/o John Crerar Lib, 35 W 33 st, Chicago Il 60616.

KUHNER, ROBERT A(LAN). b nyc 21 Ag 37. 5: Hunter Col 55-59 (Art) BFA, 60-63 MA; Rutgers 64-66 MLS. 6: Fr. 7: Hunter Col Lib 60-61, Lecturer 62-63; Libn Queens Borough Pub Lib, NY 64-67; Arch libn CCNY Sch of Arch 67-. 9: ALA; Amer Assn of Arch Bibliogr; SLA (NY Chap; Picture Div; Soc Sci Div). 14: Arch & urban studies libnship. 15: 792 Columbus ave, New York NY 10025.

KUHNS, FREDERICK IRVING. b Dayton Ohio 19 Mr 03. 4: Kathryn Zaharee Taylor. 6: Fr, Ger. 7: Asst Prof of Religion Drake U 48-50; Research assoc State Hist Soc of Iowa, Iowa City Iowa 50-55; Dean of the Chapel, Rocky Mountain Col 52-55, Dir of the Lib 55-60; Head libn Ohio No U 60-67, Ref libn 67-. 8: Del, Reg Coun of Internat Educ UPittsburgh 65-66. 9: ALA; Amer Soc Church Hist; OhioLA. 10: Presbyterian Hist Soc, Phila. 12: "A History of Illinois Congregational and Christian Churches," with others (44); "A History of Iowa," with others (52); "A History of Montana," with others (57); "The American Home Missionary Society in Relation to the Antislavery Controversy in the Old Northwest, 1826-1861(59). 13: Yes. 14: Ref, a-v aids, lib programming & design. 15: 620 Conley ave, Ada Oh 45810.

KUHNS, MYRLE RUTH. b 1 Ja 29. 5: Kutztown State Col 46-50 (Educ, LS) BS in Ed; American U 52-56 (Pub Admin) MS; Rutgers 59-64 MS in LS. 7: Lib asst US Civil Serv Commsn Wash DC 51-55, Ed clerk 55-56; Asst libn Lock Haven State Col 57-58; Co-libn Butler High Sch, Butler NJ 58-60; Libn Catasauqu High Sch, Catasauqua Penn 61-. 9: NEA; ALA; AASchL; PennStateEA; PennLA. 10: Lutheran Church Women. 14: Ref. 15: Rte 3, Allentown Pa 18104.

KUIPER, JOHN BENNETT. b Ann Arbor Mich 22 Je 28. 4: Ellen Tredway. 5: UKy 46-50 (Art) BA; UMiami 55 (Fr-Dramatic Art); UIpwa 55-60 (Dramatic-Art-Speech) MA 57, (Radio-TV- film) PhD. 6: Fr. 7: US Army Signal Corps-Photo Off 51-53; Cinematographer Reela Filma, Miami Fla 53-55; Film supv UIowa (Iowa City) 58-65, Assoc Prof of film & TV 60-65; Adj Prof of film AmerU (Wash DC) 65-; Hd Motion Picture Sect LC 65-. 8: Sec Soc of Cinematologists 6-64, Pres 65-67; Chm Curriculum Com Univ Film Assn 61-. 9: Univ Film Assn; Soc of Cinematologists; Speech Assn of Amer; SAA; Wash Film Coun. 11: Dir of prize winning short film "Autumn" (60). 13: Yes. 14: A-v archives & ref wk, research in mass media. 15: 6305 Stoneham rd, Bethesda Md 20034.

KUJAWSKI, WILMA F(RANCES). b Rochester NY. 5: URochester 32-36 (Chem) BA; Columbia 38-39 (LS) BS. 6: Ger, Russian, Fr, Ital, Sp. 7: Catlgr Columbia U 38-39; Libn Brooklyn Pub Lib 39-40; Libn Rochester Pub Lib, Rochester NY 40-44; Libn Manhattan Eng Proj URochester 44-46; Libn Distillation Products Ind, Rochester NY 46-. 9: ACS (Rochester, NY, Sect; Sec, ed & bus mgr of publs); ASIS; MedLA; SLA (chm, sec-treas Pharmaceut Sect; Bus mgr unlisted drugs, Rochester, NY Chap; sec-treas); Monroe Co NY Lib Club (chm, sec). 10: AAUW. 12: "Annotated Bibliography of Vitamin E," v 1-7. 13: Yes. 14: Ref, bibliog. 15: Distillation Products Industries, Rochester NY 14603.

KULA, SAM. b Montreal 11 O 32. 4: Eleanor Phillips. 5: Sir George Williams U 49-53 (Hist) BA; McGill 53-54 (Hist); U Coll(London) 58-59 Diploma Lib; USoCal 63- (Cinema). 6: Fr. 7: Archivist Dominion Archives of Canada, Ottawa 54-57; Immigration Off Dept of Cit & Immig, Ottawa 57-58; Deputy curator Nat Film Archive, London 59-62; Libn USoCal 62-67; Producer/writer med info project 67-68; Archivist Amer Film Inst 68-. 9: ALA; CALLA; SMPTE; Soc of Cinematologists; Wash Film Coun. 12: "Bibliography of Film Libnship," (67). 14: Catalog & preserv of motion pictures. 15: 3942 Harrison st NW, Washington Dc 20015.

KULAS, THADDEUS ALAN. b Westmoreland Co Penn 28 Jl 40. 4: Cherie Pitsch. 5: Clarion State Col 59-63 (LS, Soc Studies) BS; UPittsburgh 65-69 MLS , 69 Advanced Certif in LS. 07: Head libn Kiski Area Sr High Sch, Vandergrift Penn 63-. 8: Adv Comm on Penn Sch Lib Standards, 68. 9: NEA; ALA; PennLA; Penn StateEA; Westmoreland Co LA Coun of Sch Libns Surburban Pittsburgh. 10: Beta Phi Mu. 14: Ref, med libs. 15: RD 2 Box 191, Leechburg Pa 15656.

KULCHYCKY, WALTER. b Kulchytzy Ukraine 19 Jl 20. 4: Alexandra Dziadiw. 5: UKrainian FreeU (Munich) 46-52 (Philol) Master; Rutgers 57-59 MLS. 6: Polish, Ukrainian, Russian. 7: Gen asst Queens Borough Pub Lib, Jamaica NY 59-60, Ref libn 60-62, Bkmob libn 62-63, Br libn 63-66, Hd bkmob div 66-. 9: NYStateLA. 14: Ref, adult serv. 15: 86-08 107th st, Richmond Hill NY 11418.

KULESZA, BERNICE R. b Seattle 13 D 17. 4: Edmund G Kulesza. 5: UWash 34-38 (Eng Lit) BA, 38-39 BA in LS. 7: Libn Seattle Pub Lib 39-42, 61-67; Phoenix Pub Lib 68-. 9: ALA;-AASchL; SRLA. 14: Ref. 15: Phoenix Pub Lib, 12 E McDowell, Phoenix Az 85004.

KULLMAN, BARRIE JACQUELINE. b Vancouver BC Can 19 Ap 45. 5: UBC 64-67 (Eng/Theatre) BA, 67-68 BLS. 7: Child libn London Pub Lib & Art Mus, Lond Ont Can 68-69; 3rd libn child adult's wk Vancouver Pub Lib, Vancouver BC Can 69-. 8: Chm Young Canada's Bk week, Lond Ont Can 68. 9: CanLA. 13: Yes. 14: Child & ya wk. 15: 20624-48th ave, Langley BC Can.

KULP, AIMEE KATHERINE. b Mercersburg Penn 28 O 24. 5: Wilson Col 42-46 (Fine Arts) AB; Drexel 47-48 BS in LS. 6: Sp, Fr, Ger. 7: Asst to alumni sec Mercersburg Acad summers 42-44; Catlg clerical asst Sterling Mem Lib Yale U 46-47; Ser catlgr Firestone Mem Lib Princeton U 48-49; Hd libn Albert M Swank Lib Mercersburg Acad 49-. 9: ALA; NCTE; NEA; Cumberland Valley LA (corr sec); PennLA; PennASchL. 10: Consul Bd: Fendrick Lib Assn, Mercersburg Penn; Albert M Swank Lib, Mercersburg Acad. 13: Yes. 14: Ref, rare bks, instr materials. 15: 33 Linden ave, Mercersburg Pa 17236.

KULP, ARTHUR C. b Ithaca NY 4 Ap 21. 4: Helen Reddout. 5: Cornell U 38-42 (Hist) AB; Columbia 46-47 BS in LS; UIll 51-54 (LS) MS. 6: Fr. 7: Cornell U: Asst circ libn 47-49, Act circ libn 49-50, Circ libn 50-. 9: ALA; NYLA (dir Col & Univ Sect 65-67); Five Associated Univ Libs (chm Access Com 68-69). 10: Cornell Pub Lib Associate; Boy Scouts; Rotary Club; Beta Phi Mu. 12: "Historical Development of Storage Libraries in America," ACRL Microcards (54). 15: 116 Irving pl, Ithaca NY 14850.

KULPA, LORRAINE A. b Buffalo NY 4 Je 39. 5: UBuffalo 57-61 (Hist) BA; SUNY (Buffalo) 61-64 LLB; Syracuse 64-65 MSLS. 6: Fr, Russian. 7: Ref libn Los Angeles Co Law Lib Los Angeles 65-67 Asst law libn for ref & circ CornellU Law Lib, 67-. 9: AALL. 10: Kappa Beta Pi. 13: Yes. 14: Legal research & ref. 15: 100 Fairview Sq apt 3d, Ithaca Ny 14850.

KUMATZ, TAD G. b Honolulu Hawaii 31 Mr 29. 5: FriendsU 48-52 (Sociol) BA; Syracuse 52-54 (LS) MS. 6: Japanese, Chinese. 7: Cadet lib ach Syracuse 52-54; Jr libn NYC Pub Lib 54; Humanities res lib Hunter Col 55-58; Res libn Hofstra Col 58-59; Circ libn pratt Inst 59-67, Asst libn 67-. 8: Lectr in libnship, Pratt Inst 65-. 9: ALA; AAUP. 10: Beta Phi Mu. 14: Admin. 15: 405 E 54th st, New York NY 10022.

KUN, LESLIE ALBERT. b Kenderes Hungary 29 S 09. 4: Matild M Posta. 05: Trenton Jr Col 61-62; Rider Col 56-64; Trenton State Col 61-63; Rutgers U 58-60 MLS. Perm certif: lib sci, Ger, soc studies tchr, NJ; Jr Col Libn, Fla; Budapest (Hungary) BS, MA. 6: Ger, Hungarian, Lat, Fr. 7: Catlgr Trenton Jr Col 59-61; Trenton Pub Schs, Trenton NJ: Asst libn 61-62, Libn 61-64, Sch Libn 64-. 9: NJ TA; NJEA; NJ second sch ta; Mercer Co EA; Trenton Tchr Educ Assn. 10: Nat Cong Parents & Tchrs 14: Second sch libnship, ref, map libnship. 15: Robert Morris apts n21, Morrisville Pa 19067.

KUNCAITIS, YADWIGA (CERNIAUSKAS). b Moscow Russia. 4: Justo Kuncaitis. 5: UKaunas (Lithuania) 37-39 (Humanities, Lit); UVilnius (Lithuania) 39-41 (Humanities, Drama); Inst of Lang (Montreux Switz) 45-47; Nat Univ of Cordoba (Argentina) 51-56 (Eng, Educ) MA; West Res 61-63 MSLS. 6: Ger, Lithuanian, Polish, Russian, Sp, Fr. 7: Tr UCordoba (Argentina) Med Sch Lib 53-57; Instr of scientific Ger UCorboda Inst Math, Astronomy & Physics 57-59; Libn-tr UCordoba Observatory 57-59; Asst catlg dept West Res Freiberger Lib 59-62, Ref libn 69-; Hd sci libn Millis Sci Ctr 63-68; Visiting prof lib sci UPuerto Rico Inst Libnship 68-69. 8: Ref libn Lib/USA Info Ctr NY Worlds Fair 64; Consul to sci lib UCuyo (Argentina) 67. 9: ALA-ACRL; SLA. 10: Cleveland Coun on World Affairs; Beta Phi Mu; Case West Res; Sch Lib Sci Alumni Assn. 13: Yes. 14: Intl libnship, Union catlgs, ref. 15: 23202 McCann st, Cleveland Oh 44128.

KUNDZINS, ILGA L. b Tartu Estonia. 5: ULatvia Riga Latvia 44 Magistur iuris; Columbia 56-58 MSLS. 6: Fr, Ger, Swedish, Latvian, Russian, Lat. 7: Libn Assembly of Captive European Nations, NYC 57-59; Asst libn Engnr Socs Lib, NYC 59-64; Libn Hydrocarbon Research Inc, NYC 64-. 9: SLA. 10: Alumni Fedn of Columbia U. 14: Ref, bibliog, transl (tech lit, chem engnr, petroleum proc). 15: 251 W 98 st, New York NY 10025.

KUNITZ, ISADORA (DEROW). b Brooklyn NY 11 O 40. 4: Dr Stephen J Kunitz. 5: Smith 59-62 (Hist) BA; UKy 64-65 MSLS. 7: Summer asst Yale Collection of Amer Lit 61; Page & desk asst Smith Col Lib 59-62; Research asst "Notable Amer Women," Smith 61-62; Child libn South Ave Br Lib Rochester Pub Lib, Rochester NY 62-64; Child Libn Tuba City Pub Lib, Tuba City Ariz 65-67; Bk reviewer Sch Lib Journal NYC 65-; Sch Lib Serv, New Haven Conn 67-68; Volunteer-Reading tutor New Haven Pub Schs, New Haven Conn 69-. 9: ALA. 14: Child serv. 15: 13 Marlen dr, North Haven Ct 06473.

KUNKEL, JOHN LEIGHTON. b Petersburg Neb 13 My 13. 4: Joyce Ann Jouvenat. 5: Doane Col 36 (Econ, Hist) AB; UNeb 59 (Educ Admin) MEd, 61 (Educ Admin) EdD; UDenver 65 (LS) MA. 7: Field engnr Aero Div Minneapolis Honeywell, Minneapolis 42-46; Self-employed McCook, Neb & WPalm Beach Fla 46-57; Instr sci math Maywood High Sch, Maywood Neb 57-58; Grad asst educ admin UNeb 58-59; Instr coordinator A-V U High Sch, Lincoln Neb 59-60; Supv A-V serv UNeb 60-64; Asst Prof Coordinating program for train sch libns, media spec Teachers Col UNeb 62-. 8: Tech Repr USAF for Honeywell 42-46. 9: NebState A-V Assn (Exec sec 63-). 10: Phi Delta Kappa; Lions Club; Lincoln Films Forum. 13: Yes. 14: Libnship educ, sch libs, tchr train, a-v, tchg machines, programmed instr. 15: 1010 Manchester, Lincoln Nb 68528.

KUNOFF, HUGO. b Tiege Russia 1 Ap 29. 4: Karla Skorsinski. 5: Mexico City Col 57-58 (Hist) BA; Columbia 59 MSLS. 6: Ger, Sp, Fr, Russian, Ital. 7: Ref asst NY Pub Lib 60-65; Libn for mod langs IndU 65-. 9: ALA. 10: Beta Phi Mu. 14: Sel, resources, akad libs. 15: 4313 Deekard dr, Bloomington In 47401.

KUNOFSKY, EDWARD. b NYC 4 Sp 40. 5: Brooklyn Col 57-61 (Mus) AB; NYU 61-62 (Mus Hist); Pratt Inst 64-68 MLS. 6: Sp, Yiddish, Hebrew, Ger. 7: Mus tchr Thomas Jefferson High Sch, Brooklyn NY 64-66; Libn Intermediate School 49, Brooklyn NY 66-. 8: Coord "Earn-a Book" prog of NYC Sch Dist 14, Brooklyn 69; Dir IS 49 Lib and Homework Ctr 68. 9: ALA; MusLA; Amer Musicol Soc; NYC Sch Libns Assn; NYC Mus Tchrs Assn. 10: United Fed Tchrs; B'nai B'rith. 14: Sch libnship, music libnship, ref. 15: 1055 E 42 st, Brooklyn NY 11210.

KUNSEMILLER, (RUTH) LUCILLE (BOLY). b Harviell Mo 23 O 17. 4: Charles Frederic Kunsemiller III. 5: Chaffey Col 35-36 (Fr) AA; UCal(Berkeley) 37-38 (Fr) AB. 6: Fr, Sp. 7: Chico State Col Lib: Circ libn 59-60, Natural & applied sci libn 60-61, Order libn 61-. 9: CalLA. 10: AAUW. 15: 1 Renee circle, Chico Ca 95926.

KUNSTMAN, JOANNE L. b Decatur Ill 21 Ja 31. 5: Concordia Col (Moorhead Minn) 51-55 (Eng) BA; Northwestern U 56-57 (Journalism); UNeb 57 (Educ); Catholic U 62-65 MS in LS. 6: Ger. 7: Bank clerk & receptionist Minneapolis 55; Ed asst DC Cook Publ Co Elgin Ill 56; Tchr Elgin Pub Schs, Elgin Ill 57; Tchr Lincoln Neb 58; Bkkeeper Montgomery Ward Williston ND & Wash DC 59-60; Lib asst Arlington Co Lib, Arlington Va 61-64, Child libn 64-66; Libn Old Charles Town Lib, Charles Town WVa 67-69; Catlgr Shippensburg State Col 69-. 9: ALA; WVaLA; Cumberland Valley LA (pres 69-70). 14: Ref, catlg, bk sel, readers adv, pub rel. 15: Ezra Lehman Memorial Lib, Shippensburg Pa 17257.

KUNTZ, HELEN HARTLEY. b Troy Ohio 19 Ja 20. 4: James Eugene Kuntz. 5: Ohio Wesleyan U 37-41 (Eng) BA; UIll summer 41 (Tchr-Libn); UWis 42-43 BLS. 7: Tchr Eng, Hist & sch libn Fairborn High Sch, Fairborn Ohio 41-42; Sub high sch libn Central High Sch & East High Sch, Madison Wis 43-44; Revisor for Lib Sch UWis (Madison) 44-45; Staff Libn First Methodist Church, Madison Wis 61-. 10: Phi Beta Kappa; Theta Alpha Phi; Kappa Delta Pi; Girl Scout ldr; Univ League Bk Club. 14: Ref. 15: 905 Harrison st, Madison Wi 53711.

KUNYCIA, MARIA B (FRELKIEWICZ). b Poland 7 D 04. 4: Serge Kunycia. 5: U Poznan3ski(Poland) 38 M PH; Drexel 57 MS in LS. 6: Polish, Ukrainian, Ger, Fr, Slavic. 7: Polskie Radio (Polish Broadcasting Corp), Warsaw 38-39; US Info Center America House, Ulm Germany 50-51; Insurance Co of North Amer, Phila 52-58; Princeton U Lib 58-62; Haverford Col Lib 62-. 8: Cataloged the Philip Ashton Rollins Collection of Western Americana, Princeton U Lib. 9: ALA-RTSD (Phila Chap). 12: "Julia Molin3ska-Woykowska,MPH thesis (Poznan3, 38). 15: 31 S Wyoming ave, Ardmore Pa 19003.

KUO, HELEN YAU-LING. b Philippines 28 S 39. 5: Chung Chi Col (Hong Kong) 57-58 (Math); St Mary Col (Xavier, Kan) 58-62 (Music Educ) BME; Kan State Tchrs Col 62-64 (LS) MS. 6: Eng, Chinese. 7: Ya libn, Council Bluffs Iowa 64-. 9: ALA; IowaLA. 14: Wk with youth & child. 15: 609 Willow ave, apt 6 Council Bluffs Ia 51501.

KUO, MARGARET JIN-SHU. b China 13 S 40. 5: Nat Taiwan U 59-63 (Foreign Langs & Lit) BA; Tex Woman's U 63-65 MLS. 6: Chinese, Fr, Japanese, Sp. 7: Stud asst Tex Woman's U Lib 65; Asst libn Aerospace Ind Assn Lib, Wash DC 65-66; Babcock & Wilcox Research Lib asst libn 66-67; Chem Abst Serv catlgr 67-. 14: Catlg, ref, adult educ. 15: B3 100 E Frambes ave, Columbus Oh 43207.

KUO, RICHARD D C. b Kwei-chow China 9 My 37. 4: Margaret P Y Kuo. 5: Nat TaiwanU 54-59 (Foreign Lang & Lit) BS; UOkla 63-65 MLS. 6: Chinese, Japanese. 7: Pol instr Reg regiment 55th Div 19th, Taiwan 59-61; Tchr Provincial Maio-li Middle Sch Taiwan 61-62; Tchr Maio-li Local High Sch, Taiwan 61-62; Asst ref coord Lake Co Pub Lib, Griffith Ind 66-67; Circ libn Tex SouthernU 67-. 10: Lake of 4 Seasons. 14: Circ, ref. 15: 6721 Plaza dr, Houston Tx 77021.

KUO, THOMAS C T. b Szechwan China 17 D 29. 4: Monica Li. 5: Nat CentralU (China) 50 (Hist) BA; UPittsburgh 58 (Pol Sci) MA; Rutgers 61 MLS; UPittsburgh 63 (Hist) MA, 69 (Hist) PhD. 06: Chinese, Fr, Japanese, English. 7: Ed-in-chief The Student Weekly Inc, Taipei Formosa 51-53; Ed "The Prelude", NYC 55-56; Catlgr UPittsburgh 61-65, Libn EAsian Lib 65-, Coun mem on Asian studies. 9: AHA; Assn Asian Studies. 11: Ford Grant for Studying The Chiense Communist Movement in Hoover Institution, StanfordU summer 67; Andrew Mellon Pre-doctoral Fellow, 67-69. 12: Com "Periodicals and Serials of the East Asian Library" (68); "The Chi nese Local History" (69). 14: Catlg, ref, admin. 15: E Asian Lib, U of Pittsburgh, Pittsburgh Pa 15213.

KUPERMAN, AGOTA (MADARAS). b Budapest Hungary 8 Ag 44. 4: David Kuperman. 5: Rutgers 62-66 (Ger Lit) BA; IndU 67-68 MLS. 6: Hungarian, Ger, Fr. 7: Bibliographic searcher order dept Indiana U 66-67; Ref libn regional campus libs Indiana U 68-. 14: Ref, adult serv. 15: 197 Walnut Grove Trailer ct, Bloomington In 47401.

KURAN, PATRICIA M. b Union NJ 28 Ag 29. 4: Jack P Kuran. 5: Rutgers 61 (Eng Lit) BA, 65 MSLS. 6: Fr. 7: Lab tech RCA Semiconductor Div, Somerville NJ 50-58; Libn RCA Electronic Cmpts & Devices, Somerville NJ 58-65; Tech doc specialist Bell Labs, Whippany NJ 66; Mgr info serv Amer Foundation for Mgt Research, Hamilton NY 67-. 9: SLA; ASIS; NMA; CPL. 14: Mgt of lib. 15: Spring st #7, Hamilton Ny 13346.

KURI, SALME (HUNERSON). b Taganrog Russia. 4: Karl M Kuri. 5: Tartu U(Estonia) 39-44 (Law); Go2ttingen U(Germany) 45-47, 48-49 (Law, Econ); Freiburg U(Germany) 47-48 (Law) IUD; Columbia U & Queens Col(NY) 50-52 (LS); Catholic U 52-55 MSLS. 6: Ger, Estonian, Finnish, Russian. 7: Catlgr-tr LC 52-55, Subj catlgr 55-59; Supv libn catlg & acquis Bur of the Census, Suitland Md 59-64; Asst libn Bur of the Census, Suitland Md 64-67; Hd post 51 imprints sect LC 67-69; Asst libn US Bureau of the Census, Wash Dc 69-. 8: Instr in Cataloging & Classification, Grad Sch, US Dept of Agric 62-67; Adjunct Prof org of Knowledge in libs, sch lib & info serv UMd 68. 9: SLA; ASIS; DCLA. 12: "Estonia, a Selected Bibliography," LC (58); "Bibliographical Guide to Estonian Studies," ACLS (63). 14: Catlg, acquis, bibliog, tchg, clsf, admin. 15: 5105 - 26 ave, Hillcrest Heights Md 20031.

KURMEY, WILLIAM JOHN. b Vancouver BC Can 7 Mr 40. 5: UBC 57-60 (Chem Math) BS; UChicago 60-61 (LS) AM. 06: Fr, Russian. 7: Research asst UChicago Grad Lib Sch 61; Libn UBC Lib circ div 62; Info spec IBM Data Systems Div Tech Info Center Poughkeepsie NY 62-64; Data processing consul Chicago Ill 65; Admin research asst UChicago Com on Human Development 65; Research asst UChicago Grad Lib Sch 65; Assoc Prof UToronto Sch Lib Sci 65-. 8: Research Consul IBM Tech Info Retrieval Center, Yorktown Heights NY 64-65; Lib Systems consul 67-68; Consul Sci Secretariat, Priry Coun Of f G & V of Can, Ottawa Ont 68. 9: ACM; SLA; STWP; ASIS; Inst Profess Libns Ont. 10: AAAS; Beta Phi Mu. 13: Yes. 14: Info storage & retrieval. 15: Sch of Lib Sci UToronto 167 College st, Toronto 2B Canada.

KURODA, ANDREW Y. b Yokosuka Japan 29 D 10. 4: Julia Noda. 5: Meiji Gakuin Col (Tokyo) 29-33 (Lit) BA (equiv); Auem 34-37 (Thwol) BTh; NY Theol Sem 37-38 (Theol) STM. 6: Japanese. 7: Minister Japanese Methodist Ch, Washington Ore 38-43; Instr of Japanese UMich (Ann Arbor) 43-44; Research analyst Off of Strategic Serv, NYC 44-45; Prin catlgr Japanese Sect LC 46-59, Bibliog & ref libn 59-64, Asst hd Orientalia Div 64-65, Hd 65-. 8: Minister Japanese

Unitarian Fellowship, Wash DC 63-. 9: Assn for Asian Studies. 11: Superior Accomplishment Award LC 52. 12: Co-tr of Masanori Ito's "The End of the Imperial Japanese Navy" (62). 14: Ref. 15: 817 Orange dr, Silver Spring Md 20901.

KURSON, PHYLLIS (GREEN). b Lowell Mass 31 O 13. 4: Kenneth Morse Kurson. 5: Wellesley 31-35 (Ger) BA; Simmons 36 (Psychiatry) BS, 56-60 MS. 6: Ger. 7: Asst libn Shady Hill Sch, Cambridge Mass 60-63; Libn Faulkner Hosp Sch of Nu libn Shady Hill Sch, Cambridge Mass 60-63; Libn Faulkner Hosp Sch of Nursing, Cambridge Mass 63-. 8: Examining com Boston Pub Lib 64-69; Memb com Mass LA 65; Careers com Mass League of Nu mass League of Nursing 65, Hist source com 65-68; Chm of libs on bldg com for New mass League of ursing 65, Hist source com 65-68; Chm of libs on bldg com for New Faulkner Hosp 68-69. 9: Mass Hosp Lib Group (sec 65-66). 14: Rare bks. 15: 20 Evelyn rd, Waban Ma 02168.

KURTH, WILLIAM H. b Union Hill NJ 4 Jl 17. 4: Ruthann Spencer. 5: UVa 37-41 (Philos) AB, 41-42 (Philos); Catholic U 55-58 MSLS, 55-62 (Econ). 6: Sp. 7: LC: Filer-searcher National Union Catalog 43-44, Head Order Sect Order Div 44-48, Asst chief Order Div 48-59; Chief circ div NLM 59-62; Latin Amer bibliogr UCLA Lib 62-63, Head acquis dept 63-65; Asst dir Washington U Libs(St Louis) 65-69, Univ lib & Assoc dir 69-. 8: Consul, VA Libs 62-. 9: ALA. 10: Phi Beta Kappa. 11: Superior Serv Award, LC 55, NLM 62. 12: "Circulation of Books in the Americas," with P Jennison (59); "Survey of the Interlibrary Loan Operation of the National Library of Medicine" (62); "Moving a Library" (65). 13: Yes. 14: Admin, lib systems analysis, math & stat applications to libs, collection devel. 15: 7008 Kingsbury blvd, University City Mo 63130.

KURTZ, ELAINE AUSTIN. b NJ 18 Jl 16. 4: Oscar J Kurtz. 5: Pratt 36 Certif in LS; Skidmore Col & NYU 40 BS. 6: Fr, Ger. 7: Child libn NY Pub Lib 36-38; Child libn, Great Neck NY 38-42; Asst to libn central circ NY Pub Lib 42-47; Assoc exec dir USBE, Wash DC 47-. 9: ALA; SLA; DCLA. 13: Yes. 15: 6640 Adrian st, New Carrollton Md 20784.

KURTZ, HELEN G. b New Castle Penn 1 Je 13. 5: State Col Iowa 31-35 (Phys EDUC, Biol) BA; UCal summer 35 (Educ); UDenver 46-48 MA (Personnel) BSLS. 7: Tchr: High Sch, Cherokee Iowa 35-37, High Sch, Worthington Minn 37-38, West High Sch, Waterloo Iowa 38-40; Supv US Nat Youth Admin, Burlington Vt 42-43; High sch libn pub schs, Burlington Vt 43-47; Revisor & tchr catlg labs UDenver summer 47; Instr of catlg URI 63; Documents libn Brown U 47-68; Chief div lib ext serv RI Dept State Lib Serv 68-. 9: RILA (sec 64-65, v-pres 68-69); NE Tech Serv Libns (mem var coms). 13: Yes. 14: Catlg, ref. 15: 181 Williams st, Providence Ri 02906.

KURZMAN, CALVIN MURRAY. b San Francisco 5 Ag 28. 4: Patricia Fry. 5: UCal(Berkeley) 46-50 (Econ, Pol Sci) AB, 58-59 MLS, 59- (Pol Sci). 6: Fr. 7: Manager Burton Furniture Co, Oakland Cal 50-54; Owner- manager Daniel Furniture Co, Walnut Creek Cal 54-58; Asst soc sci & bus libn San Francisco State Col 59-66, Docs libn 66-67; Lib dir Col of Marin (Cal) 67-. 8: Lib/USA, NY Worlds Fair, 64. 9: CalLA; CalASchL. 10: UCal Lib Schs Alumni Assn; ACLU; Assoc Democ Club of San Francisco. 14: Ref, docs, admin. 15: 2115-28th ave, San Francisco Ca 94116.

KUSLER, ALAN. 5: Syracuse (Psych) BA, (LS) MA. 6: Sp. 7: A-v dept asst Rochester (NY) Pub Lib 54-57, Hd fiction div 57-61, Dir pub rel 61-. 9: ALA; -LAD (chm Pub Rel sect 68-69); NYLA. 13: Yes. 15: 115 South ave, Rochester NY 14604.

KUTHEIS, SISTER M FERDINAND CPPS. b St Louis Mo 28 Ap 21. 5: Harris Tchrs Col 39-40; St Marys Jr Col 40-43; Quincy Col 47-48 summers; St LouisU 49-58 summers (Eng) BS; Rosary Col 62-67 summers MLS. 6: Fr. 7: Tchr parochial sch syst in several states 23 yrs; Tchr-libn, hd libn Bishop DuBowe High Sch, St Louis Mo 64-68; Hd libn St Marys Col (O'Fallon) 68-. 8: Mem Archdiocese of St Louis Lib Coun 66-67; Mem team high sch lib consul for Archdiocese of St Louis 67-68. 9: NCEA; NCTE; ALA; CatholicLA (sec Elem Div 62-63); MoLA; St Charles Lib Coun. 10: Amer Assn Jr Cols; Adult Educ Coun of Greater St Louis. 14: Ref, tchg lib sci. 15: 204 North Main, O'Fallon Mo 63366.

KUTTEROFF, ETHEL (COX). b Phila 1 Ap 28. 4: Donald R Kutteroff. 5: TempleU 56 (Eng) BA; Drexel 62 MLS. 6: Fr. 7: Child libn Free Lib of Phila 45-57; Dir Cherry Hill Free Pub Lib, Cherry Hill NJ 59-62; Sch libn Randolph Elem Sch, Dover NJ 62-; Instr Newark State Tchrs Col 68-. 8: Com wk for Drexel Inst Tech Lib Sch; Surveyor Elem Sch Lib Collections. 9: ALA (CBC Com); NJLA (com duties); NJSchLA (Memb Chm 68-69, treas 68-70). 10: Col Club of Dover; LWV; Beta Phi Mu. 13: Yes. 14: Child bks. 15: 16 Mile dr, Chester NJ 07930.

KUTTNER, KAY. b Detroit 13 My 42. 5: Wayne State U 60-64 (Art) BFA; UMich 67-68 AMLS. 6: Ger, Fr. 7: Tracer & letterer Tech Illustrators, Warren Mich 64-66; Wk-study scholar UMich (Ann Arbor) 67-68; Av libn St Clair Co Lib, Port Huron Mich 68-. 9: ALA. 14: A-v. 15: 11752 Rynn, Emmett Mi 48022.

KUZEL, MRS INA M COOK. b Milwaukee 11 Ja 13. 5: UWis 30-32 (Home Econ); Cardinal Stritch Col 42-47 (Eng) PhB; UChicago 58-59; Rosary Col 56-59 MALS. 6: Fr. 7: Libn I Milwaukee Pub Lib 37-47; Libn GE X-Ray Corp, Milwaukee 47-49; Libn S C Johnson & Son, Racine Wis 49-53; Ref libn Portland Cement Assn, Skokie Ill 53-57; Libn Little Co of Mary Hosp, Evergreen Park Ill 57-58; Libn Chicago Heights Pub Lib, Chicago Heights Ill 58-63; Lib dir Moline Pub Lib, Moline Ill 63-. 9: ALA; IllLA. 10: Altrusa Club; Moline C of C. 13: Yes. 14: Admin, ref. 15: Moline Pub Lib, 504-17th st, Moline Il 61265.

KWON, MYOUNG-JA (LEE). b Seoul Korea 21 F 43. 4: Young Uk Kwon. 5: Seoul NatU 61-65 (Hist) BA; Brigham Young 66-68 MLS. 6: Ger, Korean. 7: Asst catlgr UNev Lib (Las Vegas) 68-. 9: NevLA. 15: 1917 Marlin ave, Las Vegas Nv 89101.

KWONG, LINDA. b Hong Kong 12 D 41. 5: UBC 61-64 (Eng, Hist) BA, 64-65 BLS. 6: Chinese. 7: Catlgr UBC Lib 65-67, Acquis libn 67-69, Bibliogr (gift & exchange) 69-. 14: Lib admin. 15: Univ of Brit Columbia Lib, Vancouver British Columbia Can.

KYKER, MARY (MAE). b Washington Co Tenn 7 Mr 25. 5: Tusculum Col 44-48 (Eng) BA; ETennState U 49, 50, 64, 65 Certif in Lib Sci, 66-69 (LS). 7: Tchr-libn Baileyron High SCH, Greenville Tenn 48-57; Libn Washington Col Acad, Washington Col Tenn 57-. 8: Asst to Dean of Girls, sh Col Acad 57-62; So Assn Evaluation Com, Chuckey-Doak High Sch, Afton Tenn 64; So Assn Eval Com, S Greene High Sch, Greeneville Tenn 66. 9: NEA; TennLA; SELA; TennEA; Wash Co (v-pres 68-69); Boone Tree Lib Club. 10: Church libn Vernon Brethren Church, Telford Tenn 67-69. 14: Sch, col libs. 15: Rte 1 Box 299, Telford TN 37690.

KYLE, HARRIET (MAY). b Cedarville Ohio 20 S 01. 5: Cedarville Col 22-23, 24-27 (Eng) AB, W Henburg summer 27; Ohio State 30-31. 7: Tchr: Ezel (Ky) Mission Sch 27-28, Dist Sch, Delhi NY 28-29, Eaton Ohio 29-30; Asst libn Columbus Pub Lib, Columbus Ohio 38-52, 53-69; Sem libn, Cairo Egypt 52-53. 9: ALA; OhioLA. 15: 2455 Summit st, Columbus Oh 43202.

KYOGOKU, YURII. b Japan 3 Ap 16. 5: UCal(Berkeley) 33-36 (Eng) BA; Fresno State Col 51-52; Ryukoku U (Kyoto APAN) 55-56 (Buddhist Studies); UMinn 61-63 (LS) MA. 6: Japanese. 7: Catlgr Ohio State U Libs 63-. 15: 577 Harley dr, Columbus Oh 3202.

L

LA BISSONIERE, WILLIAM R. b Minneapolis 1 Ag 29. 4: Margaret, LaBissoniere. 5: UMinn 48-49 (Liberal Arts); San Francisco St Col 54-55 (Liberal Arts; UMinn 55-57 (E Asia Area Studies) BA, 59-62 (LS) MA. 6: Fr, Ital. 7: Salesman, Minneapolis 48-50; (Cpl) surveyor USArmy Korea, Japan 51-52; Salesman Minneapolis 53-59; Staff Minneapolis Pub Lib Summer 60; Jr libn UMinn 60, Documents libn & instr 63-, Hd docs div 68-. 9: ALA. 14: Ref, documents. 15: 716 5th ave, se Minneapolis Mn 554 14.

La CROIX, FREDERIC SKELTON. b Milwaukee 13 Ja 33. 4: Louise Lesher. 5: William & Mary 51-55, (Hist) AB; 58-59 (Educ) Tchrs Certif; UWis (Milwaukee) summer 61 (LS); UNC 61-63 MSLS. 6: Sp. 7: Clerk/typist (Spec 3rd class) Army Security Agency, Ft Devens & Tokyo 55-58; Tchr Fairfield Jr High Sch, Highland Springs Va 59-60; Tchr Soc Studies Pocomoke High Sch, Pocomoke City Md 60-61; Ref libn May Mem Lib, Burlington NC 63; Asst libn acquis dept, receiving sect UNebLibs 63-67, Ref libn 67-68; Ref & doc libn Grinnell Col Lib 68-. 9: ALA; (Jr mem RT 66-68); NebLA; (Sec-treas Col & Univ Sect 67-68). 10: Lib Sci Club UNC Sch Lib Sci; Beta Phi Mu; Lincoln Lib Assn (Lincoln Neb); AAUP; ACLU. 14: Ser, ref, doc. 15: 1516 Spencer st, Grinnell Ia 50112.

LA FOND, NOBEL S(TANLEY). b Martinton Ill 6 Je 07. 4: Mary Francis (Jones). 5: UDenver 47-49 (Radio & Television) BA, 50 (LS) MA; UCal (Los Angeles) 55. 6: Fr. 7: USMarine Corps 26-32, 42-45, 46-50; Truck Driver Louisville Ky 33-42; Stud asst Mary Reed Lib, Denver 49-50; Asst libn West NMU Miller Lib 50-. 9: ALA; NMLA (treas 48); NMEA (pres 58-59). 10: Newman Club; Faculty Adv. 11: Grant Co (NM) Vet of the Year 64. 12: "Seven Short Plays" (26). 14: Catlg supv, southwest bks. 15: 410 Indiana st, Silver City Nm 88061.

LAAI, YI-FAAI. b Sekadau Pontianak Borneo 4 S 06. 4: Evelyn Loh. 5: Lingnan U 27-31 (Bus, Admin) BA; UCal 45-50 (Hist) PhD; UWash(Seattle) 52-53 MLS. 6: Chinese. 7/ libn San Francisco State Col Lib 53-. 13: Yes. 14: Catlg. 15: San Francisco State Col Lib, San Francisco Ca 94132.

LAAKSO, LILA MARTHA. b Windsor Ont Can 24 Ag 28. 4: Raymond Laakso. 5: Queen's U 61 (Eng) BA; UToronto 64 BLS. 7: Ref libn The E J Pratt Lib, Victoria U (Toronto) 64-. 9: CanLA; OntLA; Inst Profess Libns Ont. 14: Ref. 15: 168 St Clements ave, Toronto Can.

LAATS, ARMILDA. b Valga Estonia 21 D 25. 5: UErlangen (Germany) 47-49 (Hist); Iowa St Tchrs Col 50-51 (Educ) BA; Columbia 52-53 (Linguistics) MA, 53-56 (LS) MS. 6: Estonian, Ger, Fr. 7: Lib trainee NY Pub Lib 53-56, Sr libn catlgr 56-61; Catlgr IM Corp Advanced Systems Development Div, Yorktown Heights NY 61-. 9: SLA; Westchester Lib Assn. 10: Kappa Delta Pi. 14: Catlg. 15: 1918 Hanover st, Yorktown Heights NY 10598.

LAATZ, MARY JANE. b Indianapolis 27 D 16. 5: Butler U 34-38 (Sociol) AB; est res 38-39 BSLS. 6: Ger. 7: Libn Ind U Ext Div 39-41; Ind U Sch Med Lib: Catlgr 41-50, Ref libn 50, Act libn 50-51, Ref libn 51-57, Med Libn 7-. Libn 57-. 8: Coun of Midwest Reg He alth Sci Lib & Coop Info Serv (chm 68-69). 9: MedLA; (pres-Ind Chap 60-61). 10: Delta Gamma rority; John Shaw Billings Hist of Med S oc. 14: Ref , admin. 15: 5226 No Delaware, Indianapolis In 46221.

LABARTHE, CARROLL (OLTON). b Newark NJ 6 My 37. 4: Jules Labarth Jr. 5: Cornell U 55-59 (Mus) BA; UPittsburgh 66-69 MLS. 6: Fr. 7: Personnel asst Williams & Co, Pittsburgh Penn 61-62; Asst mgr staff serv UPittsburgh Lib 67-68, Acting mgr staff serv 68-. 9: ALA; PennLA. 10: Phi Beta Kappa. 14: Ref, admin, music. 15: Shady lane, Pittsburgh Pa 15215.

LABELLA, REV ROBERT. b Cleveland 1 N 27. 5: John CarrollU 46-47; Sacred Heart Sem 47-49 (Philos); St Mary Sem 49-54 (Theol); John Carroll U 60-61 (Philos) AB; West Res 61-62 MS in LS. 6: Lat, Ital. 7: Asst pastor Holy Rosary Church, Cleveland 55-56; Asst pastor St Peter Church, Lorain Ohio 56-60; Prof Libn Borromeo Sem (Wickliffe Ohio) 60-. 9: ALA; CathLA. 15: 28700 Euclid ave, Wickliffe Oh 44092.

LABOUNTY, MAXINE. b Orange Mass 20 F 05. 5: Simmons Col 28 BS. 7: Gen asst Wheeler Mem Lib, Orange Mass 21-24; DC Pub Lib: Asst child libn SE Br 30-31, Asst child libn Mt Pleasant Br 29-30, Asst dir wk with child 30-31, Child libn & asst, Central 31-34, Child libn Mt Pleasant Br 34-37, Child libn Central 37-39, Supv of wk with sch 39-48, Coordinator child serv 48-. 8: Consul AAUW-Assn Childhood Educ Internat Com on Child Bks in Lib Congress, 52-63; LC Adv Com on Sel of Child Bks for Blind Child 58-63, 65-. 9: ALA; NEA; DCLA. 10: DC Coun of Admin Women in Educ. 13: Yes. 14: Child serv. 15: DC Pub Lib 499 Pennsylvnia ave, NW Wash DC 20001.

LABOURE, SISTER MARY (PARTRIDGE). b Queens NY 2 Ap 29. 5: St John's U 57-61 (Educ) BLS, 64-67 MLS. 7: Tchg: St Patrick Sch Brooklyn 49-51, Little Flower Sch, Brooklyn 51-53, St Patrick Sch, Bay Shore 53-56, Our Lady of Mercy, Hicksville 56-61, Holy Innocents, Brooklyn 61-63; Libn Our Lady of Mercy Acad, Syosset NY 63-. 9: ALA; CathLA; Nassau-Suffolk SchLA. 10: Film Club. 14: YA bk sel. 15: Our Lady of Mercy Acad, Convent rd, Syosset NY 11791.

LaBRAKE, ORLYN (BARRON). b Bridgeport Conn 2 S 30. 4: Richard F LaBrake. 5: Skidmore 48-51, 54-55 (Psych) BA; SUNY (Albany) 66-67 (LS) MS. 6: Fr. 7: Reading dept libn SUNY (Albany) 66-67; Catlg libn Rensselaer Polytech Inst 67-68; Hd catlgr 68-. 9: ALA. 15: 13 Hidley ext, Troy NY 12180.

LaBRECHE, RAYBOURNE E (CUSHMAN). b Ladysmith Wis. 5: Superior (Wis) State Col 22-28 (Educ) High Sch Tchrs Certif; UMinn 28-29 BS in LS; Emory summer 52 Med Lib Certif; UWis summers 54,56,57 MS in LS; NY State Pub Libns Prof Certif. 6: Fr. 7: Asst libn Superior State Col 45-48; Head adult loan dept Hackley Pub Lib, Muskegon Mich 48-49; Libn VA Hosp, Battle Creek Mich 49-50; Chief libn VA Hosp, Iron Mtn Mich 50-57; Ref & circ libn Edwards Air Force Base Edwards Cal 57-58; Chief libn VA Hosp, Madison Wis 58-60; Chief libn VA Hosp, Buffalo NY 60-. 9: MedLA; ALA. 10: Town Club, Civil Def Com, Beta Phi Mu, several VA awards for work simplification and improvement suggestions. 14: Admin, ref. 15: 3495 Bailey ave, Buffalo NY 14215.

LaBUDDE, KENNETH JAMES. b Sheboygan Wis 20 Ja 20. 5: UWis 37-41 (Comparative Lit) BA, 41-42 BLS; UChicago 43-44 ASTP-Foreign Area & Language Certif; UMinn 47-48 (Amer Studies) MA, 48-50, 54 (Amer Studies) PhD. 6: Fr. 7: Sr lib asst Milwaukee Pub Lib 42; Tech 4th gr Army of the US 42-44; Libn Sheboygan Press, Sheboygan Wis 45-46; Instr in Eng Milton Col 46-47; Instr in Humanities UMinn (Minneapolis) Summer 49, Greater u fellow 49-50; UMo (Kan City): Dir of Libs 50-, Lectr in hist 50-57, Asst Prof 57-61, Assoc Prof 61-62, Prof 62-. 8: Adv, Tedrow Transportation Lib Assn, Kansas City Ecumenical Lib. 9: ALA-ACRL; MoLA (chm Col & U Div 54-55); BSA; Central MsALER Studies Assn (pres 63-64). 10: Amer Studies Assn; Amer Soc Aesth; European Assn for Amer ISIRGICTS; AAUP; Westerners (Kansas City Posse); Orgn Amer Hist; Beta Phi Mu, Phi Alpha Theta, Delta Phi Lmbda, Phi Kappa Phi; Soc Archit Hist. 11: Ed "Trail Guide," 58; Kansas City Posse of Westerners (57-58); Arts Ed "Mid-Continent Amer Studies Journal" (59-63). 13: Yes. 14: Admin, Americana. 15: UMo (Kansas City) 5100 Rockhill rd, Kansas City Mo 64110.

LACEY, ELAINE (HAHN). b Berwick Penn 2 Ag 45. 4: R B LACEY. 5: Penn StateU 63-66 (Eng) BA; Rutgers 67-68 MLS. 7: Tchr Hazleton Sch Dist, Penn 66-67; Catlgr RutgersU Lib (New Brunswick) 68-. 10: MENSA. 14: Automation, systems analysis. 15: 1115 Orange st, Berwick Pa 18603.

LACEY, SAMUEL A(NDREW). b Brownwood Tex 21 Jl 26. 5: Howard Payne Col 47 (Eng) BA; N Tex State 50 BSLS; UMich 55 MALS. 7: Period libn Southern Methodist U 50-52; Ref libn UMich 52-55; Queens Borough Pub Lib, Jamaica NY: Gen br wk 55-58, Br libn 58-60, Asst rec libn 60-64, Dept asst ext serv 63-64, Asst Chief ext serv 64-69, Chief 69-. 9: ALA; NYLA. 15: 35 W 74 st, New York NY 10023.

LACHENDRO, LEONARD L. b Pittsburgh 16 S 29. 4: Audrey Leon. 5: UPittsburgh 55-58 (Eng) BA (magna cum laude); Carnegie 58-59 MSLS. 6: Sp. 7: Fire direction control chief USMC (PFC) Korea 51-53; Ref asst Carnegie Lib Pittsburgh 59-61; Head Libn Bethel Park Pub Lib Bethel Park, Penn 61-63; City Libn Lodi Pub Lib, Lodi Cal 63-. 8: Mem Exec bd Coop Lib Syst , Cal 67-. 09: ALA; CalLA; Pub Lib Admin; Assn No Cal. 10: League of Cal Cities. 14: Admin, ref. 15: 531 Virginia ave, Lodi Ca 95242.

LACHER, JEAN STAHLIN. b Mt Vernon NY 10 Ap 41. 4: Robert J Lacher. 5: Bates Col 59-63 (Hist) AB; Rutgers 64-65 MLS. 7: Libn QUeens Borough Pub Lib, Jamaica NY 65-66; Catlgr St Cloud State Col 66-67, Hd catlg dept 67-68; Asst ref libn Colorado State Col Lib 68-. 14: Ref, catlg. 15: P167 Jackson blvd, Greeley Co 80631.

LACITIS, IRENE (ZOMMERS). b Russia 15 F 12. 4: Erik Lacitis. 5: U Latvia Law Sch (Riga, Latvia) 30-37 Magister iuris; UWash 63-64 MLibnship. 6: Latvian, Ger, Russian, Sp. 7: Russian-Latvian tr Labor Dept Riga Latvia 42-44; German-Russian tr English Mil Govt, Graz Australia 45-47; Catlgr I Seattle Pub Lib 65-. 9: WashLA. 10: Far West Slavic Conf. 14: Catlg. 15: 4611 Eastern ave N, Seattle Wa 98103.

LACKNER, IRENE VILMA. b Montreal 15 Ap 29. 5: Carnegie Tech summer 50 carleton U 53 BA; Gill 56 BLS, 64. 6: Fr, Ger, Hungarian. 7: Tech staff Pub Printing & Stationery Dept Ottawa 47-52; Clerical staff Nat Research Coun, Ottawa 53-55, Circ, Catlgr, br libn 56-64; Chief Libn Econ Coun of Can, Ottawa 64-. 9: CanLA; SLA; (Bus Finance GP Program Chm 1969 Conf); Internat Assn of Documentalists; Inst Prof Libns, Ontario (Dist Chm 59); OttawaLA past sec-treas; pres 68-69); ASIS. 10: Prof Inst of the PUB Ser of Can; UWomen's Club; Ottawa Ski Club; Nat Galley Assn Ottawa; McGill & Carleton Alumni Assns. 14: Ref. 15: 257 McArthur ave, Eastview Ont Can.

LACY, DAN (MABRY). b Newport News Va 28 F 14. 4: Hope Leiken. 5: UNC 30-33 (Hist) AB, 33-35, 38-39 (Hist) AM. 6: Sp. 7: Instr in hist UNC 35; Asststate supv, state supv, reg supv, nat dir Hist Res Survey Wks Projects Admin, Wash DC 36-41; Exec sec Commsn on Conservation of Cultural Resources Nat Resources Planning Bd, Wash DC 41-42; Asst to archivist Nat Archives, Wash DC 42-43, Dir of operations

43-46, Asst archivist of the US 47; Asst dir LC Processing Dept 47-50; Asst admin Intl Info Admin Dept of State, Wash DC 51-53; Managing dir Amer Bk Publishers Coun, NYC 53-66; Sr v-pres mcGraw-Hill Bk Co, NYC 66-. 8: Mem President's Nat Adv Commsn on Libs 66-68. 9: ALA; Amer Bk Publrs Assn. 10: Coun on For Rel; Century Assn. 11: Litt D 68, UNC; Sup Serv Medal, Dept of State 52. 12: Co-ed "The Historical Records of North Carolina", 3 v (38-40); "The Library of Congress, A Sesquicentenary Review" (50); "Books and the Future - A Speculation" (56); "Freedom and Communications" (61); "The Meaning of the American Revolution" (64). 13: Yes. 15: McGraw-Hill Book Co 330 W 42nd st, New York NY 10036.

LADD, BARBARA ELOISE. b Claridon Ohio 19 N 12. 5: Kent State 30-32 (Speech). 6: Sp. 7: Personnel mgr Chardon Rubber Co, Chardon Ohio 36-44; Hosp RC staff Amer Red Cross, MTO-Italy 44-45; Housing mgr Pub Housing Admin, Michigan, Ohio 46-58; Libn Amer Soc for Metals, Metals Park Ohio 59-. 9: SLA. 10: Amer Overseas Assn; Bus & Profess Women's Club; Women's Equality Action League. 14: Ref, rare bks. 15: 13721 Mayfield rd, Chardon Oh 44024.

LADD, DOROTHY P(IERCE). b Brooklyn NY 16 Ja 17. 4: Ralph E Ladd. 5: Col of William & Mary 33-37 (LS) AB; Columbia summers 40-43 (LS) BS. 6: Fr, Sp, Lat. 7: Libn Col of William & Mary(Norfolk) 37-48; Libn St Helena Ext Col of William & Mary(Berkley Va) 46-48; Chenery Lib BostonU: Asst ref libn 48-49, Asst catlg libn 49-55, Chief catlg dept 55-61; Chief catlg div Boston U Libs 61-, Act asst dir for tech serv 69-. 9: ALA (Memb Com);-RTSD (Chm catlg & clfst Sect 67-68); MassLA (chm &/or mem var coms); NELA (pres Col Libs Sect 65-66); NETechServLibns (pres 57-58). 10: AAUW; Delta Kappa Gamma. 14: Catlg, ref, rare bks. 15: 1575 Tremont st, Boston Ma 02120.

LADD, FRANCES ROBERTA. b Rochester NY 28 Ap 17. 5: URochester 36-39 (Eng Lit) BA; Columbia 40-41 BS in LS. 6: Fr, Ger, Lat, Sp. 7: Sr asst Rochester Pub Lib, Rochester NY 41-44; URochester: Catlgr 44-52, Asst head catlg dept 53-62, Head catlg dept 62-. 9: ALA; NYLA. 14: Catlg. 15: Univ of Rochester Lib, River Campus Sta, Rochester NY 14627.

LADD, JAY LOUIS. b St Louis 26 Mr 32. 5: Fla State U 49-53 (LS) BA, 53-54 (LS) MA. 7: USArmy (Pfc) Army War Col Lib 54-56; Asst acquis libn UNM 56-57, Asst ref libn 57-60; Circ desk libn Ohio State U 60-61, Admin asst to dir 61-65, Head, Com Lib 65-68, Hd sept libs 68-. 9: ALA; NM StateLA; OhioLA. 10: Beta Phi Mu. 14: Admin, pub serv, ref. 15: 2111 Iuka ave, Columbus Oh 43201.

LADENDORF, JANICE MARIE. b Minneapolis Minn 1 Ja 42. 5: UMinn 59-63 (Hist) BA, 64-66 (LS) MA. 6: Fr. 7: Libn N Star Research & Devel Inst 64-. 8: Organiz lib facilities at US stations in Antarctica 66-68; Provided info serv to UMinn, Exp City Proj 67-. 9: SLA (Memb Chm 66-68). 10: Sigma Epsilon Sigma. 12: "The Revolt in India, 1857-58: an Annotated Bibliography of English Language Materials" (67). 14: Lit searching, selective dissem of info, info transfer, systems analysis. 15: 8700 - 2nd ave So, Minneapolis Mn 55420.

LADENSON, ALEX. b Russia 25 S 07. 4: Inez Sher. 5: Northwestern U 28-29 (Law) BSL, 29-32 (Law) JD; UChicago 34-35 (Hist) MA, 35-38 (Hist) PhD. 6: Fr. 7: Supv WPA Lib Om nibus Project , Chicago 38-43; Asst dean Schurz Even Jr Col 38-48; Exec asst Chicago P ub Lib 43-44, Asst libn 44-67, Act libn 67-; Lecturer Rosary Col Dept of Lib Sci 65-. 8: Took part in a coun of lib resources study which resulted in "A Proposal for a Nat Code Number System for Current Pub"; Ill State Lib Adv Com 59-; Jt Com for the Recodification of Ill Lib Laws 63-; Consul: Study of Kan State Lib 68, Study of state lib legis Fla StateU 69; Chm IllState Lib Adv Com 66-. 9: ALA; IllLA (pres 59-60); Chicago Lib Club (pres 50-51); Chicago Reg Group of Catlgrs & Clsfrs (chm 46 -47). 10: Nortown Civic League (Chicago); Ill State Hist Soc. 11: 1965 Libn Citation Award (IllLA); Doctor o f letters Rosary Col 68. 12: Ed "American Library Laws" (3rd ed), First Supp 63-64, Second Supp 67. 13: Yes. 14: Catlg, lib govt & legis, pub lib admin. 15: Chicago Pub Lib, 78 E Washington st, Chicago Il 60602.

LADLEY, WINIFRED CLAIRE (SHERMAN). b Spokane Wash 26 N 04. 5: Whitman Col 22-24 (Eng); East Wash Col of Educ summers 23-26 Tchg Certif; UWash 26-27 (Eng) BA, summer 28 (Eng) Life tchg Certif, summers 50-55 MLS. 6: Fr. 7: Tchr Cowiche Elem Sch, Cowiche Wash 24-26; Tchr of Eng & Libn Union High Sch, Two Rivers Wash 27-40; Libn Ruth N Upson Elem Sch, Jacksonville Fla 44-46; Libn Central Grade Sch, Monroe Wash 48-52; Libn Central Grade Sch, Snohomish Wash 52-53; Supv of sch libs Mercer Island Sch Dist, Mercer Island Wash 53-57; Asst Prof of Lib Sci UOre 57-61; Assoc Prof of Lib Sci Grad Sch of Lib Sci UIll 61-67, Prof 67-. 8: Storyteller for pub libs, 53-54, & over TV stations 56-59; Visiting Asst Prof UWash Grad Sch of Libnship, summers 56, 57, 65; Visiting Prof Lib Sci Portland State Col summer 68; Visiting Prof Col of Libnship, Aberystwyth Wales summer 69. 9: ALA (Council 4-68); -AASchL (sec, Subs Bks Bul Com 56-62 & 64-65); -LED (Bd 62-65); NEA; NCTE; IRA; AALS; IllLA; Ill ASchL (program Chm 66). 10: AAUP, Pi Lambda Theta. 12: Ed "Current Trends in Pub Lib Serv to Children," Library Trends (Jl 63). 13: Yes. 14: Storytelling, child lit, lib serv to child & yp. 15: 804 W Florida, Urbana Il 61801.

LADOF, NINA SYDNEY (BAKER). b St Louis 23 Je 20. 4: Leonard G Ladof. 5: Pratt 43-44 BSLS; Rutgers U 56-59 (Pol Sci) BA. 6: Fr, Ger. 7: Catlgr, Great Neck Lib, Great Neck NY 44-46; Period libn John Crerar Lib, Chicago 46-47; Acquis sst UIll Lib (Urbana) 47-49; Order libn Adelphi Col 49-50; Dir Moorestown Free Lib, Moorestown NJ 60-65; Dir St Charles Co Lib, St Charles Mo 67-. 8: Pres Bd of Trustees, Levittown (NY) Pub Lib 51-53. 9: ALA; NJLA; MOLA. 10: League of Women Voters; Greater St Louis Freedom of Residence Com. 13: Yes. 14: Admin, pub libs, adult serv, com rel. 15: 619 N Lockwood ave, Webster Groves Mo 63119.

LADY, IRMA FAYE. b McMinnville Ore 3 O 25. 5: Linfield Col 46-50 (Pre-med Bio) BA; USoCal 61-63 MSLS. 6: Ger. 7: Med stenographer Barnes Gen Hosp, Vancouver Barracks Wash 42-45; Med secy Vancouver Clinic, Vancouver Wash 46; Med secy Emanuel Hosp, Portland Ore summers 47-49; Med secy Seattle 50-53; Secy Tidewater Oil Co, Seattle, Los Angeles 56-63; Tech libn Aerojet-Gen Corp, Sacramento Cal 63-68; Sci & tech ref spec Ore State Lib 68-. 9: SLA; OreLA. 10: AAUW; Pi Gamma Mu; Beta Phi Mu. 14: Ref wk in chem lib & in sci & tech. 15: 667-16th st, NE Salem Or 97301.

LAFAYETTE, PATRICIA E. b Detroit 1 O 30. 4: Louis J Lafayette. 5: MichStateU 48-52 (Sociol) BA; UMich 62 (LS) MA. 6: Fr. 7: Bkmob Lib Aid, Wayne Co Pub Lib, Wayne Co Mich 58-62; Child libn Southgate Pub Lib, Southgate Mich 60-62; Libn Trenton Pub Lib, Trenton Mich 62-. 9: ALA; MichLA. 10: Beta Pi Mu; Mich Mineralogical Soc; Mich Hist Soc. 14: Pub lib admin. 15: Trenton Pub Lib 2790 Westfield, Trenton Mi 48183.

LaFORGE, EDITH ANN (SWAN). b Ft Worth Tex 28 F 42. 4: William Garrett LaForge. 5: Oklahoma State U 60-63 (Lib Sci) BS in Ed uc; UOkla 66-68 MLS. 7: Stud asst Engnrg & Phys sci area Okla State U Lib 61-63; Prof asst gen ref dept El Paso Pub Lib, El Paso Tex 63-64; Adult serv asst libn Be lle Isle br Okla Co Libs, Okla City 66; Asst libn Presb Hosp, Okla City 66-67; Elem fld libn Okla City Pub Sch, 67-68; Dir of media ctr Harding Jr High Okla City 68-. 8: Mem Worship & Soc Concerns Commsns Lakeside (Okla) M ethodist Ch, chm Worship Commsn 67-68; MLA certif as med libn. 9: ALA (Jr Mems Round Table 67-69); SLA; SWLA; OklaLA; OklaEA. 10: Okla City EA; Okla City Lib ns Assn (Sec-treas 6 9-70); AAUW; Beta Phi Mu; Zeta Tau Alpha; Phi Kappa Phi; Alpha Beta Alpha. 12: "Treasure Hunt" Jr high sch lib unit for Okla City Pub Schs with Beverly Ryan. 14: Sch libs, ref serv in med libs. 15: 2713 NW 66th, Oklahoma City Ok 73116.

LAFORTUNE, FRANCOIS. b Montreal 9 Mr 21. 4: Suzanne Caron. 5: UMontreal 44 (LS). 6: Fr, Eng. 7: Catlgr & Clsfr Bibl municipale de Montreal 47-48; Chief Libn Bibliotheque publique de Quebec 49-59; Asst dir Serv des Bibliotheques scoalires de la ville de Quebec 60; Asst Dir Serv des Bibliotheques pub de la prov de Quebec 60-. 9: Assn canadienne des Bibliotheques; Assn Canadienne des Bibliothecaires de langue francaise. 12: Photog "OU la lumiere chante" de Gilles Vigneault (Quebec 66). 14: Ref, rare bks. 15: Ministere des Affaires Culturelles, Serv de Biblioths Pub Hotel du Government, Quebec Can.

LAFRANCHI, WILLIAM. b Brookville Penn 6 D 26. 5: Clarion State Col 45-49 (LS) BS in Ed; UIll 49-52 MS LS; UPittsburgh 54-57. 7: Sgt Maj Army of US, Korea 45-46; Libn Clarion Jt Sr High Sch, Clarion Penn 49-53; Head Libn Ind U Penn 53-. 8: Middle States Com eval teams, 52, 64, 67; chm Penn State Col Proposed Standards for Libs Com 63-65; Penn State Col eval team 65, 66. 9: NEA; ALA-ACRL (pres Tri-State Chap); PennLA (pres Col & Ref Lib Div; pres SW Chap). 10: AAUP; Rotary Club; Ind Free Lib Bd 60-; Pi Gamma Mu; BPOElks. 13: Yes. 14: Admin, ref, acquis. 15: 351 S 13th, Indiana Pa 15701.

LAGE, ALICE MARY. b NYC 14 D 25. 5: Gettysburg ol 43-47 (Hist) BA; NYU 47-51 (Hist) MA; Columbia 51-53, 60 (LS) MS. 6: Fr, Sp, Malay, Portu. 07: Circ asst NYU Sch of Com 47-49; Ed asst H W Wilson Co, NYC 49-52; Lib clerk W L Maxson Co, NYC 52-53; Libn Control Instrument Co, Brooklyn NY 53-54; Libn US Army Spec Serv Libs, France & Germany 54-59, Libn US Army Spec Serv Libs, Camp Drum NY & Ft Tilden NY 59-61; Asst libn Carnegie Endowment for Internat Peace, NYC 61-62; Libn U S Peace Corps Volunteer, Malaysia 63-65; Asst dir USIS Benjamin Franklin Lib, Mexico City 65-66; USIS-Binat Ctr Lib off, Brazil 66-. 9: ALA. 14: Admin, catlg, staff train. 15: 106-24 98th st, Ozone Park New York, Ny 11417.

LAGE, LOUISE CATHERINE. b Davenport Iowa. 5: Augustana Col (Fr) BA; UMich 43 BS in LS. 6: Fr, Ger, Sp. 7: Asst ext dept Davenport (Iowa) Pub Lib 40-42, Head ext dept 43-45; Asst libn Eli Lilly Research Labs, Indianapolis 45-51, Asst chief libn 51-56; Chief Libn Sci Lib, Eli Lilly & Co 56-. 9: MedLA (sec 52-53, chm Subcom on Recruitmt 51-52, chm Subcom on Curriculum 55-56, chm Pharm Group 57-58; Midwest Gp; Exec Com 63, chm Interlib Loan Com 66-67); SLA (chm Pharm Sect 59-60, pres Ind Chap 67-68); ASIS; ALA; IndLA; Drug Info Assn. 10: Bd of Dirs Starlight Musicals; PEO Sisterhood. 13: Yes. 14: Admin, info retrieval. 15: 5307 Primrose ave, Indianapolis In 46220.

LaGRAVE, VIRGINIA Z(OE). b St Louis 2 Ag 03. 5: Col of the Visitation 21-22; St Louis Pub Lib Sch 26 Certif. 6: Fr. 7: Asst catlgr St Louis Pub Lib 26-28; Catlgr pub lib, Enid Okla 28-29; Organizer Okla N Central Jr Col 29; Asst Catlgr Okla City Pub, Okla City Okla 29-42; Asst libn Tinker Air Force Base, Okla City Okla 42-46, Base libn 46-. 8: Okla Coun on Libs 63-67 , 67-71 (appointed by Governor for 4-year terms). 09: ALA; SLA (pres Okla Chap 63-64); OklaLA (pres 53-54); SWLA. 10: Okla Chap Nat Fed Bus Prof Women; Cath Daughters of Amer. 11: Outstanding AF Logistics Command Libn 68. 13: Yes. 14: Admin, catlg. 15: 1008 NW 33d st, Oklahoma City Ok 73118.

LAGUATAN, CARMEN SALVADOR. b Laoag Philippines 17 F 23. 5: St Williams Col (Philippines) 45-46 (Soc Sci) AB; U of St Thomas (Philippines) 47-49 (LS) BSE; Chicago 51-52 Certif Libnship; UIll 64 (Med Lit). 6: Philippine, Sp. 7: Catlg clsf asst UST Thomas (Philippines) 47-49; Lib asst uchicago Grad Sch 51-52; Instr-libn St Williams Col (Philippines) 49-50, 53-61; Asst libn The Chicago Med Sch 62-65; libn St Mary Nazareth Hosp Med Lib 65-. 9: ALA; MedLA; SLA; IllLA. 10: Philippine Nortenian Assn; Phil-Amer Youth Club of Cihcago; Phil Womens Club Chicago. 14: Catlg, ref, research. 15: 4300 S Keating ave, Chicago Il 60632.

LaHOOD, CHARLES GEORGE Jr. b Omaha 29 Ag 22. 4: Susanne Bracken. 5: St Lawrence Col 40-43 (Classics) AA; Catholic U 43-44 (Philos) BA, 44-45 (Philos) MA, 46-49 MS in LS. 7: Head ser record LC Wash DC 52-53, Asst Chief Photoduplication Serv 53-61, Chief, Ser Div 61-68, Chief photoduplication serv 68-; Adj lecturer Sch of Lib & Info Serv UMd. 8: Consul on Photocopying. 9: ALA (Interlib Loan Com);-RTSD (Copying Methods Sect, chm Ser Sect); Mem USASI PH5 -2,3; ARL (Adv Com Microform Tech Project); NMA; DCLA. 13: Yes. 14: Ref, preservation, photocopying. 15: 10102 E Bexhill dr, Kensington Md 20795.

LAI, PETER TIENPEI. b China 23 N 40. 5: SoochowU 58-62 (Pol Sci) BA; UPittsburgh 67-68 MLS. 6: Chinese. 7: Ed Fu-shin Broadcasting Inc, Taipei Taiwan 62-65; Off Ministry of Educ of Rep of China, Taipei Taiwan 65-67; Libn Elizabeth Pub Lib, Elizabeth NJ 69-. 14: Ref. 15: 1368 Fremont pl, Elizabeth NJ 07208.

LAIBLIN, KATHERINE HUNDLEY MRS. b Salem Va 5 Je 10. 5: UNC 31-32. 6: Sp. 7: Asst libn Olivia Raney Lib, Raleigh NC 29-35; Chief file clerk Govt Off, Raleigh NC 36; Child libn Danville Pub Lib, Danville VA 36-42; Libn Forest Hills Elem sch, Danville Va 45-46; Reg hosp libn Regional Hosp, Camp Blanding Fla 4 ; Libn Bellevue Elem Sch Danville Va 47-49; City Libn Ketchikan Pub Lib, Ketchikan Alaska 49-60; City Libn Petersburg Pub Lib, Petersburg Va 60-64; City Libn Astoria Pub Lib, Astoria Ore 64-65; City Libn Auburn Pub Lib, Auburn Wash 65-68; Consul inst & The physically handicapped Alaska State Lib 68-. 9: ALA; WashLA; PNLA; AlaskaLA (sec). 10: CofC; Alas lca Co Hist Soc; Sons of Norway; Angora Hiking Cl ub; SCCA; Nat Wildlife Assn; Pioneers of Alaska Aux. 14: Rare bks, acquis, catlg, instns, bkmo. 15: 504 Fifth apt 4, Juneau Ak 99801.

LAICH, KATHERINE (W S). b Bridgeton NJ 24 Ja 10. 5: Wilson Col 26-30 (Lat-Eng) AB; USoCal 40-42 BS in LS. 7: Asst Pub Lib, Bridgeton NJ 33-40; Pub Lib, Los Angeles: Stud libn 41-42, Child libn 42-44, Libn 44-46, Asst dept libn 46-47, Admin asst 47-60, Asst city libn 61-. 9: ALA (Exec Bd 64-68, Coun 58 & 63-68, chm Com on Org 61-64, chm Nom Com 69-70); -LAD (Bd Dirs 58 & 63-66, sec personnel admin sect 62-63); SLA (pres So Cal Chap 47); CalLA (chm 3 coms 56-57, 65). 10: Amer Soc Pub Admin; West Govtl Research Assn; Libraria Sodalitas; Pub Lib Execs Assn, So Cal. 13: Yes. 14: Pub lib admin. 15: Los Angeles Pub Lib 630 W Fifth st, Los Angeles CA 90017.

LAIDLAW, SHEILA MARGARET. b Edinburgh Scotland 2 D 31. 5: UEdinburgh 50-53 (Eng, Hist) MA; Toronto 59-60 BLS. 6: Fr, Ger. 7: Lib asst Univ Edinburgh (Edinburgh) 53-57; Lib asst UToronto 57-60; Libn UToronto 60-67; Libn Church Army in Can, Toronto 67-68; Libn UToronto Lib 68-. 9: CanLA; ALA; Lib Assn (Gt Brit); OntLA; Inst of Prof Libns, Ont. 10: Beta Phi Mu. 14: Circ, undergrad serv, readers serv. 15: 65 High Park ave apt 2101, Toronto 9 Ont Can.

LAING, JENCIE (BALES). b Coolidge Ga 22 N 29. 4: Robert Edward Lee Laing. 5: Fla State U 48-52 (LS) AB. 6: Sp. 7: Sch libn Havana Pub Schs, Havana Fla 52-. 9: ALA; Fla Assn Sch Libs; Fla Educ Assn. 14: Sch lib wk. 15: POBox 496, Havana FL 32333.

LAIR, LILA MARIE (GIYER). b N Miami Okla 16 Ap 11. 5: Northeastern Okla A&M Col AA; Kan State Col (Pittsburg) 60 BS in Ed; UOkla 64 MLS, Northwestern State Col summer 30; UKan summer 58. 06: Fr. 7: Clk typist flight dept Brit Flying Train Sch #3 Spartan Sch of Aeronautics 43-45; Yp libn Miami Pub Lib, Miami Okla 54-59; Asst libn Northeastern Okla A&M Col 60-. 8: ERIC A pplications Consul Research Wkshop Neas Okla A&M Col 69. 9: ALA; NEA; OklaLA; OklaEA; (chm Nom Com NE Lib Sect, Off). 10: Reviewers Club; Phi Theta Kappa; Kappa Delta Pi; Beta Phi Mu. 13: Yes. 14: Ya, catlg. 15: 909 J st NW, Miami OK 94354.

LAIR, NANCY (CHAMBERS). b Maben WVa 5 S 26. 4: E John Lair. 5: Longwood Col 44-48 (Chem, Biol) BS; Columbia 55-56 (LS) MS; ULondon summer 62 (Eng Lit); UKy 61-63. 6: Fr. 7: Lab tech Merck Co Inc (Elkton Va) 48; Tchr (Sci, Biol) Great Bridge High Sch (Norfolk Co Va) 49-51; Asst dean of women Longwood Col 51-55; Catlgr UKy Lib 56-62; Asst head acquis dept 62-66; Hd acquis dept 66-. 8: Tchr hist of bks, UKy summer 61. 9: ALA; Ohio Valley Group Tech Serv Libns (Chm 66). 10: Northside Neighborhood Assn, Lexington. 14: Ser, catlg & acquis. 15: 480 W Sixth st, Lexington Ky 40508.

LAIRD, ELEANOR CHILDS (LEONARD). b Lebanob Conn 15 Ap 08. 4: Donald Anderson Laird. 5: Pembroke Col 24-28 (Lat) AB; UNC 31-32 AB in LS. 6: Fr, Sp. 7: Asst to ref libn Brown U Lib 28-35; Organizer RI lib ext, Providence RI 35-36; Libn & organizer Arlington Co Libs, Arlington Va 37-39; Co-author (with husband) 40-; Adjunct research libn UDubuque 65-. 10: LWV. 12: Numerous books (with husband) on psychology and its practical applications. 14: Biog. 15: 3030 North River rd Rte 2, Lafayette In 47906.

LAIRD, LESBIA (REESE). b Winfield Ala 24 O 18. 4: Dennis Elvin Laird. 5: Tex Col of Arts & Ind 36-37 (Eng) Tex Women'sU 39-41 BS in LS. 6: Sp. 7: Libn high sch, Mercedes tex 41-44; Libn USN, Corpus Christi Texas 44-46; Libn US Army: Ft Lee Va 46-47, Europe 47-52; Base libn USAF: Mineral Wells Tex 52-55, Brooks AFB Tex 55-. 9: TexLA; SWLA; BexarCoLA. 10: Pecan Valley Country Club. 11: Beta Sigma Phi; Several Sustained Superior Performance Awards. 14: Ref (gen & recreational). 15: 5702 Wales ave, San Antonio Tx 78223.

LAIRD, MARGUERITE JANE. b Coquille Ore 22 S 05. 5: San Jose Col 24-26 (Eng) Jr col certif; UCal (Berkeley) 26-29 AB, 29-30 Gen Secondary Tchrs Certif, 30-31 Certif in Libnship. 6: Ger, Sp, Fr. 7: UCal (Davis) Lib 31; Act asst libn Marshfield Pub Lib, Coos Bay Ore 34-35; Ore State Lib Order Dept, Salem 35-37; Oakland (Cal) Pub Lib: Jr libn 41-45, Asst order libn 45-54, Supv libn lit div ref dept 54-62, Prin libn dept spec serv 62-. 9: ALA; AEAUSA; CalLA; Golden Gate Dist LA; Bay Area Ref Libns Coun (past sec & chm). 10: AAUW; Phi Beta Kappa; College Womens Club; Oakland Museums Assn; San Francisco Symphony Assn; San Francisco Opera Guild; Commun Betterment & Cultural Advancement; C of C. 14: Ref. 15: 2550 Dana st, Berkeley Ca 94704.

LAIRD, W(ILBUR) DAVID JR. b Kansas City Mo 15 Mr 37. 4: Linda Tusler. 5: UWichita 59-61 (Psych) UCLA 62-66 (Eng, LS) BA, MSLS. 6: Sp. 7: Aviation electronics tech (PO 2d) USN, Pacific 55-59; Mailroom clk UWichita 59-60; Guard & operator Dist Telegraph, Wichita Kan 60; Painter Boeing

Aircraft Corp, Wichita Kan 60-61; Tech Amer Electronics Inc, Culver City Cal 61-62; Lib asst UCLA Music Lib 62-66; Gen ref libn UCal(Davis) 66-67; Order libn UUtah 67-. 9: ALA; UtahLA. 10: Beta Phi Mu. 13: Yes. 14: Tech serv (esp acquis). 15: 1528 S 16th E, Salt Lake City Ut 84105.

LAITE, BERKLEY (HARRISON). b St John's Newfoundland Can 2 D 43. 4: Carol Schumacher. 5: Shippensburg State Col 62-66 (Eng, Fr) BS in Ed; UPittsburgh 67 MLS; UMd 69- (Educ Tech). 6: Fr. 7: Catlg asst UPittsburgh 67; Ref libn Shippensburg State Col 68, Dial acess dir 69-. 9: PennLA. 14: Dial access, ref. 15: 577 Nelson st, Chambersburg Pa 17201.

LAITE, CAROL A(NN SCHUMACHER). b Summit NJ 16 Ja 44. 4: Berkley Laite. 5: Shippensburg State Col 62-65 (Eng) BS in Ed; UPittsburgh 67-68 MLS. 7: Tchr sr high sch, Chambersburg Penn 65-66; Ref asst UPittsburgh 67; Catlgr Wilson Col 68-. 10: Beta Phi Mu. 14: Catlg, ref. 15: 577 Nelson st, Chambersburg Pa 17201.

LAKE, ALBERT CHARLES. b Vancouver BC Can 21 Jl 12. 4: Dorothea Olive Mackintosh. 5: UBC 29-31, 36-38 (Eng) BA; UCal 38-39 (LS) Certif. 6: Fr. 7: Libn I Kern Co Free Lib, Bakersfield Cal 39-41; Co Libn Trinity Co Free Lib, Weaversville Cal 41-43; Co Libn Sacramento Co Free Lib, Sacramento Cal 43-47; Lib Dir Riverside Pub Lib & Riverside Co Free Lib, Riverside Cal 47-. 8: Instr USoCal; Sch of Lib Sci. 9: ALA; SLA; CalLA; Pub Lib Execs Assn, SoCal (Past pres). 10: Rotarian; Riverside Breakfast Forum; Town & Gown. 13: Yes. 14: Admin, bk sel. 15: Riverside Pub Lib, Riverside CA 92502.

LAKE, JEANETTE M (STEIN). b Oakfield NY 27 My 13. 4: Ernest G Lake. 5: Mt Holyoke Col 30-34 (Psych) BA (magna cum laude); Harvard 34-35 (Educ); USoCal 62-64 MLS. 6: Fr. 7: Research asst Harvard U Grad Sch Educ 34-35; Testing spe Burdette Col 34-35; Catlgr Cal State Col (Fullerton) 64-. 9: ALA; CalLA; Orange Co Libns; So Cal Tech Proc Assn. 10: AAUW; Cal State Col (Fullerton) Faculty Women; Fullerton Jr Col Faculty Wives; Friends of Pub Lib; Patrons Lib; Friends of Col; N Orange Co Cultural Arts Forum. 14: catlg. 15: 409 E Las Palmas dr, Fullerton CA 92632.

LAKE, MARY REID. b Tenn 3 Mr 15. 4: Gildon Louis Lake. 5: Lane Col 48 (Eng) AB (magna cum laude); Peabody summer 61-63 MA in LS, summer 67. 06: Fr. 7: Elem tchr Palmer-Turner, Henning Tenn 37-49; Eng tchr Lauderdale High, Ripley Tenn 50-, Libn 55-; asst libn Lane Col 66-. 09: ALA; -RSD (chm Term Chap 68-69); TennLA; (life mem); Tenn Ed Congress; TennEA. 10: Alpha Kappa Alpha; Girl Scouts; Records Com Bd of Christ Educ; Ripley Housing Authority Com. 11: Meritorius Services Award, Lane Col 68. 14: Catlg, ref. 15: 212 Spring, Ripley Tn 38063.

LAKHANPAL, SARV KRISHNA. b India 31 Jl 28. 4: Usha Bali. 5: Panjab U (India) 42-46 (Eng) BA; E Punjab U (India) 46-49 (Eng) MA; UMich 61-62 AMLS. 6: Persian, Hindi, Urdu, Panjabi. 7: Lecturer in Eng Educ Dept Punjab, India 49-61; Hd S Asia unit UMich Lib (Ann Arbor) 61-66; Sr catlgr USask Lib 66, Hd ser dept 67-. 8: Chm, Job Evaluation Com, Saskatoon, 69-. 9: CanLA; ALA; SaskLA; SaskatoonLA. 10: India Can Assn (Saskatoon Sask). 12: "India Women: a Bibliography" (67). 13: Yes. 14: Catlg, ser, lib admin. 15: 424 11th st E, Saskatoon Saskatchewan Can.

LALLI, SARAH (MEDURI). b White Plains NY. 4: Fred Lalli. 5: NYU 42-52 (Eng Lit) BA; Columbia 39-42 (LS). 6: Fr, Sp, Ital. 07: Pub Lib, White Plains NY: Lib clerk 39-52, Jr libn 52-65, Sr libn I 65-. 7: Pub Lib, White Plains (NY) Lib clerk 39-52, Jr libn 52-65, Sr libn I 65-. 9: ALA; NYLA; WestchesterLA. 10: Civil Serv Employees Assn; Col Club, White Plains NY. 14: Ref. 15: 70 Coralyn ave, White Plains NY 10605.

LALLY, JOHN A. b Detroit Mich 3 Ap 19. 4: Aileen Dove. 5: Aquinas Col 46-48 (Fr) AB; UMich 49-50 AMLS; Mich StateU 53-55 (Educ) Certif. 6: Fr. 7: Chief warrant off Army af & Signal Corps, ETO 41-46; Bkmob libn Kent Co Lib, Grand Rapids Mich 50-51; Ref asst Mich State Lib, Lansing 51-56; Libn Belding High Sch, Belding Mich 56-64; Asst libn Grand Rapids Jr Col 64-67, Dir lib serv 67-. 9: Mich Commun Col Lib Admins. 14: Ref, a-v, admin. 15: RFD 3, Belding Mi 48809.

LALONDE, EMILE S J. b Marcellin Sask Can 3 N 18. 5: Col St-Ignace 32-36; Col Jean-de-Brebeuf 36-38; Scholasticat de l'Immaculee-Conception 42-45, 49-52 BA, LPh, LTh, BBibl. 6: Fr, Eng, Lat. 7: Prof of Lat & Fr Colle5ge de Saint-Boniface (Man) 45-48, 53-60, Libn 60-68; Libn Ctr des Etudes Univ de Trois-Rivieres 68-. 9: CanLA; Assn Canadienne des Bibliothecaires de Langue Francaise. 10: Societe Historique de Saint-Boniface. 14: Period, ref in philos. 15: 821 St-Francois-Xavier cp 548, Trois-Rivieres PQ Can.

LAM, LETITIA ELLEN. b Harrisonburg Va 11 Mr 37. 5: Madison Col 55-59 (LS) BS; UWis summers 61-66 (LS) MS. 7: Libn Washington-Lee High Sch, Arlington Va 59-. 9: ALA; NEA; VaEA; ArlingtonEA. 15: 3804 N 13th st, Arlington Va 22201.

LAMAR, EMILY (HELEN) CARR. b California 12 F 15. 4: Robert E Lamar. 5: Women's Col UDel 33-37 (Eng) AB; Drexel 38-39 BS in LS. 7: Child libn NYC Pub Lib 39-41; Libn Keystone Jr Col 41-42; Child libn Enoch Pratt Free Lib, Baltimore 42-43; Catlgr Johns Hopkins U Lib 45-46; Hosp libn VA Hosp, Palo Alto Cal 49-51; Ref libn Los Angeles Pub Lib 51-52, Supv sch libs Palo Alto Unified Sch Dist, Palo Alto Cal 53-55; Dist libn Mt Pleasant Sch Dist, San Jose Cal 67; Libn Cupertino Jr High Sch, Cupertino Cal 67-. 9: ALA; CalLA; CalSchL; CalTA; CalEA. 10: Stanford Women's Club. 14: Sch lib wk. 15: 925 Casanueva pl, Stanford Ca 94305.

LAMAR, MARILYN (LAESSER). b Buffalo NY 7 My 36. 4: James A Lamar. 5: UBuffalo 54-58 (Phil) BA; Columbia 58-59 (LS) MS. 6: Ger. 7: Asst libn Bronx Commun Col 59-60; Catlgr Buffalo & Erie Co Pub Lib, Buffalo NY 61-62; Gen catlgr NYC Pub Lib 62-63, Catlgr Schomburg Collection 63-67, Asst chief catlg off 67-68, Automation specialist 69-. 14: Automation, tech serv. 15: NY Pub Lib, 8 E 40th st, New York NY.

LAMB, SISTER AVILA CSJ. b Buffalo NY 26 Ag 13. 5: Col of St Catherine 31-35 (Hist) BA, 35-36 BS in LS. 06: Fr, Sp, Ger. 7: Libn St Joseph's Acad, St Paul 38-55; Libn Acad of the Holy Angels, Richfield Minn 55-. 8: Adv bd, Teen Age Book Club (Scholastic Bk Services) 62-65; Com on Cath Supp "Wilson Standard Catalog for High Sch Libraries" 64-. 9: CathLA. 13: Yes. 14: Use of "paper backs." 15: Acad of the Holy Angels, 6600 Nicollet ave, Richfield Mn 55423.

LAMB, R REBECCA. b Detroit 29 S 33. 5: Wayne State U 51-54 (Eng Lit); UMich 58-60 (Eng Lit) BA, 60-62 MA in LS. 7: Communications tech Petty Off 2nd Class US Navy Security Div 54-58; Child libn Detroit Pub Lib 60-64; Child libn Bloomfield Twp Pub Lib, Bloomfield Hills Mich 64-68, Coord youth wk 68-, Asst dir 68-. 9: ALA-PLA (program chm ChildRT); MichLA. 14: Child & yp wk. 15: 1099 Lone Pine rd, Bloomfield Hills Mi 48013.

LAMB, REV FR JOHN EARL. b Phila 31 O 26. 5: Temple U even 54-59; Divinity Sch of the Protestant Episcopal Church in Phila 59-62 (Theol) STB; Drexel 62-64 MS in LS. 6: New Testament Grk. 7: Toolmaker, Westinghouse Elec Corp, Lester Penn 43-45; Rifleman & Statistical Clerk, USArmy & Air Force, US & Panama CZ 45-48; Home off correspondent-Penn Mutual Life Insurance Co, Phila 48-51; Asst to reg stockkeeper Sherwin Williams Paint Co 51-53; Serv & sales correspondent Machinery Assoc, Wynnewood Penn 53-54; Prod expediter Amer Pulley Co, Phila 54-59; Assoc libn Divinity Sch of the Protestant Episcopal Church in Phila 62-. 8: Priest in the Episcopal Church. 9: ATheolLA. 14: Theol, church hist. 15: Apt C-102 4300 Spruce st, Phila Pa 19104.

LAMB, ROBERT SCOTT II. b Wash DC 1 Jl 29. 5: Cornell U 48-52 (Eng) AB; Portland State Col 53-54 (Fr); UCal(Berkeley) 54-57 (Eng) Gen Secondary Credential, 60-61 MLS. 6: Ger, Fr, Lat. 7: Pub info off 1st Lt USAFR 2343rd AFRCTC, Portland AFB, Portland Ore 52-54; Eng tchr Los Altos High Sch & Corcoran Jt Union High Sch, La Puente & Corcoran Cal 57-66; Asst libn "Oakland Tribune," Oakland Cal 61-62; Period libn Cal State Polytech Col(Pomona) 62-63, Asst catlgr 63-64; Ref libn Orange Coast Col 64-65; Assoc catlgr NY State Sch of Ind & Labor Rel, Cornell U 65-67; Hd res bk dept North western U Lib (Evanston) 67-68, hd circ div 68-. 9: IllLA. 10: Cal Lib Sch Assn; Northwestern U Lib Staff Assn. 14: Circ. 15: 1732 W Juneway terr apt 3d, Chicago Il 60626.

LAMBERT, ALLOYD PATRICK JR. b New Orlenas La 11 F 35. 5: SEast La Col 53-58 (Bus Admin) BA; LSU 62-64 MS in LS; Columbia 67-68 (Med Lit) Certif. 6: Fr, Ital. 7: Messenger West Union, New Orleans 52-58; Legal asst Gulf Oil Corp, New Orleans 58-61; Asst New Orleans Pub Lib 62; Grad fellow LSU (Baton Rouge) 62-64; Catlgr & ref libn LSU (New Orleans) 64-67; Asst libn SUNY (Stony Brook) 67-. 8: Supv New Orleans City Archives 62; Constr Indus Orient & Exper La & Miss 45-62; Assisted in planning the automation of card prod, circ, and acquis LSU (New Orleans) 64-67. 9: ALA; MedLA; LaLA; NY Tech Serv Libns. 10: SEast La Col Alum

Assn; Concert Choir of NO; NO East Optimist Club Orator Contest. 13: Yes. 14: Admin, devel new univ libs, current lib practice, machines. 15: PO Box 375, E Setauket NY 11733.

LAMBERT, GUY ROYAL SR. b Bangor Me 18 Ja 36. 4: Dorothy Apple. 5: Elon Col 55-59 (Philos) BA; UNC 59-60 (LS). 6: Sp. 7: May Mem Lib, Burlington NC: Page 56-58, Gen asst 59, Catlg libn 60-61; Assoc libn Campbell Col 61-63; Assoc libn Elon Col 63-. 9: ALA; NCLA. 10: Sigma Mu Sigma; Alpha Psi Omega. 14: Serv to undergrad studs. 15: 1111 McPherson rd, Burlington NC 27217.

LAMBERT, MARIAN ELAINE (WALKER). b Abilene Tex. 4: Edward D Lambert. 5: Hardin- simmonsU 42-46 (Eng, Educ) BA; UTex 53-59 MLS. 7: Tchr Tex high sch: Abilene 46-50, Iraan 51-53; Libn: Sweetwater High Sch, Sweetwater Tex 53-56, Abilene High Sch, Abilene Tex 56-57, Goliad Elem Sch, Odessa Tex 58-59, 60-65, Bonham Jr High Sch, Odessa Tex 66-. 9: TexStateLA; TexStateTA. 14: Sch libs. 15: 2100 Redbud, Odessa Tx 79760.

LAMBERT, NOEL P. b Birmingham Ala 24 D 18. 5: William & Mary 36-40 (Fr) BA; Emory 57-59 (LS) MA. 6: Fr. 7: Catlgr US Nat Med Lib Communicable Disease Ctr Atlanta 57-. 9: ALA; GaLA; Metro Atlanta LA. 10: Atlanta Mem Arts Center. 14: Catlg, ref. 15: 96 Montgomery Ferry dr NE, Atlanta Ga 30309.

LAMBERT, PATTIE ANN. b Brodnax Va 11 Ap 30. 5: William & Mary 47-50 (Eng) BA; UNC 50-51 BS in LS. 7: Catlgr & gen asst Braswell Pub Lib Rocky Mount NC 51-; Corr Rocky Mt Evening and Sunday Telegram, Rocky Mt NC 57-. 9: ALA; NCLA. 10: Rocky Mount Chap (NC) Symphony Soc; Rocky Mount Arts & Crafts Ctr; Rocky Mount Motorcycle Club; Downtown Deskworkers; Therapeutic Swimming League; St Mary's Guild; European Friends Exch Soc. 14: Pub rel, readers adv, bk reviews, Sunday newspaper bk col. 15: 311 Arlington ter, Rocky Mount NC 27801.

LAMBERT, ROBERT (ALLEN). b Hagerstown Md 30 S 36. 4: Gladys Long. 5: UMd 54-59 (Hist) AB; CatholicU 59-63 MSLS. 7: Catlgr Doc Lib Applied Physics Lab, Silver Spring Md 59-63; Supv tech info serv Electromagnetic Compatibility Analysis Center, Annapolis Md 63-66; Chief libn Tech Info Ctr Fairchild-Hiller Corp, Germantown Md 66-67; Asst libn US Naval Acad Lib, Annapolis Md 67-. 9: SLA. 10: USNaval Inst; Nat Rifle Assn; Jr C of C; Cape St Claire Improvement Assn; USNA Spokesmariners Toastmasters Club. 12: Assoc ed, "US Naval Institute Procesings" (67-). 14: Mgt & man/machine systems; info retrieval & corresponding catlg techniques, tech proc. 15: RFD 4 985 St Margarets ave, Annapolis Md 21401.

LAMBKIN, CLAIRE (ALICE). b Brooklyn NY 16 N 25. 5: Brooklyn Col 44-53 (Hist) BA; St John's U 54-57 MLS. 7: Tchr of Lib Bd of Educ, NYC 53-57; Admin libn HQ US Army, Europe 59-61; Libn Amer Mgt Assn, NYC 61-. 9: SLA. 10: Kappa Delta. 14: Ref, info storage & retrieval systems. 15: 904 E 38 st, Brooklyn Ny 11210.

LAMERS, CARL (FRITZ). b Malang Dutch East Indies 20 Ag 21. 5: ULeiden 47-54 LLM; UTex 59-64 MLS. 6: Dutch, Ger, Fr, Sp, Afrikaans. 7: Foreign correspondent Rotterdamsche Bank, Amsterdam Netherlands 55-57; Manager Oriental Imports, San Antonio Tex 57-; Salesman Joske's of Texas, San Antonio Tex 57; Multilith operator City Water Bd, San Antonio Tex 58-59; Lib asst UTex Law Lib 59-63; Head gifts & exch Yale U Lib 63-64, Soc sci bibliogr 64-. 8: Consul So Conn State Col 67-68. 9: BSA; NY Lib Club. 14: Bibliog. 15: 318 Elm st apt a5, New Haven Ct 06511.

LAMKIN, BURTON EMANUEL. b San Antonio Tex 30 Jl 34. 4: Kathryne Marie Stephens. 5: UDenver 51-55 (Chem) BS, 55-56 (LS) MA. 7: Page San Antonio Pub Lib, San Antonio Tex 47-51; Page UDenver 52-53, Lib asst 53-56; Research libn Honeywell Research Center, Hopkins Minn 56-61; Libn IBM Corp, San Jose Cal 61-62, Manager IBM DL Lib 62-65; Chief Lib & Info Retrieval Br Fed Aviation Agency, Wash DC 65-69; Lecturer dept of Lib Sci Catholic U 68-; Adj Prof Sch of Lib & Info Serv UMd (College Park) 68-; Asst Dir pub serv Nat Agric Lib, Wash DC 69-. 8: John Cotton Dana Lect Atlanta U 64; IBM Lib Systems Task Force 65; Fed Lib Com Wash DC Rep Dept of Trans 65-69; FIC Automation Ta sk Force 66-; Panel on Operational Techniques and Systems COSATI 66-67; Role of Libraries in Info Systems Task Force FIC 67-68; Exec Sec Task Gp on Lib Prog, COSATI Wash DC 69-. 9: SLA (Bd Dirs 68-71, Rep to AFIPS 67-69 (Engng Div) Nom Com 69, Trans Div v-chm & chm-elect 68; San Fran Circs Chap; Dir 63-65; Minn Chap; pres 60-61); Amer Mgt Assn (Adm Mgt Adv Com); Amer Fed of Info Proc Soc (Bd Dirs); ASIS. 10: Kiwanis; Phi Mu Alpha; Sinphonia; Boy Scouts. 12: Ed Literature Notes sect of "American Documentation" 64-65; Ed, "Documentation Abstracts" 66. 13: Yes. 14: Lib mgt, systems analysis , lib automation, info ret. 15: Nat Agric Lib, US Dep of Agric, Beltsville Md 20705.

LAMM, GAIL (MR). b Los Angeles Cal 29 D 18. 5: UCLA 47-51 (Geog) BA, 52; USoCal 61-63 (LS) MS. 7: Third off US Maritime Serv 42-46; Photogrammetric eng US Army Map Serv, Wash DC 52-55; Tchr Los Angeles & Santa Ana Schs 55-63; Libn Mt San Antonio Jr Col 63-65; Libn Santa Ana Col 65-67; Libn Long Beach City Col 67-68; Libn Cypress Jr Col 68-. 9: NEA; CalTA; CalLA. 10: Bruin Bench; Trojan Club. 14: Ref, a-v resources. 15: 116 St Joseph ave, Long Beach Ca 90803.

LAMON, SARA LOUISE. b Macon Ga 31 O 06. 5: Wesleyan Col (Macon Ga) 25-29 (Hist) AB; Columbia 35 BSLS. 6: Fr, Sp. 7: Libn Lanier High Sch for Girls, Macon Ga 29-31; Libn A L Miller High Sch 31-41; Act libn Mercer U 41; Asst libn Mary Washington Col 41-43; Asst libn The Infantry Sch, Ft Benning Columbus Ga 43-46; Asst libn Wesleyan Col (Macon Ga) 46-58; Libn Lanier Jr High Sch Macon Ga 46-. 9: ALA; NEA; SELA; GaEA; GaLA. 10: AAUW; DAR; UDC; Magn a Charta Dames; Middle Ga Hist Soc; F riends of Lib. 14: Ref & research, Gencal. 15: 923 North ave, Macon Ga 31201.

LaMONICA, MARVADENE (BOYTE). b Leesburg Fla 29 Ag 15. 4: Ralph LaMonica. 5: John B StetsonU 33-37 (Math, Educ) BS; Fla State Col for Women summer 40 (Statistics); So Conn State Col 63-66 (LS). 6: Fr. 7: Tchr Jackson Co Bd of Educ, Marianna Fla 37-38; Tchr Day Sch, Day Fla 38-40; Statistician Fla Ind Commsn, Tallahassee 40-42; Statistician US Employment Serv, Tallahassee Fla 42-46; Statistician Conn Labor Dept, Hartford 46-47; Libn (staff) New Haven Free Pub Lib, New Haven Conn 48-. 9: ConnLA. 10: Pi Kappa Sigma; Sigma Pi Sigma. 14: Adult, ref, readers serv. 15: 6 Lincoln pl, West Haven Ct 06516.

LaMONT, BARBARA GIBSON. b Huntington Ind 8 N 25. 5: William & Mary 43-47 (Classics) AB; Radcliffe 47-49 (Classical Philol) MA; Simmons 52-54 MS in LS. 6: Grk, Lat, Fr. 7: Latin tchr Mary C Wheeler Sch, Providence 49-51; Clerk Lamont Lib, Harvard 51-53; Catlgr Widener Lib Harvard Col 53-56, Chief of gifts & exch 56-61, Admin asst resources & acquis 61-64; Libn Douglass Col 64-67; Libn Vassar 67-. 8: Consul: Kauka Col, Kauka Park NY 68; St Thomas Acquinas Col, Sparrid NY 69. 9: ALA;-ACRL;-RTSD; SEast (NY) Lib Resources Coun (Bd Trustees). 14: Admin, resources. 15: Vassar Col, Poughkeepsie Ny 12601.

LAMPEN, ALYCE M. b Elwood Kan 25 Ag 13. 4: Lathan H Lampen. 5: SUNY (Brockport) 65 9educ) BS in Ed; SUNY (Geneseo) 65-68 MLS. 6: Fr. 7: Sec Admissions Off SUNY (Brockport) 61-65; Asst libn SUNY (Brockport) 65-. 9: SUNYLA. 10: West Monroe Hist Soc; Alumni Assn SUNY (Brockport); Fac Women SUNY; Grand Offrs Assn Monroe Dist. 14: Pub serv. 15: 99 South ave, Brockport NY 14420.

LAMPERT, HARRIET J. b Santa Ana Cal 5 N 32. 5: Fullerton Jr Col 50-52 AA; UCal(Berkeley) 52-54 (Eng) BA, 54-55 MLS. 6: Ger. 7: Catlgr Orange Pub Lib, Orange Cal 55-59; Child libn Long Beach Pub Lib, Long Beach Cal 59-65, Br libn 65-. 9: ALA; CalLA; Sch & Childs Libs Assn SoCal (v-pres 65). 10: Beta Phi Mu; PEO Sisterhood. 14: Childs serv, br admin. 15: 2741 E DeSoto st apt 1, Long Beach Ca 90814.

LAMPMAN, LOUISE (FLETCHER). b Albany Ore 23 Ap 13. 4: William M Lampman. 5: Ore stateU 30-31 (Educ); WillametteU 31-34 (Educ) BA; UWash stateU 30-31 (Educ); WillametteU 31-34 (Educ) BA; UWash summers 38-39, 41, 57 (Eng, LS); UOre summers 52-53, 59, 61 MS in LS. 7: Tchr: Mill City High Sch, Mill City Ore 36-38, Elmira Union High Sch, Elmira Ore 38-40; Tchr & libn Cal Young Jr High Sch, Eugene Ore 53-55, Libn 55-61; Libn T Roosevelt Jr High Sch, Eugene Ore 61-67; Asst prof of libnship & libn campus lab sch Central Wash State Col 67-69, Assoc Prof of libnship & curriculum libn 69-. 8: Staff (Inst Leader, Asst Dir) UOre summer NDEA Inst in Libnship 65, 66; Consul Governor's Conf on Libs, Wash. 9: ALA (Coun); AASchL; NEA-DAVI; OreEA (Exec Com, past v-pres & pres Lib Dept, chm Scholarship Com, Memb Com); Ore Inst Materials Assn; WashEA; WashASchL; Wash DAVI; AAUW; AAUP. 14: Sch libnship, curr materials. 15: 1711 College pl, Ellenburg Wa 98926.

LAMPMAN, WILMA (ABBEY). b Joice Iowa 13 D 21. 4: Duncan Lampman. 5: State Col of Iowa summer terms 39-44 (Kindergarten, Prim); SoIllU 59 (Elem Educ, LS) BS in Educ,

62 (Instr Materials) MS in Educ. 7: Elem tchr Rural Sch, Worth & Winnebago Counties Iowa 39-42; Elem tchr City Sch, Lake Mills & Hanlontown Iowa 42-45; Church sec First Presbyterian, Rochester Minn 45-46; Lib asst Talladega Col 46-47; Playground supv Pub Schs, Ottumwa Iowa summer 50; Cafeteria cashier UHouston summers 59-60; Libn & supv Voc Tech Inst, SoIllU 62-. 9: IllLA (Citation Com, Nat Lib Week Coun 67). 10: Girl Scout Leader; Univ Women's Club; PTA; Women's Soc for Christian Serv; Bus & Profess Women. 14: Ref. 15: RR #2, Carterville Il 62918.

LAMSEY, SARA CORNELIA (TIPTON). b Ashland City Tenn 16 O 13. 4: Chester H Lamsey. 5: Athens Col 32-36 (Eng) AB; Peabody 41 (LS) BS. 6: Sp, Lat. 7: Tchr & libn Monterey High Sch, Monterey Tenn 36-46; Libn ETenn State U 46-48; Libn Abraham Lincoln Elem Sch, Kingsport Tenn 47-48; Libn Monterey High Sch, Monterey Tenn 50-52; Supv sch lib serv Hamilton Co Schs, Chattanooga Tenn 52-. 8: Chattanooga Area Lib Assn (past pres); AV Sect ETenn EA (past chm); Sch Libs Sect TennLA (past chm). 9: NEA; ALA; TennEA; TennLA. 10: Alpha Delta Kappa; PTA. 11: Woman of the year; Colonial Dames of the XVII Century 63. 14: Bk seln, a-v materials. 15: 4416 Murray Hills dr, Chattanooga Tn 37416.

LAMSON, MERLE EDWIN. b Yakima Wash 10 Ag 30. 4: Norma Roberts. 5: Yakima Jr Col 49-50, 52-53 (Math) AAS; Brigham Young U 53-55 (Math) BS; Colo Col summer 56; Columbia 57-60 (LS) MS; Brigham Young U 62-68 (Educ Admin); USoCal 68- (LS). 6: Ger, Fr. 7: Tchr math, electronics Weber Co High Sch, Ogden Utah 55-57; Math libn Columbia U 57-60; Young adults libn So Puget Sound Reg Lib, Olympia Wash 60-61; Ser libn Brigham Young U 61-63, Sci & tech catlgr 63-66, Instr dept of Lib & Info Sci 66-. 09: UtahLA; Utah Acad Arts, Scis & Letters. 10: AAUP; Phi Delta Kappa; Boy Scouts; Sigma Pi Sigma. 13: Yes. 14: Tchg, ref, catlg. 15: 4155 N Crestview ave, Provo Ut 84601.

LANCASTER, J(OHN) HERROLD. b Nelsonville Ohio 5 S 1898. 4: Florence Stinchcomb. 5: Ohio Wesleyan U 16-20 (Math) BS; OhioU summer 21 (Educ, Bio); OhioStateU summers 22, 23, 24, 26, 29 (Sch Admin) MA; Columbia 32-33 summers 28, 30, 31, 33 (Educ of Tchrs) PhD, summers 38-41 BS (LS). 6: Fr, Ger, Sp. 7: Off Train Ft Sheridan Ill & Camp Perry Ohio 18; USArmy Rifle Instr 2nd Lt Infantry SATC Oberlin Col 18; Tchr coach adminstr Ohio schs, Wauseon 20-24, Oak Harbor 24-25, Old Fort 25-27; Dir of stud tchg Heidelberg Col 27-39, Libn 39-43; Asst Prof Lib Sci & Physics UIll (Urbana) 43-45; Libn & Assoc Prof Lib Sci Peabody Col 45-49; Dir of the Lib Ohio WesleyanU 49-64; Head Libn Baldwin-Wallace Col 64-68, Lib consul 68-. 8: Supv ESMWT Col of Engng U of Toledo 41-43 (Tiffin Ohio); Summer tchg Peabody Lib Sch 55, 56, 57, 59, 61; Syracuse Lib Sch 51, 52; Kent State U Dept of Lib Sci 65; Lib bldg consul Ohio Wesleyan U -66. 9: ALA; ACRL (chm Tchr Training Sect); AALS (chm Com on Recr); NEA-DAVI; OhioLA (chm Col & U Sect); Ohio Col Assn (chm Libs Sect); A-V Coun of Ohio; Midwest Acad -libns Conf. 10: AAUP; Nashville Lib Club; Delaware Co Hist Soc; PTA; Kiwanis; Methodist Church (Steward, Trustee, Lay Delegate to Ann Conf); C of C; Amer Red Cross; Boy Scouts; Bd Trustees Delaware Co (Ohio) Dist Lib Phi Delta Kappa; Kappa Delta Pi. 11: Columbia Tchrs Col Fellow; Red Cross Medal of Serv. 12: "Use of the Library by Student Teachers" (41); Ed bd, "Lincoln Library of Essential Information". 13: Yes. 14: Admin, tchg, planning Col Lib Bldgs. 15: 49 Mason ave, Delaware Oh 43015.

LANCASTER, LUCY LEE. b Elliston Va 28 Je 05. 5: Va polytech Inst 25 (Biol) BS; NY State Lib Sh 26 (LS) Certif; Columbia 31 (LS) MS. 7: Va Polytech Inst Lib: Stud asst 23-25, Asst libn 26-29, Assoc libn 29-55, Assoc libn in &hg of readers' serv 55-. 9: ALA; SELA; VaLA. 10: AAUW; AAUP; Phi Kappa Phi; Delta Kappa Gamma; Blacksburg Reg Art Assn; Blacksburg Music Club. 14: Ref, interlib loans. 15: 303 W Washington st, Blacksburg Va 24060.

LANCASTER, RICHARD (FALLON). b Roanoke Va 10 Ag 37. 5: Roanoke Col 55-59 (Hist) BA; UNC 63-64 MSLS. 7: Stud asst UNC Med Lib 63-64; Lib asst Roanoke Pub Lib, Roanoke Va 60-63, Head tech serv 64-65; Catlgr Va Mil Inst 65-66; Coord Lib Serv Va West Commun Col 66-. 9: ALA; VaLA; SELA. 14: Catlg. 15: 2522 Crystal Spring ave SW, Roanoke Va 24014.

LANCE, DAVID IRWIN. b Dunellen NJ 27 N 28. 4: Marilyn E Walters. 5: Rutgers 46-50 (Educ) BS in Ed (with highest honors), 54-55 MLS. 7: Tchr Cranford High Sch Cranford NJ 50-51, 53; Personnel Mgt (Spec Sgt) USArmy 51-53; Timekeeper Aluminum Co of Amer, Garwood NJ 53-54; Catlgr Hunter Col 55-60, Soc sci libn 60-63; Sr libn Plainfield Pub Lib, Plainfield NJ 63-65, Asst lib dir 65- 67, Hd tech serv 67-. 8: Instr NJ State Lib, Regl Ref Wkshops 67-68; Instr Introd to Li b Wk, Plainfield Adult Evening Sch 68-; Mem NJ State Lib Adv Com For Statewide Proc Study 68-. 9: ALA-ACRL; -RTSD; NJLA; (Tech Serv Sect: v-pres 67-68, pres 68-69); Lib Assn City Col NY v-pres 62-63. Lib Assn City Col NY (v-pres 62-63). 10: Phi Beta Kappa. 14: Ref, admin, lib educ, tech serv. 15: 1213 Cambridge ave, Plainfield NJ 07062.

LANCOUR, HAROLD. b Duluth Minn 27 Je 08. 4: Marie McClellan. 5: Institut Universitaire de Hautes Etudes Internat 30-31; UWash 30-35 (Internat Rel, Law) AB; Columbia 36-40 BS in LS; MS in LS, 46-48 (Admin of Higher Educ) EdD. 6: Fr. 7: Ref asst NY Pub Lib 35-37; Mus libn Cooper Union 37-39, Libn & Prof of Bibliog 39-47; Instr Army Sch for Unit Libns (Cpl), Paris & Oberammergau 45-47, Assoc dr & Prof of Lib Sci UIll Grad Lib Sch(Urbana) 47-61; Dir USIS Libs in France, Paris 52-53; Dean & Prof of Lib Sci UPittsburgh Grad Sch of Lib & Info Scis 61-. 8: Dir USIS Libs in France, State Dept FSO-3 52-53; Mem UNESCO Internat Com on Soc Sci Documentation, Conducted Survey of Libraries in Gi, Nigeria, Sierra Leone and Gambia (Carnegie Corporation) 57; Consul on Lib Educ, Pratt Inst 59; Consul on Libs, Dept of Pub Instr in Liberia 60-61 (Ford Foundation); Dir Neb State Survey of Libs 61-62; AID Consul; Ministry of Educ, Mali 63; USan Carlos, Guatemala 64-65; USAID Consul on survey of bk production and distribution in Iran; Consul SUNY 66, bk survey of Chile 66; Consul on Libs; USan Carlos, Guatemala, 4 Ill libs 66, 68; Consul on Lib Educ; Kent State U 67, Iowa State U 69. 9: ALA (Coun rep IllLA; chm Bd of Educ for Libnship 54-56, chm Com on Accredit 56-57); -ACRL (Bd Dirs 46-49, chm Egnr Sch Libs Sect 46);-AALS (pres 54-56); Amer Antiq Soc; PennLA; Pittsburgh Lib Club. 10: Grolier Club(NY); Caxton Club(Chicago); Pittsburgh Bibliophiles; Archons of Colophon; Univ Club of Pittsburgh; Pittsburgh Junta; Phi Delta Phi; Alpha Beta Alpha (Hon); Beta Phi Mu; Amer Antiq Soc. 11: Fulbright sr Scholar, Eng 50-51; Richardson Lectr, Geneseo State U 67. 12: "Passenger Lists of Ships Coming to North America 1607-1825" (38, 3rd ed 63); "Heraldry; A Guide to Reference Books" (38); "American Art Auction Catalogues, 1705-1942" (44); "Issues in Library Education" (49); "The Dillard University Library; Survey Report" (60); Ed "Library Trends" (52-62); "The School Library Supervisor" (56); "Libraries in British West Africa" (58); "The University of Liberia Library; Report of a Survey" (60); Ed "Journal of Education for Librarianship" (60-63); "Nebraska Libraries Face the Future; a Comparative Survey" (62); "Report of a Survey Mission to Mali" (63); "The University of San Carlos Library and Library School" (64); Jt ed "Encyclopedia of Library Information Science" (69-). 13: Yes. 14: Admin, educ for libnship, bibliog, internat libnship. 15: 429 Morrison dr, Mt Lebanon Pa 15228.

LAND, BRIAN (REGINALD). b Niagara Falls Ont Can 29 Jl 27. 4: Edith Eddis. 5: UToronto 45-49 (Pol Sci & Econ) BA, 52-53 (LS) BLS, 56 MLS, 63 (Pol Sci) MA. 6: Fr. 7: Copy ed, T Eaton Co Ltd 50-51; Ref libn ref div Toronto Pub Lib 53-55; Catlgr UToronto 55-56; Head bus & ind div, Windsor (Ont) Pub Lib 56-57; Asst ed Canadian Business Montreal 57-58, Assoc ed 58-59; Asst libn UToronto Lib 59-63, Assoc libn 63-64; Exec asst to Minister of Finance, Govt of Canada 63-64; Prof & Dir Sch of Lib Sci UToronto 64-. 8: Research consul UToronto (Can) Dept of Labour Research Project 56; Lib consul to Ontario Centenn Centre of Sci & Tech 66; Consul on Bldg Prog; Sch of Lib & Info Serv UMd 67, Peabody Lib Sch Geo Peabody Col 68. 9: CanLA (Coun 62-63); ALA; AALS; (dir 66-69) OntLA (First v-pres 62-63); SLA Inst Prof ess Libns Ont (pres 62-63); Can ALS, (pres 66-67); Can Lib Res & Devel Coun (v-pres 65-67); Ont Prov Lib Coun; Ont Certif Bd. 10: Beta Phi Mu; Arts & Letters Club of Toronto; Bibliog Soc Can Fac Club, UToronto. 11: Kenneth R Wilson Memorial Award for best article on Merchandising Trade, Gen Bus of Finance, 59; Distinguished Achievement Award, Ont Lib Trustees Assn 68. 12: Eglinton (65); "Avenues of Research: A Guide to Sources of Business Informat ion," (62); "Directory of Business, Trade and Professional Associations in C anada, Montreal, Canadian Business," (59, 2d ed 62); "A Cr itical Evaluation of The Index of The Labour Gazette, 1900-1955" (57); "A Student's Guide to the University Library," (59 2d ed 61, 3d ed 62). 13: Yes. 14: Admin, ref. 15: Sch of Lib Sci UToronto, Toronto 181 Can.

LAND, ROBERT HUNT. b Surry Va 7 D 12. 4: Elizabeth Dillard Waterman. 5: Tyler Jr Col 31-32 AA; William & Mary 32-34 (Eng) AB; UVa 35-36, 40-41 (Hist) MA; Columbia 38, 39, 40 (LS) BS. 6: Fr. 7: Jr hist Jamestown Archeological Project, Jamestown Va 36-38; Instr in hist & archivist William

& Mary Col 38-42; Lt US Naval Res, Atlantic & Pacific 42-45; Assoc libn & libn William & Mary Col 45-51; Asst chief mss div LC 51-58, Asst chief gen ref & bibliog div 58-64, Chief gen ref & bibliog div 64-. 8: Instr & Visit Prof (hist & lib sci): No Va Ext UVa 59, George Washington U 61, Richmond Profess inst, Richmond Va 65, 67, UMd (College Park) 66, 67; Asst dir for Bibliog and Ref Serv, LC 66; LC Coord LC, George Washington U Jt Grad Prog in Amer Thought & Culture 67-; Lectr on mss curtorship at several insts 54-60. 9: ALA (Coun 46-48); Amer Studies assn (sec-treas 52-54, pres of Chesapeake Chap 57); DCLA. 10: Phi Beta Kappa. 11: LC; Super Accomplishment Award 53. 12: "Bacon's Castle, Surry Co, Va", "Historic Sites survey Report", Nat Park Ser (37); "National Union Catalog of Manuscript Collections" (54). 13: Yes. 14: Ref, mss. 15: 220 Virginia ave, Alexandria Va 22302.

LAND, ROY. b Henry Co Va 13 Mr 08. 5: Averett Col 23-25 (Eng); UVa 29-30 (Educ) BS, 30-31 (Eng) MS; UMich 42-43 (LS) BA. 7: Eng tchr Spencer-Penn High Sch, Spencer Va 26-29; Sec Bureau of Sch & Community Drama UVa 31-39; Circ libn Alderman Lib UVa 31-. 8: Lib Consul for United Bd for Christian Higher Educ in Asia, Hong Kong & Taiwan 59-60. 9: ALA (Coun 60-64, reg chm mem com 56-59); SELA (Exec Bd 56-60); VaLA (PRES 55-56, Activities Coun 65-68). 10: LWV; AAUW; Va Players; Fortnightly Bk Club; hi Beta Kappa; Phi Kappa Phi; Beta Phi Mu. 12: Ed: "Virginia Drama News," (32-39); "Plays for Amateurs" (35); Catalogue of the Makiam Library." 13: Yes. 14: Circ, readers serv, ref. 15: 3 Dawson's row, Charlottesville Va 22903.

LANDAU, HERBERT BERNARD. b NYC 24 O 40. 4: Barbara Carol Greenberg. 5: Hunter Col 58-63 (Chem) AB; Columbia 63-64 (LS) MS; Drexel 68 (Info Sci). 6: Fr, Ger. 7: US Army Reserve 61-67; Stud asst Hunter Col Lib 62-63; Stud asst Columbia U Engng Lib summer 63; Lit analyst Bell Telephone Labs, Murray Hill NJ 64-65; Ref libn Bell Telephone Labs, Holmdel NJ 65; Lib operations supv Bell Telephone Labs, Murray Hill NJ & Naperville Ill 65-67; Lib systs analyst Auerbach Corp Philadelphia 67-. 8: Presented 10 prof devel seminars on info retrieval for ACM 68; Planning com Annual Info Retrieval Colloquium. 9: SLA; ASIS; SLA (chm Finance Com NJ Chap 64-65); ACM; Spec Lib Coun of Phila (treas Sci-Tech Gp). 10: Beta Phi Mu. 12: Asst ed "Bulletin of the NJ Chapter, Special Libraries Association"; "State of the Art Survey of Computer Assisted Placement Systems" (68). 14: Consul on computer applications in libnship, info syst design & analysis. 15: 30 Springhouse la, Media Pa 19063.

LANDER, DOROTHY E (JOHNSON). b Oshtemo Mich 9 Jl 05. 4: A L Lander. 5: Kalamazoo Col 23-26 (Fr); West Mich U 57-59 (Eng) BA, 61-63 (LS) MA. 6: Fr. 7: West Mich U; Clerk 59-63, Asst order dept 63-65, Res libn 65-, Ref 65-. 9: ALA; MichLA. 10: AAUW; Beta Phi Mu; Audubon Soc; Kalamazoo Camera Club. 14: Tech serv, res bks, ref. 15: 3219 Magnolia cir, Kalamazoo Mi 49001.

LANDER, DOROTHY JOAN. b Mt Kisco NY 20 Ap 29. 5: Washington Square Col NYU 46-51 (Eng) BA; Simmons 60-61 MLS. 7: Catlgr Wellesley Col 61-62; Fine art libn Greenwich Lib, Greenwich Conn 62; Fine Arts Libn Yonkers (NY) Pub Lib 62-64, Ref libn 64-66; Dir Ossining Pub Lib Ossining NY 66-. 8: Consul Med Lib, Stony Lodge Hosp, Ossining NY. 9: ALA; NYLA; WestchesterLA. 14: Fine arts collections, bldg phono record collections. 15: 25 Old Post rd, Armonk NY 10504.

LANDERS, LORA. b Maplewood NJ 14 Mr 27. 5: Mt Holyoke 45-49 (Econ) BA; Columbia 50-53 (LS) MS. 6: Sp. 7: Clerk libn I libn II NY Pub Lib 49-54; Field libn asst command libn US Army Spec Serv, Europe 54-56; Libn II coordinator of young adult serv, Minneapolis Pub Lib 57-65; Coordinator of adult & young adult serv Hennepin Co Lib, Minneapolis 65-. 9: ALA-YASD (Bd 63-, Lib Serv to Disadvantaged 64-, chm Best Bks for YA Com 66, 67);-ASD (m em var coms); MinnLA (chm Recr Com, chm Mem Com, chm Child & YP Sect). 12: "Young Adult Services in the Sma ll Public Library". 13: Yes. 14: Adult & young adult ser, ref, pub libs. 15: 95 Walden, Burnsville Mn 55378.

LANDGRAF, MARY (NORTON). b San Francisco 7 Ag 37. 4: David Leonard. 5: San Francisco Col for Women 55-58 (Hist); San Francisco State Col 58-60 (Psych) AB; UCal 61-62 MLS, 62-63 (L.S). 6: Sp., Fr. 7: Jr libn San Francisco Pub Lib, Chinatown Br 58-59, Jr libn Anza Br 60-63; Research asst Grad Sch of Libnship ucal(Berkeley) 62-63, Reviser 63-64. 9: ALA; AALS; Assn Col Res Libs; CalLA (sec-treas No Cal Tech Processes Group 63-64). 10: Women's Faculty Club; UCal(Berkeley); Beta Phi Mu; Viking Ski Club (San Francisco). 13: Yes. 14: Classif, catlg, educ for libnship, sch libnship. 15: 119 LaVerne ave, Mill Valley Cal 94941.

LANDIKUSIC, TOMISLAV H. b Gornj Ivakuf Yugoslavia 7 Mr 33. 4: Laura Lee Langebaugh. 5: UZagreb 52-54 (Econ); E Carolina Col 59-61 (Bus & Admin) AB; Ind U 62-65 (LS) MS. 6: Serbo-Croatian, Russian, Bulgarian, Slovenian, Scandinavian, Slavic, Ger, Swedish. 7: Off in the US Army Res, Bloomington Ind currently; Sp/4 (Artillery) US Army, Ft Bragg NC 57-59; Asst to head of period LC 61-62; Slavic catlgr Ind U 62-66; Hd catlg libn Tex Christian U 66-68; Hd catlg libn & Asst Prof Utah U 68-. 9: ALA; TexLA; UtahLA. 10: Soccer Assn Utah; US Army Reserve. 14: Catlg, tech serv, admin, spec collections. 15: 2045 Wilmington ave, Salt Lake City Ut 84109.

LANDIS, MARTHA. b Champaign Ill 22 N 35. 5: UIll 54-57 (Hist) BA, 58-59 (LS) MS. 6: Fr, Ger, Sp, Ital. 7: Asst undergrad libn UIll(Urbana) 59, Union browsing room libn 60-63; Asst ref libn Cornell U 63-. 68; Assoc ref libn UIll (Urbana) 68-. 9: ALA. 14: Ref. 15: 609 W Oregon st, Urbana Il 61801.

LANDIS, RUTH (MAY). b Wisconsin Rapids Wis 20 N 23. 4: George E Landis. 5: UWis Ext Div 41-42; Valparaiso 42-45 (Hist) BA; Rosary Col 45-47 BALS. 7: Catlgr McHenry Pub Lib, Modesto Cal 47-51; Catlgr Lane Pub Lib, Hamilton Ohio 51-55; Asst libn Framingham State Col Lib 58-62; Catlgr Seattle Pub Lib 63; Catlgr Penn Military Col 64-66; Libn Provident Hosp Sch of Nursing, Baltimore 67; Libn educ dept Seattle Pub Lib 67-. 14: Catlg, ref. 15: 4463 Glenn way SW, Seattle Wa 98116.

LANDMANN, REBECCA (JONES). b Lexington Ill 4 Ag 19. 4: Wendell A Landmann. 5: UIll 37-40 (Hist, Fr) AB, 40-41 BS in LS. 6: Fr, Ger. 7: Libn Clinton High Sch, Clinton Ill 41-43; Libn for War Info Center Purdue U summer 42; High sch libn Leyden High Sch, Franklin Park Ill 43-44; Circ libn Anacostia Br DC Pub Lib 44-45; Ser & tr Naval Research Lab, Wash DC 45-46; Sch lib supv River Forest(Ill) Pub Schs 51-64; Libn consul Bryan(Tex) Pub Schs 65-. 8: Libn consul supv in chg sch library system & cent-proc center for 15 pub schs. 9: IllSchLA (Bd, chm 1964 spring meeting); River Forest EA (pres). 10: Blackhawk Heights Wom en's Club; Phi Beta Kappa. 13: Yes. 14: Sch lib admin. 15: 1602 Dominik dr, College Station Tx 77840.

LANDO, FAY. b Winnipeg Manitoba Can 9 Ag 38. 5: UManitoba 56-60 BA; McGill 64-66 MLS. 6: Fr. 7: Lib asst Winnipeg Pub Lib, Winnipeg Manitoba Can 56-61; Lib asst Lambeth Borough Council, London England 61-62; Asst libn Manitoba Dept of Health, Winnipeg Manitoba Can 62-64; Asst libn Royal Victoria Hosp, Montreal 64-66; Research libn Urwick, Currie & Partners Ltd, Toronto Ont Can 66-68; Libn Ont Dept of Agric & Food, Toronto Ont Can 69-. 9: SLA. 14: Ref, spec libs. 15: Apt 103 23 Oriole rd, Toron to 7 Can.

LANDO, JOAN. b Canton Ohio 16 Ja 31. 5: Ohio State U 50-53 (Hist) BA; Columbia 54-56 MSLS. 7: Child libn Mamaroneck Free Lib, Mamaroneck NY 56-57, Dayton Pub Lib, Dayton Ohio 57-60; Cleveland Pub Lib, Cleveland Ohio 60; Ref libn for Tech Div Lib, Wright-Patterson AFB Ohio 60-63; Ref libn Ohio State U Lib (Columbus) 63-64; Ref libn US Info Agcy Lib, Wash DC 64-69; Ref libn Dept of Defense, Wash DC 69-. 9: SLA; DC Pub LA. 14: Ref. 15: 520 N St SW #S232, Wash DC 20024.

LANDQUIST, AUDREY DOLORES. b Minneapolis 29 N 18. 5: UMinn 36-40 (LS-Lat) BS; MacPhail Col of Music 36-40 (Music, Piano) BMusic, 40-44 (Piano) MM. 6: Swedish, Norwegian, Ger, Danish. 7: Asst libn Bd of Educ Washburn 40-; Asst Libn Edison, Minneapolis 40-41; Head Libn Sheridan, Minneapolis 41-. 8: Producer of radio prog on Sweden and Swedish music. 10: Lambda Alpha Psi; Minneapolis Fedn of Tchrs; Mu Phi Epsilon. 14: Sch lib wk. 15: 4505 No Abbott, Minneapolis 55422.

LANDRAM, CHRISTINA (OLIVER). b Paragould Ark 10 D 22. 4: Robert E Landram. 5: Tex Woman'sU -45 (Hist) BA, 45-46 BS in LS, 51 MLS; Emory 58 (Med Libs). 7: Prelim catlgr LC 46-48; Catlgr Civil Info & Educ sect GHQ, Tokyo 48-50; Catlgr Tex Tech Col 50-52; Catlgr US Dept Agric Lib Wash DC 53-54; Libn USAF Base Lib, Yokota Japan 54-55; Med libn St Mary's Hosp, W Palm Beach Fla 57-58; Libn Jacksonville High Sch, Jacksonville Ark 59-61; Co-ordinator Shelby Co Libs, Memphis Tenn 61-62; Head catlg dept Ga State Col Lib 62-. 9: ALA; SELA; GaLA (sec-treas Resources & Tech Serv Sect 67-69); Metro-Atlanta LA (pres 67-68). 14: Catlg. 15: 2143 Kilarney rd, Decatur Ga 30032.

LANDRUM, ELIZABETH ANN. b Fresno Cal 21 Ap 09. 5: Fresno State Col 26-30 (Soc Sci) AB; UCal 31-32 (LS) Certif, 37-38 (LS) MA. 7: Sr ref libn Fresno State Col Lib 32-37, 38-43; Libn Sierra Summer Sch, Huntington Lake summer 37-42, 48-49; USNaval Reserve (LCdr) Northampton Mass 43, Washington DC 43-46; Libn Army and Navy Staff Col (Wash DC) 43-46; Sr ref libn Fresno State Col 46-53, Libn III Head ref dept 53-68, Libn IV Hd ref dept 68-. 9: ALA-ACRL;-RSD; CalLA (Col Univ & Research Lib Div & State Col Libns Div). 10: AAUW; World Affairs Coun. 14: Ref. 15: 1543 No Wishon ave, Fresno Ca 93728.

LANDRUM, JOHN HINTON. b Greenwood SC 25 N 44. 5: Clemson 62-64; Erskine Col 64-66 (Hist) BA; UNC 66-67 MS in LS. 6: Sp. 7: Ammunition storage specialist US Army Res 67-; Ref libn SC State Lib Bd, Columbia 67-. 9: ALA; SCLA; SELA. 10: Beta Phi Mu; S Caroliniana Soc; SC Hist Assn. 12: "Telefacsimile Communication with the Xerox magnavox Telecopier in Reference and Interlibrary Loans: a Report" (67). 14: Ref. 15: 5526 Lakeshore dr, Columbia SC 29206.

LANDSBERG, JANET (LOUISE). b Detroit 28 Mr 36. 5: Central Mich U 54-56 (Math); Wayne State U 57-59 (Math, LS) BS in Ed; UMich 60-62 MALS; Mich State U 68-. 7: Libn Bd of Educ, Detroit 59; Libn S Redford Sch Dist, Redford Twp Mich 59; Libn Congregation B'nai Moshe, Oak Park Mich 62-. 9: ALA; MichEA; MichASchL (chm Recr Com 65); NEA-DAVI; ASCD. 14: Catlg, instrnal materials centers. 15: 18350 Lahser, Detroit Mi 48219.

LANDSVERK, JANET PATRICIA (BOLDT). b Milwaukee Wis 7 N 31. 5: Milwaukee State Tchrs Col 49-50; UValencia (Spain) 61-62 Diploma in Hispanic Studies; UWis (Art, Hist) BA, (LS) MA. 6: Sp. 7: Libn asst UWis Lib (Madison) 57-60; Eng tchr: Amer Cultural Ctr, valencia Spain 61-62, Amer Sch in Valencia 61-62, Amer Eng Speaking Soc of Kokogaguin U, Tokyo 63, Hibashi Bus Ctr, Tokyo 63; Project assoc UWis Engring Lib (Madison) 64; Libn Wis State U (Platteville) 67-. 9: ALA; WisLA. 10: Wis State Univ Faculty Assn; Fac Woman Assn; Gamma Phi Beta. 11. Wilson scholarship grant. 14: Ref. 15: 2557 Root River pkwy, W Allis Wi 53227.

LANE, ALFRED H(ENRY). b Albany NY 30 My 16. 5: UMinn 40 (Eng) BA; NY State Tchrs Col (Albany) summer 40 (Educ); Columbia 43-44 (LS) BS, 50 (LS) MS. 6: Fr, Sp, Ger. 7: Page Albany (NY) Pub Lib 39-40; Clerk transportation dept Delaware & Hudson RR Albany NY 40-43; Page philos read room Columbia U Libs 43-44, Sr asst gifts & exch 44-46, Supv gifts & exch 46-64, Head gifts & exch 64-. 8: Consul; Syracuse U Lib March-May 62, Engrg Socs Lib (NY) 67; Guest lectr Columbia U Sch Lib Serv 45-. 9: ALA-RTSD;-ACRL (Com on Dupl Exch Union 56; Cost of lib materials index com 63-66; Ser sect Bylaws Com 65-67);-AS (Repr Com 65-70, chm 69-70; Nomin Com 68); NY Tech Serv Libns (chm Program Com 63-64, Nomin Com 65-66); NY Lib Club (various com). 10: Melvil Dui Chowder & M arching Assn; Beta Phi Mu. 12: Ed "Library Service News," Columbia U (60-). 13: Yes. 14: Gifts & exch. 15: 19 Barrow st, NYC 10014.

LANE, BERNARD B. b Sedro-Wooley Wash. 4: Ina Lane. 5: UWash 30-34 (Chem) BS, 34-35 (Chem) MS, 38-40 (LS) BS. 7: Asst tech dept Seattle Pub Lib 38-46; Libn Monsanto Chem Co West Div, Seattle 46-49; Gen Electric Co, Richland Wash: Lib supv 49-58, Spec info 58-63, Engnr info & repts 63-65; Sr spec info systems Battelle-Northwest, Richland Wash 65-, Sr sci qual assur & std 68-. 8: Instr, Sch of Libnship, UWash; Lectr Ctr for Grad Study, Richland. 9: SLA (pres Puget Sound Chap 47-48). 13: Yes. 14: Tech ref. 15: 1934 Davison, Richland Wash 99352.

LANE, CAROLYN ANNE (DE VOE). b Boston Mass 5 Ag 39. 4: Robert Lane. 5: Trinity Col 9wash DC) 57-61 (Hist, Govt) AB; Simmons 62-63 (LS) MS; UTenn (Knoxville) NDEA Inst 66. 7: Libn Dept of Defense: Misawa High Sch, Japan 63, Karamursel Elem-Jr High, Turkey 64, Augsburg High Sch, Germany 65-66; Libn Catalina Foothills Sch Dist, Tucson 66-. 9: ALA (Jr Mem RT); NEA; ArizSchLA; ArizEA; Ariz Assn A-V Educ; Catalina Foothilss EA; Tucson A-V Assn. 10: Delta Kappa Gamma. 14: Sch libnship. 15: 203 S Bella Vista dr, Tucson Az 85705.

LANE, DAVID O. b Flint Mich 17 O 31. 5: Flint Jr Col 50-52; Mich 56-58 (Eng) BA, 58-59 AMLS; Chicago 68 (LS). 6: Ger. 7: Acct exec (advertising) Wimble & Assoc Inc Flint Mich 52-56; Circ ref libn Flint Col, UMich (Flint) 59-60; Head govt pubs dept No Ill U 60-62; Head of pub serv Polytechnic Inst (Brooklyn NY) 62-63; Asst dir for reader serv Boston U 63-64, Asst dir of Libs 64-67; Dir acquis study & ALA, Chicago 67-68; Asst univ libn UCal (San Diego) 68-69; Col libn Hunter Col 69-. 9: ALA-ACRL; NELA; Boston Area Libns. 10: Beta Phi Mu. 13: Yes. 14: Admin, acquis. 15: Office of Librn, Hunter Col CUNY, 695 Park ave, New York NY 10021.

LANE, DORIS A (BRUNER). b Syracuse NY 29 Ap 11. 4: Charles Nelson Lane. 5: Elmira Col 28-32 (Math, Lat) AB; American U 53-54; Catholic U 54-64 (LS). 7: Libn elem schs, Fairfax Co Va 53-. 9: NEA; ALA; VaEA. 10: Bus & Prof Women's Club. 14: Elem sch libnship. 15: 1445 Pathfinder lane, McLean Va 22101.

LANE, ELIZABETH A(DAMS). b Ozark Ark 30 Jl 15. 4: Malcolm Victor Lane. 5: Duke 33-34; Conn Col for Women 34-37 (Dietetics) BA; NY State Tchrs Col 37-38 (Educ); Columbia 61-63 (LS) MS, (A-v materials). 6: Fr. 7: Lib aid High Sch, Scarsdale NY 62-63; Libn Ridge St Sch, Portchester NY 63-. 9: ALA; NYLA; NY Tchrs Assn; WestchesterLA. 10: AAUW; Jr League of Amer; Fox Meadow Tennis Club; Scarsdale Woman's Club; Girl Scouts leader; Family Serv Bur; Red Cross; PTA; Church Libn Hitchcock Presbyterian Church. 14: Child serv, curr devel, coop between pub & sch libs, study skills. 15: 2 Claremont rd, Scarsdale NY 10583.

LANE, FRANCES (HOUSTON). b Pittsburgh 18 D 06. 4: Clarence Bronson Lane. 5: UWis 35-36 (LS); Bethany Col (Bethany WVa) 26-32 (Eng) AB. 6: Lat, Fr. 7: Eng & soc studies tchr Walton Central Sch, Walton NY 56-57; Elem libn Townsend Sch, Walton NY 58; Lib dir Ramsey Free Pub Lib, Ramsey NJ 59-60; Child libn Pease Mem Lib, Ridgwood NJ 60; Eng tchr Watertown High Sch, Watertown NY 61; Child libn N Country Lib System, Watertown NY 61-62; Ref libn Flower Mem Lib, Watertown NY 63-. 10: Alpha Xi Delta. 13: Yes. 14: Ref, child. 15: 278 Ontario dr So, Watertown NY 13601.

LANE, SISTER M CLAUDE, OP. b Dobbin Tex 7 F 15. 5: UTex Correspondence Div 34-47 (Lat); UHouston Ext 36-39; Sacred Heart Dominican Col summers 45-53; Our Lady of the Lake Col summers 48-53 (Lat) BA; UTex summers 53-61 MLS. 6: Lat. 7: Tchg elem && high schs of Dominican Sisters, Tex 33-60; Archivist Catholic Archives of Texas, Austin Tex 60-61; High sch tchr, Tex & Cal 61-64; Tchr-libn 53-60, 61-64; Archivist Catholic Archives of Tex-in absentia 61-64; Archivist 64-67 in absentia 67-; Libn-AV Coord St Pius X High Sch, Houston 67-. 8: Principal St Mary's Elem Sch, Orange Tex 58-60; Shelter Mgr Austin-Travis Co Dept of Civ Def 65-; Lib consul, Off of Educ Diocese of Austin 64-. 9: ALA; CathLA (chm 2 Tex units); SAA; TexLA (v-chm Archives RT 69-70); Tex Assn Educ Tech. 10: Tex old missions restoration assn Tex Hist Found; AASLH; Amer Museum of Nat Hist; Tex State Hist Assn. 12: Catholic Archives of Texas History & Preliminary Inven tory (61). 13: Yes. 14: Sch libs, archival wk ref, rare bks, documents & artifacts. 15: St Pius X High School, 811 Donovan st, Houston Tx 77018.

LANE, MARGARET. b Cambridge Mass 7 Ap 05. 5: Wellesley 22-26 (Math,Bot) AB; Columbia 27-28 (LS) BA, 37-38 (LS) MA; NY State Sch Lib Certif 28. 6: Fr. 7: Asst Brookline Pub Lib, Brookline Mass 26-27; Libn Plattsburg High Sch, plattsburg NY 28-31; Libn High Sch & elem schs, Delmar NY 31-37; Libn Potsdam State Normal Sch Practice Sch, Potsdam NY 38-40; Asst in lib Albany State Tchrs Col(NY) 41-42; Libn Brockton High Sch, Brockton Mass 42-45; Child libn Mem Hall Lib, Andover Mass 45-63; Libn Amer Acad for Girls, Uskudar Istanbul Turkey 63-67; Elem sch libn, Haverhill Mass 67-; Trustee Boxford Pub Lib, Boxford Mass 33-. 9: ALA; MassLA; NELA; MassSchLA; NE Sch LA; Mass Lib Trustees Assn; MassTA. 10: Mass Audubon Soc; Nat Wildlife Fed. 13: . 14: Sch & child serv. 15: Main st, Boxford Mass.

LANE, MARGARET T (TAYLOR). b St Louis 6 F 19. 4: Horace C Lane. 5: LSU 39 (Govt) BA; Columbia 41 BS in LS; LSU 42 JD. 6: Ger, Fr. 7: Ref & circ libn La StateU Law Lib 41-42; Ref & circ asst Columbia law Lib 42-44; Law Libn UConn Law Lib 44-46; Research asst La StateU Law Sch 46-47; Law Libn La StateU Law Lib 47-48; Recorder of documents La Sec of State's Off, Baton Rouge La 49-. 8: Lecturer Govt publs; La State U Lib Sch 62. 9: ALA; La State Bar Assn; LaLA. 10: Phi Delta Delta. 12: Ed "Louisiana Union Catalog, 1959-1962," (suppt 63; Comp Suppl & Index to above (66). 13: Yes. 14: Documents, law libs. 15: 7545 Richards dr, Baton Rouge La 70809.

LANE, ROBERT BROOKS. b San Francisco 6 D 30. 4: Edith Heibel. 5: San Francisco City Col 48-51 (Humanities) AA; UCal (Berkeley) 52-54 (Eng) AB, 56-57 MLS. 6: Ger, Fr. 7: US Army spec 3d class court reporter 54-56; Mgr-Listener Serv

Station KPFA-FM, Berkeley Cal 57-58; Asst libn Whitman Co Lib, Colfax Wash 58-59; Reg libn Santa Clara Co Lib, San Jose Cal 59-61; Base libn Hahn Air Base (USAFE), Germany 61-62; Area libn South Ruislip Air Base (USAFE) London 62-65; Command libn Hq Tuslog (USAFE), Ankara Turkey 65-67; Chief reader serv Air U Lib 67-. 9: ALA; SLA (chm Military Lib ns Div 69-70); AlaLA. 14: Admin. 15: 2571 Churchill dr, Montgomery Al 36111.

LANE, ROSEMARY (VOGEL). b Little Rock Ark 11 Jl 27. 4: Larry M Lane. 5: UCal(Riverside) 56 (Hist) AB; Columbia summer 56 (LS); UCal(Berkeley) 57 MLS. 7: Elem sch libn Long Beach Unified Sch Dist Cal 57-58; Br libn Long Beach Pub Lib, Long Beach Cal 58-61; Libn period San Francisco Pub Lib 63; Art & arch libn UColo (Boulder) 64-66; Asst to the chief div for the blind & physically handicapped LC 67-68; Chief pub serv Fairfax Co Pub Lib, Fairfax Va 68-. 8: Instr in bibliography, UColo 65. 9: ALA; VaLA; DCLA. 10: Beta Phi Mu; Bd Dir Fairfax Co Commun Action Program. 14: Admin, pub rel. 15: 11475 Washington Plaza West, Reston Va 22070.

LANG, REV JOVIAN PETER OFM. b Sioux City Iowa 2 Je 19. 5: Our Lady of Angels Sem 39-43 (Philos) AB; St Joseph Sem 43-47 (Theol); West Res 48-50 (LS) MS, 51-55 (Speech & Hearing Therapy) MA. 6: Lat, Ger. 7: Asst libn Quincy Col 47-50, Libn asst prof of speech 50-55; Asst prof of speech St Joseph Sem (Westmont Ill) 55-57; Asst prov libn & archivist St Louis-Chicago Prov 55-68; Asst prof of speech Villa St Joseph (St Louis) 57-60; Libn assoc prof of speech Quincy Col 60-. 8: Series of 8 TV Shows on Speech and Hearing Therapy Quincy Ill 55; Amer Franciscan Liturgical Commn Hq Wash DC 64-; Chm Franciscan Liturgical Commn of the Sacred Heart Province (St Louis) 64-; ALA Conf 63; Discussion leader, Conf within a conf. 9: ALA (Coun); CathLA (Parliamentarian, chm Constitution & By-laws Com, chm Catlg & Clsf sect; chm Col Sect, Ill Unit 54-55); Speech Assn of Amer; Amer Speech & Hearing Assn; Coun for Exceptional Child; Cath Homiletic Soc; Midwest Acad Lib Conf (Steering Com 55-57). 10: Beta Phi Mu; Kappa Sigma Kappa; NAm Liturgical Conf; MoLA; Central States Speech Assn; Mo Speech and Hearing Assn. 12: "Ordo," (58-); "Ordo for Religious and the Laity," (58-); "Guide for the Priest during Parish Service," (64 2nd ed 65); "The Liturgy of Vatican" II, 2 vols (66). 13: Yes. 14: Catlg, tchg, lib sci. 15: Quincy Col, Quincy Il 62301.

LANG, NORMA L F. b NYC 12 Ja 28. 4: Elliot R Lang. 5: Brooklyn Col 45-49 (Econ) BA; So Conn State Col 62-66 (LS) MS. 7: Circ asst Swarthmore Col 49-51; Lib asst Quinnipiac Col 61-65, Asst libn 65-. 9: ALA; ConnLA. 10: AAUP. 14: Admin, tech serv systems analysis, automation. 15: 65 Braeside dr, Hamden Ct 06514.

LANG, SISTER MARY FRANZ OP. b Detroit Mich 7 S 21. 5: Siena Heights Col 51-59 (Eng) BA; UMich 60-64 AMLS. 7: Tchr & libn: St Joseph Elem Sch, Pt Huron Mich 52-56, Bishop Quarter Military Acad, Chicago 56-62; Asst libn Siena Heights Col 62-63; Libn Saint Dominic Col 63-. 8: Vis lect Rosary Col, River Forest Ill summer 66, 68, 69. 9: ALA; -ACRL; CathLA (Cath Period and Lit Index Com 69-; v-chm & chm-elect Catlg Sect 69-; Ad hoc Com on Goals 67-; treas No Ill Unit 68-69); IllLA. 10: LIBRAS; St Charles Human Rel Coun. 14: Admin. 15: 1405 Fifth ave N, Saint Charles Il 60174.

LANG, ROBERT PEREGRINE. b Hope ND 25 Mr 12. 4: Elizabeth Whitehead. 5: Occidental Col 29-30 ; UCLA 30-33 (Eng) AB, 33-34 (Eng) MA; Columbia 34-35 BS; UMinn 44 (Swedish Area Program); Harvard 48-49, 52 (Art Hist). 7: Asst ms dept Henry E Huntington Lib, San Marino Cal 35; Asst ref libn Oberlin Col Lib 35-41; Libn Col of Arch Cornell U 41-43; US Army Info & Educ Div (T/Sgt) 43-46; Asst Prof of fine arts & Sec Col of Arch Cornell U 47-51; Libn State U Col (New Paltz NY) 51-63; Asst u libn 66-, UCal(Riverside) 63-65, Act u libn 65-66. 8: Dir For Study Program in Art, SUNY 55-58; Fulbright Prof, Univ of the Panjab, Lahore Pakistan 60-61. 9: ALA; Col Art Assn; CalLA; Soc Arch Hist; Asia Soc. 10: Phi Beta Kappa. 12: "The Book: IX-XX Centuries" (38); "The Map, XV-XIX Centuries" (39); Ed "Outfit Magazine" (45) & "Newsmap" (45-46); "In a Valley Fair: A History of New Paltz," with E Lang (61); "Land and People of Pakistan" (68); "A Victorian in Bengal," with S McKenna (70). 13: Yes. 14: Admin, rare bks, lib bldgs. 15: 2008 Prince Albert dr, Riverside Ca 92507.

LANG, ROSALIE ANN. 5: Boston U 46-51 (Hist) BA; Simmons 51-53 (LS) MS. 7: Boston Pub Lib; Asst 42-57, Ref libn 57-60; Chief gen ref dept & curator of the pub catlg 60-67, Coord of humanities 67-. 9: ALA; CathLA; MassLA. 14: Ref. 15: Boston Pub Lib, Boston Ma 02117.

LANGDON, HOPE (HOWELL). b Boston 15 D 15. 4: Courtney Langdon. 5: Smith 33-37 (Music) AB (cum laude); Radcliffe 37-38 (Music); Eastman Sch of Music summer 39; UPittsburgh 63-65 MLS. 6: Fr. 7: Instr of music Colby Jr Col 38-41; Libn Penn State U Fayette Campus 65-66; Asst libn Keene State Col 66-. 9: ALA; NHLA. 10: AAUP; Beta Phi Mu. 14: Catlg. 15: RFD Nelson, Munsonville NH 03457.

LANGE, CLIFFORD ELMER. b Fond du Lac Wis 29 D 35. 4: Janet LeMieux. 5: St Norbert Col 54-57 (Hist); Wis State U (Oshkosh) 58-59 (Hist) BS; UWis 59-60 (LS) MS, 68- (LS). 7: Ext libn Pub Lib, Oshkosh Wis 60-62; Asst dir Jervis Lib, Rome NY 62; Ref libn Pub Lib, Oshkosh Wis 63; Dir Pub Lib, Eau Claire Wis 63-66; Asst dir Lake Co Ind Pub Lib 66-68. 8: Dir Nat Lib Week; Wis 65-66, Ind 67-68. 9: ALA; WisLA (chm &/or mem 5 coms & sects 60-66); IndLA (chm Trustee Citation Com 67-68). 10: Beta Phi Mu. 14: Admin, pub rel, publicity. 15: 1325 Tompkins dr Apt f, Madison Wi 53716.

LANGE, HELEN (MARY). b Chicago 10 Ap 13. 5: Mundelein Col 30-34 (LS) AB. 7: Libn Pub Lib, Waukegan Ill 35-39; Libn VA Cheyenne & Sheridan Wyo 39-44; Patients libn VA, Hines Ill 44-54; Patients libn VA, Chicago 54-. 9: ALA. 14: readers adv. 15: 2004 W Greenleaf ave, Chicago 60645.

LANGER, ELISABETH MARIANNE (PFALZNER). b Vienna 9 Ap 12. 5: UVienna 31-38 (Pol Sci) PhD. UGeneva summer 39 (Fr); Columbia 40-41 (LS) BS. 6: Ger, Fr. 7: Asst libn Western Col 41-43; Bibliogr & ref libn StanfordU & Hoover Lib 43-45; Dir League of Nations Catlg Proj Woodrow Wilson Mem Lib NY 45-50; Ref Libn UN 50-51; In chg of ref center of the soc welfare div UN 51-56; Ref libn UN, Geneva 56-57; Assoc Libn UN, NYC 57-. 9: SLA; Assn Internat Libs. 10: AAUW. 12: "Die Diplomatischen Beziehungen Zwischen England und Oesterreich unter dem Ministerium Schwarzenberg" (Vienna 37); Comp "Index to the UN Treaty Series" (62-); Comp "League of Nations Commissions and Committies" (46-50). 13: Yes. 14: Catlg, bibliog, research in internat law, internat documents, editing, indexing. 15: 30 West 60th st, NYC 10023.

LANGER, FRANCIS ANTHONY. b Elizabeth NJ 2 Mr 22. 4: Barbara Nelson. 5: Drake Bus Col 40-41 (Bus) Certif; UMiami 48-51 (Eng) AB, 51-53 (Eng) MA; Fla State U 53-55 (LS) MA. 6: Sp, Fr. 7: SK3c & ENS Coast Guard, Brooklyn, Miami 42-46, 50; Circ & catlg Ohio State 55-56; Asst libn UIda 58-59; Ref libn U Miami(Fla) 56-67, Instr in Eng 60-62; Instr in Eng Homestead AFB 62-67; Lib Sch tchr Fla State U 67-68; Hd libn Berry Col 68-. 8: Lib & univ coms 55-. 9: ALA; FlaLA. 10: Lib Staff Assn Ohio State U; Lib Staff Assn UMiami; Phi Kappa Phi. 13: Yes. 14: Ref, admin. 15: PO Box 594, Mt B erry Ga 30149.

LANGHORNE, DOROTHEA (DISMEUKE). b Cambridge Mass 1 S 07. 4: Joseph Leon Langhorne. 5: UChicago 28-29 (Fr) PhB; NYSch of Soc Wk 44-46 (Child Welfare); Columbia 60-63 (LS) MS; Chicago Tchrs Col 29-30 Tchrs Certif. 6: Fr. 7: Case wker Ill Emergency Relief Bur, Chicago 30-36; Case wker Cook Co Dept of Welfare, Chicago 36-38; Case wker Edwin Gould Found for Child NYC 38-43; Supv of metropolitan dist NYState Train ing Sch for Girls 43-48; Tchr of common brs PS 46 NYC Bd of Educ, 48-60, Sch libn PS 28 60-64, Dist Libn Off of Dist Supt 64-. 9: ALA; NEA; NY Soc Exper Study of Educ (NYSESE). 10: Delta Sigma Theta. 14: Libs for child & yp. 15: 555 Edgecombe ave, NYC 10032.

LANGLEY, FRANCES (HOWELL). b Ethelville Ala 27 D 17. 4: William G Langley. 5: Fla State Col for Women 35-39 (Sp) BA; UNC 39-40 BS in LS. 6: Sp. 7: Libn Palm Beach Jr col 40-45; Libn US Naval Air Sta: Vero Beach Fla 45, Banara River Fla 45-46; Libn USMC Air Sta, Cherry Point NC 45-49; Libn Tryon Mall Br Charlotte Pub Lib, Charlotte NC 68-. 9: ALA; NCLA; SELA; MecklenburgLA; Staff Organiz Pub Lib. 14: Ref. 15: 800 Berkeley ave, Charlotte NC 28203.

LANGNER, MRS MILDRED (CROWE). b Chattanooga Tenn. 5: UChattanooga 29-33 (Eng) BA; Peabody 44-45 BS in ls& vanderbilt U 44-45 (Med Lib Internship). 6: Fr. 7: Various Chattanooga Pub Lib Chattanooga Tenn 33-40; Libn Chattanooga Pub Lib, Med Soc Lib Chattanooga Tenn 40-44; Intern & asst Vanderbilt U Sch of Med 44-45; Libn UAla Med Ctr Lib 44-55; Libn UMiami Sch of Med Lib (Miami Fla) 55-61; Chief ref serv div NLM 61-62; Libn UMiami Sch of Med Lib (Miami Fla) 63-, Libn & Prof Med Bibliog 68-. 8: Consul Dent Lib Bur of Lib & Indexing Serv; Amer Dent Assn 53; Lectr on Med Libnship & Sci Writing 45-. 9: MedLA (sec, chm Standards Com, Publ Com etc; pres 66-67); SLA (pres-elect Ala Chap 55); ALA; FlaLA. 10: Amer Assn Hist

Med; Amer Med Writers' Assn; UMiami Med Faculty Wives Club; U (of Miami) Women's Club; Alpha Hon Soc. 11: MedLA, Editor's Award. 12: Ed "Bulletin of MedLA" (57-61). 13: Yes. 14: Med lib admin, med hist, sci writing. 15: 1408 S Bayshore dr, Miami Fl 33131.

LANGWORTHY, DONALD L. b Winnebago Minn 24 Mr 37. 4: Sylvia Davis. 5: UMinn 55-59 9agric) BS, 63-65 (LS) MA. 6: Fr. 7: State performance supv USDA, St Paul 56-58; Sr high Eng tchr, Balaton Minn 61-63; Admin fellow UMinn (Minneapolis) 63-65, Tchg asst 64-65; Sr high libn, Northfield Minn 65-68; Asst Prof UIowa 68-. 9: ALA; -AASchL; IowaStateEA; IowaASchL. 14: Materials sel, hist of bks, ref. 15: 1030 Muscatine, Iowa City Ia 52240.

LANIER, DONALD (LEE). b Shawnee Okla 11 Ap 39. 4: Margaret Barrett. 5: Okla Baptist U 57-60 (Educ) BS; UOkla summers 60, 61; UIll 63-64 MSLS; SW Baptist Theol Sem 64-66. 6: Lat. 7: Bonding press operator Jonco Aircraft Corp, Shawnee Okla 57-60; Tchr Tulsa (Okla) Pub Schs 60-62; Tchr Choctaw (Okla) Pub Schs 62-63; Acquis libn UTex(Arlington) 64-66; Lay-missionary So Baptist Convention, Hong Kong 66-67; Lib sci libn UIll(Urbana) 67-69; Acquis libn Okla StateU 69-. 14: Bk sel, ref, educ for libnship. 15: c/o John Barrett, 605 S Third st, Fisher Il 61843.

LANIER, GENE DANIEL. b Conway NC 13 Mr 34. 4: Susan Roberts. 5: ECarolina Col 52-55 (Soc Sci) BS; UNC (Chapel Hill) 55-57 MSLS, 64- (Higher Educ) PhD. 6: Fr, Sp, Ger. 7: Tchr Hillsboro High Sch, Hillsboro NC 57; Counterintelligence spec USArmy, Europe 57-59; ECarolina Col; Asst order libn 59-60, Head order libn 60-63, Assoc Prof Dept of Lib Sci 63-64; Instr Sch of Educ UNC (Chapel Hill) 65-66; Assoc Prof lib sci E Carolina U 63-67, chm Dept of Lib Sci 67-. 8: Com duties on lib educ, NC Dept of Pub Instr 63-; Consul, 3 NDEA & Higher Educ Act Lib Insts. 9: ALA; NCLA (chm Com on Educ for Libnship); SELA; NCASchL (dir). 10: Phi Delta Kappa; Kappa Alpha; Phi Sigma Pi; Alpha Beta Alpha. 12: "The Library & Television; A Study of the Role of Television in Modern Library Service" (59); "The Transformation of School Libraries into Instructional Materials Centers" (68). 13: Yes. 14: Admin, ref, govt docs, lib educ. 15: Dept of Lib Sci E Carolina Col, Greenville NC.

LANIGAN, CLARICE. b NYC 26 Je 14. 4: Matthew J Lanigan. 5: Hunter Col 33 (Eng) AB; Queens Col 52 (LS) MA. 6: Lat, Fr, Ger. 7: Ed Union Carbide Corp, NYC 35-42; Libn John Adams High Sch, NYC Bd of Educ 65-. 9: NYLA; NYCSchLA; NY Lib Club; ALA. AAUW. 10: AAUW. 13: Yes. 14: Bk reviewing, sel, ref. 15: 160 Renison dr, Westbury NY 11590.

LANNAN, MARGARET JANE. b Columbus Ohio 22 F 19. 5: St Mary of the Springs 37-39 (Eng); Rosary Col 39-41 BS in LS; UKy 63 MS in LS. 7: Lib asst Columbus Pub Lib, Columbus Ohio 41-43; Lib asst Bexley Pub Lib, Bexley Ohio 43-45; Libn Cassingham Jr High Sch, Bexley Ohio 45-50; Ref libn Bexley Pub Lib, Bexley Ohio 50-. 8: Sch lib consul bd, Diocese of Columbus 61-64; Libn St Catherine's Parish Lib 67-; Tchr Confirnaty of Christian Doctrine. 9: ALA; CathLA; OhioLA; Franklin Co LA. 14: Ref. 15: 2812 Sherwood rd, Columbus Ohio 43209.

LANPHEAR, LUCY M. b Dansville NY 10 O 18. 5: SUNY (Geneseo) 45-48 (LS) BS in Ed; Fla State U 50-56 (LS) MS. 7: Asst to libn UTampa 48-53; Libn Lealman Jr High Sch, St petersburg Fla 53-54; Hd libn NE Sr High Sch, St Petersburg Fla 54-65; Libn in charge tech serv St Petersburg Jr Col 65-. 9: ALA; FlaLA; Fla Assn Pub Jr Cols. 10: Nat audubon Soc. 13: Yes. 14: Tech serv. 15: 3719 15th ave N, St Petersburg Fl 33713.

LANSBERG, WILLIAM R(OSS). b Boston Mass 24 Je 16. 4: Eunice Walmsley. 5: Dartmouth 34-38 (Romance Lang) AB; UNC 38-45 (Romance Lang) MA 40, Ph D 45; Simmons 48-49 (LS) BS. 6: Fr, Sp. 7: Tchg Fellow (Fr) UNC (Chapel Hill) 38-40, Supv lib res room 40-42, Fr instr 42-45; Fr instr SW Mo State Col 45-46; Fr instr Boston U 46-48; Indexer H W Wilson Co, NYC 49-51; Asst to libn Dartmouth Col 51-52, Hd acquis 52-53, Dir div acquis & preparations 53-60; Dir libs Elmira Col 60-63; Libn Hobart & William Smith Col 63-67; Dir libs Roosevelt U 67-. 8: Mem Hobart Col survey team at Voorhees Col, Denmark SC 65; Mem Middle States Assn vis team: Col of Mount Saint Vincent, NYC 66; The King's Col, Briarcliff Manor NY 67; Exec dir Nat Lib Week: NH 59, NY 63. 9: ALA; -ACRL; NE Col libns (Gen Com Chm 45th Anniv Meeting 52; NELA (treas 59-60). 10: Phi Beta Kappa; Deacon Church of Christ, Dartmouth Col. 13: Yes. 14: Admin, pub rel. 15: 505 N Lake Shore de, Chicago Il 60611.

LANTIS, HELEN ELIZABETH (FISHER). b Franklin Co Kan 28 Ag 17. 4: David W Lantis. 5: USoCal 50-54 (Educ) BS, MS; Chico State Col 57, 60, 61, 64; San Jose State Col summers 62, 64. 7: Clk Armour & Co Meat Packing, Los Angeles 40-43; Storekeeper USN (WAVES), Hutchinson Kan 43-46; Jr clk accounting clk Los Angeles City Sch Dist 46-50; Tchr: Los Angeles Sch Dist 54-55, Chico (Cal) Unified Sch Dist 58-60; Libn Bidwell Jr High Sch, Chico Cal 60-. 9: NEA; ALA; CalTA; CalASchL. 10: Phi Beta Kappa; Kappa Delta; Gamma Theta Upsilon; AAUW. 14: Sch libn. 15: Rte 3 1616 Oak Park ave, Chico Ca 95926.

LANTZ, ANNA E. b Oil City Penn 20 S 25. 5: Penn State 45-49 (Psych) BS; Carnegie 55-56 MLS. 6: Sp. 7: Ref libn Carnegie Lib of Pittsburgh 56-59, Sr catlgr 60-61, Asst head ctlg dept 61-63; Head tech serv Chautauqua Cattavaucus Lib System, Jamestown NY 63-65; Dir of lib serv Oil City Pub Lib, Oil City Penn 65-68; Hd catlg dept Carnegie Lib of Pittsburgh. 9: ALA; PennLA. 14: Tech serv, ref, admin, catlg. 15: 4733 Center ave, Pittsburgh Pa 15213.

LANTZ, DOROTHY (F). b Lebanon Penn 22 My 11. 4: B Boyd Lantz. 5: Lebanon Valley Col 28-31; Syracuse U 31-32 BLS; Lebanon Valley Col (Educ). 7: Lib asst Harrisburg Pub Lib, Harrisburg Penn 42-47; Libn Alexander Hamilton Mem Lib Waynesboro Penn 47-50; Libn Franklin Co Lib, Chambersburg Penn 50-63; Libn Venice Area Pub Lib, Venice Fla 63-66; Co libn Sarasota Pub Lib 66-. 9: ALA; FlaLA. 15: 629 Cornwell-on-the-Gulf, Venice Fl 33595.

LANTZ, NORMA LEE. b Mountain Home Ark 21 Mr 25. 5: WTex State U 43-47 (Home Econ) BS, 53 (Educ) MA; Tex Woman's U 66 Lib Certif. 7: Co home demon agent USDA, Channing Tex 47; Home econ Southwestern Appliance Co, Amarillo Tex 48; Elem Tchr Hopkins Pub Sch, Pampa Tex 48-49; Home econ tchr Lefors High Sch, Lefors, Tex 49-56; Elem tchr Lefors Pub Sch, Lefors Tex 56-57; Jr high sch soc studies tchr, Lefors Tex 57-64; High sch libn Lefors High Sch, Lefors Tex 64-. 9: NEA; Tex State Tchrs Assn; TexLA. 10: DAR, Delta Kappa Gamma. 14: Small high sch libs. 15: Box 4492 215 W Seventh, Lefors Tx 79054.

LANZANO, GEORGIA MAY (URBANO). b NYC. 4: Michael Robert Lanzano. 5: Conn Col 64-68 (Eng Lit) AB; Columbia 68-69 MLS. 6: Lat, Fr. 7: Asst (order dept) Southampton col Lib LIU summer 66; Asst in catlg (reclsf project) SUNY Maritime Col Lib summer 67; Asst in circ, ref & catlg Palmer Lib CONN Col 65-68; Ed of galley proofs & bibliog checker Simon & Schuster, & McGraw Hill Publ Co 68-69. 9: ALA; SLA. 10: Tudor singers, ColumbiaU. 14/ ref in spec or acad libs. 15: 75 Centerport rd, Greenlawn LI NY 11740.

LAPIDES, LINDA (FISHMAN). b Baltimore Md 12 Ja 36. 4: Julian Lee Lapides. 5: UMd 54-57 (Eng) BA; Columbia 57-58 MSLS. 7: YA libn in br Enoch Pratt Free Lib, Baltimore 58, Sr ya libn in br 59, Asst coord wk with ya 62. 9: ALA (var coms); MdLA (chm Child & YA Serv Div 60-61, chm Recr Com 63-64). 10: Friends of the Osborne Collection (TornXX (Toronto Pub Lib); Soc Preserv of Federal Hill; Baltimore Heritage; Baltimore Museum of Art; Walters Art Gallery; Peale Museum; Print Club of Baltimore. 12: Mem ed com -maryland Libraries" (65). 13: Yes. 14: Wk with ya. 15: 1528 Bolton st, Baltimore Md 21217.

LAPIERRE, MAURICE EDMOND. b Woonsocket RI 21 My 34. 5: Boston Col 55-59 (Mod Langs) AB; UCLA 59-62 (Fr, educ, LS) MLS; MLS; Case West Res 69-. 6: Fr. 7: Legal Yeoman (YNT3) USN USS Hornett CVA-12 53-55; Bibliog searcher UCLA Lib 62-63, Admin asst to head of acquis 63-65; Ser catlgr Ohio State U 65-66; Hd acquis dept 66-68; Assoc libn tech serv McGill U Lib 68-. 8: Survey of Acquis Dept, Ohio State U 66. 9: ALA (chm Ser Sect Discussion Gp for Large Univ & Research Libs 66-68; v-chm & chm-elect Coun on Reg Gps 69-); OhioLA; QueLA (v-chm Col & Research Lib Sect 68-69). 10: AAUP. 14: Tech serv, admin. 15: School of Lib Sci, Case Western Reserve Univ, Cleveland Oh 44106.

LAPORTE, NICOLE (LETENDRE). b Drummondville Quebec 21 D 44. 4: Paul R Laporte. 5: College St Maurice 66 BA; UMontreal 68 BLS. 7: Fr libn St Thomas High Sch, Poin pointe Claire Que Can 68-. 9: CanLA; QueLA; Assn Canadienne des bibliothecaires de langue francaise. 14: Ref. 15: 69 Pardo ave, Pointe Claire Quebec Can.

LAPPALA, JANE (LESTER). b Albany NY 4 Je 12. 4: Risto P Lappala. 5: UWis 29-33 (Econ) BA, 41-42 BLS. 7: Research assoc Wis Legisl Ref Lib, Madison 42-50; Acquis libn RiceU Lib 66-. 10: LWV. 15: 271 5 University blvd, Houston Tx 77005.

LAPSANSKY, ELIZABETH MARY. b Scranton Penn 7 N 19. 5: Marywood Col 37-41 (Eng, Hist) AB, 41-42 BS in LS, summer 68 (LS); Columbia summer 58 (LS). 7: Circ asst State Lib, Harrisburg Penn 42-43, Genealogical asst 43-44; Sub libn Marywood Sem (Penn) 45; Br libn Osterhout Free Lib, Wilkes-Barre Penn 45-55; Head circ dept Scranton Pub Lib, Scranton Penn 55-67; Ser libn UScranton Lib 68-. 9: CathLA (chm Scranton Unit); NEPennLA (chm, sec-treas, mem Nomin Com). ; PennLA. 14: Adult circ. 15: Box 51, Elmhurst Penn.

LAPWORTH, PHYLLIS. b Revelstoke BC Can 9 Ap 22. 5: UBC 42-44 (Eng) BA; UToronto 44-45 BLS. 6: Fr, Ger. 7: Bkmob libn Fraser Valley Reg Lib, Abbotsford BC 45-48; Gen libn Brantford Pub Lib, Brantford Ont 48-53; Br head libn Calgary Pub Lib, Calgary Alta 53-56; Chief Libn Medicine Hat (Alta) Pub Lib 56-68; Asst & ref dept Ohawa Pub Lib, Ottawa Ont 69-. 8: Tutor (59-61) for Corres Course for Custodians in Small Libs sponsored by Govt of Alta; wrote sect on Pub Rel. 9: CanLA (Coun 60-63, 65-68; chm Young Canada's Bk Week 61-63); Candn Assn Child Libns (sec-treas 65-66); AltaLA (pres 61-62; Sch of Lib Sci rep on Adv Coun 67-69). 10: Victorian Order of Nurses; Coun Soc Serv; YM-YMCA; Soroptimist Club; UWomen's Club; C of C; Allied Arts Coun; Overture Concerts Assn; Mus Festival Com, Nominated Woman of the Yr 62 by Quota Club; Ottawa U Women's Club; Can Fed Univ Women. 13: Yes. 14: Pub rel, adult serv, adult educ, ref. 15: 77 Cartier st apt 1009, Ottawa 4 Ont Can.

LARAMY, LARAMIE AN. b Bryn Mawr Penn 18 Ja 35. 5: Bucknell 53-57 (Elem Educ) BS; Penn State U 58-61 (Elem Ed) M Ed; Villan penn State U 58-61 (Elem Ed) M Ed; Villanova 63-64 MSLS. 7: Tchr elem sch, Penn 57-63; Asst libn Penn State U Agric Lib 64-65; A-v & period libn York Jr Col 65-66; Asst libn Harford Jr Col 66-67; Hd bkmob libn Montgomery Co Pub Lib, Norristown Penn 68-. 9: ALA; PennLA. 14: Bkmob serv. 15: 2444 Merwood lane, Havertown Pa 19083.

LARASON, LARRY D. b Shattuck Okla 7 N 35. 4: Katherine Shaefer. 5: UOkla 54-60 BA (Anthropology), MLS. 6: Sp. 7: Soc studies libn UNeb 61-63, Order libn 63-65; Ser libn Ariz State U 65-68, Systs Coord 68-. 9: ALA; Ariz State LA. 12: "Intermountain Union List of Serials" (69). 15: Rt 2, Shattuck Okla.

LARCHE, THELMA (BEASLEY). b Gainesville Fla 30 N 12. 5: Fla State U 30-31 (Home Econ); UFla 54-56 (Educ) BAE; Fla State U Summers 56-58 (LS) MA. 7: Libn Gainesville High Sch, Gainesville Fla 56-63, Child libn summer 59; Libn P K Yonge Lab Sch, Gainesville Fla 63-. 9: NEA; FlaEA; FlaStateLA. 10: Fla State U Lib; Alumni Assn; Sigma Kappa; Phi Kappa Phi; Kappa Delta Pi; Beta Phi Mu; Pi Lambda Theta. 14: Sch libs, catlg. 15: 704 NE Third ave, Gainesville Fla 32601.

LARGEY, JEAN FRANCES (MURPHY). b Boston Mass 7 Ap 12. 4: James Joseph Largey. 5: Harvard 40-45 (Liberal Arts); Burdett Col 58 (Real Estate); Amer Inst of Banking 59 (Econ); Emmanuel Col 68-69 (Theol). 6: Lat, Fr. 7: Lib asst Boston Pub Lib 29-45, Credit union MIT 54-56; Credit ref Nat Bank of Plymouth City 57-58; Info file State St Bank & Trust Co 58-59; Med lib Commonwealth of Mass 60-. 9: MedLA; NELA (pres Hosp Sect 63); MassLA (Exec Com). 10: Hosp Lib Group; Nutrition Com for Lit; Beth Israel Hosp. 11: Citation for Rehabilitation Wk. 12: Ed "Bostho-News" (60-63). 13: Yes. 14: Admin libnship, ref wk, ed wk. 15: Boston State Hospital-Med Lib 591 Morton st, Boston Ma 02124.

LARGO, ANDREW OLIVER. b Jersey City NJ 12 My 26. 5: Colgate U 47-51 (Soc Psych) BA; Rutgers 57-59 MLS. ; State of Cal Standard Tchg Credential. 7: Tech Fifth Grade USArmy (Infantry) 44-46; Travel couns Automobile Club of NY NYC 52-57; Libn II San Jose State Col 59-. 8: Lib USA NYWorld's Fair 64. 9: CalLA. 10: HE-Libs (Male Libns in San Francisco Bay Area). 14: Catlg. 15: 793 Elm st, San Jose Cal 95126.

LARICK, E(LLEN) LOUISE. b Covina Cal 31 Jl 11. 5: La Verne Col 34-37 (Eng Educ) BA; USoCal 45-47 BSLS, 56-58 MSLS; Claremont Grad Sch 61-64 (Educ). 6: Sp, Ger. 7: Libn & Asst Prof Eng & Lib Sci La Verne col Lib 37-53; Dist Libn Azusa City Schs, Azusa Cal 53-58; Libn Bonita High Sch, La Verne Cal 58-61; Ref Libn SS & AV, Mt San Antonio Col 61-62; Dist Libn Claremont Unified Schs, Claremont Cal 62-. 9: ALA; NEA; AASchL; CalLA; CalTA; SchLibAssnCal (Membersp Chm So Sect 2 yrs). 10: Dist Historian, Church of the Brethren. 13: Yes. 14: Catlg, establishing new libs. 15: 2242 Seventh st, La Verne Cal 91750.

LARIMORE, CONSTANCE (FLUHR). b Arcadia Fla 9 Ag 43. 4: Harry Larimore. 5: Fla State U 61-64 (Hist) BA, 64-65 (LS) MS. 6: Sp. 7: Catlgr Fla State U Lib 65-66; Catlgr Miami-Dade Jr Col central tech processing 66-. 9: SELA; FlaLA. 10: Soltas; Sigma Sigma Sigma; Hollywood Panhellenic. 14: Pub lib wk with child & yp. 15: 780 NE 139 st, N Miami Fl 33161.

LARISEY, JULIAN C (LARRY). b Ga 4 Ap 17. 4: Elizabeth Ray. 5: UFla 39-41 (Bus Admin); Fla State U 49-51 (LS) BA, MA. 6: Fr. 7: Glider pilot USArmyAirCorps (S/Sgt), US 42-45; Airline agent Eastern Air Lines, Orlando Fla 46-48; Head ext dept Charlotte (NC) Pub Lib 51-53; Br libn Jacksonville (Fla) Pub Lib 54-55; Libn Duval Co Pub Sch System, Jacksonville Fla 55-68; Libn Orange Co Pub Sch Syst, Orlando Fla 68-. 9: NEA; ALA; FlaLA; FLAASch Libns; FlaEA. 14: A-v, ref, circ. 15: 515 Griffin ave #81, Orlando Fl 32807.

LARKIN, ANNE R. b NYC 13 Jl 04. 5: Douglass Col 22-26 (Physics, Math) BS; Columbia 27 (Educ), 31-32 MLS. 7: Asst at charging desk Rutgers U Lib 27-29; Libn Cliffside Park Jr-Sr High Sch Lib, NJ 29-31; Asst Teaneck Pub Lib, Teaneck NJ 33-34; Libn Englewood Jr High Sch Lib, Englewood NJ 35-64; Libn Edward Williams Col 64-65; Miami-Dade Jr Col 67-. 9: NJEA; NJSchLA. 10: Bergen Co(NJ) Hist Assn; DAR. 14: Sch libs, catlg. 15: 39 Santillane ave, Coral Gables Fla 33134.

LARKIN, CHARLES A. b Springdale Conn 3 Ja 06. 5: ClarkU 26-30 (Eng) AB; Columbia 33-38 (Speech) AM; UKy 54-57 MSLS. 6: Fr, Sp. 7: Eng tchr Georgetown High Sch, Georgetown Del 30-35; Eng tchr Cloonan Jr High Sch, Stamford Conn 35-42; (Cpt) Adjutant Gen Dept USArmy, Ft Worth 42-46; Eng tchr Cloonan Jr High Sch, Stamford Conn 46-59; Libn Dolan Jr High Sch, Stamford Conn 59-65; Circ libn Sacred HeartU 65-67; Ref libn Pace Col 67-68; Libn Stamford Cath Lib 68-. 9: CathLA (treas Conn Unit). 10: Stamford-Greenwich Cath Interracial Coun. 11: Army Commendation Ribbon. 14: Ref, rare bks. 15: 655 Hope st, Springdale Conn 06879.

LARKIN, PATRICK J. b Huntington NY 6 Mr 29. 4: Mary Ann. 5: Georgetown U Sch of Foreign Serv 48-50 (Pol Sci For Serv); St Mary's (Baltimore) 54-56 (Philos) AB; Cath U 58-62 MSLS. 6: Fr. 7: Lib asst Mullen Lib Cath U 58-60; Ref libn & lecturer in Lib Sci Gaulladet Col 60-61; Info off Nat Capital Transportation Serv Wash DC 61-62; Tchr-libn Ascension Acad Alexandria Va 62-63; Lib dir George Mason Col of UVa 63-. 8: Var consultantship on lib bldgs and operations. 9: ALA; VaLA. 14: Admin ref, rare bks, tech serv. 15: 1327 Newton st NE, Wash DC 20017.

LaROCHE, FRANCIS EDWARD. b Detroit 5 Ap 28. 4: Charlotte Beebe. 5: UMich 45-46, 49-53 (Journalism) BA. 7: US Army Info spec (Cpl) 46-49; Reporter/Photographer "Ironwood(Mich) Daily Globe" 53-54; Research asst UMich 54-58; Research assoc Stanford U 58-60; Missile specifications spec Lockheed Missiles 60-62; Head of Publ & Lib Computer Sciences Corp 62-. 8: Designed several computer-based indexing systems, including the "PILL" KWIC-type program for the UNIVAC 1107, written in COBOL. 9: SLA; ADI; AssnComputMech; STWP. 10: Sigma Delta Chi. 14: Computer-aided indexing. 15: 650 N Sepulveda blvd, El Segundo Cal 90245.

LAROUCHE, LEO OMER. b Nashua NH 18 Jl 38. 5: Oblate Fathers Col & Sem 58-62 (Philos) BA; Catholic U 63-65 MSLS. 6: Fr. 7: Chm libn Catholic U 63-67; Tech libn Operations Research Inc, Silver Spring Md 67-68; Sci libn Georgetown U 68-. 14: Sci & tech collections, pub serv, pub rel. 15: 1933 Kennedy dr 204, McLean Va 22101.

LARRIMORE, ETHYLANNE (DIDION). b Sacramento Cal 27 Je 40. 4: William Larrimore. 5: Sacramento City Col (Eng Lit) AA; Dominican Col (San Rafael) (Eng Lit) BA; UCal (Berkeley) MLS. 6: Fr. 7: Ref libn bus dept Sacramento City Lib, Sacramento Cal; Post libn USA Special Serv 2nd Infantry Div Korea; Post libn USA Special Serv N Bava libn USA Special Serv 2nd Infantry Div Korea; Post libn USA Special Serv N Bavaria Dist Germany; Base libn USAF Personnel Serv 13th AF Taiwan (ROC) 68-. 14: Ref, acquis, publicity. 15: Mrs G Francke 1328 Palmetto ave, Toledo Oh 43606.

LARSEN, A DEAN. b Provo Utah 23 Ag 30. 4: Jean Maycock. 5: Brigham Young U 54 (Hist) BS; UMich 60 (LS) MA. 6: Fr, Ger. 7: Lib asst Brigham Young U 53-54; Libn Research Div CIC USArmy, Europe 55-56; Brigham Young U: Asst circ 56, Documents libn 57-58, Ser libn 59-60, Order libn 61-. 9: ALA (Memb chm, Utah 67); UtahLA (pres Col & U Sect 61-62). 10: Orem Lib Bd; Beta Phi Mu; Utah Hist Soc;

Utah Westerners. 14: Acquis. 15: 844 E 400 So, Orem Utah 84057.

LARSEN, SISTER HELEN. b Sioux City Iowa 22 S 20. 5: Briar Cliff Col 38-42 (Eng) BA; CatholicU summers 42-53 (Eng) MA; Rosary Col 52-53 MALS. 7: High sch tchr, N Washington Iowa 45-47; High sch tchr, Pocahontas Iowa 47-48; High sch tchr, Stacyville Iowa 48-52; Col libn & tchr, Mt St Francis Iowa 53-69; Ssst libn Briar Cliff Col (Iowa) 69-. 9: ALA; CathLA; Franciscan Tchg Sisterhoods (Lib Sect). 15: Library-Briar Cliff College, Sioux City Ia 51104.

LARSEN, JOHN CHRISTIAN. b Mich 1 Ag 29. 5: UMich 50 (Design) BDes, 51 (Hist of Art) MA, 55 MALS, 67 PhD. 6: Fr. 7: Ref asst Detroit Pub Lib 54-57; Art & music libn Mich State Lib 58-61; Assoc libn Towson State Col 61-64; Instr & Asst Prof Lib Sci UMich (Ann Arbor) 65-68; Asst Prof lib sci UKy (Lexington) 69-. 9: SLA; ALA; KyLA. 10: AAUP; Phi Kappa Phi. 14: Ref. 15: Sch of Lib Sci UKentucky, Lexington Ky 40506.

LARSEN, WILLIAM PAUL. b Chicago Ill 15 Je 40. 4: Joanne Cilluffo. 5: Lake Forest Col 60-63 (Philos) BA; UChicago 64-66 (LS) MA. 7: Stack supv Lincoln Pub Lib, Lincoln neb 63-64; Lib trainee Chicago Pub Lib 64-65; Catlgr Skokie Pub Lib, Skokie Ill 65-67; Catlgr Wash State Lib 67-. 10: Phi Beta Kappa; Thurston Demo Coun. 14: Catlg. 15: 2350 Cain rd 20, Olympia Wa 98501.

LARSGAARD, MARY LYNETTE. b Dickinson NDak 4 Ag 46. 5: Macalester Col 64-68 (Geol) BA, UMinn 68-69 (LS) MA. 6: Sp. 7: Docs & map libn Central Wash State Col 69-. 10: Phi beta Kappa. 14: Maps, geol, ref. 15: 232 Kent rd, Hoyt Lakes Mn 55750.

LARSON, ARLENE (MILLER). b Milford Neb 9 Ap 28. 4: William P Larson. 5: UNeb 49-53 (Eng, Educ) BS; UDenver 53-54 (LS) MA. 7: Stud asst Soc Studies Lib UNeb 51-53; Asst libn bus & ind dept Omaha Pub Lib 54-56; Asst libn circ dept El Paso(Tex) Pub Lib 56-57; High sch libn Jeff Co Schs, Denver 57-60; Br asst Jeff Co Pub Lib, Denver 63-67; Asst catlgr Ore Col of Educ 67-68; Jr high sch libn Jeff Co Schs, Denver 68-. 8: Ref & acquis libn Central Colo Lib System 66-67. 9: ALA. 14: Ref, govt docs, catlg. 15: 1374 S Drexel wy, Denver 80226.

LARSON, BERKLEY GENE. b Frederic Wis 8 Je 32. 4: Eleanor Ruth Ford. 5: Wis State U (River Falls) 50-54 (Geog) BA, 58-59 (Educ, LS) BS; UKan 54-56 (Geog); West Mich U 65-66 MSL. 6: Sp. 7: Quality control operator Stokely-Van Camp, Frederic Wis summers 50-59; Map processing asst LC Map Div summers 54-55; Tchg asst & map curator UKan 54-56; Instr geog & geol W Tex State U 56-57; Tchr & libn Beloit (Wis) Pub Schs 59-65; Asst libn Rock Valley Commun Col, Rockford Ill 66-68; Hd libn Milton Col 68-69; Coord learning materials El Paso Commun Col, Colo Springs Colo 69-. 8: Sch lib consul Morgan sch; Beloit Wis 61. 9: ALA; WisLA. 14: Admin, acquis, ref, maps. 15: El Paso Community Col, 5 W Las Vegas ave, Colorado Springs Co 80903.

LARSON, EDGAR R(AYMOND). b Ethridge Mont 18 Jl 14. 5: Pacific Lutheran Col 31-34 (Educ); UWash 36-39 (Educ) BA, 40 (Fr), 49-50 (LS) BA. 6: Fr. 7: Bibliogr-searcher LC 50-51; Visiting Faculty Japan Lib Sch KeioU (Tokyo) 51-52; Ref asst LC 52, Ref libn 52-53; Head reader serv USNaval Radiological Def Lab, San Francisco 53-54; Head ref libn ASTIA SF Off Oakland Cal 54-59; Chief reader serv dept USNaval Postgrad Sch (Monterey Cal) 59-. 9: ALA; SLA; (treas San Francisco Bay Reg Chap 58-59); CalLA. 10: Phi Beta Kappa; Phi Sigma Iota. 12: "Abstracting & Indexing Services for Periodical Literature" (65). 13: Yes. 14: Ref. 15: 122 Dune crest, Monterey Ca 93940.

LARSON, EDITH MOODY. b Chicago 25 Ja 09. 4: Gertis E Larson. 5: UIll, Chicago Northwestern, NoIllU. 07: Asst libn Ottawa Pub Lib, Ottawa Ill 29; Asst libn VA, Hines Ill; Head Libn Ft Custer, Ft Custer Mich; Br libn Maywood Pub Lib, Maywood Ill; Libn Rochelle Jr High Sch, Rochelle, Ill; Libn DeKalb Pub Lib, DeKalb Ill 66-. 8: Research writer for adver firm Beaumont & Homan; Lecturer on Eng cathedrals and abbeys. 9: ALA; IllLA (chm Com on Resolutions, Comm oh Hosp & Instl Libs); Ill State Hist Assn; Ill State Archaeol Soc. 10: Anglo-American Friendship League; Vivisection Investigation League. 15: DeKalb Pub Lib 309 Oak st, DeKalb Il 60115.

LARSON, EDNA (SEABERG) MRS. b Pittsburgh 6 Ap 04. 5: Denison U 23-27 (Eng) PhB; UPittsburgh 30-31 (Eng); West Res summers 32-33 (LS); UBuffalo summer 55 (Educ); SUNY(Geneseo) summers 59-61 MLS; Syr acuse U summer 68 (Lib as an info ctr LS. 06: Fr, Swedish. 7: Eng tchr BelleVernon High Sch, Belle Vernon Penn 28-30; Eng tchr & libn Bridgeville High Sch, Bridgeville Penn 30-34; Eng tchr & asst to libn Cleveland Hill High Sch, Cheektowaga NY 55-59; Libn Williamsville High Sch, Williamsville NY 59-. 8: Team Leader, Instructional Materials Team 68-69. 9: NEA; NYLA; NY State Tchrs Assn. 14: Ref wk with high sch studs. 15: 317 Walton dr, Buffalo NY 14226.

LARSON, EVVA LORRAINE. b St Louis Mo 11 Ag 23. 5: WashU 47 (Eng) AB, 48 (LS) BSEd, 65 (Educ) Life Certif Secondary Tchg; LSU 53 MLS. 6: Fr. 7: Cpl USMC Women's Res, San Diego 42-45; Child libn Univ City (Mo) Pub Lib 47-48; Sec Mary Bush Sec Serv 48-52; Asst readers' serv St Louis (Mo) Pub Lib 53-54, Child libn 54-57; Br libn St Louis Co (Mo) Lib 57-61; Dir libs Mellville Sch Dist, St Louis Co (Mo) 62-. 8: State Chm Recr Com, Mo State Lib 63-65; Consul wkshop for Student Assts, Mo 68. 9: ALA; -AASchL; NEA; MoLA; MoASchL; St Louis Sub Libns Assn; Sec, St Louis Lib Club (sec). 10: Mo Certified Tchrs Assn; Beta Phi Mu. 14: Wk with child & ya, admin. 15: 1 Fawnwood dr, St Louis Mo 63128.

LARSON, GERTRUDE MARTHA. b Oscar Twp Otter Tail Co Minn 26 Ag 20. 5: Moorhead State Col 39-43 (Eng) BS in Educ; UMinn 47-48 BS in LS; UDenver summers 64, 65, 66 (Lib) MA. 6: Norwegian, Fr. 7: Eng tchr & libn High Sch, Underwood Minn 43-44; Eng tchr Jr High Sch Crookston Minn 44-45; Eng tchr & libn High Sch Morris Minn 45-47; Sch libn Kindergarten-12 Pub Schs Fergus Falls Minn 49-62; Sr high sch libn Fergus Falls Minn 62-67; Asst libn Pub Lib, Escondido Cal 67-. 9: ALA; NEA; CalLA. 10: Delta Kappa Gamma; AAUW. 14: Ref. 15: 239 S Kalmia, Escondido Ca 92025.

LARSON, JOAN (KEILHOLZ). b Champaign Ill 29 Ag 29. 4: David Hathaway Larson. 5: UPenn 47-51 (Hist of Fine Arts) AB; Drexel 51-52 MS in LS. 7: Stud asst UPenn Lib 50, 51; Asst libn in chg res bks & circ Radcliffe Col 52-56; Libn I Burlingame Pub Lib, Burlingame Cal 65-66; Libn I San Matco Co Lib 66-68; Libn II Burlingame Pub Lib 68-. 9: CalLA. 10: PTA; LWV; Burlingame Citizens Action Forum. 14: Catlg, ref. 15: 1216 Cortez ave, Burlingame Ca 9 4010.

LARSON, JULIAN RALPH. b Aberdeen SD 26 Ap 35. 4: Patricia. 5: No State Col 53-57 (Second Educ) BS; West Res 60-61 (LS) MS. 7: Tchr Browns Valley (Minn) Pub Sch 57-58; Lab techn Mallinckrodt Chem, St Louis 59-60; Research libn Pittsburgh P late Glass Co Akron Ohio 61-. 8: Vis instr, Kent State U 68. 9: SLA (chm Scholarship Com 68-69; Cleveland chap: sec & Bull ed, pres 67-68); Acron Area LA (pres 69); ACS div Chem Lit. 10: Toastmasters. 14: Admin. 15: 159 25th st NW, Barberton Oh 44203.

LARSON, MAXINE (BOW). b Detroit Mich 17 Jl 22. 5: Albion Col 39-40 (Educ); Ohio Wesleyan U 40-43 (Sociol) BA; Wayne State 43-44 (Educ) Secondary Certif; West Mich U 61-64 (LS) MA. 7: Admin asst WAC-AAF Wright Field, Dayton Ohio 44-45; Tchr Michigan schs 47-60; Libn & a-v dir Hartford Pub Schs Mich 61-63; Libn & a-v coord Vine Sch, kalamazoo 63-65; Asst supv sch lib serv Kalamazoo Schs 65-68; Visiting instr Dept of Libnship West Mich U 68; Tchr Berry Sch Detroit 68-69. 8: Consul Knapp Sch Lib Proj, Allisonville summer 64; Consul Elem Sch Libs, Michigan City (Ind) Pub Schs 67; Mem Instr Materials Com, Mich State Bd of Educ. 9: ALA; NEA-DAVI; MichASchL; Mich A-V Assn; MichEA. 10: Beta Phi Mu; Delta Kappa Gamma. 14: Sch libnship (esp elem). 15: 7534 Bingham, Dearborn Mi 48126.

LARSON, MIRIAM ADELINE (TURNER). b Burke Vt. 4: Bernard A Larson. 5: Middlebury Col 26-30 (Biol, Eng) BA, 30-31 (Bacteriology) NS; SUNY (Albany) 32 (Educ); Henry Ford hosp Sch of Med Tech 33-35 (Med Tech) MT (ASCP); UMich 66 (LS); Wayne State 66-67 MSLS. 6: Fr. 7: Instr in bacteriology Middlebury Col 30-31; Tchr Deposit Secondary Schm Deposit NY 31-32; Instr in bacteriology Henry Ford Hosp Sch of Nursing, Detroit 32-34; Bacteriologist Henry Ford Hosp, Detroit 34-35; Supv clinical labs Cottage Hosp of Grosse Pointe Mich 35-42; Asst Prof Dept of lib sci Wayne StateU 68-. 9: SLA; AALS. 10: AAUP. Registry Med Technologists. 14: Lib educ, subj ref, sci & tech, gen ref. 15: 141 Parkhurst pl W, Detroit Mi 48203.

LARSON, RICHARD FARREL. b Seattle 26 Ja 23. 5: Harvard 48 (Romance Lang) AB, 49 (Romance Lang) AM; UStockholm 49-50 (Swedish Lit); UCal 51-52 BLS. 6: Fr, Swedish, Ger, Sp, Ital, Norwegian, Danish. 7: Pvt to Tech 5th Grade US Army Infantry, Signal Corps, Mil Police Intelligence

43-46; Libn Stanford U Libs 52-56; Libn UCal(Berkeley) 56-. 11: King Gustaf V of Sweden Fellow, 49-50. 14: Acquis. 15: 94 Rock lane, Berkeley Ca 94708.

LARSON, SALLY ANN. b Portland Ore 11 Ja 41. 5: Portland State Col 58-63 (Eng) BA; UPortland 63-65 MLS. 7: Libn The Port of Portland Commsn, Portland Ore 64-65; Libn St Helen's , Hall - Bishop Dagwell Hall, Portland Ore 65-67; Spec serv libn Lewis & Clark Col 67-. 9:Portland Area Spec Libns Assn; ALA. 10: Alpha Phi; AAUP. 14: Sch libnship, educ. 15: 4035 NE Laurelhurst pl, Portland Or 97223.

LARSON, WILLIAM LAWRENCE. b El Dorado Ark 18 Jl 40. 4: Dorothy Bing. 5: Ouachita Baptist U 58-62 (Gen Sci) BSE; Peabody Col 67 MLS. 7: Bkmob libn N Ark Reg Lib, Harrison summers 62, 63; Asst libn & a-v coord Hall High Sch, Little Rock Ark 62-65; Asst libn Ark Polytech Col 65-67; Asst libn Hendrix Col 67-. 9: ALA; NEA; ArkLA; ArkEA. 10: Kiwanis Club. 14: Ref, reader serv, govt docs. 15: 1209 Harton, Conway Ar 72032.

LARUDEE, GRACE EMMA (WILDER). b Surry NH 18 D 11. 4: Faze Larudee. 5: Middlebury Col 29-33 (Home Econ) BS; Andover-Newton Theol Sch 35-37 (Relig Educ) MRE; Glassboro State tchrs Col 55-56 (Elem Educ); UMich 61-63 AMLS. 6: Persian, Fr. 7: Tchr COEMAR, Iran 37-44; Libn ETS, Princeton NJ 53; Tchr Pittsfield Twp Sch, Daretown NJ 55-56; Tchr Bettendorf Schs, Bettendof Iowa 56-58; Lib asst UMich Libs (Ann Arbor) 61-63; Hd educ lib 64-65; Eng tchr Jordan-Amer Soc, Amman Jordan 65-66; Hd & area libn Inter Amer U, San Juan PR 66-68; Libn act hd tech serv Amer U Cairo, UAR 68-. 9: ALA. 10: Phi Beta Kappa. 14: Admin, acquis, circ, ref. 15: American Univ in Cairo, Cairo United Arab Republic.

LASH, DAVID BARRY. b Pittsburgh Penn 6 Jl 30. 4: Mary Lou Hirchert. 5: Westminster Col (Penn) 48-52 (Ger) AB; Pittsburgh Theol Sem 52-55 (Theol) BD; UPortland 65-66 MLS. 6: Ger. 7: Pastor United Presbyterian Ch, Garner Iowa 55-60; Assoc pastor Wallace Mem Presbyterian Ch, Greentree Pa 60-64; Pastor Laurelhurst Presbyterian Ch, Portland Ore 64-66; Catlgr Reed Col Lib 67-68; Hd catlgr Milne Lib SUNY (Geneseo) 68-. 14: Catlg. 15: 21 Melody lane, Geneseo NY 14454.

LASH, HENRY (LIVINGSTON). b NYC 4 D 10. 4: Loretta Williams. 5: Harvard 28-32 (Psych) BS; Columbia 32-33 (Eng) MA; USoCal 37-38 BDLD; UCLA 50-55 (Educ). 06: Fr. 7: Libn Greeley High Sch, Greeley Colo 36-37; Libn hist dept Los Angeles Pub Lib 38-40; Libn Cal State Polytech Col 40-42; (Cpt) USArmy Air Force Train Command 42-44; Combat Intelligence Staff Lib Off 20th AF 44-46; Libn Los Angeles Trade-Tech Col 46-68 Coord instr serv ctr 68-. 9: ALA; Los Angeles SchLA. 10: Libraria Sodalitas; Harvard Club of SoCal . 12: "Famous People" (64); Other bibliogs publ by LA City Schs; "The Paperback Rack" weekly col in "Los Angeles Herald-Examiner" (60-); "Santa Monica Evening Outlook" 68-. 13: Yes. 14: Paperbacks, ref, bibliog, commun col libs. 15: 10501 Wilshire blvd, Los Angeles Ca 90024.

LASHER, ESTHER LU (PIM). b Denver Colo 1 Je 23. 4: Donald T Lasher. 5: Temple Buell Col 41-43 (Mus) Assoc Fine Arts; Denver U 43-45 (Mus) BA, 66-67 (LS) MA; East Baptist Theol Sem 46-48 (Relig Educ) MRE. 6: Fr. 7: Tchr Denver Pub Schs 45-46; Christian educ dir First Baptist Ch, Evansville Ind 48-50; Circ libn Evansville Pub Lib, Evansville Ind 50-51; Mus tchr Dubois Co Schs, Dubois Ind 52-53; Br libn Jefferson co Lib, Golden Colo 63-65; Ref libn Penrose Pub Lib, Colo Springs Colo 65-67; Libn Harrison High Sch, Colo Springs Colo 67-68; Hd mus libn Butler U 68-. 9: ALA; MusLA; IndLA. 10: Sigma Alpha Iota. 14: Ref, non-bk materials catlg. 15: 4646 Carvel ave, Indianapolis In 46205.

LASHLEY, MIRIAM. b Tulsa Okla 20 O 21. 5: Tulsa U 37-38; Wellesley 38-42 (Pol Sci) BA; Yale Law Sch 42-44 LLB; UOkla 63-66 (LS) MA. 6: Fr. 7: Attn Tax Sect Appellate Div Dept of Justice 44-45; Staff asst Amer Red Cross 45-46; Lecturer pol sci UTulsa 47-48; Atty (priv practice) 48-50; Attn Sinclair Oil & Gas Co 50-60; Atty (priv practice) 60-62; Lib asst Tulsa City-Co Lib 62-66, Libn bus & tech 66-. 9: ALA; SLA; Okla Bar Assn; OklaLA; SWLA. 10: LWV. 14: Serv (bus & tech). 15: 3 Woodward blvd apt 215, Tulsa Ok 74114.

LASKOWSKI, SENO. b Poland 8 F 34. 4: Ingrid M Schaffer. 5: UAlta 58-62 (Hist) BA; UBC 62-63 BLS. 6: Ger. 7: Catlgr UAlta 63-65; Head catlgr Simon Fraser U 65-. 9: EdmontonLA (treas); CanLA; ALA . 10: Can Assn Univ Tchrs. 14: Catlg. 15: 140 Sea ave, Burnaby BC Can.

LASKY, BEN. b Poland 23 Ap 13. 4: Sarah G Lubo. 5: UMd 58-61 (Sociol); SophiaU (Japan) 61-63 (Sociol) BS; UCLA 63-64 MSLS. 6: Fr. 7: M/Sgt USAF 40-61; Br libn Tachikawa AB, Japan 64-65; Staff libn 7th AF, Vietnam 66-68; Base libn: Ching Chuan Kang AB, Taiwan 68-69, U-Tapao AB, Thailand 69-. 15: Base Lib, APO San Francisco Ca 96330.

LASSANYI, MARY ELIZABETH. b Versend Hungary 31 Jl 38. 5: USoCal 54-58 (For Lang, 9foreign Rel) BA, 61-63 (LS, Foreign Lang) MS. 6: Hungarian, Ger, Sp, Portug, Ital. 7: Circ libn Immaculate Heart Col 59-60; Asst ref libn Cal Tech Gen Lib 60-61, Aero libn 63-67; Ref libn USMA 67-68; Admin libn 50th CSG personnel serv br, Hahn AB Germany 69-. 8: Adv and pub rel wk, Internat Telecommunication Consultative Com, 9th Conf, Los Angeles 59. 9: SLA. 10: Alpha Mu Gamma; Delta Phi Alpha; Internat Club; Cath Alumni Club; Fed Women's Coord; Equal Employment Opport Com. 14: Ref, research, trans, bibliog. 15: 50th Combat Support Group, Pers Serv Br, APO NY 09109.

LASSLO, ANDREW. b Czechoslovakia 24 Ag 22. 4: Wilma E Reynolds. 5: UIll 46-48 (Pharm Chem) MS, 48-52 (Pharm Chem) PhD, 60-61 MSLS; MedLA Certif Med Libn 62. 06: Czech, Ger, Hungarian, Russian. 7: USA Res Med Serv Corps (1st Lt-Capt) 53-62; Res chem organic chem div Monsanto Chem Co, St Louis 52-54; Asst Prof Dept of Pharmacology Div of Basic Health Sci, Emory U 54-60; Prof & Chm Dept of Med Chem, Col of Pharmacy, UTenn Med Units 60-. 8: Dir: PHS Res Grant 58-64, Geschickter Med Res Grant 59-65, NSF Res Grant 64-66; US Army Med Res & Devel Com Res Contract 64-67; NLM Supported Postgrad Train Prog for Sci Lib 66-; Chm Lib Sci & Serv Com for NIH Designated Memphis Reg Med, Prog 67-. 9: ACS; Amer Inst of Chem (Fellow); ALA; Amer Pharmaceut Assn; Amer Soc for Pharmac & Exper Therapeutics; Drug Info Assn (Bd Dirs 68-69); MedLA. 10: Beta Phi Mu; Rho Chi; Sigma Xi. 12: "The reformatsky Reaction in the Synthesis of Compounds Having Potential Amebacidal Activity," PhD diss UIll (52). 13: Yes. 14: Chem constitution & biochem response, sci info storage & retrieval, acquis. 15: Dept of Med Chem, Col of Pharmacy, Univ of Tenn Med Units, Memphis Tenn 38103.

LASWELL, JANE B. b Milwaukee Wis 27 Ag 38. 4: H Reginald Laswell. 5: UWis (Milwaukee) 56-60 (Eng) BA; UIll 60-61 MSLS. 7: Asst ref libn Mead Pub Lib, sheboygan Wis 61-64; Hd of adult serv W Allis Pub Lib, Allis Wis 64-65; Asst ser libn UWis (Milwaukee) 65-67; Asst catlgr MarquetteU 67-. 14: Catlg. 15: 4454 N Cramer st, Milwaukee Wi 53211.

LASWELL, REGINALD HARRY. b Brodhead Ky 25 Je 40. 4: Jane Baumbach. 5: UKy 58-63 (Hist) BA, 63-65 MSLS. 7: Map catlgr UKy Lib 64; Admin asst UWis (Milwaukee) 65; Head ser dept 65-66; Ser coord Marquette U 67-. 9: ALA-ACRL; WisLA. 10: Beta Phi Mu; AAUP; Wis State Hist Soc; Ky Hist Soc; Marquette Fac Assn for Interracial Justice. 14: Tech serv, col & univ lib admin, automation. 15: 4454 N Cramer st, Milwaukee Wi 53211.

LASWORTH, EARL JAMES. b Chicago Ill 15 Ag 26. 4: Virginia White. 5: NorthwesternU 43-49 (Marketing, Advertising) BS; UNotre Dame 44-45 (Journalism, Gen Bus); UChicago (Communications); UOkla 65-66 MLS. 6: Sp, Ital, Lat, Polish. 7: F 1/c (EM) USN Submarine Serv 44-46; Asst ed & advertising sales Geyer Publ, Chicago 49-51; Asst advertising mgr Automatic Electric Co, Northlake Ill 51-53; Advertising mgr Chicago Pump Co 53-55; Account supv Calkins & Holden Inc, Chicago 55-59; Consul: Don L Baxter Inc, Dallas Tex 59-62, Research & Communications 9co-partner), Dallas Tex 62, MAGNUSSEN Advertising Agcy, Ft Worth 63; Free-lance pub rel consul, Albuquerque 63-64; Tech ed Ken Cook Publ Co, Milwaukee 64-65; Libn (sci div) Portland State Col 66-68; Assoc libn & dir lib sci East Wash State Col 68-. 8: Consul pres Evergreen Col New Lib Bldg 69; Adv Whelcom Lib Budget Analysis & Formula State of Wash 68-69; Consul Wash Jr Col Libn Conf 69; Adv Joint Coun of Econ Educ 69; Tchr; Tech Ed & Bibliog Portland State Col Div of Continuing Educ, Advertising Adult Educ Program, Arlington Hts Ill 49-50. 9: PNLA; NW Assn Acad Libns. 10: AAUP; Amer Soc for Engring Educ. 13: Yes. 14: Lib admin, educ & pub rel. 15: Associate Lib & East Washington State College Dir of Lib Serv John F Kennedy Mem Lib, Cheney Wa 99004.

LATEINER, HAROLD. b Brooklyn NY 3 S 12. 4: Helen R Morenstein. 5: NYU 36-39, 46-49 (Journalism) BA; Columbia 39-41 Prof Certif in Lib Serv. 7: Time Inc, NYC: Ed off boy 27-29, Lib clerk 30-35, Ref asst 36-38, Research libn 39-. 9: SLA. 14: Ref in nat affairs, bus & fin & mil affairs. 15: 56-23 Clearview expressway, Bayside NY 11364.

LATHAM, DORIS (STOFFREGEN). b NYC 7 F 34. 5: Hope Col 52-56 (Biol) AB; Pratt Grad Lib Sch 67-68 MLS; Montclair State Col 68-69 (Educ). 7: Jr pharmacologist Johnson & Johnson, New Brunswick NJ 56-58; Sch libn Robert Fulton Elem Sch, N Bergen NJ 68-. 9: ALA; NEA; NJLA; NJEA; Hudson CoASchL. 10: Beta Phi Mu. 14: Child wk. 15: 400 68 st, Guttenberg NJ 07093.

LATHROP, ALAN KENNETH. b Sioux Falls SD 24 Ja 40. 4: Peggy Dunnette. 5: Augustana Col 57-61 (Hist) BA; UMinn 61-64 (Hist) MA, 64-66 (LS) MA. 6: Fr. 7: Soc sci libn Ariz state U 66-67, Hd arch lib 67-68; Mss libn UIowa 68-. 9: ALA; AHA; SAA. 14: Ref, mss, archives, bibliog. 15: Special Collections Dept, Univ of Iowa Libs, Iowa City Ia 52240.

LATHROP, EVA M (KISSELL). b Herrick Twp Penn 18 Ja 13. 4: Cecil D Lathrop. 5: Mansfield State Col 30-34 (Eng) BSEd; Penn StateU 35-38 (Eng) MSEd; Marywood Col 61-63 MSLS. 7: Tchr Laceyville High Sch, Laceyville Penn 34-37; Tchr Elkland Twp High Sch, Estella Penn 42-43; Sec Elk Lake Joint Schs Sch Bd, Dimock Penn 50-61; Libn Elk Lake Joint Schs Dimock Penn 61-. 9: ALA; NEA; PennLA; PennStateEA. 14: Young adults & child collections, ref. 15: Dimock Penn 18816.

LATIAK, DOROTHY (VIOLET) (SCHER). b Sault Ste Marie Mich 27 Jl 20. 4: David Florian Latiak. 5: Wilson Jr Col 38-40 (Pre-legal) AA; Chicago Pub Lib Train Class 41-42; Col of Jewish Studies (Chicago) 48-50 06: Fr. 7: Jr lib asst Chicago Pub Lib 42-43; Army of the US (WAC) Clerk-typist (Pvt) 43-46; Child libn Chicago Pub Lib 46-, Child libn Gr II Pullman Br 53-. 9: ALA; IllLA. 10: Ridge Art Assn; Child Reading RT. 13: Yes. 14: Child. 15: Pullman Br Lib 11001 S Indiana ave, Chicago Il 60628.

LATIMER, FLOY MARIE. b Clio Iowa. 5: Kendall Col 56-58 (Educ); RooseveltU 58-60 9educ); BA; LoyolaU 61-63 (Educ) MEd; Rosary Col 67-69 MALS. 7: Typesetter "Chicago sun Times"; Tchr, Ind: Gary, Hammond & Elmhurst; Proofreader "Chicago Tribune"; Dist libn Dist 68 Du Page co, Woodridge Ill. 9: NEA; ALA; IllLA; IllEA. 10: Intl Typographical Union. 15: 6800 S La Grange rd, La Grange Il 60525.

LaTOURETTE, JOANNE (DOBSON). b Kittanning Penn 4 D 30. 4: E E LaTourette. 5: Waynesburg Col 47-51 (Eng) BA; West Res 62-63 MSLS. 7: Adult serv libn E Cleveland Pub Lib, East Cleveland Ohio 63-65, Catlg libn 65-. 9: OhioLA; No Ohio Tech Serv Libns (sec 69). 10: College Club of Cleveland. 14: Catlg, ref. 15: 2909 Washington blvd, Cleveland Heights Oh 44118.

LATTA, ANN (WAHLUND). b Eureka Cal 3 My 43. 4: Kurt nthony Latta. 5: UCal (Davis) 61-65 (Intl Rel) BA; UCal (Berkeley) 65-66 MLS. 6: Sp. 7: State & mun docs libn StanfordU 66-67, Fed docs libn 68-. 14: Govt docs. 15: 531 Lassen, Los Altos Ca 94022.

LATTIMER, ELEANOR (PHILLIPS). b Oneonta NY 12 N 17. 4: Everett C Lattimer. 5: Buffalo 35-39 (Hist, Govt) BA, 39 BS in LS; Ohio State U 63-64 (Supvn, Curriculum) MA. 7: Libn Cooperstown Village Lib, Cooperstown NY 39-42; Libn Gilboa Central Sch, Gilboa NY 42-47; Dir of Lib New Hartford Central Sch, New Hartford NY 47-60; Elem libn Schalmont Central Sch, Schenectady NY 60-61; High sch libn Colonie Central Sch, Albany NY 61-63, Jr high sch libn 64-65; High sch libn E Greenbush Central Sch, E Greenbush NY 65-66; High sch libn Colonie central Sch, Albany NY 66-. 8: Consul NYState Educ Dept summers 61-62; Assoc Prof NDEA Inst for Sch Libns SUNY summer 65; Vis Assoc Prof SUNY (Albany) 67-. 9: NEA (Legis Chm, Congress, Dist); ALA (Mem com); NYState Tchrs Assn; NYLA (pres Sch Lib Sect 61, Coun 63-65); Central NY Sch Libns Assn (pres). 10: AAUW; Delta Kappa Gamma. 13: Yes. 14: Sch lib. 15: Magee rd, Glenmont NY 12077.

LATTIMER, JOHN MANGAN. b Stamford NY 7 Ap 43. 5: Universidad Veracruzana (summer) 61; USoFla 61-65 (Chem) BA; Fla StateU 68-69 (LS) MS. 6: Sp, Visayan. 7: Tchr Peace Corps capiz High Sch, Roxas City Philippines 65-67; Instr Tampa Tech Inst 67; Ref libn US Dept of Interior, Wash DC 69. 9: ALA; SLA; ASIS. 10: Beta Phi Mu. 14: Ref. 15: 1111 Arlington blvd M-925, Arlington Va 22209.

LATUS, SHEILA E (HORN). b Brooklyn NY 6 My 42. 4: John E Latus. 5: Brooklyn Col 60-64 (Biol) BA; Immaculate Heart Col 67-69 MSLS. 6: Ger. 7: Libn Ayerst Labs, NYC 64-66; Libn Rocketdyne, Canoga Pk Cal 66-68; Libn Harbor Gen Hosp, Torrance Cal 69-. 9: SLA; CalLA. 14: Lib searching. 15: 1923 Gates ave, Redondo Beach Ca 90278.

LATZKE, HENRY RAYMOND. b Janesville Wis 3 Jl 31. 4: Laura Rahe. 5: Concordia Tchrs Col 54-56 (Elem Educ) BS; West Res 56-59 MS in LS; IndU 63- (A-V Communication). 7: Tchr libn Ala Lutheran Acad & Col 56-58; Libn Los Angeles Lutheran High Sch, Los Angeles 58-60; Asst libn & a-v dir Concordia Tchrs Col (River Forest Ill) 60-. 9: ALA; IllA-V Assn; NEA-DAVI. 14: A-v. 15: 1701 No 15th ave, Melrose Park Ill 60160.

LAUBACH, ALICE F(RANCES). b Easton Penn 30 S 13. 5: Sweet Briar Col 31-35 (Chem) BA; UHawaii 35-37 (Chem) MA. 6: Fr, Ger. 7: Analytical chem Buckeye Cotton Oil Co, Memphis Tenn 40-42; Control chem Casein Corp of Amer, Bainbridge NY 42-44; Research chem Amer Enka Corp, Enka NC 44-51, Libn 51-. 9: SLA (Paper & Textile Sect: sec-treas 59; v-pres 60, chm 61); ACS (sec West Carolinas Sect) 49; NCLA. 10: Bus & Prof Women (Asheville). 13: Yes. 15: 366 Lakeshore dr, Asheville NC 28804.

LAUCUS, JOHN PAUL. b Cambridge Mass 30 D 33. 4: Carol DesRoches. 5: Harvard 51-55 9eng Lit) AB; Rutgers 55-56 MSLS. 6: Fr, Ger. 7: Pvt E2 US Army 56-57; Hd transportation collection Harvard Bus Sch 57-58, Hd collating & binding 58-59, Selection off 59-60; Hd Bus Lib BostonU 60-62, Hd gen educ fine & applied arts lib 62-64, Hd gen lib (undergrad serv) 64-66, Asst dir, act dir 66-. 8: President's Commsn for Univ Goals (self-study gp), BostonU 61-62; Adv to BostonU African Studies Ctr in establ of tech lib, Conakry Guinea 63. 9: ALA. 14: Admin, pub serv. 15: 20 Hutchinson st, Cambridge Ma 02138.

LAUDERDALE, KENNETH WAYNE. b Cushing Okla 18 Je 23. 4: Muriel Chinn. 5: UCal(Berkeley) 40-41, 46-49 (Econ) AB, 49-50 BLS. 7: Clerk JCPenny Co Vallejo Cal 41-42; Aircraft armorer AF 42-46; Prof asst Shasta Co Lib, Redding Cal 50-52; Tech libn Naval Ordnance Test Station, China Lake Cal 52-55; Bibliogr asst Air ULib (Montgomery Ala) 55-58; Info spec Gen Elec TEMPO, Santa Barbara Cal 58-65, Manager-tech info center 64-. 8: Bd Lib Trustees; Santa Barbara Pub Lib 63-65; Bd of Freeholders (to write a new city charter) 65-66. 9: SLA; ASIS; CalLA. 14: Info research, ref. 15: 3411 Madrona dr, Santa Barbara Cal 93105.

LAUER, EVELYN GERDA. b Vienna Austria 15 S 38. 5: UBuffalo 56-60 (Fr) BA; Columbia 60-61 (LS) MS. 6: Ger, Fr, Hungarian, Ital, Russian. 7: Ref libn ColumbiaU 6-163, 65-68, Libn Sch Lib Serv Lib 68-. 12: Contrib "Selected Reference Notes, Col & Research Libs, "Slavic Review; Comp "Index to Little Magazines, (64-65 and currented). 14: Ref, admin. 15: 535 W 113 st, New York NY 10025.

LAUERSON, ILSE. b Pirna Germany 15 Jl 41. 5: Kutztown State Col 63 BS; Drexel Inst 66 MSLS. 06: Ger, Latvian. 7: Lib asst Allentown Pub Lib, Allentown Penn; Hd child dept 63; Child consul Dist Serv FLP, Phila 66. 9: ALA-CSD (Arrangements Com 69; Devel Com 69-72); PennLA (Chm Resolutions Com; Exec Bd 68-69; SE Chap: Memb Chm 68; sec 68-69); Ad Hoc Com of Lib Pub Rel Assn (chm 68-69). 10: Drexel Alumni Assn; Phila Child Reading RT; Beta Phi Mu. 14: Admin, child serv. 15: 352 S Smedley st, Phila Pa 19103.

LAUFFER, ANNA (TINKEL). b NYC. 5: Hunter Col 28-35 (Biol) AB; Columbia 36-40 MLS. 6: Fr, Ger. 7: Ref wk H W Wilson Co, NYC 30-40, Indexer 52-. 9: ALA; NY Lib Club. 10: Sierra Club. 13: Yes. 14: Catlg, ref. 15: 150 W 96th st, New York NY 10025.

LAUGHER, CHARLES (THEODORE). b Worcester Mass 5 Je 28. 4: Ann Fischer. 5: UNH 48-51 (Ger Lit) BA; West Res 52 MS in LS, 60 (Eng) MA, 63 (Eng LS) PhD. 6: Ger, Sp. 7: Head of reader ser Bowdoin Col Lib 52-54; Asst libn ECarolina Col 54-57; Asst dir of libs West Res U 58-64; Assoc libn Amherst Col Lib 64-, Act dir 66-67. 9: BSA; NELA; NE Col Libns. 13: Yes. 14: Admin. 15: Amherst Col Lib, Amherst Ma 01002.

LAUGHLIN, MILDRED (KNIGHT). b Glasco Kan 23 Mr 22. 4: William Allen Laughlin. 5: Ft Hays State 43-46 (Eng, Hist) AB; WichitaU 49-52 (Educ) MA; SUNY (Geneseo) NDEA 65 (LS); UOkla 68- (LS). 7: Tchr Downs (Kan) High Sch 46-47; High sch tchr & libn, Kan: Glaseo 47-48, Mulvane 48-50, Trousdale 50-51, Dighton 51-52; Elem libn, Wichita Kan 52-68; Tchr Child Lit Inst Wahburn U 66; Asst dir NDEA Lib Inst UOkla 67, Instr bks & materials for child 68; Resource dir Kennedy Sch, Norman Okla 68-. 8: Stearman Sch State Demonst Lib 66-68; Lib consul, Pauls Valley Okla Hilltop Sch for Retarded 68-69. 9: NEA; -DAVI; ALA (Com to Prepare Non-Bk Catlg k-Schs; OklaLA. 10: Okla Sequoiah. 12: Ed "Administrative Technique for the School Library Supervisor"

(68). 13: Yes. 14: Child lit. 15: 1206 Cherry Laurel, Norman Ok 73069.

LAUMAN, FRANCES W(HEELER). b Ithaca NY 24 Mr 14. 5: CornellU 31-35 (Ger Lit) AB; Carnegie 35-36 BS in LS. 7: Asst libn Agric Lib Penn State Col 36; Catlgr Pub Lib, Easton Penn 36-38; Catlgr High schs div Carnegie Lib of Pittsburgh 38-42; Catlgr Depauw U Lib 42-43; Tech Sgt USMarine Corps 43-45; Assoc ref libn, CornellU 46-61, Ref libn Undergrad Lib 62-, Curator Cornelliana Collection 67-. 9: ALA; NYLA. 14: Ref. 15: Uris Lib CornellU, Ithaca NY 14850.

LAUNDRY, MARION SUZANNE (TEEUWS). b Berwyn Ill 21 Ap 33. 4: Melburn Edward Laundry. 5: Rosary Col 54-56 (Bus Econ) BA, 59-61 (LS) MA; Loyola U 63-66 (Educ) MEd; All Grade Supervisory Certif 65; Alliance Francaise Sch (Paris) summer 66 (Fr). 06: Lat, Fr, Sp, Ger. 7: Jr Investment Analyst Continental Casualty & Assurance Co Chicago 56-58; Elem sch tchr Garfield Sch Maywood Ill 59-61; Sch libn William Beye Sch, Oak Park Ill 61-, Sch libn & lib consul USAF, Wiesbaden Germany 66-67; Instr of lib sci NEast Ill State Col 67-; Prof lib asst Northwestern U summer 69. 8: Lib consul in organizing a spec lib (cerebral palsy), Chicago 68-69; Tech consul for Ill activities, 1970 White House Conf on Child and Youth, Springfield Ill 67-70. 9: NEA; ALA (Election Com);-ACRL; -LED;-RTSD; AASchL; IllLA (Delegate to the Ill Commsn on Child 65-67); IllEA (Legis Com 60-61, delegate to Rep Assembly 59-60); IllASchL (Exec Bd, chm Publ Com 68-70). 10: Alpha Phi; Beta Sigma Phi; Pi Gamma Mu; Child Reading Round Table (Chicago); AAUP; Eng-Speaking Union; Chicago Coun For Rel; AAUW; Chicago Opera Lyric Guild. 12: "A Basic Reference List for Junior High School Libraries" (69); Ed "News for You," IllASchL (68-70). 13: Yes. 14: Internat libnship, sch libnship, publ, bk reviewing, catlg. 15: 330 W Diversey pkwy apt 2607, Chicago Il 60657.

LAUPACIS, BENEDICT. b Prov of Latgalia Latvia 1 Ap 10. 5: URiga(Latvia) 37-41 (Law) Magister Iuris; August-Georg U (Gottingen Germany) 45-47 (Law); LavalU (Que) 51-52 Diplome de Bibliotheconomie; Ottawa U 60-62 BLS. 6: Fr, Ger, Russian, Latvian. 7: Magistrate Ministry of Justice, Latvia, Daugovpils Latvia 43-44; Camp Leader UNRRA T208 Esslingen Germany 45-48; Bibliothecaire asst Dept of Fisheries, Prov of Que 51-56; Asst catlgr Royal Mil Col of Can 56-65; Chief catlgr & dir of tech serv Dept of Nat Defence Dept Lib, Ottawa 65-, Act libn 66-. 9: CanLA. 12: "La Bibliograpie du droit naturel dans la philosophie Cretienne Diplom thesis (52). 14: Catlg. 15: 174 Powell ave, Ottawa Can.

LAURITZEN, ROBERT L. b Rio Vista Cal 13 Ag 29. 5: UCal 47-51 (Fr) BA, 51-52 BLS. 6: Fr. 7: Jr libn Richmond Pub Lib, Richmond Cal 53; San Jose State Col Lib: Libn I 53-55, Libn II 55-58, Soc sci libn 58-62, Ref serv libn 62-68, Act col libn 65, Bibliogr control libn 68-. 9: SLA; CalLA. 10: AAUP. 13: Yes. 14: Collection bldg. 15: 42 N Tenth st, San Jose Ca 95112.

LAURSEN, ALLAN R. b Chicago 4 D 10. 4: Helen C Brown. 5: Wash State U 28-33 (Econ) AB; UMich 33-34 ABLS, 34-37 AMLS. 6: Fr. 7: Asst order & circ depts UMich Lib (Ann Arbor) 34-37; Libn Ill Wesleyan U 37-43; Act libn Knox Col 43-45; Libn Pacific U 45-46; Libn Col of the Pacific 46-60; Libn Stockton Col 48-63; Libn San Joaquin Delta Col 63-. 9: ALA; ACRL; NEA; CalLA (pres Golden Empire Dist 51, chm No Div 52, chm Col & U & Research Libs Sect 55); Cal Tchrs Assn. 10: AAUP; Phi Kappa Phi; Les Voyageurs (UMich). 14: Admin, ref. 15: 1564 W Princeton, Stockton Cal 95204.

LAUTENSCHLAGER, ELISABETH. b Phila. 5: BucknellU 36-39 (Pre-Med); UPenn 41-43 (Biol) AB; Drexel 62-63 MSLS. 6: Fr. 7: Microbiologist-serologist Misericordia Hosp, Phila 41-42; Metrologist Frankford Arsenal Phila 42-45; Microbiologist-Biochemist Rohm & Haas Phila 45-61; Asst libn TempelU 63-65; Lib consul Daniel Yankelovitch, Bala-Cynwood Penn 65-, Supv tech & info ctr Riegel Paper Corp 66-. 9: SLA; ASIS. 10: AAUW; Pilot International. 14: Admin, lit searching, info sci. 15: Madison Arms, 155 Broad st, Flemington NJ 08822.

LAUX, PETER J. b New London Wis 7 Ja 22. 4: Bernice E Dorn. 5: St Norbert Col 45-48 (Educ) BS; Marquette U 49 (Eng) MA; UWis 52 MSLS. 7: Specialist 3/c Chem-warfare USCoast Guard 42-44; Jr libn, libn III Milwaukee Pub Lib 52-54; Assoc libn Georgetown U (Washington DC) 54-60; Dir of Lib Canisius Col 60-. 08: Spec consul on periods - US Info Agency 59-60; Educ Col & Univ Sect, WNYCath Libns Conf 61-63; Trustee & v-pres, West NY Lib Res Coun 67-. 9: ALA; CathLA (chm Publ Com 65, Fin Com 67). 12: Contrib ed "Catholic Library World," "A Man's Home Is His Hassle" (69). 13: Yes. 14: Admin. 15: 251 Parkside ave, Buffalo NY 14214.

LAUZON, MAURICE G. b New Bedford Mass 22 F 26. 4: Carol Crompton. 6: Fr. 7: Off asst "Standard-Times" New Bedford Mass 43-55, Asst libn 55-65, Libn 65-. 9: SLA. 10: Union St Jean Baptist d'Amerique; Cath Order of Foresters. 15: 555 Pleasant st, New Bedford Mass 02740.

LAVAYNA, CARMELITA L. b Manila Philippines 6 My 37. 5: UPhilippines 53-55 (Liberal Arts), 55-57 (Biol, Home Econ) BSE, 62-65 (LS). 6: Philipino (Tagalog), Sp. 7: Tchr: UP High Sch, Diliman, Rizal, Quezon City 56-57, Araullo High Sch, Manila Philippines 57; Lab asst & lib helper Inst of Sci, Manila 57-58; Sci demonstrator UNESCO Travel Exhibits & NSDB, Manila 58; Abstract indexer Mission (Bd) UN, Manila 58-59; Jr libn Doc Div NIST-NSDB, Manila 59-67; Grad asst IDEP Sch of Educ UPittsburgh 67-68, Dir (admin specialist) 68-. 9: ALA; ASIS; SLA; SLA Philippines (secy 66-67). 10: Legion of Mary; Alum Student Cath Action; Pittsburgh Coun for Internat Visitors. 11: Fulbright-Hays grant 67-. 14: Info sci, spec libnship. 15: IDEP 400 S Craig st, Pittsburg Pa 15213.

LaVERDI, ADELAIDE (LUTEYN). b E Aurora NY 15 F 37. 4: Leo L LaVerdi. 5: State U Col of Educ (Geneseo NY) 54-58 (LS) BS in Educ, 60-64 MLS. 6: Sp, Ger. 7: Asst libn Milne Lib State U Col (Geneseo NY) 59-. 9: ALA. 10: Faculties Assn of State Univs of NY; Civ Serv Employees Assn. 14: Catlg. 15: Gateway Motel, Leicester NY 14481.

LAVERGNE, RODOLPHE C(HARLES). b Prince-Albert Sask Can 25 F 26. 4: Ingrid Smith. 5: UMontreal 47 BA; McGill 49 BLS, 59 MLS. 6: Fr. 7: Libn Engnr Inst of Can, Montreal 49-53; Command libn USAF, St Johns Newfoundland 53-56; Chief Libn Canadair Ltd, Montreal 56-63; Chief Libn Med Lib McGill U 63-66; U assoc libn sci McGill U 66-, Assoc dir Grad Sch Lib Sci McGill U 68-. 9: ALA; SLA; CanLA; QueLA. 15: Med Lib McGill Univ, 3655 Drummond st, Montreal Can.

LAVOIE, MONIQUE (CLAUDETTE). b Valleyfield Que Can 12 Mr 42. 5: UOttawa 61-64 BA; McGill 64-65 BLS. 6: Fr. 7: Asst libn International Cellulose Research Ltd, Hawkesbury Ont 65-66; Asst libn Grad Sch of Lib Sci McGill U 66-. 9: CanLA. 14: Catlg. 15: 530 Nelson W, Hawkesbury Ont Canada.

LAVRSEN, DORTHE G. b Balle Denmark 13 F 43. 5: Silkeborg Seminarium 62-65 (Tchg); Simmons 67-69 (LS) MS. 6: Danish, Swedish, Norwegian, Ger. 7: Catlgr Harvard Law Lib 67-. 15: 83 Hammond st, Cambridge Ma 02138.

LAW, LEAH H. b Des Moines Iowa 23 Je 1899. 4: C G Law. 5: Central State Col 18-19 (Span); UOkla 20-22 (Span) AB, 52-53 BS in LS. 6: Sp, Fr. 7: Tchr-libn Carnegie Pub Schs, Carnegie Okla 42-52; Readers adv Okla State Lib 53-56, Legal & gen ref 56-59; Sch libn Carnegie Pub Schs, Carnegie Okla 62-. 9: ALA; OklaLA (Recr Com); OklaEA; SW OklaEA (chm Lib Div). 10: Delta Kappa Gamma; PTA; Delphian Fed Club. 14: Ref, readers adv. 15: 11 Hilltop dr, Carnegie Okla 73015.

LAWRENCE, DELORIS (MAGNOLIA). b Nashville Tenn 3 Jl 34. 5: Tenn A&I State U 52-56 (Bus Admin) BS; Peabody Col 63-64 (LS) MA; La Salle Ext 66-68 (Law). 6: Fr. 7: A/2C WWAF USAF 56-59; Recreation dir Army Spec Serv, Germany 60-62; Army program dir (Spec Serv), Korea 62-63; Army libn (Spec Serv), France & Germany 64-66; Br libn Steele Mem Lib, Elmira NY 66-68; Ref libn San Diego Pub Lib 68, Br libn Valencia Park 68; Base libn USAF 348th Combat Support, Japan 68-. 14: Admin. 15: Box 1067 348th Combat Suppor Group, APO San Francisco Ca 96529.

LAWRENCE, EMILY (SOUTHALL). b NC 12 Jl 15. 5: Chowan Col 32-36 (Hist) BA; UNC 55 BS in LS. 7: Tchr, NC 36-42; Computer NACA Langley Field VA 42-45; Clerk Eastern Airlines NYC 45-53; Libn Richmond Pub Lib, Richmond Va 55-. 9: ALA; VaLA. 10: Child Bk Coun (Richmond Va). 14: Child. 15: 300 W Franklin st, Richmond Va 23220.

LAWRENCE, EMMA LUCILE. b Tehuacana tex 3 D 06. 4: Jay B Lawrence. 5: TrinityU 24-28 (Eng, Educ) AB; W Tex State Tchrs Col summer 25; Tex WomensU summers 31-3 (LS) BS; Stephen Austin Tchrs Col summers 40-42 (Eng, Educ) MA. 6: Sp. 7: Stud libn: TrinityU (Tex) 27-28, Texas WomensU summers 31-33; Libn Tex high sch: Borger 33-38, Kilgore 38-44; Circ libn Okla ChristianU 54-56; Pub serv libn Okla

City Pub Lib 56-59; Bibliog Central State Col, Edmond Okla 60-. 8: Hd USAF Dependents Sch, Goose Bay Labrador 59-60. 9: ALA; SWLA; OklaLA (life mem). 10: AAUW; AAUP; AABA; Alpha Beta Alpha; Beta Sigma Phi. 14: Bibliog, pub serv, ref. 15: PO Box 94192, Okla City Ok 73109.

LAWRENCE, GEORGE H M. b E Greenwich RI 19 Je 10. 4: Miriam Boothby. 5: URI 28-32 (Botany) BS, 32-33 (Botany) MS, 52 Honorary DSc; Cornell U 36-39 (Taxonomic Botany) PhD. 6: Fr. 7: Asst Prof botany CornellU 39-42, Prof Botany 45-60, Dir Bailey Hortorium 50-60; Dir Hunt Botanical Lib Carnegie-MellonU 60-. 8: Sec Amer Hort Coun 47-57; Internat Commsn for Nomenclature Cultivated Plants (UNESCO) 52-64; Fairchild Tropical Garden 64- (res, Bd Dirs 69-). 9: Amer Soc Plant Taxonomists (pres 64); Amer Inst Biol Scis (Bd Governors 64-69); Mem Bd Dir Hort Soc NY (Bd Dirs 68-). 12: "Taxonomy of Vascular Plants" (51); "Introduction to Plant Taxonomy" (55); Founder and ed: of "BAILEYA" (54-60); of "HUNTIA" 62-: Sr ed "Botanico-Periodicum-Huntianum" (68); Comp many art exhib, catlg (63-). 13: Yes. 14: Bot bibliog, catlg rare bks of the plant scis, hist of bot. 15: Hunt Botanical Lib Carnegie-Mellon Univ, Pittsburgh Pa 15213.

LAWRENCE, JOAN (M). b London Ont Can 11 F 30. 4: Robert G Lawrence. 5: UWest Ont 48-50; U New Brunswick 50-52 BA; UWis 55-56 MS in LS. 7: Ref libn Victoria Pub Lib, Victoria BC 56-57; Catlgr Victoria Col Lib (BC) 57-58, Ref libn 59-61; Catlgr UVictoria (BC) 61-66, Coord compilation of biog dict of 20th cent Canadians in the creative & performing arts 67-. 9: CanLA; Inst Victoria Libns. 10: Beta Phi Mu. 14: Catlg, ref. 15: 2911 Mt Baker View rd, Victoria BC Canada.

LAWRENCE, JOHN (PETER). b Sudbury Ont Can 17 S 42. 5: Victoria Col UBC 59-63 (Classics) BA; Harvard 63-64 (Ling); UToronto 65-66 (Classics) 67-68 BLS. 6: Fr, Sp, LAT, Ital, Rumania. 7: Bibliogr YorkU Libs 68-. 14: Bk sel, acquis procedures, ser, collection devel in foreign-lang fields. 15: York Univ Lib, Toronto Can.

LAWRENCE, MARGARET. b Stillwater Okla 4 O 05. 5: UNeb 22-26 (Eng) BA, 28-30 (Eng) MA; UIll 38-39 BS in LS. 6: Lat, Fr. 7: High sch, tchr Paxton Neb 26-28; Asst in Eng UNeb (Lincoln) 29-38; Asst Prof & asst Libn for ser & docs ILL State U 39-60, Asst libn for reference & docs 61-63, Asst libn docs 64-. 9: ALA; IllLA. 10: AAUP. 14: Docs. 15: 815 S Fell ave, Normal Il 61761.

LAWRENCE, MARIE K. b S Bend Ind 11 D 03. 5: Ind U 21-23, 26-27 (Eng) AB; UMich 34-35 ABLS; Columbia 49 (LS) MS. 6: Fr, Lat. 7: Circ asst U Notre Dame Lib (Notre Dame Ind) 24-26, Circ head 27-34, Catlgr 35-37, Ref head 37-42; Bibliogr acquis dept UIll Lib (Urbana) 43-44; Rare bk catlgr U Notre Dame Lib, Notre Dame Ind 44-45; Law Libn Notre Dame Law Sch (Notre Dame Ind) 45-66; Hd soc scis dept Mem Lib U Notre Dame 66-. 9: AALL; ALA. 10: Altrusa Internat; AAUW; Phi Beta Kappa; Dig & Delve Club (South Bend Ind); No Ind Hist Soc; AAUP. 14: Ref. 15: 1406 Lincoln Way W, South Bend Ind 46628.

LAWRENCE, PHILIP DRAKE JR. b Burlington Vt 1 Mr 19. 4: Annie Gilliam. 5: URichmond 36-40 (Chem, Physics) BS; UPenn 40-41 (Chem). 7: Chem Allied Chem Co, Hopewell Va 41-46; Chem Merck & Co Inc, Elkton Va 46-52; Engnr Chemstrand Co, Decatur Ala 52-56; Tech info coordinator Chemstrand Research Center, Durham NC 56-63; Engnr info analyst Lockheed-Georgia Co, Marietta Ga 63-65; Res info spec Lockheed-Georgia Co, Marietta Ga 66-. 09: ACS (Div Chem Lit); ASIS; SLA. 10: Sigma Pi Sigma; Amer Radio Relay League. 14: Application of automation to lib procedures. 15: 1197 Spring Mill lane NE, Atlanta Ga 30319.

LAWRENCE, SOPHIE ELIZABETH. b Lyons Falls NY 3 D 36. 4: Karl C Lawrence. 5: SUNY(Albany) 58 (SS) BA, summers 58-62 MSLS; Syracuse Ext 64 (Psych); UMinn summer 65 NDEA Lib & AV; NY State Permanent Certif in Libnship 62. 6: Hungarian, Fr. 7: Youth seminar adv Lewis Co 59-61; Eng III & IV Port Leyden (NY) Central Sch 59-62, 64-65, Libn 58-; Libn Lowville Acad & Central Sch 69-; Catlg supv Col of Educ for Tchrs, Albany NY summer 67. 9: NEA; ALA; NY State Tchrs Assn; NYLA. 10: Trionis; PTA; Alpha Epsilon. 13: Yes. 14: Catlg, bk sel, ref, wk with yp, a-v. 15: RD 2, Lowville NY 13367.

LAWRENCE, STUART E. b Detroit Mich 9 N 21. 4: Margaret Waterston. 5: UMich 60-66 (Sociol) BA, 66-67 MALS. 6: Fr. 7: Off mgr B&W Distributing, Grand Rapids Mich 50-56; Owner & mgr Waterston Inc, Flint Mich 56-61; Off mgr Midwest Packing Co, Flint Mich 61-62; Juv court admin Geneseo Co Probate Court, Flint Mich 62-65; Coord commun serv Geneseo Co Lib, Flint Mich 65-66; Research asst Ctr for Research in Utilization of Scientific Knowledge, Ann Arbor Mich 66-67; Circ libn Iowa State U (Ames) 67-. 9: ALA; ASIS; IowaLA. 10: Amer Sociol Assn; Soc Study of Soc Problems. 14: Pub serv, automation. 15: 310 Westwood dr, Ames Ia 50010.

LAWRENCE, THERESE (MADELEINE). b Tacoma Wash 27 Ja 15. 5: San Francisco Col for Women 35-36; Tacoma Catholic Col 44-45; USan Francisco 58-64 (Eng) BA; UCal(Berkeley) 64-65 (LS) MA. 7: Clerk Kaufer Co, Tacoma Wash 42-44; Clerical asst circ Tacoma Pub Lib, Tacoma Wash 44-45; Billing, then bk dept Benziger Bros, San Francisco 45-47; Sec-receptionist Alfred J Schwarz MD, San Anselmo Cal 47-57; Sec to dean Sch of Nursing USan Francisco 57-67; Tm bd & reg sec St Marys Hosp, San Francisco 63; Libn I Cal State Lib 65-67, Libn II 67-. 9: CathLA; CalLA. 14: Proc (non-bk material, ms bks & Californiana). 15: 1017 14th st, Apt 17, Sacramento Cal 95814.

LAWSON, A(BRAM) VENABLE. b SBoston Va 9 Ja 22. 5: UAla 39-42, 46 BA; Emory 49-50 MLibn ship; Columbia 62-63 (LS). 7: ArmyAF 42-46; Auditor Socony-Mobil Oil Co Denver 47-48; Teller First Nat Bank Altavista Va 48-49; Asst ref dept Atlanta Pub Lib 51; Lib asst Harvard Col Lib 51-54; Head ref serv Atlanta Pub Lib 54-56, Coordinator of pub serv 56-60; Asst Prof Lib Sch Fla State U 60-65; Dir Lib Sch Emory U 65-. 8: Instr AtlantaU Lib Sch 58-60; Visiting Prof Emory U Lib Sch summer 58; Lib consul Ga Power Co 56. 9: ALA; AALS; FlaLA; GaLA; SELA. 10: AAUP. 11: George Virgil Fuller Award, Columbia U 64. 13: Yes. 14: Ref, educ for libnship. 15: Lib Sch Emory U, Atlanta Ga 30322.

LAWSON, CLINTON DAVID. b Montreal 14 Ja 28. 4: Minnie G Farquharson. 5: Victoria Col UToronto 47-51 (Hebrew & Phil) BA; Emmanuel Col UToronto 51-54 (Theol) BD; UToronto 63-64 BLS. 7: Minister United Church of Can, Cochrane Ont 54-57; Minister United Church of Can, Larder Lake Ont 58-61; Libn UWaterloo (Waterloo Ont) 63-64, Head of bibliogr searching 65-66; Catlgr Waterloo Lutheran U 66-67; Hd of processing Midwestern Reg Lib Syst 67-. 9: ALA; CanLA; OntLA; Inst Profess Libns Ont. 14: Acquis, lib systems. 15: 27 Cardill cres, Waterloo Ont Canada.

LAWSON, CONSTANCE. b Constantinople Turkey 6 F 25. 5: Wilson Jr Col 42-44 (Liberal Arts); Northwestern 45 (Liberal Arts); UChicago 56 (LS); Tex Woman's U 64 (LS). 6: Russian. 7: Libn Chicago Pub Lib 45-58; Catlgr Tex Instruments Inc App Div, Dallas Tex 59-64, Asst libn SSD Div 64-65, Libn SSD Div 65-67, Catlgr 68-. 9: ALA; TexLA (chm Spec Lib Div 65); SLA (Tex Chap: bulletin ed & 2nd v-pres 65-66; 1st v-pres & program chm 68-69; pres 69-70); DallasCoLA. 10: Toastmistress Club of Amer; TACA. 14: Ref, documentation of report lit, catlg. 15: 3762 Rockdale dr, Dallas Tx 75220.

LAWSON, ESTHER (ELMER). b Hebron ND 14 S 24. 4: Sam Lawson. 5: Westmar Col 42-46 (Eng, Hist) BA; Dickinson state Tchrs Col summer 48 (Speech); UMinn summer 52 (Speech, Eng); Peabody 56, 57, 59, 62, 63 MLS. 6: Ger. 7: Red Bird Settlement Sch, Beverly Ky: Eng tchr & libn 46-54, Bkmob driver & emerg High Sch libn 55-62, Qualified libn High Sch & Bkmob 63-. 8: Spec assignment to reach schs & homes in a tri-co area of SE Ky 54-. 9: ALA; KyASchL. 14: Catlg. 15: Beverly Ky 40913.

LAWSON, RICHARD WILLIAM. b Warren Penn 2 Mr 32. 4: Dorothy Bloomster. 5: Clarion State Col 50-54 (LS, Soc Studies) BS Educ; UIll 54 (LS); West Res 56-58 MSLS; PennStateU 59 (Educ, Hist), IndU 66-69 (LS, Higher Educ). 6: Fr, Ger. 7: Libn Sch Dist of Girard Penn 54-58; Asst libn Mansfield State Col 58-60; Asst libn Alanar Bk Processing Center, Williamsport Penn 60-61; Asst libn Slippery Rock State Col 62-64; Lib Sci Instr East IllU 64-66; Asst Prof Lib Sci East Ill U 69-. 9: Penn StateEA (past-chm NW Group). 14: Lib sci educ, catlg, admin, mgt. 15: 1617 Douglas dr RD4, Charleston Il 61920.

LAWTON, JAMES NORBERT. b Chicago Ill 6 Ag 39. 5: St Procopius Col 57-61 (Lit) AB; UMich 63-66 (Eng Lit) MA, 65-67 (LS) MA. 6: Fr, Lat. 7: Tchr Hamady High Sch, Flint Mich high Sch, Flint Mich 61-63; Lib asst Rare Bk Dept UMich (Ann Arbor) 63-67; Rare bk bibliogr SyracuseU Lib 67-68; Curator of mss Boston Pub Lib 68-. 9: BSA. 14: Rare bks. 15: Rare Book Dept Boston Pub Lib Copley sq, Boston Ma 02117.

LAWYER, CARLITA (FREBERG). b Chicago Ill 5 My 27. 4: John L Lawver. 5: NorthwesternU 44-48 (Hist) BS; Rosary Col 67-69 MALS. 6: Fr. 7: Tchr Central Sch, Wilmette Ill 49-51; Tchr Fairview Sch, Skokie Ill 51-53; Sch libn Everett Sch, Lake Forest Ill 66-. 9: ALA; IllLA (Sch Libns). 14: Child lit, sch libs. 15: 1283 W Deerpath rd, Lake Forest Il 60045.

LAWYER, W ROBERT. b Des Moines Iowa 31 Jl 19. 4: Jane Snyder. 5: UWash 50-53 (Gen Studies) BA, 53-63 (Eng) PhD. 6: Fr. 7: Major AUS 42-46; Owner Chelan Appliance Co, Chelan Wash 46-50; Assoc Prof & Dir Freshman Eng West Wash State Col 60-67, Dir Wilson Lib 67-. 9: ALA; MLA; Wash State Coun Tchrs of Eng; PNLA; WashStateLA. 12: Ed "Washington State English Notes" (65-67). 13: Yes. 14: Lib admin. 15: 1993 Yew st rd, Bellingham Wa 98225.

LAXTON, ELIZABETH (EHRENZELLER). b Philadelphia Penn 7 D 11. 4: Richard R Laxton. 5: UBuffalo 32-37 (Eng) BA, (LS) BS. 7: Libn, Lancaster NY 37-40, 45-48, Lib dir 60-. 9: ALA; NYLA. 14: Ref, pub rel. 15: 59 Burwell ave, Lancaster NY 14086.

LAYNE, JAMA LOIS (HALE). b Grayson Co Va 1 D 35. 4: Don Phillip Layne. 5: Ky Christian Col 53-54 (Relig); Marshall U 54-57 (LS, Eng) AB; VPI summers 59-61 (Sch Admin & Supv) MEd; RPI 68. 6: Ger. 7: Libn C-K High Sch Wayne Co Schs, Ceredo W Va 57-58; Libn Parkway Jr High Broward Co Schs, Ft Lauderdale Fla 58-61; Tchr York High Sch York Co Schs, Yorktown Va 61-62; Tchr Ferguson High Sch Newport News Sch, Newport News Va 62-63; Libn Galax Elem Sch Galax City Sch, Galax Virginia 63-65; Libn Spencer- Penn Elem Henry Co Sch, Martinsville Va 65-66; Supv libs Charlotte Co Schs, Charlotte C H Va 66-. 9: ALA; NEA (life Mem); VaEA; VaLA; ASCD. 10: Delta Kappa Gamma; Bd dirs Charloote Co Red Cross. 14: Elem libs. 15: Keysville Va 23947.

LAYNG, WILLIAM FREDERICK. b Brooklyn NY 16 My 28. 4: Doris Dunphy. 5: Hofstra 52-57 9sociol) BA; LIU 60-67 MSLS. 7: Cpl USMC; Printer, NY 48-61; Sch libn, NY 61-68; Libn for the blind & physically handicapped, NJ 68-. 8: ESEA Title II adv on spec lib projs. 9: ALA. 13: Yes. 15: 1700 Calhoun st, Trenton NJ 08638.

LAYTHE, ROSAMOND OLIVE (SINCLAIR). b Carlyle Ill 12 Jl 13. 5: Shurtleff Col 31-35 (Eng, Langs) BA; UWash 63-64 MLS. 6: Fr, Ger. 7: Asst libn Shurtleff Col 31-35; Supv & Instr O F Schoeck Schs, Alton Ill 36-39; Clerk-steno Treasury Dept San Antonio Tex 39-42; Admin asst to pres Field-Parker Co, El Paso Tex 42-50; Corp bkkeeper Sheple Coal Co, Waterbury Vt 50-51; Corp bkkeeper Western Wood prod, Spokane Wash 58-62; Child libn Walla Walla Pub Lib 62-65; Libn Alton Ctr SoIllU 65-. 9: ALA; IllLA. 11: Henry award UWash Sch of Libnship. 13: Yes. 14: Admin, ref, bk sel. 15: Rte 2 Box 302, Godfrey Il 62035.

LAYTON, (ANNA) JEANNE. b Kaysville Utah 12 F 30. 5: UUtah 48-52 (Marketing) BS, 64-67 (LS, Educ) Sch libn & tchg certif. 7: Various Barnes Banking Co, Kayville Utah 52-59; Libn in charge High Sch Br Davis Co Lib, Kaysville Utah 60-64; Hd circ Davis Co Lib, Farmington Utah 64-68, Asst libn 68-. 9: ALA; MPLA; UtahLA (chm Pub Lib Sect). 14: Ref, lib admin. 15: 95 South 1st E, Kaysville Ut 84037.

LAZEAR, ELIZABETH A. b Tampa Fla 3 D 29. 5: Fla StateU 47-51 (LS) BS, 60-61 (LS) MA. 7: High sch libn Fernandina High Sch, Fernandina Beach Fla 51-53; Asst ref libn Pub Lib, St Petersburg Fla 53-60; Ref libn NC State Lib 61-62; Reader's consul Jacksonville Pub Lib, Jacksonville Fla 62-65, Chief bus sci ind 65-. 9: ALA; FlaLA; SELA. 10: AAUW; Beta Phi Mu. 14: Ref. 15: 1650 Mallory st, Jacksonville Fl 32205.

LAZENBY, FRANCIS D. b Hopewell Va 21 O 16. 5: UVa 33-37 (Lat) AB, 37-39 (Lat) AM, 39-41 (Lat) PhD; UMich 54-55 AMLS. 6: Lat, Fr, Ital, Sp, Ger, Gk. 7: US Army (T/Sgt), US 42-46; Instr, Asst Prof of Classics UIll 46-54; Libn, Mediaeval Inst, Asst Prof of Classics UNotre Dame (Ind) 55-61, Asst dir o f libs, humanities div, Assoc Prof of Classics 61-. 9: Amer Philol Assn; ALA; Ind Classical Assn. 10: Phi Beta Kappa; Phi Beta Mu; Caxton Club (Chicago). 13: Yes. 14: Ref, rare bks, bibliog, Gk archaeol, mythology, classical lit. 15: 1115 N Notre Dame ave, South Bend Ind 46617.

LAZEROW, SAMUEL. b Baltimore 29 Jl 12. 4: Sylvia Sugar Lazerow. 5: Johns Hopkins 30-32, 36-38 (Langs) BS; Columbia 39-41 (LS) MS; US Dept of Agric Grad Sch 50-56 (Pub Admin); American U 64- (T chr of Mgt). 6: Fr, Ger. 7: Catlg asst Enoch Pratt Free Lib, Baltimore 41-42; US Army adj gen's off 42-46; Capt asst chief Army Lib Serv, NY 46; Chief acquis div Nat Agric Lib, Wash DC 47-52; Chief acquis div NLM 52-60; Chief tech serv div NLM, Bethesda Md 60-65; Asst chief catlg maintenance & catlg pub div LC 65-66, Chief ser recreation div 66-; Chm US Nat Lib Task Force on Automation 67-. 8: Visit to USSR to study Soviet Med Lib System, 61; Del, Latin-Amer Assn of Med Schs, Pocos de Caldas Brazil, 64; Consul to Pan Amer Health Org on Latin-Amer Reg Med Lib Ctr, 65; Adv Com del White House Conf on Int Coop 66. 9: MedLA (Rep JCULS 61-, Adv mgr Bull of the MedLA 67-); ASIS (treas Baltimore Chap 68-); USBE (treas 60-64, pres & bd chm 64-67); Fed Lib Com (chm Task Force on Procurement 65-, mem Task Force on Role of Libs in Info Systems 67-); ASA (Subcom on Period Title Abbrev Z39 65-; Subcom on Coden Com on Num Ref Data, Amer Soc Test Mat 66-; COSATI Panel on Mgt Info Systems 68-; Adv Com to Proj Ballots, Stanford U Libs 69-). 13: Yes. 14: Tech serv, computer applications, admin. 15: 5909 Eastcliff dr, Baltimore Md 21209.

LAZOR, MICHAEL. b Pittsburgh 28 S 17. 4: Helen E (Zavadil). 5: Our Lady of the Lake Col 62-63 (LS) BA. 07: Asst libn San Antonio Pub Lib, San Antonio Tex 64; Libn Schertz-Cibolo Ind Sch Dist, Cibolo Tex 64-66; Libn Off Training Sch Lackland AFB, Tex 66-69. 14: Ref, catlg. 15: 125 Scott ave, Randolph AFB Tx 78148.

LE CROISSETTE, JILL CAMPBELL (McLEAN). b Campbelltown NSW Australia. 2 My 33. 4: Dennis Harlow Le Croissette. 5: USydney 50-52 (Hist) BA; Drexel 60-61 MSLS. 6: Fr. 7: Accessions libn Commonwealth Scien & Ind Research Org Sydney NSW 53-56; Ser order libn UKan 57-58; Libn Pembroke Col 58-60; Catlgr Fed Reserve Bank of Phila 61-62; Acquis libn Cal State Col (Los Angeles) 62-63, Head ser dept 63-66, Act chief tech serv 66-67, Asst to Col libn 67-. 8: Cal State Col Libns Standing Com on Program Budgeting 67-; Cal State Col Circ Subsyst Task Team 68-. 9: SLA; CalLA (sec State Col Libns Div 68); ALA. 10: English-Speaking Union; Beta Phi Mu; Phi Kappa Phi. 11: Spec Libs Coun of Phila & Vicinity Award 62. 13: Yes. 14: Lib automation, syst analysis, admin. 15: 140 S Mentor ave, Pasadena Ca 91106.

LeKERNEC, WILLIAM J. b Lancaster Penn 9 Ap 29. 4: Frances Yeager. 5: Ursinus Col 48-52 (Eng) BA; Drexel 52-53 MS in LS; Rutgers 62-63 LS. 6: Fr, Sp. 7: USN Hosp Corps HM 3 46-48; Supv libn Summit Free Pub Lib, Summit NJ 53-55; Vice-pres Vineland Optical Labs, Vineland NJ 55-59; Dir Glassboro Pub Lib, Glassboro NJ 56-59; Dir Somerville Free Pub Lib, Sommerville NJ 59-63; Dir Middletown Two Lib, Middletown NJ 63-. 9: ALA; NJLA (chm Exh Com 64-). 14: Admin. 15: 51 Nottingham way, Middletown NJ 07748.

LEACH, MAURICE DERBY JR. b Lexington Ky 23 Je 23. 4: Virginia Baskett. 5: UKy 41-45 (Hist) AB; Chicago 45-46 BLS. 6: Fr, Ger, Arabic. 7: Asst libn Tex Col of Arts & Ind 46-47; Libn US Dept of State, Wash DC 47-50; US Army 48-49; Asst attache US Foriegn Serv & USIA, Egypt, Lebanon, and other Near East countries 50-57; Program of USIA, Wash DC 58-59; Prof & Chm Dept of Lib Sci UKy 59-68; Reg program adv (Lib) Ford Foundation, Near East (Beirut); Prof & libn Washington & Lee U 68-. 8: Adv to the Egyptian Ministry of Educ 53-56; Bd EgyptianLA 53-57; Mid-Career Program, US Dept of State 59; Ky Chm State Lib Survey Com 65-66. 9: ALA (Coun 63-67); VaLA. 10: AAUP; Rotary. 13: Yes. 14: Lib educ, internat lib affairs. 15: Washington and Lee Univ, Lexington Va 24450.

LEACH, SALLY (SPARKS). b Iowa City Iowa 21 Ap 35. 4: Thomas Monroe Leach. 5: UTex 53-57 (Liberal Arts) BA, 64-67 MLS. 07: Lib asst Miriam Lutcher Stark Lib UTex (Austin) 64-65, Sr lib asst 65-66, Libn I 66-. 9: TexLA. 10: Austin Yacht Club; ACLU; Phi Beta Kappa. 12: "British Heritage-Catalogue of an Exhibit" (67). 14: Rare bks, mss, mss catlg. 15: PO Box 5370, Austin Tx 78703.

LEACH, SALLY ANN. b Owatonna Minn 23 D 23. 5: MacMurray Col 43-44; Carleton Col 44-47 (Zoo sci) BA; USoCal 47-48 BS in LS. 7: Free Pub Lib E Orange NJ: Jr libn 48, Sr libn, Prin libn 63-. 9: ALA; NJLA. 14: Catlg. 15: 221 Freeway dr E, E Orange NJ 07018.

LEACH, THEODORE EDWARD. b Spartanburg SC 10 Ap 37. 5: UTex 55-56; Palm Beach Jr Col 56-58 (Pre-Engring) AA; UMiami (Fla) 58-61 (Eng) AB; George Washington U 61-63 (Math). 6: Ger, Fr. 7: Admin specialist US Army Ft Beloir Va 61-62; Tech ed & writer, Vitro Labs, Wash DC 62-63; Computer engr So Railway System, Wash DC 63-65; Syst analyst & tech winter Wolf Research & Development Corp, Wash DC 65-66; Sr computer syst analyst LC 66-. 9: ACM;

ASIS; ALA; STWP. 13: Yes. 14: Info sci. 15: 8501 Washington ave, Alexandria Va 22309.

LEACY, RICHARD (CHARLES). b Cambridge Mass 15 Jl 35. 5: BostonU 53-59 (Pol Sci) AB; Emory 63-65 (Libnship) MA. 6: Fr. 7: Student asst MIT 50-63; Lib asst HarvardU 61-63; Gen studies libn Ga Inst of Tech 64-65, Govt docs libn 65-. 9: SELA. 10: AAUP. 14: Ref, pol sci, admin. 15: Georgia Inst of Tech Lib, Atlanta Ga 30332.

LEAH, SISTER M (KREITZ). b Akron Ohio 22 D 08. 5: Marygrove Col BA; Wayne State U M Ed; UMich MALS. 7: Elem tchr parochial schs, Detroit, Wyandotte, Dearborn & Flint Mich 29-50; Libn Immaculata High Sch, Detroit 50-51; Elem tchr St Matthew Sch, Flint Mich 51-54; Libn Marygrove Col(Detroit) 54-59; Libn Marygrove Col(Monroe) 59-. 9: ALA; CathLA; MichLA. 14: Catlg. 15: Marygrove Col Lib, Monroe Campus, 610 W Elm ave, Monroe Mich 48161.

LEAMAN, GLADYS L(UCILLE). b Chicago 29 Ag 13. 5: Bluffton Col 31-33; UIll 35-37 (Eng) AB, 37-38 BS in LS. 07: File asst Newberry Lib, Chicago 39-40; Libn Pestalozzi Froebel Tchrs Col 40-41; Catlgr Tuberculosis Inst of Chicago & Cook Co 41; Libn Town Sch for Girls, Chicago 41-42; Asst ref libn Central YMCA Col (Chicago) 42-45; Chief ref libn Roosevelt U 45-64, Chief ser libn 64-67, Chief periods libn, 67-. 8: Consul for World Bk Encyclopedia Dictionary, 54; Consul Libn for Pestalozzi Froebel Tchrs Col, Chicago Ill 61-62. 9: ALA; IllLA; Chicago Lib Club. 10: Chicago Illinae Club; Geog Soc (Chicago), Art Inst Chicago; AAUP. 11: Ten yr Volunteer Award, Travelers Aid Soc 62. 14: Period. 15: 4216 Greenview ave, Chicago Il 60613.

LEARMONT, CAROL (LOUISE). b Meriden Conn 5 S 27. 5: Duke 45-49 (Hist) BA; Wesleyan U 62 (Liberal Studies) MA; Rutgers 65 (LS) MA. 6: Sp, Fr. 7: Tchr Jonesboro High Sch, Sanford NC 49-51; Tchr Lago Commun Sch, Aruba Netherlands West Indies 51-60; Tchr American Sch, Athens Greece 60-61; Ref asst Columbia U Libs NYC 65-, Asst libn Bus Lib 65-67, Hd circ 67-. 10: Phi Beta Kappa; Beta Phi Mu. 14: Ref, adult & young adult serv. 15: 28 E 95th st, New York NY 10028.

LEARN, MARGARET SUE. b Indiana Co Penn 28 Ap 07. 4: Neal Paul Tie. 5: Juniata Col 31-34 (Eng) BA; Penn State U summers 47-50; Travel Credits Ind U, U West Ill & Upper Montclair Tchrs Col Masters Equivalent Certif; Peabody 65 MLS. 7: Elem tchr New Germany Penn 36-41; Elem tchr S Fork Schs, S Fork Penn 41-45, Jr-sr high sch tchr 45; Tchr-libn S Fork High Sch, S Fork Penn 47-50, High sch libn S Fork-Croyle High Sch, S Fork Penn 50-61; Libn Triangle Area Schs, Sigman Penn 61-65; Jr High Sch libn Forest Hills Schs Sidman Penn 65-. 9: NEA; ASCD (sec-treas Central West Region of Penn 62); PennStateEA; Triangle Area Tchrs Assn (pres 61-62). 10: PTA; YWCA; Cambria Co Sch Libns Assn; Cambria Co Schs Fed Credit Union. 14: Ref. 15: 428 Maple st, S Fork Penn 15956.

LEARY, MARGARET A (ROELLINGER). b Oberlin Ohio 2 Jl 42. 4: James B Leary. 5: Cornell U 60-64 (Pol Sci) BA; UMinn 64-66 (LS) MA. 6: Fr. 7: UMinn (Minneapolis): Libn 65-67, Instr & libn 67-68, Instr, libn & hd catlg dept Law Lib 68-. 9: ALA; AALA; MinnLA. 10: Beta Phi Mu. 14: Catlg, info stor & retr. 15: 6 Barton ave SE, Minneapolis Mn 55414.

LEASE, JANE ETTA (OMER). b Kansas City Kan 10 Ap 24. 4: Richard Jay Lease. 5: UAriz 43-57 (Home Econ) BS; IndU 61-62 (Educ) MS Ed; UDenver 66-67 (LS) MA. 6: Ger. 7: Asst home agt USDA, Tucson 57; Homemaking tchr Accomodation Sch, Ft Huachuca Ariz 57-60; Clk Ariz State U Lib 64-66; Ed psych libn NM State U 67-. 9: ALA; NEA; NMEA; NMLA. 10: PEO; DAR. 14: Ref, curr materials ctr. 15: 2145 E Boise, Las Cruces NM 88001.

LEASURE, MARILYN (FRANCES). b Pittsburgh 30 Ap 31. 5: Duquesne U 49-53 (Eng) BA; Drexel 53-54 MSLS. 7: DuPont: Lib asst Lavoisier Lib, Wilmington Del 54-61, Ref libn Tech Lib 61-62, Br libn Tech Lib-Chestnut Run Br 62-65, Br libn Tech Lib Louviers Br 65-. 9: SLA; ASIS. 14: Ref. 15: E I duPont de Nemours & Co Tech Lib Louviers, Wilmington Del 19898.

LEATHEN, KATHLEEN (MARY). b Pittsburgh 27 O 22. 5: Carnegie 47-50 BS, 50-51 MLS. 7: Staff NYPub Lib 51-53; Staff Carnegie Lib of Pittsburgh 53-55, Br libn West End Br 55-57; Miami Pub Lib, Miami Fla: Staff 57-59, Libn Fla Collection Lib & Genealogy Collection 59-. 9: ALA; FlaLA. 10: Bronte Soc. 14: Ref, adult serv, genealogy, loc hist. 15: 4980 SW Westwood Lake dr, Miami Fla 33165.

LEATHERMAN, DONALD GEORGE. b Glendive Mont 2 Je 28. 4: Nancy MacKean. 5: Mich State U 46-50 (Hist, Pol Sci) BA, 54 (Educ) MA; West Mich U 54-55 (LS) Certif; UMich 64-65 MALS. 6: Sp, Ger. 7: (Pvt) Nat Guard, Lansing Mich 48-50; Jr high tchr Riverdale Sch, Riverdale Mich 50-51; Hist tchr Clarenceville High Sch, Livonia Mich 51-54; Ref asst Pub Lib, Saginaw Mich 55-59; Asst div libn educ div Mich State U Lib 60-65; Educ libn IV UMich Lib 65-68, Educ-ext libn 69-. 9: ALA; MichLA (chm Ref Sect 61). 10: UMich Staff Assn, Ann Arbor Lib Club. 14: Educ, ref. 15: 434 Cloverdale rd, Ann Arbor Mi 48105.

LEATHERS, JAMES A. b Moberly Mo 21 Ja 31. 5: Columbia 54 BA, 57- (LS) MSLS. 6: Fr. 7: Asst libn Moberly Pub Lib Moberly Mo 49-51; USArmy intelligence Analyst (Sgt) 53-55; Salesman Salter's Col Textbk Store, NYC 51-53, 55-57; NY Pub Lib: Libn Intern 57-58, Br libn 58-59, Roving libn 60-61; Dir Cass, Jackson, Platte Co Libs, Independence Mo 61-65; Mid-Continent Pub Lib, Independence Mo 65-. 9: ALA; AMA; MoLA (sec 63) chm Legis Com 62); Jackson Co Sch Admins Assn. 10: Rotary Internat; Jackson Co Hist Soc. 13: Yes. 14: Admin. 15: 605 N High, Independence Mo 64050.

LEAVENWORTH, COMAN. b Rye NY 14 Ap 20. 5: Yale 39-41 (Eng); Columbia 46-48 (Eng) BA, 60-61 (LS) MS. 7: US Army Air Force 1st Lt Squadron Adj 41-45; Various jobs in publ, bkselling & summer theatre 49-52; Lib asst Museum of Modern Art, NY 53-60; Ref & exhibits libn spec collections dept Columbia U Libs 61-. 14: Rare bks, art materials. 15: 154 E 61st st, New York NY 10021.

LEAVITT, DONALD LEE. b Annapolis Md 2 S 29. 4: Nadine Slater. 5: AmericanU 47-51 (Mus) BA; IndU 51-56 (Musicology). 6: Ger, Fr. 7: Ch organist choirmaster var chs 48-68; Research asst Archives of Folk & Primitive Music IndU 53-56; Ref libn Archive of Folk Song LC 56-61; Ref libn Music Div LC 64-. 8: Music critic Wash "Evening Star" 56-63. 9: MusicLA; Amer Musicological Assn; Assn for Recorded Sound Collections (1st v-pres); Intl Assn Music Libs (sec Jt Com on Phonorec Catlg); Intl Fed Rec Libns; Soc for Ethnomusicology; DCLA. 10: Bd Dir Prince Georges Symphonic Assn. 12: Asst rec Ed MusicLA "Notes" (62-65). 13: Yes. 14: Music ref, phonorec catlg & ref, ethnomusicology. 15: Music Div Lib of Congress, Washington DC 20540.

LEAVITT, EDWARD PARKER. b Newton Mass 23 Mr 18. 5: Boston U 37-41 (Hist) BS; Simmons 47-48 BLS. 6: Ger. 7: USArmy Signal Corps 42-46; Ref libn NYPubLib 48-53; Ref libn Boston Col 54-55; Prin documents libn Stanford U 55-57; Ref libn Lamont Lib Harvard Col 57-60; Libn Tufts U Med-Dental Lib 60-. 9: ALA; MedLA. 13: Yes. 14: Ref, acquis, admin. 15: 151 Pearl st, Newton Ma 02158.

LEBER, MICHELE (MATHEWS). b Appleton Wis 30 Jl 38. 4: Theodore T Leber. 5: UWis 56-57 9applied Art); Northwestern U 57-60 (Eng Lit) BA; UWash 67-69 M Lib. 6: Fr. 7: Reporter Food & Family Sect "The Independent", San Diego Cal 60; Reporter Womens news "The Press Courier", Oxnard Cal 62-63; Newspaper reporter "The Post Crescent", Appleton Wis 61, 64-66. 14: Info sci, sci-tech libs. 15: 16728 39th ave NE, Seattle Wa 98155.

LEBO, SHIRLEY CAROLINE (BYSTROM). b Los Angeles. 5: UCLA 38-42 (Hist) BA; UCal(Berkeley) 51 (Hist) MA, 52 BLS. 7: Communications clerk USAAF, Alameda Cal 44-46; Ed Com Clearing House, Chicago 47-48; Clerk tech info div UCal Radiation Lab(Berkeley) 49-51; LC: Spec recruit 52-53, Head Accessioning Unit 53-55, Head European Exch Sect 55, Documents expediter 56-59, Prin evaluations off 59-. 9: ALA; DCLA; Ms Soc. 10: Phi Beta Kappa. 14: Appraisals. 15: 221 "E" st SE, Wash DC 20003.

LEBOWITZ, ABRAHAM I. b NYC 7 Ag 31. 4: Shulamith Waxman. 5: Brooklyn Col 48-52 (Sci) BA; CatholicU 52-66 MSLS; UBaltimore 56-58 (Law). 6: Hebrew, Yiddish, Ger. 7: Ref libn Hebraic Sect LC 52-55; Libn Baltimore Hebrew Col 55-59; Admin libn USNaval Personnel Research Activity Wash DC 60-62; Sci research spec Sci & Tech Div LC 62-63, Sci Spec Nat Referral Center for Sci & Tech 63; Asst to the chief Hdqrs Lib usaec wash DC 63-66, Dep libn 66-68; Adj lectr UMd Sch of Lib & Info Sci 68-; Asst to dir Nat Agric Lib 68-69, Assoc dir for resources development 69-. 9: SLA (sec-treas Documentation Div 64-66; chm Wash Sci-Tech Group 64-65). 12: Ed "Documentation Progress" (64-66). 13: Yes. 14: Mech of lib processing, admin, tech serv, abstracting, indexing, info retr. 15: 5818 Narcissus ave, Baltimore Md 21215.

LeBUS, BETTY VIRGINIA. b Bremerton Wash 8 My 23. 5: UWash 42-49 BS in Law 47, LLB 48, BA in Law Libnship 49. 7: Asst law libn UWash 49-50; Law Libn IndU 50-. 9: AALL; IndLA (pres 61-62). 13: Yes. 14: Law libnship. 15: IndU Law Lib, Bloomington Ind 47405.

LeBUTT, KATHERINE LILLIAN (FAWTHROP). b Cornwall Ont Can 28 Mr 26. 4: Paul Le Butt. 5: McMaster U 46-49 (Eng) BA; TorontoU 51-52 BLS. 7: Childs libn Pub Lib, Sault Ste Marie Ont 52-62; Bkmob libn Reg Lib Reg Lib, York Co NB 62-63, Reg Libn 63-. 9: CanLA; APLA; CanASchL (past chm). 15: 363 University ave, Fredericton NB Canada.

LECHICH, GEORGE PAUL. b Hermon NY 2 Ap 10. 5: Stanford 28-32 (Speech) AB; UCal 39-41 (LS) Certif. 6: Ger. 7: Ref libn educ Stanford U 41-48; Research chem Paraffine Co, Emeryville Cal 41-48; Ref libn Burlingame Pub Lib, Burlingame Cal 48-50, City Libn 50-. 10: Audubon Soc; Lions Club. 14: Rare bks. 15: 480 Primrose rd, Burlingame Cal 94010.

LECHNER, MARIAN G. b Butler Co Penn 19 D 15. 5: Grove City Col 33-37 (Soc Studies) AB; Columbia 48 BS in LS. 6: Fr, Ger. 7: Interviewer Penn Dept of Pub Assistance, Butler Penn 38-43; Libn Butler Co Travel Lib, Butler Penn 43-50; Libn USN Med Acceleration Lab, Johnsville Penn 50-55; Libn Conn Gen Life Insurance Co, Hartford Conn 55-. 8: Sec Conn Governor's Com on Libs 62-63; Mem Conn State Lib Research Adv Com 65-. 9: SLA (chm Non-ser Publs Com 62-63, chm Pub Rel Com 63-67, var offs at loc level); ConnLA (chm Ref Sect 65-66, Prog Chm, Pres 68-70). 10: AAUW. 12: Ed "Insurance Literature." 13: Yes. 14: Ref, lib admin. 15: 60 Robin rd, West Hartford Ct 06119.

LECKIE, JAMES JOHN. b Mineola NY 6 Ag 28. 4: Ruth Randall. 5: Pace Col 46-50 (Accountancy) BBA; Pratt 50-51 MLS; Hofstra U 57-59 A-V Certif. 7: (Cpl) US Army Trieste 51-53; Ref libn Queens Borough Pub Lib, Queens Village NY 53-56; High sch libn Massapequa UFSD #23, Massapequa NY 56-; Libn Levittown Pub Lib, Levittown NY 59-65; Libn Seaford Pub Lib Seaford NY 65-. 14: Ref. 15: 41 Sunset rd, Massapequa LI NY 11758.

LECKRONE, JOYCE (GRIFFITHS). b Manistee Mich 17 S 20. 5: Manchester Col 54-57 (Hist) BS; IndU summers 60-63 (LS) MA. 6: Sp, Fr. 7: Tchr Manchester High Sch, N Manchester Ind 57-62; Libn circ & Acquis Manchester Col 62-. 9: ALA-ACRL; IndLA. 10: Beta Phi Mu. 14: Bk sel, childs lit. 15: 404 E 9th st, No Manchester Ind 46962.

LEDBETTER, BONNIE (LYNNE) (MEYER). b Ripon Wis 14 D 42. 4: James M Ledbetter. 5: Beloit Col 61-65 (Russian Studies) BA; Fla StateU 65-66 (LS) MS. 6: Russian. 7: Catlgr AirU, Maxwell AFB Ala 67-68; Catlg libn Birmingham-So Col 68-. 9: ALA; AlaLA; SELA. 10: AAUP. 14: Catlg, Govt docs. 15: 2316 Tenth ct S apt 101, Birmingham Al 35205.

LEDDEN, MILDRED M. b Albany NY. 5: NY State Col for Tchrs (Albany) 39-43 (Eng, Hist) AB; Syracuse 49-50 MSLS. 7: Lib asst BrownU 43-46; Asst hd & hd readers serv (Mt Holyoke Col Lib) 50-60; Asst libn (catlg) NY State Lib, Albany 60-61, Sr libn (rare bks) 61-68, Assoc libn (gen ref) 68-. 14: Rare bks. 15: 501 State st, Albany NY 12203.

LEDENBACH, THELMA MARIE (BRUNKAN). b Dyersville Iowa 31 Ag 22. 4: Richard O Ledenbach. 5: Briar Cliff Col 39-40; Clarke Col 40-43 (Econ) BA; UIowa 63-64 (Lib Educ) MA. 7: Dist libn West Dubuque Co Commun Sch, Epworth Iowa 64-67; Ref libn Ellsworth Col 67-69. 9: NEA-DAVI; ALA; IowaStateEA; IowaLA; Iowa A-V EA; Iowa Assn Jr Col Libns. 10: Bus & Profes Women. 14: Ref, circ. 15: 324 Ohio, Iowa Falls Ia 50126.

LEDET, BROTHER QUINTIN. b Thibodaux La 26 F 10. 5: Rutgers 29; Loyola of the South 29-34 (Hist) PhB; Springhill Col 41; LSU 49-52 BS in LS. 6: Sp, Fr. 7: Tchr Brothers of the Sacred Heart: Metuchen NJ 29, New Orleans 30-36, Metuchen NJ 36-39, 39 Montreal, New Orleans 39-42, Mobile Ala 41-42, New Orleans 42-47, Baton Rouge la 47-48, Bay St Louis Miss 48-49; Libn Cath High Sch, Baton Rouge La 49-63, Head Libn Bishop Dunne High Sch, Dallas 63-. 9: CathLA; ALA. 14: High sch libs. 15: Libn Bishop Dunne High Sch 3900 Rugged dr, Dallas Tex 75224.

LEDGER, SALLY LEE (SHOEMAKER). b Philadelphia Penn 6 N 39. 4: Frank Wilman Ledger. 5: Brandeis 57-61 (Anthrop) BA; Simmons 62-65 (LS) MS. 7: Pre-prof child wk Boston Pub Lib 61-64, Pre-prof catlg dept ref div 64-65, Catlg catlg dept ref div 65; Child libn Wilmington Inst Free Lib, Wilmington Del 65-66; Br libn New Castle Co Free Lib Concord Pike Br, Del 66-67, Br libn Kirkwood Highway Br 67-. 8: State Com on Nat Lib Week 68-69. 9: ALA; DelLA. 14: Pub lib serv, ref, catlg. 15: 2723 Barnsley rd, Wilmington De 19808.

LEDGER, SUSAN PETRY. b Chicago Ill 6 My 40. 4: Ike Franklin Ledger. 5: SWestU (Georgetown Tex) 58-62 (Eng) AB; So MethodistU 62-63 (Eng); CatholicU 64-65 (LS); Tex woman'sU 65-68 MLS. 6: Sp. 7: Tchr Scurry-Rosser Independent Sch Dist, Scurry Tex 62; Inventory controller Collins Radio Co, Dallas Tex 62-63; Child libn Montgomery Co Dept of Pub Libs, Md 64-65; Tchr Springtown Independent Sch Dist, Springtown Tex 66-67; Child libn Enoch Pratt Free Lib, Baltimore 68-. 9: ALA; TexLA; MdLA. 14: Child wk, lib applications of automation. 15: 4601 Marble Hall rd, Baltimore Md 21212.

LEDLIE, MARY ELIZABETH. b Carlisle Iowa 23 F 18. 5: Monmouth Col 35-39 (Eng) BA; Carnegie Lib Sch 39-40 (LS) BLS. 7: Libn Iowa State Traveling Lib, Des Moines Iowa 40-43; 1st asst child dept Pub Lib, Des Moines Iowa 43-44, Br libn 44-46, Hd child dept 46-56; Supv child wk Pub Lib, Toledo Ohio 56-62; Coord youth serv Pub Lib, milwaukee Wis 62-. 8: ALA Dialogue on Manpower, Chicago 68; Participant ALA discussion meeting on "Barriers to Interlib Coop" Wis Ctr, Madison 68. 9: ALA (Coun 60-64; Grolier Soc Award Com 61; E P Dutton-John Macrae Award Com 62; Subscription Bks Bulletin Com Mem 62-65); -ChildLA (P bks Bulletin Com Mem 62-65); -ChildLA (Program Chm Trans-Miss Reg Conf 49; Publicity Com 50; reporter "Top of the News" 55); -CSD (Melcher Scholarship Com 59-60; Newbery- Caldecott Com 59-60, 66-67; Bk Eval Com 66-69; chm Jaycee Adv Com 60-65; Exec Bd 60-64; chm "Child in Trouble" Com 60; Spec Com for NY Conf 65-66; v-pres & pres-elect; chm Newbery-Caldecott Com 69-70); IowaLA (chm Child & YP Sect 52); OhioLA (Exec Bd Child & yp sect 57; NW Dist Program Chm 57; Exec Bd 60-63); WisLA (Scholarship Com: mem 63, chm 64; NLW Steering Com 64). 10. Delta Kappa Gamma; Soroptimist Club, Des Moines; Zonta Club. 13: Yes. 14: Serv to child & ya. 15: 814 W Wisconsin ave, Milwaukee Wi 53233.

LEDLOW, ELAINE (ADAMS). b Denton Tex 29 Je 12. 5: N Tex State U 27-30, 54-56 (Eng) BA; Tex Woman's U 32-33, 50-51 MLS; Columbia summers 39, 55. 6: Ger, Fr, Lat. 7: N Tex State U: Asst catlgr acquis 30-39, Asst catlgr 39-43, Instr Lib Serv Dept 47-51, Head catlg dept 52-65, Asst Prof Lib Serv Dept 65-. 9: ALA; TexLA; SWLA; Tex Reg Group of Catlgrs (chm 58-59). 10: AAUW; Tex Assn Col Tchrs. 14: Catlg, lib educ. 15: 713 Crescent, Denton Tex 76201.

LeDOUX, MARJORIE (ELIZABETH). b Breaux Bridge La 21 Ap 20. 5: USWLa 37-41 (Fr, Span) BA; Tulane 49-51 (Latin Amer Studies) MA; LSU 51-52 (LS) MS. 6: Fr, Sp. 7: Tr Intl Gen Electric Co, Schenectady NY 47-48; Instr USWLa 48-49; Ref libn Loyola U (New Orleans) 52-54; Ref asst USWLa summer 54; Ref asst Tulane 54-56; Readers serv libn LSU Med Sch 56-62; Head Latin Amer Lib Tulane 62-. 8: Seminar on acquis Lat Amer lib materials. 9: ALA; LaLA (Conv Hospitality Chm 65); La Col Conf (Sec Libns Sect 65-66); New Orleans Lib Club. 10: LWV. 14: Lat-Amer materials, ref. 15: 7301 Plum st, New Orleans La 70118.

LEE, ANITA TSE-WEN (CHEN). b Chungking China 2 S 41. 4: Norman E Lee. 5: Nat Taiwan u 60-64 (For Lang & Lit) BA; UCal (Berkeley) 64-66 MLS. 6: Chinese, Fr, Ger, Russian, Sp. 7: Lib asst ITTE Lib, Richmond Cal 65-66; Adult serv libn Orange County Lib, Tustin Cal 66; Hd ser recs sect UCal (Irvine) 67-68, Hd ser catlg sect 68-. 9: ALA; CalLA. 14: Catlg, ser, ref, rare bks. 15: 502 Verano pl, Irvine Ca 92664.

LEE, ANN (RICHEY). b Lava Hot Springs Ida 9 Ag 23. 4: Thomas S Lee. 5: Scripps 40-44 (Psychology, Eng) BA; UCal 45-46 (Social wk), 64-65 (Tchg); UChicago 49-51 (Lit) MA; USoCal 65-66 (LS) MA. 6: Fr, Ital. 7: Social wkr Amer Red Cross, Oakland Cal 45; Psychologist Hennepin Co, Minneapolis 48-49; Info serv New Standard Encyclopedia Co, Chicago 51-52; Ed Benefic, Chicago 52-54; Tchr LA Pub Sch 64-65; Libn LA Pub Lib 62-. 9: ALA; CalLA. 10: Westside Poets. 13: Yes. 15: 8001 Chase ave, Los Angeles Ca 90045.

LEE, ANNABELLE W. b Szechuan Chungching China. 5: Providence Col (Taiwan) (Western Lang) BA; UPittsburgh MLA. 6: Chinese. 7: Catlgr YaleU Lib 69-. 14: Catlg. 15: Yale Univ Lib, New Haven Ct 06515.

LEE, BYUNG IN. b Korea 31 Ag 43. 5: Ewha WomansU 61-65 (Eng Lit) BA; UOre 67-69 MLS. 6: Korean, Fr. 7: Tr World Vision Inc, Seoul Korea 65-67; Catlgr Lane Commun Col 69-. 9: ALA. 10: For Stud Org of UOre. 14: Catlg.

LEE, CAROLINE (McDOWELL). b NYC 22 F 08. 4: Norman Lee. 5: Mich State Normal Col 25-29 (Fr) AB; West Reserve summer 30 (Fr); UParis (Sorbonne) 30-31 (Fr Civilization) Superieur; UPittsburgh 64-66 MLS. 6: Fr. 7: Tchr (high sch) Mich: Morenci 29-30, Northville 31-32; Salesgirl, Detroit: Hudson's 36-38, Nu-Enamel Paint Co 38-39; Store Owner-mgr Color Shop, Pittsburgh Penn 40-66; Child libn Carnegie Lib (Woods Run), Pittsburgh Penn 66-. 9: ALA; PennLA; Pittsburgh Lib Club. 10: Friends Meeting North hills; Paint and Wallpaper Assn of Amer; Carnegie Lib (Pittsburgh) Staff Assn. 14: Child serv, storytelling. 15: 479 Perrysville ave, Pittsburgh Pa 15229.

LEE, CHARLES DONALD. b Benson NC 17 F 29. 5: Col of Wm & Mary 53-54 (Eng); UAla 54-56 (Eng); UDenver 56-58 (Eng) BA; Mont State U 59 (Eng); LSU (Baton Rouge) 65-66 (LS) MS. 6: Ger. 7: Sgt USAF Air Weather Service weather observer 47-50; Lib asst lit & lang Denver Pub Lib 58-59; Grad asst Eng Mont State U 60; Stud asst NC State U Lib 65; Stud asst LSU Lib, Baton Rouge 65-66; Asst dir Cumberland Co Pub Lib, Fayetteville NC 66-68; Hdqts libn Chesapeake Pub Lib System, Chesapeake Va 68-. 9: ALA; VaLA; Cape Fear LA (pres-elect 68). 13: Yes. 14: Catlg, ref, pub, admin. 15: 5757 W Hastings Arch, Virginia Beach Va 23451.

LEE, CLARENCE C JR. b Brompton Ala 22 My 23. 5: UAla 42-45 (Hist) AB, 48-49 (Eng) MA; Peabody Col 63-65 MLS. 6: Sp, Fr. 7: Tchr St Clair Co Bd of Educ, Pell City Ala 49-; Consul St Clair Co Lib Bd, Pell City Ala 65-. 9: ALA; AATSP; NEA; AlaLA; AlaEA. 10: Beta Phi Mu. 14: Lat Amer studies, acquis. 15: 1709 2nd ave N, Pell City Al 35125.

LEE, DAVID JENNINGS. b Morristown Tenn 5 O 37. 4: Rose Anne Sherar. 5: St Petersburg Jr Col 55-57 (Liberal Arts); Fla StateU 58-59 (Hist) BA, 59-60 (LS) MS; UTex 64-66 (Lat Amer Rel). 6: Sp. 7: Asst in soc sci & catlg UGa 60-61; Asst ser libn UFla 62-63; Libn Escuela Agricola Panamericana, Zamorano Honduras 63-64; Admin asst to the dir UFla (Gainesville) 66-67; Dir Lib Inst Colombiano Agropecuarion, Colombia 67-. 9: ALA; FlaLA; SELA. 14: Latin Amer ref, agric lib sci. 15: Rockefeller Foundation, Apartado Aereo 58-13, Bogota Colombia.

LEE, EDWARD H F. b Honan China 15 S 37. 4: Alice Ai-Lian Ley. 5: Chung HsingU 60 (Law) LLB; UOkla 68 MLS. 6: Chinese, Japanese. 7: Asst instr Chung HsingU, Taipei Taiwan 62-65; Asst law libn (catlg) KanU Law Lib 68-. 9: AALL. 10: AAUP; KyU Lib Assn. 12: "A Survey of Law Classification in the United States". 14: Catlg. 15: 425A W 87th pl, Kansas City Mo 64114.

LEE, ELSIE J (PERSON). b Big Lake Minn 2 S 16. 4: Ralph H Lee. 05ENG, LS) BS in LS; NDakota StateU 63-64 (Educ) MS. 5: UMinn 37-40 (Eng, LS) BS in LS; NDakota State U 63-64 (Educ) MS. 6: Fr. 7: Sch libn, Sauk Rapids Minn 40-41; Sch libn, Litchfield Minn 41-43; Libn AF, Dodge City Kan 43-45; LibnTTC 47-48; 5-5 Campus Sch Moorhead Minn 59-63, 64-. 9: ALA; MinnEA (sec West Div). 10: AAUW; IFO. 14: High sch lib serv, ref, recr, tchg child lit. 15: 1311-14th Ave S, Moorhead Mn 56560.

LEE, ETHEL MAY (DAVENPORT). b Providence 11 Ap 26. 4: Robert Henry Lee. 5: Simmons 43-47 (LS) BS. 6: Fr, Ger. 7: Catlgr Brown U 47-48; Lib asst Westminster Col (New Wilmington Penn) 49; Catlgr Brown U 50-, Docs libn 68-. 9: RILA; NE Tech Serv Libns. 14: Catlg. 15: Pole Bridge rd RFD 2, N Scituate RI 02857.

LEE, FELICIA WEBSTER. b Palm Beach Fla 19 O 38. 4: Thomas Lee. 5: UMe 56-60 (Eng) BS; LSU 61-62 (LS) MS. 6: Fr, Ger, 7: Libn La State Dept of Highways, Baton Rouge La 62-64; Ref libn Hollins Col 64-65; Libn NASA Inst for Space Studies Columbia U 65-. 8: Consul Cybertype Corp, NYC 68-69. 9: ALA. 12: "Library Usage, A Programmed Textbook (67). 14: Tech libs, lit searching, lib orient. 15: NASA Inst for Space Studies, 2880 Broadway, New York NY 10025.

LEE, FRANCES. b Dawson gory summers 40-42 BALS. 5: Agnes Scott Col 34-38 (Eng Hist) BA; Emory summers 40-42 BALS. 7: Tchr Jr-Sr High Sch, Ga Pub Schs 38-40; Tchr elem schs Atlanta(Ga) Pub Sch System 40-42; Child libn brs Enoch Pratt Free Lib, Bld room Youngstown Pub Lib, Youngstown Ohio 47-50; Dir of child wk Fresno Co Free Lib, Fresno Cal 50-55; Ref libn San Diego Pub Lib 55-56; Supv child libn San Diego Pub Lib 60-65, Prin libn tech serv div 65-. 8: Tchr of child lit & storytelling at Fresno State Col summers 52-54; Tchr of lib serv to childaln Youth 54. 9: ALA (Child Wk Adv Com 52-53); -CSD (Child Bk Eval Com 62-65, Child Bk Lists Com 65-68, Newbery-Caldecott Aw64); CalLA (Standards for Lib Serv to Child Com 58-61, Subcom on Quantitative Standards 58-61; Lib Devel & Standards Com 64-65, chm Nomin Com 62; Chilhm Resource cm SoCal Coun on Child Lit; Assn Child Libns No Cal (pres 58-59); SoCal Tech Proc Gp; SLA. 10: Municipal Employees Assn of San Diego; Eta Sigma Phi. 13: Yes. 14: Child serv, admin, ref. 15: San Diego Pub Lib, 820 E st, San Diego Ca 92101.

LEE, GERTRUDE W. b Peiping China 8 Mr 41. 4: Chia-chuan Lee. 5: Nat TaiwanU 62 BA; UMinn 64 MA. 6: Chinese, Sp. 7: Asst libn acquis West MichU 64; Asst libn ref Evansville Pub Lib 65; Catlgr Col of Mt St Joseph on the Ohio 66; Asst catlgr SUNY (Stony Brook) 67-. 15: 108 Vineyard pl, Port Jefferson NY 11777.

LEE, HSING CHU. b China 1 Jl 23. 4: Rita J Y Ho. 5: Nat Chengchi U(China) 43-47 (Econ) BA; UMo 58-60 (Journalism) MA; Rutgers 61-63 MLS. 6: Chinese. 7: Sr libn Jersey City(NJ) Pub Lib 63-. 15: 219 W 106 st, Apt 1W, New York NY 10025.

LEE, HWA-WEI. b Canton China 7 D 33. 4: Mary Frances (Kratochvil). 5: Taiwan Prov Normal U 50-54 (Educ) BEd; UPittsburgh 57-59 (Educ) MEd; Carnegie 59-61 MLS; UPittsburgh 59-64 (Educ Found) PhD. Japanese. 7: (1st Lt) Chinese ROTC Pol Instr, Taipei China 54-55; Dean of Stud Affiliated Elem Sch of Taipei Normal Sch, Taipei 55-56; Asst to dean of Stud Taiwan Prov Noib trainee & 1st asst in auis, UPittsburgh Lib 59-62; African Libn & head of tech serv, Duquesne U Lib, 62-65; Asst Prof of Lib Sci & dir of tech serv, Edinboro State Col 65-66, Assoc Prof Lib Sci & Chief libn 66-68, Prof Lib Sci & Chief libn 68-; Lib Dir Asian Inst Tech, Bangkok Thailand, 68- (under contract of USAID/Colo State U). 8: Lib specialist USAID thru Colo State U. 09: PennLA; PennStateEA;-ACRL (Tri-State Chap dir 68-69); ALA-ACRL; ChineseLA. 10: Rho Psi; Beta Phi Mu; Phi Delta Kappa. 12: "Educational Development in Taiwan, Republic of China under Nationalist Government 1945-1962" (66). 13: Yes. 14: Educ for libnship, tech serv, documentation, admin, automation. 15: Amer Embassy (AIT), APO San Francisco Ca 96346.

LEE, JAMES. b Macon Ga 31 O 16. 4: Lelia Blockson. 5: Va Union U 36-40 (Pre-Law) BA; Howard U Sch of law 40-43, 46-47 LLB. 6: Fr, Ger. 7: (1st Sgt) Legal Assistance Off US Army 43-6 pub Acct, Hartford Conn 49-57; Law Libn Hartford Br Lib, Hartford Conn 57-. 15: 95 Washington st, Hartford Conn 06106.

LEE, JAMES DANIEL. b Asheville NC 11 Mr 33. 4: Mary Bell. 5: Asheville-Biltmore Col 63-66 (Hist) BA (cum laude); UNC (Chapel Hill) 66-67 (LS) MS. 6: Sp. 7: Pfc US Army Inf 50-53; Tours conductor Smoky Mt Tours Co, Asheville NC 64; Asst libn Asheville- Biltmore Col 67-. 10: Buncombe Libns. 14: Catlg. 15: Rte #1 Box 525, Candler NC 28715.

LEE, JANE YU. b China 28 Ag 33. 4: Yun Chuan Lee. 5: HunanU 48-52 (Eng Lit) BA; UDenver 53-54 (LS) MA. 6: Chinese. 7: Asst libn Downers Grove Pub Lib Downers Grove Ill 65; Libn Automatic Elec Labs Inc Chicago 65-. 9: ALA; SLA. 14: Ref. 15: 6730 Fairmount ave, Downers Grove Il 60515.

LEE, JEAN (STOKES). b Cochran Ga 19 Ap 35. 4: Daniel R Lee. 5: Woman's Col of Ga 52-56 (Hist, Soc Sci) BS; Emory 56-57 MLibnship. 6: Fr. 7: Chief of acquis A W Calhoun Med Lib Emory U 57-64, Chief of tech serv 65-68, Asst libn 68-. 8: Instr, Amer Hosp AssnInst Lib Serv. 9: MedLA (So Ore Gp; sec-treas 65-66, Nomin Com 67-68). 13: Yes. 14: Acquis. 15: 717 Farrar ct, Decatur Ga 30032.

LEE, JOE BILL. b Kirbyville Tex 26 Ja 29. 4: Elaine Augustinus. 5: Tex Col of Arts & Ind 48-52 (Eng) BA; UTex 52-53, 55-58 MLS. 7: Tchr Taft Independent Sch Dist, Taft Tex 52; (Cpl) USArmy 53-55; Sr lib asst UTex (Austin) 55-56; Asst libn Tex Col of Arts & Ind 56-60; Asst libn SWTex State Col 60-63; Libn, Angelo State Col 63-. 9: TexLA (chm Col & Univ Div 68). 10: Kiwanis Club. 13: Yes. 14: Admin. 15: 2519 Colorado, San Angelo Tx 76901.

LEE, JOAN ELAINE. b Kingston Penn 12 N 31. 5: Penn State U 49-53 (Psych) BS, 58-62 (Hist) MA; UMich 62-63 MALS. 6: Fr. 7: Elem tchr Tunkhannock Jt Schs, Tunkhannock Penn 53-55; Elem tchr Upper Moreland Twp Schs, Willow Grove Penn 55-58; Penn State U; Grad asst Dept of Hist 58-60, Typist, sec Dept of Philos summers 58-6, 61, Asst to Dr Kinsley Smith Dept of Psych 61; Internat documents libn Stanford U 63-65; Asst ref libn Penn State U 65-. 10: Psi Chi; Phi Alpha Theta. 14: Govt docs, ref. 15: Mehoopany Pa 18657.

LEE, JUNG WON. b Korea 21 Ja 34. 5: Sung Kyun KwanU (Korea) 55-59 (Eng Lit) BA; Peabody Col 63-65 MLS. 6: Chinese, Japanese, Korean, Ger. 7: Libn & instr, Seton HallU 65-68; Libn & Asst Prof Southampton Col LIU 68-. 14: Catlg. 15: Southampton Col Lib LI Univ, Southampton NY 11968.

LEE, LOUISE HARPER (MAE). b Bainbridge Ga 3 Ap 10. 4: Ernest Lee. 5: Albany State Col (Ga) 44-48 (Educ) BS Ed; Florida A&M U 54-62 (LS) B Ed. 7: Libn & tchr Hutto Sch, Bainbridge Ga 30-; Libn SW Ga Reg Lib Br, Bainbridge Ga 52; Libn Bainbridge High & hutto High, Bainbridge Ga 68-. 8: Lib consul Wkshop 56. 9: ALA; NEA; GaLA; GaTA (Lib sect); GaEA; Decatur Co EA. 10: NAACP; Nat Baptist Educ Dept of the Youth; Cancer Crusade Area Chm; OES; Cornucopia Civic & Soc Club; Republ Civic Club; Mental Health Assn; Dir Youth Dept, First African Baptist Church, Bainbridge Ga. 14: Catlg, ref. 15: 920 Albany st, Bainbridge Ga 31717.

LEE, LUTHER EMMETT. b Birmingham Ala 23 F 27. 4: Glenna Stringer. 5: UAla 50-52, 58-59 (Pub Admin) MS in C&BA, 59-60 (LS) MA. 7: Catlgr AirU Lib, Maxwell AFB Ala 60-61, Circ libn 61-63, Authority libn 63-64, Acquis lobn 64-67, Indexer 67-. 9: SLA (pres A&a Chap 68-69, Ed Chap Bull 62-); AlaLS (ed "The Aabama Librarian" 61-); SELA. 10: Toastmasters Internat; Res Offrs ssn; Ala Hist Assn; Air Force Assn. 14: Acquis, indexing, automation, admin. 15: PO Box 6184, Montgomery Al 36106.

LEE, MADELEINE (CHEN). b Taipei Taiwan 28 F 41. 4: Peter N Lee. 5: Nat TaiwanU 59-63 (Eng) BA; IndU 64-65 (LS) MA. 6: Chinese, Sp. 7: Libn Queens Borough Pub Lib, NYC 65-66; Chinese catlg YaleU Lib 66-67; Chinese catlg IndU Lib 67-68; Chin 65-66; Chinese catlg YaleU Lib 66-67; Chinese catlg IndU Lib 67-68; Chinese catlg NorthwesternU Lib 68-69; Catlg John Crerar Lib, Chicago 69-. 14: Catlg. 15: #B-3 1649 W Pratt, Chicago Il 60626.

LEE, MALINDA (CARPENTER). b Memphis Tenn 15 Ag 27. 4: Joshua A Lee. 5: Xavier U 45-48 (Eng Lit) BA; NYU 49-52 (Eng Lit) MA; Catholic U 54-57 MSLS. 7: Jr libn Mt Vernon Pub lib, NY 57; Catlgr Arctic Inst of N Amer, Wash DC 57-58; Asst br libn Los Angeles Pub Lib 59; Asst law libn Georgetown U 60-61; Libn Burroughs Elem Sch, Wash DC 66-68; Asst law libn Howard U 68-. 9: ALA; AALL. 14: Tech serv, ref. 15: 8301 E Beach dr NW, Washington DC 20012.

LEE, MAMIE RUTH (BLACKSHEAR). b Marianna Fla 17 D 25. 5: Fla A&M U 49-59 (Bus Educ) BSLS. 6: Sp. 7: Tchr Bd of Pub Educ, St John Elem, Marianna Fla 49-50; Tchr Bd of Pub Educ Union Grove, Marianna Fla 50-53; Libn Bd of Pub Educ Jackson Co Train, Marianna Fla 53-61; Libn Jackson Jr Col 61-65; Marianna High libn 67-69. 9: ALA; Fla State Tchrs assn; ClrmTA. 10: White Orchard Club; Les Charms Social Civic Club; Reading Club. 13: Yes. 14: Catlg, ref, circ. 15: PO Box 214, Marianna Fl 32446.

LEE, MARGARET HSIAO-YING (CHANG). b Chung-king China 23 Mr 40. 4: David Tong-Yong Lee. 5: Taiwan Prov Chung-Hsing U (Taiwan China) 57-61 (Land Econ & Admin) BA; Peabody 63-64 MLS. 6: Chinese. 7: Sr clerk Taichung Mutual Savings & Loan Co, Taichung Taiwan China 61-63; Asst catlg libn Lincoln Meml Lib SDState u6; Catlgr Ingham Co Lib Syst, Mason Mich 66-. 14: Catlg, ref. 15: 145 W Ash st, Mason Mi 48854.

LEE, MOLLIE HUSTON. b Columbus Ohio 18 Ja 07.03033 5: Howard U 29 (Sociol) AB; Columbia 34 BLS. 7: Libn Shaw U 30-35; Supv NC Negro Pub Libs, Raleigh NC 46-53; Tchr Lib Sci Atlanta U summer 39; Tchr Lib Sci NC Col(Durham) summer 41; Tchr Lib Sci Shaw U summer 41; Supv Negro Pub Sch Libs, Raleigh NC 42-47; Libn Richard B Harrison Pub Lib, Raleigh NC 35-69, Prof 69-. 8: Delegate to UNESCO Boston 1960; NC Delegate to 1961 White House Conference on Aging; Delegate to NC Mental Health Conference, Raleigh NC 1963; Recommendations Committee for Institute on Materials by and about the Negro 1967; Member of National Library Week Committee 68-70; Member NC LSCA Title IV-B Advisor Council 68-72; Supv of the Delta National Library Project in Franklin County and instrumental in establishing the Delta Public Library in Louisburg NC 1949; Mid-Atlantic Teen-Age Regional Dir Jack & Jill of America 56-58. 9: ALA (Coun mem State elected 46-50, at large 50-54; NC Negro LA (Founder & first pres 34); SLA; NCLA. 10: NC Adult Educ Assn; NC Folklore Soc; Delta Sigma Theta; Bus or Prof League, Mayors Com on United Nations; NC Federation of Women's Clubs. 11: Elected "Raleigh Woman of the Year" for outstanding service in field of Adult Education 54; WPTF Radio Station "Hats Off" 55; Honorary member Association of NC High Sch Lib Clubs 55; NC Negro Libns citation for Outstanding Contributions in Inspiring Negroes in the field of Library Service 54; Cited in Wilson Bulletins as one of the six most distinguished Negro librarians in the country 55; Scholarships from Columbia U Sch of Lib Serv, Certificate of Recognition for 25 years of serviced by Friends of Raleigh and Wake County NC 61. 12: Author "Securing the Branch Library" (Opportunity Magazine); Author "Development of Negro Libraries in NC" (NC Libraries) 44; Co-author "Public Library Service for NC Negroes" (Libraries in NC) 48; Auth "NC Negro Library Association, 1934-54" (Library Service Review) 55; Book Reviews; Library Journal, Phylon, newspapers etc; Compiler of bks by and about the Negro 50-56, 57-66. 13: Yes. 14: Bks by & about the Negro. 15: 130 Nelson st, Durham NC 27707.

LEE, ROBERT (ELLIS). b Greensboro NC 7 S 24. 4: Helen Anderson. 5: Guilford Col 46-50 (Eng) BA; UNC 50-51 BSLS, 51-52 (Creative Writing) MFA; Chicago 57-60 (Adult Educ) PhD. 6: Sp, Fr. 7: (Sgt) USArmy US, Europe 43-46; Head adult educ dept Greensboro Pub Lib, Greensboro NC 52-5 consul Amer Heritage Proj, ALA 54-55; Consul Lib-Commun Proj ALA 55-57; Educ Consul Chicago 57-58; Research assoc proj dir Industrial Rel Center UChicago 58-63; Prof Chm Dept of XDept of Libnship Kan State Tchrs Col (Emporia) 63-. 8: Consul: Div of Lib Exten State Dept of Educ Baltimore Md 57; U Col, UChicago 58; Labor Educ & Res Div UChicago 58. 9: ALA (Coun 68-71);-LED (pres 65-66, Com on Accredit 67-72); NEA; Nat Assn Pub Sch Adult Educrs; KanLA; KanASchL; IllLA. 12: "Continuing Education for Adults Through the Public Library," (65); "The Library-Sponsored Discussion Group," (57); "Getting the Most out of Discussion," (56). 13: Yes. 14: Lib educ, pub lib, adult serv, admin. 15: Dept of Libnship Kan State Tchrs Col, Emporia Kan 66802.

LEE, THOMAS H(SUEH-PO). b Honan China 2 N 30. 4: Yvonne Liu. 5: Nat Taiwan U 53-57 (Eng Lit) BA; Nat Chengchi U 57-60 (Educ); UWis 63-65 (LS) MA. 6: Chinese, Japanese, Fr. 7: Tchr Panchiao Middle Sch, Taiwan China 58-59; Ed Govt Info Off Taipei China 59-63; Tchg asst Chinese Dept UWis (Madison) 63-64; Proj asst UWis Lib (Madison) 64-65, Catlgr 65-. 12: Ed "China Yearbook 1960-61" & "China Yearbook 1962-63"; "American Farm Life," Translated into Chinese (58). 14: Catlg, ref, acquis, rare bks. 15: Mem Lib UWis, Madison Wi 53706.

LEE, VICTORIA CHINN. b Canton China 2 N 18. 4: Victor Chinn Lee. 5: Hunter Col 33-37 (Pol Sci) BA; Pratt 37-38 BLS; St John's U summer 51, 52; Hunter Col summer 53. 6: Chinese, Fr. 7: Staff NY Pub Lib 37-50; Libn Brooklyn Tech High Sch, Brooklyn NY 50-51; Libn Graham Jr High Sch, Mt Vernon NY 51-55; Libn Seely Place Sch, Scarsdale NY 61-; Libn Woodlands High Sch, Hartsdale NY summer 64, 65. 9: NEA; NYState Tchrs Assn, Woodlands Ctr TA; Woodlands LA. 10: Alpha Xi Alpha. 14: Sch wk. 15: 161 Moorland dr, Scarsdale NY 10583.

LEE, WEI-CHENG. b Luho China 4 O 32. 4: Nancy Liu Lee. 5: Nat Taiwan U 50-54 (Hist) BA; SoIll U 57-61 (Hist) MA; UIll 61-63 MALS; UKan 64-65 (Hist). 6: Chinese, Sp. 7: Res 2d Lt Chinese Army, Formosa China 54-55; UIll (Urbana): Stud asst Educ, Psych & Philos Lib 61-62, Stud asst Lib Sci Lib 62-63; Asst circ libn UKan Libs 63-64, Catlgr 64-66; Info analyst Bus Info Ctr Dow Chem Co, Midland Mich 66-67; Libn Bus Info Ctr Dow Corning Corp, Midland Mich 67-. 9: ALA; SLA. 10: Kan Univ Lib Staff Assn. 14: Catlg, ref. 15: 2011 Lambros dr, Midland Mi 48640.

LEE, WILLIAM M. b Newark NJ 31 My 29. 4: Marilyn E Lee. 5: George Washington U 47-51 (Amer Civilization) BA; UIll 54-55 MSLS. 6: Fr. 7: Lib asst Wash DC Pub Lib 45-54; Personnel admin & Cpl US Army, Ft Gordon Ga 51-53; Libn Enoch Pratt Free Lib, Baltimore 55-56; Ref libn US Info Agency, Wash DC 57-61; Chief Libn Research Inst for Advanced Studies, Baltimore 61-64; Head Engnr & Phys Sci Lib UMd 64-66; Asst dir for Perv UKy Libs 66-. 8: Consul ACRL Grants Com 68. 9: ALA; SLA (pres Baltimore Chap 62-63); KyLA. 14: Admin, ref. 15: 973 Holly Springs dr, Lexington Ky 40504.

LEECH, SARA (HADDIX). b Lexington Ky 4 F 23. 4: James H Leech. 5: Northwestern 41-44 (Psych) BS; UKy summer 46-47 (Psych), 61-62 MS in LS. 6: Fr. 7: Psychometrist Armed

Forces Induction Center, Chicago 44-46; Grad Instr UKy 46-47; Clinical psychologist Child Guidance Clinic, Lexington Ky 47-48; Inventory control Lexington Distributing Co, Lexington Ky 52-55; Catlgr King Lib UKy 62-. 9: KyLA (Col & Ref Sect); Ohio Valley Group of Tech Serv Libns; Lexintonl& aaup. 14: Catlg. 15: 718 Brook Hill dr, Lexington Ky 40502.

LEECH, WILMER ROSS. b Baltimore 17 Jl 1883. 4: Grace K Waterbury. 5: George Washington U 03-07 (Hist, Law) LLB. 7: Ms div LC 1900-08; Ed wk State Histn's Off, Albany NY 08-14; Ms div NY Pub Lib 14-48; NY Hist Soc NYC 49, Curator of mss 56-. 8: Active in salvaging mss following the fire which destroyed the NY State Lib. 12: Var Calendars of Presidential Papers in LC. 13: Yes. 14: Catlg & clsf mss. 15: New York Hist Society, 170 Central Park West, New York NY 10024.

LEEDECKER, ESTHER (SPAHR). b Lebanon Penn 30 Jl 16. 4: Charles Leedecker. 5: Wilson Col 32-36 BA; Drexel 36-37 BS in LS. 6: Fr. 7: Circ asst Penn State U 37-38; Sch libn Manheim High Sch, Manheim Penn 38-39; Sch & ref asst NY Pub Lib 39-41; Ref asst & ser libn Penn State U 41-59; Ser libn Penn State Lib 60-. 9: ALA; PennLA. 14: Ref, ser, bibliog. 15: Box 1601, Harrisburg Penn 17126.

LEEPER, DENNIS P. b Charleroi Penn 19 N 41. 5: Millersville State Col 59-63 (LS, Soc Studies) BS in Ed; UPittsburgh 64-66 MLS, 67- (LS). 6: Sp. 7: 1st asst circ dept UPittsburgh 63-64, Admin asst to dir of libs 64-65, Chem libn 65-66, Gift libn 66-67; Ref libn Edinboro State Col 67-6, Readers' serv libn 68-. 8: Coord of sci libs, UPittsburgh 65-66; Edinboro State Col: Asst Prof of Lib Sci 67-; Instr in Title II Inst on "Elem Sch Lib Planning" summer 68. 9: ALA; SchLA; Tri State ACRL; PennLA (v-chm Bldgs & Equip Sect 69-); Penn State EA. 10: Beta Phi Mu; Staff Assn Edinboro state Col (chm 68-); Arts Coun of Erie; Col Senate, Edinboro State Col (Parliamentarian 68-). 13: Yes. 14: Admin, ref, pub serv. 15: RD 2 Box 464, Belle Vernon Pa 15012.

LEET, HERBERT LAWRENCE. b Ontario Co NY. 4: Mildred Colwell . 5: Syracuse 40 (Eng, Soc Sci) BA, 46 (LS) BS. 6: Fr, Ital. 7: Libn Gilbertsville Central Sch, Gilbertsville NY 42-44; Libn New Berlin Central Sch, New Berlin NY 44-46; Libn Ovid Central Sch, Ovid NY 46-47; Libn Triple Cities Col Syracuse U (Endicott NY) 47-50; Libn Harpur Col SUNY (Endicott NY) 50-53; Circ libn Ferguson Lib, Stamford Conn 53-54; Asst dir Binghamton Pub Lib, Binghamton NY 54-59; Dir So Tier Lib System, Corning NY 59-. 8: Trustee So Finger Lakes ETV Coun; Trustee So Tier Regl Educl Ctr; Trustee S Cent Regl Res Coun. 9: ALA (mem &/or chm Recr Netwk, NY); NYLA (chm &/or mem 5 coms). 12: Ed "Finger Lakes Northern Pennsylvania Travel-Recreation Guide", Ed "Tier Talk" (54-59); Ed "Tier Topics" (59-). 13: Yes. 14: Processing, admin, field serv to mem libs, New Yorkiana. 15: 215 W Pulteney st, Corning NY 14832.

LEFEBVRE, LOUISE. b Ottawa 18 Je 06. 5: Marguerite-Bourgeoys Col (UMontreal) 24-28 (Fr Lit) BA; McGill 32-33 BLS. 6: Fr, Eng. 7: Libn Ecole des Beaux-Arts, Montreal 33-36; Dept libn grade I, Dept of Agric Ottawa 37-42; Libn Pulp & Paper Research Inst of Can Montreal 42-. 8: Sec, Com to Establish the Corp of Profess Libns of Quebec 67-69. 9: CanLA (2nd v-pres); ALA; SLA; QueLA (pres 63-65, chm 2 coms 62, 64, Memb sec 67-, Com on Rules & Regulations 69); Inst Profess Libns Ont. 10: L'Association des Femmes Diplomees des Universites (Montreal); University Women's Club (Montreal). 12: Ed "Quebec Library Association News Bulletin," (65-66). 15: 26 Robert ave, Outremont Montreal 257 Can.

LEFFALL, DOLORES C(APITOLA). b Orlando Fla 23 O 31. 5: Fla A & M Col 47-51 (Eng) AB; IndU 51-52 MS(LS); Wash DC Tchrs Col 60-. 6: Fr. 7: Asst ref libn Lincoln U 52-53; Jr catlgr Atlanta U 53-55; Asst spec collections Howard U 55-60; Libn Hine Jr High Sch, Wash DC 60-66; Libn Anacostia Sr High Sch, Wash DC 66-. 8: Asst dir Wkshop on Bibliography of the Negro, Howard U 68. 9: ALA; NEA; DCLA; DCEA; Sr High Sch Tchrs Assn. 10: Alpha Kappa Alpha; Wash Tchrs Union. 12: Index "Negro History Bulletin," Bibl in "Journal of Negro Education," (56-60). 14: Catlg. 15: 2705 13th st NE, Apt 506, Wash DC 20018.

LEFFLER, NADINE E (DIETERICH). b Huntington Park Cal 11 Jl 20. 5: Los Angeles City Col 38-41 AA; UCLA 41-43 (Hist) BA; UCal (Berkeley) 45-46 Libnship Certif. 7: Lib acquis UHawaii 46-47; Ref libn Santa Ana Pub Lib, Santa Ana Cal 53-66; Supv ref serv Orange Co Pub Lib, Orange Cal 66-. 8: Lectr, Ref & Bibliog Resources, Chapman Col spring 68. 9: CalLA; Orange CoLA. 15: 1225 Glenwood pl, Santa Ana Ca 92707.

LEFFLER, NELL (FOUST). b Humboldt Tenn 25 D 22. 4: John Edward Leffler. 5: Lambuth Col 40-42, 43-44 (Soc Sci, Chem) BA; Vanderbilt U 42-43; Fla State U 50-51 (LS) MA. 7: Asst libn Fla State U 51-52; Asst libn Colquitt-Thomas Co Reg Lib Moultrie Ga 52; Ref libn Legis Ref Bureau Tallahassee Fla 55-63; Res libn Fla Bd of Regents, Tallahassee Fla 63-65; Asst libn Fla StateU 65-. 9: ALA; FlaLA; SELA. 10: Pi Beta Phi; Beta Phi Mu. 14: Catlg, ref. 15: 2413 Miranda ave, Tallahassee Fla 32304.

LEFKOWITZ, ROBERT J. b NYC 16 Ap 28. 5: UVt 47-51 (Bot) BS; Syracuse 51-52 (Genetics) MS; UConn 53-56 (Cytology); Central State Col 65-(LS). 6: Fr. 7: Research tech in Zoology UConn 53-58; Research libn May Inst for Med Research, Cincinnati 59-65; Med libn St Anthony Hosp & Sch of Nursg Okla City, Okla 65-; Libn Okla City Aquarium Soc, Okla City 67-. 9: Amer Inst Biol Scis; SLA (Okla Recr Chm 68); OklaLA (Recr consul 69-). 10: AAAS; Sigma Xi; Okla City Aquarium Soc. 13: Yes. 14: Lit searching & abstracting, catlg. 15: Med Lib St Anthony Hosp 601 NW 9th st, Oklahoma City Okla 73102.

LEFTERUK, BORIS (EDWARD). b Selkirk Manitoba Can 7 Ag 37. 4: Pollyanna Tessie Bobula. 5: UMan 64 (Eng) BA, 68 (LS) BEd. 7: Tchg, Whytewold Beach Man 56-58; Tchg, Flin Flon Man 58-60; Tchg, Charleswood Man 60-67, Tchr-libn 67-. 9: ManASchL; Assiniboine So Div Assn of Man Tchrs' Soc (pres Resolutions Chm; Salaries Chm). 10: Lang Arts Curriculum Revision Com; Red River Valley Hist Soc. 14: Sch libs. 15: Box 247 66 Lord ave, St Norbert Manitoba Can.

LEFVENDAHL, GEORGIE (L INABINET) ADAMS. b Calhoun Co SC 6 Jl 04. 4: Peter Anton Lefvendahl. 5: Winthrop Col 21-23 (Educ) Certif; UNC summer 39, 40 (LS); Winthrop Col 47-48 (LS) AB; USoCar 52-65 (Educ); SC Tchrs Certif 23-28, 39-. 6: Fr, Ger. 7: Lib supv WPA, Orangeburg Co SC 35-38; Libn Orangeburg Co Free Lib, Orangeburg SC 38-58; Libn Berkeley Co Lib, Moncks Corner SC 58-60; Rare bks libn McKissick Mem Lib, USoCar 60; Sub tchr Orangeburg City Schs, Orangeburg SC 60-61; Libn Cataloguing Center City Schs, Orangeburg SC 61-63; Libn Mullins High Sch, Mullins SC 63-66; Libn Orangeburg Reg Hosp Libs, Orangeburg SC 45-; Libn Williston-Elko High Sch, Williston SC 66-67; Supv of libs Mullins Sch Dist #2, Mullins SC 67-. 8: Organized several libs (pub, sch, spec). 9: ALA; NEA; SCLA (sec 53, sect sec 59); SCEA. 10: SCSoc Colonial Dames XVII Cent; DAR, Orangeburg Co Hist Soc; PTA. 12: Var general records of SC. 13: Yes. 14: Lib org, ref, guidance, catlg, geneal res. 15: 176 Adden st NW, Orangeburg SC 29115.

LEGER, JOSEPH L. b Canada 27 Ag 09. 4: Claire C (Freiberg). 5: UCal(Berkeley) 34-38, 44-45, 63, 64 (Biol, Sci, LS) BA (45); Georgetown U 38-39 (Biol Sci); San Jose State Col 56-60 (LS) MA; Sacramento State Col 64-65 (Educ). 7: Ind lib clerk, Cal; Bkbinder, Cal; Libn St Francis High Sch, Mountain View Cal 56-60; Sch lib consul Sonoma Co Supt Schs, Santa Rosa Cal 60-64; Asst libn Sierra Col 64-65; Libn Col of the Redwoods 65-68; Dir Learning Resources Ctr Linn Benton Commun Col 68-. 8: Sch lib consul in San Francisco vicinity 60-65; Spec consul Cal Dept of Educ 66-68; Cal Adv Com on Lib Tech 66-68. 09: ALA-AASchL; CalLA; CalASchL (Adv Coun, Exec Bd, var coms). 10: Friends of the Santa Rosa Pub Lib; Active in local lib and sch promotional activities. 12: Ed "California School Libraries". 13: Yes. 14: Admin & operation of small instr inst libs. 15: Dir LRC, Linn Benton Commun Col, Albany Or 97231.

LEGG, JEAN MILLER. b Hamilton Ont Can 15 D 21. 5: Mich State Col 39-44 (Eng) BA; UCal 51-52 BLS. 7: Research libn Cal Research Corp, La Habra Cal 52-61; Sci coordinator Milwaukee Pub Lib 62-63; Head Eng Libs, Ohio State U 64; Consul Mich State Lib 64-68; Consul Wis Div Lib Serv 69-. 8: SLA consul 64-. 9: ALA; SLA (chm Petroleum Sect 57-58, v-pres Wis Chap 63-64); WisLA. 10: Adv Coun on Educ for Libnship; UCal 59-61; Phi Kappa Phi. 13: Yes. 14: Admin, ref. 15: 222 Merry, Madison Wi 53704.

LEGGE, CHRISTOPHER A. b London 27 S 11. 4: Kari Brebeck. 5: Oxford 30-33 (Jurisprudence) BA, 30-33, 38 (Jurisprudence) MA; Columbia 53-54 (LS) MS. 6: Ger, Fr. 7: Tchr Dublin Sch Dublin NH; USArmy Cpl Ordnance Dept 42-45; Dir Amerika Haus (USState Dept) Berlin Germany 46-52; Head libn American Univ of Beirut Lebanon 54-57; Head libn Bradford Jr Col Bradford Mass 57-66; Base Libn (GS-11) US Air Force 66-. 9: ALA. 10: Lecture extensively on Berlin and the German question. 13: Yes. 14: Admin, acquis. 15: Hq 81 Combat Support Gp (USAFE), APO NY 09755.

LEGO, JANE THOMPSON (BURKE). b Barrington NJ 26 O 28. 4: James Melvin Lego. 5: UPenn 45-49 (Educ, Eng) BS; Drexel 64-65 MS in LS. 7: Sec Agric Lib Penn State U 49-50; Libn Four Co Lib System, Binghamton NY 65-68; Catlgr-Hd tech serv Somerset Co Lib, Somerville NJ 68-. 8: Certif pub libn NY & NJ. 9: ALA; NYLA; NJLA. 10: Alpha Omicron Pi. 14: Catlg of juvenile & film materials, tech serv. 15: 16 Logan dr, Somerville NJ 08876.

LeGREE, CHARLOTTE (PEMBERTON NEEDHAM). b Wells Mich 30 D 09. 4: Wilburn Lawrence LeGree. 5: Flint Jr Col 28-30 (Eng); UMich 58-60 (Eng) AB, 61-65 AMLS. 6: Fr. 7: Asst libn Central High Sch, Flint Mich 30-32; Libn, Flint Mich; Zimmerman Jr High 33-39, Emerson Jr High 60-62, Holmes Jr High 62-66; Asst libn Ferris State Col 66-67; Libn Lowell Jr High, Flint Mich 67-68; Libn Grand Blanc High Sch, Grand Blanc Mich 68-. 14: Ref, bk selection, coord lib with curriculum & sch activities. 15: 1271 Kra-Nur dr, Davison Mi 48423.

LEHMAN, LOIS (JOAN). b Danville Penn 25 Ap 32. 5: Penn State U 50-54 (Eng) BA; Columbia 57-59 (LS) MS. 7: Asst adv dept, Daffin Mfg Co, Lancaster Penn 54-55; Tchr Sunbury Jr High Sch, Sunbury Penn 55-58; Libn Med Lib Lankenau Hosp, Phila 59-66; Ref libn UPenn Med Sch 66-68; Hd pub serv Col of Med Penn State U (Hershey) 68-. 9: MedLA (chm Phila Reg Group); SLA. 10: Buck Ridge Ski Club; Delta Sigma Rho. 14: Med, ref. 15: 24 Talisman, Briarcrest Gardens, Hershey Pa 17033.

LEHMANN-HAUPT, HELLMUT E. b Berlin Germany 4 O 03. 4: Ingeborg Pfeifer. 5: UBerlin 25 (Fine Arts); UVienna 25-26 (Fine Arts); UFrankfurt 24, 26, 27 (Fine Arts) PhD. 6: Ger, Fr, Ital. 7: Jr curator Gutenberg Museum, Mainz Germany 27-29; Curator of rare bks Columbia U 30-37; Asst Prof of bk arts Lib Sch Columbia U 37-50; Lecturer New Sch of Soc Research 50-52; Research prin Rockefeller grant, NY 50-52; Bibliogr consul H P Kraus, NY 52-68; Research assoc Yale U 65-67; Prof of bibliog Sch of Lib & Info Sci & Consul Rare Bks Lib UMo (Columbia) 69-. 8: Civil arts admin, Off Monuments, Fine Arts & Archives, Off US Mil Govt, Berlin 46-48; Info Control Off, SHAEF, Germany 45; Deputy Chief German Policy Desk, OWI, London 44-45. 9: Amer Inst Graphic Arts (var offs & activities 30-50); Gutenberg gesellschaft; BSA. 10: Grolier Club, NY; Century Assn, NY. 12: "Schwaebische Federzeichnungen" (29); "Fifty (later SEVENTY & ONE HUNDRED) Books about Bookmaking" (33, 41, 49); Ed "A Catalog of the Epstean Collection" (37); Ed & Co-auth "The Book in America" with Ruth S Granniss & Lawrence C Wroth (39, rev ed 51); Ed & Co-auth "Bookbinding in America" (41); Co-auth "An English 13th Century Bestiary" with Samuel Ives (42); "The Terrible Gustave Dore" (43); "Peter Schoeffer of Gernsheim and Mainz" (50); "Art Under a Dictatorship" (54); "The Life of the Book" (57); "Gutenberg and the Master of the Playing Cards" (66); Ed "Homage to a Bookman," H P Kraus (67). 13: Yes. 14: Rare bks, hist of bks & printing, hist of sci. 15: 914 Fairway dr, Columbia Mo 65201.

LEHNUS, DONALD JAMES. b Lyons Kan 7 N 34. 5: UKan 52-56 (Sp) BA; UCal (Berkeley) 56-57 MLS. 6: Sp. 7: Libn (staff) Queens Borough Pub Lib, Jamaica NY 57-58; Asst dir Franklin Sq Pub Lib, Franklin Sq NY 58-62; Libn San Leandro Pub Lib, San Leandro Cal 62-63; Prof Escuela Interamericana de Bibliotecologia, Medellin Colombia 64-66; Asst Prof West Mich U 67-. 9: ALA. 12: "Principios de catalogacion y clasificacion para bibliotecas pequenas" (66). 13: Yes. 14: Catlg. 15: 1822 Academy st, Kalamazoo Mi 49007.

LEHR, ROBERT MERLIN. b Alexandria S Dak 15 N 22. 4: Helen Haug. 5: Sioux Falls Col 53-55 (Biol); Augustana Col 55-57 (Hist) BA, 57-58 Secndary Tchg Certif; U S Dak 61-62 (LS); UDenver 62-63 (Libnship) MA. 6: Ger. 7: Farming, Alexandria S Dak 40-51; Serv sta attendant Lehr's Conoco Serv, Emery S Dak 51-53; Tchr Centerville (S Dak) Pub sch 58-59; Biochem lab asst S Dak State Col 59-61; Sci ref libn Wash State U Lib 63-67, Catlgr 67-. 9: ALA. 14: Catlg, ref, clsf schemes, hist of sci, med lit. 15: 611 Michigan, Pullman Wa 99163.

LEHTINEN, MARY KATHERINE (MOUNTFORD). b Lowell Mass 28 D 15. 4: T Edwin Lehtinen. 5: Simmons 34-38 (LS) BS. 7: Catlgr Lowell City Lib, Lowell Mass 38-42; Libn Lowell Gen Hosp, Lowell Mass 63-. 8: Consul libn, Lowell Vocat Sch, Sch of Practical Nursing Lib 65-. 9: ALA; MassLA; NELA (Hosp Sect). 10: Alum Assn Simmons Col. 14: Ref. 15: Forrest st, Dunstable Ma 01827.

LEIBL, ANNE (LINDNER). b Denmark 10 F 41. 4: Raymond Leibl. 5: UManitoba 58-62 (Fine Arts) BFA; UToronto 63-64 BLS, 68-69 MLS. 6: Danish, Fr. 7: High sch tchr, Roland Man Can 62-63; Libn Educ Faculty UMan 64-65; Ref libn Winnipeg Pub Lib, Winnipeg Man Can 65-67; Ref libn Sci & Med UToronto 67-68; Med libn Toronto West Hosp, Toronto Ont Can 69-. 9: CanLA; ALA; Inst Prof Libns Ont; OntLA; ManLA. 13: Yes. 14: Ref, adult educ, research, spec libs, med libnship. 15: 40 Alexander st apt 806, Toronto 5 Can.

LEIBOLD, MARY LOUISE (McCLUSKEY). b Wheeling W Va 10 Ap 16. 4: Robert W Leibold. 5: Conn Col 34-36, 37-38 (Eng) AB; Duke 36-37; UPittsburgh 39-41 (Eng) MA; UWis summers 66 MALS. 6: Sp. 7: Libn Ohio Co Sch Syst Wheeling High Sch 41-42; Libn Ohio co Sch Syst Madison Jr High 65; Libn W Liberty State Col, wheeling W Va 66-. 9: ALA; -ACRL; W Va LA. 10: Beta Phi Mu; LWV; Wheeling rea Hist Soc. 14: Ref 15: 25 Poplar ave, Wheeling W Va 26003.

LEIBOWITZ, SHIRLEY M (KIRSHBAUM). b NYC. 4: Leonard L Leibowitz. 5: Hunter Col (Art) BA; Drexel MS in LS. 7: Ref libn Willingboro Pub Lib Willingboro NJ 66-. 8: Conducted wkshops on basic ref for non-profess libns: Sussex Co 67, Burlington and Camden Cos 68 auspices of NJ State Lib. 9: ALA; NJLA. 10: Beta Phi Mu. 14: Ref. 15: 941 Temple ave, Burlington NJ 08016.

LEIBROOK, GRACE STEIGER. b Hamilton Ohio 21 Jl 18. 4: Mark S Leibrook. 5: MiamiU 36-40 (Eng, Phys Educ) BS in Ed; UWash 67-69 Master of Libnship. 15: 3013-34th ave W, Seattle Wa 98199.

LEICHTMAN, DOROTHY (MOORE). b Berlin NH 28 F 15. 5: Simmons 32-36 (LS) BS; Cornell U 38-39 (Amer Lit) MA; Harvard 40 (Educ); Catholic U 54-57 (LS); American U 63-65 (Philos of Educ, Lit); UVa 61 (Guidance), 66 (Tchg of Reading), 68-69 (A-V). 6: Fr. 7: Lib asst Boston Pub Lib 36-37; Ref libn Rollins Col 37-38; High sch libn Danbury High Sch, Danbury Conn 40-41; Libn & Eng instr Endicott Jr Col 41-42; Libn Bristol High Sch, Bristol Conn 42-43; Elem sch libn Fairfax(Va) pub schs 9 yrs; Libn Longfellow Intermediate Sch, Falls Church Va 58-. 8: Spec com to adv Arlington Schs on Sch Libs, 52-54. 9: NEA; VaEA; Fairfax EA. 10: AAUW; PTA. 14: Bk sel, ref, giving bk and travel talks. 15: 1707 Randolph st, Arlington Va 22201.

LEIDE, JOHN E(DGAR). b Minneapolis Minn 1 N 43. 5: MIT 61-65 (Math) SB; UWis 65-66 (LS) SM; UChicago 66- (Hist, Relig). 7: Period asst Army Materials Research Agcy, Watertown Mass 65; Asst circ libn UChicago Lib 67-. 9: ALA. 14: Automation, rare bks. 15: 1919 Farnam st, LaCrosse Wi 54601.

LEIGH, CARMA (RUSSELL ZIMMERMAN) MRS. b McLoud Okla 15 N 04. 5: Okla Col for Women 20-25 (Hist) AB; UCal (Berkeley) 29-32 (LS) Certif, (Hist) MA; Columbia summer 50 (LS). 7: Asst circ dept, Berkeley (Cal) Pub Lib 30-31; Libn Watsonville (Cal) Pub Lib 31-35; Co Libn Orange Co Lib Santa Ana Cal 38-42; Co Libn San Bernardino Co Lib San Bernardino Cal 42-45; State Libn Wash State Lib 54-; State Libn Cal State Lib 51-. 8: Consul to State Lib of Victoria and Lib Coun of Victoria, Melbourne 69. 9: ALA (Coun 45-51, 58-59, 67-68, 2nd v-pres 67-68; Com on Legis, com on accredit, & other coms); -AAStateL (pres 57, chm Planning Com 64-66); PNLA (pres 51); CalLA (pres 55, pres So Dist 40); WashLA (hon life mem 68-). 11: Doctor of Humane Letters (LHD), UPAC 5. 12: Ed "Washington Library News Bulletin," (45-51). 13: Yes. 14: Admin, lib legislation at all levels. 15: 3353 Eleventh st, Sacramento Cal 95818.

LEIGHTIZER, SISTER MARION PENELOPE. b Moncton NB Can 28 Je 09. 5: Marianopolis Col ext 55-63 (Eng) BA; UToronto 63-64 BLS. 6: Fr. 7: Tchr Notre Dame Convent, Kingston Ont 29-39; Tchr Pub Schs, Prince Edward Island 30-39; Tchr Catholic Schs, Montreal 41-44; Tchr Notre Dame Convent, Ottawa 47-52; Tchr Notre Dame High Sc , Toronto 52-58, Libn 58-63; Lib supv Metro Separate Sch Bd, Toronto 64-. 9: CanLA (Standards Com); CathLA (Ont Unit, chm Elem Set 65-67); Inst Prof Libns; Ont (chm Sch Lib Standards Com); OntLA. 10: Ont Eng Cath Tchrs Assn. 12: Ed "OntLA Review. 14: Sch libs. 15: Notre Dame Convent 750 Kingston rd, Toronto 13 Canada.

LEIN, VALERIE M (PROODIAN). b Sommerville Mass 5 Jl 27. 4: Kurt Lein. 5: Clark U 47-51 (Romance Lang) BA; Simmons 51-52 MSLS. 6: Sp, Fr. 7: Catlgr Boston Col Bus Sch 52-53; Libn USArmy Lib Serv, Ulm Germany 53-55; Libn Assumption Prep Sch, Worcester Mass 57-60; Circ libn Clark

U Lib 61-64; Sch libn St Paul's Sch, San Pablo Cal 67-69; Vol libn, Richmond Cal 67-69. 9: ALA; CalLA. 10: PTA. 15: 1220 Kind dr, El Cerrito Ca 94532.

LEINBACH, PHILIP EATON. b Winston-Salem NC 17 S 35. 4: Nancy Yocom. 5: Duke U 52-6 (Pol Sci) AB; IndU 61-64 (Hist) AM, 61-64(LS) AM. 6: Fr, Russian, Polish. 7: Budget analyst GSA Wash DC 56-57; (Lt) USNavy, Naval Security Group 57-61; Admin asst dept of resources & acquis, Harvard Col Lib 64-66, Asst libn acquis 66-67, Specialist bk sel 67-. 8: Attended USArmy Language Sch Monterey Cal for study of Rusian 58-59. 9: ALA; AHA; Amer Assn for Advancement of Slavic Studies. 10: Beta Ph Mu; Pi Sigma Alpha; Phi Alpha Theta; Omicron Delta Kappa. 13: Yes. 14: Acquis, bk sel (East Europe), collection bldg. 15: 397 Huron ave, Cambridge Ma 02138.

LEISINGER, ALBERT H JR. b NYC 15 Mr 15. 4: May Rawitch. 5: Cornell U 33-37 (European ist) AB, 37 (Amer Hist) MA, 38-41 (Amer Hist). 6: Sp, Fr. 7: Archivist Nat Archives, Wash DC 41-43; Intelligence off Foreign Econ Admin, Wash DC 43-46; Nat Archives, Wash DC; Archivist 46-51, Head Documentary Publs & Exhibits Unit 51-57, Chief Exhibits & Publ Br 57-61, Dir Archival Serv Div 62-63, Dir Exhibits & Publ Div 63-68, Spec asst to Archivist of US 68-. 8: Consul Com on Documentary Reprod of AHA; Ford Foun 63-64 (Mexican Archives); NJ State Lib 57 & 62-64; NY State Lib 62; Penn Hist & Mus Commsn 63-64, Puerto Rico, 65. 9: SAA (Fellow). 12: Ed "National Archives Accessions (57-68); List of National archives Microfilm Publications" (50, 53, 57, 61, 65); "Microfilming for Archives" (68). 13: Yes. 14: Exhib , microfilming, archival org. 15: 5312 Wriley rd, Wash DC 20016.

LEITH, ANNA (RUTH). b Prince George BC Can 22 N 23. 5: UBC 40-45 (Bacteriology & Preventive Med) BA; UWash 58-59 MLibnship. 7: Bacteriologist Head of Dept of Vet Affairs, Vancouver BC 45-51; Bacteriologist Stanford U 52-54; Med tech Clinical Lab, San Francisco 54-55; Bacteriologist prov Mental Hosp, Essondale BC 51-52, 56-58; UBC: Jr libn ref div 59-60, Jr libn Biomed Lib 60-61, Head sc div lib 61-67, Biomed libn Woodward Biomed Lib 67-. 8: Lib Adv BC Inst of Tech Burnaby BC 62-; Part-time lecturer Sch of Libnship UBC 62-. 9: ALA; CanLA (coun Research & Spec Libs Sect 68-69); MedLA; SLA; PNLA (sec 63-64); BCLA (chm Hosp Libs Com 62-63, pres 68-69); PNLA (chm-elect Ref Div 67-69; sec 63-64); Assn BC Libns; Can Assn Col & Univ Libs. 10: Vancouver Jewish Commun Centre. 13: Yes. 14: Ref, med. 15: apt 301 4665 W 10th ave, Vancouver BC Can.

LEIVESTAD, KRISTY ANN. b Port Townsend Wash 11 N 41. 5: UWash 59-63 (Hist) BA, 64-65 MLibnship. 6: Fr. 7: Sec CARE Seattle 63; Asst United Control Corp Lib, Redmond Wash 63; Asst libn Washington Room Wash State Lib 65-66, Research asst local lib development div 67-. 9: ALA; WashLA; PNLA. 10: AAUW. 14: Ref, archives. 15: 1510 SE 46th apt G-2, Lacey Wa 98501.

LEJUNE, EUGENIA DICKSON. b Portsmouth Va 14 F 04. 5: Nat Cathedral Sch (Jr Col) 23& columbia summer 40 (LS); William & Mary even 50-57; AmerU summer 51 (Preservation & Admin of Archives). 6: Fr. 7: Lib asst legis ref serv LC DC 26-29; Lib asst Norfolk Pub Lib, Norfolk Va 39-42; Off-in-chg record sect & lib Marine Corps Schs, Quantico Va 43-46, Chief libn 47-49; Ref libn Armed Forces Staff Col (Norfolk Va) 49-57; Archivist-libn George C Marshall Research Lib, Lexington Va 57-, Wash DC 57-66, Lexington 66-. 9: SLA; SAA; VaLA; SELA. 10: Nat Soc of Colonial Dames in Amer; Marine Corps Women's Res (Major); AHA; Va Hist Assn. 14: Mil libs. 15: 13 Jordan st, Lexington Va 24450.

LEMAITRE, WYNIFRED (EVELYN EAVES). b Montreal 21 Ap 08. 5: McGill 27-31 (Fr) BA, 46-47 BLS. 6: Fr, Ger. 7: Catlgr Wellesley Col Lib 47-53; Head catlgr Amer Lib in Paris 5051; Catlgr Widener Lib Harvard 53-57; Catlgr Vassar Col 58-61; Head of tech serv Wheaton Col 61-62; Catlgr Wellesley Col 62-. 9: ALA; NE Tech Serv Libns (corr sec). 10: Salon francais de Boston. 14: Catlg. 15: 19 Appleby rd, Wellesley Ma 02181.

LEMANSKY, JULIUS. b Brookln NY 12 Jl 10. 4: Hannah Leibowitz. 5: City Col (NY) 27-31 (Hist) BA; Columbia 31-33 (Hist) MA; Pratt 64-65 MLS. 6: Fr, Yiddish. 7: Tchr soc studies Boys High Sch, Brooklyn NY 34-52; Off manager Sparco Steam Laundry Inc, Brooklyn NY 52-59; Tchr soc studies Rhodes Sch, NYC 59-64; Tchg asst Grad Lib Sch Pratt Inst 64-65; Asst ref libn LIU 65; Adult serv libn Brooklyn Pub Lib 65-66; Dir lib Brookln Col of Pharmacy 66-. 9: ALA; MedLA (rep to Jt Com of Pharm Col Libs); SLA; Acad Libs of Brooklyn (sec). 10: Beta Phi Mu. 13: Yes. 14: Med, ref. 15: 115 Ashland pl, Brooklyn NY 11201.

LeMASTER, CHARLES R. b Sioux City Iowa 4 Ap 27. 4: Clarice Sommers. 5: US Army specialized Res Train Program 44-45 (Pre-engring); Morningside Col 47-48 (Pre-engring), 61-62 (Soc Sci) BA; San Diego State Col 60-61 (Hist); West MichU summer 67, 68-69 MSLS. 6: Sp. 7: T-3 Signal Corps US Army, US & Italy 45-47; Journeyman electrician: Pub serv co, Sioux City Iowa 48-52, Gas & Electric Co, San Diego 52-56; Salesman John Hancock Insurance Co, San Diego 56-61; Tchr secondary Community Sch Dist, Sioux City Iowa 62-64; Asst libn instr Morningside Col 64-, Asst libn asst prof 69-. 9: ALA; IowaLA. 10: PTA; Friends of Lib (Sioux City Iowa). 14: Circ, ref, a-v. 15: 3821 6th ave, Sioux City Ia 51106.

LeMAY, FRANCOIS (R). b Ottawa Can 13 Mr 45. 4: Diana Methot. 5: Ottawa U 67 BA; Toronto U 68 BLS. 6: Fr. 7: Ref libn Lib of Parliament, Ottawa Can 68-. 14: Ref. 15: 125 Rue Bruyere, Ottawa 2 Ont Can.

LEMBO, DIANA (MacDONOUGH). b Waterbury Conn 22 F 25. 5: CornellU 42-46 (Sci) BS; LIU 57-59 (Educ) MS, 59-61 (LS) MS; NYU 65- (Educ Communication). 06: Fr. 7: Sch libn Pub Schs, Locust Valley NY 58-65; Assoc Prof Palmer Graduate Lib Sch liu 65-. 9: NEA-DAVI (Archives Com); ALA (Bk Week Com); NYLA; Nassau-Suffolk Sch Lib Assn (pres 62-63); NYSECA; LIECC. 10: Kappa Delta Pi; Pi Lambda Theta; AAUP. 12: Co-auth "The Research Paper ." (64); "Junior Plots," (67); "The Secondary Scool Library" (66). 13: Yes. 14: Sch libnship child & young adults lit, research. 15: 96 Forest ave, Locust Valley NY 11560.

LEMEL, ARLENE. b NYC 21 Ja 46. 5: Elmira Col 63-67 (Hist) BA; Columbia 67-69 MLS. 6: Sp. 7: Sec & clk Solow Building Corp, NYC 65; Govt internship program Dept of Defense, NYC 66; A-v asst Elmira Col 66-67; Admin & research asst Buttenbeim Publ Co, NYC 67; Libn (trainee) Queens Borough Pub Lib, NYC 68-69; Sec Mus of Mod Art, NYC 69. 8: Asst Station Mgr, Elmira Col Radio Station 64-67. 14: Ref, bibliog. 15: 81-27 192 st, Jamaica NY 11423.

LeMESURIER, MARY S. b Montreal Can 18 N 25. 5: Mc Gill 43-47 (Fr) BA; Columbia 62-64 (LS) MS. 6: Fr. 7: Libn Trainee NYC Pub Lib 62-63; Ref libn UToronto 64-67, Hd Govt Publ Sect 67-. 9: CanLA; ALA; OntLA. 10: Intrnat Assn of Documentalists. 14: Ref. 15: 25 Cluny dr, Toronto 5 Ont Can.

LEMKE, ANTJE (BULTMANN). b Breslau Germany 27 Jl 18. 5:Leipzig U(Germany) 41-44 Diploma in Lib Sci; Bryn Mawr 49-50 (Pol Sci); Syracuse 52-5 MSLS. 6: Ger, Fr, Lat. 7: Asst libn & Instr State Lib, Thuringia Germany 45-7; Ed asst to Ricarda uch, ena, Thuringia Germany 44-47; Dir Serv Bur for Citien Org, Wiesbaden Germany 50-52; Syracuse U: Music libn 52-60, Instr Sch of Lib Sci 61-63, Asst Prof of Lib Sci 63-, Asst Dean Sch of Lib Sci 65-67, Assoc Prof 66-. 8: Tr & ed for German & US publishers. 9: ALA; SLA; ADI; AALS; NYLA (Recr Com). 10: World Affairs Con, Syracuse NY; Friends of Chamber Music; Beta Phi Mu. 11: Guggenheim Fellow,60-61. 12: Co-auth "Almanach der Unvergessenen" (46); Auth "Mitarbeiten, aber wie" (49); Tr "Aldus Manutius and his Thesaurus Cornucopiae" (59); Ed "Librarianship and Adult Education" (63). 13: Yes. 14: Lib educ, adult educ, lib hist, bibliog. 15: Indian Oven Farm, Fayetteville NY 13066.

LEMKE, DARRELL H. b Oshkosh Wis 16 N 35. 5: UWis 53-57 9hist) BS, 59-60 MSLS; Ind 66- (LS). 6: Fr. 07: (Capt) US Army-Mil Police active 58, (Capt) res 58-65; Br libn Milwaukee Pub Lib 60-62; Asst ref libn UIll Chicago Undergrad Div 62-65; Admin asst to the libn UIll(Chcago Circle) 65-66; Hd pub serv IndU Reg Campus Libs 66-67. 9: ALA Chicago Lib Club; ASIS. 10: Beta Phi Mu. 14: Ref, admin, lib hist. 15: 416 W Barry st, Chicago Il 60657.

LEMOINE, BARBARA (PIERCE). b Mich 15 O 05. 5: UCal(Los Angeles) 24-28 (Eng) AB; San Francico State Col 39-40. 6: Fr, Sp. 7: Oakland Pub Lib, Oakand Cal: Jr libn 40-42, Asst childs libn & wk with schs 43-53, Supv libn 54-57, Prin libn order dept 58-. 9: ALA; CalLA. 14: Acquis. 15: 125 - 14th st, oakland Cal 94612.

LEMON, GERTRUDE. b Parsons Kan 4 F 05. 5: Parsons Jr Col 23-25; Kan State Tchrs Col (Emporia) 37-39 (LS BS in Ed, 47-54 (Eng) MS; Amer U summer (Archives) Certif. 7: Sch libn Wichita City Lib, Wichita Kan 39-40, Circ asst 40-43; Libn Parsons Pub Lib, Parsons Kan 43-47& ext libn Kan State Tchrs Col (Emporia) 47-50, Circ libn 50-59, Ref libn 59-. 9: ALA; NEA; KanLA; KanStateTchrsAssn. 10: AAUW; Bus &

Prof Women's Club. 14: Ref. 15: 1734 W Wilman ct, Emporia Kan 66801.

LEMON, SHELLEY L. b Indianapolis 30 Ag 35. 5: Col of Wooster 53-58 (Eng) BA UEdinburgh 57-58 (Eng); UCal 63-64 MLS. 7: Ed sec Oxford U Press Inc, NYC 58-60; Lib asst Peoria PUB Lib, Peoria Ill 60-2; Libn lit dept san Francisco Pub Lib 64-. 14: Ref. 15: San Francisco Pub Lib, Civic Center, San Francisco Ca 94102.

LEMOYNE, BERYL (ROBINSON). b Montreal 7 My 28. 4: Roy E LeMoyne. 5: McGill 45-49 BA, 49-50 BLS; Sorbonne 51-52. 6: Fr. 7: Circ libn Wellesley Col 50-51; Tchg asst McGill U Grad sch of Lib Sci 64-. 9: CanLA; QueLA; CanALS. 14: Ref. 15: 4141 Wilson ave, Montreal 260 Can.

LENFEST, DONNA (DUFF). b Duluth Minn 21 O 32. 5: UMinn (Duluth) 49-53 (Eng) BS; UIll 56-57 MS in LS, 69-. 7: Tchr-libn Mora Schs, Mora Minn 53-54; Sr lib clerk Edu Lib UCal (Berkeley) 54-56; Tchg asst UIll Lib Sch 56-57; Ref libn UIll Chicago Undergrad Div 57-59; Supv libn US Army Spec Serv, Germany 59-61; Order libn UMich Lib 61-62; Ref libn in chg of res Undergrad Lib UMich 63-67; Res Assoc Lib Research Ctr UIll 68-69; HEA II Fellowship Lib Sch. 14: Ref & gen pub serv duties, lib, educ. 15: 1408 Joann lane, Champaign Il 61820.

LENGNICK, MARCIA ELLEN (LANGFORD). b Susquehanna Penn 21 O 37. 4: Guenther Fritz Lengnick. 5: Grove City Col 55-59 (Christian Educ) BA; Syracuse 62-63 (LS) MS. 7: Libn Jr-Sr High Sch, Montrose Penn 60-62; Libn Bowsher High Sch, Toledo Ohio 64-65; Circ libn Adrian Col 65-66, Acquis libn 67-. 10: Beta Phi Mu. 14: Sch lib wk. 15: 3957 Wildwater Beach, Manitou Beach Mi 49253.

LENKEY, MARYLL I. b Budapest Hungary 16 Ag 32. 5: Budapest 50-55 (Museology-archeology) PhD; Yale 57-58 (lassics) MA; UCal (Berkely) 59-61 MLS. 6: Hungarian, Ger. 7: Asst curator Hungarian Nat Museum, Budapest Hungary 54-5; Curator Hist Museum of Budapest 55-56; Asst catlgr YaleU Lib 58-59; Bibliogr UCal (Berkeley) 6163; Visiting Prof Classics dept Stanford U 63; Catlgr Cal State Col (Hayward) 63-64; Asst Prof San Francisco State col 64-65; Head ref UCal Lib (Irvine) 65-6, Hd of acquis 66-, Ext lecturer 65-. 9: Archeol Inst Amer; ALA; CalLA; So Cal Tech Proc Gp. 13: Yes. 14: Acquis, ref, catlg. 15: 1007 Flamingo rd, Laguna Beach Ca 92651.

LENKEY, SUSAN V. b Budapest Hungary 8 N 10. 5: Pazmany U (Budapest) 34 (Ger, Fr) Tcrs Diploma, 46 (Hist of Art & archeol) PhD. 6: Eng, Hugarian, Ger, Fr, Ital, Lat. 7: Tchr Hist of Art in own sch Budapest 34-44; Asst Prof Hist of Art Dept PazmanyU (Budapest 46-50, Lcturer in museology 50-56; Prof staff mem Agric Museum udapest 54-57; Research wk Municipal Museum of Hist BUDAPEST 5; Asst catlgr YaleU Lib 58-60; Sr rare bk lib Stanford U Libs 60-, lecturer in history 66-. 8: Tchg "History of the Book" at Stanford U; Tchg Hist of Art at UCal Ext. 9: Archaeol inst Amer; Col Art Assn. 12: Publications in Hungarian on history of art & museology. "An Unknown Leonardo Self-portrait," (63). 13: Yes. 14: Rare bks. 15: 275 San Luis dr, Menlo Park Cal 94025.

LENNEBERG, HANS (H). b Olpe Germany 16 My 04 Sylvia Kolk. 5: Columbia 48-51 (Music); Brooklyn Col 52-53 (Music) AB; NYU 53-56 (Musicology) AM; Pratt 58-60 MLS, 60-61 (Musicology). 6: Ger, Fr, Dutch, Ital, Lat, Sp. 7: Fellow Dept of Music BROOKLYN Col 54-56, Lecturer 56-58; Lib trainee Brooklyn Pub Lib, Brooklyn NY 58-60 Asst chief art & music 61-63; Music libn & Asst Prof Lecturer in music UChicago 63-. 8: Adv Mus of Music, Scarsdale NY 60-; Chm to Survey musical Instrment Collection 62-68; Reprint com, Amer Musicological Soc/Music LA 62-. 9: MusLA (chm NY Chap 61-63); Amer Musicological Soc; Internat Mus Lib Assn. 12: Assoc ed "Aspects of Medieval & Renaissance Music" (66). 13: Yes. 14: Music, bibliog. 15: UChicago Music Lib, Chicago Il 60637.

LENNON, SISTER GERTRUDE MARIE OP. b Jersey City NJ 16 My 11. 5: Caldwell Col for Women 48 (Eng) BA; Villanova 56 MS in LS. 6: Fr, Sp. 7: Libn: Lacordaire Sch, Upper Montclair 45-50, St Mary High Sch, Rutherford NJ 51-56, St Dominic Acad, Jersey City NJ 57-63, Mt St Dominic Acad, Caldwell NJ 68-. 8: Mem Archdiocesan Lib Coun (Newark NJ); Ext courses Caldwell Col for Women. 9: ALA; CathLA (chm, No NJ Unit); NJLA; EssexCoLA (v-pres); Second Tchrs Assn of NJ. 14: Child lit, ref. 15: Mt Saint Dominic Academy, Caldwell NJ 07006.

LeNOIR, BARBARA F. b Greenwood Mass 22 My 13. 5: Tufts U 31-35 (Fr) AB; Simmons 40 BSLS; NYU 55,56,57. 7: Libn Lucius Beebe Mem Lib, Wakefield Mass 35-40; Libn Garland St Jr High ch, Bangor Me 40-43; Libn Melrose High Sch, Melrose Mass 43-50; Head Lbn Scarsdale High Sch, Scarsdale NY 50-. 8: ALA-CBC Jt Cm 63-; World Hist Bibliog Com, Nat Coun for Soc Studies 60. 9: ALA; NYLA; WestchesterLA. 10: Scarsdale Tchrs Assn; Westchester Tufts Club. 13: Yes. 14: Sch libs. 15: 174 Garth rd, Apt 6Q N, Scarsdale NY 10583.

LENOX, GARY (JOHN). b La Crosse Wis 26 My 42. 5: UMinn 60-64 (Eng) BA; UWis 64-66 (LS) MA. 6: Fr. 7: Page &sr clk UMinn Biomed Lib 62-64; Lib tech Mendota State Hosp (Wis) Patients Lib 64-65; Libn Rock Co Campus UWis 66-. 10: So Wis Acad Libns Organiz; Assn Janesville Libns (pres 68-69). 13: Yes. 14: Acquis, rare bks, bibliog. 15: 500 E Court st apt 2B, Janesville Wi 53545.

LENTZ, DIANA (DeMARCO). b Warren Penn 21 Mr 32. 5: Slippery Rock State Col 50-54 (Eng, Soc Studies) BS in Ed; Bary Col 61, 63 (LS); UMiami(Fla) 63, 64 (LS); Fla State U Ext 62 (Av). 07: Eng tchr Townville Consolidated Sch, Townville Penn 54-57; Eng tchr N Miami Sr High Sch Dade Co, Miami Fla 58-59; Tchr-libn Carol City Jr High Sch Dade Co, Miami Fla 60-63; Libn Horace Mann Jr High Sch Dade Co, Miami Fla 63-. 8: Materials Center Spec, Horace Mann Jr High Sch, 63. 9: NEA-DAVI; ALA; FlaEA; FlaASchL; Dade Co(Fla0 clr Tchr Assn; Dade Co SchLA. 10: Sigma Tau Delta; Beta Sigma Phi. 14: Instructional materials centers, catlg, clsf. 15: 55 NE 184 terr, N Miami Beach Fl 33162.

LENTZ, MARY ELLEN (CONE). b Eureka Kan 2 N 18. 4: Paul L Lentz. 5: WashburnU 36-40 9art, Fr) AB; State UIowa 40-41 (Art Hist) MA; Inst of Fine Arts NYU 41-42 (Art Hist); UMd 66-69 MLA. 6: Fr. 7: Asst libn Menninger Clinic, Topeka Kans 42-43; Staff mem nat Fungus Collections, Beltsville Md 59-68; Libn Spalding Jr High Sch, Suitland Md 68-. 13: Yes. 14: Sch & univ libs, ref. 15: 5 Orange ct, Greenbelt Md 20774.

LENTZ, ROBERT T. b Thorofare NJ 13 Mr 10. 4: Marjorie Kirby. 05 Temle 48 (Educ) BS; Drexel 51 MS(LS). 07: Jefferson Med Col: Asst libn 31-49, Libn 49-, Prof of med bibliog 65-. 8: Instr, Drexel Inst Grad Sch of Lib Sci 59-. 9: MedLA (pres 60-61, Bd Dirs 54-57 & 59-62, Placement Adv 58-59, chm 3 coms 54-58 & 62-). SLA (pres Phila Chap 55-56); ALA; ASIS. 13: Yes. 15: 1025 Walnut st, Phila Pa 19107.

LENZE, OTHMAR JOSEPH. b Mt Jewett Penn 18 S 19. 4: Jeanne Marie Fahy. 5: St LouisU 46-50 (Hist) BS; WashingtonU even 51; SW (Mo) State Col summer 52 (LS); Geneseo State Col 53-60 (LS) MS. 7: Staff Sgt8th Air Force USAF 42-45; Tchr Christian Brothers High Sch, St Louis 50-51; Tchr-libn High Sch, Westzville Mo 51-53& libn Sr High Sch, Hoopeston Ill 53-57; Libn East High Sch, arden City Mich 57-. 9: NEA (Life mem); MichLA (Pub Rel Com 62-64); MichASchL; MichEA (chm &/or mem var state& reg groups & coms 61-67). 14: Highsch libnship. 15: 31103 Merritt ave, Westland Mi 48185.

LEOBOLDTI, HELEN ELIZABETH (FLADLIEN). b La Crosse Wis 9 N 23. 4: Charles C Leoboldti. 5: La Crosse State Col 41-45 (His, Eng) BS & Secondary Ed; UWis 49-50 BLS. 6: Sp. 7: Libn Black River Falls (Wis) High Sch 45-46; Libn Neenah (Wis) High Sch 46-49; Libn Enoch Pratt Free Lib Baltimore 50-53; Libn San Diego Pub Lib 53-60; Reg Supv Libn San Diego Pub Lib 60-. 9: ALA; CalLA. 14: Admin, adults & youg adults serv. 15: 4830 College ave, Sn Diego Ca 92115.

LEON, SOLOMON J. b Philadelphia 29 D 18. 4: Sylvia Coopersmith. 5: Temple 35-39 (JOURNALISM) BS; UPenn 46-49 (Eng it) MA; UParis 55-56 (Fr Lit); Dreel 56-57 (LS) MS. 6: Fr, Ger, Yiddish. 7: Asst Prof of Eng Fisk U 50-52; Asst Prof of Eng Dillard U 52-53; Asst Prof of Eng Tougaloo Christian COL 5#'55; Free Lib of Phila: Prof asst 57-60, Admin asst lib for the blind 60-62, Head Wadsworth Br 62-63; Head Northeast Reg Lib 63-. 9: ALA. 12: Ed "A Foods Encyclopedia." 14: Humanities. 15: 807 66th ave, Phila Pa 19126.

LEONARD, BRADLEY W(HEELER). b Bradford Vt 27 S 14. 4: Gladys Hesselbach. 5: Fitchburg (Mass) State Tchrs Col 34-38 (Educ) BS in Ed; Pratt 38-39 BLS. 07: Page Fitchburg Pub Lib, Fitchburg Mass 30-38; Libn I Brooklyn Pub Lib 39-41; Ref libn UNH Lib 41-42; 2d Lt ArmyAF 42-45; Newark Pub Lib, Newark NJ: Jr libn 45-46, Sr libn 46-47, Prin libn 47-56, Chief lending & ref dept 56-62; Asst dir Phoenix Pub

Lib 62-64; Chief adult serv Flint Pub Lib, Flint Mich 64-. 8: Prepared & graded written exam for lib positions for NYState Dept of Civil Serv (49-50); Instr Pratt Inst Evening Lib Sch. 9: NJLA (chm var coms 48-62); Ariz State LA (pres-elect Pub Libs Div 63-64); ALA (chm Nominat Com Sci & Tech Div 48, Subscription bks Com 62-64); NJLib Films Circuit (pres 60-61). 10: Newark Lions Club. 12: Ed "NPL News," Newark Pub Lib (47-48); Ed "New Jesey Library Association News" (48-49); Ed Newark Lions Club Bulletin (52-53). 13: Yes. 14: Admin, bk sel, reader serv. 15: Flint Pub Lib, 1026 E Kearsley st, Flint Mi 48502.

LEONARD, CAROLYN M (TURNER). b Lincoln Neb 11 S 36. 4: Lawrence E Leonard. 5: Hastings Col(Neb) 54-58 9eng, Educ) BA; UDenver 58-59 (LS) MA; USoCal 63-4 (LS). 6: Sp, Fr. 7: Stud asst Hastings Pub Lib, Hastings Neb 54-58; Stud asst UDenver Lib 59; Jr high libn Riverside City Schs, Riverside Cal 59-60; Catlgr Hastings Pub Schs, Hasings Neb summer 60; Jr high libn Denver Pub Schs 60-61; Catlgr San Diego State Col 61-63; Head catlgr Riverside City & Co Lib, Riverside Cal 63-64; Head ser dept UColo Lib 64-68; Ser catlgr Ill Lib (Urbana) 68-. 9: ALA; CalLA; ColoLA; IllLA. 10: Beta Phi Mu. 14: Catlg, ser, tech proc, mechanization. 15: 709 S Mattis ave, Champaign Il 61820.

LEONARD, CHARLOTTE CORRINNE. b delaware Ohio 16 Mr 22. 5: Ohio State U 39-40; Heidelbeg Col 40-43 (Eng) AB; West Res 49-50 MSLS. 6: Fr, Ger. 7: Clerk War Price & Rationing Bd, Delaware Ohio 43-44; Clerk-typist Wright Patterson, Dayton Ohio 44-47; Order clerk Specialty Papers, Dayton hio 47-48; Asst libn Monsanto Chem Co, Dayton Ohio 48-49; Dayton & Montgomery Co Pub Lib, Dayton Ohio: Chid libn 50-59, Head bkmob 60-62, coordinator of child serv 63-. 8: Instr Wright State U 62-68. 9: ALA (chm Jr Mem Round Table 580& ohioLA (Exec Bd 58-61, chm Ext Round Table 63, chm Serv to Schs RT 67. 10: Soroptimist Club; YWCA; AAUW. 14: Child lit. 15: 204 Niagara ave, Dayton Ohio 45405.

LEONARD, GLADYS. b NYC. 4: Bradley W Leonard. 5: CornellU (Soc Sci) BA; Pratt Inst 38-39 BLS. 7: Libn grade 1 & 2 Queens Borough Pub Lib, Jamaica NY; Br libn & educ ref libn Newark Pub Lib, Newark NJ 46-62; Ref libn C S Mott Lib, Flint Mich 69-. 10: Phi Beta Kappa; Pi Lambda Theta. 13: Yes. 14: Ref. 15: 2101 E Second st, Flint Mi 48503.

LEONARD, IRENE E. b Chickasha Okal 9 Ja 08. 4: Roger E Leonard. 5: Okla Col for Women 24-28 (Lat) AB; UDenver summers 51-54 (LS) MA. 7: Libn Lakewood High Sch, Jefferson Co Colo 54-60; Supv of lib serv Jefferson Co pub Schs, Colo 60-. 8: Colo Coun for Lib Development 61-68. 9: ALA-AASchL; NEA; ColoLA; ColoASchL; ColoEA. 10: Delta Kappa Gamma; Delta Omicron. 14: Sch libs. 15: 1031 Balsam, Lakewood Colo 80125.

LEONARD, JEAN (MOVERMAN). b Brooklyn NY 6 D 26. 4: Harold Leonard. 5: CUNY 44-48 (Bus) BBA; C W Post Col of LIU 60-66 (LS) MS. 6: Ger. 7: Elem lib aide Starthtown Cental Schs, St James NY 59-60; Elem libn; Sachem Sch Dist, Lake Ronkonkoma NY 62-66, 3 Village Sch Dist, etauket NY 66-68, Sidney (NY) Central Sch Dist, 69-. 8: Recipient ESEA, Title II Grant to set up a Multi-Media ctr. 14: Child lit. 15: 3 E st, Oneonta NY 13820.

LEONARD, LAWRENCE EDWARDS. b Hartford Conn 15 Ag 34. 4: Carolyn May (Turner) Leonard. 5: Colo Sch of Mines 52-53 (Geol); UColo 53 (Geol); UIll (Champaign) 54-56 (Geol) BS; UDenver 58-59 (LS) MA; USoCal 63-64 (LS); UIll (Champaign) 68- (LS). 6: Ger. 7: Lib asst Ill Geol Survey Champaign Ill 55-56; Lib asst Post Lib Ft Leonard Wood Mo 57-58; Regimental clerk (Sgt) USArmy Ft Leonard Wood Mo 56-5; Circ asst UDenver Lib 58-59; Lit searcher Denver Research Inst 59; Research libn The Martin Co Denver 59-61; Asst libn Gen Atomic San Diego 61-63; Ref libn Naval Ordnance Lab Corona Cal 63-64; Chief Libn Natl Bur of Standards Boulder Labs Boulder Colo 64-67; Project dir NSF Lib Research Study Bk Processing Ctr 67-68; Research assoc UIll (Urbana) Lib Research Ctr 68-. 9: ASIS (sec-treas San Diego Chap 62-63); SLA (sec Colo Chap); MPLA; ColoLA (pres-elect 67-68); IllLA; ALA. 12: Comp "Magnetoresistance in Metals, Semiconductors, and Alloys: A Bibliography," (64); other bibliographies; Co-auth "Centralized Processing" (69). 14: Admin, tech serv, doc retrieval, lib syst analysis. 15: 709 S Mattis ave, Champaign Il 61820.

LEONARD, RUTH S(HAW). b Boston 24 Ag 06. 5: Simmons 28 (LS) SB; Columbia 44 (LS) MS. 7: Circ asst Brockton(Mass) Pub Lib summers 26-28; Catlgr MIT summers 29, 37; Tchg asst Simmons Col Sch of Lib Sci 28-30; Research Dir Bentley Col of Accounting & Finance 30-37; Simmons Col Sch of Lib Sci: Instr 37-41, Asst Prof 41-48, Assoc Prof 48-. 8: Chm in chg of org Civilian Defense Lib Serv Mass Com on Pub Safety 42-43; Consul in org Sch of Nurs Lib NE Deaconess Hosp, Boston 44; Dir Wkshop on Libs for Schs of Nurs: Simmons Col summer 45, URI summer 54; Org lib and was lib consul for Mass Fed of Taxpayers Assns 45-46; Tchg Catlg & Clsf UNC summer 48. 9: ALA-ACRL (Hosp Lib Standards Com 68-69); -LRTS (chm Nomin Com 68-69); -LED; -PLA; AALS (chm Recr Com 45-47, chm Com on Instr & Tchg Method 51-52); SLA (chm Train & Prof Activities Com 43-45, 2d v-pres 46-47; Chap Liaison Off & chm Chap Rel Com 47-48; Consul to Prof Standards Com 63-66, chm 66-69); NELA; MassLA; NETechServLibns (sec-treas 44-45 (chm 54-55); MedLA. 10: AAUP. 11: SLA 1965 Prof Award. 12: Auth "Bibliography of Works on Accounting by American Authors," with H C Bentley (2 v 34-35); Auth "Library Profession," with M P Hazen (2d ed 54); Comp "Profiles of Special Libraries" (66). 13: Yes. 14: Tchr, courses in the lib as a soc institution, catlg & clsf, org & admin of spec libs. 15: Simmons Col Sch of Lib Sci, Boston Ma 02115.

LEONARD, VIRGINIA (DAMM). b Cleveland 14 F 14. 4: Vincent C Leonard. 5: West Res U-Flora Stone Mather 31-35 (Fr) AB; West Res 37 (Fr) MA, 40 BS in LS. 6: Fr, Sp, Ital. 7: Prof asst Detroit Pub Lib Monteith Br 40-42, Prof asst soc sci dept 42-44, 47-51; Prof asst Grosse Pointe (Mich) Pub Lib 52-64, Chief processing dept 64-. 9: ALA; MichLA (sec-treas Tech & Resources Div 64-65); NEA. 10: AAUW; Phi Beta Kappa. 12: Weekly Library Column, "Grosse Pointe News" (62). 13: Yes. 14: Catlg, processing, rare bks. 15: 10676 Duprey, Detroit Mi 48224.

LEONARD, WILLIAM P. b Schenectady NY 9 Ap 15. 4: Kathryn Allen. 5: Union Col 33-37 (Soc Sci) BA; Fletcher Sch of Law & Diplomacy 37-38 (Internal Rel) MA; UIll 39-41 (LS) BS; Albany Law Sch 51-55 LLB; SUNY 60-64 (Public Admin. 6: Ger, Fr. 7: Stud asst Union Col Lib (Schenectady NY) 33-37; Lib asst UIll (Urbana) 39-41; Ref asst NY Pub Lib 41-42; US Army (1st Lt) Mil Govt, Europe 42-46; Asst law libn NY State Lib 46-47, Legis ref libn 47-. 8: Councilman, City of Schenectady 56-57, 59; mem City Planning Commsn 58. 9: Amer Soc Pub Admin. 10: Civil Serv Employees Assn. 14: Govt research. 15: 1234 Waverly pl, Schenectady NY 12308.

LEONDAR, JUDITH C. b Boston 8 F 31. 5: Alfred U 48-52 (Chem) BA; Rutgers 57-60 MLS; Columbia 59 (Abstracting & Indexing). 7: Tech research libn Amer Can Co tech serv div, Newark NJ 52-55; Tech libn RCA Internat Div, Clark NJ 55-56; Research libn Ethicon Inc, Somerville NJ 56-61; Sci info off Inst of Naval Studies, Cambridge Mass 61-65; Research assoc Asst Prof Rutgers Bur of Info Sci Research 65-66, Sr info research sci 66-68; Lib operations mgr Squibb Inst Med Research, New Brunswick NJ 68-. 8: SLA Profess consul. 9: ADI NE Chap (v-chm 62-65, chm by-laws com 64-65); ASIS (SIG/BC sec-treas 66-67, SIG/LA chm Educ Com 68-); SLA (chm Conv Info Com 58-59, chm Engrg Div 66-67, Pub Rel Com 69-; Boston Chap: chm Placement Serv 62-65, chm Sci-Tech Div 63-65; NJ Chap: v-pres 66-68, pres 68-69); ALA; MedLA; ACS. 12: Ed SLA "NJ Chap Bulletin" (59-61); "Bibliography of Research Relating to the Communication of Scientific and Technical Information," (67); Mem ed bd curr cont phys sci (68). 13: Yes. 14: Planning & org, & admin of spec libs, info centers in sci & tech, research in info sci. 15: 734 Park ave, Plainfield NJ 07060.

LEONHARD, G(EORGE) RUSSELL Jr. b Passaic NJ 30 Ap 17. 4: Viva Ruth Breuel. 5: UChicago 59 (LS). 7: Clerk Carlisle Mellick & Co, NYC 33-39; Assembler 40-45; Pvt USAGF USA 45-46; Millwright 46-58; Libn Twp Lib of Lower Southampton, Feasterville Penn 56-67; Maintenance Millwright Crown Cork & Seal, Phila 59-. 8: Vol Twp Lib of Lower Southampton; PLA provisional lib certif. 9: ALA; PennLA. 10: Internat Assn Machinists. 14: Org libs. 15: 37 Mary la, Orangewood Park apts, Levittown Pa 19057.

LEOPOLD, CAROLYN C. b Chicago 21 F 18. 4: Luna B Leopold. 5: Col of William & Mary 35-36; UMd 36-39 (Eng) BA; Catholic U 57-59 MS in LS. 6: Fr. 7: Libn Maret Sch, Wash DC 59-60; Libn Holton-Arms Sch, Wash DC 60-64; Libn St Albans Sch, Wash DC 64-66; Libn educ materials Lab, Rockville Md 66-. 9: ALA; DCLA; Montgomery Co (Md) LA. 10: Beta Phi Mu; Kappa Kappa Gamma. 13: Yes. 14: Ref, readers adv, child lit. 15: 5705 Springfield dr, Wash DC 20016.

LEPIE, RUTH (SLOBODKIN). b Malden Mass. 4: Myron P Lepie. 5: UNC 43 (Eng) BA; State Col (Boston) 59 (Educ) MEd; Simmons 65 (LS) MS. 6: Fr. 7: Tchr Eng soc stud Newton Pub Schs, Newton Mass 57-65; High Sch libn

Arlington Pub Schs, Arlington Mass 65-. 9: ALA; NEA; Mass Tchrs Assn; MassLA; MassSchLibns. 14: Sch libs. 15: 18 Travis dr, Chestnut Hill Mass 02167.

LEPINE, JOHN JOSEPH. b Toronto 14 Mr 20. 5: UMontreal 39-43 (Philos) BA; UToronto 43-46 ; Regis Col (Toronto) 47-51 (Theol) STL; (Hist) MA; UCal (Berkeley) 60-62 MLS. 6: Fr, Ger, Ital, Lat, Gk. 7: Asst Prof UManitoba 47-49; Prof Campion Col USask 52-; Major (Staff) Canadian Army (Militia) Regina Sask 53-; Tchr libn Campion Col High Sch, Regina Sask 52-54; Gen libn Campion Col Lib (Regina Sask) 54-60, Chief Libn 61-. 8: Dir of Music & col organist, Regis Col 44-52; Lib Consul to Separate Secondary Sch System, Regina 65-; Dir music Campion Col 53-. 9: ReginaLA (pres 62-63); SaskLA (chm Legis & Certif Com, pres 64-65); CathLA; ALA; CanLA; Can Assn Col & Univ Libns; SaskASchL. 10: Regina Symphony Soc. 11: Can Defence Medal. 12: Ed "Newsletter," YP's Sect CandnLA (55-60); Ed "Saskatchewan Library." 13: Yes. 14: Col lib admin, acquis, bk selection. 15: Campion Col USask, Regina Sask Canada.

LEPP, WILBUR NORMAN. b Saskatoon Sask Can 29 My 36. 5: USask 55-58 (Music, Art) B Ed, 61-62 (Music, Art hist) BA; UWis summer 63 (Art); UWash 63 (LS); UBC 64-65 BLS; Carleton U (Ottawa) 68 (Archival Admin) Archives Diploma. 06: Fr. 7: Art Instr USask (Saskatoon) 56; Art Instr USask (Regina) 57; Tchr Sch Bd, Saskatoon Sask 59-61; Art Instr YWCA, Saskatoon Sask 61-62; Music & record libn Pub Lib, Saskatoon Sask 64; Head Fine Arts Lib USask (Regina) 65; Local hist libn Pub Lib, Saskatoon Sask 66-. 09: CanLA; SaskLA; SaskatoonLA (pres 68-69). 14: Catlg, music & art bibliog, mss, rare bks, local hist. 15: 501 Dufferin ave, Saskatoon Sask Canada.

LEPPLA, MARTHA BOND (MRS). b Richmond Ind 8 Jl 12. 5: UArk 29-33 (Math) BA; UIll 33-35 BS in LS. 7: Clerk UArk Lib 30-33; Catlgr UIll Lib (Urbana) 34-36; Catlgr UIll Med Lib (Chicago) 36-37; Catlgr Los Angeles Co Museum Lib, Los Angeles 55-57; Head tech serv & asst libn Palos Verdes Lib Dist, Palos Verdes Peninsula Cal 57-. 9: ALA; CalLA; SoCalTech Processes Group. 10: Amer Field Serv; Commun Arts Assn; YWCA; Amer Contract Bridge League. 14: ech processes. 15: 3313 Palos Verdes dr N, Palos Verdes Estates Cal 90275.

LERITZ, HELEN AUGUSTA (SWIERCZEK). b Chicago 4 Ag 05. 4: Albert Francis Leritz. 5: UIll 23-27 (Eng) AB, 58-62 MSLS; West Mich U 64-65 (Instr Materials). 6: Fr, Ger. 7: Tchr-libn Kendall High Sch, Kendall Wis 27-28; Tchr-libn Carlinville High Sch, Carlinville Ill 28-34, 42; Instr women's pe Blackburn Col 44-45, Dramatics Dir 53-55; Tchr-libn Girard High Sch, Girard Ill 55-57; Libn Southwestern Commun Unit 9, Piasa Ill 57-. 8: Mem Sch Bd, Carlinville Commun Unit #1 53-56; Ill State Visit (Eval for Recog) COM, 68. 9: ALA (Recr Com); NEA; Nat A-V Assn; IllLA (chm pub Com, chm Memb Com); IllEA. 10: Citizens' Adv Com for the Pub Schs; PTA; Woman's Club; AAUW; Beta Phi Mu. 13: Yes. 14: Sch libs. 15: 337 E Second South st, Carlinville Ill 62626.

LERNBERG, ROSE (MATYCHAK). b New Windsor Orange Co NY 19 Je 27. 4: Ronald Lernberg. 5: NYState Col for Tchrs (Albany) 43-47 (Sci) BA, 47-51 (Guidance) MA; UCal (Berkeley) 61-62 MLS. 7: Clerk supv NY Telephone Co, Albany NY 47-55; Supv Engnr Pacific Telephone, San Francisco 55-59; Engnr Western Electric Co, NYC 59-61; Engnr Pacific Telephone, San Francisco 61- Sch libn Hoover Jr High Sch, Oakland Cal 62-64; Child libn San Francisco State Col Frederic Burk Sch, San Francisco 65-66; Sch libn Hillside Sch, Berkeley Cal 67-69. 9: ALA-AASchL; CalLA; CalASchL; Assn Child libns No Cal (sec 68-69). 14: Wk with child. 15: 831 Balra dr, El Cerrito Ca 94530.

LERNER, FREDERICK A. b Mt Vernon NY 27 D 45. 5: Columbia 62-66 (Hist) AB, 68-69 (LS) MS. 6: Ger, Anglo-Saxon. 7: Pre-prof libn Alesco, Glen Rock NJ 66; US Army 66-68. 8: Chm 1st Annual Conf on the Bibliog of Sci Fiction (ColumbiaU) 69. 9: Sci Fiction Res Assn (exec sec); Kipling Soc; Tolkien Soc of Amer; East Sci Fiction Assn. 12: "An Annotated Checklist of Science Fiction Bibliographical Works". 13: Yes. 15: 98-B Blvd, E Paterson NJ 07407.

LESH, NANCY. b Anchorage Alaska 25 My 44. 5: WillametteU 62-66 (Eng) BA; Simmons 66-67 MLS. 7: Clk Bk Cache Bkstore, Anchorage Alaska summers 64-66, fall 67-68; Asst libn Anchorage Commun Col 68-. 9: AlaskaLA. 10: Girl Scouts. 14: Ref, Alaskana, acquis. 15: 1802 11th ave, Anchorage Ak 99501.

LESKO, JOHN. b Rudanci Ukraine 14 Ja 18. 5: Col of Com(Vienna) 41-44; Leopold-Franzens U(Innsbruck) 49-51 Dr rer pol; West Res 60-61 MS in LS. 6: Ukrainian, Ger, Polish, Lat, Gk. 7: Catlgr Canton Pub Lib, Canton Ohio 61-68; Catlgr Rider Col Lib 68-. 14: Catlg. 15: 486 West State st, Trenton NJ 08618.

LESLEY, MIRIAM (LUCKER). b Minneapolis 30 Je. 5: Wells Col 32-36 (Medieval Hist) BA; UMunich 36-38 (Fine Arts); UMinn 39-42 (Fine Arts) MA, 55 BS in LS; Radcliffe 60 (rchival & Hist Mgt) Certif. 6: Ger, Fr, Ital. 7: Art libn ULouisville 48-49; Asst art dept Minneapolis Pub Lib 49-57; Archivist Archives of Amer Art, Detroit 57-62; Head art print & picture depts Free Lib of Phila 62-. 9: ALA (sec Art Subsect 60-62, chm Mus Div 61-64); SLA (var com duties in 3 chaps). 10: Soc Arch Hist; Phila Mus of Art; Print club (Phila). 13: Yes. 14: Art ref. 15: Art Dept Free Lib of Phila, Logan Square Phila Pa 19103.

LESLIE, PHILIP. b Easton Penn 20 Jl 20. 4: Olga Mae Holden. 5: Lafayette Col 37-41 (Math) AB; UIll 50-52 (LS) MS. 7: Export expediter E I duPont de Nemours & Co, Wilmington Del 44-45; Libn Rumford Chem Co, Rumford RI 45-46; Div libn Brown U 46-50; Head Libn Sandia Corp, Albuquerque NM 52-54; Chief Libn Goodyear Atomic Corp, Portsmouth Ohio 55-57; Chief TIS Ryan Aeronautical Co, San Diego Cal 57-64; Asst dir publ dept NASA Facility Documentation Inc, College Park Md 64-68; Mgr info proc dept Leasco Systs & Research Corp, Bethesda Md 68-. 9: ASIS; SLA. 12: Ed "Documentation Progress," SLA (60-62). 13: Yes. 14: Mechanized publ, data proc, lib automation, vocabulary mgt. 15: 12921 Neola rd, Silver Spring Md 20906.

LESLY, RUTH (LILIENFELD). b Stephentown Center NY 22 S 28. 4: Joe Lesly. 5: NYState U (Albany) 43-47 (Eng) BA; Columbia 48-52 (LS) MS. 7: Asst child libn NYPub Lib 48-49; Research libn Anti-Defamation League NYC 49-51; Asst libn Geyer Advertising Inc, NYC 51-55; Child libn Hastings-on-Hudson Pub Lib, Hastings-on- Hudson NY 62-68, Lib dir 68-. 9: ALA; NYLA; WestchesterLA. 10: LWV; Commun Resources Com; Hastings Com for Pub Educ. 14: Admin, bk sel. 15: 20 Villard ave, Hastings-on-Hudson NY 10706.

LESNAK, STEPHEN R. b Bakersfield Cal 24 Je 44. 4: Georgette Fontana. 5: St Vincent Col 62-66 (Hist) BA; Kent StateU 66-67 (Hist); Peabody Col 68-69 MLS. 7: Apprentice libn Youngstown Pub Lib, Youngstown Ohio 67-68; Adult serv libn Rochester Pub Lib, Rochester NY 69-. 9: ALA; NYLA; OhioLA. 13: Yes. 14: Adult serv, lib educ. 15: 12-16 Lee Garden Apts Chili ave at Westside dr, Rochester NY 14624.

LESSEN, GRACE (LEOLA PLUNKETT). b Pleasant Plains Ill 7 Ag 11. 4: W G Lessen. 5: UIll 42 (Educ) BS, 47 (Educ) MS, 62 (LS) MS. 6: Sp, Lat. 7: Eng-math tchr Lincoln High Sch, Lincoln Ill 53-54; Libn Lincoln Col(Ill) summer 64; Eng-libn Beason High Sch, Beason Ill 55-66; Asst Prof of Eng Lincoln Col (Ill) 66-69, Lib staff 69-. 9: NEA; IllEA; IllLA. 10: Kappa Delta Pi; AAUP; AAUW. 14: Child serv, ref. 15: 707 N Union st, Lincoln Il 62656.

LESSENHOP, DOROTHY W (MRS). b Toledo Ohio 7 Mr 10. 5: UMich (Ann Arbor) 26-30 AB in LS. 6: Fr, Ger. 7: Neb Pub Lib Commsn, Lincoln: Ref libn & asst sec 30-43, Act exec sec 44, 49-50, Asst exec sec 50-60, A-v & interlib loan 60-65, Hd circ dept 65-; Asst ref dept Lincoln City Lib, Lincoln Neb 45-47. 8: Bd mem Bibliog Ctr for Research, Denver 66-68. 9: ALA; MPLA (Neb rep on Bd 67-); NebLA (pres 53-54). 14: Ext, ref, interlib loan. 15: 1718 G st, Lincoln Nb 68508.

LESTER, BARBARA J (FLENNIKEN). b Santa Barbara Cal. 4: William Edward Lester. 5: Orange Coast Col 60-63 (Liberal Arts); Santa Ana City Col 61-62 (Liberal Arts); UMiss 63-65 (LS) BAE, 64-65 MLS. 7: Asst libn Orance Co Lib System Westminster Br, Westminster Cal 61-62; Libn Norfolk (Va) City Schs, Granby High Sch 65-; Inst Old Dominion Col, 66; Libn Norfolk Va City Schs, Monroe Elem 66-67; Libn Tetzlaff Jr High, Cerritos Cal 67-68; Ch Libn LA Co syst Angelo M Iacoboni Lib, Lakewood Cal 68-69, Ref Libn 69; Libn LA Co Lib Syst Paramount City Lib Paramount Cal 69-. 9: ALA; NEA; CalLA; CalASchL; CalTA. 10: Kappa Delta Pi. 15: 5336 Village rd, Long Beach Ca 90808.

LESTER, DANIEL W. b Long Beach Cal 5 F 43. 4: Marilyn A Guthrie. 5: Bakersfield Col 60-62; Monmouth Col (Ill) 62-63; No Ill U 64-67 (Eng) BA, (LS) MA; UChicago 67-68 91s0. 6: Ger. 7: Asst Ed "73 Magazine" Peterborough NH 63-64; Asst syst & procedures libn Bowling Green St U Lib 68, Hd libn 68-69; Assoc libn syst & automation Mankato State Col 69-. 9:

ALA; SLA; CanLA. 14: Lib automation, admin, systems analysis, lib hist. 15: Rte 1 Box 87, Bowling Green Oh 43402.

LESTER, LILLIAN (TAUBE). b Brooklyn NY 26 My 26. 4: Howard Lester. 5: Brooklyn Col 44-48 (Home Ecom) BS 68 (Home Econ, Educ) MA; Pratt Inst 65 MLS. 7: Soc investigator NYC Dept of Welfare, Brownsville 49-51; High sch tchr NYC Dept of Educ, Midwood & Tilden 61-64; Instr Brooklyn Co home econ 64, Lecturer adult educ 65-66, Acquis libn 65-68, Spec collections libn 68-. 8: Home econ consul "Cookbook of the United Nations" NY 64. 9: Amer Home Econ Assn; ALA; ASA; Oral Hist Assn. 10: Beta Phi Mu; AAUP; Summerhill Society; Soc Gen Semantics. 14: Archives, rare bks. 15: 730 E 23 st, Brooklyn NY 11210.

LESTER, MARY P. b Worthington Mass 14 D 15. 4: Howard B Lester. 5: SUNY (Albany) 33-37 (Fr, Eng) AB; McGill 38 (Fr); SUNY (Geneseo) 49-50 (LS) Certif. 6: Fr. 7: Tchr libn Canaseraga (NY) Central Sch 46-50; Dir Hornell (NY) Pub Lib 50-64; Child consul So Tier Lib System, Corning NY 64, Asst dir 65-. 9: ALA; NYLA. 14: Child bks. 15: 266 E Franklin st, Horseheads NY 14845.

LESTER, RICHARD HENRY JR. b Charlottesville Va 30 N 31. 5: William & Mary 50-53 (Hist); San Jose State Col 53-54 (Hist) BA; Madison Col 56, 59-60 LS certif. 6: Ger. 7: Libn: Walton Sch, Prince George Va 60-62, Green Oaks Sch, E Palo Alto Cal 62-63, George Fox jr High Sch, Pasadena Md 63-65, M M Washington High Sch, Wash DC 65-66, Giano Sch W Covina Cal 67-68, Brooklyn Park Sch, Baltimore 68-. 8: Mem Lib Sci Curr Com, Anne Arundel Co Schs Md 64-65. 9: ALA; Tchrs Assn of Anne Arundel Co; Md State TA; MdASchL. 10: Phi Alpha Theta. 14: Devel of instr materials ctrs. 15: 1533 Bolton st #2, Baltimore Md 21217.

LESTOURGEON, MARTHA (HOLMAN). b Richmond Va 25 Ag 25. 4: George Hugh LeStourgeon. 5: Longwood Col 42-46 (Hist) BS; Peabody 50-54 (LS) MA. 6: Fr. 7: Tchr libn Worsham High Sch, Worsham Va 46-47; Asst libn Longwood Col 48-. 9: SELA; VaLA. 14: Catlg, acquis. 15: Rt 1 Box 173, Farmville Va 23901.

LESUEUR, CHARLES ROBIN. b Sarnia Can 8 Je 23. 5: Sch of Practical Sci U Toronto 46-49 (Mech Engnr); UCol UToronto 49-50 BA; Sch Soc Wk UToronto 50-51 BSW; Columbia 57-59 MLS. 6: Fr. 7: Lt Royal Canadian Navy 41-45; Mgt trainee Imperial Oil Refinery, Sarnia Ont 46-48; Soc wker Child Aid Soc, Toronto 51-53; Wage & Salary spec Can Gen Electric, Toronto & Guelph Ont 53-55; Libn assoc NYU Lib 55-56, Engnrg libn 56-59; Ref libn Engnrg Soc Lib, NYC 60; Libn Engnrg & Sci Lib NYU 61-68; Libn Stevens Inst Tech, Hoboken NJ 68-. 9: ALA; NYLA; ASIS; NYLib Club. 10: Archons of Colophon; AAUP. 14: Admin. 15: Lib Stevens Inst Tech, Hoboken NJ 07030.

LETHBRIDGE, JACKSON. b St Thomas Ont 4 D 36. 5: UWest Ont 55-58 (Hist) BA, 58-59 (Hist); Rutgers 62-65 MLS; UToronto 59-65 (Educ). 6: Fr. 7: Tchr-act dept hd Harrow (Ont) Dist High Sch 59-60; Tchr-libn Trenton (Ont) High Sch 60-61; Libn Delta Secondary Sch, Hamilton Ont 61-64; Asst libn Newark State Col 65-69; Acquis libn Commonwealth Campus Penn State U 69-69; Acquis libn, Commonwealth Campuses Penn State U 69-. 9: CanLA; ALA; Hamilton Sec Sch Libns Assn (pres 62,64); SLA; Ont Sec Sch Tchrs Fed; OntEA; NJEA. 14: Acquis, ref, readers serv. 15: 15 Woodsdale Park, State College Pa 16801.

LETTS, (ANNE) ALBERTA. b British Columbia. 5: UWest Ont 37 BA; Toronto 39 BLS. 7: Asst child dept London Pub Lib, London Ont 39-40; Libn Middlesex Co Lib, London Ont 40-43; Libn Simcoe Co Lib, Barrie Ont 43-46; Bkmob libn Warder Pub Lib, Springfield Ohio 46-47; Lecturer UToronto Lib Sch 47-49; Asst dir Prov Lib, Halifax NS 49-54, Dir 55-. 8: Consul on libs to Indian Govt under Columbo Plan, 58-59. 9: CanLA (pres 57-58); ALA; Can Assn for Adult Educ; APLA. 10: Can Fed of Univ Women; Zonta Internat. 13: Yes. 14: Admin, legis, lib educ. 15: Prov Lib, Prov Bldg, Halifax NS Can.

LETITIA, SISTER CLARE SSJ (MARY E MEEHAN). b Philadelphia Penn 12 D 11. 5: Col of chestnut Hill 48 (Eng) AB; VillanovaU 65 MS in LS. 7: Tchr: Holy Infancy Sch, Bethlehem Penn 31-39, St Vincent de Paul Sch, Phila 39-41, St Michael Sch, Phila 41-46, Our Mother of Sorrows Sch, Phila 46-48, St Vincent de Paul Sch, Bayonne NJ 48-52, Visitation Sch, Phila 52-57, Sacred Heart High Sch, Vineland NJ 57-64; Tchr-libn 64-. 9: ALA; CathLA; NJSLA; NCET; NJ Secondary Sch Assn. 14: Catlg, ref. 15: Sacred Heart Convent 414 S Eighth st, Vineland NJ 08360.

LEUNG, SHUET-KEUNG. b Hong Kong China. 5: Gratham Train Col 57-58 Tchrs' Certif; Hong kong Baptist Col 59-63 (For Lang & Lit) BA; UCal (Berkeley) 64-66 (Educ, Libnship) MLS. 6: Chinese, Ger, Japanese. 7: Clk Hong Kong Govt Kowloon Canton Railway 56-57; Tchr Taipo Pub Sch, New Territories Hong Kong 58-59; Primary sch master Sycamore Primary Sch, Kowloon Hong Kong 59-64; Libn II UCal (Santa Barbara) 66-. 14: Acquis, Orientalia, rare bks. 15: 705 Via Miguel, Santa Barbara Ca 93105.

LEUSCHNER, LUCILLE (KLINE). b Beloit Wis 25 S 11. 4: Robert E Leuschner. 5: Beloit Col 29-31 (Eng); UWis 33-34 (Eng) summer Certif of Libnship. 7: Lib asst Beloit Pub Lib Beloit Wis 34-44; Libn P-1 USNavy Hosp Portsmouth Va 44-46; Libn P-1 USNavy Camp Le Jeune NC 46; Libn act chief VA Tomah Wis 47-48; Head Libn Pub Lib Tomah Wis 53-57; Libn II State of Cal Agnews State Hosp San Jose Cal 58, Libn III 58-. 9: ALA-AHIL; MedLA; CalLA (Hosp & Inst Div: v-pres 69, pres 70). 10: PTA; Cal Employees Assn; Assn of Autistic Child. 12: Contrib auth 'Bibliotherapy and Patient Libraries' in "Administration of Activity Therapy Services," ed by Gerald O'Morrow (65). 14: Ref, bibliotherapy, readers guidance. 15: 1970 Minna Way, San Jose Cal 95124.

LEUTHER, SISTER MARY HILARIA SSND. b Wanda Minn 8 S 05. 5: Mt Mary Col (Milwaukee) 40 (Eng) BA; Rosary Col MA of LS. 6: Ger. 7: Libn Loyola High, Mankato Minn 60-64; Prin & libn Notre Dame High, Cresco Iowa 64-68; Libn Emmons Central, Strasburg N Dak 68-. 8: Tchr Lib Ref Courses, Mount Mary Ext Mankato Minn summers 65-67. 12: "A Guide to the Writings of School Sisters of Notre Dame in the United States" (60). 14: Second sch lib as a resource ctr in modular scheduling. 15: Emmons Central High Lib, Strasburg ND 58573.

LEVECK, RUTH DOTTERER (ARNOLD). b Little Rock Ark 3 S 04. 4: Donald Leveck. 5: UIll 21-25 (Eng, Pub Speaking) BA; Okla State summers 40,41 (Creative Writing); UArk 52-54 (Eng, writing) MA; Peabody 60-62 MALS; Hendrix Col 57 (Photography). 6: Fr, Sp. 7: Tchr Fr, Lat Bethany (Ill) High Sch 25-26; Sec Fidelity Savings & Loan, Little Rock Ark 27; Free lance writer 31-; Pub rel dir J H Leveck & Sons 43-58; Creative writing instr even div Little Rock U 58-59; Libn Joe T Robinson High Sch 59-62; Libn Ark Baptist Hosp 62-; Ed Ark League of Nursing "Chart" 62-; Instr Lib Sci even div Little Rock U 63-65. 9: MedLA; ArkLA. 10: Nat League Amer Pen Women; Altrusa Internat; Kappa Delta; Order of Bookfellows; Ark Writers' Conf; Ark Author's & composers Soc; Poets' Round Table of Ark; Zeta Phi Eta. 12: Free-lance writing. 13: Yes. 14: Med lib. 15: 121 Normandy rd, Little Rock Ark 72207.

LEVENE, CAROL ANN (CHILDRESS). b Oklahoma City 27 D 43. 4: David Arthur Levene. 5: Metropolitan Jr Col 62-64 AA; UMo (Kan City) 64-66 (Eng) BA; UKy 66 (LS); UPittsburgh 67-68 MLS. 6: Sp. 7: Catlgr DuquesneU Lib 68-. 9: MoLA. 15: 5541 Hays st, Pittsburgh Pa 15206.

LEVERETTE, CLARKE EDWARD. b Montreal. 4: Dora I Howell. 5: McGill 53-57 BEd, 62-63 BLS. 6: Fr. 7: Tchr montreal 57-62; Libn UWest Ont 63-67, in charge leader serv 67-. 12: "Guide to Government Procurements" (3d ed 68). 13: Yes. 14: Govt documents, microforms, circ. 15: 764 Dalkeith ave, London Ont Canada.

LeVESQUE, ELAINE (MARIE). b St Croix Wis. 5: UMinn 38 BS; CathU 52-53. 6: Fr. 7: Libn Pub Sch, Wis 28-34; Nat Youth Admin, Minneapolis & St Paul 38-43; USDept of State Lib, Wash DC 43-48; Law Libn USDept of Health Educ & Welfare, Wash DC 48-52, Catlgr tech processing 52-62; Catlgr tech processing USDept of Housing & Urban Development 62-. 9: SLA; CathLA; DCLA; DCLaw Lib Soc; Potomac Tech Processing Libns. 10: AAUW. 14: Catlg, rare bks. 15: 1028 Conn ave NW; Wash DC 20036.

LEVESQUE, JULIE-ANNE. b Saint-Honore PQ Can 20 Mr 08. 5: Tchrs Col (Fredericton NB) 25-26 Tchg license; Sacred Heart Col (Bathurst NB) 36-40 (Fr) BA; Syracuse 42-45 BLS. 6: Fr. 7: Elem prin Edmundston Sch Bd, Edmundston NB Can 26-27; Tchr Edmundston Sch Bd, Edmundston NB Can 27-58; Libn Tchrs Col (Fredericton NB) 59-61, Fr tchr 61-66; Dir sch libs Commsn Scolaire Regionale du Golfe, Sept-Iles Que Can 66-67; Libn St Patrick High Sch Commission des Ecoles Catholiques de Que 67-68; Libn Quebec High Sch Protestant Sch Bd of Greater Que 68-. 8: Mem Lord Beaverbrook's Com selecting NB tchrs for overseas scholarships 52-62; Mem Royal Comsn on Sch Fin in NB 53-55 (MacKenzie Report 55). 9: Can Assn Col Libns (chm Award Sel Com for best child bk, French sect 65-66); NBTA (Exec Bd); EdmundstonTA (pres 2 terms). 10: Bus & Profess Women's Assn. 11: Member of Lord Beaverbrook's NB Tchrs United Kingdom tour 51. 14: Catlg, ref. 15: 2590 Plaza st apt 418, Quebec 6 Quebec Can.

LEVIN, WILLIAM HAROLD. b Bentleyville Penn 30 S 26. 5: UPitt 44-49 (Fr, Sp, Secondary Educ) AB, 49-50 (Span, Fr) MLitt, 63-64 MLS. 6: Fr, Sp, Ital. 7: Tchr: Wisner (Neb) High Sch 50-51, springdale (Penn) High Sch 51-53, Prospect Jr High Sch, pittsburgh Penn 53-55, Allerdice High Sch, Pittsburgh Penn, Schenley High Sch, Pittsburgh Penn 62-66; (Priv) USA, Ft Knox Ky 55; Libn Rodf Shalom Temple, Pittsburgh penn 57-59, 67-68; Lecturer Fr & Sp Point Park Col 62-68; Libn, Pittsburgh Penn: Conroy Jr High Sch 66-67, Peabody High Sch 67-. 9: NEA; Penn State EA. 10: Beta Phi Mu; Metropolitan Opera Guild; Amer Fed Tchrs; Pittsburgh Fed Tchrs; Mod lang Assn; Pittsburgh Mod Lang Assn. 13: Yes. 14: High sch libnship, synagogue libnship. 15: 6109 Stanton ave, Pittsburgh Pa 15206.

LEVINE, BERNICE UTAL. b Orange NJ 22 D 28. 4: Bernard S Levine. 5: Douglass Col 47-49 (Speech); Wash State U 49-51 (Psych) BS; NYU 53-60 (Elem Educ) MA; Paterson State Col 64-65 (LS) Certif. 7: Tchr Teaneck Bd of educ, Teaneck NJ 60-64; Libn Teaneck Bd of Educ Ben Franklin Jr High Sch 64-. 9: ALA; NJSchLA; NJEA; TeaneckTA; Bergen Co Sch LA. 10: LWV; Phi Beta Kappa. 13: Yes. 14: Serv to yp. 15: 1651 Irene ct, Teaneck NJ 07666.

LEVINE, ESTHER (SARAH). b Boston 10 N 08. 5: Simmons 30 BS in LS; Columbia 51 MS in LS. 7: Catlg & publicity asst Providence Pub Lib 36-42; Libn Harbor Defenses LI Sound 42-44; Head Libn New Sch for Soc Research, NYC 44-. 9: ALA; SLA; NYLA; NYLib Club. 15: New Sch Lib, 65 Fifth ave, New York NY 10003.

LEVINE, HENRIETTA (FINK). b Brooklyn NY 9 Mr 32. 4: Richard Levine. 5: Brooklyn Col 54 (Eng Lit) BA; Pratt 64 MLS. 6: Ger, Fr. 7: Libn Queens Borough Pub Lib Arverne Br 64-66, Howard Beach Br 67-. 9: ALA. 10: NYLib Club; Beta Phi Mu. 14: Child lib serv, ref. 15: 161-34 96 st, Howard Beach NY 11414.

LEVINER, PEGGY (GREENE) TISDALE. b Deep Gap NC 26 F 34. 4: William Porter Leviner. 5: Gallaudet Col 53-58 (LS) AS & BS; Queens Col (Charlotte NC) 66-68 (Fr). 06: Sp, Fr. 7: Stud asst Gallaudet Col Lib 55-58; Sr lib asst Pub Lib of Charlotte & Mecklenburg Co, Charlotte NC 58-. 9: ALA; NCLA; Mecklenburg (NC) LA. 10: Gallaudet Col Alumni Assn; Nat Assn for Deaf; NC Assn for Deaf; Idlewood Olympic Club; Phi Kappa Zeta. 13: Yes. 14: Catlg, research, revising. 15: 116 Heathwood rd, Charlotte NC 28212.

LEVIS, JOEL E. b Toronto Ont 13 S 44. 5: UToronto 63-67 (Hist) BA; SUNY (Albany) 67-69 MLS. 6: Fr. 7: Ref libn Chalk River Nuclear Labs Atomic Energy of Can Ltd, chalk River Ont 69-. 9: ALA; Inst Profess Libns Ont. 10: Boy Scouts of Can. 12: Chief bk reviewer, "RQ". 13: Yes. 14: Ref, ser. 15: Forest Hall, Deep River Ontario Can.

LEVITON, ALICE J. b Chicago. 5: UIll 35-39 (Hist) BA, 39-40 BS in LS. 6: Ger, Fr. 7: Lib asst Chicago Pub Lib 41-43; Army libn USArmy Spec Serv ETO Ga NC 43-46; Libn Jewish Voc Serv Chicago 47-61; Ref libn Joint Ref Lib PAS, Chicago 61-66; Libn Amer Warehousemen's Assn 66-. 9: SLA (Soc Welfare chm 55-56, Pub Rels chm of Soc Scis Div 63-64); LWV; Chicago Archaeol Soc. 14: Ref, admin. 15: American Warehousemen's Assn, 222 W Adams, Chicago Il 60606.

LEVSTIK, JOSEPH. b Prigorica Yugoslavia 14 S 16. 5: ULjubljana(Yugoslavia) 37-43 (Law) Diploma; West Mich U 62-63 (LS) MA. 6: Slovenian, Serbo-Croatian, Ital, Fr, Sp, Russian, Lat, Portu. 7: Catlgr Harvard Law Sch Lib 63-64; Instr & foreign law libn Law Sch Lib UMinn(Minneapolis) 64-. 9: AALL; MinnALL. 10: Beta Phi Mu. 14: Acquis, catlg, ref. 15: Law Sch Lib Univ of Minn, Minneapolis Mn 55455.

LEVY, BETTY E (EMMERGLICK). b Newark NJ 5 S 17. 4: Arthur L Levy. 5: Hunter Col 35-39 (Econ) AB; Queens Col 57-65 MLS. 7: Soc Stud tchr NYC 59-61; Tchr & libn Woodrow Wilson Voc High Sch, Jamaica NY 61-62; Tchr & libn Francis Lewis High Sch, Flushing NY 62-. 9: NYCLibns Assn. 10: Queens Col LEA. 14: Ref. 15: 6909A, 186 lane, Flushing NY 11365.

LEVY, DOROTHY (GARBOSE). b Gardner Mass 23 Mr 16. 4: S Arthur Levy. 5: Wellesley 34-38 (Hist of Art) BA; Drexel 59-61 MS in LS. 6: Fr, Ger, Hebrew. 7: Catlgr Drexel Lib, Phila 61-63, Head catlg dept 63-66; Catlgr Camden C o Col 67-68; Libn Buten Mus of Wedgwood 61-. 9: ALA; PennLA; Phila Area Tech Serv Libns (pres-elect 65-66). 10: Assoc curator, Buten Mus of Wedgwood. 14: Catlg. 15: Northgate apts 15-L, Camden NJ 08102.

LEVY, EVELYN. b Boston 15 S 09. 5: Radcliffe 26-30 (Eng Lit) AB; Simmons 47 (LS) BS; Johns Hopkins U 68 MA. 07: Child libn, Br libn Boston Pub Lib, Asst coordinator adult serv Enoch Pratt Free Lib, Baltimore 56-65, Supv lib commun action program 65-. 8: Training consul in res proj "Library Materials in Service to the Adult New Reader," UWis Lib Sch ; Mem summer fac Lib Sch: Fla State U, UWis (Madison); Adv Bd res proj UMd Lib Sch. 9: ALA (Council); ASD (Bd; Intell Freedom Com, Program Policy Com); MdLA (pres). 10: Adult Educ Assn ; Md Assn Adult Educ; ACLU; ADA. 13: Yes. 14: Adult serv . 15: Enoch Pratt Free Lib 400 Cathedral st, Baltimore Md 21201.

LEWANDOWSKI, THOMAS. b Hamtramck Mich 31 Mr 39. 4: Margaret Ann Kopacki. 5: Henry Ford Commun Col 57-60 AA; Wayne State 60-62 (Soc Sci) BS in Ed, 63-66 MSLS. 7: Tchr Garden City Schs, Garden City Mich 62-65; Assoc dean Learning Resrces Ctr Oakland Commun Col, Union Lake Mich 65-. 14: Automation, info ret. 15: 3256 Cero dr, Sterling Heights Mi 48659.

LEWIN, ELIZABETH (NEUBURGER). b 13 Ap 32. 4: Martin Lewin. 5: William Smith Col 49-53 (Mod Lang) BA; UMich 54-55 AMLS. 6: Fr, Ger. 7: Ya & ref libn NYC Pub Lib 55-56; Med libn Boswell Park Memorial Inst, Buffalo NY 57-59; Libn Kenmore Pub Lib, Kenmore NY 63-. 14: Ref. 15: 202 Abbington ave, Buffalo NY 14223.

LEWIN, MARTIN. b Kassel Germany 24 Jl 25. 4: Elizabeth Neuburger. 5: Syracuse 46-50 (Lit) AB, 50-51 MSLS. 6: Ger. 7: Ref asst Grosvenor Lib, Buffalo NY 51-54; Buffalo Erie Co Pub Lib, Buffalo NY: Personnel asst 54-55, Br libn 55-56, Br head 56-64, Head of the bk care dept 64-68, Asst deputy dir 68-. 9: ALA (Reg rep Memb Com); NYLA (chm Scholarship & Recr Com 56-57, mem Personnel Admin Com 59-61; Bd Resources & Tech Serv Sect 65-67). 12: Ed, "Buffalo and Erie County Public Library Bulletin." 14: Tech proc, pub rel. 15: 202 Abbington ave, Tonawanda NY 14223.

LEWIS, ALAN DARRELL. b Ottumwa Iowa 25 Mr 35. 4: Leilani L Moore. 5: Iowa StateU 53-54; UIowa 54-55, 67-69 (LS) MA; Parsons Col 61-63 (Educ) BA. 6: Korean. 7: Data processing machine operator John Morrell & Co, Ottumwa Iowa 56-57; Lang specialist USAF, KOrea 57-61; Mgr trainee John Morrell & Co, Ottumwa Iowa 63-67; Consul Prairie Hills Lib Syst, Ottumwa Iowa 67-69; Building consul Iowa State Traveling Lib 69-; Dir Burlington Pub Lib, Burlington Iowa 69-. 9: ALA; IowaLA. 10: Jr C of C. 11: Outstanding Iowa Jaycee 66-67. 14: Admin, lib bldgs. 15: Burlington Pub Lib, Burlington Ia 52601.

LEWIS, BENJAMIN M. b Buffalo NY 8 Ja 20. 4: Lois Maujer. 5: Wesleyan U 37-38; Ohio Wesleyan U 38-41 (Hist) AB; UMich 46-47 (Hist) MA, 48-51 (Hist, LS) AMLS, 56 (LS) PhD. 7: Gen asst & Lib Sci Instr East Ill U 51-55; Libn Hamline U 55-64; Libn Denison U 64-66; Libn Ohio Wesleyan U 66-. 9: Midwest Acad Libns Conf. 12: "Register of Editors, Printers, Publishers of American Magazines, 1741-1810" (57); "Guide to Engravings in American Magazines, 1741-1810" (59); "Introduction to American Magazines, 1800-1810" (61). 15: Denison U Lib, Granville Ohio 43023.

LEWIS, BETTY JANE. b Bridgeport Ohio 14 F 16. 5: Antioch Col 36-41 (Lit) AB; Columbia 41-42 BS in LS. 6: Fr, Ger. 7: Asst Pub Lib, Wheeling WVa 36-43; Asst Pub Lib, Dayton Ohio 39-40; Pub Lib, Cincinnati: Child libn 43-50, Br libn 50-61, Asst ext off 61-63, Asst chief of ext 63-. 9: ALA (Life mem; chm Staff Orgs Round Table 56-57); OhioLA. 10: Women's City Club. 14: Adult serv, ext. 15: 8623 Monroe ave, Cincinnati Oh 45242.

LEWIS, CAROL V. b Cold Spring NY 12 Je 41. 5: SUNY(Geneseo) 59-64 (LS) BS. 06: Sp. 7: Elem libn Fulton & Euclid Elem Schs, Schenectady NY 64; High sch libn Haldane Central Sch, Cold Spring ny 64-; Elem libn Altamont Elem Sch 66-69; Co libn St Basil's Acad, Garrison NY 65-. 9: ALA; NYLA; NY State Tchrs Assn. 10: DAR. 14: Bibliog, research, reading interests. 15: 29 Victor st, Albany NY 12206.

LEWIS, CATHERINE (HENIFORD) MRS. b Richmond Va 24 F 24. 5: Coker Col 40-43 (Eng, Lat) AB; UNC 44-45 (Eng) MA, 46-48 BS in LS. 7: Ref asst UNC 44-48; Instr Lib Sci NW State Col (Natchitoches La) 48-49; Bibliogr LC 49-50; Asst libn Sch of Advanced Internat Stud, Johns Hopkins U 50-51; Bk appraisal spec USDept of State & US Info Agency,

Wash DC 51-54; Libn Coastal Carolina Jr Col 58-60; Head libn Horry Co Mem Lib, Conway SC 60-. 9: ALA; SCLA; SELA. 14: Ref. 15: 1004 Sixth ave, Conway SC 29526.

LEWIS, CHESTER M. b 12 Ja 14. 4: Isabelle J Finch. 5: Columbia 34. 7: "New York Times" Lib, NYC; Asst mgr morgue 41-45, Ed ref lib supv 46-47, Chief libn 47-64; Gen serv mgr New York Times, NYC 64-. 8: Dir Microfilming Corp of Amer, Hawthorne NJ 67-; Chm adv coun Grad Sch Lib Sci CW Post Col 65-; Lectr Pratt Grad Sch Lib Sci 56-58; Visiting lecturer Grad Sch Bus Admin CornellU 59-60; SLA prof consul. 9: SLA (pres 55-56); Nat Microfilm Assn (Fellow); ASIS. 10: Admin Mgt Assn. 11: 1st Recipient Jack K Burness Mem Award, 65. 12: Co-auth "Microrecording - Industrial & Library Applications" (54); "Special Libraries - How to Plan & Equip Them" (64); Ed Bd "American Documentation". 14: Admin, microphotography, info mgt. 15: New York Times, 229 W 43rd st, New York NY 10036.

LEWIS, CLARK (SAMUEL). b Steubenville Ohio 9 Jl 19. 4: Maye Coffee. 5: Miami U 39-41; Baldwin-Wallace Col 46-47 (Hist) AB; Columbia 47-48 BSLS, 48-49 (Hist) MA. 7: Maintenance off Ordnance USAR (Maj) 41-65; Circ asst, UFla 49-53; Asst in sociol Cleveland Pub Lib 53-59; Cuyahoga Co Pub Lib Cleveland: Parma br libn 59-61, Reg supv 65, Br supv 65-66, Asst co libn 66-67, Deputy dir 67-68. 9: ALA; OhioLA (chm Intel Freedom Com 67-68, chm Memb Serv Com 68-69). 10: Friends of the Brunswick Lib (Brunswick Ohio). 12: Ed "SORT Bulletin," (64-66). 14: Ref, admin. 15: 1511 Andrea dr, Brunswick Ohio 44212.

LEWIS, DORIS EILEEN (PRINGLE). b Toronto 20 Jl 11. 4: Marshall E Lewis. 5: UToronto 29-33 (Eng, Hist) BA, 33-34 (LS) Diploma, 62 BLS. 6: Fr, Ger. 7: Gen libn circ UToronto Lib 34-36; Libn Waterloo Col & Waterloo Lutheran Sem 51-57; Lecturer Lib Sci Waterloo Col 49-57; Chief Libn UWaterloo 58-69, Collections development libn 69-. 8: Chm, Adv Jt Coun on Coord of Ont Univ Lib Research Facilities 67; Mem, Spec Subcom on Assessment of Grad and Res Requirements in Univ Libs of Ont 69-; Consul on Brief to Architects, Trent U 66; Consul Trinity Col, UToronto 69; Vis lectr Sch Lib Sci, UToronto fall 69. 9: CanLA-Can Assn Col & Univ Libs (pres 64-65, dir 65-66); ALA; OntLA; Ont Assn Col & Univ Libs; Inst Prof Libns Ont; Ont Coun of Univ Libns (chm 67). 11: LLD, Trent U. 13: Yes. 14: Acquis, bibliog, collections. 15: UWaterloo Lib, Waterloo Ont Canada.

LEWIS, DOROTHY GERALDINE. b Detroit Mich 31 O 38. 5: Siena Hts Col 56-60 (Fine Arts) PhB; UMich 62-65 (LS) MA. 6: Fr, Sp. 7: Lib trainee pub lib, E Detroit Mich 61-62; Libn Detroit News Lib 62-65; Libn Pub Rel Lib General Motors Corp, Detroit 65-. 9: SLA; ASIS. 15: 5758 Lakewood, Detroit Mi 48213.

LEWIS, ELIZABETH (HUGER MATTHEW). b Charleston SC 3 D 16. 5: Purdue 60-65 (Fine Art) BA; ULondon summer 64 (Eng Criticism); Barry I Wales summer 66 Glamoran Art Coun Certif; Cornwall Tech Col 65-66 (Sculpture); Pratt Inst 66-67 MLS. 6: Fr. 07/ statistical draftsman Pan Amer Airways 41-43; QM US Merchant Marine, Miami Fla 43-44; Tchr Miami Art Sch, Miami Fla 49-50; Instr in art IndU Ctr (Kokomo) 50-57; Fine arts libn & art instr USMA 67-. 8: Asst Program Planner, Photohraphy Show, ITV, West Point 69; Juror, Prizewinning Films in Sculpt and Arch, Amer Film Fest 68, 69; Designer, Mural for Loeb Mem Theater, PurdueU 58; V-pres Lewis Wkshop Studios (design firm) Ind & Mich 50-60. 9: ALA; SLA; ASIS; NAEA; Amer Craftsmen's Coun; Amer Inst graphic Arts; Amer Assn Museums; EFLA; Inst of Contemp Art and London Film-Makers Coop (UK); Lafayette Art Assn, Lafayette Ind (Bd Dirs 62-64). 10: Women's Club; Victoria Soc of Amer; Channel 13 NYC. 11: 4 One-Man Shows, Paintings & Sculpt; Regl prizes; 1st Prize & 2nd Prize, Essay and Drama, Purdue Writers Club 61-62. 13: Yes. 14: Automated indexes for computer info ret, art lib, a-v equipment. 15: 167 Main st, Highland Falls NY 10928.

LEWIS, ELIZABETH M(ARCKWORTH). b NYC 25 F 13. 5: UCincinnati 31-35 (Eng) BA; Columbia 37 (LS) BS. 6: Fr. 7: Pub Lib, Cincinnati Child libn 37-47, Br libn 47-59, Head fiction div 59-61, Head wk with schs dept 61-63, Hd br ext serv 63-. 9: ALA; OhioLA. 10: Zonta Internat; AAUW; Women's Rotary Club. 14: Br libs. 15: 310 Bryant ave, Cincinnati Oh 45220.

LEWIS, ELOISE C(MRS). b Iron River Mich 15 D 19. 7: Bkkeeper & cashier Mich Dept of State, Detroit 51-56; Asst libn Ross Roy Inc, Detroit 56-. 9: SLA. 15: Ross Roy Inc 2751 E Jefferson ave, Detroit Mi 48207.

LEWIS, GENEVIEVE (MARY). b Vincennes Ind 28 Ag 11. 5: Northwestern U 29-33 (Eng) BA, 33-35 (Eng) MA; Columbia 37-38 (LS) BS. 7: Ref asst Oak Park Pub Lib, Oak Park Ill 35-37, Ref libn 38-43; WACS in recruiting photo intelligence & co wk Army Air Corps (Capt), US & ETO 43-45; Head ref dept Oak Park Pub Lib, Oak Park Ill 45-50; Instr Eng head of dept Warren Wilson Col 50-61; Ref libn Stetson U 61-. 9: ALA; FlaLA. 10: Friends of the DeLand Pub Lib; Fla Audubon Soc. 14: Ref. 15: 135 W Minnesota apt 10, DeLand Fla 32720.

LEWIS, GEORGE (RUSSEL). b Eupora Miss 15 Jl 29. 4: Bobbie McClain Lewis. 5: Clarke Mem Col 48-50 Certif; Miss Col 50-52 (Eng) BA; LSU 54-56 MSLS. 6: Sp. 7: Eng tchr Forest City Schs, Forest Miss 52-54; Grad asst LSU 54-56; Asst pub servs libn Baylor U 56-57; Catlgr 58; Head circ dept Auburn U 58-62; Head Libn KySoCol 62-63; Dir of Libs Miss State U 63-. 8: Lib Planning Com, Auburn U Lib 60-62; Consul to var libs; Mem Bd of Commsnrs, Miss Lib Commsn. 09: ALA (Recr Netwk Miss 64); -ACRL; MissLA (Recr Com 64-65, chm Legisl Com 68-69, chm Scholarship Com 67-68). 10: Lions Internat; Phi Delta Kappa; C of C. 14: Admin, ref. 15: POBox 723, State College Ms 39762.

LEWIS, GILLIAN (HOLLINGWORTH). b London England 27 Ag 41. 4: Thomas S W Lewis. 5: UNC 58-62 (Eng) BA; McGill 62-63 BLS. 6: Fr. 7: Ref libn & catlgr Westmount Pub Lib, Westmount Que Can 63-64; Libn (staff) NYC Pub Lib 64-65, Asst readers' adv 65-66, Sr libn in off adult serv 66-68; Ref libn Skidmore Col Lib 68-. 14: Ref. 15: 192 Circular st, Saratoga Springs NY 12866.

LEWIS, GRACE S(HELDON). b Yarmouth NS Can 16 Je 1890. 5: Simmons 16 (LS) certif; Queen's U 25 (LS) Certif. 06: Fr. 7: Clerk Western Union Telegraph Co, Yarmouth NS 12; Asst Yarmouth Pub Lib, Yarmouth NS 13-14, Libn 14-20; Libn Dominion Bur of Statistics Ottawa 20-50; Trustee & Chm pr & pub Yarmouth Pub Lib, Yarmouth NS 52-; Organized Libs Cent Sch, Yarmouth NS 68, Vol 68-. 9: CanLA; SLA; OntLA (chm); Ont Reg Group of Catlgrs; Lib Assn Ottawa (chm). 10: Bibliog Soc Can; Soc of Indexers; Yarmouth Art Soc; Yarmouth Co Hist Soc; Kritosophian Club of Yarmouth. 12: Articles on western Nova Scotia counties in "Encyclopedia Canadiana." (57); contrib to "Dictionary of Canadian English" (69). 13: Yes. 14: Catlg, ref, bk sel. 15: 6 Lewis ave, Yarmouth (S) NS Canada.

LEWIS, JEROME T(HEODOLPH). b Boston 17 Mr 22. 5: Colby Col 41-45 (Hist, Govt, Econ) AB; Boston U summer 45 (Econ); Simmon 48-49BS in LS; Harvard summer 55 (Hist). 6: Fr. 7: Harvard U: Reading rm asst Widener Lib 46-49, Gen asst Lamont Lib 49-50, Ref & catlg asst Lamont Lib 50-51, Ref asst Widener Lib 51-54, Circ asst Widener Lib 54-55, Lib asst (Faculty member) Lamont Lib 55-59; Head of processing Newton Free Lib, newton Mass 59-67, Asst libn & Act libn 67-68; Hd libn Bryant & Stratton Jr Col 68-. 15: 47 Parker st, Cambridge Mass 02138.

LEWIS, JOAN. b Salem Ore 31 Mr 44. 5: Pepperdine Col 61-64 (Pol Sci) BA; USoCal 65-66 MS in LS. 7: Ref libn Los Angeles Pub Lib 66-68; Hd ref dept Orange Pub Lib, Orange NJ 68-. 14: Ref. 15: 348 Main st, Orange NJ 07050.

LEWIS, JOHN D JR. b NYC 15 S 27. 4: Billie B Street. 5: UOmaha 59-60 (Mil Sci) BGE; UOkla 66-68 MLS. 6: Sp. 7: Varied US Army (Maj) 46-66; Admin asst Sch of Lib Sci UOkla 67-68; Admin asst Okla State U Lib 68-. 9: ALA; LAD (Com on Statistics for Col & Univ Libs); OklaLA (Com on Lib Automation); Recruitment Committee); SWLA. 10: Beta Phi Mu; Assn of the US Army. 14: Admin, automation. 15: Rte 4 Quail Ridge, Stillwater Ok 74074.

LEWIS JR, G GORDON. b Youngstown Ohio 1 Ja 45. 4: Judith A Yek. 5: CapitalU 63-66 (Eng) BA; UPittsburgh 68-69 MLS. 6: Ger. 7: Off clk USMC Res, Camp Lejeune NC 66-67; Ref libn Youngstown Pub Lib, Youngstown Ohio 67-69; Ya libn Ext Div Free Lib of Phila 69-. 9: ALA. 10: Delta Sigma Rho; Tau Kappa Alpha. 15: Free Lib of Phila YA Div, Philadelphia Pa 19103.

LEWIS, KATHRYN A DIBBENS (MRS). 5: William Woods Col for Girls 32-34 (Eng) AA; UOkla 34-36 BA in LS, 54-58 MA in LS. 6: Fr, Sp. 7: Libn Pub Lib, Seminole Okla 37-39; Libn Houston Sch Dist 46-48; Personnel clerk Shell Oil Co, Houston 44-46; Asst order libn UOkla 51-60; Bibliogr head of order dept SoMethodist U 60-61; Period libn Tex Tech Col 61-. 9: Tex Assn Col Tchrs; TexLA. 10: AAUP. 14: Ser, acquis. 15: Tex Tech Col, Box 4079, Lubbock Tex 79409.

LEWIS, MARY (STUMREITER). b Richmond Ind 6 N 45. 4: Richard E Lewis. 5: Northland Col 63-67 (Eng) BA; UWash 67-68 M Lib. 6: Ger. 7: Libn US Dept of the Interior FWPCA Nat water Quality Lab Lib, Duluth Minn 68-. 9: ALA; SLA; MinnLA; NoShoreLA. 10: PTA; Friends of the Duluth Pub Lib. 14: Catlg, admin of govt. libs. 15: 620 N 57th ave W, Duluth Mn 55807.

LEWIS, MICHAEL HARRY. b Brooklyn NY 2 Je 40. 5: Hofstra 60-63 (Soc Sci) BA; Drexel 65-66 (LS) MA. 6: Sp, Russian. 7: Acquis libn Frostburg State Col 66-67; Acquis libn LIU 67-. 9: ALA; NYLA. 10: Sierra Club; Amer Youth Hostels; NY Ramblers. 14: Acquis. 15: 333 Lafayette ave apt 23A, Brooklyn NY 11238.

LEWIS, MURIEL J. b NS Can 4 Ja 22. 5: Calvin Coolidge Col 40-45 (Eng) AB; Simmons 45-46 (LS) BS. 7: Catlgr MIT 46-. 9: ALA; SLA. 14: Catlg. 15: 52 Windsor st, Arlington Mass 02174.

LEWIS, MYRTIS BISHOP. b Cleburne Tex 13 My 09. 4: Paschal D Lewis. 5: Decatur Baptist Col 25-26 (Span) Certif; Baylor Col 28-29 (Span) BA; UColo summers 29, 30, 36, 37 (Span, Eng); Sul Ross State Tchrs Col summer 38 (LS); UWash summers 57, 62-64 (LS) ML; So Ore Col of Educ summer 60 (LS). 6: Sp, Fr, Ger. 7: Prin Mary's Hill Elem Sch, Joshua Tex 27-28; Tchr Decatur Jr Col 29-30; Tchr Pyote Pub Schs, Pyote Tex 37-38; Libn tchr Forsan Pub Schs, Forsan Tex 38-42; Tchr Vancouver Pub Schs, Vancouver Wash 42-45; Libn Jefferson Co Sch Dist, Madras Ore 45-. 9: NEA; ALA; OreEA; OreSchLA. 10: Study Club; Amer Heritage Assn; Delta Kappa Gamma. 14: Ref, ya, reader serv, dist lib co-ord. 15: PO Box 104, Madras Ore 97741.

LEWIS, ROBERT FRENCH. b Broken Arrow Okla 26 N 18. 05: UOkla 37-42 (Chem) AB, MS; USoCal 48-49 MS in LS. 7: USArmy Air Corps (Capt) 42-46; Catlgr USoCal 49-50, Catlgr Biomed Lib 50-52, Head pub serv div Biomed Lib 52-63, Asst biomed libn Biomed Lib 63-66; Biomed libn Biomed Lib UCal (San Diego) 66-. 09: MedLA (pres So Cal Group 62-63); CalLA; SLA. 10: Sierra Club. 13: Yes. 14: Med lib admin. 15: 7623 Eads ave, La Jolla Ca 92037.

LEWIS, ROBERT W. b Portland Ore 20 S 02. 5: Princeton 20-24 (Hist, Pol) BS; Harvard 24-27 LLB; Columbia 46-47 (LS) BS. 7: Pasadena Pub Lib 47-48; Ref asst Los Angeles Co Law Lib 48-49; Law libn O'Melvent & Myers 49-59; Law lib serv & legal indexing free lance for law firms 60-. 8: Admitted to practice of law in NY, Mass, & Cal. 9: AALL; Amer Bar Assn; State Bar of Cal; Los Angeles Co Bar Assn; Lawyers Club of Los Angeles. 15: 1425 Mission st, S Pasadena Cal 91030.

LEWIS, RONALD A. b Cleveland 5 S 31. 4: Claire (Brown). 5: London Col of Bible & Missions 50-53 (Theol) certif; Wheaton Col 54-56 (Philos) BA; Wheaton Col Grad Sch of Theology 56-60 (Theol) BD; UChicago & Kent State U studies in Grad sch of Lib Sci. 6: Fr, Lat, Gk, Hebrew. 7: Circ mgr Br London Free Press, London Ont 51-54; Bus driver DuPage Motor Coach, Glen Ellyn Ill 56-59; Libn Grad Sch of Theol Wheaton Col (Wheaton Ill) 57-60; Asst libn Divinity Sch UChicago 60-64; Asst libn & catlgr Bexley Hall Divinity Sch Kenyon Col 64-68; Libn for tech serv Colgate Divinity Sch - Bexley Hall 68-; Sec for Bexley Hall Faculty. 8: Lib Construction Com for Bexley Hall. 9: ATheolLA. 10: Pinnacle Investment Club; President, Sambier Coop Nursery Sch. 14: Admin, tech processing. 15: Colgate Rochester Divinity Sch/Bexley Hall, 1100 S Goodman st, Rochester NY 14620.

LEWIS, S(UNIE) MADGE. b Abilene Tex 16 Jl 10. 5: Hardin Simmons U 28-30; UOkla 30-31; Central State Col 32-33 (Chem & Educ) Secondary tchg certif & BS; San Francisco State U part time 53-56; UMich summers 54-56 AMLS; Mary Hardin-Baylor Col part time 61 Art; Tex Woman's U 65 Lib Sci. 7: Child libn Carnegie Pub Lib Guthrie Okla 34; Tchr Kelton Independent Sch Dist Kelton Tex 36-39; Assoc Missionary Haywood Baptist Assn, Waynesville NC 42-45; Assoc Missionary Baptist Gen Conv of NC, Brushy Mt Assn, N Wilkesboro NC 45-48; Act libn Golden Gate Baptist Theol Sem 51-52, Libn 52-56, Supv tech & reader's serv 56-57; NM State Lib Commsn Clovis NM: Asst reg libn East Plain Reg Lib 58, Reg Libn NE Region Cimarron NM 58-60, Act field libn Santa Fe NM 60; Asst libn & instr Mary Hardin-Baylor Col 60-61, Libn & Assoc Prof 61-. 9: ALA; NEA; TexLA; Tex State Tchrs Assn. 10: AAUP; Kappa Pi; Central Tex Dinner Club; UMich Lib Sci Alumni Assn. 14: Catlg, lib hist. 15: PO Box 767, Belton Tx 76513.

LEWIS, SAMUEL F. b Lodi Wis 4 Ag 15. 4: Muriel Jackson. 5: UWis 35-39 (Eng Lit) BA, 39-40 BLS; UMich 46-50 AM LS. 6: Fr. 7: Circ asst Pub Lib, Madison Wis 41; Prof asst Pub Lib, Cleveland 41-45; Div libn UMich Lib (Ann Arbor Mich) 45-62; Sci & bus bibliogr SoIllULib 62-65; Assoc dir Center System Libs UWis (Madison) 65-69, Assoc dir Steenbock Mem Lib Col of Agric & Life Sci 69-. 9: ALA-ACRL (Com on Appointments 66 & Nomin 67); WisLA (Col & Univ Sect: chm Com on Coop). 13: Yes. 14: Acad libs, sci & tech bibliog, lib pub. 15: 4806 Tocora lane, Madison Wis 53711.

LEWIS, STANLEY T. b NYC 14 Ag 26. 4: Rosalie LoGerfo. 5: Washington Sq Col NYU 46-49 (Fine Arts) BA cum laude; Inst of Fine Arts NYU 49-51 (Fine Arts); Ohio State U 51-53 (Fine Arts) MA, PhD; Columbia 57 (LS) MS. 6: Fr, Sp. 7: US Army (Pfc) Infantry Med Dept 44-45; Instr educ div Brooklyn Museum, NY 50-51; Instr Sch of Fine & Applied Art Ohio State U 51-55; Head Libn Dover High Sch, Dover NY 55-56; Lecturer Sch of Lib Serv Columbia U 59-64; Lecturer Queens Col(NY) 65-; Art libn Paul Klapper Lib Queens Col (NY) 56-66; Assoc Prof dept of lib sci Queens Col 67-. 8: Lecturer Columbus Gallery of Fine Arts 51-52; Fellow Brooklyn Col 50-51; Commsn for Relief in Belgium Fellow (participant in Brussels Art Seminar) 51; Consul Bro-Dart Industries (art program) 64; Adv Com of NY publisher, & consul to NY art educ materials mfgr & distributor 65. 9: ALA (past mem Subscript Bks Com); -ACRL (past chm Exec Com of Art Group of Subject Specialists Sect); SLA (past chm NY Picture Group; Memb Chm Picture Div). 10: Chm of Libns Chap, Fed of Col Tchrs, Amer Fed of Tchrs; V-pres United Fed of Col Tchrs. 12: 'Periodicals in the Visual Arts' in "Library Trends," v 10 (Ja 62). 13: Yes. 14: Lib educ, col & univ libnship, spec libs, fine arts, admin. 15: Queens Col Lib, Flushing NY 11367.

LEWIS, SUSAN HATHAWAY. b Pasadena Cal 4 Ja 44. 4: Hartley Vanstone Lewis. 5: Pomona Col 61-65 (Zool) BA; UBC 68-69 BLS. 6: Ger. 7: Libn BC Med Lib Serv, Vancouver BC Can 69-. 8: Registered cytotechnologist CT (ASCP) 01724. 10: Beta Phi Mu. 14: Med ref & catlg. 15: 3149 W 24th ave, Vancouver 8 BC Can.

LEWIS, VIRGINIA E(LNORA). b Sault Ste Marie Ont 7 Ap 07. 5: Wellesley 26-28; UPittsburgh 30-31 AB; Carnegie 32-33 (Lab Press) Certif; UPittsburgh 35 MA; Harvard 37,40. 6: Fr, Ital, Lat. 7: Proofreader Carnegie Inst Press Carnegie Inst of Tech 31-33; UPittsburgh: Lecturer, Instr, Asst Prof, Assoc Prof, Prof Fine Arts Dept, 34-, Instr Eng 44-46, Curator of exhibitions Henry Clay Frick Fine Arts Dept 46-65, Act head of Fine Arts Dept 54, 57-58, Head libn Henry Clay Frick Fine Arts Lib 63-65, Asst dir of Henry Clay Fine Arts Bldg adv to the Henry Clay Frick Fine Arts Lib 65-67, Dir The Frick Art Mus (under construction) 70-. 8: Dir Dennis Art Gallery, Dennis Mass 53; Consul dir Westmoreland Co Mus of Art, Greensburg Penn 54-57; Ohio & Miss River Valley Arts Festival 61. 9: Amer Fed Arts; Natl Trust for Hist Preservation (chm session in Wash DC); Col Art Assn Amer (loc chm 56); Soc of Arch Histns (Bd Dir natl sec, chm Pittsburgh Chap); Amer Assn of Museums (Program chm Natl meeting Pittsburgh); SLA (Mus Dir); Print Coun Amer; Hist Soc West Penn; Pittsburgh Bibliophiles (Program Com & Memb Com); Internat Coun of Museums. 10: Women's Press Club of Pittsburgh; Pittsburgh Symphony Soc; Women's Assn. Pittsburgh Symphony; Monday Luncheon Club; Wellesley Club of Pittsburgh; Pittsburgh Playhouse; Participation Art Juries: Natl Scholastic Art; Zonta Internat; Carnegie Inst Soc; Women's City Club. 11: Woman of the Year 56 Pittsburgh Post-Gazette. 12: "Russell Smith: Romantic Realist" (57); "Andrey Avinoff: The Man," (53); Exhibitions Catlgs: Henry Clay Frick Fine Arts Gallery, Carnegie Inst; Westmoreland Co Mus of Art (40); Contrib: "New Catholic Encyclopedia" "The Printed Book" & "Graphic Arts"; Co-auth "None Can See the Limits of its Reach" (64) - a catalogue descriptive of significant books in the Henry Clay Frick Fine Arts Library, University of Pittsburgh (63-64). 13: Yes. 14: Fine & early printed bk, prints & drawings, Amer Art & arch, catlg, correspondence. 15: 401 S Dallas ave, Pittsburgh Pa 15208.

LEWIS, WILLIAM RICHARD. b Boston 20 Ag 22. 5: UCal (Santa Barbara) 46-47 (Hist); BostonU 48-49 (Hist) AB, 50 (Hist) AM; Simmons MS in LS. 7: Asst hist dept Boston Pub Lib Boston 50-62, Ref libn hist dept 62-65 Off-in-chg reader serv 65-67, curator period & newspaper dept 67-68, research lib spec (to develop Afro-American & African collections) 68-. 9: MassLA. 14: Ref. 15: 65 Morton Village dr, Mattapan Ma 02126.

LEWTON, LUCY OLGA. b Yalta Crimea Russia 23 Je 1900. 5: Barnard 18-22 (Chem) BS; Courtauld Inst of Biochem (England) 30 (Sci Techniques); Columbia 32-34 (Teaching Sci)

MA; Columbia (Abstracting & Bibliog) 30-31; Amer Inst of Metals 35-36 (Metallurgy). 6: Fr, Ger. 7: Abstractor USRubber Co NYC 22-24; Research bacteriologist Fleischmann Yeast Co, NYC 24-26; Research chem libn Pease Labs, NYC 26-32; Head libn Lehn & Fink Inc, Bloomfield NJ 32-35; Head Libn Int Nickel Co NYC NY 35-42; Statiscian & libn Freeport Sulfur Co, NYC 42-45; Research libn & Head Celanese Corp Res Labs, Summit NJ 45-54; Admin asst to med research div Hoffmann-LaRoche, Nutley NJ 54-62; Head tech lit sect Riker Labs Northridge Cal 62-67, Consul 67-. 8: Consul to Arcyrol Corp NY 31-32 & to Standard Brands, Inc; USWar Production Bd Com of Libns to advise on clsf of ordnance Res Documents 42-44; Guest Lecturer, Columbia Sch of Lib Sci 40; Consul on lib policies, Riker Labs, Northrid ge 67-; Holder of 2 US Patents. 9: SLA (chm Sci-Tech Div 47-49; chm &/or mem 4 coms 42-47); ACS (chem Lit Div). 10: AAUW; Barnard Col Club (Los Angeles); Alliance Francaise; Sigma Delta Epsilon. 12: 'Library Bulletins,' chap in "Special Libraries and their Organization," ed by L Jackson. 13: Yes. 14: Ref, tech writing, admin, bibliog, editing, translating. 15: 4900 E Telegraph rd apt 719, Ventura Ca 93003.

LEYTE-VIDAL, CELIA (HERNANDEZ). b Havana Cuba 21 O 20. 4: Jesus Leyte-Vidal. 5: Inst de la Habana 34-38 (Sci) Bachelor; U de la Habana 38-42 (Med) Certif 4 years med studies; Kan State Tchrs College 64-66 (LS) MS. 6: Sp, Ital, Portug, Fr. 7: Prof anatomy & Physiology High Sch, Havana Cuba 52-56; Asst catlgr Kan State Tchrs Col 65-66; Catlgr Duke U Lib 66-67, Subj catlg in sci 66-68, Descr catlg romance lang 66-, Catlgr Mazzoni Col (Hist of Ital Lit) 67-. 9: ALA. 10: Kan State Tchrs Col Alum Assn; Kan State Tchrs Col Endowment Assn; Duke U Lib Staff Assn. 14: Med libnship, rare bks, automation. 15: 2007 House ave, Durham NC 27707.

LEYTE-VIDAL, JESUS. b Santiago de Cuba Cuba 2 S 20. 4: Celia Hernandez. 5: Inst de la Habana 34-38 (Arts) Bachelor; U de la Habana 38-43 (Civil Law) Doctor of Law; Kan State Tchrs Col 64-66 (LS) MS. 6: Sp, Ital, Portug, Fr. 7: Law practice, Havana Cuba 43-61; Asst catlgr Kan State Tchrs Col 65-66; Catlgr Duke U Lib 66-67, Subj catlgr 67-68, Lat Amer bibliog & subj catlgr 68-. 9: ALA; Cuban Bar Assn in Exile. 10: Kan State Tchrs col Alum Assn; Kan State Tchrs Col Endowment Assn; Duke U Kub Staff Assn. 14: Law libnship. 15: 2007 House ave, Durham NC 27707.

LI, MARJORIE (HSU). b Fukien China 27 Jl 42. 4: Peter Li. 5: Nat TaiwanU 60-64 (Eng Lit) BA; UChicago 65-68 (LS) MA. 6: Fr, Chinese. 7: Stud asst UChicago 66-68, Research project asst 67-68, Med info project trainee 67-68; Ser catlgr NorthwesternU 68-. 8: Proj trainee for Sel Dissem of Info 67-68. 9: ALA. 14: Catlg, clsf. 15: 817 Hamlin st, Evanston Il 60201.

LI, ROSE NANA (YUAN). b Szechwan China 10 Ap 41. 4: Gregory S L Li. 5: Taiwan NormalU 58-62 (LS) B Educ; UMich 65-66 MALS. 6: Chinese. 7: Asst libn SoochowU Lib (Taipei Taiwan) 62-64; Wk-study scholar UMich Lib (Ann Arbor) 65-66; Staff libn NY Botanical Garden Lib, Bronx NY 67-. 9: ChineseLA. 14: Catlg. 15: 400 E Mosholu pkwy apt B66, Bronx NY 10458.

LI, SHIH-KUEI. b Hopei China 25 O 14. 4: Rachel Cheng-jung Li. 5: Northwest Tchrs Col(China) 39-44 (Educ) BA; Grad Sch of Journalism (China) 44-55 (Journalism) Diploma; Columbia 47-48 (Educ) MA, 61-65 (LS) MS. 6: Chinese. 7: Ref libn Chinese News Serv, NYC 50-65; Catlgr Gest Lib Princeton U 65-. 13: Yes. 14: Ref & catlg (soc scis), periods, govt docs, newspapers, reg studies. 15: Apt 3, 110 Prospect ave, Princeton NJ 08540.

LI, TZE-CHUNG. b Kiangsu China 17 F 27. 4: Dorothy In-lan Li. 5: SoochowU 44-48 LLB; SoMethodistU 56-57 (Law) LLM; Harvard 57-58 (Law) LLM; New Sch for Soc Research 58-63 (Pol Sci) PhD; Columbia 64-65 (LS) MS. 6: Chinese, Japanese, Fr. 7: V-pres Atlantic Fiscal Corp NYC 62-64; Asst Prof of Lib Sci & Asst libn Ill State U 65-. 9: Amer Soc Internat Law; Amer Assn Pol Sci; Assn Tchrs Chinese Lang & Culture; ALA-ACRL. 11: Taiwan Prov Govt Acad Award 56; Chinese Govt Citation 63. 12: "Treatise on Military Criminal Law," in Chinese (55). 13: Yes. 14: Catlg, ref. 15: Milner Lib Ill State U, Normal Ill 61761.

LIANG, DIANA T (FANG). b Shanghai China 10 Je 38. 4: Joseph Liang. 5: Nat TaiwanU 56-60 (Eng Lit) BA; Peabody Col 62-64 (LS) MA. 7: Acting libn Fairfield Co Dist Lib, Lancaster Ohio 64-66; Asst ed Chem Abstracts Serv, Columbus Ohio 67-. 14: Ref, child wk. 15: Chemical Abstracts Service Ohio State University, Columbus Oh 43210.

LIANZI, THERESA L(OUISE). b Sycamore Ill 23 O 39. 5: No Ill U 57-61 (Hist) BA, 62-65 (Educ) MSE; Fla State U 66-67 (LS) MS. 6: Ger. 7: Tchr; Pub Schs, Leland Ill 63-64, Pub Schs, Sandwich Ill 64-65, Carson City-Crystal Area Schs, Carson City Mich 65-66; Libn asst Fla Keys Jr Col 67-. 9: FlaLA; SELA. 10: Waterfront Playhouse. 14: Ref. 15: 2417 Staples ave, Key West Fl 33040.

LIAO, JANE CHEN-HSING. b Taiwan Free China 1 Jl 36. 5: Nat Taiwan U 55-59 (Law) BA; Tex Woman's U 62-64 MLS. 6: Chinese, Japanese, Sp, Ger, Fr. 7: Tchr Chin-ling Girls' Middle Sch, Taipei Taiwan 59-62; Catlg libn simpson Col Lib 64-. 9: ALA; IowaLA. 10: AAUW; Simpsonia; Simpson Guild; Des Moines Civic Music Assn; Alpha Mu Gamma. 14: Catlg, ref. 15: 113 E Salem ave, Indianola Iowa 50125.

LIBBEY, DAVID CARLETON. b Detroit Me 29 Ag 16. 5: Colby Col 35-39 (Hist) AB; Columbia 39-40 BS in LS; Chicago 46-47 (LS) MA; Columbia 51-54 (Amer Hist) MA; Rutgers 63-64 (LS). 6: Fr. 7: Asst libn Washington Col (Chestertown Md) 40-42; Ref asst NY Pub Lib 42-43; Cryptographer US Army Air Forces, Europe 43-46; Chief ref dept Wash State U 47-51; Head ref Newark Colleges Lib Rutgers U 54-63; Asst Prof Div of Lib Sci SoConn State Col 64-. 9: ALA; BSA; Amer Assn State Loc Hist; ConnLA. 14: Ref, bibliog, lib hist. 15: So Conn State Col, New Haven Conn 06515.

LIBBEY, F(LORENCE) ELIZABETH. b Augusta Me 8 Je 06. 5: Colby Col 25-29 (Latin-Eng) AB; Columbia 30 BS in ls, columbia 66 MS in LS; Alliance Francaise (Paris) 68. 6: Fr. 07: City Park Br Brooklyn Pub Lib summer 30; Dir Bur of Lib Ext State Lib, Augusta Me 30-42; Libn State Tchrs Col (Farmington Me) 42-45; Colby Col: Ref Libn (Instr 47-49) 45-47, Asst Libn (Asst Prof 49-56) 47-51, Act Libn 51-54, Assoc Libn (Assoc Prof) 56-. 8: Asst Dir Sch Lib Workshop UMe, Orono Me summer 50; Taught Bibliography Colby Col 47-57; Reference Lib Sci Wkshop Colby Col summers 61-64. 9: ALA (Coun 50-54); -ACRL (state rep 59-62); MeLA (pres 33-35, chm Certific 58-59; chm Exh 50-51); Me Sch Lib assn; NECol Libns; NELA (sec 59, Bibliog Com 63-67). 10: Columbia Sch of Lib Serv Alum Assn; Delta Kappa Gamma; AAUW; AAUP; Larger Libs of Me; Colby Lib Assoc (sec 51-54; Colby Alumni Assn. 12: Me State Lib, Biennial reports, Bur of Lib Ext (30-42); Ed Nov issues "Me Lib Assn Bulletin" (50-53). 13: Yes. 14: Col & Univ lib admin, ref, & spec libs, adult educ, research. 15: 45 Winter st, Waterville Me 04901.

LIBBEY, MIRIAM (HAWKINS). b Ga. 4: Frederick Libbey. 5: Shorter Col 38-42 BA; Emory 49-50 MA. 6: Sp. 7: Ref libn, Hd serv to Pub A W Calhoun Med Lib Emory U 50-55; Ref libn, Hd spec projects sect, Hd subject analysis sect, Hd subject analysis sect, Asst hd ref Nat Lib of Med, Bethesda Md 55-63; Libn Health Sce Lib SUNY (Buffalo) 63-66; Libn A W Calhoun Med Lib Emory U 66-. 8: Instr Med Libnship, Div of Libnship, Emory U 66-. 9: SLA (S Atlantic Chap, Projects Com 67-); ASIS; MedLA (Internship Com 67-; Instr Contin Educ Courses in Ref 65-). 12: Co-ed "Proceedings of the Second International Congress on Medical Librarianship" (63). 13: Yes. 14: Ref. 15: A W Calhoun Med Lib Woodruff Research bldg Emory Univ, Atlanta Ga 30322.

LIBBY, EDITH M(ARGARET). b Auburndale Mass 21 O 14. 5: Central Methodist Col (Mo) 32-36 (Eng) AB; UWis 36-37 (LS) Certif; UMich summers 45-47 AMLS. 7: Asst Ind State Tchrs Col (Terre Haute) 37-38, Order asst 38-42, Catlgr 42-47; Head of order dept Smith Col Lib 48-. 9: ALA-ACRL; MassLA. 10: AAUW; Appalachian Mountain Club; Amherst Camera Club. 15: 26 Bedford terrace, Northampton Mass 01060.

LIBBY, MARGARET SHERWOOD. b Fairfield Conn 4 O 1898. 5: Smith 15-19 (Eng) BA; Columbia 22-23 (Hist) MA, -36 (Hist thought & Culture) PhD, (LS) MA. 6: Fr, Ger, Ital, Lat. 7: Hist tchr Spence Sch NYC 20-34; Supv libs in Norwich Elem Schs, Norwich Conn 48-. 9: NEA; ALA; ConnEA; ConnLA. 10: Phi Beta Kappa; Delta Kappa Gamma. 12: 'Book Week' in "NYHerald Tribune" (56-66); "The Attitude of Voltaire to Magic and the Sciences." 14: Child & yp bks. 15: Coit lane, Norwich Ct 06360.

LIBBY, RALPH STEVEN. b Los Angeles 7 Mr 24. 4: Jean Titus. 5: UCal 42, 46-50 (Hist, Anthropology, Mus) AB; IndU 58-59 (LS) MA. 6: Ger, Fr. 7: Message center chief USArmy, US Europe 43-46; Org & methods examiner Navy dept, Wash DC 51-54; Asst to libn "Washington Post," Wash DC 55-56; Asst engnrg libn, Head of tech info serv, soc sci libn, map libn, & pol sci libn, Stanford U Libs 59-67; Br libn & Ref libn Palo Alto City Lib 67-. 9: MusLA; CalLA. 13: Yes. 14: Ref, soc scis libs, music libs. 15: 1222 Fulton st, Palo Alto Ca 94301.

LIBEL, MARIE A (SNOOKS). b St Joseph Mo 25 S 08. 5: Maryville Col (St Louis) 28-31 (Fr) BA; UWis 58-59 (LS) MA. 6: Fr. 7: Asst in circ Pub Lib St Joseph Mo 50-58; Asst br libn Detroit Pub Lib 59-63; Catlgr Pub Lib, St Joseph Mo 63-68; Libn in charge of tech resources Mo West Col, St Joseph Mo 68-. 09: ALA; MoLA. 14: Catlg. 15: 2710 Sacramento st, St Joseph Mo 64507.

LIBERSKY, FRANK. b Velky Osek, Czechoslovakia 13 Ap 17. 4: Barbara J Souter. 5: UPrague 38, 45-47 (Animal Husbandry) BS; UZurich 50-51 (Zootechnics); UIda 53-56 (Dairy Husbandry) BS; UIll 56-59 (LS) MS. 6: Czech, Ger, Polish, Slovak. 7: Asst mgr Agric Experiment Station Prague Czechoslovakia 47-48; Lab tech UZurich 0-51; Lab tech UIda 53-56; Lab tech USDA Research Serv, Urbana Ill 56-59; Catlg libn NLM 59-61, Acquis libn 61-. 9: MedLA; DCLA; Potomac Tech Processing Libns. 10: AAAS; Fed Profes Assn; Czechoslovak Soc of Arts & Sci in Amer; Coun of Higher Educ (Chicago); Alpha Zeta. 14: Acquis, bibliog, data processing. 15: 3950 Langley ct NW, Wash DC 20016.

LIBERTY, JOHN JOSEPH. b Sacramento Cal 14 D 27. 4: Irma E Madsen. 5: Grant Tech Col 48-50 (Eng) AA; Sacramento State Col 50-53 (Soc Sci) BA; UDenver 62-63 (LS) MA. 7: Staff member Levinson's Bk Store, Sacramento Cal 46-52; Sr law lib clerk Cal State Lib 53-62; Asst acquis libn Sacramento State Col Lib 63-65, Asst soc sci libn 65-. 9: CalLA (Col Univ Research Libs Sect, State Coll Libns Div). 14: Soc sci, ref. 15: 5231 Carrington st, Sacramento Ca 95819.

LiBRIZZI, ROSE MARIE (MEOLA). b Newark NJ 15 Ap 40. 4: Vincent LiBrizzi. 5: Newark State Col 58-59 (Elem Educ); Bloomfield Col 63-65 (Soc Sci) BA, Tchg certif; Rutgers 65-67 MLS, Certif. 6: Lat, Fr, Ital. 7: Libn trainee Newark Pub Lib, Newark NJ 65-66; Hd child serv Belleville Pub Lib, Belleville NJ 66-69; Asst dir Kearny Pub Lib, Kearny NJ 69-; Dir Matawan Jt Free Pub Lib, Matawan NJ 69-. 9: ALA; NJLA (Recr Com, Regist Com). 10: AAUW; Essex Co Women's Club; Phi Alpha Theta; Bloomfield Col Alum Assn; Rutgers U Alu Assn. 13: Yes. 14: Catlg, ref, child serv, tech serv. 15: Free Pub Lib, Matawan NJ 07747.

LICHTENWANGER, WILLIAM (JOHN). b Asheville NC 28 F 15. 4: Carolyn Creson. 5: UTenn 33-34; UMich 34-37 (Pub Sch Music) BM, 37-38, 40 (Musicology) MM; Ind U 43-44 (Army) (Balkan, Turkish) ASTP Diploma; Georgetown 44 (Army) (Japanese). 6: Turkish, Ger, Fr, Russian. 7: Head Music Lib UMich 37-40; Asst ref libn Music Div LC 40-41; Army of the US Infantry & Signal Corps (Intelligence) Tech Sgt 41-45; Asst ref libn & asst head Ref Sect Music Div LC 45-61, head Ref Sect Music Div 61-. 8: Music ed "Collier's Encyclopedia" 46-51; Musical adv & ed to ACLS Russian Translation Proj 48-50. 9: Amer Musicological Soc (Exec Bd, Coun; Chap head; chm of coms etc); MusLA (Exec bd, Coun; chm of coms etc); Soc for Ethnomusicology. 12: Assoc ed & ed "Notes," MusLA (46-64); Ed & contrib to v 3, pt 2 "Church Music & Musical Life in Pennsylvania in the 18th Century" (47). 13: Yes. 14: Ref, admin. 15: 7510 Gateway blvd SE, Wash DC 20028.

LICHTMAN, ELLEN HEIT. b Brooklyn NY 18 Je 43. 4: Louis Jack Heit. 5: Brooklyn Col 61-65 (Pol Sci) BA; Pratt Inst 65-66 MLS; UMe 67- (Pol Sci). 7: Adult serv libn brooklyn Pub Lib, Brooklyn NY 66; Acquis libn UMe Lib (Orono) 67, Ref libn 67-. 9: MeLA. 10: Beta Phi Mu. 12: Ed "Raymond H Fogler Library, University of Maine Orono: A Guide to Resources and Services" (68). 14: Soc sci, ref, African affairs. 15: 23-A University pk, Orono Me 04473.

LIDDELL, LEON M. b Gainesville Tex 21 Jl 14. 5: UTex 33-37 (Pol Sci) BA, 37 LLB; Chicago 46 BLS; Columbia 48 (Pol Sci). 6: Fr, Sp. 7: Claims rep Hartford Accident & Indemnity Co, Houston 37-38; Priv practice of law, Gainesville Tex 38; Claims rep Pacific Mutual Life Insurance Co, Kan City Mo 39-41; 2nd Lt to Maj Army of US 41-46; Asst dir Conn Lib Survey, Hartford Conn 46; Asst Prof of law & Law Libn UConn 46-47; UMinn: Asst Prof of law & Law Libn 49-50, Assoc Prof of law & Law Libn 50-54, Prof of law & Law Libn 54-60; Law Libn & Prof of Law UChicago 60-. 9: AALL; SLA; AmerBarAssn; Tex State Bar. 12: "Connecticut Library survey," with E Wight (48). 13: Yes. 15: Univ of Chicago Law Lib, 1121 E 60th st, Chicago Il 60637.

LIDDLE, ERNEST VICTOR. b Enniskillen N Ireland 10 Je 23. 4: Grace Edith Macmurchy. 5: Edinburgh U 47-51 (Hist) BA; Asbury Theol Sem 51-52 BD, 53-54 (Church Hist) ThM; No Baptist Theol Sem 54-56 (Church Hist) ThD; Bucknell U 59-60 (Hist) MA; Drexel 64-66 (LS) MS. 7: (Sgt) Code & Cypher Duties Royal AF, Europe 41-46; Clerical off British Civil Serv Enniskillen 46-47; Pastor Methodist Church, Clarissa Minn 52-53; Asst ed "Watchman-Examiner," NYC 57-58; Pastor Baptist Church, Blanchard Penn 58-60; Asst Prof Grand Rapids Baptist Col & Sem 60-63; Asst Prof East Baptist Col & Sem 63-65; Libn Undergrad Lib UPenn 65-66; Hd libn, Prof Seattle Pac Col 66-69; Acquis libn & bibliogr Western Ill Univ, Macomb. 9: ALA. 10: Amer Soc Church Hist; Evang Theol Soc. 13: Yes. 14: Admin. 15: 202 NW 201st st, Seattle Wa 98177.

LIEB, ARTHUR JOSEPH. b Detroit 27 Ja 38. 4: Jean Baughman. 5: Wayne State U 56-60 (Music Theory) BM; UMich 63-64 MALS. 6: Fr. 7: LC: E European exch spec Exch & Gift Div LC summer 64, Outstanding Lib Sch Grad Program 6 month orientation/train program 64-65, Info systems research asst Info Systems Spec Off 65, Documents catlgr Eng Lang Sect Descr Catlg Div 65-, Admin off Processing Dept 65-66, Exec asst processing dept 66, Hd sheld listing sect subj catlg div 66-. 9: ALA; DCLA; Potomac Tech Proc Libns (treas 68-71). 11: LC Recr Prog 64. 13: Yes. 14: Tech proc, automatic data proc. 15: 3208 Woodbine st, Chevy Chase Md 20015.

LIEB, JEAN B. b Roseville Mich 23 Mr 40. 4: Arthur Joseph Lieb. 5: Alma Col 57-58; UMich 58-61 (Eng, Educ) BA Ed, 63-64 MLS. 6: Fr. 7: Asst child libn Oak Park Pub Lib, Oak Park Mich 61-62; Tchr Redford union Schs, Detroit 62-63; Libn Prince George's Co Schs, Hyattsville Md 64-. 9: ALA; MdLA; DCLA. 13: Yes. 14: Juvenile lit. 15: 3208 Woodbine st, Chevy Chase Md 20015.

LIEBENBERG, IRENE (RUTH). b Denver Colo 24 N 41. 5: UCal (Riverside) 59-63 (Mus) BA; UCal (Berkeley) 63-64 MLS. 7: Catlgr & mus libn UCal (Riverside) 64-67; Ref libn Riverside Pub Lib, Riverside Cal 67-. 9: CalLA. 14: Ref. 15: 3138 Panorama rd, Riverside Ca 92506.

LIEBENOW, WALTHER M. b Racine Wis 18 Ap 22. 4: Elvera Hornung. 5: Biarritz Amer U 45 (Educ); Concordia Tchrs Col 47 (Educ) BS; Chicago Mus Col 50 (Mus) Mus M; Immaculate Heart Col 59 (LS) MA. 6: Ger, Fr, Sp. 7: Ger interpreter (T/3) 1st Allied Airborne Command, Europe 44-46; Choirmaster Lutheran Ch, Kankakee Ill 50-51; Organist & choirmaster St Philip Lutheran, Chicago 52-55; Clk LA Pub Lib 56; Sr bus admin clk, prin acquis clk, libn I, II, & III UCLA 56-66; Chief circ libn UMinn (Minneapolis) 67-. 9: ALA; MinnLA. 13: Yes. 14: Circ pub serv. 15: Wilson Lib Univ of Minn, Minneapolis Mn 55455.

LIEBER, WINIFRED MARGARET. b NYC 11 F 19. 5: NYU 36-40 (Eng) BA; Simmons 4950 MLS; Columbia summer 50 (Med Lit); MLA Certif 53. 7: Meteorologist's asst East Airlines LaGuardia Field 42-43; Info clerk PennRR, NYC 43-45; Travel clerk Nat Travelers Aid Assn & Nat Bd-YWCA 46; Lib asst Tchrs Col Columbia U 47-48; Hosp libn Hines VA Hosp, Hines Ill 50-51; Ref libn Westport (Conn) Pub Lib 51-52; Asst libn NYU Col Dentistry 52-53; Med libn Meadowbrook Hosp, Hempstead NY 53-57; Ref dept NYAcad Med, NYC 57-58; Med libn USNaval Hosp St Albans NY 58-59; Libn Dept Med Seton Hall Col of Med Jersey City NJ 60-62; Med libn Roosevelt Hosp NYC 62-. 8: Consul Shell Surgical Group, Freeport NY 56; Consul Med Economics Inc 59-60. 9: MedLA; SLA. 10: Phi Beta Kappa. 14: Med libs, ref. 15: 435 W 57 st, New York NY 10019.

LIEBERMAN, IRVING. b Newark NJ 6 Ja 14. 4: Lillian Kasner. 5: NYU 35 (Accounting) BS; Columbia 39 BS (LS), 50 (Adult Educ) MA, 55 (Educ, Admin) EdD. 6: Fr, Ger. 7: Lib asst Pub Lib, Newark NJ 35-38; Br lib wk Pub Lib, Detroit 39-41; Lib off (USArmy) European Theatre of Operations (Maj) 42-46; Head ext div Mich State Lib 46-48; Consul position State Prison of SoMich, Jackson Mich 48; Consul position ALA 59; Spec asst supt of central serv exec asst Pub Lib, Brooklyn NY 49-52; Research assoc in chg A-V Proj UCal (Berkeley) 52-54; Assoc in Lib Serv Columbia U Sch of Lib Serv 54-56; Dir & Prof U Wash Sch of Libnship 56-. 8: Chm Gen Policy & Exec Coms, PNLA Lib Dev Proj 56-60; Prin Investigator, Contract between the U Wash & USOff Educ on Recruitment & Training of Staff & Support of Staff Dissemination Activities at Library 21 Exhibit, Seattle World's Fair 62; Adv dir Inst of Libnship U of Ibadan Ibadan Nigeria 63-64; Surveyor Pub Lib City of Lagos Nigeria 63-64; Co-dir NDEA Inst for Sch Libns: "The Sch Lib Supv in the Modern Educ Program," contract between the UWash & USOff Educ summer 65; Mem, Survey Team for Army Lib Prog, Hdq US Army, Europe 64; Dir & lectr at two one-week wkshops for Army and AF Libns, Hdq US Army, Europe, Aug 64; Dir, Conf on Educ for Health Scis Libnship Sept 67 (PHS Grant); Dir & lectr at one-week skshop for Army, AF and Navy

Libns, Hdq US Army Pacific, Mar 68; Dir, Title II-B HEA Inst: "Lib Exec Develop Prog" Grant to UWash by US Off of Educ, Ap 69. 9: ALA (past mem Bd Dirs, past chm &/or mem 4 sects or coms); PNLA (past pres); Wash State Bd for Certif of Libns; Wash State Lib Commsn. 10: Anti-Defamation League; Boy Scouts of Amer; Col US Army Res (Ready); Life mem PTA (Seattle). 11: Three USArmy citations. 12: "Audio-Visual Instruction in Library Education" (55); "Survey of the Lagos City Library" (Lagos Nigeria 64); Ed "Proceedings of an Invitational Conference on Education for Health Sciences Librarianship" (68). 13: Yes. 14: Lib educ, lib devel, lib adult educ, lib a-v materials & serv. 15: Sch of Libnship U Wash, Seattle Wa 98105.

LIEBERT, HERMAN WARDWELL. b NYC 24 Mr 11. 4: Laura Brace Pierson. 5: Yale Col 29-33 (Eng) BA (cum laude). 6: Gk, Lat, Ital, Fr. 7: Reporter & columnist & ed Block Newspapers, NYC 33-41; Sr econ ed act chief Econ Div Research & Analysis Br OSS, Wash DC 42-45; Research asst Yale U Lib 48-51, Asst to libn 51-58, Curator rare bk rm 58-63, Libn Beinecke Rare Bk & MS Lib 63-; Act libn Conn Acad Arts & Scis 68-. 08: Sec Drafting subcom Pres com on Foreign Aid 47; Ed Com Yale Ed of boswell Papers 48; Chm Yale Ed wks of Johnson 50-; Adv Com Yale; Ed of Walpoles Correspondence 63-. 9: Bibl Soc Amer (pres 64-66); Com on BAL 69-. 10: Grolier Club. 12: "Authors at Work" (57) "Esto Perpetua" (63). 13: Yes. 14: Rare bks & mss. 15: Box 1630A Yale sta, New Haven Ct 06520.

LIEBMAN, ROY (SETH). b Brooklyn NY. 4: Judith Port. 5: Brooklyn Col 54-58 (Eng) AB; Pratt 58-61 MLS. 6: Fr. 7: Libn Brooklyn Pub Lib 58-60; Clerk-typist USArmy (Spec 4th class) 59-60; Sch libn ASSomers Jr High Sch, Brooklyn NY 60-61; Ref libn hist div NYPub Lib summer 61; Catlgr Arcadia Pub Lib, Arcadia Cal 61-62; Head ref dept Buena Park Dist Lib, Buena Park Cal 62-64; Head acquis Cal Inst of Tech 64-69; Chief acquis serv Cal State Col (Los Angeles) 69-. 9: CalLA. 14: Acquis, catlg. 15: 165 N Michigan ave, Pasadena Ca 91106.

LIEDBERG, MARIE ANN (CASIANA). b Freeport Ill 26 Je 41. 4: Donald Liedberg. 5: UIll (Champaign) 65 (Fr) BA; Rutgers (New Brunswick) 68 MLS. 6: Fr. 7: Gift & exchange clk UIll Lib (Urbana) 62-64; Catlg clk Allentown Pub Lib, Allentown Penn 65; Docs libn Kutztown State Col 68-. 9: ALA; PennLA. 14: Tech serv. 15: Mountain Park rd, Allentown Pa 18103.

LIEFELD, WALTER LINK. b Hackensack NJ 2 My 35. 4: Judith Brown. 5: Yale 54-57 (Psych); U Del 58-60 (Psych) BA; Rutgers 61-64 MLS; U Penn (NDEA Inst in Educl Media) 68. 07: Act libn St Andrews Sch, Middletown Del 53-54; Attendant Del State Hosp, Farnhurst Del 57-59; Operations sgt 404th Civil Affairs Co (USAR), Trenton NJ 60-63; Libn Lawrenceville- Rutgers summer session Lawrenceville NJ 65-67, 69-; Libn Pennington Sch, Pennington NJ 60-. 9: ALA-AASchL-YASD; NJLA; NJSchLA (Exec Bd 69-); NJIndependent Sch Tchrs Assn. 10: Deputy Dir of Civil Defense for Shelters (Pennington NJ); Pennington Fire Comp; Amer Assn of Sex Educrs & Counsrs. 14: Sch libnship. 15: Pennington Sch, Pennington NJ 08534.

LIESENER, JAMES WILL. b Cedarburg Wis 29 Ap 33. 4: Edith M Baderschneider. 5: Wartburg Col 51-55 (Educ, Psych) BA; Wartburg Theol Sem 55-56 (Theol Studies); State Col of Iowa 56-57 (LS) Guidance) Certif K-12, 58-60 (Guidance) MA; UMich 61-62 AMLS, 62-64, 64-67 (LS) PhD. 06: Ger, Fr. 7: Libn & guidance dir Manchester (Iowa) High Sch 58-61; Libn & supv tchr Lincoln Consolidated Lab Schs East Mich U 61-62; Visiting Lecturer EastMichU 64; Chief position analyst UMich Lib System (Ann Arbor Mich) 64-65; Instr Lib Sci Dept UMich (Ann Arbor) 65-67; Lecturer & Chm lib sci dept in Col of Educ Sch of Lib & Info Serv UMd 67-68, Assoc Prof 68-. 8: Consul, Ind Lib Studies Proj 69; Dir, Inst on Middle Mgt in Libnship, UMd Je 69; Md State Com on Sch & Pub Lib Relationship 69-; Md Adv Coun on Interlib Coop 68-. 9: ALA;-AASchL;-LAD (Lib Organiz & Mgt Sect: Statist Com for Sch Libs 68-70);-LED (Info Sci & Automation Div: Jt Com on Educ, Subcom Curr Devel 69-); ASIS; AALS (Com on Curr & Instr 66-71); NEA-DAVI; Amer Educl Res Assn; Assn Sch L Md; MdStateTA. 10: Phi Delta Kappa; Phi Kappa Phi; Beta Phi Mu; AAUP. 12: "An Empirical Test of the Core Concept in the Preparation of University Librarians" (67). 14: Admin, info systems & educl environments, sch libs. 15: 1125 Norman pl apt 5, Ann Arbor Mi 48103.

LIESINGER, PATRICIA JANE. b Buffalo NY 17 My 44. 5: SUNY (Buffalo) 61-66 (Sociol) BA; SUNY 66-67 MLS. 6: Ger, Sp. 7: Asst libn SUNY (Buffalo) Lockwood Mem Lib 67-. 9: ALA. 14: Ref, automation of libs. 15: 484 Norwood ave, Buffalo NY 14222.

LIETMAN, MARGARET (CAROLINE). b Pittsburgh Penn 5 O 16. 5: Monmouth Col 33-34, 35-38 (Eng) BA; Carnegie Lib Sch 39 BS in LS. 7: Inspector Joseph Horne Co, Pittsburgh Penn 34-35; Vacation libn Mercy Hosp Staff Lib, Pittsburgh Penn 39, Libn 44-48; Pittsburgh Acad of Med Lib 39; Asst libn Med & Dental Libs UPittsburgh 40-42, Catlg asst Applied Soc Sci Lib 42-44, Acquis asst 54-54; Asst catlgr E Car Col 49-52; Libn Sch of Nursing Ref Libn Columbia Hosp, Pittsburgh Penn 55-. 9: MedLA; ALA; -ACRL; Tri-State ACRL; PennLA; Pittsburgh Reg Med Gp (past treas). 10: YWCA. 14: Ref. 15: 717 Wallace ave, pittsburgh Pa 15221.

LIETZ, RICHARD J. b Bristol Conn 12 Mr 30. 5: UFla 48-50 (Liberal Arts; St Petersburg Jr Col 52-53 (Liberal Arts) AA; Oglethorpe U 53-54 (Liberal Arts) AB; Emory 54-56 (Educ); Fla State U 57-58, 62-63 (LS) MS. 7: Eng instr St Martins Sch; Metairie La 56-57; Eng instr Seminole High Sch, Sanford Fla 59-60; Eng instr Ceres High Sch, Ceres Cal 60-61; Eng instr Tustin High Sch Tustin Cal 61-62; Ref libn bus admin & soc sci div, UNC Lib (Chapel Hill) 63-66; Col libn St Andrews Presbyterian Col (Laurinburg NC) 66-. 8: Team-tchg experiment, Ceres High Sch (participated in 60-61); Consul to: Duke U 66, Regl Educl Lab for the Carolinas & Va 68; Pembroke State Col 68, "Random House Dictionary of the English Language" (66). 9: ALA; BSA; Archaeol Inst Amer; Amer Studies Assn; SELA; NCLA. 10: Phi Delta Kappa; AAUP; Kiwanis; Toastmasters. 11: Smith Fund Res Award, UNC 65. 13: Yes. 14: Admin, lib systems, bibliog, lib environment & culture. 15: PO Box 1837, Laurinburg NC 28352.

LIFSEY, JUDITH LOVE. b Jackson Tenn 6 Mr 46. 4: David Burke Lifsey. 5: Lambuth Col 64-67 (Eng) BA; Peabody Col 67-68 MLS. 6: Fr. 7: Catlg libn Joint Univ Libs, Nashville 68-. 14: Catlg. 15: 914 Winthorne dr apt D-13, Nashville Tn 37217.

LIGGETT, SUZANNE L. b Syracuse NY 28 F 39. 4: Malcolm H Liggett. 5: Harpur Col 57-61 (Econ) AB; Cornell U 61-63 (Econ); UCLA 66-67 MLS. 6: Portu, Sp. 7: Lib asst III UCal 9santa Barbara) Lib 64-66; Catlgr Standard Oil Co of Cal Lib, San Francisco 67-. 9: ALA; CalLA. 14: Catlg. 15: 1813 Union st, San Francisco Ca 94123.

LIGHTBOURN, REV FRANCIS C(HESEBROUGH). b Warwick Bermuda 15 Ap 08. 4: Marion Griffith. 5: Hobart Col 26-30 (Philos); Gen Theol Sem 30-33 STB; Seabury-West Theol Sem 57-59 STM; Rosary Col 63-66 MALS. 06: Lat, Gk, Fr, Ger. 7: Tutor Seabury-West Theol Sem 33-34; Parish ministry Episcopal Church, various 34-49; Living Church, Milwaukee Wis: Managing ed 49-52, Literary ed 50-62, Asst ed 52-57; Libn Seabury-West Theol Sem 62-64; Libn U Club of Chicago 64-. 8: Examining Chaplain Diocese of Lexington 42-& Me 45-49. 10: ATheolLA; AAUP. 11: Translation awards, Christian Res Found 61, 63, 67. 13: Yes. 14: Ref, rare bks, areas where theol & libnship meet. 15: 1436 Forest ave, Wilmette Ill 60091.

LIGHTFOOT, EVELYN LAMPREY (LYONS). b Haverhill Mass 25 My 10. 4: Robert M Lightfoot Jr. 5: WVa Wesleyan Col 28-31 (Lat) BA; UVa 31-32 (Hist); Emmanuel Col 34 (Lat); Marywood Col 38-39 (LS) ; Syracuse 44 BS in LS. 7: Lib asst Keystone Jr Col 37-39; Lib asst Raleigh (NC) Pub Lib 42-43; Asst libn Montgomery Co Lib, Montgomery Ala 52-55; Asst ref libn Bradley U 55-69, Act ref libn 69-. 9: IllLA; IllValleyLA. 14: Ref. 15: 1109 N Maplewood ave, Peoria Il 61606.

LIGHTFOOT, ROBERT MITCHELL JR. b Fayetteville NC 23 Ja 10. 4: Evelyn Lyons. 5: Wake Forest Col 27-29; NC State Col 31 (Eng, Hist) BS; UVa 32 (Sociol) MS; Syracuse 40 BS in LS. 7: Prof of soc sci Spartanburg Jr Col, Spartanburg SC 33-35; Prin St Davids Acad, Society Hill SC 35-36; Libn Keystone Jr Col 36-41; Circ libn NC State Col 41-42; Army serv 42-43; Field dir Amer Red Cross, South Pacific, Japan 44-46; Asst libn La Polytech Inst 46-48; Libn Mo Valley Col 48-52; Libn Air War Col, Maxwell AFB Ala 52-55; Dir of Lib BradleyU 55-. 9: ALA; IllLA; IllValleyLA (pres 59-60). 10: AAUP; Kiwanis; Phi Kappa Phi. 11: Commendation for Meritorious Civilian Serv USAF 55. 12: "Negro Crime in a Small Urban Community" (35); Ed "MoLA Quarterly," (51-52); Ed "Alabama Librarian" (53-55). 13: Yes. 14: Admin. 15: 1109 N Maplewood ave, Peoria Ill 61606.

LIGHTSEY, NORMA L. b Pinetta Fla 31 My 36. 5: Valdosta State Col 54-58 (Eng) AB; Emory 60-63 (LS) ML. 7: Page S Ga Reg Lib, Valdosta Ga 54-58; Eng tchr Valdosta High Sch, Valdosta Ga 58-60; Act child libn S Ga Reg Lib, Valdosta Ga summer 60; Circ asst Emory U Lib 60-63; Prof asst SC State Lib Bd, Columbia SC 63-64, Field serv libn 64-66; Dir York

Co Lib, Rock Hill SC 66-. 9: ALA; SELA; SCLA (sec 65-67). 10: SC Com on Welfare of Child & Youth; AAUW. 14: Ext, child & ya. 15: 813-1/2 Evergreen lane, Rock Hill SC 29730.

LIGHTWOOD, MARTHA B. b Natrona Heights Penn 24 Ja 23. 4: Milton H Lightwood. 5: UPittsburgh 40-43 (Pol Sci) BA; UPenn Wharton Sch Grad Div 43-44 (Public Admin); Drexel 62-63 MLS; UPenn 64-67 (Pol Sci) MA, 69-. 7: Wage economist USWar Labor Bd, Phila 44-45; Claims asst USSocial Security Admin, Phila 45-48; Cost analyst E I DuPont de Nemours & Co, Inc, Phila 48-54; Exec sec Phila League of Women Voters, Phila 60-62; Hd ref serv Lippincott Lib, Wharton Sch UPenn. 9: SLA. 10: LWV; Pub Admin Soc. 11: Drexel Inst Alumni Award for Original Work in Lib Sci 63. 13: Yes. 14: Ref, spec collection of corporation pubs. 15: 121 Upper Gulph rd, Wayne Pa 19087.

LIH, JUNE Y (TSUN-PING YOUNG). b Shanghai China 5 Je 37. 4: Marshall M Lih. 5: UPuget Sound 61 (Lit) BA; UWis 62 (LS) MS. 6: Chinese. 7: Stud asst UPuget Sound Lib 59-61; Stud asst UWis Lib (Madison) 61-62; Catlgr SUNY (Buffalo) Lib 62-64. 9: ALA. 14: Catlg. 15: 3819-64th ave, Landover Hills Md 20784.

LIIV, IRENE (VEDLER) (MRS). b Tartu Estonia 23 N 09. 5: Tartu U(Estonia) 28-33 (Philol), 30 Certif in Lib Sci; UMo 50-51 (LS) BA. 6: Estonian, Ger, Russian, Fr. 7: Catlg & period libn Tartu U Lib(Tartu Estonia) 29-33; Tr Estonian Publ Co, Tartu Estonia 36-42, Ed 42-44; Libn Bayrisches Staatsarchiv, Neuburg/Donau Germany 45-46; Sec interpreter UNRRA camps, Neuburg/Donau Germany 46-47; Tr admin asst IRO US Zone Hdqrs, Heidelberg/Bad Kissingen 47-49; Lang libn Stephens Col 49-52; Head of catlg proc sect Columbia U Libs 52-. 9: NY Tech Serv Libns; NYLibClub. 12: Tr Zischka, Anton "Teadus purustab monopolid" ("Wissenschaft bricht Monopole") Tartu (42); Tr Cervantes "Don Quijote" Tartu (40); "Searching Routines of the Processing Unit," mimeo Columbia U Libs (57). 14: Catlg. 15: 2352 Linwood ave apt 6g, Fort Lee NJ 07024.

LIIVAK, ANN (OJAMAA). b Tallinn Estonia 15 Ag 41. 4: Arno Liivak. 5: Douglass Col 61-65 (Eng) BA; Rutgers 65-67 MLS. 6: Estonian. 7: Lib trainee NY Pub Lib 65-66; Interlib loan & gen ref Drexel Inst 67, Lib sci libn 68-. 9: SLA; Spec Libs Coun Phila. 14: Ref, lib sci. 15: 18-F Northgate apts 7th & Linden sts, Camden NJ 08102.

LIKINS, JOHN (ROBERT). b Winchester Mass 31 Ja 42. 5: Colgate 61-64 (Eng) BA; Rutgers 64-66 (Eng); Simmons 68-69 MLS. 6: Sp, Portu, Ger, Fr. 7: Catlgr Widener Lib HarvardU 67-. 9: ALA. 14: Catlg, rare bks. 15: 19 Campbell park, Somerville Ma 02144.

LILES, ANNETTE LUCILLE. b Woodbine Ga 18 My 23. 5: Coker Col 40-44 (Eng) BA; UNC 46-47 (LS) BS in LS; Northwestern 53-54 (Eng) MA. 6: Fr. 7: Eng tchr Hartsville High Sch, Hartsville SC 44-46; Instr of Eng Coker Col summers 45 & 46, UFla: Asst in Lib circ dept 47-49, Asst in Lib ref & bibliog 49-50, Asst libn & humanities libn 50-62; Humanities Libn on exch UColo 51; Chm Dept of Ref & Bibliog UFla 62-. 8: Asst Prof lib sci UFla 58-. 9: ALA; SELA; FlaLA (chm Div of Col & Spec Libs 65-66). 10: AAUP; AAUW; Univ Women's Club; Univ Faculty Club; Friends of the Lib. 12: Ed "Thailand Bibliography" by J B Mason & H C Parish (58). 13: Yes. 14: Ref. 15: 1205 NW 10th ave, Gainesville Fla 32601.

LILLARD, EUGENE (PATTERSON). b Bowie Tex 6 O 06. 5: RiceU 23-28 (Eng) BA; UTex 36-40 (Eng); SoMethodistU 51-52 (Counseling) MEd; UTex 63-65 MLS. 6: Fr. 7: Tchr Houston Pub Schs, Houston Tex 28-30; Tchr Kaufman Pub Schs, Kaufman Tex 30-31; Tchr Tex Mil Col 31-34; Tchr Forney Pub Schs, Forney Tex 34-36; Tchr Edingurg Jr Col 37-42, 45-51; Control Tower Operator in Air Force (Sgt) 42-45; Dir div of com Pan American Col 52-63; Catlgr UTex 64-. 9: ALA; TexLA. 14: Catlg, mss & rare bks. 15: 7802 Mullen dr, Austin Tex 78757.

LILLEY, DOROTHY. b Towanda Penn 30 Mr 14. 5: UVt 52-56 (Eng) BA; Columbia 57-60 (LS) MS, 69 DLS. 06: Fr, Sp, Ger. 7: Asst med libn UVt Med Col Lib 54-55; Libn New Paltz State Tchrs Col at Farmingdale summers 57-59; Libn Wallkill Central Schs, Wallkill NY 56-60; High sch libn Farmingdale Pub Schs, Farmingdale NY 60-62; Libn & consul Agnes Russell Sch Tchrs Col Columbia U 62-63; Libn Tororo Girls Sch, Tororo Uganda 64-65; Coordinator of lib serv Patchogue Medford Schs, Patchogue NY 65-. 9: ALA; ASIS; NYLA. 13: Yes. 14: Innovation in lib furniture, subj clsf, circ systems. 15: Apt 1D, Sea Bldg, 234 River ave, Patchogue NY 11772.

LILLEY, OLIVER LINTON. b California Penn 26 N 08. 4: Elsie Martel. 5: Dartmouth 26-30 (Eng Lit) AB; Columbia 33-36 (LS) BS, 49-50 (LS) MS, 50-59 (LS) DLS. 6: Fr. 7: Dartmouth Col Lib: Circ asst 31-33, Sr ref asst 33-40, Ref libn 40-43; Instr dept graphics & engnr Dartmouth Col 43-49; Sch of Lib Serv columbia U: Tchg Fellow 49-50, Assoc in Lib Serv 50-59, Asst Prof 59-60, 60-66, Prof 66-. 8: Consul to Ref Dept Penn State Lib; Columbia U Adv Com of the Faculties 60-65; Columbia U Coun 60-65. 9: ALA (Subject Headings Com 55-61); ASAZ85 (60-65); ASAZ39 (65-). 12: "Feasibility Study Regarding the Establish ment of an Educational Media Research Information Service," with M F Tauber (60). 13: Yes. 14: Bibliog, ref, hist of printing. 15: Sch of Lib Serv Columbia U, New York NY 10027.

LILLY, AUDREY (ALLY). b Drake N Dak 2 O 35. 4: Donald F Lilly. 5: Minot State Col 53-56 (Eng) BS; UMinn 66- (LS). 7: Libn Erik Ramstad Jr High Sch, Minot N Dak 60-. 9: NEA; ALA; NDEA; MinotEA; Minot Lib Club. 15: 18 Vista dr, Minot ND 58701.

LIMERICK, ZADA. b Troy NY 31 Mr 14. 5: Mt Holyoke 33-37 (Eng Lit) BA; Syracuse 38-39 (LS) BS. 7: Catlg asst Russell Sage Col 39-40; Ref asst Springfield Pub Lib, Springfield Mass 40-44; Chg of Picture collection Newark Pub Lib, Newark NJ 44-45, Ref asst 45-46; Catlg asst Australian News & Info Bur NYC 46-48; Indexer "Readers' Guide to Periodical Literature" HW Wilson Col, NYC 49-61, Ed "Readers' Guide to Periodical Literature" 61-. 9: ALA; Tech Serv Libns, Greater NY; NYL Club. 15: 395 Riverside dr, New York NY 10025.

LIMONCZENKO, VALENTINA D. b Ukraine 1 O 37. 5: Wayne State 56-60 (Fr, Russian) AB, 60-61 (LS) ME & tchg certif. 6: Ukrainian, Fr, Russian. 7: Sub libn Los Angeles City Schs 61-62; Child libn Los Angeles Pub Lib 62-64, Ref libn 64-65, 66-67; Libn Dept of Defense Schs, Wiesbaden Germany 65-66; Catlgr Hughes Aircraft Co, Culver City Cal 67; Ref libn Hughes Aircraft Co, Canoga Park Cal 67-. 9: CalLA. 14: Ref serv. 15: 6952 Enfield ave, Reseda Ca 91335.

LIMPER, HILDA KATHARINE. b Blackburn Mo 29 Jl 07. 5: ULouisville 25-26; Elmhurst Col 33-35 (Eng) AB; Carnegie 50-51 MLS. 6: Fr, Ger. 7: Lib asst Louisville Free Pub Lib, Louisville Ky 27-30; Lib asst & act libn Shawnee High Sch Lib, Louisville Ky 30-33; Libn Riverside pub schs, Riverside Ill 35-44; Child libn Dayton Pub Lib, Dayton Ohio 44-50; Child libn Cleveland Heights Pub Lib, Cleveland Heights Ohio 51-53; Child libn Pub Lib of Cincinnati & Hamilton Co, Cincinnati 53-59, Spec exceptional child 59-. 8: Dir Demonstration of Lib Serv to Exceptl Child, Pub Lib Cincinnati & Hamilton Co 66-68. 9: ALA (chm The Troubled Child Com, mem Bibliotherapy Com & participant in Bibliotherapy Wkshop 64); Coun for Except Child; Nat Assn for Gifted Child (chm Bk Awards Com); OhioLA (mem-at-large Round Table for Serv to Child & YA). 11: Dutton-Macrae Award, ALA, 60. 13: Yes. 14: Child serv. 15: 3424 Brookline ave, Cincinnati Oh 45220.

LIN, EILEEN SIU-TSUNG (CHEN). b China 15 Ja 24. 4: Paul T K Lin. 5: UMich 42-44 (Sociol) BA; McGill 67-69 MLS. 6: Chinese. 7: Lib asst McGill U 66-67, Libn I 69-. 9: ALA; CanLA. 14: Lib admin, area studies. 15: 236 Corot Park, Nuns' Island Montreal Que Can.

LIN, KATY CHENGMEI. b Japan (Nationality: Republic of China). 5: Nat Taiwan U 57-61 (Eng) BA; Atlanta 62-63 MSLS; UIll(Chicago) summers 64 & 65 (Med Lit, Ref, Chem); Northwestern U 68 (Lang & thought). 06: Chinese, Japanese. 7: Libn St Bernard's Hosp Sch of Nursing, Chicago 63-65; Asst libn-catlgr Chicago Med Sch, Chicago 65-68; Asst catlgr Capital U Lib, Columbus Ohio 68-. 9: ALA; MedLA; OhioLA. 14: Catlg & clsf, lib automation. 15: 1414 E 59th st, Chicago Il 60637.

LIN, ROBERT KWAN-HWAN. b Kwangchow Canton China 7 Jl 37. 4: Deborah Shock-Kai Shieh. 5: Nat Taiwan U 56-60 (Eng Lit) BA; UOkla 63-65 MLS. 6: Fr, Chinese, Japanese. 7: Tchg Taiwan Prov Chung-li Commercial High Sch, Taiwan 60-63; Assoc libn & Instr of LS Culver-Stockton Col 66-. 9: MedLA. 10: Round Table Club. 13: Yes. 14: Catlg, ref, lib admin, tchg lib sci. 15: No 1 1492 Silver Lake blvd, Los Angeles Ca 90026.

LIN, SHIANG C (SHARON CHIEN). b Nanking Kiangsu China 22 Ag 33. 4: Duoliang Lin. 5: Nat Taiwan U 52-56 (Eng Lit) BA; UMinn 58-60 (LS) MA. 6: Fr, Chinese. 7: Catlgr Yale U Lib 60-64; Period libn State U Col (Buffalo NY) 65-; Visiting libn Stanford U Lib 66. 14: Catlg, ser. 15: 217 W Maplemere rd, Williamsville NY 14221.

LIN, WEN-CHOUH. b Shanghai China 10 O 33. 4: Anita C S Wang. 5: Taiwan Normal U 50-54 (Eng) BA; Kwansei Gakuin U 57-59 (Eng) MA; LSU 61-62 (LS) MS; UMd 67-68 (lib & info serv). 06: Chinese, Japanese. 7: Tchr sr dept Taipei Prov Fuh Shing Middle Sch 55-56; Tchr Kobe Overseas Chinese Sch, Kobe Japan 56-59; Asst mgr Nam Chow Co Ltd, Kobe Japan 59-61; Catlgr Tulane U Lib 62-67; Catlgr Duke U Lib 68-. 9: ALA. 14: Ser catlg, lib automation, info sci. 15: 920 Lambeth circle, Durham NC 27705.

LINCOLN, ELIZABETH (REEVE). b Fort Washington Penn 21 F 14. 4: John W Lincoln. 5: Rutgers Ext 38-39; NJ Lib Sch Trenton State Tchrs Col 41 Pub Lib Certif. 7: Ref asst Orange Free Pub Lib, Orange NJ 37-42; Ref libn S Orange Pub Lib, S Orange NJ 42-44; Ref catlgr Verona Free Pub Lib, Verona NJ 58-68; Hd tech serv dept Livinston Free Pub Lib, Livingston NJ 68-. 8: Instr State Sponsored Workshops: Ref 67, 68; Basic Procedures 69. 9: ALA; NJLA. 10: Trustee, Roseland Pub Lib. 14: Catlg, ref. 15: 25 Mitchell ave, Roseland NJ 07068.

LINCOLN, (CAROL) JOANNE. b Dallas Tex 17 O 38. 5: Wheaton 56-60 (Sp) AB; Emory 66- (LS). 6: Sp. 7: Lib asst Wheaton Col Lib 56-60; Clerical asst gen ref dept Dallas Pub lib, Dallas Tex 60-61, Prof asst sci & ind dept 61-64, Libn sci & tech dept 64-66; Staff libn Prof Lib Atlanta Pub Schs 66-. 9: GaLA; SELA. 13: Yes. 14: Lib applications fo data proc, ref, acquis, admin. 15: 1420 Foxhall lane SE, Atlanta Ga 30316.

LINCOLN, MARJORIE H. b Des Moines Iowa 29 O 16. 4: S A Lincoln. 5: State U Iowa 33-37 (Eng) BA; UChicago 47-48 BLS. 6: Fr, Ger, Sp. 7: Lib asst Des Moines Pub Lib, Des Moines Iowa 46; Asst catlgr UIowa 36-37; Catlgr UChicago 48-50; Lib Dir Wheaton Pub Lib, Wheaton Ill 50-. 8: Act dir DuPage Lib System 66-67; Adv Com, Col of DuPage. 9: ALA; IllLA (v-chm Pub Lib Sect); Lib Admin Conf, No Ill (sec-treas). 10: AAUW; Drama Club of Wheaton; Phi Beta Kappa; Ill Sesquicent Com, Wheaton. 13: Yes. 14: Admin, bk reviewing, pub rel. 15: 225 N Cross, Wheaton Ill 60187.

LINCOLN, SHIRLEY H. b Walton NY. 4: Philip H Lincoln. 5: Syracuse 53-57 (Eng, LS) BA; Syracuse 57-58 MS in LS. 6: Fr, Ger. 7: Clk & page Educ Lib Syracuse U 56-57, Lib clk Bus Lib 57-58; Lib dir Solvay Pub Lib, Solvay NY 58-59; Sr catlgr Syracuse Pub Lib, Syracuse NY 60-. 9: ALA. 14: Catlg, info sci. 15: Robert dr RD2, Jamesville NY 13078.

LINCOLN, SISTER ELEANOR. b Minneapolis 13 My 24. 5: Col of St Catherine 42-46, 49-50 (Eng, LS) BS, BA; UMinn 52-55 (Amer Studies) MA, 55-58 (Amer Studies) PhD. 6: Fr. 7: Lib asst & Eng Instr Col of St Catherine 47-49; Eng tchr Acad of the Holy Angels, Minneapolis 49-50; Col of St Catherine: Lib asst & Instr in Lib Sci 50-55, Chm of Dept of Lib Sci 58-62, Asst Prof of Eng & Lib Sci 62-64, Assoc Prof of Eng & Lib Sci 64-. 9: Amer Studies Assn; Minn CTE. 10: Phi Beta Kappa & 3 other nat hon socs. 12: "Cultural Significance of the Minneapolis Public Library; Its Origins and Development (58). 13: Yes. 14: Ref, reading interests. 15: 2004 Randolph, St Paul 55116.

LIND, CAROL C(ONKLIN). b Iroquois Co Ill 12 Ap 04. 4: Charles Eugene Lind. 5: Wheaton Col (Wheaton Ill) 23-27 (Hist) AB; Chicago 28-30 (Hist); UIll summers 32, 33, & 35 BS in LS. 7: Stud asst Wheaton Col (Wheaton Ill) 23-27, Asst to libn 27-33; Supv & lib tech WPA, E St Louis 36-38; Catlgr Ill State Hist Lib, Springfield Ill 38-47; Hist asst in chg of genealogy Seattle Pub Lib 49-. 9: ALA (Hist Sect: Geneal Com 68-71); Nat Geneal So; Wash State LA; Seattle Geneal Soc; Northwest Lineage Researchers. 10: DAR; Women Descendants of the Ancient & Hon Artillery Comp. 14: Geneal. 15: Seattle Pub Lib, Seattle Wa 98104.

LIND, HAROLD J JR. b Kansas City Kan 31 Jl 20. 5: UKan 40-42, 60-62 (Pol Sci) AB; Columbia 46-50, 62-64 (Govt, Art Hist); Catholic U 66-67 MSLS. 6: Fr. 7: Tec 5 Med Dept A US, MTO 42-45; CIA, Wash DC 53-60; Ref libn Prince George's Co Mem Lib, Oxon Hill Md 67-. 9: ALA. 10: Beta Phi Mu. 14: Ref, art lib serv, rare bks, music libnship. 15: 6631 Wakefield dr, Alexandria Va 22307.

LINDAUER, DINAH (EPNER). b Brooklyn NY 25 My 26. 4: Albert Lindauer. 5: Hunter Col 43-47 (Sociol, Psych) BA; Columbia 48-49 MLS. 7: Ya libn Enoch Pratt Free Lib, Baltimore 49-50; Asst coordinator, wk with ya Brooklyn Pub Lib 50-56; Instr serv to ya Pratt Lib Sch summer 58; Dir pub lib sch rel proj Nassau Lib System, Hempstead NY 65-67, Coord of programs & serv 67-. 8: Lib consul Encyclopedia Brittanica-New Dimensions in Learning Exhibit, NYC fall 63, Mem NY Commsnr of Educ's Com on Lib Devel 67-; Mem NY State Adv Com on ESEA Title II 66-. 9: ALA; NassauCoLA; Nassau-SuffolkSchLA; NYLA. 14: Pub lib progs & serv. 15: 81 Marion ave, Merrick NY 11566.

LINDBERG, LOIS ANNE. b St Paul 20 D 26. 5: Col of St Catherine 45-49 (Eng, LS) BS in LS. 6: Ger. 7: Libn Mercy Hosp Sch of Nursing, Cedar Rapids Iowa 49-50; Army Libn USArmy, Japan, France, Germany 51-55; Catlgr Carleton Col Lib 55-63; Ser catlgr Oberlin Col Lib 63-. 14: Ser, catlg. 15: Oberlin Col Lib, Oberlin Oh 44074.

LINDBLOOM, PAULINE (FUNK). b Hazen Ark 31 D 11. 4: Harold S Lindbloom. 5: UKan 33 (Hist) BA; UDenver 59 (LS) MA. 7: Libn Boulder High Sch, Boulder Colo 59-; Instr in Lib Sci USask, Can summer 69. 9: NEA;-DAVI (Eval 1969 Coms); ALA; ColoLA; ColoEA (chm Lib Div 64-65); ColoASchL (pres-elect 65-67; v-chm State Adv Com for Title II ESEA 65); Colo AV Assn. 10: AAUW; Pi Lambda Theta. 14: Pub sch libs, instrnal materials centers. 15: 1950 Dartmouth, Boulder Colo 80302.

LINDEKEN, DANIEL F. b Cedar Rapids Iowa 21 D 39. 4: Thelma P Robinson. 5: Central Mo State 67 (Eng) BSEd, 68 (A-v) MSEd. 7: Motion picture photography (Sgt) USAF 62-65; Grad asst (lib asst) Central Mo State Col 66-67, Grad asst (a-v lab) 67-69; Chm a-v dept Florissant Commun Col 68-. 9: NEA-DAVI; Ill A-V Assn& instr Film Lib Assn Greater St Louis (pres-elect 69-70). 10: PTA; Amer Legion; St Sabina Men's Club. 14: A-v, tv, audio tutorial methods of tchg. 15: 2186 Aristocrat dr, Florissant Mo 63031.

LINDELL, RUTH (DRAPER). b O'Brien Co Iowa 1 S 02. 4: Ernest L Lindell. 5: Taylor U 23-27 (Math) AB; SUNY (Geneseo) 62 MLS. 6: Sp. 7: Libn & tchr Albion Area Jt Sch, Albion Penn 46-48; Asst libn Taylor U 49-51; Staff Prendergast Free Lib, Jamestown NY 51-52; Head Libn Frewsburg Central Sch, Frewsburg NY 53-. 9: NEA; NY State Tchrs Assn. 10: Delta Kappa Gamma. 14: Catlg, ref. 15: 305 N Main, Russell Penn 16345.

LINDEMAN, KATHERINE J(ANE). b Chicago Ill 3 D 21. 5: MacMurray Col 40-44 (Lang) BA; UIll 44-45 (LS) BS. 6: Ger. 7: Asst Sweet Briar Col 45-46; Ref asst Ill State Lib, springfield 46-49; Asst order libn Fla State U 49-50; Ref libn Glenview Pub Lib, glenview Ill 52-. 9: ALA; IllLA. 10: Zonta Internat. 14: Ref. 15: 850 Eldorado st, Winnetka Il 60093.

LINDENFELD, JOSEPH F. b Syracuse NY 22 My 42. 5: Boston U 59-63 (Amer Hist) AB; Columbia 63-64 (LS) MS; UPenn 64-66 (Amer Civilization) MA. 6: Sp. 7: Libn I Free Lib of Phila 64-65, Libn II 65-66; Assignment spec US Army (Spec 5) 66-68; Hd Girard Ave Br Free Lib of Phila 68-. 8: ALA Rep to Amer Acad Pol & Soc Scis 66. 9: ALA-ACRL;-ASD;ISAD;-PLA;-RSD;-RTSD; PennLA. 10: Alpha Phi Omega; Korea Stamps Soc; ACLU; Amer Topical Soc (UN Study Unit). 14: Ref, bibliog. 15: 927 Pine st, Phila Pa 19107.

LINDENMEYER, HAROLD FRED (LOUIS). b Peru Ill 5 Ap 13. 4: Jane Copeland. 5: UColo 30-31, 32-35 (Romance Langs) AB; U Denver 36-37 (LS) BS; Stanford 38-40 (Ger); UCal (Berkeley) 40-41 (LS); Harvard 42 (Bus Admin). 6: Fr, Sp, Ital. 7: Tchr High Sch, Sheridan Wyo 35-36; Ref & circ asst U Denver Lib 36-37; Asst ser div Stanford U Lib 37-39, Asst ref libn 39-42; (Maj) Statistical Control Off US Army Air Corps US, Hawaii, Africa 42-46; Asst ref libn Stanford U Lib 46; Ref libn asst chief, actg chief, ref serv Off of Tech Serv US Dept of Com, Wash DC 47; Asst chief lib sect Air Documents Div Intelligence Dept Air Material Command Wright-Patterson AFB, Dayton Ohio 48-49; Deputy civilian chief, document requirements sect & chief acquis br Central Air Documents Off, Dayton Ohio 49; Asst libn US Patent Off Sci Lib, Wash DC 49-57, Deputy chief libn 58-68; Act hd tr & for patent processing br Patent Off Search Ctr 68-. 8: Pub Rel Off 28th Sub-Depot USAF Ellington Field Houston 42-43; Safety Off US Patent Off 58-61; Lt Col USAF (Ret). 9: SLA (Chief teller sci-tech div 52; DC Chap: chm &/or mem 2 coms 53-55 & 58-67, dir 67-69; Sci-Tech Group: treas 54-55, group chm 56-57, chm 2 coms 53-57); DCLA (chm elections com 54-55). 10: Kappa Delta Pi; Phi Sigma Iota; PTA; Patent Off Soc; Amer Legion. 12: 'Machine Methods in Library and Research Work' in "Proceedings of the Conference on Problems of Centralized Documentation," (49); "The Patent Office Scientific Library; Services for Patent Examining" (60); Ed "28th Sub-Depot Plane Platter," Ellington AFB Tex (42-43). 13: Yes. 14: Ref, admin. 15: 4046 Doveville lane, Fairfax Va 22030.

LINDER, DOROTHY GERTRUDE (AMESBURY). b Minneapolis 8 Je 08. 5: UMinn 25-29 (Music, LS) BS. 6: Fr, Ger, Ital. 7: Prof asst music dept Pub Lib, Minneapolis 29-34,

Head of music dept 34-47; Music libn UMinn (Minneapolis) 47-50; Asst chief music div DC Pub Lib 50-53, Chief music div 53; Asst head Music Sect Copyright Catlg Div LC 53-57, Head Music Sect Copyright Catlg Div 57-68, Asst chief copyright catlg div 68-. 9: MusLA (var com duties; chm Wash-Baltimore Chap 51); DCLA. 12: Ed "Index of Folk Dances and Singing Games," ALA (36). 13: Yes. 14: Mus catlg & ref, admin. 15: 5904 Hanover ave, Springfield Va 22150.

LINDER, GEORGE RICHARD. b Calumet Mich 27 Jl 19. 4: Carolyn Templeton. 5: Wis StateU (Superior) 36-37 (Eng) BS in Ed; Emory 47-48 BS in LS; UNC (LS). 7: Libn Catawba Iredell, Lincoln Commun Libs, Newton NC 48-50; Med supply off 7th Inf Div USArmy (Cpt), Korea 51-52; Libn Catawba-Lincoln Co Libs Newton NC 52-56; Dir Spartanburg Co Lib, Spartanburg SC 56-65; Dir Durham (NC) Pub Lib 65-. 9: ALA; SCLA (treas)& NCLA (chm Pub Lib Sect); SELA (Legis Com). 10: Kiwanis; Soc Serv Org (Spartanburg Co SC). 14: Admin, bldgs. 15: 3014 Buckingham rd, Durham NC 27701.

LINDER, GLORIA (ANN). b La Salle Ill 1 Ja 43. 5: UIll 60-64 (Hist) BA, 64-65 (LS) MS. 6: Fr. 7: Typist G L Herbolsheimer Law Off, LaSalle Ill 61; Stud asst UIll Lib(Urbana) 61-62; Policy typist Duncan Insurance Off, La Salle Ill summer 62, Sec summer 63; Stud asst UIll Lib (Urbana) 64; Tchg asst UIll Lib Sch 64-65; Lib trainee Mich State U 65-67; Ref libn Hoover Institution, Stanford Cal 67-69; Catlgr Lane Med Lib, Stanford Cal 69-. 9: ALA; MedLA; SLA; CalLA. 10: Beta Phi Mu. 14: Ref, catlg. 15: 220 Curtner st, Palo Alto Ca 94306.

LINDER, LeROY HAROLD. b Minneapolis 6 F 17. 4: Phyllis Eleanor Franklin. 5: UMinn 35-39 (Fine Arts) BA, 39-40 (LS) BS, 41, 49 (Hist of Sci) MS; Chicago 49-52, 58 (LS) PhD. 6: Ger, Fr. 7: Lib asst UMinn Lib (Minneapolis) 40-43; Tr & libn US Army SHAEF G-2, Europe 43-46; Prin libn ser div UMinn Lib (Minneapolis) 46-49; Libn Nat Reactor Test Station USAEC, Idaho Falls Ida 52-54; Asst Prof Grad Sch of Lib Sci UTex 54-58; Assoc Prof Sch of Lib Sci USoCal 58-59; Manager tech info serv Aeronutronic Div Philco-Ford Corp, Newport beach Cal 59-. 8: Lib sci adv com: Orange Coast Col 65-66, Fullerton Jr Col 66-67; Cal State Lib Adv Coun for Interlib Coop 67-69; Adv coun on libnship educ UCal 68-; Ext tchg UCLA 67-68; John Cotton Dana lecturer UCal (Berkeley) 67. 09; ALA-ACRL; ASIS (rep 1967 fall Jt Computer Conf); SLA (Govt Info Serv Com 61-64; Educ Com 62-65; So Cal Chap: pres 66-67, consultation off 68-). 10: Friends of the Costa Mesa Pub Lib, Friends of the UCal Irvine Lib; Amer Soc for Metals; Sci Research Soc Amer; Nat Security Ind Assn; Phi Alpha Theta; Beta Phi Mu. 11: Croix de Guerre Avec Palme (Belgium), 45. 12: "The Rise of Current Complete National Bibliography" (59). 13: Yes. 14: Admin, info storage & retrieval, automation. 15: 2566 Oxford lane, Costa Mesa Ca 92626.

LINDER, LORENE (MATHWIG). b Dunnell Minn 18 My 11. 5: Gustavus Adolphus Col 29-33 (Lit, Hist) BA; UMinn 38-47 BS in LS; Chicago 47-48 (Comparative Lit); UMinn 60-65 (Amer Studies); MA. 06: Swedish. 7: Tchr-libn Sherburn Minn, Martinsdale Iowa, Thompson Iowa, New Richland Minn, Renville Minn 34-41; Clerk US Navy Yard, Norfolk Va 42; Tchr-libn Ceylon Minn, Winnebago Minn, Pat Henry High Sch Minneapolis 43-47; Libn Col Lib UChicago 47-48, Asst readers serv 48-50; Head of readers adv serv Minneapolis Pub Lib 51-59; Asst ref libn NoIllU 59-64, Libn in chg humanities ref room 65-. 9: ALA; IllLA. 10: Great Books Discussion Groups. 14: Ref. 15: Swen Franklin Parson Lib, No Ill Univ, DeKalb Il 60115.

LINDERMAN, MARION (ARNOLD). b Syracuse NY 30 Ja 20. 5: SEast Col 37-41 (Eng) BA; LSU 61-62 MS in LS. 7: Tchr: Pine Forest Acad, Chunky Miss 41-42, Baton Rouge Jr Acad, Baton Rouge La 42-43, 55-61, Natalbony Elem, Natalbony La 43-48; Asst libn hd of pub serv & asst prof of lib sci So Missionary Col 62-. 9: ALA; TennLA. 14: Ref, govt docs. 15: PO Box 455, Collegedale Tn 37315.

LINDERMAN, WINIFRED B. b Harmony Minn. 5: Carleton Col 15-19 (Eng) BA; Columbia 33-35 (LS) BS, 37-40 (LS) MS, 54-59 (US Hist) PhD. 6: Fr, Ger. 7: Instr in Eng High Schs in Minn, ND, SD 19-24; Libn Central Schs Lib, Fresno Cal 24-26; Libn Tech High Sch, Fresno Cal 26-29; Asst Brooklyn Pub Lib 29-30; Asst ref & sch wk NY Pub Lib 31-36; Head Libn High Sch, Garden City NY 36-44; Ref libn Vassar Col Lib 44-45; Cultural off US Dept of State For Serv Res & Dir of Lib US Info Serv, Cape Town Africa 45-47; Visiting Instr UIll Lib Sch summers 39-41, 43, 44; Visiting Instr Emory Lib Sch summer 42; Columbia U Sch of Lib Serv: Assoc 47-59, Assoc Prof 59-65, Prof 65-66, Emeritus Prof 66-; Vis Prof Emory Div of Libnship 67-68; Vis Prof UIll Lib Sch 68-69. 9: ALA-RSD; -ASD; -ACRL; -LED (sec 50-52, Bd Dirs 52-55); AALS; NY Lib club. 10: AHA; AAUW; AAUP; Phi Beta Kappa; Beta Phi Mu. 12: "History of the Columbia University Library, 1876-1926" (59); Ed "The Present Status and Future Prospects of Reference/Information Service," Proc of a Conf at ColumbiaU Sch of Lib Serv (67). 13: Yes. 14: Ref, bibliog, adv serv, soc sci lit. 15: Hotel Ansonia, Broadway at 73rd st, New York NY 10023.

LINDEROTH, RUTH (ELIZABETH WITHERBEE). b Woodbury Heights NJ 16 Jl 07. 5: Simmons 24-28 BS in LS; Columbia 32 Advance courses in Catlg & Bibliog. 7: Catlg asst UPenn Lib 28-31; Catlgr Lessing Rosenwald Col Free Lib, Phila 32; Supv Union Lib Catlg, Phila 35-37, Consul 37-44; Catlgr Woodbury Pub Lib, woodbury NJ 57-58, Libn 59-. 9: ALA; NJLA. 10: AAUW. 12: Contrib "Philadelphia Libraries: A Survey of Facilities, Needs and Opportunities" (42). 14: Catlg, pub lib wk. 15: 416 Oak ave, Woodbury Heights NJ 08096.

LINDGREN, WILLIAM DALE. b Peoria Ill 8 Mr 36. 5: BradleyU 58 BA, 60 MA; UIll 68 MSLS. 6: Fr. 7: Hd libn Limestone Commun High Sch, Bartonville Ill; Assoc libn Illinois Central Col hd tech proc & acquis. 8: Concert singer. 9: IllEA; IllLA; ISLA. 10: Beta Phi Mu; Phi Sigma Pi. 15: 504 E Washington st, E Peoria Il 61611.

LINDGREN, WILLIAM FRANK. b Wadena Minn 27 F 27. 4: Katherine Howard. 5: UMinn 44-47 (Hist) BS, 47-48 BS in LS, 54-55 (Hist) MA. 6: Fr. 7: Catlg libn UOre Lib 48-50, 53-54; Sgt E-5 Admin spec USArmy, Pusan Korea 51-52; Catlg libn UAriz Lib 55-60; Head catlg dept Col State U Libs 60-. 9: ALA (chm mem com, Colo 63-65); ColoLA; MPLA (chm Reg Group of Tech Serv Libns 63-65); ArizLA (treas 57-58). 10: AAUP. 12: Co-auth "A Guide to Theses at Colorado State University, 1920-1961," (63). 14: Catlg, ser. 15: 1517 Lakeside ave, Fort Collins Co 80521.

LINDHORST, CHARLOTTE. b Clinton Ky 25 Ag 25. 4: Ellis H Lindhorst. 5: Murray State Col 45 (LS) BS in Ed; Kan State Tchrs Col 66 MSLS. 7: High sch libn, Mo: Hannibal 54-59, Carthage 60-66, Joplin 66-. 9: NEA; ALA; MoLA; MoStateTA; MoASchL. 14: Bk sel, catlg, bks for ya. 15: 2520 Kansas ave, Joplin Mo 64801.

LINDLEY, MARGARET A. b Mansfield Ohio 25 S 30. 5: Oberlin 48-52 (Hist) BA; West Res 52-54 (Educ) MA; UMich 59-60 (LS). 7: Elem tchr Mansfield (Ohio) Bd of Educ 53-58, Elem libn 58-60, Sch lib coord 60-. 9: ALA; NEA; OhioEA; OhioASchL (Bd Dirs). 10: LWV. 15: 709 Coleman rd, Mansfield Oh 44903.

LINDNER, ALDEN LOUIS. b Hamilton Ohio 8 Jl 17. 5: Capital U 34-36, 45-48 (Hist) BA; Miami U 50-51 (Educ); UIll 53-54 MSLS. 6: Ger. 7: Ref asst Dayton Pub Lib, Dayton Ohio 51-53; Catlgr Lane Pub Lib, Hamilton Ohio 55-58, Ref libn 59-60; Libn Ft Hamilton Hosp, Hamilton Ohio 59-61; Acquis libn Capital U Lib 61-. 9: ALA; ASIS; OhioLA. 10: Toastmasters Internat. 14: Tech serv, admin, ref. 15: 515 Oakland Park ave apt 218, Columbus Oh 43214.

LINDNER, SALLY ANTOINETTE. b Milwaukee 5 Jl 39. 5: UWis(Milwaukee) 57-61 (Hist, Educ) BS; Drexel summers 61-63, 65, 66, 67 MSLS. 06: Lat, Ger. 7: Head high sch libn W Bend High Sch, W Bend Wis 61-62; Elem libn Edgewood Elem Sch, Oak Creek Wis 62-. 9: NEA; ALA; WisEA; WisLA; Wis Clr Tchrs Assn. 10: Phi Alpha Theta; Beta Phi Mu. 14: Catlg, sch libnship. 15: 106 W Center st, Milwaukee Wi 53212.

LINDSAY, ANN R(UTH). b Phila 8 Ja 21. 4: Albert E(ugene) Lindsay. 5: Bryn Mawr Col 37-41, 45 (Eng Lit) AB; Catholic U 58-61 (LS). 6: Fr, Ger, Sp, Ital, Med Russian. 7: Health educator USArmy Ind Med Program, San Francisco Cal 42-46; Info spec USPub Health Serv Wash DC 46-48; Lib asst Div of Health Affairs Lib UNC 52-54; Lib asst USArmy Lib Pentagon Wash DC 56-58; NLM: Catlg asst 58-60, Catlgr biol & med sci 60-63, Supv libn-catlgr biol & med sci 63-. 9: MedLA (News ed "Bulletin" of Potomac Group); Potomac Tech Processing Libns. 12: Publns Com 2d Internat Congress on Med Libnship; ed of its "Proceedings"; Free-lance ed wk (60); Ed "NLM News" 67-68. 14: Catlg, computerized serv in libs, hist of med. 15: 8200 Wisconsin ave apt 1414, Bethesda Md 20014.

LINDSAY, BESS M. b Waynesburg Penn 13 Ja 09. 5: Carnegie 29-33 (Music) AB, 58-59 MLS. 7: Libn music div Carnegie Lib of Pittsburgh 59-. 9: Internat Assn of Mus Libs; MusLA. 15: 5617 Dunmoyle st, Pittsburgh Pa 15217.

LINDSAY, GWENOLYN JO (TAYLOR). b Quincy Ill 25 Ap 41. 4: Gene K Lindsay. 5: UIowa 59; Culver-Stockton Col 60-63 (Eng) BA; UMich 64-66 AMLS. 07: Lib wk-study scholar UMich (Ann Arbor) 65-66, Ref libn 67-. 9: ALA. 14: Ref. 15: 2786 Page st, Ann Arbor Mi 48104.

LINDSEY, JOHN M. b Okla City Okla 5 Ag 31. 4: Susan (Bush). 5: SoIllU 48-51 (Eng) BA; UIll 55-58 LLB, 62 MSLS, 68 JD. 07: (S/Sgt) Personnel USAF 51-55; Grad asst UIll Lib (Urbana) 58-59; Private law practice, Lawrenceville Ill 59-60; Bibliog Morris Lib SoIllU 60-61; Asst law libn UIll 61-64; Law Libn & Assoc Prof of Law, Cal West U 64-. 9: AALL; Amer Bar Assn; Ill State Bar Assn; Chicago ALL; San Diego Co Bar Assn; Amer Judicature Soc. 10: Phi Alpha Delta; Beta Phi Mu; Selden Soc. 13: Yes. 14: Ref, acquis, bibliog, law libnship. 15: 1883 Froude, San Diego Ca 92107.

LINDSEY, WILLIMINA (SNYDER) SCHULTZ. b Archbold Ohio 2 F 06. 4: William Guy Lindsey. 5: Ariz StateU 40 (Bus Educ) BA in Educ, 44 (Bus Educ) MA in Educ; Peabody 50 BS in LS. 6: Sp, Ger. 7: Lib asst Phoenix Union High Sch 34-37; Libn Thatcher High Sch, Thatcher Ariz 40-42; Libn Litchfield High Sch, Litchfield Park Ariz 43-44; Asst registrar Ariz State Col 45-46; Head Libn Tolleson Union High Sch, Tolleson Ariz 47-. 8: Adv Stud Lib Assn of Ariz. 9: ALA; NEA; ArizEA; ArizStateLibAssn; Salt River Valley Lib Assn. 10: Woman's Club; Delta Kappa Gamma; Pi Omega Pi; Kappa Delta Pi; Tolleson Pub Lib Bd. 11: Ariz Tchr of the Year, 58. 13: Yes. 14: Promoting reading among teen-agers. 15: 9404 W Fillmore, Tolleson Ariz 85353.

LINDSLEY, THOMAS F. b Buffalo NY 21 Ja 33. 4: Margarete Weisbrod. 5: Bethany Col 9w va) 50-54 (Physics) BS; Columbia 54-56 (LS) MS. 6: Ger. 7: Lib trainee (circ) NYC Pub Lib 54-55, Libn (sci & tech) 55-56, 58-59; Physicist US Army, Aberdeen Md 56-58; Resident libn IBM, Poughkeepsie NY 59-62; Mgr tech info searching IBM, Armonk NY 62-. 9: SLA; ASIS; ACM. 13: Yes. 14: Mechanized info ret. 15: RFD 1, Fishkill NY 12524.

LINDVALL, MARTHA EMMA (LIVINGSTON). b Kan City Mo 19 N 12. 5: UKan, UMo 32; Kan City U 33; UDenver 37 BSLS; UCal 51-52 (Educ). 6: Ger, Sp. 7: Libn Colo State Health Dept Lib, Denver 46-47; Libn Oakland (City) Health Dept, Oakland Cal 47-50; Asst libn Hayward High Sch Lib, Hayward Cal 50-52; Br asst Oakland Pub Lib, Oakland Cal 52-58; Sr libn, head ref dept in San Leandro Commun Lib, San Leandro Cal 58-. 9: CalLA; Bay Area Ref Libns Coun. 10: Bus & Prof Women's Club. 14: Ref, rare bks, Cal & loc hist materials, govt docs. 15: Commun Lib 300 Estudillo, San Leandro Cal 94577.

LINE, BRYANT WINCHESTER. b Gadsden Ala 5 Jl 17. 4: Aphrodite Chresand. 5: UAla 34-38 (Journalism) AB; Catholic U 64-65 MSLS. 6: Sp, Fr, Ital. 7: Clerical US Civil Serv Commsn, Wash DC 39-42; Yeoman 2d US Navy, Navy Dept, Wash DC 42-43; Naval Off US Navy, Wash DC, Hawaii, Japan, Italy 43-63; Ref libn Arlington Co (Va) Pub Lib (Central) 65-, Libn I 65-66, Libn II 66-, Libn III 66-. 9: DCLA. 10: Lib Bd, Falls Church Va. 14: Ref. 15: 305 N Maple ave, Falls Church Va 22046.

LINEHAM, THOMAS U JR. b Groton Conn 7 Ja 19. 4: Marguerite Mooney. 5: Bowdoin 40 (Ger) AB; Catholic U 68 MSLS. 7: Colonel USAF 28 yrs; Executive off Directorate of communication-Electronics Org of Jt Chiefs of Staff, Pentagon, Wash DC 68. 9: ALA; FlaLA. 14: Catlg, ref. 15: 266 Chase ave, Winter Park Fl 32789.

LINEHAN, JANICE E. b Lowell Mass 14 My 43. 5: Merrimack Col 60-64 (Hist) AB; Rutgers 67-68 MSLS. 6: Fr. 7: Info research analyst Nat Security Agcy, Ft Meade Nd 64-67; Ref libn Batten, Marton, Durstine, Osborn NYC 68-. 9: SLA. 14: Ref, bibliog. 15: 225 W 70th st apt 2C, New York NY 10023.

LINEWEAVER, JOE REHERD. b Rockingham Co Va 28 Je 38. 4: Betty Leona Baumgartner. 5: UWis 60 (Math, Psych) BA; UDenver 68 (Libnship) MA. 6: Russian. 7: Tchr Swedru Secondary Sch, Agona Swedru Ghana 62-64; Research asst Central Asian Research Centre, London UK 65-67; Catlgr Iowa StateU Lib (Ames) 68-. 14: Catlg. 15: 412 8th, Ames Ia 50010.

LINGO, CYNTHIA (MATTHEWS). b Los Angeles Cal 5 Mr 46. 4: Thomas Irvin Lingo. 5: UOre 63-66 (Eng) BA; USoCal 67-68 MLS. 7: Libn I Long Beach Pub Lib, Long Beach Cal 66-68; Libn I Orange Co Pub Lib, Orange Cal 68-. 9: CalLA. 14: Ya wk, rare bks. 15: 32205 Vista De La Luna, S Laguna Ca 92677.

LINHARDT, AGNES VICTORIA (SARLO). b Budapest Hungary 30 Mr 31. 4: Anthony Linhardt. 5: Eotvos LorantU (Budapest Hungary) 49-53 (Hist) Diploma; UCLA 68-69 MLS & high sch tchr's certif. 6: Hungarian, Ger, Russian. 7: High sch tchr Landler Jeno gymnasium, Budapest Hu gymnasium, Budapest Hungary 53-56; Travel coun Automobile Club of So Cal, Century Club 64-65; Clk-typist Los Angeles Pub Lib 67-68. 8: Free-lance reporter for Radio Budapest 50-56. 9: ALA; CalLA. 14: Ref. 15: 10617 Kinnard ave, Los Angeles Ca 90024.

LINK, ELVA C (BOBST). b Schenectady NY 18 Ag 13. 4: Gordon P Link. 5: Conn Col 32-36 (Math) AB; SUNY (Albany) 59-61 MSLS; Siena Col 63-65 (Educ). 07: Ref libn Schenectady Co (NY) Pub Lib 61-62; High sch libn Burnt Hills-Ballston Lake Central Schs, Burnt Hills NY 63-67; High sch Av libn Arlington Central Sch 67-69. 9: NYLA; Hudson MohawkLA. 15: 112 No Toll st, Scotia NY 12302.

LINK, VERNA MAE (HAHN). b Big Lick NC 24 Ag 10. 4: John William Link Jr. 5: Mt Amcena Sem 24-27 (Music) Diploma; Mt Pleasant Collegiate Inst 27-29 (Diploma); Lenoir Rhyne Col 29-30 (Math, Chem); Duke U 30-31 (Gen Sci, Chem) AB; UNC (Chapel Hill) 31-32 (Music & Educ) Tchrs Certif, 38-39 MS in LS. 7: Tchr NC Pub Schs 33-38, 44-53; Libn Va Polytechnic Inst 40-42; Libn-instr Cabarrus Memorial Hosp, Concord NC 64-67; Libn Cabarrus Memorial Hosp, Sch of Nursing, Concord NC 67-. 9: NEA; ALA; MLA; NLN; ACRL; NCEA; NCLA; NCLN. 13: Yes. 14: Catlg & admin, psych, child devel, sociol (tchg). 15: 205 Lee st, Mt Pleasant NC 28124.

LINKE, FRANCES BAUR. b Buenos Aires Argentina 3 My 24. 4: Raymond Joseph Linke. 5: Los Angeles City Col 58-62 (Psych) AA; UCLA 63-64 (Psych); USoCal 63-65 (LS); Los Angeles State Col 67 BS; USoCal 69 (LS). 6: Sp, Fr. 7: Pub rel & actress Comet Prod, Hollywood Cal 50-54; Pub rel exec Scoffield Assn, Hollywood Cal 55-58; Libn pub rel Cleary, Strauss, & Irwin, Hollywood Cal 58-61; Libn engnr-physics Mincom Div 3 M Co, Camarillo Cal 62-64; Libn health insurance Blue Cross of SoCal, Los Angeles 64-. 8: Lib Adv for Lib of Instruments sect, 3 M Co; Lib adv for Blue Cross Plans. 9: ALA; SLA (Insurance Div: Insurance Subj Hdings Com); CalLA; MedLA. 12: TV Journalist 50-54. 14: Spec libs mgt. 15: 1721 La Barranca, La Canada Ca 91011.

LINKHART, EDWARD GLENN. b Wilmington Ohio 26 Je 22. 4: Lyda (Sexton). 5: Wilmington (Ohio) Col 39-42 (Eng); Ohio StateU 46-47 (Eng) BA; UIll 47-48 BS in LS; 48-49 MS in LS. 6: Ger. 07: Armorer (Sgt) USAF, SPacific 42-46; Bibliog UIll Lib (Urbana) 49-51; Head Libn Logan Co Dist Lib, Bellefontaine Ohio 51-55; Head Libn New Castle-Henry Co Pub Lib, New Castle Ind 55-63; Head Libn Nez Perce Co Free Lib, Lewiston Ida 63-. 8: Admin Lewis-Clark (Ida) Lib Demonstration; Nat Lib Week 65-, chm 61. 9: ALA;-PLD (Constit & Bylaws Com); OhioLA (chm Adult Educ 52-53, meetings 55); IndLA (chm Standards Com 57); PNLA (mem Spec Proj's Com); IdaLA (Com chm Standards Com 64, pres 67-68, chm Nomin Com 68, chm Constit & Bylaws Com 68). 10: Kiwanis; Boy Scouts; United Fund; Credit Union; Lewis-Clark Coun. 13: Yes. 14: Admin, bk sel, intel freedom. 15: 1306 Ripon ave, Lewiston Ida 83501.

LINN, BOBBYE (STEELE). b Statesville NC 7 Ag 31. 4: Robert Arlen Linn. 5: Duke 49-52 (Pol Sci) AB; Winthrop Col summers 62, 63, 64, 67 (LS). 7: Libn Charlotte-Mecklenburg Schs Nation Ford Sch Lib 63-. 9: NCEA; CTA. 14: Sch libnship. 15: 336 Hillside ave, Charlotte NC 28209.

LINNENBRUEGGE, GERTRUDE ROSALIE IDA. b Buffalo NY 8 S 12. 5: State Normal Sch (Geneseo NY) 32-36 (Educ, LS) diploma; UBuffalo 37-39 (Hist, Ger) BA, 39-48 (Hist) MA; UChicago 46-48 (LS); West Res 57-58 MS in LS. 6: Ger, Fr. 7: Tchr libn Portville High Sch, Portville NY 35-38; Tchr-libn Orchard Park Central Sch, Orchard Park NY 39-43; USNavy Storekeeper second class; Libn Asst Prof OhioU 48-; Lib spec Ohio U US AID Ibadan Nigeria 65-66, Libn & Asst Prof OhioU 66-. 8: Adv to OhioU, US AID prog in West Nigeria 65-66. 9: ALA-YASD (Bd 57-58); OhioLA; OhioASL (pres 62-63, mem of Bd several terms). 10: Girl Scouts (Reg II Com); AAUP; AAUW. 14: Admin, Africana. 15: 77 W State st, Athens Ohio 45701.

LINSCHEID, CHESTER H. b Busby Mont 3 F 11. 4: M Elizabeth Wiebe. 5: Bethel Col (Newton Kan) 28-32 (Eng) BA; UOkla 33-34 BALS; UIll summer 38 (LS); UMich summer 39, 40-41 MALS. 6: Ger. 7: Libn, Instr in soc sci Panhandle A&M Col 35-36; Asst libn SD State U 36-44, Act libn 44-46; Libn Col of Agric UNeb 46-48; Libn NM State U 49-, Head Dept of Lib Sci 50-. 9: ALA (Coord for NM 54-55, Memb Chm for NM 58-62, Coun 60-64); -ACRL; Assn Higher Educ; NEA; BSA; SWLA; NMLA (pres 52-53); NMEA; SWLA (Constit Com 56-58, chm Policy Com 66-68). 10: AAUP. 13: Yes. 14: Admin. 15: 221 Oxford dr, Las Cruces NM 88001.

LINSLEY, PRISCILLA M (KAHN). b Girard Penn 20 Mr 34. 4: Paul E Linsley. 5: UNH 56 9eng) BA; No IllU 64 (LS) MA. 7: Catlgr No IllU 64-66; Catlgr Educ Testing Serv, princeton NJ 66-68, Libn 68-. 9: ALA; SLA (Com wk Princeton-Trenton Gp); ASIS; NY Educ & Behav Scis Libns. 14: Documentation. 15: Educational Testing Service, Princeton NJ 08540.

LINSTROM, OLIVE (CATON). b Valentine Neb 24 O 04. 5: Black Hills State summer 42-62 (Educ) BS; Emory summer 57 & 63 (LS). 7: Tchr, SD 24-59; Tchr, Wyo 60-63; Sch libn, Jackson Wyo 63-64; Chief Libn VA, Ft Meade SD 64-. 9: ALA; Nat Hosp LA; SDLA. 10: Old Ft Meade Museum Assn; AAUW; Amer Legion Aux; Fed Bus Assn. 14: Ref, rare bks, wk with neuro-psychiatric patients. 15: Box 162, Fort Meade SD 57741.

LINTON, MILDRED FRANCES (McCUTCHEON). b St John NB Can 29 My 07. 4: John Linton. 5: Acadia U 23-27 (Biol) BA; Toronto 47-48 BLS. 7: Tchr Regional High Sch, Plaster Rock NB 28-30; Tchr Pub Sch, Kentville NS 30-31; Catlgr UToronto Lib 48-64, Head catlg dept 64-. 9: CanLA (chm Tech Serv Sect 64-65); ALA; Inst Prof Libns Ont; OntLA (chm Tech Serv Sect 64-65). 10: Univ Women's Club of Toronto. 14: Catlg, bibliog. 15: 131 Bloor st W, apt 904, Toronto 5 Can.

LINVILLE, DORIS M. b Beloit Kan. 5: Ft Hays Kan State Col 36-41 (Speech) AB; Kan State tchrs Col 60, summers 55, 56; SUNY (New Paltz) 61; Boston U summer 63; SUNY (Albany) 63-66 MLS. 7: Eng tchr Rondout Valley High, Accord NY 61-62; Libn Rondout Valley Schs, accord NY 62-64; Libn Kingston City Schs, Kingston NY 64-67; Libn Slippery Rock State Col 67-. 8: Instructor in reading, art, & children's literature in Teachers' Institutes in Kansas Su's 42-50. 9: ALA (life mem); NEA; PennStateEA; NYLA. 10: Delta Kappa Gamma; AAUW; Woman's Club; US Capitol Hist Soc; Butterfield Trail Hist Assn; Ft Wallace Hist Assn; Pony Express Hist Assn; Old Stone House Associates; Plimoth Plantation; Slippery Rock Col Fac Assn. 14: Establ & improv sch libs, child lit. 15: Box 26, Slippery Rock Pa 16057.

LINVILLE, HERBERT. b Paris Ky 5 Je 28. 5: SW at Memphis 46-50 (Fr) BA; Columbia 50-51 (LS) MS. 6: Fr, Sp, Ger. 7: Processing asst Army Med Lib, Wash DC 51; (Sgt) US Marine Corps 51-53; Catlgr UCal (Santa Barbara) 53-59, Head govt pub ser dept 59-. 9: ALA; CalLA; SoCal Tech Processes Group (sec-treas 63-64, chm 67-68). 14: Govt pub, ser, catlg. 15: 807 Moreno rd, Santa Barbara Cal 93103.

LIPETZ, BEN-AMI. b Fargo N Dak 14 Mr 27. 4: Carolyn Aikin. 5: Cornell U 43-48 (Mech Engring) BME, 50-53 (Pub Admin) PhD. 6: Ger, Russian. 7: Electrician's mate 3/c USN 45-46; Ed researcher "Sports Illustrated" McGraw-Hill Publ Co, NY 48; Ed Brookhaven nat Lab, Upton NY 48-50; Ed consul UN AEC 48; Ed Nat Research Coun Committee on Nuclear Sci, Wash DC 48-49; Research assoc Hist of Sci Dept Cornell U 51-52, Research asst Lab of Nuclear Studies summer 52; Asst chief Info Mgt Div Battelle Mem Inst, Columbus Ohio 53-59; Hd Syst Applications Sect Itek Corp, Lexington Mass 59-62; Independent counsul on info mgt & research, Carlisle Mass 62-66; Hd research dept Yale U Lib 66-. 8: Consul: AEC 66-, Off of Educ 68-, NIH 69-. 9: ASIS (chm Boston Chap 65-66); ALA (Exec Com, Lib Res RT 68-69); Amer Soc Indexers (foundling mem); Amer Soc Pub Admin; SLA; Fed of Amer Scientists. 10: Tau Beta Pi; Pi Delta Epsilon; Phi Kappa phi; Carlisle (Mass) Conserv Assn. 12: "The Measurement of Efficiency of Scientific research" (65); "A Guide to Case Studies of Scientific Research" (65); Ed "Information Science Abstracts" (66-); "Guide to Russian Scientific Periodical Literature" (48-50); "Cornell Engineer" (44-48). 13: Yes. 14: Lib mgt, lib research & devel. 15: Yale Univ Lib, New Haven Ct 06520.

LIPNEY, MARJORIE A. b Mobile Ala 16 Je 11. 4: Max Lipney. 5: UCLA 34 (Eng) BA; USoCal 58 (LS) MS. 6: Fr. 7: Sr libn Ventura Co & City Lib, Ventura Cal 59-64, Supv libn 64-66, Coord adult serv 67-. 9: ALA; CalLA. 14: Adult serv. 15: 1199 Church st, Ventura Ca 93001.

LIPPENCOTT, MARGARET E. b Zanesville Ohio. 5: Yale 30 (Hist, Music) MusB. 6: Fr. 7: Asst Yale U Sch of Mus Lib 30-39; Research asst NY Hist Soc Lib, NY 39-43; Libn The Union League Club Lib, NY 43-. 9: ALA. 10: Nat Arts Club. 13: Yes. 14: Res, hist, early Amer music. 15: The Union League Club Lib, 38 E 37 st, New York NY 10016.

LIPSCOMB, LINDA A (WAGNER). b Cleveland Ohio 10 F 43. 4: John F Lipscomb. 5: Marietta Col 61-65 (Eng) AB; West Res 65-66 MSLS. 6: Fr, Sp. 7: Jr libn E Cleveland Pub Lib, e cleveland Ohio 65-66; Sr libn lit research TRW Syst, Redondo Beach Cal 66-67, Info specialist 67-68, Configuration & data mgt specialist (CADM) 68-. 9: SLA. 10: Phi Delta theta. 12: Ed "CADM Standard Practices". 14: Data mgt. 15: 356 Hillcrest st, El Segundo Ca 90245.

LIPSON, BINNIE CYNTHIA. b Pittsburgh Penn 24 N 42. 5: Jr catlgr DuquesneU Lib 67-68, ref asst (docs libn) 68-. 6: Sp. 7: Duquesne 60-64 (Elem Educ) BS; UPittsburgh 64-65 9spex Educ) MEd, 66 MLS. 9: ALA; SLA; PennLA. 10: Phi Delta Gamma. 14: Ref, bk sel. 15: 5548 Forbes ave, Pittsburgh Pa 15217.

LISBON, PETER WALLACE. b NYC 26 My 33. 5: Brown 51-55 (Philos) AB; NYU Law Sch 55-56 (Law); Brown 56-57 (Psych); Simmons 58-60 MS in LS. 6: Fr, Ger, Ital, Sp. 7: Harvard U: Asst for ref & circ Lamont Lib 58-60, Admin asst 60-61, Subj catlgr Widener Lib 61-65, Chief subj catlgr 65-. 9: ALA. 10: Phi Beta Kappa. 14: Catlg, ref, acquis. 15: 24 Woodbridge st, Cambridge Ma 02140.

LISS, CYNTHIA (DEE) ROSEN. b NYC 14 N 46. 4: Barry Liss. 5: CCNY 63-67 (Bio) BS; Rutgers 67-68 MLS. 6: Fr. 7: Lab tech & researcher Albert Einstein Col of Med summers 63-64; Salesgirl NYC 65-66; Receptionist NYC 66-67; Bio sci libn ColumbiaU 68-. 14: Libnship in deptal sci libs, ref, info systems. 15: 1326 Grand Concourse, Bronx NY 10456.

LIST, PHILLIP (JOHN). b Seattle 29 O 16. 4: Eloise Weaver List. 5: UWash 39-47 (Far East) BA, 57-58 MLS; UMd 68 (Lib Admin) Certif. 6: Sp, Russian. 7: King Co Lib, Seattle: Bkmob libn 58-60, Br head Kent Wash 60-61, Br dept head Seattle 61-62, Act dir Seattle 62-63, Asst dir Seattle 62-63, Asst dir Seattle 63-. 9: ALA (Com on Interlib Cooperation 62-65); WashLA (Legis Com 64); PNLA (chm Exec Com on Pacific NW Bibliog Ctr). 10: Optimist Club (Seattle); Alumni Assn, UWash Lib Sch; Puget Sound Lib Club. 14: Admin. 15: 1434-11th ave W, Seattle Wa 98119.

LISTFELDT, HANS-GUENTHER. b Brandenburg Germany 23 N 19. 4: Mary Shover. 5: Loyola Col (Baltimore) 56 (Hist) BS; Catholic U 60 MS in LS, (9hist) BS; Catholic U 60 MS in LS, (Philos) PhL. 06: Ger, Fr, Lat. 7: Asst ser libn UMd Health Sci Lib, Baltimore 60-65, Ser ref libn 65-67, Hd ser dept 67-. 9: SLA. 14: Ser, ref, admin. 15: Rte 3 Box 16-E, Westminster Md 21157.

LISTFELDT, MARY S. b Albany NY 12 Jl 22. 4: Hans-Guenther Listfeldt. 5: SUNY (Albany) 40-44 (Ger) BA; UWis 46-47 BLS; CatholicU 63- (LS). 6: Ger. 7: Gen lib asst usntc lib, Sampson NY 45-46; Period ref asst UWis Lib (Madison) 46-47; Child libn Enoch Pratt Free Lib, Baltimore 47-56; Libn Md State Legis Ref Lib, Baltimore 56-58; Act hd ref dept UMd Health Sci Lib, Baltimore 68-. 10: UWis Alumni Assn. 14: Ref serv, spec lib admin. 15: 428 Sullivan rd, Westminster Md 21157.

LITCHFIELD, MEREDITH CHARLES. b Emporia Kan 20 Ja 28. 4: Colleen McAllister. 5: Kan State Tchrs Col 45-50 (Phys Educ) BS in Ed, 61, 67 MLS. 7: Tchr Kan high sch: Burns 50-52, Bazine 55-57; Sgt US Army: Artillery 52-54, Spec Serv 57-60; Libn Riley co High Sch, Riley Kan 60-67; Admin asst Kan State U Lib 67-. 9: NEA; KanLA; KanStateTA; KanASchL. 10: Lions Intl; Amer Legion. 15: Rte 4, Manhattan Ks 66502.

LITCHFIELD, RUTH B (REED). b Whitman Mass 13 D 12. 4: Elwood Litchfield. 5: Tufts Col 30-34 (Eng, Educ) AB; Simmons summer 35 (Catlg). 6: Fr, Lat. 7: Ref libn & asst catlgr Tufts, Weymouth 35-38; Catlgr Lucius Beebe Lib, Wakefield Mass 63-. 9: ALA; MassLA. 10: Girl Scouts of Amer; Phi Beta Kappa. 14: Catlg, ref, loc hist. 15: 23 Cordis st, Wakefield Mass 01880.

LITTLE, AGNES EASTMAN (MRS). b Colerain Mass 12 Ag 16. 5: Smith 34-38 (Hist) AB; UNC 59-62 MS in LS. 7: Asst humanities ref UNC 62; Asst Chapel Hill (NC) Pub Lib 63; Asst ref period Providence Pub Lib 63-66; Libn Pembroke Col Lib (Providence). 14: Ref. 15: 7 Benefit st, Providence RI 02904.

LITTLE, ANN. b Tuxedo NY 8 D 31. 5: Beaver Col 49-52 (Span); UConn 52-53 (Span) BA; Queens Col CUNY 66-69 MLS. 06: Sp. 7: Manufacturers Hanover Trust, NY: Clerk 53-55, Asst ed 55-57, Asst libn 57-59, Libn 59-. 9: SLA (NY Chap: Treas 67-68, chm Auditing Com 68-69); NY Lib Club. 12: Co-ed "Special Libraries of Greater New York" (10th ed 63). 14: Ref. 15: 217-34 51st ave, Bayside NY 11364.

LITTLE, CECILY (JOHNS). b Wichita Kan 5 O 39. 4: Stephen James Little. 5: UKan 57-61 (Eng, Fr) BA, 62-63, 66 (Eng) MA; UCLA 67-68 MLS. 6: Fr. 7: Sec & libn Wichita Guidance Ct, Wichita Kan 61-62; Research asst UKan Eng Dept 62-63; Clk stud UKan Lib 63; Sr typist clerk UCLA Lib 63-66, Lib asst II 67, Clerk stud 67-68; Ref libn UTex Lib (Austin) 68-. 10: Sierra Club; ACLU. 14: Ref. 15: 7303 Grand Canyon, Austin Tx 78752.

LITTLE, DORIS PETTIGREW. b Telfair Co Ga 23 Mr 32. 5: Paine Col 49-53 (Eng) BA; Atlanta summers 54, 56, 57-59 MSLS. 6: Fr. 7: Eng tchr Carver High Sch, Dawson Ga 53-56; Tchr-libn Florence Elem Sch, Savannah Ga 56-58; Libn Caylor Jr High Sch, Savannah Ga 58-60; Libn Johnson High Sch, Savannah Ga 60-62; State lib consul State Dept of Educ, Atlanta 62-63; Child libn Pub Lib, Savannah Ga summers 60-62; Spec libn Fed Aviation Agency, Atlanta 64-. 9: SLA; NEA; Ga Tchrs & Educ Assn (past pres Libns Sect). 10: YWCA. 14: Ref. 15: 1390 Sharon st NW, Atlanta Ga 30314.

LITTLE, ELIZABETH (WINDEN). b Toole Co Mont 30 Ap 14. 4: Cyril Little. 5: No Mont Col 32-34, summer 35, 41 (Educ) Tchg Certif; Mont State U summer 54-57 (Elem Educ) BS; UMont summer 63, 64; UWash summer 67. 7: Prim tchr Pub Sch, Ingomar Mont 35-38; Prim tchr Pub Sch, Wilsall Mont 43-44; Rural tchr Dist 4, Sidney Mont 54-57; Elem tchr Pub Sch, Sidney Mont 57-60; Libn Jr High Sch, Sidney Mont 60-. 8: Mem of Mont Lang Arts Course of Study Com 57-60; Mont Reading Coun 57-60. 9: NEA; ALA; MontEA (Dist Lib Sect chm 64-65); MontLA; MontASchL (chm 65-66). 10: Delta Kappa Gamma. 14: Serv to young adults, admin. 15: 812 3rd st SW, Sidney Mont 59270.

LITTLE, GRETCHEN D. b High Bridge NJ 7 N 13. 5: Duke 32-36 (Chem) AB; Columbia 37 (LS); Drexel 46-49 BS in LS. 7: Asst libn US Rubber Products, Passaic NJ 36-37; Libn Mead Corp, Chillicothe Ohio 37-43; Libn Atlas Chem Ind, Wilmington Del 43-. 9: ASIS; MedLA; SLA (pres 54-55; Chm Sci-Tech Div; Pres Cincinnati Chap; Chm 50th Annual Convention; John Cotton Dana Lectr); DelLA. 10: AAAS; ACS; Zonta Club; Girl Scouts. 13: Yes. 15: Atlas Chem Ind, Wilmington Del 19899.

LITTLE, JO. b Bay City Mich 23 Ag 29. 5: Saginaw Bus Inst 46-48; Harper Hosp (Detroit) 62 Internship. 7: Act chief operator Michigan Bell Tel Co, Saginaw 46-56; Program coord XETV Television, San Diego 56-57; Chief med sec Pathology Dept St Luke's Hosp, Saginaw Mich 57-62, Chief med libn 62-. 8: Lib consul, var hosps in Saginaw-Bay City 9mich) area. 9: MedLA; ALA; Med Record Libns (E Central Dist Assn). 10: Mich Alcohol and Addiction Assn. 12: Mng ed "Staff Medical Bulletin" St Luke's Hosp, Saginaw (62-). 14: Ref. 15: St Luke's Hosp Med Lib, 705 Cooper st, Saginaw Mi 48602.

LITTLE, MARGARET L(INDSAY). b Prince George BC Can 4 D 20. 5: UBC 38-42 (Fr) BA; Toronto 42-43 BLS. 7: Catlgr Victoria Pub Lib, Victoria BC 43-45; Catlgr UBC 45-50; Catlgr Wash State U 51-53; Catlgr UBC 53-55, 56-61; Asst hd catlg div UBC 61-. 9: ALA; CanLA; BCLA; PNLA. 14: Catlg. 15: 4651 W 5th ave, Vancouver 8 BC Can.

LITTLE, MARY (ENGLAND). b Sparta Tenn 22 Je 16. 4: Joe Little. 5: Tenn Tech U 35-38 (Eng) BS; Peabody 46 (Eng) MA, 57 MA in LS. 6: Sp, Fr. 7: Eng tchr White Co High Sch, Sparta Tenn 38-39; Eng tchr Stewart Co High Sch, Dover Tenn 41-44; Eng tchr White Co High Sch, Sparta Tenn 44-45; Eng tchr Central High Sch, Murfreesboro Tenn 45-51; Class room tchr Sparta City Schs, Sparta Tenn 52-56; Reg Libn Pub Libs, Sparta Tenn 57-. 8: Tenn State Dir, Nat Lib Week 62. 9: NEA (Life mem); ALA; SELA; TennLA. 10: Tenn Congress Parents & Tchrs; AAUW; Alumni Assn of Tenn Tech U; Delta Kappa Gamma; Phi Gamma Mu. 13: Yes. 14: Catlg, ref. 15: Rt 4, Sparta Tenn 38583.

LITTLE, NANCY STONER. b Asheville NC 25 Mr 11. 4: Lonnie Marcus Little. 5: UNC(reensboro) (Greensboro) AB(LS); Northwestern 38-40 (Promotional Sales, Radio). 6: Sp, Ital. 7: Head Libn Lee Edwards Sr High Sch, asheville NC 31-34; Asst dir sch lib div NC Dept of Pub Instr, Raleigh NC 34-36; Head promotional sales dept Laidlaw Publ, NYC & Chicago 36-41; Promotional sales mgr Nat Peanut Coun 44-45; Sales manager Eastern Radio Supply, Fayetteville NC 45-47; Asst advertising dir Coca-Cola Bottling Co, Asheville NC 47-50; Head Libn Iredell Co Lib, Statesville NC 54-57; Head Libn Statesville Pub Lib, Statesville NC 58-67. 9: ALA; NCLA (Pub Lib Sect, A-V Com 61-63; co-chm Bldg Inst 63); SELA; NCEA. 10: Piedmont Pub Lib Coun; Iredell Co Libns Coun; Iredell Friends of the Lib, Statesville NC; Dogwood Garden Club; Statesville Womans Club; Altrusa Club; 21 Investment Club; Arts & Science Mus; Statesville Little Theatre; Girl Scout Coun; Iredell Hist Soc; Iredell Med Aux. 12: ED "Nutrition New Nat Peanut Coun (45): Ed "Bubbling BOTTLE," Coca-Cola; Ed "Book Nook, Laidlaw Publrs. 13: Yes. 14: Admin, a-v, ref, pub rel. 15: St Andrews rd, Shannon Acres, Statesville NC 28677.

LITTLE, ROBERT DAVID. b Milwaukee 11 Jl 37. 5: UWis(Milwaukee) 55-59 (Educ, Hist, Soc Studies) BA; UWis (Madison) summers 60-64 (LS) MA, 67-69 (LS). 06: Lat. 7: Tchr-libn Sevastopol Schs, Sturgeon Bay Wis 59-62; Libn Highland Park High Sch, Highland Park Ill 62-63; Supv of Instr materials Sevastopol Schs, Sturgeon Bay Wis 63-65; Supv of Instr materials Gibraltar High Sch, Fish Creek Wis 63-65; Pub instr supv lib serv Wis Dept of Pub Instr, Madison Wis 65-. 9: ALA; NEA; Amer Classical League; WisLA (Sch Libns Sect: sec 63-64, v-chm 65-66, chm 66-67); WisEA. 10: Wis Alumni Assn; Wis Lib Sch Alumni Assn; Eta Sigma Phi; Phi Alpha Theta. 13: Yes. 14: Sch libs, admin, supvn, adolescent lit. 15: 4817 Sheboygan ave apt 709, Madison Wis 53705.

LITTLE, ROSEMARY (von STORCH) ALLEN. b Newark NJ 14 Je 38. 4: John Edwin Little. 5: Douglass Col 56-60 (Eng) AB; Rutgers 60-61 MLS. 6: Fr. 7: Page Rutherford Pub lib, Rutherford NJ 55-56; Asst Fairleigh Dickinson U Lib summers 57-60; Asst Douglass Col Lib 60-61; Asst ref libn Princeton U Lib 61-64, Libn pub admin collection 64-. 8: Staff, Lib/USA, NY World's Faor 64. 9: ALA; SLA (sec-treas Princeton-Trenton Chap 68-69); NJLA; NY Lib Club. 10: Friends of the Princeton Univ Lib; Metro Museum of Art. 14: Ref, acad lib admin. 15: 1 Grandview ave, Lawrenceville NJ 08648.

LITTLE, RUTH ALICE (OGILVIE). b Lynn Mass 22 N 19. 4: J Gordon Little. 5: Radcliffe 35-39 (Govt) AB; Simmons 39-40 (LS) BS; UCal (Santa Barbara) 62-63 (Pol Sci) MA. 7: Catlgr Baker Lib, Harvard Bus Sch 40-42; Tech libn & histn, Boston Ordnance Dist 42-45; Base libn, Hamilton AFB Cal 49-53; Researcher Legis Ref Serv, LC 57; Fed Proj Dir Santa Barbara (Cal) Pub Lib 58-59; Head Libn Santa Barbara City Col 59-. 9: CalLA (pres Commun Col Div). 10: AAUW; Intl Soc Sci Inst. 14: Ref, admin. 15: 2521 Calle Galicia, Santa Barbara Ca 93105.

LITTLE, THOMPSON M. b Watertown Mass 26 F 30. 4: Barbara A Meade. 5: Bowdoin Col 47-51 (Hist) AB; Columbia 55-57 (LS) MS. 6: Fr. 7: Asst supt US Envelope Co, Rockville Conn 51-54; Trainee NY Pub Lib 55-57; Ref libn Stanford U Lib 57-62; Libn Sch of Lib Serv Columbia U 62-65; Assoc dir of lib serv Hofstra u 65-68; D ir of libs Ohio U 68-. 8: Lecturer lib sci, Columbia Sch of Lib Serv, 62-68. 9: ALA. 11: Joseph Towne Wheeler Award, Columbia U Sch of Lib Serv. 12: Major contrib "Sources of Information in the Social Sciences," ed by C M White (64). 13: Yes. 14: Admin, ref. 15: 10 North May, Athens Oh 45701.

LITTLEFIELD, PATRICIA . b Melrose Highlands Mass 17 Ja 14. 5: Middlebury Col 31-35 (Amer Lit) AB; Simmons 55-63 (LS) MS. 6: Fr. 7: Tchr The Misses Scully Sch, Concord NH 35-37; Sec Campbell Metal Window Corp, Boston 37-39; Sec MIT 40-49; Circ asst Harvard Law Sch Lib 52-55, Circ supv 55-63; Acquis libn Bentley Col of Accounting & Finance 63-, Asst dir Baker-Vanguard Lib 69-. 9: ALA-ACRL; NELA; NE Tech Serv Libns. 14: Acquis. 15: 14 Remington st, Cambridge Ma 02138.

LITTLETON, I(SAAC) T(HOMAS) III. b Hartsville Tenn 28 Ja 21. 4: Dorothy Young. 5: UNC 39-43 (Sociol) AB; UTenn 47-50 (Psych) MA; UIll 50-51 MS in LS, 61-68 PhD. 6: Fr, Ger. 7: (Lt jg) US Navy 43-46; Train off VA, Knoxville Tenn 46-47; Train off Knoxville Trade Sch, Knoxville Tenn 49-50; Head circ dept UNC Lib (Chapel Hill) 51-53, Asst to libn 53-58; Asst dir tech serv NC State U Lib 58-64, Act dir 64-67, Dir 67-. 8: Instr Peabody Col Lib Sch summer 58; Consul & surveyor NC Agric & Tech Col 59-60; Consul Nat Agricul Lib of Peru 67. 9: ALA (Jt Com on Union List of Ser); NCLA (chm 2 coms 53-57); SELA (chm Recr Com 56-62, treas 58-60). 10: AAUP; Beta Phi Mu. 12: Ed "North Carolina Union List of Scientific Serials" (65); "The Bibliographic Organization & Use of the Literature of Agricultural Economics," (Res Report and PhD Diss 68). 13: Yes. 14: Admin, tech proc. 15: 4813 Brookhaven dr, Raleigh NC 27609.

LITTLEWOOD, JOHN MILES. b La Moille Ill 8 S 31. 5: N Central Col (Naperville Ill) 49-53 (Eng, Pol Sci) BA; UIll 59-61 (LS) MS. 7: (SP3) Finance Corps US Army 53-56; UIll Lib (Urbana): Bkstacks deck supv 60-61, Asst chem libn 61-62, Bibliog ser dept 62-64, Documents libn 64-. 9: ALA; IllLA. 10: Beta Phi Mu; Pi Gamma Mu; Sigma Tau Delta. 15: 311 W U niv ave, Champaign Il 61820.

LITZ, CAROL (JOY). b Winnipeg Manitoba Can 24 Jl 44. 5: UBC 62-66 (Microbiol, Zool) BS, 67-68 BLS. 7: Bio sci libn Simon FraserU Lib, Burnaby BC Can 68-. 14: Ref. 15: #208 2226 W 8th, Vancouver 9 BC Can.

LIU, ALBERT CHENG-AN. b Kiangsi China 11 F 38. 4: Ruth Shan-shang Ho. 5: Tamkang Col (Taiwan) 59-63 (Eng) BA; Atlanta U 66-67 MSLS. 6: Chinese. 7: 2nd Lt Chinese Army, Taiwan 63-64; Tchr Chungli High Sch, Taiwan 64-65; Asst catlgr AM&N Col, Pine Bluff Ark 67-68; Instr & hd catlgr Hampton Inst 68-. 9: ALA. 14: Catlg, ref, lib arch. 15: Box 6626 Hampton Inst, Hampton Va 23368.

LIU, DAVID TA-CHING. b Kwangtung China 6 D 36. 4: Agnete3 Mei-Cheng Liu. 5: Tamkang Eng Col (Taiwan) 54-55 (Eng); Nat Taiwan U 55-59 (Eng Lit, Foreign Langs) BA; Eng Research Inst of Taiwan Normal U 60-61 (Eng); UWash 62 (Pol Sci); Peabody 62-63 MALS. 6: Chinese, Fr, SP. 7: Interpreter-off (2nd Lt) Chinese Air Force Hdqrs, Taipei City Taiwan 60-61; Catlgr Chicago Pub Lib 63-64; Chief of adult serv & readers adv Joliet Pub Lib, Joliet Ill 64; Dir of Lib Bay de Noc Commun Col 64-. 8: Del of UWash to Internat Stud Conf, Vancouver BC 62. 9: ALA; Nat Assn Higher Educ; Mich Assn Higher Educ. 10: Internat Cong of Orientalists; Chinese Culture Assn. 13: Yes 14: Catlg, circ, ref, Oriental bks, C hinese art, lib planning. 15: 33315 8th ave, Escanaba Mi 49829.

LIU, GEORGE BIE. b Changsha Hunan China 21 S 12. 5: Central Police Col (Nanking China) 32-33 (Criminology) Certif; Fresno State Col 48-50 (Criminology) BA; UIll(Urbana) 50-53 (Pol Sci) MA, 57-59 MLS. 6: Chinese. 7: Instr Nat Army Acad Sixth Br, Kwelin China 38-40; Dir personnel off Central Police Col (Chungking & Nanking) 40-47; Research asst Bacteriology Dept UIll(Urbana) 55-57; Libn I Cleveland Pub Lib 59-61; Libn II-III Cal State Col (Fullerton) 61-67; Catlgr GS11 LC 67-. 9: ALA. 14: Catlg. 15: 4831 36th st NW #203, Washington DC 20008.

LIU, KATHLEEN SU. b Taiwan China 1 Mr 39. 4: Sam Liu. 5: Taiwan NormalU 57-61 (Eng) BA; UPittsburgh 66-67 MLS. 6: Chinese. 7: Tchr Yen-ping High Sch, Taiwan 61-65; Child libn J Lewis Crozer Lib, Chester Penn 67-. 14: Wk with child, catlg. 15: 838 Haverfird rd, Ridley Park Pa 19078.

LIU, NATHANIEL SHIH-HSIANG. b Hupei China 8 N 33. 4: Peggy Woo. 5: Tamkang Eng Col (China) 54-57 (Eng) AA; Hofstra U 61-63 (Journalism) BA; LIU 64-65 (LS) MS; NYState Pub Libns Prof Certif 68-69, Sch Libns Prof Certif. 6: Chinese. 7: Ed asst United Daily News, Taipei Taiwan 57-59; (2nd Lt) Chinese Army, Taipei Taiwan 59-60; UN Correspondent Union News Agency, Taipei Taiwan 60-63; Asst libn period dept C W Post Col 64-66; Ref libn Plainedge Pub Lib, Massapequa NY 66-68; Libn in chg of IMC Straight Path Sch, Wyandanch NY 68-. 8: UN Spec Corres assigned by Union News Agency of Taipei Taiwan & stationed in NY 60-63. 9: Nassau Co LA. 10: LIU Grad Lib Sch Alum Assn. 11: Appreciation Certif of Hempstead Lions Club. 14: Catlg, a-v materials. 15: 33 Dikeman st, Hempstead NY 11550.

LIU, SUSANA JUH-MEI (CHEN). b Fuchien China 16 O 42. 4: Gerald Chien-wu Liu. 6: Chinese, Fr. 7: Soc wkr Guidance Ctr Ministry of Educ, Taipei Taiwan 63-64; Asst catlgr Cleveland StateU Lib 66; Jr libn UMo Lib (Columbia) 66-69; Catlg libn RiceU 69-. 9: ALA. 14: Catlg. 15: 6525 Hillcroft apt 510, Houston Tx 77036.

LIVELY, GERTRUDE (HOWARD). b Jefferson Co Ky 10 Jl 02. 5: Simmons 29 (Home Econ); Ky State Col 30-35 (Educ) AB; IndU 45-50 (Educ) MS; Catherine Spalding 55-58 MSLS. 7: Tchr Jefferson Co Sch System 30-54; Libn Jefferson Co Sch Libs, Newburg Ky 54-60; Asst libn Tenn State U summer 59; Lib wkshop consul Ky State col 63; Libn Simmons U 58-65; Libn adult educ Jefferson Co, Ky 65-. 9: NEA; KyLA; KyEA. 10: AAUW; Alpha Kappa; YWCA; NAACP; Ky State Col Alumni Assn; Mi-Dear Social Club. 11: Tchr of Year (Newburg Sch); Distinguished Alumni Award Ky State Col 64. 15: 1027 South Western parkway, Louisville Ky 40211.

LIVELY, GLADYS M. b E St Louis Ill 22 Jl 08. 5: Ind Central Col 25-29 (Eng) AB; UIll 41-43 summers BS in LS; Chicago summer 47 (LS). 7: Tchr Mendon & Kansas High Schs, Ill 30-37, 40-43; Libn Ottawa Twp High Sch, Ottawa Ill 43-47; Instr UKy Lib Sch summer 49; Libn E St Louis (Ill) High Sch 47-52; Madison Pub Schs: Libn E High Sch 52-56, Catlgr 56-65, Head catlg & processing serv 65-. 9: ALA-AASchL;-RTSD (Sch Lib Catlg Com); NEA; WisEA; WisLA. 13: Yes. 14: Catlg, centralized processing for sch libs. 15: Bd of Educ, 545 W Dayton st, Madison Wi 53703.

LIVENGOOD, EDWARD BRUCE. b Redlands Cal 16 Jl 24. 4: Jane Crane. 5: UPittsburgh 46-50 (Eng) AB; USoCal 59-60 MSLS. 6: Sp. 7: Pfc USA Med Corps, LeMans France 44-46; Asst order libn Col State Col (Long Beach) 59-60; Ref libn Cal State Col (Fullerton) 60-67, Hd ref dept 67-. 9: OrangeCoLA (Exec Com). 10: Sigma Tau Delta. 14: Ref. 15: 9901 Garrett cir, Huntington Beach Ca 92646.

LIVERITTE, RUDY H. b Hattiesburg Miss 9 Ja 34. 4: Susana Conde. 5: USoMiss 52-61 (Eng) BA; UWash 63-64 MLS. 6: Sp. 7: MP US Army, Korea & US 53-56; Spec agt CIC US Army, US & Europe 58-60; Eng & Sp instr USo Miss 60-61; Tchr Bellingham High Sch, Bellingham Wash 61-63; Asst ser & photocopy libn UWash 64-66; Consul sch lib & a-v serv Idaho Dept of Educ, Boise 66-. 8: Chm Title III Adv Coun to Idaho State Lib Bd. 9: ALA; -AASchL (State Assembly Planning Com, Reg VII rep); NEA-DAVI; IowaLA; Iowa A-V Assn. 10: Beta Phi Mu; Kappa Delta Pi; Board Member and Treasurer of the Urban Coalition of the City of Boise, Inc. 12: "Book Selection and Weeding in School Libraries" (66); "Guidelines for Instructional Materials Programs in Idaho Schools" (67); "Suggestions for Teaching Library and Bibliographic Skills in Elementary and Secondary Schools" (67); "School Library Survey" (67); "The School Library Program" (68); "Suggestions for School Library Facility Planners" (68), (All publ by Idaho Dept of Educ). 13: Yes. 14: Admin, lib educ. 15: 7023 Ashland dr, Boise Id 83705.

LIVINGSTON, FRANCES G. b Chicago 25 S 36. 4: James F Livingston. 5: Knox Col 54-58 (Fr, Eng) BA (cum laude); Chicago 58-60, 63 (LS) MA. 6: Fr. 7: Ser & catlg asst ULouisville 60-62; Sr libn for Tech Serv ULouisville Med Sch 62-67; Assoc libn 67-. 8: Lecturer in Lib Sci Catherine Spalding Col Grad Lib Sch (summer session instr in catlg) 64-; Instr of MLA course in "Punched Card Applications" 64-; Instr med bibliog ULouisville Med Sch 64-66; Asst Prof 66-. 9: ALA; SLA; MedLA (chm Com on Cont Educ 69-); KyLA. 10: Phi Mu; Sigma Alpha Iota; Louisville Lib Club; Beta Phi Mu. 13: Yes. 14: Tech serv, tchg, data processing, admin & mgt. 15: 3439 Newburg rd apt 2, Louisville Ky 40218.

LIVINGSTON, HELEN M (SHANOSKY). b Lynn Mass 27 S 09. 4: William J Livingston. 5: UNH 53-62 (Bus) BS; No Essex Commun Col 63-65 (LS). 6: Polish. 7: Bkkeeper Creamery Package Mfg Co, Boston 27-28; Bkkeeper & acc Lynn Specialty Co, Lynn Mass 28-37; Acc Keezer Mfg Co, Plaistow NH 47-53; Circ libn Haverhill Pub Lib, Haverhill Mass 55-. 10: Friends of the Haverhill Pub Lib. 15: Hemlock ave, Atkinson NH 03811.

LIVINGSTON, HELEN P(ORRITT). b Montreal Que Can 12 F 32. 4: Daniel Livingston. 5: Bishop's U 49-52 (Eng) BA; Simmon's 53-54 (LS) MS. 6: Fr. 7: Child libn Detroit Pub Lib 54-57; Child libn Akron Pub Lib, Akron Ohio 60-62; School libn Akron Pub Schs, akron Ohio 65-. 9: ALA; -AASchL; OhioLA. 14: Child, elem sch, pub lib wk. 15: 731 Frank blvd, Akron Oh 44320.

LIVINGSTON, WILLIAM (OLIVER). b Palatka Fla 11 Ja 23. 4: Julie Downing. 5: Spring Hill Col 51-55 (Eng) BA; Fla State U 55-60 MALS. 7: Chief Yeoman (personnel) US Navy 41-49; Libn Jr High Sch, St Petersburg Fla 55-60; Ref libn Mobile Pub Lib, Mobile Ala 63-66; Ref & adult serv libn Spring Hill Col 60-. 9: NEA; ALA; FlaLA; AlaLA; CathLA; PinellasCoLA. 10: Mobile Art Assn. 14: Ref, catlg. 15: 202 Stillwood lane, Mobile Al 36608.

LLEWELLYN, MARY EMMA (LEACHEY). b Lancaster Penn 20 Je 19. 4: Joseph B Llewellyn. 5: Millersville State Tchrs Col 36-40 (LS) BS; UPittsburgh 67-68 MLS. 7: Libn: Ellsworth High Sch, Ellsworth Pa 40-42, E Donegal Twp High Sch, Maytown Pa 42-45, 51-54, 54-68; Stud tchr supv Lib Educ Dept Millersville State Col 68-. 9: ALA; NEA; PennLA; PennStateEA; LancasterCoLA. 10: Beta Phi Mu; Millersville State Col Fac Assn; Alpha Beta Alpha. 14: Lib educ, catlg. 15: Box 409A RD #2, Mt Joy Pa 17552.

LLEWIS, R VIOLIAI M. b Sealy Tex 7 Jl 30. 5: Del State U 44-45 (Eng); Lincoln U (Mo) 45-48 (Journalism) BJ; Columbia 52-55 (Social Psych) MA, 54-55 (LS); Rutgers 56-57 MLS; Columbia 61-62 (Educ); St Johns U (NY) 63-64; Columbia 66-.

6: Fr. 7: Newspaper ed "Metropolitan Civic News, Houston 49-52, Publisher & ed 50-52; Founder, publisher, ed "The People's Institute Weekly," Houston 51-52; Founder of an adult sch People's Institute of Learning, Houston 51-52; Lib tech NY Pub Lib 53-54; Lib trainee & stud Brooklyn Pub Lib 55-57; Child libn Queensboro Pub Lib, NYC 57-58; Tchr & libn NY Pub Sch System, NYC 58-. 8: Tchr, NYC summer vacation Day Sch 60-; Coord of Teen's Program, NYC Bur of Commun Educ, 64-65; Tchr of Remedial reading, NYC Pub Sch System, summer 67; Libn & tchr of Eng & reading, Intermed & Jr High Sch summer 68; Instr, Even Div, Acctg Dept, NY City Community Col 68-. 10: United Fed Col Tchrs; United Fed Tchrs. 14: Ref, catlg. 15: PO Box 201 Brevoort Sta, Brooklyn NY 11216.

LLOYD, GWENDOLYN (DOROTHY). b Glasgow Mont 23 O 12. 5: Fla State U 29-32 (Educ) BA; UIll 32-33 (LS) BS, 41-42, 43 (LS) MA. 7: Libn Dixie Co High Sch, Cross City Fla 33-34; Period & binding libn UFla 34-39, Head ref dept 39-41, 42-43; Ensign to Lt USNR Div of Air Nav Hydrographic Off, Wash DC 43-46; H Head ref dept Baylor U 46; Act libn Hist & Pol Sci Lib UIll(Urbana) 47; 1st asst ref dept USoC al 47-48; Libn Inst of Ind Rel UCal(Berkeley) 48-. 9: ALA; SLA (chm Ind Rel Sect 50-51; San Francisco Bay Reg Chap; treas 53-55, Bul ed 51-52); chm Com Univ Ind Rel Libns 61, 68. 10: Beta Phi Mu; Phi Kappa Phi; Kappa Delta Pi; Beta Pi Theta; Phi Alpha Theta. 12: Co-ed "Industrial Relations Theses and Dissertations." 13: Yes. 14: Spec libs, ref (ind rel). 15: 1685 Euclid ave, apt 4, Berkeley Ca 94709.

LLOYD, H ROLLIN. b Ambridge Penn 11 O 17. 4: Hilda V Chequer. 5: Ohio No U 36-40 (Chem, Biol) AB; UPittsburgh 64 MLS. 7: Sgt Army Signal Corps, USA & ETO 42-45; Cost acct & budget analyst Amer Window Glass Co, Pittsburgh Penn 48-53; Budget analyst Crucible Steel Co, Pittsburgh Penn 53-61; Marketing consul, Pittsburgh Penn 61-62; Salesman Brown & Bigelow, Pittsburgh Penn 62-63; Libn Penn State U (New Kensington) 65-66, (Univ Park) 66-. 9: ALA; PennLA. 14: Admin, statistics analysis & eval. 15: 505 E Prospect ave, State College Pa 16801.

LLULL, HARRY P. b White Plains NY 14 O 45. 5: Marion Inst 63-65 (Math) AS; AuburnU 65-67 (Math) BS; UMich 67-68 AMLS. 7: Sci libn-instr Ralph Brown Draughon Lib Auburn U 68-. 9: AlaLA. 10: Auburn Alumni Assn; Mich Alumni Assn. 14: Ref. 15: 18 Kingston ct, Auburn Al 36830.

LO, GRACE CHENG-TSENG (HSU). b Republic of China 23 O 37. 4: Wen-so Lo. 5: Nat Taiwan U 55-59 (Hist) BA; Kan State Tchrs Col)Emporia) 60-62 (LS) MS. 06; Chinese, Fr. 7: Catlgr Nat Central Lib, Taipei Taiwan China 59-60; Res bk room libn Ore State U Lib 62-. 9: PNLA; OreLA. 14: Catlg, circ. 15: Ore State Univ Lib, Corvallis Or 97331.

LO, LYDIA. b Manila 1 Jl 43. 5: UPhilippines 60-64 BSLS; Columbia 66-68 MSLS. 6: Chinese. 7: Libn St Stephen's High Sch, Manila Philippines 64-65; Asst libn St Andrew's Theol Sem, Quezon City Philippines 65-66; Hd catlgr Gen Theol Sem, NYC 68-. 9: ALA; ATheolLA. 10: UPhilippines Madrigal Singers. 14: Catlg, ref. 15: 175 Ninth ave, New York NY 10011.

LOAR, BARBARA. b Greenville Miss. 4: Warren N Loar III. 5: UNC 45-47 (Psych) AB; UDenver 53 (LS) MA. 7: Dir tech processes Mun Lib, Jackson Miss 55-58; Humanities div asst LSU Lib 58-60; Base libn, Westover AFB Mass 60-63; Staff libn Hdqrs Second Air Force, Barksdale AFB La 63-67; Asst command libn Hdqrs SAC, Offutt AFB Neb 67-68; VA Hosp libn, Omaha Neb 68-. 8: Lib 21, Seattle Worlds Fair, 62; Exec dir La Nat Lib Wk Com 67. 9: ALA; LaLA (Recr Com); MissLA (Publ chm); PLA (pres-elect Armed Forces Libns Sect 69). 15: 1403 Lawrence la, Bellevue Nb 68005.

LOBENSTEIN, DeLAURA V (WHIPPLE). b Manhattan Kan 26 F 16. 4: Charles W Lobenstein. 5: Cottey Jr Col 34-36 AA; Kan StateU 37-39 (Soc Sci) BS; So IllU 55-62 (Educ); UIll 65-69 MSLS. 7: Tchr elem schs, Carbondale Ill 55-60, 62-65; Jr prof libn PurdueU (Lafayette) 60-62; Lib asst UMo (Columbia) 66-67, Jr libn 67-. 9: MoLA. 14: Tech proc. 15: 2007 Crestridge, Columbia Mo 65201.

LOCATELLI, JANET ANN. b Laurium Mich 7 O 36. 5: Mich Tech U 54-58 (Med Techn) BS; UMich 64-65 (LS) MA. 07: Med tech (ASCP) St Joseph Hosp, Flint Mich 58-61; Med tech (ASCP) Badger Reg Blood Center, Madison Wis 61; Med tech (ASCP) Calumet Pub Hosp, Laurium Mich 62-63; Ref libn & Instr Mich Tech U 65-. 9: ALA. 14: Ref. 15: 327 Iroquois st, Laurium Mi 49913.

LOCHHEAD, JOHN L. b Winthrop Mass 26 Ap 09. 5: Bowdoin 27-31 AB; Harvard 31-32 AM; Columbia 46-47 BS in LS. 7: Libn Mariners Museum, Newport News Va 46-. 15: Mariners Museum, Newport News Va 23606.

LOCK, MARY LOU (POSEY). b Dallas 31 Ag 29. 4: James Curtis Lock. 5: E Tex Baptist 46-47; Sam Houston State 54-57 (LS) BS; Baylor U 57; UHouston 62; Tex Woman's U 65-; Sul Ross State Tchrs Col supv certif. 7: Tchr-libn pub sch, Calvert Tex 57-58; Libn pub sch, Brookshire Tex 61-63; Tchr pub sch, Harlingen Tex 63; Libn pub sch, Longview Tex 64-. 8: Consul & dir lib wkshops 57, 65, 68, 69; Media Spec Reg VII Educ Serv Ctr; Lib consult & spec educ materials consult Reg VII Ed serv ctr at Kilgore. 9: ALA; TexLA; Tex State Tchrs Assn (Chm Lib Div of Dist 8, past sec of dist 6); Classroom Tchrs Assn. 10: PTA. 13: Yes. 14: Sch libs. 15: 1311 Stanford, Longview Tx 75603.

LOCKE, EDWARD. b NY 9 N 28. 4: Elisabeth Hildesheimer. 5: NYU 45-49 (Eng) BA, 49-50 (Eng) MA; Columbia 54-56 (LS) MS. 7: (Pfc) US Army Artillery 51-53; Libn Brooklyn Pub Lib 55-58; Libn Elmont (NY) Pub Lib 58; Dir E Paterson (NJ) Pub Lib 59-61; Dir Paramus (NJ) Pub Lib 61-64; Asst dir Mid-Hudson Libs, NY 64-. 8: Act dir SEast NY PLib Resources Coun 67-68; Exec sec Mid-Bergen Fed 62-63. 9: Amer Lib Trustees Assn (Intellectual Freedom Com); NYLA (Intellectual Freedom Com). 10: Intel Freedom Com, NJ; Mid-Bergen Fed, NJ. 13: Yes. 14: Admin. 15: 6 Miller rd, Poughkeepsie NY 12603.

LOCKE, GENEVIEVE A. b Buffalo NY. 5: Rosary Col 41-45 (Fr) BA, 61-65 (LS) MA. 6: Fr, Sp. 7: Research analyst US Army, Wash DC 45-49; Grad stud, dorm coun, sec Sch of Educ UWis(Madison) 50-51; Personnel rep Schuster's, Milwaukee 51-53; Libn G M Simmons Lib, Kenosha Wis 53-60; Libn Lincoln Jr High Sch Lib, Kenosha Wis 60-66; Catlgr Deming Instr Ctr, Kenosha Wis 66-68; Tchr & consul instr materials 68-. 9: WisLA; WisEA; KenoshaLA (charter mem, sec, treas 66-67). 10: St Catherine's Hosp Auxiliary. 14: Readers adv, tech processes, ref. 15: 7221 Second ave, Kenosha Wi 53140.

LOCKE, JOHN WILLIAM. b Chicago Ill 30 Jl 38. 4: Judith Rehnquist Locke. 5: Ill Wesleyan U 56-60 (Sociol) BS; UChicago 63-64 (LS) MA. 6: Fr. 7: Libn & a-v dir Morgan Pk Acad, Chicago 64-68; Dir of info Planned Parenthood Assn, Chicago 68; Asst libn Loop Col 68-. 9: ALA; -ACRL; IllLA. 10: Soc of Archl Histns; Nat Trust for Hist Preserv. 14: A-v, automation, acquis. 15: 2635 Central dr, Flossmoor Il 60422.

LOCKE, MARY E. b Winchester Mass 16 Ap 25. 5: Boston U 46-50 (Hist) AB; Syracuse 50-51 MLS. 7: Asst Pub Lib, N Attleboro Mass 47-49; Asst Lib Maxwell Sch of Pub Affairs Syracuse U 50-55; Ref libn Morrill Mem Lib, Norwood Mass 55-65; Libn Walpole Pub Lib, Walpole Mass 65-. 9: ALA; NELA; MassLA. 10: LWV. 14: Ref, catlg, admin. 15: Walpole Pub Lib, Walpole Ma 02081.

LOCKE, ODEAL (MISS). b Allen Indian Territory 19 Jl 02. 5: UOkla 20-24 (Eng) AB, 40 (Eng) MA, 53 (LS) MA. 6: Fr, Ger. 7: WAC US Army, US & New Guinea 43-45; Instr of Eng UOkla 40-53; Asst Prof of Eng & Lib Sci So State Col (Magnolia Ark) 53-57; Head Libn Cameron State Col 57-. 9: ALA; OklaEA; OklaLA. 10: AAUW. 14: Ref, admin, catlg. 15: 2703 A, Lawton Ok 73501.

LOCKE, WILLIAM NASH. b Watertown Mass 28 Je 09. 4: Antoinette Fortin. 5: Bowdoin Col 27-30 BS; Middlebury Col Fr summer sch 35; Ecole de Preparation des Professeurs de Francais a l'Etranger 35-36 Certif d'Etudes; Institut de Phonetique (Paris) 36 Diplome; Harvard 36-41 MA & PhD. 6: Fr, Ger. 7: Fr Instr Harvard U 38-43; Asst in phonetics & dramatics Middlebury Col Fr Summer Sch, Middlebury Vt 37-41; Fr Instr Radcliffe Col, Cambridge Mass 41-43; Fld Rep Off of War Info 43-45; Prof & Head Dept Modern Langs MIT 45-64; Prof comm on ext courses Harvard U 46-; Asst dir Eng summer sch French Assn Modern Lang Tchrs 47; Dir of Libs MIT 56-. 8: Lib consul to Penn State U 64-65; chm No East Conf on the tchg of For Langs 57; Sci Info Coun, Nat Sci Found 58-60; Trustee Phillips Exeter Acad 59-64; Sec-gen 9th Internat Cong of Linguistics 62; Dir French Lib of Boston 56-68. 9: Amer Assn Tchrs of French (pres Boston Chap 47-48); Alliance Franc6aise of Boston (pres 52-54); Amer Acad Arts & Scis (Fellow) 57-; Mass Coun for Pub Schs (Dir 59-, chm Exec Com Mod Lang Proj 58-); NE Mod Lang Assn (pres 60-61); Internat Fed of Documentation (Com on Ling Problems 63-); Amer Soc Engnr Educ (chm Subcom on Future of Engnr Sch Libs 64-); ARL (dir 64-66); Internat Assn Tech Univ Libs (v-pres 64-66); NE Deposit Lib (v-pres 62-). 10: Sigma Psi;

Boston Fulbright Com. 11: French Legion of Honor; French Order of the Psalms. 12: "La Guerre Moderne" with Sullivan (42); "The French Spoken at Brunswick Me" (49); Ed "Machine Translation of Languages," with Booth (55); "Scientific French" (57); Co ed "Mecanca 4-59). ES. 14: Info sci, application of computers to l transl. 15: Room 14S-216 MIT Libs, Cambridge Ma 02139.

LOCKER, ERROL A. b Portland Ore 14 D 42. 5: Birmingham-So Col 66 (Eng) AB; UWash 68 m lib. 6: Fr. 7: Catlgr Portland StateU 68-. 14: Catlg. 15: 1124 NE Tillamook st, Portland Or 97212.

LOCKERBY, BETTY J. b Ellsworth Wis 1 Ja 21. 5: UMinn 38-42 BLS. 6: Ger. 7: Child libn pub lib, Eau Claire Wis 42-45; Child libn Roosevelt Br, Minneapolis 45-49; Bkmob libn Minneapolis Pub Lib 49-68, Commun libn (bkmob) 68-. 9: ALA; WisLA (treas 45); MinnLA. 14: Child bks. 15: 6145 Thomas ave S, Minneapolis Mn 55410.

LOCKERBY, ROBERT WILLIAM. b Detroit Mich 5 N 39. 5: Citrus Col 57-60 (Engring); Cal state Polytech Col 60-65 (Soc Sci) BS; Immaculate Heart Col 66-67 MLS. 7: Asst a-v libn Portland State U 67-. 9: ALA" NEA-DAVI; Ore Instrl Media Assn. 15: 2744 NE 26th ave, Portland Or 97212.

LOCKETT, ELIZABETH MARY (THEOBALD). b Ootacamund S India 18 Je 26. 4: Wilfred George Lockett. 5: UBristol (Eng) 44-47 (Civil Engnr) BSC; McGill 61-62 BLS. 7: Engnr asst Sir William Halcrow & Partners, London 47-49; Br libn Niagara Falls Pub Lib, Ont 59-61; Chief catlgr Westmount (Que) Pub Lib 62-64; Asst libn Brock U (St Catharines Ont) 64-65; Pub sch libn Niagara Falls Dist (Welland Co) Bd of Educ 65-. 9: ALA; CanLA; OntLA. 14: Tech processes, sch libs. 15: 357 Portage rd N, Niagara Falls Ont Can.

LOCKHART, ADELAIDE B. b Boston 1 Jl 16. 5: Boston U 46-50 (Pol Sci) AB; Simmons 50-51 (LS) MS. 6: Fr, Ger. 7: Lib asst Brockton Pub Lib, Brockton Mass 41-43; (S/Sgt) USAAF 43-46; Lib asst yp room, Boston Pub Lib 46-50, Ref asst 50-52; Mgt res asst to assoc libn Yale U Lib 52-60; Asst libn Dartmouth Col Lib 60-. 15: Dartmouth College Lib, Hanover NH.

LOCKROW, DOROTHY (SEARLE). b Athol Mass 23 S 15. 4: Charles R Lockrow. 5: Simmons 33-37 (LS) BS; So Conn State Col 50-54 (Educ) MA. 7: Catlgr Yale Law Lib 38-42; Asst libn New Haven State Tchrs Col 46-57; Catlgr Bridgeport Pub Lib, Bridgeport Conn 57-58; Catlgr New Haven Free Pub Lib, New Haven Conn 58-61, Supv tech processing 61-63; Catlgr Phoenix Pub Lib 63-64; Asst libn New Haven Col 64-. 9: ALA; ConnLA; Conn Catlgrs. 14: Catlg. 15: 370 Drummond rd, Orange Conn 06477.

LODGE, CONSTANCE. b Colo Springs Colo 6 N 07. 5: UCLA 26-30 (Eng) BA; UCal(Berkeley) 30-31 (LS) Certif. 6: Fr. 7: Henry E Huntington Lib, San Marino Cal: Asst admin div 31-39, Order libn 40-43, Bibliogr asst Americana dept 43-45, Head catlgr 45-49, Head preparations dept 49-. 9: ALA; CalLA (chm Col & Univ Research Sect). 10: Phi Beta Kappa. 14: Acquis, catlg, rare bks. 15: Henry E Huntington Lib, San Marino Ca 91108.

LODGE, LOUISE FINLEY. b Paris Ill 2 Jl 02. 5: Hanover Col 20-22; UIll 22-24 (Span) BA, 30-31, 31-37 (Span) MA, PhD; Centro de Estudios Histo3ricos summer 28; UIll 44-46 BS in LS. 6: Sp, Fr. 7: Tchr of Fr, Lat High Sch, Salem Ill 24-25; Tchr of Span & Lat High Sch, Conneaut Ohio 25-29; Span tchr High Sch, Argo Ill 29-30; Asst in Span UIll(Urbana) 31-37; Asst Prof Span, Fr, Lat Lake Forest Col 37-41; Span tchr High Sch, Alton Ill 41-42; Instr of Span Northwestern U 42-45; Catlgr, asst catlg libn UIll Lib 46-. 9: ALA. 10: Phi Mu; Sigma Delta Pi. 12: Jt ed "Una Moneda de oro y otros cuentos mexicanos modernos" (46). 14: Catlg. 15: 806 Fairlawn dr, Urbana Il 61801.

LOEBER, GERTRUDE V (PALMI). b Wallern Austria 30 Ja 46. 4: Wilfried A Loeber. 5: CUNY (Queens Col) 63-67 (Hist) BA; Rutgers 67-68 MLS. 6: Ger. 7: Asst soc studies libn UNeb (Lincoln) 68-. 8: Analysis of reserve system in Love Mem Lib UNeb. 14: Ref, system analysis of lib operations. 15: 501 S 13th st, Lincoln Nb 68508.

LOEHR, BROTHER PETER DONALD. b Fond du Lac Wis 11 Ja 31. 5: St Mary's U (Tex) 54-57 (Eng) BA; Catholic U 60-65 MSLS. 7: Tchr McBride High Sch, St Louis 57-61, Libn 61-65; Libn Roncalli High Sch, Pueblo Colo 65-. 8: Established High Sch Lib: (Pueblo Colo) 64-65, Omaha Neb 67-68; Forum dir, repres the libns of the St Louis Prov of the Soc of Mary. 9: ALA; CathLA (chm High Sch Sect, Bd mem & v-chm Greater St Louis Unit); MoLA; ColoASchL. 12: Ed "Library Notebook," Soc of Mary Province Bull 66-. 14: High sch libs. 15: Box 3A Beulah Star rt, Pueblo Co 81004.

LOEWENHERZ, BEATRICE G. b Chicago 13 D 20. 4: Walter B Loewenherz. 5: Northwestern 38-42 (Educ) BS in Ed, 43-44 (Hist) MA; UDenver summer 62 (LS); Northwestern summers 58,59,60,63 (A-V, LS); Chicago summer 64- (Reading, Educ). 6: Fr, Ger, Sp. 7: Tchr Evanston Twp High Sch, 42; Tchr Jr High Sch, Lawton Okla 42-43; Instr Materials Coordinator Sch Dist 29, Northfield Ill 58-67, Dir of instr materials 67-. 8: Guggenheim Grant, Northwestern U 62; Elem sch study in Japan (Ministry of Educ); Consul, Encyclopedia Britannica Filmstrip Series on Using the Elem Sch Lib. 9: NEA-DAVI; ALA; IllEA; IllLA; Ill AV Assn (AV Suburban RT). 10: Phi Lambda Theta; Winnetka Woman's Clb; PTA; Boy Scouts; Cub Program; Girl Scout Bd. 14: Media and the reading prog in the elem sch. 15: 568 Hill ter, Winnetka Il 60094.

LOFF, KATHRYN (REYNOLDS). b Kenyon Minn 21 Mr 16. 4: Raymond L Loff. 5: Hibbing Jr Col 33-35; UMinn 35-37 (LS) BS. 7: Br child libn Pub Lib, Hibbing Minn 37-39; Child libn Pub Lib, Grand Forks ND 39-42; Child libn Pub Lib, Monterey Cal 42-44; Personnel interviewer Amer Red Cross, San Francisco 44-46; Off manager US Navy Ship Serv, Seattle 46-49; Stock supv VA Hosp, Ft Snelling Minn 53-54; Child libn dakota-Scott Reg Lib, W St Paul Minn 59-66, Serv Coord 66-68, dir 68-69; Dir Dakota Co Lib, W St Paul Minn 69-. 9: MinnLA. 13: Yes. 14: Lib admin. 15: 10333 Washborn ave S, Minneapolis Mn 55431.

LOFTIN, LEOLA (HUNTER). b Coushatta La 14 S 18. 4: William H Loftin. 5: NWest State col 35-38 (Eng, Lib) BA; LSU 46-47 BS in LS. 6: Fr. 7: Tchr & libn (pub schs): Rapides Parish La 38-43, Red River Parish La 45-63; Docs libn readers serv Russell Lib nwest State Col, Natchitoches La 63-. 9: ALA; LaLA; LaTA; La Hist Assn. 10: Delta Kappa Gamma. 14: Ref. 15: Rt 2 Box 262, Coushatta La 71019.

LOFTS, WILLIAM PETER. b Harwich Eng 25 N 23. 7: Asst Essex Co Lib, Harwich Eng 47-54; Reg libn W Sussex Co Lib, Chichester Eng 55-57; Child lib Lethbridge Pub Lib, Alberta Lethbridge 57-60; Okanagan Reg Lib, Kelowna BC: Catlgr 60-63, Asst libn 63-64, Reg Libn 64-. 9: CanLA; BCLA; ABCL. 10: Arts Coun; Kelowna Art Exh Soc; Kelowna Film Soc; Kelowna Museum & Archives Assn. 14: Admin, org. 15: 480 Queensway, Kelowna BC Can.

LOFTUS, HELEN E. b N Vernon Ind 22 My 21. 5: Ind U 39-42 (Psych) AB, 49-50 (Bus Admin) MBA; Drexel 51 (LS); Ind U Law Sch 57-59. 7: Interviewer US Employment Serv, Anderson Ind 42-49; Asst libn Eli Lilly & Co, Indianapolis 50-51, Supv 51-68, Dept hd 68-. 9: SLA (dir; chm 2 coms; chm Bus Div; v-pres Ind Chap). 10: Ind U Women's Club; Soc of Ind Pioneers; Tri Kappa; Beta Gamma Sigma. 14: Ref, admin. 15: 4306 Westbourne dr, Indianapolis In 46205.

LOFTUS, MARTIN L. b Sand Creek Wis 9 Je 11. 4: Isabel Orr. 5: UWash 28-32 BS in LS, 33 (Hist) AB, 34-36 (Hist). 6: Fr, Ger, Norwegian. 7: Jr libn UWash Lib 33-37; Ref asst NY Pub Lib 37-42, 46; US Army, US, Europe 42-45; Tech libn US VA, NYC 46; Libn Internat Monetary Fund & Internat Bank for Reconstruction & Development, Wash DC 46-. 8: USBE: Bd Dirs 63-64, treas 64-65; Trustee Pub Affairs Info Serv 64-. 9: SLA (treas 51-52); ALA; ASIS; DCLA. 10: Phi Beta Kappa. 13: Yes. 14: Admin, ref. 15: Jt Bank Fund Lib, Internat Monetary Fund 19th & H sts NW, Wash DC 20431.

LOGAN, DOROTHY (LOCKHART). b Hot Springs Ark 14 O 18. 4: Alphonso Logan. 5: St Augustine Col 35-39 (Eng) BA; Atlanta 57 (LS) MA. 6: Fr. 7: Tchr of Eng & Fr Langston High Sch, Hot Springs Ark 40-57, Libn 57-. 9: ArkLA; NEA; ArkEA; Hot Springs EA. 10: PTA; Health & Welfare Org; Youth Leader; Auxiliary of Men's Bus & Progressive Club; Hot Springs (Ark) Tchrs Coun. 14: Sr High Sch lib serv. 15: 212 Silver, Hot Springs Ar 71901.

LOGAN, GWYNNE (GRAVETT). b Roanoke Va 28 Mr 31. 4: Harry Martin Logan. 5: UTenn 48-52 (Eng) BA; Emory 52-53 (LS) ML. 7: Asst in serv to the pub A W Calhoun Med Lib Emory U 53-54; Asst post libn (GS 5), Ft McPherson Ga 54-57; Hosp libn (GS 7) Spec Serv Libs, Ft Bragg NC 57-64, Ext libn (GS 9) 64-66, Catlgr 66-67; Docs libn USA Spec Warfare Sch, Ft Bragg NC 66-67; Libn II Hadley Br Denver Pub Lib 67-68; Libn IV Waimea Area Hawaii Pub Lib 68-. 9: ALA; HawaiiStateLA. 10: Phi Kappa Phi; Alpha Lambda Delta. 14: Ext wk, collection devel, staff train. 15: PO Box 475, Kamuela Ha 96743.

LOGAN, KATHRYN (PALMER). b Rochester Minn 3 Ap 41. 5: UMinn 60-65 (Hist) BA, 67-69 (LS) MA. 7: Resident adv Interlochen Arts Acad, Interlochen Mich 62-64, Asst libn 62-64; Lib asst (mus) UMinn (Minneapolis) 64-68; Lib asst (hist) Minneapolis Pub Lib 68; Asst mus libn UNC (Chapel Hill) 68-. 9: MusLA. 10: Coaching student string quartets UNC Music Dept. 14: Ref, catlg (primarily music). 15: Music Lib Hill Hall Univ of NC, Chapel Hill NC 27514.

LOGAN, MADELINE (WARD). b Buffalo NY 26 N 16. 4: Samuel Frank Logan. 5: SUNY(Buffalo) 34-38 (Hist) AB; Permanent life lib sci certif. 7: Libn Bradenton High Sch, Bradenton Fla 38-40; Libn N Charleston High Sch, N Charleston SC 40-43; Circ libn Conn Col for Women 43-45; Catlg libn Converse Col 57-67, 68-. 9: SCLA. 14: Catlg. 15: 202 Lakewood dr, Spartanburg SC 29202.

LOGAN, MARY KENNEDY. b NYC 1 Jl 1900. 5: Simmons 18-22 (LS) BS. 7: Lib asst Ore State U 22-24; Lib asst UND 24-28; 1st asst br NY Pub Lib 28-42; Head catlgr Mechanics' Inst Lib, San Francisco 42-. 9: ALA. 14: Catlg. 15: 1105 Bush st, San Francisco Ca 94109.

LOGAN, VIRGINIA . b New London Conn 3 S 21. 5: UPR 40-44 (Eng) AB Ed; West Res 48-49 MSLS. 06: Sp. 7: Period libn UPR 44-51; Post libn Camp Losey, Ponce PR 51-52; Sr asst libn ser div UNeb 52-54; Libn Central High Sch Pub Lib Santurce PR 54-57; Period libn Carnegie Lib, San Juan PR 57-60; Asst documents libn UPR 60-62, Head circ dept 62-. 9: ALA-ACRL; Sociedad de Bibliotecarios de Puerto Rico. 14: Ser, documents. 15: 1115 Piccioni st apt 3A, Santurce PR.

LOGSDON, GUY WILLIAM. b Ada Okla 31 My 34. 4: Phyllis Landers. 5: E Central State (Ada Okla) 52-56 (Eng) BA; UOkla 63-64 MLS. 7: Photographer Logsdon Studio, Ada Okla 54-56; Tchr Norwalk Elem Sch, Norwalk Cal 56-57; Eng tchr Burbank High Sch, Burbank Okla 57-58; Life insurance salesman Great Southern Life, Ardmore Okla 58-60; Sch libn & Eng tchr Payson High Sch, Payson Ariz 60-63; Ref libn Okla State U 64-67; Dir of libs UTulsa 67-. 9: ALA; OklaLA (chm Recruitment Com 65-67; chm Univ & Col Div 66-67; chm Intel Freedom Com 67-68); SWLA. 10: Okla Hist Soc; Amer Folklore soc; Cal Folklore Soc; Okla Acad Sci; West Hist Assn; Indian Territory Posse of Okla Westerners. 14: Ref, rare bks, archives, admin. 15: 4645 S Columbia, Tulsa Ok 74105.

LOGSDON, IRENE K. b Scio Ohio 23 Je 10. 4: Richard H Logsdon. 5: Oberlin Col & Flora Stone Mather Col West Res 28-32 (Bot) AB; West Res 33-34 (Bot) MS; UKy 43-44 (Educ); Rutgers 60 (LS) MS. 7: Libn Chagrin Falls Pub Lib Br Cleveland Pub Lib 30-32; Garden Club of Cleveland 32-34; Consul Rockingham Pub Lib, Harrisonburg Va 41; Sci tchr Lafayette High Sch, Lexington Ky 43-44; Libn Demarest (NJ) Pub Sch 54-61; Libn No Valley Reg High ScmtlsCenter Ridgewood High Sch, Ridgewood nj 64-. 9: ALA (Ed com Period for Sch Libs); NJSchLA (pres 66-67); NJEA. 10: Amer Red Cross; Civic Conf (Leonia NJ); Elem Sch Coun; AAUW. 12: "Library Careers," with R H Logsdon (63). 15: 199 Knickerbocker rd, Demarest NJ 07627.

LOGSDON, RICHARD H(ENRY). b Upper Sandusky Ohio 24 Je 12. 4: Irene Kupfer. 5: West Res 29-33 (Econ) AB, 33-34 (LS) BS; Chicago 37-42 (LS) PhD. 7: Libn, Instr in Lib Sci Adams State Col 34-39; Libn & Assoc Prof of Lib Sci Madison Col 39-43; Prof & Head of Dept of Lib Sci UKy 43-45; Chief Libn US Off of Educ 45-47; Asst dir lib serv div USVA 47; Asst dir of tech serv Columbia 47-48, Assoc dir of libs 48-53, Dir of libs 53-69; Dean of Libs CUNY 69-. 08: Participated in evaluations & surveys of col & univ libs: Me, NH, NY, Penn, Md, Wash DC, Kan, Mich, Afghanistan, & PR; Adv on Lib arch & admin, Kabul Afghanistan 59; Chm Coordinating Com for Slavic & East European Lib Resources 61-62; chm Lib Adv Com, NYC 60-63; NY State Regents Adv Coun; NY State Commsnrs Com on Lib Devel. 9: ALA (Bd of Educ for Libnship 46-51, chm 50-51; chm Commsn Nat Plan for Lib Educ 62-64); ACRL; Commsn on Higher Inst Middle States Assn of Cols & Sec Schs 51-58; ARL (Bd 62-65, chm 64); US Off of Educ Adv Com 59-62; NYLA (pres 65-66); NY State Regents Adv Coun on Libs; Bd NY Metro Ref & Res Lib Agency (Bd Dirs). 10: Leonia (NJ) Bd of Educ 53-55; Grolier Club; Archons of Colophon. 12: "The Columbia University Libraries, a Report on Present and Future Needs," with others (58); "Library Careers," with I K Logsdon (63). 13: Yes. 14: Admin. 15: 199 Knickerbocker rd, Demarest NJ 07627.

LOHF, KENNETH A. b Milwaukee 14 Ja 25. 5: Northwestern 47-49 (Eng Lit) BA; Columbia 49-50 (Eng Lit) MA, 51-52 MS in LS. 6: Fr. 7: (1st Lt) USAAF, India, West Europe 43-46; Ref asst Sch of Lib Serv Lib Columbia U 52-53; Sr ref asst ref dept Columbia U Libs 53-57, Asst libn dept of spec collections 57-68; Lecturer Sch of Lib Serv Columbia U 59-64, Libn for rare bks & Mss. 09: BSA; Ms Soc. 10: Grolier Club; Assn Internationale de Bibliophilie. 12: "Joseph Conrad at Mid-Century: Editions and Studies, 1895-1955" (57); "The Achievement of Marianne Moore: A Bibliography" (58); "Yvor Winters: A Bibliography" (59); "Frank Norris: A Bibliography" (59); "Sherwood Anderson: A Bibliography" (60); "An Index to The Little Review, 1914-1929" (61); Co-auth "Index to Little Magazines, 1953-1955," & 4 2-yr issues (57-64); "The Collection of Books, Manuscripts & Autograph Letters in the Library of Jean and Donald Stralem" (62); Ed "Seven Lyrics by Hart Crane" (66); "The Literary Manuscripts of Hart Crane" (67); "XXX for Time," poems (66). 13: Yes. 14: Rare bks, mss, bibliog. 15: 560 Riverside dr apt 21B, New York NY 10027.

LOHRER, (MARY) ALICE. b Chicago 29 Ja 07. 5: Chicago 25-28 (Eng) PhB; UIll summers 31, 32, 36, 37 BS in LS; Chicago summers 41-45 (LS) AM. 6: Fr, Ger. 7: Asst libn Oak Park & River Forest Twp High Sch, Oak Park Ill 28-38; Libn Hinsdale Twp High Sch, Hinsdale Ill 38-41; Instr Purdue summer 39-42; Prof UIll Grad Sch of Lib Sci 41-; Summer tchg UWVa 52; Summer tchg USoCal 53; Fulbright lecturer Chulalongdorn U (Bangkok Thailand) 55-56; Rockefeller Grant Japan Lib Sch Keio U (Tokyo) 59; Summer tchg UWis 60; Dir Title VII Rch Grant US Off of Educ 61-62; Summer tchg UDenver 64, 66; Fulbright lecturer UTehran (Iran) 66-67. 8: Dir, Indianapolis Sch Lib Survey, 53-54; Mem Mo Pub Lib Survey Team, Serv for Child & YA 60-61; Dir, USOE status study of sch libs functioning as instr materials centers, 61-64; Summer tchg: Purdue U 39-42, UWVa 52, USoCal 53, UWis 60, UDenver 64, 66; Fulbright lecturer, Chulalongkorn U (Bangkok Thailand) 55-56; Visiting Prof, Japan Lib Sch, Keio U (Tokyo) 59. 9: ALA (Coun & chm var coms); NEA; Ill Assn High Sch Libns (pres); IllLA; IllASchL. 10: AAUP; AAUW; Delta Kappa Gamma; Urbana League; Beta Phi Mu. 11: Fulbright lecturer, Thailand & Iran; Rockefeller grant, Japan Lib Sch; USOE grant. 12: Co-auth "Planning Guide for High School Library Programs," ALA (51); Issue ed "Library Trends 1" (Jan 53); Ed "Allerton Institute: The School Library Materials Center" (64). 13: Yes. 14: Sch lib admin, pub lib wk with child & ya, for libnship. 15: 1905 N Melanie lane, Champaign Ill 61821.

LOIZEAUX, MARIE D(UVERNOY). b Plainfield NJ 16 Je 05. 5: Columbia 28-30; 27-36. 7: Var New Rochelle Pub Lib, New Rochelle NY 24-39; Assoc ed Wilson Lib Bulletin, Bronx NY 39-41, Ed 41-59; Ed Loizeau Bros Inc, Neptune NJ 59-. 9: ALA (several coms); NJLA; NY Lib Club. 10: Christ Bus & Profess Women's Coun; Pub Rel Planner. 12: "Publicity Primer: an abc of "telling all" About The Public Library" (37, 4th ed 67); Comp "Library on the Air" (40). 13: Yes. 14: Pub rel. 15: 418 Redmond ave, Oakhurst NJ 07755.

LOKKE, MARGARET JEAN. b Minneapolis 19 D 17. 5: Lyons Twp Jr Col 35-37; UIll 37-39 (Eng) AB, 40-41 BS in LS, 42-48 MS in LS. 6: Fr. 7: UIll Lib (Urbana): Binding asst 41-47, Asst binding libn 47-55, Union browsing room libn 55-56, Asst circ libn 56-65, Phys educ libn 65-. 9: ALA. 10: AAUP; Eng Speaking Union. 14: Pub serv (spec libs), ref. 15: Room 146 UIll Lib, Urbana Il 61801.

LOLLEY, JOHN LOUIS. b Shreveport La 24 N 37. 5: La Tech 56-60 (Geog) BA; LSU 64-65 MLS. 6: Sp, Fr. 7: (Sp/4) US Army Armored Crewman 60-63; Catlgr young adult libn Tempe Pub Lib, Tempe Ariz 65-66; Libn St James Parish Lib, Lutcher La 66-68; Ref libn Tarrant Co Jr Col (Ft Worth) 68-. 9: TexLA; LaLA. 14: Admin. 15: 3605 Carriage Hill dr, Ft Worth Tx.

LOMAGA, MARY (MOCH). b Lwin Ukraine 08 My 44. 4: Andrew Walter Lomaga. 5: UToronto 62-66 (Hist) BA, 66-67 Tchg Certif, 68-69 BLS. 6: Ukrainian. 7: Hist tchr Dept of Educ, Toronto Can 67-68, Tchr & libn 69-. 9: ALA; CanLA; Ont Secondary Sch Tchrs' Fed. 14: Sch libs. 15: 6 Churchill ave, Toronto Ont Can.

LOMBARDI, MARY. b Los Angeles 21 Je 40. 5: Occidental Col 57-61 (Music) BA; UCal(Berkeley) 63-64 (LS); UCal(Los Angeles) 64-65 MLS. 6: Sp, Ital. 7: Ref libn UCal(Los Angeles) 64-65; Ref libn NY Pub Lib 65-66; Catlgr Julliard Sch of Mus, NY 66-67; Indexer lib lit H W Wilson Co, NY 67-. 9: ALA; CalLA; NY Lib Club. 14: Indexing, info retrieval, bibliog, ref. 15: 248 E 50th st, New York NY 10022.

LOMER, GERHARD B. b Montreal Can 6 Mr 1882. 5: McGill 1899-1903 (Philos) BA, 03-04 (Eng) MA; Columbia

05-07 (Educ) PhD, Doctor's Diploma in Educ. 6: Fr. 7: Instr McGill U 06-09, summers 07, 10, 13, Libn 20-48, Dir Lib Sch 27-49; Instr UWis 09-12; Instr Sch of Journalism Columbia U 12-20; Prof & asst dir UOttawa Lib Sch 59-. 8: Consul Redpath Mus McGill U; Lib Com Montreal Mus of Fine Arts; Carnegie Lib Survey of Prince Edward Island; Adv Com Lib of the West Indies. 9: ALA (Coun 30-32, Com on Bibliog 25, Com on Lib Ethics 32); CanLA (Founding mem, Coun, Scholarship Com); QueLA (Founding mem, pres 32-33, hon pres 37-); OntLA; OttawaLA; BSCan; SLA; Assn Canadienne des Bibliothe3caires de Langue Francaise (Hon Life mem). 10: Faculty Club, McGill U; Phi Kappa Sigma; Sigma Delta Chi; Sigma Tau Delta. 11: Membre d'Honneur Acade3mie latine, Paris 28; Fellow Lib Assn (Gt Britain) 36. 12: "Concept of Method" (10); "Study & Practice of Writing English" with M Ashmum (14); "Writing of Today," with J W Cunliffe (15, 23); Asst ed "Warner Library of the World's Best Literature," 30 vols; Assoc ed "Chronicles of America," 50 vols (18-21); "Catalogue of Scientific Periodicals in Canadian Libraries," with M S Mackay (24); "Stephen Leacock: A Checklist and Index" (54). 13: Yes. 14: Admin, rare bks, tchg. 15: 51-286 Wilbrod st, Ottawa 2 Can.

LONBERGER, ROSE EVA. b Boalsburg Penn 16 D 11. 5: Penn State U 29-33 (Liberal Arts) BA; Drexel 35-36 (LS) MS. 6: Ger. 7: Circ asst Penn State U 33-35; Asst libn Westminster Col Lib (New Wilmington Penn) 35-38; Research libn RCA Victor Co, Camden NJ 38-41; Research libn Radio Corp of Amer Labs, Princeton NJ 41-47; Tech libn Towne Sci Lib UPenn 47-. 8: Bibliogr, NASA contract 68-. 9: SLA; ACS; Spec Libs Coun of Phila. 10: Pilgrim Gardens Civic Assn. 14: Admin, ref. 15: 300 Pilgrim lane, Drexel Hill Pa 19027.

LONDON, GERTRUDE J (ROSENTHAL). b Oestrich/Rhein Germany. 5: UFrankfort/Main & UMunich 29-33 (Ger, Geog); UParis 33-36 (Doct Univ Paris Dipl Prof Franc); Univ Col (London) 55-56 Diplome Libnship. 6: Ger, Fr. 7: Asst lecturer Dept of German King's Col ULondon 40-46; Libn Israel Meteorological Serv, Tel Aviv (47-56); Chief IGY Meterological Data Centre WMO, Geneva Switzerland 56-61; Libn WMO, Geneva Switzerland 62; Chief of research MGA Amer Meteorological Soc, Wash DC 63-64; Research spec Rutgers U Grad Sch Lib Serv 65-69; Assoc Prof Sch Lib Sci UNC (Chapel Hill) 69-. 9: ASIS; Lib Assn (Gt Brit); USNC FID/UDC. 10: Audubon Naturalist Soc; AAAS. 11: Recipient of NSF Grant 65. 12: "Le ro4le du monde exte3rieur dans les oeuvres en prose d'E Moerike" (35); "Classification for Information Storage and Retrieval; Microcards of IGY Meteorological Data" (62); "A Classed Thesaurus as an Aid to Indexing, Classifying, and Searching" (66). 13: Yes. 14: Clsf research, info retr. 15: School of Lib Sci, Univ of No Carolina, Chapel Hill NC 27514.

LONERS, RUTH (NORRIS). b Seattle 2 Ag 07. 4: Edwin Loners. 5: UWash 25-29 BS in LS. 7: Seattle Pub Lib: Asst libn br dept 29-34, Br libn 34-46, Sub 46-. 9: ALA; PNLA. 10: PTA; Washington Alpine Club. 14: Br lib wk. 15: 3229 Alki ave SW; Seattle Wa 98116.

LONG, CALVERTA ELNORA (DAVIS). b Johnsonville SC 15 S 32. 4: Willie H Long. 5: SCar State Col 49-53 (LS) BS; Atlanta summers 55-58 MSLS. 6: Fr. 7: Eng instr Carver High Sch, Lake City SC 53-54, Libn 53-60; Head Libn Barber-Scotia Col 60-62; Ref libn SCar State Col Lib 62-. 9: ALA; SCLA; SELA. 10: Alpha Kappa Mu; Beta Phi Mu; Delta Sigma Theta; Nat Assn Col Women. 14: Ref, documents. 15: Box 1572 SC State Col, Orangeburg SC 29115.

LONG, CATHERINE (D). b Paducah Ky 19 N 22. 5: Tillotson Col 40-44 (Sociol) AB; Kan State Tchrs Col (Emporia) 57-58 (LS) MS. 7: Elem tchr, Caruthersville Mo. 45-50; Period libn Col Lib Lincoln U (Mo) 50-62, Asst libn in chg of processing 62-. 9: ALA; MoLA. 10: Alpha Kappa Alpha. 14: Catlg. 15: 1109-1/2 E Atchison st, Jefferson City Mo 65101.

LONG, CHARLES R(OBERT) (BOB MARK). b Long Beach Cal 20 S 36. 4: Marie Giacoppe. 5: Fordham 54-55; UToronto 55-59 (Botany) BA; UMass 59-61 (Botany) MA; UHawaii 66-67; Simmons 67-68 MSLS. 6: Fr, Ital, Ger, Lat. 7: Tchg asst UMass 59-62, Instr summer 60; Instr Windham Col 62-64; Research Ctr Pacific Program US Nat Mus 64-66; Grad asst UHawaii 66-67; Stud asst Beatley Lib Simmons Col 67-68; Asst dir Nashua (NH) Pub Lib 68-69; Libn Gray Herbarium & Arnold Arboretum Harvard U 69-. 8: Co-chm, Pub Rel Wkshop, Boston, sponsored by NELA, etc Apr 69; NH State Lib del to SE Dist Adv Coun 68 (Planning Com 69-). 9: ALA; NHLA; NELA (Co-chm Pub Rel Com 69-70). 10: AAAS. 11: Res Grants: UWis 59, Hawaii Bot Soc 66. 12: Assoc ed Hawaii Bot Soc "Newsletter" 66-67. 13: Yes. 14: Admin. 15: 17 Ayer st, Nashua NH 03060.

LONG, DOROTHY. b Forsyth Co NC. 5: UNC(Greensboro) (Eng) AB; UWis 42 (Eng) MA; UIll 46 (LS) BS; Columbia summer 50. 6: Fr. 7: Br libn, Camp Lejeune NC 43-46; Chief Libn VA Hosp, Martinsburg WVa 47-49; Ref libn Pub Lib, Winston-Salem NC 50; Asst ref libn UKy 50-52; Health Affairs Lib UNC (Chapel Hill): Catlgr 52-53, Ref libn 53-64, Asst libn 64-. 9: ALA; MedLA (Publs Com 63-65, Gottlieb Prize Com 67-); NCLA. 11: Murray Gottlieb History of Medicine Prize, 54. 12: Co-auth "100 Year History NC State Board of Medical Examiners" (59). 13: Yes. 14: Ref. 15: 102 Jone s Chapel Hill NC 27514.

LONG, EDITH (BURKEY). b Lebanon Penn 24 Ap 16. 4: John B Long. 5: Millersville State Col 36-40 (Elem Educ) BS 64-69 (Lib); Temple 58-62 (Elem Educ) Ed M. 6: Fr. 7: Elem tchr Palmyra Schs, Palmyra Penn 40-62; Elem libn Milton Hershey Sch, Hershey Penn 62-. 9: ALA. 10: AAUW; Palmyra Pub Lib Bd. 13: Yes. 14: Child lit, bringing child and bks together. 15: 313 W Oak st, Palmyra Pa 17078.

LONG, FERN. b Cleveland Ohio. 5: Radcliffe (Eng Lit) AB (magna cum laude); Charles U (Prague Czechoslov akia) (Comparative Lit) PhD; West Res BS in LS. 6: Czech, Fr, Ger. 7: Exec sec Ames Soc Serv League, Ames Iowa 34-38; Cleveland Pub Lib: Lib asst 39-41, Field wker adult educ dept 41-44, Head adult educ dept 44-, Act deputy dir 68-. 8: US Del to UNESCO seminar on role of pub libs in adult educ, Malmo Sweden 50; On staff of ALA to write 3 ed bk lists on US & the war 43; Instr of course, Library in the Commun, West Res U Sch of Lib Sci 44-63; Consul West Res U Sch of Lib Sci 63-; Mem Adv Bd, Lib Materials Res Proj, U Wis 67-; Staff mem, Inst Serving Disadvantaged Adults, Col of St Catherine 69. 9: ALA (chm Adult Educ Bd 53);-ASD (pres 64-65, chm Com on Lib Serv to an Aging Population 58-61); OhioLA (chm Com on Aging 60-62). 10: Adult Educ Coun of Cleveland; Anti-Tuberculosis League of Cuyahoga Co (Ohio); numerous local civic bds & coms; Phi Beta Kappa. 11: Radcliffe Achievement Award 60; Woman of Achievement, Cleveland 61. 13: Yes. 14: Adult educ. 15: Cleveland Pub Lib, Cleveland 44114.

LONG, HARRIET (KENNEDY). b St Louis 4 Ja 13. 4: ELMER C Long. 5: Wash U 46-49 (LS). 7: Lib asst St Louis Pub Lib 30-44; Manuals clerk Emerson Electric Co, St Louis 44-45; Wash U Libs, St Louis: Lib asst circ dept 45-46, Asst libn Engnr Lib 46, Libn Earth Sci Lib 46-. 9: SLA (Petrol Div Rep to St Louis Conv 64; Greater St Louis Chap: Prog chm 48, chm Lib for a Day 69); Washington U Libs Assn (pres 65-66); Geosci Info Soc (treas 65-66). 12: "Manual of Reference Sources in Geology," mimeo (50, ref ed 64); "Bibliography of Bibliographies of Geology of the States of the United States," Geoscience Abstracts vol 7, no 7 Spec Suppl (65). 14: Geol, geog, maps. 15: Earth Sci Lib Washington U, St Louis Mo 63130.

LONG, HELEN (ROBINSON). b Tescott Kan 26 Jl 22. 4: J Walling Long. 5: Kan Wesleyan U summers 43-45; Kan State Tchrs Col (Emporia) 46-49 (LS) BS in Ed, AB; UPittsburgh summer 65; Drexel summer 67; Peabody Conservatory of Mus & West Md Col summer 68. 7: Ref libn N Central Col (Naperville Ill) 49-51; Gen asst Washington Co Free Lin, Hagerstown Md 51-54; Sch libn St James Sch, St James Md 56-62; Catlgr Franklin Co Lib System, Chambersburg Penn 63-64; Sch libn Williamsport High Sch, Williamsport Md 64-. 9: ALA; MdLA. 10: Washington Co (Md) Hist Soc; Washington Co Hosp Auxiliary; Washington Co Mus Fine Arts; Civic Music Assn; Nat Found of Meth Musicians. 13: Yes. 14: Hist research, reading adv. 15: P O Box 353, Hagerstown Md 21740.

LONG, HENRY C. b Cana NC 27 My 28. 4: Gearldyne Lee. 5: Howard U 48-52 (European Hist) BA; Ohio State U 54-55 (Eng Const Hist) MA; Catholic U 58-61 MSLS. 7: Young adult asst Enoch Pratt Free Lib, Baltimore 59-61; Asst libn Morgan State Col 61-63; Assoc libn Md State Roads Comms, Baltimore 63-, 67; Ref libn sci-tech US Naval Acad, Annapolis Md 67-. 9: ALA-ACRL; AHA. 10: Phi Alpha Theta. 14: Ref, bibliog. 15: 3703 Nortonia rd, Baltimore Md 21216.

LONG, ILZE BAIBA (DIKIS). b Livani Latvia 28 P 42. 5: Ohio State U 62-65 (Hist) BA; UMich 66 (LS) MA. 6: Latvian, Fr. 7: Catlgr Ohio State U 67-69, Catlgr Center for Vocational and Tech Educ Ohio State U 69-. 9: ALA. 10: UMich Assn Lib Sci Alumni. 14: Catlg, lib admin, lib automation. 15: 315 E 18th ave, Columbus Oh 43201.

LONG, JOAN Y(OUNG). b Arnold Penn 30 D 28. 4: Edward L(ee) Long. 5: Muskingum Col 47-50 (Span, Eng) BA; UPittsburgh summer 52 Perm tchg certif; Carnegie 55-56 MLS; West Mich U 68-69. 06: Sp. 7: Tchr Franklin Area Sch Dist Franklin Twp, Murrysville Penn 51-53; Tchr Freeport Pub Schs, Freeport Penn 53-54; Libn Monroeville Jr High Sch, Monroeville Penn 56-. 9: ALA-AASchL; -YASD; Coun of Sch Libns of Suburban Pittsburgh. 10: Beta Phi Mu. 14: Instr matls cent, child & yp bks. 15: 5311 Sardis rd, Murrysville Pa 15668.

LONG, LAURETTE (HENSON). b Cleveland Miss 5 D 34. 4: Robert J Long. 5: Miss State Col for Women 53-5 (LS) BS; UMiss 63-64, 66-67 MLS. 7: Jr libn UMiss 57-58, 59-60, Sr libn 61-64, Catlg libn Law Sch 66-67, Catlg libn Law Sch & asst prof lib sci 67-68, Asst prof of lib sci 68-; Asst libn, Greenville AFB Miss 59-60; Catlg libn Wash Co Lib, fayetteville Ark 60-61; Libn I Ouachita Parish Pub Lib, Monroe La 64-66. 9: ALA; MissLA. 13: Yes. 14: Catlg. 15: PO Box 478, University Ms 38677.

LONG, MARGARET. b Cincinnati 12 S 13. 5: UCincinnati even 40-45 (Eng) . 6: Fr. 7: Clerk Cincinnati Pub Lib 33-43, Child asst 43-. 9: CathLA (Adv Coun; chm Regina Award Com 67-68, chm Child Libs Sect 69-71, Greater Cincinnati Unit: chm 3 terms). 10: Libs & Lit chm, St Aloysius Altar Soc. 13: Yes. 14: Child wk. 15: 6386 Revere ave, Cincinnati Oh 45233.

LONG, MARIANNA. b Statesville NC 19 N 06. 5: Mitchell Col 23-25; Woman's Col of UNC(Greensboro) 25-27 (Romance Lang) AB; Emory 27-28 BS in LS. 6: Sp, Fr. 7: Duke U Law Lib: Catlgr 28-31, Asst law libn 31-42, 46-47, Act law libn 43-45, Law Libn 48-52; Libn Iredell Co Lib, Statesville NC 52-53; Law Libn Duke U Law Lib 53-. 9: ALA; AALL; NCLA (treas 46-55, 2nd v-pres 55-57); SELA. 10: DAR;NC L; NC Assn Preserv of Antiquities. 13: Yes. 14: Catlg, ser. 15: 2739 Sevier st, Durham NC 27705.

LONG, ROSALEE (VINCENT). b Concordia Kan 27 Ag 31. 4: Robert E Long. 5: UWichita 49-50 (Music); Kan State Tchrs Col (Emporia) 50-53 LS AB. 6: Fr. 7: Libn Kan City (Mo) Pub Lib 53; Catlg libn San Jose State Col 54-58; Head catlg libn Stanford U Law Lib 58-. 9: AALL. 12: Co-auth "Author Notation" (66); "Stanford Law Library Classification" (68). 13: Yes. 14: Catlg law & music. 15: Stanford U Law Lib, Stanford Ca 94305.

LONG, RUSSELL (EUGENE). b Fullerton Cal 8 N 43. 5: Fullerton Jr Col 61-63 (Hist) AA; Cal State Col 63-65 (Hist) BA; USoCal 65-67 MSLS. 6: Fr, Sp. 7: Y-a libn Santa Ana Pub Lib, Santa Ana Cal 67; Govt Publ Libn Orange Co Pub Lib, Orange Cal 67-. 9: ALA; CalLA. 14: Ref. 15: 6521 Kingman ave, Buena Park Ca 90620.

LONG, RUTH EDWARDS. b Brooklyn NY 18 Jl 15. 4: Fremont C Long. 5: State Tchrs Col 35-38 (Elem Educ) Tchrs Certif; UAla 39-41 (LS) BS; UMiss 65- (LS). 7: Libn High Sch, Collinsville Ala 41-42; Aircraft Inspector Grumman Aircraft, Bethpage NY 42-44; Libn St Lawrence U 44-46; Elem sch tchr, Selden NY 46-47; Libn Rollins Col 47-49; Libn Pinecrest Elem & Jr High Sch, Sanford Fla 56-62; Coordinator of Libs Seminole Co Schs, Sanford Fla 62-. 9: FlaEA; FlaASchL; FlaLA. 10: Alpha Delta Kappa. 15: Box 92, Enterprise Fl 32763.

LONG, SARA ELLEN. b LA County 27 D 42. 5: Ill WesleyanU 60-64 (Elem Educ) BS; UIll 68-69 MSLS. 6: Fr. 7: Elgin Pub Schs, Elgin Ill: Elem tchr 64-68, Jr high libn 69-; Grad asst (catlg dept) UIll 68-69. 9: ALA; NEA; IllEA. 10: Girl Scouts; AAUW; Beta Phi Mu. 14: Sch libs, ref. 15: 401 E Chicago st, Elgin Il 60120.

LONG, SARAH ANN (SANDERS). b Atlanta Ga 20 My 43. 4: James Allen LongIII. 5: Oglethorpe Col 60-66 (Educ) AB; EmoryU 66-67 (Libnship) MLn. 7: Libn Atlanta Pub Schs (Atlanta) 67-. 9: NEA; GeEA (Lib Dept). 10: AtlantaEA. 13: Yes. 14: Child lit. 15: Rte 2 Haralson Mill rd, Atlanta Ga 30207.

LONGAIR, MARGARET ELEANOR (RITCHIE). b Banff Alberta 20 S 28. 4: Arthur Nelson Longair. 5: UAlberta 47-49; UCalgary 66-67 (Soc Studies) B Ed; 68-69 (Sch Libnship) Grad Diploma. 7: Tchr Calgary Sch Bd 55-66, Elem Lib Consul 67-. 9: Internat Reading Assn; Can LA; Can Coun of Eng Tchrs; AltaTA (Lib coun, soc studies coun). 12: "Transportation in Early Calgary". 13: Yes. 14: Sch libs (elem grades). 15: 5912 Buckthorn rd NW, Calgary 47 Alberta Can.

LONGHENRY, RUTH A. b Brooklyn NY 19 Ja 20. 5: State Tchrs Col (New Paltz NY) 37-40 (Educ) Certif; State Tchrs Col (Geneseo NY) 40-41 (LS) BS; Columbia 47-49 (Liberal Arts). 7: Chief AG Records Sect US Army, Governors Island NY 41-45; Libn Hq Ref Lib US Army, Governors Island NY 45-48; Catlgrs US Armed Forces Staff Col Lib, Norfolk Va 48-50; US Army War Col Lib, Carlisle Barracks Penn: Chief bibliog sect 51-53, Chief processing br 53-55, Chief serv br 55-69, Dir Lib 69-. 8: USAWC ADP Steering Com; Com for 12th Milit Libns Wkshop 68. 9: ALA; SLA (sec-treas Milit Libns Div 67-68); CathLA; ASIS. 10: AAUW; Girl Scouts Leader. 12: "Guide to Student Research Elements" USAWC, annual (60-); "Subject Index to Periodicals Currently Received," annual (60-). 14: Admin, ADP applications. 15: 146 W High st, Carlisle Penn 17013.

LONGINO, NAN (SMITH). b Miller Co Ark 23 Jl 15. 4: James Franklin Longino. 5: So State Col 31-33; Ouchita Baptist U 34-36 (Fr, Eng) BA; E Tex State U 54 (LS) MS; UTex 64 (Journalism). 06: Fr, Sp. 7: Libn & Eng tchr, Fouke Ark 48-54; Libn & Eng tchr, New Boston Tex 54-62, Libn 62-. 9: TexLA (chm Dist 6); Tex State Tchrs Assn (Dist 8: chm, Welfare Com); Teen-Age LA (Exec Bd); Tex Clrm Tchrs. 10: Bus Women's Garden Club; Bus & Prof Women's Club; AAUW; Pub Lib Bd. 15: Box 594, New Boston Tex 75570.

LONGLAND, JEAN ROGERS. b Boston 11 Ja 13. 5: Wheaton Col (Mass) 30-35 (Fr) AB; Simmons 35-36 (LS) SB. 6: Portu, Fr, Sp. 7: Hispanic Soc of America, NYC: Catlgr 36-46, Asst curator of Portuguese bks 46-53, Curator of the Lib 53-. 9: SLA (NY Chap: chm Archives Com 63-64, chm Museum Gp 68-70); Amer Transl Assn; Amer Assn Tchrs of Spanish & Portu; NY Tech Serv Libns; Latin Amer Studies Assn. 10: Phi Lambda Beta; Hispanic Soc of Amer. 12: Ed & tr "Selections from Contemporary Portuguese Poetry" (66). 13: Yes. 14: Luso-Brazilian culture. 15: Hispanic Soc of Amer, 613 W 155th st, New York NY 10032.

LONGLOIS, MARY LEE. b Natchitoches La 3 D 42. 5: Gallaudet Col 60-65 (LS) BS. 6: Fr. 7: Asst in lib Gallaudet Col 65-68, Instr in lib sci 68, Circ libn 68-. 14: Catlg, circ, ref. 15: Box 980 Gallaudet College, Washington DC 20002.

LONGO, JOY PAULINE. b Albany NY 6 Ag 31. 5: NY State Col for Tchrs (Albany) 50-54 9eng) BA; SUNY (Albany) 64- (LS). 7: Lib clk NY State Lib, Albany 50-54; Soc wker Catholic Charities, Troy NY 54-58; Casualty rater Travelers Ins Co, Albany NY 59-63; Libn Nat Com Bank & Trust Co, Albany NY 63-. 9: SLA; ALA. 14: Ref. 15: 1217 Central ave, Albany NY 12205.

LONGSTREET, CHRISTINE L (REB). b Frankfort Kan 28 Ja 14. 4: Gilbert W Longstreet. 5: Baker U 30-34 (Eng, Span) AB; UIll 37-41 (LS) BS in LS, MS. 6: Sp. 7: Tchr Beattie (Kan) High Sch 34-35; Asst libn Baker U 35-41, Libn 41-43; Asst in lib sci UIll Lib Sch 38-41; Libn Winter Gen Hosp US Army, Topeka Kan 43-45; Jr ref libn UChicago 46-47; Asst libn Topeka Pub Lib, Topeka Kan 47-48; Asst libn & ref libn Art Inst of Chicago 48-52; Ser catlgr UMd 54-56; Hd ref libn UChicago 56-, Lectr Grad Lib Sch 57-67. 9: ALA (chm Subs Bks Com 61-62); IllLA; Chicago Lib Club (pres 59-60). 10: AAUW; Beta Phi Mu; Phi Kappa Phi. 14: Ref. 14: Ref. 15: 5734 Kimbark, Chicago Il 60637.

LONGSTREET, DONNA MAE. b Covington Ky 8 Ja 37. 5: UCincinnati 56-62 (Econ) BS Com; UColo 62 (Psych); UDenver 62-64 (LS) MA; San Francisco State 64 (Fr). 7: Lib clerk Procter & Gamble Co, Venice & Cincinnati Ohio 58-60, 61-62; Abstract libn Standard Oil Co of Cal, San Francisco 64-65; Adult ref libn Anaheim Pub Lib, Anaheim Cal 65-68; Sers & docs libn Cal State Col (Long Beach) 68-. 9: ALA; SLA; Orange Co (Cal) LA. 10: Sierra Club. 14: Adult ref. 15: 9643 Westminster blvd apt B, Garden Grove Ca 92641.

LONIE, CLARA ANN (FONTAINE). b Ossian NY 3 Jl 21. 4: Louis Carlyle Lonie. 5: Geneseo State Tchrs Col 37-41 (Educ) BS; West MichU summer 60-65 (LS) MA. 7: Asst libn Keene Tchrs Col 42-43; Libn Sch of Veterinary Med UPenn 43-48; Libn S Bend Med Foundation, South Bend Ind 48-52; Adult libn Niles Pub Lib, Niles Mich 60-65; Head bus & econ dept Memorial Lib UNotre Dame 65-. 14: Ref. 15: 2 6414 Brush trail, South Bend In 46628.

LOOFF, ETHEL (HOLMES). b Chicago 29 Ap 01. 4: Henry Byron Looff. 5: Chicago 18-19 (Bot, Math); UCal (Berkeley) (Eng, Educ, Soc Studies) BA; UWash summers 57-59 MLS, 61 (Libnship). 06: Fr, Ger, Sp. 7: Bot research, self- employed, Kodiak Island Alaska -42; Eng tchr Anacortes High Sch, Anacortes Wash 54-57, Libn 57-66; Hd libn Peninsula

Commun Col, Ft Angeles Wash 66-. 08: Dept of Psychology & Educ Research, Los Angeles City Schs Supv of Soc Studies 22-25. 9: NEA; WashEA; Wash State aschL (com chm 64-65; chm Area I); NWLA (sec-treas 65-66); Port Angeles EA. 10: Pi Lambda Theta; Beta Phi Mu. 13: Yes. 14: Commun Col libnship & consul. 15: Rt 2 Box 588F, Oak Harbor Wa 98277.

LOOMIS, DOROTHY (HELEN). b Cleveland 1 N 12. 5: West Res Flora Stone Mather Col 31-35 (Hist, Eng) BS; West Res 50-56 MSLS. 7: Asst to catlgr & sec to head libn E Cleveland Pub Lib, East Cleveland Ohio 37-42; Asst catlg libn Fenn Col 50-51; Asst catlg libn Battelle Mem Inst, Columbus Ohio 52-53; Catlg libn Fenn Col 53-56; Head catlg libn Cleveland Heights Bd of Educ, Cleveland Heights Ohio 56-65; Head catlg libn Cuyahoga Co Pub Lib, Cleveland 65-. 9: No Ohio Tech Serv Libns (chm). 14: Catlg. 15: Cuyahoga Co Pub Lib, 4510 Memphis ave, Cleveland Oh 44144.

LOOMIS, ELIZABETH (McCONNELL). b Greenfield Mass 1 Ja 15. 4: Frederic B Loomis. 5: Mt Holyoke 31-35 (Zool) AB; UDenver 60-61 (LS) MA. 7: Clk Sacramento City Lib, Sacramento Cal 59-60; Research libn UColo Med Ctr 61-63, Interlib loan & ref 63-65, MEDLARS searcher 65-68; Period & ref libn Houston Acad of Med Lib, Houston Tex 68-69; Asst sci libn UHouston 69-. 9: MedLA; SLA. 10: UDenver Grad Sch of Libnship Alum Assn. 14: Ref, info ret, research. 15: 570 Trianon st, Houston Tx 77024.

LOOMIS, LOUISE. b Jefferson Tex 16 My 12. 5: Tex Women's U 29-31, 33-35 (Chem) BS; UTex summers 36, 39-41 (Educ) MA; UDenver summer 58 (LS). 6: Chem Ger. 7: Elem tchr Jefferson Ind Sch Dist, Jefferson Tex 31-34; Sci tchr Sourlake High Sch, Sourlake Tex 35-41; Chem Instr Southwestern La Inst 41-42; Tech aide USDA, New Orleans 42; Chem, blender, clerk Ark Fuel Oil Co, Jefferson Tex 42-43; Sci tchr Sourlake High Sch, Sourlake Tex 43-44; Mobil Oil Co Refinery, Beaumont Tex: Chem 44-57, Libn 57-63, Operations analyst 63-64; Lit chem Mobil Chem Co Research & engnrg & development div, Beaumont Tex 64-. 8: Organized Mobil Oil Lib. 9: ACS; SLA (Tex Chap: chm By-Laws Com, sec 66-67, chm Nomin Com 67-68). 10: LWV; AAUW; Alpha Chi; Beaumont Lib Commsn. 14: Ref (chem & chem engnr). 15: 2255 Primrose, Beaumont Tx 77703.

LOOMIS, LYNN ANNE. b Wash DC 21 F 44. 5: Ohio Wesleyan 62-67 (Relig) BA; UMich 67-68 (LS) MA. 7: Child libn Fairfax Co Pub Lib, Hdqrs Lib Br 68-. 9: VaLA. 14: Child bks, rare bks. 15: 9617 Beachmill, Great Falls Va 22066.

LOOMIS, ZONA (KEMP). b Marquette Mich 26 D 11. 4: Charles P Loomis. 5: Kalamazoo Col 29-32 (Eng, Hist); Simmons 32-33 (LS) BS; UChicago 48-49 (LS) MA; Mich State U 55-62 (Sociol). 6: Sp, Ger. 7: Catlgr, child libn, Br libn Maywood Pub Lib, Maywood Ill 36-41; Br libn Wayne Co Lib, Wayne Co Mich 41-42, Hd bk Order Dept 42-44; Consul Lib ext serv Mich State Lib 44-48; Coord adult serv Enoch Pratt Free Lib, Baltimore 49-50; Prog Specialist Ford Foundation Nat Inst of Community Devel, India 64-66; Instr Soc Sci Mich State U, East Lansing 62-63, Ref Libn 67-68, Hd monographs sect acquis 68-. 9: ALA (Publ Com, var lib ext panels, coms etc); MichLA (Annual Conf Com); Tri-State 9mich Wis & Minn) Depressed Areas Lib Coun (Prog Chm). 10: Upper Peninsula State Officers Org; Phi Kappa Phi; fellowship awardee. 12: Co-auth "Modern Social Theories" (61). 13: Yes. 14: Bk sel, acquis. 15: 1155 Sabron dr, E Lansing Mi 48823.

LOONEY, ROBERT FAIN. b Rocky Mount NC 20 Jl 25. 5: UNC 49-53 (Eng) BA, 53-55 (Eng Lit) MA, 58-60 (LS) MS; Middlebury Col 56, 57 (Eng Lit). 06: Fr, Ger. 7: Armed Forces Infantry 43-46; Eng Instr Berry Col 55-58; Lib asst UNC 58-60; Libn Free Lib of Phila 60-, Curator of Prints 64-. 9: SLA. 10: Nat Trust for Preservation Hist Bldgs; Soc Arch Histns. 15: 2123 Cypress st, Phila Pa 19103.

LOOS, WILLIAM HENRY. b N Tonawanda NY 26 F 37. 5: SUNY (Buffalo) 57-65 (Hist) BA; Syracuse 67-68 MS in LS. 6: Ger. 7: Lib trainee City of Tonawanda Pub Lib 65-67; Jr libn Buffalo & Erie Co Pub Lib 68-. 9: ALA; BSA; Bibliographical Soc of Amer. 10: Beta Phi Mu; Libns Assn Buffalo & Erie Co Pub Lib. 14: Rare bks. 15: 295 Grove st, Tonawanda NY 14150.

LOPEZ, CELIA A. b Placetas Cuba 25 Ap 23. 5: UHavana 42-46 (Humanities), 59-60 (LS). 6: Sp. 7: Sp prof Havana High Sch 56-58; Libn (staff) Havana Nat Lib 60-64; Asst libn UFla 65-. 14: Ser. 15: 1716-C NW 2nd ave, Gainesville Fl 32601.

LOPEZ, JEANNE (BARWIS). b Elmira NY 13 N 12. 5: Syracuse U 29-30; Penn State Col 30-33 (Journalism) AB; Pratt 45-46 BSLS. 7: Asst circ libn Penn State U 46; Asst libn Warren Pub Lib, Warren Penn 46-48; Ref libn Jamestown Pub Lib, Jamestown NY 48-49; Libn Warren Pub Lib, Warren Penn 49-53; Asst to ref & archives libn URochester 53; Catlgr Cornell U Lib 53-55; Asst libn Princeton Pub Lib, Princeton NJ 55-56; Fine arts libn Allen Art Mus, Oberlin Col 56-60; Readers serv libn Brandeis U 60-63; Browsing room libn Ohio State U 63-65; Head adult div Pub Lib Oberlin Col Lib 66-. 8: WOSU (Ohio State U campus radio) bk talks 64-65. 9: ALA; OhioLA. 10: LWV; ACLU. 13: Yes. 14: Bk sel, readers adv, ref. 15: Oberlin Col Lib, Oberlin Oh 44074.

LOPEZ, KATHERINE (KEELAN). b Santurce PR 21 Jl 20. 4: Julio B Lopez. 5: Simmons 35-39 BLS; UPR 36-. 6: Sp, Fr, Ger. 7: Asst supv PR Hist Index Carnegie Lib, San Juan PR 39-40; Libn Tropical Forest Experiment Station, Rio Piedras PR 40-42; Asst libn UPR Gen Lib, Rio Piedras PR 41-43; Post libn US Army, Gurabo PR 43-45; UPR: Asst libn Gen Lib 47-50, Libn Schs of Med & Dentistry 55-60, Order libn Gen Lib 60-. 8: Adv wk with nursing, psychiatric & hosp libs of PR Dept of Health 55-60; Org of dental collection in UPR Sch of Dentistry 55-60. 9: Sociedad de Bibliotecarios de PR (treas 68, 69). 10: PTA; Simmons Col Alumni. 15: J-5 Violeta, Santa Mari3a, Rio Piedras PR 00927.

LOPEZ, LILLIAN. b Salinas Puerto Rico 24 Je 25. 5: Hunter Col 55-59 (Sp) BA; Columbia 60-62 (LS) MA. 6: Sp, Fr, Ital. 7: Bkkeeper, NYC 44-59; Lib trainee NYC Pub Lib 60-62, Libn I 62-64, Libn II 64-67, Libn III 67, Admin S Bronx Project 67-. 08; ALA (Adult & ya subcoms for Materials for Spanish-Speaking Peoples). 10: Educ Com: Associated Bronx Commun Organizs, NY Urban Coalition. 14: Readers' adv. 15: 111 Wadsworth ave, New York NY 10033.

LOPEZ, LILLIAN CASAS DE. b Cayey PR 31 O 24. 4: Guillermo Lopez. 5: UPR 46-51 (Eng) BA, Educ; Syracuse 57-58 MSLS; Columbia 64 9med Libnship). 6: Sp. 7: Libn US Army (Ft Bundy PR) 48-49; Tchr Dept of Educ (Dorado PR) 51; Asst libn UPR Sch of Med 52-60; Dir UPR Sch of med & Dentistry 61-. 9: MedLA; Sociedad de Bibliotecarios de Puerto Rico (pres 65). 10: Bus & Prof Women (Nat Fed). 13: Yes. 14: Ref, admin. 15: U Puerto Rico Sch of Medicine Lib, San Juan PR 00905.

LOPEZ, ROBERT ANTHONY. b Fayetteville NC 27 Je 25. 5: UFla 46-48 (Journalism); Emory 48-50 (Journalism) BA. 6: Sp. 7: (Yeoman 1c) US Navy Intelligence 42-46; Ed "New Smyrna Beach News," New Smyrna Beach Fla 50-53; Night supv libn Minneapolis Star and Tribune, Minneapolis 53-59, Hd libn 59-. 9: SLA. 10: Sigma Delta Chi; Delta Tau Delta; Minn Press Club. 14: Ref, admin. 15: Minneapolis Star & Tribune Co, 425 Portland ave, Minneapolis Mn 55415.

LORANTH, LESLIE Z. b Celldomolk Hungary 4 F 29. 4: Alice Nagypatky. 5: UBudapest 47-48 (Econ); Pazmany Peter U 48-53 (Hungarian, Ital Lang & Lit) MA; West Res 64-67 MS in LS. 6: Hungarian, Ital, Ger, Russian, Lat. 7: Lexicographer Nat Acad of Sci, Hungary 52-56; Tchr Corvinus High Sch, Budapest 52-56; Chem libn Millis Sci Ctr, Cleveland Ohio 66, Period libn 66-67; Ref & acquis libn Lorain Co Commun Col 67-68, Act libn 68, Head libn 68-. 9: ALA-ACRL (Tri-State Chap); SLA; OhioLA. 14: Ref, period. 15: 1005 N Abbe rd, Elyria Oh 44035.

LORD, DOROTHY A. b NYC 16 F 04. 5: NYU 24-31 (Biol) BS; Columbia 32-34 (Biol Sci) MA, 36-40 (LS) BS. 7: NYU: Sec to libn 26-38, Supv Sci Libs 38-42, Act chief ser dept 42-43, Ref asst 43-49, Asst libn Med Center 49-64; Jr libn Mt Vernon Pub Lib, Mt Vernon NY 64; Libn Grasslands Hosp & Westchester Sch of Nursing, Valhalla NY 64-. 9: ALA; MedLA. 14: Ref. 15: 1 Waverly pl, Valhalla NY 10595.

LORD, ISABELL EDITH. b Tampa Fla 17 O 30. 5: UTampa 48-52 (Elem Educ) BS; UFla 53-54 (Art); USoCal 58-59 (LS) MS. 7: Elem sch tchr Hernando Co Schs, Brooksville Fla 52-53; Elem sch tchr Hillsboro Co Schs, Lutz Fla 54-55; Elem sch tchr Hillsboro Co Schs, Tampa Fla 55-57; Elem sch tchr Compton City Schs, Compton Cal 57-58; Asst educ & curriculum libn Cal State Col (Long Beach) 59-. 10: Beta Phi Mu; Sigma Sigma Sigma. 13: Yes. 14: Catlg, ref. 15: 1312 E 215th pl, Torrance Cal 90502.

LORECK, RICHARD. b Milwaukee. 4: Kathleen Helgason. 5: Beloit Col 46; MSTC 46-47; Marquette U 47-49 (Hist) PhB; Drexel 50-51 MS in LS. 7: Page Milwaukee Pub Lib 41-42; US Coast Guard 42-45; Aide, libn II & I, archives libn Milwaukee Pub Lib 46-60; Rep Com Clearing House, Milwaukee 60-65; Asst acquis libn, Coord collections dev, Asst dir of libs for collections dev UWis (Milwaukee) 65-. 9: ALA; SLA. 10: Soc of Tympanuchus Cupido Pinnatus. 14: Rare bks, acquis. 15: 3031 N Prospect ave, Milwaukee Wi 53211.

LORENZ, DENIS (MARTIN). b New Haven Conn 21 Ap 39. 4: Harriet Fennster. 5: Yale 57-61 (Eng) BA; Simmons 61-62 MLS. 6: Fr. 7: Asst "Yale's Selective Bk Retirement Program" 60-61; Acquis libn New Haven (Conn) Free Pub Lib 62-67; Hd circ dept Bridgeport Conn 67-68, Asst libn 68-. 9: ALA; ConnLA; NELA; NNEA (Prog chm 67-68, sec-treas 69-). 11: Selected for assignment Library USA/NY World's Fair 64. 12: Co-ed (with Lee Ash) "Subject Collections" (3d ed 66). 13: Yes. 14: Bldg bk collections, pub rel, urban commun service s. 15: 685 Church Hill rd, Bridgeport Ct 06604.

LORENZ, JOHN G. b NYC 28 S 15. 4: Josephine Trumbull Lorenz. 5: City Col of NY 35-39 (Hist) BS; Columbia 39-40 BLS; Mich State U 48-51 (Pub Admin) MS. 07: Ref asst Queens Borough Pub Lib, Jamaica NY 40-41; Head bus & tech div Schenectady Pub Lib, Schenectady NY 41-44; Head ref div Grand Rapids Pub Lib, Grand Rapids Mich 44-46; Asst state libn Mich State Lib 46-57; Dept of Health Educ & Welfare Off of Educ, Wash DC: Asst dir lib serv br 57-58, Dir lib serv br 58-63, Dir div of continuing educ 63-64, Dir div of lib serv 64-65, Dir div of lib serv & educ facilities 65; Deputy libn LC 65-. 8: US expert to UNESCO (Paris) to consult with reps from 10 countries in devel "International Guide to Educ Documentation" 60-61; Dir, Sem on Pub Lib Devel in Africa 62; Pres Com on Lib Statistics of IFLA 64; Adv Com to Columbia U Sch of Lib Serv 64; Observer at meetings of Fed Lib Com at request of Libn of Congress 65; US consul to UNESCO Expert Mtg on Nat Planning of Lib Serv in Asia, Colombo, Ceylon 67. 9: IFLA (chm Com Stat & Standards 64-); ASIS; ALA (chm Panel on UNESCO); AAStateL (Mem-at-Large, Com to Aid Ital Libs); ARL (chm For Newspaper Microfilm Com); Com on Sci & Tech Info (Exec Off of the Pres); Nat Bk Com Exec Com; Nat Lib Week Steering Com (chm 69); USBE (v-pres 67-68, Exec Com 67-); US Dept of Agric Grad Sch (chm Critical Issues & Decisions Com); US Nat Commsn for the Internat Fed Document (Exec Com); DCLA. 11: Superior Service Award, HEW. 12: Ed issues of "Wilson Library Bulletin"; Contrib to ICMA publ; etc. 13: Yes. 14: Lib admin. 15: Library of Congress, Washington DC 20540.

LORENZO, GLADYS (SAHADI). b Brooklyn NY 24 Jl 26. 5: Brooklyn Col 45-49 (Eng) BA; UWash 62-63 MLS. 6: Fr. 7: Sec CARE, NYC 51-52; Sec Nat Coun of Churches, NYC 52-54; Sec US Dept of the Army, Paris 54-56; Recreation dir Spec Serv, Ft Lewis Wash 57-58, Lib asst 58-60; Catlgr Orange Co Pub Lib, Orange Cal 63-64, Child libn 64-66, Child coord 66-67, Br libn 67-. 14: Child serv, ref, pub libr. 15: 2868 Hickory pl, Costa Mesa Cal 92626.

LORMAND, ROBERT LEON. b Syracuse NY 7 D 37. 4: Ruth Martini. 5: Lawrence Inst Tech 56-60 (Electrical Engring); East MichU 64-67 (Math) BS. 7: Asst in research UMich willow Run Labs 63-67, Research asst 67-68; Tech info specialist Lawrence Radiation Lab, Liverm lab, Livermore Cal 68-69, Br lib supv 69-. 8: Principal Investigator of the VELA Seismic Info Analysis Ctr (VESIAC), UMich Willow Run Labs 67-68; Helped update the UDC schedule in seismology (550.34) while at VESIAC). 12: Asst ed "Earthquake Notes" 66-67. 14: Info ret. 15: 527 Rose st, Livermore Ca 94550.

LORT, JOHN (CECIL ROLSTON). b Victoria BC Can 18 My 14. 4: Faith Elizabeth Elm. 5: Victoria Col 31-32; UBC 32-35 (Hist) BA; UWash 37-38 BLS. 7: Lib asst BC Provincial lib, Victoria BC Can 40-46; Sgt Canadian Army (Inf) 42-46; Libn Ketchikan Pub Lib, Ketchikan Alaska 47-49; Libn Oakalla Prison Farm, Burnaby BC Can 49-50; Libn Vancouver Is Reg Lib, Nanaimo BC Can 50-53; Asst libn Greater Victoria Pub Lib, Victoria BC Can 53-54, Libn 54-. 9: CanLA; Inst Victoria Libns; BCLA (sec 42 & 46, treas 50-53, pres 61-62); PNLA. 10: Rotary Club; Art Gallery of Greater Victoria; Commun Arts Coun of Greater Victoria; Univ Ext Assn of Victoria; Saanich P-T Coun. 13: Yes. 15: 1312 Blanshard st, Victoria BC Can.

LOSEE, MADELEINE (WECKEL). b Kenney Ill 1 N 10. 4: Gordon Carroll Losee. 5: UIll 29-33 (Educ) BS, 33-36 (Pol Sci, Pub Law) MA; Catholic U 61-62 (LS). 7: LC: Law order libn 43-45, Chief Amer Law Sect Law Lib 45-46, Act chief Amer & Brit Exch 51; Law Libn AEC, Wash DC 51-61, Chief Hdqrs Lib 61-62; Nat Aero & Space Admin, Wash DC: Chief Legis Ref Br 62-63, Asst to Dir Tech Serv Div OSTI 63-64, Head Lib Programs 64-68, Program coord 68-. 8: Adv Com, Brookings Survey of Fed Dept Libs, Wash DC, 60; Com on Sci & Tech Info Task Gp on Dissem of Info 67-; Fed Lib Com Task Force on Automation 65-. 9: ASIS; AALL (chm Com on Fed Agencies Activs 57-59 & 62-65); Com on Automation & Sci Devel: chm 64-68, mem 68-; SLA; Law Libns Soc, Wash DC (pres 59-61). 10: AAUW. 12: Comp "Legislative History of Atomic Energy Act of 1954" (55); Comp "AEC Rules and Regulations" (58); Ed "Doorway to Legal News" (55-62). 13: Yes. 14: Admin, coord. 15: 6166 Leesburg Pike, Falls Church Va 22047.

LOSHER, SUSAN (EHRLICH). b Ulm Germany. 5: City Col of NY 47-53 (Personnel Admin); Fairleigh Dickinson U 58-60 (Eng Lit) BA; Columbia 61-63 MLS; Hunter Col 66-67 (Ling); NY State Pub Libns Prof Certif 68. 06: Ger, Fr. 7: Corr clerk order div Amer Tobacco Co, NYC 47-54; Clerical asst searching & preliminary catlg dept Firestone Lib Princeton U 54-56; Desk asst lending serv Butler Lib Columbia U 57-58; Subprof Philosophy Lib Columbia U 61-63; Asst to libn humanities & acquis divs City Col of NY 63-65, Instr Educ Lib City Col of NY 65-. 08: Transl into Ger for UNIVAC, Library/ USA 64. 9: ALA. 10: NY Lib Club; French Inst; Goethe House. 14: Ref, acquis, rare bks, computer applications to libs. 15: 6 Horizon rd, Fort Lee NJ 07024.

LOSIE, GERTRUDE L. b Elmira NY. 5: Cornell U 27-30, 33 AB; Columbia U Sch of Gen Studies & Col of Pharmacy 42, 47-49, 56; UMich 62. 6: Fr, Ger. 7: Sec asst & trainee Cornell U Lib 31-34; Admin sec NY State Dept Health, Albany NY 34-41; Tech adv Merck & Co Inc, Rahway NJ 41-44; Head Libn Wallerstein Co, NYC 44-57; Research libn Parke Davis & Co, Detroit 57-58; Head of research libs Parke Davis & Co, Ann Arbor Mich 58-. 9: SLA (Pharmac Sect): Asst ed "Unlisted Drugs," 58-59; Chemistry Sect: Moderator Wk Standards, Conv Prog 59; Nomin Com 60, chm chap Consult Com 61-63; Biol Sci Div: sec-treas 63-64, ed "Reminder" 64-65, Exec Com 63-65; Pharmac Div: v-chm 66-67, chm 67-68, Spec rep to Amer Assn of of Cols of Pharmacy Jt Comm on Pharmacy Col Libs, 67-69, Wkshop lectr 67; Mich Chap: chm Biol Scis 58-59, Chap consul 64, dir 62-63; Detroit Med Lib; Ann Arbor Lib Club (v-chm 62-63, chm 63-64; MedLA (Midwest Reg Panel Interlib loans 63, Exec Com 69-71. 10: AAUW; Friends of Ann Arbor Pub Lib. 13: Yes. 14: Admin, ref, med lit, company hist. 15: 715 S Forest, Ann Arbor Mich 48104.

LOSINSKI, JULIA M. b Baltimore 9 S 24. 5: Col of Notre Dame of Md 42-46 (Music, Educ) BA; Columbia 47-48 (LS) MS. 6: Polish. 7: Young adult libn, Br libn Enoch Pratt Free Lib, Baltimore 48-55; Br libn Dallas Pub Lib 55-56; Asst coordinator wk with young adults Brooklyn Pub Lib 56-59; Young adult serv consul Westchester Lib System, Mt Vernon NY 59-66; Coord sch & pub lib rel Prince George Co Mem Lib, Hyattsville Md 66-67, Coord ya serv 67-. 9: ALA-YASD (pres 68-69); NYLA; WestchesterLA (chm Young Adult & Child Libns Sect 64-65); MedLA (chm Child & YA Serv Dir 67). 10: Staff Assn Prince George Co Mem Lib; Delta Epsilon Sigma. 13: Yes. 14: Young adult serv, commun serv. 15: 6532 Adelphi rd, Hyattsville Md 20782.

LOTHIAN, HELEN (MARY MENZIES). b London England. 5: McMaster U 31-34 (Eng) BA, 54 (Eng) MA; Toronto 35 BLS. 7: Sec Law Office, St Cathaunes Ont Can 36-39; Boys & girls libn Niagara Falls Pub Lib, NF Ont Can 39. 9: CanLA (chm Young Canada's Bk Week, chm Child Lib Sect); OntLA (chm Child Libns Sect). 14: Child wk. 15: 3516 Portage rd S, Niagara Falls Ont Can.

LOTZ, MARIAN S(TEARNS). b Wash DC 28 Ja 19. 4: Dr James Wendell Lotz. 5: Wellesley 36-40 (Music) BA; WEST Res 41-42 BS in LS; Kent U (Pub lib admin). 6: Fr. 7: Page Wellesley Col Ref Lib 38-40; Clerk Yonkers Pub Lib, Yonkers NY 40-41; Cashier Tea-Caddy Restaurant, Cleveland 42; Jr libn Fine Arts Div Cleveland Pub Lib 42-43, Jr libn Miles Park br 43; Dental asst, Hartville Ohio 54-61; Br libn Hartville Br Lib, Hartville Ohio 61-67; Br coordinator Canton Pub Lib, Canton Ohio 64-68; Libn asst Walsh Col Lib 68-69. 9: OhioLA. 10: Hartville Jr Woman's Club; Hartville Park Assn; Hartville Kindergarten Commsn; Legis Com NE Ohio; Woman's Guild United Church of Christ; PTA. 14: Catlg, readers adv, br coordinating, admin. 15: 260 Overbrook dr, Columbus Oh 43214.

LOTZ, PATRICIA ANN. b England 20 O 30. 4: James Robert Lotz. 5: Sir George Williams 54-58 (Eng Lang & Lit) BA; McGill 58-59 BLS. 6: Fr. 7: Desk asst Redpath Lib McGill U 55-58; Staff libn Vancouver Pub Lib 59; Asst ed Canadian Period Index, Ottawa 63-68; Hd Pat Lotz Assocs, Ottawa 69-. 8: Research in bibliog & edl serv, Pat Lotz Associates, 69-. 9: CanLA. 14: Indexing, research. 15: 304 Second ave, Ottawa Ont Can.

LOUCKS, (LOLO) WENDY. b St Thomas Ont Can 19 Ja 44. 5: Bishop's U 61-65 (Chem) BS; McGill 65-67 MLS. 6: Fr. 7: Ref libn Town of Mt Royal Lib, Montreal 67-68; Libn Ind Acceptance Corp Ltd, Montreal 68-. 9: CanLA; SLA. 15: 2450 Athlone rd, Montreal 305 Quebec Can.

LOUDEN, JONATHAN E. b Painesville Ohio 12 F 42. 4: Beverly Yarnell. 5: Defiance Col 60-65 (Hist) BS; West Mich U 65-66 MSLS. 7: Bkmob libn State Lib of Ohio, Napoleon 62-65, Supv of bkmobs 66-67, Inst consul (Columbus) 67-68; Dir Gallia Co Dist Lib, gallipolis Ohio 68-. 9: ALA; OhioLA. 14: Ref, ext. 15: 2 Willow dr, Gallipolis Oh 45631.

LOUDERMILK, LOIS ADELINE. b Bigelow Ark 25 Ag 11. 4: Hayden Clifford Loudermilk. 5: Ark State Tchrs Col 29-48 (Eng) BSE; Peabody 62-65 MLS. 6: Sp. 7: Jr high sch tchr Bigelow High Sch, Bigelow Ark 31-32; Jr high sch tchr Adona High Sch, Adona Ark 32-34; Eng tchr-libn Perryville High Sch, Perryville Ark 39-61; High sch libn Joe T Robinson High Sch, Little Rock Ark 62-. 9: ALA; NEA; ArkLA; ArkEA. 10: Nat Cong Parents & Tchrs; Pulaski Co Tchrs Assn; Alpha Delta Kappa; Perryville Garden Club (Ark); Wesleyan Service Guild. 14: High sch libnship, ref. 15: Perryville Ark 72126.

LOUET, SANDRA. b Peterborough Ont Can 25 Ap 37. 4: Etienne Louet. 5: UToronto 56-59 (Fr) BA, 59-60 BLS. 6: Fr. 7: Libn James Lovick & Co Ltd, Toronto Can 60-63; Research Cockfi eld Brown & Co Ltd, Toronto Can 63-64; Libn MacLaren Advertising Co Ltd, Toronto Can 64-. 9: SLA (chm Advert Gp). 14: Ref. 15: 630 Roselawn ave apt 912, Toronto Can.

LOUGH, MARGARET E(LEANOR). b Phila 9 Ap 06. 5: Hood Col 24-28 (Hist) AB; Drexel 30-31 BS in LS. 7: Johns Hopkins U Lib: Asst in Hist & Soc Sci Lib 31-36, Head of Hist & Soc Sci Lib 36-64, Ref libn humanities & soc sci 65-. 9: ALA-ACRL; MdLA (corr sec 55-57). 10: Hist Soc of Frederick Co (Md); Baltimore Hood Club; Johns Hopkins Faculty Club. 14: Ref. 15: Homewood Apts 2 TA, Baltimore Md 21218.

LOUGHBRIDGE, NANCY J. b Beaver Falls Penn 30 S 30. 5: Antioch 48-53 (Eng) BA; UMich 55-57 MALS. 7: Catlg libn I UMich (Ann Arbor) 57, acquis libn II 57-59; Hd bk order sect USoCal 59-60; Hd readers serv Dickinson Col 60-68; Bibliogr UCincinnati 68-. 15: Pine rd, Mt Holly Springs Pa 17065.

LOUGHIN, ESTHER (WARREN). b Edmore Mich 8 Ja 05. 4: Everett Loughin. 5: Reed Col 26-29; UMich 33 BA, 35 BA in LS. 7: Ed asst ALA, Chicago 35-40; Assoc ref libn Mich State U 40-41; Mich State Lib: Documents libn 41-42, Ref libn 43-44, 46, Chief local hist 47-54, Chief Mich sect 55-65; Ref libn Mich State U 65-. 9: ALA; MichLA. 10: Hist Soc of Mich; Hist Soc of Greater Lansing. 12: Ed "Michigan in Books" (58-). 13: Yes. 14: Ref. 15: Mich State U Lib, East Lansing Mich 48823.

LOUGHIN, MARY JEANETTE. b Boyne City Mich 27 S 02. 5: UMich 20-23, 24-25 (Langs) AB, 26-32 AMLS. 6: Fr, Sp. 7: Asst sec to libn UMich 25-26; UMich: Sec Dept of Lib Sci 26-33, Sec to libn 33-41, Sec to dir Lib 41-54, Recorder Dept of Lib Sci 54-. 9: ALA; MichLA. 14: Educ for libnship. 15: 709 Dewey ave, Ann Arbor Mich 48104.

LOUP, JEAN LOUISE (ZIMMERMAN). b Council Bluffs Iowa 18 Ap 41. 4: Roland J Loup. 5: Iowa State U 59-63 BS; UOkla 63-65 MA (Hist) MLS; Drake U 66. 7: Asst ref libn & central area field consul Iowa State Travel Lib, Des Moines Iowa 65-66; Instr & order libn Iowa State U Lib 66-67; Instr & catlgr 67-. 9: Org of Amer Histns; IowaLA (R & TS Sect sec-treas 68-69); MusLA. 10: Sigma Alpha Iota; Beta Phi Mu. 13: Yes. 14: Acquis, catlg. 15: 2634 Lincoln way, Ames Ia 50010.

LOVAS, JoANNE E. b Sewickley Penn 30 O 42. 5: St Francis (Loretto Penn) 60-64 (Eng) BA; UPittsburgh 64-65 MLS. 6: Fr. 7: Libn Robert Morris Jr Col 65-. 8: Consul catlgr, Cath Info Ctr, Diocese of pittsburgh. 9: ALA; PennLA; Tri-state ACRL. 14: Catlg, circ. 15: 15 State st, Baden Pa 15005.

LOVE, DOROTHY SANFORD. b Dayton Ohio 13 My 08. 4: G Robert Love. 5: Wayne State U (City Col) 23-26 (Hist) AB, 26-27 Tchr Certif; UMich summers 40-43 ABLS; UMiami 63-67 (Clinical Reading) M Ed. 6: Fr, Sp. 7: Child 1st asst West Reg Lib, Dayton Ohio 38-43; Ref libn Dayton Pub Lib, Dayton Ohio 43-46; Circ libn Dillard U 46-48; Br libn Dorsey Pub Lib, Miami 48-49; Libn Liberty City Elem Sch, Dade Co Fla 49-54; Libn Dunbar Elem Sch, Dade Co Fla 54-63; Head Libn Mays Jr-Sr High Sch, Dade Co Fla 64-. 8: Visiting Prof Dept of Lib Serv FlaAMU, Tallahassee Fla 54; Evaluation Com, North Dade High Sch 59; Consul S Fla Desegregation Ctr UMiami 66; NDEA lectr AV Sch Lib Serv 66. 09: ALA; NEA; IRA; ASCD; ATA; FlaLA; SELA; FlaASchL (sec-treas 61-); FlaEA; Fla State Tchrs Assn. 10: Delta Sigma Theta; Fla Reading Coun; Phi Lambda Pi. 13: Yes. 14: Child ref. 15: 3273 NW 48th Ter, Miami Fla 33142.

LOVE, ERIKA. b Berlin Germany. 5: Heidelberg 47-48 (Eng) Dolm Dipl; IndU 49-50 (Musicology, Lit) BA, 51-53 (LS) MA. 6: Ger, Fr. 7: Jr libn Pub Lib, Indianapolis 50-51; Asst libn Ind U Sch of Law 51-53; Libn Larue D Carter Mem Hosp, Indianapolis 53-67; Chief libn Bowman Gray Sch of Med, Winston-Salem NC 67-. 09: MedLA (Rep Jt Com on Hosp Libs, Coun of Nat Lib Assns 65-; Midwest Reg Group: Exec Bd 59-62, sec 60-61). 12: Ed Ind "Slant" 56-57. 14: Inserv educ, lit hist of psychiatry. 15: Chief Lib, Bowman Gray Sch of Med, Winston-Salem NC 27103.

LOVE, MARILYN (McSHANE). b Sacramento Cal 28 F 41. 4: John M Love. 5: UCal 58-62 (Amer Civilization) BA, 62-63 MLS. 7: Ref libn UIowa 63-66; Consul title III LSCA Colo State Lib, Denver 67-69; Admin asst title II HEA Inst UDenver Grad Sch Libnship 69. 9: ALA; ColoLA. 14: Ref serv, lib educ. 15: 1670 Newport st, Denver Co 80220.

LOVE, MARY EMELINE. b McAdams Miss 6 My 11. 5: Miss State Col for Women 28-32 (Eng) BA; LSU 49 BS in LS; UMiss 50; USoCal 53. 6: Fr. 7: Tchr & libn Miss pub schs 33-45; Libn Cleveland High Sch, Cleveland Miss 45-47; Field libn Jackson Pub Schs (Elem), Jackson Miss 47-59; Assoc dir Miss Lib Comsn, Jackson Miss 59-67, Dir 68-. 8: Member 0f State Advisory Council, ESEA, Title III, Jackson Miss 68-69. 9: ALA (Coun 58-63); MissASchL (pres 50-52); SELA (Nomin Com 69); MissLA (pres 55-57; Lib Educ Com 69). 10: Delta Kappa Gamma. 13: Yes. 15: 567 Warrior Trail, Jackson Ms 39216.

LOVE, PAULINE J (URIAH) (SHIPP) (MRS). b Herrington Tex 22 Ap 11. 5: Kan State Col summers 30, 31, 33; Kan State Tchrs Col (Emporia) 34-37 BS in Ed, Lib Certif. 7: Elem tchr Dist 91, Wabaunsee Co Kan 29-31; Elem tchr Dist 43, Wabaunsee Co Kan 31-34; Stud asst circ dept Kellogg Lib Kan State Tchrs Col(Emporia) 34-36; Asst libn Baker U 37-38; Libn Atchison High Sch, Atchison Kan 38-40; Reviser Index Medicus, AMA, Chicago 41-42 ALA, Chicago; Ed asst 42-43, Ed of publ 43-51, Chief of publ dept 51-57, Dir of publ dept 58-68, Mgr spec pub projects 68-70. 9: ALA; IllLA; Chicago Lib Club; Chicago Bk Clinic. 10: Kappa Delta Pi. 15: 50 E Huron st, Chicago Il 60611.

LOVE, ROBERT MATTHEW. b Cleveland 14 N 27. 4: Jean Yeager. 5: Oberlin Col 45-50 (Hist) BA; UWis summer 49, 52; West Res 60-61 MS in LS; UPittsburgh summer 67, 68. 06: Sp, Ger. 7: (Cpl) US Army 46-47; Reporter "Cleveland Plain Dealer" 51-52; Reporter Steel Magazine, Cleveland 52-59; Reporter "Cleveland Press" 59-60; Acquis libn Carnegie Inst of Tech 61-63; Catlgr Carnegie Pub Lib, Pittsburgh 63-64; Catlg libn Slippery Rock State Col 64-. 9: ALA-ACRL (Tri-State Chap); PennLA. 10: AAUP; Dickens Fellowship (Pittsburgh Chap). 14: Catlg. 15: 338 E Cooper st, Slippery Rock Penn 16057.

LOVE, WAYNE. b Dothan Ala 14 S 36. 4: Gerutha Crowley. 5: Troy State Col 54-58 9eng) BS; Peabody Col 61-63 (LS) MA. 7: Bkmob libn Houston Mem Lib, Dothan Ala 56-61, Child libn 62-64, dir 64-. 8: Exec dir Nat Lib Week, Ala 68. 9: ALA; SELA; ALALA (Recr Com Chm 66-67, mem Scholarship & Loan Com 67, pres 68-69, Mem Exec Coun 66-70; Pub Lib Div pres 66-67). 10: Rotary Club. 11: Phi Delta Kappa; Recipient of the first ala Pub Lib Serv Award. 14: Admin, acquis, child wk. 15: PO Box 1369, Dothan Al 36301.

LOVEJOY, EUNICE GENE (GOWL). b Harrisonburg Va 18 Ap 24. 4: Albert Edwin Lovejoy. 5: Marion Col 39-41 (Eng); Madison Col 41-43 (Eng) BA; UNC 43-44 BS in LS. 7: Circ asst Goucher Col 44-45; Asst libn Rockingham Pub Lib, Harrisonburg Va 45-46; Asst period dept UNC Lib (Chapel Hill) 46-48; Libn sociol anthropology City & Reg Planning & Soc Wk Lib UNC (Chapel Hill) 48-50; Air Force Proj Inst for Research in Soc Sci UNC summer 52; Asst libn Lynchburg Col 52-53; Asst order dept UNC Lib (Chapel Hill) summer 57; Ohio State U: Ref libn Educ Lib summer 58, Research libn Bur of Educ Research & Serv 58-59, Ref libn Educ Lib 59-60, Lib Soc Wk Lib 60-63, Asst to supv of dept libs 63-65, Head dept libs 65-66; Abstract index ed ERIC Clearinghouse for Vocational & Tech Ed 66-68; Spec libn for serv to state govt State Lib of Ohio 69-. 9: SLA; ALA; ASIS; OhioEA. 13: Yes. 14: Pub serv, dept libs, info sci. 15: 172 W Main st, Westerville Ohio 43081.

LOVEJOY, JANET MILDRED. b Alhambra Cal 11 Ja 44. 5: Cal State Col (LA) 61-66 (Hist) BA; San Jose State Col 66-67 (LS) Credential. 7: Libn W Wilson Jr High Sch, Glendale cal 67-. 9: ALA; NEA; CalLA; CalASchL; CalTA. 14: Lit for child & yp. 15: 1420 B E Wilson ave, Glendale Ca 91206.

LOVERING, VIRGINIA ELIZABETH. b Hinsdale Ill 26 O 28. 5: No Ill U 46-47; UMo 47-50 (Journalism) BJ; No Ill U 52-53 (Eng) MSE; UMich 60-61 AMLS. 7: Advertising "DeKalb Daily Chronicle," DeKalb Ill 50-52; Tchr Somonauk High Sch, Somonauk Ill 53-59; Catlgr Parson Lib No Ill U 61-. 9: ALA; IllLA. 10: AAUP; AAUW; Beta Phi Mu; Pi Lambda Theta; Gamma Alpha Chi. 14: Catlg, rare bks. 15: 627 N First st apt 11, DeKalb Il 60115.

LOVETT, MARJORIE C (CASSELBERRY). b Phoenixville Penn 13 Ag 27. 4: Robert E Lovett. 5: Yale Sch of Mus 45-49 (Mus) BMus; Drexel 63-64 MLS. 6: Fr, Ger. 7: Instr Wilkes col Mus Dept 61-62; Ref libn (soc sci & hist dept) Phila Free Pub Lib 64; Hd circ dept Bloomfield Pub Lib, Bloomfield NJ 67-. 9: ALA. 10: AAUW. 14: Bk sel (esp collection bldg). 15: 709 S Maple ave, Fairfield Ia 52556.

LOVETT, ROBERT W. b Beverly Mass 18 S 13. 4: Dorothy T Merrow. 5: Harvard 31-35 (Hist) AB, 35-36 (Hist) MA; Columbia summers 40-41, 46-47 (LS) BS; American U summer 48 Archival Certif. 6: Fr. 7: Asst Harvard U Archives 37-42; US Army clerk Med Battalion (Cpl) 42-45; Sr asst Harvard U Archives 45-48; Head of mss div Baker Lib, Harvard Bus Sch 48-. 8: Catlgd Kendall Collection of SC material, Camden SC 52; Consul on Lexington Room, Lexington Pub Lib 58. 9: SAA (Fellow, Coun 64-68, chm Bus Archives Comm 67-). 10: Appalachian Mountain Club; Beverly Hist Soc, Essex Inst. 11: Hon Phi Beta Kappa (Harvard) 60. 12: Comp "List of Business Manuscripts in Baker Library" (51). 13: Yes. 14: Archives & mss (esp bus). 15: 27 Conant st, Beverly Mass 01905.

LOVING, PATRICIA MARIE. b Albert City Iowa 4 Mr 39. 5: UNo Iowa 57-61 (Jr High Sch Educ) BA; UMinn 65-66 (LS) MA. 7: Tchr White Bear Lake Minn 61-65; Asst ref libn cowles Lib DrakeU 66-68; Instr Lib Sch UMinn (Minneapolis) 68-. 9: ALA; AALS; Minn Assn Sch Libns. 10: Beta Phi Mu. 14: Ref, sch libs. 15: 614 Huron SE, Minneapolis Mn 55414.

LOW, EDMON. b Kiowa Okla 4 Ja 02. 4: Mayme C Low. 5: E Central State Col 22-26 (Math) BS; UIll 29-30 BS in LS; UMich 37-38 MALS. 6: Fr, Ger. 7: Asst libn E Central State Col 27-37; Libn Bowling Green State U 38-40; Libn Okla State U 40-67; Visiting lecturer UMich (Ann Arbor) summers 39-46, 50-66; Prof of lib sci 67-. 8: Adv Com Commsnr Educ on Lib Serv Act, 56-60; Chm Okla Coun on Libs, 64-67; Consul on many col & univ lib bldgs. 9: ALA (v-pres 61-62 & 64-65; Com on Legis: mem 58-62 & 64-68, chm 67-68);-ACRL (pres 60-61; chm Subcom on Copyright Issues 68-); OklaLA (pres 49-50); SWLA (pres 50-52). 11: Distinguished Serv Award OklaLA 58; Silver Book Award, Lib Binding Inst 66; Lippincott Award ALA 67; D Litt East MichU 67. 13: Yes. 14: Catlg, admin. 15: 1456 Glastonbury, Ann Arbor Mi 48103.

LOW, GLORIA. b Sherman Tex 8 F 46. 5: Okla State U 63-67 (Eng) BS; LSU 67-68 (LS) MS. 6: Sp. 7: Clk-typist Okla State Lib summer 64-66; Libn specialist West Plains Lib Stst, Clinton Okla 68-. 9: ALA; OklaLA; SWLA. 10: Great Bks leader. 14: Child & ya serv. 15: 814 1/2 B Frisco, Clinton Ok 73601.

LOWDEN, ARLENE M (PANZER). b Ivanhoe Ill 1 S 19. 4: William Lowden. 5: Cornell Col 38-42 (Sociol) BA; Garrett Theol Sem 42-43 (Religious Educ); Northwestern 42-43 (Sociol). 6: Fr, Sp. 7: Libn drs & patients libs Southwestern State Hosp, Marion Va 43-45; Sec med soc wk dept Strong Mem Hosp, Rochester NY 45; Volunteer libn First Methodist Church, Des Plaines Ill 58; Libn research & development div, lib Nuclear-Chicago Corp, Des Plaines Ill 59-. 9: SLA. 10: Cornell Col Alumni Club; Mortar Board. 14: Ref, bibliog (radioisotopes & nuclear instrumentation). 15: 2129H Ash st, Des Plaines Ill 60018.

LOWE, DORIS J. b Hartford Conn. 5: UConn (Chem) BS; Columbia 66 MSLS. 06: Fr. 7: Chem analytical Pratt & Whitney Aircraft, E Hartford Conn 41-44; Research asst Synthetic Organic Chem Schering Corp, Bloomfield NJ 44-48; Med research libn Bristol-Myers Co, NYC 48-52; Dir tech info serv Nepera Chem Co, Yonkers NY 52-54; Dir tech info serv Labs for Pharmaceutical Development Inc, Yonkers NY 54-57; Assoc libn Winthrop Labs, NYC 57-62; Ref libn Cornell U Med Col 62-. 9: ACS; MedLA; SLA. 13: Yes. 14: Ref. 15: 124 E 24th st, New York NY 10010.

LOWE, MILDRED (RABINOWITZ). b NYC 4 Ap 27. 4: Rubin Lowe. 5: Brooklyn Col 43-47, 57-60 (Sociol) BA; Pratt Inst 64-65 MLS; Columbia 68- (LS). 6: Ger, Yiddish. 7: Voice coach dance accompanist self-employed, Massapequa NY 49-57; Music dir commun theatre Steinberg & Lowe, Massapaequa NY 57-65; Govt docs libn SUNY (Farmingdale) 65-. 8: SUNY Task Force for Academic Status 66-. 9: ALA; NYLA Nassau CoLA (Col Div); NY Lib Club (Coun 68-); SUNY-FarmingdaleLA (Rep to SUNYLA 68-). 10: Pratt Inst Alum Assn; Beta Phi Mu; Demo Coalition Com Woman. 11: Title IIB Grant 68 (doctoral prog). 14: Govt publ, tech serv, personnel. 15: 120 Glengariff rd, Massapequa Pk NY 11762.

LOWE, WILLIAM C. b Brooklyn NY 18 S 30. 4: Irene Stoll. 5: Colgate U 48-52 (Amer Civilization) BA; SUNY(Geneseo) 57-60 (LS) MS. 7: Supply Off (1st Lt) USAF Strat Air Command, Columbus Ohio 52-53; Physicist Xerox Corp, Rochester NY 53-57, Libn 57-; Dir tech info ctr D H Hill Lib NC State U (Raleigh). 09: SLA (NC Chap: Bulletin ed, dir 67-69, v-pres & pres-elect 69-70). 13: Yes. 14: Acquis, ref, reprography. 15: 4708 Woodbridge dr, Raleigh NC 27609.

LOWE, WINNIE M. b Godley Tex 10 Ja 10. 4: John Willace Lowe. 5: N TexU 28-29; Henderson State Tchrs Col 45-47 (Eng); Ouachita BaptistU 56; Arkansas State Col 47-51 (Lib, Eng) BSE. 7: Tchr: New Hope Sch, Mansfield Tex 28, Carroll Hill Sch, Grapevine Tex 29, Kirby High Sch, Kirby Ark 42-44, Enola High Sch, Enola Ark 48, Willisville High Sch, Wa sch, Waldo Ark 45-47; Libn & tchr Fourche Valley High Sch, Briggsville Ark 48-. 9: ALA; ArkLA (chm Sch Sect, 2 terms); ArkEA. 10: Beta Gamma Chapter; Kappa State; Delta Kappa Gamma; Yell Co Lib Bd; Ark River Regl Lib Bd. 13: Yes. 14: Ref. 15: Bluffton Ar 72827.

LOWELL, MILDRED (HAWKSWORTH). b Chicago 11 N 05. 4: Wayne Russell Lowell. 5: UPuget Sound 23-27 (Eng) AB; UWis 27-28 (LS) Certif; Chicago 38-39 (LS) AM, 40-42, 57 (LS) PhD. 7: Asst libn Bradley U 28-30; Libn & Asst Prof East Ore Col of Educ 30-40; Research asst to Dean UChicago Grad Lib Sch 40-42; Lecturer & libn ICA-Thailand Proj Div of Lib Sci Ind U 54-60; Assoc Prof Grad Lib Sch Ind U 60-. 8: Lib consul Inst for Sex Research summer 63; Res grant, Coun on Lib Resources 66. 9: ALA (Internat Rel R T, treas 64-66; Panel on UNESCO 66-68);-ACRL (v-chm Tchr Educ Sect 64-65, Bd Dirs 64-66);-LED (Pub Com 59-61, chm Nomin Com 65-66); AALS (Curr & Instr Com 66-71); PNLA (sec 37, chm Reorg Com 40); E OreLA (pres 35). 10: Beta Phi Mu; Pi Kappa Delta. 12: "College and University Library Consolidations" (42); Jt auth (with L R Wilson & S Reed) "The Library in College Instruction" (51); "Key Word - Analytic Subject Index to The Library of Education" (67); "Management of Libraries and Information Centers " (3 v 68); Comp & ed "Proceedings of the Twenty-Eighth Annual Conference of the Pacific Northwest Library Association" (37); "Indiana University libraries, 1829-1942" PhD dirs UChicago, on microfilm (57). 13: Yes. 14: Mgt, acad libs, personnel mgt, res libs. 15: 1248 East Wylie, Bloomington In 47401.

LOWELL, VIRGINIA LEE (GREENE). b San Jose Cal 21 N 40. 4: Arthur Lowell. 5: Reed Col 58-61; UCal (Berkeley) 61-62, 63 (Eng) BA; West Res 64-65 MSLS. 6: Fr, Ger. 7: Asst catlg libn Wittenberg U 65-66, Hd catlg dept John Carroll U 66-68; Hd catlg dept cuyahoga Commun Col 68-. 9: ALA. 10: Beta Phi Mu. 14: Catlg. 15: 2588 Mayfield rd apt 6, Cleveland Heights Oh 44106.

LOWENFELS, DORIS (BECKER). b NYC 14 Je 28. 4: Dr Albert B Lowenfels. 5: UVt 49 (Hist) BA; Columbia 52 (LS) MS. 6: Fr. 7: Ref libn Manhattanville Col 65-. 14: Ref, sch wk. 15: 95 Soundview ave, White Plains NY 10606.

LOWENS, IRVING. b NYC 19 Ag 16. 4: Margery Louise Morgan. 5: Columbia 39 (Music, Music Educ) BS; UMd 57 (Amer Civilization) MA, currently (Amer Civilization). 6: Fr, Ger. 7: Contrib music critic "Washington Evening Star" 53-61, Chief music critic 61-; Ref libn for sound recordings Music Div LC 61-62, Asst head ref sect Music Div 62-66. 9: MusLA (chm Amer Music Hist Project Com 58-64; mem-at-large Exec Bd 63-64, pres 65-66); Amer Musicological Soc (Nat Coun mem 63-64, 69-71, mem-at-large Exec Bd 64-66); Music Critics Assn (treas 62-); Inter-Amer Inst for Musical Research, Tulane U (Adv Bd 62-); Moravian Music Foun (res consul 59-); Conf Bd of Associated Research Councils (Adv Screening Com in Music, Com on Internat Exch of Persons 62-64); Amer Studies Assn; Amer Folklore Soc; Soc for Ethnomusicology; BSA; Internat Musicological Soc; Internat Assn of Mus Libs; Internat Folk Music Coun; Amer Antiq Soc (Fellow); Chm Bd Dir Amer Musical Digest 67-; Bd Dir Amer Music Ctr 66-. 10: Cosmos Club (Wash DC). 11: UMd research fellow, Amer

Civilization Prog 56-58; Dunbarton Col lecturer in music, 58-59; Moramus Award (for distinguished service to American Music), 1960; ACLS; Travel grant Germany 62; res grant 65; Martha Baird Rockefeller Fund travel grant Austria 64, Romania 67; Pro Helvetia res grant 64, 67; US State Dept travel grant, Venezuela 68. 12: Auth "The Hartford Harmony: a Selection of American Hymns from the Late 18th and Early 19th Centuries" (53); Ed "John Tufts' 'Introduction to the Singing of Psalm-Tunes' (1726)" a facs ed (54); Auth "We Sing of Life," with V Silliman (55); Ed "Benjamin Carr's 'Federal Overture' (1794)" a facs ed (57); Ed "John Wyeth's 'Repository of Sacred Music, Part Second' (1813)" a facs ed (64); Ed " 'A Bibliography of Early Secular American Music' by O G Sonneck and W T Upton (1945)" a facs ed (64); Ed "Critical & Historical Essays by edward MacDowell" (69); Auth "Music and Musicians of Early America" (66). 13: Yes. 14: Ref, acquis (espec rare materials & mss). 15: 145 W 55 st, New York NY 10019.

LOWENTHAL, JANE E. b Los Angeles 10 O 16. 5: Barnard Col 34-38 (Zool) BA; Bank Street Col of Educ 53-55 (Educ) MS; Columbia 63-64 (LS) MS. 7: Lab tech Killian Research Labs, NYC 38-40; Nursery sch tchr NY Hosp, NYC 47-50; Instr child study dept Vassar Col 50-55; Libn trainee & libn Countee Cullen Br NY Pub Lib 63-64; Asst libn Carnegie Endowment for Internat Peace, NYC 64-66; Libn Res Inst for the Study of Man NYC 66-. 9: SLA; Sem for the Acquis of Latin Amer Lib Materials; BSA. 10: Victorian Soc in Amer. 14: Catlg, ref. 15: 132 E 19th st, New York NY 10003.

LOWENTHAL, RUTH (HUEFTLE). b Wichita Kan 17 Ap 23. 4: Al Lowenthal Jr. 5: Ft Hays Kan State Col 41-45 (Eng) AB; UIll 45-46 BS in LS. 7: Catlgr Ft Hays Kan State Col 46-49; Catlgr Oakley Pub Lib, Oakley Kan 52-55; Dir lib serv Colby Commun Jr Col 66-. 9: ALA; NEA; KanLA; KanStateTA. 10: Phi Kappa Phi; AAUW. 14: Admin, catlg. 15: Rt 1 Box 10K, Colby Ks 67701.

LOWER, DOROTHY MARGARET. b Monroeville Ind 5 F 14. 5: West Col for Women 32-36 (Fr, Span) AB; Ind U summers 58-60 (LS) MA. 6: Fr, Sp. 7: Gen asst Ind State Lib 38-39; Gen asst Warsaw Pub Lib, Warsaw Ind 41-42; Ft Wayne Pub Lib, Ft Wayne Ind: Br libn 52-53, Ref asst 57-58, Bus & tech asst 59-60, Libn-genealogy 61-. 8: Instr adult educ non-credit genealogy com PurdueU 69. 9: ALA (Geneal Com Hist Sect Ref Div); IndLA. 10: DAR; Soc of Colonial Dames of the 17th Cent; Allen Co-Ft Wayne Hist Soc; Soc of Ind Pioneers; Beta Phi Mu. 14: Ref, geneal. 15: 530 W Berry st No 606, Ft Wayne Ind 46802.

LOWERISON, JEAN (ANNE). b San Diego 4 Je 41. 5: San Diego State Col 59-61 (Fr); UCal(Berkeley) 61-63 (Fr) BA, 63-64 MLS. 6: Fr, Ger. 7: Libn Carlsbad High Sch, Carlsbad Cal 64-66; Libn Anatolia College, Thessaloniki, Greece 66-68; Libn Nisky Demonstr libn Nisky Demonstration School, St Thomas, Virgin Islands 68-69. 9: Cal Tchrs Assn. 10: San Diego Symphonic Chorale. 15: 1726 Montecito way, San Diego Ca 92103.

LOWERY, CHARLOTTE. b Sanborn Iowa. 5: Morningside Col 23-25; West Res 28-30 BSLS; USoCal 51 (Ger) MA. 6: Ger, Fr. 7: Bkkeeper credit off Pelleteer's Dept Store, Sioux City Iowa 25-26; Elem sch tchr, Iowa 26-28; Catlgr Rochester U 30-32; Catlgr Buffalo Pub Lib, Buffalo NY 32-39; Music catlgr USoCal 39-64; Catgr Fresno State Col 64-. 9: ALA; MusLA; CalTA. 10: AAUP; Phi Kappa Phi; Audubon Society; Cal State Employees Assn. 14: Catlg, mus. 15: 3219 E Harvey ave, Fresno Cal 93702.

LOWERY, CLORENE (BERNECE). b Daisy Ark 10 Ja 19. 5: So State Col 36-38 Diploma in Educ; Henderson State Tchrs 45-47 (Soc Sci) BA; Peabody 48-49 (LS) MA. 7: Prim tchr Pub Schs, Boughton Ark 40-43; Clerk (Cpl) Army Air Force, US 43-45; Eng tchr High Sch, Magnet Cove Ark 47-48; Libn W Side Jr High, Little Rock Ark 49-. 8: Mus Libn First Christian Church 64-. 9: ALA; NEA; ArkLA; ArkEA; Little Rock Clr TA. 14: Ref, catlg. 15: 1400 Willow, N Little Rock Ark 72114.

LOWMAN, MARGARETT GLADYS (GRAEBER). b Lawrence Kan 7 Jl 01. 5: UKan 18-22 (Entomology) AB; Kan State Tchrs Col summers 50-55 (LS) MS. 6: Ger. 7: Tchr Overbrook High Sch, Overbrook Kan 24-25; Tchr Linwood High Sch,. Linwood Kan 25-27; Tchr BOSWELL Jr High Sch, Topeka Kan 27-31; Tchr Topeka High Sch, Topeka Kan 31-36; Tchr Lawrence High Sch, Lawrence Kan 42-45; Libn Lawrence Jr High Sch, Lawrence Kan 45-54; Libn Central Jr High Sch, Lawrence Kan 54-60; Libn West Jr High Sch, Lawrence Kan 60-. 8: Consul, NDEA Wkshop, Kan State Tchrs Col, summer 65; Coord of lib serv in Lawrence (Kan) Dist #497. 09: NEA; ALA; Kan State Tchrs Assn; KanASchL; KanLA. 10: Kappa Kappa Iota; Delta Kappa Gamma; AAUW; Lawrence Educ Assn. 13: Yes. 14: Catlg, wk with yp. 15: 1102 W 22nd terrace, Lawrence Kan 66044.

LOWMAN, MATTHIAS P II. b Chicago 21 Je 38. 5: Carleton Col 56-60 (Philos) BA; Chicago 60-68 (LS) MA. 06: Lat, Ger. 7: Asst curator of rare bks Newberry Lib, Chicago 62-65, Curator of rare bks & asst head of spec collections 65-67, Curator of rare bks & hd of spec collections 67-. 9: BSA; Bibliog Soc (London); SAA; ALA; Bibliog Soc UVa. 10: Caxton Club. 14: Rare bks, modern poetry. 15: 60 W Walton, Chicago Il 60610.

LOWRIE, JEAN E. b Northville NY 11 O 18. 5: Keuka Col 36-40 (Eng, Hist) AB; West Res 40-41 BSLS, 59 PhD; West Mich U 56 (Elem Educ) MA. 6: Fr, Ger. 7: Child libn Pub Lib, Toledo Ohio 41-44; Elem sch libn Oak Ridge (Tenn) Pub Schs 44-41; West Mich U: Campus sch libn 51-56, Prof Dept of Libnship 58-63, Head Dept of Libnship 63-. 8: Exch tchr-libn, Nottingham Eng, 48-49; US Del to WCOTP, Paris 64; Vancouver 67; Dublin 68. 9: ALA (Coun 67, Exec Bd 69);-AASchL (sec 50-51, Bd Dirs 52-53, pres 63-64; chm Internat Rel Com 54-55 & 65); Assn of Higher Educ; TennLA (sec-treas 47); MichLA (chm sch & child sect 55). 10: AAUP; Altrusa; Delta Kappa Gamma; Dutton Macrae Award, 57; Alumna Prof Achiev Award, Keuka Col 63. 12: Ed "School Libraries" (59-62); Ed "Elementary School Libraries" (61). 13: Yes. 14: Elem sch libs, child lit, lib educ. 15: 1006 Westmorland, Kalamazoo Mi 49007.

LOWRY, LINA (MARTIN). b Danville Va 31 My 35. 5: Temple 53-57 (Hist) BA; Drexel 57-60 (LS) MS. 6: Ger. 7: Sr libn Brooklyn Pub Lib 60-. 14: Ref. 15: 29 Moore st, Brooklyn NY 11206.

LOWRY, W KENNETH. b Waynesburg Penn 17 My 14. 4: Jane Kern. 5: Penn State U 32-38 (Gen Studies) BA; Columbia 38-39 (LS) BS. 6: Fr, Ger. 7: Ref libn Bowdoin Col 39-43; (Lt) USNR (Navigator) MATS, Alameda Cal 44-45; Chief ref serv OTS Dept of Com, Wash DC 46-47; Chief Navy Res Sect LC 48-49; Dir Army Lib, Wash DC 49-52; Dir tech info & intelligence ARDC-USAF, Baltimore 52-56; Manager Tech Info & Libs Bell Telephone Labs, Murray Hill NJ 56-68, Dir libs & info syst 69-. 8: Trustee Engnr Index Inc 62-; US-Japan Sci Coop Group visit to Tokyo 63; US mem FID/TI Com 62-65; V-chm Engnrs Jt Coun Info Com 62-65; Mem of Info Coms of NAS-NRC, ASM, HRB, AAAS, FID, USAF, NSF, etc. 9: Internat Fed Documentation (pres 65-68); US mem NATO-AGARD Documentation Com (53-57); Sci Info Coun 66-69 (chm 69). 10: Bd Visitors UPittsburgh Grad Sch of Lib & Info Sci 68-. 11: Fellow, Inst of Info Scientists; NATO Distinguished Serv Citation 57, USAF Superior Performance awards 54, 55; Silver Medal from Pope Paul VI, Rome 67. 13: Yes. 14: Info systems. 15: Bell Telephone Labs, Murray Hill NJ 07971.

LOWY, GEORGE. b Budapest Hungary 17 My 24. 4: Livia Gyepes. 5: U of Econ Sci (Budapest) 48-52 (Econ) BA; Columbia 59-61 (LS) MS. 6: Hungarian, Ger, Russian. 7: Researcher UBudapest 52-54; Asst Prof of econ Univ Econ Sci (Budapest Hungary) 54-56; Searcher Columbia U Libs 58-61, Bibliog 61-64; Bibliog ed International Encyclopedia of the Soc Scis, NY 64-67; Dir bibliog & indexing serv Crowell-Collier-Macmillan 67-68; Asst hd of acquis Columbia U Libs 68-. 8: Adv Bd, Collier's Encyclopedia. 9: SLA; ALA. 10: Columbia U Alumni Assn. 12: "A Searcher's Manual" (65). 13: Yes. 14: Bibliog. 15: 110-26 68 rd, Forest Hills NY 11375.

LOWY, GERHARD. b Berlin Germany 4 Je 07. 4: Irma Wolf. 5: Harpur Col 50-55 (Soc Sci) AB; Columbia 55-56 9ls0 ms. 6: Ger, Fr. 7: Catlgr Columbia U 56-. 8: Org in-serv program for libns of SC held annually 46-51; Spec consul Southeastern Coop Study, which publ "Southeastern Libraries; SC Lib Devel Com; SC Lib Educ Planning Com; Adv to SC Lib Bd on sel of bks & materials for Negro libs Adv mem Marquis Biog Lib Soc, 69. 9: ALA& NY Lib Club. 10: Leo Baeck Inst 9ny0& beta Phi Mu; NYCLU. 14: Catlg, ser, univ libs. 15: 15 W 72nd st, New York 10023.

LOY, ELEANOR (CHASE). b Kokomo Ind 25 My 05. 5: DePauw U 23-27 (Biol, Econ) AB; Ind U Ext 45,49 (Educ) MS; Ball State U summers 45, 46; Ind U summers 56, 59 (LS) MA. 6: Sp, Fr. 7: Biol, Eng, math, sci tchr Greentown High Sch, Greentown Ind 44-55; Libn Alexandria High Sch, Alexandria Ind 55-60; Asst libn Anderson Col 60-64; Libn Mt Vernon Community Schs, Mt Vernon High Sch, Fortville Ind 64 (Started & organized new High Sch Lib). 9: NEA; Ind State Tchrs Assn; IndLA. 10: Bus & Prof Women; Pi Lambda Theta;

Delta Kappa Gamma. 14: Ref, periods, catlg. 15: 215 E Broadway, Alexandria In 46001.

LOYA, JACK ARNOLD. b Johnstown Penn 26 D 40. 5: Clarion State Col 58-62 (LS) BS; UDel 65; WVU 66 (LS & A-V) MA; Temple U 67. 7: Libn, Asst basketball & Asst football coach, Asst guidance coun Greater Gallitzin High Sch, Gallitzin Penn 62-63; Hd libn, AV coord, Hd basketball coach & Asst football coach Delmar High Sch, Delmar Del 63-67; AV Coord, Asst Prof Commun Col of Baltimore 67-69; Asst Data production mgr & Hd Basketball Coach Frederick Commun Col, Frederick Md 69-. 8: Av lib consul Del State Lib 66; Eval Com, Middle States Assn 67; Water safety consul, Md Dept of Forests & Parks 68; Adv to Sen Ralph Yardborough (Tex) on Educ Tech Act 69; Mgt & res consul, AV media Md 69. 9: Del State EA; Sussex Co EA (treas); NEA-DAVI; Penn State EA; Cresson-Gallitzin EA. 10: Mem var athletic coaches and athletics organizations. 12: "Basketball Players Handbook" (66); "Wealth of the School District in Relationship to the Quality of the Library" (67); "Lifeguard Manual", Dept of Forests & Parks Md (68). 13: Yes. 14: A-v media, dial access, T-V. 15: 1433 Wm Penn ave, Conemaugh Pa 15909.

LU, DIANA CHOI PING (YUE). b Hong Kong China 27 N 43. 4: Eugene Y C Lu. 5: DalhousieU 63-66 (Biol) BSc; Ealing Tech Col 66-67 (Libnship). 6: Chinese. 7: Gen asst Cambridgeshire and Isle of Ely Co Lib, Cambridge England 66; Asst docs libn State Lib of Ohio, Columbus 68-. 9: The LA. 14: Catlg, ref, info storage & retr. 15: 3011 Stadium dr, Columbus Oh 43202.

LU, PETER. b SHANGHAI China 12 S 36. 5: SUNY (Albany) 66 MLS. 6: Ger, Sp, Chinese, Japanese. 7: Lib asst SUNY Lib (Albany) 65-67; Catlgr Pub Sch Dist, Schenectady NY summer 65; Asst libn SUNY A&T Col (Cobleskill) 66; Asst libn SUNY (Cortland) 66-. 9: ALA. 14: Catlg, ref, bk sel. 15: 7 Van Hoesen st, Cortland NY 13045.

LUBAHN, HARRIET C(RAUN). b St Louis 12 N 20. 4: Jack Douglas Lubahn. 5: Ohio U 38-42 (Elem Educ) Diploma; UColo 62-63 (Elem Educ); Ohio U 63 (Elem Educ) BS in Ed (cum laude); UDenver 63-65 (LS) MS. 6: Fr. 7: Libn Denver Pub Schs 65-68, Jefferson Co Schs 68-. 9: ALA; NEA; ColoLA; ColoASchL. 10: Foster Parents of Lakewood; Fortnightly Club; Kappa Delta Pi. 15: 409 19th st, Golden Co 80401.

LUBANS, JOHN JR. b Riga Latvia 15 Je 41. 4: Judith Abbe. 5: Lebanon Valley Col 60-64 (Eng) BA; UMich 64-66 MALS; SUNY (Albany) 68- (Mgt). 7: Lib wk-study scholar UMich (Ann Arbor) 64-66; Hd circ dept Rensselaer Polytech Inst 66-68, Hd reader serv div 68-. 9: ALA. 11: T P Sevensma Prize (2d) 67. 13: Yes. 14: Reader serv, systems and analysis, lib netwks, lib automation, hist of sci & tech. 15: 2 Conway ct, Troy NY 12180.

LUBAR, LISBET (GOLDENBERG). b Czechoslovakia 15 F 16. 4: Harry Lubar. 5: N Hudson Hosp Sch of Nursing 37-40 (Nursing) RN; UMiami 46-48, 49-51 (Sociol) BA; NYU 50-52 summer 50 MA; Rutgers 63-66 MLS. 6: Ger. 7: Staff nurse (1st Lt) Army Nurse Corps, S Pacific 41-45; Grad asst dept human rel UMiami 50-51; Libn Morristown Sch Syst, Morristown NJ 65-. 9: ALA; NEA; NJEA; NJSchLA; MorrisCoLA. 10: Human Rel Coun; Maroon & White Music Booster's Club; Alpha Kappa Delta. 11: Human Rel Award 50 (UMiami). 14: Juvenile lit & ref. 15: 45 Early st, Morristown NJ 07960.

LUBETSKI, EDITH (ESTA). b 16 Jl 40. 4: Meir Lubetski. 5: Bar Ilan U 58-59; Brooklyn Col 59-62 (Hist) BA; Yeshiva U, Bernard Revel Sch of Jewish Studies 62-64 (Jewish Hist) MA; Columbia 64-65 (LS) MS. 6: Hebrew. 7: Lib asst Yeshiva U 63-65; Asst libn Stern Col 65-. 9: Jewish LA; ALA; NYLA. 14: Ref, Judaica & Hebraica. 15: 1462 E 21 st, Brooklyn NY 11210.

LUBETZKY, SEYMOUR. b Zelwa Poland 28 Ap 1898. 4: Beatrice Charnas. 5: UCal(Los Angeles) 28-31 (Ger) BA; UCal(Berkeley) 31-34 MA; 32 Gen Secondary Tchrs Credential; 34 Certif of Libnship. 6: Ger, Fr, Russian, Hebrew, Yiddish, Polish. 7: Catlgr & clsf UCal(Los Angeles) 36-42; Chief catlg maintenance div, consul on bibliog & catlg policy, LC 43-60; Prof UCLA Sch of Lib Serv 60-69. 8: Ed Catalog Code Revision 56-61. 10: Delta Phi Alpha; Beta Phi Mu. 11: Margaret Mann Award, 55. 12: "Cataloging Rules and Principles" (53); "Code of Cataloging Rules," unfinished draft (60). 13: Yes. 14: Catlg. 15: Sch of Lib Serv UCal, Los Angeles Ca 90024.

LUBIAK, REV CASIMIR JOSEPH . b Wilkes-Barre Penn 7 O 15. 5: Cathedral Col 35-37; St Mary's Sem 37-39 (Philos) AB, 39-43 (Theol) STB; West Res 50-55 MSLS. 6: Polish. 7: Head Libn Gannon Col 19-. 9: ALA; CathLA; PennLA. 14: Catlg, admin. 15: 109 W 6th st, Erie Pa 16501.

LUBIN, LLOYD G. b Brooklyn NY 31 My 27. 5: NYU 45-49 (Psych) BA; Columbia 49-51 (LS) MS. 7: Catlg asst Bridgeport Pub Lib, Bridgeport Conn 51-57; Ref libn & circ libn (interlib loan) UMich (Ann Arbor) Lib 57-60; Ref libn Pacific Aerospace Lib, Los Angeles 60-62; Sci & tech ref libn Cal State Col (Long Beach) Lib 62-63; Lib research analyst N Amer Aviation SID, Downey Cal 63-64; Hd conversion unit (tech serv dept) Orange Co Pub Lib, Orange Cal 65-66; Sr libn (catlg) Free Pub Lib of Woodbridge, woodbridge NJ 66-. 9: NJLA. 14: Catlg, ref. 15: 49 Melbourne ct, Woodbridge NJ 07095.

LUBOV, RICKI (GERMANSKY). b NYC 8 D 43. 4: Michael T Lubov. 5: Wheaton Col 61-62; NYU 62-64 (Hist) BA; Columbia 64-65 MLS. 6: Fr. 7: Hd child serv Oceanside Free Lib, Oceanside NY 65-. 9: ALA-CSD. 10: Phi Beta Kappa. 14: Child serv. 15: 8 Broadway, Lawrence NY 11559.

LUBOVITZ, FRANCES RHEA. b Chelsea Mass 2 Jl 28. 5: Westbrook Jr Col 46-48 (Liberal Arts); UMe 48-50 (Eng Lit) BA; Simmons 52-54 (LS) MS. 6: Fr. 7: Asst hd descr catlg div Yale U Lib 54-59, Supv selective bk retirement program 59-62, Sr catlgr 62-64; Hd catlg dept MIT Libs 64-66, Act asst dir 67, Hd catlg dept 68-. 9: ALA-RTSD (Desc Catlg Com; Catlg & Clsf Sect: Exec Com Secy; Edl Com Subcom on ALA Rules for Filing cat Cards; Mem Com, Exec Bd); NY Tech Serv Libns (sec). 12: "Selective Book Retirement Program Manual of Procedures" (64); ALA Rules for Filing Catalog Cards (68). 14: Catlg, admin. 15: 14E-210 MIT Libraries, Cambridge Ma 02139.

LUCAS, AURELIA LYNNE. b Homestead Penn 1 N 38. 5: UPittsburgh 57-61 (Educ) BS, 65-66 MLS; Duquesne 61-63 (Educ). 6: Sp. 7: Tchr W Jefferson Hills Sch Dist, Pleasant Hills penn 61-65& catlgr Carnegie Lib of Pittsburgh 66-68; Libn Armstrong Co Ctr Indiana UPennsylvania 69-. 9: PennLA. 10: Beta Phi Mu; Alpha Beta Gamma; Zeta Tau Alpha. 14: Admin, catlg. 15: 127 N McKain st, Kittanning Pa 16201.

LUCAS, BARBARA (MARY). b Amsterdam NY 6 Mr 44. 5: Emmanuel Col (Boston) 62-65 (Biol) BA; Simmons 66-69 (LS) MS. 6: Ger. 7: Asst libn US Army Terrestrial Scis Ctr, Hanover nh 65-. 9: ASIS; SLA. 14: Info analysis ctrs, automated catlg & indexing. 15: US Army Terrestrial Sci Ctr PO Box 282, Hanover NH 03755.

LUCAS, E LOUISE. b Middletown Ohio 31 Ag 1899. 5: Radcliffe 18-21 (Eng) AB; Simmons 24-25. 6: Fr, Ger, Ital. 7: Brookline (Mass) Pub Lib 21-27; Libn Fogg Museum of Art, Harvard U 27-63, Fine arts libn 63-65; Consul, Rockport Mass 65-. 8: Adv wk with Toledo Mus of Art, Winterthur & col & univ art depts throughout the country; Grad bibliog conf for fine arts dept at Harvard; Simmons Col faculty assoc 44-65; Art Index Com (H W Wilson) 29-34. 9: ALA (chm Art Ref Round Table, Mem Com); Amer Assn of Museums (chm Lib Group 30-36); SLA (var coms, Museum Group 30); MassLA (var coms); Harvard U Lib Club (pres 39). 10: Radcliffe Club; Phi Beta Kappa; Friends of Lib Bd (Rockport). 11: Traveling fellowships 37, 54, 60; Phi Beta Kappa Alumnae Award 46. 12: "Books on Art" (36, 38); "Guides to the Harvard Libraries: Fine Arts" (49); "Harvard List of Books on Art" (52); "Art Books: A Basic Bibliography" (68). 13: Yes. 14: Bibliog, ref (fine arts). 15: Straitsmouth way, Rockport Ma 01966.

LUCAS, JEAN M. b Huntington WVa 20 My 41. 4: Delbert E Lucas. 5: Marshall U 59-63 (Secondary Educ) AB; Case-West Res 63-64 MSLS. 7: Purdue U: Asst ref libn 64-65 Ref libn sci & tech 65, Libn Sch of Aeronautica, Astronautical & Engnr Sci 65-66, Asst engr libn (supv electrical & mechanical engring libs66-68; Hd libn Rentschler Lib Miami U (Ohio) 68-. 9: ALA sec-treas Jr Mem Round TABLE 65-66. 10: Alpha Beta Alpha, Altrusa. 14: Ref, engnr lib, admin. 15: 5510 Hamilton ave, Cincinnati Oh 45224.

LUCAS, JOHN E. b Munhall Penn 26 Je 13. 4: Aurelia V Toplin. 5: Grove City Col 32-33 (Chem); UPittsburgh 33-36 (Chem) BS, 38-39 (Metallurgical Engring), 67 MLS, 68-. 7: Tchr Homestead High Sch, Homestead Penn 36-37; Engring expediter Westinghouse electric, E Pittsburgh Penn 37-38; Metallurgical observer US Steel, Pittsburgh Penn 38-41; Supv US Steel, Homestead Penn 41-50, Gen supv 52-66; Research asst UPittsburgh 66-67; Ext libn Ind UPenn Rhodes R Stabley

Lib 68-. 8: Adv Lib Study Com Armstrong Co 68. 9: PennLA (SW Chap Scholarship Com). 10: Beta Phi Mu; Kappa Phi Kappa. 14: Ref, lib ext wk, lib sci tchg. 15: 818 Oak st, Indiana Pa 15701.

LUCAS, LINDA LUCILLE. b California 22 Ap 40. 5: San Jose State Col 57-61 (Eng) BA, 62-68 (Libnship) MA. 7: Materials tech Livermore Sch Dist, Livermore Cal 62-64; Libn mission San Jose High Sch, Fremont Cal 64-. 9: ALA; NEA; CalTA; CalASchL (No Sect publ Chm; A-V EA Cal). 14: YA serv. 15: 4848 Golden rd, Pleasanton Ca 94566.

LUCAS, LINDA SUE. b Creston Iowa 5 N 39. 5: UNoIowa 58-61 (LS) BA; UWash 65-66 MLib. 7: Libn Sidney Sr High Sch, Sidney Mont 61-62; Asst libn Minot Sr High Sch, Minot N Dak 62-65; Ref libn Iowa State U Lib (Ames) 66-. 9: ALA. 10: Beta Phi Mu. 14: Ref. 15: 2925 Woodland, Ames Ia 50010.

LUCAS, LYDIA (ANN). b San Francisco Cal 27 Ag 45. 5: Fresno State Col 63-64 (Hist); UMo 64-67 (Amer Hist) BA; UIll 67-69 (LS) MA. 6: Sp, Ger. 7: Mss catlgr Minn Hist soc, St Paul 69-. 10: Phi Beta Kappa; Beta Phi Mu. 14: Mss proc, archival wk. 15: 1320 Mississippi st apt 103, St Paul Mn 55101.

LUCAS, MARCELLA (AHNER). b Chicago 2 Je 37. 4: James Richard Lucas. 5: St Xavier Col 55-59 (Chem) BS; UIll 59-60 MSLS. 7: Head libn Amer Can Co Research & Devel Dept, Barrington Ill 60-64; Staff libn Amer Oil Co Research & Devel Dept, Whiting Ind 65-. 9: SLA. 14: Ref, computer mechanism of lib procedures. 15: Amer Oil Co, 2500 New York ave, Whiting In 46394.

LUCCHESI, JANE C. b Superior Wis 27 S 12. 4: Geno Lucchesi. 5: Col of St Scholastica 54 (Eng, Sci) BS; UMich 65 MALS. 6: Fr. 7: Off mgr Stella Cheese Co, Baltic Mich 32-37; Adams Twp Schs: Elem tchr So Range Mich 48-59, Tchr-libn secondary Painesdale Mich 59-65, Libn Jeffers High Schs, Painesdale Mich 65-68, Libn secondary 68-69. 9: NEA; ALA; MichEA; MichLA (chm Dist VII 63); michASchL; Mich A-V Assn. 10; Mich Hist Soc; PTO; AAUW; Nat Wildlife Assn. 13: Yes. 14: Ref. 15: Box 247, South Range Mi 49963.

LUCE, HELEN MARIE. b Pasadena Cal 17 O 12. 5: Ventura Jr Col 30-32 AA; UCLA 32-34 (Psych) BA; Pratt 35-36 BLS. 7: 1st asst Plumas Co Lib, Quincy Cal 36-38; 1st sst Solano Co Lib, Fairfield Cal 38-42, Act libn 42-45; County Libn San Bernardino Co Lib, San Bernardino Cal 45-57; Lib ext spec US Off of Educ, Wash 57-67. Lib program off, US Off of Educ, San Francisco. 9: ALA (treas Lib Ext Sect 52-55); CalLA (Dist pres 44, sec-treas 54). 10: Pub Lib Execs Assn So Cal (pres 55); Kappa Phi Zeta. 12: Jt ed "State Plans Under the Library Services Act, Supplement 2." 13: Yes. 14: pub lib ext & admin. 15: 1845 Green st Apt 201, San Francisco Ca 94123.

LUCE, SISTER KATHLEEN CSJ. b Milwaukee Wis 12 Mr 44. 5: Col of St Catherine 62-66 (LS) BA. 6: Ger. 7: Hd libn St Joseph's Acad, St Paul 68-69; Catlgr Col of St Catherine, st Paul 69-. 9: ALA; CathLA. MinnLA. 13: Yes. 14: Catlg. 15: Col of St Catherine, st Paul Mn 55116.

LUCE, MARGARET M. b Bridgeport Conn 5 Ja 13. 4: Sheldon R Luce. 5: Bryn Mawr 30-34 (Hist) AB; UCal 9berkeley) 59-60 MLS. 6: Fr. 7: Catlgr UCal(Davis) 60-62; Projs libn J Hugh Jackson Lib Grad Sch of Bus, Stanford U 62-, Hd tech serv 66-. 9: SLA (Bay Area Chap chm of Dupl Exch 65-66). 14: Catlg (espec ser), ref. 15: 1850 Willow rd apt 2, Palo Alto Ca 94304.

LUCE, MARILYN (DALLAS). b Little Rock Ark 28 Ag 37. 5: Hendrix Col 55-59 (Eng) BA; UArk 59-60 (Eng); Drexel 63-64 MS in LS. 7: Lib page Little Rock Pub Lib, Little Rock Ark 53-55, Desk asst summers 55-59; Desk asst Hendrix Col Lib 55-58; Grad coun UArk 59-60; Lib trainee DC Pub Lib 60-63; Libn I, Libn II, Free Lib of Phila 64-. 9: ALA; PennLA. 14: Ref, govt docs. 15: Free Lib of Phila, Logan circle, Phila Pa 19103.

LUCE, RICHARD WAYNE. b Meadville Penn 29 S 24. 5: Col of UChicago 46-50 BA; Chicago 53-55 (LS) MA. MA; Chicago Music Col 52-53 (Musicology). 6: Fr, Ger. 7: Prof asst Jt Ref Lib Pub Admin Clearing House, Chicago 55; Asst libn J Walter Thompson Co, Chicago 56-58; Libn Continental Nat Amer Group, Chicago 59-63; Asst dir Lib Tech Proj ALA, Chicago 64-68; Ref libn Montana State U Lib (Bozeman) 69-. 8: Mem, ALA/LTP Conserv of Lib Materials Adv Com 65-. 9: ALA; Assn for Recorded Sound Collections; MusLA; SLA (chm Insur Div 62-63); MontLA; PNLA. 14: Lib admin, music libnship. 15: 717 S 17th ave, Bozeman Mt 59715.

LUCHA, MARGARET M. b Rome NY. 5: Cornell U 38-42 (Human Ecology, Journalism) BS; Pratt 60-62 MLS. 7: Ed pub rel Amer Tel & Tel, NY 42-47; Writer pub rel Young & Rubicam Advert Agency, NY 47-61; Sr libn NY Pub Lib 61-64; Tchr of Lib Sci NYC Sch System (elem) 64-65; Libn Garden City Sr High Sch, Garden City NY 65-68; Supv libn Ward Melville Sr High Sch, E Setauket NY 68-. 9: ALA; NYLA; NY State Tchrs Assn; Nassau-Suffolk SchLA (pres 68-69); LI Educl communications Coun; NEA-DAVI. 10: Beta Phi Mu; Theta Sigma Phi. 14: Child & ya lit. 15: P O Box 263, Northport NY 11768.

LUCHECHKO, JOHN. b Ukraine 22 O 28. 4: Yaroslawa Ostapiak. 5: UMd 54-55 (Pol Sci); Trinity U (San antonio Tex) 55-56 (Pol Sci); Columbia 56-59 (Pol Sci) BS, 59-61 MLS; Hunter Col 63-69 (Pol Sci) (Russian Area Stud) MA. 6: Ukrainian, Ger, Polish, Russian. 7: Asst to acquis libn Law Lib Columbia U 59-60, Head of circ 61-62; Head of readers serv Jersey City State Col 62-. 8: Jersey City State Col: Com on A-V Aids 64-65; Prof Day Com on Faculty Assn 65; Com on Lib Instr 65; Com on Lib Personnel 62-69; Com on Lib Planning; Grad Study Com of the Fac Senate 68-69; Com for the Middle State Self-Eval 68-69. 09: NJEA. 10: Jersey City state Col Faculty Assn; Mem, "Plast," Ukrainian Youth Org Inc; Mem, Ukrainian Chorus "Dumka" (NYC). 12: "Russia and the Soviet Union: Bibliography of Materials at Jersey City College Library" (65); "Soviet Political Reportage: Pravda and the Ukrainian Problem, 1917-1918". 14: Admin, circ, ref. 15: 359 Fulton ave, Jersey City NJ 07305.

LUCHKIW, VASYL. b W Ukraine 29 O 30. 4: Mary Luby. 5: UMinn 53-55 (Chem Engnr); UOttawa 55-58 (Slavic Studies) MA, 59-61 (Educ) M Ed, 61-62 BLS. 6: Ukrainian, Polish, Russian, Ger, Slavonic, Bulgarian, Czech, Croatian, Fr. 7: Supply clerk US Army 51-52; High sch tchr Catholic Sch Commsn, Arylmer Que 59-60; High sch tchr Separate Sch Bd, Trenton Ont 60-61; Catlgr Russian materials UIowa 62-64, Slavic libn 65-66; Assoc dir of lib SUNY (Brockport) 66-68; Dir of lib serv Rockland Commun Col 68-. 8: Spec consul, Corallville Pub Lib, Coralville Iowa 65-66; Assoc Prof Dept of Mod Lang (Russian) SUNY (Brockport) 67-68. 9: Amer Assn Adv Slavic Studies; ALA; NEA-DAVI; SEast NY Lib Resources coun (Bd Dirs 69); Lib Assn Rockaldn Co (Exec Coun 68-); NY State Educl Communication Assn. 10: AAUP; Assn of Libns of Ukrainian Descent; Amer Assn Jr Cols. 12: Comp "Russia: Bibliography of Materials at SUNY-Brockport Library" (67). 13: Yes. 14: Admin, acquis, catlg (Slavic & East European materials), a-v, tech serv. 15: 49 Windmill lane, New York NY 10956.

LUCHSINGER, DALE FREDERICK. b Ripon Wis 10 S 41. 4: Arlene Edith. 5: Wis StateU (Oshkosh) 59-63 9hist, LS) BS; UMich 63-64 AMLS. 6: Ger. 7: Bibliog searcher UMich (Ann Arbor) 64-65; Libn Sewanee Mil Acad, Sewanee Tenn 65-67; Libn Wis StateU (Fond du Lac) 67-69; Asst prof libnship EmoryU 69-. 9: ALA; WisLA. 10: Amer Philatelic Soc. 13: Yes. 14: Ref, bk selection, admin. 15: Apt 1404D Druid Valley dr, Atlanta Ga 30329.

LUCIOLI, CLARA ELIZABETH. b London England 25 Je 10. 5: Pratt Inst 30-31 Pub Lib Certif; NYU 34-39 (Sociol); Mather Col Eest Res 39-41 (Sociol) BA; Pratt Inst 41-42 BLS. 6: Fr, Ital. 7/ jr asst S Brooklyn Br Cleveland Pub Lib 29-30, Div hd Judd Fund Div 42-46, Div hd Hosp & Judd Fund Div 46-55, Dept hd hosp & inst dept 55-; Child libn ny pub Lib 31-34, Asst libn, Scarsdale 34-39; Asst Mather Col Lib 39-41. 8: President's Com on Employment of the Handicapped; Chm LSCA Title 1VA Adv Coun to State Lib Bd of Ohio 67-69; Instr Case West Res U Sch of Lib Sci 46-; Lect UWash Lib Sch summer 67; Inst on Hosp & Inst Libs, Wayne State U Sch of Libnship 68; UWis summer 68; Consul Veterans Admin Libs 56; Amer Hosp Assn 61. 9: ALA (Coun Mem-at-Large 64-69; Com on Organiz 61-65); -AHIL (pres 58-59, Bk Sel Criteria Com 64-66; Spec Projects Com 67-69); -LED (chm Subcom on Educ for Hosp & Institl Libs); OhioLA (chm Institl Libs Com; chm Com on Organiz of Med Lib Assn of No Ohio; WestchesterLA (charter mem; co-chm Standards Com). 10: Women's City Club; Welfare Fed of Greater Cleveland; Mayor's Com on Employment of the Handicapped; NAACP; Cleveland Pub Lib Assn. 11: ALA-AHIL Exceptional service Citation 61; Named Libn in Residence, UIowa Sch of LS 68. 12: Ed and script writer, "The Winged Bequest" (sound film) (55); Guest ed "ALA Bulletin" (April 64). 13: Yes. 14: Lib serv to the handicapped, homebound and institutionalized, adult educ, lib educ. 15: 1225 Hathaway ave, Lakewood Oh 44107.

LUCKER, JAY K. b Brooklyn NY 23 F 30. 4: Marjorie Stern. 5: Brooklyn Col 48-51 (Sci) AB; Columbia 51-52 (LS) MS; NYU 55-57 (Public Admin). 6: Fr, Ger. 7: Stud asst ref dept Brooklyn Col Lib 48-51, Fellow acquis dept 51-52; Instr (Cpl) US Army Signal Corps Electronics 52-54; Head procurement sect acquis br NY Pub Lib 54-57, 1st asst sci & tech div 57-59; Asst libn for sci & tech, Assoc Prof Princeton U Lib 59-68; Assoc U libn Prof 68-. 8: Consul inst for Defense Analyses, Communications Research Div Princeton NJ 59-; Stevens Inst of Tech Lib, Hoboken NJ 65-67; Ingersoll-Rand Inc, Bedminster NJ 62-64; Visiting Lecturer Grad Sch of Lib Sci, Drexel Inst of Tech Phila 64-68; Spec consul, Nat Plan for Lib Statistics, ALA-LAD 68-. 9: ALA-ARCL (chm Subj Specialists Sect 63-64); SLA; NJLA (pres Col & Univ Sect 68-69); NJ Lib Resources Com 66-; NJ Lib Devel Com 67-. 10: AAUP; AAAS; Phi Beta Kappa; NJ Acad Sci. 12: Assoc ed "Ulrich's Periodical Directory," 9th & 10th eds; Assoc ed "Bibliographic Index" (57-69); Ed "Bibliography of Princeton Publications" (60-). 13: Yes. 14: Admin, bldgs, statistics, sci & tech ref, hist of sci. 15: 9 College rd, Princeton NJ 08540.

LUCKETT, GEORGE RIDGELY. b Baltimore 18 F 11. 4: Florence Emilie Meeth. 5: Columbia summers 39-41, 45 (LS); Johns Hopkins 43-49 (Langs, Hist) BS; Catholic U 49-51 MSLS. 6: Sp, Fr. 7: Cost & profits clerk W A Frey & Sons, Baltimore 28-30; Lib page & asst Enoch Pratt Free Lib, Baltimore 30-34; Assoc libn US Naval Acad 34-50; Prof & Libn US Naval Postgrad Sch (Monterey Cal) 50-. 8: Consul; Firestone Engnr Lab (Monterey Cal) 57-60; Dalmo Victor Co, Monterey Cal 58-60; Lab for Electronics 63-64; Data Dynamics Inc, Monterey Cal 64-67; Instr in libnship San Jose State Col, Monterey Cal 55-67; Trustee Monterey Pub Lib, Monterey Cal 59-68. 9: SLA (chm Mil Libns Div 62-63; V-chm Engnr Sect, Sci-Tech Div 65-66, v-pres, pres-elect San Francisco Bay Reg Chap 68-70); Coun of Libns; West Coast Navy Labs (chm var yrs). 13: Yes. 14: Catlg, ref, info retrieval (computer), admin. 15: 31 Dorey Way, Monterey Cal 93940.

LUCKHARDT, VIRGINIA ETHEL. b Pittsburgh 5 F 15. 5: Westminster Col 32-34 (Eng) ; UPittsburgh 34-36, 38-45 (Eng) AB, MA; Carnegie 48-49 MLS; Goethe Universita2t, Frankfurt/Main 54-55 (Eng). 6: Fr. 7: Tchr McDonald High Sch, McDonald Penn 38-48; Libn Cal State Col (California Penn) 49-. 8: Tchr Ziehen Frankfurt/Main Germany 54-55 (Fulbright grantee). 9: ALA-ACRL. 10: AAUP; Phi Kappa Phi; Pi Lambda Theta. 11: Buhl Found scholarship. 14: Acquis. 15: 3254 Wainbell ave, Pittsburgh Pa 15216.

LUCY, MARY LOU. b Lebanon. 5: East Ky State Col 39-43 (Eng) AB; Peabody 43-44 BS in LS; Columbia 53 MS in LS. 7: Adult asst br Cincinnati Pub Lib 44-45; Ref asst br NY Pub Lib 45-46; Ref asst Sch of Lib Serv Columbia U 46-50; Ref asst ref dept Columbia U 50-52; Asst circ libn UNC(Chapel Hill) 52-53, Circ libn 53-61; Head circ dept Columbia U 61-67; Butler libn 67-. 9: ALA; NY Lib Club. 14: Circ, ref, readers serv. 15: Columbia Univ Libs, New York 10027.

LUDDEN, BENNET (RAGAN). b Salem Ore 1 Jl 14. 5: Pasadena Jr Col 32-35 (Eng); DePauw U 35-38 (Eng, Music) AB, BM; Liszt Acad of Music (Budapest) 38-40 (Piano); DePauw U 40-42 (Musicology) MM; Columbia 55-57 MS in LS. 6: Ger. 7: Asst Prof of piano Willamette U 43-50; Circ libn, records catlgr Music Lib Columbia U 50-56; Libn Juilliard Sch 57-. 9: MusLA (NY rep to "Notes" 59-61). 10: Pi Kappa Lambda; Phi Mu Alpha; Lambda Chi Alpha. 13: Yes. 14: Music catlg & ref. 15: Juilliard Sch Lincoln Center, New York NY 10023.

LUDLOW, SISTER JEAN I SSJ (SISTER JOSEPH THERESE). b Penn Yan NY 1 Ag 15. 5: Mt St Joseph Col 35-41 (Educ) BS in Ed, 56 (Eng) MS in Ed; Rosary Col 42-45 MLS. 7: Hd libn: Mt St Joseph Acad, Buffalo NY 45-49; St Mary's High Sch, Dunkirk NY 49; Our Lady of Victory Acad, Lackawanna NY 50-56; Medaille Col 50-. 9: ALA; CathLA; NYStateLA. 13: Yes. 14: Ref, child lit. 15: Scholastica Lib Medaille Col 18 Agassiz cir, Buffalo NY 14214.

LUDLOW, VIRGINIA FELICY. b Toronto Can 27 Ag 19. 5: Toronto 37-39, 40-42 (Eng) BA, 42-43 BLS. 7: Libn in corc dov & wl with yp Toronto Pub Libs 43-56, Libn-in-chg, Travelling Br 56-. 09; CanLA; ALA-AHIL; The Lib assn (Handicapped readers); OntLA; Inst Prof Libns, Ont. 14: Hospls, instns, aged. 15: Toronto Pub Lib 40 St Clair ave E, Toronto 7 Ont Can.

LUE, MONA (HC). b Shanghai China. 4: Dun Lue. 5: Caldwell Col 60 (Biol) BA; Rosary Col 63 MA in LS. 6: Chinese, Sp. 7: Asst med libn Organon Inc, W Orange NJ 6061; Asst libn-catlg NY Life Insurance Co NYC 63-67, Libn 67-. 9: SLA; ALA; MedLA. 14: Catlg, admin, ref, circ. 15: 41-05 74th st apt 4D, Elmhurst NY 11373.

LUELLA, SISTER M(ARY) (POWERS). b Mukwonago Wis. 5: Marquette U 21-24 (Bot); Rosary Col 24-25, summer 27 (Bot) AB; UMich 30-31, summers 32-34 BA in LS, MA in LS; UIll summers 30, 40; Chicago 40-42, 45 (LS) PhD; Columbia summer 49 (LS). 6: Fr, Ital. 7: Tchr Trinity High Sch, Bloomington Ill 26-30; Asst Prof Rosary Col Dept of Lib Sci 31-41, Prof 44-59; Lecturer Catholic U Dept of Lib Sci 42-44; Dir Rosary Col Dept of Lib Sci 49-59; Libn Pius XII Inst, Florence Italy 59-62; Prof UPortla Dept of Lib Sci 62-65; Libn Dominican Educ Center, Sinsinawa Wis 65-67; Visiting lecturer UWis(Madison) 66-67; Prof Rosary Col Dept of Lib Sci 67-. 9: ALA; CathLA; IllLA. 12: Ed "Catholic Booklist" (45-49, 57-58). 13: Yes. 14: Catlg, hist of libs. 15: Dominican Educ Center, Sinsinawa Wi 35824.

LUESING, LOIS L. b Leverning Mich 4 Je 33. 5: Bethel Col 55-59 (Theol) BS; IndU 61-65 (LS) MA. 7: Sec United Missionary Ch, Port Huron Mich 52-55; Libn Bethel Col, Mishawaka Ind 60-. 9: ALA; -ACRL; Christ Libns Fellowship; IndLA. 10: YWCA. 13: Yes. 14: Admin, ref. 15: 17552 Parker dr, South Bend In 46635.

LUETHE, MARIE K (BRAKER). b Cal 22 Mr 21. 4: Reinhold H Luethe. 5: Sierra Col 39-41 (Liberal Arts); Cal State Col (Hayward) 60-64 (Elem Educ) BS in Ed; UWash 64-65 M Libr. 6: Sp. 7: Clerk-typist Lib Lawrence radiation Lab, Livermore Cal 57-59; Clerk-typist Lib Cal State Col (Hayward) 59-64, Libn Educ-Music Lib 65-68; Catlgr 68-. 9: CalLA; ACSCP; CSEA. 14: Catlg. 15: 43687 Ellsworth st, Fremont Ca 94538.

LUFKIN, PATRICIA (LANG). b Buffalo NY 3 S 28. 4: Howard Lufkin. 5: Fredonia State Tchrs Col 46-47 (Mus); UBuffalo 47-50 (Eng) BA; SUNY Col (Geneseo) 65-66 MLS. 6: Ger, Fr. 7: Lib clk UBuffalo Lockwood Lib 50-51; Reservation agt Amer Airlines, San Francisco Cal 52-54; Catlgr SUNY Lockwood Lib (Buffalo) 66-68, Asst circ libn 68-. 9: ALSUNY (Buffalo). 14: Circ. 15: 21 Kirkwood dr, W Seneca NY 14224.

LUFT, WILLIAM. b Providence 28 F 38. 5: Col of the Holy Cross 56-60 (Pre-Law) BS; UDenver 62-63 (LS) MA. 7: Ref libn Hd soc sci, Asst Undergrad Lib Mich State U Lib 63-68; Hd ref & ext Macomb Co Lib, Mt Clemens Mich 68-. 9: ALA; MichLA. 14: Soc sci, ref. 15: 325 N Groesbeck, Mt Clemens Mi 48043.

LUHDE, JUTTA. 5: Simmons 59-61 (LS) MS. 7: Grad asst Simmons Col Sch of Lib Sch 59-60; Libn Child Hosp Sch of Nursing, Boston 60-63; Libn Crotched Mountain Found, Greenfield NH 63-64; Libn Berkshire Med Ctr the Lib of the Pittsfield Gen Unit, Pittsfield Mass 64-. 9: MEDLA. 15: Berkshire Medical Ctr The Lib of the Pittsfield General Unit 725 North st, Pittsfield Ma 01201.

LUKENBILL, SHIRLEY HEBERT. b Mamou La 29 Ja 40. 4: Willis Bernard Lukenbill. 5: U Southwestern La 57-61 (Eng, LS) BA; LSU 61-62 (LS) MS. 06: Fr. 7: Sch libn N Shore Sr High Sch, Houston Tex 62-64; Instr in Lib Sci U Southwestern La 64-; Asst libn Hamilton Lab Sch U Southwestern La 64-68; Asst libn Sandel Lib NE La State Col 68-. 9: LaLA; LaASchL; SWLA. 10: AAUW; Beta Phi Mu; Kappa Delta Pi; Phi Kappa Phi; Sigma Tau Delta. 14: Lib educ, wk with child & yp. 15: 509 Second ave, Ruston La 71270.

LUKENBILL, WILLIS BERNARD. b Lindale Tex 27 Mr 39. 4: Shirley Ann Hebert. 5: Tyler Jr Col 57-59 (Hist); N Tex State U 59-61 (Hist, LS) BS; UOkla 62-64 MLS. 6: Sp. 7: Libn Seguin High Sch, Seguin Tex 61-63; Ref libn Austin Col 64; Instr of Lib Sci La Polytech Inst 64-. 9: ALA; LaLA (Scholarship Com 65-); SWLA; La Tchrs Assn; Mem La Lib Survey Study Com 68-69; La Col Tech Lib Sci (chm 67-68). 10: Phi Alpha Theta; Kappa Delta Pi; Alpha Beta Alpha; La Tech Concert Assn. 13: Yes. 14: Lib educ. 15: 509 Second st, Ruston La 71270.

LUKENS, BEATRICE L(ONNING). b Milnor ND 8 F 18. 04; Harold C Lukens. 5: Col of St Catherine 35-39 (Chem, Math) BA; UCal (Berkeley) 56-62 MLS. 7: Tchr math & sci Villa Maria Acad, Frontenac Minn 39-40; Tchg asst chem Col of St Catherine 40-41; Tchr physics Derham Hall Acad, St Paul 40-41; Tchr math & bus Grey Eagle Schs, Grey Eagle Minn 41; Sci aide lib US Bureau of Mines, Salt Lake City 41-43, Chem lab 43-45; Chem res lab Minn Mining & Mfg Co, St Paul 46; Lib asst US Navy Electronics Lab, San Diego 47-48; UCal Lib(Berkeley): Sr lib asst 50-51, Prin lib asst 51-62, Libn math, astronomy, statistics 62-63, Libn earth scis 63-. 9: SLA; CalLA; Geosci Inf Soc; West Assn Map Libs. 10: UCal Lib Schs Alumni Assn. 14: Subj ref. 15: 238 Overhill rd, Orinda Ca 94563.

LUKENS, LUCILE (CHRISTINE). b Beloit Kan 3 Mr 01. 5: Sterling Col 19-23 (Math) AB; Stanford 25-26 (Classical Lit) MA; UDenver summers 50-54 (LS) MA. 6: Lat. 7: Eng tchr High sch, Summerfield Kan 23-25; Eng tchr High sch, Randall Kan 26-29; Eng tchr High sch, Lenora Kan 29-34; Eng tchr High sch, Downs Kan 34-43; Eng tchr & libn High sch, Frankfort Kan 43-50; Libn Sterling 50-67; Assoc Prof Lib Sci 67-. 8: Dean of Women Sterling Col 53-61. 9: ALA; KanLA; KanASchL; MPLA. 10: Delta Kappa Gamma; Women's Fed Clubs; DAR; AAUP; IRC; AAUW; Pi Kappa Delta. 11; Sterling Col Alumni Award, 67. 13: Yes. 14: Admin, catlg, tchg. 15: Kelsey Lib, Sterling Ks 67579.

LUKER, ELLEN LEWIS (WILLIAMS). b Pittsburgh 5 Mr 20. 4: Norman P Luker. 5: Swarthmore 37-41 (Fr) BA; Drexel 41-42 BS in LS; UMich 63. 6: Fr. 7: Jr asst Enoch Pratt Free Lib, Baltimore 42-46; Hosp, br, & ref libn Lansing Pub Lib, Lansing Mich 46-47; Org of elem sch libs Red Wing (Minn) Schs 49; Circ, order, selec libn U Libs UMich 54-57; Undergrad libn III UMich 57-62; Asst libn Concordia Lutheran Jr Col Lib (Ann Arbor Mich) 62-. 8: Reviewer for 'The Book Review' in "Library Journal" 60-. 9: ALA; MichLA. 10: Beta Phi Mu. 13: Yes. 14: Catlg. 15: Concordia Luth Jr Col Lib, Ann Arbor Mi 48105.

LUKKASON, RACHEL (GROVER). b Grafton ND 8 Ap 10. 4: Melvin Lukkason. 5: UMinn 28-31 (LS) BS, 45 (Eng) BA. 6: Fr, Sp. 7: Catlgr UMinn(Minneapolis) 32-44; Ser catlg USoCal 44-45; Catlgr Minn State Lib 45-48; Catlgr UMinn(Minneapolis) 48, Instr Catlg 51; Libn J A Hamilton Assoc, Minneapolis 58-60; Instr libn UMinn(Minneapolis) 60-. 9: ALA; MinnLA. 14: Catlg, ser. 15: 3335 Johnson st NE, Minneapolis Mn 55418.

LUND, BERNARD ALONZO. b St Paul 28 F 09. 5: UMinn 49 (Art Educ) BS, 54 BS in LS. 7: Clerk Minn Mutual Life Insurance Co, St Paul 28-42; Signal serv US Army, S Pacific 43-45; St Paul Pub Lib: Lib asst 51-57, Jr libn 57-60, Libn I 60-. 9: ALA. 14: Catlg Code rev. 15: 42 Winter st, St Paul Mn 55103.

LUND, VIRGINIA ANN (DEROSIER). b Milwaukee 13 Je 31. 4: Gaar Todd Lund. 5: UWis(Milwaukee) 48-52 liberal Arts) BA; UWis(Madison) 53 MA in LS. 6: Lat, Fr. 7: Br libn W Allis Pub Lib, W Allis Wis 53-55; High sch libn S Plainfield NJ 55-56; Asst libn Bound Brook (NJ) Pub Lib 56-57; Lib Dir Middlesex (NJ) Pub Lib 63-65; Jr high sch libn Franklin Jr High Sch, Somerset NJ 65-68; Libn Sampson G Smith Sch, Somerset NJ 68-. 8: Tchr of lib volunteer course at franklin (NJ) night sch. 9: ALA (Recr Com); NEA; NJEA; SommersetCoEA. 10: Franklin Twp EA; Eta Sigma Phi; Franklin Twp Hist Soc. 14: Wk with child & yp, devel of small pub lib. 15: RD 3 Box 383C, Somerset NJ 08873.

LUNDEEN, DOROTHY (NELSON). b Ishpeming Mich 20 Ap 18. 4: Vincent D Lundeen. 5: North Park Col 36-38 AA; UMinn 38-41 BS in LS. 6: Swedish. 7: Ref libn Knox Col 41-42; Ser asst UMinn(Minneapolis) 43-44; Ref asst, catlg asst Augustana Col (Rock Island Ill) 51-, Catlg 65-. 15: 1528 - 28th st, Rock Island Il 61201.

LUNDGREN, KATHLYN KING. b Clark SD 24 O 19. 4: George A Lundgren. 5: Mankato State Col 37-41 (Elem) BS; UDenver 65- (LS), 68 MA, Libr. 6: Fr. 7: Tchr pub sch, Danube Minn 41-42; Adult & child libn McCook Pub Lib, McCook Neb 60-62; High sch libn Hannibal high Sch, Hannibal Mo 62-64; Elem libn Scottsbluff Pub Schs, Scottsbluff Neb 64-, Dir Lib-Media Serv Ctr, Scottsbluff Neb 65-; Libn Neb West Col summer 69. 8: Bd of Consul for 11th ed of "Children's Catalog." 09: ALA; MPLA; NebLA (Lib Devel Com, sec & chm Sch Sect); ScottsbluffEA (sec NebEA, sec Dist 6); Lub Media Consul: Scott Co Educl Unit, Scott Neb; Agnes Sch, Scottsbluff Neb. 9: ALA; MPLA; NebLA (Lib Devel Com, sec & chm Sch Sect); NebEA (sec Dist 6); Scottsbluff EA (sec). 10: Beta Phi Mu; AAUW; St Andrew's Episcopal Choir. 14: Elem sch libs, catlg, proc ctrs. 15: 710 E 28th st, Scottsbluff Nb 69361.

LUNDQUIST, SISTER JOAN THERESE SND. b Brooklyn NY 10 Ja 22. 5: Trinity Col (Wash dc0 40-63 (Educ) BSEd; Villanova 64-68 MSLS. 7: Elem sch tchr Sisters of Notre Dame schs Brooklyn, Wash DC, Md, Penn 41-66; Elem sch consul Baltimore Schs 66-67; Dev reading skills program reading lab Notre Dam High Sch, Penn 67-68; Elem sch lib consul Sisters of Notre Dam, Md Province 68-69; Child libn Brooklyn Pub Lib Grand Army Plaza 69-. 8: Consul for Sisters of Notre Dame for elem sch libs. 9: CathLA (Baltimore sect for Elem Sch Libs: chm 67, Prog Chm 66); ALA; NEA. 14: Child bks. 15: St Mary's Convent 5th & Locust sts, Philadelphia Pa 19106.

LUNDY, FRANK ARTHUR. b Decatur Ill 16 Jl 05. 5: USoCal 23-25; Stanford 26-28 (Eng) AB; UCal(Berkeley) 29-30 (LS) Certif; Chicago 42-44 (LS) Fellow; UCal(Berkeley) 41-42, 48 (LS) MA. 7: Act ref libn UAriz 30-31; Ref asst Sci & Tech Dept, Los Angeles Pub Lib summer 31; Bibliog UCal(Berkeley) 31-33, Prof asst accessions dept & life sci lib 33-36; Head catlg W A Clark Mem Lib UCal(Los Angeles) 36-39; Act head 39-40; Head accessions dept UCal(Berkeley) 40-42; Visiting Lecturer UIll Lib Sch summer 43; Dir of U Libs UNeb 44-; Dir UNeb Press 55-58. 8: Consul LC Conf on Descr Catlg 45; Adv Com Nat Agric Lib 62-65; Bd Dirs Ctr for Res Libs 66-69; Admin consul, Kent StateU; Bldg consul Neb WesleyanU. 9: ALA (Coun 59-63);-LAD (Bd Dirs 59-61, chm Lib Org & Mgt Sect 59-61);-ACRL (chm Univ Libs Sect 50-51); MPLA (pres 50-51); NebLA (pres 49-50). 10: AAUP; Unitarian Laymen's League of Lincoln; Lincoln Rotary Club; UChicago Grad Lib Sch Alumni Assn; UNeb Faculty Club; Beta Phi Mu; Phi Kappa Tau. 11: Centennial Lib Award 1967, Nebr Libr Assn. 12: Co-auth "Survey of Notre Dame University Library" (52). 13: Yes. 14: Admin & mgt. 15: 2236 A st, Lincoln Nb 68502.

LUNGYS, JULIA (MACKEVICIUS). b Panevezys City Lithuania 5 Jl 14. 4: Benedict Lungys. 5: UVilnius 38-42 (Hist) AB; State Sch of Libnship (Vilnius) 51-54 MSLS. 6: Lithuanian, Fr, Ger, Russian, Polish. 7: Instr & asst libn Jr Col, Vilnius Lithuania 38-45; Libn Vilnius Musicol Col (Vilnius Lithuania) 45-59; Period libn DePaul U Lib 62-68, Ref libn 68-. 9: ALA; CathLA; MusLA; IllLA. 15: De Paul U Lib, 25 E Jackson blvd, Chicago Il 60604.

LUNIN, LOIS F. b Schenectady NY. 4: Dr Martin Lunin. 5: Radcliffe 42-45 (Psych) AB; Drexel 63-66 (Info Sci) MS. 7: Ed asst Pub Rel Dept Grace-New Haven Commun Hosp, New Haven Conn 45-46; Copy ed The C V Mosby Co, St Louis 47-48; Ed asst Washington U Sch of Dentistry (St Louis) 48-50; Research asst, ed asst Columbia U Faculty of Med 50-55; Research admin Med Research Dept William Douglas McAdams, NYC 55-59; Research assoc Dept of Pathology UTex M D Anderson Hosp & Tumor Inst 59-65; Systems analyst Human Communication Info Center Johns Hopkins Med Inst, Welch Med Lib 65-66; Program dir Info Ctr for Hearing, Speech & Disorders of Human Communication; Instr laryngology & octology Johns Hopkins Sch Medicine 66-. 8: Consul; Herner & Co 65-, UMd Sch Dentistry Dept Pathology 64-, Nat Acad Sci Nat Research Coun Task Force on Med Subj Headings 67; NY Hosp Radioisotope Lab 67-; US mem Com on Train, Documentalistic Regulations, Assn Intl des Documentalistes 64-. 9: ASIS (sec Adv Bd 64-65; chm Memb Com 65; Spec Interest Gp for Info Analysis Ctrs; sec 68, v-chm 69; Award of Special Merit Com 69; sec So Tex Chap 63-64); MedLA (Ida & George Eliot Prize Essay Com 68-); ACS (Div Chem Lit); Amer Med Writers Assn; ACM; Amer Assn Hist Med; Inst Info Scientists. 10: AAAS; PhiKappa Phi; Beta Phi Mu. 13: Yes. 14: Org & development of med info centers, computer info, retrieval systems. 15: 30 Bouton Green, Baltimore Md 21210.

LUNN, JEAN (ALICE) (ELIZABETH). b Montreal Can. 5: McGill 28-32 (Hist) BA, 32-34 (Hist) MA, 39-40 BLS, 34-42 (Hist) PhD. 6: Fr. 7: Catlgr McGill U Lib 40-46; Chief Libn Fraser Inst Lib, Montreal 46-50; Dir catlg br Nat Lib of Can 50-. 9: CanLA; Assn canadienne des bibliothecaires de la langue francaise. 12: Ed "Canadiana," Nat Bibliog of Canada. 13: Yes. 14: Catlg. 15: 188 Patricia ave, Ottawa 3 Ont Can.

LUNNON, BETTY S (MRS). b Montgomery Ala 29 My 08. 5: Huntington Col 26-27 (Lit); UAla summers 27-34 (Soc Sci, LS); George Washington U 38 (Educ) AB; Appalachian State Tchrs Col 57 (LS) MA. 7: Tchr & tchr libn Ala pub schs, Hayneville Ala 27-32; Soc case wkr, Coosa Co Ala 33-36; Statistical catlgr soc res div WPA, Wash DC 37-38; Dade Co Pub Schs, Miami Fla: Libn Miami Edison Sr High Sch 38-42, Libn Fairlawn Elem Sch 52-54, Coordinator lib servs 54-59, Supv lib servs 59-68; Supv libs Dept of Educ Amer Samoa, Pago Pago 68-. 8: Prof, Night classes UMiami, Coral Gables Fla 60-68; Dir Wkshop in Bk Sel Drexel Inst 63; Mem Lib Com Field Educ Corp, Chicago 64-68; Consul Fore Corp Jacksonville U, Ala spring 68. 9: ALA (Conv Program Com 62);-AASchL (Bd 62-64, chm Supv Sect 66-67, Prof Rel Com 64-66); FlaASchL (pres 56; Bd Dist 3 62-64); FlaLA (pres 61-63); Dade Co(Fla)SchLA; DadeCoLA; FlaSCD. 10: Quota Club(Coral Gables); Kappa Delta Pi; Delta Kappa Gamma; DAR; Hist Soc SoFla. 13: Yes. 14: Sch libnship, bk sel, sch lib devel. 15: 1002 Granada blvd, Coral Gables Fl 33134.

LUNSFORD, ADRIANNE (WILLS). b Greensboro Ga 18 Ap 13. 4: Emory S Lunsford. 5: Woman's Col of Ga 30-33 (Eng) AB; UGa 34 (LS); LSU 39 BS in LS. 7: Tchr-libn

Swainsboro High Sch, Swainsboro Ga 33-35; Libn Statesboro High Sch, Statesboro Ga 35-37; Libn Moultrie High Sch, Moultrie Ga 37-39; Libn Tallapoosa High Sch, Tallapoosa Ga 40-41; Asst sch lib supv Ga State Dept Educ, Atlanta 41-45; Health educator Ga State Dept Pub Health, Atlanta 45-47; Libn & Asst prin Roswell Elem Sch Fulton Co, Roswell Ga 53-. 9: ALA (Elem Sch Lib Com); GaLA (past sec-treas, Scholarship Com); NEA; GaEA; SELA. 10: Delta Kappa Gamma; PTA. 12: "Frank Visits the Dentist" (47); "Everybody Smile" (48). 14: Elem sch libs. 15: 188 N Coleman rd, Roswell Ga 30075.

LUNSFORD, EFFIE BELLE. b Sylvester Ga 20 N 08. 5: Bessie Tift Col 25-29 (Math, Span, Educ) AB; Peabody 36-37 BS in LS; UGa(Atlanta) even 53-55 (Fr, Ger). 7: Tchr Pub Schs of Ga 30-33; Tchr-libn Meigs Ga 33-34; Tchr-libn Ellaville Ga 34-36; Libn Park Jr High Sch, Knoxville Tenn 37-43; Clerk US Army Air Force; Materiel Command SE Procurement Div, Atlanta 43-45; Clerk USAAF Retirement Records br, Atlanta 45-47; Clerk US VA 47-48; Period libn USPHS Communicable Disease Center, Atlanta 48-58, Ref libn 58-. 9: MedLA; SLA (Biol Sci Div; sec-treas 59-60, chm 61-62; Ga Chap; co-chm Spec Proj Com 56, 2nd v-pres 62-); SELA; GaLA; Atlanta Lib Club (sec 52-53, treas 56-57). 14: Ref. 15: 2457 Drew Valley Rd NE, Atlanta Ga 30319.

LUPIEN, HELENE (MARIE-ROSE). b Montreal Can 2 Ag 45. 5: Regina Assumpta 62-66 BA; UMontreal 66-68 BB. 6: Fr. 7: Bibliothecaire de reference Nationale du Can Ottawa 68; Catlg USherbrooke 68-. 9: Assn canadienne des bibliothecaires de langue francaise. 15: 2533 Davidson, Montreal Quebec Can.

LUPTON, CAROLYN (HURLBURT). b Toronto Can 22 My 39. 4: Austin Lupton. 5: McMaster U 57-60 (Geog) BA; UToronto 60-61 BLS. 6: Fr, Sp. 7: Child libn Hamilton Pub Lib, Hamilton Ont 61-62; Catlgr UAlta 62-63; Catlgr McMaster U 64; Catlgr UAlta 64-, Catlg maintenance libn 68-. 9: CanLA; Assn Col & Univ Libns. 10: Univ Prof Libns Group, UAlta. 14: Catlg, systems planning, data proc. 15: 3504 - 117 st, Edmonton 73 Alta Can.

LUPTON, DAVID WALKER. b Madison Wis 12 O 34. 4: Judith Larson. 5: UWis 52-53, 54-56 (Zool) BS; UMiami (Fla) 53-54 (Zool); UWis 58-60 (Entomology) MS, 61-63 (LS) MS. 7: UWis: Lib asst Biol Lib 55-56, Proj asst Bot Dept 56-58, Proj asst Vet Sci Dept 58, Tchg & research asst Entomology Dept 59-60; Asst in Entomology B P Bishop Museum, Honolulu 60-61; Lib asst Med Lib UWis 61-62; Asst life sci libn Life science Lib, Purdue U 63-66; Tchg asst Lit of Horticulture 65-68; Asst serls libn 67-68; Hd serls unit, Colo State U 68-. 8: Consul Westat Research Inc 67. 10: Beta Phi Mu; Ft Collins Bird Club. 11: Nat Lib Week Publ Award, 62. 14: Bibliog (entomology), ser. 15: 1313 Alford st, Ft Collins Co 80521.

LURYE, JOAN BETTY. b NYC 3 Ja 27. 5: Washington Square Col NYU 43-47 (Psych) BA; NYU 47-49 (Philos); Columbia 58-59 (LS) MS. 7: Research asst Cunningham & Walsh, NYC 51-53; Research asst Benton & Bowles, NYC 54-55; Research asst Headley-Reed, NYC 55-57; Nat Ind Conf Bd, NYC: Order libn 59-60, Ref libn 60-61, Head Libn 61-66; Libn Samson Assocs 66-67; Libn Copley Internatl 67-68; Libn The Diebold Group 68-. 9: SLA. 14: Ref. 15: 333 E 79th st, New York NY 10021.

LUSHINGTON, NOLAN. b Jamaica BWI 15 F 29. 4: Gertruda Vroom Brooks. 5: Columbia Col 45-50 (Eng) AB; Columbia U 52-53 (Hist) MA, 55-58 MLS. 7: US Marines (Lt) 50-52; Master in hist St Andrews Sch, Middletown Del 52-53, Libn & hist master 53-61; Roving libn Free Lib of Phila 61-62; Greenwich Lib, Greenwich Conn: Asst dir 63-65; Dir 66-. 8: Lib evaluator Lawrenceville Sch NJ 59; Lib consul Smyrna Schs, Smyrna Del 59; Lib consul Cathedral Choir Sch, nyc 63. 9: ALA (Memb Com); PLA (Activities Com); ConnLA (chm Legis Com); NELA (Reg Planning Co). 10: Lt Col, USMC Reserve; Greenwich Bullseye Fleet; Cos Cob Rifle Club; Rotary Club. 13: Yes. 14: Lib admin, bldgs. 15: 247 Riverside ave, Riverside Ct 06878.

LUSKAY, JACK RICHARD. b North Charleroi Penn 29 Ap 42. 5: Clarion State Col 60-63 (Eng, LS) BS in Ed; UPittsburgh 64-66 MLS; Oxford U 67 (Eng Novel) Certif. 6: Fr. 7: Eng instr Butler Area Schs, Butler Penn 63-64; Libn Ligonier Valley Schs, Ligonier Penn 64-; Lib sci instr Clarion State Col 67-. 9: ALA; NEA; PennLA; PennASchL; Pittsburgh Suburb Coun of Sch Libns; PennStateEA. 10: Amer Field Ser. 14: Ref, readers serv, curr consul. 15: 72 Center dr, Monessen Pa 15658.

LUSSKY, WARREN ALFRED. b Chicago 16 Ap 19. 4: Mildred Island. 5: Wright Chicago City Jr Col 37-40 (Gen Sci) Diploma; UColo 40-41, 45-46, 53, 63 BA; UIll 41-42; UDenver 47-48 (LS) MA. 6: Ger. 7: Instr in electronics USAAF, Chanute Field Rantoul Ill 41-45; Asst libn Pacific Lutheran Col 48-49; Libn in West Hist dept Denver Pub Lib 49; Act libn art & music dept San Jose State Col 50; Libn Hopkins Transp Lib Stanford U 50; Head Libn Rocky Mountain Col 50-55; Head Libn Neb Wesleyan U 55-56; Lib Dir Tex Lutheran Col 56-. 8: Inspection team on col accred, Tex Educ Agency 61. 9: AA; PNLA (Mont rep Personnel Admin com 51; TexLA (chm Dist 8 66); SWLA. 11: ALA grant lib bldg consul Blumberg Mem Lib, Tex Luth Col 68. 13: Yes. 14: Col lib admin. 15: 357 Irvington dr, San Antonio Tx 72701.

LUST, VERNON GEORGE. b Fresno Cal 16 Jl 28. 4: Mary Austin Lust. 5: UCal 46, 50-55 (Music) BA, 56-58 MLS. 6: Ger. 7: UCal Lib (Berkeley): Stud asst loan dept 52-55, Train supv loan dept 55-57, Circ supv loan dept 58-59, Asst head loan dept 59-63; Asst head acquis dept UCal Lib (Davis) 63-65, Head acquis dept 65-. 9: ALA; CalLA. 10: AAUP. 14: Admin, automation & mechanization, acquis. 15: Lib UCal, Davis Ca 95616.

LUSTER, ARLENE DOONG CHOW (LEONG). b Honolulu Hawaii 11 Ja 36. 4: Gilbert Norman Luster. 5: Ottumwa Hts Col 53-54 (LS); UHawaii 54-55 (Liberal Arts); Our Lady of the Lake Col 55-56 (LS); Immaculate Heart Col summer 56 (Liberal Arts); USoCal summer 56 (LS); Tex Women'sU 56-57 (LS) BA; West Res 57-58 (LS) MS; UHawaii 61-62 (Lang); SophiaU 59-60 (Educ). 6: Chinese. 7: Hosp libn Los Angeles City Lib Harbor Gen Hosp 58-59; Base libn USAF (Civil Serv) Fuchu Base Lib 59-61; Asst order libn UHawaii Gregg M Sinclair Lib 61-63; Asst base libn USAF (Civil Serv) Hickam Base Lib 63-65, Base libn 65-68, Base libn Wheeler Base Lib 68-. 9: ALA (Armed Forces Sect: Recr Com 63-64); Hawaii;A (chm Armed Forced Sect 63-64; chm Gift Com 68 Spring Conf). 10: VITA. 11: Outstanding Super Perform Award 63-64. 12: PACAF Basic Bibliographis: "Community Recreation", annual (59-61); "China and Taiwan", annual (63-). 13: Yes. 14: Ref, hosp and med wk, acquis, bibliog. 15: 3501 Kepuhi st, Honolulu Hi 96815.

LUSTIG, JOHN. b Vienna 13 Ag 31. 4: Anne Baumann. 5: Columbia Col 49-53 (Hist) BA; Columbia 53-54 (Hist), 54-56 MALS. 6: Ger. 7: Libn Queens Borough (NY) Pub Lib 54-57; Libn, Sr libn San Diego Pub Lib 57-63; Consul in adult serv N Bay Cooperative Lib System, Santa Rosa Cal 63-66; Lib consul Wash State Lib 66; Admin asst Redondo Beach Pub Lib 67; Chief libn Monrovia Pub Lib 67-. 09; ALA; CalLA; PLEASC; Pub Lib Film Circuit (v-pres). 10: B'Nai B'rith; Kiwanis; Monrovia Arts Festival; Family Service; Coord Coun. 13: Yes. 14: Ref. 15: Chief Libn Monrovia Pub Lib, Monrovia Ca 91016.

LUSTYIK, SOPHIE ELIZABETH. b Lyons Falls NY 3 D 36. 5: SUNY(Albany) 58 (SS) BA, summers 58-62 MSLS; Syracuse ext 64 (Psych); UMinn summer 65 NDEA Lib & AV; NY State permanent certif in libnship 62. 6: Hungarian, Fr. 7: Youth seminar adv Lewis Co 59-61; Eng III & IV Port Leyden (NY) Central Sch 59-62, 64-65, Libn 58-. 9: NEA; ALA; NY State Tchrs Assn; NYLA. 10: Trionis; PTA; Alpha Epsilon. 13: Yes. 14: Catlg, bk sel, ref, wk with yp, a-v. 15: Box 147, Port Leyden NY 13433.

LUTE, HARRIET. b Paxton Neb 30 Ja 14. 5: Neb Wesleyan 31-34 (Eng); Neb State Tchrs Col (Kearney) 35-36, 39 (Eng, Educ) BA; UColo 40 (Eng); Colo State Col 48 (Eng); UDenver 50-54 (LS) MA. 7: Eng tchr Mitchell Jr High Sch, Mitchell Neb 39-41; Eng tchr Wheatland High Sch, Wheatland Wyo 41-45; Eng tchr Paxton High Sch, Paxton Neb 45-48; Eng tchr Ogallala Sr High Sch, Ogallala Neb 48-49; Eng tchr N Platte Sr High Sch, N Platte Neb 49-50, Sch lib supv 50-60; Supv xonsul Neb Pub Lib Commsn, Lincoln Neb 60-. 69; Dir of Libs Englewood Co 69-. 9: ALA; NebLA (pres 60-61); MPLA. 10: Altrusa; AAUW; PTA; Delta Kappa Gamma; Alpha Gamma Delta. 13: Yes. 14: Pub lib serv. 15: Englewood Pub Lib, Englewood Co 80110.

LUTES, VIRGIL C. b Brownstown Ind 13 O 28. 4: Marie E Kennally. 5: Ind U 53-56 (Comparative Lit) AB, 58-59 (LS) MA. 6: Fr. 7: (Sgt) USAF, US 50-53; Bkmob libn Gary Pub Lib, Gary Ind 56-58; Dir Frankfort Pub Lib, Frankfort Ind 58-59; Dir Field Serv Lib Cen US Govt Dept of AF, Europe 59-62; Head popular lib dept Gary Pub Lib, Gary Ind 62-64; Dir Eastchester Pub Lib, Eastchester NY 64-. 9: ALA; NYLA (A-V Materials & Serv Com); WestchesterLA (treas). 10: Beta Phi Mu. 13: Yes. 14: Admin, rare bks. 15: Garth Woods Apts, 3-E Drake House, Scarsdale NY 10583.

LUTHER, JAMES LEROY. b Patton Penn 22 N 40. 4: Patricia Stiller. 5: Clarion State Col 59-63 (LS, Soc Studies) BS in Ed; Kent State U summers 64, 65- (LS). 7: Sr high libn Beaver Falls Area Sch Dist, Beaver falls Penn 63-68; Hd libn Cumberland Co Col, Vineland NJ 69-. 8: Tri State Area Sch Study Coun, UPittsburgh 64-. 9: Penn State EA. 13: Yes. 14: Admin. 15: 1005-07 Dock st apt 15, Millville NJ 08332.

LUTHIN, PATRICIA (EMILY). b Yonkers NY 21 Ap 44. 5: Fairleigh Dickinson 62-64; Columbia 64-68 (Hist) BS; Syracuse 68-69 MLS. 6: Fr, Ger. 7: Libn (staff) St John's Winterbottom Lib, Yonkers NY 62-; Bibliog asst Columbia U 64-. 9: ALA; ASIS; NY Tech serv Libns. 10: Libn for local church lib. 14: Catlg, automation, sci bibliog. 15: 383 Warburton ave, Yonkers NY 10701.

LUTTROPP, EVELYN B. b Hartford Wis 30 D 09. 5: UWis 40 Lib Certif; Utah State U 58; Sonoma State Col 62; UDenver 63. 6: Ger, Sp. 7: Head Libn Hartford Pub Lib, Hartford Wis 33-50; Libn II Cudahy Pub Lib, Cudahy Wis 51; Libn I & bkmob libn Sacramento Pub Lib, Sacramento Cal 51-53; Libn II Santa Maria Pub Lib, Santa Maria Cal 53-. 9: WisLA; CalLA. 10: Milwaukee Acapella Chorus; Hartford Commun Chorus; Exec Club, Santa Maria Cal. 14: Ref, music. 15: 629 E Cook st, Santa Maria Cal 93454.

LUTZ, JOAN KELLEY. b Oceanside NY 25 Ag 45. 5: UColo 63-67 (Educ) BS; UCLA 67-68 MLS; Adelphi 64. 6: Ger, Fr. 7: Hd libn Honeywell Inc Marine Syst Ctr, W Covina Cal 68-. 9: ALA; SLA; CalLA. 10: Alpha Chi Omega; UColo Alum Assn; Alum Assn UCal Lib Schs. 13: Yes. 14: Admin, spec libs, ref. 15: 16835 E San Bernardino rd apt 41, Covina Ca 91722.

LUTZ, R SYLVIA (FIRTH). b Southampton NY 7 Je 33. 4: Robert E Lutz. 5: SUNY (Geneseo) 51-54; Millersville State Col 59-62 (LS) BS, summer 64; Kutztown State Col summers 66, 68. 7: Elem tchr: W Lebanon Sch Dist, Lebanon Penn 58-59, E Earl Twp, Blue Ball Penn 62-63, Twin Valley Schs, Elverson Penn 63-65; Elem libn Rwin Valley Schs 65-. 9: NEA; ALA; PennStateEA; Twin Valley EA; PennLA; BerksCoLA. 10: Morgantown Woman's Club; Alpha Beta Alpha. 14/ child lit. 15: RD 2, Elverson Pa 19520.

LUTZKY, SVITLANA. b Ukraine 1 Ja 43. 5: Hunter Col 61-65 (Hist) BA; Pratt 66-68 MLS. 6: Ukrainian, Russian. 7: Ref libn Batten Burton Durstine & Osborn, NYC; Slavic catlgr Brooklyn Col Lib. 9: LACUNY. 10: Research Coun of Museum of Ukrainian; Folk Art in NYC. 14: Ref. 15: 39-26 65th st, Woodside NY 11377.

LUXNER, RICHARD M. b Newark NJ 29 S 23. 4: Ann Redgofe. 5: Franklin & Marshall 41-48 (Eng) AB; Rutgers 64-67 MLS. 7: Libn trainee Canarsie Br Brooklyn Pub Lib 64-65, Adult serv libn sci & ind div Grand Army Plaza 65-69; Ref libn IBM TJ Watson research Ctr, Yorktown Hts NY 69-. 9: ALA; ASIS; SLA (sec NY Chap Dpcumentation Gp 69-); BSA; Bibliographical Society of America. 10: NY Lib Club. 14: Ref (sci-tech), lib automation, info sci. 15: 40 So Highland ave, Ossining NY 10562.

LUZADER, Jo ANN. b Glenville WVa 2 My 44. 5: Glenville State Col 62-65 (Elem Educ) AB; Peabody Col 66-69 MLS. 7: Circ libn Glenville State Col 65-68; Ref libn CapitalU 69-. 9: OhioLA. 14: Ref. 15: 645 Neil ave apt 208, Columbus Oh 43215.

LYBECK, CAROLINE G. b Petersburg ND. 5: Concordia Col (Moorhead Minn) 32 (Hist) BA; UDenver summers 37, 40, 41 BS in LS; UMich 56-57 MA in LS. 7: Tchr & tchr-libn pub schs 32-42; Admin asst War Dept Off of Dependency Benefits 42-47; Asst bus & tech Pub Lib, Kan City Mo 47-48; Head of circ UND 48-53, Asst libn 53-62; Head circ libn Ore State U 62-63, Educ fine arts libn 63-. 9: ALA; PNLA. 10: Beta Phi Mu; Pi Lambda Theta; Phi Kappa Phi. 14: Ref. 15: 145 N 16th st, Corvallis Ore 97330.

LYBECK, PAULINE ELIZABETH. b Bayshore NY 7 Jl 29. 5: Tufts U 50 (Eng) BA (magna cum laude); Columbia 51 (LS) MS; Drexel 67-68 (Info Sci). 06: Ger. 7: Libn & pub rel dir US Army Spec Serv 51-54; Ref libn & pub rel asst Dayton Pub Lib, Dayton Ohio 55-57; Admin asst Time Inc, NYC 57-58; Ref libn J Walter Thompson Co, NYC 58; Libn Television Bureau of Advertising, NYC 58-62; Dir of Info Serv Papert Koenig Lois & Osborne, NYC 62-67; Hd Info & Microfilm Ctrs Batten, Barton, Durstine, NYC 68; Dir info systs Interpub Group of Cos, NYC 68-. 8: Mem, Bd Dirs, Documentation Abstracts Inc; promotion engr, Info Sci Abstracts; Staff, Ballard Sch, YWCA, NYC, courses for lib aides; Consul NY Times on pilot news research proj 67-68. 9: SLA (chm Advert & Market Div 63-64, Rep to Nat Lib Week Program 65-66, Recr & Train Chm NY Chap 65-66); ASIS; Assn Records Execs & Adminrs; NMA; LPRC; NY Lib Club. 10: Amer Women in Radio & TV; Amer Market Assn; Phi Beta Kappa; NY Tufts Club; Metropolitan Museum of Art. 12: Contrib ed "Advertising Today, Yesterday, Tomorrow" (63); Ed "What's New in Advertising and Marketing" (59-60); Auth "Guidelines for Standards for Advertising Agency Libraries" (64). 13: Yes. 14: Consul in design & devel of info systems, admin & promotion of info serv. 15: 225 First 79th st, New York NY 10021.

LYDAY, AMELIA (BRAUN). b Beaver Falls Penn 11 Ja 16. 5: UPittsburgh 33-37 (Biol) BS; Geneva Col 38 (Elem) Certif; UFla 63 (Educ) AM of Ed, 64 Certif in Lib A-V. 7: Tchr Harmony Twp, Beaver Co Penn 38-42; Tchr Patterson Twp, Beaver Falls Penn 43, 47-48; Searcher LC 43-44; Tchr Army Dependents Sch, Munch Munich 52-54; Tchr Bensalem Twp, Andalusia Penn 55-56; Tchr Brevard Co, Merritt Island Fla 56-61, Sch libn 61-. 8: Consul libn, Merritt Island Pub Lib 65-; Lib Bd, Cocoa Fla, 57-58; Merritt Island Lib Bd 65-. 9: NEA; ALA;Clr Tchrs Assn; FlaEA; FlaSchLA. 10: AAUW; Classial League. 14: Ref, classics. 15: 626 Fifth st, Merritt Island Fla 32952.

LYDERS, RICHARD ARNOLD. b Minot N Dak 16 Je 34. 4: Gay Ann Gustafson. 5: UMinn 61-63 (Eng) BA; USoCal 64-66 MLS. 6: Ger. 7: Navigator (Capt) USAF 56-60; Ref libn Long Beach (Cal) Pub Lib 64-66; Ser libn UMinn Biomed Lib (Minneapolis) 66-68; Asst circ libn Macalaster Col 66-68; Dir Assoc Cols of the Midwest Central Lib, Chicago 68-. 9: ALA. 14: Admin, lib coop, tech proc, lib hist. 15: 60 W Walton, Chicago Il 60610.

LYLE, GUY R. b Lloydminster Sask Can 31 O 07. 4: Margaret Elizabeth White. 5: UAlta 24-27 (Classics) AB; Columbia 27-29 (LS) BS, 30-32 (LS) MS. 6: Fr. 7: Libn Antioch Col 29-35; Libn Woman's Col of UNC (Greensboro) 36-44; Dir of Libs LSU 44-54; Dir of Libs Prof Emory U 54-. Tchg positions: UIll Lib Sch, Urbana 35-36, 42-43; UNC Lib Sch, Chapel Hill summers 38, 53; Columbia U Sch of Lib Sci, NY summers 46, 47; Cal Sch of Libn Berkeley 68. 8: Keio Univ Tokyo 57 (4 months), first appointee to Japan Lib Sch Rockefeller Found Lecture Series; Consul: Adrian Col, Mich; Armstrong Col, Ga; Mitchell Col, NC; Dillard U, La; Hendrix Col, Ark; Lambuth Col, tenn; Mary Baldwin Col, Ohio; USoFla; Manchester Col, Ind; Bethel Col, Ind; Queen's Col, NC; Mitchell Col, NC; ClaflinU, SC and others (lib admin or lib bldg); Served on visiting teams of So Assn of Cols & Univs. 9: ALA-ACRL (chm 49-50); NCLA (pres 41-42). 11: LLD UAlta, 64. 12: "Administration of the College Library" (3d ed 61); "Bibliography of Christopher Morley" (52); "The President, the Professor, and the College Library" (63); "I am Happy to Present: a Book of Introductions," with Kevin Guinagh (53, 2nd ed 68). 13: Yes. 14: Col & Univ lib, admin, lib bldgs, ref. 15: 2229 Tanglewood rd, Decatur Ga 30033.

LYLE, JACK WARD. b Rochester Ind 25 F 34. 5: DePauw U 52-56 (Hist) AB; Ind U 57-59 (LS) MA. 6: Fr. 7: Tchr High Sch, Logansport Ind 56-57; Personnel spec US Army, Ft Hood Tex 59-61; Ref libn Fresno State Col 61-62; Catlgr Ind State Col 62-64; Ref libn Ind State U 64-. (Terre Haute) 64-66; Hd circ 66-68; Docs libn 68-. 9: ALA; IndLA. 10: AAUP; Phi Beta Kappa. 14: Ref. 15: 700-1/2 So Eighth st, Terre Haute In 47807.

LYLE, KATHY CH'IU. b China 02 Jl 39. 4: Edgar R Lyle II. 5: TunghaiU 56-60 (Eng Lit) BA; Syracuse 61-62 (LS) MS. 6: Chinese. 7: Catlgr E Asian Collections YaleU Lib 62-64; Catlgr Cornell Med Lib Col, NYC 64-65; Libn in charge Nat Com on Maternal Health, NYC 66-67; Libn in charge & bibliogr Bio-Med Div The Population Coun, NYC 67-. 8: Lang Instr; NYU 64-66, ColumbiaU, Chinese, 67-68; Free-lance transl. 9: MedLA; Chinese Lang TA. 10: China Concerns Com; AAUW. 12: "Chinese Fables" (67). 14: Catlg, ref, info ret system. 15: Bio-Medical Div The Population Council 2 E 103rd st, New York NY 10029.

LYMAN, HELEN H(UGUENOR) (MRS). ORNELL NY 16 Mr 10. 5: UBuffalo 29-32 BA, 40 BS in LS; UChicago Grad Lib Sch 55-56. 6: Fr. 7: Circ asst Buffalo Pub Lib, Buffalo NY 32-35, Co-hd readers' bur 35-42, Admin asst 43-44, Hd adult educ dept 44-52; Dir ALA Adult Educ Survey, Chicago 52-53; Adult serv libn Hild Reg Br Chicago Pub Lib 57-59; Pub lib consul (adult serv) Wis Free Lib Commsn, Madison Wis 59-63; Dir ref dept Lockwood Memorial Lib SUNY (Buffalo) 64-65; Pub lib specialist for adult serv Lib Serv Br Off Educ HEW 65-67; Asst Prof UWis Lib Sch (Madison) 67-; Dir & prin investigator research project "Lib Materials in Serf v to Adult

New Reader" UWis Lib Sch 67-. 8: Spec lectr in Lib Educ Ref Serv and Materials, Buffalo Instl Br State U Col, Geneseo NY summer 64; Vis lectr, Adult Serv and Adult Bks, Sch of Grad Lib Studies SUNY (Buffalo) 67; Dir & consul Reading Guidance Inst, Lib Sch, UWis summer 65; Consul & eval, Adult Educ Proj, Pub Lib, Terre Haute Ind 65-. 9: ALA (Coun Mem-at-Large 62-65); -ASD; pres 69-70; Consul Com on Reading Improv for Adults 65-67; Consul Com on Pub Lib Serv to an Aging Pop 65-67; Study-Discuss Prog Proj 64-65; chm Nomin Com 63; chm Miami Beach Conf Prog 62; Publ Com 62-63; Reading Guide Proj Promot Com 61; -RSD (Standards Com 64-67); AEAUSA (Com on Soc Philos 51-52); WisLA (Adult Educ Com 61-63; Consul Ref Sect 59-63); Adult Educ Assn Wis; Adult Educ Assn, Greater Wash (treas 65-67). 12: "Adult Education ac Activities in Public Libraries: A Report of the ALA Survey in Public Libraries and State Library Extension Agencies of the United States," ALA (54); "How to Use the Reading for an Age of Change Series: A Handbook for Librarians," ALA (63). 13: Yes. 14: Adult serv, ref, readon ing interests of adults, readng guidance, art and lit. 15: 3209 Stevens st apt #3, Madison Wi 53705.

LYMAN, JESSIE W. b Duluth Minn 26 O 10. 5: Hibbing Jr Col 28-30; UMinn 31-32 (LS) BS, summers 49-51 (Educ) BS. 7: Asst catlgr Pub Lib, Hibbing Minn 33-35; Ref libn High Sch Lib, Hibbing Minn 45-61; Head Libn Alvah N Belding Lib, Belding Mich 61-65; Head Libn Joseph Mann Lib, Two Rivers Wis 65-. 9: ALA; WisLA. 14: Ref. 15: 2530 - 34th st, Two Rivers Wi 54241.

LYNAS, LOTHIAN (EMILY). b Cambridge Eng 25 F 20. 5: Chelsea Polytech London U 37-38 Inter BS; Newnham Col (Cambridge) 38-40 (Natural Sci) MA; Columbia 62-65 MSLS. 6: Fr, Ger. 7: Photo interpretation Royal Air Force, UK, N Africa, Italy 40-45; Libn Botanical Garden, Singapore 56-57; Asst under libn U Lib Cambridge 58-62; Acquis libn Amer Museum of Natural Hist, NYC 62-65; Ref libn Albert Einstein Col Med 66; Med libn Morrisania City Hosp 66; Asst libn NY Botanical Garden 67-. 8: Res for Grolier Info Ser 66-. 9: SLA; MedLA. 14: Ref, mss, incunabula, early printed bks, ser, exch. 15: 260 Audubon ave apt 28E, New York NY 10033.

LYNAUGH, ETHEL M(ALEC). b Madison Wis 7 O 05. 4: Peter C Lynaugh. 5: U Wis 23-27 (Fr) BA, 26-27 (LS) Diploma. 6: Fr. 7: Asst libn Central State Tchrs Col (Stevens Point Wis) 27-28; Libn Eau Claire High sch, Eau Claire Wis 28-29; UWis(Madison): Asst circ dept 29-47, Circ libn 47-65, Spec asst 65-67, Emeritus UWis 67-. 9: ALA; WisLA. 10: AAUP; Wis Lib Sch Assn; Delta Zeta; AAUW; Woman's Club. 14: Circ. 15: PO Box 5687, Sun City Center Fl 33570.

LYNCH, BEVERLY (PFEIFER). b Fargo ND 27 D 36. 4: John A Lynch. 5: ND State U 53-57 (Music, Eng) BS; UIll 57-59 (LS) MS. 6: Fr, Ger. 7: Sr ref asst City of Plymouth Pub Lib, Plymouth Eng (on exch) 60-61; Libn philos & theol collection Marquette U Lib 59, Asst catlgr Marquette U Lib 62-63; Asst head ser div Yale U Lib 63-65, Head ser div 65-68; Fellow UWis (Madison) 68-. 9: ALA;-RTSD (sec sers sect 67-70); BSA. 15: 709 N 66th st, Milwaukee Wi 53213.

LYNCH, DOROTHY N (MRS PHILLIPS). b Knoxville Tenn 16 N 07. 5: Stephens Col 25-26; Hood Col 27-30 (Bot) AB; Columbia 32 BS in LS, 53, 56-57 (Adult Educ). 6: Fr. 7: Child libn Brooklyn Pub Lib 33-37, 40-49; Child libn Geo L Pease Mem Lib, Ridgewood NY 38-39; Adult serv libn 1st asst Brooklyn Pub Lib, Flatbush NY 50-53; Reader's consul Queens Boro Pub Lib, Jamaica NY 53-56, Coordinator adult serv 56-59; A-V consul Westchester Lib System, New Rochelle NY 59-64; A-V consul Nassau Lib System, Garden City NY 64-. 9: ALA; -ASD (Adv Com 67-, chm 69-); LPRC (Bd, treas); NYLA (A-V Materials & Serv Com); NY Lib Club (Coun mem, sec). 10: NY Film coun; LI Film Coun, Sec 65-. 13: Yes. 14: A-v serv, adult serv. 15: 164 Wolfpit ave, Norwalk Ct 06851.

LYNCH, EVANGELINE MILLS. b Oil City La. 5: LSU 48 BS in LS, 56 (Educ) MA. 6: Fr, Sp. 7: Libn Springhill High Sch, Springhill La 48-49; LSU Lib (Baton Rouge): Res libn 49-53, Circ libn 53-56, Ref libn 56-58, Louisiana & rare bk room libn 58-64, Louisiana room libn 64-. 9: ALA; SWLA; LaLA; LA Hist Assn; Baton Rouge Lib Club. 10: Phi Kappa Phi; Phi Sigma Iota; Found for Hist La. 13: Yes. 14: Res & ref in loc hist. 15: Box 17031 LSU, Baton Rouge La 70803.

LYNCH, FLORENCE (VON FREMD). b Norfolk Conn 11 Jl 34. 4: John Richard Lynch. 5: Wellesley Col 52-56 (Mus) BA. 6: Fr, Ger, Ital. 7: Catlgr Widener Lib HarvardU 56-59, Catlgr Music Lib 59-. 14: Catlg. 15: 5 Fernald dr, Cambridge Ma 02138.

LYNCH, ISOBEL PHELPS. b Vergennes Vt 18 Ag 15. 5: Goucher 36 AB; Johns Hopkins 53-54 (Pub Admin); Columbia 41 BLS. 7: Br asst ref dept Enoch Pratt Free Lib, Baltimore 37-38, 38-40; Head adult dept Kanawha Co Pub Lib, Charleston WVa 41-42, Act libn 42-45; Post libn Army Lib Serv, Japan 46-47; Post libn Army Lib Serv, Wetzlar Germany 47-48; Field serv libn Army European Command, Germany 48-49; Command libn Army European Command 49-52; Exec asst dir Enoch Pratt Free Lib, Baltimore 53, Libn Pimlico Br 54-57, Asst chief ext div 57-64, Chief ext div 64-67; Supv interlib coop & planning div lib ext Md State Dept Educ 67-. 9: ALA; MdLA (Exec Bd 61-64, pres 62-63, Ref Serv Div); SLA; Educl Media Assn Md. 13: Yes. 14: Ref, admin, interlib coop. 15: 4 Upland rd, apt 35, Baltimore Md 21210.

LYNCH, LAWRENCE P. b Dayton Ohio 5 Ap 37. 5: Meramec Community Col 63-64 (Eng); UMiami 64-67 (Eng) AB; UKy 67-69 (LS). 6: Sp. 7: X-ray tech Med Center of Florissant, Florissant Mo 62-64; Acquis searcher UMiami Lib 67; Lib trainee VA Hosp, Lexington Ky 68-. 9: ALA. 10: Amer Registry of Radiologic Tech; Disabled Amer Veterans. 14: Med ref, lib automation, spec libs. 15: Box 2076 Cooperstown B, Lexington Ky 40508.

LYNCH, LINDA KAY. b Jacksonville Fla 17 Mr 46. 5: Fla So Col 61-67 (Speech, Drama) BA; LSU 68-69 MSLS. 6: Sp. 7: Asst libn Fla Jr Col 69-. 9: ALA; LLA. 14: Ref, reading guidance, child lit. 15: 124 W 67th st, Jacksonville Fl 32208.

LYNCH, MARGIE RUTH. b Long Beach Cal 8 Je 25. 5: McNeese Jr Col of LSU 43-45 (Eng) Certif; LSU 46-48 (Eng) BS, 48-49 BS in LS. 7: Br libn Ouachita Parish Pub Lib, Monroe La 49-50; Asst libn Auoyelles Parish Lib, Marksville La 50-51; Asst libn circ Lake Charles Pub Lib, Lake Charles La 51-54; Parish Libn Vermilion Parish Lib, Abbeville La 55-56; Demonstration libn La State Lib Vernon Parish, Leesville La 56-57; Parish Libn Vernon Parish Lib, Leesville La 57-60; Parish Libn Calcasieu Parish Lib, Lake Charles La 61-. 8: Com on La Pub Lib Standards (chm Com on Org & Operation 62-64). 9: ALA; -ALTA (Publ Com 67-69); SWLA; LaLA (sec-treas 68-69, Exec sec Lib Development com 65-66). 10: Delta Kappa Gamma; Bus & Prof Women; Calcasieu Libns Assn; ALTRUSA. 12: "Proceedings, Library Trustee Institute," ALA (61). 14: Lib ext, admin, lib bldgs, pub rel. 15: 616 Louie st, Lake Charles La 70601.

LYNCH, MARY JOSEPHINE. b Detroit 3 Je 39. 5: Marygrove Col 57-61 (Eng) BA; UMich 61-62 AMLS; UDetroit 62-66 (Eng) MA. 7: Ref libn UDetroit 62-; Hd ref dept 66-; Instr in dept of lib sci Wayne StateU 68-69. 9: ALA; CathLA; SLA; MichLA (chm Jr Mem RT 68-69). 10: Kappa Gamma Pi; Pi Lambda Theta; Beta Phi Mu; AAUP. 14: Ref. 15: 16720 Greenlawn, Detroit Mi 48221.

LYNCH, SISTER MARY DENNIS SHCJ. b Phila Penn 23 Ap 20. 5: Temple 37-41 (Sociol) BA; Drexel 41-42 (LS) BS; CatholicU 51-55 (LS) MS; Villanova 66- (Pol Sci). 6: Fr. 7: Tchr & libn Sch of the HCJ: Sharon Hill Penn 42-45, 53-62, Summit NJ 45-47; Tchr W Catholic High Sch, Phila 47-53; Libn Rosemont Col 62-. 8: Cath U Prog of Affiliation, exam & textbk consul 58-67; Instr Lib Sci VillanovaU summers 64, 65; St Charles Sem Adv com 68-; Lib Consul Serv. 9: ALA-ACRL (dir-at-large Phila Dist 65-69); CathLA (Loc Arrts Com Natl Conv 65; East Penn Unit: Memb Chm 64-66, chm Col Sect 66-68; Nat Adv Coun 69-71); Amer Acad Pol and Soc Sci; Amer Pol Sci Assn; Amer Forensic Assn; PennLA; Middle State Coun for Soc Studies; Tri-State Col Lib Coop (exec sec 68-69). 10: Beta Phi Mu; Natl Cath Forensic Assn (High Sch); Moderator Rosement Col Debating Soc. 13: Yes. 14: Readers serv, admin, lib educ, lib consul serv. 15: Rosemont College, Rosemont Pa 19010.

LYNCH, MICHAEL PATRICK. b San Rafael Cal 10 N 37. 5: USan Francisco 55-59 (Eng) BS; UDenver 62-63 (LS) MA. 7: (Sp 5) US Army, Japan 59-62; Ref libn S Puget Sound Reg Lib, Olympia Wash 63-65; Asst dir N Central Reg Lib, Wenatchee Wash 66-67, Dir 68-. 8: Ref consul, Timberland Lib Demonstration, Wash State Lib 64-65. 9: ALA; PNLA; WashLA (Exec Bd 65-, Co-chm Conv Program 65; Statewide Programs Com 67-). 14: Ref & ext in pub libs, admin, mail order lib techniques. 15: 1714 Jefferson, Wenatchee Wa 98801.

LYNCH, (MINNIE-LOU CHITTICK). b Flora Ind 28 F 16. 4: Dr Weldon J Lynch. 5: Maryville Col (Speech). 7: Desk asst Flora (Ind) Pub Lib 30-34; Chm ALA-ALTA Wkshops, Montreal & Cleveland 60-61; Pres ALA-ALTA 61-63; Mem Adv Com to ALA-LAD Small Libs Proj 61-63; Mem Adv Com to Recr Proj (ALA) 62-64; Chm ALTA Com on Governor's Confs 63-65; NLW Chm, La 65; Chm of Lib

Development Com of La 64-67; Mem GALA(ALA)PRS Com (LAD) Jury Cit of Trustees (ALTA) 64-66; Conferee IFLA (The Hague) 66. 8: Addressed a Jt Session of Gen Assembly of State of SC at request of SCLA, 65; Addressed CanLA 64; have addressed sate & reg lib assns 40 plus times; Consul for Trustee Wkshops in many states; frequent spkr at Governor's Confs; Commencement Spkr Okla Col Women 65; Lectr NDEA Inst, LSU Lib Sch 67, 68; Coord for Spec Progs, La State Lib 68-; Consul La Central Dist Libs 68-69. 9: ALA (Exec Bd, Memb Com 66-, chm Subcom on J Morris Jones Award Proposal 69; Nat Bd Nat Bk Com 66-). ; (pres 61-63, Bd 64); LaLA (chm Trustee Sect 60); Allen Parish Lib Bd of Control (pres 57-69, v-pres 69-). 10: Pi Kappa Delta; Internat Platform Assn. 11: ALA Trustee Citation of Merit 64; Modisette Award for Trustees, LaLA 61; Citation, Lib Devel Com LaLA 69. 12: "Guidelines on Holding a Governors Conference," ALA-ALTA (62, rev ed 68); Contrib "The Library Trustee" (64, rev ed 69). 13: Yes. 14: Lib development trustee educ. 15: 404 E Sixth ave, Oakdale La 71463.

LYNDEN, FREDERICK (CHARLES). b San Jose Cal 20 Ja 39. 4: Deborah Oehler. 5: Stanford 56-60 (Internat Rel) BA, 60-61 (Hist) MA; UMinn 62-63 (LS) MA. 6: Ger, Sp. 7: Ref libn UCal Bancroft Lib 64-66; Libn II ref Meyer Undergrad Lib Stanford 66-67; Admin asst acquis U Libs 67-68, Libn III, Asst chief acquis U Libs 68-. 8: Consul Stanfprd Research Inst 67. 9: ALA; He-Libs (San Francisco Bay Area). 10: Org Amer Hists. 13: Yes. 14: Ref, admin. 15: 271 Leland ave, Palo Alto Ca 94305.

LYNG, SISTER JEAN ELIZABETH CSJ. b Albany NY 27 Ap 06. 5: Col of St Rose summers 31-50 (Hist) BA; St John's U summers 55-59 MS in LS. 6: Lat, Fr. 7: Loan desk clerk NY State Lib 21-28; Libn Catholic Central High Sch, Troy NY 31-34; Libn St Mary's Hosp, Amsterdam NY 43-53; Libn St Mary's Sch, Glens Falls NY 53-57; Libn St Aloysius Sch, Rome NY 57-59; Asst libn Col of St Rose 59-60; Libn St Patrick's High Sch, Syracuse NY 60-62; Libn Catholic Central High Sch, Binghamton NY 60-, Libn Diocesan Sch Syst, Binghamton NY 63-. 9: CathLA; ALA; NYLA. 10: Women's Profess Bk Assn. 14: Ref. 15: 73 Chestnut st, Binghamton NY 13905.

LYNG, MYRNA (DALZELL). b Langdon N Dak 30 D 39. 4: Merwin John Lyng. 5: Layville State Col 57-61 (Comparative Lit) BS; UMinn summers 63-68 (LS) MA. 7: Libn & Eng tchr Portland High Sch, Portland N Dak 65-66; Libn Columbus Pub Schs, Columbus Ohio 66-67; Asst libn & instr in Lib Sci Mayville State Col 61-64, 68-. 9: ALA; NEA; NDLA; NDEA. 14: Ref. 15: Mayville ND 58257.

LYNN, CATHERINE (GAFFIN). b McMinnville Tenn 10 N 06. 4: Ollie James Lynn. 5: Carson-Newman Col 25-29 (Eng) BA; Peabody 56-57 (LS) MA. 6: Lat, Sp. 7: Warren Co (Tenn) Sch Bd: Tchr, prin, McMinnville 25, 26, Tchr, Centertown High Sch 29, Tchr, Morrison High Sch 32-34, Tchr, McMinnville High Sch 34-36; Home demonstration agent Agric Ext Serv Stewart & Giles Cos, Tenn 36-38; Attendance tchr, Hickman Co Tenn 47-48; Libn & tchr of Lat & Span, Hickman Co High Sch, Centerville Tenn 48-; Libn at Shorter Col (Rome Ga) 67, 68. 9: NEA; TennEA; GaLA. 10: UDC; AAUW; Central Ill Geneol Soc. 12: "Gaffin Family, Statistical and Biographical Sketches" (69). 14: Readers guidance, rare bks. 15: 140 N Central ave, Centerville Tn 37033.

LYNN, CLETUS LAWRENCE. b Princeton Ind 19 Ap 09. 4: Jeannette Murphy. 5: UNotre Dame 29-32 (Econ) BA; Peabody 39-41 (LS & Jr Col Admin) BS in LS, MA; Chicago summer 42 (Jr Col Admin). 6: Fr, Ger, Sp. 7: Store manager F W Woolworth Co, Ind, Ill, Miss, Tenn 32-36; Research & manufacturing Keedoozle Corp, Memphis Tenn 36-39; Supv of assembly M P Heinz Corp, Chicago summer 43; Asst to supt Gen Bottlers Corp, Chicago summers 44-47; Dir of personnel Schurz Even Jr Col even 42-47; Educ dir Com Trades Inst, Chicago 51-52; Libn Wright Jr Col 41-68, Prof of Lib Sci 68-. 8: Lib Study Com North Central Assn of Schs & Cols. 9: ALA-ACRL (dir Jr Col Sect 48-51); IllEA; Ill Assn Higher Educ. 10: AAUP; Boy Scouts Coun (Park Ridge Ill); Pi Gamma Mu. 11: Peabody Fellowship in Tchg 39-41. 13: Yes. 14: Admin, ref. 15: 631 Austin, Park Ridge Il 60068.

LYNN, JEANNETTE (MURPHY). b Boulder Mont 27 S 05. 4: Cletus Lawrence Lynn. 5: Tabor Col 22-26 (Sociol) BA; UWis 22-28 (LS) Certif; Chicago 33-35 (LS) MA; UIll (Educ). 6: Ger, Fr. 7: Music libn Tabor Col 22-26; Asst libn Omaha Pub Lib 26-27; Head catlgr UNotre Dame (Ind) 28-32; Libn St Mary's Col (Notre Dame Ind) 32-33; Head catlgr Cossitt Lib, Memphis Tenn 35-37; Libn Siena Col 37-39; Exec sec Catholic LA 52-54; Chief catlg & clsf Crerar Lib, Chicago 54-59; Catlg libn Dist 64, Park Ridge Ill 59-. 12: "Alternative Classification for Catholic Books" (37, 3rd ed 64); "Alternative Classification for Catholic Books" (37, 3rd ed 64); Ed "Catholic Library World" (52-54). 13: Yes. 14: Clsf. 15: 631 Austin, Park Ridge Il 60068.

LYNN, LOIS JEAN (TURKES). b Pittsburgh Penn 21 Jl 44. 4: Harold Jeffery Lynn. 5: UPittsburgh 62-65 (Ger) BA, 65-66 MLS. 6: Ger. 7: Libn sci & tech dept Carnegie Lib of Pittsburgh 66-68; Assoc libn Westinghouse Bettis Atomic Power Lab, W Mifflin Penn 68-. 9: SLA; PennLA. 10: Beta Phi Mu. 14: Ref, ser. 15: 32 Oakmont ave, Duquesne Pa 15110.

LYON, CHARLOTTE (HELEN GODSMAN). b Topeka Kan 1 Mr 18. 4: LaVerne Dean Lyon. 5: UDenver 36-40 (Fr) BA; UCal (Los Angeles) 64-65 MLS. 6: Fr, Sp. 7: High sch tchr Wheatridge High Sch, Wheatridge Colo 40-42; High sch tchr So Denver High Sch, Denver 42-47; Exec sec to pres Morrison Engnr Co, Temple City Cal 51-53, 55-57; Exec sec LWV Cal, Pasadena Cal 59; Lib clerk Arcadia (Cal) Pub Lib 64; Ref libn Los Angeles Co Lib System, Hawthorne Cal 65-67; Readers asst (adult) & ya libn Pomona Pub Lib 67-. 9: ALA; CalLA. 10: UCal Lib Schs Alumni Assn; LWV; So Cal Friends of Libs Wkshop. 12: Ed "This is Arcadia" (62); Asst ed "Arcadia Health Services" (64); Asst ed "Facilities for Handicapped Children" (61). 14: Ref, ya serv. 15: 115 S Marywood ave, Claremont Ca 91711.

LYON, DOROTHY (MATHEWS). b Winter Haven Fla 24 O 30. 4: Eugene Lyon. 5: Fla State U 48-52 (LS) BA. 7: Asst br libn Denver Pub Lib 52-53; Dir St Lucie-Okeechobee Reg Lib, Ft Pierce Fla 62-. 9: ALA; FlaLA. 10: Fla State Univ Alumnae Sec. 14: Child area. 15: 124 N Indian River dr, Ft Pierce Fl 33450.

LYON, EUNICE M. b Wash DC 12 F 18. 5: Howard U 45 (Pol Sci) BA, 50 (Hist) MA; Catholic U 62 MSLS. 6: Sp, Fr, Ger. 7: Program dir Amer Red Cross, Far East, Philippines, Japan 45-48; Club dir USA Spec Serv, Europe 51-60; Med libn USAF Hosp, Andrews AFB Wash DC 62-. 9: ALA. 10: Neighbors Inc; Zeta Phi Beta. 12: Comp "Medical Bibliography f or Air Force Medical Libraries" 4 cum vols (62-66). 14: Spec libs, med, hist. 15: 8138 W Beach dr NW, Wash DC 20012.

LYON, GENYA (LEE). b Berkeley Cal 9 N 26. 4: Ben A Lyon. 5: UCal(Berkeley) 53 (Slavic Lang & Lit) AB, 58 MLS. 6: Russian, Czech, Slovak, Serbo-Croatian, Ger, Lat, Ital, Bulgarian. 7: Sr lib asst UCal(Berkeley) 55-58; Ref libn I & II Cal State Lib 58-60; Catlgr libn I UCal(Berkeley) 60-61; Ref libn III Cal State Lib 61-67; Libn IV bus & mun dept Sacramento City-Co Lib 67-. 9: ALA; CalLA. 10: Amer Rose Soc. 14: Ref, Slavic lang materials, bk sel in foreign langs, bus ref. 15: 2249 John Still dr, Sacramento Ca 95832.

LYON, MARY DURAND. b White Plains NY 16 My 09. 5: Mt Holyoke 29-33 (Eng) AB; Columbia 48-50 MS in LS. 7: Asst catlgr Providence Pub Lib 50-51; Asst libn Rye Free Reading Room, Rye NY 51-. 9: ALA; NYLA; WestchesterLA (sec Ref Sect; treas YA & Child Sect). 10: Audubon Soc. 14: Ya, catlg. 15: 8 Jennifer lane, Port Chester NY 10573.

LYON, RALPH JR. b Englewood NJ 20 Ag 11. 5: Menlo Jr Col (Cal) 30-32 (Hist); Stanford 32-34 (Ger) AB; UCal 47-48 BLS; Stanford 52-53 (Hist) MA; USoCal 55-56 (Hist). 6: Fr, Ger, Sp, Swedish, Dutch, Portu. 7: Tech 5th grade US Army Ordnance 40-46; Donald Craig Certif Pub Acct, San Francisco 46-47; Hoover Lib Stanford U 47-51; UCLA Lib 51-. 9: CalLA. 10: Phi Beta Kappa. 14: Catlg. 15: 1328 Westwood blvd, Los Angeles Ca 90024.

LYONS, CATHERINE (O'BRYAN). b Kingston NY 28 Jl 18. 4: James J Lyons. 5: NY State Col for Tchrs (Albany) 37-41 (Eng) BA, 45 BS in LS. 6: Fr. 7: Tchr-libn Edmeston Central Sch, Edmeston NY 41-42; Tchr-asst libn Wappingers Central Sch, Wappingers Falls NY 42-45, Libn 46; Pub libn Albany Pub Lib, Albany NY 46-48; Libn Marlboro Central Sch, Marlboro NY 48-49; Libn Columbus Elem Sch, Poughkeepsie NY 49-50; Elem libn James S Evans Elem Sch, Wappingers Falls NY 58-. 8: Chm Soc Studies Dept, Wappingers Central Sch, 44, 45; Readers adv serv, Pine Hill Br Albany Pub Lib, 46-48; Adv wk in org of St mary Sch Lib, Wappingers Falls 64; Lib dept chm WCS 65; Lib Coord for ESEA Title II in Wappingers Sch Dist 65-68; Assisted in organiz new sch libs 63-66. 9: NYLA; NY State Tchrs Assn;Dutchess Co (NY) Libns Assn; Sch Libns SE NY. 10: Cath Daughters Amer; Wappingers Faculty Assn; St Mary Sch Lib Com, Wappingers Falls NY; Dutchess Co Pistol Assn; PTA. 14: Child bks, catlg, ref, lib instr, reading guidance. 15: 15 W Academy st, Wappingers Falls NY 12590.

LYONS, GRACE J. b NYC 22 Je 32. 5: St John's U 50-54 (Chem) BS; Columbia 57-60 (LS) MS; NYU Mgt Inst 65. 7: Proofreader Amer Tobacco Co, NYC 55-57; Bibliog Amer Cancer Soc, NYC 57-60; Supv libn Kings Park State hosp, Kings Park NY 60-. 9: MedLA; SLA; ALA (Bd 65-66) -AHIL (chm Spec Proj 67-68, chm Lib Standards Com 68-69); NYLA (chm Spec Com for Inst Libs 65-66); SuffolkCoLA (Bd 69). 13: Yes. 14: Med lib serv, lib serv to emotionally disturbed child & adult. 15: 147-64B Lake Shore dr, Lake Ronhonpoma, Long Island NY 11779.

LYONS, SISTER RITA CLAIRE CSC. b Chicago 7 Ap 09. 5: Ste Mary's Col (Notre Dame Ind) 26-30 (Eng, Soc Sci) BA; Col Ste Catherine 33-34 (LS) BS; UMich summers 47-50 (LS) MA; Ind U summer 68, 69. 7: Asst libn Saint Mary's Col (Notre Dame Ind) 34-38, Libn 38-. 8: Assoc Prof of child lit, Saint Mary's Col, Notre Dame Ind. 9: ALA; CathLA; IndLA; Midwest Acad Lib Conf. 14: Ref, rare bks. 15: Lib Saint Mary S Col, Notre Dame In 46556.

LYONS, PATRICIA LOUISE. b Wash DC 11 O 42. 5: Rosemont Col 60-64 (Math) BA; Amer U 65 9computer Tech); Villanova 65-67 MSLS; Wash U 67-68 (Computer Sci). 6: Fr. 7: Statistical clk Nat Inst of Health, Bethesda Md summers 61-63, Statistician 64-65; Circ asst Rosemont Col 65-67, Gen asst libn summers 66, 67; Trainee computer libnship Wash U (St Louis) 67-68; Asst libn & instr in lib sci Quincy Col 68-. 8: Lib consul, Sch of the Holy Child, Sharon Hill Penn 67. 9: ALA; CathLA; MedLA; ASIS. 10: AAUP. 14: Ref, lib admin, lib educ, computer applications in lib. 15: Quincy College Lib, Quincy Il 62301.

LYONS, SISTER ROSE IRMA (MARY CATHARINE). b Great Falls Mont 5 Ja 1899. 5: Creighton 22-26 (Educ) BA; UWash 30-34 (Romance Lang) MA; Rosary Col 44-48 (LS) BA; Catholic U 64-65 (LS) MS. 6: Fr, Ger, Lat, Sp. 7: Elem sch prin St Francis Xavier Missoula Mont 29-31; High sch prin: St Thomas, Great Falls Mont 33-46, Sacred Heart Acad, Missoula Mont 46-52; Supt Lourdes Acad, Wallace Ida 52-58; Exec v-pres Col of Great falls 58-60, Chm exec committee bd of trustees 61-64, Act pres 60-61, Asst libn 64-. 9: Nat Cath Educ Soc (chm Regl Com); ALA; CathLA; MontLA. 13: Yes. 14: Catlg, ref. 15: Col of Great Falls, 1301 20th st S, Great Falls Mt 59401.

LYSEK, PAUL. b Jaworzynka Poland 27 Ag 14. 5: UCracow (Poland) 36-39 (Hist, Sociol, Polish) Equiv BA; Birmingham U (England) 41-42 (Eng, Hist) Certif; Tchrs' Course (London) 45-46 (Pedagogy, Hist, Lit) Certif; Kent State 49-51 (Hist, LS) MA, MALS. 6: All Slavonic except Russian, Ger, Gk, Lat. 7: Polish Army in Eng 40-49; Educ organizer Polish Min of Educ, England 45-49; Dir & tchr in Polish High Sch, Eng; Libn foreign collection Cleveland Pub Lib 51-52; Asst to libn, head of Res Lib Queens Col (NY) 52-. 8: Serving on Ed Bd for Veritas Publ in London (transl of Summa Theologica by St Thomas Aquineas). 9: NY Lib Club. 10: V-pres of Polish Popular Univ in NY; Phi Beta Kappa; Polish Inst Arts & Scis, NY & London; Mem of Polish Writers Assn in Exile. 12: "Z Istebnej w swiat," From Istebna into the World (London 60); "Poszlo na marne," Gone with the Dust (London 65); "Przy granicy," Next to the Border (London 66). 13: Yes. 14: Ref. 15: Queens Col Lib, Flushing NY 11367.

LYTLE, MARGUERITE SARAH. b Phila 2 Je 24. 5: Ursinus Col 42-46 (Eng) AB; Drexel 55-58 MS in LS. 7: Libn: Ambler Pub Lib, Ambler Penn 46-60; Shady Grove Jr High Sch, Ambler Penn 60-62; Wissahickon Sr High Sch, ambler Penn 62-; Lib coord Wissahickon Sch Dist 68-. 8: Lib/USA, NY World's Fair 65. 9: ALA; NEA; PennLA; SchLA of Montgomery & Chester Cos; Phila Dist LA (pres 55-56); PennEA; Lib Pub Rel Assn Greater Phila; Phila Bksellers' Assn. 10: Beta Phi Mu; Phi Kappa Phi. 14: Child & yp serv, ref. 15: Morgan House 9B, Stenton ave & Mermaid lane, Phila Pa 19118.

M

MA, FRED Y M. b Kwangtung China 7 Ap 21. 4: Harriet Kwang. 5: Sun Yat-sen U (China) 42-45 (Law) BLL; UMinn 50-52 (Pol Sci) MA, 52-53 BSLS. 6: Chinese. 7: Law clerk Mei-hsien Dist Court, China 45-46; Law clerk Tungkwan Dist Court, China 46-47; Tchr Kwang-ya High Sch, Canton China 47-49; Catlgr Kan State U Lib 53-56, Order libn 56-57; U Libn Kan Wesleyan U 57-60; Head catlgr UNoIowa 60-. 9: ALA; IowaLA. 10: AAUP; United World Federalists. 13: Yes. 14: Catlg. 15: Univ of Northern Ia Lib, Cedar Falls Ia 50613.

MA, HUNG-HSIANG (HARRY). b China 1 Je 34. 4: Hsin-Kai L Mia. 5: Nat TaiwanU 54-58 (Hist) BA; Seton HallU 63-65 (Asian Studies) MA; Columbia 67-69 MLS. 6: Chinese, japanese, Ger. 7: Interpreting off Liaison Bureau Min of Natl Def, Taiwan 58-60; Asst ed Continental Biweekly, Taiwan China 60-62; Research fellow Hist Dept Queens Col 65-66; Lib asst East Asian Lib Columbia 66-67; Libn Recording for the Blind, NYC 69-. 9: ALA. 10: Chinese Student Club; Hist Soc of Nat TaiwanU. 13: Yes. 14: Ref, admin. 15: 215 E 58th st, New York NY 10022.

MA, JOHN T. b Wenchow China 22 F 20. 4: May Hoo. 5: Nat Central U 39-44 (Foreign Lit & Lang) BA; Post- Grad Sch of Journalism 44-45 (Journalism) MJ; UWis 47-48 (Journalism) MA; Columbia 56-58 MLS. 6: Chinese. 7: (1st Lt) Interpreter-codeman Amer Volunteers' Group, China 40-41; Ed Internat Dept, Chinese Ministry of Info 44-47; Peiping rep Govt Pub Rel Off 45-46; Assoc libn Missionary Research Lib, NYC 58-61; Chinese bibliog-catlgr Cornell U Lib 61-65; Curator-libn E Asian Collection Hoover Inst Stanford U 65-. 8: Ed Chinese Hist Proj UWash 55-56; Tech consul Douglas Advanced Res Lab, McDonnell-Douglas Corp 68-. 9: Assn Asian Studies (Com of East Asian Libs; chm Subcom on Chinese Materials). 12: "Current Periodicals in Missionary Research Library" (61); "Elementary Chinese for American Librarians" (63). 13: Yes. 14: East Asian collection. 15: East Asian Collection Hoover Inst, Stanford Ca 94305.

MAAG, ALBERT F. b Newark NJ 24 Ja 41. 7: Tchr Newark NJ Bd of Educ 62-65, Libn 65-67; Asst libn Lucerne Co Community Col 67-69; Lib dir Harcum Jr Col 69-. 9: ALA. 14: Admin acad libs. 15: Harcum Junior College, Bryn Mawr Pa 19010.

MAAR, GEORGIANA. b Wallkill NY 15 My 06. 5: State U Col of Educ (Albany NY) 23-27 (Eng) AB, summers 27-35 BS in LS; NYU 43 (Childhood Educ) MA. 7: Tchr of Eng & libn Brownville-Glen Park High Sch 27-29; Tchr of Eng & libn Red Hook High Sch, Red Hook NY 29-35; Libn Stratford Ave Sch, Garden City NY 35-; Instr UBuffalo summer 39-40; Instr St John's U (Brooklyn NY) summer 45-47; Instr Queens Col (NY) summer 58, 63, 65. 8: Consul for "Junior Libraries" 54-60. 9: NEA; ALA; NY State Tchrs Assn; NYLA (pres 62). 10: AAUW; Friends of Garden City Lib. 14: Child wk. 15: 205 Whitehall blvd, Garden City NY 11530.

MAAS, NELL STUART (STOY). b Leitchfield Ky 29 Ag 07. 4: Harold A Maas. 5: UWash 24-29 (Hist) BA Tchg Certif, 61-62 MLS. 6: Fr, Sp. 7: Asst libn Seattle Pub Lib Greenwood Br 62-65, 1st asst libn University Br 65-, Hd libn Columbia Br 66-67, Sr libn lit dept Centr al Lib 68-69. 9: PNLA; Wash State La. 12: Ed "Flash," SPL publ (67-69). 14: Ref wek with young adults. 15: 1720 Magnolia way W, Seattle Wa 98199.

MAASS, ELEANOR GRACE (ANDERSON). b Champaign Ill 17 S 19. 4: Alfred R Maass. 5: UIll 37-41 (Chem) BA, 41-42 (Chem) MS; UWis 42-43, 46-49 (Biochem) PhD; Drexel 64- (Info Sci). 6: Russian, Fr, Ger. 7: (Lt jg) USNR (WR) US Naval Reserve 43-46; Asst in chem Swarthmore Col 53-55; Abstractor & ed Medical Literature Inc, Phila 60-63; Asst in chem Haverford Col 61-63; Sci libn Swarthmore Col 63-. 9: ACS; ALA-ACRL; SLA. 12: Tr Oparin's "Genesis and Evolution Development of Life" (69). 13: Yes. 14: Sci libnship, lib automation. 15: 415 Cornell ave, Swarthmore Pa 19081.

MAASS, ERNEST. b Stettin Germany 29 My 14. 4: Ann Blum. 5: Heidelberg, Munich, Berne, Perugia Us 32-33 (Langs); Brooklyn Col 38-40 (Eng) BA; Columbia 40-41 BLS, 51-52 (Pol Sci); NYU 52-55 (Pol Sci) MA. 6: Fr, Ger, Ital, Sp, Hebrew. 7: Ed asst Bompiani Publishers, Milano 34-36; Off asst CIT Travel Agency, Jerusalem 36-38; Ref & catlg asst Zionist Archives & Lib, NY 41-43; Magazine ed El Indicador Industrial, NY 46-48; Magazine ed Amer Jewish Com, NY 49; Research asst Japan Intern Christ U, NY 50; UN Lib: Ser records reviser 51-53, Libn Security Coun Lib 53-56, Gifts & exch libn 56-60, Interlib loan libn 61-63, Indexer 64-. 10: Columbia Lib Sch Alumni Assn; Amer Name Soc; Propylaea Soc Brooklyn Col. 12: Free-lance writing. 13: Yes. 14: Bibliog. 15: 150-76 Village rd apt GB, Jamaica NY 11432.

MABIE, MARGARET IRENE (HUME). b Oxnard Cal 28 Jl 16. 5: URedlands 33-37 (Econ) AB; So Ore Col 49-53 (Elem Educ) BS; UWash 59-64 MLS. 7: Coos Co Dist: Clerk, Bridge Ore 47-49, Prim tchr, Broadbent Ore 49-50; Prim tchr, Myrtle Point Ore 50-60, High sch libn, Myrtle Point Ore 60-65; Libn Lane Co Dist McKenzie River Schs, Finn Rock Ore 65-68; Libn Lathop High Sch, Fairbanks Alaska 68-. 9: NEA-DAVI; ALA; OreLA; OreEA; OreASchL (chm dist 5); Ore Lib trustee Assn (pres); AlaskaLA; AlaskaEA; PNLA. 14: Sch. 15: 655 - 11th ave, Fairbanks Ak 99701.

MABLEY, ELWOOD L(ENOIR). b Roseburg Ore 14 Jl 23. 4: Virginia Miller. 5: Walla Walla Col 42-48 (Modern Lang) BA; USoCal 57-59 MS in LS. 6: Sp. 7: Tchr Auburn Acad, Auburn Wash 48-51; Tchr-libn Glendale Union Acad, Glendale Cal 51-56; Asst libn La Sierra Col 56-58; Dir Libs Walla Walla Col 68-. 9: ALA; NLA. 14: Tech serv, admin. 15: 512 SE 5th st, College Place Wa 99324.

MABSON, REV ROBERT L. b New Orleans 17 Ap 31. 4: Minnie Lewis. 5: Tulane 49-52 (Hist) BA; Union Theol Sem 52-55 (Theol); Presbyterian Sch of Christian Educ 54-55 MRE; LSU 63-64 (LS) MS. 6: Sp, Grk. 7: Pastor Mt Pleasant Presbyterian Church, Sinks Grove WVa 55-57; Coordinator of Barbee Mem Larger Parish, Mexico Mo 57-59; Missionary to Choctaw Indians, Talihina Okla 59-63; Head Libn Methodist Col (Fayetteville NC) 64-66; Pastor Eastland Presbyt Ch, Memphis Tenn 66-; Asst libn (catlg) Memphis Theol Sem, Memphis Tenn 67-. 9: ALA; NCLA; SELA; ATheolLA; TennLA. 10: Ordained minister, Presbyterian Church US; Nat Assn for Retarded Child. 12: "History of Presbyterian Mission Work in Kiamichi Valley, Oklahoma". 14: Catlg, ref. 15: 3940 Pikes peak, Memphis Tn 38108.

MACALL, SUSAN AYERS. b Detroit Mich 4 N 44. 6: Fr. 7: Departmental libn (Philos) UWis 68; Libn Col Stud Personnel Inst, Claremont Cal 68-. 9: ALA; SLA; ASIS. 10: Phi Alpha Theta. 14: Soc scis, ref, info ret, acquis. 15: 1250 N Harvard apt C, Claremont Ca 91711.

MacALPINE, HEATHER. b Reading Penn 24 N 41. 5: UKan 59-63 (Spanish, Ed) BS; UCLA 63-64 (Lib serv) MLS. 6: Sp, Fr, Ger. 7: Br libn Ventura Co & City Lib, Simi Cal 64-65; Asst city libn Oceanside Pub Lib, Oceanside Cal 65-67; Ref libn Okla State U Lib 68-. 9: ALA; OklaLA (sec Ref Div 68-69). 14: Ref, child lit, Latin America. 15: 1015 W 4th, Stillwater Ok 74074.

MACAREE, MARY W (ALEXANDER). b Scotland 28 S 22. 4: David Macaree. 5: Aberdeen U 39-43 MA; Aberdeen Train Col for Tchrs 43-44 Tchrs Certif; UBC 58-59, 62-63 BLS. 6: Fr, Lat. 7: Tchr: Stirling (Scotland) Educ Com 44-48, 49-55, Quebec Sch Commsn, Quebec City 48-49, Vanderhoof Sch Dist, BC 56-57, 57-58; Libn UBC 63-68, Hd Forestry-Agric Lib 68-. 9: CanLA; Educ Inst of Scotland; BCLA; PNLA. 10: BC Tchrs Fed. 14: Catlg, ref. 15: Univ of BC Forestry/Agric Lib, Rm 360 MacMillan Bldg, V ancouver 8 BC Can.

MACARTHUR, D JUNE. b Montreal 4 Ag 45. 5: UAlta 63-64 (Sci); U West Ont 65-67 (Eng) BA; McGil 67-69 MLS. 6: Fr, Ger. 7: Libn Mt Allison U summer 68; Libn's asst Loyola U (Montreal) summer 69. 15: 654 Roslyn ave, Westmount Que Can.

MacARTHUR, FRANCES ELIZABETH (MacBAIN). b Seneca Falls NY. 4: Charles A MacArthur. 5: RI Col 36-39 (Elem Educ) BEd; UWis summer 41 (Phys Educ); Kutztown State Col 63-65 (LS) Certified for Elem & High Sch. 7: Tchr Warwick Schs, Warwick RI 39-41, High sch phys educ 41-42; Tchr phys educ Portland Schs, Portland Ore 43-44; Tchr Parkland Sch Dist, Orefield Penn 55-63, Elem libn 63-. 9: NEA; ALA; IRA; Penn State EA; PennSchLA. 10: LWV; YWCA; PTA; Girl Scouts. 14: Elem educ in lib skills. 15: 245 S Whitehall ave, Allentown Pa 18104.

MacARTHUR, ISABELLE (MAY). b Martintown Ont Can. 5: UToronto 41-44 (Hist) BA, 45-46 BLS, 50 (Educ) High Sch Assts Certif, 52-53 (Educ) B Ed. 6: Fr, Sp, Ital, Ger, Lat. 7: Asst libn Ont Dept of Health, Toronto 46-48; Libn on staff Can Dept of Agric, Ottawa 48-50; Tchr-libn Elmvale Dist High Sch, Elmvale Ont 50-52; Tchr-libn Pickering Dist High Sch, Pickering Ont 52-53; Libn Brantford Collegiate Inst, Brantford Ont 53-61; Libn Emery Collegiate Inst, Weston Ont 61-64; Chief Libn Emery Jr-Sr High Sch, Weston Ont 64-. 9: ALA; CanLA; OntLA; Inst Prof Libns Ont. 10: Ont Secon Sch Tchrs Fed; YWCA. 13: Yes. 14: Sch libs. 15: P O Box 161, Richmond Hill Ont Can.

MacARTHUR, MARIT (SINNESS). b Old Hickory Tenn 4 Je 44. 4: Robert William MacArthur III. 5: EmoryU 62-64; UNC (Chapel Hill) 64-66 (Hist) AB (honors); Peabody Col 66-67 MLS. 6: Fr. 7: Ref libn Georgia State Col Lib, (Atlanta Ga) 67-. 9: GaLA; SELA. 14: Ref, bibliog. 15: 658 Clifton rd NE, Atlanta Ga 30307.

MacBRIDE, HARVEY. b Plainfield NJ 4 Ag 31. 4: Ruth Jean Parkerson. 5: Houghton Col 61-62; Pace Col 62 (Hist); Queens Col (NY) 63; State U Col (Geneseo NY) 63-65 (LS) BS Ed; SUNY (Albany) 66-67 MLS; ColgateU 68 (Sch Admin). 7: Systems analyst Bankers Trust Co, NYC 56-61; Elem libn Schenectady Sch System, Schenectady NY 65-66; Libn Curriculum Enrichment Ctr, Norwich NY 67-69. 9: East Libns Assn; NYLA. 14: Data processing. 15: West Onenta NY 13861.

MacCALLUM, ALICE (POST). b Highland Park Mich 24 My 21. 4: Frederick J MacCallum. 5: Hillsdale Col 38-42 (Sociol) AB; UMich 62-65 MALS. 7: Draftsman (Detailer) Ford motor Co, Detroit 42-48; Clerk Chrysler Corp, Highland Park 48-51; Pre-prof libn Detroit pub Lib Redford Br 62-65, Libn I 65-67, Libn II Redford & Edison Br 67-. 8: Instr St Johns U 51-52; Visiting lecturer USoCal summer 58; Expert-Consul Lib Serv Br Off of Educ, Wash DC summer 60; Ed Adv Bd "Science Quarterly 64; ALA Observer, Conf of Non-Govtal Orgs, US Mission to UN 54-57 Mem NDEA Inst, Simmons Col 66. 9: ALA. 14: Ref. 15: 17259 Beaverland, Detroit Mi 48219.

MacCAMPBELL, JAMES C. b Plain City Ohio 17 O 16. 4: Barbara Barrett. 5: Ohio Wesleyan U 35-39 (Eng) BA; Ohio State U 46 (Eng, Educ) MA, 50-53, 57 (Eng, Educ, Admin) PhD; Simmons 61-62 (LS) MS. 6: Fr. 7: Tchr Delaware City Schs, Delaware Ohio 39-43; Prin Lucas Co Pub Schs, Holland Ohio 43-44; Prin Erie Co Pub Schs, Sandusky Ohio 44-46; Supv Painesville City Schs, Painesville Ohio 46-48; Asst dir-Asst Prof of educ U Sch Kent State U 48-50; Instr in educ Ohio State U 50-52; Dir of elem educ Cleveland Heights City Sch Dist, Cleveland 52-56; Prof of Educ UMe 57-65; U Libn 62-; Prof of Lib Serv & Chm Dept of Lib Serv. 8: Consul to State Depts of Educ in Ohio & Maine. 9: ALA-ACRL; NEA; Ohio Assn for Supv & Curr Development (pres 49-51); MeLA (pres 65-67); NELA. 10: AAUP; NE Reading Assn. 12: Readings in the Language Arts in the Elementary School (64); Focus on Reading, New England School Development Council (with Eleanor Peck) (64); Ed New England Reading Association Newsletter, 58-65. 14: Ref, tech serv, admin. 15: 12 Mainewood ave, Orono Me 04473.

MacCANN, DONNARAE (THOMPSON). b Culver City Cal 24 O 31. 4: Richard Dyer MacCann. 5: Santa Monica City Col 49-51 (Music); UCLA 51-54 (Internat Rel) BA; UCal(Berkeley) 54-55 MLS. 7: Child libn Los Angeles Pub Lib, La Cienega Br 55-57; Head Libn U Elem Sch UCLA 57-66; Instr Arts & Humanities Ext 59-65, Lectr dept Eng 63-64; Child libn Los Angeles Pub Lib, Los Angeles C al 55-57. 8: Instr child lit Univ Ext UCLA 61, 62, 65; Lecturer Eng Dept fall 63; Consul: UCal Wr iter's Consultation Serv 64-; Addison-Wesley Publ Co, Reading Mass 67-. 9: ALA-CSD (Preconf Group Leader 65 Convention); Newberry-Caldecott Prize Com; CalLA (program chm, child & yp sect, 64) 09; ALA-CSD (Preconf Group Leader 65 Convention); Newberry-Caldecott Prize Com; CalLA (Program chm Child & Yp Sect 64). 11: ALA Dutton-Macrae Award 63. 12: "The Child, the Artist and the Book" (62). 13: Yes. 14: Child lit. 15: 1015 Avalon rd, Lawrence Ks 66044.

MacCONOMY, EDWARD N(ELSON) JR. b Munith Mich 19 N 16. 4: Alma Deane Fuller. 5: William & Mary 34-38 (Pol Sci) BA; UMd 38-40, 43 (Pol Sci) MA; UMich 48-49, 51 MALS, 55-58, 62 (Pol Sci) PhD. 6: Fr, Ger, Classical Gk. 7: Lib asst LC 40-45, Analyst in Amer Nat Govt 45-60; Libn Albion Col 61-63; Chief Stack & Reader Div LC 63-65, Asst chief Gen Ref & Bibliog Div 65-. 8: Assoc Prof of Pol Sci Albion Col 62-63. 9: Amer Pol Sci Assn; Amer Hist Assn; ALA-ACRL; Lib Assn (Gt Brit); BSA; Bibliog Soc (London); DCLA; Bibliog Soc UVa. 10: AAUP; Episcopal Church; Phi Beta Kappa; Omicron Delta Kappa; Beta Phi Mu. 12: "The Political Thought of William Temple, Archbishop of York, 1928-1942"; "Archbishop of Canterbury, 1942-1944" (63). 13: Yes. 14: Ref, admin, col & univ libs. 15: 507 Woodland ter, Alexandria Va 22302.

MacDONALD, BERNICE. b Beacon NY 30 Ap 30. 5: Simmons 48-52 (LS) BS; Columbia 55-56 (Adult aduc) MA. 7: Libn NYC Pub Lib 52-54, Sr libn 54-59, Supv libn 59-62, Prin libn 62-66, Coord libn 66-. 9: ALA; AEAUSA; NYLA; NY Lib Club. 12: "Literary Activities in Public Libraries" (ALA 66). 13: Yes. 14: Adult serv, pub lib, adult educ. 15: 1245 Park ave, New York NY 10028.

MacDONALD, BEVERLEY JOAN. b Hamilton Ont Can 20 Ap 42. 4: R Douglas MacDonald. 5: McMaster U 60-63 (Eng, Hist) BA; UToronto 64-65 BLS. 6: Fr. 7: BA asst McMaster U 63-64, Catlgr I 65-66; Catlgr I Brock U 66-67, Catlgr II (dept hd) 67-. 9: ALA; Inst prof Libns Ont. 10: Beta Phi Mu. 14: Catlg. 15: 14 Springbank dr, St Catharines Ont Can.

MacDONALD, CHAS WILLIAM. b Cornwall Ont Can 29 S 23. 5: Sir George Williams 57-61 (Eng) BA; McGill 61-62 BLS. 7: Ref London Pub Lib (Ont) 62-63, Head bkmobs 63-65; Ser libn Simon Fraser U 65-. 9: CanLA; ALA; Inst Profess Libns Ont; BCLA. 12: "Report on a Survey of Mobile Library Service" (64). 14: Ser, computer applications. 15: Lib Simon Fraser U, Burnaby 2 BC Can.

MacDONALD, ELSIE SINCLAIR. b Pittsburgh 20 S 04. 5: Purdue U 23-27 BS; Carnegie 28-29 BS in LS. 7: DC Pub Lib: Ref child libn 29-33, Asst child libn 33-35, Asst to dir, wk with child 35-48, Supv schs div 48-52, Bibliog consul schs div 52-56, Asst coordinator child serv 56-. 15: DC Pub Lib, Wash DC 20001.

MACDONALD, FRANCES (BARNETT). b Homer Ind 7 N 11. 5: Detroit City Col 29-32; UMich 32-36 (Pre-Lib) AB; West ResU 37 BS in LS. 6: Ger, Fr. 7: Stud asst Catlg Div UMich 34-36; Asst to Dean West ResU summer 37; Catlgr Mich State Col 37-41; Clerk typist Detroit Pub Lib 29-32, Catlgr 42; Treasurer sec First Christian Church, Shelbyville Ind 50-61; Mss libn Ind State Lib 62-. 9: IndLA. 10: Internatl Travel Study Club. 14: Mss, ref, Indiana hist. 15: 1807 N Layman, Indianapolis In 46218.

MacDONALD, GRACE (N). b Syracuse NY 13 O 11. 4: John W MacDonald. 5: Syracuse 29-32 (Lat, Eng) AB, 32-36 BLS. 6: Fr, Lat. 7: Eng tchr-libn Warners High Sch, Warners NY 32-33; Eng tchr-libn Elbridge High Sch, Elbridge NY 33-36; Libn-ref circ Binghamton Pub Lib, Binghamton NY 36-38; Libn Jr-Sr High Sch, Syracuse (NY) 56-57; Ref libn Syracuse U Sch System 57-59, Rare bk catlg libn 59-62; Dir of Lib Onondaga Commun col 62-. 8: Informal consulships with Libns of beginning 2-yr cols of NY. 9: ALA; SLA; NYLA; NY State U Libns Assn; Central NY Ref & Resources Coun. 10: Bus & Prof Women's Club; Women of Rotary; Faculty Wives Assn; AAUW; Civic Morning Musicals; Crouse-Irving Auxiliary; Eng Speaking Union; Frie nds of Reading; Amer Assn Jr Cols. 14: Ref, rare bks, admin. 15: Onondaga Commun Col Lib 700 E Water st, Syracuse NY 13210.

MacDONALD, HARRIET P. b SI, NY 29 S 29. 5: UMd 51-52 (Admin & Supv); Wagner Col 47-51 (Elem Educ) BS, 57-59 (Elem Educ) MS; Rutgers 65-68 MLS. 7: Tchr Bridgewater Township Bd of Educ, Finderne NJ 52-55; Tchr NYC Bd of Educ PS 28, Staten Island NY 55-64; Tch of Lib NYC Bd of Educ PS 23, Staten Island NY 64-. 9: NEA; ALA; NYCLA; SITA; SI Reading Assn. 10: Wagner Col Alum Assn. 14/ child bks. 15: 281 Decker ave, Staten Island NY 10302.

MACDONALD, HUGH. b Oneonta NY 30 Mr 42. 5: Yale 60-64 (Eng) BA; Columbia 65-66 MLS. 6: Fr. 7: Asst ref libn Columbia 66, Ref libn for rare books 66-. 10: Friends of ColumbiaU Libs. 13: Yes. 14: Rare bks & mss. 15: 654 Butler Lib Columbia Univ, New York NY 10027.

MacDONALD, JANET ANN. b St Paul Minn 21 Ap 42. 5: LawrenceU 59-63 (Classics) BA; Simmons 66-67 (LS) MS. 6: Gk, Lat, Ger. 7: Classics libn UCincinnati 67-. 9: OhioLA. 10: UCincinnati Lib Staff Assn. 14: Research collections, rare bks. 15: 2805 Stratford, Cincinnati Oh 45220.

MacDONALD, LORNA (JEAN). b Montreal Can 16 Jl 27. 5: McGill 44-48 BA, 48-49 BLS. 6: Fr. 7: Ref libn Brooklyn Pub Lib 49-50, Ref libn sci & ind 50-54, Asst chief sci & ind 54-60, Chief sci & ind 61-62; Libn NY Med Col Psychiatry Lib 68-. 9: SLA; MedLA. 14: Ref. 15: 140 Willow st, Brooklyn NY 11201.

MacDONALD, MARGOT. b NYC 19 Ap 19. 4: Dorsey L. 5: Pomona Col 36-40 BA. 6: Fr, Sp, Ger. 7: Period & documents libn Pomona Col Lib 40-41; Chief travelers censorship div US Off of Censorship, Los Angeles 41-45; Asst job printing div Pomona Progress Bulletin, Pomona Cal 45-46; Ser & documents libn Pomona Col Lib 46-52; Asst libn in chg of pub serv Honnold Lib for the Claremont Cols 52-57, Documents libn 57-. 9: ALA (Dupl Exch Union Com 52-56; chm 53-54); -ACRL; CalLA (State Documents Com 55, Regl Resources Coord Com 53-55). 10: AAUW. 14: Documents. 15: 1070 Cascade pl, Claremont Ca 91712.

MacDONALD, MARY JANE. b Springfield Ill 11 Ag 25. 5: UIll 43-46 (Pol Sci) BA, 47-48 BS in LS. 7: Jr asst bus & econ dept Enoch Pratt Free Lib, Baltimore 48-50; Ref libn Yakima Valley Reg Lib, Yakima Wash 50-52; Research libn Fed Reserve Bank of Kan City, Kan City Mo 52-56; Com libn UIll Lib (Urbana) 56-62; Asst ref dept Ill State Lib 62-63, Head documents unit 63-66, Chief research & ref sect 66-68, Hd doc unit 68-. 9: ALA; SLA (2d v-pres 54-55); IllLA. 10: Beta Phi Mu. 14: Bus libs, documents. 15: 2825 So Lincoln, Springfield Il 62704.

MacDONALD, RODERICK. b Minneapolis 13 Mr 31. 4: Joanne Gaffney. 5: Macalester Col 49-52 (Pol Sci) BA; UMinn 58-59 (LS) MA. 6: Fr. 7: (Cpl) Steno Med Div Communications Sect US Army, Orleans France 54-55; Documentation clerk Internat Milling Co, Minneapolis 55-56; Cryptographer US Dept of State, Paris 56-57; City Libn Free Pub Lib, Kaukauna Wis 59-61; Ref libn Macalester Col 61-66; Dir Anoka Co Lib, Blaine Minn 66-69; Dir Pub Lib, Des Moines Iowa 69. 9: MinnLA (chm Ref Sect; pres 67-68); ALA. 10: Friends of Minneapolis Pub Lib. 14: Ref. 15: 4817 Second ave So, Minneapolis Mn 55409.

MacDONALD, RUTH (LAKE). b Buffalo NY. 4: Ernest R MacDonald. 5: UBuffalo 30-34 (Hist, Govt) BA, 35-37 (LS) BS; SUNY (Buffalo) 55-57 Masters in Higher Educ; Syracuse, Temple Columbia 60-67. 6: Fr. 7: Libn Gowanda High Sch, Gowanda NY 35-37; Supv libn Vestal Central Sch Syst, Vestal NY 37-41; Investigator USA, Buffalo NY 42-43; Libn Buffalo & Erie Co Pub Lib, Buffalo NY 43-44; Head libn Amherst Central High Sch, snyder NY 45-47; Instr & Field Supervisor SUNY (Geneseo) 40-57; Lect SUNY (Buffalo) 66-; Lect Erie Commun Col 66-; Hd libn Erie Co Tech Inst 47-. 8: In-Serv Training Prog, Pioneer Lib System 69, Lib Tech Program, SUNY 67, Consul; Reading Task Force, Amherst Sch Syst 66, Adv Com SUNY Presidents Lib Com 63. 9: SLA (chm Metals/Materials Div 68-69; pres Upstate NY Chap 56-57); ALA (Jr Col Div); IRA Exec Bd Niagara Frontier Chap; Col Reading Assn; NYLA (Col & Univ Sect; secy-treas 68-70). 10: Pi Lambda Theta; Amherst Bus & Profess Womens' Club. 13: Yes. 14: Admin, jr col devel in libs, lib tech prog, reading improvement. 15: 85 Yorktown rd, Snyder NY 14226.

MacDONALD, VIRGINIA. b Fitzgerald Ga. 5: UAla 33-34 (Hist, Eng) AB; UWis 34-35 (LS) Diploma; UCal(Berkeley) summer 39 (LS). 6: Fr, Sp. 7: Asst libn Mansfield State Tchrs Col 35-37; Chief Libn Missouri Valley Col 37-41; US Govt Army & Navy Libs 41-61; Nat Cancer Inst NIH, Bethesda Md 61-63; Ref libn NLM 63-. 9: MedLA. 10: Alpha Phi. 14: Ref, admin. 15: 4949 Battery lane apt 420, Bethesda Md 20014.

MacDONALD, VIVIAN J. b Greenfield Ind 25 Ap 1897. 4: James F MacDonald. 5: IndianaU 15-16, 27 (Eng); Carnegie Lib Sch 27-28 Certif; Carnegie Inst 28-37 (Liberal arts); Penn State U 39 (Russian); UPittsburgh 44-45 (Hist). 6: Ger, Fr, Ital, Russian. 7: Tchr, Braeburn Penn 17-19; Shipping clk Aluminum Co of Amer, New Kensington 19-27; Libn: Alcoa Research Labs, New Kensington 28-62, West Oenn Conservancy, Pittsburgh 67-. 9: SLA (chm Chem Sect); Pittsburgh SLA (pres, Bull ed, sec). 10: Bus & Prof women; Girl Scouts; Concert Assn; Civic Theater. 13: Yes. 14: Ref. 15: 1225 Taylor ave, New Kensington Pa 15068.

MacDONALD, ZULA ZON (FOSTER). b Gonzales Co Tex 30 Je 04. 5: Stephen F Austin State Tchrs Col 28, 29; Our Lady of the Lake Col 30-31; Tex Woman's U 32-33 (LS) BS; St Mary's U 39-40 (Educ) MA; Peabody 65-66 MLS. 6: Fr. 7: Tchr pub schs of Tex 23-28; Libn San Antonio Ind Sch Dist, San Antonio Tex 33-63; Assoc Prof Dept of Lib Sci Baylor U summers 54-63, 63-67, Prof & Chm of Dept of Lib Sci Baylor U 67-. 8: Ext Div of San Antonio Pub Lib summers 45-47. 9: ALA-AASchL; Am Lib Educ Assn (sec-treas); SWLA; TexLA (Nat Lib Week Com Dist 8, sec-treas Dist 7); Tex Coun Lib Educ. 10: AAUP; Beta Phi Mu. 13: Yes. 14: Catlg, ref, child & yp lit. 15: 304 Guittard dr, Waco Tx 76706.

MacDONELL, PHYLLIS A. b Olean NY 9 D 27. 4: Herbert L MacDonell. 5: SUNY (Geneseo) 46-50 (LS) BS; Milton Col 53 (Eng, Speech) BA; Whitewater State Col (Wis) summer 53. 7: Asst libn Alfred U 50-51; Sec to pres Milton Col 52; Elem tchr Milton Sch Dist, Milton Wis 53-54; Documents libn URI 54-56; Act head circ dept Swarthmore Col Lib 56-57; Catlg & ref libn Corning Glass Wks, Corning NY 57-64, Libn ext info 64-65; Libn Col Center of the Finger Lakes, Corning NY 65-. 9: ALA; SLA; ADI; NY State LA. 10: AAUW. 13: Yes. 14: Catlg. 15: Box 1111, Corning NY 14830.

MacDONOUGH, HELEN MARIE. b Brooklyn NY 8 N 13. 5: Adelphi 29-33 (Sp) BA; Columbia 38-40 (Libnship) MLS. 6: Sp, Fr. 7: Asst Freeport Memorial Lib, Freeport NY 33-38; Child libn Baldwin Pub Lib, Baldwin NY 38-40, Lib dir 40-. 8: Interviewer on regular radio program of local authors, Station WHLI 48-50. 9: ALA; LPRC; NYLA; NassauCoLA (sec 43-44, pres 45-47). 10: Bladwin Civic Assn; Friends of the Baldwin Pub Lib. 12: Ed "Odds and Book Ends," NassauCoLA (48-50). 13: Yes. 14: Child & adult serv. 15: 159 Smith st, Freeport NY 11520.

MacDOUGALL, FRANK CHATTERTON. b Detroit 6 Ja 28. 4: Nathalie Tonkonogy. 5: Mich State U 47-51 (Art) BA;

UMich 57-60 MALS; Mich State U 65- (Art). 6: Fr. 7: S 1/c (radioman) US Navy, USS Shannon 46-47; Clerk Mich State U Lib 51-54; Commercial artist Grafek Art Forum, Lansing 54-55; Head Mich State U Lib fine arts div 55-60, Libn humanities div 60-63; Head Continuing Educ Lib, E Lansing Mich 63-. 8: Highway Research Bd (TO-6(5) Com (traffic safety libns) mem Temporary Steering Com 69-. 9: ALA-ACRL (chm ACRL/ULS Ext Lib Serv Com 68-); SLA; MichLA (chm Personnel Policies Com 67-, chm Ext Lib Serv RT 68-); Coun Planning Libns. 10: Internat Soc for Commun Development; Lansing Art Guild; Lansing Commun Art Gallery; Metro Lansing Fine Arts Coun. 12: "Readings for Michigan's Active Citizens; A Select Bibliography on P olitics and Government" (64). 13: Yes. 14: Info ret, computerized lib serv. 15: 707 Garfield Rt 5, Lansing Mi 48917.

MacDOUGALL, RONALD JOSEPH. b Berlin NH 21 Je 31. 5: Plymouth Tchrs Col 49-53 (Eng) B Ed; UNH 56-58 (Eng); Rutgers 61-62 MLS. 6: Fr, Ger. 7: Tchr Weare High Sch, Weare NH 53-54; Personnel admin spec US Army, Japan 54-56; Tchr Bethlehem High Sch, Bethlehem NH 59-60; Lib asst UNH 60-61; Asst libn & Instr of Eng Gorham State Col 62-. 9: ALA; MeLA. 10: AAUP. 14: Catlg, acquis. 15: Rt 2, Scarborough Me 04074.

MACDOWALL, TRASZHA (RIESS). b Oakland Cal 3 D 25. 4: Fergus Day Hort Macdowall. 5: Stanford 46-49 (Psych) AB; UMich 50-51 (Math); McGill 59-60 BLS, 62-65 MLS. 7: Chief Libn City View Pub Lib, Nepean Twp Ont 56-61; Chief Libn Nepean Twp Pub Lib, Nepean Twp Ont 61-. 9: CanLA; OntLA; Inst Prof Libns Ont. 15: 16 Rowley ave, Ottawa 5 Can.

MacDUFFIE, BRUCE (LINCOLN). b Newburyport Mass 22 My 36. 4: Mary Pauline Slattery. 5: Blackburn Col 54-55, 57-59 (Eng) BA; BostonU 68-69 MEd. 6: Ger. 7: Eng tchr norwood-Norfolk Central Sch, Norwood NY 59-60; Libn Lawrence Acad, Groton Mass 60-63; Eng tchr Elizabethtown-Lewis Central Sch, Elizabethtown NY 63-65; Libn Lenox Sch, Lenox Mass 65-66; Dir lib serv Berk Hills Reg Sch, Gt Barrington Mass 67-69; Dir media serv pub schs, Walpole Mass 69-. 8: Reviewer "Library Journal"; NESDEC (NESLA Jt Com). 9: NEA-DAVI; ALA; BerkshireLA (founder & chm); MassSchLA; NELA; MassLA. 13: Yes. 14: Sch media services, design facilities, development programs. 15: Box 181, Housatonic Ma 01236.

MACE, MARY B. b Detroit 22 S 13. 4: Cyrus L Mace. 5: Smith 31-37 (Hist Art) AB, MA; SUNY(Albany) 65-66 MLS. 7: Asst to dir Smith Col Museum of Art 35-42; Libn St Luke's Hosp Sch of Nursing, Pittsfield Mass 57-63; Libn Med Sci Lib St Luke's Hosp, Pittsfield 63-69; Libn Research & development ctr Sprague Elec Co, N Adams Mass 69-. 08: Memb consul gp for lib serv, Albany Reg Med Prog 68-. 9: SLA; MedLA. 15: Canaan rd, Richmond Ma 01254.

MacEACHERN, JOHN. b Phila 8 Mr 14. 4: Dorothy Hilgert. 5: City Col of NY 32-37 BA; Columbia 46-47 BSLS; Wash State U 51-56 (Hist) MA. 06: Ger. 7: Asst Dept of Pub Wks, NYC 37-46; T-4 US Army 42-46; Desk asst Columbia U 46-47, Sr catlgr 47-48; Head catlgr St Lawrence U 48-50; Chief tech serv div Wash State U 51-65, Asst to the Dir of Libs 66-. 13: Yes. 14: Admin, automation. 15: Rt 2 Box 112-A, Pullman Wa 99163.

MACEY, JOHN FRANCIS. b Marguerite Penn 16 Ja 34. 4: Virginia Kralik. 5: St Vincent Col 52-57 (Philos) BA; UPittsburgh 63-64 MLS, 65- (LS). 7: Tchr Lat, Eng Bellmarette Jt Schs, Belle Vernon Penn 60-64; Catlgr St Vincent Col 64-. 14: Catlg. 15: 242 Monastery dr, Latrobe Pa 15650.

MacFARLAND, KENNETH H. b Rensselaer NY 30 S 04. 4: Lillian F Wilde. 5: SUNY(Albany) 22-26 (Hist) BA; Yale summer 31 (Educ); SUNY(Albany) 33-34 (Educ) MA, 64- (LS). 6: Lat, Fr. 7: Prin Jefferson High Sch, Jefferson NY 27-29; Prin Sharon High Sch, Sharon Conn 29-31; Prin VanRensselaer Jr High Sch, Rensselaer NY 31-43; Supt of Schs, Rensselaer NY 43-64; Asst libn Albany Inst of Hist & Art, Albany NY 64-, ny 31-43; Supt of Schs, Rensselaer NY 43-64; Asst libn Albany Inst of Hist & Art, Albany NY 64; Libn 66-. 9: NEA; SAA; Amer Assn for State & Loc Hist; NY State Tchrs Assn; Rensselaer Co Hist Soc. 10: Rensselaer Co TB & Pub Health Assn; Rensselaer Co Mental Health Assn; Capital Area Sch Development Assn; NY State U Alumni Assn; Rensselaer Kiwanis Club; Amer Red Cross; Kappa Phi Kappa. 14: Mss, archives, loc hist. 15: 705 Wash ave, Rensselaer NY 12144.

MACFARLANE, JOAN (AKIRA). b Los Angeles 15 Je 38. 4: Alexander T Macfarlane. 5: UCal(Los Angeles) 58-60 (Eng Lit) BA; UIll 60-61 (LS) MS. 6: Fr, Ger, Sp. 7: Staff NY Pub Lib 61-62; Catlg libn Columbia U Sch of Soc Wk 62-65; Lib consul Verona Elem Schs, Verona NJ 65-66; Catlg libn Montclair State Col 66-. 9: NY Tech Serv Libns. 10: Beta Phi Mu; NJ State Col Fac Assn. 12: "Subject Headings in Social Welfare" (65). 15: 11 Carlisle rd, Upper Montclair NJ 07043.

MacGREGOR-GREER, MARY (COLEMAN). b Montclair NJ 4 Mr 13. 4: Stephen MacGregor-Greer. 5: McGill 31-35 (Hist, Eng) BA; Lond U Eng 35-36 Lib diploma. 6: Fr. 7: Indexer Imperial Chem Inds, Lond Eng 36-39; Catlgr Seronautical Lib Nat Research Coun, ottawa Ont 60-63; Ref libn Nat Lib, Ottawa Ont 63-66; Libn dept Fisheries & Forestry Forest Research Lab, Victoria BC 66-. 15: Lib Forest Research Lab, 506 W Burnside rd, Victoria BC Can.

MACH, MARGARET (HORA). b Babylon NY 5 Jl 18. 4: Frank J Mach. 5: State U (Albany NY) 35-39 (Eng) BA, 39-45 BS in LS; Columbia 58-61 MS in LS. 6: Fr, Czech. 7: Tchr Oswegatchie High Sch, Oswegatchie NY 39-41; Tchr Stony Point High Sch, Stony Point NY 41-42; Tchr-libn W Babylon Schs, W Babylon NY 42-. 8: Middle States Evaluating Com; Dir of Libs, W Babylon Sch System; Trustee, Islip Pub Lib. 9: ALA; NEA; NYLA; NY State Tchrs Assn; Nassau-Suffolk LA. 10: AAUW. 14: Ref. 15: 228 Cedar ave, Islip NY 11751.

MACHAN, WINIFRED E. b Carlisle Penn 18 Je 11. 4: Leon Machan. 5: Wooster Col 29-33 (Eng, Hist) BA; West Res 54-55 (Child serv) MLS. 7: E Cleveland Pub Lib summer 55; Cleveland Pub Lib summers 56 & 57; Publix Bk Store 57; Libn Cleveland Hts Sch Bd May Hill Arbuthnot Lib Taylor Elem Sch 55-; Instr child lit Case West Res summer 58; Instr child lit Cleveland State U summers & nights 59-. 9: ALA (mem var coms); OhioASchL; NEOhioTA. 13: Yes. 14: Child lit & a-v materials. 15: 3100 Coleridge rd, Cleveland Hts Oh 44118.

MACHOVEC, CHARLES R. b Wahoo Neb 17 N 16. 4: Geraldine Elieff. 5: UNeb 38-47 (Psych) AB, 48 (Psych) MA; UIll 50 (LS) MS; UCLA 59 (Info Storage & Retrieval). 7: (Sgt) Army Air Force, Middle East, China, Burma, India 41-45; Catlgr Penn State U 50-52; Dept libn physics Ohio State U 52-57; Assoc head libn Los Alamos Sci Lab, Los Alamos NM 57-. 8: Ext Educ Rep UNeb, for Men's Reformatory, Lincoln Neb 48. 9: SLA (Rio Grande Chap: Exec Bd, var coms); ALA; ADI; SWLA; NMLA. 13: Yes. 14: Info sci, admin. 15: 3016 B Orange, Los Alamos NM.

MACHOWSKI, RUTH (McHENRY). b Williamsport Penn. 4: Edward Machowski. 5: Allegheny Col 35-36; Carnegie Inst of Tech 36-39 (Ger) BS; Carnegie Lib Sch 40 BLS. 6: Ger. 7: Libn Tarentum High Sch, Tarentum Pa 40-42; US Coast Guard 42-46; Libn Loyola Dental Sch, Chicago 46-50; Libn of PR Dept Standard Oil Co (Ind), Chicago 50-52; Asst libn Niles Pub Lib, Niles Ill 62-. 10: PTA. 13: Yes. 14: Book sel, catlg. 15: 5931 NW cir, Chicago Il 60631.

MACHTLEY, PEGGY JANE (BELL). b Phila Penn 30 Mr 43. 4: Kenneth Austin Machtley. 5: WittenbergU 60-64 (Fr) BA; VillanovaU 65-68 MSLS. 6: Fr, Russan. 7: Sec-linguist Budd Co Intl, Phila 64-65; Asst libn (catlgr) Westchester State Col 65-. 9: PennLA. 14: Catlg (col level). 15: Sankanac Farm RD 1, Elverson Pa 19520.

MACIAS, JULIA. b Lamar Col 12 Ap 27. 5: Mesa Col 48-49 (Nursing). 6: Sp. 7: Asst libn Delta Pub Lib 49-54, Hd libn 55-. 9: ALA; MPLA. 10: Bus & Profess Women. 14: Acquis, catlg, ref. 15: 745 Grand, Delta Co 81416.

MACIOROSKI, SHANNON KAY. b Terry Mont 1 Mr 38. 5: St Mary Col (Xavier Kan) 56-60 (Eng) BA (magna cum laude); Catholic U 60-62, 63 MSLS, 63- (Eng). 6: Fr. 7: Out patient desk receptionist St Vincents Hosp, Billings Mont summers 57-59; Stud asst St Mary Col Lib (Xavier Kan) 56-60; Grad Lib asst Catholic U: Bibliog searcher 60-61, Col Lib asst 61, Act head Col Lib & Head Col Lib 61-64; Head ref & Col Lib Catholic U 64-. 9: DCLA. 10: Delta Epsilon Sigma; Kappa Gamma Phi; Beta Phi Mu. 14: Ref, bk sel, col & univ libs. 15: 1007 Bunker Hill rd NE No 3, Wash DC 20017.

MACIUSZKO, JERZY (GEORGE) J. b Warsaw Poland 15 Jl 13. 4: Danuta Maria Jablonowska. 5: UWarsaw (Poland) 32-37 (Eng Lang & Lit) MA; West Res 52-53 MS in LS, 54-62 (LS, Philos) PhD. 6: Fr, Ger, Polish & other Slavic. 7: Tchr secondary schs, Warsaw Poland 37-39; Sch inspector British Ministry of Educ, London 46-51; Instr Polish Lang & Lit Alliance Col 51-52; Cleveland Pub Lib: Asst for lit dept 53-54, Asst head for lit dept 54-63, Head John G White dept 63-69;

Chm Dept Slavic Studies, Alliance Coll Cambridge Springs Pa 69-. 8: Lecturer Slavic Dept West Res U, Cleveland Ohio 64-. 09; ALA-ACRL (chm Slavic Subsect 67-68); Mod Lang Assn; Amer Assn Tchrs Slavic & East European Langs (pres Ohio Chap 65-66); OhioLA. 10: Polish Inst Arts & Scis; The Kosciuszko Found; Polish Amer Hist Assn; Pres, Cleveland Pub Lib Staff Assn; The Ronfant Club; Slavic Honor Soc. 11: Internat award for best short story, 43, while a prisoner of war in German hands; The Kosciuszko Found Award for Doctoral Diss 67. 12: "The Polish Short Story in English: A Guide and Critical Bibliography" (68). 13: Yes. 14: Ref. 15: 2125 Westburn ave, Cleveland Oh 44112.

MACK, EDNA BALLARD. b Gilmanton NH 23 Ja 09. 4: William Harrison Mack. 5: Chicago 30-32 (Educ) PhB; Syracuse summers 38-41 BS in LS; Chicago 44-47 (LS) MA; UMich 52-57 MA (Ed), PhD (LS). 7: Tchr elem & secondary schs, NH & Conn 26-30, 31-34; Spec asst NH State Lib 34-35; Bk buyer Edson C Eastman Co, Concord NH 35-38; Asst libn & Instr New Haven State Tchrs Col 38-44; Libn Tappan Jr High Sch, Ann Arbor Mich 44-47, & Sr High Sch 51-52; Dir Sch Libs, Lansing Mich 47-50; Visiting Faculty Mem UTenn summers 48, 51; Visiting Faculty Mem West Mich Col of Educ Dept of Libnship summer 49; Lecturer UMich Dept of Lib Sci 52-58, summers 52-61; State U Col (Geneseo NY) Div of Lib Educ: Assoc Prof 58-60, Prof 60-, Act Dir 61-62. 8: Dir NDEA Inst for Sch Libns, SUNY(Geneseo), summer 65; Mem Eval Com for 1965 NDEA Insts for Sch Libns. 9: ALA-AASchL (treas 44-47);-LED (Tchrs Sect: dir 62-64, chm By-Laws Com 64-65); NESchLA (chm 42-44). 10: Delta Kappa Gamma; Pi Lambda Theta ; Beta Phi Mu. 13: Yes. 14: Sch lib serv, pub rel, lib educ, documentation in educ. 15: Sch of Lib Sci Stat e Univ Col, Geneseo NY 14454.

MACK, JAMES DECKER. b Bethlehem Penn 13 Mr 16. 4: Helen Stan ding. 5: Lehigh U 34-38 (Econ) BA; Harvard Law Sch 38-39; Columbia 47-48 (LS); Lehigh U 48-49 (Hist) MA. 6: Fr, Ger. 7: Credit clerk Bethlehem Steel Corp, Bethlehem Penn 39-42; US Navy, Pacific Fleet (Lt) 42-46; Lehigh U: Asst to libn 46-48, Asst libn 48-50, Libn 50-. 8: Middle States Assn evaluation teams. 9: ADI; ALA; CNLA; IATUL (Pres). 10: AHA; Royal Australian Hist Soc; Sixma Xi. 12: "Matthew Flinders" (66); Ed "American Documentation" (62-64). 13: Yes. 14: Info sci, rare bks. 15: Lehigh Univ Lib, Bethlehem Pa 18015.

MACK, SARA (ROHRBACH). b Topton Penn 20 N 21. 5: Kutztown State Col 39-43 (LS) BS; Columbia 50-55 (LS) MS; Temple U 54; UPenn 60, 67. 6: Ger. 7: Elem tchr Chalfont Pub Schs, Chalfont Penn 43-45; Libn Mt Penn- Lower Alsace Jr-Sr High Sch, Reading Penn 49-58; Asst Prof Lib Educ Kutztown State Col 58-. 8: Consul Penn Dept of Pub Instr 63-65; Penn Governor's Com on Quality Educ 65; Encyclopedia Britannica Awards Com for Penn 64-65; W kshop dir, Drexel summer 68; Penn Student Lib Career Wkshop dir 67, 68, 69. 09; ALA-AASchL (Stud Assts Com 60-64); NEA; PennS chLA (sec-treas 59-61, pres 63-65); Penn Stud Lib Assts Assn (Founder 62); PennLA (Nat Lib Week Com 61-62, Recr Com 63-65, 66-69); Penn State EA (Dept of Supv & Curr, East Dist; Prog Com 61-62, chm Nom Com 62). 10: AAUW; Alpha Beta Alpha; Penn German Folklore Soc; Woman's Club; Kappa Delta Pi. 11: Kutztown State Col President's Award for Superior Tchg 62. 12: "Inspirational Readings for Elementary Grades" (64); Ed "Drexel Library Quarterly" (Jl 69). 13: Yes. 14: Bk sel, ref, storytelling. 15: 125 W Palm dr, Topton Pa 19562.

MACK, WILMETTA MAE (STAKE). b Burchard Neb 24 D 19. 4: Harold L Mack. 5: UWyo 57-60 9ls, ed) BS; Catholic U 64-67 MLS. 7: Bkkeeper Lincoln Continental Bank, Lincoln Neb 38-40; Clk Govt, Wash DC 40-43; Receptionist, Pensacola Fla 43-45; Clk typist Soil conservation Serv, Lincoln Neb 46-48; Libn UWyo 60-62; Libn Florissant Jr High Sch, Florissant Mo 62-64; Libn Bacroft Elem Sch, Arlington Va 64-. 9: ALA; Elem Arlington libns (chm 67); ArlingtonEA (Bldg dir 68-69). 10: Wesleyan Serv Guild. 14: Ref, child libn. 15: 5412 No 26th st, Arlington Va 22207.

MacKAY, (GRACE) KAREN. b Shelburne Nova Scotia 3 Jl 42. 5: Acadia 61-65 (Chem) BA; McGill 65-67 MLS. 7: Catlgr Halifax City Reg Lib, Halifax NS 67-. 9: CanLA; HalifaxLA. 14: Catlg, ref. 15: Shelburne, Nova Scotia Can.

MacKAY, JEAN (BERNICE) (REID). b Shelburne Ont Can. 4: George S MacKay. 5: Shaws Bus Sch (Toronto); Toronto even U & sch. 7: Catlgr Toronto Pub Lib 29-39, Order chief order dept 39-42; Maclean Hunter Pub Co, toronto: Asst libn 42-50, Head Libn 51-. 9: SLA; Eaton's Club; Paudash Shores Assn; Mil Engnrs Assn Can Wives Div. 14: Ref. 15: Maclean Hunter Lib 481 University ave, Toronto Ont Can.

MacKELLAR, MARGARET FERGUSON. b Santa Barbara Cal 10 My 20. 5: Santa Barbara State Col 37-41 (Eng Lit) BA; UCal(Berkeley) 41-42 (LS) Certif. 6: Fr. 7: Lib asst Richmond Pub Lib, Richmond Cal 42-43; Asst libn Metropolitan Life Insurance Co, San Francisco 43-47; Libn Anglo Cal Nat Bank, San Francisco 47-51; USIS: Libn Lahore Pakistan 51-53, Reg libn Africa 54-56, Dir of lib serv Tehran Iran 56-58; Ref libn USIA, Wash DC 59-61; Dir of lib serv ACAO USIS Cairo UAR 61-66; Dir lib serv ACAO USIS, Athens Greece 67-. 9: SLA (pres San Francisco Bay Reg Chap 49-50). 15: USIS American Embassy, APO NY 09223.

MacKELLAR, MARILYN (JOY). b Windsor Ont Can 30 Ap 40. 5: U West Ont 59-62 (Eng) BA; Toronto 62-63 BLS. 6: Fr. 7: Libn I London Pub Lib & Art Mus, London Ont 63-65; Libn I Vancouver Pub Lib, Vancouver BC 65-67; Libn Apt III Walworth Secondary Modern Sch, London England 68-69. 9: CanLA; OntLA; Inst Prof Libns, Ont (Asso mem). 14: Child & sch libs. 15: Rt 2, Belmont Ont Can.

MacKENZIE, ALBERTA (ENGLE). b McClure Ohio 20 Ag 18. 4: Arthur J MacKenzie. 5: Otterbein Col 36-40 (Eng) BA; West ResU 40-41 BS in LS. 7: Asst libn Pub Lib, Westerville Ohio 36-40, Child libn 42-44; Stud asst Pub Lib, Cleveland Ohio 40-41; Child libn Pub Lib, Medina Ohio 40-41; Ref libn Otterbein Col Lib (Westerville Ohio) 55-. 9: ALA; OhioLA. 14: Ref. 15: Otterbein College Lib, Westerville Oh 43081.

MacKENZIE, FLORA HELEN. b Calgary Alta Can 20 Jl 18. 5: UCal 41 (Fr) BA, 42-43 (LS) Certif; UDenver summers 59-61 (LS) MA; UDubuque Theol Sem 65-66. 06: Fr, Ger. 7: Asst catlgr Henry E Huntington Lib, San Marino Cal 43-44; Catlgr Huntngton Beach Pub Lib, Huntington Beach Cal 44-46; Catlgr Sutro Br (Cal) State Lib, San Francisco 46-49; Research asst HICOG, Bad Nauheim Germany 49-50; Asst catlgr Los Angeles Co Law Lib, Los Angeles 50-57; Libn Mary Holmes Jr Col 57-64; Catlgr U Dubuque Theol Sem 64-66; Asst catlgr Cal State Polytech Col (San Luis Obispo) 66-. 9: ALA; ATLA; CalLA. 10: AAUW. 14: Catlg. 15: 256 N Chorro st apt 18, San Luis Obispo Ca 93401.

MACKENZIE, LOUISE (LASLEY). b Anderson Ind 16 Jl 08. 5: Phillips U 50-53 (Soc Sci, Rel Educ); George Washington U 63-65 (Psych); UColo Multi-Media Inst 69 (Instl Lib Serv). 07: Libn ref Enic Pub Lib, Enid Okla 55-58; Lib asst Smithsonian Inst, Wash DC 58-59; Lib asst Area Pub Wks Off, Navy, Wash DC 59-61; Libn Naval Med Center, Bethesda Md 61-62; Libn Fed Bur of Prisons, Wash DC 62-68; Libn US Bur of Prisons Fed Youth Ctr, Englewood Colo 68-. 9: Amer Correctional Assn (Com on Institutional Libs, chm Subcom on Institutional Staff Libs). 10: USAF Civil Air Patrol. 13: Yes. 14: Ref, admin. 15: 1190 S Allison st #5, Lakewood Co 80226.

MacKENZIE, REV VINCENT SJ. b Grand Falls Newfoundland Can 6 Jl 18. 5: Loyola Col (Montreal) BA; Rosary Col summers 54, 55 (LS); Catholic U summers 56-59 MLS. 6: Lat, Fr. 7: Chief Libn Regis Col Lib (Toronto) 53-. 9: ALA; CathLA (chm Ont Unit); CanLA; OntLA. 14: Catlg. 15: Regis Col Lib 3425 Bayview ave, Willowdale Ont Can.

MacKENZIE, RONALD J. b Weston Ont 13 D 34. 4: Evelyn. 5: Carleton 59 (Eng) BA; McGill 62 BLS. 7: Bkmob libn Cape Breton Reg Lib, Sydney NS 62-65; Chief libn Simcoe Co Lib Co-op, Barrie Ont 66-67; Supv Georgian Bay Reg Lib Ssyst, Barrie Ont 68-. 9: CanLA; OntLA. 15: RR 4, Barrie Ont Can.

MacKENZIE, RUTH C(AMPBELL) (SULLIVAN). b boston. 5: Simmons (Biol, Chem) BS, 62 MS in LS. 7: Sec Mass Gen Hosp, Boston 36-42& sec Harvard Sch of Pub Health 48-53; Sec Harvard Sch Dental Med 53-57; Acquis libn Francis A Countway Lib of Med, Boston 58-. 9: MedLA. 13: Yes. 14: Med & sci libs. 15: 1891 Beacon st, Waban Ma 02168.

MACKEY, LYLA (THRASHER). b Highway Ky. 04; Alexander B Mackey. 5: Central State Col (Edmond Okla) 32-34 (Soc Studies) AB; Peabody 35-37 (Hist) MA, 42-43 BS in LS. 6: Fr. 7: Tchr Co System, Albany Ky 27-31; Tchr Trevecca Col 35-43, Libn 43-. 9: ALA; NEA; TennLA. 10: Ladies Hermitage Assn. 14: Admin, ref. 15: 333 Murfreesboro rd, Nashville Tn 37210.

MACKIN, ALYCE L (NANTZ). b Cal 12 Ja 09. 4: J Gordon Mackin. 5: San Mateo Jr Col 27-29 (Eng) AA; Ore State Col 29-31 (Home Econ) BS; UCal 39-41 BLS. 6: Fr. 7: Circ libn Burlingame Pub Lib, Burlingame Cal 33-41; Order libn Kern Co Free Lib, Bakersfield Cal 41-44; Documents libn San Mateo Co Free Lib, Belmont Cal 49-59; Head Libn Philco Corp Western Development Labs, Palo Alto Cal 59-67; Hd libn EIMAC div of Varian Assocs 67-. 9: SLA (San Francisco

Chap: dir 66-68; Hospitality Chm 1971 Nat Conv); CalLA (Doc Com). 10: San Mateo Commun Coun; Panhellenic Bd; Child Welfare Com; Homemaker Serv Bd; AAUW; Alpha Xi Delta; AIAA. 14: Pub docs, electronics, spec libs (space sci). 15: 1325 Cabrillo ave, Burlingame Ca 94011.

MACKIN, MARGARET ELIZABETH (McCUAIG). b Toronto Can 24 My 26. 4: Richard Leland Mackin. 5: UToronto 45-49 (Modern Hist) BA, 49-50 BLS. 7: Libn Toronto Pub Lib, Toronto Ont 50-56; Libn (Ref) Montana StateU 66-. 14: Ref. 15: 524 South 5th ave, Bozeman Mt 59715.

MACKLER, LEONA (THOMAS). b NYC 17 Ja 25. 4: Cyril Lee Mackler. 5: UCLA 42-45 (Internat Rel) BA; Pratt 61-64 MLS. 6: Fr, Sp. 7: Libn trainee Queens Borough (NY) Pub Lib 60-64; Libn & research assoc Mental Health Materials Center, NY 64-. 9: ALA; NY Lib Club. 10: Pi Sigma Alpha; Beta Phi Mu. 14: Ref, computer info ret. 15: 280 Ninth ave, New York 10001.

MACKLIN, JAMES ROBERT. b Toronto 20 D 35. 4: Shirley Haynie. 5: Jacksonville U 56-60 (Psych) BA; West Res 61-62 MSLS. 6: Fr. 7: Circ asst Jacksonville Pub Lib, Jacksonville Fla 60-61; Ref asst Shaker Heights Pub Lib, Shakes Heights Ohio 61-62; Asst ref libn Jacksonville Pub Lib, Jacksonville Fla 62-63; Ref libn Swisher Lib Jacksonville U 63-64, Coordinator of pub serv 64-68; Asst Prof of Lib Admin, Coord of resource serv & Hd ref libn Wright State U 68-. 9: ALA; FlaLA; OhioLA. 12: Ed "A Checklist of the Publications of Local Government", DuvalCoLA (67). 14: Admin, ref. 15: 2917-C County Line rd, Dayton Oh 45430.

MACKSEY, JULIA ANN (ROZIER). b St Louis Mo 7 S 21. 5: Webster Col 39-42, 56-63 (Chem) BS; San Jose State Col 67-69 (Libnship) MA. 6: Fr. 7: Lab tech: Nat Lead Co titanium div, St Louis 50-53, Mallinckrodt Chem Wks, St Louis 53-61, Petrolite Corp, St Louis 61-63; Chem R/D Petrolite Corp, St Louis 63-66, Tech libn 66-67; Tech libn Kaiser Aluminum & Chem Corp, Permanente Cal 67-. 9: ACS; SLA; ASIS. 14: Lib automation. 15: 2595 Raven rd, Pleasanton Ca 94566.

MacLAREN, MILDRED LOUISE (DAVIDSON). b Isaac's Harbour NS 9 Jl 16. 5: UToronto 45-50 (Hist) BA, BLS. 07: Steno to Cashier Confederation Life Ins Co, Halifax NS 35-41; Sec Wartime Prices & Trade Bd, Toronto Can 42-45; Libn Halifax City Reg Lib, Halifax NS 51-58; Libn Pub Archives of Nova Scotia Halifax 58-67; Libn W K Kellogg Health Sci Lib DalhousieU 67-. 9: Csn 09: CanLA; APLA. 10: Nova Scotia Hist Soc. 14: Pub serv, ref. 15: 1333 S Park st apt 100 2, Halifax Nova Scotia Can.

MacLAURIN, (EVELYN) MARGARET. b Revelstoke BC Can 7 Jl 10. 5: Victoria Col 27-29 (Arts & Sci); UWash 29-34 (Home Econ) BS, 53-54 M Lib. 6: Fr, Sp. 7: Tchr jr & sr high schs, Vancouver BC 34-53; Ref & bkmob libn Kitsap Reg Lib, Bremerton Wash 55-57; Libn Seattle Pub Lib 57-. 9: ALA; PNLA; WashLA. 14: Ref. 15: 805 Warren ave N, Seattle Wa 98109.

MacLEAN, ELLEN G. b Canton Ohio 17 S 36. 4: William Plannette MacLean III. 5: UPenn 62-64 (Amer archaeology); Catholic U of Amer 65-66 MSLS; Radcliffe 54-58 (Lat) BA. 6: Sp. 7: Libn I (adult ref) Chicago Pub Lib 66-68, Libn II (loaned to Model Cities) 68, Libn III commun coord 69. 9: ALA; IllLA. 10: Beta Phi Mu. 14: Adult literacy, disadvantaged. 15: 4900 S Greenwood, Chicago Il 60615.

MACLEAN, HILDA I. b Vancouver BC Can. 5: UBC 36-40 (Eng, Hist) BA; McGill 62-63 BLS, 65-67 MLS. 7: Libn Royal Victoria Hosp, Montreal 63-67; Libn Nat Sci Lib, Ottawa 67-. 9: CanLA (Adv Coun 67-70); MedLA; SLA (pres Montreal Chap 67-68); Biol Scis Div: v-chm 68-69, chm 69-70). 14: Ref, med libnship. 15: 124 Springfield rd apt 708, Ottawa 2 Can.

MacLEAN, VIRGINIA. b Muskegon Mich 13 Jl 07. 4: Stuart MacLean. 5: UMich 30 AB in LS. 7: Asst Hackley Pub Lib, Muskegon Mich 27-28; Head catlg dept Cincinnati Art Museum Lib 30-36; Asst lib consul State Lib, Columbus Ohio 58-59, Head travel lib 59-68, Supv of field operations 68-. 9: ALA; OhioLA. 13: Yes. 14: Child bks, lib admin. 15: State Lib 65 S Front st, Columbus Oh 43215.

MacLELLAN, AUDREY (TERRILL). b Des Moines Iowa 7 My 28. 4: George O MacLellan. 5: Central Col(Pella Iowa) 49 (Hist) BA; Simmons 52 (LS) MS. 7: Br asst Detroit Pub Lib 52-53; Child libn Toronto Pub Lib 53-55; Br asst Toronto Twp Pub Lib, Cooksville Ont 60-62; Sch libn Weston Bd of Educ, Weston Ont 62-67; Chief libn Humber Col of Applied Arts & Tech 67-. 15: 10 St George blvd, Weston Ont Can.

MacLEOD, CELESTE (LIPOW). b Phoenix Ariz 27 N 31. 5: UCal (Berkeley) 49-53 (Eng) BA, 66-67 MLS. 7: Archivist West Jewish Hist Ctr Judah Magnes Mus, Berkeley Cal 67-. 9: SLA; SAA. 10: ACLU; Bk Club of Cal; Amer Jewish Hist Soc. 13: Yes. 14: Archives, spec collections, ref. 15: 2838 Woolsey st, Berkeley Ca 94705.

MacLEOD, FLORA MacLENNAN. b Calgary Alta Can 25 Ap 13. 5: UAlta 32-37 (Eng) BA, 38-39 ma& utoronto 39-40 (Eng), 41-42 BLS. 6: Fr. 7: Lib asst UWest Ont 42-43; Ext libn UAlta 45-56; Ref circ libn UCalgary 61-62; Lib asst Calgary Pub Lib, Calgary Alberta 43-45, Hd ref dept 56-61, Admin asst 62-66, Asst dir 66-. 9: CanLA (Coun 50-53); Bibliog Soc Can; AltaLA (pres 49-50 & 59-60). 10: Can Fed Univ Women; Alta Hist Soc. 14: Admin. 15: 3214 8 st SW, Calgary Alberta Can.

MacLEOD, MARJORIE W. b Springfield Mass 12 Ap 17. 5: Vassar 35-39 (Econ) AB; Simmons 59-62 MSLS. 7: Lib asst Harvard Law Lib 59-60; Lib intern Radcliffe Col Lib 60-62; Asst catlgr Boston U 62-63; Lib dir Babson Inst, Babson Park Mass 63-68; Curry Col, Milton Mass 68-. 9: ALA; NELA; MassLA; NECL; NETSL; SLA (sec Boston Br). 10: AAUW. 15: 7 Concord ave, Cambridge Ma 02138.

MacMILLAN, GARY D(UANE). b Long Rapids Mich 25 S 32. 5: Kalamazoo Col 50-54 (Psych, Sociol) BA; UMich 54-55 AMLS. 7: Libn I Detroit Pub Lib 55-56; Head Libn US Army Hosp, Ft Chaffee Ark 56-58; Libn II Detroit Pub Lib 58-61; Head Libn Detroit Inst of Tech 61-65; Tech adv ULiberia, Monrovia Liberia 65-68; Asst acquis libn & ser libn M ich State U 68-. 9: ALA; MichLA. 14: Admin. 15: 9 Woodland Apt 408, Detroit Mi 48202.

MACMILLAN, LEONARD J(OSEPH). b Boston 10 Ag 14. 4: Mary Sammon. 6: Ger. 7: Bk purchasing asst Boston Pub Lib 32-43; US Army Combat medic, surgical tech ETO 43-45; US Army Libn Lovell Gen Hosp (Tech 5th grade); Ft Devens Mass 45-46; Boston Pub Lib: Acquis of newspapers & period 47-62, Asst acquis of foreign bks 63, spec lib asst acquis of ser & spec lib materials 64-66, Spec lib asst acquis of ser 66-. 9: SLA (Bus & Fin Div: chm 62-63; Publ Program Com 66-70; Boston Chap Exec Bd 52-53, pres 58-59, ed 53-55, Employment chm 55-57 & 65-); NELA (treas 60-61). 10: Mass Men's Libns Club. 12: Ed, "Boston Chapter Bulletin," SLA 53-55; Ed, "Business & Finance Div Bulletin," SLA 61-62; "Bank Letters," SLA Bus & Fin Div (62). 13: Yes. 14: Ser. 15: Boston Pub Lib, Copley sq, Boston Ma 02117.

MacMULLIN, KATE (ESTHER L). b Rochester NY 9 D 25. 4: Robert John MacMullin. 5: URochester 47 (Eng) BA; UAriz, Ariz StateU 61- (LS, AV, Art). 6: Fr. 7: Design asst A M Baird Co, Phila 49-50; Libn AV Coord Phoenix Elem Sch Dist #1, Phoenix Ariz 63-68; Media specialist Mesa Sch Dist Lowell Sch, Mesa Ariz 68-. 8: Adv on picture bks Ariz State Wkshop State Lib Dept 67; Adv Kindergarten Assn, Casa Grande Ariz spring 69. 9: ALA; ArizLA; Maricopa Co Elem Sch LA; Ariz Assn for A-V Educ; Ariz SchLA (Elem Sch Chm, "Info" Chm, summer course chm, Memb Chm). 14: Elem sch media, storytelling, arts programs. 15: 4001 E San Juan, Phoenix Az 85018.

MacNAIR, ANNETTE (GOODFRIEND). b NYC 28 Ja 29. 5: CCNY 46-50 (Educ) BS in Ed, 52-55 (Educ); UCal (Berkeley) 66-68 MLS. 6: Sp, Gk, Hebrew. 7: Libn San Francisco Pub Lib 67-68; Dept Bibliogr UCal Med Ctr (San Francisco) 68-. 9: CalLA; Libns Assn UCal. 10: Sierra Club. 14: Ref, spec collections, rare bks, ya. 15: 1676 Funston ave, San Francisco Ca 94122.

macNAUGHTON, MARGARET ELIZABETH (HALL). b West Chester Penn 2 Jl 32. 4: Robert H MacNaughton. 5: Mary Washington Col of UVa 49-53 (Eng) BA; Ind U 57-59 (LS) MA. 7: Circ desk libn Ohio State U 59-60; Ref libn Ind U Undergrad Lib 63-64; Asst libn Ohio No U Lib 60-66; Ref libn Undergrad Lib Ind U (Bloomington) 63-64; Asst to child libn Cuyahoga Co Pub Lib, Cleveland 68-. 9: ALA; OhioLA. 10: Cosmopolitan Club; Faculty Wives Club; Cleveland State U Women's Assn. 14: Ref. 15: 4046 Northfield rd, Cleveland Oh 44122.

MACON, MYRA (FAYE). b Slate Springs Miss 29 S 37. 5: Holmes Jr Col 55-57 (Bus Educ) Diploma; Delta State Col 57-59 (Bus Educ) BSE; LSU summers 62-65 (LS) MS; UAkron 65. 6: Sp. 7: Libn Jr High Sch, Greenwood Miss 59-62; Libn High Sch, Greenwood Miss 62-63; Libn High Sch, Grenada Miss 63-64; Libn High Sch, Cuyahoga Falls Ohio 64-66; Supv elem lib serv, Cuyahoga Falls Ohio 66-. 9: NEA; OhioEA; OhioASchL; Northeast Ohio Tchrs Assn. 14: Lib educ, sch libs. 15: 431 Stow st, Cuyahoga Falls Oh 44221.

MACPHERSON, JOHN FINLAY. b Oban Scotland 12 Ja 23. 5: UWest Ontario 59-62 (Hist) BA, 64-67 (Hist) MA. 6: Fr, Sp. 7: Lib asst Mitchell Lib, Glasgow Scotland 40-56; Libn kingston Lib, Glasgow Scotland 56-57; Asst libn pub lib, Port Arthur Ont 57-59; Asst in lib UWest Ont 59-63, Chief readers' serv 63-65, Deputy chief libn 65-. 9: CanLA; Can assn Col & Univ Libs (Com on Automation); OntLA; Ont Assn Col & Univ Libs. 10: Humanities Assn of Can. 13: Yes. 14: Admin, systems devel. 15: 127 Regent st, London Ont Can.

MacQUARRIE, CATHERINE OLGA (BOEGE). b Anaheim Cal 14 My 06. 5: UCLA 24-28 (Hist) AB; UCal(Berkeley) 29 (LS) Certif. 6: Sp, Fr. 7: Head catlgr Merced Co Lib, Merced Cal 29-31; Chief tech serv Fed Trade Commsn, Wash DC 35-42; Law Libn Fed Security Agency, Wash DC 42-48; Chief tech serv Los Angeles Co Lib, Los Angeles 48-64; V-pres lib serv Econolist Inc, Los Angeles 64 los Angeles 48-64; V-pres lib serv Econolist Inc, Los Angeles 64-65; Chief lib consul Xerox Prof Lib Serv 66-68, Lib consul self-employed 68-. 8: Consul on lib coop in Colo for State of Colo 67. 09: ALA; SLA; ADA; LARC (dir). 10: Toastmistress; Writers Club, Whittier Cal. 11: Margaret Mann Citation in Catlg. 12: Ed "LARC" 68-. 13: Yes. 14: Catlg, automation of lib procedures, lib coop bk catlgs. 15: 416 Emerald Bay, Laguna Beac h Ca 92651.

MacQUARRIE, (ELINOR) DIANE. b Westville NS Can 6 O 36. 5: Acadia U 54-57 (Hist) BA; Toronto 59-60 BLS. 7: Sec Sun Life Assurance Co Ltd, Montreal 57-58; Bkmob libn Halifax Co Reg Lib, Armdale Halifax 60-62; Br libn Scarborough Pub Lib, Scarborough Ont 62-63; Asst libn Halifax Co Reg Lib, Armdale Halifax 63-64, Chief Libn 64-67; Supv of pub libs Prov of NS 67-. 9: CanLA (Coun: Adult Serv Sect & YP Sect); HalifaxLA (pres); APLA. 10: Beta Phi Mu; Can Club. 14: Adult serv, co & reg lib admin. 15: Apt 33 David Plaza, 6080 Pepperell st, Halifax NS Can.

MacQUOWN, VIVIAN (JOHNSON). b E Liverpool Ohio 14 Mr 19. 4: William C MacQuown Jr. 5: Allegheny Col 36-40 (Fr) AB; UKy 62-64 MS in LS. 6: Fr. 7: Sec Cornell U 40-43; Asst libn ref dept UKy Lib 64-; Order libn U Ky Law Lib 69-. 14: Ref, acquis. 15: 641 Beth lane, Lexington Ky 40503.

MacRAE, LACHLAN FARQUHAR. b Vancouver BC Can 7 O 14. 4: Irene (Macham). 5: UBC 35 (Chem) BA, 36 (Hist) BA, 37 (Hist) MA; UWash 38 BA in Libnship. 6: Fr. 7: Asst Lib Assn of Portland Ore 39-40; Asst libn Pub Lib, New westminster BC 41-44; Asst Sci-Ind Div Vancouver Pub Lib, Vancouver BC 44-45; Chief Libn Pub Lib, Ft William Ont 45-51; Dir Sci Info Serv Defence Research Bd of Can, Ottawa 51-65; Chief Libn UGuelph (Ont) 65-70; Assoc Natl Libn of Canada 70-. 8: Leader UNESCO, Seminar in Role of Lib in Adult Educ, Malmo Sweden 50; UNESCO adv to Govt of egypt on proposed pilot lib proj 56; NATO adv to Greek Nat Defence General Staff on Info Ctr 61, 64; Chm Assoc Com on Sci Info, Nat Res Coun, Ottawa 65-; Chm Bibliog Ctr Com, Ont Coun Univ Libns 67-69. 9: CanLA; SLA; ALA; OntLA (pres 48-50). 10: Can Film Inst (hon treas 53-65, dir 49-). 13: Yes. 14: Sci info dissemination, lib application of automatic data proc. 15: Natl Lib of Can, 395 Wellington st, Ottawa 4 Ont Can.

MacVEAN, DONALD S. b Kalamazoo 25 O 19. 4: Ruth West. 5: West Mich U 38-42 (Hist) AB; UMich 46-47 (Educ) AM, 52-53 AMLS, 53-58 (LS) Ed D. 7: Clerk (T/4) US Army, US, Britain 42-45; Tchr of govt Marshall High Sch, Marshall Mich 47-52; Curriculum lab libn Ball State U 53-58, Asst libn reader serv 58-65; Dir of Libs West Ill U 65-. 8: Lib consul ESEA Title II Proj, Hancock Co Ill 67-68. 9: ALA; NEA; IllLA; IllEA. 10: ACLU; AAUP; US Trotting Assn. 13: Yes. 14: Reader serv, intell freedom, sociol of reading, admin. 15: RFD 1, Macomb Il 61455.

MACWAY, LILA NELSON (CHRISTIE). b Walla Walla Wash 18 Je 06. 5: UCal (Berkeley) 32-36 (Educ) AB, 36-37 (Hist, Eng) Tchr Cred, 37-38 (LS) Certif, 52-54 (A-V Educ). 7: Tchr-libn Tulare High Sch, Tulare Cal 38-39; Asst chief communications & records US Dept Agric, San Francisco 39-43; Sub tchr Berkeley Pub Schs, Berkeley Cal 44-45; Child libn Berkeley Pub Lib, Berkeley Cal 46-60; Lib consul Napa Co Schs, Napa Cal 60-; Instr Napa Col lib tech 68-69. 9: ALA; CalLA; Assn Child Libns No Cal; CalASchL; Cal Tchrs Assn; Cal Assn for Supv & Curric Development; Cal Supv & Admin Assn. 10: Pi Lambda Theta; Delta Kappa Gamma; Toastmistress. 14: Child lit, sch libs. 15: 453 Seminary st, Napa Ca 94558.

MACY, (RACHEL) LOUISE. b Elmwood Ill 18 Ap 07. 5: Ill Wesleyan U 24-28 (Eng) AB; UIll 36-42 (Eng) MA, 47-48 BS in LS. 7: Tchr High Sch, Grant Park Ill 29-32; Tchr High Sch, Gridley Ill 32-37; Tchr High Sch, Tallula Ill 39-41; Tchr High Sch, Tuscola Ill 41-47; Libn Shimer Col 48-53; Catlgr UIll(Urbana) 53-55; Libn High Sch, Rochelle Ill 55-. 9: ALA; NEA; IllLA; IllEA. 15: 625 Woolf ct, Rochelle Il 61068.

MACZKOV, MELANIA E. b Beaverdale Penn 16 O 28. 5: Hazleton Center of Penn State 47-49; Seton Hill Col 49-51 (Eng) BA; West Res 53-55 MSLS. 7: Cleveland Pub Lib: Asst Child Lib South Br 51-53, Act child libn Edgewater Br 53-55, Child libn E 79 Br 55-57, Child libn W Park Br 57-. 9: ALA; CathLA; OhioLA. 13: Yes. 14: Child wk, educ. 15: 17443 Woodford ave, Cleveland 44107.

MADAN, RAJ (CHAUDHRY). b Sitpur Punjab India 22 F 36. 4: Bhim Madan. 5: Punjab U 51-55 BA, 55-56 BS in Ed; UMo 57-60 (Sociol) MA, 58-59 BSLS; Rutgers 62-64 MLS. 6: Hindi, Punjabi, Sanskrit, Multani. 7: Sr high sch tchr S D High Sch, Delhi 56-57; Bibliog UMo (Columbia) 59-62; Circ & res libn Rutgers 62-64; Bibliogr SUNY Col (Brockport) 65-66, Hd acquis dept 66-. 9: ALA; Monroe CoLA. 10: AAUP. 13: Yes. 14: Admin, acquis, searching, catlg, ref. 15: 82 Valley View dr, Brockport NY 14420.

MADDEN, DOREITHA (ROBINSON). b Baltimore Md. 4: Edward W Madden. 5: Hampton Inst 43-47 (Soc Studies) BS; Atlanta 48-49 BS in LS; UWash 62 (Train "Library 21"). 7: Res libn Hampton Inst 47-48; Child libn Enoch Pratt Pub Lib, Baltimore 49-50; Ref libn coordinator lending ser Pub & Sch Lib Serv NJ State Lib 57-. 8: Staff, Lib 21, Seattle World's Fair 62. 9: ALA; NEA; NJLA (Human Rel Com, Scholarship Com, Interlib Loan Com; NJEA. 10: YWCA Bd; Delta Sigma Theta; PTA. 14: Ref, child wk, documentation. 15: 97 Browning ave, Trenton NJ 08638.

MADDEN, ETHEL (CLARKE). b Brooklyn NY 21 Mr 10. 5: St Joseph's Col(Brooklyn) 26-30 (Eng) BA; Fordham 31-34 (Eng) MA; West Res summer 50 (LS); Columbia 51-53 (LS) MS; Rutgers 63- (Eng). 6: Fr, Ger. 7: High sch tchr of Eng NYC Bd of Educ, Brooklyn & Queens 33-49; Ref libn pub lib Ft Wayne & Allen Co, Ft Wayne Ind 50-54; Ref & ser libn UDayton 54-56; Catlgr St Francis Col(Ft Wayne Ind) 57; Catlgr Manhattanville Col 58-59; Circ libn Manhattan Col, Bronx NY 59; Ref libn & Instr in Lib Sci Seton Hall U 60-65, Asst Prof & chief ref libn 65-68, Assoc Prof & Chief ref libn 68-. 8: Asst ed, lib publs (local hist) Ft Wayne Pub Lib 53-54; Research asst to art catlgr Ft Wayne Pub Lib 50; Org'n & orderg of govt publs UDayton; Instr LS 15-hr Freshman course Seton Hall 60-64; Mem Acquis Com Seton Hall 60-. 9: ALA-ACRL; Mod Lang Assn; NCTE; NJLA; Col Lib Assn; CathLA. 10: AAUP. 14: Acquis, ref, instr. 15: 354 S Orange ave (Apt 2B), S Orange NJ 07079.

MADDEN, HENRY MILLER. b Oakland Cal 17 Je 12. 5: Stanford 31-34 (Hist) AB; Columbia 34-36 (Hist) PhD; UBudapest 36-37 (Hist); Columbia 43 (Internat Admin) AM; UCal 46-47 BLS. 6: Ger, Fr, Hungarian. 7: Instr in hist Stanford U 37-42; Lt Commander US Naval Reserve 42-46; Act Asst Prof of hist Wash State Col 48; Resettlement off Internat Refugee Org, Linz Austria 48-49; Col Libn Fresno State Col 49-. 8: Fulbright lecturer Austrian Nat Lib 53-54. 9: ALA; AHA; CalLA (pres 57); CalHistSoc. 10: Phi Beta Kappa; Roxburghe Club of San Francisco; Wine & Food Soc of Fresno; Cal Fed of Mem & Funeral Socs. 11: H W Wilson Co Lib Period Award (63) as ed of "California Librarian." 12: "Xantus, Hungarian Naturalist in the Pioneer West" (49); "German Travelers in California(58); Ed, "California Librarian" (63-). 13: Yes. 14: Admin. 15: 4687 Wishon ave, Fresno Ca 93704.

MADDEN, JEAN F. b Boston Mass 3 Ja 44. 5: Simmons Col 61-65 (Commun wk) SB, 65-66 (LS) SM. 7: Libn Sch of lib sci Simmons Col 66-, Lecturer 68-. 9: ALA; MassLA. 10: Simmons col, Sch of Lib Sci Alum Assn. 13: Yes. 14: Catlg, special lib. 15: Sch of Lib Sci Simmons Col 300 The Fenway, Boston Ma 02115.

MADDEN, MICHAEL JOSEPH. b Chicago Ill 8 O 38. 4: Patricia Giemza. 5: Marquette 56-60 (Eng) BA; Loyola U 61-63 (Eng) MA; UChicago 62-67 (LS) MA. 6: Ger. 7: Libn Ridgewood High Sch, Norridge Ill 63-65; Prof asst ALA, Chicago 65-67; Libn Schaumburg Twp Pub Lib, Schaumburg Ill 67-. 9: ALA (chm One Minute Bk Talk Com); IllLA; LACONI (chm Lib Pract Com). 13: Yes. 14: Admin. 15: 1405 Churchill rd, Schaumburg Il 60172.

MADDEN, SUSAN BROOKS (MARTHA CECILIA). b Portland Ore 7 Ag 44. 4: John Michael Madden. 5: UPortland 62-66 (Eng) BA; UDenver 66-67 MA in LS. 6: Sp. 7: Clk-page UPortland Lib 62-63; Clk-page Multnomah Co Lib Assoc Hollywood Br, (Portland) Ore 63-66; Asst to the Dean UDenver Lib Sch 66-67; Ref libn Clackamas Co Pub Lib, Oregon City Oregon 67-. 9: ALA (Recr rep); OreLA. 14: Ref, bkmob service, child wk. 15: 4454 SE Milwaukie ave, Portland Or 97045.

MADDOX, (FRANCES) EUGENIA. b Columbus Kan 28 N 08. 5: UTulsa 26-27 (Eng); Kan State Tchrs Col (Pittsburg) 28-29 (Eng); UWis 29-31 (Eng) BA; UMich summers 35, 39, 40 AMLS. 6: Fr, Ger. 7: Tulsa Pub Lib, Tulsa Okla: Asst circ dept 26-28, 1st asst catlg dept 31-32, Head catlg dept 32-43; Head Libn UTulsa Libs 43-67; Hd libn Mo Botanical Garden, St Louis 67-. 08: Visiting Prof, lib sci, Tex Woman's U Sch (Denton) summers 56, 57, 58-62, sch year 62-63; Visiting Prof UOkla Sch of Lib Sci summer 64. 9: ALA; BSA; NEA; SLA; OklaLA (2nd v-pres & Program Chm 51; pres 53; chm Nomin Com 58); SLA (Okla Chap: dir 56-57, ed Newsletter" 58-59); SWLA (sec Col & Univ libs Div 50-52 & 60-62); Greater St Louis Lib Club. 10: AAUP; Tulsa Town Club; Friends of the Tulsa Pub Lib; Delta Kappa Gamma. 13: Yes. 14: Admin, catlg, ref. 15: 4119 Magnolia apt 2A, St Louis Mo 63110.

MADDOX, BENNIE (FARRIOR). b Clayton Ala 6 Ja 34. 4: John Earl Maddox. 5: Ala State Col 50-55 (LS) BS; UMd 66 (LS). 6: Ger. 7: Libn US Army Spec Serv, Heidelberg Germany 61-63; Libn US Army Defense Lang Inst, Wash DC 66-68; Libn US Army Coastal Engring Research Ctr, Wash DC 68-. 9: SLA. 14: Ref. 15: 4510 Kinmount rd, Lanham Md 20801.

MADDOX, HELEN JEAN (BRANT). b Sumter SC 5 My 34. 4: Craig Miller Maddox. 5: Gallaudet Col 53-55, 61-64 (LS) BS; Catholic U 64-69 (LS) MSLS. 06: Ger. 7: Sewing-machine operator Eastwill Sportswear Co, Greenwood SC 56-57; Gift-wrapper Collins Store Dept, Forest City NC 58-59; Sewing-machine operator Orangeburg Mfg Co, Orangeburg SC 59-61; Furniture sander & inspector Korn Furn Co, Sumter SC 52-53; Stud asst Gallaudet Col Lib 62-65; Circ asst Catholic U 64; Asst catlgr & ref libn Gallaudet Col 65-66; Libn-supv USMC Hqs Hist Br, Ref Lib & Arch, Wash DC 66-. 9: ALA; SLA; DCLA. 10: Nat Assn of the Deaf; SC Assn of the Deaf; Palmetto Club for Deaf; Scott Key Club for Deaf; Potomac Silents Club; Phi Kappa Zeta. 14: Catlg, libnship instr, ref, tchg lib skills to deaf child. 15: 31 Cammer ave, Greenville SC 29605.

MADDOX, JOHN (DAVID). b Ottawa 17 Je 27. 5: Queens U 47-48; Carleton U 48-50 (Eng, Hist) BA; Toronto 59-60 BLS. 6: Fr. 7: Sch tchr, Daventry Ont 51-52; Tech off Can Hydrographic Serv, Ottawa 52-57; Catlg libn Mt Allison U 60-64; Bibliogr Can Coun on Urban Research, Ottawa 64-65; Catlg libn Dept of Trade & Commerce, Ottawa 65-67; Catlg libn Nat Gallery of Can, Ottawa 67-. 9: CanLA; Lib Assn Ottawa; APLA. 12: Ed "Urban and Regional References: 1st Bibliog Supp 63-64" (65). 14: Catlg, tech serv, bibliog. 15: 46 MacLaren st (Apt 6), Ottawa Can.

MADDOX, TREAN A. b Tulsa Okla 12 Ja 12. 5: UTulsa 30-31 (Eng); UMo 31-32 (Eng) ; Okla State U 32-34 (Eng) BS; West Res 34-35 BS in LS; Columbia summers 44-46, 47 MS in LS. 6: Fr. 7: Libn co-organizer Rogers High Sch Lib, Tulsa Okla summers 39, 40; Clerk-typist Fed Works Authority Grand River Dam Proj, Tulsa Okla 41; Br asst NY Pub Lib Riverside Br 47; Libn Wilson Jr High Sch Lib, Tulsa Okla 36-52; Libn Bell Jr High Sch Lib, Tulsa Okla 52-. 8: Lib org Bell Jr High Sch, Tulsa Okla 52; Visiting Prof: West Mich U 60; Tex Womans U summers 54-58, 61-64; Okla Coun on Libs 63-; Co-organ of Sch Lib Sect of OklaLA 56; Dir, Inserv Lib Course Tulsa Pub Schs 60. 9: NEA; ALA-AASchL (Bd Dir, SW Reg Group 55-58, State Assembly Rep for SW Reg 63-66); OklaLA (pres 63-64); OklaEA; OklaSchLA (sec 56-58); SWLA (sec Sch Libns Sect 54); Tulsa Clr TA. 10: Alpha Beta Alpha; Kappa Kappa Iota; Delta Kappa Gamma; Alpha Delta Pi; AAUW. 12: "School Library Services in Tulsa Public Schools" (60, rev ed 65); Consul "Basic Book Collections for Jr high Schools" (3d ed 60). 13: Yes. 14: Sch libnship, lib educ. 15: 2906 E 26th pl, Tulsa Ok 74114.

MADDOX, VIVIAN (RUTH). b Harrisburg Ark 14 My 16. 5: Ark State U 38-39, AB; LSU 44-46 BS in LS; Rutgers 58-59 MLS. 6: Fr. 7: Legal sec Maddox & Greer, Harrisburg Ark 39-44; Head Libn Poinsett Co Lib, Harrisburg Ark 44-46; Head Libn Natchitoches Parish Lib, Natchitoches La 46-47; Head Libn Southeast Ark Reg Lib, Monticello Ark 47-49; Head Libn Garland Co Lib, Hot Springs Ark 49-52; Chief Libn Springfield (Mo) Pub Lib 52-57; Pub lib consul Mo State Lib 58; Research asst Rutgers U Grad Sch of Lib Serv 58-59; Asst city libn Milwaukee Pub Lib 59-. 8: Instr for course on Pub Libs, UWis (Milwaukee) 66-67. 9: ALA (Spec Com on Copyright Issues 67-68, Memb 9memb Mo Chm 55-59, Memb Wis Chm 61); -LAD-LOMS (sec 62-64); -PLA (Subcom for Revising Costs Supplement for Pub Lib Serv 68-69); ArkLA (chm Pub Libs Sect 50-51); MoLA (Legis Com 55-57); WisLA (Awards Com 60-61, chm &/or mem Develop & Legis Com 61-). 10: Mo Libs Film Coop; SW Mo Lib Serv; Beta Phi Mu; AAUW; Delta Kappa Gamma; LWV; Milwaukee Area Soc Pub Admin; Adult Educ Assn; Milwaukee Research Clearinghouse; Milwaukee Art Center; Milwaukee Coun for Adult Learning; World Affairs Coun of Milwaukee. 11: 1963 Achievement Award of Milwaukee Women's Club. 13: Yes. 14: Admin, automation, budgeting, legislation. 15: 2281 N Lake dr, Milwaukee Wi 53202.

MADIGAN, KAREN (SORENSEN). b Chicago Ill 24 Mr 45. 4: John J Madigan. 5: Grand View Jr Col 62-64; Augustana Col 64-66 (Chem) BA; UCal (Berkeley) 68-69 MLS. 6: Fr, Danish. 7: Sci tchr Tri Co High Sch, Thornburg Iowa 66-67; Claims examiner Blue Cross-Blue shield, Chicago 67-68; Libn catlg dept Richmond Pub Lib, Richmond Cal 69; Libn catlg dept NorthwesternU Lib 69-. 14: Catlg, ref, acquis. 15: 735 1/2 Hinman, Evanston Il 60202.

MADISON, DILYS ELIZABETH (MORRIS). b London Eng 10 N 42. 4: Kenneth Glenn Madison. 5: UIll (Urbana) 61-64 (Hist) AB, 64-65 (LS) MS. 6: Fr. 7: Browsing rm libn & dept hd UIll Lib (Urbana) 65-67; Catlgr Iowa State U Lib 67-. 10: Phi Alpha Theta. 14: Circ, catlg. 15: 2337 Donald st, Ames Ia 50010.

MADISON, MARY JEAN. b Amarillo Tex 5 S 13. 5: So Methodist U 32-36 (Commercial Art) BA; UTex 46-53 BLS; 57 MLS. 6: Sp. 7: Volunteer lib wk So Methodist U 32-36; Memb chm TexLA Spec Libs 63; Asst dir First Methodist Church Lib, Dallas 46-52; Consul for Methodist Church Libs, Dallas 52-. 8: Dale Carnegie leadership wk 53-; Dallas Co Coun of Church Libs 52-. 9: ALA-LAD; -ACRL; TexLA; SWLA; TexPL; DallasCoLA. 10: Beta Phi Alpha. 14: Organ, catlg, rare bks, ref. 15: 8417 Santa Clara dr, Dallas Tx 75218.

MADSON, LORETTA (HARTWIG). b Denmark Wis 21 S 12. 4: Robert Cornelius Madson. 5: UWis 30-36 (Pol Sci, Econ) BA; Radcliffe 44 US Naval Officers' Supply Corps Sch; UWis 46-47 BLS. 6: Fr. 7: Accounting dept Mirro Aluminum Co, Manitowoc Wis 36-38; Market Research A C Nielsen Co, Chicago 38-41; Accounts Payable Dept Manitowoc Shipbuilding Co, Manitowoc Wis 41-43; Disbursing Off US Navy (WAVES) Lt jg (SC) 43-46; Manitowoc Pub Lib, Manitowoc Wis: Catlgr 47-48, Asst ref libn 54-62, Head ref dept 62-, Adult serv libn 68-. 8: Libn First Luth Church Lib 64-. 9: WisLA. 10: AAUW; Mem Hosp Auxiliary; Manitowoc Co Wis Alumni Assn; Manitowoc Co Hist Soc. 14: Ref, Wis bks. 15: 712 N 11th st, Manitowoc Wi 54220.

MAGARO, JOHN DAVID. b Natrona Heights Penn 14 Ja 40. 4: Kathleen Roach. 5: Clarion State Col 58-62 (LS) BS; Penn State U 62-63; UPittsburgh 65-66 MLS. 6: Ger. 7: Libn Kiski Area Sch System, Vandergrift Penn 62-63; Libn Prince george's Co (Md) 63-64; Lib coordinator Highlands Sch System, Tarentum Penn 64-; Asst Prof Lib Educ Shippensburg State Col. 8: Adv on design & constr of sch lib facilities, Highlands Sch Dist. 9: ALA; NEA; PennEA; PennSchLA; PennLA. 10: Assn Penn State Col & Univ Facs. 14: Sch libs, sch lib spec. 15: RD 3, Shippensburg Pa 17257.

MAGAVERO, GERARD. b Buffalo NY 25 Mr 35. 5: Chicago 51-54 (Econ) BA; Chicago-Kent Sch of Law 54-57 LLB; Pratt 62-64 MLS. 6: Lat, Sp, Ital. 7: Libn Pennie, Edmonds, Morton, Barrows & Taylor, NYC 60-61; Asst libn NY Co Lawyers Assn 61-62; Asst libn Law Lib Brooklyn Supreme Court 62-63, Libn 64-66; Libn & Asst Prof of Law Drake U 66-67; Libn & Asst Prof of Law UMiss 67-69; Libn & Asst Prof of Law Cal West U 69-. 8: Admitted to the Bar, NY & Ill. 9: AALL; ALA; MissLA. 10: The Lambs Club (NYC); Phi Delta Phi. 14: Admin. 15: Law Lib, Supreme Court Bldg, Brooklyn NY 11201.

MAGEE, ELEANOR EILEEN. b Sillsville Ont Can 21 N 19. 5: Sir George Williams 48-51 BA, BSc; McGill 53-54 BLS, 59-66 MLS. 7: Pub sch tchr, S Fredericksburg Ont 41-43; Lab tech Inspection Bd of UK & Can, Cherrier Que 43-47; Lab tech Frank W Horner Pharmaceuticals, Montreal 47; Lab tech chem lab supv libn, Monsanto Chem Co, Montreal 48-53, 54-57; Libn Can Marconi Co, Montreal 57-59; Chief libn Sun Life Ins Co of Can, montreal 59-63; Hd catlg dept McGill U

63-64, Asst prof 64-66, Visiting lecturer 66-67, Assoc libn tech serv 66-67; Chief libn Mt Allison U Lib 67-. 8: Lectr in Eng Sir George William U evenings 59-65; Lectr lib sci: Summer Sch of Educ MacDonald Col summer 65, St Anne de Quebec summer 66. 9: ALA; APLA; CanLA (treas 68; sec-treas Res & Lib Sect 63-64); SLA (treas, v-pres, pres 59-62, chm Com on Stand 62-63; Conventions Chm for -969 Convention 65-67; QuebecLA (treas 63-64, pres 64-65. 14: Admin, tech serv, collection bldg. 15: PO Box 218 Sackville, New Brunswick Can.

MAGEE, ELIZABETH P. b Spokane Wash 26 Ja 11. 4: R Willis Magee. 5: UColo summer & ext 30-39 (Eng Lit); UDenver summers 40-43 (LS) Certif. 6: Sp, Ger. 7: Asst libn Colo Springs High Sch, Colo Springs Colo 30-32; Libn North Jr High Sch, Colo Springs Colo 34-43; Child & yp libn Pikes Peak Reg Dist Lib, Colo Springs Colo 43-67, Child libn 67-. 8: Bk review & evaluation com for State Lib Reading List 63-65. 9: ALA; ColoLA (pres 51-52, Scholarship Com 62-64). 10: Altrusa Club; Child Reading RT; Area Libns. 14: Bk sel for child & yp, ref wk with child. 15: 1842 Arroya st, Cold Springs Co 80906.

MAGEE, LOIS (COWGILL). b De Smet SD 14 F 12. 5: UWash 29-30 (Psych); UCLA 30-34 (Psych) BA; USoCal 55-56 (LS) MS. 7: Ref libn Kern Co Lib, Bakersfield Cal 56-57; Asst state ext libn State of Ariz, Phoenix 57-58; Supv adult ext Kern Co Lib, Bakersfield Cal 59-62, Coordinator ext servs 62-67, Kern Co libn 68-. 9: ALA; CalLA (Black Gold Dist: v-pres 67-68, p res 68-69). 10: AAUW; ASPA; Kern Co Hist Soc; C of C Women's Div; Libraria Sodalitas. 14: Ext serv, bk sel, admin. 15: Kern Co Lib 1315 Truxtun ave, Bakersfield Ca 93301.

MAGENAU, MARY (STUBBS). b Wellfleet Mass 8 Jl 10. 4: William Magenau. 5: Radcliffe 31 (Sociol) AB; Simmons 32 (Soc wk) BS, 65 (LS) MS. 6: Fr, Lat. 7: Soc case wker State of NH, Manchester & Laconia 33, 35; Circ libn Howard Whittemore Mem Lib, Naugatuck Conn 56-57; Yale U: Catlg trainee Sterling Mem Lib 58-60, Catlgr subj div 60-62; Catlgr Economic Growth Center 62-63, Head catlgr 63-, Asst libn 67-. 9: ALA. 10: Radcliffe Club of New Haven; Naugatuck Women's Study Club; AAUW; Conn Com for the Equal Rights. 12: "A Bibliography of Development Plans in Africa, South of the Sah ara" (66). 14: Bibliog. 15: 132 Willard st, New Haven Ct 06515.

MAGER, JOHN GEORGE. b Cleveland 21 Mr 18. 4: Anna Maria Helfrich. 5: Concordia Col 36-38 (Liberal Arts); Concordia Sem 38-43, 48-58 (Practical Theol) BA, BD, STM; Washington U 48-49 (Hist) MA; UCal Lib Sch 63-65 MLS; Chicago 66. 06: Ger, Lat, Gk. 7: Asst pastor St Peter's Lutheran Church, Reedsburg Wis 43-48; Pastor & founder Good Shepherd Lutheran Church, Akron Ohio 48-57; Asst Prof Cal Concordia Col 57-65; Assoc Prof- catlgr Clarion S catlgr Clarion State Col 65. 9: PennLA. 10: Kiwanis; Luth Acad for Scholarship; AAUP. 13: Yes. 14: Ser, catlg. 15: 19 Fairview ave, Clarion Pa 16214.

MAGES, JANICE (BUTTERFIELD). b Winterport Me 2 S 27. 5: Westbrook Jr Col 45-47 (Liberal Arts); UMe 47-50 (Eng) BA; Simmons 51-52 MS in LS. 7: Field libn Army Spec Serv, Germany 53-56; Catlgr State Lib, Augusta Me 56-57, Field adv libn 58; Asst catlgr Pub Lib, Brookline Mass 59; Field adv libn State Lib, Augusta Me 60-64; Catlgr Pub Lib, Warwick RI 64-65, Asst libn 65-. 8: Chm No Country Libs Film Coop, 63-64; Dir RI Lib Film Cooperative 67-. 9: ALA; NELA; RILA. 10: Warwick Arts Foundation. 13: Yes. 14:Catlg, adv wk with other libs, a-v wk in pub libs. 15: 2281 W Shore rd, Warwick RI 02886.

MAGG, MARIAN SPATER. b Detroit. 5: UWis 23-27 (Sociol) BA; Catholic U 57-59 MSLS. 6: Fr, Ger, Ital. 7: d bus & tech dept New Britain Pub Lib, New Britain Conn 38-42; Libn China-America Coun of Com & Ind, NY 43-44; Econ analyst Foreign Econ Admin, Cairo Egypt 44-45; Div asst Div of Libs, Dept of State 45-46; Ed Coun on Lib Resources, Wash DC 57-58; Dir Corning Pub Lib, Corning NY 59; Ref libn Brookings Inst, Wash DC 60-68; Libn US-Japan Trade Coun 68-. 8: Career interrupted by residence (as wife of US Foreign Service off): Eng 28-34, Egypt 44-45, Austria 4 6-47 & 50-52, Hungary 48-50, Japan 52-53, & Italy 54-56; Organ Cairo (Egypt) Lib Assn and served as its first sec 44-45. 9: SLA (pres Conn Chap 41-42); DCLA. 10: English Spea king Union; Japan-Amer Soc, Austrian-Amer Soc, etc; Alpha Kappa S Delta; New Britain (Conn) Housing Authority 39-42. 12: Co-auth "State Standards for Public Libraries," US Off of Educ (60). 13: Yes. 14: Admin. 15: 2737 Devonshire pl NW, Wash DC 20008.

MAGGIO, PAULINE (GARRETT). b St Louis 20 Ap 11. 4: Anthony T Maggio. 5: Wash U 28-32 (Eng, Pol Sci) BA; Pratt 33-34BLS; Columbia summers 50-56 MS in LS. 7: Br asst St Louis Pub Lib 34-42; Asst circ libn Lawson McGhee Lib Knoxville Tenn42-44; Catlgr Wash Tech 3/C Army & Navy Staff Col, Wash DC 44-46; Ref asst Pratt Inst Lib 46-48, Ref libn 48-60; Coord of LibInstr Jersey City State Col Lib 60-61, Period & docs libn 61-. 9: ALA (New Ref Tools Com 64-66); NEA; NJEA; NJLA. 10: AAUW; Birmingham Art Assn; Bus & Prof Women. 14: Govt ref, catlg, ref. 15: 279 Washington ave, Brooklyn NY 11205.

MAGILL, MRS MARGARET (LOUISE). b 23 O 05. 5: UTenn 33-34 (Eng); Maryville Col 34-35 (Eng) AB; Northwestern 35-36 (Eng) MA; Peabody summers (LS). 6: Fr. 7: Tchr Sullins Col 38-43; Head of compensation dept So Fire & Gas Co, Knoxville 43-53; Tchr & libn Johnson Bible Col 53-57; Libn Webb Sch of Knoxville(Tenn) 57-66; Libn Highlands Sch, Naples Fla 67-. 9: ALA; TennLA; NEA; FlaEA; FlaLA; Collier City EA. 14: Catlg. 15: 108 Woodrush ave, Knoxville Tn 37918.

MAGLADRY, GEORGE CHARLES. b Seattle 9 S 29. 4: Barbara Klingele. 05; St Martin's Col 46-48; Seattle U 52-53 BA; UWash (Seattle) 53-54 MLib. 7: Bkmob libn Mid-Columbia Lib, Kennewick Wash 54-56; Asst libn Reg Pub Lib, Olympia Wash 56-59; Co libn Humboldt Co Lib, Eureka Cal 59-64; Coordinator of tech serv Humboldt State Col 64-. 9: ALA; CalLA (pres Redwood Dist 60). 13: Yes. 14: Lib devel. 15: 1131 Hoove st, Eureka Ca 95501.

MAGNER, MARY JO. b Detroit 22 S 34. 5: St Mary-of-the-Woods Col 52-53 (Journalism); Ursuline Col(Cleveland) 53-56 (Eng) AB; Western Res U 57 MSLS. 06: Fr. 7: Asst libn Cleveland Heights(Ohio) Pub Lib 57-60; Ref libn Nat Agric Lib, Wash dc 60-62; Asst libn St John Col of Cleveland 62-65, Head Libn 65-. 9: CathLA (No Ohio Unit: v-chm 69-); ALA-ACRL (Tri-State Chap). 10: Cath Alumni Club of Cleveland. 14: Ref. 15: 3264 Belvoir blvd, Cleveland Oh 44122.

MAGNUSON, MARY (FOWLER). b Bayonne NJ 16 Jl 11. 4: John Arthur Magnuson. 5: SUNY(Oswego) 53-61 (Eng) BS (cum laude); SUNY(Geneseo) 61-65 MLS. 7: Libn Mexico Acad & Central Sch, Mexico NY 49-. 9: ALA; NEA; NCTE; NY State Tchrs Assn; NY State LA; Onondago-Oswego Sch LA; Oswego Coun Internat Reading Assn. 10: AAUW; Delta Kappa Gamma. 14: Bks for child & ya. 15: Box 246, Mexico NY 13114.

MAGOON, CAROLYN (TOWNHILL) (MRS). b Cleveland. 5: Col of Wooster 49-51; Mich State U 51-53 (Lang, Lit) BA; UMich 55-60 MALS. 6: Sp. 7: Reader's adv Grand Rapids Pub Lib, Grand Rapids Mich 54-55, Child libn 56-57; Young adult libn Lansing Pub Lib, Lansing Mich 61-65; Young adult supv Arlington Co Pub Lib, Arlington Va 65-69; Br libn Prince Georges Co Md 69-. 9: ALA; MichLA; VaLA (sec Pub Lib Sect). 10: AAUW; E Grand Rapids (Mich) Friends of the Lib Bd; Amer Topical Assn; Beta Phi Mu; Greater Lansing (Mich) Youth Coun; Alpha Chi Omega; Arlington Co Youth Coun Adv. 14: Pub lib wk. 15: 8150 Lakecrest dr, Greenbelt Md 20770.

MAGRAW, SISTER MARY CONCEPTA. b Erie Penn 2 O 02. 5: Edinboro State Col 20-22 (Kindergarten Primary) Certif; UPittsburgh 33 BS in Ed; CatholicU 40-41 BS in LS. 6: Fr. 7: Tchr Erie (Penn) Pub Sch 22-37; Tchr St Catherines High, Cornwells Hgts Pa 38, 40; Libn St Catherines Col (Cornwells Hghts Pa) 41-44; Libn catlgr XavierU (New orleans) 44-49, Libn 49-56, Libn catlgr 56-, Hd libn -68, Assoc libn 69. 9: ALA; CathLA; NEA-DAVI; LaLA. 10: Xavier Aux. 14: Tech serv. 15: 3912 Pine st, new Orleans La 70125.

MAGRILL, ROSE MARY. b Marshall Tex 8 Je 39. 5: E Tex State Col 57-60 (Math) BS, 60-61 (Elem Educ) MA; UIll 63-64 MS in LS. 7: Asst in dean of women's off E Tex State Col 60-61, Asst catlgr 61-63; Asst in Grad Sch of Lib Sci UIll 63-64; Instr in Lib Sci E Tex State U 64-65, Asst Prof of Lib Sci 65-67; Doctoral Fellow UIll 67-69. 9: ALA; SWLA; TexLA. 10: Tex Assn Col Tchrs; AAUW; Alpha Phi; Beta Phi Mu; Alpha Chi; Kappa Delta Pi; Alpha Lambda Delta. 14: Ref, lib educ. 15: 311 Caddo, Marshall Tex 75460.

MAGUIRE, MARY VIRGINIA. b Providence RI 20 Je 18. 5: Trinity Col Wash DC 36-38, 39-40 (Fr) AB; Sorbonne 38-39 (Fr civilization) Degre superieur; Simmons 58-59 (LS) MS. 6: Fr. 7: Engring record draftsman New England Tele, Providence 40-43, 46-58; WAVES USNR 43-46; Child libn Providence Pub Lib 58-59; Curriculum ctr libn RT Col 59-61; High sch libn

Cumberland Sch Syst, Cumberland RI 61-66, Coord sch libs 65-, Coord ESEA Title II 66-. 8: Consul ESEA Title II RI State Dept of Educ Prov 66. 9: ALA; NESchLA; CathLA; RILA; RISchLA (pres); A-V Assn RI. 10: RI Hist Soc. 14: Sch lib devel, child lit. 15: 125 Hope st, Providence RI 02906.

MAGUIRE, PATRICIA V(IRGINIA). b Mt Vernon NY 3 Ap 37. 5: Regis Col (Weston Mass) 55-59 (Biol) AB; Simmons 63-65 (LS) MS. 7: Ref asst Boston Pub Lib 62-67; Ref libn Bentley Col 68-. 14: Ref. 15: 39 Milo st, W Newton Ma 02165.

MAHAFFEY, NINA JEAN. OLDSMITH Ind 27 My 19. 5: Ind U 37-39, 44-46 (Educ) BS; Peabody 49-50 (LS) MA. 7: Libn Columbus High Sch, Columbus Ind 46-49; Libn Bloomington High Sch, Bloomington Ind 50-52; Asst libn Rose Polytech Inst 52-56; Libn Scottsdale Elem Sch, Scottsdale Ariz 57-62; Head Libn Alhambra High Sch, Phoenix 62-65; Sch lib consul State Dept of Pub Instr, Phoenix 65-. 9: ALA; NEA; Ariz State LA; ArizEA. 14: Sch libs. 15: 8601 South 16th pl, Phoenix Az 85040.

MAHALINGAM, VAITHILINGAM. b Telok Anson Malaysia 8 Jl 31. 4: Thanalakshmi Nadarajah. 5: CalcuttaU 52-56 (Eng) BA (Hons); McGill 57-58 BLS; Columbia 65-68. 6: Tamil. 7: Lectr in Eng Hartley Col (Point Pedro Ceylon) 56; Asst libn Ceylon Inst of Sci & ind Research, Colombo Ceylon 57, Chief libn 58-65; Lectr catlg & classification Ceylon Lib Assn (Colombo) Ceylon 61-65; Asst Hd Catlg Div Douglas Lib Queen'sU 68-. 8: Lib adv: Vidyodaya UCeylon 61-65, Ceylon Nat Commsn for Unesco 62-65, Educ Dept of Ceylon 61-64; Nat rep Unesco Documentation Sem, Delhi 61. 9: CeylonLA (sec 60-61, Educ Offr 61-62 & 63-64; mem Exec Com 61-64). 11: Fulbright Scholar, 65-68 (Columbia). 13: Yes. 14: Tech serv. 15: Apt 1 41 York st, Kingston Ont Can.

MAHAR, ELLEN (PATRICIA). b Washington DC 15 Ja 38. 5: St Joseph Col 55-59 (Biol) BA; UMd 67-69 (LS) MLS. 07: Asst to libn Navy Dept Bur Ships Nuclear Propulsion Br, Wash DC 59-62; Catlgr Inst for Defense Analyses, Wash DC 62-63, Chief catlg sect 63-64; Chief classified lib Inst for Defense Analyses, Arlington Va 65-67. 9: ASIS; SLA (Wash DC Chap, Documentation Gp: treas 68-69, sec 69-70). 10: Beta Phi Mu. 14: Tech serv, govt docs. 15: 4341 Nebraska ave NW, Wash DC 20016.

MAHAR, MARY HELEN. b Schenectady NY 12 F 13. 5: SUNY(Albany) 30-35 (Eng) AB, ext 40-44 BS in LS; Columbia ext 45-50 MS in LS. 7: Tchr of Eng & Libns Pierson High Sch, Sag Harbor NY 35-40; Asst libn Mem High Sch, Pelham NY 40-42; Libn Scotia High Sch, Scotia NY 42-44; Libn Garden City High Sch, Garden City NY 44-54; Exec Sec ALA-AASchL 54-56; Prof Div of Lib Educ State U Col (Geneseo NY) 56-57; Spec for sch & child libs US Off Exec, Wash DC 57-63, Coordinator of sch lib serv 63-65, Program adv sch hist supv & serv 65-66, Chief sch libs sect 66-67, Chief internat resources br 67-68, Chief west program operations br 68-. 8: Visiting Instr: St Johns U(Brooklyn NY) 48, State U Col(Geneseo NY) Div of Lib Educ 49-50, Columbia Sch of Lib Sci 52-53, UDelaware(Wilmington) 64-65; Fulbright Fellowship, United Kingdom 51-52; Consul: Study Commsn of Chief state sch offs 60-62, AASchL Standards Com 59-60. 9: ALA; NEA; CathLA; DCLA. 10: Wash DC Child Bk Guild. 12: "Certification of School Librarians" (58); "State Department of Education Responsibilities for School Libraries" (60); Ed "The School Library as a Materials Center: Educational Need of Librarians & Teachers in Its Administrative Use" (63); Co-auth "Library Facilities for Elementary & Secondary Schools" (65); Ed "School Library Supervision in Large Cities" (66). 13: Yes. 14: Sch libs. 15: US Office of Education, Wash DC 20202.

MAHER, KATHLEEN ESTELLE (FORRESTER). b Detroit Mich 1 Mr 23. 4: Thomas E Maher. 5: AirU 57-59 (Comptroller) Certif; UCLA Ext 58 (Math); UOkla 68 (Humanities) BLS, 69 (Info Sci) MALS. 6: Fr. 7: Asst engineer Land-Air, NM 51-54; Asst systems analyst Hq 5th AF, Japan 55-57; Programmer Air Force, Los Angeles 57-59, Chief data processing 60; Charm sch & fashion show Coord, Brussels 62-65; Lib systems analyst UOkla 66-. 8: Lib automation consul UWisc (Green Bay) 68. 10: Mil Wive's Club; Univ Women's Club; Toastmistress. 12: Comp "Union List of Current Periodical Titles" OklaU & Okla stateU; "University of Oklahoma Libraries Serial Holding". 14: Info stor & ret. 15: 11702 E Noriwo dr, Whittier Ca 90601.

MAHESHWARY, AVINASH CHANDRA. b Amritsar Punjab India 18 Ag 34. 4: Indu R Maheshwary. 5: PunjabU (Chandigarh India) 49 (Honours in Hindi) Prabhakar, 54 (Pol Sci) BA, 59 (Hindi Lit) MA; NagpurU (Nagpur India) 58 (LS) Diploma. 6: Bengali, Gujarati, Hindi, Marathi, Punjab, Urdu. 7: Libn Municipal Lib, Kotkapura Punjab India 56-59; Sr tech asst Nat Lib of India, Calcutta 59-63; Prod exec Kalpanalok Motion Picture Producers, Bombay 63-67; Exec producer Maheshwary Pictures Motion Picture Producers, Bombay 63-67; S Asia libn DukeU Lib 67-. 8: Consul publ dept Chetana Ltd Bksellers & Publ, Bombay 65-66. 9: IndianLA; Indian Assn Spec Libs & Info Ctrs. 12: Jt comp "A Bibliography of indian Scientific an indian Scientific and Technical Publications" (60); Jt comp "A Bibliography of Dictionaries a dictionaries and Encyclopaedias in Indian Languages" (64). 14: Ref, bibliog. 15: Duke University Lib, Durham NC 27706.

MAHIN, REV PHILIP OSB. b Richmond Ind 16 Je 25. 5: St Meinrad Sem Col 44-48 (Philos) AB; St Meinrad Sem Sch of Thel 48-51 (Theol); Catholic U 51-52 (Theol) STL; UMich 59-63 AMLS. 6: Lat, Fr. 7: Priest St Meinrad Archabbey, St Meinrad Ind 51-; Catlgr Archabbey Lib, St Meinrad Ind 52-55; Manager Abbey Press & Grail Publ, St Meinrad Ind 55-58; Head catlgr Archabbey Lib, St Meinrad Ind 58-; Dir of news serv St Meinrad Archabbey, St Meinrad Ind 64-66; Asst Prof Lib Sci Ind State U (Terre Haute) summers 68-. 9: ALA; CathLA; IndLA. 14: Catlg. 15: St Meinrad Archabbey, St Meinrad In 47577.

MAHLER, JEANNE HULL (ELIZABETH). b Kingston NY 9 Ja 16. 4: Wm Mahler. 5: UPenn 33-37 (Soc Sci) BS in Ed, 37-38 (Ed) MS in Ed; Drexel 39-40 BS in LS. 6: Fr. 7: Free Lib of Phila; Asst Circ Dept 40, Sr asst Pub Documents Dept 40-48, Act head Pub Documents Dept 48, Head Pub Documents Dept 49-. 9: ALA; SLA; PennLA; Phila Dist LA; ASIS; Lib Pub Rel Assn Greater Phila. 10: Alumni Assn of UPenn & Drexel; Pi Labda Theta; Pi Gamma Mu. 13: Yes. 14: Ref, govt publs. 15: 1246 Johnston st, Phila Pa 19148.

MAHMOODI, SUZANNE (HOEGH). b Chariton Iowa 5 Ag 35. 4: Parviz Mahmoodi. 5: Ottumwa Heights Col 53-55; Col of St Catherine 55-57 (Amer Studies) BA; UMich 57-58 MALS. 7: Acquis clerk UMich Law Lib 57-58; Jr libn in ref UMinn Lib(Minneapolis) 58-59, Jr libn in circ 59-60; Reader serv libn St Catherine Lib Col of St Catherine 62-66, Instr Dept of Lib Sci 66-67, Asst Prof 67-. 9: ALA; CathLA; MinnLA. 10: AAUP; Pi Gamma Mu; Kappa Gamma Pi; Phi Beta Kappa; Beta Phi Mu. 14: Ref, readers adv, circ. 15: 2111 Roth pl, White Bear Lake Mn 55110.

MAHONEY, FRANCES (WINGERD). b Rochester Ind 20 Ja 07. 4: Claude A Mahoney. 5: DePauw U 25-29 (Eng) BA; George Washington U 36-38 (LS). 6: Fr, Ger, Russian. 7: Circ asst Ind State Lib 30-35; Catlgr & ref libn WPA Admin Lib, Wash DC 36-40; Bibliogr Pub Roads Admin Lib, Wash DC 41-43, 45; Research asst WAVES, Wash DC 43-45; Elem sch libn Fairfax(Va) Co Schs 61-. 9: ALA. 12: Ed & comp "The Observer Scrapbook," a weekly column in "The National Observer" (62). 14: Child's lit, hist research. 15: 4708 Ox rd, Fairfax Va 22030.

MAHONEY, RONALD JEROME. b Toledo Ohio 5 Jl 34. 4: Martha Wallach. 5: Defiance Col 58-59 (Hist); Mexico City Col 59-62 (Anthrop) BA; UCal (Berkeley) 55-65 MLS. 6: Sp. 7: Catlgr Defiance Col 66-68; Hd spec collections Cal State Col, Fresno 68-. 14: Rare bks. 15: 1845 East Thomas st, Fresno Ca 93701.

MAHOOD, RAMONA (MADSON). b Brigham City Utah 7 Je 33. 4: Harry R Mahood. 5: Utah State U 51-55 (Retailing) BS; UIll summers 55-59 (LS) MS, summer 68 (LS); UMich summer 66 (LS). 6: Ger. 7: Ref libn Weber State Col 55-62; Instr lib sci Memphis State U 64-. 8: Coord of Learning Resources, NDEA Eng Inst, Memphis State U 67. 9: ALA; TennLA. 10: Phi Kappa Phi; Kappa Delta Pi. 12: "Manual for Cataloging With Sample Cards" (68). 14: Tchg ref, catlg, child lit. 15: 264 Patterson, Memphis Tn 38111.

MAIER, JOAN MARCIA DAVIS EATON. b Columbus Ohio 28 N 32. 4: Carl Edwin Maier. 5: Centre Col 50-54 (Math) BA; UNC 54, 56-57 MSLS; UDenver 67- (Higher Educ). 6: Fr, Ger, Sp. 7: Libn Tchr Train Sch Winthrop Col 55-56; Catlg asst UNC Lib (Chapel Hill) 56-57, Ref asst 57-60; Chief Libn Base Lib System, Toul-Rosieres Air Base France 60-62; Libn Dependent Schs Landstuhl Army Med Center, Germany 63-64; Libn Ramstein Elem Sch, N Ramstein AFB Germany 64-65; Libn Metropolitan State Col (Denver) 65-67; Asst Dir Colo Acad Libs Bk Processing Ctr Project 67-68, Dir 68-. 8: Speed reading instr Educ Center, Ramstein AFB, Germany, 64-65. 9: NEA; ColoLA (Contin Educ Recr Chm); SLA; ColoEA. 11: Outstanding performance rating (US Civil Serv, 62, 69). 12: Co-auth "Colorado Academic Libraries Book

Processing Center" (69). 13: Yes. 14: Documentation, developl reading, higher educ, media, communication. 15: 743 9th st, Boulder Co 80302.

MAIER, MARY CLARA. b Roanoke Va 6 Ag 19. 5: Radford Col 61-63 (LS, Eng) BS, 64-67 (Eng) MS. 06: Ger. 7: Stenogr Hafleigh & Co, Buchanan Va 41-43; Sec Atlantic Greyhound, Roanoke Va 43-53; Sec-bkkeeper Roanoke Surgical Supply, Roanoke Va 53-61; Libn Norfolk City Schs, Norfolk Va 64; Libn Roanoke City Schs, Roanoke Va 64-; Tchr Eng 11 & 12) night sch. 9: NEA; VaEA; RoanokeEA; ALA; VaLA; RoanokeLA. 10: LWV. 14: Sch libnship. 15: 2609 Hillcrest ave NW, Roanoke Va 24012.

MAIER, PATRICIA (W) COKER. b Iuka Miss 30 N 41. 4: Harvey Edwin Maier Jr. 5: Northeast Jr Col 60-62 (LS) AA; USoMiss 62-64 (LS) BS. 7: Asst libn Cossitt Ref Lib, Memphis Tenn summers 61, 62; Libn & a-v coordinator Ocean Breeze Elem Sch, Indian Harbour Beach Fla 64-65; Libn Meridian Pub Schs, Meridian Miss 65-67; Libn Union Pub Schs, Union Miss 67-68. 9: FlaLA; MissLA. 10: Delta Psi Omega; AAUW. 14: Ref, technology, geneal. 15: 450 Belair ave, Merritt Island Fl 32952.

MAIHL, VIOLA R(UTH). b Paterson NJ 11 Mr 03. 5: Simmons (LS); Columbia (LS); Chicago (LS); Rutgers (LS). 7: Lib asst Paterson Pub Lib, Paterson NJ 20-27; Hosp libn USVA, Maywood Ill 27; Asst libn Bridgeton Pub Lib, Bridgeton NJ 28; Dir Linden Pub Lib, Linden NJ 28-68. 8: Consul; Berkeley Heights Pub Lib, Berkeley Heights NJ 52-54; Lansdale Pub Lib, Lansdale Penn 59; Pennsauken NJ 69; Nutley Pub Lib, Nutley NJ 69. 9: ALA (Coun 51-55); LPRC (pres 52); NJLA (pres 44-45 & 58-59). 10: Bus & Prof Women's Club; Linden Col Club; PTA. 11: Americanism Citation for Meritorious Serv, Linden B'nai B'rith. 13: Yes. 14: Admin. 15: 30 E Elm st, Linden NJ 07036.

MAILLARD, JOSEPHINE (DIKE). b N Dak 28 Ap 23. 5: Waukon Jr Col 40-42; Macalester Col 42-44 (Speech) BA; UCal (Berkeley) 45-46, 62-63 (Libnship) MLS; UCal (Davis) 55 (Ed). 7: Sec Walsh Co State Bank, Grafton N Dak summer 44; Eng & drama tchr Hoople High Sch, Hoople N Dak 44-45; Stenographer FE Booth Co, San Francisco 45; Research asst UCal (Berkeley) 45-46; Stenographer Corn Products Sales Co, San Francisco 46-47; Lib asst UCal (Davis) Lib 47-48, 56-62; Ref libn UOre (Eugene) 63-65; Asst dir Napa City Co Lib, napa Cal 65-. 9: ALA; CalLA. 10: Sierra Club; Siskiyou Trail Assn; ACLU; Nature Conserv. 14: Ref, spec collections. 15: 2396 Bohen st, Napa Ca 94558.

MAINE, JOHN STACY. b Trade Tenn 26 S 21. 4: Kathern Jaynes Maine. 5: Tasculum Col 45-48 (Bus admin) BA; Peabody Col 50-51 MALS; Temple 61-62. 7: Rm Ye USN 41-45; Hd libn Tuscalum Col 54-57; Hd libn Shepherd Col 57-61; Lib dir Millersville State Col 61-. 8: Served on Evaluation Team for College Libraries for Dept of Public Instruction for State of Penna. 9: ALA; -ACRL; PennLA (chm S Central Div, mem Exec Com). 10: Lions Club; Univ Club; Veterans of Foreign Wars. 14: Col lib admin, col & Univ Bldgs. 15: 65 Brenner st, Millersville Pa 17551.

MAIR, REBECCA. b Scotland 6 O 11. 4: William M Mair. 5: UGlasgow 32-35 LLB; Drexel 63- (LS). 7: Law practice, Glasgow Scotland 36-47; Law Libn Law Lib of Montgomery Co, Norristown Penn 65-. 9: AALL. 14: Ref, research. 15: Montgomery Co Law Lib, Norristown Pa 19401.

MAIZELL, ROBERT E(DWARD). b Baltimore 3 Ag 24. 4: Mona Fox. 5: Loyola Col (Baltimore) 42-45 (Chem) BS; Columbia 46-47 (LS) BS, 48-49 (LS) MS, -57 (LS) DLS. 6: Ger, Fr. 7: Chem Manhattan Proj and other assignments 45-46; Ref asst NY Pub Lib 47-48; Research asst NY State Lib Assn summer 49; Tchg asst Columbia U 50; Tech libn Olin Mathieson Chem Corp, Niagara Falls NY 50-58; Dir Doc Res Proj Amer Inst of Physics, NY 58-60; Supv tech info serv Olin Mathieson Chem Corp, New Haven Conn 60-65, Manager tech info serv 65-. 9: ACS (Div of Chem Lit, chm Long Range Planning Com); ASIS (organ memb NY Chap); Sci Res Soc Amer; Amer Inst Chemists (Fellow); Nat Sec Ind Assn (Tech Info Adv Group). 10: PTA. 12: "Introduction to Abstracting of Scientific Literature" (69). 13: Yes. 14: Ind chem, tech intel, data processing, cont educ. 15: 163 Hearn lane, Hamden Ct 06514.

MAJID, MOHAMMED ABDUL. b Hyderabad India 4 Ap 34. 4: Azra Ruksana. 5: Urdu Col 51-55 (Econ & Pol Sci) BA; Karachi Lib Assn 55-56 (LS) SLCC; UKarachi 56-57 DLS, 63-64 MALS. 6: Urdu, Hindi, Russian, Bengali, Persian, Sindhi, Ger, Fr. 7: Libn Karachi Polytechnic Inst, Karachi 56-57; Libn Govt Col of Com & Econ, Karachi 57-58; Libn Pub Sch, Karachi 58-60; Catlgr USind (Hyderabad India) 60-63; Catlgr UKarachi 63-67; Catlgr Mem UNewfoundland, St Johns 67-. 8: Part-time lect, Sch of Lib Sci, UKarachi 66-67. 14: Catlg. 15: Apt 102-146 Torbay rd, St John's Nfld Can.

MAJOR SHIRLEY (BORNWASSER). b Louisville Ky 5 Ap 22. 4: William C Major. 5: ULouisville 39-41 (Biol & Chem); Purdue 41-42 (Biol, Chem); Skidmore 42 (Bil, chem) BS; Catharine Spalding 58-60 (LS). 6: Fr, Lat. 7: Lab tech Ellis Hosp Lab, Schenectady NY 43-45; Asst to Dept hd Biol Dept ULouisville 62-63, Catlgr lib 63-. 10: LWV; Citizens Metro Planning Coun ULouisville Staff Assn. 14: Catlg. 15: 806 Alden rd, Louisville Ky 40207.

MAJOR, AUDREY S (SOLLIDAY). b Corbin Kan 17 D 03. 5: Kan State Tchrs Col 33 (Hist) AB, (LS) Certif. 7: Circ-readers adv City Lib, Wichita Kan 35-36; First asst ref City lib, Des Moines 46-48; First asst ref Ya libn a-v catlgr Lincoln Lib, Springfield Ill 48-. 10: Cathedral Altar and Rosary Soc; St Louise de Marillac Guild; Springfield Lib Club. 14: Ref, music. 15: PO Box 1115, Springfield Il 62705.

MAJOR, MURIEL (KELLY). b NYC 15 Jl 12. 5: Barnard 29-33 (Lat, Gk) BA; Columbia 33-34 BLS. 6: Fr, Ger. 7: Lib asst, Bk bus libn, sch libn, Libn in chg of sub-br, ref libn Queens Borough Pub Lib, NY 34-42; Lib Dir Williston Park Pub Lib, Williston Park NY 54-56; Ref libn Mineola Mem Lib, Mineola NY 56-69; Ref libn Garden City Pub Lib, Garden City NY 59-. 9: NassauCoLA. 10: LI Choral Soc; Sperry Country Dance Club; Recorder Soc. 13: Yes. 14: Ref. 15: 599 Foch blvd, Williston Park NY 11596.

MAJURI, KATHRYN (SYLVIA WRIGHT). b Coloma Ind 8 Fe 33. 4: Leonard L Majuri. 5: Ind U 51-53, 54-56 (Ger) AB, 60-61 (LS) AM; UTubingen 56-57 (Ger); Ind Central Bus Col 58 (Sec sci). 6: Ger, Sp, Fr. 7: Long distance operator Ind Bell Tele Co, Indianapolis 53-54, summer 55; Sec Classics Dept Ind U (Bloomington) 58-60; Asst acquis libn San fernando Valley State Col 61-63; Admin libn USA Spec Serv 7th Inf Div, Korea 63-65; Catlgr Bates Col 65-66; Asst catlgr Villanova U 66-. 9: ALA; PennLA. 10: Phi Beta Kappa. 14: Catlg, acquis. 15: PO Box 64, Spring House Pa 19477.

MAKI, JOAN M (STAMPEE). b Shennandoah Penn 17 My 38. 4: Roland Maki. 5: Drexel 56-60 (Educ) BS; UMich 62-63 (LS) MA. 7: Home Econ tchr Trenton Pub Sch, Trenton NJ 60-61; Dorm counselor UMich 62-63; Libn Detroit Pub Lib 63; Tchr-libn Dept of Defense, Adana Turkey 63-64, Rhein-Main Germany 44-66; Ref libn General Motors, Warren Mich 66-68, Hd libn-styling 68-. 9: SLA. 14: Ref. 15: G M Styling Lib G M Tech Center, Warren Mi 48090.

MAKOVICS, LESLEY ELIZABETH (SCHULTZ). b Rugby Eng 3 Ja 41. 4: Lajos Sandor Makovics. 5: Carleton U 58-62 (Hist) BA; McGill 63-64 BLS. 6: Fr. 7: Catlgr Westmount Pub Lib, Westmount Que 64-68; Libn Co of San Mateo Health & Welfare Lib, San Mateo Cal 68-. 09: ALA; CalLA. 14: Catlg. 15: P O Box 769, El Cerrito Ca 94530.

MAKUCH, ANDREW LUBOMIR. b Jaroslaw Poland 14 Ja 28. 5: UGoettingen 47-49 (Romance Langs); UIll 49-51 (Sp) AB; UMich 54-55 (LS) MA, 61-62 (Romance Langs) MA. 6: Ger, Sp, Polish, Ukrainian. 7: Readers' adv Detroit Pub Lib 55-56; Hd libn NMex Mil Inst 56-58; Bk selection libn UMich 58-64; Acquis libn UAriz 64-. 9: ALA; Ariz StateLA. 10: Mod Lang Assn. 14: Latin Amer and Slavic acquis. 15: 1587 E Edison, Tucson Az 85719.

MALBY, HELEN (BAIRD). b Omaha 28 Ja 42. 4: Robert J Malby. 5: Col of St Catherine 60-64 (Fr, LS) BA. 6: Fr. 7: Clerk Pub Lib, S St Paul Minn 59-64; Young adult libn Detroit Pub Lib 64-65; Br libn Riverview Br, St Paul 65-66; Commun rel staff libn 66-67; Admin asst 67-. 9: ALA; MinnLA. 14: Reading guidance in pub libs, pub lib admin. 15: 90 West Fourth ave, St Paul Mn 55102.

MALCOLM, JANET (ADELE). b Pittsburg Kan 31 Mr 25. 5: Kan State Col (Pittsburg) 42-45 (Eng) BS. 7: Bus Off Rep Bell Telephone Co, Kansas City Mo 46-47; Hd libn Gulf R&D Co, Pittsburg Kansas & Merriam Kansas 47-. 9: SLA (Heart of Amer Chap: past sec, v-pres, pres, Memb Chm). 14: Ref wk in chem (agricultural & polymer fields). 15: 9009 W 67th st, Merriam Ks 66202.

MALCOLM, LYDIA (SMITH). b Dolgeville NY 22 Ag 08. 4: David Gray Malcolm. 5: State Tchrs Col(Albany NY) 24-25 (Eng); Albany Bus Col 25-56 (Accounting); UNev 55- (Eng, LS); Equivalency Test from UCal 63 Grade III certif. 6: Sp. 7:

Bkkeeper Waldorf Lunch Systems, Boston 27-29; Bkkeeper Bird-Speakman Inc, Wilmington Del 42-46; Circ desk Wilmington Pub Lib, Wilmington Del; Circ desk Henderson Pub Lib, Henderson Nev 46-48, Head Libn 48-. 9: ALA (Coun 64-65, 66-67); NevLA (pres 63-65); Pub Lib Assn of Nev (chm 63-65). 10: Beta Sigma Phi; Nev Fed Garden Clubs. 11: Woman of the year (55) Beta Sigma Phi Sorority, Henderson Nev; Libn of the year (63) NevLA; Dist Pub Lib received the Dorothy Canfield Fisher Award of the Book of the Month Club, 63. 13: Yes. 14: Ref, child. 15: 531 Fairway rd Box 203, Henderson Nv 89015.

MALCOLM, MARY F. b St Petersburg Fla 20 S 24. 5: George Washington U 41-43; Fla State U 59-64 (Eng) BA, MS (LS). 07: Clerk-stenogr War Prod Bd, Wash DC 42-44; Clerk-stenogr War Dept, Miami Fla 44-45; Sec Fla Ind Commsn, Miami Fla 45-58; Admin asst Fla Ind Commsn, Tallahassee Fla 58-63; Libn SW Miami High Sch, Miami Fla 64; Libn Miami-Dade Jr Col 65-. 9: ALA; FlaLA. 10: Beta Phi Mu; Fla Assn Pub Jr Cols. 14: Ref. 15: 77 NW 109 st, Miami Fl 33168.

MALEADY, ANTOINETTE (KIRKPATRICK). b Powell Wyo 9 D 18. 4: Thomas J Maleady. 5: West Va Wesleyan 36-39 (Bus Admin) BS; Sonoma State Col 67; UCal (Berkeley) 67-68 MLS. 6: Sp, Ger, Japanese. 7: Coll correspondent & collection mgr Sears Roebuck & Co, Kan City Mo 40-43; Payroll computer US Army, Los Angeles 43-44; Control Tower Operator US Navy, Anacostia Va 44-45; Dept of State Foreign Serv, Japan, Thailand, Ecuador, Brazil 46-54; Phonotrvo ecuador, Brazil 46-54; Phonorecord & mus libn Sonoma State Col 68-. 9: ALA; MoLA; CalLA. 10: AAUP; Marin Soc of Artists; Mill Valley Outdoor Art Club. 14: Rare bks, music. 15: 533 Robin dr, Corte Madera Ca 94925.

MALECKI, PAUL MARTIN. b Buffalo NY 17 F 40. 4: Marian Behrens. 5: Syracuse 57-61 (Psych) AB, 61-62 (LS) MS, 62-63 (Art Hist); Chicago 63-64 (Adult Educ). 7: Art br, Syracuse U Libs 61-63, Head Engnr br 63; 1st asst Gen Reading Dept Flint Mich Pub Lib 64-66; Dir Lapeer(Mich) Pub Lib 66-68; Asst dir Jervis Lib, Rome NY 68-. 9: MichLA (Pub Rel Chm 67-68); NYLA. 10: Psi Chi; Beta Phi Mu; Kiwanis. 14: Adult educ, art hist. 15: 613 N Washington st, Rome NY 13440.

MALGERI, DINA (GLORIA). b Chicago Ill 19 Ag 29. 5: Harvard 56-63 (Humanities) BA; Simmons 64-65 MS in LS. 6: Fr, Ital, Sp. 7: Statistical clk Off Commsner Probation, Court House, Boston 51-65; Admin asst Mass Bur of Lib Ext, Boston 65-67; Army libn, Germany 67-. 9: ALA (Armed Forces Libns Sect); MassLA. 14: Adult serv, admin. 15: P O Box 83, Boston Ma 02113.

MALIN, JOYCE ELAINE. b Campbell Mo 8 Ap 36. 5: East MichU 54-58 (Biol, Eng, Pol Sci, Educ) AB; UMich 63 AMLS. 6: Ger. 7: Faculty-tchr Birmingham (Mich) Bd of Educ 58-64; Faculty-asst to libn Macomb Co Commun Col 64-65; Libn Detroit Osteopathic Hosp Corp 65-67; Dir Med Lib Henry Ford Hosp, Detroit 67-. 9: MedLA; Mich Assn Higher Educ (sec macomb Co Commun Col Chap 64-65). 13: Yes. 14: Admin. 15: 1022 E Sixth st, Royal Oak Mi 48067.

MALINOWSKY, HAROLD ROBERT. b WaKeeney Kan 7 D 33. 4: Mary Dresser. 5: Midland Col 51-52 (Pre-engnr); UKan 52-55 (Geol-Engnr) BS, 60-61 (Geol); UDenver 62-63 (LS) MA. 6: Fr, Ger. 7: Prod engnr Gulf Oil Corp, Odessa Tex 55-57; Spec 4th class US Army, Tacoma Wash 57-59; Prod engnr Gulf Oil Corp, Monahans Tex 59-60; Stud asst UKan Lib 61-62; Stud asst UDenver Lib 62-63; Asst sci libn UKan 63-64; Sci engnr libn UDenver 64-67; Sci & engnr libn UKan (Lawrence) 67-. 9: SLA (Educ Com; pres-elect Heart of Amer Chap 69-70); MPLA. 10: Tau Beta Pi; Geosci Info Soc; MPLA. 12: Ed "Columbine," Colo Chap, SLA; "Science and Engineering Reference Sources" (67). 13: Yes. 14: Sci, engring & map lib admin. 15: 2214 Hillcourt, Lawrence Ks 66044.

MALINSKI, RICHARD (MARCIN). b Broty Ferry Scotland 23 F 44. 5: YorkU 63-67 (Geog) Honours BA; UToronto 67-68 BLS. 7: Map libn YorkU 68-. 9: Assn Can Map Libns. 14: Maps. 15: 56 Proctor ave, Thornhill Ont Can.

MALKIN, MARY ANN (O'BRIAN). b Altoona Penn 13 Mr 13. 4: Sol M Malkin. 5: Penn State 31-37 (Eng, Hist, Educ) BA, 37-40 (Econ); Columbia 47-48 (Publ); NYU 48-49, 63-64 (Publ); New School 40- (Econ). 7: Economic researcher NY Publishers' Assn 40-42; Exec sec to proj dir NDRC-OSRD 42-46; Ed asst "Publishers' Weekly" 46-50; "Antiquarian Bookman" 50-; Bk review ed, Libn assoc publisher 63-. 9: MusicLA; Internat Assn Mus Libs; Amer Folklore Soc; Amer Musicological Soc; Soc State & Loc Hist; Soc Ethnomusicology; Asia Music Soc; Nat Assn Bk Editors; Women's Nat Bk Assn; ALA; BSA; Internat Folk Music Coun; SLA; NY Lib Club; Manuscript Soc; Booksellers League of NY; AAUW; Amer Bible Soc; NJ Hist Soc; Internat Soroptimist Club; Delta Gamma; NYC Panhellenic. 12: Ed asst "Publishers' Weekly" 46-50; "Antiquarian Bookman" (50-). 14: Rare bks, antiquarian bks, bk reviewing, editing. 15: Box 1100 Newark NJ 07101.

MALKUS, HUBERT PAUL. b NYC 19 Mr 26. 4: Betty Anne Jones. 5: UMich 43, 46-49 (Eng) BA, 49-50 (Eng) MA; Columbia MS in LS. 6: Fr. 7: Tchr Nott Terrace High Sch, Schenectady NY 50-51; Lib trainee E Orange Pub Lib, E Orange NJ 51-53; Br libn Free Pub Lib, Elizabeth NJ 54; Gen libn VA Hosp, E Orange NJ 54-62; Med libn VA Hosp, Castle Point NY 56; Chief Libn VA Hosp, Richmond Va 62-. 9: SLA; VaLA (Spec Libs Sect: Program Chm 63-64). 10: US Army Reserve, Ridgmond Area Spec Libs Club. 14: Admin. 15: 1547 Yeardley dr, Richmond Va 23225.

MALLERY, MARY (SILCOX). b Utica NY 9 N 36. 4: Richard C Mallery. 5: Simmons 54-58 (LS) BS; Drexel 62-67 (LS) MS. 7: Br libn USA, Ft Chaffee Ark 58-59; Bkmob libn USA, Valley Forge Penn 59-60; Dir Lansdale Pub Lib, Pansdale Penn 60-67; Ext libn montgomery Co Pub Lib, Norristown Norristown Penn 67-. 9: ALA; PennLA (corr sec SE Chap 65, chm Publ & Pub Rel Com 69). 14: Adult serv. 15: 301 W Eighth st, Lansdale Pa 19446.

MALLETT, MARGARET ROSE. b Seattle Wash 12 F 43. 5: UWash 61-64 (Swedish) BA, 64-68 MLS. 6: Swedish, Danish, Norwegian, Ger. 7: Subject Specialist I UWash Lib 65-68; Catlgr LC 68-. 8: Participant summer sem in Sweden, Soc Advanc Scand Studies, 68. 9: ALA; Soc Advanc Scand Studies (Bibliog Com 68-). 14: Catlg, bibliog. 15: 7330 Dibble ave NW, Seattle Wa 98107.

MALLICK, EVELYN (REAGHART). b Strattanville Penn 17 N 22. 4: Lewis Mallick. 5: Clarion State Tchrs Col 40-44 (LS) BS; Peabody 45 (LS); Villa Maria Col 46 (Eng); Edinboro State Col 57-61 (Educ) Ed M. 6: Fr, Lat. 7: Libn Ambridge Sr High Sch, Ambridge Penn 44-45; Libn Gridley Jr High Sch, Erie Penn 45-. 10: Erie Fed of Tchrs (AF of L). 14: Catlg, sel. 15: 619 Lowell ave, Erie Pa 16505.

MALLING, GERALD V. b Rochester ny 17 F 26. 4: Audrey J Miller. 5: BradleyU 49-51 (Bus Admin) BBS; Columbia 51-53 (Intl Affairs) MLA; UMich 64-65 MLS. 6: Sp. 7: Export Traffic Dow Chem Intl, New York NY 53-54; Sales Rep Intl Latex Corp, NYC 54-57; Sales rep Exquisite Form Industries, Chicago 57-60; Sales Rep Geneseo Corp, Greenville Mich 60-65; Legislative libn State Lib of Mich 65-. 9: ALA; (Legisl Ref Com); MichLA (chm Intel Freedom Com). 10: Pres St Paul Lutheran Church, Lansing Mich. 14: Ref serv to legislators. 15: 1720 N Fairview ave, Lansing Mi 48912.

MALLINO, KATHERYNE (YVONNE) (TOMSON). b Henrico Co Va 3 My 38. 4: John R Mallino Jr. 5: Clarion State Col 56-60 (LS) BS in Ed; Drexel 61-62 MS in LS; UPittsburgh 64-65 Advanced Certif in LS. 6: Fr. 7: Libn Carnegie Sr High Sch, Carnegie Penn 60-61; Circ libn UPittsburgh 62, Admin asst to dir of libs 63, Coordinator of sci & reg libs 63-64; Asst libn Indiana U of Penn, Indiana Penn 64-. 8: Adv com, Lib Resources Development Bd, Center for Lib & Educ Media Studies U Pittsburgh 63-64. 9: ALA-ACRL (Nat Lib Week Com 64-65); PennLA (Educ & Certif Com 64-65). 10: Nat Campers & Hiker's Assn. 13: Yes. 14: Ser, archives, child rare bks. 15: 548 Water st, Indiana Pa 15701.

MALLISON, GLENN (S). b Cortland NY 10 D 18. 4: Carolyn Weddell. 5: Earlham Col 46-49 (Sociol) BA; Ind U 49-50 (Soc wk); Syracuse 53-54 MSLS. 7: Civilian pub serv Royalston Mass & NYC 41-45; Probation off Marion Co Juvenile Ct, Indianapolis 49-50; Dir week-end wk camp, Harlem NYC 50-51; Br asst Rochester Pub Lib, Rochester NY 54-56; Libn Herkimer Free Lib, Herkimer NY 56-59; Head of tech serv N Country Lib System, Watertown NY 59-67; Hd of adv serv 67-. 9: ALA (Recr Com 3 yrs); NYLA (Bd Dirs, Film Com 2 yrs, Recr Com 3 yrs; 2nd v-pres RTSS Sect); Herkimer-Montgomery(Co)LA (pres 2 yrs). 13: Yes. 14: Admin, serv to rural areas, tech serv. 15: 724 Myrtle ave, Watertown NY 13601.

MALLISON, KATHLEEN (DONAHUE). b Detroit 4 Ap 15. 4: William C Mallison. 5: Hope Col 32-36 (Eng) AB; UNC 37-38 BSLS. 7: Jr ref asst tech dept Detroit Pub Lib 38-41; Libn Bomac R & D Varian Assn, Beverly Mass 61-64; Catlgr

New Haven Free Pub Lib, New Haven Conn 64-66; Supv proc 66-. 9: ConnLA. 14: Catlg, tech serv. 15: New Haven Free Pub Lib, Elm st, New Haven Ct 06511.

MALLON, ANNE (McGEORGE). b Ambridge Penn 12 S 23. 6: Fr, Ger. 7: Ins investigator Liberty Mutual Ins, NY 45-46; Libn Nutley Free Pub Lib, Nutley NJ 68-. 9: ALA; NJLA. 10: Montclair Fair Housing; Operation Understanding; Red Cross - Open Heart Surgery Blood Bank. 14: Ref, adult & ya serv, lib sci educ, child serv. 15: 27 Pkwy, Montclair NJ 07042.

MALLON, NEWMAN FRANCIS. b Toronto 14 Jl 06. 4: Shirley Howe. 5: Toronto 25-29 BA; Rutgers 61-62 MLS. 6: Fr. 7: Trust off Toronto Gen Trusts Corp, Toronto 29-56; Army COTC (Cpt), Toronto 40-45; Exec asst to chief libn & sec-treas Toronto Pub Lib 56-62, Asst chief libn & sec-treas 62-; Guest lectr UToronto Lib Sch 63-. 8: Pres Can Lib Res & Devel Coun 62-; Libns certif bd, Ont 62-, chm 65-. 9: ALA (Coun 69-70; ALA-CanLA Liaison Com); CanLA (treas 62-65; sec 65-68; Trustees Sect 47-48; chm Pensions Com 58-62; chm Budget & Finance Com 63-66; Lib-Publisher Rel Com; mem 65-66, chm 66-67); Inst Prof Libns Ont; OntLA (chm Trustee Sect 43-44; Coun 45-47; Legis & Grants Com 61-65). 10: Royal Can Yacht Club; Hart House, UToronto; Toronto Pub Lib Bd; Bd Dir Newman Foun Toronto; Royal Can Mil Inst. 11: CanLA Trustees Merit Award (65). 13: Yes. 14: Admin. 15: Toronto Pub Libs 40 St Clair ave E, Toronto 7 Ont C an.

MALLORY, R(OBERT) PATRICK (JOHN). b Urbana Ill 25 S 39. 4: Judith Ann Spall. 5: UNotre Dame 57-61 (Gen Sci) BS; UIll 61-62 (LS) MS. 7: Asst sci libn UNotre Dame(Ind) 62-63, Biol libn 63-66; Acquis libn UMont (Missoula) 67-. 9: AAUP; ASIS; LARC Assn; PNLA; MontLA. 14: Ref, sci-tech br admin, tech proc, purchasing, systems devel & mgt. 15: 126 Woodford st, Missoula Mt 59801.

MALLOY, MARY ANN JANE (SCHWARZKOPF). b Hoboken NJ 28 My 32. 4: John Francis Malloy Jr. 5: Douglass Col 50-54 (Eng) AB; Rutgers 54-56 (LS) MA. 6: Ger, Fr. 7: Trainee Newark Pub Lib, Newark NJ 54-55; Child libn Pease Lib, Ridgewood NJ 56-57; Child libn Providence Pub Lib 58-59; Prin child libn Elizabeth (NJ) ub Lib 59-. 9: NJLA (treas Child Sect 63-64). 14: Child wk, storytelling, puppetry. 15: 89 Meadow rd, Clark NJ 07066.

MALNAR, MARY SUSAN. b Nashwauk Minn. 5: UMinn 30-34 (LS) BS, 35 (Educ) BS. 6: Jugoslav (Croatian), Ger. 7: Child libn Buhl Pub Lib, Buhl Minn 35-40; Child libn Hackley Pub Lib, Muskegon Mich 40-42; Child libn Appleton Pub Lib, Appleton Wis 42-45; Child libn Pub Lib, Walla Walla Wash 46-47; Child libn Oshkosh Pub Lib, Oshkosh Wis 47-. 9: ALA; WisLA (chm &/or mem Child Sect, Awards & Honors Com, Memb Com); Fox Valley LA (sec, chm). 10: Amer Field Serv; AAUW; Cath Women's Club; LWV; Altrusa; Internat Readg Assn; C of C (Women's Div); Bus Women's Club. 14: Child wk. 15: 615A Algoma blvd, Oshkosh Wi 54901.

MALONE, ALTON (HODGE). b Plant City Fla 4 Ap 34. 4: Carol McGary. 5: Carson-Newman Col 53-56, 60-61 (Hist-Pol Sci) BA; UIll 64-65 MSLS. 7: IBM operator US Army, Tex, Europe 56-59; Bkmob libn Cherokee- Pickens Reg Lib, Canton Ga 60; Circ libn Kinchafoonee Reg Lib, Dawson Ga 62; Bkmob libn Nolichucky Reg Lib, Morristown Tenn 62-64; Circ-ref libn Undergrad Lib USoCar 65-68; Ref libn Mem lib Mars Hill Col 68-. 9: ALA; SELA; NCLA. 10: Civitan Club. 14: Ref, circ. 15: P O Box 202, Mars Hill NC 28754.

MALONE, ELIZABETH MARGARET. b Jonesboro Ark 5 Mr 02. 5: Wesleyan Col (Ga) 20-24 (Eng) AB; UIll summer 32,34,35,36 BS in LS. 6: Sp. 7: Tchr-libn Annie Camp Jr High Sch, Jonesboro Ark 24-37; Libn asst child dept, Cossitt Lib, Memphis Tenn 37-40; Libn Craighead Co Lib, Jonesboro Ark 40-66; Dir Crowley Ridge Reg Lib, Jonesboro Ark 66-. 9: ALA (past State Recr Rep); SWLA (chm Pub Lib Div 63-64); ArkLA (pres 44); NEArkLA. 10: Craighead Co Hist Soc; 20th Century Club; Wesleyan Serv Guild; NE Ark Mental Health Assn. 13: Yes. 14: Readers adv, pub rel, ref. 15: 624 Warner ave, Jonesboro Ar 72401.

MALONE, MAUREEN JULIA. b Hartford Conn 30 Jl 41. 5: Albertus Magnus 59-63 (Hist) BA; Pratt Inst 65-67 MLS. 7: Lib asst Olin Mathieson Research Lib, New Haven Conn 63-65; Catlgr Sacred Heart U, Bridgeport Conn 65-67; Catlgr Boston Pub Lib 67-68; Asst humanities libn MIT 68-. 9: ALA. 10: Albertus Magnus Alum. 14: Catlg, ref. 15: 94 Brainerd rd, Boston Ma 02134.

MALONE, RICHARD SANFORD. b Lima Ohio 20 O 09. 4: Marjorie Green. 5: Oberlin Col 27-33 (Eng) BA; Columbia 46-47 MLS. 7: Divisional sales mgr Bloch Bros Tobacco, S Bend Ind 35-43; (Lt) US Navy Seventh Fleet, S Pacific 43-46; Head bus & tech dept Pub Lib, Trenton NJ 47-50; Pub Lib, Detroit: Asst chief tech dept 50; Chief Downtown Lib 50-63; Coordinator Downtown Lib 63-. 8: Libn Detroit Athletic Club 61-. 9: ALA (chm For Lang Bk Sel Com 51-59); MichLA. 13: Yes. 14: Pub lib serv (bus & com), hist of printing & bk illus. 15: Downtown Lib 121 Gratiot ave, Detroit Mi 48226.

MALONE, ROBERT M. b Trenton NJ 24 Ag 24. 5: Rutgers 42-43, 46-48 (Hist) AB; Columbia 49-50 (LS) MS. 7: US Army Med Corps (Sgt) 43-46; Lib asst Trenton Pub Lib, Trenton NJ 48-49; Lib asst Brooklyn Pub Lib 50-51; Lending serv libn NJ State Lib 51-56; Dir Mercer Co Lib, Trenton NJ 57-. 15: 2152 Pennington rd, Trenton NJ 08638.

MALONE, ROSE MARY. b Stillwater Minn 9 Ja 02. 5: Col of St Catherine 18-21 (Eng) BA; UMinn 24-25 (Educ) MA; UDenver summers 47-49 (LS) MA. 7: Tchr Eng & hist High Sch, Long Prairie Minn 21-24; Proofreader West Publ Co, St Paul 25-26; Tchr Eng & hist High Sch, Geyser Mont 26-27; Tchr Eng & hist City Col (Asheville NC) 27-29; Tchr Eng, hist, math High Sch, Douglas Wyo 29-41; Prin High Sch, Douglas Wyo 41-44; Tchr Eng Natrona Co High Sch, Casper Wyo 44-47, Libn 47-67; West hist libn Casper Col 67-. 08: Mem of Governor's Com on Educ 64-65. 9: NEA; ALA; AASchL; MPLA; WyoEA (pres Centr Dist 65); WyoASchL; WyoLA (pres 55). 10: Wyo Hist Soc, Delta Kappa Gamma; Bus & Prof Women. 12: "Wyomingana" (50). 13: Yes. 14: Rare bks (Wyoming & the West). 15: 1504 S Ash, Casper Wy 82601.

MALONEY, RUTH KAY (MURRAY). b Connersville Ind 25 S 32. 4: Gerald P Maloney. 5: IndianaU 50-53 (Fr) AB; Rutgers 65-68 MLS, 68- (LS). 6: Fr. 7: Undergrad asst School of Lib Sci IndU 52-53; Hd circ Roanoke Pub Lib, Roanoke Va 53-55; Catlgr DrewU, Madison NJ 57-60. 10: Beta Phi Mu. 14: Info sci, ref. 15: 54 Elm st, Madison NJ 07940.

MALTBY, FLORENCE HELEN (GARLAND). b Sumner Iowa. 4: George Robert Maltby. 5: State Col Iowa 50-54 (Elem ed, LS) BA; UIll 59-60 MSLS, 66-67 Certif Adv Study in Libnship. 07: Elem libn Barrington Elem Schs, Barrington Ill 54-57; Elem libn USAFE Dep Sch, Sculthorpe Eng 57-58; Elem libn USAFE Dep Sch, Ramstein Germany 58-59; Grad asst Lib Sci Lib, UIll 59-60; Elem libn USAFE Dep Sch, Wiesbaden Germany 60-61; Ref asst & Instr of Lib Sci Central Mich U 61-63; Asst Prof of Lib Sci Southwest Mo State Col 63-64, Supply Instr of Lib Sci 64-; Tchg asst Grad Sch Lib Sci UIll 66-67. 10: AAUP; Beta Phi Mu. 14: Sch libs, lib educ. 12: "Rules for Full Cataloging v 3 in "Code International de Catalogage de la Musique (69) Contrib to & tr of v 1-2. 15: 819 E Linwood dr, Springfield Mo 65804.

MALTBY, GEORGE ROBERT. b Herington Kan 8 Je 30. 4: Florence Garland. 05: St Benedict's Col 49-51 (Bus); UOkla 55-57 (LS) BA; LSU 60-61 (LS) MS; UIll 66-67 Certif of Advanced Study in libnship. 07: Storekeeper 2d Class US Navy 51-55; Catlgr Rosenberg Lib, Galveston Tex 57-60; Catlgr & Instr of Lib Sci Southwest Mo State Col 61-67; Catlgr UIll (Urbana) 66-67; Catlgr & Asst Prof of Lib Sci SW Mo State Col 67-. 9: ALA. 10: AAUP; Beta Phi Mu. 14: Catlg (subj headings). 15: 819 E Linwood dr, Springfield Mo 65804.

MAMALAKIS, MARIE J. b Shreveport La 15 S 13. 5: USouthwesternLa 30-33 (Eng, Hist) BA; LSU 41 BS in LS; Chicago 48; Tulane U 51; LSU 62. 6: Gk. 7: Interviewer ERA, Opelousas 34; Tchr Pub Schs St Landry Parish, La 34-41; Head circ dept USouthwesternLa 41-65; Editor "Lafayette Progress" weekly newspaper 51-61; Prof of Lib Sci & Dir of Publs USouthwesternLa 65-. 9: ALA; Nat Fed Press Women (treas 3 yrs); LaLA. 10: Phi Alpha Theta; Sigma Tau Delta; Phi Kappa Phi; Omicron Delta Epsilon. 12: Asst ed (several yrs) "Louisiana Lib Assn Bulletin"; Brochures on people and events of Southwest La. 13: Yes. 14: Ref, circ. 15: 1018 Auburn ave, Lafayette La 70501.

MANALEY, SHIRLEY (LOGAN) KEYES. b Nashville Tenn 18 O 31. 4: Roy N Manaley. 5: Middle Tenn State Col 50-54 (Elem ed) BS; Peabody Col 57-58 (LS) MA. 7: Tchr: Dalewood Sch, Nashville 54-55, Rigdon Rd Sch, Columbus Ga 55-56; Lab tech US Tobacco Co, Nashville 56; Libn Cajon Valley Jr High Sch, El Cajon Cal 57-59, 60-64; Libn nurnberg American Elem Sch, Nurnberg Ger 59-60, Libn IBM Corp FSD, Huntsville Ala 65-. 9: SLA; SLA; Ala;A; SELA. 12: "A Library of Literary Criticism: Modern American Literature (1st ed 60, 2nd ed 61, 3rd ed 63); Ed "Bay State Librarian (60-61); "A Library of Literary Criticism; Romance Literature" (67). 15: 210 Skyline rd, Madison Al 35758.

MANCINI, SISTER M OP PhD. b Brooklyn NY 9 O 1883. 5: Brooklyn Tchrs Train Sch (NY) 02-04 License No 1; Col of New Rochelle 08-10 BA; St John's U (NY) ext 10-14 MA; Fordham 25-28 PhD; MedLA Certif 65. 6: Fr, Ger, Gk, Lat. 7: Elem tchr Pub Schs City of NY, Brooklyn NY 04-06; High sch tchr Queen of Rosary Acad, Amityville NY 06-08; High sch tchr St Agnes Academic Sch, College Point NY 08-13; Prin St Nicholas Com High Sch, Brooklyn NY 13-22; Prin St Bartholomew High Sch, Elmhurst NY 22-28; Prin elem schs, Queens Co NY 28-57; Med libn Mary Immaculate Hosp, Jamaica NY 62-. 9: Nat Art Assn; MedLA; CathLA; East Art Assn (consul). 12: "Art for Elementary Schools" (43). 14: Ref, bibliog. 15: Med Lib Mary Immaculate Hosp, 152-11 89th ave, Jamaica NY 11432.

MANDELL, EDWARD. b Pittsburgh 26 O 35. 4: Phyllis Grossman. 5: Slippery Rock State Tchrs Col 54-58 (Soc Sci) BS; Drexel summer 61 (LS); UPittsburgh 63-64 MLS. 7: Tchr Zanesville Sch Dist, Zanesville Ohio 50-60; Tchr Hillel Acad of Pittsburgh 61-64; Libn, Br Head Dayton & Montgomery Co Lib, Dayton Ohio 64-. 9: ALA; OhioLA. 10: Phi Alpha Theta. 14: Ref, catlg. 15: Westwood Lib 3207 Hoove ave, Dayton Ohio 45417.

MANDERSON, FRANCES (POWER). b Plainfield NJ 26 S 18. 4: Frank A Manderson. 5: NJ State Tchrs Col 38-42 (Elem Educ) BS; Rutgers 61-63 MLS. 7: Dist clerk Prudential Insurance Co of Amer, Plainfield NJ 36-38; Tchr Plainfield Pub Schs, Plainfield NJ 42-43; Clerk-steno Tide Water Associated Oil Co, NY 44; Sch libn Evergreen & Stillman elem schs, Plainfield NJ 63-65; Sch libn Evergreen & Emerson schs, Plainfield NJ 65-69; Sch libn Emerson Sch, Plainfield NJ 69-. 9: ALA; NEA; NJSchLA; NJEA. 10: Beta Phi Mu. 14: Child lit. 15: 1252 Cambridge ave, Plainfield NJ 07062.

MANDEVILLE, ELIZABETH (MEYER). b Madison Wis 11 S 12. 4: Charles Mandeville. 5: UWis 29-33 (Ger) BS, 36-37 (LS) Diploma. 6: Ger. 7: Asst libn Employer's Mutuals Insurance, Wausau Wis 37-39; Sr lib asst State Tchrs Col (Oshkosh Wis) 39-40; Lib asst Wis State Hist Soc, Madison Wis 40-41; Lib asst Jacksonville Naval Air Station, Jacksonville Fla 41-42; Libn Glenview Naval Air Station, Glenview Ill 42-45; Libn US VA Hosp, Mendota Wis 45-48; Asst UWis Med Lib 49-54; Catlgr Edgewood Col Lib 62-. 9: WisLA. 14: Catlg. 15: 2604 Arbor dr #227, Madison Wi 53711.

MANFREDI, DOROTHY A. b NYC 24 F 37. 5: Queens Col 53-57 (Chem) BS; UVt 57-59 (Chem) MS; Fla State U 59-60 (LS) MS; Case West Res 65- (Chem, LS). 6: Fr, Ger. 7: Tchr UVt 57-59; Tech libn FMC Corp, Princeton NJ 60-62; Hd libn Ft Knox Post Lib, Ft Knox Ky 62-63; Research libn Tenneco Chem, Pensacola Fla 63-65; Instr Case West Res 67-69; Mgr tech info serv Glidden-Durkee Div, Strongsville Ohio 69-. 9: ACS; ALA; SLA; ASIS; OhioLA. 10: AAAS; Beta Phi Mu. 14: Bibliog of sci, lit of sci & tech, chem info systems, communication behavior. 15: 12000 Fairhill rd, Cleveland Oh 44120.

MANG, JAMES. b Buffalo NY 7 My 39. 5: St Bonaventure 59-61 (Phil) BA; Diocesan Prep Sem 57-59 (Classical lang); Catholic U of Amer 63 (Relig ed); SUNY (Geneseo) 66- (LS). 6: Sp, Lat. 7: Parish priest Catholic Ch, Puerto Rico 65-66; Libn Catholic Sch, Buffalo NY 67-. 9: West NY Catholic Libs (Treas). 13: Yes. 15: 564 Dodge st, Buffalo NY 14208.

MANHEIM, THEODORE. b Detroit 21 Jl 21. 5: Wayne State 39-43 (Educ, LS) BA; UMich 46-47 ABLS, 47-48 AMLS. 6: Fr. 7: Tec 4 US Army XVI Corps HQ, US, Europe 43-45; Lib asst US Army, Shrivenham (Eng) American U 45; Sr u asst Wayne State U Lib 46, Jr asst libn emerg sub 47, Jr asst libn 48-49, Asst libn head Educ Lib 49-60, Libn IV head Educ Lib 60-. 8: Coop faculty Lib Sci Wayne State U 61-; Visiting Prof Lib Sci USoFla summer 64; Consul Com on Prof Materials MichASchL 62; Trustee John H Trybom Mem Collections Wayne State U 60-; Mem Exec Bd Detroit Children's Bk Fair 63-68; Consul Curr Lab Facilities & Uses Wkshop Detroit Bd of Educ 65. 9: ALA-ACRL; MichLA (Spec Com on Coop Lib Serv 60-). 10: AAUP. 12: "The Cul turally Disadvantaged: A Bibliography and Keyword-out-of-Context Inde x" (66); "Sources in Educational Research " (69). 13: Yes. 14: Educ libs, ref, bk sel. 15: 20230 Annchester rd, Detroit Mi 48219.

MANIER, MARY LEE (MATHEWS). b Nashville 22 O 24. 4: William Rucker Manier III. 5: Vanderbilt 42-46 (Chem) BA; Peabody 64-65 MLS. 7: Elem sch libn Nashville Pub Schs 65-67; Libn Harpeth Hall Sch for Girls. 14: Child lit. 15: 1045 Overton Lea rd, Nashville Tn 37220.

MANLY, VIRGINIA (LUDEKENS). b Phila 24 Je 14. 5: West Chester State Tchrs Col 46 BS in Ed; Drexel 48 BS in LS, 68 MS in LS. 07: Elem sch tchr, E Lansdowne Penn 34-44; Aerographer 3/c US Navy WAVES, NAS, Patuxent River Md 44-45; Drexel Inst of Tech Lib: Desk asst 47, Circ libn 48-62, Ser libn 62-65, Lib sci libn 62-66; Act hd libn Cheyney State Col, Penn 68; Ser libn Phila Col of Textiles & Sci 68-. 09: ALA; PennLA. 10: Beta Phi Mu. 15: 7373 Ridge ave apt 107, Philadelphia Pa 19128.

MANN, AMY S. b Brooklyn NY 29 Ja 43. 4: Jeffrey R Mann. 5: Queens Col 60-64 (Ed) BA; Drexel 65-68 MSLS. 7: Elem sch tchr: Phila Schs 64, Upper Merion Area Schs King of prussia Penn 64-66, Elem sch libn 66-68. 9: ALA. 14: Child lit, sch libnship. 15: 194-01A 64 cir, Flushing NY 11365.

MANN, CAROL ANN. b Coopersburg Penn 26 Ag 41. 5: Kutztown State Col 59-63 (LS) BS in Ed; Syracuse U summers 64, 65 (LS), 67 MSLS. 07: Libn Berean Bible Sch, Allentown Penn 63-64; Libn Nazareth Area Sr High Sch, Nazareth Penn 63-. 9: NEA; PennLA; Penn State EA. 10: Beta Phi Mu. 14: Ref. 15: 148 E Lawn rd, Nazareth Penn 18064.

MANN, CHARLES WILLIAM. b Altoona Penn 29 D 29. 4: Nan Gullo. 5: Penn State U 48-52 (Soc Studies) BA, 52-54 MA; Rutgers 60-61 MLS. 6: Sp, Fr. 7: Bibliogr searcher Penn State U Lib 54-57, Curator of rare bks & mss 57-67, Chief rare bks & spec collections 68-. 8: Asst with Fitzgerald Newsletter & PMLA Annual Bibliog; Asst Prof of Eng; Teach graduate course in Bibliography; Adv UPittsburgh Series in Bibliog 68-. 09: BSA; Mss Soc; Milton Soc; Penn Hist Assn. 10: Pittsburgh Bibliophiles; Grolier Club. 11: Cited by faculty for services to Univ(Penn State) 63. 12: Co-comp "The Hemingway Manuscripts: An Inventory," (69). 13: Yes. 14: Rare bks, Eng & Amer lit, art & arch hist. 15: Pattee Lib, University Park Penn 16801.

MANN, CLAUD (STANNARD JR). b Wash DC 16 N 24. 5: UNM 46-47 (Eng); So Methodist U 47-48 (Eng); New Sch of Soc Research 48-50 (Comparative Lit) BA; USeville 51 (Span) Certif; UMadrid 51-52 (Span) Certif; Pratt 58-60 MLS. 6: Sp. 7: (T/Sgt) US Army 43-46; Catlg trainee Brooklyn Pub Lib 58-60; Catlgr Engnr Societies Lib, NYC 60-61; Pratt Inst: Head catlgr 61-63, Head of tech serv 63-64, Instr Grad Lib Sch 63-64, Asst Prof Grad Lib Sch 64-67, Assoc Prof UDenver Grad Lib Sch 69-. 9: AALS; ALA; -LED (Com on Equiv and Reciprocity); NY Tech Serv Libns; NY Lib Club. 10: AAUP. 15: 594 2nd st, Brooklyn NY 11215.

MANN, ELIZABETH (BROWN). b Yale Okla 6 Mr 24. 4: Robert T Mann. 5: Fla State U 41-45 (Hist) AB, 68-69 Post master's Fellow; Carnegie 45-46 BSLS. 7: Asst child libn Pub Lib, Wash DC 46-48; Libn J J Finley Elem Sch, Gainesville Fla 48-49; Libn Cork Elem Jr High Sch, Plant City Fla 57-62; Coordinator of lib serv Polk Co Bd of Pub Instr, Bartow Fla 62-. 8: ALA-AASchL rep on adv bd of "The Paperback Goes to Sch"; Asst dir NDEA Inst for sch libns, UGa 67; Instr summer session UGa 67, 68. 9: ALA (Coun 67-71; mem Chap Relationship Com);-AASchL; FlaASchL (life mem, chm 60-61); FlaLA (pres 66-67; chm Sch & Child Sect 62-63). 10: PTA; Delta Kappa Gamma; Alpha Delta Pi. 14: Sch & child. 15: PO Box 417, Seffner Fla 33584.

MANN, JANE EDITH (PODOLIN). b Buffalo NY 29 Mr 39. 5: UBuffalo 56-58 (Eng); NYU 59-62 (Eng) BA; Columbia 64-65 MLS. 7: Research asst Skadden, Arps, Slate, Meagher & Flom, NYC 59-60, Managing clerk 60-61, Receptionist 61-64; Catlgr & ref libn Union Carbide Corp Bus Lib, NYC 65-67; Catlgr & Ref libn Metro Mus of Art Lib 67-. 9: SLA. 15: 2 Pinehurst ave, New York NY 10033.

MANN, MARIE (WHITEAKER). b Newtown Ind 25 O 17. 4: Phillip Mathews Mann. 05: Va Intermont Col 35-37 (Educ) Educ diploma; Radford Col 38-39 (Eng) BS in Ed; Peabody Col 41-43 BS in LS. 7: Tchr Washington Co Bd of Educ, Abingdon Va 37-38, Libn 39-42; Libn Bedford Co Bd of Educ 42-43; Libn Pub Lib, Kalamazoo 43-46; Tchr-libn Meriwether Co Bd of Educ, Greenville Ga 46-48, 49-50; Dir Meriwether-Talbot-Upson Reg Lib, Manchester Ga 50-55; Ext libn Pine Mt Reg Lib, Manchester Ga 61-66; Lib supv Meriwether Co Bd of Educ, Greenville Ga 66-. 8: Participated in N DEA Inst at Appalachian State U 67. 9: NEA; ALA; SELA; GaLA; GaEA. 14: Child lib serv. 15: Gay Ga 30218.

MANN, RUTH (JACQUETTE). b Rochester Minn 2 N 20. 5: Rochester Jr Col 36-37; UMinn 37-40 (Hist) BA, 40-41 (LS) BS. 6: Fr. 7: Brown U: Asst catlgr 41-42, Asst circ 42-43, Biol sci dept libn 43-44; P-1 ref & circ US Army Med Lib, Wash DC 44-45; Bindery & spec collections libn Mayo Clinic Lib,

Rochester Minn 46-55, Catlgr 55-64, Hd hist med dept 65-. 9: MedLA (sec 61-62). 13: Yes. 14: Catlg, rare bks, ref, med hist. 15: 605 11th st SW, Rochester Minn 55901.

MANN, SALLIE (EASTERLING). b Maxton NC 19 Ag 32. 4: Thomas Jefferson Mann III. 5: E Carolina U 52-56 (Eng, LS) BS, 59-60 (Eng, LS) MA. 7: Asst libn Pub Lib, Greenville NC 56-59; Asst circ libn Lib E Carolina U 60-64, Periods libn 65-67, Acquis libn 67-. 9: ALA; NCLA (Sec-treas Jr Mem Sect). 10: AAUW. 14: Period, circ, acquis. 15: PO Box 344, Winterville NC 28590.

MANN, SHERRILL ROBIN (CARTT). b Sacramento Cal 18 Ja 43. 4: David Mark Mann. 5: Whittier Col 60-64 (Chem) BA; UCal (Berkeley) 64-65 MLS. 6: Ger, Fr. 7: Sci catlgr catlg dept UCal (SB) 65-67, Projects libn sci engring lib 67-68, Asst hd sci engring lib 68-. 8: Superv of preparation of a br lib catlg & shelflist for Sci- engrg Lib. 9: ALA; SLA; CalLA; Libns Assn UCal (sec 69). 10: UC (SB) Lib Staff Assn offr. 14: Lib admin, tech processing. 15: Sci Eng Lib Univ of Cal, Santa Barbara Ca 93106.

MANNION, MARCELLA (McDONALD). b Keewautin Minn 27 S 20. 4: George W Mannion. 5: Eveleth Jr Col 38-40 (Pre-lib) AA; Col of St Catherine 40-42 (LS) BS; Cal State Col(Hayward) 59, 60 (Educ). 7: Catlgr UNotre Dame(Ind) 42-44; Libn Hayward Unified Sch Dist, Hayward Cal 58-; Dist elem libn 66-. 9: CalASchL; Cal Tchrs Assn. 10: Girl Scouts. 14: Catlg. 15: 5098 Northampton ct, Newark Ca 94560.

MANOOGIAN, SYLVA (MAHY). b Royan France 5 Ag 37. 4: Khachig Evan Manoogian. 5: Radcliff 55-59 (Lat) BA; USoCal 65-69 MLS. 6: Armenian, Fr. 7: Child libn LA Pub Lib Arroyo Seco Br 68-. 9: ALA. 10: PTA. 14: Child wk. 15: 5324 Aldama st, Los Angeles Ca 90042.

MANOSH, KATHERINE M (MACKEY). b Keene NH 26 Ag 43. 4: Larry Wayne Manosh. 5: UMass 61-65 (Zool) BA; Simmons 65-69 (LS) MS. 7: Pre Prof ya libn Boston Pub Lib 65-68; Asst libn Quinsigamond Commun Col Lib, Worcester Nass 69-. 14: Ref, acquis, catlg. 15: Great rd, Stow Ma 01775.

MANSBACH, CAROLYN EDITH (BILLITZER). b Bronx NY 5 S 38. 4: Judah Mansbach. 5: City Col(NY) 56-60 (Biol) BS; West Res 60 (LS) Columbia 60-61 (LS) MS. 6: Hebrew. 7: Hebrew tchr Young Israel, Bronx NY 56-60; Lib fellow City Col (NY) Music Lib 60-61; Temp asst to libn Columbia U Geol Lib 61; Assoc libn Mem-Sloan Kettering Cancer Center, NY 61-62, Med bibliogr 62-63; Med libn Jamaica Hosp, Jamaica NY 63-. 9: MedLA. 10: Assn of Orthodox Jewish Scientists. 14: Ref. 15: 67-30 Clyde st, Forest Hills NY 11375.

MANSBRIDGE, GEORGIA (ST CLAIR MULLAN). b NYC 31 O 09. 4: F Ronald Mansbridge. 5: Barnard 30 (Eng) BA; So Conn State Col 65 (LS) MS. 6: Fr, Sp. 7: Lib asst Ferguson Lib, Stamford Conn 63-64; Ref libn Danbury State Col 65-66; Ref libn & Interlibrary loan Sacred Heart U Lib, Bridgeport Conn 67-. 9: ALA; ConnLA (Bd Ref Sect 67-70). 14: Ref. 15: Lyons Plain rd, Weston Ct 06880.

MANSBRIDGE, JOHN. b Uxbridge Middlesex Eng 13 N 35. 5: Notre Dame Col(Wilcox Sask) 53-56 (Liberal Arts) BA; McGill 63-64 BLS. 6: Fr, Sp. 7: Soc wker Dept of Soc Welfare, Yorkton Sask 56-57; Prod mgr Robin Hood Flour Mills, Moose Jaw Sask 58-60, IBM supv 60-61; Lib asst Moose Jaw Pub Lib, Moose Jaw Sask 61-63, Libn 64-; Asst libn Selkirk Col, Castlegar BC 65-67; Libn 67-. 9: ALA; CanLA; SaskLA (sec 65-66)& BCLA. 14: Ref, catlg, a-v. 15: Moose Jaw Pub Lib, Moose Jaw Sask Can.

MANSFIELD, AGNES A. b Spartanburg SC 29 S 07. 5: Converse Col 25-29 (Eng, Fr) BA; UVa summer 38; Appalachian State Tchrs Col summer 54 (Ed); Peabody 54-55 (Elem Educ) MA; Rutgers summers 56-60 MLS. 6: Fr. 7: Tchg & sec NC, SC, Augusta Ga 29-49; Sec to radiologist Spartanburg(SC) Gen Hosp 49-52; Ref & catlg Greenwood Pub Lib, Greenwood SC 56-62; Documents libn Clemson Col 62-63; Catlgr Clemson U Lib 64-. 9: ALA; SCLA; SELA. 10: AAUW; Found for Hist Restoration in the Pendleton Area; Oconee Hist Found; AAUP; Nat Trust; Clemson Music Club. 14: Catlg, ref, child bks, child reading. 15: Daniel dr, Apt 7-c, Clemson SC 29631.

MANSFIELD, JULIET IDA (VERDIER). b Hebronville Mass 2 Ap 12. 4: Robert Risley mansfield. 6: Fr. 7: Libn Blanding Pub, Rehoboth Mass 39-, Libn Sturdy Mem Hosp Sch of Nursing, Attleboro Mass 62-. 15: Bay State rd, Rehoboth Ma 02769.

MANSON, CLARA (SUE). b Reno Nev 13 Ja 06. 5: UNev 23-24, 24-25; UAriz 25-26, 26-27 (Hist) AB; USoCal summers 31-36 (Hist) MA; UCal(Berkeley) 37-38 (LS) Certif; Columbia 40 (Med Libnship). 7: Tchr, Yucca Ariz 27-29; Tchr-libn, Kingman Ariz 29-37, 38-40; Med lib intern Tulane U 41-42; Catlg libn Col of Physicians, Phila 42-48; Chief Libn Stanford U Med Lib 48-. 9: SLA; ALA; MedLA; CalLA; Med Libns San Francisco Bay Area. 15: 180 Pecora way, Menlo Park Ca 94326.

MANTERNACH, ALBERT V. b Cascade Iowa 25 S 18. 5: Loras Col 44-48 (Philos) BA; Catholic U 51-52 (Educ) MA; UMich 52-53 MA in LS. 6: Fr. 7: Libn Loras Col 53-63; Libn Mt St Bernard Sem, Dubuque 63-68; Dir of admissions Loras College 68-. 10: Amer Legion. 15: Loras College, Dubuque Ia 52001.

MANTEUFEL, GARY L. b Oxford Wis 10 S 39. 5: Wis StateU 57-61 (Eng) BS; UWis 66-67 (LS) MS. 6: Fr, Turkish. 7: Tchr Antigo High Sch, Antigo Wis 61-63; Tchr Dept of State, Konya Turkey 63-65; Libn Queensborough Pub Lib, Queens NY 67-. 8: Organizer, sch libs Konya Turkey 63-65. 10: Beta Phi Mu. 11: Fulbright Scholarship to Turkey 63-65. 14: Ref, ya, serv to disadvantaged. 15: 159 W 75th st, New York NY 10023.

MANTHE, MARTIN G (GILBERT). b Hardin Montana 29 S 32. 4: Elizabeth Belschart. 5: UPortland 51-59 (Hist) BA; Fresno State Col 60-63 (Ed); UOre 65-68 MLS. 7: S/Sgt instr auto pilot USAF, Chanute AFB 53-57, Tchr Bakersfield Schs, Bakersfield Cal 59-64; Soc studies tchr Springfield Schs, Springfield Ore 64-68; Lib consul Lincoln Co Schs, Newport Ore 68-. 9: ALA; NEA-DAVI; OreASchL; Ore Instr Media Assn; OreEA. 10: Kiwanis Club. 14: Instr media. 15: 1012 SW 8th st, Newport Or 97365.

MANTHORNE, MARY E (ARNOLD). b Haverhill Mass 5 O 09. 4: Gordon Clarke Manthorne. 5: Russell Sage Col 28-32 (Eng) AB. 7: Pres The Horn Book Inc, Boston 62-. 8: Chm Bd of Trustees Stevens Pub Lib, Ashburnham Mass 50-. 9: Mass Lib Aid Assn (pres 60-). 15: Main st, Ashburnham Ma 01430.

MANTLER, EDWARD LOVETT. b Baltimore 27 N 37. 4: Judith S Mantler. 5: Johns Hopkins 55-57 (Hist); Washington Col 57-60 (Hist) BA; UPittsburgh 63-64 MLS. 7: Page Johns Hopkins U summer 57-61; US Army, Ft Knox Ky 62; Ready res USAR Sheridan Ar Spec E-5, Baltimore -67; Enoch Pratt Free Lib, Baltimore: Preprof 62-63, Libn 1 64-65, Libn 2 65-67, Libn 3 67-, (Supv Hd of Tel Ref Serv). 9: ALA; MLA (Ref Serv Div). 14: Admin ref. 15: 1507 E 35th st, Baltimore Md 21218.

MANUEL, MARY E. b NYC 14 Jl 15. 4: Joseph M Manuel. 5: NJ Col for Women 33-36 9psych); UMinn 56 (LS); Rutgers 57 (LS). 6: Fr. 7: Bkkeeper Seifert-Rees Co Summit NJ 37-38; Lib asst pub lib, Springfield NJ 54-57, Asst dir 57-62, Hd tech serv 62-. 9: ALA; NJLA. 10: LWV; DAR; Hist Soc (Springfield NJ). 14: Catlg, ref. 15: 24 Country Club lane, Springfield NJ 07081.

MANUEL, MELBAROSE (HUNTER). b New Orleans 1 Je 23. 4: Cyril C Manuel. 5: Xavier U(La) 41-45 (Home Econ) BS; UWis summers 51-56 MS in LS. 6: Fr. 7: Tchr Xavier U Prep Sch, New Orleans 4548; Lib asst New Orleans Pub Lib 49-52, Libn II 5364; Ser libn Southern U(Baton Rouge) 65, Asst law libn 65-, Gov doc lib summer 68. 9: ALA; CathLA (New Orleans Chap) LaLA; Assn Law Libns La. 10: Alpha Kappa Mu; Alpha Kappa Alpha. 14: Ref, circ, child libnship, catlg, proc. 15: PO Box 9242 Southern U, Baton Rouge La 70813.

MANY, FLORENCE (L). b Bayonne NJ 22 Ap 15. 4: Robert H Many Jr. 5: Fairleigh- Dickinson 58-62 (Eng) BA; Columbia 62-64 (Hist, Eng lang) MA; Rutgers 65-68 MLS. 7: Libn Morristown-Morris Twp Pub Lib, Morristown NJ 67-. 9: ALA. 10: Amer Name Soc. 14: Ref, child. 15: Rte 1 Box 221, Chester NJ 07930.

MANZER, BRUCE MONROE. b Ballston Spa NY 8 Ap 36. 5: Union Col Schenectady NY 55-59 (Chem) BS; UMich 59-60 AMLS. 6: Ger. 7: Catlg & ref asst Battelle Mem Inst, Columbus Ohio 60-62, Order libn 62-64; Tech libn The Glidden Co Inorganic Research Center, Baltimore 64-66; Asst libn tech proc UCal Lawrence Radiation Lab, Livermore Cal 66-67; ACCESS, ed Chemical Abstracts Serv, Columbus Ohio 67-. 9: SLA; ACS. 10: AAAS; Beta Phi Mu. 14: Tech proc, ser catlg, bibliog control of ser. 15: 574 Franklin ave, Columbus Oh 43215.

MANZI, LUCY M. b Everett Mass 20 O 26. 5: Boston U 43-47 (Eng) AB; Simmons 48 BS in LS. 7: Catlgr Boston Pub Lib 48-50; Radcliffe Col Lib: catlgr 50-58, Ref libn 58-64, Asst libn 64-. 10: Phi Beta Kappa. 14: Pub sev. 15: 30 Florence ave, Arlington Mass 02174.

MANZONI, JOSEPHINE THERESA. b St Charles Mich 21 Mr 25. 5: Bay City Jr Col 57-59; Wayne State 59-62 (Span & Ital) BA; West Mich U 62-64 (LS) MA. 6: Sp, Ital, Rr. 7: Audit clerk Seitner Brothers, Saginaw Mich 50-57; Off clerk Jacobsons Dept Store,Kalamazoo 62-64; Ref pub lib, Port Huron Mich 64-65; Ref libn Adrian Col 66-67; Sch libn SS Peter & Paul High Sch, SaginawMich 67-. 9: ALA; MichSchLA. 14: Ref, circ, readers adv, for bibliog, sch libs. 15: 415 Charles st, St Charles Mich 48655.

MAPES, JOSEPH L. b Des Moines Iowa 30 S 35. 4: Jo Pullen. 5: US Merchant Marine Acad 53-55; Cornell Col 56-58 (Eng)BA; UMinn 58 (LS); UDenver 60-61 (LS) MA; UColo 65- (Higher Educ). 6: Fr. 7: Ref libn Lycoming Col 58-59; Eng tchr SAC CommunSchs, Sac City Iowa 59-60; Pub serv libn Parsons Col 61-63; Asst libn So Colo State Col 63-64; Assoc libn order dept UColo Libs64-65, Circ libn 65-67, Hd educ lib 67-. 9: ALA;-RSD (Rep to ALA Memb Com 67-); ColoLA (chm Col & Univ Div 67-68); MPLA. 10: AAUP; PDK. 12: Co-comp "Research Studies in Education, 1953-1963," "Research Studies in Education, 1964"; Co-ed ColoradoAcademic Library" (68-). 15: 1700 Lombardy dr, Boulder Co 80304.

MAPP, EDWARD CHARLES. b NYC. 5: City Col NY 46-53; EN; BA; Columbia 55-56;LS; MS NYU 64-70 (Mass communications) Ph D. 6: Sp, Fr. 7: Lib asst ref dept NY Pub Lib 48-55; Asst libn NYC Commun Col 56-57; Libn Washington Irving High Sch, NY summer 59, 60;Libn ref dept NY Pub Lib summer 62; Tchr of lib Alexander Hamilton High Sch, Brooklyn NY 57-64; Chief libn & chm of lib deptNYC Commun Col 64-. 8: Faculty adv Stud Publs Alexander Hamilton High Sch, Brooklyn 62-63; Mem Evalua teams, Middle States Assn 66-; SUNY Chancellor's Adv Com on Lib 66-69. 9: ALA; -ACRL; NY Lib Club; LACUNY; Coun Chief Libns CUNY. 10: AAUP; Assn Study of Negro Life Hist; NY State Educl Communications Assn; Columbia U Sch Lib Serv Alum Assn. 13: Yes. 14: Admin, acad libs. 15: NY City Community Col, 300 Jay st, Brooklyn NY 11201.

MAPP, ERWIN E JR. b LaGrange Ga 13 S 23. 4: Elizabeth Beavers. 5: UGa 46-47; LSU 47-51 (Eng Lit) BA, 50-51 BS in LS Columbia 53-54 (LS). 7: US Navy 43-46; Asst libn b&i div Atlanta Pub Lib 51-53; Asst libn Brs Brooklyn Pub Lib 53-54; Dir Lanier Lake Reg Lib, Lawrenceville Ga 54-62; Head Libn SUNY Agric Tech Col (AlfredNY) 62-65; Libn research div W Point-Pepperell Co, Shawmut Ala 65-66; Dir Jackson Mun Lib Jackson Miss 66-. 9: ALA; GaLA (Treas 61-62); SELA; NYLA; MissLA (chm IF Com 68-69). 10: Lions; Kiwanis. 13: Yes. 15: 506 S 15th ave, Lanett Ala 36863.

MARAVILLA, CARINA SETZER. b Manila Philippines 22 Ja 44. 5: UPhilippines 59-62; UGuam 62-66 (Soc Sci) AA, BA; UPittsburgh 66-67 MLS. 6: Pampango, Pilipino, Sp. 7: Tchr Dept of Educ, Guam 63-66; Stud lib aide UPittsburgh 66-67; Instr Lib Sci UGuam 68-69; Libn George Washington Sr High Sch, Guam 67; Instr Adult Basic Educ, Guam 68-. 9: GuamLA. 10: AAUW. 13: Yes. 14: Ref. 15: PO Box 2202, Agana Guam 96910.

MARBERRY, ROBERT B. b Gilman Ill 9 D 09. 5: UIll28-30, 32-34 (Hist AB; UInd 36; San Diego State Col 39; UIll 40 BA in LS. 7: Labor statistician Resettlement Admin, Indianapolis 36-38; Supv of army-navy parts div Aeronautical Aronautical Co, San Diego 38-39; Radio-radar tech US Armed Forces, US Air Force 42-45; Timekeeper Consolidated-Vultee, San Diego 46-48; Sr libn San Diego Pub 49-62 4962; Sci libn Sonoma State Col 63-. 14: Ref. 15: Sonoma State Col Lib, Cotati Cal 94928.

MARBLE, MARTHA (SMITH). b Uniontown Penn 20 Je 08. 5: Millersville State Col 29-33 (Eng) BS Ed; UPittsburgh summer 37; Carnegie 42-43 MLS. 7: Dental asst, Uniontown Penn 33-34; Libn Lafayette Jr High Sch, Uniontown Penn 34-38; Libn Green Free Lib & High sch tchr of Eng, Canton Penn 38-41; Assoc ed Canton Independent Sentinel, Canton Penn 42; Child libn Peter White Pub Lib, Marquette Mich 43-44; Libn Talbot Co Free Lib, Easton Md 44-46; Libn Chamberlain br Akron Pub Lib, Akron Ohio 46-52; Supv of elem sch libs Elyria Ohio 52-55; Child dept head White Plains Pub Lib, White Plains NY 55-64; Libn Greenwich High Sch, Greenwich Conn 64-. 9: ALA; ConnEA ConnSchLA; MdLA; v-pres exec bd 46; OhioLA; exec bd 54-55, nomin com 54-55; Westchester NY Young Adult & Child Libns chm 57-58. 10: Col Club of White Plains (NY); Wainwright House Assocs (Rye NY); Spiritual Frontiers Fellowship. 11: E P Dutton-John Macrae Award, 54. 14: Wk with child & YP. 15: 11 Mountain View ave, Ridgefield Ct 06877.

MARCELLUS, JUNE (FLORINA) (DAVIDSON). b Warrensburg Mo. 5: Miltonvale Wesleyan Col 34-36; Kan State U summers; Kan State Tchrs Col (Emporia) 60-62 (Soc Sci) BS, 63-64 (LS) MS. 7: Tchr Kan Rural Schs, Cloud & Douglas Cos 36-43; Tchr Mankato Grade Sch, Mankato Kan 43-45; Libn Roosevelt High Sch Kan State TchrsCol (Emporia) 63-64; Libn Bonner Springs High Sch, Bonner Springs Kan 64-65; Libn Central Col (McPherson Kan) 65-. 9: ALA; NEA; KanSchLA. 10: AAUW; Homemakers Club. 14: Ref. 15: 1200 S Maple, Mc Pherson Kan 67460.

MARCH JOHN A. b Lawton Okla 25 O 04. 5: UOkla 22-26 (Chem) BS, 29-30 (LS) AB; Columbia 34-35 MLS. 6: Fr. 7: Tchr of Chem & Math High Sch, Hobart Okla 26-29; Asst ref libn UOre 30-42; US Army Med Corps 42-43; Asst libn UOkla 44-52;Libn Ft Sill Lib, Ft Sill Okla 52-53; Ref libn Collier's Ref Serv, NYC 55-. 9: SLA. 14: Ref, bibliog. 15: 70 W 85th st, New York NY 10024.

MARCHAND, LOUISE. b Montreal 4 Jl 16. 5: Normal Sch(Pedagogy) 32-34; UMontreal 40-41 (LS). 6: Fr, Eng. 7: Libn (bibliotheque St Sulpice Bibliothque Nationale du Quebec, Montreal 43-48, SE 48-64, admin off 64-67, Attachee dadmin 67-. 9: CanLA; Les Ecrivains pour la jeunesse (sec 50-56); Assn canadienne des bibliotheaires de langue francaise (ed-sec of "Bulletin 55-60). 12: Books (in French) for children and teen-agers). 13: Yes. 14: Admin. 15: 8739 Souligny st, Montreal Can.

MARCHANT, MAURICE P. b Peoa Utah 20 Ap 27. 4: (Gerda) VaLoy Hansen. 5: US Naval Acad 45-46; UUtah 44-45, 47-49 (Eng) BA, summers 50, 52, 53 (LS) MS; UMich 66 AMLS, 65-69, 68 (Higher Educ) MA. 6: Fr. 7: Midshipman US Navy 45-46; Tchr Altamont High Sch, Altamont Utah 49-50; Libn Preston High Sch, Preston Ida 50-52; Libn Jackson Jr High Sch, SALT Lake City 52-53; Chief Libn Tech Lib Dugway Proving Ground, Dugway Utah 53-58; Libn Carnegie Free Lib, Ogden Utah 58-66; Br libn Nellie S Loving Br Pub Lib, Ann Arbor Mich 66-69; Asst Prof lib & info sci Brigham Young U 69-. 8: Utha State dir, Nat Lib eek, 2 yrs. 9: UtahLA (pres 64-65, chm &/or mem 4 coms). 10: Phi Kappa Phi; Sons of Utah Pioneers; Utah Hist Soc. 13: Yes. 14: Admin, pub serv. 15: 3005 Plymouth rd, Ann Arbor Mi 48105.

MARCHESSEAULT, SISTER ROSE EDMOND FSE. b Moosup Conn 13 O 15. 5: St Joseph (West Hartford) 38-48); Annhurst Col 49-50 (Eng) BA; CatholicU summer 50-58 MS in LS. 6: Fr. 7: Elem sch tchr Daughters of the Holy Spirit, Chicopee Mass 35-36; Tchr, Hartford Conn 37-48, 55-56; Secondary sch tchr Holy Ghost Acad, Tupper Lake NY 48-55; Tchr-libn St Bernard's High Sch, New London Conn 56-62, Vice prin-superior-Dean of Girls 62-64; Tchr-guidance counselor libn Cathedral High Sch, Bridgeport Conn 64-. 9: ALA; -AASchL; CathLA (High Sch Sect; Com Unit: Exec Bd); ConnSchLA. 14: Lib admin. 15: Cathedral High School 33 Calhoun pl, Bridgeport Ct 06604.

MARCHMAN, WATT P(EARSON). b Eatonton Ga 1 S 11. 4: Martha J Dawson. 5: Rollins Col 29-33 (Amer Lit) AB, 35-37 (Amer Hist) MA; Duke U 36 (Amer foreign rel). 7: Instr Ga Military Acad, Mountain Lake NC summer 34; Sec Rollins Press Inc, Winter Park Fla 34-40; Archivist Rollins Col 35-40, Dir Alumni Placement Serv 37-40; Libn, exec sec Fla Hist Soc, St Augustine Fla 39-42; US Army Signal Corps spec Troops ETO 43-46; Dir of research The Rutherford B Hayes & Lucy Webb Hayes Found, Fremount Ohio 46-; Dir The Rutherford B Hayes Lib, Fremont Ohio 46-. 9: AHA; Amer Assn State & Loc Hist; SAA; The MSS Soc (past v-pres); OhioLA (Exec Bd 52-53); Ohio Lib Trustees Assn; Ohio Hist Soc; Fla Hist Soc; BirchardLA (sec Bd Trustees 53-). 10: Rotary Club of Fremont; Rowfant Club(Cleveland). 11: Award for Historical Achievement for 1968, Ohio Acad of Hist. 12: "The Rutherford B Hayes State Memorial (62); Ed bd "Northwest Ohio History. 13: Yes. 14: Rare bks, ref, research. 15: Rutherford B Hayes Lib Hayes ave, Fremont Oh 43420.

MARCHI, MARGARET (McKEE). b F lorence Ala 26 F 15. 4: Louis E Marchi. 5: U Ala 33-37 (LS) BS in Educ, (Eng) AB; UIll 39-40 BS in LS. 6: Fr. 7: Libn Opp High Sch, Opp Ala 37-38; Libn Ramer High Sch, Ramer Ala 38-39; Asst libn Tuscaloosa High Sch, Tuscaloosa Ala 39-40; Head catlg dept UMiami (Fla) 40-41; Head catlg dept Ga Sch of Tech 41-42; Libn-tchr Richmond High Sch, Richmond Ill 61-62; Head libn

Woodstock Pub Lib, Woodstock Ill 62-. 8: Consul McHenry (Ill) Pub Lib summer 65. 9: IllLA; Lib Admins Conf of No Ill. 14: Catlg, admin. 15: 414 W Judd, Woodstock Il 60095.

MARCINKO, DOROTHY (KIZER). b Asheville NC 7 D 36. 4: Stephen C Marcinko. 5: UNC 54-56 (Nursing); UPhilippines 58-61 (Hist) AB; Tex Woman'sU 66-68 MLS. 6: Fr. 7: Catlg libn & instr R B Draughn Lib AuburnU 68-. 9: ALA. 10: USAF Offrs Wives' Club. 14: Ref, libnship. 15: 240 Pine Hills ave, Auburn Al 36830.

MARCO, GUY ANTHONY. b NYC 4 O 27. 4: Karen Csontos. 5: DePaul U 47-50; Amer Conservatory of Music (Chicago) 47-51;(Music Theory & Composition) B Mus; Chicago 52-56 (LS) MA(Musicology) MA, PhD. 6: Ital, Fr, Ger. 7: US Army Med & Transportation Corps (Cpl), US, Italy, Germany 45-47; Asst Classics LibU Chicago 52-53; Libn & Instr in Musicology Chicago Musical Col 53-54; Circ-ser libn Wright Jr Col 54-56; Libn Amundsen Jr Col 56-60 Dean & Prof Sch of Lib Sci Kent State U 60-. 8: Summer tchg in lib schs; SUNY(Albany) 56, 58; UWis 55; UDenver 59; UOkla 60; Ref libn Chicago Tchrs Col summer 57. 9: ALA (Coun 69-); -LED; chm nomin com 65-66; mem research com 62-68; chm Internat Lib Sch Com 68-); AALS; research com 64-, chm 66-); OhioLA devel com, Nomin com 63-64, Contin Educ Com Chm 68-); MUSLA; recr com 64-66, pres Midwest Chap 65-67.40030 10: Beta Phi Mu; Lang Assn; Amer Msicological Soc; Internat Assn Mus Libs; AAUP. 12: "Syllabus for Bibliography (53); "An Appraisal of Favorability in CURRENT Book Reviewing (59); "The Earliest Music Printers of continental Europe (62), Co-auth "The Art of Counterpoint (69); Ed "Explorations in Music Librarianship (66-). 13: Yes. 14: Mus libs, mus bibliog, lib media sel humanities in the lib, compar libnship. 15: Sch of Lib Sci Kent State Univ, Kent Oh 44240.

MARCOCCI, ANN E. b Roberstsdale Penn 12 O 16. 5: Juniata Col 35-39 (Fr) AB; Millersville State Col 60-63 (LS) MA. 6: Ital. 7: Eng & Lat tchr Wood Twp, Robertsdale Penn 39-59; Libn Tussey Mountain High Sch, Saxton Penn 60-. 9: ALA; NEA; Penn State EA; PennLA. 10: Womens Civic lub, Penn Fed of Womens Club. 14: Ref, high school libn. 15: 54 S Main, Robertsdale Penn 16678.

MARCONI, JOSEPH VALENTINE. b Flint Mich 25 Ag 34. 4: Barbara Leeseberg Marconi. 5: Flint Jr Col 52-54 (Hist) AA; UMich 55-57 (Econ) BA, 65 MALS; UIll 57-59 (Labor rel) MA. 7: Claims Rep Soc Security, Dearborn Mich 59-61; Disability Claims Examiner Soc Security, Baltimore 61-63; Claims Repr Soc Security, Flint Mich 63-64; Ref Asst Detroit Pub Lib 65-. 9: Indust Relat Res Assn; SLA. 10: ACLU. 14: Ref. 15: Apt A4 1913 W McNichols, Highland Park Mi 48203.

MARCUM, (LILLIAN) LOUISE. b Easley SC 28 Je 31. 5: Furman U 50-54 (Art) BA; LSU 64-65 (LS) MS. 6: Sp. 7: Art tchr Anderson Jr Col 54-56; Elem sch tchr Sch Dist #5, Anderson SC 56-64; Co Libn conee Co, Walhalla SC 65-. 9: ALA; SCLA. 10: Pilot Club; Oconee Co Planning Bd. 14: Co lib serv. 15: Oconee Co Lib 301 S Spring st, Walhalla SC 29691.

MARCUS, RUSSELL. b NYC 2 Ag 42. 5: Earlham Col 60-64 (Sociol) AB; USoCal 65- MA in LS. 6: Finnish, Sp, Lao, Thai. 7: Lib asst Columbia U Bus Lib 64-65; Lib consul USo Cal Film Lib 65-, Owner Books Marc-Us 65-; Internat Voluntary serv 66-68; Asia Found 68. 12: Comp & publ Eng-Lao, Lao-Eng Dictionary (68). 14: Catlg in spec libs, libs in devel countries. 15: Box 188, Ojai Cal 93023.

MARCY, HENRY ORLANDO. b Boston Mass 27 Ag 38. 4: Carmen Rickard. 5: Harvard 56-60 (Hist) AB; Columbia 60-62 (Tchg of hist) MA; Simmons 63-66 (LS) MS. 7: Clerical Cambion Electronics Co, Cambridge Mass 62; Sub tchr, Arlington, Medford, Lexington Mass 62; Hist tchr Newton High Sch, Newton Mass 62-63; Clerical Harvard U Lamont Lib 63; Chief processing dept Harvard Law Sch Lib 63-66; Ref libn Harvard U Widener Lib 66; Instr in lib sci Simmons Col 66-. 8: Consul Vt Free Pub Lib Serv 68, Harbridge House 68, Boston City Hosp Med Lib 67. 9: ASIS; ALA; SLA; AALS; NELA; MassLA. 10: AAUP; Simmons Sch of Lib Sci Alum Assn. 13: Yes. 14: Info systems, machine applications to libs, tech serv, catlg, clsf. 15: 54 Linden st, Reading Ma 01867.

MARET, SARAH ELIZABETH. b Lavonia Ga 11 Ap 07. 5: Converse Col 25-29 (Hist) AB; Emory u summers 40-41-42 BA in LS. 7: High sch tchr: Comer Ga 30-33, Greenwood SC 34, Lincolnton Ga 35-37; Tchr-libn High Sch, Swainsboro Ga 37-41; Supv WPA (Atlanta & Albany Ga) 41-42; Dir Cherokee Reg Lib, LaFayette Ga 43-49; Dir Athens Reg Lib, athens Ga 50-. 8: Chm, Ga State Bd for the Certif of Libns 60-. 9: ALA (Fed Rel Com 55-56); SELA (Ga rep Exec Bd, 60-64); GaLA (pres 53-55). 10: PTA; Delta Kappa Gamma; Pilot Club Internat. 11: Woman of Year in Professions, Athens Ga 62. 14: Pub lib serv to child & adults. 15: 280 Stanton Way, Athens Ga 30601.

MARFIELD, JEANNIE S. b New Orleans La 27 F 17. 5: Goucher 34-38 (Eng) AB; Carnegie Lib Sch 46-47 BS in LS. 6: Fr. 7: Asst DC Pub Lib Child Dept 41-51; T/5 WAC 45-46; Field & dist libn USA Spec Serv, Ger 52-54; Libn Bolling AFB USAF Wash DC 54-56; Asst libn & chief catlf FHA Lib Wash DC 56-65; Ref libn Army Lib Pentagon 65-67; Chief law br dept of com lib Wash DC 67-. 9: SLA (life mem; Mil Libns Gp, DC Chap); DCLA (life mem); Potomac Tech Proc Libns; Law Libns Soc of DC. 14: Ref, law, catlg, child. 15: 4869 S 28th st apt A2, Arlington Va 22206.

MARGADANT, WILLEM D. b Wijk aan Zee en Duin Netherlands 28 My 16. 5: UAmsterdam 33-49 (Bot); Rijksuniversiteit Utrecht 67 (Bot) Doctor. 6: Dutch, Ger, Fr. 7: Student asst UAmsterdam 40-43; Asst Instituut v Landbouwk, Onderz Wageningen 43-49, Lib supv 47-49, Sci off 49-51; Sci off Bot Lab Rijksuniversiteit Groningen 51-61; Asst libn Hunt Bot Lib Carnegie Inst Tech 62-. 8: Mem Nomenclature Com for Bryophytes, nomiated at the Internatl Botanical Congress, Edinburgh 64. 9: Amer Bryological Soc; Amer Inst Biol Scis; Botanical Soc West Penn. 10: Internatl Assn Plant Taxonomists; Koninklijke Nederlandse Natuurhistorische vereniging. 12: "Mossentabel" (2nd ed 44, 3rd ed 55); co-auth "Index Muscorum" (v 1-4 59-68); "Early Bryological Literature" (69). 13: Yes. 14: Taxonomy of bryology, bibliog of bryology, botany in general, bibliog of botanical biog. 15: 4700 Sylvan dr, Allison Park Pa 15101.

MARGALITH, HELEN M (FLEIHER). b NYC. 5: Hunter Col 31-36 (Hist) AB, 37-44 (Hist, Educ) MS in Ed; Columbia 55-58 MS in LS; NYU 62- (Religion, Psych). 6: Fr, Ger. 7: Supv & correspondent Book of the Month Club, NYC 36-47; Tchr of Lib Wadleigh Jr High Sch NYC Bd of Educ 55-57; Tchr in charge of Lib Eleanor Roosevelt Jr High Sch, NYC Bd of Educ 57-. 8: Consul, Lib of Amer Foun of Religion & Psychiatry; Libn Stephen Wise Free Synagogue (NYC). 9: ALA; NY Stat LA; NYC Sch LA. 10: Columbia Univ Alumni Assn; Red Cross, Speakers Bur; Nat Conf of Christians & Jews; ewish Tchrs Assn (Delegate). 11: Spec Award Hebrew Culture Foun NYU. 13: Yes. 14: Sch libs, ref. 15: 17 W 67th st, New York NY 10023.

MARGISON, SUSAN HAVENS. b Santa Maria Cal 19 N 43. 5: State U Col(Geneseo NY) 61-65 (LS) BS in Educ; UWyo (Laramie) summer 68; State U Col (New Paltz) 69. 7: Elem libn Whitehall Elem Sch, Whitehall NY 65-66; Elem Libn Clarkstown Central Sch Dist '1, New City NY 66-. 9: NY State TA; NYLA; Clarkstown TA. 14: Child lit. 15: 87 Salisbury d, Delmar NY.

MARIA, SISTER CONSOLATA (DUNLEAVY). b Phila. 5: Chestnut Hill Col 56 (Hist) AB; Catholic U 65 (LS) MS. 6: Fr. 7: Tchr Mt St Joseph Acad, Flourtown Penn 65, Libn 65-. 13: Yes. 14: Ya. 15: Lib Mt St Joseph Acad, Flourtown Penn 19031.

MARIE SISTER THERESA RSM. b Brookville Penn. 5: Villanova AB, 58 MSLS. 7: Tchr (elem) Archdiocesan Schs 40-55; Tchr-libn St Hubert High Sch, Phila 55-62, Libn 68-; Tchr-libn John W Hallahan High Sch, Phila 62-68. 09: ALA; CathLA (East Penn Unit; sec, ed Newsletter); PennASchL. 10: Sch Libns Assn of Phila & Vicinity. 15: St Hubert High Sch Lib 7320 Torresdale ave, Philadelphia Pa 19136.

MARILLA, THEOPA COLLINS. b Natchitoches La 30 S08. 4: Esmond L Marilla. 5: Northwestern Col (La) 29-46 (Eng) BA; Tulane 49 (Eng) LSU 49-50 (Eng) MA, 50-51 BSLS. 7: Tchr Pub Schs, La 45-50; Libn Zachary High Sch, Zachary La 50-52; Libn LPI, Ruston La 52-53; Ref libn API, Auburn Ala53-56; Ref libn McNeese State Col 56-58; Libn Mandeville High Sch, Mandeville La 59-61; Libn Doyle High Sch, Livingston La64-65; Med libn US Public Health Serv Hosp 65-. 9: ALA; LaLA. 15: 626 Kimbro dr, Baton Rouge La 70808.

MARINELLI, ANNE V. b Hibbing Minn. 5: Hibbing Jr Col 25-27 diploma UWis 27-29 BA; Columbia 30-31 (LS) BS, even 34-35, (LS) summer 37, (Ital)summer 40; UI11 48 MA; USDA Grad Sch (LS) 50; U per Stranieri (Perugia Italy) 51 Diloma; UMich 52-53, 54-56 summers 58,59. 6: Ital, Fr, Sp. 7: Instr Hibbing High Sch & Jr Col, Hibbing Minn Jr Asst libn, Sr asst libn & asst br libn, NY Pub Lib; Hd libn & instr of lib sci Col of SST Theresa Lib; Hd of catlg dept Scoville Mem Lib

Carleton Col; in chg of libs Chisholm Pub Schs Chisholm Minn Bibliog UIll; Urabana; Asst prof Fla State U Sch of lib sci; Hd libn Assoc Prof Tex Woman's U Sch of Lib Sci; Head libn Hibbing State Jr Col Lib. 8: Spec participant, Internat Rel Round Table Ron Lib Serv Abroad, 48; Spec assignment, Pan Amer Union Lib, Wash DC, 49; Spec asst to Libn of Cong, 50; ALA rep, Commsn on Occupied Areas, 2nd Internat Conf, Wash DC,50; Observer, US Dept of State & LC Point FourCom, 50; Del to 7th Cong of Assn for Italian Libs, Milan Italy & Lugano Switzerland, Nov 4-7 51; Org & chm, Seminars on US Libs & Libnship, Rome, Florence & APLES, Del to US Nat Commsn of Unesco Conf, 59; Admin asst to Amer chm of IFLA 50. 9: AALS; ALA Table on Lib Serv Aboard; mem & chm Recr Com 49-51, mem Exec Bd 49-51, v-chm Round Table 50-51, mem Nomin 53-54, Com on Aid to Italian Libs 67-); -ACRL (RT on Lib Serv Abroad); mem Intercult Action Com 53-54)-ACRL; Associazione per le Biblioteche Italiane; BSA; MinnLA (chm Catlgrs Div 44-45;Tex Coun on Lib Educ (Memb Com 56-58); Exch Tchrs Club of Minn; Minn Jr Col Faculty Assn; Minn Jr Col Faility Assn (chm Lib Com);) (Minn State Jr Col Assn (chm Lib Com 65); MinnEA. 10; AAUP; Columbia Sch of Lib Serv Alummni Assn; Iota Kappa Gamma; Alpha Beta Alpha: Pi Lambda Theta. 11: Fulbright lecturer & Consul for Italian Libs & to Italian libns, Sept 51- dec 52. ; Horace Racklam Fellow, UMich 54-56; Amer Italian Award for libnship Distinction, 66; DIB certificate of Merit for disting serv International libnship 68; Hibbing State Jr Col Alum Assn Award of merit 67. 12: Ed, contrib & jt tr "Seminari di biblioteconomia (52); Comp "Bibography of US Literature Dated 1901-1952 Concerning Italian Liraries, Books and Related Phases (54) (As US contributor); Comp "Don Luigi Sturzo; a Bibliographical Contribution of Unied States Published Works to January 1, 1954 (54). 13: Yes. 14: Col & Univ Libs, Internat Lib Serv, Lib Sci Instr. 15: 909 Minnesota st, Hibbing Minn 55746.

MARINER, LEONORA (CONWAY). b Far Rockaway NY 17 Jl 16. 4: Eugene M Mariner. 5: Hunter Col 33-37 (Ger) BA; Columbia 62-65 (LS) MS. 6: Ger. 7: Libn trainee mt Vernon (NY) Pub Lib 62-65, Jr libn catlg & ya 65-67; Sr libn-readers adv & ya libn white Plains (NY) Pub Lib 67-. 9: NYLA; WestchesterLA; Westchester YA & child libns (corr sec). 10: Beta Phi Mu; AAUW; White Plains Civil Serv Employees Assn; Assn for the Study of Negro Life & Hist. 12: "The Grammar of Subject Headings (57); Ed "Pittsburgh Studies in Library and Information Science". 14: Readers adv, ya. 15: 6 Rutgers pl, Hartsdale NY 10530.

MARINO, MICHAEL. b Pittsburgh 27 F 40. 5: U Pittsburgh 58-62 Hist BA, 63 (LS) MLS. 6: Ital. 7: Ref libn Carnegie Lib of Pittsburgh 63-65; Ref libn UPittsburgh 65-67, Hd bus lib 67-. 9: SLA; PennLA. 10: Amer Youth Hostel. 14: Ref, periods, govt docs, bus. 15: 124 Oakland ave, Pittsburgh Pa 15213.

MARINO, SAMUEL JOSEPH. b New Britian Conn 29N16. 4: Dorothy Quinney. 5: LSU 36-40 (Fr) AB, 40, 46-48 BSLS, 49 (Fr) MA; UMich 52 AMLS, 62 (LS) PhD. 6: Ital, Fr. 7: Mil Censorship Off US Army (1st Lt) 43-44; Spec serv off (Capt) 44-46; Asst LSU 46-48; Ser & bind Auburn U 49-51; Asst dir UMiss 52-54; Dir Ind State U 54-58; Head Libn McNeese State Col 58-67; Prof Tex Womans U 67-. 8: Ch choir dir. 9: ALA; LaLA (2nd v-pres 65-66); La Lib Devel Com. 10: Civitan Club of Greater Lake Charles; Steering Com, Calcasieu Train & Eval Center; Beta Phi Mu; Phi Mu Alpha Sinfonia; Phi Sigma Iota. 12: Sup to "French Travelers in the United States, by F Monaghan (60). 13: Yes. 14: Fr lang printing in Amer, hist libs, admin. 15: 3205 Darby lane, Denton Tx 76201.

MARIONNEAUX, (RITA VICTORIA) SISTER MARIE EYMARD O CARM. b Plaquemine La 31 O 08. 5: Northwestern State (La) 26-28; USWLa 28-30 (Eng) BA, 39-40, summers 55, 59, 60, 61 Certif for Lib; LoyolaU (New Orleans) summers) summers 34, 37; Incarnate Word Col summer 38; Dominican Col (New Orleans) summers 58, 65, 66 Certif to tch rel; Our Lady of the Lake Col summers 67, 68 (LS). 7: Asst libn & tchr Mt Carmel High & Normal, New Orleans 31, 33-34; Asst libn & tchr Mt Carmel High Sch, Lafayette La 33-41; Tchr libn Mt Carmel High Sch, New Iberia La 42-43; Tchr libn Mt Carmel High Sch, Abbeville la 43-45; Tchr libn St Joseph High Sch, Rayne La 45-50; Tchr libn Mt Carmel High Sch, Lafayette La 51-58; Tchr libn St James Major High & Elem Sch, New Orleans 6 yrs 58-68, Libn 68-. 8: Also served as 4-H leader in all schools except here in New Orleans. 9: ALA; LaLA; LaSchLA. 13: Yes. 15: 3800 Gentilly blvd, New Orleans La 70122.

MARK, RANDY. b Oshawa Ont Can 24 Je 41. 5: Queens U(Ont) 59-63 (Eng, Lat) BA; McGill 63-64 BLS. 6: Fr. 7: Catlgr Ontario New Universities Lib Proj UToronto Lib 64-67, Libn engrg lib 68-. 9: ASIS; SLA. 10: . 14: Catlg, ref, circ. 15: Engineering Lib UToronto, Toronto 5 Can.

MARKE, JULIUS J(AY). b NYC 12 Ja 13. 4: Sylvia Bolotin. 5: City Col (NY) 30-34 (Hist, Govt) BS; NYU 34-37 LLB; Columbia 40-42 BS in LS. 6: Fr. 7: Lib asst art & arch NY Pub Lib 30-42; Infantry (Sgt) US Army, European Theatre 42-45; Asst libn NYU Sch of LAW 46-50, Law libn & Prof of Law 50-. 8: Consul for LC on Class K (Law); Adv to several law libs; Lecturer on soc cis & law libnship, Columbia U Sch of Lib Serv; Lib counsul & lecturer on legal research, Princeton U 65-; Consul on World Legal Codes Exhibit, Wash DC 65; Admitted to practice law in NY; Consul to Ford Found on Copyright Law. 9: AALL (pres 62-63, v-chm Coun of Nat Lib Assns 63-64); Law LA Greater NY (pres 49-50); Proj Law Search (chm 61-); Jt Com on Lib Educ (chm 50-52, 60-61, 63-). 10: Faculty Club NYU; Order of the Coif; ABA. 12: Comp & ed "A Catalogue of the Law Collection at NYU, with Selected Annotations (53); Ed "The Holmes Reader (55, 2nd ed 64); Comp "Deans List of Recommended Reading for Pre-Law and Law Students (58); Ed "Benders Legal Business Forms (NY), 4 v (61); Ed (with John Lexal) "International Seminar on Constitutional Review, (63); Co-auth "The Law in the United States of America; A Selective Bibliographical Guide (65); Auth "Vignettes of Legal History (65) "Copyright and Intellectual Property (67). 13: Yes. 14: Bibliog, ref, legal hist, law libnship, lib educ, info retrievalby computers. 15: 4 Peter Cooper, New York NY 10010.

MARKEL, J LOUISE. b Somerset Penn 12 My 24. 5: Cedar Crest Col 42-46; Hist; BA; Drexel 46-47 BS in LS. 7: Libn US Army, Germany 47-49; Libn Oak Ridge Inst of Nuclear Srudies, Tenn 49-56; Head lib dept Oak Ridge Inst of Nuclear Studies, Oak Ridge Tenn 56-66; Hd lib dept Oak Ridge Assoc US 66-. 8: Bd Dirs, Col of Oak Ridge; Mem, Study Group for Educ, Res & Communication,TennMid-South Reg Med Prog 69-71. 9: ALA; SLA; Tenn LA. 10: Recording for the Blind; Col of Oak Ridge Trustee. 14: Admin, catlg, ref. 15: 157 N Seneca rd, Oak Ridge Tenn 37830.

MARKER, BONNIE (LOU CATES). b Toledo Ohio 11 Ap 36. 4: Viktor Marker. 5: Harding Col 54-57; UWash 58-59 (Eng) BA, 59-60, summer 61 (LS) MA. 6: Sp. 7: Bkmob libn Columbia River Reg Lib Demonstration, Moses Lake Wash 60-61; Film interlib loan & ref libn, gen serv dept Tacoma Pub Lib, Tacoma Wash 61-68, Hd libn Fern Hill Br 68-. 9: WashLA; PNLA. 10: . 14: Ref, reader serv, film. 15: Tacoma Pub Lib Fern Hill Branch 765 S 84th st,Tacoma Wa 98444.

MARKETOS, NICOLETTA (CATHERINE). b Syracuse NY 9 Mr 14. 5: Elmira Col 31-35 Fr AB; UMich 35-6 ABLS. 6: Fr, Sp, Gk. 7: Catlgr UMich Lib 36-40; ;67, Asst hd Romance Langs Sec descr catlg div 67-69, Hd Romance Lang Sect descr catlg div 69-. Temple U 40-43; Catlgr LC 43-. 9: ALA; Potomac tech Processing libns; DCLA. 10: Daughters of Penelope. 14: Catlg. 15: 3001 Veazey ter NW apt 804, Wash DC 20008.

MARKEY, LOIS R. b Beverly Mass. 5: Simmons Col (LS) BS. 6: Fr, Sp, Ger. 7: Chld libn Brooklyn Pub Lib; Libn Reading High Sch, Boise Ida; Child Libn Lynn Pub Lib, Lynn Mass; Libn Wellington Pub Lib, Wellington Ohio; Child & yp libn, Concord NH; State Consul, Conn; Ed of Jr & Sr Bklist for Nat Assn of Ind Schs, Boston; Lib Dir Concord Pub Lib, Concord NH. 8: Consul, WENH-TV. 9: ALA; Nat Assn Indep Schs; AEA; NELA; NHLA. 13: Yes. 14: Admin, child serv. 15: Concord Pub Lib 45 Green st, Concord NH 03301.

MARKFIELD I NATHANIEL. b Rochester NY 29 Ag 09. 4: Margaret K Markfield. 5: George WashingtonU 31-37 AB in LS, 46-47 (Ger); CatholicU 49-50 (LS), 61 (LS). 6: Fr, Ger, sp, Ital, Russian. 7: Various positions Army Medical Lib, Wash DC 31-42; 1st Lieut US Army, US & Europe 42-46; Hd circ Army Med Lib, Wash DC 46-48, Hd ser sect 48-54, Hd gift & exchange 54-57; Bk selection Nat Lib of Med, Bethesda Md 57-60, Catlgr med & biol 60-. 15: 17-C Ridge rd, Greenbelt Md 20770.

MARKLE, SUSAN STUSSY. b Detroit Mich 28 Ap 45. 4: Carl Markle. 5: OaklandU (Mich) 63-67 BA; Wayne StateU 67-68 MSLS. 7: Asst catlgr SUNY (Stony Brook) 69-. 11: BA (magna cum Laude). 12: Ed "Geography & Map Division BULLETIN" SLA (56-62); Ed "Dartmouth College Library Bulletin (57-59); "Marine Atlases in the Dartmouth College Library (50); Co-ed SW Union List of Serials (65). 14: Catlg. 15: 305 Main apt D, Roslyn NY 11576.

MARKLEY, ETHELYN ANNE. b Bracken Co Ky 19 F 08. 5: Okla Col for Women 24-27 (Hist) BA; UOkla 30-31 BA in LS;UIll 43-44 MA in LS. 6: Fr. 7: Ref libn Pub Lib, Muskogee Okla 31-35; Head Libn Pub Lib, Wewoka Okla 35-37; Catlgr LSU 37-38; Catlgr Tulane U 38-40; Head catlgr UAla 40-43; Visiting Lecturer UIll Sch of Lib Sci summer 44; Ref libn Boeing Airplane Co Lib, Wichita Kan 44-45; Asst Prf UOkla Lib Sch 45-46; Asst Prof UCal Sch of Libnship (Berkeley) 46-49, Assoc Prof 49-. 8: Prof, Ankara U Turkey, Inst of Libnship, 59-61 Nuerous consultantships on catlg problems; participant in lib surveys in San Francisco Bay Area. 9: ALA (Mem Catlg Code Rev Com 53-57);-ACRL;-RTSD; AALS; BSA; CalLA; No Cal Tech Serv Group (many offs & com mem in above orgs). 10: Book Club of Cal; Womens City Club of San Francisco; AAUP; Eng-Speaking Union. 11: Beta Phi Mu Award for Good Teaching, 63. 12: "Official Publications of the State of Alabama (48); "Library Records for Government Publications (51). 13: Yes. 14: Catlg, clsf, bibliog. 15: 2533 Durant ave Apt 21, Berkeley Ca 94704.

MARKLEY, MARGARET. b Post Tex 26 D 11. 5: Southwest Mo State Col 29-33 (Span) AB; UIll 40-41 BS in LS. 6: Sp, Fr, Russian, Polish. 7: Libn Ark Col 38-40; Circ libn De Pauw U 41-42; Circ libn UIll Lib(Urbana) 42-44; Circ libn UGa Lib 44-45; Sr catlg libn UOre Lib 45-. 9: OreLA. 10: Natural Hist Soc (Eugene Ore); Obsidians Inc; Fed West Outdoor Clubs; Nature Conservancy; Wilderness Soc; NoCascades Conservation Club; AAUP. 14: Catlg. 15: 1924 Orchard st, Eugene Or 97403.

MARKOVICH, STANISLAVA (POPOVICH). b Krusevac Yugoslavia 24 N 19. 4: Vukasin. 5: Inst of Ed 46-49 (Serbo-Croatian, Russian) Tchg certif; UWindsor 59-61 (Eng) BA; UMich 62-65 AMLS. 6: Serbo-Croatian, Russian. 7: Tchr, Yugoslavia 39-50; Clerical asst Windsor Pub Lib, Windsor Ont 57-61, Sub-prof asst 61-65, Libn home reading 65-66, Asst chief libn 66-. 9: CanLA; ALA; OntLA; Inst Prof Libn Ont. 10: Windsor Pub Lib staff Assn; Can Fed of Univ Women; Local Coun of Women; United Commun Serv; Commun Forum Planning Com; Music Lit & Art Club; Women's Assn of The Windsor Symphony Soc. 14: Admin. 15: 8240 Menard st, Windsor 16 Ont Can.

MARKOWETZ, MARIANNA (CATHERINE). b Milwaukee 6 Jl 25. 5: Marquette U 54-58 (Hist LS; UWis 62-65 (LS) MS. 6: Ger. 7: High sch tchr New London Pub Schs, New London Wis 58-59; High sch tchr Delavan-Darie Pub Schs, Delavan Wis 59-61; Elem libn W Allis Pub Schs, Wallis Allis Wis 62-64; Libn Instr Media Lab Center UWis (Milwaukee) 64-. 9: MetroSchLA (Progrm Chm); WisLA (sec Child & YP; Sect). 14: Curr & non-book materials. 15: 814 S 57 st, W Allis Wis 53214.

MARKS, BARBARA S. b NYC 7 F 18. 5: Radcliffe 34-38 (Fine Arts) BA Magna cum laude; Columbia Sch of Soc Wk 40-41 MS; Columbia 59-60 (LS) MS. 7: Libn Isaac Young Jr High Sch, New Rochelle NY 60-61; Libn Valhalla High Sch, Valhalla NY 61-64; Libn, Head Educ Lib NYU 64-. 8: Scarsdale Dist Bd of Educ 57-63; Consul Julius Wile & Sons Co Inc - setting up bus lib 64; Consul; Commun Col Ctr Mt Vernon NY 69-, NY State survey, Lib Serv for the Disadvantaged in Buffalo, Rochester & Syracuse. 9: ALA; -ACRL (chm Educ & Behav Sci Subsect 68-69); NYLA SLA; ASIS; Mem Rev Com H W Wilson "Education Index 68-69. 10: Phi Beta Kappa. 12: Ed "New York University List of Books in Education (68). 14: Ref & res serv in educ on the behav scis. 15: Mamaroneck ave, Harrison NY 10528.

MARKS, ESTELLE (HOROWITZ). b NYC 28 N 24. 4: George P Marks III. 5: NYU 43-50 (Secondary ed) BS in Ed; Columbia 50-51 MLS; UWash NDEA Inst 65; Rutgers 68- (Ed admin). 7: Clk WAC Army AF 45; Period checker NYC Pub Lib 46-50; Ser catlgr Columbia U Lib 51; Y-p & 1st asst Brooklyn Pub Lib, NY 51-53; Libn: Morris Hills Reg High Sch, Rockaway NJ 53-55, Cranford High Sch, Cranford NJ 55-56, Woodbridge High Sch & Colonia Jr High Sch, Woodbridge NJ 57-63; Elem lib coord Woodbridge Twp Schs, Woodbridge NJ 63-. 9: ALA; NEA-DAVI; NJEA; NJLA; NJSchLA; MiddlesexCoSchLA (pres 66-68). 14: Sch libs. 15: Admin Bldg School st, Woodbridge NJ 07095.

MARKS, RUTH (ANN NEWMAN). b Sydney NS. 4: Alan David Marks. 5: UToronto 52-53 (Eng Lang & Lit) 65-66 BLS; Dalhousie U53-55 (Eng) BA. 7: Child libn Toronto Pub Libs 66-69; Curriculum libn Ontario Inst for Studies in Education, Toronto 69-. 14: Child literature, collection devel, curriculum. 15: 432 Broadway ave, Toronto 350 Ont Can.

MARKS, SANDRA LEE. b Dayton Ohio 10 Je 45. 5: Penn StateU 65-67 (Liberal Arts, Hist) BA; UPittsburgh 67-68 (Ref) MLS. 6: Fr. 7: Asst order libn Penn StateU 68-. 9: ALA. 14: Ref (acad, pub, ya). 15: 1000 Plaza dr 210C, State College Pa 16802.

MARKUS, FLORENCE. b Duluth Minn 6 Ag 06. 5: Butler U 41 (Eng) BA; West Res 52 MS in LS; UIll 64 Certif Med Libn. 7: Jr lib asst Chicago Pub Lib 28-31; Chief Libn VA 31-68; Dwight Ill, Lincoln Neb, Hot Springs SD, Indianapolis, Northampton Mass, Wood(Milwaukee) Wis; Visiting lecturer UWis Sch Lib & Info Sci (Milwaukee) 69-. 9: ALA (chm Publs Adv Com); -AHIL (rep Interassn Hosp Libs; chm Bibliog Com; chm Publ Adv Com); SLA (Wis Chap: (pres, Program Chm, Nat Lib Week Chm); Tri-State Hosp Assembly (Patients Lib Sect Program Chm). 10: Beta Phi Mu; AAUW. 13: Yes. 14: Admin, tchg lib sci. 15: 2528 N Maryland ave, Milwaukee Wi 53211.

MARLEY, S(AMUEL) BRANSOM. b Henderson NC 30 O 16. 4: Frances Woody. 5: Oak Ridge Mil Inst 33-35; UNC 35-37 (Hist) AB, 37-38 (Hist). 6: Fr. 7: Project supv Hist Records Survey WPA, Raleigh NC 38-41; Hd Dept of Soc Sci & Prof of Hist Oak Ridge Mil Inst 42-43; Archivist War Prod Bd, Wash DC 43-47; Records Management Off Govt Reports, Wash DC 48; Asst mgr VA Records Ctr, Phila 48; LC: Bus economist Defense Research Div 49-51, Sect hd 51-59, Asst chief 59-68, Chief ser div 68-. 9: ASIS; DCLA. 14: Ser, govt publ, lib admin. 15: 1524 Crestwood st, McLean Va 22101.

MARLOW, SISTER MARY BARTHOLOMEW. b Ireland. 5: Trenton grad 33 State tchr cert; Fordham 36 BS in Educ; Villa Nova 43 MA in Educ, 47 LS; Columbia 59 (Med lit). 7: Tchr Givernaud Home, Union City NJ 26-30; Tchr St Josephs Sch for Blind 31-38; Tchr Englewood Grade Sch 38-43; Libn (med & nurses) Holy Name Hosp, Teaneck NJ 43-. 9: ALA; CathLA; (Memb Com); MedLA; NJLA; Greater NY Lib Unit. 14: Ref, catlg. 15: Holy Name Hosp, Teaneck NJ 07666.

MARQUARD, CATHERINE. b Easton Penn. 5: Moravian Col 34-38 (Eng Lit) AB; Lehigh 41; Columbia 41-42 BLS. 6: Fr, Sp, Ger. 7: Lib asst Easton Pub Lib, Easton Penn 39-41, Ref libn 42-44; Ref asst NY Pub Lib 44-46; LibnUS VA Hosp, Bronx NY 46-47; Ref libn info div NY Pub Lib 47-59, Supv ref libn info div 59-. 9: NYLiclub. 14: Ref. 15: 45 Tudor City pl, New York NY 10017.

MARQUARDT, DOROTHY (ANN). b Edina Mo 26 Ag 21. 5: Washington U (St Louis) summer 49 (Child Lit). ; Quincy Col 69. 7: Topographer Army Map Serv, Quincy Ill 44-45; Credit mgr Montgomery Ward Co, Quincy Ill 45-47; Jr lib asst Fre Pub Lib, Quincy Ill 47-. 8: Libn, Third Order of St Francis, St Francis Church, Quincy Ill 61-64 (Coun mem 61-64). 12: Co-auth "Authors of Books for Young People, with M E Ward (64), 1st suppl 67). 14: Child lit, puppetry. 15: 3421 Lawrence rd, Quincy Il 62301.

MARQUARDT, SISTER MARY GREGORY. b Urbana Ill 2 O 03. 5: UIll 22-25, 29-30 (Eng) AB, summers 44, 46-49 (LS) MS summers 61-63, 65 (LS) MS. 6: Fr, Sp. 7: Tchr St Marys Acad, Nauvoo Ill 25-30; Tchr-libn St Marys High Sch, Moline Ill 30-43; Tchr-libn St Marys Acad, Nauvoo Ill 44-64, Libn 65-; Lib tchg staff West Ill State U summer 69. 9: CathLA; ALA; IllLA. 10: Nauvoo Hist Soc; Hancock Co Film Lib Bd; Amer Benedictine Acad, Lib Sci Sect;Beta Phi Mu. 14: Ref, catlg. 15: St MaryPriory, Nauvoo Ill 62354.

MARQUART, MARGARET (MARKLE). b State College Penn 5 Mr 22. 4: H L Marquart. 5: Penn State U 37-41 (Music Educ) BS; UIll 44-46 (LS) BS. 7: Music tchr Harris Twp Sch Dist, Boalsburg Penn 41-42; Tchr of music, Eng, Warriors Mark Penn 42-43; clerk-typist Penn State U Lib 43-44; Catlgr Enoch Pratt Free Lib, Baltimore 46-64, Asst head catlg dept 64-67, Head catlg dept 67-. 9: ALA; Potomc Tech Processes Libns (chm 65-67). 14: Catlg. 15: Enoch Pratt Free Lib 400 Cathedral st, Baltimore Md 21201.

MARQUIS, ELEANOR (BAGLEY). b Cambridge Wis 10 My 02. 5: UWis 18-22 (Hist) AB, summer 22 (LS); Ind U Ext 38-63 (LS). 7: Libn High Sch, Benton Wis 22-26; Hist tchr High Sch, Wenatchee Wash 26-27; Libn High Sch, Mishawaka Ind 27-28; Gen asst Pub Lib, Elkhart Ind 29-35, 49-63, Ref asst 63-. 9: ALA; IndLA (sec Reg Group 64-65). 10: AAUW. 14: Ref. 15: 1500 Strong ave, Elkhart Ind 46518.

MARQUIS, ROLLIN P(ARK). b Badin NC 29 N 25. 4: Marian Horton Bonstein. 5: Bard Col Columbia U 42-44, 46-48 (Langs) AB; St Catherines Soc Oxford U 48-50 (Romance Linguistics); Art Students League (NY) 50-52 (Painting);

Carnegie Inst Tech 57-58 MLS. 6: Lat, Gk, Ger, Dutch, Fr, Ital, Sp, Portu. 7: (Pic) Army, USA 44-46; Catlg asst Lib of the Col of Physicians and Surgeons Columbia U 52-53; Chief correspondent Central Dept of Church World Serv, Nat Coun of Churches of Christ, USA, NYC 53-56; Admin asst Friends Com on Nat Legis, Wash DC 56-57; Dir Citizens Lib, Washington Penn 58-59; Dir Free Pub Lib, River Edge NJ 59-63; Dir Allegany Co Lib, Cumberland Md 63-64; Chief Libn Dept of Libs Dearborn Mich 64-. 9: ALA; Michla. 10: Rotary Internat; Fellowship of Reconciliation; Soc of Friends. 14: Admin. 15: Henry Ford Centennial Lib, 16315 Michigan ave, Dearborn Mi 48126.

MARR, EILEEN AGNES (McKENNA. b Sharon Penn. 5: UCLA 41 (Hist) BA; Immaculate Heart Col 56 MA in LS. 6: Ger. 7: Hist researcher Air Force, Santa Ana Cal 46; Libn Orange Co Free Lib, Santa Ana Cal -56; Supv tech serv Fullerton Pub Lib, Fullerton al 56-. 9: ALA; CalLA. 10: Zonta Club; AAUW. 14: Bk sel, adult, catlg. 15: 221-C N Acacia ave, Fullerton Ca 92631.

MARRON, HARVEY. b NYC 27 N 24. 4: Beatrice A. 5: City Col(NY) 45-47 (Physics); NYU 47-48 (Physics) BA; union Col(NY) 48-50 (Physics) MS. 7: Physicist Xerox Corp, Rochester NY 51-5; Physicist Atlanta Res Corp, Alexandria Va 52-53; Physicist Naval Ordnance Lab, White Oak Md 53-54; Phys sci Dept of Defense, Pentgon 54-56; Sr documentalst AEC, Wash DC 56-62 Asst dir Sci Info exch Ech Smithsonian Inst, WASH DC 62-67; Chief ERIC US Off of Educ 67-. 9: ASIS; SLA. 10: Sigma Xi; AAAS. 13: Yes. 14: Mechanized storage & retrieval, info ctr mgt. 15: 7712 Beech Tree rd, Bethesda Md 20034.

MARSH, ELEANOR (HILL). b Wash DC 25 Jl 18. 4: Robert T Marsh. 5: Madison Col 35-37 (Chem); Simmons 37-39 LS BS; UPittsburgh 41-42 (Fine Arts). 7: Lib asst Clark U 39-40; Research bibliogr Mellon INST, Pittsburgh 41-42; Asst libn, catlgr Burke Surdam Lib Green Mountain Col 56-. 9: VtLA. 10: Poultney Womans Club; MidVt Artists Inc; So Vt Art Assn. 14: Catlg. 15: 13 Bentley ave, Poultney Vt 0576410509

MARSH, ELIZABETH (MARY) (DAVENPORT) (MRS). b New Orleans 22 My 11. 5: Sophie Newcomb 28-32 (Biol) BS; Tulane 32-34 (Botany, Zool); Simmons 39-40 SLS. 7: Asst lab tech Surgery Dept Tulane U 35-39; Spec asst NY Acad of Med Lib, NYC 40-41; Libn Bassett Hosp, Cooperstown NY 41-44; Libn Baylor U MedSch 44-45; Asst in chg tech processes Tulane U Med Lib 45-49; Libn UArk Med Sch 49-56; Head catlgr Tulane U Matas Med Lib 56-. 9: MedLA (So Reg Group); LaLA; New OrleansLib Club. 13: Yes. 14: Catlg. 15: 1607 Napoleon ave, Apt O, New Orleans 70115.

MARSH, JOHN SEAWELL. b Guilford Co NC 12 F 32. 5: Berea Col 50-54 (Eng) AB; Princeton 54-55, Robt K Root Fellow in Eng; UNC 59-60 LS; Columbia 61-62 LS; NYU Sch of Law 66 LLB. 6: Fr. 7: Ext libn Pub Lib, High Point NC summer 59; Lib asst UNC Lib (Chapel Hill) 59-60; Prof Intern Columbia U Lib 61-62; Asst libn Cahill Gordon Reindel & Ohl, NYC 62-63; Libn Cleary Gottlieb Steen & Hamilton, NYC 63-66; Ref libn Columbia U Law Lib 66-67; Libn Cadwalader Wickenham & Taft 67-69; Admin dir, LSU Law Lib 69-. 9: AALA; SLA; Law Lib Assn Greater Y. 10: Phi Kappa Phi; Selden Soc. 14: Ref (Law. 15: Louisiana State Univ Law Sch, Baton Rouge 70803.

MARSH, MARTHA MAE. b Antigo Wis 18 D 06. 5: Kan Wesleyan U 24-28 summer 35 (Eng, Hist) BA; USoCal summers 30, 38; UColo summer 39; Peabody summers 32, 40-42 BS in LS; Kan State Tchrs Col (Emporia) ext 57. 6: Fr. 7: Tchr Eng, hist Pub Sch, Culver Kan 29-35; Eng tchr Pub Sch, Newton Kan 35-43; Secondary libn Pub Sch, Newton Kan 43-50; Asst Educ Lib UColo summer 48; Secondary libn Pub Sch, SALINA Kan 50-68; Hd libn Marymount Col (Salina Kan) 68-. 8: Lib consul for Arch Firm Anderson, Johnson, Srack (Salina Kan) 57; Visiting lecturer UColo summers 49-54; Visiting lecturerKan State Tchrs Col(Emporia) summers 58-61; Consul N Central Kan secondary level lib, Field Enterprises. 9: ALA-AASchL; NEA; KanLA; KanASchL; Kan State Tchrs Assn. 10: Pi Gamma Mu; Sigma Tau Delta; Altrusa; AAUW; Delta Kappa Gamma; Salina City Tchrs Assn; Asbury Hosp Aux. 13: Yes. 14: Ref, sch lib serv. 15: 1017 Osborne, Saline Kan 67401.

MARSH, PATRICIA E. b St Louis Mo 28 S 46. 5: UMo (St Louis) (Eng) BA 64-68; Case West Res (Med LS) MSLS 68-69. 6: Fr. 7: US Govt, St Louis; Clk-stenographer 64, Clk-typist 65-66, Spec proj asst 67; Lib asst UMo Lib (St Louis) 68;Lib asst Allen Memorial Med Lib, Cleveland Ohio 68-69; Ref libn Ohio State U (Columbus) 69-. 9: ALA; MedLA; MoLA. 14: Med ref, reg med program, ser. 15: 8624 Deborah Jean dr, St Louis Mo 63134.

MARSH, VIRGINIA (MOORE). b Lansing Mich 15 F 20. 4: William E Marsh. 5:Mich Mich Col 38-42 9eng, Eng, Fr) BA; UMich 51-52 AMLS; Mich State U, UMich, West Mich U, East Mich U 45- MichSecondary Certif. 7: Tchr Capac High Sch, Capac Mich 47-51; Libn Ann J Kellogg Sch, Battle creek Mich 52-59; Libn Northwestern Jr. High Sch, Battle Creek Mich 59-. 8: Instr Bowling Green State U, summer 65. 9: ALA; NEA; MichLA; chm sch & child sect MichASchL; MichEA (life mem); Battle Creek EA (sec 2 yrs). 10: Bldg rep on coun; Ticker Tape Investment Club; Battle Creek Area Libs. 13: Yes. 14: Sch lib admin. 15: Northwestern Jr High Sch Lib, 176 Limit st, Battle Creek Mich 49017.

MARSHALL, ADELINE (MORRISSEY). b S Walpole Mass 18 F 15. 4: Edward F Marshall. 5: Simmons 32-36 (LS) BS; Boston U 37-38 (Educ). 6: Fr, Ger. 7: Lib asst Brookline Pub Lib, Brookline Mass 36-38; Libn Jr Col of Conn(Bridgepor) Bridgeport Catlgr Milton Pub Lib, Milton Mass 62-63; Catlgr Northeastern U 63-64; Libn Andrew Alford Consulting Engrs, Boston 64-. 10: LWV; Nat Trust Hist Preservation; Cohasset Hist Soc; Commun Garden Club; South Shore Art Ctr. 14: Catlg. 15: 181 Jerusalem rd, Cohasset Mass 02025.

MARSHALL, ALBERT P(RINCE). b Texarkana Tex 5 S 14. 4: Ruthe Langley. 5: Lincoln U 34-38 (Hist, Eng) AB; UIll 38-39 BSLS, 48-50 Hist) MA; UMo 59- (Hist). 6: Ger, Fr. 7: Asst libn Lincoln U 39-41; Libn State Tchrs Col (Winston-Salem NC) 41-50; U Libn Lincoln U 50-69; Dir of lib East Mich U 69-. 8: Mem NC Lib Survey Team, TVA, 47-48; Consul Ark AM & N Col 67; Adv Com, Off Educ Title II, Higher Educ Ast. 9: ALA (chm Nomin Com (65-67) mem Subs Bks Com 63-66); -ACRL (chm Adv Com 67-69); NC Negro LA (Exec Bd 46-48); MoLA (sec 54-56 pres 61-62; Col & Univ Lib Devel Com 64-65; chm RECR Com 54-60; chm Col & Univ Div 51-52); Mo State Tchrs Assn. 10: NAACP; Boy Scouts; Delta Phi Delta; Alpha Phi Alpha; Community Center Assn,Jefferson City; AHA; AAUP; Internat Platform Assn. 11: Alumni Achievement award, Lincoln U, 65; Alpha Phi Alpha Hall of Fame 64. 12: Ed MoLA "Quarterly (52-54; "Pictorial History of Lincoln University (66). 13: Yes. 14 Admin, surveys. 15: Dir, Eastern Michigan Univ Library, Ypsilanti Mi 48197.

MARSHALL, CAROLYN CALDWELL. b tmidland Tex 26 Jl 02. 5: Sullins Col 19-21 (Liberal Art) Certif; Tex Womens Col summer 24; Chicago Art Inst summer 25; NM State U 59 LS). 7: Tchr pub schs, El Paso Tex 22-26; Libn Pub Lib, Deming NM 58-. 8: Trustee Deming Pub Lib 2758; NMLib Commsn 56-57. 9: ALA; NMLA (pres 62). 10: Luna Co Hist Soc; PTA; Pan Amer Round Tble; City Planning Commsn, Deming NM. 11: Dorothy Canfield Fisher award 60. 14: Admin. 15: 200 S Nickel ave, Deming NM 88030.

MARSHALL, DORIS BINKLEY. b Troy Ohio 27 Je 18. 4: Fred Taylor Marshall. 5: Ohio StateU 35-40 (Chem) BA; UChicago 40-41. 6: Fr, Ger, Russian. 7: Asst libn Universal oil Products, Chicago 40-41; Tech libn Monsanto Chem Co, Dayton Ohio 41-44; Abstractor (patents) Alien Property Custodian (mail) Dayton 44-45; Libn Amer Zinc lead & Smelting Co, Kirkwood Mo 56-60; Self-employed Kirkwood Mo 63-65; Tech sales corresp Nuclear Consul Div of Mallinckrodt Chem Co, St Louis 66; Research libn Ralston Purina Co, St Louis 66-. 9: ACS; Greater St Louis LA; SLA (bulletin ed "The Slate". 10: Metropolitan St Louis Bd; Soc of Mayflower Descendants in Mo. 12: "Studies in Enterprise; A Selected Bibliography of American and Canadian Company Histories and Biographies of Businessmen (57), and 6 annual supps to above in "Business History Review (59-64); Baker Lib "Reference Lists, No 20 (60), No 21 (63), No 24 (65); Coll "Sources of Commodity Prices" (SLA 59); "Literature of Executive Management" (SLA 64). 13: Yes. 14: Lit searching. 15: Res Lib Ralston Purina Co Checkerboard Sq, St Louis Mo 63199.

MARSHALL, EDITH MAY. b Bedford Va 16 O 1900. 5: Farmvill State Tchrs Col (Va) 19-21, 27-28 (Eng) BS; UVa summers 24-27 (Eng); Columbia 30-31 (Eng) MA, 37-38 BS in LS. 6: Fr. 7: Prin Guinea Sch, Guinea Va 22; Tchr Diskinson Mem & Ind High Sch, Clintwood Va 22-23; Tchr Stuart High Sch, Stuart Va 23-24; Tchr Amelia High Sch, Amelia Va 25-26; Tchr Townesville High Sch, Townesville NC 26-27; Asst Libn & Instr State Tchrs Col, Farmville Va; 28-30; Lib Asst Tchrs Col Columbia U summers 31-37, 30-31; Tchr Pittsfield High Sch, NH 31-37; Loan asst UArk 38-43; catlgr UIll; Urbana 43, catlg reviser (present) & Asst Prof. 9: ALA; IllLA. 10: Photographic Soc MER: Champaign Co (Ill) Camera Club;

UIll Staff Assn. 13: Yes. 14: Calg. 15: 1108 W Nevada st, Urbana Ill 61801.

MARSHALL, ELIZABETH (CHESTNUTT). b Persia Tenn. 4: Robert A Marshall. 5: Lincoln MemU 35-39 (Eng) AB; Peabody Col 39-40 BS in LS. 7: Libn Pittsburgh Sr High, Pittsburgh Kan 40-43; Libn Hinter Air Force Base Lib, Savannah Ga 49-66; Libn Henderson Co Pub Lib, Hendersonville NC 66-. 9: ALA; SELA; NCLA. 15: 1810 Windsor dr, Hendersonville NC 28739.

MARSHALL, ESTELLE (ISOBEL). b Sherrooke Que Can. 28 O 30. 5: UBC 49-51 (Hist) BA, 52-53 (Geog); Toronto 53-54 BLS. 6: Fr. 7: Sr clerical Okanagan Reg Lib, Kelowna BC 51-52; Head ref dept Sudbury Pub Lib, Sudbury Ont 54-59; Gen libn Central Lib Metropolitan Borough of Lewisham, London Eng 60; Ref libn Calgary Pub Lib, Calgary Alta 60-65; Reg libn Can Nat RR, Edmonton Alta 65-. 9: CANLA; AltaLA; ALA; SLA; EdmontonLA; Inst Prof Libns Ont. 14: Ref. 15: 9E-9820 104 st, Edmonton 14 Alberta Can.

MARSHALL, FLORENIA (WEAVER). b Edgefield SC 6 D 19. 4: Alexander Marshall. 5: Benedict 47 (Eng) AB; S Car State Col 57 (Elem ed) MS; UUtah 68. 6: Fr. 7: Elem tchr Aiken Co dept of Educ, SC 38-54; Elem tchr-libn Pinecrest Sch, Aiken SC 54-68; Libn Pinecrest Elem & Aiken Grade Sch 68-. 9: ALA; NEA (life mem); SCLA; SC Dept of A-V Instr So EA; AikenCoTA (var offs). 10: Red Cross First Aid Instr; Friends of Aiken Co Pub Lib. 11: Certificates of appreciation, Ga-Carolina Coun of BSA. 14: Sch lib. 15: Rte 3 Box 99, Aiken SC 29801.

MARSHALL, FRANCES AINSLIE (BAIRD). b Port Huron Mich 17 My 22. 4: George L Marshall. 5: Denison U 40-44 (Eng) BA; Columbia 45 (LS) BS; UMich summer 47, 48 (Educ). 6: Fr, Ger. 7: Libn Port Huron Jr Col 45-53; Ref libn St. Clair Co Lib, Port Huron Mich 65-. 10: Can Fed Univ Women; Sarnia (Ont) Glf & Curling Club; Sarnia (Ont) Riding Club. 13: Yes. 14: Ref. 15: 1320 Rex st, Sarnia Ont Can.

MARSHALL, HARRIETT (LOUISE) DOUGLASS. b Portland Ore 26 S 16. 4: Donald Ross Marshall. 5: Lewis & Clarke (Albany) 35-36 (Lit); UOre 37-40, 47-48 (Mus) BS in Mus; UWash 63-67 MLS. 7: Mus record libn UWashington 63-. 9: MusLA; Assn Recorded Sound Libs. 15: Univ of Washington 19 Music Bldg, Seattle Wa 98105.

MARSHALL, MRS IDA JO (HILLIN). b Rockdale Tex 15 Mr 03. 5: Baylor Col 28-29; Sam Houston State Tchrs Col 32-38 (Hist) BS; Sul Ross State Tchrs Col 44-45; UTex 46-48 (Educ) M of Ed;UDenver 57. 7: Tchr, Milam Co Tex 20-29; Tchr, Burleson Co Tex 29-30; Tchr, Lee Co Tex 30-42; Soc studies tchr Rockdale (Tex) High Sch 42-44, Libn 44-. 8: Mem of Milam Co, Tex State Hist Survey Com 64-69; Mem Eval Coms for area high schs. Lib Club. 9: ALA; NEA; TexLA; Tex State Hist Assn; Tex State TA; Milam Co TA. 10: PTA; Tex Reading Assn; Friends of Lib. 13: Yes. 14: Catlg, ref, remedial reading, sch lib wk, soc sic, govt. 15: 615 N Main st, Rockdale Tx 76567.

MARSHALL, JOHN DAVID. b McKenzie Tnn 7 S 28. 5: Bethel Col 47-50 (Hist, Eng) BA; Fla State U 50-51 (LS) MA, 51-52 Hist, LS). 7: Stud asst Bethel Col Lib summer 49; Grad asst Fla State U Lib Schs 51-52 Ref libn Clemson Col Lib 52-55; Head ref dept Auburn U Lib 55-57; Head acquis div & Asst Prof of Lib Sci UGa Lib 57-, 67; U libn (Assoc Prof) Middle Tenn State U (Murfreesboro) 67-. 8: "Alabama Librarian ed bd 56-57; "Library Journal bk reviewer 53-64 "Library Journal Ref Checklist Com 56-57; "Journal of Library History bk review ed 66-; "Southern Observer contrib ed 53-; Gen ed, Shoe String Press "Contribs to Lib Lit Ser 63-. 9: ALA (Life Mem);-ACRL (Publ Com 57-62);-RTSD; BSA; SELA (So Bks Compet Com 66-70); SE Reg Group of Resources & Tech ServLibns (chm 68-70); Amer Lib Hist RT; TennLA (chm Intel Freedom Com 69); Tenn Hist Soc; TennEA. 10: Phi Kappa Phi; Beta Phi Mu. 12: "Books in Your Life 59; "Louis Shores; A Bibliography 64; "A Fable of Tomorrows Library 65; Ed, with Wayne Shirley and Louis Shores "Books, Libraries, Librarians 55; "Of, By, and For Librarians 60; "An American Library History Reader 61; "In Pursuit of Library History 62; "Mark Hopkins Log and Other Essays by Louis Shores 65; "Approaches to Library History (65); "The Library in the University (67). 13: Yes. 14: Acquis, lib hist, lib educ. 15: Riviera apts No 34 802 E Main st, Murfreesboro Tn 37130.

MARSHALL, JOHN M(AITLAND). b Winnipeg Man Can 5 Ag 19. 4: Christine Smith. 5: USask 38 (Eng) BA, 39 (High Sch Certif), 45 (Eng Lit) MA; Toronto 52 (BLS). 7: Educ dir Peoples Cooperative Ltd, Winnipeg Man 46-51; Sch & child libn Fraser Valley Reg Lib, Abbotsford BS 52-53; Bkmob supv Victoria Pub Lib 53-54 libn-helping tchr Yorkton Sch Unit, Yorkton Sask 54-58; Head Libn Kitimat Pub Lib, Kitimat BC 58-60; Adult serv libn N York Pub Lib 60-61, Head Bathurst Heights Br 61-66; Asst Prof UToronto Sch of Lib Sci 66-. 9: ALA; CanLA; Prof Libns Com 56-59, chm Subcom on Training of Lib Technicians 68-69); Sask Helping Tchrs Assn (pres 57-58); Inst Prob Libns Ont (pres 64-65); OntLA; Can Assn & Adult Educ; Ont Assn Contin Educ; Steering Com on Negotiation Rights for Profess Staffs 68-. 10: N York Area Coun, Soc Planning Coun of Metro Toronto 62-63. 12: Ed "IPLO Newsletter 62-64. 13: Yes. 14: Bk sel, reader adv, adult educ, ext, soc sci (bibl, lit). 15: 22 Braeside rd, Toronto 12, Can.

MARSHALL, JOSEPH WILLIAM. b Dorchester Mass 16 N 22. 4: Doris Jackson. 5: Northeastern U 41-43 (Chem); Tufts Col 47-49 (Hist) AB; Syracuse 50-51 MS (LS). 7: (T/Sgt) US Army 43-46; (2nd Lt) US Army Reserve 50-52; Lib asst Boston Med Lib 49-50; Readers adv hist div DC Pub Lib 51-57; Tech libn US Naval Ordnance Station Indian Head Md 57-59; Supv libn Franklin D Roosevelt Lib, Hyde Park NY 59-. 9: SLA; SENY Lib Resources Coun (Bd Dirs); Dutchess Co LA; Lib Trustees Found (NY), AHA. 10: Beta Phi Mu; Trustee Hyde Park (NY) Free Lib. 14: Ref, mss. 15: 23 Caywood pl, Hyde Park NY 12538.

MARSHALL, (KENNETH) ERIC. b Kings Lynn Norfolk England 25 O 30. 4: Dorothy Kindred Edgar. 5: ULondon Kings Col 48-52 (Zool) BSc. 6: Fr. 7: Radio mechanic Royal Corps of Signals, Engl 53-55; Libn Freshwater Biol Assn, Ambleside Eng 55-64; Senior asst libn Royal Holloway Col ULondon, Englefield Green Surrey, England 64-67; Libn Fisheries Research Bd of Can Freshwater Inst, Winnipeg Man 67-. 9: SLA; Aslib; LA (UK). 12: Comp Index of "Journal of Ecology" V 21-52. 14: Ref, computerized info ret, educ of lib users. 15: Fisheries Research Board of Can Freshwater Institute 501 Univ Crescent, Winnipeg 19 Manitoba Can.

MARSHALL, MARION BARBARA. b Moline Ill 9 S 33. 5: UChicago 51-53 (Liberal arts); Carleton 53-55 (Govt & Intl rel) BA; Catholic U of Amer 65-66 (LS) MA. 7: Mgt Intern Analyst computer applications programmer Dept of Navy Bur of Aeronautics, Wash DC 55-58; Asst to legis assoc AAUW Wash DC 61-64; Sec to v-pres Kerr McGee Oil Co, Wash DC 64-65; Catlgr Arlington Co Pub Lib, Arlington Co Va 67-69; Child libn Fairfax Co Pub Lib, Fairfax Co Va 69-. 15: 2112 Columbia pike, Arlington Va 22204.

MARSHALL, ROBERT D. b Oso Wash 23 O 16. 4: Amanda Lee Reed. 5: Wash State U 35-36 (Chem Engnr); UWash 36-40 (Econ) BA; USan Francisco 51-52 U Cal Berkeley BLS; UOre 54-56. 7: Accounting clerk Puget Sound Power & Light Co, Seattle 40-42; US Army Air Force Communications (Cpl), Europe 42-45; Accounting clerk Puget Sound Power & Light Co, Seattle 45-46; Orchid grower & photographer E W McLellan Co, San Francisco 46-51; Soc sci libn UOre 53-57; Ref libn Cal State Polytech Col 57-68, Lib Admin asst 68-. 9: CaLA. 10: Sierra Club; UCal Lib Schs Alum Assn. 12: "A Bibliography of Bibliographies of Instructional Aids to Learnin (55). 13: Yes. 14: Ref, docs, archives. 15: 20623 Stephanie dr, Covna Cal 91723.

MARSHALL, RUTH ANN. b Hazleton Penn. 5: Penn State U 38-42 (Educ) BA; Carnegie 45-46 BS in LS. 7: Catlgr Carnegie Inst Tech 46-51, Head catlgr Hunt Lib 51-. 9: ALA; PennLA. 12: Co-ed "Penn Lib Assn Bulletin (4849). 15: 5744 Kentucky ave, Pittsburgh Pa 15232.

MARSHALL, RUTH VIRGINIA. b Boston 19 O 27. 5: Radcliffe 45-49 (Eng) AB; Simmons 51-53 (LS) MS. 7: Boston Pub Lib: Probationary asst 50-53; Asst 53-57, Prof lib asst 5863, Ref asst 63-65, Ref libn 65-. 9: ALA; MassLA. 14: Ref. 15: 194 Franklin st, Cambridge Mass 02139.

MARSHALL, RUTHE H (LANGLEY). b Appleton City Mo 12 S 16. 4: Albert P Marshall. 5: Lincoln U (Mo) 35-40 (Home Econ) BS; UIll 48-50 (Child Development); UMo 67 (LS). 7: Tchr Douglass High Sch, Lexington Mo 40-41; Nursery dir Champaign-Urbana kindergarten, Champaign Ill 48-50; Nursery dir Commun Ctr, Jefferson City Mo 52-55; Lib clk Mo State Lib 58-67, Doc libn 67-. 9: ALA; MoLA. 10: Delta Sigma Theta; Exec Boars; Day Nur & Child Devel Ctr. 14: Ser, docs. 15: 1209 Whittier, Ypsilanti Mi 48197.

MARSHBURN, MARGARET (COMBS). b Chicago 6 S 20. 5: Whittier Col 39-42 (Chem) AB; UCal 59-60 MLS. 7: Abstract libn Standard Oil Co of Cal, San Francisco 60-64,

Geology Libn 64-. 14: Ref, catlg, acquis (earth scis). 15: Standard Oil Co of Cal Lib 225 Bush st room 2265, San Francisco Ca94120.

MARSTEN, CLAIRE (ANGEL). b Salt Lake City 30 Je 09. 5: UUtah 25-28 BS; Simmons Col 28-29 (Libnship) BS. 07: Asst libn Aberdeen Pub Lib, Aberdeen Wash 29-32; Libn Olympia Pub Lib, Olympia Wash 32-33; UWash Lib: Philosophy br lib 47-50, Ref div 54-55, Bind processes libn 55-57, Educ br libn 57-62, Soc sci ref div 62-68; Hd soc sci ref 68-. 09: ALA; PNLA (chm Col Div 66-68); WashLA; WashASchL. 14: Ref, educ. 15: 5527 17th ave NE, Seattle Wa 98105.

MARTEL, FRANKLIN (ROY). b Yonkers NY 16 N 31. 4: Jean Backus. 5: UNotre Dame 50-55 (Great Bks) BA; Syracuse 64- (Systems & Info Sci). 7: Personnel clk US Army, San Francisco 55-57; Mgt trainee P&C Food Mkts, Syracuse NY 58; Inventory control Carrier Air Conditioner Co, Syracuse NY 58-61; Syst programmer System Development Corp, Santa Monica Cal 61-64; Research programmer SyracuseU Research Corp 64-68; Syst programmer gen Electric Co, Syracuse NY 68; Asst dir Lib Educ Expansion Project Sch of Lib Sci SyracuseU 68-. 9: ACM; ASIS. 14: Automated retr, lib automation, lib sci educ. 15: 318 Jamesville rd, Dewitt NY 13214.

MARTEL, LUCILLE A (GIGUERE). b Concord NW 30 Jl 20. 4: Romeo G Martel. 5: Trinity Col Wash DC 37-38 (Liberal arts); Syracuse 38-41 (Eng, Hist) BA; John Carroll U summer 40 (Eng); Immaculate Heart 67 (LS) MS. 6: Fr. 7: Libn Brotherhood of RR Trainmen, cleveland Ohio 42-44; Advertising McCann-Erickson, Cleveland Ohio 45-47; Sec Equitable Life Ins Soc, Cleveland Ohio 47-49; Libn Orange Co Pub Lib, Orange Cal 68-. 8: Bd mem So Cal Coun on Lit for Chils & YP Los Angeles & Orange Cos 68. 9: ALA; CalLA; OrangeCoLA; OrangeCoSchLA. 10: YA Reviewers of So Cal; Orange Co Employees Assn. 13: Yes. 14: Child, ya. 15: 13192 Silver Birch dr, Tustin Ca 92680.

MARTEL, MARILEE NORLING. b Denver 11S31. 4: Leon C Martel Jr. 5: Mills Col 49-53 (Philos) BA, 53-54 (Humanities); Columbia 54-56 (Russian Studies), 57-58 (LS) MS; US Naval Intelligence Sch Lang Div 61-62 (Russian (Russian) Russian Certif Interpreter/Tr. 6: Russian, Fr. 7: Head Libn US Naval Air Sta Lib, Port Lyautey Morocco 59-61; Intelligence research tech Nat Security Agency, Ft Meade Md 62-64; Spec asst to the dean Sch of Lib Serv Columbia U 64, Asst to the dean 64-. 11: Outstanding Performance Award from Nat Security Agency. 14: Educ for libnship, Soviet area studies collections. 15: 600 W 111 st apt 9E-1, NYC 10025.

MARTELLE, HAROLD D JR. b St Joseph Mich 10 Ag 21. 4: Eletha A Welcher. 5: UMich 47-50 (Oriental Studies) AB; West Mich 50-51 (LS) Certif of Lib; Peabody 51-52 MALS. 6: Japanese. 7: (Cpl) US Army, USA, Philippines, Japan 40-46; Admin asst Wayne Co Lib, Mich 52-56; Dir Bacon Mem Pub Lib, Wyandotte Mich 56-62; Dir Dearborn Pub Lib, Dearborn Mich 62-64; Asst dir San Francisco Pub Lib 64-. 9: ALA (Coun); -PLA (Bd Dirs); CalLA. 13: Yes. 14: :Lib bldgs, admin. 15: San Francisco Pub Lib, San Francisco Ca 94102.

MARTENS, ALICE (ANDERSON COCKS). b Trenton NJ 22 D 20. 4: Stanton C Martens. 5: Vassar 38-42 (Geol) AB; So Conn State 57-61 (LS) MS. 6: Fr. 7: Geologist Godfrey L Cabot Inc, Charleston WVa 42-43; Sales correpondent Berger Brothers, New Haven Conn 43-44; Asst circ & ref Yale Divinity Sch Lib 52-58; Catlgr So Conn State Col 58-61; Lib Branford Braford Jr High Sch, Branford Conn 61-. 9: ConnLA; ConnSchL; ConnEA. 10: AAUW. ; Delta Kappa Gamma. 14: Sch libs. 15: 126 Lawncrest rd, New Haven Ct 06515.

MARTENSEN, MARILYN RUTH (NEBEN). b Rochfort Bridge Alta Can 28 S 39. 5: Chadron State Col 57-60 (Eng, Elem Educ) BS in Educ; UDenver 61,63 MS in Libnship. 6: Ger. 7: Tchr Norflk Neb 60-61; Libn Poudre Rl Schs, Ft Collins Colo 63; Asst catlg Libn Colo State U 64-66, Asst acquis libn 64-67; Instr Ed Media Colo State Col (Greeley) 67-. 09: AL. 9: ALA; NEA-DAVI; ColoASchL; Colo A-V Assn. 14: Lib educ, multi-media approach (sch libs). 15: 2200 37th st, Greeley Co 80631.

MARTHALER, SISTER MARGARET OSF. 5: Col of St Benedict (Minn) 37-40; St Johns U (Minn) 56-58 (Adult Educ); Col of St Catherine summers 58-62 (LS) BS; Fla State Usummer 66; NDEA Inst supv Sch Lib; Rosary Col summer 67-. 7: Libn St Gabriel Sch of Nursing, Little Falls Minn 43-44; Libn StFrancis Sch of Nursing, Breckeride Minn 43-44; Tchr St Cloud Childrens Home, St Cloud Minn 44-45; Libn St Gabriel Sch of Nursing,St Francis Sch of Nursing 45-50; Tchr, off St Cloud Childrens Home, St Cloud Minn 50-58; Sch lib consul Elem Schs ofSisterhood 58-65; Sch lib consul Diocese of St Cloud, Central Minn 65-. 8: Instr, Col of St Benedict Minn Lib Wkshop summer65. 9: ALA; CathLA (Minn-Dak Unit; chm 68-, chm Elem Sect 65-68); MinnLA. 12: Ed "The Catholic Librarian, Newsletter of Minn-Dak Unit (68).. 14: Supvn (sch libs). 15: Mary Hall, 8th ave & 2nd st SE, Little Falls Mn 56345.

MARTIN, ABBOTT W. b Baltimore Md 13 Jl 34. 5: Johns Hopkins 58-62 (Math) BS; Catholic U 64-66 (LS) MS. 6: Ger. 7: Pilot (Lt Cmdr) USN 54-58; Tchr Hartwack Sch, Berlin Germany 62-64; Bibliogr & sci libn LC 64-66; Dir Tech Info Center Coca-Cola Co, Atlanta 66-68; Owner Infonet, Atlanta 69-. 14: Advanc of sci through lib linfo, systems & serv. 15: 1734 Manor rd, Baltimore Md 21222.

MARTIN, AGNES (HUDSON) MACQUEEN). b Hummelstown Penn 3 Ja 1900. 5: Carnegie 30 LS Certif UPittsburgh 34-36; Eng. 7: Asst Sewickley Penn 18-29; catlgr boys & girls dept Carnegie Lib of Pittsburgh 29-38; catlgr Priv Lib Mr E A Woods, Sewickley Penn 26-43; Libn D T Watson Home for Crippled Child, Leetsdale Penn 42-44; Asst Roselle Pub Lib, Roselle NJ 59-60; Child libn Orange Pub Lib Orange NJ 60-. 9: ALA; NJLA. 14: Serv to child, catlg, ref. 15: 1280 Shetland dr, Union NJ 07083.

MARTIN, ALLIE BETH. b Annieville Ark 28 Je 14. 4: Ralph F Martin. 5: Arkansas Col 35 BA; Peabody 38 BS in LS; Columbia 49 MLS. 6: Fr. 7: Libn Pub Lib, Batesville Ark 35-36; Libn Little Rock Jr Col Lib 36-37; Asst to Exec sec Ark Lib Commsn, Little Rock Ark 37-39, 45-48; Libn Miss Co Lib. Osceola Ark 42-43; Head child & ext dept Tulsa (Okla) Pub Lib 49-61; Spec Lecturer in Lib Sci UOkla Lib Sch 58-; Head ext div Tulsa City- Co Lib, Tulsa Okla 62-63, Dir 63-. 8: Spec Lecturer Sch of Lib Sci UOkla 58-. 9: ALA (chm, Com for a Greater ALA Coun);-CSD (Exec Bd); OklaLA (past pres); ArkLA (past pres); SWLA (pres). 10: Delta Kappa AMMA: LWV; Tulsa Com for UN; Tulsa Urban League SW Art Assn. 11: Women of Year Award 64; Presented by Okla Chap of Amer Women in Radio & TV; Distinguished Serv Award, OklaLA. 13: Yes. 14: Child serv, lib admin, lib bldgs. 15: Tulsa City-Co Lib System 400 Civic Center, Tulsa Okla 74103.

MARTIN, ANN BERNARD. b Memphis Tenn. 5: Agnes Scott Col 32-32 (Chem) BA; Vanderbilt U 43-46 (Bacteriology) MA; Emory 56-59 MLn. 7: Tchr biol & Gen Sci St Marys Sch, Sewanee Tenn 36-39; Med tech neuropathological rsearch Grady Hosp, Alanta 40-41; Med tech St Elizabeths Hosp 42-43; Med tech Vanderbuilt UMed Sch 46-47; Med tech Emory Margaret Hall Sch, Versailles Ky 47-48, U Med tech Jewish Hosp, Brooklyn NY 49-50; Tchr biol, chem & algebra 51-53: Tchrs St tchrSt Marys Sch, Sewanee Tenn 55-56, Libn 56-58; Head adult serv Ida Williams Br Alanta Pub Lib 60-65; Med libn St Josephs Infirmary, Atlanta 65-. 9: ALA; MedLA; GaLA; SELA. 10: Eng-speaking Union. 14: Pub & med libnship, ref, sch libnship, lib admin. 15: 274 Rumson rd NE, Atlanta Ga 30305.

MARTIN, ANNABELLE (VILLERE). b Fairport NY 22 my 27. 4: Henry A Martin Jr. 5: Cornell U 45-49 Hist) BA; State U (Geneseo) 61-62 MLS. 7: Off equip demonstrator Friden Corp, Rochester NY 51-57; Sec TKM Electric Corp, Rochester NY 57-61; High sch libn Wayne Central Sch, Ontario Center NY 62-66; High Sch Fairport Central Sch Fairport NY 66-. 9: NYLA; NY State Tchrs Assn; Pentad. 10: Print Club of Rochester (NY). 14: Sch libnship. 15: 19 Strathallan Park, Rochester NY 14607.

MARTIN, ANTHONY A. b Pittsburgh 18 Ag 20. 4: Julia Wallace. 5: Duquesne 38-42 (Eng, Hist) B Ed; Carnegie 45-46 BSLS; UPittsburgh 46-9 (Pol Sci). 6: Ger. 7: Stud asst Carnegie Lib of Pittsburgh 36-43; Pilot (1st Lt) US Air Corps, US, Europe 43-45; Asst, sr asst ref dept Carnegie Lib of Pittsburgh 46-48; Mgr of Restaurant, Pittsburgh 49; Asst head ref dept Carnegie Lib of Pittsburgh 49-52; Purchase analyst Westinghouse Air Brake Co, Swissvale Penn 53-54; Admin asst Carnegie Lib of Pittsburgh 54-55; Libn US Bureau of Mines, Pittsburgh 55-56; Chief libn N Side Brs Carnegie Lib of Pittsburgh 56-64, Asst dir 64-69, Dir 69-. 8: Consul lib bldgs: Tionesta Penn 63; Uniontown Penn 63; an addition to Lebanon Penn lib 63. 9: MARLA (treas 58-); PennLA (treas 61-64, 2nd v-pres 65-66). 10: City of Pittsburgh No SIDE Parking Corp YMCA; Rotary. 12: Ed "Technical Bk Review Index (Sept 56-)56-Je 69. 14: Admin. 15: 4400 Forbes ave, Pittsburgh Pa 15213.

MARTIN, BEVERLY (BRESLOVE). b Chicago 28 F 20. 5: UChicago 36-39 (Bacteriology) BS, 39-40 Ms; Rosary Col 61-63 MALS. 6: Fr. 7: Bacteriologist Merck & Co, Rahway NJ 41-43; Bacteriologist Northwestern U 43-44; Lib clerk Oak Park High Sch, Oak Park Ill 60-63; Catlg Lib of Med Scis UIll(Chicago) 63-68; Lib Jewish Vocational Serv, Chicago Ill 68-. 9: ALA; IllLA; SLA. 10: AAUW. 15: 312 Linden ave, Oak Park Ill 60302.

MARTIN, BILLIE (HUDDLESTON). b Export WVa 29 My 13. 4: John H Martin. 5: URochester 31-32; Eng; WVa Inst of Tech 32-35 (Eng, Fr) AB; WVaU summers 35, 38, 39 (Eng) MA; Catholic U 55-56 MSLS. 6: Fr, Ger. 7: Tchr-libn Woodrow Wilson High, Beckleh WVa 35-43; Communications, admin registered publs US Navy LCDR, Norfolk Va, Newport RI, San Diego 42-54; Asst libn US Naval Ordnance Lab, Corona Cal 56-61; Post libn US Army, Ft Holabird Baltimore 61-63; Post libn US Army, Ft Monroe Va 63; Ref asst Army Lib Pentagon, Wash DC 63-64, Chief gen ref 64-67; Chief Gen ref US Dept Labor Lib, Wash DC 67-. 9: ALA; DCLA. 14: Ref. 15: 1700 35th st NW, Wash DC 20007.

MARTIN, BLANCHE MARY. b Harriet Ark 18 D 10. 4: Lonnie R Martin. 5: Ark State Tchrs Col 50-53 (Educ) BSE; Peabody 58-59 MA(LS); Wichita State U 65 (LS). 7: Tchr, Marshall Ark 25-50; Libn Marshall High Sch, Marshall Ark 50-55; Elem libn Wichita Pub Schs, Wichita Kan 55-57; Libn lib tech proc dept, Wichita Kan 57-61; Libn Jr High Sch, Wichita Kan 61-. 9: ALA; NEA; KanASchL; Kan State Tchrs Assn; Wichita Lib Club. ; Wichita Ctr TA (Deleg 61-62); Wichita Jr High Sch Libns (chm 66-69). 10: PTA; Beta Phi Mu; Kappa Delta Pi; Phi Alpha Theta; Alpha Chi. 13: Yes. 14: Sch libn. 15: 1721 SVolutsia, Wichita Kan 67211.

MARTIN, BROTHER DAVID. b Chicago 8 Mr 01. 5: UPortland 36 AB; UOre 36 Certif in LS; UWash 38 BLS; UPortland 40 MA; Chicago 55 MS(LS). 6: Fr. 7: Libn UPortland 28-; V-dir Rosary Col Lib Sci Ext, Portland Ore 43-52; Head Dept of Lib Sci UPortland 52-64, Univ archivist 6 6-, Prof lib sci 66-. 9: CathLA (past mem Exec Coun, var chmships NW Chap); NW Col Libns; ALA; PNLA; OreLA. 10: UPortland Friends of the Lib. 12: "American Catholic Convert Authors" (44); "Catholic Library Practice" 2 v (47-51); Ed "School Library Institute Papers"; Ed UPortland "Bookman" (40-). 13: Yes. 14: Admin, period. 15: 5000 N Willamette blvd, Portland Or 97203.

MARTIN, CARMEL G (BURNS). b Newfoundland Can 9 My 13. 4: John U Martin. 5: St Brides Col 28 Tchg) St Michaels Col 29 (Tchg); Memorial U 30-31 (Tchg) 1st Class Diploma; NBIT (Moncton NB) summer 68 (Voc & Tech Ed). 6: Fr. 7: Tchr Regional Schs, Newfoundland 32-33; Libn Arm-Air Force (Amer), Newoundland 43-47; Libn Air Force (Amer), Newfoundland 47-57; Libn Strategic Air Command, Newoundland 57-66; Tchr-Libn adult educ ctr, Stephenville Nfld 67-. 8: Fr tchr Fr USAFI courses 45-48; Set up lib in Argentia 54; Supvd libs in Narsarssuak (Greenland), St Anthony (Newfoundland), Grander (Newfoundland), and remte sites, Set up Lib, Adult Educ Ctr, Stephenville 67-. 9: ALA; CanLA. 10: Division Commnr, Can Girl Guide Assn, Bay St George Div Nfld 67-. 11: Outstanding performance citation as a mil libn from Gen Robert Harper, Gen William Tunner & Brig CV Haynes 47; 8AF Award for Pub Scrap Bk, Entered in John Cotton Dana Contest 65. 14: Research, acquis, catlg, publ. 15: P O Box 48 Hansen hwy, Stephenville Nefoundland Can.

MARTIN, DAVID LANE. b Tampa Fla 30 Jl 37. 5: UTex 55-60 (Eng) BA, summer 61 Libn Certif; NTex State U summer 65, 67, 68 (LS). 7: Libn multiple sch West so Ind Sch Dist, Corpus Christi Tex 60-. 9: Tex State Tchrs Assn; TexLA. 14: Sch libnship, child lit. 15: 2825 LAWNVIEW, Corpus Christi Tex 78404.

MARTIN, DOHN H(ANNAH). b 30 Je 42. 5: UNC (Chapel Hill) 64 (Math) AB, 67 MSLS. 7: Catlgr IBM, Durham NC 67; Trainee in computer libnship WashU Sch of Med Lib, St louis 67-68, Aquis libn 68-69; Syst analyst UTex Med Br Lib & Serv Computation Ctr, galveston Tex 69-. 9: MedLA; ASIS. 10: Buttonwood Club. 14: Lib automation. 15: Box 253 Univ of Tex Medical Br Lib, Galveston Tx 77550.

MARTIN, DOROTHY ETHEL HITCHOCK. b Oakland Cal 14 My 13. 4: LLOYD Milo Martin. 5: UCal(Berkeley) 31-35 (Fr) AB, 35-36 Certif in Libnship. 6: Fr, Sp. 7: Sub br dept Oakland Pub Lib, Oakland Cal 36; Asst museum libn Los Angeles Co Museum, Los Angeles 36-43; Libn I ref dept Los Angeles Co Pub Lib, Los Angeles 50; Asst libn Hancock Lib USoCal 50-51, Asst libn Med Lib 51-52; Museum libn Los Angeles Co Museum, Los Angeles 52-. 9: So Cal Acad Scis, Los Angeles (lib chm). 14: Ref (SW hist, biol & earth scis). 15: Lib Los Angeles Co Mus 900 Exposition blvd, Los Angeles Ca 90007.

MARTIN, ELEANOR. b Belfast No Ireland 2 O 42. 5: Queen's U 62-66 (Classics) Honours BA; UBritish Columbia 66-67 BLS. 6: Lat, Gr, Fr, Ger. 7: Libn I Queen's U 67-. 10: Alcuin Soc (Vancouver BC). 14: Catlg. 15: 824 Victoria st, Kingston Ont Can.

MARTIN ELIZABETH (BETTY) DuVERNET). b Greenville SC 12 Ja 10. 5: Erskine Col 27-28; UNC 31 (LS) AB; Furman U 62 (Educ) MA; Rutgers 58 (LS); UMich 60-61 (LS); UDenver 62 (LS). 6: Fr. 7: Libn Parker High Sch, Greenville SC 31-45; Dir materials bur Parker Sch Dist, Greenville SC 3445; Instr Lib Sci Fiske U summer 39-40; Instr Lib Sci USCar 62-64; Instr Lib Sci Furman U 65-66 Dir of lib serv Sch Dist of Greenville Co, Greenville SC 58-. 8: SC State Exec Dir, Nat Lib Week, 63; State Chm Elem Sch Lib Implement Com, 63 Consul Pickens (Ala) Sch 67-68, Camden (SC) Pub Sch 69, Jr High Sch Lib Catlg, H W Wilson Co. 9: ALA-AASchL (Exec Bd 64-65, chm Supvrs Sect 68-69); SCLA (pres 64); NEA; SELA; ASCD; SCDAVI. 10: Dellwood Commun Club. 13: Yes. 14: Sch libs. 15: 48 Conventry land, Greenville SC 2609.

MARTIN, ELIZABETH (RASOR). b Columbus Thio 28 D06. 5: Ohio State U 24-28 (Eng AB; LInstitut Universitaire de Hautes Etudes Internat (Geneva) 29-30 (Internat Studies) Diploma; Ohio State U 32 (Pol Sci, Econ, Fr); UIll 51-52 (LS) MA. 6: Fr. 7: Eng tchr Columbus Sch for Girls, Columbus Ohio 28-29; Supv libn Pasadena Br US Naval Ordnance Testing Sta, Pasadena Cal 46-51; Head Libn Ohio Hist Soc, Columbus Ohio 52-. 9: ALA; SLA; OhioLA. 10: Nat League Amer Pen Women; Altrusa; Jr League of Amer; Kappa Kappa Gamma; Phi Beta Kappa; Beta Phi Mu. 14: Admin. 15: 1594 Neil ave, Columbus Ohio 43201.

MARTIN, ELIZABETH ANN. b Waverly Iowa 30 Je 31. 5: Wartburg Col 49-50, 54-56 (Eng) BA; State Col Iowa summer 57; UMinn summers 58-61 (LS) MA; UMich summer 64, 67 (LS); UChicago summer 68. 6: Sp. 7: Eng tchr Oelwein Commun Schs, Oelwein Iowa 56-57; High sch libn Dubuque Commun Schs, Dubuque Iowa 57-60; Asst libn Wartburg Col 60-62; Asst Prof of Lib Sch State Col of Iowa 62-. 9: ALA; AASchL NEA; IowASchL; Iowa State EA; AVEduc Assn Iowa. 10: AAUP. 14: Sch libnship. 15: 1922 Campus, Cedar Falls Iowa 50613.

MARTIN, ELIZABETH CLARK. b Council Bluffs Iowa 26 Jl 08. 4: Nathan B Martin. 5: Gardner Sch (NYC) 28; NY Pub Lib Train Class 29; Columbia Ext Lib Courses 30-31; Pratt 32 (LS) Certif. 7: Child libn NY Pub Lib 32-46; Asst dir Englewood (NJ) Pub Lib 47-57, Dir 57-. 9: ALA; NJLA. 10: Bergen-Passaic Lib Club. 15: 49 John st, Englewood Cliffs NJ 97632.

MARTIN, EMMA (AVERILL). 5: UWis 29-33 (Eng) AB; Columbia 35-36 BLS. 7: Circ libn Aurora Pub Lib, Aurora Ill 40-42; Head of order & stockroom Fuller-Merriam Co, West Haven Conn 42-43; Chief catlg libn Post Lib, Ft Monmouth NJ 44-46; Post libn Post Lib, Ft Dix NY 48-50; Lib Dir W Orange Pub Lib, W Orange NJ 51-57; Head Libn Va State Lib for the Blind, Richmond Va 58-61; Lib Dir Red Bank Pub Lib, Red Bank nj 61-. 9: ALA; NJLA; NJ Adult EA; Monmouth Libns Assn (past pres). 10: Red Bank Commun Adult Sch Exec BD. 15: 59 Hubbard ave, Red Bank NJ 07705.

MARTIN, FRANK. b England 21 N 17. 4: Helen Lautard. 5: UBC 48-52 BSA, 68-69 BLS. 7: Commentator Canadian Broadcasting Corp, Vancouver 54-56; Tchr Brentwood Col 61-66, Libn 66-68. 14: Sch serv. 15: PO Box 8, Cobble Hill BC Can.

MARTIN, GERARD. b Saint-Leon 15 Ja 11. 4: Yvette Ferron. 5: College de Saint-Laurent 26-34 BA; Universite de Montreal 44-45 Dipl Bibl. 6: Fr. 7: Sec Dept of Colonisation, Quebec 37-43; Chief libn Provincial Archives, Quebec 43-60; Dir Quebec Pub Lib Serv 60-. 8: Poet and Novelist, Radio and TV writer, Quebec 37-60; Prof Lib Sci, Montreal 62-. 9: Societe des Ecrivains canadiens (sec, chm); Assn canadienne des bibliothecaires de langue francaise; CanLA; QueLA. 10: Inst of Pub Admin Can. 11: Prix David (Poetry) Medaille du Centenaire de la Confederation. 12: Le Temple" (39); "Tentations" (43); "Coherence et Logique de la classification decimale Dewey" (47); "Bibliographie sommaire du Canada francais" (54); Ed "Bulletin bibliographique" (56-59). 13: Yes. 15: Quebec Pub Lib Serv Dept of Cultural Affairs Parliament Buildings, Quebec Can.

MARTIN, GORDON P. b Frankfort Mich 16 Jl 18. 5: Fenn Col even 36-39 (Bus Admin); Chicago 40-41, 46-47 (Gen Educ) PhB, 48-52 (LS) MA. 7: Asst to sales mgr Gen Electric Lamp Dept, Cleveland, Chicago 36-41; (M/Sgt) AAA US Army, Tex, Cal, SWPA 42-46; Head res bk room UChicago Lib 48-51; Head circ desk serv UMinn Lib 51-52; Order libn San Jose State Col 52-53; Ref libn UCal (Riverside) 54-63; ALA Proj Dir Lib 21 Exhibit, Seattle Worlds Fair 62; Asst univ libn UCal(Riverside) 57-63; ALA Proj Dir Lib/USA Exhibit,NY Worlds Fair 63-66; Col libn Sacramento State Col 66-. 9: ALA; CalLA. 10: Riverside Art Assn, Torch Club. 12: Ed "Academic News Notes, column in "California Librarian, (3 rs); Co-auth, wth D M Berry, "Term Paper & Thesis Writing (56, 59); off reports of Library 21 & Library/USA exhibits (63, 66). 13: Yes. 14: Acad lib admin, bldg planning, automation of lib serv. 15: 2249 Sierra blvd, Sacramento Ca 95825.

MARTIN, HAROLD B. b Cambridge Penn 8 M 16. 5: UNM 4546 (Eng) BA; USo Cal 46-47 BS in LS; UPenn 49-50 (Eng), 66 (Planning). 6: Fr, Sp. 7: Curator of mss Hist Soc of Penn, Phila 48-62; Libn City Planning Commsn Lib, Phila 63-. 9: Coun of Planning Libns, ALA; SLA (Phila Chap: Coun & Soc Sci Group). 14: Catlg, clsf. 15: 1928 Delancey pl, Phil Pa 19/03.

MARTIN, HELEN HEATHER. b Cumberland Md 26 Jl 24. 5: Conn Col 42-46 (Hist) BA; Columbia 46-47 BLS. 7: Asst Central Circ NY Pub Lib summer 45; Lib asst (child) Huqueнot Pk Br New Rochelle Pub Lib, NY 47-53; Libn Charlotte Col 53-54; Br libn Pub Lib of Charloote, Charloote NC 55-. 9: ALA; MecklenburgLA. 14: Ref & bk sel (adults & child). 15: 2528 Cornell ave, Charlotte NC.

MARTIN, HELEN L (EVERALL). b Monona Iowa 6 N 13. 5: Carleton 30-32; UIowa 32-34 (Lat, eng) BA; UNo Iowa 60-64 Libn certif; UWis 66-69 MALS. 6: Lat, Fr. 7: Instr high sch, La Porte City Iowa 42-48; High sch libn & instr MFL Commun, Monona Iowa 60-69. 8: Mem Lib Bd, Pub Lib, La Porte City Iowa 41. 9: ALA; NEA; IowaStateEA; IowaSchLA. 10: Woman's Club; Eta Sigma Phi; Delta Delta Delta. 14: Sch libs, ref. 15: 307 N Page st, Monona Ia 52159.

MARTIN, JAMES F JR. b Wilmington Del. 4: Nancy C Hogoboom. 5: La Salle Col 49-53 (Eng, Educ) AB; UDenver 53-55 (LS) MA. 6: Ger. 7: Asst circ UDenver 54-55; Asst libn & Instr West State Col (Gunnison Colo) 55-56; Sci libn San Jose State Col 56-67, Research & development libn 67-. 9: CalLA; CalTA. 10: Humane Soc; Cal Col & Univ Fac Assn (CCUFA). 13: Yes. 14: Ref, statist control, lib planning. 15: 2914 Rossmore lane, San Jose Ca 95122.

MARTIN, JESS A. b Picher Okla 2 My 26. 4: Betty Todd. 5: San Diego State Col 48-53 (Hist) AB; USoCal 54-55 MSLS. 7: Med libn San Diego Co Med Soc, San Diego 52-57; Head of Tech Processes Convair-Astronautics, San Diego 57-58; Assoc Med libn & instr UKy Med Center 58-60; Med libn & asst prof of lib admin Ohio State U 60-63; Chief Lib Br Nat Insts of Health, Bethesda Md 63-68; Dir Temple U Health Scis Ctr Lib 68-. 8: Adj lectr UMd Sch Lib Sci; Sub lectr Drexel; US Civil Serv Commsn Career Serv Bd for Libns; Visiting Com for Col Physicians, Phila. 9: SLA (Wash DC Chap, chm Bio Sci Gp 67-68); MedLA (chm Memb Com 62-63; chm Com on Intl Coop 64-65; chm Com on Certif 66-67; chm Com on Internship 67-68; Midwest Reg Gp Exec Bd Dir 61-63); Med Lib Gp So Cal (pres-elect 57); KyLA (Exec Bd Dir 58-59). 10: Wash DC Area Lib Gp; Toastmasters Intl; Phi Alpha Theta; USoCal Lib Sch Alumni Assn; Beta Phi Mu. 13: Yes. 14: Admin, readers serv. 15: 445 W Valley Forge rd, King of Prussia Pa 19406.

MARTIN, JOHN H. b NYC 29 Ag 22. 4: Phyllis Greife. 5: Brooklyn Col 40-42, 45-46 (Eng) BA; Columbia 46-47 (Eng) MA; Chicago 49-53 (Church Hist) BD, PhD, Columbia 64 (Far EastCivilization). 6: Fr. 7: (S/Sgt) USAAF Cryptographer, Europe 43-46; Instr Eng URichmond 47-49; Assoc Prof Eng Wilmington Col 53-58; Dir of Lib, Prof of Humanities Corning Community Col 58-. 8: Consul Corning Glass Co 64, Catonsville (Md) Community Col 65. 9: ALA; Japan Soc; Mod Lang Asn; Assn Asian Studies; Col Eng Assn; NYLA. 10: AAUP. 11: NY State Awards for Study: Chinese Civilization 65, Japanese Civilization 64; NY State Fac Scholar in Internat Studies 66-67. 13: Yes. 14: Rare bks. 15: 313 WALL ST, Corning NY 14830.

MARTIN, JUNE (HOPKINS). b Garrard County Ky 27 Je 42. 4: Roy Franklin Martin. 5: East KyU 60-64 (Elem Educ) BS; UKy 65-68 MS in LS. 6: Fr, Sp. 7: Circ libn East KyU John Grant Crabbe Lib 64-65, Asst hd-catlgr 66-. 9: KyLA. 14: Catlg, rare bks. 15: POB 190, Richmond Ky 40475.

MARTIN, JUNE ROBERTSON. b Charleston WVa 9 O 22. 5: WVa U 39-43 (Hist) BA; UWis 43-44 (Hist) MA, 62-63 (LS) MA. 6: Fr. 7: Tchr Ill State Normal U 45-47; Tchr Sarah Dix Hamlin Sch, San Francisco 47-49; Exec sec Kanawha Co Soc for Crippled Child, Charleston WVa 51-61; Ref asst Kanawha Co Pub Lib, Charleston WVa 63-, Ref libn & Interlib loan libn 63-. 8: Exec Dir Nat Lib Week 66, 67-. 9: ALA (sec treas Jr Mem RT 66-67); WVaLA (sec 65-66). 10: AAUW; Quota Club; Phi Beta Kappa; English Speaking Union; YWCA; Beta Phi Mu; Kappa Delta Pi. 11: Adams Fellowship in Mod Hist UWis. 13: Yes. 14: Ref, adult serv. 15: 1627 Quarrier st, Charleston WV 25311.

MARTIN, KATHLEEN ANNE. b Rochester NY 19 Ag 42. 5: Marygrove 60-64 (Chem) BA; UMich 64-65 MALS. 7: Pre-prof libn Detroit Pub Lib 64-65, Libn I 65-66; Libn Eastman Kodak Co Lab Ind Med Rochester NY 66-; Bibliog URochester Med Lib 69-. 9: SLA; ASIS. 10: Monroe Co Lib Club. 14: Ref, lit searching in med and related fields. 15: 1704 Stone rd, Rochester NY 14615.

MARTIN, LAURA KATHERINE. b Springfield SD 28 Ja 06. 5: Los Angeles Pub Lib Sch 24-25 Diploma; UCLA 22-24, 28-29, (Eng) AB; Stanford 39-40 (Educ) MA; Chicago summers 38, 42 (LS). 7: Child libn Pub Lib, Los Angeles 25-30; Sch libn Pub Schs, Long Beach Cal 30-31, 32-35; Asst child libn Lib of Hawaii, Honolulu 31; Sch libn Jr High Sch, Ventura Cal 35-38 Instr & act dept head San Jose State Col 38-39; Visiting Instr Ind U summer 40; Visiting Instr UDenver 51; Assoc Prof UKy 40-. 8: Chm State Bd of Certif for Pub Libns 61-67; Staff of State Lib (Ky) summer 65; Mem, Governors Com on Libs 68-. Consul on sch & pub lib surveys (Ky). 9: ALA (2nd v-pres 53-54); -AASchL (pres 51-52); AALS; SELA (lib educ com 58-61); KyLA (var coms); Lexington LA. 10: AAUP; AAUW; LWV; ACLU. 13: Yes. 14: Pub & sch libs, magazine sel. 15: 442 Oldham ave, Lexington Ky 40502.

MARTIN, (RALPH) LAWRENCE. b Palo Mich 31 Ja 36. 5: UMich 54-58 (Art Hist) AB, 58-60 (LS) AM. 6: Fr. 7: Asst libn Ferris State Col Lib 60-. 9: MichLA. 14: Catlg, a-v. 15Rte 3 Box 96B, Big Rapids Mi 49307.

MARTIN, LOUIS EDWARD. b Detroit 16 S 28. 4: Barbara Heinrich. 5: UDetroit 47-51 (Eng) PhB, 51-54 (Eng) MA; UMich 58-60 AMLS. 7: USMC (Pfc), Quantico Va 46-47; UDetroit: Tchg Fellow 51-53, Instr in Eng 53-58, Circ libn 58-60; Asst libn Oakland U 60-62; Assoc dir URochester Libs 62-68 Assoc exec dir, Assoc of research libs Wash DC 68-. 8: Consul on lib bldgs,; Pres, Five Associated Univ Libs 67-68. 9: ALA. 10: Metro-Art (Rochester NY); Diocesan Ecumenical Commsn (Rochester). 14: Admin. 15: 2119 Ellis st, Silver Spring Md 20910.

MARTIN, LOWELL ARTHUR. b Chicago 12 Mr 12. 4: Bella Strauss. 5: Ill Inst of Tech 33-37 BS; UChicago 37-41, 45 AM, PhD. 6: Sp. 7: Gen asst Lane Tech High Sch Lib, Chicago 33-35; Asst libn Wright City Col 35-37; Exec asst to libn Chicago Pub Lib 41-43; Instr & asst prof UChicago 43-46; Assoc Dean Sch of Lib Serv Columbia U 47-53; Dean Grad Sch of Lib Serv Rutgers U 54-58; V-pres Grolier Inc, NY 59-68; Prof Columbia U 69-. 8: Survey-Dir Los Angeles 48; Mo 54, Penn 58 & 67, NY 64, Cal 65, Balitmore 61-68, Phila 67, Chicago 68. 9: ALA; Amer Bk Publrs Coun; NJLA. 12: "Public Administration and the Library (41); "Personnel Administration in Libraries (46); "Library Response to Urban Change (69). 13: Yes. 14: Lib org. 15: 89 Rose st, Metuchen NJ.

MARTIN, MARGARET (ELIZABETH). b Toronto 22 Ag 29. 5: Toronto 52 (Eng) BA, 53 BLS. 6: Fr. 7: Catlg Harvard Col Lib 53-55; Catlgr Halifax Mem Lib, Halifax NS 55-61, Yp libn 61-. 9: CanLA (chm YP Sect 63-64); APLA. 10: Heritage Trust of NS; Girl Guides. 12: Ed and contrib "Founded Upon a Rock; Historic Buildings of Halifax" (67). 15: 6230 Oakland rd, Halifax NS Can.

MARTIN, MARGARET (NORMAN). b Nevada Mo 6 Je 12. 5: Cottey Col 30-32 AA; UMo 49-53 (LS) AB; UIll 64-53 (LS) AB; UIll 64-65 (LS) MS. 7: Lib asst Columbia Pub Lib, Columbia Mo 53-54; Lib asst UMo Agric Lib 54-56; Asst libn UMo Med Lib 56-61; Libn admin US Army Spec Serv, Okinawa 61-63; Asst libn UMo Sci Lib 63-64; Ed research lbn Field ENTERPRISES, Chicago summer 64; Libn admin US Army Spec Serv, Vitry le Francois, France 65-66, Nurnberg Germany 66-67; Libn US Naval Acad, Annapolis Md 67-. 9: ALA. 10: Phi Beta Kappa; PEO. 14: Ref, readers adv serv, admin. 15: Apt 23-670 Americana dr, Annapolis Md 21403.

MARTIN, MARGARET W. b Schenectady NY 2 My 13. 5: Cornell U 30-36 (Home Econ) S; Syracuse 58-59 MS in LS. 7: Cornell U Asst libn Engnr Lib 59-61, Assoc libn Engnr Lib 61-62, Act libn Physics Lib 65, Libn Chem Lib 62-65, Libn Phys Sci 65-. 9: NY State LA. 10: Kappa Kappa Gamma; Beta Phi Mu. 14: Readers serv. 15: Phys Sci Lib Clark Hall, Cornell U, Ithaca NY 14850.

MARTIN, MARITA C MARINE. b Hartford Conn 4 Jl 22. 4: William T Martin. 5:Long Beach city Col 49-51 AA; UHawaii 51-52 (Eng); San Diego State 58-60 (Eng) BA, 60-63 (Educ) Certif Second ed, 63-64 Certif Lib Sci. 6: Fr, Sp. 7: Libn San Diego City Schs, San diego Calif 63-64; Acquis libn Naval Ship & Research Develop Lab, Panama City Fla 64-. 14: Acquis. 15: PO Box 2171, Panama City Fl 32401.

MARTIN, MARJORIE JEAN (MacPHEE). b Youngstown Ohio 31 Ag 24. 4: Hyer Martin. 5: Col of Wooster 42-46 (Eng, His) BA; West Res 61 MS in LS. 6: Fr. 7: Tchr-libn Boardman High Sch, Youngstown Ohio 46-51; Libn Lincoln Jr High Sch, Mt Prospect Ill 60-61; Residence centers libn Ind U 62-63;Libn Harry E Wood High Sch, Indianapolis 63-. 9: ALA; IndLA; IndSchLA; Ind State Tchrs Assn. 10: AAUW; Indianapolis Coun of Admin Women in Educ; Gamma Phi Kappa; Bus and Profess Women. 14: Young adult serv. 15: 974 Ellenberger Pwy, W dr, Indianapolis 46219.

MARTIN, MARTHA ANNE McINNIS. b Rosedale Miss 19 My 25. 5: Miss State Col for Women 43-46 (Math) BS; ; Delta State Col summer 56 (LS); UMiss 56-57 MLS; La Polytech Inst 60-64 (Fr, Span); Rollins Col summer 65 (Span); Fla State U 68- (LS). 6: Fr, Sp. 7: Lab asst Johns Hopkins U 46-47; Tchr Oldfields Priv Sch, Towson Md 47; Jr catlgr UMiss 57; Asst Prof & humanities libn La Polytech Inst 57-66, Asst Prof & Coord admin servs (Lib) 66-68, Assoc Prof & Coord admin servs 68-. 8: Adv fac Ctr Comparative Intl Studies La Polytech Inst 67-68. 9: ALA; LaLA; La Tchrs Assn; SWLA. 10: AAUP; Alpha Beta Alpha; Kappa Mu Epsilon; Kappa Pi. 14: Ref, admin, tchg. 15: Box 5138, Ruston La 71271.

MARTIN, MARY (LYDDAN). b Webster Ky 6 O 20. 4: Charles Martin. 5: Ky Wesleyan 37-41 (Eng) AB; Peabody Col 41-43 BS in LS. 7: Ref libn UCincinnati 43-45; Hosp libn US Govt, Ft Knox Ky 45-47; Decorator Gilded Cage, New Canaan Conn 63-65; Decorator Forlino builders, Elkhart Ind 66-67; Ref libn Charlotte-Mecklenburg Co Lib, Charlotte NC 68-. 9: ALA; MecklenburgCoLA. 10: Beta Phi Mu; Delta Sigma Theta; Pi Lambda Theta. 14: Ref. 15: 2118 Wendover rd, Charlotte NC 28211.

MARTIN, MARY J. b Sedan Kan 9 Mr 41. 5: Kan State Tchrs Col 59-63 (Eng) BS in Ed, 65-67 MS in LS. 6: Fr. 7: Eng instr Sherman Co High Sch, Goodland Kan 63-65; Catlgr Midwest Research Inst Lib, Kan City Mo 67-68, Hd libn 68-. 9: SLA (sec Heart of Amer Chap); ALA. 14: Catlg. 15: 7249 Eby dr apt 301, Shawnee Mission Ks 66204.

MARTIN, MARY MERNELLE. b Alamance County NC 25 D 28. 05/ bennett Col 45-49 (Elem Educ) AB; N Car Col summer 49 (A-v);IndU summer 51-52 (A-v Educ) MS, 53-55 (LS) MA; A & T State U summer 60 Renewal of Certif. 7: Lib sci instr a-v dirBennett Col (Greensboro NC) 49-57; A-v Dir Fort Valley State Col 57-58; Libn Dudley High Sch, Greensboro NC 59-64; Libn MorrisonTraining Sch, Hoffman NC 67-68; Ref libn Greensboro (NC) Pub Lib 69-. 9: Educ Film Lib Assn. 10: Beta Phi Mu; Delta SigmaTheta; Pi Lambda Theta. 14: Ref. 15: 2102 McConnell rd, Greensboro NC 27401.10589

MARTIN, MURRAY SIMPSON. b Lower Hutt New Zealand 21 Jl 28. 4: Noelene Phyllis Ax). 5: UNew Zealand (Auckland) 46-49 (Eng) MA; UNew Zealand (Wellington) 52-58 (Accounting, Econ) B Com; New Zealand Lib Sch 50 Dip NZLS. 6: Fr. 7: Lib asst Sch Lib Serv, Palmerston North New Zealand 51-53; Lib asst Sch Lib Serv, Auckland New Zealand 53-54; 1st asst Country Lib Serv, Palmerston North New Zealand d54-57; 1st asst order sect Nat Lib Centre, Wellington New Zealand 57-61, Head order sect 61-63; Br co-ordinator USask 63-64, Ser libn 64-66; Ch acq libn Penn State U (Univ Park) 67-68, Asst dir tech proc 68-. 9: CanLA; Tech Serv Com; ALA-RTSD (Acquis Sect Bkdealer Lib Rel Com 68-); New Zealand La (mem & chm Fiction Com 58-63); Saskla Convenor Com on Union List of Sask Periods; Com Reporting on Provincial Lib Org 66); PennLA. 10: Assoc Registered Accountant of New Zealand; MENSA; Sask Nat Hist Soc; Saskatoon Camera Club; Sierra Club; New Zealand Forest & Bird Protection Soc; Wilson Ornithological Soc. 14: Acquis & bk sel, ser, admin. 15: 1413 Curtin st, State College Pa 16801.

MARTIN, NINA (REA) NIX. b Laurel Miss 12 F 32. 4: Gerald L Martin. 5: U So Miss 55 (LS) BS; LSU 65 MSLS. 6: Sp. 7: Tchr Mobile Pub Schs, Mobile Ala 51-55; Libn Semmes High Sch, Mobile Ala 55-56; Libn Vigor High Sch, Mobile Ala 56-57, Tchr 57-59; Tchr Milton High Sch, Milton Fla 60-61; Libn Rain High Sch, Mobile Ala 61-. 66; Lib consul, Coord ESEA Title II State Dept Educ, Montgomery Ala 66-. 8: Consul; Purdue U (Lafayette) 68-69, Miss State Col 68, USoMiss 67. 9: ALA; AlaLA (bus mgr "Alabama Librarian"); AlaEA; NEA-DAVI; AlaASchL (corresponding sec 67-); Ala Educ Media Assn; SELA. 10: PTA; Beta Phi Mu. 13: Yes. 14: Sch lib devel. 15: 3235 S Hull st, Montgomery Al 36105.

MARTIN, NOELENE PHYLLIS (AX). b Palmerston N NZ 14 D 29. 4: Murray S Martin. 5: Canterbury U New Zealand 48-50 (Fr) BA, 52 (Fr) MA. 6: Fr. 7: Lib asst: country lib serv, Palmerston N NZ 50-52, sch lib serv, Palmerston N NZ 53-57; Sr libn sch lib serv, Wellington NZ 57-64; Br libn Veterniary Med Lib USask 65-67; Asst agric & bio sci libn Penn State U 67-. 9: CanLA; MedLA; ALA. 10: Royal New Zealand Forest & Bird protection Soc; Saskatchewan Nat Hist Soc; Sierra Club; AAUW. 14: Acquis, research libs, child & yp wk. 15: 1413 Curtin st, State College Pa 16801.

MARTIN, NORMAN DALE. b Chaseburg Wis 19 O 32. 4: Beth Helwig. 5: Wis State Col (Superior) 50-54 (Hist, Eng) BA; Peabody 57-58 (LS) MA. 6: Ger. 7: US Army 54-56; Eng tchr Port Wing High Sch, Port Wing Wis 56-57; Ref libn Wis State U (Whitewater) 58-. 9: ALA; WisLA. 10: Beta Phi Mu. 14: Ref. 15: 135 Lindsey ct, Whitewater Wis 53190.

MARTIN, PLEASENT WEBSTER (PETE). AMBURG Ioa 13 Je 10. 5: Mercer U 52-56 (Eng) AB; Rutgers 60-61 MLS. 6: Fr, Ger. 7: Mgt intern USAF, Robins AFB Ga 56-59; Tchr Bibb Co Sch System Macon Ga 59-60; Procedures asst Queens Borough Pub Lib, NY 61-63, Sch liaison consul 63-64; Asst dir Summit (NJ) Pub Lib 64-65; Asst dir Levittown (NY) Pub Lib 65-. 8: Mem Coadjutant faculty Grad Sch Lib Serv Rutgers, spring & fall 65. 9: ALA; NYLA; NCLA. 10: Beta Phi Mu. 13: Yes. 14: Ref. 15: 61-15 97th st apt 14, Rego Park NY 11374.

MARTIN, RACHEL S(ANGSTER). b Mount Olive NC 18 Ag 18. 5: Brenau 36-39 (Eng, Hist) B; UNC 49 BSLS; State U Iowa 54-55 (Hist, Govt) MA. 6: Sp. 7: Tchr Morehead City High Sch, Morehead City NC 39-40; Tchr Princeton High Sch, Princeton NC 40-42; Tchr Tarboro High Sch, Tarboro NC 42-45; Tchr Kinston High Sch, Kinston NC 45-46; Libn Lindley Jr High Sch, Greensboro NC 46-49; Asst ref libn Auburn U 49-51; Libn Mary Baldwin Col 51-56; Head humanities div Fla State U Lib 56-57; Libn Womans Col of Furman U 57-58; Ref & ser libn Furman U 58-. 9: ALA-RSD (com men 60, chm 64-66); SCLA (sec 59, chm Mem Com 60-61); SELA (chm Nom Com); chm Ref Serv Div 64-66; Mem reg & Subser Bks Review Com 68-70). 10: AAUP; Altrusa Club; Beta Phi Mu; Zeta Tau Alpha. 12: Comp index to "Furman Studies (59). 14: Ref, ser. 15: 219 Courtney Circle, Greenville SC 29609.

MARTIN, ROBERT LEE. b Pomeroy Ohio 15 S 16. 5: Bethany Col WVa 36-40 (Eng Lit) BA; Peabody 40-42 BLS. 6: Fr. 7: Circ ref asst Joint U Libs, Nashville 40-42; Loan libn UNH 42-43; (Sgt) US Army 44-45; Ref bibliog libn Army War Col (Wash DC) 45-46; Catlgr Bethany Col Bethany WVa 46; Chief tech processes sect QM Res & Dev Labs, Phila 46-47, Chief Tech Lib 48-54; Dir Tech Lib Army Natick Labs, Natick Mass 54-. 8: Army Ad Hoc Group on Sci & Tech Info, 62-63; Steering Com, Army ATLIS Proj (STINFO) 63-68; Army Tech Info Support Acts Proj 69-. 9: SLA (chm Mil Libns Div;pres Boston Chap). 10: Phi Delta Kappa; Pi Gamma Mu. 13: Yes. 14: Admin. 15: 43 Fisher st, Natick Ma 01760.

MARTIN, ROGER McQUEEN. b Stamford Tex 8 Jl 28. 5: UTex 47-49 (Chem) BS, 50 (Chem), 52-54, 58 MS in LS. 6: Fr, Sp, Ital, Ger. 7: US Army Chem Corps (Sgt) 51-52; John Crerar Lib, Chicago: Stud intern 54, Admin asst to libn 55, Research assoc research info serv 56-57, Asst manager research info serv 58-59, Chief tech dept 60; Chef Libn Shell Development Co, Emeryville Cal 61-68; Mgr info ctr, Amer Express Investment Mgt Co, San Francisco 69-. 9: ALA (chm Transl Acts Coun 66-68); ALA; ASIS; ACS; IllLA; CaLA. 14: Admin, subj ref. 15: PO Box 7650, San Francisco Ca 94119.

MARTIN, ROSEMARY. b Johnsville Ky 3 F 01. 5: UCincinnati 20-23, 28 (Eng) BA; UIll 28-29 BS in LS. 6: Fr, Ger. 7: Catlgr Pub Lib, Cincinnati 25-41, Ref libn 41-55, Map libn 55-. 9: SLA; OhioLA. 14: Geog, maps. 15: Cincinnati Pub Lib,8th & Vine sts, Cincinnati Oh 45202.

MARTIN, ROSETTA (POACHES). b Charleston SC 20 Je 30. 4: George E Martin. 5: Morgan State Col 48-53 (Hist) AB; Boston U 57-58 (Advance Educ Studies); Simmons 59-62 (LS) MS. 6: Fr. Sp, Ger. 7: Asst child libn Boston Pub Lib; So End 58-60, Bkmob 60-62, Mem br 62-63; Asst ref libn Tufts U 63-, Supv curriculum Lab 65-. 9: MassLA. 10: Zeta Phi Beta; Consul to Youth Group; Child Storyteller; Fellowship Youth Coun. 14: Afro-Amer bibliog, educ ref, bibliog. 15: 86 Harvard ave, West Medford Ma 02155.

MARTIN, STEPHANIE (FRASER). b Dayton Ohio 27 Ja 32. 5: Del State Col 49-50 Morgan State Col 50-53 (Eng) AB; Simmons 53-54 MS in LS. 6: Fr. 7: Child libn Enoch Pratt Free Lib, Baltimore 54-59; Ref libn Howard U 59-; Child libn Coppin State Col 63-. 9: ALA-CSD; Md State Tchrs Assn; MdLA; MdASchL. 10: Alpha Kappa Alpha; NAACP. 14: Child wk, tchg child lit. 15: 2049 Wheeler ave, Baltimore Md 21216.

MARTIN, SUSAN KATHERINE (OROWAN). b Cambridge Eng 14 N 42. 4: David Standish Martin. 5: Tufts 59-63 (Fr) BA; Simmons 64-65 (LS) MS. 6: Fr, Ger, Sp, Ital, Russian. 7: Intern Harvard Lib 63-65, Specialist in data processing 65-68, Syst libn 68-. 9: ALA (Memb Com); -ISAD (chm ISAD/LED Interdiv Com for Educ in Lib Automation); ASIS (mem SIG/LA Educ Com; sec NE Chap 69). 10: Phi Beta Kappa. 14: Lib automation. 15: Harvard Univ Lib, Cambridge Ma 02138.

MARTIN, WILLIAM A JR. b Burlingame Kan 11 My 22. 5: Col of Emporia 40-49 (Bus) AB; Kan State Tchrs Col 52-53 MSLS. 7: (Cpl) Qtrmstr Corps US Army 42-45; Theater manager Fox Midwest Amusement Corp, Emporia Kan 52-53; Stack supv UKan Lib 53-55, Head Undergrad Lib 55-58; Head circ dept UMo Lib 58-68; Libn Okla Col Liberal Arts 8: Consul St Gregorys Col 69. 9: ALA-ACRL (Recr Network); MoLA (v-pres Col & Res Libs Sect); pres-elect); NEA; OklaLA hd Resolutions Com; Lib Devel Com); OklaEA; SWLA. 10: Assn for Mental Health; Lions Club; Sight Conservation Com. 13: Yes. 14: Pub serv, machine methods, pub rel, rare bks. 15: 504 S 6th st, Chickaha Ok 73018.

MARTINDALE, JAMES ANTHONY. b Richmond Ind 28 S 21. 4: Eunice Hueter. 5: Wabash Col 40-44 (Hist) AB; UMich 48-49 Hist) MA, 51-52 AMLS. 7: US Navy (S 1/c) 45-46; Instr Hist Dept Earlham Col 49-51; Libn Agric Experiment Station Lib Purdue U 52-54; Libn period serv dept Ball State Tchrs Col 54-56; Libn Phoenix Mem Lib UMich 56-58; Ref libn Undergrad Lib UMich 59l; Head Libn Roy O West Lib DePauw U 62-. 8: Adj Prof of Lib Sci, Ind State U, Terre Haute 67-68. 9: ALA; IndLA (chm Col & Univ Round Table 64-65). 14: Admin, ref. 15: 425 E Franklin, Greencastle Ind 46135.

MARTINEZ, ANGELINA. b Ponce PR 27 Ag 20. 5: Inter-Amer U 39-43 (Eng) BA; LSU 44-45 BSLS: UIll 56-57 MSLS. 6: Sp, Portu, Fr. 7: Asst libn Inter-Amer U; PR 43-44, 45-46; Jr catlgr Pan American Union, Wash DC 46; Head libn Inter-Amer Inst Agric Sci, Turrialba Costa Rica 46-59; Documents libn & Subj spec in biol sci UCal Davis 59-63, Head ref dept subj spec in biol sci & agric 63-64; Dir reader serv div Nev State Lib 64-66; Hd pub serv Cal State Polytech Col 66-. 8: Dir reader serv train courses for Latin Amer libns at Inter-Amer Inst of Agric Scis, OAS 53-59; Ala com to study org & arrangement of USDAs "Bibliography of Agriculture 62. 9: ALA. 10: Toastmistress Club; Beta Phi Mu. 12: Co-comp for Inter-Amer Inst Agric Scis: "Coffee Bibliography (53); "Cacao Bibliography (54); & "Corn Bibliography (60). 13: Yes. 14: Ref, bibliog. 15: 300 Luneta dr, San Luis Obispo Ca 93401.

MARTINEZ, ANNA M. 4: Julius Martinez. 5: De PauwU 61-65 (Ger) BA; UMunich 64; UMich 67-68 MALS. 6: Ger, Sp. 7: Sch libn L'Anse Creuse Sch Syst, Mt Clemens 66-67; Ref libn UMinn 68-. 9: ALA. 10: Phi Beta Mu. 14: Ref. 15: TATAR 1630 Ravine lane, Highland Park Il 60035.

MARTINEZ, EMMA (SCHWEIZER). b Phila 25 Ag 15. 4: Raphael Martinez. 5: NYU 37 (Eng) BA; Columbia U 38 (Eng) MA; State U Col (Geneseo NY) 64 (LS) MS. 6: Fr, Sp. 7: Case wker Pub Welfare Off, Peekskill NY 38-39; Tchr of secondary Eng St Andrews Priory, Honolulu 39-40; Asst libn Balboa High Sch, Panama Cz 55-56; Libn Horseheads Free Assn Lib, Horseheads NY 58-59; Asst libn Southside High Sch, Elmira NY 59-60; Libn elem schs, Elmira NY 59-60; Libn Geo M Diven Sch, Elmira NY 60-64; Libn Ernie David Jr High Sch, Elmira NY 64-65; Asst catlg libn State U Col (New Paltz NY) 65-67; Hd of tech serv Elmira Col Lib 67-. 8: Col Ctr of the Finger Lakes Lib Com. 9: NYLA. 10: Episcopal Church Womens Guild. 14: Catlg, rare bks. 15: 313 Westinghouse rd, Horseheads NY 14845.

MARTINEZ, JULIA (JARAMILLO). b Vallecitos NM 3 Ja 26. 4: Jose Ramon Martinez. 5: Adams State Col 47-50 (Secondary educ, Eng, Soc studies) BA, summer 66 (LS); UNM summers 52-57 (Sch admin, Elem educ) MA; UUtah 64-65 (LS); Our Lady of the Lake Col 67 (LS) Certif. 6: Sp. 7: School tchr No Normal Col, El Rito NM 49-55; Tchr Bur of Indian Affairs, San Ildefonso NM 55-56; Jr high Eng tchr Rio Arriba Co Schs, Espanola NM 56-61; Dir instr Rio Arriba Co Schs, Tierra Amarilla NM 61-62; Libn Jr high sch Espanola Mun Schs, Espanola NM 62-. 9: ALA; NEA; NMLA; NMEA (coun); Rio arriba TA (pres 52-54); Espanola EA (pres 66-68). 10: Aux Veterans of Foreign Wars; Woman's Internat Bowling Congress. 13: Yes. 15: Box 37 Fairview sta, Espanola NM 87532.

MARTINEZ, JULIUS A. b Santiago Cuba 4 O 31. 4: Anna Martinez. 5: So IllU 58-63 (Fr) BA; UMich 66-67 MALS; UMich 69- (Philos). 6: Fr, Sp. 7: Ref Genesee Co Lib, Flint Mich 66; Ref & catlg St Clair Pub Lib, St Clair Shores Mich 67, 68. 9: MichLA. 10: Philosophy Club; UMinn; St Clair Shores Pub Lib Staff Com. 12: "Estudio Espanol" (61). 13: Yes. 14: Ref (humanities). 15: 20 NW 48 place, Miami Fl 33125.

MARTINEZ, PAT. b Alameda NM 24 Ja 33. 5: Catholic U 64-66 MSLS; American U 60-63 (Hist) BA. 6: Sp, Fr. 7: S/Sgt Lang Specialist US Air Force, usa abroad 52-60; Lib asst Wash Hosp Ctr, Washington DC 60-63; Counselor Episcopal Home for Child, Washington DC 63-66; Ser catlgr LC 66, Research asst Info Syst Off 66-67; Hd info serv Arts & Sci Lib PahlaviUM Shiraz Iran 67-68, Hd libn Col of Agric Lib 68-. 14: Catlg. 15: Pennsylvania Team Office PO Box 232, Shiraz Iran.

MARTING, ISABEL. b Ironton Ohio 1 Ag 07. 5: Barnard Col 26-30 (Music) AB; Columbia 32-34 (LS) MS. 6: Fr, Ger. 7: NY Pub Lib; Asst ref wk Bronx Ref Center 33-34, Asst Music Lib 34-40, Catlgr Music & Art Bks 40-45; Chief libn Juilliard Sch of Music 46-57; Spec consul on projs 57-. 8: Spec Lib Consul, mainly on catlg & org. 9: ALA; MusLA. 13: Yes. 14: Org catlg, ref. 15: 2 E 88th st, NYC 10028.

MARTULA, CHRISTOPHER A. b Boston Mass 19 N 46. 5: Tufts Col 64-68 (Hist) AB; Columbia 68-69 (LS) MS. 6: Fr, Sp. 14: Catlg, ref, a-v materials. 15: 86 College Farm rd, Waltham Ma 02154.

MARTZ, GLENNA JEAN. b Sioux Rapids Iowa 26 Ap 29. 5: Morningside Col 46-50 (Speech) BA; UWash 65 (LS) M Lib. 7: Libn Multnomach Sch of Bible 60-64; Libn I Seattle Pub Lib 65-. 10:UWash Alumni Assn of Sch of Libnship; Christian Bus & Prof Womenof Women of 14: Young adult. 15: 4200 SW Atlantic, Seattle Wa 98116.

MARUSKIN, ALBERT F. b Harmarville Penn 8 Ja 33. 4: Helen Balkunowa Maruskin. 5: Penn StateU 52-58 (Gen Arts and Letters) BA; DuquesneU summer 59, 61; Dartmouth Col summer 60; San Francisco State Col summer 63; UPittsburgh 63- (LS) MLS, Advanced certif. 6: Russian, Fr. 7: US Army Med Serv Specialist 3rd Class 53-55; Tchr highlands Sch Dist, Natrona Hts Pa 55-59; Acad adv UPittsburgh 64-66; Lit libn Cal state Col (California Pa) 66-. 9: ALA. 10: Beta Phi Mu; Federated Russian Orthodox Clubs. 14: Ref. 15: 16 Center dr, Monessen Pa 15062.

MARUYAMA, LENORE S(HIZUKO). b Honolulu Hawaii 16 Ap 40. 5: UHawaii 57-59; UWis 59-61 9eng) BA, 61-62 (LS) MA. 7: Catlgr UHawaii Lib (Honolulu) 62; Spec recruit LC 62-63, Ser catlgr 63-64, Ed monthly checklist of state publns 64-65, Ser catlgr 65-67, Lib info syst specialist 67-. 9: ALA. 14: Catlg. 15: 4465 MacArthur blvd NW, Wash DC 20007.

MARVIN, FLORENCE (FAY). b Du Quoin Ill 30 S 12. 5: Emmanual Missionary Col 31-34 (Sec sci); UArk summers 58-61 (Bus ed); La Sierra Col 62-64 (Eng) BA; USoCal 64-67 BSLS. 6: Ger. 7: Tchr Ozark Acad, Gentry Ark 54-62; Lib clk La Sierra Col, La Sierra Cal 62-67; Asst libn Loma Linda U 67-. 9: ALA; CalLA. 14: Catlg, ref. 15: 12101 Indiana ave Space 46, Riverside Ca 92503.

MARVIN, JAMES CONWAY. b Warroad Min 3 Ag 27. 4 Patricia Moe Marvin. 5: UMinn 46-50 (Econ, Pol Sci) BA, 51-52 MALS. 6: Sp. 7: US Naval RESERVE (S 1/c) 45-46; Dir Pub Lib, Kaukauna Wis 52-54; Dir Pub Lib, Eau Claire Wis 54-56; Dir Pub Lib, Cedar Rapids Iowa 56-. 8: Taught Lib Admin course for U Wis Ext Div 55-56; On leave from Cedar Rapids 7/64 - 8/65 as ALA/Rockefeller Found Visiting Prof, UPhilippines Grad Lib Sch Proj. 9: ALA (Coun 64-68, Internat Rel RT; v-chm & chm-elect 68-70); -PLA (Publ Com 65-70);

IowaLA (pres 61-62); KanLA. 10: ALA Commsn on Nat Plan for Lib Educ; Mem Reading for an Age of Change (Reading Guide Proj Eval Com); Governors Commsn on State & Loc Govt (Iowa). ; Johnson Soc; Saturday Night Lit Club; Rotary. 11: Silver Bk Award, Amer Bdg Inst 66. 12: Co-Auth "Publicity on a Shoestring" (57); "A Plan for Library Cooperation in Missoula County, Montana" (68). 13: Yes. 14: Adult serv, internat rel, ref, rare bks. 15: 2730 Second ave SE, Cedar Rapids Iowa 52401.

MARVIN, PATRICIA (HARMON). b Idabel Okla 21 S 27. 4: John Robert Marvin. 5: UDenver 45-47 (Eng) BA, 49 (LS) MA. 6: Sp. 7: Circ libn UNeb 50-51; Res room libn UDenver Lib 51-53; Catlgr libn Johns Hopkins U 53-54; Head circ dept Notre Dame U Lib (Ind) 61-63; Supvr of circ Newton Free Lib, Newton Mass 67-. 9: ALA; MassLA. 13: Yes. 14: Circ procedures, bk sel, reviewing. 15: 60 Anthony Circle, Newtonville Ma 02160.

MARWICK, LAWRENCE. b Poland 16 S 09. 4: Claiew Sklaroff. 5: UChicago 30-31 (Ancient hist) PhB, 31-32 (Semitic Lang) MA; Egyptian NatU (Cairo) 35-36 (Arabic & Islamics); Dropsie Col 33-37 (Arabic & Islamic) PhD. 6: Hebrew, Arabic, Ger, Fr, Yiddish, Russian, Aramic, Syriac. 7: Research asst Dropsie Col 37-40; CIC US Army 41-45; Asst dir Bd of Jewish Educ, St Louis Mo 47-48; Hd Hebraic Sect LC 48-; Adjunct Prof of Arabic & Islamic Studies Dropsie Col 55-. 9: Amer Oriental Soc; Amer Acad of Jewish Res. 10: Amer Friends of the HebrewU, Jerusalem. 12: Co-ed "Bloch Memorial Volume, a handbook of Diplomatic Hebrew"; Ed of texts in Judeo-Arabic. 13: Yes. 14: Ref, rare Hebraica, reprints. 15: 3221 Brooklawn ter, Chevy Chase Md 20015.

MARX, MARION FRANCES (CAPEL). b Lachine Que Can 18 Je 38. 4: Victor (Ferenc) Marx. 5: McGill 55-59 (Fr, Lat) BA; MacDonald Col McGill U 59-60 Class I Diploma in Tchg; UBC 62-63 BLS. 6: Fr. 7: Tchr Arvida High Sch, Arvida Que 60-61; Tchr Lakeside Heights Elem Sch, Pte Claire Que 61-62; Child libn Seattle Pub Lib64-65; Sch libn Hebeler Elem Sch (CWSC), Ellensburg Wash 65-67; Reviewer Horn Bk Magazine 67-68; Libn Schlesinger Lib RadcliffeCol 67-68; Visiting lecturer Salem State Col 69. 9: Wash State ASchL. 14: Wk with child. 15: 19 Bellevue st, Medford Ma 02155.

MARX, VICTOR (FERENC). b Szentbekkalla Hungary 18 Ja 34. 4: Marion F Capel. 5: Col of Horticulture (Budapest) 52-56 (Horticulture); UBC 59-61 (Horticulture) BSA, 61-64 (Horticulture) MSA; UWash 64-65 (LS) M Lib. 6: Hungarian, Russian. 7: Instr of Libnship, head acquis dept Central Wash State Col Lib 65-67; Libn Libs of Arnold Arbortetum & Gray Herbarium Harvard U 67-. 9: ALA; SLA. 10: AAUP; Beta Phi Mu. 14: Acquis, ref, automation, , admin, Lib netwks, rare bks. 15: 22 Divinity ave, Cambridge Ma 02138.

MARY, SISTER MARGARET OSU. b Lacolle Que Can. 5: Fordham summers 28-29 Libns Certif; Catholic U 31-32 AB; Nazareth Col summers 53-55 Libns Certif. 6: Fr, Lat. 7: Tchr & libn St Josephs Acad, Malone NY 45-. 9: CanLA; NYLA; Diocesan LA (chm 2 yrs, sec 4 yrs, co-chm Cath Bk Week Contest Com); RegLA (Legis chm). 15: 111 Elm st, Malone NY 12953.

MASHBURN, GLORIA. b Yakima Wash 1 Ag 23. 5: Stanford 45 BA; UWash 58 MLS. 7: Catlgr Skagit Valley Col 65-, Hd lib 68-. 15: 3403 W Chestnut st, Yakima Wash 98902.

MASLENIKOV, EMILY L. b Stowe Twp Penn 12 Je 09. 4: Oleg A Maslenikov. 5: UPittsburgh 27-31 (Lat) AB; Karlova (Prague) 33-35 (Phil); UCal 38-40 (Slavic lang & lit), 45-46 Certif in LS. 6: Fr, Czech, Slovak, Russian, Polish. 7: Catlgr (libn III) UCal Lib (Berkeley) 47-, Hd Slavic div catlg dept 63-. 9: ALA; CalLA. 10: Cal Native Plant Soc; Save-the-Redwoods League; Save San Francisco Bay Assn. 14: Catlg. 15: 18 Claremont Crescent, Berkeley Ca 94705.

MASLYN,DAVID C. b Geneva NY 11 Ag 36. 4: Sandra Holland. 5: St Bonaventure U 56-60 (Hist) Syracuse Syracue 62-63 (Hist) MA, 66-67 (LS) MS. 6: Fr. 7: Sales & foreman L S Lee & Co Oaks Corners NY 60-62; Research asst Syracuse U 63; High schchr Gorham Central Sch, Gorham NY 63-64; Asst archivist Syracuse U 64-65, Mss assoc 65-67; Asst to the assoc libn for archives & mss Yale U 68-. 8: Staff, Sch of Lib Sci, Syracuse U summers 67, 68; Staff, Sch of Lib Sci, UIll summer 69. 9: SAA (Com on Educ & Train of Archivists 67-69, Com on Automated Techniques for Archival Agencies 67-69). 12: Asst ed "Syracuse University Faculty & Staff Publications & Creative Works (64, 65); Ed " Sawyer Falk: A Register of His Papers (65). 14: Archives, mss. 15: 89 Ridgetop rd, Wallingford Ct 06492.

MASON, ALBERT GEORGE RAPHAEL. b Binghamton NY 24 O 12. 4: Irene Eleanor Owens. 5: Kenyon Col 46-48 (Hist) BA; Gen Theol Sch 48-52 (Ecclesiastical Hist) STB; Geneseo State Tchrs Col 59-60 (LS) MS. 6: Gk, Lat, Fr, Ger. 7: Vicar St Andrew's Church, Bronx NY 52-54; Chaplain Willard St Hosp, Willard NY 54-59; Bkmob libn So Tier Lib System, Corning NY 60-61; Catlgr Olin Lib Cornell U 61-63; Head catlgr St Mark's Lib Gen Theol Sem (NY) 63-68; Acquis libn Southampton Col Lib 69-. 8: Catlgr for LC. 9: ATheolLA; NYLA; ALA; Metropolitan Tech Serv. 10: Asst rector at Church of the Resurrection, Richmond Hill LI NY. 14: Tech serv, rare bks. 15: Southampton Col Lib Montauk rd, Southampton NY 11968.

MASON, ALEXANDRA. b Greenfield Mass 17 Mr 31. 5: Mt Holyoke 48-52 (Greek) AB; Carnegie Lib Sch 52-55 MLS. LS. 6: Lat, Fr, Sp, Ital. 7: Clerical asst catlg dept Carnegie Lib of Pittsburgh 52-55; Ref libn World Bk Encyclopedia Lib, Chicago 56-57; Visiting rare bks catlgr, UDurham Lib (Durham England) 61-62; Asst spec collections libn UKan Lib 57-59, Assoc spec collections libn 59-63, Spec collections libn 63-. 9: ALA-ACRL (sec Rare Bks Sect 69-70); BSA. 10: Phi Beta Kappa; Mediaeval Acad Amer; Renaissance Soc Amer; AAUP; Johnson Soc Kan; Mediaeval Soc Kan. 12: "A Guide to the Collections," Lawrence Kan (64, 2nd ed 69). 13: Yes. 14: Rare bks, mss. 15: 737 Lawrence ave, Lawrence Ks 66044.

MASON, BARBARA GAREY. b Melrose Mass 19 Jl 09. 5: Denison U 32 (Psych) AB; Simmons 33 (LS) BS; Colby Jr Col 29-30 AA. 07: Circ libn Melrose Pub Lib, Melrose Mass 34-43, Asst libn 43-. 9: ALA; MassLA; N ShoreLA. 10: Melrose Commun Coun. 14: Ref. 15: 111 First st, Melrose Ma 02176.

MASON, CHARLES W. b Bear Lake Mich 20 Je 14. 5: Wheaton Col (Ill) 40-43 (Philos) AB; UDelaware 48-51 (Philos) MA; Johns Hopkins 52-54 (Philos); UPenn 55-56 (Philos); NYU 56-59, 66- (Philos). 6: Ger, Fr, Sp. 7: Instr Philos: King's Col (Briarcliff Ma or NY) 48-51; UDel Ext Div 52-53, 55-60, 62-; LincolnU (Penn) 57-58; PurdueU Ctr (Ft Wayne) 61-62; Ind Inst of Tech 61-62; Monmouth Col (NJ) summers 64-66; Del State Col 66; Lib asst Ft Wayne Pub Lib, Ft Wayne Ind 60-62; Doc libn Morris Lib UDel 62-. 14: Govt docs. 15: Government Documents Morris Lib Univ of Delaware, Newark De 19711.

MASON, EDA N (EISEN). b NYC 2 F 32. 4: William D Mason. 5: Goddard Col 49-51; UDenver 59-6 (Humanities) BA, 62-63 (LS) MA. 6: Fr, Sp. 7: Lib asst Denver Pub Lib 51-54; Lib asst Nat Farmers Union, Denver 55-56; Admin asst Dept of Communication UDenver 62; Internat Rel Libn Grad Sch of Internat Studies UDenver 63-. 8: Consul in communication (admin & mgt wkshops). 9: SLA; ALA. 10: Phi Beta Kappa; Great Books Discussion Group. 13: Yes. 14: Internat rel, acquis, ref, internat exch. 15: 429 Salem st, Aurora Co 80010.

MASON, ELEANOR (WILLIAMS). b Denver Colo 6 N 25. 4: Andrew J Mason. 5: Santa Monica City Col 44-46 (Liberal Arts) AA; UCLA 46-48 (Eng) BA; Immaculate Heart Col 62-65 MALS. 7: Jr-sec clk Santa Monica Bd Educ, Santa Monica High Sch 48-49; Sub libn LA Bd of Educ, Los Angeles Trade Tech Col 67; Hd libn LA Bd of Educ Los Angeles SW Col 68; Coord of Lib Serv 68-. 9: CalLA. 14: Ref, child wk. 15: 811 Iliff st, Pacific Palisades Ca 90272.

MASON, ELEANOR M. b Kalamazoo Mich 14 Ag 17. 5: West Mich Col of Educ 34-38 (Art) BS; UMich 41-42 BS in LS; Wayne U summer 48. 6: Fr. 7: Asst Kalamazoo Pub Lib 38-41; Asst libn Chrysler Engring Lib, Highland Park Mich 42-43; Asst Detroit Pub Lib 43-46; Chief of art dept Kalamazoo Pub Lib 46-49; Sr Asst fine arts dept Enoch Pratt Free Lib, Baltimore 49-51, Admin asst fine arts dept 52-57, Libn picture collection 57-66; Art libn Johns Hopkins U Lib 66-67; Asst ref libn UBaltimore Lib 67-. 9: SLA (dir Baltimore Chap 69-71); MdLA (treas 59-61). 10: Walters Art Gallery; Baltimore Heritage. 14: Art, pictures, ref. 15: 192 Hollen rd, Baltimore Md 21212.

MASON, ELLSWORTH GOODWIN. b Waterbury Conn 25 Ag 17. 4: Joan Shinew Mason. 5: Yale 38 (Econ) BA, 42 (Eng) MA, 48 (Eng) PhD. 6: Fr, Ger, Ital, Sp. 7: Stud asst Yale U Lib 35-38, Ref asst 38-42; License off Bd of Econ Warfare, Wash DC 42-43 Automotive mechanic US Navy CBs (MM 1/c) 43-46; Instr of Eng Williams Col 48-50; Humanities Div Marlboro Col 51-52; Ser libn UWyo Lib 52-54; Ref libn Colo Col 54-58, Libn 58-63; Dir of Lib Serv Hofstra U 63-. 8: Planned new lib bldgs at Colo Col 60, and Hofstra U 63-64; Lib bldg consul for more than 60 high sch, prep sch, col & univ libs 62-; lectr in Eng Colo Col 54-63; Visit lectr, Syracuse

U 65, 69, Columbia U 66, 68, Elmira Col 66, Colo Col 66, U of Ill (Urbana) summer 68, Lincoln U 69; Spec week lectr, UBC 69; lectr, Conf on Acad Lib Bldgs, Grad Sch of Lib Sci,Drexel 66; chm, Conf on Univ Lib Standards, Boston U 67; Dir, Wk-study sem, Can Assn of Col & Univ Libs, Jasper 68; chm, Translations Sect, 2nd Internat James Joyce Symposium, Dublin 69. 9: BSA; Mod Lang Assn; ALA (ed Bd for Serial Slants 53-57); -RTSD (ed Bd for Ser Sect 57-59), Ser Policy & Res Com 62-63); -ACRL (Com on Standards 62-68, chm Ad hoc Subcom to Consider Poss Univ Lib Standards 67-68; ed Bd Col & Res Libs 69-; ed Bd Choice 62-65; ACRLARL Jt Com on Lib Standards 68-; Bibliog Ctr for Res Denver (v-pres & pres-elect 61-63); Colo Counc for Lib Devel (chm 62-63); ColoLA (Legis Com 61-62, Exec Bd 61-62), chm Intel Freedom Com 62-63; v-pres & pres So Dist 60-62); NYLA (Intel Freedom Com 66-, Bldgs Com, 66-; Nassau CLA. 10: Caxton club; Ghost Town Club (Colo Springs); Grolier Club; Nassau Co Hist Soc; James Joyce Found; Archons of Colophon; LI Bk Collectors; Sigma Kappa Alpha; Alpha Sigma Lambda. 11: Coun of Lib Resources, Fellow 69-70. 12: Transl "Stanislaus Joyce, "Recollections of James Joyce, (50); Ed (with Stanislaus Joyce) "The Early Joyce:the Book Reviews (55); Ed (with Richard Ellman) "The Critical Writings of James Joyce (59 &64) "Essais Critiques de J Joyce (66); "Portrait of the Artist as a Young Man (crit commen) (66); Co-auth "Impact of Technology on the Library Building (67). 13: Yes. 14: Ref, ser, acquis, rare bks, bldgs. 15: 71 Meadow st, Garden City NY 11530.

MASON, HAYDEN. b Westfield NJ 1 Ag 18. 4: Jean Trace. 5: Haverford Col 36-40 (Fr) BA; Harvard 40-41 (Romance Langs) MA, Tching Fellow in French 52-54; Universite de Poitiers, L'Institut de Touraine 49 (Fr) Diploma. 6: Fr, Sp. 7: Tch Romance Lang secondary sch; Serv in WWII Commanding Off of Intelligence Unit in Pacific; Subsection chief Korean War Eastern Br Gen Staff, Pentagon; Colonle in Mil Intelligence, US Army res; Libn Fire Protection Assn, Boston 63-. 8: Consult, Army Intell, researching docs summer 62. 9: SLA (chm Boston Chap pub rel 68). 10: Seaman, US Power Squadron. 13: Yes. 15: NFPA Tech Ref Lib, 60 Batterymarch st, Boston Ma 02110.

MASON, HELEN (HATHCOCK). b Locust Bayou Ark 1D04. 5: UArk 22-26 (Zool) BA; Carnegie 50-51 MLS. 6: Fr, Ger. 7: Tchr Smead Sch, Smead Ark 21-22; Tchr Miss Fines Sch, Princeton NJ 28-29; Libn UPittsburgh Dental & Med Lib 51-52; Libn Union Carbide Nuclear Co Oak Ridge Nat Lab, Oak Ridge Tenn 52-62; Hd Y-12 tech lib Oak Ridge Nat Lab, Oak Ridge Tenn 62-68, Hd civil defense research project 68-. 9: SLA (treas, pres S Appalachian Chap); ASLIB; ALA. 10: AAUW; Nat Com on Sci; UN USA (Oak Ridge pres, Tenn Div pres): 12: "Synchronistic Tables of Selected Journals in the Oak Ridge National Laboratory Libraries, 1880-1950 (54). 12: "Synchronistic Tables of Selected Journals inthe Oak Ridge National Laboratory, 1880-1950. 14: Ref, mgt. 15: Rt 17, Knoxville Tenn 37921.

MASON, JEAN (EDWARDA). b Hodgenville Ky 7 Jl 07. 5: West Col for Women 25-27 (Eng); Purude 27-28 (Eng); Ind U 28-29 (Eng) BA; LSU 37-38 BS in LS. 6: Fr. 7: Catlgr La State Lib, Baton Rouge La 38-42, Hd tech processes ext dept 42-68, La union catlg libn 68-. 9: ALA; SWLA; LaLA. 10: Beta Phi Mu; Baton Rouge Lib Club; Altrusa Club; Inter-Civic Club Coun; Bus Women's Circle. 14: Catlg. 15: 439 N Fifth st apt 43, Baton Rouge La 70801.

MASON, MARY (BROOK). b Hood River Ore 1S20. 5: Pomona Col 38-42 (Eng) BA; UWash 42-43 BSLS. 7: Child libn Pub Lib, Boise Ida 43-45; Child libn Pub Lib Multnomah Co, Portland Ore 45-48; Child libn Pub Lib, Honolulu 48-49; Child libn Pub Lib, Portland Ore 49-. 8: Newbery- Caldecott Com. 64. 9: ALA; PNLA (v-chm & chm child serv div 66-69). 15: Southwest Hills Br 1515 SW Sunset, Portland Ore 97201.

MASON, MILDRED (IRENE). b Mobile Ala 16 D 31. 5: Newcomb Col 49-52 (Music) BA; Columbia 54 (LS). 6: Fr. 7: Libn, asst libn The Hanover Bank, NY 53-56; Libn & personnel manager Richmond Symphony Inc, Richmond Va 57-; Libn Reynolds Metals Co Exec Off Lib, Richmond Va 57-. 8: Consult, Chesapeake Corp West Point, Va, 68-69;chm Inst Mgt Devel Sem for Libns Va Commonwealth U Mar-Ap 69. 9: SLA (Va Chap; consul Offr 67-69, pres-elect 69-70); AALL (Private Law Lib Com); VaLA; Law Libns Soc Wash. 10: Richmond Area Spec Libs Club; Symphony Wpmens Com.14 Admin. 14: Admin, ref. 15: Reynolds Metals Co Exec Off Lib 6601 W Broad st, Richmond Va 23218.

MASON, ORA M. b Manchester Conn 2 Ap 04. 7: Lib asst W Haven Pub Lib, W Haven Conn 23-29, Child libn 29-36, Hd libn 36-. 9: ConnLA (treas). 10: West Haven Hist Soc; West Haven Garden Club. 11: Woman of the Year, West Haven Jr C of C. 14: Child wk, admin. 15: 300 Elm st, W Haven Ct 06516.

MASON, PHILIP PARKER. b Salem Mass 28 Ap 27. 4: Henrietta Dow. 5: Boston U 50 AB; UMich 51 MA, 56 PhD. 6: Fr. 7: USNR 44-46; Research asst UMich Hist Collections 50-53; Dir State Archives of Mich, Lansing 53-58; Prof OF Hist Wayne State U60-, U Archivist 58-. Dir Labor Hist Archives 60-, Dir Archives of Labor Hist & Urban Affairs 8: Consul on Col & Univ Archives, Archives and Records Mgt progs & archival bldgs. 9: SAA; sec 63-68, Fellow 63-, Hist Soc of Mich (pres 65-, Detroit Hist Soc; Histn & Trustee 63; Amer Assn State & Loc Hist (trustee 68-). 10: Prismatic Club of Detroit. 12: "Schoolcrafts Expedition to Lake Itasca; The Discovery of the Source of the Mississippi River" (58); "Schoolcrafts Literary Voyager" (62); "Harper of Detroit; The Origin and Growth of a Great Metropolitan Hospital," with Frank B Woodford (64); "From Bull Run to Appomattox; Michigan's Role in the Civil War" (61); "Detroit, Fort Lernoult and the American Revolution" (64). 13: Yes. 14: Archives, hist. 15: Archives of Labor Hist and Urban Affairs, Wayne State U, Detroit Mi 48202.

MASON, SHARON L (WISCH). b Kearney Neb 7 Ag 40. 4: Gary I Mason. 5: Kearney State Col 58-62 (Eng) BA; UDenver 62-63 (LS) MA. 7: Ser libn Kearney State Col 63-66; Asst libn Homewood-Flossmoor High Sch, Flossmoor Ill 66-68; Ser bibliogr Ohio State U Libs 9columbus) 68-. 9: ALA. 14: Ser, govt docs. 15: 964 E No Broadway, Columbus Oh 43224.

MASSEY, MARY (J). b Laurel Miss 17 My 20. 5: Southeast Mo State Tchrs Col 43 (Eng) BS in HS; Peabody 59 MLS. 7: Eng tchr MOREHOUSE High Sch, Morehouse Mo 43-47; Egn tchr-libn DeWitt High Sch, DeWitt Iowa 47-60; Libn Pleasant Valley Iowa 60-; 9: Iowa State Assn; Iowa LA. 10: Beta Phi Mu; Delta Kappa Gamma; PTA. 11: Louis Shores Award, George Peabody Lib Sch 59. 14: High sch lib admin. 15: 505 23rd st, Bettendrf Iowa 52722.

MASSEY, WILLIAM CLAYTON. b Tulsa Okla 18 Je 27. 5: UTulsa 45-49 (Pre-Ministry, Eng Emph) BA; West Theol Sem 49-51 (Theol); UOkla 51-52 BA in LS. 7: Libn ref asst Milwaukee Pub Lib 52-56; Libn catlgr Research Lib Detroit Inst of Arts 57-58; Lib sub spec ref Detroit Pub Lib 58-61; Hd of adult serv Hd Libn Park Ridge Pub Lib, Park ridge Ill 61-62; Lib ref adult serv Brooklyn Pub Lib, Brooklyn NY 62-63; Supv processing New Haven Free Pub Lib, New Haven Ct 63-66, Spec projects 66-69, Dir of pub rel 69-. 9: ConnLA (Exh Chm 67-69). 14: Pub lib serv, bldgs, pub rel. 15: 278 Orange st, New Haven Ct 06510.

MASSIE, ANN LURYE. b Scottsbluff Neb 9 F 44. 5: UWyoming 62-66 (Eng) BA, 66-67 (Eng) MA; Rutgers 67-68 MLS. 7: Indexer Bibliogr Index H W Wilson Co, Bronx NY 68-. 9: ALA; NY Lib Club. 10: Phi Beta Kappa; Phi Kappa Phi. 14: Bibliog, catlg. 15: 225 W 70th st apt 2C, New York NY 10023.

MASSINGILL, ALBERTA RUTH. b Urich Mo 12 Jl 14. 5: Park Col 36 (hist) AB: UDenver 37 BS in LS; UMich 54 MALS. 7: 1st catlg dept pub lib Kan City Kan 37-41; Pub lib Grand Rapids Mich; Sr asst adult serv 41-44, chief circ dept 44-51,personnel dir & coordinator of lending serv 51-62, assoc dir 62-. 9: ALA (chm Sect on Personnel Admin 65); MichLA (chm Com 64-65. &65). 10: Grand Rapids Prog Planning Inst: Zonta Internat; Women's Nat Bk Assn; Church Lib & Synagogue Assn; Beta Phi Mu. 13: Yes. 14: Adult serv, personnel. 15: Pub Lib 111 Library st NE, Grand Rapids Mich 49502.

MASSMANN, ROBERT ERNEST. b Pittsburg Kan 2 Ap 24. 4: Eloise Coon. 5: Kan State Tchrs Col Pittsburg) 41-47 (Modern Langs) AB; UMich Law Sch 47-48 (Law); UMich 48-50 AMLS. 6: Sp, Fr. 7: Lt (Jg) Communications US Naval 43-46; Stud asst engnr lib UMich 49-50; Asst law Fed Res Bank of NY, NY 50-51; Asst libn Central Conn State Col 51-57, Dir of lib serv 57-. 8: Spec Adv Com on Standards for Lib Furniture, Com State Purchasing Dept, 61-. 9: ConnLA. 10: AAUP; Kiwanis Club; Hist Soc New Britain. 13: Yes. 14: Admin, lib bldgs. 15: Central Conn State Col, New Britian Conn 06050.

MASSONNEAU, SUZANNE. b NYC 24 F 26. 5: George Washinton U 43-46 (Psych) BA; Fla State U 51-52 (LS) MA. 7: Insurance accountant Atlantic Mutual Insurance Co. NYC 47-50; Libn Lib Sch Fla State U 52-53, Catlgr Lib Purdue U 55-57; Catlgr Lib Fla State U 57-60, Head catlg dept 6-67,

Asst Prof Sch Lib Training & Serv 67-. 9: ALA; FlaLA (chm Tech Serv Round Table 63-64). 10: AAUP; Beta Phi Mu. 14: Catlg, automotive of tech serv, acad lib admin, lib educ. 15: 1108 Linwood dr, Tallahassee Fla 32304.

MAST, JANE ELIZBETH. b St Louis 22 My 10. 5: Radcliffe 28-32 (Romance Langs) BA; Tex Womens U 58-59 (LS) MA. 7: Actress Whalom Stock Co, Lake Whalom Mass 32; Actress Biehl Sisters Stock Co, Kan, Okla 35; Actress Old Town Hall, Kan City Mo Lib N Parsons; Head Lib Parsons Pub Lib, Parsons Kan 59-. 9: ALA KanLA. 10: . 14: Admin. 15: 1727 Morgan, Parsons Kan 67357.

MASTEJ, SHERYL (WILLOWS). b Pontiac Mich 7 Ja 44. 4: Robert A Mastej. 5: OaklandU 62-66 (Eng Lit) BA; UMich 66-67 MLS. 6: Fr. 7: Ref catlgr Macomb Co Lib, Mt Clemens Mich 68-. 9: MichLA. 14: Ref. 15: 47780 Jefferson, New Baltimore Mi 48047.

MASTERS,FRED N JR . b Webster City Iowa 21 Ap 34. 4: Frances Wagner. 5: UTenn 52-58 (Hist) BA; West Res 60-61 MSLS. 6: Sp. 7: Engnr libn UTenn 58-60; Ref Libn Ohio State U 61-62; Head tech libn Amer Mach & Foundry Co Research & Development Div, Springdale Conn 62-65; Head tech libn C H Dexter & Sons, Windsor Locks Conn 65-. 9: SLA. 14: Info retrieval. 15: C H Dexter & Sons , Windsor Locks Conn 06096.

MASTERS, ROBERT GENE. b Hundred W Va 4 Ja 37. 4: May Elizabeth Wilson. 5: W VaU 56-60 (Eng) BS; Peabody Col 63-64 (Lib) MA. 7: Ref libn Fairmont State Col 60-66; Libn Alderson-Broaddus Col 66-. 9: WVaLA. 10: Beta Phi Mu; Kappa Delta Pi; Jr C of C. 13: Yes. 14: Admin. 15: A-B College, Philippi WVa 26416.

MASTERSON, WILLIAM F. b Little Blue Mo 17 F 42. 4: Lola Lynne Gossett. 5: UArk 60-66 (Psych/Arch) BA; UOkla 67-68 MLS. 7: Circ libn SWest State Col 68-. 9: ALA; SLA; OklaLA. 14: Automation, admin, ref. 15: 1306 Washington apt 1, Weatherford Ok 73096.

MATARAZZO, JAMES MICHAEL. b Stoneham Ma 1 Ap 41. 4: Alice M Keohane. 5: Boston Col 59-63 (Hist, Educ) BS, 66- (Pol Sci); Simmons 63-65 (LS) MS. 7: Ser asst Boston Col 62-65; Asst sci libn MIT 65-67, Docs libn 67-68, Sers libn, Hd tech reports 68-69; Instr Simmons Col Grad Sch Lib Sci 69-. 9: SLA (Boston Chap Memb Chm 67-). 14: Admin, sci & tech lit, tech ref, docs. 15: 146 Cottage Park rd, Winthrop Ma 02152.

MATE, ALBERT VALENTINE. b Walkerville Ont Can 1 Ja 31. 4: Eileen Elizabeth McDonald. 5: Assumption Col (Can) 49-52 (Eng) BA; UMich 52-54 (Eng) AM, 57-58 AMLS. 6: Fr, Hungarian. 7: Tchr Assumption High Sch, Windsor Ont 54-55; Instr U Du Sacre de Coeur; Tathurst NB 55-57; Humanities & Soc Sci Div 61-66; Asst libn pub serv 66-. 9: ALA; CanLA; Inst Prog Libns Ont; OntLA; sec-treas col & univ sect. 10: Windsor Symphony Orchestra. 13: Yes. 14: Ref. 15: 111 Riverside dr, E Windsor Ont Can.

MATEER, CAROLYN (SNYDER). b Baltimore Md 2 Jl 25. 5: Penn State 41-45 (Liberal Arts) AB; Drexel 67 (LS) MS. 6: Fr. 7: Libn Steelton-Highspire High Sch, Steelton Pa 62-67; Asst libn Harrisburg Area Commun Col, Harrisburg Pa 67-68; Asst libn Capitol Campus- Penn StateU 68-. 9: PennLA; CapitolAreaLA (past pres). 14: Bk sel, ref. 15: 223 N 40th st, Harrisburg Pa 17111.

MATEER, MILDRED G. b Kittanning Penn 25 Ag 10. 5: Thiel Col 27-31 (Eng) AB; Drexel 31-32 BS in LS; UMich 38; UWyo 48-50 (Educ) MA; UColo 54. 7: Libn Kittanning High Sch, Kittanning Penn 33-48; Libn Grants Pass High Sch, Grants Pass Ore 48-58; Libn Redwood High Sch, Larkspur Cal 58-66; Ref libn Rohrbach Lib Kutztown State Col 67-. 9: NEA; PennLA; PennStateEA; CalLA (No Sect: chm Sr High Sch Div 65, 66). 10: Delta Kappa Gamma. 14: Ref, lib edu 14: Ref, lib educ. 15: 448 Benner rd apt 102, Allentown Pa 18104.

MATER, WILMA (SHAFFER). b Fultin Kan 18 S 11. 4: Dan H Mater. 5: UNM 29-35 (Eng) BA; UChicago 38-43 (LS) MA. 7: Libn Hyde Park High Sch, Chicago 40-42; Libn USN, Arlington Va 43-45; Libn in charge of adult educ Portland Lib Assn, Portland Ore 46-48; Tchr Montgomery Co Pub Sch, Rockville Md 56-60, Elem sch libn 60-64, High sch libn 64-. 8: Consul, H W Wilson Co, "High Sch Catlg". 9: NEA; ALA; MdSchLA; MSTA; MontgomeryCoSchLA; Montgomery CoEA. 13: Yes. 14: Sch libs. 15: 8101 MacArthur blvd, Bethesda Md 20034.

MATHENY, PATRICIA L. b Bemidji Minn 28 Jl 45. 5: Macalester Col 63-67 (Mus) BA; UDenver 67-68 (LS) MA. 6: Sp. 7: Catlgr-instr SW Minn State Col 68-. 9: MinnLA. 14: Catlg, fine arts. 15/ 1302 Birch st apt 29, Marshall Mn 56258.

MATHER, ALMA PHELPS (SKINNER). b Kinston NC 7 Ag 36. 5: Smith 54-56; UAriz 57-59 (Anthrop) BA; UNC 60-61 MS in LS. 7: Libn (trainee) LC 61-62, Ref libn serial div 62-65, Asst hd African Asian exchange sect 66-68, Hd and ed US Govt Pub Bibliog Project 68-. 10: Beta Phi Mu. 14: US govt, publ (acquis, preparation of bibliog). 15: 415 6th st NE, Washington DC 20002.

MATHER, DAN. b Burlington Flats NY 16 Ja 25. 4: Karyl M. 5: UWash 48-50 (Eng) BA, 58-59 MLS. 7: Navy (Radioman 2/c) 43-46; Salesman Wholesale Columbia Records, San Francisco 51-55; Employment coun Wash State Employment Serv, Vancouver Wash 55-59; Acquis libn UIda Lib 60-65; Acquis libn Simon Fraser U Lib, Burnaby BC 65-66, Asst libn for processing 66-69; Asst dir for TS & Lib Syst West Wash State Col 69-. 8: Survey of T.S. Brandeis U Lib 67. 13: Yes. 14: Tech serv, data proc. 15: Lib Western Washington State Col, Bellingham Wa 98225.

MATHES, MIRIAM (SNOW). b Fall River Mass 3 Mr 05. 5: SUNY (Albany) 22-26 (Eng) AB; Columbia summers 27-30 (LS) BS, 32-34 (LS) MS, 33-34 (Eng) MA. 6: Fr. 7: Libn High Sch, Pleasantville NY 26-28; Instr U of NY (Albany) 28-30; Instr Peabody Col 30-32; Instr U f NY (Geneseo) summer 32; Campus Sch Libn West Wash State Col 34-60, Assoc Prof of Lib sch 60-. 9: ALA-AASchL(chm, mem numerous coms); NEA; PNLA (chm Sch Sect); WashEA; Wash State ASchL (several coms). 10: AAUP; AAUW; Soroptimist Internat; Twentieth Century Club. 12: Ed "Basic Book Collection for Elementary Grades, ALA (51, 56, 60); Ed "Right Book for the Rght Child (40). 13: Yes. 14: Child bks, elem sch libs, lib educ. 15: 102 Highland dr, Bellingham Wash 98225.

MATHESON, NINA W(OO). b Seattle 25 Je 33. 4: John William Matheson. 5: U Wash 51-56 (Eng) BA, 57-58 MLS. 7: INTERN NY Pub Lib 58; Sel off NLM 59-61; Bibliog for Asian Studies Ind U 61-62; Libn Mo Inst of Psychiatry 62-. 8: Principal Investigator PHS Grant LM00079 66-68. 9: MedLA; SLA. 10: Amer Inst Graph Arts; Guild of Bookworkers; Phi Beta Kappa; Beta Phi Mu. 14: Info retrieval, binding. 15: 1219 Waldron, Univerity City Mo 63130.

MATHESON, WILLIAM (JOHN). b Montreal Can 14 Je 27. 4: Nina Matheson. 5: UWash 47-50 (Eng) BA, 50-51, 55 (Eng) MA; Chicago 56-57 (Eng); UWash 57-58 MLS. 6: Fr, Ger. 7: (T/Sgt) US Army 45-46; University Bk Store, Seattle 52-55; LC: Spec recr 58, Asst head European Exch Sect 59, Bibliog Gen Ref 7 bibliog Div 60, Head Orientalia Exch Sect 61; Lilly Fellowship Lilly Lib, Ind U 61-62; Chief rare bk dept Washington U (St Louis) 62-. 8: Consul Cleveland State U Rare Bk Dept 66; Consul, St Louis Pub Lib Rare Bk Dept 67. 9: Manuscript Soc; BSA; Bibliog Soc UVa; ALA. 10: Phi Beta Kappa; Beta Phi Mu. 14: Rare bks, bibliog, bk sel, rare phonorecords. 15: 1219 Waldron, University City Mo 63130.

MATHEWS, ANNE (JONES). b Phila 5 F 28. 4: Frank S Mathews. 5: Wheaton Col (Ill) 46-49 (Speech) AB; UDenver 63-65 (LS) MA. 6: Sp. 7: Asst ref libn Ore State U Lib 65-; Spec projects dir Central Colo Pub Lib Syst 68-. 8: Part-time fac, UDenver Grad Sch of Libnship 69. 9: ColoLA. 15: Rte 3 Box 566, Golden Col 80401.

MATHEWS, KATHLEEN RUTHERFORD. b Hamilton Ont Can 21 S 20. 5: UToronot 39-40 Diploma in LS; McMaster U ext 38-39, 40-43, 46-47 BA; Columbia 47-48 (LS) MS. 7: Child libn Hamilton Pub Lib, Hamilton Ont 40-44; Naval libn WRCNS, Halifax & Victoria 44-46; Libn: Victoria Col 48-51, Sch of Nursing Hamilton Gen Hosp 51-52; Br hd Hamilton Pub lib, Hamilton Ont 52-68, Hd main lib 68-. 9: Inst Prof Libns Ont (pres 67-68). 10: Zonta Club. 15: 90 Haddon ave S, Hamilton 15 Ont Can.

MATHEWS, ROBERT CHARLES. b Independence Mo 13 Mr 40. 4: Mary Lynne Hannah. 5: Luther jr Col 59-61 (Soc sci) AA; Peru State Col 61-63 (Soc sci, LS) AB; IndU (LS). 6: Ger. 7: Tchr & libn Laurel Pub Schs, Laurel Neb 63-64; Ref libn USA Command & Staff Sch, ft Leavenworth 63-67; Base libn USAF, Grissom AFB Ind 67-. 9: ALA. 10: Phi Alpha Theta. 14: Ref. 15: 1414 W Havens, Kokomo In 46901.

MATHEWS, VIRGINIA HOPPER. b NYC 9 Mr 25. 5: Goucher Col; UGeneva; Columbia. 6: Fr, Ger. 7: Head child bk dept Brentanos 4450; Contrib ed PW 46-50; Literary scout West Europe 49-50; Tchr of seminars & courses in Child Lit

46, 52-56; Dir of sch & lib promotion & ed Longmans, Green & Co 50-57; Dir of advertising & publicity, Longmans reen & David McKay Publ 52-57; Dir reading development serv Amer Bk Publ Coun 57-; Staff ssoc Nat Bk Com & Deputy dir Nat Lib Week Porgram 57-. 8: Exec producer of "Gateway to Ideas 64-65; Governors Coun on Libs in Conn, 62; Chm, Conn Elem Sch Lib Demonstration Proj, 64-. 9: ALA (mem var coms); NCTE (mem var coms); Nat Coun for the Soc Studies (mem var coms); Nat Assn of Educ Broadcasters. 10: KNAPP Sch Libs Proj Adv Bd; Womens Nat Bk Assn. 11: Constance Lindsay Skinner medal for significant contribution to world of books. 13: Yes. 14: Devel of libs, implementation of standards, sch libs, child serv. 15: Nat Lib Week Program, One Park ave, NYC 10016.

MATHEWS, WILLIAM HOWARD II. b Baltimore Md 16 N 38. 5: Towson State Col 57-61 (Geog) BS; Loyola Col 61-65 (Europ Hist, Educ) MA; UMd 66-68 (LS) MS. 6: Ger. 7: File clk US Soc Sec Admin, Baltimore summer 57; Cashier Read's Drug Co, Baltimore summer 58; Mus salesman Sears & Roebuck Co, Baltimore summer 60; Tchr secondary sch, Baltimore Co 61-64; Tchr, Baltimore City 64-66; Recreation asst UMd summer 67; Libn-asst prof of Eng Anne Arundel Community Col 67-, Acting hd libn 69-; Libn Enoch Pratt Free Lib, Baltimore 69-. 9: ALA; -ACRL; Md Assn Jr Cols (Learning Resources Div); MdStateTA. 10: Towson Club 20-30 Ltd. 14: Admin, ref, exhib & displays, lib educ instr. 15: 3839 Loch Raven blvd, Baltimore Md 21218.

MATHIA, MARIA L. b NYC 21 D 17. 5: Hofstra Col 39 (Eng) BA; Columbia 45 (LS) BS. 7: Eng tchr Hempstead NY 39-40; Pub libn Roosevelt Commun Lib, Roosevelt NY 40-42; Pub libn Elmont Pub Lib, Elmont NY 42; Asst pub libn Yorkville Br Ny Pub Lib 42-43; Libn Franklin Roosevelt High Sch, Hyde Park NY 43-44; Libn Washington Jr High Sch, Mt Vernon NY 44-46; Libn Alex Hamilton High Sch, Elmsford NY 46-48; Libn Greenville Central Sch, Greenville NY 48-55; High sch libn Sauquoit Central Sch, Sauquoit NY 55-57; Elem sch libn Massena Central Sch, Massena NY 57-. 9: CathLA; (pres 67-69); NYLA; NY State Tchrs Assn. 10: Col Club. 14: Elem sch libs. 15: 228 Main st, Massena NY 13662.

MATHIS, ELIZABETH (ROLLIN DASHER). b Savannah Ga 24 Jl 17. 4: Malcus Bryan Mathis. 5: David Lipscomb Col 34-35; Valdosta State Col 35-39 (Eng, Fr) AB; LSU 41, 42-43 BS in LS. 6: Fr. 7: Elem chr Crisp Cons Sch, Lanier Co Ga 37-38; Elem tchr & high sch libn Ty Ty Con Sch, Tift Co Ga 39-40; Libn Valdosta High Sch, Valdosta Ga 40-67; Act libn Norman Col 68-69. 8: Tchr: LSU lib, summer 60, Valdosta State Col Lib summer 61; Elem lib consul Valdosta City Schs, 62-; Summer elem lib program, State Dept of Educ, Valdosta Ga 62, 63, 64. 9: NEA; GaEA (Child & YP Lib Div); ALA;-ACRL; Assn Nr Cols. 10: AAUW, DAR. 15: 2202 Williams st, Valdosta Ga 31603.

MATHIS, MARGARET (HARSHBARGER). b West Salem Ill 27 Je 22. 4: Leroy L Mathis. 5: McKendree Col 40-44 (Eng) AB; UIll 45-46 BSLS. 7: Hd catlg dept John McIntire Pub Lib, Zanesville Ohio 46-51; Br libn Dept of Army, Ft Leonard Wood Mo 51-53, Post libn 53-58; Ref libn NMex Inst of Min & Tech, Socorro NM 60-62; Tech libn USA CDC Air Defense Agency, Fort Bliss Tex 63-67; Libn El Paso Pub Schsm El Paso Texas 67-68, Hd catlg dept 68-. 9: ALA; TexLA, BorderRegLA. 14: Catlg. 15: 9901 Cork dr, El Paso Tx 79925.

MATHIS, MARY L TELLIER. b Frederick Okla 13 Jl 10. 5: Okla Col for Women 28-30; Okla State U 30-32 (Eng) BS; USoCal summer 41 (LS); Okla U 42-43 BS in LS. 7: Tchr pub schs, El Reno Okla 38-42; Post libn post libs syst spec serv: Ft Sill Okla 43-49, Ft gordon Ga 50-52, Chief libn, Ft Hood Tex 52-54, Chief libn, Ft Sill 54-65; 1st asst Kan City Mo Pub Lib Westport br 49-50; Hd libn Morris Sweet Tech Lib, Ft Sill Okla 65-. 9: ALA (life mem; chm Achievet citation com AFLS); OklaLA. 10: Kappa Delta. 11: John Cotton Dana Award; Sustained Superior Performance Award (2). 14: Admin. 15: 1207 Gore apt 6, Lawton Ok 73501.

MATHIS, MIRIAM LILES. b Spartanburg SC 5 Ja 27. 4: Stanley Mathis. 5: Converse Col 45-47 (Hist) AB; Emory 47-48 AB in LS; UFla 65 Certif. 7: Bkmob libn Spartanburg (SC) Pub Lib summer 48; Head Libn Pub Lib, Moultrie Ga 48-49; Asst libn Madison Col (Va) 49-50; Ref libn UFla 50-52; Libn Sidney Lanier Elem Sch, Gainesville Fla 66; Asst ibn Gainesville High Sch, Gainesville Fla 66-. 9: NEA; FlaEA; ClrTA. 10: AAUW; First Meth Church Commsn on Educ. 14: Ref. 15: 1643 NW 14 ave, Gainesville Fla 32601.

MATHIS, RUBY MADELEINE. b Stewart County Tenn 15 Ag 29. 5: David Lipscomb summers 47, 48 (Elem ed); Austin Peay State 48-60 (Elem ed) BS; Peabody Col 60-62 (LS) MA; ULouisville summer 68. 7: Tchr Stewart Co Bd of Educ: Ctr Point Sch 47-48, Bear Spring Sch 48-49; Tchr Christian Co Bd of Educ: Lacy Consol Sch 52-58, Sinking Forks Consol Sch 58-59; Libn Sinking Fork Consol Sch 59-68; Asst libn & Asst Prof of Lib Sci Ky wesleyan Col 68-. 9: NEA; ALA; -AASchL; KyEA (Deleg Assembly); KyLA; SELA; Ky A-V Assn; KyASchL (Mem Chm 67-69). 10: Kappa Delta Pi; Nat Cong Parents & Tchrs; Sec Dist EA; Ky Sec Dist LA; ChristianCoTA; Christian Co Libns Club; PTA; Ky Hist Soc; Ky Wesleyan Col Womans Club. 14: Admin of Educ Materials Ctr. 15: 1706 Tamarack rd, Owensboro Ky 42301.

MATHIS, TREVA (WILKERSON). b Randleman NC 20 Mr 13. 4: William Sam Mathis. 5: Womans Col UNC 29-33 (LS) AB; UNC(Greensboro) 60-65 (Eng); UNC(Chapel Hill) 65- MS in LS; Emory U summer 68 (Archives Inst) Certif. 6: Fr, Lat. 7: Asst circ libn Womans Col UNC (Greensboro) 4-45; Catlgr Guilford Col Lib 50-64, Act libn 54-56, 60-66, Assoc dir libs 66-. 9: SELA; NCLA (chm Col & Univ Sect 61-63). 10: Greensboro Lib Club; Guilford Col Art Appreciation Club. 12: "North Carolina Composers Represented in the Holograph Collection, of unc womans Col (45). 14: Catlg, ref, spec collections (archives, rare bks, music), admin, Quaker bks. 15: 1200 Double Oaks rd, Greensboro NC 27410.

MATHISEN, ALICE (STANDISH). b Klamath Falls Ore 14 My 12. 4: Fritjof Mathisen. 5: UOre 29-32 (Eng); Chico State Col 51 (Eng) AB; UCal 53-56 MLS. 6: Fr, Ger. 7: Jr libn Klamath Co Lib, Klamath Falls Ore 32-35; Asst libn Klamath Falls Pub Lib, Klamath Falls Ore 35-39; Child libn Tehama Co Lib, Red Bluff Cal 53-61, Co Libn 61-. 9: ALA; ; Amer Soc Pub Admin; CalLA (pres Mt Shasta Dist 62). 10: Beta Phi Mu; AAUW; Soroptimist; Bus & Prof Womens Club. 14: Readers serv, child lit admin. 15: Tehama Co Lib 909 Jefferson st, Red Bluff Cal 96080.

MATHISON, RUTH FEASEY. b Burlingame Cal 12 Ag 11. 4: John Kenneth Mathison. 5: Col of San Mateo 28-30 (Eng); UCal 30-33 (Eng, Fr) AB; USoCal 40-41 (LS). 6: Fr. 7: Co of San Mateo, Redwood City Cal: Clerical asst tax collector 33-36, Legal typist recorder 36-38, Desk attendant Lib 38-40, Br supv Lib 41-43 Catlgr Lib 44, Br supv Lib 5465, Asst co libn 65-. 9: CalLA (mem Coms on Legis, Bldgs & Conf Planning); Pub Personnel Assn; San Mateo Co Employers' Credit Union. 10: Soroptimist Club; Cal Scholarship Fed (Life mem). 14: Lib sci, ref, lib bldgs &furnishings. 15: 25 Tower rd, Belmont Ca 94002.

MATHISON, RUTH MARION (HENDERSON). b Hoboken Penn 9 N 11. 5: UPittsburgh 29-33 (Zool) BS, 62-64 MLS. 7: Ref libn Carnegie Lib of Pittsburgh 63-65; Asst libn McGill Lib Westminster Col (Penn) 65-. 9: PennLA. 10: AAUP. 14: Re, periods. 15: 502 Waugh ave, New Wilmington Pa 16142.

MATHY, MARGARET ANN. b Toledo Ohio 14 N 30. 5: Col of St Mary of the Springs 48-62 (Elem Educ) BS in Elem Ed; UKy 62-63 MS in LS. 6: Fr. 7: Tchr Newark city schs, Newark Ohio 52-55 & 60-62; Tchr Amer Dependent Schs: Okinawa 55-56, Newfoundland 57-58, Rota Spain 58-59; Tchr Christ the King Sch, Columbus Ohio 59-60; Child libn Dayton & Montgomery Co Pub Lib, Dayton Ohio 63-65, Br libn 65-68, Hd main child rm 68-. 9: ALA; OhioLA. (v-chm & chm-elect serv to child RT 68-69). 10: Dayton & Montogomery Co (Oho) Pub Lib Staff Assn. 13: Yes. 14: Child serv. 15: Dayton Montgomery Co Pub Lib, 215 E Third st,Dayton Oh 45402.

MATHYS, NEL. b Beaver Falls NY. 5: Utica Col Syracuse U 55-64 AA. 7: Libn in chg Beaver Falls Pub Lib, Beaver Fall NY 38-42; logistics off Rome Air Materiel Command, Rome NY 42-49; Lib asst Watson Lib Watson Labs, Redbank NJ 49-51; Libn ref Tech Lib RADC, Griffiss AFB NY 51-53; Chief TECH Lib Rome Air Development Center, Griffiss AFB NY 53-56; Chief Lib Serv RADC, Griffiss AFB NY 56-. 9: SLA (Mil Libns: USAF STINFO Program). 10: Griffis AFB Exec Club 14: Mgt of spec libs supporting sci res & devel. 15: 140 Glen rd S, Rome NY 13440.

MATLACK, ROBERT K. 5: UPittsburgh BS; Carnegie-Mellon U MLS. 7: Trainee UPittsburgh Libs 60-61; Libn Free Lib of Phila 62-68; Libn Carnegie Lib of Pittsburgh 68-. 9: ALA; SLA; PennLA. 15: Carnegie Lib of Pittsburgh 4400 Forbes ave, Pittsburgh Pa 15213.

MATLOCK, FAYE (BENNETT). b Lake Valley Cal 27 Jl 21. 5: Sacramento City Col 63-64 (Gen ed) AA; Sacramento State Col 64-66 (Eng) BA; UWash 66-67 MLS. 6: Fr. 7: Lib asst USN Naval Air Sta, Guam 55-60; Asst libn USAF Anderson

AFB, Guam 60-63; Catlgr Sacramento City Lib, Sacramento Cal 64-66; Sr ref libn Boeing Co, Seattle 67-68; Base libn USAF, Tan Son Nhut AB, RVN 68-. 8: Devised a modified catlg system for special coll, Long-Range Planning Office, UWash & catlgd the coll 66-67. 9: SLA; ALA; PNSLA. 14: Catlg, admin. 15: 377th Combat Support Gp, Box 11453, APO San Francisco Ca 96201.

MATON, JOANNE (THOMPSON). b Jersey Shore Penn 23 N 28. 4: Gilbert L Maton. 5: Dickinson Jr Col 46-49; Dickinson Col 49-51 (Eng). 6: Sp. 7: Libn John I Thompson & Co, Wash DC 53-. 9: SLA (Sci-Tech Div: Engnr Sect Conv Liaison 62). 12: Ed "Experimental Statistics, Nat Bur Standards Handbk 91 (63); "Users Guide to Library Services, (65 reved 67); Ed "Cataloging Manual, Library, Office Chief of Engineers, Dept of Army (68). 13: Yes. 14: Technical reports and documents. 15: 3702 Bent Branch rd, Falls Church Va 22041.

MATOVICH, RICHARD MARK. b McKees Rocks Penn 14 Ag 36. 5: Cal State Col 55-59 (Ind arts) BSEd; Duquesne 60-62 MEd in LS; W Va U 63 (Ed); UDenver 66 (LS); UPittsburgh 67-69 MLS. 7: Tchr Westinghouse Jr High Sch, Pittsburgh Penn 59-61; Chef (Priv) USA 59; Libn Carnegie High Sch, Carnegie Penn 61-68; Admin adv Andrew Carnegie Free Lib, Carnegie Penn 65-67; Ind arts & interlib loan libn Cal State Col 68-. 9: ALA; Amer Col & Res Libns (Tri-State Chap). 10: Assn Penn State Col & Univ Facs. 14: Automation, tech proc. 15: General Delivery, Stockdale Pa 15483.

MATSEN, WILLETTA (BRIEN). b Corbin Mont 25 N 04. 4: Robert Matsen. 5: State U mont 24-31 (Lib Admin) BA; Columbia 55 (Med Bibliog); Anchorage Commun Col 55 (Russian); Portland Ctr Continuing Educ 67-68 (Norwegian). 6: Sp, Fr, Ger, Russian, Norwegian. 7: Chief acquis State U Mont 31-34; Asst libn Deschutes Co Lib, Bend Ore 41-44; Libn Anchorage Pub Lib, Anchorage Alaska 45-46, Arctic Health Res Center; USPHS, Anchorage Alaska 51-59, Alaska Meth U 59-63, Alaskan Reg Fed Aviation Agency, Anchorage Alaska 63-65, Sci libn Portland State U 68-. 8: Dir Alaska Crippled Child Assn 52-57; Com to establish Alaska territorial lib 55. 9: ALA; SLA; Alaska State LA; Spec Libns Portland Area. 10: AAAS; Delta Kappa Gamma; LWV. 13: Yes. 14: Acquis, admin, sci ref. 15: 1540-A S E Bush st, Hillsboro Or 97123.

MATSON, MOLLY (HOFFMAN). b Cleveland Ohio 14 O 21. 4: Kenneth H Matson. 5: NorthwesternU 39-40; UMich 40-43 (Eng lit) BA; Rutgers 66-67 MLS. 6: Ger, Lat. 7: Hd bibliog searching Goldfarb Lib BrandeisU 67-68; Ref libn UMass (Boston) 68-. 10: Beta Phi Mu. 14: Ref. 15: 101 Monmouth st, Brookline Ma 02146.

MATSON, PAMELA JANE. b Evanston Ill 10 Mr 43. 5: UMinn 61-65 (Elem ed) BS, 65-66 (LS) MA, 66-68 (Hist). 7: Res asst Soc Wel Hist Archives Ctr UMinn 66-68; Bibliog Iowa State U Lib (Ames) 68-. 14: Bibliog, soc scis. 15: 309 Lynn ave, Ames Ia 50010.

MATSUI, MASATO. b Okayama Japan 19 O 29. 4: Adelina Vilela de Souza. 5: DoshishaU (Japan) 48-53 (Jurisprudence) BA (Law); Syracuse 56-58 (LS) MS. 6: Japanese, Chinese. 7: Soc sci libn DoshishaU Lib (Kyoto Japan) 53-56; Senior catlgr HarvardU 58-60; Asst libn UWash Far Eastern Lib 61-64; Coord & Japanese Specialist Oriental Collections East West Center Lib, Honolulu Hawaii 64-. 8: Consul Okinawa Lib System 65. 12: "urvey and Recommendations of the Development of Libraries in Okinawa", East West Ctr (65); Co-auth "Research Resources on Hokkaido, Sakhalin and the Kuriles at the East West center Library," East West Ctr Lib (67). 13: Yes. 14: Bk sel, lib admin. 15: East West Center Lib, Honolulu Hi 96822.

MATTE, PIERRE. b Shawinigan Que Can 31 Jl 18. 4: Clothilde Lessard. 5: Sem of Trois-Rivie Res 35-42 BA; Laval U 43 (Philos); UMontreal 44 (Pharmacy), 48 BLS, 48 (Statistics). 6: Fr, Lat, Eng. 7: Prof St Mary Col (Shawinigan Que) 46; Script, speaker & operator CHLN Radio Sta, Irois-Rivieres 47; Plans INSRUMENTS RECORDER Shawinigan Chem Ltd, Shawinigan Que 4 Chief of tech serv Maison Bellarmin Liz, Montreal 50; Ed of a plan organ (bilin) Shawinigan Chem Ltd, Shawinigan Que 51-57; Chief of mun lib City of SHAWINIGAN Que 57-60; Asst dir Quebec Pub Lib Serv 60-. 8: Mem, Quebec Pub Lib Commsn, 60. 9: Association Canadienne des Bibliothecaires de Langue Francaise (pres 59-60); CanLA (Coun 62-63, mem Prov Lib Com, Mem JtALA-CanLA Com); Lib Res & Devel Coun; ALA (Coun by affil 65-70); Provincial Libs Com. 12: Ed "Shawinigan Chemicals Limited Bulletin (51-57). 13: Yes. 14: Admin, ref, adult serv, legisl, state libs. 15: 1228 De Repentigny, Quebec 6 Can.

MATTERN, DAVID CARL. b Buffalo NY 31 Mr 37. 4: Nancy Eggleston. 5: Rensselaer Polytechnic Inst 55-58 (Civil Eng); WesleyanU (Middletown) 58-61 (Relig) BA; USC 61-62 MS in LS. 7: Jr libn Anaheim Pub Lib, Anaheim Cal 62-63; Catlg libn Prof Lib Serv, Santa Sna Cal 63-64; Lib Cal State Polytech Col: Period libn 64-67, Asst acquis libn 67-68, Hd acquis 68-. 9: ALA; CalLA. 14: Acquis, admin. 15: 353 St Bonaventure ave, Claremont Ca 91711.

MATTERN, MARGARET (MARY). b Rochester NY 27 My 30. 5: Nazareth Col (Rochester NY) 48-52 (Hist) BA; URochester summers 55-58 (Secondary Educ) MA; UMich 61-62 MALS. 7: Tchr jr high soc studies Lyons Cental Sch, Lyons NY 52-53; Elem tchr St Margaret Mary Sch, Rochester NY 53-55; High sch tchr world hist Wayne Central Sch, Ontario NY 55-57; Tchr world hist, guidance counselor St Agnes High Sch, Rochester NY 57-61; Libns replacement Rochester Pub Lib, Rochester NY 61; Educ libn URochester Lib 62-. 9: ALA; Monroe Co (NY) LA. 14: Admin, tech proc. 15: 115 Manor pky, apt 3, Rochester NY 14620.

MATTESON, JAMES SIGURD. b Grand Rapids Mich 10 S 36. 5: Mich State U 58-62 (Pol sci) BA; UMich 63-65 MALS; West Mich U 67-68 (Libnship). 6: Ger, Russian. 7: Radio operator USAF (security serv) Ger 54-58; Lib asst Grand Rapids Pub Lib, Grand Rapids Mich 62-64; Catlgr Mich State Lib, Lansing Mich 65-67, Ser libn 68-. 9: ALA; MichLA. 14: Catlg, ser. 15: 618 High st, Grand Rapids Mi 49509.

MATTHEW, JEANNETTE M. b St Louis 6 Mr 22. 4: Neil E Matthew. 5: Park Col 42-46 (Psych) BA. 6: Sp, Fr, Ger. 7: St Louis Pub Lib 42; Bkmob libn Denver Pub Lib 46-48; Columbia U Lib zool geol 48-50; Br libn NY Pub Lib 50-51; Tech libn Adjutant Gens Sch Lib, Ft Harrison Ind 51-56; Ind U Indianapolis Campus Lib & Soc Serv Lib Libn 56-. 8: Exec dir Nat Lib Week, Ind, 63-64. 9: SLA (chm Memb Com 57-61, mem Personnel Com 62-; Ind Chap: pres 56-57); ALA; IndLA. 10: Adult Educ Coun of Indianapolis; Commun Manpower Planning Com; YWCA; Ind Hist Assn. 13: Yes. 14: Admin, tech proc. 15: Ind Univ, 518 N Delaware st, Indianapolis In 46204.

MATTHEW, SISTER MARY (WACHA) OP. b Montcalm Co Mich 16 Je 1897. 5: Western State Col 20, 46 (LS); Aquinas Col 25 Life Certif; UNotre Dame 36; Central State Col 45 BS. 7: Tchr Dominican Sisters (Mich) 18-, Libn & tchr 61-65, libn 65-. 9: ALA; CathLA; MichASchL. 14: Rare bks, ref. 15: 723 Rosewood SE, Grand Rapids Mich 49506.

MATTHEWS, (GERTRUDE) ANN (URCH). b Jackson Mich 16 Jl 21. 5: Jackson Jr Col 39-41 (Eng) AA; Albion Col 41 (Eng); UMich 56-58 (Pol Sci) BA, 56-59 MS LA. 6: Fr. 7: Adult serv Jackson Pub Lib, Jackson Mich 56-64 Asst dir Franklin Sylvester Lib, medina Ohio 64-. 9: ALA (past mem Memb Com); MichLA (past mem Legis Com, Off Dist Div). 10: AAUW; LWV; Medina Co (Ohio) Hist So. 13: Yes. 14: Ref, pub rel. 15: 750 Weymouth rd, Medina Ohio 44256.

MATTHEWS, DONALD NATHANIEL. b Allentown Penn 20 Ag 30. 4: Elaine C Steinmetz. 5: Lafayette Col 49-53 (Philos) AB; Princeton Theol Sem 53-56 BD; Drew U 56-57 (Phil of Rel); Rutgers 57-59 MLS. 7: Sr clerk Rutgers U (Newar) 57-59; Catlgr & prof asst Lutheran Theol Sem (Gettysburg Penn) 59-61; Asst libn Lafayette Col Lib 61-66; Libn Lutheran Theol Sem (Gettysburg Penn) 66-. 9: ALA-ACRL; -ALTA. 10: AAUP. 13: Yes. 14: Admin, ref. 15: Lutheran Theological Sem, Gettysburg Pa 17325.

MATTHEWS, DONNA MAE. b Canby Mnn 20 Ap 33. 5: Drake U 53-57 (Sociol) BA; West Res 57-58 MS in LS. 6: Sp. 7: Asst Des Moines Pub Lib, Des Moines Iowa 51-57; Child libn Enoch Pratt Free Lib, Baltimore 58-60; Army libn Spec Serv, Stuttgart Germany 60-62; Asst under dir of child wk Arcadia Pub Lib, Arcadia Cal 62-63; Head of boys & girls dept Reg Lib, Hyattsville Md 63-65;Child libn Dist Lib, Wash DC 65-68; Spec wk with childs Ya Bur Lib Ext, Boston Mass 68-. 9: ALA (Good Reading for Youth Com 64-); MassLA; NELA. 10: AAUW. 14: Child serv. 15: 648 Beacon st, Boston Ma 02215.

MATTHEWS, ELIZABETH (WOODFIN). b Ashland Va 30 Jl 27. 4: Sidney E Matthews. 5: Randolph Macon Col 44-48 (Eng) BA; UIll 51-52 (LS) MS, 63 MedLA Certif. 6: Fr, Ger, Lat. 7: Asst order dept Va State Lib, Richmond 48-49; Asst browsing room UNC (Chapel Hill) 49-50; Asst order VPI 50-51; Catlgr (sci & med) Ohio StateU (Columbus) 52-59; Act hd catlg dept Battelle Memorial Inst, Columbus Ohio 56; Catlgr UIll (Urbana) 62-63; Catlgr Va Military Inst 63-64; Catlgr So IllU 64-67, Instr in catlg Dept Instr Materials 67-. 8:

Instr pub libns wkshop in processing Ill State Lib UIll 68; Visiting lecturer UIll (Urbana) summer 64. 9: VaLA; IllLA. 10: AAUW; Beta Phi Mu. 14: Catlg, instr in catlg, med libnship. 15: 811 Skyline dr, Carbondale Il 62901.

MATTHEWS, FRED W. b Newfoundland Can 27 N 15. 4: Phyllis McLeod. 5: Mt Allison U (NB) 36 (Chem) BS; McGill 41 (Phys Chem) PD. 6: Fr. 7: Can Industries Ltd: Group leader research dept 41-55, Asst gen manager chem dept 55-5, Spec studies & lib serv development dept 57-60, Head tech lit center research dept 61-. 9: Chem Inst of Can (Dir 55-60); Internat Union of Cristallography (chm Data Commsn 54-60). 13: Yes. 14: Electronic data proc for info storage & retrieval. 15: 235 Richelieu S, Mont St Hilaire Que Can.

MATTHEWS, GERALDINE ODESSA. b Memphis Tenn 18 Mr 31. 5: FiskU 49-53 (Hist) BA; AtlantaU 64-65 MSLS. 6: Fr, Sp. 7: Record tm clk Cuyahoga Co Welfare, Cleveland Ohio 54; Lib asst Cleveland (Ohio) Pub Lib 55-61; Sr lib asst UCLA 62-64; Hd libn Bluefield State Col 65-66; Act libn Bishop Col 67; Asst ed LC 68, Decimal clsf specialist 69-. 9: ALA. 14: Catlg. 15: 1669 Columbia rd NW apt 217, Washington DC 20009.

MATTHEWS, MARGERY I (HARRINGTON). b Foster RI 8 S 23. 4: Thomas J Matthews. 5: UR 41-44 (Home Econ) BS, 64-68 MLS; Rhode Island Col 68- (Educ). 7: Home econ Bristol- myers, NYC 44-45; Libn Ponaganset High Sch, Glocester RI 64-. 9: ALA; NEA; NESchLA; RISchLA (treas 65-69); RILA; RIEA. 10: Bd Trustees Tyler Free Lib, Foster RI. 15: Box A 30 RFD 2 Cucumber Hill rd, Foster RI 02825.

MATTHEWS, MARY ELIZABETH (HAMMER). b Sidney NY 12 F 44. 4: J Brian Matthews. 5: Hillsdale Col 61-62; URochester 62-65 (Hist) BA; Columbia 65-66 (LS) BS. 7: Lib trainee NY Pub Lib 65-66; Asst catlgr UAlaska 66-. 9: ALA; LARC; PNLA (Loc Arrts Chm, 1969 conf); AlaskaLA (chm loc chap 68-69). 12: Programmer and chief ed UAlaska's automated ser record (69). 14: Catlg, tech serv, automation. 15: PO Box 5-685, College Ak 99701.

MATTHEWS, RICHARD PERRY. b Milwaukee 2 O 20. 4: Merlena Gibbs. 5: Chicago 39-42 (Econ) AB; Yale 46-48 BSLS; ; UNC 48-49 BSLS; Columbia 51-55 MSLS. 7: Radar operator Signal Corps & USAAF 43-46; Catlg libn Rollins Col 49-51; Engnr libn Princeton U 51-59, Psych libn 59-61; Catlg libn Bowdoin Col 61-62; Catlgr US Mil Acad (W Point) 62-63; Readers adv Trenton State Col 63-. 9: NJLA. 15: 33 Patton dr, Trenton NJ 08618.

MATTHEWS, SIDNEY E. b Staunton Va 28 F 20. 4: Elizabeth Luck Woodfin. 5: Dunsmore Bus Col (Staunton Va) 39-40 (Accounting) Diploma; Randolph-Macon Col 41-43, 46-48 (Soc Sci) BA; UNC 49-50 BS in LS; UIll 52 MS in LS, 62-63 (LS). 6: Fr, Ger. 7: (S/Sgt) Admin US Army, US & Eng 43-46; Ref & circ libn Va Polytech Inst 50-51 Circ asst UIll(Urbana) 51-52, Bibliogr 52; Head ser div Ohio State U 52-53, Asst acquis libn 53-55, Acquis libn 56-59; Dir of Libs Va Mil Inst 59-64; Asst libn So Ill U 64-. 8: US Army QM Corps Res (Lt Col ret) 41-64; Consul Ball State U 68; Adv com lib aidtech program Sauk Valley Col 67-. 9: ALA (treas Com on Lib Automation 66-); RTSD (Com on Cost of Lib Materials Index; chm Duplicate Exchange Union); IllLA (treas 68-69; Automation Com; For Exchange Program; Com on Coop Col & Research Libs Sect). 10: AAUP; Rotary Internat; Beta Phi Mu; Kappa Alpha Order. 13: Yes. 14: Tech serv, automation, admin. 15: 811 Skyline dr, Carbondale Il 62901.

MATTHEWS, WINTON E(AHEART) JR. b Baton Rouge La 18 D 43. 5: Kemper Mil Sch & Jr Col 60-63; Rose Polytech Inst 63-64 (Math); LSU 64-66 (Educ) BS, 66-67 (LS) MS. 7: Subject catlgr LC 67-68, Decimal clsf specialist 68-. 14: Catlg. 15: 201 Mass ave NE #305A, Washington DC 20002.

MATTHIS, RAIMUND EUGEN. b La Grande Ore 3 Je 28. 5: UPuget Sound 53-58 (Fr) BA; UWASH 58-60 (LS) MA. 6: Fr, Ger. 7: (Sgt) US Ary, US, Europe 50-53; Psychiatric aide VA Hosp, Tacoma Wash 53-57; Lib trainee Tacoma Pub Lib, Tacoma Wash 57-60; Pub rel libn Pierce Co Pub Lib, Tacoma Wash 60-63; Tech serv libn UPuget Sound 63-. 8: Consul for conversion to LC Clsf Scheme: Pacific Luth U, 65-; Tacoma Commun Col, 65-. 9: Wash State LA. 14: Catlg, clsf. 15: 1502 N Mason, Tacoma Wash 98406.

MATTISON, DELIA (MAY). b Clyde Kan 25 Ap 13. 5: UArk 30-32, 35-37 (Eng, Lat) BSE: USoCal 47-48 MS in LS. 6: Sp. 7: Tchr Decatur High Sch, Decatur Ark 37-40; Tchr Springdale High Sch, Springdale Ark 40-42; Aircraft wker Douglas Aircraft(El Segundo Cal) 42-45; Tchr Bentonville High Sch, Bentonville Ark 46; UArk Lib; Jr asst 46-47, Lib asst 48-64, Asst libn Headof catlg dept 64-. 9: ALA; ArkLA; SWLA. 10: Beta Phi Mu. 14: Catlg. 15: 305 Kate Smith, Prairie Grove Ar 72753.

MATTISON, ELISABETH ROSA (TOWNE). b Schenectady NY 4 S 08. 4: Charles Wesley Mattison. 5: Cornell U 26-30 (Hist) AB; SUNY (Albany) 35-36 BS in LS. 7: Catlgr catlg sect USDA Lib Wash DC 46-49, Asst chief catlg & records sect 49-51, Bibliog 51-53; Head tech proc So Adirondack Lib System, Saratoga Springs NY 59-. 9: NYLA; Hudson-Mohawk LA. 10: AAUW, Phi Beta Kappa. 14: Catlg. 15: P O Box 29, Middle Grove NY 12850.

MATTISON, HELEN S. b Cloyds Landing Ky 2 S 17. 4: Howard S Mattison. 5: West Ky State Tchrs Col 34-38 (Eng) AB; Bowling Green Col of Com 42 Typing Fla State U 49-52 (LS) MA. 7: Tchr rural sch, Ky 38-41; Com tchr Tompkinsville High Sch, Ky 41-47; Tchr Millville Elem Sch, Panama Cty Fla 47-49; Libn Blountstown High Sch, Blountstown Fla 49-51; Libn Crawfordville High Sch, Crawfordville Fla 51-53; Libn Lakeland Jr High Sch, Lakeland Fla 53-57; Libn McArthur High Sch, Hollywood Fla 57-63; Dir of Resource Centers Nova High Sch, Ft Lauderdale Fla 63-68; Libn Prof Lib Broward Co Bd of Pub Instr 68-. 8: Eal coms, 3 Fla high schs, 60, 61, 65. 9: ALA; NEA; FlaEA; FlaSchL (sec 69-70); Fla A-V Assn; FlaLA; Broward Co Assn Media Spec. 13: Yes. 14: Ref. 15: 3641 SW 21st ct, Ft Lauderdale Fl 33312.

MATTISON, LESTER. b Melrose Minn 29 O 19. 4: Claudine Tiffany. 5: UMinn 57 BA, 61 (LS) MA. 6: Ger. 7: UMinn(Minneapolis): Libn 58-59, Asst to dir 59-61, Chief circ libn 61-; Dir Bemidji State Col 66-. 9: ALA; MinnLA. 10: ACLU; Delta Phi Lambda; Beta Phi Mu. 14: Admin. 15: 123 12th st, Bemidji Mn 56601.

MATTOX, EDNA EARLE (CANTER). b Houston 8 My 27. 4: Joseph Bluford Mattox. 5: Lamar Jr Col 44-46 AA; N Tex State Col 47-48, summer 50 BA in LS. 6: Fr. 7: Asst Jefferson Co Lib, Beaumont Tex 46-47; Libn Murray State Sch of Agric (Okla) 48-49; High sch libn Port Neches Ind Sch System, Port Neches Tex 49-51; Asst Jefferson Co Lib, Beaumont Tex 59-60; Libn Silsbee Jr High Sch, Silsbee Tex 60-68; Forest Pk High Sch Lib, Beaumont Tex 68-. 9: TexLA; Tex Clr Tchrs. 14: Ref, ya. 15: 3020 Minglewood dr, Beaumont Tex 77703.

MATTSON, LOIS ILENE (TEACHOUT). b Grand Rapids Mich 5 N 37. 4: Athur Mattson. 5: West MichU 57-59 (Eng) BA, 60-64 (Libnship) MA. 7: Libn Greenville High Sch, Greenville Mich 59-65; Libn Rudyard High Sch, Rudyard Mich 65-67; Elem libn Sault Area Pub Schs Sault Ste Marie Michigan 67-69; Asst libn catlg & acquis Lake Superior State Col 69-. 9: NEA; MichLA; MichASchL; MichEA. 14: Catlg, acquis. 15: 106 W 19th, Sault Ste Marie Mi 49783.

MATYAS, MADELEINE SUZANNE. b Montreal Can 12 S 39. 5: Syracuse 57-61 (Internat rel) BA; UCLA 62-63 MLS. 6: Fr. 7: Typist-Receptionist Wis Dept of Taxation, Madison Wis 61-62; NY Pub Lib 63-65; Art Lib UCLA 66-. 10: Japan Soc of NY. 14: Acquis, ref, catlg. 15: 19 Majestic ave, Lincroft NJ 07738.

MATZEK, RICHARD A. b Milwaukee Wis 18 N 37. 4: Ann Lynne (Erickson) Matzek. 5: Marquette 55-59 (Eng, Lat) BA (Cum Laude); UWis 60 (LS) MA. 6: Lat, Fr. 7: Libn I Wis Free Lib Commsn 60; Sgt USA 32nd div, Ft Lewis Wash 61-62; Libn I Marquette U 62-63; Asst libn Sacred Heart U, Bridgeport Conn 63-66, Hd libn 66-. 8: Assoc Editor, Catholic Bookseller & Librarian 67. 9: ALA; CathLA; NELA; Tri-Univ Libns (chm A-V Coop Com). 10: Eta Sigma Phi. 12: Co-auth "Reward of Reading"; Ed "Subject Guide to new Catholic Books" 67-. 13: Yes. 14: Lib bldg, coop, admin. 15: 4977 Main st, Bridgeport Ct 06606.

MAUDSLIEN, CLIFTON NORRIS. b Seattle Wash 6 My 43. 4: Linda Evelyn Kowing Maudslien. 5: Pacific Lutheran U 61-64 (Hist); UWash 64-66 (Hist) BA in Ed, 66-67 MLS. 7: Libn Highline High Sch, Seattle 67-. 10: Amer Field Serv Sch Adv. 13: Yes. 14: Microfilm. 15: 16923 - 32nd SW, Seattle Wa 98166.

MAULDIN, ELLEN (DRANE). b Mayhew Miss 25 Ag 34. 4: Thomas A Mauldin. 5: Miss State U 52-56 (Hosp Admin) BS; Fla State U 56-57 (LS) MS. 7: Stud asst Mitchell Mem Lib Miss State U 52-56; Off clerk Gen Hosp, Greenville Miss summers 53-55; Grad asst Fla State U Lib 56-57; Asst acquislibn acquis libn Lib 57-58; Ser libn Pub Lib of Charlotte & Mecklenburg Co, Charlotte NC 58-67; Ser libn Mitchell Mem Lib Miss State U. 8: Spec assignment (for the

Mecklenburg LA) to compile a Union List of Period Holdings in Mecklenburg Co by Using g data processing procedures. 9: ALA; MecklenburgLA (chm spec projs com 64-66); SELA; MissLA. 10: Pilot Club Starkville. 12: Ed "Down Library Lane; (59-). 14: Ser, ref. 15: 503 Green st, Starkville Ms 39559.

MAULDIN, EUGENIA EFFIE. b Baldwyn Miss 4 N 16. 5: Millsaps Col 34-38 (Eng, Soc Sci) BA; UMiss -50 (Guidance) M Ed; UIll -56 (LS) MS. 7: Eng tchr Carmichael High Sch, Carmichael Miss 38-39; Tchr Ashland Elem Sch, Ashland Miss 39-41; Tchr Glen Allan Elem Sch, Glen Allan Miss 41-42 Tchr Guntown Elem Sch, Guntown Miss 42-43; US Navy WAVES Hosp Corps 43-45; Tchr New Albany Elem Sch, New Albany Miss 46-47; Libn Baldwyn High Sch, Baldwyn Miss 47-51; US Navy WAVES Navy Recruiting 51-54; Tchg asstship UIll Lib Sch 55-56; Libn Corinth High Sch, Corinth Miss 65-57; Asst Prof Lib Serv & A-v Educ UTenn Col of Educ Dept of Lib Serv 57-. 9: ALA; Coun rep of TennLA 66-69; Recr rep for Tenn 66-69; -AASCHL; NEA-DAVI; TennLA chm Recr Com, chm Recr for Libnship Com 69-70); MissLA; TennEA; SELA. 10: AAUP; Pi Lambda Theta; Alpha Beta Alpha; Wesleyan Serv Guild; UTenn Wesley Found. 12: Act ed "Tennessee Librarian (58-59). 13: Yes. 14: Child & yp, admin, a-v methods & tech. 15: UTenn Claxton Ed Bldg 308, Knoxville Tenn 37916.

MAUNEY, GLORIA (JUANITA MEANS). b SC 26 F 28. 4: Percy E Mauney. 5: Allen U 45-49 (Ed) BS in Ed; Catholic U 56-68 MSLS; DC Tchrs Col 68- (Ed). 6: Fr, Sp. 7: Tchr Harbison Jr Col, Irmo SC 49-50; Lib asst: US DA Lib, Wash DC 53-54, USN Bur Ord Lib, Wash DC 54-56, Smithsonian Inst Lib 56-60; Ref libn Smithsonian Inst Lib 60-65; Libn Burdick Voc High DC Pub Sch 65-66; Br libn dept of entomology lib Smithsonian Inst 66-68; Libn Eugene A Clark Elem Sch, Wash DC 68-. 9: ALA; NEA; DCLA; DCASchL. 10: DC Cong of Parents & Tchrs; Alpha Kappa Alpha; Alpha Wives of Wash DC; NAACP; Urban League; YWCA. 13: Yes. 14: Child bks, sch libs, ref. 15: 23 Jefferson st NE, Wash DC 20011.

MAUPIN, ALFRED J. b Knoxville Tenn 24 Ap 31. 4: Lily Malik. 5: UChattanooga 49-52 (Sp) BA; UIowa 52-53 (Sp); Emory U 59-61 MLS. 6: Sp, Fr, Russian. 7: USA Military intelligence 53-56; Advertising copywriter WATE-TV, Knoxville Tenn 56-59; Acquis libn Stanislaus State Col 61-63; Tech processes libn Ampex Corp, Redwood City Cal 63-64; Sr libn bus & econ dept LA Pub Lib 64-68; Chief libn Development Research Assocs, LA 68-. 8: Buenos Aires Convention Fellowship in Honduras 53. 9: SLA (Prog Chm Transp Div 68; Adv Coun SoCal Chap 68-69); CalLA (pres Bus & Indus Div 68-69); Coun Planning Libns (Memb Chm 68-69). 13: Yes. 15: 731 S Flower st, Los Angeles Ca 90017.

MAURER, CHARLES D(ELBERT) JR. b Malden Mass 15 Jl 26. 4: Alice Woodbury. 5: Boston U 43-45, 46-47 (Hist) AB, 47-48, 53 (Tchg, Soc Studies) M Ed; Simmons 49-50 MS. 7: Pre-aviation cadet US Army Air Corps, US 45; Life Insurance salesman John HANCOCK Mutual Life, Boston 48-49; Bkmob libn Columbiana Co, Lisbon Ohio 50-51; Ext libn in chg of Keene Br Off BrOff NH State Lib, Keene NH 51-60; Col libn Plymouth Tchrs Col, Plymouth NH 60-63; Dir Rutland Free Lib, Rutland Vt 63-. 9: ALA; NELA (Reg Planning Com); VtLA (Exec Bd). 10: Phi Beta Kappa. 13: Yes. 14: Ext, ref, bk sel, admin. 15: 107 Church st, Rutland Vt 05701.

MAURER, ESTHER JUNE. b Mt Carmel Penn. 5: Houghton Col 46-50 (Eng) AB; UPenn 51-52, 53 (Eng) MA; Drexel 52-53 MS in LS. 7: Free Lib of Phila; Libn I Circ Dept & Main Reading Room 53-54, Libn I Educ Philos & Religion Dept 54-57, Asst Off of Wk with Adults 57-60, Admin asst Educ Philos & Religion Dept 60-. 9: ALA; PennLA (chm Conf Eval Com 63). 10: Phila Art Alliance. 14: Ref, adult serv. 15: 2309 Green st, Phila Pa 19130.

MAURER, ETHEL JANE. b Beaver Corssing Neb. 5: UNeb 36 (Eng) AB; Columbia summers 38, 39, 43, 45; West Res 49 BSLS. 6: Fr. 7: Tchr Walnut Jr High Sch, Grand Island Neb 36-44; Libn 44-47; Ref asst Lincoln City Libs, Lincoln Neb 47-57; Ref libn Neb Pub Lib Com, Lincoln Neb 57-59; Ref libn Lincoln City Libs, Lincoln Neb 59-68; Hd ref dept 69-. 9: NebLA (treas 51). 14: Ref, theater lib. 15: 3123 South st, Lincoln Nb 68502.

MAURICE, JEWELL. b Palo Pinto Tex 1 O 15. 5: N Tex U 33-36 (Biol) BS; LSU 37-38 (LS) BS; Chicago summer 42 (LS). 7: Lib asst Southwestern La Inst 3842; Ref libn LSU Med Sch 43-44; Chem libn Ind U 44-46; Supv of Tech Processes Sci Lib Eli Lilly & Co 46-. 9: MedLA; SLA (Reg Rep Memb Com 54-56; Pharmaceutical Sect; Pub Rel Proj 53, chm Memb Com 53-54, v-chm 54-55, chm 55-56; Ind Chap; Research Projs Com 49-62, Archives chm 60-). 12: Co-comp "Bacteriological Reviews, Index to Authors and Subjects" (Vols 1-10, 37-46). 13: Yes. 14: Tech processes. 15: 5324 Carrollton A6, Indianapolis In 46220.

MAUS, JUSTINA B. b Watkins Mn 13 F 10. 5: UCal(Berkeley) 46-48 (Psy, Psych, Hist) Col of St Catherine 52-53 BS in LS. 6: Ger. 7; auc wac mil Intelligence, ETO (Capt) 44-46; Libn Col St Joseph (Albuquerque NM) 53-55; Ref & research Dept of Hist & World Affairs, San Diego Cal 55-58; Libn Archbishop Murray High Sch, St Paul 58-59; Sr catlgr Pius XII Mem Lib, St Louis U 59-64; Asst libn Prospect Park Br Lib, Albuquerque NM 64-65; Libn Erna Fergusson Br Lib, AlbuquerqueNM 66-; Gen asst libs Visitation Monastery, St Paull 66-68; Art ref libn UNo Ill (DeKalb) 68-. 8: Tchr Amer Dependent Schs, Japan 48-50. 9: CathLA (sub-chm for Publicity, 1961 Conv); Albuquerque LA (treas 54-55). 10: NM Hist Soc. 13: Yes. 14: Ref, display wk. 15: 443 College ave apt 2B, DeKalb Il 60115.

MAUS, SISTER SCHOLASTICA OSB. b Cold Spring Minn 3 S 01. 5: State Col Dickinson ND 37-38; State Col (St Cloud Minn) (Elem Educ); Col of St Benedict (St Cloud Minn); Col of St Catherine 54(LS) BS; Col of St Thomas 59 (Sec Sch Admin) MA; NDEA Inst U Minn summer 65. 6: Ger. 7: Elem tchr, St Cloud Minn 29-37, 39-43; Elem tchr & prin, Richmond Minn 43-48; Jr high tchr, prin, Stillwater Minn 48-55; Jr high tchr, Robbinsdale Minn 55-56; Jr high tchr, prin St Huberts Sch, Chanhassen Minn 56-59; Libn Archbishop Murray Mem High Sch, St Paul 59-. 9: ALA; CathLA (chm Minn-Dakota Unit 61-62, chm Legis Com 64-66); MinASchL; Amer Benedictine Acad (rec Lib Sect 66-67). 10: Amer Benedictine Acad (Nat). 14: Ref, rare bks. 15: St Pauls Priory 2675 Larpenteur ave E, St Paul Mn 55109.

MAUSETH, BARBARA J(OANNE). b Mt Vernon Wash 29 S 30. 5: Pacific U 48-52 (Journalism) BA; UWash 54-56 MALS. 7: Intern Ketchikan ub Lib, Ketchikan Alaska summer 56; Asst bkmob libnYakima Wash 56-60; Cooperative processing center libn Nv State Lib 60-61, Lib consul 61-, Dir field serv div 61-. 9: ALA (State Recr Com chm; State Mem Com chm); NevLA (sec 63-65); MPLA (Rec sec 63-65, State rep from Nev 61-). 11: Special Citation, NebLA 68. 12: Ed ""Nevada Library Notes; Ed ""Nevada Libraries. 14: Ext of lib serv, development of programs. 15: P O Box 736, Carson City Nev 89701.

MAUSETH,JAMES O(LIVER). b Rice Lake Wis 18 Je 27. 5: Macalester Col 48-52 (Internat Studies, Span) BA; UMinn 52-53 (LS) MA. 7: Asst libn catlg Carthage Col 53-59; Asst libn tech serv N State Tchrs Col Aberdeen SD 59-61; Assoc dir of lib N State Col (Aberdeen SD) 61-66, Act dir of lib 66-67, Dir of lib 67-. 9: ALA; Geneal Soc NJ; MPLA; SDLA. 10: Phi Delta Kappa; AAUP; Elks; Geneal Soc NJ. 14: Catlg. 15: No State Col Lib, Ab erdeen SD 57401.

MAUTER, GEORGE A. b Brooklyn NY 3 Je 42. 4: Amy Forsman. 5: Muhlenberg Col 60-63 (Sociol); Hofstra 64-65 (Sociol) BA; Pratt Inst 66-67 MLS. 7: Ref asst Freeport Memorial Lib, Freeport NY 64-65, Libn trainee 65-66; Libn Urban Amer Inc, NYC 66; Doc libn Grumman Aircraft Engring Corp, Bethpage NY 67-. 9: SLA. 14: Info stor & retr, lib automation, lib admin. 15: 90 Jervis ave, Farmingdale NY 11735.

MAUTNER, ROBERT W. b Los angeles 24 S 25. 4: Helen Gluck. 5: George Washington U Psych) (Psyc); UCal(Berkeley) 48-49 (Psych) BA, 51-52 BLS. 7: Asst law libn Cal State Lib 52-55; Ref libn Hollywood Pub Lib, Los Angeles 55-56; Engnr libn Rocketdyne, Canoga Park Cal 56; Period libn Los Angeles State Col 56-60; Head sci & tech Sacramento State Col 60-65; Chief sci libn UAriz 65-, Act asst libn for brs 68-. 9: ALA; Ariz State LA (past pres) & Univ Div); chm Lib Adv Serv Com. 10: AAUP; ACLU; AAUP; Ariz Acad Sci. 14: Admin, ref. 15: 2122 E Mitchell, Tucson Az 85719.

MAVITY, JOAN (PUMPHREY). b San Francisco Cal 5 S 22. 5: UCal (Berkeley) 40-45 9zoology) BA; UWash (Seattle) 61-62 MLS. 7: Libn: NYC Pub Lib 62-63, Nat Lib of Med, Bethesda Md 63-65, Nat Clearinghouse for Mental Health Info, Bethesda Md 65-66, Herner & Co, Wash DC 66-67, Nat Inst of Health, Bethesda Md 67-. 14: Info retr, lib systems. 15: 6702 Hillandale rd #22, Chevy Chase Md 20015.

MAVROMATIS, ELINA (HANNULA). b Glens Falls NY 19 Je 43. 4: John Mavromatis. 5: Keuka Col 61-65 (Hist) BA; UPittsburgh 66-67 MLS. 7: Libn child rm Carnegie Lib of pittsburgh 67-. 9: ALA. 10: Beta Phi Mu. 14: Child lit. 15: 4350 Murray ave, Pittsburgh Pa 15217.

MAW, VIRGINIA (BOOKAMER). b Elwood City Pa 8 Ag 14. 5: Anderson Col 3-41 (Eng) AB; IndU 41-42, 43 (Educ) MA; Buena Vista Col 42 (practice tchg); Slippery Rock State Tchrs Col summer 54 (Hist); Westminster Col 55- (AV); UCal(Berkeley) summers 59-62 MLS. 6: Fr. 7: Tchr Alta Consolidated High Sch, Alta Iowa 42-43; Tchr Addison Road Sch, Durban S Africa 44-45; Tchr Penhale Road Girls Sch, Portsmouth Eng 46; Tchr Lincoln High Sch, Ellwood City Penn 46-47; Tchr Ventura Col 48-52; Prin Ewing Park Sch, Ellwood City Penn 54-55; Tchr Mercer High Sch, Mercer Penn 55-57; Tchr-libn Cuyama Valley High Sch, New Cuyama Cal 57-62 Libn Ernest Righetti High Sch, Santa Maria al 62-67; Libn Sacramento City Col 67-68; Instr lib educ UVictoria (BC) summers 67-68; Assoc Prof & Dir of program in Lib Sci, Sacramento State Col. 8: Santa Barbara Co Schs Lib Coun, 64; Santa Barbara Co Schs A-V Adv Coun 64-. 9: ALA, CalLA; CalASchL; ClrTA. 10: Beta Phi Mu. 14: Ref, acquis. 15: 5831 Fair Oaks Blvd apt 14, Carmichael Ca 95608.

MAWHIR, PRISCILLA (WHITE). b Moravia NY 18 My 28. 4: George Mawhir. 5: Geneseo State Tchrs Col 45-49 (LS) BS in Educ; Syracuse 63-. 7: Libn Brocton Central Sch, Brocton NY 49-51; Libn Moravia Central Sch, Moravia NY 54-55, 59, 63-. 10: Moravia Commun Theatre. 15: 21 S Main st, Moravia NY 13118.

MAX, GEORGE DONALD. b Cleveland 4 My 14. 4: Jane Miller. 5: Hiram Col 32-36 (Ger, Eng) BA; Ohio State U 38 (Amer Lit); West Res 39 (Amer Lit); Pratt 46-47 (LS) BS; Simmons 54 (LS) MS. 6: Ger. 7: Chief searching sect ref dept NY Pub Lib 46-48; AFCRL-USAF, Cambridge Mass: Asst libn Geophysics Research Lib 48-53, Chief sci lit 53-56, Chief tech info & intelligence 56-60; Mgr tech info serv Sperry Rand Res Center, Sudbury Mass 60-. 9: ASIS. 15: 30 Magnolia dr, Sudbury Ma 01776.

MAXFIELD, DAVID K(EMPTON). b Waterville Me 12 My 13. 4: Grace Kline. 5: Haverford 36 (Hist) BS; Columbia 37 (Univ lib admin) BS in LS, 46 (Univ lib admin) MS in LS. 6: Fr, Ger. 7: Asst libn School of Journalism Columbia Univ (NYC) 37-39; Asst libn The Cooper Union, NYC 39143, Act hd libn 43-44; Pharmacists Mate, US Navy 44-46; Libn UIll Chicago undergrad div 46-55; Asst to dir UMich Lib (Ann Arbor) 56-59, Med ctr libn 59-. 9: ALA; BSA; MedLA. 10: Washtenaw (Co) Lib Club; Beta Phi Mu; Amer Philat Soc; Mich Hist Soc. 12: Ed "ACRL Monographs" 52-56. 13: Yes. 14: Lib automation. 15: 2217 Manchester rd, Ann Arbor Mi 48104.

MAXFIELD, GRACE (KLINE). b Amsterdam NY 1 Je 14. 4: David K Maxfield. 5: NY State U Col (Albany) 32-36 (Fr) AB (cum laude); Columbia 36-37 BS in LS. 6: Fr, S. 7: Jr catlgr Columbia U Lib 37-41; catlgr Columbia U Med Lib 44-46; Catlgr John Crerar Lib, Chicago 48-49; Sr catlgr UChicago Lib 49-56; Asst libn UMich Law Lib 56-57, Ser catlgr 57-58; Asst catlg libn East Mich U 58-67, Hd catlg libn 68-. 9: ALA; Ann Arbor Lib Club. 14: Catlg, ref. 15: 2217 Manchester rd, Ann Arbor Mi 48104.

MAXIAN, M BRUCE. b Flushing NY 7 Ag 37. 4: Constance Buell. 5: UMich 55-56; Tulane 56-61 (Eng) BA; Hofstra U 61-62; Carleton & Winthrop Palmer Grad Lib Sch of LIU 62-64 MS in LS. 6: Ger, Sp. 7: Grad asst res bk room C W Post Col Lib 62-63, Catlgr 63-66; Instr Carleton & Winthrop Palmer Grad Lib Sch of LiU 64-. 66, Asst Prof ofLib Sci 66-. 9: ALA; NYLA; NCLA (Exec Com); SCLA. 10: Va Mus ofFine Arts, AAUP; NY Lib Club. 13: Yes. 14: Tech procesing, ref, computer sci, documentation, materials 15: 7 Janes la, Huntington NY 11743.

MAXIM, BRADLEY CLARENCE. b Winslow Me 3 Ap 22. 4: Barbara Jackson. 5: Bowdoin Col 41-42; Colby Col 44-47 (Eng) BA; Bread Loaf Sch of Eng 50; Columbia 50-53 MS(LS); Chicago 61-63 (LS). 7: Volunteer Amer Field Serv 42-44; Tchr Ft Fairfield High Sch, Ft Fairfield Me 47-48; Tchr Lawrence High Sch, Fairfield Me 48-50; Libn preprof & grade II Brooklyn Pub Lib 50-54; Catlg & order libn UMich 54-55; Catlg libn East Mich U 55-58; Catlg libn East NMU 58-64; Asst Prof Grad Sch Lib ib Sci UTex 64-67, Catlg libn 67-. 9: ALA; ASIS; SWLA; TexLA (chm 68-69, catlgrs & clsfrs RT). 10: ACLU; Phi Beta Kappa; Beta Phi Mu. 14: Tech serv, automation. 15: Lib Univ Tex, Austin Tx 78712.

MAXIMENA, DELORES ELEANOR. b Detroit 2 Ja 29. 5: UMCH 46-50 (Chem BA, 63-67 (LS) MLS. 7: Research reports libn GM Research Labs, Warren Mich 50-, Ref libn. 9: SLA (Mich Chap: Program & Hospitality Coms), (chm Lehigh Valley Chap 68-69). 10: ACS. 14: Ref, ext wk. 15: Lib GM Res Labs 12 Mile & Mound rds, Warren Mi 48090.

MAXTON, PAULINE LAURA. b Birdsboro Penn 15 Mr 20. 5: Kutztown State Col 38-42 (LS, Eng) BS in Ed; Columbia summer 44 (Sci); Albright Col summer 45; Drexel 49-50 MS in LS. 7: Tchr-libn High Sch, Mt Union Penn 42-43; Tchr High Sch, Spring City Penn 43-45; Tchr-libn Oley High Sch, Oley Pa 45-47; Pub Lib, Reading Penn: Asst ref libn 47-49, Head ref dept 49-61, Asst dir & head ref dept 61-65, Act dir 65-66, Asst dir 66-. 9: ALA; PennLA (chm Lehigh Valley Chap 68-69). 14: Ref. 15: Pub Lib 5th & Franklin sts, Reading Penn 19602.

MAXWELL, BARBARA A. b Pittsburgh 9 Je 37. 5: Wilson Col 55-59 (Fr) AB; Drexel 59-60 MS in LS. 6: Fr. 7: Ref, Catlg E I duPont de Nemours & Co, Wilmington Del 60-61; Asst ref libn Duquesne U Lib 61-63, Head of ref serv 63-66; Ref libn UDel 66-. 9: ALA-ACRL; SLA; PennLA; DelLA. 10: Beta Phi Mu. 14: Ref. 15: Apt E7 Park Place Apts, 655 Lehigh rd, Newark De 19711.

MAXWELL, BARBARA. b Greeley Col O 41. 4: Douglas L Maxwell. 5: Pomona 58-62 (Mus) BA; UCal (Berkeley) 62-65 (Mus) MA, 65-67 MLS. 6: Fr, Ger. 7: Lib asst UCal 9berkeley) 63-66, Ref libn 66-. 9: ALA; CalLA; Libn's Assn UCal. 10: Amer Musicol Soc. 14: Ref. 15: 2420 Virginia st 106, Berkeley Ca 94709.

MAXWELL, JAMES GEORGE. b Junction City Ore 7 N 36. 4: Dolores Kowsun. 5: Ore State U 55-59 (Ed) BS; UOre 61-65 MLS; Wayne State 66-67 (LS). 7: Tchr Knox Butte Sch Dist, Albany Ore 59-63; Elem sch libn Parkrose Sch Dist, Portland Ore 63-66, 67-68, Jr High Sch libn & a-v coord 68-. 8: Instr in NDEA A-V Inst summer 66; Consul Ore Div Cont educ; ITV Ser on Self-Learning Skills, Ore Bd of Educ summer 68. 9: NEA; -DAVI; ALA; -AASchL; OreEA; Ore Instr Media Assn; OreASchL. 14: Educ media. 15: 310 NE 147th st, Portland Or 97230.

MAXWELL, JOHN J. b Rome NY 1 Ja 09. 4: Barbara Brown. 5: UNotre Dame 29-32; URochester 32-35 (Eng) BA; USoCal 57-60 MS in LS. 7: Asst order libn UCal(Riverside) 60-62, Asst ref libn 63-. 9: ALA; CalLA. 14: Ref. 15: 3597 Pine st, Riverside Cal 92501.

MAXWELL, LITTLETON MILLER. b Lynchburg Va 24 O 40. 4: Mary McCormick. 5: Randolph-Macon Col 58-62 (Hist) AB; UVa 62-63 (Law); UKy 67-68 MS in LS. 7: Page & Page Foreman Richmond Pub Lib, Richmond Va 64-66; Library asst Lynchburg Pub Lib, Lynchburg Va 66; Lib asst in charge Campbell Co Pub Lib, Rustburg Va 66-67; Adult serv libn, acting br hd Henrico Co Pub Lib, Richmond Va 69-. 9: ALA; VaLA; SELA. 10: Kappa Alpha. 14: Ref, adult serv. 15: 6 Camelot cir, Richmond Va 23229.

MAXWELL, LOLA E. b Penn 23 N 29. 5: Clarion State Col 47-51 BSLS; UPittsburgh 54 9educ) MEd; Rutgers 67 MLS. 7: High sch lib, Vandergrift Penn 51-54; Army libn US Army, Nurnberg Germany 54-56; Asst libn Alcoa Research Lab, New Kensington Penn 56-61; Elem libn Bloomsburg State Col 61-67; Elem lib California State Col (California Penn) 67-. 9: ALA; NEA; PennStateEA. PennLA. 14: Child wk. 15: 2845 Leechburg rd, New Kensington Pa 15068.

MAXWELL, MARGARET (FINLAYSON). b Schenectady NY 9 S 27. 4: Dr WleGrand Maxwell. 5: Pomona Col 44-48 (Eng) BA; UCal 50 (Berkeley) BLS; George Washington U 50-54 (Eng) MA; UMich 68- (LS). 7: Intern, staff LC 50-56; Assoc libn Upper Iowa U 56-66, Asst Prof 66-68. 8: Consul Fayette (Iowa) Elem Sch Lib summer 67. 9: ALA. 10: Amer Guild of Organists; Phil Beta Kappa. 12: "Finlayson, Man of Destiny" (60); "Pioneer Plains Sorghum Cook Book" (63). 13: Yes. 14: Catlg, lib educ. 15: 1124 Olivia st, Ann Arbor Mi 48104.

MAXWELL, MARY (McCORMICK). b Danville Va 16 Mr 44. 4: Littleton Miller Maxwell. 5: Emory & Henry Col 62-66 (Eng) BA; UNC 66-67 MS in LS. 7: Stud asst Emory & Henry Col Lib 64-66; Lib asst Lynchburg Pub Lib, Lynchburg Va 66; Hd libn Wood ford Co Pub Lib, Versailles Ky 67-68; Ref libn Henrico Co Pub Lib, Richmond Va 69-. 9: ALA; SELA; VaLA. 10: Beta Phi Mu. 14: Ref, child wk. 15: 6 Camelot cir, Richmond Va 23229.

MAXWELL, NORRIS KNOX. b El Paso Tex 4 Ag 20. 4: Katherine Marian Bridges. 5: Tex West Col 38-40 (Educ); UTex 61-63 (Educ) BS in Ed, 63-65 MLS. 7: US Army Lt Col Infantry 40-61; Intern UNM Lib 64-65, Readers serv libn 65-. 9: ALA; NMLA. 14: Lib admin. 15: Zimmerman Lib UNM, Albuquerque NM.

MAXWELL, SHEILA CORINNE. b Toronto Ont Can 31 D 32. 5: UToronto 50-54 (Household Econ) BA, 61-62 BLS, 65-67 MLS. 7: Lab tech Newlands Co Ltd, Galt Ont 54-55; Bell Tele Co of Can, Toronto: Asst engring 56-61, Libn co lib 62-63, chief libn co lib Montreal, Que 63-65; Libn engring lib UToronto 65-67; Libn Ont Med Assoc, Toronto 68-. 9: SLA (Toronto Chap; sec 66-68, pres-elect 68-69, pres 69-70); MedLA; Inst Prof Libns Ont (Bd 68-69). 14: Ref. 15: 86 Delemere ave, Toronto Ont Can.

MAXYMUK, REYA (AUDREY RHINE). b Boston Mass 25 S 38. 4: Walter O Maxymuk. 5: William & Mary 56-61 (Fr) AB; Drexel 63-64 MSLS. 6: Fr. 7: Lib asst MIT Engring Lib 61-63; Asst libn Chester Co Lib, W Chester Penn 64-65; Gen ref libn Drexel Inst 65-67; Asst libn Lib for the Blind Free Lib of Phila 67; Catlgr Reg Campus Libs IndU (Bloomington) 67-69. 9: ALA. 14: Ref, catlg. 15: 3008 Fenwood ave, Terre Haute In 47803.

MAY, CORNELIA ETHEL. b Six Lakes Mich 3 D 21. 5: Owosso Bible Col 50-51; Greenville Col 51-53 (Eng) AB; UMich 54-57 (LS) AM; Ohio State U 66-69 (Eng) MA. 7: Tchr-Libn Vandercock Lake High Sch, Jackson Mich 53-54; Catlgr & Asst libn Greenville Col Lib 54-65; Ser catlgr Ohio State U Libs 65-68; Libn Greenville Col 68. 9: ALA; IllLA; OhioLA. 10: Christian Libns Fellowship Beta Phi Mu. 14: Catlg. 15: Greenville Coll Lib, Greenville Il 62246.

MAY, F CURTIS . b Santa Maria Cal 28 Ap 30. 5: City Col (San Francisco) 48-50 AA; 50-53 0-53 (Pol Sci) AB, Gen Secondary Credential; UDenver 57-58 (LS) MA, 67-68 (Higher Educ & LS). 7: US Army Ft Hood Tex 53-55; Tchr Delano High Sch, Delano Cal 55-57; Libn Highlands High Sch, N Highlands Cal 58-60; Hd Libn Sequoia Hgh Sch, Redwood City Cal 60-; Instr UDenver Grad Lib Sch summers 63, 65. 8: Lib 21 staff, summer 62; Ad hoc consultant Cal State Dept of Educ for ESEA Title II 65-67. 9: ALA Memb chm No Sect); Cal Tchrs Assn; Sequoia Dist Tchrs Assn (treas 4 yrs). 10: AAUP; Phi Delta Kappa, Kappa Delta Pi. 14: Sch libnship. 15: 216 Swett rd, Woodside Ca 94062.

MAY, JOANNE M. b Green Bay Wis 12 F 42. 5: Chestnut Hill Col 60-64 (Bio) BA; Villanova U 64-67 MSLS. 7: Tech libn: Shell Chemical Co, Woodbury NJ 66-69, West Electric Co Corp Educ Ctr, Princeton NJ 69-. 9: ALA; SLA. 14: Tech libs. 15: 8309 Cadwalader ave, Phila Pa 19117.

MAY, JOHN RYAN. b Cross Plains Ind 30 Je 15. 4: Felicia Markulis. 5: IndU 34-38 (Hist) AB, UIll 42-52 (summer) MSLS. 7: Libn Butler U Col of Pharmacy 38-47; Libn anderson Sr High Sch, Anderson Ind 47-50; Libn & a-v dir Pub sch, Crawfordsville Ind 50-53; Hd ser unit Purdue U Lib 53-58; Libn Van Zoren Lib Hope Col 58-69; Dir of lib Ctr Col of NY 69-. 9: ALA (past Sec Circ Serv Sect); MichLA (past chm Col Sect, past chm Dist IV). 10: Beta Phi Mu. 14: Admin, ref, tech serv. 15: Grace Doherty Lib Centre Col, Danville Ky 40422.

MAY, MARGARET (MERCER). b W Union Iowa 1 Mr 17. 5: Stephens Col 34-36 AA; UKy 36-38 (Psych) AB; UMich 52-55 AMLS; Wayne State U 46-50 (Soc Wk). 7: Soc wker State of Iowa, Des Moines Iowa 40-45; Soc wker Amer Red Cross, Detroit 45-47; Soc wker Assn for the Blind, Grand Rapids Mich 47-49; Wayne Co Lib: Libn Juvenile Detention Home 50-58, Libn Harper Woods 58-61, Libn Ill Allen Park 61-. 13: Yes. 15: 7662 Robinson, Allen Park Mich 48101.

MAY, PEGGY (JANE). b Collinsville Miss 26D 37. 5: E Miss Jr Col 56-58 (Liberal Arts) AA; U So Miss 58-60 (LS) BS; UMiss summers 61-64 (Guidance) MEd. 7: Jr libn Eng Dept Seattle Pub Lib summer 62 Libn E Miss Jr Col 60-68; Coord consul serv Miss Lib Com 68-69. 9: MissLA (Sec Col Sect 62). 14: Ref, young adults, rare bks. 15: 405 State Office Bldg, Jackson Ms 39205.

MAY, RUTH (NICKELSEN). b Clinton Iowa 27 S 30. 4: Harold E May. 5: Mt St Clare 48-50; UIowa 50-52 (Mus) B of Mus; UOre 66-67 MLS. 6: Fr. 7: Catlgr UManitoba 67-. 9: CanLA; ALA; ManitobaLA. 14: Catlg, ref. 15: 831 Wicklow st, Winnipeg 19 Manitoba Can.

MAY, SUSAN LYNNE (McCORD). b Boise Ida 25 Ja 42. 5: St Joseph Jr Col 60-63 (Eng) Certif; UMo 63-65 BA in LS; UWash 67-68 (LS). 6: Sp. 7: Page, ref asst libn, circ asst St Joseph Pub Lib, St Joseph Mo 58-63; Look-up girl UMo Lib, Columbia Mo 63; Demonstration libn Ida State Lib, Pocatello Ida 65-67; Consul Title IV LSCA Ida State Lib, Boise Ida 67-. 9: ALA; CLR (Home Serv Com); IdaLA. 10: LWV; Ida Mental Health Assn. 14: Serv to residents of state insts, mentally retarded, handicapped, blind. 15: 1611 W State #2, Boise Id 83702.

MAYDEN, PRISCILLA (MALTBY). b Boston 2 S 18. 5: Simmons 37-41 (LS) BS; Columbia summers 64, 65, 64-67 (LS) MS; UUtah 65 (Psych). 7: Libn Bus & Tech Br Hartford (Conn) Pub Lib 41-42 Air Base Cal 45-46; Stewardess American Airlines, NY 46; Chief Libn VA Hosp, Bedford Mass 46-52; Chief Libn VA Hosp, Salt Lake City 52-66; Med Scis libn UUtah (Salt Lake City) 66-. 9: MedLA (chm Med Sch Gp 67-68); ALA; UtahLA; pres 61-62; chm Spec Libs Gp 63-64; MPLA. 10: Utah Assn Metal Health; Trustee First Unitarian Church; Utah Assn for UN. 13: Yes. 14: Med, inst libs, admin, bldgs. 15: 830 Sixth ave apt 1, Salt Lake City Ut 84103.

MAYDIAN, PEGGY WITHROW (STOCK). b Clifton Forge Va 17 F 29. 4: Thomas Carlyle maydian. 5: Milligan Col 47-49 (Phys ed, Recreation); E Tenn State U 49-51 (Phys ed) BS; Peabody Col summers 56-59 (LS) MA. 7: Tchr Henry Co Pub Sch, Martinsville Va 51-52; Asst serv club dir: USA spec serv, Indiantown Gap Penn 52-53, USAF spec serv, korea 53-54; Serv club dir USAF spec serv, Duluth Minn 55-56; Tchr & libn pub schs, Key West Fla 57-58; Libn: State Voc Train Sch, Nashville 58-59; USA Dependent Schs, Ger; Asst libn a-v dept Dabney S Lancaster Commun Col 67-. 9: ALA; VaLA; State Commun Col A-V Com. 10: Beta Phi Mu. 14: A-v, ref. 15: Box 28, Selma Va 24474.

MAYE, BEATRICE (JONES) CARR. b Warren Co NC 23 Ap 16. 4: John W Maye. 5: A & T Col 37 (Eng) BS; NC Col 47 BSLS; E Car U 68 Lib Inst certif. 6: Fr. 7: Tchr & libn W H Robinson Sch, Winterville NC 44-66; Libn Ayden High Sch, Ayden NC 66-67; Libn Greenville Jr High Sch, Greenville NC 67-69. 8: Chm Bldg Better Libs, Pitt Co Schs 66-67. 9: NEA; ALA; ATA; NCLA; NCTA (pres Lib Div 47-49). 10: Delta Sigma Theta; Bk Club; Pitt Co Mental Health Assn. 13: Yes. 14: Sch lib. 15: 1225 Davenport st, Greenville NC 27834.

MAYER, GEORGE LOUIS. b Somerville NJ 17 S 29. 5: NYU 49-52 (Music) BA; Columbia 53-54 MS in LS; Universitat zu Koln (Germany) 60-61. 6: Ger. 7: NY Pub Lib: Clerk, trainee & libn Melrose Br 53-55, Libn & 1st asst Music Lib 55-65, Music spec Gen Lib of Performing Arts, Lincoln Center 65-. 9: MusLA. 12: Record Reviewer & Feature Articles for "American Record Guide"; Bk reviewer "Library Journal" (57-); "Saturday Review". 14: Mus, danc, circ. 15: Gen Lib of the Performing Arts, Lincoln Center, 111 Amsterdam ave, New York NY 10023.

MAYER, HARRIET. b Newark NJ 14 Mr 31. 5: Newark Col Rutgers U 48-52 (Eng) AB; Rutgers 60-61 MLS, 62-64 (Chem). 7: Supv photoduplication serv John Crerar Lib, Chicago 57-59; Asst libn Pub Serv Electric & Gas Co, Newark NJ 61-. 9: ALA; SLA; ASIS. 10: Amer Nuclear Soc. 15: 1253 Waverly pl, Elizabeth NJ 07208.

MAYER, SUZANNE. b Chicago Ill 8 Ap 39. 5: UCincinnati 62 (Eng Lit) BA; UPortland 63 mls. 6: Sp. 7: Libn Ore State Bd of Health, Portland 63-65; Asst libn Bonneville Power Admin, Portland Ore 65-67; Admin libn Fed Water Pollution Control Admin, Wash DC 67-68; Chief bibliog Serv US Dept Int (Wash DC) 68-. 8: Hd Task Force to Develop Lib for Nat Fisheries Ctr & Aquarium 69-. 9: SLA. 12: "Electric Vehicles, A Bibliography, 1928-1966" (66); "Underground Cables, An annotated Bibliography, 1960-1965" (66); "AC Power Transmission at 600KV and Avove; An Annotated Bibliography, 1960-1967" (67); "The Job Corps, An Annotated Bibliography of Publications Related to the Civilian Conservation Center Program and the Department of the Interior" (68). 14: Ref, bibliogr. 15: US Dept of Interior Lib, Wash DC 20240.

MAYER, THELMA ROSE (REHNER). b Rossford Ohio 23 Ap 18. 4: Robert Hillis Mayer. 5: Mather Col of West Res 34-38 (Hist) AB (cum laude); UMich 38-39 ABLS. 6: Ger, Fr. 7: Stud asst Mather Col Lib 36-38; Stud asst Med Lib UMich 38-39; Lib asst Winthrop Col Lib 50-58; Libn Rock Hill High Sch, Rock Hill SC 58-59; Acquis libn & Instr Dacus Lib, Winthrop Col 59-. 9: ALA. 10: Hemerocallis Soc, SC (bot); PTA. 14: Bk sel, ref. 15: 1050 Ridge rd, Rock Hill SC 29732.

MAYERS, IRWIN. b Brooklyn NY 20 My 28. 4: Dorothy Levitt. 5: LIU 46-49 (Hist) BS; Columbia 49-51 (Slavic Studies); UCal 52-54 (Slavic Studies,Tchr Train Credential, 56-57 MLS. 6: Russian, Ger. 7: Libn San Jose State Col 57-58; Head Libn Merritt Col 58-, 9: CalTA. 10: Amer Fed of Tchrs. 14: Sel, acqui, ser, ref. 15: 77 Stratford rd, Kensington Ca 94707.

MAYES,BLANCHIE GRAY. b Bigelow Ark 8 Ap 33. 4: Robert I Mayes Sr. 5: Kan State Tchrs Col (Pittsburg) 50-54 (LS) BS in Ed; UOkla 57-58 MLS. 6: Sp. 7: Libn Northeast Jr High Sch, Kan City Kan 54-57; Tchr-libn Douglass Elem Sch, Tulsa Okla 59-61; Libn Woods Elem Sch, Tulsa Okla 65-. 9: NEA; OKlaEA. 10: Les Belles Amies; City Federated Club; Alpha Kappa Alpha. 14: Ref, child bks. 15: 1728 E Mohawk blvd, Tulsa Ok 74110.

MAYESKI, JOHN K. T Louis Mo 12 Ja 41. 4: Francis Gelven. 5: St LouisU 58-62 (Eng) BS; UMich 65-66 MALS. 6: Sp. 7: Tchr St Pius X High Sch, Festus Mo 62-63; Tchr Mercy High Sch, St Louis Mo 63-65; Ref libn St Louis (Mo) Pub Lib 66; Admin Off US Air Force Fairchild AFB, Washington 67-68; Exec Off Lib, USAF Acad 68-. 14: Admin. 15: 4247 N Chestnut, Colorado Springs Co 80907.

MAYFIELD, DORIS (WIDENER). b Knoxville Tenn 13 O 15. 4: Frank L Mayfield. 5: Berea Col 34-38 (Eng) AB; Peabody 40-41 BS in LS. 7: Lib: Pfeiffer Jr Col 41-42; Simpson-Morgan Co Lib, Mc Connelsville Ohio 42-44; Fayetteville-Cumberland Co Lib, Fayetteville NC 44-46; Sever-Clark Co Lib, Kahoka Mo 46-52; Omaha Pub Lib 60-. 8: Sever Lib Bd, Kahoka Mo 58-60. 9: ALA; NebLA. 10: PTA. 14: Adult home loan serv. 15: 4321 N 55th st, Omaha Nb 68104.

MAYLES, WILLIAM. F. b Flint Mich 2 Ap 24. 4: Anne Reynolds. 5: West Res 46-49 (Sociol) BA, 56-59 MSLS. 7: Radio operator USN 43-46; Record clk Cleveland Electric Illuminating co, Cleveland Ohio 51-56; Lib asst Case Inst 56-59; Asst ref libn Union Col (Schenectady) 59-60; Sci & engring libn Tufts 60-65; Act engring libn Purdue U 65-66; Libn Purdue U (Indianapolis) 66-. 9: ALA; SLA; ASIS; IndLA. 10: Beta Phi Mu. 14: Admin, ref, lit of sci & tech. 15: 1201 E 38th st, Indianapolis In 46205.

MAYLONE, R(OGER) RUSSELL. b Brockton Mass 16 Ja 40. 4: Theresa Meyer. 5: Syracuse 57-61 (Internat Rel) BA; UWash 64-65 (LS) ML. 6: Fr, Ital, Ger. 7: Manager Mannys Bkstore, Syracuse NY 61-62, 62-63; Clerk Shorey Bkstor, Seattle 64-65; Ref Libn Rare bk dept Free Lib of Phila 65-69; Curator spec collections Northwestern U, Evanston Ill 69-. 9: BSA. 10: American Field Service 56; Philobiblon. 14: Rare bks, educ for libnship. 15: 3301 Hartzell st, Evanston Il 60201.

MAYNARD J(AMES) EDMUND. b Lee Co SC. 4: Lois McAllister. 5: Berry Col 59-63 (Eng) BA; LSU 66-67 (LS) MS. 6: Fr. 7: Page & clk Carnegie Pub Lib, Sumter SC 57-59; Eng tchr Rockmart High Sch, Rockmart Ga 63-66; Circ asst catlgr The Citadel 67-. 9: ALA; SCLA. 14: Catlg. 15: The Citadel, Charleston SC 29409.

MAYO, JOYCE (WILKES). b Lyons Ga 11 S 16. 4: Garnette E Mayo. 5: Ga State Col for Women 33-38 (Ed) BS; Fla State U summers 51-54 (LS) Certif. 7: Elem tchr Centerville, Elberton Ga 38-39; Toms Co, Lyons Ga: High sch tchr 39-41, 48-50, High sch tchr & libn 45-48, Tchr & prin 41-42; Elem tchr Sidney Lanier, Brunswick Ga 43-45; Elem libn: USAF, Eglin AFB Fla 50-54, Elem sch Ft Walton Beach Fla 54-55; Tech libn Eglin AFB, Fla 55-58, Base libn 58-66; Tech libn SE Sig Sch, Ft Gordon Ga 66-67; Sch libn USA Military Police sch, Ft Gordon Ga 67-. 8: Charter mem & trustee, City Lib, ft Walton Beach Fla 53-65; Adv-consul to sch libns, Okaloosa Co Fla 51-66. 9: ALA-PLA (Chm Orient Com, Armed Forced Libn Sect 63-); GaLA; SEasternLA; Central Savannah River LA. 14: Ref. 15: 4115 Windsor Spring rd, Hephzibah Ga 30815.

MAYO, JULIA CHRISTINE. b Cartersville Va 3 N 43. 5: Va State Col 60-64 (LS) BS; Drexel 65-(LS). 6: Ger. 7: Lib asst Johnston Mem Lib, Pertsburg Va 61-63; Libn L P Jackson High Sch, Cumberland Va 64-65; US Army Lib Program Spec Serv 66-. 9: NEA; Amer Tchrs Assn; Va Tchrs Assn. 10: Delta Sima Theta; Kappa Delta Pi. 14: Ref, med libnship. 15: 914 Croton rd, Wayne Pa 19087.

MAYO, MYRA (MORTON). b Aberdeen Scotland 1 Je 11. 4: Edward Leslie Mayo. 5: Macalester Col 29-32 (Eng Lit); UMinn 32-33 Journalism, (Eng Lit) BA, 58-61 MA in LS. 6: Fr, Ger, Lat, Gk. 7: Lib asst Des Moines Pub Lib, Des Moines Iowa 55-59, Libn 59-63; Libn Iowa Commsn for the Blind, Des Moines Iowa 63; Libn Iowa Methodist Sch Fr Nursing, Des Moines Iowa 65-; Libn U Ore Lib 66-67; Libn Iowa Methodist Sch of Nursing 67-. 9: ALA; IowLA (chm Johnson Brigham Plaque Com 59-61); Des Moines Area LA; Health Scis Libns Iowa. 10: Beta Phi Mu; Amer Recorder Sob. 14: Ref. 15: 1532 Twenty-Fourth st, Des Moines Ia 50311.

MAYO, WAYNE. b Chicago 1 O 31. 4: Gail Rote. 5: UIll 53-56 (Sociol) BS; UOkla 58-60 MSLS. 7: Photographer (Cpl) US Army 51-53; Insurance underwriter Firemans Fund Insurance Co, Chicago 56-57; Field agent Fidelity & Deposit Co, Okla City Okla 57-58; Ref asst Okla City Pub Lib, Okla City Okla 58-60; Head bus & Tech Sect Lansing Pub Lib, Lansing Mich 60-63; Head Libn Lawerence Lawrence Pub Lib, Lawrence 63-; Admin lib NE Kan Lib 66-68. 8: Consul on acquis of Bus & Tech material for Mcomb Co Lib, Mich 62. 9: ALA; KanLA (chm Pub Lib Sect 64-65, cham var coms). 10: Lawerence Coun of Soc Agencies ; C of C. 11 Ed "Business Briefs, a quarterly bus & tech publ distrib in the Lansing Mich area (60-63); Ed "Broadside NE Kan Lib newsletter (66-68). 14: Admin, ref. 15: 845 Vermont, Lawrence Ks 66044.

MAYS, FAYRENE (NEUMAN). b Smithville Tex 13 Mr 32. 4: David May. 5: Prairie View A&M Col 51 (LS) BS; Atlanta 64 MLS. 6: Fr. 7: Libn Glenwood Elem Sch, Panama City Fla 54-56; Circ libn Prairie View Col 56-58; Libn Emore High Sch, Houston 58; Sr asst libn Prairie View Col summer 65. 8: Career consul in Lib Serv, Prairie View Co 68; Spec adv on Sel of Jr Lib Materials for Settegast Jr High Sch 68-69. 9: ALA; NEA; TexLA; Tex State TA (House of Deleg 69); ClrTA. 10: Southeast YWCA (Houston); Sunnyside Civic Club (Houston). 14: Ref, circ. 15: 4903 Mayflower st, Houston Tx 77033.

MAYS, BLANCHE. b Amherst Va 6 Jl 34. 5: Madison Col 51-55 (LS) BS in Ed; Catholic U 63-64 MS in LS; UVa 65 (LS). 6: Fr. 7: Libn Nelson Co High Sch, Lovingston Va 55-57; Libn Washington-Lee High Sch, Arlington Va 57-65, Head Libn 65-. 8: Coordinator of Lib Sch Ext courses UVa 65-66; Instr of Catlg & Clsf UVa Ext 64-. 9: NEA; AEA; ALA; AST; VaLA (chm Sch Lib Sect 64-65). 10: Beta Phi Mu. 14: atlg, admin. 15: 3804 N 13th st, Arlington Va 22201.

MAYWHORT, HELEN MARGARET (WOOTEN). b Chattanooga Tenn 24 D 15. 4: John Arthur Maywhort. 5: UChattanooga 34-36 UTenn 36-38 (Fr) BA; Drexel 41-42 MLS.)06: Fr, Lat. 6: Fr, Lat. 7: Libn Tyner High Sch, Tyner Tenn 38-41; Circ asst Free Lib, Phila 42; Period asst, catlgr Temple U 43-46; Libn Chattanooga High Sch, Chattanooga Tenn 49-51; Catlgr Hamilton Co Schs, Chattanooga Tenn 51; Bibliog So Newspaper Publishers Assn, Chattanooga Tenn 52; Indexer Chamber of Com, Chattanooga Tenn 55; Libn The McCallie Sch, Chattanooga Tenn 59-. 8: So Assn of Secon Schs, Evaluation Com; Castle Heights Mil Acad, Lebanon Tenn 64; Columbia Mil Acad, Columbia Tenn 65; Org Brainerd Presbyterian Ch Lib, Chattanooga Tenn 51; Comp bibliog for So Newspaper Publs Assn 51. 9: ALA; SE Independent Schs Assn (chm Lib Sect 62); Chattanooga Area LA (past sec & pres). 10: PTA; Booster Club; Commun Concerts Org; Fac Distaff Club; Bk Club; Garden Club; Bus Womens Circle; Bridge Club. 13: Yes. 14: Bk sel, ref, bibliog. 15: 309 Belvoir ave, Chattanooga Tn 37411.

MAZAHER, ABBAS. b Tehran Iran 1 Jl 33. 4: Kay Halliburton. 5: N Tex State U 58-63 (Eng) BA, 64-67 (LS) MLS. 6: Persian (Farsi). 7: Tr Point 4, Babosar Iran 56-57; Customs ship clerk US Embassy in Iran, Tehran Iran 57-58; Cashier attendant Pershing Square Garage, Los Angeles 67-68; 61 Page Dallas Pub Lib 62-63, Libn 63-66, First asst Casa View Br 67-68; Assoc dir Tehran Bk Processing Ctr, Tehran Iran 68-. 9: TexLA; ALA; SWLA; Dallas Co (Tex) LA. 10: Pi Kappa Alpha. 14: Ref, catlg, admin. 15: co 437 Monssen dr, Dallas Tx 75224.

MAZAR, JOY SUSANNE (MENCHYK). b Butler Penn 14 O 46. 4: John Andrew Mazar. 5: Slippery Rock State Col 64-67 (LS) BS in Ed; UPittsburgh 68- (LS). 7: Libn Peters Twp Jr-Sr High Sch, McMurray Pa 67-68; Catlgr Butler Co Commun Col 68; Libn butler Area Jr High Sch, Butler Pa 68-. 9: PennStateEA. 10: Butler Co Learning Resource Assn. 14: Sch libnship. 15: RD 7, Butler Pa 16001.

MAZEFSKY, GERTRUDE TAMARA (MESSEROFF). b Bessarabia 20 AG '. 4: William H Mazefsky. 5: UPittsburgh 36-40 (Eng) BA; Carnegie 56-59 MLS. 6: Hebrew, Fr, Yiddish. 7: Asst lib UPittsburgh Lib 38-44; Readers asst & catlgr Carnegie Lib, Pittsburgh 56-. 8: Adv to synagogue & parochial Sch-Libs, & wk with Y libs. 10: Ladies Hosp Aid Soc; Nat Coun Jewish Women; Pittsburgh Coun of PTA; Amer Red Cross; Theta Sigma Phi. 14: Ref, readers asst. 15: 5548 Wellesley ave, Pittsburgh Pa 15206.

MAZURA, IRENE C. 4: Christopher C Mazura. 5: Colonial Col (Rendsburg Germany) 38-40 (Educ) BA; UBerlin & Bonn (Germany) 40-43 (Econ) Masters Econ; Tchrs' Col (Buchen Germany) 46-48 (Educ) Tchr. 6: Fr, Sp, Ger. 7: Price analyst Price Stabilization Bd, Berlin Germany 43-44; Analyst (Supply

& Demand) Austrian Supplies Dept, Vienna Austria 44-45; Tchr Steinbach & Sennfeld Baden Sch Dist, Germany 45-51; Research libn Kauser Industries Inc, Oakland Cal 57-64; Hd libn White Labs (Schering), Kenilworth NJ 65-66; Ref libn Azusa Pub Lib, Azusa Cal 67-. 8: Official interpreter & guide (Eng & Fr), Olympic Games, Berlin 36. 10: YWCA; Zonta; Bus & Profess Women; PTA; Kaiser Pub Speaking Club; Kaiser Internatl Club (Oakland). 11: Luther Medal City of Berlin. 14: Ref (classical music & arts, for lang lit, hist). 15: 623 Jalapa dr, Covina Cal 91722.

MAZUROWSKI, MARIE CECILE. b Bay City Mich 26 Jl 08. 5: Nazareth Col 27-38 (Eng) AB; UDetroit 38-45 (Eng) MA; UMich 64-66 MALS; UIll 67-68 (Eng Educ) Advance Certif. 6: Lat, Fr, Ger. 7: Instr-libn: St Mary High, Flint Mich 49-52, St Agnes High, Flint Mich 54-57, St Augustine High, Kalamazoo 57-58, St Gertrude High, St Clair Shores Mich 58-62; Eng chm-a-v coord St David High, Detroit 62-66; Eng chm-instr St Rita High, Detroit 66-67; Asst Prof Clarion State Col 68-. 9: ALA; CathLA; NCTE; Contemp Theatre assn; MichLA. 10: Metro Eng Club, Detroit. 11: Experienced tchr fellowship grant UIll 67-68. 13: Yes. 14: Catlg, bk sel, film criticism, literary criticism. 15: Clarion State Col, Clarion Pa 16214.

MAZZARELLA, DENISE (LeCLAIR). b Hartford Conn 16 Mr 31. 4: John A Mazzarella. 5: St Joseph Col (W Hartford) 49-53 (Eng) BA; UWash 66-69 M Lib. 6: Fr. 7: Asst W Hartford (Conn) Lib 46-48; Lib asst "The Hartford Courant". Hartford Conn 48-49; Contract underwriter Travelers Insurance Co, Hartford Conn 49-56. 9: ALA; SLA. 10: LWV. 14: Ref. 15: 16775 - 16th ave NW, Seattle Wa 98177.

McABEE, JUNE (LESLIE) PECK. b Petros Tenn 9 Ap 17. 4: William H McAbee. 5: Young Harris Jr Col 36-38 Diploma; UChattanooga 39-41 (Sociol) AB; Emory summers 60-61 (LS); Fla StateU summer 62 (LS); Wash StateU 51-54 (Educ) MEd; UNTex 64-67 MLS; DeKalb Tech col 69- (Data Processing). 6: Sp, Fr, Ger. 7: Cashier Trion Dept Store, Trion Ga 34-40; Stud asst bus off UChattanooga 39-41; Sears Credit Dept, Chattanooga Tenn 40-41; Recreation staff & confirmation clk Ted Hiltons Vacation Camp summers 42 & 43; Tchr: Trion Schs, Trion Ga 41-43, Bartow Schs, Bartow Fla 43-45, Elgin AFB Fla 50-51, Pullman Schs, Pullman Wash 53-54, Hillview Sch, Los Altos Cal 54-55, Tyndall AFB Fla 55-56, Bay Co Schs, Panama City Fla 56-57; Tchr-libn Elgin AFB Fla 58-61; Libn Edge Elem, Okaloosa Fla 62; Ref Tex ChristianU summer 63; Tchr-libn Country Day Sch, Ft Worth 64-66; Libn Trinity Valley Sch for Boys, Ft Worth 66-67; Libn Heritage Sch, DeKalb Co Ga 67-68; Coord Lib Proc Ctr, DeKalb Co Ga 68-. 8: Grey lady lib serv for hosp patients. 9: ALA; NEA; TexLA; GaLA; Ga A-V Assn; SELA. 10: Officers' Wives Club; Ceramic Club. 14: Ref, catlg, readers' guidance, tech serv. 15: 3540-1 Old Chamblee Tucker rd, Atlanta Ga 30340.

McADAMS, NANCY REEVES. b Kansas City Mo 28 Jl 29. 4: Kelly R McAdams. 5: UTex 46-51 (Arch) B of Arch, 62-65 MLS. 7: Architectural draftsman Niggli & Gustafson Architects, Austin Tex 51-56; Architect Kelly R McAdams AIA, Austin Tex 56-61; Architectural researcher Page Southerland Page Architects, Austin Tex 62; Arch libn UTex 65-. 8: Registered architect, Tex; Bibliog Tex Archit Survey, Austin 64. 9: ALA; SLA; Coun Planning Libns; TexLA (Ref RT; sec-treas 69-70). 10: Soc Archit Histns; Soc UTex Libns. 13: Yes. 14: Subj bibliog, ref. 15: 2607 Great Oaks parkway, Austin Tx 78756.

McALISTER, CLARA LOIS. b Fayetteville Tenn 10 Ag 06. 5: Florence State Normal 25-26 (Eng); Middle Tenn State Tchrs Col 29-31 (Eng) BS; Peabody summer 35, 36, 37 BS in LS; UMiami 48, summer 50; Peabody 62 MA in LS. 6: Lat. 7: Elem tchr Albright Elem Sch, Lincoln Co Tenn 26-27; Int & high sch Lat McBurg Sch, Lincoln Co Tenn 27-29; Lat & Eng tchr Grundy Co High Sch, Tracy City Tenn 31-36; Tchr & libn Trousdale Co High Sch, Hartsville Tenn 36-37; Libn Miami Beach Jr & Sr High Sch, Miami Beach Fla 37-50; Libn P K Yonge Lab Sch UFla 50-51; Libn Miami Shores Elem Sch, Miami Shores Fla 51-61; Libn Ludlam Elem Sch, S Miami Fla 62-. 8: Tch lib sch summer courses Fla State U 49, UMiami 52; Tchr Elem Lib Wkshop UMiami & Dade Co Bd of Pub Instr, summer 62; Tchr, NDEA Lib Inst UKy, summer 65; Consul NDEA Libr Inst, E Ky StateU & Okla StateU summer 66. 9: NEA; ALA; -AASchL (chm Sch & Child Sect); ALEE; FlaEA; FlaLA (chm Sch & Child Sect); FlaASchL (sec). 10: Delta Kappa Gamma; Internat Congress Parents & Tchrs. 13: Yes. 14: Child wk. 15: 106 Mendoza ave, apt 3, Coral Gables Fl 33134.

McALISTER, DOROTHY (CROUT). b Kappa Ill 11 Ja 13. 4: Kenneth C McAlister. 5: Ill State (Normal) U 36 (Educ) B Ed; UIll 42 BS in LS. 6: Fr, Ger, Russian. 7: Catlgr Purdue U 42-45; Catlgr UIll 45-46; Libn Hawaii Co Lib, Hilo Hawaii 46-47; Libn Lib Hawaii, Honolulu 47-48; Catlg libn UHawaii (Honolulu) 48-55, Head catlg dept 56-. 9: ALA; HawaiiLA (treas 53-54). 12: Ed J of Hawaii LA (51). 13: Yes. 14: Catlg. 15: 640 Hindiuka dr, Honolulu Hi 96821.

McALISTER, MARJORIE M (KEITH). b Des Moines Iowa 25 S 15. 4: Ned W McAlister. 5: Drake 32-36 (Fr) BA; UDenver summers 38-40 BS in LS. 6: Fr, Ger. 7: Tchr-libn Radcliffe Independent Sch, Radcliffe Iowa 36-38; Libn Cowles Lib Dr akeU 38-43; Libn US Arny, Ft Des Moines Iowa 43-46; Libn VA Hosp, Des Moines Iowa 47-48; Libn circ pub lib, Des Moines Iowa 50-51, Asst ref 52-56, Asst to dir 56-. 9: ALA; IowaLA; Iowa Adult EA. 10: Des Moines Lib Club; Bus & Prof Women's Club. 15: 100 Locust st, Des Moines Ia 50309.

McALLISTER, CARYL K(OERPER). b Moline Ill 14 S 38. 4: A Stratton McAllister. 5: Cornell U 56-60 (Chem) AB; UCal(Berkeley) 64-65 MLS. 6: Ger. 7: Research assoc Lakeside Labs, Milwaukee summers 58-60; Prin lib asst Cornel U Engnr Lib 60-61; Chem Gen Electric, San Jose Cal 61-62; Libn Fairchild Semiconductor, Palo Alto Cal 62-64; Assoc libn IBM Corp, San Jose Cal 65-68; Assoc Programmer, Los Gatos Cal 68-. 9: ACS; SLA; ACL; ASIS (San Francisco Chap: sec 68-69, pres 69-). 10: Peninsula Symphony Orchestra. 14: Indexing, lib automation. 15: IBM ASD PO Box 66, Los Gatos Ca 95030.

McALPINE, ELAINE. b Wellsburg W Va 22 Ap 31. 5: W Liberty State Col 53 (Elem educ) AB; UPittsburgh 63 (Elem educ) ME, 67 MLS. 7: Tchr Hancock Co Bd of Educ, Weirton W Va 53-61, Prin in training 61-64, Dir instr materials ctr 64-67, Prin 67-68; Libn Pelham Schs, Pelham NY 68-. 9: NEA; ALA-AASchL; HancockCoEA (pres 1 yr); PelhamEA. 10: Goodwill Grange; W Va State Grange; Nat Grange. 14: Sch libnship. 15: 124 Oregon ave, Bronxville NY 10708.

McALPINE, NELLIE L. b Detroit Mich 29 O 22. 5: Wayne StateU 40-44 (LS) BA; Case West ResU 44-45 (LS) BS. 6: Fr, Ger. 7: Asst libn Wakeman Gen Hosp Camp Atterbury (Ind) 45-46, Post libn 46; Bkmob libn Hq US Air Forces in Europe (Wiesbaden Germany) 46-47; Libn Berlin Airlift Taskforce Rhein Main Air Force Base (Germany) 48-49; Base libn Burtonwood Air Depot (Lancs England) 49-51; Staff libn Tenth Air Force Selfridge Air force Base (Mich) 51-55; Staff libn First Air Force Mitchell Air Force Base (NY) 55-58; Staff libn Fourth Air Force Hamilton Air Force Base (Cal) 58-60; Command libn Continental Air Command Mitchell Air Force Base (NY) 60-61; Chief libn Fort Ord lib system, Fort Ord (Cal) 61-. 9: ALA (pres Armed Forces Sect 60-61); CalLA. 10: AAUW. 13: Yes. 14: Admin. 15: 216 Crocker ave, Pacific Grove Ca 93950.

McANALLY, ARTHUR M. b Delaware Ark 4 Ja 11. 4: Lucille McGeorge McAnnally. 5: UArk 28-29; UOkla 30-33 (Eng) BA, 33-35 BA in LS, 33-35 (Eng) MA; Chicago 38-41, 51 (LS) PhD. 6: FR, Sp. 7: Supv of libs Edinburg (Tex) Jr Col & publ sch 35-38; Asst libn Knox Col 39-41; Libn Bradley Tech 41-44; Libn Wis State Tchrs Col (Milwaukee) 44-45; U Libn UNM 45-49; Asst dir pub serv UIll(Urbana) 49-51; Dir UOkla Libs 51-. 08: Supv Univ Nacional Mayor Mayor de San Marcos, Lima Peru Biblioteca Central 48; Visiting Prof Chair of Libnship Ankara Univ, Ankara Turkey 63-64; Consul on lib bldgs U of Wichita 60; Univ of San Marcos, Lima peru 63; Ankara Univ 63-64. 9: ALA-ACRL; SWLA (pres 60-62); NMLA (pres 47); OklaLA (pres 67-68). 10: Okla Westerners; Centennial (Wyo) Rod & Gun Club; Rotary; AAUP. 13: Yes. 14: Univ lib admin, higher educ, lib bldgs, status of libns. 15: Univ of Oklahoma Lib, Norman Ok 73069.

McANELLY, EDWIN C. b Devine Tex 26 S 18. 4: Bess Jane (Watkins) McAnelly. 5: St Mary'sU 35-37 (Pre-Engrg); Texas A&M Col 38-41 (Mech Engrg); Florida So Col 55-56 (Physics) BS, Physics; Middle Tenn State Col 64 (LS); Our Lady of the Lake Col 66-67 msls. 6: Sp. 7: Pilot Meteorologist USAF Lt Colonel 41-64; Libn Post Lib, (Ft San Houston Tex) 66-68; Instit Consul Texas State Lib, (Austin Texas) 68-. 8: Grad of Air command & Staff Sch, Maxwell AFB La 54. 9: ALA; Air Force Assn; Retired Offrs Assn; TexLA; BexarCoLA. 10: San Antonio A&M Club. 11: Distinguished Flying Cross; Air Medal. 14: Instl libs, spec libs. 15: 2338 W Kings hwy, San Antonio Tx 78201.

McANINCH, LILLIAN L. b Chicago 16 Ag 32. 5: Col of St Teresa (Minn) 50-52; Chicago 54 (LS). 7: Asst libn Dearborn Chem Co, Chicago 52-53, Libn 54-63; Libn Moffett Tech Lib

Corn Products Co, Argo Ill 63-. 9: SLA; ACS (Chem Lit Div); NMA. 14: Admin. 15: 9402 S 55th ave, Oak Lawn Il 60453.

McANULTY, ELEANOR (MARY) SHERIFF. b Blairsville Penn 3 Jl 10. 5: SusquehannaU 28-32 (Sp) BA; UPittsburgh 66-69 MLS. 6: Sp, Fr, Ital. 7: Tchr Pub Sch, (Blairsville Pa) 32-38; Soc Wker Pa DPA, (Johnstown Pa) 40-43; Insurance Agent-Self-employed, (Barnesboro Pa) 43-65; Tchr, (Elders Rodge Pa) 66-67; Libn Jr-Sr High Sch, (Saltsburg Pa) 67-. 9: NEA; PennStateEA; PennSchLA (v-pres Central-West Dist). 14: Ref. 15: 235 So Liberty st, Blairsville Pa 15717.

McAULAY, LOUISE)STARR) (SALZMAN). b Chicago Ill 20 Ag 40. 4: David L McAulay. 5: Texas Woman'sU 58-59 (journalism); Penn StateU 59-60 (journalism); UIll 60-62 (hist) BA, 62, 65 (LS) MS. 6: Fr. 7: Recreation dir special serv, Paris France 63-64; Asst libn Gen Atomic/Gen Dynamics, La Jolla Calif 65-67; Catlgr UTenn, Knoxville 67-. 9: SLA. 14: Info ret, ref. 15: 5612 Chapman highway, Knoxville Tn 37920.

McAVIN, JOHN F JR. b Omaha Neb 20 N 19. 4: Martha Jane Woodbridge. 5: UOmaha 37-41 (Pol Sci) BA; UNeb 46-49 (Pol Sci); UIll 55-56 MSLS. 6: Ger. 7: Cpl US Army Signal Intelligence 42-45; Asst Com Dept Lib UIll (Urbana) 55-56; Lib asst Omaha Pub Lib (Omaha Neb) 51-55, Asst br libn 56, Asst ref libn 57; Dir Freeport Pub Lib, Freeport Ill 57-64; Dir Allentown Pub Lib, Allentown Penn 64-68; Consul & Admin LSCA Title II Div of Lib Development NY State Lib 68-. 9: ALA; NYLA; PennLA (Lib Devel Com, chm Adult Serv Com; chm Lehigh Valley Chap 68); IllLA (Lib Devel Com, Intel Freedom Com). 13: Yes. 14: Lib arch, admin, educ, personnel, adult serv. 15: 42 Steuben st, Albany NY 12224.

McAVOY, GEORGE E. b Grundy Ctr Iowa 21 Je 07. 4: Bernadette Condon. 5: Winona State 33-37 (Soc studies) BS; Peabody Lib Sch 57-58 MALS. 7: Ref libn Ft Wayne Pub Lib, Ind 55-58; Dir pub lib, Wadswirth Ohio 58-60; Pub lib ref libn; LA 61-63, San Bernardino Cal 63-68, Long Beach Cal 69-. 9: ALA; CalLA. 15: 40 Alamitos, Long Beach Ca 90802.

McBATH, OLGA (LAKE). b Gardner Mass 31 Ag 09. 5: Simmons 27-31 BS; Montclair State summer 65 (Educ); Paterson State fall 66, summer 67 (Educ) Certif sch libn. 6: Finnish, Fr. 7: Child libn NYC Pub Lib 31-36; Catlgr & asst libn Hillsdale NJ 55-58; Sch libn Bd of Educ, Hillsdale NJ 65-. 9: ALA; NEA; NJLA; NJEA; HillsdaleTA. 13: Yes. 14: Wk with child. 15: 4 Bergen st, Westwood NJ 07675.

McBENNETT, SISTER MARY ANNETTE RSM. b Fayetteville NC 10 S 19. 5: Sacred Heart Col 36-37, 40-42 (Educ); Catholic U 42-44 (Educ) BA, summers 51-56 MS in LS. 07: Asst libn Sacred Heart Jr Col (Belmont NC) 58-65, Libn 65-. 9: ALA; CathLA (chap sec-treas); SELA; NCLA. 10: NC Cath Hist Assn. 13: Yes. 14: Ref. 15: Sacred Heart Convent, Belmont NC 28012.

McBIRNEY, RUTH CAMPBELL. b Boise Ida 16 Ja 18. 5: Whitman Col 36-39 (Fr) AB; UWash 39-40 BA in Lib; Columbia 42-46 (Musicology). 6: Fr. 7: Catlgr Boise Jr Col 40-42; Ref asst Boise Pub Lib, Boise Ida 40-42; Searcher, catlgr NY Pub Lib 42; Asst libn Columbia U Music Lib 43-46; Ref libn American Lib in Paris 47-49, Libn 49-53; Libn Boise State Col 54-. 9: ALA; PNLA; Pacific Northwest Bibliog Center Coun (Exec Com); IdaLA. 10: AAUP; Soroptimist Club. 11: "Palmes Acade3miques" (Paris 53). 14: Admin. 15: Boise Col Lib, Boise Id 83701.

McBRIDE, HARRIET F(RENCH POSTLE). b Chicago 13 My 14. 4: George McBride. 5: Northwestern 30-34 (Chem) BS; Union Col NJ) 66- (Bus). 06: Fr, Ger. 7: Chem libn Princeton 47; Asst libn Armstrong Cork Co, Lancaster Penn 48-52; Lib asst Calco Chem Co, Bound Brook NJ 53; Asst libn Westfield Free Pub Lib, Westfield NJ 54-56; Libn Amer Smelting & Refining Co, S Plainfield NJ 56-58; Libn Nat Starch & Chem Corp, Plainfield NJ 69-. 9: SLA. 14: Sci & tech. 15: 523 Clark st, Westfield NJ 07090.

McBRIDE, HELEN (ANNE). b Newark Del 13 Ap 06. 5: Ohio U 25-29 (Langs) AB; UKy summer 33 (LS); George Washington U summer 34 (LS); West Res 35-39 BS in LS; UPittsburgh 42-45 (Econ). 7: Pub Sch, Steubenville Ohio: Elem tchr 30-, Jr high libn 40-42, Libn elem sch 43-. 9: NEA; OhioEA; East OhioEA; OhioASchL. 10: Delta Kappa Gamma; AAUW; LWV; Civic Music Assn; Steubenville Players; PTA. 14: Elem sch libnship. 15: 200 Braebarton blvd, Steubenville Oh 43952.

McBRIDE, MARGUERITE (POOR). b Sherborn Mass 14 O 13. 4: D Eldridge McBride. 5: Simmons BS in LS. 6: Fr, Ger, Sp. 7: Catlgr John Crerar Lib, Chicago 35-39, Classifier 42-44; Libn Shimer Col 51-. 10: AAUW. 14: Catlg, clsf, admin. 15: Shimer Col, Mt Carroll Il 61053.

McBRIDE, PATRICIA (ANNE) CRAMER. b Butler Penn 20 Ap 23. 5: Col of New Rochelle 40-44 (Eng) BA; UPittsburgh 64-66 MLS; Slippery Rock State 67-68 (Ed). 7: Advertising copy girl Halle Bros Co, Cleveland Ohio 44-45; Advertising copywriter-mgr Stearn Co, Cleveland Ohio 45-47; Libn VA Hosp, Butler Penn 66; Libn Butler Area Sr High Sch, butler Penn 66-. 9: ALA; PennStateEA. 10: Beta Phi Mu; AAUW; Girl Scout Coun. 15: 225 W Fulton st, Butler Pa 16001.

McBRIDE, ROBERTA (ALLEN). b Circleville Kan. 4: J Andrew McBride. 5: Baker U 31-35 (Eng) AB; UIll 39 BS in LS; Northwestern 45 (Pol Sci) MS. 7: Libn Elmwood Park Pub Lib, Elmwood Park Ill 39-44; Asst libn Detroit Pub Lib 44-47; Libn UAW Research Dept, Detroit 48; Legis ref libn Kan State Lib 49-57; Sr libn Detroit Pub Lib 57-62; Libn Labor Hist Archives, Wayne State U 63-. 9: ALA (chm Jt Com on Lib Serv to Labor Groups 60-64). 10: Wayne Co (Mich) AFL-CIO Educ Com; Wayne Co Pub Lib Bd. 12: Ed "Library Service to Labor," Periodical (58-60). 14: Lib serv to labor groups, labor archives. 15: 4408 Bishop, Detroit Mi 48224.

McCABE, GERARD BENEDICT. b NYC 22 Ja 30. 4: Jacqueline Maloney. 5: Manhattan Col 48-52 (Eng) BA; UMich 52-54 AMLS; Mich State U 57-59 (Eng) MA. 6: Fr, Ger, Lat, Sp. 7: Lib serv scholar & fellow UMich Lib 52-54; Asst acquis dept UNeb Lib 54-56; Chief bibliog acquis dept Mich State U Lib 56-58; Libn Inst for Community Development & Serv Mich State U 58-59; Acquis libn U of So Fla 59-66; Assoc dir UArk 66-67; Asst dir for planning & devel USoFla 67-. 9: ALA (Life mem)-RTSD (Exec Com Acquis Sect 64-66, chm Info Com Acquis Sect 57-58); BSA; SELA; FlaLA; Fla Hist Soc. 10: Friends of the Lib, Hillsborough Co Fla. 13: Yes. 14: Acquis, automation, admin, lib bldgs. 15: U So Fla Lib, Tampa Fl 33620.

McCABE, JAMES FRANCIS. b Newcastle Neb 6 D 31. 5: St Joseph's Col 49-50; Dayton U 51-52 (Philos) BA; UDetroit 58-59 (Educ); Catholic U 59-60 MS in LS; American U summer 61 (Archives) Certif. 7: Head Libn St Charles Sem 61-65; Hed Libn St Joseph's Col (Rensselaer Ind) 65-. 14: Catlg (philos & theol). 15: St Joseph's Col, Rensselaer In 47979.

McCABE, JAMES PATRICK (BROTHER). b Philadelphia Penn 24 My 37. 5: UNiagara 61-64 (Eng Lit) BA; UMich 65-68 (Eng Lit) MA, MALS, (LS) PhD. 6: Fr, Lat. 7: Tchr Salesian High Sch, Detroit 64-65; Libn Allentown Col, Center Valley Pa 68-. 9: ALA. 14: Admin. 15: Allentown Col, Center Valley Pa 18034.

McCABE, PATSY (NELSON). b Seattle 14 F 31. 4: Hugh McCabe. 5: Lewis & Clark 55 (Eng) BS; UWash 55-58 (LS) ML. 7: Head Libn Vancouver High Sch, Vancouver Wash 54-55; Head Libn Hudson's Bay High Sch, Vancouver Wash 55-56; Eng tchr Bellingham High Sch, Bellingham Wash 58-59; Dist Libn Lopez Pub Schs, Lopez Wash 59-65; Dist Libn Centralia Pub Schs, Centralia Wash 65-. 9: NEA; Wash State ASchL; Wash EA. 10: Beta Phi Mu; Grange. 14: Lib supv, central proc. 15: 904 Johnson rd, Centralia Wa 98531.

McCABE, SISTER MARY CONCEPTA. b Superior Wis 10 Ja 10. 5: Webster Col 31-32 (Eng) AB; St Louis U 37-38 (Lat) MA; Col of St Catherine summer 53, 54 BSLS; UMich summer 62, 64, 65 MALS; Mo Prof Libn's Life Certif 60. 06: Lat, Sp. 7: High sch tchr Lat, Eng, Sp various high schs: Springfield Mo 30-31, 32-34, 42-46, New Orleans 34-37, Little Rock 39-42, 46-48, University City Mo 48-51; Libn Mercy Jr Col 52-60; Libn St John's Sch of Nursing (Springfield Mo) 60-63, 64-; Libn Sisters of Mercy Generalate, Bethesda Md 63-64. 9: CathLA (Greater St Louis Unit: Bd 4 yrs, chm 2 yrs); ALA; MoLA. 13: Yes. 14: Catlg, pub rel. 15: 1930 S National ave, Springfield Mo 65804.

McCABE, WILLIAM J. b Newark NJ 7 N 14. 5: Seton Hall 32-36 (Eng) AB; Columbia 49 9fr) MA; Rutgers 67-69 MLS. 6: Fr. 7: US Army, US, Europe Med Corps Tech Sergeant 42-46; Salesman Newark News, Newark 36-42; Tchr Seton Hall, S Orange 46-66, Libn 66-. 9: NJLA (treas Ref Sect 68-69). 10: Amer Assn Tchrs French; Mod Lang Assn. 14: Ref. 15: Apt 14J 65 Manor dr, Newark NJ 07106.

McCAFFERTY, MARY E. b Cortland NY 15 My 19. 4: John P McCafferty. 5: Geneseo State U Col 38-42 (LS) BS Ed, 48-51 (Educ) MS Ed. 7: Libn Brighton Schs No 1, Rochester NY 42-. 8: Instr in Child Lib, URochester 57-60. 9: NEA; NYLA; NY State Tchrs Assn. 14: Child wk. 15: 7 Rollingwood dr, Pittsford NY 14534.

McCAFFERY, MARY BELLE (BRANSON). b Zenda Kan 26 F 06. 4: William H McCaffery. 5: Friends U 27-29 (Modern Lang) AB; UDenver summers 58, 59, 60 (LS) MA. 6: Fr, Sp. 7: Tchr Deerfield High Sch, Deerfield Kan 29-31; Tchr Spivey High Sch, Spivey Kan 31, 32; Libn East High Sch, Wichita Kan 51-69. 09: NEA; Kan State Tchrs Assn; KanASchL. 15: 5204 S Hydraulic, Wichita Ks 67216.

McCAHILL, MICHAEL JAMES. b Victoria BC Can 6 Je 26. 5: Victoria Col 43-45; UBC 46-47 (Hist, Eng) BA; Toronto 58-59 BLS. 6: Fr. 7: Priv Can Army Infantry Corps, Can 45-46; Inspector Sidney Roofing & Paper Co, Victoria BC 48-51; Asst Scott & Reed Ltd, London Eng 51-55; Supv Bathurst Containers Ltd, Toronto 55-58; Ref libn Victoria Pub Lib, Victoria BC 59-60; Catlgr Victoria Col (BC) 60-61, Head of catlg dept 61-63; Head of Tech Serv Sir George Williams U (Montreal) 63-67; Asst to chief libn Building Planning UToronto 68-. 9: ALA; CanLA (chm Tech Serv Sect 67-68; Liaison to ALA-RTSD 67-69); Inst Profess Libns Ont. 13: Yes. 14: Admin, tech serv, bldgs. 15: Univ of Toronto Library, Toronto 5 Ont Can.

McCAIN, ELLA BYRD. b Dothan Ala 8 Mr 25. 4: Dr John H McCain. 5: Ala A&M Col 41-45 (Home Econ) BS; UMich summers 49-53 AMLS. 6: Fr. 7: Tchr East Street High Sch, Opelika Ala 45-47; Tchr Wenonah High Sch, Birmingham Ala 47-49; Instr lib educ SC State Col summer 54; Instr Sch of Lib Serv Atlanta U summers 55-69; Libn Wenonah High Sch, Birmingham Ala 49-68; Libn Gardendale Area Voc Sch, Gardendale Ala 68-. 8: Evaluation Com for sr high sch accreditation by So Assn of Schs & Cols; Conf consul on the Ga Child's Access to Materials Pertaining to Amer Negroes AtlantaU 67; Member Ad Hoc Comm of AASL, Elem Mag Articles Bibliography Committee. 9: ALA (Sec Schs Lib Com, State Mem Com); -YASD; -AASchL (Mem Ad Hoc Com, Elem Mag Articles Bibliog Com); Amer Tchrs Assn; SELA; AlaLA; AlaASchL (pres 56-57); Ala State Tchrs Assn; Jefferson Co Libns Assn (pres 68-). 10: Illuminators Civic (Prof Club). 14: Child serv, readers adv. 15: 1 Greensprings ave SW, Birmingham Al 35211.

McCALIB, CLYTIE ALINE. b Utica Okla 17 O 09. 5: Southeastern State Col 25-28 (Eng, Lat) BA; Okla A & M Col summers 34-36 (Eng) MA; Okla U summers 49-52 BA in LS. 6: Lat, Sp. 7: Eng Secondary Sch, Grady Okla 28-30; Eng & Lat Secondary Sch, Stringtown Okla 30-32; Eng, Lat, Sp Secondary Sch, Ringling Okla 33-46; Eng & lib Secondary Sch, Healdton Okla 46-50; Lib secondary sch, McAlester Okla 51-53; Asst libn E Central State Col (Ada Okla) 53-. 8: State Chm of Sequoyah Child Bk Award 63. 9: NEA; OklaLA; OklaEA. 10: Bus & Prof Women's Club; AAUW; Delta Kappa Gamma. 14: Ref, govt documents, acquis. 15: 431 W First, Ada Ok 74820.

McCALL, MARGARET RUTH. b Maryville Tenn 7 N 15. 5: Maryville Col 35-39 (Eng) AB; Peabody summers 47-49 BS in LS; UWash NDEA Inst 65. 7: Eng tchr Walland High Sch, Walland Tenn 39-42; Libn & Eng tchr Friendsville High Sch, Friendsville Tenn 42-48; Libn Lakeview High Sch, Winter Garden Fla 48-54; Libn Howard Jr High Sch, Orlando Fla 54-55; Libn William R Boone High Sch, Orlando Fla 55-62; Curric asst in Lib Serv Bd of Pub Instr, Orlando Fla 62-. 9: ALA; NEA; SELA; FlaLA; FlaASchL; Fla A-V Assn; FlaEA. 10: AAUW; Delta Kappa Gamma. 14: Sch libs. 15: 1418 Georgia blvd, Orlando Fl 32803.

McCALLA, NELLE (MARIE). b Tenn. 5: Bryson Col 21-24 (Eng, LS) AB; Peabody summers 25, 26, 30, 31, 33, 35, 37 BS in LS; Chicago summer 47 (LS); Columbia U summers 50, 52, 53-54 MS in LS. 6: Fr. 7: Elem tchr Shelby Co Schs, Shelby Co Tenn 24-26; Jr high tchr Taylor Co Schs, Perry Fla 26-27; Tchr libn Shelby Co Schs, Shelby Co Tenn 27-37, Libn 37-43; Instr Ind State Tchrs Col summer 39-43; Visiting Asst Prof UDenv Grad Lib Sch summer 55; Act libn Beirut Col for Women (Beirut Lebanon) 56-57; Lecturer Specialist Tchr Train Inst, Kuala Lumpur Malaysia 62; Assoc Prof Lib Sci Ind State U 43-69. 8: Consul to sch libs State of Ind 48-61; Act Libn Beirut Col for Women, Beirut Lebanon 56-57; Lecturer on sch libs Specialist Tchrs Train Inst, Kuala Lumpur Malaysia 62; Asst Prof of Lib Sci UDenver summer 55. 9: ALA-AASchL; IndLA; IndSchLA (past chm Sch Lib Develop Com; v-pres & pres 67-68) ; Ind State Tchrs Assn; MalaysianLA (non mem). 10: AAUW; Delta Kappa Gamma; Faculty Women's Club; Alpha Omicron Pi; AAUP; Alpha Beta Alpha; Women's Symphony Central Presby Church,Terre Haute; Elder 66-69. 11: Smith-Mundt Award to visit Kuala Lumpur Malaysia as lecturer 62. 12: Jt author "Asia; A Guide to Books for Children," Asia Soc (66). 13: Yes. 14: Sch lib prog, hist of the bks, admin, sel of materials. 15: Ind State Univ, Terre Haute In 47809.

McCALLION, PETER W. b Boston Mass 23 N 42. 5: State Col at Boston 60-64 (Eng) BS in Ed; Simmons 64-69 MLS. 6: Sp. 7: Sch libn Sachem Central Sch System, NY 64-68. 14: Ref. 15: 77 Hamilton st, Readville Ma 02136.

McCALLUM, ELIZABETH ILENE (CARSON). b Tring Alta Can 19 S 19. 4: Finlay McCallum. 5: UAlta 42-45 (Eng) BA; Toronto 48-49 BLS. 7: Tchr Vermilion Sch Div, Vermilion Can 39-42; High sch instr Correspondence Sch Br, Edmonton Can 45-48; Libn Edmonton Pub Lib, Edmonton Can 49-56; Sch libn Edmonton (Can) Pub Sch Bd, Victoria Composite High Sch 63-67; Libn Ext Lib UAlta 68-. 8: Instr in sch lib serv, UAlta summer 65, 66. 9: CanLA; AltaLA; Alta Tchrs Assn (Sch Lib Coun). 10: Alta Hist Soc; Delta Kappa Gamma. 14: Sch libs, ref, rare bks. 15: 11917-90 st, Edmonton Alta Can.

McCALLUM, HEATHER. b Toronto Can 11 Ap 27. 5: Toronto 45-49 BA, 56-57 BLS. 7: Publ Cos, Toronto & London Eng 49-55; Libn Imperial Oil Ltd, Toronto 55-60; Head theatre sect Toronto Pub Lib 61-. 9: SLA (pres Toronto Chap 65-66); Can Theatre Centre. 15: Toronto Pub Lib College & St George sts, Toronto 2B Can.

McCAMENT, PAUL H. b Albuquerque NM 24 Mr 31. 5: UAriz 49-50 (Bus Admun); UNM 50-54 (Anthrop) BA; N Tex StateU 67-69 MLS. 6: Sp. 7: Tech libn Albuquerque Div ACF Industries, Albuquerque 59-61; Admin Specialist USAF A/1c 62-66; Spec Collections UNM 67-, Acting Soc Sci Ref Libn 68; Asst loan libn Tex ChristianU 69-. 9: ALA; SLA. 10: Alpha Lambda Sigma. 14: Circ, ref. 15: 2917 McCart apt 8, Fort Worth Tx 76110.

McCANDLESS, NAN (PALMER). b Hamilton Ohio 14 O 10. 5: Western Col for Women 28-29 (Liberal Arts). 7: Asst libn Free Pub Lib, Middletown Ohio 30-35; Libn Douglas Aircraft Co Inc, El Segundo Cal 51-59; Corporate libn Douglas Aircraft Co Inc, Santa Monica Cal 59-64; Dir Pacific Aerospace Lib, Los Angeles 64-68; Dir Pacific Tech Info Lib Northrop Inst Tech, Inglewood Cal 68-. 8: ASTIA Thesaurus Revision; Consul DDC 62. 9: SLA (sec Local Chap 69); ASIS. 13: Yes. 14: Indexing, mgt, aviation hist. 15: 1119 W Manchester ave, Inglewood Ca 90301.

McCANLESS, CHRISTEL LUDEWIG. b Peenemuende Germany 20 N 39. 4: George F McCanless Jr. 5: Ala Col 57-61 (Eng) BA; UNC (Chapel Hill) 61-63 (LS), 66 MSLS. 06: Ger, Sp, Fr. 7: Lib asst ref Redstone Sci Info Center, Redstone Arsenal Ala summers 58-61; Libn UAla(Huntsville) 63-68; Consul, non-textbk materials Bkstore 68-. 9: SLA; AlaLA (Nomin Com 68-69). 10: Bd Dirs Friends of the Huntsville Pub Lib; Water Safety Com; Amer Red Cross; Huntsville Appraisal Com; Ala Space Sci Ctr; Mu Alpha Theta; Beta Phi Mu. 14: Admin, ref, tchg. 15: 1320 Monte Sano blvd SE, Huntsville Al 35801.

McCANLESS, ROSAMOND. b Asheville NC. 5: Converse Col 23-27 (Eng) BA; UNC 34-35 (Eng) MA, 36, 38 BA in LS. 6: Fr. 7: Catlgr Sondley Ref Lib, Asheville NC 36-37; Libn Richmond Prof Inst 38-68; Libn Va Commonwealth U Acad Div 68-69, asst to dir of libs 69-. 9: Archaeol Inst Amer (Richmond Chap: rec sec); VaLA; Conf East Col Libns. 10: Va Mus of Fine Arts. 14: Admin. 15: 901 W Franklin st, Richmond Va 23220.

McCANN, ESTHER N. b Delphi Ind 14 Mr 18. 4: Franklin T McCann. 5: Ind State U 36-40 (Eng) BS; UDenver 43-45 BSLS. 7: Asst libn Evanston Twp High Sch, Evanston Ill 40-42; Asst catlgr Denver Pub Lib 43-45; Asst catlgr White Plains Pub Lib, White Plains NY 45-47; Libn Auburn Pub Lib, Auburn Ala 48, 52; Act catlg libn Auburn U 55-57, Act ref libn 58-59; Catlgr Horseshoe Bend Reg Lib, Dadeville Ala 59-64; Catlg libn Auburn U 64-. 9: ALA; AlaLA. 10: LWV; Friends of the Auburn Pub Lib. 15: P O Box 325, Auburn Al 36830.

McCANON, MARILYN. b Quincy Ill 4 Jl 23. 5: MacMurray Col 40-42; Culver-Stockton Col 42-44 (Pol Sci) BS in Ed; Ind U 57 Lib Sci MAT. 7: Pre-prof asst Purdue U Lib 46-48; Indianapolis Pub Lib: Pre-prof asst 48-51, Prof br asst 52-57, Bkmob libn 57-60, Supv of ext serv Indianapolis-Marion Co, Indianapolis 60-. 9: ALA; IndLA (Dist Off 3 yrs, mem Lib Educ Com). 10: Indianapolis Pub Lib Staff Assn (past pres); Beta Phi Mu. 14: Admin. 15: Indianapolis Pub Lib 40 E St Clair, Indianapolis In 46204.

McCARGAR, SUSAN ELAINE. b Medina NY 11 Mr 45. 5: UArizona 62-66 (Anthrop, Hist) BA; Syracuse 66-67 MSLS. 06: Fr. 7: lib aide Tucson Pub Lib, Tucson Ariz summer 66; Asst libn Drake Mem Lib SUNY (Brockport) 67-. 14: Catlg. 15: 45 Chappell st apt 3, Brockport NY 14420.

McCARTHY, CATHERINE RITA. b Lawrence Mass 12 O 17. 5: Simmons 35-39 (LS) BS. 7: Catlgr Boston Pub Lib Recatlg Proj, Boston 40; Gen asst MIT 41; Libn English High Sch, Boston 42; Mass State Lib: Jr asst 43-46, Sr asst 47-54, Ref asst 55-60; Supv of tech processing Mass Bur of Lib Ext, Boston 60-. 9: ALA; NELA; SLA (Boston Chap: sec 62-63, chm Soc Sci Sect 63-64); MassLA (Fin Com 62-64, Recr Com 64-65); NE Tech Serv Libns (chm Pub Rel 64-65, treas 65-67, v-pres 67-68, pres 68-69). 12: "Bibliography on the Negro in American Life" (63 suppl 68). 14: Catlg, ref. 15: 63 Avalon rd, W Roxbury Ma 02132.

McCARTHY, DAVID J. b Phila 21 Ag 15. 4: Elaine McCarthy. 5: La Salle Col 34-35 (Bus); Temple 49-52 Assn in LS. 7: Reporter "Phila Record" 38-42; (Lt) US Army 42-45; Libn Gray & Rogers Inc, Phila 52-. 9: SLA. 10: Disabled Amer Veterans & Offs. 14: Ref. 15: Gray & Rogers Inc 12 S 12th st, Phila Pa 19107.

McCARTHY, GEORGE EDWIN. b Bayonne NJ 16 N 14. 4: Minerva MacGillis. 5: St Peter's Col 32-36 (Liberal Arts) AB; Columbia 36-37 BS in LS. 6: Fr. 7: Libn Xavier High Sch, NYC 36-39; Libn Fordham U Manhattan Div 39-42; Libn Middletown Air Serv Command, Middletown Penn 42-46; Libn Jersey City Jr Col 46-50; Libn Geigy Chem Corp, Ardsley NY 51-. 9: SLA; ASIS; BSA; ACS (Div Chem Lit); NY Lib Club. 13: Yes. 14: Admin, tech libs & info centers. 15: 3 Somerstown rd, Ossining NY 10562.

McCARTHY, INEZ (SHAW). b E Cleveland Ohio 28 F 13. 5: Wheaton Col (Norton Mass) 34 (Eng) AB; Rutgers 63 MLS. 6: Fr, Ger. 7: Asst Pub Lib, Hamden Conn 52-54, Br libn 54-59; Trainee NY State Lib 62; Dir Free pub Lib, New Brunswick NJ 63-. 9: ALA; NJLA. 14: Admin. 15: 116 Livingston ave, New Brunswick NJ 08902.

McCARTHY, MARION ADELINE. b Wash DC 9 D 40. 5: Boston U 58-62 (Ger) AB, 62-63 (Ger) AM; Simmons 64-66 (LS) SM. 6: Ger, Fr, Lat. 7: Boston Pub Lib; Pre-prof asst educ dept 63-66, Prof asst educ dept 66; Ref libn Sci Dept 66-67; Libn Jr High, E Arlington Mass 67-. 9: ALA; -AASchL; MassSchLA; MassTA. 14: Sch libs, ref. 15: 2 Pacific st, S Boston Ma 02127.

McCARTHY, MARY CONSTANCE. b Potsdam NY 7 My 28. 5: State U Col (Potsdam NY) 44-48 (Educ) BE; UDenver 50-51 (LS) MA; SUNY (Buffalo) 62-66 (Soc Scis) MS; Chicago 68- (Libnship). 07: Field libn US Army in Germany, Nurnberg, Bayreuth 51-53; Asst libn Niagara U Lib 53-57; Asst libn State U Col (Potsdam NY) 57-62; Circ libn SUNY(Buffalo) 62-68. 9: ALA; NYLA. 10: AAUP. 14: Acad libs. 15: 1450 E 55th pl apt 627S, Chicago Il 60637.

McCARTHY, MARY E. b Friendship NY 2 O 20. 5: Alfred U 39-43 (Eng) BA; Albany State Tchrs Col summers 45-49 (Eng) MA; Geneseo State Tchrs Col summers (LS) Certif; ULondon summer 54. 7: Eng tchr-libn Belfast Central Sch, Belfast NY 43-65, Libn 65-. 9: NY State Tchrs Assn. 15: 18 Queen Anne st, Friendship NY 14739.

McCARTHY, PAUL H(ENRY) JR. b Rochester NY 16 O 39. 4: Lucy Anne Knefley. 5: St John Fisher Col 57-62 (Hist) BA; Syracuse 62-64 (LS) MS; UAlaska 65- (Hist); Amer U 66 (Archival Admin) Certif. 07: Asst stack supv Syracuse U 62-63, Ms assoc 63-64; Asst readers serv libn UAlaska 64-65, U archivist 65-. 9: ALA; SAA; Alaska Lib Assn (pres); Internat Coun Archives; Amer Records Mgt Assn; Alaska Hist Soc (Bd Dirs, sec Exec Bd). 12: Ed "Anthony J Dimond Papers: An Inventory" (68). 14: Archives, mss. 15: Box 5-687, College Ak 99701.

McCARTHY, SISTER RITA OF JESUS FSE. b Jewett City Conn 14 F 1897. 5: Albertus Magnus 25-28 (Philos, Eng) BA; Boston Col summers 35-41 (Eng) MA; CatholicU 46-47 BSLS. 6: Fr, Sp, Lat. 7: Tchr Putnam Catholic Acad, Putnam Conn 32-42; Tchr Ker Anna Jr Col 43-46; Tchr & prin Holy Ghost Acad, Tupper Lake NY 49-60; Tchr & libn Rice Mem High Sch, Burlington Vt 60-63; Prin Putnam Cath Acad 63-68, Hd libn 68-. 8: Tchr, eng & Span in private girls' sch, Landerneau France 47-49. 9: ALA; CathLA; NCTE; NELA; ConnLA. 14: Catlg, ref. 15: Putnam Catholic Acad 18 Maple st, Putnam Ct 06260.

McCARTHY, STEPHEN A(NTHONY). b Eden Valley Minn 7 O 08. 4: Mary Louise Wedemeyer. 5: St Thomas Col 25-28; Gonzaga U 28-30 AB, MA; McGill 31-32 BLS; Chicago 35-37, 41 PhD. 7: Tchr Gonzaga High Sch, Spokane wash 29-31; Asst libn & catlgr St John's U (Minn) 33-34; Ref asst Chicago-American 34-35; Libn U Col northwestern U 35-37; UNeb Lib: Asst dir 37-41, Assoc dir 41-42, Dir 42-44; Asst dir Columbia U Libs 44-46; Dir Cornell U Lib 46-60; Dir Cornell U Libs 60-67; Exec dir Assoc of Research Libs 67-. 08; Fulbright Lecturer & Consul Egypt 53-54; Surveyor &/or Gen & Bldg Consul: UNH 49, 65; York U Toronto 62-; McGill U 63-64; Hunter Col 64; Ohio U 64-65; Dalhousie U 65; Loyola Col Montreal 64; Loyola Col Baltimore 64; Midwest Inter-Lib Center 63-64; and others; Project Intrex 65; Fulbright lectr ULondon 67. 9: ALA (Coun several terms, var coms);-ACRL;-RTSD (chm Copying Methods Sect 58-59); AR (Exec sec 60-62); NebLA (prs 40); NYLA (pres 51-52). 10: Cornell Club of NY. 12: "Survey of University of New Hampshire Library" (49); "Survey of McGill University Libraries," with R C Logsdon (63); "The Midwest Inter-Library Center," with R C Swank (64); Final Report(s) to the Rector(s), Alexandria, Cairo, and Ibrahim universities (54); "Report on a Proposed Union catalog in the Field of American Studies in Britain" (67). 13: Yes. 14: Admin, lib bldgs, catlg, clsf. 15: 4500 Connecticut ave NW, Washington DC 20008.

McCARTNEY, HILDA MARIE (HERMANSEN). b Baker Ore. 4: Bruce Robert McCartney. 5: UCLA 48 (Soc Sci); Long Beach State Col 49-50 (Soc Sci) BA, 50-52 (Educ) MA; USoCal 53-55 MSLS, 55-60 (Educ) Ed D. 7: Teletype operator Press Telegram, Long Beach Cal 40-43; Instr Frank Wiggin's Trade Sch, Los Angeles 47-48; Self employed, Long Beach Cal 43-47; Costa Mesa Union Sch Dist, Costa Mesa Cal: Tchr 50-52, Libn 52-53, Dist libn 53-58, Dir of lib serv & curriculum consul 58-66; Coord Instr Media Serv Newport-Mesa Unified Sch Dist 66-. 8: Tchg child & adolescent lit at UCal(Irvine) 65-; Assignments within Costa Mesa Sch Dist; chm A-V Com, Lib Com, Title III, Fed Aid to Educ; Americanism Com, Adv Com for Educ Materials, & Soc Studies tchg Educ Psych math for tchrs, Curr So Cal Col; Ed Media Chapman Col. 9: Nat Soc Study Educ; Assn; Assn Supv & Curr Development; NEA; ALA; Nat Assn Tchg Eng; Internat Reading Assn; Sch Lib Assn; Assn Childhood Educ; CalASchL; Cal Tchrs Assn; A-V Assn Cal; Cal Assn Supv & Curr Development; DAVI; NSSE; NASP; CalASSA; CalASA; OCESAA. 10: AAUW (Ed of Bulletin); Delta Epsilon; USoCal Assn for Doctors in Educ; Sigma Kappa; Alumni Assn of USC; Phi Beta Mu; Alumni Assn of USoCal Lib Sch; Alpha Mu Gamma; Bus & Prof Women's Club; PTA (Hon life mem); Ebell Club; Zonta Club; Friends of Lib; C of C Town & Gown. 12: "Selection of Instructional Materials in the Elementary Schools of California." 13: Yes. 14: Child & adolescent lit. 15: 2916 Redwood ave, Costa Mesa Ca 92626.

McCARTNEY, MARGARET (O'CONNELL). b NYC. 4: W Scott McCartney. 5: Hunter Col 38-41 (Hist) BA; Pratt 42 MLS. 06: Sp. 7: Clerk NY Pub Lib 41; Ref asst Queensborough Pub Lib, Astoria Br 42; Documents libn British Info Serv, NYC 43-47; Chief Libn Nat Ind Conf Bd, NYC 48-49; Head gifts & exch dept Ohio State U 49-51; Libn Ohio Acad of Sci, Columbus Ohio 49-51; Libn St Raphael Sch, E Meadow NY 62-68; Libn Ho ly Family Sch 67-68; Libn Holy Trinity Diocesan High Sch, Hicksville 68-. 8: Trustee E Meadow Pub Lib 65-; Bibliog Town & Country Planning Brit Info Serv, NY 43-47; Pres E Meadow Lib Bd of Trustees 68-. 9: ALA; CathLA; SLA; NYLA; NassauLA; NY Tt rustees Assn. 10; Mercy Hosp League; Rosary Soc; E Meadow Lib Trustee Bd; Amer Cancer Soc; Colum biettes. 12: "Bibliography of Town and Country Planning in England," (45). 14: Ref, admin. 15: 2089 Longfellow ave, E Meadow NY 11554.

McCARTNEY, V FAY (BRADLEY). b Ottawa Can 6 O 25. 5: UToronto 44-47 BA; Ontarion Col of Educ 47-48 High Sch Asst Certif, 64 Specialist Sch Libnship. 7: Tchr Lansdowne Continuation Sch, Lansdowne Ont Can 48-50; Tchr S Carleton Dist High Sch, Richmond Ont can 54-64; Tchr & libn Collegiate Inst Bd of Ottawa, 64-. 9: CanLA; CanSchLA (sec 67). 10: Ont Sec Sch Tchrs Fed). 14: Sch libs. 15: 414 Fraser ave, Ottawa 13 Ont Can.

McCARTY, EILEEN K. b Lima Ohio 31 O 44. 5: Bluffton Col 62-66 (Elem Educ) BSEd; UIll 9urbana) 67-68 (LS) MS. 6: Fr. 7: Elem tchr Kettering City Schs Kettering Ohio 66-67; Child libn St Charles Co Lib, St Charles Mo 68-. 9: ALA; MoLA. 10: Beta Phi Mu; Pi Delta. 14: Child serv. 15: St Charles Co Lib, 1900 Merrill dr, St Charles Mo 63301.

McCARTY, PATRICIA J. b Sheldon Iowa 18 Mr 34. 5: Col of St Benedict (St Joseph Minn) 53-57 (Music) BA; Col of St Catherine 59-60 BS in LS. 7: Jr libn UMinn(Minneapolis) 60-62; Libn UMinn Engnr Lib 62-64; Instr & Libn UMinn (St Paul) 64-. 9: SLA. 15: 1969 Asbury N, St Paul Mn 55113.

McCAULEY, ELFRIEDA B. b Milwaukee 11 Ag 15. 4: Leon McCauley. 5: UWis 32-35, 37-38 (Lat) BS; Columbia 63-65 (LS) MS, 68-69 (LS). 06: Fr, Ger. 7: Child libn Milwaukee Pub Lib 35-40; Reporter Religious News Serv, NYC 41-43; Free lance publicity Elfrieda McCauley Publicity, Brooklyn NY 43-46; Exec McCauley Enterprises, Greenwich Conn 59-64; Exec Town & Country Books, Greenwich Conn 62-64; Libn Greenwich High Sch, Greenwich Conn 64-; Coord Secondary Sch Libs, Greenwich Conn. 8: Free lance ed. 9: ALA; ConnEA; ConnSchLA; NELA. 10: PTA; Beta Phi Mu. 12: "Book of Prayers" (55); "Treasury of Faith" (57); "Book of Family Worship" (58); "Prayers for Girls; "Day Book of the Bible; "Day Book of Prayers" (60). 14: Pub rel, child & yp serv, sch lib admin. 15: 32 Longmeadow rd, Riverside Ct 06878.

McCAULEY, SHIRLEY ELIZABETH. b Portland Ore 26 Ja 36. 5: Willamette U 54-57, 59 (Journalism, Soc Sci, Educ); UOre 57-58 (Eng Lit) BA; Ore Col of Educ 60, 61 (Educ); UWash 63, 64 (LS); Ore State U NDEA Ed Media Inst sum 65; UWash 66, 67 MALS. 6: Fr, Lat. 7: Capitol guide State of Ore, Salem Ore summers 57, 58; Eng Instr N Salem Sr High Sch, Salem Ore 59-60; Exec sec Young Republican Fed, Ore 60-61; Senate page Ore Legis, Salem Ore 61; Libn & a-v coordinator Central High Sch, Independence Ore 62-. 8: Central Dist 13J Curriculum Com 64-; Central Dist 13J A-V Com 64-. 9: ALA-AASchL; NEA; OreEA; OreStateLA; MPYSLA; CEA; CTA; OAVI. 10: Chi Omega Alumnae; Pentacle Theater; Ore Hist Soc; Salem Mem & Gen Hosp Charities; Marion Co Hist Soc; Friends of Salem Pub Lib. 12: "OreStateLA Newsletter" (64-). 14: Sch libnship, ya. 15: P O Box 3051, Salem Or 97302.

McCAULEY, WALTER THOMAS. b E St Louis Ill 5 O 28. 5: Murray State Col 48-49, 54-57 (Hist, LS) BA; Peabody 57-58 MALS. 6: Fr, Sp. 7: US Army, Ft Leonard Wood Mo 51-53; US Army asst libn, Ft Leonard Wood Mo 52; Ref libn Ind State Col 58-61; Tchg materials libn Ind State U 61-63; Head pub serv Nev State Lib 63-65; Head ext serv Tucson Pub Lib 65-66; Asst soc sci libn UIda 66-69, Soc scis libn 69-. 8: Exec Dir Nat Lib Week, Ida 68-69. 9: ALA; ArizStateLA; NevStateLA; MPLA; IdaLA; PNLA. 10: AAUP; Civil Defense Shelter Program; Eagle Scout, Order of Arrow; Alpha Beta Alpha; Sierra Club; Alpha Beta Alpha. 14: Admin, ref. 15: PO Box 3252 Univ Sta, Moscow Id 83843.

McCAULLEY, MARION ROBERT. b Carroll Iowa 12 S 23. 5: UWyo 43-44; UIowa 41-43, 46-47, 48-50 BA (Journalism), MA (Amer Civilization); UIll 51-52 Ms in LS. 6: Sp. 7: Army Infantry 43-46; Tchr-libn Eagle Grove (Iowa) Pub Schs 50-51; Head Undergrad Lib UTex 52-55; Head ref libn UNeb (Omaha) 55-. 8: Assoc Prof Lib Sci UNeb (Omaha). 9: ALA; NebLA; MPLA. 10: AAUP; Beta Phi Mu. 12: Former guest ed "Texas Library Journal." 13: Yes. 14: Ref. 15: 6625 No 65th st, Omaha Nb 68112.

McCHESNEY, KATHRYN MARIE (SPENCER). b Curwensville Penn 14 Ja 36. 4: Thomas David McChesney. 5: UAkron 57-62 (Hist, Classics) BA in Ed; Kent State 64-65 MLS. 6: Fr, Lat. 7: Tchr Springfield High Sch, Akron Ohio 62-63; Grad asst Kent State U Sch, Kent Ohio 64-65; Libn Springfield High Sch, Akron Ohio 63-68; Inst & Asst to dean Kent State U Sch Lib Sci 68-. 9: NEA; OhioEA; ALA; AALS; OhioLA; OhioASc hL; YLA. 10: Uniontown Jr Woman's Club; AAUP. 14: Ya wk. 15: 3611 Edison st NW, Uniontown Oh 44685.

McCLAIN, ALICE. b Telluride Colo 20 Ap 18. 5: Mont State U 35-37; State U Iowa 38-39 (Eng); UDenver 39-40 (LS) BA with Certif; West State Col Colo 40-42 (Eng) MA. 7: Asst libn West State Col (Colo) 40-43, Libn 43; US Army libn, Hill Field Utah 43-45; US Army libn, Germany 45-47; Sr asst circ Seattle Pub Lib 48-51; Ref libn Ida State U 52-53, Assoc libn 53-66; Assoc dir Mont State U 66-69, Dir 70-. 8: Lib 21, Seattle World's Fair 62. 9: ALA; PNLA (sec 55-56; St ate rep 57-59; 2nd v-pres 61-62; pres-elect 65-66; pres 66-67; var coms); IdaLA (pres 62-63; chm &/or mem var coms); MontLA. 10: AAUW; PEO; AAUP; Delta Kappa Gamma. 13: Yes. 14: Ref, admin. 15: 411 1/2 W College st, Bozeman Mt 59715.

McCLAIN, EDITH (THOMPSON). b Mobile Ala 6 Ja 04. 4: Isaiah McClain. 5: St Augustine's Col 28-32 (Hist) AB; Hampton Inst 32-33 bls. 6: Fr. 7: Tchr Pub Sch System, Mobile Ala 22-28; Libn: Jr Col, Fort Valley Ga 33-35, Livingstone Col 35-36, Sch System, Lexington NC 36-43, Pub Lib Br, Lexington NC 36-43; Asst libn St Augustine's Col 43-44; Libn: Pub Sch System, Mobile Ala 46-49, Pub Br, Mobile Ala 49-50, Pub Sch System, Mobile Ala 50-. 9: NEA; ALA; AlaLA; AlaSchLA. 10: YWCA; Alpha Kappa Alpha. 14: Ref. 15: 504 Weinacker ave, Mobile Al 36604.

McCLAIN, EUGENE WILSON. b Omaha 16 Mr 24. 5: UVt 44 (Col Trng Det, AS); UCal(Berkeley) 46-49 (Music) BA; San Francisco State Col 49 (Educ) Cred; UCal(Berkeley) 49-51 (Musicology) MA, 53-55 BLS. 6: Ger, Fr. 7: Tech Sgt (T/4) US Army, European African Mid East Theater 43-46; Music tchr Reedley Col 51-53; Libn Pleasant Hill High Sch, Pleasant Hill Cal 56-. 8: Chm Pleasant Hill High Sch Lib Com 56-; Lecturer in Byzantine hist, Pleasant Hill High Sch 64. 9: NEA; Cal Tchrs Assn; CalASchLA. 10: Cal Alumni Assn; UCal Lib Sch Alumni Assn; Mediaeval Acad Amer; Internat Musicological Assn; Gesellschaft fuer Musikforschung; Phi Delta Kappa; Alpha Mu. 14: Ref, bibliog, catlg, rare bks in musicology. 15: 776 Duke Circle College Park, Pleasant Hill Ca 94523.

McCLAIN, HELEN (MILES). b Durham NC 18 Ja 27. 4: Arnold G McClain Sr. 5: N Car Col 55-58 (Commercial Educ) BS; UPittsburgh 62-63 MSLS. 6: Fr. 7: Mgr Bk Store N Car Col 58-60; Br hd Carnegie Lib, Pittsburgh Pa 63-. 9: ALA; PennLA; PittsburghLA. 10: Delta Sigma Theta. 14: Adult and yp serv. 15: 6962 Lemington ave, Pittsburgh Pa 15206.

McCLAIN, IONE WILLIAMS. b Russellville Ark 14 O 04. 5: Hendrix Col 22-25 (Fr) AB (magna cum laude); UIll 30-31 BS in LS. 6: Fr, Sp, Lat, Portu. 7: Lang tchr Elaine High Sch, Elaine Ark 25-26; Lang tchr Col of the Ozarks 27-30; Libn Sue Bennett Col 31-37; Libn Faulkner Co Lib, Conway Ark 37-38; Libn-in-chg of period UWyo Lib 38-42; Libn Sheridan Col 48-66; Humanities libn UWyo Lib 66-. 9: ALA; NEA; MPLA (treas); WyoLA (pres, treas); WyoEA. 10: Beta Phi Mu; Delta Kappa Gamma; AAUW; Wyo Press Women; Nat Press Women. 13: Yes. 14: Ref, admin (humanities). 15: 1626 Garfield, Laramie Wy 82070.

McCLARREN, ROBERT ROYCE. b Delta Ohio 15 Mr 21. 4: Margaret Aileen Weed. 5: Antioch Col 38-40; Muskingum Col 40-42 AB; Ohio State U 47-49, 50-51 (Eng) MA; Columbia 53-54 (LS) MS. 7: Armored unit cmdr (NCO) 14th Armored Div, Continental US & European theater 42-45; Armored unit cmdr (2d Lt) 14th & 20th Armored Div, US & European theater 45-46; Registration off VA, Cincinnati 46-47; Eng instr Gen Motors Inst, Flint Mich 49-50; Armored unit cmdr & communications off (1st Lt) 3d Armored & 40th Infantry Div, US & Korea 51-52; Various units US Army Reserve 46-51, 52-(Major, Armor); Tech asst prep div ref dept NY Pub Lib 53-54; Head circ dept Oak Park (Ill) Pub Lib 54-55, Act head libn 55; Head Libn Crawfordsville (Ind) Pub Lib 55-58; Head Libn Huntington (WVa) Pub Lib 58-62; Head Libn West Cos (WVa) Reg Lib 60-62; Dir Ind State Lib 62-67; Exec dir N Suburban Lib Syst, Morton Grove Ill 67-. 8: Governor's Commsn on Arts, State of Ind 63-65; Ind Sesquicentennial Commsn 63-66; Sec Ind Certif Bd 62-67; Fac Lib Sch UWis summer64; Dept Lib Sci, Rosary 68-. 9: ALA (chm circ serv discussion group 64-65);-ASD (sec 64-66);-AAStateL (sec 64-65; chm ALA-NEA Jt Com 67-68, Coun 68, treas 68-72); ASIS; IllLA; IndSchLA (life mem); WVaLA (pres 61); Ind Adult Educ Assn (pres 65). 10: Indianapoli s Literary Club; The Portfo lio (Indianapolis); Beta Phi Mu; Deerfield (Ill) Hist Soc; Chicago Lib Club. 11: Joseph Towne Wheeler Award, Sch of Lib Serv Columbia, 54. 12: Ed "Indiana Lives" (67). 13: Yes. 14: Admin, legisl, profess educ. 15: 1560 Oakwood pl, Deerfield Il 60015.

McCLASKEY, HARRIS CLARK. b Trenton NJ 4 Ap 31. 4: Maud Berninger. 5: Col of Wooster 49-53 (Philos) BA; Princeton Theol Sem 53-54 (Theol); UWash 55-56 MLS, 67-(Educ). 06: Fr. 7: Proof reader Gallup Polls, Princeton NJ 53-54; Research consul & ed "Letter Magazine" Character-Intelligence Researchers, Tucson 53-54; Sub-prof asst Seattle Pub Lib 56; Asst libn Renton Pub Lib, Renton Wash 56-57, Head Libn 57-62; Lib consul Wash State Lib 62-65, Dir inst lib serv 65-. 8: Library -21 Training & Standby, Seattle World's Fair 62; Dir wash Lib Film Circuit 62-. 9: ALA-LAD (Wash State rep 59-61, Reg rep for Pacific Northwest 61-66); -CSD (chm Com Lib Serv to Exceptional Child 64-66; Bldgs Com for Hosp, Inst & Spec Libs 64-65)-AHIL (chm Bibliotherapy Com Sub-Com on Research 64-67, Troubled Child Com 64-, chm Com on Research Activities 65-67); Amer Correctional Assn (Lib Com 63-); Nat Assn for Retarded Child; PNLA (chm Legis Com 59-62, chm Recr Com 62-65); WashLA (Exec Bd 59-61, chm &/or mem 3 coms 59-); Northwest Dist LA (pres 58-59); Puget Sound Lib Club (pres 61-62). 10: Wash Assn for Retarded Child; Rotary; Lower Puget Sound Development Center; Beta Phi Mu; Phi Delta Kappa. 12: "A Study Recommending Establishment of a Cooperative Library Program Between the Washington State Department of Institutions and the Washington State Library" (64); Ed "Letter Magazine" (54-55); Ed "Library News Bulletin" (64-). 13: Yes. 14: Instl & hosp lib serv, pub lib development, child serv. 15: Wash State Lib, Olympia Wa 98502.

McCLASKEY, MAUD (BERNINGER). b Abington Penn 9 Ag 29. 4: Harris C McClaskey. 5: UPenn 48-49 (Music); Col of Wooster 49-53 (Eng) BA; UAriz 52 (Eng); UWash 58-59 MLS. 6: Fr, Ger. 7: Sub asst Free Pub Lib of Phila summer 52; Stud asst UAriz Lib 52; Stud asst Col of Wooster Lib 50-53; Sec Educational Testing Serv, Princeton NJ 53-54; Catlg libn UWash Lib 59-61; Catlg libn Wash State Law Lib 62-63, Catlg & ref libn Timberland Lib Demonstration 63-67; Catlg libn King Co Lib Syst 68-. 9: ALA; AALL (Exch Com); PNLA (Nom Com of Cat Div 65); (Com on Reorgan 66); WashLA. 10: Beta phi Mu; Wash Assn foe Retarded Child; ACLU; AAUW. 13: Yes. 14: Catlg, ref. 15: 527 E 13th apt 12, Olympia Wa 98502.

McCLAUGHRY, HELEN C (OSELKA). b Chicago 29 F 24. 4: Donald McClaughry. 5: Morton Jr Col 41-43; Rosary Col 43-45 (Hist) BA, 45 BALS. 6: Czech, Ger. 7: Page-asst br libn Pub Lib, Berwyn Ill 39-45; Asst libn US Army Hosp, Santa Fe NM 45-46; Libn US Army, Schofield Barracks Hawaii 46-47; Child libn Pub Lib, Riverside Ill 47-49; Libn VA Hosp, Hines Ill 49-50; Chief Libn VA Hosp, Dwight Ill 50-52; Asst libn USAF, Lowry AFB Colo 55-57, Base libn 57-. 8: Denver Com for Nat Lib Week 60-65. 9: ALA (sec Armed Forces Sect 64-65); ColoLA; MPLA (Nom Com, Pub Rel Com). 10: AAUW; LWV; Bus & Prof Women's Club. 15: 3493 S Dallas court, Denver Co 80222.

McCLEARN, NORMA JEAN (FISCHER). b Pittsburgh Penn 3 S 44. 4: L Thomas McClearn Jr. 5: Edinboro State Col 62-66 BS in LS; Shippensburg State Col 68- (LS). 7: Libn Aliquippa Sr High Sch, Aliquippa Penn 66-67; Catlgr B F Jones Memorial Lib, Aliquippa penn 66-67; Circ Coyle Free Lib, Chambersburg Penn 67; Libn J F Faust Jr High Sch, Chambersburg Penn 67-. 9: ALA; ChambersburgEA. 10: Kappa Delta Pi; Chambersburg Commun Theatre; Chambersburg Film Classic Soc. 14: Child lib, ref. 15: 115 Brumbaugh ave, Chambersburg Pa 17201.

McCLEARY, WILLIAM (ERNEST). b Alexandria La 29 My 27. 5: Centenary Col (La) 44-48 (Humanities) BA; LSU 48-50 (Journalism) MA, 57-58 (LS) MS; UIll 66- (LS). 07: (Cpl), clk USMC 45-46, 50-51; Tchr Caddo Parish Schs, Shreveport La 50-57; Lib trainee LSU 57-58; Documents & inter-lib loans libn Shreveport Mem Lib, Shreveport La 58, Head catlg & acquis dept 58-59; Libn Union Producing Co (Pennzoil United Inc), Shreveport La 60-66; Ref libn LSU (Shreveport) 66-. 8: Consul Murphy Oil Corp, El Dorado Ark 64. 9: SLA (pres La Chap 66-67); ALA; LaLA (treas 64-65). 10: Caddo-Bossier Lib Club; AAUP. 11: City of Oslo Scholarship, Univ of Oslo 53. 12: Ed "Bulletin of the LaLA" (65-66). 13: Yes. 14: Ref, tchg, admin. 15: 6147 Creswell rd, Shreveport La 77106.

McCLELLAN, MISS NORRIS. b Ind 27 Jl 05. 5: LSU 25 BA; Columbia 40 BS in LS, 42 (LS) MS. 7: Tchr Morgan City High Sch, Morgan City La 25-28; Asst catlgr LSU 28-29; Asst libn La Lib Commsn 29-30; Libn Sch Lib Lab Tchrs Col Columbia U 32-33; Libn High Sch, Port Washington NY 33-35; Libn High Sch, Scarsdale NY 35-39; Instr LSU 39-43; NY State Col (Geneseo) summer 42; Amer Red Cross Serv, China-Burma-India 43-47; Asst Prof & coordinator lib serv LSU 43-51; Asst Prof UNC summer 52; Asst Prof Mexico City Col summer 52; Assoc Prof LSU 51-62; Prof LSU 62-; Prof U of Ankara Turkey 58-59. 8: NDEA Inst dir summer 65-67; Consul on sch libs in Turkey 58-59; HEA Inst dir summer 68, acad yr 68-69. 09: NEA; ALA-AASchL (chm Internat Rel Com); La Tchrs Assn; LaLA (Program Chm 64, Parliamentarian 65-66, Lib Study Subcom, Lib Devel Prog). 10: YWCA; Red Cross. 12: Ed "School Libraries" (54-58). 13: Yes. 14: Elem & sec sch libs. 15: La State U Lib Sch, Baton Rouge La 70803.

McCLELLAN, WILLIAM MONSON. b Groton Mass 3 Ja 34. 4: Jane Muir. 5: Colo Col 52-56 (Music) BA; UMich 58-59 AMLS; Colo Col 61 (Musicology) MA. 6: Fr, Ger. 7: Choral dir Alamosa High Sch, Alamosa Colo 56-58; Music libn UColo 59-65; Music libn UIll 65-. 9: Amer Musicological Soc; MusLA; Internat Assn Mus Libns; Assn for Recorded Sound Collection. 13: Yes. 14: Music crit, music in Amer culture, gen music bibliog, period indexing. 15: Mus Lib UIll, Urbana Il 61803.

McCLELLAND, MARJORIE (COOK). b Pittsburgh 14 S 21. 4: William T McClelland. 5: Westminster Col 39-43 (Chem) BS; UPittsburgh 63-64 MLS. 7: Chem Mellon Inst, Pittsburgh 43; Ref libn sci & tech dept Carnegie Lib of Pittsburgh 64-. 9: SLA. 10: Beta Phi Mu. 12: Comp "Review of Iron and Steel Literature," annual (66-). 14: Ref, sci & tech. 15: 34 Shannopin dr, Pittsburgh Pa 15202.

McCLENDON, IDA A(LICE). b Kan City Kan 25 My 17. 4: William H McClendon. 5: Spelman Col 35-38; Portland State Col 55-57 (Humanities) BS; UWash 58-62 (LS) ML. 6: Lat, Fr. 7: Lib Assn of Portland, Ore: Cadet libn 58, Jr libn 61, Sr libn 64-, Br libn 66-. 9: ALA; PNLA; OreLA. 10: Amer Friends Serv Com; Jack & Jill of Amer; Alpha Kappa Alpha; Family Coun serv. 14: Readers adv serv, fiction & lit. 15: 4140 NE Holman st, Portland Or 97211.

McCLOSKEY, OWEN T. b Columbus Ohio 23 Jl 09. 5: Ohio State 27-32 (Bus admin) BS; George Washington 48-50 (Govt) MA; Rutgers 64-66 MLS. 7: US Army 31-64; Ref & circ libn UFla Lib 66-67; Ref libn Kenyon Col Lib 67-. 9: ALA; OhioLA. 14: Ref. 15: Kenyon Col, Gambier Oh 43022.

McCLOUD, EARNESTINE (TATE). b La Grange NC 17 F 43. 4: Demark A McCloud. 5: Winston-Salem State Col 60-64 (Eng) BA; NC Col 66-67 MLS. 6: Fr. 7: Eng tchr Southside High, Blairs Va 64-65, Libn 65-66; Tech serv libn Winston-Salem State Col 67-68; Docs libn NC A&T State U 68-. 9: ALA. 10: Greensboro Lib Club. 14: Catlg, govt docs. 15: 412 Stedman st apt C, Greensboro NC 27401.

McCLOY, THOMAS RENNIE (PAT). b Meskanaw Sask Can 4 F 06. 4: Doreen Woodford. 5: USask 34-37 (Eng) BA; Toronto 38-39 BLS. 7: Lib asst USask 39; Can army RCASC WO I(SM) 40-46; Libn Khaki U (Leavesden Eng) 45-46; Asst catlgr Prov Lib Victoria BC 46-47; Asst catlgr UBC Lib 47-49; Catlgr Pub Archives Lib, Ottawa 49-53; Asst catlgr Nat Lib, Ottawa 54-56; Chief Libn Glenbow Found Lib, Calgary Alta 56-. 9: CanLA; AltaLA. 10: Can Hist Assn; Alta Hist Soc. 13: Yes. 14: West Canadiana, catlg. 15: Glenbow Foundation 902-11th ave SW, Calgary 3 Alta Can.

McCLUNG, CLOYD HARRELL. b Waco Tex 11 S 16. 4: Doris L Wilson. 5: Baylor 34-38 (Ed Rel) AB; Southwestern Baptist Theol Sem 41-42 (Rel Ed) MRE; Fla State U 50-53 MALS. 6: Ger. 7: Sch tchr La Vega Sch, Waco Tex 38-41; Air Force Navigator 42-46; Religious educ dir First Baptist Church, Panama City Fla 49-54; Libn Baylor U Tidwell Bible Lib 54-64; Libn Dir of Libs Polk Jr Col 64-68; Ref pub serv Fla Presby Col 68-. 8: Library/USA NY World's Fair 65. 9: ALA (Memb Com chm, Tex 58-64); ATheolLA; TexLA (Publ chm 56-61); FlaLA; SWLA. 10: Ridge Orchid Club. 13: Yes. 14: Ref, admin, lib educ. 15: P O Box 1832, Winter Haven Fl 33880.

McCLURE, FRANCES LESTER. b Montgomery Ala 10 O 42. 4: Charles Hume McClure. 5: West Ky State Col 60-63 (LS, Eng) AB; UKy 63-64 MSLS; Columbia 68-69 (LS). 6: Sp. 07: Elem libn Fayette Co Schs, E Lexington Ky 64-65; Asst ref libn West Ky State Col summer 65; Br libn Chesapeake Pub Lib, Chesapeake Pub Lib, Chesapeake Va 65; Br libn Jacksonville Pub Lib, Jacksonville Fla 66-67; Chief child serv 67-68; Child libn Miami Pub Lib, Miami Fla 68, Br libn 68; Asst ref libn Columbia U Libs 68-. 9: ALA-AASchL; -ACRL; NEA; SELA; FlaLA; DuvalCoLA. 10: Beta Phi Mu. 15: 4 W 101st st apt 59A, New York NY 10025.

McCLURE, JANE SCOTT. b Donora Penn 27 My 11. 5: Oberlin Col 29-31; UPittsburgh 32-34 (Fine Arts) AB; Carnegie 37-40 BS in LS. 7: Asst lending UPittsburgh 36-38; Asst lending Carnegie Lib, Pittsburgh 38-40, 1st asst fine arts 40-43; Army libn US Govt, Hawaii 43-45; Lib supv Far East Com, Tokyo 45-49, Command libn 49-50; Dir Pub Lib, Princeton NJ 51-53; Coordinator wk with ya Free Lib of Phila 53-61; Dir Pub Lib, Summit NJ 61-. 8: Guest Lecturer, Columbia Sch of Lib Serv 59-61; Consul "Our Wonderful World" (54-56). 9: ALA (Coun 58, 60-64);-YASD (pres 57-58; chm Asia Proj 58-61); Middle Atlantic Reg Lib Conf (Program chm 63); NJLA. 10: Soroptimist Club; Commun Serv Wkers. 13: Yes. 14: Pub lib, ya, adult serv. 15: Summit Pub Lib 75 Maple st, Summit NJ 07901.

McCLURE, JOHN DAVID III. b St Joseph Mo 8 D 30. 5: Long Beach City Col 50-52; Long Beach State Col 52-54 (Soc Sci) BA; UCal(Berkeley) 57-58 MLS. 7: Asst libn Modesto Jr Col 58-59; Sacramento State Col: Inter-lib loan bibliog 59-60, Inter-lib, res bk rm 60-61, Soc sci & bus admin asst ref libn 61-65, Soc sci & bus admin ref libn & col archivist 65-. 9: CalLA. 10: ACLU. 14: Ref, maps. 15: 2215 K st apt B, Sacramento Ca 95816.

McCLURE, LOIS (CARTER). b Tipton Co Ind 11 Ag 03. 5: DePauw U 23-27 (Biol) AB; UIll 38-39 BS in LS. 7: Head Libn Peabody Free Lib, Columbia City Ind 39-41; Ref libn El

Paso (Tex) Pub Lib 42-43; Sch libn Orange Co Free Lib, Orange Cal 43-50; Ref libn Orange Pub Lib, Orange Cal 50-53; Ref libn Fullerton Jr Col 53-61, Head Libn 61-66; Ref libn & Asst Prof Lib Sci Chapman Col 66-. 8: Instr Lib train Fullerton Jr Col; Asst Prof Lib Sci Chapman Col. 9: CalLA; Cal Jr Col Assn; Cal Tchrs Assn; Orange Co LA (past pres). 10: AAUW; BPW; Presby Church Bd of Deacons. 14: Ref, instr, educ for lib serv. 15: 253 Magnolia, Orange Ca 92667.

McCLURE, LUCRETIA WALKER. b Denver 2 Ja 25. 4: Arnold Leroy McClure. 5: Neb Wesleyan U 41-43; UMo 43-45 (Journalism) BJ; UDenver 63-64 (LS) MA. 7: Edward G Miner Lib URochester Sch of Med & Dentistry, (NY) 64-67, Ser libn 67-68, Readers serv libn 68-; Instructor in catlg UDenver summer 67. 9: MedLA. 12: Comp "Selected List of Periodicals and Serials Currently Received by the Edward G Miner Library" (68). 14: Catlg. 15: 164 Elmore rd, Rochester NY 14618.

McCLURKIN, JOHN B(RAXTON). b Neenah Ala 2 Ja 12. 4: Margaret Lawson. 5: UAla 28-32 (Hist) AB, 34, 39 (LS, Educ) Certif in LS, MA; National U of Mex summer 44 (Econ) Chicago MALS 66. 6: Sp. 7: Tchr-libn Tupelo Mil Inst, Tupelo Miss 32-34; Lib asst reading rms LC 35, Ref asst Legis Ref Serv 36-43; Economist ed US Bur Labor Statistics, Wash DC 43-44; Economist libn US Alien Property Custodian, Wash DC 44; Economist libn US Fed Home Loan Bank Admin, Wash DC 45; Ref libn Civics Dept Chicago Pub Lib 46-47; Research libn Legis Ref Bureau, Honolulu 47-50; Dir SCAP CIE Info Center US Army, Okayama Japan 50-52; Air U Lib, Maxwell AFB Ala: Bibliog asst 52-58, Tech asst to dir 58-62, Circ libn 62-65; Med serv sch libn Air U Lib, Gunter AFB Ala 65-66; Chief libn Breckinridge Lib Mari ne Corps Educ Ctr 66-. 9: SLA (chm Mil Libns Div 68-69); (Ala Chap: dir 53-54, sec-treas 56-57, pres 60-61); SELA; AlaLA (treas 62-63); VaLA. 10: Kappa Delta Pi. 12: Ed "Bulletin," Ala Chap SLA (55-56); Ed "The Alabama Librarian," (57-59). 13: Yes. 14: Ref. 15: RR 1 Box 125B, Dumfries Va 22026.

McCLURKIN, MARGARET (LAWSON). b Woodbine Ky. 4: John B McClurkin. 5: East Ky State Col 38 (Hist, Eng) AB; Peabody 46 BS in LS. 7: USNR (WR) LTJG 43-46; Sr libn Indianapolis Pub Lib 46-50; Dir Amer Cultural Center, Takamatsu Japan 50-53; Act dir & asst libn Montgomery Pub Lib, Montgomery Ala 54-55; Libn Base Lib Gunter AFB, Montgomery Ala 55-56; Child libn Base Lib Maxwell AFB, Montgomery Ala 64-66; Libn Marumsco Hills Elem Sch, Woodbridge Va 66-. 9: ALA; AlaLA. 10: AAUW. 14: Ref. 15: RR 1 Box 125B, Dumfries Va 22026.

McCOLL, MARGARET CALDWELL. b Port Deposit Md 1 Ap 24. 5: UPenn 41-44 (Ger) BA, 44-46 (Ger) MA; Drexel 52-55 MS in LS. 6: Ger, Fr, Sp, Portu, Russian. 7: Sub-prof catlgr UPenn Lib 49-55; Catlgr Temple U Lib 55-. 9: ALA-ACRL; Phila Area Tech Serv Libns. 10: Delta Phi Alpha. 14: Catlg, rare bks. 15: 229 E Front st, Media Pa 19063.

McCOLLUM, ROBERT (EDMUND). b Glendale Cal 29 Jl 22. 4: Jean Wiesner. 5: Colo State Col 42-43 (Forestry); OklaU 46-49 (Lang) BA; ULille France 50-52 (Russian) Diplome d'etudes russes. 6: Fr, Russian, Ger. 7: Subject catlgr trans LC 52-57, Tech writer 57-59, Slavic sci bibliogr 60-62, Subject catlgr 62-; Lectr in Fr AmericanU (Washington DC) 66-. 9: Soc Federal Linguists. 14: Subj catlg. 15: 6511 Parkwood st, Hyattsville Md 20784.

McCOLM, CONSTANCE (LEE). 5: UCal (Berkeley) 45 AA; Reed Col 47 (Econ) BA; UCal (Berkeley) 51 (Eng Hist) MA, 51 BLS. 7: Tchr A to Zed Sch, Berkeley 47-48; Spec recruit LC 51-52, Asst head Amer & British Exch Sect 52, Head Amer & British Exch Sect 52-55; Cal State Lib: Supv libn govt pub sect 55-57; Supv libn ref sect 57-60, Prin libn reader serv bur 60-. 9: ALA; CalLA (Standards & Dev Com). 10: Sierra Club of Cal; UCalSch of Libnship ALUMNI; Save the Redwoods League. 12: "California. Senate. Fact-finding Committee on Commerce and Economic Development. Business and Population Statistics Relating to California in Government Publications," Supp to First Partial Report, with Mary Schell, (57). 13: Yes. 14: Ref, admin. 15: 801 Carro dr apt 2, Sacramento Cal 95825.

McCOMB, M LOIS (MARTIN). b Doniphan Mo 7 Ap 14. 4: Ralph W McComb. 5: SW Mo State Col 31-35 (Elem Educ) BS in Ed; UIll (Urbana) 36-37 BS in LS. 7: Asst Pub Lib, Springfield Mo 32-36; Asst libn SE Mo State Col (Cape Girardeau Mo) 37-; Catlgr Illinois state Lib 37-40, Hd Collections Dept 40-42; Libn US Army, Camp McCoy Wis 42-44; Libn bolton High Sch, Alexandria La 44-45; Libn US Med Ctr, Springfield Mo 45-46; Sub tchr State Col Area Schs, State College Pa 61-66, Elem libn 66-. 9: NEA; PennLA; PennStateEA; PennSchLA; StateColAreaEA. 10: Sigma Sigma Sigma; Pub Lib Bd of Trustees. 13: Yes. 14: Admin, elem libs. 15: 737 Storch rd, State College Pa 16801.

McCOMB, RALPH WENDELL. b Manquin Va 11 F 07. 4: M Lois Martin. 5: Crane Jr Col 24-26 (Pre-Law) AA; Chicago 27-29 (Psych) PhB; UIll 31-32 BS in LS, 33-36 (LS) MA; Chicago 42, 46 (LS). 6: Fr. 7: Adjustment & credit depts Marshall Field & Co, Chicago 26-27; Ref asst Newberry Lib, Chicago 29-31; Circ asst, catlgr UIll(Urbana) 33-36; Ref libn Tulane U 36, Act libn, asst libn 36-42; US Army Med Corps (2d Lt) 42-45; Penn State U: Assoc libn 47, U Libn 48-65, Libn Fred Lewis Pattee Lib 66-, Dir Summer Lib Sch 48-60. 8: Chm New Orleans Gutenberg Anniversary Com (40); Co-chm Penn State Bibliog Conf 60-64. 9: ALA (chm Univ Libs Sect);-ACRL (Coun); New Orleans Lib Club (pres); LaLA; PennLA (pres, Exec Bd, var coms). 10: Pi Gamma Mu; ASEE; Phi Kappa Phi; Torch Club; AAUP. 12: "Guide to the Resources of the Regional Library Resource Centers of Pennsylvania" (67). 13: Yes. 14: Admin, lib resources. 15: 737 Storch rd, State College Pa 16801.

McCOMBS, ELIZABETH E. b Pittsburgh 12 Ja 19. 5: Hampton Inst 37-41 (Fr) BS; Carnegie 46-47 BLS. 6: Fr, Sp. 7: Tchr-libn Mary N Smith High Sch, Accomack VA 41-43; Tchr Brooks High Sch, Prince Frederick Md 43-44; Libn asst Army Med Lib, Wash DC 44-46, Stack supv 46; Carnegie Lib of Pittsburgh: Asst libn 47-49, Child libn 49-61, Br libn 61-67, Coord Project Outreach 67-. 9: ALA (Distinguished Child Bk List Com 49-50, Newberry-Caldecott Com 49-50; Com on Reading Improvement 68-; Bibliog Com Lib Serv to the Disadvantaged Child Com 68-); PennLA (chm Pub Libs Sect 62-63, Exec Com 62-63). 10: Alpha Kappa Alpha; NAACP. 14: Child wk. 15: 128 Penn circle W, Pittsburgh Pa 15206.

McCONKEY, THOMAS (WINSTON). b Pittsburgh 26 Jl 13. 4: Irene Wells. 5: UPittsburgh 32-35 (Pol Sci) AB, 36, 48, 49 (Econ); American U 36-37 (Pub Admin); UPenn 56 (Pol Sci) MA. 7: Admin analyst US & Penn State Emp Serv, Penn & Wash 36-46; T/5th Gr US Army Med Dept, US & Europe 40-45; Employment manager Portsmouth Steel Corp, Portsmouth Ohio 47-49; Employment manager Sun Ray Drug Co, Phila 49-53; Chief admin serv Bus Manager Free Lib of Phila 53-. 8: Bldg & consul to Hazleton, Conshohocken, Grundy (Bristol), Lansdale, Upper Cheltenham Penn pub libs. 9: PennLA. 10/ com for a Sane Nuclear Policy; United World Federalists. 12: Ed "Portsmouth Steel Corp News" (47-49); Products Ed "Lib Jour(56-). 14: Admin, planning, bldg constr & layout. 15: 408 W Price st, Phila Pa 19144.

McCONNELL, CAMDEN WILLIAM. b Clearfield Co Penn 23 Je 08. 4: Julia Elizabeth Chevallard. 5: US Mil Acad West Point 27-31 BS; UCal(Berkeley) 64-65 MLS. 6: Portu. 7: US Army: 31-61, Col 45-, Col Ret 61-; Asst hd circ UCal Lib (Santa Barbara) 65-. 9: ALA; CalLA; LA UCal (Santa Barbara). 15: 746 Santecito dr, Santa Barbara Ca 93103.

McCONNELL, DOROTHY (DURRETT). b Winnfield La 13 O 46. 4: John Jones McConnell. 5: LSU 64-68 (Fr) BA, 68-69 (LS) MS. 6: Fr, Sp, Ital. 7: Research asst Higher Educ Facilities Commsn, Baton Rouge 68-69; Ref libn E Baton Rouge City-Parish Lib, Baton Rouge 69-. 9: ALA; LaLA. 15: 2136 Ferndale, Baton Rouge La 70808.

McCONOUGHEY, SAMUEL S. b Solon Ohio. 5: Adelbert Col West Res U 29-33 (Hist) BA; West Res 33-34 BS in LS; UToledo 39-41 (Eng). 6: Fr. 7: Asst ref & circ depts West Res Lib 34-37; Toledo Pub Lib, Toledo Ohio: Asst tech dept 37-39, Head hist div 39-46, Head of ref & soc sci dept 46-. 9: OhioLA. 14: Ref, Amer hist, rare bks. 15: Toledo Pub Lib 325 Michigan st, Toledo Oh 43624.

McCOOEY, MARY ENNIS. b NYC 27 Ag 06. 4: Everett D McCooey. 5: Col of New Rochelle 28 (Hist) AB; Pratt 60 MLS. 7: Tchr in train NYC Bd of Educ 28-29, Sub 29-31, 56-61; Tchr of lib John Adams High Sch, Ozone Park NY 61-. 8: Libn in chg of Prof Lib of NYC Bd of Educ, summers 61-62 & 64-65. 9: NYS Sch Libns Assn. 10: Col of New Rochelle Alumnae Assn; Lady of Equestrian Order of the Knights; Ladies of Holy Sepulchre of Jerusalem. 14: Catlg. 15: 142-10 Roosevelt ave, Flushing NY 11354.

McCOOL, MAUDE ESTELLE (CRAVER). b Memphis Tex 8 Je 04. 4: Walter Derwood McCool. 5: UTex 21-24; UColo summers 24; Tex Tech Col summers 33, 39, 42, 43 (Educ) BS; N Tex State U summers 48-50 BS in LS; W Tex State U even 55-56 (Creative Writing). 7: Prin Baylor Sch, Hall Co Tex 23-24; Tchr Memphis Ind Sch, Memphis Tex 42-46; Tchr Webb

Sch, Gray Co Tex 46-48; Libn Lefors High Sch, Lefors Tex 48-51; Libn catlgr Bivens Mem Lib, Amarillo Tex summer 52; Libn Dumas High Sch, Dumas Tex 51-. 9: ALA; Tex Tchrs Assn; TexLA. 10: Alpha Lambda Sigma; AAUW; Nat Bd of Missions of United Presbyt Women (Life mem). 14: Ref. 15: 216 N Meredith, Dumas Tx 79029.

McCORD, CHARLES E. b Lewisburg Tenn 20 Ag 25. 5: AuburnU 46-49 (Secondary Educ, Soc Sci) BS; Peabody Col 50-52 (Elem Educ) MA, 55-59 MLS. 7: Prin Mooresville Elem Sch, Lewisburg Tenn 51-52; Tchr Tenn Prep Sch, Nashville Tenn 52-55; Tchr Glencliff High Sch, Nashville Tenn 54-60; Libn Middle Tenn StateU, Murfreesboro Tenn 61-. 9: TennEA; TennLA; SELA. 15: 3310 E Main st, Murfreesboro Tn 37130.

McCORD, JOHN GAREL WILLIAM. b Farmer City Ill 26 S 18. 4: Esther June Pirka. 5: UIll 37-41 (Span) AB, 46-47 BS in LS, summer 63 & 67 (Info Retrieval). 6: Sp, Fr. 7: Clerk typist statistical clerk USAF 42-46; Order libn Roosevelt U 48-50; Chief order dept So Ill U 51-59; Chief tech serv Ill State Lib 59-64, Chief pub serv 64-65; Order libn Ind State U 65-67; Chief tech servs Lake Co Pub Lib, Griffith Ind 67-. 8: Consul in automation So Ill U 59. 9: ALA; IllLA (chm tech Serv Sect 62-63); IndLA. 13: Yes. 14: Acquis, catlg. 15: Lake County Pub Lib 221 W Ridge rd, Griffith In 46307.

McCORISON, MARCUS ALLEN. b Lancaster Wis 17 Jl 26. 4: Janet Knop. 5: Ripon Col 46-50 (Eng) AB; UVt 50-57 (US Hist) MA; Columbia 53-54 (LS) MS. 7: S 1/c (SM) USNR, Pacific Theater 44-46; (1st Lt) Inf USAR, Korea 51-52; Libn Kellogg-Hubbard Lib, Montpelier Vt 54-55; Chief rare bks dept Dartmouth Col 55-59; Head spec collections State U of Iowa 59-60; Libn Amer Antiquarian Soc, Worcester Mass 60-; Dir 67-. 9: ALA-ACRL (chm rare Bks Sect 65-66); BSA (chm NE Reg 69-); Assn Amer Histns; Amer Antiq Soc; NHLA (pres 55, 59); Vt Hist Soc (Trustee 56-66); Colonial Soc Mass; MassLA; Mass Hist Soc. 10: Grolier Club (NY); Club of Odd Volumes (Boston). 12: "Vermont Imprints, 1778-1820" (63); "Three Autobiographical Fragments by Isaiah Thomas" (62); "The 1764 Catalogue of the Redwood Library at Newport, RI" (65). 13: Yes. 14: Americana. 15: Amer Antiq Soc, Worcester Ma 01609.

McCORMICK, ADOREEN MARY. b Helena Mont 20 Ag 36. 5: Seattle U 54-58 (Pol Sch, Philos) BA; Georgetown U 58-62 (Pol Sci) MA. 6: Fr. 7: LC: Info & ed asst 58-59, Info & ed spec 59-60, Admin sec to asst libn pub affairs 60, Admin asst to asst libn 60-62, Spec asst to asst libn 62-65; Legis liaison off 65-. 9: ALA; DCLA. 10: Mont State Soc; Kappa Gamma Pi. 13: Yes. 14: Pub rel, lib legis. 15: 4000 Tunlaw rd NW, Wash DC 20007.

McCORMICK, ANNA ROSEMARY. b Renfrew Ont Can. 5: Toronto 35-38 (Arts) BA, 59-60 BLS, various years (Eng). 6: Fr, Sp. 7: Sec various firms 38-42; sec-clerk Can Pacific RR Co, Toronto 42-44, Asst accountant 44-59; Law Soc of Upper Can, Toronto: Libn catlgr 60-62, Asst libn 62-65, Chief Libn 65-. 9: SLA; CanLA; AALL; CanALL; Inst Prof Libns Ont; OntLA. 10: Pro Aliis Club. 14: Ref, admin, lib planning, catlg. 15: 8 St Thomas st, apt 22, Toronto 5 Can.

McCORMICK, HENRY J. b 2 Jl 19. 4: Mary Jane Heenan. 5: Syracuse 36-40 (Classical Lang) BA, 46-47 BS in LS, 46-47 (Classical Lang) MA. 07: Tchr Fla Mil Acad, St Petersburg Fla 40-41; US Army (Capt) 42-46, 51-52; Ref asst Grosvenor Lib, Buffalo NY 47-48; Dir Olean Pub Lib, Olean NY 48-54; Asst dir Pub Lib, Syracuse NY 54-61, Dir 62-. 8: NY State Pub Libns Certif Examination Com 62-67. 9: ALA; NYLA (pres Adult Serv Div 66-67). 10: Beta Phi Mu. 15: Syracuse Pub Lib 335 Montgomery st, Syracuse NY 13202.

McCORMICK, PETER (JOSEPH). b San Francisco 9 Jl 09. 4: Prudence Billings. 5: USan Francisco 28-32 (Philos) BA; UCal 46-47 BLS. 6: Fr, Ger. 7: Jr libn various depts San Francisco Pub Lib 38-42; Mil leave 42-45; Sr libn ref dept San Francisco Pub Lib 45-48; Milwaukee Pub Lib: Asst head of ref dept 48-49, Mun ref libn 49-53, Chief of ref serv 53-57, Coordinator of gen materials & serv 57-. 8: Past chm & consul to Milwaukee Mayor's Com on Cost of Living. 9: ALA (Sub Bks Com: chm Sub-Com on SCOPE);-RSD (past 2nd v-pres, past chm Org & Activ Com); SLA (past pres Wis Chap); WisLA (past chm Ref Serv Sect, past chm Spec Com on Reg Ref Systems, past chm Com on Inter-Lib Coop of Col & Ref Sect). 10: Research Clearinghouse of Milwaukee; Milwaukee Co Citizenship Commsn; Economic Research Coun; Milwaukee Assn of Commerce; Econ Coun of Milwaukee; UN Assn; ACLU World Affairs Coun. 12: 'Identifying the Library's Public and Community' in "The Library as a Community Information Center" (59); Ed "Our City Government: Milwaukee Wisconsin" (53); Ed "Milwaukee City and County: A Statistical History" (58); Ed "A Statistical Almanac of Milwaukee: City, County, Metropolitan Area" (63); Ed "Periodical Holdings List, Milwaukee Public Library" (67). 13: Yes. 14: Ref, regl ref systems, govt docs, periods, aps, documentation. 15: 7113 W Park Hill ave, Milwaukee Wi 53213.

McCOSKEY, VERA M. b Wash Co Ind 25 D 21. 5: Ball State Tchrs Col 39-43 (LS, Art, Hist) BS, (Educ, Eng) MA; IndU 58 MALS. 6: Norwegian. 7: Tchr-libn Vernon Twp Sch, Crothersville Ind 43-44; Libn-tchr Roverton Sch, Delaware Co Ind 44-58; Catlgr Ball StateU 58-62, Tchg materials serv libn 62-. 8: Consul & dir wkshop for establishing central instr materials ctr, Anderson Ind; Consul materials ctr, Knightstown & shelbyville Ind. 9: ALA-ACRL; IndStateLA; IndASchL; IndStateTA. 10: Beta Phi Mu. 13: Yes. 14: A-v instr materials. 15: 15 Colson dr, Muncie In 47304.

McCOTTER, MARGARET (ROSEMOND) PALMER. b Thomasville NC 7 N 21. 4: Burney Richard McCotter. 5: CATAWBA Col 38-42 (Hist, Eng, Lat) AB; UNC 43-44 BS in LS. 6: Fr, Lat, ger. 7: Tchr-libn Rockwell High Sch, Rockwell NC 42-43; Libn So Pines Sch System, So Pines NC 44-47; Post libn Ft Story, Ft Story Va 50-51; Libn Occidental Life Ins Co of NC Raleigh NC 56; Lib consul NC Dept of Pub Instr, Raleigh 63-65; Libn LeRoy Martin Jr High Sch, Raleigh NC 59-62, 65-. 9: NEA; NCEA; NCLA. 10: Beta Phi Mu. 12: Ed "Reference Materials for School Libraries" (2nd ed 65). 14: Organiz & admin, bk sel, ref. 15: 332 Buncombe st, Raleigh NC 27609.

McCOURT, FLORENCE K. b Mass. 5: Emmanuel Col 24 (Lat, Fr) AB; Drexel 38 BS in LS. 7: Ref libn Boston Med Lib, Boston 38-47; High sch libn Holbrook High Sch, Holbrook Mass 63-. 9: NE SchLA; Mass SchLA; Mass Tchrs Assn. 10: Drexel Alumni Assn; Emmanuel Col Alumnae Assn. 14: Sch libs. 15: 11 Norfolk rd, Holbrook Ma 02343.

McCOURT, JOSEPH ARNOLD. b Cornwall Ont Can 29 N 24. 4: Theresa Valade. 5: U West Ont 47-50 BA; UOttawa 62-63 BLS. 7: Telegraphist RCNVR, Can & N Atlantic 43-45; Tchr Morrisburg High Sch, Morrisburg Ont 52-55; Tchr Dept of Nat Defence (Can), Zweibrucken Germany 55-57; Tchr Mining & Tech Sch, Sudbury Ont 57-58; Tchr Morrisburg High Sch, Morrisburg Ont 58-62; Tchr-libn Laurentian High Sch, Ottawa 63-. 14: Sch libnship. 15: 629 Brierwood ave, Ottawa 13 Can.

McCOWAN, LAURA (BARCUS). b Austin Tex 10 Ja 38. 5: SWestU 55-56; UTex 62-64 (Elem educ) BS, 66-69 MLS. 7: Clerical 57-62; Tchg elem sch, NH 64-66; Coord of Adult Serv Austin Pub Lib, Austin Texas 68-. 9: ALA; SWLA; TexLA. 10: Austin Lib Club. 14: Adult serv. 15: 2711Bowman rd, Austin Tx 78703.

McCOWN, LEONARD JOE. b Port Lavaca Tex 9 S 42. 4: Marjorie Ann Hoyle. 5: Victoria Col 60-62; N Tex State U 62-64 (LS) BA, 67-68 MLS. 07: Lib asst ya dept Dallas Pub Lib 63, Libn ya dept Pleasant Grove Br 64-66, Libn ya dept S Oak Cliff Br 66-67, Libn Ad Dept 67-68; Libn N Tex State U Lib Serv Dept summer 68; Ref libn Dallas Bapt Col 68-. 9: ALA; TexLA (YART: chm Nomin Com 65, v-chm 68-69, chm 69-70); SWLA; DallasCoLA; SLA; Amer Assn State & Loc Hist. 10: Alpha Beta Alpha; Tex State Hist Assn; Alpha Lambda Sigma; Scottish Clans of N Tex. 14: Tex hist, geneal, ya wk, archives, ref. 15: 1704 Lindy lane, Irving Tx 75060.

McCOY, BETTY JOE. b Catlettsburg Ky 5 Ag 28. 5: Ashland Jr Col 46-47; Carson-Newman Col 54-57 (Bible, Religious Educ) BA; Peabody 57-60 MA in LS; Electronic Computer Programming Inst 68-69 Certif. 07: Sec-bkkeeper Hearne Block Co, Catlettsburg Ky 48-50; Sec-bkkeeper First Christian Church, Ashland Ky 50; Church sec Latonia Baptist Church, Covington Ky 51-54; Church sec First Baptist Church, Jefferson City Tenn 55-57; Asst to dean of women carson-Newman Col summers 56-57; Ref research libn Baptist Sunday Sch Bd, Nashville 57-60; Circ libn So Bapt Sem (Louisville Ky) 60-. 9: ATheolLA; Ky Baptust LA. 10: Long Run Assn Lib Coun; So Baptist Hist Soc. 14: Circ, ref. 15: 2901 Meadowlark ave apt 1, Louisville Ky 40206.

McCOY, IOLA FULLER. b Marcellus Mich. 5: UMich 35 (Eng, Ger) AB, 40 (Eng) AM, 62 AMLS. 6: Fr, Ger. 7: High sch libn in var schs in Mich & NM 54-64; Free-lance writer 40-; Lib sci lecturer UMich 62-64; Assoc Prof of Eng Ferris State Col 64-69; Assoc Prof of Lib Sci Clarion State Col 69-. 8: Fiction leader UKan Writers' Conf 63, 65; UKan Literary Lectr 63. 9: Nat Assn Press Women; Lit Com Mich Coun for the Arts 68. 10: Phi Beta Kappa. 11: Avery Hopwood Award for Creative Writing; Distinguished Alumni Award UMich 67. 12: "The Loon Feather" (40); "The Shining Trail" (43); "The Gilded Torch" (57); "All the Golden Gifts" (67). 14: Lib sci tchg. 15: Div of Lib Sci Clarion State College, Clarion Pa 16214.

McCOY, JAMES FRANK. b N C 4 Ag 24. 5: Lincoln U 48-52 (Soc Sci) BA; Rutgers 54-55 MLS. 7: (Sgt 4/c) US Army Supply Sgt 44-46; Clerk VA, Phila 46-47; Clerk Fourth Naval Dist, Phila 47-48; Cost accounting clerk Frankford Arsenal, Phila 52-54; Lending libn NJ State Lib 56; Sr ref libn Elizabeth Pub Lib, Elizabeth NJ 56; Libn Trenton Jr Col 56; Dir lib serv Mercer Co Commun Col 67-. 8: Consul Amer Col in Paris 65; Trent House Comm sn, Mayor's Adv Com for Model Cities. 9: ALA (Constit Com Jr Col Sect); NJLA (Bd, var offs); NJ Jr Col Assn (sec-treas). 10: Rutgers Lib Sch Alumni Assn; Citizens Action Coun; Trenton (NJ) Tercentenary Commsn; Trenton Urban Renewal Adv Com; Kappa Alpha Psi; AAUP. 13: Yes. 14: Ref. 15: 141 Kirkbride ave, Trenton NJ 08638.

McCOY, MABEL (MADDEN). b Wash DC. 4: Cleo M McCoy. 5: Howard U 29-33 (Eng) AB; Columbia 36-37 BSLS; Howard U 34-36 (Eng) MA. 7: Libn Sch of Religion Howard U, Wash DC 39-42; Catlg libn F D Blaford Lib A&T Col (Greensboro NC) 55, Ref libn 55-; Coord Tchr Educ Materials Ctr 66-; Asst Prof Sch Educ & Art 64-; Readers adv 66-. 9: ALA; NCLA. 10: Greensboro Lib Club. 12: Ed "Library Newsletter" (64-67); Ed "Student Library Handbook" (66). 14: Ref, educ media. 15: 1009 Martin st, Greensboro NC 27406.

McCOY, RALPH E(DWARD). b St Louis 1 O 15. 4: Melba McKibben. 5: Ill Wesleyan U 37 (Hist) AB; UIll 39 BSLS, 50 (LS) MS, 56 (LS) PhD. 6: Ger. 7: Libn Marissa (Ill) Twp High Sch 37-38; Asst libn Col of Agric UIll 9urbana) 38-39; E d of publ Ill State Lib 39-43; US Army (Capt) 43-46; Libn Quartermaster Tech Lib, Ft Lee Va 46-48; Libn Inst of Labor & Ind Rel UIll 48-55; Dir of Libs So Ill U (Edwardsville & Carbondale Ill) 55-. 8: Spec Asst to v-pres for planning So Ill U 63-64; Adv Com "Works of John Dewey." 09: ALA (chm Jt Com on Lib Serv to Labor 53-54);-ACRL (pres 66); BSA; IllLA (pres 56); Ill Hist Assn; Ill Lib Development Com. 10: Phi Kappa Phi; Beta Phi Mu; AAUP; ACLU; Caxton Club; Shawnee (Ill) Systems Lib Bd; Carbondale (Ill) Pub Lib Bd. 11: Award for Outstanding Contribution to Lib Profession IllLA 61. 12: "Personnel Administration for Libraries" (53); "History of Labor & Unionism; a Bibliography" (53); "Freedom of the Press; a Bibliography" (68); Ed -illinois Libraries" (39-43); "IllLA Record" (48-50). 13: Yes. 14: Univ lib admin, bibliog. 15: 1902 Chautauqua, Carbondale Il 62901.

McCRACKEN, BONNIE L. b Altoona Penn 6 My 40. 5: Shippensburg State Col 58-62 (Elem Educ) BS; Drexel 62-63 (LS) MS. 7: Libn Donegal Union Sch Dist, Mt Joy Penn 63-65; Asst libn Elizabethtown Col 65-66; Curriculum libn Millersville State Col, Millersville Penn 66-. 9: ALA; PennLA; NEA; PennStateEA; LancasterCoLA (pres). 10: Beta Phi Mu; AAUP. 14: Curr materials. 15: 139 Cedar st, Elizabethtown Pa 17022.

McCRACKEN, RONALD (WALTER). b Toronto Can 11 Ja 40. 4: Carol. 5: Toronto Tchrs' Col 58-59; Waterloo LutheranU 63-. 6: Fr. 7: Tchr: Scarborough Bd of Educ, Agincourt Ont 59-63, N Gwillimbury Twp Sch Area, Keswick Ont 63-66; Libn: N Gwillimbury Twp Sch Area, Keswick Ont 66-69, York Co Bd of Educ, Keswick Ont 69-. 8: Libn Ont Dept of Educ Summer Sch Staff, Lakehead Centre Port Arthur Ont summer 69. 9: CanLA; ALA; NEA-DAVI; OntLA; York CoLA. 10: Pub Lib Trustee CLTA; ALTA; OLTA. 11: 67 Encyclopedia Britannica Award. 13: Yes. 14: Prof devel, pub rel. 15: 32 Queensway N Box 160, Keswick Ont Can.

McCRADY, MARIAN (MULDER). b Mich 27 S 23. 4: John W McCrady. 5: West Mich U 41-45 (Eng) AB; UMich 50-52 MALS. 7: Tchr-libn Carman Schs, Flint Mich 47-51; Libn Central High Sch Lib, Flint Mich 52-. 9: ALA-AASchL; NEA; MichASchL (past pres); MichLA (chm Sch Lib Div); MichEA; FlintLA. 10: Altrusa. 14: Sch lib wk. 15: G4315 Woodrow ave, Flint Mi 48506.

McCRARY, (ANNA) MONTGOMERY. b Wash DC 8 Ja 04. 5: Toronto 22-27 (Lat, Fr) BA; George Washington U 30-31 (Lat, Fr) AM; UNC 44-45 BS in LS. 6: Lat, Fr. 7: High sch tchr 27-35; Tchr Oldfields Sch, Glencoe Md 36-41, Libn 41-44; LC: Catlgr For Lang Sect Descr Catlg Div 45-53, Head Catlg Unit & act head Prel Catlg Sect Descr Catlg 53-61, Asst head Eng Lang Sect Descr Catlg Div 61-65, Research asst Descr Catlg Div 65-. 9: ALA; DCLA. 10: NCU Lib Sch Alumni Assn. 14: Catlg. 15: 4851 Reservoir rd NW, Wash DC 20007.

McCRAY, MARY ANNICE. b Waterford Penn 24 My 18. 5: Mercyhurst Col 36-40 (Eng) BA; West Res 40-41 BS in LS. 6 Fr. 7: Asst ref Toledo Pub Lib, Toledo Ohio 41-43; Asst re Warder Pub Lib, Springfield Ohio 43-49; Child & ref Brooklyn Pub Lib 50-53; Head ref dept Erie Pub Lib, Erie Penn 54-. 9: ALA; PennLA (chm NW Chap 64-65). 14: Ref. 15: 9 E 33d st, Erie Pa 16504.

McCREADY, REYBURN R. b Corvallis Ore 21 F 25. 4: Doris R Naslund. 5: Ore State 46-47; UOre 47-48; John Brown U 48-50 (Religious Educ) BA; UDenver 60-61 (LS) MA. 6: Japanese. 7: (Cpl) USMC 44-46; Missionary Far Eastern Gospel Crusade, Okinawa 51-57; Libn UOre 61-. 9: ALA; PNLA; OreLA. 10: AAUP. 14: Ref. 15: 476 Louis lane, Eugene Or 97402.

McCREEDY, JO ANN. b Enid Okla 3 Jl 24. 5: Our Lady of the Lake Col 42-46 (Eng) BA, 46-49 BS in LS; Columbia 55-58 MS in LS, 60-63 (LS) DLS. 6: Fr, Ger. 7: Libn Providence Central High Sch, Alexandria La 48-51; Libn Providence High Sch, San Antonio Tex 51-58; Instr Dept of Libnship Our Lady of the Lake Col 58-60, Asst Prof 63-66, Assoc Prof 66-. 8: Dir NDEA Sch Libnship Inst Our Lady of the Lake Col summer 65; Cath Supp Com, "Standard Catalog for High School Libraries" 65-67; Dir HEA Inst for Lib Personnel summer 68. 9: CathLA (Educ Sect; v-chm & chm-elect 69-; sec San Antonio Unit 64-66); ALA-AASchL;-LED;-YASD;-RTSD; TexLA (v-pres & pres-elect 68-69, pres 69-70; sec Young Adult Round Table 65-66, chm 67-68, Publ Com 64-65). 10: Tex Coun on Lib Educ; AAUP; Beta Phi Mu. 12: "The Selection of School Librarianship as a Career" (doctoral diss); Ed 'Young Adult Column' in "Catholic Library World." 13: Yes. 14: Ref, lib educ, sch lib wk. 15: 315 Vance Jackson apt C29, San Antonio Tx 78201.

McCRIMMON, BARBARA (JEANETTE) SMITH. b Anoka Minn 3 My 18. 4: James M McCrimmon. 5: UMinn 35-39 (Fine Arts) BA; UIll 59-61 MS in LS. 6: Fr, Ital. 7: Asst libn Ill State Natural Hist Survey, Urbana Ill 61-62; Research assoc UIll Bur of Commun Planning (Urbana) 62-63; Libn Ill State Water Survey, Urbana Ill 64-65; Libn Amer Meteorological Soc, Boston 65-67; Ed asst Jour Lib Hist Sch of Lib Sci Fla State U 67-69. 9: ALA-ACRL; Mss Soc. 10: Beta Phi Mu. 12: "Antonio Panizzi as Administrator" (63). 13: Yes. 14: Tech libs, admin, lib hist. 15: 1330 W Indian Head dr, Tallahasse Fl 32301.

McCROSKY, JANET ELLEN. b Springfield Ohio 2 Mr 33. 5: Wittenberg U 50-54 (Eng) AB, BS in Educ; Carnegie 54-55 MS in LS. 6: Fr, Ger. 7: Ref asst Warder Pub Lib, Springfield Ohio 55-56, Order libn, tech processing dept 56-68, Order libn Asst hd Tech Serv Dept 68-. 9: ALA; OhioLA. 10: Glen Helen Assn; Springfield Symphony Orchestra; Fortnightly Musical Club; Clark Co Hist Soc; Animal Welfare League; Beta Phi Mu; Na t Audubon Soc; Nat Wildlife Assn. 14: Catlg, ref, admin, personnel mgt. 15: 480 Forest dr, Springfield Oh 45505.

McCROSSAN, JOHN ANTHONY. b Duluth Minn. 5: UMinn 57-60 (Humanities) BA, 60-61 (LS) MA; UIll 63-66 (LS) PhD. 6: Fr, Ger. 7: Asst ref dept UMinn Lib (Minneapolis) 58-61; Head Libn Eau Claire Pub Lib, Eau Claire Wis 61-63; Research asst Lib Research Center UIll (Urbana) 63-65; Research assoc Lib Research Center 65-66; Asst Prof Kent State Lib Sch 66-68; Asst Prof UMich Lib Sch (Ann Arbor) 68-. 8: Instr of Lib Sci UWis Ext Div 62-63; Consul on lib serv for the Handicapped; Dir of several insts. 9: ALA-ASD;-RSD;-PLA;WisLA (chm Pub Rel Com 62-63, Com on Standards for Pub Libs in Wis); IllLA; MichLA (chm Spec Libn Div). 10: ACLU; Toastmasters; Phi Beta Kappa; Beta Phi Mu; Lambda Alpha Psi; AAUP. 12: Ed Newsletter of the ALA-ASD (65-). 13: Yes. 14: Adult serv, research in libnship, educ for libnship, collection bldg, serv to the handicapped. 15: Univ Mich Lib School, Ann Arbor Mich 48104.

McCUE, BROTHER WILLIAM SC. b Prichard Ala 23 Ag 31. 5: Spring Hill Col 50 (Com ed) BSC; LSU (Baton Rouge) summers 61-66 (LS) MS; LSU (New Orleans) summer 68 La sch lib certif. 6: Fr. 7: Tchr: St Aloysius High Sch, Vicksburg Miss 54-55, Catholic High Sch, Baton Rouge La 56, Ascension Catholic High Sch, Donaldsonville La 57-65; Tchr & libn Menard Memorial High Sch, Alexandria La 66; Libn: St Stanislaus High Sch, Bay St Louis Miss 67-68, 70, Cor Jesu High Sch, New Orleans 69. 9: ALA; CathLA; MissLA. 11: Citizen Award, VFW, Donaldsonville La 65. 14: High sch lib (espec ref wk with students). 15: St Stanislaus Lib, S Beach st, Bay St Louis Ms 39520.

McCULLAH, MARGUERITE JACKSON. b Sycamore Ill 22 Ja 04. 5: No IllU 43 (Elem Educ) BE, 63 (LS) MA; UChicago

54 (Educ) MA; OxfordU summer 62. 6: Fr. 7: Elem tchr Pub Schs, Western Springs Ill 23-27; Asst Co Supt Schs DeKalb Co, Sycamore Ill 40-53; Jr high sch tchr Pub Schm Sycamore Ill 53-56, Lib supv 56-; Lib sci instr NoIllU 63-64, summer 65, 68-69; Lib sci instr WestIllU summer 66. 8: Consul Off of Supt Public Instr (Ill); Adv Com Div of Instr Materials, Off of Supt Pub Instr (Ill). 9: NEA; ALA; -AASchL; IllEA; IllLA; IllASchL (Com on Standards 65-67). 10: Amer Field Serv. 12: "Illinois School Library Standards". 14: Sch libs, child lit, adolesc lit. 15: 322 W Exchange st, Sycamore Il 60178.

McCULLOCH, MARILYN (RUTH) (HILTON). b Amherst NS Can 8 D 35. 4: Lawrence E McCulloch. 5: Mt Allison U 53-57 (Eng, Lat) BA; Toronto 58-59 BLS. 6: Fr, Ger. 7: Bkmob libn Colchester-E Hants Reg Lib, Truro NS 59-61; Child libn Ottawa Pub Lib 61-. 8: Bk Sel Com OntLA (Child Sect) 61-62, 62-63; V-chm Can Assn Child Libns 65-66, chm 66-67. 9: CanLA; ALA; OntLA; Inst Prof Libns, Ontario; OttawaLA. 10: Ottawa Volunteer Bureau (Hosp wk); Ottawa Little Theatre. 14: Child wk. 15: 68 Somerset st W #1, Ottawa 4 Ont Can.

McCULLOCH, MARY KATHERINE (HERCULES). b Union City Ind 30 N 13. 4: William R McCulloch. 5: Youngstown Col 34 (Biol Sci) AB; Carnegie 37 (LS) BS. 7: Page Carnegie Pub Lib, Kokomo Ind 26-27; Clerk Reuben Macmillan Free Lib, Youngstown Ohio 31-36; Br libn Flint Pub Lib, Flint Mich 37-39; Supv child wk Hamtramck Pub Lib, Hamtramck Mich 39-41; Hosp libn Lansing Pub Lib, Lansing Mich 43-45; Child libn Cleveland Heights Pub Lib, Cleveland Heights Ohio 48-49; Dir Fairfax Co Pub Lib, Fairfax Va 53-. 8: Consul on Lib Bldg in Charles Town WVa 63; State Bd for Certif of Libns (59-65, 64-69). 9: ALA(Coun 64-68); -PLA; (Bd Dir 64-68; Pub Lib Activities Com 65); VaLA; DCLA; (Coun of G ovt Lib Tech Com). 10: Bus & Prof Women's Club; Lincolnia Women's Club; Hist Landmarks Preservation Commsn; Fairfax Co Cultural Assn. 13: Yes. 14: Admin. 15: 3915 Chain Bridge rd, Fairfax Va 22030.

McCULLOUGH, FRANCES LOUISE (SUGG). b Carlisle Ky 16 Ag 13. 4: Raymond R McCullough. 5: Berea Col 32-36 (Fr) BA; UCincinnati Evening Col 38-42, 46. 6: Fr. 7: Period libn UCincinnati 37-43, Engnr & com libn 44-45, Ref libn 46-47; Libn Mercy Sch of Nursing, Hamilton Ohio 60-; Med libn Mercy Hosp, Hamilton Ohio 67-. 13: Yes. 15: 1025 Oakmont ave, Hamilton Oh 45013.

McCULLOUGH, MARY T. b Penn. 4: Paul T McCullough. 5: State Tchrs Col (Kutztown Pa) 41 BS in Ed; Drexel 45 BS in LS. 7: Lib asst Free Lib of Phila 45-48; Lib asst Pub Lib, so Bend Ind 49-51; Lib asst Pub Lib, Reading Penn 51; Lib asst Lib, LoyolaU (Chicago) 52; Adult libn Carnegie Lib of Pittsburgh (Penn) 52-57; Base libn USAF, (Japan) 62-. 15: APO San Francisco Ca 96323.

McCULLOUGH, RUTH. b Boston Mass. 5: MIT 34-38 (Engring admin) SB; Rutgers 55 (Lib admin) Certif. 6: Fr, Ger. 7: Statistician Liberty Mutual Ins Co, Boston 38-39; Br libn Anne Arundel Co Pub Lib, Glen Burnie Md 53-61; Tech libn Westinghouse, Baltimore 61-63; Supv tech Info Ctr Westinghouse Defense & Space Ctr, Baltimore 63-. 9: SLA (pres Baltimore Chap 68-69); Soc of Women Engrs (chm Baltimore-Washington Sect 65-67); MdLA. 10: Nat Security Indus Assn; Md Acad of Sci; MIT Alum Assn. 14: Info ret methodology, mgt of I/R systems. 15: Westinghouse Defense and Space Ctr Box 1693, Baltimore Md 21203.

McCUNE, LOIS KATHRYN (MAUGHAN). b Morris Minn 12 S 41. 4: Jerry McCune. 5: Wilmington Col 59-63 (Eng, Art) BA; UMinn 62; Ind U 63-64 (LS) MA. 6: Fr, Ital. 7: Punch press operator Textron Inc, Wilmington Ohio 59-63; Catlgr Ind U Lib 64-. 14: Catlg. 15: Box 1125, Bloomington In 47402.

McCURDY, CHARLES R. b Nampa Ida 28 F 26. 5: UDenver 46-49 (Art Hist, Humanities) AB, 49-50 (Art Hist, Oriental Studies) MA; NYU 69 (Art & Archaeol). 06: Fr, Sp. 7: Cadet Program US Army Air Corps, Tex, Neb, Colo 44-46; Asst in chg visual materials Museum of Modern Art, NYC 51-58; Head art ref dept Pratt Inst 58-65; Lectr Met Mus of Art NYC 66-67; Asst Prof Dept of Lib Sci Queens Col CUNY 67-. 10: Delta Phi Delta. 13: Yes. 14: Art ref, consul, info mat ctr, systems anal, data proc. 15: 404 E 65th st, New York NY 10021.

McCUSKER, HONOR (CECILIA). b Providence 20 O 09. 5: Pembroke Col 26-30 (Eng) BA; Bryn Mawr 30-32 (Eng) MA; University Col ULondon 32-34 (Eng) MA; Bryn Mawr 34-35 (Eng) PhD. 6: Fr, Dutch, Gk, Ger, Ital, Lat. 7: Trainee Providence Pub Lib 35-36; Asst rare bk dept Boston Pub Lib 36-41; Curator of Eng lit 41-43, 45-47; (Lt jg) CNO US Naval Reserve, Wash DC 43-45; Dir of lib serv USIS, The Hague 47-50; Dir of lib serv USIS, Rome 50-52; Dir of lib serv USIS, New Delhi India 53-57; Dir of lib serv USIS, Athens 57-67; & Intl info specialist for Near E & S Asia USIA (ICS) 67-68, Ctrs program adv f or Afr 68-. 8: Lecturer on hist of writing, XEN Lib Sch Athens 61-. 9: ALA; SLA. 10: AAUW. 11: Meritorious Service Award USIA 62; Bicentennial Medallion Brown U 65. 14: Ref, rare bks. 15: 1836 Belmont rd NW, Washington DC 20009.

McCUSKER, SISTER MARY LAURETTA OP. b Sillery Que Can 18 Ja 19. 5: West Md Col 39-42 (LS, Hist, Educ) BA; Johns Hopkins 45-46 (Educ); Columbia 46-48, 50 MLS, 52-53 (LS), 62-63 DLS. 6: Fr. 7: Libn Annapolis High Sch, Annapolis Md 42-44; Libn McDonogh Mil Sch, McDonogh Md 44-47; NY Pub Lib 47-48; Asstship Columbia U Lib Sch 47-48, 52-53; Asst Prof of Lib Sci Iowa State Tchrs Col 47-59; Instr UMinn Lib Sch summers 58, 59; Assoc Prof Rosary Col Dept of Lib Sci 63-67, Dir Dept Lib Sci 67-. 8: Consul to Iowa schs, Bur of Ext, Iowa State Tchrs Col, 47-49. 9: CathLA (past chm var coms); NEA; ALA-LED (chm Tchrs Sect, chm Bogle Mem Award Com 62-); IowaLA; Iowa State EA (Bk Sel Com 48-59); IllLA; Iowa SchLA. 10: Bus & Prof Womens Club; Nat Honor Soc; Beta Phi Mu. 13: Yes. 14: Child lit, catlg, automation. 15: Rosary Col 7900 Division st, River Forest Ill 60305.

McCUSKEY, JEAN. b Canton Ohio 10 Je 10. 5: Col of Wooster 27-31 (Eng) AB; West Res 31-32 BS in LS. 6: Fr. 7: Libn McKinley High Sch, Canton Ohio 35-. 9: ALA; NEA; OhioASchL; OhioEA. 10: Delta Kappa Gamma; Canton Col Club; Canton Scholarship Found; AGO Festival Choir. 14: Adolescent reading interests. 15: 3502 Parkhill circle NW, Canton Oh 44718.

McDADE, CHRISTINE (CAMERON). b Pictov Nova Scotia 25 Ja 24. 4: Eugene L McDade. 6: Fr. 7: Libn YMCA, Boston 46-47; Asst libn Halifax Herald Mail, Halifax Nova Scotia 47-48; Libn Prot Sch Bd Gtr Montreal, Montreal PQ 63-68; Libn Trafalgar Sch for Girls, Montreal PQ 68-. 9: CanLA; QueLA. 10: Pi Beta Phi. 14: Child lit. 15: 56 Fifteenth ave, Roxboro Que Can 900.

McDANIEL, CARSE OREN. b Shelby NC 25 Ap 41. 5: Lenoir Rhyne Col 59-63 (Eng) AB; UNC 64-65 MS in LS. 7: Eng tchr Page High Sch, Greensboro NC 63-64; Asst catlgr Furman U Lib 65-67; Hd soc sci & humanities div Clemson U Lib 67-. 9: ALA; SCLA; SELA. 10: Alpha Psi Omega; SC Coun on Human Rel; AAUP. 14: Admin, ref. 15: Clemson Univ Lib, Clemson SC 29631.

McDANIEL, JAMES E. b Detroit 5 O 30. 4: Marilyn Parmly. 5: East Mich 56 (Eng) BA, 60 (Educ) MA; UMich 64 AMLS. 7: Bkmob operator Wayne Co, Romulus Mich 55-58; Lib aid Wayne Co, Southgate Mich 58-59; Sch libn Cherry Hill Sch Dist, Inkster Mich 59-60; Sch libn Crestwood Sch Dist, Dearborn Heights Mich 60-64; Br libn Monroe Co, Monroe Mich 64-65; Curriculum materials libn Clarion State Col 65-. 9: PennLA. 14: Ref, child wk. 15: RD 2 Box 113, Summerville Pa 15864.

McDAVID, LUCY ELIZABETH. b Pelzer SC 11 Ag 09. 5: Greenville Woman's Col 26-27; Chicora Col for Women 27-30 (Lat) BA, Certif in Piano; Winthrop Col summer 38 (Educ); Furman U summer 45 (Educ); Duke summers 46, 47 (Psych); USC summer & fall 57 (LS); UNC summers 58-62 MSLS. 7: Tchr Eng, Lat Holly Springs High Sch, Inman SC 30-34; Tchr elem & piano Fork Shoals Sch, Pelzer SC 34-36; Elem tchr Berea Sch, Greenville SC 36-44; Tchr of lang arts, soc stud, sci Simpsonville Elem Sch, Simpsonville SC 44-46; Elem tchr Greenville City Sch, Greenville SC 46-56; Tchr-libn Ellen Woodside High Sch, Pelzer SC 56-62, Libn 62-65; Libn Woodmont High Sch, Piedmont SC 65-. 8: Inst Lib Sci: Winthrop Col summer 67, USC (Conw ay) summer 67, USC Ext Div, Greenville 67-68. 9: ALA; NEA; SCLA (Sch Lib Div: sec 66-67, v-pres 67-); SCEA (sec-treas Sch Lib Sect 65-66). 10: Friends of the Library, Greenville Co Lib Greenville SC; Delta Kappa Gamma; Girl Scouts Leader. 14: Bk sel, sch lib programs. 15: Rt 3, Pelzer SC 29669.

McDERMOTT, BEATRICE (SCHMULLING). b Hoboken NY. 4: Cyril L McDermott. 5: Col of New Rochelle (Eng, Hist) BA; Fordham U Sch of Law 46-50 LLB. 7: Libn Dwight Harris Koegel & Caskey, NYC 37-42; Libn Dewey Ballantine Bushby Palmer & Wood, NYC 42-. 9: AALL (Com on Placement); SLA; Law Lib Assn, Greater NY (pres 51-52); Assn Law Libs, Upstate NY; ABA. 12: Ed "Manual of Procedures for Private Law Libraries," AALL Publ No 5 (62);

Contrib to "Proceedings, Third Annual Inst on Law Libnship" (60); co-auth "Government Regulation of Business Including Antitrust" (67). 15: c/o Dewey ballantine, Bushby, Palmer & Wood 140 Broadway, New York NY 10005.

McDERMOTT, CYRIL LAVELLE. b NY. 4: Beatrice Schmulling. 5: NYU 25 (Eng) AB; Fordham Law Sch 29 LLB; NYU 55 (Law) LLM; Columbia 61 MLS. 6: Sp, Ancient Gk, Lat. 7: Practice of law, NYC 30-37; Law sec to Hon Joseph W Keller, NYC 37-45; Prin Libn Civil Court of the City of NY for all 5 boroughs 45-47; Prof of law & Law Libn St John's U (Brooklyn NY) 47-. 8: Chm Sub-Com for Law Lib of New Bldg Com, St John's U (Brooklyn Center); Consul for law firm libs, NYC. 9: AALL (chm Com on Placement 64-65, cm &/or mem many other coms); ALA; SLA; Law Lib Assn, Greater NY (pres 50-51). 10: Assn of the Bar City of NY; Brooklyn Heights Assn; Univ Club; Lawyers Club; Assn of Ex-Members of Squadron A NYC. 12: "Government Regulation of Business," with Coleman (66); "Re, Brief Writing and Oral Argument" (65). 13: Yes. 14: Admin, legal ref. 15: 160 Henry st, Brooklyn NY 11201.

McDERMOTT, FRANCIS X. b Richmond Hill NY 17 S 08. 4: Kathleen Mulrooney. 5: St John's U 30 (Phil) BA; Columbia 40-42 BS IN LS. 7: Clerk Bank of the Manhattan Co, NYC 32-39; Libn Cathedral Col of the Immaculate Conception 39-. 8: Ed Com, Cath Child Bk Club. 9: CathLA (chm Brooklyn LI Unit 58-60); Metropolitan Cath Col Libns (chm-elect 67-69). 14: Ref, readers serv. 15: 7200 Douglaston pkwy, Douglaston NY 11362.

McDERMOTT, MOLLY E. b Mitchell SD 21 Je 31. 5: Rosary Col 49-53 (Econ) BA; UDenver 63-64 (LS) MA. 7: Copy writer Naegele Advertising Co, Minneapolis 54-56; Ed house organ Graphic Arts Inds, Minneapolis 56-58; Office manager C J McDermott Co Inc, Sioux Falls SD 58-61; Sec asst to manager Holiday Inns of Amer, Minneapolis 61-63; Lib asst Westminster Pub Lib, Westminster Colo 63-65, Child libn 65-67; Br lib serv child specialist stockton-San Joaquin Co Lib Syst & Child consul 49-59; Lib Syst 67-69; Coord child serv Santa Rosa-Sonoma Co Pub Lib 69-. 9: ALA; CalLA. 14: Child wk, storytelling, puppetry. 14: Child wk, storytelling, puppetry. 15: 8083 Raleigh st, Westminster Co 80030.

McDERMOTT, WILLIAM S. b Omaha Neb 24 F 30. 4: Carol Wiegand. 5: Creighton 57-63 (Marketing) BSBA, 62-65 (Sociol) AB; Omaga U summer 65; Kan State Tchrs Col 66-68 (Libnship) ML. 6: Sp. 7: Machinist apprentice Union Pacific RR, Omaha Neb 48-51, Machinist 51-53, 55-66; Machinist (Spec 3) USA Ordinance 53-55; Act hd libn Fremont Pub Lib, Fremont Neb 68-69, Hd libn 69-. 9: ALA; NebLA. 10: Optimists. 14: Ref. 15: 1700 Mayfair ave, Fremont Nb 68025.

McDILL, EDWIN BRANDAO. b New Orleans La 11 Je 36. 4: Lucinda Lanning. 5: Spring Hill Col 54-58 (Hist) BS; LSU 58-60 MSLS. 6: Fr. 7: Libn Cranwell Sch, Lenox Mass 60-62; Ref libn Holy Cross Col 62-64; Ref asst Greensboro Pub Lib, Greensboro NC 64-67; Libn Guilford Tech Inst 67-. 9: ALA; NCLA; SELA; Greensboro Commun Col Libns Assn. 10: Buten Mus of Wedgwood (Merion Penn); Wedgwood Internat Sem; Preserv Soc. 13: Yes. 14: Ref, admin, rare bks. 15: 2301 W Pisgah Church rd, Greensboro NC 27408.

McDILL, JOHN LEE. b New Haven Conn 30 Ja 33. 5: Stanford 52-56 (Pol Sci) AB; Columbia 58-59 MSLS. 6: Ger, Fr. 7: Descr catlgr Harvard U 59-63; Ser catlgr Dartmouth Col 64-67; Reclsf & ser libn Mont State U 68-. 10: Phi Beta Kappa. 14: Catlg. 15: P O Box 392, Bozeman Mt 59715.

McDONALD, BEVERLY (JANE). b Prospect Hts Ill 20 Je 41. 5: Ill Col 60-64 (Eng) BA; IndU 64-65 (LS) Masters. 6: Fr, Ger. 7: Catlgr Ohio State U (Columbus) 65-. 9: ALA; Ohio Valley Gp of Tech Serv Libns; OhioLA; FranklinCoLA (treas). 10: AAUW; Phi Beta Kappa. 14: Catlg. 15: 306 W Lane ave apt 1, Columbus Oh 43201.

McDONALD, DOROTHY (HOWARD). b Thomaston Ga 18 S 11. 5: Ga State Col for Men 29-32 (Romance Langs) AB; Peabody summers 53-56 (LS) MA, 64-65 (LS) 6th yr. 6: Fr, Sp. 7: Elem tchr Tift Co Schs, Tift Co Ga 32-34; Tchr Span, Eng, Math R E Lee Inst, Thomaston Ga 42-44; Libn LaGrange Mem Lib, LaGrange Ga 50-, Asst dir 57-. 9: ALA-Pub Lib Div; SELA; GaLA. 10: AAUW; LaGrange Theatre Guild; Chattahoochee Valley Art Assn. 14: Ref, young adult serv, tech serv. 15: 315 Hill st, LaGrange Ga 30240.

McDONALD, GERALD D(OAN). b Wilmington Ohio 5 Je 05. 5: Wilmington Col 24-27 (Eng) AB, 53 Lit D; Haverford Col 27-28 (Eng) AM; Columbia 29-30 BS in LS. 6: Fr. 7: Asst lit div Cleveland Pub Lib 28-29; NY Pub Lib: Asst info div 30, Head rare bk room 31-40, Chief rare bk div 41-45; (Sgt) Signal Corps US Army 42-45; NY Pub Lib: Chief Amer hist & gen div 45-69, Act ed of publs 54-56, Act chief map div 47-57, Chief of spec collections, Adviser to the Spencer Collection & Keeper of mss 69-. 8: Survey of lib use of films (Rockefeller Grant) 40-41. 9: ALA; NYLA; NYC Lib Club. 10: Grolier Club; Amer Antiq Soc; Friends Hist Assn; BSA; Soc Preservation of Covered Bridges; Nat Bd of Review of Motion Pictures; The Typhophiles; Rounce & Coffin Club; Arehons of Colophon. 11: LHD, Wilmington Col. 12: "Educational Motion Pictures and Libraries" (42); "A Way of Knowing" (59); "Poems of Stephen Crane" (64); "The Films of Charlie Chaplin" (65); Ed "N Y Pub Lib Bulletin" (54-56); poetry ed "Library Journal" (48-58). 13: Yes. 14: Ref, rare bks. 15: 36 W 10th st, New York NY 10011.

McDONALD, JOHN PETER. b Phila 17 O 22. 4: Josephine Herring. 5: UVa 40-43, 46 (Eng) AB; Drexel 50-51 MSLS; Rutgers 58. 6: Sp, Fr. 7: US Naval Reserve (Lt jg) 42-46; Instr of Eng Drexel Inst 46-47; Head res bk dept ref asst UPenn 49-54; Wash U Lib (St Louis): Chief ref dept 54-56, Asst to dir 56-58, Asst dir for readers serv 58-60, Assoc dir of libs 60-63; U Libn UConn 63-. 8: Lib Bldg Consul: Marymount Col, Westchester Commun Col, Annhurst Col, F ordhamU; US Off Educ Adv Com on Lib Research & Train Projs 68-. 9: ARL (Bd Dir 69-72; Shared Catlg Com 68-; Adv Com Univ Lib Mgt Study 69); ALA (Coun 62-66; Nominating Com 67-68); -ACRL (Adv Com on Coop with Educ & Prof Orgs 61-64, 65; U Libs Sect: Urban U Libs Com 61-63, Res & Devel Com 63-65);-LAD (Bd Dir 62-66); MoLA (chm Col & Univ Div 61); Greater St Louis Lib Club; ConnLA (chm Col & Univ Libs Sect 66-67; chm Devel Com 67-69); East Col Libns Conf (treas 64); BSA; NELA. 10: Phi Kappa Phi; Archons of Colop hon. 11: Educ Facil Lab Travel Grant 64. 12: 'The Rutgers University Library: A Study of Current Problems of Organization and Service in a Decentralized University' in "Studies in Library Administrative Problems" (60). 13: Yes. 14: Univ lib admin, univ lib bldgs & equipt. 15: 18 Westwood rd, Storrs Ct 06268.

McDONALD, JOSEPHINE (AGNES) K(ASHETA). b Branford Conn 22 Jl 16. 4: William Charles McDonald. 5: State Col at Worcester (Mass) 33-37 (Educ) BS; Simmons 41-42 (LS) MS. 6: Fr, Lithuanian. 7: Asst Worcester (Mass) Free Pub Lib 37-42; Camp libn, Camp Edwards Mass 42-44; Arsenal libn Watertown Arsenal, Watertown Mass 44-45; Army libn US Army, Eng, France, Berlin Germany 45-46; Base libn USAF, Westover AFB Mass 51-60; Sch libn Sch Dept, Longmeadow Mass 60-; Coord of sch libs, Longmeadow Mass 65-; Instr State Col (Westfield) 65-; Instr of lib sch State Col (Worcester Mass) summer 64; Tchr of lib skills Ursuline Acad summer 65. 8: Consul libn Ursuline Acad, Springfield Mass 63-; Mem Adv Com on Certif of Libns 66-. 9: NEA; ALA; NESchLA (pres 6 6-68); Mass State LA; Mass Tchrs Assn. 10: Simmons Col Club; Women's Club. 12: "School Library and You" (64). 13: Yes. 14: Clsf, org of sch libs. 15: 79 Roosevelt ave, Springfield Ma 01118.

McDONALD, JUDITH LOUISE. b Rockville Neb 17 Ja 39. 5: UNeb 61-65 (Eng) BS, 65-68 9ed media) MEd; West Mich U 68- (Libnship). 6: Ger. 7: Jr libn Lincoln City Libs, lincoln Neb 58-65; Sch libn Milford Pub Schs, Milford Neb 65-68; Asst libn Chadron State col 68-. 8: Adv Great Plains Sch Dist Reorgan Proj, Lincoln Neb 67-68. 9: ALA; NEA-DAVI; NebLA; Neb Educ Media Assn; NebEA. 10: Chadron State Col Fac Assn; Neb State Hist Soc; Willa Cather Mem Found. 14: Educ media, lib educ, admin. 15: Faculty Hall apt 9 CSC, Chadron Nb 69337.

McDONALD, MARGERY ANNE. b Brockton Mass 20 Ap 37. 5: Simmons 55-59 (LS) BS. 7: Libn Christ Hosp Inst for Med Res, Cincinnati 59-60; Asst libn Rockefeller U 60-68; Libn San Diego Pub Lib 68-. 9: MedLA. 14: Ref. 15: 240 E 76th st, New Y ork, NY 10021.

McDONALD, MARIE-LOUISE. b Chester Penn 17 Jl 12. 5: Rosemont Col 30-34 (Eng) AB; Villanova U 60-63 (LS) MS. 6: Fr, Lat. 7: Eng tchr Chester High Sch, Chester Penn 51-60; Libn Pulosk Jr High Sch, Chester Penn 60-. 9: CathLA; PennLA. 10: AAUW. 14: Catlg, ref, reading guidance. 15: 19th & Chestnut sts, Chester Pa 19013.

McDONALD, MARY JO (BOYD). b Cooper Tex 3 My 30. 4: Reuben B McDonald. 5: E Tex State U 48-52 (Eng) BA (Eng) BS in LS; UTex 58-59 (LS); Tex Woman's U 61-62 (LS). 6: Fr. 7: Tchr-libn Rosebud High Sch, Rosebud Tex 51-52; Libn Yoe High Sch, Cameron Tex 52-55; Eng tchr New Braunfels High Sch, New Braunfels Tex 55-56; Ref libn

Southwest Tex State Col Lib 56-58, Circ libn 58-66; Libn New Braunfels High Sch 66-. 9: TexLA; SWLA; Tex Assn Col Tchrs; TexStateTA. 10: AAUW. 14: Circ, ref. 15: 587 Lakeview circle, New Braunfels Tx 78130.

McDONALD, MARY LUCY RSM. b Grand Rapids Mich 9 Ap 11. 5: UNotre Dame summers 39-41 (Lat); Mercy Col of Detroit 45 (Lat, Eng) AB; UMich 45-48 ABLS, summers 62-64 AMLS, summers 65-68 (Eng) MA. 6: Lat, Fr. 7: Instr Mercy Col of Detroit summer 55; Libn & tchr: Our Lady of Mercy High, Detroit 56-60, St Michael High Sch, Pinconning Mich 62-65, St John High Sch, Independence Iowa 65-68; Libn Mt Mercy Acad, Grand Rapids Mich 68-. 8: Chm Saginaw Diocese Eng Coun 61-65. 9: NCTE; CathLA; ALA. 13: Yes. 14: Catlg, ref. 15: Mt Mercy Acad, 1425 Bridge NW, Grand Rapids Mi 49504.

McDONALD, MURRAY FRANK. b Hartsville SC 6 Ag 36. 4: Timothea F Allen. 5: Coker Col 53-57 (Eng, Span) AB; UNC 57-58, 59-60, 63 (LS) MS; Boston U 67-. 06: Sp. 7: Child libn Brooklyn Pub Lib 60-67; Devotion Elem Sch Libn Pub Lib of Brookline, Brookline Mass. 9: ALA. 10: Beacon Hill Civic Assn (Boston). 14: Child bks & programs. 15: 31 Mt Vernon st, Boston Ma 02108.

McDONALD, ODALIE SMITH. b Monroe La 22 S 07. 4: William J McDonald. 5: Huston-Tillotson Col 37 (Eng) AB; UDenver 44 BS in LS; Tex So U 62 (Elem Educ) M Ed. 6: Fr. 7: Libn Kealing Jr High Sch, Austin Tex 37; Libn Houston Col 44; Libn Anderson High Sch, Austin Tex 46; Libn Carroll High Sch, Monroe La 48; Libn Carver Br Pub Lib, Monroe La 49; Libn Boley High Sch, W Monroe La 53; Asst libn & Assoc Prof Lib Educ grambling Col, Grambling La 56-; State supv sch libs S tate Dept of Educ, 66-. 8: Instr, Inst for Training in Libnship, Central State Col, Edmon d Okla summer 69; Coord of Lib Educ Program Grambling Col. 9: ALA; LaLA; LaEA; LaTA; SWLA. 10: AAUP; Alpha Kappa Alpha; Altruistic Club. 13: Yes. 14: Lib educ. 15: P O Box 366, Grambling La 71245.

McDONALD, ROBERT HENRY. b Providence RI 30 Ap 12. 5: Providence Col 29-31 (Humanities); Col of St Thomas Aquinas 32-35 (Philos) BA; CatholicU 40-41 BS in LS. 6: Lat, Fr. 7: Asst order libn BrownU Lib 41-42; T/Sgt US Army Airways Comm Serv USAF (Cryptographer) ETOUSA 42-45; Asst libn Dumbarton Oaks Lib & Collection, Wash DC 46; Ed P J Kennedy & Sons, NYC 47-51; Asst libn Inst of the Aeronautical Sci, NYC 54-56; Asst Supv Rural Libs Serv State of RI 58-59; Ref libn Tech Lib US Army Natick Libs, Natick Mass 59-60, Chief readers serv 60-64, Chief doc unit 64-69, Hd tech doc gp 69-. 9: SLA (Boston Chap: chm Pub Rel Com 63-64). 10: Friendship House of Harlem. 14: Docs. 15: 40 West Central st, Natick Ma 01760.

McDONNELL, ANTHONY MICHAEL. b Birkenhead England 24 Mr 21. 04 Carole Graham. 5: Cathedral Col 38-43 (Philos) BA; Columbia 47-48 BSLS. 6: Fr, Ital, Sp, Lat. 7: Libn Immac Conception Sem (Huntington NY) 48-67; Chief catlg Suffolk Coop Lib System, Bellport NY 67-. 14: Catlg, tech serv. 15: 59 Price st, Patchogue NY 11772.

McDONNELL, AUDREY. b Seattle 29 Je 06. 5: UWash 23-27 (Fr, Eng) BA, 27-28 (LS) BA in Lib; summers 29, 31 Life Tchg Certif; Trinity Col (Dublin Ireland) 62. 6: Fr. 7: Tchr White Bluffs High Sch, White Bluffs Wash 27-29; Tchr Chiloquin High Sch, Chiloquin Ore 29-33; Tchr E Wenatchee Jr High Sch, E Wenatchee Wash 34-35; Libn Clover Park High Sch, Tacoma Wash 38-40; Dir of Libs Clover Park Schs, Tacoma (Lakewood) Wash 40-. 8: Consul Trump Wkshop, U Puget Sound summer 61; Asst Prof UWash Sch of Libnship summer 63. 9: NEA; ALA; Wash State Assn Sch Libns (pres 60-61); WashEA. 10: Phi Beta Kappa; DAR; AAUW; Admin Women Educ. 13: Yes. 14: Sch libnship. 15: 6402 100th st SW, Tacoma Wa 98499.

McDONNELL, FRANCES GERTRUDE (ADAMS). b Bristol Me 22 Ja 17. 4: Harold Francis McDonnell. 5: Simmons 34-38 (LS) BS. 6: Ger, Fr, Sp, Ital, Russian. 7: Stud asst Peabody Lib, Georgetown Mass 31-37; Catlgr Peabody Mus Lib Harvard U 38-45; Ger tchr Ft Leonard Wood Army Post, Mo 54-56; Sec St Michael's Episcopal Church, Arlington Va 61-64; Circ libn George Washington U 65-67, Bindary preparations libn 67-. 10: Madison Manor Citizens Assn; Home hospitality for Internat Centre, Wash DC. 14: Admin, lib automation. 15: 874 N Nottingham st, Arlington Va 22205.

McDONNELL, JOHN J. b Castlebar Co Mayo Ireland 15 Jl 25. 4: Toy McDonnell. 5: Sch of Libnship Co of Com (Leeds Eng) 54-55 (LS) A.L.A.; Iona Col 59-62 (Eng) BA; Pratt 62-64 (LS) MA. 6: Fr. 7: Lib asst Eccles Pub Lib, Manchester Eng 51-52; Lib asst Bedfordshire Co Lib, Bedfordshire Eng 53-55; Lib asst Siena Col 56-57; Lib asst Iona Col 58-60; Lib asst Malverne Pub Lib, Malverne NY 60-61; Libn South High Sch, Valley Stream NY 61-. 13: Yes. 14: Ref. 15: 15 Greenlawn blvd, Valley Stream NY 11580.

McDONOUGH, EAMON (EMMETT). b Boston 25 Ag 19. 4: Phoebe Stone. 5: Boston Col 42-47 (Soc Sci) BS; Simmons 46-48 (LS) BS; Adelphi Col 57-62; LIU (C W Post) 64. 06: Fr, Ger. 7: Ref libn Boston Pub Lib 36-57; Sch libn E Hampton High Sch, E Hampton NY 57-. 9: NEA; NY State Tchrs Assn; NYLA; Suffolk Co Sch LA. 10: Guild Hall Players; East Hampton Dem Com. 13: Yes. 14: Sch libs, ref. 15: 39 Buell lane, E Hampton NY 11937.

McDONOUGH, GEORGE EDWARD. b Bridgeport Conn 25 Mr 24. 4: Roxy Elizabeth Jensen. 5: UCal (Berkeley) 47-49 (Eng, Psych) AB; Johns Hopkins U 49-50 (Eng) AM; UWash 61-63 9ls0 ml& chicago 65- LS; Catholic U 67; Certif MLA. 06: Lat, Fr, Ger. 7: Instr in humanities Johns Hopkins U 49-50; Instr in humanities Lewis & Clark Col 54-55; Instr in Eng Portland State Col 55; Assoc Prof of Eng Cascade Col 57-62; Assoc Prof of Eng & Libnship, Chm Dept of Libnship Seattle Pacific Col 62-; Visiting Asst Prof of Lib Sci, ref libn Chicago State Col 65-66; Asst Prof of libnship & Dir of Admissions & student affairs UMd 66-67; Asst Prof of libnship UWash 67-68; Assoc Prof of Eng & libnship & Dir of learning resources Seattle Pacific Col 68-. 8: Chm Wash (State) Sch Lib Educators Com 65; Co-chm Pac nw sect C onf on Christianity & Lit 64; Bogle Awards Com, Lib Educ Div, ALA 67-70. 9: ALA; LED (Bogle Awards Com 67-70); NCTC; Wash (State) LA; Wash SchLA. 10: AAUP; Seattle Art Museum; PTA; View Ridge Comm Club. 11: Emily Chamberlain Cook Prize in Poetry UCal (Berkeley) 47. 12: Collected Poems (47); "The Farmington Plan; An Informative Study" (64). 13: Yes. 14: Lib sci edu, ref, admin. 15: 6638 57th ave NE, Seattle Wa 98115.

McDONOUGH, JEAN R (ROBERTS). b Jerome Ida 24 Ap 20. 4: Roger H McDonough. 5: Wilson Col 38-42 (Eng) BA; Columbia 42-43 BS in LS; Rutgers 54-57 (LS) MS. 6: Ger. 7: Ref asst Undergraduate Lib Columbia U 43-44; Catlgr Baker Lib Harvard 44-46; Asst libn fortune Magazine, NYC 46-48; Lib Dir W Orange Pub Lib, West Orange NJ 48-51; Libn Miss Fine's Sch, Princeton NJ 53-55; Libn Princeton High Sch, Princeton NJ 55-57; Educ media coord Princeton Reg Sch, Princeton NJ 66-. 8: Instr: Summer Ext in Lib Sci, UVt, Ext Div, Trenton State Col Trenton. 9: ALA; NEA; NJSchLA (Exec Bd); NJEA. 10: LWV. 14: Sch lib. 15: 43 Bainbridge st, Princeton NJ 08540.

McDONOUGH, MARTIN PATRICK. b Chicago 28 Ja 14. 4: Barbara June Scarborough. 5: Villanova U 34-38 (Eng) BA; Rosary Col 40-41 BA in LS; Chicago 41, 47-48 (LS); U Houston 66, 68 (Mgt). 7: Libn St Rita High Sch, Chicago 39-41; USAAF Personnel (S/Sgt) 42-45; Asst libn Wright Jr Col 46, 50-51; Research libn Dept Subways & Superhighways, Chicago 46; Head Libn Food & Container Inst for Armed Forces, Chicago 47-49; Dir Lib Sch E Tex State U 49-50; Base & tech libn Ellington AFB, Houston 52-54; Chief Libn The Houston Post, Houston 54-62; Chief Libn US Army Artillery & Missile Sch, Ft Sill Okla 62-64; Head processes sect Tech Lib Manned Spacecraft Center, Houston 64-. 10: San Jacinto Assn for Retarded. 13: Yes. 14: ADP STINFO stor & ret. 15: 1103 Wedgewood cir, Pasadena Tx 77502.

McDONOUGH, ROGER HENRY. b Trenton NJ 24 F 09. 4: Jean E Roberts. 5: Rutgers 34 AB; Columbia 36 (LS) BS. 6: Fr. 7: Page Trenton Pub Lib, Trenton NJ 26-28; Stud asst RutgersU (New Brunswick) 30-34, Ref libn 34-37; Dir Free Pub Lib, New Brunswick NJ 37-47; USAF 42-46; Dir (state libn) NJ State Lib, Trenton 47-. 8: Consul: US Off Educ (survey Fed lib programs in 5 So states), state libs of Tex, Me, NH, Conn & Fl; Sec Com to Study Arts in NJ; Adv bd Rutgers U Grad Sch Lib Serv. 9: ALA (pres 68-69; Exec Bd 58-62; Coun 56-62; chm Fed Rel Com 56-60); -AA State L (pres 51-52). 10: RutgersU Press Coun; Trustee NJ Hist Soc; Trustee Westminster Choir Col. 11: Litt D, Rutgers U 56. 13: Yes. 14: Admin, ref. 15: 43 Bainbridge st, Princeton NJ 08540.

McDOWELL, GAYLORD KEITH. b Phila 21 Ap 33. 5: UMiami(Fla) 50-52; UPenn 52-54 (Ger) AB, 55-56 (Ger); Drexel 57-60 MS in LS; Marquette U 66- (Ger). 06: Ger, Fr, Sp, Ital, Russian, Classical Gk, Norwegian, Czech, Chinese. 7: Subprof searcher Temple U 57-60; Catlgr, tech inst Northwestern U 60-61; Catlgr DePaul U Campus Lib 61-66; Series catlgr Marquette U 66-67; C atlg libn Carroll Col (Waukasha, Wis) 67-69; Supv tech serv Decatur Pub Lib, Decatur Ill 69-. 9: ALA. 10: Phi Beta Kappa; Beta Phi Mu;

Delta Phi Alpha; AAUP. 14: Catlg, clsf. 15: Decatur Public Lib, Decatur Il.

McDOWELL, MARY L. b Lansing Mich 21 Ap 33. 5: Siena Heights Col 51-53; Mich State Col 53-55 (Elem Educ) BA; Western MichU 64-65 (Libnship) MA. 7: Tchr Lansing Sch Dist, lansing Mich 55-57; Tchr Stockton Sch Dist, Stockton Calif 57-59; Tchr US Army Schs, heidelberg Germany 59-61; Tchr San Bruno Sch Dist, San Bruno Calif 62-63; Libn Birmingham Sch Dist, Birmingham Mich 65-. 9: NEA; MichASchL; MichEA. 14: Child lit, a-v materials. 15: 4833 Woodland #202, Royal Oak Mi 48073.

McDOWELL, ROBERT L. b San Francisco Cal 30 N 21. 4: Maria Zamarripa. 5: OmahaU 60-61 (Mil Sci) BGE; UAmericas 64-65 (Intl Rel) MA; San Jose State Col 67-68 (Libnship) MA. 6: Fr, Sp. 7: Admin NCO (Put to M/Sgt) USAF various locations 42-51; Libn (M/Sgt) USAF Mather AFB & Smoky Hill AFB, Cal & Kan 47-48; Admin off (Capt) USAF various locations 51-59; Liaison off (Capt) USAF Redstone Arsenal, Huntsville Ala 59-63; Bkstore mgr UAmericas 65-66; Ref libn Santa Clara Pub Lib (Cal) 67-68; Tech serv libn Boise State Col 68-. 9: ALA; IdaLA. 14: Tech serv. 15: 2003 N 26th st, Boise Id 83702.

McDUFFIE, SARAH W. b Lawrence Mass 1 Mr 29. 5: Hood Col 47-51 (Eng) BA; Columbia 54-55 (LS) MS. 06: Fr. 7: Catlgr Brooklyn Museum Lib, Brooklyn NY 55-58; Head catlg dept UAlaska Lib 59-60, Head reader serv dept 61-65; Assoc libn Biol Labs Lib Harvard U 65-68; Info sci Potlatch Forests, Lewiston Ida 69-. 8: Ref libn Lib/USA NY World's Fair 64. 9: SLA. 15: Wood Products Research Potlatch Forests Inc, Lewiston Id 83501.

McELDERRY, STANLEY. b Fairfield Iowa 19 O 18. 4: Bernice Ingram. 5: USoCal 40 AB, 41 BS in LS; Chicago 47-49, 56 (LS). 7: Engnr libn Lockheed Aircraft Corp, Burbank Cal 41-47; Circ libn & Asst Prof UMinn 50-52; Asst dir of libs & Assoc Prof UOkla 52-55; Visiting Lecturer UTex 54, 55; Visiting Lecturer USoCal 58, 62; Visiting Lecturer UTex 65; Col Libn San Fernando Valley State Col 57-68; Coord Lib Serv Cal State Cols, Cal 67-68; Dean's Prof Lib Sci Grad Sch L ib Sci, Austin Tex 68-. 8: Adv coun UCal Sch Libnship 58-61, 62-; Chancellor's lib devel com Cal State Col 64-68; Higher educ lib com Coord Coun for Higher Educ, Cal 65-68. 9: ALA (Coun 62-; Recruitment Com 62); -LAD (In-serv Train Com Personnel Admins Sect 59-60; chm Bldg & Equipment Sect 67); -ACRL (Standards Com 68-); CalLA (pres Col, Univ & Research Libs 64; chm So Dist Col, Univ & Research Libs); ASIS; TexLA; SWLA. 10: AAUP. 12: Co-auth "The Implications of Modern Technology for the Small College Library". 13: Yes. 14: Acad libs, admin. 15: 2615 Pembrook trail, Austin Tx 78731.

McELRATH, EDITH ANN. b St Paul 9 F 27. 5: UMinn 44-48 (LS) BS. 7: Asst Owatonna Pub Lib, Owatonna Minn 48-51; Asst to head circ dept Davenport Pub Lib, Davenport Iowa 51-59; 1st asst U Br Lib Seattle Pub Lib 59-63; Br libn Columbia Br 63; Br libn W Seattle Br 66-. 9: ALA; WashLA; PNLA. 10: Civil Serv League; Seattle Mountaineers. 15: 3636 Fremont ave N, Seattle Wa 98103.

McELRATH, MARGARET MARY (LANE). b Sioux City Iowa 1 O 12. 5: Morningside Col 29-34 (Eng Lit) BA; UIll 34-36 BLS. 6: Fr. 7: Asst catlgr Sioux City Pub Lib, Sioux City Iowa 36-39; Libn Woodbury Co Lib, Moville Iowa 56-60; Ref asst Sioux City Pub Lib, Sioux City Iowa 60-63, Head adult serv 64-69; Hd tech serv 69-. 9: ALA; IowaLA; Iowa Authors Bibliog Com (chm). 10: Libn, Calvary Episcopal Church; AAUW. 14: Ref, catlg, local hist in lib. 15: Sioux City Pub Lib 705 - 6th st, Sioux City Ia 51105.

McELROY, MRS AUDREY M (FRAISER). b Shamrock La 8 Mr 21. 4: Weldon W McElroy. 5: La Polytech Inst 38-42 (Liberal Arts) BA; LSU 58-59 (LS) MS. 7: Tchr-libn Grand Cane High Sch, Grand Cane La 42-43; Tchr-libn Sibley High Sch, Sibley La 43-44; Tchr-libn Doyline High Sch, Doyline La 44-45; Circ libn Bradley U 46-47; Libn I E Baton Rouge Parish Lib, Baton Rouge La 60-. 9: LaLA. 10: Baton Rouge Lib Club. 14: Ref. 15: 476 Maxine dr, Baton Rouge La 70808.

McELROY, ELIZABETH (WARNER). b Dixon Ill. 4: Robert McElroy. 5: Carleton (Chem) BA; UChicago 65-67 (LS) MA. 7: Research (chem) Container Corp of Amer, Chicago; Asst libn J Walter Thompson Co, Chicago 67-68; Contractor libn Goddard Space Flight Ctr, Greenbelt Md 69-. 9: ALA; SLA. 10: LWV. 13: Yes. 14: Ref. 15: 8484 Sixteenth st, Silver Spring Md 20910.

McELROY, FLETA JOHNSON. b Dekalb Miss 6 Ag 32. 4: James Alvin McElroy. 5: Miss State Col for Women 50-54 (LS) BS; U So Miss 58; Miss State U 62-63; U Miss 66-67. 07: Amer hist & Eng tchr Kate Griffine Jr High Sch, Meridian Miss 54-55, Asst libn 56-59; Head Libn Northwest Jr High Sch, Meridian Miss 59-67; Hd libn Highland Elem Sch 68-69; Enrichment materials consul for three jr high schs 68-69. 8: Wk in adv capacity to two other jr high sch libs; chm of Lib Dept in Meridian Pub Schs. 9: NEA; MissLA; MissEA. 10: AAUW; Meridian Little Theatre; Northwood Country Club; C of C Wives; Alpha Beta Alpha; PTA; Garden Club. 14: Org of new libs, admin., acquis, curr enrichment. 15: 1505 52nd, Meridian Ms 39303.

McELROY, GILLIAN (CARTER). 4: Philip P McElroy. 5: Ursinus Col 57-61 (Hist) AB; Rutgers 67-68 MLS. 6: Fr. 7: Sales rep REA Express co, NYC 62-66; Jr lib asst Jersey City Pub Lib, Jersey City NJ 66-67; Child libn NY Pub lib 68-69, Programmer and sy lib 68-69, Programmer and systems analyst trainee 69-. 9: ASIS. 10: Beta Phi Mu. 14: Lib automation. 15: 41 Huntington st, New Brunswick NJ 08901.

McELVEEN, HASSIE. b Brooklet Ga 6 N 13. 5: Ga Southern Col 31-35 (Math) BS in Ed; Peabody 37-40 BS in LS; Columbia 45 (LS). 6: Sp, Fr. 7: Jr high tchr Wadley Pub Sch, Wadley Ga 35-37; Ga Southern Col: Child libn 37-44, Act libn 44-46; Libn 46-. 9: ALA; GaLA (v-pres); SELA. 10: AAUW; Delta Kappa Gamma; Pilot Club. 14: Admin, ref. 15: 3 Lindberg st, Statesboro Ga 30458.

McENROE, MARY ANN. b Wellsville NY 26 F 37. 5: SUC (Geneseo) 54-58 (LS, Educ) BS; West Res 63-64 MLS. 7: Libn Pittsford Central Schs, Pittsford NY 58-63; Libn Kamehameha Schs, Honolulu 64-66; Sch lib consul NJ Dept of Educ, Trenton 66-68, Research assoc Tech for Child Project 68-. 8: Participating sponsor Hawaii's First Gov's Conf on Libs 66. 9: ALA; AVA; ASCD; NEA; NJEA; NJLA; NJSchLA. 13: Yes. 14: Sch libs. 15: 2030 Riverside dr, Trenton NJ 08618.

McENTEE, HELEN S. b Brooklyn NY 30 Mr 15. 5: Ladycliff Col 44-46 (Eng) AB; St John's U (NY) 46-48 BLS; Vassar 50 (Eng); Columbia 53-54 (Developmental Psych) MA, 67, 68. 06: Fr. 7: Eng tchr & libn Maybrook High Sch, Maybrook NY 48; Libn South Jr High, Newburgh NY 48-54; Libn Scarsdale Elem Schs, Scarsdale NY 54-55; Asst libn Tchrs Col Columbia U 55-56; Libn Glenrock Sr High Sch, Glen Rock NJ 56-65; Instr Paterson State Col, Wayne NJ 64; Instr St John's U (NY) 58-65, Asst Prof 65-. 8: Planning Com, St John's U Lib Congress 58-61, 63-64; Libns Com on the Negro in NJ 64-65. 9: ALA; CanLA; CathLA (sec Lib Educ Sect 69-72, sec High Sch Lib Sect 69-72); NJSchL; NYLA. 10: AAUW; West Point Women's Assn; Constitution Island Assn; Col Club; Fair Housing Commsn; CORE; NAACP; Amer Bk Women; Marquis Biog Lib Soc. 13: Yes. 14: Catlg, ya lit, serv to handicapped. 15: 209-02 - 34th ave, Bayside NY 11361.

McEVOY, RUTH MELVINA. b Merrimack NH 1 Jl 06. 5: Colby Col 24-28 (Lat) BA; Columbia 33-36 BLS; UBuffalo 58 (Eng) MA. 7: Libn, child libn, yp libn Brooklyn Pub Lib 32-45; Asst Richmond Mem Lib, Batavia NY 45-62, Dir 62-. 9: ALA. 10: AAUW; Zonta Internat. 15: Richmond Mem Lib 19 Ross st, Batavia NY 14020.

McEWAN, SUSAN. b NYC 14 Mr 42. 5: Fla Presbyterian Col 60-64 (Fr) BA; Emory 64-65 (LS) ML. 6: Fr, Russian. 7: Typist Carnegie Lib, Rome Ga summers 62-64; Tchg asst Fla Presbyterian Col 63-64; Asst catlgr U So Fla 65-. 9: ALA; FlaLA. 14: Catlg. 15: U So Fla, Tampa Fl 33620.

McFADDEN, MARILYN. b Paris Tenn 22 My 33. 5: Murray State Col 52-55 (Eng, Hist) BA, 55-57 (Educ) MA; Peabody 61-63 MA in LS; UIll summers 67-. 07: Tchr Atkins-Porter Sch, Paris Tenn 55-58; Tchr Grove Jr High Sch, Paris Tenn 58-63; Asst catlgr Murray State Col 63-. 9: KyLA. 10: Kappa Delta Pi; Beta Phi Mu. 14: Catlg. 15: 714 N Poplar, Paris Tn 38242.

McFADDEN, RUBY E(LIZABETH). b Greencastle Penn 15 My 28. 5: Juniata Col 46-50 (Eng) BA; Drexel 51 MS in LS. 6: Fr, Ger. 7: Asst libn Sch of Nursing Lib Phila Gen Hosp 50-51; Catlgr White Plains Pub Lib, White Plains NY 51-52; Catlgr Penn State U Lib 53-57; Catlgr asst libn Standard Vacuum Oil Co, White Plains NY 57-58; Ref libn Wilson Col 59-62; Catlgr Johns Hopkins U Lib 62-65; Catlgr SUNY (Stony Brook) 66-. 9: ALA-ACRL (Resources & Tech Serv Div); NYLA (sec Col & Univ Libs Sect, sec Resources & Tech Serv Sect); NY Tech Serv Libns; NY Lib Club. 14: Catlg, ref. 15: 50-165B Piedmont dr, Port Jefferson Station NY 11776.

McFADDEN, WILMOT CURNOW. b Lead S Dak 30 O 19. 4: John Stinson McFadden. 5: S Dak State U 38-41 (Journalism); UMinn 39 (LS). 6: Fr. 7: First Nat Bank, Rapid City S Dak 42-44; Asst libn Carnegie Pub Lib, Rock Springs Wyo 47-48, Hd libn 53-. 8: Wyo State lib Archives & Hist Bd 59-65, 67-71; Treas Sch Dist #4 Bd Trustees 66-69; Exec dir Wyo 9nat Lib Week) 58, 61, 69; Adv Bd West Wyo Col 67-. 9: ALA (Coun 59-63, Memb Chm 62); -ALTA (Memb Chm 61-64); WyoLA (v-pres 57, pres 58, Rep to MPLA 65-69); MPLA (sec Pub Lib sect 59, chm 68-69). 10: Wyo Adv Coun; Federal Commsn on Civil Rights; Adv Coun Visually Physically Handicapped, Wyo; Fed Woman's Club; Amer Leg Assn; Demo State Com Woman. 11: Lib received 1 of 10 Dorothy Canfield Fisher Awards 65; WyoLA Pub Award 67. 12: "Manual for Wyoming Library Trustees" (62). 13: Yes. 14: Adult & spec serv. 15: 28 Cedar, Rock Springs Wy 82901.

McFARLAND, ANNE (SOUTHWORTH). b Cleveland 12 Mr 40. 4: Charles W McFarland. 5: Oberlin Col 58-62 (Eng Lit) AB; West Res 63-64 MLS; NM State U 65- Art; Case West Res U 67- (Gen Stud). 06: Ital, Ger. 7: Asst ref libn NM State U Lib 64-65, Asst catlg libn 65; Libn Sch Lib Sci Case West Res U 66-; Dir Bibliog Systs Ctr 67-. 9: ALA (chm Discussion Gp for Lib Sci Libns 68-69); AALS. 10: Las Cruces Commun Theater; Beta Phi Mu; AAUP. 13: Yes. 14: Ref, catlg. 15: 10510 Park lane N 505, Cleveland Oh 44106.

McFARLAND, KAY (ROSALYN). b Batesville Miss 11 Ap 24. 5: Nat Col of Chiropractic (Chicago) 47-51 (Chiropractic) Doctor of Chiro; Northwestern State Col (Natchitoches La) 55-58 (Educ, LS) BS; UDenver 58-59 (LS) MA; Columbia 65-66 (LS). 6: Ger, Fr, Sp. 7: Phys therapist WAC, Landstuhl Germany 52-54; Chiropractic physician, Shreveport La 54-55, Montpelier Vt 51-52; Tchr Calcasieu Parish Sch Bd, Lake Charles La 58; Acquis libn UDenver Lib Sch 58-59; Chief acquis libn UTulsa 59-62; Dir Dept of Lib Sci State Col (Shippensburg Penn) 62-. 9: NEA; ALA; PennLA (chm CYPLS 64-65); PennStateEA; PennSchLA. 10: AAUW; Delta Kappa Gamma; Pub Lib Bd (Shippensburg Penn); State Col Profs. 14: Lib educ, wk with child & yp, sch lib wk. 15: Rt 2, Newville Pa 17241.

McFARLAND, SARAH CAMPBELL. b Anderson Ind 7 My 38. 4: Earl McFarland Jr. 5: PurdueU 56-60 (Pol Sci) BS; Columbia 66-68 MLS. 6: Sp. 7: Circ asst Bus Lib Columbia 64-68; Circ libn & asst ref libn Lib Williams Col 68-. 9: ALA. 14: Ref, docs, admin. 15: Stetson rd apt G, Williamstown Ma 01267.

McFARLAND, WILMA LYNN. b Locust Grove Okla 20 Ja 37. 5: NEast State Col (Okla) 55-59 (Hist) BA i n Ed, summers 63, 64 (Lang); UMo 61 (Langs); Okla State U summer 65 (LS); Okla U summers 67, 68 (LS). 6: Fr, Ger, Sp. 7: Stud libn NEast State Col (Okla) 55-59; High sch libn W Plains Pub Schs, W Plains Mo 58-64; Tchr-libn Hominy Pub Schs, Hominy Okla 64-67; Jr high sch libn Independence Pub Schs, Independence Kan 67-. 8: Independence TA; Independence Oratorio Soc; Messiah Chorus. 9: Participated in OklaEA Leadership Conf, Stillwater; NDEA Lib Sci Inst, Stillwater Okla 65; NEA; ALA; KanStateTA; KanASchL (asst dir Dist 2). 14: Catlg, ya. 15: 410 North 11th st, Independence Ks 67301.

McFATTER, DOROTHY (MOSES). b DeRidder La 14 Ja 26. 4: William W McFatter. 5: Northwestern State Col 42-46 (LS) BA; LSU 47-48 BS in LS. 6: Fr, Sp. 7: Asst libn Natchitoches High Sch, Natchitoches La 46-47; Libn LaGrange High Sch, Lake Charles La 48-53; Libn LaGrange Sr High Sch, Lake Charles La 54-64, Head Libn 64-. 8: Instr Lib Sci McNeese State Col summer 68. 9: NEA; ALA; LaLA; La Tchrs Assn; LaSchLA; Calcasieu Libns Assn (v-pres 69-70). 10: PTA; Delta Kappa Gamma; Lake Charles Ballet Soc; Actors Civic Theater & Studio. 14: Sch lib wk, ref, catlg. 15: 4318 Dean st, Lake Charles La 70602.

McFERRAN, ROSEMOND (IRENE BUSBY). b Omaha 28 Ap 28. 5: UMich 45-46 (Fr); UCLA 46-49 (Fr) BA, 61-62 MLS; Cal State Col 63-64. 6: Fr, Sp. 7: Sr lib asst catlg dept UCal (Berkeley) 49-50; Typist-clerk Gates Rubber Co Billing Dept, Denver 50-52; GS 3, 4, 5 VA, Denver 52-53; Sr lib asst catlg dept UCal (Berkeley) 53-55; Catlg libn I-II Cal State Col (Los Angeles) 62-64; Catlgr to head catlgr Econolist Inc, Los Angeles 64-65; Ser catlg libn II-III UCal(Davis) 65-. 9: CalLA. 10: UCal Lib SSScchs Alumnae Assn. 14: Catlg. 15: 1518 Tulane dr, Davis Ca 95616.

McFERRAN, WARREN ALDEN. b Detroit 16 F 24. 4: Elizabeth Condron. 5: Wayne State U 46-50 (Sociol) AB; UMich 50-52 MALS. 6: Fr. 7: Personnel clerk Vickers Inc, Detroit 42-43; Clsf spec (S/Sgt) USAF 43-46; Libn I & II Enoch Pratt Free Lib, Baltimore 52-55; Head Libn Essex Br & Bkmob Hq Baltimore Co Pub Lib, Towson Md 55-59; Asst dir N Country Lib System, Watertown NY 59-65; Head Libn Muskegon Co Lib, Muskegon Mich 66-. 8: Survey Com, Baltimore Co Pub Lib 57-5 8; Instr Mich State Lib summer wkshops 68. 9: ALA; NYLA; No Country Ref, Res & Resources Coun (v-pres 64-65); MichLA (Recr Com); Lakeshore LA (chm Recr Com); Muskegon Adult EA. 10: Muskegon Geriatrics Coun; Lions Club; Torch Club. 12: Co-ed "Directory of Major Manufacturers in Eastern Baltimore City and Eastern Baltimore County" (59). 13: Yes. 14: Pub lib wk (except catlg). 15: Muskegon Co Lib, Muskegon Mi 49440.

McFERRIN, JAMES B(LAKELY). b Fayetteville Tenn 2 Jl 20. 4: Jessie Stewart. 5: Erskine Col 38-42 (Math) BA; UIll 47-48 BS in LS; UIll 50-51 (LS) MS. 6: Fr, Sp. 7: (Lt) US Navy 42-46; Circ asst DePauw U 48-50; Documents libn Emory U 51-58; Head Libn Union Col (Barbourville Ky) 58-. 9: ALA; KyL A; Mid-Appalachia Col Coun Lins Gp (chm 67-). 14: Admin, Catlg. 15: 110 College Park dr, Barbourville Ky 40906.

McGARITY, MARY SUE (JOHNSON). b Kingsport Tenn 25 Mr 24. 4: Marvin James McGarity. 5: UAla 41-45 (LS) BS; LSU summer 46 (LS), 59-60 (LS) MS. 6: Fr. 7: Asst libn Northington Army Hosp, Tuscaloosa Ala 45-46; Asst circ libn UAla Lib 46-49; Head Libn Tuscaloosa Sr High Sch, Tuscaloosa Ala 49-51; Asst ref libn UAla Lib 51-53, Catlgr 54-56, 58-59; Jr libn LSU Lib 60-61; Catlgr UAla Lib 61-62; Jr high tchr Our Lady of Sorrows Parochial Sch, Birmingham Ala 62-63; Asst catlgr Birmingham Pub Lib, Birmingham Ala 63; Libn Brooke Hill Sch for Girls, Birmingham Ala 63-. 8: Lit searches for Reichold Chemicals Inc 54, 57; Sub tchr of catlg LSU Lib Sch summer 60; Instr Lib Sci UAla summer 65, part-time instr 66-; Asst Prof Lib Sci LSU summer 67; Consult filmstrip catlg, Educ Serv Inc 69. 9: ALA; AlaLA. 14: Ref, catlg. 15: 1416 Sutherland pl, Birmingham Al 35209.

McGARTY, JEAN (ROSS). b Cleveland Ohio 21 S 22. 5: Mt Mary Col 40-42; UDetroit 59-63 (Eng) AB; UMich 64-65 AMLS. 7: Libn III UDetroit 65-. 9: ALA; MichLA. 14: Ser, catlg. 15: 17580 Greenview rd, Detroit Mi 48219.

McGARVEY, ALAN R. b Phila 11 My 14. 4: Louise Houser. 5: UPenn 36 (Chem Engnr) BS, 43 (Chem Engnr) ChE. 7: Armstrong Cork Co, Lancaster Penn: Research engnr 36-42, Field engnr 42-44, Research engnr 44-58, Manager Insulations & Cellular Prods 59-63, Manager tech info serv 63-. 8: Nat Acad of Scis, Bldg Research Adv Bd on Thermal Insulations & Vapor Barriers 61-63. 9: ACS (Div of Chem Lit); ASIS. 10: Registered Prof Chem Engnr in Penn; Lancaster Twp Sch Dist Authority. 12: About 12 US patents. 13: Yes. 14: Tech info serv, info retrieval systems design, ind research. 15: Armstrong Cork Co Research & Development Center 2500 Columbia ave, Lancaster Pa 17604.

McGAW, HOWARD F(RANKLIN). b Nashville 5 O 11. 4: Lorraine Welch. 5: Vanderbilt 28-29, 30-33 (Eng) AB; Peabody 38-39 (Soc Sci) MA, 39-41 BS in LS; Chicago 42-43 (LS); Columbia summers 47 & 48, 49-50 (Admin) Ed D. 6: Sp. 7: Tchr Eng & hist Cohn High Sch, Nashville Tenn 37-40; Head Libn Memphis State Col 40-42; Head Libn Herzl Jr Col 42-43; Asst educ dir Amer Friends Serv Com, Phila 44; Educ & personnel sect Civilian Pub Serv, Orlando Fla 45; Dir of Lib Ohio Wesleyan U 46-49; Dir of Libs UHouston 50-61; Prof of Educ Tex So U 62-63; Dir of Lib & Chm Dept of Lib Sci West Wash State Col 63-67; Prof of Lib Sci 67-. 08: Summer faculty (Lib Sci): Peabody 46; Ky 49; NC 52; NY(Albany) 59; Denver 61; Dir of survey sponsored by NY City Bd of Higher Educ in 50, of lib resources (as related to tchr educ) in four municipal cols: Brooklyn, City Col, Hunter & Queens. 9: ALA (Life mem); NEA (Life mem); TexLA (Exec Bd 56-57, chm 2 coms & 1 div 52-53, 55-59); SWLA; WashLA (treas 66-67); PNLA; Houston Lib Club (pres 52-53). 10: AAUP; ACLU; Houston Inst of Internal Rels; Amer Humanist Assn; Planned Parenthood Center; UN Assn; United Good Neighbors; Beta Phi Mu; Phi Delta Kappa; Kappa Delta Pi; NAACP. 12: "Marginal Punched Cards in College & Research Libraries" (52); Comp Bibliog for "Shipstead of Minnesota" (40); Chm Ed Bd UHouston "Forum" (56-58); Ed "Aldus," Friends of the Lib UHouston (58-61). 13: Yes. 14: Pub rel, admin, bk sel, mechanization, ref, intel freedom. 15: 120 Underhill rd, Bellingham Wa 98225.

McGEE, ROBERT (STUART). b Wash DC 29 N 41. 5: Wilmington Col 59-61 (Liberal Arts) AA; UNC(Chapel Hill) 61-63 (Pol Sci) AB, 63-65 MSLS; Chicago 65-66, 67- (LS); Glasgow U (Scotland) 66-67 Diploma Computing Sci. 06: Fr.

7: Lib asst I, II UNC(Chapel Hill) 63-65; Asst ref libn UIll(Chicago Circle) 65-66; Asst systs development UChicago 67-. 8: Vis instr UIll (Urbana), Lib mech & automation summer 69. 9: ALA-ISAD (Interface Newsletter Com 68). 10: ACM. 14: Lib systems analysis and automation, univ lib admin. 15: Univ of Chicago Lib, Chicago Il 60637.

McGEEHAN, THOMAS J. b Hazleton Penn 25 Jl 41. 4: Cecelia Smitrovich. 5: King's Col 59-63 (Biol) BS; Drexel 63-64 MSLS, 68-. 7: Adult serv libn Free Lib of Phila 64-68; Asst hd Lib for the Blind, Phila 67-68; Tech docs libn Smith, Kline & French Labs, Phila 68-. 9: SLA; ASIS; PennLA (Lib Devel Com 66-68). 14: Automation, admin, ref. 15: 21 Heatherwood hills, Norristown Pa 19401.

McGILL, (GLENN) WILBUR (JR). b Camden Tenn 28 Ap 29. 4: Esther E Ebersole. 5: Murray State Col 47-50 (Hist) AB; UMich 54-55 AMLS. 7: Jr asst circ libn Evansville Pub Lib, Evansville Ind 50-51; (Cpl) US Army 51-52; Readers adv Evansville Pub Lib, Evansville Ind 52-55; Enoch Pratt Free Lib, Baltimore: Br gen asst 55-57, Br adult asst 57-60, Br admin asst 60-. 8: Instr (gen ref) Md State Div Lib Ext, lib aide train program 64-68; Bus manager "Union List of Serials in Md." 09: ALA (sec-treas Jr Mem Round Table 59-60, sec-treas 59-60, Exec Bd 60-63);-RSD (Chap Com 61-62); MdLA (chm Exhibits Com 60-61, Prog Com-Exh 61-63, treas 63-65); Md Chap RSD (sec-treas 59-60, chm 60-61). 10: All America Chorus (European Tour 58). 14: Ref. 15: 223 E Belvedere ave, Baltimore Md 21212.

McGILL, BARBARA JOAN (MATHISEN). b Brooklyn NY 28 N 40. 4: Lynn Ray McGill. 5: State U Col (Geneseo) 57-61 (Elem Educ) BS; C W Post Col 62-64 (LS) MS; Alfred U 65. 7: Elem tchr Caroline G Atkinson Sch, Freeport NY 61-62; Elem tchr Tooker Ave Sch, W Babylon NY 62-63; Elem tchr Trumansburg Central Sch, Trumansburg NY 63-65; Sch libn Chateaugay Central Sch, Chateaugay NY 65-67; Libn Seaway Baptist Bible Inst, Cornwall Ont Can 68-. 9: NY State Tchrs Assn. 14: Ref. 15: 50 Wells st, Canton NY 13617.

McGILL, THEODORA. b Orlando Fla 30 O 21. 5: Miner Tchrs Col 37-41 (Ed) BS in Ed; Howard U 41-42 (Ed); Catholic U of Amer 50-52 MS in LS. 7: Recreation wkr Smer Red Cross, Europe 45-49; Lib asst Catholic U of Amer 49-51; Libn Nat Catholic Sch Soc Serv, Wash DC 51-55; Post libn Dept of Army Spec Serv, Korea 55-56, Area libn 56-67; Ref libn Dept Health, Educ & Welfare, Wash DC 67-68; Libn Export-Import Bank of the US, Wash DC 68-. 9: ALA; SLA; DCLA. 11: Certif of Achievement 60, Outstanding Award 64 & 67, Dept of Army citation for Merit Civ Serv 66. 14: Ref. 15: Export-Import Bank of the US, 811 Vermont ave NW, Wash DC 20571.

McGINN, HOWARD FRANCIS. b Mount Carmel Penn 21 D 10. 4: Sarah Louise Briggs. 5: Mt St Mary's Col 30-32; St Vincent Col (Latrobe Penn) 32-36 (Philos) BA. MA; Drexel 37-38 BSLS; UPittsburgh 50-57 (Educ) Ed D. 6: Lat. 7: Tchr-libn Phila Bd of Educ 38-39; Tchr-libn N Catholic High Sch, Pittsburgh 39-48; US Army 8th Armored Div (Cpl), ETO 43-45; Prof-chm Secondary Educ Duquesne U 48-60; Prof-chm Lib Sci Villanova U 60-. 9: CathLA; PennLA. 10: Main Line Family Serv Agency. 14: Lib sci educ. 15: 609 E Darby rd, Havertown Pa 19083.

McGINNIS, DANIEL (WILSON). b Tiffin Ohio 9 Jl 27. 4: Patricia Gary. 5: Bowling Green State U 46-48, 60-63 (Eng) BA; UMich 63-66 AMLS. 7: Radar Man US Navy USS Robert L Wilson (DD847) 45-46; Asst McClean Pub Lib, Fostoria Ohio 58-60; Ref Lib Bowling Green State U 60-63; Consul State Lib of Ohio 63-67; Coord adult serv Toledo (Ohio) Pub Lib 67-68, Coord br & ext 68-. 9: ALA; OhioLA. 14: Ref, bibliog. 15: 819 Jefferson dr, Bowling Green Oh 43402.

McGINNIS, ESTHER (WALLACE). b Flint Mich 29 My 18. 4: W Bryce McGinnis. 5: Central MichU 35-39 (Com) BS; UMich 57-63 AMLS. 7: Libn Millington High Sch, Millington Mich 57-60; Libn Davison High Sch, Davison Mich 60-62, Dir lib serv Davison Commun Schs 62-; Lectr in lib sci UMich (Flint) 69-. 9: NEA; ALA; -ASchL; MichEA; MichASchL (Record sec 66-69, 1st v-pres 69-70); Mich A-V Assn. 10: Bd Dors, Davison Br of Genesee Co Lib. 15: 2477 S State rd, Davison Mi 48423.

McGINNIS, JANET (ANNE). b Kingston Ont 25 Ag 24. 5: Queens U 42-46 (Hist) BA; Metzler Bus Col 46-47 (Secretarial) DIP; McGill 53-55 (Journalism) DIP. 6: Fr. 7: Ref libn Aluminium Labs Ltd, Kingston Ont 47-50; Ref libn Canadian Industries Ltd, Montreal 50-54; Ref libn ICI of Can Ltd, Montreal 54-56; Libn Can Industries Ltd Textile Fibres Div, Kingston Ont 56-64; Libn Millhaven Fibres Ltd, Kingston Ont 65-. 9: SLA; AS Lib. 14: Ref wk. 15: 457 King st W, Kingston Ont Can.

McGINNISS, DOROTHY AGNES. b Schenectady NY 11 Ap 11. 5: NY State Col for Tchrs 32 (Eng, Lat) AB, 36 BS in LS; Columbia 51 MS in LS. 7: Tchr Union Sch, Rensselaerville NY 34-36; Tchr-libn Tivoli High Sch, Tivoli NY 36-39; Libn Central Sch, W Winfield NY 39-44; Educ libn & head of child wk Pub Lib, Newark NJ 44-52; Tchr of Lib Sci So Ill U 52-58; Supv of lib serv Bd of Educ Baltimore Co, Towson Md 58-62; Exec sec AASL ALA Hdqrs 62-66; Assoc Prof Sch Lib Sci Syracuse U 66-. 8: Summer tchg in lib sci: Trenton State Tchrs Col, NJ; Grad Sch of Lib Serv, Rutgers U NJ. 9: ALA; NEA-DAVI; NYLA. 10: Delta Kappa Gamma. 13: Yes. 14: Sch libs, child & ya lit. 15: 1108 E Genesee st, Syracuse NY 13210.

McGINTY, THOMAS PATRICK. b Phila 1 S 18. 4: Mary Frances Tully. 5: Fla State U 46-48 (LS) AB, 49 (LS) MA; Ind U summer 50 (Educ); Fla State U 53-54 (Educ). 6: Sp. 7: USAAC Radio Operator & Mech (S/Sgt) 41-45; Ref libn, A-v coordinator St Petersburg (Fla) High Sch 49-51; A-v coordinor Lee Co Ft Myers Sch System 51-53; Elem tchr Tallahassee Fla 53-54; Head libn US Navy Mine Defense Lab, Panama City Fla 54-57; Head libn Pratt & Whitney Aircraft, W Palm Beach Fla 57-64; Chief libn NASA Kennedy Space Center, Cocoa Beach Fla 64; Head libn Pratt & Whitney Aircraft, W Palm Beach Fla 64-66; Chief libn LTV Aerospace Corp, Vought Aeronautics Div, Dallas Tex 66-. 8: Visiting Lectureship Fla State U Lib Sch summer 53. 9: SLA; ALA; FlaLA; FlaEA-DAVI (chm 53-54). 10: Fla Lib Sch alumni Assn. 14: Admin, info retrieval. 15: 746 Flamingo way W, North Palm Beach Fl 33403.

McGIRT, LOIS BLAKE. b Richmond Va 4 S 19. 4: Zebulon Vance McGirt Jr. 5: URichmond 36-40 (Eng) BA; UNC 41-42 BS in LS, summer 63-65 MS in LS. 6: Fr, Sp. 7: Asst child dept & catlg dept Richmond Pub Lib, Richmond Va 40-41; Libn Chandler Jr High Sch, Richmond Va 42-44; Sec to libn & supv station libs, Richmond (Va) Pub Lib 44-46; Descr catlgr Duke U Lib 46-48; Libn Bethany High Sch, Rockingham Co NC 48-49; Libn Lewisville Sch, Lewisville NC 49-56; Libn Southwest High Sch, Clemmons NC 56-64; Libn West Forsyth High Sch, Clemmons NC 64-66; Coord instl materials Winston-Salem/Forsyth Co Schs, NC 66-67; Instr UNC (Greensboro) 67-. 8: Ref asst Pub Lib of Winston-Salem & Forsyth Co NC summer 61; Libn Sch Lib Sci UNC summer 65. 9: ALA; SELA; NCLA; NCEA. 10: Beta Phi Mu. 14: Catlg, ref, lib in soc. 15: Box 176, East Bend NC 27018.

McGLADE, JAMES ECCLES. b Phila 27 Ag 35. 5: West Chester State 53-57 (Soc Studies) BS in Ed; Villanova U 62-65 MS in LS; So Ill U (Media Inst) 68-69. 7: Tchr Council Rock High Sch, Newtown Penn 60-64, Libn 64-69, Libn Newtown Intermed Sch 69-. 9: NEA-DAVI; ALA; Penn State EA; PennLA; Bucks Co Sch Libns (pres 64). 14: Admin, a-v materials. 15: 150 Fern rd, Southampton Penn 18966.

McGLINN, FRANK C P. b Philadelphia Penn 19 N 14. 4: Louise Lea. 5: UNC 37 AB; UPenn 40 LLB. 7: Trustee Free Lib of Phila 48-, Dir 58-, Dir Friends of Theatre collections, Museum of NYC 67-. 10: Dir Nat Repretory Theatre; Penn Coun on the Arts. 14: Rare bks relating to theatre & performing arts. 15: 135 S Broad st, Phila Pa 19109.

McGOEY, NOELLE THERESA. b New Orleans 25 D 27. 5: Newcomb Col 43-47 (Eng) BA; Tulane 48-50 (Educ) MA. 7: Tchr Orleans Parish Sch Bd, New Orleans 47-53; Libn New Orleans Pub Lib 54-. 9: ALA; LaLA. 14: Acquis. 15: 4110 Fontainebleau dr, New Orleans La 70125.

McGOUGH, BERNARD (L). b Holyoke Mass 8 O 30. 4: Elsie Spence. 5: Amer Internat 56-59 (Hist) BA; Westfield State Col 59-61 (Educ) MEd; URI 64-65 (LS) MS. 7: Diver Diesel Eng En2 US Navy, Korea 50-54; Educ spec USAFR, Springfield Mass 54-58; Hist, Eng libn Somers High Sch, Somers Mass 59-60; Libn Ralph C Mahar Reg High Sch, Orange Mass 60-63; Libn North High Sch, Worcester Mass 63-64; Libn State Col (Worcester Mass) 64-. 8: Asst Prof of Lib Sci, Grad Sch, State Col (Worcester Mass) 63-. 9: MassLA; Mass State Col Assn. 10: West Mass Fencing Club; AAUP. 14: Ref, catlg. 15: 32 Olga ave, Worcester Ma 01605.

McGOWAN, FRANK (MALCOLM). b Portland Ore 29 D 31. 4: Afaf Sabeh. 5: U Wash 50-53 (Gen Lit) BA, 53-54 MS in LS. 6: Sp, Fr. 7: Order libn Amer U of Beirut 54-57; Bibliog UPittsburgh 57-60, Libn Grad Sch of Pub & Internat Affairs

60-65; Asst chief Overseas Operations Div LC 66-. 8: Head of US Exh UN Conf on Applications of Sci & Tech, Geneva 63; Consul: Inst of Admin, Zaria Nigeria 63; Inst of Nat Planning, Cairo UAR 63; Universidad Central, Quito Ecuador 65. 9: ALA (Internat Rel Round Table, chm Near & Middle East Com). 12: "Selected List of US Readings on Development," with Saul Katz (63). 14: Tech proc, admin. 15: 10521 Bucknell dr, Silver Spring Md 20902.

McGOWAN, JOHN (PATRICK). b NYC 11 My 26. 4: Eileen P Durkin. 5: Hunter Col 46-50 9arts, Pol Sci) BA; Columbia 50-51 (LS) MS; NYU 59-65 (Ind Engring & Operations research) BE. 7: Rifleman (Sgt) USA Inf W Europe 44-46; Libn Engring & Sci Lib NYU 51-55; Libn Tech Inst NorthwesternU 55-59; Dir Lib Franklin Inst, Phila 59-66; Assoc univ libn NorthwesternU 66-. 8: Bd of Trustees EDUCOM (Interuniversity Communications Coun) 67-; Chm Engrs Jt Coun Com on Engring Info 64-66; Consul Tripartite Com Engrs Jt Coun 67-. 9: ASIS (pres Dela Valley Chap); ALA-RSD (v-pres & pres-elect). 10: Amer Soc Engring Educ. 13: Yes. 14: Sci info serv, sci & tech info serv & facilities. 15: Technological Inst Lib Northwestern Univ, Evanston Il 60201.

McGOWAN, OWEN THOMAS PAUL. b Fall River Mass 9 Ap 22. 4: Patricia MacGill. 5: Maryknoll Col 40-45 (Philos); Catholic U 45-47 (Theol), 59-63 MS in LS, 67- (Intl Educ). 06: Fr, Sp, Lat. 7: Owner-manager Catholic Book Shop, Fall River Mass 49-56; Tchr Morton Jr High Sch, Fall River Mass 56-57, Libn 57-62; Libn B M C Durfee High Sch, Fall River Mass 62-64; Head Libn Bridgewater State Col 64-. 9: NEA; ALA; MassLA; NELA; State Col Libns. 10: AAUP. 12: "The School Library," 10 film strips, Eye Gate Publ House, J amaica LI. 13: Yes. 14: Admin, ref. 15: 80 Underwood st, Fall River Ma 02720.

McGRATH, DANIEL FRANCIS. b NYC 20 Je 35. 4: Anne Frances DePorry. 5: UVa 55-59 (Ger) BA; UMich 59-61 (Ger) MA (Ger), MALS, 61-66 (LS) PhD. 6: Ger, Fr. 7: Reconnaissance Sgt US Army, Germany 53-55; Instr Lib Sci UVa 62; Catlgr Paul Mellon Lib, Upperville Va 62-64; Curator rare bks Duke U 64-66; Visting lecturer Lib Sci UNC(Chapel Hill) 65; Assoc Prof Sch Lib & Info Serv UMd (College Park) 67-. 9: ALA; BSA; Bibliog Soc (London); Bibliog Soc UVa. 10: AAUP; Beta Phi Mu; Delta Phi Alpha; Phi Beta Kappa; Phi Kappa Phi; Raven UVa); Nat Trust Hist R Preserv. 12: Ed "Bookman's Price Index." 13: Yes. 14: Rare bks, bibliog, area studies. 15: Univ of Maryland Sch of Library & Info Serv, College Park Md 20742.

McGRATH, WILLIAM ERNEST. b Somerville Mass 27 N 26. 4: Shirley Hathaway. 5: UMass 48-52 (Eng) AB; UMich 54-56 MALS. 7: Stud asst UMass 50-52, Lib asst 52-54, 55; Stud asst UMich 54, 56; Plant & animal sci libn UNH 56-58; Br libn UNH 58-64; Head Libn SD Sch of Mines & Tech 64-68; Hd libn USowestLA (Lafayette) 68-. 8: Vis lectr UMinn summers 67, 68. 9: ALA; SLA; ASIS. 10: AAUP. 14: Lib admin, automation of libs, computers and lib proc, info sci, lit & sci, statist analysis of lib problems. 15: Dupre Lib USowestLA, Lafayette La 70501.

McGRAW, ANTHONY F. b Kansas City Mo 26 N 15. 4: Judy L Walter. 5: U Kan City 33-36 (Eng Lit); Marquette U 36-39 (Eng Lit) PhB; So Methodist Law Sch 45-47 (Law), 48-51 (Eng Lit) MA; West Res 57-58 MSLS. 6: Ger. 7: USMC Machine Gun NCO (Sgt) 51-52; Head ref dept Dallas Pub Lib 52-55, Head lit & hist 55-57; Ref libn Cleveland Pub Lib 57-58, Head sci & tech 58-60; Chief lib div USAF Aero Research Lab, WPAFB Ohio 60-63; Chief lib div US Army Command & Gen Staff Col, Ft Leavenworth Kan 63-. 10: Kiwanis. 12: Assoc ed "Machine Design." 13: Yes. 14: Admin, Mil sci, Mil hist. 15: RR 1 Box 189, Leavenworth Ks 66048.

McGRAW, CHARLOTTE MARIE (BALE). b Okla City Okla 4 Ja 30. 5: So Methodist 52 (Home econ) BS; UOkla 63 MLS. 7: Asst libn US Grant High Sch, Okla City 65-67; Libn SE High Sch, Okla City 67; Instr lib sci UOkla summer 67, Asst prof lib sci summer 68; Libn wro asst prof U Sch, Norman Okla 67-. 9: NEA; ALA; OklaEA; OklaLA (chm Sch Libns 67-68). 13: Yes. 14: Sch lib, ya lit. 15: 800 Elmwood, Norman Ok 73069.

McGRAW, DONALD (FREDERICK). b Warren Co Ohio 23 S 29. 4: Barbara L Bedsworth. 5: Olivet Nazarene Col 47-51 (Eng lit) AB; Kan State Tchrs Col 66-67 (Libnship) ML. 6: Gr, Lat, Ger. 7: Rare bk - rare bible consul Wagon Wheel Bks, Overland Pk Kan 61-; Instr libnship Kan State Tchrs Col 66-69, Summer faculty libnship 67; Instr libnship UMo (Columbia) 68-69; Chief tech serv UMo (Kan City) 67-. 8: Rare bk consul: Col of Emporia Kan 66, Washington (DC) Cathedral 66-68; Baker U Baldwin City, Kan 65-67; Rare Bible Consul Amer Bible Soc, NY 65-. 9: ALA; SLA; MoLA. 10: Amer Guild of Organists; Antiquarian Bksellers Assn of Amer. 14: Tech serv, rare bks. 15: 6300 W 66th ter, Overland Park Kan 66202.

McGRAW, ELIZABETH A. b Davenport Iowa. 5: Principia Col 32-36 (Eng) BA; Art Center Sch (Los Angeles) 49-50 (Art & Photography); UWash 57-58 MLS. 7: Lib asst Naval Electronics Lab, San Diego 47-49; Engnr aid Scripps Inst of Oceanography, La Jolla Cal 51-55; Motion picture prod asst Convair, San Diego 56-57; Art & music libn San Diego Pub Lib 58-59; Ref libn Ore State U 59-60; Ref libn Lib Assn of Portland, Portland Ore 60-61; Head of order dept New Campuses Program UCal(San Diego) 61-65; Ref and music libn 65-. 9: MusLA; CalLA. 10: Beta Phi Mu. 14: Music ref. 15: 1331 Park row, La Jolla Ca 92037.

McGRAW, JANITH CORRINE (ROOT). b Greensburg Ind 16 Je 12. 4: Howard F McGraw. 5: DePauw U 34 (Eng) AB; UWis 60 MSLS. 6: Fr. 7: Tchr-Eng & hist Fulton High Sch, Fulton Ind 35-37; Tchr-Eng & hist Greensburg High Sch, Greensburg Ind 37-44; Tchr-libn Munster Jr High Sch, Munster Ind 48-54; Head libn Libertyville High Sch, Libertyville Ill 54-. 9: ALA; NEA; IllLA; IllEA; Chicago Area Libns Assn. 10: Beta Phi Mu; Delta Kappa Gamma; Beta Sigma Phi;AW. 15: 424 Arbor court, Libertyville Il 60048.

McGRAW, MARIETTA (HORTON). b Whitesville NY 1 F 08. 4: Harold McGraw. 5: State U Col (Geneseo NY) 24-27, 50-51 (LS) BS; Alfred U Ext 27-29 (Sci, Fr). 6: Fr. 7: Tchr Hornell Sch System, Hornell NY 27-29; Buffalo Pub Lib, Buffalo NY: Asst br libn 46-49, Head William St Br 49-50, Head N Jefferson Br 51; Coordinator of storytelling Buffalo & Erie Co Pub Lib, Buffalo NY 51-56, Head Kensington Br 56-60; Dir Amherst Pub Lib, Town of Amherst, Erie Co NY 61-. 9: NY State LA. 10: Quota Club. 14: Admin, lib bldg & equip. 15: 39 Argonne dr, Kenmore NY 14217.

McGRAW, MARY DRUE (FANN). b Van Lear Ky 20 My 14. 4: Leo A McGraw. 5: Berea Col 31-35 (Eng) AB; Emory 35-36 AB in LS. 6: Fr. 7: Libn Ashland Jr Col 38; Libn USAAFB, Orlando Fla 42; Libn catlg bkmob Albertson Mem Lib, Orlando Fla 39-41, 43-44; Dir Libs 22 elem schs, Charlotte NC 45-50; Libn ref br head Miami Pub Lib, Miami Fla 52-59; Libn Miami News," Miami Fla 59-60; Ser libn Miami-Dade Jr Col 60-64; Libn Sandhills Commun Col 65-67; Hd libn Col of The Mainland 67-. 9: ALA; SWLA; TexLA; Tex Jr Col TA. 10: AAUW. 13: Yes. 14: Bibliog, bldg collections. 15: Box 1206, Texas City Tx 77590.

McGREGOR, JAMES WILSON. b Bartlesville Okla 21 Ag 35. 5: UOkla 54-57 (Hist); Chicago 60-63 (LS) MA; Loyola 68- (Hist). 06: Sp, Lat, Fr. 7: Law catlgr UChicago Law Lib 62-64; Sr catlgr Lib SUNY(Stony Brook LI) 64-65, Asst head of catlg 65-66; Instr of Lib Sci NEast Ill State Col 66-67, Act Hd of Catlg 68-. 9: NY Tech Serv Libns; IllLA (sec Tech Proc Div 68-). 10: Beta Phi Mu; Acacia. 13: Yes. 14: Tech processes. 15: 3639 N Wilton ave, Chicago Il 60613.

McGREGOR, JANE ANN. b Shelby NC 25 My 26. 5: Coker Col 42-46 (Eng, Hist) AB; UNC 46-47 BS in LS. 7: Child libn Spartanburg Pub Lib, Spartanburg SC 47-55; Br child libn Pub Lib of Cincinnati & Hamilton Co Ohio 55-63, Supv of child wk 63-. 8: Instr, UCincinnati, 65. 9: EV TOEenal Child 65-); -CSD (Bd); OhioLA (Chm Round Table for Serv to Child & Young Adults 66-; dir). 10: Consul & wkshop leader in Presbytery of Cincinnati on child wk; Pre-sch EducCU OF Greater Cincinnati; Bd of mgt, Mem Commun Center, Cincinnati; Woman's City Club; Bd Cincinnati Assn for Educ Young Child. 13: Yes. 14: Child bks. 15: 922 Ludlow ave, Cincinnati Oh 45220.

McGUCKIN, REV DENIS A. b Phila 1 My 18. 5: St Bonaventure U 37-39, 40-42 (Philos) BA, summers 42-45 (Sociol) MA; Holy Name Col 42-45 (Theol); Villanova U summers 46-50 BLS; Columbia 54-55 MLS. 6: Lat, Fr, Sp. 7: Tchr-libn Bishop Timon High Sch, Buffalo NY 46-52; Tchr-libn St Joseph's Sem (Callicoon NY) 52-58; Libn Holy Name Col 58-. 8: Prov archivist, Franciscan Fathers, Holy Name Province NYC 65-68, Prov libn 68-; Lib Chm Wash (DC) Theol Coalition. 9: CathLA; ALA; ATheolLA. 13: Yes. 14: Catlg, rare bks. 15: Holy Name Col 14th & Shepherd sts NE, Wash DC 20017.

McGUIRE, ALICE BROOKS. b Phila 9 Ag 02. 4: Dr John Carson McGuire. 5: Smith 19-23 (Span) AB; Drexel 25-26 (LS) BS; Columbia 31-32 (LS) MS; Chicago 44-49 (LS) PhD. 6: Fr, Ger, Sp, Lat. 7: Asst libn State Tchrs Col (Slippery Rock

Penn) 23-28; Asst Prof Drexel Sch of Lib Sci 28-44; Instr UChicago 44-49; Libn Casis Elem Sch, Austin Tex 51-68; Assoc Prof UTex 68-; 8: Wkshops: USoCal 50, UOre 53, West MichU 62, Drexel 63, West Wash State Col 65; summer tchg: USoCal 37, UTex 57, UA riz 58, Columbia 64; Consul NDEA Inst: Okla State U, NTex State U, Tex Woman's U, etc. 9: ALA (Coun, Awards Com, Bd of Educ for Libnship);-AASchL (pres 53-54, Bd Dirs, Sch Lib Devel Proj, chm Standards Com);-CSD (Newberry-Caldecott Com, Nomin Com); TexLA; NCTE (Lib Com); SWLA. 12: Jt ed "Youth Communication and Libraries," ALA (49). 13: Yes. 14: Child lit, elem sch libs. 15: 3415 Foothills terrace, Austin Tx 78731.

McGUIRE, EUGENE THOMAS. b NYC 13 O 20. 4: Esther Ries. 5: Benjamin Franklin U (Accounting) BCS. 7: USAAF (Cpl), US, India, CBI Theater 42-45; Shipping supv Amer Bk Center for War Devastated Libs, LC 46-48; Asst dir for operations USBE, Wash DC 48-. 15: 3319 Kilkenny st, Silver Spring Md 20904.

McGUIRE, LAURA HOLSTE. b Ludell Kan 24 F 19. 4: Benjamin F McGuire. 5: UKan 37-41 (Eng) BA; Tex Woman'sU 67-69 MLS. 6: Ger. 7: Biol libn UKan (Lawrence) 41-42; Docs libn East NMexU 69-. 9: ALA. 10: Phi Beta Kappa; Beta Phi Mu; AAUW. 14: Govt docs. 15: 921 N Howard st, Carlsbad NM 88220.

McGUIRE, MARGARET MARY. b Morton Minn 8 S 11. 5: Col of St Catherine 29-33 (Educ) BA; UMinn 35-37 BLS. 07: Child libn Minneapolis Pub Lib 34-42; Naval off (Ensign to Lt Cmdr) convoy & routing wk 42-45; Research libn Time Inc, NYC 45-47; Asst libn Minneapolis Pub Lib 47-55, Spec asst in chg of visual aids serv 55-59, Head visual aids dept 59-. 9: ALA (Labor/Lib Com, A-V Com); -PLA (A-V Com); -LAD (Pub Rel, Film Coun); FLIC; MinnLA. 10: Twin Cities Naval Reserve; Municipal Employees Retirement Assn; AFL-CIO. 11: Several awards for pub employee civic & pub rels activities. 13: Yes. 14: A-v, pub rel. 15: 1954 Kenwood parkway, Minneapolis Mn 55405.

McGUIRE, ORA (SPADAFORA). b Chicago 18 Je 24. 4: Thomas McGuire. 5: No Ill U 41-45 (Fr) BS; Purdue 59-64 (Educ) MS. 6: Fr, Sp. 7: High sch tchr Earl Park High Sch, Earl Park Ind 45-46, 59-61; Tchr Oxford High Sch, Oxford Ind 61-63, Libn 63-; Supv of Benton Commun Schs 65-69; Staff at Purdue U Tchg Lib Sci summer 68, 69. 9: NEA; Ind State Tchrs Assn; IndLA (sec 68). 10: AAUW. 14: Bk sel, story-telling. 15: 206 W Benton, Oxford In 47971.

McGUIRE, WALTER J. b Scotts Bluff Neb 14 S 14. 4: Esther Ross. 5: UMinn 39-41, 43-46 (LS) BS; UWash summer 51; UMinn 54-55 (Amer Hist) MA. 6: Fr. 7: Sr asst Minneapolis Pub Sumner Br 46-47; Head pub serv Pub Lib, Eau Claire Wis 47-48; Libn West Mont Col of Educ 48-57; Ref Ariz State U 57-58, Chief ref 58-59; Asst Prof Lib Sci & asst ref NM State U 59-. 8: Instr Pol Sci 49-54 & Asst Prof Hist 54-57 in addition to work as libn at Dillon Mont. 9: ALA; NMLA. 10: AAUP. 14: Ref, catlg, spec collections. 15: 2090 Austin dr, Las Cruces NM 88001.

McGUIRL, MARLENE (CALLIS). b Hammond Ind 22 Mr 38. 4: James F McGuirl. 5: IndU 56-59 (Pol Sci) AB; DePaul Col of Law 59-63 (Law) JD; Rosary Col 63-65 MA in LS. 7: Asst law libn DePaul Law Lib 61-65; Ref law libn Boston Col Sch of Law Lib, Newton Mass 65-66; Law libn DC Bar Assn Lib, Wash DC 66-. 8: Admitted to Practice of Law; Ill 63, Ind 64; Lib consul; Nat Clearinghouse on Poverty Law 67-68; Nat Inst for Educ in Law & Poverty; N West U 69; Prof Grad Sch, Dept of Agric (Law Libnship). 9: AALL; SLA; Wash Soc Law Libns (treas 67-69, v-pres 69-70); Amer Bar Found (Lib Serv Com). 10: Delegate Ind Democratic Convention 64; Ill Bar Assn; DC Bar Assn; Women's Bar Assn. 13: Yes. 15: 1068 30th st NW, Wash DC 20007.

McGUNIGLE, FLORENCE (ESLIN). b Wash DC 22 S 15. 4: . 5: Simmons 33-38 (LS) BS; Hofstra U 62-65 (Educ); C W Post Col 65 (LS). 6: Fr. 7: Asst child libn NY Pub Lib 38-39; Child libn Providence Pub Lib 39-41; Sch libn Rushmore-Cherry Lane, Carle Place NY 64-. 9: NY State Tchrs Assn; Nassau-Suffolk Sch LA. 14: Wk with child. 15: Rushmore Sch, Carle Place NY 11514.

McGURK, PATRICIA H. b Beacon NY 24 S 31. 5: Dutchess Commun Col 58-61; SUNY Col (New Paltz) 61-63 (Ed) BS; SUNY (Albany) 64-67 MLS. 7: Howland Circ Lib, Beacon NY 49-59; Readers serv div Vassar Col Lib 59-61; Multi-media sch libn Wappingers Falls Central Sch Dist, Wappingers Falls NY 64-. 8: Estab a multi-media ctr in a new elem sch (Myers Rd Sch) under a Spec Purpose Grant, 66-67. 9: ALA; NEA; NYLA; NYStateTA; Sch Libns of SENY (1st v-pres); Dutchess CoLA. 14: Child serv, multi-media learning ctrs. 15: 8 W Center st, Beacon NY 12508.

McHALE, MARGARET (SEIFRING). b Archbald Penn 11 O 28. 4: Thomas J McHale. 5: Marywood Col 46-50 (LS) AB; Penn State U 50-51; Marywood Col 65-67 (LS) MS. 6: Fr. 7: Asst libn Penn State U Agric Lib 50-52; Asst libn Marywood Col 52-54; Asst libn Scranton Pub Lib, Scranton Penn 55-56; Sub Douglass Col Lib 57; Asst libn Marywood Col Lib 57-59; Libn S Scranton Catholic High Sch Lib, Scranton Penn 59-. 9: CathLA; (sec-treas Scranton Diocesan Unit); ALA; PennLA. 10: Kappa Gamma Pi; Delta Epsilon Sigma. 14: Ref. 15: 2712 Pittston ave, Scranton Pa 18505.

McHALE, THOMAS JOSEPH. b Scranton Penn 24 O 19. 4: Margaret C Seifring. 5: UScranton 37-41 (Educ) BA, 52-55 (Educ) MEd; Rutgers 56-57 MS in LS. 6: Fr. 7: Pilot Army Air Force (1st Lt) 42-45; Scranton Pub Lib, Scranton Penn: Assoc ref libn 57-60, Bkmob libn 60-62, Assoc ref libn 62-. 8: Tchr-catlg Marywood Col summer 69. 9: ALA; PennLA (chm NE Chap 65-66). 14: Ref, catlg. 15: 2712 Pittston ave, Scranton Pa 18505.

McHENRY, NANCY (AEBERLY). b Chicago 30 D 27. 5: UAriz 45-48 (Math); Purdue 49-51 (Gen Sci) BS; Northwestern summers 56, 57 (Educ); Loyola U (Chicago) summer 57 (Educ); UIll 58-59, 61 (Counseling, Guidance) MEd. 7: Hostess, personnel manager Gene Doyle Steak House, Tucson; Gen off Calco Chem Co, Chicago 48-49; Soc case wker Bur of Pub Asst, Long Beach Cal 53; Mathematician N Amer Aircraft, Downey Cal 54-55; Elem tchr Arlington Heights Pub Sch, Arlington Heights Ill 56-57; High Sch math & sci Chicago Bd of Educ 56-58, 59-63; Sci tchr E Prairie Elem Sch, Skokie Ill 63-64; Picture libn Encyclopaedia Britannica Films Inc. Wilmette Ill 64-66; Research libn Armour & Co Food Research Div, Oak Brook Ill 66-. 8: Initialed and coordinated writing, photographing & producing of a 13-min color sound filmstrip. 9: SLA; Inst Food Technologists (chm Educ Com 67-69; chm Nat Career Guidance Com 69-70); Amer Marketg Assn; Nat Sci Tchrs Assn; Amer Personnel and Guidance Assn. 10: Mem, Alumni Assns: Purdue, Ill, Ariz. 14: Lit searches. 15: 4601 Washington st, Downers Grove Il 60515.

McHONE, MRS MILDRED E(DITH). b Rolfe Iowa 8 N 11. 4: Raymond C McHone. 5: Iowa State U of Sci & Tech 33 (Home Econ, Educ) BS. 7: Home econ tchr, Greenville Iowa 33-34; Home econ & Eng tchr, Bradgate Iowa 34-35; Iowa State U: Ref asst & tchr freshman lib 46-47, Circ dept asst 47-49, Asst circ libn 49-53, Ref libn 53-. 9: ALA; Iowa;A. 10: Elder, Collegiate Presbyt Church. 14: Ref. 15: 330 Crane ave, Ames Ia 50012.

McILROY, WILLIAM R. b Abington Penn 4 Ap 27. 5: St Joseph's Col (Phila) 47-51 (Psych) BA; Drexel 59-60 MSLS. 7: Free Lib of Phila: Libn: trainee ya wk, brs 59, educ dept 60, lit dept 61, gen info dept 62, educ films dept 62, fiction dept 63-. 10: Beta Phi Mu. 14: Fiction. 15: Free Lib of Phila, Logan Square, Phila 19103.

McILVAINE, DAVID WILLIAM. b Philadelphia Pa 4 Ja 40. 4: Patricia Ferguson. 5: Wheaton Col (Wheaton Ill) 58-61 (Bible) AB, 61-63 (New Testamen 05: Wheaton Col (Wheaton Ill) 58-61 (Bible) AB, 61-63 (New Testament) UIll 65-66 (LS) MS. 6: Fr, Sp, Portu, Ger. 7: Asst libn Trinity Evangelical Divinty Sch, Deerfield Ill 64-65; Circ asst UIll (Urbana) 65-66; Subject catlgr LC 66-69; Dir- Learning Resources Ctr Frederick Commun Col 69-. 9: ATheolLA; MdAJrCol (Learning Res Div). 14: Admin, subj catlg, theol libnship. 15: 520 N Market st, Frederick Md 21701.

McINNES, D(OUGLAS) N(ORMAN). b Melita Man Can 22 S 33. 4: Emily Janet Campbell. 5: UBC 51-55 (Eng, Fr, Ger) BA; Sorbonne 56-57 (Cours de Civilisation Francaise); UBC 57-58 (Tchrs Train), 62-63 BLS. 6: Fr, Ger. 7: Tchr So Okanagan Secondary Sch, Oliver BC 57-61; Tchr Windsor High Sch, N Vancouver BC 61 -62; Libn Spec collections div UBC 63-64, Biomed libn Woodward Biomed Lib 64-67, Asst libn for Pub Serv 67-. 9: ALA; CanLA (Coun 67-, chm CanLA (ACBLF Liaison Com, chm Educ for Lib Manpower Com);MedLA; BCLA (Bus Manager of Quarterly). 11: Ruth Cameron Medal in Libnship. 14: Rare bks, med libnship, ref, admin. 15: 3171 W 26th ave, Vancouver 8 BC Can.

McINNIS, RAYMOND G. b Wishart Sask Can 11 Ja 36. 4: Karen Ewbank. 5: UAlberta 55-56 (Pre-dentistry); UBC 58-60 (Hist, Eng) BA; UWash 60-61 MLS. 7: Bibliog UWash 61-62; Co libn Grays Harbor Co, Montesano Wash 62-65; Ref libn West Wash St Col 65-68, Hd ref libn 68-. 9: ALA; WashLA.

12: Co-auth "Anti-democractic Trends in Twentieth Century Americam" (69). 13: Yes. 14: Ref, bibliog. 15: 1003 14th st, Bellingham Wa 98225.

McINTIRE, GERTRUDE IRENE (ADRIANCE). b Paw Paw Mich 15 N 02. 4: William R McIntire. 5: UMich 26 (Fr & Soc Stud) AB; Mich State 52 (Counseling & Guidance) MA. 6: Fr, Sp. 7: Tchr & libn Pub Sch, Paw Paw Mich 21-22; Tchr & libn Pub Sch, Romeo Mich 26-30; Tchr, counselor Pub Sch, Lansing Mich 30-33, 38-61; Prin Jr High Sch, Lansing Mich 38-41; Libn Pub Lib, Lake Park Fla 66-. 9: FlaLA. 10: AAUW; Gold Coast Woman's Club. 15: 120 Celestial way, Juno Beach Fl 33403.

McINTOSH, LAWRENCE DENNIS. b Bendigo Victoria Australia 19 Ap 28. 4: Pamela Pascoe. 5: UMelbourne (Australia) 51-54 (Philos) BA; DrewU Theol Sch 60-62 (Hist Theol) BD (summa cum laude), 62-66 (Hist Theol) PhD. 6: Ger, Fr, Lat. 7: Minister Methodist ch of Australia 53-56; Dir of Rel Radio/TV Australian Broadcasting Commsn 56-60; Sr Hist Master Ballarat Col, Australia 66-68; Theol libn DrewU 68-. 9: ATheolLA. 11: Fulbright Scholar; Dempster Grad Fellow; Rockefeller Doctoral Fellow. 12: "The Nature and Design of Christianity in John Wesley's Early Theology," PhD diss DrewU (66). 13: Yes. 14: Theol acquis & ref. 15: Drew University Lib, Madison NJ 07940.

McINTYRE, MARGARET (IONE). b High Point NC 3 My 24. 5: Appalachian State U 41-45 (LS, Soc studies) BS; Peabody Col summer 46; Appalachian State U summers 52, 53 (LS) MA, summer 57; USCar summer 66. 7: Libn Appalachian High Sch, Boone NC 45-48; Intr lib sci dept Appalachian State U 45-48; Libn Ferndale Jr High Sch, High Point NC 48-68; State supv Ctr for Learning Resources Dept of Pub Instr, Raleigh NC 68-69; Libn T Wingate Andrews High Sch, High Point NC 69-. 8: Instr Lib Sci, Winthrop Col, Rock Hill SC summer 58; Instr NDEA Inst for Adv Study for Sch Lib Personnel, USC summer 67; Instr Lib Sci, E Carolina U, Greenville NC summer 68; Visit lectr Inst for Training in Libnship, Appalachian State U Boone NC summer 68. 9: ALA; NEA; NEA; NCLA (sec; dir & chm Sch Libs Sect); NCEA (chm & sec Sch Lib Sect). 10: Amer Bus Women's Assn; Bus & Prof Club of YWCA. 14: Admin, tchg lib sci. 15: 307 Louise ave, High Point NC 27262.

McINTYRE, MARGARET R. b Jackson Mich 13 Je 10. 5: Jackson Jr Col 29-31; UMich 31-33 (Hist) AB, 33-34 AB in LS. 6: Fr, Ger. 7: Catlgr Jackson Pub Lib, Jackson Mich 34-. 9: ALA; MichLA. 10: AAUW; Ella Sharp Museum; LWV. 14: Catlg. 15: 914 SW ave, Jackson Mi 49203.

McINTYRE, PATTIE BARTEE. b Reidsville NC 2 F 17. 4: Kenneth Murchison McIntyre. 5: High Point Col 32-36 (Eng) AB; UNC 38, 40 AB in LS. 6: Fr, Sp. 7: Elem tchr Williamsburg Sch, Reidsville NC 36-37; Tchr Fr & Eng Reeds High Sch, Lexington NC 37-39; Ref libn Charlotte Pub Lib, Charlotte NC 40-43; Libn Valley Forge Gen Hosp, Phoenixville Penn 43; Ref asst UNC(Chapel Hill) 49-57, Asst ref libn 57-. 9: ALA; SELA (sec Ref Servs Div 68-); NCLA (treas 61-65, Dir Exec Bd 65-67). 10: Beta Phi Mu. 12: Contrib "Medieval and Renaissance Studies: A Location Guide to Selected Reference Works and Source Collections in the Libraries of UNC and Duke . (65). 13: Yes. 14: Ref. 15: P O Box 86, Chapel Hill NC 27514.

McISAAC, CHARLES AUGUSTINE. b Boston 30 O 18. 4: Barbara Shaughnessy. 5: Boston Col 36-40 (Ger) AB; St st John's Sem 40-44 (Theol); Simmons 60-62 MS LS. 6: Ger, Fr, Lat, Grk. 7: Asst Pastor St Joseph's Church, Hyde Park Mass 44-48; Instr in Theol St Michael's Col (Vt) 48-50; Asst Pastor Sacred Heart Church, Malden Mass 50-59; Catlgr Creagh Research Lib, Brighton Mass 59-60; Rare bks catlgr Brandeis U Lib 60-63; Chief acquis div Boston U Libs 63-. 9: ALA; NELA; NE Tech Serv Libns; MassLA. 10: ACLU; SCLC; NAACP; Watertown (Mass) Fair Housing Com; Boston Museum of Fine Arts; Simmons Col Lib Sci Alumni; Boston Libs Staff Assn. 13: Yes. 14: Acquis, catlg, rare bks, admin, personnel. 15: 1002 Belmont st, Watertown Ma 02172.

McIVER, VIVIAN (DOWNES). b Needham Mass 14 Jl 21. 4: Gavin R McIver. 5: Simmons 39-43 (LS) BS. 6: Ger. 7: Lib asst YMCA, Boston 42-43; Needham Free Pub Lib, Needham Mass: Catlgr 43-44, 46-57, Asst libn 57-59, Libn 60-. 9: ALA; MassLA; Greater Boston Lib Admins Group (pres 62-63, chm Study Com on Org & Control for Mass "Willis Report on Educ; chm Adult Educ Com 65-). 10: Monday Club of Needham; New Century Club of Needham;Needham-Wellesley Simmons Club. 14: Catlg. 15: 1139 Highland ave, Needham Heights Ma 02194.

McIVOR, MOIRA (MARION). b Winnipeg Man Can 24 S 39. 5: United Col UMan 58-59 (Eng); UAlta 60-62 (Eng) BA; UBC 63-64 BLS. 6: Fr. 7: Lib asst grad UCalg 62-63, Ref libn I 64, Circ libn 65-68, Hd info ctr 68-69, Project off 69-. 9: CanLA; ALA; AltaLA (coun). 10: Beta Phi Mu. 14: Ref, bldgs, admin, automation. 15: 301 Leduc apts 640-14th ave SW, Calgary 3 Alta Can.

McKANN, MICHAEL R. b Franklin Va 2 N 41. 4: Virginia Ann Jacobs. 5: Col of William & Mary 60-64 (Eng) AB; UMich 65-66 AMLS. 6: Fr, Russian. 7: Bibliogr Col of William & Mary 64-65; Analyst Nat Security Agency, Ft Meade Md 66-. 8: Assigned to the situation Room, The White House, to Devise Retr System for the Presidential collection of Nat Security Coun Papers 67-68; Assigned to Intel Staff, HQS, US Mil Assist Command, Vietnam (Saigon) as Civilian Analyst. 14: Ref. 15: 8033 Woodholme cir, Pasadena Md 21122.

McKAY, MILDRED P(ETERSON). b Nashua NH 19 Jl 05. 4: Austin B McKay. 5: Wheaton Col 29 AB; Simmons 33 (LS) BS. 7: Asst Nashua Pub Lib, Nashua NH 29-32; Libn Colby Jr Col 34-42; Dir NH State Lib 42-64; Consul Governor's Adv Com, Hartford Conn 64-. 8: Consul Conn State Lib 64-. 9: ALA (coun 62-64); -AAStateL (pres 58; Survey & Standards Com 59-66); -ALTA; NHLA (v-pres & pres 36-40); N ELA (dir 39-40); ArizSLA (sec Trustees Assn 68-). 11: Hon M A Wheaton Col 61; Hon DHL UNH 64. 13: Yes. 14: Systems, admin, pub rel. 15: 2045 E Cerrada Nopal, Tucson Az 85718.

McKEE, CHRISTOPHER (FULTON). b Brooklyn NY 14 Je 35. 4: Linda Mitchell. 5: U St Thomas (Houston) 53-57 (Eng) BA; UMich 57-60 AMLS. 6: Fr. 7: Catlg libn Washingotn & Lee U 58-62; Soc sci libn So Ill 62-66, Bk sel off 67-69, Asst dir 69-. 10: Appalachian Mountain Club; Naval Hist Found; US Naval Inst; Organ Amer Histns; Amer Mil Inst. 13: Yes. 14: Acquis, bk sel, lib admin. 15: 204 S Charles st, Edwardsville Il 62025.

McKEE, ELEANOR JUNE. b Shannon City Iowa 2 Je 24. 5: Drake U 42-46 (Span) BA; Colo State U summer 48 (Eng); Peabody 54-55 MA in LS. 6: Sp. 7: Tchr Orient High Sch, Orient Iowa 46-47; Tchr So Christian Inst (Miss) 47-53; Libn Spirit Lake High Sch, Spirit Lake Iowa 55-57; Asst circ libn Iowa State U of Sci & Tech 58-60, Asst ref libn 57-58, 60-68; Asst Prof & Hd search unit Order Dept 68-. 9: ALA; IowaLA. 10: Beta Phi Mu; Phi Sigma Iota; Beta Gamma Kappa; AAUW. 14: Ref. 15: 4412 Ross rd, Ames Ia 50010.

McKEE, MARY (SHANNON). b New Castle Penn 12 Je 11. 4: Walter S McKee. 5: Carnegie 32 (LS) BS; Westminster Col (New Wilmington Penn) 58 (Educ) MS. 7: Child libn Free Pub Lib, New Castle Penn 47-52; Libn Sr High Sch New Castle Area Schs, New Castle Penn 52-65; Head Libn Miami Jackson Sr High Dade Co Schs, Miami Fla 65-. 15: 1362 NE 116 st, N Miami Fl 33161.

McKEE, WILBUR R. b Parkers Prairie Minn 29 Jl 05. 4: Elizabeth Williams. 5: Des Moines U 23-26 (Hist) AB; UWash 28 (Hist) AM, 33-34 AB in Lib; UMich 34-37 AMLS, 39-44 (Hist). 6: Fr, Ger. 7: Hist, music Bozeman (Mont) High Sch 26-27; Hist Gooding Col 28-29; Hist McKendree Col 29-30; Libn Linfield Col 34-37; Gen Lib UMich 37-44; Ref libn "St Louis Post-Dispatch" 44-. 14: Ref, catlg. 15: 23 Orchard dr, Florissant Mo 63033.

McKELVEY, MARY SUSAN. b Rockford Ill 17 S 43. 5: OhioU 61-65 (Eng) AB; UIll 65-66 (LS) MS. 7: Y-a libn Free Lib of Phila 66-68, Y-a specialist commun serv 68-. 9: ALA; PennLA. 14: Ya serv. 15: 1727 Spruce st, Phila Pa 19103.

McKELVEY, SISTER MARY JOANNE. b Holtwood Penn 11 Jl 19. 5: Millersville State Col 37-41 (LS, Soc Studies) BS; Franklin & Marshall summer 42; Drexel 51-54 MSLS. 7: Libn Hawley High Sch, Hawley Penn 41-45; Libn Sr High Sch, Long Branch NJ 45-47; Libn Immaculata Col 52-55; Libn Villa Maria Acad, Malvern Penn 55-61; Libn O'Connell High Sch, Arlington Va 61-. 8: Tchr Phila Diocesan Sch, Phila 50, 51. 9: ALA; CathLA; NCEA; VaLA. 10: Beta Phi Mu. 14: Sch libnship. 15: Little Falls rd & Underwood st, Arlington Va 22213.

McKENNA, F(RANCIS) E(UGENE). b Globe Ariz 29 Jl 21. 5: UCal(Berkeley) 41 (Chem) BS; UWash 44 (Phys Chem) PhD. 6: Ger, Russian, Fr. 7: Research chem SAM Labs (Manhattan Proj) Columbia U 44-45; Research supv SAM Labs (Manhattan Proj) Carbide & Carbon Chem Corp 45-46; Post-doctoral research fellow Inst for Nuclear Studies UChicago 46-47; Air Reduction Co Inc: Sr chem 48-53, Sr info spec 53-59, Supv info center 59-67; Ed "Special Libraries" & mgr publs dept SLA, NYC 68-. 09: ASIS; SLA (pres 66-67; Dir Liaison Off 62-65; mem 9 coms 58-65; NY Chap: chm Sci-Tech Gp 58-59; chm Bylaws Com 59-60; var other assignments 58-60; NJ Chap: pres 59-60; chm &/or mem 2 coms 57-58 & 59-60; var other assignments 58-65; Metals Div: chm 60-61; mem 3 coms 55-61; Sci-Tech Div; Adv Com 58-59). 10: ACS; Amer Inst Min, Metal & Petrol Engnrs; Amer Soc Met; Amer Soc Testing & Materials; Aslib; Chem Soc of Japan; Electrochem Soc; Inst Info Scis; Sigma Xi; Phi Lambda Upsilon. 12: Auth &/or co-auth of 3 chapters in Nat Nuclear Energy Series v 1 (50); Co-auth 'The Industrial Information Department' in "Information and Communication Practice in Industry," ed by T E R Singer (58), tr into Japanese (62); Holder of 8 patents, US, Can, & France. 13: Yes. 14: Info & communication techniques, cryoscopy, fluorine & fluorocarbons, phys properties of gases, chem reactions in the solid phase. 15: Special Libraries Association 235 Park ave S, New York NY 10003.

McKENNA, FLORENCE MARY. b Homestead Penn 5 My 30. 5: Duquesne 48-52 (Bio) BEd; Carnegie Inst 52-53 MLS. 7: Asst sci-tech dept Carnegie Lib of Pittsburgh, Penn 53-54; Libn Hagan Chemicals & Controls Inc, Pittsburgh Penn 54-61; Supv tech lib Westinghouse Astronuclear Lab, Pittsburgh Penn 61-67; Natural sci biblio UPittsburgh 67-. 9: ALA; SLA; ASIS; PennLA. 14: Tech lib. 15: 4517 Parade st, Pittsburgh Pa 15207.

McKENNA, JOHN R. b Ottawa Can 19 My 17. 4: M Constance Duclos. 5: Queen's U (Can) 47 BA; McGill 48 BLS. 6: Fr, Sp. 7: RCAF (Sgt) Air Gunner 42-45; Ref asst UMe 48-49; Head readers serv Bowdoin Col 49-53, Asst libn 53-57; Libn Colby Col 57-64; Libn Middlebury Col 64-. 8: Bus mgr, Colby Col Press 57-64. 9: MeLA (pres 57-59, chm Com on Standards 62-63); NELA (treas 62-63, v-pres & pres-elect 68-69). 10: Waterville Skating Club. 13: Yes. 14: Admin, lib bldgs, rare bks. 15: 6 Chipman park, Middlebury Vt 05753.

McKENNA, RITA M(ARIE). b Rock Rapids Iowa 6 Mr 10. 5: UMinn 39-42 (Bus Admin); Ariz State U 59-60 (Econ) BS; USoCal 61-62 MS in LS. 7: Legal sec, Phoenix Ariz 43-52; Legal sec Attorney Gen of Ariz, Phoenix 52-55; Legal sec Phoenix 57-60; Elem sch libn Coolidge Pub Schs, Coolidge Ariz 60-61; High sch libn Ajo Pub High Sch, Ajo Ariz 62-63; Libn I Phoenix Pub Lib 63-. 9: ALA; Ariz State LA; SWLA. 10: LWV; Municipal Employees Assn, Phoenix; Libraria Sodalitas; Phi Kappa Phi. 14: Ref, period, adult serv. 15: 130 W Pierson st, Phoenix Az 85013.

McKENRY, COLETTA. b Pittsburgh Penn 13 Ja 13. 5: Ind State Tchrs Col 31-35 (Fr, Eng) BS in Ed; UPittsburgh 41-43 (Educ) MEd, 62-65 MLS. 6: Fr. 7: Research asst US Steel Corp, Pittsburgh Penn 41-62, Supervisor ref bureau 62-, Libn 68-. 9: ALA; SLA; PennLA. 10: Womans City Club; Aliquippa Country Club. 14: Ref. 15: US Steel Corp 525 William Penn pl, Pittsburgh Pa 15230.

McKENZIE, JAMES TRUEMAN. b Hamilton Iowa 2 D 32. 5: Bob Jones U 52; State Col Iowa 56-60 (LS) BA; UDenver summers 63-65 (LS) MA. 7: Communications USAF (A/1c) 52-56; Libn Charles City Commun Schs, Charles City Iowa 60-63; Head Libn Davenport Central High Sch, Davenport Iowa 63-65; Dir Charles City Pub Lib, Charles City Iowa 65-66; Lib supv SoEast Polk Schs, Runnells Iowa 66-. 9: ALA; NEA; IowaLA (Recr Chm 68); IowaASchL (chm Budgeting Com 68-69; chm Central Dist 68); IowaStateEA. 14: Ref. 15: 205 - 4th st SW, Altoona Ia 50009.

McKENZIE, KAREN (LEE). b Regina Sask Can 22 F 46. 5: USask 63-66 (Psych) BA; UMinn 66-69 (LS) MA. 6: Fr. 7: Tchg asst UMinn Lib Sch (Minneapolis) 67-68, Admin asst 68, Hd libn Journalism Sch 68-. 9: SLA. 14: Spec libnship, ref. 15: 5405 25 ave S, Minneapolis Mn 55417.

McKENZIE, MARY A(GNES MUDD). b Olton Tex 6 Ag 28. 4: Terence J McKenzie. 5: N Tex State Col 45-48, 60 (Eng) BA; American U even 58-59; Catholic U 60-61 (LS). 6: Sp, Fr. 7: LC: Accessioner, Serial Record & Order Div 49-51, Asst head Ordering Unit 51-52, Head Ordering Unit 52-53, Sr ed reviser E European Accessions Index Project 53-61, Asst head Amer-British Exch Sect, Exch & Gift Div 61-62, Head Monthly Checklist Sect, Exch & Gift Div 62-63, Pub info spec Info Off 64-65, Asst info off Info Off 65-67; Conn Col: Asst libn 67-68, Col libn 68-. 9: ALA-LAD (Publs Com of Pub Rel Sect 65-67); DCLA (Publ Com 64-65; Com on DCLA Manual 65-66); ConnLA (sec Col & Univ Sect 68-70); NELA. 10: Alpha chi; Antiq & Landmarks Soc Conn; New London Co Hist Soc. 12: Ed "Monthly Checklist of State Publications" (62-63); Ed "Proceedings of the Third assembly on the Library Functions of the States" (64); Ed "LC Information Bulletin (65-67); Ed "Palmer Periscope" (67-). 14: Pub rel, bibliog, admin. 15: River rd, Essex Ct 06426.

McKENZIE, PATRICIA ALICE. b Dunedin Fla 17 Mr 39. 5: Chicago 56-58; UFla 58-61 (Eng Lit) BA; Fla State U 63-64 (LS) MS. 6: Fr. 7: Asst to assoc ed Civil Engineering, NYC 59-60; Ed asst Oxford U Press, NYC 61-62; Sch libn Clewiston Elem Sch, Clewiston Fla 62-63; Grad asst Fla State U Lib 63-64; Ref libn New Col Lib 64-65; Instr Div of Libnship Emory U 65-68; Sr ed ALA Publ 68-69. 9: ALA; NCTE. 13: Yes. 14: Publishing, ref, child lit. 15: 722 Clark st, Evanston Il 60201.

McKENZIE, ROBB. b Bridgeport Conn 2 Ap 32. 5: ClarkU 53-59 (Eng, Sociol) BS; Rutgers 59-61 MLS. 7: Libn trainee, sr libn Newark Pub Lib, Newark NJ 59-64; Sr libn Queensborough Pub Lib, Jamaica NY 64, Hd circ div 64-66, Hd Popular Lib 66; Hd acquis liu lib, Brooklyn 67-. 8: Memb consul team, Chicago Pub Lib Dec 68. 9: NYLA; NY Tech Serv Libns. 10: AAUP; United Fed of Col Tchrs; SANE. 14: Acquis, automation, collection devel. 15: 175 Willoughby st apt 15M, Brooklyn NY 11201.

McKEON, NEWTON F(ELCH). b Paterson NJ 21 D 04. 4: Mary Maury Fitzgerald. 5: Amherst 22-26 (Eng, Math) BA; Emmanuel Col Cambridge U 33-34 (Eng). 7: Master LawrencevilleSch, Lawrenceville NJ 26-27; Actuarial dept Metropolitan Life Insurance Co, NYC 27-28; Clerk Merrill Lynch & Co, NYC 28-30; Clerk Nat City Bank, NYC 30-31; Amherst Col: Eng Instr 31-37, Asst Prof Eng 37-41, Assc Prof Eng 41-48, Prof Eng 48-, Asst Dir Lib 35-39, Dir Lib 39-. 8: Act Dean Amherst Col 36-37; Math tchr USAF Pre-Meteorology 43-44; Evaluation Com NE Assn of Cols & Sec Schs 53-63; Adv Coms Lilly Endowment, Indianapolis 59, 60; Consul Dickinson col 64; Adv Com Bucknell U 65. 09; ALA (Coun 58-61); -ACRL (dir 58-61); BSA; Hampshire INTER"LIB CTR (Bd Dirs 51-; sec 52-53, 55-56, 56-57, 59-60; treas 58-59, 60-61). 10: Phi Beta Kappa; Grolier Club (NYC). 12: Ed "Amherst Massachusetts Imprints, 1825-1876, (46); Contrib "The Place of the Library in a University" (50); "The College Library in a Changing World" (53); "The Function of the Library in the Modern College" (54). 13: Yes. 14: Admin, rare bks, bldgs. 15: 32 Hitchcock rd, Amherst Ma 01002.

McKEOWN, SUSIE NORWOOD. b Rock Hill SC 17 Ag 14. 5: Winthrop Col 32-36 (Fr, Eng) BA; Emory 39-40 BA in LS; UMich summers 52, 53, 56 MA in LS. 6: Fr. 7: Tchr Campobello High Sch, Campobello SC 36-39; Libn Laurens High Sch, Laurens SC 40-41; Libn of Lib Sch Emory U 41-43; Asst ref libn Emory U 44, Act documents libn 45-46; Head catlg dept Winthrop Col Lib 46-. 9: ALA; NYLA; NYCSchLA; NY Soc forExper Study of Educ; Cath Tchrs Assn. 10: AAUW; Delta Kappa Gamma. 14: Child wk. 15: 965 Cherry rd, Rock Hill SC 29730.

McKIE, DONALD S. b Los Angeles Cal 21 Ap 30. 5: UTex 47-51 (Fr) BA; UCal 52-53 BLS. 6: Fr, Sp, Ger. 7: Catlgr Amherst Col Lib 53-54; Ref libn (sci) San Diego Pub Lib 54-60; Forestry libn Colo State U 60-62; Supv spec serv dept Oakland Pub Lib, Oakland Cal 62-67; Ref libn USan Diego 67-68; Ref libn UCalifornia (San Diego) 68-. 9: ALA; CalLA. 10: ACLU; UN Assn. 12: Co-ed "San Diego: a 200th Anniversary Bibliography" (69). 14: Ref, govt pub, maps. 15: 4502 del Monte ave, San Diego Ca 92107.

McKILLOP, ANNABELLE. b W Lorne Ont Can. 5: Queen's U (Eng, Fr) BA; Toronto BLS. 7: Br libn Pub Lib, Walkerville Ont; Head child dept Pub Lib, Windsor Ont. 9: ALA-CSD; CanLA; Can Assn Child Libns (v-chm, mem var coms); Young Canada's Bk Week (chm, chm &/or mem var coms); OntLA (chm Child Libns Sect); Inst Profess Libns Ont. 10: Delta Kappa Gamma; Can Fed Univ Women; Women's Nat Bk Assn. 13: Yes. 14: Child wk. 15: 1616 Ouellette ave, Windsor 14 Ont Can.

McKINLAY, JANET (ZIMMERMAN). b Toronto Can 30 Jl 06. 4: Duncan E McKinlay. 5: Syracuse 25-30 (Lit) AB; Columbia 32 BS in LS. 7: Asst libn Pub Lib, Glen Rock NJ 32, Libn 32-41; Post libn Post Lib, Ft Monmouth NJ 41-46; Command libn 2nd Serv Command, Governor's Island NY 46; 1st army libn First Army, Governor's Island NY 46-47, Chief army lib & serv club br 47-48; Pub lib supv Pub & Sch Lib Serv Bur Div of State Lib Archives & Hist, NJ State Dept of Educ 48-49, Act head 49-52, Head 52-. 8: Adv Com, Prof Libns Certif 57-; Rutgers U Grad Sch Lib Serv Adv Coun 53-; Adv Com, Small Libs Project, Wk Simplification in Small Pub Libs 62. 9: ALA (Bd mem & chm 5 groups & coms 37-40, 48, 59-69); -LED (treas 50-52, chm 3 coms 59 & 63-65); -Friends of Libs (chm 52-53);-PLD (chm 2 coms 56-58);-LAD (chm State Lib Personnel Practices 59); Grolier Soc Award Jury (chm 60); Scarecrow Press Award Jury for Lib Lit (chm 62);-ALTA;-AASchL;-AAStateL (dir 60-61); SLA; NJLA (pres 61-62, ALA Coun 49-53, chm 5 coms 34-35 & 45-54); Middle Atlantic States RegLA (chm 2 coms 51, 60); LPRC (Exec Bd 44-46, pres 47-48); NJEA; NJSchLA; NJ Lib Trustees Assn. 10: Friends of NJ Libs; Amer Cancer Soc; Women's Serv Org; Women's Nat Bk Assn; AAUW; Delta Delta Delta; Theta Sigma Phi; Beta Chi Alpha; Zonta Internat; Girl Scouts. 11: Decoration for Exceptional Serv rendered to Armed Forces 49; Governor's appointment to State Employees Awards Com 59-61; Commsnd Ky Col for cooperation with lib officials in Ky 65. 13: Yes. 14: Lib ext, pub & sch libs. 15: 10 Woodland rd, Sylvan Glen, Bordentown NJ 08505.

McKINLEY, ALICE E. b Champaign Co Ohio 23 F 21. 5: Blackburn Col 38-40 (Eng Lit) Associate BA; Park Col 40-42 (Eng Lit) BA; UDenver 42-43 BS in LS. 6: Ger, Fr. 7: Child libn Minot Pub Lib, Minot ND 43; Asst libn Park Col Lib 44-46; Yp asst Kan City(Mo) Pub Lib 46-47; Libn US Army, Germany, France, Austria 47-55; Lib consul Mich State Lib 56-65; Lib spec USOE Lib Serv Br, Wash DC 65-67; Exec dir Dupage Lib Syst, Wheaton Ill 67-. 8: Tech adv to Macomb Co Planning Commsn, Mt Clemens Mich 59. 9: ALA (var com assignments); AEA-USA. 12: Public Library Service in Oakland Co, Mich" (60). 14: Educ for libnship, adult educ. 15: P O Box 682, Wheaton Il 60187.

McKINLEY, JIMMIE JOE. b Williamson Co Tex 23 Jl 34. 5: Kilgore Col 51-53; UTex 53-55 (Journalism) B Journalism; UKy 62, 63-64MSLS. 7: Asst libn Bethel Col, McKenzie Tenn 61-63, 66-. 9: ALA; TennLA. 10: Sigma Delta Chi. 14: Ref, catlg. 15: 745 Tenn st, McKenzie Tn 38201.

McKINNEY, ELEANOR RUTH. b Comstock Neb 6 Ag 18. 5: Trenton State Col 35-39 (Hist, Eng) BS; UWis summer 44 (LS); Columbia 47-49 BS in LS; West Mich U 66-67 Ed S. 7: Libn Jr High Sch, Oaklyn NJ 39-41; Libn High Sch, Neptune NJ 41-46; Libn Nassau & Elmwood Elem Schs, E Orange NJ 46-49; Asst libn Columbia High Sch, S Orange, Maplewood NJ 49-54; Libn Montclair High Sch, Montclair NJ 54-56; Head Libn Hanover Park High Sch, Hanover NJ 56-66; Asst Prof West Mich U 67-. 8: Tchr Rutgers U Sch of Lib Serv, summers 64, 65; Tchr Newark State Col Lib Sci Ext, 64-65. 9: ALA-AASchL (Com on Second Sch Libs 65-71); NEA; NJLA (Exec Bd mem-at-large 3 yrs); NJSchLA (pres 56-58); MichSchLA. 10: Amer Yourh Foun Camp Leader; Chm NJ Sch Lib Assn Lib Devel Proj 60-62; Beta Phi Mu. 13: Yes. 14: Sch lib devel, lib educ, reading interests of yp, child serv in pub lib, sch lib admin. 15: 3226 Tamsin ave, Kalamazoo Mi 49001.

McKINNEY, GAYLE (NORMA). b Troy Ala 7 S 39. 5: Auburn U 57-60 (Eng, Educ) BS; Fla State U 60-62 (LS) MS; Emory 62-64 (Russian). 7: Ref libn Emory U Lib 62-66; Gen serv libn Ga Inst Tech Lib 66-. 8: Ref libn Montgomery Pub Lib, Montgomery Ala summer 61; Libn Lib/USA NY World's Fair (65). 09: GaLA; Metro Atlanta LA. 10: Phi Beta Mu; Ga Tech Lib Staff Assn. 14: Ref, interlib loan. 15: Ga Inst Tech Prince Gilbert Memorial Lib, Atlanta Ga 30332.

McKINNEY, JEAN BRABHAM. b Batesburg SC 29 S 14. 4: Walter Pennell McKinney. 5: Winthrop Col 36 (Eng) AB; UNC 39 (Dramatic Art) MA, 49 BSLS; NYU (CBS Radio wkshop) summer 46 Certif. 6: Fr. 7: Tchr Monetta High Sch, Monetta SC 36-37; Dramatic art tchr Batesburg Leesville Sch, Batesburg SC 39-40; Counselor Camp Saint Mary's, Ridgeland SC summer 40, 41; Asst dir USO NCCS, Columbia SC 42-44; Tchr Dentsville High Sch, Dentsville SC 41; Continuity writer Radio Station WIS, Columbia sc 44-48; Hd circ Richland Co Lib, Columbia SC 48-49; Child libn Enoch Pratt Pub Lib, baltimore 49-51; Libn Anderson Pub Lib, Anderson SC 51-54; Sch libn Anderson Dist Five, Anderson SC 59-. 9: SCLA; SCEA; AndersonCoEA; Anderson Dist 5 Sch Libns (chm 68-69). 10: AAUW; St Joseph's Women's Club; Internatl League of Child Poets. 13: Yes. 14: Child & yp. 15: 421 Central ave, Anderson SC 29621.

McKINNEY, MAE BELLE (SINGLETON). b Eubank Ky 12 Ja 19. 4: Edison B McKinney. 5: Berea Col 37-41 (Eng) AB; UKy summers 52-57 (Eng) MA, summers 59-63 MSLS. 6: Fr. 7: Navy gunsight calibrator Crosley Corp, Cincinnati 43-44; Lab inspector Formica Corp, Cincinnati 44-45; Eng tchr Waynesburg Sch, Waynesburg Ky 45-46; Elem tchr Ottenheim Grade Sch, Waynesburg Ky 48-49; Elem tchr Waynesburg Sch, Waynesburg Ky 49-51; Tchr-libn Mem High Sch, Waynesburg Ky 51-59; Libn Eubank High Sch Lib, Eubank Ky 62-63; Libn Mem High Sch Lib, Waynesburg Ky 59-62, 63-. 9: NEA; ALA; KyEA; KyLA; KyASchL. 10: Kappa Gamma. 14: Ref, bk sel, wk with child & yp. 15: Eubank Ky 402567.

McKINNEY, MARGOT ELIZABETH (SINGER). b Mannheim Germany 10 S 22. 5: Leipzig Lib Sch 44 Dipl Bibl. 6: Ger, Fr, Ital. 7: Circ asst German Pub Lib, Olmu2tz Czechoslovakia 44-45; Circ asst J V Brown Lib, Williamsport Penn 53-58; Research libn Glyco Chem, Williamsport Penn 59-62; Asst libn ref Green Mountain Col Lib 62-. 8: Instr Ger: Williamsport High Sch 52-53, Green Mountain Col 63-64, Fair Haven High Sch, Fair Haven Vt 65-66. 9: VtLA. 10: Creative Writers' Forum, Williamsport Penn; Poultney Hist Soc. 13: Yes. 14: Ref. 15: 38 Church st, Poultney Vt 05764.

McKINNON, HELEN J(ESSIE). b Kerrobert Sask Can 14 S 29. 5: USask 47-50 (Hist) BA; Toronto 50-51 BLS; McGill 65-66 MLS. 6: Fr. 7: Ref libn Pub Lib, Regina Sask 51-54; Ref libn Pub Lib, Saskatoon Sask 54-58; Ref libn Pub Lib, Calgary Alta 59-61, Head ref dept 61-65; Asst to libn UWaterloo Lib 66-68, Hd pub serv, Arts Lib 68-. 9: CanLA (com mem, coun Adult Serv Sect; coun Info Serv Sect); ALA; AltaLA (sec; chm Certif Coun); SaskLA (com mem); Inst Prof Libns Ont; Can Assn col & Univ Libs (treas); OntLA. 10: Univ Women's Club. 13: Yes. 14: Ref, admin. 15: 165 Neeve st, Guelph Ont Can.

McKINSTRY, ELIZABETH JEAN. b Glasgow Scotland 27 F 34. 5: UToronto 62-65 (Eng) BA, 66-67 BLS. 6: Fr, Ger. 7: Steno Surveying & Drawing Supply Co, Toronto 52-54; Accounting clk Canadian Broadcasting Corp, Toronto 54-61; Lib asst UToronto Lib 65-66, Libn 67-. 9: ALA; CanLA; Inst Profess Libns Ont. 10: Royal Ont Museum. 14: Bk sel, ref. 15: 69 Lorraine dr, Willowdale Ont Can.

McKIRDY, COLIN. b Cardiff, Wales 28 Ag 34. 4: Judith Gillette. 5: Harpur Col SUNY (Binghamton) 56-63 (Eng lit) AB; Syracuse 64-65 MLS. 7: Pfc USA, US, Ger 54-56; Time study engr Fairbanks Valve Co, Binghamton NY 60-62; Lib intern SUNY (Binghamton) 64-65; Acquis libn 65-66; Specialist data processing Harvard U 67-68, Act hd data processing dept 68-. 9: ALA. 14: Tech serv, data processing, lib admin. 15: Widener Lib Harvard Univ, Cambridge Ma 02138.

McKISSICK, MABEL F (RICE). b Union SC 12 Je 22. 4: Wallace T McKissick. 5: Knoxville Col 39-43 (Sociol) AB; Allen U 46-47, 47-48 (Prof ed); SC State Col summers 49, 50 (Lib serv); Columbia summers 52, 53, 54 (Curr & tchg, Youth ed) MA, summers 59-66 (Lib serv to child & Ya) MS. 6: Fr, Ger. 7: Soc study tchr Sims High sch, Union SC 43-48, Tchr & libn 48-54, Libn 54-68; Libn Bulkeley Jr High Sch, New london Conn 68-. 8: Participant in num wkshops & coms sponsored by S Car State Dept of Educ, Div of Lib Serv; Participant in several wkshops sponsored by the Lib Serv Dept of SC State Col; Supvg libn for practice libns from the Lib Serv Dept of SC State Col for several years; Mem of SC Lib Planning Com, Sch Lib Devel Proj sponsored by ALA; Served on numer State Visiting Com repres the State Com of So Assn of Sch & Cols; Mem A-V & Libns Com on a-v equipment & materials in the Union Co Sch 68-69 (Title III Proj). 9: ALA; -AASchL; NEA; SCLA; SEA; CEA; NLEA; Conn Sch LA (Standards Com 68-). 10: Delta Sigma Theta; PTA; Gayettes. 14: Sch libnship, admin, child & Ya serv. 15: 201 Hempstead st PO Box 1122, New London Ct 06320.

McKUSICK, ROSA A. b Heber Cal 12 N 06. 5: Whittier Col 24-28 (Sociol, Educ) AB; Columbia 28-29 (Sociol) MA; UCal(Berkeley) 41-42 (LS) Certif. 6: Fr. 7: Registrar & Dir of Admissions Whittier Col 29-31; Eng tchr Citrus High Sch, Azusa Cal 31-37; Libn in ref & catlg Berkeley Pub Lib, Berkeley Cal 42-48; Catlg libn Riverside City Col 51-67; Sr catlg libn Cal State Col (Fullerton) 67-. 9: ALA; CalLA; Cal Tchrs Assn; So Cal Tech Proc Gp; OrangeCoLA. 10: LWV; Sierra Club; NAACP; United world Federalists; AAUP; Assn Cal State Col Profs. 14: Catlg (ser). 15: 433 Melody lane, Placentia Ca 92670.

McLAIN, JUANITA JANE (BOHNSTEDT). b Zanesville Ohio 27 N 10. 4: Ralph E McLain. 5: Muskingum Col 31-35 (Eng, Ger) AB; Peabody 35-36 (Eng) MA; Columbia summer 40; UChicago summer 41; UNC 50, summers 51, 52 (LS). 6: Ger, Fr. 7: Interim tchr Meredith Col 50; Libn Needham Broughton High Sch, Raleigh 52-53; Libn Josephus Daniels Jr High Sch, Raleigh 54-. 9: ALA; NCEA; NCLA. 10: Sigma Kappa Phi; Raleigh Woman's Club; AAUW. 14: Sch libnship. 15: 3400 Lake Boone trail, Raleigh NC 27607.

McLAIN, SWAN (MARTIN). b Monroe Ga 14 Jl 12. 4: Dr Ernest Karl McLain. 5: UFla 37 (Eng, Educ) BAE; Peabody 42 BSLS; US Army Civil Affairs Sch 66. 06: Sp, Fr. 7: Tchr-libn Alachua Co Pub Schs, Gainesville Fla 29-41; Libn

Haines City Schs, Haines City Fla 41-43; Post libn US Army: Ft Barrancas Fla, Camp Croft SC, Welch Convalescent Hosp, Daytona Beach Fla, Ft McClellan Ala 43-47; Staff libn Hdqrs Third US Army, Ft McPherson Ga 47-51; Chief Libn, med libn VA Hosp, Forest Hills Div, Augusta Ga 51-63; Dir Marquat Mem Lib for Civil Affairs Research USA Civil Affairs Sch, Ft Gordon Ga 63-. 9: ALA; MedLA; SLA; SELA; GaLA; Central Savannah River Area Lib Assn (pres 65). 10: AAUW; Med Auxiliary, Richmond Co Med Soc; Augusta Country Club; Ft Gordon Officers Club. 11: Meritorious Service Award, Certificates of Achievement, Certificate for Twenty Years of Federal Civil Service. 12: Ed, US Army Civil Affairs Sch "Book Review Digest." 13: Yes. 14: Admin, med ref, civil affairs & civic action research, rare bks. 15: 748 Lancaster rd, Augusta Ga 30904.

McLANE, (KATHLEEN) ANN (BLAYNEY). b Nanaimo BC Can 1 Mr 38. 5: UBC 56-60 (Eng) BA; UWash 60-62 (LS, Eng) ML, 66 MA. 7: Libn I Seattle Pub Lib 62-63; Libn I & II UWash 63-67; Libn III Nat Lib, Ottowa Can 67-, Hd for docs sect. 9: ALA; CanLA. 10: UWash Sch Libnship Alumni Assn. 11: Woodrow Wilson Fellow, 60-61. 14: Ref, govt docs. 15: 1505 Lawson ave, West Vancouver BC Can.

McLANE, EUGENE GORDON. b Ortonville Minn 25 Mr 27. 4: Kathleen Riley. 5: UMinn 50-51 (LS) BS, 46-50 (Hist) BX. 7: Dir Martin Co Lib, Fairmont Minn 51-54; Dir Cadillac- wexford Lib, Cadillac Mich 54-55; Asst dir Minneapolis Pub Lib 55-56; Dir Fond du Lac Pub Lib, Fond du Lac Wis 56-. 9: ALA; WisLA; Fox River Valley LA. 10: Jr C of C; Rotary Internat. 14: Admin. 15: 32 Sheboygan st, Fond du Lac Wi 54935.

McLAREN, (HENRY) DUNCAN. b Toronto Can 29 O 39. 4: Ketha Clemons. 5: UToronto 57-60 9eng) BA, 67-68 BLS. 6: Fr. 7: Col traveler: McClelland & Stewart Ltd, Toronto 60-64, Collier-Macmillan (Can) Ltd, Toronto 64-65; Col sales mgr Pergamon of Can Ltd, Toronto 65-66, Gen mgr 67; Ref libn Ryerson Polytech Inst, Toronto 68-. 9: CanLA; ASIS. 14: Acquis, ref. 15: 43A Castle Frank rd, Toronto 5 Ont Can.

McLAREN, DOROTHY (NIX). b Olton Tex 15 S 20. 4: J Calvin McLaren. 5: W Tex State 40-42 (Educ) BA; UTex summers 48-50 (Educ) M Ed, summers 53-61 MLS. 7: Clerk typist US Govt, Kelly Air Field 42-44; Clerk- accountant Walker's Austex Chili Co, Austin Tex 44-46; Elem tchr Taylor Ind Sch Dist, Taylor Tex 46-50; Elem tchr Corpus Christi Ind Sch Dist, Corpus Christi Tex 50-54, Jr high libn 54-61; Libn W B Ray High sch, Corpus Christi Tex 61-67; Ref libn Del Mar Col 67-68, Asst libn & Coord pub serv 68-69. 9: ALA; NEA-DAVI; Tex State Tchrs Assn; TexLA; CBLA. 14: A-v (Materials Ctr Approach to Libnship). 15: Box 6267, Corpus Christi Tx 78411.

McLAREN, LYNNE ALBERTA (HIPSKIND). b S Bend Ind 11 D 42. 4: James Philip McLaren. 5: Moody Bible Inst 60-61; Bethel Col 61-64 (Eng) BA; West Mich U 65-66 (Libnship) MSL. 6: Fr. 7: Eng tchr & libn Union-North Pub Schs, Lakeville Ind 64-65; Libn: Squires Elem 65-66, Cassopolis High 66-68; Eng tchr Jefferson Jr High Sch, South bend Ind 68-. 14: Catlg. 15: RR 2, Decatur Mi 49045.

McLARTY, (MARY) ADELAIDE. b Memphis Tenn 3 Ag 25. 5: UNC 47 (Hist) AB, 49 (Hist) MA, 53 BS in LS. 6: Fr. 7: Tchr-libn The Shaw Sch, Shaw Miss 49-51; Ext libn Wilson Pub Lib, Wilson NC 53-57; Libn Onslow Co pub Lib, Jacksonville NC 57-67; Dir Davidson Co Pub Lib, Lexington NC 67-. 9: ALA; SELA; LPRC; NCLA. 10: NC Lit & Hist Assn; Onslow Hist Soc; Pilot Club; Bus & Profess Women; Onslow Co Hist Soc. 11: Commun Woman of the Year 64 (Jr C of C). 14: Pub rel, ref, hist. 15: P O Box 249, Lexington NC 27292.

McLAUGHLIN, BEULAH (GOODY). b Watertown SD 5 S 20. 4: Kenneth Floyd McLaughlin. 5: Burlington Jr Col 38-40 Diploma; State U Iowa 40-42 (Hist) BA; LSU 44-45 BS in LS; State U Iowa 48-50; UVa Ext 61. 6: Fr, Ger. 7: Elem & high sch libn Morris Pub Schs, Morris Minn 42-43; High sch libn Bessemer High Sch, Bessemer Mich 43-44; Ref asst LSU 44-45; Readers' adv DC Pub Lib 45-46; Asst libn Anne Arundel Co Lib, Annapolis Md 46-47; Head ser & res State U Iowa 48-50; Asst libn Leon Co Pub Lib, Tallahassee Fla 55-57; Elem sch libn Arlington Co Pub Sch, Arlington Va 61-68, High sch libn 68-. 8: Readers adv for Teen-agers for Main Lib, DC Pub Lib & at Anne Arundel Co Pub Lib. 9: ALA; VaEA; VaLA. 10: PTA. 13: Yes. 14: Ref, catlg, readers adv. 15: 871 N Madison st, Arlington Va 22205.

McLAUGHLIN, CECILE. b Kamsack Sask Can 8 D 12. 5: Col of St Benedict (St Joseph Minn) 29-33 (Hist) BA; State Tchrs Col (St Cloud Minn) 33-34 (Elem Educ); Col of St Catherine 41-42 BS in LS; UMinn (LS) MA. 6: Ger. 7: Tchr Pub Sch, White Earth Minn 34-36; Postal clerk, Eden Valley Minn 36-41; Libn High Sch, Pine City Minn 42-43; Libn High Sch, New Ulm Minn 43-. 9: NEA; MinnASchL; MinnEA. 10: AAUW. 15: 19 S Franklin st, New Ulm Mn 56073.

McLAUGHLIN, DONALD JOSEPH. b Newburgh NY 6 Ap 27. 4: Helen Hudson. 5: Fordham 47-51 (Psych) AB; Yeshiva 57-58 (Guidance) MS; LSU 63-64 MLS. 7: Company clerk (Pfc) US Army 44-47; Staff Brooklyn Pub Lib 64-66; Staff New Rochelle (NY) Pub Lib 67-. 14: Ref, rare bks, admin. 15: 254 M artine ave, White Plains NY 10601.

McLAUGHLIN, HILDA S. b Harda India 2 Ja 23. 5: N Tex State U 61 (LS) BA. 7: Libn Anson Jones Sch, Dallas 61-66; Libn Alex Sanger Sch, Dallas 66-. 9: ALA; NEA; TexLA; Tex State Tchrs Assn. 10: Alpha Lambda Sigma. 14: Child bks. 15: 6709 Avalon ave, Dallas Tx 75214.

McLAUGHLIN, JANET (SHAFFER). b Mercersburg Penn 23 Mr 25. 4: Robert L McLaughlin. 5: Penn State U 42-45 (Hist, Ger) BA; West Res 45-46 BS in LS. 6: Ger. 7: Asst ref libn Penn State 46-49; Asst libn Cleveland Electric Illuminating Co, Cleveland Ohio 49-50; Period libn Glassboro State Col 59-61; Libn Millburn High Sch, Millburn NJ 61-65; Soc sci libn New Trier High Sch-West, Northfield Ill 65-. 8: Lib adv Woodbury Friends Sch, Woodbury NJ 58-59. 9: IllEA; IllLA. 10: Mich Shores Club; Wilmette-Kenilworth Club; Phi Beta Kappa; Pi Gamma Mu. 14: High sch. 15: 2333 Schiller ave, Wilmette Il 60091.

McLAUGHLIN, RUTH AGNES. b Clarks Hill Ind 16 Je 12. 5: St Mary's (Ind) 30-34 (Bus) AB; Butler U 38 & 43; Purdue U 41 & 62; Ind U 47 & 48 (LS) MS; UDenver 63. 6: Sp. 7: Bus tchr High Sch, Clarks Hill Ind 34-35; Sec L S Ayres Dept Store, Indianapolis 35; Bus tchr High Sch, Oaklandon Ind 36-41; Bus tchr High Sch, Pendleton Ind 41-43; Sec US Govt, Ft Harrison Ind summer 41; Libn High Sch, Lebanon Ind 43-. 8: Libn, US Dependents Schs, Kaiserslautern Germany 60-62. 9: Ind Sch Libns (v-pres & sec). 10: Jr Welfare League; Red Cross. 13: Yes. 14: Reading interests of yp. 15: 216 E North st, Lebanon In 46052.

McLAUGHLIN, TERRY LEE. b Martins Ferry Ohio 3 Mr 37. 4: Doris Bryson. 5: Ohio U 55-57 (Bus); Ohio State 57-64 (Ed) BSEd; Kent State 65-69 (LS). 7: Lib asst Ohio State u 9columbus) 57-59; Tchr: Fredericktown Schs, Fredericktown Ohio 60-61, Warren consolidated Schs, Tiltorsville Ohio 61-63, Mayfield Hts Schs, Mayfield Hts Ohio 63-66, mentor Pub Schs, Mentor Ohio 66-67; Tchr & libn Brown Local Schs, Malvern Ohio 67-68; Asst ext hd Canton Pub Lib, Canton Ohio 69-. 9: ALA; OhioLA; OhioEA. 14: Admin, ya. 15: RD 1, Mineral City Oh 44656.

McLAURY, HELEN C. b Harpersfield NY 9 Ja 08. 5: West Mich Col 25-29 (Educ) AB; Columbia 32-33 (LS) BS; Northwestern 48-53 (Law) JD. 7: Catlgr, supv ser sect Princeton U Lib 36-48; Head catlgr Law Sch North western U 48-53; Libn & Asst Prof Law Sch Mont State U 53-55; Ref libn Law Sch Northwestern U 48-53; Libn & Asst Prof Law Sch Mont State U 53-55; Ref libn Law Sch UCLA 55-57; Asst libn Tax Court of the US, Wash DC 57-63, Libn 64-. 9: AALL; Law Libns Soc Wash DC. 12: "List of Subject Headings for Small to Medium Sized Law Libraries" (56). 15: Rm 2112 Int Rev bldg, Wash DC 20044.

McLEAN, AUSTIN JERSEY. b Lansing Mich 10 O 30. 4: Susan H Hunter. 5: Mich State U 48-52 (Eng) BA; UMich 58-59 MALS. 7: 1st Lt Communications USMC Res 52-55; High sch Eng tchr Hillsdale Commun Schs, Hillsdale Mich 57-58; Asst ref libn Chicago Pub Lib 59-60; Asst humanities libn Mich StateU (E Lansing) 60-62; Humanities libn Colo StateU, Ft Collins Colo 62-66; Chief of spec collections UMinn (Minneapolis) 66-. 9: ALA; MinnLA. 14: Rare bks. 15: Spec Collections Dept Univ of Minn Libs, Minneapolis Mn 55455.

McLEAN, HARRIETTE GILBERT. b Spokane Wash 9 Ja 08. 4: Allan G McLean. 5: Simmons 25-29 (LS) BS. 6: Fr. 7: Libn Libby Jr High Sch, SpokaneWash 29-31; Lib asst Seattle Pub Lib 31-32, 49-57, Sub asst 58-67, Admin asst for personnel 67-. 9: ALA; WashLA; PNLA. 15: 3520 28th ave W, Seattle Wa 98199.

McLEAN, MARGUERITE ESTHER. b Creelman Sask Can 15 F 16. 5: Prov Normal Sch(Calgary Alta) 35-36 (Educ) Certif 1st class; Pratt 46 (LS) Certif; UWash 67 BA; UWash 68-. 7:

Tchr prov schs, rural Alberta Can 36-41; Tchr Calgary(Alta) Sch Bd 41-45; Asst br libn Calgary Pub Lib, Calgary Alta 41-45; Asst ref libn Pratt Inst Lib 46-47; Bus libn New World Life Insurance Co, Seattle 47-56; Asst ref libn Seattle Pub Lib 57; Tech libn US Navy Bur of Yards & Docks, Seattle 57-66; Assoc in libnship UWash Sch of Libnship 67-. 8: SLA consul for spec libs in Seattle area 61-. 9: SLA (Admiss Com 63-66); Puget Sound Chap: pres 57-58, var offs in Insurance Div 48-56); PNLA; AALS. 11: Employee of Year Award Seattle Fed Bus Assn, 62; US Navy Sup Accomp Award 60. 12: "Northwest Log" (60-61). 13: Yes. 14: Ref, spec libs organiz & mgt. 15: 1617 Yale ave, Apt 203, Seattle Wa 98101.

McLEAN, MARILYN T. b Brookline Mass 8 My 41. 5: Simmons MS in LS; Stonehill Col 59-63 9bio) BS. 7: Research asst biochem Harvard U 63-65; Ref & catlg libn Raytheon Co wayland Lab, Wayland Mass 66-68; Libn Raytheon Co Spencer Lab, Burlington Mass 68-. 9: SLA. 15: 245 Walnut st, Braintree Ma 02184.

McLEMORE, ANDREW JACKSON. b Memphis Tenn 6 Fe 32. 4: Willie Scott. 5: Morehouse Col 50-54 (Econ) AB; Atlanta U 57-60 MS in LS. 6: Fr. 7: Lobn & spec serv Atlanta U, Atlanta Ga 58-62; Libn Miles Col 62-66; Libn Savannah State Col 66-. 8: Chm "Faculty Research Bulletin" Savannah State Col. 9: ALA; SELA; GaLA. 10: Savannah Commun leadership Sem; Alpha Phi Alpha. 14: Mgt ref. 15: 3118 Gilbert st, Thunderbolt Ga 31404.

McLENDON, ETHEL (LOUISE MATTHEWS). b St Augustine Fla 7 O 16. 4: Lewis McLendon. 5: Peabody 35-39 (Phys Educ) BS; Fla State U 55 (LS) MA. 6: Sp. 7: Phys educ tchr high schs, Fla & Ala; Libn Crestview High Sch, Crestview Fla 51-55; Visiting prof Lib Sci Albany(NY) State Col summer 58; Visiting Prof Lib Sci Jacksonville U 59; Visiting Prof Lib Sci UOkla summers 59-60; Libn Paxon & Kirby-Smith Jr High Schs, Duval Co Fla 55-60; Head Libn Duval Co Bd Pub Instr, Jacksonville Fla 60-64; Asst Prof Lib Sci UFla 65-. 9: ALA; FlaLA; FlaASchL (sec 63-64); FlaEA; Fla A-V Assn. 10: Arlington Lioness; Red Cross Alpha Delta Kappa; Beta Phi Mu. 14: Sch libs. 15: 5836 Oliver st, Jacksonville Fl 32211.

McLEOD, CECIL RODERIC. b Maymont Sask Can 26 F 18. 5: Jamestown Col 35-37 (Educ) Tchrs Certif; W Wash summers 38-41; UCLA 46-47 (Hist) BA; West Res 48-49 MSLS; UMich 60-64 (Hist) MA. 7: Tchr, Lankin ND 37-38; Tchr, Loma ND 38-42; 70th Gen Hosp N Africa, Italy 42-45; Ref asst West Res U 48-49; Ref asst Fla State U 49-52; Ref asst Detroit Pub Lib 52-55; Ser libn NC State, Raleigh NC 55-56; Acquis libn East Mich U 55-, Bk & Card process 68-. 12: "Directory of Secondary Schools in Michigan" (54). 14: Acquis. 15: 111 N Normal, Ypsilanti Mi 48197.

McLEOD, DOROTHY (LAMB). b Sulphur Springs Tex 18 Ja 20. 4: David C McLeod Jr. 5: Texas Tech Col 37-40 (Bus Ad); Texas Woman'sU 40-42 BA in LS. 7: Tchr-libn Shamrock (Tex) Pub Sch, 42-45; Libn Magnolia Petroleum Co, Beaumont Tex 45-51; Libn Rust Engineering Co, Birmingham Ala 57-. 9: SLA. 15: 921 Beech lane, Birmingham Al 35213.

McLEVIGE, ANNA ELIZABETH (NORDLIE). b Rice Lake Wis 16 Ap 10. 4: John McLevige. 5: Concordia Col (Moorhead Minn) 28-32 (Lat) BA; UWis 35-36 (LS) Diploma. 7: Catlgr La Crosse Pub Lib, La Crosse Wis 38-41; Catlgr Ann Arbor Pub Lib, Ann Arbor Mich 41-45; Libn Hamilton Jr High Sch, Rockford Ill 62-. 9: NEA; IllEA. 15: 715 Harlem rd, Rockford Ill 61111.

McMAHON, ELIZABETH VONDELLE (OSBORNE). b Summitt Ga 16 Ag 07. 5: UGa 27-28 (Speech) Diploma; Fla So Col 35-36 (Eng) BSE; UFla 37 Auburn 52. 6: Fr, Ger. 7: Speech tchr Norman Jr Col, Norman Park Ga; Supv pub sch mus Brandon Elem & High Sch, Brandon Fla; Govt recreational dir, European Theater 42-52; Tchr world geog Jr High Sch, Moorestown NJ 52-53; Tchr Amer dependent schs, Straubing Ger 57-58; Tchr, Junction City Kan 58-59; Libn & tchr Polk Co Kingford Sch, Mulberry Fla 59-. 9: NEA-DAVI; ALA; FlaASchL (chm Area 9); Fla A-V Assn (past dir, Memb Chm); FlaEA; PolkCoEA; PolkCoLA (pres 66-68); PolkCoSchLA (2nd v-pres 68-70). 10: Coord Coun of Women's Orgs; Lakeland Bus & Profess women's Club. 11: Key to the City of Lakeland for Civic work. 14: Material ctr for elem schs. 15: 415 Garden dr, Lakeland Fl 33803.

McMAHON, HELEN (MARIE). b Norristown Penn 14 Ja 44. 5: Cabrini Col 62-63; Villanova 62-65; Chestnut Hill Col 65-67 (Bio) BS; Drexel 67-68 MSLS. 7: Tchr Holy Saviour sch, Norristown Penn 63-65; Lib asst Norristown Pub Lib, Norristown Penn 66-67; Libn Reg Resources Spec Educ, King of Prussia Penn 68-. 9: SLA. 14: Catlg, indexing. 15: 325 W 11th ave, Conshohochen Pa 19428.

McMAHON, LUCILLE M (KEATING). b Wellesley Mass 7 Ap 10. 4: John P McMahon. 5: Wellesley 26-30 (Math) BA; Columbia 35-40 (LS) BS. 7: Asst Wellesley Col Lib 30-41; Ref libn Wellesley Free Lib, Wellesley Mass 63-. 14: Ref, govt docs. 15: 98 Oak st, Wellesley Ma 02181.

McMAHON, ROSEMARY. b Kenton Ohio 12 Je 31. 5: Ohio No U 49-50 (Elem Educ); Col of St Mary of the Springs 51-52 (Elem Educ); UDayton summer 61 (Elem Educ); Col of St Mary of the Springs even 56-62 (Elem Educ, LS) BS in Elem Educ; Ohio Dominican Col 69. 06: Fr. 7: Receptionist & PBX operator San Antonio Hosp, Kenton Ohio 53-55; Receptionist & PBX operator Catholic Welfare Bur, Columbus Ohio 55-61; Tchr St Augustine Sch, Columbus Ohio 61-62; Catlgr State Lib of Ohio 62-. 9: ALA; CathLA; OhioLA; OhioASchL. 10: Gypsies Club. 14: Catlg. 15: 1407 Doten ave, Columbus Oh 43212.

McMANIS, DOROTHY VIRGINIA. b Palo Alto Cal 11 Ap 02. 5: UCal(Berkeley) 22-26 (Econ) AB, 26-27 (LS) Certif. 7: Child libn UCLA 27-29, Circ asst 29-35, Acquis asst 35-47; Acquis libn US Navy Electronics Lab, San Diego 47-. 9: SLA. 14: Acquis, period. 15: 3502 Tennyson st, San Diego Ca 92106.

McMANUS, HELEN (OLIVA). b NYC 15 F 11. 4: Aloysius McManus. 5: Trinity Col 28-32 (Eng, Lat) BA; Columbia 32-33 (Lat) MA, 37-38, BS in LS. 7: Libn NY Pub Lib 38-43; Catlgr Bergen Jr Col 50-51; Asst libn Fort Lee Free Pub Lib 59-65 Dir 65. 9: ALA; NJLA. 14: Ref. 15: 2022 Center ave, Fort Lee NJ 07024.

McMARTIN, RUTH (CROSSMAN). b Lansing Mich 12 Je 15. 4: Wallace McMartin. 5: Mich State Col 32-36 (Fr) AB; UIll 36-38 BS in LS, 38-40 MS in LS; West Mich U summer 68 Instrl Media Wkshop. 06: Fr. 7: Catlgr, head of separates' sect UTex Lib 40-43; Elem tchr Coldwater Pub Schs, Coldwater Ohio 54-55; High sch libn Celina Sr High Sch, Celina Ohio 55-66; Dir of instrl resources Fargo Pub Schs, Fargo ND 66-. 09: ALA; -AASchL; NEA; NDEA; NDLA; MPLA. 10: Delta Kappa Gamma; Soroptomist; LWV. 14: Catlg, admin. 15: 2431 S 9th st, Fargo ND 58102.

McMASTER, FLORENCE RIMAN. b Chicago 6 Jl 16. 5: UToledo 33-37 (Hist) PhB; UIll 39-44 BS in LS; Ind U 56-61 LLB. 6: Fr. 7: Asst to libn UToledo 37-43; Asst documents div UIll(Urbana) 43-44, Asst law libn 44-46; Law Libn Ind U 46-. 8: Co-chm, Inst on Channels of Communication for Spec Libs (sponsored by SLA Ind Chapt) 60; Adv Com, Com to Study Lib Needs of the State(Ind) 65-66. 9: SLA (Adv Coun 57-58; Ind Chap: several offs 48-49 & 56-59 & 61-62, chm 3 coms 50-51 & 62-65); AALL (mem of many coms); Chicago ALL (Exec Bd 56-57). 10: Coun on World Affairs; Amer Bar Assn; Ind Women Lawyers Assn; Ind State Bar Assn; Amer Judic Soc. 14: Law lib admin, ref, catlg. 15: 102 W Mich st, Indianapolis In 46204.

McMEEN, FRANCES ELISABETH. b Lewistown Penn 9 Ja 43. 5: Penn State U 61-64 (Hist) BA; UPittsburgh 64-65 MLS. 6: Fr, Sp, Lat. 7: Staff Enoch Pratt Free Lib, Baltimore 65-67; Program asst Intl Studs & World Affairs SUNY (Oyster Bay) 67-68; Asst libn Carnegie Endowment for Intl Peace (NYC) 68-. 9: ALA. 10: Beta Phi Mu. 14: Ref, collection bldg, admin. 15: 788 Columbus ave, New York NY 10025.

McMICHAEL, JANET G. b Montreal 7 Ag 41. 5: McGill 58-62 BA, 62-63 BLS, 66-68 MLS. 06: Fr. 7: Asst catlgr Med lib McGill U 63-64, Chief catlgr 64-66, Hd pub serv 67-. 9: CanLA; MedLA; SLA. 14: Catlg. 15: Med Lib McGill Univ, Montreal Can.

McMILLAN, ADELLE JEANNE (MEHAFFEY). b Urbana Ill 18 O 45. 4: Kenneth C McMillan. 5: UIll (Urbana) 63-67 (Eng) BA, 67-68 (LS) MS. 6: Fr. 7: Clerk/page Urbana Free Lib, Urbana Ill 62-68; Hd libn Flossmoor Pub Lib, Flossmoor Ill 68-. 9: ALA; IllLA; Lib Adminrs No Ill; So Suburban Libns Assn. 15: 2801 School st, Flossmoor Il 60422.

McMILLAN, MARGARET. b Eaglegrove Iowa. 5: Central Mo State Col (Hist) BS; UNeuchatel (Switzerland) (Internat Law); UMo (Hist) MA. 6: Sp, Ger. 7: Tchr Christian Col, Dir of Lib; Ref libn State Hist Soc of Mo, Columb ia Mo; Ref dept Mid Continent Pub Lib Serv, Independence Mo. 9: ALA; MoStateLA. 10: Mary Paxton Study Club; Womens City Club; Pi Lambda Theta; Delta Kappa Gamma; Alpha Pi Zeta. 13: Yes. 14: Ref. 15: 2525 Lees Summit rd, Independence Mo 64050.

McMILLAN, PATRICIA ANN. b Kendallville Ind 1 Ja 40. 5: Butler 58-60 (Elem ed); Ind U 60-62 (Elem ed) BS; UDenver 63-65 MLS. 7: Libn I UNotre Dame Ind 63-66; Ref libn Wisc State U (Eau Claire) 66-67; Libn I St Paul Pub Lib 67-68; Asst ref libn No Ill U 68-. 9: ALA. 14: Ref. 15: 805 Emerson ave, S Bend In 46615.

McMILLEN, CAROLYN J. b Newark Ohio 16 Ag 27. 5: Western Col for Women 45-49 (Span) BA; UMich 55-57 MALS. 6: Sp, Ger, Ital, Portu. 7: Sec Vapo Gas Co, Leesburg Fla 49-50; Asst manager Mid-Florida Gas Co, Leesburg Fla 51-54; Asst libn Leesburg Pub Lib, Leesburg Fla 54-55; Lib serv fellowship UMich 55-57, Catlg libn 57-62; Asst catlg libn Colo State U 62-65; Ser libn Mich State U 65-66; Hd catlg dept 68-. 9: ALA; MichLA. 10: Beta Phi Mu; Bus & Prof Women's Club; Mich State U Fac Club; AAUW. 14: Ser, coop catlg, clsf, admin. 15: 750 Pine Forest dr, E Lansing Mi 48823.

McMULLAN, THEODORE NEWTON. b Jackson Miss 25 Je 08. 4: Hortense Corynne Shearer. 5: LSU 27-31 (Electric Engnr) BS, 31-32 (Physics, Engnr) MS, 33-34 (LS) BS. 7: Head circ dept LSU 34-41; Lt Col Gen Hdqrs AFPAC 41-45; LSU: Head circ dept 45-55, Act dir of libs 55-56, Assoc dir of libs 56-61, Dir of Libs 61-. 8: Lib bldg consul several La cols 56-65; Consul on univ libs, US Dept of Health Educ & Welfare; Assisted in evaluating applications: Ind U, Northwestern, UMinn, NYU, Stevens, Yale Law Sch (For & Internat Law Lib Annex), UWis & others. 9: ALA; SWLA; SELA; LaLA. 10: Baton Rouge Lib Club; Kiwanis Club; Key Club wk (sponsored by Kiwanis Club); Pres of Honor Court, Boy Scouts. 13: Yes. 14: Admin. 15: 544 Magnolia Woods, Baton Rouge La 70808.

McMULLEN, (CHARLES) HAYNES. b Tarkio Mo 3 Mr 15. 5: Centre Col 31-35 (Fr) AB; UIll 35-36 BS in LS, 36-40 (LS) MS; UChicago 43-45, 49 (LS) PhD. 6: Fr. 7: Ref asst UIll Lib (Urbana) 36-41; Libn West State Col (Gunnison Colo) 41-43; Libn & Prof of Lib Sci Madison Col 45-51; Assoc Prof of Lib Sci Ind U 51-58, Prof of Lib Sci 58-. 8: Consul, Lib Inst of Pub Admin, Thammasat U, Bangkok Thailand 61; Ind Lib Certif Bd, 55-63. 09; ALA; -LED (dir 65-68); AALS; IndLA. 10: Beta Phi Mu; AAUP. 13: Yes. 14: Lib educ, hist of Amer libs. 15: 617 S Fess ave, Bloomington In 47403.

McMULLEN, ELIZABETH. b Okla City Okla 14 S 14. 5: Park Col 32-36 (Math) BA; Okla City U summers 36, 37 (Educ Music); Columbia summers 39-41 (Tchg of Math) MA; Fla State U 63 (LS); Rutgers 63-64 MLS. 6: Fr. 07: Dir Manville Pub Lib, Manville NJ 64-65; Dir St Peters Gen Hosp Sch of Nursing Lib 64-66, Hosp libn St Peter's Hosp, New Brunswick NJ 67-. 9: MedLA; NJLA. 14: Med libnship, admin. 15: St Peters Hosp Sch of Nursing, New Brunswick NJ 08903.

McMULLEN, JOHN OSB (WILLIAM DAVID). b Washington Ind 13 My 40. 5: St Meinrad Col 58-60 (Philos); Blue Cloud Abbey Sem 60-63 (Philos) BA, 63-65 (Theol); UMinn 64-66 (LS); St Bede Abbey Sem 65-67 (Theol, Priesthood); Catholic U 67-69 MS in LS. 7: Stud asst Central Catholic High Sch, Vincennes Ind 54-55; Asst libn Blue Cloud Abbey, Marvin SD 60-66, Hd libn 66-, Catholic priest (Benedictine) 66-. 9: ALA; CathLA; SLA; SDLA. 10: Assn Amer Indian Affairs; Amer Benedictine Acad; Amer Soc for Ethnohist; Amer Soc Indexers. 14: Catlg, indexing, ref (Amer Indians, Benedictine) rel life). 15: Blue Cloud Abbey, Marvin SD 57251.

McNABB, CHARLES A. b Joliet Ill 23 Mr 04. 4: Ruth Sawyer. 5: Chicago 22-27 (Law, Econ) PhB, 28 (Law) JD, 46 BLS. 7: Lawyer, Chicago 29-37; Ref libn UChicago Law Lib 37-40; Catlg ed Union Law Catalog, Chicago 40-64; Exec Libn Chicago Bar Assn 43-64; Libn Appellate Division Law Lib, Rochester NY 64-. 9: Amer Bar Assn; AALL (chm &/or mem 3 coms); Chicago Bar Assn; ChicagoALL (pres 50, chm var coms); Assn Law Libs Upstate NY pres 66). 10: Delta Theta Phi. 13: Yes. 14: Catlg, clsf, admin. 15: 525 Hall of Justice, Civic Center Plaza, Rochester NY 14614.

McNABB, EDITH (METHAM). b Nellie Ohio 12 Ag 1893. 4: LeRoy C McNabb. 5: Ohio U 11-12 (Educ); Muskingum Col 12-15 (Math) BA; Ohio Wesleyan 23-24 (Speech) MA. 6: Gk, Lat. 7: High sch tchr Ohio 15-23; Instr in speech (Ohio Wesleyan) 23-25, Asst Prof 25-28; Asst Prof speech Millikin U 36-48, Assoc Prof 48-63; Hd of commun info Decatur Pub Lib, Decatur Ill 63-66; Hd of Communications Rolling Prairie Libs Syst, Decatur Ill 66-. 8: Produced Col Credit telecourses on commercial TV sta for 8 yrs. 9: ALA (Friends Com 4 yrs); IllLA (Pub Rel Com 2 yrs; Nat Lib Week Com). 10: AAUW; AAUP; Altrusa Club; Delta Kappa Gamma; LWV; Phi Kappa Phi. 13: Yes. 14: Use of radio, t-v films, art reproductions, records as part of lib serv. 15: 746 W Harrison, Decatur Il 62526.

McNABB, KATHERINE C. b Wewoka Okla 14 Jl 04. 5: Hood Col 24-27 (Eng) AB; Columbia 29-30 (LS) BS. 7: Catlgr Queensborough Pub Lib, NY 30-31; 1st asst catlg dept Kan City(Mo) Pub Lib 31-44, Chief catlg dept 45-47; Head catlg dept UCal(Santa Barbara) 47-59, Asst U Libn 59-68, Assoc U libn 68-. 9: ALA; CalLA (sec Col, Univ & Res Libs Sect 49-50); SoCal Tech Processes Group (chm 63-64). 10: Cal State Employees Assn; Altrusa. 14: Acquis, processing, personnel. 15: 3647 Sunset dr, Santa Barbara Ca 93105.

McNAIR, JEANENE (ALICE) (ZIEGLER). b Findlay Ohio 15 Mr 42. 4: Donald Howard McNair. 5: USFla 60-63 (Pol Sci) BA; Ind U 64-65 (LS) MA. 7: Asst catlgr USFla 65-. 9: SLA (Map Div); ALA; FlaLA. 14: Catlg (ser & maps). 15: Rte 1 Box 22JH, Thonotosassa Fl 33592.

McNAIR, JAMES. b Fordyce Ark 24 Je 29. 4: Lizzie Eads. 5: Tuskegee Inst 53 (Elem ed) BS, 53-55 (Ed admin) MEd; UDenver summers 56-58 (Libnship). 7: Tchr & libn Jeffersonville High Sch, Jeffersonville Ga 54-55; Ser libn Prairie View A&M Col 55-56; Br libn Gary Pub Lib, Gary Ind 58-61; Tchr Gary Pub Schs, Gary Ind 61-64, Libn Gary Pub Schs, Gary Ind 64-. 9: ALA-AASchL; NEA; IndLA; IndStateTA. 14: Child serv, ref serv. 15: 2084 Roosevelt st, Gary In 46404.

McNAIR, MARIAN (BOYCE). b Batavia NY 15 Ap 23. 4: Robert John McNair. 5: SUNY(Fredonia) 41-45 (Elem Educ) B Ed; UBuffalo 47-53 (Elem Sch Admin) M Ed; SUNY(Geneseo) 57-62 MLS. 6: Fr. 7: Elem sch tchr, Niagara Falls NY 45-53; Elem sch tchr, Madison Wis 53-56; Elem sch libn, Niagara Falls NY 56-59; Libn Westwood First Presbyterian Church, Cincinnati 63-66; Supv libn Cincinnati Pub Schs, Cincinnati 66-. 8: Co-op tchr UWis 54-56; Organ Lower Sch Lib, Col Prep Sch, Cincinnati; Tchr Lib Sci: Miami U 67, UCincinnati 68. 09: ALA; OhioLA; OhioASchL (Elem Sch Lib Com). 10: Women's com Cincinnati Symphony Orchestra; Friends of the Pub Lib, Cincinnati. 14: Child bks, lit, media ctrs. 15: 5624 Hickory Ridge lane, Cincinnati Oh 45239.

McNALLY, SISTER MARY ELIZABETH SND. b Boston Mass 31 My 08. 5: Emmanuel Col 27-31 (Latin & Hist) AB; VillanovaU 50-55 (summer session) MS in LS; MarquetteU 65-70 9speech). 6: Fr, Ger. 7: Sch libn Acad of Notre Dame, Villanova Penn 44-65; Sch libn Acad of Notre Dame, Villano libn Acad of Notre Dame, Villanova Penn 44-65; Sch libn Holy Trinity High Sch, Glen Burnie Md 65-66; Sch libn Martin Spalding High Sch, Severn Md 66-67; Readers serv & acquis MarquetteU (summer) 68, 69; Acquis libn Trinity Col (Wash DC) 67-. 9: ALA; CathLA; DCLA. 15: Trinity College Michigan ave, Wash DC 20017.

McNALLY, MIRIAM E. b Edgar Neb 5 Ag 06. 5: Grinnell Col 25-27, 28-30 (Eng) BA; UDenver 42 BS in LS. 7: Ed & manager Herald Printing Co, Marshalltown Iowa 27-28; Sec to adv, legal educ & admissions to bar Amer Bar Assn, Denver 31-35; Asst exec sec Adult Educ Coun of Denver 35-40; Dir of pub rel & lib publs Denver Pub Lib 41-52; Ed & publ pub rel planner (Lib Serv Info), Denver 52-. 8: Consul: Lib Interpretation Nev State Lib 58; Trustees Wkshops NM State Lib 58, 60, 62; Wkshop on Lib Interpretation Mont State Lib 60; Lib Info Neb Pub Lib Commsn 59. 9: MPLA (chm Intel Freedom Com 49-50); ALA-ASD (chm Com on Guides to Adult Educ Lit 62-63);-ALTA (Action Development Com 60-64, Pub Rel Com 44-45, 53-54);-LAD (Pub Rel Sect, Exec Bd 62-64); ColoLA (Publ Chm 45). 10: Adult Educ Coun Metro Denver; Phi Beta Kappa; Theta Sigma Phi; Mortar Board. 11: Freedoms Foun George Washington Honor Medal Award for Lib Info Serv 64. 12: "Bibliographical Center for Research, Rocky Mountain Region" (44); "The Library Image: a Manual of Library Interpretation" (60); Ed "News Letter," Adult Educ Coun of Denver (35-36); Ed "Educ Opportunities in Denver" (37-40); Ed "MPL Quarterly" (56-60). 13: Yes. 14: Lib serv info & interpretation. 15: PO Box 9132 S Denver sta, Denver Co 80209.

McNALLY, PETER F. b Tillsonburg Ont Can 21 D 41. 5: UWest Ontario 60-64 (Hist) BA; McGill 64-65 BLS, 65-66 MLS. 6: Fr. 7: Ref dept McGill U 66-68, Acquis dept McLennan Lib 68-. 9: CanLA. 14: Ref, bk sel, coll bldg. 15: Acquis Dept, McLennan Lib, mcGill Univ, Montreal PQ Can.

McNALLY, RUTH (PANTRIDGE). b Passaic NJ 24 Je 19. 4: Richard McNally. 5: NYU 37-41 9eng) BA; Rutgers 66-69

MLS. 6: Fr. 7: Asst libn Simmons-Boardman Pub Co, NYC 47-51; Libn Mountainside Hosp Sch of Nursing, Montclair NJ 64-66; Libn Fairfield Pub Lib, Fairfield NJ 64-66; Youth libn E Orange Pub Lib Franklin Br, E Orange NJ 67-. 9: ALA; NJLA. 10: Phi Beta Kappa. 14: Ref, youth serv. 15: 77 Mountain ave, N Caldwell NJ 07006.

McNAMARA, BERNADETTE. b Albion Ont Can 29 O 06. 5: D'Youville Col 25-29 (Eng) BA (cum laude); UBuffalo 38-39 (Eng); Canisius Col 40-41 (Eng) MA; SUNY (Geneseo) 62-63 MLS; Permanent Certif in sch & pub libs for State of NY. 6: Fr, Lat. 7: Elem tchr, Buffalo NY 29-30; Fr, Lat, & Eng tchr St Joseph's Col High Sch, Emmitsburg Md 30-31, Head of Eng dept 31-32; Eng tchr Hamburg (NY) High Sch 32-34; Eng tchr Buffalo (NY) Pub High Sch system 34-62; Libn Bennett High Sch, Buffalo NY 62-. 9: NYLA (del Buffalo Tchrs Fed, Sch Libns Sect); NYStateTA; Buffalo Pub Sch LA. 10: Kenmore Bus & Prof Women's Club; Bennett Commun Assn. 15: 17 Moore ave, Kenmore NY 14223.

McNAMARA, EDWARD P. b Brooklyn NY 4 Jl 31. 4: Mary Ann Greeley. 5: Niagara U 49-55 (Classical Lang) BA; Columbia 55-58 (Eng); St John's U 59-61 MLS; Nassau Commun Col 63 (Fr); URennes(France) summer 63 Fr; Queensborough Commun Col 68-69 (Ger). 06: Ger, Fr, Lat. 7: US Navy (Personnel PO/3d Class), Newport RI 56-57; Eng tchr Chaminade High Sch, Mineola NY 58; Libn W Tresper Clarke High Sch, Westbury NY 59-. 8: Lib supv (even div) Nassau Commun Col 62-64; Adj Instr Dept Lib Sci, St John's U 66-67; Asst ref libn (part-time), Levittown (NY) Pub Lib. 9: ALA; NYLA; Nassau-Suffolk SchLA; CathLA. 10: Dept Lib Sci Alum Assn, St John's U 68-69. 14: Acquis, rare bks, ref, tchg. 15: 42-30 Douglaston pkwy, Douglaston NY 11363.

McNAMARA, ELISABETH ANN. b Brooklyn NY 20 Ag 46. 5: Webster Col 63-67 (Eng) BA; Columbia 67-68 (Eng) MA; Simmons 68-69 MSLS. 6: Fr, Lat. 7: Page Valhalla Pub Lib Sec-acct J A McNamara Atty CPA, Valhalla NY 63-; Sec clerk Edward Fiske Pub Rel, White Plains NY 62-63; Traffic clerk NY Telephone Co, White Plains NY summer 63-67; Circ desk asst Harvard Law Sch 67-. 14: Tech serv, ref. 15: 20 Pine rd, Valhalla NY 10595.

McNAMARA, HAZEL F(ULLER). b Cortland NY 7 S 26. 4: Dennis C McNamara. 5: SUNY(Geneseo) 44-48 (LS) BS, summers 49-53 MS in LS; SUNY(Cortland) summer 52 (Educ). 6: Fr. 7: Libn SUNY(New Paltz, Farmingdale) summers 54, 56; Libn Bd of Educ, Geneva NY summer 60; Libn Bd of Educ, Gorham NY 48-64; Lib consul for Ontario-Seneca-Yates BOÇES 68-. 8: Trustee, Gorham Free Lib 60-; Trustee, Ontario Co Lib Coop Bd 61-66; NCCW; Rochester Diocesan Chm of Lib & Lit 62-. 9: ALA; CathLA (Regina Awards Com 68-69); NYLA; NY Tchrs Assn (Chm Lib Sect of Central West Zone); Finger Lakes LA; Lib Trustees Foun of NY State. 10: Gorham Hist Soc; Yates Co Hist Soc; Ontario, Seneca-Yates Deanery; St Theresa's Rosary Soc; Home Ext Unit (sec 64-). 13: Yes. 14: Sch lib. 15: RD 1, Stanley NY 14561.

McNAMARA, HELEN M. b New Richmond Wis 7 Je 22. 5: River Falls State Col 39-48 (Educ) BS; Rosary Col 59-63 (LS) MS. 6: Fr. 7: Classrm tchr Berwyn Pub Schs, Berwyn Ill 44-63; Libn La Grange Dist 102, La grange Ill 63-. 9: ALA; NEA-DAVI; IllLA; IllEA; Ill Assn Col Tchrs; Ill A-V Assn. 10: Delta Kappa Gamma. 14: Ref, classrm instr. 15: 925 Chicago ave, Oak Park Il 60302.

McNAMEE, BERNARD (JOSEPH). b Kingston Ont Can 3 Ag 38. 5: UOttawa 56-60 B Com; Sir George Williams 61-63 BA; McGill U 67-69 MLS. 6: Fr. 7: Pub Rel Off Forster McGuire & Co, Montreal 60-61; Personnel Off Hudson Bay Co, Montreal 61-63; Supv Train Personnel Bell Can, Montreal 63-67; Dir Lib Ser Dawson Col, Montreal 69-. 9: CanLA; ALA; SLA; QueLA. 14: Admin. 15: 3335 Ridgewood ave apt 7, Montreal 247 Que Can.

McNAMEE, DONALD WEBSTER. b Los Angeles 21 My 34. 5: USoCal 52-56 (Zool) AB, 63-64 MSLS. 6: Lat, Gk, Ger, Russian. 7: Lab tech US Army Chem Corps, Dugway Utah (Pfc) 56-58; Med tech Scripps Clinic, La Jolla Cal 59-61; Med tech UCLA Med Center 61-63; Staff USoCal Lib 64-65; Staff Cal Inst of Tech Lib 65-. 9: ALA. 14: Catlg, rare bks. 15: 232 S St Andrews pl, Los Angeles Ca 90004.

McNAMEE, GILBERT W. b Harrisonburg Va 6 Ag 18. 5: George Washington U 48-53 (Hist) AB; USan Francisco 61-62 (LS, Ital); UCal 63-64 MLS. 6: Sp, Ital. 7: US Army Air Force Instr in Radio (M/Sgt) 41-45; Documents libn Air Coordinating Com, Wash DC 48-50; Internat Civil Aviation Libn, Wash DC 50-56; Admin asst Airport Use Panel, Wash DC 56-58; Libn San Francisco Pub Lib (var brs) 59-62, Libn circ dept 62-63, Bus libn 64-66, Hd doc dept 66-67, Asst dir Bay Area Ref Ctr 67-. 8: Participates in lib radio programs; Dir ref wkshops; Participates ref panels. 9: ALA; Cal LA (pres Ref Div 69-, Coun 69-); Bay Area Ref Libns. 10: Telegraph Hill Neighborhood Assn; Phi Beta Kappa; Cal Arts Soc. 13: Yes. 14: Ref. 15: 1315 Montgomery st, San Francisco Ca 94133.

McNEAL, ARCHIE LIDDELL. b Ruleville Miss 3 S 12. 5: Memphis State Col 28-32 (Math) BS; Peabody summers 34-36 BS in LS; Chicago 48-51 (LS) PhD. 7: Ref asst Cossitt Lib, Memphis Tenn 32-34; Libn Millington High Sch, Millington Tenn 34-36; Libn E Tenn State Col 36-43, 46-48; US Air Force (Communications) (1st Lt) 43-46; Chief readers serv div UTenn 48-52; Dir UMiami Lib 52-. 8: US State Dept Consul on Gen Educ, India 57; Tchg: Columbia Sch Lib Serv 64, Fla State U 54, 55, 57, UNC 59, 61. 9: ALA (Coun 55-65, Exec Bd 61-65, 68-69, 2nd v-pres 68-69, chm Com on Intel Freedom 59-64); -LAD (pres 60-61); -ACRL (pres 64-65); TennLA (pres 40-42); FlaLA (pres 58); SELA (pres 64-66). 12: "Rural Reading Interest: Needs Relating to Availability" (51). 13: Yes. 14: Univ lib admin. 15: Univ of Miami Lib, Coral Gables Fl 33124.

McNEE, JOHN C. b Blairsburg Iowa 20 Ag 25. 4: Dorothy Law. 5: Cornell Col 46-49 (Hist) AB; UMich 50-51 AMLS; Iow State U 59-60 (Econ Hist) MS. 6: Fr, Ger. 7: Staff Sgt US Army, US & Germany 43-46; Order dept asst Cornell Col 49-50; Order dept asst UMich 50-51; Iowa State U: Ref asst 51-53, Circ libn 53-56, Head circ dept 57-. 8: Faculty Adv to Ward System, Iowa State U 58-60; Consul Hertzberg New Method bindery, Jacksonville Ill 62-66, Marshalltown Iowa Commun Col, N Central Assn High Sch Eval at Lemars, Audubon, Mason City & Des Moines Iowa 66-69; Pres J D Assocs. 9: ALA (chm for Iowa Recr Com 65-66, Iowa Chm 64-); IowaLA (chm Univ & Col Div 65-66, chm Pub Serv Div 65). 10: Lions Club; AAUP; Iowa State U Fac Coun. 13: Yes. 14: Pub rel, soc & phys scis bibliogs, admin. 15: 3511 Oakland, Ames Ia 50010.

McNEESE, MERLE (ELKINS). b Medicine Mound Tex 15 Ap 16. 4: Charles Howard McNeese. 5: N Tex Agric Col 33-35; Tex Christian U 35-37 (Eng) BA; N Tex State U 47-50 BS in LS, 66 MLS. 06: Fr. 7: Libn Ft Worth (Tex) Ind Sch Dist, Stripling Jr High Sch 47-51; Libn Hurst-Euless-Bedford (Tex) Ind Sch, Hurst Jr High Sch 60-. 9: NEA; TexLA. 10: Delta Kappa Gamma. 14: Child lit. 15: 805 Cardinal Cr, Bedford Tx 76053.

McNEIL, DON WILLIAM. b Ames Iowa 18 Jl 29. 4: Joanne Cockrell Ralston. 5: Buena Vista Col 48-49, 55-57 (Hist) BA; UKy 57-59 MS of LS. 7: Clerk typist US Air Force, Eng 50-54; Lib Dir S Central Reg Lib, Glasgow Ky 59-61; Gifts exch & rare bks libn Berea Col Lib 61-62, Asst libn 62-63; Adult serv libn Kauai Pub Lib, Lihue Hawaii 63-66; Asst Prof of Lib Studies & Asst Lib Spec UHawaii Lib 66-68; Hd libn Leeward Commun Col (Pearl City Hawaii) 68-. 08: Developed a spec buyer-product file system for the Div of Purchases State of Ky summer 58; Consul UKy Radio Arts Dept 58-59. 9: ALA (Recr rep for Kauai Co Hawaii; Reg XII Memb Chm); SELA; HawaiiLA (dir 66-68); KyLA (chm Col & Ref Sect 63). 10: Kiwanis Club. 12: Ed "Hawaii Lib Assn Journal" (64-65). 13: Yes. 14: Admin, mgt, bk selection, pub serv. 15: 563 2 Kawaikui st, Honolulu Ha.

McNEIL, MARGUERITE R. b Somers Wis 18 My 22. 5: UWis 46-49 (Eng Lit) BA, 49-50 BLS. 7: Comptometer operator Simmons Co, Kenosha Wis 41-42, 45-46; WAVE US Navy 42-45; Libn Smith Col, Northampton Mass 50-52; Libn Pub Lib Cincinnati & Hamilton Co, Cincinnati 52-59; Libn Mun Ref Lib City of Cincinnati 59-66; Libn Wis State U (Whitewater) 66-. 9: WisLA. 10: UWis Alumni Assn; AAUW; Delta Kappa Gamma. 14: Catlg. 15: 201 N Esterly ave, Whitewater Wi 53190.

McNEILL, LESLIE GRAY. b Wilmington NC 26 Ag 41. 5: Duke 59-63 (Eng) AB; UNC 63-64 (LS) MS. 6: Sp. 7: Stud asst UNC Med Sch Lib(Chapel Hill) summer 64; Asst catlgr UGa Lib 64-. 9: ALA; GaLA. 14: Catlg. 15: Univ Ga Lib, Athens Ga 30601.

McNEILL, NOEL (JOHN THOMAS). b Lond Eng 18 D 39. 4: Deena Stephanic. 5: Full Gospel Inst 58-61 (Theol) GTH; Queen's U 65-69 (Eng) BA. 7: Minister Apostolic Ch, Haliburton Can 61-66; Libn Haliburton Secondary Sch 64-69; Libn Pub Lib, Haliburton 64-69. 8: Lib Com, Richmond Col, Toronto. 14: Pub serv. 15: Box 287, Haliburton Ont Can.

McNEIR, CORINNE (CRAWFORD). b Childress Tex 11 Ja 10. 4: Waldo F McNeir. 5: Rice Inst 26-30 (Arch, Eng) BA; N Tex State Col 41-42 (Educ) High Sch Certif Math; LSU 55-57 (LS) MS. 6: Fr, Ger. 7: Registrar, publ sec, act libn Museum of Fine Arts, Houston 30-35; Instr in art hist Ext Div & Sec in chg of exhibitions in Art Dept UNC(Chapel Hill) 35-40; Instr Math Leland Jr High Sch, Chevy Chase Md 42; Act curator Museum of Fine Arts, Houston 43-45; Instr Dept of Educ Art Inst of Chicago 46-49; Instr in Fine Arts LSU 49-56, Ref libn, Head ref libn 56-58, Head humanities libn 58-61; Documents libn UOre Lib 61-. 9: ALA; PNLA; OreLA. 10: Beta Phi Mu; Phi Kappa Phi. 12: "Louisiana Paintings of the 19th Century," Exhibition Catlg (59). 14: Ref, govt publ. 15: 490 W 26th ave, Eugene Or 97405.

McNERNEY, JAMES J. b Brooklyn NY 24 Ja 14. 4: Gladys Pearce. 5: Fordham 35 BA; Columbia 37 BLS. 7: Reg libn Queens Borough Pub, Jamaica NY 59-. 9: ALA; NYC Lib Club. 15: 14-24 30th rd, Astoria NY 11102.

McNEW, EVE. b Esther Mo 24 Mr 28. 4: H L McNew. 5: SE Mo State Col 47-49 (Soc sci, Hist, Eng & Sp) AB; Peabody Col 65-66 MALS. 7: Libn: Univ City Pub Schs, Univ City Mo 55-65, Clayton Pub Schs, Clayton Mo 66-67, Berkeley Pub Schs, Berkeley Mo 67-. 9: NEA (life mem); ALA; MoStateTA; MoLA; MoASchL; SLSTA. 10: Phi Alpha Theta; Beta Phi Mu. 14: Adol lib serv. 15: 8906 Shawnee lane, Overland Mo 63114.

McNIERNEY, MARY ALICE. b Newark NJ. 5: Trenton State Col 48 BS in Ed; Douglass Col 50 BLS; Columbia 60 MLS. 7: Ref asst Bus Info Bur Cleveland Pub Lib 50-52; Libn Spec Serv USAREUR, Germany, France 52-56; Ref libn Standard & Poor's Corp, NYC 56-60; Libn Bache & Co Inc, NYC 60-67; Supv lib & res Gen Motors Corp, NYC 67-. 9: SLA (NY Chap: chm Bus & Fin Group 63-64, 68, Adv Bd 64-65). 12: Ed Directory of Business and Financial Services," SLA (6th ed 63). 13: Yes. 14: Ref. 15: 100 W 12th st, New York NY 10011.

McNIFF, PHILIP JAMES. b Cambridge Mass 10 F 12. 4: Mary Stack McNiff. 5: Boston Col 29-33 (Philos) AB; Columbia 40 (LS) BS. 06: Fr, Lat. 7: Stud asst Brookline Pub Lib, Brookline Mass 26-33; Asst Newton Free Lib, Newton Mass 33-35, Hd catlg dept 40-42; Libn West newton Lib, W Newton Mass 35-40; Ref asst Harvard Col Lib 42-43, Supt reading room 43-48, Libn Lamont Lib 48-56, Asst libn 49-56, Assoc libn 56-65, Mem Fac Arts & Sci 54-65, Archibald Cary Coolidge bibliogr Harvard U Lib 62-65; Dir & libn Boston Pub Lib 65-. 8: Consul: pub & private libs, Emerson Col, boston Museum Sci, Case Inst, Southern U, SoIll U, Merrimack Col, Providence Col, SEast Mass Tech Inst, Our Lady of the Elms Col, Andover Acad, Villanova U, Gorham State Tchrs Col, St Paul's Sch (Concord Mass); Admin lib commsn studying state aid to pub libs; Mass Lib Devel Com; Adv Bd Cambridge Ctr for Adult Educ; Pres Coun of Boston Col; Adv Bd: Newton Col of the Sacred Heart; Boys Club of Boston Lib Com, Boston Col Lib, Newton Jr Col. 9: ALA (Coun; chm & mem var coms); -ACRL (pres); -ARL (chm Farmington Plan; chm For Acquis Com; chm Adv Com Ctr for Chinese Research Materials; Bd of Dirs); CathLA; NELA (Bd of Dirs); MassLA (past sec; past v-pres, past pres). 10: Club of Odd Volumes. 11: Hon degree Doctor of Humane Letters Boston Col 69. 12: "Catalogue of the Lamont Library, Harvard Col"; "List of Book Dealers in Underdeveloped Countries". 13: Yes. 14: Admin, ref & res, area serv. 15: Boston Pub Lib, Boston Ma 02117.

McNITT, MORRIS E. b Kalamazoo Mich 2 Ap 37. 4: Bonnie Pomeroy. 5: AndrewsU 55-62 (Mus Educ) BME; West MichU 63-65 MALS. 6: Fr. 7: Mus tchr Mt Pisgah Acad, Chandler NC 59-60; Mus tchr Cedar Lake Acad, Cedar Lake Mich 62-63; Asst libn Portage Oub Lib, Portage Mich 64; Catlgr Tucson Pub Lib, Tucson Ariz 65-. 9: ArizStateLA. 10: Tucson Pub Lib Staff Assn. 14: Catlg. 15: PO Box 1296, Tucson Az 85702.

McNIVEN, JEAN. b Shawinigan Que Can. 5: McGill 43 (Lat, Fr) BA; Simmons 61 MSLS. 6: Fr, Sp. 7: Catlgr Nat Lib, Ottawa 61-62; Libn Consul Protestant Sch Bd of Greater Montreal 62-63, High sch libn 63-. 9: QueLA (Coun 65-66); Lib Assn Prot Schs (pres 64-66). 12: Ed "Quebec Library Association Newsletter" (64-65). 14: Sch libs. 15: 5025 Clanranald ave, Apt 4, Montreal 248 Can.

McNULTY, LEIGHTON (EDGAR) JR. b Carlisle Penn 4 D 29. 5: Gettysburg Col 47-51 (Eng) AB; Columbia 53-54 (LS) MS; West Res 64 (Documentation). 7: US Air Force (2nd Lt), US 52-53; Acquis asst Army War Col (Carlisle Penn) 54-55; Ref asst Enoch Pratt Free Lib, Baltimore 55-57; Bkmob asst Harrisburg Pub Lib, Harrisburg Penn 57; Ref asst Free Lib of Phila 58-60; Asst libn State Tchrs Col (Frostburg Md) 60-61; Head tech processes WVa Lib Commsn, Charleston WVa 61-63; Act head catlg dept Southampton Col of LIU 64-65, Head catlg dept 65-; Catlgr Mt St Mary's Col (Emmitsburg Md) 68-. 10: Air Force Reserve; Amer Fed Musicians. 14: Catlg. 15: 33 South Pitt st, Carlisle Pa 17013.

McNUTT, DOROTHY (CONGER). b Cincinnati 17 Ja 03. 5: Ohio Wesleyan U 22-26 (Chem) BA; Cincinnati Pub Lib Training Class 26-27; Cincinnati U 27, 29, 34; UCal summer 40 (LS). 6: Ger, Fr. 7: Asst pub documents dept Cincinnati Pub Lib 34-36, Asst sci & ind dept 27-34, 36-52, Head sci & ind dept 52-. 9: ALA (chm ALA Reading Guide Project-Author Sel, Biol Com 64-65); SLA (chm Pub Rel Com Convention 53, chm Nat Lib Week 62-63, chm Scholarship & Stud Loan Fund Com 64-65, Adv to Dayton Chap 63-65, pres Cincinnati Chap 58-59); ASIS; OhioLA (Exec Bd 55-58, Bulletin ed 56-58, Conf Pub Rel Chm 61). 10: DAR; Alpha Chi Omega; Alliance franc6aise; Cincinnati Col Club; Bus & Prof Womens Club; Soroptimist Club. 13: Yes. 14: Tech ref, pub rel. 15: Cincinnati Pub Lib 800 Vine st, Cincinnati Oh 45202.

McPARTLAND, REGINA ANN. b Hamden Conn 29 S 25. 5: Albertus Magnus Col 42-45 (Eng) BA; Columbia summers 56-61 MS in LS. 6: Fr. 7: Yale U Lib: Reserve bk room asst 47-51, Circ desk asst 51-52, Personnel asst 52-54, Supv card processing catlg dept 54-56, Purchase supv order dept 56-63, Head purchase sect order dept 63-, Asst hd acquis dept 66-. 9: ALA; ConnLA. 14: Acquis. 15: P O Box 376, Milford Ct 06461.

McPHAUL, DOROTHY (ROSSELAND). b Chicago Ill 30 Ja 17. 4: Hugh Walter McPhaul. 5: UNC 35-39 (Fr, Hist) AB; UCal (Berkeley) 42; Pembroke State Col (NC) 55; NC State Col 59; UNC 62-63, 64-67 (LS) Certif. 6: Fr. 7: Tchr: Clayton High Sch, Clayton NC 39-40, Oxford Orphanage High Sch, Oxford NC 40-41, Cary High Sch, Cary NC 55-56, Apex High Sch, Apex NC 59-62, Rolesville High Sch, Rolesville NC 62-63; Elem libn Clayton Sch, Clayton NC 63-66; Libn Broughton High Sch, Raleigh NC 66-. 9: NEA; NCEA. 10: Phi Beta Kappa. 14: High sch libnship. 15: 1323 Duplin rd, Raleigh NC 27607.

McPHEETERS, ANNIE L (WATTERS). b Rome Ga 22 F 08. 5: Clark Col 25-29 (Eng) AB; Hampton Inst 33 BS in LS; Columbia summer 56 MS in LS. 6: Fr. 7: Libn Phyllis Wheatley Br, Greenville SC 33-34; Libn Auburn Br Atlanta Pub Lib 34-39, Libn W Hunter Br 49-66; Libn Ga State Col ref dept 66-. 8: Tchr of Pub Lib course Atlanta U Sch Lib Serv. 9: ALA; AEAUSA; SELA; GaLA. 10; YWCA; Ga Coun on Human Rel; Metro Atlanta Assn for the Blind; Alpha Kappa Alpha; Utopian Lit Club; Wesleyan Serv Guild. 11: Ford Foun Grant, Adult Educ, Columbia (1 summer); Bronze Woman of the Year 53, awarded by Iota Phi Lambda Sorority, Delta Chap. 12: "Negro Progress in Atlanta Ga 50-60: A Selective Bibliography on Human Relations from Four Atlanta Newspapers" (64); "Scarcity of Children's Librarians in the Public Library: A Study" (60). 13: Yes. 14: Adults, br lib serv, ref serv. 15: 1365 Mozley pl, SW Atlanta Ga 30314.

McPHERSON, KENNETH FREDERICK. b Winnipeg Man Can 9 S 25. 4: Beryl Anne Reid. 5: UBC 43-47 (Zool) BA, 47-48 (Philos, Eng); McGill 48-49 BLS. 6: Fr. 7: Brooklyn Pub Lib: Br asst 49, Personnel dir 51-53, Asst br libn 53-54; Asst dir Bloomfield Pub Lib, Bloomfield NJ 54-59, Lib Dir 59-68; Dir Morris Co Lib, Whippany NJ 68-. 8: Lib consul: Hillside NJ (58); Williamsport Penn (62); Easton Penn (63); New Providence NJ (63); Lakewood NJ (64); Moorestown NJ (64); S Brunswick NJ (65); Lincoln Park NJ (65); Bogota (65); N assau Co, NY (67); City of Clifton (68); Sparta NJ (68); Allendale NJ (68); River Vale NJ (69). 09: ALA; LPRC (pres); NJLA (pres 64-65). 10: C of C; Bloomfield Hist Soc. 13: Yes. 14: Admin, fin, lib bldgs. 15: Morris County Free Lib, Whippany NJ 07981.

McPHERSON, MARY ELLEN (CAMERON). b Chicago 26 F 16. 4: Donald B McPherson. 5: J Sterling Morton Jr Col 33-35 (Pre-legal) Certif; Cornell Col 35-37 (Hist, Pol Sci) BA; UWis 63 MALS; UDenver summer 65 (Young Adult Lit). 7: Sec to pres Vaughan Co, Chicago 37-41; Sec to pres Elmhurst Col 41-43; Sec Amer Bar Assn, Chicago 43; Tchr Elvira Cons High Sch, Elvira Iowa 55-56; Lib, tchr Tampico Twp High Sch, Tampico Ill 57-60; Libn Freeport Sr High Sch, Freeport Ill 60-. 9: NEA; IllEA; FreeportEA; IllASchL. 10: Boy Scout & Girl Scout orgs. 14: High sch libnship. 15: 1025 S Benson blvd, Freeport Il 61032.

McPHERSON, VENITA JEAN. b Phoenix Ariz 25 N 45. 5: UCal (Santa Barbara) 63-67 (Hist) BA; UCLA 67-68 MLS. 7: Asst ref libn U C Riverside Lib, (Riverside Cal) 68-. 14: Ref. 15: Conway Summit, Lee Vening Ca 93541.

McQUITTY, EDITH (ZELLE). b St Louis Mo 16 N 12. 4: Joseph Guy McQuitty. 5: UMo 30-34 (Soc studies) AB; Harris Tchrs' Col summer 56; WashU 56; UMo ext div 67. 7: Clk St Louis Pub Lib 55-57, Sub-prof libn 57-63; Asst libn St Louis Police Lib 63-65, Libn 65-. 9: SLA (sec Greater St Louis Chapter 68-69). 15: St Louis Police Lib 1200 Clark ave, St Louis Mo 63103.

McRAE, JOYCE MARGARET (BEGGS). b Peterborough Ont Can 22 Jl 32. 4: Daniel Hugh McRae. 5: Queen's U 50-53 (Eng, Fr) BA; McGill 55-56 BLS, 67-69 MLS. 06: Fr, Russian, Sp. 7: Lib consul Protestant Sch Bd, Montreal 56-60; Child libn Fraser-Hickson Inst, Montreal 60-65; High sch libn Protestant Sch Bd, John Grant High, Montreal 65-. 9: CanLA. 10: Queen's Alumnae. 14: Ya sch lib wk. 15: 4199 Kensington ave, Montreal 28 Can.

McRAE, MARY. b El Centro Cal 29 Je 43. 5: UAmericas 61-62 (Anthrop); UAriz 60-65 (Anthrop) BA; San Jose State Col 66-68 (LS) MA. 6: Sp, Farsi. 7: Mus asst Ariz State mus 64; Stud asst San Jose State Col Lib 67; Catlgr UIsfahan (Isfahan Iran) 68-. 10: Guild mem, Triton Art Museum, San Jose Cal. 14: Bibliog, museum ref. 15: Iran-America Society, Isfahan Iran.

McREYNOLDS, FLORIS (FLAM). b NYC 19 Ag 45. 4: Michael McReynolds. 5: Barnard Col 61-65 (Govt) BA; Columbia 65-66 MS. 6: Fr. 7: Asst acquis libn Ctr for Research Libs, Chicago 66-67; Asst ref libn UIll (Chicago) 67-. 9: ALA. 10: Beta Phi Mu. 14: Ref. 15: 1451 E 55th st, Chicago Il 60615.

McSWEENEY, JOSEPHINE. b NYC 5 My 31. 5: SUNY(Plattsburgh) 48-51 (Soc Stud) BA (magna cum laude); Columbia 51-52 (Educ) MA; Pratt 59-60 MLS. 7: Tchr Bd of Educ, Huntington Station NY 51-54; Dependent Sch System: Tchr, Japan 54-55, Tchr, Philippine Islands 55-56, Tchr, Germany 56-58, Tchr, Italy 58-59; Head ref dept Pratt Inst Lib 60-. 9: ALA; Metro Col Inter-Lib Assn (sec-treas 64-66). 10: Pratt Inst Grad Lib Sch Alumni Assn; Beta Phi Mu; Bksellers' League of NY; NY Lib Club; AAUP. 14: Ref, govt docs, ser, lib sci. 15: 279 Washington ave, Brooklyn NY 11205.

McTAGGART, JAMES. b Dayton Ohio 10 Ap 14. 4: Margaret Ellen Beebe. 5: Ohio State U 35-38 (Hist) BA; UMich 49 ABLS, 55 AMLS. 7: Circ asst Dayton Pub Lib, Dayton Ohio 32-35; Stud asst Ohio State U Lib 35-38; Ref asst Dayton Pub Lib, Dayton Ohio 38-42; Stock clerk Abbott Labs, N Chicago Ill 45-48; Stack supv Ohio State U 48-49; Acquis libn Central Mich U 49-. 9: MichLA; Mich Assn Higher Educ. 13: Yes. 14: Tech processes. 15: 1307 E High, Mt Pleasant Mi 48858.

McTAGGART, JOHN BARNEY. b Dayton Ohio 9 My 18. 4: Bertha Tower. 5: East Baptist Col 47-51 (Pre-Theol) BA; Drexel 53-55 MS in LS. 7: Asst libn Union Theol Sem(NYC) 55-56; Libn Berkeley Baptist Divinity Sch (Cal) 56-60; Libn Methodist Theol Sch in Ohio 60-. 9: ATHeolLA (Exec Com 58-60). 14: Admin. 15: 701 W Central ave, Delaware Oh 43015.

McTIGHE, MARIANNE. b Scranton Penn 24 Ag 23. 5: Marywood 41-45 (LS) BS in Ed, 52-54 9ls0 ma in Libnship; UScranton 54-. 7: Asst order libn Catholic U 45-46; Asst catlgr UScranton 46-47, Hd circ & ref depts 47-51, Act libn 51-54, Libn 54-. 8: Mem ALA Lib 21 exhib, Seattle W0rld's Fair 62; Mem eval com Middle States Assn of Col & Second Schs Comsn on Second Schs, 57, 61, 63. 9: ALA; PaLA (sec-treas NE Chap 50-62); Jesuit Lib Assn. 10: AAUP; Amer Red Cross Nurse Aide Corps. 14: Col lib admin, tech processing. 15: 217 Wheeler ave, Scranton Pa 18510.

McWHIRTER, DAVID IAN. b Tonawanda NY 5 Je 37. 4: Donna Hoyt. 5: SUNY (Geneseo) 55-59 (LS) BS; The Col of the Bible (Lexington Ky) 59-62 (Theol) BD; Syracuse 65-67 (LS) MS. 6: Ger. 7: Asst minister Central Christian Church, New Albany Ind 59-62; Asst libn Christian Theol Sem(Indianapolis) 62-. 9: ATheolLA. 10: Chaplain, WFBM Gordon Pipers; Disciples of Christ Hist Soc; Disciples Libns Fellowship Chm. 13: Yes. 14: Admin, bks of Disciple of Christ interest, mss wk. 15: 4935 Graceland, Indianapolis In 46208.

McWHORTER, JIMMIE JEAN (McCONNELL). b Pine Hill Ala 12 Ag 25. 4: William Bert McWhorter. 5: UAla 43-44 (Educ); Spring Hill College 56-60 (LS). 6: Fr, Sp. 7: Asst libn Brookley AFB, Mobile Ala 45-59, Base libn 50-61; Chief libn Mobile Air Material Area, Brookley AFB Ala 60-69; Hd commun serv Mobile Pub Lib, Mobile Ala 69-. 9: ALA (Coun 66-70; Armed Forces Libns Sect: sec, chm); -PLA (Devel Com; Legis Com); SELA (Lib Devel Com; Nominating Com; Program Chm); AlaLA (Program Com; Memb Com; Convention Com; pres Col, Univ & Spec Libs Com); SLA (pres & dir Ala Chap). 10: Friends of Mobile Pub Lib; Air Force Assn; Prof & Bus Women's Assn. 11: USAF Superior Performance Award. 13: Yes. 14: Admin, pub rel, adult serv, rare bks. 15: 306 Brawood dr, Mobile Al 36608.

McWILLIAMS, EMILIE (TAYLOR). b Chester Penn 24 Ap 27. 5: Carnegie Inst 44-48 (Chem) BS; UPittsburgh 61-63 (Sci-Tech) MLS. 6: Sp, Fr, Russian, Ger. 7: Analytical chem Amer Viscose Corp, Marcus Hook Penn 48-49; Chem USQM Depot, Phila 49-50; Research chem Consolidated Coal Co, Library Penn 50-54; Lit searcher Carnegie Inst 57-58; Libn Carnegie Lib of Pittsburgh 63-65; Libn Col of Earth & Mineral Sci Penn State U 66-. 9: SLA. 14: Ref. 15: 712 Jackson st, State Col Pa 16801.

MEAD, CATHERINE MARGARET (SMITH). b Sharon Springs NY 11 Jl 24. 4: John Gower Mead. 5: NY State Col for Tchrs 40-44 (Eng) BA, summers 44-47 BS in LS. 6: Fr. 7: Tchrlibn Germatown-Clermont Central Sch, Germantown NY 44-46; Libn Corinth High Sch, Corinth NY 46-47; Libn Trenton Pub Lib, Trenton J 47-48; File clerk Enemy Prisoner of War Info Bur, Ft Holabird Md 48-49; Libn Army Lib: Yokohama Japan 53-54, Tokyo 54-55, Ft Hood Tex 7-63; Staff UMd 63; Staff Penn State Lib 64-65; Staff Ohio State Lib 65-67, Hd info resources & serv div 67-.09: ALA; OhioLA (Com on Intel Freedom). 15: 088 Cherry Hill dr, Columbus 13 Ohio 43213.

MEADE, BARBARA ALDEN (PRINCE). b Hamden Conn 28 N 18. 4: Walter Ryan Meade. 5: UMass 9bridgewater) 36-40 (Ed) BSEd; UDenver 47-50 (Libnship) MA. 6: Fr, Sp. 7: First Lt (communications) USMC, Wash DC 43-45; Libn USVA Hosp, Submount NY 46-50; Chief libn USVA Hosp: Wilkes-Barre Penn 51-53, W Haven Conn 54-56; Base libn Nouasseur AB, Morocco 57-59; Staff libn HQ Second AF, Barksdale AFB La 60-62; Base libn Andersen AFB, Guam MI 63-64; Staff libn HQ Sixteenth AF, Spain 64-65; Deputy chief lib div HQ USAF in Europe, Ger 65-66; Asst agency libn Dept of Defense, Wash DC 67-. 9: ALA-PLA (Pres Armed Forces Libns Sect 63-64). 14: Mgt, automation. 15: 4501 Arlington blvd, Arlington Va 22203.

MEADOR, CLAIRE WINDSOR. b Winter Haven Fla 30 S 09. 4: Rev Horace Clifton Meador. 5: Stetson U28-29 (Rel Educ); New Orleans Baptist Sem 29-32 (Rel Ed) MRE; Fla So Col summers; Fla State U 48-49 (Elem Educ) AB, summers (LS) MA. 7: Tchr Leon Co Pub Sch, Woodville Fla 49-55; Libn Leon Co Pub Sch, Tallahassee Fla 55-. ; Itinerant libn for co rural schs 66-68; Libn Woodville Sch 68-69. 8: Eval Com for Jefferson Co Schs, 65; Chm Handbook com for CO Lib 67-68. 9: NEA; FlaEA; FlaASchL; Fla a-V Assn; Co Sch Libns. 10: Womens Missionary Union Baptist Chuch; AAUW. 14: Child lit, a-v materials. 15: P O Box 692, Tallahassee Fla 32302.

MEADOWS, KATHERINE (McBRIDE). b Lone Oak Tex 25 Ag 07. 5: E Tex State U 27-32 (Eng) BA; Tex Tech Col 50-52 (Educ) M Ed; N Tex State U summers 56-59 BS in LS. 7: Tchr Tom Green Co Schs, San Angelo Tex 27-41; Tchr Lubbock Pub Schs, Lubbock Tex 50-53; Tchr Duncanville Pub Schs, Duncanville Tex 55-57; Dallas Pub Schs: Elem libn 57-60, Jr high libn 60-65, Sr high libn 65-. 9: ALA; NEA; Tex State Tchrs Assn; Tex Classroom Tchrs Assn; TexLA. 10: Delta Kappa Gamma. 15: 6109 Morningside, Dallas Tx 75214.

MEAGHER, JOSEPHINE JANE. b Chicago 26 Je 22. 5: Rosary Col 40-44 (LS) BA; Loyola U (Chicago) 60; Rosary Col 59-61 MALS; No Ill U 64. 6: Sp. 7: Asst libn Sears Roebuck & Co, Chicago 44-47; Libn Booz Allen & Hamilton, Chicago 47-50; Engnr libn UNotre Dame (Notre Dame Ind) 50-52; Asst Libn Needham Louis & Brorby, Chicago 52-55; Libn TATHAM Laird, Chicago 55-58; Asst libn Morton High Sch, Berwyn Ill 58-67; Lib Willow Brook High Sch, Villa Park Ill 67-. 8: Ref libn Lib/USA, NY Worlds Fair 65. 9: ALA; IllLA; Ill ASchL; High Sch Libns Chicagoland (sec 69-70). 10: Amer Fed of Tchrs. 14: Ref. 15: 328 S Harvey ave, Oak Park Il 60002.

MEAKER, MARGARET L(ARAMY). b Jackson Ohio 14 Mr 04. 5 Moravian Col for Women (Bethlehem Penn) 20-21; Wellesley Col 21-25 (Lat, Gk, Hist) BA; Columbia 25-26 Hist) MA, 29-30 BS in LS. 6: Lat. 7: Hist & math tchr Belvidere

High Sch, Belvidere NJ 26-27; Math & Lat tchr· Lewes High Sch, Lewes Del 27-29; Catlgr Lehigh U 30-39; Indexer The HW Wilson Co, NYC 41-43; Asst Physics Lib Columbia U 43; Indexer The New York Times, NYC 43-46; Asst ref & circ George Washington U Lib, Wash DC 52-65, Asst ref 65-. 9: ALA; DCLA. 10: Phi Beta Kappa. 14: Ref, catlg. 15: 4658 Cedar Ridge dr SE, Wash DC 20021.

MEAKIN, DOROTHY DEANE. b Kettering Eng. 4: John Blanchard Meakin. 5: Simmons 36-40 BLS: Montclair State Col 59-60 Certif Sch Lib. 7: Elem sch libn Montclair (NJ) Schs 48-61; High Sch Libn Groton Schs, Groton Mass 62-. 9: ALA; MassLA; NESchLA. 14: Child & young adults serv. 15: Common st, Groton Mas 01450.

MEAKIN, FAITH ANNE. b Phila Penn 15 O 43. 5: Coe Col 61-63 (Bio); Syracuse 63-65 (Eng, Bio) BA, 65-66 MLS; UCLA 66-67 Certif in Med Libnship. 6: Sp, Fr. 7: USPHS Intern UCLA Biomed Lib 66-67; Ref libn UCal (San Diego) Biomed Lib 67-. 9: MedLA; ASIS; Med Lib Group of So Cal. 13: Yes. 14: Med, bio, ref. 15: Biomedical Lib Univ of Cal San Diego, La Jolla Ca 92037.

MEANLEY, CAROLYN ANN (MIKKELSON). b Shelby Mich 14 F 44. 4: Edward Scripps Meanley. 5: Central Mich U 61-62 (Bio); Muskegon Commun Col 62-63 (Bio); UMich 63-65 (Bio) BA, 65-66 MALS. 7: Pre-print libn UMich Physics Dept 65-69; Asst sci-tech libn East Mich U 66-. 13: Yes. 14: Ref. 15: 3725 Green Brier apt 185A, Ann Arbor Mi 48105.

MEANS, FRANCES CORRY. b Colmbia SC 9 Jl 14. 5: Winthrop Col 34-35; USCar 5-38 (Eng) AB; Columbia 38-41 BS in LS. 6: Fr, Ger. 7: Asst dept libn USCar 38-41, Catlgr 41-47; Asst circ libn UDenver 47-50; Order libn USCar 50-67, Hd order dept 68-. 9: SELA; SCLA. 10: Phi Beta Kappa. 14: Acquis. 15: 1614 Senate st, Columbia SC 29208.

MEANS, JUANITA (JULIA). b Dale Okla. 5: UOkla 25-33 (Eng, Educ) BS; UDenver summers 49-52 (LS) MA. 6: Fr. 7: Tchr Tecumseh Pub Schs, Tecumseh Okla 26-31; Tchr Maud Pub Schs, Maud Okla 31-32; Tchr Graham Pub Schs, Graham Okla 33-37; Tchr Nicoma Park Pub Sch, Nicoma Park Okla 37-43; Jr accountant Douglas Aircraft Co, Okla City Okla 43-45; Circ asst Okla City Libs, Okla City Okla 45-49, Ref asst 49-50; Ref libn Okla City U 50-. 9: ALA; OklaLA (sec 62); SWLA. 13: Yes. 14: Ref, col & univ libnship. 15: 1501 Northwest 31, Oklahoma City Okla 73118.

MEANS, RAYMOND B. b Des Moines Iowa 4 Ja 30. 4: Rebecca Chartier. 5: UDenver (LS) MA. 7: US Army; Tri-Ctr Pub Schs; UOmaha; UNeb. 9: ALA; NebLA (past pres). 14: Admin, catlg, educ. 15: 5626 Leavenworth st, Omaha Nb 68106.

MEANY, PHILIP AUGUSTUS BARTHOLOMEW. b Oakland Cal 20 O 38. 5: St Marys Col (Cal) 56-60 (Hist) BA; UWash61-63 (LS) ML. 7: Clerk St Marys Col Lib (Cal) 60-61; Lib asst UWash Sci Lib 62-63; Asst libn Centralia col 63-. 9: NEA; Wash State LA; Wash State ASchL; WashEA. 14: Catlg. 15: 303 N Rock, Centralia Wa 98531.

MEARES, ROBERTA (JORDAN). b Snow Hill NC 19 Mr 10. 4: Dr Guy Maurice Meares. 5: UNC(Greensboro) 26-30 AB in LS; USCar 56, 57, 58 (Educ); Columbia Col summer 62 (Educ); USCar summer 66 NDEA Inst Lib Sci. 6: Fr, Sp. 7: Libn Parker High Sch, Greenville SC 30-31; Sch dept head Richland Co Pub Lib, Columbia SC 31-39; State wide lib supv WPA, Columbia SC 40; Sch libn Columbia ub Schs, Columbia SC 54-56, Elem sch libn 58-; Instr Lib Sci Columbia Col summer 67-69. 8: Consul with Lib Serv of SC State Dept of Educ summer 65, 66; Supvr, Columbia Pub Schs central proc of lib bks under Title I 66. 9: NEA; SCEA (Lib Div), SCA-V Assn; Richland CoEA. 10: Wistaria Garden Club (Columbia SC); PTA; Girl Scouts Coun; Red Cross Gray Lady. 14: Elem sch libs. 15; 2843 Sheffield rd, Columbia SC 29204.

MEARNS, DAVID CHAMBERS. b Wash DC 31 D 1899. 4: Mary Richardson Mearns. 5: George Washington U 16-17; UVa 18. 7: LC 18-, Supt of Reading Rooms 39-41, Chief ref libn 41-43, Dir ref dept 43-49, Asst libn 49-51, Asst libn for Amer Collections, Chief Mss Div & incumbent of the chair of Amer Hist 51-67, Honorary consul in humanities 69-. 8: Windson lecturer UIll 53; Lecturer var cols & univs; Symposium on Ms Sources of Amer Hist, held by Amer Philos Soc 53; Mem: US Abraham Lincoln Sesquicentennial Commsn (Hon mem); US Civil War Centennial Commsn; Bd of Dir of Civil War Centennial Assn; Coop Com for papers of Benjamin Franklin; Jt Com on Hist Mss; US Nat Hist Publs Commsn; Ulysess S Grant Assn (v-pres); Adv Co of Alexander Hamilton Bicentennial Commsn; White House Lib Com; Lib Coun UNotre Dame; Ed Adv Bd, the PAPERS OF Woodrow Wilson; Civil War Round Tble, Chicago (Hon life mem). 9: AHA; BSA Fellow DCLA (past pres); Ms Soc (past pes); Amer Inst of Arch (Com on Arch Archives); SAA; Cosmos Club; Ampersand Club. 10: NAACP. 11: LC Distinguished Service Award 58; Ltt D Lincoln Col 60; Phi Beta Kappa UVa 61; US Abraham Lincoln Sesquicentennial Commsn Medal of Honor 60; Diploma of Honor Lincoln Mem Univ 6; National Abraham Lincoln Distinguished Service Award 62; US Civil War Centennial Commsn Medallion of Honor 65. 12: Auth The Story Up To Now (47); "The Lincoln PAPERS" (48); "The Declaration of Independence The Story of a Parchment (50); "The Story of the Queens Letter (52); "Lincoln and the Image of America (53); "Three Presidents and Their Books, with A E Bestor & J Daniels (55); "Herbrt Herbert Putnam Librarian of the United States "Books and Publishing, with C E Sunderlin & F L Spain (55); "Historical Manuscripts (57); "Largely Lincoln (61); "Long Remembered, with L A Dunlap (63); "Lincoln and the Gettysburg Address, with A Nevins and others (64). 13: Yes. 14: Ref, Americana. 15: Library of Congress, Wash DC 20540.

MECH, EUNICE (SAMSON). b Duryea Penn 19 Mr 10. 5: Bucknell U 28-32 (Hist, Eng) BA; Central Wash State Col 57 (Bus Educ) MEd; UWash 62 (LS) ML. 6: Fr, Ger. 7: Bus educ tchr, tchr libn Mabton Sr High Sch, Mabton Wash 52-55; Libn & tchr of Eng Prosser Sr High Sch, Prosser Wash 55-63; Libn Pullman High Sch, Pullman Wash 63-66; Prosser Sr High Sch libn 66-. 9: ALA; NEA; Wash State Sch L; WashEA; Pullman Educ Forum; Prosser EA. 10: Mu Phi Epsilon; AAUW, DAR. 15: 1051 Yakima ave, Prosser Wa 99350.

MECHANIC, SYLVIA (GERTRUDE). b NY 4 Ag 20. 5: Hofstra Col 38-42 (Eng) BA; Columbia 42-43 (LS) BS. 7: Brooklyn Pub Lib: Lib asst hist div 43-45, Lib asst Chief Soc Sci ci div 46-53, Chief sci & ind div 53-61, Bus libn Bus Lib 62-. 8: ALA Worlds Fair Com 64-65; Instr Columbia Sch Lib Serv 67-. 9: ALA; SLA; NY Lib Club; NYLA. 12: "Annotated Bibliography on Government Documtnts. 13: Yes. 14: Ref. 15: Brooklyn Pub Lib Bus Lib, Cadman Plaza W,Brooklyn NY 11201.

MECINSKI, ADAM M. b Baltimore 25 N 28. 4: Irene Piekarski. 5: Loyola Col (Baltimore) 47-48, 49-50, 54-56 (Hist) BS; Rutgers 56-58 MLS. 6: Polish, Sp. 7: Regular clerk US Post Off Dept, Baltimore 48-49; Sr supply spec (S/Sgt) US Air Force, Tex, Eng, Kan 50-54; Enoch Pratt Free Lib, Baltimore: Roving asst 58-59, Sr asst bus & econ dept 59-63, Admin asst Herring Run Br 63-68, Br libn Fells Point Br 68-. 9: ALA; MdLA. 14: Ref, readers adv. 15: 2101 Echodale ave, Baltimore Md 21214.

MECKEL, CLARA LOUISE. b Emporia Kan 13 S 15. 5: Col of Emporia (Kan) 33-36 (PSYCH, Eng) AB; Peabody 46-47 BS in LS. 7: Libn Menninger Found, Topeka Kan 40-46, 48-49; Asst libn UMd Health Sci Lib 49-54; Asst libn UNeb Col of Med Lib 54-56; Asst libn circ, ref UIll Lib of Med Sci (Chicago) 56-. 8: Org MD Psychiatric Inst Lib, Baltimore 52-54; Org Neb Psychiatric Inst Lib, Omaha 54-56. 9: MedLA (chm Subcom on Internship 58). 13: Yes. 14: Ref. 15: 2951 So King dr, Chicago Il 60616.

MECKFESSEL, HARRIET (LILLIAN). b St Louis 4 D 22. 5: Mo Valley Col 45-47; Washington U (St Louis) even 47-54; UMo 55-56 (LS) BA. 7: Lib asst ref St Louis Pub Lib 48-50; Asst libn Ft Leonard Wood (Mo) 50-52; Jr libn ref St Louis Pub Lib 52-55; Jr libn ref acquis documents UMo 55-59; Ref (G-9) ser to catlgr (G-10) St Louis Pub Lib 59-61; Documents libn Ariz State U 61-63; Ser catlgr Johns Hopkins U Lib 63-65, Documents libn 65-68; Ref libn in chg govt docs Drury Col (Mo) 68-. 9: SLA; MoLA. 14: Govt documents. 15: 1852 E Bennett, Springfield Mo 65804.

MEDER, MARYLOUISE DUNHAM. b Danbury Conn. 5: Mary Washington Col of UVa 45-47 (Hist) BA; Carnegie 48-49 MLS; Trinity Col (Hartford Conn) 59-62 (Hist) MA; UMich 60-64 (LS) PhD. 6: Fr, Ger. 7: Catlgr Ohio State U 49-63; Asst libn Central Conn State Col 53-62 Lecturer Drexel Inst of Tech summer 64; Asst Prof Grad Sch of Lib Serv Rutgers U 64-66; Prof Sch of Lib Sci Tex Womans U 67-. 9: ALA; AALS; BSA; TexLA; SWLA. 10: AAUP; Medieval Acad Amer; Conn Hist Soc; AAUW. 14: Bibliog, ref, catlg, his of printing. 15: 13 Abbott ave, Danbury Conn 06810.

MEDER, REV STEPHEN A SJ. b Cleveland 2 S 11. 5: Loyola U (West Baden Col) 34-36 (Eng) AB; Catholic U summers 48-53 MSLS. 6: Ger. 7: Libn St Xavier High Sch, Cincinnati 46-55; Libn St Ignatius High Sch, Cleveland 55-63;

Libn Colombiere Col 63-. 9: CathLA (chm High Sch Sect 56-57; chm Greater Cincinnati Unit 52-55; No Ohio Unit; sec-treas 60-62, v-chm 62-63; Mich Unit; Adv Bd 68-71); ALA; Diocesan LA (Bk Review Ed 57-60). 12: Gen ed "Recommended Titles for the High Schools (53), suppl (55); Gen ed "Recommended Titles for the Primary and Elementary Grades (53), suppl (55). 14: Catlg. 15: Colombiere Col Lib, Clarkston Mich 48016.

MEDIGOVICH, STELLA ALEXANDRIA. b San Pedro Ca 23 F 20. 5: Sawyer Col of Bus 50-52 (Sec Sci); Pasadena City Col 52-54; USoCal 59-63 (LS). 6: Serbian. 7: Clerical Barden Co Los Angeles 40-46; Clerical & sec Reynolds Aluminum Co, Pasadena Cal 48-51; Libn Hycon Co, Monrovia Cal 53-. 9: SLA; Spec Libs of So Cal; LARC Assn. 14: Catlg, ref. 15: Hycon Co 700 Royal Oaks dr, Monrovia Ca 91017.

MEDINA, KAY ANN (BECK). b Trenton Mo 24 Ap 39. 04. Epifanio Medina Jr. 5: Bethany Col (Lindsborg) 57-59 (Mus ed); Kan City, Kan Jr Col 59 diploma; UKan 59-62 (Journalism) BS; UOkla 64-66 MLS. 7: Libn II Kan City Mo Pub Lib soc sci 62-64; Ref US Naval Oceanographic Off Lib, Suitland Md 66-67; Supv Defense Intelligence Sch Lib, Wash DC 67-69; Dept hd spec collections Tampa Pub Lib, Tampa Fla 69-. 8: Mem Fed Lib Com Task Force on Pub Rel 67-69. 9: ALA; FlaLA. 14: Docs, pub rel, ref. 15: Tampa Public Lib 900 Ashley st, Tampa Fl.

MEDLEY, LAWRENCE D. b 15 D 24. 4: Lucy Neal. 5: UWis 44-49 (Bot) BA; Emory 51, 55 (LS) MA. 7: Milwaukee Pub Lib; Libn I 51-52, Libn II 53-58, Libn III 58-59; Asst libn Abbott Labs, No Chicago Ill 59-62; Libn A O Smith Corp, Milwaukee Wis 62-. 9: SLA (Metals/Materials Div, Program chm 66 Conv; Pres Wis Chap 62-63). 15: A O Smith Corp Box 584, Milwaukee Wi 53201.

MEDLEY, PAUL JR. b San Angelo Tex 9 Mr 36. 4: Sue (Robbins) Medley. 5: So Methodist U 54-58 (Psych) BA; UTex 61-62 (Law), 64-66 (LS). 7: Prof asst Dallas Pub Lib 59-61; Clk Humanities Research Ctr, UTex (Austin) 61; Salesman VariTyper Corp, Austin Tex 62-63; Lib asst Undergrad lib UTex (Austin) 64-66; Hd pub serv Abilene Pub Lib, Abilene Tex 66-67; Dir Waco-McLennan Co Lib, Waco Tex 67-. 9: ALA; SWLA; TexLA (chm Nomin Com, Pub Lib Div 69). 10: UTex Lib Sch Stud Assn; Waco Lib Club; Bd Dirs W Tex Film Circuit; Rotary Club. 14: Admin, ref. 15: 1717 Austin ave, Waco Tx 76701.

MEDSKER, MAURINE (JEANNETTE) D(URHAM). b Sullivan Co Ind 21 Ap 09. 4: Carl William Medsker. 5: Ward-Belmont Jr Col 27-29; UWis 29-31 BA; UKy summers 36-43 (Bus); Ind State U 57-64 (LS) MA. 6: Fr. 7: Eng tchr Decker High Sch, Decker Ind 31-32; Bud educ Kentland High Sch, Kentland Ind 43-45; Bud educ & Eng tchr Graysville High Sch, Graysville Ind 45-48; Sch libn & tchr Hutsonville High Sch, Hutsonville Ill 59-. 9: ALA; NEA; IllASchL; IllEA. 10: Kappa Kappa Kappa; Womans Club of Sullivan Ind; Amer Assn Tchrs French. 14: High sch libs. 15: Rt 2. Sullivan In 47882.

MEECE, MARY LOU (McFARLAND). b Cross Creek Penn 31 My 16. 5: Santa Ana Jr Col 34-36 (Sci) AA; USoCal 37-38 (Phys Educ) BA, 66-67 MS in LS. 6: Fr. 7: Libn Elem Sch Huntington Beach Cal 44-46; Co-libn Morgan Jr High Sch, Casper Wy 65-66, 68, Hd Libn 68-. 8: Libn Wyoming State Child Home, Casper Titles I & IV-A 68-69. 10: ALA; NEA; Alpha Delta Kappa; Libraria Sodalitas; WyoLA; WyoASchL; WyoEA; Casper City TA; Casper Repub Womens Club. 14: Ya lit, child lit, ref. 15: 251 E Twelfth, Casper Wy 82601.

MEEDER, MILDRED (HENNEY). b Alton Ill 25 D 06. 5: Lindenwood Col 24-28 (Fr) BA; UIll 28-29 BS. 6: Fr, Sp. 7: Catlgr UIll Lib, Urbana 29-31; Libn Natural Hist Mus, San diego 47-62; Catlgr US IntlU (San Diego) 67-. 9: ALA. 14: Catlg. 15: 6060-68 Clairemont Mesa blvd, San Diego Ca 92117.

MEEHAN, JAMES E JR. b Chicago Ill 12 Ag 35. 5: DePaul 57 (European hist) BA; Rosary Col 65 MALS. 6: Ger. 7: Period libn DePaul U Lib 64; Asst circ libn Loyola U, Chicago 64-65, Circ libn 65-66, Asst dir libs 66-. 8: Consul Lewis Col Lib, Lockport Ill 67. 9: ALA; CathLA. 14: Lib admin, pub serv. 15: Loyola Univ 6525 N Sheridan rd, Chicago Il 60626.

MEERDINK, RICHARD EDGAR. b Sheboygan Wis 19 Ap 37. 5: UWis 55-59 (Span, Eng) BS, 63-64 MALS. 6: Sp, Ger. 7: Tchr Span, Eng Bd of Educ, Waupun Wis 59-60; Span tchr Bd of Educ, Manitowoc Wis 60-63; Order libn UWis(Milwaukee) 64-67; Latin Amer bibliog for NDEA Latin Amer Center 64-67. 8: Latin Amer Bibliogr, NDEA Lat Amer Ctr 64-67. 9: ALA-ACRL;-RTSD; WisLA Recr Com 65-68). 10: Sigma Delta Pi; Beta Phi Mu. 14: Acquis, tech serv. 15: 2675 N 61st s, Milwaukee Wi 53213.

MEGGETT, JOAN M. b Los Angeles 30 S 09. 5: USoCal 45-48 (Eng Lit) BA, 48-49 MS in LS, 52-(Music). 6: Fr, Ger. 7: Lib clerk Los Angeles Pub Lib 30-43; WAC Army Med Admin Corp (S/Sgt) 43-45; Libn Art & Music Dept Los Angeles Pub Lib 49-55; Music libn USoCal 55-. 8: Lecturer, Intro to Grad Studies in Music, Sch of Music USoCal 56-; Lectr USoCal; Sch of Music & Lib Sci; adv music doctoral cand. 9: Amer Musicological Assn; MusLA (chm Publ Com 68-); Internat Assn Mus Libs; CalLA (CURLS sec). 10: Los Angeles Commun Concerts; Samuel Pepys Recorder Consort; So Cal Recorder Soc; Mu Phi Epsilon. 14: Music ref & paleography. 15: Sch of Music Lib USoCal, Los Angeles 90007.

MEHL, WARREN ROY. b St Louis Mo 18O 20. 4: Lucy Ann Heitmann. 5: UTex 44-46 (Bus) BBA; Eden Theol Sem 46-49 (Theol) BD; UOkla 57-58 MLS. 6: Ger. 7: Pastor Zion Evangelical & Reformed Church, Mayview MO 49-51; Pastor Federated Church, Kingfisher Okla 51-58; Catlgr Washington U (St Louis) 58-59; Libn Eden Theol Sem (St Louis) 59-. 9: ATheoLA; MoLA. 10: Beta Gamma Sigma; Sigma Iota Epsilon; Beta Phil Mu. 13: Yes. 14: Admin. 15: 119 Bompart, Webster Groves Mo 63119.

MEHLER, VIRGINIA (SLOCUM). b Morrestown NJ 7 Ag 23. 4: John Sauter Mehler. 5: Lake Erie Col 40-44 (Math) AB; Drexel 56-59 MSLS. 7: US Army; WAC, USAF Admin & Intelligence (Capt) 44-52; Report catlgr Sperry Gyroscope Co Engnr Lib 52-53; Report catlgr Radio Corp of Amer, Camden NJ 56-58; Libn RCA, Moorestown NJ 58-60; Asst libn Rutgers So Jersey Lib (Camden) 61-63; Head catlg dept UAlaska 63-64; Sr catlgr Rutgers U Lib 64-65, Head order dept 65-. 9: ALA. 10: USAF Reserve (Maj); Kappa Alpha Sigma; Wilderness soc. 14: Tech serv, machine procedures in lib serv. 15: Webb Gdns Clifton ave, New Brunswick NJ 08901/

MEHNE, NETTIE A. b Duluth Minn. 5: UMinn 33-37 (Eng, Hist) BA, 37-38 BS in LS. 7: Child libn Rochester Pub Lib, Rochester Minn 38-42; Lib asst Mayo Clinic Lib Rochester Minn 42-44; Libn Wesley Mem Hosp Sch of Nursing, Chicago 44-46; Med Libn Jones Gen Hosp, Battle Creek Mich 46-50; Med indexer, Searcher Tech Lib Upjohn Co, Kalamazoo Mich 50-. 8: Consul, "Handbook of Medical Library Prctice (3rd ed 65). 9: SLA; MedLA (sec 58-60, Bd of Dirs 58-60, Nom Com 62-65; Pharmacy Group: sec 54-55 & 64-65, chm 61-62; Midwest Reg Group: sec 52-53, chm 53-54). 13: Yes. 14: Indexing of med lit & documentation (machine info & retrieval) . 15: Tech Lib The Upjohn Co, 301 Henrietta st, Kalamazoo Mich 49001.

MEHRER, SOPHIA B. b St Louis 8 O 09. 4: Eugene Mehrer. 5: Vassar 27-31 (Hist)BA; Columbia 31-35 (LS) BS; Hunter Col 65 (Educ). 6: Fr. 7: Libn ny pub Lib 31-41; Queens Borough Pub Lib, Jamaica LI NY: asst libn Dalton Schs, NYC 65-66; Libn Little Red Sch House 66-. 9: ALA; LPRC; NY Lib Club. 14: Sch libs. 15: 501 W 123, New York NY 10027.

MEI, VONG-HYIH NYI. b Hangchow CHina 6 My 02. 4: Yi-pao Mei. 5: Smith 21-24 (Soc Sci) BA; Chicago 24-25 (Sociol) MA; West Res 54-55 (LS) MS. 6: Fr, Chinese. 7: Instr sociol Ginling Col (China) 26-27; Asst Prof, Prof sociol Yenching U (China) 28-35, 40-45; Catlg libn Iowa U 55-, Hd Oriental Collection. 9: ALA; IowaLA. 10: Chm Nat Com YWCA in China (45-47); Beta Phi Mu. 14: Catlg. 15: 1201 Ginter ave, Iowa City Iowa.

MEICHELBECK, SISTER MARY JOSEPH SSJ. b Watertown NY, 05: SUNY (Potsdam) 30-33, summer 46, 47 (Educ) BEd; SyracuseU summer 44, 45, 48, 49, 50 MS in LS. 7: Elem tchr pub schs, jefferson Co NY 33-39; Early secondary tchr parochial schs, Diocese of Ogdensburg NY 39-63; Libn Mater Dei Col 63-. 9: ALA; Nat Catholic Assn; CathLA (Diocesan Unit; past pres N Country Ref & Resources Coun). 10: Pi Lambda Sigma. 14: Ref. 15: Mater Dei College Riverside dr, Ogdensburg NY 13669.

MEILI, JANET. b New Holstein Wis 7 Ap 29. 5: Mission House Col 46-50 (Eng) BA; UWis 50-51 (LS) MA; UMich summers 55, 59. 7: Br libn Mead Pub Lib, Sheboygan Wis 51-54; Libn Lakeland Col 54-56; Child libn Appleton Pub Lib, Appleton Wis 56-59; Libn Farnsworth Jr High Sch, Sheboygan Wis 59-. 8: Child bk reviewer, ALA booklist, summers 63, 64, 66. 9: NEA; ALA; WisEA; WisLA. 10: Wis Lib Sch Alumni Assn; Beta Phi Mu. 14: Young adult. 15: 2808 S 8th st, Sheboygan Wi 53081.

MEINECKE, KAREN ELIZABETH. b Long Beach Cal 13 Ja 45. 5: UCal (Santa Barbara) 62-66 (Hist) BA; UCLA 66-67 MLS. 6: Sp, Ger. 7: Catlgr UCal (Irvine) 67-. 9: ALA; CalLA; So Cal Tech Proc Gp. 14: Catlg. 15: 2455 apt A Tustin ave, Costa Mesa Ca 92627.

MEINERS, BETTY (FULLER). b Syracuse NY 17 Ag 24. 4: Rev Harry H Meiners Jr. 5: Hope Col 42-47 (Hist) AB; Albany State Tchrs Col 58-59; UDenver summers 62-65 (LS) MA. 6: Sp. 7: Asst to libn HOPE Col 47; Asst to libn Westminster Theol Sem (Phila) 48-50: Sub tchr Duanesburg Central Sch, Duanesbur NY 58-59; Sub tchr Las Cruces High Sch, Las Cruces NM 59-61, Head Libn 61-. 9: ALA; NEA-DAVI; NMEA (Lib Sect); Las Cruces EA; NM A-V Assn. 10: Delta Kappa Gamma. 15: 1818 Missouri ave, Las Cruces NM 88001.

MEINKE, DARREL M . b Plymouth Neb 19 Je 29. 4: Lois Koeng. 5: Concordia Tchrs Col summers 48-49, 51, 52 LTD; UNeb 49-1 (Eng) BS Ed, summers 51-55 (Secondary Educ) M Ed; UDenver summers 56-59 (LS) MA; UNeb 66 DEd. 7: Prin & tchr Grace Lutheran Sch, Platte Center Neb 51-54; Libn & Eng Supv Concordia High Sch, Seward Neb 54-60; Libn & Assoc Prof of Eng Concordia Tchrs Col 60-. 8: Tech Lib Consul, Neb Tech Sch Milford Neb; Lutheran Church, Mo Synods Lit Commsn. 9: ALA; NEA-DAVI; LUTH Acad for Scolarship; NebLA; MPLA; Neb Educ Media Assn. 10: Kiwanis; Seward Country Club; Seward City Lib Bd. 12: "From Box to Bookshelf" (62). 13: Yes. 14: Admin, ref, media. 15: Concordia Tchrs Col, Seward Nb 68435.

MEIROSE, LEO H. b Cincinnati 25 O 22. 4: Ruth Ruddell. 5: Xavier U 43-45 (Eng) AB; West Res 47-51 MSLS. 6: Sp. 7: Asst libn Xavier U; Cincinati 47-52; Cincinnati Pub Lib; 1st asst films & recordings 52-56; Head wk with schs 56-61, Personnel Off 61-62, Chief ext serv 62-63; Admin libn Xavier U (Cincinnati) 63-64; Chief libn Ft Lauderdale (Fla) Pub Lib 64-. 9: ALA; OhioLA; FlaLA (Standards Com), chm Legisl & Planning Co; chm Pub Lib Div 68-69). 10: Rotary. 14: Admin. 15: 6271 NW 16th pl, Ft Lauderdale Fla.

MEISELS, HENRY R. b Vienna 26 Mr 20. 4: Joy Daspit. 5: Hochschule fuer Welthandel (Vienna) 45-48 (Econ) Diplomkaufmann; Columbia 54-56 MLS. 6: Ger. 7: Bkkeeper Garod Radio Corp, Brooklyn NY 50-53; Off mgr Champion Toggs, Brooklyn NY 53-54; Libn I Brooklyn Pub Lib 55-56; Libn Goethe House, NYC 57-58; Dir Bethpage Pub Lib, Bethpage NY 58-66; Dir Corn Belt Lib Syst, Bloomington Ill 67-. 8: Chm Subcom on Tech Processing, Nassau Lib System 61-63. 9: ALA; NYLA; McLeanCoLA. 11: 1st annual Journal of Library History Award for best mss of year 66. 13: Yes. 14: Hist of libs. 15: 412 Eldorado rd, Bloomington Il 61701.

MEISSNER, AROLANA MARIANNE (JOHNSON). b NYC 9 Ag 43. 4: David Courter Meissner. 5: Ripon Col 62-65 (Eng) BA; AdelphiU 65-66 Certif; UMe 67-69 MLS. 7: Clk circ div R H Fogler Lib UMe 66-67, Curriculum materials libn 67-68, Ref libn 68-. 9: MeLA. 10: Phi Beta Kappa; The Laural. 14: Ref, spec libs. 15: 20 Myrtle st, Orono Me 04473.

MELAMED, DOROTHY (BRAUFF). b Vandergrift Pa 19 Ja 30. 5: Carnegie 47-51 (Home Econ) BS, 61-62 MLS. SLA. 7: Tchr Pittsburgh Pub Schs 52-54; Ref libn Carnegie Lib of Pittsburgh Sci & Tech Dept 62-66; Asst libn Penn State U Agric Lib 66-67; Asst libn US Bur of Mines, Pittsburgh Penn 67-. 9: SLA. 14: Govt tech reports, sci & tech. 15: 1700 Wight st, Pittsburgh Pa 15217.

MELANCON, HELEN ALENE. b Boyce La 22 S 29. 5: Northwestern State (La) 46-49 (Elem Educ) BA; LSU 61 (LS) MS. 6: Fr. 7: Elem tchr, Iota La 51; Welfare visitor La State Dept of Pub Welfare, Jena La 51-53; Asst libn Vermilion Parish Pub Lib, Abbeville La 56-59; Elem tchr, Delcambre La 60; Asst libn order dept & Instr Lib Sci Nicholls State Col 61-. 9: ALA; LaLA. 10: Cath Daughters of Amer; John Henry Cardinal Newman Honor Soc. 14: Acquis. 15: 521 Forest st, Thibodaux La 70301.

MELANSON, LLOYD (JOHN). b Halifax Nova Scotia 10 D 44. 5: St Mart's U (Halifax) 62-65 (Eng Lit) BA; McGill 65-67 MLS. 6: Fr. 7: Catlgr St Mary's U Lib (Halifax) 67-. 9: CanLA; ALA; APLA (treas 68-). 15: 5250 Smith st, Halifax Nova Scotia Can.

MELDRUM, LAWRIE G. b Chicago Ill 27 D 27. 5: Hanover Col 46-50 (Soc Sci) BA; IndU (Bloomington) 58-59 (LS) MA; UDenver 68 (Archival Studies) Certif. 7: Laborer Amer Kitchens, Connersville Ind summer 42; Laborer Rex Mfg, Connersville Ind summer 52; Messenger Cpl US Army Infantry, US 1 Japan 50-52; Sgt US Army Active Res, connersville Ind 52-55; Clk Amer Kitchen Mfg Co, Connersville Ind 53-58; Asst archivist Ind State Lib, Indianapolis 59-67, Acting head archives div 67-. 13: Yes. 14: Mss, mil recs. 15: Archives Division Ind State Lib 140 North Senate ave, Indianapolis In 46204.

MELICK, MARVIN E. b Atalissa Iowa 29 Ja 18. 4: Erma Miller. 5: Gustavus Adolphus 47-50 (Eng) BA; UMich 50-51 AMLS. 7: Circ Ore State Col 51-53; Ref LaCrosse Pub Lib, laCrosse Wis 53-56; Hd libn Elisha D Smith Pub Lib, Menasha Wis 57-60; Hd libn New Ulm Pub Lib, New Ulm Minn 61-65; Hd libn Blue Earth Co Lib, Mankato Minn 65-67; Dir Minn Valley Reg Lib, Mankato Minn 67-. 9: ALA; MinnLA. 10: Rotary Intl. 14: Admin. 15: 123 Dolph rd, Mankato Mn 56001.

MELINAT, CARL H. b Odessa Minn 30 S 12. 4: Ellen Morgan. 5: Valpariso U 31-35 (Eng) AB; West Res 35-39 (Eng) MA, 35-36 (LS) BS; Syracuse 42-49 (Pol Sci) MA. 6: Ger. 7: Ref libn West Res U 36-39, Pub Serv libn 39-42; Asst Prof of Lib Sci Syracuse U 42-49; Aerographers Mate US Navy 44-46; Assoc Prof of Lib Sci Syracue U 49-54, Prof of Lib Sci 54-. 8: Consul Gaylord Bros Inc 42-. 9: ALA; AALA (pres 54-55); NYLA (pres 55-56). 10: Beta Phi Mu; Gamma Mu. 12: "Subject Guide of United States Government Publiaions, with H S Hirshberg (47); Ed "Librarianship and Publishing (63); "Educational Media in Libraries (64). 13: Yes. 14: Ref, admin. 15: 707 Kirkpatrick, Syracuse NY 13208.

MELIUS, CHARLOTTE BARBER. b Baton Rouge La 12 N 44. 4: Harold W Melius. 5: LSU 62-66 (Eng) BS in Secondary Educ, 66-67 (LS) MS. 7: Lib trainee LSU Chem Lib (Baton Rouge) 66-67; Libn I NY Pub Lib 67-68; Asst catlgr LSU Law Lib (Baton Rouge) 68-. 9: ALA; LaLA. 14: Ref. 15: 960 Texas st, Livingston La 70754.

MELLARD, KATHERINE EIZABETH. b Andalusia Ala 6 N 29. 5: Brevard Col 47-49 AA; High Point Col 49-51 BA; UNC summers 57-65 MS in LS. 6: Lat, Sp. 7 Tchr Old Fort Sch, Old Fort NC 52-55; Tchr Mecklenburg Co Schs, Charlotte NC 55-56; Tchr Knox Co Schs, Asheville NC 58-; Libn Instr Mars Hill Col summers 68-69. 9: NEA; ALA; SELA; NCEA (sec 59); NCLA. 10: Internat Reading Assn. 14: Sc libs. ref. 15: 42 Weschester dr, Asheville NC 28803.

MELLINGER, SYDNEY (SHERWIN). b White Plains NY 14 Ag 31. 4: James E Mellinger. 5: BucknellU 49-52 (Pol Sci) AB; Rosary Col 67-68 (LS) MA. 6: Sp. 7: Libn Hawkins Delafield & Wood, NYC 52-54; Catlgr Picatinny Arsenal, Dover NJ 54-56; Asst libn Lake Forest Pub Lib, Lake Forest Ill 68-. 9: ALA; IllLA. 10: Commun Concert Assn; Town & Tennis Club; Girl Scouts; Beta Mu Phi. 14: Tech serv. 15: 325 Blodgett ave, Lake Bluff Il 60044.

MELLON, BETH (DENNING). b Spencer Wyo 3 Mr 41. 4: Richard M Mellon. 5: Orlando Jr Col 59-61; Fla State U 61-63 (Eng, LS) BA,63-64 (LS) MS. 7: STUD ASST OJC Lib, Orlando Fla 59-61, Act libn 62; Grad asst FSU Lib Sch 63; Ref & info dept Orlando Pub Lib, Orlando Fla 64-65; Libn Maitland Fla 65-68; Ref libn Orlando Jr Col, Orlando Fla 68-. 9: FlaLA; SELA; ALA. 14: Pub libs, ref. 15: 525 Griffin ave apt 127, Orlando Fl 32807.

MELNICOE, NORMA (HENDERSON). b Deming NM 27 Ag 18. 4: Melvin Melnicoe. 5: UCal 35-39, Household Art, AB, 39-40; Decorative Art, Gen Secondary; San Francisco State Col 58; UCal 61-62 MLS. 7: Tchr Ceres Union High Sch, Ceres Cal 40-41; Off Nurse, San Francisco 41-43, Rating Examiner Fed Civil Serv, San Francisco 43; Child libn Walnut Creek Br lib, Contra Costa Co Cal 62-64; Br libn Sanramon Valley Br Lib, Contra Costa Co Cal 64-66; Sch libn Marina Elem Sch Pittsburg Unif Sch Dist, Pittsburg Cal 66-. 9: NEA; CalLA; CalASchL; CalTA. 10: Beta Phi Mu; Sierra Club; Alum Assn UCal Lib Schs. 14: Child wk, elem sch libs. 15: 2950 Cherry lane, Walnut Creek Cal 94598.

MELSON, IRENE (WALLING). b Woodbridge NJ 19 My 06. 4: Dr Davis P Melson. 5: Wilson Col 23-27 (Math) AB; Hartford Theol Sem 29-30 (Missions); Union Theol Sem (NYC) 35-36; Emory summers 50-54 (LS) M Ln. 6: Fr. 7: Tchr St Agnes Sch, Albany NY 27-28; Tchr Woodbridge High Sch, Woodbridge NJ 28-29; Tchr Northern Star Sch, Sapporo Japan 30-31; Tchr Joshi Gakuin, Tokyo 32-35, 36-40; Libn LaGrange Col 50-. 9: ALA; SELA; GaLA. 10: AAUW. 14: Admin, catlg, bk, sel, ref. 15: 119 College ave, LaGrange Ga 30240.

MELTON, HELEN (BOND). b Seminole Tex 28 Mr 12. 5: Kidd Key Col 29-30; UNM 30-33 (Hist) BA; UDenver 53-55 (LS) MA. 7: Tchr elem schs, Hope & Vaughn NM 33-34,

37-38; Eng tchr high schs, Vaughn & Roswell NM 34-35, 35-37; Asst libn Carlsbad Pub Lib, Carlsbad NM 46-53, Chief Libn 53-. 9: NMLA (chm Pub Libs Sect 62-63), v-pres & pres-elect 68-69). 10: AAUW. 14: Admin. 15: Carlsbad Pub Lib Halagueno Park, Carlsbad NM 88220.

MELTON, SISTER MARIE RSM. b Bay Shore NY 29 Je 26. 5: St Johns U (NY) 55-60 (Educ) BS in Ed; Pratt 60-61 MLS. 7: Elem sch tchr Sisters of Mercy, Brooklyn NY 47-57; Asst libn Bishop McDonnell High Sch, Brooklyn NY 57-60; Head Libn Mater Christi High Sch, Astoria NY 61-. 9: ALA; CathLA (chm Brooklyn-LI Unit 66-68); NYLA. 10: Beta Phi Mu. 14: Ya lib serv. 15: 21-21 Crecent st, LI City NY 11105.

MELTZER, LESTER. b Brooklyn NY 19 D 19. 4: Eva Nelson. 5: The Citadel 37-39 (Bus Admin); US Mil Acad (West Point) 39-43 (Engnr) BS; Fla State U 64-65 (LS) MS. 7: Pilot, admin off, personnel off, USAF (Lt Col) 43-63; Lib manager R & D Dept Phillips Petrolem Co, Bartlesville Okla 65-. 9: SLA. 10: Beta Phi Mu. 14: Ref, info storage & retrieval. 15: 1416 Lariat dr, Bartesville Ok 74003.

MELTZER, MORTON F. b New Bedford Mass 15 Ap 30. 5: Boston U 55-57 (Journalism) BS (summa cum laude); Rollins Col 62-64 (Mgt) MBA. 6: Fr. 7: Journalist "Standard- times", New Bedford Mass 49-53; Info specialist USA, Nuernberg Ger 53-55; Tech writer USA Ordnance Command, Joliet Ill 57-58; Tech ed Raytheon Corp, Bedford Mass 58-59; Mgr tech info ctr Martin Marietta Corp, Orlando Fla 59-. 8: Professor of Bus Communication, Crummer Sch of Fin and Bus Admin, Rollins Col; Consul to Engnrs Jt Coun in prepar of "Thesaurus of Engineering and Scientific Terms" 67; consul to Dept of Defense on "Project Lex" to help them prepare their tech thesaurus; 1968 session chm of the Amer Mgt Assn's 14th annual Mgt Info and EDP Conf. 9: SLA; ALS; ASIS; Internat Soc for Gen Semantics; Nat Soc for the Study of Communication. 10: Kappa tau Alpha. 11: 1964 George Washington Honor Medal recipient, Freedoms Found, Valley Forge Pa. 12: "The Information Center: Management's Hidden Asset," (67). 14: Info ctr admin. 15: Suite A 2722 Paseo st, Orlando Fl 32805.

MELTZER, NANCY (JANE) (SWANLAND). b Superior Wis 8 Ja 16. 4: Theodore Meltzer. 5: UWash 33-37 (Econ) BA, 37-38 BA in Libnship. 6: Fr. 7: Lib asst Seattle Pub Lib 38-39; Army libn McCaw Gen Hop, Walla Walla Wash 43-45; Asst libn Seattle Pub Lib 45-48; Head circ dept Queens Col Lib City U of NY 48-. 9: NYLA; LACUNY; NY Lib Club. 10: Phi Beta Kappa; AAUP. 14: Circ, col & univ libs. 15: 28 School House lane, Lake Success LI NY 11020.

MELUM, VERNA V. b Chicago Ill 14 Ja 08. 5: St Olaf Col 26-30 (Eng) BA; UColo summer 40; UMinn 35-36 BS, summers 41, 53-56 (LS) MA. 7: Tchr High Sch Chokio Minn 30-34; Tchr & libn elem & high sch, Granite Falls Minn 36-41; Libn elem jr & sr high sch, Stillwater Minn 41-46; Circ & ref libn Stephens Col 46-57; Ref libn & tchr of lib orientation & instr No Ill U 57-. 8: N Central Eval Coms for High Schs (2 Ill high schs) 66; Consul wk in lib orient and instr (1 high schs, 2 cols) 69. 9: ALA; IllLA. 10: Delta Kappa Gamma; LWV. 13: Yes. 14: Lib orien & instr, educ materials ctr, ref. 15: Parson Lib No Ill Univ, DeKalb Il 60115.

MELVIN, SISTER M CONSTANCE IHM. b Pittston Penn 28 O 18. 5: Marywood Col 36-40 (Soc Sci) AB (magna cum laude); Columbia 40-41 BS in LS; Chicago 51-62 (Educ for Libnship) PhD. 6: Fr. 7: Sch libn high sch, Eastport LI NY 41-43; Sch libn high sch, Mt Kisco NY 43-46; Gen asst pub lib, Scranton Penn summer 42; Asst libn Marywood Col Lib 46-48; Tchr Diocesan High Schs, Scranton Penn 50-60; Lecturer Dept of Libnship Marywood Col 48-60, chm & prof dept of libnship 60-. 8: Adv Com on Implementation of Elem & Secon Educ Act, Penn Dept of Pub Instr, 65-; Consul in child lit, proj Head Start, Scranton Bd of Educ, 65-. 9: ALA (mem ALA-CathLA Jt Com 63-65); CathLA (Adv Coun 60-); PennLA (Exec Bd 65-66, chm Resol Com 65-); NE Penn LA; Penn State EA (Dept of Supv & Curr Devel); SELA; NCLA. 10: AAUW; Kappa Gamma Pi; Beta Phi Mu. 12: ""A History of Public School Libraries in Pennsylvania, PhD diss (62). 13: Yes. 14: Educ for libnship. 15: Marywood Col, Scranton Penn 18509.

MELVIN, MARY BELLE (CRAVER). b Murphysboro Ill 4 Ja 17 . 4: Joseph K Melvin. 5: So Ill U 34-38 (Hist, Eng) B Ed; UIll summers 39-42 BS in LS. 7: Tchr Murphysboro Grade Sch, Murphysboro Ill 38-42; Libn Marshall High Sch, Ill 42-43; Libn Johnston City High Sch, Johnston City Ill 43-45; So Ill U Asst & ref libn, Period Libn 47-56, Asst libn U Sch 58-60,Libn Vocational Tech Inst 61, Libn U Sch 61-; Asst sci lib 68-. 9: IllLA; IllSchLA. 15: Rt 2, Murphysboro Ill 62911.

MEMMOTT, BARBARA A. b Cranston RI 9 S 12. 5: Pembroke 29-33 (Biol) PhB. 7: Circ & ref William H Hall Lib, Edgewood RI 29-36; Circ dept Welles-Turner Mem Lib, Glastonbury Conn 55-57; Catlgr United Aircraft Corp, E Hartford Conn 57-65, Br libn Middletown Conn 60-. 9: SLA; (treas Conn Valley Chap). 10: PTA; Visiting Nurse Assn; Girl Scout Leader; Phi Beta Kappa. 14: Catlg, ref. 15: 186 House st, Glastonbury Ct 06033.

MEMORY, MARJORIE WHITTINGTON. b Durham NC. 5: UNC (Greensboro) 45-48 (Hist) AB; UNC (Chapel Hill) 68 MSLS. 6: Sp, Fr. 7: Managr Col Bk Store Campbell Col 42-43; Tchr NC Pub Sch, Randleman NC 48-49; Circ asst UNC (Greensboro) 49-63, Ser libn 63-, Hd ser libn 68-. 9: SELA; NCLA. 14: Ser. 15: 134 N Main, Randleman NC 27317.

MENCER, FRED JAMES. b E Smethport Penn 17 F 24. 4: Corinne Mencer. 5: Wheaton Col 52 9greek) AB; Dallas Theol Sem 52-56 (Bible Exposition) TaM; UWis 62-63 MS in LS. 6: Greek. 7: Mechanic Army Air Corps 42-46; Missionary appointee, Missionary Baptist Mid-Missions, Cleveland Ohio 56-61; Ext & asst libn Vaughn Pub Lib, Ashland Wis 63-65; Asst catlgr Wis StateU (Eau Claire) 65-68, Hd original catlg 68-. 9: WisLA. 10: Assn Wis StateU Fac; Beta Phi Mu. 14: Catlg, ref. 15: 509 Keith st, Eau Claire Wi 54701.

MENDELOFF, NATHAN NORMAN. b NYC 9S 14. 5: LIU 31-33; NYU even 33-37 (Hist) BA; Catholic U even 50-54 MS (LS). 6: Romance & Cyrillic langs. 7: T/Sgt (Sgt Major Off Personnel) QM Sch, Camp Lee Va; LC; Head Receiving & Routing Exch & Gift 48-51, Asst ed NST 51-53, Sr sub catlgr EEAI 53-56, Asst ed of Catlg Pbl 56-62, Ed of Catlg Publ (includes the Nat Union Catalog; Bks; Subjs; Music & Phonorecords; Motion Pictures & Filmstrips; NLM Catalogs) 62-, Asst hd Nat Union Catlg Publ Proj 67-. 9: ALA; SLA; DCLA; Potomac Tech Processing Libns. 11: Meritorious Service Award, LC 63. 12: "Checklist of Rhode Island Imprints, 1821-1830, with a Historical Introduction (54). 14 Publ of a lib nature, e.g. bibliogs. 15: 2014 Evansdale dr, Adelphi Md 20783.

MENEES, EILENE CORNWALL. b Seattle 1 D 14. 5: UWash 32-37 (Hist) BA, 37-38 BA in Libnship. 7: Lib asst Seattle Pub Lib 38-42, Br libn 43-45; Pomona Pub Lib; order libn 47-50 Br libn 51-56,Bibliog order libn 56-63, Dir tech serv div 63-. 9: ALA; CalLA; PNLA. 10: AAUW. 14: Ref, child wk, Californiana. 15: 1280 Casa Vista dr, Pomona Cal 91766.

MENEGAUX, EDMOND A. b NYC 14 Ap 38. 4: Sandra Cushman. 5: SUNY (Albany) 57-62 (Chem) BA, 66-67 MLS. 6: Fr. 7: Chem Albany Med Col 62-66; Sci libn Rensselaer Polytech Inst 67-68; Asst sci bibliogr SUNY (Albany) 68-. 9: ALA; ASIS; SUNY Libns Assn. 14: Sci ref & bibliog. 15: RD 2 Vischer Ferry rd, Rexford NY 12148.

MENENDEZ, MARIA DE LOS ANGELES (ACOSTA). b Matanzas Cuba 9 My 28. 4: Benjamin Menendez. 5: U de la Habana 45-53; PhD, 53-56 Bibliotecario. 6: Sp, Eng, Fr. 7: Libn dept of art U de la Habana 54-57; Dir of lib Bancode Desarrollo Economico y Social (Bandes), Havana Cuba 57-60; Libn Banco Nacional de Cuba, Habana 60-61; Asst to catlgr UMiami (Fla) Lib 64-. 8: Adv wk; El espiritu en Marti 53; Panorama de la Civilizacion Occidental 54. 9: ALA; FLA; Dade Co LA; UMiami LA. 10: (Agrupacion Bibliografica Jose Toribio Medina. 13: Yes. 14: Catlg. 15: 2770 SW 22 ave, Miami Fl 33133.

MENG, TE-SHENG (TIMOTHY). b Hupeh China 12 S 30. 4: Leah Lee. 5: Nat Taiwan U 50-54 (Pol Sci) BA; Nat Chengchi U 54-57 (pol Sci) MLL; Carleton U 63-64 (Pub Admin); UOttawa 64-65 BLS. 6: Chinese, Eng, Japanese. 7: Instr Nat Chengchi U (Taiwan) 57-61, Assoc Prof 62-63; Order libn UAlta 65-68; Asst libn Okanagan Reg Col (BC) 68-. 8: Acting Dir of Nat Chengchi Univ Press, Taiwan 57-63. 9: CanLA; AltaLA. 10: Dance Club, UAlta; Chinese Culture Assn, Palo Alto Cal. 12: "Business Management (Taiwan 60); "John F Kennedy and His Administration (Taiwan 62). 13: Yes. 14: Acquis, ref, catlg. 15: c/o Mr James Cheng, Box 550, Kelowna BC Can.

MENGEL, MILDRED MILLER. b Leesport Penn 23 Ag 07. 5: Kutztown State Col 24-26, 45-46 (Lib Educ) BS; Peabody 47-49 (LS) MA. 6: Sp, Russian, Ger. 7: Pub sch tchr Ontelaunee Twp, Leesport Penn 26-45; Asst libn Beaver Col 46-47; Asst libn Kutztown State Col 47-52, Asst Prof of Lib Educ 52-. 9: ALA; NEA; PennLA; Penn State EA. 10: AAUW. 14: Catlg, lib educ. 15: 496 W Walnut, Kutztown Penn 19530.

MENGES, GARY L. b Garrison Iowa 11 S 37. 5: Cornell Col (Iowa) 55-59 (Hist, Pol Sci) BA; UMich 59-61 AMLS. 6: Ger. 7: Lib wk-study scholar order dept UMich Lib 59-61; US Army (Reserve Active Duty) (Pfc) 61-62; Asst libn Undergrad Lib Cornell U 62-65, Res bk libn Undergrad Lib 65-66, City planning libn & assoc libn Fine Arts Lib 66-. 8: Library/USA NY Worlds Fair 64-. 9: ALA; Coun of Planning Libns (histn 69-). 10: ACLU; Sierra Club. 12: Bibliogs, Coun of Planning Libns; "Model Cities" (68); "Historic Preservation" (69). 14: Ref, soc sci libs. 15: 413 Dryden rd, Ithaca NY 14850.

MENIHAN, LUCILLE RUTH. b Honeoye NY 21 My 17. 5: State U Col (Geneseo NY) 34-38 (Educ) BS; Columbia 39-38 (Educ) BS; Columbia 39-48 (Educ) MA. 7: Elem libn Scotia Pub Schs, Scotia NY 38-45; Elem libn Great Neck Pub Schs, Great Neck NY 45-48; Libn campus sch State U Col (Geneseony) 48-53; Elem libn Great Neck Pub Schs, Great Neck NY 53-. 8: Consul, Child catlg; Lib sch tchg: Nazareth Col (Rochester), State U Col (Geneseo NY), West Wash Col of Euc (Bellingham Wash), St Johns U (Jamaica NY); Wkshops Directed; (Albany) State Col of Educ (NY); Queens Col, NYC. 9: NEA; ALA; NY State Tchrs Assn; Nassau-Suffolk Sch Libns. 14: Elem sch libs. 15: 29 W Mill dr, Greak Neck NY 11021.

MEOLA, MARJORIE (NEWTON). b Rochester NY 4 N 14. 4: . 5: State U (Geneseo NY) 32-34, summers 35-41 (LS) BS. 7: Libn: Sodus High Sch, Sodus NY 34-35; Franklinville High Sch, Franklinville NY 35-37; Memorial Sch, Middletown NY 37-59; Anthony J Verali, Middletown NY 59-. 9: NEA; NY State Tchrs Assn. 10: University Club. 15: 15 South st, Middletown NY.

MERBAUM, MARK E. b Chicago Ill 8 S 37. 5: UCLA 59 (Hist) BA; USoCal 65-67 MSLS. 6: Ger, Sp. 7: Computer operator bank, Los Angeles 60-64; Jr programmer Management Applied Programming, Los Angeles 64-65; Coder Electronics Personnel Research Group, Los Angeles 66; Libn Dept of Chilf PSYCH Mt Sinai Hosp, Los Angeles 66-67; Current acquis libn UCal (San Diego) Lib 67-68, Systems libn 68-. 9: CalLA. 14: Info storage & retr, syst analysis, acquis. 15: PO Box 2362, La Jolla Ca 92037.

MERCER, ELEANOR (BROWN). b Rosedale BC Can 21 Ja 14. 5: UBC 30-37 (Hist) BA, MA; UWash 37-38 BA in Libnship. 6: Fr, Sp. 7: UBC Asst circ 38-37, 1st asst circ 47-51, Head acquis 5163, Ext libn 63-66, Bibliogr 66-. 9: CanLA (Coun 50-53 BCLA (pres 50-51); ALA; PNLA; Bibliog Soc Can. 14: Collection bldg. 15: Univ of BC Lib, Vancouver 8 BC Can.

MERCER, HANNAH FAITH. b Harbour Breton Newfoundland Can 11 Ja 20. 5: ULondon 38-40 (Intermediate Arts); Toronto 43-44 Diploma in Libnship; ULondon 52-55 BA. 6: Fr. 7: Custodian Joseph Clouter FreePub Lib, Catalina Nefoundland 39-41; Lib asst Gosling Mem Lib, St Johns Newfoundland 41-43, Child libn 44-46, Catlgr 46-52; Catlgr Mem U of Newfoundland Lib 52-54; Catlgr Pub Lib Sers of Newfoundland, St Johns Newfoundland 5461, Head of tech serv 61-. 8: Actg Deputy Libn, Gosling Mem Lib, 50. 9: CanLA; APLA (v-pres for Newfoundland 60-61),66-67). 14: Child libs, catlg. 15: 08 Kent pl, St Johns Newfoundland Can.

MERCER, JOHN HERBERT. b Fredericton NB Can 6 F 32. 4: Mary Alice Smith. 5: Dalhousie U (Halifax NS) 50-54 (Hist) BA, 56-57 (Educ) B Ed; Toronto 62-63 BLS, summers 69- (LS). 6: Fr. 7: High Sch tchr Halifax Co Mun Sch Bd, Oyster Pond Halifax Co NS 57-58; High sch tchr Colchester Co Mun Sch Bd, Tatam agouche NS 58-62; Catlgr Dalhousie U Law Lib (Halifax NS) 63-64; Asst catlgr & ref libn Halifax City Reg Lib, Halifax NS 64-67; Asst catlgr & govt docs libn Acadia U, Wolfville NS 67-. 9: CanLA; APLA. 10: Beta Phi Mu. 14: Catlg, ref, govt docs. 15: PO Box 614, Wolfville NS Can.

MERCER, LEOLYN S(MITH). b Ansonia Com 21 N 1896. 4: George C Mercer. 5: Barnard 15-19 BA; Columbia 34-49 BSL, 34-36 (Educ); Rutgers 36. 6: Fr, Ger, Sp, Lat. 7: Libn High Sch, Hackensack NJ 33-62; Ref libn & org Maywood Pub Lib, Maywood NJ 55-62: Lib Dir Englewood-Charlotte Pub Lib, Englewood Fla 62-. 9: ALA; NJLA; NJSchLA; FlaLA; NJEA. 10: Altrusa Internat; Fla Hist Assn; Charlotte Co Civic Assn; Barnard Almnae Assn; NJ Retired Educators Assn. 14: Admin (wk with schs at loc level). 15: Box 5002 Grove City Rural Sta, Edgewood Fl 33533.

MERCIER, SISTER J M. b Quebec City Can 19 Ap 08. 5: Laval U 60-62 (LS) Diploma. 6: Fr, Eng. 7: OR nurse supv Hotel Dieu Hosp. ARTHABASKA Que 35-45; OR nurse supv Hotel-Dieu Hosp, Bathurst NB 46-54; Med libn Hotel- Dieu HOSP, ARTHABASKA Que 61-. 9: CanLA; MedLA; CathLA; Association Canadienne des Bibliothecaires de Langue Francaise. 14: Catlg, ref. 15: Hotel-Dieu Hospital, Arthabaska Que Can.

MERCURE, ROSEMARY P. b Bostic NC 24 Ap 28. 5: Lincoln MemU 46-50 (Fr) AB; E Tenn StateU 65-66 (LS) High Sch Certif; UKy 67-68 MSLS. 6: Fr, Sp. 7: Tchr Unicoi Co High Sch, Erwin Tenn 50-51; Psychiatric aide Inst of Living, Hartford Conn 51-53; Hd Start tchr Unicoi Elem Sch, Erwin Tenn 65; Asst libn Unicoi Co Pub Lib, Erwin Tenn 63-66; Asst libn clinch Valley Col, Wise Va 66-67, Libn 68-. 9: ALA; SELA; TennLA; VaLA. 10: Beta Phi Mu; AAUW; Pi Delta Phi; Sigma Delta Pi. 14: Ref, catlg, admin. 15: Clinch Valley College of the Univ of Va, Wise Va 24293.

MEREDITH, WILLIAM B. b Piqua Ohio 8 Jl31. 4: Mary Burson. 5: Ohio U 48-51 (Fr, Lat) AB; UMich 51-54 (Fr, Span) MA; Columbia 55-56 MSLS. 6: Fr, Sp, Lat, Ger, Ital. 7: Lib asst NYU Com Lib 54-55; Lib asst NYU Grad Lib Bus Admin 55-56; Asst dir acquis Dartmouth Cl Lib 56-60, Dir of acquis 60-66, Asst col libn 66-. 9: ALA-RTSD (Acquis Sect, ad hoc Bk Disposal Com, Nom Com); NE Col Libn; NELA. 10: Phi Beta Kappa. 14: Tech serv, acquis. 15: Box 563, Hanover NH 03755.

MERHEMIC, FADIL I. b Sarajevo Yugoslavia 29 Je 19. 4: Adela Hairlich. 5: UZagreb 38-41 (Pre-Med); Col for Bus Admin (Vienna) 41-46 (World Trade); West ResU 58-59 MSLS. 6: Serbo-Croatian, Ger, Fr. 7: Mgr Summit Square Deal, Lakewood Ohio 57-58; Ref libn Health Ctr Lib, Ohio StateU (Columbus) 59-61, Hd Veterinary Med Lib 61, Hd Bot & Zool Lib 67-; Supv Tech Info Ctr Chrysler Corp Detroit 61-62; Mgr Lakeside Labs inc Milwaukee 62-66; Supv Tech Info Ctr A O Smith, Arlington Hts Ill 66-67. 9: SLA. 13: Yes. 14: Med & bio sci libnship, ref. 15: 2647 Bristol rd, Columbus Oh 43221.

MERIAM, PHILP WITHINGTON. b Lincoln Mass 26 N29. 4: Ellin Fairkax Fuller. 5: Alfred U 58 (Pol Sci) BA; Rutgers 59 MLS. 7: Yeoman 2/c US Coast Guard 52-56; Ya libn Brooklyn Pub Lib 59-60; Lib-speech writer Harris Kerr Forster & Co, NYC 61-62; Asst dir Wellesley Free Lib, Wellesley Mass62-66; Dir Dedham Pub Lib, Dedham Mass 67-. 9: MassLA; Greater Boston Pub Lib Adminrs. 14: Admin, personnel, ref. 15: Wellesley Free Lib, 530 Washington st, Wellesley Ma.

MERICLE, REBECCA (STUTSMAN). b Grand Traverse Co Mich 3 Je 15. 5: Wayne State 32-36 (Eng) BA; Simmon 36-37 BS in LS. 7: Jr asst libn Detroit Pub Lib 37-38; Act libn Penninsula Twp Commun Lib, Old Mission Mich 57-60; Asst libn Traverse City Pub Lib 60; Asst libn Mark Osterlin Lib Northwestern Mich Col 60-. 9: MichLA. 14: Catlg. 15: Northwestern Mich Col, Traverse City Mi 49684.

MERITHEW, DORIS. b Los Angeles 9 Ag 11. 5: USoCal 28-32 (Lat) AB, 32-33 (Lat) MA, 30-33 (Educ) Secondary Credential, 46-47 BS in LS, 47-58 (Classics) PhD. 6: Fr, Sp, Ger, Ital, Portu, Russian Lat. 7: Cargo sec Wholesale Lumber E K Wood Lumber Co, Los Angeles 35-42; Ensign to Lt Cmdr US Navy 42-46; Catlgr-libn USocal 47-. 10: USN Reserve in various capacities; Personnel Officer NR Composite Co 11-05, Pomona Cal. 14: For lang catlg. 15: 4249 E Lynd ave, Arcadia Ca 91006.

MERKL, ANTHONY EDMUND. b St Paul 3 Jl 19. 4: Jeanette Biribauer. 5: Col of St Thomas 38-42, 46-47 (Philos) BA; Fordham 47-48 (Psych); Juilliard Sch of Music 49-52 (Conducting); Columbia 54-56 (LS) MS. 6: Ger. 7: Lib page St Paul Pub Lib 35-37, Lib asst 38-42; (Pvt) Tech 5 US Army Signal Corps Radio Operator 42, (2d Lt, 1st Lt) Radio Intelligence 43-46; Asst libn Fordham U Lib 52-58, Chief pub serv 58-67; Asst libn ed ref lib "New York Times," NYC 59-; Supv libn Jersey City Pub Lib 67-68; Dir S Orange Pub Lib, S Orange NJ 68-. 9: ALA-ACRL; NJLA. 10: Archons of Colophon; Melvil Dui Chowder & Marching Assn. 14: Lib admin, ref. 15: 394 Hall Court, S Orange NJ 07079.

MEROLA, LOIS A (GOODMAN). b Brooklyn NY 7 S 44. 4: Frank Merola. 5: Brooklyn Col 61-65 (Art) BA; Pratt 66-67 MLS. 6: Sp. 7: Insurance expediter Sterling Drug Inc, nyc 65-66; Grad asst Pratt 66-67; Asst ref libn LIU 67-. 9: ALA. 10: AAUP; Pratt Inst Alum Assn; Beta Phi Mu. 14: Ref, bibliog. 15: 1854 Ocean ave, Brooklyn NY 11230.

MERREL, MARY MARGARET (SYDNOR). b Orlando Fla 7 Jl 45. 4: (Louis) Gregory Merrel. 5: Whittier Col 63-67 (Eng, Sociol) BA; USoCal 67-69 MSLS. 7: Child libn LA Co, W

Covina 69-. 9: ALA. 14: Child. 15: 2308 Merced, W Covina Ca 91790.

MERRIAM, HAROLD EDWIN. b Baldwinville Mass 6 Je 02. 4: Nina (Hunt). 5: Comm of Mass univ Ext 59-60 (LS) Certif. 7: Boston Edison Co: Sec 25-41, Supv 41-42, 44-56, material coord 56-62, Supv tech lib 62-67; Chief yeoman USN (Seabees) 42-44; Tech info specialist USA Natick Labs, Natick Mass 68-. 9: SLA; ASIS. 10: Amer Legion. 14: Info storage & retr, info anal ctrs. 15: 1281 Great Plain ave, Needham Ma 02192.

MERRIAM, JOYCE. b Worcester Mass 17 Mr 36. 5: UMass 53-57 (Hist) BA; UWis 58 (Hist) MA. 6: Fr, Ger, Sp. 7: Dist dir New London Area Girl Scout Coun, New London Conn 58-60; Ref asst UMass Lib 60-65, Ref libn 65-. 10: Girl Scouts; Phi Kappa Phi. 14: Ref. 15: 196 Triangle st, Amherst Ma 01002.

MERRIGAN, PAUL GERARD. b NYC 1 Jl25. 4: Helen Pratt. 5: Fordham 51 (Educ) BS Ed; Columbia 55 MSLS. 6: Ger, Fr. 7: Libn Hoagland Lib LICH, Brooklyn NY 55-60; Libn Nassau Acad of Med, Garden City NY 60-; Libn St Clare's Sch Nursing 67-. 9: MedLA (TREAS NY Reg Group); CathLA (Rep on Interagency Counon Lib Tools for Nursing; Greater NY Unit: sec-treas & chm Hosp Sect); Med & Sci Libns of LI (chm; NY Lib Club (treas). 15: 101 W 80 st, NYC 10024.

MERRITT, BETTY JO ROUNTREE. b Springfield Mo 10N 25. 4: Harold Andrew Merritt. 5: Memphis State U 58-61 (Art, LS, Fr, Educ) BA. 7: Lab tech Kraft Foods Co, Springfield M0 43-46; Accounting clerk Gen Motors AccepCorp, Alton Ill 50-58; Asst libn Memphis Pub Lib, Memphis Tenn 62; Libn St Jude Child Research Hosp, Memphis Tenn 63-67; Acquis libn Mooney Mem Lib UTenn Med Units, Memphis Tenn 67-. 9: MedLA. 15: Mooney Mem Lib UTenn Medical Units, Memphis Tn 38103.

MERRITT, CATHERINE WAGUETTE. b NYC 23 D 10. 4: James Krom Merritt II. 5: Douglass Col Rutgers U 26- 30 (Hist) AB; Columbia 31-33 (LS) BS. 6: Fr, Ger, Lat, Russian, Ital, Sp. 7: Lib asst Rutgers U Lib 30-34; Circ asst Princeton U 35; Lib asst Rutgers U Lib 35, Ref libn, head catlg dept 38-. 10: Phi Beta Kappa. 14: Admin. 15: Rutgers U Li, New Brunswick NJ.

MERRITT, FLOYD SAMUEL. b Northampton Mass 27 D 28. 5: Amherst 47-51 (Eng Lit) BA; Cambridge U (Eng) 51-53 (Eng Lit) AB; Harvard 53-57 (Eng Lit) MA; Simmons 62-65 (LS) MS. 6: Fr. 7: Asst sales manager Wilson Farms Inc, E Lexington Mass 58; Asst ref libn Amherst Col Lib 58-62, Admin asst 62-66, Asst ref libn 67, Ref libn 68-. 9: ALA; MassLA. 14: Ref. 15: 219 Amity st, Amherst Mass 01002.

MERRITT, GERTRUDE (ELIZABETH). b Goldsboro NC 23 Jl 09. 5: Duke U 27-31 (Hist) AB. 6: Fr, Ger, Sp. 7: Duke U: Searcher order dept 31-37, Ser catlgr 38-39, Head ser dept 40-42, Head tech processes 43-46, Asst libn tech serv 66-. 9: ALA; SELA; NCLA. 14: Acquis, catlg, ser. 15: Duke Univ Lib, Durham NC 27706.

MERRITT, PAULINE (ROQUEMORE). b Taylor Co Butler Ga 15 Je 34. 4: John E Merritt. 5: Morris Brown Col 50-54 (Sociol) BA; Atlanta 56-61 MSLS. 7: Tchr-libn Baldwin Co Bd of Educ, Milledgeville Ga 55-61; Libn Chatham Co Bd of Educ, Savannah Ga 61-. 9: NEA; ALA; ATA; Ga Tchrs & Educ Assn. 10: Delta Sigma Theta; Alpha Kappa Delta. 14: Ref. 15: 825 W 5th st, Savannah Ga 31405.

MERRITT, SYLVIA (STERN). b Chicago Ill 24 Mr 24. 4: John F Merritt. 5: UIll 43-46 (Law) BSL, LLB; Immaculate Heart Col 65 MALS. 7: Ed (trade regulation reports) Com clearing House, Chicago 47-49; Rules tech Los Angeles City Schs 49-53, Admin policy coord 53-56; Ref libn UCLA Law Lib 65-. 9: AALL; So Cal Assn Law Libs. 10: Mem Ill bar; Amer Soc Indexers. 14: Ref (law). 15: 3300 S Sepulveda, Los Angeles Ca 90034.

MERRY, SUSAN A (CARNEGIE). b Toronto Can 7 Ja 38. 4: Christopher W E Merry. 5: UToronto 59 (Phil) BA, 61-62 BLS, 62 (Piano) ARCT. 6: Fr. 7: bibliogr acquis dept utoronto lib 62-63, ontario new univs Lib Proj 63-67; Chief of Lib Serv Dept of Sec of state, Ottawa 67-. 9: CanLA. 10: Prof Inst Pub Serv Can. 13: Yes. 15: Dept Sec of State 130 Slater st, Ottawa 2 Ont Can.

MERSEREAU, JOSEPH EDGAR. b Cherrydale Va 27 Mr 25. 4: Mary Bundy. 5: Amer U 46-50 (Hist) BA; Syracuse 51-53 MLS. 6: Fr. 7: Reader's adv DC Pub Lib 53-54; Ref libn HEW Lib, Wash DC 54-56; Asst chief libs sect USAF, Wash DC 56-62; Chief circ sect NIH Lib, Bethesda Md 62-64; Dir Laurel Pub Lib, Laurel Del 64-66; Supv of ref serv Fair Pub Lib, Fairfax Va 66-. 8: Adv Com for Survey of Del Pub Libs; Scholarship Adv Com for Del State Lib Commsn. 9: ALA; DelLA; VaLA. 10: Atlantic Naturalist Soc. 14: Ref. 15: 3738 Chain Bridge rd, Fairfax Va 22030.

MERSHON, MARIANNA JENKINS. b Brooklyn NY 26 F 15. 5: NJ State Col (Montclair) 33-37 (Eng) BA; NJ State Col Trenton) 43; Columbia 50-53 (LS) MS; Rutgers 60-61 (LS. 6: Fr. 7: Tchr in NJ secondary schs, 6 yrs; Asst libn Hunterdon Co Lib, Flemington nj state Col Lib (Montclair) 49-51; Libn Boonton High Sch Lib, Boonton NJ 51-53; Head of circ dept Orange Pub Lib, Orange NJ 53-55; Asst libn Upsala Col Lib 55-. 9: ALA-RSD (chm Essex Co Chap); NJLA (sec 55, Col Sect sec, Lib Devel Com 2 yrs). 10: Olivet Congregatioal Church (Livingston NJ) Bd of Deacons 3 yrs & State Soc Action Com; Kappa Delta Pi; AAUP. Montclair. 14: Ref, govt documents, instr methods of research. 15: 53 Linn dr, Verona NJ 07044.

MERSKY, ROY (MARTIN). b NYC 1 S 25. 4: Deena Hersh. 5: UWis 48 (Labor Econ) BS, 52 LLB, 53 MALS; Oxford U 49 (Brit Labor Hist). 6: Fr, Ger, Sp, Hebrew. 7: (Cpl) US Army 44-46; Govt documents catlgr UWis Law Lib (Madison) 51-52; Stud asst UWis Educ Lib (Madison)summer 52; Ref asst Madison Free Lib, Madison Wis 52; Law practice, Wis 52-54; Readers adv ref & catlg libn Miwaukee Pub Lib & Mun ref libn at City Hall 53-54; Asst libn, chief of readers & ref serv Yale Law Lib 54-59; Dir Wash State Law Lib, Olympia Wash 59-63; Exec sec of Judicial Coun & Cmmsnr for Wash Court Reporters, Olympia Wash 59-63; Prof of Law & Law Libn UColo 63-65; Prof of Law & Law Libn UTex 65-. 8: Assoc Prof New Haven State Tchrs Col 55; Lib consul for Nat Col of State Trail Judges, Reno Nev. ; Consul; UHouston Law Lib, ABA Law & Tech Com 68-69. 9: ALA (pres-elect Law & Pol Sci Subsect; past Coun mem, Subcom on Micropublishing Projs, Internat Rel Round Table, Law & Pol Sci Subsect SSS/ACRL, Lib Legis Com);-LAD (Recr Com);-ACRL (Commsn on Nat Lib Week); AALL (mem 3 coms); Amer coms; chm Spec Pres Com to Establish Guidelines for Law Libs); Assn; AAStateL Assn (Com on Research); on on By-,laws); By-laws); on Info Retrieval); ColoLA (chm Intel Freedom Com); Southwest Wash LA (pres 61-62); Tex Assn Col Tchrs (2nd v-pres UTex Chap). 10: ACLU; AntiDefamtion League; AAUP. 12: Co-ed "Index to Periodical Articles Related to Law" (58-65); Bk review ed "Law Library Journal" (60-65); Ed "American Law of Water Rights" (65); Ed "Classics in Legal History" (vols 1-). 13: Yes. 14: Rare bks, admin. 15: 2500 Red River, Austin Tx 78705.

MERTENS, PATRICIA (FURLONG). b Trenton Mo 27 S 44. 4: John F Mertens. 5: Trenton Jr Col 62-64 AA; NW Mo State 64-66 (Elem Educ) BS; UMich 66-67 AMLS. 6: Sp. 7: Clerk Grundy Co Jewett Norris Lib, Trenton Mo 62-64; Child libn Daniel Boone Reg Lib, fulton Mo 67-. 9: ALA; MoLA. 10: AAUW. 14: Child & yp. 15: Rte 2 Churchill manor, Fulton Mi 65251.

MERVIS, SARAH. b Baltimore 25 Ag 09. 5: Geneva Col 28-29; Carnegie 29-30 Certif. 7: Child libn Pottsville Pub Lib, Potts ville Penn 30-36; Br libn New Castle Free Pub Lib, New Castle Penn 36-44, Child libn 44-45; Child libn Van Nuys Br Lib, Van Nuys Cal 45-50; Br libn Sherman Oaks Br Lib, Sherman Oaks Cal 50-. 9: ALA. 15: 14318 Dickens st, Sherman Oaks Cal 91403.

MESA, ROSA QUINTERO. b Havana Cuba 14 O 23. 4: Danilo F Mesa. 5: UHabana 41-45 (Pharmacy) Doctor in Pharmacy, 59 (LS) Master. 6: Sp, Portu, Fr, Ital. 7: Asst libn Biblioteca Nacional, Havana 59-60; Asst libn Ruston Acad, Marianao Cuba 60-61; Asst libn UFla 61-. 12: Comp "Latin American Serial Documents" v 1, Colombia, v 2 Brazil (69); "Sources of information of the Governmental Organization of the Countries of Latin America" (65). 14: Latin Amer off publ, Latin Amer bibliog. 15: 1070 SW 11th st, Gainesville Fl 32601.

MESCHERIN, EUGENE. b Moscow Russia 2 My 13. 4: Xenia Meshkova. 5: Timiriazev Agric Acad (USSR) fall 33, 39 (Horticulture) BS Agronomy; UCal (Riverside) fall 64, summer 66 (Ger) MA; UCLA summer 66, 67 MLS. 6: Russian, Ger, Fr, Sp, Rumanian. 7: Russian instr Army Lang Sch, Monterey Cal 63; Libn Brain Info Ctr UCLA 66; Catlg Fresno State Col 67-. 9: CalLA. 10: Sierra Club. 14: Catlg, tech tr. 15: PO Box 4441, Pasadena Ca 91106.

MESEROLL, IDA ADELE (GIAIMO). b Lyndhurst NJ 8 N 12. 5: Albright Col 29-30, 31-33 (Fr) BA; NYU 30-31; Catholic U summer 56, 57; Rutgers 57-62 MLS. 6: Fr, Ital, Sp. 7: Tchr Bd of Educ, Lynhurst NJ 33-37; Sub-tchr Monmouth & Ocean Cos, NJ 37-52; Tchr US Armed Fores Inst, Japan 52-53; Asst libn US Army Int Sch, Baltimore 56; Core tchr Bd of Edu, Baltimore Co, Baltimore 54-56, Jr high sch libn 56-. 9: NEA; ALA; Md State Tchrs Assn; MdLA; Baltimore Co ASchL; Baltimore Co T 14: Ref. 15: 907 Marksworth rd, Baltimore Md 21228.

MESERVE, JANET R. b Chicago 24 My 42. 5: UIll 60- 64 (Geol) BS, 64-65 (LS) MS. 6: Ger, Fr. 7: Catlgr UIll Lib (Urbana) 65-67; Subj catlgr LC 68-. 9: Soc verteb Paleont; Geo Sci Info Soc. 14: Catlg, ref (sci materials). 15: 618 A st SE, Washington Dc 20003.

MESERVE, SAMUEL EDWARD. b Hawesville Ky 12 O 32. 4: Mary Catherine Arnold. 5: West Ky U 50-54 (Geog) BS, 58-62 (Educ), LS) MA; Catherine Spalding Col 61-63 (LS); UKy 65 (LS), Purdue 68 (Educ media). 7: Secondary tchr Beechmont High Sch, Hawesville Ky 55; Clerk typist US Army Spec Third Class 55-57; Secondary tchr Rineyville High Sch, Rineyville Ky 57-61, Secondary libn 61-62; Elem libn Elizbethtown City Sch, Elzabethtown Ky 62-; Headstart div City of Elizabethtown summer 69. 8: Com mem KLA Com for NLW 1968-69. 9: NEA; KyLA; KyASchL (Scholarship Com 63-69); KyEA; Fourth Dist Libn Assn (pres 63-64). 10: Hardin Co Hist Soc. 11: Outstanding Young Educator 65. 14: Sch libn (instr materials spec). 15: 107 Westwood dr, Elizabethtown Ky 42701.

MESSENGER, PAULINE OLIVE. b Roxbury Kan 3 F 14. 5: Bethany Col (Lindsborg Kan) 4649 (Eng) AB; Kan State Tchrs Col (Emporia) (LS) MS, summer 60 (LS); UAlaska summer 64 (Hist). 7: Elem tchr McPherson Co, Roxbury Kan 34-46; High sch tchr Dickinson Co, Hope Kan 49-56; Libn El Dorado Jr Col 56-61; Libn Mesa Col 61-. 8: Consul, State Lib Wkshop, Mesa Col 61. 9: EA; ALA; ColLA; MPLA (chm Col & Univ Div 68); Colo EA. 10: Delta Kappa Gamma. 13: Yes. 14: Ref, period. 15: 1704 N 15th st, Grand Junction Colo 81501.

MESSER, VIRGINIA ADELENE. b Dalby Springs Tex 4 Ap 24. 4: Don Messer. 5: Texarkana Col 41-43 AA; UTex 43-44 (Span) BA; Tex State Col for Women 50-51 summer 54 MLS. 6: Sp, Fr. 7: Receptionist, sec Young Hosp, Roscoe Tex 46-50; Receptionist, sec Young Med Center, Sweetwater Tex summers 51-52; Jr High Sch libn Gladewater Independent Sch Dist, Gladewater Tex 51-57; Spec serv libn US Dept of the Army, Germany 57-60; 1st asst lit & hist dept Dallas Pub Lib 60-61, Head lit & hist dept 61-. 9: ALA; TexLA (chm Publ Libs Div 65-66). 10: Beta Phi Mu. 14: Ref. 15: 3222 S Tyler, Dallas Tx 75224.

MESSERLI, SUSAN (ROEHRS). b Wausau Wis 30D 30. 4: Carlos R Messerli. 5: Valparaiso U 48-53 (Music) BA; UMich 64 MALS. 6: Ger. 7: Tchr & choir dir Lutheran Church of St Luke, Chicago 54-58; Instr child lit Tchrs chrs Col (Seward Neb) 61-62; Asst libn humanities div UNeb 62-63, 64-65, Assoc catlg 66-67; Music ref libn UIowa 67-. 9: MusLA. 10: Lutheran Soc for Worship, Music & the Arts. 13: Yes. 14: Child lit, catlg. 15: 112 Lowell st, Iowa City Ia 52240.

MESSICK, FREDERICK (MORTON). b S Bend Ind 20 Ap 35. 5: Ind U 53-55, 57-59 (Sociol) AB, 62-63 (Soc Sci) AMT; UMich 64-65 AMLS.07: Sales correspondent Dodge Mfg Corp, Mishawaka Ind 55-57, 60-62; J C Penney Co, Springfield Ill 59-60; Soc Soc Studies tchr Elkhart High Sch, Elkhart Ind 63-64; Ref & circ Ann Arbor Pub Lib, Mich 64-65; Ref libn American U 65-67; Ref libn Central Mich U 67-69, Soc Sci libn 69 6: Sp. 7: Sales correspondent Dodge Mfg Corp, Mishawaka Ind 55-57, 60-62; J C Penney Co, Springfield Ill 59-60; Soc Studies tchr Elkhart High Sch, Elkart Ind 63-64; Ref & circ Ann Arbor Pub Lib, Mich 64-65; Ref libn American U 65-67; Ref lib Central Mich U 67-69, Soc Sci libn 69-. 9: ALA; Amer Sociol Assn. 10: Beta Phi Mu; AAUP. 14: Ref, soc sci bibliog. 15: Central Michigan Univ Lib, Mt Pleasant Mi 48858.

MESSICK, VIRGINIA F K. b Phila Penn 26 N 09. 4: Samuel Sherwood Messick. 5: Wilson Col 27-31 (Fr) AB; Rutgers 55-59 MLS. 6: Fr. 7: Med rec libn Kent Gen Hosp, Dover Del 52-53; Hd libn State Lib Commsn, Dover Del 53-64; Libn Wesley Col 64-. 9: ALA; DelLA. 10: Beta Phi Mu; 20th Century Club; Friends of Old Dover; Duck Creek Hist Soc; DAR; AAUW. 13: Yes. 14: Acquis, bk sel. 15: Lib Wesley Col, Dover De 19901.

MESSIMER, JEAN D(EMAREST). b Hackensack NJ 20 O 21. 5: Mt Holyoke 39-43 (Zool) AB; Rutgers 60-63 MLS. 6: Fr. 7: USNR WR (Communications) LT 43-48; Analyst Communications Armed Forces Security Agency, Wash DC 48-51; Sci ed NSF, Wash DC 51-54; Lib trainee Pub Lib, Hackensack NJ 61-63; Assoc libn UColo Libs 63-67, Engnrg libn 67-. 9: SLA; ColoLA; ColoSchLA. 10: AAUP. 14: Engnrg. 15: Univ Colo Libs, Boulder Colo.

MESSIMER, NELL (MAE). b Bluff City Tenn 1 O 38. 5: Atlanta Christian Col 56-60 (Bible) BA; EmoryU summers 60-61; E Tenn StateU summer 65. 7: Asst libn Atlanta Christian Col 60-62, Libn 62-. 9: ALA; Christian Libn's Fellowship. 14: Ref, rare bks. 15: 2605 Ben Hill rd, E Point Ga 30344.

MESSINEO, ANTHONY. b Rochester NY 15 D 33. 4: Violet Totilas. 5: UMiami (Fla) 56-60 (Psych) BA; Syracuse 61-62 MSLS. 6: Sp. 7: Jr libn Rochester Pub Lib, Rochester NY 62-63, Act head libn Edgerton Br 64-66; Hd adult serv Ferguson Lib, Stamford Conn 66-68; Lib Dir N Tonawanda Pub Lib, N Tonawanda NY 68-. 9: ALA; NYLA. 10: ROCHESTER Sport Divers Inc; Kiwanis. 14: Adult & yp reading guidance, pub lib serv. 15: 1522 Jamaica Square, N Tonawanda NY 14120.

MESSMAN, HOWARD A. b Tolono Ill 17D 16. 4: Marjorie Stewart. 5: UIll 34-39 (Chem Engnr) BS, 46-48 (Chem Engnr) MS, 60-62 LS MS. 6: Ger, Fr. 7: Tech trainee Union Oil Co (Cal), Oleum Cal 89-40; Off USAR Research & Development 40-60; 4060; Math libn UIll(Urbana) 62-. 8: Consul Materials Research, Materials Lab, Wright Field Ohio 60-. 9: ASIS; IllLA. 14: Acad lbnship, documentation of research, storage & retrieval. 15: 1214 Julie dr, Champaign Il 61820.

MESZAROS, IMRE. b Budapest Hungary 2 Jl 34. 4: Patricia Kerns. 5: UNM 57-60 (Sp); Johns Hopkins 60-64 (Eng) BS; UMd 64-66 (Eng) MA; CatholicU 68-69 MLS. 6: Hungarian, sp, Fr. 7: Pre-prof libn Enoch Pratt Free Lib, Baltimore 66-68; Instr Eng Essex Commun Col, Essex Md 68; Assoc libn I McKeldin Lib UMd 69-. 9: ALA. 10: Mod Lang Assn. 14: Humanities ref, rare bks. 15: 6223 Springfield ct, Greenbelt Md 20770.

METALLO, CHARLOTTE. b Munich Germany 23 Ag 24. 4: Pat Metallo. 5: Lyceum (Munich) Abitur; Business Col Dr Sabel i (Munich) Abitur. 6: Ger, Fr, Eng. 7: Med libn Hosp for Women of Baltimore, Baltimore 60-65; Med libn Greater Baltimore Med Ctr 65-. 9: MedLA; Baltimore Hosp Libns Assn (v-pres 63-65). 14: Ref. 15: Greater Baltimore Med Center, 6701 N Charles st, Baltimore Md 21204.

METCALF, GERTRUDE R. b Oley Penn 9 S07. 4: Charles O Metcalf. 5: Ursinus Col 24-28 (Eng, Hist) AB; Drexel 49-51 (LS) BS. 6: Pennsylvania Ger. 7: Eng tchr Oley Twp Sch Dist, Oley Penn 28-36; Tchr Eng, Chem Mohnton High Sch, Mohnton Penn 44-46; Tchr Eng, Math Wilson High Sch, W Lawn Penn 46-52; Libn Bellwood-Antis High Sch, Bellwood Penn 52-. 8: Central Penn Rep on State Sch Lib Coun; Pres Co Lib Bd; Pres Bellwood-Antis Pub Lib Bd. 9: ALA;-AASchL; NEA; PennEA (Supvn & Curr Dept; Exec Com). 10: AAUW; Bus & Profess Women. 14: Reader adv, ref. 15: 104 S Second st, Bellwood Penn 16617.

METCALF, KEYES D(eWITT). b Elyria Ohio 3 Ap 1889. 4: Elinor Gregory. 5: Oberlin 07-11 (Hist) BA; Lib Sch of NY Pub Lib 11, 13-14 Certif & Diploma. 7: Page to act libn Oberlin Col 02, 05-11, 12, 16-17; Jr asst to chief of ref dept NY Pub Lib 13-37; Dir of Libs Harvard U 37-55, Prof of Bibliog 45-55; Adj Prof Rutgers U 55-58; Lib Consul, Belmont Mass 55-. 8: Consul for over 400 lib problems in Europe, Africa, Asia, Austrlia, New Zealand, Latin America, as well as Canada and 41 states of the Union. 9: ALA (pres 42-43);-ACRL (Exec sec 4yrs). 10: Trustee of Boston Athenaeum & Belmont Pub Lib; Coun of Amer Antique Soc; Mass Hist Soc; etc. 11: NY Pub Lib 50th Anniversary Award: 10 hon doctorates. 12: "Planning Academic and Research Library Buildings (65). 13: Yes. 14: Admin, personnel, lib train, cooperation, bldg planning. 15: 68 Fairmont st, Belmont Mass 02178.

METCALF, LOUISA SOHIER. b Winthrop Mass 18 JI 09. 5: Smith Col 28-32 (Eng) AB; Columbia 32-33 (LS) BS. 6: Fr, Sp. 7: Boston Pub Lib: Asst in brs 36-44, 1st asst div 44-50, Readers adv for adults 50-. 9: ALA; MassLA. 10: Womens Nat Bk Assn; Womens City Club of Boston; Boston Pub Lib Prof Staff Assn. 13: Yes. 15: 38 Harbor View ave, Winthrop Mass 02152.

METCALF, MARJORIE. b Saugus Mass 31 Mr 34. 5: Simmons 52-56 (Chem) BS, 62-67 (LS) MS. 7: Chem Tufts U Med Sch 56-60; Chem W R Grace & Co, Dewey & Almy Chem Div, Cambridge mass 60-62, Libn 62-. 9: SLA. 14: Ref. 15: 457 Pleasant st, Melrose Ma02176.

METTERNICH, VIOLA B. b Cincinnati 9 S 07. 5: UCincinnati 26-30 (Hist) BA, 40 (Geol) MA; West Res 41 BS in LS. 7: Pub Lib, Cincinnati: Asst 30-39, Br libn 39-42, Area br libn 42-56, Supv of brs 56-62, Personnel off 62-. 9: ALA (chm Circ Control Com 62-). 10: Quota Club; Womens Personnel Assn of Cincinnati. 14: Personnel, admin, lib educ. 15: Pub Lib 8th & Vine sts, Cincinnati Oh 45202.

METTS, DANIEL LAMAR SR. b Pulaski Tenn 9 Je 25. 4: Evelyn Bates. 5: Emory 42-44, 46-47 (Eng) BA, 47-48 (Eng) MA; UNC 48-49 (Eng); Emory 49-50 (LS) MLn. 7: Asst in acquis Fla State U 50-56; Asst head acquis dept UMinn 56-63; U Libn Mercer U 63-. 9: ALA; GaLA; SELA. 15: 3020 Clairmont ave, Macon Ga.

METZ, T JOHN. b Erie Penn 5 N 32. 4: Dorothy Page Neff. 5: Heidelberg Col 50-54 (Violin) B Mus; MIAMI U 54-55 (Music) MA: UMich 57-59 AMLS. 6: Ger. 7: Lib serv scholar & Fellow UMich 57-59; Libn II circ UWis(Madison) 59-62; Ref libn Lawrence U 62-64, Asst libn 64-; Humanities libn UWis (Green Bay) 67-68, Act dir 68-69, Dir of Libs 69-. 9: ALA; WisLA; NEWis Intertype Libs. 10: Performer with Green Bay Symphony Orchestra; ACLU; Amer Humanist Assn; Beta Phi Mu; Kappa Delta Pi. 14: Ref, admin, rare bks. 15: 2457 Leslie dr, Green Bay Wi 54302.

METZDORF, ROBERT F. b Springfield Mass 2 Jl 12. 5: URochester 29-33 (Eng) AB, 33-35 (Eng) AM, 35-39 (Eng) PhD. 6: Ger, Fr. 7: Curator rare bks URochester 34-49, Instr Eng 39-49; Catlgr Houghton Lib Harvard U 49-52; U Archivist, curator mss Yale U Lib 52-61, Sec Boswell ed com Yale U 52-61; V-pres, Dir Parke-Bennet Galleries, NYC 61-64; Appraiser Properties, Conn 64-. 64-. 8: Sec Yale Ed of Works of Samuel Johnson 58-; Co-founder, Partner The Shoe String Press 52-55. 9: Ms Soc (dir 54-57 & 63-); BSA (ed, PBSA 59-67). 10: Trustees Coun of Alumni Advisors URochester 64-66; Trustee URochester 66-; Grolier Club (NYC); Century Assn (NYC); Rowfant Club (Cleveland); Elizabethan Club (New Haven); Phi Beta Kappa. 12: "The Tinker Library (59); ed "R H Dana Autobiographical Sketch (53). 13: Yes. 14: Rare bks. 15: Route 183, North Colebrook Ct 06021.

METZGER, ARTHUR B (BRYAN). b Gordon Neb 19 N 34. 4: Chlovena Beth Byrd. 5: Hastings Col 53-57, 58-59 (Hist, Eng) BA; UWo 58 (Ed); UMo 59-60 (Ed, Psych) Tchg certif; West Mich U 63-65 (LS) MA. 6: Fr. 7: Tchr Pine Bluffs Schs, Pine Bluffs Wyo 60-61; Patient libn Wyo State Hosp, Evanston Wyo 61-63; Rancher Metzger Cattle Co, Merriam Neb 63; Asst docs libn Ft Vancouver Reg Lib, Vancouver Wash 65-. 14: Ref, docs. 15: 5714 NE 40th st, Vancouver Wa 98661.

METZGER, BARBARA R. b Summit NJ 11 F 45. 5: Mt Holyoke Col 62-66 (Eng) BA; Simmons 68-69 MS in LS. 6: Fr. 7: Initiator Newark Tutorial Project, Newark NJ summer 63; Asst to dir Georgetown U Col Orientation program summer 66; Prod asst WGHH-TV, Boston 66-67; Lib aide Driscoll Elem Sch Brookline Mass 67-68; Libn Runkle Elem Sch Brookline Mass 69-. 9: New England Film EA. 11: Carnegie Grant for Study & Research, Woodrow Wilson Sch. 14: Child lit, film & other joyful media. 15: 19 Shepard st 22, Cambridge Ma 02138.

METZGER, CLARISSA (MARTIN). b Alexandria La 15 S 16. 4: Herbert Asher Metzger. 5: LSU 32-37 (Eng, Fr) BA; N Tex U 61 BS in LS. 6: Fr. 7: Libn Haltom Jr High Sch, Ft Worth Tex 55-60; Richland High Sch, Ft Worth Tex 61; Hamlin Jr High Sch, Corpus Christi Tex 63-67; Jeff Davis High Sch, Houston Tex 68; Westchester High Sch, Houston Tex 69-. 14: Sch libs. 15: 2522 Southwick dr, Houston Tx 77055.

METZGER, LUDWIG (CONRAD CHARLES). b E Rutherford NJ 22 Mr 18. 4: Perpetua Cross. 5: Fairleigh Dickinson Jr Col 47-48 (Liberal Arts); Montclair State Tchrs Col 49-51 (Soc studies) AB; Trenton State Tchrs Col summer 51-54 BLS; Rutgers 51-56 (Guid & personnel) EdM. 6: Ger. 7: Supply clk, unot hist, lecturer, libn USA, US ETO 42-45; Receiving & shipping Trubek Labs Inc, E Rutherford NJ 46-48; Tchr & libn Voc & Tech High Sch, N Brunswick NJ 51-53; Asst libn Thomas Jefferson Jr High Sch, Fair Lawn NJ 53-54; High sch libn: E Rutherford NJ 54-57, E Patterson NJ 61-63, Lyndhurst NJ 63-67, Franklin Lakes NJ 67-68, Newark NJ 69-; Ref-circ unit Tech Info Sect Picatinny Ars, Dover NJ 57-59; Libn: Cleveland-Sherman Jr Schs, Cranford NJ 59-61 R Frost Jr High Sch, Deer Park LI 68. 9: ALA; SLA; NEA; NJSchLA (treas 56-58); NJEA; NJAV Coun, bergen CoSchLA (treas 66-67), EssexCoSchLA; BergenCoEA (rep 65-67); NewarkTA, Alumni assoc-MSC. 10: Hist Soc of Wood-Ridge NJ. 11: Montclair State C Alum Assn; Phi Delta kappa. 12: "A History of Wood-Ridge" (64); "Jerseyana in Bergen County", a Bibliog (64). 14: Ref. 15: 288 Sussex rd, Wood-Ridge NJ 07075.

MEYER, ANNE CLAYTON (ROBBINS). b Jackson Tenn 9 O 38. 4: Merwin Eugene Meyer. 5: Lambuth Col 56-60 (Hist) BA; Peabody 60-61 MALS. 7: Ya libn Dallas Pub Lib 61-62; Ref libn Memphis Pub Lib, Memphis Tenn 63-64; Br libn Whitehaven Pub Lib Shelby Co Libs, Memphis Tenn 65-66; Br libn Parkway Village Br Lib Memphis Pub Lib, Memphis Tenn 66-. 8: Ref libn, Lib/USA, NY Worlds Fair, 64. 9: ALA (Jr Mems Roundtable); TennLA (sec Pub Libs Div 65-66). 10: Memphis Opera Theater; Alpha Omicron Pi; Beethoven ,club. 14: Ref, readers adv serv, bk sel. 15: 4655 Knight Arnold rd, Memphis Tenn 38118.

MEYER, BETTY JANE. b Indianapolis 20 Jl 18. 5: Ball State U 36-40 (Hist) BA; West Res 44-45 BS in LS. 6: Fr, Ger. 7: Stud asst Muncie Pub Lib, Muncie Ind 36-40; Lib asst Ohio State U Lib 40-42; Lib asst Grandview Heights Pub Lib, Columbus Ohio 42-44; Stud asst Case Inst of Tech 44-45; Ohio State U: Catlgr 45-46, Asst circ libn 46-51, Act circ libn 52, Admin asst to Dir of libs & Instr of Lib Admin 52-57, Act assoc ref libn 57-58, Catlgr in chg of ser & Instr in Libn Admin 58-63, Head ser div, Catlg Dept & Asst Prof in Lib Admin 63; Assoc Prof in Lib Admin 67-, Hd acquis dept 68-. 9: ALA (pres Ser Sect 69-70);-ACRL; OhioLA; Ohio Valley Group of Tech Serv Libns (sec 64-65); Ohioana LA. 10: AAUP; Beta Phi Mu. 14: Catlg, ref, govt docs, acquis, ser. 15: 189 W Weber rd, Columbus Ohio 43202.

MEYER, CHRISTINE (LOUISE). b S Natick Mass 2 Ja 11. 5: Ohio State U 28-32 (Fr) BA & BS in Ed, 32-33 (Fr) MA, 36-41 (Romance Lang) PhD; Columbia even 45-49 BS in LS. 6: Fr, Sp, Ital. 7: Research asst Internat Auxiliary Language Assn, NY 41-50; Jr catlgr Columbia U 50-54, Catlgr 54-. 9: ALA; NY Tech Serv Libns; NY Lib Club. 10: Citizens Union (NYC). 13: Yes. 14: Catlg, col & research libs. 15: 28 E 92nd st, New York NY 10028.

MEYER, DOROTHY (HORTON). b Mayaguez pr 6 D 08. 5: Syracuse U 31 BS in LS. 6: Sp. 7: Head filing dept Fed Land Bank, Baltimore 32-33; Head filing dept Nat Recovery Admin, San Juan PR 33-35; Instr of Eng UPR (Rico Piedras) 37-38; Circ asst Syracuse U Lib 39-41; Ref asst City Lib, Springfield Mass 41-47; Head ref dept Wichita City Lib, Wichita Kan 47-53; Asst libn Fairmont State Col 53-55; Ref libn Bethesda Lib, Bethesda Md 55-64; Head ref libn Montgomery Co Dept of Libs, Bethesda Md 65-. 9: ALA; MdLA. 14: Ref. 15: Montgomery Co Dept of Pub Libs, 6400 Democracy blvd, Bethesda Md 20034.

MEYER, ELAINE EDNA. b Wolsey SD 3 My 15. 5: Huron Col 34-38 (Math) BA; UDenver 53-54 (LS) MA. 7: Math tchr High Sch, Ideal SD 38-41; Math tchr High Sch, Highmore SD 41-43; Math tchr, libn High Sch, Vermillion SD 43-48; Math tchr High Sch, Lemmon SD 49-53; Libn High Sch, Los Alamos NM 54-55; Field wkr SDak State Lib summer 55; Libn high sch, Lead SD 55-60; Ref libn & Asst Prof of Lib Sci USD 60-. 9: ALA (Recr Netwk);-AASchL;-RSD;-YASD; MPLA; SDLA (Scholarship Com); SDEA. 10: Delta Kappa Gamma; ANTA. 13: Yes. 14: Ref, educ for libnship. 15: 854 Eastgate dr, Vermillion SD 57069.

MEYER, HILDA. b Taylor Penn. 4: Richard Kempter Meyer. 5: Marywood Col 38-42 (LS) BS in Ed; Seton Hall 60-63; COLUMBIA 64- (LS). 6: Fr. 7: Adult libn Green Free Pub Lib, Canton Penn50-53; Child libn, yp libn S Orange ub Lib, E OrangeNJ 54-57; Circ libn Seton Hall U 57-. 9: ALA; NEA; IllEA; IllLA. 10: Beta Lambda Tau. 15: 10 St Lawrence ave, Maplewood NJ.

MEYER, JANE RUTHERFORD. b Evanston Ill 24 My 45. 4: Wayne Henry Meyer. 5: BradleyU 63-64; Grinnell Col 64-67 (Eng) BA; UWis 67-69 (LS) MA. 6: Fr. 7: Patients' libn Central Wis Colony, Madison Wis 69-. 15: 103 N Randall ave, Madison Wi 53715.

MEYER, JANET (WIDDOWSON). b Punxsatawney Penn 1 O 18. 4: Kurt H Meyer. 5: UIll 36-40 (Eng) BS, 40-41 MLS. 7: Libn Libertyville Twp High Sch, Libertyville Ill 41-43; Head libn Maine Twp High Sch East, Park Ridge Ill 43-. 9: ALA; NEA; IllEA; IllLA. 14: Ref, catlg. 15: 519 Creekwood dr, Barrington Woods, Palatine Il 60068.

MEYER, MARY CLAIRE (WILLMOTT DUNN). b Detroit 22 Je 22. 5: UKy 40-41 (Eng); UMich 41-42 (Eng); MichState U (Eng); UMinn 58-61 (Eng, LS) BA, MA. 6: Fr, Sp. 7: File clerk & clerk-typist War Dept, Tex, Utah, Neb; Teletypist & clerk-typist Excello Corp, Detroit 45-46; Clerk-typist, Minneapolis 54-58; Bkmob libn Minneapolis Pub Lib 61; Soc sci libn UOre 61-63, Head circ libn 63-. 8: Devel of a proposed circ system, using a computer,Univ Lib Automation Com; Automated inventory of Res Bk Rm. 14: Circ, automation of libs, recr. 15: 741 E 21st ave, Eugene Ore 97405.

MEYER, PRUDENCE (SCHMIDT). b Milwaukee 8 Jl 39. 4: Raymond F Meyer. 5: Milwaukee-Downer Col 56-60 (Chem) BA; UMinn 60-61 (LS) MA. 6: Ger. 7: Asst libn ref General Mills Research Labs, Minneapolis 62-65; Free lance lib wk businesses in Minneapolis area 65-. 9: SLA (sec Minn Chap). 14: Ref, subj analysis. 15: 3400 Shepherd Hills dr, Minneapolis Mn 55431.

MEYER, ROBERT STANLEY. b Cincinnati 9 Ap 22. 4: Nellie Weier. 5: Chicago 40-43, 46-47 (Math) BS; UFla, UPittsburgh, UCincinnati 43-44 (Elec Engnr) Certif; Chicago 50-53 (LS) MA; American U 53-55 (Fr); UCal(Berkeley) 58-59 (LS). 7: Elec engnr US Army (T/5) Tenn Eastman Corp, Oak ridge Tenn 44-46; Manager Langdon-Meyer Labs, Cincinnati 47-50; Math & phys libn UChicago Lib 51-53; Research asst Documentation Inc, Wash DC 53-55; Tech info spec Atlantic Research Corp, Alexandria Va 55-56; Partner Herner Meyer & Co, Wash DC 56-57; Research asst UCal Lib Sch (Berkeley) 58-59; Head Libn Lawrence Radiation Lab, Berkeley Cal 59-67; Lib consul, Walnut Creek Cal 68-. 8: Lecturer UCal Lib Sch (Berkeley) 60-62; Course Coordinator UCal Ext Div (Berkeley) 62-65; Lecturer Wkshop for Lib Assts USan Francisco 62-69 Chm Adv Com to U Ext & Lib Sch UCal(Berkeley) 64-65. 9: SLA (San Francisco Bay Reg Chap: Bulletin Ed 59-60, Educ Com Chm 59-60); CalLA (Prof Educ Com Chm ASIS ADI (San Francisco Bay REG Chap: v-pres 62, pres 63-). 10: Lions Club; Guide Dogs for the Blind, Inc. 13: Yes. 14: Spec libs, lib mgt, lib educ. 15: 1984 Tice Valley blvd, Walnut Creek Ca 94595.

MEYER, ROGER (LEON). b Soultz, France 24 Mr 26. 5: UStrasbourg 45-47 Licence es sc; UParis 47-49 Licence es let. 6: Fr, Ger, Russian, Ital, Sp, Swedish. 7: Documentalist usine Dielectriques SA, Delle France 51-56; Mgr tech info Heurtey SA, Paris 56-59; Research libn Evans R&D Corp, NYC 59-60; Hd tech info sect Celanese Research Co, Summit NJ 60-. 9: SLA (co-chm Paper & Textile Grp); ASIS; Association Internationale des Documentalistes et Techniciens de l'Information. 10: Amer Transl Assn. 13: Yes. 15: Regency Village apt 12F, N Plainfield NJ 07060.

MEYER, ROSALIND (WILLIAMS). b Rock Island Ill 4 O 13. 4: Gerald H Meyer. 5: Marycrest-St Ambrose 47-52 (LS, Educ) BA; State U Iowa 59-65 (Educ, LS) MA. 7 Tchr, Buffalo Iowa 48-49; Tchr, Scott Co Iowa 49-52; Libn Bettendorf High Sch, Bettendorf Iowa 52-. 9: NEA; Iowa State EA; Bettendorf EA (past pres). 10: Trustee, Bettendorf (Iowa) Pub Lib; AAUW. 14: Admin, establ new libs. 15: 1102 33rd st, Bettendorf Iowa 52722.

MEYER, ROSALYN SHEPS. b Pittsburgh Penn 15 Ag 41. 5: UPittsburgh 58-62 (Elem Educ) BS, 66-69 MLS. 6: Fr. 7: Tchr Kenmore Sch Dist, Kenmore NY 62-63; Tchr Sweet Home Sch Dist, Buffalo NY 63-64; Libn staff Carnegie Lib of Pittsburgh, Penn 69-. 14: Ref, child serv. 15: 5851 Solway st, Pittsburgh Pa 15217.

MEYER, URSULA. b free City of Danzig 6 N 27. 5: UCLA 45-49 (Internat Rel) BA, 50-51 (Hist) Secondary Tchg credentials; USoCal 52-53 MSLS; UWis 68-69 (LS). 6: Ger. 7: Ref circ libn Thurston-Mason Reg Lib, Olympia Wash 53-54; Bkmob libn Yakima Valley Reg Lib, Yakima Wash 54-59; Br libn Contra Costa Co Lib, Martinez Cal 59-60; Co libn Butte Co, Oroville Cal 61-68. 8: Lib Adv Co of Co Supvs Assn of Cal 62-; Adv Com of the Cal State-Wide Survey of Pub Lib Serv 65; No Sacramento Valley Lib Coop (Coun of libns 65-68, chm 66-67). 9: ALA; PNLA; WisLA; CalLA (pres Mt Shasta Dist 65). 10: Soroptimist; AAUW. 14: Admin, readers serv. 15: 4817 Sheboygan ave #218, Madison Wi 53705.

MEYER, VALERIE D. b Leipzig Germany 21 Jl 10. 5: UFrankfurt/Main Leipzig Grenoble 30-31; UWis 54-55 (Fr, Ger) BA; UWis(Madison) 55-56 MALS. 6: Ger, Fr, Swedish. 7: Catlg revision Harvard U 42-44; Libn Layton Sch of Art, Milwaukee 51-3; Asst libn Shorewood High Sch, Milwaukee 53-54; Order libn UMich 56-58, Ref libn at Undergrad Lib 58-68, Fine Arts libn 68-. 10: Ann Arbor Lib Club; LWV; Beta hi Mu; Col Art Assn. 14: Ref, fine arts. 15: 1311 Iroquois pl, Ann Arbor Mich 48104.

MEYER, WILLIAM PAUL. b Okla City Okla 6 N 23. 4: Rose Taylor Meyer. 5: ALBRIGHT Col 49-52 (Eng) AB; Drexel 52-53 MSLS. 7: US Army 46-49; Libn I Free Lib of Phila 53-56; Libn US Army Intelligence Sch, Ft Holabird, Baltimore 56-58; Libn Nat Security Agency, Ft Geo G Meade Md 58-. 9: SLA; MdLA. 15: 1723 Inverness ave, Baltimore Md 21222.

MEYERHOFF, ERICH. b Braunschweig Germany 24 N 19. 4: Inge Zuber. 5: City Col of NY 37-43 (Sociol) BS; Columbia 49-51 MSLS. 6: Fr, Ger. 7: Med ref libn Med Lib Columbia 51-57; Libn & asst prof SUNY (Brooklyn) 57-61; Dir Med Lib Ctr of NY, NYC 61-67; Health sci libn SUNY (Buffalo) 67-. 8: Consul: Metro Lib Agcy, NYC 68, Col of Physicians of Phila 68-69, UMich 69. 9: MedLA (Upstate NY Reg Group); AAAS; Assn Amer Dental Schs; NY Acad Med. 13: Yes. 14: Med libnship, hist of med. 15: 449 Richmond ave, Buffalo NY 14222.

MEYERS, ARTHUR S. b NY 14 D 37. 4: Marcia Indianer. 5: UMiami 55-59 (Hist) BA; Columbia 59-61 (LS) MS; Wayne State 64-65 (Hist). 7: Lib trainee NY Pub Lib 59-60, Libn I 61; US Army (Pfc), Frankfurt Germany 61-63; Libn II Detroit Pub Lib 63-67; Adult & Ya spec Commun Action Program Enoch Pratt Free Lib, Baltimore Md 67-. 9: ALA-YASD One-Minute Bk Talk Com 65-66);-AASchL; MichLA. 10: ACLU; NAACP. 13: Yes. 14: Ext serv for shut-ins adults & nursing homes, inner city neighborhood libs, wk with adult basic educ & job train programs. 15: 6130 Fairdel ave apt 1C, Baltimore Md 21206.

MEYERS, DOROTHY (CARPENTER). b Newark NJ 10 S 17. 4: Robert Meyers. 5: Douglass Col Rutgers U 35-39 (LS) BA. 6: Fr. 7: Child libn Free Pub Lib, E Orange NJ 39-41; Asst acquis dept Baker Lib Harvard Grad Sch of Bus Admin 42; Libn Miss Fines Sch, Princeton nj 60-65; Libn Princeton Day Schs, Princeton NJ 65-. 8: Visiting Com Middle States Assn of Second Schs & Cols, March 64 & March 65. 9: ALA; NJLA; No NJ Assn of Independ Sch Libns. 10: Rutgers Grad Sch of Lib Serv Alumnae Assn; Douglass col Alumnae Assn; Friends of Princeton Pub Lib. 14: Admin of sch libs. 15: 95 No Main st, Cranbury NJ 08512.

MEYERS, JUDITH ANN (KEARNS). b Columbus Ohio 18 Ap 34. 4: Ronald Ellwood Meyers. 5: Ohio Wesleyan U 52-56 (Hist) BA; UGa 56-57; UUTah Ext 59; Kent State 60-63 (LS) MA; Miami U 62-63; UWashington 65; Fla State U 67-68. 7: Asst dir of educ Ohio Hist Soc 57-58; Tchr-libn Martinsville High Sch, Martinsville Ohio 58-60; Libn Wilmington Jr High Sch, Wilmington Ohio 60-63; Libn Wilmington Sr High Sch, Wilmington Ohio 62-63; Asst supv sch dept Cleveland Pub Lib 63-; Instr Dept of Lib Sci Kent State U 65-; Coord of lib serv Tuscarawas Valley Educ Serv Ctr 66-67; Asst dir Grad Sch of Lib Sci UIll 68-. 9: ALA-AASchL; NEA-DAVI; WNBA; OhioASchL (sec 67-68); OhioEA; Educ Media Coun Ohio. 13: Yes. 14: Sch libs, lib educ, non-bk materials. 15: 8285 Wiese rd, Brecksville Oh 44141.

MEYERS, LOIS BYRON. b Bellingham Wash 7 F 29. 4: Andrew Laurence Meyers Sr. 5: UWash 48-54 BA, 55-61 M Libnship. 7: Forest Pk Br libn King Co Lib Syst 65-67, area supv 6 -68, child libn 68-. 9: ALA-Jr Mem RT; -CSD; -Intl Rel RT; WashLA; PNLA. 10: PTA; Friends of Lib (Bothell); Pacific NW Writers Conf; Delta Zeta. 14: Child wk, storytelling, author-libn relationships, writing. 15: 18530 92nd ave NE, Bothell Wa 98011.

MEYERS, PATTY J. b Santa Fe NM 5 F 30. 5: Central Mo State Col 48-50; UMo (Kan City) 54-58 (Psych) BA; Peabody 59-60 MALS. 7: Lib asst Kan City (Mo) Pub Lib 58-59; Reg libn Blue Grass Reg Lib, Columbia Tenn 60-64; Consul Tenn State Lib & Archives 64-66; Hd ext div Tucson Pub Lib, Tucson Ariz 66-. 9: ALA; SWLA; Ariz State LA. 14: Ext serv. 15: 3935 N Country Club, Tucson Az 85716.

MEYERS, ROSA MAE (MILLER). b Torras La 18 Ag 18. 4: Richard Caswell Meyers Jr. 5: LSU 57-61 (Educ) BS, 61-64 (LS) MS, 66-67 (LS) Post Master's Fellowship. 7: E Baton Rouge (La) Parish Lib: Lib asst child room 61, Lib asst circ dept 61, Stud libn ref dept 61-64, Libn ref & interlib loan libn 64-; Instr Lib Sci, LSU 69; Ref & Interlib loan libn E Baton Rouge Parish Lib 64-. 9: ALA; LaLA (Lit Award Com 64-65); Baton Rouge Lib Club. 10: Phi Kappa Phi; Phi Alpha Theta; Alpha Beta Alpha; Beta Phi Mu. 14: Ref, young adult wk. 15: 944 Magnolia Wood ave, Baton Rouge La 70808.

MEYHOEFER, IDA (THEIS). b Cos Cob Conn 15 O 09. 4: Daniel Meyhoefer. 5: URochester 27-31 (Ger) BA; Columbia summers 41-44 (LS) BS. 6: Ger. 7: Catlgr URochester 31-47; Catlgr USoCal 48-. 9: ALA. 10: Delta Phi Alpha. 14: Catlg. 15: 4650 1/2 W 18th st, Los Angeles Ca 90019.

MEZGAR, LAJOS. b Debrecen Hungary 16 F 30. 4: Zsofia Schindler. 5: Eotvoes Lorant U (Budapest) 48-52 (Law) LD; Columbia 62-64 (LS) MS. 6: Ger, Hungarian, Fr, Lat. 7: Legal sec Godollo Hungary 2-53; Dist judge 13th Dist Ct of Budapest 53-56; Lab asst Standard Oil A G, Cologne Germany 57-59; Mutual fund salesman Industrial Incomes Inc, NY 60-62; Searcher Columbia U Lib 63-64; Head of tech serv Free Pub Lib, Summit NJ 64-66, Asst dir 66-. 14: Info retrieval systems, A-v resources & equipment, tech services. 15: 970 Florida Gr rd, Perth Amboy NJ 08861.

MIAH, ABDUL JALIL. b Dacca Pakistan 2 Je 37. 4: Sakina Khanum. 5: Sch of Libnship (Karachi) 58 Certif; Islamia Col (Karachi) 61 (Econ) BA; Islamia Law Col (Karachi) 63 (Law) LLB; KarachiU 64 (LS) Diploma; LIU 68 (LS) MS. 6: Urdu, Bengali, Sp. 7: Circ (in charge) Karachi U Lib 56-59; Chief libn Pakistan Standards Inst, Larachi 59-60; Hd libn UN Info Ctr, Karachi 60-66; Libn Brooklyn Pu hd libn UN Info Ctr, Karachi 60-66; Libn Brooklyn Pub Lib, NY 66-68; Asst to libn LIU 68-69; Chief libn Manitoba Col of Applied Arts & Tech, Winnipeg Can 69-. 8: Honourary libn Nazrul Acad, Karachi 57-59. 9: PakistanLA; ALA; CanLA; ManLA. 13: Yes. 14: Ref, catlg, a-v instr material ctr. 15: 301-520 Burnell st, Winnipeg Manitoba 10 Can.

MICHAEL, REV JAMES JOSEPH. b Waukesha Wis 4 N 27. 5: Concordia Sem (Springfield Ill) 47-53; UWis 61 (Hebrew Studies) BA; UIll 63 (LS) MS. 6: Ger, Hebrew, Gk. 7: Pastor Our Redeemer Lutheran Church, Madison Wis 53-61; Ref libn Concordia Sem Lib (St Louis) 61-63, Lib Dir 64-67; Supv Commun serv St Louis Pub Lib 67-68, Chief sup of brs 68-. 9: ALA; ATheolLA; Soc for Bib Lit & Exeg; MoLA. 12: Ed MoLA "Bulletin" 65-67. 13: Yes. 14: Admin, rare bks, bldg. 15: 2317 Cleek ct, St Louis Mo 63131.

MICHAEL, KAY M. b Bakersfield Cal 1 D 38. 4: Charlene Murray. 5: Bakersfield Col 56-59 Internat Rel) AA; UCal(Berkeley) 59-61 (Hist Hisp Amer AB, 61-63 MLS, 64 (Educ) Sch Lib Certif, UPacific 67- (Educ). 6: Sp. 7: Ref libn San Joaquin Delta Col 64-; Ref libn Stockton Pub Lib, Stockton Cal 65. 9: ALA; CalLA. 10: Phi Delta Kappa; ACLU; Amer Fed Tchrs. 14: Ref, period. 15: 148 San Fernando ave, Stockton Ca 95207.

MICHAEL, MRS MARJORIE L (BRODY). b Three Rivers Mich 15 Jl 09. 5: Mich State U 26-29 AB; UMich 29-30 ABLS. 6: Fr. Ger. 7: Asst catlgr Pub Lib, Flint Mich 30-32; Head catlgr Pub Lib, Lansing Mich 32-38; Sr catlgr Pub Lib, Detroit 38-48; Supv tech processing Pub Lib, Lansing Mich 48-. 9: ALA (Descr Catlg Com 63-65); MichLA. 10: Pilot Club of Lansing; YWCA. 14: Catlg. 15: 401 S Capitol ave, Lansing Mi 48914.

MICHAELS, LEOLA ROSE. b St Louis 20 Ja 11. 5: St Louis Pub Lib Sch 29 (LS) Certif; St Louis U 35-37 (Soc Sci) BS; UIll 38-42, 45 (Hist) MA. 7: Libn Webster Col 37-38; Libn Champaign (Ill) Jr High Sch 38-42; Camp libn USAF, Mich & Wis 42-44; Libn Engnr Sch Washington U (Mo) 44-46; Asst libn Chrysler CORP, Mich 46-47; Libn Dearborn Motors, Mich 48-50; Libn GE Co Metallurgical Prod Dept, Mich 51. 9: SLA (Meals/Materials Div: var offs & ssignments; Mich Chap: var offs & asignments). 10: UIll Alumnae. 13: Yes. 14: Ref. 15: Box 237 GPO, Detroit Mi 48232.

MICHALAK, JO-ANN (OSBORN). b Bremerton Wash 17 Ap 43. 4: Thomas J Michalak. 5: Syracuse 61-65 (Art Hist) BA; UIll 65-66 (LS) MS. 6: Ital, Ger, Sp. 7: Ref chicago Pub Lib Art Dept (summer) 66; Acquis bibliog UIll Lib (Champaign & Urbana) 66-67; Asst ser libn IndU (Bloomington) 67-. 9: Ohio Valley Tech Serv Libns. 10: Beta Phi Mu; UIll Alumni Assn of Lib Sch. 14: Ser, acquis. 15: 1316 No Maple st, Bloomington In 47401.

MICHALAK, THOMAS JOHN. b Chicago Ill 18 My 40. 4: Jo-Ann Osborn. 5: Loyola U 59-63 (Pol sci) BS; UIll 63-66 (LS) MS, 63-67 (Pol sci) MA. 6: Fr. 7: Ser asst UIll Lib (Urbana) 64-66, Ser bibliogr 66-67; Libn for econ & govt Indiana U Lib (Bloomington) 67-. 8: Chm Ind U Lib Ad Hoc Com on Acad Status 68-. 9: ALA; Ohio Valley Tech Serv libns. 10: Beta Phi Mu; Amer Pol Sci Assn. 12: "Bibliography of Reference Tools in political Science" (68); Supplement I (68); "Economic Status and Conditions of the Negro", (Bibliog) (69). 13: Yes. 14: Bibliog, ref, ser, technical serv. 15: 1316 N Maple, Bloomington In 47401.

MICHALIK, ANN (FLORENCE PAULY). b Brooklyn NY 21 My 43. 4: Michael B Michalik. 5: Duke 61-65 (Fr) BA; Simmons 66-69 MLS. 6: Fr, Sp. 7: Nat risk analyst Liberty Mutual Ins, Boston 65-66; Buyer trainee Capwell's, Oakland Cal 66; Ya asst Boston Pub lib 66-67, 68-; Adult libn Danbury Lib, Conn 67-68. 9: ALA; YA Coop Bk Review Group; RT of YA Wkers. 14: Ya serv. 15: 19 Frawley st apt 9, Roxbury Ma 02115.

MICHALOVA, DAGMAR. b Prague Czechoslovakia 15 D 23. 5: Charles U (Prague) 45-46 (Eng); University Col (London) 47 (Eng); NJ Col for Women 47-49 (Eng) BA; Wheaton Col (Ill) 49-50 (Christian Educ); UIll 51-52 (LS) MS, summer 56 (Med Bibliog) Certif Grade 1, MedLA. 6: Czech, Ger, Russian, Lat. 7: Grad fellow UIll(Urbana) 51-52, Instr Lib Sci summer 52, Catlg sst Asst 52-56; Asst Med Lib ref Div Labs & Research, NY State Dept Health, Albany NY 56-61, Sr med libn ref 61-62, Head Assoc libn 63-, Dept libn 65-. 9: MedLA. 10: Nat Geog Soc; Phi Beta Kappa; Beta Phi Mu. 14: Med lib admin, ref, catlg. 15: Lib NY State Dept of Health, New Scotland ave, Albany NY 12201.

MICHALSKE, ROBERT S. b San Francisco Cal 9 Mr 31. 5: City Col San Francisco 50-51, 55-56 (Eng) AA; USan Francisco 56-58 (Eng) BS; USoCal 61-62 MSLS. 6: Fr, Ger, Sp, Ital, Lat. 7: Lib page San Francisco Pub Lib 47-51, Libn II & III 56-61; US Navy 51-55, Asst to libn Naval Air Sta Lib, Agana Guam 52-54; Prin libn TSD Anaheim Pub Lib, Anaheim Cal 62-66; Dir catlg & lib serv Bro-Dart Industries Leibel Div, City of Industry Cal 66-. 8: Consul in Tech Serv to Libs Anaheim Pub Lib & Bro-Dart 62-; Wked with youth groups San Francisco Pub Lib 58-60. 9: ALA; CalLA; CASL; So Cal Tech Proc Group (chm 64-65). 13: Yes. 14: Technical serv. 15: 17282 Norwood Park pl, Tustin Ca 92680.

MICHAUD, TREFFLE. b Sherbrooke Que Can 27 Mr 34. 4: Yolande Labrecque. 5: Sem de Sherbrooke 46-54 BA; USherbrooke 56-61 (Electrical Engring) B Sc A; UMontreal 64-65 BLS, 65-66 (Electrical Engring) M Sc A. 6: Fr. 7: Sales engr: Klockner-Moeller Can, Granby-Quebec 61-63, Allen-Bradley Can, Quebec-Sherbrooke 63-64; Dir Faculte des Sci Lib USherbrooke 66-. 9: Eng Inst of Can; Association des bibliothecaires de langue francaise; Eng Corp of Que; Association des bibliothecaires du Que. 13: Yes. 14: Sci ref, lib syst, analysis & automation. 15: 525 blvd Jacques-Cartier nord apt 1, Sherbrooke Que Can.

MICHEL, NORMA FLORENCE. b Ottawa Can 10 Ag 31. 5: Ottawa Tchrs Col 49-50 1st Class Interim Certif; Phila Col of Bible 51-54, 58-59 BSc in Bible; Columbia U 63-65 (LS) MS. 7: Elem tchr, Ontario 50, 54 Clerk Civil Serv of Can, Ottawa 55, Clerk Toronto 55-58; Asst dean of women Phila Col of Bible 60-61; Clerk & steno Civil Serv of Can, Ottawa 61-63; Trainee NY Pub Lib 63-65, Staff 65-68; Ref libn St Patrick's Col Lib Carleton U, Ottawa 68-. 10: Delta Epsilon Chi. 14: Ref. 15: 1801 Riverside dr, Ottawa 8 Ont Can.

MICHEL, VICTOR J JR. b St Louis 2 F 27. 4: Margaret Renaud. 5: St Louis U 47-49 (Bus Admin). 7: Catlgr McDonnell Aircraft Corp, St Louis Mo 49-53; Libn Pastushin Avia Corp, Los Angeles 53-55; Chief tech info center Autonetics Div of NAA Inc, Anaheim Cal 55-. 9: SLA; Orange Co LA. 10: City of Placentia Cal; Mayor; Councilman; Planning Commsn; C of C; Kiwanis Internat. 12: Pictorial History of the West Atwood Yacht Club (69). 14: Admin, catlg, lib automation. 15: 419 Somerset dr, Placentia Ca 92670.

MICHELS, AUDREY J (HARRINGTON). b Elkhart Ind 23 Je 20. 4: Harry M Michels. 5: Goshen Col 36-38; Jordan Col of Music 38-40 (Music Educ) BM, 55-57 (Music Hist & Lit) MM; Butler U 59-61 (LS) Certif. 7: Music tchr Pike High Sch, New Augusta Ind 53-55; Music tchr & libn White River Sch, Wash Twp, Indianapolis 55-60; Music tchr & libn Allisonville Sch, Wash Twp, Indianapolis 60-64, Head libn 64-. 8: Particiant in Knapp Sch Libs Proj as head libn in a phase II sch (Allisonville). 9: ALA; NEA; Ind State Tchrs Assn; Ind State LA. 10: St Marthas Guild. 13: Yes. 14: Sch libs. 15: 2157 East 67th st, Indianapolis In 46220.

MICHELSEN, JAMES T(HEODOR) ANSKAR. b Port Clinton Ohio 15 Mr 38. 4: Sandra Weaner. 5: U Toledo 56-58 (Liberal Arts); Concordia Sr Col (Ft Wayne) 59-61 (Philos) BA; Concordia Sem (Springfield Ill) 61-64 (Religion); West Res 64-65 MSLS. 6: Ger, Classical Gk. 7: Sr asst Toledo Br Lib 65-66; Soc sci libn Mich Bur Lib Serv, Lansing Mich 66-67, Prof educ libn 67-68, Hd gen ref unit 68-. 8: Ordained deacon in Lutheran Church. 9: ALA; MichLA. 10: Central Mich Philatelic Soc. 14: Ref, catlg. 15: 212 E Point lane, E Lansing Mi 48823.

MICHELSON, AARON I. b Cleveland 3 O 27. 4: Fairlie A Brown. 5: West Res 46-49 (Psych, Math) BS, 49-50 MSLS; Chicago 56-58 (LS). 6: Ger. 7: Readers serv Detroit Pub Lib

50-51; US Army (Sgt) 51-54; Libn ND State Tchrs Col (Ellendale) 55-56; Ref asst UChicago Lib 57-58; Dir Okla Lib Community Proj, Okla City Okla 59-60; Asst Prof Sch of Lib Sci UOkla 60-65; Head Libn Scott-Foresman & Co, Chicago 65-66; Lib dir US Alabama (Mobile). 9: ALA; Adult Educ Assn; SELA; AlaLA. 10: AAUP. 12: Ed "Oklahoma Library-Community Project Newsletter (59-60). 13: Yes. 14: Admin, ref. 15: 634 Maple ct, Mount Prospect Ill 60056.

MICHENER, DAVID HASTINGS. b Englewood NJ 15 D 42. 4: Celia Eugenia Archambeault. 5: UKan 60-64 (Hist) BA; UCLA 66-68 (African Hist) MA; UDenver 68-69 (Libnship) MA. 7: Vol US Peace Corps, Cameroon 64-66; Catlgr NorthwesternU 69-. 10: Phi beta Kappa; Phi Alpha Theta. 14: Africana. 15: 710 Hinman st apt A, Evanston Il 60202.

MICHNA, JAMES THOMPSON. b Racine Wis 19 My 34. 4: Mary Blanchard. 5: U Wis (Racine) 52-53, 56-57 (Hist); UWis(Milwaukee) 57-59 (Hist) BS; UWis 59-60 MSLS. 6: Sp. 7: US Army (Sp3) Sound Ranging Computer, Karlsruhe Germany 54-56; Ref libn Kalamazoo Pub Lib 60-62; Libn UWis(Green Bay) 2-65; Asst to dir UWis-Center System Lib (Madison 65-; Lib dir Rockford Col 68-. 10: AAUP; Phi Alpha Theta; Beta Phi Mu. 14: Ref, admin. 15: Howard Colman Lib, Rockford Col, 5050 E State st, Rockford Il 61101.

MICHNIEWSKI, HENRY J. b Derby Conn 25 D 29. 4: Helen Huckins. 7: Personnel US Army Artillery, US & Europe 52-54; Lib asst Brooklyn Pub Lib 55-57; Dept head Flint Pub Lib, Flint Mich 57-62; Coordinator LSCA NJ State Lib 62-69; Coord planning & development 69-. 8: Consul on patterns of service, site sel, etc. 9: ALA; MichLA; NJLA. 15: 500 Maple ave, Trenton NJ 08618.

MICKELBERG, DEENA. b Philadelphia Penn 16 Mr 46. 5: Temple 64-67 (Econ) BA; UPittsburgh 67-68 MLS. 6: Fr. 7: Hd tech serv Usarhaw Schofield Barracks, Hawaii 68-. 9: HawaiiLA. 14: Acquis, catlg. 15: 61741 Papailoa rd, Haleiwa Hi 96712.

MICKENBERG, FANNIE (KLEINSIEC). b NYC 27 Mr 14. 4: Edwin Mickenberg. 5: Hunter Col 30-34 (Biol) BA; NYU summer 58 (Educ); St Johns U 60-61 (LS); Queens Col 62-65 (LS) MA. 7: NYC Bd of Educ: Tchr PS 164, Brooklyn 51-54, Tchr PS 173, Queens 54-55, Elem tchr PS 154, Queens 55-62, Reading imrovement tchr PS 154, Queens 62-64, Elem libn PS 154, Queens 64-. 14: Elem sch lib. 15: 73-10 178th st, Flushing 66 NY.

MICKEY, ETHEL MARIE (KISER). b Cedar Co Iowa 2 N 21. 4: Charles Otha Mickey. 5: Parsons Co 39-40 (Ed); Clark Col (Vancouver, Wash) 55 (Ed) AA; UPortland (Portland) 63 (Ed) BA in Ed, 67 MA in LS. 7: Elem sch tchr, Jefferson Co Iowa 40-41, Wapello Co Iowa 41-42, Vancouver Dist #37, Vancouver Wash 59-65; Elem sch libn Vancouver Dist #37, Vancouver Wash 65-69. 9: ALA; NEA; WashLA; WashASchL; WashEA. 10: Alpha Delta Kappa. 15: Rte 2 Box 245, Ridgefield Wa 98642.

MICKLE, EDWARD BUXTON. b Winston-Salem NC. 5: UNC 44-47 (Comparative Lit) AB; UDENVER 57-58 (LS) MA. 6: Fr, Ger. 7: Asst libn U Neb 58-60; Order libn Colgate U 60-63; Asst to libn City Col (NY) 63-. 9: ALA; NY Lib Club. 10: AAUP; NY Shavians Inc. 14: Ref, gift & exch, bk sel & elimination. 15: Ansonia Hotel apt 15-155, Broadway & 73rd st, New York NY 10023.

MICKLEY, MABEL (DAVIS). b Porter Okla 1 D 10. 5: Okla A&M Col 27-29 (Educ); Northeastern State Col 29-32 (Hist) AB; UOkla 59-62 ML. 7: Pub sch tchr 20 yrs; Ref libn Southwestern State Col (Okla) 62-. 8: Lib Sci instr 62-. 9: NEA; OklaLA; OklaEA. 14: Ref. 15: 706 N 5th st, Weatherford Okla 73096.

MICUDA, VLADIMIR. b Croatia 26 Ja 26. 4: Martha Nauman. 5: University of Zagreb (Croatia) 46-52 (Forestry); Sch of Agric (Wageningen Netherlands) 55-56 (Forestry); Ind U 60-61 MA in LS. 6: Ger, Croatian, Russian, Polish, Dutch. 7: Asst libn Mann Lib Cornell U 61-64, Assoc libn 64-66; Agric & Biol scis libn Penn State U (State College) 66-. 9: ALA. 10: Beta Phi Mu; The Croatian Acad of Amer, NY. 14: Acquis, admin. 15: 445 Waupelani dr apt L-6, State College Pa 16801.

MIDDLEMISS, ROBERT (WILLIAM). b Eng 24 Ap 38. 4: Deborah Louise Cass. 5: Sir George Williams u 59-63 (Philos) BA; McGill 63-64 BLS; Adelphi U (Bus Admin). 7: Lab techn Armstrong Cork Co, Montreal 53-54; Prod clerk United Aircraft Corp, Montreal 54-56; Stud engnr marine & naval arch Fed Dept of Transport, Ottawa 56-59; Asst acquis libn York U (Toront) 64-65; Acquis libn Adelphi U 65-67, Hd acquis dept Ind State U (Terre Haute) 67-. 8: Asst prof (ext) selection lib materials Ind State U Lib Sch. 9: ALA; IndLA; Ind Jr Libns RT (pres). 14: Acquis, antiquarian bks, admin, automation. 15: 1200 S Center, Terre Haute In 47802.

MIDDLETON, BERNICE BRYANT. b Orangeburg SC 11 N 22. 4: Earl M Middleton. 5: Claflin Col 38-42 (Eng) AB; Atlanta 43-44 BLS, summers 52, 54, 57 MS in LS; UIll(Champaign) summer 65; UPittsburgh summers 67, 68 Advanced Certif in LS. 6: Fr. 7: Tchr-libn Granard High Sch, Gaffney SC 42-43; Asst catlgr Atlanta U 44-46; SC State Col: Asst libn 47-48, Circ libn 48-52, Instr Dept of Lib Serv 52-57, Chm Dept of Lib Serv 57-. 8: Visiting Com So Assn Cols & Schs, 57-63. , 66; Mem, Statewide Standing Com on Lib Educ. 9: ALA; SCLA; SELA. 10: AAUP; Nat Assn of Col Women; Beta Phi Mu; Delta Sigma Theta; Wesleyan Serv Guild. 13: Yes. 14: Catlg, child lit. 15: Box 1868 SC State Col, Orangeburg SC 29115.

MIDDLETON, BETTY MARIE (DIXON). b Englewood Tenn 23 My 29. 4: Robert H Middleton. 5: E Tenn State U 47-51 (Eng) BS; Peabody summers 52-54 (LS) MA. 7: Libn Polk Co High Sch, Benton Tenn 51-58; Libn Jefferson Sch, Alexandria Va 58-62; Admin asst to reg libn Ft Loudoun Reg Lib, Athens Tenn 62-64, Reg libn 64-. 9: SELA; TennLA. 10: AAUW; Alpha Omicron Pi. 14: Pub rel, catlg, bk sel, bkmob wk. 15: Box 254, Englewood Tn 37329.

MIDDLETON, CALVIN V. b Grants Pass Ore 20 S 24. 4: Josephine R. 5: Willamette U 50 (Biol) BA; UDENVER 58 (LS) MA. 7: Tchr-libn Glide High Sch, Glide Ore 51-57; Libn Marshfield High Sch, Coos Bay Ore 57-59; Field serv State Lib, Salem Ore 59-61; Libn Sr High Sch, Oregon City Ore 61-. 8: Instr in lib sci So Ore Col summer 68. 9: NEA; ALA; OreEA; OreASchL (ed; OreLA (pres). 10: Ore City Friends of the Lib. 14: Sch libnship. 15: 131 Barker ave, Oregon City Or 97045.

MIDDLETON, DALE R(OBERT). b Great Falls Mont 20 My 35. 4: Helene Patricia OKeefe. 5: Reed Col 53-57 (Philos) BA; San Francisco State Col 57; Columbia 58-60 MSLS; UWash 67. 7: NY Pub Lib, libn trainee 58-60, child libn 60-64, br libn & child libn 66; Instl libn Wash State Lib Rainier Sch 66-68; Interlib loan UWash Health Sci Lib (Pacific NW Reg Health Sci Lib) 68-. 14: Devel & admin of readers serv. 15: 603 20th E, Seattle Wa 98102.

MIDDLETON, RICHARD DELANEY. b St Louis 22 O 27. 5: UDayton 44-48 (Chem) BS Educ; St Louis U summer 51 (LS); Our Lady of the Lake Col summers 52-56 BS LS, summer 68. 7: Libn Assumption High Sch, E St Louis 52-54; Libn Cathedral High Sch, Belleville Ill 5463; Libn Vianney High Sch, Kirkwood Mo 63-67; Libn Central Cath High Sch, San Antonio Tex 67-. 9: CathLA (St Louis Unit; pres 58-60, sec 64-66; San Antonio Unit; sec 67-68, pres 68-69); ALA; MoLA (treas 66-67); St Louis Suburban Sch Libns; Bexar Co LA. 14: Sch lib. 15: Central Catholic High School Lib, 1403 N St Mary's st, San Antonio Tx 78215.

MIDENCE, MARTITA. b Charleston W Va 28 Jl 46. 5: Randolph-Macon Woman's Col 64-68 9pol Sci) AB; ColumbiaU 68-69 MS in LS. 6: Sp, Fr. 7: Gen asst Intl Affairs Lib ColumbiaU 68-. 9: ALA; SLA; NYSLA. 10: Stud Forum on Intl Order & World Peace. 14: Ref, intl rel, acquis, ser, admin. 15: 521 W 122nd #64, New York NY 10027.

MIDGETT, ADELAINE (STILLINGS). b Frazee Minn 28 O 10. 4: J Kent Midgett. 5: UMont 29-33 (LS) BA. 6: Fr, Ger. 7: Asst libn Chouteau Co Free Lib, Ft Benton Mont 33-35; Libn Teton Co High Sch, Choteau Mont 36-38; Libn St Patricks Sch of Nursing, Missoula Mont 56-57; Asst catlg libn UMont 57-. 8: Cataloged high sch lib, Harlowton Mont 39. 9: ALA; ONLA (Memb Com); MontLA (pres 68-69; mem &/or chm var coms). 10: Friends of Missoula Pub Lib. 14: Catlg, ref. 15: 141 W Beckwith, Missoula Mt 59801.

MIELKE, FRANCES SARA. b Sedgewick Alta Can 2 Ag 26. 5: UMan 44-47 BA; Toronto 49-50 BLS. 6: Fr. 7: Dept of Educ, Man Govt, Winnipeg Man: Steno 47-49, Asst libn 50-55, Libn 55-61; Asst libn Ed Lib UAlta 61-67; Interlib loan libn UAlta (Edmonton) 67-. 9: CanLA; AltaLA; EdmontonLA. 14: Circ, ref. 15: Ref Dept Cameron Lib Univ of Alberta, Edmonton Alta Can.

MIELKE, THELMA (JANE). b Rochester NY 16 D 14. 5: Elmhurst Col 33-37 (Sociol) AB; URochester 37-39 (Philos) MA; Columbia U & Union Theol Sem 41-45 (Philos)

Columbia 60-61 (LS) MS; NYU 54- (Govt). 6: Ger, Sp, Fr. 7: Asst Dept of Philos URochester 37-39; Group wker Baden St Settlement House, Rochester NY 39-41; Libn Harlem Boys Club, NYC 44-45; UN Correspondent, Revista PR 45-50; Pub Rel Hill & Knowlton, NYC 52-54; Ref asst - Sr ref libn NYU 54-63; Ref libn, Asst Prof LIU 63-65, Ref libn, Assoc Prof 65-. 9: ALA; SLA; Amer Polit Sci Assn; East States Hist Clearing House (Exec sec 65-). 10: War Resisters League; NAACP; ACLU; AAUP. 13: Yes. 14: Ref, info retrieval systems, admin. 15: 175 W 12th st, New York NY 10011.

MIERZWINSKI, REV THEOPHIL THOAS. b Torrington Conn 9 Mr 24. 5: St Bernards Sem Col 43-45 AB; St Bernards Theol Sem 45-48; Columbia 48-49 (LS) MS. 6: Fr, Polish, Lat. 7: Head Libn St Thomas Sem (Bloomfield Conn) 48-. 9: ALA; CathLA; ConnLA. 13: Yes. 14: Ref. 15: 467 Bloomfield ave, Bloomfield Conn 06002.

MIGLIORE, ROSEMARY A. b NY 17 Jl 44. 5: Harpur Col 63-66 (Hist) AB; UMich 67 AMLS. 6: Ital, Fr. 7: Acquis lib UMich (Ann Arbor) 68-69; Libn Malcoln Pirnie Consulting Engrs, White Plains 69-. 9: ALA. 10: Beta Phi Mu. 14: Acquis, spec libs. 15: 1925 Mulliner ave, Bronx NY 10462.

MIH, DORA H(SIA). b Nanking China 12 O 35. 4: Walt er C Mih. 5: Nat Taiwan U 53-57 (Foreign Lang & Lit) BA; UCal 58-60 MLS; Chicago 62-63 (LS); UWis 68 (Sp). 6: Chinese, Fr, Ger, Sp. 7: Libn Tech Lib Beloit Corp, Beloit Wis 60-62; Libn S Beloit Pub Lib, Beloit Ill 63-65; Circ libn Janesville Pub Lib, Janesville Wis 65-67CHIF RomanceLang catlgr UWis Gen Lib 67-. 9: ALA. 13: Yes. 14: Catlg, admin, tech. 15: 608 L Eagle Heights Apts, Madison Wi 53705.

MIHALCIK, THERESE (KRAJSA). b Allentown Penn 15 Jl 15. 4: Joseph A Mihalcik. 5: Kutztown State Col 32-36 (LS) BS; PennLA Libn Certif 40; Temple 59 (Educ). 6: Slovak. 7: Lib asst Pub Lib, Allentown Penn 36-42; Elem sch libn elem schs, Allentown Penn 61-. 9: NEA; Penn State EA; PennSchLA; Penn Dept Supv & Curr. 10: AAUW; Women Tchrs Club; Womens Club of Allentown; Allentown Art Museum. 14: Ref, child bks. 15: 1830 W Congress st, Allentown Penn 18104.

MIKKELSEN, JOHN HENRY. b Brooklyn NY 4 O 29. 4: Christine May. 5: Champlain Col 47-49 (Hist); Alfred U 49-51 (Hist) BA; SUNY 63-67 MLS. 7: IBM, Poughkeepsie NY: Programmer 61-62, libn DS Lib 62-63, Libn Info ret center 63-64, Libn Documentation 64-65; IBM Burlington Vt 65-, Mgr IBM Burlington Lib 68-. 9: SLA; VtLA. 10: Jr C of C. 14: Info retrieval, documentation, admin, catlg. 15: 8 Sebring rd, S Burlington Vt 05401.

MIKUS, DONALD AARON. b Pittsburgh Penn 5 F 44. 4: Jacqueline (Abrahms). 5: Clarion State Col 62-66 (Ed, LS) BS; Duquesne 66; Penn State 68; UPittsburgh 67-69 MLS. 6: Sp. 7: Libn Chartiers Valley Schs, Pittsburgh Penn 66-69. 9: ALA; PennStateEA; PennLA. 14: A-v, sch libn. 15: 13C Chartier ter, Carnegie Pa 15106.

MILAC, METOD MARJAN. b Prevalije Solvenia Yugoslavia Yugoslavia. O 24. 4: Herta Schiffer. 5: Karl-Franzen-U (Graz Austria) 46-48 (Law); Landeskonservatorium (Graz Austria) 48-50 (Piano); Cleveland Inst of Music 53-57 BM in Theory, 57-60 MM in Musicology; West Res 60-62 MS in LS. 6: Slovene, Croatian, Ger. 7: Music libn Syracuse U 62-65, Head ref dept 65-67, Coord pub serv 67-68, Asst dir libs, pub serv 68. 8: Conductor Singing Soc Korotan, Cleveland 51-62; Choral & solo performances, Choral dir & piano accompanist for 3 LP records of Slovenian Folk & art songs; Grant to attend 10th Congress Intl Musicological Soc, Ljubljana Slovenia Yugoslavia 67. 9: MusLA (NY State Chap: Program Chm); ALA; Assn Recorded Sound Collections. 14: Ref, music, Slavic, lib admin. 15: Rm 208, Carnegie Lib Syracuse Univ, Syracuse NY 13210.

MILAM, VICTORIA (S) P(OTTS). b Jacksonville Fla 30 O 43. 5: Fla StateU 63-65 Ger BA, 65-66 (LS) MS. 6: Ger. 7: Acquis libn VanderbiltU Med Lib 66-68; Admin asst NW Reg Lib, Panama City Fla 68-. 9: MedLA; SLA; FlaLA. 14: Admin, ref. 15: 1708 Arthur ave, Panama City Fl 32401.

MILBERG, DENISE (BANKS). b Toronto Can 5 N 41. 4: Marvin Milberg. 5: UToronto 60-64 9hist) BA, 65-66 BLS. 7: Clerk Toronto Pub Lib, Toronto Can 64; Sub-Professional N York Pub Lib, Toronto Can 65, Libn 66-. 14: Pub serv. 15: 103-6000 Bathurst st, Toronto Ont Can.

MILCZEWSKI, MARION A (MR). b Saginaw Mich 12 F 12. 4: Anabel Robb. 5: UMich 36 (Eng) AB; UIll 38 BSLS, 40 MSLS. 6: Sp, Fr, Portu. 7: Lib interne TVA, Wilson Dam Ala 38-39; Ala Asst to exec sec (Chicago) 40-42; Exec asst to bks for Latin America, Wash DC 42-44; Asst to dir Internat Rel Off, Wash DC 44-46; Dir Internat Rel Off, Wash DC 46-47; Dir SoEast States Coop Lib Survey 47-49; Asst U libn UCal (Berkeley) 49-60; Dir UWash Libs 60-; Prof UWash Sch of Libnship 67-. 8: Assisted in estab biblioteca, Benjamin Franklin, Mexico City 41; Esta Ala Internat Rel Off, Wash DC 42; Rep Ala at Mexican bk fair & Congress of libns & archivists, Mexico City 45; Lib consul Universidad Del Valle, Cali, Columbia, summer 62, 68; Universidad de Oriente, Cumana, Venezuela, summer 63; Pontificia Universidad Javeriana, Bogota, Colombia 64, Univ de Brasilia, Brazil summer 67. 9: ALA (Exec Bd 69-; chm Internat Rel Com 62-68); PNLA; WashLA; PugetSoundLA; PAC; Northwest Bibliog Center (Bd of Dirs); Bks for the People Fund, Inc (Bd of Dirs); ARL (chm Adv Com Slavic Bibliog & Documentation Ctr, v-chm For Acquis Com); Latin Amer Studies Assn; Sem acquis of Latin Amer Lib Materials; AALS. 10: AAUP; Beta Phi Mu. 11: Fulbright Research Grant, Birmingham Eng 54-55. 12: ""Libraries of the Southeast (49); ""Report of a Survey and Recommendations for Administration, Collections and Services of Libraries of the Universidad del Valle (62); ""Staffing, Collections and Services of the Libraries of the Universidad de Oriente (63); ""The Libraries of the Pontificia Universidad Javeriana, Their Present State and Some Recommendations for the Future (64); ""Estructura de La Biblioteca Universitaria en La America Latina (67). 13: Yes. 14: Admin, internat lib rel & devel. 15: 3621 Northeast 100t, Seattle Wa 98125.

MILES, CHARLES HOWARD. b Baltimore 27 Ag 08. 4: Frances Rankin. 5: St Johns (Annapolis) 28-32 (Eng) AB; Columbia 37-39 BLS, 40-42 (Adult Educ) MA. 7: Asst to libn City Col (NY) 37-; Asst Prof Bernard M Baruch Col CUNY 67-. 10: Kappa Delta Pi. 15: Bernard M Baruch Col, CUNY, 17 Lexington ave, New York NY 10009.

MILES, CLARA ANN (McCLURE). b Ord Neb 1 Je 42. 5: UTex 60-64 (Math) BA; UWash 66-68 MLS. 7: Bkmob libn Beyan Pub Lib, Beyan Tex 64-65; Hematology lab tech Tex U of A&M 65, Histology lab tech 65-66; Lib asst III UWash 66-67, Libn of prev med 67-68; Ref libn Seattle Pub Lib 68-. 14: Ref. 15: 7340 24th ave NE, Seattle Wa 98115.

MILES, GERTRUDE E. b Waverly NY. 5: Syracuse 31-35 (Fr) AB, 36-37, 39-40 (Fr) AM, 43-44 BS in LS; Middlebury Summer Sch 35 (Fr). 6: Fr. 7: Fr tchr high sch, Cattaraugus NY 37-39; Eng tchr high sch, New Paltz NY 41-43; Circ libn & ref asst BucknellU 44-. 14: Circ, ref. 15: Bertrand Lib Bucknell Univ, Lewisburg Pa 17837.

MILES, JACK FREDRIC. b El Reno Okla 23 S 29. 5: UOkla 47-50 (Pre-law), 55-58 (Law) BA, LLB, 67-68 MLS. 7: Pilot USAF 51-55; Prosecutor Kiowa Co Okla 58-60; Priv law practice, Okla 60-66; Docs libn UWis (Green Bay) 68-. 8: Pub rel Nat Aircraft Show, Okla City 56; Survey specialist Dept of Educ, Colo 67. 14: Docs, ref. 15: 506 S Lahoma, Norman Ok 73069.

MILES, LAURA ANN. b Huntington W Va 16 Jl 12. 5: Marshall 30-34 (Fr) AB; Drexel 34-35 BS in LS; Columbia summers 39-45. 6: Fr, Sp. 7: Asst libn Glenville State Col 35-38; Sch libn Marshall U 38-39, Ref libn 39-46; Reader's adv DC Pub Lib 47-51; Libn US Bur of Naval Personnel 51-55, Bur libn 55-60; Ref libn, Wash DC: US Off of Tech Serv 60-61, US Civil Serv Commsn 61-, US Dept of Health, Educ, & Welfare. 9: SLA. 14: Ref. 15: 4416 N 4th rd, Arlington Va 22203.

MILES, MARY LOUISE. b Indianapolis Ind 10 O 42. 4: Donald D Miles. 5: ButlerU 60-64 (Sociol) BA; IndU 64-65 (LS) MA. 6: Fr, Sp. 7: GS II Indianapolis Pub Lib 63-64; Prof libn 65-, Br libn 67-. 9: ALA; IndLA. 10: Phi Kappa Phi. 14: Ref, admin, ya. 15: 1038 S Reisner st, Indianapolis In 46221.

MILES, PAUL M. b Denver Col 14 Mr 17. 4: Perla Virginia Carrasco. 5: Regis Col (Denver) 35-37; Denver U 38-40 (Hist) BA; UCal (Berkeley) 47-50 (Hist) MA, BLS; Mexico City Col 49 (Sp). 6: Sp, Fr, Portug. 7: Journalist Associated Tradepaper Writers, Denver 36-37; Page Denver Pub Lib 38-40; S/Sgt US Air Corps, Puerto Rico, 41-45; Tchg asst hist dept UCal (Berkeley) 47-48; Ref libn UCLA Lib 50, Geoly libn 51-52, UN & intl docs libn 52-54, Ind rel libn 54-58, Bus admin libn 58-59; Asst univ libn 59-. 8: Lib planning consul, Nat U of Colombia Bogota 62; Lib prog Coord, U of Chile (UCal Exch Prog 65-); Lib bldg consul: Ariz State U 62, UCal (Davis) 64, UCal 9irvine) 62, Occidental Col 68-69. 9: ALA (Internatl Rel RT, Bldgs & Equip Inst); CalLA (Internat Rel RT). 10: UCal

Lib Sch Alum Assn. 12: Ed "Ed "Industrial Relations Theses and Dissertations," SLA (55-58); Ed "Calibrarians" (UCal Lib Sch Alum Assn 53-55); "Las Bibliotecas de la Universidad de Chile" (65); "Las Bibliotecas de la Universidad de Colombia" (62). 13: Yes. 14: Lib bldgs, tech proc. 15: UCLA Lib, Los Angeles Ca 90024.

MILES, PAULINE (MECKLEY). b Columbus Ohio 8 Jl 14. 4: William C Miles. 5: UToledo 32-36 (Hist) BA; West Res 36-37 BS in LS. 7: Libn WPA union catlg proj, Toledo Ohio 37-38l Sr asst Toledo Pub Lib, Toledo Ohio 38-. 9: ALA; OhioLA. 14: Catlg. 15: 2115 Berdan ave, Toledo Ohio 43613.

MILFORD, CHARLES C. b Berlin 13Jl 27. 4: Patricia Shannon. 5: UBerlin 46-48; Free U of Berlin 48-50; Columbia 50-51 (LS) MS; UWash 59-61 (Pol Sci) MA. 6: Ger. 7: Libn US Army Korean Base Sect 52-53; Libn II Gen serv div Tacoma Pub Lib, Tacoma Wash 53-59; Asst head readers serv div Ore State Lib 61, Head readers serv div 62-64; Libn Food Reasearch Inst Stanford U 64-. 9: ALA-ACRL; OreLA (Local Conv Arrangements Chm 64). 13; yes. 14: Ref, admin. 15: 280 Waverley st, Menlo Park Cal 94025.

MILLAR , BARBARA (PEARLE). b Montreal Can 14 My 27. 5: McGill 44-48 (Biol Sci) BS; UIll 63-64 MSLS. 6: Fr. 7: Research tech McGill U 48-51; Lab supv Papanicolaou Cancer Research Inst, Miami Fla 5163; Catlg UIll Med Center (Chicago) 64-68, Catlg libn 68-. 9: ALA; Chicago Lib Club. 10: Beta Phi Mu. 14: Catlg. 15: 2851 S Parkway apt 1406, Chicago Il 60616.

MILLAR, LEOLA (FAUDREE). b Evansville Ind 4 D05. 5: Stephens Col 23-25 (Eng, Langs) AA; Mo Sch of Mines 26; UMo summers 51-52 (LS). 7: Libn Rolla High Sch, Rolla Mo 50-54; Libn Rolla Mo 54-. 9: ALA-ASD (com chm); MoLA (chm Legis Com 67-68, chm Pub Lib Div 63-); Mo Adult Educ Assn. 10: Arthritis Found. 11: Lib received John Cotton Dana Publ Award 61; Dorothy Canfield Fisher Award for Mo 63. 13: Yes. 14: Adult serv, ref, pub rel. 15: 1400 Pine st, Rolla Mo 65401.

MILLAR, YVONNE JANE (MANZ). b Pasadena Cal 19 D 42. 4: Donald James Millar. 5: Brigham YoungU 65 (Eng); Cal State Col (Los Angeles) 65-67 (Eng) BA; USoCal 67-68 MSLS. 7: Lib clerk City of Pasadena Dept of Lib, Pasadena Cal 61-62; Lib clerk Jet Propulsion Lab, Pasadena Cal 62-66; Tech libn AiResearch Mfg Div of the Garrett Corp, torrance Cal 68-. 8: Sec USoCal Sch pf Lib Sci 67-68. 9: SLA. 13: Yes. 14: Catlg. 15: 24035 Ocean ave apt 34, Torrance Ca 90505.

MILLARD, EUGENIA L(UCY). b Albany NY 5 My11. 5: NY State Col for Tchrs (Albany) 30-33 (Eng) AB 33-34 (LS) BS, 34-35 (Eng) AM; Cornell U summer 41-51 (Amer Lit) PhD. 6: Sp, Fr. 07 libn Albany Pub Sch, Albany NY 35-; Asstship Dept of Eng Cornell U 47, 48; Libn Albany Pub Libs, Albany NY summers; Tchr Albany Adult Even Sch, Albany NY 63-65. 8: Consul: NY State Eng Coun 53-; Loc Hist Com, Albany NY. 9: ALA; Nat Conf Amer Folklore for Youth (Consul & Bibliog); NYLA; East NY SchLA (treas, v-pres, pres); Hudson- Mohawk LA; Cornell (U) LA; NY Flklore Soc. 10: Center Square Assn; Albany Obedience Club (dogs); Albany Cat Franciers Club. 13: Yes. 14: Sch libs, catlg, ref, miniature bks, lib aides & instr. 15: 157 Chestnut st, Albany NY 12210.

MILLEN, GEORGE ALBERT. b Tacoma Wash 10 N 41. 4: Jean Jordan. 5: UPuget Sound 61-65 (Hist, Pol Sci) BA; UWash 65-66 M Libn. 6: Fr. 7: Catlg libn Buena Vista Col, Storm lake Iowa 66-67; Asst ref libn S Dak StateU 67-68, Asst acquis libn 69-. 9: ALA; SDakLA. 14: Tech proc. 15: 1427 6th st, Brookings SD 57006.

MILLEN, JEAN VERA JORDAN. b Sturgis SC 12 Ag 40. 4: George A Millen Jr. 5: Black Hills State Tchrs Col 58-59; State U of SD 59-62 (LS) BA; UDenver 62-63 (LS) MA. 7: Catlgr & ref Buena Vista Col 63-64, Catlgr 64-66; Catlgr Black Hills State Col 66-68; Asst libn Brookings Pub Sch 68-. 9: ALA; SDLA. 10: AAUW. 14: Catlg. 15: 1427 6th st, Brookings SD 57006.

MILLENDORF, CAROLE DIANE. b Phila Penn 5 My 46. 5: Temple 63-68 (Elem ed) BS in Ed; Drexel (LS) MS. 7: Lib page Free Lib of Phila 62-63; Lib asst Sch Dist of Phila 65-68, Stud tchr 68, Lib asst 69. 9: ALA; -AASchL; PennLA. 14: Sch lib wk. 15: 7919 Bayard st, Phila Pa 19150.

MILLER, ALICE ANN (BLACKWELL). b Taunton Mass 25 D 26. 4: Robert Humphrey Miller. 5: Simmons 44-50 (LS) BS. 6: Fr, Sp, Ger. 7: Lib aide Taunton (Mass) Pub Lib 42-8; Lib aide Simmons Col 46; Head libn Raynham Pub Lib, Raynham Mass 60-67, 69-. 9: Raynham (Mass) LA (sec). 14: Adult wk, catl. 15: 185S Main st, Raynham Ma 02768.

MILLER, ANN. b Los Angeles Cal 10 Ja 31. 5: UCLA 48, 50-52, 68 MLS; Brigham Young 53-55 (Eng) BA; UCal (Berkeley) 56-58 (Educ, Lib). 6: Fr, Sp. 7: LA Pub Lib: Clk-typist 53, Ref libn 58-, Y-a libn 60-65, Serv to shut-ins 66; Apprentice libn Richmond Pub Lib, Richmond Cal 57-58; Y-a libn Woodland Hills Br 66-67, Dub libn 68-; Sub sch libn LA City Schs 69-. 8: YA Adv Com, Los Angeles Pub Lib 61-63. 9: ALA; CalLA. 14: Ref, child lit, sch libs. 15: 5654 Saloma ave, Van Nuys, Ca 91401.

MILLER, ARTHUR H(AWKS) (JR). b Kalamazoo Mich 15 Mar 43. 4: Janet C Schroeder. 5: Kalamazoo Col 61-65 (Eng) BA; U deCaen France 63-64; UChicago 65-68 (Eng) MA (Libnship) MA; Northwestern U 67- (Eng). 6: Fr. 7: Ref lib Newberry Lib, Chicago 67-68, Supt main reading room 68-. 9: ALA. 10: Caxton Club; Mod Lang Assn. 14: Ref, Amer lit. 15: Newberry Lib, 60 W Walton st, Chicago Ill 60610.

MILLER, BARBARA (SIMMONS). b Chattanooga Tenn 19 Ag 12. 4: Thomas Rowland Miller. 5: UMich 293 (Pub sch mus) Mus B; Catherine Spalding Col 50-51 BS in LS, 52-53 MA. 7: Mus tchr Madison Jr High Sch, Louisville Ky 33-35; Child lib: West Br Lib, Louisville 51-57, Main Lib, Louisville 57-59; Hd child dept Main Lib, Louisville 59-60; Dir child serv Louisville Free Pub Lib 61-. 8: Con Storytelling Wkshops for Ky State Lib. 9: ALA (consul Com on Stand for Wk with child in Pub Libs 63-64); KLA (past chm Pub Libs Sect); SELA. 10: Louisville Lib Club; YWCA; WICS. 11: Outstanding Pub Libn of 1967, Ky LA. 14: Storytelling, child prog. 15: 215 N 46th st, Louisville Ky 40212.

MILLER, BELLE. b Charlestown NH 23 My 15. 5: UNH 33-37 (Eng) BA; Simmons 38-39 (LS) BS. 7: Asst in bk selection Harvard 40-. 15: 84 Prescott st, Cambridge Ma 02138.

MILLER, BETTYE ELAINE. b Evansville Ind 3 O 17. 5: Evansville Col 35-39 (Eng) AB; Simmons Col 46-47 BSLS; Ind U 57-2 (Educ) MS in Ed. 7: Child libn E Br Lib, Evansville Ind 39-44; Petty Off 3/c US Navy, Wash DC 44-46; Order libn Central Pub Lib, Evansville Ind 46; Br libn & Supv E Br Lib, Evansville Ind 47-; Br libn & supv Glenwood Br Lib, Evansville Ind 58-69; Coord of adult serv, Evansville Pub Lib & Vanderburgh Co Lib 69-. 9: ALA; IndLA. 10: Evansville Mus of Arts & Sci; Harmonic Assoc of New Harmony (Ind); AAUW. 11: Herbert Goldhor Award 66. 13: Yes. 14: Pub rel, ref, bk sel, rare bks. 15: 1013 Bayard Park dr, Evansville In 47714.

MILLER, BEVERLY ANN. b Tulsa Okla 22 D 41. 5: Thiel Col 60-64 (Eng) BA; UDenver 64-65 (LS) MA. 6: Fr. 7: Period libn Minot State Col 66-67; Asst libn, Ref & readers serv Rocky Mountain Col 67-68; Circ libn Boise State Col 68-. 9: ALA; MPLA; IdaLA. 14: Ref, circ, period. 15: 1001 1/2 E Jefferson, Boise Id 83702.

MILLER, C(LAYTON) MARTIN. b Danville Ill 12 Ja 41. 4: Ruth Guldner Miller. 5: UIll 58-62 (Hist) BA, 62-64 MSLS. 6: Sp. 7: Grad asst UIll Lib (Urbana) 62-64; Bkstacks libn UIowa Lib 64-65; Circ libn UVt Lib 65-68; Head of circ MiamiU Lib (Ohio) 68-. 9: ALA; SAA. 10: Beta Phi Mu. 14: Pub serv archives, admin. 15: 602 Glenview dr, Oxford Oh 45056.

MILLER, CAROLYN V. b Rochester NY 18 Ag28. 4: Edward P Miller. 5: UMich 45-48; UBuffalo 48-50 (Hist) BA; W Tex State U 63; UOkla 64-65 MLS. 6: Fr. 7: Grad asst UOkla Bizzel Lib 64-65; Asst chief of bkmobs Tulsa City- Co Lib, Tulsa Okla 65-66, Chief Sheridan Br 66; Libn Pub Serv Co of Okla 67-. 9: ALA; SLA; OklaLA. 10: Discussion leader, Great Bks Found; Beta Phi Mu. 14: Young adult, bkmob, ref, spec libs. 15: 2102 E 25th st, Tulsa Ok 74114.

MILLER, CAROLYNNE L. b Crown Point Ind 17 Ap 29. 4: Howard W Miller. 5: Butler U46-52 (Zool, Sociol) BS; Ind U 51-58, 59 (LS) MS. 7: Stud asst Crown Point Pub Lib, Crown Point Ind 45-46; Stud asst Nurses Lib, Methodist Hosp, Indianapolis 47-48; Ind State Lib: Stud asst 46-48, Clerk-typist 48-51, Asst libn loan ref Genealogy Divs 52-55, Act head genealogy div 56-59, Head genealogy div 59-. 9: ALA; Amer Assn State & Loc Hist; IndLA; IndHist Soc. 10: Beta Phi Mu. 12: "Aids to GENEALOGICAL Research (rev ed 58); "Aids for Genealogical Searching in Indiana (62). 13: Yes. 14: General. 15: Ind State Lib, 140 N Senate, Indianapolis 46204.

MILLER, CHARLES E. b Bridgeport Conn 3 Ag 38. 4: Alice Phillips. 5: UHawaii 57-58; McNeese State Col 59-64 (Eng)

BA; LSU 65-66 (LS) MS. 6: Fr. 7: Lib stud asst Lake Charles Pub Lib, La 61-62; Tchr Lake Charles High Sch 64-65; Catlgr LSU (Baton rouge) 667, Hd order dept 67-68, Hd acquis 689; Assoc med libn Tulane Sch Med lib 69-. 9: ALA; AAHE; SLA; SWLA; LaLA. 10: Beta Phi Mu; Phi Kappa Phi; Sigma Tau delta; Baton Rouge Lib Club; LSU Lib Staff Assn. 12: Asst ed "LaLA Bulletin" (67). 14: Tech serv, acquis, catlg. 15: Tulane Univ, School of Med Lib, 1430 Tulane ave, New Orleans La 70112.

MILLER, CLAIRE (BRECKENRIDGE). b Ingram Tex 16 N 10. 4: Wilson S Miller. 5: Wash U 27-31 (Ed) AB, 55-57 Certif in LA. 7: Lib Asst St Louis Co Lib 54-57, Hd Rock Rd br 57-59, Hd Natural Bridge br 59-61, Hd child ext 61-. 14: Child wk. 15: 7511 Milan, St Louis Mo 63130.

MILLER, CLARA (GERTRUDE). b St Johns Newfoundland 20 Je 13. 5: Newfoundland Mem U Col 30-32 Diploma; Acadia U 32-34 (Organic Chem) BS; Toronto 43-44 BLS. 7: Typist Bowring Bros Ltd, St Johns Newfoundland 35-37; Circ, ref libn Gosling Mem Lib, St Johns Newfoundland 37-40, Head child dept 40-42; Clerk codes & cypher RCAF Civil Serv of Can, St Johns Newfoundland 42-43; Libn & reviser in catlg UToronto Lib Sch 44-45; Libn Imperial Oil Ltd pub rel dept, Toronto 45-57, Chief Libn Central Lib 57-. 9: SLA (Bd 53-56, pres Toronto Chap 49-50); CanLA (Coun 59-62). 15: 340 Lonsdale rd, Toronto 10 Ont Can.

MILLER, DOLORES. b Memphis Tenn 18 Jl 38. 5: Fla So Col 56-60 (Chem) BS; Fla State u 65-66 (LS) MS. 7: Research libn Jim Walter Research Corp, St Petersburg Fla 66-. 9: SLA; ACS; Tech Assn Pulp & Paper Indus; Fla LA. 14: Lit searching, ref, indexing. 15: Jim Walter Research Corp, 10301 Ninth st North, St Petersburg Fl 33702.

MILLER, DONALD WILLIAM. b Cornwall Ont Can 19 Jl 33. 4: Patricia Marie Kirk. 5: Toronto 54-57 (Eng) BA; UBC 63-64 BLS. 7: Research asst Robt Simpson Co, Toronto 57-59; Lib asst Scarboro Pub Lib, Scarboro Ont 61-63; Br head Calgary Pub Lib, Calgary Alta 64-65, Ref dept head 65-66; Asst dir London Pub Lib & Art Mus, London Ont 66-. 9: CanLA (Coun, Adult Serv Sect); OntLA; Inst Profess Libns Ont. 10: Kinsmen Club; C of C; Humanities Assn. 14: Ref, admin, adult serv. 15: 305 Queen's ave, London Ont Can.

MILLER,DWIGHT MERRICK. b Keosauqua Iowa 25 Jl32. 4: Frances Olney. 5: State U Iowa 55-59 (Sociol) BA; Northwest Mo State Tchrs Col 59-61 (Hist) MA; American U 63-64 (Archives Admin). 6: Sp. 7: Army Ammunition Spec (Sgt 1/c) 52-54; Archivist Ms Div LC 61-64; Sr archivist Herbert Hoover Presidential Lib, W Branch Iowa 64-. 9: SAA. 10: Nat Capitol Hist Soc; State Hist Soc Iowa; W Branch Heritage Found; Lions Internat; Univ Athletic Club (Iowa City Iowa). 14: Arranging & describing mss, ref. 15: 226 Wetherell, West Branch Iowa 52358.

MILLER, EDNA SMOCK. b New Haven Ky. 4: Robert J Miller. 5: Catherine Spalding Col 57-58, 69 MLS; ULouisville 58-65 (Eng) AB. 6: Sp, Fr, Lat. 7: Asst lign Louisville (Ky) Free Pub Lib; Libn ULouisville Sch of Dentistry 58-. 9: ALA (Mem Chm 59-61); SLA; KyLA (sec 62-63); SELA; Louisville Lib Club (pres 57). 10: Univ of Louisville Women;s Club; AAUW; AAUP. 11: Certif of Merit, Founders of Ky Libs. 14: Ref, rare bks. 15: Univ of Louisville, Sch of Dentistry, 129 E Broadway, Louisville Ky 40202.

MILLER, EDNA. b Thorntown Ind 12 My 06. 5: Ind Central Col 24-28 (Math) AB; UIll Lib Sch 31-32 BS in LS; Butler U 46 (Hist) MA. 7: Libn Ind Central Col 35-37; Ref libn Butler U 37-40, Circ libn 40-43; Asst local hist & documents dept S Bend (Ind) Pub Lib 43-44; Asst Ind div Ind State Lib 45-46; Libn Ind Central Col 46-. 9: ALA; IndLA. 10: Phi Kappa Phi; ACLU; AAUW; Ind Hist So. 15: 1424 Mills ave, Indianapolis In 46227.

MILLER, EDWARD P. b Catharines Ont Can 10 My24. 4: Carolyn Vicinus. 5: UMich 43-44 (Aeronautical Engnr); Toronto 45-46 (Aeronautical Engnr) BAS; Kenyon Col 50-53 (Divinity) BD (cum laude); UOkla 64-65 MLS; Okla State U (Computer sci, Mgt Info). 6: Fr, Ger. 7: Flutter analyst Cornell Aero Lab, Buffalo NY 47-50; Episcopal Church Ministry, NY Cal, Okla, Tex 5363; Program assoc adult educ Amer Inst of Discussion, Oklā City Okla 63; Tech writer UOkla Research Inst 64-65; Head bus & econ dept Tulsa City-Co Lib, Tulsa Okla 65-66, Coord adult serv 66-. 8: Exec dir Nat Lib Week, Okla 66. 9: SLA (Okla Chap Bd 67-70); ALA;-ASD (chm Bylaws Com); OklaLA; SWLA. 10: AAAS; Soc Tech Writers & Publishers; Amer Inst of Discussion. 12: Ed "Make Up Your Own Mind, study-discussion manual (64); "Info, newsletter of Sci-Tech/Bus-Eco, Tulsa City-Co Lib (65-66); Ed SLA Okla Chap "Newsletter" (65-); Ed SWLA "Proceedings" (68). 14: Info retrieval, lib automation, adult serv, bus-econ & sci-tech lit, mgt info. 15: 2102 E 25th st, Tulsa Okla 74114.

MILLER, EDWIN FORREST JR. b Binghamton NY 2 Ja 27. 5: Syracuse 45-49 AB, 49-50 (LS) MS. 7: Ref asst Rochester Pub Lib, Rochester NY 50-53; Br libn Binghamton(NY) Pub Lib 53-59, Asst ref libn 59-65, Coord of ref serv 65-. 8: Pres Binghamton Pub Lib Unit Broome Co Chap, Civil Serv Employees Assn 68-. 9: NYLA. 14: Ref serv, adult serv. 15: 78 Exchange st, Binghamton NY 13901.

MILLER, ELIZABETH (KUBOTA). b Dairen USSR 9 Ag32. 5: Wheaton Col 54 (Eng Lit) BA; UMinn 57 (LS) MA; Harvard 58 (Amer Studies). 6: Fr, Japanese. 7: Jr libn UMinn (Minneapolis) summers 56, 57; Col Libn & Eng Instr Bethel Col (St Paul) 56-59; Base libn USAF, Pacific 60-63; Chief Libn Fairchild Hiller Corp, Rockville Md 64-66; Chief libn Mount Vernon Jr Col 66-68; Chief libn Urban Inst, Wash DC 68-. 9: ALA; NCTE; SLA; Coun Planning Libns; AIP. 10: AAUW; AAUP; Lambda Iota Tau. 12: "Tell Me About Tokyo (54); "Pacific Area Bibliography: China Section (62, 63); "Seven Lucky Gods and Ken Chan" (69). 13: Yes. 14: Ref, lib sci educ. 15: 9406 Linden ave, Bethesda Md 20014.

MILLER, ELIZABETH (LEWIS). b West Point Miss. 5: Miss State Col for Women 26-30 (Fr) BA; UIll 31-32 BS in LS. 6: Fr. 7: High sch libn, Miss 32-43; Base libn Columbus Army Air Field, Miss 43-46; Asst libn Tech Lib, Randolph Field Tex 46; Air U Lib, Maxwell AFB Ala: Catlgr 46-49, Chief circ libn 49-59, Bibliogr 59-64, Chief ref libn 64-. 9: SLA; AlaLA. 10: AAUW. 14: Ref. 15: 1813 S Hull st apt B-3 Montgomery Ala 36104.

MILLER, ELIZABETH. b Orange NJ 26 Jl 13. 5: Pratt 42-44 (LS) Certif. 7: Gen asst City Lib, Springfield Mass 33-37, Br child libn 37-42; Asst child room NY Pub Lib 42-44; Br child libn Pub Lib, Brookline Mass 44-49, Head of child serv 49-53; Libn Child lib, Westbury NY 53-. 9: ALA; NYLA. 15: Child Lib, School st, Westbury LI NY 11590.

MILLER, ELSPETH MARGARET. b Milngavie Dunbartonshire Scot 31 D 33. 5: Scottish Sch of Libnship 55-56 ALA, 62-63 Fla; USask 67-69 BA. 7: Lib asst Glasgow Pub Libs, Glasgow Scotland 53-59, Sub libn 57-59; Deputy libn Airdrie Pub Lib, Airdrie Scotland 59-62; Ext libn Prov Lib, Regina Sas 64-66; Supv reg libs 66-67. 15: #204-505 Clarence ave S, Saskatoon Sask Can.

MILLER, ERNEST IVAN. b Harvard Nb 27 F07. 4: Elinor Ross. 5: Elmhurst Col 28-31 (Hist) AB; UIll 31-32 BS in LS; UTenn 39-41 (Sociol) ma. 7: Page Elmhurst Pub Lib, Elmhurst Ill 29-31; Ser asst UNeb Lib 33-34; Asst libn TVA Tech Lib, Knoxville Tenn 34-41; Tech libn Detroit Pub Lib 41-47; Asst libn Pub Lib, Cincinnati 47-55, Libn 55-. 8: Consul on bldgs for a umber of libs, includ Wayne Co (Mich), Ft Wayne (Ind), Nashville (Tenn), Coral Gables (Fla), Clayton (Mo), & DUBUQUE (Iowa). 9: ALA (chm Bldg Com 44-47);-PLA (chm Bldg Com 47-49, chm Nom Com 64-65); MichLA (pres 44-45): OhioLA (pres 51-52). 10: Cincinnati Hist Sco; Cincinnati Literary Club; Engnr Soc; Rotary; Cincinnaus Assn; Civil War Round Table 11: LL.D, Elmhurst Col 62; LHD Xavier U 66. 13: Yes. 14: Admin. 15: 6955 Nolan circle, Cincinnati Oh 45227.

MILLER, FLOYD WALDO. b Findlay Ohio 18 F16. 4: Mildred Dailey. 5: Findlay Col34-38 (Hist) AB; West Res 38-39, 40-41 (Hist) MA, 39-40 BS inLS; UIll summers 51-54 MS (LS). 6: Fr. 7: Jr ref libn Cleveland Pub Lib, 40-43; I-E spec Army of the US (T/Sgt) 43-46; Libn Trumbull Co Serv, Warren Ohio 46-49; Libn & Assoc Prof of Glenville Sci Gleville State Col 49-58; Chief ref libn WVaU Lib & Libn Assoc Prof of Lib Sci Shepherd Col 62-. 9: ALA-ACRL; NEA; Assn Higher Educ; WVaLA (pres 55-56); WVaEA; Tri-State Chap ACRL. 10 Elder, Presbyt Church; Beta Phi Mu. 12: Ed "West Virginia Libraries (53-55). 14: Admin, catlg, ref. 15: P O Box 72, Shepherdstown WVa 25443.

MILLER, FRANCES (ASHTON). b Iowa 25 F18. 4: Robert Miller. 5: Drake U 37-41 (Eng) BA; Columbia 46-47 BSLS; Drake U 48-54; Washington U 52; UMinn summer 58 (LS); UIowa 64. 6: Fr. 7: Tchr Leland pub schs, Leland Iowa 41-42; Tchr pub schs, Guthrie Center Iowa 42-43; USNR (W/R) Spec (S) 2/c 43-45; Jr libn Des Moines Pub Lib, Des Moines Iowa 45-46, Asst circ libn 47; Asst circ & asst humanities libn Drake U 47-51; Catlgr Cushing Lib Tex A&M 51-52; Tchr pub schs, Webster Groves Mo 52-58; High sch libn Minnetonka Schs, Excelsior Minn 58-60; Libn Lyons Twp High Sch, La Grange

Ill 60-61; Asst resarch libn Field Enterprises Inc, Chicago Lib Curriculum Schs, lb pub shcs, Cedar Rapids Iowa 62-64; Catlgr Coe Col 64-65; Educ bibliog SUNY (Albany) 65-. 8: Supv of libs, Minnetonka Schs, Dist #276, Minn 58-60; Lib consul Commun Pub Schs, Cedar Rapids Iowa 62-64; Mem, Iowa (State) Com for the Devel of Sch Libs 63-64. 9: NEA; ALA (Recr Com 63-65); NY State LA; NYLA; SUNYLA. 13: Yes. 14: Ref, bk sel, catlg.5 15: 4 Colonial ct Country Knolls, RR #2, Ballston Lake NY 12019.

MILLER, GEORGE A. b Penn N Dak 14 Jl 14. 4: Vona Bjorgo. 5: UNotre Dame 32-36 (Eng) BA; UND 40-41; UOre 55-62; Alaska MethodistU 67; UAlaska 65-68. 6: Sp. 7: Tchr high sch, Oslo Minn 41-42; Welder Butler Ship Builders, Superior Wis 42-45; Welder rohl-Connelly, Haines Alaska 45; Asst prin Blackduck Minn Sch Dist 46-47; Prin Penn sch Dist, Penn N Dak 48-52; Asst prin Hampden Sch Dist, Hampden N Dak 53-55; Tchr Redmond Union Sch Dist, Redmond Ore 55-62; Tchr-libn Anchorage Independent Sch Dist, Anchorage Alaska 62-. 8: Eng & lib curriculum courses, Anchorage Alaska. 9: NEA; Nat Eng Coun; MinnEA; NDakEA; OreEA; AlaskaEA. 10: Lions Club; Boy Scouts. 14: Rare bks. 15: 2437 Susitna dr, Anchorage Ak 99503.

MILLER, GLENN FREDERICK. b Saginaw Mich 5D 37. 4: Janice Gase. 5: UMich 60-62 (Pol Sci) BA 62-63 MALS. 7: Laborer Central Foundry Div Gen Motors, Saginaw Mich 55-57; Dispatcher Lufkin Rule Co, Saginaw Mich 58-60; Ref asst Ann Arbor Pub Lib, Am Arbor Mich 60-63; City Libn Southfield Pub Lib (Wayne Co System), Southfield Mich 63-67; Dir Genesee Co Lib Syst, Flint Mich 67-69; Asst dir Orlando Pub Lib, Orlando Fla 69-. 9: ALA (chm JMRT 68-69); MichLA (chm Co & Reg Sect 67-68). 10: Dir Southfield (Mich) Jr C of C; Dir Southfield Fair . 14: Admin. 15: Orlando Pub Lib, 10 N Rosalind, Orlando Fl 32801.

MILLER, GLENN E. b Chicago 27 My34. 4: Jacqueline. 5: Seattle U 52-56 Biol)BS; UWash 56-58 (LS) MA; UChicago 62- (LS). 6: Ger. 7: Annex libn Seattle Pub Lib 56-57; Ser libn Chicago Pub Lib 58; Chief of circ Newberry Lib, Chicago 58-60: Dir of Lib Inst for Psychoanalysis, Chicago 60-. 8: Rsearch Asst, Dept of Psychiatry, UIll 63-; Mem Standing Com Amer Psychoanalytic Assn, indexing & clsf 62-. 9: MedLA; ASIS. 12: "Pyychoanalytic Library Index Monthly Guide to the Literature, Ed "Bulletin of the Chicago Psychoanalytic Society. 13: Yes. 13: Yes. 14: Indexing & clsf. 15: 180 N Michigan, Chicago Il 60601.

MILLER, GORDON (FREDERICK). b Edmonton Alberta Can 17 N 46. 5: Red Deer Jr Col 64-65; UCalgary 65-68 (Hist) BA; UBC 68-69 BLS. 6: Fr. 7: Catlgr UAlberta 69-. 9: CanLA; ALA; Can Assn Col & Univ Libns; AltaLA. 10: Beta Phi Mu. 14: Catlg, archives. 15: Box 1420 Drumheller, Alta Can.

MILLER, GORDON WAYNE. b Wellman Iowa 27 F 38. 4: Gail Brown. 5: Iowa State U 57-58 (Farm Op); Iowa Wesleyan Col 59-63 (Hist) BA; Peabody Col 65-66 MLS. 7: Hist tchr Pella High Sch, Pella Iowa 63-65; Libn Niles High Sch, Niles Mich 66-67; Hd libn mcKendree Col 67-68; Hd libn Iowa Wesleyan Col 68-. 9: ALA. 10: American Rifle Assn. 11: Who's Who in American Universities & Colleges - 1963 cum laude BA. 14: Admin ref. 15: 203 E Broad st, Mt Pleasant Ia 52641.

MILLER, GRACE B. b Lititz Pa. 5: Millersville State Col 29-33 (LS, Soc Studies) BS Ed. 7: Elem tchr Marietta Sch Dist, Marietta Pa 33-34, Warwick Two, Rothsville Penn 34-38, Tchr & libn Warwick Twp 38-43, 46-56, Middletown Pa 43-46; Elem libn Warwick Union Sch Dist, Lititz Pa 56-60, Manheim Twp Sch Dist, Neffsville Pa. 9: ALA; PennLA; Penn State EA. 10: Church Sch tchr, Church Coun. 15: Box 298 Kissel Hill rd, RD 3, Lititz Pa 17543.

MILLER, HANNAH E(LLIOTT). b DicksonCity Dickson City 23 F 04. 5: West Chester Normal Sch 20-22 Tchg Certif; Penn State Col 31-32; UPenn 33-34; Marywood Col 34 BS in Educ) NYC 34-36; Bucknell U 35; UScranton 50; Marywood Col 52 MS in LS; Gen Ext UFla 50-56, 65; State Dept of Educ Certif for Life Penn, Cal, & Fla (72). 6: Sp. 7: Libn Bd of Educ, Dickson City Penn 22-42; Head Libn Bd of Educ High Sch, Sarasota Fla 49-62, Ref libn 62-63; Head catlgr Central Processing Bd of Educ, Sarasota Fla 63-, Previewed lib bks Random House 66; Adj instr lib sci U So Fla 66-67; Prof libn Research Educ Media Ctr, Sarasota Fla 64-69. 8: Lib Consul on Evaluation Team for So Assn of Schs & Cols. 9: FlaASchL (Dist chm). 10: Bus & Prof Womens Club; University Womens Club. 14: Ref, catlg, research. 15: 2306 Gull lane, Sarasota Fla.

MILLER, HARRIET F. b Akron Ohio 8 N40. 5: Kent State 59-63 (Sociol) BA, 64-65 MLS. 6: Fr. 7: Teletype operator Babcock & Wilcox Co, Barberton Ohio 58-59; Sec pool Pittsburgh Plate Glass Co, Barberton Ohio 60; File clerk Kelly Girl Serv, Akron Ohio 61, summer replacement 62; Bkmob libn Wadsworth Pub Lib, Wadsworth Ohio 63-64; Hd of Ext Rodman Pub Lib, Alliance Ohio 65-68, Hd libn 69-. 9: ALA; OhioLA (Memb Com, chm-elect of ext RT). 10: Alpha Lambda Delta; Pi Gamma Mu; Alpha Kappa Delta; Beta Phi Mu. 14: Lib ext, lib admin. 15: Rodman Pub Lib, 215 E Broadway, Alliance Oh 44601.

MILLER, HEATHER (SWAN). b Buffalo NY 23 Je 42. 4: Norton G Miller. 5: Grove City Col 60-64 (Eng) BA; UMich 66-67 (LS) MA. 6: Fr. 7: Stud asst Eng dept Grove City Col 62-64; Sr lib clk, lib Mich State U (E Lansing) 64-66; Libn Mich biological sta (Pellston) summers 67,68; Libn undergrad lib Mich State U (E Lansing) 67-. 9: ALA. 10: Pi Gamma Mu; Beta Phi Mu. 14: Univ lib wk. 15: 1630 C Spartan Village, East lansing Mi 48823.

MILLER, MRS HELEN (ESTEY). b Ryegate Mont 18 Ja 15. 4: J Vance Miller. 5: UWyo 33-37 (Eng) BA; UMinn 40-41 (LS) BLS. 6: Fr. 7: Libn Tracy High Sch & Jr Col, Tracy Minn 41-43; Libn hoenix Pub Lib 44-45; Libn Phoenix Elem Dist 1 45-46; Child libn Tucson Pub Lib 46; Libn Phoenix Pub Lib 49-50; Libn Gilbert High Sch, Gilbert Ariz 52-57; Libn Phoenix Pub Lib 59-, Head of adult ref 62-68, Hd Acacia Br Lib 68-. 9: ALA; Ariz State LA; Salt River Valley LA. 14: Ref. 15: 750 E Townley, Phoenix Az 85021.

MILLER, HELEN M. b Conway Mo 13 S 18. 5: Drury Col 36-40 (Eng) AB; UDenver 40-41 BS in LS. 7: Engnr libn UArk 41-43; Circ libn Springfield Pub Lib, Springfield Mo 43-45; Army libn, Ft George G Meade Md 45-46 Libn Cole Co Lib, Jefferson City Mo 47-49; Libn Jefferson City & Cole Co Libs, Jefferson City Mo 49-55; Air Force libn USAF in Europe, Germany & Eng 55-58; Consul WVa Lib OMMSN, Charleston WVa 59-61; State Libn Ida State Lib 62-. 9: ALA (Coun 52-53 & 63-67); 9sec 62-63);-alta 92nd v-pres 65-66); MoLA (pre 52-53); WVaLA (pres ub Lib Div 60-61); IdaLA (Exec Bd 62); PNLA. 12: Ed WVa Lib Commsn "Newsletter (60-61); Ed "The Idaho Librarian (62-). 14: Ext, publs, bldgs. 15: 2410 State st, Boise Id 83702.

MILLER, HESTER (MARCIA). b Morenci Mich 3 N 20. 4: Ransom A Miller. 5: Mich State U 37-41 (Eng Lit) BA; UMich 41-42 (Eng Lit) MA, 42-43 BLS. 7: Summer asst theater collection NY Pub Lib 43; Asst, 1st asst music & drama dept Detroit Pub Lib 43-51; Br ref asst NY Pub Lib 52-54; Engnr lib asst Johns Hopkins U 54-55; Ref asst Amer Assn of Accountants, NYC 55; Ref asst Mich State U Lib 55-56; Ref asst, 1st asst Detroit Pub Lib 56-57; Ref asst Albuquerque NM 58-67, Art libn Albuquerque Pub Lib 67-. 9: ALA; NMLA (pres 65-66); MichLA; TheatreLA; Albuquerque LA. 10: NM Opera Guild; Phi Kappa Phi; Phi Beta Kappa. 14: Ref (music, theater, fine arts). 15: 3607 Calle del Ranchero NE, Albuquerque NM 87110.

MILLER, HOWARD E. b Elmira NY 12 Ag 39. 4: Penny (Ames) Miller. 5: Alfred U 57-61 (Eng) BA; Syracuse 61-63 MS in LS. 7: Ref libn N Country Lib Syst, Watertown NY 63-66; Asst dir Morril Memorial Lib, Norwood Mass 66-68; Reg ext lib Boston Pub Lib 68-. 9: MassLA; NYLA. 10: Beta Phi Mu. 14: Ref, bkmob, ext serv. 15: 45 Monroe st E, Norwood Ma 02062.

MILLER, IDA MAE (GOOD). b Indianapolis Ind 25 Mr 19. 4: John C Miller. 5: Ind Central Col 35-41 (Mus, Eng, Home econ, Soc sci) AB; Columbia 47-48 BSLS; Butler U 48-52 (Voice) B Mus. 7: Home econ tchr Indianapolis Pub Schs 41-43; Sgt WAAC & WAC USA, Me, Lond & Cincinnati 43-45; Lib asst Manual High Sch, Indianapolis Pub Lib 46-47, Sr libn tchrs & bus br 48-52; Hist libn Plainfield Pub Lib, Plainfield Ind 67-. 9: ALA; IndLA. 10: Sigma Alpha Iota; Hymn Soc of Amer; Choristers' Guild; Ind Hist Soc; Hendricks Co Hist Soc; Indianapolis Choir Directors' Assn. 12: Ed "Quaker Life," music. 13: Yes. 14: Ind & loc hist. 15: 525 E Main st, Plainfield In 46168.

MILLER, INGRID O. b Askov Minn 26 Ja 12. 5: Grand View Col 29-30; UMinn 31-34 (LS, Eng) BS; Macalester Col 51-54 (Soc studies) M Ed. 6: Danish. 7: Tchr & libn: Kerkhoven Schs, Kerkhoven Minn 34-37, Cokato Schs, Cokato Minn 37-39; Libn: Litchfield Schs, Litchfield Minn 39-41, W High Sch, Waterloo Iowa 41-43; Ref & circ libn Central Washington Col of Educ 43-44; Jr-Sr High Sch Libn Whiting Schools, Whiting Ind 44-46; Libn: Mt Clemens Schs, Mt Clemens Mich 46-48, Edina Schs, Edina Minn 48-49; Consul for dist lib serv & sr high sch libn, Edina Schs 49-67; Consuk kib serv Edina Schs 67-. 9: ACE; NEA; ALA (Coun 57-58); AASchL (Rec sec 57-58, Bd mem 68 & 69; Internat Rel Com, Legisl Netwk); -YASD; MinnEA; MinnASchL (pres 50-51, Legisl chm); Hennepin Co Suburban LA; EdinaEA. 14: Sch libs. 15: 5008 W 40th st, Minneapolis Mn 55416.

MILLER, J(AMES) GORMLY. b Rochester NY 5 Ja 14. 4: Mildred Bevan. 5: U Rochester32-36 (Eng) AB; Columbia37-38 BS in LS; Ecole des Chartes UParis 45. 6: Fr. 7: Asst libn Rochester Pub Lib, Rochester NY 38-42; Hist research analyst US War Dept, Rochester Ordnance Dist 42-43; Tech 4th grade aus, eto 43-46; Supv Bur of Adult Educ NY State Educ Dept, Albany NY 46; Libn NY State Sch of Tech & Labor Rel, Cornell U 46-64, Prof 56-; Asst dir personnel &budget & Prof ind & labor rels Cornell U Libs & NY State Sch of Industrial & Labor Rels 62-. 8: External Expert Internat Labor Off, Geneva Switzerland 64; Consul US Dept of Labor, Wash DC 64-68; Lib Consul Puerto Rico Dept of Labor, San Juan PR 65; Chm Ithaca City Charter Rec Commsn. 9: ALA; SLA (pres West NY Chap 51); Ind Rel Res Assn; NYLA. 10: Ithaca NY (Alderman) Common Coun 59-63, 68; AAUP. 14: Admin, info documentation. 15: 401 Turner pl, Ithaca NY 14850.

MILLER, JACQUELINE E. b NYC 15 Ap 35. 5: Va State Col 52-54 (Eng); Morgan State Col 55-57 (Eng) BA; Pratt 58-60 MLS. 6: Fr, Sp. 7: Dir of young teens Brooklyn Pub Lib, Br libn Cypress Hills Br. Br libn Bedford Br 64-68; Head ext serv New Rochelle Pub Lib, New Rochelle NY 68-. 9: ALA; NYLA; NY Lib Club (Coun). 10: LWV. 13: Yes. 14: Wk with yp, ext serv. 15: New Rochelle Pub Lib, 662 Main st, New Rochelle NY 10805.

MILLER, JAMES PRESLEY. b Somerset Ky 30 My 38. 5: Berea Col 56-60 (Hist) AB; UMich 60-62, 64-65 MALS. 6: Ger. 7: Wk-study schoar UMich Lib 60-62; Catlg libn St Louis Pub Lib 62; US Army clerk-typist Spec 4/c 62-64; Supv publ University Microfilms Inc, Ann Arbor Mich 64-66; Asst catlg libn & Instr lib sci Berea Col Lib 66-. 9: ALA; SELA; KyLA. 14: Catlg, info retr, tchg. 15: Box 1308, College Station, Berea Ky 40403.

MILLER, JANET. b Spokane Wash 10 Ja 16. 5: Walla Walla Col 34-40 (Music) BA; USoCal 42-50 (Musicology) M Mus; UDenver 47-48 (LS) MA. 6: Fr. 7: Music tchr, libn Mt Ellis Acad, Bozeman Mont 40-43; Music tchr Lynwood Acad, Los Angeles 43-47; Asst Prof of music Walla Walla Col 47-54; Libn Spokane Pub Lib, Spokane Wash 54-, Music & fine arts libn 63-. 10: Choral dir various church & civic orgs; Pi Kappa Lambda. 14: Music catlg, record & tape libs. 15: 523 W Mansfield, Spokane Wash 9205.

MILLER, JEAN RUTH. b St Helena Cal 4 Ag 27. 5: Occidental Col 48-50 (Psych) BA; USoCal 51-52 MS in LS. 6: Sp. 7: Base libn USAF, Long Beach Cal 50-51; Libn I Glendale Pub Lib, Glendale Cal 51-52; Base libn USAF, Wethersfield Eng 52-55; Sta libn USMC Air Station, Santa Ana Cal 55-63; Libn Data Systems Autonetics, Anaheim Cal 63-65; Chief libn Beckman Instruments, Inc, Fullerton Cal 66-. 8: Consul, 2 Marine Corps Libs 55-63. 9: SLA (Bylaws chm 68-69); ASIS; Inst Electric & Electron Engnrs; Orange Co LA (Corr sec 68-69). 14: Info stor & retr, SDI progs, systems analysis mgt. 15: 15501 Pasadena ave #204, Tustin Ca 92680.

MILLER, JEROME K. b Great Bend Kan 18 Ap 31. 5: St Benedict's Col 51-55 (Econ); Kan State Tchrs Col 63-65 (Hist) BA; UMich 65-66 MALS; UKan 66-67 (Hist). 7: Instr libnship (catlgr) Central Wash State Col 67-. 9: ALA; PNLA. 10: AAUP; Kiwanis; Organ Amer Histns. 14: Catlg, rare bks, archives, lib orient. 15: 200 E Ninth, Ellensburg Wa 98926.

MILLER, JOHN. b Trenton NJ 12 Ap 22. 4: Sarah Jordan. 5: Fisk U 41-43; Rutgers 46-47 (Hist, Pol Sci) AB; Columbia 50-51 (Pub Law, Govt) AM; Oslo U Summer Sch 51 Norwegian Pol Inst Certif; Columbia 55-58 (LS) MS. 6: Fr, Ital. 7: Infantryman (Pfc) US Army, Italy 43-45; Instr hist A&T Col (Greensboro NC) 51-52; Instr pol sci Tex So U 52-53; Clerk NY Pub Lib 53, Tech asst 53-61, 1st asst bk delivery div Central Stack 62-67, Exec Asst Research Libs 67-69, Chief Amer Hist Div Research Libs 69-. 14: Reader serv. 15: 549 W 123rd st apt 11B, New York NY 10027.

MILLER, JOSEPH A. b Chicago 27 Jl 33. 4: Frances Griffith. 5: UMinn 51-55 (Hist) BA, 55-57 Hist) MA, 60-64 (LS) MA, 64- (Hist). 7: Econ analyst Central Intelligence Agency, Wash DC 57-58; US Army Counter Intelligence Corps (E-4) 58-60; Research assoc Forest Hist Soc, Yale U 60-69; Libn Henry S Graves Mem Lib & Lect in Forest Hist, Yale Sch of Forestry 69-. 9: AHA; SLA. 12: Assoc ed "Forest History" (64-68), Ed (68). 14: Bibliog, info retr of natural resources lit, spec libnship. 15: 131 Briarcliff rd, Hamden Ct 06518.

MILLER, JUDITH ANN. b St Peter Minn 6 Ag 41. 5: Macalester Col 59-61; Mankato State Col 61-63 (Elem ed) BS. 7: Period libn Mankato State Col, Mankato Minn 64; Elem libn Independent Sch Dist #706, Virginia Minn 64-. 9: ALA; NEA; MinnASchL; MinnEA. 10: Wednesday Musicale; Ventura Club. 15: 218 W Jefferson ave, St Peter Mn 56082.

MILLER, JUDITH HELEN. b Montreal Can 2 S 43. 4: Hugh Miller. 5: McGill 61-64 (Eng) BA, 64-65 BLS; UWaterloo 68-69 (Eng). 6: Fr. 7: Asst libn Waterloo Pub Lib, Waterloo Ont 65-68; Circ libn Waterloo Lutheran U, Waterloo Ont 68-. 9: Inst Profess Libns. 10: United Church Kairos (Nat Exec mem). 15: 330 King st N, Waterloo Ont Can.

MILLER, JUNE (LABB). b Gary Ind 14 Je 12. 4: Clarence E Miller. 5: UWis 30-31 (LS); Ind U 35-38 (Eng) AB; UIll 38-39 BSLS, 48-50 MLS. 7: Ext dept Gary Pub Lib, Gary Ind 29-30, 31-35; Catlgr Ind U Lib summers 39-45; Jr high sch libn Pub Schs, Michigan City Ind 39-45; Libn Lew Wallace High Sch Gary Pub Schs, Gary Ind 45-55 Materials Center Ambridge Sch, Gary Ind 65-. 9: ALA-AASchL (treas); Ind SchLA (pres & treas). 10: Phi Mu; Delta Kappa Gamma; Kappa Kappa Kappa; Gary Col Club; AAUW; Gary Tchrs Union. 13: Yes. 14: Sch libs. 15: 267 Arthur st, Gary Ind 46404.

MILLER, KATHRYN N(AOMI). b Ada Ohio 12 Ja 1900. 5: Fla So 24 (Fr) BA; Columbia summers 24-27; Chicago 28-29 (Fr) MA, 35 (LS) MA. 7: Tchr Fla, NY & NJ schs 17-18, 24-26; sec 18-20,26-27, 29-30 & summers 20-24; Tchr typing Fla So 21,Stud asst in lib 21-24; Instr Fr & Eng Lander 27-28; Asst to assoc dir UChicago 30-33, Catlr ser 33-34, Libn & sec UChicago Grad Lib Sch 34-36; Catlgr Ohio State U 36-37; Catlgr Mo 37-46; Ohio State U 46-, Catlgr & Instr 63-. 9: ALA;-ACRL (Univ Sect);-RTSD (Catlg & Clsf Div); OhioLA; Ohio Valley Reg Group of Tech Serv Libns; Franklin Co LA. 10: Fac Women's Club; Worthington Hist Soc. 12: "Selection of US Serial Documents for Liberal Arts Colleges (37); Ed "Missouri Library Association Quarterly (40-42). 13: Yes. 14: Catlg, govt docs. 15: 109 W Granville rd, Worthington Ohio 43085.

MILLER, KENT EDWARD. b Holton Kan 17 S 41. 4: Clara Ruth Burnette. 5: Kan State Tchrs Col 59-63 (Hist) BA; UKan 63-65 (Hist) MA, 66-67 (Libnship) ML. 6: Sp, Ger. 7: Admin off USAF Res, Richards-Gebaur AFB Mo 66-; Catlgr UKan Libs 67-. 9: ALA; KanLA. 10: AAUP. 14: Catlg, tech processes. 15: 1023 Illinois, Lawrence Ks 66044.

MILLER, LAURENCE ALAN. b Bloomsburg Penn 19 Ja 40. 4: Carole Bissinger. 5: Kutztown State Col 58-62 (LS) BS Ed; Fla State U 62-63 (LS) MS. 7: Stud supv Campus Elem Sch Lib, Kutztown St Col 59-61; Grad asst Strozier Lib Fla State U 62-63; Act libn Bertrand Lib Bucknell U 65, Acquis libn 63-65; Area dir libs Inter Amer U, San German PR 66-. 9: ALA; PennLA. ; Sociedad de Bibliotecarios de PR. 14: Acad libnship, admin, reader serv. 15: Box 433 Inter Amer Univ, San German PR 00753.

MILLER, LAURENCE HANSON. b Iola Kan 23 S 32. 4: Mary Cohen. 5: UKan 50-54 (Eng) AB; Ind U 58-59 MA (LS). 6: Russian, Ger, Fr, Czech. 7: USAF (Linguist) 54-57; UIll Lib (Urbana): Slavic catlgr 59-61, Slavic bibliog 62-64, Head spec langs dept 64-. 9: AL-ACRL (chm Slavic & E European Subsect). 10: Amer Assn Adv Slavic Studies; AAUP. 13: Yes. 14: Non-Western area studies, acquis, catlg. 15: 1304 Mumford dr, Urbana Ill 61801.

MILLER, LEANNE MAE. b Wauseon Ohio 3 Je 42. 5: Goshen Col 60-64 (Eng) BA; UMich 64-65 AMLS. 6: Ger, Sp. 7: Catlgr Shipman Lib Adrian Col 65-68; Prin libn, Wolfner Lib for the Blind & Physically Handicapped, St Louis 68-. 9: ALA (Lib Serv to the Blind RT); MoLA. 14: Lib serv to the blind & physically handicapped. 15: 4388 McPherson, St Louis Mo 63108.

MILLER, LINDA. b Flandreau SD 28 D 40. 5: Augustana Col 58-62 (Eng) BA; UWis 62-65 (LS) MA. 6: Fr. 7: Eng tchr Ind Sch Dist, Council Bluffs Iowa 62-65; Libn Omaha ub Sch System 65-66; Lib coord Council Bluffs Commun Schs, Council Bluffs, Iowa 66-69. 9: NEA; ALA; IowaLA; Iowa State EA; Council Bluffs EA; A-V Educ Assn Iowa; ACEI 10: AAUW. 14: Sch libs. 15: 220 Bluff st, Council Bluffs Ia 51501.

MILLER, LOIS BELL. b Green Bay Wis 21 My 06. 4: Eldredge Miller. 5: Lawrence Col 24-26; UWis 27-29 (Eng) BA, 29 Certif in LS. 7: Catlgr E Chicago (Ind) Pub Lib 29-30; Clsf

John Crerar Lib, Chicago 31-37; Catlgr Nat Archives, Wash DC 38-45; Free lancing, NYC 46-48; Libn Amer Journal of Nursing Co, NYC 49-. 9: MedLA (Bd Dirs 64-67, many coms; NY Reg Group: chm 59-60, Exec Com 58-59, 60-61); SLA; ALA. 10: Nat League Nursing; Interagency Coun on Lib Tools for Nursing. 13: Yes. 14: Catlg, clsf. 15: 7 Peter Cooper rd, New York NY 10010.

MILLER, SISTER M TERESINA IHM. b Spokane Wash 27 Mr 05. 5: Immaculate Heart Col 24- (Eng, Music) BA (41); Cal Gen Secondary Credential 42; Cal Libnship Credential 58. 6: Fr, Ger, Sp. 7: Eng tchr Immaculate Heart High Sch, Los Angeles 41-43; Eng tchr Bisop Conaty Mem High Sch, Los Angeles 43-47; Eng tchr Immaculate Heart High Sch, Los Angeles 47-53; Libn Mary Star of the Sea High Sch, San Pedro Cal 54-58; Eng tchr St Anthony High Sch, Long Beach Cal 59-62; Libn Mission High Sch, San Luis Obispo Cal 62-63; Music libn Immaculate Heart Col 63-. 9: MusLA. 14: Catlg. 15: 2021 N Western ave, Los ANGELES Ca 90027.

MILLER, MARCIA JEAN. b Clevland 28 D 19. 5: Swarthmore Col 38-42 (Hist) BA; Columbia 46-47 BS. 6: Fr, Ger. 7: Asst gift sect LC 42-46; Asst libn Freer Gallery of Art, Wash DC 47-51; Catlgr US Dept of Labor Lib, Wash DC 51-59, Head catlg sect 59-63, Chief div of catlg & acquis 64-67, Asst libn tech processes 67-. 9: ALA;-ACRL (chm-elect Subj Spec Sect); SLA; DCLA; Potomac Tech Processing Libns. 14: Catlg, acquis. 15: 5524 Trent st, Chevy hase Md 20015.

MILLER, MARCIA MUTH. b Ft Wayne Ind 27 S 19. 5: UMich 44-49 (Eng) AB, 49-53 AMLS. 6: Fr. 7: Lib asst Ft Wayne Pub Lib, Ft Wayne Ind 40-43; Jr catlgr UMich 44-53; Asst catlgr Warder Pub Lib, Springfield Ohio 54; Sr documents libn UMich Law Sch Lib 55-61; Asst libn UMo 61-62; Asst law libn UMo Law Sch Lib 63-66; Docs libn NM State Lib 67-68, Coord LSCA Titles 68, Hd SWest & Rare bks room 69-. 9: ALA; AALL; Internat Assn Law Libs; MoLA; Southwestern Assn Law Libs (pres 65-66); NMLA. 10: AAUW; Bus & Prof Women. 12: Comp "Directory of Law Libraries in the Chapter Area, Southwestern Assn Law Libs (64). 14: Law libnship, ref, rare bks. 15: New Mexico State Lib, Santa Fe NM 87501.

MILLER, MARGARET (COLLEEN PUCKETT). b Denver Col 7 O 42. 4: Richard Warner Miller. 5: Colo State U 60-64 (Eng) BA; UIll 66-67 (LS) MS. 7: Sales clk Carson Pirie Scott & Co, Urbana Ill 64-65; Lib clk II law lib UIll (Urbana) 65-66, Grad asst 66-67, Bibliogr 67-68; Ref libn UMo (Rolla) 68-. 9: ALA. 10: Beta Phi Mu; Rolla Arts Assn. 14: Ref, catlg, ser. 15: Rte 4 Box 247, College Hills Rolla Mo 65401.

MILLER, MARGARET (K). b Thompsonville Conn 24 Jl 14. 5: Amer Intl Col 61 Certif. 6: Fr. 7: Sec Bigelow-Sanford Carpet Co, Thompsonville Conn 45-57; Sec Combustion engineering NRD, Windsor Conn 57-59, Admin supv & libn 59-. 8: Records Mgr "Combustion engineering," NRD 63-. 9: SLA. 10: Enfield Choral Soc. 14: Ref. 15: 66 Elm st, Thompsonville Ct 06082.

MILLER, SISTER MARIAN (ALMA). b St Marys Ohio 5 Je 25. 5: Athenaeum of Ohio 45-53 (Eng) BS in Ed; Xavier U (Cincinnati) 57-60 (Ed) M Ed; Catherine Spalding Col 62-68 MSLS. 7: Music tchr & organist St Joseph Home, Dayton Ohio 45-46; Tchr: Precious Blood, Ft Wayne Ind 46-47, St Margaret Mary, N Col H Ohio 48-50, Sts Peter & Paul, Norwood Ohio 50-53, St Francis Xavier St Joseph Mo 53-56; Libn Regina High Sch, norwood Ohio 56-57; Tchr & libn Russia Local Sch, Russia Ohio 67-. 9: ALA; CathLA (Cincinnati Unit; registrar 60-62, treas 62-66, chm 66-67); OhioASchL. 14: Ref. 15: Box 98, Russia Oh 45363.

MILLER, MRS MARGUERITE (NAHIGIAN). b Povidence 6 Ap 09. 4: Frank John Miller. 5: Pembroke 27-31 (Sociol) AB; Columbia 31-32 BS in LS; 67 NY State Pub Lib Certif. 6: Fr. 7: Soc wker Dept Pub Welfare, PROVIDENCE 33; Child libn Providence Pub Lib 34-44; Child libn Pasadena (Cal) Pub Lib 44; Camp libn US Army, Camp Roberts Cal 44-45; Sch libn Dolgeville Central Sch, DolgevilleNY 55-56; Sec to prin Dobbs Ferry Pub Sch, Dobbs Ferry NY 58-65; Ref libn Marymount Col (Tarrytown NY) 65-. 8: V-pres Bd Trustees Dobbs Ferrry Pub Lib (NY) 58-. 9: ALA; Westchester LA. 10: Alumni Assn Sch of Lib Serv, Columbia; Amer Field Serv. 14: Ref. 15: Sussex Hall2, Dobbs Ferry NY 10522.

MILLER, MARILYN L(EA). b St Joseph Mo 9 O 30. 5: Graceland Col 48-50 AA; UKan 50-52 (Eng, Lang, Arts) BS; UMich 56-59 AMLS; UMinn 65. 6: Fr. 7:Tchr-libn Tchr-libn High Sch, Wellsville Kan 52-54; Tchr-libn Arthur Capper Jr High Sch, Topeka Kan 54-56; Head Libn Topeka High Sch, Topeka Kan 56-62; Sch lib supv State Dept Pub Instr, Kn 62-66; Asst Prof West Mich U 66-. 8: Lib sci instr: Kan State Tchrs Col summers 59, 63, 66; UMinn summer 64 & spring 65; H W Wilson Standard Catlg Consul, 62-. 9: NEA; ALA-AASchL (Bd Dirs 62-64, chm Adv Com Ency Brit Elem Sch Lib Award 69, Newbery-Caldecott Com; KanASchL (pres 62); MichASchL (2nd v-pres 68-70); Mich Assn Higher Educ; Mich A-V Assn. 10: Beta Phi Mu; Delta Kappa Gamma. 11: Valley Forge Freedoms Found Clr Tchrs Award. 12: Ed "Newsletter, KanASchL (58-61). 13: Yes. 14: Sch libs, child & yp bks & reading, sch lib admin. 15: 4410 Canterbury, Kalamazoo Mi 49007.

MILLER, MARJORIE EILEEN. b Oak Park Ill 10S 26. 5: UIll 45-50 (Eng) AB, 51-55 MLS. 6: Sp. 7: Eng tchr Ogden Com High Sch, Ogden Ill 50-53; Asst libn Glenbard Twp High Sch, Glen Ellyn Ill 53-57; Libn UIll U High Sch (Urbana) 57-60; Head Libn Ridgewood High Sch, Norridge Ill 60-. 8: Instr NDEA Inst in Instr Materials, UKy summers 65, 69; Consul NE Mississippi Conf on Ed Innovation Dec '67, Feb '68; Consul Marine City, Michigan May '68, Antioch Ill Jan '69. 9: NEA (Life mem); ALA (Life mem);-AASchL; IllEA; IllLA; IllASchL. 11: John Hay Fellowship in Humanities, 63. 12: Ed IllASchL "News for You" 56-60. 13: Yes. 14: High sch libnship, instr materials centers. 15: Ridgewood High Sch 7500 W Montrose, Norridge Ill 60634.

MILLER, MARJORIE ELAINE. b Howison Miss 15 D 19. 5: WHITWORTH Col 37-38 (Eng); Millsaps Col 38-41 (Eng) BA; UNC 47-48 BS in LS; UMich summers 53, 57, 58 AM in LS. 6: Ger, Fr, Sp. 7: Catlgr Southeastern La Col 48-. 9: ALA; LaLA (treas 67-68); La Tchrs Assn. 10: Phi Kappa Phi; Beta Phi M. 14: Catlg. 15: 610 W Charles st, Hammond La 70402.

MILLER, MARJORIE HELEN. b Pittsburgh Penn 7 Ja 25. 4: J Lee Miller. 5: Grove City Col 42-43; UPittsburgh 43-46 (Com ed) BS, 66 MLS. 7: Elem libn Fox Chapel Area Schs, Pittsburgh Penn 66-. 9: ALA; NEA; PennStateEA. 10: AAUW. 15: 725 Field Club rd, Pittsburgh Pa 15238.

MILLER, MARVIN A. b NC 25 O 02. 4: Violet Lanneau. 5: UNC 22-26 (Eng) BA; Columbia 28-29 BS in LS, 39-40 (LS) 30 hrs. 6: Sp, Fr. 7: Stud asst UNC(Chapel Hill) 23-26; Eng tchr Leaksville (NC) High Sch 26-27; Stack supv NY Pub Li Lib Ref asst info desk 29-32; Libn UNH 32-40; Libn UArk 40-, Dir of Libs 47-. 9: ALA (pastmem var coms); -ACRL; ArkLA (pres 46-47); SWLA (treas 49-50, pres 53-54). 0: Ark Hist Assn; Washington Co (Ark) Hist Assn. 13: Yes. 14: Admin. 15: Rte 5, Rogers Ar 72756.

MILLER, MARY (LUCENTE). b Meyersdale Penn 16 Jl 11. 5: NYU 29-32 (Music Educ) BS; Carnegie 60-62 MLS. 6: Fr. 7: Music supv Stonycreek Twp Consol Schs, Shanksville Penn 34-35; Bkmob asst Carnegie Lib, Pittsburgh 60-62, Music libn 62-. 9: MusLA; Internat Assn Mus Libs. 14: Music libnship. 15: 311 N Neville st, Pittsburgh Pa 15213.

MILLER, MARY (McGREGOR). b Springfeld Ohio 8 Ag 05. 5: Smith 22-26 (Landscape gard) AB; Parsons Sch of Fine & Applied Arts 26-27. 7: Sec McGregor Bros Co, Springfield Ohio 28-29; Sec Vitaglass Corp, NYC 29-30; asst Warder Pub Lib, Springfield Ohio 53-59, Head ref dept 61-. 12: "Warder Family, a Short History (57). 13: Yes. 14: Genealogy, local hist. 15: 1502 Garfield ave, Springfield Ohio 45504.

MILLER, MARY CELINE (BOYER). b O'Hara Township Penn 20 Ap 31. 4: Ronald Dale Miller. 5: Duguesne 50-59 (LS) BEd, 59-63 (LS) MEd. 6: Ger. 7: Tchr St Joseph Sch, Braddock penn 52-56; Tchr St Anne Sch, Pittsburgh Penn 56-59; Head libn La Roche Col, Allison Park Penn 59-66; Dir of lib serv Robert Morris Jr Col 66-. 8: Dir wkshop for school libns at LaRoche Col 65. 9: ALA-PLA; CathLA; PennLA. 10: AAUW; Pittsburgh Lib Club. 14: Admin. 15: Robert Morris Jr College 610 Fifth ave, Pittsburgh Pa 15219.

MILLER, SISTER MARY LEON. b Milwaukee Wis 14 Jl 21. 5: Mt Mary Col 38-42 (Sociol) BA; St LouisU 43 (Sociol) MA; Rosary Col 49, 54-57 MA in LS; CatholicU 50 (Rel Educ); UChicago 65. 6: Ger, Fr. 7: Tchr-libn St Mary High Sch, Menasha Wis 45-51; Tchr Acad of Our Lady, Chicago Ill 51-56; Libn-tchr Notre Dame of the Lake, Mequon Wis 56-59; Libn Mt Mary Col, Milwaukee Wis 59-62; Libn Acad of Our Lady, Chicago 62-65; Libn MarquetteU 66-. 8: Dir Relig Ctr, Wonder Lake Ill 65-66. 9: ALA; CathLA; WisLA. 10: Bel Canto Chorus; Marquette Faculty Assn for Interracial Justice; NAACP; Delta E-silon Sigma. 13: Yes. 14: Ser. 15: 722 N 13th st, Milwaukee Wi 53233.

MILLER, MAXINE ANTOINETTE. b Helena Ark. 5: Spelman Col 43-47 (Sci) AB; Atlanta 64 (LS) MS. 7: Tchr, North End, Helena Ark 50-53; Sch libn South Side, Helena Ark 53-. 9: ALA; NEA; ArkLA; Amer Tchrs Assn; Ark Tchrs Assn. 10: Girl Scouts; Goodfellows; Beta Phi Mu. 13: Yes. 14: Child bks. 15: 121 Don, Helena Ark 72342.

MILLER, MICHAEL MARTIN. b Strasburg N Dak 3 Jl 43. 5: Valley City Statet Col 61-64 (Eng) BS; UNDak 66-67 (Educ) MEd, 67-69 MSLS. 6: Ger. 7: Lib asst Valley City State Col, Valley City N Dak 62-64; Tchr-libn pub schs, Kulm N Dak 64-65; Tchr-libn pub schs, Dickinson N Dak 65-66; Asst to exec sec UN Dak Alumni Off, Grand Forks N Dak 66-67; Hd circ dept N Dak State U 67-. 8: Rep & researcher Title III of Lib Serv & Construction Act for N Dak State Lib Commsn 67-68. 9: NDakStudEA (past State Ed). 13: Yes. 14: Circ, pub rel, a-v, display, instr materials. 15: North Dakota State Univ Lib, Fargo ND 58102.

MILLER, MILDRED VIRGINIA. b Dayton Va 26 S 15. 5: Madison Col 34-38 (Eng) AB in Ed; Peabody 43-44 BS in LS. 7: Elem tchr Rockingham Co Pub Schs, Harrisonburg Va 38-43; Asst catlgr Cuyahoga Co Pub Lib, Cleveland 44-46; Rockingham Pub Lib, Harrisonburg Va: Asst libn 46-56, Act libn 56-59, Asst libn 59- 09: ALA; VaLA (Sect sec & chm); SELA. 9: ALA; VaLA (Sect sec & chm); SELA. 10: AAUW. 14: Catlg, ref. 15: 760 Chestnut dr, Harrisonburg Va 22801.

MILLER, MIRIAM E. b Davis WVa 10 O 17. 5: WVaU 34-38 (Phys Educ) BS; UCLA 61-62 MLS. 7: Phys therapist AUS MDPT, US, Pacific 39-47; Supv phys therapist Johns Hopkis Hosp, Baltimore 48-53; UAriz: Ref asst 60-61, Ref libn 62-63, Ref libn sci div 63-65, Acquis libn Col of Med 65-. 9: MedLA; ALA; SLA; ArizLA; CalLA. 13: Yes. 14: Acquis.15: Lib Col of Med Univ of Ariz, Tucson Az 85721. 15: Lib Col of Med Univ of Ariz, Tucson 85721.

MILLER, NANCY (ELIZABETH). b Campbellsville Ky 17 S 16. 5: SD State Col 34-36; UKy 36-38 (LS) AB; UIll summers 39-42 BS in LS, 46-47 MS; West Res 51-58 (Amer Culture) MA. 6: Fr. 7: Libn Campbellsville High Sch, Campbellsville Ky 38-40; Libn-sec-reviser Dept of Lib Sci UKy 40-43; Head ref dept Canton Pub Lib, Canton Ohio 43-49; Assoc Prof Lib Sci Kent State U 49-55; Head Chamberlain Br Akron Pub Lib, Akron Ohio 55-56, Head ext dept 56-59; Asst dir Ohio State U Law Lib 59-. 8: Instr in catlg, Wkshop of InstAALL, Chicago 55. 9: AALL (chm Catlg & Clsf Com 62-64, 67-68); ALA; OhioALL (sec 60-64, pres 64-65); OhioLA. 10: Pilot Internat; Kappa Delta Pi; Beta Phi Mu. 13: Yes. 14: Catlg, ref. 15: 1995 Tewksbury rd, Columbus Oh 43221.

MILLER, NORMA L. b Greenville SC 10 Ap 28. 4: Louis V Miller. 5: So Ill U 46-48; UIll 48-50 (Art Educ) BFA; So Ill U 50-52 (Eng) MA; Ind U 62-65 (LS) AM. 7: Jr high libn U High Sch, Bloomington Ind 65-66; Documents asst Ind U Lib 58-65; Libn U High Sch, Bloomington Ind 65-. 9: ALA; Ind State Tchrs Assn; Ind Sch LA. 14: Ref, bk sel, docs. 15: 509 Pleasant Ridge rd, Bloomington In 47401.

MILLER, OSCAR J. b Saginaw Mich 11 S 26. 5: UMich 53 AB, 56 LLB, 58 AMLS. 7: Tank Corps/CIC US Army, US, Germany 45-49; Research asst UMich Law Sch 56-57, Circ ref dept 57-61; Assoc libn Cornell U Law Lib 61-63, Assoc libn & Asst Prof 63-65 Law Libn & Assoc Prof UColo Law Sch 65-68, Law libn & Prof 68-. 9: AALL chm Com on Chaps 65-66, pres Upstate NY Chap 64); Intrnat Asn Law Libs. 13: Yes. 14: Admin, ref. 15: 250 S 39th st, Boulder Colo 80302.

MILLER, RICHARD ANDERSON. b Bowling Green Va 31 O 41. 4: Carmen Marian Orork. 5: Orlando Jr Col 60-62 AA; Fla State U 62-63 (Eng, LS) BA, 64-65 MSLS. 6: Ger. 7: Lib asst Orlando Jr Col 61-62; Waterfront dir Red Arrow Lodge, Tomahawk Wis 61; Circus performer & recreation leader Callaway Gardens, Pine Mountain Ga 64; Lib asst Fla State U Materials Center 64-65; Asst libn Med Col of Va Tompkins-McCaw Lib 65-. 9: SLA; MedLA; VaLA. 14: Admin, ref (med). 15: Tompkins-McCaw Lib Med Col of Va, Richmond Va 23219.

MILLER, RICHARD ELROY. b New Haven Conn 1 O 31. 4: Eugenia Clayton. 5: So Conn State Col 49-52, 52-57 (Educ, LS) BS; San Diego State fall 57 (Educ); USoCal 62-67 MSLS. 6: Fr. 7: S/Sgt Med Corps USAF 52-56; Employment serv State of Conn 58; Tchr-libn us maag, phnom Penh Cambodia 58-59; Tchr-libn Pine River Schs Wis 59-60; Br libn San Bernadino Pub Lib, Cal 60-63; Libn Aerospace Corp Tech Lib, San Bernardino Cal 63-64; City libn Veterans Mem Pub Lib, Bismark ND 64-66; City libn Port Angeles Pub Lib, port Angeles Wash 66-. 8: Lib consul New Haven Conn 56-57. 9: ALA; WashLA; WashStateASchL; PNLA. 10: Kiwanis Intl; United Good Neighbors; American Cancer Soc; Order of Runeberg; Citizen's Com for Better Schls; Libraria Sodalitas. 11: General's Commendation Letter Cambodia. 14: Ref, lib educ, lib pub rel. 15: 306 E Lopez ave, Port Angeles Wa 98362.

MILLER, ROBERT A(LEXANDER). b Elk Horn Iowa 19 Ap 07. 4: Eleanor Gough. 5: State U Iowa 25-29 BA; Columbia 29-30 BS; Chicago 34-36 PhD. 7: Clsf NY Pub Lib 30-31; Supv dept libs StateU Iowa 31-36; Dir of Libs UNeb 36-42; Dir of Libs IndU 42-. 15: Ind Univ Libs, Bloomington In 47401.

MILLER, ROBERT ALFRED. b Flushing NY 20 Jl 27. 4: Mary Beall. 5: UNC 46-50 (Span) AB, 50-53 (Romance Langs) MA, 51-53 BSLS; Chicago 58-59 (LS). 6: Sp, Fr. 7: US Navy 45-46; Circ asst UNC Lib (Chapel Hill) 50-53; Visiting Instr UNC Sch of Lib Sci summers 53; Libn Goldwin smith Lib Cornell U 53-55; Asst Prof UNC Sch of Lib Sci 55-. 9: SELA; NCLA. 10: Phi Beta Kappa; Beta Phi Mu. 14: Ref, bk sel, bibliog, hist of bks & printing, humanities lit. 15: Sch of Lib Sci UNC, Chapel Hill NC.

MILLER, ROBERT C. b Evanston Ill 9 My 36. 4: Ellen Reynolds. 5: Marquette U 54-58 (Hist, Phil, Pol Sci) BS; UWis 58-59,62 (Hist) MA; Chicago 61-66 (LS) AM. 6: Fr. 7: Mss asst LC 59, Head telephone ref sect 59-60; Reader serv libn Marquette U 60-62, Acquis libn 62-66; Hd tech serv Parsons Col (Iowa) 66-67, Libn 67; Hd acquis UChicago 68-. 8 ALA (chm Law & Pol Sci Subsect 61); Org Amer Histns. 10: AAUP. 11: Woodrow Wilson Fellow. 13: Yes. 14: Acquis, rare bks, bibliog, lib resources. 15: 1644 Idlewild lane, Homewood Il 60430.

MILLER, ROSS E. b Syracuse NY. 5: Syracuse 46-50 (Hist, LS) BA, 50-51 MS in LS. 7: USAF 42-45; Ref, circ Allegheny Col 51-52; Ref, asst br libn, br libn Queensboro Pub Lib, NY 52-59; Head lending dept Hartford Pub Lib, Hartford Conn 59-. 9: ConnLA. 15: Hartford Pub Lib 500 Main st, Hartford Conn 06103.

MILLER, ROY DANIEL JR. b Sharon Penn 12 F 29. 5: Gettysburg Col 54-58 (Sociol) AB; Columbia 60-62 MLS. 6: Fr. 7: Hosp corpsman (HM2) US Navy 50-54; Asst to dir Alumni Rel Gettysburg Col 58-60; Brooklyn Pub Lib: Lib trainee 60-62, Libn (Gr 2) 63-64, Sr libn (Gr 3) asst div chief hist div 64-67, Div chief hist trav rel biog 67-. 8: Library/USA (Standby) NY Worlds Fair 64; Couns, Ind U Wkshop for High Sch Lib Assts, Bloomington Ind 65; Assoc dir & dir Purdue U Conf for High Sch Lib Assts, Lafayette Ind 66-68; Dir NESchLA Student Leadership Conf, UNH 68, 69. 9: ALA; NYLA; NY Lib Club; LPRC; NESchLA (hon mem). 14: Pub rel, recr, pub serv. 15: 48 Pierrepont st, Brooklyn NY 11201.

MILLER, RUBIN R. b NYC 15 Ap 06. 4: Ruth Manella. 5: Brooklyn Col 27 (Pharmacy) PhG, 40 (Educ) BA; NYU 47 (Educ) MA, 52 (Educ Admin) CAS. 6: Yiddish. 7: Lab asst Far Rockaway High Sch, Far Rockaway NY 32-40; US Army Tilton General Hosp, Fort Dix NJ 40-46; Lab asst Erasmus Hall High Sch, Brooklyn NY 46-50; Tchr High Sch of Fasion Ind, NYC 50-58; Supv A-V Instr Bd of Educ, NYC 58-67; Prof Lib (IRC) Staten Island Community col 67-. 9: NSTA (Bus-Ind Com); AASA; AAUF; ASCD; NEA-DAVI; NY State A-V Assn. 12: "History of the 302nd Medical Regiment" (36); Co-auth "Laboratory Experiments in Chemistry" (50). 14: Educ tech in instr media ctr. 15: Staten Island Commun College 715 Ocean Ter, Staten Island NY 10301.

MILLER, RUTH (BICKETT). b Altoona Penn 11 N 18. 5: Muskingum Col 6-40 (Hist) BA; Carnegie 40-41 BS in LS. 6: Sp, Ger. 7: Period room asst Penn State U 42-45; Catlgr Carnegie Lib of Pittsburgh 45-50; Catlgr Altoona Pub Lib, Altoona Penn 63-69. 9: ALA; PennLA. 14: Catlg, tech serv. 15: 502-52nd st, Altoona Penn.

MILLER, RUTH E. b Akron Ohio 25 O 08. 4: Charles D Miller. 5: UAkron 26-30 (Span, Eng) BE. 6: Sp. 7: B F Goodrich C, Akron Ohio: Asst libn & file clerk 34-37, Libn & supv files 3748, Libn & supv microfilm & files 48-47, Libn & histn 57-. 9: SAA; SLA. 10: Pioneer Investment Club; Wesleyan Serv Guild for Prof Women. 14: Bus bks & periods. 15: 1148 Overton dr, Akron Ohio 44319.

MILLER, RUTH GULDNER. b Broken Bow Ne b 25 Ap 39. 4: (Clayton) Martin Miller. 5: State U Iowa 57-61 (Elem Educ) BA; UIll 62-63 (LS) MS. 7: Documents asst UIll(Urbana) 63-64; Law lib asst State U Iowa 64-65; Catlgr UVt 65-68; Catlgr Miami U (Ohio) 68-. 10: Miami Newcomers Assn. 14: Catlg, doc, tech serv. 15: 602 Glenview dr, Oxford Oh 45056.

MILLER, SARAH (JORDAN). b Pittsburgh 4 N 24. 4: John Miller. 5: Fisk U 42-43 (Soc Sci); UPittsburgh 43-46 (Soc Sci) BA; Columbia 50-51 (Public Law & Go vt) MA, 54-55 (LS) MS 67-. 6: Fr. 7: Tchr of Soc Sci Washington High Sch, Raleigh NC 46-47; Instr Pol Sci Southern U 48-49; Libn Frederick St Br Lib, Houston 53; Columbia U Libs; Head documents acquis 55-56, Head ser & documents acquis 56-58, Ref asst lib serv Lib 60-61, Head ser & documents acquis 61-67. 9: ALA; ASIS; NY Tech Serv Libns. 10: Nat Assn Col Women; Alpha Kappa; Beta Phi Mu. 11: Joseph Towne Wheeler Award, 55. 14: Tech serv, govt docs. 15: 549 W 123rd st apt 11 B, New York NY 10027.

MILLER, STEPHEN ARNOLD. b St Louis Mo 4 Ap 42. 5: Cornell Col 60-62; Westminster Col 9mo) 62-65 (Econ) BA; West Res 65-67 MS in LS. 6: Ger, Lat. 7: Ser catlgr & ser libn Iowa State U (Ames) 67-69; Acquis libn Rockford Col 69-. 9: ALA; SLA. 10: AAUP; Assn for Evolut Econ; Lions Internat; Pi Delta Epsilon; YMCA. 11: William Allen White Award (twice); Medal of Merit (Pi Delta Epsilon). 14: Acquis, ser, catlg, admin. 15: 1731 Logan apt 1, Rockford Il 61103.

MILLER, STEPHEN ROGERS. b Asheville NC 2 My 33. 4: Priscilla North Charlton. 5: Baldwin Wallace Col 56-60 (Relig Educ) BA; BostonU 60-61 (Theol); UPittsburgh 64-65 MLS. 7: Off wker West Auto Supply Co, Cleveland Ohio 51-54; Radar maintenance US Army 54-56; Youth dir Broadway Methodist, Cleveland Ohio 58-60; Processor Campbell & Hall, Boston 62-64; Prof lib asst Boston Pub Lib, 65-66; Ref libn Cary Memorial Lib, Lexington Mass 66-. 9: ALA; NELA; MassLA. 10: Beta Phi Mu. 11: August Alpers Annual Award 65. 12: ""A Century of Service (69). 14: Acquis, ref. 15: 72 Bow st, Lexington Ma 02173.

MILLER, VIRGINIA (MAYE) (TAYLOR). b Harold SDak 16 Ap 22. 4: V Crandall Miller. 5: Asbury Col 40-46 (Psych) BA; Appalachian StateU summers 61, 62, 64, 65 (LS); S FlaU 68-69 (LS). 7: Tchr Dade Co Schs, Miami Fla 48-50; Tchr Manatee Co Schs, Bradenton Fla 54-60; Tchr Collier Co Schs, Immokalee Fla 60-63; Tchr Co Schs, Brevard NC 63-64; Libn seast Bible Col 64-. 9: NEA; ALA; FlaEA; FlaLA. 15: 2030 Irving st, Lakeland Fl 33801.

MILLER, VIRGINIA (STAUB). b Hampstead Md 13 My 09. 4: Herman S Miller. 5: William & Mary 32 (Eng) BA; Columbia 40 BS (LS). 6: Fr. 7: Lib asst Richmond Pub Lib, Richmond Va 26-29, summers 30-32; Libn (catlg) Med Col of Va, Richmond 32-43; Libn (catlg) William & Mary 43-50, 53; Libn (catlg) NASA, Langley Field Va 51-52, 54-60; Hd libn US Army Transportation Sch Lib, Ft Eustis Va 60-. 9: SLA; VaLA. 11: Dept of Army Meritorious Civilian Serv Award. 14: Catlg, ref, admin. 15: 6 Shore Park dr, Newport News Va 23602.

MILLER, WILLENE (EVELYN) McDUFFIE. b Savannah Ga 13 F 31. 5: William & Mary 49-51 (Liberal Arts) AA; UVa 51-53 (Educ) BS in Ed; UNC 61-63 MS in LS. 7: Tchr, Norfolk Va 55, 59; Dance instr, Norfolk Va 57-58; Lib asst circ Kirn Memorial Lib, Norfolk Va 60-61, Asst libn circ 63-. 9: ALA; VaLA; SELA. 10: Chi Omega. 14: Fiction. 15: 1423 Morris crescent, Norfolk Va 23509.

MILLER, MRS ZELDA (GRUVER). b Cleveland Ola 27 Ag 05. 5: Central Col for Women (Lexington Mo 23-25 (Hist) AA; Northwestern 25-27 (Educ, Hist) BA; Kan State Tchrs Col (Emporia) summer 49-50 (LS); Wichita State U 60 (Educ) M Ed. 6: Sp. 7: Libn Augusta High Sch, Augusta Kan 49-52; Libn elem schs, Wichita Kan 52-. 9: NEA; ALA; Kan State TA; KanSchLA; ACEI; IRA. 14: Elem sch libs. 15: 1113 Dearborn, Augusta Ks 67010.

MILLETT, JOANNA R(UTH). b Portland Ore 18 F 28. 5: Huntington Col 46-50 (Eng,Hist) BA; Peabody 50-51 MA in LS. 7: Period libn, asst in pharmacy UMd Med, Dental Pharmacy 51-54; Asst in circ Atlanta Pub Lib 54-55; Asst catlgr Miami Pub Lib, Miami Fla 55-57; Catlgr Eugene Pub Lib, Eugene Ore 58-. 9: ALA; PNLA; OreLA (past ed of "Newsletter). 14: Catlg. 15: 1313 Lincoln st apt 501, Eugene Or 97401.

MILLICAN, ANNIE RUTH. b Deerford La 19 Ap 20. 5: UDenver summer 66; LSU 37-41 (Educ) BA, summer 42, 43, 44, 45 BS in LS, 67-68 MS. 6: Fr. 7: Libn Pride High Sch, Pride La 41-55; Libn Glasgow Jr High Sch, Baton Rouge La 55-59; Libn I East Baton Rouge Parish Lib, Baton Rouge La summers 61, 62, 63; Asst prof LSU Lib Sch, Baton Rouge summer 64; Asst summer Inst LSU Lib Sch summers 65, 67, 68; Libn Robert E Lee High Sch, Baton rouge La 59-. 9: ALA-AASchLA; LaLA; LaASchL; LaTA; CTA. 10: Baton Rouge Lib Club; Delta Kappa Gamma; Phi Kappa Phi; Mu Sigma Rho; Kappa Delta Pi; Alpha Lambda Delta. 13: Yes. 14: Sch libnship, rwading guidance. 15: 144 Atkinson st, Baton Rouge La 70806.

MILLICH, EUGENE J. b So St Paul Minn 26 Jl 24. 4: Lorraine Pribyl. 5: Col of St thomas 46-50 (Soc Sci) BA; UMinn summers 47, 50, 58, 50-51 BS in LS; UMich 52-54 AMLS, 65-66 (LS). 6: Ger. 7: Non-commissioned off US Navy 43-46; Ref libn Ann Arbor Pub Lib, Ann Arbor Mich 51-54; Ref asst Minneapolis Pub Lib 54-56; Asst br libn 56-57; Ref period libn Wis StateU (La Crosse) 57-64, Reader's adv 66-67, Assoc Prof lib sci 61-. 8: Med lib consul Gundersen Clinic-Lutheran Hosp, La Crosse Wis 57-58; Nursing lib adv Gundersen Clinic-Lutheran Hosp, St Francis Hosp, Viterbo Col, Wis stateU, La Crosse Wis 69-. 9: ALA; WisLA. 14: Ref, lib sci tchg, miniature bks, priv press bks. 15: 2003 So 29th st, La Crosse Wi 54601.

MILLIGAN, LOUISE (MARGUERITE). b Cedar Rapids Iowa 7 My 07. 5: UAriz 26-30 (Eng) BA; LA Pub Lib Sch 31-32 (Catlg) Certif; Columbia 39-40. 6: Sp. 7: Catlg asst UAriz Lib 30-31, 32-34; Doc libn & circ asst 34-37; Ref libn & circ hd 37-39, 40-43; Hd ref libn 43-46; Circ asst Ore State U 46-47; Hd circ dept 47-49; Asst ref libn 49-59; Asst catlg libn 59-62; Asst ref libn Tucson Pub Lib 62-64; St catlgr 62-66; Asst catlg libn UAriz Lib 67-. 9: ALA; -ACRL; (Interlib Loan Code Rev Com 50-51); ArizLA (sec-treas 36-37, 2d v-pres 44-45); OreLA; PNLA; (chm Catlg Div 59-60). 10: Delta Zeta. 12: Ed "Arizona Library News" (44-45); Auth (Jt comp) "Oregon State College Serial Publications, 1938-50) (50). 14: Catlg, ref. 15: 4131 E Lee st apt B, Tucson Az 85716.

MILLIKEN, CALLIE FAYE. b August Tex 13 Ag 17. 5: Abilene Christian Col 34-38 (Eng) BA; UTex summers 40-43 (Eng, LS) MA; Peabody summer 44 (LS); Fla State U summer 50 (LS); UDenver summer 64 (LS. 6: Sp. 7: Eng tchr Weldon High Sch, Weldon Tex 38-39; Eng tchr Grapeland High Sch, Grapeland Tex 39-42; Jr high sch libn Gaston Jr High Sch, Joinerville Tex 42-43; Jr high sch libn Houston Schs, Houston 43-53; Libn Abilene Christian Col 53-. 9: ALA; TexLA (sec 58-59, dist chm 65-66). 10: AAUW; Delta Kappa Gamma. 15: 1134 Washington blvd, Abilene Tex 79601.

MILLIKEN, SISTER KATHLEEN R b Elmira NY 2 My 27. 5: Nazareth Col (Rochester) 44-50 (Eng) BA; Catholic U summers 54-59 MS in LS; NYU summer 65 NDEA Inst in Eng. 6: Lat, Fr. 7: Elem tchr St Marys Sch, Corning NY 47-52; Tchr Eng, Lat Our Lady of Mercy High Sch, Rochester Ny 2-54, Libn 54-62; Lin & Eng tchr Notre Dame High Sch, Elmira NY 62-67; Libn Cardinal Mooney High Sch, Rochester NY 67-. 8: Chm Eng Dept, Notre Dame High Sch, 64-, Pub rel dir 64-; Mem evaluation coms Middle States Assn 5762, 68, Directing staff of Elmira Ecumenical Service Project, 1967-1968. 9: CathLA; ALA; NYLA. 10: Western NY Cath Libns Conf; Beta Phi Mu. 13: Yes. 14: Reading guidance for studs, adv wk with tchrs, Inner city wk with teenagers & adults, theol, pub rel. 15: 800 Maiden lane, Rochester NY 14615.

MILLING, CHAPMAN JAMES JR. b Darlington SC 7 F 27. 5: USCar 45-50 (Fr) AB; Emory 53-55 MLS. 6: Fr. 7: Clerk Richland Co Pub Lib, Columbia SC summer 53; Dir Carnegie Pub Lib, Sumter SC 55-. 9: SCLA (Standards Com); SELA. 10: Bd, Sumter Little Theatre. 13: Yes. 14: Admin, bk sel. 15: Sumter County Lib, Sumter SC 29150.

MILLOY, ELLA M. b Ca. 5: UToronto 3142, 43 BA; U Toronto 29-30, 46 BLS. 6: Fr. 7: Toronto Pub Lib: Catlgr 30-33, Br libn & circ libn 33-46, Br head 46-56, Bk sel 56-61, Hd acquis 61-67, Act hd tech serv 67-68, Hd tech serv 68-. 9: CanLA; Ont LA; Inst Prof Libns Ont; ALA. 10: Univ Women's Club of Toronto. 12: Consul on Can lit Comptons Pictured Encyclopedia (52). 13: Yes. 14: Canadiana, tech serv, automation. 15: 214 College st, Toronto 2B Can.

MILLS, ANNIE ELIZABETH. b Oxford Miss 2 D 24. 5: UMiss 42-46 (Soc Studies) BAE, 57 (Hist) MA, 63 MLS; EmoryU 46-47 AB in LS. 7: Catlg dept UMiss (Univ) 47-49, Order libn 49-52, Docs libn 53-. 9: MissLA; SELA. 10: Oxford Pilot Club; Phi Kappa Phi; AAUW. 14: US govt publ. 15: P O Box 495, Oxford Ms 38655.

MILLS, DOROTHY J M. b Jamaica NY 21 O 28. 5: Hofstra U 46-50 (Eng) BA; New Paltz State Tchrs Col 1-53 (Elem Educ) MS in Ed; Pratt 60-61 MLS. 6: Fr. 7: Elem tchr Prt Jefferson Pub Schs, Port Jefferson NY 51-55; Elem tchr Huntington Pub Schs, Huntington NY 55-60; Lib trainee Huntington Pub Lib, Huntington NY 60-61; Libn Syosset High

Sch Lib, Syosset NY 61-64; Lib Dir Babylon Pub Lib, Babylon NY 64-65; Lib Dir Jericho Pub Lib, Jericho NY 65-. 9: ALA; NYLA; Nassau Co LA; Suffolk Co LA. 14: Pub rel, bk sel, catlg. 15: 4 Nursery rd, Melville NY 11749.

MILLS, DOUGLAS E. b Portland Ore 3 Mr22. 4: Betty Ramsdell. 5 San Jose State Col 39-41; UCal 41-43 (USHist) BA, 45-47 (Hist, Educ), 50-51 BLS, MA. 6: Fr. 7: US Army Cpl), European Theatre 43-45; Tchr Orland Jt Union High Sch, Orland Cal 47-50; Libn I UCal(Davis) 5156; Libn II & IIICal State lib 56-60; Head tech processs & acquis UMont 60-66, Dir tech serv 66-. 9: ALA; PNLA; Mont LA. 10: Off in UMont Fed Credit Union; Campus Christ Found. 13: Yes. 14: Tech processes, acquis. 15: 604 E Central ave, Missoula Mont 59801.

MILLS, FORREST LAIRD. b Helena Mont 15 Ag 13. 4: Ave Ezelle. 5: Willamette U 31-33; Stanford U 33-35 (Philos) BA;UCal (Berkeley) 35-36 Certif; Chicago 50-51 (LS) MA. 7: Asst libn Willamette U 36-38; Ref asst Enoch Pratt Free Lib, Baltimore 39-41; USF 41-45; Retail clerk J K Gill Co, Portland Ore 46-48; Asst Prof State Col (Starville Miss) 48-50; Grad Stud & tchg asst Chicago 51-53; City Libn Racine Pub Lib, Racine Wis 53-. 9: ALA (Coun rep from WisLA 64-68); WisLA (past pres). 10: Rotary Club. 11: Wis Libn of the Year 60. 15: 311-16th st, Racine Wis 53404.

MILLS, HAZEL E(MERY) (MRS). b Pomona Cal 29 O 10. 5: Long Beach (Cal) Jr Col 27-29; UCal (Berkeley) 29-31 (Hist) AB, 32-35 (Hist)MA; UWash 52-53 (LS) ML.40648 6: Sp, Fr, 07: Asst ref dept UOre 43-45; Asst sci & tech div Seattle Pub Lib 52; Ref asst Ore STATE Lib 53-5; Ref asst Mulnomah Co Lib, Portland Ore 55-56; Oregoniana libn Ore State Lib 56-59; Research consul & Washington Room libn Wash State Lib 59-. 9: ALA; PNLA (chm Pacific Northwest Authors Proj Com 55-57, chm Bibliog Com 57-59); WashLA. 10: Pi Lambda Theta; AAUW; Wash State Hist Soc; Ore Hit Soc; State Capitol Hist Assn. 11: Research Grant-in-aid Amer Assn State & Loc Hist, 63, to use in researc on biog of Frances Fuller Victor. 12: Ed "Whos Who Among Pacific Northwest Authors, Ref Sect of PNLA (57). 13: Yes. 14: Ref, mss, rare bks. 15: 1517 Capitol way apt 212, Olympia Wa 98501.

MILLS, JOHN (WLLSON). b Lewes Del 16 D33. 5: Swarthmore Col 51-55 (Fr) BA; UParis 53 (Fr); MIDDLEBURY Col 54 (Fr); Columbia 57-59 (LS) MS; UMich 62 (LS). 6: Fr, Ger. 7: Troop info & educ (Pfc) USArmy Artillery 55-57; Aduly asst Detroit Pub Lib 59-. 15: 3740 Commonwealth, Detroit Mi 48308.

MILLS, MARGIE (INGRAM). b Enola Ark 17 S08. 4: T M Mills. 5: Ark State Tchrs Col 33 (Soc Studies) BSE; UArk 46 (Educ Admin) MS; UMiss 60 (LS MS. 6: Fr. 7: Elem tchr Faulkner Co 25-30; Sci tchr 30-32; Math tchr 33-36; Math tchr 36-38; Math tchr 38-39; Math & Phys Educ 39-48; Math & Phys Educ 48-49; Math & libn Elaine Ark 49-, Lib sup Elaine Ark 64-69. 8: Tchr of Phys Educ, Ark State Col. 9: NEA; ArkEA; ArkLA. 10: PTA; Kappa Delta Pi; Delta Kappa Gamma; Bus & Prof Womens Club; Mark TwainSoc; Phillip's Co Hist Soc. 12: "Turn South for Arkansas"; "Second Fiddle. 13: Yes. 14: Catlg, ref, lib clubs, Ark hist, folklore. 15: Elaine Ar 72333.

MILLS, THEODORA T B. b Wyoming NJ 4 My 13. 5: Antioch Col 30-33; UChicago 33-34 9pol sci) BA; UChicago 37-38 (Hist); Catholic U of Amer 61-65 MSLS. 6: Fr, Russian. 7: Researcher Encyclopedia Britannica, Chicago 38-39; Various jobs with Fed govt 40-65; Catlg Russian URochester 65-69, Ref 69-. 9: ALA; NYLA. 10: Phi Beta Mu. 13: Yes. 14: Ref, Slavic colls. 15: 41 Winbourne rd, Rochester NY 14611.

MILNOR, JEAN C(AMPBELL). b Mildred Penn 15 D04. 5: Goucher Col 21-25 (Hist) AB; Syracuse 53-55 MSLS. 7: Catlgr Lycoming Col 48-52; Ref libn Towson State Col 52-65; Libn Md State Dept of Educ Prof Lib, Baltimore 65-. 9: ALA-RSD (chm Md Chap 62); MdLA; SLA. 10: Beta Phi Mu; AAUW. 14: Ref. 15: 909 Dulaney Valley ct, Towson Md 21204.

MILONAS, MARY (CONDARAS). b Greece 2 O 09. 4: John C Milona. 5: Pratt 36-37 (LS) Diplomas; UMe summers 40, 43; NYU 46-48 (Educ) BS. 6: Gk. 7: Libn WAC, Ft Robinson Neb & Qm Sch Camp Lee Va (T-3) 44-46; Head catlgr Greenwich Lib, Greenwich Conn 37-44; Gk lang spec NY Pub Lib 46-49 Head catlgr Scranton Pub Lib, Scranton Penn 49-51; Head catlgr NY Soc Lib, NYC 53-54; Head catlgr Darien Lib, Darien Conn 55-68, Hd tech serv 68-69. 9: ConnLA (Catlg Div); NY Tech Serv Libns. 10: Pratt Alumni Assn. 15: 115 Prospect st, Greenwich Conn 06830.

MILSOM, DEREK SIDNEY. b Bath Eng 5 My 16. 5: UAla 57-60 (LS) BS; Columbia 63-64 MSLS. 6: Fr. 7: Bank Off Bank of Eng, London 35-40; Flying Off RAF 40-46; Circ libn Friedman Lib, Tuscaloosa Ala 59-60; Field rep Ala Pub Lib Serv, Montgomery Ala 60-63; Ref libn UAla 64-. 14: Ref. 15: 1220 Queen City ave, Tuscaloosa Al 35401.

MILSTEAD, AGNES (McDOW). b Covington Tenn 23 Jl 15. 4: James Brooks Milstead. 5: UWyo 59 (Elem ed) BA; NE La State Col 65; LSU 66 msls& colo U 68. 6: Sp. 7: Tchr Laramie Co Schs, Cheyenne Wyo 53-59; Tchr Cheyenne Pub Schs, Cheyenne Wyo 59-60; Libn Ouachita Parish Schs, Monroe La 60-66; Tchr of lib sci UWyo 66-. 9: NEA; ALA; -AASchL; WyoEA; MPLA; WyoASchL. 10: Beta Phi Mu; Phi Kappa Phi; Faculty Women's Club; Kappa Delta Pi. 13: Yes. 14: Educ. 15: 715 Gerald pl, Laramie Wy 82070.

MILTON, BETTY LANE (McINTOSH). b New Orlans 29 D32. 4: Earl D Milton. 5: Miss State Col for Women 50-54 (LS, Eng) BS; LSU 54-55 (LS) MS. 6: Fr. 7: Child libn Brookln Pub Lib 55-56; Head of ext serv bkmobs & new br survey Dallas Pub Lib 56-59; Church libn Churchill Presbysteian Church, Dallas 61-. 8: Adult educ survey in Dallas for ALA, 58. 9: TexLA. 10: Beta Phi Mu. 14: Child bks, ref, bkmob. 15: PO Box 30343, Dallas Tx 75230.

MILTON, JOHN THOMAS. b Los Angeles 14 Jl27. 4: Anneliese Beate Reinhard. 5: San Francisco State Col 61 (Internat Rel) BA (magna cum laude); SUNY (Albany) 65 MLS. 6: Ger, Sp. 7: (Sgt) USArmy 46-48; SMSGT US Air Force 51-. 14: Ref. 15: 7901 Woodman ave, Van Nuys Ca 91402.

MILTON, LEWIS. b Mass 31 Jl 20. 5: UNH 38-42 (Eng) BA; Columbia 49-51 (Eng) MA, 68-69 (LS) MS. 6: Fr, Ger. 7: Military Intelligence US Army, US & Europe 42-46; Libn Dept of Defense, Germany 46-47; Chief entries Combined Travel Bd US Govt, Europe 47-49; Tchr Mass & NY 53-68; Libn Harrison High Sch, NY 68-. 9: ALA; Westchester Co 9ny0 tchrs of Eng (pres); NYStateTA. 14: Sch libnship. 15: 151 Fenimore rd, Mamaroneck NY 10543.

MIMS, DOROTHY (HART). b Memphis Tenn 19 Mr22. 4: Benjamin Lovick Mims Jr. 5: Winthrop Col 40-44 (Eng, LS) BA; UNC 46-47 BS in LS. 6: Fr. 7: Cartographic Draftsman Tenn Valley Authority, Chattanooga Tenn 44-46; Asst circ libn SCar Lib 47; Ref libn Med Col of Ga Lib 63-.14: Med bibliog & research, interlib loan. 15: PO Box 489, Edgefield SC 29824.

MINADAKIS, NICHOLAS J. b Island of Chios Greece 22 Ja 24. 5: oston U 5862 (Econ) BA; Simmons 62-64 (LS) MS. 6: Modern Gk, Fr, Ital. 7: (2nd Lt Interpreter-tr, Greek Armed Forces 50-51; Interpreter-tr Pierce Mgt Inc, Aliverion Greece 51-53; Deptl mgr United Africa Co Ltd, Ghana 53-57; Tchr of Modern Gk 58-62;Circ supv Harvard U Baker Lib 62-64; Libn Greek Orthodox Theol Sch (BrookineMass) Brookline Mass 67; Dir Chelsea PubLib, Chelsea Pub Lib, Chelsea Mass 68-. 10: Off, Pancretan Assn of Amer; Helicon Inc; Bd Trustees Greek Orthodox Commun of Cambridge Mass. 14: Circ, ref, admin. 15: 8 St Paul st apt 1, Cambridge Ma 02139.

MINEMIER, BETTY (ANN) MITCHELL. b Dansville NY 1 Jl 28. 4: Robert Stansbury Minemier. 5: SUNY (Geneseo) 57-61 (LS) BS in Ed (summa cum laude), 61-65 MLS. 6: Fr. 7: Libn Central Sch, Arkport NY 61-64; Libn Jr High Sch, Dansville NY 64-. 9: NY State LA; NY State Tchrs Assn; Genesee Valley Tchrs Assn. 10: Girl Scout Council; Hornell Symphony Chorus; Kappa Delta Pi; Amer Field Serv. 13: Yes. 14: Sch libnshp. 15: 20 Chestnut ave, Dansville NY 14437.

MINESINGER, SARA KATHRYN. b New Manchester W Va 5 Ag 23. 5: Madison Col 42-44 (Eng); Columbia Union Col 44-46 (Eng) BS; MiamiU 49; West Liberty State Col 56-58; UPittsburgh 66-68 MLS. 6: Sp. 7: Dean of Women Arizona Acad, Phoenix Ariz 46-47; Dean of Women sheyenne River Acad, Sheyenne River ND 47-48; Tchr Dayton SDA Church Sch, Dayton Ohio 49-51; Priv sec Coop Extension Serv, New Cumberland W Va 54-65; Hd libn Swaney Memorial Lib, New Cumberland W Va 65-. 9: WVaStateLA. 10: Hancock Co Farm Women's Coun; Hancock co 4-H Leaders Assn. 14: Admin. 15: RD 1 Box 343, New Cumberland W Va 26047.

MING, MARIAN SHIH-KING. b Chiang-Su China 22 Ja 40. 5: Law Sch Nat Taiwan U 57-61 (Law) LLB; Law Sch UChicago 62-63 Grad Fellow;Rosary Col 63-65 MA in LS. 6: Chinese, Fr. 7: Asst libn Amer Bar Found Lib, Chicago summer 64; Asst acquis libn Center for Research Lib, Chicago 65-66; Catlgr-bibliogr Amer Bar Found Lib, Chicago 66-. 9: AALL (Comm on Internat & For Law); Women's Bar Assn Ill

(Jr mem). 14: Ref & catlg in law libs. 15: Apt 201, 5550 S Dorchester, Chicago Il 60637.

MING, V LESLIE (THOMPSON). b Toronto Ont Can 3 Mr 25. 4: Carlos M Ming. 5: McGill 42-47 (Sociol) BA; Cornell U 47-48 (Sociol); Fla State U 56-58 MALS. 6: Fr. 7: Asst ref (soc sci) Fla State U 60-63; Asst ref Bailey Lib, UVt 63-64; Hd ref Sir George Williams U 64-67; Hd ref UCan Francisco 67-68; Catlgr Sir George Williams U 68-. 9: ALA; CanLA; QueLA. 14: Ref, admin, catlg. 15: 1900 Lincoln ave apt 38, Montreal Que Can.

MINGLEDORFF, JOYCE (SANDS). b Montgomery Ala 16 Ja 27. 4: Dr Ernest Beckwith Mingledorff. 5: Huntingdon Col 43-47 (Biol, Math) AB; Emory 57-58 (LS) MLn, 61-62 (Med Libnship) Certif. 6: Sp. 7: Asst in biol Huntingdon Col 47-48; Med tech US Pub Helth Serv, Atlanta 48-56; Asst libn Emory U Sch of Dentistry 58-65; Hd ref circ Col of Physicians of Phila 66-67, Hd reg ref serv 68-. 9: MedLA; ALA; SLA (Ga Chap; v-pres 64-65, memb chm 60-62, hosp chm 59-60 &62-64); SELA; GaLA. 13: Yes. 14: Ref, ser. 15: 900 Coopertown rd, Bryn Mawr Pa 19010.

MINICK, RACHEL. b Was DC 9 D07. 5: Wilson Col 29 AB; UIll 30 (LS) BS; Columbia 48 (LS) MS; Colubia U Sch of Fine Arts archaeol 53 MA. 6: Fr, Ger, Ital. 7: Catlgr Eoch Pratt FREE Lib, Baltimore 31-43; Head catlgr Brookln NY 43-50; NY Hist Soc, NYC: Head catlgr 50-57, Bibliog 57-64, Asst curator maps & prints 64-66; Asst libn NY Geneal & Biog Soc, NY Geneal & Biog Soc, NYC 67-. 9: ALA; SLA (chm NY Picture Div 66-67); NY Lib Club. 10: DAR; College Art Assn; Civil War Round Table, NY. 12: "History of Printing in Maryland 1791-1800 (48). 13: Yes. 14: Ref, rare bks, fine arts. 15: 1995 Sedgwik ave, Bronx NY 10453.

MINITER, JOHN JOSEP. b Hamden Ct 9 Je 24. 4: Helen Bondarowicz. 5: U Conn 46-50 (Romance Langs) B Ed; UMass 1-52 (Romance Langs) MA; Columbia 55-56 MSLS. 6: Fr. 7: Bk&period libn U Nvy Underwater Sound Lab, New London Conn 56-60; Chif Libn Collins Radio Co, Richardson Tex 60-64; Asst Prof Tex Woman's U 64-. 9: SLA; Inst of Electronics & Elec Engnrs; ASIS. 13: Yes. 14: Catlg, spec lib admin, automation. 15: 13511 Heartside pl, Dallas Tx 75234.

MINK, ARTHUR DeWITT. b E Liverpool Ohio 9 Ja09. 4: Geraldine Ryan. 5: Mt Union Col 27-31 (Eng) BA; West Res 41-42 BS inL, 48-52 (Eng) MA. 6: Romance langs. 7: Asst libn Pub Lib, Orrville Ohio 38-42; Head newspaper div Ohio State Archaeol & Hist Soc 42-46; Asst catlg dept West Res U Lib 46-47, Sr catlg dept 47-59, Head catlg dept 59-68, Asst chief catlg dept 69-. 8: Consul Com to Study Phila Bibliog Center, 63. 9: ALA (Subcon on ALA Rules for Filing Cards 62); No Ohio Tech Serv Libns (v-pres & Program Chm 60-61). 10: Prof Mens Club of Clevland. 12: "TITLE List of Ohio Newspapers (45); "Union List of Ohio Newspapers (46; "History of Alliance Newspapers (46; Ed "Atlanta Correspondence, by Finley Foster & Margaret Mitchell (61); Comp "Some Resources in Microtext in the Cleveland area" (66). 14: Catlg, bibliog, rare bks. 15: 1884 Forest Hills blvd, Cleveland Oh 44112.

MINK, GERALDINE (RYAN). b Mt Filead Ohio 5 O10. 4: Arthur DeWitt Mink. 5: Ashland Col 28-2 (Fr, Lat, Eng) AB; Ohio State U (Eng: Ohio U 36 (Spec course for Deans of Women); West Res U BS in LS; MLA Certif as Med Libn 67. 6: Fr, Lat. 7: Tchr & Dean of Girls Loudonville High Sch, Loudonville Ohio 32-42; Libn pharmacy, bacteriology & fine arts Ohio State U Lib 42, Asst to supv f dept lib 43, Head ser div 44-46; Libn Frances Payne bolton Sch of Nursing West Res U 46-. 8: Consul Hist Source Material, Coun & League for Nursing; Occasional lecturer, West Res U Sch of Lib Sci, on Nursing Libs & Lit; Mem Ed AdvCom, Adv Com, Internat Nursing 65-6771. 9: ALA-AHIL (chm bk sel com 63);-LAD (Com on Statis 66-67); Nat League Nursing (Coun & League Nursing; Bd Dirs 62-64); No Ohio Tech Serv Libns (sec 65-66); MedLA. 13: Yes. 14: Hist materials in spec field. 15: 1884 Forest Hills blvd, E Cleveland Ohio 44112.

MINK, JAMES VANTINE III. b Wisconsin Rapids Wis 3 Je 23. 5: Occidental Col 41-43 9chem); UCLA 45-49 (Hist) BA (honors), (Hist) MA; UCal (Berkeley) 50-52 (Hist) BLS; AmericanU 53 Certif in Archival Admin. 7: US Army Air Forces 42-45; Instr UCal Hist Dept, LA 47-49; Asst to catlgr UCLA Bancroft Lib 50-51; Stack supervisor Lib UCLA 45-46, Univ archivist 52-, Dir Oral Hist Program 65-. 8: Consul archives & lib program Automobile Club of SoCal; Consul spec collections Los Angeles State Col Lib. 09; SAA (Com on Col & Univ Archives); UCLA Libns Assn (pres 68-69). 10: Pi Gamma Mu; Phi Alpha Theta; Oral Hist Assn Inc. 12: "Papers of General William S Roseceans & the Rosecrans Family" (61). 13: Yes. 14: Archives, oral hist, spec collections. 15: 2365 Stanley Hills dr, Los Angeles Ca 90046.

MINNERATH, GARY R. b Bowdle S Dak 8 S 38. 5: Woodbury Col 62 (Bus Admin) BBA; Immaculate Heart Col 66 (LS) MA. 7: Jail libn Laco Lib Laco Central Jail, Los Angeles 64-65; Ref libn Laco Lib, S Gate Cal 66; Libn-in-charge Bell Flower Br Laco Lib, Bell Flower Col 66-67; Asst inst libn Los Angeles Co Lib 67-. 9: CalLA. 14: Admin. 15: 13324 Merkel ave, Paramount Ca 90723.

MINNICH, DAVID WILLIAM. b Rochester NY 13 Ap31. 4: Mary Douglass. 5: SUNY NY (Geneseo) 51-55 (Lib BS S; State U Col (Plattsburgh NY) 62-66 MS; NY State Permanent Certifs as Sch libn &Pub libn. 7: ef-catlg libn Carnegie Pub Lib, Bradford Penn 55-57; Libn Wead Lib, Malone NY 57-. 9: ALA; SLA; NYLA; N Country 3R Coun. 10: Kappa Delta Pi. 14: Ref, adv serv, admin, bk sel. 15: 5 Clay st, Malone NY 12953.

MINNICH, MARY (DOUGLAS). b Waterloo NY 13 Mr 32. 4: David W Minnich. 5: SUNY (Geneseo) 50-54 (Speech, Dramtic Arts) BS in Ed with certif in speech correction. 7: Libn Harison Jr High Sch,Malone NY 60-67; Wead Lib asst 67-. 9: ALA-AASchL; NYLA. 14: Child & ya serv, child lit. 15: 5 Clay st, Malone NY 12953.

MINNICK, MIRIAM SHARP. b Eaton Ind. 4: Kenneth C Minnick. 5: Mather Col West Res 34 (Eng, Hist) AB; UPittsburgh 42 (Eng); West Res 51 MS in LS. 6: Fr, Russian, Ger. 7: Jr high tchr Mentor Pub SCHS, Mentor Ohio 44-46; Ed asst Mcgraw-Hill Publs, Cleveland 46-47; Instr in Eng Wilmington Col 47-51; Libn Wellington Pub Lib, Wellington Ohio 51-52; Ref libn Bowling Green State U Lib 52-57; Interlib loans Ore State U Lib -. 9: PNLA. 10: AAUP. 13: Yes. 14: Interlib loans, ref. 15: 3550 Harrison st, Corvallis Ore 97330.

MINNIK, NELLE F(RANCES). b Spokane Wash 24 S20. 5: UNM 37-41 (Hist) BA; UDenver 41-42 BS in LS; Chicago 45-46 (LS) MA. 7: Denver Pub Li ; asst circ dept 42-43, Asst west hist dept 43-45, 1st asst west hist dept 46-48; Jr libn Cal sect Cal State Lib 48-50; Adult serv libn ext dept Fresno Co FreeLib 50-60, Coordinator of br operations 60-. 9: ALA; CalLA (Yosemite Dist; sec 55, pres 68). 10: Fresno Co Hist Soc; AAUW; Amer Soc Pub Admin. 13: Yes. 14: Pub lib ext. 15: 146 E Simpson ave, Fresno Ca 93721.

MINOR, LILLIAN G(RACE) SUTTER), b Akron Ohio 20 Ag32. 4: Ross A Minor. 5: UAkron 49-54 (Natural Sci) BS. 7: Stud asst UAkron 51-54; Libn div of rubber chem ACS UAkron 54-59; Asst libn Goodyear Tire 7 rubber Co, Akron Ohio 59-62;Libn Dow Chem Co Roky Flats Div, Golden Colo 63-. 9: SLA. 10: Boulder ,commun Hosp Axiliary. 12: Sect ed ""Bibliography of Rubber Literature. 13: Yes. 14: Ref, machine applications. 15: PO Box 938, Golden Co 80401.

MINTON, ANN M (DIONNE). b St Johnsbury Vt 4 S36. 4: Henry J Minton. 5: Danbury State Col (Conn) 54-57 (Chem); Rutgers 62-63. 6: Fr. 7: eh libn Schlumberger Well Surveying Corp, Ridgefield Conn 57-62; Libn Lever Brothers Research, Edgewater NJ 62-63; Researcher & libn World Book Sci Serv,Houston 63-64; Tech libn Dow Chem Co, Houston 65-. 9: SLA; NMA; ASIS; ARMA. 10: Jr Achievement. 14: Documentation, info storage & retrieval. 15: Dow Chemical Co, 3636 Richmond ave, Houston Tx 77027.

MINUDRI, REGINA URSULA. b San Francisco Cal 9 My 37. 5: San Francisco Col For Women 54-58 (Eng) BA; UCal (Berkeley) 58-59 MLS. 7: Ref libn Menlo Park Pub Lib, Menlo Park Cal 59-62; Reg libn Santa Clara Co, Saratoga Cal 62-68; Coord Fed Y-A Lib Serv Project, Santa Clara Cal 68-. 9: ALA; CalLA (chm YASD Bklist Com 64-67); Bay Area Young Adult Libns (pres 66-68). 10: Sar Bus & Prof Womens Club. 12: Ed "Adult Books for Young adults," in "School Library Journal")67-). 13: Yes. 14: YA serv, bk reviewing, adult serv. 15: 470 Wraight ave, Los Gatos Ca 95030.

MINVIELLE, VIRGINIA LEE. b New Iberia La 1 Ap 30. 5: LSU (Baton Rouge) 47-51 (Ed) BS; SWest La Inst 55-56; U SWest La, Lafayette 65-66 (LS) Certif. 6: Sp. 7: Lib asst LSU Nursing Sch Lib (New Orleans) 51; Lib asst Loyola U Lib (New Orleans) 51-52; Woman's page ed "The Daily Ibeuan", New Iberia La 52-54; City libn Iberia Parish Lib, New Iberia La 54-57; Jr admin Humble Oil & Refining Co, New Orleans & Lafayette La 57-65; Libn Gulf S Research Inst, New Iberia La 66-. 9: SLA; ALA; LaLA. 10: Iberia Concert Assn. 14: Ref. 15: 127 Prairie ave, New Iberia La 70560.

MION, NANCY (WRIGHT). b Rockville Centre NY 21 Mr34. 4: John Mion. 5: Hofstra U 51-55 (Mgt) BBA; cum laude; SUNY Albany 56-58 MSLS; Hofstra U 59-69. 7: Production expeditor Bulova Watch Co, Flushing NY 55-6; Lib Asst NY State Lib 56-57; Libn Brentwood Jr-Sr High Sch, Brent00d NY 57-58; Libn Merrick Ave Jr High Sch, Merrick NY 58-60; Libn MacArthur High Sch, Levittown NY 64-65; Libn Bay Shore Pub Lib, ,bay Shore NY 65-66; LibnSycamore ave Sch, Bohemia NY 66-. 9: NYSchLA. 12: "Adventures in Research" (69). 14: Yp serv. 15: 1420 N Penataquit ave, Bay Shore NY 11706.

MIRACLE,F HUNTER. b Tulsa Okla 13 Ja 15. 5: UTulsa 33-35 (Eng Lit); U Okla 35-37 (Eng Lit) BA, 63-64 MLS; UPittsburgh 66-. 6: Fr, Ger. 7: Accounting clerk Carter Oil Co, Tulsa Okla 37-42; Yeoman USN (Seabees), S Pacific 42-44; Accounting clerk Okla Pipe Line, Tulsa Okla 44-45; gr Tulsa Bk & Record Shop 45-52; Head circ Tulsa Pub Lib 52-64; Head Ref Tulsa City- Co Lib 65-. 9: ALA; OklaLA; SWLA; Okla Adult Educ Assn. 10: Southwestern Art Assn; Tulsa Little Theater; Friends of the Tulsa Lib; Univ Club of Tulsa; Beta Phi Mu. 14: Ref, readers serv, a-, loc hist, info retrieva, documentation, admin, tech proc. 15: 1407 South Newport, Tulsa Ok 74120.

MIRANDA, ALTAGRACIA. b San Pedro de Macoris Dom Republic 23 N 23. 5: UPuerto Rico 40-43, 45-46 (Bio) BS; Syracuse 49-50 MSLS. 6: Sp, Fr, Portu. 7: Censorship clerk-tr US Censorship, San Jaun PR 43-45; Lib asst Sch of Tropical Med, San Juan PR 46-49; Libn Payne Whitney Clinic NY Hosp Cornell U Med Ctr 51-66; Libn Sch of Med UPR (San Juan) 50-51; Head dept org of info & catlg UPR (Rio Piedras) 66-. 9: AALL; Sociedad de Bibliotecarios de PR)chm Memb Com). 10: Women's Col Club. 12: Contributor "Mental Health Book Review Index" (56-66); Bibliog ed "Journal of the History of the Behavioral Sciences" (66). 14: Computerization of legal info, catlg, legal research, admin of research lib, behavioral sci. 15: Calle Jose R Acosta 524 Urb Ingenieros, Hato Rey PR 00918.

MIRCHUK, PETRO. b Ukraine 26 Je13. 4: Anisia Makovska. 5: J K U (Lviv) 32-33, 37-39 (Law); Karls U (Prague) 40-41 (Law); Ukrainian Free U Prague 40-41 (Law) JD; Drexel 59-60 MS in LS; Ukrainian Free U (Munich) 60-61, 68-69 (Hist) PhD. 6: Ukrainian, Ger, Russian, Polish, Czech, Ital, Lat. 7: Ed Ukrainian Press, Lviv Ukraine 33-39; Ed Ukrainian Press, mmunich Germany 45-51; Attorney at law, Munich Germany 45-51; EdUkrainan Press, US & Canada 52-59; Catlgr UDel 60-61; Catlgr Ursinus Col 61-63; Catlgr LaSalle Col 63-67. 8: Legal adv & rep of Ukrainianvictims of Nazism. 9: CathLA; Shevchenko SC Soc; Ukr Congress Com. 10: 16 bks in Ukrainian (52-69). 14: Catlg. 15: 5012 N Marvin Stn, Phila Pa 19141.

MIRSKY, PHYLLIS (SIMON). b Israel 18 D 40. 4: Edward Neal Mirsky. 5: Ohio State U 59-62 BS in Soc Welfare; Columbia 62-63 (Soc Wk); UMich 64-65 AMLS. 6: Fr. 7: Receptionist Dr Abraham Arons, Cleveland 59; Casewker Child Aid Soc, NYC 62-63; Hosp libn Cleveland Pub Lib 63-64; Ref libn UCLA-Biomed Lib 65-68; Ref acquis libn II 68-. 9: Med Lib Group So Cal. ; MedLA. 14: Ref. 15: Biomedical Lib Ctr for the Health Sciences UCLA, Los Angeles Ca 90024.

MIRTH, KARLO . b Otocac Croatia Yugoslavia 15 Jl 17. 4: Mecedes Velarde. 5: UZagreb 36-42 (Civil Engnr; URome 46-47 (Liberal Arts); UBarcelona summer 51 (Span lang0; Columbia 60-62 (LS) MS. 6: Croatian, Span, Ital, Ger, Fr, Russian. 7: Tech draftsman Babcock & Wilcox Co Engnr, Cleveland 52-53, Checker 53-56; Designer Foster Wheeler Corp Engnr Design, Livingston NJ & NYC 56-64; Head libn Foster Wheeler Corp Research Lib, Cartaret NJ 64-68; Mgr Research Info Ctr & Lib Foster Wheeler Corp, Livinston NJ 68-. 9: SLA; ADI. 10: Croatin Acad of America9pres 59-65); Amer Assn ofTchrs of Slavic & East European Langs. 12: Croatia Press (founder, publ & ed): Rome 47-48, Madrid 48-52, Cleveland 52-56, NY 56-; Ed ""Journal of Croatian Studies(60-). 14: Info retrieval, documentation, ref. 15: 12 Peachtree Hill rd, Livingston NJ 07039.

MISCHLER, IRENE B. b Danvers Ill 23 Ag 12. 5: Ill State U 31-33, 36-38 (Eng, Educ) BE; UIll 38-39 BLS. 6: Fr. 7: Circ asst & registration libn Hoyt Pub Lib, Saginaw Mich 39-43; Br libn Butman-Fish Lib, Saginaw Mich 43-51; Asst head circ dept Indianapolis Pub Lib 51-53; Ref asst Grosse Pointe Pub Lib, Grosse Pointe Mich 53-59; Ref asst Indianapolis Pub Lib 59-61, Head soc Sci div 61-. 9: ALA; IndLA. 14: Ref. 15: 1434 N Delaware st apt 31, Indianapolis In 46202.

MISH, JOHN L. b Poland 4 Ja 09. 4: Lucy Kent. 5: UBreslau 26-30 (Classics); UBerlin 30-34 (Sinology) PhD. 6: Over 20 langs. 7: Prof Warsaw Oriental Inst 34-39; China rel off Govt of India, Bombay 41-46; Chief Oriental div NY Pub Lib 46-, Chief Slavonic div 55-. 8: Prof Asia Inst, NY 46-51; Visiting Prof Dropsie Col 61-63; Adjunct Prof Seton Hall U 63-. 9: Amer Oriental Soc; ALA; NY Oriental Club (pres twice). 11: Guggenheim fellow (Italy) 58; Fulbright Research Fellow (Rome) 59-60; Kings Medal for Service in the Cause of Freedom 46. 13: Yes 14: Oriental & Slavic collections. 14: Oriental and Slavic colls. 15: NY Pub Lib, Fifth ave at 42nd st, New York NY 10018.

MISIAK, FREDA MARY. b Oshawa Ont Can 25 Je 30. 5: UToronto 48-51 (Fr) BA; Columbia 64-65 MS in LS. 6: Fr, Polish. 7: Libn Can Packers Ltd Research Labs, Toronto 51-. 9: SLA (Toronto Chap: treas 67-68, sec 68-69). 15: Canada Packers Ltd Research Labs, 2211 St Clair ave W, Toronto 9 Ont Can.

MISSNER, MICHELE WENDY (GOLDSTEIN). b Flint Mich 7 O 44. 4: Marshall H Missner. 5: UMich 62-66 (Hist) BA, 67-68 MLS. 6: Hebrew, Fr. 7: High sch tchr Carman Sch dist, Flint Mich 66-67; Libn (staff) UChicago 68-. 8: Org lib for Polhemus Assoc, Ann Arbor Mich 68. 14: Research. 15: 924 Somerset lane, Flint Mi 48503.

MITCHELL, ALICE (TOLK). b NYC 12 Mr 44. 4: Daniel J B Mitchell. 5: Barnard 60-64 (Fr) AB; Columbia 64-65 (tchg of Fr), 65-66 MLS. 6: Fr. 7: Sub Fr tchr NYC Schs, Brooklyn 64-65; Libn trainee Brooklyn Pub Lib, NY 65-66; Ref asst Town Lib of Brookline, Mass 66-68; Asst libn Acad of Motion Pictures Arts & Sci, LA 68-. 9: ALA. 14: Ref. 15: 1437 Euclid st, Santa Monica Ca 90404.

MITCHELL, ANN ELIZABETH. b Bessemer Ala 30 My 27. 5: UAla 47 (Eng, Educ) BS; Vanderbilt 55 (Eng) MA; Peabody 58 MA in ls. 7: Case wker Dept of Pub Welfare, Ft Payne Ala 49-50; Tchr Williamson Co Tenn 53-54; Asst Prof Jacksonville State Col 56-57; Asst info desk Mobile Pub Lib, Mobile Ala 58; Ref libn Stetson U 58-61; Undergrad ref libn UTenn 61-62, Asst ref libn 63-. 9: ALA; TennLA; SELA. 14: Ref. 15: 1631 Laurel ave, Knoxville Tenn 37916.

MITCHELL, ANN MARIE (DORWART). b Pasadena Cal 25 Ag 38. 4:John Ronald Mitchell. 5: UCal(Berkeley) 55-60 (Span) AB, 63-65 MLS. 6: Polish, Sp, Fr, Ital, Russian, other romance & Slavic langs. 7: UCal(Berkeley): Research asst-tr 62-65, Lib asst Inst of Transportation and Traffic Engnr 65, Libn acqus dept exch div 65; Tr US Govt Joint Publ Research Serv, San Francisco 62-. 9: ALA; AMER Transl Assn; CalLA. 14: Exch, Slavic acquis. 15: 2509 Stuart st apt 1, Berkeley Cal 94705.

MITCHELL, BARBARA J (KOPP). b NYC 3 Ag 46. 4: Peter J Mitchell. 5: Marietta Col 63-67 (Phil) BA; Rutgers 67-68 MLS. 6: Fr. 7: Jr libn Free Pub Lib of Woodbridge, NJ 68; Hd circ Medford Pub Lib, Mass 68-. 9: MassLA. 10: Phi Beta Kappa; Beta Phi Mu. 14: Adult serv. 15: 200 Swanton st #728, Winchester Ma 01890.

MITCHELL, BASIL MANLEY. b Elysian Fields Tex 11 O 16. 5: UTex 36-40 (Eng Lit) BA; Columbia 44-45 (LS) BS; Fordham 55-57 (Eng Lit) MA. 6: Ger, Fr. 7: Ref asst art div NY Pub Lib 45-46; Libn Grad Sch of Journalism Columbia U 46-53; Head a-v dept The Greenwich Lib, Greenwich Conn 53-55; Catlgr Adriance Mem Lib, Poughkeepsie NY 57-61; Lib Dir Orange Co Commun Col 61-65; Academic & research libs consul NY State Lib 65-. 67; Exec dir SEast NY Lib Resources Coun 68-. 9: NYLA. 13: Yes. 14: Col & res lib admin. 15: 18 Davies pl, Poughkeepsie NY 12601.

MITCHELL, (BETTY JO). b Coin Ioes 2 My 31. 5: SW Mo State Col 49-52 (Sociol) BA; USoCal 66-67 MS in LS; San Fernando Valley State Col 69- (Bus Admin). 6: Fr, Sp. 7: Hd cashier Menger Hotel, San Antonio Tex 52-53; Teller Central Nat Bank, carthage Md 54-54; Cost accountant Carthage Marble Corp, Carthage Mo 54-61; Hd accounts received Truog-Nichols, Kan City Mo 61-62; Hd accounts payable Pacific Finance Corp, LA 63-66; Acquis libn San Fernando Valley State Col 67-. 9: ALA; CalLA; SoCal Tech Proc Assn. 10: Assn Cal State Col Prop. 14: Acquis, catlg. 15: 9127 Geyser, Northridge Ca 91324.

MITCHELL, BONNIE J(EAN) (ODELL). b Chicago Ill 18 S 44. 4: Loyal R Mitchell Jr. 5: Grove City Col 62-66 (Eng, Hist) BA; UPittsburgh 66-67 MLS. 6: Fr. 7: Circ libn Mohawk Valley Commun Col 67-. 9: ALA; NYStateLA; NY State A-V Assn. 10: Lambda Iota tau; Pi Gamma Mu; Phi Beta Mu. 13: Yes. 14: Circ. 15: 3 Hart's Hill pkwy, Whitesboro NY 13492.

MITCHELL, CHARLOTTE (STUDER). b Milwaukee 26 S 17. 04 Philip J Mitchell. 4: Philip J. Mitchell. 5: Milwaukee-Downer ol 35-39 (Eng Lit) AB; USoCal 39-40 BS in LS; Chicago 49-50 (LS) MA. 7: 2nd asst libn Berwyn Pub Lib, Berwyn Ill 40-43; Clerk US Off of Censorship, Chicago 43-44; Libn Michael Reese Hosp Sch Nursing, Chicago 44-51; Libn Miles Laboratories Inc, Elkhart Ind 51-. 9: ALA-AHIL (Coun 53-55; ed "Quarterly" 50-53); MedLA; SLA (Pharmaceutical Sect;ed "COPNIP" 56-61, treas 61-63, v-chm 64-65, chm 65-66; chm Hosp & Nursing Gp48-49, chm Adv Coun 68-69). 10: Altrusa Club of Elkhart Co; Elkhart Concert Club Bd of Dirs. 11: Spec Serv Award, AHIL 64. 12: Ed "AHIL Quarterl, formerly Hosp Book Guide. 13: Yes. 14: Admin, documentation, info retrieval. 15: Miles Labs Inc, Elkhart In 46514.

MITCHELL, COLLEEN. b San Francisco Cal 29 Ap 39. 5: Col of The Holy Names 57-61 (Eng) BA; WashU 61-63 (Eng) MA; UCal (Berkeley) 67-68 MLS. 6: Fr. 7: Libn II acquis Fresno State Col 68-. 14: Acquis. 15: 1304 N Wishon ave apt D, Fresno Ca 93728.

MITCHELL, DAVID LEE. b Highland Park Mich 30 S 36. 4: Mary Lee Armao. 5: Harvard 54-58 (Eng) AB; Brandeis 58-59 (Eng); SUNY (Albany) 61-62 MLS. 6: Ital, Fr. 7: trainee gen ref Boston oston Pub Lib 59-60; Asst libn Siena Col 60-61, 62-63; Instr Sch of Lib Sci SUNY (Albany) 63-65, Head lib lab collection 65-68, Asst Prof 68-. 8: Chm, Conf on Bibliog Control of Lib Sci Lit, Albany 68. 9: ALA;-LED (chm Com on Rel of Lib Sch Libs 67-68). 14: Bibliog. 15: 936 Livingston ave, Schenectady NY 12309.

MITCHELL, ELEANOR. b Orange NJ 4 Ap 07. 5: Douglass Col 24-28 (Art, Langs) BA; Columbia 28-29 (LS) BS; Smith 36 (A rt) MA. 6: Sp, Fr, Ital. 7: Asst curator books & photographs Smith Col Art Dept 29-36; Asst to dir The Graduate House, Florence Italy 36-37; Libn fine arts dept UPittsburgh 37-42; Lib consul Biblioteca Publica del Estado de Jalisco, Guadalajara Mex 42-43; Chief art div NY Pub Lib 43-51; Arts & museum spec Spec Cult Activ Dept Unesco, Paris 48-49; Dir of Lib Serv USIS,-Italy,Rome Italy 51-53; Consul on fine arts LC 54-55; Consul Montclair Pub Lib, Montclair NJ 55; US spec Int Educ Exch Serv, Dept of State Consul, Biblioteca Publica Departamental, Cali Colombia 55-56, Consul Escuela Interamericana de Bibliotecologia, Universidad de Antioquia, Med ellin Colombia 56-57; Exec Dir Fine Arts Com People-to-People Prog, Wash DC 57-61; Sec Pro Tem Bks for the People Fund Inc, Pan Amer Union, Wash DC 61-62; Bibliog asst Bibliog Proj for Internat Rice Research Inst, Wash DC 62-63; Consul Hispanic Found LC 63; Lib consul Universidad Catolica del Ecuador (St Louis U AID Contract), Quito Ecuador 6 3-. 9: ALA-ACRL; SLA (chm NY Chap Mus Group 46-47; v-chm Wash Chap Picture Group 58-59). 10: Soc of Woman Geographers. 13: Yes. 14: Lib org & admin. 15: USAID/Quito c/o Amer Embassy, Quito Ecuador SA.

MITCHELL, ELOSIA E. b MKeesport Penn 24 D 39. 4: John A Mitchell. 5: Roberts Wesleyan Col 57-61 (Eng) AB; UPittsburgh 64-65 MLS; UMd 67 Certified Med Libn. 6: Sp. 7: Eng tchr Greece Olympia High Sch, Rochester NY 61-62; US Peace Corps Volunteer, PI 62-64; Med libn McKeesport Hosp, McKeesport Penn 64-66; Ref libn Nat Insts of Health 66-67; Tech libn The Boeing Co 67-69; Acquis libn West Ill U 69-. 9: MedLA; SLA. 10: YMCA; Beta Phi Mu. 14: Ref. 15: 138 Kurlene dr, Macomb Il 61455.

MITCHELL, GLADYS. b Ottawa Ont Can 12 Mr 19. 5: Carleton U (Ottawa) 51 (Eng, hist) BA; UOttawa 68 BLS. 7: Stenographer, clk & non-prof libn Fed Govt, Ottawa Ont 37-; Prof ref libn Dept of Nat Defence, Ottawa Ont 68-. 9: CanLA. 14: Ref. 15: 595 Fraser ave, Ottawa 13 Ont Can.

MITCHELL, HELEN L. b Kan City Kan 14 Ja 29. 5: UMo (Kan City) 59-63 (Eng lit) BA; UIll 63-64 (LS) MS. 6: Fr. 7: Clk Com Trust Co, Kan City Mo 46-49; Bkkeeper City of Kan City Mo 49-52; Clk & stenographer Studebaker-Packard, Kan City Mo 52-59; Ref Kan city (Mo) Pub Lib 64-65; Bibliogr & catlgr UKan 65-. 14: Catlg. 15: 1726 Tennessee, Lawrence Ks 66044.

MITCHELL, HESTER L(OUISE). b Plainfield NJ 8 D 15. 5: UVa ext 37 (Liberal Arts); Regent Inst (London) ext 37 (Journalsm);UNH 39, 40, 48, 51 (LS); Harvard 41, 42 (LS); Boston U 41, 46, 50, 52, 53, 61 (Liberal Arts); UOkla 61-64 (Prof Writing). 7: Asst Beverly High Sch Lib, Beverly Mass 33-34; Child asst Beverly Pub Lib, Beverly Mass 35-40, Adult asst 40-48; Literary staff Springfield (Mass) Rep Newspaper 41-45; Head child dpt Pub Lib, Everett Mass 48-51; Head Libn Pub Lib, Ipswich Mass 51-67; Libn Addison-Wesley Publ Co, Inc, Reading Mass 67-. 9: SLA; ALA (Com on Labor Serv); NELA; NESchLA; MassLA (Memb Com 61-64,Educ Com 58-59, Exec Bd 52, 53, 56, Nom Com 54, Lib Admin Sect); MerrimackValleyLA (pres 52-54, Exec Bd 51-60). 10: Cable Mem Hosp Auxiliary; DAR; Womens Nat Bk Assn; Amer Red Cross; Wayfarer's Travel Club; Internat Platform Assn. 13: Yes. 14: Ref, juvenile. 15: Holen Gardens Apts, Danvers Mass 01923.

MITCHELL, JOY. b Rome Ga 29 Mr 25. 5: Tenn Temple Col 51-54 (Bible) BA; Peabody 57-60 (Eng) BA, (LS) MA; Certif in Eng & Libn. 7: IBM proof machine Operator Bank, Rome, Chattanooga & Nashville 9 years; Circ desk Pub Lib, Nashville 58-59; Ref dsk Vanderbilt Lib, Nashville 59; Head Libn tenn Temple Col 54-57, 60-64; Libn Dalewood Jr High Sch, Chattanooga Tenn 64-66; Hd libn Franklin HighSch Franklin Tenn 66-. 9: ALA; NEA; TennLA; TennEA. 10: Woman's Nat Bk Club. 14: Ref, readers adv, admin. 15: 2406 Blair blvd, Nashville Tn 37212.

MITCHELL, LEANNE (DYKE). b Livermore Falls Me 12 Je 39. 4: Larry D Mitchell. 5: UMe 57-61 (Psych) BA; Case West Res 63-64 MSLS. 7: Employment interviewer NY State Employment Serv, Buffalo 62-63; Asst ref libn UNH 64-65; Sci libn UDel Lib 66-68, Sr libn Div of tech serv & asst sci libn 68-69, Info specialist Div of tech serv 69-. 9: SLA; ASIS. 10: AAAS; AAUP. 14: Sci & tech, ref, info ret, info systems, computer application. 15: Div of Tech Ser Univ of Delaware, Newark De 19711.

MITCHELL, MARTHA MAUDE (WILSON). b Clinton SC 31 My 36. 4: James Otto Mitchell. 5: Erskine Col 54-57 (Bus Educ) BS; Emory 60-66 (LS) MA. 6: Fr. 7: Tchr Greenville Co Pub Schs, Greenville SC 57-60; Libn Parker High Sch, Greenville SC 60-65; Catlgr Greenville TEC Lib, Greenville SC 68-. 9: ALA; SCLA. 10: Beta Phi Mu. 14: Sch libs, ref, catlg. 15: 9 East Parkins Mill rd, Greenville SC 29607.

MITCHELL, MARY (FRIEDRICH). b Jasper Minn 23 D 19. 4: James Mitchell. 5: St Olaf Col 36-40 (Eng) BA; UMinn 41 BLS. 6: Ger. 7: Ref libn UMinn(Minneapolis) 41-44; Ref ibn Libn Bur of Budget, Wash DC 44-47, Admin asst 47-48; Detroit Pub Lib: Gen asst 48-49, Chief Mun Ref Lib 49-53, Chief gen info dept 53-63, Personnel dir 63-67, Ref serv dir 67-68; Assoc dir 68-. 9: MichLA (pres 65-66). 10: Zonta Internat. 13: Yes. 14: Admin, personnel. 15: Detroit Pub Lib, 5201 Woodward ave, Detroit Mi 48202.

MITCHELL, MARY JANE (DYBDAHL). b Pequot Minn 27 N 15. 4: Robert H Mitchell. 5: Columbia Union Col 40 (Eng) BA; Catholic U 44 (LS) BS in LS; Andrews U 57 (Church Hist) MA; West Mich U summer 65 (LS). 6: Fr. 7: Asst Libn Norwalk Pub Lib, Norwalk Conn 51-53; Libn Seventh-day Adventist Theol Sem, Wash DC 53-60; Libn ANDREWS U 60-. 9: ALA; ATheolLA. 10: Bus & Prof Womens Club. 14: Catlg, admin. 15: Box 211 Andrews Sta, Berrien Sprigs Mich 49104.

MITCHELL, MILTON EDWARD. b Wausaukee Wis 2 Ja 45. 4: Barbara Johanek. 5: UWis (Green Bay) 62-64; UWis (Madison) 64-66 (Hist) BA; UWis (Milwaukee) 67-68 MALS. 6: Fr. 7: Libn Milwaukee Pub Lib 68; Libn (Instr) Wis StateU (Oshkosh) 68-. 9: WisLA. 14: Ref, bibliog. 15: 808A Washington st, Oshkosh Wi 54901.

MITCHELL, PAMELA MERLE. b Montreal Can 28 Ja 41. 5: UWest Ont 60-63 (Hist) BA; Toronto 63-64 BLS. 7: Libn UToronto 64-66; Libn Faculty of Arch, Urban & Reg Planning & Landscape Arch UToronto 66-. 9: CanLA; Can Assn Col & Res Libs; Coun Planning Libns. 14: Circ. 15: 368A Bloor st W, Toronto 4 Ont Can.

MITCHELL, PETER (DORLAND). b Toronto Can 7 Mr 21. 5: Nat University (Ireland) 47-48 (Philos); U West Ont 55-57 (Eng) BA; McGill 57-58 BLS. 6: Fr. 7: Libn ref dept London Pub Lib, London Can 58-59; Lecturer Lib Sci Col of Christ the King (London Can) 59-62; Chief libn King's Col, London Can 59-. 9: CanLA; ALA; OntLA; Cath LA (Hon life mem, past pres Ont Unit). 12: "Index to Macleans Magazine, 1914-1937," CanLA Occas Paper No 47 (65). 13: Yes. 14: Catlg, admin. 15: King's Col Lib, Waterloo st, London Ont Can.

MITCHELL, W(ILLIAM) H(INCKLEY). b E Orange NJ 5 Je 03. 4: Janet MacDonald. 5: Rutgers 21-25 (Math) BS; Harvard 25-29 (Biol) MA, PhD; Columbia 38-39 BS in LS. 6: Fr, Ger, Span, Ital. 7: Research entomology USDA, Orlando Fla & Honolulu30-33; Instr zool Rutgers U 33-35; Catlgr Rutgers U Lib 35-38; Lib consul Union Club of NY, NYC 39-43; Indexer

H W Wilson Co, NYC 41-43; Bibliog USDA Lib, Wash DC 43-51; Supv Libn The Adj Gens Off US Dept of the Army, Wash DC 51-64; Chief of tech processing Fairfax Co Pub Lib, Fairfax Co Va 64-. 8: Fairfax Co Lib Bd Trustees 62-64. 9: ALA; VaLA; DCLA; Potomac TECH Processing Libns (Coun 66-68). 10: Clermont Woods Commun Assn; Delegate to Fairfax Co Fed of Citizens Assns; Phi Beta Kappa. 14: Catlg, comp & ed bk catlgs. 15: 4421 Upland dr, Alexandria Va 22310.

MITCHELL, WILLIAM LAWRENCE. b Kan City Mo 2 Je 32. 4: Virginia Jean Cox. 5: UKan 50-52, 56-59 (Eng) BA; UIll 59-60 MS in LS. 7: Engineman2/c US Coast Guard 52-56; UKan Lib 60, Head catlgr 63-. 10: Beta Phi Mu. 14: Catlg. 15: 1201 Emery rd, Lawrence Kan 66044.

MITLIN, LUCEILLE (LISTON). b Clarksburg WVa 7 Je 18. 4: Norman Mitlin. 5: WVaU 36-40 (Zool) AB, 41 (Secondary Educ); UMd 59-61 (Elem Educ); Miss State U 68- (Geog). 7: Sci ci tchr WVaU Demonstration High Sch, Morgantown WVa 41; Research Pharmacologist Hynson Wescott & Dunning, Baltimore 41-42; Chem Lever Brothers Co, Baltimore 42-44; Chem "Good Housekeeping, NYC 44-45; Entomologist Shaff Labs, Brooklyn NY 45-47; Sub elem tchr Montogomery Co Sch Bd, Rockville Md 53-58, Elem tchr58-61; Sci libn ref Mitchell Mem Lib Miss State U 62-. 9: ALA; MissLA. 10: AAUP; So Appalachian Bot Club. 13: Yes. 14: Sci ref. 15: 513 Poplar rd, Starkville Ms 39759.

MITRA, HIMANSU BHUSAN. b Calcutta India 6 Ja 28. 4: Gita. 5: Calcutta U 53-57 BA; Lib Assoc 58-60 Assoc of Lib Assoc. 6: Bengali, Hindi. 7: Inst of Jute Tech, Calcutta 50-57; Jay Engring Wks Ltd, Calcutta 57-58; Hendon Pub Libs, Lond Eng 59-60; B M Inst, Ahmedabad India 61; Indian Inst of Tech, Delhi India 61-66; Mt Allison U, Sackville N B 67-. 9: Lib Assn (Gt Brit); CanLA; APLA. 14: System analysis. 15: Box 1088, Sackville NB Can.

MITRENGA, REV EDWIN F CR. b Chicago 9 O 30. 5: St Louis U 49-53 (Eng) BA; Rosary Col 58-60 (LS) MA. 6: Polish, Ital, Lat, Fr. 7: Resurrection Sem, St Louis. 14: High sc libs. 15: 3689 W Pine blvd, St Louis Mo 63108.

MITRISIN, SOPHIE (SPEIGLMAN). b Berdichev Russia. 5: West Res 41 (Psych) BA; Rutgers 60 MSLS; New Sch for Soc Research 69 (Philos,Arts) MALS. 6: Yiddish, Fr, Ger. 7: Libn NY Pub Lib 60-65; Dept supv libn City Planning & Housing Lib, NYC 65-. 8: Inst on Law Libnship, Milwaukee Wis 69; Adv Proj URBANDOC, NYC 67, NY Times "Quotations" 65, Frances Christoph "Salerno Sculpture" NYC 64; Franklin Watts Inc,NYC 62; Consul, Amer Soc Consul Planners, Berkeley Cal 68, B'nai B'rith Voc Serv,NYC 62. 9: SLA (sec Planning, Bldg & Hous Sect 67-69); PrivLA; ALA; ASIS. 14: Ref, child serv. 15: 605 Water st apt 2D, New York NY 10002.

MITTELGLUCK, ELAINE (ROTHBERG). b Brooklyn NY 5 S 33. 4: Eugene Leon Mittlegluck. 5: Hunter Col 50-54 (Sociol) AB; Columbia 55-58 MSLS. 7: Tchr Bd of Educ, NYC 54-55; NY Pub Lib; Lib trainee 55-58, Ya libn 58, Sr libn ya 58-62, Sr libn ya & asst br libn 62; Exch libn Notts Co, Eng 62-63; Sr libn ya & asst br libn NY Pub Lib 63-67; Hd circ dept New Rochelle Pub Lib, New Rochelle NY 67, Asst dir 68-. 9: ALA-YASD (Com on Sel of Bks & Other Materials, chm Subcom Outstanding Theater List); NYLA; NY Lib Club; Westchester LA. 10: Friends of the City Center, NYC; Columbia Sch of Lib Serv Alumni. 14: YA serv, adult recr rding. 15: 640 Pelham rd, New Rochelle NY 10805.

MITTELGLUCK, EUGENE LEON. b NYC 27 N 30. 4: Elaine Rothberg. 5: Brooklyn Col 49-53 (Sociol) BA; Rutgers 58-60 MLS. 6: Ger. 7: (Lt jg) USNR (Active duty) Deck watch off USS Ticonderoga (CVA 14) 53-56; A-v coordinator Hunter Col 56-57; Soc studies tchr Jr High Sch 115, NYC 57; Soc investigator Dept of Welfare, NYC 57-58; Lib asst Bd of Higher Educ, NYC 58-60; Libn adult serv & a-v Free Pub Lib, E Orange NJ 60-65; A-v consul Westchester Lib Sysem, New Rochelle NY 65-67; Adult serv consul Westchester Lib Syst, Mt Vernon NY 67-; Instr Sch LibsInfo Sci Pratt Inst 69-. 8: V-chm NJ Lib Film Circuit; Pre-screening panel for Amer Film Festivl; Evaluation panel for Educ tfilm LA; Pub Rels Liaison for Lib Devel Com of NJ LA; Adv panel for revision of; Goldstein a-v serv in NY State 67, adult servstandards in NY 68. 9: ALA-PLA (A-V Com); NYLA (past chm & mem A-V Com; Conf Program Com 68);Westchester(NY)LA (Exhibits Chm). 10: Nlvil Dui Chowder & Marching Soc; USNR (Lt); Beta hi Mu; Film Lib Info Coun. 13: Yes. 14: A-v materials & methods, adult serv. 15: 640 Pelham rd, New Rochelle NY 10805.

MITTEN, ELEANOR MARY. b Syracuse NY 18 O 17. 5: Cornell U 38-42 (Home Econ) BS; Syracuse 48-49 (LS) BS; Columbia summer 58 (Med Lit & Libnship) Certif. 6: Fr, Ger, S, Russian. 7: File clerk Kemper Insurance Co, Syracuse NY 36-38; Sales clerk W I Addis Co, Syracuse NY 39; Sec to mgr Mohawk Hotel, Old Forge NY 40; Clerk Crouse-Hinds Co, Syracuse NY 41; Sec-steno Phoenix Mutual Life Insurance Co, Syracuse NY 42-4; Stud Boot Training Hunter Col, USNR WAVES Appren Seaman 43; Personnel yeoman Naval Air Sta, Pensacola Fla, USNR WAVES Yeoman 3/c & Yeoman2/c 43-44; Stud Off Indoctrination Train Smith Col, Northhampton Mass USNR WAVES Appren Seaman & Midshipman 44; Stud Radio/Radar Admin Sch Naval Air Tech Train Center, Corpus Christi Tex USNR WAVES Ensign 44; Asst Radio/Raar Admin Off Aviation Supply Off, Phila, USNR WAVES Ensign & Lt jg 44-46; Steno Gen Electric Co, Syracuse NY 46-47; Sec-steno Cine Simplex Corp, Syracuse NY 47; Sec-steno Funda-Austin Construction Corp, Syracuse NY 48; Sr asst libn Harper Hos, Detroit 49-54; Asst libn NY State Vterinary Col Lib, Cornell U 54-59; Health Sci Lib UMd: Head catlgr 59-63, Head bk acquis & catlg63-65, Asst libn for readers serv 65-. 9: MedLA (By-laws Com 67-69); SLA (Coun 64-65, sec Mich Chap 53-54, BaltimoreChap Pres 64-65, Dir 65-67); ALA. 10: Cornell Univ Womens Club. 14: Admi, ref, circ, catlg, acquis. 15: UMd Health Sci Lib, 111 S Greene st, Baltimore Md 21201.

MITTON, HALINA G. b Lodz Poland 23 Ag 40. 4: David Mitton. 5: UBC 61-65 (Intl Studies, Ger) BA, 66-67 (Ref, Spec Libs) BLS. 6: Ger, Fr, Russian. 7: Lib asst UBC 66; Libn (in charge) MacMillan Bloedell Research Corp, Vancouver BC 67-68; Hd interlib loan & ref libn UCal (Santa Barbara) 68-. 9: CanLA. 14: Spec libs, catlg, ref in sci. 15: 2235 W 14th ave, Vancouver BC Can.

MITTWEDE, FRIEDA PAULA (MRS). b Fulton M 1 d 02. 5: William Woods Col 23 (Liberal Arts) AA, Certif in Piano; Westminster Col 44; UMo summer 45; UDenver 47 (LS) AB. 6: Ger. 7: Music tchr Geneva Co High Sch, Hartford Ala 23-24; Music tchr Morgan Co High Sch, Hartselle Ala 24-26; Asst libn William Woods Col 37-57; Libn Fulton Pub Lib, Fulton Mo 57-. 9: ALA; MoLA (Pub Lib Div: chm &/or mem var com). 14: Ref. 15: 710 Jefferson, Fulton Mo 65251.

MIX, BETTYE JO (ROGERS). b Sandersville Ga 17 N 29. 4: J Valery Mix. 5: Wesleyan Col 46-48; 4; UGa 48-50 (Journalism) ABJ; Tex Womans U 60-63 (Eng, LS) MLS. 7: Tchr Tennille High Sch, Tennille Ga 50-53; Stewardess & asst stewardess supv Delta Airlines, Atlanta 53-58; Libn II UTex Southwestern Med Sch Lib 63-68; Libn Washington Co High Sch, Sandersville Ga 69-. 9: ALA; GaLA. 10: Theta Sigma Phi; Sigma Tau Delta; Alpha Beta Alpha. 14: Ref, ser. 15: 525 Lee st, Sandersville Ga 31082.

MIXER, CHARLES W(ILSON). b Salt Lake City 29 Ja 06. 5: Harvard 24-28 (Eng) AB, 32-33 (Educ); Columbia 33-34 (LS) BS. 7: Ed asst Ginn & Co Publ, Boston 28-31; Circ asst Tchrs Col Lib Columbia U summer 34; Catlg asst LC 34-35; Ref asst, asst chief ref dept DC Pub Lib 35-38; (Lt jg) USN libn US Naval Acad 42-45; Libn US Naval Acad (Annapolis) 38-46; Asst dir of libs Columbia U 46-. 8: Sec, Md Com for Conservation of Cultural Resources 42-45; Coun on "Whos Who in Library Service 52-55; Accredit teams, Middle States Assn of Cols & Sec Schs 50; Adv Com Lib Tech Proj, of f Fire & Protection Portection of Lib Resources 61-62. 9: ALA (Coun 64-67, chm &/or mem 3 coms 50-57)-RTSD (chm 2 coms 56-58)-LAD (Bd Dirs 60-62, chm &/or mem 4 coms 56-63); Md LA (Exec Bd 43-45, pres 45-46); NY Reg Catlg Group (pres 54-55); NY Lib Club (Coun 60-61); NY Tech Serv Libns. 0: Friends of the Columbia Libs; Archons of Colophon; Melvil Dui Chowder & Marching Soc. 12: Ed "DC Libraries, Jrl of DCLA (36-38); Ed "Between Librarians, Jrl of MdLA (41-45); Asst ed "Columbia Library Columns, Friends of Columbia Libs (51-). 13: Yes. 14: Lib insur, friends of libs, exhibits, ed & publ. 15: 35 Claremont ave, New York NY 10027.

MIXON, JOYCE (MINOR). b Baton Rouge La 31 Mr 43. 4: Gene Mixon. 5: SouthernU 60-64 9bus Educ) BS; LSU 66-68 (LS). 6: Fr. 7: Libn Buena Vista High Sch (Saginaw Mich) 64-. 9: NEA; MichSchLA; MichEA. 10: Sigma Gamma Rho. 14: Catlg, rare bks. 15: 638 South 16th st, Saginaw Mi 48601.

MLEYNEK, DARRYL. b Wash DC 6 Ja 40. 4: Sherryll Mindell. 5: UIll 58-59, 60-61 (Pol sci) BA; Cal State Col (LA) 66 (Psych); USoCal 66-67 MSLS. 7: Ref libn LA Pub Lib 67-. 10: Amwe Fed State, Co & Mun Employees. 13: Yes. 15: 1166 N Normandie ave #4, Los Angeles Ca 90029.

MOAKLEY, GERTRUDE (CHARLOTTE). b Pittsburgh 18 F 05. 5: Barnard 22-26 (Classics) BA; Columbia 27-28 (LS) BS. 6: Fr, Ger, Sp. 7: Catlgr circ dept NY Pub Lib 28-65; Short-term occasional assignments in bibliog or research for individuals & orgs 65-66; Catlgr Pratt Inst 66-. 9: ALA (chm Subcom on Filing Rules 53-54); NY Tech Serv Libns (past sec-treas, pres 57-58); NY Lib Club. 10: ACLU; MENSA; Liberal Party (Co Com Woman). 12: "Basic Filing Rules for Medium-Sized Libraries" (57); "The Tarot Cards Painted by Bonifacio Bembo" (67). 13: Yes. 14: Catlg, bibliog, research. 15: 411 W Twenty-second st, NYC 10011.

MOATS, RUBY (WILSON). b Boonville Ind 25 Ag 03. 4: John S Moats. 5: Evansville Col 22-23, summers 24, 25; Ind U 26-27 (Hist) AB; UIll 31-32 BS in LS. 7: Asst Evansville ub Lib, Evansville Ind 27-29; Catlgr USDA Lib, Wash DC 30-36; Asst libn US Soil Conservation Serv,Wash DC 36-41; Bibliog USDA Lib, Wash DC 42-46, Chief bibliog of Agric 47-61; Bibliog Biol Scis Communication Proj of George Washington U 61-. 9: SLA (Biol Scis Div, Wash DC Chap; v-chm 56-57, chm 58-59); DCLA. 12: Ed "The Millets; a Bibliography of the World Literature Covering the Years 1930-1963" (67); Ed "Sorghum; a Bibliography of the World Literature Covering the Years 1930-1963" (67). 14: Bibliog. 15: 5100 Dorset ave apt 213, Chevy Chase Md 20015.

MOBBS, PATRICIA ANN (BURGER). b Etowah Co Ala 1 Ap 38. 4: Charles A Mobbs. 5: Jacksonville State U 62-63 (Elem educ); Auburn U 63-65 (Elem educ) BS, 66-67 (LS) MEd. 7: Asst libn Gadsden Pub Lib, Gadsden Ala 57-62; Tchr & reading consul Lee Co schs, Opeika Ala 66; Dir materials ctr & instr &ib sci Auburn U 67-. 8: Co-dir of Conf for Pub Sch Libns, E Central Ala 68-69. 9: ALA; NEA-DAVI; AlaLA (chm By-Laws Com); Ala Educ Media Assn. 10: Nat Beta Club. 15: 1327 So Gay st, Auburn Al 36830.

MOBERG, BARBARA (SIGRID). b Portland Ore 10 O 11. 5: UWash 29-32 BS in LS. 6: Fr, Ger. 7: Ore State Lib: Ref libn 51-59, Documents libn 59-64, Documents & ser libn 64-66, Hd of catlg sect 66-. 9: ALA; SLA; OreLA. 10: LWV. 12: Ed "Oregons Documents Depository Law and Policies, Past and Present" (65). 14: Tech processes, ref. 15: E State Lib, Salem Or 97310.

MOBERG, F ALDEN. b Harris Minn 28 D 32. 5: John Muir Col 50-52 (Music) AA; Bethel Col (St Paul) 53-56 (Lit) BA; USoCal 61-62 MS in LS. 7: Postal clerk US Post Off, Los Angeles 59-61; Hist libn Ore State Lib 62-. 67, Hist & Oregoniana libn 68-. 9: ALA; PNLA; OreLA. 10: Salem City Club; Salem Civic Choir. 14: Ref. 15: 236 25th st NE, Salem Or 97301.

MOBERG, JANE MARIE (BEYER). b Boston Mass 14 S 44. 4: Guy H Moberg Jr. 5: Thiel Col 62-64, 65-66 (Ger) BA; UMunich (Germany) 64-65 (Ger); Simmons 66-67 MSLS. 6: Ger. 7: Asst ref libn Penn StateU 67-. 14: Ref. 15: 1357 Pennsylvania ave, State College Pa 16801.

MOBERLY, FLORENCE L(ALLY). b Chicago 28 Jl 08. 5: Carleton Col 26-30 (Eng) BA; Rosary Col 43-49 MA in LS. 6: Fr. 7: Head adult circ Oak Park Pub Lib, Oak Park Ill 42-52; Head Libn Josephine Co Lib, Grants Pass Ore 52-. 9: ALA; OreLA (chm Legis Com); PNLA. 10: PEO; Amer Field Serv; Human Rights Coun. 13: Yes. 14: Admin. 15: 1331 NW Washington blvd, Grants Pass Ore 97526.

MOBLEY, EMILY RUTH. b Valdosta Ga 1 O 42. 5: UMichigan 60-64 (Sci) AB Ed, 65-67 AMLS. 6: Ger. 7: Tchr Ecorse Pub Sch, Ecorse Mich 64-65; Engring libn Chrysler Corp, Detroit 65-. 9: SLA (chm Resolutions Com 69-71). 14: Lit searches (sci materials). 15: 4134 Seventeenth, Ecorse Mi 48229.

MOBLEY, JOYCE ELIZABETH. b Minden La 2 D 44. 5: LSU 62-66 (Secondary Educ) BS, 66-68 (LS) MS. 6: Fr. 7: Asst catlgr USouth Ala Lib, Mobile 68-. 9: ALA; AlaLA. 10: Alpha Beta Alpha. 14: Catlg, clsf. 15: Catalog Dept Univ of South Alabama 307 Gaillard dr, Mobile Al 36608.

MODEMANN, HARRIETT FIELD. b Paterson NJ 11 Jl 25. 5: Douglass Col Rutgers U 43-47 (LS) BA; Columbia 50-53 (LS) MS; Rutgers 60-64 (Eng Lit). 7: Libn Mitchell Col 47-49; Libn Oradell Hub Lib, Oradell NJ 49-50; Head catlgr & Asst Prof Paterson State Col 50-. 9: NJLA. 10: Assn NJ State Col Faculties; Paterson State Col Faculty Assn; Col Club of Ridgewood NJ; BEvening Dept of Ridgewood Womans Club. 14: Catlg, acquis. , ser. 15: 23 Christopher p, Ridgewood NJ 07450.

MOEDRITZER, ANNE (MIDDLEBROOK). b St Paul Minn 11 Mr 32. 4: Kurt Moedritzer. 5: UAriz 50-51; UMinn 51-55 (Phil) BA, 55-57 (LS) MA. 6: Ger. 7: Asst sci libn USoCal 57; A-v & curriculum libn Webster Col 65-68; Asst libn Country Day Sch, St Louis 69-. 10: LWV. 14: Ref, a-v. 15: 408 Belleview, St Louis Mo 63119.

MOELK, MILDRED (ELIZABETH). b Rochester NY 25 My 15. 5: URochester 35-43 (Eng) AB; Columbia 44-45 (Catlg) BS in LS; NYU 47-50 (Eng) MA. 6: Fr, Ital, Ger, Old Eng, Middle Eng, Middle High Ger. 7: Hd ser acquis dept Harvard U Grad Sch of Bus Admin Lib 45-46; Ser catlgr NYU Wash Sq Lib 46-47; Catlgr Vassar Col Lib 47-51; Catlgr State U of Iowa Libs (Iowa City) 52-53; Catlgr Colo U Lib 53-55; Asst lit dept Cleveland Pub Lib, Ohio 55-57; Catlgr & circ asst Bridgeport (Conn) Pub Lib 57-58; Catlgr Ferguson Lib, Stamford Conn 58-61; Catlgr Union Col Lib, Schenectady NY 61-64; Catlgr Worcester Polytech Inst Lib 64-67; Catlgr UMass 67-. 9: ALA. 10: Phi Beta Kappa. 13: Yes. 14: Catlg. 15: 362C Northampton rd, Amherst Ma 01002.

MOELLER, PEARL L. b New Haven Conn. 5: Mount Holyoke Col 34-38 (Sociol) BA (Honors); William & Mary Col 38-40 (Fine Arts) BFA. 6: Fr, Sp. 7: Museum of Modern Art, NYC: Sec in film lib Latin Amer Program 41-44, Asst in charge negatives & slides 44-54, Supv photographic serv 54-59, Supv rights & reproductions (dept head) 59-69, Supv special collections 69-. 9: SLA (chm NY Chap Picture & Museum Div 59-60). 13: Yes. 14: Fine arts, photographic reproductions, spec collections lib, rights of reproduction. 15: Museum of Modern Art 11 W 53rd st, New York NY 10019.

MOEN, LOUISE (FREDRICSON). b Soldier Iowa 20 Je 07. 5: Des Moines U 27-29 (Educ); UOmaha 45-53 (Educ); Lewis & Clark 57-60 (Educ) BS; UPortland 63-66 MLS. 7: Tchr: Valley Pub Schs, Valley Neb 52-53, N Platte Schs, N Platte Neb 53-57, District #48, portland Ore 57-60, Dist #1, Portland Ore 60-65; Libn Dist #48, Beaverton Ore 66-67; Tchr Dist IJ, Scappose Ore 67-68; Libn Dist IJ, Scappose Ore 68-. 9: ALA; NEA-DAVI; OreASchL. 10: AAUW. 14: Elem sch libs. 15: 14205 SW Jenkins rd #40, Beaverton Or 97005.

MOEN, BARBARA J (STRATTON). b Springfield Mass 26 Ag 32. 4: Clifford H Moen. 5: Simmons 50-54 (LS) BS, 54-56 (Psychiatric Soc Wk) MS; UMinn 67-68 (Sch Lib Wk) MA. 6: Fr. 7: Br child libn Springfield Mass Pub Lib summers 54-56; Circ Wheelock Col 54-56; Bibliog div UMinn(Minneapolis) 57; Sch libn Minneapolis Pub Lib 57-59; Bkmob libn Dakota-Scott Reg Lib, W St Paul Minn 60-61, Br libn 61-67; Jr High Lib Hastings Minn Sch Syst 68-. 9: MinnASchL. 10: Clear Air, Clear Water. 14: Child wk. 15: Rt 2, Hastings Minn 55033.

MOENCKMEIER, ANNA LOUISE (HUNT). b Des Moines Iowa 22 Jl 24. 4: Ernest O Moenckmeier. 5: Burlington Jr Col 43-44; Coe 44-46 (Soc sci) BA; UIll 52-53 MSLS. 7: Tchr high sch, Buck Creek Iowa 46-47; Libn Burlington High & Tr Co, Burlington Iowa 47-52; Hd circ dept Cedar Rapids Pub Lib, Cedar Rapids Iowa 53-59; Asst libn Pub serv Elec & Gas Co, Newark NJ 59-. 9: ALA; SLA; NJLA; IowaLA (past sec). 10: Phi Kappa Phi; Beta Phi Mu. 14: Adult serv, ref, govt, docs, catlg. 15: 55 E Park st, E Orange NJ 07017.

MOFFAT, EDWARD STEWART III. b Pasadena Cal 19 Jl 23. 5: Stanford U 45-47 (Hist) BA, MA; Columbia 53-54, 59-63 (LS, Hist) MS, PhD. 6: Fr. 7: Tch asst hist UWash 47-48; Instr hist Everett Jr Col 48-49; Instr hist Glendale Col 49-51; Instr hist MIT 52-53; Lib trainee NY Pub Lib (Riverside Br) 53-54; Libn tchrs Central Lab Hunter Col Lib 54-59; Instr hist CCNY 58-60; Asst libn Tchrs Col Columbia U 60-64; U libn Ohio Wesleyan U 64-66; Assoc Prof Grad Lib Sch LIU 66-. 9: ALA; -LED (rep to ALA Mem Com); AHA; NYLA; NY Lib Club. 10: Kiwanis. 14: Hist of libs, col lib admin. 15: Grad Lib School Long Island Univ, Greenvale NY 11548.

MOFFAT, HELEN (MOORE). b Garland Utah 26 Ap 17. 5: Weber Col 38-40 (Eng); UUtah 40-42 (Eng) BA; Ariz State U 48-55 (Educ) MA; UDenver 55-58 (LS) MA. 6: Sp. 7: Eng chr Wever High Sch, Ogden Utah 43-48; Eng tchr Mesa High Sch, Mesa Ariz 48-55; Guest instr UUtah 60; Guest instr Ariz State U 58-59; Head Libn Mesa High Sch, Mesa Ariz 55-62; Head Libn Westwood High Sch, Mesa Ariz 62-67; Dir lib serv The Church Col of Hawaii, Laie Ha 67-. 9: ALA; NEA; Ariz State LA(chm var coms); ArizEA (chm var coms); HawaiiLA. 10: Delta Kappa Gamma; Phi Kappa Phi. 14: Instr, reader guidance, catlg. 15: PO Box 113, Laie Ha 96762.

MOFFIT, INEZ (WALTON). b Alden Iowa 8 Je 06. 5: UNoIowa 24-28 (Eng) BA; UMinn 47-48 BLS; UDenver 49-50 (Educ) MA. 7: Libn Ellsworth Col 41-53; Asst Prof Ariz

StateU 53-. 9: ALA; ArizStateLA; SWLA (Ariz coun to SWLA). 10: Beta Phi Mu; Alpha Beta Alpha. 13: Yes. 14: Sch libs. 15: 523 W 13th st, Tempe Az 85281.

MOHAN, SAHOTA. b India 24 Ag 17. 4: Lajja Mohan. 5: Punjab U 33-37 (Econ) BA; Colo U 40-43 (Eng) MA; Penn U 43-46 (Eng) PhD; Toronto U 65-66 MLS. 6: Fr, Persian, Urdu, Hindi, Punjabi. 7: Asst pub dept Lippincott Publ Co, Phila 46-47; Chief ed March of India Govt of India, New DlXX India Govt of India, New Delhi 48-56; Eng specialist Bd of Educ, Kingston Ont 57-61; Libn UN & Intl Docs Queen's U 63-65, Sr ref libn 66-. 9: CanLA. 12: "Basic Hindustani" (43); "Modern One Act Plays" (New Delhi 55); Ed "March of India" (48-56); "Douglas Library Notes" (66-); "Factotum" (66-). 13: Yes. 14: Ref. 15: 36 Collingwood st, Kingston Ont Can.

MOHN, WALLACE D. b Buffalo NY 30 Ap 35. 4: Ruth Johnson. 5: UBuffalo 53-61 (Geog) BA; UKy 62-63 MSLS. 7: Asst libn ref dept SUNY(Buffalo) 65-66, Assoc libn Sci & Engring Lib 66-67; Lib trainee Bu Engring Lib 66-67; Lib trainee Buffalo & Erie Co Pub Lib, Buffalo NY 62, Jr libn Sci & Tech Dept 63-65, Sr libn II 67-. 9: Libns Assn Buffalo & Erie Co Pub Lib Syst (pres). 10: Phi Beta Kappa. 12: Co-auth "Selected Serials in Western New York" (66). 14: Catlg, ref. 15: 2904 Bowen rd, Elma NY 14059.

MOHRHARDT, CHARLES M(ARTIN). b Hubbardston Mich 3 Ag 04. 5: Mich State U 22-26 (Mechanical Engnr) BS; Columbia 27-28 (LS) BS; Wayne State U 56-57 (Mgt Seminar) Certif. 7: Stud asst Mich State U Lib 23-26; Engnr Exec Group Olds Motor Works,Lansing Mich 26-27; Chief Tech Dept Toledo (Ohio) Pub Lib 28-30; Chief TechDept Detroit Pub Lib 30-41, Assoc dir 41-67; Dir 67-. 8: Lib bldg consul Amer Mem Lib, Berlin; US Dept of State 51-52, 53;Freie Universitat Bibliothek, Berlin 51-52; Biblioteca Publica Piloto de MedellinColombia (UNESCO) 55 and for more than 50 pub libs in the US, 51-. 9: ALA (Coun 49-53, chm &/or mem 6 coms & sects 36-60); (chm Spec Com on Nat Def Serv 40-42); PLD (Lib Arch Com 53-54); SLA (pres Mich Chap 33-34); MichLA (chm &/or mem numerous coms); Engnr Soc of Detroit (chm Lib Com 40-52, 56-58). 10: Friends of the Detroit Pub Lib; Detroit Hist Soc; AAAS (Fellow); Kresge-HookerSci Lib Associates; Automotive Old Timers; Torch Club of Detroit. 11: Citation for lib bldg planning by Senate of Berlin, 54. 12: "Survey of Wright Field Tecnical Libraries (45); "Survey of Ford Motor Company Libraries (47); Co-auth "Industrial Research Service for the Metropolitan Detroit Area (47); "Survey of Springfeld (Mass) Public Library (50); "Building Remodeling Feasibility Study, San Francisco Public Library (64); "Central Library of Los Angeles (Cal) 13: Yes. 14: Admin,lib bldg planning, automation & data proc. 15: 3996 Lincoln dr, Birmingham Mich 48010.

MOISTER, JEAN GILBERT. b Pine Bliff Ark 8 F 15. 5: Rutgers 51-54 (Hist) AB; Emory 64 mln. 6: Fr. 7: Secondary sch tchr, elem sch libn, asst to coord of libs Atlanta Pub Schs 55-65; Lib development specialist Coun of So Mts, Beren Ky 65-66; Asst Prof div of libnship Emory U 66-. 9: ALA; SELA; GLA. 10: Rutgers Honor Society. 13: Yes. 14: Sch libnship. 15: 222 Rumson rd NE, Atlanta Ga 30305.

MOLINES, ISABEL MARY. b New Bedford Mass 20 S 07. 4: Angel P Molines. 5: Simmons 27-32 (LS) BS; Boston U 45-48 (Educ); Syracuse 50-51 (LS) MS. 6: Ger, Fr, Sp. 7: Spec catlgr Sch of Landscape Arch Harvard U 32; Gen asst New Bedford Pub Lib, New Bedford Mass 34-37; Tchr, Apponang RI 37-38; Tchr Standish Manor, W Bridgewater Mass 38-39; Tchr & head of lower sch Perkins Sch, Lancaster Mass 38-43; Tchr Training Sch, Elwyn Penn 43-44; Tchr-spec class, Turners Falls Mass 44-45; Tchr elem sch, Mattapoisett Mass 45-46; Tchr Training Sch, Vineland NJ 46; Libn & lib tchr Bd of Educ, Norwich Conn 46-47; Ref & circ Boston U Sch of Educ 46-48, Catlgr & assoc libn 48-50; Catlgr & assoc libn State Tchrs Col (Keene NH) 50; Sr stud asst Syracuse U 50-51; Catlgr Pub Lib, Bridgeport Conn 51-52; Sr catlgr Princeton U 52-54; Org research med lib Princeton Hosp, Princeton NJ 53-54; Head Libn Towanda Pub Lib, Towanda Penn 54-58; Ser libn Sch of Agric & Biol Sci Penn State U 58-59; Elem sch libn & lib tchr De La Warr Dist #47, New Castle Del 60-. 9: NEA; DelEA; DelLA; New Castle Co EA; DelASch L. 14: Catlg, sch libs. 15: 45 LaSalle ave, Wilmington Manor Gardens, New Castle De 19720.

MOLL, BONIFACE EDMUND. b Lawton Okla 13 O 08. 5: St Benedicts Col (Atchison Kan) 25-30 (Lat) AB; Columbia 37-38 (LS) MS, 38-39 (LS) MS; US Army Chaplain Sch (Cambridge Mass) 43 Basic Course; US Army Chaplain Sch (Carlisle Bks Penn) 48 Assoc Basic Course; US Army Chaplain Sch (Ft Slocum NY) Off Adv Course. 6: Lat. 7: Asst libn St Benedict s COL (Atchison Kan) 30-37, Libn 39-43; Chaplain (Maj) US Army India, China, Burma 43-46; Libn St Benedicts Col (Atchison Kan) 46-48; Libn US Army Chaplain Sch (CARLISLE Bks Penn) 48-50; US Arm: Chaplain (Lt Col), Germany 50-53, Korea 54-55, Ft Polk La 56, 4th US Army 57-59, Hawaii 60-63, Ft Sill Okla 63-65, Chaplain (Col) Ft Sill Okla ret; Dir of relig educ (GS-7) Ft Sill, Okla 66-. 8: Reorg & recatgd Libat US Army Chaplain Sch, Carlisle Barracks Penn 48-50; Ordained Priest, 33. 9: ALA; CathLA; KanLA. 10: Prot-Cath-Jewish Chaplain Team rep Nat Coun Christs & Jews; Mem St Benedict's Abbey, Atchison Kan. 13: Yes. 14: Relig educ, texts, journals & films. 15: PO Box 1583, Lawton Ok 73502.

MOLL, WILHELM. b Vienna 2 Je20. 4: Margot W Weith. 5: Denison U 40-43 (Hist) BA; Chicago 43-45 (Law) JD; Catholic U 52-56 MS in LS. 6: Ger, Fr. 7: Pol Off War & State Depts, Germany 45-51; Research assoc War Documentation Proj, Alexandria Va 51-55; Asst documents libn Ind U Lib 56-60; Asst med libn UKy Med Center 60-62; Med libn & assoc prof of Preventive Med UVa Med Sch 62-. 9: ALA; MedLA (chm Wash DC Reg Group 65-66; VaLA. 10: Amer Assn Hist Med; Phi Beta Kappa. 13: Yes. 14: Med hist & edu, internat cultural affairs, med econ, pub health. 15: 2217 Greenbrier dr, Charlottesville Va 22901.

MOLLER, JOHN JOSEPH. b Jersey City NJ 25 Je28. 4: Michiko Watanabe. 5: UColo 53-56 (Geog) BA; Rutgers (LS) MA. 6: Fr, Ger. 7: Tech asst NY Pub Lib 48-50; US Army Parachutist (Pfc) 50-52; Sr lib asst Elizabeth Free Pub Lib, Elizabeth NJ 56-59, Sr libn ref 59-60; Assoc libn UColo Law Lib 60-65; Law Libn Col Cl of State Trial Judges, Reno Nev 65-. 9: AALL. 14: Ref. 15: Nat Col of State Trial Judges UNev, Reno Nv 89507.

MOLLESON, MARIANNE (BUCZKOWSKI). b Milwaukee Wis 27 F 30. 4: Lester L Molleson. 5: MarquetteU 46-50 (Eng, Philos) PhB; UWis 51-52 (Eng), 65-67 MSLS. 7: Asst ref libn pub lib, W Allis Wis 57-66, Hd catlg dept 66-67; Dir libn Cudahy Pub Lib, cudahy Wis 68-. 8: Tech Adv Com SEast Wis Reg Planning Commsn's Comprehensive Lib planning Program 68-. 9: WisLA. 10: Milwaukee Area Lib Bds Assn; Bus & Prof Women's Club. 14: Pub lib admin, ref. 15: 3965 E Dale ave, Cudahy Wi 53110.

MOLNAR, JOHN EDGAR. b Cincinnati 12 S42. 5: William & Mary 60-64 (Hist) BA; UMich 64-65 AMLS; URichmond 66-68 M Humanities. 7: Asst period dept, Lib William & Mary 61-63; asst Catlg Dept 63-64;libn Kelsey Museum of Archael UMich 65; Asst libn Longwood Col 65. 10: Beta Phi Mu; SAR; Assn Preserv Va Antiqs; Confed Hist Soc (Gt Brit). 14: Catlg, bibliog, music libnship. 15: 900 High st, Farmville Va 23901.

MOLOD, SAMUEL E. b Trenton NJ 27 Ag21. 4: Hannabelle Heller. 5: LIU 39-43 (Hist) BS; Clark U 45-46 (Hist)MA; UMich 47-52 (Hist) 52-53 (LS) MALS. 6: Fr, Ger. 7: (S/Sgt) Intelligence US Army, Italy 43-45; Bk buyer Wahrs Book Store, Ann Arbor Mich 47-53; Tchg Fellow UMich 47-52; Instr East Mich U 49-5; Asst Pub Lib, Ann Arbor Mich 52-53; Consul Mich State Li, Escanaba Mich 5362; Dir James V Brown Lib, Williamsport Penn 62-66; Assoc state libn Conn State Lib 66-. 8: Consul, Surveys, Mifflin Co (Penn) Lib 64; Tchr Lib Sci UMich Ext 55-62, UOkla summrs 55-57, Peabody Col summer 65, Penn State U 62-66, So Conn State Col summers & ext 67-. 9: ALA; PennLA (2 coms, Chap pres, Sect chm); NELA (chm Ext Libns); ConnLA. 14: Pub lib admin, ext wk. 15: 47 Huntington dr, West Hartford Ct 06117.

MOLONEY, LOUIS C. b Trenton NJ 26 N20. 4: Doris Lee Pettit. 5: Trenton (NJ) State Col 38-42 (Hist, Eng) BS in Educ, summers 39-40, 47-48 BLS; Chicago 49-50 (LS); Tex Col of Arts & Inds 55-58 (Eng, Hist) MS in Eng; Columbia 61-(LS). 7: Aviation Radio Tech 1/c US Nvy 42-46; Head libn Bishop Mem Lib, Toms River NJ 47-50; Head Libn Trenton Jr Col 51-52; Asst libn Tex Col of Arts & Ind 52-64; Assoc libn Southwest Tex State Col 64-65, Head Libn 65-, Assoc Prof 65-. 8: Lib Consul for Welder Wildlife Found, Sinton Tex 58-61. 9: ALA; TexLA (Publ Chm 55-56; Program Chm & Chm of Dist 4); Coun State (Tex) Col Libns. 12: Comp "Union List of Scientific Serials in The Corpus Christi Area (3rd ed 61). 13: Yes. 14: Admin, ref, lib coop. 15: 616 Conway dr, San Marcos Tex 78666.

MOLOSO, PHILLIP J III. b Colville Wash 1 S 36. 5: Reed Col 55-59 (Liberal Arts) BA; UWash 58 (Liberal Arts); Yale 59-63 (Anthropology, Linguistics); UDenver 64-65 (LS) MA; U New Mex 59 (Az Stud) 65-. 6: Fr, Ger, Sp, Papiamentu, Gk.

7: Reed Col Scholarship Fellow Woodrow Wlson Found 59-60; Fellow Yale U 60-61, Grad asst 59-61; Fellow Amer Coun of Learned Socs 61-62; Fellow NIH 63; Clerk Phoenix Pub Lib 64; Grad research asst UDenver 64-65; Libn Glendale Commun Col 65-66; Acquis libn 66-68, Dir lib tech servMaricopa Co Jr Col Dist 68-. 9: ALA; Salt River LA; ArizStateLA. 14: Acquis, ref, catlg, automation. 15: 9251 N 35th dr, Phoenix Az 85021.

MOLTON, ERNA (HOPIN). b NYC 10 Mr23. 4: Lewis Molton. 5: Trenton State Col 41-45 (Bus Educ) BS; Rutgers 59-60 MLS. 6: Fr, Sp. 7: Sec Trenton State Col Lib 45, Various positions to head Receiving sect Preparation iv NY Pub Lib 45-58; Libn Hubbard Jr High Sch, Plainfield NJ 60-. 9: NEA; NJSchLA. 10: Kappa Delta Pi; Phi Beta Nu. 14: Sch lib wk. 15: 43 Linden ave, Springield NJ 07061.

MOLZ, JEAN-BARRY. b Baltimore 11 O 26. 5: Johns Hopkins 44-48 (Hist) BS; Drexel 49-50 MS in LS. 7: Enoch Pratt Free Lib, Baltimore; Jr asst 50-52, Sr asst 52-55, Admin asst 55-58, Exec asst to dir 58-63, Br libn 63-64; Assoc Dir Baltimore Co Pub Lib, Towson Md 64-. 9: ALA; MdLA (Rec sec 62-66). 14: Ref, admin, pub libs. 15: 4 E 30 st apt 306, Baltimore Md 21218.

MOLZ, REDMOND KATHLEEN. b Baltimore 5 Mr28. 5: Johns Hopkins 45-49 (Eng) BS, 49-50 (Eng) MA; UMich 52-53 MA in LS. 6: Fr. 7: Libn I Enoch Pratt Free Lib, Baltimore 53-54, Libn II 54-56; TV spec Free Lib of Phila 57-58, Pub rel off 58-63; Ed "Wilson Library Bulletin, Bronx NY 63-68; Chief lib planning & development br div of lib programs US Off of Educ 68-. 9: ALA (Jt Com on Reading Devel, Nomin Com 69-70, ALA/ABBC-70); LPRC (pres 67-68). 10: Phi Kappa Phi; UMich Sch of Lib Sci Alum Assn. 11: Leadership Training Award, Fund for Adult Educ 56-57. 12: Ed "Wilson Library Bulletin" (63-68); "Portraits in Print" distributed by Nat Educ, Television & Radio Assn. 13: Yes. 14: Pub libs, lib devel. 15: 700 7th st SW Apt 703, Wash DC 20024.

MONAGHAN, FLORENCE C (OGDEN). b Somerset Ky 7 My 05. 4: Patrick Monaghan. 5: Ohio wesleyan 22-25; UKy 26 (Eng) BA; Pratt 64-66 MLS. 6: Fr, Sp. 7: Asst Sunday ed "Louisville Herald-Post", Louisville Ky 27-29; Child libn Harrison Pub Lib, Harrison NY 66-. 9: ALA; NYStateLA; Westchester (NY) Lib Syst. 14: Ref, storytelling, bk talks. 15: 150 Theo Fremd ave, Rye NY 10580.

MONAHON, RUTH C. b Liverpool Ohio 3 Jl 19. 5: Greenville Col 37-41 (Biol, Modern Langs) AB; UPittsburgh 43, 45; USoCal 46-53, 55 MS in LS. 6: Fr. 7: Tchr Patton Twp Jr High, Turtle Creek Penn 42; Tchr Harbrack Union High Sch, Brackenridge Penn 42-45; Tchr Los Angeles Pacific Col 45, Libn 47-55; Pub serv & ser libn USoCal Sch of Med 55-68, Ref libn 68-. 9: MedLA; Med Lib Gp So Cal (treas 64-66). 10: Alpha Kappa Sigma; Beta Phi Mu; USoCal Med Fac Assn. 14: Ser, ref, rare bks. 15: 5619 Monterey rd apt 12, Los Angeles Ca 90042.

MONDELLO, OMAH H. b Colon Panama 7 Ja 25. 4: Anthony L Mondello. 5: Mater Dei Rome Italy 35-44 (Classical lyceum); Barnard 45-47 (Foreign area studies) BA; Catholic U 65-67 MSLS. 6: Ital, Sp, Fr. 7: Interpreter & sec to dir of clubs Amer Red Cross, Rome Italy 44-45; Exec trainee B Altman Dept store, NYC 47-48; Off wkr lib sci dept Catholic U 67, Asst libn humanities lib 67-. 8: Lib consul, Washington DC summer 67. 9: ALA (Recr Com); DCLA. 10: Internat Visitors Info Serv (Wash DC); Md Democ Assn. 14: Univ libs, mod langs, ref, admin, computer info ret. 15: 5608 Namakagan rd, Wash DC 20016.

MONDOLFO, VITTORIA. b Ancona Italy 14F 16. 4: Lucio F Mondolfo. 5: URome 32-38 (Chem) PhD. 6: Ital, Fr, Sp, Ger, Russian, Lat, Gk, Portu. 7: Asst libn Classics Lib UChicago 50-57, Libn Chem Lib 57-66; Lit sci Bristol Labs, Syracuse NY 66; Hd tech serv Hamilton Col (NY) 67-. 9: SLA (Ill Chap Memb Chm); ALA; NYLA. 14: Chf, lit searching, tech serv. 15: Hamilton College, Clinton NY 13323.

MONET, MARION (CRENSHALL). b Los Angeles 23 Ap 19. 4: Gilbert P Monet. 5: UKan 37-41 (Chem) BA; MIT 41-43 MS in Chem Engnr; Drexel 57-59 MS in LS; UDel 56-60 (Educ) M Ed. 6: Fr. 7: Jr engnr E I DuPont de Nemours, Wilmington Del 43-44; Jr engnr Manhattan Proj, Chicago & Oak Ridge Tenn 44-46; Lit Sci Sun Oil Co, Marcus Hook Penn 60-. 9: ACS; Amer Inst Chem Engrs; SLA; Soc Women Engrs. 10: Sports Car Club of Amer. 14: Lit searching, esp in chem engrg. 15: 727 Nottingham rd, Wimington Del 19805.

MONGER, GEORGE ANNE (McCUNE). b Houston 27 Je25. 4: Gene Clyde Monger. 5: Baylor U 42-46 (Eng) BA; West Res 46-47 BS in LS. 7: Order libn UTex 47-48; Ref libn Tyrrell Pub Lib, Beaumont Tex 48-50; Engnr libn Lamar State Col of Tech 51-52, Documents libn 59-. 15: 885 Heather lane, Beaumont Tex 77706.

MONHEIT, ALBERT. b Kan City Mo 6 Je23. 4: Linda Babbit. 5: LIU 46-49 (Eng) BS; Columbia 51-53 MLS. 7: Libn II Brooklyn Pub Lib 51-54; Dir of wk with child & young adults Greak Neck NY 54-62; Dir Wantagh Pub Lib, Wantagh NY 62-. 9: ALA; NY State LA; Nassau Co LA. 10: C of C; Wantagh Planning Com. 12: "Picnic in the Park, a juvenile (60). 13: Yes. 14: Pub lib admin. 15: Wantagh Pub Lib, 3366 Park ave, Wantagh NY 11793.

MONICAL, CAROL J. b Lodi Ohio 27 My 44. 5: Col of Wooster 62-66 (Pol Sci) BA; UMich 66-67 (LS) MA. 7: Ref & bus libn Arlington Co Pub Lib, Arlington Va 67-. 9: SLA; VaLA; DCLA. 14: Ref, bus. 15: 1111 Arlington blvd M411, Arlington Va 22209.

MONK, JOANNE (THOMPSON). b Carrsville Ky 6 Ap 31. 4: John Colburn Monk Jr. 5: Murray State Col 48-51 Span, L) BA; Peabody 51-52 (Span,LS) MA; Okla 65-68 MLS. 6: Sp. 7: Asst libn Southwestern State Col 52-54lLibn Labette Co Commun High Sch, Altamont Kan 5-57; Educ area Okla State U Lib summers 56, 57; Ref libn George Washington U Lib 57-61; Acquis libn Okla City U Lib 64-68; Supv of acquis Fairfax Co Pub Lib, Fairfax Va 68-. 9: ALA; VaLA. 10: Beta Phi Mu. 14: Acquis, ref. 15: 3949 Fairfax Sq, Fairfax Va 22030.

MONK, VIRGINIA KERR (SKINNER). b Brownwood Tex 15 Ap14. 5: Daniel Baker Col 31-34 (Eng) BA, (Speech) Diploma; Trinity U 32-33; UTex 34-35 (Eng) MA; Tex State Col for Women summers 38-42 BS in LS. 7: Libn Daniel Baker Col 42; Libn Spec Serv US Army, Camp Bowie Tex 42-46; Asst to libn Rice Inst 48; Catlg libn, head of tech serv Del Mar Col 58-. 9: ALA; TexLA; SWLA; Tex Reg Group Catlg & Clsfs (sec 64-65); Tex Jr Col TA;Del Mar Col EA. 10: AAUW. 14: Catlg. 15: 501 Coral pl, Corpus Christi Tex 78411.

MONKE, ARTHUR. b Regent N Dak 30 Mr 25. 4: Jytte Petersen. 5: Gustavus Adolphus 46-50 (Eng) BA; Columbia 54-58 MS in LS. 6: Fr. 7: USA 44-46; Libn Fallsburg Central Sch, Woodridge NY 54-58; Ref libn Colgate U 58-63; Asst libn Bowdoin Col 63-68, Libn 68-. 9: ALA; NELA; MeLA (pres 68-). 10: AAUP; Brunswick Pub Lib Assn. 13: Yes. 14: Acquis, catlg, admin. 15: 2 Page st, Brunswick Me 04011.

MONROE, HAROLD CHARLES. b Waterbury Conn 16 Ag10. 4: Frances Cronin. 5: Middlebury Col 28-32 (Chem) AB; Columbia 32-33 (LS) BS. 6: Fr, Sp, Ger. 7: Lib asst circ dept Sterling Mem Lib Yale U 37-40; Lib asst US Dept of State Lib 40-43; US Army 895th Chem Co Air Operations 43-46; Catlgr US Navy Dept Bur of Ordnance Tech Lib 46-50; Subj catlgr LC Tech Info Dv 50-52, Sr subj catlgr E European Accessions List 52-61, Subj catlgr Subj catlg div 61-68; Tech info spec, Nat Heart Inst, extramural programs,analysis & reports sect 68. 12: Comp "List of Subject Headings Used for Naval Ordnance," LC, Navy ResSect (52). 14: Catlg. 15: Apt 614 5101 River rd, Chevy Chase Md 20016.

MONROE, MABEL ESTHER. Sanford NC. 5: Winston-Salem State Col 36-40 (Elem Educ) BS; Temple 48 (Guidance); NC Col (Durham) 51-55 (LS) MLS; Caholic U 56 (LS). 7: Inspector Triumph Explosive, Elkton Md 43; Accuracy control clerk Montgomery Ward, Baltimore 44; Tchr Johnston Co Bd of Educ 45-60, Libn lib supv 61-. 8: Visting team So Assn Schs & Cols 63-64. 9: ALA; NEA; NC Tchrs Assn; NCLA. 14: Vertical file, ref, catlg. 15: 800 Leak ave, Sanford NC 27330.

MONROE, MARGARET ELLEN. b NYC 21 My14. 5: NY State Col for Tchrs (Albany) 33-35 (Eng) BA, 35-36 BS in LS; Columbia 38-39 (Eng) MA, 54-62 DLS. 6: Fr. 7: Readers adv NY Pub Lib 39-52; Dir Amer Heritage Proj ALA, Chicago 52-54; Asst Prof, Assoc Prof in Lib Serv Rut gers U 54-63; Prof Lib Sch UWis 63-, Dir 63-70. 9: ALA (Coun 68-; Com on Accred 65-);-ASD (pres 60-61); WisLA (chm IntelFreedom Com 64-65, chm Scholarships Com 65-66); AEAUSA. 10: AAUP; Altusa Club. 11: Fund sor Adult Educ Fellowship, 54-55. 12: "Alcohol Education for the Layman" (59); "Library Adult Education" (63). 13: Yes. 14: Reader serv, adult educ, lib educ. 15: 2620 Arbor dr, Madison Wis 53711.

MONROE, PAUL JORDAN. b Delaware Ohio 21 N 15. 4: Aline Virginia (Norenson). 5: Pasadena Jr Col 34-35 (Eng); UCLA 36-38 (Eng) BA, 39-40 (Eng); NYU 43-44 (Ger lang & area studies); USoCal 48-50 MSLS. 6: Ger, Fr. 7: Proofreader Ward Ritchie Press 40-41; S/Sgt USA, US & Europe 41-45;

Staff writer & ed Lorenz Pub Co, Dayton ohio 46; Hd tech report sect USN Rocket Test Sta, China Lake Cal 47-48; Humanities libn Cal Tech 50; Libn II USoCal 51-53; Libn II LA Co Lib 53-57; Catlg libn Lockheed Aeronautical Corp, Burbank Cal 57-58; Libn Belmont High Sch, LA 58-. 8: Mem Text Bk sel Com, Los Angeles City Schs 66-. 9: ALA; -ACRL; CalLA; CalSchLA. 14: Second libs, catlg. 15: Belmont High Sch 1575 W 2nd st, Los Angeles Ca 90026.

MONSMA, MARVIN EUGENE. b Jasper County Iowa 14 My 33. 4: Elaine Gross. 5: Calvin Col 52-57 (Eng) AB Gen; Mich StateU 59-61 (Secondary Educ) MA; UMich 65-67 MALS. 7: Tchr (jr high sch) Muskegon Christian Sch, Muskegon Mich 57-60; Tchr Grand Rapids Christian High Sch, Grand Rapids Mich 60-63; Amer lit speech & debate Unity Christian High Sch, Hudsonville Mich 63-65; Hd gen serv Calvin Col & Sem Lib 65-68, Asst dir libs 68; Lecturer lib sci UMich Ext (Grand Rapids) 69-. 8: Sch lib consul to Christian schs in grand Rapids Mich area 66-. 9: ALA; MichLA (chm Local Arrangements Com for Annual Conf 68). 13: Yes. 14: Tchg, lib admin, ref. 15: 1316 Dickinson st SE, Grand Rapids Mi 49507.

MONSON, DONALD M. b Minneapolis Minn 28 D 36. 4: K Joyce Watson. 5: UMinn (Minneapolis) 58-61 (Psych), 62-63 (Gen psych) BA, 66- (Pub admin); Rutgers 64-66 MLS. 6: Ger. 7: USN Communications Lt (jg) USN, Japan 54-57; Circ res libn Wis State U (River Falls) 66-67, Ref libn 67-68; Instr materials libn UMinn (Minneapolis) 68-. 9: ALA; NEA-DAVI; MinnLA; MinnEA; A-V Coordinators Assn Minn; Minn Adult Educ Assn (Prog Chm). 10: PTA. 13: Yes. 14: Automation (computer application in lib), a-v materials, ref. 15: 2008 Seabury ave S, Minneapolis Mn 55406.

MONTAGUE, ELEANOR ANN. b Phila Pa 24 S 41. 04. Richard Mark Montague. 5: UChicago 60-64 (Anthrop) BA, 64-67 (LS) MA. 7: Stud research asst UChicago Grad Lib Sch 64-66, law catlgr Law Sch summer 66, Chem libn 66-67; Research asst Stanford U Libs Automation Div 67-. 9: ALA; ASIS; CalLA. 11: NSF Grant UChicago 64-66. 14: Lib automation, info sci. 15: Stanford U Libs, Stanford Ca.

MONTAGUE, HENRY (STARBUCK) JR. b Starville Miss 12 My16. 5: Miss State U 34-38 (Bus Admin) BS; LSU 38-40 BS in LS; West Res summers 54-57 MS in LS. 6: Ger. 7: Catlgr Miss Dept of Archives & Hist, Jackson Miss 40; Asst libn Govt Documents Clemson U 41-43; Prof Asst tech dept Pub Lib, Bridgeport Conn 43-46; Fed govt serv, Wash DC 47-51; Ref libn Pub Lib, Columbus Ohio 52-54; Asst libn Heidelberg Col 54-63; Head catlg dept Va Polytech Inst 63-. 8: Bibliog Consul, Presidents Temporary Waler Policy Commsn. Wash DC 49. 9: VaLA. 10: 14: Catlg, acquis. 15: Box 276, Blacksburg Va 24060.

MONTANA, EDWARD J JR. b Jamaica Plain Mass 27 O 33. 5: Boston Col 51-53, 54-55 (Hist, Govt) BS; Georgetown U 53-54 (Foreign Serv); Boston Col 55-57 (Hist) MA; Simmons 58-62 (LS) MS. 6: Fr. 7: Boston Pub Lib: Pre- prof 57-60, Prof lib asst 60-61, Ref asst 61-64, Lib Publs off 64-69, Asst to reg admin East Mass Reg Lib Syst 69-. 8: Exec dir Nat Lib Week, Mass. 9: ALA; NELA; MassLA; Charles River Lib Club (treas). 12: Ed "Boston Pub Lib News"; Ed "Eastern Region News". 13: Yes. 14: Pub rel, reg systems, publ. 15: Boston Pub Lib, Copley Sq, Boston Ma 02117.

MONTAVON, ROBERT E. b Akron Ohio 6D 32. 4: Carolyn Bussan. 5: St Charles Col 51-55 (Philos) BA; Columbia U 59-62 (Educ) MA, 62-65 MS in LS. 7: US Army Sp/44th Armd Div, Germany 57-59; Asst sch libn & tchr Carroll High Sch, Wash DC 61-64; Ref libn Dayton & Montgomery Co Pub Lib, Dayton Ohio 64-65; Acquis libn Air Force Inst of Tech 65-66; Hd acquis UDayton 66-. 8: Mem, Task Force on Parochial Sch Consolidation, Dayton 68-69. 9: OhoLA. 10: Assumption Sch Bd; AAUP. 14: Ref, tech serv. 15: 1650 Ruskin rd, Dayton Ohio 45406.

MONTAVON, SISTER MARY JAMES PAUL BVM. b Maytown Ill 27 N05. 5: Clarke Col 25-43 (Math) BA; Rosary Col 45-49 BA in LS; Marquette U 52-53; UColo 56-57; Queens Col 66. 7: Tchr Our Lady of Victory, Waterloo Iowa 28-30; Tchr Immaculte Conception, Rapid City SD 30-38; Tchr St Patrick Sch, Lead SD 38-42; Lib asst St Mary High Sch, Chicago 42-45; Tchr St Joseph Acad, Dubuque Iowa 45-47; Tchr-libn St Dorothy, Chicago 47-51; Libn St Joseph Acad, Des Moines Iowa 51-55; Libn Mt St Gertrude Acad, Boulder Colo 55-. 9: ALA; CathLA. 15: 845 Tenth st, Boulder Colo 80302.

MONTEE, MONTY L. b Newton Kan 3 Mr 38. 5: UWichita 56-58 (Piano, Mus educ); UKan 58-62 (Mus hist) BM; UMich 62-63 MLS. 6: Fr, Ger. 7: Asst catlg libn Cornell U 63-66; Asst hd des cath div Yale U 66-67; Hd catlgr Yale Med Lib 67-. 9: ALA; MusLA; NY State Tech Serv Libns. 14: Catlg, tech serv, admin. 15: 12 Court, New Haven, Ct 06511.

MONTESINOS, MARY JANE (CURRY). b Fairmont W Va 16 My 19. 4: Miguel J Montesinos. 5: W Va U 37-41 (Chem) BA; Ga Inst of Tech 64-65 (Info sci). 6: Fr, Sp. 7: Chem Celanese Corp of Amer, Cumberland Md 41-42; Chem Tenn Corp research & development, college Park Ga 56-64, Libn 62-68; Scientist libn Ga Inst of Tech 68-. 9: SLA. 13: Yes. 14: Ref. 15: 4155 Lesley dr, College Park Ga 30337.

MONTGOMERY, BEATRICE. b Knoxville Tenn 4 Ja19. 5: UTenn 35-36; Randolph-Macon Womans Col 36-39 (Eng) AB; Emory 43-44 AB in L; UNC 53-57 MS in LS. 6: Fr, Russian. 7: Sch libn Knoxville Pub Sch, Knoxville Tenn 44-48; Catlgr Kingsport Pub Lib, Kingsport Tenn 49-52; Asst catlg dept UNC(Chapel Hill) 52-58; Head catlgr Baylor U 58-59; Had Head Ga State Col 59-60; Asst catlg dept UCal(Davis) 61-63; Asst acquis UNC(Chapel Hill) 63-66, Hd catlg maintenance 66-67, Hd catlgdept 67-. 9: ALA; SELA; NCLA. 14: Catlg, acquis. 15: 90 Hamilton rd, Chapel Hill NC 27514.

MONTGOMERY, CHRISTOPHER (TRUMP). b Buffalo NY 29 Mr31. 4: Ruth Shimony. 5: Swarthmore Col 49-53 (Psych) BA; Princeton 55-58 (Music) MFA; Pratt 58-60 MLS. 7: Music catlgr Brooklyn Col 60-64; Music & art catlgr Wesleyan U (Middletown Conn) 64-. 9: MusLA. 14: Catlg (music). 15: Oln Lib Wesleyan U, Middletown Ct 06457.

MONTGOMERY, EDWARD B(ENJAMIN). b Louisville Ky 15 Je15 . 4: Mary Louise Lynch. 5: ULouisville 33-35, 37-39 (Physics) BA. 6: Ger. 7: Gen Electric Co; Info spec Hanford Atomic Prod Oper, Richland Wash 53-56, Manager Systems Analysis Computer Dept, Schenectady NY 56, Manager Systems Analysis Computer Dept, Phoenix 56-57, Prod Planning Consul, Phoenix 57-59, Consul Physicist Computer Dept, Phoenix 59-61, Proj Engnr Syracuse NY 61-63; Research consuSyracuse U 63-65, Dean Lib Sch 65-68, U Prof info sci & dir Florence Bioinformation Ctr UTex Southwestern Med Sch (Dallas) 68-. 9: Amer Phys Soc; Inst of Electric & Electron Engnrs. 10: AAAS. 14: Info sci. 15: 6720 Greenwich lane, Dallas Tx 75230.

MONTGOMERY, GOLDIE GREIG. b Ville Platte La 2 My20. 4: Thomas W Montgomery. 5: Southwestern La Inst 36-38, 49-51 (Elem Educ) BA; LSU summers 51-54 (LS) MS. 6: Fr. 7: Prim tchr Acadia Parish Sch Bd, Crowley La La; Prim tchr E Baton Rouge Parish, Baton Rouge La; Iberia Parish Lib, New Iberia La 2-53; Sch libn Plaquemines Parish Sch Bd, Buras La 53-54; Head Libn St Tammany Parish Lib , Covington La 54-59, 62-63; Asst Prof LS Southeastern LA Col 65-. 9: ALA; SLA. 14: Ref, catlg. 15: Rt 2 Box 10E, Hammond La 70401.

MONTGOMERY, HELEN KATHERINE (GIBLER). b Topeka Kan 30 Mr13. 4: Paul Jarboe Montgomery. 5: UMo 31-35 (Journalism) BJ; Rutgers 57-60 MLS. 7: Asst dir Fanwood Mem Lib , Fanwood NJ 57-61, Dir 61-64; Dir Piscataway Twp Libs, Piscataway NJ 64-67; Dir Free Pub Lib, Berkeley Heights NJ 67-. 9: ALA; NJLA (sec 67-68). 10: Rutgers Alumni Fed Bd of Governors. ; Alum Assn, Grad Sch of Lib Serv, Rutgers U; AAUW; Bus & Profess Women. 13: Yes. 14: Admin, ref. 15: 290 Plainfield ave, Berkeley Heights NJ 07922.

MONTGOMERY, HUGH. b Cambridge Mass 10 Je 11. 4: Elizabeth Beal. 5: Harvard 30-34 (Amer Govt & Amer Colonial Hist) BS; Columbia 38-39 BS in LS, 40-42, summers 47, 48. 7: Ref asst info div NY Pub Lib 39-40, Econ div 40-42; T/4 US Army Field Artillery 42-45; Asst in chg of Gift Exch Sect Harvard Col Lib 46; Asst ref libn Baker Lib Harvard Grad Sch of Bus Admin 46; Sr asst Harvard Col Lib & Asst libn in chg of Grad Sch of Pub Admin Lib, Harvard U 46-52; Libn UMass 52-67; Assoc lib Wentworth Inst, Boston 67-68; Acquis lib Southeastern Mass Tech Inst 68-. 9: ALA (Com on Pub Docs 49-55);-ACRL (sec Law & Pol Sci Subsect SSS 67-70);-RSD;-RTSD; AALL; SAA; SLA (Sci-Tech Div, Geog & Maps Div, Engring Div; Dir Boston Chap 68-70); BSA; MassLA (Com on Intel Freedom 57-60). 10: Hist Assn (London); Assoc John Carter Brown Lib; Appalachian Mountain Club; Crown Point Road Assn; Organ, Amer Histns; Amer Assn State & Loc Hist; West Hist Assn; Old Dartmouth Hist Soc; Mass Archaeol Soc; Map Circle (London); Flintshire Hist Soc (Wales); Cumberland & Westmoreland Hist Soc (UK). 13: Yes. 14: Admin, catlg, acquis, Govt publ, maps, law, pub admin. 15: 174 Rockland st, S Dartmouth Ma 02748.

MONTGOMERY, ISABELLA. b NYC 20 O 19. 4: James L Montgomery. 5: Wellesley 37-41 (Psych) BA; Columbia 64-67 (LS) MS; Montclair State Col 68 NJ educ certif. 6: Fr. 7: Correspondent Amer Bk Co, NYC 41-42; Engine tester Wright Aeronautical, Patterson NJ 43-44; Libn Ridgewood Pub Schs, Ridgewood NJ 67-. 9: ALA. 15: 494 Hanks ave, Ridgewood NJ 07450.

MONTGOMERY, JAMES HOUSTON. b Greensboro NC 22 O 30. 4: Lois Lee. 5: Guilford Col 49-53 (Span) BA; UNC 55-57 (Romance Lang) MA; UCLA 57-59 (Romance Lang); Peabody 62-63 MA in LS. 6: Sp, Fr, Portu, Ital. 7: Tchr Boydton High Sch, Boydton Va 53-54; Tchr Escuela Eugenio Maria de Hostos, PR 54-55; Tchg asst UNC (Chapel Hill) 55-57; Tchg asst UCLA 57-59; Asst Prof Carson-Newman Col 59-60; Asst Prof Bloomsburg State Col, Penn 60-61; Bibliog & catlgr Jt U Lib, Nashville 64-66; Asst hd tech serv UCal (Irvine) 66-67; Hd tech serv Rutgers U 67-68; SrLat Amer & Catlgr UFla 68-. 8: Consul to Nat Univ of Colombia, Feb 69, Ford Found. 9: ALA; SELA. 10: Beta Phi Mu. 13: Yes. 14: Catlg, bibliog. 15: 2120 E Univ ave apt 1, Gainesville Fl 32601.

MONTGOMERY, MARY (ELLA). b Detrot 6 D 25. 5: Wayne U 44-48 (Hist, Govt) AB; UMich 50-51 MALS. 7: Bkmob libn Dearborn Pub Lib, Dearborn Mich 50-56; Ref libn Gen Motors Research Labs, Warren Mich 56-62; Corp libn Burroughs Corp, Detroit 63-66; Research libn Eaton Yale & Towne Inc Research Ctr 67-. 9: SLA (Metals/Materials Dir; Fall chm 65-68; Mich Chap; pres 61-62, chm ProgCom 59-60, chm Union List 63-64, chm Recr Com 65-66, chm By-laws Com 67-68, chmNomin Com 68-69, chm Regis Com 70; many com memberships. 10: Walnuts & Wine Club; Philosophical Com. 14: Ref, admin. 15: Eaton Yale & Towne Inc, Research Ctr Lib, 26201 Northwestern hwy,Southfield Mi 48075.

MONTGOMERY, MILDRED CARTER. b Parkin Ark 28 D 15. 5: Ark State Col 34-37 (Eng) AB; UArk 56-58 (Zool) MA; UIll 58-59 MSLS. 6: Fr. 7: Catlgr & Instr in Lib Sci Ark State Col 59-63; Catlgr Memphis State U Lib 63-, Head Catlgr 65-. 9: ALA; TennLA; SELA. 14: Catlg, tchg (lib sci). 15: 646 Graham, Memphis Tenn 38111.

MONTGOMERY, PAULA KAY. b Omaha Neb 23 S 46. 5: Fla State U 64-67 (Eng, LS) BA, 68 (LS) MS. 6: Sp. 7: Sch libn Montgomery Co Pub Schs, Rockville Maryland 69-. 9: ALA; NEA; Montgomery Co (Md) SchLA; Montgomery Co (Md) EA. 14: Sch libs (reading guidance). 15: 856 College pkwy apt T-2, Rockville Md 20850.

MONTWILL, MARIA (HUSZCZA). b Wilno Poland 13 Je 10. 5: U Fribourg (Switzerland) 29-30 (Fr Lit); Rensselaer Polytech Inst even 52-55; Russell Sage Col even 62. 6: Polish, Fr, Ger, Russian, Lithuanian. 7: Sec-interpreter UNRRA, Landshut Germany 45-47; Co-ed "Kronika. weekly, Frankfurt/M Germany 47-49; Sec-interpreter WRS - NCWC, Frankfurt/M Germany 49-50; Typist Behr-Manning, Troy NY 51; Asst libn Behr-Manning Div Norton Co, Troy NY 51-55, Libn 55-. 9: SLA; ASIS. 14: Indexing. 15: 17 Summit ave, Troy NY 12181.

MONTY, MARY I (QUINN). b Ottawa Can 9 Ap 10. 4: Gerard Monty. 5: UToronto 27-31 (Modern lang) BA; Ontario Col of Educ 31-32 (High sch); MacDonald Col 65-66 Tchr & libn certif. 6: Fr, Sp. 7: Tchr Sudbury Ont High Sch 32-37; Fr specialist Ottawa Nepean high Sch 37-39; Sp tchr adult educ High Sch Com, Ottawa 43-44; Tchr Bishop Whelan High Sch, Lachine Can 60-64, Libn 64-. 9: CanLA; QueLA. 10: Can Fed Univ Women; Montreal coun of Women; UToronto Alumnae. 14: Ya reading (gist & biog). 15: 249 Clement ave, Dorval Que Can.

MOODY, KENNETH E. b Nashville Ark 6 Ap 35. 5: Mich StateU 53-57 (Art/Eng) BA; Eastern michU 61-62 (Educ); UMich 63-66 MALS. 6: Fr. 7: Admin asst US Army, USA, Korea, Japan 57-60; Lib asst (catlg) UMich (Ann Arbor) 60-61, Lib asst (order) 61-63, supervisor (admin) 63-64, Libn (med) 64-66; Hd ref dept Lib of Sci and Med RutgersU (New Brunswick) 68-. 9: MedLA (NY Reg Group). 14: Ref, bk selection, hist of med. 15: 10 Landing lane #1F, New Brunswick NJ 08901.

MOODY, MARGARET (MAE). b Rochester Minn 16 My 18. 5: UMinn 35-38 (Eng, Foreign Lang) BA, 38-39 BS in LS. 6: Fr, Ger, Ital, Lat, Sp, Portu, Russian, Turkish, Old Eng. 7: Catlgr Minneapolis Pub Lib 39; Catlgr Bismarck Pub Lib, Bismarck ND 40-41; Asst libn Harvard U Law Lib 42-. 9: AALL; ALA; SL; SLA; NE Law Libns; NELA; MassLA. 13: Yes. 14: Catlg. 15: 17 Prince ave, Winchester Mass 01890.

MOODY, MYRTLE A(NNETTE). b Rochester Minn 9 My 15. 5: UMinn 37 (LS) BS. 6: Fr, Sp. 7: Steno Chamber of Com, Rochester Minn summer 33-34; Bkkeeper Olmsted Co Bank & TRUST Co, Rochester Minn summer 3-36; Reviser UMinn Lib Sch (Minneapolis) summer 37; In chg order wk UMinn Law Lib (Minneapolis)37-42; Head of acquis dept Harvard Law Sch Lib 43-. 9: ALA; AALL; Internat Assn Law Libs; Law Libs of NE. 10: Bd Dirs Harvard U Employees Credit Union. 13: Yes. 14: Tech processing. 15: 17 Prince ave, Winchester Mass 01890.

MOODY, PAULINE (MARIE). b Waterbury Vt 16 My 01. 5: Boston U 22-24 (Eng)B Sec Sci; McGill 35-36 BLS. 7: Head Libn Waterbury Pub Lib, Waterbury Vt 25, 30-37; Head Libn Fletcher Mem Lib, Ludlow Vt 37-42; Head, ref & wk with schs, Geo Bruce Br NY Pub Lib 42; Head Libn Springfield Town Lib, Springfield Vt 42-51; Dir Pleasantville Pub Lib, Pleasantville NY 51-57; Instr in lib UNH summer 56; Dir Bay Shore Pub Lib, Bay Shore LI NY 58-63; Libn Waterford Pub Lib, Waterford Conn 64-65; Maine Hist Soc Lib 66-68; Catlg private sch& home libs 69-. 8: Mem Adv Bd 62 Congress for Libns, St JOHNS Univ; Lib consul Eaglebrook Sch, Deerfield Mass 64-65. 09: VtLA (pres 34); Better Library Movement of Vt (sec 34-44); Suffolk Co LA (v-pres, pres, dir 59-63); NYLA (dir Adult Serv Sect 61). 10: Vt Fed of Womens Clubs; Vt Congress of Parents & Tchrs; League Vt Writers. 12: "Vermonts School Children Need More Library Service" (45), suppl withBarbara Douglas (51); "Come and Get it at Your Public Library". 13: Yes. 14: Ref. 15: Sheraton-Eastland Motor Hotel, Portland Me 04101.

MOODY, ROLAND HERBERT. b Manchester NH 17 Jl 16. 4: Ethel Corwin. 5: Dartmouth 34-38 (Econ) AB; Columbia 40-41 BLS. 7: Asst reserve desk Dartmouth Col Lib 38-39; Asst ref & circ libn Middlebury Col Lib 39-40; Gen asst Harvard Col Lib 41-43; (Sgt Maj) 3rd Bn 86th Mtn Inf 10th Mtn Div 43-45; Keeper of collections Harvard Col Lib 46-48; Circ libn Lamont Lib Harvard Col 48-53; Dir Northeastern U Lib 53-. 9: ALA; MassLA. 10: Deacon First Congregational Church, Winchester Mass. 11: Bronze Star Italian Campaign 45. 14: Mgt. 15: 11 Crescent rd, Winchester Mass 01890.

MOOMAW, JUDITH ANNE. b Lincoln Neb 27 O 39. 5: UNeb 57-61 (Fr) BA; UMich 64-65 MALS. 6: Fr, Ger. 7: Jr libn Love Mem Lib UNeb 61-62, 63-64; Ref libn UOre Lib 65-66, Asst ser catlgr 66-67; Ref libn Hofstra U Lib 67-69; Catlgr Stanford ULib 69-. 9: ALA; Nassau Co LA; NY Lib Club. 10: Sierra Club. 11: Chi Omega; Alpha Lambda Delta; Phi Sigma Iota. 14: Ref, catlg, child lit. 15: 451 Fulton ave Apt 606, Hempstead NY 11550.

MOOMAW, THELMA C. b Saluda SC 12 F 08. 4: W A Moomaw. 5: Converse Col 25-29 (Chem) BS, 62-63 (Chem); UCincinnati 29-31 (Chem) MS. 6: Ger, Fr. 7: Stud asst in chem Converse Col 27-29; Grad asst chem UCincinnati 29-31; Chem faculty Shenandoah Jr Col 31-34; Chemistry fac Richmond Prof Inst evening sch Richmond Va 51-54; Lit scientist research labs Amer Tobacco Co, Richmond Va 37-62; Libn (staff) UVa, Charlottesville Va 64-. 9: ACS; ASIS; Richmond-Hopewell SLA (chm gp). 14: Admin. 15: McKim Hall Box 2 Univ of Va, Charlottesville Va 22903.

MOON, ERIC (EDWARD). b Yeovil Eng 6 Mr 23. 4: Diana Mary Simpson. 5: Loughborough Col of Further Educ Sch of Libnship (England) 47-49 FLA. 6: Fr, Ger. 7: Asst Southampton Pub Lib, Southampton Eng 39-48; Area libn Hertfordshire Co Lib, Eng 49-51; Dist libn Finchley Pub Lib, Eng 51-54; Deputy borough libn & curator Brentford & Chiswick Pub Lib, Eng 54-56; Head of tech processes Kensington Pub Lib, Eng 56-58; Dir of pub lib serv & sec of pub libs bd, St Johns Newfoundland 58-59; Ed "Library Journal" NY 59-68; Dir R R Bowker Co, NY 65-67; Dir of ed development R R Bowker Co 69-. 8: Corr Course tutor, Assn Asst Libnship, London 52-54; Lecturer in Lib Display &Publ, Brit Army Inst of Educ, London 53-54; Examiner (Brit) Lib Assn 56-58. 9: ALA (Coun 67-70); Lib Assn UK (Coun 55-58); Can LA (Fed Aid Com 58-59, Compar Lib Educ Com 58-59; Pensions Com 59-60); Assn Asst Libns (Coun 53-58, sec 55-57, v-pres 58); NY Lib Club (Coun 61-64); LPRC (v-pres 64-65). 11: Savannah State Col Lib Award, 1966, for distinguished serv in Libnship. 12: "Pennsylvania Politics, 1872-1877: A Study of Political Leadership (66); "Modern Methods of Arrangement of Archives in the United States" (Coun Brussels 69). 13: Yes. 14: Bk sel, pub rel, bibliog, lib educ. 15: R R Bowker Co, 1180 Ave of the Americas, New York NY 10036.

MOON, MARTHA LOUISE (MORGAN). b Omaha Ga 23 N 30. 4: John Comer Moon. 5: Troy State U 55-60 (Eng) BS; Auburn U 60-64 (Educ in LS) MEd, 65 (LS). 7: Libn:

Crenshaw Co Bd of Educ, Luverne Ala 60-62, Barbour Co Bd of Educ, Louisville Ala 62-65, (Hd) Enterprise State Jr Col, Enterprise Ala 65-67, Muscogee Co Bd of Educ, Columbus Ga 67-68, Media Ctr Dothan City Schs, Dothan Ala 68-. 9: ALA; NEA; AlaEA (pres local gp); AlaLA; AlaSchLA; Ala Jr Col LA (sec). 10: Alpha Delta Kappa; Altrusa Club. 14: Admin, ref. 15: 504 Peachtree st, Headland Al 36345.

MOON, MYRA JO. b Emporia Kan 26 D 31. 5: UOkla 50-53 (Med Tec) BS Med Tech, 63-65 MLS. 7: MedTech St Johns Hosp, Tulsa Okla 54-60; Med Tech St Francis Hosp, Tulsa Okla 60-63; Asst catlg libn Colo State U 65-. 9: ALA; ColoLA. 14: Catlg. 15: 1412 Constitution, Ft Collins Co 80521.

MOONAN, WILLARD JAMES. b Portland Ore 23 Mr 34. 4: Jean Axtell. 5: UMinn 52-55, 58-59 (Psych) BA, 59-63 (Educ Psychol) MA, 66-69 (LS) MA. 7: Med tech US Army 55-57; Instr Col of Educ UMinn (Minneapolis) 62-63; Psychologist Independent Sch Dist #281, Robbinsdale Minn 63-69; Period libn Ill StateU (Normal) 69-. 14: Ref, bibliog. 15: Milner Lib Ill State Univ, Normal Il 61761.

MOONEY, HARRY J JR. b Hackensack NJ 18 F 22. 5: UTex 50-54 (Mus) BS (cum laude), 54-55 MLS. 7: Captain USAF, US & England 42-49; Libn I art & mus dept Denver Pub Lib 55-56, Libn II 56-58, Libn III & spec collections libn 58-63, Hd Park Hill Regional Br 64-65, Bk selection libn 65-. 9: ColoLA (chm Intell Freedom Com 68-70). 10: Beta Phi Mu. 14: Admin, rare bks. 15: 1601 Krameria st, Denver Co 80220.

MOONEY, SANDRA TAYLOR. b Wichita Kan 20 Je 43. 4: Rex Oliver Mooney Jr. 5: Ark StateU 61-65 Eng BSE; LSU 65-67 (LS). 7: Catlgr Ark State U Lib (Jonesboro) 67-68; Supv bk orders LSU Lib (Baton Rouge) 68-. 8: LSU Lib Exhibit Com: mem 68-69, chm 69, v-chm 70. 9: ALA; LaLA. 14: Tech serv, ref. 15: Box 16258 La State Univ, Baton Rouge La 70803.

MOONEY, THOMAS. b Pittsburgh 16 O 21. 4: Betty Jane Cox. 5: Findlay Col 4246 (Hist, Soc Sci) BA: Hartford Theol Sem 47-49 BD; Ohio State U 54-55; Portland State Col 59-60; UWash 60-61 (LS) ML. 6: Fr. 7: Minister First Congregational Church, Plainfield Conn 49-53; Minister N Congregational Church, Columbus Ohio 53-56; Minister First Community Congregational Chruch, Clackamas Ore 56-60; Head Libn Peninsula Col 61-66; Dir Learning Ctr Ft Steilacoom Commun Col 66-. 8: Mem, Governor's regional Lib Conf. 9: ALA; PNLA; Wash Commun Col LA; Tacoma-Pierce Co Lib Coun. 14: Ref, readers adv, acquis. 15: 11 Columbia Circle SW, Tacoma Wa 98499.

MOORACHIAN, ROSE. b Buffalo NY 21 D 29. 5: Simmons 47-51 (LS) BS; Northeastern U 62-67 (Hist) MA. 6: Fr, Armenian. 7: Asst Boston ub Lib 51-56, Young adults libn 56-62, Br libn 62-65, Readers adv for young adults 65-. 8: Reviewer, "Adult Books for Young People in "Library Journal 59-63; UNH Pub Lib Techniques, Lecturer in Porgrams & Serv for Young Adults 64. 9: ALA-YASD (chm Magazine Eval Com 65-68, chm Best Bks for YA Com 68-); MassLA (Exec Bd 56-59); Mass Round TABLE OF Libnsfor Young Adults (chm 56-59); Young Adult Coop Bk Review Group of Mass (Steering Com 65). 10: Womens Nat Bk Assn. 14: Young adult wk. 15: Boston Pub Lib Copley Square, Boston Ma 02117.

MOORE, ALICE C. b Sunbury Penn 9 Mr 18. 5: Bucknell U 36-40 (Eng) AB, 40-41 (Lit) MA; Columbia 41-42 BS in LS. 6: Fr, Ger. 7: Br asst Brooklyn Pub Lib, NY 42-46; Libn Sunbury High Sch, Sunbury Penn 46-47; Hd libn John R Kauffmann Jr Pub Lib, Sunbury Penn 47-53; Hd circ Osterhout Free Lib, Wilkes Barre Penn 53-57; Reader's adv Trenton State Co, Trenton NJ 57-58; Br hd Nicetown-Tioga Br Free Lib of Phila 58-62, Adult specialist off of wk with adults and ya Free Lib of Phila 62-. 9: ALA (Adult Serv Com on Lib Serv to an Aging Population 68-71); AEAUSA; PennLA (pasy pres Pub Lib Sect); Penn Assn Adult Educ; Adult Educ Coun of Phila. 10: YMCA; Acad Nat Sci; Phila Mus of Art. 14: Lib serv for the aging. 15: The Plaza 8M Parkway at 18th st, Philadelphia Pa 19103.

MOORE, ANN (MOSKOUIS). b Akron Ohio 21 Ap 27. 4: Clifford W Moore. 5: West Res 45-46; UAkron 47-49 (Hist, Eng) BA; West Res 49-50 MS in LS. 6: Fr, Ger, Modern Gk. 7: Libn Akron Pub Lib, Akron Ohio 50-56; Libn Shaker Heights Bd of Educ, Cleveland 56-58; Libn Cleveland Pub Lib 58-. 9: ALA; NEA; OhioLA. 10: LWV; YWCA; PTA; Women's Com Cuyahoga Commun Col. 14: Ref, yound adults, pub lib. 15: 3122 Standish ave, Cleveland Oh 44134.

MOORE, BESSIE B. b Owensboro Ky 2 Ag 02. 5: Ark State Tchrs Col BES: UConn MA. 7: County sch supv, Jefferson Co Ark 26-32; Staff Ark Dept of Educ 33-37; Supv of elem schs, N Little Rock Ark 37-42; Pres The Moores Cafeteria Inc, Little Rock Ark 42-58; State supv of elemeduc Ark Dept of Educ 58-; State co-ordinator of econ educ Ark Dept of Educ 61-. 8: Ark Lib Commsn 42-; Crusade for Freedom sponsored by Radio Free Europe, 61; US Com for UNICEF; Defense Adv Com on Women in the Servs 61-64; Guest of W German Republic, 64, as mem of com to evaluate Marshall Plan; Delegate to IFLA 64 & 65, 67. 9: ALA (Legis Com, Com for a Greater ALA);-ALTA (pres 57-59); Nat Assembly of Lib Trustees (chm 60 & 61); ArkLA. 10: Delta Kappa Gamma; Soroptomist Internat. 11: ALA Trustee Citation 54; Ark Woman of the Year 54; Hon doctorate in laws UArk 59. 13: Yes. 14: Trustee affairs & functions. 15: 1807 Battery st, Little Rock Ar 72202.

MOORE, BETTY ROSE. b Cincinnati Ohio 27 D 28. 5: UCincinnati 47-51 (Amer hist) BA; UTenn 64 (LS); Columbia 65-67 MSLS. 6: Sp. 7: Tchr & libn Friendsville Acad, Friendsville Tenn 63-64; Sub-prof Columbia U Med Lib 65-67; Libn Francis Delafield friendsville Tenn 63-64; Sub-prof Columbia U Med Lib 65-67; Libn Francis Delafield Hosp & Inst of Cancer Research of Columbia U 67-. 9: ALA; MeLA. 10: AAUW. 11: High honors in history. 14: Ref, bio-med lit. 15: 10 Bennett ave apt 6C, New York NY 10033.

MOORE, CAROLYN A. b Pittsburgh 18 Mr 39. 5: Thiel Col 57-61 (Hist) BA; Chicago 61-63 (LS) MA. 7: Asst ref libn Municipal Ref Lib, Chicago 63; Army libn Spec Serv US Army, Europe 63-66; Ref libn Municipal Ref Lib, Chicago 66-67, Asst libn 68-. 9: SLA; ASIS; AALL. 10: Beta Phi Mu. 14: Ref. 15: Rt 2 Box 145, Apollo Pa 15613.

MOORE, DAVID G. b Portland Ind 2 Jl 40. 5: Col Ida 58-62 (Hist) BA; USoCal 62-63 MSLS. 6: Fr, Ger. 7: Catlg libn Wardman Lib Whittier Col 63-66, Asst libn 66-69; (Sgt) Admin Man USMC Reserve 64-; Acquis libn UNevada (Las Vegas) 69-. 9: ALA; CalLA. 10: ACLU. 14: Catlg, acquis. 15: 1603 N Cogswell, El Monte Cal 91733.

MOORE, DAVID LEWIS. b Peking China 27 O 11. 4: Alice Wardwell. 5: Harvard 29-36 9eng) AB; George Washington 50-52 (Law) JD, 55 (Pol Sci) MA; National U 57 (Law) LLM. 6: Fr, Sp, Ger, Ital. 7: Asst libn intl rel George Washington U 52-56; Ref libn NYU Sch of Law 56-60; Libn Hastings Col of Law 60-. 13: Yes. 15: 198 McAllister st, San Francisco Ca 94102.

MOORE, DELIA GENE (MORGAN). b Philip S Dak 10 Ap 26. 4: Warren F Moore. 5: UMich 43-46 (Design) B of Design; SUNY (Albany) 65-68 MLS. 7: Ref libn Schenectady Co Pub Lib, Schenectady NY 66-67; Catlgr Union Col (Schenectady) 67-. 9: ALA. 14: Catlg. 15: 20 Puritan dr, Schenectady NY 12306.

MOORE, EDYTHE. b Coxton Ky. 5: Penn State U 43 (Physics) BS; USoCal 65 (LS) MS. 6: Ger. 7: Engnr Brewster Aeronautical Corp, Hatbo Penn 43-44; Patent liaison L P Graner Inc, NYC 44-45; Admin Tech Info Center Philips Labs Inc, Irvington-on-Hudson NY 46-48; Research libn Hydrocarbon Research Inc, NYC 48-53; Research libn Behr Manning Corp, Troy NY 53-55; Head Tech Info Center Amer Potash & Chem Corp, Whittier Cal 56-62; Lit research analyst Aerospace Corp 58, El Segundo Cal 61, 62-64, Manager Lib Serv 64-. 8: Instr, Immaculate Heart Col Grad Sch of Lib Sci, Los Angeles 65-; Adv Bd,UCal Grad Sch of Lib Sci, Los Angeles 63-64; Co-dir, Cal State Lib Sem on Resources& Serv for Bus & Indus, Sacramento 68; Sem leader, American Records Mgt AssnSem on Mgt of Tech Report Lit, UCLA 65. 9: SLA (chm Memb Com 67-69, Spec Com on Memb Requirs 67-68, Chem Sect; chm61-62; Engrg Sect; Nomin Com 62-63; Aerospace Sect; sec 63-64; So Cal Chapt;v-pres & program chm 63-64, pres 64-65; Dir chm 59-61; sec 58-59; Memb chm 57-58,66-68); ASIS; ACS (Dir Chem Lit); CalLA (Lib Stand & Devel Com 69); Los Angeles LA. 10: AAUW; Alpha Lambda Delta; LWV; Humanitarian Serv. 13: Yes. 14: Admin & mgt. 15: Aerospace Corp, Bldg A4/10, PO Box 95085, Los Angeles Ca 90045.

MOORE, ELEANOR (MARGARET) (MARCHMAN) (MRS). b Pinckard Ala 6 N 13. 5: Fla State Col for Women 36 (Arts & Sci) AB; Peabody 47 (LS) BS, 62 (LS) MA. 7: Tchr Alva High Sch, Alva Fla 38-40; Tchr Wacissa Jr High Sch, Wacissa Fla 40-43; Libn Bartow Sr High Sch, Bartow Fla 43-45; Libn Bartow Pub Lib, Bartow Fla 45-48; Libn Bartow Sr High Sch, Bartow Fla 48-67; Catlgr Roux Lib Fla So Col 67-. 9: NEA (Life Mem); FlaLA. 10: Delta Kappa Gamma; Beta Phi Mu. 14: Catlg. 15: Lake Morton Apts 61-g, 175 Lake Morton dr, Lakeland Fl 33801.

MOORE, ELEANOR DEWALD. b Emlenton Penn 28 Ag 20. 4: James D Moore. 5: Clarion State Tchrs Col 38-42 (LS) BS in Ed; Alleghey Col 44; UPittsburgh 48-50 (Educ) M Ed; Columbia 55 MSLS. 7: Tchr-libn Elders Ridge (Penn) Jt Vocational High Sch 42-44; Tchr-libn Verona Pub Schs, Penn 44-48; Libn Penn Jr High Sch, Penn Hills, Pittsburgh 48-56; Libn Clarion State Col 56-65, Assoc Prof of Lib Educ 65-. 8: Mem, Evaluation Coms for Middle States; Mem Penn Nomin Com for Ency BritSch Lib Awards 66; Mem, Penn Sch Lib Resources Bk Sel Adv Comm, ESEA Title II65-66. 9: ALA; NEA; PennLA; Penn State EA; ASCD; Penn Assn STATE Col Faculties. 10: Clarion Civic Club. 14: Sch lib educ. 15: Clarion State Col, Claron Penn 16214.

MOORE, ERDEAL (AULTMAN). b Ala 1 D 24. 4: D C Moore. 5: UAla 43-47 (Educ, (LS) bs certif in Lib, 52 (Secondary Educ, LS) MS. 6: S, Lat, Fr, Ger. 7: Libn W Blocton High Sch, W Blocton Ala 47-48, 48-49; Catlgr UAla Col of Educ Lib 49-53, Ser libn Med Center Lib 53-. 9: MedLA: SLA (Ala Chap: dir 58-59, chm &/or mem 4 coms 57-59 & 61-63); AlaLA (Nom Com Col & Univ Div 65). 10: Birmingham Lib Club. 14: Med ser, catlg, automation in libs. 15: 2961 Old Rocky Ridge rd, Birmingham Ala 35243.

MOORE, EVELYN ALICE. b Houston Tex 15 S 36. 5: UDenver 54-58 (Chem) BS in Chem; West Res 59-61 MS in LS. 6: Ger. 7: Research asst chem div Denver Research Inst 57-59; Libn trainee Monsanto Co, St Louis 59-61; Libn trainee LC, Wash DC 61-62, Ref libn & bibliog 62-63; Ref libn Battelle Mem Inst, Columbus Ohio 63-64; Research asst in machine methods, Washington U Sch of Med (St Louis) 64-65; Asst Prof UIll (Chicago Circle) 65-69), Asst ref libn 69; Researchengr Northwestern U (Evanston) 69-. 9: ACS; ASIS; SLA. 12: "Directories in Science and Technology, a Provisional Checklist (LC (63). 13: Yes. 14: Ref, info serv, computer applications, admin, educ. 15: IE/MS Dept Northwestern Univ, Evanston Il 60201.

MOORE, EVERETT T(HOMSON). b Los Angeles6 Ag 09. 4: Jean Macalister. 5: Occidental Col 31 (Eng) AB; Harvard 33 (Eng) AM; UCal(Berkeley) 39 (LS) Certif. 7: Tchr Webb Sch of Cal, Claremont Cal 34-38; Jr libn ref & accessions depts UCal(Berkeley) 39-41; Ref asst UIll(Urbana) 41-42; US Army (Pvt to Maj) Educ Off 42-46; Head ref dept UCal(Los Angeles) 46-61; Asst univ libn & Lecturer in Sch of Lib Serv UCLA 61-. 8: Visiting Faculty: Japan Lib Sch, Keio U (Tokyo) 52-53; uwash Sch of Libnship summer 57, 62; Ed Bd "Wilson Library Bulletin 64-; Fulbright lectr, Japan 67-68. 9: ALA (Coun 62-66; chm Publish Bd 65-); (chm Univ Libs Sect 65-66); ACRL (chm Univ Libs Sect 65-66);-RSD (pres 58-59); CalLA (pres 64). 10: Zamorano Club (Los Angeles); Rounce & Coffin Club (Los Angeles); ACLU; Phi Beta Kappa. 12: Auth "Issues of Freedom in American Libraries (64); Ed "Newsletter on Intellectual Freedom (60-61). 13: Yes. 14: Ref, intel freedom, lib publs. 15: Univ Res Lib UCLA, Los Angeles Ca 90024.

MOORE, FLORENCE (AGNES). b Cobalt Ont Can30 S 22. 5: UOttawa 40-43 BA, 49 BLS. 6: Fr. 7: Catlgr Lib of Parliament, Ottawa 49-50, Chief catlgr 51-. 9: CanLA; OntLA; LA Ottawa. 10: Prof Inst Civil Serv Can. 14: Catlg. 15: Lib of Parliament, Ottawa Ont Can.

MOORE, GAY (GARRIGAN). b Blytheville Ark 13 O 31. 4: Waddy William Moore. 5: Lindenwood Col 49-50; UArk 50-53 (Hist) BSE; UNC 59 MSLS. 7: Tchr Springdale Jr Hogh, Springdale Ark 53; Asst libn (catlgr) State Col of Ark 67-. 9: ALA; ArkLA. 14: Catlg. 15: 2601 Robinson, Conway Ar 72032.

MOORE, MRS HAZEL (STAMPS). b Learned Miss 10 Ja 24. 4: Wilbur Daniel Moore. 5: So Christian Inst 43-45 (Sociol) Certif; Tougaloo So Christian 45-47 BA (um laude); Atlanta summer 49-54 MSLS. 6: Fr. 7: Tchr-libn Oakley Train Sch, Oakley Miss 47-49; Tchr-libn Tougaloo Prep, Tougaloo Miss 49-50; Asst libn Tougaloo Col 50-57; Libn, chm B T WashingtonSch, New Orleans 57-61; Libn St Louis Pub Lib 61-62; Libn, chm B T Washington Sch, New Orleans 62-. 9: ALA; LaLA; CathLA. 10: Delta Sigma Theta; Snacirema Club. 12: "The School Library in a Changing World" Catholic Library World February 1962. 13: Yes. 14: Catlg, ref. 15: 5931 Congress dr, New Orleans La 70126.

MOORE, HELEN-JEAN. b Falls Creek Penn. 5: UPenn 34-38 (Eng) BA; UPittsburgh 38-41 (Eng) MA, 45-52 (Eng) PhD; Carnegie 56-57 MLS. 6: Fr, Ger. 7: Tchr Pittsburgh Bd of Educ Even Div 38-45; Instr in Eng UPittsburgh 41-43, 45-52; Instr in Eng Sophie Newcomb Mem Col 43-44; Instr in Eng Chatham Col 44-45; Ref asst, libn in chge of faculty & commun rel, bibliog UPittsburgh 55-62; Dir of Libs & Prof Point Park Col 62-. 8: Tchr Carnegie Lib Sch, Pittsburgh 60-62; Indexer, UPittsburgh Press; Ed consul, UPittsburgh Press and others. 9: ALA; PennLA. 10: Mod Lang Assn; College Club of Pittsburgh; AAUP. 13: Yes. 14: Ref, bibliog, admin. 15: 228 Parkman ave, Pittsburgh Pa 15213.

MOORE, HELEN M (COCHRAN). b 1 Mr 06. 4: Raymond O Moore. 5: Northwest Mo State Col 51 (Prim Educ) BS; UMo 54-9 (Guidance, Counseling) M Ed; UDenver summer 63. 7: Rural sch tchr, Clinton Co Mo 26-29; Elem tchr, Albany Mo 46-53; Tchr-libn, Albany Mo 53-59; Jr high libn, N Kansas City Mo 59-. 8: Curric Com Dept of Educ, Mo 62-63. 9: ALA (Mem of State Assembly rep Mo for 3 rs); Mo Northwest Dist Sch Libns (pres 54-55); MoASchL (pres 59-60). 13: Yes. 14: Train jr high sch studs to use & wk in lib. 15: 5415 N Wayne, Kansas City Mo 64118.

MOORE, HILDA E(LIZABETH). b Stapleton Va 20 Mr 14. 5: Randolph-Macon Womans Col 32-36 (Hist) AB; Emory 36-37 AB in LS. 7: Asst libn Va Polytech Inst 37-38, 40; Asst libn Norfolk Va Pub Lib 38;Asst libn Fla State U 39-40, 41-44; Asst libn UMd Lib of Med Dentistry Pharmacy44-52, Assoc libn Health Sci Lib 52-65, Asst Prof of Lib Sci 56-65, Libn & AssocProf of Lib Sci 65-. 9: ALA; SLA (pres Baltimore Chap 51-52); MedLA (chm Bylaws Com 63-); MLA. 10: AAUP. 13: Yes. 14: Admin, ref, rare bks. 15: 928 Belgian ave, Baltimore Md 21218.

MOORE, IVY PEARL (SIMMONS). b Collingsworth Tex 13 Ja 32. 4: William R Moore. 5: Wayland Baptist Col 49-52 (Speech); W Tex State Col 54-55 (peec) BS; Tex State Col for Women 55-57 MLS. 7: Typist Hesperian Publ Co, Floydada Tex 51; Lib asst Floyd Co Pub Lib, Floydada Tex 53-54,Act libn 54-55; Catlgr Hardin-Simmons U 57-58; Asst catlgr N Tex State U 58-62; Catlgr San Diego Pub Lib 62-65; Chief lib br Fed Aviation Agency Alaskan Region, Anchorage Alaska 65-. 9: SLA (sec 67, treas 68); AlaskaLA. 10: Nat Rifle Assn; Alpha Chi; Alpha Beta Alpha. 14: Catlg, spec lib. 15: 7800 De Barr rd No 309, Anchorage Alaska 99504.

MOORE, JANE (ROSS). b Phila 24 Ap 29. 5: Smith 47-51 (Zool) BA; Drexel 51-52 MS in LS; NYU 59-65 (Mgt) MBA; Columbia summer 53; SUNY(Geneseo) summer 61; Med libn certi f Grade I from MedLA 58. 6: Fr. 7: Catlgr Yale U Lib 52-54; Chief tech serv group Lederle Labs Lib Amer Cyanamid Co, Pearl River NY 54-58; Brooklyn Col Lib: Catlg libn, chief ser catlg libn 58-64, Act chief catlg libn 65, Chief catlg libn 66-. 8: Visiting fac Syracuse U Lib Sci Sch summers 67 & 69; Lecturer Queens Col CUNY Dept Lib Sci 67-69. 9: ALA (Memb Com 67-);-RTSD (chm Coun Reg Gps 68-69; Bd Dirs 68-69; ed adv "Library Resources and Technical Services" 68-69; Ad Hoc Com on Reg Gps 66-67; Conf Program Com 65-66; Catlg & Clsf Sect: Nominating Com 64-65); ASIS; LA (Gt Brit); SLA (chm NY Chap Bio Sci Gp 55-56); NYLA (coun 67-68; Resources & Tech Serv Sect: dir 67-68, pres 66-67, v-pres 65-66, c hm Com on Objectives & Org 68-, chm Nominating Com 67-68); NY Lib Club (Coun 66-; chm Flight Com 66-69; sec Exec Com 64-66; chm Memb Com 62-64); NY Tech Serv Libns (pres 63-64; v-pres 62-63; sec-treas 61-62; chm Nominating Com 64-65); LACUNY (Brooklyn Col del 59-62). 10: AAUP; Phi Kappa Phi. 11: Spec libs Coun Phila & Vicinity, Award in Spec Libnship 52. 14: Tech serv, catlg, automation, admin, sci lit. 15: 35 Schermerhorn st, Brooklyn NY 11201.

MOORE, JEAN (BEIGHLEY). b Zelienople Pa 28 Ja 19. 4: Musser M Moore Jr. 5: Allegheny col 36-40 (Modern Lang) AB; Syracuse 40-41 (LS) BS. 6: Fr, Sp. 7: Adult ref & hd circ lockport Pub Lib, Lockport NY 41-43; TSgt organized aviation Eng lib USMC WR, 2nd Marine Corps air sta 43-45; Ref & bibliogr United Aircraft Corp, E Hartford Conn 46-48; Volunteer organizer Marple-Newton Pub Lib, Broomall Penn 54-56; Area ref libn Ridgewood pub Lib, Ridgewood NJ 61-66; Ref wkshop instr NJ State Lib, Trenton 67; Adult serv ref libn Paramus Pub Lib, Paramus NJ 67-. 9: ALA; NJLA; Small Libs Gp, Bergen & Passaic Cos. 14: Ref, adult serv. 15: 639 Alanon rd, Ridgewood NJ 07450.

MOORE, JEAN (MACALISTER). b E Orange NJ 21 Jl 07. 4: Everett T Moore. 5: Barnard 25-29 BA; Columbia 29-30 (LS) BS. 7: Lib asst Sch Bus Lib ColumbiaU 30-38, Lib asst, assoc ref libn ref dept 38-51; Visiting Prof ReioU Lib Sch, Tokyo 52-53; Instr Immaculate Heart Lib Sch (Los Angeles) 54; Art libn UCLA 57-. 14: Ref. 15: 11320 Joffre st, Los Angeles Ca 90049.

MOORE, JERROLD NORTHROP. b Paterson NJ 1 Mr 34. 5: Swarthmore 51-55 (Eng) BA; Yale 55-56 (Eng) MA, 56-59 (Eng) PhD. 6: Fr, Ger. 7: Instr URochester 58-61; Curator Hist

Sound Recordings Program Yale 61-. 9: MusLA. 12: "An Elgar Discography" (63). 13: Yes. 14: Early recordings by important performers. 15: Hist Sound Recordings Yale U Lib, New Haven Ct 06520.

MOORE, JOHANNA L. b Ossining NY 3 S 06. 5: Richard Wagner Oberlyceum Berlin 22-24; Prussian State Lib Sch Berlin 27-28; Berlin U 28-29 BLS. 6: Ger, Fr. 7: Catlgr Lib of the Govt Ministry of Labor, Berlin Ger 29; Asst jr catlgr Sterling Mem Lib Yale U 31-33; Catlgr Brooklyn Mus Art Ref Lib, 38-40; Dir Beaman Mem Pub Lib, W Boylston Mass 49-50; Asst libn hd tech serv Rose Mem Lib Drew U 50-. 9: ALA; NJLA. 14: Catlg, clsf, lib organ & mgt, personnel. 15: 46 Green Village rd, Madison NJ 07940.

MOORE, JOYCE (WALLINGFORD). b Welch W Va 30 Jl 31. 5: Stephens Col 49; UKy 50-53 (Eng) BA, 64-65 MSLS. 7: Child libn Baltimore Co Pub Lib, Towson Md 65-67, Child specialist 67-68; Libn UKy Maysville Commun Col 68-. 9: ALA; SELA; KyLA. 10: AAUW; Delta Delta Delta. 14: Admin, ref. 15: Edgemont rd, Maysville Ky 41056.

MOORE, JULIA LEE (LOUISE). b Sioux City Iowa 11 S 41. 5: UDenver 59-62 (Bot, Anthropology) AB, 62-63 (LS) MA; U So Cal 68-69 (Automation in Libs). 6: Sp, Fr. 7: Clerical I Mary Reed Lib UDenver 60-63; Sci & TECH Lb UNeb 63-65; NY Bot Gard Lib Bronx NY 66-; Fish & Game Indexer Conserv Lib Ctr, Denver 66-68. 9: SLA; NebLA; CalLA; Amer Soc Indexers. 10: San Diego Soc of Natural Hist; Amer Transl Assn; Amer Inst Bio Sci; Intl Union for Conservation of Nature; Amer SocMammalogists; Wildlife Soc. 12: Jt comp "US Sport Fish & Wildlife Thesarus" (68). 14: Bibliog, abstracting, info retrieval, automation, indexing (bio). 15: 3789 Menlo ave, Los Angeles Ca 90007.

MOORE, KATHRYN (WILLIAMS) MRS. b Hartford Ky 5 Jl 06. 5: LSU 24-27 (Eng) BA, 28 (Eng) MA; Columbia 33 BS in LS. 7: Libn Lyon High Sch, Covington La 28-32; Libn & Sch Lib Supv Sabine Parish Lib, Many La 33-35; Libn Many High Sch, Many La 37-55; Instr lib sci Northwestern State Col (Natchitoches La) summer 40-42; Asst Prof Lib Sci LSU summer 52; Asst Prof Lib Sci Southeastern La Col summer 54, 55, Assoc Prof lib sci 55-. 8: Dir Sch Lib Wkshop, La State U summer 50; Consul Sch Lib Wkshop, Miss So summer 53. 9: ALA; LaLA (pres 42, Fed Rel Com 57-58, Pub Rel Com 58-60); La Tchrs Assn. 10: Sch Improvement League; PTA; Womans Club; Bk AAUW; AAUP; Delta Kappa Gamma. 13: Yes. 14: Sch lib wk, tchg. 15: Box 717 College Sta, Hammond La 70401.

MOORE, KAY KIRLIN (MR). b Pembina ND 26 N 10. 4: Louise Winsor. 5: Mt Union Col 8-32 (Eng) AB; Columbia 32-33 (LS) BS, summers 36-40 (LS. 6: Fr, Ger, Russian, Lat, Gk, tal, Sp. 7: Page Carnegie Pub Lib, Alliance Ohio 29-32; Inventory asst state documents, desk asst Tchrs ,col Lib Columbia U 33-34; Asst catlg dept Mt Union Col Lib 33; Libn Norwich U 34-45; Chief catlg libn Brown U Lib 45-. 8: Trustee, Greenville Pub Lib, Greenville RI; RI Legis Commsn on Libs. 9: ALA-ACRL;-RTSD; VtLA (pres 39-40, Exec Bd 38-45); RILA (past pres, chm Com on Govt Rel .7-63); NE Tech Serv Libns (past pes). 10: Amer Guild Organists. 12: "Checklist and Index of the University of the State of New York Bulletins nos 255-1094 (38); Ed "List of Latin American Imprints before 1800, Selectd from Bibliographies of Jose Toribio Medina (52); Ed "Contribution to a Union Catalog of Sixteenth Centruy Imprints in Certain New England Libraries (53; Ed "Report of the Legislative Commission on Libraries to the General Assembly of the State of Rhode Island and Providence Plantations (64). 14: Catlg, small pub libs, lib ext. 15: 73 Austin ave, Greenville RI 02828.

MOORE, KENT ALLEN. b Charlottesville Va 27 My 35. 4: Janice Quigley. 5: UVa 55-58; UMiami 58-60 (Eng) BA; UOkla 62-64 (LS) Masters. 7: Adult libn Enoch Pratt Free Lib, Baltimore 64-66; Films libn Prince Georges Co, Md 66-. 8: Audio-visual Committee ASD-ALA; Audio-visual Committee YASD-ALA. 9: ALA-ASD (A-v Com); -YASD (A-v Com); MdLA. 14: Films. 15: 6532 Adelphi rd, Hyattsville Md 20782.

MOORE, KENT UNDERHILL. b Madison Wis 4 F 14. 4: Charlotte Russell. 5: Yale 33-37 (Eng) AB; Columbia 37-38 (Eng) MA, 41-42 (LS) BS. 6: Fr. 7: Stack attendant LC 40-41; Govt Documents asst Columbia U 42; US Army, New Caledonia 42-45; Exch asst Yale U 45-46; Asst libn, act libn Kenyon Col 46-52; Chief catlg dept So Ill U 52-. 9: ALA; IllLA. 14: Catlg. 15: 1000 Emerald lane, Carbondale Il 62901.

MOORE, L A. b Plainfield Iowa 25 Jl 17. 5: State Col Iowa 34-38 (Eng) BA; State U Iowa 39 (Eng) MA; UWis 42-43 Army Specialized Training Program; Columbia 51-52 MSLS. 6: Ital. 7: Ed asst Iowa State Supreme Court Reporter & Code E, Des Moines Iowa 39-42; US Army 42-46; Eng dept pub schs, Ft Dodge Iowa 46-51; Br libn, coordinator of performance standards & admin asst Brooklyn Pub Lib 52-57; Dir Plainfield Pub Lib, & Area Ref Ctr, Plainfield NJ 57-. 8: Coadjutant Faculty mem Grad Sch of Lib Serv, Rutgers 60-. 9: ALA (Life Mem); LPRC (Exec Bd, var offs); SLA; AEAUSA; NJLA (var offs); NJAdult Educ Assn. 10: Plainfield Adult Evening Sch Coun; Kappa Delta i; Sigma Tau Delta; Gamma Theta Upsilon. 13: Yes. 14: Admin, adult educ, lib educ. 15: Plainfield Pub Lib, Eighth st at Park ave, Plainfield NJ 07060.

MOORE, LILLIAN B. b Mt Joy Penn 27 D 09. 4: Joseph D Moore. 5: Wilson Col 27-31 (Hist) AB; Millersville State Col summer 30-33 (LS); West Chester State Col summer 61. 6: Fr. 7: Tchr of hist Swatara Twp High Sch, Oberlin Penn 31-32; Libn Gloucester City Jr-Sr High Sch, Gloucester City NJ 32-37; Libn Riverside High Sch, Riverside NJ 38; Libn Darby Jr-Sr High Sch, Darby Penn 59-60; Libn Lower Merion High Sch, Ardmore Penn 60-68; Libn Dover AFB High School 68-. 9: NEA; Del State EA; Del State LA. 10: AAUW. 14: Catlg, ref. 15: 19 Candlewicke, Dover De 19901.

MOORE, LOUISA JOHNSTON. b Marion SC 24 Mr 16. 5: Winthrop Col 34-39 (Eng, LS) AB; UNC (Chapel Hill) 39-40; Peabody Lib Sch 40-41 BSLS. 7: Libn: Fitzgerald High Sch, Fitzgerald Ga 41-42, St Cloud High Sch, St Cloud Ga 42-47, Marion High Sch, Marion SC 49-. 9: SCEA; SCLA. 11: Mary Mildred Sullivan Award from Winthrop Col 64. 14: Catlg, high sch lib wk. 15: 102 Willcox ave, Marion SC 29571.

MOORE, M(ADGE) JOSEPHINE. b Portland Ore 1 S 28. 5: West Col for Women 5-49 (Eng) BA; UIll 51-52 MS in LS. 7: Gen asst New Castle-Henry Co Lib, New Castle Ind 49-51; Br libn Lib Assn of Portland, Portland Ore 52-54; Br supv & admin asst Yakima Valley Reg Lib, Yakima Wash 54-59; Field libn US Army Spec Serv, Germany 59-61; County libn Plumas Co Free Lib, Quincy Cal 61-64; City libn Longview Pub Lib, Longview Wash 64-. 9: ALA; PNLA; WashLA. 10: Soroptimist Club; Delta Kappa Gamma; AAUW; Lower Columbia Commun Action Coun. 14: Admin, ext. 15: 1808 Florida st, Longview Wash 98632.

MOORE, MARY L. b Okla City Okla. 5: Tex State Col for Women 44-48 (Fine Arts) BA-BS. 7: Libn Tidewater Oil Co, Houston 56-63; Libn Humble Oil & Refining Co, Houston 63-. 9: SLA (treas Petrol Sect 68-70; Tex Chap: Pub Rel Com 61-62, Memb Com 62-63 & 65-66, treas 66-67; Recr and Educ Com 67-68). 15: Humble Oil & Refining Co Box 2180 rm 4120, Houston Tx 77001.

MOORE, MARY McCulloch. b Norfolk Va 29 Ap 37. 5: Agnes Scott Col 55-59 (Eng) BA; UNC 59-60 (Eng) MA; EmoryU 66-67 MLS. 6: Fr, Ger. 7: Tchr St Catherine's Sch, Richmond Va 60-63; Asst libn Norfolk Acad, Norfolk Va 63-66; Asst ref libn Birmingham-Southern Col 67; Circ libn Winthrop Col 68-. 9: ALA; SELA. 10: Beta Phi Mu. 14: Ref. 15: 930 College ave, Rock Hill SC 29730.

MOORE, MATTIE RUTH. b Marlin Tex 2 F 03. 5: So Methodist U 25 (Drama, Speech) BA; Peabody 42 BS in LS; UTex 54 (Educ Supv & Admin) M Ed. 6: Sp. 7: Dallas Schs: Tchr Elem Sch 25-29, Libn 29-37, Critic tchr 37-41, Libn Jr High Sch, 41-46; Lib consul Tex Educ Agency, Austin Tex 46-52; Lib consul Dallas Schs 52-. 8: Tchr of Lib Sci during summers: Tex, 49, 51, 59; No Tex State U 52, 58; UWVa, 54; Adams State Col 59, 65. 9: ALA (chm &/or mem of Awards Coms 9 yrs);-AASchL (Exec Bd 57); TexLA (pres 50-51); SWLA (pres 62-64). 10: AAUW; Delta Kappa Gamma; Zeta Phi Eta; Altrusa Club. 11: Tex Libn of the Year, 65. 13: Yes. 14: Bks for child & yp, sch lib devel. 15: 3533 Normandy, Dallas Tx 75205.

MOORE, MILDRED ALLEN. b Louisville Ky 9 D 24. 5: UKy 42-46 (Hist) AB; Peabody 46-47 BS in LS. 6: Ger, Fr. 7: Ref asst KAN State Col (Manhattan) 47-49; Ref asst Auburn U 49-52; Engnr libn UKy 52-68, Ref libn 68-. 9: ALA; KyLA (past chm Col & Ref Sect). 10: Zeta Tau Alpha; AAUP; Friends of the Lexington Pub Lib; UKy Lib Staff Assn;Deaconess Crestwood Christ Church. 13: Yes. 14: Ref. 15: 341 Henry Clay blvd, Lexington Ky 40502.

MOORE, MILTON CYRIL. b Yucaipa Cal 31 Ja 21. 4: Loretta Adams. 5: U of Redlands 45-51 (Eng) AB; UCal (Berkeley) 51-52 BLS; So Ill U 65- (Eng). 6: Fr, Ger, Sp. 7: Asst ref libn UKan 52-54; Asst ref libn Duluth Pub Lib, Duluth Minn 55; Catlg libn & asst ref libn Canton ton Pub Lib, Canton Ohio 55-60; Ref re libn Sacramento State Col

60-61; Asst head catlg sect Cal State Lib 61-64; Head catlr So Ill U 64-. 9: ALA. 10: YMCA; Cooper Ornithological Soc. 13: Yes. 14: Catlg, ref. 15: PO Box 341, Glen Carbon Il 62034.

MOORE, NANCY. b Huntington NY 30 Ap 39. 5: UMass 56-58, 62-64 (Eng) BA; Simmons 65-66 (LS); UHawaii Inst on Asian materials 68. 7: Ref asst & govt doc libn northeastern U 64-67; Libn Hawaii Loa Col 67-. 9: ALA; HawaiiLA. 10: AAUW. 14: Ref, govt, docs. 15: PO Box 64, Honolulu Hi 96810.

MOORE, NORMAN B. b Sterling Mass 12 J 11. 4: Mary L Carleton. 5: Clark U 31-35 (Hist) AB; Simmons 46-47 BS in LS. 7: Lib asst Millicent Lib, Fairhaven Mass 46; Ref sci & tech Rochester Pub Lib, Rochester NY 47-48, Head Reynolds a-v dept 48-62; Dir Waterville Pub Lib, Waterville Me 62-; A-V libn Waterville Sr High Sch Model Lib, Waterville Me 66-. 8: Ed "Films for Public Libraries for "ALA Booklist, 53; Fculty Syracuse U Lib Sch summer 54; Consul Syracuse U Lib Sch 54-. 9: ALA; Educ Film LA; NYLA; NELA (Adv Coun); MeLA (v-pres); Rochester (NY) A-VAssn; MeTA. 10: Kiwanis Internat; No Kenebec Co Commun Action Coun. 13: Yes. 14: Admi. 15: 42 Winter st, Waterville Me 04901.

MOORE, PATRICIA (STRONG). b Champaign Ill 4 My 27. 5: UIll 45-50 (Eng) BS in LS, 56-58 MS in LS. 7: Libn Pascagoula High Sch, Pascagoula Miss 52-53; Child libn Champaign Pub Lib, Champaign Ill 53-56; Tchr-libn Unity High Sch, Tolono Ill 56-57; Libn Edison Jr High Sch, Champaign Ill 57-60; Supv of brs Mobile Pub Lib, Mobile Ala 60-64; Dir The Emmet ONeal Lib, Mountain Brook Ala 64-. 8: Library/USA 64 (6 wks telling stories). 9: ALA; SELA (v-pres Pub Lib Div); AlaLA. 10: Birmingham Libns; Ill Alumni Club of Birmingham (sec-treas); Beta Phi Mu. 14: Pub lib mgt. 15: 613 Winwood dr, Birmingham Al 35226.

MOORE, RICHARD E(UGENE). b Abilene Kan 21 My 32. 4: Marjorie Hipp. 5: Ft Hays Kan State Col 55-58 (Hist, Eng) AB; UKan 58-60 (Latin Amer Hist) MA; Universidad de San Carlos (Guatemala) 59 (Anthropology); UOkla 60-62 MLS. 6: Sp. 7: Airman US Navy 51-54; Asst acquis libn State U Iowa 62-64; Head of acquis Pottland State Col 64-65; Head of acquis UCal(Santa Cruz) 65-68; Hd acquis So Ore Col 68-, Asst Prof of LS 68-, Asst dir Lib 69-. 8: Coord, So Ore Lib Fed, "Union List of Serials" 68-. 9: PNLA (co-chm ann conv 70); OreLA; Cal Univ LA (v-chm 68; By-laws Steering Com 67; chm Com on Libns Status 68). 10: Santa Cruz Peace Center; Co Com, Peace and Freedom Party, Cal. 12: "Historical Dictionary of Guatemala" (67). 13: Yes. 14: Acquis, catlg, bibliog, Guatemalan hist. 15: 1060 Emma st, Ashland Or 97520.

MOORE, ROSEMARY (MENGISEN). b Franklin Penn 6 S 18. 4: Edward John Moore. 5: Mt St Scholastica 36-40 (Eng) AB; Carnegie 41-43 BS in LS. 6: Ger, Fr, Swiss. 7: Carnegie Lib f Pittsburgh: Br asst Homewood Br 41-42, Asst Cental 42-43, Asst Wylie 42-43; Asst Cumberland Lib, Cumberland Md 44; Head St Patrick Parish, Woodbury NJ 60-62; Org & head St Patrick Elem Sch, NJ 60-64; Asst Woodbury Pub Lib, Woodbury NJ 66-. 8: Com for Lib Serv for Gloucester Co; Consul Gloucester Cath High Sch, Gloucester NJ 65-. 9: CathLA; ALA; NJLA. 10: Exec Bd, St Patrick Sch, Woodbury NJ; Bd, St Joseph Prep Sch, Phila; Gloucester Co Visiting Nurse Assn. 14: Sch lib wk. 15: 30 S Evergreen ave, Woodbury NJ 08096.

MOORE, SARAH (HUNT). b Winchester Tenn 25 My 09. 5: UTenn 27-28 (Eng); Peabody 28-31 (Eng, Hist) BS, 46 BS in LS. 6: Fr, Ger. 7: Jr high sch tchr Sewanee Pub Schs, Sewanee Tenn 31-36; Elem prin Franklin Co Schs, Winchester Tenn 36-39, High sch lib supv 39-43; Aviation supply USNR WAVES 43-45; Libn S Side High Sch, Memphis Tenn 45-48; Dir lib serv Memphis City Schs, Memphis Tenn 48-52; Libn Murfreesboro City Schs, Murfreesboro Tenn 52-55; Catlg Libn Middle Tenn State U 55-. 9: ALA; SELA; TennLA; TennEA (chm Lib Sect 51-52). 10: AAUW; Delta Kappa Gamma; YWCA; Tenn Hist Soc. 14: Catlg, So hist, Tennesseana. 15: Middle Tenn State U, Murfreesboro Tenn 37130.

MOORE, VERNA (PARCHER). b Blackwell Okla 3 D 07. 4: Harry C Moore. 5: Northwestern State Col 2655 (Elem Educ, Home Econ) BS; Okla State summers 60-62 (LS). 7: Tchr Park Elem Sch, Blackwell Okla 26-30; Tchr Lone Elm Sch, Grant Co Okla 31-34; Tchr Triumph Sch, Kay Co Okla 40-41; Tchr Braman Elem Sch, Braman Okla 45-47, Tchr-Prin 47-48; Tchr Lincoln Elem Sch, Blackwell Okla 55-56; Libn Lovett Jr High Sch, Blackwell Okla 56-63; Libn Blackwell igh Sch, Blackwell Okla 63-. 9: NEA; OklaEA; OklaLA. 14: Ref. 15: 509 E Bridge, Blackwell Okla 74631.

MOORE, WALDO H(AWTHORNE). b 20 D 21. 4: Telma Patterson. 5: George WashingtonU 46-49 (Law) LLB; NationalU 52-53 (Law) MPL. 7: Hd materials control sect serv div Copyright off LC 53-57, Hd Bk Sect examining div 58-61, Asst chief 61-63, Chief ref div 63-. 9: BSA. 10: Amer Bar Assn; Fed Bar Assn; Trustee of Copyright Soc of the USA. 14: Copyright & its relationship to libs. 15: Copyright Office Lib of Congress, Washington DC 20540.

MOORE, WOODY (STURDIVANT). b Marion Ala 1 Ag 17. 4: John C Moore. 5: Judson Col 35-39 (Bus Admin) AB; UAla 60 Certif in LS; UMich 61 (LS); UAla 62 (LS) MA. 7: Asst Birmingham PubLib, Birmingham Ala 40-41; Clerk So Bell Telephoe Co, Birmingham Ala 42-43; Clerk Agric Adjustment Agency, Marion Ala 43-44; Asst sec-treas Nat Farm Loan Assn, Marion Ala 44-51; Libn Marion Inst 59-. 9: ALA;-Jr Col LA (pres 65-66); SELA; AlaLA (chm Legisl & Fed Rel Coms 66-68);AlaASchLA. 10: Triad Study Club; Antiq Soc. 14: Admin. 15: 213 Polk st, Marion Al 56756.

MOORES, MARJORIE (JUDD). b Tacoma Wash. 4: Merwin Moores. 5: Col of Puget Sound 29-31 (Hist); Wash State U 31-33 (Hist) BA; UMich 35-36 BALS. 7: Asst libn Alma Col 36-37; Libn Girls PolytechHigh, Portland Ore 37-40; Libn Brooklyn Br Lib Assn of Portland, Portland Ore 40-43; Stacks libn UWash Lib 43-45; Libn Hill Co Rural Li, Havre Mont 48-63; Area libn King Co Pub Lib System, Seattle 63-65, Coord of adult serv 65-. 8: Instr Educ Dept, tchg Story-telling No Mont Col summer schs; Story Book Lady on Radio Sta KOJM, Havre Mont; Org first Friends of Lib Group in Mont, 48. 9: ALA; PNLA (sec 62-63, Bd Dirs (Mont), chm Nom & Adult Educ Coms); MontLA (past pres & sec); WashLA. 10: AAUW; LWV; Bus & Prof Women; Havre City Planning Commsn; Altrusa Internat. 14: Adult & child serv. 15: 16412 SE Ninth st, Bellevue Wa 98004.

MOORES, MERWIN MARION. b Puyallup Wash 29 Je 13. 4: Marjorie Judd. 5: Wash State Col 31-32 (Eng Lit); UWash 32-37 (Eng Lit) BA, 37-38 BALS, 57-61 MALS. 7: Libn Sabin High Sch, Portland Ore 38-43; (S/Sgt) USArmy 63rd Div 253rd Inf, France, Gerhany 43-46; Reg Libn Fed Pub Housing Authority, Seattle 46-47; Libn No Mont Col 47-63; Asst chief ref libn UWash Lib 63-67, Asst dir of lib for personnel & budget 67-. 8: Admin Com No Mont Col. 9: ALA; NEA (Life mem); MontLA (pres 51-52); PNLA (Bd 56-58, chm Col Div 58-59, pres 62-63); WashLA. 10: . 13: Yes. 14: Ref. 15: 16412 SE 9th st, Bellevue Wash 98004.

MOORMAN, HENRY (DABNEY). b Stigler Okla 1 F 19. 4: Virginia Hawkins. 5: UColo 46-47 (Geol); UOkla 48-51 (Geol, LS) BS, BA; URichmond 62 (Mgt Train; Sheridan Col 67-68 (Accounting). 7: Air Traffic Controller US Army Air Corps (S/Sgt), US & Alaska 40-45Lib asst ref UOkla 49-51; Asst libn USAF (Res), Rapid City SD 51-52; LibnSupv Tech Info Prod Dev Div Reynolds Metals Co, Louisville Ky & Richmond Va52-67; Libn Purchasing agent, Staff asst to mgr Wyoming div, Reynolds MiningCorp, Buffalo Wyo 67-. 8: Asst to Admin Dir PRODUCT Devel Div, Reynolds Metals Co 60-; Lib ComChm & Head Libn Westhampton Baptist Church, Richmond Va. 64-. 9: SLA; Amer Soc for Metals; Amer Inst Min, Metall & Petrol Engnrs. 12: Ed "Reynolds Aluminum Digest (53-60). 14: Ref, bibliog, lit research, admin. 15: 583 Walters st, PO Box 593, Buffalo Wy 82834.

MOOSE, VIVIAN (CATHERINE). b Hildebran NC 24 Jl 07. 5: Lenoir Ryne Col 25-29 (Math) AB; UNC summer 38-40 BS in LS. 6: Fr. 7: Math tchr Tryon High Sch, Bessemer City NY 29-30; Math tchr Aurora High Sch, Aurora NC 30-38, Math tchr & libn 38-41; Libn Sanford High Sch, Sanford NC 41-45; Libn Boyden High Sch, Salisbury NC 45-47; Asst catlg libn Womans Col UNC(Greensboro) 47-61; Hd libn UNC(Greensboro) 61-. 8:Visiting instr in Lib Sci, Lenoir Rhyne Col summer 41. 9: ALA; SELA (chm Catlg Sect 52-54); NCLA (Catlg Sect: chm 57-59, dir 63-65); Luth Church LA. 10: AAUP; Greensboro Lib Club. 13: Yes. 14: Catlg. 15: 225 Kensington rd, Greensboro NC 27403.

MOOSSY, YVONNE (REESE). b McComb Miss 11 O 27. 4: John Moossy. 5: LSU 45-47 (Pre-nursing); Charity Sch of Nursing & LSU Med Sch 47-50 (Nursing) BS; Tulane 51-52, 55; LSU (New Orleans) 60-61, 64-65; UPittsburgh 65-67 MLS. 6: Fr. 7: Bkkeeper Ford Motor Co, Franklinton La 43-45; Hd nurse Charity Hosp, New Orleans 50-51; Priv duty nursing New Orleans 51-53; Asst libn Salem Col 68-. 9: ALA; NCLA. 10: Amer Acad of neurology; Womans Aux; Phi Delta Gamma. 14: Catlg. 15: 335 Fairfax dr, Winston Salem NC 27104.

MOQUIN, O LEONARD. b Hartford Conn 15 F 09. 6: Fr. 7: Holyoke Pub Lib, Holyoke Mass: Lib asst 33, Br supv 51, Asst libn 60, Assoc libn 62-. 9: ALA; MassLA (Legis Com 62); West Mass Lib Club (pres 64-65). 14: Admin of pub libs. 15: 17 Columbus ave, Holyoke Ma 01040.

MORAN, IRENE E. b Jersey City NJ 25 Je 27. 5: NYU 44-51 (Journalism) BS. 7: Ed asst "The American Banker, NY 44-51& Publicity rep DuMont TV Network, NY 51-55; Press ed WOR Radio & TV, NY 55-59; Asst pub rel & dir Brooklyn Pub Lib 62-65, Dir of pub rel 65-. 9: ALA (Memb Com, Brooklyn 64-); NYLA; LPRC (chm Archives Com 65); Pub Rel SocAmer; Pub Rel Offrs Soc (NY). 13: Yes. 15: Brooklyn Pub Lib Grand Army Plaza, Brooklyn NY 11238.

MORAN, JOHN F(RANCIS JR). b Pittsfield Mass 18 N 27. 5: Tufts Col 46-50 (Econ, Hist) AB; Columbia 53-54 MS IN LS; Rutgers 61 (Documentation); SUNY (Fredonia) 67-69 (Hist). 6: Fr. 7: US Army Inf & Personnel (Cpl), US, Japan 50-52; E Orange Pub Lib, E Orange NJ: Jr libn 54-56, Sr libn 56-58, Prin libn 58-60, Supv libn 61-65;Assoc libn readers serv Daniel Reed Lib SUNY (Fredonia) 66-. 9: ALA; NYLA. 10: Amer Com for Irish Studies; AAUP. 13: Yes. 14: Ref, adult serv, fin admin. 15: E Orange Pub Lib, 291 Main st, E Orange NJ 07018.

MORAN, LEILA (PADGETT). b Wash DC 11 Ap 24. 5: Hood 42-46 (Eng lit) BA; Drexel 46-47 BSLS; George Washington 49-51 (Eng lit) MA. 6: Fr. 7: Lib asst Georgetown br DC Pub Lib, Bethesda Md 47; Circ & ref asst Goucher Col Lib 47-48, Catlgr 48-49; Asst libn for catlg Georgetown U Lib 49-54; Selection off asst chief, chief div of acquis Nat Agric lib USDA Wash dc 54-. 8: Instr USDA Grad Sch 64-. 9: SLA (Wash DC Chap; sec Biol Scis Gp 61-62). 10: Montgomery Co Art Assn; Rehoboth Art League. 13: Yes. 14: Acquis, pub rel, graphics, rare bks. 15: 3703 Chevy Chase Lake dr, Chevy Chase Md 20015.

MORAN, MARGARET (SARAH). b oodland Ind. 5: Northwestern 30 (Lat, Fr) AB; UIll 43 BS in LS, 51 (LS) MS; Columbia summer 63 (LS). 07: Tchr of Eng & Lat Indiana High Schs, 9 yrs; Libn E Detroit High Sch, E Detroit Mich 44-45; Asst libn Thornton Twp High Sch, Harvey Ill 5-46; Circ dept asst Norhwestern U summer 46; Loan libn No Ill State Tchrs Col 46-48; Asst libn Santa Ana High Sch, Santa Ana Cal 48-50; High sch libn San Bernardino Co Lib, San Bernardino Cal summer 51; Instr Tex State Col for Women summer 52; Instr San Jose State Col summer 53; Instr Ill State Normal U summer 54; Instr Ariz Stat Col summer 57; Libn Pomona High Sch, Pomona Cal 51-58; Libn Ganesha High Sch, Pomona Cal 58-. 9: AL-AASchL; NEA; Cal Tchrs Assn; CalASchL. 10: Beta Phi Mu. 15: 422 Grinnell dr, Claremont Ca 91711.

MORAN, MARGUERITE K. b Pringle Penn. 5: College Misericordia Chem) BS (cum laude); Columbia (Chem); (MS); Rutgers 60 MLS. 6: Fr, Ger. 7: Research chem Richhold Chem, Elizabeth NJ 43-49; Tech info supv M&T Chem Inc 49-. 8: Consul, Med Lib Elizabeth Gen Hosp 57-64; J.F. Kennedy Hosp 68-. 9: ACS (Advert mgr, Chem, Lit Div); Soc of Plastics Engnrs; Com on Guide to Litof Polyvinyl Chloride 62-; SLA (chm &/or mem 4 coms 59-63 (NJ Chap) sec 55-57, dir 63-64, pres 65-66, chm &/or mem 14 coms 53-65); ASIS. 12: Ed "Putting Knowledge to Work - the Profession of the Special Libraran, (SLA rev ed 60). 13: Yes. 14: Tech info. 15: 13 Longfellow dr, Colonia NJ 07067.

MORAN, PAUL FRANCIS. b Scranton penn 30 Ag 16. 4: Muriel Block. 5: UScranton 34-38 (Educ) AB; Drexel 46-47 BSLS. 7: Army Air Force, Air Force Supply (T/Sgt) 42-45; Sr lib asst Rochester (NY) Pub Lib 47-50; Ref libn Villanova Col Lib 50-51; Asst ref libn US Weathr Bureau, Wash DC 51-53, Libn catlgr 53-60; Libn US Bureau of Mines, College Park Md 60-. 13: Yes. 14: Catlg, ref. 15: 9524 51st ave, College Park Md 20740.

MORAN, VIRGINIA L. b Brooklyn NY. 5: Mt St Vincent 35-39 (Hist) AB; Columbia 40-41 BS(LS); NYU 41-45 (Admin) MA, 49-57 (A-V Programs). 6: Fr, Sp. 7: Ref libn Hunter Col 4154; Dir Massapequa Pub Lib, Massapequa LI NY 54-60; Dist libn Syosset Pub Schs, Syosset LI NY 60-61; Dir Half Hllow Hills Commun Lib, Melville LI NY 61-64; Dir Seaford Pub Lib, Seaford LI NY 64-68; Proj libn Research Found Inc NY State Dept of Mental Hygiene 68-. 8: Consul: NY State Lib, 50-53; City Sch Dist of New Rochelle, 62-63. 9: NEA-DAVI; ALA; NY LA. 10: Womans Club of Massapequa; Internat Fed of Cath Col Alumnae; Nassau Shores Civic Assn. 11: BNai BRith award of Year 58. 13: Yes. 14: Admin, ref, bibliog. 15: 107 Unqua rd, Massapequa LI NY 11759.

MORATZ, RUSSELL F. b Wis. 5: Wis State U (Oshkosh) 45-48 (Educ) BS; UMinn summers 52-56 (Educ admin) MA; UDenver 62-63 MA in LS. 6: Ger. 7: US Armed Forces, Europe 42-45; Tchr Beaver Dam Sch Syst, Beaver Dam Wis 48-62; Libn Wis Lib Commsn 63-65; Libn asst dir libs & Assoc Prof Wis State U (Whitewater) 65-. 8: Tchr and adminr Amer dependents' Schs in Austria 50-51. 9: ALA; WisLA; OverseasEA. 10: Phi Delta Kappa; Assn Wis State U Facs; AAUP; Phi Delta Kappa; Wis State Hist Soc; Wis Acad of Scis, Arts & Letters. 12: Co-comp (with others) "Publications of the Faculty" Wis State U, Whitewater (68). 13: Yes. 14: Col & univ lib admin, hist of libs, hist of bks & bk making. 15: PO Box 182, Whitewater Wi 53190.

MORECOCK, DONALD LEE. b Richmond Va 14 Ag 33. 4: Jewel C Morecock. 5: URichmond 51-55 (Span) BA, 55-57 (Pol Sci) MA. 7: US Army 57; US Army (Reserves) 5763; Archivist Va State Lib archives div 58-. 14: Docs, microfilm. 15: 4801 Leonard pkwy, Richmond Va 23226.

MOREHEAD, BEBE (BEHNKE). b Wild Rose Wis 20 My 40. 4: Joseph Morehead. 5: UWis 58-62 (Hist) BS, 62-63 MLS. 7: Sr libn San Francisco Pub Lib 63-. 9: ALA. 14: Ref. 15: 3049 Sacramento st, San Francisco Ca 94115.

MOREHOUSE, HAROLD G. b Covina Cal 27 Jl 28. 4: Edwina Knivila. 5: San Francisco State Col 47-48 (Music); UCal 53-56 AB, MLS. 6: Fr. 7: Catlgr Cal State Lib 56-58, Ref libn 58-59; Asst libn Aerojet-Gen Corp, Sacramento Cal 59-61; Sci libn UNev 61-63, Asst dir of libs 63-69, Dir of libs 69-. 9: ALA; NevLA (pres). 10: AAUP. 13: Yes. 15: Box 8937, Reno Nv 89507.

MOREHOUSE, RICHARD ELLIOTT. b Kingston NY 12 Je 11. 4: Marjorie Gallup. 5: Columbia 28-32 (Geol, lit) BA; Centenary Col 59 (Petroleum law); UDenver 65-66 (LS) MA. 6: Fr. 7: Geologist (exploration) Standard Oil Co, NYC 32-41; Intelligence off (major) USA Corps of Engrs, US & S Pacific 41-46; Geologist (research & exploration) Standard Oil co, US & S Amer 46-65; Lib UColo sci lib 66-. 8: Consul Photogeomorphologist 65-. 9: SLA; Amer Geol Inst Geosci Info Soc; ColoLA. 10: AAAS. 14: Automation of libs. 15: 1445 Judson dr, Boulder Co 80302.

MOREL, GRACE. b Kankakee Ill 4 Je 01. 5: Pacific Union Col 19-23 (Eng) BA; USoCal 48-49 MS in LS. 7: Tchr-libn Los Angeles Academy, Los Angeles 23-27; Eng tchr Pacific Union Col 27-28; Tchr-libn Glendale Acad, Glendale Cal 29-35; Tchr-libn Mt View Acad, Mt View Cal 36-39; Tchr-libn Lynwood Acad, Lynwood Cal 40-48; Tchr-libn Lodi Acad, Lodi Cal 49-62; Libn Rio Lindo Acad, Healdsburg Cal 63-. 8: Taught lib sci classes Pacific Union Col summers 51, 62. 9: ALA; NCTE. 14: Sch libs. 15: 3200 Rio Lindo ave, Healdsburg Ca 95448.

MORELAND, CARROLL COLLIER. b Edgewood Penn 20 D 03. 4: Sara Lacy. 5: Princeton U 20-24 (Eng) AB; UPittsburgh Law Sch 24-27 LLB; Johns Hopkins 31-35 (Eng); Carnegie 36-37 BS in LS. 6: Fr. 7: Assoc Thorp Reed & Armstrong, Pittsburg 27-31; Reading room asst LC 35-36; Ref asst NY Pub Lib 37-38; State Law Libn Mich State Lib 38-43; Asst libn Assn of the Bar of the City of NY 43-46; Biddle Law Libn UPenn Law Sch 46-62; Visiting Prof Lib Sci UDacca (E Pakistan) 62-64; Libn The American Bar Found 64-. 8: Amer legal adv Inst of Advanced Legal Studies ULondon, spring 54; Lib Adv Inst of Pub & Bus Admin UKarachi & Hon lib adv The Asia Found, 59-61; Hon lib adv Pakistan Army Libs 60; Pakistan Air Force Acad & Planning Commsn, Govt of Pakistan 61; Spec consul Indian Law Inst, New Delhi 60; Lib Adv, spec adv, or spec lib adv to The Rep, The Asia FOUND: Pakistan, 62-64; Korea, summer 63 & spring 64; Thailand, spring 64; Dir Nat Sem on Lib Devel, Pakistan 67. 9: AALL (pres 55-56); ALA; SLA (chm Constit & Bylaws Com); Amer Bar Assn. 12: "Legal Research, with Sidney B Hill(46); "Research in Pennsylvania Law, with Erwin C Surrency (53); "EQUAL Justice Under Law: the American Legal Sysem System" 13: Yes. 14: Admin. 15: 1155 E 60th st, Chicago Il 60637.

MORELAND, GEORGE B(OULTON). b Edgewood Pittsburgh Penn 25 Jl 01. 4: Mildred Conklin. 5: Princeton 19-23 (Eng); UPittsburgh 25-26 (Eng) AB; Carnegie Lib Sch 35-36 BSLS. 6: Ger. 7: Child libn, supv y-a DC Pub Lib 36-42; Lt US Maritime Serv 42-46; Hd circ DC Pub Lib 46-48; Libn Cambria Free Lib, Johnstown Penn 48-51; Dir Montgomery Co (Md) Dept of Pub Libs, Bethesda 51-. 8: Consul Lancaster Co (Pa) Commsnrs 62; Bldg consul Ayne Avunlel Co (Md) 64; Consul: Somerset Co (NJ) Hist Commsn 65, libs & trustees Newark (Del Pub Lib 68); Lib Adv to Pakistan 57-58. 9: ALA (mem var coms); MdLA (pres 56); DCLA (pres 60); Md Lib Adminrs (pres 62); Montgomery Co Adminrs Assn (pres 60). 10: Libns Tech Com Coun of Govts, Wash DC; Cap and Gown Club, Princeton NJ. 12: "Star and Crescent: an Annotated Bibliography of Pakistan" (58); "Government of Pakistan Publications, 47-57 (58); "a Report On Public Library Service in Somerset county NJ (66); Ed "Open Look" (monthly house organ). 13: Yes. 14: Admin, bldgs, automation. 15: 4411 Knowles ave, Kensington Md 20795.

MORELAND, SARA (LACY). b Sioux City Iowa 24 Jl 10. 4: Carroll Collier Moreland. 5: Long Beach Jr Col 29-31 Cal jr certif; UCLA 31-34 (Am hist) AB; Carnegie Lib Sch 36-37 BS in LS. 6: Sp, Fr, Ger. 7: Asst to hd adult dept Youngstown Pub Lib, Youngstown Ohio 37-39; Libn Eastern High Sch, Lansing Mich 40-42; Catlgr & classifier UPenn 50-56; Acquis libn Swarthmore Col Lib 56-59; Bks program asst Asia Foundation, Karachi Pakistan 59-61; Asst hd acqios UChicago 66-68; Resources bibliogr Midwest Reg Med Lib Serv John Crerar Lib, Chicago 68-. 8: External examiner in Catlg & Clsf, Grad Lib Sch, UDacca E Pakistan 63-64. 9: ALA; MedLA; E PakistanLA (life mem). 10: Delta zeta; Kappa Phi Zeta. 12: "Directory of Health Science Research Collections in illinois, Indiana, Iowa, Minnesota, Wisconsin" (69). 14: Tech proc. 15: 20617 Promethian way, Olympia Fields Il 60461.

MORELOC, MOLETE JOSEPHINE. b Ruski Tenn 13 D 09. 5: Murray State Col 26-29 (Phys Sci) AB; Peabody 39-43 BS in LS; UMo 45-52 (Pys Sci) MS. 7: Tchr pub schs, Tenn, Ky 29-42; Libn Hillcrest High Sch, Burlington NC 42-43; Sci lib Stephens Col 43-47; Engnr libn UMo 47-54; Libn II Detroit Pub Lib 54-56; Assoc libn Parke Davis & Co, Detroit 56-58; Coordinator reg campus libs Purdue U 58-. 9: ALA; SLA (chm Engnr Sect 65-66, pres Ind Chap 64-65); Amer Soc Engrg Educ; IndLA (chm Col & Univ Round Table 62-63). 46-48). 10: AAUP. 13: Yes. 14: Ref, admin. 15: 1025 Hillcrst rd, W Lafayette Ind 47906.

MORELOCK, EUGENIA B(ROWNE). b Shreveport La 6 S 21. 4: James C Morelock. 5: Nat Park Col 39-40; LSU 40-42 (Eng) BA, 43 BS in LS. 7: WAC (Pfc) Lib asst Luke Field AAF, Phoenix Ariz 43-45; Catlgr UMo 46-47; Catlgr UFla 51-52; Catlgr Auburn U 53; Asst libn Sullins Col 57-58; Catlgr King Col 58-60; Catlgr Mary Washington Col 61; Catlgr Huntsville Pub Lib, Huntsville Ala 65-68, Hd dept of tech processes 69-. 10: DAR; Church libn, First United Meth Church. 14: Catlg. 15: 2917 Garth rd SE, Huntsville Al 35801.

MORELOWSKI, JAN. b Cracow Poland. 4: Janina Maciulska. 5: Piaristengymnasium (Vienna) 10-12; Gimnazjum (Cracow) 14-18 Matric Exam; Jagiellonian U (Cracow) 18-22, 25 DL; Columbia 53-56 MLS. 6: Eng, Polish, Ger, Fr, Russian. 7: Polish Ministry of Justice: Judge, Cracow 25-32, Presiding judge of a district court, Skawina & Zolkiew 32-39; V-chm of the Delegation ofPolish Ministry of Justice (in exile), Teheran Iran, Jerusalem 44-47; Searcher Butler Lib Columbia U 53-56; Asst law libn St Johns U (NY) 56-. 8: Assoc of Columbia U Sem on the Hist of Legal & Polit Thought, 64-. 9: SLA; AALL; Internat Law Assn, Amer Br; Internat Assn Law Libs. 10: Polish Juridical Soc US (sec-gen 53-69, v-pres 69-); Polish Inst Arts ; Scis in Amer (Bd Dirs 65-66). 12: "A Judge Behind the Prison Bar: Personal Reminiscences 1930-1943, in Polish (64). 13: Yes. 14: Catlg. 15: St Johns U 96 Schermerhorn st, Brooklyn NY 11201.

MORENO, ERIN (LASSITER) MRS. b Gibson Co Tenn 20 N 09. 5 Lambuth Col 27-31 (Eng Lit) AB; Peabody 35 BS in LS; UIll summers 37, 40 (LS). 7: Vaired tchg jobs in W Tenn 31-35; Lbn Carbondale Community High Sch, Carbondale Ill 35-38; Libn Crosby-Ironton Jr Col 38-41; Libn Army Lib Serv, Ft Riley Kan 41-45; Libn Oceanside Jr High Sch, Oceanside NY 54; Libn Merrick Elem &Lake Shore Elem Scs, Merrick NY 55; Libn Messick High Sch, Memphis Tenn 55-. 9: TennLA; TennEA; W TennEA (chm Lib Sect). 10: Memphis Little Theater; Sigma Kappa. 14: Sch lib wk. 15: 756 Prescott st, Memphis Tenn 38111.

MOREY, BARBARA (LOUISE). b Shrewsbury Mass 11 S 16. 5: UPenn 34-38 (Eng) BA; Simmons 38-39 BS in LS. 7: Child libn Rochester Pub Lib, Rochester NY 9-44; Head child wk Elemwood Pub Lib, Providence 44-46; Child libn Berkshire Athenaeum, Pittsfield Mass 46-48; Reg bkmob libn West Reg Pub Lib System, •Pittsfield Mass 48-. 9: MassLA; West Mass Lib Club. 10: Berkshie Co Hist Soc; Richmond Pub Lib; Com to Rewritè Richmond (Mass) Town By-laws; Richmond CEMETERY Com; Richmond Sch Bldg Com; etc. 13: Yes. 14: Bkmob serv, child wk. 15: Canaan rd, Richmond Ma 01254.

MOREY, THOMAS J. b Hornell NY 10 D 20. 4: Delores J. 5: UBuffalo 46-49 (Biol); Canisius Col 49-51 (Bio-chem) BS. 6: Ger, Fr, Russian. 7: Capt USAF 42-45; Physiologist Stanley Aviation, Buffalo NY 51-53; Asst libn Cornell Aeronautical, Buffalo NY 53-57; Chief libn Hooker Chem, Niagara Falls NY 57-58; Sr libn Continental oil Co, Ponca City Okla 58-65; Mgr corporate lib serv Xerox Corp, Rochester NY 65-. 9: SLA; ACS; ASIS; ALA; RRRLC (Adv Bd). 13: Yes. 14: Lib serv, automation, lib materials proc. 15: 646 Cumberland way, Webster NY 14580.

MORFORD, (JOSEPHINE STELLA) IONE. b Haviland Kan 19 D 14. 5: Ft Hays Kan Sate Col 3344 (Eng, Hist) BS; Kan State Tchrs Col (Emporia) 60-62 (LS) MS; UOkla (Norman) 67. 7: Tchr rural schs, Kiowa & Stafford Cos Kan 34-39; Tchr & prin Mullinville Elem Sch, Kan 39-43; Hist tchr Jr High Sch, Pratt Kan 44-62; Libn Sr High Sch, Pratt Kan 62-. 8: Mem, Rev & Eval Bd, Kans State Reading Circle. 9: NEA; Kan State Tchrs Assn; KanASchL; PrattTA. 10: Commun Concert Assn; Wesleyan Serv Guild. 14: Circ. 15: 421 E Third, Pratt Ks 67124.

MORGAN, BARBARA (JEANETTE). b Lyndon Ohio 10 O 16. 5: Capital U 35-39 (Chem) BS; West Res 51-52 MS in LS. 7: Clerk-typist Ohio Div of Highways, Chillicothe Ohio 40-42; The Mead Corp, Chillicothe Ohio: Analytinal chem 42-51, Asst libn 52-64, Libn 64-. 9: SLA (Papr & Text Div); ALA. 10: AAUW; Chillicothe Hosp guild. 14: Admin, ref, catlg. 15: The Mead Corp, Central Research Labs, Chillicothe Oh 45601.

MORGAN, CARMAN H (HEAD). b Eglin AFB Fla 2 D 42. 4: James E Morgan. 5: Fla StateU 63-65 (Hist, LS) BA, 65-66 (LS) MA. 6: Sp, Fr. 7: Asst libn Western Piedmont Jr Col Morganton NC 66; Sch lib supervisor Hancock Co, Sparta Ga 67-. 9: SELA; GaLA; GaEA. 10: AAUW; Beta Phi Mu. 15: PO Box 257, Milledgeville Ga 31061.

MORGAN, DEURENE (ALMA). b Shamrock Tex 8 Ja 19. 4: John H Morgan. 5: N Tex State U 38 (Bus Admin) BA, 50 (LS) BA; UHouston 55 (Elem Curriculum, Supv & Admin) MA. 6: Ger, Sp. 7: Tchr, Victoria Tex 48-50; Lib supv, Victoria Tex 50-55; Elem sch supv, Victoria Tex 55-57; High sch libn & Col ref lib, Victoria Tex 57-60; Jr high sch libn, Taft Tex 60-62; Bus high sch tchr, San Benito Tex 62-64; Supv elem curriculum, Brownsville Tex 64-; Second curr supvr NE, San Antonio Tex 67-. 8: Eval Com, Woodville Tex 54; Sci Wkshop Consul, Orange Tex 56; Soc Studies Guide for Tex Imporvement of Educ Servs Com 56. 9: NEA; ALA (Memb, Stae Committeeman); TexASchL (pres, chm); Tex State Tchrs Assn. (chm Dist XII); ASCD; NCTE. 10: Tex Assn of Curric Supvs; Tex Assn of Admin & Instrl Supvs; Tex Assn of Elem Principals; Delta Kappa Gamma; Pi Omega Pi; Kappa Delta Pi; AAUW; Pilot Internat; Nat Coun of Soc Studies; Alpha Lambda Sigma. 13: Yes. 14: Sch & yp libs. 15: 1118 Curlew, San Antonio Tx 78213.

MORGAN, ELLA (PARKER). b Salisbury NC 30 My 23. 4: Booker Taliaferro Morgan. 5: Bennett Col 40-44 (Eng) AB; Atlanta 44-45 BSLS. 6: Ger. 7: Demonstration Agent, Salisbury NC summer 45; Asst libn St Pauls Polytech Inst 46-48; Libn CLAFLIN U 48-50; Catlgr G Lamar Harrison lib Langston U 50-. 8: Sec County Home summer 45. 9: ALA; OklaLA; OklaEA. 10: Great Books Discussion Group; Zeta Phi Beta. 14: Catlg. 15: Box 777, Langston Ok 73050.

MORGAN, ELLIOTT. b Los Angeles 26 S 06. 5: UCLA 23-27 (Eng) BA; Oxford U 29-31 (Eng); UCal(Berkeley) 47-48 BLS. 6: Fr, Sp. 7: Research asst MGM Studios, Culvr City Cal 37-41; US Army (S/Sgt) 41-45; Research asst MGM Studios,Culver City Cal 45-46; Research asst Universal Studio, Universal City Cal 50-55; Head research dept MGM Studios, Culver City Cal 55-. 9: CalLA. 15: 502 Palisades ave, Santa Monica Cal 90402.

MORGAN, ELOISE (WOOTEN). b Bristol Va 5 D 29. 04. Namon McDuffie Morgan Sr. 5: Va Intermont Col 47-48 (Liberal arts); UAla 48-52 (Hist) BS; E Tenn State U 61-62 (LS); Peabody Col summers 63-66 MLS. 7: Tchr pub schs Bristol Tenn 54-55, 58-60; Libn elem sch, Bristol Tenn 62-63; Libn Furst Presbyterian Ch, Bristol Tenn 63-64; Assoc libn Va Intermont Col 64-66; Catlgr UAla 66; Libn Enterprise Jr Col 68-. 9: NEA; ALA; AlaLA; AlaEA. 10: Beta Phi Mu. 14: Admin, circ. 15: PO Box 985 2506 Stonebridge rd, Dothan Al 36301.

MORGAN, ELOISE LENA (FRY). b princeton WVa 26 Jl 13. 5: Concord State Col 31-35 (Eng) AB; Peabody 36-37 BS in LS 06: Fr. 7: Libn Douglas High Sch, Douglas Ga 37-38; Libn Kingsport High Sch, Kingsport Tenn 38-40; Tchr Blue Ash

Elem Sch, Cincinnati 53-54; Libn Maderia High Sch, Cincinnati 54-56; Child libn St Louis Pub Lib 56-57; Libn Riverview Gardens Sr High Sch, St Louis 57-. 9: ALA; NEA; MoLA; Mo State SchLA; Mo State Tchrs Assn; Classroom Tchrs Assn; St Louis Sub SchLA. 10: PTA Coun; Apalachian Girl Scout Coun. 13: Yes. 15: 10813 Hallstead dr, St Louis Mo 63136.

MORGAN, ELSIE (ELIZABETH) (SACHS). b New Prague Minn 27 N 16. 4: Robert J Morgan. 5: Col of St Catherine 32-36 (Art, Lit) BA; Sch of Art Inst 38-40 (Art); Northwestern 40 (Journalism); UMinn 62-64 MA in LS. 6: Fr, Japanese. 7: Pub rels asst Art Inst (Chicago) 39-42; Pub rels asst Mc-Cann-Erickson, Chicago 42-43; Pub rels dir Ruthrauff & Ryan, Chicago 3-45; Feature writer "Nippon Times, Tokyo 47-50; Pub rels dir Walker Art Center, Minneapolis 52-60; Br libn Dakota-Scott Reg Lib, W St Paul Minn 60-63, Adult serv coordinator 63-66; Dir Scott Co Lib Syst 68-. 9: Pub Rels Soc Amer; Overseas Pres Club; Minn Adult Educ Assn (Bd mem 65-68); Min Press Club; MinnLA; NEA. 10: Ikebana Internat; Arts Councl; AAUW. 13: Yes. 14: Adult serv, pub rels, ref, reading guidance. 15: 310 First ave NW, New Prague Minn 56071.

MORGAN, ERMA JEAN. b Columbus Ohio 23 S 39. 5: Bowling Green State U 57-61 (Eng) BA; UMich 61-62 MALS. 7: Catlgr Bowling Green State U 62-67; Asst hd catlgr No Ill U 67-. 9: ALA; IllLA. 10: Bus & Profess Women. 14: Catlg. 15: 1537 Rogers ct, DeKalb Il 60115.

MORGAN, FLORENCE B(LANCHE). b Galva Ill 27 S 1900. 5: UColo 25 (Eng Lit) BA; UIll 29 BS in LS; Columbia 36 (LS) MS. 6: Fr. 7: Asst Pub Lib, GalvaIll 22-3; Tchr High Sch, Hooper Colo 25-26; Order asst UIll Lib (Urbana) summers 28, 29; Catlr Queens Borough Pub Lib, Jamaica NY 29-41; Ser catlgr Tex A&M Col 41-43; Jr libn Colo A&M Col 43-44; Catlgr UNM Lib 44-49; Catlgr Ariz State U Matthews Lib 50-. 9: ALA; Ariz State LA. 10: Beta Phi Mu. 13: Yes. 14: Catlg, clsf. 15: 1162 S Mill ave, Tempe Az 85281.

MORGAN, GERTRUDE ANN. b Cambria Wis 23 Ag 13. 5: UWis 35 (Bot) BA, 48 BSL. 7: Tchr Cambria High Sch, Cambria Wis43-47; Br libn Racine Pub Lib, Racine Wil 8-52, Head ext dept 52-. 9: ALA; WisLA. 14: Serv to pub. 15: 1754 Grange ave apt 102, Racine Wi 53403.

MORGAN, INA KATHRYN (MIDDLETON). b Hawthorne Fla 11 S 32. 4: Edward Lewis Morgan. 5: UFla 50-54 (Elem Educ) BAE; Peabody summer 57; Fla State U summers 58-62 MS in LS. 7: Tchr Winter Garden Elem Sch, Winter Garden Fla 54-58; Sch libn Winter Garden Elem Sch, Dillard Elem Sch, Tildenville, Winter Garden Fla 58-63; Sch libn Winter Garden Elem Sch & Dillard Elem Sch, Winter Garden Fla 63-66; Coord elem libs & sch libn Hickory Hills Elem Sch,Marietta Ga 66-68; Libn Madison Jr High, Titusville Fla 68-. 9: ALA-AASchL; NEA-DAVI; ACEI; FlaLA; FlaEA; FlaASchL; Fla A-V Assn Classroom Tchrs; GaLA; SELA. 10: Alpha Delta Kappa; Friends of Lib; PTA; AAUW. 14: Child wk, Church libs. 15: Box 171, Windermere Fla 32786.

MORGAN, JAMES EARL. b Wheeling W Va 30 Je 41. 4: Carman Head. 5: Otterbein Col 59-61; Ariz State Col 62-65 (Soc sci) BS in Ed; Fla State U 65-66 MSLS. 6: Fr. 7: Grad asst Fla State U 65-66; Hd pub serv Ga Col Milledgeville Ga 67-. 9: ALA; SELA; GaLA. 10: Kappa Delta Pi; Phi Alpha Theta; AAUP. 14: Ref, archives. 15: PO Box 257, Milledgeville Ga 31061.

MORGAN, JEAN M. b Bellefontaine Ohio 29 Mr 26. 5: USan Diego 53-57 (Sp) BA; San Francisco Col for Women 62 (Sp) MA; Immaculate Heart Col 67 MALS. 6: Sp, Fr, Portu. 7: Tchr Cal Schs, San Diego, San Francisco, Los Angeles, Eureka 57-60; Libn Bernard High Sch, Eureka Cal 60-64; Libn Bernard High Sch, Playa Del Rey Cal 64-68; Assoc libn Ventura Col 68-. 8: Consul CathLA 67-68; Sec Lib Com; Archdiocese of Los Angeles 67-68, Ventura Col 68-69. 9: ALA; CalLA; CalASchL. 10: Ventura Co Hist Soc. 14: Catlg, ser. 15: 632 Empire ave, Ventura Ca 93003.

MORGAN, JOE LEE. b Mars Hill NC 14 My 31. 5: Berea Col 50-54 (Hist & Pol Sci) AB; Northern Ill U (spring) 55 (nights) (Educ); UHawaii (spring) 66 (nights) (Ancient Hist); UColo (summers) 57-58 (Pol Sci); UNC 57-58 (nights) (Educ); Duke 59 (summer) (Asian Studies); East Tenn State U (summers) 60, 61, 62, 63, 68 (LS). 6: Fr. 7: Tchr Sedgefield Jr High Sch (Charlotte NC) 57-59; Tchr-libn Madison Co Sch (Marshall NC) 59-65; Hd libn Truett McConnell Col (Cleveland Ga) 65-66; Libn-tchr Georgia Industrial Inst (Alto Ga) 66-67; Libn-tchr Riverside Mil Acad (Gainesville Ga) 67-. 15: R-2, Marshall NC 28753.

MORGAN, JOHN F(RANCIS). b Astoria LI NY 17 Je 23. 4: Mary Morgan. 5: NYU Washington Sq 45-49 (Eng) BA; Columbia 49-50 (LS) MS. 7: Infantry (Lt) US Army, ETO & US 40-45; Asst libn Col of Med UNeb 51-52; Patent-Searcher Self employed, NYC 53-54; Libn Gr II Queensboro Pub Lib, Astoria & Jamaica NY 54-56; Asst libn Republic Aviation Corp, Farmingdale LI NY 56-58; Chief libn Filtron Co Inc, Flushing NY 59-61; Sr libn ref E Meadow Pub Lib, E Meadow NY 62; Lib supv Fairchild Stratos Inc, Wyandanch LI NY 62-63; Industrial lib consul 64-; Assoc libn & Assoc prof Acad of Aeronautics, LaGuardia Field, Flushing NY 67-. 9: ALA; SLA. 10: AAUP. 13: Yes. 14: Admin, ref, info retrieval systems, tech proc. 15: P O Box 854, Point Lokout NY 11569.

MORGAN, JOHN MATHEW. b Toledo Oho 12 Ja 28. 4: Helen Pershing. 5: St John's Col (Annapolis) 43-47; U Toledo 47-50 (Educ) BA in Educ, (Hist) MA; UMich 52-57 (Hist, LS) MALS. 6: Fr, Russian. 7: US Army Signal Corps Cryptography 50-52; UToledo: Asst circ libn 56-57, Asst ref libn 57-62, Ref libn 62-, Asst Prof Lib Sci 62-. 9: ALA; OhioLA. 10: Ohio Hist Soc; Maumee Valley Hist Soc. 14: Ref, info retrieval, clsf theory, govt docs, hist Amer printing. 15: 3112 Kenwood blvd, Toledo Oh 43606.

MORGAN, LA VERA ANNE. b Albertville Ala. 5: Woman's College of Ga 29-32 BS; UAla 35 9ls0 5th Yr Degree. 7: Libn: Thomson High Sch, Thomson Ga 35-36, Cullman High Sch, Cullman Ala 36-42; Libn Guided Missiles div CNO, Wash DC 48-50; Asst libn & deputy libn Naval Research Lab, Wash DC 50-65, Hd libn 65-. 9: SLA; ALA; ASIS; DCLA. 10: Bus & Profess Woman's Club; Mil Libns Wkshop; Coun of Libns; East Council Naval Labs. 15: Naval Res Lab, Wash DC 20390.

MORGAN, MARIANNE. b Muncie Ind 13 O 40. 5: Ball State 58-61 (Pre-Med); Cal State Col (Long Beach) 61-63 (Geog) BA; USoCal 66-68 MSLS. 7: Lab tech Ball Mem Hosp, Muncie ind 56-61; Lab Tech Boyd Med Clinic, Long Beach Cal 61-62; Sr lib asst Anaheim Cal 63-68; Asst libn Orange Coast Col 68-. 9: SLA; ALA; CalLA; OrangeCoLA; OrangeCoSchLA. 10: CalTA; Alpha Sigma Tau; Beta Phi Mu. 14: Ref, ser, catlg. 15: 480 Schooner way, Seal Beach Ca 90740.

MORGAN, MARTHA JANE. b Panama City Fla 12 O 41. 5: Gulf Coast Jr Col 59-61 AA; Fla State U 61-63 (Soc sci) BA, 64-65 (LS) MS; UFla 68 (Bus admin). 7: Tchr Mowat Jr High Sch, Lynn Haven Fla 63-64; Libn Brunswick Jr Col 65; Ref libn Atlanta Pub Lib 66; Ext libn NW Reg Pub Lib, Panama City Fla 66-67; Ref libn Eng & Physics Lib UFla 67-. 9: ALA; -PLA; -ACRL; SLA; SELA; FlaLA (Pub, Col & Spec Ref RT). 10: Gulf Const Jr Col Alum Assn; Fla StateU Alum Assn; AAUW; Le Moyne Art Found. 14: Ref, personnel, lib educ. 15: Box 12408 Univ sta, Gainesville Fl 32601.

MORGAN, MARY SUE (SIMPSON). b Cleveland Miss 17 N 40. 4: James Patrick Morgan. 5: Millsaps Col 58-59; Southwestern (Memphis) 59-60; UNC 60-62 (Eng) BA, 63-64 MSLS. 7: Eng tchr high sch, Vazoo City Miss 62-63; Child libn pub lib, Arlington Co Va 64-65; Sch libn elem sch, Va Beach Va 65-66; Asst Prof UMiss Lib Sci Dept (Oxford) 68, Catlgr 68-. 14: Child lit, catlg. 15: 208 Williams st, Oxford Mi 38665.

MORGAN, PAULA MARGARET. b Modesto Cal 11 Ag 35. 5: Mills Col 53-57 (Msic) AB; Columbia 57-59 (Musicology) MA; UCal(Berkeley) 59-63 (Musicology), 63-64 MLS. 6: Fr, Ger, Lat. 7: Mus libn Princeton U 64-. 9: Amer Musicological Soc; MusLA (chm Contemp Amer Composers Libs Com 68-; sec-treas NY Chap 67-69). 10: Phi Beta Kappa. ; Bk Club of Cal. 14: Music libnhip. 15: Princeton Univ Lib, Princeton NJ 08541.

MORGAN, ROBERT J(AMES). b Chicago. 4 Elsie Sachs. 7: Trustee Dakota-Scott Reg Lib System, W St Paul 60-69. 8: (Lt Col) USAF 42-46, Pacific Theatre. 9: ALA (Coun 68-69; Jt ASD-RSD Com on Orientation Proj 64-69);-ALTA (pres 68-69; Action Devel Com 63-65, Del Assembly 63, Alternate Del 64-65, Admin Coun III 65-66, Dir Reg VI 65-66); Minn Lib Trustee Assn (pres 64-66). 10: World Affairs Center UMinn; Minn Com for Nat Lib Week; New Prague Lib Found; New Prague Lib Bd; Minneapolis Great Bks Coun. 13: Yes. 15: 310 First ave NW, New Prague Minn 56071.

MORGAN, VIVIAN (HOFF). b Collegeville enn 2 F 04. 5: Ursinus Col 21-25 (Eng, Hist); Drexel MS in LS. 7: Libn Pub Lib, Wyomissing Penn 56-59; Ref dept Pub Lib, Reading Penn 60-62; Catlgr Pub Lib, Reading Penn 63-. 9: PennLA. 10: LWV. 14: Catlg, ref. 15: 1560 Delaware ave, Wyomissing Penn 19610.

MORGAN, WHITNEY N(ORCROSS). b Worcester Mass 28 Je 11. 5: Harvard 29-33 (Art Hist) BA, 33-34 (Musum wk); Pratt 41-42 BLS. 6: Fr, Ger. 7: Catlgr E Weyhe's Art Bkstore, NY 34-35; Volunteer Mus Wker Soc for Preserv of NE Antiquities, Boston; Res wker WPA Index of Amer Design, Boston 36-37; Sec Gallery of Mrs Cornelius J Sullivan, NY; Ed asst College Art Assn, NY 37-38; Bk-selling, antique dealing, volunteer wk Worcester Free Pub Lib, Worcester Mass 39-41; Ref dept asst in Main Reading Room, Exhibitions asst NY Pub Lib 42-44; Catlgr University Club Lib, NY 44-47; Shop asst B T Batsford Ltd, London & NY 47-49; Museum libn Cooper Union (NY) 50-55; Libn Nat Recreation Assn, NY 55-57; Catlgr NY Sch of Soc Wk Columbia U 57-58; Ref asst W Hartford Pub Lib, W Hartford Conn 58-59; Catlgr UHartford 60-. 9: SLA (pres Conn Valley Chap 63-64; sec-treas icture Group of NY Chap 55-57). 14: Catlg, rare bks. 15: 22 Townley st, Hartford Ct 06105.

MORGENSTERN, SALI (WEIDENFELD). b Romania 6 Ap 18. 4: Jacob Morgenstern. 5: Czernoutz (Romania) 37 H S Baccalaureat Diploma; UCzernoutz Faculty of Phylosophy & Linguistics 37-39 (Ger-Fr). 6: Ger, Fr, Lat, Romanian, Hebrew, Russian. 7: Asst libn Acad of S R Romania, Bucharest 49-52, Libn 52-56; Chief libn Israel Med Assn, HaifaU 60-67; Rare bk catlgr NY Acad of Med, NYC 67-. 8: Adv wk for org of Hosp Libs in Haifa, hedera & Naharija Israel 64-67. 9: MedLA. 14: Ref, catlg, rare bks. 15: 142-20 84th dr, Jamaica NY 11435.

MORGENTHALER, EVELYN (DEARISO). b Sylvester Ga 5 Ag 09. 5: Ga State Womans Col 26-30 (Lat, Edu) AB; Emory 31-32 AB in LS. 7: Ga State Womans Col; Asst libn 30-31, Act libn 32-33, Libn 33-40; Lib asst FWA Ref Lib, Wash DC 42-43; Libn E C Glass High Sch, Lynchburg Va 50-52; Asst ref libn USC 54-56; Asst libn Mitchell-Baker-Worth Reg Lib, Camilla Ga 56-62; Asst libn Valdosta State Col 62-. 9: ALA; SEL; GaLA; GaEA. 10: AAUP. 14: Catlg, ref. 15: 1104 Thomwal st, Valdosta Ga 31603.

MORIARTY, JOHN H(ELENBECK). b Waterbury Conn 9 N 03. 4: Helen Jean Merritt. 5: Columbia 22-26 (Eng) BA, 33-34 (LS) BS, 34-35 (LS) MS; Chicago 45 (LS). 6: Fr. 7: Off manager NY Telephone Co, Buffalo NY 26-33; Libn & Lecturer in philos Cooper Union (NYC) 35-39; Asst to dir Columbia U Libs Process 39-41; Asst dir acquis & dept dir processing, chief Access Div LC 41-44; Dir of Libs Purdue U 44-, Dir of Libs & A-v center 50-. 8: Assoc, Columbia U Sch of Lib Serv, 37-41; Interdeptl Com for Acquis of publs, OSS 41-44; Chm, Interdeptl Com on indexing Combat film, Bur of the Budget, 43-44; Visiting lecturer, UIll Lib Sch, summers 50, 53, 56. 9: ALA (Coun 47-49 & 64-67; (chm AV Com 66-69, chm bd of Resources 53; chm Subcom on Punched Card Procedure 44-46); -ACRL (chm Agric Libs Sect 48-49; chm Pure & Appl Sci Sect 52); SLA (pres Ind Chap 47-48); Amer Soc Engnr Educ (chm Libns Com 54-55); Univ Film Producers Assn (pres 58-60); IndLA (chm Col Libns Round Table 45; pres 52-53); Ind Sch Bds Assn (chm Dist 4 56). 10: Rotary; Torch Club; Ind Legisl Adv Commsn, Lib Adv Com; Ind Dept Pub instr Lib Adv Com; W Lafayette Bd of Educ; Phi Beta Kappa; Beta Phi Mu. 12: Auth "Directory Information for New York City Residents, 1626-1786 (42). 13: Yes. 14: A-v serv, lib bldgs, lib admin. 15: 168 Drury lane, W Lafayette In 47906.

MORIARTY, PAUL V. b Jacksonville Ill 22 Mr 40. 4: Judith Essie Moriarty. 5: Pepperdine Col 63-65 (Hist) BA; UWis 65-66 (LS) MA. 6: Fr. 7: Acquis libn Wis State U 66-. 14: Acquis wk. 15: 915 Eastman st, Platteville Wi 53818.

MORIER, YVAN. b 19 O 31. 5: UMontreal 58 BA, 61 L Ped, 65 B Bibl. 7: Dir period dept Bibliotheque Nationale du Quebec. 9: Association canadienne des bibliothecaires de langue francaise. 14: Ref. 15: 1700 St Denis, Montreal 129 Que Can.

MORIN, WILFRED LAURIER. b Troy NH 1 D 11. 5: UNH 34 (Hist, Eng) BA; UVa 43 (Civil Affairs) Certif; Stanford 44 (Far East Studies) Certif; Columbia 46 BS LS; Maxwell Sch of Syracuse U 56 (Pub Admin) MPA. 6: Fr, Portu, Japanese. 7: (Capt) S Atlantic Wing, Purchasing Off, Rio de Janeiro Brazil 41-43; (Maj) G-5 US War Dept Far East Affairs, Monterey Cal 43-46; Asst NY Pub Lib 39-41; Asst to Exec Sec ALA, Chicago 46-47; Head circ dept Cornell U Lib 47-49; Pub lib supv NY State Educ Dept, Albany NY 49-57; Lib Ext Spec US Off of Educ, Wash DC 57-60; Dir Freeport Mem Lib, Freeport NY 60-. 8: Assoc Prof of Lib Sci, St Johns U 60-; Lecturer in lib sci Pratt Inst 60-66. 9: ALA; SLA; AEAUSA; NRTA; NCCM; LPRC (Exec Bd); NYLA (Legis Com); DCLA (Exec Bd); WestchesterLA; NCLA (Exec Bd). 10: Echange Club; Rotary Club; Can Econ & Hist Assn; Amer Mgt Assn; C of C; Commun Coun; Freeport Hist Soc. 12: "State Library Extension Services with N Cohen (60); "American Laws Governing State Aid to Public Libraries, Library Trends (60); 13: Yes. 14: Admin, tchg. 15: Freeport Mem Lib, S Ocean ave & W Merrick rd, Freeport LI NY 11520.

MORISSET, AUGUSTE-M OMI. b Fall River Mass 27 O 1900. 5: UOttawa 21-28 (Priesthood), 29-30 (Canon Law) LJC, 29-36 (Fr Lit) BA; UMich summer 35 (LS); Columbia 36-39 BS (LS), 48 MS (LS). 6: Fr. Lat. 7: Bursar & curate St Pierre-Apotre, Montreal 28-29; Prof of Fr & Lat Juniorat du Sacre-Coeur, Ottawa 29-30; Curate Sacre-Coeur Parish, Ottawa 30-34; Libn UOttawa 34-58, Founder & Dir Lib Sch 38-. 8: Can del, Internat Congress of Libs & Documentation Centers, Brussels 55; Lecturer, Ecole de Bibliothecaires, UMontreal 37-62; Com on Can Bk Center, Jt Bk Proj Com (Ottawa) 48-50; Nat Lib Adv Com, 49-52; Nat Lib Adv Coun, 53-59; Adv Com, Bibliothegionale du Nord de L'Outaouais, Hull Que 61-64. 9: Internat Assn of Documentalists; Bibliog Soc Can (pres 50-52; ALA; SLA; CanLA (Com on Lib Educ 64-66 chm CLA-ALA Liaison Com 53-54; CLA-ACB Coun mem 61-62); Can Mus LA (chm 61-62); Association Canadienne des Bibliothecaires de Langue Francaise (pres 60-61): hon life mem 68; Lib Assn Ottawa (pres 43-44); QueLA; OntLA; Ont Reg Group of Catlgrs (chm 48-49); Inst Prof Libns Ont. 10: Can Writers Foun. 11: Centennial Medal 67. 12: "La Bibliotheque de lUniversite dOttawa: Son role et ses initiatives (45). 13: Yes. 14: Lib educ, catlg. 15: Lib Sch, UOttawa, Ottawa Can.

MORITA, JAMES R. b Salem Ore 13 Je 31. 4: Ichiko Takagi. 5: Okayama U (Japan) 50-54 BA; UMich 57-59 (Far East Studies) MA, 59-60 (LS) MA; PhD Chicago 61-68 (Far East Langs & Civilizations). 6: Japanese, Fr, Chinese. 7: Sr catlgr Harvard-Yenching Inst Harvard U 60-61; UChicago: Japanese bibliogr Lib 61-62, Asst libn Far East Lib 62-66, Lecturer Dept of Far East Langs & Civilizations 64-67, Instr Deptof Far East Langs 67-68 , Asst Prof 68-. 9: Assn for Asian Studies; ALA; JapanLA. 13: Yes. 14: Japanese lit, bibliog (espec for Asian studies), area studies & libs. 15: 921 E 54th pl. Chicago Il 60615.

MORITZ, CHARLES FREDRIC. b Cleveland 23 Ja 17. 5: Ohio State U 36-42 (Eng) BA; Columbia 47-48 BS in LS; Harvard 46-47 (Eng); Middlebury Col 48-50 (Eng) MA. 6: Fr, Ger, Sp. 7: Asst ref rare bk room Yale U Lib 48-50; Asst libn Woodstock Br NY Pub Lib 50-52; Reviewer of bks for adults ALA "Booklist, Chicago 52-55; Asst Prof Grad Sch of Lib Serv Rutgers U 55-58; Ed "Current Biography, H W Wilson Co, NYC 58-. 9: ALA ("Booklist Staff 52-55); BSA; NJLA; NY Lib Club. 12: Ed NJLA "Newsletter (57-58). 13: Yes. 14: Ed wk. 15: 518 W 232 st, New York NY 10463.

MORITZ, WILLIAM DEAN. b Tyler Minn 21 S 35. 4: Phyllis Y Hackett Moritz. 5: Northwestern Col (Minneapolis) 53-54; Mankato State Col 54-57 (Eng) S; UDenver summers 63-65 (LS) MA; USD 65-66. 7: Tchr West Jr High Sch, Sioux City Iowa 57-58; Libn Central High Sch,Sioux City Iowa 58-66; Admin asst to dir libs UWis (Milwaukee) 66-. 9: ALA; NEA; IowaLA (pres NW Dist 59-60); WisLA. 12: "History of the Sioux City Public Library (65). 14: Admin, pub serv, personnel. 15: 1934 Cedar dr, Grafton Wi 53024.

MORLEY, MAE (GRIGG). b Montreal Can. 4: William Morley. 5: McGill 42-47 (Psych & Sociol) BA; Toronto 52-53 BLS. 6: Fr, Ger, Sp. 7: Libn Allan Mem Inst of Psychiatry, Montreal 54-57; Catlgr McGill U 57-58; Ser asst Providence Pub Lib 60-63; Ref asst Queens U (Ont) 64-65, Ref asst Health Scis Lib 65-. 10: YM-YWCA. 14: Med lib wk, soc sci. 15: 147 Norman Rogers dr, Kingston Ont Can.

MORLEY, WILLIAM F(ELIX) E(DMUND). b London 25 S 20. 4: Mae L Grigg. 05: UToronto 48-52 (Philos, Eng, Hist) BA, 52-53 BLS. 5: UToronto 48-52 BA (honors), 52-53 BLS; Brown 59-60. 6: Fr. 7: Flight engnr (Flight Sgt) RAF, Europe, W Indies, N Amer 40-46; Proprietor advertising concern, London Eng 46-47; Chief Libn YM-YWHA, Montreal 53-54; Chief Libn Can Pacific RR Co, Montreal 54-59; Bibliog John Carter Brown Lib Brown U 59-64; Bibliog Queens U (Kingston Ont) 64-66, Curator of spec collections 66-. 9: Bibliog Soc Can (2nd v-pres); RILA (chm Program Com); Inst Profess Libns Ont. 10: Prof Libns Assn Queens Univ; Can Hit Assn. 12: "Canadian Local Histories to 1850; a Bibliography" v1 (67); Ed "Canadian Notes & Queries" (68-). 13: Yes. 14; bibliog, rare bks & spec collectons, Canadiana, admin. 15: Duglas Lib Queens Univ, Kingston Ont Can.

MORLINO, PASCHAL ANTHONY OSB. b Portsmouth Va 3 My 38. 5: Belmont Abbey Col 57-62 9hist) AB; Belmont

Abbey Sem 62-63; Saint Maur's Sem 64-66 (Theol) STB; UPittsburgh 67-69 MLS. 6: Fr. 7: Lectr Belmont Abbey Col, Belmont NC 62-63; Lectr & admin asst benedictine Mil Schs, Savannah Ga 63-64, Dir pub rel & alumni 66-67; Prep libn & asst to dir St Vincent Col Lib, Latrobe Pa 67-. 8: Mem for curriculum planning St Vincent Prep School. 9: ALA; CatholicLA; PennLA. 14: Rare bks, spec collections. 15: St Vincent Archabbey, Latrobe Pa 15650.

MORRILL, WALTER DUNLAP. b Pittsburgh 11 Ja 36. 4: Marcia Simpson. 5: Monmouth Col 53-57 (Eng) AB; UIll 57-60 (LS) MS; UInd 67. 6: Gk, Fr, Lat. 7: UIll(Urbana); Rhetoric Instr 57-59, Asst catlg libn 5-60, Bind libn 60-61; Col Libn Muskingum Col 61-65; Asst dir of libs Kent State U 65-66; Dir of col libs Hanover Col 66-. 8: Admin consul, Lib Serv Center of East Ohio, Barnesville Ohio 65-66. 9: ALA-ACRL (chm Nomin Com Tri-State Chap 64); Amer Mgt Assn; OhioLA (chm Col & Univ Round TABLE 64-65); Ohio Col Assn (Spec Lib Coop Com 62-65); Ind LA (Adv Coun, Ind State Lib & Hist Bd). 10: Beta Phi Mu; AAUP. 13: Yes. 14: Admin, catlg, tech proc. 15: Box 53, Hanover In 47243.

MORRIS, BETHEL (RYLAND). b Stockton Cal 14 Ap 16. 4: Charles Russell Morris. 5: UCal(Berkeley) 34-38 (Lat) BA; UCal 39-40 Certif in LS. 7: Bibliogr asst UCal Lib (Berkeley) 40; Br libn Concord Br Contra Costa Co Lib, Concord Cal 51-65; Br libn Lafayette Br Cal 66-. 9: CalLA; LafayetteLA. 10: Concord Lib League; Phi Beta Kappa; pi Sigma. 15: 224 Jeanne dr, Pleasant Hill Ca 94523.

MORRIS, CAROLINE (STEWART). b Ridley Park Penn 14 S 23. 5: Drexel 46-50 (Ret Mgt) BS Com, 62-64 MS LS. 6: Fr, Sp. 7: MaM 2/c USNR(WR) Post Office 43-35; Personnel interviewer John Wanamaker, Phila 46-50; Sec to pres & acct Cliton Heights Penn 57-58; Accountant Lybrand Ross Bros & Montgomery, Phila 58; Accountnt George Young Co, Phila 60-64; Ser libn Penn Mil Col 64-65; Libn Penn Hosp Sch of Nursing, Phila 65-, Libn Penn Hosp Med Lib, Phila 67-. 9: MedLA; SLA; ALA; Lib Prof Assn. 10: Bus & Prof Women; DAR; AAUW; AAUP; Drexel Inst, Lib Sch Alum Assn. 14: Med libnship, med hist. 15: 555-13th ave, Prospect Park Penn 19076.

MORRIS, DAVID DAVIS. b Cedar Rapids Iowa 1 D 10. 4: Portia Marie Glindoman. 5: Northwestern U 30-35 (Hist) BA, MA; UIll 36-37 (Hist); UWis 47-48 BLS. 6: Fr. 7: Math tchr Lake Forest Acad, Lake Forest Ill 36; Libn "The Rotarian Magazine, Chicago 37-44; US Army Artillery Surveyor (Pvt), Ft SILL Okla & Ft Bragg NC 44; Eng tchr & libn Tekoa High Sch, Tekoa Wash 45; Bkstore clerk John W Graham & Co, Spokane Wash 45-46; Bkstore manager Whitworth Col 46-47; Acquis asst UWis Lib 47-48; Hist & period Whitman Col Lib 48-50; Ref, acquis Albion Col Lib 5063; Adult serv Jackson Co Lib, Jackson Mich 63-. 9: MichLA. 10: Phi Beta Kappa. 12: "The Greatest Queen of France (56). 13: Yes. 14: Ref, acquis. 15: 1046 Lilac st, East Lansing Mi 48823.

MORRIS, DOROTHY F. b Raymond NH 16 S 16. 5: Simmons summers 56-58 (LS). 7: Lib asst Dartmouth Col Lib 39-46; Lib asst VA Hosp, White River Jct Vt 46-47; Supv libn US Navy Underwater Sound Lab, New London 47-. 9: SLA; NELA. 14: Catlg, ref. 15: Navy Underwater Sound Lab, Ft Trumbull, New London Ct 06320.

MORRIS, EFFIE LEE. b Richmond Va. 5: Chicago 38-41 (Soc Sci); Flora Stone Mather Col West Res U 44-45 (Soc Sci) BA; West Res 45 (Amer Culture), 45-46 BLS, 56 MSLS. 7: Child libn Cleveland Pub Lib 46-55; Instr child serv Sch of Lib Serv Atlanta U 54; Child libn NY Pub Lib 55-58; Child pec Lib for the Blind NY Pub Lib 58-63; Coordinator child serv San Francisco Pub Lib 63-. 8: Field wk supv, 49-55, & Spec lecturer 53-55, West Res Sch of Lib Sci; Consul Amer Foun for the Blind, 59-63; Judge, juvenile bks 59 & child bks 63; LC Adv Com of Child Libns on the Sel of Child Bks for the Blind, 58-63; Consul child serv Chicago Pub Lib Survey 68-69; Adv com State of Cal ESEA Title II 66-. 9: ALA (Exec Bd Jr Mem RT 53-55; Coun 67-71; chm San Francisco Conf Local Arrangements 67; Newberry-Caldecott Com 50-56, Laura Ingalls Wilder Award Com 53-54, 59-60; chm Pub Com 59-60; Adv Mgr "Top of the News" 57-58; Mem Publ Sub-com 61-62);-Child Lib Assn (chm Bk Eval Com 52-54; sec 55-56; chm Nomin Com 55-56; Bd Dirs 63-66; Mem Adv Com to Bkstores 63; Lib serv to Except Child 65-68); CalLA (Com on For Libns Exch 63; pres-elect Golden Gate Dist 64-66); Assn of Child Libns No Cal (Inst Com 63-64; Coun mem-at-large 64-65); NCTE (mem 2 coms 65). 10: Nat Braille Club; Womens Nat Bk Assn; YWCA; Coun on Civic Unity; LWV; Bay Area Urban League; NAACP; AAUW; Beta Phi Mu; Alpha Kappa Alpha; Altrusa. 11: E P Dutton-John MacRae Award, 58; Outstanding Volunteer Serv, Nat Aid to the Visually Handicapped, 64; Bay Areas Outstanding Negro Woman, Iota Phi Lambda, 64. 13: Yes. 14: Child serv. 15: San Francisco Pub Lib, Civic Center, San Francisco Cal 94102.

MORRIS, EUGENE S. b Sterling Col 10Jl 26. 5: Whitman Col 46-48; UDenver 48-51 (Psych) BA, 55-56 (Personnel) MSBA, 61-62 (LS) MA. 6: Ger. 7: US Navy Sonar 3/c P O 44-46; Voc coun UDenver 52-53, Psychometrist 53-55; Test tech Colo Merit System,Denver 55-57; Psychometrist UDenver 57-61; Catlgr Colo Womans Col, Temple Buell Col 62-. 9: ALA; ColoLA; MPLA. 10: Denver Metropolitan Libns; Theatre Guild-Amer Theatre Soc. 14: Catlg. 15: 2512 So Univ blvd apt 301, Denver Co 80210.

MORRIS, IRVING. b Brooklyn NY 31 Mr 27. 4: Joan Amdur. 5: Brooklyn Col 45, 47-50 (Hist) BA, 59; Columbia 50-52 (LS) MLS; NYU summers 54, 55; Hunter Col summers 56, 60. 6: Sp. 7: (Pfc) US Army, US & Europe 45-47; Prof libn Gr 1 & 2 Brooklyn Pub Lib 50-52; Tchr-libn R L Stevenson High Sch, NYC 52-60, 62; Tchr of lib F K Lane High Sch, Brooklyn NY 54-55; Tchr of lib Flushing High Sch, Flushing Queens NY 55-64; Tchr of lib John Bowne High Sch, Flushing Queens NY 64-; Tchr NYC Bd of Educ summers 64-66. 8: Tchr-libn, R L Stevenson Sch, reorg lib into spec collection for 12-18 yr old "under-achievers, 62; Bk rev for Bur of Libs, NYC Bd of Educ, 55-; Consul UFT, planning li-ref collection, 63-; Consul UFT, More Effective Schools Com 63. 9: ALA-AASchL, & other divs & sects; NEA; LPRC; NCSS; NYLA (Merchanization Com); NY Lib Club. 10: Amer Fed of Tchrs; NYC Sch Libs Assn; PTA; Nat Coun for the Social Studies. 13: Yes. 15: United Fed of Tchrs Lib, 260 Park ave S, New York NY 10010.

MORRIS, JOHANNA SMITH. b Wash DC. 5: Fisk U 44-48 (Hist) BA; West Res 48-49 MSLS; Wayne State 55-57 (Educ) Tchg Certif; UMinn (NDEA Inst) 65 (LS); George Washington U 68-69 (Supervision). 7: Readers adv DC Pub Lib 49-53; Adult asst Detroit Pub Lib 54-56; Tchr & Libn Detroit Pub Schs 57-60; Libn DC Pub Schs 60-65, Asst dir lib serv 65-. 8: Lectr DC Teachers Col, spring 67; Consul UMinn (Minneapolis) NDEA summer inst 67. 9: ALA (Ad hoc Com on Treatment of Minorities in Lib Bk); -AASchL; -Yasd& -CSD; -ASCD; NCTE; DCLA; DCASchL (pres 63-65). 10: Sigma Upsilon Pi; Delta Kappa Gamma; Coun of Admin Women in Educ. 12: "Thr Black American: a Selected List of Books of Significance for School Libraries" (68). 13: Yes. 14: Sch libs (admin & supv). 15: 14 Logan cir NW, Wash DC 20005.

MORRIS, JUNIUS H. b Tonica Ill 22 Mr 22. 4: Vera Campbell. 5: UIll 40-43, 47-48 (Biol) BS, MS; UMd 50-54 (Child Study); Columbia 51-52 (A-v Educ); UWash 58-60 MLS; Wash 61-68 (Higher Educ) PhD. (Higher Educ). 6: Russian, Fr, Sp. 7: (T/5) 223rd Army Hosp Ship Com, European & Asiatic 43-46; Sci tchr Newman Sch, New Orleans 48-50; Head sci dept Damascus High Sch, Mongomery Co Md 50-52; Jr physicist Ordnance Engnr Corp, Rockville Md 52-54; Homesteader Columbia Basin Irrigation Project, Eltopia Wash 54-60; Sci libn Wash State U 60-64; Head Libn Highline Col 64-. 9: ALA; PNLA; WashLA. 10: AAUP; Rotary; ACLU. 13: Yes. 14: Jr col & undergrad libs. 15: 23147 20th ave S, Des Moines Wash 98188.

MORRIS, KENNETH HARLAN JR. b Dayton Ohio 16 Ja 38. 5: Ohio Wesleyan U 56-60 (Fr) BA; Stanford 60-63 (Fr) MA; UMich 64-65 MLS. 6: Fr, Sp, Ital, Esperanto. 7: Asst catlgr Bradley U Lib 65-68; Catlgr Presentation Col Lib, Aberdeen SDak 68-. 9: ALA. 10: Esperanto Assn of N Amer; Phi Beta Kappa. 14: Catlg. 15: 570 W William st, Delaware Ohio 43015.

MORRIS, LESLIE R. b Sewickly Penn 18 D 35. 4: Sandra Chass Morris. 5: Geneva Col 53-57 (Eng) BS Ed; Duquesne U 60-61 M Ed LS; Rutgers 64-67. 6: Fr, Sp. 7: High sch Eng tchr, Penn & Tex 57-61; (Sp/4) US Army Radar operator 60; Catlgr St francis Col (Penn) 61-64; Catlgr Ind State Col 61-63; Head catlgr E Stroudsburg State Col 64-. 9: ALA-ACRL; PennLA. 10: AAUP. 12: "A Newman Bibliography" (64). 13: Yes. 14: Catlg, rare bks, IBM bk catlgs, tech serv. 15: 400 Quentin rd, Stroudsburg Pa 18360.

MORRIS, MARGARET (SINCLAIR). b Pontiac Ill 5 Mr 08. 4: Warren M Morris. 5: Frances Shimer 25-27; Knox Col 27-29 (Eng) BS. 7: Asst circ libn Galesburg Pub Lib, Galesburg Ill 44-45, Catlgr 46-62, Hd libn 63-. 9: ALA; IllLA. 10: Pi Beta Phi; PEO; Altrusa. 14: Admin, catlg. 15: 170 W N st, Galesburg Il 61401.

MORRIS, MARGARET ANN. b Parsonsburg Md 5 Ap 31. 5: East Pilgrim Col 57-59; Kutztown State Col 59-61 (LS) BS; Syracuse 65-66 (LS) MSLS. 7: Bkkeeper Salisbury Nat Bank, Salisbury Md 48-47; Libn Lower Shore Area Lib, Salisbury Md 61-62; Libn East Shore Bk Processing Center, Salisbury Md 62-66; Libn Owosso Col (Mich) 66-. 9: ALA; MichLA. 10: Kappa Delta Pi; Beta Phi Mu. 14: Catlg, tech proc. 15: 115 Oakwood ave, Owosso Mi 48867.

MORRIS, MARGARET FRANCINE. b Gilmer Tes 26 Je 38. 5: UTex 56-61 (Eng) BA; E Tex State 62-63 MS in LS. 6: Fr. 7: Bkmob libn Tex State Lib 64; Libn I ref & interlib loan Arlington State Col UTex 64-67, Libn II, Ref libn 68-. 8: Dallas Regl Planning Com for a State-wide Communications Netwk 68-. 9: ALA; TexLA. 10: AAUW; AAUP; Tex Assn Col Tchrs; Ft Worth Corral of Westerners. 14: Ref, interlib coop, collection devel. 15: Univ of Texas at Arlington, Arlington Tx 76010.

MORRIS, MARTHA. b Phila 14 D 09. 5: Womens Col UDel 28-32 (Chem, Educ) AB; UVa summers 33-35 LS); UNC 38-39 AB in LS. 7: Ref libn UDel 35-42; Hosp libn US Navy, Bainbridge Naval Train Sta, Md42-47; Co Libn Wicomico Co, Salisbury Md 47; Tech libnNaval Engnr Expt Sta, Annapolis Md 47-54; Chief Libn Vet Hosp, Wilmington Del 54-. 9: ALA; SLA; MedLA; DelLA. 14: Ref, readers adv serv to hosp patients. 15: 507 Nottingham rd, Newark Del 19711.

MORRIS, MARY EUGENIA. b Sylva NC 12 Je 37. 5: UNC (Greensboro) 55-59 (Eng) AB; UNC (Chapel Hill) 61-62 MSLS. 6: Fr. 7: Tchr & libn Princess Anne Co Schs, Va 59, Sch libn 59-61; Order libn West Carolina U Lib 62-. 9: ALA; NCLA (RTS; sec-treas 66-67; dir Jr mems RT 66-67); SEast Regl Gp of Resources and Tech Serv Libns (Nomin Com); SELA. 14: Acquis. 15: Box 295, Sylva NC 28779.

MORRIS, MARY FRANCES. b Portsmouth Va 20 Ag 29. 5: Agnes Scott Col 46-50 (Music) BA; UNC (Chapel Hill) 54-56, 60-61 MS in LS. 7: Ref libn Duke U Lib 56-64; Act head ref dept Womans Col Lib Duke U 64-65; Ref libn Duke U Lib 65-. 68; Asst ref libn Joyner Lib ECarolina U 68-. 9: NCLA; SELA. 10: AAUW; Beta Phi Mu, Mortar Board. 14: Ref. 15: Joyner Lib, E Carolina Univ, Greenville NC 27834.

MORRIS, MARY SUE (TATUM). b Homestead Fla 29 N 15. 4: Harry A Morris. 5: Phoenix Jr Col 34-35 (Liberal Arts); Ariz State (Flagstaff) 36-38 (Educ) BA. 7: Tchr, Nogales Ariz 38-41; Clerk Lockheed Aircraft, Burbank Cal 42-43, 49-51; Admin asst Mesa Pub Lib, Los Alamos NM 51-53; Los Alamos Sci Lab, Los Alamos NM; Lib buyer 53-56, Asst Procurement & Distrib Sect Leader 56-60, Asst order libn 61-62, Asst report libn 62-66, Report libn 67-. 9: SLA. 14: Reports. 15: 24 Royal Crest Trailer ct, Los Alamos NM 67544.

MORRIS, NED CORLEY. b Laneville Tex 3 My 24. 4: Betty Jean Spiller. 5: Kilgore Jr Col 46-48; N Tex State U 48-50 (LS) BA. 6: Ger. 7: US Army Air Corps Mil Police Unit (Pfc) 42-45; Ref libn Tex Col of Arts & Ind 50-51, Act head libn 51-64, Acquis libn & ser supv 64-. 9: TexLA(sec-treas Col Div 53-54; v-chm Dist 4 53-54). 10: Robert J Kleberg Pub Lib, Kingsville Tex (Charter mem); Alpha Lambda Sigma. 13: Yes. 14: Acquis, ser. 15: 1205 W Richard, Kingsville Tx 78363.

MORRIS, R(AYMOND) PHILIP II. b New Haven Conn 4 D 42. 4: Karen Louise Morris (nee kraus). 5: Central Methodist Col 60-64 (Eng Lit) AB; Pratt 64-65 MLS. 7: Sgt US Army, NYC 65-68; Dir lib Central Methodist Col 68-. 9: ALA. 15: 317 N Mulberry st apt O, Fayette Mo 65248.

MORRIS, RAYMOND PHILIP. b Garnett Kan 16 Mr 04. 4: Jean Louise Kelly. 5: Baker U 26 (Hist) BA; Garrett Theol Sem 29 (Hist) BD; Columbia 30 (LS) BS, 32 (LS) MS. 6: Hebrew, Gk, Lat, Ger, Fr. 7: Libn Garrett Biblical Inst Theol Sem 31-32; Yale Divinity Sch: Asst libn 32-34, Libn 34-, Asst Prof 41-49, Assoc Prof 49-51, Prof of Religious Lit 51-. 8: Consul: Lib Program, World Coun of Churches, 56, Nat Coun of Churches, Interchurch Center 58-64, Nanking BD OF ounders 58, Nat Coun of YMCA; Presbyt Bd of Ecumenical Missions 58, Meth Bd of Missions 68, Ecumenical Inst for Advanced Theol Studies,Jerusalem 67; Inst of Cult & Ecumenical Res, Collegeville Minn 67-; Mem, Commsnon Accred, Am Assn Theol Schs 66-68. 9: ALA; Amer Church Hist Soc; SAA; ATheolLA (pres 51-53, chm Bd of Microtexts,chm Lib Devel Program 61-). 10: Lambda Chi Alpha. 11: MA (Hon, Yale 51); Litt D (Baker U 52); DD (Drake U 65). 12; libraries of Theological Seminaries (34); "A Theological Book List (60); "Aids to Theological Libraries" (69). 13: Yes. 14: Admin, bibliog, consul (theol libs). 15: 409 Prospect st, New Haven Conn 06511.

MORRIS, RITA LOUISE (AUERBACH). b NYC. 4: Joseph Morris. 5: Hunter Col 41-45 9journalism) BA; GeorgetownU 45 (Admin Law); C W Post 65-68 MLS. 7: Indexer- abstractor Nat Archives, Wash DC 45-46; Copywriter Barkow Advertising, NYC 46-50; Hd catlg Nassau Commun Col, Garden City NY 66-. 15: Lib Nassau Community College, Garden City NY 11530.

MORRIS, THELMA J. b Evanston Ill 4 Je 32. 5: Oberlin Col 50-54 (Eng Lit) BA; Simmons 54-56 MS in LS. 6: Fr. 7: Asst in lib Simmons Sch of Soc Wk 54-56; Ref asst Baker Lib Harvard Bus Sch 56-61& Asst libn UWash Bus Admin Lib 61-62; Ref libn Fed Res Bank of Cleveland 62-64; Ref libn govt, educ, soc sci dept Cleveland Pub Lib 64-. 8: Staff, Lib 21, Seattle Worlds Fair, 62. 9: ALA; Ohio LA. 12: "Executive Compensation, Selected Preferences (60). 13: Yes. 14: Ref. 15: 11807 N Lane dr, Lakewood Ohio 44107.

MORRIS, VERNA (TOLLESON). b Gaffney SC 19 Ja 08. 5: Limestone Col 26-29; UNC (Greensboro) 29-31 (LS) AB, summer 35; Appalachian State Tchs Col summer 48 (LS); West Carolina Col summer 63 (LS); UNC (Chapel Hill) summer 64 (LS). 7: Libn Blue Ridge Sch for Boys, Hendersonville NC 35-64; Order libn Furman U 64-. 9: ALA; SELA; SCLA. 10: AAUW. 15: Furman Univ, Greenville SC 29613.

MORRIS, WARREN. b Viola Ill 14 Je 18. 4: Margaret Sinclair. 5: Knox Col 36-39, 41 (Hist) AB; UDenver 48-50 (LS) AM. 7: US Army Cavalry 42-46; Circ libn Galesburg Pub Lib, Galesburg Ill 46-48; Knx Col: Ref libn 49-51, Catlgr 51-58, Libn 59-66, Report libn 67-. 9: ALA; IllLA. 14: Admin. 15: Know Col Lib, Galesburg Ill 61401.

MORRISEY, MARLENE D. b St Marys Kan. 4: John A Morrisey. 5: BakerU 31-35 (Eng, Music) AB (highest honors); AmericanU summer 49 (Television writing); CatholicU 52-54 (LS). 6: Fr, Ger. 7: Asst Registrar BakerU 31-35; Asst to Registrar UMo(Columbia) 36-37; Asst to vice president Page Mill Co, Topeka Kan 37-40; Special asst to chief asst libn LC 41-46; Exec asst Admin Dept 46-48, Special asst to libn of Congress 48-51, Ed & participant Project East River, NYC on Detail Form LC 51-52, Historian & special asst to libn of Congress 52-53;xec asst to libn of Congress 53-. 8: Ed, writing & conf wk with variety of prof groups. 9: DCLA. 10: League of Women Voters. 11: Meritorious Service Award for Superior Service, LC. 12: Ed "Project East River" (10 vols). 14: Admin. 15: 5023 N Washington blvd, Arlington Va 22205.

MORRISON, ALAN EDWARD. b Albany NY 30 Je 32. 4: Amy Vezzoli. 5: Ill Wesleyan U 56-59 (Eng) BA; Rutgers 65-66 MLA. 7: Jr libn Newark Pub Lib, Newark NJ 65-67; Asst libn Cornell U Libs 67-. 9: ALA. 14: Art, arch. 15: 117 Winston dr, Ithaca NY 14850.

MORRISON, CAROLINE (MARY) (ATTEBERRY). b East Prairie M0 5 My 35. 4: Jack William Morrison. 5: Greenville Col 53-57 (Elem Educ) BS; UIll 57-58, summer 59 MA. 6: Fr. 7: Child catlgr Lincoln Lib, Springfield Ill 58-63, 1st asst catlg dept 63-. 9: ALA; IllLA. 14: Catlg. 15: 1904 S Glenwood ave, Springfield Il 62704.

MORRISON, CHARLES ALEXANDER JR. b Rochester NY 2 Ja 34. 5: URochester 52-56 (Pol Sci) AB, 59-60 (Educ) AM; SUNY (Geneseo) 63-67 (LS) NY State Sch Libn Certif. 6: Fr. 7: Personnel clk (Sp/4) US Army USARELM Air Passenger Center, Frankfurt Germany 56-58; Tchr Irondequoit High Sch, Rochester NY 60-63, Libn 63-. 8: Consul Lib Sect Genesee Valley Sch Development Assn 68. 9: ALA; NYStateLA; NYStateTA; NY State A-V Assn; Rochester A-V Assn; IrondequoitTA; NEA-DAVI. 12: "Design for Cataloging Non-Book Materials: Adaptable to Computer Use" (69). 13: Yes. 15: 39 Radcliffe rd, Rochester NY 14617.

MORRISON, CHRISTINE (CATTO MACKENZIE). b London Ont Can 23 Ap 37. 4: Kevin Morrison. 5: UToronto 59 (Psych, Eng) BA; UBC 64 BLS. 6: Fr, Ger, Sp. 7: Spec libn Boy Scouts of Can, Ottawa 60-63; Spec libn Imperial Oil Ltd, Ioco BC 64; Catlgr UVictoria (Victoria BC) 64-66; Asst libn Air Canada, Montreal 66-68; Libn Ministry ofAgric, Jamaica 68-. 9: CanLA. 14: Catlg, spec libs. 15: Lib Min of Agric, PO Box 480, Kingston Jamaica.

MORRISON, DORIS (BRACKEN). b Dallas. 5: S Park Jr Col 23-25; UHouston summer 47; Sam Houston State Tchrs Col summer 53-54 (LS) BS; LSU summers 62-65 (LS) MS. 6: Sp. 7: Jr high tchr Liberty Ind Sch Dist, Liberty Tex 45-46, Sec to supt 46-53; Jr high libn Beaumont Ind Sch Dist, Beaumont Tex 54-. 8: Tchr, lib sci, Sam Houston State Col, summer 61. 9: ALA; NEA; Tex LA; Tex State Tchrs Assn; Tex Clr Tchrs

Assn. 10: Delta Kappa Gamma; Phi Kappa Phi; AAUW; Wesleyan Serv uild; E Tex Nature Club; Music Study Club; Beaumont ClrTA. 14: Sch libs. 15: 2236 Victoria, Beaumont Tex 77701.

MORRISON, DOROTHEA A (MEYER). b NYC 26 Mr 06. 4: George Morrison. 5: NYU 32-37 (Elem Educ) BS, 37-41 (Sup, Admin) MA; Columbia 55-57 MSLS. 6: Ger. 7: Tchr NYC Sch System, Whitestone NY 24-41; Tchr Manhasset Pub Schs, Manhasset NY 43-44; Elem sch libn UFSD 4, Northport NY 54-60, Jr high sch libn 60-. 8: Rep to Metro(NY) Sch Study Coun. 9: NEA; ALA; NY State Tchrs Assn; NYLA; Nassau-Suffolk SchLA. 10: Suffolk Co Hist Assn; St Charles Aux. 14: Ya reading material, sch ref, bibliog. 15: 300 Ocean ave, Northport NY 11768.

MORRISON, DOROTHY MAE (FREEMAN). b Ft Worth Tex 9 Jl 26. 4: Frank Morrison, Jr. 5: Tex Woman's U 43-47 (LS) BA, 67- (LS); E Tex State U 66-67 (LS). 6: Sp. 7: Dtud asst Tex Woman's U Lib 43-47; Asst libn Tex Wesleyan Col Lib summer 47; Asst libn in child dept Ft Worth Pub Lib 47-49; Jr libn Jarvis Christian Col Lib 65-. 8: Church libn, First Baptist Church, Hawkins Tex 53-. 10: Hawkins Study Club; PTA; East Tex reading Coun. 14: Circ, ref, child lib wk. 15: Box 16, Hawkins Tx 75765.

MORRISON, EILENE M(AY). b Bellingham Wash 19 N 12. 5: West Wash Col 30-35, summers 37-38 (Elem Educ) BA; Columbia summer 45, 46-48 (Curriculum, Tchg) MA, spring 61 (LS); UWash 49-50 (LS) BA. 7: Elem tchr, Wash pub schs; Shelton 35-37, Bellingham 37-46; Instr in educ San Francisco State Col 48-49; Lib supv & high sch libn Aberdeen Pub Schs, Aberdeen Wash 50-54; Asst Prof lib sci Mont State U summers 53-54, 54-60; Dist libn (supv) Bremerton Pub Schs, Bremerton Wash 61-. 8: Mont State Sch Lib Com 56-60; Mont State Reading Coun 56-60; Co-dir, two lib wkshops to devel a Mont Sch Lib Guide summers 58, 59; Consul for Mont Sch 56-60; Vis prof Lib Sci UOre summer 60; Asst prof Ext UWash winter 63; Asst prof in Educ, Pacific Luth U summers 63-64; Asst dir NDEA Lib Inst UOkla summer 66. 9: NEA; ALA; -AASchL (Bd Dirs 65-67, mem of an awards com 65); WashEA; PNLA (chm-elect Lib Educ Div 59-60, chm Lib Educ Div 63-65); WashStateASchL (pres 68-69, treas 63-65, histn 51-53); Wash Div A-V Inst; Wash State Assn Supv & Curr Devel. 10: Kappa Delta Pi; Pi Lambda Theta; Soroptimist Club. 13: Yes. 14: Sch libs. 15: 2775 Marine dr, Bremerton Wa 98310.

MORRISON, (HELEN) FRANCES. b Saskatoon Can 28 S 18. 5: USask 36-39 BHSc; UToronto 47 bls. 7: Lib asst Saskatoon Pub Lib, Saskatoon Can 43-46, Asst child libn 47-48, Ref libn 48-51, Asst libn & hd of circ 51-61, Chief libn 61-. 9: CanLA; ALA; SaskLA (past pres) SaskLA (past pres). 10: Bus & Profess Women's Club; Univ Women's Club. 15: 318 cumberland ave, Saskatoon Sask Can.

MORRISON, JANE H (OLLENBERG). b Newark NJ 5 Ja 10. 5: NYU 27-32 (Sociol) BA; Rutgers 58-63 MLS. 7: Libns sec Pub Serv Corp of NJ, Newark NJ 31-40; Libn Alfred Vail Sch, Morris Plains NJ 56-63; Libn Sussex Ave Sch, Morristown NJ 63-65; Libn The Frelinghuysen Sch, Morristown NJ 65-. 8: Coord of Libs, Morris TWP (Morris Co, NJ) Schs, 63-. 9: ALA; NJSchLA. 10: AAUW; Green Mountain Club of NY. 14: Wk with child, admin. 15: 94 Burnham pky, Morristown NJ 07960.

MORRISON, LILLIAN. b Jersey City NJ 27 O 17. 5: Douglass Col 34-38 (Math) BS; Columbia 40-42 BS in LS. 6: Fr. 7: NY Pub Lib: Sub-prof 39-41, Ya libn Seward Park Br 41-42, Ya libn Aquilar Br 42-47, Libn in chg of wk with voc high schs, sch wk off 47-52, Asst coordinator ya Serv 52-68, Coord ya serv 68-. 8: Tchr, Lib Sci, Rutgers summer 61, Columbia U spring 62, summer 63. 9: ALA; NYLA. 10: Authors League of Amer; Phi Beta Kappa. 12: "Yours Till Niagara Falls (50); "Black Within and Red Without (53); "A Diller A Dollar (55); "Touch Blue (58); "Remember Me When This You See (61); "Sprints and Distances (65); Gen ed for Crowell Poets Series (64-); "The Ghosts of Jersey City" (67); Co-auth "Miranda's Music" (68). 13: Yes. 14: Pub lib serv to the teen-ager. 15: 106 Cabrini blvd, New York NY 10033.

MORRISON, MILDRED E. b Dover NH 30 S 03. 5: Posse 21-24; Syracuse summer 38 (LS); UNH 55-58. 7: Pub Lib, Dover NH: Circ asst 29-44, Asst libn 44-60, Libn 60-. 9: ALA; NELA; NHLA. 10: Dist Nurs asn; Bus & Prof Womens Club; Womens Serv Coun. 15: Dover Pub Lib, Dover NH 03820.

MORRISON, PERRY DAVID. b Minneapolis 30 N 19. 4: Catherine Jean Gushwa. 5: Pasadena City Col 38-40 (Soc Sci) AA; Whittier Col 40-42, 46-47 (Soc Sci, Hist) AB, MA; UCal(Berkeley) 48-49, 58-61 BLS, DLS. 6: Fr, Ger, Sp. 7: Personnel off US Army (Capt), Ft Knox KY 42-46; Acquis clerk Henry E Huntington Lib, San Marno Cal 47-48; Admin asst UOre Lib (Eugene) 49-50, Head soc sci libn 50-63, Asst univ libn & head soc sci libn 59-63; Col Libn Sacramento State Col 63-65; Assoc Prof Sch of Libnship UWash 65-67; Prof Sch of LibnshipUOre (Eugene) 67-. 8: Dir HEA Inst on Lib Materials for Vocat and Tech Progs in Commun Cols (69). 9: ALA (Life mem; chm Binding Inst Scholarship Jury 63-64, Del to Internat Fed Lib Assns Congress, Helsinki 65); PNLA (chm Conf Com 61); OreLA (pres 61-62); CalLA; SLA. 12: "Career of the Academic Librarian," ACRL Monograph 29 (69); Ed "PNLA Quarterly" (67-). 13: Yes. 14: Ref, admin, lib sci, tchg (admin, ref, bibliog, govt publs & research methods). 15: Sch of Libnship, Univ of Oregon, Eugene Or 97403.

MORRISON, SIBYL ANNE (PIRTLE). b Comanche Tex 17 Je 19. 4: Ernest E Morrison. 5: Tex Tech Col 37-40, & 46 (Educ) BS in Educ; UCal 47 BLS. 7: Tchr High Sch, Anson Tex 41-42; Tchr High Sch, Post Tex 43; US Navy WAVES 43-45; Circ libn Tex Tech Col 47, Ref libn 48-53; Libn tech processes Boeing Airplane Co, Wichita Kan 54-55; Ref libn Tex Tech Col 56-63, Order libn 64-. 9: TexLA; Tex Assn of Col Tchr. 15: 4812 43rd st, Lubbock Tx 79414.

MORRISSEY, ELEANOR (FLEMING). b Baton Rouge La 5 N 12. 5: Ward-Belmont Col 29-31 Certif; Vanderbuilt U 31-33 (Fr) BA; Columbia 42-43 (LS) BS. 6: Fr. 7: Asst docs div Columbia Lib summer 43; Admin asst & hd ser, docs, gifts & exch Joint Univ Libs, Nashville 43-62, Hd acquis libn 62-67, Systs analyst 63-67, Systs libn 67-68, Act hd tech serv 68-. 9: ALA; SELA; TennLA (Memb chm 62-63); Nashville Lib Club (chm Col Sect 48, v-pres 50, Bd 60). 10: Nat Soc Colonial Dames of Amer; Query Club; Tenn Botanical Garden & Fine Arts Center; Nashville Symphony. 12: Assoc ed "Bulletin of the Medical Librar Association, (57-62); Ed pro tem (65-66); Comp "Cumulative Indxs, 1-40 & 41-50; Co-ed "Handbook of Medical Library Practice (3d ed 69). 13: Yes. 14: Tech serv, designing automated lib procedures. 15: Joint Univ Libs, Nashville Tn 37203.

MORRISSEY, KATHLEEN M. b Livonia NY 26 Mr 16. 5: URochester 37 (Eng) BA; State Tchrs Col (Geneseo NY) 41 (LS) BS; Middlebury Col 53 (Eng) MA. 7: Narrowsburg Central Sch, Narrowsburg NY 37-42; Ten Broeck Acad, Franklinville NY 42-43; Caledonia High Sch, Caledonia NY 43-45; Guild Bk Shop, NYC 45-47; Goldwater Hosp, NYC 47-48; Oceanside Sr High Sch, Oceanside NY 48-. 9: NYLA Scholarship & Recr Com); NY State Tchrs Assn; Nassau-Suffolk SchLA. 15: 37 Clinton ave, Rockville Centre NY 11570.

MORRONE, KAY (OSHEA). b Altoona Penn 4 F 37. 4: Samuel Donald Morrone. 5: Col of Notre Dame (Md) 55-59 (Hist) BA; Drexel 59-60 MS in LS. 7: Baltimore Co Pub Lib, Baltimore: Gen prof asst 60-61, Child libn 61, Interlib loan libn 61-62, Br libn 62-64, Area br libn 64-. 9: ALA; MdLA. 10: Beta Phi Mu. 15: 1212 Brook Meadow dr, Baltimore Md 21204.

MORRONI, JUNE (ROSE). b Smithmill Penn 8 Ja 38. 5: Lebanon Valley Col 55-56 (Mus); Penn State U 56-59 (Educ) BS; UChicago 59-60, 66 (Libnship) AM. 6: Ger. 7: Asst UChicago Libs 59-61; Ref & a-v libn Steele Mem Lib, Elmira NY 61-67; Libn Elmira City Schs, Elmira NY 67-69; Asst ref libn Penn State U 69-. 9: ALA; MusLA; NYStateLA; PennLA. 10: AAUP; Mu Phi Epsilon. 14: Ref, arts, child lit. 15: 201 Pattee Lib, University Park Pa 16802.

MORROW, ALICE (PER LEE). b Peoria Ill 25 Mr 13. 4: Harry M Morrow Sr. 5: William Jewell Col 3034 (Eng) AB; Peabody 34-35 BS in LS, 62, 64 (LS) MA. 7: Tchr-libn High Sch, Troutville Va 35-36; Tchr-libn High Sch, Gilbert La 36-37; Libn Sr High Sch, Longview Tex 37-40; Catlgr Pub Lib, Kan City Mo 40-41; Catlgr William Jewell Col 59-65; Catlgr Central Mo State Col 65-. 9: ALA; MoLA; Mo State Tchrs Assn. ; MoASchL. 10: AAUP; AAUW; DAR; Mo Hist Soc; Heart of Amer Geneal Soc; W Central Mo Geneal Soc. 14: Catlg. 15: Rural Rte 1, Lathrop Mo 64465.

MORROW, ELLEN B. b Phila Penn 15 My 23. 5: Dickinson Col 41-45 (Chem) BS; Drexel 47-48 (LS) BS. 7: Chemist Monad Paint Co, Phila summers 41-42; Chem McNeil Pharmaceutical, phila 45; Chem Cochrane Corp, Phila 47; Asst libn Rohm & Haas Co, Phila 48-52; Libn tuaber Chem Corp, Conshohoeken Penn 52-. 9: SLA; ACS; Spec Lib Coun Phila. 10: Pilot Internat. 14: Ref, admin. 15: 22 Alene rd, Ambler Pa 19002.

MORROW, LOUISE R. b Baden Penn. 5: UPittsburgh 46 (Chem) BS, 50 (Chem) MS; Carnegie 59 (Tech Libr) MLS. 7: Chem Mellon Inst (Corn Products Fellowship), Pittsburgh Penn 47-60; Info coord Corn Products Co, Moffett Tech Ctr, Argo Ill 60-66; Tech libn Corn Products Food Tech Inst 67-. 15: 12 Russell ave, Watertown Ma 02172.

MORROW, WYNDOL J. b Konawa Okla 29 S 39. 5: E Central State Col 57-60 (Eng) BA Ed; UOkla 65-66 MLS. 7: Reporter USAF, San Antonio Tex, Madison Wis, Osan Korea 61-64; Libn USA, Pusan Korea 66-67; Libn USAF: Phu Cat AB Vietnam 67-68, Nha Trang AB Vietnam 69-. 9: ALA (life mem). 14: Admin, ref. 15: Box E 14CSG, APO San Francisco Ca 96205.

MORSE, A(RTHUR) LOUIS. b Peekskill NY 29 Je 17. 4: Anne Skelly. 5: Catholic U 36-39 (Eng) BA; Manhattan Col 39-45 (Eng Lit) MA; St Johns U 42-49 BLS; Columbia 51-54 MS in LS. 6: Fr. 7: Tchr Priv elem & Secondary schs, NYC 39-47; Head catlgr & asst libn Iona Col 47-54; Libn E Meadow Pub Schs, E Meadow NY 54-57; Libn W T Clarke High Sch, E Meadow NY 57-58; Supv of lib E Meadow Pub Schs, E Meadow NY 58-62, Dir of Libs 62-. 8: NY State Educ Dept; Adv Com on Handbk for Second Sch Lib 65-66, Ad hoc advCom on Title II ESEA 65-, Consul-coord LOIS projs 66-67, Adv Com on State Contracts for Sch Lib Purchasing 68-69; Adv Bd; St John's Univ Lib Cong 59, 60, 63, 67; Nassau Co Com on Co Ref Lib 63-67; Nassau Tuberculosis and Health Assn 60-63; Mem Exec Coun, Libns Unit, Metro Cath Col 53-55; Adv Com on Catlg & Clsf 53-55; Rep to CNLA, Z-39 Subcom on Indexing 60-63; Mem Exec Bd Sch Lib Supvrs Sect 69-; Vis lectr; St John's U summer 60, Queens Col spring 60, Asst prof, LIU Grad Lib Sch, 60-63, Assoc Prof 63-. 9: ALA-AASchL;-LED; CathLA (chm catlg & clsf sect 51-52); Sch Lib Supv Assn; NYLA (Sch lib sect; Non-bk materials, standards rev com 59-60; Bd Dirs 62-64, Publ Dir 62-64, Publ Com 62-64, chm Awards Com 67-68, chm Sch Media Supvrs of NY State 66-68); Nassau Co LA (chm Sch Pub Lib Rel Com 64-66); Nassau-Suffolk SchLA (chm Dir Com 55-56, chm Nomin Com 58, pres 59-60, chm Publ Com 60-63, Liaison Offr, CNLA 60-63, chm Legis Com 66-68); NY State TA; NY Lib Club; LIASCD; LI Educ Communications Coun. 10: Tri-Co Tchrs Retirement Coun; Cath Youth Org; Signum Fidei Alumni Assn; Queen of the Rosenavy Acad; Phi Delta Kappa. 13: Yes. 14: Sch libs, lib educ, ref. 15: 3778 Lincoln st, Seaford NY 11783.

MORSE, ALFRED WINSLOW. b Amherst Mass 24 Mr 19. 4: Dorothea Cloud. 5: Bates Col 36-40 (Fr) AB; Middlebury Col summers 39, 41 (Fr); Brown U 40-41, 42 (Romance Langs) MA; Drexel 49-50 MS in LS. 6: Fr, Ger, Sp. 7: Tchr of Fr & Span Kents Hill Jr Col 41-42; Cryptographer spec agent USAAF, US Army 42-45; Tchr of Fr & Eng Tower Hill Sch, Wilmington Del 47-49; Intern descr, subj catlgr LC 50-54; Catlgr Free Lib of Phila 54-56; Catlgr Longwood Lib, Kennett Square Penn 56-58; Catlgr Temple U Lib 59-. 9: ALA-ACRL;-LRTS (Catlg & Clsf Sect). 10: Phi Beta Kappa. 14: Catlg, rare bks. 15: Box 39, RD 3, Kennett Square Pa 19348.

MORSE, CLARENCE RALPH. b Kan 7 S 21. 4: Joan Blakiston. 5: Kan State Tchrs Col (Emporia) 41-47 (Sociol) AB, Lib Certif, 54 (Eng) MS; UWash 60-61 (LS) ML. 7: Ref asst St Louis Pub Lib 47-49; Asst libn U of Puget Sound 50-51; Ref libn US Civil Serv, Siver Spring Md 51-52; Libn Multnomah Col 53-55; Circ libn West Wash Col 55-60; Circ libn San Jose State Col 61-; Libn Pershing Col (Neb) 66-67. 9: ALA; OreLA; PNLA; CalLA; NebLA. 10: AAUP; Kappa Delta Pi. 14: Circ, ref. 15: 2424 Fairoak ct, San Jose Cal 95125.

MORSE, ELIZABETH COATES. b NYC 3 Ag 18. 4: Harold Grant Morse. 5: Wilson Col 36-40 (Psych, Philos) BA; Rutgers 58-61 (lem Educ) M Ed, 61-65 MLS. 6: Fr. 7: Elem sch tchr Bd of Educ, Piscataway Twp NJ 60-61, Elem sch libn 61-64; Elem sch libn Bd of Educ, Plainfield NJ 64-; Coord elem sch libs, Plainfield NJ 66-. 9: ALA; NJSchLA (v-pres 69, (Exec Bd, Pub Rel 64-65); NJLA (Sch Sect); NJEA. 10: AAUW. 13: Yes. 15: 827 Madison ave, Plainfield NJ 07060.

MORSE, ELLIOTT H(OW). b New Haven Conn 9 N 16. 4: Helen Louise Moore. 5: Haverford Col 34-38 (Ger) BS; Drexel 38-39 BS in LS; UPenn 40-43 (Ger) MA. 6: Ger, Fr, Sp. 7: Ref asst UPenn 39-41; Ref asst & period asst Temple U 41-43, Act ref libn 43-44; Ref libn UPenn 44-49; Col ofPhysicians of Phila: Admin asst libn 49-52, Admin assoc libn 52-53, Libn 53-. 9: MedLA (Bd Dirs 58-60, v-pres & pres-elect 68-69, chm &/or mem 8 coms 50-; chm Phila Reg Group 52-53); Spec Libs Coun, Phila & vicinity (pres 49-50); PennLA (chm Col & Univ Sect 44-45). 10: Drexel Lib Sci Alumni Assn; Trustee, Narbert Pub Lib. 12: Co-ed PennLA "Bulletin" (45), Circ mgr 46-48; Ed "Bulletin" Spec Libs Coun Phila (45-49). 13: Yes. 14: Med libnship, admin, ref, ser. 15: Col of Physicians of Phila, 19 S 22nd st, Phila Pa 19103.

MORSE, GRANT WESLEY. b Fredonia NY 20 O 26. 4: Jocelyn G Carlson. 5: Ottawa U 47-51 (Sociol) BA; East Baptist Theol Sem 51-54 (Missions) BD; NY State Col of Educ (Albany) 57-58 MS in LS. 7: US Army Signal Corps (Sgt), US & Japan -47; Various chruch wk, NY State & Ind 54-57; Head Libn Findlay Col 58-60; Head Libn Ottawa U (Kan) 60-61; Asst libn Carthage Col61-62; Head Libn Grove City Col 62-64; Head Libn Wagner Col 64-66; Hd libn Stout State U, Barron Co Campus 66-. 9: ALA; WisLA. 10: AAUP; Assn Wis State Univ Faculties. 12: "Concise Guide to Library Research" (66, rev paperback 68). 14: Col lib admin, ref. 15: 932 Craite ave, Rice Lake Wi 54868.

MORSE, HELEN LOUISE (MOORE). b Wynnewood enn 5 Ja 20. 4: Elliott H Morse. 5: Wilson Col 37-41 (Eng) AB; Drexel 41-42 BS in LS. 6: Fr. 7: Catlgr Curtis Publishing Co, Phila 42-46, Libn 46-50; ib asst Narberth (Penn) Community Lib 62-; Libn Main Line Project Learning Lower Merion High Sch, Penn 65-. 9: Phila Area Catlgrs Group (chm 46-47); Amer Marketing Assn. 10: PTA. 14: Ref, catlg, readers adv serv. 15: 304 Powell rd, Wynnewood Penn 19096.

MORSE, JOAN (BLAKISTON). b Tacoma Wash 12 Jl 25. 4: C Ralph Morse. 5: UWash 42-46 (Eng) BA, 46-47 (LS) BA. 7: Circ libn Wellesley Col Lib 47-49; Documents libn UMo 49-51; Asst libn Col of Pget Sound 51-52; Base libn McChord AFB, Tacoma Wash 52-53; Br libn Multnomh Co Lib, Portland Ore 53-55; Sch libn Blaine Pub Sch Dist, Blaine Wash 58-60; Bkmob libn King Co Pub Lib, Seattle 60-61; Documents libn Santa Clara Co Free Lib, San Jose Cal 64-66, 67-; Asst libn Pershing Col (Neb) 66-67. 9: ALA; PNLA; MoLA; OreLA; Wash State SchLA; WashLA; WashEA. ; NebLA; CalLA. 10: AAUW; PTA. 14: Documents, ref, sch libs. 15: 2424 Fairoak ct, San Jose Cal 95125.

MORSE, JOAN EILEEN (BROWN). b St John NB Can 5 Ja 42. 4: Lawrence Bacon Morse. 5: Mount AllisonU 59-63 (Mus) BA; Simmons 66-67 MS in L Sc. 7: Libn's asst Mt AllisonU 63-66; Curator mss Francis A Countway Lib of Med HarvardU 67-. 9: ALA. 14: Rare bks & mss, reference wk, catlg. 15: 10 Shattuck st, Boston Ma 02115.

MORSE, JUNE ELIZABETH (NICKERSON). b Halifax NS Can 16 Jl 34. 4: Charles A Morse. 5: AcadiaU 51-55 (Econ) BA; UToronto 68-69 BLS (with honours). 6: Fr. 7: Libn DuPont of Can Ltd, Montreal 57-68; Libn St Albans City Elem Sch, St Albans Vt 69-. 9: ALA; CanLA; SLA. 13: Yes. 14: Ref, sch lib. 15: PO Box 462, St Albans Vt 05478.

MORSE, MARTHA ELIZABETH. b Kewanee Ill 4 D 1900. 5: Smith 19-23 (Eng) AB; West Res 27-28 BLS; Chicago 35-39 (Soc Wk) MA. 7: Asst & Eng tchr Fancis Parker Sch, Chicago 23-26; Libn Pub Lib, Geneseo Ill28-30; High sch libn Pub Lib, Kewanee Ill31-34; Case aide Fed Relief Off, Kewanee Ill 34; Case wker Ill Childs Home & Aid Soc, Chicago 39-44; Case wker Family Serv Assn, Rockford Ill 44-47; Adult educ libn Pub Lib, Rockford Ill 48-53; Head Libn Herrick Mem Lib, Willington Ohio 53-68; Hd child libn Elyria Pub Lib, Elyria Ohio 68-. 10: LWV; Ohio Fed of Womens Clubs; Wellington Hist Soc; Friends of Art of Oberlin Col Art Museum; Lorain Co Arts Coun. 14: Child & ya serv. 15: One Orchard lane, Wellington Ohio 44090.

MORSE, PHYLLIS C. b Painted Post NY 23 F 27. 5: State U Tchrs Col (Geneseo NY) 45-49 (Elem Educ) B Ed; Syracuse 53-58 MSLS. 7: Tchr Dist 10, Corning NY 49-50; Elem tchr Riverside Sch, Elmira NY 50-51; Clerk Elmira Bank & Trust, Elmira NY 51-52; Steele Mem Lib, Elmira NY: Jr lib clerk 52-53, Prin lib clerk 53-58, Sr libn II 58-. 9: ALA; NYLA (Ref serv Div: mem 2 coms). 10: YWCA; Nat Parks Assn; Nat Wildlife Fed; Zonta Club. 14: Ref. 15: 456 Riverside ave, Elmira NY 14904.

MORSE, THELMA E. b Artemas enn 21 D 07. 5: Juniata Col 24-26, 28-29 (Math) BA; UMe 38; Penn State U 49; Clarion State Col 58-60 (LS) Masters Equivalent. 6: Fr, Lat. 7: Elem tchr Bedford Twp Schs, Bedford Co Penn 26-28; Secondary tchr Manns Choice High Sch, Manns Choice Penn 29-39, Prin 39-40; Secondary tchr Schellsburg-Napier High Sch, Schellsburg Penn 40-48; Secondary tchr Everett Southern High Sch, Everett Penn 48-61, Libn 61-. 9: NEA (life mem); PennLA; Penn State EA (life mem; Exec Coun 62 & 63, Dept Supv & Curr); Future Tchrs of Amer Com (56-62 & 64-67, 69-); Everett Area EA.

10: Delta Kappa Gamma; Penn Citizens Coun, Governors Com of 100,000 Pennsylvanians. 14: Ref, ya. 15: 335 E Pitt st, Beford Penn 15522.

MORTENSEN, MARJORIE LEE. b Reno Nev 4 N 34. 5: UNev 52-56 (Homemaking Educ) BS; UDenver 59-60 (LS) MA. 7: Sch libn & homemaking tchr Pershing Co High Sch, Lovelock Nev 56-59; Field consul Wyo State Lib 60-. 9: ALA; Nv 56-59; Field consul Wyo State Lib 60-. 10: ALA; NevLA (sec 57-58); MPLA (Exec Bd 61-65, rec sec 69); WyoLA. 13: Yes. 14: Ext serv. 15: 215 W 26th No 7, Cheyenne Wyo 82001.

MORTIMER, RUTH. b Syracuse NY 16 S 31. 5: Smith 49-53 (Eng) AB; Columbia 54-57 (LS) MS. 6: Fr, Ital. 7: Proofreader Lawyers Co-operative Publ Co, Rochester NY summer 50-52; Pre-prof libn Brooklyn Pub Lib 53-54; Asst in ser Smith Col Lib 54-56; Rare bk catlgr for printing & graphic arts Harvard Col Lib 57-. 9: ALA; BSA; Renaissance Soc Amer. 11: Guggenheim Fellow 66. 12: Comp "Catalogue of Books and Manuscripts, Part I: French 16th Century Books (64). 13: Yes. 14: Rare bk catlg. 15: Houghton Lib Harvard Univ, Cambridge Mass 02138.

MORTIMER, WILLIAM J(OHN). b Randolph Vt 30 Mr 25. 4: Marion Thomann. 5: Amherst Col 43-47 (Hist) AB; Cornell U 47-48 (Soc Studies) MA; Columbia 50-51 (LS) MS. 7: Lib asst Life Insurance Agency Mgt Assn, Hartford Conn 51-52, Libn 52-, Mgr lib & ref serv 65-. 9: SLA. 14: Ref. 15: 170 Sigourney st, Hartford Conn 06105.

MORTON, ANN (WHITE). b Atlanta 27 S 39. 4: Jack W Morton. 5: Tift Col 57-61 (Eng) BA; Emory 62-65 MS in LS. 7: Eng tchr Griffin High Sch, Griffin Ga 61-62; Asst to the res libn Emory U 62-65; Asst to the libn Agnes Scott Col 65-66; Circ Asst Emory 68-. 9: SELA. 14: Ref, readers serv. 15: 492 Eastland dr, Decatur Ga30030.

MORTON, DONALD JOHN. b Brooklyn NY 11 Ja 31. 4: Ann Tilden Morton. 5: UDel 48-52 (Biol) BS; LSU 52-54 (Biol) MS; UCal (Berkeley) 54-57 (Biol) PhD; Simmons 68-69 MLS. 7: Biologist: NM StateU 57-58, NDak StateU 59-61, US Dept Agric, Tifton Ga 61-65; Biol Assoc Prof UDel 65-68; Libn NortheasternU 68-. 9: ASIS; SLA; ALA; MedLA. 10: Sigma Xi; Phi Kappa Phi; Mycological Soc Amer; Phi Sigma. 13: Yes. 14: Sci-tech, info syst, admin. 15: 5 West st, Natick Ma 01760.

MORTON, DOROTHY JEAN. b Madisonville Ky 14 My 39. 5: Rice Inst 57-58; UKy 58-61 (Chem) AB, 61-62 MS in LS. 7: Ref libn DuPont Tech Lib, Wilmington Del 62-67, Info chemist 67-. 9: SLA; DelaLA. 10: ACS (Chem Lit Div). 14: Ref. 15: Apt 46C, 2601 Jefferson st, Wilmington De 19802.

MORTON, ELIZABETH HOMER. b Tunapuna Trinidad WI 13 F 03. 5: Dalhousie U (Halif) 22-26 (Eng, Hist) BA; Nova Scotia Normal Sch 26 A Certif; Ont Lib Sch (Toronto) 26 A Certif; Toronto 31-32 (Bibliog); Chicago 45-47 (LS, Adult Educ). 6: Fr. 7: Tchr Pub Sch, Oban NS 24; Catlgr Pub Lib, Toronto 27-28; Tchr & libn Voc Sch, St John NB 28-30; Exec-sec NB Lib Comm, St John NB 30-31; Ref libn Pub Lib, Toronto 31-44; Exec-sec & ed Can Lib Coun, Ottawa 44-46; Exec-Dir & Edin-Chief Can LA, Ottawa 46-68; Free lance lib consul, ed, compiler, 68-. 8: Consul, Nat Lib Adv Coun, 52-68. 9: Can Assn Adult Educ; CanEA; OntLA (sec-treas 36-43). 10: Can Citizenship Coun; Can Centenary Coun; Can Fed of Univ Women; Nat Coun of Women; Chelsea Club, Ottawa; Univ Womens Club of Ottawa. 11: Merit Award of the Can Lib Trustees Assn, 63; Centenary Medal 63; Order of Can (Memb of Service Medal 69); LLD (hon) UAlta 69. 12: Ed "Canadian Library" (44-68); Ed "Feliciter" (56-68). 13: Yes. 14: Lib ext, sel Canadiana. 15: 150 MacLaren st, apt 413, Ottawa 4 Can.

MORTON, FLORRINELL (FRANCIS). b Pollock Tex 20 D 05. 4: Charles Hester Morton. 5: W Tex State Col 21-23; UCal(Berkeley) 23-25 (Eng) BA, 26-27 (LS) Certif, 30-31 (LS) MA. 7: Eng tchr La high schs 25-26, 28-29; Catlgr N Tex State Col 27-28, 29-30, summer 31; instr of Lib Sci UIll 31-33, summer 37; LSU Lib Sch: Instr 33-38, Asst Prof 38-42, Asst to dir 40-41, Asst dir 41-43, Assoc Prof 42-47, Act dir 43-44, Prof 47-, Dir 44-. 8: Dir Wkshop on Educ for Sch Libnship, Tex 49; Survey Miss Lib Educ, 50; Survey Lib Serv for the Blind 56; Consul, Wkshop on Lib Educ, Kan 60; Inst on Lib Educ n the Southeast, 61; Var La sch & pub lib wkshops. 9: ALA (pres 61-62, Life mem of Coun, Exec Bd 59-62, chm Bd of Educ for Libnship 51-52; Coun 49-52 & 60-);-LED (pres 56-58, chm Jt Com on Lib Wk as a Career 51-52); AALS (pres 46-47); SWLA (pres 60-62); LaLA (pres 41-42); La Tchrs Assn. 10: AAUP; Quota Club; Delta Kappa Gamma; AAUW; Phi Kappa Phi; Alpha Beta Alpha; Beta Phi Mu. 11: Beta Phi Mu Award for Contrib to Educ for Libnship; Essae M Culver Award for Contribution to La Lib Devel. 13: Yes. 14: Lib educ, catlg & clsf, hist of bks & libs. 15: Lib Sch La State Univ, Baton Rouge La 70803.

MORTON, JESSIE (HILL). b Randolph County NC 2 Ap 28. 4: A Glenn Morton. 5: High Point Col 47-50 (Eng, Sp) BA; Peabody Col 61-68 MLS. 6: Acquis Huntingdon Col 67-68; Indexer Air Univ Lib, Maxwell AFB Ala 69-. 9: ALA; SLA; AlaLA. 14: Indexing, military docs. 15: 3175 Lexington rd, Montgomery Al 36106.

MORTON, MARY D(ANIELS). b Tunapuna Trinidad WI 27 O 12. 5: Toronto 33 BHS, 37 BLS. 6: Fr. 7: Libn Ayerst McKenna & Harrison, Montreal 37-39; Asst libn Acad of Med, Toronto 39-42; Sci intelligence off Can Dept of Nat Defense, OTTAWA 42-46; Dept libn Can Dept of Nat Health & Welfare, Ottawa 46-69; Sr consul sci info div Can Dept of Nat Health & Welfare 69-. 8 Tech Adv, Can Colombo Plan Med Bk Scheme, 58-61. 9: Internat Assn of Documentalists; CanLA; MedLA; Lib Assn Ottawa. 14: Health sci libs. 15: Sci Info Div, Dept of Nat Health & Welfare, Ottawa 3 Can.

MORTON, REBECCA E. b Stowe Vt 19 F 01. 4: Albert E Morton. 5: Colo Col 17-19 (Eng Lit); UColo 19-21 (Eng Lit) AB. 6: Fr, Sp. 7: Child libn McClelland Pub Lib, Pueblo Colo 21-23, Br libn 27-44; Corwin Hosp Med Lib 44-55; St Mary Hosp Med Lib 50-56; Parkview Hosp Med Lib 59-. 9: MedLA; ColoLA. 10: DAR; Colo Archeol Soc; Pueblo Metro Museum. 15: 2209 Seventh ave, Pueblo Colo 81003.

MORTONSON, SISTER MARY SHEILA OSF. b Minneapolis Minn 18 Ja 17. 5: Col of St Benedict 34-38 (Eng Educ) BA; UChicago 39-40 (Eng); CatholicU 64-66 MSLS; OxfordU (England) 69 (Eng lit). 6: Ital, Fr. 7: Eng instr St Francis High Sch, Little Falls Minn 43-53; Med libn: St Francis Hosp, Breckenridge Minn 53-55, St Gabriel's Hosp, Little Falls Minn 55-56, 61-64, St Francis & St Gabriel's 56-61; Libn (theol) N Amer Col, rome Italy 66-. 8: Weekly radio broadcast program to Africa conducted for Vatican radio 67-; Lib consul: Eng col Rome Italy 66-67, Intl Propaganda Fide Col Rome Italy 69-. 9: CathLA (v-chm 63-64, Nat Chm Hosp Sect 64-65); ALA. 10: Intercontinental Club (Rome Italy); Beta Phi Mu. 13: Yes. 14/ admin, ref, catlg. 15: Via Nicolo V 35, Rome Italy 00165.

MOSCA, ANN (MALNAR) MRS. b Nashwauk Minn 5 N 13. 5: Hibbing Jr Col 32-34 Diploma; UMinn 34-36 (LS) BS, MI, 36 (Hosp & Med) Diploma; Chicago summer 42 (Hist). 6: Ger. 7: Head Libn Monticello Pub Lib, Monticello Iowa 37-41; Sch libn, Muskegon Heights Mich 41-43; Tech & gen libn AAF, Hastings Neb 43-45; Reg libn, European Theatre 45-47; Head Libn Chisholm Pub ib, Chisholm Minn 48-. 8: Chm, Minn Governors Planning Coun on Mental Retardation; Bd Dirs, St Louis Co (Minn) Econ Opportunity Agency. 9: MinnLA. 10: Forty-miners Club; Chm Commun Econ Opportunity for Chisholm (Minn); LWV; Chisholm Day Care Ctr; Mem, Adv Coun to Governing Bd of Arrowhead Lib System. 14: Ref, for bks, readers adv serv, child. 15: Pub Lib, Chisholm Mn 55719.

MOSELEY, KATHERINE (JORDAN). b Jacksonville Ill 13 Ag 07. 5: MacMurray Col for Women 25-29 (Phys Educ, Biol) BS; UIowa summers 31-32; Fla State U 51-58 (LS) MS. 7: Tchr phys educ & biol Marion Twp High Sch, Marion Ill 29-30; Tchr phys educ & biol E Peoria High Sch, E Peoria Ill 30-37; Supv phys educ E Aurora Elem & High Sch, E Aurora Ill 37-38; Tchr phys educ Cedar Falls High Sch, Cedar Falls Iowa 41-42; Clerical wk Fla State U Lib 51-54; Libn Sopchoppy Elem & High Sch, Sopchoppy Fla 55-56; Libn Caroline Brevard Elem Sch, Tallahassee Fla 57-. 9: NEA; FlaEA; FlaASchL. 10: Tallahassee Kennel Club. 14: Sch libs. 15: 702 Truett dr, Tallahassee Fla 32303.

MOSELY, OMAR HARRY JR. b Chattahoochee Fla 3 Ja 24. 5: USC 41-44 (Chem) BS, 49-52 (Pharmacy) BS; Rutgers 55-56 MLS. 6: Ger. 7: (S/Sgt) Infantry US Army 44-46; Chem Seagram-Calvert Distilling Co, Relay Md 47-48; Pharmacist Central Drug Co, Columbia SC 52-55; 1st asst bus sci & tech div Queens Borough Pub Lib, NYC 56-59; Sr ref libn sci & tech div NY Pub Lib 59-61; Asst ref co-ordinator Nassau Lib System, Garden City NY 61-. 9: SLA; ALA; NYLA; Nassau co LA; NY Lib Club. 10: Melvil Dui Chowder & Marching Assn. 14: Ref. 15: 33 Greenwich ave, apt 14h, New York NY 10014.

MOSER, BERYL RITA (PEARLMAN). b Winnipeg Can. 4: William Oscar Jules Moser. 5: United Col 49-50; UManitoba 50-53 (Eng, Psych) BA; UToronto 53-54 (Soc wk); McGill 66-69 MLS. 6: Jewish, Fr. 7: Catlgr McGill Faculty of

Dentistry Lib 68-. 9: CanLA. 15: 7798 Kildare rd, Montreal 268 Que Can.

MOSER, EDWARD RANDOLPH. b American Falls Ida 26 S 19. 4: Ruth Crippin. 5: Wheaton Col (Ill) 43 (Biol) AB; Cornell U 44 (Vertebrate Zool) MS; USoCal 54 MSLS. 7: Catlgr Long Beach State Col 54-55; Libn Div of Biol Cal Inst of Tech 55-67, Assoc dir libs 67-. 9: MedLA. 14: Catlg, ref. 15: Millikan Lib Cal Inst of Tech, Pasadena Ca 91109.

MOSER, MABEL (YOUNG). b Spencer NC 9 Ag 07. 4: Artus Monroe Moser. 5: UNC 23-27 (Eng) AB; Appalachian State U 58-61 (LS) MA. 6: Fr, Sp. 7: Libn Lincoln Mem Lib, Harrogate Tenn 32-35; Tchr Swannanoa Sch, Swannanoa NC 45-47, Libn 58-62; Libn Claxton Sch, Asheville NC 63-67; Asst Prof of lib sci Mars Hill Col 67-. 8: Dir Curr Lab, Mars Hill Col 67-69. 9: ALA; NEA; SELA; NCLA; NCEA; NC Clrm Tchrs. 10: AAUP; Delta Kappa Gamma. 14: Sch libnship, catlg, ref, child lit. 15: Mars Hill Col, Mars Hill NC 28754.

MOSER, MARGARET LOUISE. b Phila 30 N 16. 5: Ursinus Col 34-38 (Eng) BA; Drexel 38-39 BS in LS. 7: Lib asst to Prin libn Camden Co Lib, Camden NJ 40-. 9: NJLA; NY Tech Serv Libns. 14: Catlg, ref, circ. 15: 6 Merrick Villa, Allan lane, Collingswood NJ 08108.

MOSES, MRS DOLORES (WILLIAMS). b Bowling Green Ky 18 F 14. 4: O Alfred Moses. 5: Fisk U 29-33 Eng AB; UIll summers 48-51 MS in LS. 6: Fr, Ger. 7: High Street Sch, Bowling Green Ky: Elem tchr 33-34, Eng tchr 34-39, High sch libn 40-65, Elem libn 65-. 9: NEA; KyEA; KyLA. 10: Bd, Carver Commun Center, Bowling Green Ky. 13: Yes. 14: Wk with yp. 15: 140 State st, Bowling Green Ky 42101.

MOSES, KATHERINE. b Clinton Iowa 23 F 1898. 5: Cornell Col 18-21 (Eng, Speech) BA; UMinn 29-30, summer 36 (Amer lit) MA; UDenver summers 51-55 (LS) MA. 7: High sch eng tchr: Algona Iowa 23-28, Little Falls Minn 29-30; Hd Eng dept Rapid City High Sch, rapid City S Dak 30-55; Libn W Jr High Sch, Rapid City 55-63; Libn Nat Col of Bus, Rapid City 64-67; Libn Cathedral High Sch, Rapid City 63-68; Lib consul Nat Col of Bus 68-. 8: Lib consul Nat Col of Bus, Rapid City 68-69. 9: ALA; SDLA; SDEA. 10: Delta Kappa Gamma; Nat Retired TA; AAUW; PEO. 13: Yes. 14: Reading guidance, acquis. 15: 4122 W Omaha st, Rapid City SD 57701.

MOSES, LOUISE JANE. b Anniston Ala. 5: Talladega Col 28-33 (Eng) AB; Atlanta 50-52 MSLS. 7: Tchr-libn Cobb High Sch, Anniston Ala 35-42; Asst club dir Spec Serv, Serv Club , Ft McClellan Ala 42-46; Club dir Spec Sev USAFE European Command, West Germany 4749; Libn Morris Col 51-54; Libn Albany State Col (Ga) 54-57; Asst circ libn Doheny Lib USoCal 57-60; Libn Reg IX Institutions Los Ageles Co ub Lib, Los Angeles 60-. 8: Ft McClellan Civillian Coun, 44-46; Hostess, Beibich (USAFE) Germany, Sp Assignment, Berlin Blockade, Roth AFB, Langsberg AFB Hostess 47-49. 9: Calla (Soc Concern Com). 10: So Cal Coun on Child & YP Lit; Juvenile Hall Coun. 11: Libn of Year, Los Angeles Co Pub Lib, 64. 13: Yes. 14: Child & yp serv. 15: 4127 Edgehill dr, Los Angeles Ca 90008.

MOSES, MARTHA WRIGHT. b Raleigh NC 22 N 07. 4: E George Moses. 5: UNC (Greensboro) 24-28 (Hist) AB; Emory 30 (LS) AB. 7: Tchr of soc sci Richard J Reynolds High Sch, Winston-Salem NC 28-29; Libn North High Sch, Winston-Salem NC 30-33; Gen asst Tchrs Col Columbia U summers 31-33; Ref asst Mott Haven Br NY Pub Lib 33-37; Concord Pub Lib, Concord NH: Catlgr 53, Supv of ext wk 54-48, Asst libn 59-. 9: ALA; NHLA. 10: NH SOC Welfare Coun. 15: Concord Pub Lib, Concord NH 03301.

MOSES, RICHARD B. b Rochester NY 1 Jl 33. 4: Elizabeth Gibb. 5: Ohio Wesleyan U 51-54 (Psych, Socio); Harpur Col SUNY 58-60 (Soc sci) BA; Rutgers 62-63 MLS. 6: Ger. 7: ;70; Hd libn Roger Williams Col 70-. 8: Annotations of Wye Inst High Sch Paperback List. 9: ALA; -YASD (Com on Serv to Disadvantaged; Econ Opport Prog Com; Recr Materials Com; Regl recr rep); MdLA (Recr Com Chm, 2 yrs). 10: MENSA; Dramatics & musical performance gps. 13: Yes. 14: A-V, small pub libs, pub serv, publicity, pub rel. 15: Roger Williams Col Lib, Bristol RI 02809.

MOSES, STEFAN B. 4: Joan Mawhorter. 5: UCal (Berkeley) 48-52 (Eng) AB; Columbia 52-53 (Eng) AM, 56-57 (LS) MS. 6: Ger. 7: ;69; Exec Dir Calif Lib Assn 69-. 9: ALA; SLA; Amer Correct Assn; Nat Coun Crime & Delinq; NYLA; NY Lib Club. 11: Helen E Vogelson Award, Columbia Sch of Lib serv 60. 13: Yes. 14: Consul, admin, mgt, state lib prog. 15: 15 Acorn Park, Cambridge Ma 02140.

MOSHER, DIANE L. b Oakland Cal 23 My 45. 5: Col of the Pacific 63-65 (Hist); Fresno State Col 65-67 (Hist) BA; UCLA 67-68 MLS. 7: Ref libn Fresno State Col Lib 68-. 9: ALA; CalLA. 10: UCal Lib Schs Alumni Assn; Phi Kappa Phi. 14: Ref. 15: PO Box 61, Farmington Ca 95230.

MOSHER, FREDRIC JOHN. b Oakes ND 19 F 14. 4: Evelyn Varland. 5: UND 31-36 (Eng) AB, AM; UIll 36-43, 48-50 (Eng) PhD; Chicago 46-48 BLS. 6: Fr, Ger, Danish. 7: Asst in Eng UND 35-36; Asst in Eng UIll(Urbana) 36-43; Clsf Spec AAF (Sgt) 43-46; Ref libn Newberry Lib, Chicago 46-48, Head Ref Dept 48-50; Assoc Prof Sch of Libnship UCal(Berkeley) 50-. 8: Fulbright lecturer, Danish Lib Sch, Copenhagen 63-64. 9: ALS. 12: "New York libraries (34-37); "Small Public Library, Pamphlet for small libs proj, Ala (42). 13: Yes. 14: Ref, bibliog, hist of the bk. 15: Sch of Libnship Univ of Cal, Berkeley Ca 94720.

MOSHIER, LOUISE MARION. b Utica NY 21 O 1897. 5: Simmons 15-19 (LS) BS; Columbia 30-31 (LS) MS. 7: Child libn NY Pub Lib 19-20; Child libn Endicott Free Lib, Endicott NY 20-22; Asst libn & Instr Skidmore Col 22-23; Dir Ilion FreePub Lib, Ilion NY 23-33; Lib ext div NY State Educ Dept: Asst lib sup 33-34, Sr li sup 3446, Assoc lib sup 46-50, Dir 50-56; Consul Health Educ & Welfare, Wash DC 56-57; Visiting Prof of Lib Sci West Mich U 58, 62; Staff assn Commsn on Standards & Accreditation of Serv for the Blind, NYC 63-65. 8: Consul reg lis, Prov Govt, NS, 46; Survey, Me State Lib, 61; Survey, ref serv So Adirondack System, 65; Consul serv: Montreal, 58; Md, 58; RI, 58; NY, 65. 9: ALA (Coun)-LED; SLA; NYLA (past pres). 10: AAUW. 11: Outstanding Achievement Award 66, Commsn on Standards & Accredit of Serv for the Blind. 12: Ed "New York Libraries" (34-37); "Small Public Library", Pamphlet for small libs proj, ALA (42). 13: Yes. 15: 8 Watso pl, Utica NY.

MOSHIER, RUTH. b Keokuk Iowa. 5: Marion Col 27 (Eng, Soc Studies) BA; Kan State Tchrs Col (Emporia) 45 (LS) BS; UMinn 52 (Eng Lit) MA; UIll (Champaign) 65 (LS) MS. 6: Fr. 7: High sch tchr of Eng Friends Acad, Haviland Kan 28-30; Supv State Sch for Child, Owatonna Minn 36-43; Civilian Personnel Hill Field Air Force Command, Ogden Utah 44; Acquis libn Hamline U Lib 45-48; Head libn Marion Col Lib 48-58; Catlg libn St Cloud State Col 58-. 8: Tchr Marion Col 45-48, St Cloud State Col 65-; Col Survey & Faculty Coms 47-58; Art Adv Com St Cloud State Col 60-63. 9: ALA-LRTS; ACRL; MinnLA; MinnEA (Acad Libs Sect). 10: AAUW; Girl Scout Coun; Lit Study Group; St Cloud State Col Faculty Assn; AAUP; Beta Phi Mu. 14: Catlg, tchg catlgs & lit. 15: 608 So 8th st, St Cloud Mn 56301.

MOSHOLDER, WILMA. b Somerset Penn 7 D 14. 5: Otterbein Col 34-38 (Sociol) AB; Carnegie 40-41 BS in LS; Middlebury Col summers 47, 52, 53 (Span)MA. 6: Sp. 7: Libn Inter Amer U (San German PR) 41-45 & 48-60; Jr catlgr Pan Amer Union, Wash DC 45-48; Libn Amer Acad for Girls, Istanbul Turkey 61-63; Libn Evangelical Sem of PR, Rio Piedras PR 63-. 15: Box C, Rio Piedras PR 00928.

MOSIER, ROSALIND (ASCH). b NYC 14 My 23. 4: Richard D Mosier. 5: Tyler Sch Fine Arts templeU 40-43 (Art); Columbia 43-44 (Art educ) BS; Inst Fine Arts NYU 44-46 (Art hist); UCal 48-50 (Art) MA, 53-54 BLS. 6: Fr, Ger, Russian. 7: Lib asst catlg dept UCal (Berkeley) 51-53; Child libn Richmond Pub Lib, Richmond Cal 54-59; Elem libn spec assignment Oakland Pub Schs, Oakland Cal 59-. 8: Taught child lit to tchrs in serv train Oakland Pub Schs summers 61, 63; Consul child lib serv Seaside Elem Schs. 9: ALA (Newberry-Caldecott Com); CalASchL (past chm Elem Sect); Assn Child Libns of no Cal (chm annual inst; Inst Planning Com); CalLA (guest speaker Child Sect); A-V EA of Cal. 10: Delta Kappa Gamma; San Francisco's Women Artists Assn; Oakland Art Assn; Richmond Art Ctr. 13: Yes. 14/ child lib serv. 15: 310 Ramona ave, Piedmont Ca 94611.

MOSIGIAN, ROSE LORAE. b Kalaazoo 12 Jl 24. 5: UWis 44-48 (Art, Eng) BS, 48-49 BSLS. 7: Libn I art & music dept Milwaukee Pub Lib 49-51; Libn I circ dept Madison Pub Li, Madison Wis 51-56; Gilbert M Simmons Lib, Kenosha Wis: Head of circ 56-59, Admin asst 59-63, Asst dir 63-. 9: ALA; WisLA (chm Pub Rel Com). ; Sr Citizens Coml; SE Wis RegLA. 10: Kenosha Art Assn; KenoshaLA. 14: Admin, pub rel. 15: Gilbert M Simmons Lib, Kenosha wis.

MOSKOWITZ, MAY (KAPLAN). b NYC 7 D 29. 4: David Moskowitz. 5: Hunter Col 47-50 (Anthropology) BA; Brooklyn Col 51-55 (Elem Educ); Wayne State U 60-65 (LS) M Ed. 7: Elem sch tchr Bd of Educ NY 50-52; Elem sch tchr Bd of Educ, Detroit 62-64; Elem sch libn Bd of Educ, Southfield

Mich 64-. 9: NEA; ALA; MichASchL; MichEA; Southfield EA. 10: PTA. 14: Sch libn, tchg, reading guidance. 15: 27450 Pierce, Southfield Mi 48075.

MOSLEY, MARY MAC (HOWELL). b Rome Ga 11 N 26. 5: Auburn U 47 (Chem, Bio) BS; Athens Col 63 (Educ); Emory 68 MLn. 7: Sci tchr E Rome Jr High, Rome Ga 64-66; Ext libn Tri-Co Reg Lib, Rome Ga 66-67; Libn & dir Shorter Col 68-. 9: ALA; NEA; GaLA; GaEA; SELA. 10: AAUW. 14: Tchg undergrad lib sci. 15: 113 Woodcrest dr, Rome Ga 30161.

MOSLEY, MATTIE (JACKS). b Manila Philippines 28 O 39. 4: Thomas H Mosley. 5: La Polytech Inst 57-61 (Eng) BA (summa cum laude); LSU 61-62 (LS) MS. 7: YA libn Sheve Mem Lib, Shreveport La 62-64; Asst parish libn Bossier Parish Lib, Bossier City La 64-65; Tchr Minden High Sch, Minden La fall 65; Libn Lowe Jr High Sch, Minden La 65-67; Catlgr LSU (Shreveport) 67-68, Instr of bks & libs 68-. 9: LaLA. 10: Quota club; Phi Kappa Phi; Beta Phi Mu; Caddo-Bossier Lib Club. 14: Catlg, lib sci tchg, child & ya lit. 15: 9221 Midvale dr, Shreveport La 71108.

MOSS, ALINE CAMPBELL. b NYC 12 D 20. 4: William J Moss. 5: Maryville Col 37-41 (Eng) BA (cum laude); TempleU summer 41; William & Mary summer 42; Columbia 57-62 MSLS (cum laude). 6: Fr. 7: Tchr & libn Clarksville High Sch, Clarksville Va 41-43; Tchr Mason Schs, Plainfield NJ 56-57; Libn Wood-Ridge High Sch, Wood-Ridge NJ 57-63; Libn child room Newark Pub Lib, Newark NJ summers 59-61, 63-65; Libn Irvington Pub Schs, Irvington NJ 63-. 8: Tchr lib sci for sch libns: Newark State Col 65-68 summer 69, Caldwell College spring 68, Paterson State Col fall-winter 68-69, Alphonsus Col spring 69. 9: NEA; NJLA; NJEA; NJSchLA; EssexCoSchLA (treas 66-67; v-pres 67-68; pres 68-70). 14: Sch libnship, ref. 15: 392 Beech st, Kearny NJ 07032.

MOSS, CAROL E (STICKLE). b Seattle 27 Ap 33. 4: Gene D Moss. 5: San Francisco State Col 50-52 (Gen Educ); San Jose State Col 54-59 (Marketing) BA, 60-65 (LS) MA. 6: Sp, Fr. 7: Sales clerk & asst to fashion coordinator The Emporium, San Francisco 52-54; San Jose Pub Lib, San Jose Cal: Lib asst 54-56, Sr lib asst 56-57, Jr libn child wk 57-59, Br libn 59-61, Asst city libn 61-; Instr lib-tech San Jose City Col 68-. 8: Staff, Lib 21, Seattle Worlds Fair 62. 9: ALA (Grass Roots Recr); CalLA (sec Golden Gate Dist 65; Conf Site Com, Recr Com); (Cal) Bay Area YA Libns; (Cal) Peninsula LA; (pres 67-68); Assn Child Libns No Cal (treas 58); Pub lib Execs No Cal (treas 66-68). 13: Yes. 14: Admin, child serv. 15: 1797 Comstock lane, San Jose Ca 95124.

MOSS, EUGENIE (LAIR). b Cynthiana Ky 20 N 21 04: Ronald A Moss. 4: Ronald A Moss. 5: Randolph-Macon Womans Col 39-41, 42-43 (Biol, Span) BA; Duke 43-45 (Bot) MA; UKy 41-42 (Biol); Ohio State U 49-51 (Plant Pathology); Uky 64-65 (LS) MS. 6: Sp, Fr. 7: Mycologist US Army Chem Corps, Ft Detrick, Frederick Md 48-50; Catlgr Agric Lib UKy 65-; Ref libn Lincoln City Lib, Lincoln Neb 66-67; Ref libn Owensboro-Daviess Co Pub Lib, Owensboro Ky 67; Asst libn Agric Lib UKy (Lexington) 68-. 9: ALA; Amer Phytopathological Soc; Amer Inst of the Biol Scis; SELA; KyLA. 10: AAAS; Mem of horticultural, ornithological & farming socs; Ky Read Sci; AAUP; Sigma Delta Epsilon; Beta Phi Mu. 14: Ref, catlg, acquis. 15: 608 Beechmont rd, Lexington Ky 40502.

MOSS, JESSIE LUKE. b Richmond Ky 22 S 10. 5: West State Col Bowling Green Ky 30-44 (Educ) BS; UKy 52-60 (LS); Ky State Dept of Educ Standard Certif in admin & supv, Standard certif for full time sch libn; Peabody 63-67 MLS. 7: lem tchr: Summer Co Scs, Tenn 36-42; Warren Co Schs, Ky 43-44; Boone Co Schs, Ky 44-45; Franklin Co Schs, Ky 45-47; Ohio Co Schs, Ky 47-48; Libn: Lawrenceburg High Sch, Ky 57-58; Kenton Co Schs, Ky 51-57; Ludlow High Sch, Ky 58-68; Current River Reg Lib Mo 68-. 9: NEA; ALA; KyEA; KyLA; KyASchL; No KyEA; No KySchLA (sec-treas 64-65) MoLA. 10: Sch Morms No Ky (KNOMS); PTA; Womans Soc Christian Serv. 14: Sch & reg libnship; ref. 15: PO Box 446, Van Buren Mo 63965.

MOSS, JULIA (NAIL). b Marathon Tex 30 My 21. 4: John M Moss. 5: Sul Ross State Col 38-39, 41-42 (Eng) BA; Drexel 47-48 BS in LS. 7: Dept Agric Lib, Wash DC 43-45; Libn Ft Bliss, El Paso Tex 46; Libn Biggs Field, El Paso Tex 47; Lib asst Free Lib of Phila 48; Libn Val Verde Co Lib, Del Rio Tex 49-50; Asst libn Sul Ross State Col 62-. 9: TexLA. 14: Catlg. 15: Box 515, Marathon Tex 79842.

MOSSER, DONALD W. b Chicago Ill 19 Mr 25. 5: PrincetonU 45-49 (Hist) AB; UChicago 66-67 (LS). 6: Fr. 7: Rifleman US Army, European Theatre 43-45; Sec of the Corp A L Webster & Co, Chicago 49-63; Libn I Chicago Pub Lib 66-. 14: Ref in hist. 15: 1516 N State pkwy, Chicago Il 60610.

MOSSUTO, MARION JEANNE (DALLMAN). b Seattle Wash 28 Je 44. 4: Robert Neil Mossuto. 7: Sr page King Co Pub Lib, Bellevue Wash 57-60; Interlib loans asst Pacific Aerospace lib (AIAA), Los Angeles 63-64, Interlib loans (libn in charge) 66-67; Bibliog checker SLA Tr Ctr John Crerar Lib, Chicago 65; Catlgr TRW Syst, Redondo Beach Cal 67-. 9: SLA; CalLA. 10: Young Republicans. 14: Ref, ser, catlg. 15: 3852 Aloha st, Los Angeles Ca 90027.

MOST, GEORGETTE KEATH (MOYER). b Schaefferstown Penn 8 My 17. 4: Ralph C Most. 5: Swarthmore 34-38 (Eng) BA; Drexel 38-39 BSLS; Columbia 40-42 (Fine arts). 6: Ger, Sp. 7: Asst ref libn Columbia U 39-45; Ref libn Fed Pub Housing Authority, Wash DC 45-47; Ref libn La Salle Col 47-. 9: ALA; -ACRL; CathLA; PennLA. 10: Phila Art alliance; Phila Mus of Art; Phila Orchestra Assn. 14: Ref. 15: 1520 Brookhaven rd, Wynnewood Pa 19096.

MOSTAR, ROMAN. b Vancouver BC Can 14 Je 13. 4: Edith Margaret Wickham. 5: UBC 36-39 (Econ) BA; UWash 39-40 BLS. 7: Catlgr Fraser Valley Union Lib, Abbotsford BC 40-42; Wireless off RCAF 42-45; Catlgr Fraser Valley Union Lib, Abbotsford BC 45-46; Stacks libn, circ asst UWash Lib 46-60; Asst City libn & head of ext Seattle Pub Lib 60-. 8: Lib bldg consul, Wash State Lib 64-. 9: ALA; PNLA (chm Exhibits Com, chm Pub Libs Div 64-66); WashLA (Exec Bd 68-70); CanLA. 10: UWash Sch of Libnship Alumnae Assn. 12: Co-comp "A Checklist of Pacific Northwest Newspapers (50). 13: Yes. 14: Pub lib admin, pub lib bldgs. 15: Seattle Pub Lib, 4th & Madison, Seattle Wa 98104.

MOSTECKY, MRS IVA (ERET). b Prague Czechoslovakia 23 N 23. 4: Vaclav Mostecky. 5: City Gym ChG (Masaryk Prague) 35-42 (Chem, Fr) BS; Charles U (Prague) 45-46 (Chem), 46-47 (Hist of Law); Columbia 50-51 MS in LS. 6: CZECH, Slovak, Ger, Fr, Russian. 7: Catlgr Folger-Shakespeare Lib, Wah DC 51-52; Catlgr Army Med Lib, Wash DC 52-53; Bk sel Armed Forces Med Lib, Wash DC 53-55, Head name estable unit 55-57; Sr catlgr Slavic Unit NLM, Wash DC 57-58; Chief of catlg Harvard Med Lib 59-. 8: MedLA (Rep to ALA Bibliog Com); SLA (Boston Chap: Program Com); Harvard Lib Club. 14: Admin. 15: 32 Tobey rd, Belmont Mass 02178.

MOSTECKY, VACLAV. b J HRADEC Czechoslovakia 29 Je 19. 4: Iva Eret. 5: Lycee Carnot (Dijon)35-38 (Liberal Arts) BA; Charles U (Prague) 38-46(Law) JUD; Columbia 39-40 (Pub Law) MA; Catholic U 43-44 MS in LS; Columbia 55-56 (LS). 6: Czech, Ger, Fr, Ital, Russian. 7: Law dictionary ed Slavic Inst, Prague 39-40; Production supv Coal Dealers Assn, Prague 40-45; Lib asst Faculty of Law, Prague 45-47; Foreign Serv Off Ministry of Foreign Affairs, Prague 47-48; Production supv Beta Shoe Co, Belmont Md 48-49; Br chief US Dept of State, Wash DC 49-53; Asst Prof Catholic U 54-58; Asst libn Harvard Law Sch 58-. 8: Part-time lecturer in lib sci, Simmons Col 59-65. 9: Internat Law Assn; ALA; AALL. 10: Phi Beta Mu. 11: Meritorious Serv Award, US Dept of State, 52. 12: Ed "Catalog Use Study ALA (60); Co-auth "Russian and East Euroean Pblications in the Libraries of the US (60); Ed "Annual Legal Bibliography (60-); Ed "Soviet Legal Bibliography (65); Ed "Index to Multilaterl Treaties (65). 13: Yes. 14: Admin, ref. 15: 32 Tobey rd, Belmont Mass 02178.

MOSTELLER, BETTE (VAUGHAN). b Amelia Co Va 1 F 37. 5: Longwood Col 54-58 (LS) BA; Peabody Col 59 MA in LS. 6: Fr. 7: Catlgr Va State Lib 59-62; Readers Adv Richmond Pub Lib, Richmond Va summer 62; Head Libn Christopher Newport Jr Col 62-. 9: VaLA. 10: Alpha Sigma Tau. 14: Admin, adv serv, lib recr. 15: 510 Bulkeley pl apt 14, Newport News Va 23601.

MOSTOW, SYLVIA A. b NYC 8 D 08. 5: City Col NY even 26-34; Eng BS in Ed; Catholic U 58-62 MS in LS UMD 62,65. 7: Libn Lone Oak elem sch, Montgomery Co Pub Schs, Montgomery Co Md 59-. 9: ALA-AASchL; NEA; MdLA; Sch Libns Md; Md State Tchrs Assn; Montgomery CEA; Montgomery Co SchLA. 10: Beta Phi Mu; Kappa Delta Pi. 14: Wk with child. 15: 8811 Colesville rd apt 908, Silver Spring Md 20910.

MOTHERAL, LINDA (ETIER CHEVES). b Iowa Park Tex 27 F 39. 4: Robert Clifton Motheral. 5: Cisco Jr Col 57-59 Assoc BA; N Tex State U 59-61 (LS) BA. 6: Sp. 7: Asst libn Southwestern U 61-67; Asst order libn Stephen F Austin State Col 67-. 9: TexLA. 14: Catlg. 15: Box 5962 SFA Sta, Nacogdoches Tx 75961.

MOTHERSHED, SPAESIO WILLARD. b Bloomburg Tex 30 Je 25. 4: Juliene Craven. 5: Jarvis Christian Col 49-52 (Eng) AB; Syracuse 54-56 (LS) MS; N Tex State U 63 (Educ). 6: Fr. 7: USN 43-46; Catlgr Michigan State Lib, Lansing Mich 56-60; Hd libn Jarvis Christian Col 60-66; Hd libn Tex So U 66-. 9: ALA; TexLA. 14: Admin, catlg. 15: 3515 Oakdale, Houston Tx 77004.

MOTLEY, ARCHIE JOHN. b Chicago 2 D 34. 5: DePaul U 53-57, 60 (Philos) BA; Loyola U (Chicago) 60-65 (Philos) MA. 6: Ger. 7: US Army (Pfc) Clerk typist 58-59; Broadside libn Chicago Hist Soc 56-57, Ms libn 60-. 14: Org & catlg mss (urban hist). 15: Chicago Hit Soc, Clark st & North ave, Chicago 60614.

MOTLEY, DRUCILLA. b Epps La 3 Je 22. 5: NE La State Col 39-65; La Polytech Inst 41-43 (Econ) BA; LSU 46-50 (Educ) MEd, 59-62 (LS) MS; Fla State U 68- (LS). 7: Tchr Delhi High Sch, Delhi La 43-44; Tchr Mer Rouge High Sch, Mer Rouge La 4-46; Bkkeeper Central Savings bank, Monroe La 46-49; Supv tchr NE La State Col 52-68; Tchr & libn Crosley Elem, W Monroe La 49-58; Libn W Monroe Jr High 58-64; Libn Ouachita Parish High, Monroe La 64-68; Visiting asst prof LSU (Baton Rouge) summers 67-69; Dir media ctr Ouachita Parish Schs, Monroe La 69-. 8: Memb NDEA Inst Fac, Ind U 45; Memb HEA Inst Fac, La State U 49. 09; ALA; -AASchL; -ISAD; NEA-DAVI; NCTE; AALS; SWLA; LaLA; LaTA; LaASchL. 10: AAUW; Beta Phi Mu. 11: HEA Doctoral Fellowship Program, FlaStateU. 13: Yes. 14: Sch libs, lib educ, automation. 15: 3903 Harrison st, Monroe La 71201.

MOTOMATSU, NANCY REIKO. b Woodinville Wash 30 Je 31. 6: Japanese. 7: Tchr Tumwater Elem Sch, Tumwater Wash 57-60; Tchr Sagamihara Elem Sch, Camp Zama Japan 60-61, Libn 61-62; Jr high libn & Head Libn DuPont-Ft Lewis Sch Dist, DuPont Wash 62-; Assoc supv of Learning resources serv Off of the Supt of Pub Instr, Olympia Wash 66-. 8: Adult Educ, Eng for the foreign born, citizenship DuPont-Ft Lewis Sch Dist, DuPont Wash 64-. 9: NEA; -AASchL (Internat Sel Com 68; Ad hoc Com Soc Studies in World Affairs 69); WashEA; Wash State ASchL (Conf Publicity chm 67-70, Jt Standards Com; see Reg VII 66-67). 10: Delta Kappa Gamma; Japanese Amer Citizens League. 14: Bks on the Far East (Japan). 15: Rt 1 Box 261, Olympia Wash 98502.

MOTT, SCHUYLER L. b NYC 16 O 28. 4: Constance M A Wiley. 5: Colby Col 47-51 (Hist) AB; Pratt 51-52 MLS. 7: Stud asst Colby Col 49-51; Summer asst New Bedford Mass Pub Lib 51; Classified documents libn E I DuPont de Nemours & Co, Wilmington Del, & Aiken (SC) Atomic Energy Div 52-54; US Army Counter Intelligence Corps, Spec Agent 54-56; Supv libn, Circ Pub Lib, Bloomfield NJ 57-63; Dir Pub Lib, Bernardsville NJ 63-. 8: Planning Adv for Somerset Hills Area Lib, 62-63. 9: NJLA (Exec Bd 62-63, pres circ sect 60-62, chm Recr Com 67-68, chm Personnel Admin Com 68-). 10: Somerset Hills C of C. 12: Co-ed "New Jersey Interlibrary Loan Code" (64); Ed "A History of Bernardsville" (66); Ed "Looking for a Challenge Try New Jersey Recruitment Booklet of NJLA" (68). 13: Yes. 14: Admin of pub libs. 15: Pub Lib, 2 Morristown rd, Bernardsville NJ 07924.

MOTYCKA, ELIZABETH (NEWBERRY). b N Rose NY 30 Jl 05. 4: Joseph Motycka. 5: Syracuse 22-26 (Eng) AB; Albany Lib Sch 27 (LS); Columbia 28-30 (LS); So Conn State Col 61-67 9ls0. 6: Lat, Fr, Greek. 7: High sch Eng tchr & libn; Holland Patient NY 26-28, Lawrence LI NY 28-31; Eng & reading tchr Bd of Educ, Coventry Conn 60-61, High sch lib tchr 61-68, Sch lib supv 68-. 9: ALA; ConnSchLA; ConnEA Coventry EA (Exec Com 2 yrs, Scholarship Com 3 yrs). 10: Alpha Delta Kappa; Pi Beta Phi; 4H Leader; Coventry Hist Assn. 14: High sch learning ctrs. 15: Rte 3 Folly lane, Coventry Ct 06238.

MOTZ, MRS MINNE R(OSENBAUM). b NYC 3 F 16. 4: Lloyd Motz. 5: Brooklyn Col 32-36 (Eng Lit) BA; CCNY 41-42 (Lit); Columbia 54-56 (LS) MS. 7: Eng tchr pub high schs, NYC 41-53; Jr high libn, NYC 53-55; High sch libn, NYC 55-58; Bd of Educ, NYC: Act supv of Libs 58-60, Supv Sch Libs 60-63, Asst dir 63-. 8: Mem of Jury, Amer Inst Graph Arts 68. 9: ALA-CSD (Pre-Conf Com 65); NYLA; NY Lib Club (Coun); ASCD (ALA-CBC Jt Com); NYC SchLA; NY Soc Experim Study Educ. 10: Womens Nat Bk Assn; Admin Women in Educ; Phi Beta Mu. 13: Yes. 14: Supv of sch libs, reading guidance for ya. 15: 815 W 181 st, NYC 10033.

MOULTON, CHARLOTTE (BREWSETER) JAMIESON (MRS). b New Haven Conn 11 F 11. 5: American U 28-32 (Eng, Soc Studies, Langs) BA; Drexel 35-36 BS in LS; Stetson U summer 61 (Philos, Child Lit); Catholic U summer 62 (Philos, Elem Educ), summer 65 (Indexing). 6: Fr, Sp, Portu. 7: Libn & dir of files Nat Fed Bus Prof Womens Clubs Inc, NY 36-42; Pan Amer Union, Wash DC: Lib asst & ed Pan Amer Book Shelf Columbus Mem Lib, Juridical div asst, Cultural rel asst 42-47; Med libn George Washington U Sch of Med 47-51; Asst libn & catlgr Nat Gallery of Art, Wash DC 51-52; Upper sch tchr in Eng, hist & Gk Mythology & sch libn Powhatan Sch, Boyce Clarke Co a 60-63; Ref libn in med & biol sci, med lit br div of med info Bur of Med Food & Drug Admin, Dept Health Educ & Welfare, Wash DC 6465; Ref libn in med & biol sci ref sect, ref serv div NLM Public Health Serv US Dept of Health Educ & Welfare, Bethesda Md 66-. 9: SLA; MedLA. 10: Audubon Soc; Friends of DC Zoo. 12: Ed & comp "Pan American Book Shelf (42-44). 13: Yes. 14: Ref (med, bio sci, behavioral sci). 15: 3914 McKinley st NW, Wash DC 20015.

MOULTON, JAMES C. b Columbia Mo 8 Jl 43. 5: Mich State U 61-65 (Soc sci) BA; UMich 65-66 MALS. 6: Fr. 7: Docs libn & instr Mich Tech U 66-. 9: ALA; MichLA. 10: AAUP. 14: Ref, govt docs, rare bks. 15: 101 W Montezuma ave, Houghton Mi 49931.

MOULTON, MARY (KENNINGTON). b Wuhu Anhwei China 28 S 13. 5: Aurora Col 32-33 (Biol). 6: Chinese. 7: Med record libn Mass Mem Hosp, Boston 36-40; Asst in Lib NEA Research div Lib, Wash DC 40-41; Dir Nature Educ House of Three Bears Camp. Green Lake Wis 42-46; Child Libn St Charles Pub Lib, St Charles Ill 44-46; Self-employed landscape designer 47-63; Libn Morton Arboretum, Lisle Ill 63-. 8: Member, St Charles Library board 12 years. Chm, Environmental Comment Committee, Mid-Central States Chapter of the American Society of Landscape Architects. 9: ALA; BSA; Bk Wkers Guild (AIGA). 10: Garden Hist Soc (Eng); Newberry Lib Assocs; var socs in conserv and landscape arch. 13: Yes. 14: Rare bks (hortic, hist of bot), ref, bot art. 15: Morton Arboretum, Lisle Il 60532.

MOULTON, MARY W. b Elwood Ind 31 O 20. 4: Benjamin Moulton. 5: Butler U 43-48 (Eng) BA; IndU 63-66 MLS. 6: Ger, Fr, Sp. 7: Catlgr Ind State U Lib (Terre Haute) 63-. 9: IndLA; Ohio Valley Gp of Tech Serv Libns. 10: AAUP; Vigo Co Park Bd; Ind State U Fac Women's Club. 14: Child bks. 15: RR 21 Box 101, Terre Haute In 47802.

MOULTON, PRISCILLA L(ANDIS). b Brooklyn NY 12 O 23. 4: Lloyd Jackson Moulton. 5: Cornell U 40-44 (Nutrition) BS; West Res 56-59 MSLS. 6: Fr. 7: Research asst Cornell U 44; Research asst Ohio State U 45; Libn Pub Schs, Mentor Ohio 55-59; Libn Pub Schs, Swampscott Mass 59-61, Coord elem sch libs 62-66; Libn Phillips Acaf Lib, Andover Mass summer 64; Dir lib serv pub schs, Brookline Mass 66-. 8: Consul "Elementary School Booklist", ALA 66-67; Adv Com "Junior High School Catalog"; Instr in child lit, Salem State Col, Salem Mass 68. 9: ALA; -CSD (Bd Dirs 65-68, Devel Com Chm 67-71); -RTSD (Com on Catlg of Child Materials Chm 68-); -YASD (Com on Africa List 61-64); NELA (chm RT of Child Libns 63-65, chm Child Sci Bk Review Com 63-65; Hewins-Melcher Lectr 67). 10: Beta Phi Mu. 11: Dutton-,acrae Award 65. 13: Yes. 14: Child lit, admin of serv to child. 15: 10 Pinecliff dr, Marblehead Ma 01945.

MOUNCE, MARVIN W. b Lufkin Tex 24 Ag 34. 5: Lamar State Col of Tech 52-55 (Hist) BS; UTex 56-58 (LS). ; U Pittsburgh 67-68 (LS) MLS. 6: Sp. 7: Sci tchr W Orange Jr High Sch, Orange Tex 55-56; Engnr Western Electric Co, Chicago 57; Sr lib asst UTex 56-58; Order libn Tex A&I 58-60; Catlgr Cal State Lib Processing Center 60-62; Research libn Cal State Lib 62-63; Coordinator of tech serv Fresno Co Free Lib, Fresno Cal 63-66; Hd tech serv New Orleans Pub Lib, New Orleans La 66-67; Dir Ingham Co Lib & Central Mich Lib Syst, Mason Mich 68-. 9: CalLA (Yosemite Dist: sec Pub Rel); ALA; MedLA. 13: Yes. 14: Tech proc, coop lib systems, a-v. 15: PO Box 212, Mason Mi 48854.

MOUNKES, KAY (CORREEN) (YOUNG). b Chanute Kan 8 Ja 34. 4: William Lee Mounkes. 5: Chanute Jr Col 51-53 (Eng); Kan State Tchrs Col (Emporia) 53-54, 59-60 (Eng) BS in Ed, 60-61 (LS) MS. 6: Fr, Sp. 7: Libn Great Bend Pub Lib, Great Bend Kan 55-57; Act libn Emporia Pub Lib, Emporia Kan 59-60, Br libn 60-61; Libn Nallwood Jr High Sch, Shawnee Mission High Sch Dist, Shawnee Mission Kan 61-68, Coord lib serv 68-. 9: ALA; NEA; KanLA (chm Chiod Div 62); KanASchL. 10: PTA; 4-H Project Leader. 12: Ed KanASchL ""Newsletter (61-63). 14: Catlg, admin. 15: P O Box 86, Stanley Kan 66084.

MOUNT, (HUSTON) ELLIS. b Connersville Ind 25 S 21 04: Katherine Lyman Mount. 5: Ind U 39-41, 42-43 (Music); Principia Col 46-48 (Physics) BS; Northwestern 48-49 (Physics)

MS; UIll 49-50 (LS) MS. 6: Fr. 7: USAAF Communications Off (1st Lt) 43-46; Ref asst John Crerar Lib, Chicago 50-51; Libn Gen Electric Aircraft Nuc Prop Proj, Cincinnati 51-53; Research assoc John Crerar Lib, Chicago 53-65; Chief libn Internat Tel & Tel Fed Labs, Nutley NJ 55-64; Sci & engnr libn Columbia U 64-. 9: SLA (NJ Chap; treas 60-62, pres 63-64; Sci-Tech Div; treas 68-70); ASIS. 10: Beta Phi Mu. 13: Yes. 14: Sci libs, info retrieval. 15: Engnr Lib Columbia Univ, New York NY 10027.

MOUNT, MARY (VIRGINIA). b Delavan Ill8 S 19. 5: Whitworth Col 36-40 (Eng) BA; UDenver 51; UWash summers 44, 45. 55-57 (LS) ML. 7: House mother Rosamund B Goddard Home, N Fork Cal 40-42; Tchr-libn Clarksfork High Sch, Clarksfork Ida 42-43; Tchr-libn Quilcene High Sch, Quilcene Wash 43-49; Libn Columbia High Sch, Richland Wash 49-60;Lib dir Lake Washington Sch Dist, Kirkland Wash 60-. 8: Adv com, Wash State Det of Educ Reading List 65-. 9: NEA-DAVI; ALA; WashEA; WashLA; Wash Org for Reading Level; Wash State ASchL (var coms); WashDAVI. 10: AAUW; Bus & Prof Women; Beta Phi Mu; Nat Campers & Hikers Assn. 13: Yes. 14: Pub sch libnship, child bks. 15: 225 First st, Kirkland Wash 98033.

MOUNTCASTLE, ANNE (WOODWORTH). b Cleveland 20 My 04. 4: Henry R Mountcastle. 5: Flora Stone Mather Col West Res 21-25 (Lit) BA; West Res 26-27 BSLS. 7: Asst lit div Cleveland Pub Lib 26-35; Carnegie Lib of Pittsburgh: Asst ref dept 53-55, Schs dept 55-56, Yp libn Homewood Br 56-. 9: ALA; Penn LA. 14: Ref, yp serv. 15: 4950 Perrysville rd, Pittsburgh Pa 15229.

MOUNTFORT, RUTH A. b Portland Me 30 Je 44. 5: UNH 62-66 (Socio) BA; Rutgers 66-67 MLS. 6: Fr. 7: Ref asst Va Polytech Inst 67-. 9: ALA. 10: Amer Sociol Assn. 14: Ref. 15: 402 Progress st, Blacksburg Va 24060.

MOUNTS, MELVIN. b Washington Penn 28 Je 40. 5: Washington & Jefferson Col 58-62 (Biol) BA; Rutgers 62-64 MLS; Seton Hall U 64-69 JD. 6: Fr. 7: Stud asst W &J Col Lib 59-62; Libn trainee art & music dept Newark Pub Lib, Newark NJ 62-64, Ref libn Bus Lib 64-69; Rules analyst NJ Div of Admin Procedure 69-. 8: Lib consul, Herculite Protective Fabrics, Newark NJ 65. 14: Ref, electron data proc, info ret. 15: 381 Broad st, Newark NJ 07104.

MOURSUND, GERALDINE BERG. b Seattle 15 Ag 09. 4: John Stribling Moursund. 5: Wash 27-31 (Fr) BA, 31-32 (LS) BS. 6: Fr. 7: Child libn Austin Pub Lib, Austin Tex 33-35; Asst child dept Tacoma Pub Lib, Tacoma Wash 35-39; Asst child dept Seattle Pub Lib 39-41; Libn US Off of Censorship, Nogales Ariz 43-44; Tchr high sch Tule Lake Relocation Center. Tule Lake Cal 44-46; Libn Tex Sch for Deaf, Austin Tex 49-. 9: Conv of Amer Instrs of the Deaf; Tex State Tchrs Assn. 10: Phi Beta Kappa. 14: Child serv. 15: 2107 Ashby, Austin Tex 78704.

MOUSHEY, EUGENE WILSON. b Ft Wayne Ind 28 D 22. 4: Grace Freeman. 5: UMich 41-42, 46-48 (Span) BA, 48-49 (Span) MA, 49-50 (Span) BS, 50-51 AMLS. 6: Sp. 7: Assoc Prof Lib Sci Wis State U (Oshkosh Wis) 51-57, Ref libn 58-62, 64-66; Hd ref unit Mich State Lib, Lansing Mich 66-68. 8: Visiting Prof of Lib Sci, Nat Univ of El Salvador, 57-58; Prof of Lib Sch, Escuela Interamericana de Bibliotecologia, Medellin Colombia, 63-64; Consul UCatolica Madre y Maestra Santiago de los Caballeros (USAID), Republica Dominica 68-70. 9: ALA; WisLA; WisEA. 10: Assn of Wis State Univ Faculties. 14: Catlg, ref. 15: 141 Gunson st, E Lansing Mi 48823.

MOUZON, KATHERINE (BRADLEY). b Forest City NC 1 My 17. 4: Olin T Mouzon. 5: Greensboro Col 34-38 (Biol) AB; Duke U 38-39 (Zool); UNC 45-47 BSLS. 6: Fr, Ger, Ital. 7: Asst ref UNC Lib (Chapel Hill) 48, Music catlgr 49-52; Ser catlgr Duke U 56-58; Libn Estes Hill Sch, Chapel Hill NC 60; Instr Child bks UNC Ext (Chapel Hill) 60. 10: AAUW. 14: Catlg, child lit. 15: 903 Greenwood dr, Chapel Hill NC.

MOWERS, LARRY (GILES). b Utica NY. 5: Ithaca Col 55 (Music Theory) BM; Boston U 60 (Musicology) MM; Simmons 64 (LS) MS. 6: Ger, Fr, Lat. 7: Asst libn Harvard U Dept of Music 57-. 14: Printed & ms music to 1700. 15: 10 Dana st, Cambridge Mass 02138.

MOWERY, BOB LEE. b Charlotte NC 22 Je 20. 4: Peggy Setzer. 5: Catawba Col 37-41 (Hist) AB; Chicago 46-47 BLS, 50-51 (LS) MA; Institute Za Strane Jezik-Belgrade 68. 6: Fr, Ger, Serbo-Croatian. 7: (Maj) Artillery US Army, Alaska 42-46; Catlg libn Dickinson Col 47-50; Head Libn Murry State Col 51-53; Head Libn McNeese State Col 53-58; Head Libn Stetson U 58-64; Dir of Libs Wittenberg U 64-. 8: Consul; Edward Waters 62; Findley 66; Lindenwood 67; chm, Com on Lib Resources; Reg Coun on Internat Educ 66-68; chm Dayton-Miami Valley Consortium, Lib Div 68-. 9: ALA; BSA; Bibliog Soc (London); Bibliog Soc UVa); OhioLA. 10: Rotarian; Com on Christian Educ & chm Constitution Com, Fla Synod, Luth Church in Amer 61-63; Trustee, Newberry Col; Arthur Machen Soc; Friends of DeLand Pub Lib; Civic Forum (Springfield); Springfield Hist Commsn. 11: ACLS fellowship 68. 12: Ed "Bulletin LaLA (56-58). 14: Admin, rare bks. 15: Thomas Lib, Wittenberg U, Springfield Ohio.

MOWERY, JUDITH KAY. b Akron Ohio 6 O 42. 5: Ohio U 60-64 (Eng) AB; Case West Res 64-65 MSLS; UAkron 67-(Eng). 6: Fr. 7: Lib aide Akron Pub Lib Ayres br, Akron Ohio 64, Libn II adult serv 65-67; Asst humanities libn UAkron 67-68, Humanities subj libn 68-. 9: ALA (Jr Mem RT); -ACRL; OhioLA (Recr Com 66-68; sec Jr Mem RT 68-69); Young Libns Assn NE Ohio (sec 67-68); Akron Area LA (chm Proj Com 68-69). 10: AAUP; ACLU; Greater Akron Arts Fed. 14: Intel freedom, recr. 15: 1808 Carter ave, Akron Oh 44301.

MOWERY, ROBERT LONG. b Rochester Penn 22 Mr 34. 4: Janet Bartholomew Mowery. 5: Purdue 52-56 (Mech Engring) BSME; Garrett Theol Sem 56-60 (Theol) BD; NorthwesternU 60-67 (Rel) MA, PhD; Eberhard-Karls-Universitat (Tubingen Germany) 62-63 9theol); UIll 67-68 MS in LS. 6: Ger, Fr, Russian, Gr. 7: Pastor Odell Methodist Ch, Odell Ill 63-66; Pastor Pesotum Methodist Ch, Pesotum Ill 66-68; Sci libn & a-v coord ill WesleyanU Lib 68-69, Humanities libn 69-. 9: ALA. 10: Phi Eta Sigma; Pi Tau Sigma; Tau Beta Pi; Beta Phi Mu. 14: Ref, automation, philos of libnship. 15: 1504 N Franklin, Bloomington Il 61701.

MOYER, MARY E(LLEN). b Russelville Ill 24 S 1899. 5: Eureka Col 20-24 (Eng Lit, Fr) AB; UIll summer 27, 28-29 BS in LS. 7: Tchr country sch, Fortville Ind 19-20; High sch tchr Livingston Acad, Livingston Tenn 24-28; Tchr-libn Robinson High Sch, Robinson Ill 29-30; Tchr Orio Sch, Allendale Ill 31-34; Tchr-libn Acad, Hazel Green Ky 35-38; Asst ctlgr Ill State Lib 38-46, Order libn 46-47; Ctlgr Ill State Hist Lib, Springfield Ill 47-. 9: IllLA. 10: Beta Phi Mu; Audubon Soc; AAUW; YWCA; Ill State Hist Soc. 14: Catlg. 15: 400 W Capitol, Springfield Ill.

MOYER, MICHAEL (ORIN). b Henderson Tex 10 Ag 37. 5: Kilgore Jr Col 55-57; N Tex State U 57-62 (LS) BA. 7: Asst libn Rusk C Lib, Henderson Tex 60; Asst libn Madison Parish Lib, Tallulah a 60-62; Asst libn US Bur of Mines Pet Res Center, Bartlesville Okla 62-63; Libn Ellington AFB, Houston 63-65; Libn phys sci & engnr Rocket Prop Lab, Edwards AFB Cal 65-. 9: ALA; CalLA. 15: P O Box 6012, Rocket Prop Lab, Edwards Cal 93523.

MOYERS, JOYCE C. b Broadway Va 21 D 27. 5: Bridgewater Col 46-48; Madison Col 48-50 (LS) BS in Ed; UNC 58-59 MS in LS. 7:Libn Brentsville Dist High Sch, Nokesville Va 50-52; Libn James Monroe High Sch, Fredericksburg Va 52-54; Head circ dept Olivia Raney Lib, Raleigh NC 54-58; Asst libn Rockingham Pub Lib, Harrisonburg Va 59-60, Libn 60-. 9: ALA; VaLA. 10: Quota Club. 15: Rte 1, Broadway Va 22815.

MOZLEY, DOROTHY. b Boston 12 Ap 16. 5: Russell Sage Col 33-37 (Eng) BA; Simmons 44-45 (LS) BS. 7: Sec Oak Grove Sch, Vassalboro Me 38-40; Ed Bellman Publ Co, Boston 40-41; Asst supv index dept Recording & Statistical Corp, Boston 41-44; Lib asst Enoch Pratt Free Lib, Baltimore 45-47; Libn Mass Mutual Life Insurance Co, Springfield Mass 47-49; Head ref dept Life Insurance Agency Mgt Assn, Hartford Conn 49-50; Ref asst in chg of local hist & genealogy Springfield City Lib, Springfield Mass 50-. 9: ALA; SLA; NELA; MassLA; West MassLA. 14: Ref. 15: 252 Union st, Springfield Ma 01105.

MOZOROSKY, TERRY HOWARD. b Walla Walla Wash 21 Je 41. 4: Zmira Kalif. 5: YeshivaU 59-61 (Sociol); Portland State Col 61-64 (Educ, Soc Sci) BS; LIU 66-68 MLS. 6: Hebrew. 7: Recreation dir Morningside Hosp, Portland Ore 63-64; Jr high sch soc studies tchr Yonkers Pub Schm Yonkers NY 65-66; High sch libn a-v coord Tarrytown Pub Sch, Tarrytown NY 66-. 8: Lib consul SUNY (Mt Vernon) Coop Col Ctr 69-. 9: ALA; NEA-DAVI (Intl Projects Com); Westchester (NY) LA; Westchester A-V Assn; NY State a-V Assn. 10: TarrytownTA. 14: A-v, ref, data proc syst, intl lib & a-v programs. 15: 131 Grand ave, Englewood NJ 07631.

MROZEWSKI, ANDRZEJ H. b Paris France 25 F 30. 4: Janina Karolewska. 5: UMontreal 53-54 (Slavic Studies) Ma

UOttawa 59-60 BLS, 6: Polish, Fr. 7: Gen libn UOttawa Lib 59-60; Head Libn Col Rouyn Lib (Rouyn Que) 60-64; Med libn Hopital dYouville, Noranda Que 62-64; Chief acquis dept USherbrooke (Sherbrooke Que) 64-65, Asst chief lbn & chief of tech serv 65-68; Asst chief libn 68-. 8: Lecturer in Polish Lit, UOttawa, summers 60-61 in Lib Sci summers 61-64. 9: CanLA; Association canadienne des bibliothecaires de langue franc24aise; QueLA (pres 67-68); ALA. 10: Can Assn of Slavists. 12: Ed quela "Newsletter (67-). 13: Yes. 14: Tchg, mechanization, rare bks, art collections. ; admin, collection bldg. 15: Univ of Sherbrooke, Que Can.

MUCHIN, JOHN SERGE. b Odessa Ukraine 25 N 20. 4: Halyna Yanchyk. 5: Pervomaisk pedagogical Inst 36-39 (Philology) BEd; Moscow Artillery Col 39-41 Lt; UOttawa 62-63 BLS; UManitoba 69 (Slavic Studies). 6: Ukrainian, Russian, Polish, Ger, other Slavic lang. 7: Artillery off USSR Army, Moscow, West front of USSR 41-43; Lecturer UNRRA Tech sch, Landshut Germany 46-47; Libn J Richardson & Sons Fin Lib, Winnipeg Can 63-64; Catlgr UManitoba Lib 64-65, Slavic libn & catlgr 65-67, Hd spec collections 68-. 9: CanLA; ManitobaLA. 10: Ukrainian Free Acad of Sci; Can Assn of Slavists; Ukrainian Cult & Educ Ctre; Ukrainian Can Com. 14: Catlg, rare bks, bk sel. 15: 165 Lansdowne ave, Winnipeg 4 Manitoba Can.

MUDD, SISTER JAMES EDWARD. 5: St Mary of the Woods Col 36-38 (Hist) AB; Catholic U 53 BS in LS. 6: Fr. 7: Tchr-libn St Charles High Sch, Lebanon Ky 39-45; Libn Brescia Col 49-. 9: ALA; CathLA; KyLA. 14: Catlg. 15: Brescia Col, Owensboro Ky 42302.

MUDGE, JOY (NORTH). b Cleveland 14 Mr 29. 4: Glen Mudge. 5: Beaver Col 47-51 (Hist) AB; Kent State U 55 (LS); Wayne State U 55-61 (LS) MS. 6: Sp. 7: Tchr, E Liverpool Ohio 54-55; Libn Wayne State U 55-57; Libn Oak Park schs, Oak Park Mich 57-; Dir Sch Libs Charlevoix Sch Charlevoix Mich. 9: ALA; MichASchL. 10: Pi Lambda Theta; Alpha Beta Kappa. 13: Yes. 14: Sch libs, child lit, bk reviewing. 15: Box 96a, Ellsworth Mi 49729.

MUEHLECK, REBECCA BREWER. b Trenton NJ. 4: J Robert Muehleck. 5: Mt Holyoke 36-40 (Eng Lit) AB (cum laude); Columbia 40-41 (LS) BS; Rutgers 42-43 (Engnr) Certif. 6: Fr. 7: Ref & sch asst br NY Pub Lib 41-42; Stud engnr, weight analyst Eastern Aircraft Co, Trenton NJ 42-44; Trenton ub Lib, Trenton NJ: Jr libn ref 57-58, Sr libn ref 58-60, Supv libn, head ref dept 60-. 8: Trenton Tercentenary Commsn 63-64. 9: ALA (Ref, Col & Univ, Hist); NJLA (chm Bibliog Com 63-68, pres Hist & Bibliog Sect 68-69). 10: NJ Hist Soc; Trenton Hist SOC: Trenton Hist Soc; Wm Trent House Assn. 13: Yes. 14: Ref, Americana, Jerseyana, Trentoniana, bibliog. 15: 322 S Main st, Pennington NJ.

MUEHSAM, GERD. b Berlin Germany. 5: UBerlin 32-33; UVienna 33-37 (Musicology) PhD; West es 41-42 BLS. 6: Fr, Ger. 7: In chg of photograph collection Cleveland Musum of Art, Cleveland 42-44; Cooper Union (NY): Catlgr 45-46, Prep libn 46-50, Assoc libn 5065; Supv libn Donnell Art Lib NY Pub Lib 65-67; Asst Prof & Art bibliog(r) Queens Col CUNY 67-. 8: Lecturer on music, Cooper Union Adult Educ Dept, 61-. 9: ALA; SLA (NY Chap: chm Mus Group 66-68). 10: AAUP; Amer Soc Aesthetics. 12: "D Edzard (48). 13: Yes. 14: Art, music. 15: Paul Klapper Lib Queens Col,Flushing NY 11367.

MUELLER, ALLEN W(ALTER). b St Louis Mo 2 Ap 43. 5: St Louis Jr Col 63-65 AA; Valparaiso 65-67 (Hist, Ger) BA; UIll 67-68 (LS) MS. 6: Ger. 7: Catlgr St Louis Co Lib 62-65; Catlgr Valparaiso U Lib 66-67; Asst Grad school of lib sci UIll (Urbana) 67-68; Ref libn LC 69-. 9: ALA; MoLA. 11: Special Recr; LC 68-69. 14: Ref, catlg. 15: 756 Reed ave, St Louis Mo 63125.

MUELLER, ANNE L (COCHRAN). b Dumas Tex 19 Ag 16. 4: Henry Mueller. 5: UTex 39 (Educ) BS; UOkla 52 (LS) BA; SMU 67. 6: Fr. 7: Libn Fairfax Co Schs (Fairfax Va) 54-56; Libn Dallas Pub Lib 56; Libn Dallas Ind Sch Dist 57-. 9: ALA; Tex State Tchrs Assn; Dallas Clr Tchrs. 10: Kappa Alpha Theta; Delta Kappa Gamma. 14: Child & ya libs. 15: 5730 Penrose st, Dallas Tx 75206.

MUELLER, DOROTHY ANN (ELIZABETH). b Birmingham Ala 10 F 38. 5: Birmingham So Col 55-59 Religious Educ) AB; Peabody 60-61 (LS) MA. 7: Intern in med libnship UCLA Biomed Lib 61-62; Ref libn Duke U Med Lib 62-65; Circ libn UAla Med Center Lib 65-66; Medlars trainee Nat Lib of Med, Bethesda Md 66; Chief searcher Ala Medlars Ctr UALa Med Ctr Lib (Birmingham) 67-. 9: MEDLA; AlaLA. 10: Beta hi Mu; AAUW. 14: Pub serv, info retr. 15: 556-19th st SW, Birmingham Ala 35211.

MUELLER, ELIZABETH. b Hinsdale Ill 7 N34. 5: Valparaiso U 52-56 (Elem Educ) BS; Chicago 61-65 (LS) MA. 7: Kindergarten tchr Trinity Lutheran Church, Hicksville NY 56-57; Nursery tchr & co-prin Holy Cross Lutheran Chruch, Mahwah NJ 57-58; Elem tchr Immanuel Lutheran Sch, Elmhurst Ill 5-60; Asst child libn Thomas Ford Pub Lib, Western Springs Ill 59-62; Research libn J Walter Thompson Co, Chicago 2-5; Head Libn La Grange Pub Lib, La Grange Ill 65-69; Admin serv lib Suburban Lib Syst, West Springs Ill 69-. 9: ALA; IllLA; Laconi. 10: AAUW; LWV. 13: Yes. 14: Ref, adult & child serv, admin. 15: 341 S Spring, La Grange Ill 60525.

MUELLER, ESTHER (EYTCHESON). b Kempton Ind 24 D 06. 5: Butler U 29 (Soc Sci) BA; UIll 33 BS in LS; Columbia summers 37-39, 40-41. 7: Ref libn Butler U 29-37 Asst catlg dept Gary Pub Lib, Gary Ind 37-39; Catlgr Enoch Pratt Free Lib, Baltimore 39-42, 1st asst 42-44; Ref asst USDA Lib, Wash DC 44-45; Catlgr descr catlg dept LC 45-46; Head tech proc dept Linda Hall Lib, Kan City Mo 46-. 9: ALA. 10: Phi Kappa Phi; Phi Mu. 15: 5802 Locust st, Kansas City Mo 64110.

MUELLER, JEANNE (GUTHRIE). b Louisville Ky 31 Jl 26. 4: Rudy T Mueller. 5: Catherine Spalding Col 44-48 (Eng) AB (magna cum laude); UKy 52-53 (LS) MA. 6: Fr. 7: Br asst Louisville Free Pub Lib, Louisville Ky 48-52; Catlgr U Louisville 53-54; Child libn Indianapolis Pub Lib 54-58; Catlgr Ind U Sch of Med Lib 58-. 9: MedLA. 10: Beta Phi Mu; Kappa Gamma Phi. 14: Catlg. 15: Ind U Sch of Med Lib 1100 W Michigan, Indianapolis In 46202.

MUELLER, MARTHA ANN. b Kansas City Mo. 5: UKan 51-54 (Eng) BS in Ed, 59-60 (Eng); Carnegie 57-58 MS in LS; UMo 59 (Eng). 7: Tchr libn Eureka Jr High Sch, Eureka Kan 54-55; Asst libn Kuhn Loeb & Co, NYC 55-57; Asst circ libn UMo (Columbia) 58-59; Monograph catlgr UKan 60-62, Serials catlgr 62-64; Ed catlgr Nat Lib of Australia, Canberra 64, Ed sec union list 64-65; Hd catlg dept OaklandU (Rochester Mich) 66-67, Hd ser dept 67-69; Asst libn SUNY Col of Ceramics (Alfred) 69-. 15: 58 1/2 S Main, Alfred NY 14802.

MUELLNER, IDA. b Austria 29 O 27. 5: Los Angeles City Col 61-65 (Philos) AA (cum laude); UCLA 65-67 (Ger) BA, 67-68 (LS) MA. 6: Ger, Fr. 7: Stud asst Los Angeles City Col 64-65; Tchr German-Amer Sch Assn, Los Angeles 64-; Reader UCLA 65-66, Stud asst 67-68; Ser libn USoCal 68-. 8: Chm German Lit Club Los Angeles City Col 64-65. 9: ALA; SLA; CalLA. 10: Phi Beta Kappa; Delta Phi Alpha; UCal Lib Schs Alumni Assn. 14: Ser. 15: 10965 Roebling ave, Los Angeles Ca 90024.

MUELLNER, J PHILLIP. b Chicago 20 Je 36. 4: June Kurz. 5: Chicago Tchrs Col 58-61 (LS) BA-ME; Loyola U 60 (Eng). 7: Tchr Beidler Elem Sch, Chicago 59-61, Libn 61-63; Libn Schurz High Sch, Chicago 63- Head Lib Schiller Park (Ill) Pub Lib 64-. 9: ALA; IllLA; IllSchLA Memb Com 68, Conf Site Com 68). 15: 405 N Lincoln ave, Park Ridge Il 60068.

MUENCH (KATTAN) ELIZABETH J. b Green Bay Wis 9 O 10. 4: George Muench. 5: UWis 27-31 (Eng) BA, 32-33 (Lib) Diploma. 6: Fr. 7: Eng tchr Green Bay High Sch, Green Bay Wis 34-38; Libn Kellogg Pub Lib child dept, Green Bay 57-65; Elem libn Green Bay Dept Pub schs 65-. 8: Wis State Com mem for handbk of lib skills 67-69. 9: ALA; WisLA; WisASchL. 10: Girl Scout leader. 14: Ref, wk with child. 15: 220 E Summit, Green Bay Wi 54301.

MUENCH, EUGENE (VICTOR). b Terre Haute Ind 2 Ja 20. 5: Ind State Tchrs Col 37-42 (Sci) BA; UParis 45-46 (Fr) Letter of Certif; UMex 47-48 (Span); Fla State U 55-56 (LS) MA. 6: Fr, Sp. 7: T/5 Army Signal Corp, USA & European Theatre 42-45; Tchr Fr & Span Harris Sch, Chicago 48-49; Tr QM Res & Devel Lab Lib, Phila 50-52; Microbiologist QM Gen Testing Lab, Phila 52-54; Asst libn sci reading room UNeb 56-60; Head of tech serv NYU Med Center Lib 60-. 8: Pan Amer Union Adv Com on Subj Headings in Span. 9: ALA (IRRT Memb Com 60-61);-RSTD (Reprint Com 62-); ASIS; MedLA (Asst bus mgr 62, adv mgr b ul 63-64, chm NY Reg Gp 67-68); ASLib; Internat Fed for Documentation FID-(61, UDC, Com 67-69); SLA; Melvil Dui Chowder & Marching Assn. 10: AAUP; Hist of Sci Soc; Amer Name Soc; Neb Folklore Soc. 13: Yes. 15: NY Univ Med Center Lib, 550 First ave, New York NY 10016.

MUENZ, MERCEDES (THERESA). b BowdleSD 29 Jl 1899. 5: Col of St Catherine 20-24 (Romance Langs) BA; UMinn 28-29 BSLS; American U 49 (Preservation & Admin of Archives) Certif. 6: Fr, Sp. 7: Libn Alfred Dickey Free Lib, Jamestown ND 35-45; Assoc archivist UNotre Dame (Notre Dame Ind)47-. 9: ALA. 14: Catlg. 15: Box 121, Notre Dame Ind 46556.

MUGNIER, CHARLOTTE. b Los Angeles 27 Ja 25. 5: H Sophie Newcomb 42-46 (Eng Lit) AB; Columbia 49-50 (Pub Health Educ) MS; Rutgers 59-60 MLS. 7: Dir of Health Educ Tuberculosis Assn of Greater New Orleans 48-53; Recreation supv US Army Spec Serv, Europe 54-58; Libn Ky State Health Dept, Frankfort Ky 60-61; Gen ref libn & asst in admin UCal(Berkeley) 61-63; Br libn, Hd Adult Educ & Info, Index dept New Orleans Pub Lib 64-68; Asst Prof UMinn 68-. 15: Lib School Univ of Minn, Minneapolis Mn 55455.

MUHVIC, ALICE AMELIA (NAGOLSKI). b Gilbert Minn 12 Mr 13. 4: John George Muhvic. 5: UMinn(Duluth) 31-33 (Elem Educ) Certif; East Mich U 50-58 (Elem Educ) BS Ed; UMich 58-61 MLS. 6: Polish. 7: Tchr St Louis Co (Minn) Sch Dist 35-42; Lib clk Bd of Educ, Flint Mich 42-47; Lib asst Flint Pub Lib, Flint Mich 56-60, 1st asst child dept 60-65, Hd child commun serv dept 66-. 9: ALA; MichLA (Child Sect). 14: Wk with child. 15: Public Library, 1026 E Kearsley, Flint Mi 48502.

MUIR, GERTRUDE (HILL). b hoenix 26 O 09. 4: Robert Muir. 5: UAriz 33-37 (Anthropology) BA, 37-38 (Anthropology) MA; UDenver 44-45 BS in LS. 7: Asst catlgr El Paso Pub Lib, El Paso Tex 28-33; City Libn Flagstaff Pub Lib, Flagstaff ariz 38-45; Tech Southwestern Nat Mt, Coolidge Ariz summer 37, Ranger histn summer 38; Head of circ dept U Lib UAriz 45-49; Catlgr & 1st asst Blanchard Mem Lib, Santa Paula Cal 49-51; Asst libn Museum of NM, Santa Fe NM 51-52, Chief Libn 52-60; Spec collections libn Ariz State U (Tempe) 60-62; Head tech serv NM State Lib 62-63; Spec collections libn Ariz State U (Tempe) 63-67, Ref libn humanities 67-. 8: Ariz Governors State Hist Adv Com, 61-62. 9: Soc for Amer Archaeol; West Hist Assn; Ariz Pioneers Hist Soc; NM Hist Soc; Archaeol Soc of NM; ArizLA. 10: Charles Lamb Soc; Thoreau Soc. 13: Yes. 14: Southwestern hist, rare bks, anthropolgy. 15: 502 Solana dr, Tempe Ariz 85281.

MULCAHY, MARGARET MILLIGAN. b Syracuse NY 8 N 18. 4: F James Mulcahy. 5: Syracuse 36-40 (Classics) AB, 40-42 (Classics) MA, 47-48 BSLS, 64 (LS); UVa 62-63 (Educ). 7: Tchr Summerville Sch Dist, Summerville Penn 41-42; Sales corr Mack Miller Candle Co, Syracuse NY 42-43; US Naval Res Lt Communications, New Orleans & Wash DC 43-46; Various assignments DC Pub Lib 48-50, Chief fiction div DC Pub Lib 50-55; Libn Lakeview High Sch, Battle Creek Mich 59-60; Libn Springfield High Sch, Battle Creek Mich 61-62; Libn Arlington Sch Bd, Arlington Va 62-. 9: ALA; NEA; VaLA; Arlington EA. 14: Devel media ctrs for students & tchrs. 15: 5211 N Washington blvd, Arlington Va 22205.

MULHOLLAND, JOHN H. b Baltimore Co Md 5 D 37. 5: La Salle 57-61 (Eng lit) BA; Drexel 64-67 MS in LS. 6: Fr. 7: Circ & ref Biddle Law Lib UPenn 64-65; Research ref asst Med Lib Phila Gen Hosp 65; Asst libn Gwynedd-Mercy Col Lib 65-67; Dir lib serv Charles Co Commun Col, La Plata Md 67-. 9: ALA; CathLA; Md Assn Jr Cols (v-chm Learning Resources Div 69-70); MdLA; Lib Pub Rel Assn Phila. 10: AAUP. 14: Jr col lib admin. 15: 9 Oak ave PO Box 685, La Plata Md 20646.

MULHOLLAND, SISTER MIRIAM OP. b Bay City Mch 7 Ap 1899. 5: UNotre Dame 37-42 (LS) AB Rosary Col 49-54 (LS) MA; St Paul Sem 61-66 (Theol) MA. 6: Ger, Fr, Sp. 7: Libn Catholic Central High Sch, Grand Rapids Mich 37-44; Libn Marywood Acad, Grand Rapids Mich 48-. 9: VATHLA. 13: Yes. 14: Snh libn. 15: Marywood Acad Lib, 2025 E Fulton, Grand Rapids Mich 49503.

MULL, MARGARET MARIE. b Minneapolis 12 F 10. 5: Milwaukee Downer Col 27-28 (Eng); UMinn 28-31 (Eng, LS) BLS. 7: Minneapolis Pub Lib: Asst Hosmer Br 31-44, Br head Hosmer Br 45-50, Supv asst circ dept 50-55 Head circ dept 55-58, Chief of Central Lib 58-, Act libn 63-64; Chief of central lib & public rel 64-. 9: ALA (Counc 67-71), (Memb Chm Minn); MinnLA. 10: UMinn Lib Sci Alumni Assn; AAUW; Zonta Internat; Womens Assn Minneapolis Symphony Orchestra; Delta Kappa Gamma; Womens Div Minneapolis C of C; Marshall U High Policy Bd. 11: Minn Libn of the year award, 64. 14: Pub lib admin. 15: 36 Orlin ave SE, Minneapolis Mn 55414.

MULLANE, WILLIAM H. b San Angelo Tex 6 O 35. 4: Judith Sandstrom. 5: UNM 53-54 (Mech engring); UNM 56-59 (Eng) BA; Kan State Tchrs Col 66-67 (LS) ML. 6: Ger. 7: Clk (Sp 3) Hdqrs 47th AAA Bn, Kaiserslautern Ger 55-56; Linotype operator; Case-Thompson Printing Co, Albuquerque NM 56-57, Sandia Composition Serv, Albuquerque 57-58, "Albuquerque Journal", Albuquerque 58-59; Linotype-teletype & monotype operator Smith-Brooks Printing Co, Denver 60-66; Asst libn humanities div UNeb Libs (Lincoln) 67-68, Admin asst to dir 68-. 9: ALA; NebLA (chm Jr Mem RT 68-69). 10: AAUP; UNeb Fac Club. 13: Yes. 14: Lib admin, educ for libnship, recr for libnship, ref. 15: 2545 Theresa, Lincoln Nb 68504.

MULLEN, EUGENE. b Carnero Kan 22 Ag 33. 4: Elizabeth Young. 5: Kan Wesleyan U 51-53 (Hist); Ft Hays Kan State Col 56-60 (Hist) AB, UDenver 61-63 (LS) MA; Ft Hays Kan State Col 60-67 Sociol MS. 6: Sp. 7: Farmer & farm laborer, Carneiro Kan 42-54; Infantryman (Pfc) US Army, US & Korea 54-56; Farmer, Carneiro Kan 56-58; Hosp orderly St JOHNS Hosp, Salina Kan 58-59; Hosp orderly Hadley Mem Hosp, Hays Kan State Col 60-65; Instr of lib sci Kearney State Col 65-67, Asst Prof of Sociol 67-. 10: Amer Sociol Assn; Midwest Sociol Assn; Soc for Study of Soc Problems. Phi Kappa Phi; Phi Gamma Mu. 12: "The Effects of Formalization on Rates of Successful Affiliation with Local Gropus of Alcoholics Anonymous" (67). 14: Hist of bks, sociology. 15: 3119 ave D, Kearney Nb 68847.

MULLEN, EVELYN DAY. b Rosemary NC 5 F 11. 5: Sweet Briar Col 27-31 (Hist) AB; UNC 31-32 AB in LS. 6: Fr. 7: Reviser UNC Sch Lib Sci (Chapel Hill) 32-37; Asst Wells Col Lib 37-38; Libn & asst prof Coker Col 38-40; Libn Halifax & Northampton Cos Libs, nc 41-43; Army libn, Aberdeen Proving Ground Md, Camp Lee Va & Germany 43-47; Lib dir Charlottesville-Abemarle Co Lib, Va 47-50; Field wker NC Lib Commsn, Raleigh 50-54; Dir Ala Pub Lib Serv, Montgomery 54-57; Lib ext specialist US Off Educ, Wash DC 57-67, Lib serv program off Reg III, Charlottesville Va 67-. 8: Mem gp Amer libns visiting Swedish libs 61. 9: ALA (past mem Coun); -RTSD (chm Reg Proc Xom; Subscription Bks Com); -LED (Awards Com; Small Libs Proj Adv Com); SELA; NCLA; VaLA; MdLA. 10: Amer Soc of Pub Admin. 13: Yes. 14: Pub libs devel & admin. 15: 103 Bennington st, Charlottesville Va 22903.

MULLEN, FRANCIS X. b Phila Penn 31 O 35. 4: Eileen Marie Fogarty. 5: St Joseph's Col 9phila) 53-57, 59-61 (Eng) BS; Drexel 63-67 (LS) MS. 6: Fr. 7: Traffic rate clk Luria Bros, Phila 53-57; Enlisted man (Specialist) USA, Ger 57-59; Asst personnel mgr Phila Police Dept 61-62; Lib trainee Free Lib of Phila 62-64, Lib tech 64-67, Libn I 67; Libn Marple Pub Lib, Broomall Penn 67-. 9: ALA; PennLA (treas SE Chap); Lib Pub Rel Assn Greater Phila. 14: Adult ref, reader's adv serv. 15: 5926 Springfield ave, philadelphia Pa 19143.

MULLEN, HELEN MAE. b Hastings Neb. 5: Hastings 46-51 (Eng) BA; USyracuse 52-53 MSLS. 7: Child libn Free Lib of Phila 53-66, Hd inservice train & commun serv child off 66-67, Asst coord of wk with child 68-. 9: ALA; -CSD (chm Jaycees Good Reading Bklist Subcom); PennLA. 10: Phila Bksellers; Phila Lib Pub Rel Assn. 14: Child serv. 15: Office of Work with Children, Free Lib of Phila, Logan Square, Phila Pa 19103.

MULLEN, JESS S. b St Louis 26 Ap 40. 4: Virginia Kettler. 5: Washington U 58-59 (Liberal Arts); UMo 59-60, 61-63 (LS) BA; St Louis U 60; UIll 63-64 (LS) MS; Ill State U (Normal) 67-68; U Ill 67 (Art Hist). 7: Asst Ref libn Ill State U 64-; Instr, Asst ref libn Ill State U (Normal) 64-67, Instr, Fine Arts libn 67-. 9: ALA; IllLA. 10: Lions Intl. 14: Ref, catlg. , art, music, theatre. 15: 1007 Dillon dr, Normal Il 61761.

MULLEN, MARION L(OUISE). b Syracuse NY 4 S 27. 5: Syracuse 46-49 (Psych, Hist) AB, 49-52 (Guidance, Coun), 61-64 MS (LS). 6: Fr. 7: Legal sec Wortman & Wortman, Syracuse NY 45; Audit dept E W Edwards & Son, Syracuse NY 45-46; Syracuse U Lib: Pub serv dept & asst to libn in chg of open shelf room 47-48, Asst to individual in chg of U Archives & asst open shelf room 48-49, Libn in charge of Archives & Asst in ser dept 49-52, Asst to libn in charge of interlib loan & pub serv dept wk 52-54, Pub serv dept, loan desk, open shelf room, res bk room, interlib loan 52-53, In chg of Interlib loan-pub serv dept 54-57, In chg of overdues, pub serv wk & interlib load 53-57, In chg of overdues-circ dept 57-58, In chg of interlib loan-ref dept & ref wk 57-. 9: ALA. 10: Beta Phi Mu; Syracuse UnivLibs Staff Assn; Libns Assn Syracuse U; AAUW. 14: Interlib loan, ref. 15: 124 Pattison st, Syracuse NY 13203.

MULLEN, MARJORIE M(cELROY). b Indianapolis 14 Jl 10. 4: John L Mullen. 5: Butler U 26-30 (Eng) BA; Tex Womens U 45-46 BS in LS. 6: Fr. 7: Fill-in for instr Tex Womans U Lib Sch 46; Reading room libn Tex Womans U Lib summer 46; Asst libn Household Finance Main Off Lib, Chicago 50-51; Asst libn abstract ed "Rehabilitation Literature Nat Soc for Crippled Child & Adults, Chicago 51-. 8: Instr, hosp libnship, Amer Hosp Assn, 64. 9: ALA-AHIL (Sec 61-63, Publ Adv Com 68-); MEDLA Midwest Reg Group; (Sec 62-63; chm Nomin Com, chm Exec Com). 12: Co-comp "Rehabilitation Literature, 1950-1955 (56); Abstract ed "Rehabilitation Literature monthly Jl (51-); Ed "Reading Aids for the Handicapped", AHIL 3rd ed (68). 13: Yes. 14: Ref, bibliog (rehab area). 15: 3923 Howard ave, Western Springs Ill 60558.

MULLER, BARBARA H (RICH). b Salem NY 21 Ja 34. 4: Alfred C Muller. 5: Geneseo STATE U 51-55 BS in LS; Columbia 58 MS in LS. 6: Sp. 7: Sch Libn Bd of Educ, Mamaroneck NY 55-66; Sch libn Bd of Educ Schuylerville NY 66-67; Sch libn Bd of Educ, Saratoga NY 68-. 8: A-v consul, Mamaroneck, 55-. 66. 9: ALA; NEA; NY State Tchrs Assn; NYLA. 10: Kappa Delta Pi; Commun Inst; Mamaroneck Elem Sch Planning Com. 12: "Field Trip Guide, used by Mamaroneck sch system (60 rev ed 65). 14: Elem sch libs, ref, a-v materials. 15: Rd 2, Gansevoort NY 10831.

MULLER, EMILY D EL MAR CHAPMAN. b NYC 25 D 18. 4: Robert B Muller. 5: UNC 57 (Hist of Art) AB, 58 MS in LS; UBridgeport 61-62 6th Year Certif. Educ. 6: Fr. 7: Libn Boblingen Elem Sch, Boblingen Germany 58-59; Desk libn Westport Pub Lib, Westport Conn 59; Coordinator of all sch libs in Wilton Conn Sch System & Libn High Sch, Wilton Conn 60-, Media Ctr coord Wilton Sr High Sch 69-. 9: ALA; NEA-DAVI; ConnSchLA Fairfield Co (Conn) Libns Assn; NELA. 10: World Affairs Center, Westport onn. 14: Wk with ya. 15: 116 Newton Turnpike, Westport Conn.

MULLER, MARGARET A. b Chicago Ill 23 O 43. 5: Rosary Col 61-65 (Ger) AB, 67-68 MALS. 6: Ger. 7: Asst to dir Off for Recruitment Amer Lib Assoc, Chicago 68; Ref libn J Walter Thompson Co, Chicago 68-. 9: SLA. 14: Ref, info retrieval. 15: 6467 N Oxford ave, Chicago Il 60631.

MULLER, ROBERT HANS. b Krotoschin Germany 12 Mr 14. 4: Martha Muller. 5: Victoria U (Manchester Eng) 33-34 (Sci); Stanford 34-36 (Philos) BA; UCal 36-37 (LS) Certif; Chicago 39-42 (LS) MA, PhD. 6: Ger, Fr, Sp. 7: Asst San Francisco Pub Lib 37; Asst Temple U Lib 37-39; Ref asst UChicago 40-42; Chief libn Air Weather Serv Lib, Hdqrs US AAF, Wash DC 42-43; (Sgt) US Army Air Corps 44-45; Chief acquis sect Lib Div Off Tech Serv US Dept Com, Wash DC 46; Hd libn BradleyU 46-49; Dir libs SoIllU 49-54; Asst dir UMich Lib 54-58, Assoc dir 59-, Prof Sch Lib Sci 69-, Research consul Univ Lib 69-. 8: Tchr, lib sci & other subjects, Bradley U 46-49; Head Lib Educ Prog, So Ill U 49-54; Visiting instr UIll Lib Sch summer 61-; Lib bldg consul; Naperville (Ill) pub sch 60; Grand Valley Col 52; Spring Arbor Col 63; USask (Regina) 64; Olivet Col 65; Loyola U (Chicago) 65; Lib consul UKy, 64. 9: ALA (Rep on Microcard Com 57-60, ed bd "Choice" 63-65, Intel Freedom Com 65-67, chm Good Tchr Award Com 64-65);-ACRL (Com on Col & Univ Lib Stat 48-51, Com on Train & Prep 48-49, chm Com on Col & Univ Lib Bldgs 49-53; Univ Libs Sect; chm 57-58; chm Com on Res & Devel 59-63, mem Com on Acad Status 64-);-Lib Org & Mgt Div (Exec Com 64-); MichLA (Sal & Ten Com 56-57, Planning Com 61-63). 10: Ann Arbor Exchange Club; Jackson Soc Welfare Fund (Ann Arbor); Ann Arbor Pub Lib Friends. 13: Yes. 14: Univ lib admin, lib bldgs. 15: Univ Lib, Univ of Mich, Ann Arbor Mich 48104.

MULLIGAN, GEORGIA (FINNIGAN). b NY 6 Ag 43. 4: Gerard A Mulligan. 5: Mary Washington Col UVa 61-65 (Hist) BA; UNC 65-66 MS in LS. 6: Ger, Fr. 7: Ref libn St Augustines Col 66-67, Tech libn UNC Undergrad lib 67-68, Res reading libn 68-. 14: Ref, circ. 15: 105 Stinson st, Chapel Hill NC 27514.

MULLIKIN, DAISY COPELAND. b Mulberry Tenn 6 F 09. 4: Houston Yost Mullikin. 5: Middle Tenn State U 29-30, summer 34, & 39; UTenn summers 49, 50; UKy 50-51 (LS) BA. 6: Lat. 7: Elem tchr Lincoln Co Sch System, Lincoln Co Tenn 30-33, 36-38; Eng & math Flintville High Sch, Flintville Tenn 41-43; Elem tchr Sewanee Pub Sch. Sewanne Tenn 43-45; Elem tchr Powell Elem Sch, Powell Tenn 47-50; Elem tchr Garth Sch, Georgetown Ky 51-52; Asst libn Georgetown Col (Ky) 52-. 9: ALA; KyLA. 10: Georgetown Col Womans Assn; Georgetown Bk Club; Scott Co (Ky) Hist Soc. 14: Catlg, ref. 15: 407 Hollyhock land, Georgetwn Ky 40324.

MULLIKIN, MRS DOROTHY GAFFNEY. b Plymouth Minn 29 My 03. 5: UMinn 21-26 (Eng Lit) AB; West Res 29-30 (LS) Certif. 7: Bkmob asst Hibbing Pub Lib, Hibbing Minn 20-21; Br child Asst Minneapolis Pub Lib 23-24, 26-27; Ref child libn DC Pub Lib 28-29; Br & sch asst Cleveland Pub Lib 29-30; Br child libn Minneapolis Pub Lib 30-31; Adv to adults DC Pub Lib 31-40; Child libn Bethesda Pub Lib, Bethesda Md 51-52; Br child libn DC Pub Lib 57-60, Ext child libn 60-. 9: ALA (sec Child Sect 32). 14: Child lit. 15: 2623-39 st NW, Wash DC 20007.

MULLINS, EVELYN JEANNETTE. b Grinnell Iowa. 5: Grinnel Col 22-26 (Lat) BA; Columbia 27-28 (LS) BS. 7: Asst Grinnel Col Lib 26-27; Libn Grand Rapids Pub Lib, Grand Rapids Mich 28-30; Circ libn Col Lib State Col Iowa 30-48, Order libn 48-. 9: ALA; Iowa State EA; iowaLA. 10: AAUP; AAUW. 14: Aquis, tech serv. 15: Univ of Northern Iowa, Cedar Falls Ia 50613.

MULLINS, LYNN SARA. b NYC 24 Je 40. 5: CUNY (City Col) 57-62 (Anthrop) BA; Columbia 64-66 MS in LS; CUNY (Hunter Col) 68-. 6: Fr, Sp. 7: Lib asst Amer Geog Soc NYC 62-65, Asst libn 65-; Ref libn NYU Law Sch 66-68. 9: SLA (sec NY Chap Geog and Map Div 67-69); NY Tech Serv Libns. 10: Phi Beta Kappa. 12: Asst ed "Current Geographical Publications" (67-). 13: Yes. 14: Bibliog, geog lit, cartog lit, ref. 15: Amer Geographical Soc Lib, Broadway at 156th st, New York NY 10032.

MULLIS, LEONARD M. b Ft Lauderdale Fla 4 S 21. 4: Lois McMurry Mulls. 5: UDenver 45-47 (Humanities Area) AB, 48-52 (LS) MA. 7: Tchr-libn Akron High Sch, Akron Colo 48-50; Libn Carnegie Pub Lib, Ft Morgan Colo 50; Admin Off (Lt Col USAF Ret) US & Japan 50-65; Asst libn Amarillo Col 65-67; Libn Arapahoe Jr Col (Colo) 68-. 9: ALA; ColoLA. 10: Toastmasters Club. 14: Admin, acquis, catlg. 15: 6174 Fairfield, Littleton Co 80120.

MULRENNAN, MARY (MASSIE). b Lee Va 18 Mr 19. 4: Timothy Mulrennan. 5: Lynchburg 36-40 (Soc studies) AB; Emory 40-41 AB in LS; USoFla summer 64, 65. 6: Fr, Ger. 7: Libn & tchr, Middletown High Sch, Middletown Va 41-42; Libn Battlefield Park High Sch, Midlothian Va 41; Libn Navy Dept, Camp Lejeune NC 42-46; Libn lib Supv's off hillsborough Co Schs Fla 64; Hd libn King High Sch, Tampa Fla 64-. 9: NEA; ALA; FlaASchL; FlaEA; Fla A-V Assn. 10: Friends of the Lib. 14: Catlg, clsf. 15: rte 1 Box 563M, Valrico Fl 33594.

MULVIHILL, JOHN (GARY). b Minneapolis 3 Mr 33. 4: Anna Marie Stubenrauch. 5: St Michaels Col 51-53; U St Thomas (Houston) 53; UCLA 53-54; U St Thomas (Houston) 54-55 BA; Rice U 55-58 MA; UWis(Madison) 57-58; UTex 58-60 MLS; St Benedicts Col (Kan) 61-62; West Res U 62; IBM Educ Center (Boston) 63 Certif, Fortran; Clark U 63-64; Harvard U (Holyoke Center) 64-65; Rutgers 69-. 6: Lat, Fr, Sp. 7: Tchg asst UWis(Madison) 51-58; (Pvt) US Army clerk-typist, Ft Chaffee Ark 58; Lib asst UTex Lib 58-59, Sr lib asst 59-60; Assoc libn St Benedicts Col (Kan) 60-62; Evaluator, Center for Documentation & Communication Res West Res U 62; Libn Astra Pharmaceutical Products Inc, Worcester Mass 62-64; Indexer Central Abstracting Serv, Amer Petrol Inst 64-66, Asst to mgr 66-. 9: SLA; ASIS. 12: "Guide to the Univrsity of Tex Library Collections, Indexes, and Catalogs Not Fully Displayed in the Public Catalog (60); "Indexers Manual . . . (65) "Amer Petrol Inst Subject Authority List" (2nd 6th ed 65-69). 13: Yes. 14: Indexing, clsf, making of Thesauri, computer searching. 15: 7 Russett rd, Somerset NJ 08873.

MUMFORD, L(AWRENCE) QUINCY. b Ayden C 11 D 03. 5: Duke U 25 (Eng) AB, 28 (Eng) MA; Columbia 29 (LS) BS. 6: Fr. 7: Hd circ dept Duke U Lib 26-28, Act chief of ref & Circ 28; NY Pub Lib: Ref asst 29-31, Gen asst in chg of dirs off 32-35, Exec asst & Chief of the prep div 36-43, Exec asst & Coordinator of the gen serv divs 43-45; Asst dir Cleveland Pub Lib 45-50, Dir 50-54; Libn of Congress 54-. 8: Org & dir, Proc Dept LC, 40; Chm, Lib Com Theodore Roosevelt Cent Commsn, 57-58; Lincoln Sesquicent Commsn, 58-60; Commsner of Educ's Adv Com on Lib Serv, 56-65; US Nat Bk Com; Fed Coun on the Arts & the Humanities; Bd of Bks USA Inc; Hon Internat Bd of Sponsors of the Bks for the People Fund Inc; Bd of Adv, Dumbarton Oaks Res Lib & Collection; Sponsors Com, "Papers of Woodrow Wilson"; Cor mem, US of Unesco's Internat Adv Com on Bibliog, Documentation, & Terminology; Chm, Bd of Visitors, Duke U; Chm ex officio, Permanent Com for the Oliver Wendell Holmes Devise; Benjamin Franklin Fellow, Royal Soc for the Encouragement of Arts, Manufactures & Commerce (London); mem ex officio; Bd of

Regents, NLM, Sci Info Coun, Bd of Trustees of the John Fitzgerald Kennedy Center for the Performing Arts; Chm Fed Lib Com; Nat Trust for Hist Preserv; Hon Fellow, Harry S Truman Lib Inst for Nat and Internat Affairs; Sec, ex officio LC Trust Fund Bd; Mem ex officio Adv Bd Natl Park Serv Hist Amer Bldgs Survey; President's Com on Libs 66-68; Amer Revol Bicentl Commsn; Bd of Trustees, Woodrow Wilson Internat Ctr for Scholars; Adv Com, Hist Amer Engrg Record; Natl Hist Publ Commsn. 9: ALA (v-pres 53-54, pres 54-55); Manuscript Soc (Bd Dirs); OhioLA (pres 47-48) DCLA; US Capitol Hill Hist Soc; Brit Museum Soc (founder-memb). 10: Phi Beta Kappa; Omicron Delta Kappa; Beta Phi Mu; Internat Club (Wash DC); Cosmos Club (Wash DC); Bd Trustees, Greater Wash T-V Assn; Adv Bd Cafritz Foun. 11: Hon degrees, LittD: Bethany Col 54, Rutgers U 56, Duke U 57, & Belmont Abbey Col 63; LLD: Union Col 55, Bucknell U 56, UNotre Dame 64, & UPittsburgh 64. 13: Yes. 15: Lib of Congress, Wash DC 20540.

MUNAZOZ DE OLMOS-BEIZAGA, SYLVIA. b Anasco PR 28 O 32. 4: Osvaldo Olmos-Beizaga. 5: InterAmerican U (San German PR) 54-57 (Zool, Chem) BA; Tex Womans U 59-60 MLS; Rutgers 63-64. 6: Sp, Fr. 7: Head order dept Col of Agric & Mechanical Arts (Mayaguez PR) 57-59, Head circ dept 60-63; Caltr UPR Gen Lib (Ro Piedras) 63; Head catlg dept UPR Humacao Reg Collection 64-67; Dir lib Sch Arch UPR 67-. 8: Tchr, lib sci courses, Col of Agric & Mech Arts & Humacao Reg Col, UPR;Adv Col Arch, Engrs & Surveyors 68-. 9: ALA; Sociedad de Bibliotecarios de Puerto Rico (Memb Com 67). 10: Faculty Club of the Humacao Reg Co, UPR. 14: Catlg, admin. 15: 2073 Hercules, Reparto Apolo Guaynabo 00657.

MUNDEN, MRS KAYE (STOUGHTON). b Battle Creek Mich 12 Je 31. 4: Thomas F Munden. 5: Okla Col for Women 48-50 (LS); N Tex State U 51-53 (LS) BS, 64-65 MLS. 6: Sp. 7: Libn Ft Worth Pub Lib, Ft Worth Tex 53-55, Gen Dynamics, Ft Worth Tex 54-55, Tex Electric Serv Co, Ft Worth Tex 56; Hd libn L D Bell High Sch, Hurst Tex 56-. 9: ALA; ArTA; TexLA; Tex State Tchrs Assn. 10: Alpha Lambda Sigma; Alpha Chi; Oak Crest Womans Club; Beta Sigma Phi. 14: Wk with yp. 15: 1302 Pebble Creek dr, Euless Tx 76039.

MUNDY, ELVA (LAYCOCK). b Montreal Can 6 Ja 35. 4: Kenneth Mundy. 5: Sir George Williams U 53-55 (Chem). 7: Libn Monsanto Canada Ltd, La Salle Que 53-66; Libn Dominion Bridge Ltd, Lachine Que 67-. 9: SLA. 13: Yes. 15: P O Box 73, Como Que Can.

MUNFORD, NORVA R (HAVENS). b Ithaca NY 25 S 29. 5: SUNY (Geneseo) 47-51 BLS; Syracuse 60-61 MLS. 7: Asst libn & libn Mohawk Valley Commun Col 51-55; Libn Spec Serv Dept of Army, Ger 55-57; Libn USA Dependents Sch, Ger 60; Asst & assoc libn SUNY Agric & Tech Col (Cobleskill) 61-. 9: ALA; NYStateLA; Jr Col Libns NY State. 10: AAUP; NY State Assn of Jr Cols. 14: Ref. 15: 14 Pleasant View dr, Cobleskill NY 12043.

MUNGER, ELIZABETH (MACK). b Nazareth Penn 28 Jl 06. 5: Chicago Normal Col 23-25 (Elem Educ) Certif; UChicago 25-27; UIll 27-28 (Eng, Educ) BS in Ed; NorthwesternU summers 41-42-43 MA in Ed; Purdue 66-67 (LS) Certif. 7: Summer asst Pub Lib, Michigan City Ind 22-23; Elem tchr Chicago Pub Schs 25-28; Hd Eng Dept Georgetown Twp High Sch, Georgetown Ill 28-30; Tchr Secondary Schs, Michigan City Ind 30-32, 41-49, 61-66; Tchr Hart High Sch, Hart Mich 55-58; Asst libn Elston Sr High Sch, Michigan City Ind 67-. 9: ALA; NEA; NCTE; IllLA; IllTA; ICTE. 10: Girl Scouts; League of Women Voters; PTA; Coun for Unity; AAUW; DAR. 12: Contrib "New Library of Catholic Knowledge, 12 v (63-65); Ed Booknotes "Peabody Journal of ducation (48-63); Ed "Current Reference Books in "Wilson Lirary Bulleti (51-52); Contrib "Catholic Encyclopedia for School and Home 12 v (65). 14: Ya & ref serv. 15: 500 Marquette trail, Michigan City In 46360.

MUNGLE, VIVIAN J. b Lawton Okla 27 Ag 03. 5: UOkla 22-23 (Mus). 7: Libn Sutonetics (N Amer Rockwell Inc), Anaheim Cal 55-. 9: SLA. 14: Ref. 15: 9341 Maxine, Pico Rivera Ca 90660.

MUNN, RALPH. b Aurora Ill 19 S 1894. 4: Anne Shepard. 5: UDenver 12-17 AB & LLB; NY State Lib Sch 19-21 BLS. 7: Ref libn pub lib, Seattle 21-26; Libn pub lib, Flint mich 27; Dor Carnegie Lib, Pittsburgh Penn 28-64, Dir Emeritus 64-. 8: Survey of libs of Australia and New Zealand for Carnegie Corp 34; Survey of lib branches, NYC for City Planning Commsn 43. 9: ALA (pres 39-40), many other duties and assignments); PennLA (pres 30-31, var other duties). 11: Hon Litt D UPittsburgh 40; Hon LLD Waynesburgh Col 6'. 12: "Australian Libraries" (35); "New Zealand Libraries" (34); "Conditions and Trends in Training for Librarianship" (36). 13: Yes. 14: Admin, lib schs. 15: Carnegie Lib, Pittsburgh Pa 15213.

MUNN, ROBERT FERGUSON. b Seattle 17 Jl 23. 5: Oberlin Col 49 AB; Chicago 50 (LS) MA; UMich 61 PhD. 6: Ger. 7: Res asst UChicago 49-50; Ref asst Penn State U 50-52; UWVa; Chief ref libn 52-53, Asst libn 53-57, Dir of Libs 57-, Asst provost 65, Act provost 66-67, Provost 68-. 8: Consul on higher educ in E Africa 64-67, 69. 12: ""The Southern Appalachians, A Bibliography (61); ""Coal Industry inAmerica, A Bibliography (65). 13: Yes. 14: Libnship in devel countries. 15: WVa Univ, Morgantown WVa.

MUNOZ, ROSA E (PRINCIPE DE). b Juncos PR 24 F 27. 4: Ernesto Munoz. 5: UPR 42-46 (Home Econ) BS, 47-48 (Med Soc Wk) Soc Wk License, Syracuse 67-68 MLS. 6: Span, Eng. 7: Med soc wker Pub Health, PR 48-52 US Navy Personnel Woman Seaman, San Diego 52-55; Asst libn in chg of music room Gen Lib UPR 59-67, Hd periods dept 68-. 9: ALA; Lib Soc, PR. 14: Catlg of records, ref. 15: 1054 19th st, Villa Neverez, Rio Piedras PR 00927.

MUNRO, DONALD M. b Ft Stanton NM 14 Je 17. 4: H Bernice Proctor. 5: Wayne U 35-39 (Eng) BA; Columbia 39-40 (LS) BS. 7: Jr libn Yonkers Pub Lib, Yonkers NY 40-41; Lib asst Hamtramck Pub Lib, Hamtramck Mich 41-42; Signal Corps & Air Corps US Army (Sgt) 42-45; Sr libn Detroit Pub Lib tech dept 46-48; Libn Train Dept Lib Ford Motor Co, Dearborn Mich 48-60; Asst head TDS Inst of Sci & Tech UMich 60-;Hd Libn, Highway Safety Research Inst UMich 66-. 9: ALA. 14: Ref, sci reports, admin. 15: 1950 Longshore, Ann Arbor Mi 48105.

MUNRO, JUNE (EDITH). b Echo Bay Ont Can 21 Je 21. 5: Carleton U 58-61 BJ; Toronto 43 (LS) Certif, 62 BLS. 6: Fr. 7: Child libn Pub Lib, Sault Ste Marie Ont 43-51; Child libn Pub Lib, LONDON Ont 51-53; Child libn Leaside Pub Lib, Leaside Ont 53-56; Hdqrs staff CanLA, Ottawa 56-61; Supv ext serv Ont Prov Lib Serv, Toronto 61-. 8: Past chm & past sec Young Canadas Bk Week. 9: ALA; CanLA (Recr Com); Can Lib Trustees Assn (sec 56-61); Can Assn of Child Libns (past sec); OntLA chm Operations Com; (Child Libns Sect: chm 65-66; Inst Prof Libns Ont. 10: May Court Club of Can; UNICEF. 12: Ed "Ontario Library Review (61-64); role the Library Trustee (62). 13: Yes. 14. Child, ext of pub lib serv. 14: Child, ext of pub lib serv, educ & train of lib technicians. 15: 4 New st, Toronto 5 Can.

MUNROE, MARY JO. b St Louis. 5: Maryville Col of the Sacred Heart (Eng) BA (magna cum laude); Washington U (St Louis) (Eng); Columbia 46-47 (Comparative Lit), 50 LS; NY Inst of Photography 64 (Com Photography) Certif. 6: Lat, Fr, Old Eng, Ger. 7: Desk asst & publicity Maryville Col Lib (St Louis), Instr in Eng, Logic & Creative Writing, Desk asst Natural Sci Libs, Asst Psychol Lib Columbia U; Catlgr & ref asst Washington U Sch of Med (St Louis) 50-53; Libn Cornell U - NY Hosp Sch Nursing, NYC 53-62; Pub serv libn in chg of ref & circ Washington U Sch Med (St Louis) 63; Libn Mt Sinai Hosp Sch of Nursing, NYC 64-66; Sr subj catlgr Yale U Lib 66-. 9: MedLA; SLA (chm Hosp Div 55-56; mem Greater NY Hosp Div 53-55)); ALA; CathLA. , ConnLA, NY Tech Serv Libns. 10: Delta Epsilon Sigma; Kirkwood Hist Soc. 13: Yes. 14: Med & nurs ref & catlg, admin, subj catlg in relig & philos, child lit. 15: 973 Townsend ave, New Haven Ct 06512.

MUNSON, BARBARA (C) (NELSON). b Salina Kan 5 S 40. 4: Bruce R Munson. 5: Rockford Col 58-60; UIll 60-63 (Eng educ) BA; UMinn 66-67 (LS) MA. 6: Sp. 7: Tchr Bd of Educ, Rockford Ill 63-64; Lib asst hist & travel dept, S Bend (Ind) Pub Lib 64-66; Libn ref & interlib loans UMinn 67-68, Libn interlib loans div 68-. 14: Ref. 15: 404 - 8th st SE, Minneapolis Mn 55414.

MUNTZ, MARGARET MILLS. b Cincinnati 28 Ap 15. 4: Ralph Wesley Muntz. 5: Col of Wooster 32-36 (Math, Soc Sci) AB; West Res 60-64 MSLS. 6: Fr. 7: Resident tchr Hudson Country Day Sch, Hudson Ohio 36-37; Catlgr Firestone Tire & Rubber Co, Akron Ohio 37-38; Ms typist, Cleveland 41-47; Bkkeeper & tech, Cleveland 41-43; Ms typist, Cleveland 48-63; Asst libn Cleveland Heights High Sch, Cleveland Heights Ohio 58-61; Libn Hilltop Elem Sch, Beachwood Ohio 62-68; Beachwood lib coord & Middle Sch libn 68-. 9: ALA; -LAD; NEA; OhioLA (Scholarship Com 68-69); OhioASchL (Loc Arrang Co-chm 68); OhioEA; NEOhioTA. 10: Nat Women's Bk Assn; PTA. 14: Creative writing for child. 15: 105 Meadowhill lane, Chagrin Falls Ohio 44022.

MUNZENMAIER, MRS GENEVIEVE (MORONEY). b Des Moines Iowa 31 D 16. 4: Harry Thomas Munzenmaier. 5: Dowling Jr Col 35-37; St Ambrose Col & Marycrest Col 38-40 (Eng) BA; UIll summers 42-44 BSLS. 7: Pub Lib, Des Moines Iowa: Apprentice 40, Jr asst catlg dept 40-42, Order libn 42-45; 1st asst order dept State U Iowa 45-49; 1st asst catlg dept Pub Lib, Des Moines Iowa 49-. 9: ALA; IowaLA Des Moines Lib Club; Lib Assn Des Moines Metro Area. 10: Raymond Blank Mem Hosp Guild; Mercy Hosp Guild. 14: Catl. 15: 1429-62, Des Moines Iowa 50311.

MUNZER, MARION PAULINE. b Grand Rapids Minn 16 Je 23. 5: SUNY(Albany) 41-45 (Eng) AB, 45-46 BS in LS; Cornell U summers 49-53 (Lit) MA. 7: Libn Greenville Central Rural Sch, Greenville NY 46-48; Russell Sage Col: Period libn 48-50, Asst catlgr 50-51, Head catlgr 51-57; Exch libn, sr catlgr UQueensland (Brisbane Australia) 57-58; Ref libn Russell Sage Col 58-65; libn U col sect U Lib SUNY(Albany) 65-67; Dir tech serv 67-. 9: ALA. 10: AAUP; Pi Gamma Mu. 13: Yes. 14: Ref, admin, tech serv. 15: SUNY, Albany NY 12203.

MURAKAMI, MOMOKO. b Los Angeles. 5: HERZL Jr Col 49-51 (Soc Sci); UWash 51-53 (Pol Sci) BA, 53-54 9ls0 ml. 7: Libn ref in br libs, catlgr Chicago Pub Lib 54-57; Libn III Acquis libn UCLA 57-. 9: ALA; AALL; CalLA. 15: 3429 Hillcrest dr, Los Angeles Ca 90016.

MURATOFF, HELEN. b Stuttgart Germany 25 N 45. 5: UBC 64-68 (Slavonic Studies) BA, 68-69 BLS. 6: Russian. 14: Ref. 15: 3076 Clark dr, Vancouver BC 12 Can.

MURDOCH, FAITH T. b Sault Ste Marie Mich 28 Ap 09. 4: James Roderick Murdoch. 5: Wayne State U 25-27, 30-34, 35-38 (Educ) BS,MA; UMich 60-63 MALS. 7: Detroit Pub Sch Elem sch libn 27-35, High sch libn 36-45, Visiting libn 50- 57, Supv of sch libs 58-63, Dir of Sch Libs 63-. 9: ALA (mem var coms);-AASchL (2nd v-pres 65-66); NCTE; MichASchL (Charter mem, mem var coms); Mich ASCD; Mich A-V Assn. 10: Delta Kappa Gamma; Womens City Club of Detroit. 12: Ed, 3 curr guide: "The Elementary School Library; "The Junior High School Library; "The High School Library. 13: Yes. 14: Devel of sch libs. 15: Dept of Sch Libs, 5057 Woodward, Detroit Mi 48202.

MURDOCH, MARION CALDER. b Oakland Cal 22 Ja 15. 5: UCal(Berkeley) 31-35 (Econ) AB, 35-36 Certif in Libnship, 40-41, 44 (LS) MA. 7: Catlgr & ref asst UCal Col of Agric (Davis) 36-43; Bibliog & admin asst Order Dept UCal Lib (Berkeley) 43-46, Asst head acquis dept 46. 15: Gen Lib Univ of Cal, Berkeley Cal 94720.

MURDOCK, J(ON) LARRY. b Provo Utah 20 D 39. 4: Romanie Neyan Rex. 5: Brigham Young U 57-59, 62-64 BS (Anthropology), 2 yr certif (Geneal Tech); UMich 64-65 AMLS. 7: Ref libn UWash 65-67; Asst doc libn UUtah 67, Asst soc scis libn 68; Catlgr hist & maps Brigham Young 68-69, Doc & Maps libn 69-. 9: ALA; Utah LA. 14: Ref, maps, docs. 15: 559 N University ave, Provo Utah 84601.

MURDOCK, MRS ALICE (BILLINGTON). b Hart Mich 8 Je 26. 4: Gerald K Murdock. 5: West Mich U 44-48 (LS) BS, 60- (LS) 67 Permanent Secondary Certif. 7: Muskegon Heights Br libn Muskegon Co Lib, Muskegon Heights Mich 44-45; Jr ref libn Hackley Lib, Muskegon Mich 52-58, Jr circ libn 59-60; Libn N Muskegon High Sch, N Muskegon Mich 60-. 8: Jr ref libn Hackley Pub Lib, Muskegon Mich summers 65, 67, 68. 9: MichEA; MichASchL; Lakeshore Libns Assn (sec 62-64); No Muskegan EA (sec 64-65). 10: PTA. 14: Ref, catlg, working with adolescents. 15: 115 W Main st, Whitehall Mi 49461.

MURDOCK, ROMANIE NEYAN (REX). b San Jose Cal 22 O 42. 4: J(on) Larry Murdock. 5: Church Col of Hawaii 62-63 (Elem Educ); Brigham YoungU 60-62 (Elem, Educ), 63-64 (Elem Educ) BS (cum laude), 66-68 MLS. 7: Tchr Nebo Sch Dist, Spanish Fork Utah 64-65; Tchr Encinitas Sch Dist, Encinitas Cal 65-66; Inst lib consul Utah State Lib 68-. 8: Consul for inst lib serv, Dir of Title IV-A OF LSCA. 9: UtahLA. 14: Inst serv, child, ya. 15: 559 No University ave, Provo Ut 84601.

MURO, ERNEST ANGELO. b Baltimore Md 18 Ag 44. 4: Oretta Sue Cecchini. 5: Clarion State 62-66 BS in LS; Villanova 67-68 MS in LS. 7: Media libn Newark Special Sch Dist, Newark Del 66-; Lib sci instr Drl Tech & Commun Col 68-. 8: Mem Curr adv com; Del Tech & Commun Col. 9: ALA; NEA; DelLA (v-pres); DelEA; NewarkEA. 14: Info stor & ret, lib educ. 15: 89 Pike Creek rd 8B, Newark De 19711.

MURPHREE, JANIE (EVANGELINE). b Buffalo Tenn 8 N 42. 5: Martin Col 60-62 AA; Vanderbilt 62-64 (Chem) MA; Peabody 67-68 MLS. 6: Ger. 7: Chem tchr Glynn Acad, brunswick Ga 65-66; Staff mem Wyandotte Chem Corp, Wyandotte Mich 66-67; Asst libn Martin Col 67-68; Catlg libn Jt Univ Libs, Nashville 68-. 10: Beta Phi Mu; Phi Theta Kappa. 14: Catlg. 15: 1107B Graybar lane, Nashville Tn 37204.

MURPHY, ANN MARIE. b Hoboken NJ 30 D 30. 5: Col of St Elizabeth 47-51 (Fr) AB (Magna cum laude); UMich 59-61 AMLS. 7: Sec Sch of Pub Health UMich (Ann Arbor) 54-55, Ed asst 56-62, Asst to dir continuing educ serv 62-64; Subj catlgr Princeton U Lib 64-66, Hd subj catlgr 66-, Asst hd catlgr 68-. 9: ALA. 10: Beta Phi Mu. 14: Catlg. 15: 180 Nassau st, Princeton NJ 08540.

MURPHY, ANNA MARIE. b NYC 24 Jl 26. 5: Col of Mt St Vincent 44-48 (Fr) AB; Pratt 49-50 BLS. 6: Fr. 7: Prof asst NY Pub Lib 50-51, Asst br libn 51-54; Asst libn Fordham U Lib 54-56, Assoc libn 56-. 9: ALA; CathLA. 14: Lib admin, ref. 15: Fordham Univ Lib, Bronx NY 10458.

MURPHY, BARBARA S(EAMAN). b Poughkeepsie NY 12 Ag 37. 4: John Charles Murphy. 5: Russell Sage Col 55-56 (Nursing); Geneseo State Col 56-59 (LS) BS. 7: Asst libn Rockefeller Inst, NYC 59-63; Libn Amphenol Corp div of Bunker Ramo Corp, Broadview Ill 63-. 9: SLA (Sci- Tech Div: Engnr Sect); (Mem Area Info Sources Com 68-69); ASIS. 10: LWV; Lib Com of First Presbyterian Ch of Oak Park Ill. 14: Circ, ref, admin, bibliog searching. 15: The Bowker-Ramo Corp 8801 S 25th st, Broadview Il 60153.

MURPHY, EILEEN M. b Brooklyn NY 22 S 23. 5: St Johns U Sch of Com (NY) 43-47; St Johns U Sch of Law (NY) 47-51 LLB; Pratt 51-52 MLS; Columbia summer 52 (LS); St Johns U (NY) 53-54 BBA. 7: Asst to registrar St Johns U Sch of Law (NY) 42-50; Asst law libn, Asst Prof of Law St Johns U Law Lib (NY) 50-54; Law Libn, Asst Prof of Law UConn Sch of Law 54-55; Libn US Dept of Justice Civil Div, Wash DC 56-59; Law Libn Gen Motors Legal Staff, Detroit 59-. 8: SLA, Counsul on law libs. 9: AALL (chm Nomin Com 63-64, chm Hdqr Fund Raising Com 64-65, Com mem placement 59-, Publ 60-, Recr 61-, Info retrieval 62-, Law Library Journal 59-); SLA (Mich Chap; sec 61-63, mem Recr Com 62); Internat Law Libs Assn. 10: Phi Delta Delta. 12: Ed staff & ed "Film Facts "Law Library Journal (59-). 13: Yes. 14: Admin. 15: 14-224 General Motors Bldg, Detroit Mi 48202.

MURPHY, ELEANOR ECKFORD. b Greenville Ga. 4: James L Murphy Jr. 5: UGa 36-40 (Eng Lit) AB; Emory 40-41 BS in LS. 6: Fr. 6: Fr. 7: Asst period libn Ga Inst of Tech 2-43; Asst ATLANTA Pub Lib 43; Asst ref libn UGa 44; Catlgr Washington Mem Lib, Macon Ga 51-54; Head Libn Huntsville Pub Lib, Huntsville Ala 58-60, Asst dir 60-68, Interim dir 69-. 8: Consul, UAla Huntsville Center Lib, 60. 10: Phi Beta Kappa; Phi Kappa Phi; Mortar Board. 15: 2206 Lytle st SE, Huntsville Ala 35801.

MURPHY, MRS ELIZABETH (HUNTINGTON) BLISS. b Springfield Mass 18 O 29. 5: Pembroke 48-52 (Eng & Amer Lit) AB; Simmons 58-59 (LS) SM; Catholic U54-56 (LS). 7: Circ asst John Hay Lib Brown U 52-53; DC Pub Lib: Lib asst catlg dept 53-54, Desk asst circ dept Central Lib 54, Desk supv circ dept Georgetown Br 54-57, Gen adv Georgetown Br 57-58, Child ibn Anacostia Br 59-60, Child libn Ft Davis Br 60-62, Asst to coordinator child serv 62-68, Asst in bk sel child serv 68-. 8: Bk Eval Com; AAAS "Science Book List for Children" (2d ed 63); Com "Childrens Books" Comp by V Haviland & L Watt (64-65, 68-. 9: ALA; DCLA. 14: Child serv. 15: DC Pub Lib, Wash DC 20001.

MURPHY, ELLEN MARY. b Milwaukee Wis 15 D 37. 5: Carroll Col (Waukesha) 56-58; UWis (Mikwaukee) 58-61 (Lower elem educ) BS; UWis (Madison) 62-63 (LS) MS. 7: Tchr Range Line Sch, Mequon Wis 61-62; Catlgr UNo Iowa 63-67; Catlgr UWis (Milwaukee) 67-68; Catlgr Northwestern U 68-. 14: Catlg. 15: 1121 Church st apt 212, Evanston Il 60201.

MURPHY, FRANCES GERTRUDE. b Napa Cal 22 O 07. 5: UCal 26-30 (Phil) AB, 30-31 (LS) Certif. 7: Asst libn Plumas Co Free Lib, Quincy Cal 31-36; Hd sch dept Sacramento co Lib, Sacramento Cal 36-45; Co libn Sonoma Co Lib, Santa Rosa Cal 45-65; Asst dir Santa Rosa-Sonoma Co Lib, Santa Rosa Cal 65-. 9: ALA; CalLA. 10: AAUW; Soroptimist Club. 14: Admin devel of lib systems. 15: 1600 Yulupa ave #30, Santa Rosa Ca 95405.

MURPHY, SISTER GERTRUDE SND. b Middletown Conn 12 Ag 05. 5: Trinity Col (Wash DC) 23-27 (Chem, Lat) AB;

Columbia summer 32-33 (Bio); Boston Col 44-49 (Eng) MA; Providence Col summer 54 (Theol); Simmons summers 55-60 MLS; FairfieldU summer 63 (Bio). 7: Tchr: Portland High Sch, Portland Conn 32-37, Roxbury Acad, Roxbury Mass 40-42, St Mary High Sch, Cambridge Mass 42-44, St Mary High Sch, Beverly Mass 44-50, Sacred Heart High Sch, Springfield Mass 50-52, Archbishop Cushing High Sch, South boston Mass 53-57; Tchr-libn St Thomas Acquinas High Sch, New Britain Conn 57-. 9: ALA; CathLA. 10: Amer Inst Bio Sci. 15: 74 Kelsey, New Britain Ct 06051.

MURPHY, GWYNETH (ROE). b NYC 5 O 13. 4: Edwin W Murphy. 5: Yankton Col 32 (Eng, Drama) BA; UWis 53 (Journalism) MA; UMich 60 (LS) BS. 6: Fr. 7: Recreation leader Nat Youth Admin Prog NY State Employment Serv; Coun Ill State Employment Serv; Placement asst Ill Art Project; Jr economist Bur of Labor Statistics Union Agreements Sect 41-42; Labor rel consul War Producton Bd Labor Disputes Off, Wash DC 42-43; Disputes review off Nat War Labor Bd, NYC 45-47; Ind program dir YWCA, Grand Rapids Mich 47-49; Reporter UWis News Serv 49-53; Asst state ed "News-Palladium, Benton Harbor Mich 53-55; Asst womans ed "Grand Rapids Herald, Grand Rapids Mich 55; Gen assignment reporter "Register-Republic, Rckford Ill 56-57; Br libn & publ adv Kent Co Lib, Grand Rapids Mich 57-58; Info off Prince Georges Co Mem Lib, Hyattsville Md 59-. 9: ALA; MdLA (chm Pub Com 61-62 & 63-64); DCLA. 11: Three John Cotton Dana Awards 61, 64, 66. 12: "The People Speak for Public Librarie in Maryland (64); "Good Libraries are Good Business for Maryland (62). 14: Pub rel, publ, adult serv & educ. 15: 6406 W Halbert rd, Bethesda Md.

MURPHY, HENRY T. b Lynn Mass 9 D 23. 4: Mary Scarseth. 5: Boston U 45-48 (Biol) AB; UNH 48-49 (Zool); UMich 49-51 MA in LS. 7: US Navy 42-44; Lib scholar UMich 49-50, Lib fellow 50-51; Ref asst USDA, Wash DC 51-52, Spec bibliog 53; Libn Animal Disease Lab USDA, Greenport NY 53-54; Libn Agric Expt Sta Purdue U 54-56; Libn Agric Lib Ohio State U 56-57; Libn Life Sci Lib Purdue U 57-69; Libn Albert R Mann Lib Cornell U 69-. 8: Consul Agric Vocabulary Proj Nat Agric Lib, Wash DC 66. 9: SLA. 12: Ed "Indiana Slant"; Co-auth "Biological and Biomedical Resource Literature" (68). 14: Agric & bio bibliog. 15: 505 Campbell ave, Ithaca NY 14850.

MURPHY, JOAN. b Detroit 4 O 18. 5: UOre 37-40 (Eng Lit) BA; Bryn Mawr 43-44 (Eng Lit); Mills Col 49-50 (Eng Lit) MA; UCal(Berkeley) MLS. 6: Ger, Fr. 7: Research asst UOre 40-42; Asst Airport traffic controller Civil Aeronautics admin 42-43; Ed McGraw-Hill Bk Co, NYC 44-46; Relief wker Amer Friends Serv Com, Phila & Germany 46-49; Ed supv McGraw-Hill Bk Co, NYC 50-52; Instr in Eng Bennett Col 52-54; Ed report serv Stanford Reearch Inst, Menlo Park Cal 55-58; Lib asst Richmond Pub Lib, Richmond Cal 58-59; ibn San Francisco State Col 59; Ed Lockheed Aircraft Corp, Palo Alto Cal 60-62; Readers serv libn Vassar Col Lib 62-. 8: Consul, "Essay and General Literature Index. 09: BSA. 13: Yes. 14: Ref, rare bks, acquis, bibliog. 15: Vassar Col, Poughkeepsie NY 12601.

MURPHY, KATHLEEN (COSTIGAN). b NYC. 4: James F Murphy. 5: CUNY (Hunter Col) 31-35 (Soc studies) BA; Pratt Inst 41-42 MLS. 7: Indexer H W Wilson Co, NY 66-. 9: ALA; NY Lib Coun. 12: Indexer "Book Review Digest" 67-. 14: Catlg, indexing, ref, abstracting. 15: 50 Norman pl, Tenafly NJ 07670.

MURPHY, REV KEVIN JOHN) OSB. b Evanston Ill 3 Mr 36. 5: St benedicts Sem 54-62 (Phil, Theol); Rosary Col summer 60 (LS). 6: Sp, Lat. 7: Asst libn St Benedicts Abbey, Benet Lake Wis 57-60; Libn Colegio Agropecuario de San Benito; Santa Clara de San Carlos Costa Rica 63-65, Prof of Eng 63-65; Libn St Benedicts Abbey, Benet Lake Wis 65-66, Prof of Eng 65-66; Ed "News & Views" 65-66; Missionary, Panama 67; Libn St Benedict's Abbey 68-69; Missionary El Salvador 69-. 8: Missionary & parish wk in Mexico & Costa Rica, 62-65, Panama 67, El Salvador 69-. 9: ALA; CathLA. ; ATheolLA. 14: Theol collectios. 15: Benet Lib, St Benedicts Abbey, Benet Lake Wis 53102.

MURPHY, LAVINIA ELLEN. b Medford Mass 30 N 39. 5: Bridgewater State Col 56-60 (Elem Educ) BS; Boston 62-65 (Sch Li) MS. 6: Fr. 7: A-v coordinator NDEA Inst in Sch Libnship Boston U summer 65; Sch lib consul, Marshfield Mass 61-65; Sr supv Mass Bur Lib Ext 65-68; Asst dir instr in sch media personnel Boston U 69. 8: Consul, Non-print Media, ALESCO, Paramus NJ 68-69; Instr NESchLA student leadership conf Aug 69. 9: NEA; ALA; AASchL (Index ed "School Libararies 63-65, & 66-69, chm Publ Com 65); YASD (dir 65-68); MdLA (v-pres 65); Assn of Sch Libns of Md; Ariz State LA (v-pres & ed "Arizona Libraries 52-54, pres 56). 10: Intercollege Club, Boston; YWCA; Kappa Delta Pi; Pi Lambda Theta. 13: Yes. 14: Elem sch libnship, a-v educ. 15: 152 Center st, HanoverMass.

MURPHY, LAWRENCE PARKE. b Columbia Mo 18 O 24. 5: Whitman Col 42-47 (Chem) AB cum laude); UWash 47-48 (Eng Lit) MA, 48-49 BA in Libr; UDel 54-55 (Chem); Columbia 57- (Eng & Comparative Lit). 6: Fr, Ger. 7: Clerical Whitman Col Lib 43-47; Ref libn UWash Lib 49-50; Libn in chg Fisheries, ceanography Lib & Oceanographic Labs Lib UWash 50-53; Bibliog & ed Jackson Lab Lib E I DuPont de Nemours & Co, Wilmington Del 53-57; Libn info div NY Pub Lib 62-66; Asst to the deputy dir 66-67, Asst to the dir 67-. 9: ALA; SLA (Pacific NW Chap: pres 52-53, Bd 52-53);-LPRC; NYLA; NY Lib Club. 10: Columbia Univ English Grad Union; UWash Sch of Libnship Alumni; Phi Beta Kappa, Internat Bach Soc. 13: Yes. 14: Ref, bibliog, admin. 15: 308 W 105 st, New York NY 10025.

MURPHY, LAYTON B(ARNES). b San Antonio Tex 27 Jl 31. 5: San Antonio Col 48-50; Hardin-Simmons U 50-52 (Math) BA; UMich 52-54 AMLS, 55-57 (Hist) AM, 59-65 (LS) PhD. 6: Sp, Fr, Ger. 7: Physics and astronomy lib UMich 52-54; Lib Hardin-Simmons U summer 52, 53; Bio Station Lib UMich summer 54; Bio & Natural Resources Lib UMich 54-55; Tching asst Dept of Lib Sci UMich 56-57, 60; Pub Health Lib UMich 57; Bio and physics Lib UTex 57-58; Lect Sch of Lib Sci USoCal summer 61; Instr Dept of Lib Sci UMich 61-65, Asst Prof 65-66; Asst Prof Dept of Lib Sci UKy 66-67; Lect Grad Sch of Lib Sci UTex 57-59, summer 60, Assoc Prof 67-. 9: ALA; -LED (Publ Com); -LAD (Com on Stat for Lib Educ); AALS; (chm of Stat Com); SWLA; TexLA (chm Catlgr's RT). 13: Yes. 14: Catlg, acquis. 15: 403 Juniper rd, Austin Tx 78746.

MURP HY, MRS LUCILE LUCAS. b Clarksville Ark 13 N 12. 5: Col of the Ozarks 30-33 (Foreign Langs) AB; UIll 33-34 BS in LS; Columbia 35-36 (LS); Middlebury Sch of Fr summer 37 (Fr). 6: Fr. 7: Libn NY Inst for Educ of B lind, NYC 35-36; Libn Rio Grande Col 36-38; Libn Sue Bennett Col 38-40; Libn WPA Lib Proj, Little Rock Ark 40-41; Libn Ozarks Reg Lib, Clarksville Ark 41-53; Libn Col of the Ozarks Lib, Clarksville Ark 53-. 8: Chm AFAC Libs; Planned Lib Bldg, Col of the Ozarks 62-63; Mem, Com on Higher Educ of Ark in survey Ark Col Libs. 9: ALA; ArkLA. 10: AAUW. 12: Ed "Periodical Holdings in Arkansas Foundation of Associated Colleges" (57). 15: Clarksville Ark 72830.

MURPHY, M PATRICIA (McCARTHY). b Wash DC 1 O 23. 5: St Mary's Col (Ind) 41-45 (Hist) BA; Immaculate Heart Col 63-64 (LS) Masters; SeattleU summer 43. 6: Fr, Ital, Sp. 7: Libn Special Serv US Army, Ft Bliss Tex 49-50; Okinawa 48-49, 50-53; Libn interlib loan, Space Tech Labs, Redondo Beach Cal 57-63; Libn circ Nat Geographic Soc, Wash DC 64-. 9: SLA (Memb Chm Geog & Map 66-68; sec Wash Chap Geog & Map Div 66-68); DC Libns. 10: St Mary's Col Alumni Assn; Immaculate Heart Alumni Assn. 13: Yes. 14: Care of gen collections, mil sci. 15: 8133 Marcy ave, W Springfield Va 22150.

MURPHY, MABEL ARDIS. b Hutchinson Kan 23 Jl 1899. 5: Kan State (Manhattan) 19-23 (Piano) BM; USoCal 40 (Musicology) MA, 46 BSLS. 7: Okla Col for Women: Instr piano 26-32, Asst Prof piano 3242, Asst libn & Asst libn & Asst Prof 42-56, Libn 56-60; Sr field libn Okla State Lib 60-63; Asst humanities & fine arts libn So Ill U 63-. 9: ALA (Coun, Okla 60-63); MusLA; (Prog chm Midwest Chap 69); TheatreLA; OklaLA; SWLA (sec 60-62); IllLA. 10: PEO; Delta Kappa Gamma; Mu Phi Epsilon; Phi Kappa Phi; AAUW. 11: Theta Sigma Phi Award, community service, Okla City 62. 14: Admin, personnel, mus, ref, theater. 15: 726 Randle, Edwardsville Il 62025.

MURPHY, MARCY. b Ogden Utah 23 S 25. 5: UUtah 43-44; Colo Col 45-48 (Eng) BA; UDenver 58-59 (LS) MA. 6: Fr, Sp, Ger. 7: Staff artist Denver Art Museum 48-52; Lib asst Colo Col 52-58; Ref asst & documents libn UDenver 58-60; Head of ser UNM 60-63; Head of ser UColo 63-65; Head of acquis Colo State U 65-67; Title II Fellow UMinn Lib Sch 67-68; Title II Fellow UPittsburgh Grad Sch Lib & Info Scis 68-. 9: ALA; PennLA. 10: AAUP; Sierra Club. 14: Acquis, ref, lib educ. 15: 5614 Walnut apt 5, Pittsburgh Pa 15232.

MURPHY, MARY (DALTON). b Lawrence Kan 31 D 17. 4: Jim Gordon Murphy. 5: Ukan 35-39 (Span) AB; Columbia 39-40 (LS) BS. 7: Acquis asst UKan Lib 40, Period libn 41; Hdqrs libn Johnson Co Lib, Merriam Kan 61-66, In-serv 66-68;

Ref libn Lawrence Pub Lib, Lawrence Kan 68-; Consul NEKL 68-. 9: ALA; KanLA; MPLA. 14: Ref. 15: Lake Dabinawa, McLouth Ks 66054.

MURPHY, MARY. b Hibbing Minn 14 Ag 17. 5: Hibbing Jr Col 35-38; St Lawrence U (NY) 38-40 (Fr) BA; Ill 40-43 BS in LS. 6: Fr. 7: Army Map Serv Lib, Wash DC: Engnr aide 43-44, Map libn 44-46, Catlgr 46-52, Supv libn 52-56, Asst chief bk & period br 56-65, Chief document br 65-68; Army Topographic Command, Wash DC, Chief info sec 68-. 9: SLA, ASIS, DCLA. 11: Sustained Superior Performance Award, 61, 66. 13: Yes. 14: Ref, catlg, automation. 15: 8102 Birnam Wood dr, McLean Va 22101.

MURPHY, PAUL H. b Davidson Co Tenn 28 Ap 28. 5: St Ambrose Col 49-52 (Phil) BA; Peabody Col 61 (Eng) MA, 63 MLS. 7: Catlge So Educ Reporting Serv, Nashville 60-62; Ref libn Jt Univ Libs, Nashville 64-66, Sci libn 67-. 9: ALA; -RSD (v-chm Tenn Chap 68-69); SLA; TennLA; SELA. 12: Ed "Tennessee Librarian" (68-). 14: Ref. 15: 107 Lea ave, Nashville Tn 37210.

MURPHY, VIRGINIA (BARDWELL). b Aliceville Ala 2 Ag 08. 5: Alabama Col 25-29 (Eng) BA; Emory 38-39 BA in LS. 7: High sch tchr pub schs, Ala 29-38; Catlgr Womans Col Lib Dke U 39-41; Ref libn Miss State Col for Women 41-43; Ref libn Roanoke (Va) Pub Lib 43-45; Libn Coordinat Col UGa 45-46; Catlgr, asst ref libn UAla 46-51; Humanities & soc sci libn UHouston 51-67, Soc sci Lib 67-. 9: ALA; TexLA. 10: Beta Phi Mu. 12: Comp "Newspaper Resources of District V, Texas Library Association; A Union List". 13: Yes. 14: Ref, US Govt docs. 15: 5701 Jackson Apt 1509, Houston Tx 77004.

MURPHY, WALTER H. b Phila 7 Je 33. 4: Mary Rule. 5: Cameron Col 51-53 (Journalism) Assoc BA; UOkla 53-55 (Eng) BA, 57-59 MLS. 7: Bus manager Cameron Col Newspaper, Lawton Okla 52-53; Housing dept UOkla 53-55; Artillery Off (1st Lt) US Army, Germany 55-57; Asst ref libn Okla City Libs, Okla City Okla 57-59; Admin asst to libn Kan City (Mo) Pub Lib 59-60; Instr Lib Sci Fla So Col 62-66; Dir of Libs Lakeland Pub Libs, Lakeland Fla 60-66; Dir Flint River Reg Lib, Griffin Ga 66-. 8: Consul; Cherokee Reg Lib, Lafayette Ga 68, Chattooga Co Ga 68, Wilkes Co Ga 69. 9: ALA; Fla LA; SELA, GaLA. 10: Beta Phi Mu; Lakeland Concert Assn; Capt US Army Rerves. 13: Yes. 14: Pub sev, ref, admin, tchg, bldgs. 15: 210 S 6th st, Griffin Ga 30223.

MURRAY, ARTHUR BEACH. b Des Moines Iowa 14 My 27. 4: Carol-Faith Platt. 5: Antioch Col 44-45, 47-50 (Hist) AB; Emory 50-51 (LS) ML; San Diego State Col 57-64 (Public Admin) MS. 7: (Pvt) med dept US Army 45, 46; Clerical asst NY Pub Lib 47-48; Ref asst Dayton Pub Lib, Dayton Ohio 51-55; San Diego Co Lib, San Diego Cal: Ref libn II 55-59, Asst co libn 59-65, Act co libn 65, Co Libn65-. 8: Adv Com on Lib Tech Prog SWest Col, Palomar Col. 9: ALA; CalLA. 10: Pacific Beach Investors; San Diego Co Exec Assn; San Diego Co Train Adv Com. 14: Ref, admin. 15: 329 Dunemere dr, La Jolla Ca 92037.

MURRAY, CATHERINE (REED). b Minneapolis 9 O 39. 4: John Stevenson Murray. 5: Iowa State U 57-61 BS; Columbia 61-62 (LS) MS. 7: Child libn Arlington Co Pub Libs, Arlington Va 62; Libn Capehart Sch Marine Corps Schs, quantico Va 63-64; Asst libn Law Sch Lib UIowa 65-68; Chief libn Paul, Weiss, Goldberg, Rifkind, Wharton & Garrison, NYC 69-. 8: Bd of Consuls, US Capitol Hist Soc, 65. 9: AALL. 10: Kappa Alpha Theta. 11: Joseph Towne Wheeler Awar, Columbia U 62; Outstanding Performance Award, Marine Corps Sch, Quantico Va 64. 14: Ref, legal libs. 15: Apt 4C 400 Central Park W, New York NY 10025.

MURRAY, FLORENCE B(EATRICE). b Huntsville Ont Can 10 F 05. 5: Toronto 22-27 (Eng, Hist) BA; Ont Lib Sch 27 Diploma; UMich 33-34 AMLS. 6: Fr, Ger, Lat. 7: Catlgr Toronto Pub Lib28-29, Ref libn 29-50; Prof UToronto Sch of Lib Sci 50-. 8: Tchr UMich Dept of Lib Sci, summer 58. 9: CanLA (Coun 59-60; Ref Sect, chm Res & Spec Libs Sect 59-60); ALA-ACRL;-LED;-RSD (Hist Sect Chm 68-69); SLA; AAS; Bibliog Soc Can (Off 54-60, pres 56-58); Inst Prof Libns Ont; OntLA (Coun 58-61); Ont Resources & Tech Serv (Group chm 39-40); Can Assn Lib Schs. 10: Ont Hist Soc; Can Assn of Univ Tchrs; Univ Womens Club, Toronto; Faculty Club, Univ of Toronto. 12: "Muskoka and Haliburton, 1615-1875" (63); "Preliminary Guide to the Manuscript Collection in the Toronto Public Libraries," with Elsie McLeod Murray (40); Jt ed & ed "Canadian Catalogue of Books, Annual" (35-40). 13: Yes. 14: Ref, bibliog,govt publs, Canadiana. 15: Univ of Toronto Sch of Lib Sci, 167 College st, Toronto 2 B Can.

MURRAY, JUDITH ANN. b Detroit 8 Ap 40. 5: UDetroit 58-61 (Geog); Wayne State U 61-62 (Geog) AB; UMich 65 MALS. 7: Map libn Wayne State U Lib 62-63; Libn Oakland Commun Col (Mich) 65. 15: 708 Lakepointe, Grosse Pointe Mich 48230.

MURRAY, LILA BERNICE (KROEGER). b Davenport Iowa 12 My 13. 4: Walter R Murray. 5: Augustana Col (Rock Is Ill) 30-34 (Nursing) RN. 6: Ger, Lat. 7: Registered Nurse - Priv Duty, Moline Ill & Davenport Iowa 34-60; Libn Davenport Municipal Art gallery, Davenport Iowa 60-. 9: ALA; Am Nurs Assn; Ill State Nurs Assn; Luth Hosp Sch for Nurs Alum Assn; Quad-City LA. 14: Art, sci, catlg, ref, rare bks. 15: 407 E 30th st, Davenport Ia 52803.

MURRAY, MARGUERITE M. b Chicago Il 21 D 17. 4: James J Murray. 5: Rockford Col 35-39 (Eng) AB; Carnegie Inst 40-41 BLS. 7: Libn Oak Park Pub Lib 39-40; Libn DC Pub Lib 41-46; Tchr Montgomery Co (Md) Pub Schs 56-58, Libn 58-68; Asst coord child serv Montgomery Co Pub Lib 68-. 13: Yes. 14: Child serv. 15: Dept of Pub Libs, 6400 Democracy blvd, Bethesda Md 20034.

MURRAY, MARY ELEEN. b Brandon Manitoba Can 15 Je 44. 5: UWest Ont 63-66 (Eng) BA; UToronto 66-67 BLS. 6: Fr. 7: Acquis libn Health Sci Lib UWest Ont 67-. 9: MedLA; ALA; Inst Profess Libns Ont. 10: Kappa Alpha Theta. 14: Ref, acquis. 15: 1 Grosvenor st apt 804, London Ontario Can.

MURRAY, OLIN BRYAN JR. b Bedford Va 12 Jl 30. 4: Margrit Scheel. 5: Ferrum Jr Col 50-51; UVa 51-53 (Langs, Sci) BA; UNC 54-57 (Germanic Langs, Linguistics); Rutgers 62-63 MLS; Yale 63 (Linguistics). 6: Ger, Slavic, Classical Gk, Lat, Sanskrit, Celtic. 7: Tchr of langs Buckroe Beach Jr High Sch, Buckroe Beach Va 53-54; Instr in Ger UNC(Chapel Hill) 54-57; Acquis asst UNC Lib (Chapel Hill) 58-62; Ref asst NY Pub Lib ref dept summer 62; Research asst Grad Sch of Lib Serv, Rutgers U 62-63; Rare bk catlgr Princeton U Lib 63; Acquis asst order dept Yale U Lib 63-64, Soc sci bibliog 64-66; Bibliogr Aricana Northwestern U Lib (Evanston) 10: Phi Beta Kappa; Beta Phi Mu. 13: Yes. 14: Org & devel of res lib collections & serv, soc & behavioral sci bibliog, area progs. 15: 2027 Pratt Court, Evanston Il 60201.

MURRAY, ROBIN (RIVERS BARDEN). b Shediac Cap NB Can 27 Ag 21. 4: Eldred (Maud) MacAlpine Murray. 5: Andrew Col 32-32 AA, Certif Piano; Emory Col 32-34 (Eng) BA; Emory U 35-36 ABLS. 6: Fr, Lat. 7: Lt Royal Can Artillery, Medium Artillery & Foreign Serv Signal Instr 38-44; Stud asst UToronto Main Lib 47-48; Stud asst Nat Research Coun of Can, Ottawa summer 48; Stud asst Law & Econ Lib McGill U 48-49; Ref libn, hist, theol, biog asst Brooklyn Pub Lib 49-51; Applied chem br libn Nat Research Coun of Can, Ottawa 51-53; Chief Libn St John Free Pub Lib, St John NB Can 53-54; Research libn Crucible Steel Co, Pittsburgh 54-59; Libn SUNY Col of Ceramics Alfred U 59-. 9: SLA; (pres Upstate NY Chap 66-67); CanLA; Aslib; ALA; Amer Ceramic Soc; NYLA; OntLA; NBLA (pres 54). 10: S Central Research Lib Coun; Col Center of the Finger Lakes Lib Com; Alfred U Lib Com; NY Forest Owners Assn; Assn for Retarded Child. 12: "A Subject Index of Figures in Greek and Roman Mythology" (50); Ed "Directory of Librarie in the Ottawa District" (52); Ed & principal contrib "Saint John Free Public Library; 50th Anniversary of the Carnegie Building" (54)12016 13,; yes. 14: Admin, ref. 15: 113 S Main st, Almond NY 14804.

MURRAY, ROCHELLE ANN. b Davenport Iowa 14 D 36. 5: Marycrest Col 55-59 (Speech, Eng) BA; UWis summer 63-67 LS MA. 6: Fr, Sp. 7: Davenport Pub Lib, Davenport Iowa: A-v libn 59-65, Yp libn 60-65, Head adult serv 64-65, Head child serv 65-, Hd tech processes 68-. 8: Lib consul, Davenport Municipal Art Gall, Davenport Iowa, 59-. 65; Asst coun Ann Emery Hall, Madison Wis summers 64-67. 9: ALA-CSD; -YASD (Mag Eval Com; Period List Subcom 65-); EFLA; IowaLA (chm Recruitment Com 65-66); Iowa A-V EA. 10: AAUW; Kappa Gamma Pi; Beta Phi Mu; Wis Alumnae Assn; Davenport Pub Lib Staff Assn; Marycrest Alumnae Assn; Civic Music Assn; Quad City LA; Davenport Park Bd Jr Theatre; Boy Scouts Amer; NCCJ. 11: Outstanding Young Woman of Amer 68-69. 13: Yes. 14: Child & yp serv, a-v, pub rel, catlg. 15: 407 E 30th st, Davenport Iowa 52803.

MURRAY, ROSEMARY FRANCES CATHERINE. b Ottawa Ont Can 11 F 47. 5: UToronto 64-67 9eng) BA, 68-69 BLS. 6: Fr. 7: Lib asst Nat Mus of Can, Ottawa Ont 67-68; Libn Royal Ont Mus, Toronto Ont summer 69. 9: CanLA; ALA. 15: St George Grad Student Res 321 Bloor st W, Toronto Ont Can.

MURRAY, RUTH C. b Baton Rouge La 4 N 23. 4: John J Murray. 5: LSU 42-45 (Bus Admin) BS, 58 (LS) MS, 62-65 (Geog). 6: Fr, Sp. 7: Accounting clerk Navy US Bur of Supplies & Accts, Wash DC summer 44; Sec LSU gen ext div 45-47; Sec La State Dept of Educ, Baton Rouge La 47-49; Sec Housing & Home Finance Agency, Baton Roue La 50-53; USDA annual disease eradication 53-58; Jr libn ser record LSU Lib 58-60; Sr libn govt docs dept LSU Lib 60-67, Res bk room 66-67, Instr bks & libs dept 67-. 9: ALA; Assn Amer Geogs; LaLA; Baton Rouge Lib Club. 10: LSU Womans Faculty Club. 14: Ref, US docs, geog. 15: 5975 Menlo dr, Baton Rouge La 70808.

MURRAY, SUZANNE HELEN. b Syracuse NY. 5: Le Moyne Col (Chem) BS; Syracuse 59-60 MSLS, 67-69 (Relig). 7: Ref, circ SUNY Upstate Med Ctr Lib 60-61, Acquis libn 62-67, Reg med program libn 69-. 8: Conaul in Adult Educ to the Confraternity of Christian Doctrine, Roman Cath Diocese of Syracuse. 11: Beta Phi Mu. 15: Library SUNY Upstate Med Center, 766 Irving ave, Syracuse NY 13210.

MURRAY, THOMAS BERNARD. b Omaha 2 D 12. 4: Jean K Foley. 5: Kearney State Tchrs Col 31-33; UCLA 38-42 (Eng); UCal(Berkeley) 45-53 AB, BLS, MLS. 6: Ger. 7: Rural sch tchr local sch dists, Custer Co Neb 30-34; Asst postmaster US Post Off, Sargent Neb 34-38; Aerial navigator (coinciding with rank in USNR as Lt jg) Pan American Airways, San Francisco 42-45; Stack supv Main Lib UCal(Berkeley) 47-49; Head Libn Diablo Valley Col 49-. 8: Consul for jr col libs (ALA-ACRL0. 9: CalLA (sec & chm Col Univ & Res libs sect, no div). 10: Sierra Club. 12: "An Evaluation of the Reference Collections in the Libraries of Seven San Francisco Bay Area Junior Colleges, ACRL Microcrad Ser, no 10 (53). 14: Bk sel & acquis, admin, personnel, automation. 15: Diablo Valley Col Lib, Concord Cal 94523.

MUSCO, MARY FRANCES. b Elizabeth NJ 2 N 28. 5: Rutgers (Newark) Eng BA, Rutgers (New Brunswick) 63-67 (LS) MLS. 6: Ger, Sp, Ital. 7: Br libn Free Pub Lib, Elizabeth NJ 46-57; Research libn White Labs Inc, Kenilworth NJ 57-64; Research libn Coca-Cola Research Div, Linden NJ 65-. 9: SLA; NY Acad of Scis; ALA; NJLA; ASIS. 14: Ref. 15: 16 Cypress dr, Colonia NJ.

MUSE, FRANCES (McDOWELL). b Waverly Hall Ga 15 N 13. 5: Andrew COL 32-32 Certif Piano; Emory Col 32-34 (Eng) BA; Emory U 35-36 ABLS. 6: Fr, Lat. 7: Tchr Mt Vernon Sch, Atlanta 34-35; Libn Thomson High Sch, Thomson Ga 36-37; Asst in chg res bks Emory U 37-41; Catlgr & asst libn US Waterways Expt Sta, Vicksburg Miss 41-42; Catlgr & asst libn US Engnrs S Atlantic Div, Atlanta 42-43; Asst in ref & circ, act head documents Emory U Lib 43-45; Asst in circ & catlg Ga Inst of Tech 45-46; Libn LaGrange Mem Lib, LaGrange Ga 46-47; Libn Emory U Bus Sch 47-57; Libn Ga Power Co, Atlanta 57-59; Head ref dept Ga State Col Lib 59-. 9: SELA; GaLA (Mem Com to Study the Distrib, Preserv & Bibliog Control of Ga State Docs; Act chm Ref Sect. Atlanta Lib Club. 10: Altrusa Internat. 14: Ref. 15: 423 Emory dr NE, Atlanta Ga 30367.

MUSGROVE, WALTER SHELDON. b Baltimore 12 Jl 33. 5: Fla State U (Lat); UFla (Eng) BA; Blackstone Sch of Law (Law) LLB; Inst Tech de Monterrey (Sp); Atlanta U 65-66 MS in LS. 6: Lat, Sp, Fr. 7: Libn Coral Shores Sch, Tavernier Fla 56-60; Libn Spring Park Sch, Jacksonville Fla 60-61; English tchr & libn Miami Mil Acad, Miami Fla 61-62; Libn Lake Forest Elem Sch, Jacksonville Fla 62-64; Catlgr Pembroke State Col, Pembroke NC 66-. 9: ALA; SELA; NCLA. 14: Catlg. 15: PO Box 481, Pembroke NC 28372.

MUSMANN, KLAUS. b Magdeburg Germany 27 Je 35. 4: Gladys Arakawa. 5: Wayne State U 59-62 (Geog, Ger) BA; UMich 62-63 (LS) MA; Mich State U 65-67 (Ger) MA. 6: Ger. 7: Libn I & II Detroit Pub Lib 62-65; Ser bibliog Mich State U 65-67; Asst order libn Cal State Polytech 67-68; Hd acquis libn Los Angeles Co Law Lib 68-. 9: ALA. 10: Amer Assn Tchrs Germ. 13: Yes. 14: Tech ser. 15: 1601 C Amberwood dr, So Pasadena Ca 91030.

MUSSER, NECIA ANN. b Grand Rapids Mich 25 N 28. 5: Grand Rapids Jr Col 46-48; UMich 48-50 (Soc Studies) BA, 51-52 (Hist) MA, 52-53 MALS, 65-67 (LS) PhD. 6: Ger, Fr. 7: Ref libn UMich 52-61; Catlg libn Mich Tech U 61-62 Catlg libn West Mich U 62-65, Acquis libn 67-. 9: ALA; MichLA. 10: AAUW; Phi Beta Kappa; Phi Kappa Phi. 14: Tech proc. 15: West Mich Univ Lib, Kalamazoo Mi 49001.

MUSSER, RUTH N. b Mount Joy Penn 1 N 24. 5: Elizabethtown Col 46 (Eng, Soc Studies) BS in Sec Ed; Drexel 47 BS in LS; UMich 55 AM LS. 6: Fr, Sp. 7: Libn Messiah Col 47-. 9: ALA; PennLA; Area Col Lib Coop Program. 10: AAUW; Grantham Oratorio Soc; Christian Libns Fellowship; Beta Phi Mu; Phi Kappa Phi. 14: Acquis, catlg, circ. 15: Grantham Penn 17027.

MUSTAIN, ADELIA PARSONS. b San Diego Cal 30 N 14. 5: San Diego State Col 31-35 (Eng) AB; UCal (Berkeley) 41-42 Certif; UMinn 47 (Hosp libn). 6: Fr. 7: Page & clk San diego Pub Lib 35-41; Jr libn Oakland Pub Lib, Oakland Cal 42-43; Army libn US War Dept hd libn Letterman Gen Hosp 43-46; Hd libn Glen Lake Sanitorium, Hennepin Co Minn 47-48; Libn I (med option) Co of San Diego Co Hosp 48-52, Libn II 52-66; Libn I ref & docs co lib San Diego 66-68, Libn II ref & docs 68-. 9: ALA; -AHIL (Awards Com 68-70); MedLA (Hosp Sect: sec 56, 62, pres 64); CalLA; Hosp & Institutions RT (pres 58 & 66, sec 62; mem Intel Freedom, Legisl Com 67). 10: LWV; San Diego Co Employees' Assn; League of Co employee Assns. 15: 3603 29th st, San Diego Ca 92104.

MUTCHOW, SUELLEN. b Milwaukee Wis 12 D 40. 5: Bryn Mawr 59-63 (Hist) BA; UWis 63-64 (LS) MS; UPenn 65-66 (Hist) MA. 6: Fr, Sp. 7: Libn I Free Lib of Phila 64-65; Research asst Houghton Lib HarvardU 66-. 8: Assisted in revision Pollard & Redgrave's "Short Title Catalogue of Books Printed in England 1470-1640". 14: Ref, rare bks. 15: 401 Broadway apt 34, Cambridge Ma 02139.

MUTH, THOMAS J. b Lyons Kan 6 N 42. 4: Kirthen Ann Brosamer. 5: Hutchinson Jr Col 60-62 (Bus) AA; Kan State Tchrs Col 62-65 (Soc Sci) BA, 67-68 (Libnship) ML. 6: Fr. 7: Asst hd adult serv Topeka Pub Lib, Topeka Kan 68-69, Hd adult serv 69-. 14: Ref. 15: 2027 Lane, Topeka Ks 66604.

MUTNICK, MARGARET (SHIRLEY CAMPBELL). b Chicago Ill 30 My 20. 4: George G Mutnick. 5: UMich 38-42 (Eng) AB, 48 (Educ); Rutgers 49 (Educ), 67-69 (LS) MLA. 6: Fr 7: Tchr Wayne High Sch, Wayne Mich 47-48; Tchr N Plainfield High Sch, N Plainfield NJ 63-66; Trainee Plainfield Pub Lib, Plainfield NJ 68, Adult serv libn 69-. 9: ALA; NJLA. 10: League of Women Voters. 14: Commun serv, ref. 15: 621 Woodland ave, Plainfield NJ 07062.

MUTSCHLER, HERBERT F. b Eureka SD 28 N 19. 4: Lucille I Gross. 5: Jamestown Col 38-41, 46-47 (Hist) BA (cum laude); West Res 48-49 (Hist) MA, 50-52 MSLS; UMich 52-53 (Marketing). 6: Ger. 7: Inf unit comdr US Army 88th Inf Div 41-46; Tchr Lemmon High Sch, Lemmon S Dak 47-48; Personnel off & (Capt) & Sp US Army Inf 50-52; Lib asst Cleveland Pub Lib 52; Head ref dept Royal Oak Pub Lib, Royal Oak Mich 52-53, Asst libn 53-55; Dir Hamtramck Pub Lib, Hamtramck Mich 55-56; Head pub serv Wayne Co Lib, Detroit 56-59, Asst libn 59-63; Dir King Co Lib System, Seattle 63-. 8: Bldg adv, 12 commun libs; Wash State Lib Bldg Consul. 9 ALA; (Coun 65-69, mem Pub com 65-66, chm Pub Rel Sect 69-70); MichLA (chm Co Lib Sect, chm Ref Sect); WashLA (chm Legis Com 64-65; Exec Bd 64-65; Statewide Lib Serv Devel Com), pres 66-69); WashStateASchL; PNLA. 10: Kiwanis; Rotary, Municipal League; Forward Thrust Com. 13: Yes. 14: Admin, bldg, pub serv. 15: 1100 E Union, Seattle Wa 98122.

MYER, ELIZABETH GALLUP. b Hyde Park Mass. 5: Conn Col 30-32 (Eng); Barnard 33-35 (Fr) BA; Simmons 40 BS in LS; Brown 47 (Eng Lit) MA; Wayne State U 56. 7: Asst Providence Pub Lib 35-39; Supv RI WPA Statewide Lib Proj 40-42; (Lt) USNR 6th Naval Dist Hdqrs, Charleston SC 42-45; Libn Phoebe Griffin Noyes Lib, Old Lyme Conn 46; Bkmob libn Enoch Pratt Free Lib, Baltimore 48-50; Ref libn Morrill Mem Lib, Norwood Mass 50-53; Tchr-libn Newton Pub Schs, Newton Mass 53-58; Supv pub lib servs in rural areas, RI 58-64; Dir RI Dept of State Lib Servs 64-. 8: EXEC DIR Nat Lib Week, RI 59; Adv Com on URI Grad Lib Sch, 62-64; Mem Adv Com on Sch Lib to RI Bd of Ed 59-62; Mem RI Legis Com on Lib 62-64. 9: ALA-AAStateL (Exec Bd 65; chm Standards Ser Com 68-69); SLA; NELA (Reg Devel Com); ConnLA; MassLA; RILA (pres 62-64); Member, Reg Develop Com; NELA. 10: AAUW; Quota Club Internat, RI Exec Bd, 64-65; 69-; Camp Fire Girls, Narragansett Council, Exec Bd 68-. 13: Yes. 14: Admin of statewide lib program. 15: 3 SUNSET DR, Barrington RI 02806.

MYER, VIOLET FRANCES. b PUEBLO Colo 19 O08. 5: UAla 25-28 (Eng Lit) BA; Columbia 28-29 BS in LS. 7: Asst Queens Borough Pub Lib, Jamaica NY 29-44; Asst dir US Info Libs, Caetown & Johannesburg, Union of S Africa 45-47; Br libn Enoch Pratt Free Lib, Baltimore 47-53; Dir sub-grant project ALA Off for Adult Educ 53-55 Hd films dept Enoch Pratt Free Lib, Baltimore 55-. 9: ALA; AEAUSA; MDLA. 10:

Phi Beta Kappa. 12: "Cooperative Film Services in Public Libraries, with P B Cory (ALA 56). 13: Yes. 15: Enoch Pratt Free Lib, 40 Cathedral st, Baltimore Md 21201.

MYERS, AGNES McKECHNIE. b St Paul 1 Ag 24. 4: Vernon Myers. 5: UCal (Berkeley) 41-45 (Physiology) B; UDenver 47 BSLS. 7: Staff libn UDenver 46-49; Ser catlgr Yale U lib 49-50 Catlgr in chg of tech process dept Loretto Heights Col 63-. 14: Catlg, acquis. 15: 2786 S Newland st, Denver Co 80227.

MYERS, ALITA. b Memphis Tenn 9 Jl 41. 4: Harry T Myers. 5: Clarke Mem Col 60-62 AA; USoMiss 62-64 (LS) BS. 7: Clerk-sec Lincoln Co Sch System, Brookhaven Miss 64-65; Libn Concordia Parish Sch Bd, Vidalia La 65-66; Accountant Orange Coast Jr Col Dist, Costa Mesa Cal 66-68; Faculty Picayune Mun Separate Sch Dist, Picayune Miss 68-. 9: Parish Libns Assn. 10: Kappa Delta Pi. 15: Rte 1 Box 37, Picayune Ms 39466.

MYERS, ALPHA BLANCHE SCOGGIN BARBER. b St Louis 27 S 12. 5: Southeast Mo State Col 31-38 (Art, Eng, Speech) BS in Ed; Peabody 44-45 BLS; Rutgers 60-64 (LS); Rutgers U Grad Sch of Educ 64-. 7: Tchr in elem schs in Mo 32-38; Ref & documents asst St Louis Pub Lib 39-42, 43-4; Ref libn Washington Lib (St Louis) 42-43; Circ & ref asst Joint U Lib, Nashville 44-45; Libn Edwardsville (Ill) High Sch Lib 46-47; Ref libn Med Col of Ala 46-47; Prin libn Popular Reading Div & Sr libn educ dept & lending & ref dept Newark (NJ) Pub Lib 47-59; Head Lbn Montclair (NJ) High Sch Lib 59-67, 68-; tchg Asst Grad Sch of Educ Rutgers 67-68. 8: Tchr, Lib Sci for Sch Libns summer or ext courses; UMd Sch of Educ 62, 63, 67-69; Paterson State Col (NJ) 65; NDEA Inst for Sch Libns on the Use of the Newer Media, UMinn Lib Sch, 65. 9: NEA; ALA (sec & chm Staff Orgs Round Table 53-54);-AASchL;-ACRL;-RD;-LED; NJLA (Ref Sect, Adult Educ Sect, Child & YP Div, chm Sch Lib Com); NJSchLA (Adult Educ Sect); NJEA. 10: NJ Oratorio Soc. 13: Yes. 14: Readers adv wk, ref, rapid reading train, a-v materials, lib educ secon lib instr. 15: 26 Chadwick dr, Nutley NJ 0711.

MYERS, ELIZABETH L. b Evanston Ill 20 S 23. 5: Monticello Col 41-42; NorthwesternU 42-45 (Hist) BS; UWis 45-47 (Hist) MA; SUNY (Geneseo) 65-68 MLS. 6: Fr. 7: Asst libn period records SUNY AB 67, Asst libn circ 67-68, Assoc libn Ridge Lea Lib 68-. 9: SUNY Libns' Assn. 10: AAUP. 14: Admin, period. 15: 16 Hardt lane, Snyder NY 14226.

MYERS, IRENE L(OIS). b Cincinnati 27Ap 28. 5: UCincinnati 46-50 (Chem) BS. 6: Ger, Fr. 7: Tech libn Procter & Gamble Co, Cincinnati 50-. 9: SLA; ASIS. 15: The Procter & Gamble Co, 6000 Center Hill rd, Cincinnati Oh 45224.

MYERS, JAMES CHRISTOPHER. b Fairmont WVa 30 Ag 18. 4: Enid Haller. 5: WVaU 36-40 (Bot) AB, 40-41 (Bot) MS; Ohio State U 40 (Bot); umich 41 (Bot); UIll 41-42, 50-52 (Bot, LS) MS. 7: Grad asst WVaU 40-41; Grad asst UIll(Urbana) 41-42; Med Tech US Army (Pfc), European Theatre 42-45; Catlgr UGa 52-55; Catlgr-libn Lockheed Aircraft Corp, Marietta Ga 55-59; Head Sci-tech div Fla State U Lib 59-. 9: SLA; SELA; FlaLA. 10: Sigma Xi; So Appalachian Botanical Club; AAUP; Fla State U Lib Staff Assn; Faculty Club, Fla State U. 13: Yes. 14: Sci ref, botany, hist of sci. 15: Fla State Univ Lib, Tallahassee Fla 32306.

MYERS, JOAN (SAWALL). b Marinette Wis 22 Ap 34. 4: Ray L Myers. 5: Monmouth Col 52-54 (Eng); Simmons 54-55 (Retailing); Ill State U 61-64 (Eng) BS; UIll summers 67, 68. 7: Libn: Mason City (Ill) High Sch 64-66, Hartsburg (Ill) High Sch 66-67, Glendale (Ariz) High Sch 67-68, Camelback High Sch, Phoenix Ariz 68-. 9: ALA; ArizStateLA. 14: Ref, catlg. 15: 2861 E Fairmount, Phoenix Az 85016.

MYERS, JOSEPH H. b Kinston Penn 11 N 22. 4: Katherine Jane Matthews. 5: LeHigh U 41-44 (Hist) BA; McGill 46-47 BSLS. 6: Sp. 7: Libn Wilkes Col 47-52; Asst libn Pub Lib Scranton Penn 52-55, Libn 55-58; Penn State Lib: Field rep 58-63, Supv of adv serv 63-64, Supv of bldg construction grants 64. 9: ALA; PennLA (treas 57-59). 13: Yes. 14: Bldgs. 15: Lib Dev Bureau State Lib Box 1601, Harrisburg Pa 17126.

MYERS, JUDITH (LENDING). b NYC 15 Ag 29. 4: Stanley Myers. 5: Westhampton Col URichmond 46-50 (Liberal Arts) BA; Columbua 66 (LS) MS. 7: Ref libn NY Med Col, NYC 66-69, Act libn 69-. 9: ALA; MedLA. 14: Ref. 15: 47-30 61st st, Woodside NY 11377.

MYERS, JUDY L. b Webster City Iowa. 5: Webster City Jr Col 59-61 AA; UIowa 62-64 (Hist) BA; UWis 66-67 (LS) MA. 7: Catlg libn UNo Iowa 67-. 9: ALA; IowaLA. 14: Catlg. 15: 319 1/2 W 22nd, Cedar Falls Ia 50613.

MYERS, KURTZ (ELIOT). b Columbus Grove Ohio 16 F 13. 5: Hillsdale Col 30-34 (Eng) AB; UMich 34-36 (Eng) MA, 34-36 ABLS; Columbia 46. 6: Ger. 7: Stud asst Arch Lib UMich 35-36; Libn Detroit News Lib, Detroit 36; Theatre Collection NY Pub Lib 37, 39; In chg Navy S Pacific Lib Bk Supply 42-45; Detroit Pub Lib 36: Chief of a-v dept 46-54, Chief of music & drama dept 54-. 8 Tchr a-v wk-shops for libns, Wayne State U. ; Staff mem music lib wkshops Eastman Sch Music URochester 67, 69. 9: Internat Assn of Mus Lib (vpres Pub Libs Sect); ALA (A-V Bd); TheatreLA; MusLA; Assn Recorded Sound Collections. 10: Greater Detroit Film Coun;Mich Coun on the ARTS; Bohemians (Detroit); Detroit Chamber Music Soc; Detroit Grand Opera Soc. 11: Detroit Pub Lib Staff Mem Award, 58. 12: ""Record Ratings, with R S Hill (55). 13: Yes. 14: Ref, spec collections. 15: 16356 Hamilton ave, Highland Park Mi 48203.

MYERS, LINDA LEE. b Wilmington Del 26 Ag 40. 5: Col of Wooster 58-62 (Sociol) BA; Drexel 62-63 MS in LS. 7: Research libn E I duPont de Nemours Co, Wilmington Del 63-, Br libn 68-. 9: SLA; DelLA. 10: Phi Kappa Phi. 14: Ref. 15: 4304 Miller rd, apt 203, Wilmington Del 19802.

MYERS, MARCIA J. b Corry Penn 6 Je 41. 5: Thiel Col 63 (Econ) AB; UPittsburgh 64 MLS. 7: Hd circ Warren Lib Assoc, Warren Penn 64-67; Asst reader's serv libn Miami-Dade Jr Col 67-. 9: ALA; SELA; PennLA; FlaLA. 10: Beta Phi Mu. 14: Ref. 15: 5500 SW 63rd ct, Miami Fl 33155.

MYERS, MARILYN S. b Manhattan Kan 29 Jl 44. 5: Kan StateU 62-66 (Hist) BA; UIll 66-68 (LS) MS. 6: Fr. 7: Acquis libn Wichita StateU 68-. 10: Beta Phi Mu; Phi Kappa Phi; Kappa Delta Pi. 15: Box 227, 4000 E 17th, Wichita Ks 67208.

MYERS, MILDRED (SOCHATOFF). b Pittsburgh Penn 11 F 43. 5: Carnegie-Mellon U 60-63 (Eng) BA; UPittsburgh 64-66 MLS, 66-67 (LS) Advanced Certif. 6: Fr. 7: Asst libn PPG Ind, Pittsburgh Penn 63-65; Tchg fellow GSLIS UPittsburgh 66-67; Libn Pittsburgh Br Fed Reserve Bank, Penn 67-. 9: SLA (chm Educ Com, Pittsburgh Chap 67-68); PennLA. 10: Beta Phi Mu. 13: Yes. 14: Catlg & clsf 9bus & fin libs), educ for libnship. 15: 5237 Fifth ave, Pittsburgh Pa 15232.

MYERS, MILDRED FONTAINE (PERKINS). b Liberty Mo 12 Jl 06. 4: John Edgar Myers Sr. 5: William Jewell Col 25-29 (Lat) AB; Kan State Tchrs Col (Emporia) 54-57 (LS) MS. 7: Tchr high sch dept Cotty Col 30-31; Tchr Purdy Rural High Sch, Purdy Mo 43; Asst libn William Jewell Col 52-54; Period libn Kan State Tchrs Col (Emporia) 57 57-. 9: ALA; KanLA; KanaSchL. 10: AAUW; Womens City Club, Emporia; La Sertoma; PEO. 14: Period (indexes). 15: 1232 Santa Fe Trail rd, Emporia Ks 66801.

MYERS, PAUL. b NYC 5 Mr 17. 4: Elizabeth Burke. 5: NYU 34-38 (Dramatic Art) BFA; Pratt 54-60 (LS) MLA. 6: Fr. 7: Theatre collection NY Pub Lib 45-, Act curator 65-67, Curator 67-. 9: TheatreLA. 10: Nat theatre conf. 12: Co-auth "A Guide to Theatre Reading. 13: Yes. 15: NY Pub Lib, 111 Amsterdam ave, New York NY 10023.

MYERS, ROSE E (HETHERINGTON). b Oakland Cal 16 D 28. 4: Ted Myers. 5: UWash (Seattle) 62-65 (Art hist) BA; UHawaii 66-67 MLS. 6: Sp. 7: Supv Pacific NW Bell, Seattle 53-60; Libn AID Far East Train Ctr, Honolulu 67; Ref libn UHawaii 67, Hd circ 68, Hd selection & search (acquis) 68-. 8: Tech abstractor, Hawaii Tech Info Ctr 68. 9: ALA; ASIS; HawaiiLA (sec). 10: Beta Phi Mu; Phi Kappa Phi. 12: Ed "Hawaii Library Assn Journal". 14: Acquis info sic. 15: 3232B Ahinahina pl, Honolulu Hi 96816.

MYERS, SARA FAY (LEE). b Shephersdville Ky 13 S 15. 4: Homer Lee Myers. 5: West Ky State Col 32-38 (Eng) AB; Catherine Spaulding Col 55-59 (LS) MS. 7: Tchr & libn 52-57; High sch libn Jefferson Co Bd, Louisville Ky 58-. 9: NEA; KyLA; KyEA; SELA. 10: Bullitt Co Homemakers. 13: Yes. 14: Catlg, ref. 15: Brooks Ky 40109.

MYNATT, ELOTIA (MOHR). b Victor Iowa 9 Je 08. 4: Robert S Mynatt. 5: Mankato State Tchrs 36-37 (Upper Elem); Drake U 42 Iowa Tchg Certif; UCLA 45; Wayne Stae U 53 (Upper Elem) BS, 65 MSLS. 6: Lat. 7: Rural tchr Dist 23, Bingham Lake Minn 28-30; Elem tchr pub sch, Bingham Lake Minn 37-41; Elem tchr pub sch, Maxwell Iowa 41-42; Elem deptl tchr pub sch, Nevada Iowa 42-43; Elem tchr Dist 4,

Dearborn Mich 43-54; Elem tchr pub sch, Allen Park Mich 54-61; Libn North Jr High, Allen Park Mich 61-63; Libn High Sch, Allen Park Mich 63-. 10: Alpha Delta Kappa. 14: Catlg, ref, yg ad serv. 15: 24712 Union ave, Dearborn Mich 48124.

MYRICE, MARY JANE. b Bowling Green Oh 6 Ag 37. 5: Bowling Green State U 55-59 (Elem Educ) BS in Ed; West Res U 60-61 MS in LS. 7: Elem tchr Anthony Wayne Local Schs, Whitehouse Ohio 59-60; Bkmob libn State Lib Serv Cente, Napoleon Ohio 61-67; Napoleon City Schs elem lib supv, Napoleon Ohio 67-. 9: NEA; OhioLA; OhioEA. 10: Soroptimist Fed. 14: Child serv, ref. 15: 1070 1/2 Willard, Napoleon Oh 43545.

N

NABORS, BIRDIE LOUISE. b Naborton La 20 S 08. 5: Mansfield Female Col 25-27 (Eng) AA; SMethodistU 27-29 (Eng) BA; Columbia 29-31 (Eng), 33-34 (LS) BS. 7: Tchr-libn Pelican High Sch, Pelican La 31-33; Reviser sch of Lib Serv Columbia U 34-35, Act head reviser 35-37, Asst browsing room Lib 36; Act libn Scarsdale High Sch, Scarsdale NY 37; Head catlg dept Brookline Pub Lib, Brookline Mass 37-39; Head circ dept LA Lib Commsn, Baton Rouge La 39-43; Libn Harding Field, Baton Rouge La 43-45; Asst libn & head catlg dept & ref Evans Signal Lab, Belmar NJ 45; Command libn Fifteenth AF, Colo Springs Colo 45-47; Command libn Air Materiel Command, Wright-Patterson AFB Ohio 47-48; Command libn Air Train Command, Randolph AFB Tex 58-. 8: Panel Mem, Interagency Bd, US Civil Serv Examiners of S Central Tex for Libns of the Air Force & Army; Adv mem, Marquis Biog Lib Soc. 9: ALA (Armed Forces Libns Sect; sec 48-49, Memb Com 51-53, Pub Rel Com 54-56, chm Nomin Com 59-60, v-pres, pres-elect & Ed of "Armed Forces Librarians Newsletter" 65-66, pres 66-67, Exec Bd 67-68); TexLA; SWLA (chm Info Co Conf 62); Bexar CoLA (pres 63-64). 10: Kappa Delta Alumnae Assn; Dayton City Panhellenic Assn; Dayton Coun of Womens Classified Serv Club; Zonta Club; Womens Gp of St George Episcopal Church. 14: Catlg & ref. 15: 7134 Blanco rd apt 211C, San Antonio Tex 78216.

NABORS, KENNETH L(EROY). b Affton Mo 24 Jl 30. 5: WashU (St Louis) 48-52 (Ger) AB; UMinn 53-56 (Ger) MA; UKiel (Germany) 56-57 (Linguistics); UIll 63-64 (LS) MS. 6: Ger. 7: Tchr Taylor Sch, Clayton Mo 57-58; Salesman Appleton-Century-Crofts, NYC 59-62; Ref asst pub lib, St Louis 62-63; Ref libn Wash U (St Louis) 64-68, Chief ref dept 69-. 8: Lect in Libnship, U Col, Wash U 66-67. 9: ALA; MoLA. 11: Fulbright Scholar (Kiel Germany). 14: Ref, bibliog. 15: Olin Lib Washington Univ, St Louis Mo 63130.

NACE, WILLIAM HOWARD. b Phila 27 S 29. 5: UPenn 53-56 (Nursing Educ) BS; Drexel 58-60 MS in LS. 6: Ger. 7: US Army Operating Room Tech (Cpl) 51-53; USAF Nurse-Supv (Capt) 56-58; Clinical instr surgery Penn Hosp Phila 59-60; Jr ref libn TempleU 60-61; Instr-libn Essex Co Hosp Cedar Grove NJ 62-64; Sch libn Morris Twp NJ; Hillcrest Ave Sch 64-67, Woodland Sch 67-68, Vail Sch 68-. 9: NEA; NJEA; NJSchLA. 10: ACLU; NJ Com for the Right-to-Read; USAF Reserve. 14: Catlg, ref, admin. 15: 22 Clover lane, Lincoln Park NJ 07035.

NACHOD, SALLIE E (CUMING). b 13 D 08. 4: Lewis P Nachod. 5: UMiss 26-30 (Fr) BA; UIll 31-32 (LS)BS. 6: Fr. 7: Eng tchr high sch, Piave Miss 30-31; Libn U High Sch, Oxford Miss 32-33; Tutor & Governess, Ygrande France 33-34; Chief file clerk Coun of Soc Agencies, New Orleans 35-36; Libn juvenile dept New Orleans Pub Lib 63-. 9: ALA; LaLA. 10: Delta Delta Delta. 14: Juvenile bks. 15: 2007 Palmer ave, New Orleans La 70118.

NACSIN, LORRAINE (CORNETTE). b Detroit Mich 16 My 25. 4: John Nacsin. 5: Albion Col 44-47 (Eng-Psych) AB; So Conn State Tchrs Col 55 (LS) BS. 6: Sp. 7: Libn NH State Hosp Med Lib, Concord NH 55; Libn Conn Mutual Life Ins Co, Hartford Conn 55-56; Libn Conn state Welfare Dept 57-59; Libn Conn State Highway Dept 59-. 9: SLA. 14: Ref. 15: 35 Canterbury st, E Hartford Ct 06118.

NADAL, ANTONIO. b Ponce PR 18 O 32. 5: Catholic U (PR) 49-54 (Educ) BA (cum laude); Columbia 56-58 MLS; UPR Sch of Law 65- (Law). 6: Eng, Sp. 7: Libn Catholic U (PR) 58-60, Prof 59-6; Staff NYPub Lib 60-61; Head Libn Supreme Ct of PR, San Juan 61-. 9: Sociedad de Bibliotecarios de Puerto Rico; AALL. 14: Ref (law) bks, civil law. 15: Commonwealth of Puerto Rico Supreme Ct of Puerto Rico Lib, San Juan PR 00903.

NADAS, ROSE J. Kecskemet Hungary. 5: UBudapest 32 Soc Sci) PhD. 6: Ger, Fr, Hungarian. 7: Libn C of C & Ind, Budapest Hungary 33-44; Libn UBridgeport Lib 51; Libn Gen Electric Co Lighting Research Lab, Cleveland 51-. 9: SLA. 15: Lighting Res Lab Lib, GE, Nela Park Cleveland 44112.

NAESETH, GERHARD (RANDT). b Valley City ND 14 Ap 13. 4: Milma Petrell. 5: Luther Col 30-34 (Hist) AB; UMich 34-36 ABLS, 36-39 AMLS, 39-40 (Hist); Okla StateU 47-48 (Hist). 6: Norwegian, Danish, Ger, Fr, Lat. , Gk. 7: Stud asst Luther Col 31-34; UMich (Ann Arbor): Asst grad reading room 34-35, Jr catlgr 35-36, Gen serv asst 36-37, Sr catlgr Law Lib 37-40; Assoc libn Okla StateU 40-48; Yeoman second class USNavy (Seabees) 43-46; Assoc dir UWis (Madison) 48-. 8: Lecturer World Conf on Recs, Salt Lake City 69. 9: ALA (Coun 49-53); WisLA; OklaLA. 10: Norwegian-Amer Hist Assn; Wis State Hist Soc; Ygdrasil Literary Soc; Phi Kappa Phi; NorwegianAmer Museum Exec Bd; AAUP. 12: "Naeseth-Fehn Family History (56). 13: Yes. 14: Tech serv, personnel, catlg, admin. 15: 4909 Sherwood rd, Madison Wi 53711.

NAFTALIN, MORTIMER LEWIS. b Fargo ND 13 N 21. 5: /02/39-46/03 6: Fr, Sp. 7: US Army 42-46; Jr libn UMinn 46-50; Lib asst in charge of for lang collection Minneapolis Pub Lib 50-51; Ref asst US Senate Lib, Wash DC 51-52; Libn Human Resources Research Off George Washington U 52-56; Asst chief research files archives sect Intl Bank for Reconstruction & Development, Wash DC 56-58; Nat Agric Lib, Wash DC Sel Off 59-62; Mem Task Force ABLE 62, Chief agency fld libs sect 62-64, Bibliog 64-66, Hist Programs Lib 66-. 9: SLA; DCLA. 12: Com; historic Books and Manuscripts Concerning General Agriculture in the collection of the National Agricultural Library (67); "Historic Books and Manuscripts Concerning Horticulture and Forestry in the Collection of the National Agricultural Library (68); Linneana in the Collection of the National Agricultural Library (68). 15: 2800 Quebec st NW, Wash DC 20008.

NAGORSKI, SANDRA JANE. b Cleveland 20 S 39. 5: Ursuline Col 57-61 (Chem & Eng) BS; West Res 61-63 MS in ls. 6: Fr. 7: Ref-circ Libn Cleveland Pub Lib 61-63; Hd ser ref Cleveland Health Scis Lib, 63-64, Asst hd libn 64-65, Hd acquis periods bind 65-69; Hd Veterinary Med Lib Iowa State U 69-. 10: Albertus Magnus Guild. 12: Ed "Selected List of Biomedical Serials in the Cleveland Area (69). 14: Ser, ref, circ, acquis. 15: 7413 Aetna rd, Cleveland Oh 44105.

NAGY, RUTH L (TANQUARY). b Severance Colo 13 O 16. 4: Joseph F Nagy. 5: Colo Col 35, 36, 38 (Fine Arts) BA; UCLA 36-37; UDenver BS in LS. 6: Sp, Fr. 7: Libn Englewood High Sch, Englewood Colo 39-40; Br libn Denver Pub Lib 40-41; Libn Keating Jr High Sch, Pueblo Colo 57-61; Libn Palmer High Sch, Colo Springs Colo 62-64; Libn & a-v Hinkley High Sch, Aurora Colo 65-68; A-v coord 68-69. 9: NEA; ColoLA (sec-treas So Div); ColoEA; ColoASchL. 14: Sch lib wk. 15: 1085 Fraser st, Aurora Co 80011.

NAHON, MARY RITA. b NYC 20 My 38. 5: Ladycliff Col 56-60 (Chem) BA; Columbia 67-69 (LS) MS. 6: Fr. 7: Lab tech RockefellerU 60-66, Libn asst 66-67, Asst libn 68-. 9: ACS; ALA. 10: Kappa Gamma Pi; Girl Scouts. 14: Catlg. 15: 446 E 85th st, New York NY 10028.

NAIRN, CHARLES E. b Columbus Ohio 26 Ag 26. 4: Margaret Prentiss. 5: Kent State 46-50 (Philos, Religion) BA, 50-51 (LS) MA; Oberlin Col Sem 53-58 (Bible, Theol) BD. 6: Fr, Ger, Gk, Hebrew, Lat. 7: USNavy -46; Ref asst in philos & religion div Cleveland Pub Lib 51-53; Ref & br libn Lorain Pub Lib, Lorain Ohio 55-60; Head Libn Upper Iowa U 60-64; Head Libn Findlay Col 64-68; Lib dir (rank of Assoc Prof) Lake Superior State Col 68-. 8: Instr of philos, Upper Iowa U 60-64; Organ mem, NWest Ohio Acad Libns 64-68. 9: ALA; MichLA; Midwest Acad Libns Assn; Amer Philos Assn; Amer Soc for Aesthetics; Assn Asian Studies; Bible Soc Amer; Renaissance Soc Amer; Soc Bibl Lit. 10: Amer Acad Rel; Fellowship of Rel Humanists; AAUP; NAACP; Mich Acad of Sci, Arts & Letters; Boy Scout Leader. 13: Yes. 14: Col & univ lib admin, a-v serv, lib automation, readers serv, ref, rare bks, spec collections. 5 15: 812 Summit st, Sault Ste Marie Mi 49783.

NAKADA, FRANK SHOZO. b Tottori Japan 10 N 31. 4: Ayako Yoshioka. 5: UMo 56-58 (Eng) MA; Columbia 6-61 MLS. 6: Japanese, Chinese, Fr. 7: Asst libn Metropolitan Museum of Art NY 61; Assoc libn UNLib 62-. 9: ALA; SLA. 14: Catlg, indexing. 15: 4 Dartmouth st, Forest Hills NY 11375.

NAKAMAE, EMIKO (HIRANO). b Hilo Hawaii 12 Ag 30. 4: Stanley A Nakamae. 5: UHawaii 48-52 BS in LS; UMinn 52-53 BS in LS. 7: Asst child libn Hawaii Pub Lib, Hilo 53-66, Ext libn 66-. 9: ALA; HawaiiLA. 15: 1788 Waianuenue ave, Hilo Hi 96720.

NALL, BETTY (REED). b White Mills Ky 19 Ag 39. 4: Donald Nall. 5: West State Col 57-60 (LS) AB. 7: Elem libn Dependent Sch, Ft Knox Ky 60-. 9: NEA; KyEA (4th Dist LA); KyLA; KyASchL. 15: Rte 2, Rineyville Ky 40162.

NAMENWIRTH, SIMON MICHAEL. b Hillegersberg Netherlands 8 S 34. 4: Hester Beatrix Meurs. 5: Muzieklyceum of Amsterdam 53-58 (Mus) MA; UMinn 58-61 (Musicology) PhD; Simmons Col 66-68 (LS) MS. 6: Dutch, Ger, Fr. 7: Instr IndU (Indianapolis) 65-66; Specialist in bk selection Harvard Col Lib 66-. 9: Amer Musicol Soc; Amer Soc for Aesthetics. 12: "Twenty Years of Schoenberg Criticism; Changes in the Evaluation of Once Unfamiliar Music" (64); "Divertiment for Toys and Orchestrea" (68). 13: Yes. 14: Acquis, admin. 15: 271 Concord ave, Cambridge Ma 02138.

NANCE, BETTY L. b Nashville Tenn 29 O 23. 5: TrinityU 53-57 (Eng) BA; UMich (Ann arbor) 57-58 AMLS. 7: Hd acquis dept Stephen F Austin State Col 58-59; Hd libn 1st Nat Bank of Ft Worth 59-62; Hd catlg dept TrinityU 62-65; Hd tech processes UTex Law Lib (Austin) 65-66; Hd catlg dept Tex A&MU 66-. 10: Alpha Lambda Delta; Alpha Chi. 14: Tech proc. 15: 904 Park pl, College Station Tx 77840.

NANGLE, SISTER CATHARINE MARIA. b Paduach Ky. 5: Nazareth Col (Bardstown Ky) (Music) AB; Catherine Spalding Col (LS) MS. 7: Med libn S S Mary & Elizabeth Hosp, Louisville Ky 63-68; Med libn St Joseph Hosp Lexington Ky 68-. 9: MedLA; ALA; CathLA; KyLA. 15: 1400 Harrodsburg rd, Lexington Ky 40504.

NAPIER, PAUL A. b Louisville Ky 1 Ja 11. 4: Marion Davis. 5: ULouisville 28-32 (Eng) BA; AmericanU 57-61 (Eng) MA; CatholicU 61-62 MS in LS. 6: Fr, Ger. 7: Spec agent Fed Bur of Investigation, Wash DC 41-61; Ref libn Arlington Co Pub Lib, Arlington Va 62-65; Head of ref AmericanU Lib 65-67, Hd of catlg 67-68; Spec Collections catlgr George Washington U Lib 68-. 8: Deciphered shorthand diary of Christopher Gadsden, delegate from SC to the First & Second Continental Congresses. 9: DCLA; VaLA. 10: Beta Phi Mu. 14: Ref, cryptanalysis, rare bks, catlg. 15: 3600 N Woodstock st, Arlington Va 22207.

NARODE, PATRICIA (MALLON). b NYC. 4: George H Narode. 5: Barnard 59-63 (Natural Sci) BA; Pratt Inst 63-64 MLS. 7: Trainee Brooklyn Pub Lib, Brooklyn NY 63-64, Adult serv libn 64-65, Tele ref libn 65-67, Asst br libn 67-68; Asst in pub lib serv Div of Lib Development, Albany 68-. 9: ALA; NYLA; NY Lib Club. 14: Ref, adult serv. 15: 41 S Main ave, Albany NY 12208.

NARTKER, BROTHER RAYMOND H (SM). b Dayton Ohio 11 Ap 20. 5: UDayton 39-43 (Soc Studies) BA; West Res summers 51-55 MS in LS; UHawaii Summer Inst 68 (LS). 07: High sch tchr Cincinnati, PR & Cleveland 43-51; Tchr-libn High Schs, Pittsburgh, Mineola, NY & Cleveland 51-62; Dir of Libs UDayton 62-. 8: Com of the Cath Suppl to the "Standard Catalog for High School Libraries" 61-62. 9: ALA; CathLA (chm High Sch Sect 60-61); OhioLA. 10: AAUP. 12: Ed "Newsletter of the High Sch Sect of the Cath Lib Assn" 60-61. 13: Yes. 14: Bk acquis, ref, admin. 15: Univ of Dayton 300 College Park, Dayton Ohio 45409.

NARY, LINDA LEE. b Pittsburgh Pa 3 Je 46. 5: Millersville State Col 64-68 (LS) BS. 6: Sp, Fr. 7: Libn E Deer Sch Dist Edera High 68-. 9: ALA. 15: RD 2 Star rd, Cheswick Pa 15024.

NASEER, SYED MOHD MR. b Patna India 3 Je 38. 5: Aligarh MuslimU (India) 5256 (Eng, Econ, Pol Sci) BA, 56-58 (Pol Sci) MA; McGill 60-62 (Pol Sci) MA, 64-65 BLS. 6: Eng, Urdu, Hindi. 7: Jr news writer Can Nat Rys Montreal 62; Lecturer in Pol Sci Aligarch MuslimU (India) 63; Sr indexer of documents Can Nat Rys, Montreal 63-64; Libn Centre for Div Area Studies McGillU 65-68, Lib acquis McGill U Lib Syst 69-. 10: Royal Commonwealth Soc. 11: Alexander Mackenzie Fellowship. 14: Bibliog on developing areas, bk sel, admin. 15: Centre for Devel Areas Studies McGillU, Montreal Canada.

NASH, ELLEN (PERRINE). b Maysville Ky 7 D 17. 4: Robert C Nash. 5: UKy 36-40 (Fr, LS) AB, 66 MS in LS. 7: Sch libn Fayette Co Bd of Educ, Lexington Ky 40-43; Libn Army Map Serv, Wash DC; Libn US Army Spec Serv, Stuttgart Germany; Libn Fayette Co Bd of Educ, Lexington Ky 59-62; Libn chem-physics UKy 63-. 9: SLA. 10: AAUP. 15: 336 Linden walk, Lexington Ky 40508.

NASH, NORMAN FREDERICK. b Brockton Mass 18 Ap 36. 5: Harvard 54-60 (Latin Lang & Lit) AB; Rutgers 63-64 MLS. 6: Lat, Fr. 7: Asst filing div catlg dept Harvard Col Lib 58-60; Tchr, Lat & Eng Franklin High Sch, Fraklin High Sch, Franklin Mass 60-63; Assoc libn I Gen Ref Room McKeldin Lib UMd 64-, Ser catlgr 67; Circ libn UIll (Urbana) 67-69, Rare bk libn 69-. 9: ALA-ACRL; -RDS. 14: Ref, bk sel, lib arch. 15: 1605 Valley rd, Champaign Il 61820.

NASH, RICHARD M. b Pittburg Kan 2 F 35. 4: Anna L McCollum. 5: UMo (Kansas City) 60-63 (Hist, Govt) BA; UDenver 64-65 (LS) MA. 6: Fr. 7: Sales corr Buttler Mfg Co, Kan City Mo 55-56; Personnel admin spec US Army, France 56-58; Sales corr Buttler Mfg Co, Kan City Mo; Soc sci ref asst Kan City (Mo) Pub Lib 62-63; Acquis libn UKan Med Ctr Lib 63-64, Asst catlgr 65, Catlgr & act libn 66-67; Asst libn M S Hershey Med Ctr Lib 67-. 9: MedLA. 12: Asst ed M S Hershey Med Ctr "Serials Catalog" (2nd ed 69). 14: Catlg, acquis, admin, data proc applications. 15: 11 Chevy Chase Briarcrest Gardens, Hershey Pa 17033.

NASH, WILLIAM VERLIN. b OGDEN Utah 7 S 28. 4: Lorene Munk. 5: Weber Col 46-48 AS; Brigham Young U 48-50 (Eng) BA; UIll 56-57 (LS) MS, 59-64 (LS) PhD. 6: Ger. 7: Libn Snow Jr Col 50; Battalion clerk USArmy, Ft Riley Kan 50-52; Missionary LDS Church, WGermany 53-55; Circ libn Brigham YoungU 57-58, Phys sci libn 58-59; Circ asst UIll (Urbana) 59-61, Bkstacks libn 61-64; Assoc dir of libs UUtah 64-66; Asst dir of libs UWash 66-68, Assoc Prof Lib Sch 68-. 9: ALA (chm LOMS 69-70). 10: Beta Phi Mu. 13: Yes. 14: Admin, automation, readers serv, lib research. 15: 19251 Ashworth N, Seattle Wa 98133.

NASHOLM, CLARA E. b Portland Ore. 5: UOre 33-37 BA, 39 (LS) Certif. 6: Swedish. 7: Stud asst UOre Lib 35-36; Eugene Pub Lib, Eugene Ore: Stud asst 36-37, Lib asst 37-39, 40-44, Asst libn 44-49, City ibn 50-. 9: ALA; PNLA (chm Cir div 63-65, Coun 7 exec Com 64-65); OreLA (sec 57-58, chm 2 coıns 63-65). 10: Zonta Internat; Eugene Fortnightly Club; Mu Phi Epsilon; AAUW; State Assn UOre Women; Bus & Prof Women. 14: Admin, ref. 15: Eugene Pub Lib 100 W 13th ave, Eugene Ore 97401.

NATALE, SAVERIO FRED(ERICK). b Connellsville Penn 17 Ag 38. 5: St Vincent 55-58 (Phil); St Mary's (Baltimore) 58-59 (Philos) AB, 59-60 (Theol); UPittsburgh 64-65 MLS. 6: Ital, Sp. 7/ clk US Post Off, Wash DC 60-61, 64, Clk Sp/4 USA, Ft jackson SC 61-63; Asst libn Monessen Pub Lib, Monessen Penn 65-. 9: ALA; PennLA. 10: Beta Phi Mu. 14: Catlg, admin. 15: 164 N 10th st, Connellsville Pa 15425.

NATH, HERBERT THOMAS. b Pittsburgh Pa 24 Mr 36. 4: Leatha Sykes. 5: IndStateU 54-58 (Soc Studies) BS; Penn State 58-62 (Hist); Drexel 62-64 MS in LS. 7: Grad asst Penn state (Univ Park) 61-62; Admin asst Drexel Lib 62-64; Ref libn Citadel 64-. 9: SCLA. 14: Ref. 15: Citadel Lib, Charleston SC 29409.

NATKIN, SADIE M(ARON). b NYC 3 O 07. 5: UHartford 57 (Lib Arts) BA; So Conn State Col 61 MSLS; Permanent Pub Libn's Certif for NY State; Certif in Med Libnship from MedLA. 7: Libn NY State Psychiatric Inst & Hosp, NYC 26-29, Sec to Dir 29-44; Med libn New Britain Gen Hosp, New Britain conn 46-63; Sr instr libn Al Prince Sch, Hartford Conn 63-. 8: Consul New Britain Gen Hosp, New Britain Conn 63-64. 9: Conn State Employees Assn; Instrs' Org (vocational sch Conn). 10: AAUW. 13: Yes. 14: Med & tech libnship. 15: 52 Federal st, West Hartford Conn 06110.

NATUSHKO, FRANCES ANNE. b Detroit 21 Ag 32. 5: Wayne State 51-53 (Educ, LS) BS; UMich 57-59 AMLS, 61-65 (Guidance, Counseling) AM. 6: Ukrainian. 7: Page & clerk Detroit Pub Lib 48-52; Staff Detroit Pub Schs 3-64; Staff summer 62-63; Libn Grosse Ponte High Sch, Grosse Pointe Mich 64-, Lib coord S High Sch 66-68, Lib coord N High Sch 68-. 8: Critic Lbn for Wayne State U 55-64; Adv wk for evaluation forms used with stud tchrs at Wayne State U 62-63; Lib Sci TV Program; Detroit Bd of Educ. 9: ALA; MichLA. 10: Ukrainian Womens Club; Womens City Club of Detroit. 11: Bk Sel Citation, Detroit Bd of Educ. 14: Young Adult wk. 15: 28225 Hughes, St Clair Shores Mi 48081.

NAYLOR, LEWIS C. b Osbornes Mills WVa 18 Ag 14. 4: Beatrice Blair. 5: Marshall U 31-33; Kent State 38-46 (Pol Sci) AB; West Res 47 BS in LS. 6: Fr, Ger. 7: Agent Nat Life

Insurance Co, Canton Ohio 36; Tester Hercules Motors Inc, Canton Ohio 37; Bk Trailer driver Canton Pub Lib, Canton Ohio 38-42; Armed Forces Army of the US 44th Inf Div ETO (1st Sgt, Europe 42-45; Head ext serv Canton Pub Lib, Canton Ohio 45-51; Chief Libn Muncie Pub Lib, Muncie Ind 51-55; Dir Cuyahoga C Lib, Cleveland 55-. 8: Consul Sch of Lib Sci, West Res U 55-; Lecturer, 63-65; Consul Canton Pub Lib 64; Adv Bd Ohio State U (Lakewood Acad Center); Adv bd Cuyahoga Commun Col 67-69; lect sch of Lib Sci, Kent State U 69; Consul other pub libs. 9: ALA (Life mem, mem 5 coms); IndLA (2 coms); OhioLA (pres 63, Bd Dirs 60-63, chm &/or mem var coms). 10: Lib Club of Metropolitan Cleveland; Ohio Lib Found; Cleveland Commsn on Higher Educ; Cleveland Metropolitan Serv Com; Kiwanis Club; Vocat Planning com, Welfare Fed of Cleveland. 11: Bronze Star, US Army ETO. 12: Ed & comp "To the County Line (54). 13: Yes. 14: Admin, bldgs, contract serv, devel programs. 15: Cuyahoga Co Lib, 4510 Memphis ave, Cleveland Oh 44144.

NAYLOR, MURIEL ALLEGRA. b Newton Mass 20 Ap 06. 5: Keuka Col 25-29 (Biol) BS; Simmons 30-31 (LS) BS. 6: Ger, Fr, Ital. 7: Asst Fre Pub Lib Newton, Mass 22-24, 30-31; Head-circ head-documents UConn 31-40; Chief legis ref dept Conn State Lib 40-58; Dept head bus-ind-sci Providence Pub Lib 58-60; Lbn Hartford Hosp Sch of Nursing, Hartford Conn 61-. 9: NELA (rep-at-large 57-58); CONNLA (treas 41 rep-at-large 45-50); Greater Hartford Libns Club. 10: LWV; AAUW; Conn League for nursing. 13: Yes. 14: Ref, admin. 15: 294 Collins st, Hartford Conn 06105.

NDENGA, VIOLA (WATSON). b Manning Ark 1 Ag 33. 4: Muga Abner Ndenga. 5: Philander Smith Col 53-57 (Home Econ) BS Iowa State Col 57 (Nutrition); UWash 59 (LS) ML. 6: Fr. 7: Receptionist-caterist Philander Smith Col 54-57; Girl supv Camp coun, Rockford Ill 58; Clerk UWash Lib 59-62; Ref libn-a-v coordinator, Lewis & Clark Col 62-63; Ref libn UWash Lib 63-67; Instr, Ref libn UMinn (St Paul) 67-. 8: Wash State UN Cult Affairs Chm, Seattle 65-66. 9: ALA; PNLA; WashLA; MinnLA. 10: AAUP; AAUW; NAACP; Alpha Kappa Mu. 14: Admin, ref. 15: 512 11th ave SE, Minneapolis Mn 55414.

NEAFIE, NELLE BLACKMER (JONES). b Iowa. 5: Ward-Belmont 27-28; Northwestern 28-29; Iowa Wesleyan 62 (Humanities) BA; West Ill 62-63 (Eng) MA; UKy 63-64 MS in LS. 7: Adult serv Bridgeport Pub Lib, Bridgeport Conn 64-66; Adult serv Cedar rapids Pub Lib, Cedar Rapids Iowa 66; Area consul Seven Rivers Lib Syst, Iowa City 67-. 9: ALA; WEA; IowaLA. 13: Yes. 14: Lib devel. 15: 1025 N Summit, Iowa City Ia 52240.

NEAL, FRANCES (POTTER). b Strong Ark 27 O 05. 5: UArk 45 (Hist) AB; UDenver 49 (LS) MA. 7: Tchr Pub Sch, El Dorado Ark 24-31; Libn Elem Sch, Warren Ark 41-47; Circ libn ref libn Ark Lib Commsn, Little Rock Ark 47-51, Exec sec 52-. 9: ALA (Coun 51-); ArkLA (pres 50); SWLA (pres 65-66). 10: AAUW; Bus & Prof Womens Club; Kappa Delta Pi; Delta Kapa Gamma. 11: Progressive Farmer Woman of Year Award 56; Ark Woman of the Year, Democrat Award 57. 12: Bus mgr ArkLA publ. 13: Yes. 14: State lib, pub lib, child serv. 15: 108 Brown st, Little Rock Ark 72205.

NEAL, JANETTE L. b Bloomington Ill 4 Ja 44. 5: Quincy Col 62-65 (Hist) BA; West Res 65-66 MSLS. 6: Sp, Ger. 7: Libn I Free Lib of Phila 66-. 9: ALA; PennLA. 14: Ref. 15: 2228 Wallace st, Philadelphia Pa 19130.

NEAL, JOAN BURKES (MILLIE). b Phenix City Ala 27 F 28. 4: Ray Verlin Neal. 5: UGa 47-51 (Recreation) BSEd, 65-67 T-4 & Libn certif. 6: Sp. 7: Dir First Baptist Kindergarten, Fayetteville Ga 60-63; Teacher Fayette Co Bd of Educ, Fayetteville Ga 63-66; Libn Fayetteville Elem Sch 66-. 9: GaEA (treas, chm 6th Dist Libns 69-71). 10: PTA; UGa Alum Assn; Fayetteville Garden Club. 14: Child bks. 15: RFD 2, Fayetteville Ga 30214.

NEAL, LOIS SMATHERS. b Canton NC 18 F 12. 4: James B Neal Sr. 5: Duke 33 (Hist, Eng) AB; UNC 39 AB in LS. 7: Libn Waynesville Twp High Sch, Waynesville NC 40-46; Asst re libn UNC (Greensboro) 46-49; Asst libn Thomas Jefferson Sr High Sch, Roanoke Va 53-56; Libn Hayes, Seay, Mattern & Mattern, Architects Engnrs, Roanoke Va 58-59; Ref libn NC State Lib 59-67; Libn Alexander Co Lib, Taylorsville NC 67-. 8: Org: Church Lib, Salem Va 52; Nurs Sch Lib, Roanoke Va 57. 9: ALA; SELA; VaLA; NCLA; VaEA; NCEA. 10: AAUW; Bd Trustees, NC State Lib. 14: Ref, NCaroliniana. 15: 924 4th st dr NW, Hickory NC 28601.

NEAL, MARY JEANNE (SCRIMGER). b Pekin Ill 6 F '6. 4: J Lawrence Neal. 5: Ill Wesleyan U 24-28 (Eng) AB; UIll 30-31 BS in LS. 7: Catlgr Agric & mech Col of Tex 30-43; Asst Sgt Major Port Battalion, New Orleans 44-45; Libn Bremen Port Command, Bremen Germany 45-46; Ser & REF LIBN Bradley U 46-47; Catlgr Howard Payne Col 47-48; Catlgr UAla 48-50; Ser libn UHouston 50-. 9: Mod Lang Assn; TexLA (Dist 5); SWLA; Tex Assn of Col Tchrs. 10: AAUP. 15: 3711 Florinda, Houston Tx 77021.

NEAL, MILDRED (GOGDELL) MRS. b Crowell Tex 30 D 07. 5: Baylor U 25-29 (Hist) BA; Sul Ross STATE Col summer 32 (Eng); UColo summer 34, 36, 56; Nat UMex summer 38; USoCal summer 39 (Hist); UTex summer 44 (Health, Phys Educ): UDenver summers 45, 47 BS in LS; Highlands U summer 51 (Psych); UNev summer 54 (LS); Colo West Col summer 59 (LS); NMState Col (Carlsbad) summer 64 (Reading). 6: Sp. 7: Prin Co Schs, Crowell Tex 29-34; Tchr Crowell High Sch, Crowell Tex 34-42; Tchr-libn Eunice High Sch, Eunice NM 42-45; Libn Sr High Sch, Carlsbad NM 45-. 8: Consul & catlgr NM StateU (Carlsbad) 50-. 9: ALA; NEA; Classroom Tchrs Assn; NMLA (past treas; chm Child & YP Sect); NMEA (past chm Lib Sect); Pecos Valley LA (past pres); NMClrTA. 10: Altrusa; Knife & Fork; Wesleyan Serv Guild; Delta Kappa Gamma; NM Lib Devel Coun. 14: Sch lib. 15: 1001 W Blodgett, Carlsbad NM 88220.

NEAL, ROBERT LOUIS. b Stewartstown Penn 5 F 26. 4: Evelyn Snyder. 5: Gettysburg 46-49 (Bio) AB; Univ Ext Schs 56-62 (Engring); Drexel 64-66 MS in LS. 6: Fr. 7: Radioman 3rd class USN, USS Sigsbee 44-46; Engring asst Rehrig Radio Sch & Lab Inc, Baltimore 49-52; Process engr Aircraft-Marine Prods Co, Glenrock Penn 52-54; Prod foreman Nat Biscurt Co, Phila 54-56; Ind engr mgt serv dept Phila Gas Wks 56-60, Tech asst to mgr customer rel dept 60-61, Asst mgr tele serv dept 61-63; Exec dir Kingston (NY) Area Lib 66-68; Dir Allegargy Co (Md) Lib Syst 68-. 9: ALA; Soc Advancement Mgt; Amer Inst Indus Engrs; MdLA; NYStateLA. 10. Lions Club. 13: Yes. 14: Admin. 15: 31 Washington st, Cumberland Md 21502.

NEASE, PAULINE (LIGON). b Durham NC 30 Ja 27. 4: Felton R Nease. 5: Duke 45-49 (Educ) AB, summers 55-56 (Educ); UNC (Chapel Hill) 66, spring 67, summer 56 (LS). 6: Fr. 7: Bio-forestry libn DukeU 49-50; Lib asst Oak Ridge Pub Lib, Oak Ridge Tenn 51-52; Tchr Ayock High Sch, Cedar Gorve NC 52-56; Instr bio dept Lovisburg Col 58-60; Subj catlgr Perkins Lib DukeU 56-57, 65, Supv bindery unit & ser 65-67, Act hd ser dept 67-. 9: NCLA. 10: Phi Beta Kappa; Kappa Delta Pi; Tau Psi Omega; AAUW. 14: Tech proc (esp ser wk). 15: 1010 Rosehill ave, Durham NC 27705.

NEBEHAY, ELISABETH H(OFFMANN). b Pecs Hungary 7 Jl 21. 5: UGraz (Austria) 40-45 (Philol,LS) PhD; UCal (Berkeley) 57-58 MLS. 6: Ger, Fr, Hungarian, SerboCroatian. 7: Tchg asst & libn Slavic dept UGraz (Austria) 43-45; Asst for Press & politics Brit Mil Govt Graz Austria 45-50; Research asst UCal Lib Sch (Berkeley) 57-58; Intern in Admin UCal Lib (Berkeley) 58-59; Exch libn NY Pub Lib 59-60; Head ser records dept UChicago Lib 60-62; Chief acquis dept UNLib 62-. 9: Assn of Internat Libs; v-pres 64-67; ALA-ACRL; subj spec sec, Slavic & East European subsect; chm nomin com 65-66; -RTSD; mem of a ser sect com 64-65; Internal Rel Com 69-; -Internat Rel Round Table; NYLib Club; NYTech Serv Libns (chm Prog Com 67-68; v-pres 68-69, pres 69-70). 13: Yes. 14: Acquis, bibliog, lib educ, compar libnship. 15: 320 E 52 st, New York NY 10022.

NEBLICK, GLADYS ANN (STYDUHAR). b Walsenburg Col 8 S 26. 4: James J Neblick. 5: Mt St Scholastic Col 44-48 (Eng) BA; Adams State Col summer 54; UDenver summers 55-58 (LS) MA. 7: Jr high soc studies tchr Pub Sch Walsenburg Colo 48-49; High sch tchr-libn pub sch, Pagosa Springs Colo 49-55; Elem sch tchr libn pub sch Dist 60, Pueblo Colo 55-58, High sch libn 59-. 9: NEA; (life mem); ColoLA (sec); ColoAssn SchL; ColoEA (pres, v-pres & sec Lib Sect); PuebloEA. 14: Sch libs, catlg, ref. 15: 2002 Ridgewood lane, Pueblo Colo 81004.

NECKER, WALTER L(UDWIG). b Hamburg Germany 27 D 13. 5: UChicago (Zool) BS, 47-52 (LS). 6: Ger. 7: Curator & Libn Chicago Acad of Sci, Chicago Ill 30-39; Rare bk asst Barnes & Noble, NY 40-41; Vertebrate zool USNR-NAMRU 2, Pacific Theater 42-45; Catlgr chief Chicago Hist Soc 54-56; Ref libn Gary Pub Lib, Gary Ind 57-58; Chief lib br Food & Cont Inst Armed Forces, Chicago 59-63; Libn-curator Wood Lib Mus of Anesthesiology, Park Ridge Ill 63-66; Bio-med libn UChicago 67-. 8: Consul USAMEDS Veter Sch Lib Chicago 62-; Vis Prof, Hist of Anesthesiology, U Mainz (Germany) summer 69-. 9: Internat Assn of Agric Libns & Documentalists

Internat Soc Hist Pharm; Schw Ges Med & Naturwiss; Soc Study of Alchemy & Early Chem; Aslib; ALA; MedLA; Assn Hist Med; Amer Inst Hist Pharm; Hist Sci Soc; Soc Hist Tech; Am Museums; Gutenberg Ges. etc. 10: AAAS; Kennicott Club. 11: Carnegie Grant, Mexico 39; Fulbright grant UK 52-53. 12: Ed "Ichtherps 39-42; "Herpetologica (39-45). 13: Yes. 14: Bibliog, rare bks. 15: 1415 Hoffman ave, Park Ridge Il 60068.

NEDILA, KATHARINA (EDITH AGNES MOSSNER). b Berlin Germany 12 N 23. 4: Emil G Nedila. 5: Freie U (Berlin) 52-57 (Publizistik) Dr phil; Columbia (LS) MS. 6: Ger, Fr, Rumanian, Sp, Eng. 7: Sec-interpreter, Delagation Francaise de la main-doeuvre fr. en Allemagne, Berlin 43-44; Fre-lance writer Bundeskorrespondenz, Berlin Frankfort 59; Catlgr Yale U Law Sch 59-67, Catlg lib Beinecke Rare Bks & Mss Lib 67-. 12: "Henri Rochefort (59). 14: Rare bks. 15: 233 Country st, New Haven Conn 06511.

NEDS, ISAAC NOLAN. b Columbus Ohio 28 F 21. 5: Ohio State U 46-50 (Intl studies) BA; West Res 50-51 (LS) Masters; UWis 65 (Lib syst) Certif. 7: S Sgt Army Air Force, India & Burma 42-45; Repairman Ohio Bell Tel Co, Columbus Ohio 46; Lib asst Ohio State U (Columbus) 46-50; Libn I Milwaukee Pub Lib 51-54, Libn II 54-59, Libn III 59-64, Libn IV 64-65, Supv Neighborhood & ext serv 65-. 8: Exec dir Nat Lib Week, Wis; Chm Tech Adv Com, Wis Lib Survey (7 SEast Cos); Chm SEasE Wis Lib Conf. 9: ALA; Adult Educ Assn Wis; WisLA (Dir Bd of Trustees, chm Scholarship Com, Pub Rel Com); Chm Scholarship Comm WisLA; Chm Public relations Comm WisLA; Chm Local Arrangements Comm, Four State Conf; Chm Tech adv Comm - Seven Southeastern Countries, Wis Lib Survey; Chm SE Wis Lib Conf; Dir WisLA, Bd of Trustees. 10: ACLU; Milwaukee Coun for Adult Learning; Research Clearinghouse of Milwaukee; Milwaukee Area Soc for Pub Admin. 14: Serv to the disadvantaged handicapped, adult activities programming, library cooperation. 15: 2534 N Prospect, Milwaukee Wi 53211.

NEE, NANCY (MORROW). b Tulsa Okla 9 Mr 27. 4: Thomas f nee. 5: Conn Col 44-48 (Philos) AB; UCal(Berkeley) 61-62 MLS. 6: Fr. 7: Registration clerk NYU 50-54; Sec Ampex Corp, San Francisco 54-57; Sec Nederland Line-Royal Rotterdam Lloyd, San Francisco 58-59; Clerk McCuthen, Doyle, Brown & Enersen, San Francisco 59-61; Libn Lit Dept San Francisco Pub Lib 62-, Sr libn 66-69, Prin libn 69-. 8: Radio interviewer "Books and Authors Program, KNBR (San Francisco 64-; Admin asst to city libn 64. 9: UCal, Sch of Lib Alum Assn; San Francisco Pub Lib Staff Assn; San Francisco Symphony Assn. 10: Friends of The San Francisco Pub Lib; Beta Phi Mu; UCal, Sch of Lib Alum Assn; San Francisco Pub Lib Staff Assn; San Francisco Symphony Assn. 14: Ref, rare bks. 15: 4345 25th st, San Francisco Cal 94114.

NEEDHAM, JOHN (RALEIGH) Jr. b Livingston Tenn 27 Ja 40. 5: Tenn Tech 5862 (Eng) BA; Peabody 62-63 (LS) MA. 7: Pub serv libn Mccormick Lib Wash & Lee U 63-. 15: 203 Jackson ave, Lexington Va 24450.

NEELEY, MARY (ELIZABETH) SIMPSON. b Kan City Mo 24 S 12. 4: Joe Robert Neeley. 5: S Methodist 29-33 (Phys Educ) BS Life Certif for all grades; Tex Womans U 58-62 MLS; Ohio State Prof Certif. 6: Fr. 7: Elem tchr pub sch, Paris Tex 34-35; Phys educ elem sch, Gladewater Tex 35-37; Phys educ elem sch, Bishop Tex 56-61; Circ libn Tex Col of Arts & Ind, Kingsville Tex 61-63; Libn Gallia Acad High Sch, Gallipolis Ohio 64-. 8: Ordering Title II bks for City Sch System. 9: ALA; -AASchL; NEA; OhioEA; Ohio ASchL. 10: AAUW; Beta Phi Mu; Gamma Phi Beta; Womans Club. 14: Ref, circ. 15: Route 1 Sandy Heights, Point Pleasant WVa 25550.

NEELY, EUGENE TRAHIN. b Greenwood Miss 20 Ag 40. 5: Davidson Col 58-62 (Eng) AB; UNC 63-64, 66 (LS. 7: Stud asst Davidson Col Lib 60-62, Asst to ref libn summer 61; Br asst Pub Lib of Charlotte & Mecklenburg Co, Charlotte NC 62-63; Ref asst Pub Lib Charlotte NC 63, 64-65; Head ref sect Pub Lib, Charlotte NC 65-. 9: ALA; SELA; NCLA; MecklenburgLA. 10: Beta Phi Mu; Staff Org Pub Lib Charlotte & Mecklenburg Co. 12: Co-comp "Bibliography on Alcoholic Beverage Control Systems" (65). 14: Ref. 15: 310 N Tryon st, Charlotte NC 28202.

NEELY, JACK WILLIAM. b Cameroon W Africa 16 S 25. 4: Patricia Hays. 5: Ohio State U 47-50 (Soc Sci) BA; Kent State 46-47, 53-55 MALS. 6: Ger, Fr. 7: Pharmacist 3/C US Navy, USA & Pacific 43-46; Statistical qual Control b f goodrich Co Akron Ohio 51-53; Manager-chem Store Rooms Akron U 53-55; Circ libn Mich State U 55-57; Libn United Automobile Wkers, Detroit 57; ref asst Detroit Pub Lib 57-66; Catlgr UAkron 66-67; Senior research libn Firestone Tire & Rubber Co, Akron Ohio 67-. 9: SLA; ASIS; NEast Ohio Tech Proc Assn. 10: PTA. 13: Yes. 14: Ref. 15: 684 Glendora, Akron Oh 44320.

NEELY, JANE (REED). b Pittsburgh Penn 13 Ag 42. 4: Bruce A Neely. 5: WVaU 60-64 (LS) BS. 7: Clk WVaU Lib 63-64; Bkmob libn Carnegie Lib of Pittsburgh Penn 64-66, Br libn 66-. 15: 416 Caryl dr, Pittsburgh Pa 15236.

NEESE, JANET A. b Sheboygan Wis. 5: Milwaukee-Dower Col 51-55 (Home Econ) BS; UDenver 63-64 (LS) MA. 7: Admissions Coun Milwaukee-Downer Col 55-58; Serv rep Wis Telephone Co, Milwaukee 58-59; Asst buyer Gimbels Dept Store, Milwaukee 60-61; Lib asst Milwaukee Pub Lib 61-63; Stud asst UDenver 63-64; Libn Phoenix Pub Lib 64-66; Catlgr SUNY(Geneseo) 66-67, Lib Sch libn 67-. 9: ALA. 10: AAUW. 14: Ref, lib educ, catlg. 15: 125 Main st, Mt Morris NY 14510.

NEFF, EVALINE (LUCY) B(LANCO). b Madison Wis 18 My 23. 4: Louis E Neff. 5: West Res 43-45; Rosary Col 46-49 BLS; Mexico City Col 49-51 (Latin Amer Studies) MA; NYU 56 (Practice of Publ); Rutgers summer 60 (Abstracting & Indexing); Columbia summer 63 (Public Relations Wkshop). 6: Fr, Sp. 7: X-ray Tech WAC Med Corps, US Army T/5 44-46; Gen asst Denver Pub Lib 51-52; Patients libn Bronx VA Hosp, Bronx NY 52-55; Catlgr Manhattan Col 55-58; Ref libn Queensborough Pub Lib Queens NY 58-59; Catlgr Naval Train Device Center Lib Pt Wash NY 59-61; Dir Wayne Co Lib Systems & Ontario Cooperative Lib YSTEMS & Ontario Cooperative Lib System, Newark NY 61-67; Exec dir Rochester Reg Research Lib Coun Rochester NY 67-. 9: ALA; (per-to-per recr netwk); SLA; NYLA (Legis Com). 10: LWV. 14: Inter lib coop (Nat, reg & loc). 15: 29 Littlebrook dr, Pittsford NY 14534.

NEFF, MARY JANE (FOWLER). b Emporia Kan 16 Ag 29. 4: Leslie A Neff. 5: Kansas State Col summer 60 (Guidance (Ndea); Kansas State Tchrs Col 46-50 (Math, Soc Sci) BS in Educ, summers 55-59 (Educ (Guidance) MS in Educ, 61-66 (Educ) Specialist in Educ, MS in Libnship. 7: Tchr Valley Falls Rural High Sch, Valley Falls Kan 50-52; Tchr Ottawa High Svh, Ottawa Kan 52-59; Counselor Sr High Sch, Emoria Kan 59-64; Counselor asst Roosevelt High Sch - KSTC, Emproia Kan 64-66; Sch libn Butcher Child Sch, Kan State Tchrs Col, Emporia Kan 66-68; Asst catlgr WAW Memorial Lib Kan State Tchrs Col, Emporia Kan 68-. 9: KanLA. 10: Pi Lambda Theta; AAUW. 14: Catlg, child bks. 15: 1724 W Wilman ct, Emproia Ks 66801.

NEFF, REBECCA SUE. b Wheeling WVa 19 S 40. 4: Arthur F Neff Jr. 5: WVA Wesleyan Col 58-62 (LS) BS; West Res 63-64 MSLS. 6: Fr. 7: Jr high sch libn Ohio Co Schs, Wheeling WVa 62-63; Child libn Grosse Pointe Schs, Grosse Pointe Mich 64-. 9: ALA; MichLA; NEA; MichEA; Grosse Pointe EA. 14: Child & ya. 15: 1126 Lakepointe, Grosse Pointe Mi 48230.

NEFT, SISTER MARY AQUINAS, OSF. b Shooks Minn 14 D 29. 5: Mt Mary Col 49-50; Col of St Catherine 50-53 (LS) BS; Catholic U summers 63-68; MS in LS. (LS). 6: Ger. 7: Act libn St Clare Col 61-64; Tchr St Francis High Sch, Little Falls Minn 53-, Libn 54-. 8: Elem Sch Lib Org, Franciscan Sisters 53-58; Bd Dirs St Clare Resource Ctr Little Falls Minn 68-. 9: ALA; CathLA (Minn-Dak Unit); MinnLA. 13: Yes. 14: Wk with young adults. 15: St Francis High Sch, Little Falls Minn 56345.

NEGAARD, HARRIET ALLENE (JORDAN). b Clarinda Iowa 7 Jl 10. 4: Raymond Negaard. 5: Graceland Col 28-30 (Liberal arts, Educ) AA; Pepperdine Col 62-63 (Eng) BA; USoCal 64-65 MSLS. 7: Catlg libn Graceland Col Lib 64-65; Asst libn FAA West reg Lib, Los Angeles 65-66; Catlg libn System Development Corp, Culver City Cal 66-67; Ref libn Los Angeles Co Pub Lib, Hawthorne Cal 67-. 9: ALA; CalLA. 10: Nat Trust for Hist Preserv; Los Angeles Co Mus Allince; Hist Soc of Centinela Valley; SoCalHistSoc. 14: Catlg, ref. 15: 536 W Hillcrest blvd, Inglewood Ca 90301.

NEGRO, ANTOINETTE CARMELA. b Passaic NJ 12 O 33. 5: Fordham 51-55 (Soc Studies) BS Ed; Rutgers 56-58 MLS; West MichU 66-67 (Instr Materials) Ed Sp. 6: Ital, Sp. 7: Tchr St Cecilia High Sch, Englewood NJ 55-57; Libn Hanover Park High Sch, Hanover NJ 57-62; For serv libn USIA, Wash DC 62-63; Lib sci instr Trenton State Col, Trenton NJ 63; Libn Central Jr High Sch, Brooklawn Jr High Sch, Parsippany NJ 63-66; Lib sci instr Newark State Col 64-65; Grad asst West MichU 66-67; Media specialist Dept Educ Media & Tech Montgomery Co Pub Schs, Rockville Md 67-. 8: Lib sci instr West MichU summer 66. 9: ALA; NEA-DAVI; ASCD; Nat

Microfilm Assn; MdLA. 10: Beta Phi Mu. 14: Instr media & tech, info retrieval, computer applications. 15: 104 Second st, Hackensack NJ 07601.

NEHLIG, MARY (ELIZABETH). b Morton Penn 4 Ag 26. 5: Wilson Col 44-48 (Pol Sci) AB; Drexel 49-52 MS in LS. 6: Ger. 7: Drexel Inst of Tech; Circ asst 49-52, Ref asst 52-57, Bus libn 57-59, Bus & Soc Sci libn 59-63, Head ref libn 63-67; Asst dir of lib serv West Chester State Col (Penn) 67-. 9: ASIS; SLA; ALA; -ACRL; PennLA; spec libs Coun of Phila & Vicin (Sec 61-63, chm soc sci group 64-65, v-pres 66-67, pres 67-68; NEA. 13: Yes. 14: Ref, admin. 15: 945 Mitchell ave, Morton Pa 19070.

NEIDERHEISER, CLODAUGH M. b New Philadelphia Ohio 17 F 17. 5: Augsburg Col 41-44 Hist BA; UMinn 53 (Hist) MA. 7: Research asst Minn Hist Soc, St Paul 47-49, 52; Research asst UMinn (Minneapolis) 50-51; Research assoc Forest Hist Soc, St Paul 53-59; Libn Archives UMinn (Minneapolis) 60-63, Instr & libn 63-66, Instr & Asst archivist 66-. 9: SAA. 12: "Forest History Sources of the United States and Canada" (56); Assoc ed "Forest History" (57-59). 13: Yes. 14: Archives & hist mss. 15: 5409 29th ave SO, Minneapolis Mn 55417.

NEIGHBORS, KATHERINE (LANDISS). b Cumberland City Tenn 13 N 26. 4: Charles E Neighbors. 5: Peabody 44-48 (Bus Educ) BS, 63-65 MLS. 7: Tchr Forrest High Sch, Chapel Hill Tenn 48-56; Tchr Giles Co High Sch, Pulaski Tenn 56-58; Tchr Cornersville SCH, Cornersville Tenn 58-59; Tchr Lebanon Jr High Sch, Lebanon Tenn 59-63; Tchr Tenn Prep Sch, Nashville 63-64 Libn 64-. 9: ALA; TennEA; TennLA. 10: Nashville Lib Club; Alpha Delta Kappa. 14: Catlg, child bks. 15: Tenn Prep Sch Foster ave, Nashville Tn 37211.

NEIL, ALICE V. b Omaha Neb 29 S 10. 5: UChicago 27-31 (Hist) PhB; Carnegie Lib Sch 31-32 BS in LS; NorthwesternU 36-41. 6: Fr, Sp. 7: Libn/statistician Infilco, Chicago 33-35; Asst libn Ill Inst Tech 35-41; Libn research lib General Electric Co, Schenectady NY 41-62, Specialist ref info ctr Daytona Beach Fla 62-64, Tech libn Bay St Louis Miss 64-66; Libn Crummer Sch, Rollins Col, Winter Park Fl 66-. 8: Commsers com on ref & research lib resources, NY State 60-61; Chm Model Lib Proj Mainland Sr High Sch, Daytona Beach Fla 63-64. 9: SLA (chm Engring Sect 53-54; Sci-Tech Div; sec-treas 56-57, treas 58; Tr Com 59-61; pres West NY Chap 49-50); Hudson-MohawkLA (pres 60-62); NYStateLA; SELA; FlaLA. 10: AAUW; Schenectady Co Hist Assn. 12: Ed ""Doc Digest of Sci Tech News (61-62). 13: Yes. 14: Ref. 15: Rollins Coll, Winter Park Fl 32789.

NEIL, JOSEPHINE. b Nashville 9 N 16. 5: Ward-Belmont Col 35-37 Diploma; Peabody 37-39 Eng BS; 39-40 BS; in LS; UChicago 49 (Med Lib Admin). 6: Fr, Sp. 7: Ref asst Newark Pub Lib, Newark NJ 40; Med lib interne Orleans Parish Med Soc, New Orleans 40-41; Asst libn Vanderbilt U Med Lib 41-43; Chief libn Thayer Gen Hosp, Nashville 43-48; Chief libn Thayer Vet Hosp, Nashville 48-51; Command libn US Army Forces Antilles, San Juan PR 51-54; Command libn, Hdqrs Command US Army Europe, Germany 54-61; Dist libn Hq Sixth Naval Dist, Charleston SC 61-. 8: Dir nat lib week, SC. 9: ALA (Internat Rel RT, Nat Lib Week Com 68-70); -PLA (Nomin Com 67-68; Armed Forces Libns Sect; Nomin om 62, chm Sect Devel Com 63, v-pres 64-65, pres 65-66; mem Achievement Citation Com 67-); SCLA; SELA. 10: English speaking union so hist soc Charleston Natural Hist Soc Carolina Art Assn Carolina Bird Club; Kappa Delta Phi; Sigma Delta Pi; Pi Gamma Mu; Freedoms Foun (Valley Forge). 11: 4 awards for Lib publicity, US Army, Europe 54-56; Outstanding Performance Rating 66. 14: Lib, admin, publicity, pub rel. 15: Sereant Jasper Apts #9G, Charleston SC 29401.

NEILL, SAMUEL DESMOND. b Port Arthur Ont Can 17 My 28. 4: Mary Greive. 5: UToronto 45-50 (Hist) BA, 50-51 BLS. 7: Hd libn Long Br Pub Lib, Long Br Ont Can 51-54; Supv brs Cape Breton Reg, Cape Breton NS Can 54-56; Chief libn Teck Twp Pub Lib, Kirkland Lake Ont Can 56-62; Chief libn NEast Reg, Kirkland Lake Ont Can 59-62; Libn & tchr: Parry Sound High Sch, Parry Sound Ont Can 62-64, York Central Dist, Richmond Hill Ont Can 64-67; Assoc Prof Sch of Lib & Info Sci, Lond Ont Can 67-. 9: OntLA (chm Sch Lib div 69). 10: Sch Trustee: Kirkland Lake, Richmond Hill. 14: Sch & pub libs. 15: 1087 Richmond st, London Ont Can.

NEILSON, DOROTHEA (RYMAN). b Pittsburgh Pa 26 S 08. 5: Chatham Col 26-27; Conley sec Sch 27-28; UPittsburgh 39-46. 7: Receptionist Equitable Gas Co, Pittsburgh Penn 28-29; Asst libn Phila Co, Pittsburgh 29-32; Libn Alle Co Bd of Assistance, Pittsburgh 39-49; Libn Ketchum, MacLeod & Grove Inc, Pittsburgh 49-. 9: SLA (Pittsburgh Chap: chm Nomin Com, chm Hospitality Com; Bus mgr chap Bull). 14: Organ & catlg materials ref wk. 15: 50 Academy ave, Pittsburgh Pa.

NEITZ, CORDELLA MILLER. b Millersburg Penn 27 Mr 11. 4: John Donald Neitz. 5: Syracuse 27-31 BS In LS Susquehanna U 34-35 (Educ); Temple 64 (Educ), 68 (Educ) MS. 6: Fr, Ger, Lat. 7: Org sch libs Penn State Lib 33-34; Advanced file clerk Governors Off, Harrisburg Penn 35-36; Lib asst US Dept of Agric, Wash DC 36; Lib asst Penn State Col 37; Catlgr US Dept of State, Wash DC 37-40; Sr catlgr Columbia U 44-63; Head catlgr Dickinson Col 63-. 9: ALA; PennLA; Cumberland Valley LA; Area Col Lib Coop Prog of 5 Central Penn. 10: AAUP; Mary Dickinson Club; Metro Opera Guild. 14: Catlg & rare bks, col & univ libs, a-v. 15: 304 S Pitt st, Carlisle Penn 17013.

NEKRITZ, LEAH. b NYC 6 Ap 32. 4: Richard Nekritz. 5: Brooklyn Col 49-52 (Eng) AB. 6: Fr. 7: Libn Prince George's Commun Col 62-66, Dir lib serv 66-. 9: ALA; MLA (Com on Intell Freedom); Md Assn Jr Col (Learning Resources Div). 10: PTA. 14: Admin, instr. 15: 4702 Teak ct, Camp Springs, Wash DC 20031.

NELIUS, ALBERT A. b Memphis Tenn 9 D 25. 4: Sigrid von Renner Nelius. 5: SWest at Memphis 43, 48-51 (Philos) BA; Univ of the South 51-53 (Theol); Episcopal Theol Sem 53-54 BD; UNC (Chapel Hill) 68-69 MS in LS. 6: Fr, Ger. 7: Yeoman 2c USN USS Bainbridge 44-46; Bking clk Matson Navigation Co, San Francisco 47-48; Dir dramatics Univ of the South 52-53; Asst rector St George's Ch, Nashville 54-57; Vicar St Barnabas' Ch, Florissant Mo 57-60; Curate St Philip's Ch, Durham NC 60-67; Subj catlgr DukeU Lib 69-. 10: Durham Art Guild. 15: 3112 Sprunt ave, Durham NC 27705.

NELMS, LOUISE (PARMENTIER). b Westville Ill 15 S 21. 4: Benton C Nelms. 5: Peabody summers 60-63(LS) MA. 6: Fr. 7 Libn Pub Lib Danville Ill 58-61; Sch libn E Park Jr High Sch, Danville Ill 61-64; Sch libn Program Development for gifted Students, Danville Ill 64-65; Sch libn E Park Jr High Sch, Danville Ill 65-; TMC Ill State U summer 66; Hd libn Danville High Sch 66-. 9: NEA: IllEA; IllLA; IllASchL (chm Prof Rel Com); Danville EA. 10: PTA; Alpha Beta Alpha; Danville Hist Soc; AAUW; Delta Kappa Gamma, Ass secon Educ. 15: 913 Colfax, Danville Ill.

NELSON, BEATRICE (JEAN) (PARKER). b Yakima Wash 8 Ap 23. 4: Merlin W Nelson. 5: State U Idaho 41-42 (Eng); UPuget Sound 42-43 (Eng); UWash 43-44 (Gen); UUtah 59-60 (Hist) BS; UIdaho 64-66 (Hist, LS). 7: Child libn Coeur d'Alene Pub Lib, Coeur d'Alene Ida 61-64; Child asst Moscow Pub Lib, Moscow Ida 64-66; Humanities asst UIda Lib 65-66; Bkmob clk Latah Co Free Lib, Moscow Ida 66; Bkmob clk Moscow-Latah Co Lib Syst, Moscow Ida 67, Child libn 67-. 9: ALA; PNLA; IdaLA. 10: AAUW; Chi Omega; Phi Alpha Theta; Fac Women's Club UIdaho; Moscow Women's Bowling Assn. 14: Child serv. 15: 320 N Coarfield, Moscow Id 83843.

NELSON, DONALD (KOFOED). b Cedarville Ida 27 Je 15. 4: Vaudys Christensen. 5: Utah state U 38 (Accounting) BS; UDenver 46 BLS, 49 (Bus) MBA. 7: Circ libn Utah State U, 39-41; Libn Col of So Utah 41-50; Hd libn East Ore Col 50-61; Assoc libn Brigham Young u 61-67, Dir of libs 67-. 8: Vice-pres & pres of Bd, Bibliog Ctr for Research, Rocky Mountain Region. 9: ALA; MPLA; UtahLA (past pres); OreLA (treas); Utah Acad Sci, Arts & Letters. 10: AAUP; Kiwanis Club. 14: Univ lib admin. 15: 324 J Reuben Clark Jr Lib, brigham Young U, Provo Ut 84601.

NELSON, EDWARD CARL. b NYC 2 N 10. 4: Polly Post. 5: NYU 48 (Amer Hist) BS, 49 (Educ) MA; Pratt 50 (LS) MS. 7: J C Penny Co Buying Off, NYC 29-42; US Army Med Dept (Sgt) 42-45; NYPub Lib 50-55; Supv libn Bronx Ref Cente r 55-59; Supv libn Donnell Ref Lib 59-. 8: Chm, NY Pub Lib Staff Com 62-63; Consul NY State Lib 66-67. 9: ALA (Com on Wilson Period Indexer 68-); NYLA; NY Lib Club. 13: Yes. 14: Ref. 15: 42-25 Layton st, Elmhurst NY 11373.

NELSON, FREDEVA (MASSENGILL). b Upatoia Ga 15 N 36. 4: Edward Ellis Nelson. 5: Ft Valley State Col 54-58 (Eng) BS; Mich State U summer 59; Fla A & M U summers 61, 64; Atlanta U 66 (LS) MA. 6: Sp. 7: Eng tchr Kennedy High Sch, Riviera Beach, Fla 59-63, Libn 63-. 9: ALA; Palm Beach Co Tchrs Assn. 14: Sch libnship. 15: 664 W Fourth st, Riviera Beach Fl 33404.

NELSON, HESTER JOAN. b Eau Claire Wis 10 My 33. 5: Wis State U (Eau Claire) 51-55 (Eng) BS; UMinn summer 60; UDenver summer 65. 7: High sch libn Viroqua Area Schs, Viroqua Wis 56-. 9: NEA; ALA; WisEA (Lib Sect: chm Standards Com); WisLA; West WisEA (past chm Lib Sect). 10: ViroquaEA. 15: 322 E Jefferson, Viroqua Wis 54665.

NELSON, JAMES B(ARTON). b Hankow Hupei China 3 O 32. 4: Sharon McFall. 5: Augsburg Col 50-52 (Eng); UMinn 52-54 (Eng) BS, 54-55 (LS) MA. 6: FR. 7: Young Adult Libn Brooklyn Pub Lib 56; US Army 2d USA MSL; CMD Court Reporter, Ft Hood Tex SP 5 57-59; Libn Hastings State Hosp, Hastings Minn 59-62; Asst to libn Mayo Clinic, Rochester Minn 62-63; Dir Cattermole Mem Pub Lib, Ft Madison Iowa 63-66; Dir Cabell Co Pub Lib & West Cos Reg Lib Syst, Huntington WVa 66-. 9: IowaLA (chm RTSD 64; chm Intel Freedom Com 66); WVaLA (Exh chm 67-68, pres Pub Lib Sect 68-). 10: Rotary Club; Cof C. 13: Yes. 14: Admin & mgt, pub rel. 15: 1768 Crestmont dr, Huntington WV 25701.

NELSON, JEAN E. (OLSON). b Los Angeles 2 S 28. 4: William G Nelson. 5: Cal State Col (Los Angeles) 63-65 (Amer studies) BA; USoCal 65-66 MALS, 68- (Pub admin). 6: Ger. 7: Period & libn Whittier Pub Lib, Whittier Cal 66-68, Br libn Whittwood br 68-. 10: ALA; CLA; AAUW. 14: Admin. 15: 9403 S Klinedale ave, Downey Ca 90240.

NELSON, JOAN GAIL (CRUSE). b Wilson Ark 28 D 36. 4: John Terry Nelson. 5: Ark StateU 57-64 (Bio) BSE; Fla StateU 65-67 (LS) MS. 7: Tchr Lepanto Elem Sch, Lepanto Ark 61-63; Tchr & libn Keiser High Sch, Keiser Ark 64-66; Ref libn Dean B Ellis Lib Ark StateU 67-. 9: ALA; ArkLA; NEArkLA. 14: Ref, lib educ. 15: 1808 Broadmoor, Jonesboro Ar 72401.

NELSON, KAREN ANNE. b Boston 8 Ja 37. 5: St Olaf 54-58 (Eng) (Cum laude); ULondon summer 62 (20th Century Drama) Certif; UCal (Berkeley) 63-64 MLS; UMinn 66- (Scandinavian). 6: Ger, Danish. 7: Coun U Lutheran Stud Center Iowa State U 58-61; Tchr asst libn John Marshall High Sch, Rochester Minn 61-63; Libn Augsburg Amer High Sch, Augsburg Germany 64-65; Libn Anoka Elem Schs, Anoka Minn 66-67; Libn Kerlan Collection UMinn 67-; Tchr child lit USask summers 66, 67. 8: Storytelling seminar, Minneapolis. 9: ALA. 11: Stipend Internat Youth Lib, Munich Germany 65. 13: Yes. 14: Hist child bks, Danish child bks, contemporary illustration. 15: Kerlan Collection Walter Lib Univ of Minn, Minneapolis Mn 55455.

NELSON, LARSANA LEE. b Cottage Grove Ore 4 Je 40. 5: Willamette 58-62 (Eng) BA; Claremont Grad Sch 62-64 (Eng) MA; UOre 68-69 MLS. 6: Fr, Ger. 7: Lib asst UCal (Santa Barbara) 64-68; Catlgr NorthwesternU 69-. 14: Catlg. 15: Main & River, Cottage Grove Or 97242.

NELSON, M HELEN ANN, SISTER. b Lafayette Ind 29 S 32. 5: St Francis Col 53-63 (soc studies) BS; St Joseph Col 62-63; DePaul U 62-63; Catholic U 63-67 MSLS. 7: Tchr elem sch 53-63; Libn Marian High Sch, Mishawaka Ind 64-. 9: CathLA; ALA. 10: Ind Coun Soc Studies; Adv Hoosier Student LA. 14: Ref. 15: 1311 So Logan, Mishawaka In 46544.

NELSON, M(ARGARET) KAREN. b Bryan Tex 5 Mr 41. 5: SWest at Memphis 58-60; UNC (Chapel hill) 60-62 (Eng) AB; Simmons 64-66 (LS) MS. 6: Fr. 7: Lib intern HarvardU Lib 63-66; Personnel libn 66-69; Asst univ libn for personnel 69-. 9: ALA. 10: Phi Beta Kappa. 14: Personnel admin, pub rel, lib educ. 15: Harvard Univ Lib, Cambridge Ma 02138.

NELSON, MARIETTA. b Benzonia Mich 16 Mr 28. 4: Sherman E Nelson. 5: Smith 45-49 (Hist) BA; UDenver 65-66 (LS); UMich 67 MALS. 6: Fr, Ger. 7: Ref libn Mich State U (E Lansing) 68-. 9: ALA. 14: Ref. 15: 1003 Delridge, E Lansing Mi 48823.

NELSON, MARION A (LYNCH). b Oak Park Ill 2 Je 20. 4: Walter C Nelson. 5: UChicago 38-39; Rosary Col 39-44 (LS) BA; Ag Sch Ft Ben Herrison (Mal Hist Spec Serv Publ). 6: Ger, Tagalog, Siamese. 7: Chief clerk & act libn Elmwood Park (ill Inst of Tech 44-45; Libn Spec Serv Libs Camp MCOY Wis Luzon 45-48; Br libm Elmwood Park Pub Lib, Elmwood Park Ill 49-50; ChiefLibn 50-58; Catlgr & post libn Spec Serv Libs Ft Ord Cal 56-58; Ref libn Monterey Pub Lib, Monterey Cal 58-59; Libn Joint US Mil Adv, Thailand angkok 59-62; Libn Spec Serv Libs, Ft Knox Ky 62-. 09: ALA; SiameseLA (Honorary mem); KyLA; Pub Libs Assn of Ky; IllLA. 8: Estab New Army Lib, called Copple Lib, Ft Knox. 10: Royal Siam Soc of Bangkok Thailand; AAUW. 11: Certif of Achievement for outstanding serv as Libn Military Libs SE Asia. 12: Many Bibliogs in Line of Duty; Latest Publ by Adjutant General Fort Knox, was a Bibliog on Military Leadership. 15: Box 126, Ft Knox Ky 40121.

NELSON, MARY LOIS. b Hampton Iowa 2 Ag 27. 5: Iowa State Tchrs Col 45-47, 49-51 (Jr High Educ) BA: UTex 55-57 (LS). 7: Elem tchr pub sch, Osage Iowa 47-48; Elem tchr Consolidated sch, Meservey Iowa 48-49; Catlgr Scott Co Lib, Eldridge Iowa State Travel Lib, Des Moines Iowa 57-58; Dir of tech processes Anoka Co Lib, Minneapolis 58-61, Asst libn 61-67; Admin asst Pub Lib Coun Bluffs Iowa 67-. 9: ALA; MinnLA; IowaLA. 14: County libs, admin, tech processes. 15: 600 Huntington, Council Bluffs Ia 51501.

NELSON, MARY LOUISE. b Oakwood Tex 16 Ag 12. 5: UTex 29-33 (Hist) BA, summers 36-42 (Govt) MA, 54-56 MLS. 6: Fr, Sp. 7: Tchr Del Rio Pub Schs, Del Rio Tex 33-39; Tchr Alpine Pub Schs, Alpine Tex 39-43; Tchr Edinburg Pub Schs, Edinburg Tex 43-44; Tchr Santa Rita Pub Schs, Santa Rita NM 44-45; Tchr New Braunfels Pub Schs, New Braunfels Tex 45-53; Staff UTex 56-. 9: TexLA (Program Chm for 66 Conf); Tex Assn Col Tchrs. 10: Phi Beta Kappa; Beta Phi Mu. 14: Ref, (soc sci). 15: 4002 Ridgelea dr, Austin Tex 78731.

NELSON, PAULINE CHESNUTT. b Atwood Okla 29 Ja 15. 4: Floyd Victor Nelson. 5: Christian Col 34; UOkla 58 (Educ) BS, 59 MLS. 6: Fr. 7: Lib sch revisor UOkla 59; Libn Aero Commander Inc, Norman Okla 63-64; Child lib Scottsdale Pub Lib, Scottsdale Ariz 66-69. 9: ALA; Ariz State LA. 10: Delta Delta Delta; Holdenville Schubert Club; AAUW; City Concert Assn; YWCA; Christ Col Alumnae Club. 15: 310 N Burns, Holdenville Okla 74848.

NELSON, POLLY POST (MARY MAXIMA POST). b Rochester NY 9 Ap 11. 4: Edward Carl Nelson. 5: Col of Wooster 29-33 (Hist) BA; West Res 34 BLS; Columbia 50 MLS. 6: Lat, Gk, Ger. 7: Asst Canton Pub Lib, Canton Ohio 34-39; Br libn Cleveland Pub Lib Maple Heights Reg 39-43; WAVES issuing libn USNR Chief of Naval Operations (Lt) Wash DC 43-46; Libn NY Pub Lib brs 46-. 9: ALA (Notable Bks Com); NYLA; NYLib Club. 10: Pub Rel Coun; Mid-Bronx Commun Coun. 14: Neighborhood & Commun gp wk. 15: 1866 Washington ave, Bronx NY 10457.

NELSON, RACHEL (WAYNE). b Cleveland 13 Mr 25. 4: Bernard J Nelson. 5: Cleveland Col West Res 43-47 (Hist) BA West Res 47-48 BS in LS. 6: Fr. 7: Young adult libn Cleveland Pub Lib 48-53, 1st asst libn 53-54; Cleveland Heights Pub Lib, Cleveland Heights Ohi: Ohio Asst dir 63-. 9: OhioLA (Asst Exec Dir & Exec Dir Nat Lib Week Program 63-66, sec Round Table for child & young adults 53-54, chm Constit Com 68-69). 10: Womens Nat Bk Assn; Jewish Bk Coun Cleveland; West Res Alumni Assn; Adult Educ Coun Greater Cleveland. 13: Yes. 14: Pub lib admin. 15: 2359 Ashurst rd, University Heights Oh 44118.

NELSON, RITA (MERCER). b Ava Mo 15 Ag 11. 4: George O Nelson. 5: UMont 29-35 (Lib Econ) BA. 7: Asst libn Missoula Co Lib, Missoula Mont 35-40; Circ libn UMont 44-45, Acquis libn 45-47, Asst acquis libn 48-57, Ser libn 58-. 9: PNLA; MontLA (treas & memb chm 61-). 14: Ser. 15: 640 S ave E, Missoula Mt 59801.

NELSON, ROSCELIA (MARY) (GRIGG). b Ironwood Mich 19 Jl 04. 5: Lewis Inst (Chicago) 22-24 (Eng) AA; UMich 24-26 (Eng, Hist) AB, 27-28 AB in LS. 6: Fr, Ger. 7: Tchr Wakefield Pub Sch, Wakefield Mich 6-27; Catlgr Mich State Col 28-35; Catlgr Hamtramck Pub Lib, Hamtramck 40-42, 46-. 9: ALA; MichLA. 10: AAUW; Detroit Assn of UMich Women. 14: Catlg, ref. 15: 17214 Evergreen rd, Detroit Mi 48219.

NELSON, RUTH WEISS. b Thomson Ga 3 0 14. 4: William Jones Nelson Jr. 5: Birmingham So Col 32-35 (Hist) AB; Emory 37-38 ABLS.06: Fr, Sp, Lat. 7: Birmingham Pub Lib, Birmingham Al: Br Lib asst 35-37, Child dept asst 38-41, Ref dept asst 61-63, Ref dept head 63-. 9: AlaLA (Handbook Com). 10: DAR; Daughters of Colonial Wars; Ala CAR. 14: Ref. 15: 1680-F Valley ave, Birmingham Ala 35209.

NELSON, VERNON HANS. b Sturgeon Bay Wis 12 Ap 33. 4: Jane Jordan. 5: UWis 51-55 Lat BA; Moravian Theol Sem 55-58 BD; UPenn 67 MA. 6: Ger. 7: Pastor Mamre Moravian Church, Watertown Wis 58-60; Asst archivist Moravian Archives, Bethlehem Penn 60-63, Archivist 63-; Asst prof Moravian Theol Sem 64-. 9: Soc AA. 10: Moravian Hist Soc. 12: " Christian David (62) "John Valentine Haidt (66). 13: Yes. 14: Mss. 15: Main & Elizabeth, Bethlehem Penn 18018.

NELSON, WESLEY JOSEPH. b Beloit Wis 13 Ag 35. 4: Annita Marie Palmer. 5: Beloit Col 53-57 (Philos) BA (cum laude); So MethodistU 59-62 (Theol) BD; Peabody Col 66-67 MLS. 6: Ger, Fr. 7: Minister Johnson Creek & Concord Methodist Ch, Johnson Creek Wis 62-63; Minister Monona Methodist Ch, Monona Wis 63-66; Act Divinity catlg libn Joint Univ Libs, Nashville 66-67, Divinity catlg libn 67-; Ref libn Trevecca Nazarene Col 67-69. 9: ATheolLA; Tenn Tech Serv Libns (sec-treas 68-69). 10: Ordained Methodist minister. 14: Catlg, ref. 15: Divinity Lib Joint Univ Libraries, Nashville Tn 37203.

NEMEC, JAROSLAV. b Orechov Czechoslovakia 23 Mr 10. 5: Sch of Law Masaryk U (Brno Czechoslovakia) 29-35 (Law, Pol Sci) Jur D; Catholic U 54-56 MS in LS. 6: Czech, Slovak, Lat, Fr, Ger, Polish, R ussian. 7: Mil Justice, Gen field prosecutor, Czechoslovak Army abroad 39-45; Sect chief Ministry of Interior, Prague 45-48; Documentalist Ministry for Unification of Laws, Prague 48-50; Var bus & banking orgs, US 52-56; Legal research libn AMA, Wash Off 56-59; Ref libn med jurisprudence NLM 59-. 10: Soc Med Jurisprud; Amer Assn Advanc Slavic Studies; Czechoslovak Soc Arts & Sci in Amer (past sec-gen, pres 68); Pittsburgh Inst Leg Med; Washington Soc Hist Med; Internat Ref Org Forensic Med. 12: "Documentation of the Czechoslovak Law" thesis Cath U (56); "How Federal Government has Expanded its Medical Care Program" (58); "Highlights in Medicolegal Relation," NLM (68); Co-comp "Medical Research Institutions Named After Medical Men," NLM (69); "International Bibliography of Medicolegal Serials, 1736-1967," NLM (69). 13: Yes. 14: Ref med jurisprud, med econ, hist of Forensic med. 15: 2067 Park rd NW, Wash DC 20010.

NEMENZO-SACRIS, CAROLINA A. b Cebu City Philippines 30 Ap 39. 4: Eduardo M Sacris. 5: UPhilippines 54-58 (LS) AB; USoCal 63-65 MSLS. 6: Philipino, Cebuano, Hiligaynon, Sp, Fr. 7: U Philippines: Grad asst Pharmacy-Chem Lib 58-60, Col Libn Col of Dentistry 60-61, Libn I on detail as Catlgr catlg dept 61-62; In-serv trainee USoCAL Lib 63-65; Libn G K Turner Assoc Lib, Palo Alto 65-66; Ref libn Stanford Research Inst Menlo Park Cal 66-66; Ref libn Stanford Research Institute, Menlo Park Cal 66-. 8: Detailed to help org the lib of the newly opened Baguio Col (Phila), A new br of the UPhilippines 63. 12: Jt comp "Index to the Philippine Social Sciences and Humanities Review". 14: Catlg, ref wk. 15: Box 4865 Stanford Cal 94305.

NEMEYER, CAROL (ANMUTH). b NYC 29 Ja 29. 4: Sheldon Nemeyer. 5: Queens Col (NY) 45-46; (Eng) Berea Col 46-48; LIU 48-49 (Eng) BA; Columbia 60-62 MSLS66- (LS). 7: Ref catlg libn McGraw Hill Inc, NYC 62-64, Asst libn 64-; 66. 9: SLA; ASIS; ALA; Private Libs Assn, Gt Brit. 10: Beta Phi Mu. 14: Admin, ref, bk trade. 15: 415 W 23nd st, New York NY 10011.

NEMOY, LEON. b Balta Russia 29 D 01. 4: Elizabeth McGinley. 5: UOdessa (Russia) 17-18 (Classical & Slavic Philol); Yale 24-29 (Semitic Langs) MA, PhD. 6: Fr, Ger, Russian, Hebrew, Arabic, Lat. 7: Catlgr Lib of the Soc for the Propagation of Knowledge, Odessa Russia 14-21; Asst libn Academic Lib Odessa Russi 19-21; Catlgr ULib Lembreg Poland 22-23; Curator of Hebrew & Arabic Lit & research assoc in Bibliog Yale U 23-. 66, Advisor in Hebrew & Arabic Lit 68-; Scholar in residence Dropsie Col 67-. 9: ALA; Amer Acad for Jewish Research. 12: Auth: "Selected Poems from the Kitab Zahr al-Kimam (30); "Checklist of an Exhibition of Judaica and Hebraica (33); "Kitab al-Anwar wal-Maraqib 5 vols (39-43); "Ibn Kammunas Arabic Treatise on the Immortality of the Soul (44); "Catalogue of the Asch-Rabinowitz Collection (45);"Karaite Anthology (52); "IScroll of Antichus (52); "Arabic Manuscripts in the Yale University Library (56); Ed "Yale Judaica Series. 13: Yes. 14: Arabic philology, Early printing; Hist of Arabic Jewish Med, hist of Karaite lit & thought, Oriental bibliog. Med. 15: Dropsie Coll Lib, Broad at York st,Philadelphia Pa 19132.

NEPHLER, MARY EMILY. b Kan City Mo 10 Ag 07. 5: Oxford Col for Women 25-27; UMich 27-30 ABLS, 37-38 ABLS, 37-38 AMLS. 6: Fr. 7: Catlgr Pub Lib, Pontiac Mich 30-32; Asst libn High Sch Lib, Pontiac Mich 33-37; Clsf Swarthmore Col Lib 38-39 Ref libn DePauw U 39-43; Head of ref & circ Goucher Col 43-46; 43c46; Libn II Pub Lib, Detroit 47-57; Libn III & US Documents spec 57-. 9: ALA; MichLA. 14: Ref, govt docs. 15: 630 Merrick ave, Detroit Mi 48202.

NERI, MARGARET (BLAIR). b Wilkinsburg 17 Ja 19. 4: Zeno Neri. 5: Grove City 36-40 (Eng) AB; Carnegie 40-41 BS in LS; UPittsburgh 42-48 (Sociol Studies) MLitt. 6: Fr, Ger. 7: Libn Bethel Twp High Sch, Bethel Twp Penn -42; Libn Monaca High Sch, Monaca Penn 43-45; Libn Wilmerding High Sch, Wilmerding Penn 45-48; Libn Wilkinsburg High Sch, Wilkinsburg Penn 48-. 9: NEA; Penn StateEA (Lib Div). 10: DAR; Pi Gamma Mu, Alpha Delta Kappa. 14: Wk with yp. 15: 353 Churchill rd, Pittsburgh Pa 15235.

NESBEITT, PHILIP LAWSON. b Kan City Kan 25 Ap 22. 5: UCal (Berkeley) 48 (Pol sci AB, 49 MA, 51 BLS. 7: Admin spec USAF, Europe 43-46 Intern in Admin UCal (Berkeley) 51-52; Ref libn Enoch Pratt Free Lib, Baltimore 52-54; Ref libn Brooklyn Col Lib 54-58; Libn United Commun Funds & Couns of Amer, NYC 59-63; Gen ref libn City Col Lib (NY) 63-. 9: ALA; SLA; NY Lib Club. 10: AAUP. 14: Ref. 15: 309 E 37th st, New York NY 10016.

NESBIN, ESTHER W (WINTER). b Denver Colo 5 Ag 10. 5: UBuffalo 27-31 (Eng) BA, 32 Certif in LS; San Diego State Col 48 (Educ). 6: Ger, Fr. 7: Lib asst Grosvenor Lib, Buffalo NY 31-42; Instr in lib sci UBuffalo 39-42; Libn Temple of the Jewelled Cross, Los Angeles 42-46; Libn & instr in lib sci Palomar Col 47-65, Hd dept of lib sci 62-65, Dir lib serv 65-. 8: Consul: devel Palo Verde Jr Col Lib, Blythe Ca 57; Monterey Cal Jr Col Lib 58; Camp Pendleton Law Lib, Camp Pendleton Cal 64. 9: CalLA (pres Jr Col Libns RT 66); CalASchL; CalTA. 10: Delta Kappa Gamma; Palomar Cactus and Succulent Soc; Escondido Garden Club; Defenders of Wildlife; Nat Wildlife Found; Wildnerness Soc; Nat Audubon Soc. 12: "Shaker Literature in the Grosvneer Library" (40, rev ed 68). 14: Ref, rare bks, admin. 15: PO Box 102, San Marcos Ca 92069.

NESBITT, DORIS (MARGARET). b Houston Tex 18 D 14. 5: Tex Womans U 31-35 (Bus Admin) BS; LSU 41-42 BS in LS. 7: Tchr-libn 35-38; Catlgr Wharton Co Lib, Wharton Tex 39; Sec-libn Schlumberger Well Surveying Corp 40-41; Gen asst Tex State Lib 42-44; Libn Howard & Waller Co Lib, Hempstead Tex 45-47; Ref libn Mo State Lib 47-50; Document ref libn Phoenix Pub Lib 50-52; Libn Hobbs Pub Lib, Hobbs NM 52-54; Catlgr Midland Co Lib, Midland Tex 54-57; Asst libn Bivins Mem Lib, Amarillo Tex 57-60; Documents period ref libn El Paso Pub Lib, El Paso Tex 60-66; Docs-genealogy libn 66-. 9: ALA; SWLA; TexLA (var com assignments; Bus Mgr "News Notes" 45). 10: Daughters of Republic of Tex; Nat Geneal Soc; Royal Neighbors of Amer; Phi Kappa Psi; UDC. 13: Yes. 14: Reg serv, catlg, govt docs, geneal. 15: 1011 Tobinson, El Paso Tex 9902.

NESBITT, OLIVE KATHRYN (BUCHANAN). b Erie Penn 28 Ja 07. 5: UPittsburgh 30-31 (Lit); UBuffalo 34 (Psych) CERTIF Soc casewk; Erie Pub Lib train course 37 State certif; Gannon Co 68 (LS) Certif. 7: Asst all depts Erie Pub Lib, Erie Penn 29-46; Pub rel Price Control Bd, Erie Penn 6; Social casewk TB Assoc & Bd of Assistance, Erie Penn 47; Sec & off mgr & libn FAMILY & Child Serv, Erie Penn 47-49; Head Libn Engnr Lord Mfg Co, Erie Penn 49-61; Head Libn med Hamot Hosp, Erie Penn 63-. 8: Volnteer Libn Soldiers & Sailors Home Erie Penn 62. 9: ALA; MedLA; SLA; ACS (Div Chem Lit); ASIS; PennLA. 10: DEMOCRATIC Womens Coun; Mental Health Assn; YWCA. 13: Yes. 14: Ref, research. 15: Med Lib Hamot Hosp, 4 E 2d st, Erie Penn 16512.

NESETH, JULIE ANN. b Waukon Iowa 31 Mr 40. 4: Bernard E Neseth. 5: Luther Col 58-62 (Bus Educ) BA; UMinn summers 64, 65. 6: Sp. 7:Sch Sch Kenyon pub schs, Kenyon Minn 62-, A-V supv. 9: ALA; NEA; MinnASchL; MinnEA. 10: Club 254 (investment club). 14: Catlg, circ, child adv. 15: Rte 1, Nerstrand Mn 55033.

NESHEIM, KENNETH MILTON. b Glendale Cal 18 O 30. 4: Roberta Jane Loy. 5: San Diego City Col 55-57 AA; UCLA 57-59 (Amer Hist) BA, 59-60 (Amer Hist), 60-61 MLS. 6: Fr, Ger. 7: Ad2 USN 51-55; Lib asst San Diego City Col 55-57; Stud asst Main Lib UCLA 57-58; Sr lib asst Wm A Clark Mem Lib, UCLA 5861; Catlgr dept of mss Henry E Huntington Lib, San Marino Cal 62-63; Asst libn The Beinecke Rare Book & Mss Lib, Yale U 63-, Act curator Amer lit 68-69. 8: Lilly Lib Fellow in Rare Bk Libnship Lilly Lib Ind U 61-62; chm, UAN Sinderin Prize Com, Yale U, 68-69; Adu, Trumbull Col Lib, Yale Lib Assn; Fellow, Trumbull Col. 9: BSA. 14: Rare bks. 15: 881 Indian Hill rd, Orange Ct 06477.

NESOM, RUTH EVELYN. b Tickfaw La 10 N 16. 5: Southeastern La Col 34-36 (Elem Tchg) 2 yr certif; Northwestern State Col 36-38 (Eng, Health & Phys Educ) BS; LSU 46-48 BS in LS; Tulane U 62-63 (Painting & Creative Writing). 7: Tchr & libn Tangipaha Parish Sch Bd, Kentwood & Hammond La 38-50; Libn Terrebonne Parish Sch Bd, Houma La 50-54; Lib supv of Frankfurt Germany Amer Schs, US Army System 54-55; Libn Forrest Sherman High Sch

NATO, Naples Italy 56-57; Base libn USAF Haneda Air Base, Tokyo Japan 57-58; Libn Plaquemines Parish Schs, Belle Chasse La 58-61; Libn Jefferson Parish Schs, T H Harris Jr High Sch, Metairie La 62-. 8: Prof of Lib Sci, Ark State Col. summer 65. 9: ALA; LaASchL (past pres). 10: AAUW; DKG; KKi. 13: Yes. 14: Ref, readers adv serv. 15: 1812 Green Acres rd, Metairie La 70003.

NESS, CHARLES H. b York Penn 7 My 24. 4: Sara Krone. 5: Penn State U 46-49 (Eng) BA; UPenn 49-51 (Eng lit) AM; Drexel 52-53 (LS) MS. 7: Aviation cadet US Army Air Corps, US 43-44; Med tech Pfc US Med Corps, US European theatre 44-46; Ref asst Free Lib of Phila 52-54, Adult asst lit dept 54-56, asst br hd 56-57, Hd lib for blind 57-61; Dir gen lib Penn State Lib, Harrisburg 61-67; Asst dir for admin & planning Penn State U Libs 67-. 8: Mem President's Com on Employment of the Handicapped. 9: ALA (chm Rd table on Lib Serv for the Blind 58,59); BSA; Amer Soc Pub Admin; PennLA. 10: Sierra Club; Middletown Twp Lib Bd; Penn Home Tchg Soc. 12: "Early Pennsylvania Imprints in the Pennsylvania State Library 1689-1750" (66). 13: Yes. 14: Admin, interlib coop, microforms, rare bks. 15: 1238 Park Hills ave E, State College Pa 18102.

NESTELL, CLIFFORD LEE. b Fletcher NC 16 Jl 41. 5: AndrewsU 61-63, 64-66 (Hist) AB; UMich 66-68 MALS; West CarolinaU 68-69 (Hist). 6: Sp. 7: Staff ref libn Charles F Kettering Med Ctr, Kettering Ohio 69-. 8: Lib adv & tchr, Fletcher Acad, Fletcher NC 68-69; Bk sel, Asheville-Buncombe Tech Inst Lib, Asheville NC 68-69. 9: ALA; NCLA. 14: Catlg, rare bks. 15: 3535 Southern blvd, Kettering Oh 45429.

NESTLEROAD, ROSEMARY (ELLEN). b Cleveland 19 Ap 08. 4: Glenn A Neslteroad. 5: Miami U (Ohio) 25-29 (Hist, Eng); Ohio) 25-29 (Hist, Eng); Ohio State U 29-30 (Hist, Eng) BS in Ed; West Res summers 52-54, 55, 56 MLS; UWis summer 65 (LS). 7: Tchr Cleveland Pub Schs 30-31; Asst libn Napoleon Pub Lib, Napoleon Ohio 46-49; High sch lib Napoleon Pub Schs, Napoleon Ohio 49-66; Hd libn Marvin Mem Lib, Shelby Ohio 66-. 9: ALA; OhioLA. 10: AAUW; Bus & Profess Women. 14: Ref, adm. 15: Marvin Memorial Lib, Shelby Oh 44875.

NETHERY, WALLACE. b Gravity Iowa 29 D 10. 5: Union Col (Lincoln Neb) 29-34 Eng ab; USOCAL 46-50; 54-55 MSLS. 6: Fr. 7: Lt JG US Navy Reserve 41-45; Libn II USOCAL 55-. 10: Charles Lamb Soc (London); Beta Phi Mu. 12: "Charles Lamb in America to 1848 (63); Ed "Coranto: Journal of the Friends of the Library USoCal. 13: Yes. 14: Philos ref, rare bks. 15: Hoose Lib USOCAL, Los Angeles Ca 90007.

NETZ, DAVID J. b Kansas City 27 O 44. 4: Phyllis Veenstra. 5: Dordt Col 62-66 (Eng) AB; West Mich U 66-67 MLS; UIowa summer 69- (Higher educ). 7: Dordt Col Lib: Catlgr 65-66, Ref libn 68-; Grad asst West Mich U 66-67; Lib intern Ohio State U 67-68. 9: ALA. 10: Jr C of C; Chm, Dordt Alum Com; Beta Phi Mu. 14: Ref, admin, lib educ. 15: 117 3rd ave SE, Sioux Center Ia 51250.

NEU, JOHN (ALBERT). b Green Bay Wis 19 O 35. 5: UWis 53-57 (Eng) BS, 58-59 MS in LS. 6: Ger, Fr. 07: Personnel clerk US Army (Pvt, Ft Sheridan Ill 57; Libn I, Libn II Mem Lib UWis 59-61; Interrogator spec 5 US Army Ft Devens Mass 61-62; Bibliog in hist of sci Mem Lib UWis 63-. 9: Hist of Sci Soc. 11: Lilly Lib Fellowship in Rare Bk Libnship, Lilly Lib IndU 62-63. 12: "Chemical Medica and Pharmaceutical Books Printed Before 1800, in the Collections of the University of Wisconsin Libraries (65), "French Political Pamphlets, 1547-1648 (69). 14: Rare bks. 15: Mem Lib UWis, Madison Wi 53706.

NEUBAUER, ADAH DARLINE. b Purdum Neb 18 Ja 25. 5: Chadron State Tchrs Col 43-44, 46-49 (Educ) BS; UNeb summers 53, 55; UDenver summers of 59-61 MA in LS. 7: Rural Sch Cherry Co Neb 44-46; Elem tchr Alliance Pub Schs, Alliance Neb 49-53; Eng tchr & libn Rock Co High Sch, Bassett Neb 53-61; Head Libn East High Sch, Aurora Ill 61-. 9: Nea; ALA; IllEA; IllLA. 10: Delta Kappa Gamma. 14: High sch libs. 15: 415 E Downer place, Aurora Ill 60505.

NEUBAUER, JANICE EVELYN (ERNEST). b Clarion Penn 21 Jl 33. 4: Richard A Neubauer. 5: Clarion State Col 51-55 (LS) BS; SUNY (Geneseo) 66 (Eng). 7: Legal sec Harris Law firm, Clarion Penn 51-52; Libn No Bedford Co Schs, Penn 58-60; Libn Hornell City Schs, Hornell NY 60-62; Hd libn Duxbury Free Lib, Duxbury Mass 68-. 13: Yes. 14: Lib publ, catlg. 15: 47 Blodgett ave, Duxbury Ma 02332.

NEUBAUER, RICHARD ARTHUR. b Meadville Penn 9 O 33. 4: Janice Ernest. 5: Clarion state 51-55 (Geog, Soc studies) BS; SUNY (Geneseo) 61-65 MLS; Kent State U 67-68 (LS) 07: Air Control Off (1st Lt) USMC, Cherry Point NC 55-57; Geog tchr FranklinPenn 57-58; Soc studies tchr: N Bedford City Schs, Penn 58-60; Hornell City Schs, NY 60-62; Libn Hornell City Schs, NY 62-65; Asst to chief libn Edinboro State Col 65-68; Asst Prof of lib sci, Edinboro State Col 65-68; Dir sch libs Duxbury Sch, Duxbury Mass 68-. 8: Higher Educ Act Institute for training in libnship, Dir Edinboro State Col, Aug 68-. 9: ALA; ACRL; AASchL. 14: Lib admin, sch libnship. 15: 47 Blodgett ave, Duxbury Ma 02332.

NEUFELD, ELDO. b Perryton Tex. 4: Grace Miller. 5: Bethel Col 48-53 (Mus) AB; Amer Conservatory of Mus 53-54 (Mus); Union Sem Sch of Sacred Mus 54-56 (Voice & Choral Conducting) SMM; Nordwestdeutsche Musikakademie (Detmold Germany) 62-63 (Choral Conducting); West Res 64-65 MS in LS. 6: Ger,Sp, Fr. 7: Dir of Music Indianola Presbyterian Church, Columbus Ohio 56-64; Asst music libn Oberlin Col Conservatory 65-. 10: Cleveland Orchestra Chorus; Cleveland Orchestra Chamber Chorus. 11: Fulbright scholarship for music study in Germany 62-63. 12: Ed "Mr & Mrs C W Best Catalog of Autographs (68). 14: Catlg. 15: Oberlin Col Conservatory, Oberlin ohio.

NEUFELD, IRVING H. b NYC 4 F 25. 4: Rachel Kurinsky. 5: Brooklyn Col 41-43, 46-47 (Psych) BA; Escuela Universitaria de Bellas Artes (Mexico) 48-49 (Fine Arts) MFA; Columbia 49-50 (LS) MS. 6: Sp, Fr, Ger. 7: US Army 44-46; Intern & catlgr LC 50-52; Bibliog-indexer US Dept of Agric Lib, Wash DC 52-57; United Aircraft Corp Lib, E Hartford Conn: Ref libn 57-59, Head ref sect 59-62, Head Libn 62-65; Act chief United Aircraft Corp Lib System, E Hartford Conn 65-. 9: SLA (pres Conn Valley Chap 68-69); ConnLA. 10: Conn Aero Hist Assn. 13: Yes. 14: Ind lib mgt. 15: 31 Woodland st apt 3L, Hartford Conn 06105.

NEUFELD, JOHN. b Vienna 20 D 25. 5: UMich 43-44, 48-50 (Math) AB, 50-51 (Hist) MA; Columbia 51-52 (Hist): UMich 57-58 MALS, 58-65 LS Ph Cand. 6: Ger, Fr. 7: Pvt T/3 US Army Intelligence, US, Europe 44-47; Interrogator Cl Off US War Dept, Germany 46-47; Instr asst dir pub serv Detroit Inst of Tech 54-55; Lib asst Detroit Inst of Art 57-58; Catlgr Dearborn Pub Lib, Dearborn Mich 58-60; Catlgr Mich State Lib 60-. 9: Amer Assn State & Loc Hist; BSA. 10: Book Club of Detroit; ACLU; ACBL; Greater Lansing Hist Soc. 12; Ed "Added Entries Michigan State Lib Newsletter. 13: Yes. 14: Spec collections, bibliog, catlg, educ, local hist. 15: 1321 W Grand River, E Lansing Mi 48823.

NEUFELD, JUDITH GINSBERG. b Brooklyn NY 7 N 35. 4: Meyer P Neufeld. 5: Queens Col (NY) 52-56 (Eng & Comp Lit) BA; Jewish Theol Sem 52-56 BHL; Columbia 56-58, 59- (LS) MS. 6: Hebrew, Fr. 7: Libn Ramaz Sch, NYC 56-57; Admin libn Jewish Theol Sem (NYC) 57-. 9: ALA; NY Lib Club; Assn Jewish Libs. 10: Hadassah, Mizrachi Women. 14: Admin, ref, rare bks, tech serv, theol lit. 15: 1000 Ocean pky, Brooklyn NY 11230.

NEUHOFER, SISTER M DOROTHY (ANNA) OSB. b St Joseph Fla 19 Je 31. 5: Sacred Heart Jr Col (Cullman Ala) summer 51; Mt St Scholastica summers 52-58; Barry College summers 53-64 (Educ) 64 (Educ) BS; Rosary Col 64-65 MALS. 6: Ger. 7: Tchr Parochial Schs, Fla 51-60, 63-64; Tchr & Prin Parochial schs, Fla 60-63; Ref libn St Leo Col Lib 65-67, Dir Readers' Serv St Leo Col Lib 67-. 8: Chm Cath Bk Week 68-; Chm doc congressional dist Nat Lib Week proj 69. 9: ALA; CathLA; FlaLA. 10: Amer Benedictine Acad. 12: Ed "The Library World of Saint Leo College," weekly bull (65-). 14: Ref, research catlg. 15: Holy Name Priory, San Antonio Fl 33576.

NEUMAN, RICHARD JOHN. b Sabetha Kan 1 S 24. 4: Jo Ann (Nelson). 5: Southwestern U 46-48 (Bus Admin) BBA; UMiami 50-52 (Bus Admin); Fla State U 52-53 MSLS. 6: Ger. 7: US Navy 43-46; priv bus 48-50; Ref asst Miami Pub Lib, Miami Fla 53-54, Bus libn 54-61; Dir Salina Pub Lib, Salina Kan 61-. 8: Financial & bldg consul 65-. 9: ALA-RSD (Chm Sci Tech & Bus Com 59-62; Com on Org 61-67; chm Org & Activities Com 64-65, 2nd v-pres 64-65); FlaLA; KanLA (pres 68-69); SELA; MPLA. 10: Beta Phi Mu; Pi Gamma Mu; Lions Internat; Curator Smoky Hill Hist Museum. 13: Yes. 14: Ref. 15: 301 W Elm, Salina Ks 67401.

NEVEU, WILMA (BARBRE). b Rayne La 25 F 26. 4 Durwood Herbert Neveu. 5: USouthwestern La 43-46 (Eng, Soc Studies) BA; LSU 46-47 BS in LS. 6: Fr, Sp. 7: Catlgr asst libn Lafayette Parish Lib, Lafayette La 47-48; Bkkeeper sales

D H Castille Sales & Ser, LAFAYETTE La 51-52; Bkkeeper acct rec Lafayette Lumber Co, Lafayette La 52-53; Enumerator Bur of the Census, Lafayette La 60; Instr-asst libn Northeast La State Col 60-64, Br libn-libn II New Orleans Pub Lib 64-66; Cir & Res libn Tulane Med Lib 66-69; Libn II New Orleans Pub Lib 69-66; Circ & Res Libn Tulane Med Lib 66-69; Libn II New Orleans Pub Lib 69-. 9: ALA; LaLA; SWLA; MedLA (Memb Com So Reg Conv 67. 14: Ref, acquis. 15: 7030 Walmsley ave, New Orleans La 70125.

NEVILL, ANN DOUGLAS (WOODWORTH). b Kentville NS 12 D 29. 4: Richard C Nevill. 5: Acadia U 47-51 (Bio) BS; UMich 67-69 (LS). 6: Fr. 7: Research asst Atomic energy of Can Ltd, Chalk River 51-55; Research asst Connaught Labs, Toronto 55-56; UMich (Ann Arbor): Research asst 56-58, Medlars searcher 66-. 10: AAAS. 12: "Effects of Human Exposure to Ionizing Radiation; a Bibliography," NP-17232 (68). 13: Yes. 14: Info serv. 15: 1067 Barton dr, Ann Arbor Mi 48105.

NEVIN, DAVID GREGG. b Pittsburgh 21 My 35. 4: Janet M Godfrey. 5: Williams 53-57 (Music) BA; Columbia 57 (Musicology); UPittsurgh 63-64 MLS. 6: Fr.)07: Group dir Mens Campaign Div United Hosp Fund NYC 57-58; Communications Watch Off LTJG, USNR, US Sixth Fleet Mediterranean 58-61; Pre-prof ref dept Carnegie Lib of Pittsburgh 63-64; Grad asst Grad Lib Sch UUPittsburgh 63-64; Prof libn asst a-v dept Boston Pub Lib 64-65; Chief a-v dept Washington U Libs (St Louis) 65-. 8: Fleet Communicaxions Liaison Officer, Cannes France 61; Lectr in Lib Sci, Washington U 66-. 9: ALA; -RTSD (chm Photocopy Com 66-67); MusLA; MassLA; NELA; MoLA (chm Regis Com 67 Conv); NMA; NEA-DAVI. 10: Beta Phi Mu; Bd of Deacons, 2nd Presby Ch, St Louis. 12: "State Plans under the Library Services Servces Act, Suppl 3 (62); "Small Library Project Sec of "Library Administration. 14: A-v, ref, catlg, microforms, photoduplication. 15: 6644 Washington ave, St Louis Mo 63130.

NEW, GREGORY RYAN. b Boston 12 O 28. 5: Harvard 45-46 (Sociol); UGa 47-48 (Pol Sci); Geroge WashingtonU 49-51 (Hist) AB; Emory 53-54 MLib. 6: Ger, Romance lang. 7: tele ref asst GR&B LC 55-56, Hd filing sect catlgr maintenance div 56-59, Asst ed Nat Union Catlg 59-60, Catlgr-ed Union List of Ser 60-61, Mss catlgr 61-63, Asst ed new ser titles 63-68, Decimal clsf specialist 68-. 10: Capitol Hill Commun Coun; DC Fed of Civic Assns. 12: News ed and chief reporter, Capitol Hill Spectator/News 68-. 14: Bibliog editing, clsf. 15: 1118 E Capitol st, Washington DC 20002.

NEWBERG, ELLEN JOYCE (HERR. b Wellman Iowa 29 S 41. 4: Alan Keith Newberg. 5: Sioux Falls Col 59-63 (Eng) B; UIll 63-64 MLS. 7: Asst libn Sioux Falls Col 64-66; Catlg libn UWyo 66-68; Catlg libn UOre 68-. 9: OreLA. 10: LWV. 13: Yes. 14: Catlg, ref. 15: Ollie Ia 52576.

NEWBERRY, DANIEL ARTHUR. b Clovis Cal 21 N 36. 5: WillametteU 54-58 (Fr Lit) BA; UOre 58-60 (For Lang) MA; ULiege (Belgium) 60-61 (Medieval Fr Lit); Harvard 62-63 (Fr Lit); Simmons 63-64 MS in LS. 6: Fr, Sp. 7: Tchg fellow UOre (Eugene) 58-60; Tchr Andover High Sch, Andover Mass 61-62; Tchg fellow HarvardU 62-63; Dental libn Harvard Med Lib 63-64; Romance lang bibliogr SUNY (Albany) 64-65, Humanities libn 65-67; Hd lib pub serv Portland StateU 67-. 9: ALA; PNLA. 10: Mod Lang Assn. 11: Fulbright Research Grant, Liege Belgium 60-61. 13: Yes. 14: Ref, bibliog acquis, admin. 15: 2030 SW Main st, Portland Or 97205.

NEWBERRY, MARIE AMNA. b Dundee Mich 8 O 1886. 5: Lib Sch of the NY Pub Lib 11-13 Diploma; UMich 16-17 BA, 31-32 (Eng) MA. 7: Libn Pub Sch Lib, Ypsilanti 07-11; Asst ref Dept NY Pub Lib 12-16 Instr No State Normal Sch (Marquete Mich) summers 13-15; Instr Lib Sch of the NY Pub Lib 17-19; Asst ALA Lib War Serv Dispatch ff, Newport News Va 19; Head lib train class Bd of Educ, Toledo Ohio 20-22; Head Lib train class Pub Lib, Toledo Ohio 22-31; Br libn Pub Lib, Racine Wis 32-36; Br libn Pub Lib, Dayton Ohio 36-41; Head of acquis dept Pub Lib, Dayton Ohio 42-54; Parish libn St Andrews Episcopal Church, Dayton Ohio 57-. 9: ALA (Life mem; chm train Class Round Table 25-26, Represented Ohio Lib Assn on Coun 25-26, 45-49); OhioLA (treas 23-2, rep to ALA Coun 25-26 & 45-49). 10: AAUW; LWV; Correctional Assn; ACLU. ; Zonta Intl; Dayton View Neighborhood Coun; Dayton View Coalition. 13: Yes. 15: 1046 Cumberland, Dayton Ohio 45406.

NEWBURG, JAMES D. b Des Moines Iowa 10 S 36. 4: Lola Minor. 5: Iowa Wesleyan Col 54-58 (Eng) BA; UIll 58-59 MS in LS. 7: Ref dept asst Gary Pub Lib, Gary Ind 59-62, Ref dept 1st asst 62-64; Ref asst So Ill U 65-66, Spec ser libn 66-. 9: SLA; IllLA; NMA. 10: Cof C. 14: Ref, Govt docs, data processing applications to libs, admin, lib arch. 15: 1415 Montclaire ave, Edwardsville Il 62025.

NEWCOMB, ANNA (MARIE HELEN). b Pittston 21 S 13. 5: Marywood Col 32-36; Eng, soc studies; AB, 52-53; LS; MA, 54; Columbia 54. 6: Fr. 7: Tchr Pittston Twp High Sch, Pittston Penn 40-52; Sr libn catlgr W Orange Pub Lib W Orange NJ 53-56; Head catlgr Osterhout Free Lib, Wilkes-Barre Penn 56-59; Rec & circ libn Kings Col Lib 59-. 9: ALA; CathLA; PennLA. 14: Ref, circ. 15: 186 Market st, Pittston Pa 18702.

NEWCOMB, DORIS (DOYLE). b Bufalo SD 10 S 11. 4: Josiah T Newcomb. 5: U Denver 30-34 (LS) AB; Colo State Col 34-35 (Secondary Educ) MA; Syracuse 60 (LS). 6: Sp. 7: Libn Lab Sch Colo State Col 35-40; Asst catlgr Colo State Colo re-catlg proj 40-41; Libn Lab Sch Colo State Col 41-45; Order Libn Associated Cols of Upper NY;Plattsburg 46-50; Act libn Champlain Col SUNY 51-52; Libn Jennie Snapp Jr High Sch 55-56; Libn Central High Sch, Binghampton NY 57-. 8: Adv Child Bks, Fenton Free Lib, Broome Co NY 57-. 9: Womens Nat Bk Assn; NYLA. 10: /07/Boys/08/ 14: Admin, bk sel. 15: RD 5, Brooks rd, Binghamton NY 13905.

NEWCOMB, JOSIAH T. b Norwalk Conn 11 Je 11. 4: Doris D Newcomb. 5: Colo State Col of Educ 33-37 (Hist, Pol Sci) AB; UDenver 39-40 BS in LS; Columbia 49-50 (LS) MS. 7: Libn Greeley Pub Lib, Greeley Colo 41-42; Captain Armour US Army 42-45; Asst libn Tchrs Col Columbia U 45-46; Libn Champlain Col 46-50; Major Infantry US Army 50-52; Lib consul SUNY(Albany) 52; Dir of libs SUNY Harpur Col (Binghamton) 53-. 8: Visiting lecturer Sch of Lib Serv Syracuse U summers 47-52. 9: ALA; NYLA. 10: Broome Co Hist Soc; Dir, Binghamton Boys Club. 11: Bronze Star (Army). 13: Yes. 14: Admin, acad libs. 15: RD 5 Brooks rd, Binghamton NY 13905.

NEWELL, DORIS JEAN. b Cedar Rapids Iowa 23 F 41. 5: Coe Col 58-62 (Eng) BA; Columbia 62-63 (LS) MS. 6: Fr. 7: Summer wker St Louis Pub Lib, St Louis Mo 60-62; Ref libn Cedar Rapids Pub Lib, Cedar Rapids Iowa 63-65; Asst dir Clinton Pub Lib, Clinton Iowa 66-67; Y-a libn Long Beach Pub Lib, Long Beach Cal 67-68, Br libn 68-. 9: ALA; CalLA. 10: Beta Phi Mu. 14: Ref. 15: 32 7th pl #502, Long Beach Ca 90802.

NEWELL, ETHEL (JOHNSON). b Mesa Ariz 31 Ag 07. 5: Ariz State Tchrs Col 24-26 (Educ) Certif; Ariz State U 58 BA, 64 (Educ, Libnship) MA. 6: Sp. 7: Mus tchr Mesa Pub Schs, Mesa Ariz 26-27; News staff Ariz Republic & Gazette Mesa office 31-39; Instr Ariz State U summer 66; Libn Carson Jr High, Mesa Ariz 58-. 8: Consul for 1970 "Jr High Catalog" of H. W. Wilson Co. 9: Internat Reading Assn; Ariz State LA (pres sch Lib Div 65-66; Jr High Chm, 5 yrs, Pub Chm; Budget Chm 62; (past pres). 10: Delta Kappa Gamma; Jr Great Bks leader and coord. 11: Alpha Beta Alpha Award for excellence in libnship, 58. 14: Lit for middle sch & jr high. 15: 1131 E Univ dr, Mesa Az 85201.

NEWELL, M JEAN. b Attica NY 1 Ap 09. 4: Kenneth J Newell. 5: Mansfield State Tchrs Col 25-28 (Educ); State Tchrs Col (Geneseo NY) & Columbia 27-30 (Educ); Hofstra State Tchrs Col (New Paltz NY) 47-50 (Educ); St. Johns U 54-57 MLS; State Tchrs Col (Geneseo) UDenver Adelphi 57-65 (Educ). 7: Tchr & libn Brentwood Pub Schs, Brentwood NY 46-60; Libn Lloyd Harbor Sch, Huntington NY 60-. 9: NEA; ALA; NY State TA, NYStateTchrsA; NYLA. 10: Huntington Twp C of C; Delta Kappa Gamma. 14: Child serv. 15: 26 Ridgewood ave, Brentwood NY 11717.

NEWELL, VERA (CLEGG). b NYC 9 My 19. 4: Francis M Newell III. 5: Adelphi Col 36-38 (Eng); Douglass Col 39-41 (Eng, LS) AB. 7: Summer sub (br libn NY Pub Lib NYC 41; Br asst Hosp libn Newark (NJ) Pub Lib 41-42; Lib asst hosp libn US Signal Corps Spec Serv, Ft Monmouth NJ 42-44; Tech copywriter press) General Electric Co, Schenectady NY 44-45; Sec ser exchg asst Rutgers U Lib, New Brunswick NJ 47; Asst libn Hercules Powder Co, Wilmington Del 48-66, Libn 66-. 9: SLA; DelaLA. 14: Ref, catlg. 15: Hercules Inc Room 963, Hercules Tower, Wilmington De 19899.

NEWHALL, JANNETTE E. b Chester NH 28 N 1898. 5: Boston U 20-24 (Soc Wk) BS, 24-25, 26-30 (Philos) MA, PhD; UBerlin 30-31 (Philos); Simmons summers 41-44 BS in LS. 6: Ger, Fr. 7: Instr philos Wheaton Col Norton Mass) 31-37; Asst Newton Free Lib, Newton Mass 37-39; Asst libn Harvard Divinity Sch 39-44 Libn 44-49; Libn Boston U Sch of Theol

49-64; Act libn & Visiting PROF Union Theol Sem (Manilla Philippines) 64-66; Act libn Mary Baldwin Col 68-69. 8: Visiting Prof of Philos & Lib Sci Ewha Womans U Seoul Korea spring sem 59; Lib consul Silliman U Col of Theol (Philippines) 65; Consul Lib Wkshops; Philippines, Taiwan, Indonesia, Sarawak, Singapore, 66; Korea & Japan, Ap-May 67. 9: ALA; ATheolLA (pres 2 yrs, many com assignments, chm Com on Relig Period Index til 62); Amer Philos Assn; Greater Boston Theol Libn; Soc for Religin Higher Educ (Fellow). ; MassLA; VaLA. 12: "A Theological Library Manual for the Seminaries of Africa, Asia, and Latin America (69). 13: Yes. 14: Admin, period, index, Overseas theol libs. 15: 38 Buswell st apt 3, Boston Ma 02215.

NEWHARD, MARGARET (ELEANOR). b Norfolk Va 3 D 16. 5: Shorter Col 35-39 (Fr) AB; UNC 48-51 (Fr) MA, 55-57, 59-60 (Sp) PhD, 63-65, 68-69 MS in LS. 6: Sp, Fr. 7: Tchr: Hawkinsville High Sch, Hawkinsville Ga 39-40, Dalton Pub Schs, Dalton Ga 40-43, westminster Schs, Atlanta 45-47; Assoc Prof for langs Shorter Col 47-58; Tchg fellow Centro Colombo-Americano, Bogota Colombia 58-59; Assoc Prof for langs Wesleyan Col (Macon Ga) 64-68; Sp instr UNC (Chapel Hill) 64-68, catlgr 64-. 9: NCLA. 10: SAtlantic Mod Lang Assn. 14: Tchg, catlg. 15: 84 Dartmouth ave, Avondale Estates Ga 30002.

NEWKIRK, PHYLLIS ASENATH (TURRITTIN). b Sauk Rapids Minn 17 S 11. 5: UMinn 29-35 (Music, Piano) BA (cum laude); UMiami 51-56 (Elem Educ) BEd (magna cum laude); Fla State U 54-58 (LS) MA. 6: Sp, Fr. 7: Spec music tchr Nautilus Elem·& Jr High Sch, Miami Beach Fla 51-52; Tchr Ojus Elem Sch, Ojus Fla 53-54; Sch libn N Miami Elem Sch, Miami Fla 54-56; Tchr Hilltop Elem Sch, Chula Vista Cal 56-58; Sch libn Lemon Grove Jr High Sch, Lemon Grove Cal 58-63; Sch libn Palm Jr High Sch, Lemon Grove Cal 63-. 10: Phi Beta Kappa; Kappa Delta Pi; Sigma Alpha Iota. 14: Sch libs, music. 15: 2613 Nida place, Lemon Grove Ca 92045.

NEWKIRK, ROBERT DEVERELL. b Germantown Penn 2 N 10. 5: UPenn 39 (Eng) AB, 51 (Hist) MA; Drexel 40 BSLS. 6: Fr, Ger. 7: Spec asst Friends Free Lib, Germantown Penn 40-41; Libn Chestnut Hill Acad, Chestnut Hill Penn 41-42, Tchr 42-43; Libn & tchr Tower Hill Sch, Wilmington Dela 43-4, Head hist dept 45-47; Sr catlgr Temple U Lib 47-53; Libn II Free Lib of Phila 53-; Reviser catlg dept 53-55, catlgr rare bk dept 55-. 9: BSA. 10: Soc Arch Histns; Athenaeum of Phila; Lib Co of Phila Art Allance Print Club of Phila; Phila Museum of Art; Friends of UPenn Lib; Zoolo Soc Phila. 15: 1810 Rittenhouse sq, Phila Pa 19103.

NEWLAND, CHESTER A. b Kansas City Kan 18 Je 30. 5: MidwesternU 51-52; N Tex StateU 52-54 (Govt) BA; UKan 54-58 (Pol Sci) MA & PhD. 6: Ger, Fr. 7: Staff Sgt USAF (instr), Sheppard AFB 48-52; Research fellow Soc Sci Research Coun, NYC 58-59; Instr dept of Pol Sci Ida StateU 59-60; Prof & dir Dept of Govt N Tex StateU 60-66; Visiting Prof School of Pub Admin USoCar, Los Angeles Ca 66-67, Prof 68-69; Prof Dept of Pol Sci UHouston 67-68; Dir Lyndon B Johnson Lib, Austin Tex 69-. 9: Amer Soc Pub Admin (pres Dallas-Ft Worth Chap 64-65); Amer Pol Sci Assn; Amer Mgt Assn; West Pol Sci Assn; Midwest Conf of Pol Sci. 10: Pub Personnel Assn; Soc for Personnel Admin. 13: Yes. 15: 1801 Lavaca apt 9B, Austin Tx 78701.

NEWLAND, ELIZABETH (WHARTON). b Greensboro NC 4 My 18. 4: Charles W L Newland. 5: Woman's Col UNC 34-39 (Hist, Pol Sci) AB; UNC (Chapel Hill) 39-40 ABLS. 6: Fr. 7: Brunswick Co Lib, Lawrenceville Va 40-42; Asst circ libn HYC Pub Lib 42; Middle- lower sch libn Brearley Sch, NYC 42-43; Circ asst Woman's Col UNC (Greensboro) 53-54; A-v catlgr Greensbory City Schs, Greensboro NC 53-57, 61-67; Asst catlg libn UNC (Greensboro) 67-. 9: ALA; SELA; NCLA. 10: Phi Beta Kappa. 14: Catlg. 15: 2403 Pinecroft rd, Greensboro NC 27407.

NEWLAND, LYDIA M. b Albany NY 4 Ag 13. 5: Skidmore Col 30-34 (Eng Lit) AB; Columbia 34-35 (LS) BS. 6: Fr. 7: Asst catlgr Skidmore Col Lib 35; Lib asst Albany Pub Lib, Albany NY 36-38; Libn Dickinson Jr Col 38-40; Lib asst Sweet Briar Col 40-42, Asst libn 42-. 8: Lib Adv Com Va State Coun for Higher Educ. 9: ALA; SELA; VaLA. 10: Bibliog Soc UVa. 13: Yes. 14: Ref, acquis. 15: 4 Woodland rd, Sweet Briar Va 24595.

NEWLON, ELOISE (FISHER) (MRS). b Walton WVa 15 My 13. 5: Ohio U 29-31 WVa U 31-35 (Eng) AB, AM; Columbia 47, summer 48 BS in LS. 7: Tchr-Roane Co Schs, Spencer WVa 35-36; Tchr-libn Roane Co Schs, Walton WVa 36-43; Sr catlgr WVa U 45-54; Catlgr Cleveland Pub Lib 54-56; Asst libn Morris Harvey Col 56-66, Act libn 58-61; Coord lib serv Kanawha Co Schs, Charleston WVa. 9: ALA; WVaLA; NEA; WVaEA. 10: AAUP, Soroptimist Club. 14: Catlg. 15: 1938 Bona Vista dr, Charleston WVa 25311.

NEWLOVE, MRS ELIZABETH (SMITH). b Syracuse NY 2 Jl 03. 4: Thomas P Newlove. 5: Syracuse 21-25 BS in LS. 6: Fr, Sp. 07x; syracuse U Lib: Catlgr 25-30, Head of catlg dept 30-65, Asst dir 65-. 9: ALA; NYLA. 10: Syracuse U Lib Staff Assn; Beta Phi Mu; Phi appa Phi. 11: Syracuse Post Award for Distinguished Serv to SyracuseU Lib 66. 14: Catlg, personnel. 15: 1832 S State st, Syracuse NY 13205.

NEWMAN, CLARE B. b Oskaloosa Iowa 5 Jl 15. 4: William H Newman. 5: William Penn Col 32-35 (Econ); UChicago 36-37 (Pol Sci) AB; Columbia 59-61 (LS) MS. 6: Fr. 7: Elem sch libn Paramus Pub Schs, Paramus NJ 61-62; Music Libn Tenafly Pub Lib, Tenafly NJ 62-. 9: ALA; MusLA. 10: Beta Phi Mu; AAUW. 14: Music libnship. 15: 152 Downey dr, Tenafly NJ 07670.

NEWMAN, EDWARD C. b NYC 9 Mr 21. 4: Nancy Bowers. 5: Columbia 49-50 MS in LS; Dartmouth Col 38-42 (Classics) BA. 6: Portu, Sp, Fr. 7: Examiner Off of Censorship, NYC 42; Tech Sgt US Army 42-46; Catlgr NY Pub Lib 46-50; Catlg libn Yakima Reg Lib, Yakina Wash 50-52; Asst libn Temple U 52-53; Br libn Free Lib of Phila 54-59; Asst Dir Omaha Pub Lib 59-. 8: Consul Nat Lib of Guatemala, Guatemala City Guatemala 58. 9: ALA (Coun 67-71); NebLA (Exec Bd 68-71). 13: Yes. 14: Admin. 15: 5201 Cass st, Omaha Nb 68132.

NEWMAN, ELMER S. b Cleveland 19 Mr 19. 4: Mary Kratt. 5: West Res 37-41 (Pol Sci) BA, 63-65 MS in LS. 7: Intelligence Off US Army Signal Corps (1st Lt) 41-45; Credit manager Electroline Sales Co, Cleveland 46-55; Pricing supv Sam Palevsky Hardware Co, Bedford Ohio 55-63; Adult serv lbn Cuyahoga Co Pub Lib, Maple HEIGHTS Ohio 65-67; Acquis libn Cleveland State U 67-. 9: OhioLA. 10: Phi Beta Kappa; AAUP. 14: Ref, acquis. 15: 858 S Green rd, Euclid Oh 44121.

NEWMAN, JOHN JAMES JR. b Morehead City NC 12 N 42. 5: UWash 60-61, 64-67 (Hist) BA, 67-68 MLib. 6: Ger. 7: Asst mss libn UIowa 68-. 10: Phi Alpha Theta& friends of the UIowa Libs. 13: Yes. 14: Mss, ser. 15: 715 Carriage hill apt 7, Iowa City Ia 52240.

NEWMAN, LILLIAN (LEE). b Middlesboro Ky 3 N 25. 5: Lincoln Mem U 45-47 (Hist) BA; Peabody 47-48 BS in LS; Emory 56-57 (LS0 MLn. 6: Sp. 7: Asst to libn Agnes Scott Col 48-51, Asst libn 51-; Ref dept Emory U summer 60. 9: ALA; GaLA; SELA; Atlanta Lib Club. 10: AAUP. 14: Col libs, ref. 15: Agnes Scott Col, Decatur Ga 30030.

NEWMAN, LOIS EDA. b Los Angeles 14 My 34. 5: Scripps Col 52-53; Marymount Col 53-56 (Theatre Arts) AB; Smith 56-58 (Theatre) AM; Immaculate Heart Col 59-61, 64-65 (Educ, LS) MALS; USoCal summers 61, 62. 6: Fr, Ger. 7: Tchr Our Lady Queen of Angels High Sch, Los Angeles 58-59; Tchr Villa Cabrini Acad, Burbank Cal 59-61; Tchr Mary Star of the Sea High Sch, San Pedro Cal 61-62; Instr Edgewood Col 62-63; Catlgr Rand Corp, Santa Monica 65-. 9: ALA; CalLA; Amer Soc Indexers. 10: Internat Wizard of Oz Club; UN Assn, Los Angeles. 13: Yes. 14: Rare bks, ref, catlg. 15: 10390 Ashton ave, Los Angeles Ca 90024.

NEWMAN, MRS MAYRELEE (FALLQUIST). b Spokane Wash 29 Je 26. 5: Mills Col 44-45; Wash State U 46-49 (Eng) BA; UWash 56-58 MLS. 7: Newspaper reporter "Spokane DAILY Chronicle Spokane Wash 44; Bk saleslady Frederick & Nelson, Seattle 55; Asst child libn King Co Pub Lib, Seattle 57-58; Juvenile serv & ext libn Washoe Co Lib, Reno Nev 58-59; Bkmob libn Columbia River Reg Lib Dem, Moses Lake Wash 60; Base libn Larson AFB Wash, Moses Lake Wash 60-65; Visiting Prof UNev summers 60, 62, 63, 64, 65; Staff libn Hq 8 AF Direct of Personnel, Westover AFB Mass 65-66; Planner learning res Dallas Co Jr Col Dist 66-. 8: Tchg lib sci courses at U of Nev; Reading for ya; Producing pub serv radio programs 4 times weekly 63-; Nat adv com AAJC Program W Devel Inst; chm JCLS Preconf Com 69-70. 9: ALA; NEA-DAVI; TexLA; SWLA. 10: Phi Beta Kappa; Phi Kappa Phi. 12: Jt auth "Tex-Tec Syllabi". 13: Yes. 14: Pub, radio, child wk, music collections, jr col. 15: 9960 Brockbank, Dallas Tx 75220.

NEWMAN, ROBERT GEORGE. b Garden City NY 25 Je 12. 5: Dartmouth 30-34 (Eng) AB; Harvard 34-35 (Eng) AM; Columbia summers 39-41, 46 BS in LS. 7: Circ ref exec asst high sch libn Berkshire Athenaeum, Pittsfield Mass 35-41; Pvt to 1st Lt AUS 42-43; Captain AUS Chief MilPersonnel Br Camp Edwards Mass Chief libn ChiefLibn Berkshire Athenaeum, Pittsfield Mass 46-. 8: Chm Pittsfield Sch Bldg Survey Commsn 49; Chm Pittsfield City Hist Commsn 54-57. 9: ALA; MassLA; (pres 68-69); West Mass Lib Club (past pres) West Mass Reg Pub Lib system v-chm Exec Com 64-; NELA (mem Adv Coun Reg Planning Com, mem Adv Com, Little Lib Planning Study for Mass). 10: Rotary; Harvard Club; Dartmouth Club; Melville Soc; Trustee & Clerk of Corporation City Savings Bank of Pittsfield; Mem Bd Govrs Berkshire Med Ctr; Trustee Hancock (Mass) Shaker Commun. 13: Yes. 14: Admin, reg pub lib serv. 15: Berkshire Athenaeum 44 Bank Row, Pittsfield Ma 01201.

NEWMAN, RUTH (MISHNUN). b NYC. 4: Seymour Newman. 5: Hunter Col (Eng) BA; Columbia (Eng) MA; (LS) BS. 6: Fr, Ger. 7: Ed asst H W Wilson Co, NYC 40-42; Libn Coles Signal Lab, Red Bank NJ 42-44; Libn Amer Smelting & refining Co, Perth Amboy NJ 44-47; Asst libn Squibb Inst for Med Research, NYC 47-54; Libn Nepera Chem Co, N Yonkers NY 54-55; Libn Sproul & Associates, Inc, NYC 55-63; Head catlgr Cornell U Med Col NYC 63-. 9: MedLA; SLA; NYLib Club; NYTech Serv Libns. 10: AMer Med Writers Assn. 12: "A Modern Flower of St Francis (39); "A. Vade Mecum for Teachrs of Religion (49); ". and Spare Me Not in the Making (52);"Beneath the Lamps Rays (61); "The Handbook of Catholic Practices (64); Ed Commun "Newsletter (49-55); Ed "Newsletter Greater NY Unit CathLA 55-58; Ed "Pro Deo Newsletter (65); Ed Col & Univ Sect Newsletter 68-. 14: Catlg, ref. 15: 501 W 123d st, NYC 10027.

NEWMAN, RUTH (TRAMMELL). b Lexington Ky 24 Je 15. 4: James A Newman. 5: UKy 35-39 (LS) AB. 7: Librarian: Harlan (Ky) High Sch 39-41, Ludlow (Ky) High Sch 41-43; Staff Margaret I King Lib, summers 39-42; Libn Lloyd High Sch, Erlanger 44-45; Reserve libn West Ky State U 46; Hd Bowling Green Pub Lib, Ky 47-48; Libn child lib Denver Pub Lib 48-49; Asst libn Denison Lib UColo Med Sch 49-51; Asst libn Woodbury br Denver Pub Lib 51-54, Head Park Hill Reg Lib 54-64, Hd literature & hist dept 64-67, Coord adult serv 67-. 9: ALA; ColoLA; MPLA. 10: Bus & Prof Women. 14: Admin, ref, lib educ. 15: 1401 Fairfax st apt #7, Denver Co 80220.

NEWMAN, WILLIAM. b Cerne Czechoslovakia 18 F 37. 4: Vivian Dowling. 5: Brooklyn Col 55-59 (Math Philos) BA; Columbia 59-60 MS in LS. 6: Ger, Czech, Russian, Yiddish. 7: Libn trainee Brooklyn Pub Lib 59-60; Personnel mgt spec (Sp/4) US Army 60-62; Adult serv libn Brooklyn Pub Lib 62-63; Ser catlgr Cornell U Libs 63-65; Ref libn UMont 65-67; Libn Fac of Admin Studies York U (Toronto Can) 67-; Asst dir pub serv York U Lib 69-. 9: ALA; SLA; ASIS. 10: AHA, Audubon Soc; Wilderness Soc.13 Yes. 14: Ref, bibliog, adm. 15: 14 Wycliffe Cresc, Willowdale Ont Can.

NEWMEYER, FRITZIE (NISENSON). b Pittsburgh Penn 12 Mr 20. 5: UPenn 37-41 (Pol Sci) BA; Bryn Mawr Col 41-42 (Econ, Politics); LIU 63-65 (LS) MS. 6/ ger, Fr. 7: Jr economist War Manpower Commsn, Wash DC 42; Asst economist War Labor Bd, Phila 43-44; Libn C W Post Col LIU 64-, Hd catlg dept 68-. 9: ALA; NassauCoLA (pres Col & Univ Div 69-). 10: Pi Gamma Mu; Delta Phi Alpha; LWV. 14: Catlg. 15: 63 Reid ave, Port Washington NY 11050.

NEWNAM, BARBARA (BONOMO). b Miami Fla 15 F 44. 4: Robert Edward Newman. 5: UNC (Greensboro) 62-66 (Sp' BA; UNC (Chapel Hill) 66-67 MSLS. 6: Sp, Ital. 7: Catlgr Pub Lib of Forsyth Co, Winston-Salem NC 67-68; Catlgr Pub Lib of Charlotte & Mecklenburg Co, Charlotte NC 68-. 9: ALA; MecklenburgLA. 10: Phi Beta Kappa. 14: Catlg. 15: 5346 Glenbrier dr, Charlotte NC 28212.

NEWNAN, MARJORIE (EVELAND) MRS. b Spokane Wash. 5: UWash 39-41 (Gen Studies) BA; San Jose State Col 60-65 (LS) MA. 6: Fr, Ger. 7: Page clerical asst Pub Lib, Spokane Wash 35-42 Clerical wk UWash Lib 40-41; Asst libn Los Altos High Sch, Los Altos Cal 59-61; Head Libn Awalt High Sch, Mountain View Cal 61-. 8: Subscr mgr "California School Libraries 65-, Assoc ed 69-. 9: ALA; NEA; CalASchL CalTA; CLA. 10: Bd of Trustees, Mountain View Pub Lib 58-64. 14: Ya serv. 15: 1044 Sladky ave, Mountain View Cal 94040.

NEWSOM, FRANCES S(UE SCHROEDER). b Portland Ore 27 Ja 06. 5: UOre 24-28 Biol Sci BA; UDenver 48-53 (LS) MA. 7: Biol tchr Ashland Sr High Sch, Ashland Ore 28-30; UOre Lib; Ref asst 30-31, Res asst 43-45, Museum of Art libn 45-47, Asst arch & allied arts libn -50, Arch & allied arts libn 50-. 9: PNLA; OreLA. 10: UOre Women; Natural Hist Soc of Eugene; Ore Acad of Sci; Fed of West Outdoor Clubs; Sierra Club; Mem of 7 Conservation and Wildlife Clubs & Coms; Ore Hist Soc; Lane Co Hist Soc; Very Little Theatre; Phi Beta Kappa; Pi Lambda Theta; AAUP; Soc Arch Histns; Arts in Ore Assn. 14: Slide processing, classification & catlg, Ore arch, natural hist of Ore. 15: 708 E 11th ave, Eugene Or 97401.

NEWSOME, LOUANE LEECH. b Orange Cal 8 S 06. 5: Santa Ana Jr Col 24-26 Jr Certif; Pomona Col 26-28 (Educ) BA; UCal (Berkeley) 30 BSLS. 6: Fr. 7: Head Libn Pub Lib, Petaluma Cal 30-43; Libn US Army Camp Lockett Cal 43-44; Libn US Navy Lib Serv NIsland San Diego Cal 44-47; Supv sch libs Pub Schs, River Forest Ill 47-50; Libn Math-Physics lib UIowa 50-58; Prof Lib Sci 58-. 8: Prof Lib Sci Mont State U, Bozeman Mont summers 68, 69. 9: ALA (chm Dorothy Canfield Fisher Com, chm Melcher Scholarship Com); CalLA (Dist Chm); IowaLA (pres 62-63, Exec Bd two 3-r terms, chm var coms). 10: Pi Lambda Theta; University Club; Delta Kappa Gamma. 14: Educ for libnship, child lit. 15: 127 Fersun ave, Iowa City Ia 52240.

NEWSOME, WALTER L. b Panama City Fla 11 O 41. 4: Carolyn H Wegner. 5: Fla State U 61-63 (Eng Educ) BS, 64-65 (LS) MS. 7: Eng tchr S Broward High Sch, Hollywood Fla 63-64; Libn Ctr for adult studies Pensacola Jr Col 65-67; Asst ref/docs libn Fla Atlantic U 67-. 9: ALA; FlaLA. 14: Govt docs. 15: 246 NE 16th st, Delray Beach Fl 33444.

NEWSWANGER, K LOUISE (MYERS). b Doylestown Penn 20 My 42. 4: Carl K Newswanger. 5: East Mennonite Col 60-64 (Hist) BA; Drexel 64-65, 66 MSLS. 6: Ger. 7: Libn Biblical Sem Lib Goshen Col 65-. 14: Ref, theol collections. 15: Biblical Sem Lib, Goshen Col, Goshen Ind 46526.

NEWTON, ALICE ELIZABETH (WATERMAN). b Athol Mass 12 Ag 11. 4: Burton E Newton. 5: Simmons 29-33 (LS) BS. 7: Asst libn Athol Pub Lib, Athol Mass 36-42, 57-60, Libn 60-. 9: MassLA; Bay Path Lib Club (v-pres). 10: Athol Hist Soc; Womens Club. 15: 285 High, Athol Mass 01331.

NEWTON, DANIEL R(ABUN). b Lyons Ga 19 Ja 31. 5: USCar 48-52 (Eng) AB, 53-54 (Eng) MA; Rutgers 55-56 MLS. 6: Fr. 7: Circ asst Richland Co Pub Lib, Columbia SC 52-53; Asst sci dept McKissick Mem Lib USCar 54-56; Research asst Grad Sch of Lib Serv Rutgers U 55-56; Gen asst br libn Queens Borough (NY) Pub Lib 56-58; Dir W Hempstead (NY) Pub Lib 58-60 Dir The Bryant Lib Roslyn NY 60-. 9: ALA; NYLA; NYLib Club; Nassau Co (NY) Lib Club. 10: Melvil Dui Chowder & Marching Soc; Phi Beta Kappa. 14: Pub lib admin. 15: The Bryant Lib, Roslyn NY 11576.

NEWTON, DOROTHY ELIZABETH. b Quincy Mass 31 Ja 14. 5: Simmons 32-36 (LS) BS. 7: Sr asst Thomas Crane Pub Lib, Quincy Mass 37-45, Catlgr 46-63, Chief catlgr 63-64, Asst libn 64-. 9: MassLA; NELA; Old Colony Lib Club. 10: Quincy Hist Soc; Womens Club. 14: Catlg. 15: 17 Howe st, Quincy Mass 0219.

NEWTON, DOROTHY H (EISE) MRS. b Columbia Penn 26 O 10. 4: Fred H Newton. 5: Syracuse 30-34 BSLS. 7: Libn sec Jr High Sch, Endicott NY 35-36; Jr libn Buffalo Pub Lib, Buffalo NY 50-52; Hosp libn Hartford Pub Lib, Hartford Conn 53; Lib tchr Bd of Educ, Hartford Conn 53-66; Lib Aide State Dept of Educ, Hartford Conn summer 61; Libn Prosser Pub Lib, Bloomfield Conn summer 62, 64; Libn Hartford Inst of Accounting, Hartford Conn 66-68; Libn Wethersfield Bd of Educ, Wethersfield Conn 66-. 8: Libn Morse Col, Hartford Conn summer 66. 9: ALA; ConnSchLA; ConnEA; WethersfieldEA. 10: Chi Omega; New Horizons,Child Museum of Hartford. 14: Yp wk. 15: 10 Carmel st, Hartford Conn 06106.

NEWTON, EARLE W. b Cortland NY 10 Ap 17. 4: Josephine A (Lyon) Newton. 5: Amherst 34-38 (Hist) AB; Columbia 38-40 (Hist) AM; UFla 67-68 (Lib Admin). 6: Sp. 7: Asst to libn Amherst Col 34-38; Libn (dir) Vt Hist Soc, Montpelier Vt 41-49; Dir Old Sturbridge Vil, Sturbridge Mass 49-54; Dir inst of hist & archival mgt Harvard- Radcliffe 54-55; Sr research fellow ULond, Eng 55-56; Dir Penn Bur of Mus & Hist Sites, Harrisburg Penn 56-59; Exec dir St Augustine Hist Preservation & Restoration commsn, St Augustine Fla 59-68; Exec dir Pensacola Hist Preservation & Restoration Commsn, Pensacola Fla 68-. 8: Consul (and Actg Dir of the Lib), Flagler Col, St augustine 67-68; Consul Rockefeller Bros Fund (Museum devel) 53; Consul on Spec collections, UWFla 68-69. 9: ALA; Amer Assn of Museums; Amer Assoc State & Local hist (exec sec 46-52); Soc of Amer Histns (sec 51-52); Inter-Amer Inst of Fine Arts (pres 65-66); Northeast Museums Assn (v-pres); NEd Mus Assn (chm 53-62).

10: Nat trust; Newcomen Soc. 11: Commander, Order of Isabella la Catolica; Order of Merit; AWARD OF Merit (Amer Inst of Graphic Arts) 50,51,52. 12: Ed-in-Chief (& founder) "American Heritage" (49-54); ed-in-chief (& founder) "Vermont Life" (46-50); ed-in- chief "Vermont Quarterly" (42-50); Auth "The Vermont Story" (49); "Before Pearl harbor" (42). 13: Yes. 14: Admin, organ of new libs, rare bks, exhibits. 15: 105 W Gonzalez st, Pensacola Fl 32501.

NEWTON, MACK DAVID. b Vicksburg Miss 13 N 39. 4: Celia Sue Walker. 5: Centralia Col 58-60 (Hist) AA; West Wash State Col (Hist) BAEd; UWash 68-69, summer 67 MLS. 6: Fr. 7: Secondary sch tchr: Ocosta Consolidated, Westport Wash 62-63, Oak Grove High Sch, Oak Grove La 63-67, Pe Ell High Sch, Pe Ell Wash 67-68; Libn Hazen High Sch, Wash 69-. 9: LaTA; WashEA. 15: 4005 15th ave NE apt 609, Seattle Wa 98105.

NEWTON, SABRON R(EYNOLDS). b W Branch Iowa 8 Mr 33. 4: Robert C Newton. 5: Earlham Col 49-50, 52-53 (Soc Sci) AB; UIll 54-55 (LS) MS. 6: Sp. 7: Asst ref libn UIll Lib (Urbana) 55-60; Ref libn readers Serv div Oberlin Col Lib 60-63; Summer libn Sheldon Jackson Jr Col summers 62, 64;Documents Docs libn Earlham Col Lib 64-66; Docs libn UChicago 66-. 9: ALA (Scarecrow Press Awardjury 66; Internat Rel Round Table);-ACRL;-RSD. 12: Contrib auth "The Student Economists Handbook (67). 14: Govt docs, ref. 15: Documents Dept Univ of Chicago Lib, Chicago Il 60637.

NEYMAN, MARK (RICHARD MARKLE). b Parkersburg WVa 17 N 40. 4: Sandra Lee Bessemer. 5: Marietta Col 58-62 (Hist) BA; West Res summers 63-65, spring 66 MS in LS. 6: Sp. 7: Tchr marietta City Schs, Marietta Ohio 62-63, Libn 63-68; Dir Wash Co Pub Lib syat, Marietta Ohio 68-. 9: ALA; OhioLA. 10: Alpha Tau Omega; Marietta Col Alum Assn; Lions Internatl; Mid-Ohio Valley Players. 14: Ref, ya, admin. 15: 128 Euclid pl, Marietta Oh 45750.

NEYMAN, SANDRA (LEE) BESSEMER. b Mansfield Ohio 16 Mr 40. 4: Richard M Neyman. 5: Marietta Col 58-62 (Hist) BA; Case West Res 67-68 MS in LS. 6: Sp, Fr, Lat. 7: Asst catlgr Dawes Memorial, Marietta Col 62-67, Sr catlgr 68-. 9: ALA; -ACRL; ASIS. 10: Beta Phi Mu; Phi Alpha Theta. 14: Catlg, rare bks. 15: 128 Euclid pl, Marietta Oh 45750.

NEYNDORFF, HANS. b Surabaya Indonesia 25 My 21. 4: Hertha Desiree Schultz. 5: Govt lyceum (Surabaya Indonesia) 34-41 (Lit, Econ) Equiv of AA; UIndonesia (Djakorta) 41-42 (Law), 46-48 (Econ, Law) BS, LLB; ULeiden (Netherlands) 50-52 (Econ of Developing countries) Doctoral; Netherlands Inst of Documentation & Research 53 Equiv MLS. 6: Dutch, Fr, Ger, Indonesian. 7: Dist commissioner Netherlands-Indies Civil Serv, Modjokerto Indonesia 48-53; Judge advocate Royal Netherlands Army, Modjokerto Indonesia 49-50; Documentalist & asst libn Central Bur of Statistics, The Hague Netherlands 53-55; Econ researcher & ref libn Econ Info Serv, The Hague Netherlands 55-57; Accountant San Diego Gas & Electric Co Construction Dept 57-61; Prof Hist Grossmont Col 61-65; Asst soc sci libn San Diego State Col 62-. 8: Sec to the Asst Governor of East-Java, Surabaya, Indonesia 48; Adv to the UN Commsn for Indonesia (Truce Observance Commsn), Field Commsn for Good Offices, Modjokerto, East-Java, Indonesia 49; Consul to the Regent of Modjokerto Indonesia 48-49; Adv wk on behalf of Dutch participation in Common Market, The Hague Holland 53-57. 9: CalLA. 10: Amer Fed Tchrs; Mem of the Session and the Board of Trustees, Chm Soc Educ and Action Commsn, Trinity Presbyterian Church; Del Synod So Cal, United Presbyt Church USA; Pres DURF Inc (Dutch-Indonesian Assn) San Diego Cal. 11: War Memorial Cross with Combat Star, awarded by the Queen of the Netherlands, Java 41-42. 14: Ref. 15: 7902 Normal ave, La Mesa Ca 92041.

NEZGODA, SALLY (KEYES). b Tomahawk Wis 11 Ag 44. 4: Thomas Nezgoda. 5: UWis(Madison) 62-63, 66-67 MLS; Northland Col 63-66 (Soc Studies) BA; Colo State U 67-68 (Accounting). 7: Asst acquis libn Colo StateU 67-68; Pub serv libn Beloit Col 68-. 15: Beloit College Lib, Beloit Wi 53511.

NG, DORA (LEE). b Fresno Cal 2 Mr 42. 4: Gene T Ng. 5: San Francisco State Col 60-64 (Sociol) AB; UCal (Berkeley) 64-65 MLS. 6: Chinese, Sp. 7: Child libn Oakland Pub Lib, Oakland Cal 65-66; Soc sci ref libn San Francisco State Col 66, Catlgr 66-. 9: CalLA. 15: 677-35th ave, San Francisco Ca 94121.

NICHOL, FLORENCE (MARIE). b Albia Iowa 11 Jl 03. 5: Monmouth Col (Monmouth Ill) 21-25 (Eng) BA; UIll 26-27 BSLS. 6: Ger, Sp. 7: Circ dept Ill State Lib, Springfield Ill 27-35, Circ & direct ref 35-50, Hd ref dept (direct & mail) 50-. 9: ALA; Amer Soc Pub Admin; IllLA. 10: AAUW; Springfield Lib Club; Amateur Musical Club; Altrusa Internat. 14: Ref. 15: 425 S 7th st apt L, Springfield Il 62701.

NICHOLAOU, MARY P. b Mytilene Greece 14 F 38. 5: Keuka Col 57-58 (Eng); SUNY Albany) 58-61 (LS) BA, 61-62 (LS) MS. 6: Gk, Fr. 7: Lib page Albany Pub Lib, Albany NY 55-57; Lib clerk Albany Pub Lib, Albany NY 58-61; Child & ya libn Delmar Pub Lib, Delmar NY 62-63; Spec serv libn Friedberg/Butzbach Germany 63-64, Libn Bamberg Germany 64-65; Main libn Vaihingen Germany 65-, Main libn Robinson Bks, Germany 66. 8: Child serv consul Mohawk Valley Lib Assn, Schenectady NY. 9: ALA; NYLA (mem bd dirrs, mem com for rev "Recording for Children; Hudson-Mohawk LA. 14: Admin, child wk. 15: 144 Lawn ave, Albany NY 12204.

NICHOLAS, MARTHA ANN (WILLIAMS). b Memphis 15 Ap 36. 4: D Jack Nicholas. 5: Ark State U 55-58 (Elem Educ) BSE; N Tex State U 61-64 (Second Educ) MEd. 7: Elem mus tchr: Gideon (Mo) Pub Schs 55-58, Ft Worth Pub Schs 58-61; Elem tchr Aubrey (Tex) Pub Schs 61-64; Elem libn Lewisville (Tex) Pub Schs 64-65; Elem tchr Riverside (Cal) Pub Schs 65-66; Libn So Baptist Col 66-. 9: Ark Foun of Associated Cols (sec 67-68). 14: Lib admin, circ, ref. 15: Box 456 College City, Walnut Ridge Ar 72476.

NICHOLDS, RUTH (SIBLEY). b Austin Tex 3 Je 17. 4: B Melvin Nicholds. 5: So Methodist U 35-40 (Comparative Lit) BA; Tex State Col for Women 50-53 MLS; UChicago even 54. 6: Lat, Fr. 7: Dallas Pub Lib: Registration clerk 37-39, Br libn Oak Lawn Br 39-41, Br libn Oak Cliff Br 41-53; Head poular lib dept Gary Pub Lib, Gary Ind 53-56; Head Libn Geneva Pub Lib; Geneva Ill 56-. 8: Tchr childs lit Elgin Commun Col 61-68. 9: ALA; IllLA; Lib Adminrs Conf of No Ill (Chm 59-61, chm In-service Train 64-65). 10: Geneva Womans Club: Zonta Internat; AAUW; No Ill Steam Power Club C of C. 14: (Admin, in-serv train, tchg. 15: Geneva Pub Lib 27 S nd, Geneva Ill 60134.

NICHOLLS, ALICE (MASTERS). b Sioux City Iowa 1D 30. 4: Edwin Alfred Nicholls Jr. 5: UTenn 48-51 (Elem Educ) MS; Fla State U 54-55 MS in LS. 7: UTenn Lib Circ asst 52-53, Documents asst 53-54, Asst order libn 55-59, Educ libn 59-. 9: ALA; TennLA; SELA. 10: Alpha Beta Alpha. 14: Pub serv, circ, ref. 15: Educ Lib, Univ of Tenn, Knoxville Tenn 37916.

NICHOLS, DIANE MARIE (PENDLETON). b Louisville Ky 27 Je 41. 4: Harold L Nichols. 5: UKy 59-60 (Eng); ULouisville 61-65 (Eng) BA; Catherine Spalding Col 67- MSLS. 6: Sp. 7: Asst libn Portlanf Br Louisville Free Pub Lib, Louisville Ky 61-68; Asst libn ULouisville Sch of Dentistry Lib 68-. 9: KyLA; Louisville Lib Club. 14: Ref. 15: 2745 Bank st, Louisville Ky 40212.

NICHOLS, DOLORES (JULIA) DUNAVIN. b Algood Tenn 17 Mr 33. 4: Earl Young Nichols. 5: Tenn Polytech Inst 51-53, 56 (Home Econ) BS; Peabody 57, 58-59 (LS) MA. 7: Clerk typist GS-3 Off Personnel Br, Ft Huachuca Ariz 54-56; Libn II Upper Cumberland Reg Lib Cookeville Tenn 57-, Asst dir 68-. 9: ALA; SELA; TennLA (sec Pub Lib Sect 68-69). 10: Algood Bk Club; Algood Wesleyan Serv Guild. 14: Bkmob, child bks. 15: Rte 6, Cookeville Tenn 38501.

NICHOLS, JAMES EDWIN. b Iowa City Iowa 3 Je 23. 5: Coe Col 46-50 (Eng) BA; UMinn 50-51 (Amer Studies); Colo State Col 51-52 (Educ); UDenver 54-57 (Educ) MA, 64-65 (LS) MA. 6: Fr. 7: USAF (Cpl), US & Europe 43-46; Tchr Denver Pub Schs 52-64; Staff consul UDenver summer 65; Libn Denver Pub Schs 65-; Instr UDenver 65-, Asst Prof UDenver 66-. 8: Educ TV French Instr, Denver 60-62; Summer wkshop consul (libnship) UDenver summer 6566. 9: NEA; NCTE; Dir Elem Div; ALA; ColoLA; ColoSchLA; ColoEA. 10: Denver Symphony Soc; Denver Lyric Theatre; Canterbury Club; Great bks discussion gps; AAUP. 13: Yes. 14: Tchg libnship, lit & guidance for ya, ref, hist of bk, sch lib admin. 15: 1568 Verbena st, Denver Colo 80220.

NICHOLS, LUCY. b Everett Mass 24 Je 12. 5: Mt Holyoke 30-34 (Eng Lit) AB; Simmons 34-35 (LS) BS; State Tchrs Col (Oswego NY) 36-37; Syracuse 38 (LS); West Res 54, 65- (Pub speaking, a-v aids). 7: Gen asst UMe Lib, Orono Me 35-36; Asst City Lib, Oswego, NY 36-42; Libn Kingsford Park Jr High Sch, Oswego NY 36-42; Libn Oswego High Sch, Oswego NY 42-43; Elem sch lib; Lakewood Ohio 43-46; Libn Emerson Jr High Sch, Lakewood Ohio 46-47; Elem sch libn, Lakewood Ohio 47-66; Libn Lincoln Learning Ctr, Lakewood Ohio 67-. 9: ALA; NEA-DAVI; OhioEA; OhioASchL (chm Elem Libs Com 59) 10: PTA; Cleveland Coun on World Affairs; Mt Holyoke

Club of Cleveland; Simmons Col Club of Cleveland. 13: Yes. 14: Child lit, educ media. 15: 1372 Bunts rd, Lakewood Oh 44107.

NICHOLS, MARIAN (CHAMBERLIN). b Bellevue Ohio 13 S 15. 4: William J Nichols. 5: Cornell Col 31-35 (Speech, Play Production) BA; UColo summer 35 (Educ); Columbia 39-40 BS in LS. 7: Jr high tchr City Schs, Muscatine Iowa 35-39; Asst libn 6 Bard Col 40-42, Ref libn 54-56, Asst libn 56-63; High sch libn Central Sch, Rhinebeck NY 63-64; Assoc libn Marist Col 64-. 9: NYLA. 10: Pres Starr Inst (Lib) Rhinebeck NY 63-65; Phi Beta Kappa. 14: Catlg. 15: 27 South st, Rhinebeck NY 12572.

NICHOLS, WILLIAM J. b NYC 0 S 18. 4: Marian Chamberlin. 5: Bad Col 36-40 (Math) BA; Columbia 40-41 MLS. 6: Fr, Ger. 7: The Franklin Roosevelt IB, Hyde Park NY: Jr museum aide 41-42, Jr archives asst 42-43, Libn 43-58; Dir Dutchess Commun Col Lib 58-. 8: Presidents Com on Lib Devel, SUNY, Consul St Mary's Col 68. 9: ALA; NYLA DCLA; SEast NY Lib Res Coun. 10: Dutchess Co (NY) Hist Assoc. 14: Admin. 15: 27 South st, Rhinebeck NY.

NICHOLSON, BARBARA ELAINE. b Franklin Tex 29 N 26. 5: Mt Alvernia Col (Eng) AB; UTex (Austin) 66-68 MLS. 7: Sec US Info Agcy, Europe, Far East, Near East 50-57; Tchr Boston schs 60-66; Intern UHouston 67-68; Physics-astronomy libn UTex (Austin) 68-. 9: SLA; TexLA. 14: Ref, admin. 15: 1518 Parkway apt 1, Austin Tx 78703.

NICHOLSON, CAROLYN (BERNICE). b Danville Ky 22 S 34. 5: Georgetown Col 53-57 (Hist) BA; Catherine Spaulding Col 58-62 MSLS. 7: Sch libn Henry Co Bd of Educ Pleasureville Ky 58-60; Elem sch libn Bullitt Co Bd of Educ, Shepherdville Ky 60-. 9: ALA; NEA; NCTE; AASchL; KyLA; kyEA; KyASchL. 10: Brownie Girl Scout Leader. 14: Sch lib, catlg. 15: Box 194, Shepardsville Ky 40165.

NICKEL, MILDRED LUCILLE. b Brazil Ind 13 F 12. 5: Ind State U 29-32 (Educ) AB; UIll summers 38-41 BS in LS; Mich State U 63-67 (Educ) MA. 6: Ger. 7: Tchr libn High Sch, Worthington Ind 35-37; Libn High Sch, Argo Ill 37-41; HeadLibn High Sch & Jr Col, LaGrange Ill 41-50; Dir sch libs State Dsupt of Pub Instr, Springfield Ill 50-58; Dir sch libs Dependent Schs, USAFE, Europe 58-60; Dir sch libs Lansing Pub Schs, Lnsing Mich 60-. 8: Conducted summer wkshops for sch libns: UMich 61; Drexel 64; UWis 65, Fla State U 66. 9: ALA (Coun 69-72, chm Planning Sch Lib Quarters Com 62-63);-AASchL (chm Stand Com 60-66, treas 63-64, chm Supv Sect 63-64); NEA; IllLA (past pres); MichASchL (sec 63-66); MichEA; ASCD. 10: Delta Kappa Gamma; AAUW; Bus & Prof Women; Beta Phi Mu; Susanna Wesley Guild; Women's Natl Bk Assoc. 12: ED "Planning School Library Quarters, (ALA 50); Consul "Michigan by R Nye (66). 13: Yes. 14: Sch libs. 15: 401 S Capitol, Lansing Mi 48914.

NICKELS, ANITA (BARTHOLY). b NYC 29 Ja 25. 5: UPittsburgh 42-46 (Chem) BS; USoCal 60-63 MS in LS. 7: Chem US Bur of Mines, Pittsburgh Penn 46-49; Libn Fullerton Pub Lib, Fullerton Cal 61-62; Libn Nogales High Sch, La Puente Cal 62-. 8: Calif Assoc of School Librarians chairman High Sch section 65, state chairman 66. 9: ALA; CalASchL (chm 66, chm High Sch Sect 65). 10: Phi Mu; Folk Dance Fed Amer; AAUW; Music Box Soc Internat; AAUW; U Pittsburgh Alumni. 14: Sch libn. 15: 1054 La Mesa pl, Fullerton Ca 92633.

NICKERSON, DAVID ARNOLD. b Fitchburg Mass 4 D 23. 4: Arline Bryce. 5: Tufts U 45-50 (Eng) BA; Columbia 59-60 (LS) MS; NYU 62-69 (Educ) AM. 06: Fr. 7: USAF (Bombardier) Lt Italy 43-45; Lib asst Tufts Col 50-51; High sch tchr St Johnsbury Acad, St Johnsbury Vt 51-52; USAF Educ Spec (Capt) Morocco & US 52-58; Lib assoc NYU 60-. 8: Pub Info Serv Offr, Ground Observer Corps, Savannah Ga 54-55. 9: ALA; NYLA; NY Lib Club. 10: Soc for the Libs NYU; AAUP; Air Force Assn. 14: Govt docs, ref, documentation, bk sel, catlg. 15: 2475 Palisade ave, Bronx NY 10463.

NICKERSON, DONNA LEE. b Kan City Kan 13 O 32. 5: FriendsU 50-54 (Eng) BA; Simmons 54-57 (LS) MS. 6: Ger. 7: Acquis clerk Baker Lib Harvard Bus Sch 54-57; Documents asst Columbia U 57-61; catlgr Manhattanville Col 61-. 9: ALA. 10: AAUP. 14: Catlg. 15: 11 Lake st apt 5T, White Plains NY 10603.

NICKERSON, MILDRED ELEANOR. b Somerville Mass 29 My 04. 5: Radcliffe Col 22-26 (Romance Lang) AB. 6: Fr, Sp. 7: Asst in charge Hispanic & Lat Amer collections Harvard Col Lib 26-42; Rare bk catlgr Houghton Lib HarvardU 42-. 13: Yes. 14: Rare bk catlg. 15: 48 Long ave, Belmont Ma 02178.

NICKEY, DOROTHY LUCILLE. b Mansfield La 31 Ag 23. 5: La Col 40-44 (Eng, Soc Studies) BA; LSU summers 5?-53 BS in LS; Northwestern State Col (Educ). 7: Eng tchr Merryville High Sch, Merryville La 44-49; Eng tchr Stonewall High Sch, Stonewall La 49-50; Tchr-libn Pelican High Sch, Pelican La 50-63; Lib Sci Instr Northwestern State Col (Matchitoches, La) summers 61-65; Libn Natchitoches High Sch, Natchitoches La 63-; Supv libn Northwestern State Col (Natchitoches La) 63-. 9: NEA; LaLA (past sec); LaASchL (past sec, past pres); LA Tchrs Assn. 10: Delta Kappa Gamma; Beta Phi Mu; Alpha Beta Alpha; Kappa Kappa Iota. 14: Lib educ, wk with teenage lib clubs, ya serv. 15: Rte 1 box 49, Mansfield La.

NICODEMUS, DOROTHY ADELAIDE. b Bucketown 1 D 06. 5: Hood Col 24-28 (Hist) AB; Simmons 28-29 BS in LS. 07L Enoch Pratt Free Lib, Baltimore Md; Asst circ dept 29-33, Asst circ & popular lib 33-35, 1st asst circ & popular lib 35-46, Head circ & popular lib 46-63, Head popular lib 64-.09: ALA-ASD (chm &/or mem Notable Bks Coun 60-62); -LAD (chm Circ Serv Disc Group 64-65); MdLA (treas 33, v-pres 46-47). 9: ALA-ASD; chm &or mem notable bks coun 60-62; Lasting Bks List Com 44-64; -LAD; chm circ serv disc group 64-65; MDLA treas 33, v-pres 46-47. 10: Hood Col Alumnae Assn; Simmons Col Alumnae Assn. 13: Yes. 14: Circ, bk sel, readers adv. 15: Homewood apts 2TA, Baltimore Md 21218.

NICOLAUS, JOHN JOSEPH. b Brooklyn NY 26 Ja 16. 4: Elizabeth Miller Nicolaus. 5: Catholic U 35-38 (Hist) B; St Johns U (NY) 38-42 BLS; Columbia 52-53 (Ind Engnr) Certif. 6: Fr. 7: Tchr & asst libn Bishop Loughlin High Sch, Brooklyn NY 38-42; Libn & tchr St Augustine High Sch, Brooklyn NY 42-44; (Lt) USNavy Gunnery off & Educ Serv Off 44-46; Insurance agent D K Tuttle Co, Brooklyn NY 46-48; HeadLibn N Y Naval Shipyard (USNavy) Brooklyn NY 48-52; Br head NY Naval Shipyard Tech Serv Br, Brooklyn NY 52-56; Asst libn Bur of Ships Tech Lib, Wash DC 56-62, HeadLibn 62-6; Dir of libs Naval Ship Systs Command 66-. 8: Pro dir 61-65, Bureau of Ships Proj SHARP, develop of an Automated Lib Info & Retrieval System; Documentation Consul 64, Off of Naval Res, development of NARDIS System (Navy Automated Res & Devel Info System); Porj Off 62-65, Devel of Bureau of Ships Tech Lib Thesaurus of Descriptive Terms; Fed Lib Com, Task Force on Automation 67-; COSATI Panel #5 Ad hoc Com for Stinfo 67-68; CSC Stinfo Course lectr 66-68; DOD Stinfo Course lectr 67-68. 9: SLA (Mili Libns Group sec-treas,v-chm Wash DC Chap Mem , Directory chm 66-68)& Dir-chm); Amer Soc Naval Engnrs; ADI; Internat Fed for Documentation; East Coast Coun of Naval Lab Libns; West Coast Coun of Naval Lab Lbns Wash DC; ASIS; ALA; DCLA. 10: Foggy Bottom Restoration Assn Wash DC; Island Investment Co, Atlantic City NJ. 11: BuShips Superior Achievement Award 66. 12: "The Automated Approach to Technical Information Retrieval-Library Applications (64). 13: Yes. 14: Admin, sci, tech. 15: Naval Ship Systems Command, Scientific Documentation Div (Ships 205), Wash DC 20360.

NICOT, SUZANNE L M. b Montreal. 5: Simmons 50-54 BLS. 6: Fr. 7: Catlgr Anglo-Saxon Harvard Law Sch Lib 54-60; Catlgr art slides & photos Harvard U Fogg Museum 60-61; Ref libn Winchester Mass Pub Lib 61-62; Ref supv Cary Mem Lib Lexington Mass 62-66, Asst dir 66-. 9: MassLA (Recr Com 64-65); MassLA (Pub Rel Com 68). 10: Assoc DeCordova Mus Lincoln; LWV. 14: Ref, admin. 15: 1387 Commonwealth ave, Boston Ma 02134.

NIDA, JANE B(OLSTER). b Chicago 19 Jl 18. 4: Dow Hughes Nida. 5: Aurora Col 36-42 (Eng) BA; UIll 42-43 BS in LS. 6: Ger, Fr, Sp, Lat. 7: Aurora Pub Lib, Aurora Ill: Lib page 35-40, Lib asst 40-42, Circ libn catlgr 43-44; Act recreation dir staff aide Amer Red Cross Eng, France 44-46; Ref libn Aurora Pub Lib, Aurora Ill 46; Order libn OhioU 47; Research libn Info Research, Detroit 51; Head Libn Falls Church Pub Lib, Falls Church Va 51-54; Asst dir Arlington Co Dept of Libs, Arlington Va 54-57, Dir 57-. 8: Exec dir Va Nat Lib Week, 64; mem, Va Adv Legis Coun Com to Rev State Lib Laws 68-69. 9: ALA; DCLA; VaLA (2nd v-pres 63-64, 1st v-pres 68-69, pres 69-70). 10: AAUW; Quota Internat; Arlington Hist Soc; Aurora Col Alumni Assn; Ohio U Alumni Assn. 11 Amer Red Cross Meritorious Service Award, World War II Overseas. 13: Yes. 14: Admin. 15: Arlington Co Pub Lib 1015 N Quincy st, Arlington Va 2220741385

NIEBALL, MARY (ROY). b Odessa Tex 28 F 29. 4: Paul R Nieball. 5: Odessa Col 54-56 (Gen Educ) AA; UTex 55-56

(LS); Sul Ross State Col 58-59 (Eng, Hist) BS; Tex Womans U 59-63 MLS; Cal Western U summer 65; Ariz State U summer 67; US Intl U (San Diego) 68. Sci). 6: Fr. 7: Lib clerk Ector Co Lib, Odessa Tex 44-49; Odessa Col Lib 50-51; Libn & sec Shannon Sch Nursing San Angelo Tex 51-52; Head dept of tech processing Ector Co Lib, Odessa Tex 53-58; Catlgr Sul Ross State Col Lib 59; Ser dept U Tex Lib 56; Libn Sam Houston Elem Lib, Odessa Tex 59-62; Libn Gonzales Elem Lib, Odessa Tex 63-64; Asst libn Odessa Col Lib 64-64-66, Hd libn 66-. 8: Consul Southwestern Coop Educ Lab. 9: ALA; Jr Col TA; TexLA (v-chm Dist II); Tex State TA; Tex Jr Col Lig Gp (chm). 10: AAUW; Polyantha Garden Club; Civic Music; Midland Commun Theatre; Odessa Col FACULTY Womens Club; Phi Delta Kappa; Kappa Delti Pi; Sigma Tau Delta; Alpha Delta Kappa; Permian Hist Assoc; LWV. 14: Tech processing, ref. 15: 1507 Cimarron, Odessa Tex.

NIEDERMAN, ADELE (SCHREIBSTEIN). b NYC 19 F 45. 4: Nicholas Niederman. 5: CCNY 61-65 (Hist) BA; Columbia 65-68 MLS. 6/ sp. 7: Claims examiner NY State Employment Serv, NYC 65-66; Libn trainee NYC Pub Lib 66-68; Ref libn State Lib Reg Serv Ctr, Napoleon Ohio 68-. 8: Tchr course in hist of Amer Negro, Defiance Col. 9: ALA; OhioLA. 14: Ref, serv in urban areas. 15: 813 Scott st, Napoleon Oh 43545.

NIELANDER, RUTH M. b Lansing Iowa 27 Ja 12. 5: UMinn 29-33 (LS) BS. 6: Ger. 7: Supv Mayo Clinic, Rochester Minn 35-43; Ref libn Nat Safety Coun, Chicago 43-51; Libn Lumbermens Mutual Casualty Co, Chicago 51-. 8: Mem Ill Adv Coun of Libns 68-71. 9: SLA (dir 65-68, Chap Liaison Offr 56-60, Nomin Com 51-52 & 61-62, chm 69-70; Insur Div; chm 56-57, Ill Chap; pres 50-52, Consul chm 62-63, Dir); AALL; IllLA. 10: PEO. 12: Co-ed "Special Libraries-A Guide for Management" (65); Co-ed "Sources of Insurance Statistics" (65); Co-ed 'Insurance Periodicals Index' monthly in "Best Review Magazine". 13: Yes. 15: 721 Gordon ter, Chicago Il 60613.

NIELL, CORA FOX (YONGE). b Post Tex 3 S 16. 4: Edwin L Niell. 5: Tex Tech Col 33-36 (Eng): Tex Womans U 36-37 (LS) BA, 61 (LS). 6: Fr, Sp, Lat. 7: Tex Tech Col: Sec to libn 37-42, Asst ref libn 61-63, Asst period libn 63-. 9: TexLA; Tex Assn Col Tchrs. 10: AAUP. 14 Ser & ref. 15: POBox 4079, Lubbock Tex 9409.

NIELSEN, DAVORA EDMUNDS. b Fairview Utah 24 Je 14. 4: Lowell Wendell Nielsen. 5: UUtah 31-33 (Gen Studies); Utah State U 33-35 (Bot) BS; UNC 52-53 (LS) BS, 60-61 (LS). 6: Sp. 7: Catlgr NC State U 53-56; Abstractor Bibliogr Tobacco Lit Serv, raleigh 56-60; Catlgr NC State Lib 61-63; Docs libn 63-64; Ref libn NC State U 65-66, libn Sch of Textiles 66-. 9: SLA; SELA. 10: Beta Phi Mu. 15: 2308 Darien dr, Raleigh NC 27607.

NIELSEN, ROY JAMES MAURICE. b San Francisco 26 O 16. 4: Betty Torosian Nielsen. 5: UCal (Berkeley) 35-39 (Geol Sci) AB, 40-41 Libnship Certif, 43-45. 6: Ger, Sp. 7: Sp3 US Army Finance Corps Heidelberg Germany 54-56; Underwriter Hartford A & I Co, NYC 56-59; Lib asst "Newsweek NYC 59-61; Ref, ya lbn Hicksville (NY) Pub Lib 61-63; Lib Dir Plainedge Pub Lib, Massapequa NY 63-. 8: Chm Coun of Libns, West Coast Navy Labs, 55-56; Coord UCal ext course, acquis of spec materials, San Francisco, 64; Mem AEC Lib OPNS Task Force 68-69. 9: SLA (ed Documentation Dir 59-61; chm Jt Meeting Com, San Francisco Bay Reg Chap 66). 13: Yes. 14: Admin, ref, sel, catlg. 15: 638 Viona ave, Oakland Ca 94610.

NIEMEIER, NORA LOUISE. b Hamilton Can. 5: McMaster U 48-49; UToronto 49-50, 51-52 BA, 52-53 BLS. 6: Fr. 7: Libn Ontario Research Found, Toronto 53-63, Libn Sheridan Park br 63-. 9: SLA; CanLA; OntLA. 14: Admin. 15: 30 Walmer rd apt 305, Toronto 4 Ont Can.

NIEMI, TAISTO JOHN. b Aurora Minn 3 D 14. 4: Arleen Bruflat. 5: Va Jr Col 33-36 (Educ) AA; UMinn 38 (Hist) BS, Lib Certif; UMich 50 AMLS, 60 (LS) PhD. 6: Finnish. 7: Adult educ tchr WPA, Aurora Minn 38-42; US Army (Cpl) 7th Inf Div 42-45; Asst libn West Mich U 47-53; Libn No MichU 53-60; Libn StateU Col (Buffalo NY) 60-63; Dir Le Moyne Col 63-. 8: Lib Lecturer: Ext Div UMich 58-60; No Mich U 55-60; Geneseo StateU Col 61-63. 9: NEA; SLA; CathLA; NYLA. 13: Yes. 14: Admin. lib educ. 15: Le Moyne Col, Syracuse NY 13214.

NIENTIMP, JUDITH A. b Rochester NY 2 Jl 38. 5: Nazareth Col 56-60 (Eng) BA; St Johns U 60-61 MLS. 7: Period libn St Johns U (NY) 61-62; Documents libn URochester 62-65, Head of ser & bind sect 65-68, Info syst specialist 68-. 8: Worlds Fair Lib/USA, NYC 65. 9: ALA; NY State LA; SLA; ASIS. 10: Mem Art Gallery; AAUW; Cath Interracial Coun, St Augustine Sch Bd, UR Womens Club. 14: Ser & Doc, automation, info sci. 15: 731 Arnett blvd, Rochester NY 14619.

NIES, RITA ANN. b Erie Penn 20 Mr 22. 5: Villa Maria Col 39-43 (Hist) BA; West Res 44-45 BS IN LS. 6: Ger, Sp. 7: Lib clk Alta Br, Cleveland Ohio 45; Circ & ref Erie Pub Lib, Erie Penn 45-47; Circ libn Gannon Col Lib 47-50, Ref libn 50-. 8: Tchr of ref course & leader of wkshop, Erie Pub Lib spring 65. 9: ALA; CathLA; PennLA. 10: St Vincent Hosp Auxiliary; St Marks Sem Auxiliary; Erie Civic Music Assn. 14: Ref. 15: Gannon Col Lib Perry Square, 607 E 24th st, Erie Pa 16503.

NIEVERGELT, TERESITA (QUIAMBAO. b Bacacay Albay Philippines 9 M 40. 4: Jurg Nievergelt. 5: USanto Tomas (Manila) 56-60 (LS) BS Ed (summa cu laude); UIll 62-63 (LS) MA. 6: Tagalog, Sp, Ger, Fr. 7: Ref libn USanto Tomas (Manila) 61-62; Catlgr UIll Lib (Urbana) 63-. 11: Fulbright-Smith-Mundt Fellowship. 14: Ref, calg. 15: UIll 220 S Library, Urbana Ill.

NIH, EMMA (COUGHLIN). b Luzerne Penn 9 Ap 1900. 4: Alfred T Nih. 5: Goucher Col 17-21 (Hist) AB; Cornell U 21-24 (Phil) MA; Columbia 39-40 (Eng), 52-53, 54 MALS. 7: Various tchg Eng & philos: Chekiang U (Hangchou China) Peiping U (Peiping China), Briarcliff Jr Col, Hampton Inst, NY State Col (Albany), Iowa State Col, Alfred U 29-52; Asst to coordinator adult serv DC Pub Lib, 53-56, Asst coordinator adult serv 56-. 8: Com on Info about Japanese encroachments (semi-off), Hangchou China 31-32; Adv to Chinese YWCA, Peiping China 38-39. 9: ALA-ASD (Philos Com 63-65). 10: AAUP. 14: Adult Serv, admin. 15: 7010 Georgia st, Chevy Chase Md 20015.

NIILUS, WALTER E(DWARD). b Tallinn, Estonia 15 Jl 13. 4: Leili Pollusaar. 5: UTartu 9estonia) 33-38, 39-40 (Estonian & Finnic Lang) Magister Philosophiae; USorbonne 38-39 (Fr Lang, Phonology). 6: Estonian, Fr, Ger, Russian. 7: Period & doc's asst Claremont Grad Sch, Honnold Lib, Claremont Cal 50-52, 52-54, Order libn 54-56, Asst libn 56-, Act libn 62-63, 67-68. 8: Orientales Vivantes, Paris 39; Sec Estonian Lang Soc, Tartu estonia 39-44; Lectr of Estonian and Finnic Linguistics Ecole Superieure pour les langues; Welfare Asst, UNRRA, Germany, 44-45; Admin (civilian) US Army Dept, Germany; Liaison Offr, US Army Dept, Germany 48-50. 9: ALA; Linguistic Soc of Amer; Estonian Learned Soc of Amer; CalLA. 10: AAUP. 14: Period & bks on linguistics, ethnol, archaeol. 15: 2485 Sierra dr, Upland Ca 91786.

NILSON, MILDRED ELAINE (GOODENOUGH). b Baraboo Wis 27 Mr 24. 4: Milton S Nilson. 5: Marion Col 43-47 (Educ) BS Ed; UWis summer 48 (Educ); Milwaukee State Tchrs Col summer 49 (Educ); UWis 61-62 MS in LS. 7: Kindergarten tchr: Escanaba (Mich) Pub Schs 47-50, Burlington (Wis) Pub Schs 50-51, New Glarus (Wis) Pub Sch 55-57, Rockford (Ill) Pub Schs 57-60; Gen off wk; Saris Auto Co, Beloit Wis 51-52, Fairbanks , Morse & Co cost dept, Beloit Wis 52-55; Tchr Beloit (Wis) Pub Schs 60-61; Ref libn N Park Col 62-. 9: ALA; IllLA. 14: Ref. 15: 5436 N Spaulding ave, Chicago Il 60625.

NIM, MYRTLE (HEATH). b Greensboro NC 21 D 19. 4: Carl John Nim Jr. 5: Greensboro Col 36-40 (Pub Sch Mus) BM; UNC (Greensboro) 44-45 (Educ); UPittsburgh 66-69 (Spec Resources) MLS. 6: Fr, Sp. 7: Mus tchr George Wythe Jr High, Hampton Va 40-42; Soloist St John's Episcopal Ch, Hampton Va 40-42; Mus tchr Carolina & Bradley Creek Schs, Wilmington NC 43; Ensemble mem WBIG radio station, Greensboro NC 44-45; Sub tchr Greensboro Pub Sch, Greensboro NC 44-45; Choir dir Woodmont Union Chapel, Woodmont Conn 51-53; Violinist Charlotte Symphony, Charlotte NC 58-60; Violist Charlotte Symphonette 58-60; Mus tchr Charlotte Pub Schs 59; Jr choir dir Caldwell Mem Presbyterian Ch, Charlotte NC 58-60; Soloist St Andrews Lutheran Ch, Pittsburgh Penn 64-; Lib asst mus lib Carnegie-Mellon U 64-69, Asst catlgr (Mus) 69-. 10: S Orange (NJ) Commun Orchestra; Wilkinsburg (Penn) Civic Symphony; Forest Hills Women's Club; Bryn Mawr Women's Club; Tuesday Musical Club of Pittsburgh. 14: Music libs, ref, catlg. 15: 33 Wilkins rd, Forest Hills, Pittsburgh Pa 15221.

NIMMO, MABEL INEZ. b Elizabeth City NC. 5:NC NC 42-46 (Hist) AB, 50-51 MALS; UDenver 56, 57, 59 MALS. 6: Fr, Ger. 7: Sch libn Sumner High Sch, St Louis 51-56; Sch libn Soldan High Sch, St Louis 56-. 8: Examining Bd for Sch Libns, St Louis City Bd of Educ 61; Ref libn LibraryUSA Worlds Fair, NYC 64; Sch libn Laclede-Chouteau Inst, St Louis 65. 9:

ALA; MoLA (chm St Louis Dist 59); MoSchL; Mo State Tchrs Assn. 10: Delta Sigma Theta. 13: Yes. 14: Reading guidance, lib pub. 15: 5475 Cabanne ave, apt 802, St Louis Mo 63112.

NISBET, EDITH. b Paris 29 Je 32. 5: Institut Social-Menager France 48-50; Home Econ BA Ecole Commerciale France 50-51; Bus Admin Diploma. 7: Exec Sec Life & Beauty Inc, Paris 51-54; Sec-TR NATRO Hdqrs, Fontainebleau France 54-56; Lib asst Ohio State U 57-59; Tr Embassy of Morocco, Wash DC 59-60; Records asst Internat Bank for Reconstruction & Development, Wash DC 60-63; Tech libn C-E-I-R Inc, Wash DC 63-66; Tech libn Computer Applications Inc, NYC 66-68; Tech libn Value Engrg Co, Alexandria Va 68-. 9: SLA; Assn Comput Mach; ASIS. 14: Admin, info retr, info systems design. 15: 1600 S Joyce st, apt A308, Arlington Va 22202.

NISETEO, ANTHONY. b Zadar Croatia 5 F 13. 4: Anna Scheer. 5: Croatian U(Zagreb) 32-37 (Law) LLB; Fordham 53-55 (E European Hist) MA; Columbia 57-58 MLS. 6: Gk, Lat, Romance Langs, Slavic, Ger. 7: Stud Lib Asst Fordham U 53-54; Lib searcher Columbia U 54-58; Assoc libn Cornell U Lib 58-. 10: Crotian Acad of Amer. 12: Bks of poetry, fiction & translations, in Croatian (34-45); Ed "Matica Hrvatska, "Bez povratka (57), "Dante i Hrvati (65). 13: Yes. 14: Catlg, bibliog, rare items. 15: 517 Warren rd, Ithaca NY 14850.

NISKERN, DIANA M. b St Cloud Minn 15 Mr 42. 5: Macalester Col 60-64 (Biol) BA; UMinn 64-65 (LS) MA. 7: Spec recruit LC 65-66; Bibliog & sci libn 66-68; Sci ref libn 68-. 9: ALA. 14: Ref, bibliog. 15: 220 C st SE, Washington DC 20003.

NISTENDIRK, VERNA (RUTH). b Wright City Mo 12 Ag 07. 5: Southeast Mo State Col 29 (Eng) BS; Peabody 34 BS in LS; Columbia 44 (LS) MS. 7: Elem tchr Neelyville & Blodgett Mo 27-29; Sch libn N Kan City Mo 29-38; W br libn Kan City (Mo) Pub Lib 38-43, Dir lib ext 43-46; Consul Mo Lib Commsn, Jefferson City Mo 46-47; Libn Dunklin Co Lib, Kennett Mo 47-52; Field libn Ala Lib Serv, Montgomery Ala 52; Libn Boonslick Reg Lib, Sedalia Mo 52-56; Dir lib Devel Fla State Lib 56-69; Libn Leon Co Pub Lib Talla hassee Fla 70-. 8: Survey of Kansas City Pub Lib brs 45; Dir Bkmob Wkshop UKy 56. 9: ALA; chm Ext Sect; -PLA; memb com; MoLA; pres Co Lib Sect, Sec certif com, mem other coms; FlaLA (pres 68, var coms); SELA. 10: AAUW; LWV; Delta Kappa Gamma. 13: Yes. 14: Ext, adult educ. 15: Leon Co Pub Lib, Tallahassee Fl 32304.

NITCHIE, MILDRED (WEST). b NYC 23 D 09. 4: Edward B Nitchie. 5: Skidmore 27-31 (Eng) BA; Rutgers 59-62 MLS. 6: Fr. 7: Catlgr Fairleigh Dickinson U 62-63; Catlgr Drew U 63-66; Br libn Hilton br Maplewood Mem Lib Maplewood NJ 66-. 10: AAUW; Beta Phi Mu. 14: Catlg, readers advy wk, ref admin. 15: 36 Plymouth rd, Summit NJ 07901.

NITECKI, ANDRE. b Sosnowiec Poland 30 Ap 25. 5: UGrenoble 43 (Fr lang) Dip; ULyon 43-44 (Law); Oxford U 45-48 (Law); Wayne State 51-52 (Eng); Chicago 55-57 (LS) MA. 6: Fr, Ger, Lat, Polish, Russian. 7: Catlgr UChicago 56-58; Catlgr Museum of Nat Hist, Chicago 58-59; Dir of tech serv Mich(Flint Col) 59-63; Sub-libn ULagos (Lagos Nigeria) 63-65; Lecturer UIbadan(Ibadan Nigeria) 64-66; Asst Prof Syracuse U 66-68; Sr Lecr UGhana (Accra Ghana) 68-; Adj Assoc Prof Syracuse U 69-. 8: Lecturer on Africa, Art appreciation, and Human relations for the Flint Bd of Educ & Mott Foun in Flint Mich 59-63; Bk reviewing for the Polish Program. WJLB Radio Sta. Detroit 52-55; Tchg African Art Syracuse U 66-, UGhana 68-; Curator of A Nitecki African Collection, Syracuse U 60-. 9: ALA (Internat Rel Round Table, mem 3 coms); Aslib; Nat Microfilm Assn; NigerianLA; Lib Assn(Bristish); Mich Coun for Better Libs; MichLA (Tech Serv Sect, chm 2 coms). ; GhanaLA. 10: AAUP; ACLU; NAACP; Flint Assn of Sch Admins; Flint Human Rel Coun; Flint Inst of Arts; Mich Acad of Science, Art, & Letters; Mich Soc for Mental Health; Urban League; UChicago Grad Lib Sch Alumni Assn. ; African Studies Assn. 12: "History of Western Ar, a syllabus (62); "The Acquisition of Polish Books in America (63); "Introduction to Cataloguing of Books (Ibadan 65); "Acquisition of Library Materials in Nigeria (Ibadan 65);"Introduction to Classification of Books (Ibadan 65); "Index to Library of Congress Classification (68); "Art of West Africa (Ghana 69). 13: Yes. 14: Tchg, tech serv. 15: 5716 S Dorchester ave, Chicago Il 60637.

NITECKI, JOSEPH Z. b Poland 31 Ja 22. 4: Sophie Zboinska. 5: Lyceum-Jr Col (Poland) 37-39 (Phys Scis) Matriculate; Naval Col (Plymouth Eng) (Naval Sci) Commsn; Wayne State 51-55 (Philos) BA; Roosevelt U 56-9 (Philos) MA; Chicago 60-61 (LS) MA. 6: Polish, Fr. 7: Lt Polish Navy under British Command, Eng 39-48; Asst chem AMIF-UChicago 55-61; Catlgr Law Sch Lib UChicago 61-63; Br libn Wilson Jr Col 62-66; Coord tech serv UWis (Milwaukee) 67-68, Asst dir for tech serv 68-. 8: Examining Milwaukee City Serv Commun 68. 9: ALA; Amer Philos Assn; Chicago Lib Club; Soc Gen Systems Res. 10: Beta Phi Mu; UChicago Grad Lib Sch Alumni; Amer Photographic Soc. 13: Yes. 14: Theory of libnship, tech serv. 15: 2562 N Prospect ave, Milwaukee Wi 53211.

NIX, LARRY T. b Mt Pleasant Tenn 7 N 43. 4: Katherine Lowry. 5: Peabody Col 61-65 (Eng) BA; UIll 65-67 (LS) MS. 7: Lib clk Pub Lib of Nashville & Davidson Co, Nashville Tenn 63-65; Lib asst UIll Lib (Urbana) 65-67; Br libn Pub Lib of Charlotte & Mecklenburg Co, Charlotte NC 67; Army Quartermaster E-5 67-69. 9: ALA. 14: Pub lib, adult serv. 15: 1951 Milton rd apt 6, Charlotte NC 28205.

NIX, MARY KATHERINE LOWRY. b Louisiana Mo 4 D 42. 4: Larry Thomas Nix. 5: So Ill U 61-65 (Hist) BA; UIll 66-67 (LS) MS. 7: Tchr O'Fallon Grade Sch, O'Fallon Ill 65-66; Gen bibliog UNC (Charlotte) 67-68, Order libn 68-. 9: ALA;-AASchL;-CSD; Mecklenburg LA. 14: Acquis, child serv. 15: 1951 Milton rd #6, Charlotte NC 28205.

NIXON, ARLESS (BARNETT). b Ben Wheeler Tex 23 F 14. 4: Margaret Hassell. 5: E Tex State Col 33-36; Hist, Govt; BA UIll 42 (LS). 6: Sp. 7: Prin & tchr Edgewood Ind Sch Dist, Edgewood Tex 36-37; Sch libn Leveretts Chapel Inc Sch, Overton Tex 37-45; Libn Kilgore Pub Lib, Kilgore Tex 45-50; Lib Dir Mobile Pub Lib, Mobile Ala 50-54; Lib Dir Ft Worth Pub Lib, Ft Worth Tex 54-64; Asst lib dir Phoenix Pub Lib 64-. 8: Helped develop two library surveys of the Ft Worth Pub Lib, Ft Worth Tex. 9: ALA-PLA (past chm Nomin Com); Ariz State LA; (past pres Pub Lib Dir), TexLA (past pres & past treas, past chm Sch Lib Div); SWLA. 10: Mineral Soc Ariz; Phoenix Symphony Assn. 11: WKRG Pub Serv Award (Mobile Ala). 14: Pub lib admin. 15: 920 W Rose lane, Phoenix Az 85013.

NIXON, EMILY C(ATHARINE). b Waterford Ohio 23 F 08. 5: Ohio U 24-28 (Span) AB; UMich 30-31 ABLS; State U Iowa 32-35. 6: Sp, Fr, Ital, Ger. 7: Asst ser div UMich 31-32; Catlgr State U Iowa 32-35; NYU: 1st asst catlg dept 35-51, Chief catlg dept 51-52, Chief catlg libn 52-66, Catlgr spec collections 66-67; Hd reclaf project CCNY 67-. 9: ALA-RSTD; -ACRL; NYC Tech Serv Group (sec, pres). 14: Catlg. 15: 440 W 34 st, New York NY 10001.

NIXON, LOUISE A. b Paradise Kan 27 Jl 1897. 5: UKan 15-19 (Hist) BA; UMin 22-24 (Hist) MA; UDenver 51 (LS) MA. 7: Asst dir Neb Legis Ref Bur, Lincoln Neb 31-39; Libn Neb Legis Coun, Lincoln Neb 39-49; Exec sec Nb Pub Lib Commsn, Lincoln Neb 50-. 9: ALA; Adult Educ Assn; MPLA; NebLA. 10: Mortar Board; University Club; English Speaking Union; Amer Fed of Arts; Neb Art Assn; LWV. 12: "Comp "Nebraska Blue Book, 1932-1948, Books for Farm People, in "Yearbook of Agriculture (US) (62) Ed "Nebraska News Letter, Pub Lib Com. 13: Yes. 14: Lib ext. , lib serv to blind & physically handicapped; instl lib serv. 15: 3136 So 30th st, Lincoln Nb 68502.

NOAK, THERESA (KOLMSCHLAG). b London Eng 27 Mr 07. 4: Fred W Noak. 5: Col of Music(Cincinnati Ohio) 23-29 (Piano) Diploma; UCincinnati 35-39 (Educ) BS; West Res 41-42 BLS. 6: Ger, Fr. 7: Asst Pub Lib of Hamilton Co, Cincinnati 30-47; Libn Col Music (Cincinnati) 48-53; Asst ref music div NY Pub Lib 54-55; Libn Col Conservatory of Music (Cincinnati) 56-65; Catlgr art and mus Pub Lib of Hamilton Co, Cincinnati 66-68. 8: Tchr, Bk sel & ref, Col of Mt St Joseph, Cincinnati summers 56-57. 9: MusLA; ALA; Internat Musicological Soc; Internat Mus Lib Assn. 14: Ref, rare bks, musicology. 15: 217 Eight Mile rd, Cincinnati Oh 45230.

NOBLE, ELIZABETH (HALLOCK). b NYC 16 Ag 09. 5: Columbia 30-39 (Elem Educ) BS; Drexel 51-52 MS in LS. 7: Tchr Cresskill Pub Sch, Cresskill NJ 30-43; Tchr Westtown Sch, Westtown Penn 43-46; Tchr Friends Central Sch, Overbrook Penn 46-51; Catlgr Northwestern U 52-54; Catlgr Bryn Mawr Col Lib 54-58; Head catlgr Biddle Law Lib UPenn 58-. 9: AALL (Com on Catlg & Clsf); ALA-ACRL. 14: New clsf scheme. 15: 326 Lincoln ave, Lansdowne Penn 19050.

NOBLE, G(EORGE) C(AMERON). b Regina Sask Can 11 A 21. 4: Jean Isabel Hewitt. 5: USask 45-48 (LatBA; McGill 48-49 BLS. 6: . 7: Flying Off RCAF, Can 39 Ottawa 49-51; Asst libn Pub Lib Commsn, Prince George BC 51-52; Dir Manitob a Lib Serv, Can 52-55; Dir UExt Lib UMan 55-. 9:

CanLA; ManLA. 12: ""Public Library Service in Manitoba, a Report and Recommendations (56); Ed ""Manitoba Library Assn Bulletin (54-56). 13: Yes. 14: Catl, pub rel. 15: 36 Thatcher dr, Winnipeg 19 Man Can.

NOBLE, HADLEY WAYNE. b Rochester NY. 4: Ella J Burger. 5: URochester 49-53 (Eng) BA; SUNY (Albany) 53-54 (Eng, Educ) MA; Syracuse U 63-64, summers 54,57,61,62,63 (Tech Processes) MSLS. 6: Lat, Fr, Ger. 7: Clk Eastman Kodak Co, Rochester NY summers 50-53; Eng & reading tchr Marion Central Sch, Marion NY 54-55; Eng tchr: Albion Central Sch, albion NY 55-59, E Irondequoit Central Sch, Rochester NY 59-61; Prof lib trainee URochester 61-63, Asst libn (ser catlg) 63-. 8: Delegate to NY State Tchrs Assn 58-59. 9: ALA; Monroe Co LA. 10: Beta Phi Mu; Rochester Fac Club; Civic Music Assn. 13: Yes. 14: Ser, catlgr, tech proc. 15: 1973 5 Mile Line rd, Penfield NY 14615.

NOBLE, VALERIE. b Cal 28 O 31. 5: Riverside Col 49-51 (Art) AA; Pomona Col 51-53 (Art) BA; West Mich 63-65 (LS) MA. 7: Exec train program The Emporium, San Francisco 53-55 Retail advertising dept "Honolulu Star Bulletin, Honolulu 55-58; Advertising dir Spence Cliff System of Restaurants, Honolulu 58-60 Self-employed Advertising, p r servs, Honolulu 60-61; Communications dir Woodrum & Staff, Honolulu 61-62; Self-employed Advertising, p r serv, Honolulu 62-63; Libn Wm John Upjohn Assoc Inc, Kalamazoo 63-68; Bus research Self employed, Kalamazoo Mich 68-. 8: Pub rel consul to Mich Interlib Scholarship Bd 67-; Coord, design of logotype for West Mich U Dept of Libnship 68. 9: SLA (Advert & Marktg Div; ed Div "Bulletin 67-69). 10: Honolulu Ad Club; Pub Rel Women of Honolulu; Bishop Museum Assn, Honolulu. 11: ANPA Award, 59, tabloid advertising. 13: Yes. 14: Research, ref, communications. 15: 313 Solon, Kalamazoo Mi 49006.

NOBLET, CHLORIS KAY. b Terrero NM 22 Jl 30. 5: TempleU 53-54 (Fine Arts); UNM 54-57 9fine Arts) BFA; UWash 62-68 MLS; Sacramento State Col 66-67. 6: Fr. 7: Sgt USAF 49-52; Libn readers asst Main Lib San Francisco City-Co 58-59, Libn asst hd art dept 60-61, Libn bus br 61-64, Br libn 64; Libn asst hd bus & mun dept City-Co Lib, Sacramento Cal 65-. 8: Served on 11 libns com with City of San Francisco studying and rewriting bk sel policy 64. 10: Air Force Assn. 14: Ref (art, arch, and other art subjects). 15: 624 N st Capitol Towers, Sacramento Ca 95814.

NOCK, MARGARET (KAPUTA). b Southwest Penn 17 Ag 12. 4: John J Nock. 5: Seton Hill Col 30-34 (Eng) BA; Columbia 39 MLS. 7: Tchr-libn Mt Pleasant Twp High Sch, M Pleasant Penn 35-40; Libn Penn Joint High Sch, Claridge Penn 56-61; Libn Ramsay High Sch, t Pleasant Penn 61-65; Libn Hurst Jr High Sch, Mt Pleasant Penn 65-. 9: Westmoreland Co Sch Libns (pres 61-63). 10: Mt Pleasant Twp(Penn) Womans Club. 15: Box 512, RD 2, Greensburg Penn 15601.

NODEN, DENYS. b Liverpool Eng 25 Ap 21. 4: Frances Grace May. 5: UCambridge 39,45-47 (Modern langs) MA; McGill 51-52 BLS. 6: Fr, Sp, Ger. 7: Pilot Royal Air Force (Flight Lt) 40-45; Articled clerk Price, Waterhouse, Vancouver 48-49; Lib asst USask 49-51; UAlta: Catlgr 52-56, Law libn 56-64, Chief catlgr 64-67; Asst libn tech serv 67-. 9: CanLA; ALA. 11: Distinguished Flying Cross. 14: Tech servs, law. 15: #13, 11608 79th ave, Edmonton Alta Can.

NOEL, DONALD CLAUDE. b Blue Island Ill 2 Ag 30. 5: St Norbert Col 48-49, 54-57 (Philos) BA; LoyolaU (Chicago) 49-50; DePaul summer 50; UWis summers 57-58, 61-63 (LS) MA. 7: Libn: Abbot Pennings High Sch, West de Pere Wis 59-60, Premontre High Sch, Green Bay Wis 60-66, St Norbert Abbey, De Pere Wis 66-68, Bishop Neumann High Sch, Phila 68-. 8: Ref wk in theol & philos, UNotre Dame Mem Lib summer 66. 9: ALA; CathLA. 14: Ya reading interests. 15: 1815 S 27 st, Philadelphia Pa 19145.

NOEL, FLORENCE (HAAS). b Cleveland 11 O 34. 5: Kent State 52-53 (Chem); Maryville Col (St Louis) 53-57 (Chem) BS (cum laude); UCal (Berkeley) 64-65 MLS. 6: Fr. 7: Sec & gen off wk 51-57; Lab tech West Res Med Sch 58-60; Sci data analyst UCal (Berkeley) Lawrence Radiation Lab 60-61; Catlg libn for Tech Div Wright-Patterson AFB, Ohio 65-66; Ref libn dayton & Montgomery Co Pub Lib, Dayton Ohio 66-67; Ref libn Syntex Corp, Palo Alto Cal 67-68; Sec Massey Off Serv, Palo Alto Cal 68; Ref libn Mt View Pub Lib, Mt View Cal 68-. 9: CalLA. 10: Beta Phi Mu; Pi Mu Epsilon; Orchesis. 12: Developing Your Dermatological Library; A Practical Guide," Syntex Labs (67). 14: Ref. 15: 2427 Marcelyn ave, Mountain View Ca 94040.

NOEL, THOMAS JACOB. b Cambridge Mass 6 My 45. 5: UTenn 63-66 (Hist); ULaval summer 64 9fr) Certif; UDenver 66-67 (Hist) BA, 67-68 (LS) MA. 6: Fr. 7: Asst libn for resources & tech serv UCal Lib (Riverside) 69-. 9: ALA. 10: Colo Hist Soc. 14: Collection bldg. 15: Apt B 3475 Lemon st, Riverside Ca 92501.

NOELTNER, ELEANOR. b Glen NY 19 Mr 26. 5: Col of Educ (Geneseo NY) 43-47 (LS) BS in Educ; Col of Educ(Albany) 60-61 (LS). 7: Child libn Schenectady Co (NY) Pub Lib 47-57; Elem libn Scotia-Glenville Schs, Scotia NY 57-60; Libn Oriskany Central Schs, Oriskany NY 61-64; High sch libn Draper Sch, Schenectady NY 64-67; Asst libn NY State Commerce Dept 68-. 9: ALA; NYLA. 14: Child & elem sch wk. 15: 496 Arthur st, Schenectady NY 12306.

NOFCIER, LENA BARBARA. b Syracuse NY 31 Ag 1895. 5: Kent State 16-23 (Educ) Certif; Asbury Col 25-27 (Eng, Fr) AB; UIll 27-48 BS in LS; Chicago summer 43 (LS); Ohio State U 56-60 (Educ) MA; Kent State 65 (Far East Educ). 7: Elem tchr Pub Sch, Sebring Ohio 17-21, Alliance Ohio 21-23, Canton Ohio 23-25; Libn Asbury Col 25-27, 28-30; Dir State Lib Ext Div, Frankfort Ky 30-45; Libn Asbury Theol Sem 45-49; Chief State Lib Ext Div, Indianapolis 49-50; Dir Pub Lib, Lima Ohio 50-65; Lib consul, Lima O 31-45; Sec-treas, Bd for Certif of Libns, Ky 38-45; Bd for Certif of Co Libns, Ohio 53-55; Ky Congress of Parents & Tchrs 32-45; Consul to Ky Fed of Womens Clubs Lib rogram 30-45; Libn Remedial Reading Lab Perry Local Sch, Lima Ohio 67-. 9: ALA (Coun, mem Fin Com, chm Jury for Trustees Citation); -Ext Div (var offs); KyLA (pres 37-39, Exec Bd many yrs); OhioLA (Exec Bd 60-63, mem var coms). 10: AAUW; LWV; Altrusa; Delta Kappa Gamma.13: Yes. 14: Admin, lib bldgs, org wk, child servs. 15: 415 12 Lincoln, Lima Oh 45805.

NOLAN, JOAN P. b Olean NY 16 S 34. 4: Kevin J Nolan. 5: Clarion State Col 52-56 BS in Ed; West Res summers 57-59 MS in LS; Westminster Col even 57-59 (Hist) St Bonaventure U summer 60 (Hist). 6: Sp. 7: Libn Linesville High Sch, Linesville Penn 56-59; Libn Cameron Co High Sch, Emporium Penn 59-62; Catlg Cameron Co Pub Lib, Emporium Penn summer 62; Libn Shady Grove Jr High Sch, Ambler Penn 62-65; Coordr lib serv N Penn Sch Dist, Lansdale Penn 68-. 8: Middle States Assn of Cols & Second Schs, Eval Coms, 60-64; Tchr (part-time) Drexel, Phila 64-. 9: ALA; NEA; Penn State EA (Dept of Curric Suv); PennLA; Phila Area LA; N Penn TA (sec 2 terms). 10: Ambler Jr High Tchrs Assn (sec); Beta Phi Mu; Pi Gamma Mu; AAUW. 11: E P Dutton-John Macrae Award 65. 14: Sch libnship. 15: 843 Lombardy dr, Lansdale Pa 19446.

NOLAN, JOHN LESTER. b Concord NH 14 Ap 09. 4: Dallas Fraser. 5: Harvard Col 27-33 (Eng) BS; Columbia 35-38 BS in LS. 6: Fr. 7: Libn Adams House Lib Harvard Col 31-34; Head searching sect ref dept, NY Pub Lib 35-38, Sr ref asst 38-40; Chif cat prep & maintenance div LC 40-43, Chief exch & gift div & act chief order div 43-45; Sel off & ed "LC Quarterly Journal 45-51; Asst dir processing dept 51-52 1-52; Dir of lib serv in the UK, USIS, London Eng 52-54; Asst dir ref dept LC 54-58, Assoc dir ref dept 58-, Dir 68-69, Hon consul in ref & bibliog; Prof lf lib studies, UHawaii 69-. 9: ALA (Coun, chm var groups). 10: . 12: Ed "Library of Congress Quarterly Journal of Current Acquisitions (45-51). 13: Yes. 14: Ref, admin. 15: Grad School of Lib Studies, Univ of Hawaii, Honolulu Hi 96822.

NOLAND, GENEVA V. b Madison Co Ind 10 Ag 07. 4: F Paul Noland. 5: Earlham Col 25-29 (Lat, Eng) AB; Ind U Ext 54-55 (LS); Butler 55-62 (LS). 6: Lat, Fr. 7: Comptometer operator Stokely Van Camp, Indianapolis 39-45; PTA volunteer wker Sch 91 Lib Indianapolis Sch System 52-56; Libn Sch 91 Indianapolis Schs 56-63; Libn Sch 101 Indianapolis Sch System 63-. 9: ALA; IndSchLA (com for Jr High Schs 65-66); IndLA. 10: Bus & Profess Women. 14: Child sch libs, esp Jr High. 15: 5021 Evanston ave, Indianapolis In 46205.

NOLAND, JON FRANCIS. b Chicago Ill 17 Mr 45. 4: Soraya Qaummaqami. 5: UKy 63-67 (Lat Amer Culture) BA, 67-68 MSLS. 6: Fr, Sp. 7: Hd circ dept Memorial UNewfoundland 69-. 9: CanLA; AtlanticProvincesLA. 14: Admin, pub serv, lib serv to non users. 15: 70 Mullock, St John's Newfoundland.

NOLL, RACHEL R(UTH). b Newark NJ 1 Ag 40. 5: Millersville State Col 58-62 (LS) BS. 7: Sr high libn Palmyra Area Sch Dist, Palmyra Penn 62-. 9: ALA; PennStateEA (Dept of Supv & Curr); PLA; Palmyra Area EA; Lebanon Co Coord Coun (sec-treas 67-68). 14: Catlg, ya serv. 15: 739 E Elm st, Palmyra Pa 17078.

NOMLAND, JOHN B. b Pasadena Cal 28 O 23. 5: Pasadena Jr Col 39-42 (Span); USoCal 42, 51-52 (Span, LS0 MSLS (cum laude); Whittier Col 43 (Span); UCLA 44-50 (Latin Amer Lit) AB, MA, PhD. 6: Sp, F, Ger. 7: Tchg asst UCLA 45-49; Arch-fine arts libn USoCal 52-54; Libn & Prof Los Angeles City Col 54-. 8: Pres, Acad Senate, Los Angeles City Col 65-66. 9: CalLA. 10: Beta Phi Mu; Sigma Delta Pi. 11: Buenos Aires Fellow in Mexico 1950. 12: ED "USoCal Lib Staff Bulletin (52-54); Jt ed "ALA Summary Reports (53). ; Auth "Teatro Mexicano Contemporaneo" (67). 13: Yes. 14: Latin Amer acquis, periods. 15: 404 S Benton way, Los Angeles Ca 90057.

NOOE, MARY A(MANDA). b Versailles Ky 24 O 11. 5: UKy 34-35 (LS) BA, 49-53, 54 (Eng) MA; Georgetown Col 35 (Math); Columbia 39 (LS). 7: Tchr-libn Black Star High Sch, Alva Ky 35-36; Libn Cynthiana High Sch, Cynthiana Ky 36-45; Catlgr UKy 45-55; Catlgr Stephen F Austin State Col 55-67, Tech processes libn 67-. 9: ALA; SWLA; TexLA; Tex Reg Group of Catlgrs & Clsfrs; Central Ky Lib Club; Ohio Valley eg Group of Catlgrs & Clsfrs (pres 53-54). 12: Ed, "KyLA Bulletin" (49). 14: Catlg. 15: 1210 Raquet st, Nacogdoches Tx 75961.

NOON, PAUL A T. b Columbus Ohio 18 Je 05. 4: Grace Rinard. 5: Ohio State U 27-30 BA & BS in Ed; Columbia 30-32 BS in LS; NYU 32-34 AM. 7: State libn Ohio State Lib 33-42; Sgt Major 119th Armored Eng Battalian US Army 42-45; Libn Lansing(Mich) Pub Lib 45-47; Assoc libn Jacksonville Pub Lib, Jacksonville Fla 47-54; Dir Canton Pub Lib, Canton Ohio 54-62; Instr in sociol & asst libn Walsh Col 62-64; Asst Prof Lib Sch Kent State U 64-. 8: Surveys; Mich State Lib, Tex State Lib, Lib Serv of WVa, 21 Co Libs in Fla. 9: ALA (Coun, chm var coms); -AAStateL (pres); FlaLA (pres & exec sec); SELA (pres Pub Lib Div). 10: Rotary; Torch Club. 12: Ed, "OhioLA Bulletin " (57-62). 13: Yes. 14: Admin, lib educ, ref. 15: 2880 Sharonwood NW, Canton Ohio.

NOONAN, EILEEN FLORENCE. b Spalding Neb 3 D 20. 5: Neb State Tchrs Col 41-45 (Educ, Hist) BA in Educ; UWash summers 48-45 (LS) ML; UMinn summer 58; UCal(Berkeley) summer 63. 7: Tchr Pub Schs, Greeley Co Neb 37-41; Tchr Pub Schs, Gering Neb 45-47; Tchr libn Pub Schs, Morton Wash 47-49; Tchr-libn Pub Schs, Summer Wash 49-52; Sch libn Pub Schs, Tacoma Wash 52-54; Periods libn State Col Iowa 54-55, Instr 55-64; Lecturer Kan State Tchrs Col 64-. 9: ALA; NEA; IowaASchL (pres 63-64); KanLA; KanASchL. 10: AAUP; AAUW. 12: Ed "Basic Book Collection for High School Libraries. 13: Yes. 14: Sch libs. 15: Dept of Lib Sci Rosary College, River Forest Il 60305.

NORBURY, ALDEN (CLAYTON). b Dawson City Yukon 1 Ap 05. 5: OxfordU 20-24 B Phil; McGill 24-27 (Anthrop' MA; Carver Intl Col (Paris) 40-42 (Mediaeval Studies) MA; Ocean FallsU 56-59 (Indian Ling) PhD; UBC 60-61 BLS. 6: Fr, Sanskrit, W Coast Indian dialects. 7: Prin Wroclaw Inst, Paris 28-40; Publ Czar Clipper, Czar Alberta 42-49; Spec lecturer Blednock Co (LondonU), England 49-53; Poet in residence Blundell Col, Dryden Ont Can 53-56; Hd catlgr Watson-Brock Lib, Powell River BC Can 61-64; Hd libn millet Pub Lib, Millet Alta Can 64-66; Spec libn (on leave) Visser Ind, Vancouver BC Can 66-. 8: Spec consul Dolittle Lib of Nat Sci Gloucester Co England 51; Design consul Watson-Brock Ext Lib Powell River NC 62. 9: Assn of Native Lang Libns (Rec sec 69-); Pac Conf on Indian Langs (chm 62-64). 10: SDS; Fraser Arms Club. 11: Watson-Brock Medal 58. 12: "Empty Glasses: Poems" (29); "L'Essence du Carverisme" (38); "Gnarled Fingers: Poems" (43); Ed "Petit Mouquet" (33-40); "Ad-Lib" (68-). 13: Yes. 14: Systems analysis, West-Coast Indian mss. 15: General Delivery, Crystal Springs PO Alberta Can.

NORDEN, MARGARET (KANOF). b Brooklyn NY 23 Jl 37. 4: Carl Norden. 5: Wellesley 54-58 (Pol Sci) BA; Simmons 58-59 MLS; West Res 64- (LS). 6: Fr. 7: Ref asst Brookline Pub High Sch, Brookline Mass 59-60; Ref libn Atlanta Pub Lib 63-64; Research asst Case West Res U 66; Ref libn Brandeis U 66-67, Docs libn 67-68; Ref libn U Rochester 68-. 9: ALA. 10: Amer Jewish Hist Soc; Nat Coun Jewish Women; PTA; Rochester Sch Vol Program. 13: Yes. 14: Ref, info retr, docs.41443 15: 3107 E Derbyshire rd, Cleveland HEIGHTS Ohio 44118.

NORDGREN, ANN-MARI RUTH. b Stamford Conn 17 Ja 32. 5: State U Col of Educ (Geneseo NY) 49-53 (LS) BS; Syracuse (LS) MS. 7: Elem sch libn: pub sch, Lindenhur st NY 53-54, Herricks Pub Schs, New Hyde Park NY 54-58, Dept of Army, Boeblingen Germany 58-60, pub sch, Manhasset NY 60, pub sch, LaGrange Ill 61-63, Dept of Defense, Tachikawa Japan 63-66, Dept of Defense, Lajes, The Azores, Portugal 66-68, Dept of Defense Hanau Germany 68-. 9: Far East EA (sec 64-66); NEA; ALA; OverseasEA. 10: Beta Phi Mu. 14: Elem sch libnship, child wk. 15: Hanau American Sch, APO NYC 09165.

NORDLIE, MARGARET. b Rice Lake Wis 17 N 12. 5: Concordia Col(Moorhead Minn) 30-34 (Lat) BA; UWis 34-35 comparative Lit) MA; UMich 42-43 BALS. 7: High sch tchr Killdeer High Sch, Killdeer ND 35-36; Eng instr Waldorf Col 36-42; Lib asst Royal Oak Pub Lib, Royal Oak Mich 43-44; Lib asst Detroit Pub Lib 44-45; Asst libn & instr in lib sci, Concordia Col 45-61; High sch tchr Zulu Lutheran High Sch, Eshowe Natal S Africa 61-64; Asst libn & assoc prof of LS Concordia Col 65-. 9: ALA; MinnLA. 10: Delta Kappa Gamma; AAUW. 14: Catlg. 15: Concordia Col, Moorhead Minn 56560.

NORDQUEST, CORRINE MARIE. b Ashtabula Ohio 10 S 22. 5: Schauffler Col 40-44 BS in Religious Educ; Simmons 58-61 MS in LS. 6: Fr. 7: Dir of Christian Educ First Congregational Church, Hyde Park Mass 44-48; Missionary Amer Bd of Commissioners for Foreign Missions, Boston 48-54; Missionary City Missionary Soc, Boston 55-58; Libn Congregational Lib, Boston 58-67; Hd catlgr Barbour Lib Pittsburgh Theol Sem, Pittsburgh Penn 67-. 9: AthTheolLA; SAA. 14: Catlg. 15: 601 N Negley ave, apt 32, Pittsburgh Pa 15206.

NORDSKOG, OLIVE (THOMPSON). b Jackson Minn 21 F 13. 4: Arne Nordskog. 5: UMinn 30-33 (LS), 35-36 BS. 6: Norwegian, Fr. 7: Circ, catlg, ref UMinn Biol/Med Lib (Minneapolis) 36-43; Catlg, gifts & exchanges, ser Iowa State U Lib (Ames) 56-58, 63-. 9: ALA. 14: Ser. 15: 3516 Oakland, Ames Ia 50010.

NORDSTROM, WILLIAM (STUART). b NYC 12 Je 31. 5: Wagner Col 50-51; Gallaudet Col 51-54 (LS) BA. 6: Ger, Sp. 7: Lib clerk NYU 54-. 10: Mem in var churches and clubs for the deaf in & around NYC. 13: Yes. 14: Highly-varied clerical assignments. 15: 364 Lincoln ave, Ft Lee NJ 07024.

NOREEN, AURORA MERCEDES (ANDERSON). b Herman Minn 2 O 14. 4: Oscar Henning Noreen. 5: Gustavus Adolphus 29-33 (Sociol, Biol) BA; UMinn summers 58-60. 7: Tchr-libn Kensington Pub Sch, Kensington Minn 57-6; Libn Elbow Lake Pub Sch, Elbow Lake Minn 64-. 9: ALA; NEA; MinnEA. 10: Sch Bd Herman (Minn) Commun Sch; Lutheran Church Women of Amer; Dir Aggassiz Little Theatre. 14: Sch libs. 15: Herman Mn 56248.

NORELL, IRENE LOUISE PALMER. b Springfield NH. 5: UMinn 56-58 (LS) MA. 6: Fr. 7: Head Libn Grand Forks Pub Lib, Grand Forks ND 50-56; Lecturer Lib Educ UND 52-56; Asst Prof NoIll U 58-59; Assoc PROF Dept of Libnship San Jose State Col 59-. 9: ALA; Amer Studies Assn; CalLA; SLA; WNBA. 10: Alpha Beta Alpha; Beta Phi Mu. 12: "Prose Writers of North Dakota (58); "Geographical Literature, a Brief Guide (69). 13: . 14: Lib educ, pub lib serv, child wk. 15: 522 South 5, San Jose Cal 95112.

NORIE, ELISABETH (IRENE) (SIMPSON). b Duncan BC Can 10 N 8. 5: UBC 35-39 (Eng, Lat) BA, 39-40 (Educ) Teaching certif; UWash 47-48 (LS) BAL, 50-53 (Eng) MA. 6: Lat, Ger, Ital, Fr. 7: Tchr BC High Schs 40-47 Catlgr UWash 48-58, Asst head catlg div 59-. 9: ALA; PNLA. 14: Catlg, rare bks. 15: UWash Lib, Seattle Wa 98105.

NORMAN, BEVERLY. b Port Chester NY 29 Mr 41. 4: Ivan H Norman. 5: Stern Col for Women 59-63 (Educ) BA; Pratt 63-66 (LS); NY State Elem Sch Libn Certif. 06: Hebrew. 7: Libn-tchr E Side Hebrew Inst (NY) 63-64; Sch libn Rye Neck Elem Schs, Mamaroneck NY 64-. 9: ALA; NY State Tchrs Assn. 10: Westchester Tchrs Assn; Rye Neck Tchrs Assn. 14: Child lit. 15: 25 Trinity pl, New Rochelle NY 10805.

NORMAN, CAROL (GAY). b Baltimore 8 N 45. 5: USask 63-66 (Fr) BA; McGill U 66-68 (LS). 6: Fr. 7: Gen libn Azusa Pub Lib, Azusa Cal 68-. 9: ALA; CalLA. 14: Ref, tech serv. 15: 1903 E Petunia st, Glendora Ca 91740.

NORMAN, EILEEN (BARR). b Lucas Kan 4 Ap 20. 4: Donald A Norman. 5: Tex Womans U 38-42 BA (Eng) BS in LS, summer 65 (NDEA); Tex A & T 65-69 (Supv). 7: Ref libn Tex Womans U 42-43; Ref libn ext loan UTex 43; Supv libn Porter Doss MEM Lib, Weslaco Tex 64; Elem sch libn Weslaco Pub Schs, Weslaco Tex 48-65; Dir of Inst materials Harlingen Pub Sch 65-. 9: ALA; Tex State LA; Rio Grande Valley LA; Tex State Tchrs Assn; Tex Classroom Tchrs Assn;

NEA-DAVI; Tex A-V Educ Assn. 14: Child wk, sch lib supv. 15: 1802 E Washington, Harlingen Tx 78550.

NORMAN, GENE (ORVAL). b Norman Ind 2 N 37. 4: Darlene (Meki). 5: Ind State Tchrs Col 55-59 (Speech) BA; Ind U 59-60 (LS) MA. 6: Sp. 7: Grad asst Ind U Div of Lib Sci 59-60; Documents & asst ref libn DePauw U 60-61; Asst ref libn Ind State U 61-65, Act head ref dept 65-66, Hd 66-. 8: Chm Bibliog and Ref course, Ind State U Lib; Asst Prof, Sci Dept 68-69. 9: ALA; IndLA. 10: AAUP; Alpha Beta Alpha; Sigma Phi Epsilon. 14: Ref, bibliog. 15: 2417 Morton st, Terre Haute In 47802.

NORMAN, GLENNIE M(AE). b Minden La 25 F 07. 5: St Vincents Col 33-35 (Educ) Teachers La Tech 38-40 (Educ Sci) BA; Peabody 41-42 BS in LS; Amer U 51-52 (Pub Admin). 7: Tchr St Marys Acad, Marshall Tex 35-39; Libn Slidell High Sch, Slidell La 41-42; Libn Anderson Col 42-43; Libn Vivian High Sch, Vivian La 43-44; Catlgr US Interstate Com Commsn, Wash DC 44-47; Libn engnr research div US Army Engnrs 47-50; Asst libn US Interstate Com Commsn, Wash DC 50-54, Libn 55-. 9: SLA; DCLA. 10: Bus & Prof Women; Nat Coun Church Women; Internat Christ Leadership. 14: Admin, legal research, bibliog. 15: 3801 Conn ave NW, Wash DC 20008.

NORMAN, LEVERETT M. b Halifax NS Can 24 O 22. 5: Dalhousie U 42-46 (Eng Lit) BA; Columbia 46-47 BSLS. 7: Catlgr Columbia U 47; Asst ser div City Col (NY) 47-55, Documents lib 55-, Asst Prof. 8: . 9: NY Lib Club (chm Bd of Scholarship & Awards 56-57. 10: AAUP. 13: Yes. 14: Ref. 15: 95 Christopher st, NYC 10014.

NORRIS, CARRIE ANN. b Gary Ind 24 Ap 41. 5: Ind U 59-64 (Govt) AB. 6: Fr. 7: Asst ref libn Lake Co Pub Lib, Griffith Ind 64, Act ref libn 64-. 66, Asst ref libn 66-67, Community libn 67-. 9: ALA; IndLA. 10: Delta Zeta; IndU Alumni Assn. 14: Ref, ya & adult serv. 15: 6 W 71st pl 4, Merrillville In 46410.

NORRIS, HELEN LOUISE. b Abingdon Ill 7 Mr 10. 5: Eureka Col 28-30; Knox Col 30-32 (Eng) AB; UIll 32-33 BS in LS, 44-45 MS in LS. 7: Asst Ill State Lib 34-35; Asst Rockford Pub Lib, Rockford Ill 35-43; Catlgr Gary Pub Lib, Gary Ind 43-44; Asst libn Oak Park Pub Lib, Oak Park Ill 45-47; Coordinator of personnel Indianapolis Pub Lib 47-65; Head tech processes Rockford Pub Lib, Rockford Ill 65-. 9: ALA; IllLA. 10: AAUW; Beta Phi Mu. 13: Yes. 14: Catlg, personnel admin. 15: 1322 Harlem blvd, Rockford Ill 61103.

NORTCOTT, JEAN. b Tottenham NSW Australia 26 Je 26. 5: USydney (NSW Australia) (Chem) BS, MS, PhD. 6: Fr. 7: Teaching Fellow USydney (NSW Australia) 49, 51-53; Grad asst Washington U St Louis 50; Chem bacteriologist Campbell Soup Co Ltd, Toronto 54-55; Research chem; Library & Patent Asst Specialty Chems Div Allied Chem Corp, Buffalo NY 56-. 9: SLA (chm-elect Chem Sect Sci-Tech Div 65-66; Upstate NY Chap Bd Dir 65-)66, 68-69; chm Chem Div 66-67. 10: AAUW; ACS; Organic Chemists Club(Buffalo); Sigma Xi; Women Chemists Club(Buffalo-Niagara Falls); Interclub Coun of Wes NY; Mental Health Assn of Erie Co; Soroptimist. 11: Susan B Anthony Award for profess achievement & community serv, Interclub Coun of West NY 69. 13: Yes. 14: Info retrieval. 15: PO Box 1069, Buffalo NY 1440.

NORTH AUDREY. b E Aurora NY 21 Ag 14. 5: Rockford Col 33-37 (Pol Sci) AB; UBuffalo 37-38 BSLS; UMich summers 40, 41, 44 MA in LS. 6: Fr, Ger. 7: Asst libn Susquehanna U 38-42, libn 42-45; Asst libn Rockford Col 45-51; Lib staff Port of NY Authority, NYC 51-52; Head Tech Serv American U of Beirut 52-55; Head order unit Purdue U Lib 55-57; Head readers servs Oberlin Col Lib 57-59; Assoc libn Oakland U 59-61; Libn Keuka Col 61-65; Asst prof sch of lib sci, Syracuse U 65-. 9: ALA; -ACRL (chm Col Lib Sect 67-68); NYLA (sec-treas Col & Univ Sect 64-66); AALS. 10: AAUP. 13: Yes. 14: Tchg catlg & tech proc, admin, bibliog of soc scis, materials sel. 15: 832 Ackerman ave, Syracuse NY 13210.

NORTH, DENNIS DARRELL. b Mason Mich 24 Jl 41. 5: Mich StateU 58-62 (Mus Theory & Composition) B Mus; UDenver 63-65 (Libnship) MA. 6: Fr, Ger, Ital. 7: Ref libn UDenver Libs 65-67, Hd ref serv 67-69; Hd libn Regis Col 69-. 9: MusLA; ColoLA (Col & Univ sect: v-chm 68-69, chm 69-70). 13: Yes. 14: Ref, catlg, hist of bks and libs. 15: 2265 S Humboldt, Denver Co 80210.

NORTH, JANICE KAY (FERGUS). b Kansas City Kan 22 My 46. 4: Edward Ray North. 5: UKan 64-67 (Hist, Psych) BA; UDenver 67-68 (LS) MA. 6: Ger, Sp. 7: Catlg libn UKan Med Ctr 68-. 10: Beta Phi Mu. 14: Catlg. 15: 2618 W 43rd, Kansas City Ks 66103.

NORTH, JEANNE B. b Independence Mo 12 F 22. 4:John W North. 5: Graceland Col 39-41 AA: State U Iowa 41-42, 47 (Eng) BA; Cornell U 43 (Aero Engnr) Certif; Columbia 47-48 BSLS. 7: Jr liaison engnr Curtiss-Wright, Buffalo NY 44; Jr liaison engnr Wilson Chem Feeders, Buffalo NY 44-45; Ref libn United Aircraft Corp, E Hartford Conn 48-56, Head Libn 56-51; Supv Palo Alto Lib Lockheed Aircraft, Palo Alto Cal 61-63; Head Engnr Lib Stanford U 63-65, Chief govt document div 65-67, Sr lib syss analyst programming serv 67-69; Res assoc Info Gen Corp 69-. 8: Visiting lecturer UTex Grad Sch of Lib Sci summers 63 & 65. 9: SLA; sec 60-63; Pres Conn Valley Chap 54-55; pres San Francisco Chap 66-67; chm Metals materials div 56-57; chm Documentation Div 69-70); Soc Tech Writers & Publrs (sec 59-61); ALA; Amer Soc Engnr Educ; Calla; ASIS; Amer Soc Indexers. 12: Ed com "Special Libraries (57-59). 13: Yes. 15: 742 Southampton dr, Palo Alto Cal 94303.

NORTH, JOHN A. b St Albans England 13 Mr 42. 5: Associate of Lib Assoc GB. 6: Fr. 7: Asst libn NRPRA, Eng 59-61; Asst libn Morgan Bros (Pub) Ltd, Lond Eng 61-63, libn 63-64; Catlgr Co-op Bk Centre Can, Toronto 64-66, Mgr catlg dept 66-67; Chief libn centennial Col 67-. 9: ALA; SLA; CanLA; Lib Assn (Gt Brit); OntLA. 14: Admin, jr cols. 15: 651 Warden ave, Scarborough Ont Can.

NORTH, (JON) FREDERICK. b Oneida NY 28 D 35. 5: Columbia 66- (Ling). 6: Ger, Fr, Sp. 7: Lib asst Enoch Pratt Free Lib, Baltimore 52-53; Asst libn Amer Friends Serv Committee, NYC 55-57; Acquis libn Amer Mus of Natural Hist, NYC 65-. 10: AASR, radio programing. 14: Acquis, ser, translation. 15: Lib Amer Museum of Natural Hist CPW & 79th st, New York NY 10024.

NORTH, ROBERT JR. b Buffalo NY 1 Mr 10. 4: Marion deMauriac. 5: Harvard 29-33 (Fine Arts) AB; UBuffalo 34-65 BS in LS. 7: Lib asst Buffalo Pub Lib, Buffalo NY 34-46; Hd ref dept Emory U Lib 46-49; Hd libn Kanawha Co Pub Lib, Charleston WVa 49-52; Deputy dir Erie Co Pub Lib, Buffalo NY 52-54, Asst deputy dir Buffalo & Erie co Pub Lib, Buffalo NY 54-. 9: ALA; NY State LA; WV LA (pres 51-52). 10: Internat Torch Club; Harvard Club of Buffalo; Buffalo Fine Arts Acad. 14: Admin, ref. 15: 16 St James pl, Buffalo NY 14222.

NORTHENSCOLD, DORIS. b Fond du Lac Wis 6 S 23. 5: UMinn 42-48 (LS) BS. 7: Ref libn ND State Lib 49; Head Libn Pub Lib, St Paul Minn 49-50; Prof asst Pub Lib, Minneapolis 50-54; Head Libn Pub Lib, Chicago Heights Ill 54-56; Prof asst Pub Lib, Minneapolis 56-58, Br libn 58-64, Br libn Experimental Unit 64-, Commun Action Prog Lib 66, Br libn 67-68, N dist libn 68-. 9: ALA; MinnLA. 10: Bus & Prof Womens Club; Jordan Area Activity Com; Altrusa Club; NAACP. 14: Br lib admin, lib ser to disadvantaged. 15: 5322 DuPont ave S, Minneapolis Mn 55419.

NORTON, ALICE (LEE). b Columbus Ohio 20 Ap 26. 5: Wellesley 43-47 (Hist) BA; UIll 61-62 (LS) MS. 7: Ed asst "The Reader's Digest," Cleveland 47-51; Ed asst National Coun Protestant Episcopal Church, Greenwich Conn 52-53; Continuity dir KLZ-TV, Denver 53-54; Asst to pub rel dir Eastman Oil Well Survey Co, Denver 54-55; Pub rel off Denver Pub Lib 55-61; Pub rel dir Westchester Lib System, Mt Vernon NY 62-66; Wellesley Col Stevens Traveling Fellow 66-67; Lib pub rel consul for own firm 68-. 8: Lib 21 staff, Seattle World's Fair 62; Pub rel consul for state libs, lib systs, pub libs & lib assns. 9: ALA-LAD (chm Pub Rel Sect 63-64); LPRC (pres 69-70); NYLA; WestchesterLA; NYLibClub. 10: LWV; Beta Phi Mu; Pub Rel Soc of Amer; NY Wellesley Club. 13: Yes. 14: Pub rel, communication, admin. 15: 392 Central Park West, New York NY 10025.

NORTON, ELIZABETH D (MRS). b Dayton Ohio 18 Jl 21. 5: Otterbein Col 53 (Hist, Govt) BA; Wes Res 54 MSLS. 7: Head circ dept Pub Libs of Saginaw, Saginaw Mich 54-55; Community Libn Willard Lib, Battle Creek Mich 55-58; Br libn Northtown-Shiloh Br Lib Dayton & Montgomery Co Pub Lib, Dayton Ohio 58-66; Circ libn Berea Col Lib 66-67; Reg consul Central Mass Reg Lib Syst, Worcester Mass 67-68; Staff devel consul State Lib of Ohio 68-. 8: Staff, Mich State Lib Wkshop, 55; Pres Adv Com ASD-Study-Discussion Programs Proj, ALA, 64; Braille Transcribing; Literacy Training PROGRAM. 9: ALA; MichLA (Salary, Staff & Tenure Com 54-55; chm Ad Educ Sect 57-58); Ohio LA (chm Staff Org Round Table62-63, chm Ad Educ Round Table 65-66). 14: Adult educ. 15: 1340 Dublin rd apt 16, Columbus Oh 43215.

NORTON, ELIZABETH F. b N Platte Neb. 5: St Teresa Col (Kan City Mo) 31-33 AA; Col of St Mary-of-the- Wasatch 34-36 (Eng, Hist) BA; Col of St Catherine 37-38 BS in LS. 7: Act libn Col of St Mary of the Wasatch 36-37; Libn Carbon Col 39-42; Tech libn Pacific Aeronautical Lib, Los Angeles 42-44; Asst engn libn Hughes Aircraft Co, Culver City Cal 44-45; UCLA: Asst in circ dept 45-47, Asst in acquis dept 47-49, Ser libn acquis dept 4963, Head ser dept 63-66; Acquis libn San Mateo Co Lib System, Belmont Cal 67; Consul libn Stacey's Div of Brodart, Palo Alto Cal 69-. 9: ALA (Memb Com SoCal Chap 47-49);-RTSD (Ser Sect; Chm 65-, Policy & Research Com 57-59, NY Conf Planning Com 65-66, Acquis-ser Jt Com to compile list of Internat Subs Agents 59-65); SLA (SoCal Chap; Union List of Periods Com 51-65); CathLA; CalLA. 10: Women of the Faculty, UCLA: Friends of the UCLA Lib. 12: Comp "International Subscription Agent, ALA (63. 13: Yes. 14: Ser, records, serv for lib users). 15: 5800 Balboa dr, Oakland Ca 94611.

NORTON, ELOISE (SPEED). b W Point Miss 14 Ag 29. 5: Miss State Col for Women 52 (LS) BS; Miss State U 61 (Counseling) MEd; Peabody summer 61 (LS); Interamerican U Mex summer 63 (Span); LSU summers 64, 65, 68 (LS), 69 MS in LS. 6: Sp. 7: Libn Harlingen Ind Sch, Harlingen Tex 51-52; Libn Fondren Lib, Rice U 54-55; Elem lib consul Spring Branch Ind Schs, Houston 55-63, Multi-Sch libn 63-. 8: Instr, NDEA Lib Inst, Okla State U summer 66; Dir Okla State Children's Lit Study Tour 67, 68, 69; Lectr, Child Lit UHouston 68,69; Spec Com for NEA Brochure on Elem Lib Serv; Producer of "Authors for Children" (21 taped interviews of Child authors available from UMich Tape Lib. 9: ALA-AASchL (Elem Lib Com); TexLA (chm Dist I, chm Child RT); Tex State Tchrs Assn (chm Dist V, Lib Div). 13: Yes. 14: Sch libs, child lit, learning media ctrs. 15: 1739 Nocturne, Houston Tx 77043.

NORTON, ESTHER (ELLIS). b Marion Ind 14 My 05. 4: Charles V Norton. 5: Purdue 23-27 (Hist, Eng) BS; UIll 28-29 BS in LS. 7: Lib asst UIll (Urbana) 29-30; Lib asst UCincinnati 30-33 Lib asst Cincinnati Pub Lib 33-35, 50-51; Libn Robert A Taft San Engnr Center, Cincinnati 51-67; Libn US Pub Health Serv, Cincinnati 67-. 9: ALA; SLA; ASIS. 10: Zeta Tau Alpha. 14: Admin. 15: 6061 Crittenden dr, Cincinnati Oh 45244.

NORTON, MARGARET ELIZABETH (MASON). b Spotsylvania Co Va 17 D 20. 4: Rolland G Norton. 5: Bridgewater Col 39-43 (Home Econ) BS; West Mich U 62-68 (Libnship) MS. 7: Hosp dietitian Grace Hosp, Richmond Va 43; Nutritionist Dairy Council of Richmond Va 43-46; Home econ tchr Bronson High Sch, Bronson Mich 46-48; Libn & a-v dir Bronson Commun Schs 63-. 9: ALA;-AASL; NEA; MichASchL; Mich A-V Assn; MichEA; BronsonEA. 10: Farm Bureau; Home Econ Ext; 4-H Club leader. 14: Ref, wk with students. 15: Rte 1, Bronson Mi 49028.

NORTON, MARIE ALLISON. b Philadelphia 30 Ap 28. 5: St Joseph's Col 63 (Soc Sci) BS; Villanova 65-66 (LS) MS. 6: Ger. 7: Med tech Lankenau Hosp, Phila 49-60; Virology tech Smith Kline & French, Phila 60-63, Med correspondent 63-65; Libn med lib Lankenau Hosp, Phila 66-. 8: Instr Sci Lit, Lib Sch Villanova U 67-. 9: MLA; SLA. 13: Yes. 14: Ref (med). 15: Med Lib Lankenau Hospital, Philadelphia Pa 19151.

NORWOOD, FLINT. b Bookman SC 18 Mr 27. 4: Elizabeth Laughridge. 5: USCar 47-50 (Ger) AB; UNC 54-55 (LS) BLS. 6: Ger, Fr. 7: PFC US Army (Mil Police), Berlin Germany 45-47; Asst ref libn Richland Co Pub Lib, Columbia SC 48-54; Young adults libn Enoch Pratt Free Pub Lib, Baltimore 54-57; Head circ Richlnd Co Pub Lib, Columbia SC 57-60; HeadLibn Chester Co Free Pub Lib, Chester SC 60-67; Libn Statesville Pub Lib, Statesville NC 67; Dir Iredell Pub Lib, Statesville NC 67-. 9: SLA; SCLA; v-pres pub lib sect 63-63; Charlotte NC trade area pub lib assn (pres 67-69); chm fine arts com, mem lib serv com; NCLA (Personnel Com, Pub Lib Sect). 10: PTA; Boy Scouts; Girl Scouts; Church Sch Super, Episcop Church. 14: Ref, adult educ. 15: 420 Summit ave, Statesville NC 28677.

NOTEHELFER, MARGARET ANN. b Vancouver Can 15 D 35. 4: Frederick G Notehelfer. 5: UBC 55-59 (Eng, Classical Studies) BA, 62-63 BLS. 7: Lib asst UBC Lib 59-62; Ref libn I UVictoria Lib 63-65; Mus asst Victoria d'Albert Mus, London 65; Ref libn I CarletonU 66; Catlg ed PrincetonU 67-. 9: ALA. 14: Ref. 15: 3D Hibben apts Faculty rd, Princeton NJ 08540.

NOTHEISEN, MARGARET A. b Chicago 24 Jl 26. 5: Col of St Francis 44-45; Rosary Col 45-48 (LS) BA; Chicago 57-58 (LS) MA. 6: Ger, Fr. 7: Order libn Ill Inst of Tech Lib 48-49; Asst libn Rush Med Col Lib 49-51; Libn Michael Reese Hosp Sch of Nursing Lib, Chicago 51-55; Libn The Armour Labs Kankakee Ill 55-57; Asst libn World Book Encyclopedia Ref Lib, Chicago 58-50; Tech libn Argonne Nat Lab High Energy Physics Lib, Argonne Ill 59-66; Tech libn Met Sanitary Dist of Grtr Chicago 66-. 9: SLA; ALA. 14: Ref. 15: 230 E Ontario pl, Chicago Il 60611.

NOTT, GOLDIE LUELLA (TILMAN). b Eugene Ore 1 Ja 13. 4: George William Nott. 5: Miami U(Oxford Ohio) 30-34 (Eng Ger) BS in Educ; UIll 38-42 BS in LS; UMich 56 MALS, 62 (Educ) MA in Educ. 7: Proofreader Standard Register Co, Dayton Ohio 34-35; Child libn, br libn Dayton Pub Lib, Dayton Ohio 35-42; Soc ed & reporter "Big Rapids Pioneer, Big Rapids Mich 43; Head Libn Sch-Pub Lib, Greenville Mich 43-46; Head Libn Ferris State Col 46-. 8: Admin Coun, Ferris State Col 53-. 9: ALA; MichLA (chm Dist 4 55; col sect; sec 57, chm 64). 10: AAUW; Bus & Prof Women; Zonta; Phi Beta Kappa; Delta Zeta; Beta Phi Mu; Kappa Delta Pi; Tau Kappa Alpha. 13: Yes. 14: Admin, catlg. 15: RR1, Rodney Mich 49342.

NOVAK, ANNE L (BERMAN). b Brooklyn NY 13 O 20. 4: Henry Novak. 5: Brooklyn Col 37-45 9eng); Sul Ross State Col 46-49 (Eng, Art, Educ) BA; Simmons Col 65-69 (LS) MS. 6: Yiddish. 7: Lab tech med asst Doctors' off, NYC 37-41; Exec sec American Red Cross, Brooklyn NY 41-43; Private sec Meat purveyor, NYC 44-46; Grad asst (Art tchr) Sul Ross State Col 49; Tchr/newspaper sponsor Martin High Sch, Laredo Tex 50-52; Publ writer, Laredo AFB Tex 53-55. 10: Alpha Chi; Kappa Delta Pi; Org pres, Friends of the Library, West Peabody Mass 61-63; LWV; AAUW. 11: Editor of College Yearbook (1st prize). 14: Art libn, tchg lib skills, adult serv, ref. 15: 53 Turning Mill rd, Lexington Ma 02173.

NOVAK, VICTOR. b Yugoslavia 6 Je 23. 4: Cirila Cesnik. 5: ULjubljana 43; UGraz (Austria) 45-49 (Pol Sci) PhD; Wes Res 54-55 MSLS. 6: Fr, Ger, Ital Slovenian, Serbo-Croat. 7: Ref libn Cuyahoga Co Lib, Cleveland 55-57; Circ libn USanta Clara 57-58, Loan & ser libn 58-64, Ser libn 64-68, Dir of Libs 69-. 8: Active in co-op efforts to prepare a union list of serials for the nine Bay Area Cath cols and univs 68-69; Survey of Cath col & univ libs with enrollment above 1,000 students regarding staff assns, staff meetings, and staff mem status. 9: ALA; CathLA (chm Col Sect NoCal Unit 59-63); CalLA. 10: Helibs. 13: Yes. 14: Ser, ref, admin. 15: Univ of Santa Clara Lib, Santa Clara Ca 95053.

NOVOSAL, BROTHER PAUL PETER SM. b St Louis 5 O 18. 5: UDayton 38-40 (Eng) BS Ed; Our Lady of the Lake Col 40-41 BSLS; St Marys U 61-65 (Eng) MA. 6: Croatian. 7: Libn & tchr Central dir St Josephs High Sch, Victoria Tex 46-47; Libn & Asst Prof of Eng St Marys U(San Antonio Tex) 47-57, Dir of Libs & Asst rof Prof Eng 57-. 9: ALA; CathLA (Adv Bd 65-66, v-chm & chm San Antonio Unit 53-54 & 58-60); SWLA; TexLA (Const Com 64-65). 10: Wisdom Soc Adv of Knowledge; Nat Cath Theatre Conf. 12: Ed "Union List of Marian Books in the Libraries of San Antonio (56). 14: Admin. 15: St Marys Univ, 2700 Cincinnati ave, San Antonio Tex 78221.

NOWAK, ILDIKO DESIREE (SINGER). b Bratislava Czechoslovakia 10 Ag 25. 4: Franz Bernard Nowak. 5: Bratislava Tech U 43-49 (Chem) MS; Charles U Lib Prague) 47-48 (Abstracting, Indexing, Clsf) Certif. 6: Ger, Fr, Hungarian, Czech, Slovak. 7: Abstractor Nat Wood & Paper Research Inst, Bratislava Czechoslovakia 49-51; Interpreter US Counter Intelligence Corps, Salzburg Austria 51-53; Research chem Helene Curtis Ind Inc, Chicago 53-55; Tr US Corps of Engnrs, Kaiserslautern Germany 55-56; Supv, Chief SLA Tr Center, Chicago 56-. 8: Free-lance abstractor for Preston Technical Abstracts Co, Evanston Ill 57-. 9: SLA. 10: German Amer Nat Cong (Chicago). 14: Tr of for sci & tech lit. 15: 838 S Michigan ave, Villa Park Il 60181.

NOWAK, STANLEY JOHN. b Buffalo NY 9 F 41. 4: Catherine M Nowak. 5: Canisius Col 58-62 (Sociol) BS; StateU Col(Geneseo NY) 62-64 MLS; SUNY (Buffalo) 65-69 MEd. 7: Libn Pub Sch No 44, Buffalo NY 63-64; Libn Woodlawn Jr High Sch, Buffalo NY 64-69; Staff Buffalo & Erie Co Pub Lib, Buffalo NY summer 6568; W Hertel Middle Sch, Buffalo NY 69-. 9: NYLA; NY State Tchrs Assn; BuffaloSchLA (treas). 10: Aircraft Owners and Pilots Assn; Buffalo Tchrs Fed. 14: Sch libs, pub libs. 15: 550 Hertel ave, Buffalo NY 14207.

NOWELL, MARY ANN (DELINSKI). b Wilkes-Barre Penn 17 Ap 41. 4: Michael Joy Nowell. 5: Col of New Rochelle 59-63 (Physics) AB; Drexel 64-65 MS in LS. 6: Ger. 7: Lib asst Math-Physics Lib UPenn 63-65; Libn USA Hosp, Heidelberg Ger 65-66; Libn Spec Serv Lib Pendleton Bks, Giessen Ger

66-67; Govt docts libn Kansas State Col of Pittsburg 68, Instr of Lib Sci 69-. 9: SLA. 14: Sci & tech libs, catlg, ref. 15: 109 E Quincy st apt 22, Pittsburg Ks 66762.

NOWICKI, LEONARD J. b Gniezno Poland. 5: UPoznan Poland 31-36 (Fr) MA; Syracuse 57-58 MLS. 6: Polish, Fr, Ger, Ital, Sp. 7: Br & ref libn Buffalo & Erie Co Pub Lib, Buffalo NY 58-64; Hd ref dept SUNY (Buffalo) 64-. 9: ALA; NYLA; Fac Assn State of New York. 10: Beta Phi Mu; AAUP; Com on East European Studies; Polish-Amer Com on Cultural Affairs. 15: 950 Fillmore ave, Buffalo NY 14211.

NOYES, SUZANNE (NISBET). b Marshfield Wis 15 D 32. 4: James L Noyes Jr. 5: Colorado Col 50-52 (Eng Lit); UWis 52-57 BS (Eng Lit), MS (LS). 6: Ger. 7: Research asst Off of Atty General, Madison Wis 57-58; Asst libn VA Hos, Madison Wis 58-60, Chief Libn 60-. 9: Mad (Wis) Lib Club (pres 64-65). 14: Med libnship. 15: VA Hosp 2500 Overlook terrace, Madison Wis 53705.

NUERNBERG, DONNA. b Wausau Wis 26 Jl 34. 5: UWis 52-56 (Hist) BS, 63-64 (LS) MS. 7: Order libn Pub Lib, Green Bay Wis 56-57; Employers Insurance Wausau Wis: Circ & order libn 57-60, Asst libn 61-64, Libn 64-. 9: SLA (sec Insurance Dir 68-); WisLA. 15: 2000 Westwood dr, Wausau Wi 54401.

NUGENT, ROBERT STEEL. b Jersey City NJ 24 Mr 26. 4: Natalie Kreinbihl. 5: Columbia 47-51 (Fr) BS; NYU 52-53 (Fr); Columbia 53-54 (French Romance Phil), 68 MA; Rutgers 55-56 MLS. 6: Fr, Lat. 7: US Navy: Seaman 1/c 44-46; Comiler & rewriter Mordys Investors Serv, NYC 51-53; Sr libn Free Pub Lib, Jersey City NJ 55-59; Jersey City State Col Dir libs & Assoc Prof 59-. 8: Ch, Lib Com, Middle States Eval Com (NEA-Secon Educ Div) 64. 9: NJLA (Pub Rel Com 58); NJEA. 10: Jersey City State Col Faculty Assn. 12: "Photographic Reproduction for Libraries (42); ed "Library Buildings for Library Servce (47); ed "The Function of the Library in the Modern College (54); Co-author "Patterns in the Use of Books in Large Research Libraries (61-69). 14: Acquis, rare bks. 15: 255 Union st, Jersey City NJ 07304.

NULTON, AGNES GALTON. b Beaver Falls Penn 21 Jl 10. 5: Geneva Col 27-31 (Eng) BA; UPittsburgh 63-64 MLS. 7: Libn Lib of Sch of Nursing Providence Hosp, Beaver Falls Penn 52-63; Asst libn McCartney Lib Geneva Col 64-. 9: ALA; PennLA. 10: Bus & Profess Women. 14: Acquis, ref. 15: 419 Seventh st, Patterson Hts, Beaver Falls Pa 15010.

NUNELEE, JOHN (PAUL). b Lindale Tex 28 N 43. 4: Paula Betts. 5: Tyler Jr Col 62-63; Tex West Col 63-66 (Educ) BS; LSU 66-67 (LS) MS. 6: Sp. 7: Chief catlg libn UTex (El Paso) 67-69; Assoc dir Miss Lib Commsn, Jackson Miss 69-. 9: ALA; Miss LA (sec Scholarship Com); Tex Regl Gp of Catlgrs & Clsfrs (v-chm 68-69). 14: Lib admin, catlg. 15: 1142 Raymond rd A-1, Jackson Ms 39204.

NUNEZ, ANA ROSA. b La Habana Cuba 11 Jl 26. 5: Academia Baldor (Habana) 40-45 Bachelor in Letters; U de La Habana 45-50 PhD, 50-52 MLS. 6: Fr. 7: Asst Prof Spanish Dept, Wooster Col Ohio 49-50; Dir lib Tribunal de Cuentas, Cuba 51-61; Asst ref libn UMiami Fla 66-. 9: ALA; FlaLA; DadeCoLA. 10: Sigma Delta Pi; Phi Alpha Theta; Cuban Womens club; UMiami Staff Assn; Agrupacion Bibliografica Jose Toribio Medina (Colombia). 12: "La vida bibliografica de Don Antonio Bachiller y Morales (58); "Aspectos de una vida entre libros" (55); "Un dia en el verso 59" (59); "Gabriela Mistral, amor que hirio" (60); "Loores a la palma real" (68); "La Florida en Juan Ramon Jimenez" (68). 13: Yes. 14: Acquis, ref. 15: 2130 SW 14 ter apt 2, Miami Fl 33145.

NUNEZ, FRANK. b Detroit Mich 27 Mr 31. 4: Patsy Orene Barnett. 5: Sue Bennett Jr Col 58-60 (Eng) Certif; East KyU 60-62 (Eng) BA; UKy 66-68 MSLS. 6: Sp. 7: A1/C USAF 51-55; Circ libn East KyU 62, Admin asst to libn 63, Acquis libn 64-68; Dir lib SW Va Commun Col 68-. 9: ALA; VaLA. 14: Acquis procedures, automation. 15: General Delivery, Lebanon Va 24644.

NUNN, THEODORE JOSEPH JR. b Albany NY 16 Ja 35. 4: Joyce L Potter. 5: UDayton 52-56 (Hist, Pol Sci) BA; West MichU 61-62 MSLS. 7: Asst base libn Naval Air Sta, Oceana Va 57-58; Ref libn Dayton Pub Lib, Dayton Ohio 59-61; Ref libn Bronson Methodist Hosp Lib, Kalamazoo 62; Ref libn AF Main Tech Lib, Wright Patterson AFB Dayton Ohio 62-64; Hd libn AF Flight Dynamics Lab Lib, Wright-Patterson AFB Dayton Ohio 64-66; Dir Nat Cash register Co Tech Lib, Dayton Ohio 66-68; Chief reader serv AF Inst of Tech Lib, Wright-Patterson AFB Dayton Ohio 68-. 9: SLA (Nat Adv Coun; Dayton Chap: treas, pres-elect & pres); ASIS (treas So Ohio Chap). 10: Dayton Area C of C. 14: Mgt, automation, ref, research. 15: 2759 Vineland trail, Dayton Oh 45430.

NUNNELEE, JANICE LESSLEY (MRS). b Gravel Hill Mo 23 F 20. 5: Southeast Mo State Col 38-41 (Eng, Hist) BS in Ed; UIll 54-58 (LS) MS. 6: Fr. 7: Eng tchr Lutesville High Sch, Lutesville Mo 41-42; Miss Co Lib, Chaleston Mo 51-56; Ref libn Southeast Mo State Col 56-. 9: MoLA; Mo State Tchrs Assn. 10: AAUP; Delta Kappa Gamma; Kappa Delta Pi; Pi Kappa Delta; Sigma Tau Delta; LWV. 14: Ref. 15: 760 Perry ave, Cape Girardeau Mo 63701.

NURKIN, RITA. b NY 15 My 31. 4: Morton Nurkin. 5: Vassar 48-52 (Psych) BA; LIU (C W Post) 64-67 MSLS. 7: Libn Central Sch Dist #2, Syosset NY 67-. 9: ALA. 14: Child lit. 15: 25 Flamingo rd No, E Hills NY 11576.

NUSSBAUM, IRWIN. b NYC 28 Je 31. 5: Brooklyn Col 50-54 (Hist) BA; Columbia 54-56 MLS. 6: Fr. 7: Fellow City Col (NYC) 54-55; Brooklyn Pub Lib: Staff 56-58; Sr libn 58-60, Supv libn 60-. 9: NY Lib Club. 14: Admin, adult serv. 15: 245 E 19 st, New York NY 10003.

NUTT, RICHARD SHERMAN. b Wakefield Mass 23 N 17. 4: Edith Woolsey. 5: Hobart Col 40-42 (Eng); Yale 45-47 (Amer Hist, Lit) AB, 50-52 (Hosp Admin) MS; Simmons 55-56 (LS) MS. 6: Fr. 7: Instr Hobart Col 47-49; Admin asst NYU Bellevue Med Center 51-52; Research asst Bibliogr Soc of Amer, Cambridge Mass 56-57; Catlgr Yale Med Sch Lib 57-60; Libn Moses Brown Sch, Providence 60-. 14: Rare bks. 15: 67 Congdon st, Providence RI 02906.

NUTTER, DANIEL LYON. b Alcester Union Co SD 16 Ja 32. 4: Elizabeth Jane Mohnkern. 5: Southeastern State Col (Durant Okla) 52-56 (Hist, Speech) BA in Ed; N Tex State U MLS. 6: Sp. 7: Libn Buna Independent Sch Dist, Buna Tex 56-61; Lib dir Clarendon Col 61-66; Libn Hamshire-Fannet Independent Sch Dist, Tex 66-67; Hd libn E Tex Bapt Col 67-68; Hd libn Southwestern Col 68-. 9: ALA; KanLA. 10: Sigma Tau Gamma; Blue Key; Alpha Lambda Sigma; Jr C of C; Friends of Tex Libs, Lions Internat; AAUP; TASK. 14: Admin. 15: 1402 E 2nd, Windfield Ks 67156.

NYE, WILLIAM J. b Keukuk Iowa 28 O 26. 4: Ida Lenore Boatman. 5: Carthage Col 47-50 (Hist, Phil, Psych) BA; Central Lutheran Theol Sem 50-53; UIll 57-59 MSLS. 7: USA Infantry US, Philippines, Korea, Alaska& pastor St James Lutheran Ch, Harvel Ill 53-56; Libn Fisher Ill Pub Schs 57-59; Libn Central Methodist Col 59-60; Spec collections libn Ill StateU 60-64; Ref serv libn Ball StateU 64-67, 68-. 9: Ind Educl Res Assn. 12: Asst ed "Steinbech Newsletter" (69-). 14: Ref, archives, spec collections. 15: 2525 Lanewood, Muncie In 47304.

NYGAARD, ANITA (STRICKLAND). b Salem Ore 4 O 24. 4: Milton S Nygaard. 5: illamette U 44-47 (Fr) AB; UWash 63-64 (LS) MA. 6: Fr, Ger. 7: Lib asst King Co Pub Lib, Seattle 62-64; Libn The Mountaineers, Seattle 60-; Libn Nat Bank of Com, Seattle 68-. 9: ALA; SLA. 10: The Mountaineers. 14: Catl, clsf. 15: 17027 33rd SW, Seattle Wa 98166.

NYHOLM, JENS (PETER). b Hj4orring, Denmark 24 Jl 1900. 4: Amy Fredericka Wood. 5: 4Osters4ogades Gymnasium (Copenhagen) 16-19 (Langs) Artium; UCopenhagen 19-20 (Philos) Filosofikum; Danish State Lib Sch(Copenhagen) 22-23 Diploma; Columbia U 27-28 (LS) BS; George Washington U 34 (Eng & Amer Lit)MA. 6: Danish, Norwegian, Swedish, Ge, Fr. 7: Asst Pub Libs, Copenhagen 19-21; Danish Army (Coast Artillery) 21-22; Asst libn Nordjyske Landsbibliotek, Aalborg Denmark 23-27; Catlgr LC 28-37; Head catlg dept UCLA 38-39; Asst libn UCal(Berkeley) 39-44; U Libn Northwestern 44-68, U libn emer 68-; Bibliog consul 68-. 8: Eight book-buying trips to Europe 33-68. 9: ALA (chm Catlg & Clsf Sect 38-39, Coun 43-47);-ACRL (chm Univ Libs Sect 46-47); ARL (chm Jt Com on African Res 59-64); Ctr for Res Libs. 10: Caxton Club, Chicago; Amer-Scand Foun; Northwestern U Press; Univ Club, Evanston; BSA; Grolier Club (New York); Rebild Nat Park Soc; Soc for the Adv of Scand Study. 11: Amer-Scand Foun Fellowship 27-28. 12: "Portal Til Amerika" (53); Ed Bd "College and Research Libraries" (46-62); "Scandinavian Studies" (47-57); "Libri" (50-). 13: Yes. 14: Admin, collection bldg. 15: 125 Canon dr, Santa Barbara Ca 93105.

NYLAND, ANNE (MARION). b Lyn Ont Can 17 F 19. 4: Herman Nyland. 5: Queens U 40 (Eng) BA; Toronto 41 BLS. 7: Jr catlgr Sun Life Assurance Co, Montreal 41-42; Libn Pub

Lib, Ft Frances Ont 43-44; Libn Pub Lib, Pembroke Ont 44-49; Libn Essex Co Lib Co-op, Windsor Ont 49-57; Asst dir Prov Lib, NS 58-60; Chief Libn Halifax Co Reg Lib, Halifx NS 60-64; Chief Libn Pub Lib, Cornwall Ont 64-. 9: CanLA (Salaries Com, Pub Lib Standards Com); OntLA (Lib Legis Com); Inst Profess Libns Ont. 10: Univ Womens Club; Stormont Yacht Club. 14: Admin. 15: PO Box 1356, Cornwall Ont Can.

NYLANDER, ENID (PEARCE). b Minneapolis 18 S 12. 4: (Erik) Ivan Nylander). 5: UMinn 31-34 (Ger) BA, summers 58, 59, 60, 62 MA in LS. 6: Fr, Ger, Swedish. 7: Clerk-typist Pub Lib, Highland Park Ill 28-31; Pub Lib, Duluth Minn: Lib asst 45-55, Act head acquis 55, Ref asst 55-63,Head child dept 63-67; Instr & Sr libn UMinn (Duluth) 67-. 9: ALA; MinnLA. 10: Phi Beta Kappa; Lambda Alpha Psi. 14: Ref, child lit. 15: 1906 Kent rd, Duluth Minn 55812.

NYLIN, MIRIAM S(PENCER). b Cornwall NY 20 My 16. 5: Barnard 34-38 (Hist) BA; Columbia 38-39, 40 LS BS. 6: Fr, Ger, Ital. 7: Ref asst Columbia U Libs 39-43; Base libn ft Dix NJ 43-44; Post libn, Camp Kilmer NJ 44-46; Command libn Air Transport Command, Wash DC 46-48; Engnr Libn Convair, San Diego 48-51; Asst Pacific Aeronautical Lib, Los Angeles 51-53; Staff Aerojet-Gen Corp, Sacramento Cal 54-65, Mgr Tech Lib 65-. 9: SLA; CalLA. 10: Unitarian-Universalist Soc; AAUW; Phi Beta Kappa. 14: Admin, ref, catlg. 15: 911 School st, Folsom Cal 95630.

NYQUIST, NORMA. b McPherson Kan 13 S 23. 5: Bethany Col(Lindsborg Kan) 41-45 (Eng) AB; UKan 47-50, 52 (Eng) MA; UCal(Berkeley) 53-54 BLS. 6: Fr. 7: Tchr soc sci Lindsborg High Sch, Lindsborg Kan 45-47; Eng Instr UKan 47-50; Tchr Eng, Latin Washington High Sch, Bethel Kan 50-51; Eng tchr Shawnee Mission High Sch, Mission Kan 51-53; Catlgr Santa Monica Col 54-67, Hd libn 67-. 10: Beta Phi Mu. 14: Catlg, ref. 15: 16565 Chattanooga pl, Pacific Palisades Ca 90272.

NYREN, KARL EDWIN. b Boston 25 N 21. 4: Judith Styles Noren. 5: Boston U 46-49 (Eng Lit) AB, 49-50 (Eng Lit) MA. Fr. 6: Fr. 7: US Army T/5 34th Inf Division, S Pacific, USA 43-46; Instr Eng & humanities Caney Jr Col 50-51; Instr Eng & humanities Bethun-Cookman Col 53-56; Ref asst Boston Pub Lib 56-59; Dir Peabody Inst Lib, Danvers Mass 60; Dir Cary Mem Lib, Lexington Mass 61-66; Assoc ed "Lib Journal 66-. 9: ALA (Leaflets Com); -LAD (Pub Rel Sect 64-65); NELA (chm Pub Rel Com 65); MassLA (chm Nat Lib Week 62, chm Pub Rel Com 64-65). 10: Lib Trustee, Hendrik Hudson Free Lib, Montrose NY. 13: Yes. 14: Admin. 15: 1 Galloway lane, Peekskill NY 10566.

O

O'BANNON, PAUL WARE. b St Louis Mo 29 D 31. 5: UCal (Berkeley) 49-53 (Hist) AB; USoCal 53-54 (LS) MS; UCLA 59-61 (Film); Automation Inst (San Diego) 61-68 Computer programming & syst. 6: Fr, Ger, Sp. 7: Jr libn San Bernardino Pub Lib, San Bernardino Cal 54-56; Libn-engrg Rocketdyne Div of N Amer Aviation, Canoga Pk Cal 57-58; Hd fine arts (a-v) d4pt Buena Pk Lib Dist, Cal 59-64; Catlgr Carl J Leibel, La Puente Cal 65-66; Catlgr Prof Lib Ser, santa Ana Calif 66; Hd a-v & lib standards div Masterlist, San diego Cal 67-. 9: CalLA (Intel Freedom Com 66). 10: Trustee, Buena Park Lib Dist; ALA; SLA; Assn for Recorded Sound. 14: A-v serv, lib automation, info sci. 15: Box 4006, San Diego Ca 92104.

O'BRIEN, COLEEN F. b Des Moines Iowa 27 Ja 29. 5: Drake 51 (Pol Sci) BA, 54 (Law) LLB; Rosary Col 69 MA in LS. 6: Sp. 7: Practice of law, Des Moines Iowa 54-; Des Moines Sch Syst in sch libs, Des Moines Iowa 63-. 15: 818 E 25th st Ct, Des Moines Ia 50317.

O'BRIEN, ELEANOR R (McLAUGHLIN). b Somerville Mass 14ag04. 4: John J OBrien. 7: Cambridge Pub Lib, Cambridge Mass: Sec 21-42, Asst libn 42-63, Act libn 46, 48-49, Assoc libn 63-. 15: Cambridge Pub Lib, Cambridge Ma 02139.

O'BRIEN, ELMER J. b Kemmerer Wyo 8 Ap 32. 5: Birmingham So Col 50-54 (Hist) AB; Iliff Sch of Theol 54-57 (Theol) ThM; UDenver 60-61 MA in L. 6: Lat, Ger, Sp. 7: Clergyman Methodist Church, Pagosa Springs Colo 57-60; Circ-re libn Boston U Sch of Theol 61-65; Asst libn Garrett Theol Sem (Evanston Ill) 65-69; Libn United Theol Sem, Dayton Ohio 69-. 9: ATheolLA; Chicago Area Theol Libns (sec-treas 66-69); United Methodist Ch; Archives Commsn (Bibliog Com 69-). 10: AAUP; Omicron Delta Kappa; Chicago Bkbinders Club. 14: Ref, acquis, Methodist Church hist. 15: 1338 Cornell dr, Dayton Oh 45406.

O'BRIEN, KATHERINE LORD. b Ellisburg NY 22O 07. 5: Wells Col 24-28 (Classics) BA (magna cum laude); Columbia 30-31 BLS. 6: Fr. 7: NY Pub Lib: Libn, asst libn 31-41, Br libn Riverside Br 41-49, Borough Coordinator Richmond Borough SI 49-55, Coordinator Donnell Lib Center 55-59, Coordinator of adult serv Off of Adult Serv 59-67; Chief, Mid-Manhattan Lib NYC 67-. 8: Formerly lecturer, Pratt Inst Lib Sch; Consul Bur of Adult Educ, NY State Educ Dept, 46-47; Past Coadjust staff Rutgers U Grad Sch of Lib Serv. 9: ALA (Coun 67-71, Exec Bd); -ASD (chm Standards Devel Com, past chm Reading Improvement Com); NYLA (past chm; memb Com, Standards Com & Legisl Com; pres Adult Serv Sect); NY Lib Club (past res). 10: AEAUSA; NCTE; NY Adult Educ Coun 13: Yes. 14: Adult serv, lib admin. 15: 400 Central Park West, NYC 10025.

O'BRIEN, PATRICK MICHAEL. b Newport RI 17 Mr 43. 4: Wendy Baldwin. 5: Merrimack Col 60-64 (Eng Lit) BA; URI 64-65 MLS. 7: Ref libn "Newsweek", NYC 65-68, Chief ref sect 68-. 9: SLA (1967 Convention Com, Local Arrments Com). 14: Ref (nat & loc politics). 15: Newsweek Magazine, 444 Madison ave, New York NY 10022.

O'BRIEN, PHILIP MICHAEL. b Albion Neb 5 Ja40. 4: Christina OBrien. 5: Whittier Col 57-61 (Sociol) BA; USoCal 61-62 MSLS. 7: Asst libn Whittier Col 62-66; Soc sci & bus libn Chico State Col 66-67; Army libn, Europe 67-. 8: Asst libn Royal Military Col (Kingston Ont) 50-55; Ed of the Editorial Page & Libn Kingston-Whig Standard, Kingston Ont. 9: ALA. 14: Rare bks, small collections. 15: AG Spec Servs Branch HQ Berlin Brigade, APO NY 09742.

O'BRYANT, MARY AMANDA. b Panola Co Miss 3O05. 5: Miss State Col for Women 22-26 (Lat) AB; Chicago 33-34; Albion Col 51 (Econ) AM; UMich summers -65 AM in LS. 6: Fr, Sp, Ger. 7: Asst treas Feild Coop Assn, Jackson Miss 27-33; Governess private family, Surigao PI 39-40; Off manager Fla Crushed Stone Co, Jacksonville Fla 40-46; Bkkeeper Albion Col 34-38, 46-55; Asst libn Lake Forest Col 55-62 Libn Crosby Mem Lib, Picayune Miss 62-64; Libn Millsaps Col 64-. 9: ALA; SELA; MissLA (chm Scholarship Com 63-64; v-chm Col Sect 64-66). 10: AAUP; AAUW; Jackson Little Theater. 14: Catlg, admin. 15: Millsaps-Wilson Lib, Jackson Miss 39210.

O'BRYANT, MATHILDA (BRUGH). b Logan W Va 2 Ap 18. 5: Mary Baldwin 35-39 (Eng) BA; Drexel 39-40 BS of LS; UMich 43-44 MA of LS. 6: Fr, Ger, Lat. 7: Catlgr UGa 40-41, Order libn 42-43; Catlgr Claremont Associated Cols 47-50; Hd acquis Pomona Pub Lib, Pomona Cal 51-52; Catlgr Montgomery Co Pub Lib, Montgomery Co Md 52-53; Hd catlgr BrandeisU 55-56; Hd catlgr SUNY (Oneonta) 57-61; Hd catlgr Union Col (Schenectady NY) 61-62; Hd catlgr PrincetonU 62-67; Hd acquis dept ULouisville 67-. 8: Taught catlg UGa summer 62; Alumnae Bd Trustees Mary Baldwin Col 66-; Exec Com ULouisville Lib Fac 67-; Agenda Com ULouisville Lib Cabinet 67-; summer fac Syracuse U 63. 9: ALA; KyLA; SELA; Ohio Valley Tech Libns (Program Com 67); NJLA (Com on Coms 65). 10: AAUP; LouisvilleLA; ULouisvilleLA; PTA; Speed Art Museum. 13: Yes. 14: Catlg, rare bks, order wk. 15: 606 Alpine way, Louisville Ky 40214.

O'BYRNE, MARGARET C(LAUDIA). b Paterson NJ 24 Mr 13. 5: George Washington U 44 (LS) AB. 7: Asst libn Georgetown U Med & Dental Schs 35-37, Libn 37-57; Libn Georgetown U Med Center 57-. 9: MedLA; SLA. 15: Georgetown Univ Med Lib, 3900 Reservoir rd NW, Wash DC 20007.

O'CONNELL, KAY (WEBB). b Greenport LI NY 11 Je 38. 4: John Joseph O'Connell. 5: SUNY (New Paltz) 56-60 (Educ) BS; Brooklyn Col 60-61 (Eng); Emory 66-69 MLibnship. 9: ALA. 14: Bibliog, rare bks, ya, readers adv. 15: 2340 Hurst dr NE, Atlanta Ga 30305.

O'CONNELL, MARGARET JANE (PHELAN). b Niagara Falls NY 1 My 30. 4: Daniel J OConnell. 5: Mercyhurst Col 47-51 (Hist) AB: Geneseo State Col summer 51 (LS); Columbia 52-57 MS in LS. 7: Libn Alden Central Sch, Alden NY 51-53; Libn Hicksville High Sch, Hicksville NY 53-59; Lecturer St Johns U (NY) 57-58; Libn W Islip Jr High Sch, W Islip NY 60-63; Lib coordinator W Islip Pub Schs, W Islip NY 63-68; High sch libn 68-. 9: NEA; NY State Tchrs Assn; Suffolk Co (NY) LA; Nassau-Suffolk SchLA; W Islip TA. 10: Cath

Daughters of Amer. 14: Sch lib admin. 15: 123 Haynes ave, W Islip NY 11795.

O'CONNELL, THOMAS FRANCIS. b Boston 5 Ap 21. 4: Margaret Delaney. 5: Boston Col 50 (Econ) AB; Columbia 51 MSLS. 7: US Army Air Force 42-45; Asst circ libn Widener Lib Harvard U 51-52, Circ dept hd 52-55, Circ & stacks chief 55-61, Asst libn 61-63; Act libn Lamont Lib, Harvard U 60-61; Dir libs York U 63-. 9: ALA; CanLA; PrivLA (London); OntLA; Ont Coun Univ Libns. 10: Fellow Atkinson Col, YorkU; Alcuin Soc. 13: Yes. 14: Acquis, admin. 15: York Univ, 4700 Keele st, Downsview Toronto Ont Can.

O'CONNOR, ALICE DALY. b Mt Carmel Ill 1 Ja 07. 4: James C OConnor. 5: St Mary-of-the-Woods Col 23-27 (Hist) BA; UIll 27-29 BS in LS; Chicago 30-32. 7: Reviser in catlg & clsf UIll(Urbana) 28-29; Lib asst in chg of mss Chicago Histo Soc 29-35; Libn Ursuline Acad, Cincinnati 62-. 9: ALA; OhioASchL; CathLA. 10: Kappa Gamma Pi; AAUW: Great Books Study Groups; LWV. 14: Catlg, clsf, high sch libs. 15: 6529 Brackenbridge ave, Cincinnati Oh 45213.

O'CONNOR, DANIEL O. b Niagara Falls NY 11 Ag 45. 5: NiagaraU 63-67 (Eng) BA; Syracuse 67-68 MSLS. 6: Fr. 7: Admin asst to dean Sch of Lib Sci SyracuseU 68-69; Ref libn SUC (Cortland) 69; Lt US Army Adjutant Gen Corps 69-71. 9: ALA; ASIS. 13: Yes. 14: Admin, libnship in the inner city, ref. 15: 1641-10th st, Niagara Falls NY 14305.

O'CONNOR, DOROTHY M. b NJ 24 My 19. 5: Fordham 64 (Eng Lit) BS Secondary Educ; Columbia 66 MS in LS. 6: Fr. 7: Libn I Theatre Research Col NYC Pub Lib 66-68, Libn II Lincoln Ctr 68-. 9: SLA; ALA; TheatreLA; ASIS. 10: Lib Club NY; CARTA; Volunteers of the Shelters. 13: Yes. 14: Ref, indexing, period. 15: 321 Park Slope, Clifton NJ 07011.

O'CONNOR, ELIZABETH (LENNANE). b Detroit 28 Mr 28. 4: Joseph A O'Connor. 5: Marygrove Col 47-51 (Hist) BA; UMich 51-52 AMLS. 7: Catlgr Dorsch Mem Lib, Monroe Mich 52-56; Head catlg dept Monroe Co Lib, Monroe Mich 56-63, A'V DIR 63-66; Catlgr Monroe Co Commun Col 66-. 09: NEA-DAVI; MichLA; Mich A-V Assn; ALA. 10: AAUW; Family Serv Div Monroe Co Bd; Commun Players; Commun Center of Monroe; Marygrove Lib Guild; UMich Alum; Monroe Hist Soc. 14: A-v materials, catlg. 15: 5997 Edgewood dr smt, Monroe Mi 48161.

O'CONNOR, GERTRUDE (PATTON). b Lorain Ohio 6Mr 02. 5: Ohio State U 18-22 (Eng) BA; Northwestern 36-37 (Educ) MA; UIll 45-46 BS in LS. 7: Critic tchr ISSCS-ISNU Children's Sch, Normal Ill 37-45; Libn Champaign Jr High Sch, Champaign Ill 46; Supv sch libs West Mich Col Train Sch 47-48; Libn Arlington Heights TWP High Sch, Arlington Heights Ill 48-50; Dir Sch Libs Glenview Elem Schs, Glenview Ill 50-55; Dir Sch Libs Carlinville Schs, Carlinville Ill 55-57; Libn Curriculum Lib, Deerling Lib Northwestern U 57-. 10: Pi Lambda Theta; Bus & Prof Women's Club. 13: Yes. 14: Curr libs. 15: 1400 Central st, apt 2 S, Evanston Ill 60201.

O'CONNOR, JOHN H. b Morristown NJ 6 Ja 36. 5: Seton Hall 54-58 (Classical Lang) BA, 67-69 (Secondary Educ) MA; CatholicU 65-66 MSLS. 6: Fr. 7: Libn Neumann Prep, Wayne NJ 66-. 9: CathLA; ALA. 15: 970 Black Oak Ridge rd, Wayne NJ 07470.

O'CONNOR, JOSEPH A. b NYC 13 Je 16. 4: Evelyn Fullam. 5: Manhattan Col 34-37 (Eng) AB; Columbia U 38-39 (Lib Admin) MS, 39-42 (Lib Admin). 7: Lib asst NYC Pub Lib 39-42; Chief abstracting & indexing counter intelligence off strategic serv 42-44; Research analyst Bendix Aviation, NYC 44-45; Pres Joseph A O'Connor Co Lib Consuls, NYC 45-. 9: SLA. 15: 22 Marwood lane, Yonkers NY 10701.

O'CONNOR, MARIE J (REINICHE). b Ashkum Ill 20 F 10. 4: Roy J O'Connor. 5: Ill State Normal 28 (Educ); Olivet Col (Educ); UIll Ext 38 (Educ); Bradley U 53-55 (Educ) MA; Ill State U 64 (LS), 68 (LS). 7: Elem tchr: Reddick Ill 30, St Anne Ill 34, Momence Ill 40; Elem prin Newton Co Ind 45; Elem tchr: Momence Ill 52, Herscher Ill 55; Unit libn Herscher Ill 65-. 9: ALA; NEA; IllEA; IllLA. 10: Bus & Prof Women. 14: Catlg. 15: 795 Hilltop, Bradley Il 60915.

O'CONNOR, MARY ALICE. b Pittsburgh 8 F 42. 5: Mt Mercy Col 59-63 (Eng) BA;UPittsburgh 63-64 MSLS. 6: Fr. 7: Catlgr Carnegie Lib of Pittsburgh 64-; 66; Libn-Fr Tchr St Francis Acad, Pittsburgh Penn 66-68; Libn Byzantine Cath Sem, Pittsburgh Penn 69-. 9: PennLA (sec-treas New Libns Sect 69-). 10: West Penn Botanical Soc; Cactus & Succulent Soc of Amer. 13: Yes. 15: 836 Country Club dr, Pittsburgh Pa 15228.

O'CONNOR, MARY C. b Kingston Ont Can. 5: Queens U (Kingston Ont) 34-38 (Eng, Hist) BA; Toronto 39 BLS. 6: Fr. 7: Ref head Queens U Lib (Kingston Ont) 39-43; Libn Nylon Div C-I-L Ltd, Kingston Ont 43-47; Catlgr USask 47-48; Chief Libn Nat Defense Col & Can Army Staff Col Ft Frontenac Li, Kingston Ont 48-. 8: Trustee Kingston Pub Lib Bd, Kingston Ont, 63-. 9: CanLA; OntLA (Trustees Sect); SLA (Mil Libns Div). 10: Prof Inst of Can; Newman club. 14: Admin, bibliog, ref. 15: 193 Earl st, Kingston Ont Can.

OCONNOR, MARY E. b Ireland. 5: Fordhamu 38-42 (Soc Studies, Hist) BS in Ed, 49-50 (Psych); Columbia 50-54 MS in LS 7: Lib asst Fordham U Sch of Educ Lib 41-44; Mortgage Serv Correspondent Home Life Insurance Co, NYC 44-52; Sr libn art Elizabeth Pub Lib, Elizabeth NJ 52-54; Asst lib dir Bayonne Pub Lib, Bayonne NJ 54-55, Lib Dir 55-. 9: ALA; CathLA; NJLA (Memb chm 57-58, chm Lib-for-the-Day Com 69); Hudson Co LA (sec 58-60, pres 64-66). 10: Zonta Club; Nat Conf of Christians Jews; UN Assn. 14: Lib educ. 15: 122 W Ninth st, Bayonne NJ 0700.

O'CONNOR, MILDRED C(ATHERINE). b Holyoke Mass 17 S 07. 5: Mt Holyoke Col 24-28 (Fr) AB; Boston U 44 (Econ) AM; Simmons 35 (LS) SB. 6: Fr, SP. 7: Boston Pub Lib: Asst catlg & clsf dept ref & res div 35-42, Asst-in-Chg 42-48, Chief catlg & clsf dept 48-57, Chief gen ref dept 57-60, Deputy supv 57-60; Lecturer Simmons Col Lib Sch summers 46-68; Act curator of educ ref & res div Boston Pub Lib 60-68; Coordinator of the soc sci & curator of soc sci 60-. 9: ALA (Memb Com 57-64);-CCS (By-Laws Com 58-59, chm Nomin Com 57, chm Catlg Code Rev Com 58-65, Com on Bk Catlgs 59-62); SLA (sec Boston Chap 64-65); CathLA (sec New England Unit 68-); Amer Econ Assn; NELA; MassLA; NE Tech Serv Libns (chm 48-49; chm Nomin Com 65-66). 13: Yes. 14: Catlg, ref, tchg. 15: 687 Washington st, Brighton Mass 02135.

O'DEA, GEORGIA (STILLMAN). b Cleveland 27 Jl 07. 5: UAkron 24-29 (Eng Lit) AB; UTAH 60-63 (Hist); UCLA 64-65 MLS. 6: Fr, Sp. 7: Sec to ed-in-chief Little Brown & Co, Boston 30-33, Mss reader & copy ed 33-39; Sec to manager pub rel Will Folsom & Smith, Boston 48-55; Asst to period libn UUtah Lib 60-63, Asst ref libn 63-64; Catlgr ser sect Research Libs NY Pub Lib 65-68; Rare bk catlgr 68-. 9: ALA; AHA; NY Tech Serv Libns; NY Lib Club. 10: Phi Alpha Theta. 14: Catlg, bibliog, data proc, ser (Amer soc hist), rare bks, fine printing. 15: 115 E 9th st, NYC 10003.

ODONNELL, BROTHER FRANCIS J SM. b Phila 6 Ag42. 5: UDayton 60-63 (Eng) BA; Cath U 63-64 MS in LS; Boston U 68. 6: Fr. 7: Libn Chaminade Prep, Marcy NY 59-60; Asst libn Marianist Col 60-63; Libn Cardinal Gibbons High Sch, Baltimore 63-. 8: Archivist, NY Prov, Soc of Mary, 64-66. 9: ALA; CathLA; MdLA; Md Educ Media Assn; NEA-DAVI. 12: "Catholic Supplement to the Senior High School Library Catalog". 13: Yes. 14: Secon sch lib serv. 15: Cardinal Gibbons High Sch, 3225 Wilkens ave, Baltimore Md 21229.

O'DONNELL, SISTER MARIE SSJ. b Detroit 13 Ag 06. 5: Nazareth Col 4(Eng) AB; UDetroit 45 (Eng) M; UMich 55 MALS. 7: Tchr-libn Sisters of St Joseph, Nazareth Mich 24-. 8: Consul for libs of the Sisters of St Joseph; summer sch Instr in Dept of Lib Sci Catholic U. 13: Yes. 14 Sch libs. 15: 8111 E Outer dr, Detroit Mi 48213.

O'DONNELL, MARY (KANE). b Troy NY 29 Mr 16. 4: Harry J O'Donnell. 5: NY State Col for Tchrs 32-36 (Eng) BA, summers 36, 39-42 (Eng) MA; SUNY (Albany) summers 64-68 MLS. 7: Tchr E Rockaway High Sch, E Rockaway NY 36-44; Tchr Knickerbocker Jr High Sch, Troy NY 44-45; Libn Algonquin Middle Sch, Averill Park NY 66-. 10: Pi Gamma Mu; Theatre Alum Assn, SUNY (Albany) 60-63. 14: Child serv. 15: Box 8, Averill Park, NY 12018.

O'HALLORAN, FRANCES MARY. b Newton Mass 22 D 07. 5: Wellesley 27-31 (Eng) BA; Boston Col 32-35 (Eng, Educ) MA; Simmons 34-35 BLS; Columbia 51-55 (LS); UHawaii 68-69 (LS). 6: Ger. 7: Staff libn Hq EUCOM, Frankford & Munich Ger 45-47; Lib instr Offs' Sch, Ft Monmouth NJ 48; Staff libn: Hq First Army, Governors Is NY 49-55, Hq USAREUR, Heidelberg Ger 55-65, Hq Eighth Army, Seoul Korea 65-67; Dir USARPAC Lib Prog Hq usarpac, honolulu 67-. 8: Conducted Libns' Training Wkshops: Nuremberg & Heidelberg Ger (for qualified libns) 56-64, Tokyo Japan 68, Okinawa 69. 9: ALA (Coun; Nomin Comm); Royal Asiatic Soc, Seoul, Korea; HawaiiLA. 10: Wellesley Col Alum Assn; Bus & Prof Women's Club; Assn of Personnel Admin, Heidelberg. 11: Meritorious Award for civilian Serv overseas; Outstanding award, Honolulu, Hq USARPAC. 13: Yes. 14:

Admin, training & consul wk & mgt. 15: apt 2108, 1350 Ala Moana blvd, Honolulu Hi 96814.

O'HALLORAN, CHARLES. b Denver 7 D 26. 4: Genevieve Miller. 5: UColo 47-50 (Soc Sci) BA; West State of Colo 53 (Eng; UDenver 53-54 (LS) MA. 6: Lat. 7: Tchr Pub Schs, Ft Morgan Colo 50-52; Tchr Pub Schs, Denver 52-53; Ref asst Kan City (Mo) Pub Lib 54-56; Readers adv Kan City (Mo) Pub Lib 56-59; Dir Rosenberg Lib, Galveston Tex 59-64; State libn Mo State Lib 64-. 8: Lectr Sch Info & Lib Sci UMo 68-. 9: ALA; MoLA; TexLA. 10: Rocky Mt Railroad Club. 13: Yes. 14: Lib org, lib pub rel. 15: 119 Douglas dr, Jefferson City Mo 65101.

O'HOGAN, KATHLEEN E. b Chicago Ill 15 Ap 31. 5: SeattleU 47-56 (Secondary Studies) BS; UWash 60-63 MLS. 7: Child libn NYC Pub Lib, Manhattan 63-68; Libn (child) Seaford Pub Lib, Seaford LI NY 68-69; Libn VA Hosp, Bronx NY 69-. 9: NY Lib Club. 10: Amer Youth Hostel. 14: Child & gen pub lib serv. 15: 142 Henry st, Brooklyn NY 11201.

O'KEEFE, RICHARD BENNETT SR. b Wash DC 11 Ag 30. 4: Mary Gingras. 5: Washington & Lee U 48-50 (Eng Lit); Catholic U 50-51, 53-58 (Eng Lit) AB, MS in LS. 6: Classical Gk, Lat, Sp, Ger. 7: Rifleman (Cl) E 4 US Army Infantry, ZI & Korea 51-53; Lib asst Catholic U Libs 54-55; Clerk & indexer US Govt Printing Off, Wa h DC 55-57; Cryptanalist Nat Security Agency, Wash DC 57: Tchr Emerg Cert Prince Georges Co Schs, Upper Marlboro Md 57-58; Assoc ed bus manager "Catholic Periodical Index, Wash DC 58-61; Libn research div Amer Legion, Wash DC 61-69; Asst dir of Lib George Mason Col 69-. 8: Index consul for var publs, 58-; Spec consul on US Isthmian Canal questions. 10: Amer Legion Sigma Chi; Confraternity of Christian Doctrine; Cub Scouts (Den Father); Cana Club; Citizens for Educ Freedom; Order of Felix Australis; Va Hist Soc; Catholics United for the Faith. 13: Yes. 14: Indexing. 15: George Mason Col Lib 4400 University dr, Fairfax Va 22030.

OKEEFFE, RICHARD LEONARD. b Boston 17 My 27. 4: Jacqueline Wilde Thompson. 5: Mt Carmel Col 45-49 (Phi;) PhB; LSU 55-56 (LS) MS; UIll 63- (LS). 7: Acquis libn Los Alamos Sci Labs, Los Alamos NM 56-58, Libn Main Tech Lib 58-60; Asst libn & sci libn Fondren Lib Rice U 60-64, Assoc libn Fondren Lib 64-68; Dir Reg Info & Communication Exch 67-, Univ libn 68-. 9: ALA; (mem Nomin Com 69-70); SLA; TexLA (past chm Spec Libs Div). 10: Houston Com for the Devel of Lib Resources; Houston Philos Soc; Beta Phi Mu. 13: Yes. 14: Sci ref, univ lib admin. 15: Rice Univ P O Box 1892, Houston Tx 77001.

O'LEARY, ANN MARIE. ORT Worth Tex 26 O 44. 5: Emmanuel Col 62-66 (Eng) BA; Simmons 66-67 MSLS, 67-69 (Eng) MA. 6: Fr. 7: Mail order dept Sears Roebuck Co, Boston summers 62-63; Typist Metropolitan Dist Commsn, Boston summer 64; Playground instr Boston Parks Dept summers 65-66; Ref libn HarvardU Countway Lib of Med 67-. 9: ALA. 14: Ref. 15: 4 Calvin rd, Jamaica Plain Ma 02130.

OLEARY, FRANCIS BERNARD. b NYC 6 O 26. 4: Antoinette Walbroel. 5: Manhattan Col 44-49 (Hist) BS; Columbia 49-51 MS in LS, 51-56 (LS); MedLA Certif Grade 1. 6: Ger. 7: Columbia U: Var positions Med Lib 45-49, Zool-bot libn 49-53, Asst libn fornatural sci 53-57; Libn Inst of Tech UMinn(Minneapolis) 57-60; Med sch libn St Louis U 60-63, Libn Med Center 63-, Assoc Prof 63-. 8: ACRL Rep to 45th Nat Conf on Health in Cols, NYC, 53. 9: SLA (Coun 63-64; pres Greater St Louis Chap 63-64); MedLA; (chm Med Schs Gp 68-69); Hist of Sci Soc; St Louis Med Libns (chm 61-62); Amer Assn Hist Med. 10: AAUP; US Naval Inst; World Ship Soc; Sigma Xi; AAAS; Naval Records Club. 12: Ed "Science Reference Notes Columbia U (54-57). 13: Yes. 14: Reg lib coop, lib admin, tchg sci bibliog. 15: 1402 S Grand blvd, St Louis Mo 63104.

O'LEARY, KATHLEEN F. b Boston 12 Ja 43. 5: Gallaudet Col 62-66 (LS) BS. 6: Ger. 7: Trainee Boston Pub Lib summer 65; George Fingold State House Lib, Boston summers 65,66; Boston Sch for the Deaf, Randolph Mass summers 67, 68; Horace Mann Sch for the Deaf, Roxbury Mass 66-. 10: Quincy Deaf Club Athletic Assn. 13: Yes. 14: Acquis, proc of child and prof bks. 15: 78 Elm st, Scituate Ma 02066.

O'LEARY, MARTHA H. b NYC 14 A- 08. 4: Austin J O'Leary. 5: Hunter Col 26-29 (Math) BA; Columbia 31-33 (Eng Lit) MA (top 5th), 46-49 BLS (with honors). 6: Fr, Swedish. 7: Asst Buyer L Bamberger & Co, (Newark NJ) 37-39; Libn Reynolds & Co, (New York City) 39-41; Libn Natl Assn of Manufacturers, (NYC) 41-44; Libn Benton & Bowles Inc, 9nyc0 44-55; Dir Info Center J Walter Thompson & Co, (NYC) 55-61, Lib Consul (NYC) 61-65; Libn Ogilvy & Mather Inc (NYC) 65-67; Lib Consul (Bus Lib Files & Archives Organization & Reorganization) 68-. 9: SLA (Nomin Com 50-51, Fin Com 53-55, Profess Standards 56-61, chm Archives Com 61-65, Advert Div: chm 49-50, NY Lib Club). 10: Beta Phi Mu; Columbia U Sch of Lib Serv; Alum Assn. 12: Ed "What's New in Advertising and Marketing" (49-50); Comp "Automated Functions in Libraries and Information Centers New York City and Vicinity, Directory" (67). 14: Ref, org & admin of bus libs, files, archives. 15: 431 E 20 st, New York NY 10010.

O'MALLEY, KENNETH GERALD CP. b Detroit Mich 30 O 36. 5: Holy Cross Province Col 54-60 9phil); Holy Cross Province Theologate 60-64 (Theol) Ordination; UMich 65-68 AMLS; ULoyola (Chicago) 64; UDetroit 64-65& st Louis U 66-68. 6: Fr, Lat, Gr. 7: Libn Holy cross Province Theologate, Louisville Ky 60-64; Libn Mother of Good Counsel Sem, Warrenton Mo 65-69; Catlgr Catholic Theol Union at Chicago 69-. 8: Coun Cath Soc Serv, Detroit 64-65; Tchr Mother of Good Counsel Sem, Warrenton Mo 65-69; Roman Catholic Priest of the Congreg of the Passion (Passionists). 9: ALA; CathLA (chm-elec to chm Sem Sect 68-70). 13: Yes. 14: Catlg, ref. 15: Catholic Theological Union, 5401 S Cornell, Chicago Il 60615.

O'MALLEY, WILLIAM THOMAS. b Boston Mass 6 Mr 43. 4: Sheila Sullivan. 5: Boston Col 61-65 (Eng) BA; URI 65-66 MLS, 68-69 (Eng). 6: Fr. 7: Asst to br libn Newton Free pub Lib, Newton Mass 65-66; Catlgr URI (Kingston) 66-69, Hd order dept 69-. 8: Instr, Ext Div URI 69. 9: ALA; RILA. 14: Tech serv. 15: 790 Kingstown rd, Peace Dale RI 02883.

O'MARA, JOAN (CARBONE). b Bronx NY 10 F 42. 4: Brian Borv O'Mara. 5: Manatee Jr Col 59-61 AA; Tex WomansU 61-63 BA, 65-66 (LS) MLS. 7: Libn I Queens Borough Pub Lib, Jamaica NY 63-64; Libn I Order State Lib of Hawaii 64-65; Libn Tex Instruments, Dallas Tex 66-68; Libn Dallas Pub Lib, Dallas Tex 68-. 9: ALA; HawaiiLA; SLA; TexLA. 10: Alpha Beta Alpha. 14: Catlg, law & other spec libs, bus ref. 15: 14042 Peyton dr #130, Dallas Tx 75240.

O'NEAL, ELLIS E(LDRIDGE) JR. b Norfolk Va 18 D 23. 4: Helen Spivey O'Neal. 5: URichmond 43-46 (Bible, Eng) BA; So Baptist Theol Sem 46-47 (Andover); Newton Theol Sch 47-49 BD; Simmons 60-62 (LS) SM. 7: Pastor Hillsboro Baptist Church, Crozet Va 49-56; Pastor Chamberlayne Baptist Church, Richmond Va 56-60; Head trans collection Baker Lib Harvard Bus Sch 60; Libn Andover Newton Theol Sch 60-. 9: ATheolLA; NE Theol Libns; Men's Libn's Club. 10: Amer Baptist Hist Soc. 15: 97 Herrick circle, Newton Centre Ma 02159.

O'NEALL, NANCE. b San Diego 22 Jl 08. 5: Tex Tech Col 26-27; UMich 27-28; UCLA 28-29; Transylvania 29-30 (Romance Lang) BA; Ohio State U summer 34: Geo Washington U summer 40; UCLA summer 38, 39 (LS); UCal 41 Lib Certif; USoCal 63 MLS. 06R. 6: Fr. 7: Libn Humboldt State Col 41-42; Libn Santa Maria High Sch & Jr Col, Santa Maria Cal 42-46; Libn Manual Arts High Sch, Los Angeles 46-52, 54-57; Libn (Fulbright) Pierce Col (Athens Greece) 52-53; Tchr-libn Anglo-Amer Sch, Athens Greece 53-54; Lecturer USoCal 50; Lecturer Immaculate Heart Col 55, 56; Dir of Libs US Info Agency, Saigon Vietnam 57-59; Lib coordinator Lib Sect of Los Angeles City Schs 59-61, 62-64; Lecturer (Fulbright) UAnkara Sch of Libn-ship (Ankara Turkey) 61-62; Libn Harbor Col (Los Angeles City Schs) 64-. 9: SchLA Cal (So Sect: Program Chm, pres); Los Angeles SchLA (treas). 14: Child & ya lit, tchg sch lib wk. 15: 1617 Campus rd, Los Angeles Ca 90041.

O'NEIL, B JOSEPH. b Boston 20 Jl 14. 4: Mary Gill. 5: Boston Col 33-35, 41-43 AB; MIT 43-44 (Meteorology) Certif; Simmons 46-8 (LS) BS; Boston U 54-57 (Bus Admin). 6: Sp, FR. 7: Prof lib asst Boston Pub Lib 37-43; Meteorologist Lt (jg) USNR, Alaska, Fla 44-46; Prof lib asst Boston Pub Lib 46; Meteorologist Lt USNR Naval Air Sta, Quonset Pt RI 50-52; Boston Pub Lib: Ref libn 46-50, 53-57, Curator of period & newspapers 57, Deputy supv ref & research serv 57-59, Coordinator of gen ref serv 59-67, Supv research lib serv 67-. 9: SLA (Boston Chap); Placement Com 59-61, Chm 61-62, Treas 63-64, Adv mgr 66-; CathLA; ALA; (Steering Com, Chm Staff Orgs RT 65-66); MassLA. 10: USNR (Commander); Meteorologist Air Wing Staff 91; Admin Off Naval Air Squadron NARMU 911; Off-coun Naval Air Res Staff Z91. 14: Ref, admin. 15: 555 Poplar st, Roslindale Mass 02131.

O'NEIL, MARY GERMAINE. b New Castle Penn 14 Mr 12. 4: Lawrence M ONeil. 5: Marywood Col 29-33 (Music) BM; UPittsburgh 63-64 MLS. 6: Fr. 7: Receipt clerk Commonwealth of Penn, Harrisburg Penn 36-40; Tchr New Castle Schs, New Castle Penn 33-35; Libn Carnegie Lib of Pittsburgh 64-65; Libn Avonworth High Sch, ben Avon Penn 65-;66; Libn Churchill Area Sch Dist, Pittsburgh Penn 66-. 9: ALA; Penn State EA; NEA. 10: AAUW; Beta Phi Mu; Phi Delta Gamma. 14: Sch libn. 15: 7723 Cannon st, Pittsburgh Pa 15218.

O'NEIL, PERRY (HUGH). b Lufkin Tex. 5: Chicago Musical Col 39-44 (Piano) BM; Chicago 45-46 (Humanities); Juilliard Sch of Music 46 (Piano); Phila Conservatory of Music 46-48 (Piano); Columbia 60-63 (LS) MS. 7: Med Corps Infantry US Army 43; Instr: Chicago Musical Col 44-46, UChicago 45-46, Dalcroze Sch of Music, NY 48-53; Tech asst II NY Pub Lib 59-63; Res asst Bibliog of Amer Lit, NY 61-; 1st asst Arents Collection NY Pub Lib 63-, Curator Arents Collections 66-. 9: BSA; NY Lib Club. 10: Beta Phi Mu; Kappa Gamma Psi; The Bohemuans; (NY Musicians Club). 12: Comp "Supplement to the Checklist of the Arents Collection of Books in Parts (63); Comp; supplement Arents Tobacco Catalog (part VIII 67, part IX 68, part X 69). 13: Yes. 14: Rare bks, ref, admin, bibliog. 15: 61 Jane st apt 17K, New York NY 10014.

O'NEILL, CATHERINE. b Corona LI NY 26 Ag 12. 5: Hunter Col 30-33 (Span) BA; Columbia (LS). 7: Libn Queensborough Pub Lib, Queens Co NY 33-43; Lib Dir NY Jr League, NYC 43-46; Libn & tchr of comparative religion Calhoun Sch, NYC 46-. 9: Nat Assn of Indep Schs; Hudson Valley LA. 14: Sch libs. 15: 400 W 119 st, New York NY 10027.

O'NEILL, EILEEN MARY. b New Haven Conn. 5: Albertus Magnus Col 33-37 (Econ & Soc) BA; Columbia 41-43 BS in LS. 7: New Haven (Conn) Pub Lib: 1st asst child room & brs 37-46, Br head Stetson Br 46-47, Chief catlg libn 48-57, Asst libn & head of ref 58-61, Asst libn & head of Main Lib 62-. 9: ALA; ConnLA (pres 60-61); CathLA. 10: Quota; New Haven Colony Hist Soc. 11: Alumna of the Year, Albertus Magnus Col, 61. 14: Ref, adult serv. 15: 281 Willow st, New Haven Conn 06511.

ONEILL, ROBERT HENRY JR. b New Haven Conn 8 Ap 25. 4: Barbara Bussiere ONeill. 5: Yale 46-50 (Fr) BA; So Conn State Col 50-51 (Elem Educ) BS; Yale 51-52 (Admin) MA; So Conn State Col 59 MLS; Chicago 60- (LS) PhD. 6: Fr. 7: (S/Sgt) US Army, European Theatre 43-45; Elem sch tchr, Meriden Conn 51-55; High sch libn, Wallingford Conn 55-57; Catlg & org Eli Whitney Tech Sch Lib, New Haven Conn summer 57; Chief catlgr Bur of Lib Serv, Hartford Conn summer 59; Ref libn So Conn State Col summer 60-63; Jr high sch libn, Wallingford Conn 57-; Lectr in lib sci So Conn State Col 65-. 8: Visiting lecturer in Lib Sci, UTex, summer 64; Org; eli Whitney Tech Sch Lib 57, Wallingford EA Prof Lib 59, Holy Trinity Parochial Sch Lib 62; Supv moving Post Jr Col Lib. 9: ALA; ConnSchLA (Pub Rel Com, Speakers Bur, Exec Bd 63-); CathLA (Exhibits Chm). 10: Wallingford Educ Assn; ConnEA; Conn Horticultural Soc. 11: Outstanding Young Conn Libn, 60. 12: Ed & originator of Conn Sch Lib Assn Newsleter, 63-. 14: Sch libnship, sch lib a-v media. 15: 336 E Main st, Wallingford Conn.

O'NEILL, SUSAN S (SNYDER). b Chicago Ill 23 S 39. 4: Richard Patrick. 5: Conn Col for women 57-60 (Govt); Boston U 60-61 (Pol Sci) BA; UPittsburgh 63-64 MLS. 6: Fr. 7: Catlgr pulmonary div UKy 66, Ref libn King Lib 66-67, Research specialist tobacco & health research program Agric Sci Ctr 68-. 10: Lexington Montessori Soc. 14: Ref, awareness in sci research. 15: Tobacco and Health Research Program, Univ of Ky, Lexington Ky 40506.

O'ROURKE, MARGARET (WALTERS). b Raeford NC 11 Ap 12. 4: William Joseph ORourke. 5: UNC(Greensboro) 29-33 (LS) AB. 7: Libn Fayetteville Pub Lib, Fayetteville NC 35-40; Libn Warwick Co High Sch, Morrison Va 48-49; Hd of tech proc Pikes Peak Reg Dist Lib, Colo Srings Colo 56-. 9: ALA; ColoLA (mem Com for Certif). 10: AAUW. 14: Catlg, ref. 15: 2821 N Jon st, Colorado Springs Colo 0907.

O'SHEA, HORACE WILLIAM JR. b Raleigh NC 7 Ja 22. 5: UNC 44 (Chem) BS, 55 MLS Columbia 56 (LS). 6: Fr, Ger. 7: Stud asst ref dept UNC(Chapel Hill) 54-55; Libn Brooklyn Pub Lib 55-56; Tech libn WVa Pulp & Paper Co, Charleston SC 56-57; Asst libn Citadel Mil Col of SC 57-60; Co Libn Rockingham Co Lib, Leaksville NC 60-66; Dir Wake Co Pub Libs, Raleigh NC 66-. 8: Ch, Nat Lib Week, NC; Lib consul, Rockingham Commun Col, 65-. 9: ALA; AEAUSA NCLA (past dir (Exec Com; chm Printed Resources Com, Steering Com Legis Coun); SELA; SCLA (past dir); SLA (dir Ga Chap). 10: A-V Resources Com; Sigma Chi; Rotary; Hope Valley Country Club; Pennrose Country Club; Rockingham Co Commun Action. 11: Yong Man of Year, Duham NC, 53. 13: Yes. 14: Admin. 15: Wake County Pub Libs 104 Fayetteville st, Raleigh NC 27601.

O'SHEA, JOHN M. b Hartford Conn 30 Mr 28. 4: Marian Ralff. 5: Columbia 54-58; Hofstra 58-65 (Hist) BA; LIU 65-68 MLS. 6: Ger. 7: Disbursing clk 1st Class USN 46-54; Mgr Aeronautical Serv Inc, Albertson NY 54-66; Asst libn Suffolk Commun Col 66-. 9: ALA; SuffolkCoLA. 14: Ref, period, circ. 15: 3 Dickey ct, Commack NY 11725.

O'SULLIVAN, JANE C(ARLSON). b Oakland Cal 25 Jl 23. 5: UCal (Berkeley) 41-48 (Liberal Arts) AB, 65-66 MLS. 6: Fr. 7: Cpl USMC Women's Res 44-46; Intermediate stenographer Sch of Pub Health Cal (Berkeley) 53-57; Sr stenographer State of Cal Dept of Pub Health, berkeley 62-65; Med staff libn John Muir Memorial Hosp, Walnut Creek Cal 67-68; Libn med & bio sci US Naval Hosp, Oakland Cal 68-. 9: MedLA; CalLA. 10: Sierra Club; UCal Lib schs Alumni. 14: Catlg (NLM), commun hosp libs. 15: 19137 Mayberry dr, Castro Valley Ca 94546.

O'SULLIVAN, MARY BOSWORTH. b Rochester NY 11 O 16. 4: George H OSullivan. 5: URochester 34-38 (Eng) BA, Tchrs Prov Certif; Columbia 40-41 BS in LS, Libns Prof Life Certif. 6: Fr, Lat. 7: Clerk child dept Rochester Pub Lib, Rochester NY 38-40; Jrlibn child room NY Pub Lib 41, 43; Child libn Rochester Pub Lib, Rochester NY 41-43; Dir patients lib Metropolitan Hosp, NYC 43-44; Ref asst White Plains Pub Lib, White Plains NY 61-64; Libn Archbishop Stepinac High Sch, White Plains NY 64-. 10: Col Club of White Plains; Red Cross Gray Lady; Womans Club of White Plains. 14: Sch libs, ref, rare bks. 15: 4 Hewitt ave, White Plains NY 10605.

O'TOOLE, ELLEN E. b Pittsburgh Penn 3 O 43. 5: Duquesne 61-65 (Educ) BS in Ed; UPittsburgh 65-66 MLS. 7: Child libn Phoenix Pub Lib 66-68; Child libn Palos Verdes lib Dist, Palos Verdes Pen Cal 68-. 9: ALA; CalLA. 10: Beta Phi Mu. 14: Child serv. 15: 21107 Amie ave, Torrance Ca 90503.

OAKES, CHARLOTTE. b Decatur Ill. 5: Millikin U 30-34 (Hist, Pol Sci) AB; UMich 37-38 ABLS; UCal (Berkeley) 49-50 (Hist) MA. 6: Fr, Ger. 7: Gen asst Decatur Pub Lib, Decatur Ill 34-37; Asst catlgr 38-43; Catlg libn URedlands44-51; Head catlg dept Pasadena Pub Lib, Pasadena Cal 51-53; Chief acquis div 53-56; Head tech processes div 56-62; Head g dept New Campuses Program UCal San Diego 62-65; Catlg libn 65-. 9: SLA; CalLA; (Curls; sec, v-chm & chm So Div 64-66, Palomar Dist Staff Org RT 59-60, sec Steering Com 59, chm Los Angeles Reg Group of Catlgrs 57-58); ALA-RTSD (Catlg &Clsf Sect, By-laws Com 67-69); UCalLA; UCal (San Diego)LA. 10: AAUW; Pasadena Lib Club; Friends of the Lib, UCal (San Diego); UMich Lib Sci Alumni Assn; Phi Kappa Phi; Phi Alpha Theta. 13: Yes. 14: Catlg. 15: Univ of Cal Lib San Diego, La Jolla Ca 92037.

OAKES, FRANK EDWIN. b Rochester NY 18Mr 14. 4: Frances Etheridge. 5: Allegheny Col 32-35 (Fr) BA; UWis 35-37 (Fr) MA; Fla State U 50-51 (LS) MA. 6: Fr. 7: Catlgr & order libn Law Sch Lib UAla 51-54; Sr catlgr Northwestern U Lib 54-57; Catlgr Chicago Pub Lib 57-58; 1st asst Catlg Dept Flint Pub Lib, Flint Mich 58-59; Head Order Dept 60-64; Supv Tech Serv St Louis Pub Lib 64-. 9: ALA; MoLA. 14: Tech serv. 15: 1301 Olive st, St Louis Mo 63103.

OAKES, VANYA (VIRGINIA) ARMSTRONG. b Nutley NJ 13 S 09. 5: UCal (Berkeley) 28-32 (Philos) BA; USoCal 58-59 (LS) MS. 6: Fr. 7: Journalist: United Press, Shanghai W China 36-39, Christian Sci Monitor, W China, SE Asia 39-41; Lecturer W Colston Leigh, nationwide in US 41-46; Instr (journalism & pol sci) Los Angeles City Col 46-58; Libn Los Angeles Pub Lib Soc Sci Dept 59-65, Hollywood Reg Lib 65-. 8: Ya Adv Bd, Los angeles Pub Lib 66-67. 9: ALA; CalLA (Docs Com 61-63). 10: Phi Beta Mu; Libraria Sodalitas. 12: "White Man's Folly" (48); 8 juvenile bks (46-60). 13: Yes. 14: Ref, ya serv. 15: 1623 N Ivar st Hollywood Lib, Los Angeles Ca 90028.

OAKLEY, ADELINE (DUPUY). b Cleveland Ohio 14S14. 4: Kenneth H Oakley. 5: Bridgewater State Col 58-62 (Secondary Sch Eng) BS ED; Simmons 62-64 MS LS; Boston U 67- (Eng Educ). 7: Psychiatric nursing asst Vet Hosp, Brockton Mass 55-61; Circ libn Canton Pub Lib, Canton Mass 62; Sch libn & tchr in guided reading program Bridgewater- Raynham Reg

High Sch, Bridgewater Mass 62-63; Head Libn Catherine Laboure Sch of Nursing, Boston 63-67; Instr in Lib Sci Bridgewater State Col 67-. 8: Consul, Org of New Lib, Plymouth-Carver Reg High Sch, Plymouth Mass 63; Massasoit Commun Col (Abington Mass) 66; Randolph Sch Syst 68-. 9: ALA; CathLA (chm-elect Health Sci Sect 69; Planning Com for Pre-Convention Conf in Lib Educ for 70 Conv, past treas Hosp Sect); NESchLA; MassASchL. 10: Ladies Lib Assn, Randolph Mass; Friends of he Turner Lib, Randolph Mass; Great Books Groups; Charter mem New Eng Screen Educ Assn; New Eng Assn of Tchrs of Eng. 14: Nursing educ, ref, ya serv, sch lib serv. 15: 24 Reynolds ave, Randolph Mass 02368.

OAKS, CAROL (VERDA). b Provo Utah 27 D 20. 5: Brigham Young U 39-43 (Drama, Elem educ) BA; UChicago 45-46 (Eng Lang and Lit) MA; Stanford U (summers) 49-50; Brigham young U summer 58 Sch lib certif, 65-68 (LS). 6: Fr. 7: Tchr Juab Sch Dist, Nephi Utah 43-44; Tchr Nebo Sch Dost, Spanish Fork Utah 44-45; Instr Eng lang & lit Brigham young U 46-55; Correspondence off wk Radiation Lab UCal (Berkeley) 55-58; Libn Morningside Elem Sch, Salt Lake City 58-59; Libn Grandview Elem Sch, Salt Lake City 59-62; Res libn & bk selection Brigham Young U Lib 62-63; Latter Day Sts Ch Mission in France 63-65; Arts & humanities libn Brigham Young U 65-67, Catlg & bk selection 67-68; Consul Utah State Lib Commsn 68-. 9: ALA; UtahLA. 10: AAUPL AAUW. 12: Ed "Utah libraries" (68-). 14: Child lib wk, child lit. 15: 677 North Univ ave, Provo Ut 84601.

OAKSFORD, MARGARET (JOHNSTON). b Gloversville NY. 4: Robert Stratton Oaksford. 5; Hartwick Col 43-47 (Eng) AB; Catholic U 63-65 MSLS; American U (Archives Admin). 6: Fr, Ger, Lat. 7: Searcher acquis Cornell U Lib 61-63; Grad lib asst Catholic U 63-64; Lib asst II UMd 64-65; Asst catlgr Cornell U Lib 65-68, 69-; CCFL Lib Ctr 68-69. 9: ALA. 10: Campus Club Cornell U. 14: Catlg, rare bks, archiv wk. 15: 203 Muriel st, Ithaca NY 14850.

OAKSFORD, ROBERT S. b Gloversville NY 1 D 20. 4: Margaret Johnston. 5: Cornell 61-63 (Ind & Labor Rel) BS; Syracuse 65-66 MLS. 7: Catlgr Finger Lakes Lib Syst, Ithaca NY 66-. 15: 203 Muriel st, Ithaca NY 14850.

OAKUM, J ALLEN. b Aristes Penn 15Ag20. 5: Millersville State Col 38-42 (LS, Eng) BS in EDD: Kent State U 50-52 (LS) MA. 7: Libn Theodore Roosevelt High Sch, Kent Ohio 42-. 9 NEA (Life mem); ALA; OhioEA (Life mem); OhioASchL (pres 59). 10: Kiwanis, Phi Sigma Pi; Beta Kappa Theta; Bd Dirs Kent Credit Union; KentEA. 12: "A Manual for the High School Library Assistant (57-); "A Guide for writing Term Papers nd Reports (62). 14: Yp serv. 15: 170 N Prospect st, Kent Oh 44240.

OAS, JUANITA ZIEGLER (ELLIOTT WILES). b Battle Creek Mich. 5: Willard Inst of Mus 30-32 (Mus, voice); Battle Creek Col 32-33 (Nutrition, Sociol); West Mich U 51-53 (Libnship) BS, 60 (Libnship) MA. 6: Sp. 7: Sec Calhoun Co Soc Serv, Battle Creek 33-35; Soc Wer Maternal Health Assn, Battle Creek 35-39; Sec & asst libn W K Kellogg Foundation, Battle Creek 47-51; Libn Leila Y Post Hosp, Med & Nurs, Battle Creek 51-53; Dir of libs Bronson Methodist Hosp, Med & Nusg, Kalamazoo 52-63; Ref libn Newport Beach Pub Libs, Newport Beach Calif 63-64; Hd libn Pub Lib, Sturgis Mich 64-. 8: Tchg: Hist of Nurs, Bronson Hosp Sch of Nurs 55; Lib Org & Admin, West Mich U, Kalamazoo 61; Inst on Hosp Libnship, Amer Hosp Assn, Chicago 59; Consul for new lib plans, Borgess Hosp, Kalamazoo 67. 9: ALA (chm Memb Com, Mich 68-70); MichLA (chm Awards Com 68-70; chm Hosp & Inst Com Sect 60). 10: AAUW; C of C (non mem); Co Hist Soc; Sponsor Creative Writing Gp; Poetry Soc of Mich. 13: Yes. 14: Pub rel, rare bks, res, bldg, tchg, writing. 15: North Nottawa at West, Sturgis Mi 49091.

OATFIELD, HAROLD. b Concord Ore 25 Ja 10. 4: Virginia Hoffer. 5: Reed Col 27-30 (Chem); Rice U 30-31 (Chem) BA; Iowa State Col 31-33 (Organic Chem) M Sc. 6: Fr, Ger, Russian. 7: Tester Control Lab Crown Zellerbach, W Linn Ore 33-34; Che Intelligence Div Chem Dept Expt Station E I DuPont de Nemours 34-35; Lib research fellow in Biol MIT 45-47; Proc assoc Div Med Sci Nat Research Coun 47-51; Lit chemist chem research & development div Charles Pfizer & Co, Brooklyn NY 51-59, Lit chem & hd tech info serv Pfizer Med Research Labs, Groton Conn 59-. 8: Exec sec Com to Consider the Future of the Army Med Lib, 51. 9: ACS Div Chem Lit; (sec Conn Valley Sect 61-62); ASIS (treas 54, chm Biol Med SIG 69); MedLA (mem & chm Periods & Ser Com 48-54); (chm Bibliog Com 53, 54, 56, chm Pharmacy Group 53-54 & 64-65); Rep to ASA Z39 59-61 & 63-66; ALA Jt Com on Union List of Ser 50-51; SLA Sci-Tech Div & Pharmaceut Sect Com on Translators & Translations 49-51;Com on Need for an Abstract Digest 65-66; NY Chap; program chm Sci-Tech Div 58-59, ASA Z39 sec-treas 58- (mem & chm sub-com to consider standardiz in period title abbrev 51-); USBE Corp 50-52; Drug Info Assn (charter mem). 10: Chemists Club, NYC; AAAS; Ledyard (Conn) Perm Elem Sch Bldg Com; Fellow Amer Inst Chemists; Friends of the NLM; NY Reg Med LA; NEng Reg Med LA 63. 12: Auth "Documentation of Current Literature, chap X in Jackson, "Technical Libraries: Organization & Management (50); Ed NRC/DOD "Symposium on Burns (51); Adv Bd "Journal of Chemical Documents (67-69). 13: Yes. 14: Info retrieval, ref, acquis, embalming lit, sci documentation, standardization. 15: Pfizer Med Res Labs, Groton Conn 06340.

OATHOUT, EVELYN LEWIS. b Hartford Conn 3 Ag 16. 4: Melvin Carl Outhout. 5: Simmons 34-38 (LS) BS; U New Zealand 48-49 (Econ) MA. 6: Fr, Sp, Ger. 7: Catlgr state documents libn Duke U Lib 38-42; Catlgr Army War Col, Wash DC 42-43; Catlgr Stanford U Libs 45-48, 49-51; Libn II Modesto State Hosp, Modesto Cal 51-53; Libn II Cal State Lib 54-55; Libn Resources Lib, Sacramento Cal 55-63; Catlgr Science Press West Coast, Ventura Cal 65-. 9: Consul, Botany Dept Lib UCal, Davis, 64. 10: LWV, Audubon Soc. 14: Catlg, spec libnship, govt publs. 15: 1778 W Chapel dr, Camarillo Cal 93010.

OBEAR, LEGARE HILL BOWLES. b Madison Ga 12 O 13. 5: George Washington U 38 (Pol Sci) AB, 41 (Law) JD. 6: Fr. 7: Asst reading rms LC 30-40, Admin asst admin dept 40-42; USA (Maj) Adj Gens Dept 42-46; Admin asst acquis dept LC 46-47, Asst chief Surplus bks project 47-48, Hd Coop acquis project 48-49, Admin off ref dept 49-50, Chief Loan div 50-. 9: ALA; DCLA (pres 54-55). 10: XIII Corps Assn. 13: Yes. 14: Ref. 15: 2 Terrace ct NE, Washington DC 20002.

OBENHAUS, ADAH MAY (ALLIN). b Steamboat Springs Colo 7F20. 4: Jake G Obenhaus. 5: UAriz 37-41 (Pol Sci) BA; UTex 61-66 (LS). 6: Sp, Fr. 7: Lib UAriz Catlg asst 41-43, 53-54, Circ asst 55-56, Catlg asst 56-58; Acquis asst lib Southwest Tex State Col 58-61, Acquis libn 62-65; San Marcos Pub Lib, Hd libn, San Marcos Tex 66-. 9: ALA; TexLA (sec Acquis Round Table), 65-66); SWLA. 10: Beta Sigma Phi. 14: Acquis, catlg, admin. 15: 517 W Hopkins, San Marcos Tex 78666.

OBERKOETTER, SISTER MARY JOACHIM. b Bloomington Ill 30 Mr 13. 5: Rosary Col 31-33 (LS) BA; Catholic U summers 42-47 (Religious Educ) MA; Rosary Col summers 51-55 (LS) MA. 6: Lat, Fr. 7: Libn Ursuline Acad, Louisville Ky 35-36; Libn Marquette High Sch, Tulsa Okla 39-41; Libn St Johns High Sch, McAlester Okla 41-45; Libn enedictine Heights Col (Guthrie Okla) 45-57; Libn Benedictine Heights Col (Tulsa Okla) 57-65; Libn Monte Cassino High Sch Okla 65-. 8: Tchr, Grad course in catlg, UOkla Ext, Tulsa 64-65; Instr Rosary Col Grad Sch of Lib Sci summers 63, 65, 66. 9: ALA; CathLA; OklaLA. 10: Friends of the Lib of Benedictine Heights Col; Bd of Dir Friends of the Tulsa Pub Lib. 13: Yes. 14: Bk sel, catlg, bldg up rare bk collection. 15: 2120 E 21st st, Tulsa Ok 74114.

OBOLER, ELI M(ARTIN). b Chicago 26S15. 4: Marcia Wolf. 5: UChicago 31-41 (Eng Lit) BA; Columbia 41-42 BS in LS; Chicago 46-49 (LS) Lib S. 6: Fr, Yiddish, Lat. 7: Asst chief Lend-Lease Expediting Bur US War Prod Bd, Wash DC 42-43; Dept Army Hist US Army (Sgt), US & Panama 43-46; Head res bk room UChicago 46-49; Libn UChicago U Col Adult Educ 47-49; Lecturer Great Bks Program UChicago 48-49; Libn Ida State Col 49-63; U Libn Ida State U 63-. 8: Bibliog consul, Great Bks Foun, Chicago 47-49; Surveyed Col Libs Col of Ida, 55; Northwest Nazarene Col 55 & 65; Mem accreditation teams, NWest Assn of Secon & Higher Schs; Pacific U 67, Utah State U 68; Seattle U 69; Mem Adv Com on Lib Training & Research Proj UF Off of Educ 66-69, chm of Com 68-69. 9: ALA (Coun 53-59; chm Lib Periods Round Table 52-53, Memb Com 54-59; Lib Legisl Com 54-56; Intel Freedom Com 65-69);-ACRL (Standards Com 54-56, chm Col Sect 63-64); PNLA (pres 55-56);. IdaLA (pres 50-53). 10: AAUP; Bnai Brith; Kiwanis. 11: ALA-H W Wilson Lib Period Award, 64, to PNLA Quarterly. 12: Ed "College and University Library Accreditation Standards, 1957" ACRL 58; Ed PNLA "Quarterly" (58-67); Ed Lib Period Round Table "Newsletter" (61-62); Ed "Idaho Librarian" (50-54, 57-58); Ed Bd "College & Research Libraries" (62-63). 13: Yes. 14: Admin, lib educ, lib stat. 15: Idaho State Univ Lib, Pocatello Ida 83201.

OCCHINO, IDA (BATTISTA). b Endicott NY 18N 14. 4: Bennie Occhino. 5: Albany State U 38-42 (SS) BS in Ed, 51-54 MSLS. 6: Ital. 7: Elem tchr Union-Endicott Schs, Endicott NY 35-47; Scotia-Glenville C Schs, Scotia NY: Jr high math tchr 47-53, Elem jr high libn 53-56, High sch libn 56-. 8: Lib Chm, Scotia Glenville Central Sch Dist, 60-65, Lib dept hd 65-67; Dir lib serv 68-; Fulbright Lecturer in lib sci UTehran, Tehran Iran 67-68. 9: NEA; NY State Tchrs Assn; NYLA; East NY SchLA. 14: Catlg, ref, bk sel. 15: 554 Mumford st, Schenectady NY 12307.

OCHAB, CHARLES S. b Utica NY 1 F 18.'5: UMich 37-41, 46 (Sci, Math) BS; UIll 47-49 (Philos) MA; NY State Col for Tchrs (Albany) 49-50 (Educ) Tchrs Certif; Columbia 52-53 LS MS. 7: Lt (jg) Aviator US Navy 42-45; Tchr Union Free Sch No 29, N Merrick NY 50-52; Abstracter Amer Petroleum Inst, NYC 53-54; Asst ref libn Yonkers Pub Lib, Yonkers NY 54-55; Cartographic survey aid Dept of Interior, Denver 56-58; Tchr S Huntington Station NY 58-60; Gen asst & bkmob libn Queens Borough Pub Lib, Jamaica NY 60-62; Asst libn mss & hist NY State Lib 62-65; Ref serv supv Ramapo Catskill Lib System, Middletown NY 65-67; Ref libn Mid York Lib System, Utica NY 67-. 9: ALA; Hudson-Mohawk Lib Assn; NYLA (Tech Com Resources & Tech Serv Sect). 10: Amer Legion; Elks. 11: Air Medal with Gold Star; Navy Commendation Ribbon; Two Battle Stars. 13: Yes. 14: Ref, interlib loan. 15: 1126 Schuyler st, Utica NY 13502.

OCHAL, MRS BETHANY J. b Flint Mich 2 D17. 4: Edward Louis Ochal. 5: Flint Jr Col 35-37; Wayne State U 44-45 BA & JD. 7: Attorney Ochal & Ochal, Detroit 45-52; Ref libn Detroit Bar Assn 52-60, Libn 60-61; Assoc libn Wayne State U Law Lib 61-62, Law Libn 62-. 8: Tchr, Legal Research, Wayne State U Law Sch 62-68; Admitted to practice before Supreme Court of Mich, the Dist Court of the US for the East Dist of Mich, the US Court of Sixth Sxth Circuit, & the Supreme Court of the US. 9: AALL (Memb chm 64-66); OhioALL (pres 68-69); Women Lawyers Assn, Mich (prea 66-67); State Bar of Mich (chm Legal Publns Com 68-69). 10: AAUP; Wayne State U Assn of Faculty Women. 15: Wayne State Univ Law Lib, Detroit Mi 48202.

OCHS, MICHAEL. b Cologne Germany 1 F 37. 4: Carol Blumenthal. 5: City Col (NY) 58 BA; Columbia 63 (LS) MA; NYU 64 (Musicology) AM. 6: Ger, Dutch, Lat, Hebrew, Yiddish. 7: Math tchr Bd of Educ, NYC 61-62; Fellow City Col (NYC) 62-63, Catlgr 63-65; Music libn Brandeis U Lib 65-68, Creative arts libn 68-. 8: Ref libn, Lib/USA, NY Worlds Fair, 64; Lectr in music City Col (NY) 64-65. 9: Amer Musicological Soc; MusLA (chm N E Chap 68-69). 12: "An Alphabetical Index to Robert Schumann Werke (67). 13: Yes. 14: Mus libnship. 15: 32 Blvd terrace, Brighton Mass 02134.

ODELL, GERTRUDE DEIRDRE. b Los Angeles 18 N 12. 5: Riverside Col 30-31 (Eng) AA; Riverside Lib Serv Sch 31-32 (LS) Certif; URedlands 46-51 (Eng) BA; USoCal 61- (LS), MSLS. 6: Fr, Sp. 7: Circ asst Riverside Pub Lib, Riverside Cal 33-38; Sec E T Wall, Riverside Cal 38-42; Asst libn San Bernardino Air Serv Command, San Bernardino Cal 42-46; Circ & ref libn San Bernardino Valley Col Lib 46-52; Libn Pacific High Sch, San Bernardino Cal 52-53; Libn Fremont Jr High Sch, San Bernardino Cal 53-54; Head ref dept San Bernardino Pub Lib, San Bernardino Cal 54-. 9: ALA-ACRL;-PLA;-RSD; CalLA (Col Univ & Res Libs Sect; Staff Orgs Round Table: Steering Com 60, 61, sec 61); Lib Hist Com 65-68). 10: Arrowhead Allied Arts Coun; San Bernardino Co Museum Assn; Malki Museum Assn; Orange Co Hist Soc; Beta Phi Mu. 13: Yes. 14: Ref. 15: 3137 N "H st, San Bernardino Cal 92405.

ODERKIRK, MARCIA L. b Rochester NY 23 Je 44. 5: Keuka Col 62-64 (Hist); Syracuse U 64-66 (Hist) BA; 66-67 MSLS. 6: Fr, Sp. 7: Asst ref Providence Pub Lib 67-. 9: ALA. 14: Ref. 15: 115 E Main st, Victor NY 14564.

ODESCALCHI, ESTHER KANDO. b Budapest Hungary 30 S 38. 4: Edmond P Odescalchi. 5: Manhattanville Col 57-60 (Eng) BA; Columbia 60-61 (LS) MS. 6: Hungarian, Ger, Ital, Russian, Fr. 7: Catlgr IBM, Poughkeepsie NY 61-62; Head ext serv Adriance Lib, Poughkeepsie NY 62-. 9: Dutchess Co (NY) LA; Md Educ Media Assn; NEA-DAVI. 14: Ref. 15: 11 Darlene dr, Poughkeepsie NY 12601.

OEDEKOVEN, PHYLLIS RAE (RICHMOND). b Denver 25 My 28. 5: Black Hills State 45-48 (Phys Sci) BS; UDenver 48-49 (LS) MA; Black Hills State summer 63-68 (Ed-Mus) BS. 6: Fr. 7: Indexing E I duPont de Nemours Co Inc, Wilmington Del; George Amos Mem Lib, Gillette Wyo 50-53; Adv & catlgr Gillette Graded Sch, Gillette Wyo. 9: ALA. 10: AAUW; Delta Zeta. 14: Ref, catlg, spec libs. 15: 1420 W Jackson, Spearfish SD 57783.

OEHL, BETTYE SUE (VOLLRATH). b Sherman Tex 7 O 24. 4: Louis Albert Oehl. 5: Austin Col 42-43; Tex State Col for Women 43-45 (LS) BA; Trinity U 50-53 (Educ) M Ed, 64-65; Our Lady of the Lake Col 63 Certif for NDEA Inst. 7: Lib asst Civil Serv Brooke Gen Hosp, San Antonio Tex 45-46; Catlgr Trinity U 46-53; Jr high libn San Antonio Pub Schs 53-64, Elem lib coord 64-. 9: NEA; ALA; Tex State TA; TexLA; Tex Assoc Ele Prin & Supv; SW LA; Bexar Co LA; Bexar LA (pres). 10: Alpha Delta Kappa. 14: Catlg, tech serv. 15: 3142 Valley View lane So, San Antonio Tx 78217.

OEHLER, EILEEN LENORE. b Lansing Mich. 5: Mich State U 43-47 (Eng Lang & Lit) AB; Central Mich U (Lit, Govt, Hist) 50, 56, 59; UMich summer 51, 53-54 (LS) MA, 62, 65, 67-69 (LS & Eng). 6: Sp, Fr. 7: Tchr high sch Eng & Sp, Alma Mich 47-50; Tchr-libn, Lake Odessa Mich 50-51; Air Force Civilian, Clerk -Steno Third Air Force Staff Judge Advocate, London 51-52, Tchr Third Air Force Sch, London 52-53; Ref libn Gen Ref Dept Enoch Pratt Free Lib, Baltimore 54-55; Ref libn Ref Sect Mich State Lib 55-58, Head Ref Sect Reader Serv Div 58-62; Chief libn Concordia Lutheran Jr Col 62-. 9: ALA; MichLA (chm Newcomers Com 61, chm Dist III 67-68); Ann Arbor Lib Club (chm 65-66). 10: Friends of the Ann Arbor Lib; LWV; Lutheran Human Rel Assn of Amer; Concordia Hist Inst; UMich Lib Sci Alumni; Delta Kappa Gamma. 14: Ref, admin, col & univ libs. 15: 312 Pine ridge, Ann Arbor Mi 48103.

OEHLERTS, DONALD ERVIN. b Waterloo Iowa 3 Ag 27. 4: Alberna Herrick Oehlerts. 5: Amherst 49-51; UWis 51-53 (Amer Studies) BS, 55-58 (LS) MS, Ind U 67-70 (LS) PhD. 7: Newspaper libn State Hist Soc, Madison Wis 53-58; Period libn SD State Col 58-60; Lfe sci libn Colo State U 60-64, Soc sci libn 65-67; Faculty Lib Sch Kan State Tchrs Col summer 67; Asst Dir for Pub Serv, U Houston Lib 70-. 9: ALA; ColoLA (chm Col & Univ Sect 63-64, pres-elect 65-66); MPLA. 12: "Guide to Wisconsin Newspapers, 1833-1957 (58); "Guide to Colorado Newspapers, 1859-1963 (64); "The Most Cited Serials in Biological Abstracts in 1960 (62); "A Study to Determine the Feasibility of Establishing a Cooperative Technical Processing Program and Direct Transmission of Interlibrary Loans (62); "The Status of Ornithological Literature, 1964, with P H Baldwin (64); "Colorado Agricultural Experimental Index, 1888-1965 (66). 14: Ref. 15: U Houston Lib, Houston Tx 77004.

OESCH, DONNA S. b Warsaw NY 10 F 40. 4: Gerald I Oesch. 5: Geneseo State U Col 57-61 (LS) BS Permanent Certif. 7: Libn W Irondequoit Central Sch, Rochester NY 61-6; Sec Wilmont Castle Co, Rochester NY summer 62-63; Domitory coun, Hathaway Brown Sch, Cleveland 63; Libn Byron-Bergen Central Sch, Bergen NY 64-. 9: NYLA (sec-treas NW Zone Conf 65-66); Genesee Co LA (pres 67-69). 10: Beta Sigma Phi; Byron-Bergen Faculty Assn. 14: Ref, bk sel, a-v. 15: 144 Bowen rd, Churchville NY 14428.

OETTING, GERTRUDE L. b Pittsburgh. 5: Chatham Col (Hist) AB; Carnegie BS in LS; UPittsburgh (Hist, Eng) Litt M. 6: Fr. 7: Tchr Jr High Sch Ross Twp, Allegheny Co Penn; Asst libn Latimer Jr High Sch, Pittsburgh; Libn: Conroy Jr High Sch, Pittsburgh, Westinghouse High Sch, Pittsburgh, Taylor Allderdice High Sch, Pittsburgh Dir Allegheny Campus Lib Commun Col of Allegheny Co currently. 8: Lectr, Carnegie Lib Sch, Carnegie Inst Tech. 9: ALA; -ACRL (Tri-State Chap; penn Chap Jr Col Sect); PennLA (SWest dist;v-pres & pres-elect); Pittsburgh Lib Club. 10: Zonta Internat. 13: Yes. 14: Jr & commun col lib wk. 15: 500 'Bunker Hill st, Pittsburgh Pa 15206.

OETTINGER, RUTH M. b Cologne Germany. 5: ULondon 28-32 (Law, Econ, Pol Sci), equivalent of BA; UHamburg; UGeneva (Switzerland); Friedrich-Wilhelms-U (Berlin); Columbia 57-58 MLS. 6: Ger, Fr, Dutch. 7: 1st asst ref dept NY Acad of Med, NYC 59-. 9: MedLA (NY Reg Gp; past chm Com on Continuing Educ, chm Memb Com); SLA. 14: Ref. 15: 245 Seaman ave, NYC 10034.

OFFERMANN, GLENN. b Waterloo Ill 20 My 36. 4: Marilyn Wirth Offermann. 5: Concordia Tchrs Col (River Forest Ill) 54-58 (Eng) BS Ed; Chicago 60-65 (LS) MA. 6: Ger. 7: Prin & tchr St Stephens Lutheran Sch, Atkins Iowa 58-60; Libn Luther High Sch South, Chicago 60-67; Hd libn Concordia Col St Paul 67-. 9: ALA; Lutheran EA; MinnLA. 10: Educ Resources RT; Coop Libs in Consortium. 14: Admin, educ libs, instr materials. 15: 1371 W Burke ave, St Paul Mn 55113.

OGBIN, FRANCES. b NYC 12 Ap 16. 5: Hunter Col 34-38 (Geol) AB; Columbia 38-40 (Geog) AM; NY State U Col (Albany) 49-50 BS in LS. 7: Sci tchr Williamstown Union Sch, Williamstown NY 42-44; Sci & soc studies tchr Newfield Central Sch, Newfield NY 44-46; Sci tchr Cincinnatus Central Sch, Cincinnatus NY 46-49; Libn Gilboa-Conesville Central Sch, Gilboa NY 50-. 9: ALA; NEA; Nat Sci Tchrs Assn; NY State Tchrs Assn; East NY Libns; Hudson-MohawkLA. 10: Grange PTA; Girl Scouts; Delta Kappa Gamma; Gilboa Fac Assn. 14: Sch lib. 15: RD 2, Gilboa NY 12076.

OGDEN, HELEN (MOSS). b Portland Me 17 Ap 41. 4: William B Ogden. 5: Smith 59-63 (Fr) AB; Columbia 63-64 MLS. 6: Fr, Ital, Ger. 7: Libn US Army Spec Serv: France 64-66, germany 66-67, Child libn Los Angeles Pub Lib Sherman Oaks Br 68-. 9: NevLA (Convention Reserv Chm 64, Exhib Chm 65, Adv Manager for "Nevada Libraries), Fin Com 68-69). 10: Beta Phi Mu. 14: Child wk (pub lib or sch). 15: 1017 Elden ave apt 6, Los Angeles Ca 90006.

OGILVIE, MARTHA M C. b Oakland Cal 16 F 18. 4: Bruce C Ogilvie. 5: Northwestern U 36-40 (Geol, Geog) BS (Honors); UWash summers 54, 56, 58 M of Libnship; UChicago summer 63. 6: Sp, Fr. 7: Tchr Vuster Sch, (Berwyn Illinois) 40-42; Map libn Off of Strategic Serv - US Govt, (Washington DC) 42-43; Research libn Campbell-Ewald Advertising Agency, (NYC) 43-44; Tchr Princeton Elem Schs, (Princeton Mass) 49; Acquis libn Chico State Col, (Chico Cal) 50-57; Libn Dept of Geogr UWash, (Seattle) 57-59; Dir IMC (Distr Level) Elem Sch Distr #65, (Evanston Illinois) 59-66; Coord Consul Serv Educ Serv Dept - Field Enterprises, Educ Corp, (Chicago) 66-. 9: ALA; ASCD; CathLA; CanLA; IllLA; IllASchL (Exec Bd 65-67). 10: Beta Phi Mu. 13: Yes. 14: Sch libnship, lib educ, ref materials. 15: Educational Services Dept Station 8, Field Enterprises Educ Corp, Merchandise Mart Plaza, Chicago Il 60654.

OGILVIE, PHILIP SMYTHE. b Savannah Ga 14 Mr 19. 4: Joan Marie Forshag. 5: St Marys U (Baltimore) 42-44 (Philos) BA; Catholic U 44-47 BS in LS; UNC 48 (Sociol); NC State Col 48 (Sociol); Loyola U (New Orleans) 50-52 (Sociol). 6: Fr, Lat. 7: Exec sec NC Catholic Laymans Assn, Nazareth NC 47-49; Exec sec Catholic Com of South, New Orleans 49-53; Asst libn Rock Hill (SC) Pub Lib 53-54; Dir Albemarle Reg Lib, Winton NC 54-56; Dir Coastal Plain Reg Lib, Tifton Ga 56-58; Dir Roanoke Pub Lib, Roanoke Va 58-61 Dir Jackson Mun Lib, Jackson Miss 61-63; Asst dir Tulsa City-Co Lib System, Tulsa Okla 63-65; State Libn NC State Lib 65-. 8: Lib consul, Northeast Reg Lib Survey, Corinth Miss 62; Budget & Program Consul, Okla State Lib, 65; Exec com NC Governor's Coord Coun on Aging. 9: ALA (Coun 6771; chm Awards Com 67-68; chm ALA-SELA Memb Com Region VII 66-69); SLA; NCLA; SELA; NCSchLA (pres 68-69). 13: Yes. 14: Admin, pub serv. 15: P O Box 2889, Raleigh NC 27602.

OGLESBY LEORA (WALDEAN). b Akron Ohio 2 F 35. 5: Ohio State 52-56 (Sp) BS in Ed; Mexico City Col 55; West Res 56 MSLS. 7: Child libn Akron Pub Lib, Akron Ohio 57-58; libn Rochester Pub Lib, Rochester NY 58-61; Ya ref libn Berkeley Pub Lib, Berkeley Cal 61-64; Coord ya serv San Mateo Co Lib, Belmont Cal 64-66; Br libn New Haven Pub Lib, New Haven Conn 66-. 8: Set up the YA Dept under a LSCA grant at the San Mateo Co Lib; Spec summer lib proj, New Haven Pub Lib. 9: CalLA; (YA Bklist Com; pres YA RT); ConnLA. 10: Rochester Oratorio Soc; Newhallville Teen Cr Exec Bd; YA Materials Discussion Gp (Conn). 13: Yes. 14: YA serv, ref. 15: 401 Mill Rock rd, Hamden Ct 06517.

OGURA, IRENE K. b Stockton Cal 22 Ja 19. 5: UColo 54-56 (Bus) BS; UDenver 57-59 (LS) MA. 6: Japanese. 7: Med rec libn Gen Rose Hosp, Denver 56-57; Med libn II UColo Med Ctr 58-. 9: MedLA. 10: Rocky Mountain Biol Lab; People-to-People. 14: Catlg, ref. 15: E 119th pl Rte 1, Denver Co 80229.

OH, GRETCHEN (BRENNEKE). b Muncie Ind 6 Jl 41. 4: Tai Keun Oh. 5: Shimer Col 58-61 (Humanities) BA; UWis 61-64 (LS) MS. 6: Ger. 7: Libn I Mem Lib UWis 64-67; Libn St Marys Sch of Nursing, Madison Wis 67-68. 8: Instr Hosp Libns Wkshop Med Lib UWis summer 68; Moderator, Panel on "Continuing Educ - The Libs Role, Lib Serv Conf 39th Tri-State Hosp Assembly, Chicago Ill.09 9: ALA; MedLA. 13: Yes. 14: Catlg, med libnship. 15: 1531 W Fargo ave, Chicago Il 60626.

OHLMAN; HERBERT (MARVIN). b NYC 6 Mr 27. 4: Sally Petty. 5: Syracuse U 48-50 (Physics) BS; Ohio State U 57 (Operations research); UCLA 59 (Info Sci); Rutgers 61 (LS); MIT 63 (Linguistics); Wash U 67-69 (Computer Sci). 7: Coordinator of tech info Carrier Corp, Syracuse NY 54-55; Sr info analyst Battelle Mem Inst, Columbus Ohio 55-57; Sr operations & mgt research analyst System Development Corp, Santa Monica Cal 57-60; Research staff Lockheed Electronics Systems Research Center, Bedminster NJ 60-61; Sr Staff analyst IBM Adv Systems Dev Div, Yorktown Heights NY 61-62; Head systems applications info sci lab, Itek Corp, Lexington Mass 63-64; Sr bus & market research analyst Xerox Corp, Rochester NY 64-67; Assoc dir Cemrel Inc, St Louis 67-69; Consul in info sci & tech, St Louis 69-. 8: Devised new system of mechanical indexing (permutation indexing), 57, Lexington Mass, & Santa Monica Cal; Wrote programmed text to teach computer simulation lang, 62, NYC; Developed system for comparison of diverse info systems (activity spectrum) 64, Rochester NY; Org & dir programs in computers in educ to St Louis 68. 9: ASIS (chm Spec Group on Educ for Info Sci 66-67; chm Spec Interest Group on Info Ret 67). 10: Sigma Pi Sigma; AAAS. 12: Ed "Proceedings of Symposium on Uses of Computers in Education (69); "Permutation Index to Reprints of International Conference on Sciencr Information (58). 13: Yes. 14: Analysis, design, eval of info systems. 15: 6952 Waterman ave, University City Mo 63130.

OHLSON, ANNETTA (DIEKHOFF). b Ann Arbor Mich 31 O 12. 4: John Edward Ohlson Sr. 5: UMich 29-33 (Geog, Hist) AB, 33-34 ABLS. 7: Staff "Detroit News," Detroit 51-54, Asst libn 54-55; Libn Nat Bank of Detroit, Detroit 55-. 9: SLA (Consultation Com 65-67, chm Bus & Fin Div 60-61, Bul ed 58-59; Mich Chap, pres 64-65, sec 60-61). 15: Lib Nat Bank of Detroit, Box 116, Detroit 48232.

OHM, BETTY (BOZARTH). b Henderson Ky 23 Jl 29. 4: Bernard M Ohm. 5: East Ill U 46-48 9eng); UIllinois 48-49 (Journalism); Ill Col 59-60 (Eng) AB; UIll 67-68 (LS) MS. 7: Sales clk Burtschi's Bk & Gift Shop, Matton Ill 49-50; Copyreader & asst publ ed Ill State Lib 57-59, asst juvenile unit 60-61; Libn Jefferson High Sch, Springfield ill 61; Asst circ Ill State Lib 63-64, asst hd catlg unit 64-67; Asst dir Lincoln lib, Springfield Ill 68-. 9: ALA (Recrt Netwk 64-67); IllLA. 10: Springfield Lib Club; Springfield Municipal Choir; People-to-People. 13: Yes. 14: Catlg, admin. 15: 818 Kenyon dr, Springfield Il 62704.

OHM, HOLLY V(AN VALKENBURGH). b NYC 22 N 36. 4: Kenneth R Ohm. 5: UColo 53-57 (Elem Educ) BA; East NMU 55-56 (Elem Educ); UDenver 63-65 (LS) MA. 7: Tchr Davidson Co Schs, Nashville 58-60; Tchr Clovis Mun Schs, Clovis NM 60; Head tchr Boulder Co Schs, Boulder Colo 61; Tchr Boulder Valley Schs, Boulder Colo 61-62, Libn 62-66; Hd libn Sheridan Col 66-. 9: ALA; WyoLA (Acad Libs Com, Nat Lib Week Com). 10: Girl Scout Leader. 14: Sch libnship, lib sci educ, jr col libs. 15: 835 Big Horn ave, Sheridan Wy 82801.

OHR, MARION (GRACE). b Staten Island NY 29 N 17. 5: Wagner Col 35-37, 39-40 (Lat) AB; Pratt 46-47 BLS; UMich 51-52 ALS. 6: Ger, Lat. 7: Typist Despard & Co, NYC 40-42; US Army WAC (Cpl) 42-45; Sec NY Adult Educ Coun, NYC 45-46; Catlgr Western Col for Women 49-53; Head catlgr State Hist Soc of Mo, Columbia Mo 53-54; Libn US Army, Europe, Germany 55-57; Catlgr UDel 58-60; Head catlgr UUtah 60-64, Catlgr 64-. 9: ALA; UtahLA. 10: AAUP; Wasatch Mountain Club. 14: Catlg. 15: 73 Elizabeth st, Salt Lake City Ut 84102.

OHTA, MRS MIWA (TSUJI). b Tokyo Japan 25 F 26. 4: Masao Ohta. 5: Kyoritsu Col of Pharmacy 44-48 (Pharmacy) B in Pharm; UCal(Berkeley) 55-56 (Chem); UAkron 56-58 (Chem) BS; West Res 58-60 MSLS; Columbia summer 63. 6: Japanese, Ger. 7: Ref asst Dayton & Montgmery Co Pub Lib, Dayton Ohio 60-61; Ref libn St Louis U Med Center Lib 61-64; Ref libn Washington U Sch of Med Lib (St Louis) 64-66; Hd pub serv 66-67; Hd ref dept 67-68; SDI libn 68-. 9: SLA; MedLA;ASIS. 14: Ref, pub serv, info retrieval, automation. 15: 4580 Scott ave, St Louis Mo 63110.

OILLE, SARA McGILL. b Kings Creek SC 25 Ag 25. 5: Montreal Col 42-47 (Soc Studies) AB; Winthrop Col 47-52 (Eng) AB; Emory 55-57 MLibnship. 7: Libn: St George Sch, St George Ga 48-52, Morgan County High Sch, Madison Ga 52-53, Stoneville High Sch, Stoneville NC 53-55, Mt Pleasant High Sch, Mt Pleasant NC 56-57, Robertsdale High Sch, Robertsdale Ala 57-68, Foley High Sch, Foley Ala 68; Libn II Atlanta Pub Lib 56. 9: ALA; AlaEA; AlaLA. 10: AAUW; Alpha Delta Kappa. 14: Sch lib. 15: Star Rte Box 375, Elberta Al 36530.

OKEY, ANNE (R). b Ann Arbor Mich 28 Ag 30. 5: UMich 48-52 (Hist) BA, 57 AMLS. 6: Sp, Fr. 7: UMich Lib: Sr circ libn 57-59, Educ libn 59-61, Asst head circ dept 61-67; Hd circ dept 67-. 9: ALA. 10: AAUW; Bd Dirs, Ann Arbor/Washtenaw Coun of Churches. 14: Pub serv. 15: 802 Jones dr, Ann Arbor Mich 48105.

OKO, DOROTHY KUHN. b Cincinnati 22 Jl 1896. 4: Adolph S Oko (dec). 5: Bryn Mawr 14-16 (Econ); Radcliffe 16-18 (Labor Econ) BA; Columbia 45-47 (LS) BS; New Sch of Soc Research 53-55 MA. 6: Ger, Fr, Sp. 7: Spec agent US Employment Serv, Cincinnati 1-19; Exec dir Ind Health Labs, Cincinnati 21-31; Labor educ spec NY Pub Lib 47-61; Consul Hist Soc, Madison Wis 63-64; Consul United Housing Assn, NYC 63-64; NY State Sch of Ind Rel, NYC 63-64; Consul Labor Dept City of NY 65-. 5-. 8: Tchr NY State Sch of Industrial & Labor Rels NYC 66-. 9: ALA (chm Jt Com on Lib Serv to Labor Groups 48-61); Amer Sociol Assn; AEAUSA; Indus Rel Assn. 10: Amer Assn for Jewish Educ; ACLU; Amer Fed of Tcrs. 12: Co-ed "Library Service to Labor (63). 13: Yes. 14: Lib serv to labor, serv to the functionally illiterate, etc. 15: 545 W 111th st, NYC 10025.

OKTAY, ELIZABETH J. b E Orange NJ 2 N 36. 4: Sevgin Oktay. 5: Antioch 54-59 9eng Lit) BA; Columbia 59-60 MSLS. 6: Turkish, Fr. 7: Asst to dir Columbia U Libs 60-63; Reader serv libn Vassar Col 66-. 9: ALA; DCLA. 10: Beta Phi Mu. 13: Yes. 14: Ref. 15: 70 Hudson View dr, Beacon NY 12508.

OLDENBURG, ADELE LOUISE. b Cleveland 11 F 25. 5: Bowling Green State U 45-48 (Eng) BA; Fla So Col 63 (LS, Child Lit); Fla State U 64-65 (LS) Masters. 6: Ger. 7: Sec to dir of acad train Bartow (Fla) AB 50-55; Exec sec IMC Research Div, Mulberry Fla 55-62, libn 62; Child libn, fine arts libn, adult serv libn, asst city libn Lakeland Pub Lib, Lakeland Fla 62-. 9: ALA (Recr Com); FlaLA. 10: AAUW; Chi Omega; Kappa Tau Delta; Lakeland Art Guild; Friends of the Lib; Symphony Guild. 14: Admin, ref, fine arts. 15: 1317 Candyce st, Lakeland Fl 33801.

OLDFATHER, MARGARET. b Evanston Ill 29 Mr 04. 5: UIll 22-26 (Hist) AB, 26-27 BS in LS, 29-32 (LS) MA. 7: Catlgr Lawrence Col 28-29; Catlgr UIll(Urbana) 29-32; Catlgr Ohio State U 32-43, Catlg reviser 43-45; Ser reviser UIll(Urbana) 46-47, Catlg libn 47-51 Head catlg dept Ohio State U 51-, Prof of Lib Admin 65-. 8: Instr San Jose State Tchrs Col, summer 30; Instr UIll Lib Sch, summer 45, 63. 9: ALA (Coun 56-57 & 61-65); -ACRL; OhioLA; Ohioana; Ohio Valley Reg Group of Tech Serv Libns (pres 44-45). 10: AAUP; Archaeol Inst of Amer Delta Kappa Gamma; Beta Phi Mu. 14: Catlg, ser. 15: 89E Henderson rd, apt C, Columbus Ohio 43214.

OLDHAM, ELLEN McQUILKIN. b Worcester Mass 13 O 22. 5: Vassar 39-43 (Lat) AB; Yale 43-45 (Classical Lang & Lit) AM; Simmons (LS) MS. 6: Fr, Lat. 7: Tchr St John Baptist Sch, Mendham NJ 45-48; Boston Pub Lib : Asst rare bk dept 50-56, Ref libn rare bk dept 56-62, Curator of classical lit 62-66; Curator of printed bks 66-. 9: BSA. 10: AAUW; Phi Beta Kappa; Mensa. 13: Yes. 14: Rare bks. 15: Boston Pub Lib Copley sq, Boston Ma 02117.

OLDHAM, PHYLLIS VIRGINIA (KIDD). b Lafayette Ind 19 Mr 26. 4: Robert Forsyth Oldham. 5: Purdue 44-48 (Fr, Sp, Sci) BS, 48-49 (Hist), 52-53 (Eng); ButlerU 64-66 (LS) MS; Certified to teach Fr, Sp, Eng, & Social Studies. 6: Fr, Sp. 7: Sales Southworth's Bkstore, W Lafayette Ind 48-49; Off wk Twp Assessor's Off, Lafayette Ind 49-50; Tchr Jefferson High Sch, Lafayette Ind 50-51; Tchr Tudor Hall Sch, Indianapolis Ind 54-61, Libn 63-. 9: ALA; MarionCo(Ind)LA (v-pres). 10: Kappa Delta Pi; Pi Beta Phi; La Sertoma Internatl. 14: Ref, ya serv. 15: 3650 Cold Springs rd, Indianapolis In 46222.

OLDSEN, CARL F. b Rockford Iowa 13 My 41. 4: Patricia Ervin Oldsen. 5: UNoIowa 59-63 (LS, Soc Sci) BA; Peabody Col 65-66 (Col & Univ Libs) MLS. 7: Libn Iowa Braille & Sight Saving Sch, Vinton Iowa 63-65; Libn & info syst coord IMC-Handicapped Child & Youth Mich State U (E Lansing) 66-. 8: Consul UMinn, Dept of Educ 68. 9: ALA; SLA; Instrl Materials Ctr Netwk for Handicapped Child & Youth (chm Libns Gp). 10: Beta Phi Mu; Phi Delta Kappa. 13: Yes. 14: Lib info ret, automation. 15: 4400 S Okemos rd, 114-H, Okemos Mi 48864.

OLECHNO, ETHEL GILLIAN. b Stockport England 1 Mr 30. 4: Czeslaw Olechno. 5: LeedsU (England) 48-51 (Soc Sci) BA; USoCal 63-64 MS in LS. 6: Fr. 7: Hd tech processes pub Lib, Inglewood Cal 61-66; Hd tech proc Med Lib Unit I Los Angeles Co/USC Med Ctr 67-. 9: ALA; CalLA; Med Lib Gp of So Cal. 13: Yes. 14: Catlg. 15: 3017 W 83rd st, Inglewood Ca 90305.

OLESNYCKYJ, OSTAP. b Uhryn Ukraine 3 Ap 17. 4: Jaroslawa Mosora. 5: ULviv (Ukraine) 37-39 (Law); ViennaU (Austria) 41, 43-44 (Law, Pol Sci); UGraz (Austria) 45-47 (Law) Absolutorium; Ukrainian FreeU (Munich Germany) 49 (Law, Econ) Master of Law. 6: Ukrainian, Ger, Polish, Russian. 7: Co-partner & mgr "OWYD" Advertising Agcy & Bk Co Inc, Lviv Ukraine 41-43; Catlg asst pub lib, Newark NJ 57-58, Catlg libn 59-67; Problem bks catlgr Alanar Bk Processing Ctr Newark Br 65-67; Hd catlg libn (assoc prof) Bloomfield Col Lib 67-. 9: ALA (Subj Hdings Com 66-68). 10: Assn Ukrainian Libns USA; AAUP; UkrainianAAUP; Ukrainian Lawyers Assn USA. 13: Yes. 14: Catlg. 15: 336 Ellery ave, Newark NJ 07106.

OLESON, DOUGLAS DEAN. b Aberdeen Wash 5 S 29. 4: Nancy Ann Buckreus. 5: IndU 61-63 (Govt) AB, 67-68 MLS; Purdue 64-66 (Hist) MA. 7: Photographer USN 51-55; Announcer-news ed KBKW Radio, Aberdeen Wash 57-59; Newsman KVOS Radio TV, Bellingham Wash 59-60; Announcer-engr WIOU Radio, Kokomo Ind 60-61; Tchr Lebanon Commun Schs, Lebanon Ind 63-66; Hd W Campus Lib Ohio StateU (Columbus) 68-69; Hd libn Davis & Elkins Coll WVa 70-. 9: ALA; OhioLA. 10: Phi Delta Kappa; Phi Beta Kappa. 14: Ref, undergrad libs, admin. 15: Davis & Elkins Coll, Elkins WVa.

OLEVNIK, PETER P. b Fort Wayne Ind 23 D 34. 4: Judith K Armstrong. 5: St Francis Col 59-62 (Liberal Arts) BA, 62-65 (Educ) MA; Rosary Col 66-68 (LS) MA. 7: Radio & tele operator (Pfc) US Army 57-59; Y-a libn Ft Wayne & Allen Co Pub Lib, Ft Wayne Ind 61-64; Ref asst libn Chicago Pub Lib 66-68; Humanities ref libn Ill StateU 68-. 9: ALA; McLeanCo(Ill)LA. 14: Ref. 15: 1320 Dogwood lane, Bloomington Il 61701.

OLINER, STAN. b Denver 13 Je 38. 4: Evelyn Smith. 5: UColo 56-60 (Pol Sci) BA; UDenver 60-61 (LS) MA. 7: Bkmob libn Freeport Mem Lib, Freeport NY 62-63; Supv libn Colo State Lib 63-64, Area libn supv 64-65; Co Libn Laramie Co Lib, Cheyenne Wyo 65-. 8: Bldg consul Wyo State Lib 67-68; Operate own private press. 9: SLA; ALA; WyoLA. 10: Nat Amateur Press Assn. 12: "Review of Cattle Business in Johnson County, Wyoming" (68). 13: Yes. 14: Ext, pub. 15: PO Box 883, Cheyenne Wy 82001.

OLIVA, JOHN J. b NYC 10 O 41. 4: Doris Ann. 5: Queens Col 59-64 (Geol) BS; Fla State U 65-66 (LS) MS. 7: Research asst Fla State U 65-66; Info sys analyst System Development Corp, Falls Church Va 66-67; Libn Sp/5 USA, Fort Lee Va 67-69. 10: Beta Phi Mu. 14: Info sci. 15: 14-31 30th dr, L I City NY 11102.

OLIVER, JAMES MICHAEL. b Detroit Mich 14 Je 42. TROIT Mich 14 Je 42. 5: Wayne State 58-63 (LS) BS, 65-66 (Instr Tech) MEd. 6: Sp. 7: Prin of adult educ VI Govt Dept of Educ 63-65, Libn & a-v coord 63-66; Coord ESEA Title II Program, St Croix 66-68, Dir lib serv & instr materials 68-. 8: Assoc dir ESEA Title I Reading Inst, Col of the VI summer 68-69; Educl Media Instr, NDEA Title XI Inst (Tchg Eng as a sec lang), Col of the VI summer 67; Coord A-V Serv, ESEA Title I, St Croix VI summer 66; Instr-Partic, NDEA Title XI Inst in Educl Media, Col of the VI summer 65. 9: NEA-DAVI; ALA; Internatl Studies Assn; Nat Assn Educl Broadcasters. 12: "Programmed Instruction" v. 1, Code #201 (65). 13: Yes. 14: Sch media progms, caribbean research. 15: PO Box 1505, Frederiksted St Croix US Virgin Islands 00840.

OLIVER, JOHN AARON. b Athol Mass 14 S 26. 4: Diana L Gallotta. 5: UMass 46-50 (Eng) BA; UDenver 51-52 (LS) MA. 7: US Navy 44-46; Lib asst UMass 50-51; Ref asst Ft Wayne Pub Lib, Ft Wayne Ind 52-54; Coordinator of educ TV Detroit Pub Lib 55-56, Asst br libn 56-62; Head Libn Oak Park Pub Lib, Oak Park Mich 62-67; Asst dir Flint Pub Lib, Flint Mich 67-. 9: ALA (Life mem); MichLA (Legis Com 62-66; chm Lib Admin Sect 65-66). ; 2nd v-pres 69). 10: Amer Contract Bridge League. 15: 14521 Leslie, Oak Park Mich 48237.

OLIVER, LEE ROY. b Amarillo Tex 27 D 26. 5: W Tex StateU 58-62 (Soc Sci) BS; E Tex StateU 66-67 MSLS. 7: USN: Bm2 44-46, BmG2 50-52; Boiler fireman SW Pub Serv Co, Amarillo Tex 50-55, Sales 56-57; Sales Armstrong Transfer Co, Amarillo Tex 55-56; Electrician Pantex Ord, Amarillo Tex 57-66; Circ libn W Tex StateU 67-69; Hd libn Amarillo Col 69-. 9: TexLA; SWLA. 10: Phi Delta Kappa; YMCA. 14: Admin, ref. 15: 3411 Ong st, Amarillo Tx 79109.

OLIVER, MARGARET W. b Pittsburg Kan 7 N 03. 5: Kan State Tchrs Col 22-27 (Soc Sci) BS, summers 34-36 (Hist) MS; UDenver summers 45-47 BS in LS; USCal summer 53. 7: Tchr-libn High Sch, Riverton Kan 4-44; Libn Sr High Sch, Pittsburg Kan 44-56; Libn Truesdell Jr High Sch, Wichita Kan 56-59; Instr in Lib Sci Wichita State U summers 54-; Libn Wichita High Sch South, Wichita Kan 59-. 9: NEA;

ALA-AASchL; Kan State Tchrs Assn (chm Sch Lib Com 60-63); KanASchL (pres 54-55). 10: AAUW; Kappa Delta Pi; Beta Phi Mu. 12: Jt auth "I Want to Buy Books for the School Library - But. with M Miller, Kan State Dept of Educ (64). 14: Sch libnship. 15: 509 S Market, Wichita Kan 67202.

OLIVER, MARY WILHELMINA. b Cumberland Md 4 My 19. 5: West Md Col 40 (Hist, Eng) AB; Drexel 43 BS in LS; UNC 51 LLB. 7: Asst circ libn NJ Col for Women 43-45; Asst in Law Lib UVa 45-47; Asst ref libn Drake U 47-48, Asst soc sci libn 48-49; Research asst Inst of Govt UNC(Chapel Hill) 51-52; Asst law libn UNC 52-55, Law Libn & Assoc Prof of Law 55-59, Law libn & Assoc Prof of Law 59-69, Law libn & Prof of Law 69-. 8: Tchr, lib sci summer course, UNC, 63, 66-68; Admitted to law practice NC 51. 9: AALL (chm Com on Chaps 55-56; chm Com on Educ 59-61, 64-65; Certif Com 64-66); , chm 67-; rep to Coun of Nat Lib Assn Jt Com on Lib Educ 65-, Jt Com AALSS-AALL 67-69); AALS (Com on Libs 68-69); SLA; NCLA (chm Const & Codes Com 64-65). 10: Amer Bar Assn; NC State Bar; NC Bar Assn; Amer Soc for Legal Hist; SELDON Soc. 12: Ed "Membership Nws in "Law Library Journal v 50-54 (57-61); Co-comp "Questions and Answers in "Law Library Journal v 49-52 (56-59). 14: Admin (law). 15: PO Box 733, Chapel Hill NC 27514.

OLIVER, PATRICIA W. b Louisville Ky. 4: Michael A Oliver. 5: Nazareth Col (Ky) 57-62 (Eng) AB; UMich 62-64 amls; ULouisville 64-65. 6: Fr, Ger. 7: Clerical & sec; Clerical asst to catlgr Catherine Spalding Col Lib 57-62; Wk-study scholar-catlg dept UMich 62-64; Ref asst libn Louisville Free Pub Lib, Louisville Ky 64-65; Ref libn Bellarmine Ursuline 65-. 9: ALA; KyLA; Louisville Lib Club. 10: LWV. 14: Ref. 15: 3311 Goldsmith lane, Louisville Ky 40220.

OLIVERI, BLANCHE (LITTS). b Bushkill Penn 13 Ag 16. 4: Ernest B Oliveri. 5: Churchman Bus Col (Easton Penn) 35; Benjamin Franklin U 42-44. 6: Fr. 7: Clerk-admin asst Francis E Walter, MC, Wash DC 38-39; Clerk-admin asst US Dept of Agric, Wash DC 39-44, 47-48; US Dept of Agric Nat Agric Lib, Wash DC; Personnel off 48-56, Chief div of admin mgt 56-61, Act asst dir mgt serv 61-63, Asst dir prog coordination serv 63-. 8: Consul US Book Exchange, Wash DC 65. 9: ALA; SLA; ASIS (chm Legis Com); DCLA (chm Standards Com). 10: PTA; Agric Employees Credit Union. 11: Superior Accomplishment Award, 52; Outstanding Performance Awards, 50-64. 14: Mgt. 15: 1006 Brooks rd, Capital Heights Md 20027.

OLLER, ANNA KATHRYN. b Waynesboro Penn 1 Jl 16. 5: Juniata Col 34-38 (Classical LANGS, Eng) AB; Drexel 38-39 BS in LS; UIll 49-51 (LS) MS; UMich 59-63 (LS, Eng Lit) PhD. 6: Fr, Ger. 7: Asst libn Huntingdon Co Lib, Huntingdon Penn 39-40; Catlgr Juniata Col 40-42; Libn Huntingdon Co Lib, Huntingdon Penn 42-45; Libn Adams Co Free Lib, Gettysburg Penn 45-48; Asst ext libn Penn State Lib 48-49; Instr Penn State U summers 48, 49, 51; Research asst Grad Lib Sch UIll 49-50, Tchg asst 50-51; Instr Lib Sch Fla State U 51-52; Asst Prof Grad Sch of Lib Sci EXEL Inst of Tech 52-55, Assoc Prof 56-68, Act Dean 67-68, Prof & Assoc Dean 69-. 9: AALS; ALA-LED; -RSD; -ACRL (Subs Bks Com 65-, Isadore Mudge Citation Jury 65-68); PennLA (Documents Com 65-, Rec sec SE Chap 65-67); ASIS. 10: Penn Hist Soc; Germantown Hist Soc; AAUP; Beta Phi Mu. 12: "A Time Study of the Urbana (Ill) Free Library (50). ; "Christopher Saur, Colonial Printer; a Study of the Publication of the Press, 1738-1758 (UMich Microfilms 63). 13: Yes. 14: Ref, lib educ. 15: 706C Alden Park manor, Phila Pa 19144.

OLM, JANE (GRAY). b Van Horn Tex 5 N 25. 4: Kenneth William Olm Sr. 5: UNM 43-48 (Bus Ad, Econ) BBA; UTex 65-66 MLS. 7: High sch libn Austin Independent Sch Dist, austin Tex 63-65; Gen ref libn UNM 66-67; Ser libn UTex Law Lib (Austin) 67-. 9: AALL; ALA; S W Law Lib Assn. 13: Yes. 14: Acquis, ser. 15: 6111 Rickey dr, Austin Tx 78731.

OLMSTEAD, ELIZABETH HIATT. b Topeka Kan 9 O 19. 5: Dickinson State Tchrs Col 36-38 (Music); UND 38-39 (Music); Eastman Sch of Music URochester 39-40 (Theory) Mus B; UMinn 44-46 (Music) AM, 48-50 SB in LS; UMd 67-68 Post masters fellow (Lib & Info Serv). 6: Fr. 7: Tchr of Eng & music High Sch, Churchs Ferry ND 40-41; Tchr of Eng & music High Sch, Declo Ida 41; Tchr of Eng &vocal music Jr & Sr High Sch, Bottineau ND 42-43; Invoice clerk UMinn Bus Off 43-44; Bk-store sales clerk Century Bk Store, Minneapolis 44-46; Prof asst music dept Minneapolis Pub Lib 46-51; Mus libn Ohio State U 54-58; Mus libn Oberlin Col Conservtory of Mus 58-. 8: Tchr of Introduction to Mus Libnship Case West Res U 69. 9: MusLA (past chm, v-pres 69, Mid West Chap). 10: Ohio State U Staff Org. 13: Yes. 14: Mus lib admin, acquis, catlg, lib netwks, coop catlg. 15: Rt 2 Peasley rd, Amherst Oh.

OLNEY, ROBERT GORDON. b Gauhati Assam India 10 O 26. 4: Anne Quin. 5: Colby Col 46-50 (Hist) BA; Syracuse 55-56 MSLS; SUC (Potsdam) NY State Sch Libn's Certif; SUC (Geneseo) NY State Sch Libn's Certif. 6: Japanese, Sp. 7: Y-a libn (br) Enoch Pratt Free Lib, Baltimore 56-59; Libn Massena Central High Sch, Massena NY 59-63; A-v libn n country Lib Syst, Watertown NY 63-66, Adv hd 66-67, Processing hd 67-68; Dir washtenaw Co Lib Washtenaw Area Lib Syst, Ann Arbor Mich 68-. 9: Pres, NoArea(NY)SchLA (pres 57-58). 10: Beta Phi Mu; PTA; Cub Scouts Leader. 14: Readers adv, ref, lib admin, system consul serv. 15: PO Box 74, Manchester Mi 48158.

OLSEN, CHARLES O. b Greenville SC. 4: Dorothy Starr Olsen. 5: Stanford 48 (Internat Rel) BA; Columbia 54 MLS. 6: Ital, Fr. 7: US Army Signal Corps 42-46; Bus analyst US Dept of Com, Wash DC 52-53; LC: Ref asst main reading room 54-55, Asst serv libn Legis Ref Serv 55, Bibliog Legis Ref Serv 55-58; Asst Chief, then Chief, research files Internat Bank for Reconstr & Devel, Wash DC 58-62; Asst libn Joint Bank-Fund Lib, Wash DC 62-. 8: LC intern. 9: SLA; DCLA; ASIS. 14: Ref, admin. 15: Jt Bank-FUND Lib, 19th & H sts NW, Wash DC 20431.

OLSEN, DAVID LOUIS. b Denver Colo 20 Ap 39. 4: Sandra A (Bissell). 5: Mesa Jr Col 57-58 (Hist); UColo 58-61 (Hist) BA; UWis (Madison) 61-64 (Hist, Educ) MS; UDenver 66-67 (LS) MA. 7: Pre-Prof asst Milwaukee Pub Lib 64-66; Ref asst Detroit Pub Lib 67-68; Acquis libn David Bishop Skillman Lib Lafayette Col 68-. 9: ALA. 10: Phi Alpha Theta. 14: Ref, acquis. 15: 312 March st apt 6, Easton Pa 18042.

OLSEN, DONALD D. b Minneapolis 7 Ag 31. 4: Miriam Olsen. 5: UMinn 59 BA, 64 (LS) MA. 6: Sp. 7: Cat;g libn UMinn(Morris) 64-65; Acquis libn Stout U 65-. 8: Ed, printer, publisher Ox Head Press, poetry pamphlets. 9: WisLA. 13: Yes. 14: Catlg, acquis. 15: 1210 15th ave, Menomonie Wi 54751.

OLSEN, GEORGE LIEBERG. b Mankato Minn 31 My 01. 5: St Olaf Col 20-23 (Econ, Hist) BA; Fla State U 48-49 (LS) MA; UOslo summer 52 Certif. 6: Sp, Ger, Norwegian. 7: Partner & manager retail food store, Mankato Minn 24-40; Asst to dean High Point Col 40-41; Food stamp off Blue Earth Co, Mankato Minn 42-43; War plant wker Kato Engnr Co, Mankato Minn 43-45; Clerk Co Auditors Off, Mankato Minn 46-47; Grad stud asst lib Sch Fla State U 48-49; Gift & exch libn UFla 49-52, Catlgr UFla Libs 52-57; Libn Newberry Col 57-65; Coordinator secondary sch libs Duval Co Bd of Pub Instr, Jacksonville Fla 65-68; Evaluator of collections Mills Mem Lib Rollins Col 68-. 9: SELA; FlaLA; SCLA (chm Col & Univ Sect 60. 10: AAUP; Civitan Internat; Lutheran Hist Conf; Lutheran Soc for Worship, Mus & the Arts; Norwegian-Amer Hist Assn; Scand-Amer Foun; Soc Adv Scand Studies; Jacksonville Beaches Chorus; Sons of Norway; Norwegian-Amer Museum. 14: Acquis, catlg. 15: 363 Henkel cir, Winter Park Fl 32789.

OLSEN, HAROLD ANKER. b St Cloud Minn 30 Ap 34. 4c; Constance Balcom Olsen. 5: UMinn 52-57 (Behavioral Sci) BA, 58, 63 (LS) MA; Princeton U 67-68. 7: UMinn Minneapolis Desk attendant Lib 52-57; Tchg asst Lib Sch 57; Jr sci admin off 58; Info off USAF Capt (Japan) 58-62; Prof asst OSIS Nat Sci Found, Wash DC 63-66; Asst prog dir 67-. 8: NSF Rep to ASA Subcom Z39, 63-65 NSF Observer ARL 63-66. 9: ALA; SLA; ASIS. 10: Amer Stat Assn; Amer Soc Pub Admin; AAAS; Econ Assn; Assn for Pub Policy Analysis. 14: Lib planning & systems devel, research in sci info, mgt, economics of info. 15: 6911 Wilson lane, Bethesda MD 20034.

OLSEN, JAMES LAWRENCE JR. b Baltimore 22 D 22. 4: Anita Cabo. 5: UMd 46-51 (Sociol) BA. 7: (T/Sgt) US Army 42-46; (1st Lt) US Army Res 50-59; Prep libn Johns Hopkins U Appl Physics Lab 51-53; Libn Smith Kline & French LaPhila 53-61; Resident consul Herner & Co, Wash DC 61; Libn NAS-NAE, Wash DC 61-. 8: Consul Nat Cancer Inst, 65-. 9: SLA (chm Pharmaceut Sect 58-59); ASIS. 10: AAAS. 13: Yes. 14: Org & admin of lib serv. 15: 10604 Brunswick ave, Kensington Md 20795.

OLSEN, JANE O. b Flint Mich 24 Je 22. 4: Gerald C Olsen. 5: N Pk Col 40-42 (Liberal Arts) Ass BS; Northwestern U 42-44 (Elem Educ) BS in Educ; National C0l of Educ 56-62; Rosary Col 66 (LS); UIll 68 (LS). 6: Swedish. 7: Tchr, Moline Ill 44-45; Tchr, Rosemont Ill 45-66, Libn 66-. 9: ALA; IllEA. 10: PTA. 14: Student serv, sch libs. 15: 2210 Cedar st, Des Plaines Il 60018.

OLSEN, VIRGINIA ELIZABETH. b Portland Ore. 5: St Helen's Hall Jr Col 33-35 AA; UOre 35-37 (Eng Lit) BA; UCal (Berkeley) 40-41 Libnship Certif. 6: Fr. 7: Tchr high sch, Grants Pass Ore 37-40; Libn Franklin High Sch, Portland Ore 41-43; Libn Ore State Col 43-45; Libn Naval Base, Bremerton Wash 45-46; Libn Naval Supply Ctr, Oakland Cal 46-49; Libn Marine Corps Air Sta, El Toro (Santa Ana) Cal 50-52; Dist libn 12th Naval Dist Hdwrs, Treasure Island (San Francisco) Xal 52-. 9: ALA; CalLA. 10: Pi Lambda Theta; Delta Kappa Gamma; Fac Women's Club Ore State Col; Coun of Libns West Coast Navy Labs. 13: Yes. 14: Admin. 15: 2500 Hillegass ave, Berkeley Ca 94704.

OLSEN, WALLACE C. b Roseglen ND 28 Mr 29. 5: State Tchrs Col (Minot ND) 47-51 (Hist, Eng, Educ) BS in Ed; UWis 55-56 BS in LS. 7: Asst libn Lawrence Col 56-57; Asst libn Acad of Natural Sci of Phila 57-59, Libn 59-62; Libn Nat Aviation Facilities Center Fed Aviation Agency US Govt, Atlantic City NJ 62-66; Asst dir for tech serv UMd 66-67; Research assoc InterU Communications coun 67-. 9: ALA; SLA (pres Sci-Tech Group of Phila Chap 63-64); ASIS; Phila Area Tech Serv Libns; DCLA; MdLA. 13: Yes. 14: Tech serv, admin, col & univ libs. 15: 4605 Brandon lane, Beltsville Md 20705.

OLSHESKI, HAZEL R (SCHAFER). b Portland Ore 5 O 13. 4: Charles Olsheski. 5: UWash 31-35 (Ger, Eng Lit) BA, 35-36 BA in LS. 7: Buyer in bk store Harry Hartman, Seattle 36-39; Libn art dept Seattle Pub Lib 39-42, Libn bus dept 51-66; 1st asst libn bus dept 66-. 9: ALA; SLA; PNLA; WashLA (Hosp & Inst Com 65-). 14: Ref. 15: 13722 Aurora ave N, Seattle Wa 98133.

OLSON, DAVID R. b Sioux Falls S Dak 7 Je 34. 4: Janice R Rosenbaum. 5: Augustana Col 52-56 (Eng) BA; UDenver summer 60, 64-66 (LS) MA. 6: Ger. 7: Instr high sch, Humboldt S Dak 56-57; Lib asst Sioux Falls Pub Lib, Sious Falls S Dak 57-59, Ref libn 60-64; Prof musician 59-60; Period libn UDenver Lib 66-67; Ref libn US Dak Lib 67-68, Hd pub serv 68-. 9: SDLA (Acad Libs Sect); MPLA. 10: Amer Fed of Musicians. 14: Ref, music, art, literature, SD hist. 15: 215 Forest ave, Vermillion SD 57069.

OLSON, EARL E. b Salt Lake City 17 My 16. 4: Verene Ellen Stott. 5: LDS Bus Col 39-41. 6: Danish. 7: Hist compiler Off of the Church Histn, Salt Lake City 33-37, 39-42; Missionary The Church of Jesus Christ of Latter-day Saints, Denmark 37-39; US Army (T/Sgt) Serv Command Unit, Stockton Cal 42-46; Supv Church Records Archives, Genealogical Soc, Salt Lake ity 46-47; Asst libn Histns Off Lib, Salt Lake City 47-48, Libn 48-. 8: Priesthood Geneal Com Church of Jesus Christ of Latter-day Saints, 63-67; Chm Church Lib Coord Com 68-. 9: SAA; ALA; Amer Assn State & Loc Hist; Amer Records Mgt Assn; Nat Microfilm Assn; UtahLA; West Hist Assn. 10: Mormon Hist Assn; Utah Hist Soc. 11: Award of Serv, Utah Hist Soc 68. 13: Yes. 14: Rare bks, docs, photos. 15: 3148 So Crestview cir, Bountiful Ut 84010.

OLSON, EDNA (HOWARD). b Dawson Co Ga. 5: Ga State Col 50 (Soc Sci) BCS; Emory 55 (LS) MLn. 6: Fr, Ger. 7: Libn Ga Agric Expt Sta, Experiment Ga 49-. 9: Internat Assn of Agric Libns & Documentalists; ALA-ALTA; SELA; GaLA (sec 61-63); Ga Citizens Lib Trustees (treas 60-66). 10: Fed Garden Clubs of Griffin; Amer Camellia Soc; Amer Rose Soc; Griffin-Spalding Co C of C; Bus & Prof Womens Club; Trustee, Flint River Reg Lib. 12: "Activities of Librarians and Trustees Under the Library Services Act Program (58). 13: Yes. 14: Ref. 15: Experiment Ga 30212.

OLSON, EUGENE GEORGE. b Regina Sask Can 22 S 40. 4: Leona Junk. 5: USask 59-62 (Eng) BA; McGill 64-65 BLS. 6: Lat. 7: Eng Instr So Alta Inst of Tech 62-63; Catlgr UAlta Lib 64, Head period dept 65-. 9: Edmonton LA (v-pres 65-66);ALA; CanLA; AltaLA. 10: Fac Club, UAlta; Assn Acad Staff, UAlta; Can Assn Univ Tchrs; Assn Prof Libns, UAlta. 14: Tech serv, catlg, ref, period acquis. 15: 5143 - 106A st, Edmonton 70 Alberta Can.

OLSON, EVELYN D ANIELSON. b Ft Dodge Iowa 27 D 10. 4: Alvin R Olson. 5: Red Wing Jr Col 27-29; St Olaf Col 29-31 (Hist) BA; Pratt 37-38 BLS. 7: Lib aide Racine Pub Lib, Racine Wis 35-37; Libn Brooklyn Pub Lib 38-40; Br libn Fairfax Co Pub Lib, Springfield Va 53-. 9: VaLA; ALA. 14: Pub lib serv. 15: 6005 Grayson st, Springfield Va 22150.

OLSON, BETTY (EVELYN NAOMI) (MANSFIELD). b Highland Twp Ohio 17 O 23. 4: Sidney Gerald Olson. 5: Defiance 41-45 (Eng, Educ) AB; Rosary Col 63-65 (LS) MA. 7: Portsmouth Pub Lib, Portsmouth Va; Lib clerk 59-62, Lib asst II 62-63, Lib asst III 63; Lib trainee Educ Dept Chicago Pub Lib 63-64, Act child libn 64-65, Child libn 65-; Asst Prof Lib Sci Baptist Col; Libn SC Hist Soc. 9: ALA; SLA; SELA; SCLA. 10: Relig Educ Bd; Brownie Scout Leader; Interfaith Church Gp. 14: Church lib, ref, child wk. 15: 1216 Orange Branch rd, Charleston SC 29407.

OLSON, IVY T. b Virgina Minn 12 F 17. 5: Va Jr Col 35-37 AA; Wheaton 37-39 (Eng Lit) BA; UMinn 40-41 (LS) BS. 6: Finnish. 7: Tchr-libn Silver Lake Pub Schs, Silver Lake Minn 41-43; Lib staff Wheaton Col 43-, Asst libn 45-. 8: Ed com ""Christian Periodical Index. 9: ALA. 11: Wheaton Col Award of Merit 66. 14: Acquis. 15: 1123 Cherry st, Wheaton Il 60187.

OLSON, LOWELL E. b Maywood Ill. 4: udrey Monsen. 5: UIll 45 (Eng) BS; UChicago 49 9psych) MA; UMinn 55 (LS) MS, 66 (Higher Educ LS) PhD. 7: Tchr pub & priv elem & secondary schs 40-48; Tchr priv high sch, Maywood Ill 48-49; Instr Bismark Jr Col 49-51; Tchr Minneapolis Pub Schs 51-55; Libn 55-64; Assoc Prof lib sch UMinn (Minneapolis) 64-. 8: Dir NDEA Inst for Elem & Second Sch Libns 65; Field-Study Inst for Sch Lib supvrs 67. supvrs 67. 9: ALA; AALS; MinnASchL. 10: AAUP. 12: "Teachers', Principals', and Librarians' Perceptions of the School Librarian's Role," UMinn (66) Ed "Libraries of Seven South Dakota Institutions of Higher Learning," by D.K. Berninghausen. (65), "Effective Book Processing," (60). 13: Yes. 14: Sch libnship, lib educ. 15: 209 Exeter pl, St Paul Mn 55104.

OLSON, NEIL BRADFORD. b Boston 26 My 29. 4: Rose Papazoglos. 5: Tufts U 50, 51-54 (Eng) AB; Simmons 60-61 (LS) MS. 6: Bibliog knowledge of most Romance Langs, Ger. 7: USMC Aviation Instr 46-49; USMC Res Platoon Sgt 50-51; Freelance writer 56-57; Sub-prof libn Widener Lib Harvard Col 58-61; Head Libn Boston U Sch of Pub Communications Lib 61-65; Head Libn Mass State Col (Salem) 65-. 8: Bibliog researcher, NE Consuls Inc for Esso Res Div, 63-64. 9: ALA; NELA; MassLA (Coun Mass State Col Libns); Mass Conf Chief Libns Pub Higher Educ Insts. 10: Simmons Col Lib Sch Alumni Assn. 12: "Death of a War Dog and Other Poems" (61). 13: Yes. 14: Lib admin, lib recr. 15: 15 Victor st, Saugus Mass 01906.

OLSON, ROBERT JOHN. b Minneapolis Minn 3 Ag 26. 5: UMinn 46-49 (Lat) BA, 49-50 (Gr); NWest Lutheran Theol Sem 50-52; UMinn 52-53 BS in LS. 6: Fr, Ger, Gr, Lat, Swedish. 7: Ph M 3/c US Naval Reserve 45-46; Jr libn ref dept UMinn Lib Minneapolis 53-55, Libn ref dept 55-56; Sr ref asst Yale U Lib 56-58, Asst ref libn 58-61, Hd order dept 61-65, Hd bibliog dept 65-68, Sr catlgr 68-. 8: Instr (part time) in Lib Sci, So Conn State Col 59-60. 9: ALA-ACRL. 10: Phi Beta Kappa; Conn Acad Arts & Scis. 14: Acquis, catlg, ref. 15: 224 Park st, New Haven Ct 06511.

OLSON, RUE E. b Chicago Ill 1 N 28. 4: Richard L Olson. 5: Herzl Jr Col 46-48 (Fine Arts) Diploma; Northwestern U 48-50 (Bus); Ill State U 63- (Bus Admin). 6: Sp. 7: Accounting FS Serv Inc, Chicago & Bloomington Ill 48-60; Asst libn Ill Agric Assn & Affiliated Cos Lib, Bloomington Ill 60-66, Libn 66-. 9: ALA; ASIS; SLA (Dir Insur div 68-69; Ill Chap: Asst ed "Informant" 67-68 & Memb Com 68-69) 68-69; IllLA; McLeanCoLA (sec-treas 67-68, pres 69-70). 14: Admin, ref. 15: 103 Radcliff rd, Bloomington Il 61701.

OLSONI, KARL EMERIK. b Kuopio Finland 29 Ag 11. 4: Elli Spiess. 5: Mil Schs in Finland 31-32, 43 Artillery, Diploma; Helsinki U 32-43 (Hist, Econ) MA; Helsinki U 32-35 (LS) Diploma; UIll 49-50 (LS). 6: Finnish, Swedish, Danish, Norwegian, Ger, Estonian, Fr. 7: Capt Artillery Finnish Army 31-32, 39-44; Helsinki U Lib 32-45; Dir State Dept of Agric Helsinki U Lib 45-47; Dir info serv State Inst for Tech Research, Helsinki 47-52; Libn catlgr LC 52-58; Asst program dir Nat Sci Found, Wash DC 58-. 8: Several Govt Coms on Libs, Stat mgt & sci & tech info in Finland Scandoc Adv Bd, Wash DC 59-; Mgr Finnish Olympic Canoe Team 48. 9: ALA; SLA; ASIS; Aslib; Ger Doc Soc; FinnishLA, Finnish Doc Soc (founder & sec 47-55); etc. 10: Finlandia Foun; AAAS. 11: Freedom Cross of Finland, 4th & 3rd Class. 12: Ed Finish ed of UDC. 13: Yes. 14: Internat sci & tech info & libnship. 15: 9504 Cable dr, Kensington Md 20795.

OLSRUD, LOIS C. b Havre Mont 21 S 30. 5: Concordia Col 48-52 (Eng) BA; UMinn summers 54, 55, 56, 60; IndU 65-66 (LS) MA. 6: Fr. 7: Eng tchr & libn Princeton High Sch, Princeton Minn 52-54; Libn Havre High Sch, Havre Mont 54-57; Libn West Jr High, Great Falls Mont 57-65; Ref libn UAriz 66-. 9: ALA; ArizStateLA. 10: Delta Kappa Gamma. 14: Ref. 15: 718 N Palo Verde, Tucson Az 85716.

OLSTEAD, PATRICIA (MAUREEN) B(RADY). b Brooklyn NY 7 S 23. 4: William J Olstead. 5: Trinity Col Wash DC 45 (Eng, Hist) AB; Simmons 48 BS in LS. 6: Fr, Sp, Ger. 7: Br asst Cambridge Pub Lib, Cambridge Mass 46-47; Catlgr Dartmouth Col Lib 48-51; Catlgr Peabody Mus Lib Harvard U 51-52; Catlgr Newton Free Lib, Newton Mass 52-53; Libn Millis Pub Lib, Millis Mass 57-61; Catlgr USA Natick Labs Tech Lib, Natick Mass 61-. 8: Consul, Millis Pub Lib 61-. 9: SLA; NELA. 14: Catlg. 15: 244 Exchange st, Millis Ma 02054.

OLTMAN, FLORINE (ALMA). b Flatonia Tex 13 N 15. 5: Southwest Tex State Tchrs Col 34-37 (Eng) BA; UDenver summers 40-42 BS in LS. 6: Sp. 7: High sch libn Eagle Lake Tex, Weslaco Tex, Pt Neches Tex 37-43; Ref libn US Naval Air Train Sta, Pensacola Fla 43-44; Libn US Naval Hosp Lib, Pensacola Fla 44-46; Catlgr Air U Lib, Maxwell AFB Ala 46-47; Libn Spec Staff Sch Air U Lib Br, Selma Ala 47-50; Air U Lib, Maxwell AFB Ala: Bibliog asst 50-55, Libn Air War Col Br 55-58, Chief Bibliog Br 58-. 8: Consul, Armed Forces Sch, Air Force of Venezuela & USAF Mission to the Sch, Caracas Venezuela, Nov 60. 9: SLA (2nd v-pres & chm of adv coun; Chap Liaison Off, Div Liaison Off; chm Mil Div; pres Ala Chap; pres-elect 69-70); AlaLA (sec). 10: AAUW; Knife & Fork Club; Partners for Alliance, Ala. 13: Yes. 14: Ref, bibliog. 15: 219 E Riding rd, Montgomery Al 36111.

OLUND, LENNART ERIK. b Chicago 1 Je 30. 4: Patricia Johnson. 5: N Park Jr Col 50-52 (Liberal Arts) AA; Augustana Col 52-54 (Psych) AB; Ill Tchrs Col 60-65 (Educ, LS) M Ed; Chicago 60-61 (Educ); No Ill U 67. 6: Swedish. 7: Chaplains asst US Army, Korea 55-57; Bldg real estate & insurance bus, Chicago 57-69 Tchr Canterbury Jr High Sch, Markham Ill 60-64, Libn 64-65; Libn Bloom Community Col 65-67; Supv instrl materials Off of Supt of Pub Instr, Ill 67-. 8: Lib Coord & consul, Dist 144, Cook Co (Ill) summer 65; Lib eval N Central Accred Assn 69. 9: NEA; ALA-ACRL; -AASchL; Chicago Rep Recr Netwk 63-67); IllEA. 10: Christian Bus Mens Com, Internat; Christian Bus Men of Evergreen Park Ill; Rotary Club; YMCA; Commun Chest Coun. 14: Admin, lib educ, ref. 15: 2851 W 101st st, Evergreen Park Ill 60642.

OLYNYK, NADIA M. b Sokal Ukraine 2 Ja 26. 4: Roman Olynyk. 5: Ukrainian Free U (Munich) 45-48 (Slavic Lang & Lit) BA; UMontreal 63-64 (Slavic Lits) MA; McGill 64-65 BLS. 6: Ger, Polish, Russian, Ukrainian. 7: Tr Canadian Scene, Toronto 55-65; Catlgr II McGill U Lib 65-. 14: Catlg. 15: 5245 St Ignatius ave, Montreal 265 Can.

OMELUSIK, NICHOLAS EDWARD. b Creston BC 1 Mr 40. 4: Judith Russell. 5: UBC 58-64 (Intl Studies) BA, 65-66 BLS. 6: Fr, Russian. 7: Acquis libn UBC Lib 66-67, Hd acquis div 67-. 9: ALA; CanLA; BCLA (treas 68-69). 10: Amer Polit Sci Assn; Can Assn of Univ Tchrs; UBC Alum Assn. 13: Yes. 14: Infor sci, automation. 15: 2236 W 16 ave, Vancouver BC Can.

ON, RUH NAOMI. b NY 12 Ja 38. 5: NY State Col for Tchrs (Buffalo) 55-57 (Elem Educ); UWash 57-59 (Eng, Educ) BA, 59-64 M of Libnship. 7: Jr high sch tchr Highline Sch Dist, Seattle 59-62, Jr high sch ln 62-67; Asst Prof of Lif Sci & educ East Wash State Col 67-69. 9: ALA; NEA; Wash State ASchL; WashEA. 14: Young adults , sch lib admin. 15: W207 Grace, Spok ane W .

ONGARO, MARIO P. b Verona Italy 7 Ap 26. 5: Athenaeum of Ohio 47-52 (Philos) BA; XavierU 59-61 (Educ Psych) MA; UMich 62-64 MALS. 6: Ital, Lat. 7: Latin tchr Sacred heart Novitiate, Monroe Mich 52-56, 62-64, Libn 62-64; Latin tchr Sacred Heart Aem, Cincinnati Ohio 58-61, 65-, Libn 65-. 15: 8108 Beechmont ave, Cincinnati Oh 45230.

ONSI, PATRICIA (WILSON). b Rockford Ill 26 Je 40. 4: Mohamed Onsi. 5: Rockford Col 58-60 (Amer Studies); UIll (Amer Civilization) BA, 62-63 MS in LS. 6: Fr. 7: Hd bus info serv Abbott Labs N Chicago Ill 63-64; Libn II bkmob Fresno Co Pub Lib, Fresno Cal 64-66; Subj analyst SUNY Biomed Communication Network (Syracuse NY) 66-67; Assoc libn for tech serv Upstate Med Ctr Lib Syracuse NY 66-. 8: Shared catlg prog with NLM 68-. 9: MedLA; SUNY Univ Libns. 10: Beta Phi Mu; LWV. 13: Yes. 14: Catlg. 15: 302 Sycamore ter, DeWitt NY 13214.

ONUFROCK, HARRY J. b Chicago Ill 17 N 41. 4: Betty Hamm. 5: Colo Col 59-63 (Sociol, Anthrop) BA; UKy 65-66 MSLS. 7: Clk-libn Shrewsbury Pub Lib, Shrewsbury Mass 63-65; Jr libn Multnomah Co Lib, Portland Ore 67-68; Jr libn MarquetteU Lib 68-. 14: Ref. 15: 2555 N Farwell ave, Milwaukee Wi 53271.

OPEM, JOHN D. b Rochester Minn 23 F 33. 4: Joyce Stefan. 5: St Olaf Col 51-55 (Chem) BA; Chicago 62-64 (LS). 6: Ger, Fr. 7: Analytical chem Swift & Co R&D Center, Chicago 55-56; Spec 4/c US Army Vet Food Inspection Serv 56-58; Research chem Swift & Co R&D Center, Chicago 58-62; Lit chem Swift & Co Research Lib, Chicago 62-65; Head libn Sci Info Serv Abbott Labs, N Chicago 65-. 9: ACS; ALA; ASIS; SLA. 13: Yes. 14: Ref. admin. 15: 1534 Alexander court, Waukegan Il 60085.

OPLINGER, PHOEBE (MARY). b Hickory NC. 5: Maryville Col (Eng) AB; Drexel 58-59 MSLS. 7: Chief engnr libn Douglas Aircraft Co, Charlotte NC 59-61; Head Libn Queens Col (NC) 61-65; Dir of Lib Central Piedmont Community Col 65-. 9: ALA; SLA; SELA; NCLA. 10: Phi Kappa Phi; Beta Phi Mu. 15: 1254 Salem dr, Charlotte NC 28209.

OPPENHEIM, ABRAM. b NYC 23 Ja 17. 4: Frnces Rosenberg. 5: Brooklyn Col 33-36 (Eng) BA; Columbia 37-39 BS in LS, 46-50 (Eng) MA; Claremont Grad Sch 51-56 (Behavioral Sci). 6: Fr, Ger, Yiddish. 7: BD&M Watch Case Mfgrs, NYC 31-36; Lincoln Road Jewelers, Miami Fla 36-37; Pioneer Watch-Case Co, Mt Vernon NY 37-40; (Sgt) Infantry 45th Div, Europe, CBI spec assign 42-45; Ref & high sch depts Mt Vernon Pub Lib, Mt Vernon NY 40-50; Ref dept Brooklyn Pub Lib 50-51; Libn Cal Inst for Men, Chino Cal 51-. 9: CalLA (pres Institut Libns). 10: PTA. 13: Yes. 14: Adult educ, ref, compar lit, group wk, pub rel. 15: 1812 N Palomares, Pomona Ca 91766.

OPPENHEIM, MICHA FALK. b Hamburg Germany 7 Ap 37. 4: Doris Sanders. 5: Yeshiva U 54-59 (Sociol) BA; Columbia 59-61 (LS) MS. 6: Hebrew, Ger. 7: Asst libn Congregation Shearith Israel, NYC 59-60; Catlg libn Brooklyn Col 61-63; Libn Nat Conf of Christians & Jews, NYC 63-65; Instr NYC Commun Col 65-66; Judaica catlgr Jewish Theol Sem, NYC 66-. 8: Comp: "Author & Subject Index to "Jewish Life, 1946-1960; "Special List of Subject Headings Used in "Jewish Life Index, 60-63. 9: ALA; JewishLA. 10: Jewish Publ Soc; YMCA & YWCA. 12: Comp of 7 bklists on human rel issued by NCCJ (63-65); "Jewish Life Index 46-65 (68). 14: Ref, bibliog, catlg, indexing. 15: 951 - 56th st, Brooklyn NY 11219.

OPPENHEIMER, ELSBETH. b Stuttgart Germany. 5: Us of Berlin, Hamburg & Tuebingen; UBerlin Lib Diploma; Columbia (LS) BS. 6: Ger, Fr. 7: Lib asst Brooklyn Pub Lib 43-45; Lib asst Queens Col Lib (NY) 47-53; Assoc libn Manhattan Sch of Music 62-. 10: Com of Friends of the Manhattan Sch of Music; Lib Com, Manhattan Sch of Music; Bd of Trustees & Mgt Com, NJ Fellowship for the Aged. 15: 45 E End ave, New York NY 10028.

OPPENHEIMER, GERALD J(ULIUS). b Frankfurt/M Germany 8 My 22. 4 Mildred Karnofsky. 5: Whitman Col 41-43; UWash 45-47 (Foreign Lang, Philos) BA, MA; Harvard 47-51 (Philos); Columbia 52-53 (LS) MS. 6: Ger, Fr, Sp. 7: Jr libn Seattle Pub Lib 53-55; Libn Fisheries-Oceanography Lib UWash 55-60; Manager Infor Serv Boeing Sci Research Lab, Seattle 60-63; Head Libn Health Sci Lib UWash 63-68; Asst dir of libs for Health Scis 68-; Dir Pacific NW Reg Health Scis Lib 68-. 9: SLA; MedLA; ;ASIS; Wash State LA. 10: Assn for Symbolic Logic; ACLU; Phi Beta Kappa. 12: Ed "Regional Medical Library Service in the Pacific Northwest" (67). 13: Yes. 14: Admin. 15: Health Scis Lib Univ of Wash, Seattle Wa 98105.

OPPENHEIMER, MARIANNE AULER (MRS). b Hamburg Germany 8 Je 08. 5: Central Mich U 52-55 (Fr, Ger) BA Secondary Tchg Certif; Drexel 62-63 MSLS. 6: Ger, Fr, Dutch. 7: Sec Amer Friends Serv Com, Phila 55-62; Temp catlgr United Gas Improvement Co, Phila 63; Circ libn & ref asst Beaver Col 63-67; Med libn Northeastern Hosp of Phila 68-. 9: ALA; PennLA; MedLA. 10: AAUP; Phi Beta Mu. 14: Ref, rare bks, for langs. 15: 441 W Carpenter lane, Phila Pa 19119.

OPPENNEER, BERNARD L(EE). b Grand Rapids Mich 5 D 8. 5: West Mich U 48-52 (Eng) BA; UMich 57, 60 MALS. 7: Radioman US Army, Pacific Area 46-48; Qtrmstr Corp US Army, European Area 52-54; Circ asst Kalamazoo Pub Lib 54-56, Bkmob dept head 56-57; Head Libn Reddicks Lib, Ottawa Ill 58-66; Dir Grand Traverse Area Lib Federation & Traverse City Pub Lib, Traverse City Mich 66-. 9: ALA; IllLA (chm Publ & Pub Rel Com 63-65, chm Constit Rev Com 62-63); Lib Adminrs Com of No Ill (pres 60); MichLA. 10: Red Cross; C of C; Kiwanis Club; Traverse City Arts Coun; Bd of Commun Concerts. 11: Distinguished Serv to the Commun Award, Jr C of C, 65. 12: Ed IllLA newsletter "ILA Reporter 64-65. 14: Admin. 15: 516 Washington, Traverse City Mi 49684.

OPPMANN, LYDIA (BRUNER). b Cleveland Ohio 12 D 44. 4: Paul Henry Oppmann Jr. 5: Smith 62-66 (Art Hist) BA; Case West Res 66-67 MSLS. 6: Fr, Ital, Sp. 7: Asst libn Rotch Lib of Arch & Planning MIT 67-. 10: Jr League. 14: Ref (art hist). 15: 13515 Shaker blvd, Cleveland Oh 44120.

ORAM, ROBERT WILLIAM. b Warsaw Ind 11 Je 22. 4: Virginia White. 5: UToledo 46-49 (Eng) BA; UIll 49-50 MS in LS; UMo 51-52 (Eng). 7: US Army, US, Europe 42-46; UMo: Bibliog 50-51, Head acquis dept 51-52, Head circ dept 52-53, Asst to U libn 53-56; Circ libn UIll(Ubana) 56-64, Circ libn & asst dir for pub serv 64-. 9: ALA-ACRL; IllLA (chm Intell Freedom Com, dir Trustees Assn); MoLA. 10: Beta Phi Mu; AAUP; Bd of Dirs Urbana Free Lib. 13: Yes. 14: Admin, trustee duties. 15: Univ of Ill Lib, Urbana Ill.

ORCUTT, ROBERTA (KIEFER). b Los Angeles Cal 29 Jl 29. 4: Richard G Orcutt. 5: UCLA 47-50 (Pre-libnship) AB; UCal (Berkeley) 50-51 BLS. 6: Sp. 7: Page LA Pub Lib 46; Clk Gen Petroleum Corp, LA 50; Jr libn Cal State Dept of Pub Health Lib, San francisco 51; Libn GS-5 US Dept of Agric Lib, Wash DC 52-53; Libn I Phys Sci Libs UCal (Berkeley) 53-55; Asst libn acquis dept UFla Lib 67-68; Asst ref libn UNev Lib 68-. 9: ALA. 10: Phi Beta Kappa. 14: Ref, automation. 15: 985 Munley dr, Reno Nv 89503.

ORENCHUK, VOLODYMYR. b Ukraine 24 O 13. 4: Yaroslava Pylypiw. 5: State U (Lviv) 33-34, 37-38 (Law) Magister Iuris; Ukrainian Free U 47-49 (Law) Dr Jur; Rosary Col 56-57 (LS) MS. 6: Ukrainian, Ger, Polish, Russian. 7: Attorney at Law, Ukraine 38-43; Interpreter, Germany 45-49; Various jobs, US 49-57; Ref libn City Hall, Chicago 57-58; Head catlgr & Lecturer USanta Clara 58-. 13: Yes. 15: 2122 Laurelei ave, San Jose Ca 95128.

ORGAIN, MARIAN (MACKEY). b San Saba Tex. 4: Henry Kellogg Orgain. 5: Mary Hardin-Baylor 35-36; Tex Christian U 36-39 (Eng, Hist) BA; Columbia 46-47 (LS) BLS; UHouston 60-65 (Eng), MA. 6: Fr, Lat. 7: Stud asst Columbia U Lib 46-47; Readers adv White Plains Pub Lib, White Plains NY 47-48; Depot libn US Army, Tokyo 48-50, Hq & Sv Gp Staff libn 50-52; For langs libn Nat Taiwan U 54-57; Ref libn Lee Col 58-60; Houston Chronicle Lib 60-67, Curator Spec collections UHouston 67-. 8: John Cotton Dana Lectr Atlanta U 67. 9: SLA (Newspaper Lib Div; chm 65-66, sec 63-64; Tex Chap; 2nd v-pres 61-62, sec 64-65, 1st v-pres 66-67, pres 67-68); TexLA (chm Dist 64); Houston Lib Club. 10: Texas Bill of Rights Found. 13: Yes. 14: Newspapers, rare bks. 15: Univ of Houston Univ Libs Special Collections Cullen blvd, Houston Tx 77002.

ORGREN, CARL FRANZ. b Saginaw Mich 5 Mr 37. 4: Bonnie Nelson. 5: UDetroit 55-59 (Eng) PhB; UMich 59-62 MALS; UDetroit 61-66 (Eng) MA; UMich 67- (LS). 6: Fr, Ger. 7: Pre-prof adult asst Detroit Pub Lib 59-60; Dir of circ dept UDetroit Lib 60-61, Ref asst 61-62, Head ref dept 62-66; Asst Prof Lib Sci Wayne State U 66-67; USOE Fellow (title 26 Higher Educ act 65) UMich 67-. 8: Visiting lecturer, Lib Sci, Wayne State U, fall 65; Bibliog demonstr Proj of Basic Communication & Computation Skills for Functionally Illit or Illit Adults, UDetroit, summer 65; Adv US Govt docs Henry Ford Commun Col 63-67. 9: ALA; CathLA. 13: Yes. 14: Ref (col & unv libs), lib educ. 15: 16811 Stoepel, Detroit Mi 48221.

ORMS, BETTY JANE. b Johnstown Penn 9 Jl 21. 5: Ind State U 40-44 (Art Educ) BA; Penn state U 49-52 (Art Educ) MEd; UPittsburgh 62-65 MLS. 7: Supv of art Ferndale Sch Dist, Johnstown Penn 44-53; Art tchr Greater Johnstown Sch Dist, Johnstown Penn 53-67, Jr high libn 67-. 8: Part-tome spec catlgr, Cambria Dist Lib, Johnstown Penn 65-67. 9: ALA; Nat art Educ Assn; PennLA; Eastern Arts Assn. 10: Associated Artists of pittsburgh; Delta Kappa Gamma; Allied Artists of Johnstown. 14: Catlg, art bks. 15: 1096 Edson ave, Johnstown Pa 15905.

ORNE, JERROLD. b St Paul 25 Mr 11. 4: Catherine Lamont Bowen. 5: UMinn 28-32 (Fr) BA, 32-33 (Fr) MA; UParis 34-35 (Fr) Certif & diplome; Chicago 36-39 (Linguistics) PhD; UMinn 39-40 (LS) BS. 6: Fr, Sp, Ital, Ger. 7:page & clerk St Paul Pub Lib 28-36; Fellow in Lib Sci LC 40-41; Libn & Prof Knox Col 41-43; US Naval Res Yoeman 3/, US Bases 43-46; Dir of Libs Washington U (St Louis) 46-51; Dir of Libs Air U, Maxwell AFB Ala 51-57; U Libn UNC(Chapel Hill) 57-. 8: Lang examiner, UChicago 37-39; Fellow, LC 40-41, Hon 41-50; Libn UNCIO, San Francisco 45; Consul; LC 42, 50; Com Dept 47; CIA 56; NASA 62-68; US Del to Iso/Tech Com 37, Berlin 60; Iso/Tech Com 46, Paris 62, Brussels 63, Budapest 64, Moscow 66, Stockholm 69; Amer Spec Grant to Vietnam for State Dept, 65. 9: ALA; SLA (Dir 55-57); Pres ALA Chap 53-55; ASA Z39 (chm 65-); ASIS (treas 53-54); USBE (Bd 60-, Pres 62-64); ASERL (chm 62-64); NCLA; AlaLA (pres 57). 10: Rotary Club; AAUP. 11: Dept of the Air Force Commendation for Meritorious Civilian Service. 12: Comp "Subject Heading List for Naval Research Libraries (46); "Subject Headings for Technical Libraries (47); "Language of the Foreign Book Trade ALA (49, 2d ed 64); Ed MoLA "Quarterl (47-51); Assoc ed "American Documentation (54-57); Consul ed "Library Journal (62-63); Ed "SE Librarian (66-). 13: Yes. 14: Admin, standards, langs. lib bldgs. 15: 529 Dogwood dr, Chapel Hill NC 27514.

ORNEE, NELL (VAN ZANDT). b Ft Worth Tex 22 F 20. 5: Tex Christian U 37-40 (Bus Admin) BS; N Tex State Tchrs Col 40-41 BS in LS; UMich 49, 50 MA in LS. 6: Sp, Fr, Ger. 7: Head catlgr Tex Christ U 41-51; Ref libn bus & tech Grand Rapids Pub Lib, Grand Rapids Mich 51-53, Head Readers Adv 53-54; Head ref libn Calvin Col & Sem 55-57; Head loan libn Tex Christian U 57-61, Act head libn 61-63; Head libn Tex Wesleyan Col 63-. 9: ALA; TexLA. 14: Admin, ref. 15: 3237 Preston Hollow rd, Ft Worth Tex 76109.

OROSZ, BARBARA J. b Glendale Cal 5 Ag 39. 5: Immaculate Heart Col 57-61 (Chem) BS & BA; USoCal 62-67 (LS) MS. 7: Asst res chem Lib Union Oil Co Research, Brea Cal 61-64, Head Libn 64-. 9: SLA; ASIS; Geosci Info Soc. 10: Iota Sigma Pi; Delta Epsilon Sigma. 14: Tech lib serv. 15: P O Box 76, Brea Cal 92621.

ORPWOOD, JEAN (DOROTHY). b Toronto Can. 5: Toronto ext 55-62 (Econ, Pol Sci) BA, 62-63 BLS. 7: Sec & asst Wheeler Newspaper Syndicate, Toronto 44-50; Sec Consolidated Press, Toronto 50-51; Imperial Oil Ltd, Toronto: Distribution asst 51-54, Graphics asst 55-62, Libn 63-67; Libn info off Indian-Eskimo Assn of Can, Toronto Can 67-68; Coord info serv, Etobicoke Pub Lib 68-. 9: ALA; Inst Prof Libns Ont; OntLA; CanLA (pres-elect Toronto Chap 69-70); SLA. 14: Ref. 15: 121 Ferrier ave, Toronto 6 Can.

ORR, ADRIANA PANNEVIS. b Albertson LI NY 30 S 23. 4: Oliver H ORR Jr. 5: Elmira Col 40-44 (Eng, Lat) AB; Harvard summer 51; UNC 53-58 MS in LS; UMd 67-68. 7: Eng tchr Wisner High Sch, Wisner Neb 44-45; Eng tchr Downsville Central Sch, Downsville NY 45-48; Eng tchr libn Lago Community Sch, Aruba Netherlands West Indies 48-53; Ref asst UNC Lib (Chapel Hill) 53-58; Lat tchr Raleigh City Schs, Raleigh NC; Libn Sch of Textiles Lib, NC State U (Raleigh) 59-65; Ref libn FAA Lib, Wash DC 68-69; Ref libn Bur of Pub Roads, Wash DC 69-. 9: SLA; ASIS; NCLA. 12: Ed "North Carolina Libraries (63-65). 14: Ref. 15: 529 Seventh st SE, Wash DC 20003.

ORR, JOELLA ALLEN. b Justin Tex 6 S 27. 4: Harold A Orr. 5: Tex Womans U 60 (LS) BS, 64 MLS, NTSU 68. 6: Sp. 7: Libn Lewisville Pub Sch, Lewisville Tex 60-; TWU Main Lib 67; Denton Pub Lib 68. 9: TexLA; Tex State Tchrs Assn; TexASchL; ALA. 10: AAUW; Altrusa; DAR. 14: Child libn, catlgr. 15: 1509 Kendolph, Denton Tex.

ORR, LOUISE. b Sarnia Ont Can 15 My 42. 5: Marianopolis Col 59-63 (Chem) BS; McGill 63-64 BLS. 6: Fr. 7: Asst libn Alcan Aluminium Ltd Lib, Montreal 64-, Archivist 67-. 9: SLA (Montreal Chap: chm Educ Com). 14: Ref, syst analysis. 15: 11795 Frigon st, Montreal 356 Can.

ORR, MARGARET H. b Columbus Junction Iowa 9 Ja 26. 5: Monmouth Col (Monmouth Ill) 43-47 (Eng) BA; UWis 47-48 BS in LS. 7: Bkmob libn New Castle-Henry Co Lib, New Castle Ind 48-53; Br libn La Crosse Pub Lib, La Crosse Wis 53-59; Order libn Iowa State U Lib (Ames) 59-60, Hd order dept 60-. 9: ALA; IowaLA. 10: Beta Phi Mu; Altrusa Club. 14: Acquis. 15: 316 11th st, Ames Ia 50010.

ORR, SISTER MARY MARK. b Beattie Kan 1 Mr 1900. 5: UKan 28 (Eng) AB, 31 (Eng) AM; UIll 33 BS in LS; U Nacional de Mex summer 44 (Span Amer Culture); Truman Lib, Kansas City Mo 59 (Archival Mgt). 6: Fr, Sp, Lat. 7: Tchr & prin elem schs, Beattie & Home Kan 18-24; Eng tchr Annunciation High Sch, Denver 28-40 Eng tchr Immaculata High Sch, Leavenworth Kan 30-32; Ref libn St Mary Col (Xavier Kan) 33-36, Head Libn 36-. 8: Head of Dept of Libnship, 50-. 9: ALA; CathLA (Midwest Unit: chm 4 terms,mem Exec Bd); Nat Coun Family Rel; Cath Biblical Assn; KanLA; Kan State Hist Soc. 10: Metro Opera Guild. 12: Ed & publ Fitzgeralds "Beacon on the Plains (39). 13: Yes. 14: Bk sel, ref, rare bks. The Bible, lib educ, Mexican culture, early Americana. 15: St Mary Col Lib, Xavier Kan 66098.

ORR, MARYDE FAHEY. b Walla Walla Wash 30 Ja 25. 5: Whitman Col 42-46 (Chem) BA; UWash 52-53 (LS) ML; UNeb 53-55. 7: Instr UNeb 53-55; Ref pec Gen Electric Co, Richland Wash55-63; Manager Whitney Lib Gen Electric Co, Schenectady NY 63-. 8: Lecturer: UWash Center for Grad Study, Richland; UWash Grad Sch of Libnship, 61-63; Instr SUNY(Albany), 63-65. 9: SLA; ACS; ASIS; Amer Soc Metals; Hudson-Mohawk (NY) LA. 10: AAAS; AAUW; Amer Mus of Nat Hist; Nat Wildlife Fed; Tri-City Folk Dancers. 14: Sci & tech info storage & retrieval. 15: 906 Bedford rd apt 8, Schenectady NY 12308.

ORR, RICHELIEU. b Pennington Gap Va 6 D 26. 5: Col of William & Mary 44-48 (LS) AB; Peabody 50-51 (LS) MA. 7: Asst libn Washington Col (Md) 48-50; Circ libn LSU 51-52; Asst libn Westmar Col 53-55; Asst libn Ark Polytech Col 55-57; Libn Alameda Co Lib, Fremont Cal 57-61; Catlgr Va Polytech Inst 61-65, Hd doc dept 65-. 9: VaLA; SELA. 14: Catlg. 15: 215 Penn st, Blacksburg Va 24060.

ORR, ROBERT McDANIEL. b Springfield Ill 21 Ag 13. 4: Edith Smith. 5: UIll 36 (Econ) BA, 37 BSLS. 7: Jr asst Detroit Pub Lib 37-39; Asst ext libn Springfield (Ill) Pub Lib 39-40; Reg lib dir WPA, E St Louis Ill 40-41; USAAF 41-45; Reg Dir Ill State Lib 45-47; Br co libn, Coldwater Mich 47-49; Dir, Pub Libs, Grosse Pointe Pub Lib, Grosse Pointe Mich 49-. 8: Pub lib Surveys W Bloomfield, Greenville, Wyoming, Sturgis, Grand Haven, Mt Clemens & Alpena Mich. 9: ALA (Coun 52-55 & 66-69 chm Friends of Libs Com 63-66 MichLA (past pres, chm Friends Com 60-63). 10: Grosse Pointe Rotary Club; Grosse Pointe Symphony Soc Bd; Boy Scouts & Indian Guides; Episcoal Lay Reader; Torch Club; Bk Club of Detroit. 13: Yes. 14: Admin, pub lib surveys, pub lib bldgs, Friends of Lib groups. 15: 16929 Village lane, Grosse Pointe Mi 48230.

ORR, ROBERT STEVENSON. b Mercer Penn 2 Jl 18. 5: Grove City Col 36-40 (Eng) AB; West Res 58-59 MSLS. 7: US Naval Res 43-46; Staff asst in purchasing Catalytic Construction Co, Phila 46-50; Materials expediter Westinghouse Electric Corp, Pittsburgh 51-55; Off manager Cleveland sales off Yale & TowneMFG Co, Phila 55-58; Ref libn Free Lib of Phila Mercantile Br 59; Commercial research libnJones & Laughlin Steel Corp, Pittsburgh 60-. 9: SLA. 10: SAR; Scenic Hudson Preserv Conf; Mt Lebanon (Penn) Tennis Assn. 14: Ref. 15: Jones & Laughlin Steel Corp 3 Gateway center, Pittsburgh Pa 15230.

ORR, ROBERT WILLIAM. b Winterset Iowa 9 Je 5. 4: Elizabeth Strohbehn. 5: Iowa State Col 26-30 (Chem Tech) BS; Columbia 38-39 (LS) MS. 7: Iowa State U; Instr & order libn 30-31, Instr & asst in Loan Dept 31-33, Instr & asst ref libn 33-35, Instr & ref libn 35-41, Asst prof & asst libn in chg of pub serv 41-43, Asst prof & asst libn 43-44, Assoc prof & assoc libn 44-46, prof & dir of lib 46-67, Prof Lib Sci 67-. 9: ALA-ACRL (pres 56-57); IowaLA (pres 47-48). 10: Phi Lambda Upsilon; Alpha Chi Sigma; Gamma Sigma Delta. 12: "A Report of a Survey of the Libraries of the Alabama Polytechnic Institute, with L R Wilson (49); "A Report of a Survey of the Lirary of Texas A and M College, with W H Carlson (50); Tuskegee Institute Self-Study; Library Consultans Report (56); "Report of a Survey of the Library of the Michigan College of Mining and Technology, with M J Voigt (60); "Library Instruction Manual, with M H Easton (6th ed rev63); "Iowa State College Centennial. Final Report (58); "The Library at Iowa State 46-68. 13: Yes. 14: Admin. 15: 919 Beach ave, Ames Ia 50010.

ORREN, LAURETTA MARIE FILIATRAULT. b Duluth Minn 17 N 05. 4: Eugene S Orren. 5: Col of St Catherine 23-27 BA (Hist), BM (Music); UMinn 32-33 BLS. 6: Fr. 7: Duluth Pub Lib, Duluth Minn: Jr lib asst 8-37, Head co lib serv 37-55, Head co & city ext serv 55-. 8: Inaugurated Co Lib Serv in So St Louis Co & Bkmob serv in Duluth (Minn). 9: MinnLA. 10: US Power Squadron; Minn Horticul Soc; Womens Assn; Duluth Symphony Orchestra; Duluth Garden Club. 14: Ext, ref. 15: 3205 Minnesta ave, Duluth Minn 55802.

ORTH, REV RAYMOND EDWARD. b Grosse Pointe Farms Mich 23 F 35. 4: Mae Ann Elg Orth. 5: Capital U 53-57 (Hist) BA; Evangelical Lutheran Theol Sem 57-61 (Exegetical Theol); UMich 61-62 AMLS; Bowling Green State U 68 (Ger). 06: Ger, Gk. 7: Asst Pastor Solomon Luth Church, Woodville Ohio 62-. 8: Oversight of the educ program of the congregation. 9: ALA; ATheolLA; Amer Luth Educ Assn. 10: Ohio Hist Assn; Sandusky Co Hist Soc; Lutheran Soc Serv of NWest Ohio. 12: "Lutheran Standard Index 1842-1848" (61); Co-ed & tr "Introits and Collects for the Sundays and Festivals of the Church Year" (unpublished). 14: Archival wk, ref, Lutheran publs. 15: 401 W Main st, Woodville Ohio 43469.

ORTIZ DE MATOS, MARIA C. b Aibonito PR 3 My 32. 4: Antonio Matos. 5: UPR 51-55 (Home Econ) BAED; UMich 58-59 MALS. 6: Sp. 7: UPR: Libn ext div 55-60, Catlgr Gen Lib 60-61, Ser catlgr Gen Lib 61-65, Libn Grad Sch of Planning 65-66; Coord ref serv & dir tech proc 66-67; Coord ref serv & dir tech proc Arecibo Reg Col, PR 67-; Instr lib sci UPR 65-. 8: Instr. lib sci UPR 65-. 9: ALA; Sociedad de Bibliotecarios de Puerto Rico (pres 64-65). 10: Asociacion de Maestros de Puerto Rico. 14: Catlg, admin, ref. 15: Univ of Puerto Rico Arecibo Regional Col, Arecibo Puerto Rico 00612.

ORTIZ, ONEIDA (RIVERA) DE. b Santirce PR 12 O 26. 4: Felix Luis Ortiz Cintron. 5: UPR 45-49 (Humanities) BA; Drexel 66 MSLS. 6: Sp. 7: Libn UPR ext dept; Libn Dept Educ, PR; Tchr PR High Sch, Rio Piedras; Tchr Mayaguez Voc Sch; Hd contact serv upr mayaguez Campus Lib 60-66, Libn In charge period sect 66. 9: ALA; Sociedad de bibliotecarios de Puerto Rico. 10: Asociacion de Graduadas de UPR; Altrusa; Cath Daughters of Amer; Garden Club; Damas ABX; Engr's Wife Club; Drexel Alumni. 14: Admin ser. 15: College Station, Mayaguez PR 00708.

ORTON, FLOYD E(MORY). b Minn 16 Jl 10. 4: Ora Mae Goldsworthy. 5: Hamline U 36 (Chem) BS; UMinn 37 (LS) Cert 9chem) BS; UMinn 37 (LS) Certif; UMich 40 AMLS. 7: Hd delivery serv John Crerar Lib, chicago 37-38; Physics libn UMich (Ann Arbor) 38-40; Libn & instr East Ore Col 40-42; Asst to hd bk dept St Paul Bk & Stationery 42-43; Chem Minn Mining & Mfg Co, St Paul 43-45; Chem & lib consul Archer Daniels Midland Co, Minneapolis 45-46; Dir Boston U 46-51; Sci libn Wash State U 51-. 8: Lib cons to Engring Sch, Cath U of Chile in Santiago 65-66 (UCal (Berkeley) Ford Found Proj). 9: SLA. 10: AAAS. 13: Yes. 14: Catlg, clsf, ref. 15: 1906 1/2 Monroe st, Pullman Wa 99163.

ORTOPAN, LeROY DONALD. b Kenmore Ohio 1 O 25. 5: UAkron 43-49 (Humanities) BA; West Res 49-50 (Eng) MA, 51-52 MS in LS. 6: Fr, Ger, Ital, Russian. 7: Aviation radioman 3/c US Navy 44-46; Catlg libn Grace A Dow Mem Lib, Midland Mich 52-56; Catlg libn Pontiac City Lib, Pontiac Mich 56-57; Head of the catlg dept Northwestern U Lib 57-65; Chief of catlgMem Lib UWis 65-. 9: ALA; Chicago Reg Group Libns Tech Serv (past pres). 14: Tech serv, photoduplication, binding prep, computer applications to lib wk. 15: Univ of Wis Lib, Madison Wis 53706.

ORTYNSKY, VERA (BEZSONIW). b Kiev Ukraine 15 Ag 18. 4: Nicholas Ortynsky. 5: Friedrich-WilhelmsU (Breslau Germany) 40-44 (Dentistry) DDS; Rutgers 62-64 MLS; Columbia 64 (Med Lit). 6: Ukranian, Russian, Polish, Ger. 7: Ref libn ColumbiaU Med Lib 64-. 9: MedLA; UlranianLA. 14: Ref. 15: Col of Physicians & Surgeons Columbia Univ Med Lib 630 W 168th st, New York NY 10032.

ORWIG, MARY H (WOOLHANDLER). b Buffalo NY 10 Ja 11. 4: Edwin Orwg. 5: St Mary of the Springs Col 58-60 (LS). 6: Ger. 7: Engnr clerk Spencer Lens Co, Buffalo NY 39-42; Ind Planner Curtiss Wright Corp, Buffalo NY 42-45; Steno-clerk Howe Scale Co, Buffalo NY 46-50; Sec Transportation Consul "Piper", Buffalo NY 52-54; N Amer Aviation Inc, Columbus Ohio; Steno-sec 55, Libn in Engnr 55-64; Lib asst Engnr Tech Lib 64-68. 9: SLA (Memb Com); OhioLA. 10: Voyagers Club. 14: Catlg, ref. 15: 1048 Bertram ave, Dayton Oh 45406.

OSBORN, ANDREW DELBRIDGE. b Launceston Tasmania Australia 14 Je 02. 4: Beatrice Waite. 5: Melbourne U -25 (Psych, Philos) AB, AM; Columbia -34 (Philos) PhD; UMich -35 AMLS. 6: Ger, Fr. 7: Sr catlgr Commonwealth Parliament Lib, Australia 20-27; Gen asst NY Pub Lib 28-38; Dir USoCal Lib Sch 35-36; Asst prof UMich Lib Sch 37-38; Visiting prof Columbia U Sch of Lib Serv summer 40-43, 58; Chief of processing UN Lib 49-50; Assoc libn Harvard U 38-58; Dir of the Lib USydney Sydney NSW Australia 58-62; Prof of Lib Sci Grad Sch of Lib & Info Sci UPittsburgh 62-66; Dean Sch of Lib & Info Sci U West Ont 66-. 8: Lib Surveys Harvard Bus Sch Lib 39 with C B Joeckel and P N Rice LC 40 with K D Mecalf & others; US Army Med Lib 43 with K D Metcalf; NY State Lib 46 with H M Lydenberg & others; UPenn 48; Buffalo Pub Lib 47; US Dept of State 45 with K D Metcalf; US Dept of Health, Educ & Welfare 53 with K D Metcalf and J D Russell; UIll Lib Sch 43. 9: ALA (Accred Com);-DCC (pres 40-41); New Zealand LA; CanLA; OntLA. 11: Margaret Mann Citation (59). 12: "Crisis in Cataloging" (41); "The Philosophy of Edmund Husserl" (34); "Program of Instruction in Library Schools, with K D Metcalf & J D Russell" (43); Tr "Prussian Instructions" (38); "Descriptive Cataloging" 63; "Languages for Librarians" (64). 13: Yes. 14: Catlg (bk catlgs), tech serv (charging systems). 15: Univ of Western Ontario, London Can.

OSBORN, JOYCELYN (BEGGS). b Dundurum Ireland 28 F 05. 5: Monmouth Col (NJ) 58-61 (Mod Lang) BA; Rutgers 62 MLS. 6: Fr, Ger, Sp. 7: Catlgr Jersey City State Col 62-63; Asst libn Monmouth Col 63-69; Acquis libn Jersey City State Col 69-. 9: ALA; NJLA; (sec tech ser div 68-); Tech Serv Libns. 10: WILPF; Mus of Modern Art; Friends of City Center. 14: Docs, catlg, rare bks, acquis. 15: 3 Slocum pl, Oakhurst NJ 07755.

OSBORN, KATHERINE H(UGHES). b Bellingham Wash 3 Je 06. 5: West Wash State Col 24-26; UWash 26-28 BS in LS; Ore State U 38-39 (Bot) MA. 7: Lib asst Seattle Pub Lib 28-29; Ore State U; Lib asst 28-39, Asst sci libn 39-41, Sci libn 41-63, Sci-tech libn 63-. 9: ALA-ACRL; PNLA; OreLA. 10: AAUP; AAAS. 13: Yes. 14: Ref. 15: 2928 NW Taylor ave, Corvallis Or 97330.

OSBORN, VELVA JEANNE. b Revere Mo 25 Ap 18. 5: Park Col 5-36; Kan State Tchrs Col (Emporia) 36-39 (LS) BS in Ed; Chicago 42-44 (LS) MA; UIll 61-65 (Philos) MA, PhD. 6: Ger, Sp, Fr, Ital. 7: Circ libn Kan City (Kan) Pub Lib 39-42; Catlgr Chicago Tchrs Col 42-45; Catlg & ref libn Columbia U Libs 45-51; Ref libn Midwest Inter-Lib Center, Chicago 51-53; Ref libn UIll at Navy Pier (Chicago) 53-54; Lib Sci Instr West Ill U 54-55; Lib Sci Instr East Ill U 55-56; Head catlg dept West Ill U 56-67; Assoc Prof of Lib Sci NoIllU 67-. 9: ALA; NEA; IllLA. 10: ACLU. 12: "Early Developments in Storage Library Processing (57). 14: Catlg, lib educ. 15: West Ill U Lib, Macomb Ill 61455.

OSBORNE, DONALD ARTHUR. b Summit NJ 2 D 33. 4: Cheryl Rutter. 5: Middlebury 52-56 (Eng) AB; Columbia 57-58 (Eng); UPenn 59-62 (Eng); Drexel 63-64 MSLS. 6: Fr. 7: (1st Lt) USAR Armor 57; Instr Mercersburg Acad 58-59; Asst instr UPenn 59-62; Libn I Free Lib of Phila 64-65; Instr RutgersU 66; Period libn Slippery Rock State Col 66-69; Hd bibliog & order sect SUNY (Stony Brook) 69-. 9: ALA. 14: Acquis. 15: 206A Jefferson ave, St James NY 11780.

OSBORNE, FRED YANTIS. b Athens Tex 1 Ja 17. 4: Eloise Lattimore Osborne. 5: Tex Wesleyan Col36-40 (Soc Sci, Educ) AB; So Methodist U 46-47 (Hist) MA; UDenver 8-50 (LS) MA. 7: Tchr Mansfield High Sch, Mansfield Tex 40-42; (Sgt) Finance Div US Air Corps 42-46; Asst Prof Hist Okla City U 47-48; Libn Pub Serv Baylor U 48-51, Act U Libn 51-53; Libn Long Beach City Col 53-59; Libn Cabrillo Col 59-. 8: Lib bldg consul, Long Beach City Col & at Cabrillo Col, Aptos Cal; Indexing wks of Joseph Wood Krutch. 9: CalLA (pres Jr Col Libs Round Table 65); Cal Tchrs Assn; CalASchL. 10: Phi Alpha Theta, UCSC Friends of the Lib. 13: Yes. 15: Cabrillo Col 6500 Soquel dr, Aptos Cal 95003.

OSBORNE, MAURICE GRIFFITH. b Richmond Va 15 My 12. 5: UCLA 29-30; Reedley Col 51-53; UNev 58-63 (Hist) BA; UCal(Berkeley) 63-64 MLS. 6: Fr, Sp. 7: Lib asst Fresno Co (Cal) Lib Reedley Br 53; Circ libn Washoe Co Lib, Reno Nev 55-58; Lib asst UNev Life Sci Br 60-63; Life sci libn UNev Lib 64-; Life Sci-Phys Sci Lobn UNeb Lib 67-. 9: ALA. 10: AAUP; Sierra Club; Alliance Francaise; Phi Kappa Phi; Phi Alpha Theta; Beta Phi Mu; Audubon Soc. 15: 955 Skyline blvd, Reno Nev.

OSBORNE, RUTH (WRIGHT). b Avon NY 30 Jl 14. 4: Bradford A Osborne. 5: UVt 32-35 (Pol Sci); Simmons 35-36 BSLS; Columbia 39 Spec Lib Admin), Emory 68 (US Govt Publications). 6: Fr. 7: Asst tech libn tech & bus dept Yonkers Pub Lib, Yonkers NY 36-41; Libn Bethel Park Pub Lib, Bethel Park Penn 55-61; Ref asst Pub Lib of Charlotte & Mecklenburg, Charlotte NC 62-64, Documents libn 64-. 9: ALA; NCLA; NELA; MecklenburgLA. 10: Pi Beta Phi; Trustee, Bethel Park (Penn) Pub Lib. 14: Ref, govt docs. 15: Pub Lib of Charlotte & Mecklenburg County 310 N Tryon st, Charlotte NC 28202.

OSBORNE, SHEILA RUTH (MacLEOD). b Bramshot Surrey Eng 24 Mr 42. 4: Brett Hawley osborne. 5: UToronto 60-64 (Eng) BA; UBC 65-66 BLS. 6: Fr. 7: Lib asst UBC Lib 64-65; Asst child libn pub lib, New Westminster BC 66-. 9: CanLA; BCLA. 15: Public Lib 716 - 6th ave, New Westminster British Columbia Can.

OSBORNE, YOST (NEWELL). b Jewett Ohio 10 N 14. 4: Mary Carson. 5: Mt Union Col 32-36 (Hist) AB; UPittsburgh 37, 38-39 (Hist) Litt M; West Res 39-40 BLS. 6: Fr. 7: Tchr High Sch, Jewett Ohio 36-38; US Army Anti Aircraft (T/5) 43-46; Libn Mt Union Col 40-. 9: ALA-ACRL (pres Tri-State Chap 60-61). 12: "A Select School; the History of Mount Union College, An Account of A Unique Educational Experiment, Scio College (67). 13: Yes. 14: Rare bks. 15: Mt Union Col Lib, Alliance Ohio 44601.

OSBORNE, ZELDA LEIGH. b Tularosa NM 23 My 10. 5: Houston Jr Col 30, 31; UTex 32; Tex Womans U 35-36 (LS) BA; UHouston 40-43 (Foreign Langs) BS; UIll 44-45 MS (6th yr degree). 6: Fr, Sp, Ger. 7: UHouston Lib: Asst libn-order libn & catlgr 36-46, Asst libn-head catlgr 46-49, Head of tech serv 49-63, Asst dir for tech serv 64-67; Asst dir for development of collections 67-. 9: ALA; TexLA; SWLA; Houston Lib Club; Tex Assn Col Tchrs. 10: SALAM; AAUW; AAUP; Mod Lang Assn; Beta Phi Mu. 14 Tech serv. 15: Univ of Houston Libs Cullen blvd, Houston Tx 77004.

OSBURN, CHARLES B(ENJAMIN). b Pittsburgh Penn 25 My 39. 4: Margaret Brimfield. 5: Grove City Col 57-61 (Fr) BA; Penn State 61-63 (Fr) MA; UWis 68 (LS). 6: Fr, sp, Ital, Ger. 7: Tchg asst Penn StateU 61-63, Instr in Fr 63-66; Asst Prof of Fr Wis StateU (Whitewater) 66-69; Humanities bibliogr INC (Chapel Hill) 69-. 9: ALA. 10: Mod Lang Assn; AAUP; Amer Assn Tchrs French. 12: "Research and Reference Guide to French Studies' (68). 13: Yes. 14: Documentation in the humanities. 15: 404 Tinkerbell rd, Chapel Hill NC 27514.

OSBURN, HARRIET S. b Marshall Minn 8 Mr 24. 5: Millersville State Col 41-45 (LS) BS; Columbia 46-49 (Curriculum) (Curriculum) MA; Drexel 53-55 MS in LS. 7: Libn W York (Penn) Pub Sch 45-48; Libn NY Pub Lib 49; Libn Bellport Union Free Sch, Bellport NY 49-52; Libn Alexis I Dupont Jr-Sr High Sch, Wilmington Del 52-55; Libn Amer Educ Publs Middletown Conn 55-60, Head Libn 60-. 9: ALA, SLA. 10: Altrusa; Beta Phi Mu. 14: Ref, admin. 15: 404 Pine st, Middletown Ct 06457.

OSER, ANITA K. b NYC 21 Ja 37. 5: UMiami 55-58 (Sp) AB; Fla StateU 58-59 (LS) MA. 6: Ger. 7: Catlgr UMiami Fla 59-61, Asst circ libn 61-. 9: FlaLA. 10: Phi Kappa phi; Delta Phi Alpha; Alpha Lambda Delta. 14: Circ. 15: 8141 SW 54 ave, Miami Fl 33143.

OSGOOD, JAMES B. b New Castle Penn 6 Ap 32. 5: Chicago 49-52 54 (Liberal Arts) BA; NYU 55-57 (Fr); Carnegie 60-62 MLS. 6: Fr, Sp, Ger, Norwegian. 7: Lib clerk UN Lib, NY 55-60; Readers asst circ Carnegie Lib of Pittsburgh 60-62, Ref asst 62-64; Law circ libn UChicago Law Lib 64-66; Hd libn Southeast Campus Chicago City Col 66-68; Asst libn 68-. 9: ALA; Chicago Assn of Law Libns. 10: ACLU; Com to Abolish Capital Punishment; Sierra Club. 12: Comp "Municipal Information List (62-64). 14: Ref, admin, catlg. 15: 5239 S Kenwood ave, Chicago Il 60615.

OSGOOD, WILLIAM E(DWARD). b Nashua NH 24 Mr 26. 4: Thelma Slabaugh. 5: UNH 47-51 (Eng) BA; Simmons 51-52 (LS) MS. 7: US Army Rifleman (Pfc), Ohio; Co Libn New Philadelphia-Tuscarawas Co Dist Lib 52-53; Ref asst Dartmouth Col Lib 53-55; Adult serv libn Vt Free Pub Lib Serv, Montpelier Vt 55-56; Libn Goddard Col 57-. 8: Vt Governors Adv Panel on Scenery & Historic Sites, 63; Lectr lib sci Tampereen Yliopisto & Svenska social och Kommunal hogskolan, Finland 68-69. 9: VtLA. 10: AAUP; Arctic Inst of North Amer; Vt Acad of Arts & Scis (former Trustee); Fellow Amer Scand Found. 12: "Ski Touring (69). 13: Yes. 14: Admin, lib planning. , info transfer experimentation. 15: Rt 1, Northfield Vt 05663.

OSINSKI, SISTER MARY THOMAS CFM. b Harrison NJ 15 N 22. 5: St Joseph Col (W Hartford Conn) 41-42, 45-48 (Bus, Econ) BS; Central Conn State Col summers 47, 48; Fordham summer 50; Boston Col summers 51-55 (Hist) MA; St Johns U (NY) summers 56-60 MLS. 7: Tchr Mary Immaculate Acad, New Britain Conn 48-, Tchr & libn 56-. 9: ALA; CathLA. 14: Catlg. 15: Mary Immaculate Acad, Osgood ave, New Britain Conn 06053.

OSIS, JANIS ARTURS. b Latvia 1 My 06. 4: Biruta Ziemins. 5: URiga(Latvia) 39 (Classical Langs) MAG PHIL; UMich 56-57 AMLS. 6: Latvian, Ger, Fr, Russian, Lat, Gk. 7: Lat tchr Duke Peter Gymnasium, Jelgava Latvia 30-44; Army of Latvia Infantry (Cpl); Tchg Lat, Ger, Fr DP camp sch, Nuremberg Germany 45-49; Factory wker, Kalamazoo 50-55; Catlgr Capital U 57-. 10: Latvian Assn. 14: Catlg. 15: 994 Euclaire ave, Columbus Ohio 43209.

OSIS, MRS BIRUTA ZIEMINS. b Saratov Russia 30 S 18. 4: Janis Arthur Osis. 5: ULatvia 38-40. 42-44 (Geog) cand rer nat; UHamburg(Germany) 46-49 (Geog) BS; UMich 64-65 AMLS. 6: Ger, Latvian, 7: Bkkeeper First Nat Bank & Trust Co,

Kalamazoo 53-55; Bkkeeper Ann Arbor Bank, Ann Arbor Mich 55-56; Clerk The Fashion Co, Columbus Ohio 60-64; Catlg Ohio State U Lib 65-66; Capital U (Columbus Ohio) 67; Ohio State U Lib 68-. 14: Catlg, ref. 15: 994 Euclaire ave, Columbus Ohio 43209.

OSMA, HELEN (MRS J M). b Mesquite Tex 29 Ja 04. 5: UKan 28 (Fr) AB, 29 (Fr) MA; Emporia State Col 52 (LS) MA. 6: Fr, Sp. 7: Lawrence Pub Lib, Lawrence Kan; Adult serv 52-54, Asst libn 54-58, Head of tech processes 58-. 9: KanLA. 10: LWV; AAUW. 14: Tech proc. 15: 1934 Alabama, Lawrence Kan 66044.

OSMAN, MARY ELLA (WILLIAMS). b Honea Path SC 15 Je 13. 4:John Osman. 5: Presbyterian Col 36-39 (Eng) AB (summa cum laude); UNC 38, 43-44 BS in LS. 6: Fr, Ital. 7: Asst to libn Presbyterian Col (SC) 36-38; Asst libn Union Theol Sem (Richmond Va 38-44; Asst libn Southwestern Col 44-52; Exec asst to pres Fund for Adult Educ (Ford Found), White Plains NY 52-61; Asst libn Amer Inst of Architects, Wash DC 62-. 13: Yes. 14: Catlg, ref. 15: 2500 Que st, NW, Wash DC 20007.

OSSEN, VIRGINIA FRANCES. b Denver 27 Mr 13. 5: Long Beach City Col 32-34 (Hist); UCLA 36-38 (Eng) AB; USoCal 45-46 BS in LS, 46-48 (Comparative Lit) MA; UCal ext 50-54 (Ind Rel) Certif. 7: Libn I USoCal 46-48; Los Angeles Co Lib: Libn I, Los Angeles 48-49, Libn II, Los Angeles 49-53, Reg libn, Bellflower 53-56, Chief central serv libn, Los Angeles 56-64, Chief tech serv libn, Los Angeles 64-. 9: ALA; CalLA; So Cal Tech Proc Gp. 10: Amer-Scand Foun. 14: Admin, acquis, bk sel, catlg. 15: 3724 Brayton ave, Long Beach Cal 90807.

OSTASHEWSKY, ROMAN (JOSAPHAT). b Lviv Ukraine 19 Ap 24. 4: Lillian Makuch. 5: URome (Italy) 45-47 PhB, 47-49 BTh; McGill 62-63 BS in LS; UDenver 67 Diploma in Archives Admin. 6: Eng, Ukrainian, Polish, Russian, Ital, Lat. 7: Catlgr Edmonton Pub Lib, Edmonton Can 61-66; Archivist Prov Archives of Alta Can 66-. 9: AltaLA (Coun); EdmontonLA (pres). 10: Ukrainian Lit & Art Club; Ukrainian-Can Com; Ukrainian Cath Coun of Edmonton Diocese. 14: Catlg, archives admin. 15: 12931-119th ave, Edmonton Alta Can.

OSTEEN, MARTHA (MAE) HUTCHISON. b Charlotte NC 25 O 11. 4: Willis Edwin Osteen. 5: UNC(Greensboro) 28-32 (LS, Sociol)AB; USoCar 54-55, 59-60, 61; Winthrop Col 57. 7: Libn McClenaghan High Sch, Florence SC 51-52, 54-58, 60-. 9: ALA; NEA; SCLA; SCEA. 10: Archibald Rutledge Lit Club; FCEA. 15: 1506 Jackson ave, Florence SC 29501.

OSTEEN, PHYLLIS. b Mansfield Mo 16 Je 04. 5: UArk 22-26 (Lit) AB, 26-27 (Fellow); Columbia 30-32 (LS) BS, 42-47 (Admin) MS. 7: NY Pub Lib: Jr asst 28-29, Sr asst 29-35, Asst br libn 36-43, Br libn 43-47, Personnel asst 48-53; Co Libn Jefferson Co Pub Lib, Golden Colo 53-58; Child asst Denver Pub Lib currently. 8: Research asst, Pub Lib Inquiry, NYC 50-52. 9: ALA (Coun 53-56); SLA; NYLA; NY Lib Club (pres); ColoLA; MPLA. 10:Personnel Club of NY; AAUW; LWV; Bus & Prof Womens Club; Color Authors League. 12: "Bears Around the World (66). 13: Yes. 14: Child bks. 15: 525 Jackson st, Denver Co 80206.

OSTEN, MARGARET ESTHER. b Mukaceuo, Czechoslovakia. 5: UPrague 36-38 (Pol Econ) Professor's Diploma; UBudapest 42-44 (Pol Econ) Ind Engnr Diploma; UPrague 45-48 (Pol Econ); UBudapest 46 (Pol Econ) PhD; Columbia 50-52 MS in LS. 6: Czech, Slovak, Russian, Ukrainian & other Slavic langs; Hungarian, Ger, Fr. 7: Prof Col (Prague) 45-48; Jr lib asst Hunter Col 51-52; Catlgr ser Columbia U Butler Lib 52-59; Head of searching div, later adult serv libn Brooklyn Pub Lib 59-62; Hd Catlgr Manhattanville Col 62-65; Catlgr in Slavic Sect Descr Catlg Div LC 65-66; Catlgr in Ger Sect Share Cat 66-67; Asst sect hd post-51; Imprints sect, catlg maintenance & catlg publ div 67-69; Chief catlg dept UGrad Div Lib of CUNY 69-. 8: Volunteer ed asst, "Whos Who in Library Service 3d ed 9: ALA; SLA; NY Reg Catlgrs; Potomac Tech Proc Libns NY Lib Club; DCLA. 10: Nat Coun of Women for a Free Czechoslovkia; AAUP; Coun of European Women in Exile; Czechoslovak Soc of Arts & Sciences in Amer; Commercial Engnrs Soc. 12: "Income Tax in Modern Tax Politics, PhD diss (46). 14: Catlg. 15: 80 La Salle st, NYC 10027.

OSTERBIND, SYLVIA. b Oldenburg Germany 28 Jl 24. 5: Carleton U (Ottawa) 57-60 (Eng) BA; McGill 60-61 BLS. 6: Ger, Fr. 7: Catlgr Ottawa Pub Lib 61-62; Ref libn Carleton U 62-65; Ref libn Brock U (Ont) 65-; Hd ref dept 66-. 9: CanLA; Bibliog Soc Can; OntLA; Inst Prof Libns Ont. 13: Yes. 14: Ref. 15: Brock Univ Lib, Glenridge Campus, St Catharines Ont Can.

OSTRANDER, CHESTER BROOKS b Clemons NY 15 Je 13. 4: Sara Reynolds. 5: Hamilton Col 31-35 (Eng, Fr) BA; SUNY (Albany) 36-40 (Educ Admin) MA; Columbia 60-61 (Educ Research). 6: Fr. 7: Eng tchr Central Sch, Schroon Lake NY 36-41; Sr clk (civilian) USA, Baldwinsville NY 41-43; Eng tchr pub sch, Corinth NY 44-45; V-prin Central Sch, S Glens falls NY 45-50, Supt 50-69; Exec dir Lib Trustees Foundation of NY State, Rochester 69-. 8: Witness for NY State re nat lib legisl before Congress com 59; Mem NY State Commsnr's com on Lib Develop 68; 69 Chm Action Dev Comm, Am Lib Trustee Assn. 9: Amer Assn Sch Admin; ALA-ALTA (chm Action Develop Com 69); Lib Trustees Found NY State (pres 66-68); NYS Coun of Sch Dist Adminrs. 10: Rotary Club; So Adironack Lib System; trustee Crandall Lib, Glens Falls; So Glens Falls Fac Assn; Kappa Delta Pi. 12: Ed "The Newsletter," Lib Trustees Foun. 13: Yes. 14: Trustees, lay participation in lib govt. 15: 149 Main st, S Glens Falls NY 12801.

OSTREM, ERNEST RAYMOND. b Viroqua Wis. 5: UWis 46-50 (Journalism) BS; UWis (Milwaukee) 66-67 MSLS. 6: Fr. 7: Jr libn Milwaukee Pub Lib 64-67; Libn MarquetteU 67-. 9: WisLA. 14: Acquis, ref. 15: 1628 W Wisconsin ave, Milwaukee Wi 53233.

OSTROFF, HARRIET (HARTZ). b NYC 14 Ja 30. 4: Jesse Ostroff. 5: CCNY 47-50 (For Trade) BBA; Columbia 50-52 (LS) MS. 6: Sp, Fr, Ger. 7: Lib fellow City Col Sch of Bus Lib, NYC 50-52; Catlgr City Col Lib, NYC 52; Catlgr Eng lang sect LC 53-59, Catlgr mss sect 59-68, Asst ed Nat Union Catlg of Mss Collections, mss sect 68-. 9: Amer Assn State & loc Hist; Jewish Hist Soc of Wash. 14: Indexing. 15: 5414 41st st NW, Washington DC 20015.

OSTROMECKI, JULIUS. b Warsaw Poland 5 Ap 09. 4: Ursula Sobczak. 5: Warsaw U Law Sch 33 lb; Columbia 55 MLS. 6: Polish, Russian, Ger, Fr. 7: Legal counsel Polish Civil Serv, Poland 29-39; (1st Lt) Polish & British Armies, Poland, Great Britain 39-48; Johnson Pub Lib, Hackensack NJ: Tech serv libn 55-58, Asst dir 58-59, Dir 59-. 8: Consul & Act Dir, River Edge NJ Pub Lib, 56-59; Consul on Reorg of Newspaper Morgue, Bergen Evening Record Corp, 60. 9: ALA; NJLA (past chm, Personnel Mgt Com), past chm Trustees Rel Com, chm Federal Rel Com. 10: Hackensack Lions Club; Trustee Commun Chest. 14: Tech serv, admin, personnel mgt. 15: 275 Moore st, Hackensack NJ 07601.

OSTROW, HELEN GASTWIRTH. b NYC 24 Ap 27. 4: Milton Ostrow. 5: Brooklyn Col 45-49 (Eng) BA; Columbia 49-53 (LS) MS; Queens Col (Educ). 7: Child libn Brooklyn Pub Lib 49-53; Libn Jr High Sch, Queens NY 63-. 9: NYCASchLA. 14: Wk with child & yp. 15: 80-76 Surrey pl, Jamaica Estates NY 11432.

OSTRUM, ROXANE MIR TULLSEN. b Taylor Tex 25 My 15. 4: Ralph L Ostrum. 5 Kent State U 32-36 (Biol, Fr, Eng) BS in Ed; UPittsburgh 62-65 MS in LS. 6: Fr. 7: Tchr Bennett Sch, Youngstown Ohio 37; Lib asst South Side Lib, Youngstown Ohio 37-38; Chem analyst & sec Carnegie Ill Steel, Youngstown Ohio 43-45; Sub tchr in Allegheny Jt Schs, Pittsburgh 58-60; Libn Avalon Pub Lib, Avalon Penn 61-67; Stud lib asst UPittsburgh 62-64; Libn St Alexis Sch Lib 67; Libn St Teresa Sch Lib 67-68; Libn Avalan Elem Sch Lib 67-. 9: ALA; PennLA. 10: Girl Scouts; PTA; Kappa Delta Pi. 14: Ref, wk with child. 15: Box 244 Bellcrest rd, Ingomar Pa 15127.

OSTVOLD, HARALD. b St Paul 4 O 14. 4: Mildred Ritt. 5: Hamline U 32-36 (Ger) BA; UMinn 38-39 BSLS, 39-40 (Ger) MA. 6: Norwegian, Fr, Ger. 7: Ser asst UMin Lib (Minneapolis) 39-40; Newspaper indexing supv Minneapolis Pub Lib 40-41; Chief clerk Signal Corps 6th Corps Area, Chicago 41-45; Sci libn Northwestern U Lib 45-47; Chief of ref Washington U Lib (St Louis) 47-49; Libn St Paul Campus UMinn 49-57; Chief ref dept NY Pub Lib 57-63; Dir of Libs Cal Inst of Tech 63-. 8: Lib consul, Seoul Nat U Lib, Seoul Korea, 56. 9: ALA-RTSD (chm Acquis Sect, Coun); MinnLA; NYLA; CalLA; ASIS. 10: Trustee Altadena (Cal) Pub Lib. 11: Oberly Mem Award 58. 12: "Literature of Agricultural Research, with J R Blanchard (58). 13: Yes. 14: Ref, admin. 15: 966 Dale st, Pasadena Ca 91106.

OSTWALD, VENICE (VARNER). b Denver Col 19 Jl 28. 5: UColo 46-50 (Soc Sci) AB; USoCal 53-54 MSLS. 7: Secondary libn Long Beach Unified Schs, Long Beach Cal 54-61; Asst prof of lib sci UOre (Eugene) 61-63; Dir of libs & a-v Hillsborough City Schs, Hillsborough Cal 63-65; Admin asst to dir San Jose State Col 65-66, Research & development libn 66-67; Asst libn DeAnza Col 67-. 9: ALA; -YASD (Nomin Com); Internat Reading Assn (Publ Com); NEA (Memb Com); CalTA; (Intell Freedom Com). 10: Beta Phi Mu. 13: Yes. 14: Ref. 15: 1373 Phelphs ave apt 13, San Jose Ca 95117.

OSWALD, SISTER THERESE. b Duluth Minn 13 F 04. 5: Col of St Scholastica (Hist) BA; UMinn (Hist) MA; Catholic U MSLS. 7: Tchr elem schs; Tchr-libn Stanbrook Hall, Duluth Minn 40-55; Asst libn Col of St Scholastica 57-66, Libn 66-. 9: CathLA; MinnLA; Lake Superior LA(v-pres 67-68, pres 68-69). 10: Phi Alpha Theta; Beta Phi Mu. 14: Catlg. 15: Col of St Scholastica, Duluth Minn 55811.

OTA, LESLIE H. b Kilauea Kauai Hawaii 18 D 31. 5: UHawaii 49-50; UDenver 50-53 (Bus Admin) BS Bus Admin; Rutgers 58-59 MS LS. 7: Jr bus libn Newark Bus Lib, Newark NJ 59-60, Sr ref libn 61-66; Asst docs libn Rutgers U Lib 66-. 9: SLA. 14: Bus ref serv. , govt docs. 15: 381 Broad, Newark NJ 07104.

OTNESS, HAROLD MATHEWS. b St Louis Mo 20 Ag 38. 4: Loretta Chiang. 5: Portland StateU 56-60 (Soc Sci) BS; UPortland 65-66 MLS. 6: Sp. 7: Ref libn So Ore Col 66-67, Hd ref libn 67-. 9: PNLA; OreLA. 10: AAUP. 14: Ref, educ of libns. 15: 451 N Main, Ashland Or 97520.

OTT, HELENE. b Salt Lake City 31 My 16. 5: Stanford 33-35; UUtah 35-37 (Sociol) BA; UWis 38-39 (Anthropology) MA; USan Francisco 61-62 (LS); UCal(Berkeley) 62-63 MLS. 6: Ger. 7: Jr info analyst Off of War Inf, Wash DC 42-43; Asst research analyst War Dept Gen Staff G-2, Wash DC 43-44; Sec Dept of Pathology UUtah Med Sch 44-45; Res asst UChicago Com on Human Development 45-46; Res asst Consolidated Bk Publishers, Chicago 46-48; Sec Martin Food Products Inc, Chicago 48-49; Sec Armour Research Found of Ill Inst of Tech, Dept of Mechanism & Dynamics Research, Chicago 49-55; Sec UCal Med Center Biomechanics Lab (San Francisco) 56-62; Catlgr UNM Zimmerman Lib 63-65; Sr catlgr Stanford U Libs 65-. 9: ALA; CalLA. 14: Catlg. 15: 2151 Williams st, Palo Alto Ca 94306.

OTT, MARGARET VIRGINIA (HALL). b Milo Iowa 14 O 17. 4: Clifford Raymond Ott. 5: Simpson Col 35-39 (Educ) BA; UMinn summers 61-66 MALS. 6: Fr, Lat. 7: Lib asst pub lib, Des Moines Iowa 39-41; Lib asst pub lib, Evanston Ill 41-44; Tchr & libn pub sch, Fonda Iowa 53-61; Libn pub sch, Humboldt Minn 65-68; Tchr & libn elem sch, Hallock Minn 68-. 8: Dir, Hallock Pub Lib 67-. 9: ALA; NEA; MinnEA. 10: Fed Women's Club; Creative Writing Group. 14: Child wk. 15: Box 256, Hallock Mn 56728.

OTTE, LAUREL (BENN). b Detroit 26 Je 39. 4: Daniel Otte. 5: UMich 57-62 (Eng) BA, 62-63 AMLS. 6: Fr. 7: Res order libn UMich Undergrad Lib 63-65, Period libn 65-. 12: "Find it - or Flunk' (Pamphlet 67). 14: Rf, undergrad lib orientation. 15: 235 South Highland dr, Dearborn Mi 48124.

OTTE, MAXINE R (ROEHL). b Savanna Ill 8 Ag 14. 4: Karl Henry Otte. 5: Stephens Col 33-35 (Liberal Arts) AA; Northwestern 35-37 (Langs) BA, 37-38 (Educ) MA; Rosary Col 62-64 MA in LS; UTex summers 40, 41; UMich summer 65 (LS). 6: Ger. 7: Headof educ dept Clifton Col 39-40; Dir of stud personnel Morgan Park Jr Col 41-43; Supv train dept Spiegel Inc, Chicago 43-44; Reg dir of operations Blecker Inc, Chicago 44-50; Libn A B Dick Co, Chicago summer 63; Catlgr Ill Tchrs Col, Chicago-North 64-. 9: ALA; IllLA; Chicago Lib Club. 10: Womans Auxiliary to Amer Soc of Mech Engnrs, Chicago Sect; Twentieth Century Club. 14: Catlg, ref. 15: 1005 S Knight ave, Park Ridge Ill 60068.

OTTERSEN, SIGNE RUH. b Cresco Iowa 6 Jl 06. 5: St Olaf Col 24-26; UWis 27-30 (Eng) AB, 28-29 (LS) Certif; UMich 36-37 (LS). 6: Norwegian. 7: Catlgr Carnegie Pub Lib, Boise Ida 30-35; Catlgr Pub Lib, Ann Arbor Mich 35-37; Libn US Forest Serv, Ogden Utah 37-42, US Forest Serv, Wash DC 41-42, San Francisco br US Dept of Agric 42-53, Beltsville Md 53-55; Bibliog Nat Agric Lib, Wash DC 55-65; Chief ref serv US Dept of The Interior Lib, Wash DC 65-67; Biol Scis Communication Proj George Washington U 68-. 9: SLA; DCLA. 15: 2712 Wisconsin ave NW, Wash DC 20007.

OTTEWELL, HAZEL MARY (BETTERIDGE). b Clifton NY 16 Ap 16. 4: John Wesley Ottewell. 5: Keuka Col 32-36 (Math, Physics BA; Geneseo State Col 37-38 (LS) BS; UMich 41-43 MALS. 7: Sch libn Bd of Educ, Marathon NY 38-40; Sch libn Bd of Educ, Belleville NY 40-41; Stud asst in catlg UMich Lib 41-43; Libn Detroit Pub Lib 43-45, 53-. 09: ALA; MichLA. 14: Br lib serv. 15: 5920 Guilford ave, Detroit Mi 48224.

OTTMERS, SELMA W. b Comal Co Tex 19 Mr 03. 4: Delbert M Ottmers. 5: Southwest Tex State Col 24-28 & 30-31, 43-44, 50-51, 56, 57 BA (Hist); UTex 51-54, 56-58, 61 MLS. 6: Ger; Sp. 7: Prim tchr Pub Sch, Bexar Co Tex 20-21; Prim tchr Pub Sch, Comal Co Tex 21-23; Prin & TCHR Pub Sch, Caldwell Co Tex 31-34; Ref libn Southwest Tex State Col summer 31; Prim tchr Pub Sch, Comal Co Tex 38-39, 41-42; Prim tchr Pub Sch, San Marcos Ind Sch 49-51; Ref libn Southwest Tex State Col 51-, Archives & spec collections libn 68-. 9: TexLA. 10: Tex Assn of Col Tchrs; AAUW; Alpha Chi; Pi Gamma Mu; Fac Womens Club. 11 Ed & comp "Faculty Publications, Research, and Creative Works: A Bibliography, Southwest Tex State Col (65), Suppl I 67, Suppl II 68, Suppl III 69). 14: Ref, archives, rare bks. 15: 401 Franklin dr, San Marcos Tex 78666.

OTTO, LANDO C E. b Omaha 15 F 12. 4: Lois M Heyne. 5: Omaha Mun U 34 (Ger) AB, 37 (Eng) AM; UMinn 50 BSLS; Concordia Sem (St Louis) 35 Diploma. 6: Ger, Lat, Gk, Hebrew. 7: Asst Pastor Trinity Lutheran Church, Portland Ore 38-39; Pastor Concordia Lutheran Church, Weiser Ida 39-41; Tchr Concordia High Sch, Portland Ore 41-42; Assoc Prof & Libn St Pauls Col (Concordia Mo) 426; Libn Concordia Sr Col (Ft Wayne Ind) 56-. 9: ALA; MoLA; IndLA (v-pres & pres Col & Univ Sect 62-64). 11: Fulbright Tchg Scholarship, Vienna Austria, 54-55. 14: Admin. 15: 6600 N Clinton st, Ft Wayne Ind 46805.

OTTO, LEROY W. b Almond Wis 28 O 17. 5: Madison Col 36-38; AndrewsU 39-41, 47-48 (Hist, Bus) BA; UMich 49-50 MALS; USoCal 55-62 (Educ) EdD. 6: Fr. 7: Sch lib supv Dist 271, Ashton Ill 50-52; Asst Prof Bus & Libn Masison Col 52-54; Hd Educ Lib USoCal 54-56; Chief libn Cerritos Col 56-58; Hd libn Loma LindaU 58-63; Col libn Pacific Union Col 64-65; Chief libn UMo Med Lib Kan City Gen Hosp, Kan City Mo 67-. 9: SLA; MedLA; MoLA. 10: Greater Kansas City Mental Health Assn. 13: Yes. 14: Admin, organ med libs. 15: 241 Cherry, Kan City Gen Hosp, Kan City Mo 64108.

OUIMET, LUCILE. b Que 18 Je 07. 5: UMontreal 43 Diploma; McGill 47 Diploma Traduction. 6: Fr. 7: Libn in charge Ecole des Beaux-Arts de Montreal 44-. 9: ALA; CanLA; SLA; QueKA; Assn Canadienne des bibliothecairs de langue francaise. 13: Yes. 14: Supv of an art library. 15: 125 Sherbrooke st W, Montreal 130 Can.

OUSTINOFF, HELEN(FICKWEILER). b NYC 21 Ag 09. 5: Brown U 27-30 (Eng) AB; Providence Pub Lib Train Class 31-32. 6: Fr. 7: Asst in chg of adult wk Providence Pub Lib 33-36, Ref asst 36-39; Head of circ dept Amer Lib in Paris 39-41; Ref asst Providence Pub Lib 41-43; Asst libn Chemists Club Lib, NYC 47-51; UVt Lib: Catlgr 51-52, Asst dir & head of tech serv 52-61, Act dir 61. 8: With Polaroid Corp developed use of its CU-5 camera for lib procedures. 9: ALA-LAD; Recr State Rep 61-66; NELA (sec Col Sect 66-67); VtLA (sec 59-62). 10: Trustee, Dorothy Alling Mem Lib, Williston Vt; Appalachian Mountain Club; PTA; Home Demonstration. 13: Yes. 14: Tech serv. 15: Williston Vt.

OUTHET, HARRIET (MITCHELL). b Toronto Can 1920. 4: Murray Outhet. 5: McGill 39-42 BA; UOttawa 64-65 BLS. 7: Libn Ref Nat Lib, Can 65-68, Union catlg div 68-69. 9: CanLA; PIPSC; LAO. 15: 513 Court st, Aylmer E Que Can.

OVEN, LOUIS. b Smartno Slovenija Yugo 8 My 23. 4: Stana Jakomin. 5: Tchrs Col (Ljubljana Slovenya) 39-44 (Educ) Diploma; Monterey Inst of For Studies 63-64 (Russian) BA, 64-68 (Russian) MA; UCal (Berkeley) summers 65-68 MLS. 6: Slovenian, serbo-Croatian, Russian, Ger. 7: Instr Defense Lang Inst, Monterey Cal 55-64; Asst libn Monterey Inst of For Studies 65-67, Hd libn 67-69; Catlg libn Naval Postgrad Sch, Monterey Cal 69-. 14: Catlg, clsf. 15: 835 Pine st, Monterey Ca 93940.

OVERBY, MILTON S(IDNEY). b Lumpkin Ga 4 Jl 24. 4: Agnes Downer. 5: Norman Jr Col 41-43; Mercer U 43-44 (Philos, Religion) AB; Southwestern Baptist Theol Sem 45-47, 55-56 BD, MRE; Tex Wesleyan Col 56-58 uc, Admin) M Ed; N Tex State U 57-58 BS in LS; UIll 66-67 MS in LS. 6: Fr. 7: Baptist Clergyman: Rhine Ga 47-48; Doerun Ga 48-52; Valdosta Ga 52-55; Mineral Wells Tex 56-58; Aimwell La 58-59; Campbellton Fla 60-62; Clifton La 62-64; Lib asst Southwestern Baptist Theol Sem 55-58; Asst libn La Col 58-59; Libn & Prof of Rel Educ Baptist Bible Int (Graceville Fla) 59-62; Head Libn & Head of Lib Sci Dept Southeastern La

Col 62-65; Head Libn & Head of Lib Sci Dept Baptist Col (Charleston SC) 65-66; Tchg asst UIll Lib Sch 66-67; Dir of tech processes & Hd of lib sci dept Central Mo State (Warrensburg) 67-. 8: Ordained as a Baptist Clergyman in 42; Trustee of Norman Col 48-54; Moderator Colquitt Co (Ga) Baptist Assn 49-51. 9: ALA; NEA; IllLA; MoLA; MoStateTA. 10: AAUP; Rotarian; Alpha Lambda Sigma. 14: Admin, tech proc. 15: 811 Laurel dr, Warrensburg Mo 64093.

OVERCAMP, LUCILLE R. b Toledo Ohio 15 My 12. 5: Mary Manse Col 47 (Eng) AB; Toledo Pub Lib Train Class 30-31. 7: Libn Toledo Pub Lib, Toledo Ohio 31-; Br libn Heatherdowns Br 68-. 9: ALA; OhioLA. 10: Cath Collegiate; Daughters of Isabella; Gradatim Study Club; Art Museum. 14: Ref, circ. 15: Toledo Heights Lib, 423 Shasta dr, Toledo Ohio 43609.

OVERHOLSER, MARGARET (McKINSTRY YOST). b Hugo Okla 12 Ap 09. 4: James Arthur Overholser. 5: Southwestern at Memphis 2730 (Eng) AB; Emory U 3132 AB in LS. 6: Fr. 7: Br lib asst NYC Pub Lib 3233; Sch libn Memphis City Sch Syst, Memphis Tenn 3339; Libn So Cal of Optometry 3940; Ref & order libn Ark Lib Commsn, Littel Rock 5158; Ser libn Memphis State U 5860; Assoc libn UTenn Med Lib (Memphis) 6167; Libn Englewood High Sch, Jacksonville Fal 68. 9: ALA; MedLA (Com on Curriculum; mem 6266, chm 6667); TennLA (sec 6163); ArkLA (5160; Ark rep to SWLA 5253). 10: Delta Delta Delta; Chi Delta Pih. 14: Ref. 15: 5228 Arlington rd, Jacksonville Fl 32211.

OVERMIER, JUDITH ANN (SMITH). b Columbus Ohio 1 Ag 39. 4: James Bruce Overmier. 5: Bowling Green State U 57-62 (Eng) AB, 57-62 (Educ) BS; Drexel 62-65 MSLS; MedLA Certif Level 1. 7: Page U Lib Bowling Green State U 57-62; Circ asst U Lib UPenn 62-64, Libn Fernberger Lib dept of psych 63; Catlg asst Phila Col of Physicians Lib 64-65, Ref asst 65; Libn Bio-Med Lib Diehl Hall UMinn 65-67; Curator Hist of Med & Rare Bks Collections 68-. 9: MedLA. 10: Amer Soc Hist Med. 13: Yes. 14: Hist of med, rare bks. 15: 1965 E River ter, Minneapolis Mn 55414.

OVERTON, ELIZABETH (FOX). b N Attleboro Mass 21 O 20. 4: Allan H Overton. 5: Simmons 38-42 (Home Econ) BS; Columbia 58-61 (LS) MS. 6: Fr. 7: Engnr records clerk Ranger Aircraft Engines, Farmingdale NY 42-47; Caseker Suffolk Co Dept Pub Welfare, Bayshore NY 48-57; Libn Westhampton Beach High Sch, 57-59; Dir Riverhead Free Lib, Riverhead NY 59-. 9: ALA; NYLA; Suffolk Co (NY) LA (cor sec), 67; v-pres 67-68; pres 69; Inst Chm 67; Exec Bd 63-); Suffolk Co (NY) Lib Dir Assn (Exec Bd 68-69; chm A-V Adv Com 68; Child Serv Adv Com, sec 68, chm 69). 10: LWV. 14: Admin, ref, adult & ya serv. 15: Main st, E Quogue NY 11942.

OVERTON, MARGARET (BRYAN) C(ASSELL). b Harriman Tenn 8 D 06. 4: James M Overton. 5: Hamilton Col (Ky) 24-25 (Fr); UTenn 25-28 (Hist, Math) BA, 31-32 (Hist). 6: Fr, Sp. 7: Sec & asst to dir King-Smith Studio Sch, Wash DC 28-29; High sch tchr Harriman High Sch, Harriman Tenn 29-30; Tchg Fellow UPenn 31-32; Sec & bkkeeper Cassell Ladd & Carson Attys, Harriman Tenn 32-40; Sec to safety engnr Maxon Constr Co Inc, Oak Ridge Tenn 52-55; Sec Reactor Div Union Carbide, Oak Ridge Tenn 55-57, Sales off isotopes div 57-59; Ref & circ Y-12 Tech Lib Oak Ridge Nat LAB Union Carbide Nuclear Co, Oak Ridge Tenn 59-. 8: Lib consul, Harriman City Schs, 65-. 9: SLA (Archivist So Appalachian Chap 66-67). 10: Nat Soc Colonial Dames Amer; Order of First Families of Va; Order of the Crown in Amer. 14: Ref, geneal material. 15: 316 Queen ave, Harriman Tenn 37748.

OWEN, AMY. b Brigham City Utah 26 Je 44. 5: Brigham Young 62-66 (Humanities) BA, 66-68 MLS. 6: Fr. 7: Grad asst Brigham Young Lib 66-68; Syst libn Utah State Lib Commsn, Salt Lake City 68-. 9: UtahLA. 14: Lib computer applications. 15: 434 2nd ave #6, Salt Lake City Ut 84103.

OWEN, BERNIECE MARIE (CAMPBELL). b Parker SD 14 S 41. 4: Carlton M Parker. 5: USDak 59-63 (LS) BS; USoCal 63-64 MSLS. 6: Fr. 7: Ref libn Phoenix Pub Lib 64-65; Asst hd ser dept Ariz StateU Lib 65-67, Asst hd catlg dept 68-. 10: Alpha Lambda Delta; Phi Beta Kappa. 14: Ser, catlg. 15: 6101 E Osborn rd, Scottsdale Az 85251.

OWEN, FLAVIA (REED). b Huntsville Ala 29 My 19. 4: Theodore G Owen. 5: Athens Col 35-36; Randolph-Macon Womans Col 36-39 (Fr) AB; Emory summers 40-42 BS in LS. 6: Fr. 7: Lib asst RMWC Lipscomb Lib, Lynchburg Va 39-42; Libn Randolph-Macon Col 42-. 9: ALA; VaLA; SELA. 10: Phi Beta Kappa. 14: Bk sel. 15: 208 Howard st, Ashland Va 23005.

OWEN, KATHERINE C(RAWFORD). b Montclair NJ 27 Ja 25. 5: Wilson Col 42-44; Fairleigh Dickinson U 53-62. 7: Asst med libn Hoffman-La Roche, Nutley NJ 44-45; Asst libn Winthrop Labs, NYC 45-56; HeadLibn Warner-Lambert Res Inst, Morris Plains NJ 57-. 9: SLA (Sci-Tech Div; chm Pharmaceut Sect 60-61). 12: Ed "Copnip List (54-56). 13: Yes. 14: Drug nomenclature, ref, indexing. 15: Warner-Lambert Res Inst, 170 Tabor rd, Morris Plains NJ 07950.

OWEN, WALTER FREDERICK. b Jamaica NY 7 My 37. 5: C W Post Col 55-59 (Eng) BA; Rutgers 59-60 MLS. 7: Catlgr-ref NYC Field Off US Dept of Com 60; Asst libn Electric Boat G D Corp, Groton Conn 60-61; (Sgt) film libn US Army 61-63; Libn Comsewogue Sch, Port Jefferson Station NY 63-. 9: ALA; NY State TchrsAssn; NEA; NYLA; Port Jefferson Station TA (corres sec 69-70). 14: Ref. 15: 655-18 Belle Terre rd, Pt Jefferson NY 11777.

OWENS, BILLIE JOY (AUSTIN). b Tipton Ola 28 N 21. 4: William D Owens Jr. 5: N Tex State 38-42 (LS) BA. 7: High sch libn Gaston Ind Schs, Joinerville Tex 42-44; Libn, catlgr Air Force, Sheppard AFB Tex 61-65, Chief Libn 65-. 9: ALA (Armed Forces Sect; chm By-Laws Com 69); SAA. 10: DAR; Co Lib Bd, Wichita Co Tex. 14: Geneal, admin. 15: Box 452, Burkburnett Tx 76354.

OWENS, GEORGE E. b Pinnacle Ark 7 Ag 16. 4: Janet Wilson. 5: UCal(Berkeley) 46-50 AB (Econ), BLS. 7: US Army Communications (Capt) 41-46; US Air Force Communications (Capt) 50-52; Catlgr David Taylor Model Basin, Wash DC 52-53; Reports libn Los Alamos Sci Lab, NM 54-57; Reports libn Convair-Astronautics, San Diego 58; Tech ed Broadview Research Corp, Burlingame Cal 59-60; Lit searcher Lockheed Missiles & Space Co, Palo Alto Cal 61; Chief Libn Stanford Linear Accelerator Center, Stanford U 62-68; Hd tech info dept 69-. 9: SLA; CalLA. 15: 863 Moreno ave, Palo Alto Cal 94303.

OWENS, MRS ELIZABETH (WAGENBRETH). b St Louis. 5: St Louis Lib Sch 18; UWis 24 AB. 6: Ger. 7: Child libn St Louis Pub Lib 19-21; Hist tchr & libn High Sch, Rolla Mo 21-22; Child libn Pub Lib, Long Beach Cal 23-25; Libn Mercantile Trust Co, St Louis 42-52; Chief Libn Union Electric Co, St Louis 52-67; Lib consul, St Louis 67-. 8: John Cotton Dana lecturer, UOkla, 63; UInd 66; Instr on Spec Libs, Washington U, St Louis 55-. 9: SLA (pres 50-51, Scholarship-Student Loan Chm; Greater St Louis Chap; Lib consul 55-67, Recr chm 55-67, Archivist 67-); ALA; MoLA. 10: Nat Assn Bank Women; Mo Hist Soc; Zonta Club; Gamma Phi Beta; Wednesday Club of St Louis; St Louis Lib Club. 11: SLA Professional Award, 57; SLA Hall of Fame 66; St Louis Prof Woman of Year 67. 12: "History of Mercantile-Commerce Bank and Trust Co 1857-1949; "History of Zonta Club 1919-1963. 13: Yes. 14: Spec libs. 15: 1140 Edward terr, St Louis Mo 63117.

OWENS, MRS KATHLEEN(MARSHALL). b Stonewall La 3 Ag 11. 5: Centenary Col (La) 28-31 (Eng) BA; LSU 9-61 (LS) MS. 7: Parish sec, assoc organist St Marks Episcopal Church, Shreveport La 28-49; Sec United Fund of Caddo & Bossier Parishes, Shreveport La 56-57; Sec Walker & Walker Architects, Shreveport La 57-59; Tchr Eng & journalism FAIR Park High Sch, Shreveport La 61; Asst libn Centenary Col (La) 61-. 9: ALA; LaLA. 10: AAUW; La Hist Assn; Va Hist Assn; Amer Guild of Organists; Nat Soc Col Dames Amer; Beta Phi Mu; AAUP; No La Hist Assn. 14: Ref. 15: 534 Slattery blvd, Shreveport La 71104.

OWENS, NOEL (ARTHUR SCOTT). b Vancouver BC Can 31 D 18. 4: Valerie Skinner. 5: UBC 35-37, 46-48 (Hist) BA; Toronto 50-51 BLS; UBC 48-49, 56-57 (Hist) MA. 6: Fr, Ger. 7: Clerk Dept of Finance, Ottawa 39-42; Gunner Artillery Surveyor Can Army, UK & NW Europe 43-46; Foreign serv off Dept of External Affairs, Ottawa 49-50; Jr & sr libn ref UBC Lib 51-57; Northwestern U Lib: Ref asst 59, Head Documents dept 60-63, Chief of ref & spec serv 63-. 9: ALA; CanLA; IllLA. 10: Can Youth Hostels Assn. 14: Ref, govt docs. 15: 2117 Noyes st, Evanston Ill 60201.

OWENS, SYDNEY JANE. b Atlanta Ga 13 Mr 43. 5: Bryn Mawr 60-64 (Chem) AB; Simmons 66-67 (LS) MS. 6: Ger. 7: Research asst Harvard Med Sch 64-66; Weekend ref libn Counway Lib of Med, Boston 67, Ref libn 67-. 10: Bryn Mawr Club of Boston. 14: Ref. 15: 10 Shattuck st, Boston Ma 02115.

OWENS, VIRGINIA LEE. b Columbus Ga 11 Jl 18. 5: Okla City U 39 (Eng Lit) BA; UIll 56 MLS. 6: Fr, Sp. 7: Asst to dir Okla City Libs, Okla City Okla 48-55, Adult serv coordinator 56-57; Pub lib consul Okla State Lib 57-66; Grants-in-aid coord

Okla Dept of Libs 67-68, Assoc dir planning & research 68-. 8: Okla del to White House Conf on Aging, 61; Chm, Okla Lib Fact Finding Com for White House Conf on Aging. 9: ALA (Coun Mem-at-Large 63-66, Memb Com Rep Pla 63); -ASD (chm Com on Lib Servtto an Aging Popul 62); -AAStateL (Bd of Dirs 67-70); OklaLA (Exec Dir, Nat Lib Week 62; Pres 68-69); OkLA; AEAUSA (sec) 59. 10: Okla Ornithol Soc; Okla Anthropol Soc. 12: Ed "Oklahoma Librarian (56-60). 13: Yes. 14: Lib devel, planning & research, automation. 15: 5304 N Hudson, Okla City Ok 73118.

OWENS, WARREN SPENCER. b Massena NY 28 D 21. 4: Pauli Hartung. 5: Kalamazoo Col 39-43 (Eng) BA; Chicago 46-49 (Eng) MA; UMich 52-53 AMLS. 7: (Sgt) USAF 43-45; Lecturer in Eng Ind U Calumet Center 47-49; Instr in Eng UND 50-52; Asst circ libn, asst engnr libn, personnel & budget off, supv br libs UMich Lib 52-61; Dir of Libs Temple U 61-68; Dir libs UIda Lib 68-. 9: ALA; PennLA (pres 67); PNLA. 10: Treas "Union Library Catalogue of the Philadelphia Metropolitan Area"; Phi Kappa Phi. 14: Admin. 15: UIdaho Library, Moscow Id 83843.

OWENSBY, MARY (POYNOR). b Columbia SC 23 D 15. 4: Othell O Owensby. 5: Coker Col 33-35; Flora MacDonald Col 35-37 (Eng) AB; UAla 37-38 (LS) Certif; USCar 39 (Educ). 7: Libn Hand Jr High Sch, Columbia SC 38-39; Libn High Sch, Grannitville SC 40; Libn High Sch, Wilkesboro NC 42-44; Asst libn Naval Train Sta, Bainbridge Md 44-46; Head of brs Albertson Pub Lib, Orlando Fla 46-47; Lib asst Houston Pub Lib 48-49; Co Libn Harris Co Pub Lib, Houston 51-. 9: ALA; TexLA; SWLA. 10: Bus & Prof Women's Club. 14: Catlg, ref, child serv. 15: 4406 Grass Valley, Houston Tx 77018.

OWINGS, ELISE R. b Edmond Okla 16 Jl 21. 4: Donnell M Owings. 5: Okla A&M Col 42(Music, Pipe Organ) BFA; UOkla 49-50, 54-55 MLS. 7: Ser libn UCal (Berkeley) 45-48; Fine arts ref Okla City Lib, Okla City Okla 49-51; Head of ref Burlingame Pub Lib, Burlingame Cal 51-52; Arch libn UOkla 54-57, 58; Consul & surveyer Wellington Central Libs, Wellington NZ 57; Head Libn NATTC Lib, Norman Okla 58-59; Libn Del City High Sch, Del City Okla 60-64; Head ref serv & adult serv Ontario City Lib, Ontario Cal 65-, Supv libn. 8: Consul for Fine Arts Collection; Made a survey of resources & redesigned the bldg of the Wellington Central Lib, Wellington New Zealand, 57. 9: SWLA; CalLA. 12: "Handbook for the Burlingame Pub Lib. 14: Ref. 15: Ontario City Lib, 215 E "C st, Ontario Cal 91761.

OWINGS, LOREN C. b San Fernando Cal 29 S 28. 4: Elizabeth Leonard. 5: UCal (Berkeley) 48-53 (Hist) AB, 53-54, 56-57 (Hist) MA, 62-63 MLS. 6: Ger, Sp. 7: Co clk Hq det 7th QM Gp USA, Ger 54-56; Sr lib asst loan dept gen lib UCal (Berkeley) 58-60; Soc sci tchr Lompoc Jr HighSch, Lompoc Cal 61-62; Asst hd loan dept gen lib UCal (Davis) 63-64, Hd 64-69, Soc sci bibliogr 69-. 9: ALA; CalLA. 10: Libns Assn UCal; Acad Staff Organ UCal (Davis); Sierra Club. 12: Ed "The Bibliograph" UCal (Davis) Lib (66-69). 14: Bk sel, bibliog. 15: 1013 Alice st, Davis Ca 95616.

OWNBY, MARGARET (CAMILLE HACKWORTH). b Maryville Tenn 8 N 40. 4: Kenneth Gene Ownby. 5: Tenn Temple Col 59-63 (Eng) BA; Peabody Col 63-64 (LS) MS. 6: Sp. 7: Catlgr LC 64-. 14: Catlg. 15: 6606 Dorset dr, Alexandria Va 22310.

OXTOBY, FRED B. b Huron So Dak 13 Mr 18. 5: Ill Col 35-39 (Eng) AB; UIll 39-40 BSLS, 40-41, 46-47 AMLS. 6: Fr. 7: Asst UIll Lib Sch (Urbana) 40-41; Admin (Capt) US Army Adjutant Gens Off 41-46; Catlgr UIll Lib (Urbana) 46-48; Hd catlgr Ill Inst of Tech 48-62; Chief acquis dept John Crerar Lib, Chicago 62-63, Chief catlg dept 64-66; Catlgr LC 67-. 9: SLA (var off Sci-Tech Div). 10: Phi Beta Kappa; Beta Phi Mu. 14: Catlg. 15: 801 A st SE, Washington DC 20003.

OYER, CHARLOTTE ANNE. b Boynton Beach Fla 19 Je 30. 5: Palm Beach Jr Col 48-50; UFla 50-52 (Elem Educ) BAE; UTex 62-63 MLS. 7: Tchr Palm Beach Co Bd of Pub Instr, Belle Glade Fla 52-53; Deputy clerk Court of Record Broward Co, Ft Lauderdale Fla 53-61; Sr lib asst UTex 63; Asst ref libn Tex Christian U 63-64, 64-65; Ref libn San Fernando Valley State Col 65-. 9: ALA; CalLA. 10: Kappa Delta Pi; Phi Kappa Phi; Phi Theta Kappa; Alpha Chi Omega. 14: Ref, interlib loan. 15: 18521 Prairie st No 207, Northridge Cal 91325.

OYLER, PATRICIA GAIL. b NYC 11 N 43. 5: Chestnut Hill Col 61-65 (Eng) AB; UPittsburgh 65-66 MLS, 66-67 (LS) Advanced Certif, 67- (LS); UStockholm 68-69 9sociol). 6: Swedish, Fr. 7: Lib asst Adams Co Pub Lib, Gettysburgh Penn 59-61; Waterfront dir Mistick Side Girl Scout Coun, Boston 63; Water Safety instr Adams Co Red Cross, Gettysburg Penn 64; Ref libn Carnegie Lib of Pittsburgh Penn mus div 66-68. 8: Studying at Statens Biblioteksskolan (Swede0 and doing research on Swedish Libs and Lib Educ 68-69. 9: ALA; ASIS; ComparEA; PennLA. 10: Amer-Scand Assn; Girl Scouts; Sveriges Allmanna Biblioteks forening. 11: August Alpers Award, UPittsburgh Lib Sch. 14: Internat libnship, lib educ, catlg. 15: RD 2 Box 362, Biglerville Pa 17307.

OYSTER, VIRGIL S. b Coalinga Cal 24 Ja 35. 5: Coalinga Col 56-58 AA; Fresno State Col 58-60 (Fr) BA; UCal(Berkeley) 60-63 (LS) MA. 6: Fr, Sp. 7: Mechanics Helper V V Oyster Motor Co, Coalings Cal 45-54; Auto Parts Salesman 55-57; Lib Page Coalinga Dist Lib, Coalinga Cal 57-59; Lib Clerk UCal Lib Phys Sci Berkeley 60-61; Research Asst Sch of Libnship UCal Berkeley 61-62; Catlgr & ref libn Hayward Pub Lib 62-67; Catlgr Cal State Polytech Col (Pomona) 67-. 9: CalLA. 10: ACLU; Sierra Club. 14: Catlg, ref. 15: Cal State Poly College K-V, Pomona Cal 91766.

OZBURN, TOMMY. b Seymour Tex 18 Ag 14. 5: Tex Tech Col 31-35 (Speech, Eng) BA; N Tex StateU 64-66 MLS. 6: Sp, Fr. 7: Libn MidwesternU 66-67; Campus libn Tarrant Co Jr Col NE Campus 67-. 9: ALA; TexLA; SWLA. 10: LWV. 14: Admin, ref. 15: 828 Harwood rd, Hurst Tx 76053.

OZOLINS, KARLIS L. b Riga Latvia 11 Mr 23. 4: Sulamit Ozolins (Ivask). 5: Philipps U (Marburg Germany) 46-49; Augsburg Col 49-51 (Langs, Hist) BA; Augsburg Theol Sem 49-52 B Th; UMinn 60-61 (LS) MA, 66 (Educ) MA; UMich 66-. 6: Ger, Fr, Latvian. 7: Pastor Lutheran Free Church, Barronett Wis 52-55; Instr of religion Augsburg Col 55-59; Fulbright Lecturer Nat Taiwan U 63-64; Head Libn Augsburg Col 60-; Lectr UMich 66-67; Lectr UMinn 68-. 8: Lecturer, lib sci, UMinn(Minneapolis) 61-; Fulbright lecturer, 63-64. 9: ALA; BSA; MinnLA; AALS. 10: Luth Hist Conf; Beta Phi Mu; Latvian Acad Soc. 11: Fulbright Award 63-64. 14: Admin, lit in humanities. 15: 2836-41st st S, Minneapolis Mn 55406.

P

PAASCH, MARY (DeVAUSNEY). b Newark NJ 30 D 04. 5: Wellesley 22-26 (Psych) BA; Pratt 49-51 (LS) Certif. 7: Lib asst Nat Probation Assn, NYC NYC 37-41, Libn 41-44; Libn Family Serv Assn of Amer, NYC 44-69. 9: SLA. 15: 46 N Arlington ave, East Orange NJ 07017.

PABLO, WINIFRED (O'CONNOR). b Houston Minn. 5: UMich (Hist) AB, (Hist) AM; Catholic U 60 MSLS. 6: Sp, Ger. 7: Div asst Dept of State, Wash DC 45-47; Assoc Prof UPhilippines 47-49; Mil Dist of Wash (DC) Pentagon 51-53; Asst libn Dunbarton Col of Holy Cross 55-. 9: ALA; CathLA. 10: AAUW. 13: Yes. 15: 800 N Florida st, Arlington Va 22205.

PACE, ETTA E. b Pleasant Grove Miss 18 F 05. 4: Noble H Pace. 5: Miss State Col for Women 22-26 (Biol) BA; Fla State U 57-58 (LS) MA. 7: Registrar Delta State Col 26-34; Owner Pace Seed & Supply Co, Cleveland Miss 50-57; Field wker Miss Lib Commsn, Jackson Miss summer 60; Asst ref libn Miss State U simmers 62-64; Assoc libn Miss State Col for Women 58-68; Act dir 68-69. 9: MissLA (pres 64); SELA (Exec Bd rep Miss 62-66). 14: Ref. 15: 1121 7th st N, Columbus Miss 39701.

PACE, GENEVIEVE YVONNE (HESS). CAlester Okla 29 Mr 14. 5: Okla Col for Women 31-33 Art; UOkla 65-67 (Lib Sci, Educ) BS, 67-68 MLS, 68 Med Libn-certif I. 6: Fr, Sp. 7: Asst libn McAlester Pub Lib, McAlester Okla 33-36, Hd libn 37-42, Assoc libn 58-63; Arch br libn UOkla 64-66, Interlib loan asst libn 67-68; Acquis libn Clendening Med Kib UKansas Med Ctr, Kansas City Kan 68-. 9: MedLA; SLA (Heart of Amer Chap). 14: Tech serv, ref, interlib loans. 15: 729 W 46th st apt 2E, Kansas City Mo 64112.

PACE, JULIAN HUGHES. b Abilene Tex 11 D 38. 4: Elizabeth Anne Mitchell Pace. 5: Baylor U 57-61 (Hist) BA; UTex 61-62 (LS); UOkla 62-63 MLS; Kan State U summer 68. 7: Page Waco (Tex) Pub Lib 54-57; Stud ser asst Baylor U Lib 57-60; Night page Waco (Tex) Pub Lib 60-61; Stud asst UOkla Lib 62-63; Admin libn Southwest Baptist Col Lib 63-. 8: Mem Adv Com to Mo State Libn on Title III of Lib Serv & Construction Act 67-; Local chm (Bolivar Mo) Nat Lib Week 67. 9: MoLA; Springfield (Mo) LA; ALA; -ACRL (Sec Mo Chap 69-70). 14: Admin. 15: Estep Lib SW Baptist Col, Bolivar Mo 65613.

PACE, RUTH C. b Allentown Penn 11 Mr 19. 5: Moravian Col 37-41 (Hist) BA; Carnegie 41-42 BLS; Lehigh 48-51 (Hist) MA. 6: Fr. 7: Asst catlg & ref depts Conn Col 42-43; Circ libn Muhlenberg Col 43-44; Act libn Moravian Col for Women 45; Libn York Jr Col 45-47; Circ libn Lehigh U 48-56, Acquis libn 56-65; Manager ed info serv John Wiley & Sons, NY 65-. 8: Consul Jewish Commun Center, Allentown Penn. 9: SLA; ASIS; ALA. 12: "A Union List of Medical Journals in Libraries of the Lehigh Valley (64). 14: Acquis, info scis, documentation. 15: Apt 10D 201 E 25th st, New York NY 10010.

PACHAL, ANN LOUISE (HOWE). b Seattle 21 Jl 38. 4: Ashley Arthur Pachal. 5: Marylhurst Col 57-61 (Hist) BA; Seattle U summer 59; UWash 61-62 MLS. 6: Ger. 7: Lib asst Marylhurst Col Lib 58-61; Ref libn Seattle U Lib 62-64; Catlg libn Edmonton (Alta) Pub Lib 64-. 9: CanLA; AltaLA; EdmontonLA (v-pres 69). 10: Edmonton Pub Lib Staff Assn; Bus & Profess Womens Assn Can. 14: Catlg, readers serv. 15: 8008 - 129 A ave, Edmonton Alta Can.

PACHECO, FELIPE RAMON. b Sagua la Grande LV Cuba 22 Ag 24. 4: Infiesta Maria. 5: UHavana 42-49 (Lang & Lit) D Phil, 50-53 (Law) LLD, 56-57 MLS; Syracuse 66-67 MLS. 6: Sp, Portu, Fr, Ital, Catalan, Ger, Lat. 7: Secondary Sch tchr, Santa Clara Cuba 47-52; Practicing lawyer, Santa Clara Cuba 53-62; Asst Prof Prof Sch of Com, Sagua la Grande Cuba 52-55; Dir Gen Lib Central U of Las Villas Santa Clara Cuba 55-61; Asst catlg libn Cornell U Libs 62-68, Assoc catlg libn 68, Asst law libn for tech serv 68-. 9: ALA; Lat Amer Studies Assn; AALL; Assn Law Libs of UpstateNY. 10: Beta Phi Mu. 12: "Jornadas Bibliotecologicas Cubanas" (56); "Informe final; recomendaciones y trabajos" (56). 13: Yes. 14: Tech serv. 15: 103 Birchwood dr, Ithaca NY 14850.

PACK, FRANCES (LEISE). b Liscomb Iowa 23 J 19. 4: Lawrence D Pack. 5: Drake U 36-39 (Pub Sch Music) B Mus Ed; USoCal summer 38 (Music); UMich summer 8 (Educ); Wayne State U 63-64 (LS) MEd. Ed. 7: Music & Eng tchr Union Consolidated Sch, Union Iowa 39-40; Music & Eng tchr Ferguson (Iowa) Consolidated Sch 40-42; Music (vocal) tchr Conrad (Iowa) Consolidated Sch 42-45; Eng & hist tchr Raleigh Co Schs, Beckley WVa 45-46; Music tchr S Redford Schs, Detroit 58-59, Sub secondary tchr 60-63; Libn Burger Jr High Sch Garden City (Mich) Schs 63-. 9: ALA; MichLA; MichASchL (Recr Com); MichEA (Reg Conference Chm 67). 14: Ref, sch libs. 15: 11377 Rockland, Detroit Mi 48239.

PACKARD HELEN L(OUISE) (EVANS). b Port Huron Mich 11 Jl 13. 4: John DeKruif Packard. 5: Kalamazoo Col 31-34 (Eng, Fr) AB; UMich 35-36 MALS. 6: Fr, Sp, Ger. 7: Head Libn Olivet Col 36-39; Head Libn Lincoln Park Br Wayne Co Mich 39-40; Libn Detroit Pub Lib 40-43; High sch libn S S Peter & Paul High Sch, Saginaw Mich 60-67; Libn Delta Col 67; High sch libn St Stephen High Sch 67-. 8: Helped establish elementary lib in Jerome Sch in Saginaw & did much of clsf & catlg. 9: CathLA; ALA. 10: Reading Club; Music Club; Swimming Club; UMich Alumnae. 15: 1723 Maine, Saginaw Mich 48602.

PACKARD, GEORGE M. b Cambridge Mass 2 My 44. 5: Calvin Coolidge Col 62-66 (Hist) BA; URI 66-68 MLS. 6: Fr. 7: Acquis libn Calvin Coolidge Col 65-68; Sp/4 post lib USA Ft Dix NJ 68-. 9: ALA; SLA. 14: Ref, acquis, admin. 15: 26 Tobey rd, Belmont Ma 02178.

PACKARD, MERLIN W(ADSWORTH). b Portland Me 10 Ap 29. 5: Haverford Col 46-50 (Mediaval Hist) BA; UMunich (Germany) 56-57 (Slavic Hist); Columbia 60-64 (Byzantine Hist). 6: Gk, Lat, Ger, Fr, Russian. 7: Research analyst US Dept Defense, Germany 50-56; Asst to libn Dumbarton Oaks Research Lib, Wash DC 64-67, Libn 67-. 9: Med Acad Amer; Amer Assn Advance Slavic Studies; Am Soc Church Hist; AHA; ALA; DCLA. 15: 1703 32nd st NW, Wash DC 20007.

PACKER, KATHERINE H. b Toronto 20 Mr 18. 4: William A Packer. 5: UToronto 37-41 (Modern Langs) BA; UMich 50-53 MA LS. 6: Fr. 7: Catlgr: Wm L Clements Lib UMich 53-55, UMan Lib 56-59, UToronto Lib 59-63; Head catlgr York U (Ont) 63-64; Chief Libn Ont Col of Educ Lib (Toronto) 64-67; Asst Prof Sch of Lib Sci UToronto 67-. 9: CanLA; ALA; Inst Prof Libns Ont; OntLA (chm Col & Univ Sect 65-66). 13: Yes. 14: Catlg, clsf, lib admin, rare bks. 15: 53 Gormley ave Toronto 7 Can.

PACKWOOD, CYRIL OUTERBRIDGE. b Pages Paget 22 N 30. 4: Dorothy I Cunningham. 5: Fisk U 49-53 (Hist) BA; West Res 53-54 MSLS. 7: Catlgr Fisk U 54-55; Sp 3 clerk-typist US Army, Stuttgart Germany 55-57; Supv libn NY Pub Lib 57-68; Acquis libn Borough Manhattan Commun Col 68-. 9: ALA; NYLA; LA CUNY. 10: Beta Phi Mu. 14: Adult serv, catlg, spec libs in transportation. , acquis. 15: 303 W 66th st & 15 F East, New York NY 10023.

PACTOR, BARBARA ANN (BYNUM). b Gadsden Ala 8 F 40. 4: Howard Sidney Pactor. 5: Jacksonville StateU 58-59; AuburnU 59-62 (Eng) BS; Fla StateU 66-68 (LS) MS. 6: Fr. 7: Tchr Charlotte Jr High Sch, Punta Gorda Fla 62-64; Tchr Manpower Train Ctr, Birmingham Sla 64-66; Docs catlgr USAF Air Univ Lib, Maxwell AFB Ala 68-. 9: SLA; AlaLA. 10: Beta Phi Mu; Kappa Delta Pi. 14: Catlg, ref. 15: 555 S McDonough apt 23B, Montgomery Al 36104.

PADDOCK, BEATRICE FRANCES. b Wichita Kan. 5: FriendsU 22-26 (Sp) AB; UMich 29-30 AB in LS. 6: Sp, Fr, Lat. 7: Ref City Lib, Wichita Kan 27-29; Libn Free Pub Lib, Beatrice Neb 30-31; Libn Incarnate Word Col, San Antonio Tex 31-34; Libn East High Sch, Wichita Kan 43-53; Head libn West High Sch, Wichita Kan 53-58; Asst libn Macomb Co Lib, Mt Clemens Mich 58-61; Libn Wichita Hts High Sch, Wichita Kan 61-62; Asst Prof & humanities ref libn Wichita StateU 62-. 9: ALA (Coun); -AASchL (Bd of Dirs); KanLA; KanASchL (1st pres; chm var coms). 10: Beta Phi Mu; Delta Kappa Gamma. 13: Yes. 14: Ref. 15: 1710 Burns, Wichita Ks 67203.

PADDOCK, CAROLINE. b Roswell NM. 5: Tex Womans Col 24-28 (Eng) AB; U Denver 36-37 BS LS; UCal (Berkeley) 52-53 MLS. 6: Fr. 7: Tchr in pub schs: Portales NM 28-30, Carlsbad NM 31-35; Gen asst Lib Assn, Portland Ore 37-43; Camp libn Camp Abbot, Bend Ore 43-44; Serv club libn Chief Camp libn, Ft Lewis Wash 44-46; Reg libn Hq EUCOM, Frankfurt Germany 46-47; Act ref libn UTulsa summer 48; Departmental libn La Polytech Inst 48-61, Sci tech libn 61-; Coord readers serv 66-. 9: ALA; SLA (Sec-treas var com assignments in LA Chap); LaLA; SWLA; LaTA. 10: AAUP; Delta Kappa Gamma; Ruston Civic Symphony Soc. 14: Ref, pub serv. 15: Box 4702 Tech Sta, Ruston La 71270.

PADELFORD, ANNE (OHORA) (MRS EDWARD A). b Scranton Penn 19 Mr 40. 5: Marywood Col 57-61 (Elem Educ) BA, 61-63 (LS) MS; Univ of Md 65-. 6: Fr. 7: Tchr sch dist City of Scranton Penn 61-64; Elem libn Montgomery Co (Md) Pub Schs 64-. 9: NEA; Md State EA; MdLA; MCEA. 10: . 14: Elem sch instr materials centers. 15: 4000 Tunlaw rd NW, Wash DC 20007.

PADGETT, FRANCES E(LIZABETH BUCHANAN). b Fordwick, Augusta Co Va 20 Jl 22. 4: Hal Lee Padgett. 5: Madison Col (Va) 41-45 (Elem Educ, LS) BS Ed. 7: Libn: Pasco High Sch, Dade City Fla 46-51; Fluvanna Co High Sch, Carysbrook Va 51-55; Immokalee (Fla) High Sch 55-58; Trenton & Bell Schs, Gilchrist Co Fla 58-59; Baker Co O High Sch, Macclenny Fla 59-. 8: Libn First Baptist Church. 9: ALA; FlaEA, FlaLA; FlaA SchL. 14: Ref. 15: P O Box 159 232 E McIver ave, MacClenny Fl 32063.

PADULA, GINEVRA LOUISE. b NYC 21 My 37. 5: Barnard Col 55-59 (Psych) BA; Columbia 59-60 (Soc Studies MA, 62-64 (LS) MS. 6: Fr, Russian. 7: Tchr NYC Bd of Educ 60-61, Tchr-libn 61-. 9: ALA; NYCSch Libns Assn. 14: Ya. 15: 2790 Arlington ave, New York NY 10463.

PADWE, MARTIN M. b NYC 15 S 10. 4: Catharine Gergely Padwe. 5: NYU 36-42 (Chem) BA. 6: Ger, Fr. 7: Pageboy circ & ref NY Acad of Med 28-42; Med Corps (Pfc) US Army 42-45; Supv tech lit sect Jefferson Chem Co Inc, Austin Tex 46-. 8: Lecturer, chem lit UTex 49-54. 9: SLA (chm Consul Com Tex Chap 64-65); ACS; Austin Lib Club. 13: Yes. 14: Indexing, chem patent validity & infringement searches. 15: Jefferson Chem Co Inc, 7114 N Lamar blvd, Austin Tex.

PADY, DONALD STUART. b Kan City Mo 17 Ag 37. 4: Carol Lee Tulloss. 5: UKan 55-59 (Eng) BA; Kan State Tchrs Col 61-62 MS LS. 6: Fr. 7: LibnAiresearch Corp, Phoenix 62; Ref libn, Ariz State U 63-66; Humanities libn Kan State U (Manhattan) 66-68; Bibliogr Iowa State U 68-. 9: ALA; ArizLA. 10: Ariz State U Lib Staff Assn. 11: Carnegie Research Grant, UKan. 13: Yes. 14: Humanities ref, spec collections. 15: 4009 Ross rd, Ames Ia 50010.

PAEGLIS, VILIS. b Grundzale, Latvia 21 Mr 12. 5: ULatvia (Riga) 31-37 Mag Phil; UMich 54-55 MA LS. 6: Latvian, Ger, Lat, Russian; Gk. 7: Tchr: Secondary Sch, Gaujiena Latvia 37-38; Elem Sch Grundzale Latvia 39-40; Secondary Sch, Neustadt Germany 46-49; Catlgr Aurora (Ill) Pub Lib 55-60; Catlgr West Wash State Col 61-. 9: ALA. 14: Catlg. 15: 227 1/2 S Forest, Bellingham Wa 98225.

PAEZ, LINDA B. b Newark NJ 4 Mr 43. 4: Mario D Paez. 5: Chatham Col 61-65 (Sp Lit) BA; Universidad Internacional (Saltillo Mex) summer 63 (Mex Hist Lang); UPittsburgh 65-67 MSLS. 6: Sp, Fr. 7: Searcher UPittsburgh Libs 65-67, Asst hd order sect 67-68, hd order sect 68-69; Out-of-print libn UNC Lib (Chapel Hill) 69-. 8: UPittsburgh: Mem Libs Policy Com 68-69, Staff rep Lib Staff Assn Exec Bd 66-67, 68-69, Sec Lib Staff Assn Exec Bd 67-68, Rep to East Col Libn's Conf 68. 10: Beta Phi Mu. 14: Acquis, bibliog. 15: 3817 Lupton cir, Raleigh NC 27606.

PAGE, BENJAMIN F. b Green Lake Wis 16 Ap 27. 5: Ripon Col 45-49 (Eng) AB; UWis 53-54 MALS; UIll 59-63, 65-66 (LS). 6: Sp, Fr. 7: Eng tchr Munising High Sch, Muising Mich 49-50; (Cpl) US Army Inf Educ Spec 50-52; Eng tchr Escanaba High Sch, Escanaba Mich 53-54, Libn 54-56; Libn NM West U Lab Sch 56-57; Ref libn NM West U 57-59; Instr UIll 60-64; Asst Prof Grad Lib Sch URI 64-65; Asst Prof libnship UWash 66-. 8: US Armed Forces Info Sch,Ft Slocum NY 51; Asst, Survey of Lib Agecies of the States, ALA 62. 9: ALA; SLA (Pac NW Chap; chm Educ Com 67-68). 10: Beta Phi Mu; Phi Kappa Phi. 14: Catlg, clsf, humanities ref, documentation. 15: 4145 11th ave NE 37, Seattle Wa 98105.

PAGE, JAMES ALLEN. b Lexington Ky 31 Ja 18. 4: Ethel Ross. 5: Roosevelt U 46-50 (Psych) AB; DePaul U 50-51 (Elem Educ); USoCal 52-53 (Elem Educ), 56-57 MSLS; Ind U 65-66 (Adult Educ) MA. 6: Sp, Fr, Danish. 7: Elem tchr Los Angeles City Schs 53-56; Adult tchr Dorsey High Sch, Los Angeles adult schs 54-59; Libn catlgr Bur Govt Research UCLA 57-59; Econ libn Planning Research Corp, Los Angeles 59-60; Br libn & reg ref libn Los Angeles Co Pub Lib, Los Angeles 61-64; Col Libn Hampton Inst 64-65; Coord adult educ Gary Pub Lib, Gary Ind 66-68; adult serv consul Mid-Hudson Libs, Poughkeepsie NY 68-. 8: Chm Lake Co Adult Educ Coord Coun (Ind) 66-68. 9: ALA; VaLA; SELA; NYLA; AEAUSA. 10: Phi Delta Kappa; NAACP. 11: 1st Prize, Annual Essay Contest, Negro Hist Week, 54. 13: Yes. 14: Admin, ref, adult literacy programs, adult serv, y-a serv. 15: 25 Sharon dr, Poughkeepsie NY 12603.

PAGE, MELDA (WALTER). b Morristown NJ 10 Ja 41. 4: Robert Leroy Page. 5: Emory 59-63 (Pol Sci) BA; Boston U 63-64 (Govt); Fla State U 67-68 (LS) MS. 6: Ger, Fr, Russian. 7: Lib clk Nasson Col Lib 64-65; Elem sch libn, Lewiston Me Sch Syst 66-67; Asst libn-instr, catlgr Fla State U Strozier Lib 68-. 9: ALA. 10: Beta Phi Mu; Phi Beta Kappa; Pi Sigma Alpha; Amer Pol Sci Assn; AAUP. 14: Tech proc admin, tchg lib sci. 15: Box 132 RFD 1, Monmouth Me 04259.

PAGE, PERRYMAN L. b Repton Ala 22 Jl 35. 4: Cecelia Frances Page. 5: UMiss 58-61 9sociol) BA; LSU 61-63 MLS. 6: Sp. 7: Sgt USAF, Cal, Greenland, La 54-58; Asst ref libn Cal State Polytech Col 63-. 14: Legal bibliog, lib orientation. 15: PO Box 39 Halcyon Ca 93420.

PAGE, WILLIAM L. b Omaha 3 D 35. 5· UOmaha 53-57 (Chem) BA; Purdue 57-59 (Chem) MS: UDenver 62-63 (Libnship) MA. 6: Russian. 7: Russian tr (SP5) US Army 59-62; Asst libn Clarkson Col of Tech 63-65. Act libn 65-66; Hd sci-tech div Drexel Inst of Tech Libs 66-. 9: SLA; NYLA; ASIS; ALA-RSD (Sci & Tech Ref Serv Com 66-); Spec Lib Coun of Phila (treas 67-69, ed Bulletin 69-). 10: AAUP; Nat Geneal Soc; Central NY Geneal Soc; Gamma Pi Sigma; AAAS. 13: Yes. 14: Ref, period, admin. 15: 1014 Spruce st, Philadelphia Pa 19107.

PAGEAU, HENRIETTA CECELIA. b Portland Ore 24 Ap 11. 5: Col of Great Falls 45 (Eng) BA; Seattle U 50 (Eng) MA; UWash 59 MLS. 6: Fr. 7: Tchr priv & pub schs, Wash 33-59; Libn Alameda (Cal) Unified District 59-. 8: Tchr grad educ evening div Seattle U. 9: NEA (Life Mem); AEAUSA (Sabbatical Leave Com); CalASchL (co-chm High Sch Com); CalLA; ClrTA; Alameda EA (Tchr Aide Com). 14: Sch libnship. 15: 210 Central ave, Alameda Ca 94501.

PAGES, INES L(ORENS). b Matanzas Cuba 19 Mr 27. 4: Hector Carlos Pages. 5: Pfeiffer Jr Col 45-46, 46-47 AA; Salem Col 47-48, 48-49 Fr & Sp BA; Columbia 49-50 MLS; U de la Hàbana summers 47-48 (Eng). 6: Sp, Eng, Fr. 7: Child libnSociedad Economica de Amigos del Pais, Habana Cuba 50-51, Lyceum & Lawn Tennis Club, Habana Cuba 51, Ramon Guiteras Pub Lib, Matanzas Cuba 51-60; Prof of Eng Inst de Matanzas, Matanzas Cuba 59-60; Child libn Miami ub Lib, Miami Fla 61; Br libn So Miami & Miami Springs Fla 61-64; Libn Academia Santa Teresita, Santurce PR 65-. 8: Mem, Middle States Assn Vis Com for Eval (Instr Materials Serv) 67, 69. 9: ALA; Asociacion de Bibliotecarios de PR. 10: Asociacion de profesionales de biblioteca (Cuba, USA). 14: Child serv, Span lit, fiction, biog. 15: 17-19 Paseo de la Alhambra, Torrimar, Bayamon PR 00619.

PAGES, SISTER M HELEN OSU. b Sauerbrunnen Germany 8 Ag 06. 5: Mt Calvary Col (Ahrweiler ger) 24-25; Minot State Tchrs Col 30-34 (Lang) BA; St Louis U 50-51 (Educ) MEd; UMo summer 45; Catholic U 62-63 MSLS. 6: Ger, Fr, Sp. 7: Tchr & prin: St Agnes Acad, kenmare N Dak 30-42, Holy Childhood High Sch, Mascoutah Ill 43-53, Holy Rosary Sch, E St Louis Ill 53-62; Libn Cathedral High Sch & Althoff Catholic High Sch, Belleville ind 63. 8: Econ Opport (Foster grandparents Sect) Adv Bd, East St Louis 68-; Coun Regl Coun of Ursuline Congreg, Belleville 45-; Adv Bd Marianist Apostolic Ctr, Glencoe Mo 67-. 9: ALA; CathLA; IllLA. 10: Belleville Fair Housing Com; Belleville Kennedy-King Ctr. 13: Yes. 14: High sch lib serv. 15: Ursuline Motherhouse 1026 N Douglas ave, Belleville Il 62221.

PAIGE, M JEAN. b Cedar Rapids Iowa 7 F 22. 5: Stephens Col 39-41: State U Iowa 41-43 (Eng) BA; West Res 46-47 (LS). 7: Asst libn US Navy Air Bas, Banana River Fla 44-45; Order libn Drake U 47-48; USVA: Libn, Hines Ill 48, Chief Libn, Clinton Iowa 48-52, Med Libn, Jefferson Barracks Mo 52-53, Med libn, Iowa City Iowa 53-58, Chief Libn, Iowa City Iowa 58-. 8: Consul Iowa Adv Coun Lib Serv & Construction Act, Title IV-B 66-. 9: MedLA; IowaLA; ALA-AHIL (Sec 64-66, v-pres 68-69, pres 69-). 10: Nat Story League; Zeta Tau Alpha. 14: Ref, reader, adv (med & patients libs). 15: VA Hospital, Iowa City Ia 52241.

PAINE, BARBARA (ANDERSON). b Evanston Ill 17 Ja 25. 5: Northwest 42-43, 45-48 (Elem Educ) BS; Catholic U 62-63 MSLS. 6: Fr. 7: Child libn Fairfax Co Pub Lib, Fairfax Va 63-. 9: ALA; VaLA; DCLA. 10: Fairfax Co Coun on Human Rel. 14: Bk sel, child serv. 15: 7412 Hastings st, Springfield Va 22150.

PAINE, CLARENCE S. b Lincoln Neb 9 Je 08. 4: Ruth Moore. 5: UNeb 33-36, 37 (Eng, Hist) AB; UIll 36-37 BS in LS; UNeb 37 (Eng) AM. 7: Dir of Libs & Prof of Lib Sci Beloit Col 38-49; Dir of Libs Okla City Libs, Okla City Okla 49-59; Chief Libn & bldg consul Lansing Sch Dist Libs, Lansing Mich 59-65; Lib bldg consul Self-employed, Knoxville Tenn 65-; Consul co libn, Blount Co Tenn 69-. 8: Consul on lib bldgs: Okla City Okla 49-53, Lansing Mich (pub sch & commun col) 59-65, Lakeland Fla 64-65; Consul on lib personnel, City of Madison Wis 41-44; Visiting lecturer on Libnship, UDenver 48 & Central State Col 58; Consul on lib bldgs; New Kensington Penn 66, E Orange NJ 66, Clayton Co Ga 67, Flint River Reg Lib Ga 67-68, Lawrence Kan 69. 9: ALA; SELA; TennLA. 10: Rotary Club; C of C; Red Cross; Nat Cowboy Hall of Fame (Life mem). 11: Res Fellow, Western Range Cattle Ind Study, Rockefeller Found, 45-46. 12: Co-auth "The Black Hills (52); Co-ed "Review Index (40-44). 13: Yes. 14: Lib bldgs & equip. 15: Box 10445, Knoxville Tenn 37919.

PAINE, ELIZABETH (CAMPBELL). b Fairland Okla 13 Ap 12. 5: NEast Okla A & M Col (Eng) AA; UOkla 32-34 (Psych) BA; UWis summer 36, 37 (Eng); UOkla 58-59 summer 56 MLS. 7: Eng instr Maud (Okla) High Sch 34-37, Miami (Okla) High Sch 37-39, Fairland (Okla) High Sch 42-45; Finance co CLIC, Miami Okla 45-48; Sec Stanolind Oil Purchasing Co, Tulsa Okla 48-51; Clk NEast Okla A & M 54-56, Libn 56-. 8: Consul: NEast Okla A & M Lib Bldg, 66 & 67, Tonkawa Jr Col Automation proc for Lib (Feb 69). 9: ALA; OklaLA. 10: LWV; AAUW. 14: Admin, ref. 15: 516 C st NW. Miami Ok 74354.

PAINE, JOAN (ERIKSON). 4: Timothy D Paine. 5: Colo Col 57-61 (Econ) BA; UWis 61-62 MSLS. 7: Ref & ser libn Colo Col 62-64; Ref & documents libn Hofstra U 64-67; Asst gen ref libn Brigham Young U 67-. 14: Ref, govt documents, catlg. 15: 381 E Center #6, Provo Ut 84601.

PAINTER, AGNES E(TTA). b Terre Haute Ind 4 Ag 06. 5: Earlham Col 23-25, 27-29 (Eng) BA; Syracuse 29-31 BLS. 7: Tchr Dist Sch, E Charlotte Vt 25-26; Catlgr U Lib, Syracuse NY 29-31; Resident adv in dormitories, Allegheny Col 32-; Allegheny Col Lib: Catlgr 31-, Asst libn 44-57, Asst libn in chg of tech processes 57-. 9: ALA; PennLA. 10: Bus & Prof Womens Club; AAUP; AAUW; Delta Kappa Gamma. 14: Catlg; rare bks. 15:Allegheny Col, Meadville Penn 16335.

PAINTER, ANN F. b Baltimore 12 S 35. 5: Middlebury Col 53-57 (European Hist) BA; Rutgers 59-60 MLS, 60-63 (LS) PhD. 6: Fr, Ger. 7: Lib asst catlg dept Johns Hopkins U 57-59; Instr Rutgers 60-63; Data processing applic analyst info tech div Nat Bur of Standards, Wash DC 63-64; Libn staff asst

Tech Serv Nat Agric Lib, Wash DC 64-65; Libn info sci Center for computer sci & tech Nat Bur of Standards, Wash DC 65-67; Asst Prof Dept of Lib Sci Indiana U 65-68, Assoc Prof 68-. 8: Consul on reclsf Wabash Col, East Ky U, Great lakes Col 67; Mem Engnrs Jt Coun (Engrg Vocabulary Panel) 65-67; Mem ASIS/SLA Com to Consider Desirability of Merger 69-. 9: ALA; SLA (Com on Lib Wk & Documentation & Subcom on Indexing 64-69); ASIS (sec 69-71; sec-treas SIG/CR 66-68; mem Info Sci Educ Com 69); IndLA (chm Lib educ Com 69); USA Stand Inst. 10: AHA (Engnrs Jt Coun) Engnrg Vocabulary Panel 65-. 12: "Analysis of Duplication and Consistency of Subject Indexing Involved in Report Handling at the Office of Tech Serv, US Dept of Comm" (63); "Role of the Library in Relation to Other Information Activities in Federal Agencies" (68). 13: Yes. 14: Tech Serv, data procg, info sci, catlg, clsf, lib educ.5 15: PO Box 1305, Bloomington In 47401.

PAINTER, MAXINE M. b Ann Arbor Mich 5 D 15. 5: UMich 34-37 AB; UMich 50-51 MALS. 6: Fr, Ger. 7: Catlgr UWis Lib (Madison) 51-52; Catlgr Upjohn Co Tech Lib, Kalamazoo Mich 52-. 9: ALA; SLA (Pharmac Div: sec, treas). 14: Catlg, clsf. 15: The Upjohn Co Technical Lib, Kalamazoo Mi 49001.

PAKULAK, JEANNETTE ELAINE. b St Catharines Ont Can 9 N 23. 5: UToronto 41-45 (Eng lang & lit) BA; Ont Col of Educ 45-46 Eng diploma; UToronto 64-65 BLS. 6: Fr. 7: Tchr & hd Eng dept: Meaford (Ont) High Sch 46-47, Palmerston (Ont) High Sch 47-48; Sec educ bk dept Ryerson Press, Toronto Ont Can 48-51; Mgr textile wkers Credit Union Ltd, Hamilton 52-53; Sec credits & collection dept Reliance Petroleum Ltd, Hamilton Ont Can 53-54; Tchr: Sturgis Sch Unit, Hazel Dell Sask 54-55, Langenberg High Sch, langenberg Sask 55-56; Libn (br asst) Mt Dennis Pub Lib, Mt Dennis Ont 65-66, Br hd libn 66-. 9: CanLA; OntLA; Inst Profess Libns Ont. 14: Circ, ref (adult and high sch levels). 15: 36 Hook ave, Toronto 9 Ont Can.

PAL, NANCY KATHLEEN (RUTHERFORD). b Toronto Can 31 D 42. 4: Gabriel Pal. 5: UWaterloo 61-64 (Sociol) BA; UBC 64-6 BLS. 6: Fr. 7: Stud asst Waterloo Pub Lib, Waterloo Ont 60-64; Stud asst UWaterloo 61-63; Libn Toronto Pub Lib Mun Ref Lib 64-65; Libn II adult serv North York Pub Lib, No York Ont 65-68; Chief libn Preston Pub Lib, Preston Ont 68-. 9: OntLA (sec Adult Serv Sect 67-68). 13: Yes. 14: Ref, circ, adult serv. 15: Preston Pub Lib 156 Argyle stn, Preston Ont Can.

PALAIS, ELLIOT SAMUEL. b Portland Me 12 S 33. 4: Nancy Cane. 5: Bowdoin Col 51-55 (Hist) BA; UMich 55-57 MA LS. 7: US Army 57-59; Ref libn Ariz State U, Tempe 59-62; Asst chief ref dept Washington U, St Louis 62-66; Hd Soc sci ref Ariz State U (Tempe) 66-68, Collections coord 68-. 9: ALA; ArizLA. 10: Phi Beta Kappa; Phi Kappa Phi. 12: Compiler "A Guide for Business Administration Students" Ariz State U Lib (68); Ed "Publications of the Faculty" (Ariz State U) (67-68). 14: Ref, collection bldg. 15: 3408 N 85th st, Scottsdale Az 85251.

PALANDRI, GUIDO. b Portland Ore 9 N 24. 4: Angela Jung. 5: UOre 46-49 (Foreign Lang) BA; UFlorence 49-50 (Ital Lit); UGrenoble 51-52 (French Lang & Lit) Diplome daptitude; UCal 52-54 BLS. 6: Ital, Fr, Sp. 7: (Cpl) USMC 43-46; Catlgr UOre 54-56; Ref libn Pub Lib of Ft Wayne & Allen Co Ind 56-57; Catlgr UDetroit 57-58; Catlgr Wayne State U 58-60; Ser catlgr UOre 60-, Asst hd catlg dept 69-. 14: Catlg. 15: Univ of Ore Lib, Eugene Or 97403.

PALANSKY, KATHLEEN (LINTON BLOWERS). b Newark NJ 22 O 30. 4: Stefan Palansky. 5: Trenton State Col 48-52 (Elem Educ) BS; Wheaton Col 57-61 (Christian Educ) MA; Rosary Col 66-67 (LS) MA. 7: Tchr Nassau Sch, E Orange NJ 52-55, Dept of the Army, Japan 55-57, Edison Sch, Wheaton Ill 60-62, Dept of the Army, Ger 62-63; Sales correspondent Silver Burdett Co, Park Ridge Ill 64-65; Libn W Leyden High Sch, Northlake Ill 67-68; Libn Niles N High Sch, Skokie Ill 68-. 9: ALA; High Sch Libns Chicagoland. 14: Ref. 15: 5960 North Odell ave, Chicago Il 60631.

PALCANIS, RICHARD M. b Plainfield NJ 10 Je 23. 5: Col William & Mary 46-49 (Philos) BA; UNC 49-50 (Sociol), 50-51 (LS) BS. 6: Fr. 7: (Pfc) Army Engnrs 43-4; Libn in soc sci div Brooklyn Pub Lb 51-54; Catlgr City Col Lib (NY) 55-59; Head catlgr UNev Lib 59-. 9: NevLA. 10: Phi Beta Kappa. 14: Catlg. 15: 5 Redstone dr, Reno Nev 89502.

PALDI, TAVOR T. b Balassagyarmat Hungary 3 Ag 18. 4: Eve Loewenstein. 5: Rabbinical & Teachers Sem 34-37 (Humanistic-Pedagogy) Teach Lic; Faculty of Agric & Nat Sci 38-41 (Agric) BS; HebrewU 58-61 (Pol Sci) MA Pol Sci, 65-67 MLS; Inst of Soc Studies (The Hague) 63-65 (Nat Dev) Diploma. 6: Fr, Ger, Hebrew, Hungarian, Dutch, Yiddish, Ital, Russian. 7: Dist info off Dept of Communications, Nathanya Israel 45-51; Libn & Nat Sci tchr Dist Sch, Nathanya Israel 51-54; Libn & prin Tech High Sch, tel-Aviv 54-64; Acquis libn Tel-AvivU Ctr Lib 65-67; Staff libn Israeli Program for Sci Tr Jerusalem 67-68; Dir sci lib Dept of Agric & Univ, Rehovot Israel 68; Sr bibliogr Encyclopaedia Judaica Jerusalem, NYC 69-. 8: Clsf & catlg adv Israel Farmers Assn Lib 66-67; Liaison off European Tr Ctr Delft The Netherlands 67-68. 9: SLA; Spec libs & Info Ctrs Assn Israel. 10: Intl Broadcasters Soc (Bussum The Netherlands); Israel Pub Opinion Research Inst; Israel Soc Sci Assn. 11: Italian Govt Study Award; University Scholarship Award. 12: Sci trans to & from Ger, Fr, Hungarian; Intl coop column in "Cooperative Economy". 13: Yes. 14: Ref, info storage & retr, computer applications to lib serv. 15: Giltedge Inc 347 Fifth ave, New York NY 10016.

PALEN, OLOANNE D. b Lakeview Ore 1 My 18. 4: Joseph Andrew Palen. 5: UOre 36-40 (Eng) BA; USoCal 40-41 BLS; Columbia 46-47 (LS). 6: Fr. 7: Ref & circ asst State Lib, Salem Ore 41-43; WAAC, WAC Asst Command libn, US 43-45; City libn Corvallis Ore 46; Ref & ya libn brs NY Pub Lib 47-49; Ref libn Great Neck (NY) Lib 49-50, Act libn 51-52; Asst libn Marin Co Free Lib, San Rafael Cal 56-66; Asst admin N Bay Coop Lib System, Santa Rosa Cal 66-. 9: ALA; CalLA (Conf Subcom 69). 14: Admin, ref, tech proc.15: 725 3rd st, Santa Rosa Ca 95404. 15: Marin Co Free Lib, Civic Center Admin Bldg, San Rafael Cal 94903.

PALFFY, HELEN. b Budapest Hungary 10 Ap 06. 5: Col of the Sacred Heart (Budapest) 20-24 (For Lang) Tchrs Certif; Col of Mary Ward (Budapest) 24-25 (Cathechetics) Tchrs Certif; Case West Res 56-58 MA in LS. 6: Hungarian, Ger, Fr, Ital. 7: Period libn Grasselli Lib Town CarrollU 58-. 10: Alumni Col of the Sacred Heart (Cleveland Ohio Chap). 14: Ref, period. 15: 3171 Washington blvd, Cleveland Oh 44118.

PALIANI, MARY ANN. b Rochester NY 31 Ja 35. 5: URochester 52-56 (Bio) BA; Syracuse 59-60 MLS; Justus LiebigU (Giessen Lahn Germany) 64-65 (Bio). 6: Ger. 7: Ref libn Rochester Pub Lib (Educ Div) Rochester NY 60-62; Army libn US Army Giessen Lahn Germany 62-64; Hd tech serv Sloan-Kettering Cancer Inst, NYC 65-; Ref libn NYC Pub Lib 9sci & tech div) 65-68; Lib supv Dow Chem Co Rocky Flats Div, Golden Colo 68-. 8: Free-lance lit searching NYC 67-68. 9: SLA; ASIS. 10: Colo Mt Club; Beta Phi Mu. 14: Ref, lib syst, automation. 15: Stratford Park apts 16B 3250 O'Neal cir, Boulder Co 80302.

PALK, DONALD (HOUSTON). b Bloomington Springs Tenn 25 Ja 28. 4: Donna Ruth Flatt. 5: Tenn Tech U 46-50 (Soc Sci) BS; Peabody Col 50-51 (LS) MA, 68. 7: Typist & personnel specialist (Sgt ES) USA, Iceland & Ft Monroe Va 51-54; Libn Jakcson Co High Sch, Gainesboro Tenn 54-63; Tchr & libn Parkview Elem Sch, Cookeville Tenn 63-65; Dir lib sci Tennessee Tech 65-. 8: Consul several lib wkshops in South. 9: ALA; (Recr Com Middle Tenn 67-); NEA; SoLA; TennLA; TennEA. 14: Sch libnship. 15: 1210 Maddux ave, Cookeville Tn 38501.

PALLAY, STEVEN GABRIEL. b Budapest 21 My 30. 5: Eotuos Lorand U (Budapest) 48-52 (Lit, Hist, LS) BA; UToronto BLS. 6: Ger, Hungarian. 7: Ref libn Lib of Szeged (Hungary) 52; Art historian Art Gallery of Budapest 52-55; Art histoian Art Hist Inst, Budapest 55-56; Circ clerk London Pub Li, London Ont 57-62; Asst libn Can Assn for Adult Educ, Toronto 63-64; Records libn Edward Johnson Music Lib, UToronto 64-. 13: Yes. 14: Research. 15: 153 St George apt 504, Toronto 5 Can.

PALLING, BARBARA R(OBERTA). b Ft Scott Kan 14 O 31. 5: Kan State Tchrs Col 49-53 (LS) BS Ed; UDenver 57-58 (LS) MA. 7: Libn Fredonia High Sch, Fredonia Kan 53-55; Catlgr Northwest Mo State Col 55-57, Ref 58-64, Instr LS 65-. 8: Instr in Lib Sci, Northwest Mo State Col. 58-. 9: ALA; MoLA; MoA of Col & Res Libs (chm 65-66); MoASchL. 10: AAUW; Gamma Sigma Sigma; Delta Kappa Gamma; Alpha Beta Alpha.5 14: Undergrad instr in lib sci. 15: Northwest Mo Stte Col Lib, Maryville Mo 64468.

PALMER, ANN F(ROUNFELTER). b Westminster Md 17 Mr 25. 4: William H Palmer. 5: West md Col 41-42; George Washington 44-45. 6: Fr, Sp. 7: Reviser of catlg Copyright Off LC 42-63, Assoc ed bks subjs Catlg Maint & Pub Div 63-66, Specialist in copyright recs utilization Copyright Off 67-. 11: Meritorious Award LC 56. 14: Catlg. 15: 221 Third st SE, Wash DC 20003.

PALMER, DAVID CHEETHAM. b Wash DC 26 Ag 25. 4: Marion Louise Chamberlin. 5: John Hopkins 43-53 ((Music) BS; Peabody Consergatory of Music 43-52 (Composition); Rutgers 55-56 MLS. 6: Fr. 7: Ref asst Enoch Pratt Free Lib, Baltimore Md 56-57; Exec sec Penn Lib Survey, Penn State Lib 57-58; Exec Dir Governors Commsn for Pub Lib Development in Penn 58-61; Asst dir lib development div Penn State Lib 61-64, Dir lib development div 64-65; Instr Grad Sch of Lib Serv Rutgers U 65-; Chief readers serv NJ State Lib 65-. 8: Consul to New Castle Penn Pub Lib Survey by R Blasingame, 65; Co-surveyor with R Blasingame, Kent-Caroline Pub Libs Assn, Denton Md 64-65; Pub & state libs consul, Nat Lib Stat Coordinating Proj of ALA, 63-64; Co-consul; Tenn State Lib & Archives, LSCA, Title III, IVA & IVB Plans 67; Penn State Lib, Title IVA Plan 68; Rockland Co (NY) Lib Survey 68; Lectr Wayne State U Lib Sch 68; Dir, ALA-LAD Nat Plan for Lib Stat Proj 9: ALA (chm Stat Coord Com LAD-LOMS 64-69, chm Stat Com for State Libs LAD-LOMS 63-67);-AAStateL (Planning Com 66-67); USA Stand Inst Z-39 Com (ALA consul); SLA; NJLA; NJEA. 10: Amer Soc PubAdmin; CLU; Nat Honor Soc. 12: Co-auth with L Martin "Library Service in Pennsylvania, Present & Proposed (58); Co-auth with Ralph Blasingame "A Study of he Kent-Caroline Public Libraries Association (65). 14: Pub lib devel, ref, State lib planning & admin.5 15: NJ State Lib, 185 W State st, Trenton NJ 08625.

PALMER, DAVID W. b Detroit 24 N 28. 4: Charlene Goldenberg. 5: Pasadena City Col 47-49 (Eng) AA; UCLA 49-51 (Eng) BA, 51-52 (Eng), 60-61 MLS. 6: Sp. 7: Troop movement control spec US Army 53-55; Insurance claims rep Royal-Globe Insurance Group 56-59; Pub info writer UCal Press(Berkeley) 59-60; Ref libn Humboldt State Col 61-64; Lib dir Rockford Col 64-68; Lib dir Baldwin-Wallace Col 68-. 9: ALA; OhioLA. 10: UCal Lib Schs Alumni Assn; AAUP. 12: Quickly, Over the Wall" Poems & Paints (66); Ed "The Beloit Poetry journal" (64-67). 13: Yes. 15: 139 E Center st, Berea Oh 44017.

PALMER, FORREST CHARLES. b Burlington Wis 17 O 24. 4: Lois Mae (Davis) Palmer. 5: Valparaiso U 42-43, 46-48 (Govt) BA; UIll 43; ASTP Prog-US Army; UPittsburgh 43-44 (ASTP Prog-US Army, Area & Lang Studies); Peabody 48-49 BSLS, summers 51-53 MSLS. 6: Ger, Fr. 7: Catlg libn Janesville (Wis) Pub Lib 49-50; Ser catlgr NC State Col, Raleigh 50-51, Ser libn 51-55; Dir of Libs, Miss State U 55-62; Libn & Head Dept of Lib Sci Madison Col (Va) 62-. 8: Mem of exec com of Adv Com on Libs, Va State Coun of Higher Educ, 64-; Jt Adv Com on Libs, Higher Educ Study Commsn (Va) 65-66; Rep on Lib Affairs, Univ Center of Va 63-. 9: ALA; SELA (SEast lib devel com 60-62, 66-68; chm col & univ sect 60-62); VaEA; VaLA (chm pub com 62-65, Mem exec & activities coms 62-65, 2nd v-pres 66, 1st v-pres 68, pres 69). 10: Boy Scouts; Alpha Beta Alpha; Pi Gamma Mu; Beta Phi Mu. 11: Golden Triangle Award (YMCA). 12: Ed "Virginia Librarian" (62-65). 13: Yes. 14: Admin, lib sci educ, sers. 15: Madison Col Lib, Harrisonburg Va 22801.

PALMER, FOSTER M(cCRUM). b Kan City Mo 19 Mr 14. 4: Doris Brown. 5: Washington & Lee U 30-34 (Eng, Fr) AB summa cum laude, 34-35 (Eng, Fr) MA; UMich 37-38 BA in LS. 6: Fr, Sp, Portuguese. 7: Instr Eng Morningside Col 35-37; Harvard Col Lib: Asst, ref & circ dept 38-41, Ref asst 41-56, Asst libn for ref 56-61, Assoc libn for ref & circ 62-65; Assoc U libn for ref & circ Harvard U Lib 65-. 8: Lectr on Computers and Libs, McGill U 66, 67; Mem Adv Bd, NELINET Proj, NE Bd of Higher Educ 68-. 9: ALA (chm Subs Bks Com 50-51 & 57-59; chm Interlib Loan Com 55-59); MassLA. 10: Coun, Cambridge Hist Soc; Trustee, N E Elect Railway Hist Soc; ACLU; United World Federalists; Phi Beta Kappa. 12: ""Punched Card Circulation System for Widener Library (65); Co-ed ""Widener Library Shelflist (Computer ser 65-). 13: Yes. 14: Ref, lib automation. 15: Widener Lib 183, Cambridge Mass 02138.

PALMER, HELEN (HANSSEN). b New Orleans 19 Je 11. 4: Arthur Macdonald Palmer. 5: LSU 52-56 (Psych) BA, 56-60 (Anthropology) MA, 60-61 (LS) MS. 6: Sp, Ger. 7: Head, humanities div LSU Lib, Baton Rouge La 61-. 9: ALA; LaLA; Baton Rouge Lib Club. 10: Phi Kappa Phi; AAUW. 12: "American Drama Criticism" (67); "European Drama Criticism" (68). 14: Ref. 15: 3753 Hyacinth ave, Baton Rouge La 70808.

PALMER, HELEN FRAYDA (KIVENKO). b Montreal Can 1 Ja 41. 4: Frederick Earl Palmer. 5: McGill 58-62 (Eng Lit) BA, 62-63 BLS. 6: Fr. 7: Sch libn Sch Bd of Greater montreal 63-64; Asst libn EdinburghU Lib 64-65; Sch libn Inner London Educ Lib Authority, London England 65-67; Bibliog supervisor UAlberta 67-. 9: Canadian Assn univ Tchrs. 10: Alta Chap Commun Planning Assn. 14: Rare bks, selection of child lit, bibliog. 15: Kivenko 4551 Michel Bibaud, Montreal Que Can.

PALMER, MARGARET KAREN. : Augustana Col (Rock Island Ill) 57-59 (Hist); Washington U (St Louis) 59-61 (Hist) AB; UIll 61-63 (LS) MS. 6: Fr, Swedish. 7: Catlgr UMo Lib 63-. 9: ALA; MoLA. 14: Catlg, automation. 15: Univ of Mo Lib, Columbia Mo 65202.

PALMER, MARY KLENNER. b Durham NC 11 D 42. 4: William J Palmer. 5: UMiss 60-64 BA; Peabody Col 65 MLS. 6: Fr. 7: Asst libn Stratford Col 65-66; Asst acquis libn U Miss 66-68; Libn Jackson Co Jr Col 68-. 9: MissLA. 14. Catlg, ref, acquis. 15: 1602 N Clairmont, Pascagoula Ms 39567.

PALMER, PAUL R. b Cincinnati 21 Ja 17. 5: UCincinnati 45-49 (Eng Lit) AB; Columbia 49-50 (LS) MS, 54-55 (Eng Lit) MA. 6: Fr, Ger. 7: (Med tech) (Cpl) US Army, Africa, Europe 42-45; Lib asst UCincinnati 49; Lib asst Brooklyn (NY) Pub Lib, 50-51; Libn Burgess-Carpenter-Classics Libs, Columbia U 51-67; Libn Sch of Lib Serv 67-, Theatre arts libn, Speech recording libn, curator Brander Matthews Dramatic Mus 68-. 8: Supv Paterno Lib, Columbia U 54-65 (Philos) Lib, Columbia U 63-65. 9: ALA (past consul on reprints); TheatreLA; Amer Inst of Graphic Arts, Amer Assn of Museums; AETH; Amer Assn for Theater Research; Internat Coun of Museums. 10: Phi Beta Kappa. 13: Yes. 14: Comparat lit, art, theatre materials, soc scis. 15: 560 Riverside dr, NYC 10027.

PALMER, RAYMOND ALFORD. b Louisville Ky 8 My 39. 5: UKy 57-61 (Bio) BA, 65-66 MSLS. 6: Sp. 7: Mgt trainee Research Dept Joseph E Seagrams & Sons, Louisville Ky 61-64, supv warehouse dept 64-65; Grad asst lib sci dept UKy (Lexington) 65-66; Admin asst to dir Welch Med Lib Johns HopkinsU 67-69; Asst libn Francis A Countway Lib of Med HarvardU 69-. 9: MedLA. 14: Admin, pub serv. 15: 50 Pinckney st, Boston Ma 02114.

PALMER, RICHARD PHILLIPS. b Milwaukee 10 Mr 21. 4: Jocelyn Wold. 5: Principia Col 46-49 (Eng) BA Highest Honors; UWis Milwaukee 62-64 (Eng) MA; UWis Madison 64-65 MA LS; UMich 66-69. 6: Fr. 7: Elem tchr Leelanau Sch, Glen Arbor Mich 41-42; US Naval Res Naval Intelligence Yeoman 1stClass 42-46; Christian Sci Practitioner, Milwaukee 49-60; Real Estate Salesman E A Purell Co, Milwaukee 60-62; Instr of Eng UWis, Milwaukee 62-64; Visiting lecturer UWis Lib Sch summer 65; Asst libn Ill State U 65-66; Lecturer UMich Lib Sch summer 67, 68; Research assoc Commun Systs Found 68-. 9: ALA; ASIS. 10: AAUP; Sigma Tau Delta; Phi Alpha Eta; Beta Phi Mu. 14: Educ for libnship, admin, application of computer tech to libs. 15: 1821 Oneida pl, Ann Arbor Mi 48104.

PALMER, ROBERT BAYLIS. b Rockville Centre NY 5 Ap 38. 5: Kenyon Col 55-60 (Classics) AB; Simmons 62-65 (LS) MS; Middlebury Col 62-65 (Eng) MA. 7: Tchr Brooks Sch, N Andover Mass 60-63, Libn 61-65; Act libn U Libs, Columbia U 65-66, Asst to the dir 66-67; Barnard Col libn 67-. 9: ALA. 10: Archons of Colophon. 14: Admin. 15: 7 W 14th st apt 20G, NYC 10011.

PALMER, RUTH E. b Greensburg Penn 15 N 09. 5: Los Angeles City Col 30-34 (Liberal Arts) AA; UCLA 34-36 (Pol Sci) BA; USoCal 36-38 BS LS; USoCal Civic Center Div 46-47 (Admin, Org, Personnel). 7: Sub-prof & clerical Los Angeles Pub Lib brs & central 29-40, Libn water & power div 40-44; Libn US Army Bimingham Hosp, Van Nuys Cal 44; Los Angeles Pub Lib: br libn Henry Adams Br 44-46, Libn water & power div 46-47, Sr libn Mun ref dept 47-50, Prin libn Mun ref dept 50-. 9: ALA; SLA (SoCal Chap: sec & mem var coms); West Govtal Res Assn; Pub Personnel Assn. 14: Admin, ref. 15: Mun Ref Lib. Rm 1003, City Hall, Los Angeles Ca 90012.

PALMER, VERNELLE(GILLIAM). b Wilkes Co NC 15 Mr 22. 4: G A Palmer Jr. 5: Appalachian State Tchrs Col 38-42 (Eng, Fr, LS) BS, summers 48, 51, 52 (LS) MA. 7: Tchr-libn FAIRGROVE High Sch, Thomasville NC 42-44; bn Henderson (NC) High Sch 44-47; Libn Lexington (NC) High Sch 47-48; Asst libn Greensboro (NC) Sr High Sch 48-50; Libn Boyden High Sch, Salisbury NC 50-59; Libn Sch of Lib Sci UNC summer 53; Libn E Rowan High Sch, Salisbury NC 61-. 8: Mem-in serv Educ Sub-com Governor's Commsn to Study Pub Schs of NC 68. 9: NEA; NCLA (pres 57-59; chm Recr Com 55-57; Mem Coun on Libnship 57-61; Chm Scholarships Com 63-); NCEA (pres Rowan Co Unit 68-69); Chm Bd of Trustees Spencer Pub Lib 63-; chm Personnel Policies Com Rowan Pub Schs 68-69. 10: Alpha Delta Kappa; Womans Missionary

Union; LWV. 13: Yes. 14: High sch libn . 15: 501 Eighth st, Spencer NC 28159.

PALMER, WILLIAM W. b Bangor Me 2 Ja 32. 4: Vivian Davidson. 5: State UIowa 55-60 (Music) BMus; UChicago 60-63 (LS) MA. 6: Fr. 7: (Sgt) Army, Ft Leonard Wood Mo 52-54; Asst libn Music Lib UIowa 58-60; Libn I Music dept Chicago Pub Lib 60-63; Head music dept Pub Lib of Des Moines, Iowa 63-67; Catlgr LC 67-. 9: ALA; MusLA. 10: . 14: Mus libnship. 15: 5074 Livingston ter apt 301, Oxon Hill Md 20021.

PALMIERI, L(UCIEN) E(UGENE). b Cambridge Mass 11 Ag 21. 4: Valerie Tremlin. 5: UWis 46-47 (Philos) BS, 48-49 (Philos) MS, 49-53 (Philos) PhD, 55-56 MSLS. 6: Fr. 7: Instr UWis (Madison) 49-51, 53-56; Hd libn Chicago Tchrs Col 56-62; Consul Ministry of Educ, Tanzània Dar es Salaam 62-66; Prof NEast Ill State 67; Hd libn SUNY (Buffalo) 67-. 8: Consul Ministry of Educ Tanzania 62-66. 9: ALA; Amer Philos Assn; West NY Lib Resources Coun (Trustee); Hd Libns Assn, SUNY. 10: AAUP; Univ Club of Buffalo. 12: "Language and Clear Thinking" (60). 13: Yes. 14: Catlg, admin. 15: 607 Auburn ave, Buffalo NY 14222.

PALONEY, ALICE (THOMPSON). b Burlington Iowa 17 My 14. 5: Coe Col 32-36 (Eng, Lat) BA (magna cum laude); Columbia 41 BS LS. 6: Fr. 7: Tchr-libn High sch, What Cheer Iowa 36-38; Tchr-libn High sch, Shelby Iowa 38-40; Libn: Omaha Pub Lib 40-41; LC 41-44; Los Angeles Pub Lib: Libn 48-58, Catlg reviser 58-62, Br libn Pio Pico Br 62-67, Br libn Palms-Rancho Park Br 67-. 9: ALA; CalLA. 10: AAUW; West LA Commun Coord Counc. 14: Ref. 15: 520 W 64th pl, Inglewood Cal 90302.

PALOTAI, OLGA MARIA (CSAKY). b Mezokeresztes Hungary 15 Jl 29. 5: U Budapest 51 (Law, Pol Sci) UNC 62 MS LS; George Washington U 68 ML. 6: Hungaria, Ger, Fr. 7: Libn UNC Inst of Govt 60-65; Asst libn Tax Court of the US, Wash DC 65-. 9: Internat Assn of Law Libs; AALL; NCLA. 10:Beta Phi Mu. 13: Yes. 14: Law (especially tax law). 15: Tax Court of the US, Internal Revenue Bldg 12th st & Constitution ave NW, Wash DC 20044.

PALUKA, FRANCIS J. b Council Bluffs Iowa 2 D 27. 5: UWyo 45; Creighton U 47-50 (Eng) AB; UConn 50-52 (Eng) MA; Fla State U 52-53 (Eng); UIowa 53-59 (Eng); UIll 60-61 (LS) MS. 7: (Pfc) 20th Air Force, Marianas slands 46-47; Instr UConn 50-52; Grad asst Fla State U 52-53; Fellow, Instr & ref libn UIowa 54-59; Research asst UIll (Urbana) 60-61; Head spec collections dept UIowa 62-. 9: Mod LANG Assn; IowaLA (chm Johnson-Brigham Com 62-65). 10: Beta Phi Mu; Phi Kappa Phi; Alpha Sigma Nu. 12: Ed "Books at Iowa; Sixty Iowa Authors; a Bio-Bibliography. 13: Yes. 14: Bibliog, rare bks, mss. 15: Univ of Iowa Libs, Iowa City Iowa 5240.

PAMMENT, MARY LORETTA (RIGNEY). b Renton Wash 10 S 14. 4: Leonard Pamment. 5: UWash 31-39 (Romance Langs) BA, 55-57 (LS) ML. 6: Fr. 7: Clerical asst Seattle Pub Lib 29-39; Eng dept libn UWash 57-60, Period rm libn 60-67, For docs libn 67-.0 9: ALA; PNLA (mem var coms); WashLA mem var coms). 10: Faculty Womens Club UWas; Phi Sigma Iota; Beta Phi Mu. 13: Yes. 14: Ref. 15: 7708 17th ave NE, Seattle Wa 98115.

PANAJOTOVIC, ELENA MARIA. b Havana Cuba 21 My 41. 4: Ilija Panajotovic. 5: Occidental Col 58-62 (Span, Ger) BA; UCLA 62-63 MLS. 6: Sp, Ger, Fr. 7: Asst ref Occidental Col 63-. 8: Org of an inforetrieval system for an engnr Prof at UCLA. 9: CalLA. 14: Ref, info retrieval, org. 15: 1615 Crest dr, Los Angeles Ca 90035.

PANCIERA, WILLIAM J. b Distant Penn 6 Ja 22. 4: Jean Gould. 5: Clarion State Col 49-52 (LS) BS; Penn State U 54 (Educ); Eastern Baptist Col 60 (Educ). 7: Laborer Bakery, New Bethlehem Penn 40-42; Rifleman US Army, S Pacific 42-45; Laborer Brick Yard, St Charles Penn 45-49; Libn Elderton Jt Sch, Elderton Penn 52-59; Libn Philipsburg-Osceola Area Sr High Sch, Philipsburg Penn 50-. 9: Penn State EA; NEA (Dept of Supv & Curriculum). 14: High sch libs (improving quality & usability). 15: 100 Fifth st, Philipsburg Penn 16866.

PANE, VIRGINIA (VIRSHEK). b Virginia Minn 8 S 24. 4: Albert J Pane. 5: Va Jr Col 41-43 (Eng, Fr, Hist) Assoc BA; Col of St Catherine 43-45 (LS) BS. 7: Jr libn Dept of Army Clinton (Iowa) Hosp 45; Catlgr USanta Clara 46-48; Libn Dept of the Army, Guam, Marianas Islands 48; Jr libn Oakland City Lib, Oakland Cal 49-50; Jr libn Stanford U Lib 50-51; Libn GS-7 VA Hosp, Oakland Cal 51-54; Libn Kaiser Aluminum & Chem Corp, Oakland Cal; Libn Kaiser Sch of Nursing, Oakland Cal 58-61; Asst libn Parks Job Corp Ctr, Pleasanton Cal 65-66, Ref libn City of Livermore, Livermore Cal 66-67; Libn II Alameda Co Lib, Hayward Cal 67-. 9: ALA; CathLA; CalLA. 14: Spec libs, med libs (catlg, admin). 15: 1713 Fifth st, Livermore Ca 94550.

PANGBORN MARK W(HITE) JR. b Indianapolis Ind. 4: Ruth Anderson Panghorn. 5: Ind U 31-35 (Geol) AB; UIll 39-40 BS LS. 6: Fr. 7: Clerk Indiana Nat Bank, Indianapolis 35-39; Ref-circ asst Purdue U Lib 40-41; Stack & r r asst LC 41-42, Photodup serv searcher 42-43; Bibliogr, Mil Geol Br US Geol Survey, Wash DC 43-49; Ref libn & map curator US Geol Survey Lib, Wash DC 49-. 9: Assn Amer Geogs; SLA; Geosci Info Soc (pres 66); Nat Assn Geol Tchrs. 10: AAAS. 12: "Earthfor the Layman (57), "Bibliography of Oceanographic Publications (63), Ed adv bd "Science Books, a Quarterly Review (6-). 13: Yes. 14: Maps, ref, popularization of Sci. 15: 5204 Brookeway dr, Wash DC 20016.

PANKAKE, MARCIA JEAN (LARSEN). b Minneapolis Minn 1 N 40. 4: Jon A Pankake. 5: UMinn 58-62 (Intl Rel) BA, 63-65 (LS) MA. 6: Fr, Ger. 7: Lib asst UMinn Walter Lib 63-64; Jr libn UMinn St Paul Campus Lib 65-67, Libn (acquis) 67-. 9: MinnLA. 10: Beta Phi Mu; Assocs of James Ford Bell Lib. 14: Bk selection, acquis. 15: 1012 23rd ave SE, Minneapolis Mn 55414.

PANKRATZ, BETH (EVALINA). b Pryor Okla 9 Jl 42. 5: Grace Bible Inst 60-62; Northeastern State Col 62-64 (Eng) BA in Ed; UOkla 65-68 MLS. 7: Tchr-libn Okla Bible Acad, Meno 64-67; Libn Connors State Col 67-. 9: ALA; OklaLA; OklaEA. 10: Delta Kappa Gamma; Alpha Chi; Rho Theta Sigma. 15: Connors State College, Warner Ok 74469.

PANNELL, GLADYS EDITH. b Lynchburg Va 11 My 31. 5: Va State Col 48-52 (LS) BS; Rutgers summers 57-61 MLS. ; Va State Col Educl Media Inst, summer 66.9 6: Fr, Sp. 7: Tchr-libn Central Elem Sch, Rustburg Va 52-53; Libn Campbell Co High Sch, Rustburg Va 53-. 9: VaEA; NEA; VaLA. 10: Twelve and One Club; YWCA. 14: Ref, catlg. 15: Route 3 Box 100, Lynchburg Va 24504.

PANNIER, PATRICIA (JEAN). b Pittsburgh Penn 3 Jl 40. 5: St LawrenceU 58-62 (Bio) BS; UPittsburgh 63-65; UDenver 65-66 (Libnship) MA; UColo 68-. 7: Med tech Allegheny Gen hosp, Pittsburgh Penn 62-63; Research tech UPittsburgh Dept of Biochem 63-65; MEDLARS searcher UColo Med Ctr Lib 66-. 9: MedLA. 10: Mortar Bd; Phi Beta Kappa. 11: SLA scholarship. 12: "Bibliographie's on Antilymphocye Serum and Human Histocompatibility" (69). 13: Yes. 14: Computerized searching of med lit. 15: 200 Pearl st #205, Denver Co 80203.

PANNU, GURDIAL SINGH. b Punjab India (now Pakistan) 2 O 30. 4: Gurbaksh Sahota. 5: Panjab U (India) 46-50 (Eng, Math) BA; UToronto 61-62 BLS (Honors), 62-65 MLS; UIll 67-68 (LS). 6: Arabic, Hindu, Panjabi, Persian, Urdu. 7: Sub Inspector Police, Punjab India 50-58; Lumber Grader Plumper Bay Sawmill, Victoria BC 58-61; Catlgr UToronto Lib 62-65; Lecturer & asst to the dir Sch of Lib Sci UToronto 65-66, Asst Prof 66-67; Assoc Prof Sch Lib Sci U Alberta 68-. 9: ALA; AALS; CanLA; Inst Prof Libns Ont; EdmontonLA. 10: Beta Phi Mu; Can Assn Univ Tchrs. 12: Co-comp "Sample Catalogue Cards Exemplifying the Anglo-American Cataloging Rules" (68). 13: Yes. 14: Catlg, research methodology. 15: 8312-68 A st, Edmonton 83 Alberta Can.

PANOFSKY, HANS E. b Berlin Germany 30 Ja 26. 4: Gianna Sommi. 5: London Sch of Econ & Pol Sci ULondon 43-44; Columbia 49-52 (Sociol, LS) BS MS; Cornell U 52-58 (Labor Econ) MS. 6: Ger, Fr. 7: (Sgt) Brit Army, Britain, Germany 44-47; Asst ref libn NY State Sch of Ind & Labor Rel Cornell U 52-58; Ref libn Oak Park (Ill) Pub Lib 58-59; Curator of Africana Northwestern U Lib 59-, Sci libn 59-62. 9: ASIS; ALA (Mem Com, Internat Rels Round Table 64-);-ACRL (mem-at-large Law & Pol Sci Sub-sect 65-66); African Studies Assn (chm Archives-Libs Com 68-); IllLA (Intel Freedom Com 69). 10: Econ Soc of Ghana (Fellow); Internat African Inst; Ind Rel Res Assn. 13: Yes. 14: Internat libnship, info retr. 15: 1229 Judson ave, Evanston Ill 60202.

PAPAJ, MARIANNE (LOUISE ELIZABETH). b Buffalo NY 4 Jl 41. 5: SUNY (Buffalo) 59-65 (Eng, Hist) BA, 65 (Hist); Columbia 67- (Hist). 6: Fr, Ger. 7: Period recs asst SUNY (Buffalo) Lockwood Mem Lib 63-65; Libn E High Sch, Buffalo NY 65-66; Libn trainee Buffalo & Erie Co Pub Lib, Buffalo 66; Docs analyst for archival materials St Marks Lib Gen Theol Sem 67-, Asst to libn 68-; Reserve asst Bus Lib ColumbiaU 67-68. 8: Org libn St Paul's Cathedral Lib, Buffalo NY 65-68; Docs analyst for archival materials Coates Hall

Theol Train Col, Edinburgh Scotland 69. 9: AHA; SAA. 10: NY Hist Soc. 13: Yes. 14: Hist & admin of archives, ch archives, hist mus archives, mss collections, priv papers. 15: St Mark's Lib Gen Theol Sem 175 9th ave, New York NY 10011.

PAPIER, LAWRENCE S. b Newark NJ 12 N 28. 4: Doris Papier. 5: Rutgers 46-50 (Chem) AB; Columbia 50-51 (LS) MS. 7: Info spec Army Chem Corps (Pfc), Edgewood Md 51-53; Libn indexing & ref Nval Research Lab, Wash DC 51-58; Head document sect Naval Weapons Lab, Dahlgren Va 58-59; Head lib div Naval Propellant Plant, Indian Head Md 59-63; Asst libn Ft Detrick, Frederick Md 63-64; Chief Libn Edgewood (Md) Arsenal 64-66; Syst coord US Off of Educ, Wash DC 66-. 8: Grad study grant NIH, in pub admin & info retrieval 62-63. 9: SLA; ASIS; Amer Rocket Soc. 10: Pi Sigma Alpha. 12: "Technical-Thesaurus (62); others. 13: Yes. 14: Sch lib wk. 15: 10121 Riggs rd, Adelphi Md 20783.

PAPILLON, LUCIEN. b Donnacona Cte Portneuf 25 N 23. 4: Gertrude Germain. 5: Michaud's Inst 45-48 (Classical) BA; Sch of lib sci 48-49 BLS. 6: Fr. 7: Asst hd Pub Lib, Timmins Ont 50-54; Hd catlg dept Lib Mil Col (St Jean Que) 54-60; Chief libn Forest Research Lab, Que 60-63; Hd catlg dept University Lib, Que 63-68, Hd tech serv 68-. 9: CanLA; Assn Canadienne des Bibliothecaires de Langue Francaise (pres tech serv sect 67-68). 12: "Cumulative Index of Bi-monthly Progress Reports" v 1-16, 45-60 (61); "Bibliography on the Elm Disease in North America" (63). 14: Tech serv. 15: 1057 de Grenoble, Ste Foy Que 10 Can.

PAPPALARDO, CHARLES. b NYC 2 S 18. 4: Annette Canary. 5: City Col(NY) 34-39 (Math) BA; Columbia 40-42 BLS, 51-54 MS. 6: Ital, Fr. 7: (Lt Col) US Army Civil Affairs, Europe Theater 4 2-46; Catlgr City Col (NY) 46-49; Chief tech serv Baruch Sch, NYC 50-59; Prof & Lib n Queensborough Commun Col 60-. 9: ALA; Mil Govt Assn (pres NY Chap 69-); LA City Univ NY (pres 55-57; Res Off Assn Dept of NYS Dist II v-pres 68. 10: Bayside Hist Soc; AAUP. 14: Tech serv, lib bldgs. 15: 169-43 25 ave, Bayside NY 11357.

PARADIS, JACQUES. b Montreal Can 16 Je 43. 5: Ecole De Bibliotheconomie U de Montreal 65 B Bibl. 6: Fr. 7: Clerk "American Encyclopedia, Chicago summer 51) Clerk Local Loan Co Exec Off Accting Div, Chicago summers 52-59; Coun UIll Dormitories (Urbana) 55-59; Bibliog researcher UIll Lib (Urbana) 59-60; Ref libn Chicago Pub Lib 60-61; Ed research libn Field Enterprises Educ Corp, Chicago 61-65, Asst ed 65-67, Ed research libn 67-. 9: Assn canadienne des bibliothecaires de langue francais. 13: Yes. 14: Library sci lit. 15: Bibliotheque Ecole De Bibliotheconomie Univ De Montreal CP 6128, Montreal 250 Can.

PARAGAMIAN, HELEN. b Braddock Penn 10 My 19. 5: Simmons 37-41 (LS) BS. 6: Armenian. 7: Child libn Shute Mem Lib,. Everett Mass 41-49, Asst libn & child libn 49-56; Head Libn Pine Manor Jr Col (Mass) 56-. 9: ALA-ACRL (Jr Col Lib Sect: sec 61-63 & 65-66, chm Constit & By-laws Com 65-66; rep to Nat Lib Week); MassLA; NELA; Round Table of Child Libns of Mass (treas 51-53). 10: Womens Nat Bk Assn; Bus Womens Fellowship. 13: Yes. 15: Pine Manor Jr Col Lib, 400 Heath st, Chestnut Hill Ma 02167.

PARALKAR, VEENA VASANT. b Nasik India 4 Jl 44. 5: St Xavier's College (Bombay) 60-64 (Eng) BA; UBombay (India) 64-65 BLS; UIll (Urbana) 66-68 (LS) MS, 68- (Journalism, communications). 6: Hindi, Marathi. 7: Ref asst "Times of India", Bombay 65; Lib asst UBombay 65-66; Asstship UIll (Urbana) 66-68, Lib asst Lib of art & arch 68-. 9: SLA. 14: Ref, newspaper commun libs. 15: c/o Foreign Student Affairs Ofc, Univ of Illinois, Urbana Il 61801.

PARAMSKAS, BALYS. b Riga Latvia 6 My 07. 4: Nathalie Lelejevaite. 5: UKaunas 9lithuania) 26-31-35 (Law). 6: Lithuanian, Fr, Russian, Polish, Ger, Lat, scandinavian. 7: Lib asst desk attend LC Law Lib 58; Prel catlg & search LC proc dept descr div 59, Sr searcher-catlg 62; Libn catlg reviser 65; Lib tech reviser 68-. 8: Dir Varpas Inc Co, Kaunas Lithuania 30-40; Mem press com of Coun of Europe 49-51; Lab tech Papeterie de la Robertsau, Strasbourg France 45-51; Lab researck wk Capitol Printing Ink Co, Wash DC 51-58. 10: Glover Park Citizens Assn; Amer Lithuanian Soc; Intl Peasant Union. 13: Yes. 14: Rare bks in Eng, Ger, Lat & Fr. 15: 3843 Beecher st NW, Washington DC 20007.

PARCH, GRACE DOLORES. b Cleveland 15 My 26. 5: Flora Stone Mather Col 43-46 (Hist) BA; West Res 47-50 (Span); McGill 50-51 BLS. 6: Sp. 7: Publicity libn US ArmySpec Servs, Frankfurt Germany 51-52; Post libn US Army Spec Servs Camp Darby, Liborno Italy 52; Br libn Cleveland Heights (Ohio) Pub Lib 54-63; Asst head ref dept Va State Lib 64; Dir Twinsburg (Ohio) Pub Lib 65-. 8: Establ first post-war Army Libraries in Italy, 52; Establ several Convents High Sch Cath Sch Libs in Ohio. 9: SLA; CathLA (past co-chm NOU); ALA (Rep ALA on ALA-CathLA Jt Com 67-70). 11: John Cotton Dana Award 67. 13: Yes./ 8rare bks, admin.5 14: Pub libs, rare bks. 15: 688 Jefferson, Bedford Ohio.

PARCHE, M(ARY) CONSTANCE (COLE). b Niagara Falls NY 10 Jl 07. 4: William Henry Parche. 5: Bryn Mawr 26-30 (Chem) AB; UBerlin 34 (Ger); Niagara U 40-41 (Ger); UBuffalo 44-45 (LS, Metallurgy). 6: Ger, Fr, 07: Acturial dept Mutual Life Ins Co of NY, NYC 30-31; Math tchr, Niagara Falls NY 31-32; Self-employed org & conductor European Tour 33-38; Libn The Carborundum Co, Niagara Falls NY 38-. 8: Guest lecturer on "The Chemical Library at ERIE Co Tech Inst, Buffalo NY 45-47. 9: CS (West NY Chap: mem-at-large 62, sec 64-66); SLA (West NY Chap: sec, treas, chm). 10: Carborundum Co Functional Staff-Mgt Club; Women Chem Group, Col Club of Niagara Falls; Nat Assn Power Engnrs; Womens Auxiliary; YWCA. 12: "Silicon Carbide in Kirk Othmer, Ency Chem Tech vol 2 (48, 64); Periodicals: "Chemistry of SiC in "Science Counselor (49); "Micro-Opaque Cards in "Special Libraries (58); Abstr "Sci-Tech News & "Chemical Literature. 13: Yes. 14: Spec libs (tech), info storage-retrieval, ref. 15: 724 Park pl PO Box 275, Niagara Falls NY 14302.

PARDEE, MARY R. b Linthicum Heights Md 13 Ag 22. 5: Stetson U40-43 (Humanities) AB; Fla So Col summer 42; Emory 44-45; UNacional Autonoma de Mex summer 58 (LS) BS; UFla 60-61. 6: Sp, Fr. 7: Catlgr instr UFla 45-61; Catlgr Jr Col of Broward Co 61-. 9: ALA; FlaLA (sec, Catlgrs Round Table 64; Nomin Com 65). 10: AAUP. 15: 1021 S W 31st st, Ft Lauderdale Fla 33315.

PARHAM, PAUL M. b Near Paris Tex 20 Ap 28. 5: Paris Jr Col 45-47; UTex 47-49 (Hist) BA, 53 MLS; UDenver 64 (Hist, LS) PhD. 7:Libn Panhandle Agric & Mech Col 49-62; Asst libn & Prof of Hist Northeastern State Cl, Tahlequah Okla 62-64, Head Libn 64-65; Libn Tex Christian U 65-. 8: Visiting instr George Peabody Col summer 58; Assoc dir NDEA Inst for Sch Libn Northeastern State Col 65. 9: ALA; SWLA; TexLA (Chm acquis RT 67, v-chm dist VII 69, Exec Bd 69-72). 10: AAUP; Phi Alpha Theta; Pi Gamma Mu. 13: Yes. 14: Admin. 15: 2633 Forest Park blvd, Ft Worth Tex 76110.

PARIS, JANELLE (AVENELL). b Houston 10 O 26. 4: Otto Paris. 5: Sam Houston State Tchrs Col 43-46 (LS) BS; Tex Womans U 48-50 BS LS; UHouston 49-56 (Educ) MEd; Tex Woman's U summer 65 NDEA Institute in Lib Sci. 7: Libn Pearland (Tex) High Sch 46-50; Libn Clear Creek High Sch, League City Tex 50-65, Hd sch libn 65-; Visiting instr in Lib Sci Sam Houston State Col ummer 68.5 9: ALA; NEA (Life Mem); TexLA; Tex State Tchrs Assn. 10: PTA. 14: Bk sel for yp, reading guidance, reading publicity. 15: POBox 382, Frindswood Tex 77546.

PARIS, JANET (FRESCH). b Baltimore Md 29 Jl 11. 4: Maurice Thatcher Paris. 5: Wilson Col 29-33 (Eng) AB; Drexel 33-34 BS in LS; Columbia 39-40 MLS. 6: Fr. 7: Catlgr Enoch Pratt Free Lib,. Baltimore 34-41; Catlgr LC 41-52; Catlgr NYC Pub Lib 53-56; Instr Nazareth College Dept· of lib sci, Louisville Ky 56-60; Catlgr Montgomery Co Dept of pub Lib, Rockville Md 60-66; Catlgr SC State Lib Bd, Columbia 66-68; Libn Georgetown Co Mem Lib, Georgetown SC 68-. 11: Superior accomplishment award LC 49. 14: Catlg. 15: Georgetown County Mem Lib, Georgetown SC 29440.

PARISEAU, EARL JOSEPH. b Methuen Mass 14 Ag 28. 4: Joyce L Womack. 5: St Petersburg jr Col 54-55 AA; UMiami (Coral Gables Fla) 48-49; UFla 55-57 (Latin Amer Studies) BA; AmerU 58-59 (Intl Rel) MA. 6: Sp, Portu. 7: Br mgr Rex Med Supply Co, Tampa Fla 50-51; Salesman Julius Schmidt Inc, NYC & Fla 51-52; Med supply tech (E-4) USA 52-54; Ed "Hdbk of Lat Amer Studies" LC 62-66, Asst dir Hispanic Foundation 64-66, 68-, Field dir LC Off Rio de Janeiro 66-68. 9: ALA. 10: Phi Alpha Theta& lat Amer Studies Assn; AHA. 13: Yes. 14: Ref & acquis of Lat Amer Lib materials. 15: 5515 Margate st, Springfield Va 22151.

PARISH, BARBARA LU (SHIRK). b Lincoln Kan 28 N 42. 4: Harlie Albert Parish Jr. 5: Fort Hays Kan State Col 60-64 (Eng) AB; UMo (Columbia) 64-68 (Eng) MA, (LS) MA. 6: Fr. 7: Catlgr & instr in lib sci ULouisville 68-. 9: AAUP. 14: Catlg, rare bks. 15: 7904 Avanti Way, Louisville Ky 40291.

PARK, BEATRICE S. b Winburne Penn 28 O 14. 4: Robert L Park. 5: Carnegie 30-34 (Pub Sch Music) BA, 60-61 MLS; Penn State Col summers 34, 36; Stetson U summer 60. 6: Fr. 7: Tchr Philipsburg (Penn) High Sch 35-39; Tchr Cooper Twp High Sch, Winburn Penn 39-49, Tchr & asst prin 49-60; Libn West Branch Area High Sch, Morrisdale Penn 61-. 9: NEA; ALA; NCTE; Penn State EA; Penn LA. 15: Winburne Penn 16879.

PARK, HWAYANG. b Seoul Korea 12 Jl 30. 5: Sacramento State Col 56-61 (Home Econ) BA; State U Col (Geneseo NY) 64-65 MLS. 6: Eng, Korean, Japanese. 7: Clerk-typist UNKRA, Pusan-Seoul Korea 53-54; Asst libn SUNY (Buffalo) 65-. 9: Upstate NY MedLA; MedLA. 14: Catlg. 15: 3214 Main st, Buffalo NY 14214.

PARK, JOHN GRAY. b Boston 15 S 08. 5: Harvard 28-29 & summers 29-32; Harvard Grad Sch of Educ 32 (Eng). 7: Eng dept Kent (Conn) Sch 30-42; (Maj) AAF CombatIntelligence 42-46; Libn Kent (Conn) Sch 46-58, Dir of Libs 58- 58-. Conn Governors Com on Libs 61-62; Sch Lib J consul 60; Dept of Health, Educ & Welfare consul rep independent schs at Title II meting, Wash DC My 65. 9: ALA-AASchL (oser ISEB Conf, mem Prof Rels Com 61-62); Nat Assn Indep Schs (past chm Lib Com); ConnLA (past chm Program Com). 12: Com chm "3000 Books for Secondary School Libraries (61). 13: Yes. 14: Secon schs. 15: Kent School, Kent Ct 06757.

PARK, LELAND MADISON. b Alexandria La 21 O 41. 5: Davidson Col 59-63 (Pol Sci) AB; Emory 63-64 (LS) ML. ; Simmons Summer 68 (Lib Automation). 7: Ref asst Pub Lib of Charlotte (NC) & Mecklenburg Co 64-65; (1st Lt) US Army: Adjutant Gen Corps; Deputy Commander of the Armed Forces Examining & Entrance Station, Raleigh NC 65-67; Hd of ref & stud personnel Lib of Davidson Col 67-.9 9: ALA; SELA; NCLA. 10: SAR; Soc of the Cincinnati; Sigma Nu; Jr C of C; Res Offs Assn; Piedmont Univ Ctr. 14: Ref, admin. 15: PO Box 2201, Davidson NC 28036.

PARK, LUCY ANN (PRITCHARD). b Asheville NC 16 Mr 22. 4: Bruce Robertson Park. 5: St Genevieve-of-the-Pines Jr Col 39-41 AA; Womans Col UNC 44-46 (Eng) BA (magna cum laude); Columbia 46-48 BS in LS, 49-51 (Eng). 6: Fr, Sp. 7: Lib asst St Genevieve-of-the-Pines Jr Col 40-41; Lib asst bkmob, ref, circ pub lib, Asheville NC 41-42; Clerk NC Shipbuilding Co, Wilmington NC summer 45; Stud aide Woman's Col UNC Lib 44-46; Columbia U Libs; Desk asst, Carpenter Lib 46-47, Jr catlgr Tchrs Col Lib 47-48, Catlgr modern langs 48-49, Supv proc unit catlg dept 49-52, Asst acquis libn Cornell U Libs 52-56; Catlgr ser, spec collections Columbia U Libs 56-57, 59-. 9: ALA. 10: Phi Beta Kappa. 14: Catlg, ser, acquis, rare bks. 15: 150 Hicks st, apt 2A, Brooklyn NY 11201.

PARK, ROBERT (MICHAEL ALEXANDER). b Winnipeg Man Can 26 S 28. 4: Lisa Ison. 5: UMan 45-50 BA, 52-58 BEd. 7: Tchr: Elphinstone High Sch, Elphinstone Man 50-52, Roland High Sch, Roland Man 52-54; Tchr & libn: Winnipeg Sch Div, Winnipeg Man 54-61, Seven Oaks Sch Div, Winnipeg Man 61-62, Ft Garry Sch Div, Winnipeg Man 62-. 9: CanLA (Coun Adv Gp); ManLA (pres 67-69); ManASchL (past pres). 14: Sch libnship. 15: 736 Townsend ave, Winnipeg 19 Man Can.

PARK, WILMER (REGINALD). b Itasca Tex 23 D 06. 5: Austin Col 24-28 (Eng) BA; UTex (Austin) 49-52 MLS. 6: Sp. 7: Catlgr Hardin-Simmons U 52-53; Ref libn pub lib, houston Tex 53-57; Ref libn pub lib, LA 58-. 9: ALA. 14: Ref. 15: 3213 1/2 W 18th st, Los Angeles Ca 90019.

PARKE, CAROL (REEVES). b Fairfield Conn 23 D 35. 4: Richard Parke. 5: Conn Col 54-58 (Eng) BA; Columbia 64-66 MS in LS. 7: NY Pub Lib 66-68; Ref asst ref dept Yale U Sterling Mem Lib 68-. 15: 383 Canner st, New Haven Ct 06511.

PARKE, KATHRYN (EMMA). b Fairport NY 12 F 15. 5: Smith 32-36 (Eng) BA; SUNY (Albany) summers 38-41 BS LS; UIll 44-46 MSLS. 6: Norwegian, other Scandinavian langs, Fr. 7: Tchr Eng & libn Norfolk (NY) High Sch 36-41; Libn Monticello (NY) High Sch 41-42; Tchr Eng & libn New London Jr Col 42-43; Libn Spencerport (NY) High Sch 43-44; Asst libn Green Mt Jr Col 45-47; Asst libn State U Col (Geneseo NY) 47-51; Libn & tchr Eng State U Agric Tech Col (Cobleskill NY) 51-52, Libn 52-. 8: SUNY Lib Devel Com 57-65; Sabbatical year study of Scandinavian folk high schs 58-59; Exec Com of SUNY Libns 66-. 9: ALA Jr Col Sect: NE Reg Chm 46-47); Hudson-Mohawk (NY) LA (pres 64-66); Capital Dist (NY) Lib Coun (Trustee 66-). 12: "Norways Folk-High-Schools (63). 13: Yes. 14: Admin, Jr Col level educ, lib tech (non-prof) training. 15: State Univ Ag-Tech Col, Cobleskill NY 12043.

PARKER, BARBARA TENNEY. b Haverhill Mass 5 N 26. 5: Simmons 44-48 (LS) BS; Rutgers summers 58, 59, 60 & 61 MLS. 6: Fr, Ger. 7: Catlgr UCincinnati Lib 48-50; Catlgr Yale U 50-52, Ref asst 52-55; Head circ & ref Yale Divinity Lib 55-62; Catlgr UVt Lib 62-63, Head catlg dept 63-. 9: ALA; NELA. 14: Catlg, ref. 15: 154 Birchcliff parkway, Burlington Vt 05401.

PARKER, EDWARD DALE JR. b Searcy Ark 19 Je 38. 4: Olive Allen. 5: Texarkana 56-57 (Pre-engr); Hardin-Simmons U 57-58 (Pre-engr); Stetson U 60-63 (Speech) BA; Fla State U 65-66 (Academic Libs) MSLS. 6: Sp. 7: A/2C Missile syst analyst USAF 58-60; Ins salesman Conn Mutual Life, San Antonio Tex 63; Loan Processor Ark Bank & Trust, Hot Springs Ark 64-65; Asst sci libn & instr in Lib Sci NM State U 67-69, Act order libn 69; Chief ref serv Trinity U 69-. 9: ALA; SWLA; NMLA. 14: Ref. 15: Trinity Univ Box 216, 715 Stadium dr, San Antonio Tx 78212.

PARKER, EDWIN BURKE. b Berwyn Alberta Can 19 Ja 32. 4: Shan Greenwood. 5: McGill 50-52; UBC 52-54 (Philos) BA; Stanford 57-58 (Communication) MA, 58-60 (Communication) PhD. 7: Staff reporter "The Vancouver Sun", Vancouver Can 54-55; Info off UBC 55-57; Research asst StanfordU 58-60, Asst Prof (communication) 62-63, Assoc Prof (communication) 63; Asst Prof (communication) UIll, Urbana 60-62. 8: Spec consul to dir of libs StanfordU on computer utilization 68-; Prin investigator Project SPIRES (Stanford Pub Info Retrieval Syst) 66-. 9: ASIS (Exec Com: Spec Interest Groups for lib Automation 67-68; Educ Com 67-); Assn for Computing Machinery (treas Spec Interest Group for Info Ret 68-69). 10: Amer Psychological Assn; Amer Sociological Assn. 11: Fellow Ctr for Advanced Study in Behavioral Sci 69-70. 12: Co-auth "Television in the Lives of our Children" (61); Co-auth "The Kennedy Assassination and the American Public" (65). 13: Yes. 14: Computer info retr syst. 15: Inst for Communication Res Stanford Univ, Stanford Ca 94305.

PARKER, ELAINE (MARIE). b New Orleans La 11 D 40. 5: Xavier U (La) 57-60 (Spanish Educ) BA; LSU 65 summers 63, 64, 65 MS in LS; USoCal summer 62, 68 (LS). 6: Fr, Sp. 7: Sp/Fr Tchr Orleans Parish Schs, New Orleans 61-66, Libn Centralized Serv 66; Ref libn Xavier U, New Orleans 66-67; Libn, Elem Sch Orleans Parish, New Orleans 67-68. 9: ALA; NEA-DAVI; CathLA (rec sec Greater New Orleans Chap 67-68); LaLA; CalASchL. 10: Beta Phi Mu; Phi Kappa Phi. 14: Sch libnship. 15: 847 Exposition blvd, Los Angeles Ca 90007.

PARKER, ELIZABETH LEE (SWITZER). b Raymond Wash 19 Jl 25. 5: UWash 43-44 (Liberal Arts); UOre 62-64 (Elem Educ) BS, summers 65-68 (LS) MS. 7: Libn Maple Elem Sch, Springfield Ore 65-67; Lib consul State Dept of Educ 67-68; Libn The Dalles High Sch, The Dalles Ore 68-69. 9: ALA; NEA; OhioASchL; OhioEA. 14: Sch libs. 15: 1878 Villard st, Eugene Or 97403.

PARKER, EMMA LOUISE (MILLER). b Newberry County SC 8 Je 18. 4: Forrest Bailey Parker Sr. 5: Spelman Col 35-36; AllenU 37-40 (Chem) BA; ColumbiaU summer 56; AtlantaU summer 59-63 MLS. 6: Fr. 7: Tchr Orangeburg Co Tr Sch, Elloree SC 40; Tchr-libn brewer High Sch, Greenwood SC 40-47; Tchr Mt Zion No 39, Epworth SC 55-56; Libn E End Elem Sch, Greenwood SC 57-. 9: ALA; NEA; SCLA; SCEA (Libn's Div; past sec). 10: Yellow Jessamine Garden Club; Museum Greenwood SC; Greenwood Co Beautification Commsn; Alpha Kappa Alpha; Beta Phi Mu. 14: Catlg, ref. 15: Power House rd, Hodges SC 29653.

PARKER, EVELYN (ABRAMSON). b Detroit Mich 1 F 18. 4: Max Parker. 5: Wayne StateU 43 (Educ) BS; UMich 66 MALS. 6: Ger. 7: Libn Detroit Pub Lib 63-69; Libn-tchr Southfield Bd of Educ, Southfield Mich 69. 9: NEA; Assn of Childhood Intl; ALA. 10: SouthfieldEA; Wayne State Lib Sci Alumni Assn. 15: 20541 Charlton sq, Southfield Mi 48075.

PARKER, GROVER P. b Santa Monica Cal 14 D 24. 5: UOmaha 61 BA; Fla State U 65 (LS) MS. 7: USAF (Capt) 51-63; Ref libn Air U Lib Maxwell AFB 65-. 14: Ref. 15: Box 405 Rt 2, Millbrook Al 36054.

PARKER, HELEN (HARRIETT). b Des Moines Iowa 19 S 05. 5: Grinnell Col 23-27 (Hist) AB; West Res 28-29 BS LS; UIll Med Sch 50. 7: Dir wk with child Pub Lib, Des Moines Iowa 33-36; Child libn br Pub Lib, Kansas City Mo 36-44; Army libn 44-47; Ref libn 1st asst Pub Lib, Des Moines Iowa

48-49; Chief Libn VA Center, Des Moines Iowa 49-. 9: ALA; Des Moines Lib Club. 10: Altrusa. 14: Med ref. 15: VA Center, Des Moines Ia 50308.

PARKER, HENRY ARTHUR III. b New London Conn 15 My 44. 5: Johnson State Col 62-66 (Educ) BS; Rutgers 66-68 MLS. 6: Fr. 7: Lib stud asst Johnson State Col 62-66; Period clk Rutgers (Newark) 66-67; Catlgr Rutgers (New Brunswick NJ) 67-68; Libn (hd) Peabody Elem Sch, Cambridge Mass 68-. 8: Consul: Stowe Elem School Lib, Stowe Vt 65-66; Educ Lib Memorial UNfld summer 69. 9: MassSchLA; NewEnglandSchLA. 10: Kappa Phi Kappa. 14: Sch lib serv, catlg. 15: 48 Beacon st, Boston Ma 02138.

PARKER, J CARLYLE. b Ogden Utah 14 O 31. 4: Janet Greene. 5: Weber Col 49-51, 53 Music; Brigham Young U 55-57 (Hist) BA; UCal(Berkeley) 57-58 MLS. 7: Chaplain's asst US Army (Cpl) 53-55; Spec serv libn Humboldt State Col Lib 58-60; Asst libn Church Col Hawaii Lib 60-62, act libn 62-63; hd pub serv Stanislaus State Col Lib 63-. 8: Staff libn USA World's Fair NYC 65; Stanislaus State Col research leave 68; Founder & volunteer libn Modesto Genealogical Lib 68-. 9: ALA; CalLA (pres State Col Libns Div 68, Redwood Dist pres 59-60); HawaiiLA (treas 62-63). 10: Assn Cal State Col Profs. 12: Comp "An Annotated Bibliography of the History of Del Norte and Humboldt Counties (60); Comp "Academic Qualifications of Librarians in The California State Colleges; A Survey Report" (67). 14: Ref, loc hist, genealogy. 15: 2115 N Denair ave, Turlock Ca 95380.

PARKER, JEWEL GRAY. b Counce Tenn 26 Mr 02. 5: Miss So U 22-23 Tchg Certif; Memphis StateU 29-33 (Eng, Geog) BS; Peabody Col summers 46, 47, 49, 50 BS in LS, summers 51-55 MA in LS. 6: Fr. 7: Tchr The Lausanne Sch for Girls, Memphis Tenn 41-46; Ref libn SWest Col, Memphis Tenn 58-59; Libn The Hutchinson Sch for Girls, Memphis Tenn 46-58, 59-68. 8: Card catlg lower sch The Hutchinson Sch for Girls 69-. 9: ALA; SELA; TennLA (chm Sch Libs Div 58). 10: Beta Phi Mu. 14: Sch libs. 15: 1185 Marcia rd, Memphis Tn 38117.

PARKER, JOHN (AUSTIN). b Philadelphia Penn 12 Je 20. 4: Betty Shoop. 5: Temple 39-42 (Fine Arts), 43-46 (Secondary Educ) BS Ed; Syracuse 49-50 (Amer Lit); Pratt Inst 54-55 MLS. 7: Army of the US 42-43; Eng tchr: Staunton Mil Acad, Staunton Va 46-48, Church Farm Sch, Paoli Penn 48-49, Haddonfield High Sch, Haddonfield NJ 50-51; Lib asst Franklin Inst, Phila 51-54; Ref libn Peabody Inst, Baltimore 55-58; Libn Catonsville commun Col 58-59; A-v Libn USMA 59-66; Libn Storm King Sch, Cornwall-on-Hudson NY 66-. 9: ALA; Hudson Valley LA. 10: Beta Phi Mu. 12: Ed "Maryland Libraries" (57-58). 13: Yes. 14: Wk with yp. 15: 90 Weeks ave, Cornwall on Hudson NY 12520.

PARKER, JOHN ALBERT. b Norfolk Va 25 Ja 44. 5: Old Dominion Col 61-65 (Eng) BA; UNC 65-66 (LS) MS, 68 (Sp). 6: Sp. 7: Shelver Norfolk Pub Lib, Norfolk Va 64-65, Libn I 68-; Clk-typist (Sp/4) US Army 66-68. 9: ALA; VaLA; SELA. 10: Amer Assn Sp & Portu Tchrs. 11: Army Commendation Medal. 14: Ref, catlg. 15: 155 W Chester st, Norfolk Va 23503.

PARKER, JOHN. b Nekoma ND 15 My 23. 4: Patricia Falstad. 5: Jamestown Col 41-43, 46-47 (Soc Sci) AB; Wayne State U 47-49 (Hist) AM; UMich 48-49, 52-53, 60 (LS) AM LS, PhD. 7: Instr in hist UND 49-52; Asst Mss dept Clements Lib, UMich 52-53; Curator James Ford Bell Collection UMinn 53-. 9: BSA; Soc Hist Discoveries (sec); Hakluyt Soc; Ms Soc. 12: "Van Meteren's Virginia, 1607-1612" (61); Ed "Merchants and Scholars" (65); "Books to Build an Empire" (66). 13: Yes. 14: Rare bks, bibliog research. 15: 2325 Minneapolis ave, Minneapolis Mn 55406.

PARKER, LOUISE (PRATT). b Wills Point Tex 4 Mr 19. 5: Tex Womans U 37-38; N Tex State U 38-41 (LS) BS. 7: Eng tchr Pub Sch, Wills Point Tex 41-42; Libn: Jr High Sch, Greenville Tex 42-44, Naval Air Tech Train Center, Norman Okla 44-45, High Sch, Vernon Tex 49-51, Pub lib, Newark NJ 52; Prin libn Pub Lib, Passaic NJ 53-58; Head of gen ref Pub Lib, Dallas 58-. 9: TexLA; ALA; SWLA. 14: Ref. 15: 6817 de Loache ave, Dallas Tx 75225.

PARKER, MABLE YVONNE. b Lancaster SC 17 N 34. 4: Ulysses Parker. 5: SCar State Col 52-56 (LS) BS; Rutgers 63-66 MLS. 7: Libn Manchester high Sch, Pinewood SC. 8: State Adv Stud Lib Assts Assn SC 66-68. 9: ALA; SCLA; SELA; GuamLA. 10: NAACP. 14: Ref, readers serv. 15: 421 E Barr st, Lancaster SC 29720.

PARKER, MALCOLM GLYNDOL. b Purvis Miss 23 Ag 30. 4: Peggy Sawyer. 5: USoMiss 52-54 (Eng, LS) BS; LSU 56-58 (LS) MS, 60-64 (Educ) MEd. 6: Fr, Russian. 7: Lib asst USoMiss summers 53, 54; Libn Gulfport (Miss) City Schs 54-56; LSU (Baton Rouge): Ref libn 58-59, Ser record libn 59-62, Head circ 62-63, Sci catlgr 63-65; Libn LSU (Shreveport) 66-. 8: Lib consul, Schuykill Products, Baton Rouge, La fall 65. 9: ALA; LaLA; SWLA; Caddo-Bossier Lib Club (chm 67-68). 14: Catlg, ref. 15: 306 Yolanda lane, Shreveport La 71105.

PARKER, MARY (LEWIS) GRAY. b Canton NY 7 Ja 13. 5: St LawrenceU 31-35 (Math) BS, 47-48 (Educ) MEd; Syracuse 50-55 MS in LS. 7: Math tchr Central Sch, Madrid NY 48-49; Libn SUNY Agric & Tech Col (Canton) 49-. 9: ALA (chm Jr Col Sect 56-58); SLA; NYLA (v-pres & pres-elect Col & Univ Sect 69; pres N Country & Research Resources Coun 67-68, sec 68-, trustee 66-). 10: CantonLA; Canton Club Womens' Bowling League; Alumnae Adv Coun for Pi Beta Phi; Canton Republican Town Com; Delta Kappa Gamma. 14: Ref, pub rel. 15: Southworth Lib State Univ Agricultural & Technical College, Cant canton NY 13617.

PARKER, RALPH H(ALSTEAD). b Bertram Tex 21 Ap 09. 4: Mary Kate Norman. 5: UTex 25-29 (Hist) BA, 29-30 (Hist) MA, 30-35 (Hist) PhD; UChicago 36-37 (LS). 6: Sp. 7: Loan libn UTex 30-35, Asst archivist 35-36; Research asst UChicago 36-37; Libn Pomona Col 37-40; Dir of Libs UGa 40-47; US Army, AGD machine records 42-46; Libn UMo 47-69; Dean Sch of Lib & Info Sci 66-. 8: Lecturer: UIll summer 63, Simmons Col summers 64, 65; Pres, Mo State Lib Cmmsn 50-51, 59-65. 9: ALA (Coun 53-57, 61-65);-ACRL (treas 55-58); MoLA (pres51-52). 10: Sigma Delta Chi; Columbia Rotary Club. 12: "Library Applications of Punched Cards 52. 13: Yes. 14: Admin, data prcessing. 15: 1104 S Glenwood ave, Columbia Mo 65201.

PARKER, RICHARD J M. b Mass 20 Jl 38. 5: State Col (Salem) 56-58 (Educ); BostonU 58-59, 60-63 (Bus & Educ) BS; Harvard summer 66 (Chem); Simmons 69- (LS). 6: Ger. 7: Admin asst to Univ Registrar BostonU 60-62; Personnel asst Harvard Trust Co, cambridge Mass 63; Asst to dean-registrar NortheasternU, Boston 63-65; Suburban campus admin NortheasternU (Framingham) 65-67; Admin asst to dir Dept of Chem HarvardU 65-68, Chem placement off 65-68, Chem libn 68-. 8: HarvardU: Asst admissions com for grad wk in chem, Mem Bd of Freshman Advs, Univ proctor. 14: Chem libs. 15: 12 Oxford st, Cambridge Ma 02138.

PARKER, RICHARD MELVIN. b Red Oak Iowa 17 My 42. 4: Charlotte Bennett. 5: SW Baptist Col 60-62 AA; SWMo State 62-64 (Fr) BS in Educ; MoU 67-68 (LS) MA. 6: Fr. 7: Sch libn linn High Sch, Linn Mo 64-67; Grad asst Missouri U Lib (Columbia) 67-68; Libn Boonslick reg Lib, Sedalia Mo 68-. 9: ALA (Jr Mem RT); NEA; MoLA (Jr Mem RT); MoTA. 14: Admin. 15: 2412 S Quincy, Sedalia Mo 65301.

PARKER, SARA ANN. b Cassville Mo 19 F 39. 5: Okla StateU 57-61 (Pol Sci) AB; UNC 61-62 (Pol Sci); Lan State Tchrs Col 67-68 (LS) ML. 7: Reg asst Barry-Lawrence Reg Lib, Monett Mo 62-66; Asst ref libn Springfield Pub Lib, Springfield Mo 66-. 9: ALA; MoLA. 14: Ref, adult serv. 15: 1106 E Elm apt 6, Springfield Mo 65806.

PARKER, THOMAS FRANCIS. b Joplin Mo 3 O 32. 4: Barbara Brennan Parker. 5: St Louis U 55-58; Tulane U 58-61 (Modern European Hist) BA, MA; UCLA 64-65 MLS. 6: Fr, Sp. 7: Aviation Bosun Mate 2d Class US Nvy 50-53; Br lbn Tulsa (Okla) Pub Lib 61-63; Libn Burbank (Cal) Pub Lib 63-65; Asst dept head ser dept U Research Lib, UCLA 66-67, Act dept hd ser dept 67, Ref libn 68-. 9: ALA; CalLA (War on Poverty Com 65). 13: Yes. 14: Ref, systs wk. 15: Univ Res Lib Univ of Cal, Los Angeles Ca 90024.

PARKER, VIRGINIA. b Brookhaven Miss 10 O 16. 5: Newcomb Col 33-37 (Fr) BA; LSU 41-42 (LS) BS; Tulane U 49 (Feature Article Writing); UChicago 56-57 (Applied Psych); UHouston 59-60 (Pub Speaking). 6: Fr, Ger, Sp. 7: Lib asst Wayne U Col of Med 42-43; Catlgr & ref libn "Detroit News" 43-46; Libn Amer Cancer Soc, New Orleans 46-49; Assoc libn UTex Med br 56-57; Libn Tex Med Center Lib (Houston) 57-67; Libn Health Scis Lib Queen's U (Kingston Ont) 67-. 9: MedLA; SLA (pres LA Chap 49); Prof Libns at Queen's (v-pres 69-70). 10: John Austin Soc of Queen's U; Phi Beta Kappa; Phi Kappa Phi; Beta Phi Mu; Audubon Soc; Kingston Field Naturalists. 12: "Index to Current Periodical Literature on Neoplastic Diseases" (47-48). 13: Yes. 14: Admin, ref. 15: Health Scis Lib, Queen's Univ, Kingston Ont Can.

PARKER, WILLIAM E. b Nelson BC 15 My 35. 4: B Louise Freeman. 5: UBC 61 (Math, Physics) BS, 63 BLS. 7: Yard clk Can Pacific Railway, Nelson BC summers 50-56; Geol asst & prospector, BC summers 57-59; Construction inspector Swan Wooster Engring, vancouver BC 59-60; Lib asst Biomed Lib UBC 61-62; Catlgr UToronto Lib 63-64; Libn to asst hd Woodward Biomed Lib UBC 64-. 9: MedLA; ALA; CanLA; BCLA. 10: UBC Fac Assn. 14: Catlg, acquis, bibliog. 15: Woodward Biomedical Lib, Univ of BC, Vancouver 8 BC Can.

PARKER, WYMAN W(EST). b Woburn Mass 31 O 12. 4: Jane Kingsley. 5: Middlbury Col 34 (Amer Lit) BS, 39 (Eng Lit MA; Columbia 35 BLS; Wesleyan 57 MA. 7: Stack supv NY Pub Lib 35-36; Libn Pynson Printers, NYC 36; Act libn Middlebury Col 36-37; Libn Bread Loaf Summer Sch 33-37; Libn Middlebury Col 38-41; US Navy Intelligence Operations, Cominch, 7th Fleet Flag 41-46; Libn Kenyon Col 46-51, Libn UCincinnati 51-56; Libn Wesleyan U (Conn) 56-. 8: Bd Dirs, Midwest Inter Lib Corp 51-56; Mem, Survey of the Possibilities of Acad Lib Coop in Ohio, Ohio Col Assn, 63; Adv Coun Columbia Lib Sch 60-. 9: ALA (chm Awards Com 59);-ACRL (pres 60); ConnLA; BSA; Bibliog Soc (London); ACLU. 10: AAUP; Archons of Colophon; Grolier Club (NY); Acorn Club (Conn printing); Columbiad Club (fine printing). 12: "Henry Stevens of Vermont (63). 13: Yes. 14: Rare bks, private presses. 15: Olin Lib, Wesleyan Univ, Middletown Ct 06457.

PARKES, HELEN A. b High Point Mo. 5: Central Mo State Col (Math) BS Ed; Kan State Tchrs Col (Emporia) 54-55 (LS) MS. 7: Retail merchandising, Cal Mo; Several years tchg in Mo & Kan; Libn Sr High Sch & Jr Col, Garden City Kan 55-57; Catlg libn Bradley U 57-. 9: ALA; IllLA (sec Tech Procs Div). 10: AAUW; Peoria Players; Amateur Musical Club. 10: AAUW; Peoria Players; Amateur Musical Club; AAUP; Delta Kappa Gamma. 14: Catlg. 15: 1027 N Elmwood, Peoria Ill 61606.

PARKHILL, JOHN TAYLOR. b St John NB Can 23 Ap 19. 4: Frances Collins. 5: Queens U 37-41 (Eng) BA, 43-44 (Eng) MA; McGill 44-45 BLS; Harvard 45-47 (Eng) AM. 6: Fr. 7: Machine operator, Can Locomotive Co, Kingston Ont 41; Asst ed Queens Review, Asst to mgr Employment Bur, Queens U (Ont) 41-52; (Lt) Infantry Can Army 42-43; Tchg Fellow & Tutor Harvard U 46-51; Head adult serv child & yp serv high sch br Pub Lib of Brookline 50-57; Consul Lib Commun Proj ALA, Chicago 57-58; V-pres Northeast Sci Corp, Acton Mass 58-61; Head central lib div Toronto Pub Lib 61-67; Dir Metro Toronto Lib Bd 68-. 8: Eng tchr eve div Northeastern U 60-61; Act Chief Libn N York Pub Lib 62-63; Survey of the St John Free Pub Lib, Bd of Lib Commsners 63. 9: CanLA (past chm Adult Serv Sect); OntLA (chm Publs Com, Exec sec Res Com). 11: Leadership Train Award, Fund for Adult Educ 56-57; CLA Ruby E Wallace Travel Fellowship 67. 12: Ed Mass LA "Bulletin & two eds of MassLA "Handbook, Comp "School Library Service in Brookline, 1917-1954 & 2 sups; Ed OntLA"News (62-65); Ed CanLA Adult Serv Sect "Newsletter. 13: Yes; Auth "Amsterdam to Westminster," CanLA Occ Paper no 75 (68). 13: Yes. 14: Sch libs & serv to yp, admin, collections, surveys, adult educ, systs, automation. 15: Toronto Pub Lib, College & St George sts, Toronto 2B Can.

PARKHILL, MIRIAM (SMULL). b Ada Ohio 8 Jl 13. 5: Ohio No U 30-34 (Eng, Foreign Langs) AB; Ohio State U 34-35 (Eng Lit) MA; Ohio No U 38; UMich 62-63 MA LS. 6: Fr, Sp, Ger. 7: Asst area supv Nat Youth Admin, Lima Ohio 39-40; Asst to the libn Ohio No U 59-62, Asst libn 63-69, Hd catlg dept 67-; Libn & Asst Prof 69-. 9: ALA; OhioLA. 10: AAUW; Alpha Phi Gamma; Zeta Tau Alpha; Cosmopolitan Club; Ohio No U, Womens Assn; Ohio No U Faculty Club. 14: Ref, admin, catlg. 15: 301 S Main st, Ada Ohio 45810.

PARKHURST, MURIEL TAYLOR. b NYC 11 F 12. 4: Hugh Haven Parkhurst. 5: NJ State Tchrs Col (Montclair) 30-34 (Eng) MA; Columbia 36-37 (Lib Admin) Certif; Rutgers 40-42, 53-54 (LS) Certif. 6: Fr. 7: Demonstration libn High Sch, NJ State Tchrs Col (Montclair) 35-37; Sch libn Jr High Schs, Hackensack NJ 37-56; Lib consul Bergen Co, Hackensack NJ 56-59; Dir Maywood (NJ) Pub Lib 59-61; Dir Broadway Br Lib, Hackensack NJ 61-64; Tech libn Bergen Co Tech High Sch, Hackensack NJ 64-. 8: Bergen Co PTA lib consul, Hackensack NJ 45-56; Paramus pub lib consul, Paramus NJ 51-53; Maywood pub lib consul, Maywood NJ 57-59; Bergen Co tech lib consul, Hackensack NJ 64-. 9: ALA; NEA; NJLA; NJEA; A-V Assn Amer; ASCD. 10: Amer First-Day Cover Soc; Pi Beta Alpha (Womens Auxiliary); Prof Bkmen of Amer; NJ Hist Soc; NJ Vocat Assn; Bergen Co NJ Col Club. 11: Rotarys "Service Above Self Award for wk with yp in Paramus NJ, PTA "Gold Key Award for wk with yp in Bergen Co NJ. 12: Co-auth "Pennsylvania Story" (51, 56, 59, 64 & 67). 13: Yes. 14: Ref, bk sel, tech serv, admin. 15: 124 E Century rd, Paramus NJ 07652.

PARKIN, MARGARET LILLIAN. b Toronto 31 Mr 21. 5: Toronto 38-40 (Engnr Physics), 40-42 (Math, Physics) BA; Ottawa U 59-60 BLS. 6: Fr. 7: Flight Off Engnr Admin RCAF, Ottawa 42-46; R esearch off Nat Research Coun, Ottawa 46-50; Tech asst Atomic Energy Control Bd, Ottawa 50-51; Flight Lt Engnr Admin RCAF, Ottawa 51-59; Libn Ottawa Pub Lib 60; Br libn Dept of Labour, Ottawa 61-62; Libn Unemployment Insurance Commsn, Ottawa 62-63; Catlgr Carleton U (Ottawa) 63- 64; Chief Libn Can Nurse's Assn, Ottawa 64-. 9: CanLA; OntLA. 10: Libns Group, Prof Inst Civ Serv Can; Women's Can Club; B us & Prof Women's Club. 12: Ed "Quarterly Bulletin of the Division of Mechanical Engineering, National Research Council of Canada" (46-50); Auth "Library Service and the Nursing Profession in Canada". 13: Yes. 14: Ref. 15: 290 Park rd, Rockcliffe Park, Ottawa 2 Can.

PARKINS, KATHERINE L. b Bozeman Mont 10 My 17. 5: Mont State U 35-38 (Hist) BA; UWash 39-40 (Hist) MA; Columbia 41-42 MSLS. 6: Ger, Fr, Japanese. 7: Libn-bibliogr Military Govt Div War Dept, Wash DC 42-45; Army lib serv, Japan 46-47; Processing USoCal 47-51; Ref (period) Cal State Polytech Col 51-53; Ref San Diego Pub Lib 54-60; Catlgr Coronado pub Lib, Coronado Cal 60-62; Tech processes Newport Beach Pub Lib, Newport Beach Cal 62-64; Y-A libn Los Angeles Pub Lib, Pacoima Cal 64-67, Br libn Sun Valley 67-. 8: Consul, Wash DC Dept of Recreation 52-55; Visiting lecturer, George Washington U, 52 Consul, Nat Instr Television-program "Cover to Cover 68-70; & "Matter of Fiction 69-70. 9: ALA; CalLA. 10: Sun Valley Commun Coord Coun; C of C. 15: 4748 Lemona ave, Sherman Oaks Ca 91403.

PARKS, AGATHA (WEAKS). b Canalou Mo 20 My 11. 5: SE Mo State summers 29-42 (Eng); Ark State summers 45-46 (Eng) BSEd; Peabody Col summers 53-56 MALS. 7: Elem tchr: Rural Sch, E Pararie Mo 30-36, Lilbourn Dist 36-38; Cons sch, Canalou Mo: Elem tchr 38-40, Elem prin 40-46, High sch soc studies tchr 46-48; Cons sch, Elvins Mo: High sch soc studies tchr 48-53, High sch libn 53-55; Re-organized sch, Hazelwood (Mo) Sch Dist: High sch libn 55-67, Consul for instr materials 67-. 8: Consul Instr Materials media Wk, Hazelwood Sch Dist 67. 9: NEA; ALA; MoStateTA; MoLA; MoASchL; ClrTA. 10: AAUW; Bus & Profess Women; Kappa Kappa Iota. 14: Ref. 15: Educ Off 4655 Parker rd, Florissant Mo 63033.

PARKS, ALTA. b Oakland Co Mich 8 D 10. 5: Mich State Col 32 (Eng) AB; Columbia 42 BS LS. 6: Fr. 7: Gen Off Parks Coal Co, Birmingham Mich 32-34; Eng tchr Big Beaver Sch, Birmingham Mich 34-38; Tchr-libn St Johns (Mich) High Sch 38-41; Libn Roseville (Mich) High Sch 4143; Head Libn Ingham Co Lib, Mason Mich 43-51; Head of ext dept Gary (Ind) Pub Lib 51-55, Asst dir 55-. 9: ALA (Coun 61-65, Recr Com 51-61, Memb Com 57-61, Chm Reg 6 61-64);-PLA (pres 65-66)-LAD (Elect Com 62-63, sec Lib Org & Mgt Sect 58-60); MichLA (pres 49-50, pres Co Libns Sect 44-45, chm Planning Com 47-48); IndLA (pres 56-57, chm Action Com 54-55, Chm Budget Com 59-60, Chm Nomin Com 59-60), Insurance Com 67-69, Constit & By-laws Com 68-69). 10: Altrusa Internat; Gary Neighborhood House Bd. 13: Yes. 14: Admin, personnel. 15: 3654 Polk st, Gary Ind 46408.

PARKS, DORA RUTH. b Seven Springs NC 12N 06. 5: UNC (Greensboro) 25-29 (LS) AB. 7: Asst libn R J Reynolds High Sch, Winston Salem NC 29-32; Bkmob libn Greensboro (NC) Pub Lib 32-38; Br libn Osterhout Free Lib, Wilkes Barre Penn 38-40; WPA Supv West NC Lib Proj 40-41; Reg libn Nantahala Reg Lib, Murphy NC 41-45; Exec Sec WVa Lib Commsn, Charleston WVa 45-. 9: ALA; WVaLA. 10: Soroptimist Club. 11: WVaLA Award for Outstanding Serv. 14: Admin, bk sel, personnel, construction, legis. 15: 2004; Quarrier st, Charleston WVa 25311.

PARKS, ETHEL G. b Chicago. 5: West Mich U 45-47 (Phys Ed, Soc Studies BS; UMich 47-52 (Guidance) MA; West Mich U 60-63 (LS) MA. 7: Phys educ instr: Kalamazoo Pub Sch 47-48, Mater Dei High Sch, Evansville Ind 48-51, N Muskegon (Mich) High Sch 51-52, Benton Harbor (Mich jr High Sch 52-60, Libn 60-62; Head Libn Waukegan (Ill) Twp High Sch-West 62-. 9: ALA; IllLA; IllEA. 10: Amer Fed Tchrs; Friends of the Lib, Waukegan Ill; Kappa Delta Pi; Phi Beta Mu. 15: 2520 N Walnut st, Waukegan Ill 6005.

PARKS, EVELYN LOUISE. b Seven Springs NC 27 F 10. 5: NC Col for Women 28-32 (LS) AB, Womens Col 32-33 (Eng) AB. 7: Sch libn Vanceboro (NC) High Sch 33-34; Sch libn Greensboro (NC) City Sch 34-37; Co Libn Stanly Co,

Albemarle NC 37-42; Libn Park Mem Lib, Asheville NC 42-44; Consul Mich State Lib 44-46, Spec trustee consul 46-49; Chief Libn May Mem Lib, Burlington NC 49-63; Reg dir Central NC Reg Lib, Burlington NC 63-. 9: ALA (Pub Rel Com 53-54); SELA (Pub Libs Sect 59-61); NCLA (Dir 58-60, Pub Libs Sect 65-67). 10: Bus & Prof Women; LWV; Altrusa Club. 15: 200 N Mendenhall st, Greensboro NC 27401.

PARKS, GARY DENNIS. b Dexter Mo 13 S 43. 5: Mineral Area Jr Col 62-63 (General Educ) AA; UMo 63-66 (Fine Arts) BS in Educ, 67-69 MALS. 6: Fr. 7: Supply clk Sp/4 US Army res, Farmington Mo 61-69; Tchr Wash Sch Dist, Washington Mo 66-67; Lib clk UMo (Columbia) 67, Lib asst 67-68; Dir lib serv E Central Mo Jr Col, 68-. 9: ALA; MoLA. 10: Delta Phi Delta; UMo Alum Assn. 14: Admin, bldg planning, multi-media facilities. 15: 1607 Sylvan lane apt 2I, Columbia Mo 65201.

PARKS, GEORGE RICHARD. b Boston 11 Ap 35. 4: Carol Richmond Parks. 5: UNH 55-59 (Eng) AB; Johns Hopkins 59-6(eng); UMich 61-62 (LS) MA. 6: Sp. 7: Enoch Pratt Free Lib, Baltimore; Pre-prof ya 60-61, Roving asst 62, Sr asst Hist Dept 63, Br libn Broadway Br 64, Admin asst to the asst dir 65; Exec asst libn URochester 66-, Asst dir 68, Act dir 68-69; Libn U RI 69-. 9: ALA; MdLA (Constit & By-laws Com 65). 10: Phi Beta Kappa; Phi Kappa Phi; Beta Phi Mu. 11: Margaret Mann Award, UMich 62. 14: Ref, admin, automation, bldgs.5 15: Univ of Rhode Island Lib, Kingston RI 02881.

PARKS, LANETTA W. b Baltimore Md 15 O 41. 4: Floyd L Parks. 5: UMd 59-63 (Eng) BA, 65-66 MSLS. 7: Pre-prof y-a libn Brs of Enoch Pratt Free Lib, Baltimore 63-65, Sr y-a libn 66-67, Hd y-a dept (central lib) 67-. 9: ALA; MdLA. 13: Yes. 14: YA. 15: 4900 Cedar Garden rd, Baltimore Md 21229.

PARKS, VIRGINIA A. b Lyndhurst NJ 17 Ap 41. 4: Robert C Parks. 5: Newark Col of Engnr 59-60; DrewU 6-163 (Eng Lit) AB; Rutgers 63-65 MLS. 7: Jr draftsman C & M Machine Co, Bloomfield NJ 62; Jr lib asst Kearny Pub Lib, Kearney NJ 63-65; Ref libn Springfield Pub Lib, Springfield NJ 65-68; Sr libn catlg Monmouth Co Lib, Freehold NJ 68-. 9: ALA; NJLA; MonmouthCoLA. 14: Catlg, tech serv. 15: Tinton Falls rd Box 237, Farmingdale NJ 07727.

PARMAN, LEE F. b Decorah Iowa 6 My 18. 4: Edith Morrissett. 5: State Col of Iowa 35-39 (Math) BA; UIowa 46-47 (Eng) MA, 47-52 (Eng). 6: Sp. 7: High sch prin, Epworth Iowa 39-40; Instr UIowa 47-52; Sandia Corp, Albuquerque NM: Tech writer 53-55, Section supv tech writing 55-57, Div supv tech writing & Lib 57-63; Dept manager tech libs 63-68; Deputy libn US Atomic Energy Commsn, Wash DC 68-. 8: Hd Tech Info, AEC "Atoms in Action" exhib, Nicaragua, 66. 9: SLA (pres Rio Grande Chap 64); NMLA (treas 63, pres-elect 65). 10: AAUP; ASIS; Soc Tech Writers (pres 57-58); SLA (Rio Grande Chap; ed 62-63, treas 62, pres 64; Pres Nuclear Sci Div 67); NMLA (pres 66); Albuquerque Coun Sci & Tech Socs (pres 68). 13: Yes. 14: Lib systems planning & admin. 15: 1131 W Univ blvd, Warwick Towers apt 1103, Silver Spring Md 20902.

PAROJCIC, JOAN (JAKES). b Chicago 19 Jl 33. 4: Vlade Parojcic. 5: Nat Col of Educ 51-54 (Educ) BE; Chicago Tchrs Col 57-59 (Sch lib) M Ed in sch libnship; Rosary Col 67-69 MALS. 7: Elem tchr Portland pub schs, Portland Ore 54-55; Tchr Oak Park elem schs, Oak Park Ill 55-57, Tchr & libn 57-61; Research ed Childcraft, The How & Why Lib, Field Enterprises Corp, Crp, Chicago 61-66, Photographs ed 66-68. 9: NEA (Life Mem); ALA. 14: Ref, child lit. 15: 4840 N Wolcott ave, Chicago Il 60640.

PARR, MARY Y(OHANNAN). b Cleveland 21 Je 27. 4: Wendell R Parr. 5: Col of Wooster 45-48 (Eng, Soc) AB; West Res 48-49 MLS; Columbia 58-60; New School 60-61; Columbia 68-69. 6: Fr. 7: Child libn Cuyahoga Co Lib, Cleveland 49-50; Head Libn Willard Mem Lib, Willard Ohio 50-51; Supt off Luna Co Bd of Educ, Deming NM 51; Cost analyst Miller Paper Co, Syracuse NY 52-53; Asst ext div San Antonio Pub Lib, San Antonio Tex 53-54; Asst libn Newark State Col 55-62; Instr Drexel Inst of Tech 61 & 62; Asst Prof Villanova U 62-63; Asst Prof Pratt Inst 63-66, Assoc Prof 66-. 9: ALA; CathLA; NJLA; NYLA. 10: Womens Nat Bk Assn. 13: Yes. 14: Lib educ, admin. 15: 63 Essex ave, Montclair NY 07042.

PARRATTO, HENRY LOUIS. b Phila 28 F 14. 4: Mary Elizabeth Bolger. 7: Lib asst ""Phila Public Ledger 31-34; Lib asst ""Phila Inquirer 34-43; US Army Artillery Field Tech Sgt, Ft Sill Okla Train Center 43-46; ""Phila Inquirer: Lib asst 46-54, Lib clsfr 54-, Asst head libn 57-. 9: SLA. 14: Ref, research, catlg. 15: 353 Central ave, North Hills Penn 19038.

PARRINO, DONNA (PINERO). b Tampa Fla. 4: Sam Parrino. 5: LoyolaU 66 (Hist) AB; Fla StateU 67 (LS) MA. 6: Sp, Fr. 7: Asst ref libn USouth Fla 67-. 9: FlaLA. 10: Beta Phi Mu. 14: Interlib loans. 15: 1311 17 ave, Tampla Fl 33605.

PARRISH, LORRAINE (MIDDLETON). b Winters Tex 29 O 22. 5: Stephens Col 39-40, 40-41 (Eng); McMurry (Abilene Tex) 50 (Eng); So MethodistU 41-42, 50-51 (Eng, Educ) BS; Tex woman'sU 69 MLS. 6: Fr. 14: Ref. 15: 1824 Ruddell, Denton Tx 76201.

PARROTT, BARBARA (GAIL). b Nassawadox Va 4 Ap 45. 5: William & Mary 63-67 (Eng) AB; UMich 67-68 MALS. 6: Fr. 7: Asst ref libn PrincetonU 68-69. 14: Ref, child libnship. 15: Box 656, Exmore Va 23350.

PARROTT, M(ARGARET) SANGSTER. b Throckmorton Tex 31 D 22. 5: N Tex State Col 43-47 (LS) AB; UNC 54-56 MS LS. 7: Asst circ libn Tex Tech Col 47; Asst circ libn N Tex State Col 47-54; Order libn Sch of Law Lib UNC 54-56; Asst circ libn N Tex State Col 56-57; Documents libn NC State Lib 57-63, Head tech serv div 63-69, Hd ref-doc serv div 69-. 8: Visiting lecturer UNC Sch of Lib Sci summer 67, 67-68. 9: ALA; SELA; NCLA (chm elect Resources & Tech Serv Sect 65-67). 10: Beta Phi Mu; UN Assn; Wake Co Hist Soc (Bd of Dir 67-70). 14: Docs, tech serv, ref. 15: 2105 St James rd, Raleigh NC 27607.

PARRY, DAVID RUSSELL. b Allentown Penn 15 Ap 32. 5: Lafayette Col 50-54 (Eng) AB; Rutgers 62-65 MLS. 7: Disbursing spec (Pfc) US Army Finance Corps, Germany 54-56; Tchr Salisbury Twp Sch, Lehigh Co Penn 58-63; High sch libn Salisbury Jr-Sr High Sch, Lehigh Co Penn 63-66; Asst libn Kutztown State Col 66-. 9: ALA; PennLA. 10: Muhlenberg Col Opera Wkshop; AAUP. 14: Acquis. 15: 18 N Parkway rd, Allentown Penn 18104.

PARRY, ELEANOR E. b Wash DC 25 Jn 16. 5: Central bible Col 35-38 (Bible) Diploma; Taylor U 38-41 (Sociol) BA; George Washington U 48-49 (Psych) MA; Cath U summers 55-59 MS LS. 7: Supv clerks War Dept US Govt, Wash DC 41-43; Tchr Central Bible Col 43-48; Tchr & registrar Great Lakes Bible Inst, Zion Ill 50-53; Tch Lanham Elem Sch, Lanham Md 53-54; Assoc Prof & Libn Central Bible Col 54-68; Ref libn Evangel Col 68-. 9: ALA; Christian Libns Fellowship; MoLA; Amer Soc of Indexers. 10: AAUW; Beta Phi Mu; AAUP; AAHE. 14: Ref, bk sel, indexing. 15: Rte 5 Box 707, Springfield Mo 65803.

PARRY, SHIRLEY. b Valparaiso Ind. 5: Valparaiso U 45-49 (Hist) BA; UColo (Hist); IndU 68 MLS. 6: Sp. 7: Tchr: Mich City (Ind) Pub Schs 50-55, Jr High Sch, Great Neck ny 55-58, High Sch, Globe Ariz 58-61; Child libn br Gary Pub Lib, Gary Ind 61-64, Asst child room 65-67, Asst ref dept 67-. 9: ALA; IndLA. 14: Ref, interlib loan, child serv. 15: Gary Pub Lib, Gary Ind 46402.

PARSELL, MIRIAM A. b Newark NJ. 5: West Md Col 45-46; Scarritt Col 46-48 (Relig educ) BA; Rutgers 47-48 MLS. 7: Dir Christian educ: 1st Methodist Ch, Waterbury Conn 48-51, St James Methodist Ch, Phila 52-60; Field wkr Methodist Bd of Missions, NYC 60-65; Libn United Mission Lib, NYC 68-. 15: Rm 1372 475 Riverside dr. New York NY 10027.

PARSLEY, BRANTLEY HAMILTON. b Baltimore 15 O 27. 4: Loyce Marie Franklin. 5: Baltimore Jr Col 48-50 AA; UMd 50-52 (Sociol) BA; New Orleans Baptist Theol Sem 52-55 (Theol) BD, 57 (Religious Educ, Libnship) MRE; Emory 60-65 MLn. 6: Sp, Fr, Gk. 7: Pastor Calvary Baptist Church, Albany Ore 56-57; Asst Broadmoor Br New Orleans Pub Lib 58-60; Libn Ernst & Ernst, Atlanta 63-65; Supt of night circ Theology Lib, Emory U 60-65; Lib Dir Campbellsville Col 65-. 9: ALA-ACRL; NEA; KyLA; KyEA; SELA; KyLA (Educ com). 10: Taylor Co Hist Soc. 14: Admin, bk sel. 15: 114 Longview dr, Campbellsville Ky 42718.

PARSLEY, GERTRUDE (MORTON). b Clarksville Tenn 15 O 10. 5: VanderbiltU 27-31 9sociol) BA, 31-32 (Sociol); Peabody Col 48-52 MA. 6: Fr. 7: Res libn Joint Univ Libs, Nashville 46-49, Asst ref libn Tenn State Lib & Archives, Nashville 49-52; Hd ref libn 52-65; Asst libn TrinityU 65-68, Assoc libn 68-. 8: Guest faculty mem Peabody Col Lib Sci Dept 57-58. 9: TexLA; SWLA; Tenn Hist Soc. 14: Ref, admin. 15: 8208 Windover, San Antonio Tx 78218.

PARSLEY, ZADA (MOORE). b Ky 14 F 11. 4: Jarvis Parsley. 5: East State Col 35 (Eng) AB; UKy 54 (LS) MS. 7: Tchr Bd of Educ, Jackson Co Ky 35-39; Tchr Bd of Educ,

Laurel Co Ky 39-41; Tchr Bd of Educ, Bracken Co Ky 42-54, Libn 54-. 9: ALA (Recr Com); KyLA (treas 66-67); KyASchL (past pres, pres-elect 69-70); AASchL (delegate 69). 10: Delta Kappa Gamma; Beta Phi Mu. 14: Child lit, folklore & folk lit. 15: Brooksville Ky 41004.

PARSLY, NANCY (LAYTON). b Phila 20 Ju 38. 5: Mary Washington Col 55-57 (Eng); Ursinus Col 57-59 (Eng) BA; Drexel 63 MS LS. 6: Fr. 7: Eng tchr Linden Hall, Lititz Penn 59-62; Catlgr East Baptist Col (St Davids Penn) 63-64; Catlgr UPenn 64-66; Asst catlgr Dickinson Col 66-67& asst libn Harcum Jr Col 67-. 9: ALA-ACRL (Del Valley Chap). 14: Catlg. 15: 8104 Eastern ave, Phila Pa 19118.

PARSONS, A(UGUSTINE) CHAPMAN. b Ripley WVa 30 Ap 22. 4: Elizabeth Eloise Hall. 5: WVaU 46-49 (Educ) BS Ed; West Res 49-50 MS LS; Syracuse 64-66, Certif Organization-mgt. 7: Lathe operator Nat Acme Co, Cleveland 40-42; USNR AEM 3/c 42-46; A-v asst WVaU 47-49; Grad asst Case Inst of Tech 49-50; Co Libn Martins Ferry Pub Lib, Martins Ferry Ohio 50-52; Libn: Gallia Co Dist Lib, Gallipolis Ohio 52-56, Alliance Pub Lib, Alliance Ohio 56-62, Rodman Pub Lib, Alliance Ohio 62-64; Exec Dir Ohio Lib Assn, Columbus Ohio 64-; Exec Dir Ohio Lib Trustees Assn, Columbus Ohio 64-; Exec Sec Ohio Lib Found, Columbus Ohio 65-68, Exec v-pres 69-. 8: Instr WVaU Dept of Lib Sci summers 54-58; Lib Serv & Bldg Consul. 9: ALA (Ohio Memb Chm 59-62, Ohio Rep to ALA Coun 61-64, chm Arch for Pub Lib Com 64, mem Coun 68-72);-PLA (chm Com on Standards 65-66, chm Com for Promotion of Standards 66-69);-LAD (Com on Lib Admin Devel); Amer Soc Assn Execs; Ohio C of C; US C of C; Ohio Hist Soc; Ohio Genealogical Soc; OhioLA (Exec dir, bus mgr "Bulletin," asst treas); Ohio Lib Trustees Assn (Exec dir, treas); Ohioana Lib Assn. 10: Rotary Club (Hon mem); Wranglers Alliance (Hon mem). 12: "History of Wranglers, Alliance Ohio (64); Ed "Ohio Library Trustees Association Bulletin. 13: Yes. 14: Admin, assn mgt, lib standards. 15: 292 Lambourne ave, Worthington Ohio 43085.

PARSONS, GERALD J(AMES). b Syracuse NY 30 Je 24. 5: Syracuse 46-49 (Hist) AB, 49-50 (LS) MS. 7: (Pfc) US Army Engnrs, US & Europe 43-46; Asst libn local hist div Rochester (NY) Pub Lib 50-53, Head educ & religion div 53-58; Head local hist & genealogy dept Syracuse (NY) Pub Lib 58-. 9: ALA; NYLA. 10: Amer Soc of Genealogists (Fellow). 12: Contrib ed "The American Genealogist. 13: Yes. 14: Loc hist, geneal. 15: 224 Arnold ave, Syracuse NY 13210.

PARSONS, HELEN RUTH (WADDELL). b Toronto 22 Mr 10. 4: James Edward Parsons . 5: McMaster 28-32 (Classics) BA; Ontaro Col of Educ 32-33 Asst tchrs certif; Toronto 60-61 BLS, 64-65 (Soc Wk) BSW, 65-67 MLS. 7: Gen libn Leaside Pub Lib, Leaside Can 61-64; Ref libn York U Leslie Frost Lib, Toronto 65-67; Ref McMaster U (Hamilton Can) 67-68; Circ SUNY (Albany) 68-. 9: CanLA; ALA; OntLA; Prof Libns Ont. 14: Ref, yp, research, automation. 15: 897 Edgewater dr, Tonawanda NY 14150.

PARSONS, JANE (WALLACE) AMOS. b Montgomery Ala 31 O 27. 4: Richard William Parsons. 5: UNC (Greensboro) 44-48 (Hist) BA; UNC (Chapel Hill) 48-49 (LS) BS. 7: Asst hist div Brooklyn Pub Lib NY 49, Asst Highlawn br 49-50, 1st asst Bay Ridge br 50-51, 1st asst Brighton Beach br 51-53, Ref asst Borough Park br 53-55, Asst to supt of brs 55-56, Adult serv libn East Parkway br 56-58; Elem sch libn Bd of Educ of Baltimore co, Towson Md 66-67; Catlgr Med & Chirurgical Faculty of State of Md Lib, Baltimore 67-. 9: ALA. 14: Ref. 15: 412 Woodbine ave, Baltimore Md 21204.

PARSONS, LELIA ROSS. b Oxford Miss 31 Ja 38. 5: UMiss 56-60 (Bus Educ) BS C 60-64 M of LS. 7: UMiss Lib: Non-prof asst 60-62, Jr libn 62-65, Sr libn 65-66; Libn Biloxi City Schs 66-. 9: Miss LA. 14: Circ, period, jr high sch libs. 15: 104 Beanland dr, Gulfport Mi 39501.

PARSONS, MURIEL W (WOOD). b Philadelphia Penn 28 D 27. 4: Earl H Parsons. 5: Dickinson Col 45-49 (Econ) BA; Drexel 62-66 MS in LS. 7: Ed asst Blakiston Co, phila 49-51; Legal sec Townsend Munson Elliott, Phila 52-54; Jr high sch libn Wissahickon Sch Dist Penn 65-. 9: ALA; NEA; PennStateLA; Chester-Montgomery Sch Libn Assn; WissahickonEA. 10: Zeta Tau Alpha; Beta Phi Mu; Wheel and Chain; Jr Colony Club of Ambler. 14: Child & ya wk. 15: Evans rd RD 1, Ambler Pa 19002.

PARSONS, MYLA (TAYLOR). b Auburntown Tenn 9 F 07. 5: Middle Tenn State U 24-41 (Eng, Soc Sci) BS; Peabody Col summers 46-48 BS in LS. 6: Fr. 7: Elem sch tchr Rutherford Co Syst, Rutherford Co Tenn 25-31, 33-44; High sch Eng tchr & libn Christiana High Sch, Rutherford Co Tenn 44-47; Libn Linebaugh Pub Lib, Murfreesboro Tenn 47-62; Ref libn Middle Tenn State U Lib 62-. 9: ALA; TennLA (treas 53-54); SELA; TennEA. 10: Delta Kappa Gamma; Linebaugh Pub Lib Bd. 14: Ref. 15: Nilewood apts 12 East Main, Murfreesboro Tn 37130.

PARSONS, RICHARD WILLIAM. b Victoria BC Can 6 N 26. 4: Jane Amos. 5: UBC 51 (Slavonic Studies) BA; McGill 53-54 BLS. 7: Bkmob libn Edmonton (Alta) Pub Lib 51-53; Brooklyn Pub Lib: Asst in brs 54-55, New bk sect, bk order dept 55-58, Adult serv libn & asst br libn 58-61, Asst coord of catlg 61-62; Coord of adult lib, Towson Md 62-. 9: ALA (chm Jt ASD/RSD Com on Orient of Adults 65-68, Publishers liaison Com 62-64; Ad hoc Com on Instr in the Use of Libs 66-67); -RSD (Dir 68-71, chm Md Chap 64-66, chm Md Chap Reprint Com 64-); MdLA (Int Freedom Com 63-65, rec sec 67-68, chm Ed Com 68-); AEA (pres Md Chap); Potomac Tech Proc Libns (Couns 62-64, chm Nom Com 64); SLA; DAVI; Md A-v Assn. 10: Md Coun for Educ Television. 11: Lib Binding Inst Silver Bk Award 66. 12: Introductions to; "Historical View of the Government of Maryland" by J V L McMahon (68), "History of Maryland" by James McSherry (68), "The History of Maryland" 2 vols by John Leeds Bozman (68). 14: Ref, adult serv, adult programming. 15: Baltimore Co Pub Lib, 25 W Chesapeake ave, Towson Md 21204.

PARTA, JUNE ARDATH (PASTORET). b Duluth Minn 5 D 16. 4: Russell O Parta. 5: UMinn (Duluth) (Elem Educ, Hist) BS; Moorhead State Col 60, 61; UMinn (Minneapolis) 62-64 5th year Lib Certif. 6: Fr. 7: Pub sch tchr: NY Mills Minn 38-40, Osakis Minn 44-46; Eng tchr & libn Bertha-Hewitt Consolidated Sch, Bertha Minn 61-64, Libn 64-. 8: Adv Com Minn Sch Lib Demon Ctr 66-68. 9: ALA; NEA; MinnASchL (Nomin Com 68); MinnEA. 10: Delta Kappa Gamma; State pres Lutheran Church Women; Nat Fed Women's Clubs; Ottertail Co Treas 44-46; Minn Press Women. 15: 201 Broadway, New York Mills Mn 56567.

PARTRIDGE, ALLAN B JR. b Worcester Mass 29 My 27. 4: Marjorie Wolf. 5: Worcester Polytech Inst 49-51; UNH 51-53 (Geol) BA; West Res 54-55 MSLS. 6: Ger. 7: Set-up man, Gen Elec Co, Somersworth 53; In chg of stacks Hamilton Smith Lib, UNH 54; Soils tech US Army Engnr Corps, Pease AFB 54; Ref libn Detroit Pub Lib tech dept 55-57; Br libn Hamilton Standard Div UAC Windsor Locks Conn 57-59; Ref libn United Air Craft Corp, E Hartford Conn 59-61, Head catlgr 61-. 9: ALA; SLA (treas Conn Valley Chap 58-59). 14: Catlg, admin, rare bks. 15: 57 Littel Acres rd, Glastonbury Ct 06033.

PARTRIDGE, CHARLES VICTOR. b Detroit Mich 3 D 29. 4: Marjorie L Barlow. 5: UDetroit 48-52 (Eng) BS; Wayne StateU 55-56 (Lib Educ) MEd; UMich 59-61 AMLS, 61-65 (Educ) EdS. 6: Fr. 7: Pub rel "New York Times, NYC 36; Br libn Queens Borough Pub Lib, Jamaica NY 62, Asst reg libn 63, Ext serv dept asst 64; Coordinator child serv Smithtown Lib System, Smithtown LI NY 64-; Asst Dir Adult servs Elmont Lib Sys, Elmont LI 68-. 9: MichASchL (pres 68-69). 12: Ed ""Forward, mag MichASchL (61-66). 14: Educ. 15: 20687 Kensington ct, Southfield Mi 48075.

PARTRIDGE, JAMES C JR. b Atlanta Ga 13 My 40. 5: Morehouse Col 57-62 (Sociol) BA; Atlanta 63-65 MLS. 6: Fr. 7: Tchr Bartow Pub Sch System, Cartersville Ga 62-63; Ya libn Enoch Pratt Free Lib, Baltimore 65; Spec libn educ systems div Litton Ind, College Park Md 65-; Libn Instrl Materials Ctr Montgomery Co Pub Sch Syst, Rockville Md 65-66; Supv of dept of mental hygiene Hosp Libs, Baltimore Md 66-; Eve libn Commun Col of Baltimore. 8: Consul for job Corps Camps, Atterbury & Camp Parks, helping to estab libs; Consul University Research Corp New Careers. 9: ALA; SLA; MLA; AAMd. 13: Yes. 14: Ref, info center admin, inst lib admin. 15: 3816 Grantley rd, Baltimore Md 21215.

PARTRIDGE, MARJORIE LOUISE (BARLOW). b Detroit Mich 20 S 33. 4: Charles Victor Partridge. 5: UMich 51-55 (Geog) AB, 58-69 AMLS. 7: Sec & bkkeeper Barlow Electric Co, Detroit 55-57; Travel coun Automobile Co of Mich, Detroit 57-58; Child libn Wayne Pub Lib, Wayne Mich 59; Child libn Garden City Pub Lib, Garden City Mich 60; Hd libn Southgate Pub Lib, Southgate Mich 60-62; Dir libs W Bloomfield Pub Lib, W Bloomfield Mich 62-65; Elem sch lib Birmingham Schs, Birmingham Mich 66; Libn W Bloomfield Jr High, W Bloomfield Mich 66-67; Coord secondary sch libs Royal Oak Pub Schs, Royal Oak Mich 67-. 8: Instr Lib Sci UMich; Adv elem sch libs, Royal Oak Mich. 9: Mich Assn sch Libns (treasurer Supv Sect 68-70; Ed Com of "Forward"; Oakland Co Chap: v-chm 67-69, chm 69). 10: Friends of the Southfield Pub Lib; Martha Cook Alumnae UMich; Founders Soc of Detroit Inst of Arts. 12: "Finger Plays and Stories for the Pre-School Story Hour" (64). 13: Yes. 14: Sch libs. 15: 20687 Kensington ct, Southfield Mi 48075.

PASCO, CARL EDWARD. b Warren Mich 28 My 38. 5: UMich 56-60 (Eng Lang & Lit) BA; LoyolaU 63 & 64; IBM Education Center (Chicago) 65 (Programming); Rosary Col 68-69 MALS. 6: Fr. 7: Jr high sch instr Cleveland Hts Schs, Cleveland Hts Ohio 60-61; Eng instr Proviso E High Sch, Maywood Ill 61-68, Libn 69-. 8: Test construction Sci research Assocs Tex Project 63. 9: ALA. 10: Beta Phi Mu. 15: 503 Aldine, Chicago Il 60657.

PASCUA, CAMERON ELAINE (BUCK). b Cortland NY 13 F 14. 4: Dominador G Pascua. 5: Syracuse 32-36 (Fr) AB; Middlebury Sch of Lang summer 37 (Fr); McGill summer 38 (Fr); Columbia 52-57 MLS. 6: Fr, Sp. 7: Tchr (Fr, Eng) Harpursville Central High Sch 36-39; Tch libn Caribbean Sch, Ponce PR 53-57; Libn Queens Borough Pub Lib, Jamaica NY 58-. 8: Tchr, Internat Child Center, Bangkok Siam 49. 9: ALA; NYLA; NY Lib Clubs. 10: AAUW; Filipino Womens Club; Phi Beta Kappa; Phi Kappa Phi. 14: Child & ya wk. 15: 115-24 217th st, Cambria Hgts LI NY 11411.

PASCUCCI, PHILIP JOSEPH. b Bronx NY 19 My 19. 5: Don Bosco Col 40-44 (Philos) BA; Salesian Col 47-51 (Theol) MA; St John's U 65-67 MLS. 6: Lat, Ital, Fr. 7: Tchr Salesian High Sch, New Rochelle NY 44-47, 51-54; Tchr Don Bosco Tech High Sch, Boston 54-60; Parish priest Corpus Christi Ch, Port Chester NY 60-61; Parish priest Sacred Heart Ch, Vancouver BC 61-64; Parish priest St Anthony's Ch, Paterson NJ 64-66; Libn Don Bosco col 66-. 9: ALA; CathLA. 13: Yes. 14: Admin, ref. 15: Don Bosco College, Newton NJ 07860.

PASKE, ARTHUR J. b Sheboygan Wis 2 D 31. 4: Mary Ann Kowalski. 5: UWis 51-53; Wis State U (Oshkosh) 53-55 (Eng, Hist, Soc Sci) BS; UWis summers 59-62 (LS) MS. 6: Fr. 7: Tchr Denmark (Wis) High Sch 55-56; Instr USAFI US Army Hq 7th Army, Stuttgart Germany 57; Tchr libn Pembine (Wis) High Sch 59-61, Tchr libn Whiteford High Sch,Ottawa Lake Mich 61-62, Head Libn Bowsher High Sch, Toledo Ohio 62-64, Hd ref dept Mead Pub Lib, Sheboygan Wis 64-. 9: Marinette Co (Wis) EA (past pres). 10: Mead Pub Lib Staff Assn. 14: Ref. 15: 3509 South 12th st, Sheboygan Wi 53081.

PASSARELLI, MARIE GRAF. b NYC 10 Je 05. 4: Robert E Passarelli. 5: SUNY 50-54 (Soc Studies) BA, 57-59 MSLS. 7: Lib asst NY State Lib, Albany 55-59, Asst libn 59-65, Sr libn 65-68, Assoc libn & Hd catlg sect 68-. 9: ALA; NYStateLA; NY Tech Serv Assn; Hudson MohawkLA. 10: Schenectady Symphony Orchestra (viola); Delmar Commun Orchestra (viola). 14: Catlg. 15: Box 427, Altamont NY 12009.

PASSINEAU, HAROLD WILLIAM. b Rochester NY 18 Ag 39. 5: URochester 57-62 (Eng) BA; Columbia 63-66 (LS) MS. 7: Lib clk URochester Lib 62-63, Lib trainee Ill 63-66, Ref libn & bibliogr 66-68, Hd bus lib 68-. 8: Mem Access Com, Five Associated Univ Libs 68-. 9: ALA. 14: Ref, bibliog. 15: Business Lib, Univ of Rochester, Rochester NY 14627.

PASSO, THELMA F. b Hibbing Minn 9 Mr 08. 5: UMinn 27-30 (Hist) BS in Ed; UIll 40 BS LS; UChicago 40-41 (LS). 7: Tchr Storden (Minn) Consolidated Sch 30-32; Sch libn Lincoln Jr High Sch, Hibbing Minn 32-39; Ref libn Quarre Corp, Chicago 40-41; Sch libn High Sch, Ottawa Ill 41-42; Head Libn Quarrie Corp, Chicago 42-45; Ref libn Kern Co Free Lib, Bakersfield Cal 45-46, 54-55; Head of ref dept Lib of Hawaii, Honolulu 46-48; Supv ref libn Stockton (Cal) Pub Lib 49-50; Dir USIS Libs, Helsinki Melbourne 50-53; City Libn San Bruno(Cal) Pub Lib 54-. 9: ALA; CalLA (chm Pub Lib Assn 59-60);PLECC (dir 61-63). 10: AAUW; Soroptimist. 14: Ref. 15: 556 W Angus ave, San Bruno Cal 94066.

PASTAN, HERBERT MARTIN EDMUND. b Boston 29 S 28. 4: Frances Kostick. 5: Burdett Col 49-51 (Bus); Hofstra U 56 (Eng); UMiami (Fla) 56-58 (Eng); UDenver 60-62 (Eng) BA, 62-63 (LS) MA. 7: Stud asst UMiami (Fla) Lib 56-58; Computyper biller R J Kremer Co Inc, Denver 58-62; Stud asst UDenver Mary Reed Lib 62-63 Head tech serv Littleton (Colo) Pub Lib 63-64; Catlgr Prince Georges Co Mem Lib, Hyattsville Md 65-. 8: Adv mgr "Maryland Libraries 65-. 9: ALA; MdLA. 14: Catlg, bk binding & repair, films. 15: Prince Georges Co Mem Lib, 6532 Adelphi rd, Hyattsville Md 20782.

PASTERNAK, ELIZABETH ANN (FUNK). b Wash DC 11 Je 44. 4: Wendell Graham Pasternak. 5: Knox Col 62-66 (Elem Educ) AB; UIll 66-67 MSLS. 6: Fr. 7: Catlgr Mich State U (Lansing) 67; Catlgr a-v materials Professional Lib Serv, Santa Ana Cal 68, Mgr catlg dept 68-. 9: ALA. 14: Catlg. 15: 7073 21st st apt B, Westminster Ca 92673.

PASTERNAK, WENDELL G. b Georgefield Ill 1 Ag 44. 4: Elizabeth Ann Funk. 5: UIll 62-66 (Soc Studies) BA, 66-67 (LS) MS. 6: Fr. 7: A-v libn Long Beach City Col 67-. 9: CalASchL. 14: A-v serv, admin. 15: 7073 21 st apt B, Westminster Ca 92673.

PASTORETT, RICHARD THOMAS. b Richmond Hill NY 2 N 34. 4: Tomma N Hill. 5: Mt St Mary 52-56 (Educ) BS; Fla State U 56-57 (LS) MA. 6: Fr. 7: Radio-teletype team chief US Army, Ft Lewis Wash 57-59; Circ libn Jacksonville U 60-61; Radio-teletype team chief US Army, Ft Hood Tex 61-62; Admin asst, acquis libn, coordinator of pub serv, Jacksonville U 62-65; Head of acquis Auburn U 65-68; Coord of resources W Va Lib Commsn 68-. 9: WVaLA. 13: Yes. 14: Tech serv, rare bks, automation. 15: 2410 Harrison ave, St Albans W Va 25177.

PASTORETT, TOMMA N HILL. b Baldwin Miss. 4: Richard T Pastorett. 5: Miss State U 52-55 (Educ) BS; Fla State U 56-57 (LS) MA; Emory 63 Med Lib Certif. 7: Tchr Pub Schs, Monroe Co Miss 52-56; Asst circ libn Miss State U 57-58; Materials center libn Fla State U 58; Bkmob libn Olympia (Wash) Pub Lib, 59; Libn of Nursing Sch St Lukes Hosp, Jacksonville Fla 60; Med libn Fla State Bd of Health, Jacksonville Fla 60-65; Sci libn & instr Auburn U 65-68; Asst lib W Va State Col 69-. 9: WVaLA. 14: Med libnship, ref. 15: 2410 Harrison ave, St Albans W Va 25177.

PATCH, WILLIAM HENRY. b Abington Penn 28 S 19. 4: Rosanna Michelassi. 5: Amherst 38-42 (Hist) AB; Drexel 46-47 BS LS; UMich 50-51 AM LS. 7: Staff Sgt US Army, Africa, Italy 42-46; Catlgr USoCar 47-50; Catlgr Flint (Mich) Pub Lib 51-53; Documents libn Mem Lib UWis 53-65, Circ libn 65-. 12: . 13: Yes. 14: Docs, circ. 15: 5817 Dorsett dr, Madison Wis 53711.

PATE, CAROLYN J (THREET). b Sheridan Ark 28 O 9. 4: Eugen F Pate. 5: Ark State Tchrs Col 47-50 (Fr, Span) BSE; UArk summers 51-53 (LS); UTulsa summer 57 (Educ), 64 (LS); UOkla summers 68, 69. 6: Fr, Sp. 7: Libn Bixby (Okla) Pub Schs 51-53; Bkmob libn Tulsa (Okla) Pub Lib 53-54; Elem libn Tulsa (Okla) Pub Schs 54-64; Temp asst libn Tulsa (Okla) City-Co Libs summer 63; Libn admin Spec Serv US Army, Ft Sill Okla 64-. 9: ALA. 10: AAUW. 14: Admin, ref. 15: 13 NW 56 st, Lawton Okla 73501.

PATE, MICHAEL B(RIEN). b Owosso Mich 8 My 37. 4: Rose Anne Pate (Curry). 5: UMich 56-58 (Liberal Arts); St Petersburg Jr Col 59-60 (Liberal Arts); West Mich U 61-63 (Hist) BA, 63-65 (LS) MA. 6: Fr. 7: Ref asst, documents Kalamazoo Pub Lib 63-66; Hd libn UWis (Waukesha Co) 66-. 13: Yes. 14: Govt docs, ref, col lib admin.41935 . 15: RR #1 Chrisie Lake, Lawrence Mich 49064.

PATER, REV THOMAS G. b Hamilton Ohio 5 N 16. 5: Mt St Marys Sem (Norwood Ohio) 38-42 BA; Cath U 44-46 STD; Col Angelico (Rome) 46-48 PhD. 6: Lat, Fr, Ital, Sp, Ger. 7: Prof of theolgy & libn Mt St Marys Sem, Norwood Ohio 49-59; Theol catlgr Cath U 59-61, Head of catlg div 61-. 9: ALA; CathLA; Cath Theol Soc Amer; Potomac Tech Proc Libns. 12: Sup, 54-65, to ""An Alternative Classification for Catholic Books, by J M Lynn & G C Peterson. 13: Yes. 14: Catlg, theol lit. 15: Curley Hall, Cath Univ, Wash DC 20017.

PATMON, MARIAN (GUEST). b Sapulpa Okla 1 Mr 33. 4: John V Patmon. 5: Langston U 50-54 (Elem Educ) BS; UOkla 59-63 MLS. 6: Fr. 7: Sch libn High Sch, Lawton Okla 54-56; Catlgr Langston U 56-59; Asst gen ref State Lib, Okla City Okla 61-63; Med libn St Anthony Hosp, Okla City Okla 64-65; Libn for the blind Okla State Lib 65; Assoc dir of spec serv br Okla Dept of Libs 67. 9: ALA; MedLA; NEA; OklaLA. 10: Urban League; NAACP; Delta Sigma Theta. 13: Yes. 14: Spec Libs. 15: 4404 Woods dr, Oklahoma City Ok 73104.

PATON, ROBERT REID. b Vila New Hebrides 24 Jl 37. 5: UMelbourne 56-59 (Eng, Hist) BA; Lib Assoc of Australia 61 ALA. 6: Fr. 7: Joint copying project off Nat Lib of Australia & Pub Lib New So Wales, London UK 64-65; Catlgr Nat Lib of Australia, canberra ACT Australia 60-63, Ref libn 66-69; Liaison off Nat Lib of Australia, NYC 69-. 9: LA (Australia); SLA. 15: Australian Consulate-General 636 Fifth ave, New York NY 10020.

PATRIC, JEANNE BROLEY. b Winnipeg Man Can 1 S 28. 4: Earl Francis Patric. 5: Queen'sU (Can) 46-48 (Zool, Eng) BA; Vassar 49-50 (Zool) MS; SUNY Col Forestry 50-59 (absentia) (Zool) PhD; Syracuse 67- (LS). 6: Fr. 7: Research asst SUNY Col Forestry (Newcomb) 53-57; Libn Newcomb Central Sch, Newcomb NY 65-67; Libn Wellwood jr High,

Fayetteville NY 67-. 9: ALA; NEA; NYStateTA; NYLA. 10: Sigma Xi. 12: "Classification and Cataloging System for Wildlife Literature" (PhD diss). 14: Sch libs. 15: 7800 Heritage cir, Manlius NY 13104.

PATRICK, CAROLYN (MAYE KELLY). b Eastland Tex 2 F 27. 5: UTex 43-47 (Textiles) BS, 63-65 MLS. 7: Film bking libn Visual instr bur div of ext UTex (Austin) 47-50; Lib intern Sandia Lab Tech Lib, Albuquerque 65-66; Ref libn 66-68; Acquis libn UTex Med sch (San Antonio) 68-. 9: SLA; NMLA; AlbuquerqueLA. 10: Alpha Omicron Pi. 14: Ref, acquis. 15: 4214 Bunker Hill, San Antonio Tx 78230.

PATTEE, ALICE (PHELPS). b Ft Spring WVa 7 Jl 05. 4: Edwin J Pattee. 5: Penn State U 23-24; UDel 24-25, 26-27 (Hist) AB; Drexel 28-29 BS LS; UMich 38-39 MA LS. 7: Catlgr Oberlin Col Lib 28-42; Head clsf & 1st asst catlg dept Cleveland Pub Lib 42-43, 47-48; Head catlg dept Okla State U Lib 47-. 8: Instr, UOkla Lib Sch summer 54. 9: ALA-DCC (Ex sec 44-47, pres 50-51); SWLA; OklaLA. 14: Catlg. 15: 105 Orchard lane, Stillwater Okal 74074.

PATTEN, FREDERICK WALTER. b Los Angeles 11 D 40. 5: UCLA 58-62 (Hist) BA, 63 MLS. 6: Sp, Fr. 7: Ref libn Los Angeles Co Pub Lib, Hawthorne Cal 63-64; Catlg libn Los Angeles Co Law Lib 64-65; Catlg libn USoCal 65-. 67; Catlg libn Xerox Prof Lib Serv Santa Ana Cal 67-68; Asst libn Xerox Electro-Optical Systems, Pasadena Cal 68-. 9: SLA; CalLA. 10: Inst for Specialized Lit; Los Angeles Sci Fantasy Soc. 14: Catlg. 15: 8943 E Arcadia ave apt 14, San Gabriel Ca 91775.

PATTERSON, ANN EILEEN. b Marquette Mich 5 O 13. 5: No MichU 30-34 (Fr, Eng) AB; UMich 40-41 ABLS, 42-43 AMLS, 54, 58 (Eng). 6: Fr, Sp, Ital, Ger, Lat. 7: Tchr: Iron Mt (Mich) Pub Schs 34-39, Grosse Ile (Mich) Pub Schs 39-40; Libn Mercy Col (Detroit) 41-42; Lib serv fellow (catlg) UMich (Ann Arbor) 42-43, Order libn 43-49, Fine arts libn 49-52; Acquis libn UMont 52-53; Ref libn Detroit Pub Lib 53-65; Ref libn No MichU 66-67; Act dir acquis Lake Superior State Col 67-68, Catlg libn & Asst Prof 68-. 9: ALA; MichLA. 10: League of Women Voters; Sault Intl Naturalists Club. 14: Ref, acquis, catlg. 15: 1500 Fourteenth st, Sault Sainte Marie Mi 49783.

PATTERSON, BETTE LUCINDA. b Indianapolis 19 Ja 42. 5: Ind U 59-61 (Botany) AB, 64-66 (LS) AM. 6: Fr. 7: Libn Aerospace Research Applications Ctr Ind U Foundation 9bloomington) 64-66; High sch libn MSD of Brookville, Brookville Ind 66-67; Catlgr Ball State U 67-. 9: ALA; Ohio Valley Gp Tech Serv Libns. 14: Catlg. 15: 2570 White River blvd, Muncie In 47303.

PATTERSON, CHARLES DAROLD. b Wahpeton ND 8 Ag 28. 5: Bemidji State Col 50 (Hist, Music) BS; UMinn 56 (LS) MA; WVa U 64 M Mus; U Pittsburgh 68 (LS) Adv certif, '68-(LS). 7: Tchr Fargo (ND) Pub Schs 50; Sgt First Class US Army, Japan & Korea 50-52; Jr ref libn UMinn, Minneapolis 54-55; Head Libn Bemidji State Col 55-58; Head Libn & Asst Prof Glenville State Col 58-62; Asst Prof of Lib Sci WVa U 62-66; Instr Lib & Info Sci UPittsburgh 66-. 8: Adv serv; WVa Lib Commsn 60; WVa Dept of Pub Instr 63. 9: ALA; AALS (WVa Recr Rep 63-66, Bogle Mem Fund Com 68-); -ACRL (Tri-State Chap, Internat Rel RT 67-); WVaLA (Exec Bd 60-61, 64-66, chm Col & Univ Sect 60-61, chm Indexing & Publns Com 62-66, chm Nomin Com 65-66); PennLA; Pittsburgh Lib Club. 10: AAUP; Amer Guild of Organists. ; Pittsburgh Bibliophiles. 12: Ed "West Virginia Libraries" (63-66). 13: Yes. 14: Educ for libnship, ref, admin, lib resources, 18th cent keyboard music. 15: Grad Sch of Lib & Inf Sci, Univ of Pittsburgh, 135 N Bellefield ave, Pittsburgh Pa 15213.

PATTERSON, CHRISTINE (BORGMANN). b Boulder Colo 11 Mr 40. 4: Robert Logan Patterson. 5: UVt 58-61, 62-63 (Eng Lit) BA; UDublin 61-62 (Eng Lit); Harvard 63-64 (Eng Educ) MAT; Simmons 68-69 (LS) MSc. 7: Tchr Millis Jr-Sr High Sch, Millis Mass 64-65; Sub tchr var sch dist, San Jose Cal 65; Tchr Fremont Union High Sch Dist, Cupertino Cal 65-66; Tchr Christopher Wren Comprehensive Sch, London Eng 66; Program libn Computer ctr Univ-Col London (London Eng) 67-68; Lib asst assigned to spec proj Boston Pub Lib 69-. 9: ALA; ASIS. 14: Tech serv, admin, lib educ. 15: 14 Dudley st, Cambridge Ma 02140.

PATTERSON, CORNELIA (EDELEN). b Seattle 10 S 10. 4: William A Patterson. 5: UWash 27-31 BS LS. 7: Circ asst Seattle Pub Lib 31-42; Censor US Off of Censorship, Seattle 42-44; Circ ref libn Longview (Wash) Pub Lib 54-59; Ref libn San Bruno (Cal) Pub Lib 60-67; Ref libn Hayward Cal Pub Lib 67-. 9: CalLA. 10: Alpha Xi Delta. 15: 4741 Sorani way, Castro Valley Ca 94546.

PATTERSON, JANET KAY (DAVISSON). b Rensselaer Ind 5 D 40. 4: James Herbert Patterson. 5: Ball State 58-62 (Eng) BS; UColo summer 62: Harding Col summer 58: Ind U 63-64 (LS) MA. 6: Fr. 7: Stud lib asst Ball State U 61-62; Jr high sch libn Columbus Ohio 62-63; Ref libn Grad Lib Ind U 64-66; Asst ref & grad res libn 66-. 9: ALA. 10: Assn of Univ Women; Pi Lambda Theta; Kappa Kappa Kappa; Beta Phi Mu. 14: Ref. 15: 806 Emilie st, Rensselaer In 47978.

PATTERSON, DEWEY (DEWART). b Chicago 24 Je 32. 4: (Margaret) Esther Kelley Patterson. 5: Antioch Col 50-55 (Educ) AB; Simmons summers 61-65 MS LS. 7: Wk-camper Amer Friends Serv Com, Mex 55-57; Self-employed farmer-woodcutter, Sharon Vt 57-59; Stack supv, later admin asst Dartmouth Col Lib 59-65; Serv libn Antioch Col Lib 65-68; Ref libn & Supv interlib loan UVictoria, Victoria BC. 9: Univ Victoria Prof Staff Assn (sec-treas 68-69). 14: Ref. 15: Rural rte 7 (Mark Lane), Victoria BC Can.

PATTERSON, LEROY ROGER. b Grand Rapids Mich 15 Ag 24. 5: Hope Col 42-46 (Hist) AB; UMich summers 47-51 (Hist) AM, 52 AMLS, summer 53. 6: Sp, Fr. 7: Tchr Fremont (Mich) Pub Schs 47-51; Libn S Haven (Mich) Pub Lib 52-54; Libn Grand Rapids Mich 69-. 8: Instr in Lib Sci UMich Ext Dept. 9: ALA; MichLA. 14: Music and art, child & ya wk. 15: 1761 Eastbrook st SE, Grand Rapids Mi 49508.

PATTERSON, MARGARET. b Central City Ky 26 Ap 33. 4: Floyd H Patterson Jr. 5: Western KentuckyU 56-57; USan Carlos 59; UTulsa 61-63 (Eng Lit) BA; UOkla 63-64 MLS; O of the Americas (summer) 65. 6: Sp. 7: Admin asst United Appeal, Atlanta 58-60; Educ sec 1st Baptist Ch, Tulsa Okla 60-61; Instr UOkla Sch of Lib Sci 65-67; Catlg libn US Bur of Budget Lib, Wash DC 67-68; Catlg instr LC 68-. 9: ALA; OklaLA; DCLA. 10: Beta Phi Mu. 13: Yes. 14: Catlg, instr. 15: 2475 Virginia ave NW, Washington DC 20037.

PATTERSON, ROBERT H. b Alexandria La 11 D 36. 4: Virginia Alice Bookhart. 5: Millsaps Col 54-58 (Hist) BA; Tulane U 58-63 (Latin Amer Hist) MA; UCal (Berkeley) 64-65 MLS. 6: Sp. 7: Lib asst Tulane U Lib 63-64; Stud asst Grad Theol Union Bibl Center, Berkeley Cal 64-65; Rare bk libn Tulane U 65-66, Chief catlgr Lat Amer Lib 66-68, Fine Arts & scis libn 68, Libn II, Assoc humanities libn 69-. 10: Tulane U Lib Staff Assn. 13: Yes. 14: Rare bks, Latin-Amer bibliog, mss & archives, spec collections, ref. 15: Tulane Univ Lib, New Orleans La 70118.

PATTERSON, ROBERT LOGAN. b Pittsburgh 12 Mr 40. 4: Christine Borgmann. 5: UVt 58-62 (Psych) BA; San Jose State Col 64-66 (LS) MA. 7: Eng tchr, Milo Me 62-63; Stud libn San Jose State Col 65; Libn IBM, San Jose Cal 65; Libn IBM United Kingdom, London Eng 66-68; Info Dynamics Corp, Reading Mass 68-. 9: ALA; ASIS; NELA. 14: Automation, systs design, admin. 15: 14 Dudley st, Cambridge Ma 02140.

PATTERSON, SARA E (ANDREWS). b Eastland Tex 8 S 22. 4: Stanley R Patterson. 5: Tarleton State Col 39-41 (Eng) AA; UTex (El Paso) 57-58 (Eng) BA; USoCal 66-67 MS in LS. 6: Fr. 7: Elem & high sch tchr Erath Co Schs, Stephenville Tex 41-42; Clerk-stenographer US Civil Serv, El Paso Tex 42-44; Sec-cashier El Paso Pub Schs, el Paso Tex 46-58, High sch tchr & libn 58-65; High sch tchr Coronado Unified Sch dist, Coronado Calif 65-66; Asst catlg libn San Diego State Col 67-68; Traveling libn Chula Vista City Sch Dist, Chula Vista Cal 68-. 9: ALA-AASchL; NEA; CalASchL; CalTA. 10: Libraria Sodalitas (USoCal); Beta Phi Mu; Phi Kappa Phi; Pi Lambda Theta. 14: Catlg, sch libnship. 15: 7130 Waite dr apt 12, Lemon Grove Ca 92045.

PATTERSON, SHEILA ANN. b Long Beach Cal 17 Ap 39. 4: Randall Patterson. 5: Cal State Col (Long Beach) 57-61 (Eng) BA; UCLA 61-62 MLS. 6: Sp. 7: Libn Loara High Sch Anheim (Cal) Union High Sch Dist 62-64; Child libn Los Angeles Co Pub Lib, Bellflower Cal 64-. 9: CalLA; So Cal Coun on Lit for Child & Ya. 14: Ref, child serv. 15: 8181 Terry dr, Huntington Beach Cal 92647.

PATTILLO, JOHN W. b Atlanta Ga 16 Ag 30. 5: Emory 47-51 (Hist) BA, 51, 55 MLn. 7: Army security agcy USA, US & Europe 51-54; Asst gen studies libn, gen studies libn, Hd ser catlgr, Asst binding libn, Archivist & display libn Ga Inst of Tech Lib 56-66; Hd libn So Tech Inst 67-. 9: ALA; SELA; GaLA (v-chm Col & Univ Sect). 10: Atlanta hist Soc; Atlanta Civil War RT. 14: Admin, ref, rare bks. 15: 701 Martina dr NE, Atlanta Ga 30305.

PATTISON, FREDERICK (WOODWORTH). b Cleveland 31 Ja 30. 5: Trinity Col 49-53 (Art Hist) AB; West Res 53-54 MS LS; Columbia 64-65 Certif by Med LA. 7: Libn Sch of Soc Wk UPittsburgh 54-56; Asst libn NYC Commun Col 57-61; Asst to the libn Queens Col (NY) 61-63; Asst libn & indexer Amer Journal of Nursing Co, NYC 63-. 9: MedLA (Adv Com on Med Lib Problems 68-, NY Reg Group; Program Chm 66-67, treas 67-69, Exec Com 67-69); SLA; NY Lib Club. 10: Grolier Club (NY); NY Geneal & Biog Soc; NY Zool Soc; English-Speaking Union; Rector's Coun Grace Ch 68-. 14: Indexing, ref, acquis. 15: 10 W 16th st, New York NY 10011.

PATTISON, MARJORIE (ROSE). b NYC 23 Jl 08. 4: Earl Barber Pattison. 5: Cornell 26-30 9classics) BA; Syracuse summers 58-62 MSLS. 6: Fr. 7: Tchr DeKalb Junction High Sch, DeKalb Junction NY 30-32; Tchr Fultonville Hogh Sch, Fultonville NY 32-34; Libn Potsdam Jr-Sr Highm Potsdam NY 54-60; Libn Potsdam Sr High 60-. 9: NYStateLA (pres Sch Lib Sect 66, chm var coms; pres No Zone Libns). 10: Beta Phi Mu. 12: Ed SLS Newsletter (64). 14: Loc hist. 15: Route 1, Potsdam NY 13676.

PATTON, AUDREY M(ARIE). b Paris Tex 25 My 14. 5: Tex Mil Col 32-34; Tex Womans U 34-36 (LS) BA; UWyo summers 45-48; Tex Womans U summer 54-58 MLS. 6: Lat, Fr. 7: Libn: Kaufman Tex 36-54; Boude STOEY Jr High Sch, Dallas 54-58; Justin F Kimball SR High Sch, Dallas 58-. 9: ALA; NEA; TexLA; Tex Assn of Sch Libns (chm 65-66); Tex State Tchrs Assn;Dallas Sch Libns (pres 56-57); Dallas Clrm Tchrs. 14: High sch libs, ya collections. 15: 500 First st, Terrell Tx 75160.

PATTON, ELIZABETH (HYDE). b Charleston SC 6 Ag 17. 5: Col of Charleston 34-38 (Eng) BS; Columbia 39-61 (LS) MS. 7: Catlg asst Charleston (SC) Free Pub Lib 38-39; Act ref libn 40; Indexer Govt Print Off, Wash DC 42; Catlgr DC Pub Lib 42-44; Head Libn New Haven (Conn) Col Lib 8-. 9: ALA-AASchL; ConnLA (Program chm 65-66); ConnSchLA. 10: Beta Phi Mu. 14: Admin, in-serv train. 15: 135 Clifford st, Hamden Ct 06517.

PATTON, GLENN E JR. b Wichita Kan 25 O 45. 5: UKan 63-67 (Organ, Mus Theory) BM, 67-68 (Musicology) MA; Columbia 68-69 (LS) MS. 6: Fr, Ger, Ital, Lat. 9: MusLA; ALA; Amer Musicological Soc; Amer Guild of Organists. 10: Pi Kappa Lambda. 14: Mus. 15: 644 Riverside dr, Cunningham Ks 67035.

PATTON, GLENNA (RAY). b Calderwood Tenn 17 Jl 29. 4: Joe Patton. 5: Berea 45-49 9elem Educ) AB; Peabody Col 66 MLS. 6: Fr. 7: Tchr: Livingston Elem Sch, Livingston Tenn 56-60, Lyles Elem Sch, Lyles Tenn 61-63, E Elem Sch, Lyles Tenn 63-65; Libn Centerville Elem Sch, Centerville Tenn 65-. 9: ALA; NEA; TennLA; Middle Tenn LA; TennEA; HickmanCoEA. 10: Beta Phi Mu; Woman's Club; Town & Country Home Demonst Club. 14: Child lib serv, catlg. 15: 1038 Highway 100, Centerville Tn 37033.

PATTON, HELEN (DORSEY). b Poseyville Ind 26 Ap 10. 4: Roy Arthur Patton. 5: Earlham Col 27-31 (Eng, Soc Sci) BA; UMont 48, 50; Peabody Lib Sch 63p64 MSLS. 6: Sp. 7: Tchr Owensville High Sch, Owensville Ind 33-40; Tchr & libn Hot Springs High Sch, Hot Springs Mont 47-54; Libn Ashland High Sch, Ashland Ohio 54-57; Libn Wellington High Sch, Wellington Ohio 57-65; Asst prof Central Wash State Col 65-. 8: Chm Profess Training Lib Com (Wash); Chm Com on Catlg of Non-Print Materials (Wash). 9: EllensburghEA (pres). 14: Catlg, sch lib admin. 15: Rte 4 Box 63, Ellensburg Wa 98926.

PATTON, IDA (R). b Clinchco Va 18 Ja 33. 5: Madison Col 51-54 (LS) BA; Fla State U 58-59 (LS) MA. 7: Asst libn Falls Church (Va) High Sch 54-56; Asst libn Mt Vernon High Sch, Alexandria Va 56-58; Pub lib adv ext div Va State Lib 59-. 9: VaLA (Sec Activities Com 67-68, Sec Pub Lib Sect 64, chm Activities Com 69); SELA. 10: AAUW. 14: Ext wk. 15: Va State Lib, Richmond Va 23219.

PATTON, JOAN (ANTHONY). b Los Angeles 19 Ja 34. 4: Roy Lee Patton. 5: Tenn Wesleyan Col 51-53 (Hist) AA; UTenn 53-55 (Hist) BS; Rutgers 58-65 MLS. 7: Hist tchr McMinn Co High Sch, Athens Tenn 55-56; Tchr Elem Jr High Sch, Berks Co Penn 57-58; Sch libn Harding Twp Sch, New Vernon NJ 58-. 8: Adv Com Title II, Elem & Secon Educ Act of 65; Tchr NDEA Inst for Sch Libns, Grad Sch of Lib Serv, IndU summer 66. 9: ALA-AASchL; NEA; NJEA; NJSchLA (pres; chm Legis Com); Harding Twp EA (pres). 13: Yes. 14: Elem sch libs. 15: Harding Township School, New Vernon NJ 07976.

PATTON, JOHN IRVIN JR. b El Dorado Kan 18 D 27. 5: UNM 45-46 (Inter-Amer Affairs); UOkla 49-52 BS LS; UChicago 55-57 (LS). 7: US Army Finance (S/Sgt) 46-49; Bibliogr Ohio State U Lib 52-53; Asst Soc Studies libn Wayne State U 53-55; Ref & circ libn Educ Lib UChicago 55-57; Libn Col of Guam (Agana Guam) 57-62; Libn CBS-TV, Chicago 63-68; Lib Standard Educl Corp, Chicago 68-69; Adv-consul libn Faculty of Med USaigon, S Vietnam 69-. 8: Pub Lib Bd, Agana Guam 60-62. 9: SLA; ALA; Chicago Lib Club. 12: Ed "What's New in Advertising and Marketing". 14: Admin. 15: Ed Project-AMA, APO San Francisco Ca 96243.

PATTON, MARGARET (E). b St Louis. 5: Hardin Col AA; UKan (Eng) BS Ed; UIll BS LS. 7: Br libn Kan City (Mo) Pub Lib; Asst ref libn Wichita Kan) City Lib; Ref asst Art Inst of Chicago Lib; Libn Louis Latzer Mem Pub Lib, Highland Ill 39-. 8: Adv Com, Ill State Lib 40-45. 9: IllLA. 14: Ref. 15: 1423 Laurel, Highland Ill 62249.

PATTON, PEGGY. b Leavenworth Kan 8 F 21. 5: UMiami 37-66 (Hist) BA; IndU 66-68 MLS. 6: Fr. 7: Reader's serv & acquis Miami-Dade Jr Col 68-. 9: ALA; DadeCoLA. 10: Miami Dental Aux; AAUW. 14: Ref. 15: 6250 Chapman Field dr, Miami Fl 33156.

PATTULLO, AMBROSE D. b Chicago 2 D 11. 4: Margaret Mooney. 5: Carnegie 43-44 Diploma; UPenn 45 (Ger); Mich State U 46-54 (Pre-med, Eng) BA & MA; UMich 53-54 MA LS. 6: Ger, Fr, Russian. 7: Asst libn "The Flint Journal, Flint Mich 54; Catlg dept Mich State Lib Tech libn Techlibn Battelle Mem Inst, Columbus Ohio 56-59; Lit sci Goodyear Atomic Corp, Portsmouth Ohio 59-60; Research libn Union Carbide Chem Co, S Charleston WVa 61-62; Head circ dept Auurn U Lib 62-63; Head Libn Avon Lake Pub Lib, Avon-on-the-Lake Ohio 63-64; Sr libn Ind State U 64-66; Head libn Rochester Pub Lib, Rochester Mich 66-67; Asst Prof Eng Adrian College 67-69. 8: Med instr US Army 41-44; Mil Intel ETO 45; Lib consul Wright-Patterson Field 56-58; German instr Morris Harvey Col 61-62; Eng Prof Adrian Col 67-69. 9: SLA (chm Wkshop on Lib Techniques, Metals Div, 62 Conv). 10: AAUP; Mich Col Eng Assn; MichLA. 11: Adrian Faculty Study Award 68. 14: Admin, tech serv, ref. 15: 1907 Pontiac rd, Ann Arbor Mich 48105.

PAUGH, MINNIE ELLEN. b Virginia City Mont 7 Ap 19. 5: Mont State U 39-41 (Hist) BA, 52 (Educ) ME; UDenver 59-60 (LS) MA. 7: High Sch Eng & Hist Tchr, Mont 41-60; Spec Collection Libn Mont State U Bozeman 61-. 9: ALA; PNLA; MontLA. 10: AAUP; AAUW; Delta Kappa Gamma; Amer Assn of State & Local Hist; Montana Inst of the Arts (Hist Group). 12: Montana Bibliog in PNLA "Quarterly" (3 yrs). 14: Ref, curator of hist mss. 15: 510 W Story, Bozeman Mt 59715.

PAUL, A CURTIS. b Monessen Penn 4 S 35. 4: Margaret M Paul. 5: Cal State Col 53-57 (Speech Therapy, Educ) BS; Northwestern Lutheran Theol Sem 57-60 (Theol) BD; Dropsie Col for Hebrew & Cognate Lang 61-62; UMinn (LS) MALS. 6: Gk, Hebrew, Fr. 7: Assoc Pastor Calvary Lutheran Church, Pittsburgh 60-61; Pastor Reedemer Lutheran Church, Phila 61-63; Libn Northwestern Lutheran Theol Sem 63-. 9: ATheolLA; MinnLA; MinnTheolLA; ALA; Lutheran Ch LA; Lutheran Histl Conf. 10: Minneapolis Inst of Art. 13: Yes. 14: Theol libnship. 15: 1501 Fulham st, St Paul Mn 55108.

PAUL, DONALD CHARLES. b Newton Iowa 17 Jl 25. 5: UCLA 45-50 (Philos) BA; USoCal 57-59 MS LS. 6: Fr. 7: Sr lib asst: UCLA 47-50; UCal (Berkeley) 54; UCLA 54-55; Operations asst Ramo-Wooldridge Corp, Los Angeles 55-58; Head Libn Hughes Aircraft Co, Solid State Research Center, Newport Beach Cal 58-67; Hd pub serv Anaheim Pub Lib, Anaheim Cal 67-68, Hd tech serv 68-. 9: SLA (chm consul serv, SoCal Chap 65-67); CalLA; Orange Co (Cal) LA (treas 66-67). 10: . 14: Admin. 15: 2761 Drake ave, Costa Mesa Cal 92626.

PAUL, GARY NORMAN. b Los Angeles Cal 21 N 43. 5: Occidental Col 61-65 (Hist) BA; UDenver 65-66 (Libnship) MA; UCal (Berkeley) 68- (LS). 6: Fr. 7: Stud asst Occidental Col Lib 65; Supv period rm UDenver Libs 65-66; Libn gen ref & soc sci div San Jose State Col 66; Basic combat & adv indiv training US Army Pfc 66-67; Intelligence analyst US Army Res Spe/4, Mt View Cal 67; Admin asst Dir of Libs San Jose State Col 67-68; Instr Dept of Lib 68. 8: Res Fellow Heritage Found, Deerfield Mass summer 64. 9: ALA (Amer Lib Hist RT); SLA; CalLA; Helibs No Cal. 10: Ephebian soc of Los Angeles; Sierra Club; Alum Assns of Occidental Col & UDenver Grad Sch of Libnship. 14: Col & univ lib admin and bldgs, acad lib hist, a-v materials. 15: 707 Cunningham Hall 2650 Haste st, Berkeley Ca 94721.

PAUL, MAY LOU (NANCE). b Tilden Neo 24 F 24. 4: Donald R Paul. 5: Meredith Col 41-45 (Soc Studies) BA; Drexel 46-47 BS LS. 6: Fr. 7: Asst circ libn Penn State U 47-50; Asst br libn Carnegie Lib, Pittsburgh 50-52; Asst catlg libn Wash & Jefferson, Wash Penn 59-61; Elem sch libn Strabane Twp, Wash Penn 61-65; Jr High Sch Trinity Area, Wash Penn 65-69; Jr High Sch, Chester Penn 69-. 9: ALA; NEA: PennLA; PennStateEA. 10: AAUW. 14: Child serv, catlg, read adv, col ref. 15: 32 Waterford way, Wallingford Pa 19086.

PAULAITIS, ARTHUR. b Lithuania 25 Ja 17. 4: Martha Elizabeth Zviliute. 5: Toronto 48-52 MA (Ger, Eng), BLS. 6: Lithuanian, Ger, Eng, Fr. 7: Staff writer "Universal Jewish Encclopedia, NYC 34-39; Indexer "Americana Encyclopedia, NYC 42-44; Researcher, libn Francis S Bushman, NYC 49-53; Libn NY Acad of Med, NYC 55-57; Libn Labs for Pharmaceutical Development, NYC 60-63; Libn Beth Jacob Schs, NYC 63-65; Libn Newark Beth Israel Hosp, Newark NJ 65-. 9: Inst Prof Libns Ont; OntLA (Ref Wkshop, past pres). 10: Greater Windsor Citizenship Coun. 13: Yes. 14: Ref, bus & tech. 15: 38 McNicoll ave, Willowdale Ont Can.

PAULI, DANIEL. b The Hague Netherlands 11 Jl 24. 4: Clementine M Spinks. 5: PBNA 53 (Chem Engng); GO-NIDER/NVB 59 (Info Retrieval), 60 (Archivist). 6: Dutch, Fr, Ger. 7: Hd documentation dept Central Tech Inst TNO, The Hague 49-66; Libn Gulf Oil Canada Limited, Calgary Alberta Can 66-. 9: Intl Assn Documentalists & Info Officers; CanLA; Geosci Info Soc; AltaLA. 13: Yes. 14: Universal decimal clsf, computerized info retrieval. 15: Gulf Oil Canada Limited Library, PO Box 130, Calgary 2 Alberta Can.

PAULIN, ALICE D. b Cleveland Ohio 17 O 08. 5: West ResU 26-30 AB, 29-30 (Law), 42-44 bs in LS; Fenn Col 54-55 (Ferrous Metallography). 7: Desk asst Cleveland Hts Pub Lib, Cleveland Hts Ohio 31-44; Libn Bus Info Bur, Cleveland Pub Lib, Cleveland Ohio 44-47; Research libn US Steel Corp-Wire Div, Cleveland Ohio 47-68; Head ref dept State Lib of Ohio 68-. 9: SLA (pres Cleveland Chap 52-53; chm Metals Div); ALA; OhioLA. 14: Gen ref, state govt, wire tech. 15: 3440 Olentangy River rd, Columbus Oh 43202.

PAULK, FRANCES. b Ocilla Ga 5 D 16. 5: GSCW 38 (Educ, Eng) BS Ed; Peabody 46 BS LS, summers 58-60 MALS. 7: Elem tchr Ocilla (Ga) Pub Sch 35-37; Elem tchr Pavo (Ga) Pub Sch 38-39; Libn Irwin Co High Sch, Mystic Ga 39-44; Libn Fitzgerald (Ga) High Sch 45-46; Libn Ocilla (Ga) High Sch 44-45, 46-51; Asst catlgr Ga State Col 51-65; Asst libn Augusta Col 65-. 8: Supvr Irwin Co Lib, Ocilla Ga 43-51. 9: ALA; SELA; GaLA; GaEA; CSRALA. 14: Ref, catlg. 15: 2110 Walton way, Augusta Ga 30904.

PAULSEN, HOWARD W. b Hutchinson Minn 1 Jl 12. 5: Macalester Col 35 (Hist, Eng, Sociol) BA; UMinn (Minneapolis) (Soc Wk) Masters; UN Dak (Educ, Hist) Masters; UWis (Milwaukee) (LS) Certified. 6: Sp. 7: Soc wkr Minn State Dept Soc Welfare, St Paul 35-50; Lt (sr grade) USNR Navy Navy Air Force 42-45; Tchr N Dak Pub Schs 50-55; Tchr & sch libn Minn Pub Schs 55-61; Tchr & sch libn Kettle Moraine Boys Sch, dept of health & soc serv, Plymouth Wis 61-. 8: Chm Dept of Soc Welfare Lib Com, St Paul 39-42; US Navy Fleet Air Wing Lib Com on Profess Lit 44-45; Mem Conf of Libns of Wis State Institns to improve liv serv in institns 67, 69-. 9: ALA; -AHIL; NEA; NCTE; Amer Corr Assn; WisEA; Wis Coun Tchrs Eng; SheboyganCoEA. 10; Wis State Employees Assn; Sheboygan Co Civic Music Assn; Amer Legion; Navy League; Univ Grad Sch Club. 11: Rockefeller Found Fellowship. 12: "History of Public Assistance Legislation in Minnesota 1930-1945" (60). 13: Yes. 14: YA ref serv, US Govt publ. 15: R Rte 2, Plymouth Wi 53073.

PAULSEN, SHEILA F. b Minneapolis 22 O 32. 4: Richard H Paulsen. 5: Mills Col 50-52 (Bot); UIll 53-55 (Hist) BA, 55-57 (LS) MS. 6: Fr, Sp. 7: Jr libn UMinn (Minneapolis) 57-63, Libn 63-68; Catlg libn St Paul Sem Lib, St Paul 68-. 8: St Paul Ramsey Hosp Volunteer serv (lib). 9: ALA; MinnLA. 10: AAUW; Ullr Ski Club. 14: Child bks, catlg. 15: 576 So Cretin ave, St Paul Mn 55116.

PAULSON, MERLE J. b Newton Kan. 5: Kan State Tchrs Col (Emporia) 52-54 (Speech, Eng) BS Ed, AB; U Denver 62 MA Libnship. 7: Ser libn Wichita State U Lib 62-66, Hd of acquis 65-. 9: ALA; KanLA; MPLA. 14: Ser, acquis. 15: 1552 N Vassar, Wichita Ks 67208.

PAULSON, PETER (JOHN). b NYC 30 Ja 28. 4: Josephine Bowen. 5: CCNY 45-49 (Hist) BSS; Columbia 50 (Hist) MA; SUNY(Albany) 55 (LS) MA. 6: Sp. 7: Lib asst NY State Lib 52-55, Head gift & exchange sect 55-64, Head catlg sect 65, Prin libn for Tech Serv 65-. 8: Asst Prof (Part Time) Lib Sci SUNY (Albany) 60-; Chm NY State Lib Com on Depository Libs 64-. 9: ALA; NYLA (Resources & Tech Serv Sect; pres 63, v-pres 62, chm Resources Com 62-65, chm Com on Pub Docs 69-); Hudson-Mohawk LA (NY) (sec 61-64). 10: Nat Railway Hist Soc; NY State Hist Assn; SUNY(Albany) Lib Sch Alumni; Phi Beta Kappa. 12: "National Exchange Centers and the International Exchange of Publications" (62); "Federal Depository Library Service in New York State" (64). 13: Yes. 14: Tech serv, hist bks & printing, intl lib devel. 15: 24 Tillinghast ave, Menands NY 12204.

PAULUKONIS, JOSEPH THOMAS. b Worcester Mass 14 F 41. 4: Mary Ann Frost. 5: State Col at Worcester 62-66 (Math) BS Ed; Case West Res Univ 66-67 BSLS. 7: Teller Worcester Co Inst for Savings, Worcester Mass 61-62; Libn Tech Inst Lib NorthwesternU 67-. 9: ALA; ASIS; LARC; Chicago Reg Gp Libns in Tech Serv (sec-treas 68-70). 13: Y 14: Automation, admin. 15: 1338 W Farwell, Chicago Il 60626.12873

PAULUS, MARGARET ISABELLE. b Milwaukee Wis 9 F 14. 5: Marquette U 31-35 (Journalism) PhB; Columbia 44-45 (LS) BS; UWis (Milwaukee) 67 (Adult Educ), UWis (Madison) 67-68 (LS) MS. 6: Ger. 7: Sec Pub Sch, Milwaukee 37-39, High sch libn 39-44; Jr high sch libn, Grosse Pointe Mich 45-46; Child libn Pub Lib, West Allis Wis 46-48, chief libn 48-66; Instr UWis (Milwaukee) 66-67; Interim Assoc Prof UFla 69-. 9: ALA; WisLA; FlaLA. 10: Theta Sigma Phi. 13: Yes. 14: Lib admin. 15: 1216 SW Second ave apt 42, Gainesville Fl 32601.

PAULUS, MARY CAROL. b Grand Rapids Mich 26 N 36. 5: Grand Rapids Jr Col 54-56 AA; UMich 56-58 (Eng Lit) BA, 58-59, 62 MA LS. 6: Fr. 7: Catlgr Sandia Corp, Albuqerque NM 59; Child libn Enoch Pratt Free Lib, Baltimore 59-63; Child spec Baltimore Co Pub Lib, Towson Md 63-. 9: ALA; MdLA. 10: Phi Kappa Phi. 14: Child serv. 15: 1207 St Agnes lane apt G, Baltimore Md 21207.

PAUTZ, MARTIN R. b Wisconsin Rapids Wis 3 Je 17. 4: Phyllis O'Hanlon. 5: Concordia Col 9milwaukee) 31-35 (Liberal Arts); UWis 38-41 (Eng) BS Ed; State UIowa 60 (Soc Sci); UNC 67-68 MSLS. 7: Lt Col USAF 41-66; Asst libn IBM Research, Triangle Park NC 67-68; Dir lib Greenville Tech Educ Ctr, Greenville SC 68-. 9: ALA; SLA; SELA; SCLA. 15: Lib Greenville TEC, Greenville SC 29606.

PAUTZSCH, RICHARD O(SCAR). b Boston 30 Ag 19. 5: Boston U 37-41 (Eng Lit) SB; Columbia 49-50 (LS) MS, 50-51 (LS). 6: Fr, Ger. 7: Asst Mass Horticultural Soc Lib, Boston 38-41; Searcher, catlgr Harvard Col Lib 41-43; Libn New Eng Deposit Lib, Allston Mass 44; Welfare spec SIC US Navy, US & Pacific 44-46; Catlgr Harvard Col Lib 46-47; Catlg supv Harvard Undergrad Lib .Proj 47-48; Supv circ dept Lamont Lib, Harvard U 49; Catlgr Brooklyn (NY) Pub Lib 50; Head catlg unit Brooklyn Pub Lib 51-55, Coordinator of catlg 56-. 8: Coun "Whos Who in Library Service 53-55; Dewey Decimal Clsf Ed Policy Com 55-57; Consul LC Catlg in SCR Survey 59; Prof consel to Dirs, Forest Press, Inc 67-68. 9: ALA activities; ALA-DCC (Com on Clsfn 52-53, Catlg Code Rev Com, Composite Wks Subcom 56-66);-RTSD (Nomin Com 60-61, CCS Nomin Com 61-62, chm Melvil Dewey Award Jury 62, Tech Serv Co & Ratio Com 63-, CCS Policy & Res Com 64-65, 68-69);-LAD (LO&MS Stat Com for Tech Serv 63-64, chm 65-66); NY Tech Serv Libns activities; (Program chm 52-53, Memb Chm 55-56, chm Nomin Com 63-64, sec/treas 66-67); NYLA; NY Lib Club; ALA-RTSD (Tech Serv Cost Com 68-69). 10: Amer Guild of Organists; Columbia Sch of Lib Serv Alumni Assn. 12: "Classification, in "Technical Services in Libraries by M F Tauber (54). 13: Yes. 14: Tech serv. 15: 34 Plaza st, apt 302, Brooklyn NY 11238.

PAVIAN, DORATHY (STOTLER). b Wilkinsburg Penn 3 F 07. 5: UPittsburgh 26-38 (Sociol) BA, 54-58 (Sociol) M Litt, 62-65 MLS. 6: Sp. 7: Sec to dean Grad Sch UPittsburgh 25-38, Hostess Heinz Mem Chapel 38-40; Libn UPittsburgh (Johnstown) 52-, Libn & instr in sociol 61-. 8: Adv com Lib Tech Asst Program Mt Aloysius Col 68-. 9: ALA; Amer Sociol Assn; Penn Sociol Assn; PennLA; Juniata-ConemaughLA (chm 62-63); CambriaLA (pres 68-70). 10: Delta Kappa Gamma; Johnstown Art League; Johnstown Area Arts Coun; AAUW; DAR; Beta Phi Mu; Pi Tau Phi; Alpha Kappa Delta. 14: Admin. 15: 347 Highland ave, Johnstown Pa 15902.

PAVLIK, MARY J. b Monongahela Penn 10 D 23. 5: Boston U 51-55 (Liberal Arts); Harpur Col 56-57 (Liberal Arts); SUNY (Geneseo) 58-60 (LS)BS; Syracuse 63-64 MS LS. 6: Russian. 7: Sch libn Spencer (NY) Central Sch 60-63; Ref libn St Petersburg (Fla) Pub Lib 65-. 9: ALA; FlaLA. 10: Beta Phi Mu. 14: AV, ref. 15: 3175 Tenth av N, St Ptersburg Fla·33713.

PAVLIN, STEFANIA A (STUKELJ). b Novo Mesto Yugoslavia 13 Ja 29. 4: Peter Pavlin. 5: Mt St Vincent Col 49-52 (Philos) BA; UToronto 53-54 BLS. 6: Slovenian, Eng. 7: Clerk Can Life Ins Co, Toronto 52-53; Libn Toronto Pub Libs 54-56; Libn Ont Dept of Highways, Toronto 57-. 9: SLA (Toronto Chap). 14. Catlg, ref. 15: 22 Islay ct, Weston Ont Can.

PAWLAK, BONNIE (ANN). b Minneapolis 8 Ja 45. 5: Col of St Catherine 63-67 (LS, Psych) BA. 7: Child & asst libn Hopkins Pub Lib, Hopkins Minn 67-. 9: MinnLA (chm Child & YP Sect 69). 14: Child & yp. 15: 5136 Vincent ave S, Minneapolis Mn 55410.

PAWLEY, CAROLYN PATRICIA (ROBERTS). b Kitchener Ont Can 21 My 39. 4: John Diarmid Pawley. 5: McMaster U 58-61 (Fr, Span) BA; UToronto 62-63 BLS. 6: Fr, Sp. 7: Catlgr; UWaterloo (Ont) 63-64, UToronto 64-65, UWaterloo (Ont) 66-, Hd catlg dept. 9: CanLA; ALA; OntLA: Inst Prof Libns Ont. 14: Catlg. 15: 95 Owen ave, Kitchener Ont Can.

PAYNE, DESSIE MAUDE. b Green Co Tenn 15 Ag 10. 5: E Tenn State U 35 (Soc Sci) BS; Peabody 45 BS LS, 58 MA. 7: Elem tchr Fall Branch Tenn 29-32; Elem tchr, Johnson City Tenn 35-37, Jr High tchr 37-39, Elem libn 39-42, Libn Sci Hill High Sch 42-. 9: NEA; TennEA; TennLA. 10: Delta Kappa Gamma. 15: 108 E 11th ve, Johnson City Tenn 37601.

PAYNE, DORIS JANE (HITCHENS). b Cincinnati Ohio 19 S 27. 4: Paul E Payne. 5: Bowling Green State U 45-49 (Eng, Soc Studies) BS in Ed; UWash 64-66 M Lib. 6: Fr. 7: Tchr Celina High Sch, Celina Ohio 50-52; Tchr Fairborn High Sch, Fairborn Ohio 52-54; Libn Redmond High Sch, Redmond Wash 66-67; Libn Lake Wash High, Kirkland Wash 66-67; Hd libn finn Hill Jr High Sch, Kirkland Wash 67-. 9: ALA; NEA; WashLA; WashStateASchL; WashEA. 10: Beta Phi Mu. 14: Libnship for child & yp. 15: 2114 N 112nd st, Seattle Wa 98133.

PAYNE, EMILY (CLEMENT). b Walker Co Ga 10 O 20. 4: Albert S Payne. 5: Shorter 58 (Eng) AB; Emory 63 (LS) ML. 6: Fr. 7: Eng tchr Model Sch, Shannon Ga 58-59; Child & yp libn Tri-Co Reg Lib, Rome Ga 59-64; Dir Tri-Co Reg Lib, Rome Ga 64-. 9: ALA; SELA; FEA; GEA; NEA; GaLA (Com on Planning for Lib Coord of Info Serv, Publicity Com, Lib Constit Adv Com). 10: Alpha Delta Kappa; Quota Club; Bus & Prof Womens Club; Farm Bur. 14: Admin. 15: 606 W 1st st, PO Box 1547, Rome Ga 30161.

PAYNE, HELEN L(OIS) MOHLER. b Columbus Ohio 13 Mr 09. 5: Marion Col 28-30; George Washington U 30-32 AB LS. 7: LC: Desc Catlg Div 31-45, Copyright Off; currently Hd, bk sect, catlg div 50-. 9: DCLA. 10: Phi Mu. 14: Catlg. 15: 1501 Ray rd apt 302, Hyattsville Md 20782.

PAYNE, NORAH (RUSSELL). b Dorking Surrey England. 4: George L Payne. 5: UWash 32-33 (LS). 6: Fr. 7: Asst fine arts dept Enoch Pratt Free Lib, Baltimore 33-40; Compiler union list of serials H W Wilson LC 40-42; Montgomery Co (Md) Dept of Pub Libs: Libn 47-62, Child libn 64-68, Ref libn 68-. 9: ALA; MdLA. 10: Amer Recorder Soc. 14: Ref, child wk. 15: 10707 Kenilworth ave, Garrett Park Md 20766.

PEABODY, BREWSTER EARL. b Plymouth Mich 18 O 34. 5: UMich 52-56 (Hist) AB, 56-57 AM LS, 57-58 (Hist) AM. 6: Ger. 7: Bibliog searcher order dept UMich 56-58; US Army & Res Company Clerk (Sgt E-5) 58-63; Ser libn UDel 59-62; Alton libn SoIll U (Edwardsville) 62-65, Asst libn 65-66; Lib dir Old Dominion U 66-. 9: ALA; VaLA; SLA. 10: Nat Railway Hist Soc; Va Hist Soc. ; Electric Railway Assn; Light Railway Transport League, Upper Can Railway Hist Soc; Can Railway Hist Soc. 14: Univ lib admin, tech serv. 15: 934 Armfield cir apt 103, Norfolk Va 23505.

PEABODY, DIANN LYNN (STERRENBERG). b Urbana Ill 26 S 44. 4: Charles K Peabody. 5: East IllU 62-66 (Sp) BS in Educ; UIll (Urbana) 66-67 (LS) MS. 6: Sp, Fr. 7: Ref & adult libn Rolling Prairie Libs Syst, Decatur Ill 67-. 10: Friends if Lib; Kappa Delta Pi; Sigma Delta Pi; Beta Phi Mu. 14: Ref, pub serv areas. 15: 403 North Pine, Decatur Il 62522.

PEACE, WILLIAM KITTRELL. b Rusk Tex 25 Mr 26. 5: Tex Christian U 46-50 (Hist) BA; UTex 60 (Educ) MEd; LSU 64 MS LS. 6: Fr. 7: Lib asst Ft Worth (Tex) Pub Lib 48-50; Lib asst UTex 50-52; Tex State Lib: Asst legis ref libn 52-53, Chief records div 53, Dir ext div 54-55, Asst state libn 55-60, Act state libn 60-62, Asst state lbn 62-. 66; Post masters fellow LSU 66-67, Libn Lee Col (Baytown Tex) 67-. 8: Pub lib bldg consul; Adv serv to small pub lib bds on lib admin. 9: ALA (v-chm RT Serv for the Blind); AAStateL; SWLA; TexLA (Exhib chm, chm dist V 68). 10: Tex State Geneal Soc; SAR; Phi Delta Kappa; LSU Lib Sch Alumni Assn; Baytown C of C. 12: Ed "Texas Libraries (54-55); Ed "National Association of State Libraries Newsletter" (55); "History of the Texas State Library with Emphasis on Period 1930-1959" (Tex State Lib 59). 13: Yes. 14: Admin, ref, US docs, serv for the blind, jr col admin. 15: 1305 Memorial dr apt 23, Baytown Tx 77520.

PEACOCK, HELEN (MILLE). b Donegal Penn 7 Ja 11. 4: William H Peacoc. 5: Lenoir Rhyne Col 28-32 (Eng, Hist) AB; UNC 39-41 BS in LS, 67 NDEA Inst for Advanced Study in Educ Media. 6: Fr, Lat. 7: High sch tchr of Eng & speech, Hickory NC 32-40; Libn Chapel Hill Sr High Sch, Chapel Hill NC 40-53, 57-. 8: Served on state com for study of materials for thegifted; Tchr: Amer Lt, Lenoir Rhyne Col, summer 39, lib sci NC Col, summers 42-45; Dir Title II Demonstration Lib 67-69. 9: ALA; NEA; NCEA; NCLA; DAVI. 10: AAUW; Delta Kappa Gamma; Beta Phi Mu. 13: Yes. 14: Ref, wk with yp. 15: Box 1023, Chapel Hill NC 27514.

PEARCE, DONALD JOSLIN. b Southampton Eng 31 My 24. 4: June Bond. 5: Sch of Oriental Studies, ULondon 41-43; Geo Washington U 50-53 (Fr) BA; Cath U 53-54 MS LS. 6: Fr. 7: (Capt) Japanese Linguist British Army Intelligence Corps 43-47; Compositor Col Printing Co, Vancouver BC 48-49; Ill asst US Dept of Agric Lib Wash DC 49-54; Circ libn Denison U 53-59; Asst acquis libn, admin asst,gift & exch asst, Ohio State U 55-59; Head Libn & Asst Prof UND 59-69, Chief bibliogr & Asst Prof of Oriental Phil 69-. 9: ALA-ACRL; OhioLA (chm SVTAFF Org Round Table 58-59);NDLA (chm Legis Com 63-65; pres 65-67). ; MPLA (v-pres 68-). 10: AAUP; rand Forks Ballet Co; Phi Beta Kappa; Beta Phi Mu. 14: Admin. 15: 110 Columbia ct, Grand Forks ND 58201.

PEARCE, GERTRUDE MARGARET (McKEON). b St Paul Minn 24 O 13. 4: Raymond C Peace. 5: UMinn 31-36 (Romance Lang) BA, 40-41 BLS. 6: Fr, Sp, Ital. 7: Libn Lockheed Aircraft Co, Burbank Cal 41-45; Art libn Metro Goldwyn Mayer Studio, Culver City Cal 45-58; Libn St John's Hosp & Daniel Freeman Hosp, Santa Monica Cal 60-62; Libn Black Foxe Military Acad, Los Angeles 63-64; Libn Cal State Lib, Orange Co 64-65; Libn Orange Co Pub Lib, Costa Mesa Cal 65-. 8: Made survey of Yorba Linda, Placentia & orange Co Pub Libs 64-65. 9: CalLA; Orange CoLA. 10: Friends of Costa Mesa Libs; Pacific Sands Cabana Club; AAUW. 14: Ref. 15: 10072 Valley Forge dr, Huntington Beach Ca 92646.

PEARCE, HARRIET M. b Lewistown Penn 28 O 28. 4: Edward D Peace II. 5: Smith 47-51 (Govt) BA; Simmons (LS) MS. 6: Fr. 7: Lib asst CIA, Wash DC 51-53; Dept registrar & libn Mus of Sci, Boston 53-55; Child bk buyer Charles E Lavliat Co, Boston 55-60; Asst buyer Campbell & Hall, Boston 60-66; Libn Beavee Country Cay Sch, Chestnut Hill Mass 66-. 9: ALA; NELA; MassSchLA. 10: YA Coop Bk Rev Gp Mass, Needham (Mass) Civil Rights Com. 15: 41 Bond st, Needham Ma 02192.

PEARCE, STANLEY KEITH. b Sprague Wash 13 Je 28. 4: Donna Mae Ince. 5: UWash 46-52 (Psych) BS, 53-56 LLB, 56-57 (Law Libnship) MLL; UCal (Davis) 66 (Computer Serv) Certif. 6: Fr. 7: Asst ref libn Los Angeles Co Law Lib, Los Angeles 57-59; Libn OMelveny & Hyers, Los Angeles 59-. 8: Inst, Summer Inst in Law Libnship, Sch of Law, UCal(Berkeley) 69. 9: AALL; ASIS; SLA; So Cal Assn of Law Libs (pres 68-69). 12: Co-auth "Order Procedures (60), Contrib "Manual of Procedures for Private Law Libraries (62). 13: Yes. 14: Ref, admin (legal). 15: 611 W 6th st, Los Angeles Ca 90017.

PEARLMAN, ELISSA (NASSIM). b Singapore. 4: Louis H Pearlman. 5: USingapore 56-60 (Hist) BA; Columbia 66-67 MS. 6: Hebrew, Malay, Fr. 7: SE Asian bibliogr Columbia 68-. 14: Area studies (SE Asia & Hebraica). 15: RD 1, Cranbury NJ 08512.

PEARLMUTTER, REGINA (SINGER). b Bronx NY 11 Mr 24. 4: Morris Pearlmutter. 5: UWis 41-42; NYU 42-44 (Psych) BA; Columbia 63-66 (LS) MS. 7: Merchandise buyer Bloomingdale bros, NYC 44-52; Libn Elem Sch Pub Sch 158 NYC Bd of Educ 65-. 9: ALA; NYCSchLA. 14: Child serv. 15: 410 E 57 st, New York NY 10022.

PEARSON, ELLEN M. b Amherst NS 25 S 37. 4: W B Pearson. 5: Dalhousie U 54-57 (Chem) BS; McGill61-62 BLS. 6: Fr. 7: Ref lbn Nat Sci Lib NRC, Ottawa 62-68; Chief search ed Can SDI Project 68-. 9: CanLA; SLA. 10: Prof Inst of Pub Serv Can; 14: Ref, research, data proc, sel dissemin of info. 15: Nat Sci Lib, 100 Sussex dr, Ottawa 2 Can.

PEARSON, FLAVAL ARLEEN. b Stanwood Wash 3 F 12. 5: UWash 36-38 (Lit) BA, 38-39 (LS) BA. 6: Fr. 7: Libn Pub Lib, Anacortes Wash 40-43; Libn Pub Lib, Chehalis Wash 43-58; Head Libn Whitworth Col Lib 58-68, Ref libn 68-. 9: ALA; PNLA; WashLA. 10: Wesleyan Serv Guild; AAUP. 14: Admin, ref. 15: W706 Providence, Spokane Wa 99205.

PEARSON, JACQUELINE VERONICA (BELL). b England 23 O 43. 4: John E Pearson. 5: UBradford Eng 62-66 (Physics) BTech; USheffield Eng 67-68 (Libnship) Diploma. 7: Grad trainee lib BradfordU 66-67; Ref libn Drexel Inst 68-. 9: BritishLA; Inst of Physics, Physical Soc. 14: Sci ref. 15: Drexel Inst of Tech Lib 32nd & Chestnut sts, Philadelphia Pa 19104.

PEARSON, JAMES EUGENE. b Okla City Okla 6 S 20. 4: Isabelle Taylor Pearson. 5: UOkla 38-41, 46-47 (Hist) BA, 47-49 (Geog) MA; Ohio State U 49-50 (Geog); UMinn 52-54 (LS) MA. 7: Chief petty off US Coast Guard 41-46; Grad asst in geog UOkla 47-49; Instr in geog Henderson State Col 50; Instr in geog Moorhead State Col 50-52; Sr cerk Bio-Med Lib UMinn 52-54; Libn soc sci Drake U 54-55; Asst dir Dodge Telfair Reg Lib, Eastman Ga 5556; Dir Troup-Harris-Cowets Reg Lib, LaGrange Ga 56-58; Center libn US Marine Corps Supply Center, Albany Ga 58-59; Force libn Commander Naval Forces Marianas, Agana Guam 59-63; Station libn US Naval Station, Keflavik Iceland 63-64; Ref libn US Mil Acad (W Point) 64-67; Supv libn USAAVNS Elem Tech Lib, Hunter Army Airfield Ga 67-69; Chief tech serv div US Mil Acad (W Point) 69-. 8: Part-time instr in geog, Col of Guam, Agana Guam 60-62. 14: Tech serv. 15: Greystone Old 9W, Highland Falls NY 10928.

PEARSON, JANET B(EATRICE WHITAKER). b Edmonton Alta Can 23 Je 10. 4: Robert Wilfred Pearson. 5: UBC 28-31 (Eng, Hist) BA; McGill 31-32 BLS. 6: Fr. 7: Victoria Pub Lib, Victoria BC: Circ asst 35-38; 1st asst ref 38-42, 52-63, Head ref dept 63-. 9: CanLA; BCLA (Bursary Loan Com 64-); Inst of Victoria Libns. 10: Victoria Pub Lib Staff Assn. 14: Ref. 15: Victoria Pub Lib, Victoria BC Can.

PEARSON, MARY D. b Kan City Mo 27 O 07. 5: UKan 30 (Hist) BA; Columbia 43 BS LS; CSCLB 59 (Educ) MA. 7: Head record sect Long Beach (Cal) Pub Lib 45-59, Head art, music & philos dept 59-. 9: CalLA (pres AV Round Table Bd 60-66, A-V chm 54, A-V recordings chm 53). 10: Long Beach Symphony Assn; Mental Health Dist Coun. 12: "Recordings in the Public Library, ALA (63). 13: Yes. 14: Ref, fine arts. 15: Long Beach Pub IB, Long Beach Cal 90802.

PEARSON, ROBERT VICTOR. b Pittsburgh Penn 7 F 38. 4: Marianna E Buck. 5: Clarion State Col 57-62 (LS) BS; Pittsburg 63-65 MLS. 6: Fr. 7: Libn Chartiers Valley Jt Schs, Bridgeville Penn 62-65; Acquis libn Xerox Corp 66-. 9: SLA. 10: Monroe Co Lib Club. 14: Acquis serv of ind & univ libs. 15: 93 Hefner dr, Webster NY 14580.

PEARSON, RUTH W(ILLIS). b Quanah Tex 28 Ja 15. 4: Fred Pearson. 5: Tex Wesleyan Col 32-33; N Tex State U 33-34; UTex 34-36 (Zool) BA; Tex Womans U summers 49-52 (Elem Educ) MEd, 63, 65; UTex 53, 54, 62 (Educ, LS); Tex Tech U; Tex Tchrs Certif, Prof Elem High Sch Libn. 6: Sp. 7: Kermit Ind Sch Dist, Kermit Tex: Elem tchr 43-44, High sch sci tchr 44-46, Elem tchr 46-52, Elem sch libn 52-. 9: NEA; ALA; TexLA (past chm & past Program chm Dist 2); Tex State Tchrs Assn; Tex Clrm Tchrs Assn. 10: Delta Kappa Gamma; AAUW; Internat Fed of Univ Women; Wesleyan Service Guild. 11: Teacher of the Year, 62. 13: Yes. 14: Ref, reading guidance. 15: Box 16, Kermit Tex 79745.

PEARSON, WALTER OSGOOD. b Dover NH 15 My 24. 5: Harvard 43, 49-51 AB (magna cum laude); Wesleyan U 44-46; Cornell U 51-53, 54-55; Glasgow U 53-54; Drexel 64-66 MS in LS. 6: Ger. 7: Civilian pub serv 43-46; Stud asst (Econ) Wesleyan U 45-46; Relief wk in europe with Amer Friends Serv Com 46-48; Grad asst (Hist, Philos of Relig, Hist of philos) Cornell U 51-53, 54-55; Instr Philos Dept Borwn U 55-56; Instr Philos Dept UN Dak 56-58; Jr asst Medford Pub Lib, Medford Mass 61-64; Asst libn Phila Gen Hosp Nurses' Sch 65-66; Asst libn SUNY (Binghamtom) 66-68; Asst libn Lehigh Co Commun Col 68-. 9: ALA. 10: Amer Philos Assn; Phi Beta Kappa. 14: Ref, philos. 15: 3430 Linden st, Allentown Pa 18104.

PEASE, KENNETH R. b Independence Iowa 1 Ja 36. 4: Kay Corson. 5: UDubuque 55-57 (Hist) AB; Harvard 58-60 (Theol) STB; UChicago 63-64 (LS) 68 MA. 6: Ger, Fr, Gk, Hebrew, Lat. 7: Lib trainee Chicago Pub Lib 63-64; Research asst libn Harvard Divinity Sch 64-, Paul Tillich Archivist 66-. 9: ATheolLA. 14: Bibliog, ref, rare bks, period. 15: 37 Langdon st, Cambridge Mass 02138.

PEASE, RUSSELL C. b Orange NJ 9 O 38. 5: Davidson Col 56-60 (Ger) AB; UNC (Chapel Hill) 60-65 (Ger) MA, 67-68 MS in LS. 6: Ger, Fr. 7: Asst Prof Ger Col of Charleston 65-67; Readers' serv libn Wilmington Col (Wilmington NC) 68-. 9: ALA; SELA; NCLA. 14: Ref. 15: Box 287, Wrightsville Beach NC 28480.

PEASE, WILLIAM ARTIS. b Rockland Me 28 Ja 34. 4: Lydia Katz. 5: Gorham State Tchrs Col 52-53 (Educ); Harvard 55-59 (Philos) AB; Simmons 59-61 (LS) MS. 6: Fr. 7: Microwave radio tech (Pfc) US Army 53-55; Acquis dept asst Harvard Col Lib 55-61; Acquis dept asst UNC (Chapel Hill) 61-62, Undergrad libn 62-66; Libn Franklin & Marshall Col 67-. 8: Consul & contrib, "Random House Dictionary of the English Language" (66). 9: ALA; PennLA. 12: Co-auth "Opening Day Collection," ALA (66). 13: Yes. 14: Admin. 15: 435 W Marion st, Lititz Pa 17543.

PEASE, WILLIAM J JR. b Long Beach Cal 22 My 29. 4: Btte Erickson. 5: Pomona Col 50 (Psych) BA; Fordham 50-52 (Psych) MA; UCal (Berkeley) 54-55 MLS; UOre 57-58; Portland State Col 61-63. 6: Fr, Ger, Russian. 7: Psychiatric med off clerk US Army, Stuttgart Germany 52-54; Ref-circ libn Reed Col 55-57; Soc sci libn UOre 57-58; Acquiscatlg libn Portland State Col 58-64; Head catlgr Reed Col 65-. 9: ALA; Portland Area Spec Libns (past chm). 14: Catlg, acquis. 15: 105 SE 84th ave, Portland Ore 97216.

PEASLEE, RUTH ISABEL. b Oak Park Ill 4 Ag 22. 5: Berea Col 40-44 (Eng) BA; Carnegie 46-47 BS LS. 7: Asst sch serv dept DC Pub Lib 47-48; Child libn Oak Park (Ill) Pub Lib 48-52; Child libn King Co Pub Lib, Seattle 52-58; Coordinator child serv Indianapolis Pub Lib 58-. 9: ALA-CSD (Melcher Scholarship Com; 62-65, chm 65; Storytelling Materials Survey Com 66-68; Subscription Bks Com 66-68); IndLA (Child & YP RT; Coun 64-66). 10: Coun of Admin Women in Educ. 14: Child serv. 15: 40 E St Clair, Indianapolis In 46205.

PEASON, TIMOTHY J. b Nukualofa Tongatapu Tonga 1 Ap 15. 4: Cecily Cardew. 5: Tchr's Train Col (Nukualofa Tonga) 23-25 (Educ) Certif; New S Wales Pub Lib Train Program 26 (Libnship) Certif; West ResU 56-60 (Hist) BA, 61 MS in LS. 6: Fr, Tongan, polynesian lang. 7: Trainee Pub Lub of New S Wales, Sydney 26-27; Ref libn Carnegie lib, Juva Fiji 27-32; Asst libn Agnes Wisdom Lib, Rabaal New Guinea 32-37; Libn Port Moresby Inst Lib, Port Moresby New Guinea 38-41; Camp libn various Japanese prisoner of war camps 41-45; Consul & adv Australian Ministry of Educ, Canberra 45-55; Libn Spring Hill Pacific Lib (priv collection), Storrs Conn 61-. 8: Consul UN Trusteeship coun on Libs in Trust Territories of Pacific Is 45-55. 9: LA (Australia); BSA. 10: Polynesian Soc. 12: Ed "New Guinea Library Club News" (35-41). 13: Yes. 14: Rare bks (Pacific). 15: Box 340 Spring Hill, Storrs Ct 06268.

PEATTIE, NOEL R(ODERICK). b Menton France 28 N32. 5: Pomona Col 50-54 (Philos) BA; Yale 54-55 (Philos) MA; UCal (Berkeley) 60-61 MLS. 6: Fr, Ger, Danish. 7: Save-the-Redwoods League, San Francisco58-59; Catlgr libn II Cal State (Los Angeles) 61-66; Humanities bibliogr Col devel libn III UCal (Davis) 66-. 9: ALA; CLA. 10: Beta Phi Mu. 14: Tech serv, acquis. 15: Rte 1 Box 216, Winters Ca 95694.

PECK, CAROL PICKERING (NIELSEN). b Cumberland Md 13 Jl 27. 4: Theodore P Peck. 5: AdelphiU 45-49 (Hist) BA; Columbia 49-51 (LS) MS; UMinn 67-69 (Educ). 7: Lib asst Brooklyn Pub Lib, Brooklyn NY 49-50; Asst child libn Rockville Ctr Pub Lib, Rockville Ctr NY 50-53; Child libn Enoch Pratt Free Lib, Baltimore 53-56; Libn escondido Pub Lib, Escondido Cal 63; Child libn James Prendergast Free Lib, Jamestown ny 66-67; Child libn Anoka Pub Lib, Anoka Minn 67-. 14: Child lib wk in pub & sch libs. 15: 638 83rd ave NE, Minneapolis Mn 55432.

PECK, FRANCES ELIZABETH. b Tannersville NY 26 F 07. 5: SUNY (Albany) 26-30 (Hist) AB, 32-33 BS LS. 7: Tchr Tannersville (NY) Central Sch 31-32, 33-36, Libn: Larson Jr Col 36-40; Stuart Hall, Staunton Va 40-42; Centenary Col (NJ) 42-44; Meriden (Conn) High Sch 44-51; New London (Conn) High Sch 51-. 8: Tchr lib sci, Larson Jr Col 36-40. 9: NEA; ConnEA; Conn SchLA; NESchLA. 10: AAUW. 14: Catlg, ref. 15: 35 Raymond st, New London Conn 06320.

PECK, JEAN MARIE. b Buffalo NY 15 N 25. 5: UBuffalo 54-56 (Nursing Admin) BS; Syracuse 60-61 (LS) MS. 7: Staff nurse: NY Hosp, NYC 46-47; Cedars of Lebanon Hosp, Los Angeles 48-49; Dartmouth Col Infirmary 49-50; VA Hosp, Buffalo NY 51-54; Nursing supv Buffalo (NY) Gen Hosp 56-60;Libn catlgr Mich State U 61-66; Libn catlgr UCal (Berkeley) 66-. 9: ALA. 10: Nat Audubon Soc; Beta Phi Mu;

Sierra Club; Golden Gate Audubon Soc; Point Reyes Bird Observ. 14: Catlg, admin. 15: 1780 Spruce st, Berkeley Ca 94709.

PECK, JOHN GROVE JR. b Lynchburg Va 19 S 30. 4: Martha F M Ehlkes. 5: Mars Hill Col 48-50 (Music) AA; Baylor U 53-55 BMus; UNC 55-57 MS LS. 7: Catlgr Vassar Col Music Lib 56-59; Libn Westminster Choir Col 59-. 9: ALA; MusLA; NJLA. 10: AAUP. 15: 205 Loetacher pl, apt 2-A, Princeton NJ 08540.

PECK, JOYCE ELAINE. b Flint Mich 10 Je 31. 5: Flint Jr Col 49-51 AA; UMich 51-53 9eng) BA, 54-57 (Eng) MA; Breadloaf Sch of Eng 60, 63 (Eng); UMich 64-66 MALS. 6: Fr. 7: High sch Eng tchr: Albion Pub Schs, Albion Mich 53-56, Flint Pub Schs, Flint Mich 56-61, AF Dependent Sch, Tokyo 61-62; Eng instr Kellogg Commun Col, Battle Creek Mich 62-63; Libn trainee Flint Pub Lib, Flint Mich 64-66, Ref libn 66-67, Furst asst bus & ind dept 67-. 8: UMich Dept of Lib Sci Ext Serv Instr (Ref Materials) Fall 68. 9: ALA; MichLA. 10: Beta Phi Mu; Flint Pub Lib Staff Assn. 14: Ref. 15: Flint Pub Lib 1026 E Kearsley st, Flint Mi 48502.

PECK, MARIAN B. b Saukcenter Minn 28 Je 20. 5: Ind StateU 39-42 (Eng). 7: Sch libn Plymouth Elem Sch, Plymouth Twp 62-64; Hd child serv Montgomery Co Norristown Pub Lib, Norristown Penn 60-62, 64-. 8: Planning & org of dist children's bk review meetings child Serv Div Bk Review Com 69-72. 9: ALA-CSD; PennLA. 14: Child bks. 15: Montgomery County Norristown Pub Lib 542 DeKalb st, Norristown Pa 19401.

PECK, MARIE D(AHL). b St Paul 10 Jl 09. 5: UMinn 27-31 (LS) BS. 6: Fr. 7: Ref asst UMinn Lib 31-35; Asst libn West High Sch, ch, Minneapolis 37-38; Sch station libn Minneapolis Pub Lib 39-40; Ref libn lib div Minn Dept Educ St Paul 40-43; St Paul Pub Lib: Ref libn 47-49, Head fine arts room 49-50, Supv libn arts & av serv 61-. 9: ALA; MinnLA. 10: Minn Artists Assn; St Paul Art Ctr; Phi Beta Kappa; Profess Employees Assn. 13: Yes. 14: Ref (art, music, film). 15: 2162 W Hoyt ave, St Paul Mn 55108.

PECK, MARIOL RUTH. b Powers Lake N Dak 11 Ja 45. 5: Linfield Col 63-67 (Eng) BA; UCal (Berkeley) 67-68 MLS. 7: Asst catlg libn Ore StateU 68-. 9: ALA; MusLA; OreLA; PNLA. 10: Mu Phi Epsilon; AAUP. 14: Catlg. 15: 145 NW 16th #205, Corvallis Or 97330.

PECK, MARY R(OSE). b Scranton Penn 22 My 24. 4: Frank G Peck. 5: Marywood Col 41-45 (LS) BA; Catholic U 65-(LS). 7: Asst libn UScranton 45-56; Libn Bel-Air Jr-Sr High Sch, Bel Air Md46-47; Asst libn Loyola Col (Baltmore) 47-51; Catlgr Army War Col Carlisle Penn 51-53; Prof asst adult wk Baltimore Co Pub Lib 62-65, Br libn 65-67; Pub serv libn Essey Commun Col 67-. 9: ALA; MdLA; Md AJC (Learning Resource Div; v-chm 68-69, chm 69-70). 14: Catlg, ref. 15: 4022 Raymonn ave, Baltimore Md 21213.

PECK, SUSAN (VENABLE). b Oneonta NY 2 My 45. 4: Donald G Peck. 5: URochester 63-67 (Eng) BA; SUNY (Geneseo) 67-68 MLS. 6: Fr. 7: Bibliogr & asst acquis libn Albert Emanuel Lib UDayton 68-. 14: Acquis. 15: 5219 Cobb dr, Dayton Oh 45431.

PECK, THEODORE PARKER. b Brooklyn NY 13 Ja 24. 4: Carol Nielsen. 5: Gettysburg Col 47-50 (Eng) BA; Columbia 50-52 (LS) MS. 7: Ref libn Brooklyn Pub Lib, Brooklyn NY 51-53; Yp br libn Enoch Pratt Free Lib, Baltimore 53-57; Doc control off System development Corp, Santa Monica Cal 57-59; Tech info specialist Gen Dynamics astronautics, San Diego 59-64; Asst dir Chautaugua-Cattaraugus Lib Syst, Jamestown NY 64-67; Dir tech info serv UMinn (Minneapolis) 67-. 9: SLA (treas Minneapolis Chap); MinnLA. 12: "Information Sources Directory for Industry" (68); "Bibliography on the Contamination and Preservation of Poultry, Meat, and Eggs (68). 14: Ref. 15: 638 83rd ave NE, Minneapolis Mn 55432.

PECK, V LADONNA. b Wells Minn 26 S 16. 4: George Peck. 5: UChicago 33-37 (Physiol) BS; Rutgers 59-62 MLS. 7: Libn Tinton Falls Schs, New Shrewsbury NJ 59-. 9: ALA; NJEA; NJSchLA; NJLA. 14: Child & ya lit. 15: 5 Wanamassa Pt rd, Asbury ark NJ 07712.

PEDDLE, (SISTER) HELEN OP. b Duluth Minn 16 Ap 20. 5: Superior State Tchrs (Superior wis) 37-39 (Liberal Arts); UWis 40-42 (Journalism-Soc Sci) BA; Col of St Catherine ss 50-54 (LS) BS; UChicago SS 56-59 (LS) AM. 6: Sp. 7: Ed Burlington Free Press, burlington Wis 42-43; Advertising copywriter Allis-Chalmers Mfg Co, Milwaukee 43-46; Instr in psych Dominican Col (Racine Wis) 51; Libn St Catherine's High Sch, Racine Wis 52-54; Libn Dominican Col Lib (Racine Wis) 55-. 8: Adv to Intl Club Dominican Col 62-65; On leave as libn at IBEAS Inst Lib, LaPaz Bolivia 69-70. 9: ALA; CathLA (co-chm Wis Unit Col Sect); WisLA. 10: Beta Phi Mu. 14: Catlg, ref. 15: 5915 N Erie st, Racine Wi 53402.

PEDERSEN, PATRICIA FLORENCE (ZAVATTERO). b Fresno Ca 22 Mr 22. 5: UCal (Berkeley) 40-42 (Eng); NM State U 63-64 (LS); UDenver summers 65-68 (LS). 7: Lib clk Far E AF, Tokyo 55-56; Acquis & processing Tech Lib, White Sands Missile Range NM 56-69; Docs catlgr 69-. 9: SLA; Border Regl LA. 14: Catlg, acquis. 15: 10045 Ontario, El Paso Tx 79924.

PEDERSON, KAROLYN ROSALIE. b Whitewater Wis 30 N 41. 5: UMich 59-66 (Near East Studies) BA, (Ling) MA, (LS) MA. 6: Fr, Ger, Arabic, Turkish, Russian. 7: Editorial wker on dictionaries, encyclopedias & textbks Consolidated Bk Publs & Follett Publ Co, Chicago 36-39; Sr ed asst ALA, Chicago 41; Asst libn Know Col 42-43; US Army libn in Troop Sch Lib, clerk in publ sect Adj Gen DEPT, PERSONNEL CLERK IN AA train unit, Camp Stewart Ga 43-44; US Army spec agent Counter-Intelligence Corps, European Theater 44-45; Asst libn then Chief Libn & Ed of "Rehabilitation Literature Nat Easter Seal Soc for Crippled Child & Adults, Chicago 47-. 9: ALA; Middle East Studies Assn; Amer Oriental Soc. 14: Catlg, bibliog (Middle East Area). 15: 251 S 7th E 16, Salt Lake City Ut 84102.

PEDERSON, VIRGIL L(YLE). b Mason City Iowa 1 O 21. 4: Darlene Spangler. 5: Mason City Jr Col 39-41; State UIowa 41-42, 46-47 (Ger) BA (magna cum laude); Carnegie Lib Sch 47-48 BSLS; Columbia 48-49 (Comparative Lit). 6: Fr, Sp. 7: Acquis libn State U Iowa Libs (Iowa City) 49-51; Research tech Inland Steel Co, E Chicago Ind 52-54; Libn amer Peoples Encyclopedia Spencer Press, Chicago 54-61; Bar docs libn Amer Bar Foundation, Chicago 61-65, Bar docs & supv catlg libn 65-. 8: Consul Nat Inst Educ on Law & Poverty, Chicago 67-. 9: SLA; NMA; AALL; Chicago Assn of Law Libs. 10: Phi Beta Kappa; Delta Phi Alpha; Soc of King Charles the Martyr. 12: "Checklist of the Standing and Special Committees of the American Bar Association" (64); "Chesklist of American Bar Association General Publications," with Section suppl (64); "Continuing Legal Education: a holdings list and supplement" (64-66). 13: Yes. 14: Archives, microfilm. 15: 1155 E 60th st, Chicago Il 60637.

PEDRO, IRENE DUNNE. b NYC 6 Ag 33. 5: CCNY 53-56 (Eng); Va CommonwealthU 66- (Eng). 6: Fr. 7: Copywriter S F Auerbach Co, NYC 53-56; Copywriter Bermuda Press Ltd, Bermuda 59-62; Libn Reynolds Intl Inc, Bermuda & Richmond 63-67; Libn Blue Cross & Blue Shield of Va, Richmond 67-. 9: VaLA. 10: Richmond-Hopewell Spec Libs Club; YWCA; Intl Club. 14: Lib admin. 15: 12 South blvd, Richmond Va 23220.

PEEBLES, MARGARETE MARY. b Winona Miss 21 Ja 13. 5: Miss State Col for Women 30-31 (Elem Educ); Miss State U 31-34 (Bus) BS, 34 (Hist); Peabody 39-45 BS in LS. 6: Fr. 7: Elem tchr Betheden Sch, Louisville Miss 34-35; Lib Miss State U: Clerical desk asst circ dept 35-45, Circ asst 45-47, Circ libn & head circ dept 47-62, Head acquis dept 62-. 08: Circ asst Peabody Col summers 39-41; Tchr lib sci, Gen Ext Div Miss State U ummers 51-55; Self-Eval Com, Miss State U Lib 60-61. 8: Circ asst Peabody Col summers 39-41; Tchr lib sci, gen ext div Miss State U summers 51-55, self-eval com, Miss State U Lib 60-61; Lib Com Chm 1st Bapt Ch, Starkvill Miss. 9: SELA (Miss rep Memb Com 52-54, Miss rep Nomin Com 62-64); MissLA (sec 62, Exec Bd 54-55 & 62-63; 67-, bus mgr & mem Ed Bd "Mississippi Library News 55-61 & 63-; mem&/or chm 6 coms52-; sec & chm Col & Univ Sect 53-55); v-pres 67; pres 68; chm handbk com 69). 10: AAUW; Faculty Club Miss State U; Sec Faculty Council 64-65, 68-69. 12: Ed "History of Mississippi Library Association 1900-1968" MLA (68). 13: Yes. 14: Ref, Miss authors, automation, bibliog, sers. 15: Box 104, Miss State Univ, State College Miss.

PEEK, ELLEN T(ANSEL). b Coffeyville Kan 10 D 04. 4: G Medwin Peek. 5: Okla Central State Col 21-25 (Home Econ) BS. 7: Tchr Pub Sch, Wyona Okla 23-24; Tchr, High Sch, Edmond Okla 25-26; Stetson U Lib: Apprentice 53-55, Asst in ref 55-59, Asst ref libn 59-. 8: Responsible for decorating ' furnishing Stetsons Sttsons $1,000,000 duPont-Ball Lib, completed 64. 9: FlaLA. 14: Ref. 15: 930 N Florida ve, De Land Fla 32720.

PEEL, BRUCE BRADEN. b Ferland Sask Can 11 N 16. 4: Margaret (Fullerton). 5: USask 40-44 (Hist) BA, 46 (Hist) MA; UToronto 45-46 BLS. 7: Canadiana libn Adam Shortt

Collection USask 46-51; UALTA: Chief catlgr 51-54, Asst libn 54-55, Act libn 55-56, Chief Libn 56-. 8: Mem of Downs Survey Team - Survey of Academic libs in Can 67. 9: Can Assn Col & Univ Libs (pres 65-66); AltaLA (pres 60-61); EdmontonLA; CanLA (pres 69-70); Bibliog Soc of Can (v-pres). 10: Hist Soc of Alta. 12: Comp "Bibliography of the Prairie Provinces to 1953" (55, sup 63); "The Saskatoon Story, 1882-1952," E Knowles (52); Ed "Librarianship in Canada" (46-47); "Essays in Honour of Elizabeth Homer Morton" (68). 13: Yes. 14: Catg, bibliog, admin. 15: 11047 - 83rd ave, Edmonton Alta Can.

PEEL, RUTH (JOHNSON). b Kinston NC 14 Ap 18. 4: William Bryan Peel. 5: Atlantic Christian Col 35-38 (Educ) AB; UNC 42 (Educ); E Carolina Col 54, 64 (Educ, Bus); UOkla ext at Tulsa U 64-65 (LS); UMich 66-67 AMLS. 6: Fr. 7: Tchr: Hookerton Pub Sch, Hookerton NC 38-41, Smithfield Pub Sch, Smithfield NC 41-42, Wheat Swamp Sch, La Grange NC 42-43, 55-56; Research analyst Dist Unemployment Compensation Bd, Wash DC 43-55; Self-employed (Auto Specialty Co), Greenville NC 56-63; Catlgr Oral Roberts U Lib 64-66, Hd catlgr 67-. 9: ALA; OklaLA; SWLA. 10: Beta Phi Mu. 14: Catlg. 15: 1851 E 57th pl, Tulsa Ok 74105.

PEELE, DAVID A. b NYC 24 Mr 29. 4: Marla Hamilton Peele. 5: Swarthmore 46-50 (Hist) AB; West Res 50-51 MS LS; Swarthmore 51-54 (Hist) MA. 7: Asst libn Swarthmore Col 51-55; Asst to libn City Col (NY) 55-62; Assoc Prof Staten Island Community Col 62-. 8: Staff, Lib/USA NY Worlds Fair 65. 13: Yes. 14: Ser. 15: 111 W 94 st apt 4-C, New York NY 10025.

PEELE, MARLA HAMILTON. b Ellensburg Wash. 4: David Arnold Peele. 5: UWash 56-61 (Sociol) BA, 62-63 (LS) ML. 7: Child libn Brooklyn Pub Lib 63-65; Child libn Merrick Lib, Merrick LI NY 65-68; Libn Barnard Sch for Boys, Riverdale NY 68-. 8: Child libn, Lib/USA N Y Worlds Fair 65. 9: ALA-CSD; NYLA. 14: Child bks, storytelling. 15: 111 W 94th st, apt 4-C, New York NY 10025.

PEELER, ELIZABETH H(ASTINGS). b Nashville 5 Ap 14. 5: Vanderbilt 35 (Amer Hist) BA, 36 (Amer Hist) MA; Emory 39 BA LS; Columbia summers 43-47, 50 MS LS. 7: Asst to act libn Southwestern at Memphis 39-42; Catlgr BirminghamSoCol 42-44; Catlgr Agnes-Scott Col 44-46; Head catlg dept UMiami (Fla) 46-60; Sr lecturer in Inst of Libnship UIbadan (Ibadan Nigeria) 60-64; Chief catlg sect UN Lib, NY 64-65; Head catlg dept SUNY (Stony Brook LI) 65-67; Lectr Emory U summer 67; Assoc dir for tech serv UW Fla 67-. 9: IFLA; Nigerian LA; ALA (var coms); FlaLA (pres 55-56); SELA (chm SE Reg Group of Catlgrs 56-58). ; LA-LED (chm Bogle Mem Fund Com 67-). 12: Ed "Florida Libraries (59-60). 13: Yes. 14: Catlg, lib educ. 15: University of W Florida, Pensacola Fl 32504.

PEERSON, ETHEL. b Florence Ala 16 My 06. 5: Florence State Col 23-25 (Educ) Diploma; Athens Col 27-28 (Eng); Radford Col 33-34 (Eng, Hist) BS; Emory 34-35 Grad degree in LS. 6: Fr, Lat. 7: Libn: Spalding Co High Sch, Griffin Ga 35-36, Savannah High Sch, savannah Ga 36-41, TVA Lib, Wilson Dam Ala 42-47; Ref & adult educ Kingsport (Tenn) Pub Lib 47-50; Dir Flint River Reg Lib, Griffin Ga 51-57; Consul Ala Pub Lib Serv, Montgomery 57-58; Dir Muscle Shoals Reg Lib, Florence Ala 58-. 8: Exec dir Nat Lib Week 91 yr) for Ala, Exper proj for Ford Found, World Affairs are Your Affairs, Great Men and Great Issues. 9: ALA; SELA; AlaLA (Pub Rel Com, chm Fed Rel Com). 10: Delta Kappa Gamma; LWV; AAUW; var loc organizs. 14: Ref, adult serv, rare bks, a-v, admin. 15: PO Box 160 North Wood ave, Florence Al 35360.

PEET, HELEN H(ANNA). b Hattiesburg Miss 7 Jl 06. 5: Miss Womans Col 26 (Eng) AB; Tulane 27 (Eng) AM. 6: Fr. 7: Eng instr Miss Womans Col 27; Head Eng Dept Blackstone Col 27-30; Head Eng Dept St Marys Jr Col, Raleigh NC 34-35; API, Auburn Ala: Sec libn Economics Dept 37-39; Instr Sociol 53-55, Ref libn 56-60; Humanities bibliog Auburn U 60-, Instr Humanities 60-. 9: AlaLA; AlaEA. 14: Bibliog (humanities). 15: PO Box 101, Auburn Al 36830.

PEGAU, RUTH M(OYER). b Fairfield Iowa 12 D 20. 4: Ernest E Pegau. 5: Parsons Col 37-41 (Eng) BA; Cal State Col (Fullerton) 62-63 (Educ); Immaculate Heart Col 64-65 MA LS. 6: Fr. 7: Prin Taipei (Taiwan) Amer Sch 52-54; Libn Foothill High Sch, Tustin Cal 65-67; Dist supv libs Tustin Elem Dist, Tustin Cal 67-69; Lectr Cal State Col (Long Beach Cal) 69-. 9: NEA; ALA; CalTA; CalASchL; OCSLA (pres-elect 69-70). 10: Theta Alpha Phi. 14: Sch libnship. 15: 13061 Wreath pl, Tustin Cal 92680.

PEGRAM, JOSEPH WALLERSTEIN. b Carson Va 17 Ap. 5: Va State Col 47-51 BS LS; USoCal 54-55 (LS) MS. 6: Fr. 7: US Army Quartermaster Corp 1st Lieut Accountable Officer for QM Sales Stores & QM Laundry; Asst catlgr Enoch Pratt Free Lib, Baltimore 53-54; Catlgr Universal Studios, Universal City Cal 55-56; Head tech processes Ramo-Wooldridge Corp, Canoga Park Cal 57-62; Catlgr & ref libn Hughes Research Labs, Malibu Cal 62-. 9: SLA. 14: Catlg, ref. 15: 1813 17th st, Santa Monica Cal 9404.

PEIFFER, PATRICIA L. b Lebanon Penn 30 Ap 45. 5: Millersville State Col 63-67 (LS) BS (cum laude); Drexel 68- (LS). 6: Fr. 7: Child libn Lebanon Commun Lib, Lebanon Penn 67; Elem libn Palmyra Area Sch Dist, Palmyra Penn 67-. 9: ALA; NEA; PennLA; PennStateEA; Palmyra Area EA (act sec). 14: Child serv. 15: 619 Hill st, Lebanon Pa 17042.

PEIRCE, LAURA S. b Arlington Mass 26 Jl 43. 5: Colby Col 61-66 (Math) BA; Case West ResU 66-67 MSLS. 6: Russian, Ger. 7: Info serv programmer Deere & Co, Moline Ill 67-. 9: ASIS. 10: Beta Phi Mu. 14: Automated lang proc, info retr. 15: 3627-43rd st apt 324, Moline Il 61265.

PEKARSKI, MARY LOUISE. b Lawrence Mass 5 My 23. 5: Emmanuel Col (Mass) 40-44 (Eng) AB; Simmons 45-47 BS LS. 7: Libn Boston Col Intown 44-48; Boston Col Sch of Nursing 48-. 8: Adv Com, Practical Nursing Program, Vocational Sch, Lawrence Mass; Free-lance Consul, Schs of Nurs Libs; Adv com for nurs, Countway Lib of Med (Harvard) 67-; Consul Leominster Hosp Sch Nurs, Leominster Mass 68-. 9: CathLA (Hosp Sect chm 59-60, Exec Bd 55-61); Med LA. 12: Ed "The Hospitaller (57-59). 14: Admin, ref, bk sel. 15: Boston Col Sch of Nurs Lib, Chestnut Hill Mass 02167.

PEKEL, KATHERINE (QUELLO). b Milwaukee Wis 16 Ag 41. 4: Rev Jon Girard Pekel. 5: St Olaf Col 59-63 (Eng) BA; UWest Mich summer 66; Rosary Col 68-69 MLS. 6: Ger. 7: Tchr Fairview Jr High, Roseville Minn 63-64; Tchr Proviso E High Sch, Maywood Ill 64-67. 8: Title II experimental "Project Push-up" tchg of disadvantaged Proviso East High Sch, Maywood Ill 65-66. 10: Phi Beta Kappa; Beta Phi Mu. 14: Sch & acad libs, media. 15: 8008 S Jeffrey blvd, Chicago Il 60617.

PELAGIA, SISTER MARY RSM. b Louisville Ky 30 Jl 30. 5: Our Lady of Cincinnati Col 48-55 (Educ) BS Ed, Standard Elem tchg certif; Catherine Spalding Col 56-59 MS LS. Standard 12 year lib certif. 6: Lat, Ger. 7: Tchr: St Aloysius Sch, Louisville Ky 53-55; Holy Family Sch, Columbus Ohio 55-58; St Paul Sch, Louisville Ky 58-60; Holy Cross Sch, Louisville Ky 60-61; Asst libn Assumption High Sch, Louisville Ky 61-63, Libn 63-. 9: CathLA; ALA; KyLA; KyASchL; SELA. 13: Yes. 14: Catlg. 15: 2170 Tyler lane, Louisville Ky 40205.

PELLETIER, REV CLAUDE (JOSEPH-MARC-ANDRE). b Sherbrooke PQ 24 Ap 24. 5: Sem de sherbrooke 39-46 BA; Grand Sem de Sherbrooke 46-50 (Theol); UMontreal 57 Tchg Brevet a, 56-58 (Pedagogy-classical letters) Licence, 56-58 (Fr Lit). 6: Fr, Latin. 7: Tchr Sem of Sherbrooke 50-56, 58-62, Chief libn 63-. 8: Consul for Col Libs, Que Ministry of Educ. 9: Assn canadienne des bibliothecaires de langue francaise (chm Col Sect 67-68); CADRE (Exec Offr Lib Commsn 67-69). 10: Corporation des bibliothecaires professionnels de la Province de Quebec; Municipal Lib of Sherbrooke Que Trustee of Bd. 14: Admin, ref. 15: Seminaire 195 rue Marquette CP 790, Sherbrooke PQ Can.

PELLOWSKI, ANNE. b Pine Creek Wis 28 Je 33. 5: Col St Teresa 51-55 (Comparative Lit) BA; UMinn summer 55 (Ger); Ludwig Maximilian U (Munich) 55-56; Columbia 57-59 MSLS. 6: Fr, Ger, Sp, Polish, Russian. 7: Instr Col of St Teresa 56-57; Child libn Winona pub Lib, Winona Minn 57; Child libn NYC Pub Lib 57-66; Lecturer UMd 65-66, UWis (Madison) summer 66, Columbia U summer 67; Child ctr dir US Com for UNICEF, NYC 66-. 8: Field Enterprises Educl Corp Lib Adv Com, Chicago 68-. 9: ALA (mem of numerous coms). 12: "The World of Children's Literature' (68); "Folk and Fairy Tales Series" (7 recordsings) 64-68). 13: Yes. 14: Child lit, storytelling, internat libnship. 15: US Com for UNICEF, 331 E 38th st, New York NY 10016.

PELT, RUTH M(ERBLER). b Pensacola Fla 21 Jl 18. 4: Jack Holland Pelt. 5: Fla State U 36-39 (Soc Studies) AB, summers 53-55 LS Certif. 7: Tchr: Myrtle Grove Elem Sch, Pensacola Fla 39-40, Clubbs Jr High Sch, Pensacol Fla 40-43, McMillen Elem Sch, Pensacola Fla 52-54, Libn: 54-56; Oakcrest Elem Sch, Pensacola Fla 56-58; Tech High Sch, Pensacola Fla 58-69, Escambia Co Sch Processing Lab, Pensacola Fla 69-. 9: NEA-DAVI; ALA-AASchL; FlaEA; FlaSchLA; FlaLA; Fla

A-V Assn; EscambiaCoSchLA (chm 56-58). 10: Alpha Delta Kappa. 14: Acquis, catlg. 15: 1221 N 13th ave, Pensacola Fla 35203.

PELTIER, EUCLID JOSEPH. b Worcester Mass 3 F 22. 4: Felicia Langdon Peltier. 5: Boston U 47-50 (Communication Arts) BS, 52, 54 (Communication Arts) MS; URI Grad Lib Sch 68 MLS. 6: Fr. 7: Proc clerk Reed & Prince Mfg Co, Worcester Mass 40-42, US Naval Reserve-Spec Q - Chief, Wash DC & Overseas 42-45; Prod asst Dekko Film Co Boston 46-49; A-v asst Boston Pub Lib 50-56, Chief, a-v dept 57-. 8: Tchr Adult Ed Classes Boston YWCA 59-64; Tchr Adult Ed Classes Boston Adult Educ Center 62-; Educational Film Lib Assoc, Program chm 09: NatA-V Assn; Educ Film Lib Assn (Program chm); ALA; MassLA; NELA; Mass AV Assn; ALA (AV Com); New Eng Screen Educ Assn; Film Lib Info Coun. 10: Friends of the Wellesley Free Lib; Boston Mus of Fine Arts; Boston Inst of Contemporary Art; Internat Inst. 13: Yes. 14: A-v serv in libs. 15: Boston Pub Lib, Copley Sq, Boston Ma 02117.

PELZ, BRUCE E. b Orange NJ 11 Ag 36. 4: Dian Girard. 5: UFla 54-58 BS; USoCal 60-63 MSLS. 6: Ger. 7: Physics libn UCLA 62-64, Phys sci libs catlgr 64-67, Engring & math sci acquis libn 67-. 8: Consul Mechanics Research Inc, Los Angeles 69-. 10: Inst for Specialized Lit Inc; Bd of Dir Sci Fantasy Soc Inc (Los Angeles). 14: Collection dev, tech proc. 15: Box 100 308 Westwood plaza, Los Angeles Ca 90024.

PENCE, LOIS H(OWARD). b Hawthone Wis 9 Jl 11. 4: Robert G Pence. 5: UWis32-33, 36-38 (Bot) BA, 38-39 BLS. 7: Asst to co libn & circ asst Racine (Wis) Pub Lib 30-32, 34-36; Catlg dept typist UWis Lib 32-33, 36-38; Ref asst Gary (Ind) Pub Lib 39-42; Libn ADTIC US Air Force, Eglin Field Fla 42; Libn Sch of Nursing Methodist Hosp, Gary Ind 56-59; Child libn Gary (Ind) Pub Lib Main Lib 59-62; Libn Sch of Nursing St Mary Mercy Hosp, Gary Ind 62-. , Hosp libn 68-. 9: CathLA (chm-elect Health Sect of NoIll Unit); ALA. 15: 341 Polk st, Gary Ind 46402.

PENCE, LORRAINE. b Hastings Neb 31 My 06. 5: Hastings Col 23-27 (Math) AB; UOre 47-51 (Educ) MEd; UDenver 52-56 MA LS. 6: Ger. 7: High sch tchr of math & bus educ, Kan, Neb, SD, Iowa, Minn 27-46; High sch tchr bus educ, Molalla Ore 46-51; High sch tchr bus educ, Aurora Ore 51-57; Libn Reynolds High Sch, Troutdale Ore 57-58; Libn Waldo Jr High Sch, Salem Ore 58-. 9: OreASchL (pres 65-66, Reg 2: rep Bus Educ 56, Tri-Co Com 63-66). 10: AAUW. 14: Sch libs. 15: 2184 Lansing ave NE, Salem Or 97303.

PENCHANSKY, MIMI B(LACK). b NYC 17 O 25. 4: Charles Penchansky. 5: Queens Col 62 (Eng Lit) BA; Columbia 64 MS LS. 6: Sp, Fr. 7: Sec Prudential Insurance Co, Brooklyn NY & Baltimore 42-45; Sec Ely Finkelstein Esq attorney, NYC 45-51; Tchr Jr High Sch 190Q, Forest Hills NY 62; Tchr Jr High Sch 145Q, Jackson Heights NY 62-63; Fellow Paul Klapper Lib Queens Col (NY) 63-64, Interlib Loan & Ref libn 64-. 9: ALA; SLA; LACUNY. 10: Phi Beta Kappa. 14: Ref, research, bibliog, interlib loans, photocopying, copyright. 15: 67-35 Kissena blvd, Flushing NY 11367.

PENDELL, LUCILLE (HUNT). b Hennessey Okla 17 Ja 02. 5: Okla State U 25 (Educ) BS, 30 (Hist) MA; Catholic U 48 BS in LS. 6: Fr. 7: Tchr pub schs, Okla 4 yrs; Documents libn Okla State U 26-31; Archivist war records off Nat Archives, Wash DC 43-7; Assoc archivist UOkla summer 49; Chief Libn Mt Alto VA Hosp Lib summer 53; Libn, Assoc Prof of Lib Sci, & Chm Dept of Lib Sci Gallaudet Col 47-. 8: Rockefeller Fellowship for Archival Research, summer 50-51; Mem, Adv Bd, Lib Serv to the Deaf 64-; Dir, NDEA Sch Lib Inst, Lib Serv for the Dear, Gallaudet Co, summers 65, 66. 9: ALA; Assn of Sch Libs of the Deaf; Conv Amer Instrs of the Deaf; DCLA. 10: Delta Zeta; Kappa Delta Pi; Beta Phi Mu; AAUP. 12: Auth of several checklists of War record groups in the Nat Archives. 13: Yes. 14: Sch libnship, admin, col & research libs. 15: Gallaudet Col, 7th & Florida ave NE, Wash DC 20002.

PENDLETON, MARILYN. b El Dorado Ark 3 Ag 40. 5: Gulf Park Col 58-60 AA; Centenary Col (La) 60-62 (Bus) BS; LSU 4-65 MLS. 6: Fr. 7: Bkkpr "Arkansas Democrat Little Rock Ak 63; Asst acquis libn UNM 65-66, Acquis libn 66-68; Catlgr Sandia Corp Lib 68-. 9: ALA; NMLA (chm Col, Univ & Spec Lib Div); SLA. 14: Acquis, tech proc, catlg. 15: 1305 Coal SE, Albuquerque NM 87106.

PENDLETON, MARY HELEN (FRANCIS). b Oakland Cal 24 Ap 05. 5: UAriz 23-27 (Econ) AB; USoCal 40-41 (LS) BS, 60-61 MS in LS. 6: Sp, Fr. 7: Catlgr mus LC 28; Gen libn Phoenix Pub Lib, Phoenix Ariz 29-30; Catlgr fiction, ref libn Long Beach Pub Lib, Long beach Cal 36-42; Libn Bell Flower Sch Dist, Bell Flower Cal 56-60; Libn Pasadena City Sch, Pasadena Cal 60-61; Libn Pasadena Jr Col Dist, Pasadena Cal 61-. 9: NEA; CalTA. 10: AAUW; Soc of Woman Geographers. 14: Ref, travel. 15: 585 N Hill apt 3, Pasadena Ca 91106.

PENDLETON, RUTH JANE. b Lee Co Ky 10 Ag 10. 5: Union Col (Ky) 28-34 (Eng, Educ) AB; Peabody 40 BS LS; UFla summer 52; UGa summers 50, 60-61. 6: Fr. 7: Tchr Elem Schs, Letcher Co Ky 35-37; Libn: Jellico (Tenn) High Sch 41-42; Homerville (Ga) High Sch 42-47; Robert E Lee High Sch, Thomaston Ga 47-. 9: NEA; ALA; GaEA; TennEA; GaLA (A-V Com); SELA. 10: Womans Club; Nat Assn for the Metally Retarded; Beta Sigma Phi. 14: Admin, bk sel. 15: Geo A Harrison Mem Lib, Thomaston Ga 30286.

PENFIELD, DORIS (REEN). b Syracuse NY. 4: George A Penfield. 5: Syracuse 29-33 BS i LS. 6: Fr. 7: Sch libn Solvay Jr-Sr High Sch, Solvay NY 34-39; Ref libn SyracuseU Lib 57-58, Arch sch libn 58-59, Bindery libn 59-64, Ref-doc libn 64-69, Ref-reserve libn 69-. 14: Ref. 15: 118 Annetta st, Syracuse NY 13207.

PENFOLD, MRS FRANCES (WATKINS). b Okla City Okla 30 My 14. 4: Charles W Penfold. 5: Okla City U 36 (Eng, Sociol) BA; UOkla BA in LS. 7: Libn Tex MilCol 37-38; Lib asst Okla City Pub Lib, Okla City Okla 38-45; Post libn Jefferson Barracks, Mo 45-46; Lib asst St Louis Pub Lib 47-48; Arch sch libn Washington U (St Louis) 48-50; Libn, Camp Atterbury Ind 50-52, Catlg libn Okla City Pub Lib, Okla City Okla 52-53; Hosp libn Tokyo Army Hosp, Tokyo Japan 53-54; Lib asst Milwaukee Pub Lib 55-56; Asst catlgr UOkla 56-57; Catlg libn Okla City U 57-64; Libn Stillwater Pub Lib, Stillwater Okla 64-67; Senior catlgr Okla State U Lib (Stillwater) 67-68; Libn I Pikes Peak Reg Lib Dist, Colorado Springs Colo 69-. 9: ALA. 15: 5127 Palmer Park bldgs, Colorado Springs Co 80915.

PENINGTON, JUDITH (MARY). b Seattle Wash 13 Ap 45. 5: IndU 63-64; UDubuque 64-67 (Hist, Soc Studies) BA; UWash 67-68 M Libnship. 6: Sp. 7: Pre prof libn Seattle Pub lib 67-68; Readers serv libn Fiske-Laird Lib UDubuque 69-. 10: Girl Scouts. 14: Ref, circ, child & ya. 15: Ficke Laird Lib Univ of Dubuque, Dubuque Ia 52001.

PENLAND, PATRICK R. 5: UBC 45-48 (Psych, Eng) BA; McGill 52-53 BLS; UMich 54-55 AMLS, 55-60 (LS) PhD. 6: Fr, Ger. 7: Head libn Parry Sound (Ont) Pub Lib, & Exec Sec Parry Sound & Dist Film Coun 53-54; Ext libn Ann Arbor (Mich) Pub Lib 55-58; Lib consul for Adult Educ NC State Lib 58-60; Statewide Dir Adult Film Proj, NC 58-60; Statewide Proj Dir of ALA Lib-Community Proj in NC 58-60; Spec instr in lib sci UOkla summer 61; Dir of ext serv & asst prof of lib sci West Wash State Col 61-62; Dir div of lib sci & prof of lib sci So Conn State Col 62-67; Visiting Prof UToronto 67-68; Visiting Prof UMinn summer 68; Assoc Prof Grad Sch of Lib & Info Sci, UPittsburgh 68-. 8: Conn State Lib Research Adv Com; Lib Sci examiner, Conn State Personnel Dept; Visiting Fellow, Dept of Philos Yale U 65-66. 9: ALA; SLA (Devel Com); BSA; ASIS; Adult Educ Assn; CanLA; NELA; NEA-DAVI; NAEB; PLA; NSSC. 10: Beta Phi Mu. 13: Yes. 14: Educ for libnship, communications, media studies. 15: Grad School of Lib & Info Sci, University of Pittsburgh, Pittsburgh Pa 15213.

PENN, MARIAN R. b Sharon Penn 10 Jl 17. 4: William L Penn. 5: Westminster Col 35-36; Oberlin Col 37-39 (Eng) BA; Carnegie 39-40 BS in LS. 7: Depauw U 41-42; UBridgeport 56-, Act hd catlg dept 67-. 14: Catlg. 15: 11 Austin dr ext, Easton Conn 06612.

PENN, VIVIAN-SUE. b NY. 4: Robert M Penn. 5: Grove City Col 45-49 (Hist, Pol Sci) AB; Rutgers 55-56 MLS; UConn (Educ, Secondary); Temple 69- (Educ). 6: Hungarian, Sp. 7: Lib asst Grove City Col 45-49; Head traffic dept Gardner Adv Co, St Louis 50-54; Asst to pres EDW Kletter Co, NYC 54-55; Ref libn Teaneck Pub Lib, Teaneck NJ 56-57; Head libn Perrot Mem Lib, Old Greenwich Conn 57-61; Libn Burdick Jr High Sch, Stamford Conn 61; Libn Darien High Sch, Darien Conn 62-67; Lib dir Ocean Co Col 67-. 9: ConnLA (sec 61; Recruitment Com 66-67); NJLA (pres Jr Col Sub-section 69-71, Recruitment Com 68-69). 10: Pi Gamma Mu; LWV; AAUW; Zonta. 13: Yes. 14: Higher educ, educ media. 15: 868 Brookside dr, Toms River NJ 08753.

PENNELL, JERE C. b Tokyo Japan 24 S 33. 4: Evadne Dianne King. 5: Jochi Daigaku 51; UPuget Sound 56-60 (Educ) BA; UWash 61-65 (Hist), 65-67 M Libr. 6: Japanese, Sp. 7: Sgt (E-6) USA 52-56; Tacoma Pub Lib 57-58; Tchr & a-v Bethel

School Dist, Spanaway Wash 59-61; Fed Way High Sch, Federal Way Wash 61-65; Bus & sci Tacoma Pub Lib, Tacoma Wash 65-67; A-V serv Highline Col 67-. 8: A-V Adv Com, State Purchasing Dept Olympia Wash 68-. 9: ALA; NEA-DAVI; WashLA; WashASchL; Wash Div A-V Instr. 14: A-V, ref. 15: 1512 North Fife, Tacoma Wa 98406.

PENNELL, LOIS G (REHL). b Lynn Ind 17 N 07. 4: Vaughn E Pennell. 5: Oberlin Col; Wittenberg Col; Carnegie 46-47. 7: Co Libn Mansfield Pub Lib, Mansfield Ohio, Head of circ; Bkmob libn Spokane Pub Lib, Spokane Wash 57-. 9: ALA; PNLA; WashLA; Wash State SchLA. 12: "The Public Library Reporter No 14; The Bookmobile - a New Look" ALA (69). 13: Yes. 15: W 1503 13th ave, Spokane Wash 99204.

PENNEY, CLARA LOUISA. b Clifton Me 23 S 888. 5: Simmons 08-12 (LS) BS. 7: Catlgr: Dept Landscape Arch Harvard U 12, UMe 12-13, Brown U 13-15, MIT 15-16, NY Pub Lib 16-18; Tech US Army, Camp Meade Md 18; Curator of mss & rare bks The Hispanic Soc of Amer, NYC 18-. 11: Mitre Medal, 37; Medal of Arts & Letters, 53. ; Hispanic Soc Silver Medal 69. 12: "Luis de Gongora y Argote (26); "List of Books Printed Before 1601 in the Hispanic Society, (29,55); "List of Books Printed 1601-1700 in the Hispanic Society (38); "Catalogue of Publications of the Hispanic Society (43); "The Book Called CELESTINA" (54); "Printed Books, 1468-1700, in the Hispanic Society (65); Ed: "Washington Irvin; Diary (26); "Prescott; Unpublished Letters (27); "George Ticknor; Letters (27); "George Edward Bonsor. The Archaeological Expedition Along the Guadalquivir (31); "George Edward Bonsor. An Archaeological Sketch-Book of the Roman Necropolis at Carmona (31); "Washington Irving in Spain; Unpublished Letters (58-59); "An Album of Selected Bookbindings", (67). 13: Yes. 14: Hispanic rare bks & mss. 15: 788 Riverside dr, NYC 10032.

PENNEY, PEARCE JOHN. b St Anthony Newfoundland 10 Mr 28. 4: Amy Parrill. 5: Mt AllisonU 57 (Philos) BA; Pine Hill Div Hall 59 (Theol) BD; Syracuse 68 MSLS. 7: Tchr UC Dept of Educ, Newfoundland 46-50; Clergyman UC of Canada, Newfoundland 59-67; Libn memorialU (Newfoundland) 68-. 9: CanLA. 10: Kiwanis Club of St John's. 14: Catlg, ref. 15: Bldg 707 apt D Pleasantville, St John's Newfoundland.

PENNIMAN, (MRS) BLANCHE L (DOWNING). b Beverly Mass 5 N18. 5: Tufts U 35-39 (Hist) AB, 39-40 (Hist) MA; Simmons summers 61-64 (LS) MS. 6: Fr, Ger. 7: Asst in treas off Tufts U 40-42; Statistical clerk US Weather Bur,)Boston 42-44; Lib clerk Bergenfield High Sch, Bergenfield NJ 60-62, Asst libn 62-. 9: NEA; NJEA; NJLA; Bergen Co (NJ) SchL. 10: Phi Beta Kappa. 14: Sch serv. 15: 12 Dick st, Bergenfield NJ 07621.

PENNINGTON, EUNICE CATHERINE (RANDOLPH). b Fremont Mo 16 F 23. 4: Daniel Douglas Pennington. 5: SE Mo State Col 40; UAriz 42; Ark State U 62 (Elem Educ) BSE; Peabody Col 67 Masters LS. 7: Tchr: Van Buren Mo 40, Fremont Mo 42; Free lance writing & reporting 44-54; Tchr: Elsinore Mo 56, Fremont Mo 56-60, Winona Mo 60-63; Reg libn Current River Ref Lib, Van Buren Mo 63-. 8: Stories, articles and features on assignment and as a free lancer during the last thirty years. 9: ALA; MoLA. 10: Mo Hist Soc; Carter Co Hist Soc; Friends of the Lib, and var others. 11: Hon Mem of the Eugene Field Poetry Soc. 12: "History of Carter County" (59); "History of the ozarks" (62); "Perry, the Pet Pig" (66); "Ozark National Scenic Riverway" (67); Editorial staff, "The Ozarks Mountaineer". 13: Yes. 14: Regl lib admin. 15: Fremont Mo 63941.

PENNINGTON, JACK G. b Clio Mich 20 Mr 39. 4: Carole Cecile Lynch. 5: Flint (Mich) Jr Col 58-60 (Mus) AA; UMich 60-62 (Eng); West Mich U 66-67 (Hist) BA, 67-68 MSLS. 7: Organist-choirmaster St Christopher's Episcopal Ch, Flint Mich 60-64; Organist-choirmaster Christ Anglican Ch, Dartmouth NS 64-65; Hd tech serv Dalhousie U Med Lib Halifax NS 64-65; Organist-choirmaster St Peter's Anglican Ch, Brockville Ont 65-66; Supv Upjohn Lib Kalamazoo Col 67-68; Ser & docs libn Jessie Ball duPont lib Univ of the South 68-. 8: Govt Publ Inst, Emory U summer 68. 9: ALA; CanLA; SELA. 10: Amer Guild of Organists; AAUP; Hymn Soc of Amer; Royal Musical Assn; Royal Sch of Church Music. 14: Govt docs, ref, archives, rare bks. 15: Jessie Ball duPont Lib Univ of the South, Sewanee Tn 37375.

PENNINGTON, WALTER WILLIAM III. b Mobile Ala 12 N 42. 5: N Fla Jr Col 60-62 (Genl Educ) AA; Fla State U 62-65 (Eng, LS) BA, 67-68 (LS) MS. 7: Libn Hamilton Co High Sch, Jasper Fla 65-67; Libn Univ Sch Fla State U 68-. 9: ALA; -AASchL; NEA-DAVI; FlaEA; FlaASchL; Fla A-V Assn. 10: Jr C of C; Leon Co Libns Assn. 14: Sch libs, ya wk. 15: 1636 Jackson Bluff rd apt 134, Tallahassee Fl 32304.

PENNINO, JOHN. b NYC. 5: NYU 55-59 (Eng Lit) BA; Columbia 59-61 MLS; NYU 64-65 (Eng Lit) MA. 6: Fr, Ital. 7: Asst to libn City Col (NY) 61-62; Catlgr Polytech Inst of Brooklyn (NY) 62-63, Order libn 63-64, Head acquis dept 64-66, Asst dir of libs & Asst Prof 66-. 9: SLA. 10: Metropolitan Opera Guild; Art Students League. 14: Admin, tech serv. 15: 434 E 58th st, New York NY 10022.

PENROSE, CHARLES. b Marietta Ohio 18 Ap 15. 4: Ruth Stevens. 5: Marietta Col 32-35 (Sci); Col of William & Mary 36-39 (Jurispudence) AB 37, 39 JD U of Geneva summer 37 (Fr); Georgetown U 40 (Econ); UMich 45-46 ABLS. 6: Fr. 7: Research asst State of Va Div of Budget, Richmond Va 39; Tech 4th grade US Army, Iran, India, Egypt 41-45; Asst libn Bethany WVa) 46-48; Head Libn Clarkston Col of Tech 48-65, Asst libn 65-. 8: Consul, bk sel, Potsdam Pub Lib, 63-64; Mem Notable Bks Coun (1 yr); Served on Middle States Evaluating Com. 9: ALA (chm Dup Exch Union); ASIS; SLA (Exec Bd Upstate NY Chap); NYLA (pres Col & Univ Sect); No Country Ref & Res Resources Coun. 10: Torch Club; Commun Concerts; PTA; Democratic Town Chm; Town Planning Bd. 13: Yes. 14: Admin. 15: Rt 2, Potsdam NY 13676.

PENSON, CLAUDINE (PRICE). b Surry Co Va. 4: Gozie E Penson. 5: Miner Tchrs 37-41 (Kindergarten Educ) BS; Va State summers 40, 41 (LS) Certif; Amer U 56-58 (Elem Educ); Peabody Col 66-67 MLS. 7: Pub sch elem tchr: Wash DC 42-48, 58, Pahokee Fla 50-53; Tuskegee Inst Lib: Nursery sch tchr 59-60, Nursery sch libn 60-63, serials asst 63-67, Ref 67-. 8: Wk with agric migrants in Palm Beach Co Fla 48-57. 9: ALA; SELA; AlaLA. 10: AAUW; Kappa Delta Pi; Beta Phi Mu; NAACP; Tuskegee Civic Assn; Women of Presbyt Ch; Homemakers Arts and Crafts Club; Girl Scouts Leader. 14: Ref, govt docs. 15: 202 Althea st, Tuskegee Inst Al 36088.

PEPLINSKI, RUTH CAROLYN. b Milwaukee 30 Ap 18. 5: UWis (Milwaukee) 36-41 (Educ) BS; UWis (Madison) 48-49 (LS) BS; Carroll Col 65. 6: Fr, Sp. 7: Eng tchr, Gresham Wis 41-43; Eng tchr, libn & Span tchr, Hancock Wis 44-46; Lat & Eng tchr, Montello Wis 46-48; Sch libn Horlick High Sch, Racine Wis 49-51; Ref libn Wausau Pub Lib, Wausau Wis 51-53; Libn West High Sch, Madison Wis 53-64; Libn Muskego High Sch, Muskego Wis 64-65; Developmental reading Edgewood Sch, Greenfield Wis 65-66; Libn Brown Deer High Sch, Brown Deer Wis 66-69. 9: Internat Reading Assn; WisEA del 3 yrs); SoWisLA (chm LibDiv); Wis State Reading Assn. 10: Sigma Pi Rho; Beta Phi Mu. 14: Sch libs, ref, readers adv. 15: 8250 N 46th st, Brown Deer Wi 53217.

PEPLOWSKI, CELIA. b Montreal Can 4 Je 18. 5: UWis(Milwaukee) 37-40 (Secondary Educ); Tex Womans U 52-53 (LS) BA, BS; UWis 54-55 MALS; Alverno Col summer 60; UWis(Milwaukee) summer 62; Wis 60 Pub Lib Certif Grade I. 6: Fr, Polish. 7: Clerk, supv Catholic Bk & Supply Co, S Milwaukee Wis 41-42, 44-46; Clerk-steno US War Dept, Japan 46-48; Clerk, admin aide US Disp Per Cm, Germany 48-50; Clerk Wis Mil Dist, Milwaukee 51-52; Unclsf Cudahy Pub Lib, Cudahy Wis 53-54; Sub libn Shorewood Pub Lib, Shorewood Wis 55; Catlg & per serv Arlington State Col (Tex) 55-56; Head Eng sect U Sacred Heart (Tokyo) 56-57; Base libn Sioux City AB USAF, Sioux City Iowa 57-59;Sub tchr libn Milwaukee Sch Bd 59-61; Head tech serv Milwaukee Downer Col 61-63; Catlg & ref libn Sterling Mun Pub Lib, Baytown Tex 64-. 67, Act City libn 64-65; Asst supv ext Mobile (Ala) Pub Lib, 67-68, Admin asst & Personnel off 68-. 9: ALA; AlaLA; SELA. 10: Beta Phi Mu; Pi Lambda Theta; AAUW; Wis Lib Sch Assn; UWis Alum Assn; Mobile League of Bus & Prof Women. 14: Catlg, ref, admin, bibliog control, clsf. 15: C-21 351 Azalea rd, Mobile Al 36609.

PEPPER, ALAN GEORGE. b London England 21 Je 33. 4: Sheila (Griffiths). 5: BritishLA 57 ALA, 62 FLA. 6: Fr. 7: Asst Surrey Co Lib, Merton England 49-55; Sr asst Winchester City Lib, Winchester England 55-59; Deputy libn Aldershot Pub Lib, Aldershot England 59-63; Asst dir NWest Reg Lib, Ft William Ont Can 63-66, Dir 66-. 9: Assn Asst Libns (nat coun 60-63). 10: Ft William Rotary Club. 13: Yes. 14: Admin, ref. 15: 910 Victoria ave, Fort William Ont Can.

PERABO, CHARLOTTE. b San Antonio Tex 3 Ag 15. 5: Maryville Col of the Sacred Heart (St Louis) 32-36 (Math) AB. 7: Monsanto Co, St Louis: Asst tech personnel recruitment 47-52, Asst pub rel dept 52-61, Pub Rel Lib 57-61, Bus libn 61-. 9: SLA (pres-elect Greater St Louis Chap). 14: Bus libs. 15: Monsanto Comp, 800 N Lindbergh blvd, St Louis Mo 63166.

PERAZA, ELENA VERZ. b Havana Cuba 22 Jl 19. 5: UHavana 37-42 (Philos, Letters) Doctor, 46-48 (LS). 6: Sp, Portu. 7: Dir Pan Amer Lib of Pan Amer Columbus Soc, Havana Cuba 43-49; Libn Nat Econ Cou, Havana Cuba 50-58; Prof UPanama summers 49-50; Inst of Lib Sci UHavana 49-52, 59-60; Prof Escuela Interamericana de Bibliotecologia, Medellin Colombia 61; Asst libn catlg dept UFla Lib 62-67; Asst Prof & catlgr Richter Lib UMiami (Fla) 67-. 8: Cuba Nat Econ Coun fellowship to study the org of econ libs, London 51. 9: ALA; FlaLA. 12: Comp; "Publicaciones de las instituciones culturales cubanas (Havana 49, 2nd ed 54); "Bibliografia bibliotecologica cubana, with Fermin Peraza (48-55); "Bibliografia Colombina (51); Directorio de revistas y periodicos de Mendelin" (62); "Directorio de revistas y periodicos de Cuba," with Fermin Peraza (68). 13: Yes. 14: Catlg. 15: 1550 Miller rd, Coral Gables Fl 33146.

PERCIVAL, MARJORIE (DORT). b Cleveland. 4: C Richard Percival. 5: West Res 38-42 (Ger) AB, 42-43 BSLS. 6: Ger, Fr. 7: Br libn Euclid Pub Lib, Euclid Ohio 43-45; Catlgr Ind State Lib 60-62; Asst Tchrs Lib Indianapolis Pub Lib 62-64, Head Tchrs Lib 64-67; Hd tchrs lib Indianapolis Pub Schs 67-. 9: ALA; IndLA. 10: Indianapolis Coun Ad Women in Educ. 15: 4014 N Pennsylvania, Indianapolis In 46205.

PERDEW, ELIZABETH B. b Los Angeles 29 Ag 12. 5: UCLA 29-33 (Hist) BA; Humboldt State Col 63-65 (LS). 7: Intermediate clerk Los Angeles Co Lib, Los ANGELES 36-44; Catlgr Humbold Co Lib, Eureka Cal 50-. 9: CalLA. 10: Bus & Prof Women. 14: Catlg. 15: 642 P, Fortuna Cal 95540.

PERDUE, HELEN. b Salisbury Md 28 D 06. 5: Johns Hopkins 50 (Hist) BS; West Res 50-53 MLS. 7: Tchr Wicomico Co Bd of Educ, Salisbury Md 25-36; Tchr Baltimore Co Bd of Educ, Towson Md 36-48, Libn 48-. 8: Instr in lib sci, West Md Col Ext, 53-57; First elem sch libn in Md. 9: NEA; ALA; Md State Tchrs Assn; Assn Sch Libns Md (pres 54-56). 13: Yes. 14: Child lit. 15: 2906 Dunmore rd, Dundalk Md 21222.

PERDUE, MARGARET (PAINTE). b Pulaski Va 15 N 08. 4: Nester C Perdue. 5: Stonewall Jackson Col 24-26; Col of William & Mary 27-29 (Eng) BA; Radford Col summer 56, 58, 59 Certif in Lib Sci. 7: Tchr: Mercer Co Sch Bd, McComas WVa 29-33, McDowell Co Sch Bd, Elkhorn WVa 34-37, Mingo Co Sch Bd, Matewan WVa 44-45, Pulaski Co Sch Bd, Pulaski Va 46-55, Libn 55-. 9: NEA; VaE: VaLA. 10: DAR. 15: Thorn Spring Farm, Rt 1 Box 38, Pulaski Va 14301.

PERDUE, PHYLLIS M. b Cleveland Ohio 2 D 26. 4: Robert T Perdue. 5: Kent State U 46-49 (Elem Educ) BS Educ, 49-51 (LS) MA. 7: Libn ref Cleveland Pub Lib 51-53; Libn Greenville Pub Schs, Greenville SC 65-66; Libn Dentsville High Sch, Columbia SC 66-. 9: ALA; SCEA; RichlandCoEA. 13: Yes. 14: Devel lib serv. 15: 6485 Bridgewood rd, Columbia SC 29206.

PEREGO, MARTHA (BROSKY). b Pittsburgh 21 Jl 26. 4: A Charles Perego. 5: Manhattanville Col (Pre-med) BA; Carnegie MLS. 7: Asst libn UPittsburgh 50-51; Asst libn Westinghouse Atomic Power Div, Pittsburgh 51-52; Asst ref libn Carnegie Lib, Pittsburgh 60-63; Catlgr UPittsburgh 63-67; Libn Taylor Allderdice High Sch 67-. 14: Supv of lib, ref. 15: 6300 Morrowfield ave, Pittsburgh Pa 15217.

PEREIRA, PRISCILLA M (McGUIRE). b Weymouth Mass 20 Ag 23. 4: Antonio D Pereira. 5: Radcliff 41-45 (Eng Lit) AB; Simmons 49-50 (LS) MS; NYU 63-64 (Eng Lit) AB. 7: Brooklyn Pub Lib 50-53; High Sch Libs 54-60; Libn Cape Cod Commun Col 61-63; Libn Div of Tchr Educ CUNY 64-. 15: 111 Thompson st, New York NY 10012.

PEREZ, ERNEST RAOUL. b San Marcos Tex 10 My 43. 5: NM State U 60-61 (Physics); Tex West Col 61-64 (Journalism) BA; UTex 67-69 MLS. 6: Sp. 7: 1st Lt US Army Med Serv Corps, Germany 65-67; Ins adjuster Aetna Casualty & Surety, San Antonio Tex 67; Lib asst UTex Lib (Austin) 68-. 9: TexLA. 14: Ref, admin. 15: 322 Bryn Mawr, San Antonio Tx 78209.

PERILLO, ATTILIA DOROTHY. b Brooklyn NY 17 F 12. 5: Hunter Col 30-34 (Fr) AB; Columbia 34-41 (Fr) MA, 38-39 (LS) BS, 44-46(LS) MS. 6: Fr, Ger, Ital, Sp. 7: Eng tchr Puerto Rican Pub Schs, Bayamon PR 36-37; Queens Borough Pub Lib, Jamaica NY: Sch libn 39-41, Ref libn 41-48, Head Ref div 48-51, Head educ Div 51-60, Head bus sci & tech div 60-64, Asst libn Central Lib 64-65, Coordinator programs & serv dept 65-. 8: Wilson Index Com to revise "Education Index, 58-60. 9: ALA (Life mem); LPRC (sec 58-69, pres 61-62); NYLA; NY Lib Club (Coun 55-56); Bksellers League of NY. 10: Coun for Soc Welfare Phi Beta Kappa; Beta Phi Mu. 13: Yes. 14: Pub lib age-level serv, in-serv training. 15: 87-19 97 st, Woodhaven NYC 11421.

PERILLO, EMILIE LUCILLE. b Brooklyn NY 17 F 12. 5: Hunter Col 30-34 (Fr)AB; Columbia 34-39 (Romance Philol) AM; Pratt 4-41 BLS; Columbia 44-46 (LS) MS. 6: Fr, Ger. Sp, Ital, Portu, Danish, Dutch, Norwegian. 7: Eng tchr Jr High Sch, Bayamon PR 36-37; Queens Borough Pub Lib, Jamaica NY: Asst to tchrs consul 41-45, Head lang div 45-64, Head lang & lit div 65-. 9: ALA-PLA (mem & chm for bk sel com 54-68);-LPRC; NYLA; NY Lib Club; Bksellers League of NY. 10: Coun for Soc Welfare; United Staff Assn. Pub Libs, NYC; Phi Beta Kappa; Beta Phi Mu. 12: Coord foreign bk sel for "The Booklist & Subscription Books Bulletin" ALA (68-). 13: Yes. 14: Adult serv. 15: 8719 97th st, Woodhaven NY 11421.

PERINCHIEF, ELIZABETH (MARREN). b Mt Holly NJ 22 Ja 13. 5: Wellesley 29-33 (Art, Eng Lit) BA; Drexel 34 (LS) MS. 7: Gen asst in lib Drexel Inst 34-35; Gen asst in lib Moorestown Pub Lib, Moorestown NJ 36-39; Catlgr Burlington Co Hist Soc, Burlington NJ 44-50; Dir of admissions St Marys Hall, Burlington NJ 56-62; Sr/ref Burlington Co Lib, Mt Holly NJ 62-. 9: ALA; NJLA. 14: Ref, loc hist. 15: 225 High st, Mt Holly NJ 08060.

PERKINS, EDNA (JEWEL) SMITH. b Belton Tex 4 Je 21. 5: Henderson Co Jr Col 51-57 (Eng) AS; E Tex State U 57-63 (LS) BS, 63-67 (LS) MSLS. 6: Sp. 7: Asst bus rep Gulf STATES Telephone Co, Athens Tex 48-58; Fied wker State Dept Pub Welfare, Dallas & Athens 58-63; Libn Dallas Indp Sch Dist, Dallas 63-65; Asst libn Henderson Co Jr Col 65-. 9: Tex Jr Col Tchr Assn. 10: Alpha Chi; Bus & Prof Women's Club; AAUW. 14: Catlg. 15: Henderson Co Jr Col, Athens Tx 75751.

PERKINS, HELEN AGNES. b Beverly Mass 23 Ja 37. 5: Wheaton Col (Ill) 56-60 (Lit) BA (magna cum laude); UColo 60-62 (Eng Lit) MA; UWash 62-63 MLS (WITH DISTINCTION). 6: Portu, Fr, Ger. 7: Circ & res asst Wheaton Col Lib (Ill) 57-60; Ref asst humanities UColo Libs 60-62; Grad asst UWash Lib Sch 62-63; Asst child libn Seattle Pub Lib 63-64; Clsf & catlgr UBrasilia Biblioteca Central (Brasilia DF Brazil) 64-66; Supv child & yp sch Concord NH Pub Lib 66-67; Research tech Taximetrics Info Retrieval Lab UColo 68, Data syst mgr 69-. 8: Adv to var Peace Corps volunteers efforts to org small libs in their communities, 64; Lecturer on libnship to the non-prof staff of the Univ Lib in Braslia, 64. 9: ALA. 12: Co-comp & co-ed "Directory of Natural History Museum and Other Related Institutions of the World" (69). 14: Info retr, child lit, educ for libnship. 15: 717-1/2 Ninth st, Boulder Co 80302.

PERKINS, JEAN (KAMERER). b Union City Penn 4 D 14. 4: Ruso H Perkins. 5: NY State Col for Tchrs (Albany) 37 (LS, Hist) BS; Syracuse 39, 57, 59 (LS) Elem Certif; NY State Col for Tchrs 56, 57, 59 Elem Certif. 7: Lib asst Schenectady Pub Lib, Schenectady NY32-37; Catlg Union Col Lib (Schenectady NY) 37-40; Sch libn Central Sch, New Berlin NY 37-44, Elem tchr 57-50; Elem sch libn Central Sch, Cooperstown NY 59-. 9: NY State Tchrs Assn; NYLA. 10: Pi Beta Phi; Nat Honor Soc. 14: Elem sch. 15: 6 Cushman st, New Berlin NY 13411.

PERKINS, JOHN W. b Toledo Ohio 30 O 17. 5: UToledo 36-42 (Hist); City Col (NY) 42-43 (Fr); UCal(Berkeley) 46-48 BA,48-49 BLS, 49-52 (Art) MA. 7: Asst head res bk dept UCal(Berkeley) 49-52; Cultural off US Foreign Serv, Naples Italy 52-53; Asst city libn San Bernardino Pub Lib, San Bernardino Cal 53; Area libn San Bernardino Air Materiel Command USAF, Norton AFB 53-55; City libn Redondo Beach Pub Lib, Redondo Beach Cal 55-62; Lib dir Inglewood Pub Lib, Inglewood Cal 62-. 8: Consul on activating city lib in Inglewood Cal, 62. 9: ALA; SLA; CalLA; Pub Lib Execs Assn of So Cal. 10: Rotary Club. 12: Inglewood Pub Lib; "Job Descriptions of Non-Professional Library Employees, Circulation Procedures, Technical Processes Procedures" (quarterly report, annual report). 15: Inglewood Pub Lib, 10 Queen st, Inglewood Ca 90301.

PERKINS, PHILIP B(ANNING). b Cleveland 5 F 20. 5 East Res 39-40 (Liberal Arts); Temple 40-41,46-48 (Eng) AB; Drexel 48-49 BA in LS; UPenn 50-52 (Ger). 6: Fr. 7: Libn: Math-Physics Lib UPenn 49-50, Naval Boiler & Turbine Lab Naval Base, Phila 50-60, Phila Naval Shipyard 60-61, Northeastern Forest Expt Sta, Forest Serv USDA, Upper Darby Penn 61-. 8: Chm Forestry Libns Second Wkshop, 65. 9: SLA (Phila Chap: past treas, mem var coms). 10: Nat Honor Soc. 14: Catlg, ref. 15: 110 Pennock pl, Media Penn 19063.

PERKINS, RALPH. b My Ayr Iowa 10 F 13. 4: Flossie M Leighton. 5: Ft Hays Kan State Col 33-37 (Soc Sci, Eng) BS; Colo State Col 38-39 (Soc Sci, Educ) AM; UDenver 58-60 MALS. 6: Sp, Ger. 7: Tchr pub schs, Ruleton Kan 33-35; Tchr pub schs, Montezuma Kan 35-37; Supt pub sch, Montezuma Kan 37-41; Supt pub schs, Hugoton Kan 41-55; Prin pub schs, DeSoto Kan 55-57; Libn pub schs, Hays Kan 57-59; Libn State Col (Hays Kan) 59-62; Dir Lib Educ UND 62-. 8: Northwest Kan Dist sch lib consul; elem lib consul. 9: NEA; ALA; NCTE; NDEA; NDLA. 10: Phi Delta Kappa. 12: "Prospective Teachers Knowledge of Library Fundamentals" (65); "New Concept Guide to Reference Books (64); "New Concept Guide to Reference in Education (65). 13: Yes. 14: Pub sch libnship, col lib orientation. 15: Dir, Lib Educ Univ of ND, Grand Forks ND 58201.

PERKINS, THEODORE EDISON. b Goldsboro NC 11 D 17. 4: Arthur F Perlin. 5: West Carolina Col 36-39 (Soc Sci) BS; Duke U Divinity Sch 43-46 (Church Hist) BD; UNC (Greensboro) 57 (Educ) M Ed; UNC(Capel Hill) 57 BS in LS, 62 MS in LS. 6: Fr. 7: TCHLIBN NC pub schs 39-43, 47-52; Libn Allen Jay High Sch, High Point NC 54-58; Libn Elon Col 58-. 8: Recorded Minister in the Religious Soc of Friends; Quakers, Del to Third Friends World Conf, Oxford Eng 52. 9: NEA; ALA; NCEA (chm lib sect NW dist); NCLA; AAUP; SELA; Greensboro Lib Club. 14: Admin, ref. 15: Box 187 Elon Col Lib, Elon College NC 27244.

PERLIN, ELINOR W (MOUER). b Lake Benton Minn 23 My 12. 4: Arthur F Perlin. 5: UMinn 31-35 (Journalism) BA, 47, 49, 58 (LS). 7: Northwestern Nat Life Insurance Co, Minneapolis: Clerk 35-43, Com corres 44-46, Libn 47-. 9: SLA. 10: Garden Coun; Minn Fed of Garden Clubs. 14: Ref. 15: N/W Nat Life Ins Co, Box 20, Minneapolis Mn 55440.

PERLMAN, EDITH (FELDMAN). b NYC 14 Jl 09. 4: Saul Perlman. 5: Hunter Col 56-59 (Eng) BA; Queens Col 59-62 (Lib Educ) MS; Columbia 64-65 (LS). 6: Fr. 7: Libn including 2 1/2 yrs as act child libn Morrisania Br NY Pub Lib, var local brs 26-35; Ref libn Educational Alliance, NYC 36-43; Eng tchr NYC Bd of Educ JHS60Bx 59-60; Libn NYC Bd of Educ Evander Childs High Sch & James Monroe High Sch 60-61; Libn Ridgefield Park Bd of Educ Ridgefield Park High Sch, NJ 61-63; Libn-in-chg NYC Bd of Educ Wm H Taft High Sch 63-. 8: Guidance Coun to Immigrants, Educ Alliance, 38-41; After-sch Study Center, remedial reading tchr, 64-65; Bk reviewer NYC Bd of Educ Lib Bur, 63-. 9: ALA; NYC SchLA (Memb Chm 64-66, Prof Com 66-69). 10: Girl Scouts; Wkshop for Principals & Parents; Nat Coun of Jewish Women; East Side Chap Womens League for Israel; PHI Beta Kappa; Kappa Delta Pi; Sigma Tau Delta. 14: Ya bks, remedial reading develops & expts. 15: 300 E 40th st, New York NY 10016.

PERODEAU, LUCILLE THERESE (LEGER). b Fitchburg Mass 12 O 30. 5: Annhurst Col 49-50; Clark U 50-53 (Romance Langs) AB; Simmons 55-57 (LS) MS. 6: Fr, Sp. 7: Asst circ dept Fitchburg Pub Lib, Fitchburg Mass 53-55; Asst med & bus sect Lederle Labs, 57-59, Head of med & bus sect 59-60; Asst libn Avco Everett Research Lab, Everett Mass 60-65; Catlgr UMe 66, Hd ref dept 67-. 9: SLA (Aerospace Div). 12: Assoc ed "Proceedings in Print," Bimonthly publ of Aerospace Div of SLA (64). 14: Ref, admin. 15: 188 Main st, Orono Me 04473.

PERPENTE, JUDITH (FULLER). b Gouverneur NY 15 Ag 30. 4: Edward J Perpente. 5: SUNY(Cortland) 48-51 (Elem Educ) BS in Ed; Fla State U summers 59-64 (LS) MS. 7: Elem tchr: Edwards Central Sch, Edwards NY 51-53, Lowville Acad, Lowville NY 3-56, Southside Elem Sch, Sarasota Fla 56-58, Brentwood Elem Sch, Sarasota Fla 58-60; Materials spec Fruitville Elem Sch, Sarasota Fla 60-68; Pine View Sch for Gifted Students 68-69. 9: ALA-AASchL; NEA; FlaASchL; Fla A-V Assn; FlaEA (Bd of Dirs); Fla Educ Research Assn. 10: NY State Grange; Nat Grange; Beta Phi Mu. 14: Sch libs. 15: 2106 Waldemere st, Sarasota Fl 33579.

PERRAULT, ANNA HEMER. b Biloxi Miss 28 S 44. 4: Joseph A Perrault Jr. 5: UMiss 62-65 (Eng) BA; LSU 65-67 (Eng) MA, 67-69 (LS) MS. 7: Lib asst LSU Lib 67-69, Sr libn 69-. 10: Mortar Bd; Phi Kappa Phi. 14: Automation, interlib loan, lib syst admin. 15: 2649 Edward ave, Baton Rouge La 70808.

PERREAULT, JEAN M. b Kan City Mo 6 Ja 31. 4: Beverly Berghoefer. 5: Rockhurst Col 48-52 (Eng, Philos) BS; Marquette U 52-54, 56-57 (Philos) MA; UWis 58-59 (LS) MA. 6: Ger, Lat. 7: US Army Signal Corps Spec 2/c 54-56; Jr libn Milwaukee Pub Lib 56-58, Libn I - II 59-63; Chif of catlg Fla Atlantic U 63-64, Head info retrieval div 64-65; Lecturer Sch of Lib & Info Serv UMd 65-68; Dir of the lib, U Ala (Huntsville) 68-. 8: Prin investigator, development of a programmed course for the training of indexers in educl documentation - USOE grant; Consul Environmental Sci Serv Admin; Consul Biol Scis Communications Project George Washington U. 9: Internat Fed of Documentation; ALA-RSD (chm Info Retrieval Com). 10: Delta Epsilon Sigma. 12: "Introduction to the Universal Decimal Classification" (69); "Towards a Theory for Universal Decimal Classification" (69); Ed "Proceedings of the International Symposium on Relational Factors in Classification" (67); Ed "Reclassification-Rational and Problems" (68). 13: Yes. 14: Catlg, clsf, computer searching strategy. 15: McKeldin Lib, College Park Md 20742.

PERRINE, DONNA CHRISTINE. b Rives Junction Mich 28 Ap 07. 5: Park Col 24-28 (Hist, Eng) AB; Columbia 30-31 BS in LS. 7: Lib asst Utica Pub Lib, Utica NY 31-35; Elem sch libn Madison Free Lib, Madison Wis 35-43; High sch libn Fint Pub Lib, Flint Mich 43-46; High sch libn Lansing Libs, Lansing Mich 46-. 9: ALA; NEA; MichLA (chm Sch & Child Sect 58-59); MichEA. 10: AAUW; YWCA. 14: Child & yp. 15: 1510 Marcus st, Lansing Mich 48912.

PERRINE, RICHARD H(OOKER). b Bloomfield NJ 2 Ja 18. 5: Rutgers 34-35; Yale 36-40 (Arch) BFA; Fontainebleau summer 50 (Arch); UTex summers 58-60 MLS. 7: Draftsman Snead & Co, Jersey City NJ 40-41; (Pvt - 1st Lt) US Army, US & Europe 41-46; Draftsman & designer var arch & engnr firms in NY, Atlanta, Birmingham, Houston, & Vnezuela 46-57; Lib asst Rice Inst Lib, Houston 58-60; Ref libn Rice U Lib 61-, Asst libn for planning & humanities ref libn 68-. 8: Staff, Lib 21, Seattle Worlds Fair, 62; Consul Lib Planning Com, RICE U 64-; Consul lib blg; Laredo Jr Col 67; Elmira Col 67, Houston Baptist Col 68, Brazosport Jr Col 69. 9: ALA-RSD (chm Catlg Use Com 63-); TexLA (pres 68-69). 13: Yes. 15: 5701 Jackson, apt 105, Houston Tx 77004.

PERRINS, BARBARA (COWGILL). b New Haven Conn 23 My 27. 4: Allen Ross Perrins. 5: Conn Col 45-49 (Econ) AB; So Conn State Col 64-67 (LS) MS. 7: Libn La Salette Sem, Cheshire Conn 66-67; Libn Cheshire Pub Schs, Cheshire Conn 68, Materials selector 69; Instr So Conn State Col 69-. 9: ALA; -AASchL; ConnLA. 14: Child lit, sch libnship. 15: 951 Sperry rd, Cheshire Ct 06410.

PERRON, HOWARD CLEMENT. b Montreal Can 4 My 28. 5:UOttawa 54-56 (Philos) B Ph, 57-60 BA, 62-63 BLS. 7: Airo-engine tech RCAF 48-53; Libn catlgr Nat Lib, Ottawa 63-64; Libn head of circ Loyola Col (Montreal) 64-. 9: CanLA; QueLA. 14: Circ. 15: 2555 Benny ave, apt 212, Montreal Can.

PERRY, DOROTHY (ADAMS). b Melrose Mass 11 S 14. 4: Walter Gleason Perry. 5: UTenn 32-37 (Sociol) AB; Simmons 38-39 (LS) BS. 7: Lib asst Lawson McGhee Lib, Knoxville Tenn 37-38; Lib asst Brooklyn Pub Lib Brownsville Br 39-40, Saratoga Br 40-41, Ft Hamilton 41; Lib asst Westfield (NJ) Mem Lib 60-. 8: Bd of Trustees Westfield Adult Sch. 10: Sr Auxiliary to Child Spec Hosp; Womans Club; DAR. 15: 144 St Paul st, Westfield NJ 07090.

PERRY, EDNA (ANNE). b Moncton NB Can 6 N 36. 5: Acadia U 55-58 (Eng Lit) BA; UToronto 61-62 BLS. 6: Fr. 7: Sec-steno Quebec Cartier MINING Co, Port Cartier Que60-61; Catlgr UNB Bonar Law-Bennett Lib 62-65, Libn ref dept 65-68, Sect hd Union Catlg U Toronto Lib 68-. 9: CanLA; ALA. 13: Yes. 14: Ref, catlg. 15: Apt 707, 50 Hillsboro ave, Toronto 5 Ont Can.

PERRY, GEORGE ELEUTHERIOS. b NYC 27 Ag 29. 4: Sophie Livadas. 5: NYU Univ Col 48-50; Cornell U 50-52 (Eng LANG ; Lit) AB; Columbia 54-56 (Russian & East European Studies, Intl Affairs) MIA. 6: Fr, Russian, modern Gr, ancient Gr, Lat. 7: Acquis libn acquis dept Columbia U Libs 56-61; Slavic libn aerospace info div LC 63-64, Curator Slavic room Slavic & central European div 64-. 8: Ford Found Foreign Area Training Fellow 9soviet Union and East European Prog) Columbia U 54-56. 9: ALA-ACRL (sec Slavic & East European Sunsect, Subject Specialists Sect 66-69); Amer Assn Advancement Slavic Studies. 10: Phi Beta Kappa; Phi Kappa Phi. 11: LC Meritorious Serv Award 65. 13: Yes. 14: Ref, bibliog, East European studies. 15: 6100 Eastview st Kenwood Park, Bethesda Md 20034.

PERRY, HELEN GUEST (WASHBURN). b NYC 1 Jl 28. 4: Thomas Whipple Perry. 5: Keuka Col 46-50 (Eng Lit) AB; Simmons 51-52 (LS) MS. 7: Asst to period catlgr Harvard Bus Sch 50-51, Ref asst 52-54, 61-64; Dir educ div lib Houghton Mifflin Co 66-. 8: Lib Trustee, Watertown Free Pub Lib (an elected off), 62. 9: ALA; SLA; MassLA. 10: Friend of

Watertown Free Pub Lib (Charter mem); LWV; FAIR Housing Com. 14: Ref. 15: 64 Russell ave, Watertown Ma 02172.

PERRY, JOHN MARK. b Ft Spring WVa 29 Jl 20. 5: Concord Col 39-42, 47-49 (LS) BS; Peabody 57-58 (LS) MA. 7: US Army CAC: Pvt 28th Gun Bn, Camp Wallace Tex & Camp Davis NC 42-43, 2d Lt 71 Gun Bn, Camp Stewart Ga 43, 2d Lt to 1st Lt 771 Gun Bn, Pacific Ocean Area 44-46; Capt: US Army ORD 82d Ordnance Bn, Pacific Ocean Area 46-47, US Army Artillery 53d AA Brigade, Ft Meade Md 50-53, US Army Artillery KCAC, South Korea 53-54; Libn Greenbrier High Sch, Ronceverte WVa 55-68; Libn Greenbrier E High Sch, Lewisburg WVa 68-. 9: NEA; ALA; SEA; WVaLA; WVaEA. 14: High sch libnship. 15: Box 21, Ft Spring WVa 24936.

PERRY, MARGARET. b Cincinnati 15 N 33. 5: West Mich U 50-54 (LS) AB; U Paris summer 56 Certif dEtudes Francais; City Col (NYC) 57-58 (Educ); Catholic U 58-59 MSLS. 6: Fr. 7: Ya & ref libn NY Pub Lib, Bronx NY 54-55, 57-58; US Army Libs, Metz, Toul-Nancy, Verdun, &Orleans France 59-63; Libn Spec Serv USAREUR, Hanau Germany 65-67; Ref lit & circ West Point Lib Dept of Army 67-70; Hd Educ Dept Lib, Univ of Rochester (Rochester NY) 70-. 9: ALA (chm Prog Com, AFLS). 10: Armed Forces Writers League. 12: Ed "Editus, Army lib j (65-66); Comp Criticism of American, British, European and Classical Authors (68). 14: Ref. 15: 131 Willow ave 5C, Cornwall NY 12518.

PERRY, MAXINE H. b Bellepoint WVa 11 Ap 22. 4: Walter W Perry. 5: Concord Col 38-40 Standard Normal, 51-52 (Educ) BS; Fla State U summers 59-62 (LS) MS. 7: Tchr Summers Co Schs, Green Sulphur Springs WVa 40-42; Tchr Pinellas Co Schs, St Petersburg Fla 55-60; Libn Azalea Jr High Sch, St Petersburg Fla 60-; Supv lib serv Educ Media Ctr Pinellas Co Schs 66-. 9: ALA; FlaASchL; FlaLA (v-chm, chm-elect, Sch & Child Div 69-70). 10: Kappa Delta Pi; Beta Phi Mu; Alpha Delta Kappa. 14: Sch libs. 15: 6766 Third ave N, St Petersburg Fla 33710.

PERRY, MICHAEL JOHN EDWARD. b United Kingdom Bradford-on-Avon Wiltshire 14 My 42. 5: Sir George Williams 60-61; UNB 61-64 (Hist) BA; McMaster U 64-65 (Hist) MA; UToronto 67-68 Secondary tchr's certif. 7: Lt Canadian Army 61-64; Asst master & libn Boulden House Trinity Col Sch, Port Hope Ont 65-. 9: CanLA; CanSchLA. 10: Can Hist Assn; Hist assn of Great Britain. 14: Sch libs, hist. 15: Trinity College School, Port Hope Ont Can.

PERRY, MYRNA (GRACE). b Vineland Ont Can 8 S 34. 5: David Lipscomb Col 53-56 (Gen Bus) BS; Peabody 57-58 MA(LS). 7: Catl libn Ottawa Pub Lib 59-61; Libn Freed-Hardeman Col 61-68; Catlg & assoc libn David Lipscomb Col Lib 68-. 9: ALA; TennLA; SELA. 10: Beta Phi Mu. 14: Catlg. 15: 1518 Grandview dr, Nashville Tn 37215.

PERRY, NENA (KATE). b Moultrie Ga 3 F 27. 5: Norman Col 44-46 diploma; Mather Sch of Nursing 46-49 diploma; Tift Col 51-52 BA; Peabody Lib Sch 65-66 MLS. 7: Hosp staff nurse Vereen Memorial Hosp, Moultrie Georgia 49-51; Sch nurse Tift Col 51-52; Hosp staff nurse So Baptist Hosp, New Orleans 52-54; Nursing instr Ga Baptist Hosp, Atlanta 54-60; Lib asst Ga Baptist Hosp Sch of Nursing, Atlanta 60-65; Ref libn A W Calhoun Med Lib EmoryU 66-. 9: MedLA. 14: Ref. 15: 528 Burlington rd NE apt A, Atlanta Ga 30307.

PERRY, PATRICIA J. b LaCrosse Kan 16 Jl 32. 5: Ft Smith Jr Col 55-57 (Journalism) AA; UTulsa 57-59 (Journalism, Elem Educ) BA; LSU 61-62 (LS) MS; UMd 68-. 6: Ger. 7: Tchr Irving Elem Sch, Irvington Cal 59-60; Tchr-libn George Washington Elem Sch, Tulsa Okla 60-61; Lib trainee LSU (Baton Rouge) 61-62; Catlgr Brooklyn Pub Lib 62-65; Army libn US Army Spec Serv, Germany 65-. 9: ALA; SLA; ERS. 14: Admin. 15: Spec Serv Lib, US Army Med Center, APO NY 09180.

PERRY, RODNEY BRITTON. b Philadelphia Penn 9 Ag 44. 4: Joyce Winslow Klein. 5: Swarthmore 62-66 (Eng Lit) BA; Simmons 66-67 (LS) MS. 6: Fr, Lat. 7: Bibliog asst HarvardU Sch Pub Health 68; Asst libn Treadwell Lib Mass Gen Hosp, Boston 68-. 14: Info sci, ref. 15: 83 Pinckney st, Boston Ma 02114.

PERSHE, FRANK F. b Croatia Yugoslavia 20 N 14. 4: Agatha. 5: UZagreb 33-38 (Forestry Engnr) Engineer of Forestry, 42-44 (Anthropogeography); UMunich 46-48 (Forestry , Geog) PhD; West Res 63-65 (LS). 6: Serb, Croatian, Polish, Ger, Portu, Sp, Fr, Russian, Ital, Czech, Eng. 7: Yugosl Artillery Reserve Off (Lt); Forest manager State Forest Serv, Crotia Yugoslavia 40-45; Chief clerk Int Refugee Org, Munich Germany 49-51; Forest manager Industrias Matarazzo, S Paulo Brazil 51-53; Forest manager Industrias Klabin, Monte Alegre Brazil 53-54; Forest manager consul priv bus, S Paulo Brazil 54-59; Forest manager State Forest Serv, S Paulo Brazil 59-63; Asst libn Mo Botanical Garden, St Louis 65-66; Assoc libn (hd tech serv) UMo (St Louis) 66-. 9: MoLA. 12: "The World of Conifers," recent bibliog (65). 13: Yes. 14: Tech serv, forestry ref, Slavic, Brazilian, Ger bibliog, indexing, abstracting. 15: 2811 Moniteau dr, St Louis Mo 63121.

PERSHE, RATIMIR MAXIMILIAN. b Lepoglava Croatia 24 My 16. 4: Irmi Dehnert. 5: UZagreb (Zagreb Croatia) 39 (Law) LLB, 40 (Law) PhD; Columbia 55 MSLS; FordhamU 62 (Law) LLB. 6: Croatian, Serbian, Ger, Sp, Fr, Russian. 7: Warrant off Judge Advocate (Belgrade Yugoslavia) 40; Legal adv Vatican Mission to Germany, Hamburg Germany 45-49; Legal adv Intl Refugee Org Area 7, Munich Germany 50-51; Research asst Law Sch Columbia 52-55; Asst law libn Law Sch RutgersU (Newark) 55-57; Research & lib dir Chadbourne Parke Whiteside & Wolff, NY 57-65; Assoc Prof & libn Law Sch UPR (San juan) 65-. 8: Spec asst Atty Gen NY State 64-65; Lib consul Legis Assembly Commonwealth of PR 66-; Lib consul Dept of Justice, Commonwealth of PR 66; Admitted to NY State Bar 64; Admitted to PR Fed Bar 67. 9: AALL; Intl Assn of Law Libs; SLA; Amer Bar Assn; Sociedad de Bibliotecarios de PR; NYC Bar Assn. 10: Fordham Law Sch Alumni Assn; ColumbiaU Alumni Assn. 13: Yes. 14: Admin of law libs, legal research & writing, legal method, theory of law. 15: Box 22251 University Station, San Juan PR 00931.

PERSON, DOROTHY HOLT. b Mebane NC 26 S 22. 4: Robert Person Jr. 5: NC Col 42 (Hist, LS) BA, 48 BS in LS. 7: Sch libn High Sch Durham NC 46-49; Bkmob libn Pub Lib, Charlotte NC 52-57; Head br libn Pub Lib of Charlotte & Mecklenburg Co, Charlotte NC 57-63, Ref libn 63-. 9: ALA; NCLA; SELA; Mecklenburg LA. 14: Ref. 15: 1712 Madison ave, Charlotte NC 28208.

PERSONETT, MARRIEL. b Ellwood City Penn 9 Mr 29. 4: Elden J Personett. 5: Citrus Col 65-67 (LS). 7: Lib clk Honeywell Inc, W Covina Cal 64, Lib asst 67, Asst libn 68. 14: Reports & govt publ. 15: 1200 E San Bernardino rd, West Covina Ca 91790.

PERSONETTE, JOAN(RATCLIFF). b Enterprise Ore 9 Ag 30. 4: Vergil (Edgar) Personette. 5: Ore State U 55-56 (Educ) BS; UWash 64-65 (LS) ML. 7: Elem tchr, Condon Ore 52-53; Elem tchr, Philomath Ore 54-57; Jr high sch, Nyssa Ore 57-58; Jr high tchr, Pitot Rock Ore 58-62; Elem tchr, Billings Mont 62-63; Elem tchr, Richland Wash 63-64; Libn chief Joseph Jr High Sch, Richland Wash 65-66; Libn Washington & Eastgate Elem Sch, Kennewick Wash 66-68; Libn Park Jr High Sch, Kennewick Wash 68-. 9: NEA; ALA; WashEA; Wash State ASchL. 14: Child serv. 15: 4315 Metaline, Kennewick Wa 99336.

PERSONS, CAROLINE CHAPMAN. b Newton Miss 1 Mr 11. 4: F S Persons II. 5: Miss State Col for Women 29-33 (Hist) AB; Peabody 33-34 BS in LS. 7: Libn: High Sch, Kosciusko Miss 34-36, Ruleville Miss 36-37, High Sch, Canton Miss 37-40, WPA Serv La Lib Com 40-41; Asst libn orehouse Parish Lib, Bastrop La 41-43; Bibliog sci & tech div Auburn U 63-. 9: SELA; AlaLA. 10: AAUW. 14: Ref, bibliog. 15: 160 Burton st, Auburn Al 36830.

PERSYK, SISTER M PAULETTE OP. b Detroit Mich 5 Ap 30. 5: Siena Hts Col 47-55 (Hist) PhB; UMich 60-66 AMLS; UWis (Milwaukee) 68 non-bk materials certif. 7: Tchr: Resurrection Sch, Lansing Mich 49-52, St Jude Sch, Detroit 52-56, St Joseph Sch, Port Huron Mich 58-61; Tch port Huron Mich 58-61; Tchr-libn; SS Peter & Paul High Sch, Ruth Mich 56-58, St Paul High Sch, Owosso Mich 61-62, Dominican High Sch, Detroiy 62-65, Tampa Cath High Sch, tampa Fla 65-66, Mount St Mary Acad, St Charles Ill 66-. 8: Chm Secondary Sect of Mich CatholicLA 62-65. 9: CatholicLA (publicity chm & newsletter ed No Ill Unit 67-); ALA; IllLA; Ill A-V Assn. 10: High Sch Libns of Chicago; Chicago-Suburban A-V RT. 13: Yes. 14: Sch libn. 15: 701 Geneva rd, St Charles Il 60174.

PERTWEE, MARGARET ENID (BARNARD). b Mistley Essex Eng 11 F 08. 5: UHeidelberg 50-54; UMontreal 59-61 (LS) Diploma. 6: Fr. 7: Libn in chg Sig C Hq US Army, Heidelberg Germany 49-51; Libn-in-chg US Army Info & Educ Sch, Munich Germany 51-52; Libn-in-chg C of Engnr Hq US Army, Heidelberg Germany 52-57; Libn-in-Chg chg Cossor Electronics, London 57-58; Catlgr Aluminum Secretariat, Montreal 58-59; Period libn Sir George Williams U 59-60;

Libn-in-chg Dental Faculty UMontreal 60-. 9: CanLA; QueLA. 14: Spec libs. 15: 2915 Bvd Edouard Montpetit, apt 502, Montreal Can.

PERUSSE, LYLE FRANCIS. b Lincoln Neb 6 O 16. 5: Beutel Bus Col 36 Sec Certif; Oberlin Col 46-50 (Art Hist) AB; magna cum laude; Harvard 50-51 (Art Hist) MA; UCal 51-52 BLS; Cal 68 Certif Co Libn. 6: Fr. 7: Statistical clerk Gen Mills Inc, Tacoma Wash 36-42; SpW1/c USNR, Pacific Theater 42-45; Libn Sch of Arch UMinn 52-54; Ref asst UCLA 55-57; Supv lbn art & music Pasadena Pub Lib, Pasadena Cal 57-64; City Libn Corona Pub Lib, Corona Cal 64-. 9: BSA; ALA (Bldg & Equip Com); LAD (sec 59); CalLA (chm Hospitality & Decorations Com for Conf 60, mem Conf Sites Com 65-67); Pub Lib Execs So Cal; Pasadena Lib Club (pres 61-62). 10: Soc Arch Histns; Kiwanis; YMCA; Phi Beta Kappa. 12: Ed "Calibrarian (56-58). 13: Yes. 14: Admin & lib arch. 15: Corona Pub Lib, 805 S Main st, Corona Ca 91720.

PERUSSINA, MARY ANN. b Galveston Tex 2 My 27. 5: UTex 43-44, 46-49 (Educ, Hist) BS Secondary Ed; Tex Woman's U summers 64, 65, 66 MLS. 6: Fr. 7: Tchr Dept of Army, Orleans France 53-54; Libn Lamar Jr High Sch, Temple Tex 55-67; Dir lib serv Galveston col 67-. 9: ALA; NEA; TexLA; Tex Assn Jr Col Tchrs; TexStateTA. 10: Galveston Hist Assn; Galveston Civic Music Assn. 14: Acquis, ref, a-v. 15: 4015 ave Q, Galveston Tx 77550.

PERZYK, ROBERT JOSEPH. b Detroit Mich 9 Ja 31. 4: Jane Baysinger. 5: UDetroit 48-53 (Eng) PhB, 53-54, 58 (Pol Sci) MA; UMich 65-66 AMLS. 7: Auto assembler Chrysler Corp, Detroit Mich 55; Personnel man 3rd USN, Atlantic theatre 55-57; Admin trainee IBM, Detroit Mich 57-62; Salesman Automobile Club of Mich, Roseville Mich 63-64; Libn II Detroit Pub Lib 65-. 14: Ref. 15: 20407 Ardmore Park dr, St Clair Shores Mi 48081.

PESKIND, IRA JAMES. b Chicago 4 Ap 21. 5: UChicago 39-43 (Pol Sci) BA, 45-46 BLS; Harvard 46-47 (Pol Sci) MA; UChicago 52-53 (LS) MA. 6: Fr, Ital. 7: US Army 43-45; Asst libn Wright Jr Col 47-62; Libn Loop Jr Col 62-. 9: ALA; NEA-DAVI; IllLA; Ill A-V Assn. 10: AAUP. 13: Yes. 14: Admin, catlg, a-v, automation. 15: 64 E Lake st, Chicago Il 60601.

PETERMAN, EDWARD. b Longmont Colo 26 O 24. 4: Clarice Stenberg. 5: Northwest Nazarene Col 43-45; Azusa Col 45-47 (Biblical Lit) ThB; Nazarene Theol Sem 47-50 (Biblical Lit) BD; West Mich U 62 (LS) MA. 6: Gk. 7: Clergyman Church of the Nazarene, Michigan Wash 50-59; Libn, Prof Azusa Col 59-. 8: Lib consul to World Vision, Monrovia Cal, 65-. 9: ALA. 14: Admin, ref. 15: Azusa Pacific Co, Azusa Ca 91702.

PETERMAN, ELIZABETH (SPARROW). b Syracuse NY 2 F 19. 4: Thomas V Peterman. 5: Syracuse 36-39 (Hist) AB, 40 (LS) BS. 6: Ger. 7: Grad asst Syracuse U 40-41; Jr libn Syracuse Pub Lib, Syracuse NY 41-45; Jr libn Contra Costa Co Lib, Martinez Cal 47-54, Head catlg dept 56-65; Head tech serv Contra Costa Co Lib, Pleasant Hill Cal 65-. 8: Lib Wking Com associated with IBM projecting the ideal lib system under automation; Consul Walnut Creek Christian Acad. 9: CalLA. 10: AAUW; Navy League. 14: Catl, tech serv. 15: 1830 S Sixth st, Concord Cal 94520.

PETERNELL, THERESE. b Fontainebleau France 30 Ag 30. 5: UParis 50 BA; UMontreal 63 BLS. 6: Fr. 7: Libn Inst de Med et de Chirurgie experimentales, Montreal 55-62; Libn bibliotheque med UMontreal 63-. 14: Ref. 15: Bibliotheque medicale Universite de Montreal, PO Box 6128, Montreal Can.

PETERS, ANDREW K. b Moscow Ida 30 J3 07. 5: Yale 29 (Eng) BA; UChicago 29-31; Columba 35-36 BS in LS. 7: Asst libn St Lawrence U (NY) 36-43; Journalism libn Columbia U 43-46; U Libn St Lawrence U (NY) 46-. 8: Trustee No Country Lib Serv, Watertown NY; Trustee, No Country Ref & Res Resources Coun. 9: NYLA; BSA; Bibl Soc of Can. 10: Trustee, Canton (NY) Free Lib; Delta Kappa Omicron. 14: Admin, rare bks. 15: St Lawrence U Lib, Canton NY 13617.

PETERS, ELAINE. b Bellville Tex 24 N 30. 5: Incarnate Word Col 47-49, 51-53 (Chem) BA; Tex Col of Arts & Ind 58 (Biol); Del Mar Col 59 (Electronics). 7: Research chem Monsanto Chem Co, Aniston Ala & Mobay Chem Co, New Martinsville WVa 53-57; Research chem Columbia So Chem Co, Corpus Christi Tex 57-58; Research libn Jefferson Chem Co, Austin Tex 59-. 9: SLA; Austin (Tex) LA; Heart OTexas Orchid Soc. 14: Indexing, lit surveys, nomenclature. 15: AquaVerde dr, Rt 7, Lake Austi, Austin Tex 78746.

PETERS, FRANCES (ELIZABETH). b Phila 25 N 15. 5: UPenn 36 (Lat) BS in Ed, 38 (Lat) MA; Drexel 40 (LS) BS, 63-66 MS in LS. 6: Fr, Lat. 7: Lib asst Free Lib of Phila 40-48; Libn Holiday Magazine, Phila 49-51; Br libn, asst in off wk with adults Free Lib of Phila 52-62; Asst libn Pedagogical Lib Phila Bd of Educ 62-63; Libn Cheltenham High Sch, Wyncote Penn 63-66; Libn Community Col Temple U 66; Asst libn Holy Family Col (Phila) 67; Libn Penn Col of Podiatric Med 68-. 9: ALA; SLA; Amer Classical League; MedLA; PennLA; Phila Classical Assn. 10: Beta Phi Mu; Eta Sigma Phi; Pi Lambda Theta; Penn Hist Soc; Eng-Speaking Union; Drexel Lib Sch Alumni Assn; AAUW; Phila Art Alliance; Phi Delta Gamma. 1: Yes. 13: Yes. 14: Ref, wk with adults & ya, readers adv. 15: 3634 Midvale ave, Phila Pa 19129.

PETERS, JEAN R. b Belleville Ill 17 Jl 35. 5: Northwestern 55-57 (Eng) BA; Columbia 58-61 MSLS. 7: Ref libn Morgan Guaranty Trust Co, NY 57-61; Ref libn McGraw-Hill Inc, NY 61-64; Libn R R Bowker Co, NY 64-67; Researcher John Tebbel's book on Hist of Book Publishing 67-69; Libn R R Bowker Co, NYC 69-. 9: SLA; ALA; NY Lib Club. 14: Ref, rare bks. 15: 322 W 77 st, New York NY 10024.

PETERS, JOHN ALBERT. b Seattle 10 Ap 38. 5: UWis 57-61 (Hist) BS; UIll 61-63 (Hist); UWis 64-65 MS in LS. 7: Tchr Monroe High Sch, Monroe Wis 63-64; Libn State Hist Soc of Wis Lib, Madison Wis 65-67, Readers serv 67-, Docs - sers libn 67-. 9: ALA. 14: Acquis. 15: 3400 Tallyho lane, Madison Wis 53705.

PETERS, MARGARET LAURA. b Cleveland 9 Ag 02. 5: Col of Wooster 21-27 (Pre-med) BS; West Res 29-30 BLS; Columbia summer 41 (Microphotography). 7: Cleveland Pub Lib: Asst Carnegie West Br 27-29, Asst tech div 30-52, 1st asst tech div 52-57, Head photoduplication div 58-. 9: ALA. 10: Cleveland Pub Lib Staff Assn. 13: Yes. 14: Photoduplication. 15: Cleveland Pub Lib, 325 Superior ave, Cleveland Oh 44114.

PETERS, MARTHA ANN. b Easton Md 21 D 19. 5: State Tchrs Col (Salisbury Md) 37-41 (Elem Educ) BS Ed Tulane U 47-49 (Hist) AM; USoCal 51-52 MSLS. 7: Tchr, Baltimore Co Md 41-43; US Army WAC 43-45; Tchr, Talbot Co Md 46-47; Sch libn, Prince Georges Co Md 49-51; Ref libn Tulane U 52-57; Gen asst Md Dept Enoch Pratt Free Lib, Baltimore 57-59, Admin asst Md Dept 59-. 9: SLA (Baltimore Chap: sec 63-64, dir 65); ALA-RSD (Md Chap 61). 14: Ref. 15: 922 St Paul st, Baltimore Md 21202.

PETERS, MARY E. b Cincinnati 30 Ap 11. 5: Col of the Sacred Heart (Cincinnati) 29-33 (Hist) BA; Columbia 36-37 (LS) BS. 6: Fr, Lat. 7: Child libn in brs & admin asst in off of coordinator of wk with child Pub Lib of Cincinnati & Hamilton Co, Cincinnati 37-58; Head child dept Lima Pub Lib, Lima Ohio 58-65; Libn Brooklyn Br, Cleveland 65-. 9: ALA (Coun 51-54);-Child LA (Pub chm 50-52, treas 55-56);-Div Libs Child & YP (chm Nomin Com 55-56);-CSD (Bd Dirs 64-67, chm 2 coms 58-, mem Publns Planning Com 67-70); OhioLA (Bd mem-at-large sect of wkers with child & yp 55; v-chm & chm Round Table on Serv to Child & YA 59-60; Nomin Com 62); Ohioana Lib Assn. 10: Delta Kappa Gamma; LWV. 12: Assoc ed & ed "Top of the News (53-55). 13: Yes. 14: Pub lib serv, child serv, adult serv. 15: 12471 Cedar rd #103, Cleveland Heights Oh 44106.

PETERS, WILLIAM EDWARD. b Pittsburgh Penn 27 Ja 32. 4: Eleanor Stanley Peters. 5: UPittsburgh 50-54 (Psych) BS, 62-63 MLS. 7: Psych tech US Army, Lompoc Cal 55-57; Pub health off Allegheny Co Health Dept, Pittsburgh 58-60; Probation off Allegheny Co Juvenile Court, Pittsburgh 60-62; Catlgr Penn State U 63-65; Sr catlgr Harvard Med Lib 65-66; Hd bibliogr UConn (Storrs) 66-. 9: ALA (reprint com). 10: Beta Phi Mu; Pi Kappa Alpha. 14: Catlg, admin, acquis. 15: 36 Timber dr, Storrs Ct 06268.

PETERSCHMIDT, MARY JOSEPHINE. b Portland Ore 12 Je 42. 5: UPortland 60-64 (Soc Sci) BA; UCal(Berkeley) 64-65 MLS. 6: Fr. 7: Ref libn UWash 65-67; Head gen ref & bibliog San Jose State Col 67-; Instr Lib I, Lib Sch 67-.13035 9: ALA; CalLA. 14: Lib orientation, ref. 15: 1050A Crestview dr, Mountain View Ca 94040.

PETERSEN JUDITH(AGERTON). b Orange NJ 0 S 42. 4: Richard O A Petersen Jr. 5: Wilson Col 60-64 (Hist) AB; Columbia 64-65 MLS. 6: Fr. 7: Elem sch libn Pub Lib, Brookline Mass 65-66; Child & ref libn Summit Pub Lib, Summit NJ 66-67; Dir Chesapeake Col Lib 67-. 9: ALA. 10: Phi Beta Kappa. ; Beta Phi Mu. 14: Child bks & serv, ref. 15: 5326 Piney Branch ct, Norfolk Va 23320.

PETERSEN, PHYLLIS ESTHER. b Syracuse NY 8 Jl 33. 5: LeMoyne Col 51-55 (Math) BS; SUNY (Geneseo) 62-64 (LS) MS; Syracuse 61-68 (LS) MS. 7: Math asst Carrier Corp, Syracuse NY 55-62; Catlg libn SUNY Agric & Tech Col (Morrisville) 62-. 9: NYLA. 10: AAUP. 14: Catlg. 15: RD 3, Cazenovia NY 13035.

PETERSIEL, BEVERLY E. b Richmond Va. 5: UAla (Educ) BS; Emory (LS) MLS. 7: Tchr, Fulton Co Ga; Libn, Arlington Va. 8: Hd libn at Glencarlyn Br in Arlington Co Pub Lib Syst. 9: NEA; ALA. 14: Adult serv. 15: 5353 Columbia Pike #708, Arlington Va 22204.

PETERSON, BENDIX L. Boston Mass. 5: Boston U 49 (Hist) AB; Simmons 50 MS in LS. 6: Fr. 7: Assoc libn Loop Jr Col currently. 9: ALA. 14: Catlg. 15: 1360 Lake Shore dr, Chicago Il 60610.

PETERSON, BETTY JO. b Paso Robles Call 22 N 32. 5: UPacific 54 (Eng) AB; UCal 56 MLS. 7: Intern libn Richmond (Cal) Pub Lib 54-56; Child libn Kern Co Lib, Bakersfield Cal 56-64, Libn Boys & Girls Br 64-68, Supv child ext dept 68-. 9: ALA; CalLA (sec Child & YP Div). 10: AAUW; UN Assn; Alumni Assn UCal. 14: Child libnship. 15: Kern County Lib, 1315 Truxtun ave, Bakersfield Ca 93306.

PETERSON, EDWARD J. b Detroit Mich 26 Ap 30. 4: Elsie R McMillan. 5: Ithaca Col 61-63 (Hist) BA; UTex 63-65 (Lat Amer Studies) MA; Columbia 65-67 (LS) MS. 6: Sp. 7: Yeoman 2nd class US Coast Guard, Boston 51-54; Searcher acquis dept SUNY (Stony Brook) 65-67; Admin asst for catlg Harvard Col Lib 67-. 14: Tech serv. 15: 97 North rd, Bedford Ma 01730.

PETERSON, ELLEN L. b Jersey City NJ 14 Jl 45. 5: Rutgers (Newark) 63-67 (Pol Sci) BA; Rutgers (New Brunswick) 67-68 MLS. 7: Jr libn Free Pub Lib of Woodbridge, Woodbridge NJ 68-. 9: ALA; NJLA. 14: Ref, adult serv. 15: 64 W 7th st, Bayonne NJ 07002.

PETERSON, ESTHER. Crookston Minn 18 S 04. 5: St Olaf Col 23-27 (Hist) BA; UIll 27-28 BS in LS. 6: Norwegian. 7: Reviser UMinn Lib Sch summer 28; Catlgr UMinn Lib (Minneapolis) 28-. 8: Fellow in Coop Catlg, LC, 43. 9: ALA; MinnLA. 14: Catlg. 15: 1471 Fulham st, St Paul Mn 55108.

PETERSON, FRED M. b Minneapolis 29 D 36. 5: UMinn 54-58 (Internat Rel) BA, 59-60 (LS) MA. 6: Ger. 7: Asst to dir lib Iowa State U 61-64, Head catlg dept & asst to dir 64-67, Asst dir 68-69; Assoc Div 69-. 9: ALA; IowaLA. 15: Iowa State Univ, Ames Ia 50010.

PETERSON, GARY TAYLOR. b Hayward Cal 18 D 39. 4: Patricia Cottam. 5: San Jose State Col 58-62 (LS, Eng) BA, Lib credentials, 65 (LS) MA; Cal State Col (Hayward) 64-65 9educ); IndU 68- (A-v). 7: Libn & a-v coord John Muir Jr High, San Leandro Cal 62-66; Eng tchr Los Cerlos, San Leandro Cal 64-65; Col libn & media dir Canal Zone Col, Balboa Canal Zone 66-68, Instr in media 66-68; Visiting Prof of media San Francisco State Col summer 68; Grad asst to dean a-v ctr Ind U (Bloomington) 68-. 8: Dir of Student Activities, John Muir Jr High Sch 64-66; Night Sch Proj consul 65-66. 9: NEA-DAVI; CalASchL (Jr High Chm 65-66); ClrTA. 10: AAUP; Profess photographer; Epsilon Eta Sigma. 13: Yes. 14: Integrated lib media. 15: 760 Paula lane, Petaluma Ca 94952.

PETERSON, GENEVA A(GNES). b Waynesburg Penn 25 O 18. 5: Waynesburg Col 36-41 (Eng); UPittsburgh 54-56 (Eng Lit) BA; Drexel 59-62 MS in LS. 6: Fr. 7: Sec nursing off Passavant Hosp, Pittsburgh 51-57; Lib asst Westinghouse E Corp, Pittsburgh 57; Lib asst Chatham Col Lib 57-60; Lib asst Temple U Lib 60-62; Adult serv libn Brooklyn Pub Lib, Brooklyn NY 62-64; Asst libn NY State Lib 64-, Sr libn 68-. 9: ALA (Jr Mem Round Table 62); NYLA. 10: Pi Tau Phi; Womens Coun; NY State Educ Bldg. 14: Ref, bk sel, reviewing, readers serv, Interlib loan. 15: 115 1/2 Chestnut st, Albany NY 12210.

PETERSON, HAROLD D(ANIEL). b Ft Dodge Iowa 21 S 10. 5: Ft Dodge Jr Col 29-31; UIowa 31-33 (Letters) BA, 33-34 (Eng) MA; Columbia 35-36 (LS) BS. 6: Swedish. 7: Libn Wm Scheerer Jr Mem Lib, Hill Sch, Pottstown Penn 36-41; Lt Col Army Med Serv Med Registrar 42-63; Asst manager Grolier Soc Inc, Portland Ore 53-56; Base lbn 337th Fighter Group USAF, Portland Internat Arpt Ore 56-63; Ext libn US Army Japan, Camp Zama Japan 64; Depot libn US Army Ryukyu Islands, Zukiran Okinawa RI 64-66; Chief libn USAF, Naha Okinawa 66-. 8: Dir Med Sect US Army Res Sch, Portland Ore, 61-63. 10: Philatelic Lit Assn; Soc of Philatelic Amers; Amer Philatelic Soc; Scandinavian Collectors Club (Chicago); The Scandinavian Philatelic Soc (London);The Ryikyu Philatelic Soc (Okinawa RI); Iowa Acad Sci; Phi Beta Kappa; Beta Phi Mu. 13: Yes. 14: Admin. 15: 1403 SE Ogden st, Portland Ore 97202.

PETERSON, HARRY N. b Arendal Norway 27 S 07. 5: NYU 24-28 (Eng) BS; Columbia 32-34 BS in LS. 7: Supv asst Mt Vernon Pub Lib, Mt Vernon NY 34-35; Asst libn Yonkers Pub Lib, Yonkers NY 35-38; Libn Ft Worth Pub Lib, Ft Worth Tex 39-47; (Maj) Army of the US 42-46; Dir DC Pub Lib 47-. 8: Surveys of 9 Pub Libs, Lib Systems & Lib Serv, Conn, Ill, Kan, La, Fla, Tex & Tenn (One with a co-wker) 58-63; Consul on 20 Proposed Pub Lib Bldgs, Va, tenn, Iowa, Ill, Wis, NY, Fla, Ind, Mo, NJ & Wash DC 57-. 9: ALA (2nd v-pres 61, Coun 49-52 & 55-63, v-chm loc com 1959 Conf, chm Lending Round Table 42, chm Lippincott Award Jury 61);-LAD (Bd Dirs 59-63); SWLA (treas 40-42, 2nd v-pres 46-47); TexLA (1st v-pres 42 & 46); DCLA (Exec Bd 58-59, Exec Dir DC Nat Lib Week Com 58-61). 10: Cosmos Club (Wash DC). 11: Govt Employees Incentive Awards: Outstanding Performance Rating, 57. 12: "Access to the DC Public Library,. . . with C M Houck (63); "Distribution and Characteristics of DC Public Library Aencies. . with C M Houck (64);"Public Library Organizations and "Public Library Management in "Public Library Administration (63); "Statement of Program for Proposed New Downtown Central Library Building in Washington D (65). 13: Yes. 14: Bldg planning, admin, mgt. 15: D C Pub Lib, 499 Pennsylvania ave NW, Wash DC 20001.

PETERSON, KENNETH GERARD. b Brooklyn NY 30 My 27. 4: Jane Elizabeth Shumaker. 5: Drew U 44-46 (Hist) BA; Yale 46-49 (Theol) BD; UCal 62-63 MLS; 63-68 PhD. 6: Fr, Ger. 7: Minister: Burton Congregational Church, Burton Ohio 49-55, Community Congregational Church, Chico Cal 55-59, United Church of Christ, Petaluma Cal 59-62; Libn Pacific Lutheran Theol Sem 63-66; Assoc libn UVa 68-. 9: ATheolLA; ALA; VaLA; SELA. 10: Pi Gamma Mu; Beta Phi Mu. 11: Certif of Outstanding Achievement, UCal Sch of Libnship, 64. 12: "An Introductory Bibliography for Theological Students (64). 13: Yes. 14: Admin, lib educ, lib hist, bk sel, theol educ. 15: 2911 Brookmere rd, Charlottesville Va 22901.

PETERSON, LAWRENCE HERBERT. b Minneapolis 2 Ag 23. 5: UMinn 41-43, 46-47 (Hist) BA, 47-48 (Hist) MA; UWis 48-51 (Hist) PhD; Columbia 56-57 (LS) MA. 6: Fr, Ger. 7: Asst catlgr Hammond Pub Lib, Hammond Ind 58-60; Libn Field Enterprises Educ Corp, Chicago 60-. 9: ALA; SLA. 15: Field Enterprises Educ Corp, Merchandise Mart Plaza, Chicago Il 60654.

PETERSON, LEROY OLIVER. b Sturgis Sask Can 14 D 10. 4: Clara Evelyn Myers. 5: USask 35-39 (Eng) BA, 39 (Educ) B Ed, 48 (Psych); UWash 62-63 (LS) ML. 6: Eng, Fr. 7: Prin Sask schs 30-39 Educ off RCAF 40-45; Educ off Dept of Soc Welfare, Regina Sask 48-50; Tchr Can Voc Train, Saskatoon Sask 46-48; Tchr Saskatoon Tech Collegiate, Saskatoon Sask 51-62; Libn Walter Murray Collegiate, Saskatoon Sask 63-68; Libn Tchrs Prof Lib, Edmonton Alberta 68-. 8: Spec lecturer USask summer 65. 9: CanLA; SaskASchL. 10: Can Welfare Coun; John Howard Soc of Sask; Sask Tchrs Fed. 12: Ed Sask ASchL "Journal. 13: Yes. 14: Centralized catlg for second & elem schs. 15: 2301 Albert ave, Saskatoon Sask Can.

PETERSON, LOIS (ELIZABETH). b Lynn Mass 18 Mr 17. 5: Mass Col of Art 35-39 (Art) BS in Ed; Simmons 46-47 BS in LS; Boston U summers 44-47 (Art, Hist) MA. 7 Tchr Stonington High Sch, Stonington Conn 39-45; Tchr Cunningham Jr High Sch, Milton Mass 45-46; Libn Wylister Jr Col 47-48; Asst libn Boston U Law Lib 48-50; Sr libn Mass State Lib 50-53; Asst libn Soc Law Lib, Boston 53-60; Libn US Court of Appeals First Circuit Lib, Boston 60-. 9: AALL (mem var coms); LL NE (past pres & sec). 12: Ed "Law Library Journal" (58-60); Comp "Directory of Law Libraries" (68-). 13: Yes. 14: Law lib wk. 15: US Court of Appeals, First Circuit Lib, 1208 P O & Court House, Boston Ma 02109.

PETERSON, MAHLON NEALE. b Moline Ill 10 Je 37. 4: Helga Maria Jendrosch. 5: Augustana Col (Rock Island Ill) -62 (Hist) BA; UIll 62-64 MLS. 6: Ger. 7: Acquis libn Lafayette Col Lib 64-66, Asst libn 66-68; Hd libn Wartburg Col 68-. 9: ALA; IowaLA. 10: Phi Alpha Theta. 15: 614 16th st SW, Waverly Ia 50677.

PETERSON, MARTHA H (PUTNAM). b Los Angeles 24 Ja 08. 4: Leo R Peterson. 5: UCal(Berkeley) 24-28 (Lat) AB, 28-29 (LS) Certif; UMich summer 31, 32 & 33 MALS. 7: Asst libn Fresno State Col 29-44; Elem schs libn Watsonville Pub Schs, Watsonville Cal 47-49; Adult circ head Great Falls Pub Lib, Great Falls Mont 49-51; Head acquis dept UCal(Santa Barbara) 53-68, Asst libn Collections 68-. 9: ALA; CalLA. 10: Pi Lambda Theta, Phi Beta Kappa. 13: Yes. 14: Acquis, collection bldg. 15: Star Route, Rosario Park, Santa Barbara Cal 93105.

PETERSON, MELVA LORRAINE. b Hamilton Co Iowa. 5: Drake U 43-47 (Music Educ) BME; Columbia 48-50 (LS) MS; New Sch for Soc Research 66- (Liberal Studies). 6: Ger. 7: Clerical asst art & music dept Des Moines Pub Lib, Des Moines Iowa 47-48; Asst George Bruce Br NY Pub Lib 48-49; Asst Music Lib NY Pub Lib 49-51; Music libn Kan City (Mo) Pub Lib 51-56; Music libn City Col Lib (NY) 56-. 9: MusLA (sec 64-70, mem Reading Com 64; chm Bibliog Com NY Chap 62-64); ALA. 10: AAUP; Sigma Alpha Iota; Alpha Lambda Delta; Kappa Delta Pi; Pi Kappa Lambda; Palisades Nature Assn; The Wilderness Soc; Monhegan Assocs; Amer Scandinavian Found; Goethe House; ACLU; SANE; UN Assn of NY. 13: Yes. 14: Music libs. 15: 900 West End ave, New York NY 10025.

PETERSON, MIRIAM E. b Chicago. 5: Augustana Col (Rock Island Ill) 25-29 (Eng) AB; Chicago Tchrs Col 30-3 (Educ) Certif; Northwestern summers 33-35, 43-46, & 52-53 MA (Eng), MA & PhD in Educ; UChicago 46-47 BLS; Columbia U summer 39; Breadloaf Sch of Eng summers 40-41; UWash summer 65. 7: Tchr Oak Terrace Sch, Highwood Ill 32-35; Tchr Old Trail Sch, Akron Ohio 35-38; Chicago Pub Schs: Tchr & libn 35-48, Supv high sch libs 48-50, Prin Funston Elem Sch 50-53, Prin Bateman Elem Sch 53-55, Dir Div of Libs 55-. 9: ALA (Coun 59-64, Exec Bd 60-64);-AASchL (Exec Bd 58-62, 2nd v-pres 66-67, chm AASchL-NEA Conf Com);-LAD (chm LAD-LOMS Com of Sch Lib Stat 62-64, chm LAD-BES Com on Planning Sch Lib Quarters 65-66); IllLA (pres 60, chm Com on Org Manual 61, mem Nomin Com 63-64, chm Child & YP Sect 49, Child Reading RT, Chicago Area, pre 63-64, chm Award Com 65). 10: Delta Kappa Gamma; Pi Lambda Theta; Beta Phi Mu; Mem Bd of Dirs Augustana Col, Rock Island Ill. 11: Child Reading RT Award 66; Friends of Amer Lit Citation 67. 12: Coauth "Reading Roundup, Bks I, II, III (56-60). 13: Yes. 14: Sch libs. 15: 5422 Wayne ave, Chicago Il 60640.

PETERSON, ODRUN E. b Waltham Mass 30 My 08. 5: Gustavus Adolphus Col 25-29 (Eng) BA; Columbia summer 38; UMinn 50 BS in LS; UDenver 54 MA. 6: Swedish. 7: Prin High Sch, Castlewood SD 30-34; Libn Pub Schs-Jr Col, Crosby-Ironton Minn 43-44; Gustvus Adolphus Col: Asst libn 44-50, Act libn 50-54, Libn 54-. 9: ALA-ACRL (Lippincott Award Com 65); MinnLA (Exec Bd 60-64; chm Col Sect 53); Midwest Acad Libns Conf. 10: Delta Kappa Gamma; AAUW; AAUP Scout Troop Leader. 14: Admin. 15: 1001 S 7th st, St Peter Mn 56082.

PETERSON, ROWENA BERYL. b Watertown NY 26 Ap 16. 5: Houghton Col 34-38 (Eng) AB; Syracuse 36-37; Geneseo State U 41 (LS) BS; Cornell U 56 (Eng) AM. 6: Fr. 7: Sch libn Gen Brown Central Sch, Brownville NY 38-46; Research analyst NY Air Brake Co, Watertown NY 47-48; Sch libn Holland Patent Central Sch, Holland Patent NY 48-52; Adv wk withchild & yp State Educ Dept, Albany NY 53-55; Instr in Eng St Josephs Apostolic Sch, Watertown NY 65; Sch lib dir Sandy Creek Central Sch, Oswego Co NY 65-68; Dir of libs Wayne Central Sch Ontario Ctr 69-. 9: NY State Tchrs Assn (House of Delegates 3 yrs; chm Pub Rel of No Central Zone 46-47); NYLA. 10: Salvation Army Women's Aux. 12: Assoc ed "York State Tradition (47-); Auth of pageant "Thus Saith the Lord. 13: Yes. 14: Sch lib admin, child bks, visual literacy. 15: 130 Stuart st, Watertown NY 13601.

PETERSON, SANDRA K. b McCook Neb 21 N 41. 5: Nebraska State Col 59-63 (Hist , Pol Sci) BA; AmericanU 65-66 (Amer Hist); UPittsburgh 66-67 MLS. 6: Fr. 7: Ref asst legislative Ref Serv LC 64-66; Readers asst y-a div Carnegie Lib of Pittsburgh 66-67; Ref libn W Va State Lib (Charleston) 67-68; Ref libn Oberlin Col Lib 68-. 9: OhioLA. 10: ACLU; Beta Phi Mu. 13: Yes. 14: Ref, bibliog. 15: 108 E College st apt 1, Oberlin Oh 44074.

PETERSON, STEPHEN LEE. b Lindsborg Kan 31 Ja 41. 4: Mabel Jean Moen Peterson. 5: Bethel Col 58-62 (Philos, Hist) AB; Colgate Rochester Div Sch 62-65 (Old Testament) BD; UMich 65-67 (Biblical Hist & Lang) AM, 67-68 AMLS. 6: Hebrew, Ger, Fr. 7: Acquis libn Div Lib Jt Univ Libs, Nashville 68-. 9: Soc of Biblical Lit; ALA. 10: Beta Phi Mu; Amer Oriental Soc. 13: Yes. 14: Bibliog, tech serv. 15: 1911 Cedar lane, Nashville Tn 37212.

PETERSON, SUZANNE (JOHNSON). b Wash DC 13 O 42. 4: Robert G Peterson. 5: UVt 60-62; UMich 62-64 (Speech) BA, 64-65 MALS. 7: Stud asst UMich Nat Sci Lib 62-65; Asst ref libn UIll (Chicago Circle) 65-68; Asst ref libn Kent State U 68-. 14: Ref, interlib loan. 15: Kent State Univ Lib, Kent Oh 44240.

PETERSON, VIVIAN A(LICE). b Blooming Prairie Minn 15 O 19. 5: Augsburg Col 37-41 (Eng) BA; Winona State Tchrs Col 41 (LS) Certif; UDenver 47-49 (LS) MA; Columbia 55, 68 (LS). 7: Tchr-libn pub high schs, Minn 41-48; Asst libn UColo Med Sch Lib 48; Instr & ser catlgr Iowa State U 49-52; Asst Prof & catlg libn Luther Col 52-60; Head Libn Midland Lutheran Col 60-. 9: ALA-ACRL; NebLA (treas 65-67); MPLA. 10: AAUW; AAUP. 13: Yes. 14: Admin, catlg. 15: 760 E Military, Fremont Neb 68025.

PETERSON, WALTER F. b Idaho Falls Idaho 15 Jl 20. 4: Barbara Mae Kempe. 5: UIowa 42 (Hist) BA, 48 (Hist) MA, 51 (Hist) PhD. 7: Sgt US Air Corps 42-45; Instr West Civilization UIowa 49-51; Instr Hist Buena Vista Col 51-52; Instr Hist Downer Col 52-54, Assoc Prof & Chm Hist Dept 54-57, Assoc Prof & Chm Soc Sci Div 57-64; Assoc Prof hist LawrenceU 64-67, Prof Hist & libn 67-. 8: Consul on hist, Allis-Chalmers Mfg Co 59-, Home Mutual Ins Co 67-; Dir Home Mutual Ins Co & Homeco Life Ins Co 68-; Peace corps Train Offr 65-68. 9: Amer Studies Assn (pres Wis No Ill Chap 62, 69; WisLA; chm Col & Univ Sect 69. 10: Phi Alpha Theta; The UN Assn of USA; World Affairs Coun of Milwaukee; Lutheran Campus Ministry of Wis, Upper Mich. 11: Citation of Merit for Scholarly Achievement in Hist 65, Milwaukee Co Hist Soc. 12: Ed "Transactions of the Wis Acad of Sci, A wis Acad of Sci, Arts & Letters". 13: Yes. 14: Admin. 15: Lawrence Univ Lib, Appleton Wi 54911.

PETERSON, WILMA M (LANDEEN). b College Place Wash 11 F 24. 4: Birger T Peterson. 5: Wash State Col 44 (Gen studies); UWash 44-45 (Gen studies) BA, 46-47 BA in LS. 7: Libn jr grade Seattle Pub Lib 47-49, summer 56, Libn II 60-. 14: Ref. 15: 11320-38th NE, Seattle Wa 98125.

PETGEN, ELIZABETH (AHERN). b Norfolk Va 24 Jl 31. 5: Owens Col 49-50; Womens Col UNC 50-51; UNC 51-53 (Elem Educ) BA; Columbia 60-61(LS) MS. 6: Sp, Lat. 7: Libn & tchr Ft Bragg Dependents Sch, Ft Bragg NC 53-56; Libn & tchr Bd of Educ, Arlington Va 57; Tchr & libn Bd of Educ, Fairfax Co Va 57-58; Libn: Bd of Educ, NYC 60-61, TV Info Off, NYC 63, Pub Lib of Charlotte & Mecklenburg Co, Charlotte NC 64-66; Med libn Med Lib of Mecklenburg Co Inc, Charlotte NC 66-. 9: ALA; SLA; MedLA; NCLA; SELA; NCSchLA; MecklenburgLA. 10: AAUW; Nature Mus; Little Theatre; Mint Mus of Art. 14: Admin. 15: 3033 Hampton ave, Charlotte NC 28207.

PETHYBRIDGE, ARTHUR E. b Leominster Mass 20 Ag 24. 4: Dorothy King. 5: Bowdoin Col (Army Spec Train Prog) 43 (Engnr); Boston U 42-43, 46-48 (Eng) AB; Harvard 48-49 (Educ); ULondon summer 49 (Eng) Certif; Simmons 50-51 MSLS. 6: Fr. 7: US Army, US & ETO 43-45; Gen asst Leominster Pub Lib, Leominster Mass 50; 1st asst ref Providence Pub Lib 51-53; Pub libn Racine Pub Lib, Racine Wis 53-56; Libn Glastonbury High Sch, Glastonbury Conn 56-65; Libn Northwestern Conn Col 65-. 8: Ed Lib Publicity Clippings 54-56. 9: ConnSchLA (sec 63-65); Hartford Libns Club (v-pres 63-65). ; ConnLA (Litchfield Hills Reg Libns Group Chm); AAUP; ALA. 10: Beta Phi Mu; Mensa; Conn Opera Chorus; Amer Recorder Soc. 13: Yes. 14: Stud lib relnships, role of lib in acad institutions. 15: RFD 3, Winsted Ct 06098.

PETRASEK, MR LEE CALVIN. b Long Beach Cal 4 Ap 26. 5: UOre 44-48 (Eng) BA; Columbia 49-50 (LS) MS. 6: Sp, Fr. 7: Stud page UOre 46-48; Lib asst City Col (NY) 49-50; UCal(Berkeley): Prof libn I 50-52, Head processing div 52-, African spec 61-. 9: ALA; African Studies Assn (Lib Archives Com). 14: Acquis, African studies spec. 15: 2468 Bancroft way, Berkeley Cal 94720.

PETRE, GRACE (CASINO). b NYC 27 F 26. 4: Salvatore J Petre. 5: Queens Col (NY) 42-45 (Bio) BS; Rosary Col 67-69 (LS) MA; St Procopius Col 69. 6: Fr. 7: Research tech flower 5th Ave Hosp, NYC 45-48; Research tech, NYC Mary Immaculate Hosp 48-51; Asst libn, Lisle Ill, Benet Scad Lib 65-. 9: IASL. 10: Elem Sch Bd mem (Lisle Ill 65-); Beta Phi Mu. 14: Child libn. 15: 5705 Clover dr, Lisle Il 60532.

PETRIE, BARBARA (TERRY. b Evanston Ill. 4: Claude Petrie Jr. 5: Northwestern 37-41 (Eng) BA; UMich 54-55 AMLS. 6: Fr, Lat. 7: Free-lance artist, Chicago 41-50; Lib asst

Evanston Pub Lib, Evanston Ill 48-50; Exhibit designer & readers adv Northwestern U 51-54; Ref asst UCal(Santa Barbara) 55-56; Libn ref Brooklyn Pub Lib 56-57; Libn ref NY Pub Lib 57-60; Libn ref Queens Borough Pub Lib, Jamaica NY 60-64; Lang & lit ref spec Queens Col Lib (NY) 64-67; Libn ref Mus of Modern Art Lib NY 67-68; Free-lance research, NY 69-. 10: ACLU; Phi Beta Kappa. 14: Ref, art & theater collections, rare bks. 15: 67-02A 188th st, Fresh Meadows NY 11365.

PETRIE, CLAUDE E JR. b Hopkinsville Ky 10 My 27. 4: Barbara Terry Petrie. 5: Vanderbilt U 46-50 (Eng) BA; UNC 50-51 BSLS. 6: Fr. 7: US Navy MAM 3 45-56; Asst circ dept LSU 51-52; Asst ref dept Northwestern U 53-55; Br wk Broolyn Pub Lib 55-57; Ref wk Time Inc, NY 57-59; Head res, head circ, then head ref Hunter Col 59-. 10: LibAssn City U NY. 14: Ref. 15: 67-02A 188 st, Fresh Meadows NY 11365.

PETRIE, TROY (JAMES). b Hopkinsville Ky 11 Ja 06. 4: Helen Starbuck. 5: Columbia intermittently 22-40 (Eng) BA, MA; London 28-29; Columbia 41-42 BS in LS. 7: Instr UMinn(Mineapolis) Minneapolis Instr UPR(Rio PIEDRAS) 30-32; Lib asst City Col (NYC) 42-43; US Army 43-45; Chief circ City Col (NYC) 45-57, Chief humanities reading room 57-. 9: ALA. 10: Phi Beta Kappa. 15: 12 Monroe st, New York NY 10002.

PETRIWSKY, EUGENE EDWARD. b Jaroslaw Poland 31 Jl 22. 4: Raisa Diatelovich. 5: UVienna(Austria) 41-42 (Econ); UBreslau(Germany) 42-44 (Econ); U Tuebingen(Germany) 44-47, 49 (Econ) Dipl Volkswirt; UBasel (Switzerland) 48 (Philos); Commercial U (St Gallen Switzrland) 48 (Com); UDenver 59-60 (LS) MA; UColo 61- (Russian 61-66 6 Ukrainian, Polish, Russian, Ger. 7: Accountant DBL, Toronto 57-59; Catlgr UColo Libs 60-63, Head catlg dept 63-66, Asst dir for tech serv 67-. 9: ALA; ColoLA. 10: Ukrainian Hist Soc. 13: Yes. 14: Catlg. 15: 2195 King ave, Boulder Co 80302.

PETRO, ELIZABETH I. b Wilke-Barre Penn. 5: Temple 32; Geo Washington U 32-33 Certif in LS; Col Misericordia 33-36 (Eng, Educ, Ger) BA; Columbia 50-51 MLS. 6: Fr, Ger, Lat, Russian, Polish Slovak. 7: Sr catlgr Penn State Law Lib 42-48; Head catlgr Penn Mil Col Lib 48-51; Head of Ser Div Notre Dame U Lib 51-53; Head of catlg dept Crosby Lib Gonzaga U, 53-60; Head libn Hoyt Pub Lib, Kingston Penn 60-61; Head of catlg dept Polytech Inst of Brooklyn 61-. 9: ALA; SLA; NEA; NYLA; NY Tech Serv Libns; NY Lib Club. 10: AAUW; Brooklyn Heights Womens League; YWCA. 14: Catlg, tech proc, ser. 15: Brooklyn Polytech Inst Lib, 333 Jay st, Brooklyn NY 11201.

PETROF, BARBARA (JEAN GAINEY). b Atlanta 18 N 37. 4: John Vasil Petrof. 5: Emory 55-59 (Fr) BA, 60 (LS) Atlanta 61-62 MSLS. 6: Fr. 7: Asst to chief of ser & bind dept Emory U Lib 59-60; Ref libn soc sci UFla Lib 62-64; Instr & asst to the Dean Atlanta U Sch of Lib Serv 64-. 9: AALS; Atlanta Lib Club. 10: Beta Phi Mu. 13: Yes. 14: Ref, acquis, catlg. 15: 1295 Lenox Circle NE, Atlanta Ga 30306.

PETROVITS, MARTHA OLDHAM. b Hutchinson Kan 26 Ja 37. 4: Richard G Petrovits. 5: Kan State Tchrs Col (Emporia) 55-60 (Home Econ, Art, LS) BS in Ed, 61-63 (Lib Educ) MS. 7: Stud libn Mary White Room Kan State Tchrs Col 55-60; Head Libn Jr High Sch, Manhattan Kan 60-66; Lawrence High Sch Hd libn 67-. 8: Chm Nat Lib Week, Kan SchLA, 63; Data Processing for High Sch Lib. 9: NEA; ALA (Nat Lib Week Com 63); Kan State TchrsAssn; KanLA; KanSchLA. 10: Sigma Kappa; Theta Epsilon; United Fund Com. 14: Sch libn. 15: 1012 Emery apt 10C, Lawrence Ks 66044.

PETRU, WILLIAM C. b San Antonio Tex 6 Jl 30. 5: Millersville State Col 47-51 (Eng, LS) BS in Ed; Drexel 55-56 MSLS. 7: P O 2 Tradesman US Navy 51-55; catlg Free Lib of Phila 56-59; Tech info spec Gen Electric, Phila 59-61; Supv lib serv United Tech Center, Sunnyvale Cal 61-66; Asst lib mgr Hewlett-Packard, Palo Alto Cal 66-. 9: SLA; CalLA; ASIS. 12: Ed "The Library; An Introduction for Library Assistants" SLA (67). 14: Catlg. 15: Hewlett-Packard Co, Corporate Lib, 1501 Page Mill rd, Palo Alto Ca 94304.

PETTENGILL, GEORGE EWALD. b Cambridge Mass 5 Je 13. 4: . 5: Bowdoin Col 29-33 (Math, Physics) AB; Columbia 33-35 (LS) BS, MS. 7: Stud asst Bowdoin Col 29-33; Summer sub NY Pub Lib 34, Ref asst 35-37; Ref libn Reading Pub Lib, Reading Penn 37-45; Asst libn Franklin Inst, Phila 45-51; Libn Amer Inst of Architects, Wash DC 51-. 9: ALA-ACRL; SLA (Phila Chap: past pres & treas; Wash DC Chap: past sec & dir); BSA; SAA; Coun of Planning Libns (past dir); Amer Inst Architects (Hon mem); DCLA. 10: Arlington Hist Soc. 12: Ed "Arlington Historical Magazine (63-64). 13: Yes. 14: Ref, rare bks. 15: Amer Inst Arch 1735 New York ave NW, Wash DC 20006.

PETTENGILL, RICHARD LITTLE. b W Reading Penn 3 N 42. 5: Bowdoin Col 60-64 (Hist) AB; Columbia 64-65 (LS) MS; Lehigh U 65- (Hist). 6: Ger, Russian. 7: Stud asst Bowdoin Col Lib 61-64; Soc sci catlgr Lehigh U 65-67; Chief circ libn Emory U 67-68, Spec asst to dir of libs 68-. 9: ALA. 10: ASIS. 14: Catlg, ref, lib automation. 15: 1111 Clairmont rd apt B-1, Decatur Ga 30030.

PETTITT, ESTHER RUBY (GREGORY). b New Castle Penn 8 Ap 28. 4: Ralph Eugene Pettitt. 5: Slippery State Col 63 (Educ) BS; UPittsburgh 69 MSLS. 6: Fr. 7: Sec Bruce & merrilees Electric Co Inc, New Castle Penn 47-50; Elem sch tchr New Castle Area Schs, new Castle Penn 63-66, Libn 66-. 8: Tchr New Castle Reading Study 63-64; Replicative & longitudinal study under US Off of Educ 64-66; Asst coord instr materials & new reading program 67-68. 9: NEA; Intl Reading Assn; PennEA. 10: PTA; AAUW; New Castle Area EA; Kappa Delta Pi. 14: Instr materials, local prod of materials, child lit. 15: RD 6 Box 385 Shenango Twp, New Castle Pa 16101.

PETTITT, KENNETH I. b Berkeley Cal 3 F 29. 4: Nancy Halloran. 5: UCal(Berkeley) 46-50 (Eng) AB, 53-54 BLS. 7: Libn 1 documents dept UCal Gen Lib (Berkeley) 54-56; Libn 6 microtext room Yale U Lib 56-58, Libn 7 sr ref asst & research asst 58-61; Cal State Lib: Admin ref libn 61, Legis ref libn 61-62, Supv libn admin-legis ref sect 62-. 9: SLA; CalLA. 10: UCal Lib Schs Alumni Assn. 15: 2420 L st, Sacramento Ca 95816.

PETTY, DONALD. b Chicago Il D 29. 5: Amer Conservatory of Music 47-55(Piano) BM; Columbia 57-63 (LS) MS. , 66 (Eng & Comp Lit) MA. 6: Fr. 7: Med Corpsman (Pvt) US Army, US & Japan 51-53; Stud asst Northwestern U 54-57; Office clerk Salomon Bros & Hutzler, Chicago 55-57; Mail clerk Geol Soc of Amer, NYC 57-60; Clerk-typist NYU Med Center 60-61, Period libn 61-63; Ref libn City Col (NY) 63-. 9: ALA. 10: United Fed Col Tchrs. 14: Ref. 15: Apt 3D, 202 W 82nd st, New York NY 10024.

PETTY, HELEN (LATHROP). b NYC 26 Mr 15. 4: William C Petty. 5: Vassar 34-38 (Psych) AB; URI 65-67 MLS. 6: Fr. 7: Sec to libn Col Lib ColumbiaU 38-40; Libn Pine pt Sch, Stonington Conn 59-66; Hd libn SE Br UConn (Groton) 67-. 14: Ref. 15: Harvey rd, Stonington Ct 06378.

PEZDA, WALTER STANISLAUS. b Newark NJ28 Ag 16. 5: NJ State Tchrs Col 33-37 (Elem Educ) BS; Columbia 39 (Educ Psych) MA, 49 (LS) BS. 6: Polish. 7: (S/Sgt) US Army Air Corps 42-46; Newark Pub Lib, Newark NJ: Lib asst 36-46, Jr libn 46-47, Br libn 4764, Supv libn educ schs dept 64-66, Chief libn brs & exts 66-. 9: ALA; NJLA. 12: Ed "Newark Public Library News (50-51); Ed NJLA "Newsletter (52-54). 15: 220 Sunset ave, Newark NJ 07106.

PEZDEK, ROBERT VICTOR. b Norman Okla 2 Je 38. 5: UPittsburgh 56-60 AB; Carnegie 60-62 MLS. 6: Ger. 7: Trainee UPittsburgh Lib; Asst acquis libn Cornell U; Asst to the libn NY State Sch of Ind & Labor Rel Cornell U. , Assoc libn. 8: Memb Cornell U Libs Com on continuing educ. 9: BSA; NYLA. 10: Beta Phi Mu; Jr C of C (Mem Bd of Dirs). 14: Admin, acquis. 15: 205 Linden ave, Ithaca NY 14850.

PFAFF, CONSTANCE A. b St Louis 9 Jl 10. 5: UMo 44 (Econ) BS in Bus Admin; Washington U 46; UMo 52. 7: St Louis Pub Lib: Stud asst circ dept & in brs 26-28, asst in circ dept 28-29; Asst incirc dept UMo Lib 29-41; Libn Williams Woods Col 41-44; Libn Baylor U Col of Dentistry 44-45; Research libn Fed Res Bank of St Louis 45-. 9: ALA; SLA (Stud Loan Fund Com 50-51, Scholarship & Stud Loan Fund Com 54-56; pres Greater St Louis Chap 50-51, mem Nomin Com 68-69). : Amer Inst of Banking; Downtown Activities Unlimited, St Louis. 10: Amer Inst of Banking; Downtown Activities Unlimited, St Louis. 14: Spec libs, microforms. 15: Fed Res Bank of St Louis, PO Box 442, St Louis Mo 63166.

PFANNER, FLORENCE M. b Lockport NY 15 Ag 07. 5: Syracuse 26-30 (Eng) AB; Geneseo State Col 51-52 BS in LS. 7: Asst libn & Asst Prof of Educ Ithaca Col Lib 59-. 14: Ref, interlib loan. 15: 100 W Buffalo, Ithaca NY 14850.

PFEFFER, VIOLA MARY (PAUL). b Jasper Co Iowa 27 Je 08. 4: Charles B Pfeffer. 5: Cornell Col 25-26 (Liberal Arts); Iowa State Tchrs Col 27-28 (Educ); UIll 29-31 (Educ) BS; Kan State Tchrs Col (Emporia) summers 59-62 MS in LS. 7: Tchr

Hunnewell High Sch, Hunnewell Mo 31-32, 33-35; Tchr Bison Rural High Sch, Bison Kan 49-54; Elem libn Wichita Pub Schs, Wichita Kan 58-2, High sch libn 62-. 9: NEA; KanASchL; Kan State Tchrs Assn, Wichita City Tchrs Assn; Wichita Fed of Tchrs.4 14: Sch libnship, ref. 15: Lot 41 - 4824 W Pawnee, Wichita Ks 67209.

PFEIFER, RUTH-ANN (F). b Wuppertal-Barmen Germany 26 Mr 27. 5: UDubuque 49-51 (Eng) BA; Marquette U 51-56 (Eng) MA; Chicago 59-61 (LS) MA. 6: Germanic & Romance Langs. 7: Instr Clarke Col 50-54; Catlgr Loyola U(Chicago) 57-61; Catlgr UChicago 61-65; Asst head catlgr UWis(Milwaukee) 65-66; Sect hd LC 66-. 14: Catlg, info storage & retrieval. 15: 4101 Cathedral ave NW, Wash DC 20016.

PFEIFFER, ROBERT M. b Kenosha Wis 9 D 40. 5: UWis (Kenosha) 59-62; UWis (Milwaukee) 62-64 (Hist) BS; Rosary Col 64-66 MALS. 7: Lib asst G M Simmons Lib, Kenosha Wis 59-66; Stud asst UWis Lib (Kenosha) 61-62; Stud asst UWis Lib (Milwaukee) 62-64; Hd ext dept Yakima Valley Reg Lib, Yakima Wash 66; Personnel sgt USA 1st Batallion 3rd Inf, Ft Myers Va 66-68; Hd borrowers' serv G M Simmons Lib, Kenosha Wis 68-. 9: ALA; WisLA; KenoshaLA. 14: Adult serv, catlg. 15: 3705-10th ave, Kenosha Wi 53140.

PFEIL, DOROTHEA SANDERSON. b Chorley Lancashire Eng 31 Ag 27. 5: UPen Undergrad wk; Drexel 59-63 (LS & Infor Retrieval). 7: Engnr Data Analyst Standard Pressed Steel Corp, Jenkintown Penn 50-55; Supv tech records & lib Compudyne Corp, Penn 55-57; Libn Honeywell Inc, Ft Washington Penn 57-62; Libn Burroughs Corp Great Valley Lab, Paoli Penn 62-64; Supv Tech Documents Lib Gen Electric Co, King of Prussia Penn 64-65; Libn Burroughs Corp Paoli Penn 65-. 9: SLA (Pub Rel Chm Phila Chap 64); ADI; ASIS; STWP; Lib Assn (UK). 10: Bus & Prof Womens Club. 12: Assoc ed, Spec Lib Coun Phila Vicinity "Bulletin" (64-66). 13: Yes. 14: Mechanized info retrieval systems. 15: Burroughs Corp, Paoli Pa 19301.

PFISTER, FRED C. b Great Falls Mont 10 A- 30. 4: Iris Sanguine. 5: No Mont Col 48-56 (Soc Studies) BA; UMont 57-59 (Educ) MEd; UMich 61- AMLS. 6: Fr. 7: Tchr pub schs, Mont 50-59; Media specialist pub schs, Livonia Mich 59-66; Asst prof Wayne State U 66-67; HEA IIB Doctoral fellow UMich (Ann Arbor) 67-. 8: Adv on videotape productions for Wayne State U Dept of Lib Sci 66-67. 9: ALA; NEA-DAVI; MichASchL. 10: Phi Delta Kappa. 14: Admin, lib educ, sch libnship. 15: 34623 Elm, Wayne Mi 48184.

PFLUEGER, MARGARET L(OIS). b Franklin Furnace Ohio 12 Ap 16. 5: Capital U 35-37 (Fr) BA; Ohio State U 39-40 (Fr) MA; Chicago 43-44 BLS. 6: Fr. 7: Lib asst Columbus Pub Lib, Columbus Ohio 42-43; Libn Metallurgical Proj Lib U Chicago 44-45; Catlgr Army Lib, Wash DC 45-48; US AEC, Oak Ridge Tenn; Libn 48-50, Chief exch & loan unit 50-52, Chief info sect 52-66, Asst chief tech serv br 66-. 8: Ref libn, US Tech Info Exhib, Internat Conf on the Peaceful Uses of Atonic Energy, Geneva 64. 9: SLA (Tr Activities Com 63-; pres Oak Ridge Chap 58-59; chm Assoc By-Laws Com 66-). 10: LWV; ASIS. 12: Co-ed "Index to Conferences Relating to Nuclear Science. 13: Yes. 14: Ref libnship (tr & conf lit), admin. 15: USAEC Div of Tech Info Ext, PO Box 62, Oak Ridge Tn 37830.

PFOUTZ, DANIEL RUFF. b Tarrs Penn 6 D 12. 4: Mary Skinner. 5: Oberlin Col 30-35 (Eng, Biol) BA; Akron U summer 35; West Res 35-36 BLS. 7: Circ & ref asst West Res U Lib 35-37; Pickaway Co ext libn Circleville Pub Lib, Circleville Ohio 38-39; Libn Circleville Pub Lib, Circleville Ohio 40-42; Head tech & bus dept Toledo Pub Lib, Toledo Ohio42-52; Instr Carnegie Lib Sch Carnegie Inst of Tech 52-62; Head sci tech dept Carnegie Lib of Pittsburgh 52-. 8: Survey & planning study of Pittsburgh Acad of Med Lib, 61; Evaluation of the collection Acad of Med Lib 67; Survey & evaluation of the collection Butler Pub Lib 69. 9: SLA; ALA; PennLA; Pittsburgh Lib Club. 10: Amer Mgt Assn; Iron & Steel Inst; Inst of Metals; Instrument Soc of Amer; Faraday Soc; Early Amer Industries Assn; Soc of Tech Writers & Publs; Audubon Soc of West Penn; Hawk Mt Sanctuary Assn; West Penn Humane Soc; Defenders of Wildlife; Penn Quarter Horse Assn; Torch Club; West Penn Conservancy. 11: "1959 Annual Award Pittsburgh Chap SLA. 12: Ed "Bulletin of the Audubon Soc of West Penn; "Toledo Naturalists Association Yearbook. 13: Yes. 14: Sci & tech, lib admin, ref. 15: 3913 Milton dr, Gibsonia Penn 15044.

PHAIR, MARY IDA (KNIGHT). b Amarillo Tex 23 D 20. 4: Robert Lynn Phair. 5: Cal State (Los Angeles) 62 (Eng) BA; USoCal 63 (LS) MA. 6: Sp, Fr, Ger. 7: Clerical So Pasadena (Cal) Pub Lib 38-62; Semi-prof Pasadena City Col Lib 59-60; Libn So Pasadena (Cal) High Sch Lib 63-. 9: NEA; ALA; Cal Tchrs Assn; CalASchL. 11: USoCal Educ Alumni Assn Award in Directed Teaching. 15: 1244 Brunwick, S Pasadena Cal 91030.

PHELAN, MARY CLAIRE (WALSH). b E Cleveland Ohio 27 Ja 43. 4: William Thomas Phelan. 5: Ursuline Col 61-65 (Chem) BA; UChicago 65-67 (LS) MA. 6: Fr, Sp. 7: Page Cuyahoga Co Lib, Euclid Ohio 59-63; Clerical asst Euclid Pub Lib, Euclid Ohio 63-65; Indexer Harshaw Chem Co, Cleveland Ohio 65; Research asst UChicago Grad Lib Sch 65-67; Ref libn Abbott Labs, N Chicago Ill 67-68; Libn UChicago Bio Lib 68-. 9: ASIS; ALA; SLA; MedLA. 10: Chicago Inst of Art. 14: Ref, automated info retr. 15: 5653 S Blackstone ave #2W, Chicago Il 60637.

PHELAN, RITA ROGERS. b Lincolnton NC 2 N 45. 4: John M Phelan. 5: E CarU 64-67 (elem Educ) BS, 67-68 (LS) MEd. 6: Lat. 7: Grad asst E Car U Lib 67-68; S Greenville Elem, Greenville NC 68; Hd libn Tarboro High Sch, Tarboro NC 68-. 9: ALA; NCLA. 10: Alpha Beta Alpha. 14: Elem & high sch libs. 15: 505 Oak st, Greenville NC 27834.

PHELPS, EDWARD CHARLES HOWARD. b Toronto Can 23 Je 39. 5: U West Ont 57-61, 61-62, 65 (Hist) BA, MA; McGill 62-63 BLS. 7: Lib asst UWest Ont 63-67, Co recs libn 69-; Collections libn & hd tech serv BrockU 67-69. 9: CanLA; Inst Prof Libns Ont. 10: Lambton Co (Ont) Hist Soc. 12: Ed "Industrial Research Laboratories of the United States (11th ed 60); Ed "Scientific and Techncal Societies of the United States and Canada (7th ed 61); Ed "The Southeastern Librarian (64-)66. 14: Catlg, Canadiana, archives. 15: 305 Picadilly, London Ont Can.

PHELPS, ELIZABETH (SPENCER). b Roswell NM 13 Je 14. 4: Allen S Phelps. 5: Kan State Tchrs Col (Pittsburg) 32-34; UDenver 34-36 (LS) AB; SUNY(Albany 64-68 MLS. 7: Libn High Sch Lib, Pratt Kan 36-37; Lib asst Pub Lib, Pratt Kan 36-37; Circ & catlg asst Northwestern U 37-40; Libn USDA No Reg Research Lab, Peoria Ill 40-42; Libn Rockland Commun Col 59-68, Ref libn 69-. 9: ALA; NYLA; SE NY Lib Resources Coun. 10: Delta Kappa Gamma. 14: Admin. 15: Rockland Commun Col, 145 College rd, Suffern NY 10901.

PHELPS, ELOISE (WARD). b Rose Hill NC 28 Jl 11. 4: Orva L Phelps. 5: UNC (Greensboro) 27-31 (LS) AB; UNC (Chapel Hill) 39-40 (Personnel wk in educ) MA. 7: Libn: Currituck Co (NC) Sch Syst 31-35, pub lib, Thomasville NC 35-36, Sr High Sch, High Point NC 36-38; Dean of studs Sr High Sch, High Point NC 38-39; Dean of women Jr Col, Lamar Colo 40-41, 42-43; Instr in psych Pueblo Jr Col 47-48; Coun Co High Sch, Pueblo Colo 56-66; Ref libn So Colo State Col 66-. 9: ALA; ColoLA. 10: AAUW; Friends of the Lib; Mental Health Assn; Faculty Women's Club; Pueblo Museum Assn; Steel City Toastmistress Club; Delta Kappa Gamma. 14: Ref, tchg the use of the lib. 15: 1604 Claremont, Pueblo Co 81004.

PHELPS, ESTHER BROOKS. b NYC 27 My 05. 5: Elmira Col 24-25, 27-28 (Eng Lit) BA; Cornell U 31-32 (Play Production); Columbia 37-38, 40 (LS) MS. 6: Fr, Sp. 7: Speech tchr & play coach Ellenville Pub High Sch, Ellenville NY 28-30; Nat Field Sec Home & Foreign Missions No Baptist Convention, NYC 30-31; Theatre dept, ref asst Museum of City of NY 32-35; Art ref libn Tchrs Col Lib Columbia U 35-42; Ref dept art div, ref libn NY Pub Lib 42-48; Head catlg dept White Plains Pub Lib, White Plains NY 48-. 8: Libn Adirondack Mus, summers 59-61. 9: ALA; SLA; WestchesterLA; NY Lib Club. 10: NH Hist Soc; Westchester Hist Soc; NE Hist Geneal Soc; NY Geneal & Bog Soc; Nat Geneal Soc. 14: Catlg, spec libs (art & hist), geneal. 15: 26 Park Circle, White Plains NY 10603.

PHELPS, GERALDINE MARY. b St Joseph Mo 30 Je 07. 5: St Louis Lib Sch 30-31; St Louis U 36-40 (Eng) AB; UMich 48 MALS. 6: Fr, Lat. 7: Elem tchr Pub Schs, St Joseph Mo; Tech serv St Louis U Lib 36-43; Fellowship UMich Lib 43-44; Catlgr UChicago 44-48; Chief of catlg dept St Louis U 48-63; Asst rare bks libn 63-. 9: ALA; CathLA; MoLA (Certif Bd). 13: Yes. 14: Rare bks, catlg. 15: 3654 Fillmore, St Louis Mo 63116.

PHELPS, IRENE (JELATIS). b Lawrence Mass. 4: Austin H Phelps Jr. 5: Simmons 36-41 (LS) BS. 6: Gr, Fr, Ger. 7: Lib asst ClarkU 41-43; Lib asst Radcliffe Col 43; Lib asst MIT 43, Asst libn 43-47; Catlgr Brookhaven Nat Lab, Upton NY 47-49; Libn-in- charge physical sci reading room Iowa State Col

(Ames) 49-51; Mod Greek catlgr UCincinnati 68; Libn Jewish Hosp Sch of Nursing, Cincinnati 68-. 9: ALA; SLA. 14: Phys sci, mod Gr catlg. 15: 972 Ligorio, Cincinnati Oh 45218.

PHELPS, MARGUERITE E (PERL). b St Paul Minn 25 Ag 15. 4: William R Phelps. 5: Col of St Catherine 32-36 (LS) BS. 6: Fr. 7: Asst libn Pub Lib, St Cloud Minn 37-39; Libn Central High Sch, Fargo ND 40-47; Libn Nativity Sch, Fargo ND 61-64; Vol libn Cardinal Muench Sem, Fargo ND 64-; Hd central process Fargo Pub Schs, Fargo ND 67-. 10: Fargo Fine Arts Club. 14: Ref, wk with child. 15: 625 17 ave S, Fargo ND 58101.

PHELPS, MARJORIE DEVERELL DUNTON. b Hillsdale Mich 30 Ap 14. 4: George Phelps. 5: Alma Col 21, 22, 24; UWash 27 (LS) BA. 7: Lib clerk Detroit Pub Lib summer 22; Sch libn Berkeley Sch, Berkeley Mich 23; Sub-br dept Detroit Pub Lib 28; Sub-br dept Flint Pub Lib, Flint Mich 28-36; Child libn Arcadia Pub Lib, Arcadia Cal 45-. 9: SoCalSchLA (sec). 10: PTA (Life mem); Zonta Internat. 14: Child wk, storytelling. 15: P O Box 741, Arcadia Cal 19008.

PHELPS, MARY POWELL (ELLIOTT). b Lexington Ky 27 My 11. 5: Sweet Briar Col 28-30; UKy 30-32 (Eng, Lit) AB, 57-59 MS in LS. 6: Fr. 7: UKy: Bibliog searcher 57-59, Asst head acquis 59-62, Agric libn 62-64, Ref libn 64-65; Head of acquis SUNY(Stony Brook) 65-68; Dir Lexington Pub Lib, Lexington Ky 68-. 9: KyLA; ALA; LexingtonLA. 14: Acquis, rare bks, systs analysis, computerization. 15: 432 W Second st, Lexington Ky 40508.

PHELPS, MERWIN CHARLES. b Manton Mich 27 Mr 23. 4: Doris Johnston. 5: UMich 41-48 (Pol Sci) AB, 48-49 (Pol Sci) MA, 49-51 AMLS. 7: Stud asst UMich Lib 49-51; Legis Ref Serv LC; Bibliog 52-58, Head subj spec sect Lib Serv Div 58-61, Serv libn & asst chief Lib Serv Div 61-. 14: Ref. 15: 411 Audrey lane, Oxon Hill Md 20021.

PHELPS, WILMA A(HRENS). b Ft Smith Ark 11 Je 07. 4: Arthur Lee Phelps. 5: UCLA 26-28 (Hist) AB; Riverside Lib Serv Sch (29 LS Certif); Ariz State U 61 (LS) MA. 7: Catlgr Maricopo Co Free Lib, Phoenix Ariz 29-32; Circ Phoenix Pub Lib 35; Asst libn Phoenix Jr Col 35-, Lib Dir 58-. 9: ALA (chm Nat Projects Com JC sect 65-67); Ariz State LA (pres). 10: Delta Kappa Gamma; Kappa Delta Pi; Altrusa; AAUW; AAUP. 12: Co-ed "Junior College Library Collection" (68). 14: Tech serv, admin. 15: 7549 N 16th lane, Phoenix Az 85021.

PHILIPPI, GRACE. b Dallas 26 D 04. 5: UTex & Our Lady of the Lake Co. 7: San Antonio (Tex) Pub Lib: Gen asst 22-31. Head catlg dept 32-40, Head circ dept 41-59, Head lit philos & religion dept 59-. 9: ALA; TexLA; (Memb Chm, chm Archives Div; chm Dist 8); SWLA. 10: San Antonio Hist Assn; San Antonio Press Club. 12: "Essence of Creative Writing (62); "John Igo on Poetry (65). 13: Yes. 14: Ref, creative writing, pub serv. 15: 1615 Hicks ave, San Antonio Tex 78210.

PHILIPPSEN, JOHN JOSEPH. b Milwaukee 24 N 15. 4: Lola Mae Johnson. 5: Marquette U 57 (Ger) MA, 47 B Ph; UWash (Seattle) 48 BA Libnship. 6: Fr, Ger, Sp. 7: (1st Lt) Infantry US Army, USA, Eng, France, Germany, Holland, Belgium 42-45; Lib asst US Patent Off Sci Lib, Wash DC 38-41; Lib asst US Pub Roads Admin, Wash DC 41-42; Lib asst Marquette U Lib 48-51; Instr Marquette U Dept of Modern Lang 54-57; Bibliog acquis dept Mem Lib UNotre Dame (Ind) 57, Asst head acquis dept 57-59, Head acquis dept 60-. 9: ALA (Life mem)-ACRL. 10: Delta Phi Alpha; Phi Eta Sigma; Wis State Hist Soc; US Army Mil Intel Res; John Henry Newman Hon Soc. 14: Acquis, nat bibliog. 15: Mem Lib Univ of Notre Dame, Notre Dame Ind 46556.

PHILLIPPS, JANET ISABELLE. b Grand Falls Newfoundland Can 23 Ap 42. 5: Memorial U of Newfoundland 59-63 (Eng) BA; UToronto 63-64 BLS. 6: Fr. 7: Asst catlgr Memorial U of Newfoundland Lib 64-67; Ref libn UNB 67-. 9: CanLA; APLA. 14: Ref, microforms. 15: 23 Roche st, St Johns Newfoundland Can.

PHILLIPS, AUDREY E. b Gt Britain. 5: NN Col (Educ, Eng) BA; UWash (Eng) BA; UCal 43•(LS) Certif; UWis (LS) UIda (Eng, Geog); UCLA (Libnship). 6: Fr, Ital, Sp. 7:Libn Libn Schs, Boise Ida; Ref libn & act head of br Pub Lib, Oakland Cal; Ref libn UCal(Berkeley) 47-. 9: IdaEA (So Sect: pres Libns Group). 14: Interlib loan, ref. 15: 2500 Durant ave, Berkeley Cal 94704.

PHILLIPS, BETTY (DAVIS). b Macon Ga 12 Je 22. 4: Richard E Phillips. 5: SW Tex State col 39-42 (Eng) BA; UTex 58-62 MLS. 7: Libn San Marcos Pub Lib, San Marcos Tex 50-51; Supv res room collection SW Tex State Col 58-59, Ser & docs 59-65, Acquis libn 65, reader serv libn 66-. 9: ALA; TexLA (chm Dist 8 64; sec-treas Col & Univ Div 67; v-chm 68). 10: AAUP; Tex Assn of Col Tchrs. 14: Ref, govt docs. 15: PO Box 387, San Marcos Tx 78666.

PHILLIPS, BRIAN FREDERICK. b New Westminster Can 9 Mr 30. 5: UBC 48-53 (Hist) BA; Toronto 53-54 BLS. 6: Fr. 7: Libn UMan 54-55; Libn Ref Lib Toronto Pub Lib 55-57; Secondary tchr Co Borough of West Ham, Eng 57-58; Libn I Vancouver Pub Lib, Vancouver BC 59-61, 63-65; Soc sci libn Simon Fraser U (Vancouver BC) 65-. 9: CanLA; Assn BC Libns; SLA; Internat Assn Documentalists & Info Offrs. 13: Yes. 14: Ref. 15: 2041 Larch st, Vancouver BC Can.

PHILLIPS, CATHERINE (MARTHA) P(ATTERSON). b Birmingham Ala 24 Je 17. 4: Norwood H Phillips. 5: Tex Tech 36-38 (Eng); UOkla 38-40 ba in LS; UOre 52-53 (LS); UWash summer 51 (Educ). 6: Fr. 7: Catlgr Tex WPA Lib Proj (Austin Tex) 40-41; Catlgr Ala WPA Lib Proj (montgomery Ala) 41-42; US Air Force Libn Gunter Field (Montgomery Ala) 42-45; Catlgr Pub Lib, (Bremerton Wash) 45-47; Order libn Texas Tech 47-48; Jr high libn Coontz Jr High Sch, (Bremerton Wash) 49-. 9: NEA; WashEA; WashStateLA. 14: Catlg, admin. 15: 1515 High ave, Bremerton Wa 98310.

PHILLIPS, DON (DONALD EVERETT). b Brinkman Okla 18 F 30. 4: Shirley Jean Studebaker. 5: Tex Tech Col 47-51 (Hist) BA; UDenver 57; UTex 58-62 (Mus Educ); No Ill U 66-68 (LS) MA. 7: Airman 1/C Cryptanalyst USAF, Wash DC 53-56; Tchr: Edcouch-Elsa Sr High, Edcouch Tex 57-59, Buckholts Sr High, Buckholts Tex 59-60, Bus Mathis Sr High, Mathis Tex 62-64, Morris Elem Schs, Morris Ill 64-68; Hd libn Cary-Grove Sr High Sch, Cary Ill 67-68; Mus libn Swen Franklin Parson Lib No Ill U 68-. 9: NEA; NCTE; IllLA; IllEA. 10: Phi Mu Alpha; Amer Assn Tchrs French. 13: Yes. 14: Ref, tchg. 15: 904 Suburban apts, DeKalb Il 60115.

PHILLIPS, DORIS (ALEXANDER). b Brownton Minn 15 N 16. 4: Ronald O Phillips. 5: Morningside Col 35-39 (Eng) BA; UIll 40-41 BS in LS. 6: Fr. 7: Circ libn USD 41-48; Ref libn Coe Col 4852; Head Libn Black Hills State Col 52-. 9: SDLA (chm Col Sect 65-66, pres 68, 69); ALA. 10: AAUW; Delta Kappa Gamma; Beta Sigma Phi. 14: Catlg, admin. 15: Box 127, Spearfish SD 57783.

PHILLIPS, DOROTHY EILEEN. b Perry Iowa 8 Ag 30. 5: Iowa State Tchrs Col 49-53 (Eng, LS) BA; UChicago 60-66 (LS) MA. 7: Tchr & libn Lyons Jr High Sch, Clinton Iowa 53-57; Ref libn Fed Reserve Bank, Chicago 57-67, Asst libn 67-. 9: SLA. 14: Ref. 15: 316 W Barry, Chicago Il 60657.

PHILLIPS, EDITH (CROWL). b Shelby Mich 24 Mr 21. 4: Clarence A Phillips. 5: East Mich U 38-42 (Eng) BA; UMich 47-49 MALS. 7: TCHRLIBN Pub Sch, Melvindale Mich 44-45; Jr libn UMich Gen Lib 46-49; Sch libn Chicago Jewish Acad, Chicago 51-52; Catlgr & asst dir Kent Co Lib, Grand Rapids Mich 53-55; Sch libn Pub Schs, Grandville Mich 58-62; Head catlg sect State Lib of Mich 62-65, Bk sel coordinator 65-68; Asst Prof dept of Lib Sci Wayne State U 68-. 9: ALA; MichLA. 10: LWV. 14: Catlg, bk sel. 15: 25301 Circle dr, Southfield Mi 48075.

PHILLIPS, HAROLD THOMAS JR. b Mt Vernon Ohio 26 Ap 28. 5: Ashland (Ohio) Col 52-53; UCincinnati Even Col 54-61 (Eng) PhB; UKy 62-63 MSLS. 7: Br libn Pub Lib of Cincinnati 64-. 9: ALA; OhioLA. 10: Beta Phi Mu. 15: 3982 S Fordham pl, Cincinnati Oh 45213.

PHILLIPS, HELEN (GORRIE). b Yonkers NY 16 Je 21. 4: Arthur Page Phillips. 5: Barnard 39-43 (Hist) BA; Columbia 43-46 (LS) BS with high honors, 46-50 (LS) MS. 6: Fr, Ger. 7: Asst libn Nat Recreation Assn, NYC 43-46; Asst reviser Columbia U Sch of Lib Serv 46-47; Asst libn Burroughs Wellcome & Co, Tuckahoe NY 47-52; Lib asst Eastchester Pub Lib, Eastchester NY 58-, Sr libn I 66-, Sr libn II 69-. 9: WestchesterLA. 10: AAUW. 14: Catlg, ref. 15: 5 Hilary wy, Tuckahoe NY 10707.

PHILLIPS, JAMES W(ILBUR). b Farmersville Tex 12 Mr 16. 5: So Methodist U 33-37 (Eng, Fr) BA; Columbia 40-41 BS in LS; Yale 47-49 (Gen Studies) MA; Trinity Col UDublin 49-52 (Modern Langs) PhD. 6: Fr, Sp, Ger, Ital. 7: Clerk Phillips Motor Line, Farmersville Tex 37-40; Circ asst So Methodist U 41; Army of the US Med Adm Corps (Capt) 41-45; Ref libn Dickinson Col 46-47; Exchanges Yale U Lb 47-49; Ref libn Rice U 52-57; Catlgr bibliogr DeGolver FoundLib 59-. 9: Bibliog Soc(London). 10: Phi Beta Kappa. 13: Yes. 14: Rare bks, catlg. 15: Box 407, Farmersville Tex 75031.

PHILLIPS, JERRY CLYDE. b Shreveport La 10 F 43. 4: Susan Lee Harper. 5: Brigham young 61-64 (Eng Lit) BA; LSU 67 & 68-69 (LS) MS. 6: Fr, Sp. 7: USN, USS Betelgeuse (AK-260) & USS Neptune (ARC-2) CYN3 65-67; Asst libn Lib Sch Lib LSU (Baton Rouge) 68-69; Catlgr non-bk material Plymouth State Col 69-. 9: ALA. 10: Young Democrats. 14: Catlg & related tech serv. 15: Lamson Lib Plymouth State Col, Plymouth NH 03264.

PHILLIPS, JILL (PAULINE). b Sherbrooke Que Can 26 N 27. 4: Gilbert (James) Phillips. 5: UBC 48-51 (Philos, Sociol) BA, McGill 51-52 BLS; Rutgers summer 64 (LS). 6: Eng, Fr. 7: Yp libn Brooklyn Pub Lib 52-54; Ref libn Vancouver Pub Lib, Vancouver BC 54-58; Catlgr Atomic Energy of Can Ltd, Chalk River Ont 58-. 8: Actg libn Whiteshell Nuclear Res Establ, Pinawa Man 69. 9: SLA. 14: Catlg, ref, period. 15: Atomic Energy of Canada Ltd, Chalk River Nuclear Lab, Chalk River Ontario Can.

PHILLIPS, JOHN RICHARD. b Plainfield NJ 20 Ag 39. 4: Leslie St John. 5: Brown 57-61 (Eng Lit) BA; UChicago 62- (LS). 6: Ger. 7: Eng tchr high sch, Grafton Mass 61-62; Asst rare bk Curator UChicago Lib 63-65, Asst mss & archives 65-67; Archivist & spec collections libn Amherst Col 67-. 9: BSA. 10: Fund Raising Com, Amherst Human Rel Coun. 14: Archives, mss, rare bks. 15: 456 S Pleasant st, Amherst Ma 01002.

PHILLIPS, LINDA (TRUSTY). b Eugene Ore 5 N 44. 4: Nelson Orvis Phillips. 5: Lewis & CLARK Col 62-66 (Pol Sci) BA; UOre 67-68 MLS. 7: Sales clk Diamond Lake Improvement Co, Diamond Lake Ore summers 61-62; Flagman C A Trusty Rd Construction, Roseburg Ore summer 64; Sec-receptionist Winter Real Estate summer 65; Filing clk Off of Senator Morse dummer 66; Sub tchr DC Pub Sch 67; Lib specialist, catlgr, tech proc dir, consul to sch libn Polk Co Intermediate Educ Dist Bd 67-. 14: Ref, incunabula, child serv. 15: Rte 3 Box 300, Roseburg Or 97470.

PHILLIPS, LORRAINE (BOBLE). b Dubuque Iowa 15 Mr 18. 4: Charles William Phillips. 5: Clarke Col 34-38 (Chem) BS. 7: Asst supv Off of Research Dir Dow Chem Co, Midland Mich 41-46; Supv tech info sect Ford Motor Co, Dearborn Mich 52-. 9: ACS; SLA. 10: AAUW. 14: Tech lit searching, current awareness serv. 15: 912 Aberdeen dr, Ann Arbor Mi 48104.

PHILLIPS, LYNNE M. b Denver 23 D 33. 5: UAriz 53-56 (Hist) BA; Tex Womans U 59-60 MLS. 7: Ref libn Ft Worth(Tex) Pub Lib 60-62; Ref libn humanities UAriz 63-65; Head ref sect Tucson Central Lib Pub Lib 65-. 9: ArizStateLA. 10: Alpha Chi Omega. 14: Ref. 15: 3401 E Monte Vista dr, Tucson Az 85516.

PHILLIPS, MARGARET (HILLER). b arion Mass 17 Ja 39. 4: David Reid Phillips. 5: Oberlin Col 56-60 (Eng Lit) BA; UCal(Berkeley) 60-61 (LS); Drexel 63-69 (Info sci) MLS. 6: Fr. 7: Film libn Amer Inst of Archs, Wash DC 61; Asst to tech ed AIAJ Amer Inst Archs, Wash DC 61-62; Libn Electronic Assocs Inc, Long Branch NJ 63-64; Bibliogr Lit Service Assn, Bound Brook NJ 64-65; Mgr J1 serv Inst for Sci Info, Phila 66-67; Asst libn Smith Kline & French 68-. 9: SLA; ASIS; MedLA. 13: Yes. 14: Info sci, systems analysis. 15: Presidential Arms C4, Lansdale Pa 19446.

PHILLIPS, MARY ELIZABETH. b Portland Ore 31 O 09. 5: UOre 26-30 (Eng) BA; UWash 30-31 (LS) BS. 7: Lib Assn of Portland, Portland Ore: Gen asst 31-37, Br libn 37-50, Head ext dept 50-53, Assoc libn 53-59, Act head libn 59-60, Chief assoc libn 60-64, Head Libn 64-. 8: Consul, Ore State Lib 62. 9: ALA (chm br lib Round Table 39, Coun 69-71); PLA (By-laws Com 63, Exec Bd 69-71; com mem Metropolitan lib serv 67-69, mem Activities com 69-71); OreLA (pres 48, chm Nomin Com 50-51, chm Lib Devel Com 51-53, Exec Bd 61-62, chm Intel Freedom Com 64-65); PNLA (Exec Bd 61-62, chm Nomin Com 64, pres 67-69). 10: AAUW; LWV; Univ Club; Portland Art Mus; Ore Hist So. 12: "Public Libraries in Oregon (62). 13: Yes. 14: Pub lib admin. 15: 801 South West Tenth ave, Portland Ore 97212.

PHILLIPS, MARY LOUISE. b Matthews NC 12 D 17. 5: Queens Col 34-38 (Hist) AB; Emory 38-39 AB in LS. 6: Fr. 7: High sch libn Glen Alpine High Sch, Glen Alpine NC 39-40; Co Libn Lunenburg Co Lib, Lunenburg Va 40-43; Co Libn Franklin Co Lib, Louisburg NC 44-45; Catlgr Olivia Raney Lib, Raleigh NC 44-45; Clerk Post Off, Matthews NC 46-54; Local hist libn Pub Lib, Charlotte NC 55-. 9: ALA; SELA; NCLA. 14: Loc hist, geneal. 15: PO Box 265, Matthews NC 28105.

PHILLIPS, RUTH H(ENRIETTA). b Baltimore 24 Jl 18. 5: Md State Tchrs Col 35-39 (Educ) BS; Johns Hopkins 44-48 (Eng) BS; Columbia 49-50 MSLS; American U 53, 62 (Personnel Admin). 7: Elem tchr pub schs, Baltimore 39-40; Salewoman Hutzler Bros Co, Baltimore 40-43; Lib asst Enoch Pratt Free Lib, Baltimore 43-49; Catlg asst Columbia U 50; Assoc libn American U 50-54; Assoc libn West Carolina Col 54; Libn US Army Spec Serv, Japan 55-58; Libn US Army Spec Serv, Ft Carson Colo 58-59; Chiek Libn US Army Command & Gen Staff Col, Ft Leavenworth Kan 59-62; Asst libn USDefense Supply Agency, Cameron Sta Alex Va 62-64; Ref libn Fairfax Co Pub Lib, Fairfax Co Va 63-64; Pub lib consul Va State Lib 64-. 8: Ref staff, Lib/USA, NY Worlds Fair 65. 9: ALA (chm Memb Com; Armed Forces Libn Sect: sec 59-60); SLA (Wash DC Chap: chm Pub Com Mil Libns Sect 63-64, mem Cons Com Va Chap 66-67, sec Va Chap 68-); VaLA (corr Pub Lib Sect 65-67, mem Nomin Com Pub Lib sect 67); SELA (Va reporter for "The Southeastern Librarian); 65-67; Potomac Tech Proc Libns. 10: Altrusa Internat; PEO. 13: Yes. 14: Admin, ref, tech proc, lib educ, serv to blind. 15: 35 Malvern ave, Apt 5, Richmond Va 23221.

PHILLIPS, RUTH M. b Rochester NY 8 My 04. 5: Carnegie 25-26 (Chil wk) Certif; Syracuse 35-45 (Eng Lit) AB. 7: In chg irc dept Reynolds Lib, Rochester NY 22-25; Head boys & girls depts Cedar Rapids Pub Lib, Cedar Rapids Iowa 26-29; Syracuse Pub Lib, Syracuse NY: Br libn 29-47, Br supv 47-49, Asst dir 49-54; Deputy dir West Lib System, New Rochelle NY 59-62; Dir New Rochelle Pub Lib, New Rochelle NY 54-. 8: Deputy dir, Westchester Lib System 59-62; Life mem, Adv Co 63-; Mem NY State Co Lib Devel 50-54; Bd Regents, Pub Libns Certif Exam Com 56-64 (chm 59-62); Conductor of Radio Program (4 mornings a week) Station WVOX 62-; Judge, John Cotton Dana Awards. 9: ALA; NYLA (Dir Adult Serv Sect 55, v-pres 67, pres 68); LPRC (treas 56-58); WestchesterLA (pres 58-60). 10: C of C; Coun Social Agencies; Prof Womens League; Citizens Adv Com on Aging; AAUW; Phi Beta Kappa New Rochelle Womans Clubs; Soroptimist Club; LWV. 13: Yes. 14: Admin. 15: New Rochelle Pub Lib, 662 Main st, New Rochelle NY 10805.

PHILLIPS, THEODORE DENTON. b Kan City Mo 13 Je 29. 4: Laurel Clarke. 5: UNM 52-56 (Gen Bus) BBA; UDenver 56-57 (LS) MA. 7: Lib asst Peabody Inst Lib, Baltimore 44-45; Lib asst Joslyn Mem Art Lib, Omaha 47-48; US Navy Clerical-personnel, classified documents, YN2 48-52; Lib asst UNM 53-56; Lib asst UDenver 56-57; Libn Fed Res Bank of Kan City, Mo 5763; Asst libn IBM Corp, Los Gatos Cal 63-65; Libn mgr SSD IBM Corp, San Jose Cal 66; Asst chief libn Queen's U, Kingston Ont 67-69, Assoc libn 69-. 8: John Cotton Dana Lecturer UBC 68. 9: SLA (Heart of Amer Chap: pres 60-62, treas 58-59, chm Nomin Com Bus-Fin Div 60-61, chm Admiss Com 63-64, act sec San Francisco Bay Reg Chap 64, Spec Com to investigate merger with ASIS 69); CanLA. 13: Yes. 14: Ref, readers serv. 15: Douglas Lib Queens Univ, Kingston Ont Can.

PHILLIPS, VIRGINIA S. b Columbus Ohio 6 Jl 23. 5: George Washington U 41-45 (Eng Lit) BA; West Res 56-57 MSLS. 7: CorrespondencedeptNat Geographic Soc, Wash DC 45-53; Recreation supv US Army Spec Serv, Straubig Germany 53-56; Readers adv Free Lib, Phila 57-58; DC Pub Lib: Readers adv 58-62, Br libn 62-64, Act coordinator spec serv 64-65, Asst to the dir 65-. 9: DCLA. 13: Yes. 14: Admin. 15: DC Pub Lib, 499 Pennsylvania ave NW, Wash DC 20016.

PHILLIPS, VIRGINIA. b Quantico Md4 N 22. 5: West Md Col 39-43 (Econ, Hist)BA; Emory 45-46 BALS; American U 56-59 (US Hist) MA; UMd 63- (Hist). 7: U M: Jr Asst libn 43-45, Asst ref libn 46-57, Soc sci libn 58-. 9: ALA; MdLA (Ref Serv Div: sec-treas 61-62, chm 62-63). 14: Ref, US & UN docs. 15: 7017 Fordham ct, College Park Md 20740.

PHILLIPS, VIVIAN (BRANCH). b Bishop Ga 16 My 15. 4: James W Phillips. 5: UGa 32-36 (Fr) BA; Emory 44-45 AB in LS; UGa 57-58 (Eng)MA. 6: Fr. 7: Tchr Bishop(Ga) Jr High Sch 43-44; Tchr High Sch, Butler Ga 37-43; Ref libn UGa Libs 45-53, Humanities libn 53-. 9: ALA; SELA; GaLA. 10: Phi Beta Kappa; Phi Kappa Phi; Beta Phi Mu. 14: Ref. 15: Bishop Ga 30621.

PHILLIPSON, JOSEPHINE LILLIAN CRUTCHFIELD). b Portland Ore 13 Ap 09. 4: Arnold L Phillipson. 5: UOre Ext 28-31 (Art); Portland State Col 62 (Sci Lit). 7: Clerical asst Lib Assn of Portland, Portland Ore 27-42; Oregon Shipbuilding, Portland Ore 43; Sylvia Holzman Advertising Agency, Portland Ore 54; Lib asst I UOre Med Sch Lib 58-65, Lib asst II 65-. 9: SLA (Portland Area). 15: 4935 SW 19th dr, Portland Ore 97201.

PHILPOTT, EMALEE ISOLA (EWING). b Charlotte NC 19 D21. 4: Earl Russel Philpott. 5: Col of William & Mary 38-42 (LS) AB; George Washington U 46-48 (Fr, Ger); UAriz summers 52-55 (Educ) MEd; UNC summer 68 (LS). 6: Sp. 7: Prof asst to libn Cocke Mem Lib, Hollins Col Va 42-43; Libn pub schs Corey Mem Lib, Oceana Va 42-43; Post libn Army Lib Serv, Camp Pendleton Va 44; Hosp libn Convalescent Hosp, Ft Story Va 44-45; Post libn Army Lib Serv, Camp Pickett Va 45; Prof ref libn gen ref & bibliog div LC 45-47; Catlgr Ind Col of Armed Forces Nat War Col, Ft Leslie J McNair Wash DC 47-48; Chief of libs Engnr Res & Development Labs, Ft Belvoir Va 48-50; Sec & tchr of Span, Hist, Govt & Soc Studies Duncan Union High Sch, Duncan Ariz 50-52; Libn & Eng tchr Pima pub schs, Pima Ariz 52-55; Libn Thatcher High Sch, Thatcher Ariz 55-. 8: Assoc in Educ, Dept of Lib Sci, Ariz State U summers 61 & 66, 67. 9: ALA;-AASchL; NEA; Ariz State LA (chm Recr Com 58-60; pres 63-64; Legis Com 68-69; Policy Chm 64-65); SLAA (chm Adv Com 69-70); NEA-DAVI (Legis Com); Thatcher Educ Assn. 10: AAUW; Beta Sigma Phi; Founder Stud Lib Assn of Ariz, 58; Marquis Biog Lib Soc. 12: Ed "Arizona Librarian (60-62); AStateLA "Policy Handbook (65). 14: Ya serv, ref, admin. 15: P O Box 233, Ducan Ariz 85534.

PHINAZEE, (ALETHIA) ANNETTE (LEWIS) (HOAGE). b Orangeburg SC 25 Jl 20. 4: Joseph Phinazee. 5: SC State Col 34-37 (Eng; Fisk U 37-39 (Modern Foreign Langs) BA; UIll 40-41, 47-48 BLS, MLS; Columbia U 53-54 DLS. 6: Fr, Sp. 7: Tchr libn Caswell Co Train Sch, Yanceyville NC 39-40; Catlgr Talladega Col 41-42; Journalism libn Lincoln U 42-44; Asst Prof Atlanta U 46-57; Asst catlgr SoIll U 57-62; Head spec serv Trevor Arnett Lib Atlanta U 62-67, Prof in Sch of Lib Serv 64-. 8: Prin investigator Feasibility Study of a centralized processing ctr for 6 cols in Ala & Miss; Ed proceedings; Inst on Materials By & About Amer Negroes 65; Conf on Ga child's access to Materials pertaining to Afro-Americans; Consul for Ford Found project to improve lib serv in Negro Cols 68-70. 9: ALA-RTSD (CCS: mem & chm Clsf Com 62-68 AALS; Atlanta Lib Club; SELA. 10: AAUP; AAUW; LWV. 13: Yes. 14: Catlg, spec materials, rare bks. 15: 4466 Bakers Ferry rd SW, Atlanta 30331.

PHINNEY, ELEANOR. b Hanover Mass 2 Mr 08. 5: Simmons 27-31 (LS) BS; Columbia 5-55 (LS) MS. 5: Simmons 27-31 (LS) BS; Columbia 53-55 (LS) MS. 7: Gen asst City Lib, Springfield Mass 26-27; Catlgr W Hartford Pub Lib, W Hartford Conn 31-40, Ref libn 40-43; Town Libn Hamden Conn 43-53; Libn grade II NY Pub Lib 53-54; Research spec Grad Lib Sch Rutgers U 54-55, Lecturer·55; Research Adult Educ ALA, Chicago 55-57; Exec Sec ALA-ASD and ALA-AHIL 58-; 57-68; Exec sec ALA-AHIL 58-. 8: Cosul in lib-community proj, ALA 55-57. 9: ALA; Adult Educ Assn; MedLA; ConnLA; New England LA. Assn. 10; nat Coun on the Aging; Amer Correctional Assn; Internat House Assn; Beta Phi Mu; Art Inst of Chicago; Old Dartmouth Hist Soc; Nantucket Hist Assn; Nor Wildlife Fed. 12: "Library Adult Education in Action (56V. 13: Yes. 14: Adult serv, pub lib serv, serv to the aging, hosp & inst lib serv, wkshop & inst planning. 15: 316 W Barry ave, Chicago Il 60657.

PHIPPEY, MARY C. b Manistique Mich 22 D 1900. 5: Colo State Col of Educ 19-23 (Romance Langs) AB; Lib Sch Los Angeles Pub Lib 26-27; UMex 44-45 (Hist of Mex, Archaeol). 6: Sp, Fr, Ital, Portu. 7: High sch tchr, Paonia & Greeley Colo 23-26; Catlgr for bks Los Angeles Pub Lib 23-43, Head Geneal Div 43; Catlgr & ref Biblioteca Benjamin Franklin, Mexico City 44-45; Lit & Philol ref Los Angeles Pub Lib 45-47; Libn Biblioteca Amer de Nicaragua Managua Nic, Dir 48-52; USIS libn, Barcelona, Johannesburg, Chile, Accra, & reg libn East Africa 53-63; Br libn Placer Co (Cal) Free Lib 63-68. 8: Catlg consul, under Ford Found & UMinn reorg plan, at U of Concepcion Chile, 66. 11: Meritorious Serv Award, USIA, 63. 14: Catlg, ref, consul. 15: Box 423, Kings Beach Cal 95719.

PHIPPS, BARBARA HELEN. b Hinsdale Ill 1 Jl 15. 5: Emmanuel Missionary Col 34-39 (Eng, Fr) BA; UMich 41-42 ABLS, summers 47-49 AMLS. 6: Fr. 7: Tchr-libn Indiana Acad, Cicero Ind 39-40; Tchr-libn Adelphian Acad, Holly Mich 42-43; Asst libn SDA Theol Sem (Takoma Park DC) 43-45; Asst libn Emmanuel Missionary Col (Mich) 45-58, Libn 59-61; Assoc libn Pacific Union Col 61-. 8: Act hd Sch Libnship Program Pacific Union Col. 9: ALA; CalLA. 14: Ref, tchg lib sci. 15: 415 Eastern ave, Anwin Cal94508.

PHOENIX, ANN (LOFTIN). b Columbia Tenn 19 F 26. 4: William David Phoenix. 5: David Lipscomb Col 44-48 (Eng) BA; UDenver 60-61 (LS) MA; Emory 64 (Med Libnship). 6: Fr. 7: Gen off Int Min & Chem Corp, Columbia Tenn 48-51; Salt Lake City pub Lib: Lib asst 51-55, Spencer Br libn 55-60, 61-62, Catlgr 62; Act med libn UUtah 62-66; Dental libn UMO (Kansas City) 66-. 8: Tchr of catlg & clsf, UUtah summer 63, spring 64, fall 65. 9: MedLA; SLA; ALA; UtahLA; MPLA; Amer Assn Dental Schs. 10: AAUP; Faculty Women's Club, UUtah; AAUW; Faculty Club; UUtah Lib Staff Assn; Utah Acad Sci, Arts, Letters. 14: Med libn ship, admin, catlg. 15: 8561 Holmes rd, Kansas City Mo 64131.

PHOENIX, DOROTHY G. b Chillicothe Mo 27 Je 16. 5: American U 45-46 (Soc Sci); Drake U 51-53 (Elem Educ) BS; UDenver 54-55 (LS) MA. 7: Pub sch tchr: Minneapolis 53-54, Kansas City Mo 55, Cherry Creek Dist Denver 56-57, Greeley Colo 57-58; High sch libn Pub Sch, Greeley Colo 58-60; Child libn Kan City(Mo) Pub Lib 60-61; Libn Rockhurst High Sch, Kan City Mo 61-65; Libn Pririe Village Elem Schs, Prairie Village Kan 65-; Tchr lib sci UMo (Kan City) 66-. 8: Taught Summer Sessions at Lib Sch UDenver 55-57, & Colorado State Col, Greeley Colo 60. 9: ALA; NEA; KanLA. ; ASCD; IRA. 15: 28 W Winthrope rd, Kansas City Mo 64113.

PHOENIX, WILLIAM DAVID. b Denver 9 Ja 30. 4: Ann Loftin Phoenix. 5: Regis Col (Denver) 49-53 (Eng) AB; UDenver 54-55 (LS) MA; UMo(Kansas City) 60-65 (Educ) PhD. 6: Lat, Gk, Russian; Fr. 7: Circ libn Colo State Col 56-60; UKan City(Mo): Acquis libn 60-61, Chief of tech serv 61-62, Adminasst to dir 61-63; Asst dir of libn UMo(Kan City) 63-65, Assoc dir of libs 65-; Assoc Prof Educ 65-. 8· Adv Joseph H Tedrow Memorial Lib; Mo prof libn life certif. 9: ALA-ACRL; -LAD; -RTSD; -LED; Assn Supv & Curr Devel; Nat Assn Study Educ; MoLA. 10: AAUP; Phi Delta Kappa; Shakespeare Assn of Amer. 12: "The Doctorate and the Univeristy Library Administrator (65). 13: Yes. 14: Admin, , tech serv. 15: 8561 Holmes rd apt 90, Kansas City Mo 64131.

PICCIANO, JACQUELINE L (CHAMBERS). b Los Angeles 19 Jl 28. 4: Eugene M Picciano. 5: Trinity Col (Wash DC) 46-50 (Chem, Pre-Med) BA; Catholic U 50-52 MS in LS; US Dept Agric Grad Sch 53 (Logic of Mechanized Info). 6: Ital, Fr, Ger. 7: Lab asst US Dept Agric, Beltsville Md48; Work fellow catlg dept Catholic U Lib 50; Ref libn Armed Forces Med Lib, Wash DC 50-55; Libn US VA NY Reg Off, NYC 55-56; Libn Hoffmann-LaRoche Inc, Nutley NJ 56-57; Libn Acad of Med of NJ Lib, Bloomfield 60-. 60. 8: Indexer, Biol Coord Ctr, NRC & Inst for Adv of Med Communication 50-. 9: MedLA; SLA (NJ Chap; Program chm 65-67; Bus mgr Unlisted Drugs 56-57, chm Educ Recruitment 67-69); ALA; NJLA (Asst chm Ref Div 68-69), mem NJ Lib Resources Com, Subcom on Med Lib Resources 68; Ad Hoc Com on Lib Serv Reg Med Program, NJ. 13: Yes. 14: Ref, admin. 15: 502 Essex ave, Bloomfield NJ 07003.

PICCIONI, CONSTANCE (LEHDE). b Boise Ida. 5: UWash 26-30 BS in LS, 30-32 (Sociol) BA. 7: Acquis asst UWash Lib 0-35; Acquis asst Ore State U 35-41; Libn US Army Lib Serv, Ft Lewis Wash 41-45; Ref libn Santa Barbára Pub Lib, Santa Barbara Cal 48-49; Libn US Army Lib Serv, Camp Cooke Cal 50; Catlgr Tacoma Pub Lib, Tacoma Wash 51-52; Catlgr King Co Pub Lib, Seattle 52-57; Acquis libn Mont State U Lib 57-67; Acquis libn Wash State Lib 67-. 9: PNLA; WashLA. 10: Mont Congress of Parents & Tchrs (Life mem); AAUP; Bus & Prof Women; Alpha Kappa Delta. 12: Co-auth "Book Repairing; New Ideas From the Mendery" (36); Co-auth "Checklist of Oregon State College Serial Publications" (38). 13: Yes. 15: 417 N Rogers, Olympia Wa 98501.

PICCOLO, VINCENT. b Somerville Mass 21 Mr 25. 4: Joan Lord. 5: Tufts Col 46-50 (Econ) AB; Simmons 50-51 MS in LS. 6: Ital. 7: Inst in Radio Repair US Army Air Forces 43-46; Head of ser unit Dept of State Lib, Wash DC 51-53; Sr catlgr Rutgers U Lib 53-56; Supv of catlg & processing Providence Pub Lib 57-64; Supv of tech processes & Instr in Lib Sci Worcester State Col 64-. 9: ALA; New Eng Tech Serv Libns (pres 69-70). 15: 100 Richmond ave, Worcester Mass 06102.

PICHETTE, BROTHER ANDRE WILLIAM. b Sturgeon Bay Wis 16 Je 37. 5: St Norbert Col 58-62 (Amer Hist) BA; UWis (Madison) 62-63 (LS) MA; UInd summer 64 (US Hist); UChicago summer 65 (US Hist); UIll summer 66 (LS). 6: Fr. 7: Instr US hist Premontre High Sch, Green Bay Wis 63-65, Guidance dir 65-67, Libn 67-. 9: ALA; CathLA; NCTE; WisLA. 10: Organiz Amer Histns. 13: Yes. 14: Sch libs. 15: 610 Maryhill dr, Green Bay Wi 54303.

PICHURKO, NICHOLAS GREGORY. b Hlyniany Ukraine 20 My 12. 4: Jaroslawa Martyniuk. 5: Univ J Kazimierz's 32-37 (Law) Master; West Res 64-66 (LS) Master. 6: Slavic langs, Ger, Latin, Gk. 7: Asst-libn Cleveland StateU 66-68, Catlg libn 69-. 8: Faculty adv Ukrainian Stud Club. 9: OhioLA; No Ohio Tech Serv Assn. 14: Catlg. 15: 3902 Sheraton dr, Parma Oh 44134.

PICKEL, HARRIET (LAUBACH). b Easton Penn 3 S 27. 4: Charles Francis Pickel. 5: Wilson Col 45-49 (Pol Sci) AB; Carnegie 51-52 MLS; UPittsburgh 54-58 (Fine Arts). 7: Lib asst ind rel sect Princeton U 49-51; Asst libn Tech Lib Westinghouse Electric Corp, E Pittsburgh Penn 52-53; Ref asst UPittsburgh Lib 53-56, Ref libn 56-59; Libn Reg Pub Lib, Levittown Penn 64-67; Libn Langhorne-Middletown Lib, Langhorne Penn 67-. 9: ALA-PLA. 10: AAUW. 14: Ref. 15: 29 Cable rd, Levittown Penn 19057.

PICKENPAUGH, TREVA A. b Canton Ohio 20 Je 44. 5: Ohio U 62-66 (Eng) AB; Case West res 66-67 MSLS. 6: Sp. 7: Child libn Dayton & Montgomery Co Pub Lib, Dayton Ohio 67-. 9: ALA; OhioLA. 10: Beta Phi Mu. 14: Child serv. 15: 127 S Third st, Miamisburg Oh 45342.

PICKENS, LYNNE ROBERSON. b Savannah Ga 17 S 44. 5: Lewis & Clark Col 62-66 (Eng) BA; Emory 66-67 (Libnship) MLn. 7: Child libn Boston Pub Lib 67-68; Child libn Atlanta Pub Lib 68-. 9: ALA; SELA; GaLA; Metro-AtlantaLA. 14: Child wk. 15: 45 Sheridan dr #19, Atlanta Ga 30305.

PICKENS, MYRA (DAVIS). b Cumberland Miss 19 Ag 10. 4: Theron L Pickens. 5: Wood Jr Col 30-32; Miss State Col for Women 34-35 (Elem Educ); Blue Mountain Col summers 37-40 (Elem Educ) AB; UMiss summers 56-60 (LS) MA. 7: Tchr: Clarkson Grammar Sch, Mathiston Miss 32-34, Springhill Sch, Grenada Miss 37-39, Egypt High Sch, Egypt Miss 39-40, Randolph High Sch, Randolph Miss 40-69; Eng tchr & libn 56-69. 9: MissEA; sponsor Randolph Sr Beta Club. 14: Ref. 15: Randolph Miss 38864.

PICKERING, JAMES H(ERMAN). b Cope SC 23 Jl 19. 4: Ann Ferguson. 5: Mars Hill Jr Col 37-39 AA; USCar 45-47 (Educ) AB Ed; Emory 47-48 ABLS; UNC 49-52 (Sociol). 7: Tchr-prin Bethera Elem Sch, Bethera SC 41-42; Tchr-prin S Willow Elem Sch, Norway SC 42-43; Surgical tech US Army Med Dept, ETO T/5 43-45; Asst libn Mars Hill Jr Col 48-49; Asst in Order Dept UNC Lib (Chapel Hill) 49-52; Interim dir Sumter Co Pub Lib, Sumter SC Dir Di Charlottesville-Albemarle Pub Lib, Charlottesville Va 53-58; Dir John McIntire Pub Lib, Zanesville 58-65; 48-65; Dir Warder Pub Lib, Springfield Ohio 65-. 9: ALA; OhioLA (Lib Devel Com, Awards & Honors Com); PLA (Standards Com). 10: Literary Club, Springfield. 14: Admin. 15: 1706 Wittenberg blvd E, Springfield Oh 45506.

PICKERING, JOANNA E. b Bluefield W Va 5 N 40. 4: C Chapin Pickering III. 5: URichmond 58-62 (Hist) BA; Syracuse 63-64 (LS) MA. 6: Fr. 7: Libn-trainee Buffalo & Erie Co Pub Lib, Buffalo NY 62-63, Jr libn 64-66, Sr libn I 66-; Asst ref libn SyracuseU Lib 63-64. 9: ALA; NYLA. 10: Libns Assn of Buffalo & Erie Co Pub Lib. 13: Yes. 14: Ref. 15: 63 Arlington pl, Buffalo NY 14201.

PICKETT, ASA STEPHEN. b Cincinnati 30 S 12. 5: UCal(Berkeley) 46-49 (Sociol) BA, 53-54 BLS, 54-58 (LS). 7: M/Sgt Personnel Sgt Major US Army 42-45; Various positions in bk, publ & printing 30-42, 49-53; Order libn San Francisco State Col 54-60, Admin asst 60-61; Col libn Sonoma State Col 61-. 9: ALA; CalLA; Assn Cal State Col Profs. 10: AAUP; Cal State Employees Assn; ACLU. 13: Yes. 14: Acquis, gift & exch. 15: Sonoma State Col Lib, Rohnert Park Cal 94928.

PICKETT, BEATRICE MARION. b Toronto Ont Can 15 My 25. 5: McMaster U 43-47 (Fr, Eng) BA; UToronto 48 BLS. 6: Fr. 7: Catlgr McMaster U 48-. 9: CanLA; Can Assn Col & Univ Libns; Can Library Trustees Assn; OntLA; Inst Profess Libns Ont. 10: Stoney Creek Pub Lib Bd. 14: Catlg. 15: 11 Jones st, Stoney Creek Ont Can.

PICKETT, ESTHER LORENA (HODSON). b Newberg Ore 4 S 07. 4: John Herschel Pickett. 5: Earlham Col (Hist, Eng) BA; UOre 45-49 (Educ) MEd; UDenver 52-55 MALS; UPacific 57 (Philos); UUtah 59-60 (Soc Hist), corres 65-67 (Educ, Phil, Art). 6: Fr, Sp, Lat. 7: Eng-math tchr Kerby Union High Sch, Kerby Ore 44-49; Tchr-libn Kiona-Benton High Sch, Benton City Wash 49-53; Eng-Sp tch-libn St Maries High Sch, St Maries Ida 53-56; Libn Mineral Co High Sch, Hawthorne Nev 56-59; Libn Antelope Union High Sch, Wellton Ariz 59-64; Libn Juneau High Scj, Juneau Alaska 64-65; Libn Sanford Naval Acad, Sanford Fla 65-66; Libn II City Lib, Sacramento Cal summers 58, 59; Asst catlgr City Lib, San Mateo Cal summer 61; City Lib, Glendora summer 62; Asst catlgr Lamson Lib, Plymouth State Col summers 65, 66; Tchr Eng math Tularosa Jr-Sr High Sch, Tularosa NM 66-67; Tchr-libn North River High Sch, Brooklyn, Wash 67-68; Libn Lagumd-Acoma Jr-Sr High Sch, Laguna NM 68-. 9: ALA; CalLA; NEA; CalEA; state Creative Writing (sec NMex 66-67); Chm Lib Recruitment (Nev 56-58; Ariz 59-64). 14: Ref. 15: 25914 Ritter st, PO Box 117, Homeland Cal 92348.

PICKETT, MARY JOYCE (BAKER). b Ottumwa Iowa 18 Jl 40. 4: Leroy Kenneth Pickett. 5: Simpson Col 58-62 (Philos, Religion) BA; UIll 62-63 MSLS. 7: Asst ref libn Jackson Co Pub Lib, Independence Mo 63-65; Jr asst Purdue U Libs 65-67; Asst ref libn 67-68; Catlgr E Lansing Pub Lib, E Lansing Mich 69-. 9: ALA. 10: Beta Phi Mu. 14: Ref. , catlg. 15: 656 Beach st, E Lansing Mi 48823.

PICKETT, MARY LOUISE (LAMBERT). b New Orleans 1 S 19. 4: Merrill C Pickett. 5: Dillard U 34-38 (Eng) BA; Valena C Jones Normal (New Orleans) 38-39 (Educ); USoCal 41-42 BLS; Chicago summer 44 (LS); UWis(Milwaukee) 51 (Eng). 6: Sp. 7: Ref asst libn Dillard U 42-43; Army libn Camp Van Dorn Miss, Centerville Miss 43-44; Child libn Chicago Pub Lib 45-46; Milwaukee Pub Lib: Asst br libn 46-48, Br libn 48-58, Child libn 58-61, Ya libn 61-. 66, Br libn 66-. 8: Child libn, Lib/USA, NY Worlds Fair 65. 9: ALA (2 ya coms); Internat Rel RT; WisLA (Child & YA Div). 10: Internat Inst of Milwaukee Co; NAACP; Urban League; Delta Sigma Theta; People-To-People Program. 14: Ref, readers adv serv, ya wk. 15: 3870 N 77th st, Milwaukee Wis 53222.

PICKRON, JOHN EDWARD. b Blakely Ga 7 F 42. 4: Judith Antonina Anselmo. 5: Birmingham-So Col 60-62; Tulane 62-64 (Hist) BA; LSU 65-67 (LS) MS. 6: Ger. 7: Lib asst Loyola U (New Orleans) 65; Lib trainee LSU Lib (Baton Rouge) 65-67; Admin asst dept of resources & acquis Harvard Col Lib 67-68, Act hd ser recs 68; Asst Prof of educ Livingston U 69-. 9: ALA. 10: Beta Phi Mu. 14: Catlg, admin, ref. 15: PO Box 261, Livingston Al 35470.

PIEDRACUEVA, MISS HAYDEE NOEMI. b Cordoba Argentina. 5: UCordoba (Argentine) 49-54 Tchg certif; Columbia 63-65 (LS) MS. 6: Sp, Portu, Fr, Ital. 07L Tchr Escuela de Profesores "A Carbo, Cordoba Argentina 56-62; Prof intern Columbia U Libs 65-. 7: Tchr Escuela de Profesores; A Carbo, Cordoba Argentina 56-62; Prof intern Columbia U Libs 65-; Catlgr 66, Lat Amer bibliogr 68-. 9: ALA; LASA; ASIS. 14: Catlg, acquis. 15: 423 W 120 st, NYC 10027.

PIEKARSKI, HALA. b Warsaw Poland 5 Mr 22. 4: Konstant Piekarski. 5: Warsaw U 38-39; UWaterloo (Ont) 62-64 (Hist) BA; Toronto 64-65 BLS. 6: Eng, Polish, Ger, Fr, Russian, Sp, Lat. 7: Sec engnr firm, Warsaw 40-45; Sec Pharmaceutical Export, London 47-50; Lib asst Oshawa Pub Lib, Oshawa Ont 52-54; Lib asst N York Pub Lib, Toronto 54-57; Head clerk acquis Waterloo U(Ont) 57-62; Catlgr Waterloo Lutheran U(Ont) 65-66; Bibliogr Heffer Bksllr, Cambridge Eng 66-67; Ed Union Catlg UCambridge, Eng 67-68; Hd bibliog dept UGuelph (Ont) 68-. 9: ALA; CanLA; Inst Prof Libns Ont. 12: "Catalog Number 809 & 827 (67). 14: Acquis, research out-of-print bks, rare bks. 15: Lakeside dr, Kitchener Ont Can.

PIER, PATRICIA (BRADDELL). b Winnipeg Man Can 24 Ap 42. 4: Foroyce C Pier. 5: QueensU (Kingston Ont) 60-63 (Pstch, Fr) BA; McGill 63-64 BLS. 6: Fr. 7: Circ order libn Sch of Educ, Boston U 64-66; Educ libn Mugar Lib 66-68; Ref libn Rotch Lib Arch & Planning MIT 68-. 10: Boston Philharmonia. 14: Ref. 15: 20 Anselm ter, Boston Ma 02135.

PIERCE, ANNA EDITH. b Bridgewater NY 10 Ag 10. 5: State U Col(Potsdam NY) 28-31; State U Col(Geneseo NY) 40-41 (LS) BS in Ed. 7: Libn & music tchr Groveland High Sch, Groveland Fla 42; US Mil Acad Lib (W Point): Lib asst 42-55, Sr catlg asst 55-58, Sr catlgr 59-63; Hd catlgr 64-; Act hd tech serv div 67-68. 9: ALA; NY Tech Serv Libns. 10: Friends of the Lib, Higland Falls Pub Lib; Constitution Island Assn. 11: Outstanding Performance Certif 69. 14: Catlg, rare bks, microforms. 15: PO Box 167, Highland Falls NY 10928.

PIERCE, BENJAMIN T(HOMPSON). b NYC 9 O 16. 4: Josephine Wells Browning. 5: Yale 35-39 (Fr) BA; Columbia 40-41 BS in LS. 6: Fr. 7: NY Pub Lib; Asst 67th st br 41-42, Stack supv ref dept 46-47, Ref asst info div ref dept 47-52; UNESCO, Paris; Documentalist 52-54, Ref libn 54-55, Chief documentation div educ dept 55-68, Chief catlg serv UNESCO Lib 68-69, Chief UNESCO Documentation Serv 69-. 8: Estab a nat-educ documentation centre in the Ministry of EDUC OF Iran, 59; Head, Unesco Reg Centre for Educ Info & Studies in Asia, Bangkok, 61-62; Trustee, Amer Lib in Paris 66-(nominated by ALA, which nominates part of Bd). 12: Ed "Education Abstracts Unesco (55-64). 13: Yes. 14: Educ libs. 15: Unesco, Place de Fontenoy, Paris 7e France.

PIERCE, ELIZABETH (GIESELER). b Alexandria Minn 14 S 11. 4: Norman A Pierce. 5: UWis 28-32 (Eng) BA, 31-32 (LS) Dploma; UMd summer 65, 68. 7: Ref libn ND State Lib Comm, Bismarck ND 32-35; Catlgr LC 35-48; Libn Bladensburg Sr High Sch, Bladensburg Md 63-68; Libn Parkdale Sr High Sch, Riverdale Md 68-. 8: Catlgr Columbia U Lib (on exch from LC) 45-46. 9: NEA; MdLA; Md State Tchrs Assn. 10: LWV; PTA. 14: Catlg, ref. 15: 5808 Carlyle st, Cheverly Md 20785.

PIERCE, MARY G. b Wenatchee Wash 28 My 29. 5: Wenatchee Jr Col 47-50, West Wash State Col 52-54 (Art) BA in Ed; UWash summers 60-64 (LS) MA; Ore State U summer 66. 7: Auburn Sch Dist, Auburn Wash: Elemtchr 54-59, Elem tchr 59-60, Elem sch libn 60-62; Jr high sch libn Puyullup Sch Dist, Puyallup Wash 62-. 9: NEA; ALA; WashEA Wash-Davi; WashStateASchL; WashStateLA. 10: Delta Kappa Gamma. 12: Ed "Library Leads, Wash State LA (67-69). 14: Child & yp serv. 15: 1018 Milwaukee ave 139, Puyallup Wa 98371.

PIERCE, MARY SYLVIA (CLARK) (MRS). b Yarmouth NS Can 26 Jl 13. 5: Acadia U 31-35 (Eng) BA; Toronto 36 BLS. 7: Jr libn ser dept Stanford U 39-41, Law Libn 41-44; Sec NoCal Baptist Convention, Oakland Cal 50-53; Ref libn U of Redlands 53-. 9: ALA; CalLA. 10: AAUW; AAUP. 14: Ref. 15: 426 W Olive ave, Redlands Ca 92373.

PIERCE, MIRIAM (DICKEY). b Berlin Penn 13 S 28. 4: William S Pierce. 5: Juniata Col 45-49 (Lat) BA; West Res summers 52-55 MS in LS. 7: Lat & Eng tchr Hollidysburg Penn 49-52; Asst libn Juniata Col 52-56; Army libn US Army, Europe, Germany 56-58; Penn State U: Ref asst 58-61, Asst engnr libn '62-64, Act engnr libn 64-65, Asst engnr libn 65, Act mineral ind libn 65-66; Act agric & biol sci libn 66; Coord academic unit working collections 67-. 8: Bibliog consul Center for Research Col of Bus Admin Penn State U 61-. 9: ALA; PennLA. 10: Beta Phi Mu; State Col Choral Soc. 12: "Bibliography of Studies on the Economic Development of Pennsylvania and Its Regions (62). 14: Ref. 15: 437 E Fairmount ave, State College Penn 16801.

PIERCE, WILLIAM SUTHERLAND. b Pittsburgh Penn 23 Jl 30. 4: Miriam Dickey. 5: WVa Wesleyan Col 48-52 (Eng, Hist, Pol Sci) AB; Carnegie 52-54 MLS. 7: Libn NY Pub Lib 54-56; Libn Commonwealth Campuses & Continuing Educ Penn State U 56-66; Asst dir of libs Commonwealth Campuses & continuing educ 66-. 8: Bldg consul. 9: ALA; PennLA (treas 64-67, chm 2 coms 62-63). 10: AAUP. 13: Yes. 14: Admin. , bldgs. 15: 437 E Fairmount ave, State College Penn.

PIERCE, NELLIE LYDIA (WHITE). b Claremont NH 19 N 1895. 4: Howard Richards Pierce. 5: UNH 12-16 (Eng) AB; Simmons 31-32 (LS) BS. 6: Fr, Ger, Ital. 7: Libn Enfield Pub Lib, Enfield NH 32-; Town histn 40-; Dartmouth Col: Catlgr map libn 32-42, Libn Tuck Grad Sch of Bus Admin 42-61, Catlgr Thayer Sch of Engnr 61-62; Libn Mascoma Valley Reg High Sch, W Canaan NH 63-64; Asst libn Canaan Col, NH 67-. 8: Chm Enfield BicentennialCelebration, 61. 9: NHLA (past pres); ALA; SLA; NELA; NH Federation of Womens Clubs. 10: NH Covered Bridge Assn; Enfield Town Budget Com; Town Planning Bd; Treas Trustees of Trust Funds; Former Dir Lebanon Col; Alpha Xi Delta; NE Hist & Geneal Soc; NH Hist Soc. 12: "100 Years for God and Man, hist of the Enfield Commun Church (52). 14: Catlg, loc hist, costume, arts & crafts. 15: Main st, Enfield NH 03748.

PIERRE-PIERRE, DENYSE (ETIENNE). b Port-Au-Prince Haiti 17 Ja 28. 4: Auguste Pierre-Pierre. 5: Ecole Normale Superieure in Port-au-Prince UHairi 45 Diploma. 6: Fr. 7: Fr composition & lit tchr, Port au Prince Haiti 48-60; Sec Haitiano-Amer geodetic Survey, Haiti 60-62; Rare bks restorer Harper Lib spec collections UChicago 63-. 9: ALA; Amer Inst Graphic Arts. 10: Women's Club League of Soc Action, Port au Prince (Haiti). 14: Rare bks. 15: 5454 Everett apt 4E, Chicago Il 60615.

PIERRON, IONE PATRICIA (FEEK). b Seattle 29 Je 15. 5: Col Puget Sound 32-36 (Fr) BA; UWash 36-37 (LS) BA; UOre 58-60 (Secondary Educ) MS; Ore State U 63-64 (Educ). 6: Fr. 7: Libn Seattle Pub Schs 37-41; Libn US Engnr Dept, Seattle 41-42; Circ libn Portland Pub Lib, Portland Ore 45-46; Catlgr & law libn Bonneville Power Assn, Portland Ore 46-48; UOre libn 49-60, Faculty Sch of Libnship 60-, Libn Center for Advanced Study of Educ Admin 64-67. 9: ALA (SBB Com 62-63); PNLA; OreLA. 10: LWV; Bus & Prof Womens Club; Pi Lambda Theta. 14: Tchg, spec libnship. 15: 1360 Ferry, Eugene Or 97401.

PIERSON, ROBERT MALCOLM. b Greencastle Ind 1 Ja 27. 4: Dolores Lehmann. 5: DePauw U 42-46 (Eng) BA; Duke 46-49, 51 (Eng) MA, PhD; Catholic U 53-55 MS in LS. 6: Fr. 7: Instr in Eng Ohio State U 49-52; UMd: Instr in Eng 52-55, Asst loan libn 55-56, Catlgr 56-57, Head humanities room Lib 57-66; Lecturer in educ 61-64; Lecturer in Lib Sci USDA Grad Sch, Wash DC 63-66; Assoc Prof Lib Sci Catholic U 66-68; Asst dir for admin UMd (College Park) 66-. 9: ALA-RSD (chm Md Chap 63-64); -RTSD; Potomas Tech Proc Libns (sec 64-65). 10: Mod Lang Assn; Beta Phi Mu. 12: Assoc ed "Sevententh Century News (57-58). 13: Yes. 14: Ref, catlg, lib bldgs, bibliog (humanities), tchg. , admin, Eng prosody. 15: 6209 Balfour dr, W Hyattsville Md 20782.

PIERSON, ROSCOE MITCHELL. b Crenshaw Miss 21 S 21. 4: Dorothy McCowan. 5: Centre Col 47 (Zool) AB; UKy 47-50 (Zool, LS) MA; Lexington Theol Sem 50-53 Theo). 6: Fr, Ger, Sp, Classical Gk, Hebrew. 7: (T/Sgt) Army Air Force Gunner B-17, ETO 41-45; Asst libn Lexington Pub Lib, Lexinton Pub Lib, Lexington Ky 49-50; Libn Lexington Theol Sem 50-. 8: Libn Union Theol Sem, io Piedras PR, during sabbatical yr, 58-59; Ordained minister of the Disciples of Christ; United Theol Col, Jamaica West Indies 67. 9: ATheoLA (pres-elect 65, chm var coms); KyLA (pres 63-64). 10: Phi Beta Kappa; Omicron Delta Kappa. 11: Outstanding Special Libn (Ky) 64. 12: "A Preliminary Check List of Lexington, Ky. Imprints, 1821-1850 (53); "Disciples of Christ in Kentucky, A Finding List . . . (62); "West Indian Church History, A Finding List (68). 13: Yes. 14: Catlg, acquis. 15: 624 Seattle dr, Lexington Ky 40503.

PIETTE, ONESIME L. b Woonsocket RI 8 Ap 16. 4: Margaret Martin. 5: UDenver 46-49 9soc Sci) BA; UPenn 49-51 (So Asia Reg Studies) MA; Syracuse 66-67 MSLS. 7: Meteorologist USAF, US, India 41-45; Research analyst Harvard U 51-52; Research analyst Dept of State, Wash DC 52-56; Second sec Amer For Serv, Amer Embassy, New Delhi India 56-58; Consul Amer For Serv, Amer Consulate Gen, Bombay India 58-61; Research specialist Amer For Serv Dept of State, Wash DC 61-66; Asian bibliogr Syracuse U Lib 67-. 10: Phi Beta Kappa; Beta Phi Mu; Amer Foreign Serv Assn. 14: Acquis. 15: 320 Greenwood place, Syracuse NY 13210.

PIETY, JOHN SCOTT. b Lampassas Tex 7 S 38. 4: Mary Ann Bollen. 5: UAriz 56-60 (Anthrop, Hist) BA; San Diego State Col 64-66 (LS); UOkla 67-68 MLS. 6: Sp, Fr, Portu. 7: Stud asst UAriz Lib 57-60; Asst to post histn US Army, Ft Lee Va 60-63; Ser specialist Gen Atomic Lib, San Diego 63-67; Lib fellow UOkla Lib 67-68; Acquis libn UWis Lib (Green Bay) 68-. 8: Lib specialist Off of Pres UOkla 68. 9: ALA; OklaLA; WisLA. 10: Beta Phi Mu. 14: Acquis, lib automation. 15: Rte 1 4260 Nicolet rd, Green Bay Wi 54301.

PIGAN, ELEANOR (FACE). b E Nassau NY 28 My 28. 4: Edward Andrew Pigan. 5: SUNY 46-50 (Eng) BA, summers 50-56 MS in LS. 7: Libn, tchr New Lebanon Central Sch, Lebanon springs NY 50-56; Volunteer libn No Amer Martyrs Sch, Monroeville Penn 66-. 8: Organized East Nassau (NY) Central Sch Lib 54; St Colman's Sch, Turtle Creek Penn 61; St Michael's Sch; Pitcairn Penn 66. 9: ALA; CathLA; PennLA. 10: AAUW; Cath Daughters Amer; PTA. 14: Sch libs. 15: 1193 Bucknell dr, Monroeville Pa 15146.

PIGGFORD, ROLAND JR. b Monongahela Penn 28 Ja 26. 4: Carole Meanor. 5: WVa Wesleyan Col 42-43, 46-48 (Eng) BA; Duke 43-44; UPittsburgh 63-64 MLS; Renss Polytech Inst (68). 6: Fr. 7: Libn Internat Lib Info Ctr UPittsburgh 65-66; Dir Internat Studies Doc Ctr SUNY (Oyster Bay) 66-67; Asst Prof Sch of Lib Sci SUNY (Albany) 67-. 8: Exec sec, First Inst on Internat Compar Libnship, 65; Campus coord AID/CENTO/SUNY Bk development survey (66); Project dir AID SUNY Bk development Guidlines Manual Project 68-69. 9: ALA-LED (Com on Equivalencies & Reciprocity 65-70. 10: Beta Phi Mu. 13: Yes. 14: Compar libnshp. 15: School of Lib Sci State Univ of NY at Albany 1400 Washington ave, Albany NY 12203.

PIGNATELLO, LEONARD JOHN. b Minneapolis 19 My 19. 4: Eugenia Stifter. 5: UMinn 41-43 AA, 46-48 (Pol Sci) BA, 46-48 BSLS; Col of St Catherine 57-60 (LS) MA. 7: (Sgt) US Army Air Forces 43-46; Prof asst Pub Lib, Minneapolis 48-52, Br libn 53-. 8: Libn Minneapolis Central Labor Union Coun. 9: MinnLA (chm Pub Libs Sect 68, 69). 10: Amer Fed of State, Co, & Munic Employees, (Off 52-, Del nat conv 7 yrs 52-68). 14: Ext, ref, ya ser. 15: 3201 Benjamin st NE, Minneapolis 55418.

PIGOTT, FRANCES (MOAK). b Covington La 31 Mr 17. 4: Charles Edgar Pigott. 5: Southeastern La Col 31-35; -35 (Eng,

Hist) Diploma; LSU 36,37 BA (Eng), BS in LS; Columbia 45 (LS) MS. 6: Fr. 7: High sch libn La High Schs 37-45; Asst libn Loyola U(New Orleans) 45-47; Instr LSU Med Sch(New Orleans) 47-50; Chief Libn Charity Hosp Sch of Nursing, New Orleans 47-50; Head Libn Livingston State Col 50-53; Libn Dept of Nursing UMiss 53-57; Asst libn LSU (Baton Rouge) 57-. 8: Coun on Careers in Nursing Miss State 53-56; Spec assignment for Nurse recruitment, World Health Organization 63. 9: ALA; SLA; (pres La Chap 68-69); LaLA; Baton Rouge Lib Club. 10: AAUW; Twentieth Century Club. 12: "High School Library Participation in the Visual Aids Program in Louisiana 1941-1942" (45). 13: Yes. 14: Ser, ref, catlg, sch lib serv. 15: 1564 Avondale dr, Baton Rouge La 70808.

PIKE, EUGENE LOREN. b Pueblo Colo 13 Ja 19. 4: Miriam T Pike. 5: UCLA 41, 46-48 (Philos, Pol Sc) BA; UCal(Berkeley) 49-50 BLS. 6: Fr, Ger. 7: (Cpl) Mil Police 84th Inf Div, US & ETO 42-46; Jr libn ref sect Cal State Lib 50-52, Asst ref libn 53-60, Supv ref libn 60-. 9: CalLA. 14: Ref, rare bks. 15: Cal State Lib, Sacramento Cal 95814.

PIKE, MARY MILLER. b Kittery Pt Me 25 O 06. 5: Bates 25-29 (Eng) AB (magna cum laude); Simmons 35-36 (LS) BS. 7: Eng tchr high sch, Rockland Me 29-33; Libn: high sch, Marblehead Mass 36-38, high sch, Williamantic Conn 38-45, Jr high sch, Providence RI 45-49; Supv wk with yp McArthur Pub Lib, Biddeford Me 49-50; Libn Westbrook Jr Col, Portland Me 50-54; Catlgr pub lib, Dover NH 54-62; Libn Spaulding High Sch, Rochester NH 62-63; Libn Wonnacunnet High Sch, Hampton NH 63-. 8: Standards Com for NH 66-67; Title II Com for NH 67-. 9: NEA; ALA-AASch; NESchLA (var offices, archivist, etc); NELA; NHLA; NHEA; MeLA; MassLA. 10: Phi Beta Kappa; Delta Phi Alpha; Kittery Hist Soc; Piscataqua Hist Club. 12: Co-auth "NESLA; a Fifty Year History" (68); Ed ConnSchLA "News Letter" (35-49). 13: Yes. 14: Sch libs. 15: Cutts Island, Kittery Point Me 03905.

PIKE, MIRIAM T. b Mt Union Iowa 14 Ag 18. 4: Eugene L Pike. 5: Iowa Wesleyan Col 35-37, 38-39 (Eng); UIowa summer 52 (Educ); UDenver 46-47 (LS) BA. 7: Tchr Pleasant Lawn Cons Sch, Mt Pleasant Iowa 37-38; Tchr Sperry Cons Sch, Sperry Iowa 39-42; Office wk Time Inc, Chicago summer 42; Tchr Albia Cons Sch, Albia Iowa 42-44; WAVES US Navy Fleet PO, NYC & San Francisco 44-46; Ref libn Kan City (Mo) Pub Lib 47-51; Libn Alamogordo High Sch, Alamogordo NM 51-56; Readers Adv & circ libn Phoenix Pub Lib 56-57; Research libn Cal Sect Cal State Lib 57-. 8: Publ, Colo Lib Assn, org State Student Lib Assts in NM. 9: ALA; NEA; MoLA; NMEA; CalLA. 10: Sacramento Bk Collectors Club; Alamogordo Jr Womens Club. 12: Ed "New Arrivals in Californiana" (Quarterly list). 13: Yes. 14: Ref, research. 15: 1400 N st apt 2, Sacramento Ca 95814.

PIKUL, THOMAS. b Warwick NY 27 F 34. 5: OhioU (Athens) 56-58 (Comp Speech) BFA; Columbia 58-59 (Speech Educ) MA; Rutgers (LS); New Paltz State U (LS); Certif in NY State in Speech & Lib. 7: Asst program dir USA, Japan 54-56; Eng tchr Goshen (NY) High Sch 60-62; Libn: Tappan Zee High Sch, Orangeburg NY 62-63, Clarkstown High Sch, new City Crock Co NY 63-66, Briarcliff High Sch, Briarcliff Manor NY 66-. 9: NYStateTA; WestchesterCoTA. 14: Bk sel, a-v, admin. 15: Castle Beacon Hill dr, Dobbs Ferry NY 10522.

PILE, ESTHER B (FOWLER). b Westerly RI 11 S 20. 4: Wilson H Pile. 5: Vassar 38-42 (Eng) AB; Radcliffe 55-56 (Amer Hist); Simmons 60-67 (LS) MS. 6: Fr. 7: Lib asst Vassar Col 42-43; Libn Milton High Sch, Milton Mass 58-. 9: ALA; -AASchL; MassSchLA (YA RT). 10: LWV. 14: Sch libs, ya serv. 15: Milton High Sch Lib, Central Ave, Milton Ma 02186.

PILLEY, CATHERINE M(OORE). b Nashville Tenn 7 Mr 14. 4: John A Pilley. 5: Vanderbilt 32-36 (Hist) BA; Villanova 64-66 MSLS. 7: Sec to v-pres & gen coun Fed Reserve Bank, NY 42-46; Lecturer lib sci Villanova U 66-67; Ed "The Catholic Periodical & Literature index" Catholic Lib Assoc, Haverford Penn 66-. 9: ALA; CathLA (Adv Coun); PennLA (chm Conf Eval Com; mem Recr Com); Lib Pub Rel Assn Greater Phila. 10: Gamma Phi Beta; DAR; Woman's Club. 12: "The Guide to Catholic Literature" (66); "The Catholic Periodical & Literature Index" (67-68). 13: Yes. 14: Catlg, ref. 15: 3 E Wilmot ave, Havertown Pa 19083.

PILLGRENE, MICHAEL JOSEPH JR. b Phila 15 Ag 36. 5: UDel 54-58 (Amer Studies) BA; Drexel 58-59 MSLS. 6: Fr. 7: Lib asst Wilmington Inst Free Lib, Wilmington Del 59-61, Head Bus & Tech Dept 61-66; Lib dir Chesterfield Co Lib, Chester Va 66-68; Dir J Lewis Crozer Lib, Chester Pa 68-. 9: SLA; DelLA (treas 62-65, chm Memb Com 61-62); PLA; ALA; VaLA. 10: Beta Phi Mu. 14: Ref, lib admin, adult serv. 15: 508 Tyrone ave, Woodcrest, Wilmington Del 19804.

PILLON, NANCY BACH. b Jackson Ky 28 Jl 17. 5: Lees Jr Col 34-36; West Ky State Col 38-39 (Eng) BA; UIll summer 41 (LS); UKy summers 56-59, 64, 65 MS in LS, 65-. (Ed)67 Ed D. 6: Fr. 7: US Navy Off (Lt) US Nav, Miami, Wash DC & Detroit 42-51; Libn Edgewood High Sch, Edgewood Md 56-57; Libn Breathitt Co High Sch 39-42, 52-56, 57-60; Instr No Ill U 60-65; Asst Prof UKy 65-. 8: Dir Ky Sch Libns Wkshop 68, 69; Dir Fed Inst for Sch Libns under Title II B Higher Educ Act 60. 9: ALA; KyLA. 10: AR; AAUP. 14: Child lit, sch lib wk. 15: Wellington Arms apt 206, Main st, Lexington Ky 40507.

PILLSBURY, STANLEY (ROLFE). b Concord NH 21 Ja 06. 5: Brown 31-32 (Romance Langs) AB; Simmons 49-50 MS. 6: Fr, Sp. 7: Desk asst NY Pub Lib, New York 27-29; Stud asst Brown U Lib 29-31, Circ desk asst 31-32; Exhibitions asst NY Pub Lib, New York 32-42; M/Sgt (Clerical) US Army Air Forces, China 42-47; Air base manager Chinese Nat Relief & Rehabilitation Assn, China 47; Atlas catlgr LC 50-. 13: Yes. 14: Rare bks, ref, catlg. 15: 348 Webster st, Needham Heights Mass 02194.

PILTON, JAMES (WILLIAM). b Hamilton Ont Can. 5: McMaster U(Ont) 46-48 (Hist); UBC 48-51 (Hist) BA, MA; UParis 51-52 (Fr Lang); Toronto 52-53 BLS. 6: Fr. 7: Royal Can AF Radar Mech LAC 42-46; Gen libn Dept of External Affairs, Ottawa Ont 53-54; Dept libn Dept of Citizenship & Immigration, Ottawa 54-59; Assoc dir Edmonton Pub Lib, Edmonton Alta 59-. 9: CanLA (Coun); CanMusicLA (v-chm); AltaLA; EdmontonLA. 11: French Government Scholarship, 51. 13: Yes. 14: Admin. 15: Edmonton Pub Lib, Edmonton Alta Can.

PIMSLEUR, MEIRA (GOLDWATER). b NYC. 4: Solomon Pimsleur. 5: Hunter Col 39-46 (Pol Sci) BA; Columbia 46-48 (LS). 6: Sp, Fr, Ger. 7: Catlgr Columbia U 42-47; Acquis libn Law Lib Columbia U 47-. 8: Indexing law books for authors & publishers. 9: AALL (chm For Law Com); Law Lib Assn Greater NY (pres 56-57); Law Lib Assn Upstate NY (Bd Dirs 65); AALL (rep Amer Standards Com Z39, 67-69). 10: Phi Beta Kappa. 12: "Law Books in Print, with J M Jacobstein (Consolid ed (65, 66, 67, 68); "Checklist of Basic American Legal Publications, loose leaf with sups (62)-64. 13: Yes. 14: Acquis, catlg, indexing,bibliog (law). 15: Columbia Univ Law Lib 435 W 116 st, New York NY 10027.

PINCHES, MARY FRANÇES. b Tarenum Penn 8 F 04. 5: Flora Stone Mather, West Res 23-27 (Chem) AB; West Res 29-30 BS in LS, 56-58 MS in LS. 7: Cleveland Pub Lib: Sub-prof asst tech div 27-30, Asst libn sch dept high schs 30-34, Libn sch dept jr high sch 34-39, Asst libn tech div 39-43; Libn Ferro Enamel Corp, Cleveland 43-47; Libn Case Inst of Tech 47-68; Assoc Prof & Libn Scars Lib Case-West Res U 68-. 8:Tchr, Instr & chem engnr lit, Case Inst of Technol 49-59. 9: ALA-ACRL (sec Subj Spec Sect 64-67; Exec Bd Tri-State Chap 62-64); Aslib; ADI; ACS (chm Pub Rel Com Cleveland Sect 51-52); Amer Soc Engnr Educ; Soc of Chem Ind; OhioLA (Exec Bd 57-58); Ohio Col Assn (Col Lib Sect: v-pres & Program Chm 54-55, pres 55-56, sec-treas 65-66). 10: Soroptimist Club of Cleveland. 11: Case Achievement Award, 64. 14: Admin, chem lit, ref, catlg. 15: 19581 Argyle oval, Rocky River Oh 44116.

PINCOE, GRACE (LILLIAN) (COCHRANE). b Toronto 22 Je 06. 4: Roland Pincoe. 5: Ont Lib Sch 26; Toronto 30 BA. 6: Fr. 7: Gen asst Toronto Pub Lib 27-37, Ref asst 40-41; Libn Art Galley of Toronto 41-46; Head catlg dept Etobicoke Pub Lib, Toronto 56-60, Head tech serv 60-67; Catlgr Secondary Sch Lib Processing Ctr Toronto Bd of Educ 67-. 9: ALA; CanLA; MusLA; CanMusLA (v-pres 66-67); SLA; OntLA (sec-treas, Ref Sect). 12: Jt comp "Musical Canadiana (67). 13: Yes. 14: Calg, ref, art, music. 15: 12 Boustead ave, Toronto 3 Can.

PINCOFFS, MAURICE C(HARLES) JR. b Baltimore Md 18 D 19. 5: Harvard 38-42 (Modern European Hist) AB; UVa 46-48 (Law) LLB. 6: Fr, Ger. 7: Field observer JHU Applied Physics Lab, Silver Springs Md 42-43; Navigator trainee Northeast Airlines Inc, Boston 43; Pfc Celestial Navigation trainer operator US Army Air Corps 43-46; Traveling judicial examiner USF&G Co, Baltimore 49-51; Night ref libn, page Lib Co of Baltimore Bar, Baltimore 58-65; Self employed attorney, Baltimore 52-; Asst law libn UBaltimore 67-. 9: AALL; Law Libns Soc Wash DC. 14: Law libnship, catlg, ref. 15: Rm 302 11 E Lexington st, Baltimore Md 21202.

PINCOTT, GEOFFREY (HUME). b Grand Forks BC 27 Ap 37. 4: Barbara Dower. 5: UBC 55-60 (Eng, Hist) BA, 61-62 BLS. 7: Ref libn Vancouver Pub Lib, Vancouver BC 62-65;

Catlgr 66; Deputy hd catlgr 67-. 8: Lib consul, Macmillan Bloedel & Powell River Co, Vancouver BC 64. 9: CanLA; BCLA. 12: Ed, BCLA "Reporter (63-65). 13: Yes. 14: Ref, catlg. 15: 7926 French st, Vancouver 14 BC Can.

PINE, PATRICIA ELEANOR. b Dayton Ohio 17 Je 25. 5: UDayton 44-45; UKy 45-47 (Lit) AB; Columbia 47-48 (Lit); Peabody Col summers 63-66 (LS) MA. 7: Tchr Mansfield High Sch, Mansfield Ohio 48-50; Clerical circ dept Dayton & Montgomery Co Pub Lib, Dayton Ohio 61-62, Pre-prof br ext 62-66, Ref libn 66-67, Br hd libn 68-. 9: ALA; OhioLA. 10: Phi Beta Kappa; Beta Phi Mu. 14: Ref, br lib wk. 15: 360 Kenwood ave, Dayton Oh 45405.

PINGS, JOAN (GILMORE). b Buckhannon WVa 22 O 27. 4: Vern M Pings. 5: WVa U 45-49 (LS) AB; West Res 49-50 MS in LS. 7: Catlgr UUtah 50-55, Catlgr Wayne State U 55-. 8: Instr Col of Educ Wayne State U spring 63. 9: ALA; MichLA. 14: Catlg. 15: 17404 San Juan dr, Detroit 48221.

PINGS, VERN M. b Sauk City Wis 10 Ap 23. 4: Joan Gilmore. 5: UChicago 44-46 PhB; UWis 46-47 (Zool) BA; Columbia 48-52 (Educ) MA; UWis 54-55 (LS) MA, 56-58 (Educ) PhD. 6: Fr. 7: Sci instr Englewood Hosp, Chicago 47-48; Wks off UN Relief for Palestine Refugees, Beirut Lebanon 49-52; Dir University Farms American U(Beirut Lebanon) 52-54; Asst engnr libn UWis(Madison) 56-58; Libn Ohio No U 59; Assoc Prof UDenver 60; Med libn Wayne State U 60-. 8: Consul NAS 63; Proj dir Amer Nurses Foun NY 64; Visiting lecturer Kent State U 61-63; Lectr UMich. 9: ALA; SLA; MedLA; NLM (mem Facilities & Resources Com). 10: AAAS. 13: Yes. 14: Med libnship. 15: 17404 San Jua, Detroit 48221.

PINKERTON, WESLEY (JOHN). b Van Lear Ky 26 Jl 20. 4: Grace Woodburn. 5: Pikeville Col 37-39 (Bus Admin) 2 yr diploma; Morehead State Col 40-44 (Com, Econ) AB; UKy 47-54 (Bus Educ) AM; UNC 55-56 BS in LS. 7: Elem tchr Van Lear Pub Sch, Van Lear Ky 41-44; Bus educ tchr Scio Pub Sch, Scio Ohio 44-47; Bus educ tchr Pikeville Col 47-55, Libn 56-64; Catlgr Wilmington Col 64-. 9: ALA-RTSD; -ACRL; OhioLA; Ohio Valley Tech Serv Libns. 10: AAUP; Clinton Co(Ohio) Hist Soc. 11: Kiwanian of the Year, 62, Pikeville Ky. 14: Catlg, bk sel, govt docs. 15: 775 Piedmont st, Wilmington Ohio 45177.

PINKNEY, GERTRUDE (GOLDSMITH). b Brooklyn NY 15 S 16. 4: Irving Pinkney. 5: City Col of Detroit 33-34; UMich 34-36 (Fr) AB, 36-37 ABLS. 6: Fr. 7: Jr asst NYC Pub Lib 37-38; Detroit Pub Lib: Jr asst 38-42, Hd mun ref lib 44-49, Ref asst 57-66, Asst lib mun ref 66-67, Chief mun ref 67-; US Bur of Budget, Wash DC: Ref asst 42-44, Chief ref, bibliog, loan 49-51; Asst libn & catlgr NICB Lib, NY 51-53. 8: Guest lectr WashStateU Lib Sch on Spec Libs 68-69; Memb Educ Subcom of Mayors Citizen Study Com on Consumer educ & Protection (69). 9: SL; ALA. 10: LWV. 12: Ed Municipal Ref Lib Bulletin. 14: Ref, munic ref libs. 15: 10725 Borgman ave, Huntington Woods Mi 48070.

PINKNEY, HELEN L(OUISE). b Decatur Ill. 5: Sch of the Dayton Rock Art Inst 40. 7: Dayton Art Inst, Dayton Ohio: Libn & Registrar of Collections 36-45, Gen curator & Libn 45-59, Libn & Assoc curator 59-. 9: Amer Assn Museums SLA; Dayton Art Inst Alumni Assn (sec & in chg of Annual Exhib 39-52). 10: DAR. 14: Art ref. 15: Dayton Art Inst, Forest & Riverview aves, Dayton Ohio 45405.

PINNEY, JOYCE (YVONNE). b Los Angeles Cal 4 Jl 42. 5: USoCal 62-64 (Lit) BA, 64-65 (LS) MA; Pasadena Jr Col 60-69 (Lit, Hist) AB. 6: Fr. 7: Libn I Pasadena Pub Lib, Pasadena Cal 65-. 9: ALA; CalLA. 14: Ref (ya). 15: 3835 Scandia way, Los Angeles Ca 90065.

PINNEY, NANCY MARGARET. b Topeka Kan 23 D 39. 5: UDenver 57-61 (Hist) BA, 61-62 (LS) MA. 7: Libn catlgr Denver Pub Lib 62-. 14: Catlg. 15: 600 Williams st, Denver Co 80218.

PINZUR, SAMUEL. b Brooklyn NY 11 N 18. 5: Brooklyn Col 36-40 (Eng) BA; Pratt 40-41 BLS; NYU 50-51 (Educ) MA. 6: Fr. 7: Ref asst NY Pub Lib Bronx Ref Center 41; US Army Post Lib, Ft Monmouth NJ 41-43; Air Force (Staff Sgt) Clsf spec 43-45; Circ asst NY Pub Lib Riverside Br 46; Queens Col Lib (NY): Ser libn 46-49, Educ libn 50-57, Chief of reader serv 57-. 9: NYLib Club. 10: AAUP. 14: Educ, ref, admin. 15: 78-10 34 ave, Jackson Heights NY 11372.

PIPER, NELSON (ALFRED). b Vacaville Cal 5 O 25. 4: Patricia L Piper. 5: UCal (Davis) 46-48 (Chem); UCal (Berkeley) 48-51 (Hist) AB, 51-53 (Hist, LS) BLS. 6: Sp. 7: Soc sci ref libn UCal (Berkeley) 53-54; Asst acquis libn UNeb Libs 54-55; Ser libn 55-56; UCal Lib(Davis): Asst head acquis dept 56-58, Head acquis dept 58-62, Asst libn tech serv 62-66; Asst U libn 66-. 9: ALA; CalLA; NoCal Tech Proc Group. 10: Phi Alpha Theta. 14: Acquis, catlg, rare bks. 15: 1001 Alice st, Davis Ca 95616.

PIPER, PATRICIA BAKER. b Norman Okla 9 Ap 29. 4: Nelson A Piper. 5: UOkla 47-51 (Journalism) BA, 56-58 MLS. 7: Law libn UTulsa 58-59; Asst law libn UOkla 59-65; Asst law libn UCal (Davis) 65-. 8: Sers Proj Task Force UCal (Davis) Lib; Instr AALL Wkshop on LC Clsf Schedule KF 68, Phila. 9: AALL (Memb chm 62-64, pres Adv Com on Memb 68-); OklaLA (sec 64-65, chm Div of Tech Serv 64-65); CalLA. 10: Friends of the Davis Pub Lib; Phi Beta Kappa; Mortar Board. 14: Catlg, law lib wk. 15: 1001 Alice, Davis Ca 95616.

PIPER, SHIRLEY CAROLYN. b Flemington Mo 8 Mr 41. 5: SW Mo State Col 59-62 (Mus) BS in Ed; NorthwesternU 62-63 (Mus) MM; UMo 65-66; UMd 67; Case West Res 68-69 MLS. 6: Ger, Japanese. 7: Stud asst music libn UMo (Kan City) 65; Vocal music tchr Independence Pub Sch, Independence Mo 63-66; Eng tchr Nippon Oil Seal, Fujisawa Japan 67-68; Vocal music tchr Dept of Defense, Yokosuka Japan 66-68; Record catlgr Cleveland Inst of Music 68-69; Stud asst music libn NorthwesternU 62-63, summer 64, Asst music libn for readers serv 69-. 9: MusicLA. 10: Mu Phi Epsilon. 14: Ref, catlg. 15: 7667 Sheridan rd, Chicago Il 60626.

PIPKIN, MICHAEL BRUCE. b Mena Ark 3 O 34. 4: Betty Jodan. 5: Peabody Conservatory of Music (Baltimore) 52-53, 56-58 (Harmony); UMd 59-61 (Eng) BA; UNC 61-62 MS in LS. 6: Ger. 7: Bandsman, Spec 3d Class US Army, Ft Meade Md 53-56; Libn I Free Lib of Phila 62-64; Libn US Air Force, Olmstead AFB Penn 64-67; Lib dir Charles Taylor Mem Lib, Hampton Va 67-. 9: ALA-PLA (Armed Forces Libns Sect: chm Sect Devel Com 65-66); Capitol Area Lib Assn, Harrisburg Penn; VaLA (Nat Lib Week Com Chm 69). 10: Hampton Hist Soc; Kicotan Chap Archaeological Soc of Va. 14: Ref. 15: 137 OCanoe pl, Hampton Va 23361.

PIRIE, EUGENIA L. b Ballinger Tex 2 N 20. 5: Tex State Col for Women 36-40 (LS) BA; UTex 40 (Eng); UScal 48 (Med Lib). 6: Ger. 7: Sch libn DeQueen Sch, Pt Arthur Tex 41; Sch libn Tomball Ind Sch Dist, Tomball Tex 41-42; Base libn Normoyle Ordnance DEPOT, San Antonio Tex 42-43; WAVES Radio-Radar Admin (Lt) 43-46; Ref libn UTex Ext Loan Lib 46-47; Med libn VA Center, Temple Tex 47-53, Chief Lib Serv 53-. 9: TexLA; MedLA. 10: AAUW. 14: Admin. 15: 903 N 7th st, Temple Tex 76501.

PIRIE, JAMES W. b NYC 22 S 13. 4: Elizabeth Waller. 5: NYU 32-39 (Music) BS; Pratt 39-40 BLS; West Res 51-53 (Amer Culture) MA. 7: Catlgr Pratt Inst Lib 40-41; US Army Infantry (1st Lt) 41-46; Harvard Col Lib: Admin asst 46-47, Chief gift & exch 47-49, Ref asst & head of Ref Lamont Lib 49-50; Libn Youngstown U Lib 50-57; Libn Charles Stewart Mott Lib Flint Commun Jr Col, Flint Col of UMich 57-66; Libn Lewis & Clark Col 66-. 8: Adv Final Review Conf on Proposed Publication "Libraries for Technician Education, US Off of Educ, 65. 9: ALA (chm Jr Col Libs Sect 65-66); MichLA (chm Jr Col Lib Sect 63-64). 10: ACLU; Planned Parenthood World Population. 13: Comp "Books for Junior Colleges, ALA (69). 14: Bk sel, admin, bibliog. 15: 3203 SW Mitchell ct, Portland Or 97201.

PISPEKY, MARY A. b Lebanon Penn 23 My 18. 5: Kutztown State Tchrs Col 35-39 (Lib Educ) BS in Ed; Simmons 44-47 (LS) BS. 7: Libn: Beaver Falls High Sch, Beaver Falls Penn 39-45; Lansford High Sch, Lansford Penn 45-65; Panther Valley Joint High Sch, Lansford Penn 64-. 9: NEA; ALA; Penn StateEA. 10: . 14: Yp serv. 15: 605 E Ridge st, Lansford Penn 1232.

PISTORIUS, MARIE. b Prague Czechoslovakia 24 Ja 23. 5: Real gymnaium (Prague) 34-52 Matura; State Libn Sch(Prague) 43-44 Diploma in Lib Sci; Charles U(Pragu) 45-48 (Fr, Hist) Statesexam (MA); Union Francaise des Organismes de Documentation, Paris 50 Certif de Documentation Gen. 6: Fr, Ger, Czech. 7: Asst catlgr Lafayette Col 61-63; Libn Sterling & Francine Clark Inst, Williamstown Mass 63-67; Art libn Williams Col Lib 68-. 8: Research for Centre National de la Recherche Scientifique, Paris 50-52. 9: ALA. 14: Catlg. 15: Cluett dr, Williamstown Ma 01267.

PITCHFORD, HARRIET DAY. b Canton Miss. 5: USoMiss 31-35 (Eng) BS; Duke summer 41; Peabody Col 58-59 MALS; Columbia summers 61, 64, 66 (LS). 6: Fr. 7: Tchr elem sch,

Brookhaven Miss 36-43; Libn Spec Serv Lib: Camp Van Dorn Miss 43-46, Camp Beale Cal 46-47, Camp Zama Japan 47-49, Ft Benning Ga 49-. 8: MARC II Inst Ga Inst Tech 68. 10: AAUW; Altrusa Intl; Amer Assn for UN. 14: Catlg, ref. 15: PO Box 1972, Fort Benning Ga 31905.

PITERNICK, GEORGE. b NYC 5 Ap 18. 5: UCal(Berkeley) 35-39 (Zool) AB; UHawaii 39-40 (Zool); UCal(Berkeley) 40-42 (Zool), 46-47 BLS. 6: Fr, Ger. 7: Catlgr, catlg analyst, lib admin analyst UCal Lib(Berkeley) 47-61; Asst dir of libs UWash Lib 61-64, Asst dir of libs & Lecturer in Libnship 64-65; Assoc Prof of Libnship UBC 65-. 9: ALA (ALA-CathLA Jt Com 65-66, 67-68, Com on Stats 56-57, Inter-Div (RSD-CCS) Com on Bk Catlgs 58-63); -ACRL (Univ Libs Sect: Res & Devel Com 65-67); -LAD (Lib Org & Mgt Sect: Exec Com 57-58, Stats Coord Com 57-58, chm Nomin Com 58-59); -RTSD (Nomin Com 62-63; Catlg & Clsf Sect: Adv Com Catlg Use Study 55-58, Com on Descr Catlg 55-59, Nomin Com 60-61; Ser Sect: Ser Pol & Res Com 62-64); -Lib Tech Proj: Adv Com on Catlg Card Reprod Study 61-64); AALS; CanLA; MedLA; SLA; BCLA; PNLA (Program Com Jt CURLS-PNLA Meeting 62); WashLA (Govt Docs Com 62-63, Legis Com 62-65, Lib Serv Act Com 64-65); Can Assn Lib Schs (pres 69-70). 10: UCal Lib Schs Alumni Assn; Phi Beta Kappa. 13: Yes. 14: Univ lib admin, tech proc, sci & tech libs. 15: Sch of Libnship Univ of Brit Col, Vancouver 168 BC Can.

PITTMAN, ELIZABETH (CHAFFIN). b Jasper Ala 1 Ag 10. 4: Kenneth C Pittman. 5: Florence State Tchrs Col 29-32 (Educ) BS; Peabody summers 35, 36 (LS). 7: Tchr-libn Cherokee Voc High Sch, Cherokee Ala 32-42; Document libn Air U Lib, Maxwell AFB Ala 46-. 9: SLA; AlaLA. 10: Pilot Club of Montgomery; Jt Legis Coun. 14: Acquis of mil docs. 15: 3347 Walton dr, Montgomery Al 36111.

PITTMAN, SHIRLEY A. b Vandrgrift Penn 29 Ag 31. 5: Grove City Col 49-53 (Soc Studies) AB; Edinboro State Col 60-62 (Soc Studies) MEd; UPittsburgh 63-64 MLS, 65 (LS). 6: Sp. 7: Tchr Washington Twp Sch Dist, Apollo Penn 53-64; Libn Slippery Rock State Col 65-66; Elem libn North Hills Sch Dist, Pittsburgh Penn 67-. 9: ALA; NEA; PennLA; PennStateEA. 10: Assn for Student Tchg; Beta Phi Mu. 12: "Pittman Learning Guides (68); Ed Pa dept of pub instr publ; guide for School Library Programs (69). 14: Sch libnship, educ for libnship. 15: 186 McIntyre rd, Pittsburgh Pa 15237.

PITTS, CYNTHIA FRANCES (ZAKES). b Chicago 22 My 35. 4: Robert S Pitts. 5: UArk 53-57 (Chem) BS; UIll 57-58 MSLS. 7: Jr lib asst UArk Lib 57; Libn I Chicago Pub Lib 58; Order libn Ark Lib Commsn, Little Rock Ark 59-. 9: ALA; SWLA; ArkLA. 10: Ark Soc of Prof Engnrs Auxiliary Little Rock Jr C of C Auxiliary Phi Beta Kappa; Beta Phi Mu. 14: Ref, bk sel. 15: 32 Lorna dr, Little Rock Ark 72205.

PITTS, EARLINE (ROSS). b Nashville Tenn. 4: Edward E Pitts. 5: Tenn A&I U BS; Fisk U MA; UMich MA in LS. 7: Libn Chattanooga (Tenn) City Schs 54-. 9: ALA; NEA; TennEA; ETennTA (sec). 10: Alpha Kappa Alpha. 14: Lib wk with teen-agers. 15: 900 Line st, Chattanooga Tn 37404.

PITTS, ELSIE M (YOST). b Adrian Mo 5 F 04. 4: A E Pitts. 5: Central State Col (Okla) 24-35 (Educ) BS; UOkla summers 39-41 (Educ) MA; UWash summers 60-63 (Libnship' MA. 7: Tchr: Gracemont (Okla) Sch Dist 25-31, Ponca City Okla 31-43, Richland Sch dist, Richland Wash 34-52; Libn Richland Sch Dist 52-. 8: Hd libn at Marcus Whitman Elem Sch for Phase 1 in the Knapp Sch Libs Proj 63-65. 9: ALA (Newberry-Caldecott Awards Com 66); WashStateASchL. 10: Delta Kappa Gamma; AAUW. 13: Yes. 14: Elem libs & child bks. 15: 9517 Richardson rd, Pasco Wa 99301.

PITTS, MARY HELEN (McCREA WEAVER). b Spokane Wash 20 Mr 1898. 5: Whitman 16-17; Wellesley 17-18; UWash 18-20 (Eng) AB; USoCal 23-24 (LS) Diploma; Gonzaga U (Educ) MA 30, 55 LLB; UWash 37 Life Diploma Chicago summer 33; Stanford 50-51; UIda summer 51; UUtah summer 54; Gonzaga U 67 JD. 6: Ger, Sp. 7: Lib asst Seattle Pub Lib 21-22; Lib asst Los Angeles Pub Lib 23-24; Sec Washington Educ Bur, Spokane Wash 24-26; Asst libn Lewis & Clark High Sch, Spokane Wash 21-22, 26-28; Libn Libby Jr High Sch, Spokane Wash 28-29; Head libn Lewis & Clark High Sch, Spokane Wash 29-40; Sec Community Survey of Educ, Hawaii 40-41; Instr. in lib sci Wash State Col 37-40; Libn 14th Naval Dist 41-43; Law libn Supreme Court State of Hawaii 43-61; Law lib consul 61-. 8: Del, 2nd Internat Lib Congress, Madrid; Hawaii Rep, AASL, 35; Admitted to law practice in Hawaii, 55. 9: Amer Bar Assn; Hawaii Bar Assn; ALA (Life mem; Chm Com on lib coop with Latin Amer 34-39, var other coms 31-40); HawaiiLA (life mem); AALL (life mem). 10: Altrusa; AAUW; Bishop Museum Assn; Honolulu Acad of Arts; Nat Assn of Women Lawyers; Phi Delta Delta; Nat League Amer Pen Women; Composers, Artists & Authors of Amer; Waikiki Bus & Prof Assn; Del Worlds Sunday Sch Assn, Rio de Janeiro, Oslo; Del Internat Fed of Univ Womens Conf, Brisbane Australia 65, Karlsruhe Germany 68; Del Internat Fed Bus & Prof Women, London 68; English Speaking Union, Del Conf Edinburgh 68. 12: "Keiki Puffer Fish" (58); Co-ed "Significance of the School Library" (37). 13: Yes. 14: Law libs. 15: E 2903 - 25th ave, Spokane Wa 99203.

PITTS, MARY LOUISE (PRICE). b Paris Ky 22 Ja 15. 4: William T Pitts. 5: Georgetown Col 33-36 (Eng) BA; UIll 42 BS in LS. 7: Libn Christian Col 45; Asst libn Col of Educ Ohio State U 46-49; Libn circ dept Fla State U 49-52; Bibliogr Air U Lib, Maxwell AFB Ala 52-. 9: SLA; AlaLA. 10: Delta Kappa Gamma. 15: Rt 1, Hopehull Al 36043.

PITTS, PAULINE D. b Palo Pinto Tex. 5: Southeastern State Col(Okla) (Lat) -30 BA; UOkla BA 47-48 in LS; UIll (LS) MS. 6: Lat, Sp, Fr, Ger, Ital. 7: Southeastern State Col(Okla) Lib; Phillips U Lib; Howard Payne Col Lib; Tex Tech Col Lib; Tyrell Pub Lib, Beaumont Tex; Tex Tech Col Lib. 9: ALA; TexLA; SWLA; TexAColTchrs. 10: AAUW; Friends of Tex Tech Lib; South Plains Geneal Soc. 14: Catlg. 15: Box 2324, Lubbock Tx 79408.

PIVONKA, SISTER SIMEON. b Timken Kan 27 Mr 06. 5: Kan State Col 47 (Chem) BS; CatholicU 57 MS in LS. 7: Instr St Theresa High Sch, Hutchinson Kan -57; Libn St mary's High Sch, Wicihta Kan 57-63; Libn St Mary of the Plains Col 63-. 8: Instr in lib sci St Mary of the Plains Col 65-. 9: ALA; CathLA; KanLA; KanASchL. 14: Ref. 15: St Mary of the Plains College, Dodge City Ks 67801.

PIZER, IRWIN H(OWARD). b Wellington New Zealan 16 O 34. 5: Antioch Col 52-57 (Biol, Pre-Med) BS; Hahnemann Med Col 57-58 (Med); Columbia 59-60 (LS) MS; Washington U 62(Hist of Med). 7: Stack supv Columbia U Butler Lib 59-60; Intern NLM, Wash DC 60-61; Asst libn for pub serv, Washington U Sch of Med (St Louis) 61-62, Research assoc for machine methods 62-64; Dir of Lib & Asst Prof of Med Hist SUNY(Syracuse) 64-; Dir SUNY Biomed Communication Network 66-. 8: Instr in ref & bibliog Cath Hosp Assn Insts on Cont Educ for Hosp Libns 62-65; Guest lecturer Syracuse U Sch of Lib Sci; Res assoc Inst for the Adv of Med Communication; Devel of mechanized circ control system at SUNY Upstate Med Center; •Mem of the State Univ Intra-Univ Communications Com & chm of its Task Force on Med Libs; Proj dir, SUNY Union List of Sers& NY State Union list of sers; Bd Trustees Central NY Ref & Research Coun 67-61. 9: MedLA (mem & chm Com on Contin Educ 63-66, mem & chm on Recrt 64-68; SLA Chm Research Com 66-69); ASIS (chm Upstate NY Reg Group 68-69); NYLA. Upstate NY Reg Group); ADI; NYLA; Mo Hist Soc. 10: AAUP; AAAS; Drug Info Assn; Mo Hist Soc. 11: Murray Gottlieb Prize, (Hist of Med), 64. 13: Yes. 14: Hist, rare bks, admin, mechanization, automation. 15: 875 Ostrom ave, Syracuse NY 13210.

PLACE, PHILIP ANDREW. b Lorain Ohio 10 My 39. 4: Diana Walthall. 5: TaylorU 58-63 9hist) AB; USoCal 65-66 MSLS. 7: Period clk Santa Barbara Pub Lub, Santa Barbara Cal 64-65; Stud asst USoCal 65, Stud libn Inst of Aerospace Safety & Mgt 65-66; Sci dept bkmob & br libn San Francisco Pub Lib 66-68; Assoc dir Cabell Co Pub Lib, Huntington w va 68-. 9: ALA; WVaLA. 14: Admin. 15: 152 Sycamore st, Huntington W Va 25705.

PLACEK, JOSEPH ANTHONY. b Detroit 14 O 29. 5: St Marys Col(Mich) 47-48; UDetroit 50-53 (Eng) AB; Catholic U 53-56 MS in LS; Georgetown U 60-65 (Russian) MS. 6: Fr, Polish, Russian, Lat. 7: Page UDetroit 51-52; Clerk Detroit Pub Lib 52-53; Lib asst DC Pub Lib 53-54; Lib asst US Weather Bur Lib, Suitland Md 54-56; Circ libn, ref libn UDetroit 57-60; Ed CatholicLA, Wash DC 60-63; Libn DC Tchrs Col Lib 63-65; Head ref dept Ohio State U Lib 65-67; Hd Slavic sect & tech serv UMich 67-. 8: Mem, Adv Com, Slavic Bibliog & Documentation Ctr, ARL, Wash DC 69-70. 9: ALA (Mem-at-Large 65-66);-ACRL (chm Slavic & E European Subsect 69-70). 10: Amer Assn Advanced Slavic Studies. 12: Ed "Catholic Periodical Index, v 11 (61-62). 14: Ref, catlg. 15: 5704 Mitchell, Detroit Mi 48211.

PLACZEK, ADOLF K. b Vienna 9 Mr 13. 4: Laura Beverley Robinson. 5: UVienna 31-34 (Med34-38 (Art Hist); Columbia 41-42 BLS. 6: Ger, Fr, Ital. 7: (Sgt) US Army 43-46; Asst libn Avery Lib Columbia U 49-60, Avery Libn 60-. 9: Soc of Arch

Histns (sec 63-67, dir 69-). 10: MUNICIPAL Art Soc. 13: Yes. 14: Arch hist, rare bks. 15: 176 W 87th st, New York NY 10024.

PLANK, MARION S. b Aurora Ill. 5: UMich 25 AB; Aurora Col 31-33 (Educ); UMich 36 AB in LS; Chicago 50 MA in LS. 6: Sp, Fr. 7: Asst Aurora Pub Lib, Aurora Ill 31-34, Asst ref libn 34-36; Asst catlgr & Instr in Lib Sci Ind State Tchrs Col 36-37; Head catlgr Aurora Pub Lib, Aurora Ill 38-39, Head Libn 39-; Sch lib devel adv, Penn 66-68; Curriculum spec, N Hills Pittsburgh Penn 8: Adv Coun of Libns, UIll Grad Sch of Lib Serv 64-. 9: ALA (Coun 54-58 & 65-; Subcom on Civil Serv Rel 46; chm Coun Nomin om 56-57; chm Jury on Citation of Trustees 53-56); -PLD (exec sec 48-51, sec-treas 51); -PLA (chm Subcom on Clsf & Pay Plans 54-56, chm Subcom on Standards for Small Libs 60-62; mem Bd Dirs 65-; mem Standards Com 63-); IllLA (pres 48-49; chm Nomin Com 57-58 & 63-64; Coord for Fed Legis 58-). 10: DAR; Midwest Early Amer Pressed Glass Club; AAUW; Aurora Ill Hist Soc; Ill Hist Soc (Life mem); Beta Phi Mu; Chi Omega. 11: Libn Citation Award, IllLA, 62. 13: Yes. 14: Admin, personnel. 15: 144 W McIntyre ave, Pittsburgh Pa 15214.

PLANK, MARION S. b Pittsburgh 2 O 19. 5: Col of Wooster 36-40 (Hist) BA; Carnegie 40-41 (Sec Studies) BS; UAriz 47-49 (Hist) MA; Duquesne 58-61 (LS) MA Equiv, UPittsburgh (Educ, Lang). 6: Sp, Fr. 7: Clerk Pittsburgh Bd of Educ 41-42; Tchr W View High Sch, W View Penn 42-46; Asst head resident dorm U Ariz 47-49; Tchr Wakefield Jr High Sch, Tucson 49-50; Legal sec Reed, Smith, Shaw, McClay, Pittsburgh 50-51; Personnel sec US Steel Corp Pittsburgh 51-52; Tchr Jr High, N Hills, Pittsburgh 52-58, Libn 59-; Sch lib devel adv, Penn 66-68; Curric spec, N Hills Pittsburgh Penn 68-. 8: Curriculum consul N Hills Schs, summer 62; Mem Penn Com for Nat Lib Week 66. 9: NEA; PennStateEA; PennLA (mem Sect Com); Suburb Libns of Pittsburgh (chm 63); NCSS; ALA (mem Period Com 67-69). 11: Frick Scholarships to Europe & Japan to study & collect materials for N Hills Schs Libs. 13: Yes. 14: Instr materials centers in schs. 15: 144 W McIntyre ave, Pittsburgh Pa 15214.

PLANT, WILLIAM H(ENRY). b Phila 10 Ja 16. 4: Anglesea Ruth Asby. 5: State U Iowa 34-37 (Music) BMus, 37-38 (Music) MA; West Res 41-42 BS in LS. 6: Ger. 7: Pub Sch Music Tchr 39-41; Lib asst Case Sch of Applied Sci 41-42; Ref asst Off for Emergency Mgt Lib, Wash DC 43; Naval Res Off (Lt JG) 43-46; Jr libn Dept of Agric Lib, Wash DC 42-46; Catlgr Off of Tech Serv Com, Wash DC 46-47; Libn catlgr Bur of Ordnance Tech Lib, Wash DC 47-48; Asst chief & ref libn Tech Lib Off; Asst sec Def & Reseach & Devel Bd 48-54, chief 54-57; Libn Diamond Ordnance Fuze Labs, Wash DC 57; Head engnr Info br Bur of Aeronautics, Wash DC 57-69; Tech libn Bur of Naval Weapons, Wash DC 60-67; Dir tech lib Naval Air Systs Command, Wash DC 67-. 8: Principal Violist with civic groups. 9: SLA (treas Wash DC Sci-Tech Group). 10: Arlington (Va) Civic Symphony; Arlington(Va) Chamber Music Orchestra; Alexandria (Va) Civic Symphony; Amer U Symphony Orchestra; George Wash U Symphony Orchestra. 12: Ed DC SLA "Chapter Notes. 13: Yes. 14: Catlg, info retrieval, glossaries & thesauri. 15: 2102 Small st, Alexandria Va 22302.

PLAPINGER, JOAN (HAASE). b NYC 4 N 26. 4: Robert Edwin Plapinger. 5: Hunter Col 43-47 (Geol, Geog) BA; Columbia 49-51 (LS) MS. 7: Libn: NY Pub Lib 49-52, Dept of the Army, Japan, Korea 52-53, NY Pub Lib 53-54, Baltimore Co(Md) Pub Lib 65, Lib Baltimore Hebrew Col 65-; Libn Bedford Elem Sch, Baltimore Co 66-. 14: Child lit, story-telling. 15: 3417 Merle dr, Baltimore Md 21207.

PLASMATI, JOHN. b NYC 3 Mr 24. 4: Valdine Plasmati. 5: CCNY 57 (BS); Pratt Inst 60 MSLS. 6: Ital, Fr. 7: Tech asst ref dept NY Pub Lib; Ref libn & automation specialist Engrg Lib Grumman Aircraft, Bethpage NY; Automation libn SUNY (Stony Brook) 66-. 9: SLA; ASIS. 10: Sayville Hist Soc; Wet Pants Yacht Club, Sayville NY. 14: Lib automation, private press printing, ref. 15: 317 Candee ave, Sayville NY 11782.

PLATE, KENNETH HARRY. b Richmond Cal 8 Je 39. 5: UCal (Berkeley) 58-62 (Eng) AB; Rutgers 65-66 MLS, 66-. 6: Fr, Sp, Ger. 7: Specialist-4 USA Med Corps (Reserve) 57-62; Chem libn Columbia U 66; Tchg asst Rutgers U 68, Research fellow 66-69; Asst prof UToronto 69-. 9: ALA; ASIS. 13: Yes. 14: Admin, educ for libnship, research in lib serv. 15: Sch of Lib Sci, Univ of Toronto, Toronto 2B Ont Can.

PLATT, CAROLINE S. b Milford Conn 31 My 10. 5: Elmira Col 27-31 (Fr) BS; Columbia (Educ) BS in LS. 6: Sp. 7: Lib Tchr Brooklyn Pub Lib System, Libn Off of Cable Censorship, NYC 41-45; Asst libn Taylor Lib, Milford Conn 45-46; Catlgr Evanston Pub Lib, Evanston Ill 46-48; Libn Taylor Lib, Milford Conn 48-53; Libn Fairfield Pub Lib, Fairfield Conn 53-67, Adult serv coord 68-. 8: Instr, lib sci summer courses, New Haven State Tchrs Col Survey of Derby Neck Lib; Instr So Conn State Col 68. 9: ConnLA (pres 54-55, program chm & mem var coms, v-pres 68-69). 10: DAR; Milford (Conn): Bd of Educ, Planning & Zoning Bd, Bd of Health. 12: Comp & ed "Consumer Education Bibliography. 14: Catlg, admin. 15: Fairfield Pub Lib, Fairfield Conn 06430.

PLATT, GLENN E(VERETT). b Ellwood City Penn 11 Mr 20. 4: Lettie Holt Henry. 5: Geneva Col 46-50 (Liberal Arts) BA; Wheaton Col (Ill) 51-53 (New Testament) MA; Simmons 65-67 (LS) SM. 6: Fr, Ger, classical Greek. 7: US Army Ordnance Corp T/5 43-45; Pastor N Darian & W Bethany Baptist Ch, Corpu NU 56-62; Pastor Ransomville Baptist Ch, Ransomville NY 62-65; Lib trainee Andover Newton Theol Sch Lib, Newton Ctr Mass 65-67, Hd catlgr 67-. 9: ATheolLA. 14: Catlg. 15: 73 Herrick rd, Newton Center Ma 02159.

PLATZ, ELLA MAE (LEWIS). b Childress Tex 23 Je 12. 4: James E Platz. 5: Okla State 30-33; UOkla 33-34 BS in LS. 6: Fr, Sp. 7: Act libn Seminole Pub Lib, Seminole Okla 36-37; Head Libn Pub Lib, Wewoka Okla 37-41; Catlg asst UNeb Lib 41-42; Asst in period UInd Lib 43; Head Libn Pub Lib, Frederick Okla 45; Child libn Pub Lib, Lubbock Tex 54-65, Act libn 65-66; Hd child serv Lubbock City-Co Lib 67-. 9: TexLA (chm Child Round Table 62-63). 14: Child serv. 15: 4315 40th st, Lubbock Tex.

PLAYER, THELMA B. b Owosso Mich 28 My 16. 5 UMich 34; Albion Col 35; West Mich U 52-54 (LS) BA. 7: Ref libn Aeronautical Chart & Info Center, Wash DC 54-57; Ref libn Navy Hydrographic Off, Suitland Md 57-58, Asst libn 58-59; Tech lib br head Spec Projects Off, Wash DC 59-68; Tech lib br hd Strategic Systems Project Off, Wash DC 68-. 9: SLA; DCLA. 14: Ref. 15: 3903 Pennsylvania ave SE, Wash DC 20020.

PLAYFOOT, MARION COOMAN. b Penfield NY 27 Ja 21. 4: Donald S Playfoot. 5: SUNY (Geneseo) 41 (LS) BS in Ed, 62 MLS; Charter Certif by MedLA. 7: Record room Strong Mem Hosp, Rochester NY 42-45; Asst med libn URochester Sch of Med 45-62; Period libn UNeb (Omaha) 62-. 9: MedLA; NebLA. 14: Periods. 15: 7512 Bauman ave, Omaha Nb 68122.

PLETTE, LORRAINE. b Gardner Mass 30 S 15. 5: Marie Anne Col 35-38; Catholic Tchrs Col 40-46; Anna Maria Col 46-48 (Educ) BS in Ed; CatholicU 48-55 MS in LS. 6: Fr. 7: Tchr: Luke Callaghan Memorial Sch, Montreal 34-35, Iroquois Indian Mission Sch, Caughnawaga PQ Can 35-38, St Joseph's Sch, Cohoes NY 39, Precious Blood High Sch, Holyoke Mass 39-43, St Anne Acad, Marlboro Mass 43-51; Libn Anna Maria Col 51-. 9: ALA; CathLA. 15: Anna Maria College, Paxton Ma 01612.

PLETZKE, CHESTER J. b Bay City Mich 26 S 41. 4: Linda M Brady. 5: Duquesne U 60-64 (Philos) AB; UMich 64-65 AMLS; Yeshiva U 65- (Educ Guidance). 6: Fr, Lat. 7: Ref libn NY Pub Lib Jl-O-65; Res libn R R Bowker, NYC 65-; Libn Info Retrieval Center for Culturally Deprived Yeshiva U 65-66; Med libn Mount Sinai Hosp Serv 66-68; Med libn Montague Mem Lib & Study Ctr, Will Rogers Hosp 69-. 8: Consul Lib Materials Price Index Com 68-69. 9: ALA; SLA; No Co Ref Research & Resources Coun; MedLA. 10: ACLU; Sarana Free Lib Assn. 13: Yes. 14: Ref, res, automation. 15: 212 Lake Flower ave, Saranac Lake NY 12983.

PLETZKE, LINDA M (BRADY). b Cleveland 18 N 41. 4: Chester J Pletzke. 5: West Res 59-63 (Eng, Psych) BA; UMich 64-65 AMLS. 6: Fr. 7: Pre-prof libn Cuyahoga Co Pub Lib, Cleveland 63-64; Adult serv libn Brooklyn Pub Lib 65-67; Consul Amer Mgt Assn, Saranac Lake NY 69-. 9: ALA. 10: Beta Phi Mu; Saranac Lake Free Lib Assn. 14: Adult ser, ref. 15: 212 Lake Flower ave, Saranac Lake NY 12983.

PLEUNE, B JOYCE. b Grand Rapids Mich 18 N 21. 5: Calvin Col 41-45 (Educ) AB; West Mich 50-51 Certif in LS; UMich 59 MA in LS. 7: Tchr Diamond Sch, Grand Rapids Mich 45-50; Kent Co Lib, Grand Rapids Mich: Bkmob libn 51-52, Head of sch serv det 52-58, Dir 58-. 9: ALA; MichLA (sec to Exec Bd 68). 10: Nat Assn of Co Officials. 14: Admin. 15: Kent Co Lib, 726 Fuller ave NE, Grand Rapids Mich 49503.

PLEXICO, ELIZABETH (NAN). b Rock Hill SC 11 Jl 15. 5: Winthrop Col 32-36 (Fr, Eng) AB; LSU 38-39 BLS. 7: Asst libn Natchitoches Parish Lib, Natchitoches La 39-40; WPA lib supv Baton Rouge Area Libs, Baton Rouge La 41-42; Asst libn Concord Pub Lib, Concord NC 46-52, Libn 53-58; Ref libn Pub Lib of Charlotte & Mecklenburg Co, Charlotte NC 58-66; Ref libn Winop Col Lib 66-. 9: SELA; ALA; NCLA; SCLA. 10: Bus & Prof Womens Club; AAUW. 14: Ref. 15: 726 Crest st, Rock Hill SC 29405.

PLOCH, RICHARD A(LLAN). b Paterson NJ 18 S 37. 5: Colgate U 54-58 (Geol) AB; UMich 58-60 (Geol) MS, 60-63 MALS. 6: Fr, Lat, Ital. 7: Lib asst rare bk room UMich 59-63; Lilly Fellow Lilly Lib Ind U 63-64; Curator of rare bks & spec collections Ohio State U Libs 64-67; Curator of rare bks & spec collections Brandeis U Libs 68-. 9: ALA; BSA; Mem RT. 10: Brandeis U Libs Staff Assn (chm 68-69). 11: Lilly Fellowship, 63-64. 13: Yes. 14: Rare bks &spec collections, admin. 15: Brandeis Univ Lib, Waltham Ma 02154.

PLOTKIN, JACK. b Los Angeles 23 S 11. 5: UCal(Berkeley) 33-35 (Hist, Pol Sci, Eng) BA, 36-37 Lib Certif, 39-40 (Hist). 6: Fr. 7: Page Henry E Huntington Lib, San Marino Cal 31-33; tud asst UCal Lib(Berkeley) 33-37; 1st asst circ dept U Ore 37-38, Act exec asst 38-39; Stack supv UCal(Berkeley) 39-42; Amer Red Cross: Asst Field Dir, San Diego 42-43, Asst reg dir, San Francisco 43-46, Budget anayst, San Francisco 46-47, Personnel clsf off, San Francisco47-48; Stanford U: Sr ref libn 48-50, Asst chief ref div 50-56, Asst chief humanities & soc sci div56-57, Chief libn circ div 57-, Lecturer in Bibliog 52-. 9: ALA; CalLA (chm Com on Internat Exch of Libns 67; mem var other coms);-CURLS (pres North Div 68); PNLA (treas 38-39). 10: AAUP; Stanford Fac Club. 12: Ed "Your Libraries at Stanford University" (64-68). 13: Yes. 14: Ref, circ, interlib loan. 15: Stanford Univ Lib, Stanford Cal 94305.

PLOTNICK, ROBERT N. b Stamford Conn 21 N 31. 4: Meryl Friedman. 5: UBridgeport 49-53 (Hist) BA; NY Law Scl 53-56 BLL; Yale Law Sch 57; Practicing Law Inst 60. 6: Sp. 7: Law clerk Plotnick & Plotnick, Stamford Conn 56-58; Libn Stamford Law Lib, Stamford Conn 58-. 8: Asst clerk Circuit Court Judic Dept, Stamford Conn-. 9: ALA; NELA; NYLA. 10: Young Professional Assn; Stamford Good Govt Assn; B'Nai BRith; Conn Valley Coun; Long View Park Assn; Conn State Employees Assn; Amer Numis Assn; UBridgeport Alumni Assn of Stamford. 12: "Connecticut Practice Annotated" (68). 14: Ref. 15: Stamford Law Lib, Hoyt st, Stamford Conn.

PLOTNIK, ARTHUR. b White Plains NY 1 O 37. 4: Meta von Borstel. 5: SUNY (Albany) 55-58 (Eng); SUNY (Binghamton) 59-60 (Eng) BA; State UIowa 60-61 (Eng-Creative writing) MA; Columbia 65-66 (LS) MS. 6: Sp. 7: Sgt E-5 US Army Res, Ft Dix NJ 62; Reporter "Albany Times-Union", Albany NY 62-63; Free-lance journalist, Albany NY 63-65; Libn (spec recruit) LC 66-67, Ed & info specialist 67, Asst ed LC Info Bulletin 67-69; Assoc ed Wilson Lib Bulletin H W Wilson Co, NYC 69-. 9: ALA; SLA; Lib Pub Rel Coun. 13: Yes. 14: Lib ed wk, pub rel, ref. 15: Apt 5F 5715 Mosholu ave, Bronx NY 10471.

PLOWITZ, ALICE (ERTLOVA). b Most Czechoslavakia. 4: Kurt M Plowitz. 5: Charles U (Prague) 30-36 (Philol) PhD; Columbia 41-42 BS. 6: Czech, Ger. 7: Catlgr Nat Lib, Prague 38-39; NYC Pub Lib: Catlgr 42-43, Ref libn 44-47, 54-67, 1st asst econ div 67-; Period libn UN, NYC 47-49. 14: Ref. 15: 40 Jefferson ave, Hastings on Hudson NY 10706.

PLOWS, GRACE (SMITH). b Brooklyn NY 21 Jl 07. 4: Herbert Curtis Plows. 5: Adelphi Col 24-28 (Classics) BA; Columbia 34 (LS) MS; Columbia 45 (LS). 6: Lat. 7: Asst libn Flushing High Sch, Flushing NY 29-33; Tchr libn Horace Greeley Sch, Chappaqua NY 33-36; Lib asst John Adams High Sch, Ozone Park NY 36-49; Tchr of lib Automotive High Sch, Brooklyn NY 49-67; Lib asst St John's U (Jamaica) 67-. 9: NYLA; NYCSchLA (pres 54-56); NYLibClub. 15: 4891 187 st, Flushing NY 11365.

PLUHAR, ANNAMARIA (S. b Bermerhaven Germany 23 S 19. 4: Edward A Pluhar. 5: Douglass Col 37-38 (Langs). 6: Ger, Fr. 7: Personnel Dept Bakelite Corp, Bound Brook NJ 42-43; Libn asst, Asst libn Biol div Tech Lib Oak Ridge Nat Lib, Oak Ridge Tenn 54-61, Interlib & period libn Tech Lib 61-66, Libn Thermonuclear Div 66-. 9: SLA (Oak Ridge Tenn Chap). 14: Ref, interlib loans, periods. 15: 312 Sevenoaks dr, Concord Tn 37720.

PLUMLEY, BOYD FULTON. b Hager W Va 6 Ag 30. 5: Berea Col 57-61 (Philos) BA; Theol Sch of St LawrenceU 61-62 (Theol) MA; UKy 66-67 MSLS. 6: Ger, Lat, Gr. 7: Asst hd adult serv Lake Co Pub Lib, Griffith Ind 67; Br hd Vigo Co Pub Lib, Terre Haute Ind 68; Dir Jacksonville Pub Lib, Jacksonville Ill 69-. 9: ALA; IllLA. 14: Ref, pub serv, lit of So Applachian Mountains. 15: 1040 College ave, Jacksonville Il 62650.

PLUMMER, EDWARD. b Towson Md 20 F 20. 4: Rosamond Krumm. 5: Antioch Col 38-39 (Eng); Mich State Col 39-43 (Animal Husbandry) BS; French State Col 65-66 (Eng) AB; UCLA 66-67 MLS. 7: Herdsman Coupens Farm, Towson Md 46-48; Cost accountant Schmidt Lithograph Co, San Francisco 48-55; Asst mgr Citizens Nat Bank, San Francisco 55-65; Bus libn Fresno Co Lib, Fresno Cal 67-. 8: Libn State Tech Serv Act Proj Fresno Co Lib 68-69. 9: ALA; SLA; CalLA. 14: Bus ref. 15: 5370 No Callisch, Fresno Ca 93726.

PLUMMER, ROSAMOND (KRUMM). b Middletown NY 5 My 16. 4: Edward Plummer. 5: Col of Wooster 34-38 (Hist) BA; West Res 38-39 (Lib wk with child) BLS. 6: Fr. 7: Child libn Toledo Pub Lib, Toledo Ohio 39-41; Elem sch libn Cleveland (Ohio) Pub Lib 41-45; Child libn Daly City Lib, Cal 54-56; Child libn Taft Kern Co Lib, Cal 58-61; Hd boys & girls room Fresno Co Free Lib, Fresno Cal 65-. 9: ALA; CalLA. 14: Wk with child. 15: 5370 N Callisch, Fresno Ca 93626.

PLYBON, LOUISE (MOORE). b Elizabethton Tenn 11 Jl 12. 4: Charles Plybon. 5: Appalachian State Tchrs Col 29-33 (Educ) BS; Peabody 37-38 BS in LS, 47-48 MS in LS. 7: Tchr Pub Sch, Granite Falls NC 33-37; Supv of Demonstration Sch Lib & Tchr of Lib Sci Appalachian State Tchrs Col 37-39, Head Dept of Lib Sci 40-49; Libn Eastover Sch, Charlotte NC 49-53; Libn Gardner-Webb Col 53-54; Head tech serv Forsythe Pub Lib, Winston-Salem NC 54; Libn Eastover Sch, Charlotte NC 55-. 8: Dir, spec proj, acquis & catlg, Charlotte Col, now UNC (Charlotte), 57-67 full time summers, part time acad yr; Instr Lib Sch UNC (Chapel Hill) summers 50-53, 67; Inst Appalachian State Col summers 68, 69. 9: ALA; NEA; NCTE; NCLA; NCEA; SELA. 10: Delta Kappa Gamma. 12: "Rainbow Reading Record for Use by Children". 14: Sch libnship. 15: 1325 Drexmore ave, Charlotte NC 28209.

POARCH, MARGARET ELIZABETH. b Louisville Ky 18 S 22. 5: Averett Col 39-41 (Liberal Arts) Jr Col Diploma; Radford Col 41-43 (Soc Studies) AB in Secondary Ed; Simmons 45-46 BS in LS. 6: Ger, Fr. 7: DC Pub Lib: Desk asst Central Child Room 43-44, Asst in schs div 44-46, 47-48, Child libn Chevy Chase Br 48-49, Child libn Southeast Br 49-50; Asst child libn King Co Pub Lib, Seattle 50-52, Child libn 52-55; Army libn US Army Europe, COM-Z & NACOM 55-57, Child libn Kings Highway Reg, Leonard Br, & Arlington Br, Brooklyn Pub Lib 57-58; Supv wk with boys & girls Berkeley Pub Lib, Berkeley Cal 58-61; Supv child libn San Mateo Co Lib System, Belmont Cal 61-. 68; Child serv consul State Lib of Ohio, Columbus 68-. 8: Tchr Child lit, Col of Holy Names, Oakland Cal spring 68. 9: ALA (Intercult Action Com 52-57); -CYAS (Nomin Com 53); -CSD (Newberry-Caldecott Com 63-64; Storytelling Materials Com 66-68, Nomin Com 68-69, Publ Planning Com 61-63, 68-70). 13: Yes. 14: Child & ya serv, bk sel, wk with inner city dwellers & minorities. 15: State Lib of Ohio, 65 S Front st, Columbus Oh 43215.

PODESVA, RUTH ELIZABETH (DECKER). b Saratoga Springs NY 7 Je 23. 5: SUNY (Geneseo) 40-44 (LS) BS in Ed. 6: Ger, Fr. 7: Libn-tchr Homer Acad, Homer NY 44-45; Libn Washington Acad, Salem NY 45-46; Preps libn & catlgr Rider Col Lib 47-. 8: Chm/libn. 9: NJLA. 10: AAUW; Mem Admin Bd Emilie United Methodist Ch, sec of Coun of Ministries. 14: Catlg, proc. 15: 261 Elderberry dr, Levittown Pa 19054.

POE, ELIZABETH H(OLT). b Phila. 4: Frank Wilson Poe. 5: Temple 36-40 (Eng) BA; Drexel 43-46, 50 BS in LS; Temple Law Sch 43-46; Wake Forest Col Law Sch 46-50; UIll Col of Law 50-52. 7: Asst law libn Temple U Law Sch 42-43, Act law libn 43-46; Law Libn Wake Forest Col Law Sch 46-50; Asst law libn UIll Col of Law 50-52; Law Libn: UNeb Col of Law 52-53, Nev State Lib 53-57, Penn State Lib 57-. 9: AALL (Recruitment com 66-); AALL-CNLA (Jt Com on Lib Wk as a Career 59-); PennLA; OhioLA. 10: AAUW. 13: Yes. 14: Law. 15: 358 Beverly rd, Camp Hill Penn 17011.

POE, JOHN E(DWARD). b Newnan Ga 31 My 35. 5: UGa 53-56, 59-61 (Classics) AB; George Washington U 58-59; UNC summer 59; Emory 62-64 (LS) MLN. 6: Lat, Fr. 7: US Army 56-59; Tchr Briarcliff High Sch, DeKalb Co Ga 61-62; Circ asst Emory U Lib 62-64; Ser libn Auburn U Lib 65-67; Asst arch libn Ga Inst of Tech 67-68, Readers' services libn 69-. 9: SELA. 14: Ref. 15: Lib Ga Inst of Tech, Atlanta Ga 30332.

POE, JULIE ANNE. b Los Angeles Cal 15 Mr 45. 5: Cal State Polytech Col 63-67 (Lang Arts) BS; UCLA 67-68 MLS, 68-69 Certif of Specialization in Music Libnship. 6: Sp, Fr. 7: Aide Los Angeles Co Lib, Temple City 64-66. 9: ALA; MusLA; CalLA. 10: Beta Phi Mu. 11: Title II-B Post MLS Fellowship. 14: Ref, readers' services, a-v. 15: 6022 N Rowland ave, Temple City Ca 91780.

POETZEL, REV RICHARD (KARL) CSSR. b Batimore 1 N 36. 5: St Marys Col (North East Penn) 55-57 (Lat); Mt St Alphonsus Sem 58-60 (Philos) AB, 60-64 (Theol); Catholic U 64-65 (LS). 6: Sp. 7: Asst libn Mt St Alphonsus Sem 58-64; Asst libn Holy Redeemer Col 64-65; Libn Mt St Alphonsus Sem 65-. 9: ALA; CathLA (Sem Sect: Memb Chm); SE(NY)Lib ResourcesCoun. 13: Yes. 14: Catlg, ref, bk sel. 15: Mt St Alphonsus Sem, Esopus NY 12429.

POFFENBERGER, KATHRYN IONE (PURCELL). b Carlisle Ind 7 O 08. 5: Ind Central Col 26-30 (Mus) BM; Ball State summers 36-41 (Lib); UIll summer 43 (Lib); IndU summer 50-52 (Mus) MM. 7: Tchr Pleasantville High Sch, Pleasantville Ind 30-33; Libn & tchr: Glenwood High Sch, Glenwood Ind 33-36, Eden Twp Sch, Topeka Ind 36-41, Wilson Sch, S Bend Ind 41-46; Libn S Bend (Ind) Community Schs: Linden School 46-51, Oliver School 51-65, Jackson High School 65-68; Dir education media processing ctr S Bend Commun Schs 68-. 8: Catlgr Fed Pub Housing Auth, Wash DC summer 44; Acquis dept, NY Pub Lib summer 45. 9: ALA; -AASchL; IndLA; IndSchLA. 10: AAUW. 14: Catlg. 15: 19551 Jewell ave, South Bend In 46614.

POGANY, ANDRAS HENRIK. b Budapest Hungary 26 Je 19. 4: Hortenzia Lers. 5: Peter PazmanyU (Budapest) 42 (Law, Pol Sci) DJ, 46 (Pol) PhD; So Conn State Col 59 MS in LS. 6: Hungarian, Fr, Ger, Lat. 7: Asst order libn & bibliogr Yale U Lib 59-60; Asst chief ref libn Seton Hall U Lib 60-63, Assoc univ libn (assoc prof) 63-. 9: ALA; AAUP; CLA; NJLA. 10: Hungarian Freedom Fighters Fed; Amer Coun for Emigrees in the Professions Inc. 11: Golden Key of the City of Rochester NY 66. 12: "A City in the Darkness" (66); "Political Science and International Relations: a Bibliography" (67); Columnist for several Amer-Hungarian newspapers in USA & Can. 13: Yes. 14: Bibliog, ref. 15: 201 Raymond ave, South Orange NJ 07079.

POGANY, HORTENZIA LERS. b Budapest Hungary. 4: Dr Andras Pogany. 5: Pazmany U(Budapest) 37-4t Lang & Lit) MA; Rutgers62-65 MLS. 6: Hungarian, Ger, Fr, Lat. 7: High sch tchr, Budapest Hungary 42-44; Research asst Hungarian Nat Archives, Budapest Hungary 51-54; Asst libn Albertus Magnus Col 58-60; Catlgr Seton Hall U 60-64, Act chief catlg libn 64-, Asst Prof 64-. 9: Amer Classical League; ALA; CLA; NJLA. 10: Hungarian Freedom Fighters Fed of Amer. 12: Co-author "Political Science and International Relations; a recommended list of books" with Andras Pogany (67). 14: Catlg, rare bks. 15: 201 Raymond ave, S Orange NJ.

POHL, EMMA (PAGE) W(ILDER). b Louisburg NC 26 N 05. 5: Randolph-Macon Womans Col 23-27 (Lat) AB; Columbia 28-29 (Finance) UNC summers 53-56 BS in LS. 7: Security analyst Irving Trust Co, NYC 29-35; Tchr, later Libn High Sch, Aberdeen NC 48-57; Ref libn NC State U 57-. 9: SELA; NCLA. 10: Beta Phi Mu; Pi Beta PHI. 14: Ref. 15: 2634 Churchill rd, Raleigh NC.

POHL, GUNTHER ERICH. b Germany 22 Jl 25. 4: Dorothy E Beck. 5: NYU 43-46 (Hist) BA, 47-48 (Hist) MA; Columbia 50-51 (LS) MS. 6: Ger. 7: Libn local hist & geneal div Research Libs NY Pub Lib 48-, Chief local hist & geneal div. 8: Comp NY State Biog, Geneal & Portrait Index (250,000 names, 900v), Consul to the Assn for Records & Census Indexing. 9: ALA; NY Lib Club. 10: Lakeville PTA & Civic Assn. 14: Ref, local hist & geneal. 15: 24 Walden pl, Great Neck NY 11020.

POHL, ROBERT KARL. b Mendota Ill 6 Ag 16. 4: Lucile Timmerman. 5: Valparaiso U 45-49 (Hist) BA; UWis 49-50 BS in LS. 6: Ger, Fr. 7: US Armed Forces, Europ Theater 40-45; Dir of bkmob serv Door-Kewaunee Reg Lib, Sturgeon Bay Wis 50-53; Chief Libn Waupun Pub Lib, Waupun Wis 53-57; Dir Joliet Pub Lib Joliet Ill 57-. 9: ALA; IllLA (treas 68); Lib Adminrs Conf No Ill. 10: Kiwanis Internat. 14: Pub lib admin. 15: 1105 Krings lane, Joliet Ill 60435.

POHORECKY, NATALIA VERA. b Saskatoon Saskatchewan Can 27 Jl 34. 5: UManitoba 53-56 9eng, Psych) BA; McGill University 59-60 BLS. 6: Ukrainian, Fr. 7: Lab tech Swift Canadian Co, St Boniface Manitoba 52-53; Lib asst Winnipeg Pub Lib, Winnipeg Manitoba 56-59, Bkmob libn 60-61; UManitoba Med Lib: Circ & ref libn 61-65, Ref libn 65-. 9: CanLA. 10: YWCA. 14: Ref, research. 15: 329 Polson ave, Winnipeg 4 Manitoba Can.

POIRIER, ROBERT JAMES. b Pittsburgh 23 Jl 39. 4: Marian Elborne. 5: Duquesne U 59-61 (Eng, Educ) BEd; UPittsburgh 63-64 MLS. 6: Fr. 7 Tchr Penn Hills Sch Dist, Pittsburgh 61-64; Tchr Point Park Jr Col 62-; Libn N Braddock High Sch, Pittsburgh 64-; Libn Carnegie Lib of Pittsburgh 65-; Dir lib S Campus Commun Col of Allegheny Co. 9: Penn State EA; PittsburghLA. 14: Col lib work, educ media. 15: 259 Oakcrest lane, Pittsburgh Pa 15236.

POKORNY, LEITHIA (MURRAY). b Coopers Plains NY 2 N 18. 4: William F Pokorny. 5: Geneseo State Tchrs Col 36-40 (LS) BS; St Lawrence U summers, Ext 46-47 (Admin); State U Col of Educ(New Paltz NY) summers 57, 58 (Educ). 7: Libn Painted Post High Sch, Painted Post NY 40-42; Asst libn Summer Session Potsdam State Tchrs Col 42-47; Consul lib n Clarkson Col of Tech 42-47, Head Lib 46-47; Libn head of circ div Hunter Col 47-51; Coordinator of libs Half Hollow Hills, Huntington LI NY 57-. 8: Consul on estab a loc pub lib 59-60. 9: NEA; NYLA; NYStateTchrsAssn; Nassau-Suffolk LA. 10: PTA; Active in tchrs assn & civic assns. 13: Yes. 14: Child lit, ref. 15: 1 Rupert pl, Melville, Huntington Sta, LI NY 11743.

POLACHECK, DEMAREST LLOYD. b Milwaukee 13 Jl 18. 4: Janet Gregg. 5: Chicago 35-47 (Eng) AA, PhB; Ohio State U 43-44 (Ital) ASTP Certif; Yale 47-50 (Drama) MFA; Kent State U 61-67 MLS. 6: Ital, Sp. 7: Army serv Med Corps (Cpl) 42-46; Dir various commun theatres 50-56; Research asst Fels Research Inst, Yellow Springs Ohio 56-59; 1st asst libn Delta Col 59-61; A-V coordinator Washington High Sch, Massillon Ohio 63-66; Tchr Massillon Local Sch Dist, Massillon Ohio 61-67; Hd adult humanities dept Canton Pub Lib, Canton Ohio 67-68, Hd adult serv 68-. 9: ALA; -RTSD; -ACRL; -AISD; OhioLA (Bd Adult Serv RT); OhioEA; E Cent Ohio Tchrs Assn. 10: Amer Assn of Physl Anthropol; Actors Equity Assn; AAUP; Urban League; NAACP. 12: Assoc ed OhioLA "Newsletter". 13: Yes. 14: Adult serv, acquis, lib automation. 15: 36 Fourth st, SE, Massillon Ohio 44646.

POLACHECK, JANET GREGG (ELIZABETH). b Cleveland 13 S 14. 4: Demarest Lloyd Polacheck. 5: West Res 38-41 (Hist) BA, 41-43 BSLS. 07: Page & yp libn Cleveland Pub Lib 30-44; Co Libn Belmont Co, Martins Ferry Ohio 44-48; Head Libn Gallia Co, Gallipolis Ohio 48-52; Head Libn Portsmouth Pub Lib, Portsmouth Ohio 52-56; Co Libn Stark co, Springfield Ohio 56-57; Act libn Wilmington Col 57-59; Head Libn Delta Col 59-61; Coordr sch libs Massillon Pub Schs, Massillon Ohio 61-67; Coord ya serv Canton Pub Lib, Canton Ohio 67-. 8: Adv Coun Kent State U Sch Lib Serv 67-69. 9: ALA-AASchL; NEA; OhioASchL; OhioEA (Life mem); Stark Co(Ohio) Libns Assn (past pres); OhioLA (YA Serv RT; chm Nomin ating Com 69; Legis Com 48; Exec Com 49). 10: NAACP; Urban League; AAUW. 11: 1st Alper Award, Kent State U. 12: " Mystery on Wheels." 14: Ya serv. 15: 47 6 st SE, Massillon Ohio 44646.

POLADIAN, SIRVART. b Aleppo Syria. 4: John Kachie Poladian. 5: UCal(Berkeley) 32-37 (Music) BA, MA, TC; Cornell U42-43, 45-46 (Musicology) PhD; Columbia 40-42 (Musicology), 53-56 BS in LS. 6: Armenian, Turkish, Ger, Fr. 7 Assoc Prof of Music Fla State U 46-48; Ref libn NY Pub Lib 53-68; Registrar-Catlgr Museum Village (Amer Hist Mus), Monroe NY 69-. 9: Amer Muicological Soc; MusLA. 10: AAUW. 12: "Armenian Folk Songs (42); "Sir Arthur Sullivan; an Index to His Vocal Works (61); Record review Column, "The Music Journal ('62-64). 13: Yes. 14: Ref, rare bks. 15: RD1 Box 41A, Craigville rd, Chester NY 10918.

POLAN, MORRIS. b St Louis 24 Ja 24. 4: Cecelia Hassan. 5: SoIll U 41-42; UCLA 46-49 (Pol Sci) AB, 49-50 (Pol Sci); USoCal 51 MSLS. 7: (Cpl) USAF, US, Guam 43-46; Libn Mun Ref Lib, Los Angeles 51-52; Ser & ref libn Hancock Lib of Biol & Oceanography USoCal 52-55; Cal State Col(Los Angeles): Period libn 55, Supv ref libn 56, Chief of reader serv 58, Act col libn 65-. 8: Adv Bd USoCal Sch of Lib Sci 66-69; Adv Coun UCal Lib Schs 67-70. 9: ALA; CalLA (pres Col, Univ & Res Libs Sect 66). 10: AAUP; Assn Cal State Col Profs. 14: Col & univ lib admin, prof educ. 15: 11130 Greenlawn ave, Culver City Cal 90230.

POLAND, GERTRUDE (KRAFT). b Chicago 18 D 24. 4: Robert R Poland. 5: UAriz 43-47 (Drama) BFA; Yale 47-51 (Drama) MFA; UTex 60-62 MLS. 6: Sp, Ger. 7: Tchr Bishops Sch, LaJolla Cal 58-59; Lib internee Yale U Lib 61-62; Mss libn UAriz 62-64; Ref libn Tucson Pub Lib 64-68, Br libn 68-. 9: ALA; ArizStateLA; Bus Mgr, "The Arizona Librarian. 10:

Beta Phi Mu. 14: Ref, fine arts, theatrical material. 15: 2026 E 5th st, Tucson Az 85719.

POLAND, ROBERT RALPH. b Arthur Ill 26 Jl 23. 4: Getrude Kraft. 5: Knox Col 43-46 (Hist) BA; UIll46-47 BS in LS. 7: Gifts & exch asst UIll Lib(Urbana) 46-48; Ser libn UNotre Dame Lib(Ind) 48-50; Order libn UTex Lib 50-55; Partner Lampl & Poland Bksellers, Costa Mesa Cal 55-57; Head tech processes Dalas Pub Dallas 57-58; Head acquis dept UAriz Lib 59-. 9: ALA; ArizStateLA (pres Col & Univ Div 63-64); SWLA (chm Constit & By-Laws Com, Resources & Tech Serv Sect 65-66). 10: ACLU. 12: Ed "Arizona Librarian (64-66). 14: Acquis. 15: 2026 E 5th st, Tucson Az 85719.

POLCARI, ANN LINDA. b NYC 19 F 43. 5: Queens Col (NY) 59-63 (Fr) BA; UPittsburgh 67-68 MLS. 6: Fr, Russian. 7: Lib asst PurdueU Libs (Lafayette) 63-65; Computer Sci Dept Penn StateU (University Park) 66-67; Libn I (ref) UConn Lib (Storrs) 68-. 9: ALA; ConnLA. 10: Beta Phi Mu. 14: Ref. 15: Univ of Conn Lib, Storrs Ct 06268.

POLCYN, BARBARA J. b Manistee Mich 25 F 30. 5: Central Mich U 48-52 (LS, Soc Sci) BS; West Mich U 55-59 (LS) MA. 7: Libn Mich Sch for the Deaf, Flint Mich 52-53; Tchr Guardian Angels Sch, Manistee MICH 53-54; Tchr Lincoln Sch, Muskegon Mich 54-58; Libn Bunker Sch, Muskegon Mich 5-; Coordr Muskegon Sch Libs, Muskegon Mich 62-. 8: Libn, Muskegon Center Lib WEST Mich U, summer 61. 9: ALA-AASchL (Subcom on Memb); NEA; Assn Childhood Educ Internat; MichLA; MichASchL (chm Supvs Sect 68-69); MichEA; Lakeshore Libns Assn. 10: AAUW; Coun of Womens Club; Polish Arts Soc of Grand Rapids, Mich; Girl Scouts Coun. 14: Sch & child serv, ya, tech proc. 15: 2142 Harrison ave, Muskegon Mich 49441.

POLCZYNSKI, JULIA. b Wiatka USSR. 5: UPoznan (Poland) 43-47 (Dentistry) DDS; Columbia 63-64 (Biochem), 64-65 (LS) 6: Polish, Fr, Lat. 7: DDS priv practice & Pub Health Serv, Warsaw Poland 48-62; Dental tech Dental Labs, Jersey City NJ 63-64; Libn Queens Borough Pub Lib, Jamaica NY 65-66; Libn NYU, Eng sci lib 67, PIB Grad Center Lib 67-. 9: SLA; NY Tech Serv Libns. 10: Columbia U Sch of Lib Serv Alumni; Polish Astron Soc; Polish Dental Soc; Polish Med Alliance; Nat Shrine of St Jude. 14: Admin, automation, ref, res reports, govy docs, bibliog. 15: 104-20 Queens blvd, Apt 19-P, Forest Hills NY 11375.

POLETTE, NANCY JANE. b Richmond Hts Mo 18 My 30. 4: Paul L Polette. 5: William Woods 9speech) AA; Wash U (Educ) BS Ed; So Ill U (Inst Materials) MS. 7: Tchr 53-54, ritenour Sch Dist, St Louis Co 53-54; Instr lib sci So Ill U 68-69; Elem materials coord Pattonville School Dist, St Louis Co 54-69. 8: Consultant Lutheran Teachers State Conference Mo 67-68; Consultant Mo Lib Assoc Storytelling Conf 69. 9: ALA; NEA; MoLA; MoASchL; MoStateTA. 10: Bd of Dirs, Leukemia Guild of Mo & Ill. 13: Yes. 14: Child serv. 15: 1190 Boulder dr, Florissant Mo 63031.

POLHAMUS, JULIA ELIZABETH (SALOWICH). b Detroit 1 F 41. 4: Royal George Polhamus Jr. 5: UMich 58-62 (Eng) BA, 62-5 MALS. 6: Sp, Fr. 7: Head Libn (stud) A C Lloyd Resid Hall 59-62; Preprof libn Detroit Pub Lib 62-63; Child libn Wayne Co(Mich) Pub Lib System Ecorse Br 63-64, Head Libn Riverview Br 64-68; Asst libn Lincoln Park Br 68-. 14: Adult readers adv, child serv. 15: 15120 Philomene, Allen Park Mi 48101.

POLICH, KATHERINE (ROTHERHAM). b Fresno Cal 8 Mr 40. 4: John Leo Polich. 5: Fullerton Jr Col 58-59; UCal(Berkeley) 59-62 (Hist) BA; Cal State Col(Fullerton) 62-63; USoCal 63-65 MS in LS; UNM 66-69 (Hist). 6: Fr, Sp. 7: Jr libn Fullerton Pub Lib, Fullerton Cal 62-63; Catlgr UNM 65-67; Libn San Diego State Col (Imperial Valley Campus - Calexico) 69-. 14: Catlg, ref, archives. 15: Imperial Valley Campus, San Diego State Col, 720 Heber ave, Calexico Ca 92231.

POLISHOOK, LOUIS. b Boston Mass 24 D 17. 4: Grace Goldman. 5: SuffolkU 35-39 (Law) LLB; Bentley Col 50-54 (Accounting). 6: Fr, Yiddish. 7: Sgt US Army, England & France 43-46; Asst prof Boston Pub Lib (br) 36-43, Asst prof (sci dept) 46-54, Chief of central charging 55-67, Asst supv readers serv 67-. 14: Ref. 15: 73 Withington rd, Newtonville Ma 02160.

POLK, BAXTER. b Santa Anna Tex 27 Ag 14. 5: Hardin-Simmons U 32-35 (Eng) BA; UOkla 35-36 BS in LS; Columbia 50-51 MS in LS. 6: Sp, Fr. 7: ULibn UTex (El Paso) 36-. 8: Lib Resources Com, Tex Commsn on Higher Educ. 9: Tex Coun State Libns. 10: NAACP; El Paso Humane Soc. 14: Admin, rare bks. 15: Tex West Col Lib, El Paso Tex 79902.

POLL, BERNARD. b Seattle 24 F 27. 4: Orabelle Connally. 5: UWash 43-47 (Philos) BA; Columbia 47-48 (Philos) MA; UMich 49-50 (Philos); UWash 51-52 (LS) MA. 6: Fr, Ger. 7: Catlgr Spokane Co Rural Lib 52-53; Libn Mltnomah Co Lib 53-56; Libn Seattle Pub Lib 56-57; Coordinator of child serv Kng Co(Wash) Lib System 57-. 8: Child program reader, KRAB Radio, Seattle; Exc dir Nat Lib Week, Wash 64; Lecturer UWash Sch of Libnship Ext 61-64; Visiting instr UBC summer 63, UVictoria summer 65. 9: ALA (Planning Com for Model Lib, Seattle Worlds Fair); PNLA (Com for Young Readers Choice Award); WashLA (Exec Com 66-67). 10: Amer Friends Serv Com; Seattle Film Assocs. 13: Yes. 14: Child serv in pub libs. 15: King Co Lib System, 1100 E Union, Seattle Wa 98122.

POLLACK, ERVIN HAROLD. b St Louis 19 Ap 13. 4: Lydia Weiss. 5: St Louis U 32-35 (Pre-law) Washington U 36-39 JD; Columbia 39-41 (LS). 6: Ger. 7: Libn Hays, Podell & Shulman, NYC 42; Sec Off of Price Admin, Wash DC 42-47; Ohio State U: Libn & Asst Prof of Law 47-50, Libn & Assoc Prof of Law 50-54, Libn &Prof of Law 54-. 8: Consul off of Econ Stabil 51; Consul LC 59-64; Consul Dept of State 66-; Numerous other consultantships. 9: Amer Bar Assn; AALL (pres 58-59); Amer Soc Polit & Leg Philos; Ohio State Bar Assn (chm Libs Com 50-60); OhioLA (pres 49-51); Internat Assn for Philosophy of Law & Soc Philosophy. 10: Trustee, Ohio Legal Center; Order of Coif; Trustee Ohio Lib Found; Fellow Ohio State Bar Assn Found. 12: "Fundamentals of Legal Research" (3rd ed 67); "Ohio Unreported Judicial Decisions Prior to 1823" (52); "Ohio Court Rules Annotated" (49); "Legal Research and Materials, Ohio Ed" (50); "OPA Service and Desk Books" 42-47; "Supplement to the Checklist of Session Laws" (41); "Brandeis Reader" (56). 13: Yes. 14: Admin. 15: 1659 N High st, Columbus Ohio 43210.

POLLACK, ROBERT JOSEPH. b Flint Mich 17 Ap 36. 4: Patricia Chema. 5: Flint Jr Col 58-60; UMich (Flint) 60-64 (Biol) BA; UMich (Rackham) 64-69 MALS. 7: Med admin specialist (A/1c) USAF 54-64; Stock clk Sears Roebuck, Flint Mich 58-60; Lib asst Genesee Co Lib, Flint Mich 60-67, Br libn 67-69, Hd pub serv 69-. 9: ALA (Jr Mem RT); MichLA. 10: Flint Lib Club. 15: 2701 Branch rd Lot 82, Flint Mi 48506.

POLLAK, FELIX. b Vienna 11 N 09. 4: Sara Allen. 5: UVienna Dr Jur; UBuffalo 40-41 BSLS; UMich 48-49 AMLS. 6: Ger, Lat, Gk. 7: Readers adv Buffalo Pub Lib, Buffalo NY 41-43, 45-48; US Army Interpreter PW Camps 43-45; Curator of spec collections Northwestern U 49-59; Curator of rare bks UWis 59-. 10: Beta Phi Mu. 12: "The Castle and the Flaw (poems) (63). 13: Yes. 14: Rare bks. 15: Mem Lib Univ of Wis, Madison Wis 53706.

POLLARD, FRANCES (MARGUERITE). b Florence Ala 7 O 20. 5: Selma U 36-38 (Elem Educ) Jr Col Diploma; Ala State Col 39-41 (Elem Educ) BS in Ed; West Res 48-49 MS in LS; Columbia 52-54 (LS); West Res 59-63 (LS) PhD. 6: Fr, Ger. 7: Tchr Waterloo Elem Sch, Waterloo Ala 38-39; Tchr Marengo Co Train Sch, Thomaston Ala 41-42; Tchr Sterling High Sch, Sheffield Ala 42-43; Lib asst Ft McClellan Ala 43-46; Lib asst Ala State Col 46-48; Stud aide child room Sterling Br, Cleveland Pub Lib 48-49; Asst libn Ala State Col 49-61; Temp asst to the chief of the publ dept ALA, Chicago 52; Head Libn & Chm of Lib Educ Dept Ala State Col 61-63; Assoc Prof of Lib Sci & admin asst Booth Lib East Ill U 63-. 8: Ill State Lib Adv Coun on Lib Devel 66-. 9: ALA (Subscription Bks Com 52-56); NEA; IllLA; IllEA. 10: Amer Tchrs Assn; Amer Sociol Assn; AAUW; AAUP; Soc for Applied Anthrop; Great Bks Discussion Gp. 12: Contrib "Major Problems in the Education of Librarians," ed by R D Leigh (54). 13: Yes. 14: Admin, ref, lib educ, col & univ libs. 15: 1330 A st, Charleston Ill 61920.

POLLARD, WILLIAM ROBERT. b Farmville NC 7 Ja 33. 4: Elizabeth Hatch. 5: UNC 51-58 (Eng, Educ) AB, 58-65 MS in LS. 6: Fr. 7: Personnel clerk US Army, Ft Eustis Va 53-55; Lib asst UNC Lib(Chapel Hill) 58-65; Catlgr NC State U(Raleigh) 65-68, Asst rf libn 68-. 9: NCLA. 14: Tech proc, ref. 15: PO Box 5214, Raleigh NC 27607.

POLLOCK, JAMES (WILSON). b Assiut Egypt 21 Mr 22. 4: Rachel Buchanan. 5: Monmouth Col(Ill) 40-43, 45 (Philos, psych) BA; Pittsburgh-Xenia Theol Sem 43-45 (Theol, Bible) BD; Andover Newton Theol Sch 51-52 (Pastoral Psych) STM; Hartford Sem Found 58-61 (Arabic & Islamic studies) MA, Ind U 61-64 (LS) MA. 6: Arabic, Fr. 7: Missionary Bd of Foreign Missions United Presbyterian Church of NA, Egypt

46-56; Clergyman United Presbyterian Church, Eskridge Kan 56-57; Period libn Hartford Sem Found, Hartford Conn 57-60; Catlgr of Near East materials, Ind U 61-65, Libn for Near E Studies 66-. 9: ALA; Ohio Valley Group Tech Serv Libns; Amer Oriental Soc; Middle East Studies Assn (mem Lib Subcom). 10: Lions Club; Amer Friends of the Middle East. 12: Comp Index of "The Muslim World, v 26-50 (36-60). 13: Yes. 14: Acquis, bibliog, catlg, ref, training of libns. 15: 221 E Chester dr, Ellettsville Ind 47429.

POLLOCK, JOHN W. b Fargo ND 11 O 21. 4: Nancy Higbee. 5: Carleton Col 39-41 (Eng); Harvard 41-43, 46 (Eng) SB; San Jose State Col 61-62, 66 (LS) MA. 7: Chief lib br NASA Ames Research Ctr, Mt View Cal 64-67; Order libn De Anza Col 68; Ref libn W Valley Jr Col 68-. 9: SLA; ASIS; CalLA; CalASchL. 14: Ref. 15: 4043 Ben Lomond dr, Palo Alto Ca 94306.

POLLOCK, LUELLA (REBECCA). b Waynesburg Penn 1 Jl 20. 5: W Va U 36-40 (Math) AB; Peabody Col 41-42 BS in LS; State UIowa 42-45 (Statistics) MS. 7: Math physics libn State UIowa (Iowa City) 42-45; Ref libn Vassar Col 45-55, Hd readers serv 55-57; Libn Reed Col 57-. 9: ALA (Coun 59-60); -ACRL (Grants Com 57-60); PNLA; OreLA (Rep to PNLA 68-69). 11: Fulbright fellowship 53-54. 14: Admin. 15: 4805 SE 36 pl, Portland Or 97202.

POLLOCK, MARGARET MARIE. b Highland Park Mich 3 N 16. 5: Penn State Col 34-35; Col of Wooster 35-38 (Hist) BA; Columbia 38-39 BLS. 7: Tchr-libn Kempsville High Sch, Kempsville Va 39-40; Child libn Baldwin Pub Lib, Baldwin LI NY 40-46; Ref libn Bard Col Lib 46-48; Akron Pub Lib, Akron Ohio: Asst main child rooms 48-50, Child libn Maple Valley Br 50-57, Head of main child room 57-. 9: ALA; OhioLA; Akron Pub Lib Staff Assn. 10: Womens Nat Bk Assn; AAUW; YWCA. ; PROCONESS (Bus & Prof Women's Group). 14: Child serv. 15: 753 W Market st, apt 201 Akron Oh 44303.

POLLOT, MICHAEL JOHN. b Peoria Ill 30 S 23. 4: Florence Roberts. 5: Fla State U 63-64 (Hist) BA, 64-65 (LS) MS. 6: Fr. 7: (Maj now Ret) US Air Force, Aircraft Commander 42-63; Catlgr Air U Lib, Maxwell AFB Ala 65-67, Chief doc syst br 67-68, Chief indexing syst br 69-. 9: SLA; AlaLA. 14: Admin, automation/mechan systems. 15: 176 Maple, Prattville Al 36067.

POLSON, BILLIE MAE. b St Louis 5 N 32. 5: UNev 50-54 (Eng) BA; USoCal 55-56 MS in LS. 6: Fr, Sp. 7: Child libn Los Angeles Pub Lib, Westchester Br 56-59; Nev So U: Catlg libn 59-63, Act libn 64-65, Head catlg libn 65-. 9: ALA (Recrt Com, So Nev); NevLA (sec-treas Acad & Spec Libs Sect); MPLA. 10: AAUW; Nev So U Faculty Women Club; AAUP; USoCal General Alum Club. 12: "Cataloging Manual, Nev So U Lib; "Library Handbook for Nev So U. 14: Catlg, child lit. 14: Catlg, child lit. 15: 1420 E Helm dr, Las Vegas Nv 89109.

POMEROY, ANNA B. b Port Royal Penn 12 O 15. 5: Wilson Col 33-37 (Fr) AB; Drexel 37-38 BSin LS. 6: Fr. 7: Ct asst libn Wilson Col 38-39; Asst libn Allegheny Col 39-42; USNR (Lt) 42-46; Libn bus br Carnegie Lib of Pittsburgh 46-. 9: ALA; SLA; PennLA: 10: Zonta Internat. 14: Bus ref. 15: 6829 Church ave, Ben Avon, Pittsburgh 15202.

POMEROY, MARJORIE JANE. b Hudson Wyo 4 Ja 20. 5: UToledo 38-39; Ohio State U 40-41, 47-48 (Hist, Eng) BS in Ed (cum laude); UColo 46; UWis 50-51 MS in LS. 7: Clerk Lucas Co Lib, Maumee Ohio 41-43; (Sgt) US Marine Corps Womens Res, San Diego 43-45; Eng tchr Brown High Sch, Conover Ohio 49-50; Co libn Malheur Co Lib, Ontario Ore 51-58; Asst state libn State Lib 58-59; Dir E Central Reg LB, Cambridge Minn 59-66; Admin serv libn Bartholomew Co Lib, Columbus Ind 67-68; Dir NW Kan Lib System, Hokie 68-. 9: ALA; KanLA. 10: Bus & Profess Women; Delta Kappa Gamma. 11: E Central Reg Lib wom 1964 Book-of-the-Month Club top National award. 13: Yes. 14: Admin. 15: Box 642, Hoxie Ks 67740.

POMNITZ, JOAN E (ROMANOUGH). b Delta Penn 14 Ap 40. 4: William E Pomnitz. 5: Chestnut Hill Col 58-62 (Art) BA; Villanova U 62-63 (LS) MS. 7: Ref circ Villanova U 63-65; Asst libn Stuart Hall, Stanton Va 66-67; Libn St Frances De Sales High Sch 67-. 12: Indexer & asst ed "Catholic Periodical Index (63-65). 14: Ref, indexing. 15: 458 Oakdale ave, Utica NY 13502.

POMPEY, H RUTH (KEYS). b Quincy Fla 9 My 23. 4: C Spencer Pompey. 5: Fla A&M Col 44-45 (Soc Studies) AB; Atlanta summers 46-48 BLS; Syracuse summer 59; Fla Atlantic U 68. 7: Tchr-libn Carver Elem Jr & Sr High Sch, Delray Beach Fla; Libn Jr & Sr High Sch, Delray Beach Fla; Libn Plumosa Elem Sch, Delray Beach Fla summer 65; Libn Hagen Rd Elem Sch, Boynton Beach Fla. 9: ALA; NEA; Amer Tchrs Assn; Fla State Tchrs Assn; FlaASchL; Sec Palm Beach Co Mass Media Assn; Sec Palm Beach Co Clrm Tchrs Assn. 10: Frances J Bright Womans Club; Naciremas Club; Alpha Kappa Alpha; LWV. 14: Catlg, child reader serv. 15: P O Box 1533, Delray Beach Fl 33444.

POMRANKA, EDWIN CARL. b Wellington Colo 31 Ja 11. 4: Marjorie Romans. 5 UColo 28-33 (Econ) BA; Fletcher Sch of Law & Diplomacy 33-34 (Internat Law) MA; USoCal 53-54 MS in LS. 6: Ger, Sp, Fr, Farsi. 7: Various positions in advertising, selling, & mgt Counselling with firms in Boston, NYC & Denver 34-54; Catlg div UWyo Lib 54-57, 59-60; Lib consul AID Contract Team, Kabul Afghanistan 57-59; Ind economist AID Contract Team, Ankara Turkey 60-62; Spec Asst to dir UWash Lib 62-. 9: ALA; NMA. 10: Phi Beta Kappa; Delta Sigma Rho; Pi Gamma Mu. 14: Admin, catlg, internat libnship. 15: 2467 42nd ave W, Seattle 98199.

POND, PATRICIA (BROWN). b Mankato Minn 17 Ja 30. 4: Judson S Pond. 5: Col of St Catherine 48-52 (Eng, LS) BA; UMinn 54-55 (LS) MA; Chicago 65- (LS) (beginning work on PhD). 6: Ger. 7: Sch libn Ind Sch Dist 21, Mt Iron Minn 52-54; Sch libn Greenburgh No 8 Schs, Greenburgh NY 55-56; Libn Robbinsdale High Sch, Robbinsdale Minn 56-62; Asst Prof Lib Sch UMinn 62-63; Tchg asst UChicago Grad Lib Sch 65-67; Asst Prof UOre Lib Sch (Eugene) 67-. 08: UMinn Lib Sch Inst Conf dir, Ap 63; Visiting instr E Wash State Col, summer 64; Visiting lecturer, Lib Sch UMinn, summer 65; UChicago Ctr for Child Bks Evaluation Com 65-67. 9: ALA; AALS; NEA; PNLA; OreASchL; OreEA; OIMA. 10: Phi Beta Kappa; Beta Phi Mu; Delta Phi Lambda; Kappa Gamma Pi. 13: Yes. 14: Sch libs, child & yp serv, lib educ, hist child lit. 15: 3540 Mill, Eugene Or 97405.

PONTIER, GRACE A (deVRIES). b Garfield NJ 27 Mr 14. 4: Peter L Pontier. 5: Newark State Col 31-35 (Educ) BS; Paterson State Col 59-61 (Educ) MA, 61-65 MLS. 6: Dutch. 7: Tchr: Comstock Mich 36-40 Midland Park NJ 40-42, franklin Lakes NJ 58-62; Sch libn Franklin Lakes NJ 62-. 8: Adv Franklin Lakes (NJ) Pub Elem Schs 63, 66. 9: NEA; ALA; NJEA; NJSchLA; Bergen Co ASchL (2nd v-pres 68-69). 10: Amer Guild of Organists. 14: Elem sch libs. 15: 187 Birch rd, Franklin Lakes NJ 07417.

POOL, JANE. b Nevada Tex 13 N 32. 5:n No State U 50-53 (LS) BA; UIll 60-61 (LS) MS; UIll 65-67. 6: Fr. 7: Elem sch libn pub schs, Wichita Falls Tex 53-57; Elem sch libn, pub schs, Dallas 57-58; Elem sch libn pub schs, Andrews Tex 58-60; Ref libn So Methodist U Sci Lib 61-65; Instr No Tex State U 67-. 8: Visitinginstr Lib Serv Dept NoTex State U 64-65. 9: SLA; ALA; TexLA. 10: Delta Kappa Gamma; Beta Phi Mu. 14: Ref, lib educ, sch media ctrs. 15: Nevada Tex 75073.

POOLE, FRAZER GLENDON. b Federalsburg Md 5 N 15. 4: Rebecca Veach. 5: Catawba Col 33-37 (Bot) BA; UNC 41-42 (Bot); US Naval Acad Post Grad Sch 43-44 (Aerological Engnr) Certif; UCal 48-49 BLS. 7: Instr of Biol Catawa Col 39-41; Lt Cdr US Naval Res, Aerological Off 42-46; Libn I UCal(Berkeley) 49-50; Head spec & serv depts UCal (Santa Barbara) 50-54; Cdr US Naval Res Aerological Off 50-52; Asst libn UCal(Santa Barbara) 54-59; Dir Lib Tech Proj ALA, Chicago 59-63; Dir Lib UIll(Chicago Circle) 63-67; Asst dir for preserv Admin Dept LC 67-. 8: Lib bldg consul. 9: ADI; ALA (chm Copying Methods Sect 65-66) -LAD (Bldg & Equip Sect: chm Equip Com 64-66); IllLA (chm For Exch-Program Com 64-66); Chicago Lib Club (pres 65-66); SAA. 10: Caxton Club(Chicago); Wilderness Society; Sierra Club; Internat Inst Conserv. 12: Issue ed "Library Trends (Ap 65). 13: Yes. 14: Tech serv. 15: 5410 Surrey st, Chevy Chase Md 20015.

POOLE, HERBERT (LESLIE). b Pittsboro NC 7 N 37. 4: Donna Ballenger. 5: UNC 59-62 (Ger Lit) AB, 62-64 MSLS. 6: Ger, Russian. 7: Spec 5, Russian Interpreter US Army, Frankfurt W Germany 56-59; Suv Interlib Center UNC (Chapel Hill) 62-63, Lib Fellow 63-64; Head circ dept UAla Libs 64-66; Dir libs Guilford Col 66-; Visiting lecturer Emory U 67; Lib coord Tri-college consort, Greensboro NC 69. 8: Lib consul, UAla Computer Center 65-66. 9: AlaLA; Ala Jr Libns (chm-elect 65-66); SELA; NCLA; AAUP (v-pres Guilford Col Chap 68-69). 10: Delta Phi Alpha; Beta Phi Mu; chm Com on Lib Affairs, Piedmont U Ctr 67-69; Greensboro Lib Club (pres 68-69). 11: Ger Embassy Bk Award, 60. 13: Yes. 14: Ref, rare bks. 15: Guilford Col Lib, Guilford Col, Greensboro NC 27410.

POOLE, KINUYE (JITODAI). b Seattle. 4: Harold A Poole. 5: So Ill U44-48 (Art) BS; UWash 51-54 (LS) ML. 6: Japanese. 7: Catlg libn UWash 53-. 9: ALA; PNLA. 10: UWash Faculty Womens Club. 14: Catlg. 15: 4223 Latona ave NE, Seattle 98105.

POOLE, MARY E(DNA). b Galveston Tex 7 Je 17. 5:UHouston 36-39 (Eng Lit, Sociol) AB; UMinn 40 (Higher Educ); State U Iowa 41, 42 (Writers Wkshop, Radio-Drama); Columbia 50-51 MLS. 6: Sp, Ital, Fr. 7: Asst Instr West World Lit remedial Eng clinics, creative writing & speech UHouston 39-42; Ed asst Gulf Publ Co, Houston 43-49, libn 48-49; Asst libn Jewish Mem Hosp Med Lib, NYC 50; Libn Amer Inst of Banking, NYC 50-51; Trust libn Army Spec Serv, Trieste FTT 51-53; Post libn USFA, Linz Austria 53-54; Head Grad Sch of Bus Lib, Columbia U 54-57; Ref asst Richmond Pub Lib, Richmond Cal 57; Adult Serv libn Washoe Co Lib, Reno Nev 58-62; Reviewer adult bks "Booklist (ALA), Chicago 62-63; Asst ed "HOIC: Books for College Libraries, Middletown Conn 63-66; Mgr lib serv dept UChicago Press 66-67; Head libn Kendall Col 67-. 8: Consul, Nev State Lib 60-61; Governors Com for the Aging (61). 9: ALA (Notable Bks Coun 61);-ACRL (Jr Col Div); Amer Assn Jr Cols; IllLA (Nat Lib Week Com 69; Col & Univ Sect). 10: Columbia Grad Sch of Lib Serv Alumni Assn. 11: Poetry Bk Award, Tex Inst of Letters, 50. 12: "Being in Night (50). 13: Yes. 14: Bldg lib collections, a-v, bk reviewing, ed, promotion. 15: 800 Hinman ave, Evanston Il 60202.

POOLE, MARY ELIZABETH. b Troy NC 20 O 14. 5: Duke 31-35 (Hist) AB; UNC 35-36 ABLS. 7: Document libn Duke U Lib 36-43; Document libn Va Polytech Inst 43-44; Ref & document libn The D H Hill Lib NC State Col(Raleigh) 44-53, Document libn 53-. 8: Currently wking on Author Index to Monthly Catlg of US Govt Publns for yrs 1947-62. 9: ALA; SLA; NCLA; SELA. 10: Delta Kappa Gamma. 12: Comp: "History References from the Idustrial Arts Index 1912-1917, Univ Microfilms 67; "Documents Office Classification, Univ Microfilms (59); Documents Office Classification Numbers for Cuttered Documents 1910-1924, pt I, A-Y3, Univ Microfilms (60). 14: US govt publns. 15: A-6 Raleigh apts, Raleigh NC 27605.

POOLE, SANDRA (LILLIAN). b New Orleans 23 Je 38. 5: Mary Washington Col of UVa 56-60 (Eng) BA; LSU 60-61 (LS) MS. 6: Sp, Gk. 7: Ref libn Kan City Mo Pub Lib 61-62; Acquis libn Park Col 62-64; Consul Mich State Lib 64-65; Catlgr UMo (Kan City) 65-, Hd of acquis 66-68; Ref libn Kan City Pub Lib, Kan City Kan 68. 13: Yes. 14: Reviewing, catlg. 15: 1323 N 77th st, Kansas City Ks 66112.

POOLER, (BENJAMIN) JACK. b Okla City Okla 9 Je 21. 5: UCal (Berkeley) 47-50 (Slavic Lang) AB, 53-54 BLS. 6: Russian. 7: Ref libn UCal Lib (Berkeley) 54-56, Asst hd physical sci libs 56-59; Chief sci div & dir TIS Stanford U Libs 60-. 9: SLA; CalLA. 10: AAUP. 12: Co-auth "Guide to Russian Reference Books, Volume V: Science, Technology, Medicine" (67). 13: Yes. 14: Sci libs, info serv to indus. 15: 530 Lowell, Palo Alto Ca 94301.

POOLEY, BEVERLEY JOHN. b London 4 Ap 34. 4: Patricia Joan Ray. 5: Cambridge U (Eng) 53-57 BA, UMich 57-60 LLM, SJD, 63-64 MALS. 6: Fr, Ger. 7: Legis analyst Legis Research Center UMich 58-60; Lecturer Dept of Law UGhana (Legon Ghana) 60-62; Instr UMich Law Sch 62-63, Asst Prof 63-66; Dir UMich Law Lib 65-; Assoc Prof 66-. 9: AALL; African Studies Assn. 11: Blackstone Scholar, Middle Temple, London. 12: "The Evolution of British Planning Legislation" (60); "Planning and Zoning in the United States" (61). 13: Yes. 14: Admin. 15: Law Lib, Univ of Mich, Ann Arbor Mich 48104.

POOLEY, ELEANOR L. b Greene Iowa 5 Jl 15. 5: Coe Col 32-36 (Hist, Sociol) BA; UColo summer 39 (Educ); State Col Iowa 57-58 (LS); Rutgers 58-59 MLS. 7: High sch tchr Kensett Pub Sch, Kensett Iowa 36-40; Sec, Commanding Off US Army AF Base, France Field CZ 41-42; Chief clerk Mil Personnel Sect US Army Admin Sch, Grinnell Iowa 42-43; Admin asst The Adjutant Gens Off, Pentagon 43-49; Sect, head, Ind adv Coms, OPS, Wash DC 51-53; Deputy clerk US Dist Court, No Dist of Iowa, Sioux City Iowa 53-55; Sec, libn State Col Iowa 57-58; Acquis libn Douglass Col 59-62; Acquis libn Ariz State U 63-67; Hd bibliog serv 68; Acquis libn Mesa Commun Col 68-. 9: ALA; ArizStateLA. 10: Faculty Womens Club; PEO. 11: Civilian Meritorious Award, US War Dept (46). 14: Acquis. 15: 837 E No Revere, Mesa Az 85201.

POPE, ANITA LOUISE. b Hillsboro Ohio 26 Ag 36. 5: Antioch Col 55-60 (Biol) BA; UMich 63-64 (LS) MA. 7: Ref libn Battelle Mem Inst, Columbus Ohio 64-67; Order libn 67-. 15: 224 E Deshler ave, Columbus Oh 43206.

POPE, LARRY JACOB. b Cincinnati 26 F 37. 4: Genevieve Scott Johnston. 5: UKy 55-59 (LS) AB, 60-61 (LS) MS. 6: Sp, Ger, Fr. Russian. 7: Ser catlgr UKy 61-64, Head circ dept 64-66, Period libn E KyU 66-. 9: ALA; KyLA; Ohio Valley Group Tech Serv Libns(Nomin Com 64-65); SELA; AAUP. 10: Spindletop Hall; Nat Opera Guild; Amer Theater Socs Theater Guild (Cincinnati Div). 14: Catlg. 15: 406 Lancaster ave, Richmond Ky 40475.

POPE, NANNETTE (McCARTHY) (MRS). b Chicago Ill 27 Ja 23. 5: Barat Col of Sacred Heart 40-44 (Eng) BA; UDenver 64-66 (LS) MA. 6: Fr, Lat. 7: Society reporter Chicago Tribune 44-46; Lib trainee VA Hosp, Denver 64-66; Order libn Nat Inst of Health, Bethesda Md 66-68; Ref libn Armed Forces Radiobiology Research Inst, Bethesda Md 68-69, Hd libn 69-. 9: MedLA. 15: 6005 Conway rd, Bethesda Md 20034.

POPE, S ELSPETH. b Montreal 14 S 26. 5: Sir George Williams U 45-50 BA; McGill 50-51 BLS; UDenver 59-60 MA. 6: Fr. 7: Libn Jameson Mem Hosp, New Castle Penn 51-53; Ref libn Vassar Col 53-55; Libn Providence Hosp Sch of Nursing, Portland Ore 55-59; Period libn UDenver 59-60; Asst libn U Puget Sound 60-63; Ref libn UWis(Milwaukee) 63-65; Asst Prof State U Col (Geneseo NY) 65-66; Instr Grad Sch of Lib & Info Sci UPittsburgh 66-. 8: Staff, Lib 21, Seattle Worlds Fair, 62. 9: ALA; -LED (sec); PennLA. 14: Tech serv. 15: 5614 Walnut st, Pittsburgh Pa 15232.

POPE, WILEY ROGER. b Cut Bank Montana 10 O 41. 4: Juanita Jones. 5: Brigham Young 59-60, 63-66 (Ger) BA, 66-68 MLS. 6: Ger, Norwegian, Danish, Swedish. 7: Docs libn Brigham YoungU 67-68, Asst gen ref libn 68-. 8: Indexing LDS Ch period 68-69. 15: RFD 2, Vernal Ut 84078.

POPECKI, JOSEPH THOMAS. b Saginaw Mich 25 N 24. 4: Jeanne Marie Gillespie. 5: Sacred Heart Sem(Detroit) 42-45 (Philos) BA; Catholic U 45-49 BSLS. 7: Catholic U: Asst order libn 47-49, Catlgr 50, Head Col Lib 51, Asst to dir of libs 52, Asst dir of libs 58-65, Act dir of libs 65-67; Dir of libs St Michaels Col, Burlington Vt 67-. 8: Pres, Mid-Atlantic Assocs Inc, Wash DC; Lecturer: A-v materials, Educ DEPT Catholic U 49-, Lib courses US Dept of Agric Grad Sch 49-. 9: CathLA; ALA; ASIS; DCLA; NELA; VtLA; Champlain Valley LA. 10: Beta Phi Mu; Vt Hist Assn; Vt Archaeological Assn; Chittenden Co Hist Assn; St Marks Mens Club. 12: "Near-print Duplication and Photographic Reproduction (54); "An Introduction to Bibliography (64); "A Thesaurus of Terms for Coordinate Indexing of Nursing Literature (66). 13: Yes. 14: Admin, tech serv, photoduplication, binding & preserv of materials, lib design, info retrieval systems, admin of acad libs, consulting. 15: 33 Woodridge dr, Burlington Vt 05401.

POPOVICH, MARY MARGUERITE (WITT). b Saginaw Mich 10 Jl 15. 4: B Robert Popovich. 5: Alma Col 33-37 (Fr, Music) AB; UMich 60-64 MALS. 06: Fr, Ger, Lat. 7: Music & Lat tchr Bd of Educ, Vanderbilt Mich 37-40; Elem & music tchr Bd of Educ, Owosso Mich 40-45; Music & math tchr Bd of Educ, Flint Mich 45-48; Bd of Educ, Comstock Park Mich: Lat, Fr, math & music tchr 48-55, Art, music tchr, libn 55-57, High sch libn 57-. 8: Lecturer lib sci, UMich Ext, Grand Rapids Mich 65. 9: ALA; MichASchL; MichEA; NEA. 10: Camp Fire Girls; Comstock ParkEA. 14: Tchg child lit to adults, catlg. 15: 1152 Park st SW, Grand Rapids Mich 49504.

PORCELLA, BREWSTER. b Cranford NJ 30 Ap 22. 4: Bonnie June Price. 5: Wheaton Col(Ill) 39-43 (Bible) AB, 46-48 (Theol) AM; UIll 63-64 MS (LS), UIll 68-. 6: Gk, Fr. 7: Sgt Maj Army Troop Transport, US Army T/Sgt 44-46; Pastor Indian Landing Church, Rochester NY 51-53; Past Ortwin City Bible Church, Urbana Ill 53-63; Asst Lib Research Center UIll 63-64; Asst acquis iibn UIowa 64-66; Hd acquis dept 66-68. 9: Evangel Theol Assn; ALA. 15: 512 6th ave, Coralville Ia 52240.

PORCHER, ELIZABETH LONG. b Charleston SC 12 N 05. 5: Converse Col 24-45; Col of Charleston 25-28 (Eng) AB; Columbia summers28-32 BS in LS. 6: Fr. 7: Libn Charleston High Sch, Charleston SC 28-36; Lib Caroliniana Collection USCar 36-42; Visitor Red Cross (Capt) N Africa 42-43; Head of circ dept Lib of USCar 43-46; Head of circ dept UDenver 46-50; Libn Greenwood Co Pub Lib, Greenwood SC 50-65; Dir of Abbeville-Greenwood Reg Lib Syst 65-. 9: SCLA (past sec & chm Pub Lib Sect). 11: John Cotton Dana Library Award 58, Dorothy Canfield Fisher Award, 61. 14: Admin. 15: 105W Henrietta st, Greenwood SC 29646.

POREMBA, FRANCES J(ANE). b Donora Penn. 5: Cal State Col 40 BS; Carnegie 47 BS in LS. 7: Asst libn Bus Br Carnegie Lib of Pittsburgh 47-51; Asst libn Central Lib US Steel Corp, Pittsburgh 51-56; Chief Libn Research Center US Steel Corp, Monroeville Penn 56-. 9: SLA; ASIS. 15: US Steel Corp Res Center Lib, Monroeville Pa 15146.

PORODA, DONALD LOUIS. b Colo Springs Colo 1 Je 21. 4: Helen C Pickerill. 5: Colorado Col 39-42, 46-47 (Eng) AA, BA; UMich 47-50 MA(Eng), MALS. 6: Ger, Fr. 7: Br lib asst Detroit Pub Lib 50, Ref asst soc sci dept 51; Sr ref libn UMich Gen Lib 51-57, Ref libn Undergrad Lib 57-. 10: Phi Beta Kappa; Phi Kappa Phi. 14: Ref. 15: 815 S First st, Ann Arbor Mi 48103.

PORRITT, RUTH KILBURN. b Goffstown NH 6 O 08. 5: Simmons 26-30 (LS) BS; Boston U 40-44 9econ) MA. 6: Fr, Ger. 7: Acquis asst Baker Lib Harvard 30-42, Ref libn 42-49; Libn radcliffe Col 49-. 8: Lib consul, Salberg seminars in Amer Studies, Salberg Austria 57. 9: ALA-ACRL; MassLA. 10: Appalachian Mountain Club; Vis Com Boston Museum of Fine Arts Lib. 13: Yes. 14: Ref, acquis, admin. 15: 20 Standish rd, Melrose Ma 02176.

PORSCHE, ELIZABETH (KOCH). b Pittsburgh Penn 28 O 18. 4: Alvin J Porsche. 5: Seton Hill Col 35-39 (Eng) BA; UPittsburgh 39-40 (Child libn) MS in LS. 6: Fr, Ger. 7: Carnegie Lib of Pittsburgh: Asst child libn 40-41, 1st asst child libn 66, Child libn 66-67, Child libn & 1st br asst 67-68; Hd catlgr Gen Serv Admin Lib, Wash DC 68-. 9: ALA. 14: Catlg. 15: 2800 Wisconsin ave NW, Washington DC 20007.

PORTAL, RICHARD J. b Kan City Mo 2 Ja 18. 4: Doreen Yorkston. 5: Willamette U 45-48 & 50-51 (Philos) BA; Oregon Col 49-50 (Educ) BS; UPortland summers 51-54 (LS): UWash 64-65 (LS) ML. 6: Lat, Fr. 7: US 13th, 7th, 4th Air Forces Cook 18 months, Air-Sea Rescue 24 months (Sgt) 42-45; Circ ref libn Willamette U 51-54; Documents catlgr Ore State Lib 54-56; Asst libn Oregon Col 56-57; Acquis libn Ore State Lib 57-64, Humanities libn 65-; Circ libn Pub Lib Medford/Jackson Co 67-68, Ref libn 68-. 9: OreLA (Exhib Chm 56 & 64 Conventions), Conference Exhibits Chm 69). 10: Salem Civic Players; Ore State Employees Assn. 14: Ref, org of materials. 15: 517 Holmes, Medford Or 97501.

PORTE, CHARLOTTE (MARTHA) (GROSSKOPF). b Indianapolis 18 O 01. 5:Sanderson Bus Col (Indianapolis) 19; Butler U 20-22 (Hist; Ind U 26 (Creative Writing). 6: Fr. 7: Pub rel dir Marion Co Ind, OCD 41-44; Dept libn Union Tribune Publ Co, San Diego 45-56; Ed research dept head Union-Tribune, San Diego 56-. 9: SLA (Chart mem San Diego Chap). 10: Scripteaser Club (San Diego); 7th Dist Fed Womens Clubs, Indianapolis; Coun Toastmistress Clubs, Cal; Bd Footlights Theater, San Diego 48-50. 11: Nat 1st Prize, NY Herald Tribune for ed excellence; 1st prize (twice) for Journ in Ind, awarded by Butler Univ,42-43. 14: Org newspaper lib, ed res. 15: 633 Sutter st, San Diego Cal 92103.

PORTE, MASHA R (UDNITZKY). b Dallas 7 Ag 14. 5: So Methodist U & Dallas Col 54-63 (Eng) Jr quiv. 6: Yiddish. 7: Gen off wk, wholesale clothing mfr, Dallas 32-41; Asst to exec sec Civic Fed of Dallas 41-46; Dir music & art Civic Fed of Dallas 46-49; Sec to manager Dallas Symphony Orchestra 50-51; Sec to exec dir Jewish Welfare Federation, Dallas 51-53; Head a-v dept Dallas Pub Lib 53-. 9: ALA; (A-V Com 61-65); -ASD (A-V Com 67-); Educl Film La; TexLA; DallasCoLA; Film Lib Info Coun. 10: Dallas Chamber Music Soc; Hadassah; Jewish Welfare Fed; Dallas Assn for the UN. 12: Coord film reviews "Booklist & SSB ALA (61-); Ed film reviews sect "Film Library Quarterly (67-,) 13: Yes. 14: Films. 15: Dallas Pub Lib 1954 Commerce st, Dallas Tx 75201.

PORTER, BARRY LaVON. b Cedar City Utah 3 O 42. 4: Gayle Willis Porter. 5: Col of So utah 60-62, 64-67 (Pol Sci) BA; Brigham Young 68-69 (LS). 7: Bkmob libn Utah State lib 67-68, Ref libn 68-. 9: UtahLA. 14: Ref, rare bks, West Americana. 15: 2150 S 2nd W Suite 16, Salt Lake City Ut 84115.

PORTER, CLIFFORD (SELLERS) HENDERSON. b Mt Kisco NY 24 Jl 29. 4: John Bowman Porter. 5: Vassar 47-51 (Child study) BA; UMd 67-69 (LS) MA. 6: Fr. 9: ALA; SLA. 14: Ref. 15: 528 Carr ave, Rockville Md 20850.

PORTER, GAIL ANN. b Niagara Falls NY 27 N 46. 5: DenisonU 64-68 (Fr) AB; UIll 68-69 MLS. 6: Fr, Ger. 7: Ref libn NorthwesternU 69-. 10: Beta Phi Mu. 14: Ref. 15: 1704 W Thome, Chicago Il 60626.

PORTER, GENEVIEVE (GATES). b Lena Ill 20 S 09. 4: Gerald M Porter. 5: Northwestern 26-30 (Fr, Hist) BS; UWis summers 32-34, 37 & 35-36 (Fr, Eng) MA; Augustana Col even 42-44 (Span; National U of Mex summers 43, 44 (Span); UDenver 44-45 BS in LS. 6: Fr, Sp. 7: Eng & Fr tchr: Lena Commun High Sch, Lena Ill 30-35, 36-37, West High Sch, Waterloo Iowa 37-42, Moline High Sch, Moline Ill 42-44; Circ libn UDenver 45-46, Asst ref libn 46-49; Catlgr SoMethodist U 51-52, Head ref dept 52-. 9: ALA; TexLA; SWLA. 10: Phi Beta Kappa; Phi Delta Gamma. 14: Ref. 15: 2805 Amherst, Dallas Tex 75225.

PORTER, JEAN F. b Danville Ill 20 F 44. 5: UIll 62-66 (Hist) AB, 66-67 MSLS. 6: Fr. 7: Ref libn LA Co Pub Lib 67-69; Ref libn No Ill U 69-. 9: ALA. 14: Ref. 15: Apt C5 1400 W Lincoln highway, DeKalb Il 60115.

PORTER, JEAN H (ASLER). b Buffalo NY 29 Ja 22. 4: Charles Hunt Porter. 5: UBuffalo 38-41 (Eng) BA, summer 41, 44 (LS); SUNY(Geneseo) summer 49, 50 (LS) Permanent Certif as Sch Libn in NY State. 6: Lat, Ger, Fr, Ital, Sp. 7: Lib-Eng tchr Castile High Sch, Castile NY 41-46; Libn Lyndonville Central Sch, Lyndonville NY 49-54; Libn Newfane Central Sch, Newfane NY 54-62; Dir Lib Resources & Tech Serv Bd of Cooperative Educ Serv, Medina NY 62-. 8: Adv com, sch-pub lib coord, Niagara-Orleans Area (NY) 64-65; Consul lib serv Bd of Educ, Hartford Conn 67; Consul on adv com, NY State Educ Dept Lib Bur 65-; Consul on adv com Lib Bur NY State Educ Dept (Title II ESEA) 65. 9: ALA; NYLA (mem Bd of Dirs 61-64; chm sch libs supvs sect 65-66, mem constit com 67-68; -RTS sect mem 69); NY State Tchrs Assn (chm lib sect West Zone 58-59, v-chm NWest Zone 65-66, chm NWest Zone 66-67, v-chm NWest Zone 67-68; pres sole supv dist Niagara Co 59-60, 60-61); Niagara-Orleans Area Assn of Sch Libns (pres 60-61); NEA-DAVI. 10: PTA. 13: Yes. 14: Catlg, ref, curr coord of lib materials. 15: Bd Coop Educ Serv, Salt Works rd, Medina NY 14103.

PORTER, LUCILLE (KEPLEY). b Rochesr NY 25 N 17. 4: Willard W Porter. 5: Ohio State U 35-39 (Eng, Fr) BS in Educ; Queens Col 59-64 MLS. 6: Fr. 7: Sch libn Weber Jr High Sch, Port Washington NY 61-66; Ref libn US Naval Acad, Annapolis Md 66-. 9: ALA; NYLA; AASL; NY State Tchrs Assn; Nassau-SuffolkLA. 10: YWCA. 14: Ref. 15: 90 Market st, Annapolis Md 21401.

PORTER, RUBY G. b Randolph Neb 9 My 06. 5 Gen Beadle Col 24-28 (Educ) BS; UWash summer 34; UMich summer 37; UIll summers 39-42 BLS. 6: Fr. 7: High sch tchr-libn City Sch Dist, Madison SD 32-42; Chief Libn Dept of the Army, Lowry AFB Colo & Ft Worden Wash 42-48; Command libn 24th Inf Div & I Corps, Dept of Army, Japan 48-50; Command libn Gen Hq Dept of the Army, Tokyo 50-54; Chief Libn Dept of the Army, Ft Bragg NC 54-56; Ships libn Bur of Naval Pers Navy Dept, Wash DC 56-58; Chief Tech Lib Off of Research Analyses, Holoman AFB NM 58-63, Chief tech info div 63-66; Chief Tech Lib Off of Research Analyses 66-. 9: ALA; SLA; NMLA. 10: Beta Phi Mu. 11: Air Force Meritorious Civilian Serv Award, 64. ; Superior Serv Award (twice). 14: Admin, ref. 15: 113 - 14th st apt 3, Alamogordo NM 88310.

PORTER, WILLIAM (HUBERT). b Hant's Harbour Newfoundland 26 Jl 21. 4: Renee Wight. 5: Memorial U Newfoundland 40-41, 42-44 (Educ, Hist); Mt Allison U 44-46 (Hist) BA; UToronto 50-51 (Educ) B Paed; Syracuse 67-68 MSLS. 6: Fr. 7: Tchr St John's Bd of Educ, St John's Nfld 46-50, 51-52; Tchr N York Bd of Educ, Metropolitan Toronto 53-67; Lib consul 68-. 9: CanLA; ALA. 10: Ont Pub Sch Men Tchrs Fed. 14: Sch libnship. 15: 35 Medina Crescent, Scarborough Ont Can.

PORTERFIELD, FRANCES GEAHEART. b Watsville WVa 5 Ag 17. 4: Birtle Oren Porterfield. 5: Radford Col 39-40, 50-54 (Elem Educ) BS, 62-65 (Educ) MA. 7: Elem tchr: Patrick Co Sch Bd, Bent Sch, Meadows of Dan Va 40-41, Floyd Co Sch Bd, Check Elem Sch, CheckVa 41-48, Roanoke Co Sch Bd, Back Creek Sch, Roanoke Va 48-49, Botetourt Co Sch Bd, Fincastle Elem Sch, Fincastle Va 49-50, Co of Warwick Sch Bd, Briarcliff Elem Sch, Newport News Va 50-54, Russell Co Sch Bd, Cleveland Elem Sch, Cleveland Va 54-57; High sch tchr Russell Co Sch Bd, Cleveland High Sch, Cleveland Va 57-61, Libn 61-68; Libn R B Worthy High Sch, Saltville Va 68-69. 9: NEA; VaEA; ALA; VaLA. 15: Box 635, Lebanon Va.

PORTERFIELD, GENEVIEVE (R). b Bunker Hill W Va 6 Jl 07. 5: W Va U 27-29; Carnegie lib Sch 29-30 (Child wk) Certif; UChicago 30-32 (Eng) PhB; Columbia 40-41 (Sch lib) MS. 7: Libn private lib, Chcago 30-31; Br libn Berwyn Pub Lib, Berwyn Ill 31-36; Child libn Ohio U Lib (Athens) 36-42; Sch libn Cleveland Pub Lib, Cleveland Ohio 42-44; Ref libn Tex Tech Col 44-46; Ref libn UNM Lib 46-. 9: ALA; SWLA; NMLA. 10: AAUW; LWV. 13: Yes. 14: Ref. 15: 231 Sycamore st NE, Albuquerque NM 87106.

PORTH, EVELYN H (KELLNER). b Merrill Wis 27 D 19. 4: Carl J Porth. 5: Lincoln Co Normal (Wis) 36-37 Certif; Central State Tchrs' Col summers 40, 41; Whittier Col 61. 7: Tchr Bay Mill Sch, Tomahawk Wis 37-41; Tchr Hartwig Sch, Merrill Wis 41-43; Clk-typist Puget Sound Navy Yard, Bremerton Wash 43-44; Clk-typist Merchandise Mart, Chicago 43; Clk-typist Naval Air Station, Terminal Is 44-45; Clk-typist Fed Res Bank, San Francisco 45; Libn Autonetics-N Amer Avia, Downey Cal 52-57; Sec Los Nietos Sch Dist, Los Nietos Cal 60-62; Sec Worley & Co, Whittier Cal 62; Libn Autonetics-No Amer Rockwell, Anaheim Cal 62-. 9: SLA; OrangeCoLA. 13: Yes. 14: Ref. 15: 5212 Cornell ave, Westminster Ca 92683.

PORTNER, DOROTHY (MARIE) (KIRK). b Chicago 17 S 24. 4: Nick Portner. 5: No Ill U 45-47 (Soc Sci) BS in Ed; Rosary Col 52-56 MA in LS. 7: Chem lab asst Reynolds Metals, McCook Ill 42-45; Lib aide NoIll U 45-47; Argo Commun High Sch, Summit Ill: Tchr 47-56, Libn 56-57, Tchr-libn 57-61, Libn 62-. 9: IllEA; IllASchL; IllLA. 14: Ref, circ. 15: 5304 S Wolf rd, Western Springs Il 60558.

PORTNOY, PEARL ELIZABETH. b St Louis 11 Ap 07. 5: St Louis Lib Sch 26-27 (LS) Certif; Washington U 25-34 (Eng, Psych) BA; UIll 57-58 (LS, Educ) MSLS; UCincinnati 36-64 (Educ). 6: Ger. 7: Asst St Louis Pub Lib 28-36; Asst & br libn Pub Lib of Cincinnati 36-57; Med libn Jewish Hosp, Cincinnati 58-60; High sch libn Deer Park High Sch, Deer Park Ohio 60-64; Sub libn Los Angeles Pub Schs 65; Libn Alondra Jr High Sch, Paramount Cal 65-. 9: AASchL; NEA; CalASchL. 10: AAUW; Hadassah. 15: 11224 Woodruff ave, Downey Ca 90241.

PORTSCH, JOANNE. b Mt Vernon NY 26 Ap 33. 5: Green Mt Jr Col 50-51 (Liberal Arts); Conn Col 51-54 (European Hist) BA; Syracuse 54-55 MLS. 7: Ref libn White Plains Pub Lib, White Plains NY 55-58; Market research libn Raytheon Co Corporate Govt Marketing, Waltham Mass 59; Libn Raytheon Co equipment div hdqtrs, Waltham Mass 60-. 9: SLA (Boston Chap Bulletin ed 66-69). 15: 58 Jacqueline rd, Waltham Ma 02154.

PORTSCHY, ARTHUR DALE. b Herndon Kan 8 Ap 24. 4: Lauretta Clinkscales. 5: Ft Hays Kan State Col 42-43, 46-47, 51-52 (Eng) AB; Southeast Mo State Col 43-44 USNR V-12; Northwestern U 44 Midshipman Commsn; UDenver 54-55 (LS) MA. 7: A/S V-12 USNR, Southeast Mo State Col 43-44; Ensign USNR, S Pacific Area 44-46; Asst manager Raychester Clo Co, Russell Kan 50-51; Tchr-libn Lane Co Commun High Sch, Dighton Kan 52-54; Readers adv Omaha Pub Lib 55-57, Head ref dept 57-67; Supv adult serv 67-. 9: ALA; NebLA. 14: Ref. 15: Omaha Pub Lib, 1823 Harney st, Omaha Nb 68102.

PORTTEUS, ELNORA (MANTHEI). b Rosendale Wis 28 S 20. 4: Paul Portteus. 5: UWis 41 (Eng) BS; Kent State U Catholic (LS) MA. 6: Fr. 7: Tchr High Sch, Marshall Wis 41-42; Libn & tchr Co Normal Sch, Racine-Kenosha Wis 42-43; Lib asst Fed Res Bank of Cleveland 43; Libn Ind Rel Counselors, NY 48; Libn Donnell Jr High Sch, Findlay Ohio 49-58; Asst Prof Lib Sci Kent State U 58-65; Directing supv of sch libs Cleveland Bd of Educ 65-67; Libn Elizabeth Seton High Sch, Bladensburg Md 68-. 8: Dir, Kent State U Annual Sch Lib Wkshop 59-65; Dir, NDEA Sch Lib Inst 65; Consul Educl Planning Serv, Columbus 60-; Consul Crestline, Warren, Boardman Pub Schs; Consul USOE for Buffalo Schs 68; memb task force on implementation of Little Hoover Commsn, Ohio Dept of Educ 68; Adv Bd Jr High Sch catlg, H W Wilson Co 69; Consul & visiting lecturer; edinboro State Col, UTenn, Appalachian State Col. 9: ALA-AASchL (mem sel of materials about minorities, mem Pub Com of Supvs Sect 68-, chm Great Cities 69); (chm AASchL-MATI Com63; Ohio Liaison for Encyc Brit Sch Lib Awards 65); NEA; ohioASchL (pres 57-58; chm Serv to Schs Round Table 59; chm Scholarship Com 65-66, chm Bk exam com 63-64, mem Rand-McNally Bd of Consuls 67-68); OhioEA. 10: AAUW; WNBA; Delta Kappa Gamma; Findlay Coun of Youth Serv Agencies; Adv Bd Lib Tech Program Cuyahoga Commun Col. 11: Distinguished Alumna Award Kent State U Sch of Lib Sci, 68; Encyclopedia Britannica Award,-67. 12: "Handbook for Volunteer Services in the Elementary School (65, 68); "Handbook for Secondary Schools (68).42451 13: Yes. 14: Sch lib admin, child & ya serv & lit, hist ofchild bks. 15: 5715 Emerson st, Bladensburg Md 20710.

POSEY, EDWIN DALFIELD. b Dallas Tex 1 Ag 27. 4: Grace Krumm. 5: So Methodist 47-48 (Engring); UHouston 53-66 (Hist) BA; Drexel 66-68 MSLS. 6: Ger. 7: Engr Texsteam Corp, Houston Tex 57-66; Libn trainee Free Lib of Phila 66-67; Asst libn Forrestal Campus Princeton U 67-68, Engring libn 68-. 9: ALA; Amer Soc Engring Educ. 10: MENSA. 13: Yes. 14: Sci-tech libnship. 15: 113 Bayard lane, Princeton NJ 08540.

POSEY, SISTER LAURETTA DC. b Greenburg Penn. 5: St Joseph Col(Md) 42 (Eng) AB; Cathoic U 56 MS in LS. 7: Tchr St Dominic Sch, Baltimore 42-44, Sacred Heart Sch, Norfolk Va 44-49, St Catherine Labouree Sch, Harrisburg Penn 49-55; Libn Immaculate Conception Acad, Wash DC 56-58; Libn Cardinal McCloskey Mem High Sch, Albany NY 58-68; Libn Elizabeth Seton High Sch, Bladensburg Md 68-. 8: Consul, St Mary Hosp Sch of Nursing, Troy NY 59-64. 9: CathLA (Bd Dirs Albany Unit 60-65, chm 68); ALA; MdLA. 14: Catlg. 15: 5715 Emerson st, Bladensburg Md 20710.

POSKA, VALENTINE JEROME. b Chicago Ill 20 My 18. 4: Mollyan Howell. 5: St Mary's Col (Winona Minn) (Eng) AB; MinnU 46 BS in LS, 53 (Speech) MA; Memphis State U 65 (Counseling) MA. 7: Tchr De La Salle High Sch, Chicago 44-46; Tchr St George High Sch, Evanston Ill 46-47; Tchr/libn Christian Bros High Sch, St Joseph Mo 47-49; Libn Christian Brothers Col, Memphis Tenn 49-65; Spec libn Houston Pub Lib, Houston Tex 65; Spec libn Eisenhower Jr High Sch, San Antonio Tex 65-67; Jr libn San Antonio Col 67-. 9: CathLA; Tex Assn Jr Col; BexarLA. 10: San Antonio Speech Arts Assn. 12: Ed Texas Junior College Libraries "Newsletter" (69-). 13: Yes. 14: Ser libn, genealogy, publ. 15: 234 Windcrest dr, San Antonio Tx 78239.

POSNANSKY, DANIEL. b Tel Aviv Israel 25 N 38. 4: Barbara Lucchi. 5: Hunter Col 63 (Philos) AB; Columbia 67 MLS. 7: Supv bk deliveries div NYC Pub Lib 65-67, Collection maintenance libn Harvard Col Lib 67-68, Chief circ libn 68-69; Assoc libn Harvard Grad Sch of Educ 69-. 15: 105 E Dunstable rd, Nashua NH 03060.

POSNER, DAVID. b NY 23 Jl 30. 4: Olivia Wedgwood. 5: Kenyon Col 48 BA; Harvard 50 MA; Oxford 53. 6: Fr, Ital. 7: Curator of Poetry Collection Lockwood Lib UBuffalo 57-. 8: Member of the Brit Mus Archaeological Expedition to Libya & Crete; Commentator, French Radio Netwk; Tr for Unesco. 10: Phi Beta Kappa. 11: Newdigabe Prize, 57. 12: "The Deserted Altar (57); "A Rakes Progress (66); "Hungary Since 1956 (66); "Dialogues (69). 13: Yes. 15: San Fernando Valley State Col Asst Professor English Dept, Northridge Ca 91324.

POSNER, WALTER H. b Rochester NY. 4: Aurora Perez-Camorlinga. 5: Ricks Jr Col 40-41 (Elem Educ) AA; Utah State Agric Col 39-40, 42-43 (Secondary Educ) BS; West State Col of Colo 47-48 (Hist, Pol Sci) MA; UDenve 61-62 (LS) MA. 6: Sp, Fr. 7: Pub elem sch tchr, various areas 9 yrs; Prof of hist Rio Grande Col 56-58; Elem tchr Washington Elem Dist, Phoenix 58-61; Libn San Diego State Col 62-. 9: CalLA. 10: Cal State Employees Assn; Phi Kappa Phi; Kappa Delta Pi; Beta Phi Mu. 12: "Bibliography of European Integration (2 eds, 65, 67). 13: Yes. 14: Catlg. 15: 4723 Soria dr, San Diego Ca 92115.

POST, CHARLOTTE KATHERINE. b S Bend Ind 9 Ag 06. 5: Olivet Col 24-28 (Modern Langs) AB; West Res 36-37 BS in LS; UIll 53-54 (LS) MS. 6: Sp, Fr. 7: Libn Washington-Clay Twp High Sch, S Bend Ind 37-40; Asst catlgr UNotre Dame(Ind) 40-47; Head catlgr NoIll U 47-68; Asst catlgr Wis State U (Whitewater) 68-. 9: ALA; IllLA; IllEA; WisLA. 10: AAUP; AAUW; PEO; DAR; Alpha Beta Alpha; Bus & Prof Womens Club; Nat Audubon Soc; NoIll U Dames Club. 14: Catlg. 15: 629 N First st, DeKalb Ill 60115.

POST, HELEN M. b Burlington Vt 8 Ag 27. 5: UVt 46-50 (Eng) BA; NY State Col for Tchrs(Albany) 51-52 (LS) MS. 7: Libn Penfield Central Sch, Penfield NY 52-60; Libn Penfield Jr High Sch, Penfield NY 60-65; Coordinator of sch libs Penfield Central Sch, Penfield NY 65-. 9: NEA; ALA; Rochester Area(NY) SchLA. 14: Sch lib materials centers. 15: 96 Hillside ave, Rochester NY 14610.

POST, JEREMIAH B(ENJAMIN). b Rochester NY 17 N 37. 4: Joyce Arnold. 5: URochester 56-60 (Philos) AB; Columbia 60-61 MSLS. 7: Page Rochester Pub Lib, Rochester NY 57-60 (Trainee 60); Page Psych Lib Columbia U 60-61; Libn I Free Lib, Phila 61; (Pfc) US Army Signal, Engnr, France 61-63; Libn I Lit Dept Free Lib, Phila 64; Map curator 65-. 9: ALA; SLA; Private Libs Assn (Brit); Spec Libs Coun Phila & Vicinity. 10: Phila Sci Fiction Soc; Philobiblon Club; ACLU.

13: Yes. 14: Intel freedom, methods of preserv, reprography, rare bk, ref, bibliog. 15: 4613 Larchwood ave, Phila Pa 19143.

POST, MARY MARGARET. b S Bend Ind 20 O 09. 5: Olivet Col 27-31 (Eng) BA; Drexel 37-38 BS in LS. 7: Lib asst S Bend Pub Lib, S Bend Ind 31-42; Asst Libn ULouisville Sch of Med Lib42-47; Libn Ramsey Co Med Soc Lib, St Paul 47-. 9: MedLA (dir 63-65; Assn Hosp & Med Libns (pres 50). 10: AAUW; Quota Internat. 15: 1500 Lowry Med Arts Bldg, St Paul 55102.

POSTAL, CYNTHIA (EAVES). b Peterborough NH 4 My 31. 5: Bates 49-53 (Hist) BA; Simmons 53-54 MS in LS. 7: Adult libn Lib Assoc of Portland, Portland Ore 54-58; Adult libn LA (City) Pub Lib 58-66; Dist lib consul NH State Lib, Keene NH 66-69; Inst lib consul NH State Lib, Concord NH 69-. 9: ALA; NHLA; NELA. 14: Ref. 15: 12 Maple st, Concord NH 03301.

POSTE, LESLIE I(RLYN). b St Catharines Ont Can 26 Ag 18. 4: Virginia Lloyd. 5: Wayne State 36-41 (Literary hist) BA; Columbia 41-42 (LS) BS; UChicago 48-49, 51-52, 58 (LS) PhD. 6: Ger, Fr, Sp. 7: Page Detroit Pub Lib 32-36, Desk asst 36-41; Stud asst Columbia U 41-42, Ref libn 42, act libn 42-43; Enlisted service (Pvt Tech 4) USA 43-45; Asst lib br spec serv, European theater 44; Coun US Armed Forces Inst, European theater 44; Libn & instr USA Info Educ Staff Sch, European theater 44-45; Commissioned serv (2nd-1st Lieutenant) USA 45-46; Libs & archives specialist off arts, monuments, and archives west military dist & land Wuerttemberg-Baden, US zone of occupation in Germany 45-56; Deputy dir pub rel, off of military govt for land Wuerttemberg-Baden 46; Chief US Info Ctrs off of military govt for Land Hesse, us zone of occupation Germany 46-47; Ed assoc A N Marquis Co, Chicago 49; Hd & prof dept of lib sci UKy (Lexington) 49-53; Dir & Prof sch of libnship, UDenver 53-55; Asst dir Toledo Pub Lib, Toledo Ohio 55-58; Arts, monuments, and archives specialist off US Army Civil Affairs Sch, Ft Gordon Ga 59-68; Dir of instr Second US Army Civil Affairs Sch, Ft Gordon Ga 68-; Consul faculty US Army Command & Gen Staff Col, Ft Leavenworth Kan 68-; Visiting Prof dept of lib serv N Tex State U summers 68, 69; Prof sch of lib sci SUNY Col of Arts and Sci (Geneseo) 58-. 8: Conducted first lib travel sem in Europe, State U Col (Geneseo) summer 61. 9: ALA; AALS (chm Com on Statistics 53-55); BSA; Lib Assn (Gt Brit); SLA; KyLA (2nd v-pres 52-53); MPLA (chm Intel Freedom Com 54-55); NYLA. 10: Beta Phi Mu; NY Lib Club; Res Officers Assn; Lt Col US Army Res (Ready). 11: Fellow Lib Assn (Gt Brit). 12: Edl Assoc "Who Knows-and What" (49); "Arts, Monuments and Archives" (59); "The Development of US Protection of Libraries affairs Sch, Ft Gordon (64): 13: Yes. 14: Admin, compar libnship, educ for libnship, lib hist, ref. 15: 4222 Lakeville rd, Geneseo NY 14454.

POSTELL, FRANCES M. b Plaquemine La 20 D 12. 5: LSU 29-33 (Math, Sci) BA, 33-34 BS in LS. 6: Fr, Sp. 7: Libn Jesuit High Sch, New Orleans 34-36; Libn Baton Rouge Sr High Sch, Baton Rouge La 36-38; Head catlgr UMiss Lib 40-43; Catlgr LSU Lib Rouge) 38-40, 43-44; Instr Sch of Lib Sci Catholic U summer 45, 46, Head catlg dept Caholic U 44-46; Libn sch dept Multnomah Co Lib, Portland Ore 46-56, Head sch serv dept 56-; Instr Lib Sci Portland State U 66-67; Instr Lib Sci UPortland 66-67; Adj Asst Prof Sch of Libnship UOre 69-. 8: Mem, Adv Bd, Knapp Sch Proj, Roosevelt High Sch, Portland Ore; Summer sch tchg, lib sci, UMiss; Catholic U bk reviewer, "School Library Journal. 9: ALA; OreLA; PNLA (Exec Bd 62-64). 10: Beta Phi Mu; Portland Area Spec Libns; E Multnomah-N Clackamas Migrant Ministry Coun. 13: Yes. 14: Child bks, sch libs, catlg. 15: 115 N Polk st, Eugene Or 97402.

POSTELL, PATRICIA L(UCK). b New Orleans 17 Mr 11. 4: Paul E Postell. 5: Ursuline Col 28-32 (Eng) ABl Loyola U(New Orleans) 30-32; LSU 32-33 BS in LS. 6: Fr. 7: Libn Xavier U New Orleans 33-35; Libn Agric Est Div LSU 36; Asst catlg La Lib Commsn Ext Div, Baton Rouge La 37-38, 39-40; Libn UAla Ext Div Montgomery 49-51; Libn St Margarets Hosp, Montgomery Ala 49-51; Oak Ridge Pub Lib, Oak Ridge Tenn; Act dir summer 57, catlgr 57-60, dir 60-. 9: ALA; TennLA; SELA. 10: PTA; Prof Staff of the City of Oak Ridge(Tenn). 14: Catlg, ref. 15: Rt 18, Yount rd, Knoxville Tenn 37921.

POSTELL, PAUL E. b Plaquemine La 15 Ap 10. 4: Patricia Luck. 5: LSU 28-32 (Hist AB, 33-35 (LS) BS, 35-36 (Hist) Am. 7: Chief acquis dept LSU Lib Baton Rouge 36-41; Asst chief & chief lib br Dept of Army, Wash DC & NYC 41-48; Chief lib div Air U Lib Maxwell AFB, Montgomery Ala 48-51; Chief catlg br & Chief ref br, Div of Tech Info Ext USAEC, Oak Ridge Tenn 51-66, Chief tech serv br Div of Tech Info Ext 66-. 9: SLA (Oak Ridge Chap: pres & other offs); SELA; TennLA. 10: Res Officers Assn. ; Amer Legion. 13: Yes. 14: Ref, documentation. 15: Rt 18, Knoxville Tn 37921.

POSTELL, WILLIAM DOSITE JR. b New Orleans La 11 D 45. 4: Lisa Payne. 5: Spring Col 63-64 (Pol Sci); TulaneU 64-67 (Pol Sci) BA; LSU 67-69 MS in LS. 6: Fr, Ger, Russian. 7: Grad asst LSU Lib (Baton Rouge) 67-69; Soc sci catlgr UTex (Arlington) Lib 69-. 10: Jr C of C. 14: Catlg, admin, lang ref, rare bks, educ for libnship. 15: 1638-D Carter dr, Arlington Tx 76010.

POSTELL, WILLIAM DOSITE. b Plaquemine La 5 O 08. 4: May Belle Andries. 5: LSU 26-30 (Geol) BS, 30-32 (Geol) MS, 32-33 BS in LS. 7: US Coast Guard, coxswain, temp res 44-45; Visiting Instr Loyola (New Orleans) summers 34, 36, 37; Asst Libn Sabine Parish Lib, Many La 33-34; Libn Mansfield Pub Schs, Mansfield La 34-38; Libn & Prof of med bibliog LSU Sch of Med(New Orleans) 38-59; Libn & Prof of med bibliog Tulane U Sch of Med (New Orleans) 59-. 8: Consul: Houston Acad of Med, 51-52, UFla, 54; Nat Taiwan U 55; VA Hosps, 57; Duke U Sch of Med, 61; DePaul Hosp, 61-; La State Dept of Hoss, 57-; Instr, refresher courses, VA Hosp libns & med libns 58-59; UPittsburgh Med Ctr; Scott & White Clinics; chm Adv Com to UTex on Reg Med Libs. 9: MedLA; SWLA; LaLA; Amer Assn for the Hist of Med. 10: La Hist Soc; Principal, High Sch of Religion, Church Parish(La); Confraternity of Christian Doctrine, Church Parish, Jesuit Sem Guild, New Orleans. 11: Marcia C Noyes Award for outstanding contributions to med libnship, 58; Certifcate of Merit, City of New Orleans, 52. 12: "An Introduction to Medical Bibliography (51); "The Health of Slaves on Southern Plantations (51); "Applied Medical Bibliography for Students (55); Ed"The Libraries of New Orleans (45); Ed "Bulletin of the Medical Library Association (46-49). 13: Yes. 14: Med libnship, hist of med, loc med hist. 15: 140 Tulane ave, New Orleans La 70112.

POTEAT, DOROTHY MAE. b Marion NC 29 O 16. 5: E Carolina Col 38-41 (Eng, Hist) AB, 48 (Eng) MA; UTenn summers; Fla State U 58-59 (LS) MS. 7: Instr Emmanuel Col(Franklin Springs Ga) 41-43; Instr & Libn Lee Col 43-50; Tchr Ringgold Elem Sch, Ringgold Ga 51-52; Libn Emmanuel Col(Franklin Springs Ga) 52-68; Libn Pleasant Gardens High Sch, Marion NC 68-. 9: NCEA. 10: Beta Phi Mu. 14: Admin. 15: Rte 1 Box 268A, Marion NC 28752.

POTENZA, PHILIP A. b NYC 10 D 42. 5: Queens Col (NY) 60-65 (Bio) BA, 65-67 MLS. 6: Sp. 7: Libn trainee Queens Borough Pub Lib, NY 65-67, Libn (staff) 67-. 9: NYLA. 14: Science ref, ya. 15: 79-11 - 41st ave apt A606, Jackson Hts NY 11373.

POTTEIGER, JOHN (FREEMAN). b Fleetwood Penn 1 S 24. 4: Hilda Antia Estep. 5: Reading Bus Inst 46-48 (Exec Sec); Juniata Col 49-53 (Hist) BS; Kutztown State Col 53 (LS); West Res summers 54-60 MS in LS; Penn State U summer 61. 6: Ger, Fr. 7: US Army 43-46 T-4 Med tech, Night supv Fleetwood Embroidery Mill, Fleetwood Penn 48-49; Clerk Reamstown Exch Bank, Reamstown Penn 47-48; Libn Williamsburg Commun Sch Dist, Williamsburg Penn 53-. 8: Bd Dirs, Williamsburg (Penn) Pub Lib; Helped org Blair Co Lib System; Blair Co Lib Bd Dirs; Designed Williamsburg New Pub Lib. 9: NEA; PLA; WEA; PTA; PennStateEA. 10: Blair Co Hist Assn; Amer Legion; F & AM; Meth Mens Organ; Veterans of Foreign Wars. 12: "175th Founder Week Historical Book of Williamsburg (65). 14: Local hist, civil war hist, art. 15: 311 Plum st, Williamsburg Pa 16693.

POTTER, ALENE B(ANNISTER). b Churchville NY 4 N 15. 4: Clayton K Potter. 5: SUNY(Brockport) 37-42 (Educ) BE; SUNY(Geneseo) 57-62 (LS) MS. 7: Tchr Chili #3, Scottsville NY 37-42; Tchr Chili #11, Rochester NY 51-55; Libn Brasser Sch, Rochester NY 55-; Organizer of lib & Libn Lyell Rd Elem Sch, Rochester NY 69-. 8: Chm Gates Chili Lib Dept 66-67. 9: NYLA; Monroe Co NY LA (sec 62); NY State Tchrs Assn; Pentad. 10: Bd, Chili Pub Lib. 12: "Meet the Authors (tapes & short biographies) (69).42469 13: Yes. 14: Wk with child. 15: Potters pl, Scottsville NY 14546.

POTTER, DONALD CARL. b Wichita Kan 21 Mr 21. 4: Mary J Warinner. 5: Friends U 39-42 (Eng: Wichita U 46-48 (Eng) BA; UMich 48-49 BA in LS. 7: Tech 4th Grade, Med Corps, US Army X-Ray Tech 42-45; Sub-prof asst Wichita City Lib, Wichita Kan 46-48; Sub-prof asst Ann Arbor Pub Lib, Ann Arbor Mich 48-49, Asst ref libn 49-51; Libn Lawrence Free Pub Lib, Lawrence Kan 51-55; Dir Duluth Pub Lib, Duluth Minn 55-62; Dir Knoxville Pub Lib Syste, Knoxville Tenn 62-65; Dir Bur of Lib Devel Penn State Lib, Harrisburg 66-. 9: ALA; PennLA. 13: Yes. 14: Admin, adult bks. 15: 3142 Brookwood st, Harrisburg Pa 17111.

POTTER, ELEANOR JOSEPHINE. b Omaha 24 N 07. 5: Columbia 45 (Fine Arts) BS; Pratt 38 BLS. 7: Lakewood Pub Lib, Lakewood Ohio 26-36; Englewood Pub Lib, Englewood NJ 38-43; Newark Museum, Newark NJ 48; Columbia U 43-47; USoCal 49-52; Detroit Pub Lib 52-. 9: ALA. 14: Catlg, ref, fine arts, admin. 15: Lafayette Plaisance, Detroit Mi 48207.

POTTER, EMILY S. b Marquette Mich 24 Jl 17. 4: William Hotchkiss Potter. 5: Smith 35-38 (Eng); UKy 63-65 (Eng) BA; NYU 65-66 (Eng) MA; Columbia 66-67 (LS) MA. 6: Fr. 7: Lib assoc NYU 67-. 9: ALA; NYLA; NY Lib Club. 10: Delta Epsilon Upsilon. 14: Ref, acquis. 15: 4920 Arlington ave, Riverdale NY 10471.

POTTER, GEORGE. b Cambridge Mass 17 My 18. 4: Wiltrud Preibisch. 5: Harvard 36-40 (FEL-Hidt) BA; UOklahoma 63-64 (LS); Simmons 64-66 MSLS. 7: Armed Forces 43-63; Circ libn Harvard-Yenching Lib 64-. 15: 87 Hammond st, Cambridge Ma 02138.

POTTER, HAZEL (PIERCE). b Weld Co Col 22 Ag 20. 4: Donald Glenn Potter. 5: Colo State Col 38-43 (Lit, Lang) AB; UOre (Eugene) summer 65 (Lib); UNevada 60-69 (Lib educ) MA. 6: Ger. 7: Eng tchr pub schs, Brighton Colo 43-44; Appt sec Pub Rel Colo State Col 40-45; Sec Speech Dept UColo 58-60; Off mgr ARS US Dept of Agric, Reno Nev 61-63; Libn Sparks High Sch, Sparks Nev 63-. 8: Tchr of Wkshop for Elem Libns Nev State Dept of Educ In-Serv Course 66; Mem State Lib Steering Com 69-. 9: ALA; NevLA; WashoeCoSchL (pres 69). 10: Alpha Delta Kappa; PEO; LWV. 14: Ref, lib educ. 15: 401 Moraineway, Reno Nv 89502.

POTTER, MARY ALICE (MINTEER). b Butler Penn 9 Mr 12. 4: Leroy Reed Potter. 5: Slippery Rock State Col 58-61 (Elem Educ) BS; UPittsburgh & West Res 65 MLS; UPittsburgh 69 Advanced Certif. 6: Fr. 7: Clerk Schusters Dept Store, Milwaukee 32-35; Clerk Willis Dept Store, Champaign Ill 39-40; Sec Bantam Car Co, Butler Penn 43-45; Receptionist Medical Asst, Butler Penn 45-57; Maltby Lib Slippery Rock State Col; Libn catlgr 61-63, Libn curr materials 64, Libn ref & circ 61-. 8: Alpha Xi Delta Fraternity, Slippery Rock Chapter - Financial Advisor,63, 64, 65, 66, 67, 68. 9: ALA-ACRL; NEA; PennLA; Penn State EA. 10: AAUP; Slippery Rock Col Faculty Assn; Sorptimist Fed Butler Co Club; Toastmistress Club; YWCA; Girl Scouts; DAR; Womens Club; People-to-People; YMCA Mothers Club; Alpha Xi Delta. 14: Ref. 15: 927 E Brady st, Butler Penn 16001.

POTTER, RICHARD CHARLES. b Davenport Iowa 9 Ag 24. 4: Dolores Pavao. 5: St Ambrose Col 46-51 (Hist, Eng) AB; Fla State U 56-57 (LS) MA. 6: Sp, Fr. 7: Fleet Marine Forces Pacific, USMC, Tinian, Guam, Japan 43-46; Line off Aircraft Carriers, Communications, USNR 52-54; Various other short tours of active duty in Res (Lt); Tchr soc studies jr high sch 51; Eng tchr sr high sch 54-55; Libn: Warrington Elem Sch, Pensacola Fla 57-64, Pensacola High Sch, Pensacola Fla 64-65, Woodham High Sch, Pensacola Fla 65-. 8: Consul libn "Pensacola News-Journal 58-; Evening libn & catlgr Pensacola Jr Col 57-58; Org, prof lib, Fleet Train Center, Charleston SC, summer 62; Statn-histn for Pensacola-Monsanto PGA Open Golf Tournament 56-; Organized model lib using original revised Dewey Schedule for elem sch, Little Flower Sch, Pensacola Fla 66-. 56-. 9: NEA; FlaEA; NWFlaEA; NWFlaLA; CathLA. 13: Yes. 14: Lib org, catlg, ref, hist bibliog. 15: 404 Clairmont dr, Forest Park, Pensacola Fl 32506.

POTTER, SALLY N. b Rochester NY 10 Ap 25. 4: Wyatt F Potter. 5: Brockport State Tchrs Col 42-45 (Educ) BE; Syracuse 61-67 MSLS. 7: Jr High Eng tchr Holley Central Schs, Holley NY 45-46; Libn & tchr Chestnut Hill Jr High, Liverpool NY 62-64; Lib trainee Liverpool Pub Lib, Liverpool NY 65-67; Asst libn & instr Onondaga Commun Col 67-. 8: Lib trustee Liverpool Pub Lib, sec & v-pres of Bd 60-65. 9: ALA; NYLA. 10: Fac Assn SUNY; Boy Scouts; Girl Scouts; Red Cross, etc. 14: Catlg, tech serv. 15: 222 Buckley rd, Liverpool NY 13088.

POTTER, SHARON (LEE). b Danville Ill 23 F 42. 5: Danville Jr Col 60-62 (Liberal Arts); Tex ChristianU 62-64 (Hist, Pol Sci) AB; UIll 64-66 MSLS. 6: Fr. 7: Libn (staff) UIll lib acquis dept (Urbana) 66-67; Libn (staff) Dallas Pub Lib, Dallas Tex 67-. 9: ALA; DallasCoLA; TexLA. 14: Ref, acquis. 15: 4112 Holland apt 209, Dallas Tx 75219.

POTTLE, MARION ISABEL (STARBIRD). b Oxford Me 23 O 1897. 4: Frederick A Pottle. 5: Colby Col 14-18 (Eng Lit) BA; Simmons 18-19 (LS) BS; Yale 33 (Eng) MA. 6: Fr, Lat, Ger, Ital. 7: Catlgr Yale Law Sch Lib 19-21; Asst ref libn UNH 22-23; Order dept act asst libn, act libn Yale Law Lib 23-29; Catlgr of the Boswell Papers, owned by Ralph H Isham, Glen Head LI & NYC 29-31; Catlgr of the Boswell Papers Yale U Lib 49-. 10: Chi Omega; Phi Beta Kappa. 11: Litt D West Col for Women, 56. 12: Comp & ed (with F A Pottle) "The Private Papers of James Boswell from Malahide Castle . . . A Catalogue (31). 14: 18th century mss. 15: 35 Edgehill rd, New Haven Conn 06511.

POTTS, ESTHER (TOPKIS). b Phila 2 Mr 14. 4: Albert M Potts. 5: Hood Col 31-32; UDel 32-35 (Eng) BA; Columbia 35-36 (LS) BS. 6: Fr, Ger, Norwegian. 7: Br asst NY Pub Lib 36; Reviewer bk inform sect NY State Lib 37; Ref asst, then catlgr of slides & photographs Chicago Art Inst 38-40; Asst catlg dept Cleveland Heights Pub Lib, Cleveland Heights Ohio 47; Reviewer of adult bks ALA, Chicago 63-. 13: Yes. 14: Bk sel. 15: 5490 S Shore dr, Chicago 60615.

POTTS, GENEVIEVE GRACE. b Wetumka Okla 3 F 37. 5: NM Highlands U 55-59 (Elem Educ) AB; UDenver 62-63 (Libnship) MA. 7: Lib aide City of Las Vegas, Las Vegas NM 52-59; Tchr Gallup-McKinley Co Sch, Thoreau NM 59-62; Libn Gallup-McKinley Co Schs, Gallup NM 62-. 9: NEA; ALA; NMEA; Gallup-McKinleyCoEA. 10: Delta Kappa Gamma; AAUW. 14: Reader guidance. 15: PO Box 874, Gallup NM 87301.

POTTS, MARY EVELYN. b Anson Tex 23 Ja 06. 5: Park Col 24-26 (Eng); UOkla 28-30 BA in LS, 42 (Eng) BA; UMich summer 47, 56 AMLS. 6: Sp, Fr, Ger. 7: Elem tchr, Grannis Ark 26-27; Tchr Pub Sch, Mena Ark 27-28; UOkla Lib: Catlgr 30-47; Act head catlgr 53, Asst head 53-54, Chief catlgr 54-67; Hd catlg dept & Assoc Prof 67-. 9: ALA; OklaLA (v-pres 47; past chm Tech-Serv Div); SWLA (v-chm Tech Serv Div 64-66), chm 66-68). 10: AAUW; UOkla Faculty Women. 14: Catlg. 15: Rt Box 96, Normal Ok 73069.

POTTS, RINEHART SKEEN. b Phila 13 Jl 27. 4: Grace Moore. 5: Temple 49-53 (Psych) AB; Rutgers 61-64 MLS. 7: US Air Force 45-49, active reserves 49-53; Air Weather Service weather observer/rawinsonde operator; airman first class; Production control, admin & planning Aero Serv Litton Ind, Phila 53-58, Chief Libn 58-64; Ref libn NJ State Lib summer 65; Asst Prof II & documents libn & Coord Curriculum Lab Glassboro Stte Col 64-68; Coord of grants 68-. 9: ALA; ADI; SLA; Aslib; NEA; Clsf Soc; SAA; NJLA (Com on Intel Freedom); NJEA; Spec Lib Coun Phila & Vicinity; Faculty Assn Glassboro State Col (pres 67-68); Faculty Senate Glassboro State Col (sec 68-). 10: AAUP; Trustee Pub Lib of Willingboro (Levittown) NJ: Deputy dir Civil Defense; Bd ofEduc. 12: "Bulletin, SL Coun Phila & Vicinity (64-); "Library Service for the Martian Exploration Expedition, Microphoto/Aero Serv(63); Co-ed "Bibliomancer, Glassboro State Col Lib (64-); Ed "Education for Information Science Newsletter ASIS (66-68). 13: Yes. 14: Educ of libns, communication among libns, studies of lib users. 15: 1223 Glen ter, Glassboro NJ 08028.

POTTS, VIRGINIA ERNESTYNE (RUSH). b Pinehurst NC 22 My 33. 4: James L Potts. 5: NC Col(Durham) 51-55 (Eng) BA; Duquesne U summer 57 (LS); Rutgers 59-63 MSLS. 6: Fr. 7: Libn W B Wicker Sch, Sanford NC 55-58; Lib trainee Newark Pub Lib, Newark NJ 58-61; Lib trainee NY Pub Lib 62-63; Ref libn Fisk U 63-. 10: Alpha Kappa Alpha; Alpha Kappa Mu. 14: Ref. 15: 640 N 5th st, Nashville 37207.

POULIN, ROGER JOSEPH. b Williamstown Vt 19 Ja 16. 4: Shirley C Ekberg. 5: Assumption Col Mass 34-38 (Liberal Arts) AB; Boston Col 40-44 (Theol); Carnegie 47-48 BSLS; Lebanon Valley 62 (A-v); Syracuse 63-69. 6: Fr. 7: US Army, Infantry (Pfc) 44-46; Eng & Latin instr Assumption Col(Worcester Mass) 46-47; Asst circ St Louis U 48; Asst ref St Louis Pub Lib 48-49; Libn Biol Lib Washington U(St Louis) 48-51; Lib plant & animal sci lib UNH 51-54; Asst libn Va, Mass & Penn 54-62; Asst libn SUNY Agr & Tech Col(Alfred) 62-65; Lib dir Vt Tech Col 65-. 9: ALA; SLA; ASIS. 13: Yes. 14: Tech serv. 15: 27 Highland ave, Randolph Vt 05060.

POULIN, ROLAND U. b Laconia NH. 5: Assumption Col 54-58 (Philos) BA; Inst Catholique (Paris) 56-57 Middlebury Col Summer Sch of French summers 58, 60; Simmons 64-65 MLS. 6: Fr. 7: Fr tchr Laconia High Sch, Laconia NH 58-60; Fr Tchrs Paulding High Sch, Rochester NH 60-62; Asst libn Assumption Col Lib (Worcester Mass) 65-66; Asst catlgr Dinand Lib Holy Cross Col (Worcester Mass) 66-. 9: ALA; MassLA; Mass Mens Club. 14: Catlg. 15: 18 Morningside rd, Worcester Ma 01602.

POULOS, ANGELA. b Kokomo Ind 8 Mr 42. 5: Ind U 60-64 (Hist) AB, 64-65 (LS) MA. 6: Fr, Ger. 7: Prof libn

Indianapolis Pub Lib 65-67; Libn Bowling Green State U Lib 68-. 8: Tchr introd libnship course Bowling Green StateU 69. 10: Beta Phi Mu. 14: Ref. 15: 822 Jefferson dr, Bowling Green Oh 43402.

POULTON, HELEN JEAN. b Warren Ohio 22 Ap 20. 5: San Jose 42 (Soc Sci) AB; UOre 46 (Hist) MA, 49 (Hist) PhD; UMich 51 MALS. 7: Asst Prof Hist Westminster Col(Utah) 48-51; Sr ref libn Okla A&M 51-52, Soc sci libn 53; Ref chief Washington U(St Louis)53-54; Ref libn Okla State U 54-58; UNev: Agric libn 58-62, Soc sci libn 62-63, Ref libn 63-. 9: ALA. 10: Pi Gamma Mu; Pi LambdaTheta; Phi Kappa Phi; Phi Alpha Theta. 12: "Analytical Index and List of Publications of the Oklahoma Agriculture Experiment Station, 1891-1956 (57); "Author-Subject Index: Oklahoma Current Farm Economics, 1927-57 (59); "Index to Angie Debos "This Week in Oklahoma History, a column in "Oklahoma City Times, Dec 52-Jl 54 (59); "James Edward Church: Bibliography of a Snow Scientist (64); "Nevada State Agencies: From Territory Through Statehood (64); "Writings on Nevada: A Selected Bibliography, with R R Elliott (63); "Index to History of Nevada (66). 13: Yes. 14: Ref, bibliog. 15: 115 Imperial blvd, Reno Nev 89503.

POUNCEY, LORENE. b N Little Rock Ark 18 O 21. 5: UTex 44-46 (Fr) BA; UCal 46-47 BLS; UIll 49-50 (LS); UHouston 58-63 (Eng) MA. 6: Fr, Sp, Ger. 7: Jr catlgr HE Huntington Lib, San Marino Cal 47-49; Catlgr UIll (Urbana) 49-51; (1st Lt) USAF, ROME NY 51-52; Bibliogr Johns Hopkins U 52-53; Bibliogr LC 54-56; Asst catlg libn UHouston 56-. 9: BSA; The Bibliog Soc(London); TexLA; Critical Quarterly Soc (Hull England); Poetry Soc of Tex. 10: Tex Assn Col Tchrs. 12: Prd "The William B Bates Collection, a CATALOG OF AN Exhibition (65). 14: Bibliog, rare bks, lithog, prints, poetry, lib exhibs. 15: 2815 Jarrard, Houston 77005.

POUNCY, MITCHELL LOUIS. b Palestine Tex 3 Ap 30. 5: Prairie View A&M Col 47-51 (Hist) AB; Atlanta 54-55 MSLS. 6: Fr. 7: (Sgt) US Marine Corps, El Toro Cal 52-54; Southern U Lib: Asst ref libn 55-59, Acquis libn 59-61, Circ libn 61-65; Catlg libn 65-. 8: Mem, Visiting Com for the eval of 3 high schs in La 58-62. 9: ALA. 10: Commun Assn for the Welfare of Sch Child. 14: Ref, circ, ser. 15: Box 10031, So Br PO, Baton Rouge La 70813.

POUND, MARY (ELIZABETH). b Houston 9 Je 32. 5: Rice U 50-54 (Eng) BA; UTex 5-56 MLS. 6: Sp, Fr. 7: Stud asst Rice U Fondren Lib 50-54; Ser catlgr U Tex Lib 55-. 9: ALA; TexLA; SWLA. 10: Beta Phi Mu. 12: "Texas Library Journal: bus mgr (57-65), ed (65-). 14: Catlg. 15: 1110 Autrey st, Houston Tx 77006.

POUNDSTONE, SALLY (HILL). b Wash DC 7 Ap 33. 4: Robert Bruce Poundstone. 5: UKy 50-54 (LS) BA, 54-55 (LS) MA. 7: Asst head ref dept Louisville Ky Free Pub Lib 55-59; Asst Folger Shakespeare Lib, Wash DC 59-60; Chief acquis dept White Plains NY Pub Lib 60-62; Libn Bedford Hills Elem Sch, Bedford Hills NY 65-66; Dir Mamaroneck Free Lib, Mamaroneck NY 66-. 8: Instr in Lib Sci NYU Ctr for Continuing Educ, White Plains NY 68-. 9: ALA (Staff Orgs Round Table; Memb Chm 59-60); KyLA (sec 57-59); NYLA; NY State Tchrs Assn; Westchester (NY) LA (Publicity Chm 68-, Admin Sect v-chm 69-). 10: Phi Beta Kappa; Beta Phi Mu; Garden Club of Mamaroneck. 13: Yes. 14: Ref, admin. 15: 129 N Ridge st, Rye Town Port Chester NY 10573.

POURCIAU, LESTER J JR. b Baton Rouge La 6 S 36. 4: May Moore. 5: LSU 59-62 (German Lang) BA, 62-64 (LS) MS; Ind U 67- (LS). 6: Fr, Ger. 7: Electronic Tech USAF 55-59; Electronic Tech LSU 60-63; Asst ref libn USCar 63-64; Ref libn Florence Co Lib, Florence SC 64-65; Dept of ref & bibliog UFla 66-67. 9: ALA; ASIS; SELA. 10: Delta Phi Alpha; Jr C of C; AAUP. 14: Lib admin, philos of libnship, info sci. 15: 1114 S Henderson st, Bloomington In 47401.

POURCIAU, MAY (MAULDIN) MOORE. b Greenville SC 26 S 40. 4: Lester John Pourciau Jr. 5: Erskine Col 58-62 (Eng, Hist) BA; LSU 62-63 (LS) MS. 7: Prof asst co dept Richland Co Lib, Columbia SC 63-64; Head ext dept Florence Co Lib, Florence SC 64-65; Hd ext dept Santa Fe Reg Lib, Gainesville Fla 66-67; Catlgr IndU Lib (Bloomington) 68-. 9: SELA; SCLA. 10: Crescent Fine Arts Club. 14: Adult readers adv serv, catlg. 15: 1114 S Henderson st, Bloomington In 47401.

POVILONIS, LOUISE EUNICE. b Hartford Conn 18 Ja 26. 5: St Joseph Col Hartford Conn) 44-48 (Eng Lit) BS; Drexel 51-52 MS in LS. 6: Fr, Lithuanian. 7: Lib asst Pub Lib, Hartford Conn 48-51; Asst libn St Joseph Col Lib (Conn) 52-53; Catlgr Pub Lib, Hartford Conn 53-64; Admin asst of the catlg dept 64-. 9: ALA (Recr Tetwk Conn rep 65-67); ConnLA (Rep-at-Large 59-60); Hartford(Conn) Libns Club (pres 65-66). 10: Phi Kappa Phi. 11: Lippincott Contest Winner, 59. 12: Ed ConnLA "News and Views (63-66), 14: Catlg, spec collections, phonograph records. 15: 700 Hillside ave, Hartford Conn 06110.

POVSIC, FRANCES FRANCKA (BOLHA). b Yugoslavia 29 S 23. 4: Boleslav S Povsic. 5: John carroll U 57-60 (Hist) BS; West Res U 61-65 (LS) MS. 6: Slovenian, Ger, Serbo-Crooition. 7: Tchr St Procop Sch, Cleveland Ohio 55-59; Tchr St Vitus Elem Sch, cleveland Ohio 59-61; Research ref libn Bowling Green State U 63-. 9: ALA; OhioLA. 14: Ref. 15: 604 Knollwood dr, Bowling Green Oh 43402.

POWELL, ALICE (THOMPSON). b S Glastonbury Conn 19 Ja 12. 4: Richard Roy Belden Powell. 5: Lake Erie Col 28-32 (Music) BMus; Oberlin col 32-33 (Fr) MA; Columbia 33-36 (LS) BS. 6: Fr. 7: Libn Sr High Sch, Concord NH 33-36; Libn So Conn State Col 36-58; Assoc Prof of Lib Serv 40-64; Libn Crystal Springs Sch, Hillsborough Cal 64-65; Child consul Burlingame Pub Lib, Burlingame Cal 65-68. 8: Instr Fla State U Lib Sch, Summers 48, 49, UMe, Summer 54, Consul Kent Sch Lib, Kent Conn, Summer 50, Columbia Bicentennial Commsn, Summer 53, Child Lit San Francisco State Col 65-. 9: ALA-LED (chm Tchrs Sect 53); ConnLA (pres 53, Hon life mem 62-); ConnSchLA (pres 39, Hon life mem 64-); CalLA; (sec Child Sect 68-69); Assn of Child Libns NoCal. 10: AAUW. 13: Yes. 14: Child lib serv, lib educ. 15: 1808 Black Mountain rd, Hillsborough Cal 94010.

POWELL, ANGELIKA SCHMIEGELOW. b Guestrow Mecklbg Germany 28 My 35. 4: Lazarus Whitehead Powell. 5: Hambrug Lib Sch 55-58 Diploma. 6: Ger, Russian, Fr, Lat. 7: Libn Borgward Automobile Factory, Bremen Germany 58-61; Libn Heidelberg Teacher col, Heidelberg Germany 61-62; Exchange libn NYC Pub Lib 62-63; Exchange libn UVa Lib (Charlottesville) 63-64, Catlgr hd Slavic sect 66-; Chief libn Intl Youth Lib, Munich Germany 64-66. 9: VaLA. 14: Catlg. 15: 302 Preston ct, Charlottesville Va 22903.

POWELL, BEATRICE (HOPPER). b Ono, Russell Co Ky 18 My 10. 4: Curtis J Powell. 5: Campbellsville Col 38-39 (Educ) Diploma & Certif; Baltimore Cty Col 44 (Com) Certif; West Ky State Col 47-49 (LS) BS; UKy 53 (Educ); West Ky State Col 60 (Educ) MA; West State U 66, 68. 6: Fr. 7: Grade tchr Russell Co Bd of Educ, Russell Co Ky 35-42; US File Clerk US Govt Dept of Soc Security, Baltimore 42-43; Grade tchr City Bd of Educ, Baltimore 43; IBM operator Glenn L Martin Aircraft, Baltimore 44-45; Russell Co Bd of Educ, Russell Co Ky; Jr high tchr 45-47, Tchr-libn 47-49, High sch libn 50-60, Elem libn 60-69. 8: Organized MCEA Dept CTA of KyEA 51; Organized Russell Co Educ Assn 50; Organized first FTA Club in MCEA 53. 9: NEA (Life mem); Cir Tchrs Assn (Bd Dirs 9 yrs); ALA; KyASchL (dir 67-69); Del to Convs State, Dist & Local Levels; KyLA; KyEA; MCEA; RussellCoEA. 10: Delta Kappa Gamma; Bus & Prof Womens Club (Charter mem); Womens Soc for Christian Serv (charter member); Russell Co Hist Soc (charter mem). 12: Jt auth "Library Quarters and Equipment" (53). 13: Yes. 14: Sch libnship, materials spec. 15: Rt 2 Box 480, Russell Springs Ky 42642.

POWELL, BENJAMIN (EDWARD). b Sunbury NC 28 Ag 05. 4: Elizabeth Graves. 5: Duke 22-26 (Hist) AB; Columbia 29-30 (LS) BS; Chicago 34-35, 45-46 PhD. 6: Ger, Sp, Fr. 7: Tchr & dir of athletics Bethel High Sch, Bethel NC 26-27; Asst circ dept Duke U Lib 27-28, Chief of circ 28-29; Asst ref dept NY Pub Lib 29-30; Chief of circ & ref dept Duke U Lib 30-37; Libn UMo 37-46; Libn Duke U 46-. 8: Consul to various agencies of US Government and to Col & Univ Libs; Visiting Prof, UNC Sch of Lib Sci, spring 61, 62 & 68. 9: ALA (pres 59-60, Exec Bd 56-61; chm 6 coms 50-63); -ACRL (sec 40-44; dir 46-47, pres 48-49; chm Nomin Com 44-45); Coop Com on Lib Bldg Plans (chm 47-48); MoLA (pres 38-39); SELA (Exec Bd 50-54, Act chm 51-52); NCLA (Exec Bd 52-54). 10: Rotary Club; Trustee Durham Pub Lib; Phi Beta Kappa; AAUP; Hope Valley Country Club. 13: Yes. 14: Admin. 15: 3609 Hathaway rd, Hope Valley, Durham NC 27707.

POWELL, DONALD M(OORE). b Yonkers NY 25 My 14 05: Swarthmore Col 32-36 (Eng) AB; Duke U 36-38 (Eng) MA; UMich 41-42 ABLS. 6: Sp, Fr. 7: Instr Colo State Col 38-41; US Army Artillery (Master Sgt) 42-45; Asst NY Pub Lib 42, 46; UAriz: Head ref dept 46-64, Chief pub serv 64-65, Asst libn 65-68, Assoc libn & prof lib sci 68-. 8: Lib consul, Iraq Col of Agric, Abu Ghraib Iraq 57. 9: ALA; ArizStateLA (pres 50); SWLA. 10: Ariz Pioneers Hist Soc; West Hist Assn; Phi Kappa

Phi. 12: "The Peralta Grant" (60); Ed "Notes of Travel Through the Territory of Arizona," by J H Marion (65); Comp "Index to Arizona News in the 'Arizona Daily Star,'" with L Higley & C Colby (52-). 13: Yes. 14: Ref, SWest Americana. 15: UAriz Lib, Tucson Az 85721.

POWELL, KAREN LOUISE. b Shelburne Nova Scotia 28 D 43. 4: Donald David Powell. 5: Acadia U 61-64 (Hist) BA; UToronto 64-65 BLS. 7: Bkmob libn Halifax Co Reg Lib, Halifax NS 65-66; Catlgr Edmonton Pub Lib, Edmonton Alberta 66-. 9: CanLA; EdmontonLA. 15: 9837 - 103 st, Edmonton 15 Alberta Can.

POWELL, LAWRENCE CLARK. b Wash DC 3 S 06. 4: Fay Ellen Shoemaker. 5: Occidental Col 24-28 (Eng) BA; UDijon 30-32 PhD; UCal 36-37 (LS) BLS. 6: Fr. 7: Acquis libn Pub Lib, Los Angeles 37; UCLA: Acquis libn 38-43, U Libn 44-51, Dean Sch of Lib Serv 60-66, Dir W A Clark Mem Lib 44-66. 8: Visiting Prof Columbia U Sch of Lib Serv 54; Lecturer in Eng UCLA 55-60; Annual lecture, Lib Assn (Gt Brit) 57; Keynote Speaker; ALA Conf, 52 & 65, SLA Conf, 61; Conducted wkshop for Air Force Libns, Tokyo 60; Founded UCLA Library Occasional Papers; Visiting Prof Simmons Lib Sch 68; Visiting lectr Loughborough Lib Sch 69. 9: ALA (Coun 49-53 & 58-62); BSA (pres 54-56); CalLA (pres 50). 10: Grolier Club (NY); Zamorano Club (Los Angeles);Phi Beta Kappa. 11: LittD, Occidental Col, 55; LittD Juniata Col, 60; LHD Carnegie Inst, 61; Clarence Day Award, 60; Guggenheim Fellow, 50-51, 66-67; LittD Lycoming Col 68; Drexel Inst Achievement Award 68. 12: Auth "Robinson Jeffers (32, 34, 40); "Manuscripts of D. H. Lawrence (37); "Philosopher Pickett (42); "Islands of Books (51); "Land of Fiction (52); "Alchemy of Books (54); "Heart of the Southwest (55); "Books West Southwest (57); "Southwestern Century (58); "The Maib, with W W Robinson (58); "Passion for Books (59); "Books in by Baggage (60); "Southwestern Book Trails (63); "Little Package (64); Ed: "Rare Books and Research, "Libraries in the Southwest, "Southwest of the Bookman, "Libros Californianos; "Clark Library Decade Reports (44, 55, 66); "Mercurius Redivivus; "Poetry of Walt Whitman; Ed Bd: "Southwest Review; Auth; bookmans Progress (68); "Fortune and Friendship (68). California Quarterly; "Augustan Reprint Society. 13: Yes. 15: 405 Hilgard ave, Los Angeles Cal 90024.

POWELL, LUCILE (EVANS). b Waco Tex 10 S 1898. 4: Roger Mills Powell. 5: Baylor U 17-21 (Math, Eng) BA; Tex Womans U summers 43, 44, 48 BSLS; UTex 48; Baylor U 58. 7: Elem tchr: Waco Ind Schs, Waco Tex 30-36, La Bega Ind Sch, Bellmead Tex 41-42, Waco Ind Schs, Waco Tex 42-43, Jr high libn 43-64; High sch libn Midway Ind Schs, Waco Tex 64-; Educ br libn UTex summer 48-55; Circ desk Baylor U summer 64. 8: Rep the South on ALA Com on Lib Bldg Plans, 50. 9: ALA; NEA; TexLA; TexStateTA; McLennanCoTA; Waco Clr TA. 10: AAUW; Delta Kappa Gamma; PTA; Waco Lib Club; DAR; Waco Hist Found; Nat Retired Tchrs Assn. 14: Catlg, ya reading prog. 15: 2100 Colcord ave, Waco Tex 76707.

POWELL, MYRL D. b Burr Oak Kan 22 F 30. 4: Josephine Emanuele. 5: UKan 48-52 (Ger) BA, 556 (Russian); CatholicU 60-67 (LS). 6: Russian, Ger, Danish, Norwegian, Sp, fr. 7: Classified US Army 52-55; Teaching asst UKan 55-56; Classified Dept of Defense, Wash DC 56-57; Asst ed MIRA LC 57-63, Subj catlgr 63-67, Sr subj catlgr (natural sci) 67-. 9: Geosci Info Soc. 14: Catlg. 15: 9220 Columbia blvd, Silver Spring Md 20910.

POWELL, PATRICIA KAY. b Port Arthur Tex 18 Jl 39. 5: Tex Christian U 57-61 (Eng) BA; UEdinburgh 63-64 (Eng Lit) Diploma in Eng Studies; LSU 64-65 (LS) MS; Lamar State Col of Tech 65-67 (Eng) MA. 6: Fr. 7: Tchr of Sophomore Eng Port Neches-Groves High Sch, Pt Neches Tex 61-63; Rotary Fellow UEdinburgh 63-64; Trainee LSU Lib (Baton Rouge) 64-65; Libn Lamar State Col of Tech 65-66; Libn Port Neches-Groves High Sch 66-. 8: Rotary Found Fellow to UEdinburgh, 63-64, HEA Inst N Tex State U 69. 9: ALA; LaLA; Tex Sch TA; Tex Clrm TA; MLA. 10: Alpha Chi; Phi Kappa Phi. 14: Pub serv humanities, ref, lib educ. 15: 6538 Washington, Groves Tex 77619.

POWELL, RUSSELL H. b Windber Penn 29 Jl 43. 4: Beverly Jean Ambrose. 5: Juniata Col 61-65 (Hist) BA; UPittsburgh 65-66 MLS. 7: Sci libn Juniata Col 66-68; Engring libn UKy 68-. 9: ALA; SLA; Amer Soc Engrg Educ; KyLA. 10: Beta Phi Mu. 14: Sci bibliog, lib admin. 15: 2233A Alexandria dr, Lexington Ky 40504.

POWELL, RUTH ANN. b Fairmont W Va 22 F 39. 5: Fairmont State Col 57-61 (Soc Sci) AB Ed; Kent State 62-67 MS in LS. 6: Fr. 7: Tchr Moody Jr High Sch, Bedford Ohio 61-65, Dept chm 63-65; Libn Mannington High Sch, Mannington W Va 65-66; Circ libn Fairmont State Col 66-. 9: ALA; Assn Amer Higher Educ; Tri-State ACRL; WVaLA (sec col & Univ Sect). 10: Kappa Delta Pi; Sigma Kappa (Fac Spons); Pi Gamma Mu; Fairmont Concert Assn. 12: "History of Fairmont State College Library, 1867-1967" (69). 14: Admin, catlg, circ. 15: 1116 Country Club rd, Fairmont WVa 26554.

POWELL, WILLIAM STEVENS. b Smithfield NC 28 Ap 19. 4: Virginia Penn Waldrop. 5: UNC 38-40 (Amer Hist) BA, 7: Reporter, Statesville Daily, Statesville NC 41; Master Sgt US Army, US, S Pacific, Japan 41-46; Ref asst, rare bk room, Yale U 47-68; Researcher NC Dept of Archives & Hist, Raleigh NC 48-51; Asst libn NC Collection, UNC(Chapel Hill) 51-58, Head 58, Lectr in Hist 64-. 9: ALA (Coun 67); So Hist Assn (Com Assignments); Hist Soc NC Coun (Com Duties); NCLA; NC Soc of Co & Loc Histns (pres 54-55); Roanoke Island Hist Assn (Histn 63). 10: Bd of Governors, UNC Press; NC Hist Markers 51; Ed Bd NC Hist Review 61; Ed Bd NC Colonial Records 62. 11: Guggenheim Fellow, 56 Grantinaid for research in England, Inst of Early Amer Hist & Culture, Williamsburg Va 50. 12: Auth "The Carolina Charter of 1963" (54); Ed "Ye Countie of Albemarle" (58); "Com North Carolina County Histories; A Bibliography" (58); "Annals of Progress, The Story of Lenoir County" (63); "The Proprietors of Carolina" (63); "Higher Education in North Carolina" (64); "North Carolina, A Students Guide to Localized History" (65); "Paradise Preserved, A History of the Roanoke Island Historical Association" (65); "The First Book of North Carolina" (66); Ed "Journal of the House of Burgesses, 1749" (49); Ed "North Carolina Fiction, 1734-1957, An Annotated Bibliography" (58); Ed "Clement Hall, A Collection of Many Christian Experiences" (61); Ed "North Carolina Lives" (62); Ed History "News", Amer Assn State & Loc Hist (49-57); Assoc ed "North Carolina Libraries" (58-68); Comp "North Carolina County Histories, A Bibliography" (58); "The North Carolina Colony" (69); "The North Carolina Gazetteer" (68); Contrib ed "American Heritage" (50-55). 13: Yes. 14: Ref, rare bks, North Carolinana. 15: 307 Plum lane, Chapel Hill NC 27514.

POWER, FLORENCE MARIE. b Detroit 16 D 07. 5: UCLA 29 (Fr) AB; Columbia 46 MSLS; Los Angeles Pub Lib 30 Lib sci certif. 6: Fr, Ger. 7: Asst Hist Dept & Brs Los Angeles Pub Lib 30-33; Period dept Detroit Pub Lib 34-39, Brs 40-41, Ref dept 42-43; Asst ref dept Pasadena Pub Lib, Pasadena Cal 43-52, Head ref serv 52-. 9: ALA-RSD (chm New Ref Tools Com 62-64); CalLA (chm Ref RT 63-64). 10: Book Club of Cal. 13: Yes. 14: Rf, rare bks. 15: 285 E Walnut st, Pasadena Cal 91101.

POWER, MARY HELEN RABUS. b Glen Ridge NJ 19 My 38. 5: Lasell Jr Col 56-57; Upsla Col 57-60 (Eng) AB; Emory 61-63 MLS. 6: Fr. 7: Eng tchr St Marys-in-the-Mountains, Littleton NH 60-61; Libn Ga Inst of Tech 63-65; Br libn Dayton Pub Lib North Town Shiloh Br, Dayton Ohio 66-. 9: ALA; OhioLA. 14: Ref, admin. 15: 51 Grafton ave apt 708, Dayton Oh 45406.

POWERS, CAROL L. b Hornbeck La 10 Je 40. 4: Charles L Powers. 5: State Col of Ark 57-60 (Educ) BSE; Peabody Col summers 63-66 MLS. 7: Libn Jr high sch, N Little Rock Ark 60-66; Lib supv N Little Rock Pub Schs 66-68; Asst libn & instr of lib sci State Col of Ark 68-. 9: ALA; NEA; ArkSchLA (past v-chm, past sec); ArkLA; ArkEA. 10: AAUW; Alpha Delta Kappa; Alpha Beta Alpha; Sigma Sigma Sigma. 14: Ref, sch libs. 15: 2329 College, Conway Ar 72032.

POWERS, JANE (BIDDLE). b Ann Arbor Mich 11 Jl 15. 5: UMich 32-36 (Hist) AB (Tchr's certif), 36-37 ABLS. 7: Libn Slauson Jr High Sch, Ann Arbor Mich 37-38; Libn River Rouge Pub Lib, River Rouge Mich 38-39; Jr libn Trenton Pub Lib, Trenton NJ 42-43, 49-59; Sr libn Hamilton Twp Pub Lib, Trenton NJ 59-64, Dir 64-. 9: ALA; NJLA. 10: LWV. 14: Admin, ref. 15: 2090 Greenwood ave, Trenton NJ 08609.

POWNALL, DAVID E. b Rochester NY 31 Ja 25. 4: Vicci Broda. 5: UWis 45-50 (Musc) BM; UWyo summer 50 (Musi); UTlsa 52-53 (Music) MM; Ind U 55-57 MALS. 6: Fr, Ital, Ger, Sp. 7: Instr Music Westky State Col 53-54; Cellist Nat Symphony Orchestra Wash DC 54-55; Asst ref & readers adv Richmond Pub Lib, Richmond Va 57-58; Asst circ & humanities libn Ore State U Lib 58-63; Asst ref libn 63-64; Hd reader serv State Col, Iowa 64-67; Hd humanities libn Simon Fraser U 67-69; Assoc dir Hofstra U Lib 69-. 9: ALA. 10: AAUP; ACLU; United World Federalists; Beta Phi Mu; CAUT. 13: Yes. 14: Bibliog, pub serv, admin. 15: Lib Hofstra Univ, Hempstead LI NY 11550.

PRAGER, HERTA (SCHILD). b Fiume Italy 30 D 09. 4: Frank D Prager. 5: UMunich 29-34 (Hist) Dr phil; Chicago 36-40 (Law) JD, 50-51 (LS). 6: Ger, Ital, Fr. 7: Libn UChicago Law Sch 39-41; Lawyer, Chicago 41-50; Libn Northwestern U Law Sch52-55; Head law & legis ref & gen ref burs NJ State Law Lib, Trenton J 56-. 9: ALA; AALL; NJLA. 13: Yes. 14: Law ref. 15: NJ State Lib, 185 WState st, Trenton NJ 08625.

PRANGE, LUCILLE M. b Granc Rapids, Mich 1 My07. 5: UMich 25-29 AB in LS,49 MA in LS. 6: Fr, Ger. 7: Lib asst Grand Rapids Pub Lib, Grand Rapids Mich 30-36; Sch libn E Grand Rapids Schs, E Grand Rapids Mich 36-, Dir of Sch Libs 50-. 8: Lecturer UMich Ext Serv, Grand Rapids 55-. 9: MichLA (chm Sch & Child Sect; E Grand Rapids Tchrs Assn (pres 2 yrs); MichASchL (chm Supv Sect); ALA; AASchL. 10: Delta Kappa Gamma. 14: Sch lib admin. 15: 1103 Lake Grove, E Grand Rapids Mi 49506.

PRATT, BARBARA FISHER. b Providence 21 Je 14. 4: Norman T Pratt Jr. 5: Pembroke 32-36 (Eng lit) AB; Ind U 55-59 (LS) MA. 6: Ger. 7: Child lit tchr Ind U Cor Bur 59-60; Elem Sch libn U Sch, Bloomington Ind 58-60; Halls of Residence libn Ind U 60-. 9: ALA; IndLA. 10: YWCA Bd; Psi Iota XI; University Club; Girl Scout Bd; Monroe Co Commun Coun; Archaeological Inst of Amer (So Ind Chap). 14: Admin of resid halls lbs. 15: 1010 E First st, Bloomington In 47403.

PRATT, BERT WILSON. b Denver 6 M 28. 5: Knox Col 45-49 (Econ) BA; Northwestern U 49-51 (Accounting) MBA; UWis 63-64 (LS) MS. 7: Finance clk US Army 51-53; Jr accountant Stewart-Warner Corp, Chicago 53-56, Budget accountant 56-58; Tax accountant Walgreen Co, Chicago 58-61, Supv tax accountant 61-63; Asst hd loan dept UCal (Davis) 64-65, Ser libn acquis dept 65-67, Chief bibliogr acquis dept 67-. 9: ALA; CalLA. 10: AAUP; Sierra Club; ACLU. 14: Acquis. 15: 958 F st, Davis Ca 95616.

PRATT, PRISCILLA E. b Plainfield NJ 21 Mr 41. 5: Wheaton Col (Ill) 59-63 (Eng) AB; Rutgers 66-68 MLS. 6: Fr, Sp, Ger, Ital. 7: Asst to period libn Fairleigh DickinsonU 65-66; Lib trainee Plainfield Pub Lib, Plainfield NJ 66-67; Asst acquis libn SUNY (Stony Brook) 68-. 14: Acquis, rare bks. 15: 4-4A Dark Hollow rd, Port Jefferso NY 11777.

PRATT, (VIRGINIA) LORRAINE. b Trenton Mich 15 Je 19. 5: Wayne State U 37-42 (Bus Admin) BS; UDenver 43-44 BSLS; Conn Col for Women summer 44; UOslo summer 55. 6: Norwegian, Sp, Fr. 7: Ref libn United Aircraft Corp, E Hartford Conn 44-45; Libn Redwood City Pub Lib, Redwood City Cal 45-48; Ref libn Stanford Research Inst, Menlo Park Cal 48-50, Manager Lib Serv 57-. 8: Lib consu l, Coun of Rectors, UChile, 57-58. 9: Internat Fed for Documentation; SLA (San Francisco Bay Reg Chap; pres 58-59); ADI; ACS(Chem Lit Div). 10: AAAS; Friends of Commun Lib of Portola Valley, Cal. 13: Yes. 14: Admin, systems analysis, lib automation, info retr. 15: 1019 Los Trancos rd, Menlo Park Ca 94025.

PRAYZICH, ELISE M. b Lakewood NJ 17 N 37. 4: Donald S Prayzich. 5: Trenton State col 55-57 & 62-63 (Elem Educ) BA; USoCal 68-69 MS in LS. 7: Tchr: NJ 57-58, 60-62, 63-64, Commerce City Colo 64-66, Redondo Beach Cal 67-68; Child libn Los Angeles Co Pub Lib S Gate 69-. 14: Child wk. 15: 3768 S Flower st, Los Angeles Ca 90007.

PRELEC, ANTONIJA (GUBERINA) (MRS). b Sibenik Yugoslavia 2 Mr 29. 4: Krsto Prelec. 5: UZagreb (Yugoslavia) 48-52 (Physics) BS, 61-63 (LS). 6: Croato-Serbian, Ital, russian. 7: Tchr high sch, Zagreb Yugoslavia 52-57; Libn inst "Rudjer Boskovic", Zagreb Yugoslavia 57-63, 65-67; Lib asst PrincetonU Firestone Lib 63-64, Libn Fine Hall Lib 68-. 14: Ref. 15: 109 Bayard lane, Princeton NJ 08540.

PRELOWSKI, MURIEL (MINNE MARY MURIEL JAMES). b London 25 Ag 07. 4: Stefan Prelowski. 5: ULondon Westminster Col 46-49 (Mental Health, Soc Studies); Chicago 55-58, 60 (LS) MA. 6: Fr, Ger. 7: Dir Supv Dept Health & Welfare London Co Coun, Eng 49-51; Exec Dir Montreal Day Nursery, Montreal 51-53; Asst libn Cook Co Sch of Nursing, Chicago 55-57; Libn Bateman Sch, Chicago 58-60; Asst libn St John's Col (Ohio) 60-61; Child libn Merrick Pub Lib, Merrick NY 61-62; Dir Sachem Pub Lib, Lake Ronkonkoma NY 62-64; Coord Instr Materials Ctr Regis Col 68-. 8: Lib consul on org, Instituto Universitario Santa Famiglia, Asmara Ethiopia, summer 65. 9: ALA; CathLA; ColoLA; Colo A-V Assn. 11: Grad scholarship, London Univ, 46-49. 13: Yes. 14: Org of new libs, promotion, bldgs, consul. 15: 2430 Eldridge st, Golden Co 80401.

PREMINGER, ALEXANDER S. b Berlin Germany 29 Jl 15. 4: Augusta Friedman. 5: NYU 46-50 (Ger) BA; Columbia 50-52 (LS) MS. 6: Fr, Ger, Lat, Gk, Hebrew. 7: Sales correspondent Somerset Tool Co, Newark NJ 40-41; US Army 42-45; Asst tech serv NYU Law Lib 46-51; Brooklyn Col Lib: Period & documents lbn 52-59, Soc sci libn 59-60, Humanities libn 60-55, Chief humanities div 65-. 8: Ed consul, Frederick Ungar Publg Co, NYC, 65-; Mem Ed Bd, "Encyclopedia of World Literature in the Twentieth Century 66-. 9: ALA-ACRL;-RSD (Bibliog Com); Amer Comparative Lit Assn; MLA; NY Lib Club. 10: AAUP; Flushing Affiliates of the Educ Broadcasting Corp; Columbia Sch of Lib Serv Alumni Assn; Bollingen Foun (Fellow); Phi Beta Kappa; Beta Phi Mu. 12: Ed "Princeton Encyclopedia of Poetry and Poetics " (65); Ed "Against the Running Tide" by H D Gideonse (67). 13: Yes. 14: Ref, bibliog. 15: 1311 Decker st, Valley Stream NY 11580.

PRENTICE, ANN E (HURLBUT). b Grafton Vt 19J133. 4: Paul N Prentice. 5: U Rochester 50-54 (Hist) AB; SUNY (Albany) 58-65 MLS; Columbia 68- (LS). 6: Fr. 7: Elem libn Kingston Sch System, Kingston NY 63-64; Dir Kingston NY 64; Jr high sch libn Arlington Sch System, Poughkeepsie NY 65-67; Instr Sch of Lib Sci SUNY (Albany) NY 67. 9: NYLA (chm Hist Com - RTSS); ALA. 10: AAUW; LWV (ed of published booklet on Hyde Park, NY). 14: Admin, tchg of lib sci. 15: 29 Lawrence rd, Hyde Park NY 12538.

PRENTISS, S(AMUEL) GILBERT. b Hinchkley NY 20 My 12. 4: Evelyn Martin. 5: Syracuse 30-34 (Eng) BS in LS; Elmira Col 44-45; UVt 44. 7: Ref asst Rochester(NY) Pub Lib 35-36; Dir Chemung Co Lib, Elmira NY 36-39; Dir Steele Mem Li, Elmira NY 39-45; Head travel libs & lib for blind NY State Lib 46-50; Head field serv NY State Lib Ext Div, Albany NY 50-54; Ref libn UVt Lib 54-56; Lib consul Div of Research NY State Educ Dept, Albany NY 56-59; Pub lib consul NY State Lib Ext Div, Albany NY 60-61, Dir 61-63; State Libn & asst comm for libs NY State Lib 63-66; Consul 66-. 9: ALA-AAStateL; NYLA. 13: Yes. 14: Statewide & reg lib devel, lib educ. 15: RD #1, Castleton-on-Hudson NY 12033.

PRESCHEL, BARBARA (MEITIN). b NYC 22 Ja 29. 4: Dr Sheldon Preschel. 5: Finch Col 45-47 (Eng Lit) AA; Columbia 47-49 (17th cent Eng Lit) BS; Columbia 59-61 MLS, 66- (LS). 06: Fr. 7: Bibliogr Info Center on Crime & Delinquency of Nat Coun on Crime & Delinquency, NYC 61-66. 9: SLA; ALA; ASIS. 10: Beta Phi Mu. 12: Ed & indexer "Current Projects in the Prevention Control & Treatment of Crime and Delinquency" (61-); Ed 'Current Projects Section' of "International Bibliography on Crime and Delinquency" (65-). 14: Ed, indexing, info retrieval, abstracting. 15: 400 E 56th st, New York NY 10022.

PRESS, RICHARD LEON. b Spokane Wash 13 N32. 4: Esther Azran. 5: City Col (San Francisco) 50-52 (Pol Sci) AA; UCAL(Berkeley) 52-54 (Pol Sci) BA; Hebrew U(Jerusalem Israel) 55-56 (Spec Study Prog); UCal(Berkeley) 58-59 MLS; Dropsie Col 61-64 (Middle East Studies). 6: Fr, Arabic, Moroccan Arabic. 7: Ref libn Humboldt State Col 59-61; US Army libn Hq SACOM, Munich Germany 57-58; Period libn Temple U 65-66; Asst libn Keneseth Israel Synagogue, Elkins Park Penn 65-66; SWANA bibliog SUNY (Binghamton) 60-68; Asst U Libn Northwestern U 68-. 8: Consul to the Planning Com for the Pub Lib of Conshohocken Penn 65-. 9: Middle East Inst; Amer Anthropol Assn. 11: NDEA- Fulbright-Hays research grant for Morocco, 64-65. 14: Ref, bldg of spec collections on AFRICA & the Middle East, area studies. 15: 1407 Elmwood ave, Evanston Il 60201.

PRESSER, CAROLYNNE. b NYC 14 Ja 41. 5: Hunter Col 58-62 (Sociol) BA; Pratt 62-63 MLS.)06: Fr. 7: Grad asst Hunter Col Lib 62-63; Ref asst Temple U Libs 63-69; Ref libn Ont Inst for Studies in Educ, Toronto 69-. 9: ALA; PennLA. 10: Beta Phi Mu. 14: REF. 15: Ontario Inst for Studies in Ed, 102 Bloor st, Toronto Can.

PRESSER, SARAH (SARAH SIMON). b Pittsburgh Penn 14 Je 19. 4: Israel Presser. 5: UPittsburgh Certif tchr, Voc educ libn. 7: Tchr Pittsburgh Bd of Educ; Hd libn Rosenbloom Lib Hebrew Inst 56-69. 8: Helped var Judaica libs organize their collections. 9: ALA; JewishLA; PennLA; Church & Synagogue LA. 14: Catlg, ref. 15: 207 McMasters dr, Monroeville Pa 15146.

PRESSING, KIRK L. b Pittsburgh 4 F 32. 5: UDel 49-53 (Hist) BA; UPR summer 52; DREXEL 53-54 MSLS. 7: Gen prof asst Wilmington Inst Free Lib, Wilmington Del 54; Mil police US Army, Ft Jackson SC 54-56; Ref asst Richland Co Pub Lib, Columbia SC 55-56; Great Neck NY; Jr libn 56-57,

Br libn 57-58, Admin asst 58-61; Dir Northport Pub Lib, Northport NY 61-69; Chief readers serv London Pub Lib, London Ont 69-. 9: ALA; Suffolk Co NY LA (v-pres 65-66, pres 67-68, past pres 69, Instr Chm 64 & 66). 10: Beta Phi Mu. 14: Ref, adult serv, admin. 15: 470 Scenic dr apt 703, London Ont Can.

PRESSLER, MARION JOAN. b Hollidaysburg Penn 24 Je 25. 5: Slippery Rock State Col 44-46 (Biol Sci, Eng, Soc Sci) BS in Ed; Penn State U 48 (Educ); Ohio State U 48-49 (Eng Lit); UMiami (Fla) 56-58 (Educ); Carnegie 58-59 MLS; Chicago 61-(LS). ; UPittsburgh summer 68 (LS). 6: Fr, Ger. 7: Eng tchr Sandy Lake Pub Sch, Sandy Lake Penn 46-47; Libn Phillipsburg High Sch, Phillipsburg Penn 47-48; Newspaper ed staff "Altoona Mirror, Altoona Penn 50-53; Tchr Eng, dramatics Conewago Jt Schs, York Penn 53-55; Tchr Eng, Dramatics Hollidaysburg High Sch, Hollidaysburg Penn 55-58; Libn Mt Lebanon Pub Schs, Mt Lebanon Penn 59-. 8: Gen chm lib serv Mt Lebanon Sch Dist 67-. 9: ALA-AASchL; NEA; PennStateEA; Sch Libns Assn of Pittsburgh (Gen Chm 67-68); PennLA. 10: Beta Phi Mu; Penn State Fed of Womens Clubs; Blair Co Hist Soc; Pi Lambda Theta. 13: Yes. 14: Wk with child & yp, sch libs. 15: Chatham Ctr apt 19E, Pittsburgh Pa 15219.

PRESSLER, WAYNE NORBEN. b Sharpsburg Penn 17 S 25. 4: Mildred Maseth. 5: UPittsburgh 46-49 (Eng) AB; UCLA 65-66 MLS. 6: Sp. 7: QM/signalman 2c USN, USS Amer Legion 9apa17)-Pacific, USS Callaghan (dd792)-Pacific 42-45; Lt (jr gr) USN, USS G K Mackenzie 9dd836) Korea 49-52; Teacher-jr high sch Sweetwater Union High Sch Dist, Chula Vista Cal 52-64, Libn SW Jr High Sch 66-67; Asst libn SWest Col (Chula Vista Cal) 67-. 8: Instr lib tech program SWest Col 67-. 9: NEA; CalTA; Cal Assn Sch Libns. 14: Catlg & ref jr col level. 15: 368 E Moss st, Chula Vista Ca 92011.

PRESSMAN, ROBERTA ANN (BRISKIN). b Phila Penn 22 My 44. 4: David Roy Pressman. 5: Goddard Col 62-66 (Fr Lit) BA; UPenn 67 (Educ); Drexel 68 (LS) MS. 6: Fr. 7: Bibliogr Mercy Doyles Hosp, Phila 67-68; Ref libn Free Lib of Phila Lit Dept 68-. 8: Aspen Writers' Wkshop in Poetry 66. 9: SLA; ALA. 14: Ref, bibliotherapy. 15: 915 William Penn House, Phila Pa 19103.

PRESSNALL, PATRICIA ELIZABETH (BULOV). b Detroit Mich 17 Mr 25. 4: Hugo Everette Pressnall. 5: UMinn 44-45 (Eng); Long Beach City Col 45-46 (Eng); UCal (Berkeley) 50-52 (Art) AB, 56-57 MLS; UPacific summers 67, 69. 6: Fr, Sp. 7: Sch libn Albany schs, Cal 57-62, Lib consul 64-66, Sch libn 66-69. 9: ALA. 10: Phi Beta Kappa; PTA; Tutoring disadvantaged youth; Wk with girl & boy scouts; Tchg folk dancing to child & adults. 14: Child & youth schs, art. 15: 1165 Shevlin dr, El Cerrito Ca 94530.

PRESTIANNI, VINCENT. b Rochester NY 25 My 40. 4: Susanne Marie Smith. 5: Fordham 58-62 (Classical Langs) AB; Rutgers 63-64 MLS. 6: Gk, Lat, Fr. 7: Libn trainee Rochester Pub Lib, Rochester NY 62-63, Jr libn 64-. 66; Asst libn Monroe Commun Col 66-; US Army Reserve Civil Affairs (2d Lt). 10: Rochester Poetry Soc; Monroe Commun Col Faculty Assn. 14: Ref, periods out of print. 15: 92 Highland ave, Rochester NY 14620.

PRESTON JEAN F(IORA). b Bournemouth Eng 12 Ag 28. 5: Bristol U Eng 48-51 (Eng Hist) BA; Liverpool U (Eng) 51-52 Diploma in Study of Records & Admin of Archives. 6: Fr, medieval Latin. 7: Asst archivist Middlesex Co Record Off, London 52-57; Ms catlgr Folger Lib, Wash DC 57-60; Ms catlgr H E Huntington Lib, San Marino Cal 60-66; Libn Osborn Collection Yale U 66-67; Asst curator of Mss H E Huntington Lib, San Marino Cal 67-. 10: Conf on Brit Studies; Brit Records Assn. ; Amer Archivists (Mss Com). 13: Yes. 14: Mss (ref & catlg). 15: Henry E Huntington Lib, San Marino Cal 91108.

PRESTON, AMY E. b Phila 9 Ja 08. 5: Ursinus Col 30 (Hist) AB; UPenn 31 (Hist); Drexel 32 BLS.)06: Fr. 7: Priv bus, Norristown 32-35; Wilmington Sch Dist, Wilmington Sch Dist, Wilmington Del 36; Abington Lib, Jenkintown Penn 37-41; Bethlehem Pub Lib, Bethlehem Penn: Child libn 41-42, Br 42-56, Dir 56-. 9: ALA; PennlLA. 10: Delta Kappa Gamma; Fortnightly Club; Hist Bethlehem Inc; AAUW; LWV. 14: Admin, mgt, bldgs (arch). 15: 11 W Church, Bethlehem Pa 18010.

PRESTON, JOHN DUNCAN. b Southhampton NY 14S21. 5: Harvard 40-44 (Eng) BA Columbia 48-49 (LS) MS. 7: Reporter US Army Yank Magazine, ETO 43-44; Ref libn Univ of Portland 49-50; Ref libn UWVa 50-54; Yp libn NY Pub Lib 54-55; Libn Univ Club, NYC 62-. 10: The Archons of Columbia Univ. 14: Readers adv serv. 15: 125 E 72 st, New York NY 10021.

PRESTON, KATHARINE HARRIS. b Pontiac Mich 28 Jl 02. 4: Ronald J Preston. 5: Vassar 21-25AB; UMich 26-27 (LS)AB, 39 (LS) AM. 6: Fr. 7: Ref libn Mich State Col (Lansing) 27-28; Asst libn Pontiac City Lib, Pontiac Mich 28-31; Head circ dept Ann Arbor Pub Lib, Ann Arbor Mich 33-36; Ref libn Mich State Normal Col Lib (Ypsilanti) 36-40; Head art dept Kalamazoo Pub Lib 40-42; Detroit Pub Li: Ref asst 42-48, Chief gen info dept 48-53, Dir ref serv 53-67; Internist lib consul, Simmons Col 68-. 9: ALA (mem 4 coms 58-63);-ACRL (sec ref libns sect 48-49);-PLD (ref sect com on reorg RD (org om 5657, pres 59-60; Prep 601, chm 759& 3-65); MichLA (Exec Bd 44-45, pres 58-59, chm & or mem 4 coms 54-65; chm ref sect 46-47). 10: Friends of Detroit Pub Lib; Womens City Club of Detritappa Phi; College Club Akron. 11: Isadore Gilbert Mudge Citation, 65. 12: Ed "Library Trends (Ja 66). 13: Yes. 14: Ref. 15: 3165 Bath rd, Akron Oh 44313.

PRESTON, KATHERINE (H). b Manchester NH 24 F 29. 5: NH Sch of Accounting & Finance 47-48 (Bus) Bkkeeping; Santa Ana Col 68-69 (LS). 6: Grk. 7: Info specialist autonetics 62-. 9: OrangeCoLA. 10: Ladies Guild; Greek Orthodox Church. 14: Info retr. 15: 1042 St Regis place, Santa Ana Ca 92705.

PRETORIUS, JEAN (NELSON). b Auburn Cal. 5: UCal (Berkeley) 38-40 (Soc Theory) AB; 40-41 (LS) Certif. 7: Libn in ext Fresno Co 41-42; Libn US Army, Wheeler Fld Hawaii 43-45; Supv child room Kern Co Lib, Bakersfield Cal 51-64, Supv child ext 64-68, Ext coord 68-. 8: Tchr child lit, Fresno State Col Ext in Bakersfield 68. 9: ALA; CalLA. 10: LWV; AAUW. 13: Yes. 14: Child serv, ext wk. 15: 1315 Truxtun ave, Bakersfield Ca 93330.

PRETTYMAN, KATHLEEN (PHYLLIS). b Cleveland Ohio 4 Je 24. 5: Baldwin-Wallace Col 40-44 (Eng) BA; Columbia 45-46 (Lit) MA; West Res 51-52 MS in LS. 7: Eng tchr Oberlin Jr High Sch, Oberlin Ohio 44-45; Eng tchr N Ridgeville High Sch, N Ridgeville Ohio 46-47; Eng instr Ohio State U 47-48; Ed asst Saalfield Publ Co, Akron Ohio 48-51; Commun libn pub rel & adult educ Willard Lib, Battle Creek Mich 54-54; Y-p libn & asst br libn Cleveland Pub Lib, Cleveland Ohio 54-57; US Army libn Dept of Defense, Germany 57-59; Asst hist dept Cleveland Pub Lib, Cleveland Ohio 59-. 9: ALA; OhioLA. 14: Hist ref (esp Latin Amer). 15: 2572 Kemper rd apt 8, Shaker Heights Oh 44120.

PRETZER, DALE H(OWARD). b Saginaw Mich 10 Ag 34. 4: Marilyn Carol Miller. 5: Central Mich U 56-50 (Eng, Speech) AB; Mich State U 60-62 (Eng); UMich 62-63 AMLS. 6: Fr. 7: Integrator clerk Mich Gas Storage, Saginaw Mich 52-55; Cmpdr product devel Dow Corning Corp, Midland Mich 55-60; Mich State U Lib: Clerk 61-62, Libn 63-64, Act div head humanities div 64-65, Asst to dir 65-68, Deputy State Libn 68-. 8: Develop automation procedures for Mich State U Lib. 9: ALA. 13: Yes. 14: Admi, automation, spec collections, info retrieval. 15: 1426 Gay lane, Lansing Mich 48912.

PREVRATIL, JUDITH. b Schenectady NY 24 S 41. 5: Syracuse U 59-63 (Eng, Journalism) AB, 65-66 MLS. 7: Ed asst Syracuse U Press 63-65; Jr libn Rochester Pub Lib, Rochester NY 66-. 10: Beta Phi Mu. 14: Ref. 15: 52 Gorsline st, Rochester NY 14613.

PRIBANIC, GEORGIA (REICHEL). b Trenton NJ 2 Ap 43. 4: Gerald J Pribanic. 5: Bethany col 61-62; Penn State 62-65 (Hist) BA; Rutgers 66-68 MLS. 6: Ger. 7: Serv rep N J Bell Telephone Co, Englewood NJ 65-66; Asst libn Westwood Pub Lib, Westwood NJ 66-68; Catlgr Bergen Commun Col 68, Reader serv libn 68-. 9: NJLA; NJEA. 10: Bergen Commun Col Faculty Assn. 14: Ref, reader serv. 15: 34 Grant ave, Dumont NJ 07628.

PRIBRAMSKA, MILENA. b Prague Czechoslovakia 1 Ja 23. 5: Charles U (Prague) 45-48 (Eng); Trenton State Col 48-50 (Eng) BS; Columbia 57 (LS) MS. 6: Czech. 7: Ref libn Maplewood Mem Lib, Maplewood NJ 50-. 9: NJLA; EFLA; NY Film Coun; Film Lib Info Coun. 13: Yes. 14: Ref, films. 15: Maplewood Mem Lib, 51 Baker st, Maplewood NJ 07040.

PRICE, ALVIS HENRY. b Tyler Tex 31O34. 4: Elizabeth Burnsid. 5: USoCal 52-56 (Bus) BS; Simmons 61-62 (LS)MS. 6: Fr. 7: Off asst Div of NeurologyUCLA Med Sch 56-57; Journalist & newspapered US Navy Seaman 57-59; Asst to dir Animal Research Center Harvard Med Sch 59; Off manager UCal Comissary (Berkeley) 60-61; Ref libn henery Lib

BOSTON U 62-63, Head Bus & Econ Lib 63-64; Ya libn Boston Pub Lib 64-65, Br libn (Mem & Mt Pleasant Brs) 65-66; Dir of lib & Asst Prof Jarvis Christian Col, Hawkins Tex 66-68; Asst hd circ dept U Research Lib UCLA 68-. 9: Mass Round Table of YA Libns (sec 65-66); TexLA; ALA. 14: Admin. 15: Circulation Dept, University Research Lib, Univ of Cal, Los Angeles Ca 90024.

PRICE, ELIZABETH (RITTER). b Chicopee Mass 17 D 10. 4: Minard W Price. 5: Middlebury Col 28-29; Our Lady of Elms Col 29; Boston U 30-37 (Educ); Mt Holyoke 32-34 (Eng) AB; Kings Col London U 35; Simmons 55-57 (LS) AM. 6: Fr. 7: Tchr & libn MacDuffie Co Day Sch, Springfield Mass 34-36; Eng tchr & dept head Orange High Sch, Orange Mass 36-39; Eng tchr Miss Hall's Sch, Pittsfield Mass 39-42; Eng tchr & drama coach Lincoln Sch, Providence 42-45; Health tchr Gorton High Sch, Warwick RI 52-55; Hd libn Warwick Vet Mem High Sch 55-. 8: Inst Simmons Sch of Lib Sci 60-63; RI Adv Coun on Interlib Coop 66-. 9: ALA; NEA; NELA; NESchLA (Conv Chm 61); RILA (chm Intel Freedom Com 65-); RI E in A; RI SchLA. 13: Yes. 14: Ya serv. 15: 2700 Warwick ave, Warwick RI 02889.

PRICE, EMILY (JOHNSON). b Baltimore 25 D 15. 4: James L Price. 5: Bryn Mawr 33-37 (Eng) BA; Columbia 51-56 (LS) MS. 6: Fr, Sp. 7: CZ Lib-Museum, Balboa CZ; Lib asst period 50-52, catlgr 52-60, chief tech serv 60-66, libn curator 67-. 9: ALA; SLA; Amer Assn Museum; Assn Grad Libns Isthmus of Panama (treas 60-61, sec 61-62). 10: Soroptimist Club. 12: Jt auth "Manual de bibliotecologia para bibliotecas rurales". 14: Catlg. 15: PO Box 1897, Balboa CZ.

PRICE, ETHEL (LOUISE). b Norwood Ohio 23 My 09. 5: UCincinnati 32-34 (Eng). 6: Sp. 7: Libn for the blind Cincinnati Pub Lib 34-. 9: ALA; OhioLA. 14: Lib wk with the blind, physically handicapped or home-bound. 15: 1756 Weyer ave, Norwood Oh 45212.

PRICE, GRETCHEN (EGGER). b Louisville Ky 17 My 43. 4: Peter Elliott Price. 5: Elmhurst Col 61-63; ULouisville 63-65 (Bio) BA; UIll 65-66 (LS) MS. 7: Catlgr Tech Serv Lib ULouisville Med Sch Lib 66-67; Tech Info Libn UKy Med Ctr Lib 68-. 9: ALA; MedLA; KyLA. 10: Phi Kappa Phi; Beta Phi Mu. 14: Catlg, ser, data proc. 15: 232 Hillsboro ave, Lexington Ky 40505.

PRICE, HELEN LOUISE. b Admire KAN 27 My 18. 5: Kan State Tchrs Col (Emporia) 35-39 (LS, Hist, Soc Sci) BS in Ed, Lib Certif; UIll 49. 6: Fr. 7: Libn Field Kindley Mem High Sch, Coffeyville Kan 39-43; Engnr libn Beech Aircraft Corp, Wichita Kan 43-46; Asst libn va center, Wadsworth Kan 46; VA Hosp: Chief libn, Muskogee Okla 46-53, Chief Libn, Okla City Okla 53-56, Asst chief lib, Topeka Kan 56-60, Med libn, Topeka Kan 60-. 9: ALA-AHIL (pres 60-61); Med LA; SLA (pres Heart of Amer Chap 58-59); KANLA; Topeka Lib Club (co-chm 65-67). 10: AAUW; VA Hosp Employees Fed Credit Union. 13: Yes. 14: Medlibs. 15: 2208 College ave, Topeka Kan 66611.

PRICE, JANET C. b Orange NJ 9 F 33. 5: Mass Col of Art 50-54 (Fine Arts) BFA; Boston U 63-64 (Fr); Simmons 62-66 (LS) SM. 6: Fr. 7: Staff artist Cambridge Engraving Co, Boston 55-57; Lib asst Brookline Pub Lib, Brookline Mass 57-64; Y-a br libn Boston Pub Lib 64-65; Asst libn Trident Lib Arthur D Little Inc, Cambridge Mass 65-66, Asst libn operations research 66-67, Libn econ development 67-68, Libn info syst 68-. 8: Lib interviewing and casewk, Arthur D Little 67-68. 9: SLA (Hospitality Com 1969 Conv; Boston Chap: Pub Rel Com; Proj Hollywood Com); ALA; ASIS; ARMA; MassLA; LPRC. 10: Nat Pilots Assn. 14: Info stor & ret, lib pub rel. 15: 780 Boylston st, Boston Ma 02199.

PRICE, JOHN J. b NYC 25 Jl 23. 4: Carol Ann Josephy. 5: Sampson Col 47-49 (Liberal Arts); Syracuse 49 (Liberal Arts); Columbia 56-59 (Hist) BS, 61 (LS) MS. 6: Fr. 7: US Navy MTB Squadrons 8 & 12, QM2/c 43-45; Lib clerk NYU Med libn Montefiore-Morrisania Affil Morrisania Hosp, Bronx ny64-66; Med libn; Grasslands Hosp, Valhalla NY 63-64, US Naval Hosp, St Albans NY 66-. 9: Med LA; SLA. 10: AAAS; Country Dance of Soc of Amer. 14: Med libnship, catlg, ref,hist of med. 15: 49 Hinsdale ave, Floral Park NY 11002.

PRICE, SISTER M CONSUELO OSU. b Wilmington NC 21D18. 5: Ursuline Col (Louisville) 56 (Eng) BA; Creighton U 50-52; Catholic U summers 57-64 MSLS. 7: Proof reader "Times-New Cumberland Md 39-41; Tchr St Boniface Sch, Evansville Ind 44-47; Tchr St Elizabeth Sch, Louisville Ky 47-49; Tchr-libn St Patrick Grade & High Sch, N Platte Neb 49-55; Tchr St Martins Sch, Louisville Ky 55-56 Tchr-libn Catholic High Sch, Columbia SC 56-58; Tchr-libn Our LADY OF Lourdes Sch, Louisville Ky 58-62; Asst libn Ursuline Col Lib(Louisville) 62-68; Libn Bishop Walsh High Sch, Cumberland Md 68-. 9: ALA-AASchL CathLA (Bk Week Com Elem Sect; Greater Loisville Unit: chm Elem Sect 58-62, chm Col Sect 64; sec-treas 65-67); KASchL; KyLA (mem Lib Educ Com 66-68); MdLA; MdASchL. 13: Yes. 14: Tchg sch lib courses, ref serv in col lib, developing lib programs for innovative secondary sch curriculum. 15: Bishop Walsh dr, Cumberland Md 21502.

PRICE, PAXTON P. b Batesville Ark 18 Je 13. 4: Ella Tarbell. 5: Nom Mil Inst 31-33 AA Peabody 36-37 (Soc Sci BS), 39-41 BS in LS; Columbia 46-47 (L Tchr high sch, Roswell NM 37-40; Libn NM Mil Inst 40-42; (Pvt-1st Lt) US ArLib 49-64; Dir lib serv br USDE, Wash DC 64-69; Libn St Louis Pub Lib 69-. 6: Sp, Fr. 7: Tchr high sch, Roswell NM 37-40; Libn NM Mil Inst 40-42; (Pvt-1st Lt) US Army ETO Mil Intell; Libn NW Mo State Col 47-49; State libn Mo State Lib 49-64; Dir lib serv br USDE, Wash DC 64-69; Libn St Louis Pub Lib 69-. 8: OAS Expert Adv on Nat Lib of Colombia SA, 60; US Expert UNESCO Internat Conference on Nat Lib Planning in Latin Amer, Quito Ecuador 66. 9: ALA (Coun 59-63; co-chm Jt Com ALA-Rural Sociol Soc; -AAStateL (cCom on Implem of Standards); MoLA (past sec & pres). 10: US Army Res Off (Lt Col). 12: "Financial Administration in "Local Public Library Adminstration (64); Ed "Library Trends (Ap 56); Co-ed "Library Trends (Ap 63). 13: Yes. 14: Admin. 15: St Louis Pub Lib 1301 Olive st, St Louis Mo 63103.

PRICE, ROSA LEE (MONTGOMERY). b Hobart Okla 3 Ap 12. 4: Robert H Price. 5: UOkla 37 BS in LS; Long Beach City Col 49-55; NM State U 63-64. 7: Ref and order libn NWest State Col, Alva Okla 37-40; Jr libn Army Industrial Col, Wash DC 40-41; Sr libn Special Serv Off, Ft Sill Okla 41-43; Jr libn Pasadena Pub Lib, Pasadena Cal 43; Ensign WAVES USN: Wash DC 43-44, San Francisco 44-45; Res bk room UChicago 46; Hd libn Ore Pub Lib, Corvallis 46-47; Coord of elem sch lib, Ore 47-49; Hd libn (bus & tech) Long Beach (Cal) City Col 55-56; Hd libn Colo Pub Lib, Duraneo 57-58; Libn Tibbetts Jr High Sch, Farmington NM 59-65; Special catlgr Tex SoU summer 65; Asst libn Lamar High Sch, Houston Tex 65-67; Libn Strake Jesuit Col Prep, Houston Tex 67-. 9: ALA. 10: Beta Sigma Phi. 14: Catlg, ref. 15: 8611 Ferris rd, Houston Tx 77035.

PRICE, SUSAN WOODRUFF. b Cleveland 28 S 37. 4: James Howard Price. 5: Oberlin Col 60 (Chem) BA; West Res62 MS in LS. 6: Fr, Lat, Russian. 7: Abstracter & coder Center for Documentation Communications Research West Res U 60-61; Order dept Oberlin Col Lib 62; Libn Winebrenner Theol Sem 64-65; Math libn Syracuse U 65-. 9: SLA; Syracuse U Libns Assn (Publ Chm). 14: Math ref. 15: Math Lib 21 Smith Hall Syracuse Univ, Syracuse NY 13210.

PRICE, SYLVIA (RECHTMAN). b NYC 20 Ap 21. 5: Hunter Col 37-41 (Econ) BA; Pratt 60-64 MLS. 6: Fr, Ger. 7: Production coordinator Circle in the Square, NYC 59-63; Ref libn New School For Soc Research64-. 8: Poetry Therapist NY Postgrad Ctr for Mental Health 69-. 9: ALA; NY Libns Round Table on the Social Responsibilities of Libns. 10: Beta Phi Mu; Pratt Inst Grad Lib Assn; Friends of Freedom Libs. 12: Ed com "Mental Health Book Review Index". 13: Yes. 14: Ref., research, bibliog (soc scis & lit). 15: 117 W 11th st, NYC 10011.

PRICHARD, HAZEL W (WILSON). b Augusta Ark 31 Mr 16. 5: Ark State Col 34-38 (Eng) BSE; UIll 38, 43-44 BS in LS. 7: Co libn Conway Co Lib, Morrilton Ark 38-43; Co libn Whitey Co Lib, Searcy Ark 45-47; Reg libn SW Reg Lib, Hope Ark 47-. 9: ALA; ArkLA (pres 58); SWLA. 10: Bus & Profess Women's Club; Delta Kappa Gamma. 15: 500 S Elm, Hope Ar 71801.

PRIDEAUX, B ELIZABETH. b Ashland Ore 26D14. 4: John A Prideaux. 5: SoOre Col 32-33 (Educ); Ore State U 33-36 (Home Econ) BS; UWash 58-64 (LS) ML. 7: High Sch tchr: Silverton Ore 36-38;Gresham Ore 38-39; Portland 39-40; High Sch libn, Stayton Ore 59-; Lib spec Ore Bd of Educ, Salem Ore 65-. 9: OreLA (sec); OreASchL (Bd). 10: PTA; Girl Scouts; Amer Friends Serv Com; Lyons Pub Lib Trustee. 12: "Open Door to Learning" (68); Ed "School Media Services", Ore Bd of Educ. 14: Child serv, pub rel. 15: 451 Waianuenue ave apt 19, Hilo Hi 96720.

PRIDMORE, PETER. b Peterborough England 26 O 32. 4: Marion Shirley Crabtree. 5: UDurham Eng 53-56 (Turkish) BA; Loughborough Lib Sch Eng 56-57 ALA. 6: Fr, Ger,

Russian, Turkish, Lat, Gr. 7: Russian lang specialist (Sgt) British Army Intelligence Corps 51-53; 1st asst Sherwood Br Lib Nottingham Pub Lib, Eng 57-58, 1st asst ref lib 58-59; Period libn Univ lib, Newcastle upon Tyne Eng 59-64; Asst libn Univ lib (Oriental sect), Durham Eng 64-67; Slavonic catlgr UAlberta Lib 67-68, Acting educ libn 68-. 9: Lib Assn (UK); CanLA; AltaLA. 10: Can Assn of Univ Tchrs. 14: Catlg, admin. 15: Univ Lib, Univ of Alberta, Edmonton 7 Can.

PRIESTLEY, VIOLET ARTA. b Pleasanton Kan 14 D 06. 5: Kan State Tchrs Col (Pittsburg) 24-31 (Biol) 31; Colo State Col of Ed 42; Wichita State U 50; UColo 54; Kan State Tchrs Col(Emporia) 58-60 MS in LS; UKan 61. 7: Tchr Eureka Pub Schs, Eureka Kan 26-37; Tchr Wichita Pub Schs, Wichita Kan 37-45, Libn Roosevelt Jr High Sch Lib 51-69. 8: Dir, Lib Filmstrip Center. 9: ALA; NEA; KanLA; Kan State Tchrs Assn; KanASchL; Kan A-V Assn. 10: AAUW. 11: The Chris Award, given by the Columbus Fil Festival 64; Educ Film LA Award, 64, 65, 66, 67, 68. 12: Producer of library filmstrips. 14: Sch lib wk, ref, research. 15: 3033 Aloma, Wichita Ks 67211.

PRIMACK, LILLIAN. b NYC 1 Ag 23. 7: Head libn Asbury Park Res, Asbury Park NJ 58-60; Asst libn "Business Week," NYC 60-61; Head libn "National Enquirer," NYC 61-64; Head libn "New York World-Telegram & Sun," NYC 64-; Ed asst Off of Publs Ford Found 66-67; Ref libn for bus & finance "Newsweek" 67-. 9: SLA (Newspaper Div: sec-treas 65-66; NY Chap: Pub Chm 61-62; v-pres Newspaper Sect 65-66). 14: Ref. 15: NY World-Telegram & Sn, 125 Barclay st, NYC 15.

PRINCE, HAROLD B(AILEY). b Easley SC 10 Ja 17. 4: Evelyn Houck. 5: USCar 35-41 AB(Journalism), MA(Eng); Emory 49-50 (LS) ML: Columbia Theol Sem 53-60 BD. 6: Fr. 07: Tchr Edmunds High Sch, Sumter SC41-42; Armed serv 42-46; Manager bking dept Eastin Pictures Inc, Chattanooga Tenn 46-49; Libn Columbia Theol Sem (Ga) 51-. 9: ATheolLA (treas 56-64); (v-pres 68-69); ALA; SELA; Atlanta Lib Club. 14: Admin, ref. 14: Admin, ref. 15: 1169 Oldfield rd, Decatur Ga 30030.

PRINCE, HELEN KENNEDY(JEAN). b Indianapolis 23 S 27. 5: Butler U 41-45 (Lat, Span) AB,48-50 (Educ) MS; Columbia 50-52 (LS) MS. 6: Lat, Sp, Ger. 7: Tchr Indianapolis Pub Schs 49-51; Yp ref asst NY Pub Lib 52-53; Yp ref asst Brooklyn Pub Lib 53-54; Libn Shriners Hosp for Crippled Children, Salt Lake City 54-57; Ref asst UUtah 54-55, catlgr 55-57; Libn Central circ Chicago Pub Lib 57-58; Asst to dir publ dept ALA, Chicago 58-68, ALA Publ Serv 68-. 10: Phi Kappa phi; Kappa Delta Pi; Phi Chi Nu. 14: Ref psych of reading, bk publg. 15: 50 E Huron st, Chicago 60611.

PRINCE, JANET. b San Diego Cal. 5: Brigham Young 63 (Humanities) BA, 67 MLS. 7: Libn San Leandro Commun Lib, San Leandro Cal 67-. 15: 4833 Kendall st, San Diego Ca 92109.

PRINCE, VIVIAN CHRISTINE. b Anderson Co SC 31 Jl 08. 5: Winthrop Col (Hist) AB: UNC summer 30 (Hist,summers 37, 38, 40 (LS)BS; Columbia summers 41, 42, 46, 47 (LS)MS. 6: Fr. 7 Tchr Gatesville High Sch, Gatesville NC 30-32; Tchr Manning High Sch, Manning SC 33-36; Tchr-libn Pageland High Sch, Pageland SC6-38; Tchr-Libn Kingstree High Sch, Kingstree SC 38-39; Tchr-libn FORT Mill High Sch, Fort Mill SC 39-41; Libn Rockingham High Sch, Rockingham High Sch, Rockingham NC 41-43; UFla: Catlgr 43-46, Head catlgr46-51, Head of tech processes 51-62, Asst Prof of Lib Sci 49-53, Assoc Prof 53-62; Visiting Prof Emory U summers 53,55, 65; Visiting Prof UNC(Chapel Hill) summers 62, 64; Lecturer UCal(Berkeley) 59-61; Visiting Prof UIll(Urbana) summer 60; Assoc Prof USoCal 62-. 8: Fulbright lectureship, Univ of Dacca Pakistan 56-57. 9: ALA-RTSD (sec Catlg & Clsf Sect 62-65; CalLA (pres Tech Processes Group 67). 10: AAUP; Phi Alpha Theta; Delta Kappa Gamma. 13: Yes. 14: Catlg. 15: 3113 S Hoover st, Los Angeles 90007.

PRINCZ, JOSEPH. b Temesvar Hungary 2 My 33. 4: Judy Ilosvai. 5: Sir George William U 59-61 (Eng) BA; McGill 61-62 BLS; Montreal 62-63 (Slavic Studies) MA, 63- (Eng). 6: Ger, Russian, Ital, Fr, Hungarian, 07: Stock ref libn McGill U 62-64; Ref libn Loola Col Lib(Montreal) 64, Deputy libn 65-. 8: Tchg Lib Tech courses 67-, Consul to high sch libs 67-. 9: QueLA; MLA; CanLA. 14: Admin, ref. 15: Loyola Col Lib, Sherbrooke W, Montreal Can.

PRINGLE, CALLAN M. b Detroit 15 Ag 25. 5: UDetroit 46-47 (Sci); East Mich U 48-52 (Fine Arts) B; Wayne State U 52-56 LLB; UMich 63-(LS). 7: Attorney Pringle & Dare, Detroit 57-61; Asst libn Detroit Bar Assn 62-63, Libn 63-. 9: SLA; AALL. 10: Nat Women Lawyers Assn; Zonta Mich Women Lawyers Assn; State Bar of Mich; Detroit Bar Assn; Womens City Club of Detroit; Phi Delta Delta. 14: Admin. 15: 77 Penobscot Bldg, Detroit 48215.

PRITCHARD, ANN (DOLORES). b Los Angeles5 Ja 28. 5: UCLA 55-59 (Pre libnship) BA; UCal(Berkeley) 59-60 MLS. 7: Ref dept UCal(Santa Barbara) 60-62; Army libn US Army Spec Serv, Germany 62-63; Catlgr System Dvelopment Corp, Santa Monica Cal 63-65; Ref dept UCal(Santa Barbara) 65-. 9: ASIS; SLA; CalLA. 15: Ref Dept Lib Univ of Cal, Santa Barbara Ca 93106.

PRITCHARD, DOROTHY MARIE. b Leon NY 31 My 14. 5: Forestville Tchr-training Class 31-32 (Elem Educ) Gods Bible Sch &Col 35-38 (Eng) AB (cum laude); Syracuse 55-59 (Bus Admin); Duquesne U 62 (LS); Syracuse 62-63 MSLS. 7: Elem tchr Dayton Dist No 8, Cattaraugus NY 32-35; Ediphone operator Merchants Mutual Casualty Co, Buffalo NY 40-44; Sec Wesleyan Methodist Missionary Soc, Syracuse NY 45-54; Registration & grades sec Grad Sch Syracuse U 54-55; Sec Wesleyan Methodist Missionary Soc, Syracuse NY 55-56; Digital computer Carrier Corp, Syracuse NY 56-59; Digital computer Elliott Co subsidiary of Carrier Corp, Jeannette Penn 59-61, Libn Engnr Lib 62; Asst libn State U Col (Brockport NY) 63-66; Asst libn State U Col (Cortland) 66-. 9: NYLA. 10: Cobblestone Soc; SUNY LA; Cortland Co Hist Soc; Beta Phi Mu. 14: Ref, catlg, acquis. 15: 30 Scammell st, Cortland NY 13045.

PRITCHARD, HUGH (CHARLES). b Winnipeg Can 30 Ja 16. 4: Joan Tinley. 5: U Wash 35-39 (Eng) BA; UNC 41-42 (Eng) MA; Columbia 49-50 MLS. 6: Fr. 7: Weather observer USAF 42-46; Instr in Eng Wash State U 46-47; Ref asst NY PubLib 48-49 ; Ref libn Amherst Col 50-53; Asst ref libn UIll (Urbana) 53-54; Ref libn UNH 54-, Instr in ref wk 62-. 12: Ed "Subscription Books Bulletin (60-65). 13: Yes. 14: Ref, lib orientaion. 15: 1 Hoitt dr, Durham NH 03824.

PRITCHARD, ZONA BELLE. b Huntsville Tex 27N13. 4: Aubrey Herman Pritchard. 5: Hardin- Simmons U 38 (Elem Educ) BA; N Tex State U 55 (Elem Educ) M Ed, 69 MLS. 6: Lat, Sp. 7: Tchr Granbury Elem Sch, Granbury Tex 50-58; Tchr Wilson Elem Sch, Corpus Christi Tex 60-; Libn Mary Carroll High Sch, Corpus Christi Tex 59-67; High sch libn, Kingsville Tex 67-. 9: NEA; Tex Stat Asn; TexLA; ALA; Coastal Bend LA. 10: Delta Kappa Gamma. 14: Ref, circ, acquis, ya. 15: Rte 1 Box 229F, Kingsville Tx 78363.

PRIVAT, JEANNETTE MARY. b Seattle 2 My 38. 5: UWash 56-60 (Bus Admin) BA, 67-69 (Libnship) MLib. 7: Asst libn United Control Corp, Redmond Wash 60-64, Libn 64-68; Lib Seattle First Nat Bank, Seattle Wash 68-. 8: Amer Mgt Assn Lecturer 67. 9: SLA (Pacific-NWest chap; sec-treas 66-67, memb chm 67-68). 15: Seattle First National Bank, PO Box 3586, Seattle Wa 98124.

PROBST, MICHAEL LOUIS. b Dayton Ohio 6 O 45. 5: UDayton 63-67 (Hist) BA; Rutgers 67-68 MLS. 6: Fr, Ger. 7: Ref asst libn Dayton & Montgomery Co Pub Lib, Dayton Ohio 68-. 10: Phi Alpha Theta. 15: 2525 Revere ave, Dayton Oh 45420.

PROCTOR, IRENE (ADAMS). b Erin Tenn 1 Ap 24. 4: James Matthew Proctor. 5: Austin Peay State Col 43-48 (Soc Sci) BS; Peabody 48-51 (LS)MA. 7: Elem & high sch tchr, High Sch Libn Houston Co Bd of Ed, Erin Tenn 45-51; Libn k-9 Bd of Educ, Ft Campbell Ky 51-54; Demonstration sch libn AUSTIN Peay State Col 54; Libn & coordinator of lib serv k-12, Ft Campbell Ky 55-. 9: ALA; SELA; KYLA (Bd Dirs, pres 2nd dist); Ft Campbell EA (past pres). 10: AAUW. 13: Yes. 14: Catlg, child reading, Storytelling, guidance. 15: Box 51, Southside Tn 37171.

PROCTOR, MARIA MARVIN. b Richmond Va 28 F 22. 5: Radford Col 40-42 (Eng) BA; UNC45-46 bs in LS; Columbia 47-51. 6: Fr, Ger. 7: Circ asst Grinnell Col 46-48; Loan libn Randolph-Macon Womas Col 48-53; Ref asst hist, travel & biog dept Enoch Pratt Free Lib, Baltimore 53-59; Archivist Mun Archives & Record Center NY Pub Lib 59-61; Sr catlgr circ dep NY Pub Lib 61-64; Catlgr NYU 65-. ; Catlgr Inst of Pub Admin, NYC 66-68; Catlgr Schomburg Col, NY Pub Lib 69-. 9: SLA; NY Tech Serv Libns. 15: 38 Livingston st, Brooklyn NY 11201.

PRODRICK, ROBERT GERALD. b Ottaa 31 Jl 20. 4: Elizabeth Smiley. 5: Toronto 38-42 (Pol Sci, Econ) BA, 46-47, 50 (Econ) MA; Columbia 49-51 (Econ), 54-55 (LS) MS. 6: Fr, Ger. 7: Capt Can Army Can & Overseas 42-46; Asst Prof

United Col UMan 47-49; Bibliogr Joint Lib Internat Monetary Fund Wash DC 55-60; Asst libn humanities & soc sci UToronto lib 61-. 9: CanLA; SLA; ALA; OntLA; Inst Pub Libns Ont. 10: Beta Phi Mu. 13: Yes. 14: Ref, bibliog. 15: 47 Allan st, Oakville Ont Can.

PROESCHEL, DIANA C. b Chicago Ill 5 F 30. 5: West Mich U 46-50 (LS) BS; Loyola U 53-55 (Educ). 6: Ger, Ital. 7: Model Johnson Pub, Chicago 53-55; Asst child libn Kalamazoo Pub Lib 50; High sch libn Chicago Bd of Educ 50-52, Child libn 52-55; US Army Spec Serv: Army Libn, Kaiserslautern 55-58, Asst Command libn, Munich Germany 58-64, Asst command libn, Verdun France 64-66, Command libn SETAF, Vicenza Italy 66-. 8: Ref libn, Lib/USA, NY Worlds Fair, 64. 9: ALA. 14: Ref, admin, child & yp wk, mgt, bk sel, publ & pub rel. 15: Spec Serv Lib, US Army Port APO NY 09221.

PROFFITT, L GRACE. b Garnerville NY 19 Je02. 5: Smith Col 20-24 (Eng) AB; NY Sch of Soc Wk 26-27; Columbia & Union Theol Sem 27-29 (Religious Educ)MA; Columbia 38-40 BS in LS. 7: Religious educ wk, NYC & NJ 28-34; Asst libn Pub Lib, Madison NJ 40-47; Readers serv libn Vassar Col Lib 47-. 9: ALA; NY LA; Dutchess Co LA; Seast NY Lib Resources Coun. 14: Circ, ref. 15: Vassar Col, Poughkeepsie NY 12601.

PROGAR, DOROTHY RUTH (WATKINS). b Bruceville Tex 14 S 24. 4: Walter L Progar. 5: Baylor 41-45 (Bus), 65, 67-68 (LS) BA; Mich State 46 (Art). 7: Lib asst Waco-McLennan Co Lib, Waco Tex 61, Circ libn 61-65, Ya libn 65-67, Ref libn 67-68, Asst dir 68-. 9: ALA; TexLA. 14: Ref. 15: 4004 Parrott, Waco Tx 76707.

PROPER, DAVID RALPH. b Stoneham Mass 22 F 33. 5: UNH 51-55 (Romance Langs) BA; UBesanc (France) 55-56 (Fr) Certif; Middlebury Col summers (Fr) MA; Simmons 60-62 (LS) MS. 6: Fr, Sp. 7: Tchr, sch libn elem, pub high sch & priv sch, NH; Staff Simmons Col Grad Sch of Lib Sci 60-62; Libn The Essex Inst, Salem Mass 63-68; Asst libn, acquis Keene State Col Lib 68-69; Lib consul Pocumtuck Valley Mem Assn & Heritage Found, Deerfield Mass 69-. 9: ALA; BSA; MassLA; Mass N Shore LA. 10: Essex Co Mass Hist Coun; NE Hist Geneal Soc; Mass Soc of Mayflower Descendants; Nat Assn of Watch & Clock Collectors; Organ Hist Soc; Hist Soc of Cheshire Co NH; Essex Inst. 11: Fulbright Scholarship grant for study in France, 55. 12: "History of the First Baptist Church, Keene NH" (64); prin contrib "Upper Ashuelot; A History of Keene NH" (68); "Salem Witchcraft, a Brief History" (67); "Bibliography of Period Articles Dealing with the American Shakers" (65-66); "A Mayflower Bibliography" (61). 13: Yes. 14: Rare bks, Amer imprints & bibliog, hist socs, geneal & loc hist res. 15: 51 S Lincoln st, Keene NH 03431.

PROPST, ESTHER (RUTLEDGE). b Demopolis Ala 26 Jl 14. 5: Judson 31-33 (Fr); UAla 33-35 (Fr) BA, summers 56-59 (Sch Lib) MA. 6: Fr. 7: Tchr pub sch systems of Ala 35-40, 47-59; Tchr-libn Demopolis High Sch, Demopolis Ala 50-59; Order libn Jacksonville State Col 59-60; Ref libn UAla 60-67; Act hd Col of Educ Lib UAla 67-68, Libn & Asst Prof 68-. 9: AlaEA; AlaLA (chm By-laws Com 67-68, mem Lit Awards Com 68-69, chm-elect Col & Univ & Spec Libs Div 68). 10: AAUW; Delta Kappa Gamma; Alpha Gamma Delta; Kappa Delta Phi. 14: Ref, rare bks, circ, res. 15: Box 2604, University Ala 35486.

PROSSER, JUDITH MARGARET. b Chicago 20 Je 38. 5: Winthrop Col 57-61 (Eng) BA; Columbia 62-63 MS in LS; UDenver summer 66 (Archival Admin) Certif; Nat Archives & Amer U summer 67 (Archival Admin) Certif; UIll summer 68 (Computer Syst); USoCal spring 69 (Info Sci) Certif. 7: Lib trainee NY Pub Lib 61; Bkmob libn Orlando (Fla) Pub Lib 61; Lib asst Bus Lib Columbia U 62-63; Asst in the lib spec collections dept UFla Libs 63-. 9: ALA; FlaLA; SAA. 10: AAUW. 14: Univ archives, computer applications to libs. 15: 1404 NW 43rd ave, Gainesville Fl 32601.

PROSTANO, EMANUEL T. b New Haven Conn 12 O 31. 4: Joyce Scala. 5: So Conn State Col 49-53 (LS, Educ) BS; So Conn-Yale Coop 53-55 (LS, Educ) MA; UConn 56-58 (Admin) Prof diploma, 58-62 (Curriculum & supv) PhD. 7: Tchr Woolsey Sch, New Haven Conn 53-54; Lib tchr: e haven High, E Haven Conn 54-56, M J Whalen Jr High Sch, Hamden Conn 51-58, S L Grant Jr High Sch, Hamden Conn 58-66; Coord lib media serv Hartford (Conn) Schs 66-69; Assoc Prof lib sci So Conn State Col 69-. 8: Consul E C Scranton Lib, Madison Conn 56. 9: ALA; ConnSchLA (Exec Bd); Conn A-v EA. 10: Hamden Pub Lib Bd. 13: Yes. 14: Educ, lib admin. 15: 42 Harrison dr, Hamden Ct 06514.

PROTACIO, ANDREA BEATRIZ. b Brooklyn NY 24 Mr 26. 4: Arthur S Protacio. 5: UPhilippines 46-48 (Secondary Educ) AA; Col of Guam 64-67 (Secondary Educ, Eng) BA; UMich 67-68 MALS. 7: Libn Dept of Educ, Agana Guam 63-67, Lib consul 68-. 9: ALA; GiamLA. 10: AAUW. 14: Sch libs, child lit. 15: PO Box 2589, Agana Guam 96910.

PROTOPOPOFF, ANNE TENNENT (PLUMMER) b Honolulu 10 Je 11. 4: Nicholas Michael Protopopoff. 5: UCal (Berkeley) 31-35 (Span) AB; San Jose State Col 39-40 (LS). 6: Sp, Ger. 7: Lib aid Alameda Free Lib, Alameda Cal 37-38; Child libn Martinez City Lib, Martinez Cal 40-43; Clerk US Army Intelligence, San Francisco & Wash DC 43-44; Latin AMERICAN SPEC US Dept Com Wash DC 44-46; Lib asst NY Pub Lib 46; Spanish-Eng clerk coffee importer, San Francisco 46-47 Sr clerk Cal Dept Employment, Oakland Cal 49-50; Research libn Cal Tchrs Assn, San Francisco 51-59, Burlingame Cal 59-. 8: Devies spec clf for educ materials 55-. 9: ALA; SLA (San Francisco Bay Area Chap; Dir 56-58; Hospitality chm & program chm); CalLA; Cal Tchrs Assn. 10: Internat Soc for Gen Semantics; Friends of the Bancroft Lib; Nat Herb Study Soc; Soc of Cal Pioneers Womans Auxiliary. ; Bath (Me) Marine Hist Soc. 12: Ed/asst "California Journal of Educational Research" (52-58). 13: Yes. 14: Clsf, bibliog, catlg. 15: Cal Tchrs Assn, 1705 Murchison dr, Burlingame Ca 94011.

PROUDFIT, CLARIBEL (SOMMERVILLE). b Des Moines Iowa 5 N 13. 4: Garnet L Proudfit. 5: Drake U 31-36 (Soc Sci) BS; UDenver summers 40-42 BS in LS. 7: Pub Lib, Des Moines Iowa: Gen asst 38, Asst U Br 38-40, Asst in chg Lincoln Heights Br 40-42 Br 40-42, Br libn Capitol Hill Br 42-43, 1st Asst catlg dept 46-49, Head catlg dept 49-52, Coordinator of tech processes 52-. 9: ALA (Coun 57-61); IowaLA (sec 51-52); Des Moines Lib Club (sec 43-44 & 47-48, treas 54). 10: Quota Internat; Prof Womens League. 12: Ed "The Catalyst, IowaLA (49). 13: Yes. 14: Catlg, pub libs. 15: 314 E 18 st, Des Moines Ia 50316.

PROULX, ADELINE L(UCILE). b Omaha 8 Ap 09. 5: Duchesne Col 26-30 (Lat, Fr) 30; Columbia 35-36 LS) 36. 6: Fr. 7: Omaha Pub Lib: Asst Benson Br 30-32, Asst child dept 32-35, Catlg & ref dept 36-37, Child libn SOUTH Br 37-41, Libn Benson Br 41-42, Supv wk with boys & girls 42-. 8: Faculty, Col of St MARY 65-. 9: ALA; CathLA; NebLA; Omaha & Council Bluffs Libns Club. 10: PTA (Hon life mem); Omaha Radio & TV Coun; United Commun Servs. 13: Yes. 14: Wk with child. 15: Swanson Mem Lib, 9101 W Dodg rd, Omaha 68114.

PRUDHOMME, BERNARD. b NYC 2F29. 4: Ruth Berl. 5: Columbia 46-50 (Liberal Arts) BA; Rutgers 58-63 MLS. 6: Fr. 7: Libn Internat Flavors & Fragrances Inc, Union Beach NJ 53-. 9: ACS (Div of Chem Lit). 14: Lib mgt. 15: 1515 Highway 36, Union Beach NJ 07735.

PRUETT, JAMES WORRELL. b Mount Airy NC 23 D 32. 4: Lillian Pibernik. 5: UNC 51-55 (Music) BA, 55-57 (Music) MA, 57-62 (Music) PhD. 6: Ger, Fr, Ital, Lat. 7: UNC Lib(Chapel Hill): Ref asst 57-59, Head res reading room 59-61, Music libn 61-63, Asst Prof & music libn 63-. 8: Consul on Lib Program: Brevard Col 67, NC Col 68. 9: Amer Musicological Soc; Music Tchrs Nat Assn; MusLA (var com duties); NC Mus Tchrs Assn. 11: Research Award, Coop Program in the Humanities, summer 65. 12: Co-ed "Opera Omnia" of Costanzo Porta; Music review ed "Notes," MusLA; Ed "Studies in Musicology" (69). 13: Yes. 14: Music bibliog, musicology. 15: Dept of Music, Univ of NC, Chapel Hill NC 27515.

PRUITT, CONSTANCE MAY B(UMP). b Beardstown Ill 9 My 39. 4: James Donald Pruitt. 5: Ill Col 57-60 (Eng) BA; OhioU 60-61 (Eng); West Ill U summer 62; UDenver summers 63-66 (Libnship) MA. 7: Tchr & libn Dallas City High Sch, Dallas City Ill 61-63; Catlgr Carthage Col 63-64; Hd libn Kenosha Tech Inst 64-66; Libn Denver Pub Schs 66-67; Catlgr No State Col, Aberdeen SD 67-. 10: AAUW. 14: Catlg, spec libs. 15: 1512 Marsie cir, Aberdeen SD 57401.

PRYOR, ELLEN A(CH). b NYC 27 N 15. 5: Smith 32-36 (Eng) BA; Pratt 60-62 MLA. 6: Fr, Ital, Lat. 7: Sec Hares Research Ltd, NYC 37-38; Ed asst "Time Magazine," NYC 38-41; Child libn Queens Borough Pub Lib, Jamaica NY 60-65; Child libn Deer Park Pub Lib, Deer Park NY 65-68, Dir 68. 9: ALA; Child Study Assn of Amer (Chil Bk Com 50-); NYLA; Suffolk Co (NY)LA. 14: Child serv. 15: 252 Puritan ave, Forest Hills NY 11375.

PRYOR, LEWIS A. b San Jose Cal 12 Ag 14. 4: Whilhelmine Wolpert. 5: San Jose State Col 32-37 (Soc Sci) AB; Seattle Pacific Col 56-57 (Educ); UWash 57-60 (LS) ML; UDenver summer 65 (Bkbind); UIowa summer 69 (Typography). 7: Employment inteviewer Cal State Empl Serv, San Jose Cal 38-42; Asst to empl dir Columbia Steel Co, Pittsburg Cal 43-47; Proprietor-Letter Shop & Mailing Serv, Pittsburg Cal 47-49; Sales repr bus forms Standard Register Co, Cal, & Wash 49-56; Libn Concrete High Sch, CONCRETE Wash 57-59; Asst libn Lower Columbia Jr Col 59-60; Ser libn Humboldt State Col 60-. 9: CalLA (Redwood Dist; v-pres, pres-elect 60, pres 70). 10: Beta Phi Mu; Brit Pntg Soc; Pntg Hist Soc. 13: Yes. 14: Typography, hist of printing, improving "home binding methods. 15: Humboldt State Col Lib, Arcata Cal 95521.

PRYSE, JOAN (ABELS). b PARIS Tex 17 O 38. 4: Scott W Pryse. 5: SoMethodist U 56-58; UOkla 58-61 (Educ, LS) BS. 7: Libn John Marshall High Sch, Okla City Okla 61-63; Libn Northeast High 64-67 Sch, Okla City Okla 64-67; Libn Webster Jr High Sch 67. 9: NEA; OklaEA; Okla City Clrm Tchrs Assn; Okla City LA. 10: Zeta Tau Alpha; Jr C of C; Jr Hospitality Club. 13: Yes. 14: Sch libn. 15: 3222 Wilshire blvd, Oklahoma City Ok 73116.

PUCKETT, (MARY) ELAINE. b Livingston Tenn 4 D 39. 5: Tenn Tech U 59-62 (Secondary Educ) BS; Peabody Col 62-63 (Eng) MA, 65-66 MLS. 7: High sch tchr Overton Co Sch Syst, Rickman Tenn 63-64; High sch tchr Metropolitan Nashville Davidson Co Sch Syst 64-65; Asst ref libn Purdue U 66-. 9: ALA (Jr MemRT); SLA. 10: Beta Phi Mu; AAUP. 14: Ref. 15: 2410 Happy Hollow rd apt E6, W Lafayette Ind 47906.

PUDDICOMBE, LULA (RIPPY). b Georgetown Ind 19 F 27. 4: Edmund C Puddicombe. 5: IndU 45-49 (Lang Arts) BS, (summers) 49-53 (LS) MA for tchrs. 7: Tchr-libn N Vernon High Sch, N Vernon Ind 49-51; Freshman libn Joliet Twp High Sch, Joliet Ill 51-55, Libn (W Campus) 65-67; Libn Joliet Jr Col 67-. 9: IllEA; IllLA. 14: Catlg. 15: 1719 W Acres rd, Joliet Il 60435.

PUFFER, KATHLEEN MARY (McCULLEY). b Oakland Cal 8 Mr 39. 4: Raymond LaBounty Puffer. 5: UMinn 57-61 (Anthropology) BA; UNC 61-63 MSLS; U NMex 67. 6: Sp, Lat. 7: Lib page St Paul Pub Lib St Anthony Park Br 56-57; Coun Camp Ojiketa Campfire Girls, St Paul 59; Sr clerk-typist Sch of Pub Health UMinn 61; Asst Sch of Lib Sci UNC 63; Libn ref dept Jacksonville Pub Lib, Jacksonville Fla 63-64; Asst acquis libn U NMex 67-68; Ref libn Lovelace Foundation for Med Educ & Research Med Lib, Albuquerque 68-. 9: ALA; NMLA; Greater Albuquerque LA. 14: Ref, acquis. 15: 637 D Charleston SE, Sandia Base Albuquerque NM 87108.

PUFFER, MICHAEL E. b Dowagiac Mich 9 Ag 43. 4: Holly Howson. 5: Adrian Col 61-65 (Bio) BS; West MichU 65-69 MSLS. 7: Dir Dowagiac Pub Lib, Dowagiac Mich 65-67; Dir Sage Pub Lib, Bay City Mich 67-. 9: MichLA (Pub Rel & Recruiting Coms). 10: Lions Club; Bay Area Child Guidance Com; Boy Scouts Com. 14: Admin. 15: 211 S Dean st, Bay City Mi 48706.

PUFFER, NATHANIEL HALL. b Nashua NH 3 F38. 4: Yvonne Smith. 5: Bates Col 57-61 (Hist) BA; UDenver 61-62 (LS)MA. 6: Fr. 7: Ref libn Brooklyn Pub Lib 62-63; US Army, Ft Gordon Ga 63-64; Asst acquis libn UDel Lib 64-68, Bibliogr 68-, Spec collections 66-. 9: ALA;-ACRL (Del Valley Chap); Del LA. 14: Acquis, rare bks, bibliog. 15: 600 Lehigh rd, Apt W-10, Newark De 19711.

PUFFER, YVONNE (SMITH). b Windsor Colo 29 S 40. 4: Nathaniel Hall Puffer. 5: Colo State Col 58-62 (Eng) BA; UDenver 62 (LS) MA. 7: Ref libn US Army Spec Serv, Ft Gordon Ga 63-64; Libn William Penn High Sch, New Castle del 64-67; Asst libn Newark Free Lib, Newark Del 68-. 8: Bk reviewer for Del State Lib 69-. 9: ALA; Del LA. 14: Ref, acquis, catlg. 15: 600 Lehigh rd, Apt W-10, Newark Del 19711.

PUGH, ELIZABETH (LaBRUCE). b Savannah Ga 30 Jl 22. 4: Albert E Pugh. 5: Col charleston 39-43 (Eng) AB; Emory 44-45 BS in LS. 7: Post libn US Army, Ft Moultrie SC 45-46; US Army libn Germany 46-48; Libn VA Hosp, Ft Howard Md 48-50; Asst libn Duke hosp Lib 61; Asst ref libn USoCar 66-. 9: ALA; SELA; SCLA. 14: Ref, med ref. 15: 1415 Sunbury lane, Columbia SC 29205.

PUGH, ELLEN (TIFFANY). b Cleveland 2 Je 20. 4: David B Pugh. 5: West Res 39-43 (Eng) AB, 43-45 BS in LS; Northwestern 45-47 (Eng) MA; Penn State U 50-51 (Eng). 6: Ger, Fr, Swedish. 7: Catlgr West Res U 43-47; Catlgr Northwestern U 45-47; Instr in Eng Queens Col (NC) 51-54; Rare bk libn USCar 54-55; Br libn Cincinnati Pub Lib 55-58; Assoc catlg libn UNeb 58-63; Sr catlg libn UOre 63-65; Assoc catlg libn URochester 65-68; Libn Ill Wash State U 69-. 9: ALA. 10: Quota Internat; AAUP; Mod Lang Assn; Delta Phi Gamma; Neb Writers Guild. 12: Auth "Tales from the Welsh Hills" (68). 13: Yes. 14: Tech proc. 15: 102 Joe st, Pullman Wa 99163.

PUGH, FRAYA JEAN. b Cumberland Md 28 Je 44. 5: WVaU 61-65 (Secondary Educ) BS; Wesley Jr Col 66-67 (Fr); UKy 68-69 MSLS. 6: Fr. 7: Coun Winchester Presbytery, 61, 62, 66, 67; Tchr-aide Headstart, Romnet WVa summer 65; Libn Caesar Rodney Spec Sch Dist, Camden Del 65-68. 8: Prof negotiations com Caesar Rodney Dist, Camden Del 66-67; Freshman adv & dorm counc WVaU 64-65. 9: ALA; NEA; DelaLA; DelaEA. 14: Child wk, supv, mgt, tchg at col level. 15: Slanesville WVa 25444.

PUGH, JULIA CAROLYN. b Amory Miss 24 N 35. 5: Miss State Col for Women 53-57 (Eng) BA;Emory 57-58 (LS) MA;Ohio State U 60-62. 6: Sp. 7: Asst reg libn NM Reg Lib 58-60; Catlgr Ohio State U 60-62; Ser libn Miss State Col for Women 62-66; Hd libn Miss Delta Expt Station 66-. 8: Establ lib for Delta Br Exper Sta, Stoneville Miss summers 63-65. 10: Phi Kappa Phi; Mortar Board; Beta Phi Mu. 14: Catlg, ref. 15: Box 215, Amory Ms 38821.

PUGHE, MARY COLLEEN (ADAMS). b Del Norte Col 23 Mr 25. 5: Colo Woman's Col 43-45 9piano) AA; San Fernando Valley State Col 58-62 (Educ). 7: Clk Rio Grande Co Courthouse, Colo 46-47; Mus tchr Del Norte & Center Colo 49-55; Mus tchr Canoga Park & Chatsworth Cal 55-66; Lib asst Bunker-Ramo Corp, Canoga Park Cal 64-66, Asst libn 66-. 9: SLA; ALA; ASIS. 14: Acquis, ref. 15: 9809 Oakdale ave, Chatsworth Ca 91311.

PUGSLEY, JAMES W. b Portland NY 21 Jl02. 4: Ruth Hook. 5: Cornell U 21-25 (Classics) AB, 25-28 (Gk) PhD; Columbia 41-42 BS in LS. 6: Gk, Lat, Fr,Ger. 7: Instr in the Classics & hist of art State U Iowa 28-29; Instr in the classics UNeb 29-32; Prof of the classics Buffalo Collegiate Center, Buffalo NY 34-37; Prof of Gk & Lat Taylor U 37-41; Libn humanities reading room Brown U 42-43; Libn Baldwin-Wallace Col 43-50; Prof of Lib Sci Jersey City State Col 50-. 9: NJEA. 10: Amer Philol Assn (Life mem); NY Classics Assn. 13: Yes. 14: Curr materials, Greek metrics, Greek & Latin lit, New Testament Greek lang & lit. 15: 2 Elena pl, Belleville NJ 07109.

PULASKA, JADWIGA. b Warsaw Poland 21 Ag 06. 5: UWarsaw 26-30 (Ling, Art Hist) MA; Columbia 51-53 (Libnship) MS. 6: Polish, Fr, Lat, Ger, Ital. 7: Archivist Polish Lib in Paris 36-49; Libn PRCU of Amer, Chicago 49-50; Independent researcher Mid-European Studies Ctr NYC 50-53; Ser catlgr Columbia U Libs 53-55; Asst libn Cooper Union Lib 55-57; Hd libn Parsons Sch of Design, NYC 57-. 8: Planning adv for Free Europe Com for organ a chain of libs in France 56; Radio talks for Radio Free Europe; Transl from Eng to Polish for "America" (CIA). 9: SLA; NYLA; NY Lib Club; NY Tech Libns. 10: The Kosciuszko Found (NY); Joseph Pilsudski Inst (for research in modern hist, NY). 13: Yes. 14: Admin, bk sel, catlg, organiz of materials, rare bks. 15: 399 E 72nd st, New York NY 10021.

PULEO, ANTHONY R. b St Albans Long Island NY 13 Je 22. 4: Helen June Puleo. 5: SoIllU 40-43; Hofstra 46-48 (Bus Admin) BS; UIll summer 50; C W Post of LIU 61-68 MLS. 7: Tech/Sgt US Army Counter Intelligence Corps 43-46; Faculty asst in lib SoIllU 49-51; Sr com loan clk Bankers Trust Co, NYC 52-60; Secondary sch libn N Babylon Pub Schs, N Babylon NY 60-. 9: NEA; ALA; NYTA; NYLA. 10: N BabylonTA. 14: Ref, sch libs (secondary). 15: 25 Ryan st, West Islip NY 11795.

PULLEN, MABLE (SPENCER). b Cumberland Co Tenn 14 F 16. 4: William W Pullen Jr. 5: Tenn Polytech Inst 51 (Educ) BS; Peabody 63 (LS) MA. 7: Putnam Co Bd of Educ, Monterey Tenn: Tchr 35-37, 48-54; Elem prin 37-40; Elem tchr Davidson Co Bd of Educ, Nashville Tenn 54-60; High sch libn Metro-Nashville, Davidson Co 60-. 9: NEA (Life mem); ALA; TennLA; TennEA; Nashville Lib Club. 10: Woman's Nat Bk Assn; Middle Tenn EA. 14: Ref. 15: 3714 West End ave, Nashville Tn 37205.

PULLING, BARTON SEBRING. b Canada 2 Ja 20. 4: Dorothy Lloyd Kissam. 5: UMinn 37-41 (Zool) BA; Army Lang Sch 47-48 (Russian) Diploma; UMich 68-69 AMLS. 6: Russian. 7: 2nd Lt-Col USAF Research & Development 41-63; V-pres Mil Radar Div Conductron corp, Ann Arbor Mich 63-67; Ops mgr Polhemus Navigation Sci, Ann Arbor Mich 67-68; Consul info mgr Adams Lafferty Madden & Moody, Detroit 69-. 9/ inst Electrical & Electronic Engrs; British

Interplanetary Soc. 10: Beta Phi Mu. 11: 2 Legions of Merit; USAF Missile Badge. 13: Yes. 14: Info mgt, data proc, syst & procedures. 15: 1610 Morton ave, Ann Arbor Mi 48104.

PULLING, HAZEL ADELE. b Edmonton Alta Can 16 Ap 02. 5: Chicago 27-30 (Hist, Eng) PhB, 30 (US Hist) MA; USoCal 38 BS LS, 44 (US & Eng Hist) PhD; Chicago 48 (LS). 6: Sp. 7: Ref libn San Jose State Col 38-40; Instr to assoc prof lib sch USoCal 40-50; NY Pub Lib & Chicago Pub Lib 48; Asst dir lib sch Fla State U 50; Visiting prof lib sch Rutgers U summer 54; Dir lib sch Tex Womans U 51-53; Assoc prof of lib sci Immaculate Heart Col 55-60; Head libn Cal West U 51-57, 60-65. 9: ALA (chm Memb Com, mem Subsc Bks Com 6 yrs); SLA (Conv Chm 49); CalLA. 10: Phi Beta Kappa; Phi Alpha Theta; Phi Kappa Phi. 13: Yes. 14: Admin, ref, bk sel. 15: 910 Cornish dr, San Diego Ca 92107.

PULS, ELAINE (MARJORY) (ALLISON). b Grand Junction Colo 14 Mr 27. 4: Dr Gerald E Puls. 5: Mesa Jr Col 45-47 (Eng) AA; Western State Col 47-48 (Eng); UDenver 48-49 BS in LS. 7: Libn I Barnum Br Lib, Denver 49-52; Libn I Ref Denver Pub Lib 52-53 Reading guidance Fitsimons Army Hosp Lib, Denver 53-55; Libn Meeker Grade Sch, Meeker Col 58-5; Libn Rangely Col 62-63; Acquis libn UColo Med Lib 63-65; Libn UWash 65-66; Asst libn VA Hosp Lib, Seattle 65-66; Lib dir Loveland Pub Lib, Loveland Colo 68-. 9: ColoLA. 14: Acquis, ref, catlg, admin. 15: 1821 Busch ct, Fort Collins Co 80521.

PULSIFER, JOSEPHINE (STURDIVANT). b Cumberland Me 27S15. 4: Herbert Gerald Pulsifer. 5: Barnard 32-36 (Psych) BA; Drexel 41-42 BS in LS.06: Sp. 7: Order asst Portland Pub Lib,Portland Me 36-41; Br libn Ench Pratt Free Lib, Baltimore 42-43; Period libn & ref asst UMe Lib 49-52; Asst head catlg dept Iowa State U 52-55; Head catlg dept SD State U 56-61; Libn Pan American Agric Sch (Tegucigalpa Honduras) 61-63; Ser catlg LC 63-65; Chief of tech serv Wash State Lib 65-. 8: Lecturer ISAD/LC MARC Inst 68-69; Mem Recon Wking Task Group, Wash DC 68-69. 9: ALA-AA StateL; -RTSD; -ISAD; WashLA; PNLA. 10: Phi Beta Kappa. 14: Tech proc, ser, data proc. 15: Rt 8 Box 336, Olympia Wa 98502.

PUNGITORE, VERNA LEAH. b ClairtonPenn 30 Ap 41. 5: BACKBURN U 59-63 (Eng) A; UPittsburgh 64-65 MLS. 6: Fr. 7: Readers asst Youngstown Pub Lib, Youngstown Ohio 63-64, Br asst 65-66, Br libn 66-67; Ref coord Clinton-Essex-Franklin Lib, Plattsburgh NY 67-68; Dir Plattsburgh Pub Lib, Plattsburgh NY 68-. 9: ALA. 10: Beta Phi Mu; Champlain Valley Bus & Prof Women's Club. 14: Ref, admin. 15: 60 Oak st, Plattsburgh NY 12901.

PURCELL, GARY R. b Idaho Falls Ida 22 Ap 36. 04L Carolyn Despain. 4: Carolyn Despain. 5: UUtah 53-57 (Pol Sci) BA; UWash 58-59 (LS) MS; Case West Res 69 (Pol Sci) MA. 7: Lib asst Ida State Lib 57-58; Lib asst Enoch Pratt Free Lib, Baltimore 59-61; Instr West Mich U 61-65; Instr West Res U 65-. 8: Consul to Ferguson Lib, Stamford Conn 68, Cuyahoga Co Pub Lib, Cleveland 68. 9: ALA (Subscription Bk Com); OhioLA; AALS; MichLA (chm Recr & Scholarship Com). 10: Afro-Amer Cultural & Hist Soc. 12: Comp "Hanbook of Scholarships for Study in Librarianship (65). 13: Yes. 14: Ref, pub docs, pub libs, soc sci lit. 15: 3014 Edgehill rd, Cleveland Heights Oh 44118.

PURCELL, DORIS (WILSON). b Bliss NY 4D 10. 5: Geneseo State Normal Sch 27-30 (Educ); URochester 34-36 (Educ) BS; State Col for Tchrs(Albany NY) 36-37. 38-39 BS in LS; New Sch for Soc Research 60-. 6: Fr, Ger. 7: Asst libState Col for Tchrs 9chadron Neb) 39-42; Lib asst Mills Col 42-44; Catlgr St Lawrence U (NY) 45-46; Lib asst Upsala Col 46-47; Catlgr Sch of Theol Boston U 55-58; Catlgr LIU 60-. 10: AAUP. 14: Catlg. 15: 60 Remsen st, Brooklyn NY 11201.

PURDY, ROBERTA. b Brooklyn NY 19 Mr 19. 5: Womans Col UNC 40 (Eng) AB; Columbia 41 BS in LS. 7: Circ asst NY Pub Lib 41-46; Catlgr Russell Sage Found Lib, NYC 46-49; Catlgr Time Inc Lib, NYC 49-52; Indexer Industrial Arts Index H Wilson Co, NYC 52-57, Ed Applied Sci & Tech Index 58-62; Catlgr Engnr Socs Lib, NYC 62-63; Catlgr & Indexer IBM, San Jose Cal 63-65; Catlgr Stanford U Libs 65-67; Catlgr UUtah Libs 67-. 9: ALA; SLA; UtahLA. 14: Catlg. 15: 123 Q st, Salt Lake City Ut 84103.

PURDY, VICTOR WILLIAM. b Milwaukee Wis 4 Mr 26. 4: Alice Thalman. 5: UWis (Milwaukee) 46-47, 50-51; Brigham Young U 51-52 (Hist) BS, 54-59 (Hist & Philos); Columbia U 52-53 (LS) MS; UWis (Madison) 59, 61-62 (US Intel Hist). 6: Fr, Ger. 7: GM 3/c US Navy, Pacific theater 44-46; Missionary N Central States Mission LDS Ch, man Can 48-50; Ser & asst circ libn Fresno State Col Lib, Fresno Cal 53-54; Ser libn Brigham Young U Lib, Provo Utah 54-58, Subject libn (Hist, Rel & Philos) 58-61, 63, Acting order libn 59, 61, Asst dir in charge of readers serv & chm of Bk Selection Com 64-66, Asst Prof Lib & Info Sci, Grad Dept Lib & Info Sci 67-. 9: AHA; ALA; Amer studies Assn; Mormon Hist Assn; Org Amer Histns; UtahLA. 14: Historiography, hist of bks & printing, Hist of libs, soc sci lit, Mormon Hist & lit sel & acquis of materials, ref, bibliog. 15: 1740 N 500 E, Provo Ut 84601.

PURIFOY JR, CECIL ERNEST. b Houston Tex 22 S 27. 5: UHouston 44-47 (Soc Sci); UTex 47-49 (Soc Sci, Eng) BS in Ed; Mich State U 50-52 (Educ Curriculum) MA, 53-54, 64-66, summers 68 & 69 (Educ Curriculum). 6: Russian, Fr, Sp. 7: Tchr houston Independent Sch Dist, Houston Tex 61-62, 63-64; Specialist Panama Canal Co, Balboa Canal Zone 62-63, 67-68; Grad tchg asst Mich State U (E Lansing) 64-66; Asst prof Col of Educ UTenn 66-67, 68-69. 9: Amer Acad of Religion; AHA; ALA; Assn Childhood Educ Internat; ASCD; Internat Reading Assn; NCTE; Nat Coun Soc Studies; Organiz Amer Histns. 10: AAUP; Phi Delta Kappa. 14: Child lit, sch libs. 15: PO Box 1853, Knoxville Tn 37901.

PURIFY, DEARTIS GENE. b Dallas Tex 4 Ag 42. 5: Prairie View A&M 59-64 (LS) BS in Ed; N Tex State U 64- (LS). 6: Sp, Fr. 7: Child libn Dallas Pub Lib, Dallas Tex 64-68; Sch libn Dallas Independent Sch Dist, Dallas Tex 68-. 9: NEA; TexStateTA; Clr Tchrs of Dallas. 10: YWCA; Delta Sigma Theta; Prairieview Alum assn. 14: Pub lib (child wk). 15: 2807 Dathe st, Dallas Tx 75215.

PURNELL, JOYCE (REACHARD). b Waynesboro Penn 2 My 22. 4: Lewis R Purnell. 5: Kutztown State Col 40-44 (LS, Eng) BS. 7: Libn: Jr-Sr High Sch, E McKeesport Penn 44-45, Waynesboro Jr High Waynesboro Penn 45-47, E Jr High Sch Waynesboro Penn 62-. 9: ALA; NEA; PennStateLA; PennStateEA; WaynesboroAreaTA. 10: Waynesboro Col Club. 14: Wk with the early adolescent. 15: 229 Park st, Waynesboro Pa 17268.

PURSHOTTAM, NATESAIER. b Kotagiri India 25 O 17. 4: Savitri Ramcharan. 5: Madras U Med Col 35-40 (Medicine) MBBS-MD; UColo Sch of Med 49-51 (Human Growth) MS; Harvard 51-52 (Pub Health) MPH; UCal (Berkeley) 66-67 MLS. 7: Asst ind health off Tatagroup of Ind, Bombay 54-57; Staff scientist Worcester Foundation for Experimental Bio, Shrewsbury Mass 57-59; Research assoc Stanford Med Ctr 59-62; Asst Prof preventive med UCal Sch of Med (San Francisco) 62-64; Physiologist health evaluation program Retail Clks Union, Hollywood Cal 64-65; Research physician (occ health) UCal (Berkeley) 65-67; Med info scientist Kaiser Foundation Research Inst, Oakland Cal 68-. 8: Consul in Med Epidemiology, State of Cal 62-64; Med Nutrition Adv Dairy Coun of Cal Sacramento 65-67. 9: Amer Pub health Assn; MedLA; SLA. 10: AAAS; Alta Siena Country Club. 13: Yes. 14: Biomed selective dissemination of info. 15: 1533 Beverly pl, Berkeley Ca 94706.

PURVIS, BRENDA (SIMONTON). b Lawrenceville Ga 12 O 42. 4: Joe B Purvis. 5: Agnes Scott 60-64 (Sociol) BA; Emory 64-67 M Lib. 7: Circ asst reserve bk mgr Emory U Theol Lib 64-66; Asst libn DeKalb Co Bd of Educ Avondale High Sch, Avondale Est Ga 66-67; Asst libn Gainesville Jr Col, Gainesville Ga 67-. 9: ALA; NEA; GaLA; GaEA; SELA. 14: Catlg. 15: Rte 1 Rebecca st, Lilburn Ga 30247.

PUTNAM, VIRGINIA KAY. b Council Bluffs Iowa 17 Je 40. 5: Graceland Col 58-60 (Liberal Arts) AA; State UIowa 60-62 (Elem Educ) BA; Rosary Col 64, 65 (LS); West Mich U summers 65-67 MLS. 6: Fr. 7: Free Pub Lib, Council Bluffs Iowa summer 62; Elem sch libn William Hatch Sch, Oak Park Ill 62-68; Instr Rosary Col 67-68; Act lib consul Oak Park Elem Schs Dist #97, Oak Park Ill 68-. 8: Lectr for NDEA Inst for Elem Sch Supvrs, Rosary Col fall 67; Selector for "The Elementary School Library Collection" (ed by Mary V Gaver) 67-. 9: ALA; -AASchL (Elem Sch Lib Com 63-66, Ad hoc Com on Sch Lib Manuals 66-69); NEA; IllEA (Del 65-68 Lake-Shore Div); IllLA; Oak Park TA (chm TEPS, chm Pub Rel). 10: Phi Beta Kappa; Pi Lambda Theta; Beta Phi Mu; Child Reading RT. 13: Yes. 14: Elem sch libs. 15: 2430 ave F, Council Bluffs Ia 51501.

PUTNEY, ELEANOR MARIA. b Ferry Mich 12O 04. 5: East Mich U 22-26 (Hist) AB in Ed; UMich 32-36 ABLS, 06: Fr. 7: Hist tchr Sand Creek Mich High Sch 26-28; Circ & catlg asst East Mich U 28-36; Catlgr UCincinnati Lib 36-39; Head catlgr DePauw U Lib 39-42; Catlgr Yale U Lib 42-44; Sr order libn UMich 45-47; Catlgr & reviser Copyright Catlg Div & Eng Lang Sect LC 47-65, Hd Eng Lang Sect 66-. 9: ALA; DCLA; Potomac Tech Proc Libns. 10: Kappa Delta Pi; Phi Kappa Phi. 14: Docs, catlg. 15: 5649 Shadyside ave, Suitland Md 20023.

PYKE, GERTRUDE V (LACKBURN). b Hanford Cal 31 Jl 07. 5: Walla Walla Col 2832 (Eng) BA; UWash 56-60 (LS) MS. 6: Sp. 7: Libn Ft Vancouver Reg Lib, Vancouver Wash 40-43, 53-58; Libn Columbia Acad, Battle Ground Wash 53-60; Libn Walla Walla Co Sch of Nursing 60-. 10: Guidance Com, Sch of Nursing, lib com, Sch of Nursing. 14: Ref. 15: 6014 SE Yamhill, Portland Or 97215.

PYLE, CLAIRE. b Johnstown Penn 17 S 17. 5 Pittsburgh 35-39, & 40 (Hist, Eng) AB; Ind U summers 50-52 (Amer Savings & Loan Inst) Grad Diploma; Carnegie 57-58 MLS. 6: Fr. 7: Tchr Johnstown Pub Sch Dist Even Sch, Johnstown Penn 40-44; Treas Cambria Savins & Loan Assn, Johnstown Penn 41-57; Ref libn gen ref div Carnegie Lib of Pittsburgh 58-64, Head of gen ref div64-66; Hd of ref dept 66-69, Hd of br serv 69-. 9: ALA; PennLA. 10: Beta Phi Mu; Phi Theta Kappa; Pi Lambda Theta; Soroptimist Internat. 13: Yes. 14: Ref, ext serv. 15: 4733 Centre ave, Pittsburgh Pa 15213.

PYLE, FRANCES LETELLIER. b Grand Rapids Mich 24 Mr 19. 5: UMich 37-41 (Eng) BA, 51-54 MALS. 6: Fr, Ger. 7: Tchr UMich Ext Serv 41-42; Asst ref libn Ann Arorpub Lib, Ann Arbor Mich 53-67, child libn 67-. 9: ALA; MichLA. 14: Ref, child, ya. 15: 4630 Midway dr, Ann Arbor Mi 48103.

PYLE, HELEN MARY. b Chester Springs Penn25Je 08. 5: State Tchrs Col(West Chester Penn) 27-31 BS in Secondary Ed; Drexel 43-44 BS in LS. 7: Tchr-libn Marcus Hook Jr High Sch; Marcus Hook Penn 31-43; Libn Wyeth Inst of Applied Biochem, Phila 44-48; Libn Sun Oil Co, Phila 48-. 9: SLA (dir52-55; pres Phila Chap): PennLA (chm Phila Dist 48-50). 10: Chester Co Penn Hist Soc. 12: Auth "Libraries for Research and Industry," SLA MN5). 13: Yes. 14: Admin, catlg, ref. 15: Sun Oil Co, Gen Off Lib, 1608 Walnut st, Phila Pa 19103.

PYLE, MARJORIE McCAUSLAND. b Cleveland 19 S 35. 4: Edward Norman Pyle. 5: Kent State U 53-57 (Span) BS in Ed. 6: Sp. 7: Bkmob libn Akron Pub Lib, Akron Ohio 57; Catlgr Hispanic Soc of America, NY 57-59; Indexer H W Wilson Co, NY 59-. 9: NY Lib Club. 14: Catlr, indexer,child serv. 15: 2347 Haviland ave, Bronx 62 NY.

PYLE, MERTICE PAULINE. b Carmi Ill 16 O 0. 5: MacMurray Col 26-30 (Music) BME; Peabody 46-47 BS in LS; George Washington U summer 32; Nortwestern summer 36; UMich 56. 7: Music tchr Grayville Pub Schs, Grayville Ill 31-49; Unit libn Com Unit Sch Dist #2, Mattoon Ill 49-67; Title I Carmi Twp High Sch 68-. 9: Internat Reading Coun; ALA (Recr Com 60-); IllASchL (Exec Bd 52-54 & 65-67); IllLA; IllEA (Del to Gen Assembly 65-67); Mem Illinois Reading Serv Basic Bk Com 66-67. 12: "Basic List for Elementary School Libraries" IllASchL. 13: Yes. 14: Sch libs. 15: Box 325, Carmi Il 62821.

PYNE, ELEANOR (GRAVES). b Lexington Mass 26 Ja 06. 4: Ralph Curtis Pyne. 5: Simmons 23-27 (LS) BS. 7: Ctlgr Ohio State U 27-29; Catlgr Harvard Col Sch of Bus Admin 30-31; Instr Simmons Col 31-38; 1st asst Redwood Lib & Athenaeum, Newport RI 38-48; Ref libn Providence Pub Lib 49-52, 57-63, Index libn 63-. 14: Ref, catlg. 15: 135 Garden City dr, Cranston RI 02920.

Q

QUARTZ, BEATRICE M(AE). b Plymouth Mass 21 My 06. 5: Smith 28 (Fr) BA; UMich 39 BALS, 48 MALS. 6: Fr, Sp, Ger. 7: Ser catlgr Yale U Lib 28-39; Catlgr Wellesley Col Lib 39-48, Assoc libn for tech serv 48-. 9: ALA-RTSD (mem nomin com DCC 49-50);-ACRL; NELA; MassLA; NE Tech Serv Libns (pres 59-60, sec-treas 45-46). 14: Catlg. 15: Wellesley Col Lib, Wellesley Mass 02181.

QUATTLEBAUM, MARGUERITE V(OGEDING). b Garrett Ind 14 O 09. 4: Charles A Quattlebaum. 5: Ind U 27-31 (Lat) AB; George Washington U 36-39 AB in LS, 49-51 (Sp). Sp. 6: Lat, Sp. 7: LC Shelflister & shelflist reviser 38-43, Asst ed of subj headings 43-48, Ed of subj headings 48-63, Head Ed Sect Subj Catlg Div 63-. 9: ALA; DCLA. 10: George Washington Univ Lib Sch Alumni Assn; Eta Sigma Phi; Pi Lambda Theta; Phi Beta Kappa; Arlington Ridge Civic Assn. 12: Ed "Period Subdivisions under Names of Places Used in the Dictionary Catalogs of the Library of Congress (50); Ed "Subject Headings Usd in the Dictionary Catalogs of the Library of Congress (7th ed 66). 14: Subj catlg & clsf, automation in LC. 15: 1022 S 26th rd, Arlington Va 22202.

QUATTRONE, BARBARA. b NYC 28 O 21. 4: Joseph Quattrone. 5: Vassar 39-43 (Sociol) BA; Pratt Inst 64-66 MLS. 6: Fr. 7: Catlgr Perrot Mem Lib, Old Greenwich Ct 64-67; Libn Greenwich Acad, Greenwich Ct 68-. 9: ALA; ConnLA. 10: Beta Phi Mu. 14: Catlg, ref. 15: 124 Lockwood rd, Riverside Ct 06878.

QUEEN, MARGARET E. b Kan City Mo 21 Ap 28. 5: Washington U (St Louis) 46-50 (Span) AB; UIll 50-56 (LS) MS. 6: Sp, Fr. 7: St Louis Pub Lib: Sub-prof libn 51-55, Intermediate libn Info desk 56-57, Prin libn ref dept 57-60, Chief libn Br for the Blind 60-62; San Diego Pub Lib: Ref libn 62-63, Sr libn lit sect 63-69, Soc Sci sect 69-. 9: ALA (Steering Com Sort 60-62, Memb Chm Palomar Dist 64-65); CalLA 64-. 10: ACLU; YWCA; San Diego Mental Health Assn; Phi Beta Kappa; Beta Phi Mu; San Diego Pub Lib Assn (pres 68). 13: Yes. 14: Adult bk sel & ref (lang & lit). 15: San Diego Pub Lib, 8th & E st, San Diego Ca 92101.

QUENEMOEN, HELEN (MOORE). b Cleveland Ohio 20 O 41. 4: Lowell R Quenemoen. 5: Cartelon Col 60-64 (Hist) BA; UMinn 64-65 (LS) MA. 7: Libn Pillsbury Co, Minneapolis 65-67, Hd libn 67-68; Libn Mental Health Research Inst UMich (Ann Arbor) 68-. 9: SLA (treas Minn Chap 67-68). 10: Ann Arbor Lib Club; Phi Beta Kappa; Beta Phi Mu. 14: Spec libs (esp bus libs), ref. 15: 702 Thomas ct, Ann Arbor Mi 48103.

QUERY, EUNICE (MARY). b Hudson NC 1 S 09. 5: Duke U 29-31 (Eng, Soc Studies) A;UNC summes 37-39 ABLS; Appalachian State Tchrs Col 53 (Educ) MA. 6: Fr, Sp. 7: Tchr Elem Sch, Reeds NC 28-29; Tchr High Sch, Hudson NC 31-36; Asst libn High Sch, High Point NC 36-38; Libn High Sch, Lenoir NC 38-46; Libn Co Lib, Lenoir NC 46-47; Instr, Assoc Prof Dept of Lib Sci Appalachian State Tchrs Col47-. 8: Act State Sch Lib Adv, NC Dept of Pub Instr 54; Numerous assignments on com for eval of sch libs, So Assn of Schs & Cols. 9: NCLA (sec 45-47, v-pres & pres elect). 14: Sch libs. 15: 204 Pine st, Boone NC 28607.

QUICK, MARY BETH. b New Haven Conn29 Ja 12. 5: Transylvania Col 36 (Eng) AB; Emory 40 AB in LS. 7: Personal serv dept Sears Roebuck, Atlanta 36-39; Circ libn Clemson U Lib 41-44; Third libn Hllins Col 44-46; Circ libn Howard Col 46-51; Period libn Henderson State Tchrs 51-54; Acquis libn Winthrop Col Lib 54-61, Asst catlgr 61-. 9: ALA; SCLA; SELA. 10: Mental Health Assn; AAUW; Bus & Prof Women. 14: Catlg. 15: 316 Aiken ave, Rock Hill SC 29730.

QUICK, RICHARD CHRISTIAN. b Montclair NJ 4 D 26. 4: Christine Merritt. 5: Kenyon Col 48-52 (Eng) A (cum laude); West Res 53-54 MS in LS. 6: Sp, Fr. 7: US Navy dental tech 45-46; Clerical Fairchild Publs Inc, NYC 47; UDel Lib: Circ libn 54-56, Asst t libn 56-59, Asst to dir 59-65; Dir of Lib Serv No Ariz U 65-68; Dir of libs SUNY (Geneseo) 68-. 9: ALA-ACRL; DelLA (pres 58-60); Middle Atlantic Reg Lib Conf (Exec Bd 62-); NYLA; Ariz State LA (pres col & univ libs sect 67). 10: Archaeol Soc of Del; Del Educ TV Inc. 11 Ed DelLA "Bulletin (69-64); Ed Archaeol Soc of Del "Bulletin & "Inksherds. 13: Yes. 14: Admin, tech proc, spec collections. 15: 9 Westview Crescent, Geneseo NY 14454.

QUICK, YOUNG HI (KO). b Milyan S Korea 11 F 25. 4: Timothy W Quick. 5: Ewha Womens U (Seoul Korea) 43 (Music) BA; Skidmore Col (NY) 49 (Music). 6: Korean, Japanese. 7: Research libn pub rel Western Electric, NYC 54-. 9: SLA. 14: Ref, archives. 15: Pub Rel, Western Electric Co, 195 Broadway, NYC 10007.

QUIER, (CHARLOTTE) ELIZABETH (METZGER). b Weissport Penn 1 N 02. 4: Kenneth E Quier. 5: Moravian Col for Women 19-23 (Eng, Sci) BA; UPenn 23-24 (Eng Lit & Philol) MA; Pratt 38 BLS. 6: Fr, Ger. 7: Supv of Eng & sch libn Hatfield Jt Consol Sch, Hatfield Penn 24-28; Faculty Penn State U summer 47; Ref asst Pratt Inst Lib 38-43; Prof of Libnship Grad Lib Sch Pratt Inst 43-. 9: ALA; NYLA; NY Lib Club. 10: AAUP; Beta Phi Mu. 14: Ref, bibliog. 15: 65 Broadway, Ocean Grove NJ 07756.

QUIGG, DOROTHY. b Livermore Ky. 5: West State Col(Bowling Green Ky) (Eng) AB; Cathlic U (LS) MS. 7: High sch Eng tchr & libn, Rutherford Tenn 41-43; LC 43-55; Libn catlg Naval Ordinance Lab, White Oak Md 55-57; Chief catlg sect Dept of Housing & Urban Development, Wash DC 57-. 9: SLA. 12: Ed ""Subject Headings Used nin Catalog of the HHFA Library (62). 14: Catlg. 15: 3515 N Washington blvd, Arlington Va 22201.

QUIGLEY, BEATRICE MAE (DRUMMOND). b Sutton WVa 3019. 5: Salem Col 37-40 (Home Econ, Phys Educ), 53 (Home Econ) BA, 59-61 (LS); WVaU 59 (LS). 6: Sp. 7: Receptionist & Payroll clerk City Lines Bus Co, Clarksburg WVa 45-50; VA Hosp, Clarksburg WVa; Switchboard operator 50-54, Admin clerk 54-56, Recreation asst 56-58, Chief libn 58-. 9: WVaLA (Sec Spec Libs Sect). 10: Employees VA Hosp Fed Credit Sunnycroft unnycroft Counry Club; Commun Concert Assn; Wesleyan Serv Guild; Altrusa Internat. 14: Ref. 15: 306 Ross st, Bridgeport WVa 26330.

QUIGLEY, MARJORIE N. b Ancon Panama CZ 6 Ap 10. 4: Dr Roscoe Murphy Quigley. 5: UOre 28-32 (Eng, Pre Lib) BA; UWash 32-33 BS in LS. 7: Temp catlg asst Ore State Lib 33; Lib dept asst J K Gill Bk Co, Portland Ore 33-35; Asst co libn Deschutes Co Lib, Bend Ore 35-37; Child libn Dept Head Boise Pub Lib, Boise Ida 37-42; Instr lib sci Altoona Campus Penn State U 60, Libn 62-. 9: PennLA; ALA. 10: AAUW; Quota Internat; DAR; YWCA. 14: Col lib admin. 15: Altoona Campus Lib, Altoona Pa 16601.

QUIJANO, CARLA HACKETT. b Genoa Italy 9 My 18. 4: Jose Santos Quijano. 5: Cornell U 36-38; NYU 38-40 (Art Hist) BA; NYU Inst of Fine Arts 40-43 (Art Hist); Harvard Fogg Museum Sch 40 (Art Hist). 6: Ital, Fr, Sp. 7: Catlgr Metropolitan Museum of Art, NYC 40-44; Researcher Maryknoll Fathers, Maryknoll NY 57-61; Libn Maryknoll Info Lib, Maryknoll NY 63-. 9: SLA (Picture & Publ & Newspaper Div). 10: LWV; PTA. 14: Researc, translating. 15: 4 Cedar lane, Croton-on-Hudson, NY 10520.

QUIMBY, GRACE. b Phila 7D 06. 5: Bryn Mawr 25-29(Lat) BA; Drexel 32-33BS in LS. 7: Ref libn Princeton Theol Sem 33-40; Ref libn DC Pub Lib 41-44, Readers adv 45-50; Nat Archives Lib, Wash DC: Documents libn 51, Head catlgr 52-5, Libn 58-66; Libn Vt Hist Soc, Montpelier Vt 67-. 8: Instr in lib sci & bibliog "Study of Cols of East NC," Asheville Col summer 42; Discussion leader Great Books Program, DC Pub Lib 47-49; Exhib & lib consul, Wash Assn for Wkers Educ, DC 47-56; Libn, Friends Serv Com, Sem for Refugee Scholars (Wolfeboro NH) summer 40; Libn & consul, Hudson Shore Labor Sch, West Park NY, summers 49-50. 9: ALA; SLA (DC hap Soc Sci Group: sec 5, chm 53,& other assignments); SAA (fellow); DCLA (chm Archives Com 64-); Tech ech Proc Libns; VtLA; NELA. 10: Potomac Appalachian Trail Club; Staff Assn DC Pub Lib; Appalachian Mountain Club; Audubon Naturalist So; Wilderness Soc; Green Mountain Club; League of Vt Writers; Poetry Soc of Vt. 11: Climbing Award, Heiligenblut (Austria Mountainerng Sch, 55; Award from Amer Artists Prof League, for Contributions to Traditional American Art 64; Meritorious Service Award (group), Nat Archives & Records Serv, 57. 12:"Writings on Archives, Current Records, and Historical Manuscripts in "The American Archivist 57-); "Labor Books i the Library weekly in "The Trades Unionist (45-49); Bibliog ed, "The American Archivist (63-). 14: Bibliog, archival lit, govt docs, Vt hist. 15: RFD #1 Montpelier Center, Montpelier Vt 05602.

QUIMBY, HARRIET B(OWMAN). b Winchester Mass 16 F 20. 5: Simmons 38-42 (LS) BS; Columbia 51 (Educ Psych) MA. 7: Brooklyn Pub Lib: Child libn 42-51, Asst br libn 51-54, Asst to supt of bs 54-55, Br libn 55-59, Coordinator of child serv 590-. 8: Lecturer, Pratt Inst, summer 62, 64 (Bk rv adv com); School Library Journal; Adj asst Prof Palmer Grad Lib Sch LIU 68, 69. 9; ALA-CSD (Exec Bd 64-67); NYLA; NY Lib Club. 10: Womens Nat Bk Assn. 14: Child serv. 15: 115 Washington pl, NYC 10014.

QUINLY, WILLIAM J. b Kan City Kan 1 O 21. 4: Clifton Wight. 5: Kansas City Jr Col 39-41; UMo (Kan City) 41-43 (Hist, Pol Sci) BA; UDenver 47-48 (LS) MA. 7: Page, clerk Kan City Pub Lib 36-40; (Lt) US Navy Navigator, Port Dir 43-47; Readers adv Grand Rapids Pub Lib, Grand Rapids Mich 48-50; Asst State libn Mo State Lib 50-52; Head A-v Center Chicago Tchrs Col 52-56; Asst prof lib sch Fla State U 56-; Dir media ctr 58-. 8: Consul Gen Ext Div State of Fla, 57-60; Visiting lecturer Lib Sch UTenn, summer 64; Consul, St Andrews Presy Col 67-69, N Fla Jr Col 67-69; Faculty U OK Inst summer 69. 9: ALA (A-V Round Table, chm Jr Mem Round Table); FlaLA; Fla A-V Assn; Chm NEA-DAVI Media Catlg Com; MLA (past v-pres). 10: Phi Delta Kappa; Lions Club. 12: "On Record" (51); Ed "Junion Members Round Table Newsletter" (49-51); "Standards for Cataloging, Coding and Scheduling Educational Media" (68). 13: Yes. 14: Admin, educ media, catlg. 15: Media Center Fla State Univ, Talahassee Fl 32306.

QUINN, EDWARD W(ILLIAM). b NYC 5 Jl 7. 4: Louise Stukart. 5: Cooper Union Inst of Tech 36-40 B Ch E; Chicago 49-50 MA in LS. 7: Ref asst John Crerar Lib, Chicago 50-51; Sci libnU Gen Electric Co Agt Div, Cincinnati 53-55; Research libn Amer Optical Co, Southbridge Mass 55-59; Libn Portland Cement Assn, Chicago 59-. 9: SLA. 14: Ref. 15: Portland Cement Assoc, Old Orchard rd, Skokie Il 60076.

QUINN, SUSANNA (BEYER). b Staten Island NY 6 Ap 09. 4: Leo D Quinn. 5: Temple of Tech 28-32 (Eng) BA; Drexel 59-60 MS in LS. 6: Fr. 7: Y-a libn Chestnut Hill Br Free Lib of Phila 60-61, Y-a libn W Oaklane Br 61-65, Adult libn & br hd Germantown Br 65-. 9: ALA; PennLA. 10: Beta Phi Mu. 14: Ref, pub lib serv. 15: 220 Sumac st, Philadelphia Pa 19128.

QUINONES-SEDA, GRACE. b San German PR 11 Ja 28. 5: Polytechnic Inst of PR 44-47 9bio) BA; Syracuse 48-50 MSLS; Ludwing-Maximilians Universitut Munchen 56-57, 61-62 (Germanic Studies). 6: Sp, Ger. 7: Circ libn Polytechnic Inst of PR 50-54, Ref libn 54-56, 57-59, Asst libn 59-61; Libn IAU of PR Rio Piedras Reg Col 62-63; Ref libn UPR (Mayaguez) 63-67, Hd readers' serv dept 67-. 9: Asociacion Interamericana de Bibliotecarios y Documentalistas Agricolas; Sociedad de Bibliotecarios de PR (coord Mayaguez Region, mem Bd of Dirs 66, sec 67-). 10: Altrusa Internatl. 13: Yes. 14: Ref. 15: Gamboa #3, San German PR 00753.

QUINT, MARY D(OROTHEA). b Worcester Mass 4 Ja 13. 5: Worcester State Col 32-36 (Fr, Eng) BSE; Simmons 51-55 MLS; Boston U 64-66 (Pub Rel) MPR. 6: Fr. 7: Libn Metropolitan State Hosp, Waltham Mass 37-46; Libn Amer Optical Co, Southbridge Mass 46-52; Ref libn MIT Proj Lincoln, Lexington Mass 52-55; Admin libn AF Cambridge Research Ctr, Bedford Mass 55-60; Libn Spec Serv, Korea 60-61; Asst dir tech lib, Holloman AFB NM 61-64; Lib research specialist SyracuseU Research Corp 66-68; Dir Lib Careers, Syracuse NY 68-. 8: Profess consul, SLA; Consul, Amer Optical Co 55; Consul NY State Div of the Budget 68. 9: ALA; SLA (Upstate (NY) Chap: Exec Bd 67-69); ASIS; NYLA. 10: Bus & Profess Women; LWV. 12: Co-auth "Library Manpower" (68); Comp "Directory of Library Resources in Central New York" (68). 13: Yes. 14: Mgt, pub rel, recr. 15: 53 Marlborough st, Boston Mass 02116.

QUIRK, MARGARET (PARKER). b Fulton NY 29 Ja 21. 4: Francis E Quirk. 5: State U Col Geneseo NY) 38-42 (LS) BS; State U Col (Oswego NY) summers 50-54 (Educ) MS. 7: Elem tchr Brooklyn Sch, Wellville NY 42-43; Libn Elem Schs East side, Fulton NY 49-65; Libn Jr High Sch, Fulton NY 65-. 9: NY State Tchrs Assn; NYLA. 10: Delta Kappa Gamma. 14: Sch lib wk. 15: 620 Highland st, Fulton NY 13069.

QUON, FRIEDA (SEU). b Greenville Miss 4 Ag 42. 4: John Paul Quon. 5: UMiss 60-63 (Educ)BAE; Delta State Col summer 61-62; UMiss 63-65 MLS; LSU 66. 7: Lib asst Dept of Lib Sci UMiss summer 65, Asst Prof of Lib Sci UMiss 67-. 9: ALA; MissLA. 14: Pub rel, libnship educ, child lit. 15: PO Box 1519, University Ms 38677.

R

RABAUT, SISTER CELESTE (SISTER PALMYRE) IHM. b Detroit Mich 22 Jl 14. 5: Marygrove Col 32-34, 37-39 Lat BA; CatholicU summers 45-51 MS in LS. 6: Lat, Fr. 7: Sec Louis C Rabaut M C, Wash DC 35-36; Tchr St Matthew Sch, Detroit 39-41; Tchr Annunciation Sch, Detroit 41-45; Lib asst Marygrove Col 45-47, Admin asst 47-52, Asst libn 52-63, Acting libn 63-66, Asst libn 66-. 9: CatholicLA (Mich Unit: sec-treas 55-57, chm Col Sect 58-60, unit chm 66-68). 13: Yes. 14: Tech serv. 15: 8425 W McNichols, Detroit Mi 48221.

RABB, BERNICE BATEN). b Jenkinsville SC 2 F 20. 4: Paul Rabb Jr. 5: Allen U 37-41 (Fr) AB; Atlanta summer 55-58 MS in LS. 6: Fr, Sp. 7: Tchr Reed Street High Sch, Anderson SC 41-42; Tchr- libn Sims High Sch, Union SC 42-49; Tchr-libn Camp Liberty High Sch, Jenkinsville SC 49-54; Tch- libn Mcrorey-Liston Sch, Blair SC 54-60, Libn 60-. 9: NEA; SCEA; SCLA; Fairfield Co Sch EA. 10: McCrorey-Liston Sch Faculty; (sec) Book Club; Beta Phi Mu, 14: Catlg, illusrs of child bks. 15: Box 21-3, Jenkinsville SC 29065.

RABBAN, ELANA (GHITMAN). b Soviet Union 4 O 22. 4: Meyer Rabban. 5: Brooklyn Col 39-43 (Psych) BA; Columbia 45-47 (LS)MA. 7: Libn Soc Serv Brooklyn Pub Lib, Grand Army Plaza 43-46, 48-51; Libn Edgewood Elem Sch Lib, Scarsdale NY 57-. 9: ALA; NEA; NY State Tchrs Assn; Westchester LA; NYLA. 10: AAUW; PTA; Scarsdale Studio Wkshop; Friends of the Pub Lib; Amer Field Serv. 13: Yes. 14: Readers adv wk with child & adults, ref, child bks. 15: 123 Brite ave, Scarsdale NY 10583.

RABER, NEVIN WILLARD. b Fowlerton Ind 18 Jl 18. 4: Dorothy Irene Lockman. 5: Purdue U 38-42 (Soc Sci) BS; Ind U 46-47 (Hist) MA, 51-52 (LS) MA. 7: Agent operator Chesapeake & Ohio RR Co, Co, Peru Ind 38-42; 38-2; (1st Lt) US Army Artillery Unit Commander 42-46; Asst traffic manager Wm H Block Co, Indianapolis 47-50; Libn bus dept Indianapolis Pub Lib 50-51, 52-53; Grad asst Ind U 51-52; Dept head bus dept Inianapolis Pub Lib 53-56, Asst dir 56-62; Bus libn & Asst Prof of Bus Admin Ind U 62-. 8: Org Info Center of the Aerospace Res Applications Center; ARAC, 63 (Tech Info Consul & Mem of the Adv Bd 63-67); Consul Ind Lib Studies 68. 9: ALA; SLA (chm Bus & Finance Div Com on Standards for Collegiate Schs of Bus 68-); IndLA (Exec sec Insur Com 53-58). 10: Delta Nu Alpha; AAUP; Major USAR-Ret; Phi Kappa Tau; Beta Gamma Sigma. 13: Yes. 14: Bus info, lib planning & lib furniture & equipt, tech & mgt info systems. 15: 3701 Morningside dr, Bloomington In 47401.

RABKIN, JUDITH ROSE. b Glen Cove NY 18 O 42. 5: Syracuse 60-64 (Hist) BA, 65-66 MSLS. 7: Asst libn Nat Council on Aging, NYC 66-67; Catlgr UMiami 68-. 9: ALA. 14: Catlg. 15: 1913 S Ocean dr, Hallandale Fl 33009.

RABKIN, SARA (JANE) (NUTTER). b Rushville Ind 21 Je 42. 4: William I Rabkin. 5: UCincinnati 60-62 (Pre-,ed); BostonU 62-64 (Bio) AB; Simmons 64-65 (LS) MS. 6: Ger, Fr, Sp, Hebrew, Grk. 7: Lib clerk MIT 63-64; Service asst Mass Gen Hosp, Boston 64; Circ desk asst Harvard Med Lib, Boston 64-65; Jr ref libn F A Countway Lib of Med, Boston 65-66, Sr ref libn 66-67, Reg ref libn NERMLS 67-. 9: SLA; MassLA. 10: Harvard Library Club. 14: Ref. 15: 1514 Beacon st Suite 33, Brookline Ma 02146.

RABNER, ELLIOT. b LaGrange Ga 11 O 38. 5: Washington Sq Col NYU 50 (Hist) BA; NYU 51 (Educ) MA; Columbia 54 (LS) MS. 6; sp. 7: Br libn Jersey City Free Pub Lib, Jersey City NJ 52-55; Sr libn Newark Pub Lib, Newark NJ 55-57; Libn Vailsburg High Sch, Newark NJ 57-63; Libn Central Sch Dist 4, Plainview NY 63-. 8: NY State Dept of Educ Com for the Rev of Sch Lib Standards 66; Curr consul, NY State Proj for Internat Prog 67. 9: GaLA; SELA. 10: LI Educ Communications Coun RECENT OF US Govt grants, India & Hawaii. 13: Yes. 14: Ref, catlg. 15: John F Kennedy High School, Plainview NY 11803.

RABOWSKI, DOROTHY M (HILL). b NYC 30 D 15. 4: Joseph S Rabowski. 5: Brooklyn Col 40-42; Queens Col (NYC) 63 (Hist) BA, 65 MLS; Hunter Col 67- (Hist). 6: Fr. 7: Clk Brooklyn Pub Lib, Brooklyn NYC 36-41; Sec Conlan Electric Corp, Brooklyn NYC 41-47; Sec Commercial Selv Corp, NYC 47-51; Sec to asst supt of schs, Levittown NY 56-59; Tchr of lib Whitelaw Reid Jr High Sch, Brooklyn NYC 63-66, Libn-in-charge 66-. 9: ALA; NYLA; NYCASchL. 10: Phi Alpha Theta; AHA. 14: Tech serv. 15: 87-40 166th st, Jamaica NY 11432.

RABURN, JOSEPHINE (RILING). b Norman Okla 6 D 29. 4: Winston Raburn. 5: Southeastern State Col summers 46-48; Okla Col for Woman 46-49; OklaU 49-50, (Nutrition) BS, 63-64 MLS. 6: Fr. 7: Asst dietician Okla Col for Women 48-49; Asst supv dining hall OklaU 49-50; Lib asst Spec Serv, Ft Sill Okla 62-63, Ref circ libn, admin libn 64-65; Ref libn USAAMS Tech Lib, Ft Sill Okla 65-66; Instr lib sci Cameron State Col 66-. 8: Part-time instr lib sci OklaU 66. 9: ALA; AALS; OklaLA; SWLA; OklaEA. 10: AAUW. 14: Ref, lib educ. 15: 511 N 40th, Lawton Ok 73501.

RABY, EVA FREDA (ROSKIES). b Montreal Can 2 N 42. 4: Jacob Israel Raby. 5: McGill U 59-63 (Hist, Pol Sci) BA; Lond Sch Econ & Pol Sci Eng 63-65 (Diplomatic Hist) MSc (Econ); Simmons 65-66 MLS. 6: Fr, Yiddish, Hebrew, Ger, Russian. 7: Catlgr McGill U Com Lib 66-67, Asst libn 67-. 9: ALA. 14: Catlg, ref. 15: 4545 Lacombe ave, Montreal 249 Que Can.

RACHOW, LOUIS A(UGUST). b Shickley Neb 21 Ja 27. 5: York Col (York Neb) 44-48 (Chem) BS; Columbia 57-59 MS in LS. 6: Ger. 7: Stud asst York Col (York Neb) 45-48, Asst libn 48-49, Acting libn 49-50, Hd libn 50-54; Catlgr Henderson High Sch, Henderson Neb 54; Battery clk (Pfc) US Army, Ft Bliss Tex 54-55; Adjutant gen libn (Spec 3d Class) US Army V Corps Hq, Frankfurt Germany 55-56; Instr lib asst Queens Col (NYC) 56-57; Ser acquis asst Columbia U Law Lib 57-58; Asst libn Univ Club, NYC 58-62; Libn Walter Hampden Memorial Library at The Players, NYC 62-. 8: Consul theatre sect: UCal (San Diego) New Campuses Program 64, Ash Survey of Bk Resources Toronto Pub Lib Syst 65, Ash Survey Queens Borough Pub Lib 69; Lib adv bd Eugene O'Neill Memorial Theatre Foundation 66-; Sec Kelcey Allen Award Com 68-. 9: Amer Educ Theatre Assn; Amer Nat Theatre Acad; Amer Soc for Theatre Research; Intl Fed for Theatre Research; SLA (NY Chap: sec-treas Museum Gp 64-66); Theatre LA (Bd Dirs 65; recording sec 66-67; pres 67-); Amer Commun Theatre Assn; NY Lib Club; NY Tech Serv Libns. 10: Melvil Dui Chowder & Marching Assn; Archons of Colophon. 12: Asst ed "American Notes & Queries" (67-). 13: Yes. 14: Ref, research, spec collections. 15: 16 Gramercy pk, New York NY 10003.

RADDIN, SARAH (FRALICH). b Dover NJ 29 Ja 09. 5: Douglass Col 26-30 (LS) AB. 7: Sr asst ref Free Pub Lib, Trenton NJ 30-37; Dir Mem Lib, Roselle NJ 37-42; Libn Dover High Sch, Dover NJ 46-47; Br libn Free Pub Lib, Trenton NJ 47-49; Dir Mem Lib, bound Brook NJ 49-56; Dir Free Pub Lib, Cranford NJ 56-. 8: Consul Bound Brook Memorial Lib Bldg Expansion Program 64. 9: ALA; NJLA (exec dir NLW 65; sec 65-66). 11: Cranford Bus & Prof Women's Club Women of Achievement Award 65. 14: Admin, ref. 15: Cranford Pub Lib, Cranford NJ 07016.

RADEMACHER, RICHARD J. b Kaukauna Wis 20 Ag 37. 4: Mary Liethan. 5: Ripon 55-59 (Econ) AB; UWis 60-61 MS in LS; UInd 62. 7: Kellogg Pub Lib, Green Bay Wis: Lib asst 59, Ext hd 61-62; Asst libn USA, Ft Harrison Ind 62-64; Dir Kaukauna Pub Lib, Kaukauna Wis 64-66; Dir Eau Claire Pub Lib, Eau Claire Wis 66-; Coord Tri Valley Lib syst, Eau Claire Wis 66-. 9: ALA; WisLA (Indianhead Dist Chm). 10: Beta Phi Mu; Rotary. 14: Admin. 15: Eau Claire Pub Lib, 217 S Farwell, Eau Claire Wi 54701.

RADFORD, NEIL ANTHONY CHARLES. b Sydney Australia 15 S 41. 5: USydney 59-63 (Econ) BEc; UNew S Wales 64-65 (LS) Dip Lib; UChicago 66- (LS) AM; Lib Assn of Australia 66 Assoc. 6: Fr. 7: Lib asst USydney (Australia) 59-65, Circ libn 66; Research asst UChicago Grad Lib Sch 66-67; Visiting lecturer in Lib Sci UIll summer 68, Visiting Asst Prof summer 69; Ref asst UChicago 67-. 9: ALA; -ACRL; Lib Assn Australia. 10: Beta Phi Mu. 13: Yes. 14: Ref, automation, educ for libnship. 15: Grad Lib School, Univ of Chicago, Chicago Il 60637.

RADMACHER, CAMILLE J(ANE). b Monmouth Ill 14 Ap 17. 5: Monmouth Col 35-36. 7: Clk Warren Co Lib, Monmouth Ill 35-43, Circ libn 43-48, Co libn 48-; Exec dir West Ill Lib Syst, Monmouth Ill 62-. 8: Exec dir for Ill NLW 59-60; Ill State Lib Adv Com 63-. 9: ALA (chm Ill Memb Com 63-65; Recruitment Com 67); IllLA (Lib Devel Com; NLW Com; Nominating Com; Recruitment Com; Memb Com; chm Libn Citation Award Com). 10: Altrusa Club of Monmouth; Monmouth Col Commun Concert Lecture Bd. 11: Ill Libn Citation Award IllLA 67. 13: Yes. 14: Admin. 15: Warren County Lib 60-62 West Side sq, Monmouth Il 61462.

RADMACHER, MARY. b Monmouth Ill 24 N 15. 5: Monmouth Col 34-36 (Math); UIll 43-45 9eng) AB, 45-46 BS in LS. 7: Child libn Warren Co Pub Lib, Monmouth Ill 36-41, Ref libn 41-43; Asst catlgr dept UIll Lib (Urbana) 43-45, Asst agric libn Agric Lib 46; Ref libn Gary Pub Lib, Gary Ind 46-51, Hd ref dept 51-56; Chief libn Skokie Pub Lib, Skokie Ill 56-. 9: ALA; IllLA (life mem); Child Reading RT; Chicago Lib Club; LACONI. 10: Women's Nat Bk Assn; Art Inst of Chicago. 13: Yes. 14: Admin, lib designing & bldg, ref. 15: 1209 Sherwin, Chicago Il 60626.

RADO, GEORGIA (ZAKONYI). b Budapest Hungary. 4: Steven Rado. 5: Manhattanville Col of the Sacred Heart 52-53 Art); UCLA 54-58 (Theatre Arts) BS, 60-61 MLS. 6: Hungarian, Ger, Fr. 7: Sr lib asst circ dept UCLA Main Lib 59-61; Catlgr Aerospace Corp PC Engnr, El Segundo Cal 61-62; Asst libn Radio Corp of Amer, Van Nuys Cal 62-63; Libn-catlgr Hughes Aircraft Corp, Culver City Cal 63-65; Head Libn US AEC Lib, UCLA 66-. 9: SLA (Program Com 68 Conv). 14: Info retrieval, indexing, catlg, admin, computer scis. 15: 900 Veteran ave, Warren Hall Library, Los Angeles Ca 90024.

RADOFF, LEONARD. b Houston Tex 9 Ja 27. 4: Lisel Ephraim Radoff. 5: Rice 44-45, 46-49 (Hist) BA; UTex 63-64, summers 61-62 MLS. 7: Seaman 1c USN 45-46; Tchr Houston

Independent Sch Dist, Houston Tex 49-53; Silk screen operator Rustproof Sign & Metal Co, Houston Tex 53-59; Tchr Aldine Independent Sch Dist, Houston Tex 59-61, Sch libn 61-63; Acad asst UTex Grad Sch Lib Sci (Austin) 63-64; Pub serv libn Abilene Pub Lib, Abilene Tex 64-65; Lib dir Pasadena Pub Lib, Pasadena Tex 66-. 9: ALA; SWLA; TexLA; Tex Mun Libns Assn (pres 68-69). 10: Beta Phi Mu. 14: Pub serv. 15: 131 W Curtis, Pasadena Tx 77502.

RADTKE, EUGENE R(ICHARD). b Milwaukee Wis 23 Jl 39. 5: UIowa 61-62 (Classics); UWis 57-61 (Lat) BA, 62-63 (Classics) MA; UMinn 63-64 (Classics); West MichU 66-69 (Libnship) MSL. 6: Lat. 7: Readers' serv libn Albion Col Lib 69-. 9: ALA. 10: Phi Beta Kappa. 14: Readers' serv. 15: 419 N Berkeley st, Kalamazoo Mi 49007.

RADY, DONALD EDMUND. b Cleveland Ohio 1 D 30. 5: UNM 48-50, 51-55 (Anthrop) BA, MA; NorthwesternU 50-51 (Anthrop); UCal 58-61, 65-68 (Hist) PhD, MLS; Inter-AmerU summer 61 (Sp, Econ); USao Paulo 61-63 (Econ, Sci, Law). 6: Portu, Sp, Lat, Fr, Polish, Ger. 7: Fellow UNM 54-55; Lt USAF, Tex, NY, Mexico 55-57; William Harrison Mills Fellow, brazil 61-62; Researcher (Bolsista) Companhia Siderurgica Nacional Brazil 62-63; Asst prof WashU (St Louis) 63-65; Fellow (pre-doctoral) UCal (Berkeley) 65-67, Fellow (post-doctoral) 67-68; Visiting Asst Prof of Hist Cal State Col (Hayward) summer 68; Assoc Prof of Lib Admin Ohio StateU (Columbus) 68-. 8: Research Liaison with the Brazilian Nat Steel Co (Companhia Siderurgica Nacional) in Bus Hist and Info Systems; Do Research, Writing, and Tchg for the Air Force through the Reserve. 9: AHA; Conf latin Amer Hist; Latin Amer Studies Assn; ALA; SLA (pres-elect Dayton-Columbus Chap); OhioLA; Ohio Valley Gp Tech Serv. 10: Toastmasters; Air Force Assn; Brazilian Metals Assn; Phi Kappa Phi; Phi Alpha Theta; Phi Sigma Iota; ASIS; Pacific Coast Coun on Latin Amer Studies. 11: Mills Traveling Fellow 61-62; NDEA Post-Doctoral Fellow in Libnship 67-68. 12: "Brazil's Volta Redonda Steel Center" (69). 13: Yes. 14: Compar libnship, soc sci-humanities bibliog, lib automation. 15: 4011 Ave La Resolana NE, Albuquerque NM 87110.

RAE, GRACE (YODER). b Middlebury Ind 16 My 15. 4: Charles Rae. 5: Bluffton Col 34-38 (En) AB; UDenver 50-54 (LS) MA. 6: Ger. 7: Tchr-libn Higginsport Ohio 41-44; Bk saleslady Steinheimer;s Bks, Tucson 44-49; Libn Tucson High Sch, Tucson 49-. 9: ALA (Memb Com); NEA; SWLA (Coun; past sec child & yp, chm); Ariz State LA (sec, Legis Com, Recr Com); ArizEA (Teps Com). 10: Alpha Delta Kappa. 14: Admin, ref, readers guidance. 15: 3417 E Pima st, Tucson 85716.

RAEPPEL, JOSEPHINE EUGENIA. b Rochester NY 22 Ag 03. 5: URochester 26-30 (For Langs) AB; Columbia 34-37 (LS) BS, 37-49 (LS) MS; NYU 36-38 (Eng Lit) MA; Ore StateU 50-55 (Educ) EdD. 7: Lib asst URochester 30-35; Lib asst Union Theol Sem 35-42; Libn War Prisoners' Aid, NYC 42-43; Libn Bergenfield Jr-Sr High Sch, Bergenfield NJ 43-45; Libn (asst prof, assoc prof, prof) Albright Col 45-. 8: Assoc prof MarshallU summers 54, 56-58, 60. 9: ALA; PennLA (past chm Nominating Com; past auditor). 10: AAUP; AAUW; Kappa Delta Pi& Phi Delta Gamma; Altrusa Intl; AAUP. 12: "History of Libraries Before the Invention of Printing" (36); "College Students' Use of Public Library" (49); "Some Traits of Certain Student-Elected College Leaders" (54). 13: Yes. 14: Admin. 15: 920 N 4th st apt 508, Reading Pa 19601.

RAFFES, HELEN F (LEVIN). b NYC 6 Ap 15. 4: Abe Raffes. 5: Hunter Col 33-38 (Eng) BA. 6: Fr. 7: High sch libn Bd of Educ, NY 59-61; Sr libn Queens Borough Pub Lib, Queens NY 61-. 10: Phi Beta Kappa; Beta Phi Mu. 14: Child serv. 15: 143-25 41st ave, Flushing NY 11355.

RAFISH, ETHELYN (MILLER). b Minneapolis Minn 1 N 07. 4: Harry J Rafish. 5: UMinn 28 (Greek) BA, 39 BSLS; UCal (Berkeley) 30 (Ancient Studies) MA, 30-31; Columbia summer 39; UChicago summer 40 (LS). 6: Fr. 7: Tchg asst Greek Dept UMinn (Minneapolis) 29-30; Lib asst UMinn Lib (Minneapolis) 35-37, Tchg asst ref dept 36-37; Libn high sch, Bessemer Mich 37-42; Gen prof libn pub lib, Beverly Hills Cal 42-48; Libn Woodbury Col 58-60; Libn Reiss-Davis Child Study Ctr, Los Angeles 60-. 9: ALA; MedLA; SLA (chm Bio Sci Div 66-67; chm Com for Study of "Reminder" 68-69; SoCal Cha p; chm Bio Sci Gp 63-64); CalLA; Med Gp So Cal (Reg Planning Com 67-68). 14: Spec lib admin. 15: Anna Freud Research Lib Reiss-Davis 9760 W Pico blvd, Los Angeles Ca90035.

RAHAL, PATRICIA (MARY). b St John's Nfld 30 Ag 42. 5: MemorialU of Nfld 59-63 (Eng) BA; McGill 63-64 BLS. 6: Fr. 7: General libn MemorialU of Nfld 64-65, Acquis libn 65-. 9: CanLA; APLA (Nfld v-pres 65-66). 14: Acquis, univ libs. 15: 20 Larch pl, St John's Nfld.

RAHILLY, MAURICE F. b Roxbury Mass 4 Ja 24. 4: Patricia Marie (Kane). 5: Boston Col 47-51 (Econ) BS; Simmons 51-52 (LS) MS; Boston U 51-52; UPittsburgh 57-58. 6: Fr, Sp, Ital. 7: Boston Pub Lib: Extra asst 47-50, Asst 50-51, A-v libn 51-52; Admin intern US Dept of State Div lib & ref serv, Wash DC 52-53; Asst libn SUNY Maritime Col 53-56; Westinghouse Atomic Power Div, Forest Hills Penn: Asst libn 57-60, Libn & doc custodian 61-63; Chief research lib AVCO Missile Syst Div, Wilmington Mass 63-67; Proj mgr Info Dynamics Corp, Reading Mass 67-68; Chief libn 1st Nat Bank of Boston 69-. 8: Lectr & instr Maritime Col, Ft Schuyler NY 53-56. 9: Soc Tech Writers & Publishers (Ed staff 65-66); Nat Security Indus Assn (Tech Info Adv Com); Amer Bankers Assn; ASIS; Amer Inst Banking; SLA (Boston Chap: v-pres & Prog Chm 68-70, pres-elect 70-71; Divisions: Regl Corresp Documentation Progress 60-61; Aerospace Div: Bus mgr Proceedings I Print 63-65). 10: Christian Family Movement; Toastmasters Internat; Boy Scouts, Troop Committeeman; Bak Officers Assn. 12: Ed & comp of Bibliogs; Lists of Periods & Docs. 14: Lib admin, systems & services, computer applications for libs, tech info serv mgt. 15: 165 Franklin st, Arlington Ma 02174.

RAINEY, LAURA J. b Benton Ill. 5: UCLA 48 (Hist, Intl Rel) BA, 50 (Hist) MA, 65 MLS. 6: Fr, Sp. 7: Libn Braun & Co, Los Angeles 50-57; Libn Foote, Cone & Belding, Los Angeles 57-65; Classified docs catlgr Rand Corp, santa Monica Cal 65-66; Ref libn TRW Systems, Redondo Beach Cal 66; Tech processing libn Sci Ctr N Amer Rockwell, Thousand Oaks Cal 66-. 8: Lecturer SLA wkshop for lib asst, Los Angeles 67. 9: SLA (So Cal Chap: advertising mgr Bulletin 57-59, chm Bus & Finance Div 62-63, recording sec 65-66, chm Aerospace Div 68-69; chm Local Arrangements Com 1968 Conf; bus mgr "Sci-Tech News" 68-; Govt Info Serv Com 67-69); ASIS. 10: UCal Lib Schs Alumni Assn. 14: Catlg, rel. 15: 14332 Riverside dr, Sherman Oaks Ca 91403.

RAINS, MARION E(dward). b Highland Ohio 24 Ag 17. 4: Mildred Hinshaw. 5: Wilmington Cpl 35-39 (Bus educ) BS in Ed; U No Iowa 64; Drake 65; UIowa 64-67 (Educ) MA; UMinn 68. 7: Bus educ tchr Winchester High Sch, Winchester Ohio 39-42; Bus educ tchr W Elkton high Sch, W Elkton Ohio 42-43; Farmer New Providence Iowa 43-66; Bus educ tchr Steamboat Rock High Sch, Steamboat Rock Iowa 63-64; Tchr-libn Hubbard High Sch, Hubbard Iowa 64-66; Circ libn William Penn Col 66-68, Libn 68-. 9: ALA; NEA; IowaLA; IowaStateEA. 10: American Friends Serv Com; Kiwanis; Farm Bureau. 14: Circ, ref. 15: 301 N 3rd, Oskaloosa Ia 52577.

RAIRIGH, SUSAN L. b NYC 14 Je 43. 5: Wilson Col 61-65 (Hist) AB; Simmons 66-67 MLS. 7: Ref libn Meyer Lib StanfordU Lib 67-68, Intl docs libn 68-. 9: CalLA. 14: Ref. 15: 5 Newell rd #6, Palo Alto Ca 94303.

RAIRIGH, WILLIAM NELSON. b Ridgely Md 8 Ja 15. 5: St John's (Md) 32-36 (Govt) AB; UNC 36-39 (Pol Sci) MA; UMd 39-41 (Pol Sci); Drexel 49-50 MS in LS. 7: Admin asst USAF Air Transport Command 42-46; Instr pol sci UMd 46-48; Asst Prof pol sci SW Tex State Col 48-49; Prof asst Enoch Pratt Free Lib, Baltimore 50-52, Admin asst to asst dir 52-59; Asst libn Jt Ref Lib of Pub Admin Serv, Chicago 59-61; Admin Kent-Caroline Pub Libs Assn, Ridgely Md 61-. 8: Resource specialist "Local Public Library Administration" 60-64; Adv com "Public Library Systems in the United States" 65-68. 9: ALA-PLA (chm Com on Interlib Coop 63-65); MdLA. 15: Ridgely Md 21660.

RAISCH, JUDITH ANN. b Altoona Penn 27 F 44. 5: Marywood 62-66 (Math) BA; West Res 66-67 MSLS. 6: Fr. 7: Ref libn Battelle Mem Inst, Columbus Ohio 67-. 9: ALA; SLA; ASIS; ColumbusLA. 14: Ref. 15: 505 King ave, Columbus Oh 43201.

RAITT, MILDRED DANDRIDGE. b Baltimore Md. 5: Goucher 43-47 (Eng) AB; Columbia 47-48 BS in LS, 54-55 (Eng) MA. 6: Fr, Ger. 7: Order libn Principia Col 48-54, Asst libn 55-57; Ref asst Folger Shakespeare Lib, Wash DC 57-58; Asst libn C of C of US, Wash DC 58-62; Asst chief acquis Smithsonian Inst 63-. 9: SLA; DCLA. 15: 3024 Tilden st NW, Wash DC 20008.

RAJCIC, JULIETTE (BIDWELL). b Troy NY 26 O 38. 4: Slavko B Rajcic. 5: SUNY(Ablany) 59-62 (Eng) BA (cu Cum Provisional Secondary Certif in Eng, 62-63 MLS Perm Certif as Sch Libn, 67 NY State Pub Libns Certif. 6: Sp. 7: Libn 1-12

Draper Schs, Schenectady NY 63-64; Eng instr SUNY Agric & Tech Col (Cobleskill) 65; Sr high libn Amsterdam pub schs. Amsterdam NY 65-66; Libn K-6 Copiaque Pub Schs, Copiaque NY 66-67; Eng instr & libn Commun Col of Allegheny Co 67-69. 14: Col ref in Eng & soc scis. 15: 404 DeWalt dr, Pittsburgh Pa 15234.

RAJEC, ELIZABETH MOLNAR. b Bratislava Czechoslovakia 31. 4: Stephen L Rajec. 5: U of Foreign Langs 53 (Ger); Columbia 63 (Ger) BS; Rutgers 64 MLS. 6: Hungarian, Czech, Slovak, Ger, Russian. 7: Interpreter, Inst of Cultural Rel, Budapest 51-53; Libn Inst of Czechoslovak Culture, Budapest 54-56; Fashion asst Frankfurter-Graf, NY 57-63; Libn City Col (NY) 64-. 14: Catlg. 15: 500 E 77 st, NYC 10021.

RAJKAY, LESLIE. b Magyarovar Hungary 26 N 16. 4: Alice von Mihalovich. 5: Royal Hungarian Ludovka Mil Acad 34-38 (Mil Sci) Diploma & Commsn; Johns Hopkins 57-63 (Chem Engnr) BS. 6: Hungarian, Ger, Fr. 7: Royal Hungarian Army (Capt) Comp Cmdr Batl Exec Off, Aide-de-Camp 38-45; Foreman Carr-Lowrey Glass Co, Baltimore 50-52; Sup Fuld Bros Inc, Baltimore 52-56; TECH LIBN Armco Steel Corp, Baltimore 56-. 8: Abstractor, Chem Abstract Serv; Abstractor & res assoc, Documentation Serv, Amer Soc for Mtals; Materials Adv Panel, Proj LEX (D of D Tech Thesaurus). 9: SLA (Baltimore Cha: past pres); Amer Soc Metals; Amer Inst Chem Engnrs 9(Materials Div). 10: Amer Translators Assn. 14: Ref, metallurgy, chem, engnrg. 15: 627 Aldershot dr, Baltimore Md 21229.

RAKOWICZ, MARY LOUISE. b McKees Rocks Penn 31 D 37. 4: Rodney Webb. 5: Upper Iowa col 55-57 (Eng); Luther Col 57-59 (Eng) BA; UWis 60 (LS); UWash 65-66 (LS) M Libnship. 6: Fr. 7: Eng tchr & libn high sch, Waukon Iowa 59-61; Libn high sch, shelton Wash 61-67; Libn & a-v coord high sch, Lacey Wash 67-69. 8: Summer fac Wash state U Holland Lib Tech Serv 66, 67. 9: NEA; ALA; WashEA; WashStateASchL. 14: Catlg, tech serv. 15: Rte 2 Box 182B, Shelton Wa 98584.

RALPH, ESTHER (RICHARDSON). b Malvern Penn 29 Jl 18. 4: Gordon Maurice Ralph. 5: State Tchrs Col W Chester Penn 36-40 (Math, Fr) BS in Ed; Drexel 40-41 BS in LS. 6: Fr. 7: Asst libn reader serv Haverford Col 41-. 9: ALA. 14: Catlg. 15: 422 Berkley rd, Exton Pa 19341.

RALPH, RUTH (BERG). b Crosby NDak 11 Ag 24. 5: Interstate Bus Col (Fargo) 42-43 (Secretarial); ND StateU 66 (LS). 6: Norwegian. 7: Sec & timekeeper Northwest Airlines, Fargo N Dak 43; Sec engring dept Northwest Airlines, Dayton Ohio 43-44; Timekeeper Northwest Airlines, Minneapolis 44; Hd personnel dept US Government, Savannah Ga 44-45; Deputy clk of court Divide Co, Crosby N Dak 52-56; Hd libn Divide co Lib, Crosby N Dak 57-. 8: State Nat Lib Week Com for N Dak. 9: NDakLA (sec 65-66). 10: Federated Women's Club; Girl Scouts; Homemakers. 12: "Divide County History Book" (64). 14: State & local hist. 15: Box 261, Crosby ND 58730.

RALSTON, CAROL (GUNDERSEN). b Brooklyn NY 3 S 42. 4: George F Ralston. 5: Beaver Col 60-64 (Eng) BA; Drexel 65 MSLS. 7: Ref asst New Haven Free Pub Lib, New Haven Conn 65-66, Child libn Fair Haven Br 66-67, Asst to hd processing catlgr 67-. 9: ConnLA. 15: 86 Dana st, West Haven Ct 06516.

RALSTON, DONALD McKENZIE. b Reed City Mich 29 D 14. 4: Tommyanne Clark. 5: LehignU 32-33 (Ind Engring); UMich 33-37 (Mech & Industrial Engring) BS; George WashingtonU 49-52 (Accounting); UCLA 65-66 MLS. 7: Communications off (Lt jg) USNR USS Melvin 44-46; Reg personnel off Off of Price Admin, San Francisco 42-44, Asst to dist dir 46-47; Asst mgr ind rel Paraffine Co, Emeryville Cal 47-49; Asst dir personnel Gen serv Admin, Wash DC 49-50; Asst chief classified sect Federal Housing Admin, Wash DC 38-42, Deputy dir personnel 50-52; For serv off Dept of State 52-64; Asst to libn UCal (Santa Barbara) 66-. 8: For serv inspector, Far East & Lat Amer 60-62; For Serv Inst 63. 9: ALA; CalLA. 10: Phi Kappa Tau; Council on For Affairs; For Serv Assn. 14: Admin. 15: 937 Roble lane, Santa Barbara Ca 93103.

RALSTON, JACK LEONARD. b Kan City Mo 13 O 29. 4: Carol Buckels. 5: Conservatory of Music of Kan City 46-50 (Music, Organ) BM, 54-56 (Music, Organ) MM; Peabody 63-67 MLS. 7: Personnelman 2/c USN San Diego, USS Consolation 50-54; Lib asst music dept Kan City (Mo) Hub Lib 57-58; Organist, asst choirmaster Dauphin Way Methodist Church, Mobile Ala 58-60; Music libn UMo (Kansas City) 60-. 8: Consul to Music Libs, Evangel Col 64, Wis State U (Whitewater) 67; Assoc dir, Inst for Studies in Amer Mus, UMo (Kansas City) 67-. 9: MusLA; Mid-West MusLA. 10: Phi Mu Alpha Sinfonia; Beta Phi Mu; Pi Kappa Lambda. 12: Composed "Come, Thou Fount of Every Blessing" (66). 14: Hymnody, 19th century Amer music. 15: Conservatory Lib, 4420 Warwick blvd, Kansas City Mo 64111.

RALSTON, PAULINE L. b Albion Penn 5 Mr 17. 5: Thiel Col 35-39 (Eng) BA; Syracuse 45-46 (LS) BS. 7: Clk pub lib, Greenville Penn 42-44; Circ asst Allegheny Col Lib 44-45; Ref libn Salem Pub Lib, Salem Ohio 46-48; Syracuse U Lib; Grad asst order dept 45-46, Ref libn 48-66, Asst hd ref dept 66-. 8: Tchr ref course Sch of Lib Sci Univ Col, Syracuse U spring terms 64, 65, 67. 9: ALA. 10: Beta Phi Mu; Syracuse U Profess Libns. 14: Ref wk. 15: Syracuse Univ Lib, Syracuse NY 13210.

RAMBLER, LINDA KAY. b Londonderry Twp Dauphin Co Penn 18 Ja 40. 5: Millersville State Col 57-61 (Eng & LS) BS; West Res 61-64 MS in LS; Lehigh 67- (Eng). 6: Ger, Fr. 7: Jr & Sr high sch libn Selinsgrove Area Sch Dist, Selinsgroce Penn 61-63; Army libn lib div spec serv sect USA civilian, Frankfurt Germany 64-66; Lehigh U: Humanities catlgr 66-68, Ref libn MART Sci & Engr Lib 68-. 9: ALA; PennLA; LehighValleyLA. 10: Alpha Beta Alpha; Beta Phi Mu; Mod Lang Assn. 14: Personnel mgt, recr, lib educ, ref. 15: rte 5, Bethlehem Pa 18015.

RAMBO, BARBARA (GRABEY). b Fracville Penn 31 Ag 34. 4: Richard W Rambo. 5: Kutztown State Tchrs Col 53-54 (LS), 63-f. (LS) BS in Ed; Drexel 66-. 6: Sp. 7: Libn Royersford Pub Lib, Royersford Penn 55-56; Libn Great Valley Sr High Sch, Malvern Penn 65; Libn Valley Forge Jr High Sch, Wayne Penn 65-. 8: Com Chester Co In Service Day.4 9: NEA; ALA;Penn State EA. 10: Yellow Springs Assn. 14: Reders adv. 15: BonnieBrae rd, Rt 1, Spring City Penn 19475.

RAMBO, HELEN MARIE). b Hutchinson Kan 29 Ja 27. 5: Northwest Nazarene Col 45,49 (Hist) A; UWash summers 53-57 (LS) ML. L. 6: Sp. 7: Tchr Emmett High Sch, Emmett Ida 50-52; Tchr-libn Merrill High Sch, Merill Ore 52-53; Tchr-libn Bly High Sch, Bly Ore 53-54; Libn Miller Jr High Sch, Aberdeen Wash 54-57; Asst libn & catlgr Northwest Nazarene Col57-. 9: PNLA; IdaLA (SEC Col & Univ Div 65-66, Dorothy Canfield Fisher Award Com 64). 10: AAUW; Bus & Prof Women. 14: Catlg. 15: Northwest Nazarene Col, Nampa Ida 83651.

RAMBO, MARJORIE. b Chester Penn 31 Jl 24. 5: Millersville State Col 41-45 (Educ) BS; Peabody Col 46-48 (LS) MA. 7: Sch libn Scott High Sch, Coatesville Penn 45-47; Field libn USA, Ger 48-53; Libn US VA, Coatesville Penn 53-57; Base libn USAF, Korea 57-58, japan 58-62; Staff libn 1st Air Force, Stewart AFB NY 62-67; Staff libn 13th Air Force, Clark AFB Philippines 67. 9: ALA (chm Noming Com, Armed Forces Sect 67-68). 12: Comp "PACAF Bibliography: Aeronautics (60, 61). 14: Admin, acquis. 15: 13AF (DPSL), APO San Francisco Ca 96274.

RAMER, FAYE (PADGETT). b Darlington Fla 10 Mr 30. 4: Maxwell Ramer. 5: Fla State U 46-47, 59-61 (Elem ed) BS, 64-66 (LS) MS. 6: Sp. 7: Tchr Bay Co Sch Syst, Panama City Fla 59-63; Libn Cive Elem Sch, Panama City Fla 63-65; Libn Cedar Grove Elem Sch, Panama City Fla 65-66; Libn Everitt Jr High Sch, Panama City Fla 66-. 9: NEA; ALA; FlaASchL; Fla A-V Assn; BayCoSchLA; BEA; BayClrTA. 10: Kappa Delta Pi; Alpha Delta Kappa; PTA. 14: Ref, a-v serv. 15: 4625 N Lakewood dr, Panama City Fl 32401.

RAMER, JAMES DAVID. b Metropolis Ill 14 Jl 27. 5: Occidental Col 48-50 (Philo) AB; Columbia 56-57 (LS) MS. 6: Sp, Fr. 7: Documents catlgr (us quartermaster Corps, Ft Lee Va 46-48, Head documents lib 52-56; Engnr libn NYU 56-57; Engnr & Phys Sci libn UMd 57-59; Engnr & phys sci libn Columbia U 59-64; Head libn UNC (Charlotte) 64-67; Sch of Lib Serv Columbia U 67-68; Assoc Prof Emory U 69-. 10: Phi Beta Kappa. 12: Comp ""Bibliography on mplasma Physics and Magnetohydrodynamics; (59). 13: Yes. 14: Admi, rare bks. 15: Div of Libs, Emory Univ, Atlanta Ga 30322.

RAMEY, MARY LOUISE (RAGLAND). b Salisbury NC 10 Ap06. 4: Vernon Grafton Ramey. 5: UNC (Greensboro) 23-27 (Educ) BA, summer 28; Emory 28-29 (LS) AB. 6: Sp, Fr, Lat. 7: Lib asst Danville Pub Lib, DANVILLE Pub Lib, Danville Va 29-43; Len asst Jones Mem Lib, Lynchburg Va 43-44; Head of catlg dept Danville Pub Lib, Danvile Va 44-66, Lib dir 66-. 9: ALA; SELA (Catlg Div); VaLA. 10: Little Theatre of Danville Va; Amer Theater Productions. 14: Catlg, ref, geneal. 15: Rt 1 Box 457, Danville Va 24541.

RAMIREZ, WILLIAM LOUIS. b San Francisco 17 Ag 25. 4: Margaret Patricia Kelly. 5: USan Francisco 44-48 (Hist) BS; UCal 52-54 BLS. 6: Sp, Fr. 7: San francisco Pub Lib: Libn ref dept 49-50, Sr libn ref dept 50-53, 55-56, Head Libn bind & Repair Deputy 57-59, Head Hea Libn Sunset Br Lib 59, Prin libn Br lib BrLib 60-63, Prin libn dept of rare bks & spec collections 63-. 8: Org & catlgd lib for Salvation Army Offs Train Col, San Francisco 59-62; Spec consul Latin Amer Lib, Oakland 66-. 9: CalLA (Loc Arr Chm 1963 Conv; Chm Cal Lib Hist Com 63-64); San Francisco Bay Area Ref Libns Coun (pres 66); CalLA (pres-elect Golden Gate Dist 69; chm Com on Soc Responsibility of Libs 68-69; Coun-at-Large 68); Pub Lib Execs Central Cal (chm Legis Com 68-69); rep UCal Lib Schs Alum Assn 69-70; CalASchL (Northern sect co-chm Human Rel Com 69). 10: Beta Phi Mu. 13: Yes. 14: Rare bks, spec collections, ref serv, Cal hist, lib serv to Spanish speaking, ethnic gps, soc concerns. 15: 515 Vicente st, San Francisco Ca.

RAMON, ADOLPH I. b San Antonio Tex 6 Je 33. 5: UTex 51-56 (Bacteriology) BA; Incarnate Word Col 59-64 (Med Record Sci) BS; TrinityU 65- (Hosp Admin); Our Lady of the Lake Col 68 (LS). 7: Hosp corpsman (HM3) USN 56-58; Lib asst San Antonio Pub Lib, San Antonio Tex 59-63, Libn (staff) 65-67; Med rec internship Santa Rosa Med Center, San Antonio Tex 63-64, Asst med rec libn 64-65, Chief med rec libn 67-. 9: Amer Assn Med Rec Libns; MedLA; ALA-AHIL; ARMA; Tex Assn Med Rec Libns (treas San Antonio Chap 64 & 69). 10: Amer Hosp Assn; Amer Col of Hosp Admin; Sigma Iota Epsilon. 14: Spec libs (sci, med, hosp). 15: 247 St Francis ave, San Antonio Tx 78204.

RAMSAUR, EDMUND (GEORGE) JR. b Lincolnton NC 4 Ap 29. 4: Barbara Meyer. 5: Mars Hill Col 47-49; Duke 49-53 (Hist) AB, MA; UNC 53-55 (Hist) MSLS. 6: Fr. 7: Circ & ref libn Mercer U 55-56; Period libn E Carolina Col 56-58; Ref asst Enoch Pratt Free Lib, Baltimore 58-62Community Col 62-63; Catlgr Frostburg State Col summer 63; Asst catlg libn URI 63-66, Tchr of catlg in ext div Feb-June 64; Catlgr Wilson Col 66-68; Libn Eaton-Burnett Jr Col 68; Libn Cecil Commun Col 68-. 9: Md Assn of Jr Cols. 14: Catlg. 15: 108 Jarmon rd, Elkton Md 21921.

RAMSAY, GRACE G. b Guelph Ont Can 4 S 11. 4: D Scott Ramsay. 5: Toronto 31-34 (Household Econ) BA. 7: Libn in chg Golden Mile Br Scarborough (Ont) Pub Lib 59-62; Libn Ont Hosp Serv Cmmsn, Toronto 62-. 9: SLA (treas Toronto Chap 65-67). 15: 2195 Yonge st, Toronto 7 Can.

RAMSEY, AUCY (MAYFIELD). b Raleigh Miss. 4: Howard Earl Ramsey. 5: USo Miss 29-32 (Sp, Fr) BS; George Peabody Col summers 54, 55, 57, 58 MALS; UDenver summer 65 (LS). 6: Fr, Sp. 7: Sp & soc sci tchr Leaf River Consol High Sch, Petal Miss 33-35; Tchr Mize High Sch, Mize Miss 35-37; Eng tchr Sem High Sch, Seminary Miss 37-38; Eng tchr Durvis High Sch, Durvis Miss 38-41; Libn Union High Sch, Union Miss 41-43; Libn Starkville High Sch, Starkville Miss 43-45; Libn Drew High Sch, Drew Miss 45-46; Libn Cleveland High Sch, Cleveland Miss 52-58; Libn Lovington High Sch, Lovington NM 58-. 9: NEA; ALA; NMEA; NMLA; LovingtonEA. 10: AAUW. 13: Yes. 14: Catlg, ref. 15: 1400 S 9th st, Lovington NM 88260.

RAMSEY, EVELYN (ADAMS). b Elizabethtown Ky 17 Ag 18. 4: Charles Ramsey. 5: Blue Mountain Col 35-39 (Soc Sci, Modern Langs) BA; West Ky State Col 39-40; Catherine Spalding 62-64 MSLS. 6: Sp. 7: Chief file clerk Armored Bd, Ft Knox Ky 41-46; Libn Army Ground Forces B 2, Ft Knox Ky 46-47, Ed asst 47-48; Libn Kyoto Japan 48-49; Libn N Hardin High Sch, Vine Grove Ky 62-. 9: NEA; KyASchL; KyEA; KyLA (pres 4th dist). 10: Duplicate Bridge Club. 14: Ref. 15: 608 Cherrywood dr, Elizabethtown Ky 42701.

RAMSEY, JACK. b Kan City Kan 12 Je 22. 4: Sue Worsley. 5: UKan 40-42, 43-45 (Pol Sci) AB; UIll 45-46 (LS) BS, 46-47 (Pol Sci) MS. 7: Libn asst ref dept NY Pub Lib 47-48; Admin asst Stockton Pub Lib, Stockton Cal 48-49; Co Libn Solano Co Free Lib, Fairfield Cal 49-82; Chief LIBN Glendale Pub Lib, Glendale Cal 52-59; Chief Lib Rel Dept H W Wilson Co, Bronx NY 59-65; Rp Carl J Leiel Inc, La Puente Cal 65-66; Chief libn Glendale Pub Lib, Glendale Cal 66-. 8: Consul Clark Co Lib Dist Nev 68. 9: ALA (Dir Exhib Round Table); SLA; CalLA; NY Lib Club (pres 63); Assn Child Libns; Pub Lib Execs Assn So Cal (v-pres 59). 10: Beta Phi Mu. 15: 3501 St Elizabeth rd, Glendale Ca 91206.

RAMSEY, MARIAN (MORGAN). b Sharon Penn 12 F 28. 4: Richard C Ramsey. UColo 46-50 (Educ, Eng BA; UDenver 53-55 (LS) MA. 5: UColo 46-50 (Educ, Eng) BA; UDenver 53-55 (Libnship) MA, 67 (Educ); UMd (Heidelberg, Germany) 60 (Ger). 7: Elem tchr pub schs, Junction City Kan 50-52; Pub schs, Portland Ore 52-53; Elem libn pub schs, Denver 53-55, Jr high libn 55-57; Child libn pub lib, Long Beach Cal 57-59; Elem libn ArmcHEEGGermany 59-61; Jr high libn pub sch, Denver 61-67; Catlg Pub Schs, Denver 68-. 8: Catlgd industrial lib, C A Norgren Co, Littleton Colo summer 63. 9: ALA;ColoLA; ColoASchL; Denver Clr Tchrs Assn; NEA. 10: Denver Symphony Soc; Friends of Denver Pub Lib; ColoEA. 14: Yp serv, sch libnship. 15: 5334 E Utah pl, Denver 80222.

RAMSEY, PAULINE CATHERINE. b Toledo Ohio. 5: Ohio State U 32-35 (Fr, Bus Admin) BSC in Ed; Columbia 40-41 BS in LS. 6: Fr, Polish, Sp. 7: Catlgr Columbia U 41-47; Catlg libn Notre Dame U (Ind) 47-48; Libn catlg & acquis Argonne Nat Lab, Chicago 48-49; Libn catlgr NLM, Wash DC 49-51; Libn catlg & ref Bur ofSHIPS (Navy, Wash DC 51-58; Libn Ordnance Tech Intelligence Agency, Arlington Va 58-60; Libn Off of Tech Serv, Sev, Wash DC 60-64; Info spec Army Lib, Pentagon, Wash DC 64-. 8: Instr in catlg, Columbia U Lib Sch 46-47. 9: SLA 12: Co-ed "Poland in the British Parliament, 3 v 4662). 14: Catlg, ref, acquis, admin. 15: 4115 Wisconsin ave NW, Wash DC 20016.

RAMSEY, VERNA MARGARET. b Los Angeles Cal 6 Ap 05. 5: UCLA 25-27 (Eng) BA; UCal (Berkeley) 37-38 (Libnship) Certif. 6: Sp, Fr, Ger. 7: Santa Ana Pub Lib, Santa Ana cal: Lib asst 25-37, Asst ref libn 37-45, Ref libn 45-60; Orange Co Pub Lib, Orange Co Cal: Asst ref libn 60-65, Hd ref serv 65-67, Hd adult serv 67-68, Hd collection mgt 68-. 9: ALA; CalLA; OrangeCoLA. 10: AAUW; LWV; Friends of Santa Ana Pub Lib. 14: Ref, acquis, catlg. 15: 1125 N Flower apt B, Santa Ana Ca 92703.

RAND, LAWRENCE W. b Port Angeles Wash 27 N 33. 5: Seattle Pacific Col 51-53, 55-57 (Music Ecuc) BA ED: Brigham Young U summer 58; UWash 60-62 M Libr. 6: Sp. 7: Musician Adj Gen Corps US Army, Ft Lewis Wash 53-55; Tchr Seattle Sch Dist 57-60; Tchr-libn San Francisco Unified Sch Dist 62-63; Libn Emery ,unified Sch Dist, Emeryville Cal 63-67; Instr So Ore Col summers 65-67; Instr UAlaska summer 68; Dist libn Fairfax Sch Dist, Fairfax Cal 67-. 8: Lib 21, Seattle World's Fair 62; Prof of Libnship, So Ore Col summer 65. 9: ALA; CalASchL; Cal TA; CalLA; Assn Child Libns (San Francisco); Sch Lib Assn of Marin. 10: ACLU. 14: Ref, catlg, geneal. 15: 31 Corte Ortega 21, Greenbrae Ca 94904.

RANDALL, ANN (MICHELLE) KNIGHT. b Brooklyn NY 19 O 42. 4: Julius T Randall Jr. 5: Barnard 59-63 (Govt) BA; NYU 63-64 (Pub Admin); Columbia 65-67 (LS) MS, 69- (LS). 6: Fr, Ger. 7: Adjustment examiner (GS 7) US Soc Security Admin, NY 63-64; Lib asst USA Spec Serv, Bamberg Ger 64-65; Libn trainee Brooklyn Pub Lib, NY 65-67; Ref libn Queens Col Lib 67-. 8: Indexer for ERIC docs, Clearinghouse on the disadvantaged, spec proj 68; Volunteer abstracting, Schomburg Collection of Negro Hist and Lit NY; consul Neighborhood Col Lib, Brooklyn NY. 9: ALA; SLA; (NY Documentation Gp Exec com); LACUNY (Spring Inst Com & Pres Offr). 10: Beta Phi Mu 67. 13: Yes. 14: Ref, documentation, admin, lib educ. 15: 114 Linden blvd, Brooklyn NY 11226.

RANDALL, AUGUSTUS (CAESAR). b Arcadia La. 4: Ercell Powel. 5: Morehouse Col 31 BA; Hampton Inst 37 (LS) BS; Miami U (Oxford Ohio) 60. 6: Fr, Gk. 7: Head libn Morehouse Col 31-32; Asst ref dept Atlanta U 32-40; Tchr-libn Lynch Colored High Sch, Lynch Ky 40-43; Civilian employee WPAFB supply sect, Dayton Ohio 43-45; Ref asst Dayton Pub Lib, Dayton Ohio 45-47; Head Libn Wilberforce U 47-50; Ref asst Dayton Pub Lib, Dayton Ohio 50-. 8: Head Libn, Payne Theol Sem, 58-64. 9: ALA; OhioLA; KY Negro EA (pres Lib Div). 10: Dayton Pub Lib Staff Assn. 11: Rockefeller Found Fellowship, 36-37. 14: Catlg, ref. 15: 109 S Monroe st, Xenia Ohio 4535.

RANDALL, BARBARA (BARTLEY). b Oak Park Ill 26 Jl 16. 4: Gordon E Randall. 5: Lawrence Col 36-38 (Eng) BA; UIll 38-39 BS in LS. 7: Personal libs Stephens Col 39-41; Br libn TVA, Chattanooga Tenn 42-46; Br libn Biol Div ORNL, Oak Ridge Tenn 50-52; Ref libn IBM-ASDD, Yorktown Heights NY 61-. 9: SLA. 14: Ref. 15: 2240 Van Cortlandt circle, Yorktown Heights NY 10598.

RANDALL, DORIS IRENE CAIRNS). b Mazomanie Wis 17 Ag 21. 4: Leon D Randall. 5: UWis 39-43 (Comparative Lit) BA, 43-44 BLS. 6: Fr. 7: Asst Ref libn Ind U 44-46; Ref libn Lansing Pub Lib, Lansing Mich 46-50; Asst educ libn USo Cal 50-51; Asst educ libn Los Angeles Pub Lib 51-52; Catlgr Mich State U 57-59;Br libn Rubidoux Br Riverside Co, Riverside Cal 60-62; Ref libn Tulare Co Free Lib, Visalia Cal 64-. 9: ALA;

CalLA. 10: AAUW. 14: Ref, catlg. 15: 2800 W Laurel lane, Visalia Ca 93277.

RANDALL, DUDLEY (FELKER). b Wash DC 14 Ja 14. 4: Vivian Spencer. 5: Wayne U 46-49 (Eng) BA; UMich 49-51 MALS. 6: Fr, Russian. 7: Lincoln U (Mo): Ref libn 51-52, Catlgr 52-53, Ref libn 53-54; Head tech serv Morgan State Col 54-55, Head pub serv 55-56; Hosp libn Wayne Co Pub Lib, Wayne Mich 56-63, Head Ref Interloan 63-. 9: MichLA (chm Hosp Sect 62-63). 10: Detroit Soc for the Adv of Culture & Educ. 11: Tompkins Award, Wayne State U, 62, for fiction & poetry, 66 for poetry. 12: Fiction, articles & poetry in magazines, poetry in anthologies; "Poem Counter Poem" (66); "For Malcolm; Poems on the Life and the Death of Malcolm X" (67); Ed "Cities Burning" (68); Ed "Broadside Press" (65). 13: Yes. 14: Ref. 15: 12651 Old Mil pl, Detroit 48238.

RANDALL, FERN AVERIL (MRS). b Westphalia Kan 22 Jl 05. 5: Winona State Col 23-25, 38-40(Elem Educ) BS; Col of St Catherine 40-41 BS in ls. 77: Elem tchr Kellogg Pub Sch, Kellogg Minn 28-31; Elem tchr St Charles Pub Sch, St Charles Minn 31-34; Lib asst child dept Cossitt Lib, Memphis Tenn 41-44; Head chid dept Winona Pub Lib, Winona Pub Lib, Winona Minn 44-45; Head child & Sch DEPT Cossitt Lib, MEMPHIS Tenn 4557; Head child serv Memphis Pub Lib, Memphis Tenn 57-66, Coord child serv 66-. 8: Bk consul Memphis Juvenile Court, 56-61, Memphis Crippled Child Hosp56-58. 9: ALA-CLA (Memb Chm Tenn 52); TennLA; SELA (Sch & Child Sect: chm 59-60, v-chm 64-65). 10: AAUW; Bus & Pof Womes Club; Altrusa Club. ; Adv mem Marquis Biograph Lib Soc. 13: Yes. 14: Child serv. 15: 2760 Harbert ave, Memphis Tenn 38111.

RANDALL, FERRIS SEAMAN. b Monterey Mex 25 My 09. 4: Dorothy Stuart. 5: Crane Jr Col 28-30 AA; Chicago 30, 46-47 AB, 47-48 BLS. 6: Sp. 7: Jr asst Newberry Lib, Chicago 2532; Salesman Horikoshi Co, Chicago 33-37; Asst manager Personal Finance Co, Tampa Fl 38-43 (Sgt) USAF 43-45; Ser libn Stanford U 48-53; Asst dir So Ill U 53-65, Head Libn 65-. 8: Survey of lib resources & serv of both SoIllU campuses, 60-61. 9: ALA; IllLA. : AAUP; Beta Phi Mu. 12: Ed IllLA "Record (54-58). 3: Yes. 10: AAUP; Beta Phi Mu. 12: Ed IllLA "Record" (54-58). 13: Yes. 14: Admin. 15: 51 Hillcrest dr, Carbondale Il 62901.

RANDALL, MICHAEL H. b Tulsa Okla 3 Ap 45. 5: UCal (Riverside) 63-67 (Eng) AB; UCLA 67-68 MLS. 6: Fr, Ital, Lat, Sp. 7: Catlgr UCal (Santa Barbara) 68-. 9: ALA; CalLA; So Cal Tech Proc Gp; Libns Assn of UCal. 10: Beta Phi Mu; UCal Lib Schs Alumi Assn. 13: Yes. 14: Catlg, tech processes, univ libs, lib hist. 15: Univ of Cal, Santa Barbara Ca 93106.

RANDALL, RUTH ESTHER (ROSS). b Garnett Kan. 5: UAlta 52 (Hist) BEd, 63 (Soc Studies) MEd; UWash 62 MLS. 6: Fr. 7: Tchr Pub sch, Alta Can 25-58; Libn high sch Edmonton Pub sch Bd, Can 58-. 9: CanLA; ALA; AltaLA; AltaTA Lib Coun. 10: Bus & Prof Women's Club; Univ Women's Club. 14: Clsf & catlg (child & ya lit). 15: 904 9915-115 st, Edmonton 10 Alberta Can.

RANDAZZO, CORRINE OHSEN. b Vidalia La 23 S 32. 4: Samuel Randazzo. 5: U Southwestern La 50-54 (Upper Elem Educ) BA; LSU summers 55-58 MS in LS; UOkla summer 66 (LS); U So Miss 68 (LS). 6: Sp. 7: Coun Camp Nakanawa, Mayland Tenn summer 54; Libn: St Martin Parish Schs, St Martinville La 54-59, USoMiss Natchez 62-65, Natchez Adams High Sch, Natchez Miss 59-66; Sch lib supv Natchez Adams Co Schs, Natchez Miss 66-; Instr in lib sci U So Miss summer 68; Instr NDEA Inst UOkla summer 68. 9: MissLA; MissSchLA (v-pres & pres); MissEA; ASCD; ALA; NEA. 10: PTA. 13: Yes. 14: Ref, bibliog, bldgs. 15: 103 Carter, Vidalia (Concordia) La 71373.

RANDEL, JANET (BELKNAP). b Franklin Ind 25 Ja 10. 4: William Peirce Randel. 5: Denison U 30 (Eng) AB; Fla State U 61 (LS) MA. 7: Ed asst "Marriage and Family Living, Tallahassee Fla 52-55; Staff Strozier Lib Fla State U 59-64; Catlgr Fogler Lib UMe 65-. 10: Beta Phi Mu; Phi Kappa Phi. 14: Catlg. 15: Fogler Lib Univ of Me, Orono Me 04473.

RANDLE, GRETCHEN (RUNGE). b Haddonfield NJ 22 O 18. 4: David S Randle. 5: Syracuse 36-40 (B us Admin, Educ) BS ; Drexel 47-49 BS in LS. 7: Sec Radio Corp of Amer, Camden NJ 41-46, Lib asst 46-49; Libn Burroughs Corp, Paoli Penn 49-65; Libn The Newcomen Soc in N Amer, Downington Penn 65-. 9: SLA; Internat Coun of Museums; Amer Assn of Museums; ALA; PennLA. 10: Phi Kappa Phi. 12: Ed "Correlation Index Document Series and PB Reports" SLA (53); Auth "Electronic Industries; Information Sources" (68). 13: Yes. 14: Ref, rare bks, ed. 15: P.O. Box 113, Downington Pa 19335.

RANDLE, LILLIAN ELIZABETH BIBB. b Booneville Ark 2 My 05. 5: Galloway Womans' Col 22-26 (Eng) BA; ColoradoU summer 26 (Eng); UCal (Berkeley) summer 28 (Eng); Ark State Col summer 52, 53 (LS). 7: Tchr Prescott Sr High Sch, Prescott Ark 26-27; Tchr Shawnee High Sch, Joiner Ark 34; Tchr-libn Booneville Jr High Sch, Booneville Ark 54-56; Libn Logan Co Lib, Booneville Ark 56-57; Tchr Booneville Sr High, Booneville Ark 28-33, Journalism libn 57-60; BHS Lib Jr-Sr high Sch Lib, Booneville Ark 60-. 8: Mem Ark Adv coun on Secondary Educ 60-64; Libn Methodist Ch 63-. 9: ArkEA (pres Sch Libs Div 67-69); ArkLA. 10: Delta Kappa Gamma; Rotary-Anns. 13: Yes. 14: Reading guidance, ref. 15: 603 N Broadway, Booneville Ar 72927.

RANDOLPH, EARL J. b Koshkonong Mo 13 O 14. 4: Lilly Renfrow. 5: Colo State U 33-37 (Chem) BS; UMich 38-39 ABLS, 45 AMLS. 7: Period libn Colo State U 37-38; Ref libn UMo (Rolla) 39-41; Ref libn Dayton Pub Lib, Dayton Ohio 41; US Army Signal Corps & Field Artillery (Capt) 41-45; Bibliog Ga Inst of Tech 45-46; Libn UMo(Rolla) 46-. 9: ALA; SLA; Amer Coc Engnr Educ; MoLA. 10: Trustee, Rolla Pub Lib; Rotary Club. 14: Admin. 15: 40 Hawthorne, Rolla Mo 65401.

RANEY, A LEON. b Charleston Ark 14 Ja 39. 4: Mary Lee Wilson. 5: Arkansas State Tchrs Col 56-60 (Hist) BSE; Ind State U 61-62 (LS) MS; UOkla 68-69; IndU 69- (LS). 06: Sp, Ger. 7: Tchr of Amer hist Paris High Sch, Paris Ark 60-61; Libn Grant Parish Lib, Colfax Ark 62-64; Asst libn Ark State Col 64-65, Dir of Lib 65-66; Acquis libn UOkla 66-67, Act asst dir for tech serv 67-. 9: ALA; SWLA; OklaLA. 10: Phi Delta Kappa; Beta Phi Mu; Sigma Tau Gamma; Lions Club. 14: Catlg, acquis. 15: 404A Wadsack, Norman Ok 73069.

RANEY, CAROL HELENA. b Spokane Wash 28 Ag 29. 5: Reed Col 47-48; Wash State U 49-52 (Hist) BA; UCal(Berkeley) 52-53 BLS. 6: Fr, Ger. 7: Catlgr UCal(Davis) 53-56; Yale U: Sr subj catlgr 56-59, Revisor ser div 59-61, Head ser div 61-65; 1st asst catlg libn Joint Bank-Fund Lib Internat Monetary Fund, Wash DC 65-66; Chief catlg div Smithsonian Lib, Wash DC 66-69; Exec sec ALA-RTSD 69-. 9: ALA-RTSD (chm Ser Sect 64-65, v-pres 68-69); SLA; Ch & SynagogueLA; CalLA; ConnLA; NY Tech Serv Libns; DCLA (treas 68-69). 10: Phi Beta Kappa; Phi Kappa Phi; Phi Alpha Theta. 14: Catlg, ser. 15: American Library Assn, 50 E Huron st, Chicago Il 60611.

RANK, JANE BRADFORD. b St Paul Minn 20 O 14. 5: Vassar 32-35 (Art); UMinn 36 (Art) BA. 7: Child libn Anoka Pub Lib, Anoka Minn 60-62, Catlgr & ref br libn Ramsey Co pub Lib, St Paul 62-. 15: 493 Portland ave, St Paul Mn 55102.

RANKEY, BROTHER EDWARD G SA. b Bethlehem Penn 26 Mr 18. 5: Moravian Col 36-40 (Hist) BA; Syracuse 48-49 BS in LS. 6: Ger. 7: Catlgr Lehigh U 43-60; Libn St Pius Xth Sem (Garrison NY) 60-. 15: St Pius Xth Sem Lib, Graymoor, Garrison NY 10524.

RANKIN, C (ATHERINE) ALICE. b NY 7 Ja20. 5: Douglass Col 37-41 (LS) BA; Columbia -56 (LS) MS. 7: Asst libn (Nopco Chem Co) Diamond Shamrock Chem Co, Nopco Chem Div, Harrison NJ 43-45, Libn 45-. 9: SLA (NJ Chap: pres 61-62, Consul Off 63-); ASIS; ACS (Chem Lit Div). 10: Zonta Club. 14: Spec libs (chem), amin. 15: Diamond Shamrock Chem Co Nopco Chem Div, Harrison NJ 07029.

RANSOM, DORIS. b Quapaw Okla 23 Ag 21. 5: Joplin Jr Col 39-41; UMo 46-48 (Eng) AB; UMich 48-49 MALS. 7: Catlgr LC 49-53; Catlgr Ore State Col 53-5; Chief catlgr Emory U 56-58; Head catlg dept UCincinnati 58-65; Unit supv, Descr Catlg Div LC 65-. 9: ALA-RTSD (chm Coun of Reg Groups; CCS: Subj Catlg Com). 14: Catlg. 15: 1652 Preston rd, Alexandria Va 22302.

RANSOM, DOROTHY (HINZ). b Meriden Conn 18 N 28. 4: Stanley Austin Ransom Jr. 5: Douglass Col 46-50 BA in LS. 6: Sp, Ger. 7: Ser catlgr & exch libn Yale U Lib 50-52; Asst libn Stevens Inst of Tech 52; Asst libn Nat Ind Conf Bd, NYC 53-55, Libn 56-57; Ref libn Patchogue Pub Lib, Patchogue LI NY 58; Catlgr S Huntington PubLib, S Huntington LI NY 62; Asst ref libn Half Hallow Hills Community Lib, Melville LI NY 64-. 9: ALA; SLA (Bus Div); Suffolk Co (NY) LA. 10: AAUW; Huntington Hist Soc; PTA; Friends of the Heckscher Mus; DAR; Friends of the Huntington Pub Lib. 14: Ref, catlg. 15: 39 Irwin pl, Huntington LI NY 11743.

RANSOM, MARY LOU (THOMASSY). 03McDonald Penn 17 Ap 15. 4: Alured Chaffee Ransom. 5: Carnegie 33-35; UPittsburgh 35-37 (Econ) BS; Carnegie 56-59 MLS; Kent State U 62-64 (Educ). 6: Fr. 7: Circ & acquis asst UPittsburgh 56-58; Supv & ref asst Sci-Tech Carnegie Pub Lib, Main, Pittsburgh 58-59; Libn TCCU Team Inst of Educ, Kabul Afghanistan 59-60; Asst catlg libn, Asst ref libn Kent State U 60-68, Chief lib & info servs Ctr for Urban Regionalism 68-. 8: Consul: Kabul, Afghanistan, Tchrs Col Columbia U Libn Spec 59-60; Kabul, Afghanistan; Consul The Asia Foundation, Wkshops with USIS. 9: ALA-ACRL; OhioLA; No Ohio Tech Serv Libns; Coun of Planning Libns. 10: AAUW; Faculty Prof of Womens Club; University Women; Rotary ANNS; Alpha Gamma Delta. 14: Ref, catlg, urban affairs. 15: 1501 Stratford dr, Kent Oh 44240.

RANSOM, STANLEY AUSTIN JR. b Winsted Conn 24 Ja 28. 4: Dorothy Hinz. 5: Yale 45-46, 48-51 BA; Columbia 51-53 MLS. 6: Fr. 7: (Cpl) Rifleman & Chaplains asst US Army Infantry, Japan 46-48; Ser asst Yale U 49-51; NY Pub Lib: Searcher & ser asst ref dept 51-52, Ser catlgr ref dept 52-55, Gen asst Bloomingdale Br 56; Asst dir Huntington Pub Lib, Huntington LI NY 56-58, Dir 58-. 8: Adv Com Annual Cong for Libs, St Johns U 63. 9: ALA (Life mem); NYLA; (chm RTSS Mem Com 68-69); Suffolk Co LA (pres 62-64; chm Inst of Coop 58; chm Inst on New Directions in Lib Serv 62); Nassau-Suffolk LA (Adv Com, Com on Ref & Res Resources 63-65); Westchester LA; ConnLA; LPRC; Long Island Lib Resources Coun Inc (trustee 65-, sec 65); Suffolk Co Lib Dirs Assn (pres 69). 10: Huntington Cof C; SAR; PTA; Friends of Heckscher Museum; Elder Old First Presbyterian Ch; Rotary. 12: Ed "Suffolk County Library Assciation Data (57-58, 61-62); Auth "Jupiter Hammon of Long Island, Americas First Negro Poet (69). 13: Yes. 14: Admin, ref, pub rel, lib bldgs. 15: Huntington Pub Lib, 338 Main st. Huntington LI NY 11743.

RANZ, JAMES. b Atlanta Neb 21 Jl21. 4: Delores Christensen. 5: Neb State Tchrs Col 38-42 (Com) BS; UMich 46-48 MALS; UIll 50-60 (LS) PhD. 6: Fr, Ger. 7: US Army Infantry 42-46; Map libn UIll (Urbana) 48-49, Catlgr 49-51; Prep libn UVa 51-53; Admin asst UIll (Urbana) 53-55; Dir of Libs UWyo 55-62; U Libn UBC 62-63; Dean of Academic Affairs UWyo 64-. 8: Educ consul on the formation of a new liberal arts col in Sun City Ariz, 64; Nat Adv Coun for Correctional Manpower & Training (67-69). 9: ALA (Coun & mem var coms): Can LA; Bibliog Center for Res, Denver (chm Exec Com 56-58); Bibliog Soc of Can; (pres 62); WyoLA (pres 59). 12: "Printed Book Catalogues in American Libraries: 1723-1900 ALA (64). 13: Yes. 14: Catlg, admin. 15: Univ Sta Box 3302, Laramie Wy 82070.

RAPETTI, VINCENT A. b Floral Park NY 26 Ja 26. 5: Rollins Col 46-50 (Fr, Hist) AB; UMich 50-52 AMLS; Laval U & &Grenoble summers 49-50 (Hist, Fr AM. 6: Fr. 7: Libn Soc of the Four Arts, Palm Beach Fla 52-57: Admin asst tech serv & ext Orlando (Fla) Pub Lib 57-61; Head catlg dept Nassau (NY) Lib System 61-62, Deputy dir 62; Records admin Launch Ops Center Kennedy Space Center 63-64; Ling -Temco-Vought libn Kennedy Space Center, Fla 64-. 9: ALA; SLA; Amer Records Mgt Assn; FlaLA. 10: Phi Kappa Phi. 14: Tech & pub serv, admin. 15: 1116 Glen Arden Way, Altamonte Springs Fla 32701.

RAPHAEL, ANNE (WAGNER). b Boston 12 Ap 41. 4: Bertram Raphael. 5: UCal (Berkley) 64-65 MLS; Mt Holyoke Col 58-62 (Physiology) BA. 6: Fr. 7: Circ, catlg clerk, Lib Mt Holyoke Col 59-62; Circ Boston U Sch of Educ Lib summers 58, 59; Indexing & filing RAND Corp Lib, Santa Monica Cal summer 62; Gifts & exch UCLA Lib summer 63; Period Operations Research Lib Arthur D Little Inc, Cambridge Mass 62-63. Ref Bus Research Lib 63-64: Ref & interlib loan NASA Ames Research Center, Moffett Field Cal 65-66; Lib systs analyst Info Gen Corp, Palo Alto Cal 66-. 9: SLA; ASIS (San Francisco Bay Chap; sec 67-68, v-chm 68-69; treas Nat Convention 69). 10: Sierra Club; Beta Phi Mu; Intercol Outing Club Alum Assn. 14: Lib automation, sci ref, info retrieval, systs analysis. 15: 176 Osage ave, Los Altos Cal 94022.

RAPP, MARIE A. b Grand Rapids Mich 16 O 05. 5: West Mich U 23-27 (Eng) AB; UMich 34-37 BLS; UMex 46. 6: Sp, Fr, Portu. 7: Eng tchr Bad Axe High Sch, Bad Axe Mich 27-29; Asst Battle Creek Pub Sch Lib, Battle Creek Mich 29-31; Catlgr & ref libn Battle Creek Col Lib 31-33; Ref libn Battle Creek Pub Sch Lib, Battle Creek Mich 33-37; Sr ref asst Detroit Pub Lib 37-46; Cryptographic tech WAC 44-45; Ref libn Benjamin Franklin Lib, Mex City Mex 46-48, Assoc dir 48-51; Dir Lib Reg Fundamental Educ Center (Unesco), Patzcuaro Michoacan Mex 51-57; Ref libn undergrad div UIll(Chicago) 57-59; Acquis libn Columbus Mem Lib Pan Amer Union, Wash DC 59-60; Circ libn UIll (Chicago Circle) 60-. 8: Lib consul to Inter-Amer Defense Col, on Ford Foun grant, in Wash DC & Latin-Amer, Dec 62 - Ap 63. 9: ALA (treas Internat Rel Round Table 60-64); IllLA; Chicago Lib Club. 10: Pan-American Bd of Educ; AAUW; Pan-American Coun. 14: Ref, circ, Lat Amer bibliog. 15: 401 Fullerton pky apt 601E, Chicago Il 60614.

RAPPAPORT, LOUISE (KOHL). b NYC 22 S 22. 4: Sidney M Rappaport. 5: Hunter Col 39-43 (Home Econ) BA; Drexel 61-64 BS in LS. 7: Asst ref libn LaSalle Col 64-. 9: ALA; PennLA. 10: United World Federalists. 14: Ref. 15: 1423 Mellon rd, Wyncote Penn 19095.

RAPPE, IDALIA (HELENA). b Mlawa Poland. 4: Zbiginiew Rappe. 5: AssumptionU (Windsor) 59-63 (Eng) AB; UMich 65-67 AMLS. 6: Polish, Fr, Ger, Sp. 7: Sec Arthur S Fitzgerald & Co, Windsor Ont 59-63; Lib asst UWindsor Lib, Windsor Ont 63-67, Sect hd ser catlg 67-. 14: Catlg. 15: 2795 Mark ave, Windsor 21 Ont Can.

RASBACH, SISTER MARY ALICE OSF. b Herkimer NY 26 Jl 25. 5: St Elizabeths Hosp Sch of Nursing (Utica NY) 42-45 RN; Catholic U 52-53 BS in Nursing, 55-56, 57 MS in LS. 7: Head nurse in maternity St Elizabeth Hosp, Utica NY 45-46; St Josephs Hosp, syracuse, NY: Head nurse in med-surgical 47-48, Dir of out patient dept 49-52, Head nurse in emergency room 54-55, Libn Sch of Nursing & Med Lib 56-68; Instr in lib tech Maria Regina Col 68-. 8: Lecturer in Health & Physiology, Maria Regina Col, 57-62. 9: CathLA (chm-elect Hosp Sect 65); Nat League for Nurs; Cemt NY League for Nurs (chm Hist Source Com). 10: Beta Phi Mu. 14: Ref, lib educ. 15: Maria Regina College 1024 Court st, Syracuse NY 13208.

RASMUSSEN, DOROTHY MARIE. b Minn 27 Ja 25. 5: Gustavus Adolphus Col 44-46, 47-49 (Eng) AB; UMinn 52-53 (LS) MA. 7: Ref libn Gustavus Adolphus Col 54-59; Asst libn in chg of adult serv Skokie Pub Lib, Skokie Ill 59-. 9: ALA; IllA. 10: Great Bks Group. 14: Ref, bk sel. 15: 1209 W Sherwin, Chicago 60626.

RASMUSSEN, GORDON EDWIN. b Highland Park Mich 13 D 32. 4: Virginia Louise Kolze. 5: N Central Col 50-54 (Eng) BA; UDenver 60-61 (LS) MA; UIll 66-67 (LS). 07: Elem tchr pub schs, Crystal Lake Ill 54-55; Elem tchr pub schs, Wheaton Ill 55-56, 58-59; Spec 3 US Army 56-58; Elem tchr pub schs, Adams Co Colo 59-60; Lib asst UDenver 60-61; Circ libn No Ill U 61-. 9: IllLA. 14: Circ-res. 15: 815 N Ninth st, DeKalb Ill 60115.

RASMUSSEN, NANCY (HAMM). b Watseka Ill 9 Mr 43. 4: Eric Rasmussen. 5: UIll 61-65 (Eng) BA; NoIllU 67-68 (LS) MA. 6: Sp. 7: Short-term missionary United Presbyterian Ch, Osaka Japan 65-66; Tchr, Kirkland Ill 66-67; Period libn No Ill U 68-. 9: IllLA. 10: Pi Lambda Theta. 14: Period, ser, catlg. 15: 912 North Seventh st, DeKalb Il 60115.

RASMUSSEN, PHYLLIS JOANNE. b Blair Neb 20 Je 42. 5: Dana Col 60-64 (Eng) BA (Magna cum laude); UMinn 64-66 MA in LS. 6: Danish, Norwegian, Swedish, Ger. 7: Libn Nordsjoellands Centralbibliotek, Helsingor Denmark 67-68; Libn Frederiksberg Kommunebiblioteker, Copenhagen Denmark 68; Asst libn Dana Col 69-. 9: ALA; NebLA. 10: Amer Scand Found; AAUW; Alpha Chi. 14: Ref, catlg. 15: 333 North 18th st, Blair Nb 68008.

RAST, ELAINE (KIRKPATRICK). b Chicago 28 Ag 33. 4: Lawrence R Rast. 5: Concordia Tchrs Col 51-56 (Educ) (BS) Ed; Rosary Col 56-63 MALS; Northwestern 59-60. 6: Ger. 7: Lib asst Concordia Col (River Forest Ill) 54-56; Libn Walter High Sch, Melrose Park Ill 56-57; Ref libn Kansas City (Mo) Pub Lib; Hd reg campus tech serv div Ohio State U (Columbus). 9: ALA; -ACRL; -RTSD; OhioLA; Ohio Valley Tech Serv Libns. 14: Catlg, ref, admin. 15: 450 Haymore ave S, Worthington Oh 43085.

RATCLIFFE, THOMAS EDWARD. b Roanoke Rapids NC 14 S 11. 5: UNC 29-34 (Amer Hist) AB; UIll 39-40, 49 BS in LS, MS; UParis 48-49 (Fr Civilization). 6: Fr. 7: Personnel Survey TVA, Chapel Hill NC 33; Credit investigator & br dept head Personal Loan Dept Nat City Bank, NYC 34-39; Asst agric libn UIll(Urbana) 40-41; Field Artillery US Army (Maj) 42-46; UIll Lib(Urbana); Asst acquis dept 46-48, Undergrad libn 49-52, Ref libn & asst prof lib admin 52-, Assoc prof 55-, Prof 69-. 8: . 9: ALA. 10: AAUP. 13: Yes. 14: Ref. 15: 604 W Nevada st, Urbana Ill 61801.

RATHBONE, MARGARET. b Latchford Ccheshire Eng 1 O 09. 5: Marot Jr Col 28-30; Conn Col 30-32 (Hist) BA; Simmons 32-33 (LS) BS. 6: Fr, Ger, Slavic. 7: Asst libn Paul Pratt Mem Lib, Cohasset Mass 34-36; Lib asst Fogg Art Museum Harvard U 36-37; Catlgr & clsf, later admin libn Dumbarton Oaks Research Lib, Wash DC 37-57; Libn Human Resources Research Off, Wash DC 57-63; Lib consul Corcoran Sch of Art, Wash DC 65-; Libn Washington Gallery of Modern Art, Wash DC 65-67; Lib consul to Corcoran Gallery of Art 68-. 9: DCLA. 14: Acquis, ref, bibliog (fine arts). 15: 3039 O st NW, Wash DC 20007.

RATHBUN, LOYD RAYMOND. b Los Angele s 2 Je 11. 4: Betty Moore. 5: USoCal 28-42 (Music) MA, 58-59 MSLS. 7: Oboist Kansas City Philharmonic Orchestra, Kan City Mo 34-41; Oboist Warner Bros Pictures, Burbank Cal 41-58; Lecturer in Oboe USoCal 41-52; Libn Hughes Aircraft Co, Los Angeles 59-61; Libn MIT Lincoln Lab, Lexington Mass 62-. 9: SLA (chm Personnel Com 62-66; Spec rep to Nat Lib Week 63-64, pres Boston Chap 67-68; Bd of Dirs 69-72); ALA; NELA; MassLA. 10: Libraria Sodalitas; Beta Phi Mu; US Power Squadron. 15: MIT Lincoln Lab Lib Lexington Mass 02173.

RATHER, JOHN CARSON. b Brooklyn NY 31 Mr 20. 4: Lucia Johnson. 5: Amherst 38-42 (Eng) AB; Columbia 50-51 (LS)MS. 6: Fr, Sp. 7: (S/Sgt) Cryptographer Army Airways Communications System, Air Corps 42-46; Managing ed; Chess Review, NYC 46-49; Exec ed Travel Magazine, NYC 49-50; Assoc ed Medical Economics, Rutherford NJ 50; Spec recruit LC 51-52; Catlgr descr catlg div LC 52-54; Assoc Sch of Lib Serv Columbia U 54-56; Asst dir UBuffalo Libs 56-58; Spec for Col & Research Off of Educ, Wash DC 58-62; Asst chief descr catlg div LC 62-67, Spec in tech proc research 67-. 9: ALA; ASIS. 11: Joseph Towne Wheeler Award, Columbia Sch Lib Serv, 51. 12: Ed "Library Research in Progress" (59-62); Jt auth "Conversion of Retrospective Catalog Records to Machine-Readable Form". 13: Yes. 14: Admin, catlg, lib automation. 15: 4114 Woodbine st, Chevy Chase Md 20015.

RATHER, LUCIA (JOHNSON). b Durham NC 12 S 34. 4: John Carson Rather. 5: URichmond 51-53 UNC 53-55 (Hist) AB, 55-57 (LS) MS. 7: Catlgr LC 57-64, Bibliog 64-66, Lib info syst spec 66-. 8: Mem staff, ISAD/MARC Inst 68-69. 9: ALA. 10: Phi Beta Kappa. 12: Jt auth "The MARC II Format" (68). 13: Yes. 14: Lib automation, catlg. 15: 4114 Woodbine st, Chevy Chase Md 20015.

RATTRAY, MARJORIE (ELIZABETH). b Newport Me 30 Je 08. 5: UWash 25-29 (Phys ed) BS, 64-67 MLS. 6: Fr. 7: Bkkeeper Sunset Oil Co, Seattle 41-55, Bkkeeper Oscar Lucks Co, Seattle 55-59; Bkkeeper Groninger Co, Seattle 59-62; UWash: Lib asst 62-66, Subj specialist 66-67, Catlgr 67-. 9: ALA; SLA; PNLA. 10: Beta Phi Mu; Viewridge Commun Club; UWash Fac Women's Club. 14: Catlg. 15: 6849 47th NE, Seattle Wa 98115.

RATZ, CAROLYN (CHANCE). b Nevada Ohio 7 Jl 39. 4: Ronald Ratz. 5: Kent State 57-61 9health & Phys ed) BS, 64-66 MLS. 6: Sp. 7: Health & phys educ tchr: Columbus (Ohio) Pub Schs 61-62, Crawford Co (Ohio) Pub Schs 62-64; Asst libn Harding High Sch, Marion Ohio 65-66; Circ libn Heidelberg Col 66-. 9: ALA; OhioLA; Ohio Col Assn. 10: AAUP. 14: Circ, ref, ya, child lit. 15: 1131 Dean st, Bucyrus Oh 44820.

RATZLOFF, MARY LOU (EKSTROM). b Burlington Iowa 23 Ja 19. 4: Dan Olin Ratzloff. 5: Kan City Mo Jr Col 35-37 AA; UKan 37-43 (Nursing) BS & RN; West Res 63-67 (LS) MS. 7: Staff nurse Crile Veteran's Hosp, Cleveland Ohio 63-64; Sch of Nursing Lib Fairview Sch of Nursing, Cleveland Ohio 67-; Med libn Fairview Gen Hosp, Cleveland Ohio 67-. 15: 9210 Evergreen dr, Parma Oh 44129.

RAUB, HAROLYN. b Kingston Penn 18 My 46. 5: Wilkes Col 64-68 (Eng) (certif elem ed) BA; Simmons 68-69 (LS) MS. 6: Fr. 7: Processing asst Harford Co Bd of Educ Lib Processing Ctr, Bel Air Md 67, Asst in child room 68. 9: ALA. 14: Sch lib, instr materials ctr. 15: 15 Lexington rd, Bel Air Md 21014.

RAUCH, JEROME S. b Jersey City NJ 31 O 25. 5: Columbia Col 43-47 (Biol Sci) AB; Columbia 52-57 (LS) MS. 7: Staff libn NY ACAD OF Med Lib, NYC 52-54; Libn, Jewish Chronic Diseases Hosp, Brooklyn NY 54-56, Acad of Med of NJ, Bloomfield NJ 56-60, Endo Labs, Garden City NY 60-61, NJ Col of Med & Dentistry, Jersey City NJ 61-66; Chief med libn UPenn Sch of Med 66-. 9: MedLA (Subcom on Recr, Program Com 1965 Meeting); SLA. 14: Admin, equip, microfilm/photocopy serv. 15: UPenn Sch of Med Med Lib, Philadelphia Pa 19103.

RAUHALA, BARBARA (FERN). b Oakland Cal 24 O 37. 505: UCal (Berkeley) 55-59 (Art) AB, 59-61 MILS. 5: UCal (Berkeley) 55-59 (Art) AB, 59-61 MLS. 7: Child libn: NY Pub Lib 61-62, San Leandro Community Lib, San Leandro Cal 63-64. Marin Co Free Lib. Marin Co Cal 64-. 9: CalLA: Assn of Child Libns No Cal (chm Bk Review Com 65-66). 14: Wk with child. 15: 5831 Huntington ave, Richmond Ca 94804.

RAULINS, IDA ELIZABETH. b Huntingdon Tenn 29 Ag 20. 5: LA Polyech Inst 39-42 (Eng) BA; UIll 42-43 BS in LS. 7: Acquis asst UIll(Urbana) 43-45; Sr order libn LSU(Baton Rouge) 45-47; Field libn US Army, Frankfurt Germany 47-49; Post libn US Army, Stuttgart Germany 49-50; Sr circ libn LSU (Baton Rouge) 50-53, Sr ref libn 53-54; Head ref dept La State Lib 54-. 9: ALA; LaLA; SWLA. 14: Ref. 15: Apt 19, 2800 July, Baton Rouge La 70808.

RAUM, HANS L. b Phila 26 J140. 5: Penn State U 58-62 (Liberal Arts) BA; Drexel 62-64 MS in LS. 06: Ger. 7: Educ libn State Lib of NJ 62-64; Air Nat Guard USAF, Wichita Falls Tex 64-65; Ref asst Pattee Lib Penn State U 65-67; Assoc undergrad libn 67-. 9: ALA; AAUP. 10: Delta Chi. 14: Ref, bldgs & furnishings. 15: 626 S Pugh st apt 18, State College Pa 16801.

RAUNIO, LEO LORENZ. b Tampere Finland. 4: Elfriede Carla Raunio (Kolling). 5: Pacific Union Col 51-53 (Theol & Biblical lang) BA; USoCal 55-57 MS in Ed, 63-65 MS in LS. 6: Finnish, Swedish, Norwegian, Danish. 7: Seventh-day Adventists: Missionary, Swedish Lapland 47-50, Sch prin, Huntington Park Cal 53-55, Sch prin, simi Cal, Missionary for Maricopa Indians, Ariz 57-60; Tchr Glendale Union Acad, Glendale Cal 60-63; Catlgr Los Angeles Pub Lib 63-65; Supv reader serv Andrews U 65-. 15: 220 University blvd, Berrien Springs Mi 49104.

RAUSCH, GEORGE JAY JR. b Aurora Ill 9 Ap 30. 4: Margaret Singleterry. 5: Aurora Col 54; N Central Col 49-51, 54-55 (Psych) BA; UIll 55-61 MA, PhD (Hist), MLA. 6: Sp. 7: Research asst Dept of Hist UIll 59-60; Acquis asst Lib UIll 61-62; Chief Soc Sci Lib & Lecturer in hist, Wash State U 62-68; Dir U Lib Drake U 68-. 8: Coord Urban Affairs Ctr Drake U 69. 9: Conf on Latin-Amer Hist; IowaLA; AAUP. 13: Yes. 14: Admin. 15: 1429 - 30th st, Des Moines Ia 50311.

RAVELO, ROBERTO MAXIMO. b Santiago Cuba 18 S 10. 4: Maria Mercedes Garrote Ravelo. 5: Instituto Santiago de Cuba 23-27 BA & S; UHavana 27-30, 33-34 Dr of Civil Law; Kan State Tchrs Col 64-65 (LS) MS. 6: Sp, Portu. 07: Judge Judiciary Power in Cuba, Oriente Prov Cuba 35-61; Justice State Supreme Court, Oriente Cuba, Santiago de Cuba 53-61; Soc wker US Cuban Refugee Asst Prom, Miami Fla 62-64; Catlgr Yale U Lib 65-69; Sr catlgr NYU Lib (Stony Brook) 69-. 8: Legal adv & Prof judge in Cuba. 9: ALA; Judicatura Cubana. 13: Yes. 14: Catlg. 15: 32 Madeley lane, Stony Brook LI NY 11790.

RAWLES, BEVERLY A. b Ohio 14 Ja 30. 4: Henry A RAWLES Jr. 5: Ohio State U 47-48, 56-59 (Geol); Capital U 48-51 (Biol) BS; Case-West Res 59-60 MS in LS. 6: Russian. 7: Battelle Mem Inst, Columbus Ohio: Bibliog 52-57, Info spec 57-62, Proj leader & Slavic libn 63-. 9: Internat Assn Documentalists. 12: "Guide to the Scientific & Technical Literature of Eastern Europe (62). 13: Yes. 14: Ref, admin. 15: 1489 Doone rd, Columbus Ohio 43221.

RAWLES, HENRY A R. b Suffolk Va 19O28. 4: Beverly Archer. 5: Va Polytech Inst 46-48 Aero Engnr); Parks Col St Louis U 48-50 (Aeronautics) BS; Washington U (St Louis) 55-58 (Hist) MA; West Res 59-60 MSLS. 7: Hydraulics tech Remmert-Werner Inc, St Louis 51-52; Design engnr Robertson Deveopment Corp, St Charles Mo 52-53; USAF Radar Maintenance Off (1st Lt) 53-55; Pre-prof lib asst Enoch Pratt Free Lib, Baltimore 59, Lib asst 60-62; Head ref dept Battelle Mem Inst Lib, Columbus Ohio 62-. 8: Adv Korean Inst of Sci & Tech, Seoul Korea & Columbus Ohio 66-67. 14: Ref, bibliog. 15: 1489 Doone rd, Columbus Oh 43221.

RAWLEY, WAYNE III. b Pittsburgh Penn 30 Ag 39. 4: Barbara Pings. 5: Washington & Jefferson 57-61 (Eng) AB; UPittsburgh 66-67 MLS. 6: Fr, Sp. 7: Ballalion adj USA Artillery, Nurnberg Ger 61-63; Tchr Wilkinsburg Sch Dist, Wilkinsburg Penn 64-66; UIowa Libs: Res bks libn 67-68, Undergrad libn 68-. 9: ALA; NCTE; IowaLA. 10: Beta Phi Mu. 14: Admin. 15: 1424 Crescent st, Iowa City Ia 52240.

RAWSKI, CONRAD HENRY. b Vienna 25 My 14. 4: Helen Orr. 5: Vienna 32-37 (Musicology, Hist) PhD; Austrian Inst for Hist Research 35-37 (LS) Diploma;Peter Pamany U (Budapest)

38-39 (Medieval Lat, Art Hist); Harvard 39-40 (Musicology); West Res 57 MS in LS. 6: Ger, Fr, Sp, Lat. 7: Asst Austrian Nat Lib, Vienna Austria 37; Visiting lecturer musicology ULouisville 40; Asst, Assoc Prof, & Prof of Music Ithaca Col 40-56, Dean Sch of Music 53-56; Head fine arts dept Cleveland Pub Lib 57-62; West Res U: Lecturer Lib Sci 57-62, Assoc Prof Lib Sci 62-65, Prof of Lib Sci 65-. 8: Co-ord PhD program, West Res U Sch of Lib Sci, 62-. 9: ALA-ACRL Amer Musicological Soc; Amer Soc for Aesthetics; MusLA; OhioLA; Medieval Acad of Amer; Philos of Sci Assn. 10: Beta Phi Mu; Friends of Cleveland Pub Lib; Cleveland Museum of Art; Rowfant Club. 11: Ford Foun, Faculty Fellowship, 52-3. 12: Ed & tr Petrarch "Four Dialogues for Scholars (67); Ed Joseph Bodin de Boismortier "Sonatas for Three Flutes or Alto Recorders, Op 7 2 v (54,57). 13: Yes. 14: Research in libnship, hist of bks & libs, lit of the humanities, Philos of sci. 15: Sch of Lib Sci Case-West Res Univ, Cleveland Oh 44106.

RAY, DAVID TRYON. b NYC 1 Ap 10. 4: Jean Elizabeth Meyer. 5 UCLA 27-31 (Econ) AB; USoCal 31-32 (Educ) Tchg Certif; Catholic U 46-47 (LS) BS; Yale 47-49 (Linguistics, Oriental Studies); SoIllU 61-67 (Philos) MA. 6: Sp, Fr, Ger, Russian, Japanese. 7: Statistical research US Cane Sugar Refiners Assn, Wash DC 36-38; Foreign serv off US Dept of State, Wash DC 38-46; Lib asst US Army Map Serv, Wash DC 49; Bibliog US Nat War Col, Wash DC 49-53; Ref asst LC 53; Catlgr Smithsonian Inst, Wash DC 53-59; Catlgr SoIllU 59-. 8: Attache, US Embassy, Tokyo, for Japanese lang study, 40-42; Typographical & printing research on var scripts of India, research proj carried out for SoIllU in India & the US, 6264; Lib Adv Ministry of Educ Republic of Mali 66-68. 9: ALAACRL; Amer Oriental Soc; IllLA; Assn for Asian Studies. 10: AAUP. 13: Yes. 14: Catlg, Orientalia (Sinology & Indology). 15: 502 Orchard dr, Carbondale Il 62901.

RAY, DEE ANN. b Tulsa Okla 28M38. 5: UTulsa 56-59 (Span) BA; UOkla 59-60 MLS. 6: Sp, Ger. 7: Field libn Okla State Lib 60-63; Dir of demonstration serv Mo State Lib 64-66; Dist libn West Plains Lib Syst, Clinton Okla 66-. 9: ALA (Exec Bd Jr mems Round Table 65-68); -YASD (Latin-Amer Bk List Com); OklaLA (Sequoyah Child Bk Award Chm 63; chm Bk Sel Wkshop 61); chm Intel Freedom Com; chm Memb Com); MoLA. 10 Beta Phi Mu. 10: Beta Phi Mu; Bus & Prof Women. 13: Yes. 14: Ext serv, pub libs, bk se, child & yp bks, lib admin. 15: 1105 W ilson, Clinton Ok 73601.

RAY, INEZ (KATHERINE) POE. b Apex NC 16 Mr 15. 4: Marl Ellis Ray. 5:' Meredith Col 31-35 (Eng) AB; UNCLBN Gilbertsville Dam Tenn Valley Authority, Gilbertsville Ky 40-42; Post libn Edgewood Arsenal Chem Warfare Center, EdgewoodM CWake Forest NC 63-65; Dir curr materials center Sch of Educ NC State U (Raleigh) 65-. 6: Fr, Lat. 7: Camp libn Gilbertsville Dam Tenn Valley Authority, Gilbertsville Ky 40-42; Post libn Edgewood Arsenal Chem Warfare Center, Edgewood Md 43; Consul sch lib serv NC Dept of Pub Instr, Raleigh NC 62; Ref asst D H Hill Lib NC State Co (Raleigh) 63; High sch libn Wake Forest High Sch, Wake Forest NC 63-65; Dir Curr Materials Center Sch of Educ NC State U (Raleigh) 65-. 9: ALA; NEA; NCLA; NCEA. 10: LWV. 15: 3401 Noel ct, Raleigh NC 27607.

RAY, JEAN (ELIZABETH MEYER). b Cambridge Mass 20 S 15. 4: David Tryon Ray. 5: Simmons 32-36 LS BS; Columbia 41-44, 45 (LS) MS; Ore State U 46-47 (Bot & Geol); Yale 48-50 (Sociol, Anthropology). 6: Fr, Sp. 7: Asst libn Paul Pratt Mem Lib, Cohasset Mass 36-38; Asst in order dept Amherst Col Lib 38-40; Catlgr Tufts U Lib 4042; Catlgr Hartford Sem Found Lib, Hartford Conn 42-45; Union catlgr Ore State System of Higher Educ, Corvallis Ore 4-47; Sr catlgr Yale U Lib 47-50; Sr catlgr Ser Sect Descr Catlg Dv LC 50-53, Head searching ,unit Prelim Catlg Sect Descr Catlg Div 53-59; Ast catlg libn SoIllU Lib 61-66; Spec asst USIS Lib, Bamako Mali 67-68; Map libn & Asst sci libn SoIllU Lib 68-. 9: ALA; IllLA. 10: AAUW; LWV. 13: Yes. 14: Catlg (espec subj headings). 15: 502 Orchard dr, Carbondale Il 62901.

RAY, JOHN GILBERT (III). b St Marys Penn 14 Mr 45. 5: Oberlin 63-67 (Hist) AB; Rutgers 67-68 MLS. 6: Sp. 7: Hd tech proc Charles Co Commun Col, Laplata Md 68-. 9: ALA; MdLA; Md Assn Jr Cols. 14: Admin. 15: 1310 Iverson st apt 12, Oxon Hill Md 20021.

RAYBURN, GLORIEUX. b Durand Wis 19 Je 30. 5: Col of St Teresa 48-52 (Eng) BA; Columbia 58-62 MSLS; NoIllU 61-62. 6: Fr, Lat, Russian. 7: Tchr-libn Winnebago High sch, Winnebago Minn 52-54; Libn Longfellow Jr High Sch, LaCrosse Wis 54-58; Libn DeKalb Sr High Sch, DeKalb Ill 58-61; Columbia U: Itern Lib Serv Lib 61-62; Libn ref Bus Lib 62-64, Asst libn Bus Lib 64-65, Libn Lib Serv Lib 65-. 68; Info spec Nat Indl Conference Bd 68-. 9: ALA; SLA. 10: Beta Phi Mu. 15: 440 Riverside dr, NYC 10027.

RAYBURN, VIRGINIA (CLARA) KEMP. b Batson Tex 23 Ja 18. 4: John Chalmers Rayburn. 5: Tex Col of Arts & I 38 (Eng) LSU LEU 39 BS in LS; Tex Col of Arts& Ind 49 (Eng) MA; UTex 5, 51 (Eng). 6: Sp. 7: Asst libn Tex Col of Arts & Ind 39-43; Lt (Jg) womens Rs USNR 43-45; Order libn Bylor U 46-48; Libn A C Jnes High Sch, Beeville Tex 48-49; Libn Presbyterian Pan Amer Sch, Kingsville Tex 49-. 9: TexLA (sec 46-48). 12: Co-ed, with J C Rayburn "Century of Conflict" (66). 14: Ref. 15: 1714 W Santa Gertrudis, Kingsville Tx 78363.

RAYMER, GITA (ROTHBARD). b Istambul 18 D 29. 4: Gene Raymer. 5: Wayne State U 44-48 (Eng) BA, 58-60 (Educ) Tchg Certif; UMich 62-64 MALS. 7: High sch libn E Detroit High Sch 61-62; High sch libn Ferndale High Sch, Ferndale Mich 62-65; Head jr high lib Melby Jr High Sch, Warren Mich 65-. 9: ALA; MichLA; Mich ASchL; NEA. 10: CLU; Girl Scouts; ADA. 14: Bk sel, ref. 15: 26389 York rd, Huntington Woods Mi 48070.

RAYMO, EVELYN (PATCHIN). b Pine Plains NY 31 Ja 19. 4: Francis Q Raymo. 5: NY State Col for Tchrs (Albany) 40 (LS, Soc Studie) BSLS,47 (Guidance) MA. 6: Fr. 7: Albany NY 40-41; Libn Finkelstein Mem Lib, Spring Valley NY 41-44; Libn Roosevelt High Sch, Hyde Park NY 44-53; Elem libn Hyde Park (NY) Central Sch Dist 57-. 9: NY State Tchrs Assn. 10: DAR; AAUW. 14: Wking with elem studs. 15: Smith d, Hyde Park NY 12538.

RAYMOND, ANNE (FARLEY) (MRS). b NYC. 5: Fordham 36-38 (Eng) BS in Ed; Columbia 38-39 MA in Tchg of Eng; Catholic U 52-54 MS in LS. 6: Fr, Sp. 7: Tchr St Francis xavier Acad, Nassau NP, Bahama Islands BWI 35; Tchr St Louis Acad, Staten Island NY 39-40; Asst rare bk room & legis ref serv LC 40-42; Tchr Ticonderoga Hgh Sch, Ticonderoga NY 42-44; Tchr W C Mempham High Sch, Bellmore LI NY 44-46; Instr Mohawk Col 46-47; Libn sr & jr high schs, Mt Raiier Md 49-57; Libn Surrattsville Sr ,high Sch, Clinton Md 57-. 8:V-chm, V-chm, Stering Com Mohawk Co, 46-47; Middle States Assn Col & Secondary Schs; Evaluation Annapolis Sr High Sch, Annapolis Md, chm Instrl Materials Lib & A-V & chm English Com. 9: ALA; NEA; d State Tchrs Assn; MdLA. 13: Yes. 14: Ref, catlg. 15: 1510 Farlow ave, Crofton Md 21113.

RAYMOND, BORIS. b Harbin China 18 D 25. 5: UCal 49 (Sociol) BA, 53 (Sociol) MA, 55 MLS. 6: Russian, Fr. 7: Russian bibliogr UCal (Berkeley) 64-67; Ser libn UNev (Reno) 66-67; Asst dir UMan 67-. 9: CanLA. 13: Yes. 15: 441 Kingston Row, Winnipeg Manitoba Can.

RAYMOND, SISTER MARY (DE SANTIS). b Reading Penn 23 S 13. 5: St John Col (Cleveland) 46 (Educ) BS Ed; West Res 57 MSLS. 6: Ital, Fr, Sp, Lat, Slovak. 7: Elem tchr Catholic Sch Bd, Cleveland 31-; Elem tchr Helena Herlihy Hall, Mex City 31-33; Tchr-libn Incarnate Wd Acad, Parma Heights Ohio 44-; Ref libn St John Col (Cleveland) 61, Asst libn 65-. 9: CathLA (No Ohio Unit; past sec-treas, past Bk Rev Ed). 14: Ref, catlg. 15: 6618 Pearl rd, Cleveland 44130.

RAYNOR, GEORGIA E. b Prnceton NJ7 My 23. 5: Chatham Col 45 (Biol) BA; Lehigh U 54 (Eng Lit) MA; Columbia 54 MS in LS. 6: Fr. 7: Jr circ libn Orange Pub Lib, Orange NJ 54-56, Sr libn in chg of ref 56-60; Humanities catlgr Lehigh U Lib 61-64, Head catlg 64-68; Asst libn for catlg 69-. 9: ALA; PennLA; NJL. 14: Catlg, ref. 15: 349 - 8th ave, Bethlehem Pa 18018.

RAZZANO, LOUIS. b Monongahela Penn 24 Je 32. 4: Virginia Gagliardi. 5: Cal State Col (Penn) 50-54 (Eng-Speech) BS; UPittsburgh 57-59 (Educ, Guidance) M Ed, 64-66 MLS. 6: Fr, Ital. 7: Hd libn Byers Memorial Lib, Monongahela Penn 55-65; Chm Eng dept Monongahela High Sch, Monongahela Penn 54-65; Hd tech serv Slippery Rock State Col 65-. 9: NEA; PennLA; Penn Reading Assn. 10: AAUP. 14: Tech serv. 15: 606 Stewart ave, Grove City Pa 16127.

RE, ARMANDO JOHN. b Gloucester Mass 11 Mr 33. 5: Northeastern U 51-52 (Hist); San Francisco State Col 57-59 (Hist) BA; Simmons 60-62 (LS) MS. 6: Fr, Portu. 7: USAF 5th Bombardment Wing (SAC), Travis AFB Cal 53-57; Catlgr Harvard U Littauer Lib 60-63; Ref consul Ramapo Catskill Lib System, Middletown NY 63-65; Asst libn Salem State Col Lib 65-. 9: ALA; Mass Coun of State Libns. 10: Diogenes Club. 14: Ref, catlg, tech serv, archives. 15: 8 Forest st, Gloucester Ma 01930.

REA, HAZEL. b Dalls Co Mo 25 Ag 01. 5: Mo State Col (Springfield) 21-25 (Math) BS; UIll 26-29 (LS) BS, MA. 7: Lib asst UIll(Urbana) 27-29; Libn Ore State Col 29-30; Lib asst Neb State Col 30-39; Asst to libn USoCal 39-48, Asst libn for Tch Processes 48-, Act libn 53-55, 58-60. 9: ALA; Mss Soc; ASIS; CalLA. 14: Catlg. 15: Univ of So Cal Lib, Univ Park, Los Angeles 90007.

REA, MARYALICE F(RANCES). b Belfast N Ireland 18 O 11. 5: UMass Ext 32-33, 38-40 (Langs) Certif; UNH 40, 41 (LS) Certif; Harvard Ext 64-67 (Humanities) BA; ULiverpool, Chester England 64 (Drama Certif); Oxford U (Oxford Eng) 67 (U & Local Hist) Certif; Scottish Lib Assn (Dalkeith Scotland) 67 (LS); URI 68-69 (LS). 7: Asst-in-chg MCHS Sch Lib, Boston 28-30; Claims asst Mass Mutual Life Insurance, Boston 29; Med claims sec Dr Harry Boland, Boston 30; Mission Parish Lib, Boston; Lib asst 28-30, Asst libn 30-32, Libn-in-chg 32-36; Boston Pub Lib; Probationary asst 30-34, Prof asst 35-58; Tchr bk ordering, in-serv train program 45-48; Libn-in-chg St Catherine's Music Lib, Norwood Mass 49-60; Tchr CLA Lecturasic Principals of Lib Sci, Boston 58; Boston Pub Lib; 2nd asst 58-64, 1st asst bk purchasing dept 64, Chief bk purchasing dept 64-66; Research catlg info off & Theater-arts subject spec 66-. 8: Co-founder Cath Bk Week, Boston, 37; Trustee Westwood Pub Lib 56-62. 9: ALA; Amer Merchant Marine LA; CathLA (Nat Nomin Com 57-58; NE Unit Publicity Dir 46-48; Bk Week Com 37-48 & 58-59, Prog Dir 48-53; chm 55-57, Bd 57-59); Theatre LA; MassLA; NELA. 10: Boston Symphony Orchestra Friends Assn; Harvard Coop Soc; NE Conserv Friends Assn; NE Theatre Conf; Federation International pour la Recherche Theatrale. 12: Asst ed "Boston Catholic Worker" (44); Ed CathLA NE Unit "Bulletin" (46-58). 13: Yes. 14: Acquis, rare bks, child lit. 15: 180 Washington st, (Islington) Westwood Ma 02090.

REA,HELEN E. b Pittsburgh 1 O 20. 5: Clarion State Col 38-42 (LS) BS in Ed; UPittsburgh 42-46 (US Hist) M Litt; West Res 49-51 MSin LS. 7: Libn Ingram Pub Schs, Pittsburgh 42-45; Jr-sr high sch libn West View High Sch, Pittsburgh 45-58; Libn N Hills Sr High Sch, Pittsburgh 58-; Visiting lectr UPittsburgh Grad Sch of Lib Sci summer 67-. 8: Mem Penn Sch Lib Resources Sel Adv Com 67-69. 9: NEA; PennStateEA; ALA; AASL. 15: 18 N Linwood ave, Pittsburgh 15205.

READ, GLENN FRANKLIN JR. b Cincinnati 13 Mr 31. 4: Marie Dennison. 5: Long Beach City Col 49-51 (Span) AA; UCal (Berkeley) 51-53, 58-59 (Latin Amer Hist) AB, 59-61 (Latin Amer Hist)MA, 61-62 MLS. 6: Sp, Portu, Ger. 7: Wire electronics repairman US Army Signal Corps (SP-5), Hawaii 53-56; Frameman PACIFIC Telephone, Cal 56-60; Sr lib asst UCal Gen Lib (Berkeley) 61-62; Ref libn NY Pub Lib Amer hist div 62-64; Latin Amer bibliog Cornell U 64-. 9: AHA; Latin Amer Studs Assn; Seminar on the Acquis of Latin Amer Lib Materials. 10: Alpha Gamma Omega; Beta Phi Mu. 13: Yes. 14: Ref, acquis, Latin-Americana, bibliog. 15: 218 Tareyton dr, Ithaca NY 14850.

READ, IDA (DUNAWAY). b Bedford Co Tenn 31 D 23. 4: William Eris Read. 5: Tenn Col for Women 42-45 (Mus, Soc Sci) AB; Middle Tenn StateU 58-59 (Educ) MA. 7: Tchr-libn Rutherford Co Christiana High Sch 58-59; Bkmob libn Tenn State Lib & Archives Highland Rim Reg 59-65; Asst catlg libn Middle Tenn StateU 65-. 9: SELA; TennLA; TennEA. 10: Chi Omega; Middle Tenn State Univ Dames Club; Middle Tenn State Univ Orchestra; Bohannan Music Club; AAUW. 14: Catlg, a-v, mus. 15: 911 Scotland dr, Murfreesboro Tn 37130.

READER, KAREN (THERIOT). b Los Angeles Cal 25 O 42. 4: Dennis J Reader. 5: UCal (Berkeley) 60-64 (Eng) BA, 64-65 MLS. 6: Fr. 7: Elem sch libn San Leandro Unified Sch Dist, San Leandro Cal 65-67; Doc & legal ref libn West IllU 67-68; Ser catlgr UCal (San Diego) 68-. 9: CalASchL. 10: Phi Beta Kappa; Beta Phi Mu. 14: Child wk. 15: 3735 Seventh ave, San Diego Ca 92103.

READING, DOROTHY T. b Evanston Ill. 5: Northwestern 34-38 (Educ) BS in Ed; UIll 41 BS in LS. 6: Swedish, Fr, Ger. 7: Ref libn White Plains (NY) Pub Lib 41-43; Ref libn Highland Prk (Ill) Pub Lib 43-44; Head circ dept Evanston Ill Pub Lib 44-60, Asst libn 60-. 9: ALA; IllLA. 10: Pi Lambda Theta; Beta Phi Mu; Zonta Internat. 14: Admin. 15: 1703 Orrington ave, Evanston Ill 60201.

READING, PAULA J. b Cambridge Mass 7 D 40. 5: West Res U 58-59 (Art); UOmaha 59-63 (Eng) BA; UDenver 63-64 (LS) MA. 6: Sp. 7: Admin libn Army Spec Serv, Korea 64-66; Hd art & mus dept Santa Barbara Pub Lib, Cal 66-67; Dir & command ref libn Saigon Area Lib Spec Serv 67-. 9: ALA. 14: Ref, research. 15: 1520 So 93 ave, Omaha Nb 68124.

READY, WILLIAM (B). b Cardiff Wales 16 S 14. 4: Bessie Dyer. 5: UWales 34-39 (Hist, Lit) BA, Diploma Paleography & Archives; Oxford U 46 Diploma Ed; UMan 47-49 (Hist) 47-49 MA; Rutgers 56 (LS); Assoc of Brit Lib Assn. 6: Fr, Lat. 7: Asst libn pub lib, Cardiff Wales 31-39; (Capt) Infantry & Staff Off Educ British Army, Overseas 39-45; Tchg fellow UMinn 48-50; Instr Grad Lib Sch UCal 50-51; Libn asst div Stanford U 51-56; Libn & assoc prof Marquette U 56-62; Libn & prof Sacred Heart U (Conn) 62-66; U Libn & Prof of bibliog McMaster U, Hamilton Ont 66-. 8: Consul:Mudelein Col 62, Marymount 65; Visiting lecturer, UIll Grad Lib Sch, 57; Consul US Naval Acad 62-63. 9: ALA; CanLA; BritLA; Amer Archives Assn. 11: Atlantic Monthly Award, 48; Clarence Day Award, 61; Thomas More Award, 62. 12: "The Great Disciple (51); "The Poor Hater (59); "Reward of Reading (65); "Tolkien Relation (68); "Understanding Tolkien (69); "Necessary Russell (69). 13: Yes. 14: Acquis, admin, tchg. 15: 170 Woodview crescent, Ancaster Ontario Can.

REAGAN, AGNES L(YTTON). b Fayetteville Ark 12 Ag 14. 5: UArk 31-35 (Math) BA; Emory 35-36 (Hist) MA, 38-39 BALS; UIll summer 41, 42-43 (LS) MS; Chicago summer 45 (LS); UIll summer 52, 53-54, summer 56, 57 (LS) PhD. 7: Tchr Rogers High Sch, Rogers Ark 36-38; Asst in lib Agnes Scott Col 39-42; Reviser Emory U Lib Sch summer 42; Sub in ref dept Carnegie Lib of Atlanta summer 42; Circ libn Wellesley Col 43-46, readers libn 46-47; Visiting lecturer UIll Lib Sch summer 47; Asst Prof Emory U Div of Libnship 47-58; Assoc Prof Emory U Div of Libnship 58-67; Asst dir ALA Off for Lib Educ & Exec sec LED 67-69; Asst dir for accreditation ALA Off for Lib Educ & Exec sec LED 69-. 8: Survey with P M Cousins & G R Lyle of Lib of Armstrong Col, 60; Visiting lecturer, Syracuse U Sch of Lib Sci summers 60, 62. 9: ALA (Coun 63-66, Subs Bks Com 62-64); -ISAD; -RSD; -ACRL -LAD; -LED (chm Nomin Com 57-58, Bd Dirs 61-64, chm Equival & Recip Com 62-65; chm Tchrs Sect 61-62); AALS (ALA Coun for AALS 63-66, chm Com on Recr & Personnel 51-53 & 56-57, chm Research Com 60-62); SLA (Ga Chap; chm Recr Com 58-59); ASIS (Ill Chap); BSA; SELA (chm Col & Univ Libns Sect 62-64); GaLA (chm Scholarship Com 57-; Sec Educ for Libnship Sect 59-63); IllLA; Atlanta Lib Club (pres 62-63). 10: AAUP; Kappa Kappa Gamma; AHA; Phi Kappa Phi; Pi Mu Epsilon; Beta Phi Mu. 11: Dogwood Award, Ga Chap SLA, 60 for Serv to the Chap in Directing a Recr Proj. 12: A Study of Factors Influencing College Students to Become Librarians--, ACRL Monograph No 21 (58); Asst ed The Southeastern Librarian-- (6164). 13: Yes. 14: Educ for libnship, ref, col libs. 15: 50 E Huron st, Chicago Il 60611.

REAM, SALLY ANN. b Bridgeport Conn 16 Ap 43. 5: Fla State U 61-65 (Lit of west cultures) BA, 65-66 (LS) MS. 6: Sp. 7: Catlgr Miami-Dade Jr Col central tech proc 66-. 9: ALA; SELA; FlaLA; DadeCoLA. 10: Beta Phi Mu. 14: Catlg (a-v materials). 15: 13210 Memorial Highway, North Miami Fl 33161.

REAMES, J(AMES) MITCHELL. b Rembert SC 31 Ag 20. 4: Mary Beall Hall. 5: Furman U 37-41 (Eng) BA; UNC 41-42 BS in LS; UMich summers 50, 51, 53 AMLS. 6: Fr, Ger. 7: Yoeman 2/c U Navy 42-46; Ref libn Clemson Col 46-52; Assoc libn & Assoc Prof of Lib Sci Northwestern State Col of La 52-58; Dir Undergrad Lib USCar 58-. 8: Mem, Eval Coms, So Assn of Cols, 7 cols 62-68. 9: ALA; SCLA (v-pres 48 & 67-69, pres 49, pres-elect 69); SELA (chm Constit & Bylaws Com 66-68; treas Col & Univ Sect 59-60); Columbia (SC) Lib Club (pres 60-61). 10: AAUP; Alpha Beta Alpha; Alston Wilkes Socl Columbia Sch of Theol Bd of Dirs. 13: Yes. 14: Admin, ref. 15: 4665 Datura rd, Columbia SC 29205.

REAMS, BERNARD D JR. b Lynchburg Va 17 Ag 43. 4: R Bridget Boyle. 5: Lynchburg 61-65 (Eng) BA; Drexel 65-66 MS in LS. 6: Ger. 7: Asst libn Rutgers U (Camden NJ) 65-69; Asst law lin UKan 69-. 9: ALA; AALL; NJLA. 10: Beta Phi Mu; Kappa Delta Pi; Pi Delta Epsilon. 14: Legal research, acquis, sel. 15: Univ of Kansas School of Law, Law Lib, Lawrence Ks 66044.

REAMS, GWENDOLYN. b Decatur Ala 11 Je 16. 5: UAla 38-40 (Eng) AB; Peabody 50-53 (LS) MA; UNC 55 (LS; Syracuse 64 (LS). 6: Sp, Fr. 7: Tchr pub schs, Ala 40-53; Libn Va Polytech Inst 53-5; Libn Bloomsburg State Col 54-. 9: NEA; ALA; Penn State EA; PennLA. 10: AAUP; AAUW. 14: Catlg. 15: 345 Fetterman ave, Bloomsburg Penn 17815.

REASON, JOSEPH H(ENRY). b Franklin La 23 Mr 05. 4: Bernice Chism. 5: Dillard U 24-28 (Hist) AB; Howard U 31-32 (Fr) AB; UPenn 32-33 Fr) MA; Columbia 35-36 (LS) BS; Catholic U 58 (Fr) PhD. 6: Fr, Sp. 7: Tchr Gilbert Acad, New

Orleans 28-29; Tchr Fla A&M U 29-31, 34-35, Libn 36-38; Howard U: Ref libn 38-46, U Libn 46-57, Dir of U Libs 57-. 8: Lib adv, Faculty of Soc Scis, U Rangoon Burma 61-62; Exec dir, DC Co, Nat Lib Week, 65; Consul CLR for acad libs 68-. 9: ALA (2nd v-pres 66-67); -ACRL; (exec sec 62-63); DCLA. 10: Amer dialect Soc; Internat Arthurian Soc. 12: "An Inquiry into the Structural Style and Originality of Chrestiens "Yvain (58: Ed Bd "Choice 65-66. 13: Yes. 14: Admi, bldgs. 15: 1242 Girard st NE, Wash DC 20017.

REASONER, BARNABAS (REV). b Whiskey Hill Ore 31 Mr 23. 5: Mt Angel Sem 41-47 (Phil) BS; Rosary 50-51 MALS; UChicago 51 (LS). 6: Lat, Ger, Fr. 7: Vice-rector Mt Angel Major Sem, St Benedict Ore 53-55; Libn Mt Angel Abbey, St Benedict Ore 52-. 9: ALA; CathLA; PNLA; OreLA. 13: Yes. 14: Rare bks. 15: Mt Angel Abbey, St Benedict Or 97373.

REAVIS, RAYMOND EDWARD. b Richmond Mo 27 Mr 22. 4: Elizaeth Steffen. 5: UNM 39-40; Col of St Joseph 53-56 (Hist) BA; UTex 64-65 (LS); LSU 65-67 (LS) MA. 7: MSGT Personnel Supervisor USA & USAF 40-61; Catlgr Tom Green Co Lib, San Angelo Tex 67; Ref asst Wilmington Inst Free Lib, Wilmington Dela 67-68; Asst libn Reading Pub Lib, Reading Mass 68-. 9: ALA; MassLA. 10: Phi Kappa Phi; Beta Phi Mu. 14: Ref. 15: PO Box 277, Redding Ma 01867.

REBADAVIA, CONSOLACION BALQUIN. b Makati Rizal Philippines 18 Je 28. 5: UPhilipines 48-52 (LS) BSE, 53-60 (Educ) M Ed; Rutgers 61-63 MLS. 6: Sp, Tagalog. 7: Sr catlg UPhilippines Lib 52-61; Libn trainee Montclair Pub Lib, Montclair NJ 61-62; Indexer "International Index H W Wilson Co, NY 63-64; Sr catlgr Rutgers U Lib 62-63, 64-. 9: Philippine LA; Bibliog Soc Philippines; ASIS; MLA (NY Reg Group). 12: "Checklist of Philippine Government documents, 1917-1949 (60). 14: Catlg, bibliog. 15: Rutgers Univ Lib, New Brunswick NJ 08903.

REBMAN, ELISABETH (HUTTIG). b Miami Fla 20 Je 41. 4: Kenneth Ralph Rebman. 5: Oberlin Col 59-63 (Music Gist) AB; Staatliche Hochschule fur Musik (Frankfurt a M Germany) 63-64 (Organ & Harpischord); UMich 65-67 MALS. 6: Ger, Fr. 7: Audio room supv Undergrad Lib UMich (Ann Arbor) 65-67; Asst humanities libn East MichU 67-. 9: MusLA; CanLA; CanMusLA; Assn for Recorded Sound Collection. 14: Mus libnship. 15: 2700 S Main rd, Ann Arbor Mi 48103.

REBENACK, JOHN H(ENRY). b Wilkinsburg Penn 10 F 18. 4: Dorothy Treat. 5: UPittsburgh 36-42 (Eng) AB; Carnegie 46-47 BS in LS. 7: US Army Infantry Duty NCO (T/Sgt) 42-45; Ref asst Carnegie Lib o f Pittsburgh 45-50; Libn Salem Pub Lib, Salem Ohio 50-53; Libn Elyria Lib, Elyria Ohio 53-57; Asst libn Akron Pub Lib, Akron Ohio 57-65, Assoc libn 65-67, Chief libn 67-. 8: Survey Adv Com State Lib Ohio 66-67; Consul, Crafton (Penn) Pub Lib 66; Review Com State Lib Ohio, LSCA Title II 67-72; Lib Com, President's Com on Employment of the Handicapped 66-69; Bd of Visitors, UPittsburgh, Grad Sch of Lib & Info Serv; Vis Com Case West Res U Sch of Lib Sci. 9: ALA (Memb Com, Ohio chm 51-57, Reg chm 57-61);-ASD (Com on Internship 61-63);-LAD (Personnel Admin Sect; Exec Com, sec 63-65, chm 66-67; In-Service Train Com 59-66; Buildings & Equip Sect; Arch Com for Pub Libs 64-69);PLA (Div Org Com 59-62; Pub Libs Activities Com 64-65); AASchL (Sch Lib Manpower Proj; Adv Com 68-70); OhioLA (Exec Bd 57-60; Adult Educ RT chm 63; Instit Lib Com chm 63; Legis Com chm 65-66; Admin Training Wkshop Com 66; Tri-State Legis Wkshop Com 66; pres 66-67; Lib Admin RT chm 68-69). 10: Greater Akron Arts Fed; Akron Torch Club; United Commun Coun; Kiwanis; Beta Phi Mu; Akron Area Adult Educ Coun. 11: United Commun Coun Commun Serv Award 67; Newton D Baker II Citation 68. 13: Yes. 14: Pub lib admin. 15: Akron Pub Lib, 55 S Main st, Akron Ohio 44308.

RECORD, PAULINE (LOWE). b Lincoln Neb. 4: Mason T Record. 5: UNeb (Hist) BA; Columbia 35-36 BS in LS, 65-66 MS. 7: Lib asst Lincoln Pub Lib, Lincoln Neb; Lib asst NYC Pub Lib 36-37; Asst libn Sweet Briar Col 37-40; Libn Bradford Jr Col 40-42; Libn Waterford High Sch, Waterford Conn 56-65; Asst dir Lib Serv Ctr, Willimantic Conn 66-69; Consul Conn State Lib div of lib development, Hartford Conn 69-. 9: ALA; Film Lib Info Coun; NELA; NESchLA; ConnLA. 10: Beta Phi Mu; ACLU; LWV; Planned Parenthood League; SANE; United World Federalists; etc. 14: Pub libs, ya serv, a-v materials in the pub lib. 15: 19 Benham ave, Quaker Hill Ct 06375.

RECTOR, RUTH (GILL). b Liberty Mo 8 Je 11. 4: Hartman Rector. 5: William Jewell Col 28-32 (Math) AB; Columbia summers 37-40 BS in LS. 6: Fr. 7: Ref libn Mo Sch of Mines & Metallurgy, Rolla Mo 34-39; Ref libn UKan City 39-40; Ref libn sci & tech div NY Pub Lib 41-42; Head libn Mont Sch of Mines 43; Libn spec serv br US Army & Air Force, Cal, PI, Korea & Germany 44-49; Metallurgy libn Oak Ridge Nat Lab Lib, Oak Ridge Tenn 50; Post libn, Ft McPherson Ga & Camp Rucker Ala 51-52; Reg demonstration libn Mo State Lib 52-53; Ref libn Jackson Co Lib, Independence Mo 54; Head libn Mexico-Audrian Co Lib, Mexico Mo 55-56; Head libn Little Dixie Reg Lib, Moberly Mo 56-58; Interlib loan libn Hist & World Affairs Sect San Diego Pub Lib 62-67, Br libn Clairemont Br. 9: ALA (Recr Com 58-60). ; SLA (treas San Diego Chap 67). 14: Ref, sci. 15: 3531 Sterne st, San Diego 92106.

REDDITT, JANEL. b Lake Charles La 30 Ag 26. 5: UAla 43-47 (Eng) BA, summers 65, 66, 67 (LS) MA. 6: Fr. 7: Sec Dantzler Lumber Export Co, Mobile Ala 47; Sec Waterman Steamship Co, Mobile Ala 48; Sec bkkeeper Mason Drug Co, Brewton Ala 49-58; Fiscal acct clerk Whiting Field NAAS, Pensacola Fla 58-65; Libn Jefferson Davis Col 65-. 9: ALA; AEA; AlaLA (pres Jr Col Libns 69). 15: 1400 Poplar ave, Brewton Al 36426.

REDDY, ANNA (MARIE). b Geneva NY 30 N 15. 5: Nazareth Col (Rochester NY) 33-37 (Eng) BA; Geneseo State Col 39-40 BS in LS. 6: Fr. 7: Libn N Arlington High Sch, N Arlington NJ 41-51; Chief catlgr Assn of the Bar of the City of NY 52-. 9: AALL; SLA (NY Chap); Law Libns Assn of Greater NY. 14: Catlg, ref. 15: 451 E 14th st, NYC 10009.

REDDY, JESSIE (NEWCOMER). b Alliance Ohio 18 F 06. 4: John A Reddy. 5: Mt Union Col 22-26 (Eng Lit) AB; Radcliffe 26-27 (Eng Lit); Kent State U summers 55-58 MA in LSc. 6: Fr, Sp. 7: High sch tchr Paris loc schs, Paris Ohio 27-28; High sch tchr Mahoning city schs, Sebring Ohio 27-28; Newspaper ed "Sebring Times, Sebring Ohio 46-55; High sch libn Sebring loc schs, Sebring Ohio 55-. 9: NEA; OhioEA; OhioLA; Mahoning City Sch Libns Assn. 10: Womans Club of Sebring; PTA; Sebring LocalEA. 13: Yes. 14: Catlg. 15: 315 W Indiana ave, Sebring Ohio 44672.

REDHEFFER, ADELINE. b Morton Penn 7 My 16. 5: West Chester State Tchrs Col 34-38 (Educ) BS in Ed; Drexel 39-42 BS in LS. 7: Circ dept Swarthmore Col Lib 38-45; Asst libn Upper Darby Pub Lib, Upper Darby Penn 45-46; Order libn Fla State U 46-49; Asst libn Jefferson Med Col 49-58; Libn Penncrest High Sch, Lima Penn 58-. 9: NEA; Penn State EA; Delaware Co (Penn) SchLA. 10: Bk Sel Com Media Pub Swarthmore Players Club; BPW. 14: Sch libs. 15: 214 Sylvan ave, Ruthledge Penn 19071.

REDMAN, HELEN (FIELD. b Boston 6 Ja 23. 4: Leslie Merrill Redman. 5: Wellesley Col 40-44 (Eng Lit) AB; West Res 46-47 BS in LS. 7: Circ clerk rare bks Houghton Lib Harvard U 44-46; Ref asst West Res Lib 46-47; Los Alamos Sci Lab, Los Alamos NM: Asst libn 47-49; Report libn 49-52, Head Libn 53-. 8: Jt (AEC-DED) Atomic Weapons Tech Infor Group, 51-; Tech Infor Panel US AEC, 55; 550; Dir Tech Infor Center, Atomos en Accion Exhibit, San Salvador, El Salvador CA, 65; : John Dana Danna lecturer, Tex Womans U, 64; Exec dir, Nat Lib Week, NM, 60-61. 9: SLA (chm Engnr Sect 62-63, chm Sci-Tech Div 64-65, chm Adv Coun 66-67; Rio Grande Chap, pres 56-58); NMLA (chm Col Univ & Spec Lib Sect 55-56, pres 57-58); NM Lib Dev Coun (chm 67-69). 11: SLA Sci-Tech Publs Award, 63. 12: Co-ed "Dictionary of Report Series Codes (62); Co-ed "Weapon Data Subject Heading List (TID-9000) var eds. 13: Yes. 14: Admin, report lit. 15: P O Box 1663, Los Alamos NM 87544.

REDMON, ALICE JANE (GARDNER). b Cedar Rapids Iowa 6 Ag 16. 4: Charles F Redmon. 5: UDenver 33-37 (Eng Lit) BA. 7: Elem sch tchr Denver Pub Schs 37-49; Sub-prof asst RiceU 57-61, Catlg reviser 61-66, Act hd catlg dept 67-68, Asst hd 68-. 14: Catlg. 15: 4567 Elm st, Bellaire Tx 77401.

REDMON, MARTHA ANN. b Lawrencebirg Ky 16 N 02. 5: East KyU 23-28 (Lang Arts, Soc Sci) AB; UKy 31-46 (LS). 6: Fr, Lat. 7: Libn & tchr Ky Pub Sch 24-46; Hd libn Lima Pub Sch (Central), Lima Ohio 46-51; Tchr-libn Chicago Pub Sch 51-53; Libn Ill Pub Sch 53-67; Libn Bateman Sch, Chicago 68-. 9: IllLA. 10: Delta Kappa Gamma. 13: Yes. 14: Ref. 15: 222 E Pearson, Chicago Il 60611.

REDMOND, DONALD AITCHESON. b Owosso Mich 19 My 22. 4: Ruth M White. 5: Mt Allison U 39-42 (Chem, Eng) BS; McGill 46-47 BLS; UIll 47-48, 50 MS in LS; Atlantic Summer Sch of Adv Bus Admin Kings Col (ailfax NS) Diploma 54. 6: Ger, Fr, Sp. 7: Libn Can Bk Center, Halifax NS 48-49; Libn Nova Scotia Tech Col (Halifax NS) 49-60; Sci

& Engn libn UKan 61-64, Asst dir of libs 65; Chief Libn Queens U (Kingston Ont) 66-. 8: Tech ib adv, Ceylon Inst of Sci & Indus Research, Colombo 57-58 (Colombo Plan); Dir of lib Middle East Tech Univ. (UNESCO). 59-60 (nesco). 9: SLA; CanLA; Chem Inst Can; Soc Tech Writers & Publrs; Amer Soc Engnr Educ; APLA. 10: Baker Street Irregulars; Nat Model Railroad Assn. 12: Ed APLA "Bulletin (52-56). 13: Yes. 14: Sci-tech, admin. 15: Queens Univ, Kingston Ont Can.

REDMOND, DOROTHY A. b Granite City Ill 30 Mr 20. 5: SoIll U 38-41 (Hist) BEd; Colo state Col of Educ summers 42-46 (Hist) MA; Fla State U 49-50 (LS) MA. 7: Elem sch tchr pub schs, East Alton Ill 41-46; Elem sch tchr pub schs, Tieton Wash 46-47; Elem sch tchr pub schs, Punta Gorda Fla 47-49; Asst catlg Fla State U 50-53; Hd tech processes Mo State Lib, 50-54; Libn spec serv lib Dept of the Army, Japan 54-56, Europe 57-68; Chief tech ref div USA Garrison, Ft Huachuca Ariz 68-. 9: ALA; SLA; ArizLA. 14: Catlg, acquis, admin. 15: Box 888, Sierra Vista Az 85635.

REDMOND, JOHN OLIVER. b Atlanta Ga 20 Ja 34. 4: Donna Jean Bell. 5: Ga Tech 51-53 (Chem, Eng); UHawaii 55-58 (Eng) BA; Ohio State 58-60 (Eng) MA; Catholic U 63-67 (LS) MS. 6: Ger. 7: Fuel observer co-op Armco Steel Co, Ashland Ky 51-53; Sig C technician artillery off (1st Lt) USA, Hawaii CONUS 53-55, Reserve duty 55-63, Commissioned 57; Grad asst Eng Dept Ohio State U 58-60; Appeals examiner US Civil Serv Commsn, Wash DC 60-63; Y-a libn Arlington Co Libs 64; Hd circ unit ref libn interior Dept Lib, Wash DC 64-68; Hd stack serv ser div & processing sect LC 68-. 9: SLA; DCLA. 10: Beta Phi Mu; Phi Beta Kappa; Phi Kappa Phi; Phi Eta Sigma. 14: Tech serv, (esp control of ser), ref. 15: 11260 Evans Trail T3, Beltsville Md 20705.

REDMOND, MARIE LUCILE DUNKELBERG POHL. b Gouverneur NY 17 F 16. 5: St Lawrence U 33-37 (Hist) AB; Columbia 37-38 BS in LS. 7: Libn: Cornwall High Sch, Cornwall NY 38-40, Scotch Plains High Sch, Scotch Plains NJ 40-42, Tide Water Associated Oil Co, NYC 48-53, Howells Rd Sch, Valley Stream NY 53, Westbury High Sch, Westbury LI NY 53-58, Hermon-DeKalb Central Sch, DeKalb Junction NY 58. 9: NYL: NY State Tchrs Assn; No Zone LA; No Country Coun of Internat Reading Assn. 10: St Lawrence Co Hist Assn. 15: 31 Sterling st, Gouverneur NY 13642.

REDWOOD, (SHEILA) ANN (ROUT). b Vancouver BC Can 22 D 29. 5: UBC 48-52 (Bot, Zool) BA; UToronto 52-53 BLS. 7: Libn Forest Products Lab, Vancouver 53-57; Bkmob libn King Co Pub Lib, Seattle 57-58; Libn I Vancouver Pub Lib Bus & Econ Div 58-60; Libn Arch co-partnership, London Eng 61; Asst libn Arch Assoc, London Eng 61-63; Br libn Bell Tele Co of Can, Toronto 63-64; Ref libn Ontario Col of Educ 64-67; Chief libn Conestoga Col of Applied Arts & Tech 67-. 9: SLA; Inst Profess Libns Ont; OntLA; Coun Libns Commun Cols Ont; BCLA (bursar 59). 14: Ref. 15: Conestoga College Lib 299 Doon Valley dr, Kitchener Ont Can.

REECE, DONNA YORK (LASKER). b Springfield Mass 14 N 39. 4: John L Reece. 5: Marietta Col 57-61 (Eng) BA; Fla StateU 61-63 (LS) MS. 7: Asst ref libn USFla 63- 68, Docs libn 68-. 9: ALA. 14: Ref. 15: Rte 4 Box 672, Lutz Fl 33549.

REECE, NANCY (JONES). b Cattarugus NY 28 Ap 18. 4: Robert N Reece. 5: Ohio State U 35-39 BA, BS in Ed; West Res 43-44 BS in LS, 50-52 MA. 7: Tchr, Wharton, Ohio 39-41; Tchr, W Jefferson Ohio 41-43; Asst libn Lakewood High Sch, Lakewood Ohio 44-54; Supv Supv tchr in Lib Sci East Mich U 54-56; Libn Lakewood High Sch, Lakewood Ohio 56-. 9: NEA; ALA; OhioEA; OhioASchL. 14: Sch lib admin. 15: 3118 W 160th st, Cleveland Oh 44111.

REED, CAROL RIDER. b Syracuse NY 5 O 41. 5: Albany State U 59-63 (Soc studies) AB. 7: Eng tchr Syracuse City Sch Dist, Syracuse NY 64-65; Jr high libn Marcellus NY 66-68; Inter lib loan libn Onondaga Lib Syst, Syracuse NY 68-. 9: ALA; -AASchL. 10: Beta Phi Mu. 14: Ref. 15: 3 Flower lane, Marcellus NY 13108.

REED, DANIEL (JOHN). b Springfield Ill 19 J122. 4: Helen De Mars. 5: St Louis U 45-47 (Hist) BS, 47-49 (Hist) MA; Chicago 49-50 (Hist) PhD. 6: Fr. 7: Instr in hist St Louis U 48-49; Instr in hist UDetroit 50-53; Dir of Libs UDetroit 53-59; Asst chief Ms Div LC 59-65; Histn-biographer Nat Portrait Gallery, Wash DC 65-68; Asst archivist Pres Lib Nat Archives, Wash DC 68-. 8: Assoc dir Nat Adv Comm. 9: AHA; SAA; Org Amer Histns; Amer Assn of Museums. 12: Auth "Portraits of Presidents (68). 14: Bibliog, ms sources for Amer hist & biog. 15: Pres Libraries Nat Archives & Records Ser, Wash DC 20408.

REED, DAVID FRANKLIN. b Milwaukee 17 D 36. 4: Sandra Jo LeGath. 5: Carroll Col 59-60 (Geog); UWis 60-64 (Geog) BS, 64-65 MS in LS67- (LS). 6: Sp, Fr. 7: SP 4 photographer US Army, Germany 55-58; Proj asst Map Div LC summer 63; Ref asst UWis (Milwaukee) 65-66; Circ libn Fla Atlantic U 66-67. 9: ALA. 10: Beta Phi Mu. 14: Tech serv, lib admin, automation, col & univ libs. 15: 2021 Lakeview ave, Middleton Wi 33362.

REED, DONALD ANTHONY. b St Bernard La 22 N 35. 5: Loyola U (Los Angeles) 53-57 (Hist) BS; USoCal 57-58 (LS) MS, 58-65 (Hist, Law); 65-68 (Law) Juris Doctor. 7: Instr of Hist Cal Inst of the Arts, Los Angeles 63-64; Lecturer in Hist Los Angeles Valley Col 64, Instr of Lib Serv 64-66; Legal asst to J B Tietz, Los Angeles 68-. 9: ALA-AASchL; CathLA; CalLA. 10: AAUP; Beta Phi Mu; Phi Alpha Theta; Count Dracula Soc; Cath Peace Fellowship. 11: The Mrs. Ann Radcliffe Award for Literature, 63; Hon PhD, 65. 12: "Th e Vampire on the Screen 1922-1965" (65). 14: Order libnship, ref. 15: 334 W 54th st, Los Angeles 90037.

REED, EDWARD V JR. b Lawrence Mass 8 S 39. 5: Nasson Col 58-62 (Hist) BA; Simmons 65-69 (LS) MS. 7: US Army Security Agcy 62-65; Br libn Cambridge Pub Lib, Cambridge Mass 65-, A-V libn (asst) 65-66, Catlgr 66-. 14: Admin. 15: 28 Gage st, Methuen Ma 01844.

REED, EMILY WHEELOCK. b Asheville NC 4 N 10. 5: Ohio Wesleyan U 28-30; Ind U 35-37 (eng) BA; UMich 37-40 ABLS. 7: Jr & sr asst Detroit 40-46; Asst in chg circ & ref & catlgr, Kauai Hawaii 46-47; Instr Fla State U Sch of Lib Serv & Train 48; Prin lib asst med sci dept Detroit Pub Lib 48-49; Asst libn Wayne U Col of Med Lib 49; Admin asst Jefferson Parish Lib Demonstration, Gretna La 49-50; Libyn Rapides Parish Lib, Alexandria La 50-57; Dir Ala Pub Lib, Montgomery Ala 57-60; Consul in Adult Educ DC Pub Lib 60-66; Coord adult serv Enoch Pratt Free Lib, Baltimore 66-. 9: Adult Educ Assn; ALA (Coun mem-at-large 65-69; co-chm Jt Com (ALA-Amer Home Econ Assn)on Consumer Info 65; rep to Nat Civil Liberties Clearing House 64-65); -ASD (chm Com on Lib Serv to an Aging Popul 65-66);DC LA (pres-elect 65-66, chm Memb Com 63-65); LaLA (sec Pub Lib Sect 54); Rep to NCOA 68-69). 10: UN Assn; Nat Coun of Aging. 13: Yes. 14: Adult serv, ref, admin, lib ext, films. 15: 1101 St Paul st, Baltimore Md 21202.

REED, ESTELLA E. b Marion Co Ind. 5: Ball State U 36-40 (Eng) AB; Butler U 42-48 (Guidance) MS Ed; George Wash U 46-47 (Reading); Ind U 58-65 (Reading & LS) EDD. 7: High sch libn-tchr; Napoleon High Sch, Ind 40-42, Mt Comfort High Sch, Ind 42-43, Center Grove High Sch, Ind 43-45, 48-49, Frankline High Sch, Ind 45-46; Libn Mt Vernon Sem & Jr Col, Wash DC 46-48, 49-50; Libn Brookville High Sch, Ind 50-55; Libn Roosevelt High Sch, Ind 55-56; Instr IndU U HighSch 56-58; Libn Washington High Sch, E Chicago Ind 58-66; Asst Prof Purdue U Calumet Campus (Hammond) 66-69. 9: ALA (chm Stud Assts Com); IndSchLA (rec sec, v-pres 68-69, pres 69-70); IRA; AASchL; NEA-DAVI; ASCD; A-v Dirs of Ind. 10: Amer Educ Research Assn; Pi Lambda Theta; Delta Kappa Gamma. 13: Yes. 14: Admin sch libs, remedial reading. 15: Purdue Univ Calumet Campus, Hammond In 46323.

REED, GERTRUDE (SCHOLL). b Jamaica LI NY 4 Je 26. 4: Charles FReed. 5: Purdue U 45-47 (LS); NJ Col for Women 47-49 (LS) BA; Rutgers 54-57 MALS. 6: Ger, Fr. 7: Ref asst Berkeley Pub Lib, Berkeley Cal 49-53; Sch libn Glencoe Pub Schs, Glencoe Ill 54-55; Circ & ref asst Syracuse Pub Lib, Syracuse NY 63-64; Circ & ref asst Bryn Mawr Col Lib 64-. 9: ALA. 10: Phi Beta Kappa. 14: Ref. 15: 665 Weadley rd, King of Prussia Pa 19406.

REED, JANET S. b Rochester NY 16 Mr 40. 5: Middlebury Col 57-61 (Amer Lit) AB; UPittsburg 67-68 MLS. 7: Ed asst Houghton Mifflin Co, Boston 61-63; Libn R T French Co, Rochester NY 63-67; Asst to dir Penn State U Lib 68-. 9: SLA; ALA; PennLA. 10: Beta Phi Mu. 14: Admin, pub rel, automation. 15: 102 Pattee Lib, University Park Pa 16802.

REED, JEANNE P (RATT). b Wash DC 21 O 28. 4: John DReed Jr. 5: Howard U 46-50 (Eng) BA; Catholic U 50-58 MS in LS; Simmons NDEA Inst Lib Serv for Acadly Talented Stud summer 67. 7: Stat coding clerk Census Bur, Wash DC 50-1; Coding clerkdept of Health, Educ & Welfare, Wash DC 51-52; Libn Diamond Ord Fuze Labs, Wash DC 52-60; Libn Alice Deal Jr High Sch, Wash DC 60-. 8: Org lib for Strayer Bus Col summer 65. 9: DCASchL (v-pres). 14: Ref. 15: 4660 Nichols ave SW Apt A-901, Wash DC 20032.

REED, JOHN FRANCIS. b Amarillo Tex 9 Mr 38. 4: Judith Ann May. 5: Columbia 56-57; UNH 57-60 (Geol) AB; UMich 60-62 AMLS, 62-65 (Conservation). 6: Fr. 7: UMich: Wk-study scholar 60-62, Asst libn natural resources & sci lib 63-65, Lib curator ny botanical Garden, Bronx NY 65-. 9: SLA; ALA; Guild of Bkwkers; Amer Inst Graph Arts. 10: Phi Beta Kappa; Phi Kappa Phi; Delta Phi Mu. 14: Admin, bibliog, bk restoration & repair. 15: Lib NY Botanical Garden, Bronx NY 10458.

REED, JOHN HENRY. b Ososso Mich 17 Mr 23. 4: Libuse Ann Lacina. 5: Heidelberg Col 47-51 (Eng, Hist, Botany) BA; West Res 51-52 MSLS 62-63; Ohio State 56 (Amer Studies). 6: Fr, Ger, Lat, Greek. 7: Act asst hd ref Ohio State U (Columbus) 57; Ref hd & asst prof Ohio Wesleyan U 52-67, Univ archivist & asst prof 68-. 8: Bldg consul; Otterbein Col 6667; Heidelberg Col 6667. 9: ALA (Div Chm Copying Methods Sect; Com on Constitution & ByLaws 59); Microfilm Assn Amer; SAA; Soc Ohio Archivists (founder 68); OhioLA (pres Col Sect 62, 64); MidWest Acad Libns Assn. 10: Nat Trust Preservation Hist Places; NY Hist Soc; Mod Lang Assn; Amer Studies Assn; AAUP. 13: Yes. 14: Rare bks, archives, ref, computerization. 15: 6 Westgate dr, Delaware Oh 43015.

REED, L E (McMURTRY). b Kosciusko Miss 17 Ag 17. 4: Walter Aaron Reed Jr. 5: Fla A&M u 48-53 (Educ, LS) BS, MS; UJaime Balmes (Mex) summers 63, 65; Kalamazoo Col 64 (Span); Interamerican (Mex) 64 (Span); SUNY Summer Inst Media (Research) for jr col libns 66; Temple U summer Inst Media for jr col libns 67; SUNY (Albany) summer Inst Media Filming as an Art 68. 6: Sp. 7: Libn Fla A&M U; Libn &Span Harris Jr Col. 8: Mem Adv Bd Universidad Jaime Balmes, Mexico 63-. 9: ALA; Mod Lang Assn; Amer Tchrs Assn; NEA (life mem); MissTA; ASCD. 13: Yes. 14: Catlg, ref, educ media, films. 15: Harris Jr Col, Meridian Miss 39304.

REED, LAWRENCE LEE. b St Paul Minn 4 Ag 40. 4: Sylvia Alexander. 5: UMinn 58-66 (Philos) BA, 67-68 (LS) MA. 7: Period libn Moorhead State Col Lib 68-. 14: Acquis, mechanization. 15: 1616 1/2 Third ave S, Moorhead Mn 56560.

REED, LAWRENCE M. b Hays Kan 6 Je 42. 5: Ft Hays Kan State Col 60-64 (Bus) BS; UDenver 64-65 (LS) MA. 6: Ger. 7: ref libn Ft Hays Kan State Col 65-. 9: ALA. 10: Sigma Phi Esilon; Faculty Assn of Fort Hays Kan State Col (sec-treas 68-69, v-pres 69-70). 14: Ref. 15: Box 401, Hays Ks 67601.

REED, MARCIA (E LLA BRIDENSTINE). b Yakima Wash 12 Mr 29. 4: Carl H Reed. 5: Northwest Nazarene Col 47-49 (Music); UWash 49-51 (M usic) BA, 51-53 M Lib. 7: Catlgr Seattle Pub Lib 53-54, UWash Lib 54-58, Seattle Pacific Col 61-66, 69-. 9: ALA; Amer Musicological Soc. 14: Music catlg, music ref. 15: 3261 10th ave W, Seattle Wa 98119.

REED, MARY JANE (POBST). b Georgetown Ohio 4 N 20. 4: Horace B Reed. 5: Antioch Col 38-43 (Soc sci) BA; Antioch-Putney Grad Sch 53-55 (Educ) MA; Rutgers 60 (Catlg); SUNY (Albany) 66-68 MLS. 7: Skidmore Col: Acquis asst 59-61, Catlg libn 61-66; Rensselaer Polytech Inst: Hd catlg dept 67-68, Coord libn tech serv 68-. 9: ALA; ASIS; NYLA. 10: ACLU; NAACP. 12: Co-auth "Nepal in Transition" (68). 14: Admin, tech serv, computer applications. 15: 42 Circular st, Saratoga Springs NY 12866.

REED, RICHARD E. b Brockton Mass 7 Jl 36. 5: Bates Col 54-55 (Hist); Gordon Col 55-56 (Relig); Conception Col (Mo) 59-61 (Relig); UMiami (Fla) 66-67 (Relig) AB; Syracuse 68-69 MLS. 6: Lat. 7: Sp/4 US Army Artillery Fire Control 56-59; Catlg Reading Pub lib, Reading Mass 61-66, Asst libn; Trainee ref dept Miami Pub Lib, Miami Fla 66-68; Bkmob Miami-Dade Lib System, Miami Fla 68; Dir of dorm libs SyracuseU 68-. 8: Resident adv SyracuseU 68-69. 9: ALA. 14: Ref, govt docs, ya wk. 15: 401 Van Buren, Syracuse NY 13210.

REED, ROBERT CAMERON. b Cambridge Mass 21 S 25. 5: Hamilton Col 46-48; Hartwick Col 51-53 (Eng) BA; UMich 58-60 MALS. 7: (Cpl) 87th Infantry Div 43-45; UNH Lib: Catlgr 60-62; Asst order libn 63-65, Order libn 65-. 9: ALA; NELA; NHLA. 10: AAUP. 14: Acquis. 15: Stone House Farm, Durham NH 03824.

REED, SARAH REBECCA. b Warren Ill 8 F 14. 5: Cornell Col 31-34, 35-36 (Eng, Music) AB; UIll summers 41-45 BLS, MA; Chicago 45-46 (LS). 6: Fr. 7: Pub sch tchr & tchr-libn, Ill, Iowa 36-41, 34-35; Bk stacks libn UIll(Urbana) 41-45; Lib sch libn, supv of induction train UChicago 45-52; Visiting faculty UDenver Grad Sch of Libnship summers 51-53; Asst Prof UNC Sch of Lib Sci 52-55; Asst Prof Fla State U Lib Sch 55-60; Exec sec lib ed div, sec Com on Accreditation ALA, Chicago 60-63; Lib educ Spec US Off of Educ, Wash DC 63-67; Dir Sch of Lib Sci UAlta (Edmonton Can) 67-. 9: ALA; ASIS; CanLA; AltaLA; ManLA; SaskLA; EdmontonLA; Alta Sch Lib Coun; CanASchL. 10: Beta Phi Mu. 12: "Library Research in Progress" (63-65); "Library Education Directory" (63, 65); "Continuing Education for Librarians" (64, 65); "Problems of Library School Administration" (65); Co-auth "The Library in College Instruction" (51). 13: Yes. 14: Lib educ. 15: School of Lib Sci, Univ of Alberta, Edmonton Can.

REED, SUSANNE A (BUSSE). b Berlin 26 Ap 18. 4: Ernst D Reed. 5: Rhediger Gymnasium 34-38 (Langs, Chem) BA. 6: Ger, Fr. 7: Head libn West Precipitation Corp, Los Angeles 51-59; Libn Lockheed Cal Co 62-. 9: SLA. 14: Ref, transl. 15: 5102 Vesper ave, Sherman Oaks Ca 91403.

REED, VIRGINIA R. b Chicago 13 Ja 37. 5: St Mary-of-the-Woods Col 54-58 (Eng Lit) BA; Chicago 58-60 MALS. 6: Fr, Ital. 7: Ref & circ libn Upjohn Co, Kalamazoo 60-67; Libn Instituto di Ricerche Farmacologiche "Mario Negri (67-69). 9: SLA. 14: Ref, info sci. 15: Via Eritrea 62, 20157 Milano Italy.

REEDER, DOROTHY WELSH. b Williamsport Penn. 5: Kellogg Sch of Phys Educ 21-24 (Phys Educ) Diploma; Susquehanna U 24-26 (Eng, Educ) AB; Drexel 36-37 BS in LS; UMich summers 42-46 MALS: Columbia U Tchrs Col summers. 7: Instr phys educ Susquehanna U 28-36; Asst libn, assoc libn Roanoke Col 37-42; Libn Matthew Whaley Sch, Williamsburg Va 42-43; US Army libn, Camp Patrick Henry Va 43-45; Libn Blackstone Jr Col 45-46; Libn Radford Col 46-47; Libn Towson State Col 47-. 9: ALA (chm Melvil Dewey Award Jury 65); -ACRL (Bldgs Inst 59); MdLA (treas, pres, mem var coms). 10: AAUP. 13: Yes. 14: Ref, bldgs. 15: Towson State Col Lib, Baltimore 2204.

REEDER, FRANCES ELLEN (FORKNER). b Athens Tex 23 S 08. 4: Roy Reeder. 5: Joliet Jr Col 25-27 (Eng); UIll 27-28 (Eng) summers 33, 34, 37, 38, 39, 40 BLS; UWis summer 33 BS. 7: Rural tchr, Ill 28-35; High sch tchr, Ohio 36-37; Jr high Eng, Eng dept head & libn, Richmond Ind 37-46; High sch libn in br lib, Lima Ohio 47-51; Bkmob libn King Co, Seattle 52; Jr & sr high libn, Wapa to Wash 52-. 8: State Textbk Com for Eng in Richmond Ind, 40; Jt Exec Bd OhioEA & OhioLA 50. 9: Washington State SchLA (past reg chm); Wapato (Wash) EA (sec 64-65); ALA; NEA. 14: Ya wk. 15: Rt 1 Box 1375, Wapato Wa 98951.

REEDER, GRACE BOGART. b Evanston Ill 26 Je 06. 4: William O Reeder. 5: UWis 25-29 (Eng lit & compostion) BA. 6: Fr. 7: Hd libn geol & geog lib UWis 29-36; Lindgren libn of Lindgren Lib MIT 36-45; Hd libn Rustless Iron and Steel Corp Baltimore 45-51; Ref libn NACA, Wash DC 51-58; Chief ref libn NASA Hdqrs Lib, Wash DC 58-. 8: Assigned to spec duties on the MANHATTAN PROJECT 43-45; Assigned also to spec projs for indus firms. 9: SLA (Metals Div: v-chm chm-elect, ed monthly bull 50-51; past record sec wash Chap, Sci Tech Div; past Prog Chm Baltimore Chap, Sci Tech Div; several terms on Nomin Com Wash Chap, Sci-Tech Div). 10: UWis Alum Club of Wash DC. 13: Yes. 14: Ref. 15: 6200 28th st N, Arlington Va 22207.

REEDER, JOYCE JUNE. b Springer NM 10 Je 32. 5: San Bernardino Valley Col 50-52 (Art); Cal Baptist Col 52-56 (Hist) BA; USoCal 62-65 MA in LS. 6: Sp. 7: Charge of art dept Stockwell-Benny, San Bernardino Cal 56-58; Lib asst Cal Baptist Col Lib 58-62, Asst libn 62-64, Asst lib in charge tech processes 64-. 8: In charge of change-over from Dewey to LC Cal Baptist Col. 9: ChristianLA; CalLA. 10: AAUW. 14: Catlg, display wk within lib. 15: 8432 Magnolia ave, Riverside Ca 92504.

REEDER, NORMAN LEE. b Maywood Cal 6 S 44. 5: URedlands 62-66 (Govt) BA; UCLA 66-67 MLS. 6: Ger. 7: Libn Anaheim Pub Lib, Anaheim Cal 67; Signal intelligence off 1st Lt USAF 6986 Scty Gp APO San Francisco 68-. 9: ALA. 10: Beta Phi Mu; Pi Gamma Mu. 14: Ref, catlg. 15: 6986 Scty Gp, APO San Francisco Ca 96270.

REEDY, RUTH (CLARK) (MRS). b Corsicana Tex 22 Jl 15. 5: Northwestern State Col 31-32 (Eng); La Col 32-35 (Eng) BA; UIll 36-37 BS in LS; LSU 50, 53 (LS). 7: Libn Rayville High Sch, Rayville La 37-42; Libn Lake Charles High Sch, LAKE Charles La 42-61; Materials center libn & Assoc PROF OF Lib Sci McNeese State Col 61-. 8: Exec dir, Nat Lib Week, La, 64; Exec Sec Lib Dev Com of La 67-; Visiting Prof LSU 67. 9: NEA (Life mem); ALA; La State Tchrs Assn (Exec Coun 50-52); LaLA(sec 53, pres 56); LaASchL (pres 48-50). 10:

Delta Kappa Gamma; Art Assocs; Lake Charles Civic Symphony; Commun Concert Assn. 11: Modisette Award for Sch Libs, 56. 13: Yes. 14: Sch libs, a-v materials. 15: 3126 Second ave, Lake Charles La 70601.

REELING, PATRICIA ANN (GLUECK). b Cincinnati 6 Je 39. 4: Glenn E Reeling. 5: Edgecliff Col 56-60 (Ger) BA; Ind U 60-61 (LS) MA; Columbia 63-69 DLS. 6: Ger. Fr. 7: Ref asst Ohio State U Libs 61-62; Asst to dir of libs Boston Col 62-63; Tchg asst Columbia U Sch of Lib Serv 64; Visiting Lecturer in Lib Sci Ind U summer 64; Lecturer Columbia U 66-67; Asst Prof Grad Sch of Lib Serv Rutgers U 67-. 9: ALA(Jr Mems Round Table, Internat Rel Round Table); ADI; NJLA; NY Tech Serv Libns. 10: Beta Phi Mu; Kappa Gamma Pi; AAUP. 14: Educ for libnship, govt publns, ref, bibliog. 15: 100 Hepburn rd, apt 6-F, Clifton, NJ 07012.

REES, ALAN M. b London 14 My 29. 4: June M Litt. 5: ULondon 47-50 (Hist) BA; UOxford 50-52 (Hist) B Litt; Ohio STATE U 52-55 (Hist, Soc Sci); West Res 56-57 MS in LS. 6: Fr. 7: Grad asst Dept of Hist Ohio State U 54-55; Lib asst Case Inst of Tech 56-57; West Res U: Research assoc Center Documentation Cocumentation & Communication Research 57-60, Proj manager AMER Soc for Metals Documentation Serv 60-62, Instr Sch of Lib Sci 61-63, Asst Prof Sch of Lib Sci 63-, Asst dir for research Center for Documentation & Communication Research 64-; Prof of Lib Sci 68-. 8: Consul to NIH, NLM, etc; Lectr Australian LA, UMelbourne, 69. 9: ASIS; (Coun 65, chm Educ Com 65-; chm Cleveland Chap 63-64); MedLA (Com on Surveys & Stats). 11: Fulbright Award, 52-55. 13: Yes. 14: Documentation, info scis, ref. 15: 10831 Magnolia dr. Cleveland 44106.

REES, FRANCES (WILLA). b Sparks Ga 12 Ja 14. 5: Wesleyan Col 30-34 (Math) AB; Emory 34-35 (Relig Educ) MA, 40-41 BLS; Columbia 47-48, summer 46 (LS) MA. 6: Fr, Ger. 7: Youth dir Methodist Ch So Ga Conf, Macon Ga 36; Sec Wesleyan Christian Advocate, Macon Ga 36-39; Asst Savannah Pub Lib, Savannah Ga 41-43, Hd child dept 43-51; Coord- child serv & asst dir, Savannah Pub & Chathaw-Effingham-Liberty Savannah Reg Lib, Savannah Ga 52-. 9: ALA-CSD (var coms); GaLA (past pres Child Sect ; past sec Pub Lib Sect); SELA. 10: Delta Kappa Gamma; Pilot Club Intl; Opera Study Club. 13: Yes. 14: Child serv, ext. 15: 2002 Bull st, Savannah Ga 31401.

REES, JOE C. b Ripley Miss 15 O 30. 5: UMiss 55-57 (Eng) BA; UNC 59-61 MS LS; NE Miss Jr Col 49-51 AA. 06: Fr, Sp. 7: (S/Sgt) electronics tech USAF 51-55; Ed asst Law Lib LC 57-59; Humanities asst UNC Lib (Chapel Hill) 60-61; Ref asst Charlotte Pub Lib, Charlotte NC 61-62; Asst document libn Duke U Lib 62-65; Humanities libn Simon Fraser U Lib (Burnaby BC) 65-66; Asst ref libn NC State U 66-67; Engring libn DukeU 67-. 9: SLA. 10: Beta Phi Mu. 14: Ref, catlg. 15: Sch of Engring Lib Duke Univ, Durham NC 27706.

REES, MARJORIE GUEST. b Reading Penn 5 Je 20. 4: John Arlington Rees Jr. 5: Kutztown State Col 36-40 (LS) BS; Marywood Col 66-67 MLS. 6: Fr. 7: Child libn hoyt Pub Lib, Kingston Penn 47-52; Hd adu&t serv Osterhout Free Lib, Wilkes-Barre Penn 55-60; Ref libn Keystone Jr Col 67-. 9: ALA; PennLA (v-pres & pres-elect NE Chap). 10: Wyoming Monument Assn. 14: Ref. 15: 116 Hilltop rd, Waverly Pa 18471.

REES, PHILIP ADRIAN. b Manitowoc Wis 19 O 31. 5: DenisonU 50-54 (Art Hist) AB; West ResU 54-55 MS in LS. 7: Ref libn Union Col (Schenectady NY) 55-58; Libn Museum of nyc 59-62; Readers' serv libn Sarah Lawrence Col 62-68; Art libn UNC (Chapel Hill) 68-. 9: ALA. 10: Soc of Arch Histns; Sierra Club; Nat Trust for Historic Preservation. 14: Bibliog, ref. 15: Ackland Art Ctr Univ N Carolina, Chapel Hill NC 27514.

REES, THOMAS HUGH JR. b Mansfield Ohio 17 F 29. 4: Janet Felle Rees. 5: Denison U 47-51 (Biol) BS; West Res 56-58 MS in LS; West Res Med Col 51-54 (Med). 7: Research assoc Center for Documentation & Communication West Res U 55-61; Med libn Dalhousie U Fac Med (Halifax NS) 61-64; Med center libn UCincinnati Col of Med 64-. 9: SLA; ASIS; MedLA; OhioLA. 10: Great Lakes Hist Soc. 12: 'Commercially Available Equipment and Supplies' in Casey, R, et al "Punched cards." (2nd ed 58). 14: Med libnship, documentation, admin. 15: 1122 Beverly Hill dr, Cincinnati Oh 45226.

REESE, ANNE (CATHERINE) OHLSON. b Niagara Falls NY 15 Jl 43. 4: Edwin Lee Reese. 5: UMich 60-64 (Hist of Art), 64-65 MALS. 6: Ger. 7: Libn Toledo Mus of Art, Toledo Ohio 65-. 9: SLA; ALA; Art Research Libs of Ohio. 14: Sel, catlg. 15: Toledo Mus Art Box 1013, Toledo Oh 43601.

REESE, BETTY JO (SEELIG). b Montezuma Co Col 30 Je 21. 4: Donald W Reese. 5: West state Col of Color 40-41 & 45-47 (Eng, Educ) AB; UColo summers 51, 58, 59 (LS); UDenver summers 63-66 (Libnship) MA. 6: Sp. 7: Tchr & libn Montezuma Co High Sch, Cortez Colo 47-49; Libn & tchr Gunnison Co High Sch, Gunnison Colo 49-50; Libn Canon City High Sch, Canon City Colo 50-53; Eng tchr Wilson Borough Area High, Easton Penn 54-57; Libn & tchr Douglass Jr High, Boulder Colo 58-60; Libn Fairview High Sch, Boulder Colo 60-. 9: ALA; NEA; ColoEA; ColoASchL (sec 66); Colo A-V Assn; ColoLA; ColoEA; BoulderValleyEA. 14: Bk sel & ref for ya. 15: 441 Harvard lane, Boulder Co 80302.

REESE, DAVID ANDREWS. b Baltimore Md 26 S 41. 4: Ronaleen Osborne. 5: Brown 59-64 (Eng lit) AB; UKy 64-65 MSLS. 6: Fr. 7: Asst libn Bethany Col (Bethany W Va) 65-67; Acquis libn Plymouth State Col 67-. 9: ALA. 10: AAUP. 14: Acquis, admin. 15: 37 Winter, Plymouth NH 03264.

REESE, EDWARD A. b San Diego 6 O 16. 4: Fay Stewart. 5: San Diego State Col 46 (Eng) BA; Columbia 47 (LS) MS. 6: Ger, Fr. 7: (M/Sgt) 217 Gen Hosp US Army, Europe 41-45; Libn; Zool Lib Columbia U 46-49, US Army Qtrmstr Corps NYC 49-50, UCal(Berkeley) 50-51, Los Angeles Co Pub Lib, Los Angeles 51-52; Research libn Hughes Research Labs, Malibu Cal 52-. 9: ALA. 14: Ref. 15: Hughes Res Lib, Box 338, Malibu Cal 90265.

REESE, GARY FULLER. b Logan Utah 2 Ag 38. 5: Brigham Young U 56-59 (hist) BS, 59-61 (Hist) MS; UWash 64-65 MLibr. 6: Finnish. 7 Histn-libn Church of Jesus Christ of Latter-day Saints Finnish Mission, Helsinki 62-64; Livn Libn Tacoma Pub Lib, Tacoma Wash 65-67; Libn II 67-; Libn Tacoma Br Geneal Lib 66-. 9: WashLA. 10: Phi Alpha Theta. 14: Hist, geneal, maps, archives. 15: 9519 - 112 SW, Tacoma Wa 98498.

REEVES, BLANCHE. b Brooklyn NY 5 Je 10. 5: Hunter Col 26-28 (Biol); UWis 29-30 (Art educ); Brooklyn Col 50-51 (Eng) BA; Long Island Col 62-63 (Elem & secondary educ); Pratt Inst 67-68 MLS. 7: Br off mgr Paulson Engring Co, Fla 51-52; Corporate personnel sec & sec to pres & v-pres Induction Heating Corp, Brooklyn NY 53-62; Tchr nyc bd of Educ 63; Tech asst PR & PI dir Kingsborough Commun Col 64-65; Sec 65-66; Brooklyn Pub Lib, NY: Trainee 66-68, Libn 68-. 9: ALA; ASIS. 10: Beta Phi Mu; Pratt Inst Alum Assn; Booksellers League. 14: Child serv, bk sel criteria, progs, storytelling, info serv, computer applications. 15: 580 Flatbush ave, Brooklyn NY 11225.

REEVES, MARJORIE (ANN). b Oceanside Cal 21 J e 35. 5: Chapman Col 52-56 (eng, Hist) AB; UCal (Berkeley) 58-59 MILS. 7: Jr ref libn Fresno State Col 59-60, Jr ser libn 60-61; Libn Chapman Col 61-64; Head acquis dept UCal(Irvine) 64-66; Hd tech proc 66-. 9: . 14: Acquis, ser. 15: 446 Seward rd, Corona Del Mar Ca 92625.

REEVES, PATRICIA ANN (EMSLEY). b Chicago 18 Ag 33. 5: Rosary Col 51-55 (Zool) BA, 55-56 MA in LS. 7: Asst libn Armor Research Lib, Chicago 56; US Army Spec Serv: Post libn 32d Inf 7th Div, Korea 56-57, Admin libn I Corps Artillery, Korea 57-59, Main post libn, Ft Benning Ga 60-64, Post Libn 5th Army Hdqs, Chicago 64-66; Command ref libn 5th Army, Ft Sheridan Ill 67-68; Chief libn post lib 69-. 9: AFLS (Army rep Mem Com). 14: Ref, catlg. 15: 115 W Hawley st, Mundelein Il 60060.

REGALBUTO, VIRGIL ROBERT. b Valguarnera Sicily 10 Mr 16. 4: Alvina Beaulieu. 5: Brooklyn Col 37-42 (Govt) BA; Columbia 47-48 BS in LS, 48-50 MS in LS. 7: Tr Off of Censorship, NYC 42-45; Clerk Consolidated Cigar Corp, NYC 45-48; Catlgr Queens Col (NY) 48-60, Head acquis dept 61-. 9: NY Tech Serv Libns; NY Lib Club. 10: AAUP. 14: Catlg, acquis. 15: 8608 Little Neck pky, Floral Park NY 11001.

REGAN, MARY MARGARET. b Detroit Mich. 5: Margrove Col 45-49 (Eng) BA; Wayne U 50 (Eng); UMich 52-53 AMLS; Pub Libn's Prof Certif from SUNY Educ Dept 68. 6: Fr, Sp, Lat. 7: Prod mgr "Design News" Magazinem Detroit 50-51; Publicity dir Berkley Jr Theatre, Royal Oak Mich 51-52; Tech libn Control Instrument Co, Brooklyn NY 53-55; Sr ref libn Young & Rubicam Advertising Inc, NYC 55-67; Advertising & Marketing specialist (Economics Div NYC Pub Lib) 68-. 8: Co-discussion leader Amer Mgt Assn sem "How to Organize and Manage the Company Library" Sept 64. 9: SLA (NY Chap: mem &/or chm 4 coms 60-63, Auth and designer of recr lit for Advertising Gp 63-64; Advert Div) (Memb chm 56-57, ed Advert Div Bull 61-62); NY Lib Club; Educl Film Lib Assn. 10: Poetry Soc of Amer; Bronte Soc. 12: Exec ed "Guide to Special Issues and Indexes of Periodicals", SLA (62). 13: Yes. 14: Ref, recr, pub rel. 15: 36 E 36th st, New York NY 10016.

REGAN, MURIEL (BLOME). b NYC 15 Jl 30. 4: Robert A Regan. 5: Hunter 47-50 (Hist) BA (cum laude); Columbia 50-52 MS in LS. 6: Ger. 7: Post libn USA, Okinawa 52-53; Researcher P F Collier & Son, NY 53-57; Rockefeller Foundation, NY: Asst libn 57-62, Libn 62-67; Deputy chief libn Manhattan Commun Col, NY 67-68; Libn Booz-Allen & Hamilton Inc, NY 68-. 9: SLA. 10: Phi Beta Kappa. 14: Ref. 15: 792 Columbus ave, New York NY 10025.

REHAK, DOROTHY (ROBERTS). b Wash DC 7 D 25. 4: Stanislav Rehak. 5: UMich 43-47 (FR) AB, 47-48 (Fr) MA, 50-51 AMLS. 6: Fr, Ger, Czech. 7: Libn UMich Willow Run Res Center 50-54; Ref libn Ann Arbor Mich 65-67; Sch libn Ann Arbor Pioneer High Sch 68-. 10: LWV; Audubon Soc; Washtenaw Assn for Retarded Child; NAACP. 14: Ref, child & yp lit. 15: 1726 Hanover, Ann Arbor Mi 48103.

REHNBERG, MARILYN J. b Albany NY 6 Jl 34. 4: Axel Upton Rehnberg. 5: Rockford Col 52-56 (Modern dance) BA; UWis 57-58 (LS) MA. 6: Fr, Lat, Ger. 7: Libn's asst Rockford Col 56-57; Rockford Pub Lib, Rockford Ill: Bus & sci libn 58-59, Asst ref libn 59-62, A-v catlgr 68-. 9: ALA; -PLA. 10: Phi Beta Kappa; LWV. 14: Ref. 15: 212 Palm ave, Rockford Il 61107.

REHRAUER, GEORGE P. b Union City NJ 26 F 23. 5: Newark Col of Engring BS; Columbia (Educ) MA, EdD. 6: Ger, Sp. 7: Asst engineer US Navy Seabees, Leonia NJ 43-46; Tchr high sch, Port Jefferson NY 49-50; Tchr jr high sch, Hartsdale NY 50-58, Asst prin 60-63; Asst prin Mattlin Jr High Sch, Plainview NY 63-65; Prin Jr-Sr High Sch, Mahwah NJ 65-67; A-v coord Prentice-Hall Inc, NYC 67-68; Assoc prof Grad Sch of Lib Serv rutgers 68-. 9: NEA; NASSP; ASSA; ALA; NJEA; NJLA; NYStateTA. 10: Chamber of Com; PTA; Lions Club; Rotary. 14: A-v. 15: Grad School of Lib Serv Rutgers State Univ, New Brunswick NJ 08903.

REHRING, MARGARET CECILIA. b Cincinnati. 5: UCincinnati 30-34 (Span, Fr)BA, 34-37 MA; UIll 34-37 BS in LS. 6: Sp, Fr, Ital, Ger, Portu. 7: Libn Withrow High Sch, Cincinnati 38-53; Libn Woodward High Sch, Cincinnati 53-56; Supv of sch libs pub schs, Cincinnati 56-65; Instr lib sci UCincinnati 58-. 8: Visiting Instr in lib sci in summer & ext: Butler U, Appalachian State Tchrs Col, UKy, Marywood Col, UCincinnati. 9: ALA (Life mem):-AASchL (Bd Dirs; var coms); OhioASchL (past pres, sec & ed of "Bulletin). 13: Yes. 14: Sch libs, tchg lib sci. 15: Cincinnati Bd of Educ, 608 Mc Millan st. Cincinnati 45206.

REIBEL, DOROTHY (ELIZABETH). b Pomeroy Ohio 20 My 17. 5: Ohio U 35-39 (Eng, Hist) AB; Columbia 40-41 BS in LS; UNC 44-47 (Eng Lit) MA. 6: Lat, Fr. 7: Asst catlgr UArk 41-43; Jr catlgr UVa Law 43-44; Asst catlgr 44-47; Asst catlgr State U Iowa 47-48; Bibliog UMo 48; Catlgr Columbus Pub Lib, Columbus Ohio 49-61; Hd of catlg div 62-. 9: ALA; Ohiola. 14: Catlg, ref. 15: 96 S Grant, Columbus Ohio 43215.

REICH, DAVID LEE. b Orlando Fla 25 N 30. 5: UDetroit 57-61 (Eng) PhB (magna cum laude); UMich 62-63 AMLS. 7: (Sgt) US Army, Ft Bliss Tex 52-53, Mainz Germany 53-55; Admin asst US Civil Serv, Orlando AFB Fla 55-57; Eng tchr Jeff Davis Jr Sch, San Antonio Tex 61-62; Prof asst Albertson Pub Lib, Orlando Fla 63; Lib dir Radiation Inc, Melbourne Fla 63-64; Asst acquis libn Miami-Dade Jr Col 64-65, Asst to dir of libs 65; Dir of instr resources, Monroe Co Community Col 65-68; Assoc dir pub serv Dallas Tex Pub Lib 68-. 8: Auth of fifty of the orig "Word for the Day" radio prog for Detroit station WJBK 59-60; Consul Ctr Campus Lib, Macomb Co Commun Col (Mich) 66-67; Participant, AAJC-ALA Conf on Jr Col Libs Je 67. 9: ALA (Coun 68-72; mem Nat Lib Week Com 68-70);-ACRL (Com on Liaison with Accred Agencies 68-70; Jr Col Lib Sect; Mich Chm Spec Proj Com 66-68, sec 68-69; Preconf Planning Co 68-69); SWLA (Com to Draft Goals Award Proposal 68-69); MichLA (Nat Lib Week Com 66-68; Jr Col Sect; chm-elect 66-68); FlaLA (Col & Spec Libs Div; sec-treas 65; Nomin Com 64); Mich Commun & Jr Col Lib Adminrs (chm 67-68). 10: UMich Lib Sci Alumni Assn; InterTask Force (Lib) Wking Gp, Goals for Dallas. 11: Wm B Calkins Found Scholarship (Fla) 63. 13: Yes. 14: Admin, personnel, catlg. 15: 4203 Avondale apt 202, Dallas Tx 75219.

REICH, KATHLEEN (J WEICHEL). b Mannheim Germany 1 My 27. 5: ULeipzig (Germany) 47-50 (hist of Art, LS); UMainz (Germany) 50-54 (Hist of Art, LS). 6: Ger. 7: Head tech proc Albertson Pub Lib, Orlando Fla 55-57; Catlgr UDetroit 57-60; Head tech proc Muskegon Pub Lib, Muskegon Mich 60-61; Head catlgr Trinity U (Tex) 61-62; Admin Book Processing Center, Orlando Fla 62-. 9: ALA; SELA; FlaLA. 14: Catlg, rare bks, coop proc of lib materials. 15: 211 Fawsett rd, Winter Park Fla 32789.

REICHER, DANIEL DAVID. b Brussels Belgium 17 S 30. 5: Toronto 52-55 (Fr) BA, 55-56 MLS. 6: Fr, Dutch. 7: Catlgr UToronto Lib 56-59, Head reclsf div 59-61; Chief catlgr UAlta Lib 61-63; Asst libn USask Lib 63-67; Dir of libs UMontreal Lib 67-. 9: CanLA (chm Tech Serv Sect 65-66); ALA; Assn Canadienne des bibliothecaires de langue francaise; QueLA. 15: 847 Rue du Calvet, Laval Quebec Can.

REICHER, ISRAEL ROSE. b Bucharest Rumania 16 Mr 24. 5: BucharestU 44-46 (Philos) MA, 48-53 (Math) BS; Columbia 67-69 (Med Lib) MS. 6: Fr, Ital, Ger, Rumanian. 7: Tr Med Doc Ctr, Bucharest Rumania 61-64; Lib trainee NYU Med Center Lib 66-. 9: ALA; ASIS; SLA; MedLA. 10: Intl Ctr in NY. 14: Tech serv, info sci. 15: NY Univ Med Ctr Lib 550 1st ave, New York NY 10016.

REICHERT, KATHERINE (TEMPLIN). b Harrisburg Penn 18 Je 41. 4: George Martin Reichert. 5: Wilson Col 59-61; Drew U 61-63 (Eng) BA; Fla State U 64-65 (LS) MS. 7: Ya asst Springfield City Lib, Springfield Mass 63-64; Asst readers consul Jacksonville Pub Lib, Jacksonville, Fla 65-; Springfield City Lib, Springfield Mass; Asst supv 16 Acres Br 66-67; Admin asst ref dept 67-. 9: ALA; NELA; MassLA. 10: Beta Phi Mu. 14: Readers adv, ref, ya wk, govt docs. 15: 19 Edendale S, Springfield Ma 01104.

REICHMANN, FELIX. b Vienna 14 S 1899. 4: Lilly Doerfler. 5: UVienna 23 (Hist of Art, Hist) PhD; Chicago 42 (LS) MA. 6: Ger, Fr, Ital, Lat, Greek. 7: Owner & manager of bkshop, Vienna 26-38; Asst curator & libn Landis Valley Museum, Lancaster Penn 39-42; Libn Carl Schurz Found, Phila 42-44; Proj spec Off of Strategic Serv, Wash DC 44-45; Chief Publs Control 45-46; Joint acquis project LC 46-47; acquis Cornell U 47-48; Asst dir for tech serv Cornell U Lib 48-64, Asst dir for the development Devel the collections 64-70. 8: Lib consul. 9: ALA-RTSD (chm Planning Com (Acquis Sect); chm & sec Research Com); NYLA (Resources Com; chm Resources & Tech Serv Sect); SALALM (chm of Acquis). 11: Fulbright Professorship; Guggenheim Fellowship 56. 12: Auth: "Gothische Wandmalerei in Niederosterreich (25), "Subject-Index to the Proceedings of the Lancaster Historical Cociety, 1895-1939 (40), "The Location of Books on the College Campus (42), "Christopher Sower, Sr Printer in Germantown, 1694-1758 (43), "Ephrata as Seen by Contemporaries, with E E Doll (53), "Sugar, Gold and Coffee (59), "Notched Cards; (61); Comp: "The Muhlemberg Family, a Bibliography (43), "German Printing in Maryland, a Checklist 768-1050 (50). 13: Yes. 14: Bk sel, acquis. 15: 217 Willard way, Ithaca NY14850.

REICHWEIN, BERNIECE. b Cincinnati 15 Jl 20. 5: UCincinnati 36-40 (Ger) BA; UMich 43-46 BA in LS. 6: Fr, Ger, Ital, Sp. 7: Steno Rash-Saville-Crawford Corp, Cincinnati 40; Clerical asst Fiction dept Cincinnati Pub Lib 40-41; Typist, Catlg Dept UCincinnati 41-42, Continuations asst 42-43; Jr catlg asst UMich 43-45, Circ asst 45-46; Catlgr UCincinnati 46-64, Catlg reviser 64-. 9: ALA; Ohio Valley Group of Tech Serv Libns. 10: Trianon Sorority; Cincinnati Histl Soc. 15: Univ of Cincinnati Lib, Cincinnati Oh 45221.

REID, BETTY (MARY ELIZABETH) (DOUGLASS). b Conway Ark 5 D 15. 4: Joseph W Reid. 5: Hendrix Col 31-32; Ark State Tchrs Col 32-35 (Eng) BS in Ed; UColo summer 37; LSU 40-43 BS in LS. 6: Fr. 7: Tchr various schs, Ark 35-41; Co libn Faulkner & Laurence Co, Ark 41-42; Asst circ dept UAla Lib (Tuscaloosa) 44-46; Asst circ dept UNC (Chapel Hill) 46-48; Ref libn Middle Ga Reg Lib, Macon 48-55; Catlgr LSU 55-59; Order libn La State Lib, Baton Rouge 59-62; Head tech serv SW Mo State Col Lib 62-. 9: MoLA; Mo Assn Col & Research Libns. 14: Catlg, selection. 15: Box 3456 Glenstone sta, Springfield Mo 65804.

REID, CECIL ALEXANDER JR. b Richmond Va 30 Ap 31. 5: Randolph-Macon Col 48-52 (Hist) BA; Peabody 53-54 (LS) MA. 6: Lat. 7: Tchr Crewe High Sch, Crewe Va 52-53; Libn WVa Lib Commsn, Charleston WVa 54-62; Head circ & asst libn Bradley Mem Lib, Columbus Ga 63-64; Dir Central Lib Arlington Co Libs, Arlington Va 64-. 9: ALA; WVaLA; GaLA; VaLA. 10: Beta Phi Mu. 14: Ref, admin. 15: 2030 N Adams st, apt 809, Arlington Va.

REID, CHARLES E. b Englewood NJ 2 O 25. 4: Elizabeth Bampton. 7: US Navy Petty Off 2/c 2 1/2 yrs; Gen contractor. 8: Mayor Boro of Paramus NJ 67-. 9: ALA-LAD (Budgeting, Acctg & Costs Com 61-64); -ALTA (Adv Coun 61-63, chm Nat Lib Week Com 60-61, mem Wkshop Com 59, chm Action Devel Com 61-64, Del Nat Assembly 62-63, pres 64-65); Nat Soc of Home Bldrs; Bur of Marketing Research; NJLA; NJ LTA (Exec Com 59-, pres 63-64; Title 40 Com 61-63, Nat Lib Week Com 59-61, chm Trustee Educ Com 60-63); NJEA (Consul on Com for Wking Conditions for Tchrs 62-63). 10: Paramus Friends of Lib; Trustee, Paramus Free Pub Lib; Pub Sch Serv Assn; Trustee, Paramus Bd of Educ. 11: Trustee of the Year Award, NJTLA 59; Paramus Rotary Award for "Service Above Self" (given for lib activities), 55. 13: Yes. 15: 620 West dr, Paramus NJ 07652.

REID, CHRISTINE JANET (MILES). b Oxted Surrey England 30 Ag 43. 4: Alan Barry Reid. 5: Univ Col of Rhodesia & Nyasaland 62-64 (Eng) BA (honors); Loughborough Col 65-66 ALA. 7: Interlib loans asst & catlgr Univ Col of Rhodesia, Salisbury 66-68; Bibliog supv (order dept) UAlta 68-. 8: Summer sch on catlg & clsf UWitwatersrand, Johannesburg S Africa 68. 14: Catlg, ref uses on automation. 15: 153 Michener pk, Edmonton 70 Alta Can.

REID, de LAFAYETTE. b Alton Ill 18 Ap 15. 4: Mildred Joyce Weaks. 5: Shurtleff Col 32-35; UMo 36-38 (Journalism) BJ; UIll 39-40 (LS) BS, 40-42, 45-48 (LS) MS. 7: Reporter "Democrat-Argus, Caruthersville Mo 38-39; Asst circ dept UIl Lib (Urbana) 40-41, Asst acquis dept 41-42; Pharmacists Mate 1/c USNR 42-45; Bibliog acquis dept UIll Lib (Urbana) 45-46; Libn UIll Undergrad Div Lib (Galesburg) 46-49; Asst dir UKan Libs 49-51; Chief of pub serv Ill State Lib 51-54, Asst state libn 54-65, Deputy state libn 65-68; Asst Prof Dept of Lib Sci No Ill U (DeKalb) 68-. 8: Consul Judson Col 69. 9: ALA; AAStateL; NEA-DAVI; IllLA (pres elect 68-69); Ill Adult EA (pres 57-59); Ill A-V Assn (pres-elect, IllLA 68-69). 10: Rotary Internat; Beta Phi Mu. 12: Co-producer-Ed UIll Lib Orientation Film "Contact with Books (42); Spec ed "Collier 64-67). (64-65). 13: Yes. 14: Admin, automation, adult educ, pub lib systs. 15: RR 1, Box 251 Ellen Oaks, Genoa Il 60135.

REID, DOUGLAS GRAHAM. b Kingston Ont Can 15 S 20. 4: Mary Bastone. 5: McGill 46-48 BA, 48-49 BLS. 7: Pilot Royal Can Air Force, Coastal Commad FLT/Lt 40-45; Br libn Brooklyn Pub Lib 49-59; Statewide Pub Lib consul Conn State Dept of Ed, Hartford Conn 59-63; City Libn Bridgeport Pub Lib, Bridgeport Conn 63-. 9: ALA (Coun Mem-at-Large); ConnLA; NELA. 13: Yes. 14: Adult serv. 15: RR 1 Black Rock Tpke, W Redding Ct 06896.

REID, JEAN (RAMEY). b Electra Tex 19 Je 31. 4: Robert J Reid. 5: Stephens Col 48-50 AA; E Tex State U 50-51 (LS) BS. 6: Sp. 7: Ref & circ libn Stephens Col 52-53; Libn Rural Sem Bible Col of Mo 55-58; Ref & circ libn Stephens Col 58-59; Head catlgr Marquette U 61-64; Sch libn Lake Bluff Ill 64-69. 9: ALA; NEA; IllLA; IllEA; AASchL; IllASchL. 10: AAUW. 14: Sch ibnship, catlg. 15: 321 Walden rd, Wilmington De 19803.

REID, JEAN (SMITH). b Mammoth Utah 15 Je 16. 4: Ray Lorenzo Reid. 5: Brigham Young 33-37 (Food & Nutrition) BS; USoCal 61-64 (LS) MS; Cal State (Long Beach) 64 (Educ); Whittier Col 65 & 68 (Educ). 7: Home econ tchr-high sch: Springville Utah 38-40, Huntington utah 37-38, San Diego 44-45; Libn Sante Fe High Sch & Whittier Union High sch, Whittier Cal 64-. 9: ALA; NEA; CalLA. CalASchL; CalTA. 14: Ya, ref. 15: 8407 Calif ave, Whittier Ca 90605.

REID, LUCILLE (ALBRECHT). b Ohio Ill 10 Jl 15. 5: UIll 33-37 (Foods, Nutrition BS; Rosary Col 60-63 MA in LS. 7: Libn St Josephs High Sch, Westchster Ill 61-62; Manager info serv Moffett Res Center Corn Products Co, Argo Ill 62-. 9: ASIS; SLA; ACS (Chem Lit Div). 10: Iota Sigma Pi; Soroptimist. 14: Sci & tech admin, tech info mgt. 15: 744 59th st, Hinsdale Il 60501.

REID, MARGARET G(RAFF) (NYBERG). b Centralia Ill 22 Jl 09. 4: N Stanley Reid. 5: Colo Col 27-31 (Eng Lit) BA; UDenver 35-36 BS in LS. 7: Act head catlg dept Coburn Lib Colo Col summer 36; Libn High Sch Lib, LaJunta Colo 36; Asst circ & ref depts Deering Lib Northwestern U 37-39; Jr libn in catlg Fed Works Agency, Wash DC 39-42; Jr libn in catlg US Army War Col, Wash DC 42; Libn US Air Sea Rescue Agency 43-47; Ref libn Colo Springs (Colo) Pub Lib 47-49, City Libn 49-63; Libn Pikes Peak Reg Dist Lib, Colo 64-. 9: ALA; MPLA (sec 57-58); ColoLA (pres 58-59; Legis Com 60-65; Exhib Chm 61-65; Coun rep to ALA 67-); Colo Coun for Lib Dev (Adv Coun to State Lib 67-). 10: Colo Springs Charter Assn; Hist Soc of the Pikes Peak Reg; Nat League Amer Penwomen; Women's Educ Soc Colo Col. 14: Admin, catlg, ref. 15: 25 Cragmor Village, Colorado Springs Co 80907.

REID, MARION (TAYLOR). b Baltimore Md 27 O 44. 4: Dr Kenneth Brooks Reid. 5: Millsaps Col 62-64; UIll (Urbana) 64-66 (Eng Educ) BS, 66-68 (LS) MS. 7: Elem sch libn Urbana Schs, Urbana Ill 66-68; Asst libn Nat Hist Survey Lib, Urbana Ill 68; Sr libn LSU (Baton Rouge) 68-. 9: ALA; LaLA. 10: Kappa Delta Pi; Beta Phi Mu. 14: Acquis. 15: 1818 Blouin ave, Baton Rouge La 70808.

REID, REBECCA (LOIS) FARRIS. b Montgomery Ala 4 N 38. 4: Herman Edward Reid Jr. 5: Bennett Col 56-60 (Sociol) BA; Tuskegee Inst summer 58; UKan summer 59; Ala State Col summer 60; Atlanta U 64-67 MSLS. 7: Asst libn Langston U 60-62; Circ libn Albany State Col, Albany Ga 62-64; Grad asst ref dept Atlanta U 64-65; Soc studies tchr & libn Cedar Hill High Sch, Cedartown Ga 65-66; Lib coord Sylacauga City Sch Syst, Sylacauga Ala 66; Monroe High Sch, Albany Ga: Soc studies tchr 66-67; Libn 67-. 9: ALA; SELA; GaTchrEA. 14: Ref, a-v materials, circ. 15: 515 S Davis st, Albany Ga 31701.

REID, RUTH MARGARET (WADSWORTH). b Boshawa Ont Can. 4: Lloyd Reid. 5: Victoria Col UToronto 45-48 BA; Toronto 48-49 BLS. 7: Libn Ont Dept of Educ, Toronto 49, 52; Libn Etobicoke Pub Lib, Rexdale 61-. 14: Circ. 15: 12 Densmore ave, Rexdale Ont Can.

REID, THELMA ELOISE. b Pueblo Colo 9 Ja 09. 5: UCal(Berkeley) (Soc Institutions) AB, 31-32 Cert in Libnship, 35-39 (LS) MA. 7: Asst brs dept Oakland Free Lib, Oakland Cal 27-30; Catlgr Contra Cost Co Free Lib, Martinez Cal 30-35; Asst libn Beverly Hills High Sch Lib, Beverly Hills Cal 35-36; CVO Libn Napa Co Free Lib, Napa Cal 36-40; State Supv of Cal WPA Lib Prog, San Francisco 41-42; 41-;2; Field rep Cal State Lib 43-53; Chief Libn Sn Diego Schs Lib, San diego 53-. 67; Prof Lib Sci San Diego State Col 68-. 8: Lecturer on Ct & Munic libs, UCal(Berkeley) 50-51; Lecturer onchild lit & reading guidance for ya, San Diego State Col 63; Instr, USoCal Ext course in ch libnship 62. 9: ALA (chm Co & Reg Lib 47)-LAD (Coun 56-60; chm Bldgs & Equip Sect 63); CalLA (pres 56). 12: Consul, J Nickelsburg California from the Mountains to the Sea, 4 v (64). 13: Yes. 14: Child lit, lib ext. 15: 1933 Alameda ter, San Diego Ca 92103.

REIFEL, LOUIE ELIZABETH (ROGERS). b Curve Tenn 1 Ag 13. 4: Alexander F Reifel. 5: Memphis State 32-33 (Lat; UHouston 46 (Lat, Educ) BS; UTex MLS, (Supv) Supv Certif. 6: Lat. 7: Tchr Aldine Ind Sch Dist, Aldine Tex 50-54, Marshall Jr High Sch, Houston 54-57, McReynolds Jr High Sch, Houston 57-59, Fonville Jr High Sch, Houston 59-61; Consul Houston Ind Sch Dist 61-63, Supv 63-. 8: Visiting lectr; NDEA Inst West Mich U (Kalamazoo) 66, NDEA Inst UOkla (Norman) 67, UHouston summer 68; New Careers Program OEO - prepared Curriculum & consul for HISD - New Careers Program 68-69; Tex-Tec Adv Com 68. 9: ALA; Grolier-Americana Scholarship Award Com (State Assembly Mem);-LAD (Recr Com);-AASchL (chm Nom Com Supvs Sect 67-68); TexLA (chm Dist 5; chm Dist Planning Com 66-68; State Assembly Del 64-65); SWLA; TexASchL (chm); Houston Lib Club. 10: Delta Kappa Gamma; Alpha Delta Kappa; Houston Assn of Supv & Curr Devel; UTex Grad Sch of Lib Sci Alumni Club; Houston ASchL; Kappa Delta Pi. 14: Supv child & ya lit, lib educ. 15: 12118 Queensbury, Houston Tx 77024.

REIFF, HARRY B. b Royersford Penn 20 Mr 30. 4: Julie Webster. 5: West Chester State Col 48-52 (Hist) BS; West Res 54-55 (LS) MS. 7: Free Lib of Phila: Ref asst gen info dept55-57, Asst dept head soc sci & hist dept 57-63, Dept head soc sci & tech dept Northeast Reg Lib63-, Bk sel spec Off of wk with adults & ya 66-. 9: ALA; PennLA. 14: Ref, bk sel. 15: 6913 Heyward st, Phila Pa 19119.

REILEIN, DEAN A. b Aurora Ill 22 N 33. 4: Bonnie Birch. 5: Aurora Col 57-61 (Eng) BA; No IllU 63-65 (LS) MA. 7: A/1C Weather Observer USAF 52-56; Caseworker Ill Pub Aid Commsn Kane Co 61-63; Ref libn W Liberty State Col 65-. 14: Catlg. 15: Box 177, W Liberty WVa 26074.

REILLY, ALICE (FIELDS). b Denver 18 S 11. 5: UDenver 28-32 (Eng) AB, 32-33 BS in LS. 7: Libn High Sch, Ft Morgan Colo 33-3; Libn High Sch, Lake Forest Ill 38-41; Post libn US Army, George Field Ill 41-43; Head Libn Pub Lib, Manhattan Kan 49-57; Consul Fla State Lib 57-58; Consul Cal State Lib 58-60; Co Fresno Freno Co Free Lib, Fresno Cal 60-; Chm

Admin Com San Joaquin Lib Syst 64-. 9: ALA; KanLA (pres 56-57); CalLA (chm Legis Com 65-67, pres Yosemite Dist 63); Chm Internat Exchange of Libns Com 68-; Co Supv Assn of Cal (v-chm Lib Adv Com 68-). 10: AAUW; ASPA; NSAL; Fresno C of C (Cultural Arts Com); People-to-People. 12: . 13: Yes. 14: Admin. 15: Fresno Co Free Lib, 2420 Mariposa st, Fresno Cal 93721.

REILLY, HEDWIG OLGA. b Pilissaba Hungary 22 Ag 20. 5: Pazmany Peter U (Hungary) 38-42 B of Pharmacy; West Res 62-63 (LS) MS. 6: Hungarian, Ger, Fr, Lat. 7: Pharmacist, Budapest Hungary 42-44; Lab tech agric biochem Ohio State U 60-61, Lab tech veterinary pathology 61-62; Catlgr Chem Abstracts Serv, Columbus Ohio 63-. 14: Ref, admin, automation. 15: 2436 Medary ave, Columbus Ohio 43202.

REILLY, JAMES HENRY. b San Francisco 2 Ap 33. 4: Beryl T Johnson. 5: USan Francisco 50-54 (Philos) BA; San Francisco State Col 54-56 (Educ) Tchrs Cred; UCa(Berkeley) 62-63MLS. 7: 3/c petty off Sk3 US Navy 56-57; Libn San Francisco Pub Lib 58-63, Sr libn Sci Dept 64-. 9: CalLA; SLA. 14: Sci, math, ref. 15: San Francisco Pub Lib, San Francisco 94102.

REIMAN, MARY. b LaCrosse Wis 3 Mr 40. 5: Col of St Catherine 58-62 (LS) BA; Atlanta U 68-69 MS in LS. 6: Fr. 7: Asst child libn Kellogg Pub Lib, Green Bay Wis 62-64; Child libn Wallingford Pub Lib, Wallingford Conn 64-. 8: Staff, Lib/USA, NY Worlds Fair, 64. 9: ALA (Memb Com rep Conn, Jr Mem Round Table Conn liaison 65); WisLA (Memb Com 63-64). 10: AAUW; Girl Scout Leader. 14: Child serv. 15: 422 So 14th st, LaCrosse Wi 54601.

REIMERS, PAUL R. b Crawford Ohio 7 Jl 17. 4: Elizabeth Jetter. 5: UBuffalo 35-39 (Eng) BA, 39-41 MA; Harvard 54-55 (Bus) MBA. 6: Ger. 7: 1st Lt Signal Corps US Army 2-I - Phillipines 42-46; Research analyst Army Security Agcy, Wash DC 47-54; Comptroller Nat Security Agency, Wash DC 55-57, chief syst eng 57-60; Mgr info syst RCA, Wash DC 60-64; Info analyst RAC, Wash DC 64-66; Coord of Info Syst LC 66-. 9: ALA; Inst of Mgt Scis; Assn Compg Mach. 10: Phi Beta Kappa; Capitol Hill Club; Capitol Hill Restor Soc. 12: Co-auth "Neutralization of Voet Cong Safe Havens," RAC Rep (65); Principal auth "Determination of Parameters of a Post Attach Radiologic reporting System," RCA Rep (63). 13: Yes. 14: Lib automation. 15: Inf Sys Off Lib of Congress, Washington DC 20540.

REINACH, GERTRUDE A (BAER). b Germany 14 Mr 11. 5: Temple 36-40 (Soc studies) BS, 40-41 (Soc group wk) MEd; Syracuse 61-63(Catlg) MSLS. 6: Ger, Fr. 7: Johns Hopkins U Lib 63-65; Temple U Lib 65-66; Wilimington Inst Free Lib 66-67; Monmouth Col Lib 67-. 9: ALA; MonmouthCoLA. 14: Catlg. 15: 123 Washington st, Long Branch NJ 07740.

REINAP, MIA. b Estonia 9 Jl 17. 5: UMass 36-40 (Zool) BS; Simmons 40-41 (LS) BS. 7: Catlgr Museum of Comp Zool Harvard U 41-43; Catlgr Brown U 43-46; Act libn biol & chem Tex 46-47; Asst libn Col of Dentistry (NY) 47-52; Asst libn NY State Veterinary Col (Ithaca) 52-54, Libn 54-. 15: NY State Vet Col, Ithaca NY 14850.

REINDL, ELLENE ANNETTE. b Houston Tex 8 Ag 34. 5: Rice U 52-56 (Fr) BA; Columbia 60-62 (LS) MS. 6: Fr, Ger, Russian, Sp, Portu. 7: Sec IBM, Houston 56-58; Sec Humble Oil, Houston 58-60; Circ asst Union Theol Sem Lib (NY) 61-62; Circ libn Rice U 62-64, Acquis libn 64-66, catlg libn 67-. 9: ALA; TexLA. 10: PHI Beta Kappa. 14: Catlg. 15: 9402 Stonehouse lane, Houston Tx 77025.

REINER, MABEL D. b Superior Wis 29 S 01. 4: Laszlo Reiner. 5: UWis 20-24 (Chem) BS, 27-28 (Chem) MS; Columbia 43 (LS) BS. 6: Ger, Fr. 7: Analytical chem C F Burgess Labs, Madison Wis 24-27; Research asst UWis Dept Agric Chem summer 28; Chem instr Lincoln High Sch, Manitowoc Wis 28-31; Research libn Burroughs Wellcome Res Labs, Tuckahoe NY 32-42; Chem abstractor Standard Oil & Develop Co, Elizabeth NJ 43; Lit searcher Gen Aniline & Film Corp, NYC 43-49; Sci lit consul (free lance) 49-54, Inst of Cancer Research Columbia U Col of Physicians & Surgeons 54-59, free lance 59-. 9: ACS; Fellow Amer Inst of Chemists. 10: AAA. 13: Yes. 14: Sci lit, searching, writing, editing. 15: 10-C Crestmont rd, Montclair NJ 07042.

REINHARDT, MARJORIE (PRISCILLA). b NY 9 Ja 47. 5: Wagner Col 64-68 (Ger) AB; Simmons 68-69 MSLS. 6: Ger. 7: Order libn Andover-Harvard Theol Lib 69-. 10: Delta Phi Alpha. 14: Ref, acquis. 15: 106 Myrtle st, Boston Ma 02114.

REINHOLD, EDNA (JONES). b Clinton Ill 15 Je 35. 4: James F Reinhold. 05: MacMurray Col 54-58 (Econ) BS; UIll summers 61-65 (LS) MS. 6: Fr, Lat. 7: Stud asst Henry Pfeiffer Lib, MacMurray Col 54-55; Decatur (Ill) Pub Lib: Circ asst 58-61; Ref dept asst 61-65, Head of ref dept 65-66, Chief central pub serv & act city libn 67, Supv adult serv 68; Prin libn circ dept St Louis Pub Lib 68-. 09: IllLA. 14: Ref, readers' adv. 15: 820 LaSalle, Collinsville Il 62234.

REINING, ELIZABETH. b Akron Ohio 11 S 06. 5: Akron U 25-29 (Educ) BA; UColo summer 44; USoCal 47-48 MLS. 6: Ger, Hungarian. 7: Tchr Akron Pub Schs, Akron Ohio 28-38, Elem Sch libn 38-46; Libn Los Angeles City Schs 48-55; Consul Riverside Co Supt Off, Riverside Cal 55-57; Dist libn & libn consul Pomona Unified Sch Dist, Pomona Cal 57-. 8: Instr, lib sci ext courses: UCLA 56, USoCal 56-62, 64-. 9: NEA (Life mem); ALA; CalLA; CalASchL (treas 54-55, chm Educ Code Com 53-63). 10: YWCA. 14: Sch libs. 15: 359 E 14th st, Upland Cal 91786.

REINISCH, LILLIAN (MACHOVER). b Brooklyn NY Ap 17. 4: Mann B Reinisch. 5: Brooklyn Col 34-38 (Eng) BA; Pratt 38-39 BLS. 6: Fr, Hebrew. 7:Asst Asst Mem Lib, Bound Brook NJ 39-40; Asst libn NY Pub Lib 40-42; Libn Metropolitan Voc High Sch, NYC 49-53; Libn Manhasset High Sch, Manhasset NY 53-. 9: NEA; ALA; NY State Tchrs Assn; NYLA; Nassau Co (NY) SchLA. 10: No Shore Child Study Assn; LWV. 14: Wk with yp. 15: 325 E Shore rd, Great Neck NY 11023.

REINKE, BERNNETT (GORDON). b Bismarck ND 27 F 41. 4: Doris Hirning. 5: Dickinson State Col 59-63 (Eng, Biol) BS; Peabody 64-65 MLS. 7: Eng tchr pub sch, Mott ND 63-64;Libn Dickinson State Col 65-. 9: NEA; MPLA; NDLA; NDEA; ALA. 14: Admin. 15: Dickinson State Col, Dickinson ND 58601.

REINKE, DORIS (HIRNING). b Elgin ND 24 S 42. 4: Bernnett Reinke. 5: Dickinson State Col 60-64 (Elem Educ) BS; Peabody 64-65 MLS. 7: Elem tchr pub Sch, Mott ND 63-64; Asst libn Dickinson Stae Col 65-. 9: NEA; MPLA; NDLA; NDEA. 10: Delta Zeta. 14: Circ, catlg. 15: Dicinson State Col, Dickinson ND 58601.

REINMILLER, ELINOR CALMBACH. b Oswego Kan 29 Ag 19. 5: N Tex U 35-37, 46-47 BS in LS, 50-54 (Hist) MA; UIowa 38-39 (Zool) BA. 7: Asst libn UTex Southwestern Med Sch (Dallas) 47-. 9: SLA; MedLA. 13: Yes. 14: Ref. 15: 5323 Harry Hines blvd, Dallas Tx 75235.

REISNER, EDITH (O GUR). b NYC 3 Jl 13. 4: Bernard J Reisner. 5: Barnard 29-33 (Econ) BA; Queens Col (NYC) 59-60 (LS; C W Post Col LIU 60-62 (LS) MS. 6: Fr. 7: Research statistician R H Macy, NYC 33-46; High sch libn UFSD 9, Wyandanch NY 60-, 8: Dir of Lib Serv, Wyandanch NY 65-. 9: NEA; ALA; NY State Tchrs Assn; NYLA; Nassau-Suffolk (NY); SchLA (v-pres); LIECC. 14: Ref, reading guidance, high sch wk. 15: 9 Overbrook dr, Centerport NY 11721.

REITAN, MARILYN JEAN (BERGLIN). b Little Falls Minn 20 O 3 5. 4: Howard M Reitan. 5: Coe Col 53-55; UMinn 55-57 (Elem Educ) BS, 65-69 (LS) MA. 6: Fr. 7: Elem sch tchr Richfield Pub Schs, Richfield Minn 57-62; Elem sch libn Robbinsdale Pub Schs, Robbinsdale Minn 62-63; Elem sch libn Edina Pub Schs, Edina Minn 64-65. 10: Alpha Gamma Delta. 14: Sch lib wk. 15: 9941 Oxborough rd, Minneapolis Mn 55431.

REITH, MARIANA K. b San Pedro Cal 10 Mr 26. 5: UWis 45-49 (Hist) BS, 50-51 (LS) MA. 7: Tchr & libn Randon Lake High Sch, Randon Lake Wis 49-50; Caterpillar Tractor Co bus libm Peoria Ill: Asst libn 51-54, Libn 54-62; Los Angeles Pub Lib bus & econ div: Libn 58-62, Asst dept hd 62-65, Dept hd 65-. 8: Vis assoc prof USoCal Lib Sch 68, 69. 9: SLA (chm Bus Div 57-58, chm Bus & Fin Div 66-67, corres sec So Cal Chap 67-68); CalLA (v-chm & chm-elect Docs Div 68-69). 13/ yes. 14: Ref. 15: 516 S Oak Knoll 9, Pasadena Ca 91106.

REITZ, CONRAD HJALMAR. b Pretoria SA 3 Ja 35. 4: Blodwen Davies. 5: U Pretoria (S Africa) 58 (Sociol, Psych) BA; UCape Town 62 Diploma in Libnship; UToronto 66 MLS. 6: Eng, Afrikaans, Dutch, Flemish. 7: Probation Off Dept of Soc Welfare (SA), Durban 59-61; Libn Cape Prov Lib Lib Serv, Cape Town 62-63; Catlgr UToronto 63-65; Head acquis dept UWaterloo (Ont) 65-66; Hd acquis dept UWindsor 66-67, Asst libn tech serv 67-. 9: SLA (Nat Exec Bd 65-68; sec of Bd 65-66, Convention chm 63; pres Colo Chap 53-54; "Bulletin ed 48-52; com chm 56-59, div chm 54-55); ALA 63-68; 63-)-RSD (com chm 64-); ColoLA (Exec Bd 61-, Legis Com 59-65); MPLA. 12: "The Reitz Family; an Annotated Bibliography; (Capetown 64); "South African Bibliography" (67). 13: Yes. 14: Tech serv, admin, research. 15: Lib Univ of Windsor, Windsor Ont Can.

REITZ, LOUIS (MARTIN) SS. b Baltimore 11 N 29. 5: St Mary's Sem & UMd 47-51 (Philos) AB, 51-55 (Theol) STL; Catholic U 51-59 MS in LS; Loyola Col (Baltimore) 58-60 (Educ) MEd. 6: Lat, Fr. 7: Asst libn St Thomas Sem (Louisville y) 55-56; Libn Sulpician Novitiate, Baltimore 56-57, St Thomas Sem (Louisville y) 57-58, St Marys Sem & U Sch of Theol (Baltimore) 58-61, St Thomas Sem (Louisville Ky) 61-; Assoc Prof St Thomas Ctr Bellarmine-Ursuline Col (Louisville) 69-. 9: CathLA (mem & past chm Ad Bd of Sem Sect); ALA-AASchL;-ACRL; KyASchL. 10: US Power Squadron. 13: Yes. 14: Catlg, a-v, circ. 15: 7101 Brownsboro rd, Louisville Ky 40222.

REITZEL, HILDA M. b Pittsburgh 9 My 21. 5: UPittsburgh 39-43 (Eng) AB; Carnegie 43-45 BS in LS; UPittsburgh 49-52 (Geog) MA. 7: UPittsburgh: Asst med libn 43-45, Asst ref dept 45-52, Research libn 52; Libn Mine Safety Appliances Co, Pittsburgh 52-54; Head ref dept UPittsburgh 54-56; Libn Mine Safety Appliances Co, Pittsburgh 56-. 9: SLA (pres Pittsburgh Chap 58-59); ALA-ACRL; PennLA; Pittsburgh Lib Club (pres 50-51). 10: Phi Delta Gamma; Sigma Kappa Phi; Pi Tau Phi; Pilot Internat. 11: Certif of Merit, PennLA 67. 12: Ed PennLA "Bulletin (61-). 13: Yes. 14: Ref, spec libs. 15: Carlton House, Pittsburgh Pa 15219.

REITZELL, VIRGINIA SCOTT. b Erie Penn 6 S 10. 5: Conn Col 27-31 (Eng) BA; West Res 36-37 BS in LS. 7: Erie Pub Lib, Erie Penn: Supv ext dept 37-40, Head adult circ ept 40-48, Head adult circ wk & Brs & asst libn 65-. 9: Penn NW Dist LA (past pres). 10: Soroptimist Club; Jr League; YWCA. ; AAUW. 14: Ext serv, adult serv. 15: Box 1583, Erie Penn 16507.

REKEY, TIBOR R(OBERT). b Budapest 23 Je 21. 4: Magda Vidor. 5: Pazmany Peter U (Budapest) 39-44 Dr Jur; Columbia 57-58 (LS) MA. 6: Hungarian, Ger, Russian, Fr. 7: Clerk to the Court County Court, Budapest 44-49; Clerk to the Court Supreme Court of Hungary, 49-51; Tech tr Taki TKI, Budapest 52-54; Tech tr United Incandescent Lamp Ltd, Budapest 54-56; Catlgr Dartmouth Col 58-. 10: Appalachian Mountain Club; Fed of Hungarian Scouts. 14: Catlg. 15: 2 E Wilder rd, W Lebanon NH 03784.

RELLEVE, ROSALIE. b Philippines 3 Ag 34. 4: Emiliano Relleve. 5: UMd 62-64 BA; Catholic U 65-66 MS in LS. 6: Fr, Tagalog. 7: Asst libn Hawaii State Lib 66-68; Asst humanities libn Cal State Col, Long Beach Cal 68-. 9: CalLA. 10: Cal State Employees Assn. 14: Ref. 15: 4396 Adenmoor ave, Lakewood Ca 90713.

REMINGTON, DAVID G. b Worchester Mass 21 Ap 37. 4: Susan Smith. 5: Wesleyan U 55-59 (Eng) BA; Rutgers 59-61 MLS. 7: Lib trainee pub lib, Plainfield NJ 59-61; Hd tech serv pub lib, Summitt NJ 61-64; Hd catlgr Alanar Bk Processing Ctr, Williamsport Penn 64-65, Dir 66-; Lecturer Lib Assoc Program Williamsport Area Commun Col 66-; Dir prof serv Bro-Dart Inc, Williamsport Penn 66-. 8: Consul RECON proj LC Info Systems Off 69-; Chm Subcom for Cost of Tech Serv, NJ Lib Devel Com 63-64; Mem US ASA 239; Subcom 15: (fling standards). 9: ALA; -AASchL; -ACRL; -PLA (var coms); NJLA (Tech Serv Div: sec 63-64. 13: Yes. 14: Lib admin, lib educ, tech serv. 15: Bro Dart 1609 Memorial ave, Williamsport Pa 17701.

REMINGTON, EDITH M (ING). b White Plains NY 29 Je 26. 4: Patrick Remington. 5: King's Col 59-63 (Psych) BA; UOre 67 MLS. 6: Sp. 7: Sec NYC; Peace Corps vol, Kabul Afghanistan 64-66; Asst libn UNeb, Lincoln 68-. 9: ALA; NebLA. 14: Ref, rare bks. 15: 6335 Walker ave, Lincoln Nb 68507.

REMLEY, A(LBERT) L(OUIS). b Granger Ind 6 Mr 17. 4: Caroline Imel. 5: Hiram Col 34-38 (Amer & Eng Lit) AB; UIll 38-39 BS in LS. 7: Asst Govt Documents Dept Northwestern U 39-41; Pvt to Lt 41-45 & Capt AGD GHQ AFPAC, Manila 45-46; Advertising manager ALA, Chicago 46-48; Libn R R Donnelley & Sons Co, Chicago 48-52; Advertising manager ALA, Chicago 52-59; Exhibits Dir The Combined Book Exhibit, Bronx NY 59-63; Dir of advertising & promotion H W Wilson Co, Bronx NY 63-. 9: ALA; NY Lib Club. 10: Amer Inst of Graphic Art; Publrs Ad Club, NY; Publrs Lib PROMOTION Group, NY; ALU. 14: Catlg. 15: H W Wilson Co, 950 University ave, Bronx NY 10452.

RENAUD, RUTH. b New Orleans 8 Je 09. 5: Tulane 44 BA; Columbia 46 BLS. 7: Pub Lib, New Orleans: Asst catlg dept 26-32, Head catlg dept 32-46, Head adult dept 46-58, Head gen serv dept 58-62; Ref libn Loyola U Lib (New Orleans) 62-68; Asst supv Centralized Lib Project, New Orleans 68-. 9: ALA; SWLA (treas 51-52); LaLA (treas 51-52); New Orleans Lib Club (pres 51-52). 14: Child, sch libs. 15: 1639 S Jefferson Davis pky, New Orleans La 70118.

RENDELL, JOSEPH WARREN. b Trenton NJ 27 Ag 16. 4: Virginia Claudia Jump. 5: Trenton State Col 34-38 (Secondary Educ) BS, 49 BLS; Columbia 51 (Curriculum, Tchg)MA, 60 (Curriculum, Tchg) EdD. 7: Tchr Hopewell Grammar Sch, Hopewell NJ 38-39; Jr asst libn bus & tech dept Free Pub Lib, Trenton NJ 40-41; (Sgt) US Army Air Forces 42-45; Libn Pennington Sch for Boys, Pennington NJ 46-47; Libn Trenton Jr Col 47-51; Asst libn Newark State Col 51-55, Col Libn & Prof of Lib Sci 55-. 8: Served with Middle States Assn of Cols & Secondary Schs eval Teams, Feb 61, Feb & Nov 65. 9: ALA; NEA; NJLA (pres Col & Univ Sect 61-62); NJEA. 10: Kappa Delta Pi. 13: Yes. 14: Admin. 15: 732 Mountain ave, Westfield NJ 07090.

RENFRO, KATHRYN R. b Horse Cave Ky 15 Ag 18. 5: Colo Col 35-38; UDenver 38-39 AB, Diploma in Lib Sci. 7: Catlg reviser UDenver Lib Sch summer 39; Asst catlgr Stephens Col Lib 39-42; Head of catlg dept Utah State Agric Col Lib 42-43; Catlgr Iowa State Col Lib 43-4; Sr asst libn catlg dept UNeb Lib 46-49, Catlg libn 49-50, Tech serv libn 50-53, Asst dir of libs for tech serv 53-64, Assoc dir of libs for tech serv 64-68, Assoc dir of libs for gen serv 68-. 9: ALA (Coun 57-61 & 65-69); - RTSD (Bd Dirs 57-61; CCS Exec Com 59-61); -ACRL (Bd Dirs 65-69; sec Univ Libs Sect 54-55); NebLA (pres 63-64); MPLA (chm Reg Catlg Group 50-51; chm Col &Univ Sect 54-55). 10: AAUP, AAUW. 13: Yes. 14: Tech serv, univ libs, admin. 15: Univ of Neb Libs, Lincoln Neb 68508.

RENGER, SISTER MARY ANNETTE. b Allance Neb 26 Ag 1889. 5: Catholic U 14-18 (Sci) AB; UIll 30-31 Bs in LS, 41-42 MA in LS. 7t; libn Mt St Francis, Dubuque Iowa 19-39; Head Libn Briar Cliff Col 42-64; Lib supv Sisters of St Francis, Dubuque Iow 64-. 9: CathLA (ch Col Sect 1952 Conf). 10: Beta Phi Mu; Phi Kappa Phi. 12: "A Manual for Cataloging School Libraries (51,55,61). 13: yes. 14: Catlg yp libs. 15: Holy Family Hall, Windsor Ext, Dubuque Iowa 52001.

RENSHAW, MARITA. b Decatur Ill 8 N 38. 5: Ill Col 56-60 (Eng) AB; No Ill U 66-67 (LS) MA. 6: Sp, Fr. 7: Libn St John's Hosp Sch Nursing Lib, Springfield Ill 60-66; Catlg libn No Ill U 67-. 9: ALA; IllLA; Profess Libn Assn No Ill U. 10: Coun for Except Child; AAUW. 14: Catlg. 15: 224 Suburban apts Glidden rd, DeKalb Il 60115.

RENSTROM, ARTHUR G(EORGE). b Willmar Minn 30 O 05. 4: Mary Long. 5: Hamline U 23-26; UMinn 26-28 BA UIll 27-28 BS in LS; Columbia 29-30 (LS) MS. 6: Danish, Norwegian, Swedish. 7: Sr asst & asst chief Aeronautics Div LC 35-45, 46-53; Libn Civil Aeronautics ADmin 45-46; LC: Bibliogr Tech Info Div 54, Curator & supv sci rm sci & tech div 54-62, Hd ref sect sci & tech div 62-63, Sci ref & Bibliog spec sci & tech div 63-65, hd aeronautics sect sci & tech div 65-. 9: SLA; DCLA. 12: Jt auth I "Subject Headings for the Aeronautical Index" (40); Jt auth "Aeronautica Americana" (43); "Earliest Swedish Imprints in the United States" (45); "United States Aviation Policy" (47); "Aeropolitics" (48); "Aeronautical and Space Serials, A World List" (62); "Bibliographical Note on the History of Rocket Technology" (64); Bibl Ed "Journal of Air Law and Commerce"; auth "Wilbur and Orville Wright; A Bibliography ." (68). 13: Yes. 14: Sci & tech ref, bibliog, aeronaut hist. 15: 5306 N Washington blvd, Arlington Va 22205.

RENTHAL, HELEN (GREENWALD). b Chicago 24 D 11. 4: Sidney Renthal. 5: UMich 30-33 (Eng) AB; Carnegie 33-34 BS in LS. 7: Libn Shaker Heights Pub Schs, Shaker Heights Ohio 34-36; Elem sch libn dist 65, Evanston Ill 36-; Instr Chicago

Tchrs Col 57-58; Instr Nat Col of Educ Evanston Ill 61-66; Elem sch lib consul State Dept of Pub Instr, Phoenix Ariz, 66-67; Asst Prof Lib Sci UAriz (Tucson) 67-. 9: ALA; Newbery-Caldecott Awards Com 63-64, Rep to NCTE Elem Sch Bklist Com 60-64; Ariz Coun 69-71; Aurianne Award Com 57-60, NC Com 67-68);-CSD (chm Lib Serv to Disadvantaged Child 68-69);-AASchL; NEA; ArizEA; ArizLA. 10: Delta Kappa Gamma. 14: Child & sch lib week. 15: 1801 E Spring st, Tucson Az 85719.

RENTSCHLER, MERRYL. b Hamburg Penn 8 D 17. 4: Pearl Rice. 5: Kutztown State Col 45-48 (Eng, Hist) BS in Ed; UDenver summers 52-54 MA in LS; Columbia 52-54 (A-v Spec) MA, 55-57 (A-v Spec). 7: Libn: Easton Jr-Sr High Sch, Easton Penn 48-61, Easton Area High Sch, Easton Penn 61-, Easton Area Summer Sch, Easton Penn 61-63; Easton Even Adult Sch, Easton Penn 62-. 9: NEA; ALA;-ACRL;-AASchL; -YASD:-RTSD; Penn STATE EA (Dept of Supv & Curr); NYLA. 10: Phi Delta Kappa; Kappa Delta Pi; Alpha Beta Alpha. 14: Ref, a-v, micro storage, catlg. 15: 4455 Charles st, Bethlehem Twp, Easton Penn 18042.

RENTZ, JOSEPHINE (WHEELER). b Kansas City Mo 18 O 10. 4: Frank A Rentz. 5: UKan 31 (Span) BA, MA; UWis 61 (LS) MA. 6: Sp, Fr, Lat. 7: Instr UWis(Madison) 34-42; Libn West Sr High Sch, Madison Wis 61-. 9: WisEA; WisLA. 10: Phi Beta Kappa; Pi Lambda Theta; Eta Sigma Phi. 12: Ed "The Madison Teacher" (42). 15: 624 Bordner dr, Madison Wi 53705.

RENZ, JAMES HENRY. b Columbus Ohio 23 O 28. 5: Ohio State U 49-53 (Ger) BA; UMich 56-57 MALS. 7: US Air Force (Capt) 53-55; Fla collection libn Miami Pub Lib, Miami Fla 57-60; Acquis libn Col of William & Mary 60-62; V-Pres Private Family-Owned Business, Ft Myers Fla 63-64; Asst libn Col of William & Mary 64-66, Act libn 66, Assoc libn 66-. 8: Visiting lectr Richmond Spec Libs Inst 65, 67; Faculty Adv Col of William & Mary; WCWM radio broadcasts on "Richard Wagner & Music Drama". 9: ALA; VaLA (chm Col & Univ Sect 66, chm Local Arrangement Com 66, Col & Univ Acquis Sect Moderator); SELA; FlaLA (chm Ref RT 60). 10: Delta Phi Alpha; Beta Phi Mu. 12: Auth "Sources for the Music Dramas of Richard Wagner" (69); auth "Richard Wagner and the Music Drama" (67). 13: Yes. 14: Acquis, admin, pub serv. 15: Heritage Inn Suite 3D, 1324 Richmond rd, Williamsburg, Va.

RENZE. DOLORES C (ALAHAN). b Denver 11 J107. 4: Walter A Renze. 5: UDenver 23-27 (Anthropology, Biol) AB BS, 46-48 (Hist); American U 52 Certif in Archival Admin. 6: Fr, Sp. 7: Archaeologist US Nat Mus Nat Geographic, Wash DC & field 27-28; Sec US Senator F E Warren, Wash DC & Cheyenne Wyo 29-30; Admin asst Lab of Anthropology, Santa Fe NM 30-33; Research supv USDA, Denver & Wash DC 34-38; Investigator US Dept of Labor 38-46; Owner & operatorDude Ranch, Estes Park Colo 46-48; State Archivist & Dir Colo State Archives 49-. 8: Assoc Prof, Dept of Hist UDenver, 52-; Dir UDenver Inst of Archival Studies, 62-. 9: SAA (Life Fellow, exec sec 56-63, v-pres 64-65, pres 65-66, mem Com Prof Standards, mem Com on Educ & Training 65-; mem Com State & Local Records 66-); SLA; SHA; American Assn State & Loc Hist; NMA; Nat Trust Preserv Hist Sites; Soc Arch Histns; Internat Coun Archives; West Conf Histns; MPLA; Colo State Hist Soc; Inter-Agency Records Coun; NARS (Reg 8; Adv Com 69- Bd Dirs); Amer Soc Pub Admin; Brit Microfilm Assn. 10: The Westerners; Unesco; UDenver Womens Faculty Club; Pub Personnel Assn. 12: Indexes & Guides to Var Archival Holdings in the Colo State Archives 1-63). 13: Yes. 14: Archival source materials. 15: 1530 Sherman, Denver Colo 80203.

RePASS, ELEANOR (WHEELOCK). b Illinois 18 D 02. 4: Paul E RePass. 5: UColo 20-24 (Romance lang) BA, BE; UDenver 52 MA in LS. 6: Fr, Sp, Ital, Lat, Ger. 7: High sch tchr Bear Creek Sch, Morrison Colo 24-25; Asst libn UColo Med Sch 25-27; Trans & ref libn NY Acad of Med NYC 27-28; Ref libn Gen Foods Lib, Hoboken NJ 44-46; Martin Co, Denver Colo: Researcher of engring lit 61-62, Admin br lib 62-63; Catlgr UColo Med Ctr 63-65; Hd &ibn N Shore Commun Col 66-. 9: ALA; SLA; MedLA; MassLA; Coun Commun Col Libns Mass; Coun Mass State Instns Hd Libns; Essex So Med Aux. 10: Colo State Med Aux; Kappa Delta Pi. 13: Yes. 14: Admin, ref. 15: 3 Essex st, Beverly Ma 01915.

RESNICK, NATHAN. b Brooklyn NY 13 Je 10. 4: Ernestine Roberts Cederholm. 5: LIU 33 (Eng) BS; Columbia 37 (LS) BS; NYU 45 (Amer Lit) MA. 7: LIU: Prof of Eng 38-52, Prof of f Art & Chm of dept 52-, Dir of LIU Press 48-, Campus planning coord 64-, Dir of Libs 39-. 8: Nat sec "Leaves of Grass Centennial Com, 55; Consul Photography in Fine Arts; Consul Fund for Concerned Photographer 67-. 9: ALA. ; aasp; AAAS; Walt Whitman Birthplace Assn. 12: "English Literature Study Guide" (48); "Walt Whitman and the Authorship of the Good Gray Poet" (48); Ed "Songbirds of America" (53); "The Third Eye" (62, photographs sent on world tour by USIA in 61 & 64); Gen ed "Ancient Peru" (65). 13: Yes. 14: Admin, campus planning. 15: 72 Barrow st, NYC 10014.

RESS,' LAWRENCE R. b Chatham NJ 2 Apt 28. 4: Lorna Marnett. 5: Mt St Marys Col 45-47 (Eng Lit); Hall U 47-48 (Eng Lit) BA (cum Fordham U 48-49 (Eng Lit); Rutgers 58-62 MILS. 6: Lat. 7: High & jr high sch tchr Oratory Sch, Summit NJ 49-51; Statistician P Ballantine & Sons, Newark NY 52; Correspondent & Dist rep Prudential Insurance Co, Newark NJ 53-58; REF LIBN Union Pub Lib, Union NJ 58-61; Research asst Rutgers U GradLib Sch 61-62; High sch libn Hackensack Pub High Sch, Hackensack, NJ 62; Ref libn Newark State Col Lib 62-; Pub serv libn 67-. 9: NEA; NJEA; NJLA; NJ Secon Tchrs Assn. 10: NJ State & Loc Faculty Assn; Newark State Col Faculty Assn Exec Coun, 68-69. 14: Ref, pub serv. 15: 677 Summit rd, Union NJ 07083.

RESSEGUIE, BRUCE. b Evanston Ill 14 Ja 19. 4: Virginia Reeve. 5: Cal State Col (Long Beach) 60-65 (Sociol) BA; San Jose State Col 66-67 (LS); Fresno State Col 66-67 (LS); Loyola U (Chicago) 66-68 (LS). 7: Chief Petty Off US Coast Guard 40-65; Pub info libn Kern Co Lib, Bakersfield Cal 65-67; Period libn ref asst 67-. 9: ALA; CalLA. 10: Kern Co (Cal) Lib Staff Assn; Episcopal Church Vestryman. 14: Ref. 15: 2912 Mt Vernon ave, Bakersfield Ca 93306.

RETAN, (EMMA) ELIZABETH. b Burlington Vt 29 Ap 07. 5: Pomona Col 28-31 (Romance Langs) AB; Columbia 32 BS in LS. 6: Fr, Sp, Ital, Portu, Ger. 7: Libn Jr Col 32-33; Catlgr LC 33-48; Catlgr & clsf Hoover Lib, Stanford Cal 48-56; Head catlgr Stanford Law Lib 58-60; Catlgr & clsf Huntington Lib, San Marino Cal 60-66; Catlgr & clsfr Cal State Col (Fullerton) 66-. 9: CalLA. 10: AAUW. 14: Catlg, clsf. 15: Cal State Col Fullerton Lib 800 No State College blvd, Fullerton Ca 92632.

RETTIE, JEAN E. b Mt Kisco NY 12 Mr 32. 5: SUNY (Geneseo) 50-54 (LS, Elem Educ) BS; SUNY (Albany) 56-57 MSLS. 6: Fr. 7: Child libn Rome Free Lib, Rome NY 54-56; Child libn Pine Hills Pub Lib, Albany NY 57-61; Libn Lisha Kill Jr High Sch, Colonie NY 61-62; Bkmob libn Mohawk Valley Lib Assoc, Schenectady NY 64-67; Br libn Schenectady Co Pub Lib, NY 62-64, Hd of circ 67-. 9: NYLA; Hudson-MohawkLA. 10: Albany Civic Symphony. 14: Circ, child wk, ya. 15: 15 Forest dr, Albany NY 12205.

RETTIG, MILDRED MAGDALENE. b Evansville Ind 3 My 06. 5: West Res 26-27 (LS) Certif, 30-32 BS; UWash summer 55 (LS); USoCal summer 60. 7: Catlg dept asst Evansville Pub Lib, Servel Inc, Evansville Ind 33-34; Evansville Pub Lib, Evansville Ind: Catlg dept 1st asst 34-50, Catlg dept head 50-52, Tech serv dept chief 52-57, Asst dir 57-, Act dir 62. 9: ALA; IndLA (chm Catlg-Wkshop 62, mem Constit & By-laws Com 64-); Ohio Valley Group of Tech Serv Lbns (pres 59). 10: YWCA; AAUW. 13: Yes. 14: Catlg, tech serv, admin. 15: 1227 E Gum st, Evansville Ind 47714.

RETZER, ELIZABETH HELM. b Baltimore 20 Ap 19. 4: William R Retzer. 5: West Md Col 36-40 (Pre-Med, Educ) BA; Columbia 45-46 (Educ) MA; Ill State U 64-65 (LS); UIll 60-61, 64-65 (LS); Bradley U 65 (Spec Educ, LS). 6: Sp, Ger. 7: Montgomery Co Bd of Educ;girls phys educ, Silver Spring Md 40-44, Rec coordinator, Rockville Md 44, Supv educ, Rockville Md 44-47; Licensing consul State of ill Dept Pub Welfare, Peoria Ill 51-53; Phys educ Bradley U 56-57; Br libn Peoria Pub Lib, Peoria Ill 56-58, Homebound libn 58-63; Libn Hines Sch, Peoria Ill 63-; 63-66; Libn Bergan High Sch, Peoria Ill 65-67; Libn R J High Sch, Peoria Ill 66-; Faculty Bradley U (Peoria) summer 66. 9: ALA; NEA; IllLA; IllEA; Ill State U Administrators Club. 10: AAUW; Bd, Salvation Army; Prof Adv Coun Crippled Child (Nat Foun). ; Intl Platform Assn; Lakeview Ctr for Arts & Scis; PeoriaEA; Entre Nous; Peoria Nursing Assn; Univ Club. 13: Yes. 14: Ref, rare bks. 15: 1317 W Moss ave, Peoria Ill 61606.

REUBER, MARLENE M. b St Paul Minn 16 Mr 31. 5: Maukato State Col 49-51; UMinn 52-54 bs in LS. 7: Asst to owner Pygmalion Charm Sch, Miami Fla 57-59; Asst libn Brockway Lib, Miami Shores Fla 60-61; Exec sec ACS, NYC 61-62; Nat Airlines spec rep, NYC & Miami 62-63; Circ mgr "The Dines Letter", NYC 63-64; Exec sec "Look Mag", NYC 64-66; Br libn St Paul Pub Lib 66-. 9: ALA; MinnLA (sec Adult Serv Div). 15: 127 Nina st, St Paul Mn 55102.

REVERE, LINNEA (SODERMAN). b Phila 24My 09. 4: George J Revere. 5: Adelphi U 28-30 (Math, Sci) BA; UWis 39 Certif for Sch Lib; St Johns U (NY) 39-42 BLS; Hofstra U 52-55 (Admin, Supv) MS in NYU 61 NYU (Educ); UIll 56, 57 (Sch Lib Supv). 6: Fr. 7: Math tchr & libn Massapequa Pub Schs, Massapequa NY 30-43; Head libn Curtiss-Wright New Products Div, Bloomfield NJ 43-44; Head libn Reynolds Metals Research Div, Glen Cove NY 44-47; Priv bus, Montclair NJ 47-50; Supv of sch libs Levittown Union Free Sch Dist 5, Levittown NY 50-. 9: NEA; ALA (NY State chm Sch Lib Standards 60-64); NY State Tchrs Assn; NYLA (chm Supv Sect of Sch Libs 58-60); Nassau-SuffolkSchLA; (Standards Chm 59-61; State Bur of Libs Com on Central Processing 66; Sch Libs Sect Com on State Contracts for Purchasing 68); NASSP; DEP; NCTE; SuffolkSchLA; NY Sch Lib Supvs (Com on Pub & Sch Lib Coop 68-69). 10: Heckscher Mus; Huntington; Nassau Co Hist Soc; NY Folklore Soc; St Johns U Lib Sci Alum Assn; Assn of Levittown Sch Admin. 12: "Library Teaching Manual, Levittownn K - 12; "History of School Library Supervision, New York State. 14: Sch libs, catlg, ref, abstracting. 15: 3700 Manchester rd, Wantagh NY 11793.

REVESZ,GABRIELLE S(TERN). b Budapest 4 My 27. 4: George Revesz. 5: U Zurich 47-50 (Chem); Temple U 56-60 (Chem) MA. 6: Ger, Fr, Hungarian, Ital. 7: Res asst Temple U Med Sch 60-61; Sr res asst Temple U Pharmacy Sch 61-62; Supv indexing ; "Index Chemicus, Phila 62-67; Managing ed 67-. 9: ACS; ASIS; Fellow Amer Inst Chemists. 10: Sigma Xi. 13: Yes. 15: Inst for Sci Info, 325 Chestnut st, Phila 19106.

REY, MARGUERITE A(NN). b New Orleans La. 5: Xavier U (New OrlenasO 58-62 (Hist) BA; Catholic U 62-64 MS in LS. 7: Grad lib asst Catholic U Lib 62-64; Catlgr Xavier U (New orlenas) 64-65; Catlgr New Orleans Pub Lib 65-68; Hd catlg Baltimore Co Pub Lib, Towson Md 68-. 9: ALA; MdLA; LaLA; Potomac Tech Proc Libns (Coun from Md 69-70). 14: Tech serv. 15: 25 W Chesapeake ave, Towson Md 21204.

REYES, AUREA L. b Philippines 24 Ag 27. 4: Gervacio T Reyes. 5: Philippine Women's U 56-61 LS BS Educ; UOkla 66; Cameron State Col 66-68; Our Lady of the Lake Col 68. 6: Filipino. 7: Patients' libn Spec Serv Hosp Lib, Ft Sill Okla 64-66, Libn 66-68; Patients' libn Spec Serv Lib Div, Ft Sam Houston Tex 68-. 9: ALA; TexLA; BexanCoLA. 14: Ref. 15: 4418 Eisenhauer, San Antonio Tx 78218.

REYMOND, MONIQUE (MARTELLY). b Marseille France 15 Je 37. 5: Sacre Coeur de Marseille. 54 Baccalaureat de l'Enseignement Secondaire; Universite d'Aix-Marseille 55-57 Licence d'Enseignement d'Anglais; Ecole Superieure de Bibliothecaires Paris 58-59 Diplome Superieur de Bibliothecaire; British Council Intl summer 60 (Libnship). 6: Fr, Sp. 7: Altachee saisonniere Bibliotheques Mejanes, Aix eu Povence (13) 59; Bibliothecaire Centre Pedagogigve Reg, Bordeaux (33) 60-61; Bibliothecaire Lycee Bernard Palioy, Agen (47) 61-62; Bibliothecaire USherbrooke 67. 9: Association de l'Ecole Nationale sufeneure de Bibliothecaire (France). 14: Ref, Fr & Eng lit. 15: 1498 Desnoyers, Sherbrooke PQ Can.

REYNAROWYCH, ROMAN. b Woroblachyn W Ukraine 15 Ag 12. 4: Helen Reynarowych. 5: Jagello U (Krakov Poland) 31-37 (Civil Law, Exec Admin) LLM; UInnsbruck (Innsbruck Austria) 45-49; So Conn State Col 58-59 MLS; Ukrainian Free U (Munich) 60-61, JSD. 6: Ger, Polish, Ukrainian, Russian. 7: Sr catlg libn Rutgers U Lib 59-60; Asst head of catlg dept Seton all U Lib 60-63,Documents libn 63-66; Docs libn St Johns U 66-. 8: Abstractor, Amer Bibliog Ctr. 9: ALA. 10: AAUP; Shevchenko Sci Soc, NY; Ukrainian Acad of Arts & Scis NY; Ukrainian Hist Assn. 13: Yes. 14: Admin, ref, documentation. 15: St Johns Univ Lib, Jamaica NY 11432.

REYNOLDINI, SISTER M OP. b Chicago. 5: Ill State Normal 36-40 (Educ); Edgewood Col 40-41 (Eng) BS; U Wis (Madison) summers 42-46 (Eng) MA; Columbia 50-51 (LS) MA; Stanford U summer 60 (Research in Eng), Florence (Italy) Research in Fine Arts 65-68. 6: Ger. 7: Tchr lang arts Edgewood Sch, Madison Wis 41-46; Eng tchr Trinity High Sch, River Forest Ill 46-50; Libn St Clara Acad, Sinsinawa Wis 56-57; Asst libn & Prof of Eng, Edgewood Col 57-58; Assoc Prof lib sci Rosary Col 51-56, 59-65; Prof bibliog of music, Villa Schifanoia Sch of Fine Arts, Florence Italy 65-68; Assoc Prof Lib Sci Rosary Col 68-. 9: ALA; CathLA (Adv Coun, chm Lib Educ Sect 63); NCTE; IllLA; IllASchl. 10: AAUP; Cath Poetry Soc Amer. Ed "Catholic Booklist" (59-65, 69-). 13: Yes 14: Ref (Humanities), cur lit,bk sel. 15: Dept of Lib Sci Rosary Col, River Forest Ill 60305.

REYNOLDS, CARROLL F. b Granville Ohio 14 O 10. 4: Erma Lewis. 5: WVaU 27-32 (Phys Educ) BS; Columbia 34-35 (LS) BS; UPittsburgh 37-40 (Hist) MA, 40-50 (Hist) PhD. 7: Asst to libn W Va Lib 35-36; Curator of documents UPittsburgh Lib 36-38; Ref libn Okla A&M Col 38-40; Asst libn & act libn UPittsburgh 40-43; Histn Proj of UPittsburgh for US Corps of Engrs, Ft Belvoir ,va 45-47; Assoc dir ext div UPittsburgh 47-57, LIbn Falk Lib of Health Prof 57-. 8: Med lib consul, Ulbadan, Ibadan Nigeria, 64 (Rockefeller Foun grant); Visiting Med Libn Faculty of Med Scis, Bangkok Thailand 67-68 (Rockefeller Found). 9: ALA; SLA (Pittsburgh Chap: var coms); MedLA (treas 63-64, Fin Com 63-4, Com on Med Lib Problems 65-). 10: Pittsburgh Bibliophiles; Amer Assn Hist of Med. 13: Yes. 14: Med libs, admin, hist of med. 15: 497 Willow dr, Pittsburgh Pa 15243.

REYNOLDS, CATHARINE JANE. b Erie Penn 3 Ap 19. 5: Villa Maria Col 37-41(Eng) BA: Columbia 46-47 LS) BS; UMich summer 50 (LS). 7: Petty Off 3/c WAVES 44-46; Ref-circ libn Allegheny Col 47-50 Head govt documents dept UIowa 50-66; Head govt docs div UColo 66-. 9: ALA; ColoLA. 12: Comp "Iowa Documents accession list no 1 (56-). 13: Yes. 14: Govt publns. 15: 830 - 20th st, Boulder Co 80302.

REYNOLDS, DORSEY JR. b Wilmington Del 6 N 34. 4: R Naomi (Eldridge) Reynolds. 5: Central Bible Inst 52-56 (Missions) BA; Drexel 59-61 (LS) MS. 6: Sp.07: Lib asst New Castle Co Free Lib, Wilmington Del 56-61; Ref asst Wilmington Inst Free Lib, Wilmington Del 61-64; Libn Northeast Bible Inst (Green Lane Penn) 64-. 9: ALA. 14: Ref. 15: Northeast Bible Inst, Green Lane Penn 18054.

REYNOLDS, ELIZABETH MURRAY LOUISE. b Towson Md 19 Ap 17. 5: Wilson Tchrs Col 34-37 (Educ); USDA Grad Sch Even (LS); UOre 57-59. 7: Lib asst US Dept of Agric, Wash DC 42-49; Catlg filer LC 49-50; Gen libn US Naval Hos, Wash DC 50-54; Med libn SGO US Navy, Wash DC 54-56; VA Hosp: Chief Libn, Roseburg Ore 56-59, en libn, Topeka Kan 59-64, Med libn, Portland Ore 64-. 9: ALA-AHIL; MedLA; OreLA. 10: Toastmistress; DAR. 14: Bibliother, publicity. 15: 5130 SW Nebraska st, Portland Ore 97221.

REYNOLDS, ELSIE ELLEN. b Brooklyn NY 29 Jl 27. 5: Hofstra 45-48 (Hist) BA; UIll 48-49 (Hist) MA; Columbia 50-52 MSLS. 6: Sp, Fr. 7: Subprof Queensborough Pub Lib, Jamaica NY 49-50; Army libn USA Spec Serv, Germany & France 52-54; Subprof Hofstra Col 50-52, catlgr 54-56, Res libn 56-58, Ref libn 58-, Asst libn 58-. 9: ALA; NYLA; NassauCoLA. 14: Univ ref serv. 15: 590 Fulton ave apt 10F, Hempstead NY 11550.

REYNOLDS, ERNA (ERNESTINE) DETERS. b Caledonia Minn. 5: Hamline 31-34 (Eng, Foreign Langs) BA; Colo State U summers 56, 57 Certif in Libnship; UDenver summers 59-61 (LS) MA; UMinn(Minneapolis) summers 56, 57; UWis(Madison) summer 65 (NDEA Inst). 6: Ger. 7: Tchr of Eng Ger & Lat High Sch, Dawson Minn 34-40; Tchr of Eng & libn High Sch, Pierre SD 55-58x; Libn Riggs High Sch, Pierre SD 58-60; Elem libn Stillwater Dist 834, Stillwater Minn 60-61; Ref libn USD summer 62; Tech libn UNIVAC, St Paul summer 64; Sr libn Stillwater Sr High Sch, Stillwater Minn 61-. 8: Dir IMC; Consul area wkshops in schs adopting mod scheduling - team tchg programs; Mem N Central Assn of Sec Schs Evaluation Team, lib , a-v fields. 9: ALA; NEA; MinnEA; MinnASchL. 10: AAUW; Delta Kappa Gamma; PEO. 13: Yes. 14: Catlg, ref, reader serv, guidance. 15: Rt 5 Garden Hills, Stillwater Minn 55082.

REYNOLDS, FLORA ELIZABETH. b San Rafael Cal 4 N 11. 5: UCal(Berkeley) 34 (Lat) AB, 35 (Lat) MA, 36 (LS) Certif. 6: Fr, Lat. 7: Co-libn Sausalito Pub Lib, Sausalito Cal 37-39; Libn Mill Valley Pub Lib, Mill Valley Cal 39-43; Libn US Army 43-45; Asst ref libn San Francisco State Col 49-50, Chief ref serv 50-53; Instr UCal (Ext) (Berkeley) 53-54, Lecturer 58, 4; Libn & Assoc Prof Mills Col 55-, 64; Libn & Assoc Prof Mills Col 55-; Lecturer UOre summers 66, 68, 69. 9: ALA; SLA; CalLA (pres Col Univ & Res Sect 60-61). 10: Bk Club of Cal; UCal Sch of Libnship Alumni Assn; Phi Beta Kappa; PI Sigma; Sierra Club. 13: Yes. 14: Ref, rare bks, col admin. 15: 1152 Amador ave, Berkeley Cal 94707.

REYNOLDS, FREDERICK JAMES. b Ft Wayne Ind 7 Ja 11. 4: Winifred Irene Hoppe. 5: Ind U 36-41 (Hist) AB; West Res 44-46 BSLS. 6: Ger. 7: Ft Wayne Pub Lib, Ft Wayne Ind: Bkmob 30-35, Head of Allen Co ext dept 35-41, Asst libn 41-59, Head Libn 60-. 9: ALA; IndLA. 10: Quest Club; Kiwanis; Fortnightly; Executive Club; Allen Co-Ft Wayne Hist Soc; Ind Hist Soc; Humane Soc; Soc of Ind Pioneers; C of C; Izaak Walton League; Junto Club. 13: Yes. 14: Admin, rare bks, local hist. 15: 4533 Wilmette, Ft Wayne Ind 46806.

REYNOLDS, GRACE ELLEN (DORIS). b Montreal Can 7 Mr 07. 5: McGill & Sir George Williams Col; McGill (LS) Certif. 7: Priv sec, Stephen Leacock, Montreal 24-27; Sec, reviser, lecturer McGill U Lib Sch 27-51; Libn Railway Assn of Can, Montreal 51-62; Asst to exec dir SLA, NYC 62-67; Chief libn Beaconsfield Pub Lib, Beaconsfield Que 67-. 9: SLA (pres Montreal Chap 40-41, past chm Transp Div). 15: 92 St Louis ave, Beaconsfield Que Can.

REYNOLDS, HELEN MARGARET. b Pratt Kan 7 Ap 16. 5: UNeb, 35-39 (Art) BFA, 39-40 (Art) BA; UIll 40-41 BS in LS, 42-46 MS in LS. 06: Fr. 6: Fr. 7: Asst libn Arch Lib UIll(Urbana) 42-61; Libn II catlg dept UCal(San Diego) 61-. 8: Visiting art bibliog Art Dept UTex; 59. 9: ALA; CalLA. 10: Alpha Lambda Delta; Delta Phi Delta; Phi Beta Kappa. 13: Yes. 14: Catlg, art bks, univ lbs. 15: Univ of Cal Lib, PO Box 109, La Jolla Ca 92038.

REYNOLDS, JEAN E. b Saginaw Mich 11 D 41. 5: Wells Col 59-63 (Rel) BA; CCNY 64-65 Amer Lit MA. 7: Sr ed child bks Prentice-Hall Inc, Englewood Cliffs NJ 63-69; Sr ed child bks McCall Publishing Co, NYC 69-. 9: ALA. 10: Child bk coun; Womens Nat Bk Assn; Child Study Assn& mensa. 13: Yes. 14: Child bk editing. 15: 747 River rd, Piermont NY 10968.

REYNOLDS, JOHN DEVEREUX. b Brooklyn NY 31 Ag 34. 4: Sally Jo Sawyer . 5: Cornell U 52-55; Columbia 56, 60-63 (Russian) BS, 63-65 (LS) MS. 6: Russian, Fr. 7: Off Clerk IBM Corp, NYC 55-57; US Army Lang Sch 57-58; US Army Russian Linguist (Sp/5) 58-60; Catlg asst Columbia U Libs 60-64; Spec Russian 64-65; Catlg Slavic Langs Sect Descr Catlg Div LC 65-67; Asst hd Slavic langs sect descr catlg div 67-68; Supv Cyrillic Unit Slavic langs sect Shared Catlg Div 68-. 9: Potomac Tech Proc Libns; DCLA. 14: Catlg, Slavic bibliog, automation. 15: 4201 Massachusetts ave NW apt 100, Wash DC 20016.

REYNOLDS, MARGARET NORENE (ALLEN) (MRS). b Moncton NB Can 15 J3 14. 5: Dalhousie U (Halifax NS) 31-35 (Econ) BA; McGill 37-38 BLS. 7: Clerk Bank of Montreal, Montreal 36-37; Libn asst Royal Bank of Can, Montreal 39-42; Chief libn Can Legion War Serv, Ottawa & London Eng 42-46; Dir Can Bk Centre Halifax NS 48-50; Chief libn Can Dept of Agric, Ottawa 50-. 9: SLA; ASIS; APLA. 10: UN Assn. 14: Admin. 15: Canada Dept of Agric Lib, Ottawa Can.

REYNOLDS, MARIE PARK. b Sherman Co Tex 30 O 15. 4: Levi Henry Reynolds. 5: W Tex state U 31-34 (Home econ) BS; Highlands U summer 34; Denver U summer 50; Peabody Col summers 51-54 (Libnship) MA. 6: Sp. 7: Home econ tchr high sch, House NM 34-35; Tchr & libn Dalhart Pub Schs 35-. 9: ALA; NEA; TexLA (past pres Dist I); TexStateTA. 10: Beta Phi Mu; Delta Kappa Gamma; 1928 Study Club; Coon Mem Home Aux. 14: Sch libn, catlg, ref. 15: Box 326, Dalhart Tx 79022.

REYNOLDS, MARTHA LOUISE. b Indianapolis 20 Ap 28. 5: Hanover Col 46-50 (Eng, Math) AB; Ind U 54-55 (LS) MS. 7: Br asst Indianapolis Pub Lib 50-54;Head of adult serv Fairbanks Lib, Vigo Co Ind 55-63; Asst coordinator adult serv Montgomery Co Pub Libs, Md 63-65, Asst chief pub serv 65-67; Dir Frederick Co Pub Libs 67-. 8: Trainer, Lib Adult Educ Proj, Ind U, Purdue Bur of Studies in Adult Educ, 56-63; Md Adv Study Com on LSCA Title I 68. 9: ALA -ASD (mem & chm Notable Bks Coun 64-65, Bd mem SORT 62-63): Adult Educ assn of Ind (Bd Dirs 62-63); IndLA (chh In-Service Educ Com 57-59, chm Lib Certif Exam Com 59-61); Ind Lib Film Circuit Adv Com (61-63). 10: Nat Ballet Soc; Friend of the NY Pub Lib Dance Collection; Frederick Arts Coun; Frederick Womans Civic Club; Friends of C Burr Artz Lib. 12: Ed "Focus on Indiana Libraries (61-63). 14: Admin, informal adult educ, bk sel, pub rel. 15: 116 Record st, Frederick Md 21701.

REYNOLDS, MARYAN E(VELYN). b Minneapolis 17 F 13. 5: UMinn 36 (Hist) AB; USoCal 40 BS in LS. 7: Circ asst Madera Co Free Lib, Madera Cal 40-41; Supt of brs Kern Co Free Lib, Bakersfield Cal 41-43; Field libn Wash State Lib 43-50; Head Libn Richland Pub Lib, Richland Wash 50-51; State Libn Wash State Lib 51-. 8: Adv Com on Retrospective Conversion Study (LC); Governor's Cabinet; Sec Governor's Commsn on Status of Women; Sec Citizen's Com on Wash Courts 66-; Public Defender Demonstration Proj Adv Com: mem, exec bd, & sec. 9: ALA (Coun 51-55, 63-67);-PLA (act exec sec summer 50);-AAStateL (pres 65-66); -ISAD (Exec Bd 67-69); Amer Assn Pub Admin; Amer Assn Adult Educ; PNLA (v-pres & pres-elect); WashLA. 10: AAUW; LWV; Soroptimist Club; Amer Red Cross. 11: 1967 State Arts Commsn Award presented to Wash State Lib. 14: Admin, coord all lib serv. 15: Rt 10 Box 670, Olympia Wa 98501.

REYNOLDS, MICHAEL M. b NYC 12 Ag 24. 4: Katherine Dean. 5: Hunter Col 47-50 (Hist) AB; Columbia 51-52 (LS) MS; American U 53-55 (Pub Admin) MA; UMich 59-64 (LS) PhD. 7: US Army Parachute Artillery 43-46; Intern LC 52-53; Asst libn for ref Georgetown U 53-54, Asst libn for catlg 54-55; Chief ref libn LSU 55-57; Asst Prof of Pol Sci WVaU 62-64, Assoc dir of libs 57-64; Asst dir of libs Ind U 64-68; Prof of Lib Sci SUNY(Albany) 68-. 9: ALA (Life mem; Ins Com 59);-RSD (Interlib Loan Com);-LAD (Com on Lib Admin Devel 62); WVaLA (pres 63). 10: AAUP; WVa Acad of Scis; Phi Beta Kappa. 12: "Forest & Forestry in West Virginia; a Bibliography" (62); "The Development of Bibliographic Center in the West Virginia Region; Current Practices and Future Directions" (63); Co-auth "Milestones of West Virginia History" (63). 13: Yes. 14: Ref. 15: 1 Coventry rd, Glenmont NY 12077.

REYNOLDS, PERLITA (NEWBY). b Los Angeles 19 J 13. 4: Col Charles Ferry Reynolds. 5: UCLA 3136(Eng) BA; USoCal 61-65 MS L.): Sp. 7: Libn San Bernardino Co Free Lib, Big Lake Br 59-64; Libn Bear VAlley Unified Sch Dist, Big Bear Lake Cal 64-. 9: ALA; NEA; CalLA; Cal Tchrs Assn. 14: Ref, stud adv. 15: Box 475, Big Bear City Ca 92314.

REYNOLDS, SALLY JO (SAWYER). b Sagniaw Mich 29 S 40. 4: John D Reynolds. 5: UMich 58-63 (Hist) BA with high distinction & honors; Columbia 63-65 (LS) MS (cum laude). 6: Fr. 7: Asst program dir Womens Residence Halls UMich 62-63; Research asst Columbia U Libs 63-64; Head of circ E Asian Lib Columbi U 65; Ser libn American U Lib65-66; Catlg libn 66-67; Acquis libn 67-68; Asst libn 68-. 9: Potomac Tech Proc Libns, DCLA. 10: Phi Beta Kappa; Phi Kappa Phi; Mort Arboard. 14: Catlg, ser, acquis. 15: 4201 Massachusetts ave NW apt 100, Wash DC 20016.

REZNICK, SYLVIA (MILLER). b Braddock Penn 10 S 27. 4: Aron Reznick. 5: UPittsburgh 45-49 (Bus educ) BS; Duquesne 65-67 MEd in LS. 7: Supv Navy Dept, Pittsburgh 51-54; Libn Swissvale High Sch, Swissvale Penn 67-. 9: NEA; ALA; PennStateEA; SwissvaleTchrsEA. 14: Catlg. 15: 221 Whipple st, Pittsburgh Pa 15218.

RHEAY, MARY LOUISE. b MontgomeryAla 8 Mr 20. 5: Ala Col 37-40 (Hist) AB;Emory 40-41 ABLS, 57-59 MSLS. 7: ATLANTA Pub Lib: Lib asst I Child Dept 41-42; Libn I Asst in chg of wk with schs 42-49, Libn II asst child dept 49-53, Libn II asst head child dept 53-56, Libn III head child dept 56-63, Asst dr 63-. 8: Instr, child & ya it, Emory U & Ga State Co, var terms, 60-69 Staff, Setle Worls FR (62). 9: ALA (Newberry Caldecott Award Com 62); SELA (act chm Sch & Child Sect 63-6, Loc Arr Ch 66); GaLA (chm Child & YA Sect 49-51, chm Pub Lib Sect 67-69); Atlanta Lib Club (pres 64-65). 10: Delta Kappa Gamma; Bus & Prof Women; Zonta Internat. 11: Woman of the Year in Professions, Atlanta (62). 13: Yes. 14: Child & ya wk, admin. 15: 4555 Meadow Valley fr NE, Atlanta 30305.

RHOADES, CAROLYN. b Stamford Conn 7 N 40. 5: Swarthmore 58-62 (Intl Rel) BA; Columbia 64-65 (Tchg of Soc Studies) MA, 66-69 (Pub lib serv) MS in LS. 6: Ger. 7: Tchr elem & high sch Peace Corps, Manila & Mindanao Philippines 62-64; Tchr Bd of Educ, Stamford Conn 65; Libn trainee Ferguson Lib, Stamford Conn 66-69, Libn (staff) 69-. 9: Westchester (NY) LA. 10: Beta Phi Mu. 14: Adult pub lib serv, serv to non-lib users. 15: 95 Alton rd, Stamford Ct 06906.

RHOADES, NANCY (LYBARGER). b Coshocton Ohio 17 S 15. 4: Rendell Rhoades. 5: Westminster Col (Penn) 34-37, 38-39 (Hist) BA; West Res summers 40-43 BS in LS. 6: Fr. 7: Sch libn Warder Pub Lib, Springfield Ohio 39-43, Ref libn 43-45; Ref asst hist div Cleveland Pub Lib 45-54; Ref asst Columbus Pub Lib, Columbus Ohio 54-56; Sc libn Starling Jr High Sch, Columbus Ohio 56-58; asst Ohio asst hio State U 58-60, Ser catlgr 60-62; Libn Ashland Theol Sem Lib (Ashland Ohio) 63-. 8: Jr libn, attending Assembly of Libns of Latin Amer, serving on Educ Com, Wash DC, 47. 9: ATHEOLLA;

SLA; OhioLA. 10: AAUW. 12: Ed SLA Cleveland Chap; "Bulletin (52-53). 14: Ref. 15: 433 Buena Vista, Ashland Ohio 44805.

RHOADS, JAMES BERTON. b Sioux City Iowa 17 S 28. 4: Angela Handy. 5: Southwestern Jr Col 46-47; Union Col (Lincoln Neb) 47-48; UCal(Berkeley) 49-52 (Hist) AB, MA; American U 5565 53-65; PhD. 7: Org Methods examiner, McClellan Air Force Base Cal 52; Archivist in var poitions Nat Archives, Wash DC 52-65, Asst archivist for civil archives 6-66; Deputy Archivist of US 66-68; Archivist of US 68-. 9: Internat Coun on Archives (mem Exec Com 68); SAA (Fellow, chm Com on Copyright Legis 67-; mem Program Com 68); Gen Serv Admin (chm Com on Career Training Programs 68-69). 10: Chm; Nat Hist Publns Commsn, Archives Adv Coun, Admin Com of Fed Register, Nat Archives Trust Fund Bd; Mem; Amer Revolution Bicentennial Commsn, Fed Fire Coun, Bd Trustees Woodrow Wilson Internat Ctr for Scholars, Bd Dirs Harry S Truman Lib Inst for Nat & Internat Affairs; Phi Alpha Theta; Phi Kappa Phi; Org Amer Histns; Amer Hist Assn. 13: Yes. 14: Archival mgt, 20th cent US pol hist. 15: National Archives and Records Serv 8th and Penn ave Room 111, Washington DC 20408.

RHOADS, JOSEPH JR. b Phila Penn 27 My 35. 4: Mary-Elizabeth Hawke. 5: Earlham Col 57 AB; Rutgers 63 MLS. 7: Free Lib of Phila: Trainee 61, Libn I 63, Libn II 64; Asst libn Rutgers U 65; Assoc libn SUNY (Binghamton) 66-. 9: ALA. 15: 1557 Rita rd, Vestal NY 13850.

RHOADS, NORMAN ELMER JR. b Somerset Penn 22 Ag 31. 5: Kent State U 56-60 (Hist) BA; Drexel 61-62 MSLS. 7: Bkmob driver Somerset Co Lib, Somerset Penn 50-52; US Army Post Off registry Clerk cerk (Cpl) 52-54; Bkmob libn Somerset Co Lib, Somerset Penn 54-56; Stud asst Kent State U Lib 56-60; Asst ref libn 60-61; Dir Gladwyne Free Lib, Gladwyne Penn 62-65; Ref libn Finkelstein Mem Lib, Sring Spring NY 65-67; Asst dir 68-. 8: Libn, Lib/USA, NY Worlds Fair 64. 09: NYLA; NY Lib Club. 9: NYLA; NY Lib Club; RocklandCoLA. 10: Nat Aid for the Visually Handicapped. 14: Tech serv, ref, admin. 15: 260 W End ave, New York NY 10023.

RHODES, AGNES (GREEN(. b Kittanning Penn 4 N 01. 4: Charles Everett Rhodes. 5: Carnegie 19-21 (Apprentice LS); Syracuse 22-25 BS in LS; West Res 27 Lib Sch Certif n Child Wk. 7: Ref libn Adelbert Col West Res 25-26; 1st asst Stevenson Room for yp, yp libn, 1st asst Hough Br Lib, sch libn, br libn, Cleveland Pub Lib 27-35; Catlgr Union Col Lib (Schenectady NY) 43-45; Libn & catlgr Central States Forest Srv, Columbus Ohio 39; Spec consul State Lib of Ohio 38; Ref libn Agric & Tech Inst SUNY (Alfred) 65-. 10: AAUW; LWV; Allen-Civic Amandine Club of Alfred U; Internat Club of Alfred U; Camp Fire Girls Coun; Alfred Hist Soc. 14: Yp libn, ref. 15: 154 N Main st, Alfred NY 14802.

RHODES, CAROLYN (LOLITA) BOLDEN. b Mobile Ala 10 Jl 26. 4: Charles Twyner Rhodes. 5:Ala State Tchrs Col 42-44 Jr Col Degree; Bennett Col 44-46 (Eng) AB; Atlanta 56-59 MS in LS; Springhill Col summer 65 (Inst in Human Rel) Certif. 6: Fr. 7: Libn Dunbar High Sch, Mobile Ala 46-47; Asst libn Fla A&M U 47-49; Asst libn Mobile Co Train Sch, Plateau Ala 49-56; Libn Williamson High Sch, Mobile Ala 56-; Libn Davidson High Sch, Mobile Ala 67-. 9: ALA; NEA; Amer Tchrs Assn; AlaLA (sec 60-62); Ala State Tchrs Assn; Mobile ASchL (Asst chm 63-65). 10: Speakers Bur of Modile Pub Sch System; Delta Sigma Theta. 14: Ref, catlg, readers adv serv. 15: 2302 Linda dr, Mobile Al 36617.

RHODES, CLAYTON E(UGENE). b Clarion Co Penn 24 My 31. 5: Clarion State Tchrs Col 49-53 (LS, Soc Studies) BS in Educ; West Res summers 56-60 MS n LS. 7: Personnel management spec & clerk- typist US Army, Ft Carson Colo 53-55; Sch libn Clarion Area High Sch, Clarion Penn 55-61; Sch libn Satellite High Sch, Satellite Beach Fla 61-63; Enoch Pratt Lib, Baltimore Adult Asst ast 64, Br libn 65, Sch liaison libn 65-66; Sch liaison libn & actg hd George Peabody Br 66-. 9: ALA (Life mem); NEA (Life mem); MeLA; MdLA. 10: Beta Phi Mu; Baltimore Bibliophiles. 11: E P Dutton - John Macrae Award (67). 14: Sch libs, wk with ya, rare bks. 15: Box 272, Rimersburg Penn 16248.

RHODES, LELIA (GASTON). b Jackson Miss 21 O 23. 4: John Dolph Rhodes. 5: Jackson State Col 44 (Elem Educ) BS; Atlanta 56 MS in LS. 7: Clerk-typist US Govt, Wash DC 44; Lib asst Jackson State Col 44-52; Libn Hill High Sch, Jackson Miss 52-56; Asst libn in chg of catlg Json State Col 57-; Assoc hd libn in charge of catlg. 9: ALA; NEA; MissLA; Miss Tchrs Assn. 10: YWCA; Alpha Kappa Alpha. 14: Catlg. 15: 1125 Winter, Jackson Miss 39204.

RHODES, MARGAREY M(ARY) G(ILLPATRICK). b Biwabk Minn 30 N 10. 4: John C Rhodes. 5: Col of Puget Sound 29-33 (Fr) BA; UWash 35-37, 38 BALS. 6: Fr. 7: Oakland Pub Lib, Oakland Cal: Jr libn circ 46-49, Ref asst lit Div 49-53, Ref asst sci & ind Div, act chief 53-54, Supv libn sci & ind div 54-. 9: ALA; Cal LA(sec, v-pres & pres ef Ref Round Table 59-61); San Francisco Bay Area Ref Libns Coun; SLA. 14: Ref. 15: 1733 Bancroft way, Berkeley Cal 94703.

RHODÈS, MYRTLE LEVONNE (JONES). b Marianna Fla 16 F 37. 4: Chester J. 5: Fla A&M U 54-58 (LS) BS; Atlanta summers 61-64 MSLS; Fl State U 67-68 (LS). 6: Fr. 7: Rosenwald Jr Col Even 59-61; Sch libn Pub Sch, Panama City Fla 58-; Tech Lib Naval Ship Research & Dev Lab, Panama City Fla. 9: FlaStateTA; Bay Co (Fla) LA. 10: Phi Delta Kappa. 13: Yes. 14: A-v, ref, docs catlg (sci). 15: 1208 E 8th courtn Panama City Fla 32401.

RHODES, MARION (DILLER). b Pittsburgh Penn 15 Mr 22. 4: Milton Rhodes. 5: UMiami Fla 39-43 (Art) AB; SUNY (Oneonta) 60-63 (Elem educ) MSEd; SUNY (Albany) 64-66 MLS. 7: Tchr Burnt Hills Ballston Lake Central Sch, Burnt Hills NY 60-61; Tchr Shenendehowa Central Sch, Elnora NY 63-64; NY State Educ Dept, Albany: Asst libn Lib Spec Serv 66-67, Sr libn Lib to the Blind 67-68, Sr libn Auxiliary Serv 68-. 9: ALA; NYLA. 13: Yes. 14: A-v materials. 15: 25 Sandalwood lane, Scotia NY 12302.

RHODES, ROBERT HUNT. b Providence 24 Ja 37. 5: URI 55-59 (Eng) BA; Simmons 59-60 (LS) MS. 6: SP, Fr. 7: Sp . Fire Direction Computer Artillery, RI Army Nat Guard 60-64; SGT E-5, Vt Army Nat Guard 64-; Asst ref libn URI 61-63, Ref & documents libn 6364; Libn Windham Col 64-. 8: Trustee Walpole NH Pub Lib. 9: VtLA; RILA; RI Hist Soc. 14: Catlg, ref. 15: P O Box 339-A, Walpole NH 03608.

RHODES, THEODORA (GERTRUDE). b Victoria BC 6 Je 12. 7: Flying control RCAF, BC 43-46; BC Tele Co, Toll settlement supv, Vancouver 46-48, Libn 48-. 9: CanLA; SLA; BCLA (past treas & pres). 10. Toastmistress Internat. 11: British Empire Medal. 13: Yes. 15: Business Lib BC Tel Co 768 Seymour st, Vancouver 2 BC Can.

RHODES, VERNIE KATHERINE (KATHERINE VERONICA). b Perth Amboy NJ 17 Ap 11. 5: NJ Lib Sch 35-38 (Pub lib) Certif; Rutgers 40-46 (Eng) BS in Ed, 62 (Sch libs) MLS. 6: Ger, fr. 7: Perth Amboy Pub Lib, Perth Amboy: Gen asst 31-34, Asst child libn 34-37, Y-p libn 37-41, Catlgr 41-46; Libn & tchr Midd Co vocational & tech high schs, Woodbridge, Perth Amboy & New Brunswick NJ 46-56; Sch libn Union Co High Sch Dist #1 Springfield High Sch, A L Johnson Reg High Sch, NJ 56-. 8: UWash; NDEA Adv Md Sch Lib Coun Assn 60-61; Lib Inst 65; Middle States Eval Team 59-66; Instr UVt summer 67. 9: ALA; CathLA; NJEA; NJLA (mem Nat Lib Wk Steering Com 64); NJSchLA; UnionCoSchL (pres 64-65. 10: Kearny Cottage Hist Soc; Damien Dutton Soc; New Brunswick; Edith Stein Guild; Rutgers Grad Sch Lib Serv Alum Assn. 14: Organiz of sch lib, media ctrs. 15: 135 Brighton ave, Perth Amboy NJ 08861.

RHODES, YVONNE MARGARET WATTERS. b Edinburgh Scotland 4 S 19. 6: Fr, Ger. 7: Sec & libn US Army Med Res & Nutr Lab, Denver 54-58, Libn 58-. 9: SLA; Colo Coun of Med Libns. 10: Eng-Speaking Union. 14: Ref. 15: 1031 Kingston st, Aurora Co 80010.

RHYDWEN, DAVID. b Toronto Can 14 Je 18. 6: Fr. 7: Chief Libn The Globe and Mai, Toronto 38-. 9: SLA (chm Newspaper Div 60-61); CanLA. 10: Com of Adjustment, Markham Ont. 11: Jack Burness Mem Award for Outstanding Newspaper Libnship. 13: Yes. 15: 140 King st W, Toronto Can.

RHYMER, MARY FRANCES. 5: Ill Wesleyan U (Eng, Ed) BA. 7: Curator prints & photographs Chicago Hist Soc 52-. 9: SLA; IllLA. 15: Chicago Hist Soc, North ave at Clark st, Chicago Il 60614.

RHYNE, JEAN (BETTY). b Roanoke Va 10 My 35. 5: USCar 53-58 (Eng) AB; NC 58-60 MS in LS. 7: Ref asst humanities div UNC Lib (Chapel Hill) 59-60; Asst lib readers serv Goucher Col Lib 60-64; Ref asst Knoxville Pub Lib, Knoxville Tenn 64-66; Hd of ref dept Pub Lib of Knoxville & Knox Co 66-. 9: TennLA. 10: AAUP; AAUW. 14: Ref. 15: 3736 Timber circle SE, Knoxville Tn 37920.

RICARD, HERBERT F(RDERIC). b Toldo Ohio 6 Je 05. 4: Elizabeth Curtis. 5: UToledo 24-26; Ohio State U 26-28 (Hist) AB; UMich 28-30 AB in LS; Columbia 30-36 MS in LS. 7:

Queens Borough Pub Lib, Jamaica NY: Gen asst 30-35, Supv inter-br loans 35-39, Libn LI collection 39-47, Supt br admin 47-55, Br libn 55-60; Ventura Co & City Lib, Ventura Cal: Br libn 60-63, Reg libn 63-65, Adult serv libn 65-67; Libn Ventura Co Hist Collection 67-. 8: Queens Borough Historian 44-53. 9: CalLA; NY Lib Club (Coun 51-54, treas 54-57, ed 57-60). 13: Yes. 14: Loc his. 15: 998 Church st apt 2, Ventura Ca 93001.

RICCARDI, SARO JOHN. b Giarre Italy 23 Je 10. 4: Sadie R DOrio. 5: NYU 27-31 (Bus Admin) BCS; Columbia 31-35 (Econ) MS, 35-38 MLS. 6: Fr, Ger, Ital. 7: Asst to ref libn art div NY Pub Lib 26-43; 739th F A Battalion US Army 43-45; NY PubLib: Ref libn Info Div, Econ div 45-46, Supv 1st asst main reading room 46-54, Chief newspaper div 54-62, Chief annex ref serv 62-; 62-65; Libn Racquet Tennis Club, NY 38-; Hd circ libn Hofstra U 66-. 9: ALA; SLA; NCLA; NYLA. 11: Jean Campbell Award for meritorious serv, NY Pub Lib, 56. 12: "English Regency Furniture and Architecture" (40); "Pennsylvania Dutch Folk Art and Architecture" (42); "739th F A Battalion History" (45); "Union List Current Newspapers, US & Foreign" (57). 13: Yes. 14: Admin. 15: 6 Harbor rd, Woodbury LI NY 11797.

RICCI, PATRICIA ROSE LAMSON. b St Paul 30 D 41. 4: Vernon Ricci. 5: Col of St Catherine 59-63 (LS) BA; UMinn 62-63, 65 (LS) MA. 6: Fr. 7: Lib asst St Paul Pub Lib 62-64; Lib asst UMinn Law Lib 64-65; Ref asst James Jerome Hill Ref Lib, St Paul 65-. 9: MinnLA. 14: Ref. 15: 722 E 5th st, St Paul 53106.

RICE, ANNA CAROLYN. b Elizabeth NJ 21 S 22. 5: NJ State Tchrs Col (Newark) 39-41; NJ Col for Women 43-45 (Eng Lit) AB; Columbia 46-47 (Educ), 48-50 BS LS; Rutgers 65- (Educ). 6: Fr. 7: Lib asst Burgess Lib Columbia U 45-50; Elizabeth (NJ) Pub Lib; Sr libn 50-60, Head of readers adv serv 54-60, Coordinator of adult program, Prin libn 60-62, Supv libn circ dept 62-. 8: V-chm, NJ Lib Film Circuit, 61; Consul, A-V Com, Nat Assn for Retarded Child;Past sec Mayors Commsn on Human Rel, Elizabeth NJ; Sec Bd of Elizabeth Adult Sch. 9: ALA; Adult Educ Assn; NJLA (chm Human Rel Com; treas Hist & Bibliog Sect; Com on the Negro Bibliog Com; past mem Adult Educ Com); NJ Adult Educ Assn. 10: Good Neighbor Coun; NAACP; Red Cross; LWV; YWCA; Com Con on Aging, Elizabeth NJ. 12: Comp "New Jersey and the Negro; A Bibliography 1715-1966 (67); Ed com "This Is Elizabeth (pamphlet 56). 14: Readers adv serv, adult educ, serv to disadvantaged. 15: 718 Pearl st, Elizabeth NJ 07202.

RICE, BARBARA A. b Northampton Mass 21 F 36. 5: UMass 53-57 (Chem) BS; UCal 9berkeley) 66-67 MLS. 6: Fr. 7: Lab tech UCLA 57-58; Libn tech files Shell Oil, Emeryville Cal 58-60; Libn Richfield Oil Anaheim Cal 60-61; Tchr 61-63; Doc libn Knolls Atomic Power Lab, Schenectady NY 68-. 10: Sigma Xi; Mensa; Beta Phi Mu; Phi kappa Phi. 14: Ref. 15: 31 Fredericks rd, Scotia NY 12302.

RICE, CECELIA (EARLY). b Endicott NY. 4: Ray E Rice. 5: CornellU 41-45 (Hist) AB; Syracuse 55-56 MSLS. 7: Tchr Mattituck High Sch, Mattituck LI 45-47; Tchr Main Central Sch, Maine NY 48-49; Asst libn SUNY-Harpur Col 53-56; Libn G A F Corp, Binghamton NY 56-65; Ref libn Xerox Corp, Webster NY 65-68; Supv Corp Lib Xerox Corp, Rochester NY 68-. 9: SLA. 10: AAUW; League of Women Voters; Beta Phi Mu; Pi Lambda Theta. 14: Ref, admin. 15: 19 Pineview dr, Penfield NY 14526.

RICE, DOROTHY. b Rochester NY 12 Je 16. 5: Nazareth Col 34-38 (Fr) BA; State U Col (Geneseo NY) 38-39 BLS; URochester 45-47 (Secondary Educ) Ed M; Fla State U 61 (LS. 6: Fr. 7: Libn Coxsakie High Sch, Coxsackie NY 40-41; Libn Livingston Manor Central Sch, Livingston Manor NY 41-44; Libn Brighton High Sch, Rochester NY 44-. 9: NEA; NY State Tchrs Assn; NYLA (sec Sch Libs Sect 57-58). ; Monroe Co Lib Club (pres 67-68). 10: BrightonTA; Nazareth Col Alum Assn. 14: Ref, curriculum. res bks, subject matter specn with tchrs & studs. 15: 71 Roslyn st, Rochester NY 14619.

RICE, JEAN ADRIENNE (STACHIW). b Detroit 9 Mr 38. 4: Albert F Rice. 5: Central Mich U (LS) BS; Murray State Col summer 66 (LS) MA. 7: Libn Farmington Sch System, Farmington Mich 60-. 9: MichEA; MichASchL; ALA. 10: PTA; Alpha Beta Alpha. 14: Ref, bk sel. 15: 31515 Delaware, Livonia Mi 48150.

RICE, JUANITA M. b Clay Co Ala 30 Ja 29. 4: Charlie H Rice Jr. 5: Lineville High Sch 47; Jacksonville State Col 51 (Eng, Hist) AB, BS; UAla 59 (LS) MA. 6: Fr. 7: Tchr Jr High Yc, Clay Co Ala 49-53; Computer, Ames Cal 53-54; Sr Eng tchr, Heflin 58-59; 58-60; Libn High Sch, Oxford Ala 60-; Girls Physical Educ Lineville High Sch 59-60. 9: ALA; NEA; AlaLA (chm Childs Sch Div); AlaSchLA (chm Nomin Com Dist pres). 10: Pilot Club. 14: Sch lib wk. 15: 16 Main st, Oxford Ala 36203.

RICE, LILA. b Wadley Ala 8 Je 21. 5: LaGrange Col 38-39; Tift Col 40-41 (Eng, Biol) AB; Peabody 51-54 (LS) MA; Emory U 66-68 (libnship) Diploma in adv studs. 7: Tchr Meriwether High Sch, Woodbury Ga 42-43; Chambers Co High Sch, Milltown Ala 43-44; Funston Cons Sch, Funston Ga 44-46; Staff Writer, Womens Ed "La Grange Daily News, La Grange Ga 47-51; Asst dir Kinchafoonee Ref Lib, Dawson Ga 54; Asst dir Flint River Reg Lib, Griffin Ga 55; Dir Pine Mountain Reg Lib, Manchester Ga 55-68; Pub lib Consul Ga State Dept of Educ 68-; Tchr lib educ UGa 66-67. 9: ALA (Memb Com, Ga); GaLA; SELS; Adult Educ Coun; GaEA; Ga Prof Lib Com. 10: Ga Gerontol Soc; Metro-AtlantaLA (Memb Com). 13: Yes. 14: Lib construction, ext, org & admin. 15: 4110 Windsor Oak dr, Doraville Ga 30040.

RICE, SISTER M MARCIA OP. b Oneida NY 15 S 07. 5: Col of St Mary of the Springs 36 (Hist) BA; Catholic U 37-39 (Hist) MA; Duquesne 64 MEd in LS. 6: Lat, Fr. 7: Hist (faculty) Albertus Magnus Col 51-56; Libn & tchr NW Catholic High Sch, W Hartford Conn 61-65; Lib Sci (Faculty) Ohio Dominican Col 66-67; Dir St Mary of the Springs Acad, Columbus Ohio 65-66; Libn Columbus Dominican Educ Ctr Lib, Columbus Ohio 66-. 9: Nat Cath EA; ALA; CathLA; OhioLA. 14: Ref, child lit, philos, relig. 15: Columbus Dominican Education Center Lib, St Mary of the Springs, Columbus Oh 43219.

RICE, MARGARETE M(cBRIDE). b Phila 20 Ag 26. 5: Bryn Mawr 42-46 (Pol Sci) BA, 49-51 (Pol Sci, Hist) MA; Drexel 54-55 MSLS. 6: Fr, Sp, Ital, Lat, Ger, Classical Gk. 7: Cartographic aide Army Map Serv, Wash DC47-49; Apprentice tchr Friends Central Sch, Ovebrook Penn 51-52; Lib Asst Ludington Mem Pub Lib, Bryn Mawr Penn 52-55; Libn catlg & ref Dept of the Interior Central Lib, Wash DC 55-56; Catlgr Princeton U Lib 60-61; Lib dir Asbury Park Free Pub Lib, Asbury Park NJ 61-62; Ref libn Post Lib, Ft Monmouth NJ 62-68; Catlgr 68-. 9: ALA; NJLA. 13: Yes. 14: Catlg, ref. 15: 243 Woodcrest rd, Oakhurst NJ 07755.

RICE, MARGARETTA GWENLLIAN apRHYS. b Southbourne England 29 Jl 17. 5: UBC 34-38 9eng, Fr) BA, 38-39 (Tchr train); UToronto 57-58 BLS; UIll 65-66 (LS) MS. 6: Fr. 7: Tchr Queen Margaret's Sch, Duncan BC 40-42, 46-49; Inspector British Admiralty Tech Mission, Ottawa & Toronto 42-45; Tchr N Saanich High Sch, Saanich BC 50-52; Tchr Royal Oak High Sch, Saamch BC 52-57; Sch libn Esquimalt Jr High, Victoria BC 59-65; Sch libn S J Willis Jr Secondary, Victoria BC 66-. 8: Summer session instr UBC 64, 66, 68. 9: CanLA; ALA; -AASchL; CanSchLA; BCLA; BCSchLA (pres 67-68, Curr Repr 63-66). 10: Victoria Inst; Beta Phi Mu; BC Tch Fed. 13: Yes. 14: Readers serv, ref. 15: 1497 Rockland ave, Victoria BC Can.

RICE, MARION (ANN). b Detroit 15 Ap 3. 5: Mt San Antonio Col 51-54 (Educ) AA; UCLA 54-57 (Psych) BA; USoCal 58-59 MSLS. 6: Ger, Fr. 7: Sr typist clerk UCLA Sch of Med 55-57; Asst statistician UCLA Agric Econ 57-58; Lib asst USO Cal Sch of Med Lib 58-59; Ref & sci libn Los Angeles State Col 59-60; Ref libn & sci bibliog San Fernando Valley State Co 60-68; Tech libn IBM Fed Systs Div/West. 9: SLA; ASIS. 10: Assn Cal State Col Profs. 14: Sci ref & bibliog. 15: IBM Federal Systems Div West P O Box 780, Westlake Village Ca 91360.

RICE, MARY LOIS. b Norfolk Va 7 Ag 15. 5: George Washington U 32-37 (Arch) AB; UDenver 47-48 (LS) MA. 7: Architect Fed Govt, Wash DC 39-43, 46-47; Ensign & Lt (jg) WAVES Pub Wks Dept, NY Naval Shipyard 43-46; Catlgr UCLA Lib 49-55; Catlgr DC Pub Lib 56-63; Chief catlg div 64-. 9: ALA; DCLA. 10: Wesleyan Serv Guild. 14: Catlg. 15: 5314 32nd st NW, Wash DC 20015.

RICE, RONALD STANLEY. b Los Angeles Cal 8 Je 33. 5: USoCal 51-56 (Advertising) BS, 64-66 MSLS. 7: Radio & cables USA, Tokyo 56-58; Owner Rice Advertising, N Hollywood cal 59-61; Salesman Olivetti-Underwood, San Francisco 61-64; Spec collections USoCal 64-65; Libn I Orange Co Free Lib, Orange Cal 65-66; Br libn Fountain Valley Br, Orange Co Pub Lib 66-. 8: Coord Santiago Coop Lib System 67. 9: ALA; CalLA; OrangeCoLA. 10: Charter mem Fountain Valley Hist Soc; Nat Exchange Club; So Cal geneal Soc. 14: Geneal. 15: 9192 Crawford cir, Huntington Beach Ca 92646.

RICE, SALLY ELIZABETH. b Short Hills NJ 9 My 44. 5: AmericanU 62-66 (Hist) BA; Rutgers 66-67 MLS. 6: Fr. 7: Lib intern E Orange Pub Lib, E Orange NJ 67-. 9: NJLA. 14: Ref, adult serv. 15: 250 Prospect st, East Orange NJ 07017.

RICE, WENDY MARY (HANSEN). b St Louis Mo 7 F 42. 4: Hugh Julian Rice. 5: Mo Valley Col 60-64 (Fr) BA; StrasbourgU (France) 65-66 (Fr); UWis 66-67 (LS) MA. 6: Fr. 7: Ref libn pub lib, Worcester Mass summer 67; Ref libn pub lib, Vallejo Cal 68-. 8: Review com mem Vallejo Cal 68-; Vertical file libn Vallejo Cal 68-. 14: Art & mus. 15: Apt 5 50 Frey pl, Vallejo Ca 94590.

RICH, ANNIE B(AILEY) F(REEMAN). b Hyde Park Mass 28 S 06. 4: HAROLD W Rich. 5: Bates Col 24-28 (Eng)BA. 7: Lt (jg) US Coast Guard, New Orleans 44-46; Libn Nathan & HenryB Cleaves Law Lib of the Cumberland Bar Assn, Co Court House, Portland Me 9-44, 46-. 9: AALL; Law Libns of NE; MeLA. 10: Zonta Clu. 15: Cleaves Law Lib, Co Court House, 142 Federal st, Portland Me 04111.

RICH, EDWARD PERCY. b Bryn Mawr Penn 16 My 31. 5: Haverford Col 49-53 (Ger) BA; UPenn 53-57 DDS; Drexel 65-67 MSLS. 6: Ger. 7: Lib asst Horace Howard Furness Mem UPenn 65-66; Dental off (Maj) Armed Forces Serv 57-60 63-65; Chief Div of Spec Collections usma lib, West Point NY 68-. 10: Orders & Medals Soc of Amer. 11: Josiah Kirby Lilly Fellow (Rare Bk Curatorship), IndU 67-68. 12: Ed "The Medal Collector". 14: Rare bks, mss. 15: USMA Lib, West Point NY 10996.

RICH, MARGARET C (HICKS). b Michigamme Mich 25 N 36. 4: Calvin Rich. 5: UMich 53-55 (Bus admin); West Mich U 63-65 (Eng) BA, MSLS. 7: Catlgr Rochester Pub Lib, Rochester ny 66-68; Curriculum libn SUNY (Brockport) 68-. 14: Curr materials. 15: 55 Clay ave, rochester NY 14613.

RICHARD, HARRIS M. b Newark NJ 1 Ap 39. 5: Rutgers 56-60 (Eng) BA, 63-65 MLS. 7: (1st Lt) US Army 60-62; Sr libn ref Plainfield (NJ) Pub Lib 65-69; Ser libn UAriz Lib 69-. 9: NJLA; ALA; ArizStateLA. 10: Printing Hist Soc (London). 14: Ref, catlg. 15: 350 N Silverbell apt 29, Tucson Az 85705.

RICHARD, JOHN B(ENARD). b Gulfport Miss 2 N 32. 5: Perkinston Jr Col 50-52 (Eng, LS); Miss So Col 52-54 (Eng, LS) BS, LSU 57-59 MS in LS. 7: Head pre dept LSU(Baton Rouge) 59-60; Head Libn LSU(Alexandria,0 60-. 8: Organized LSU Alexandria Lib; Spec Instr LSU Lib Sch (Baton Rouge); Exec Dir La Nat Lib Week 68. 9: ALA; SWLA; LaLA (pres 69-70; chm Col & Ref Sect 68-69); (chm La Lit Award Com 64-66). 10: Rotary Club; Beta Phi Mu. 14: Admin, ref. 15: La State Univ Li, Alexandria La 71303.

RICHARD, JOHN M. b Rahway NJ 28 D 41. 5: Elizabethtown Col 61-64 (Hist) BA; LSU 65-66 MLS. 6: Ger. 7: Ref libn UAriz 66-67m 69-; Finance clk USA, Ger 67-69. 9: ALA; ArizStateLA. 14: Ref. 15: 114 W Laguna st D7, Tucson Az 85705.

RICHARDS, ARNE HJORT. b Harvey Ill 18 O 32. 5: Yankton Col 50-54 (Psych, Hist) BA;Chicago 54-58 (Soc Sci, Educ); UIll 59-60 (LS) MS, 63-65 (LS). 6: Fr, Danish. 7: Bkkeeper Cedar Co Treasurer, Hartington Neb 49-50; Ed col newspaper Yankton Col 52-53; News release writer pub rel off Yankton Col 53-54; Clerk-typist UChicago 54-59; Postal clerk MAIN Post Off, 57; Asst ref libn Northwestern U 60-61, Asst documents libn 61-63; Tchg asst Grad Sch of Lib Sci UIll 63-65; Documents libn Kan State U 65-. 8: Consul Ref Bks Gale Res Co summer 65. 9: ALA-ACRL; -LED; -RSD; -RTSD; KanLA; MPLA. 10: Internat Soc for Gen Semantics Central Electric Railfans Assn; ACLU; AAUP; W Kan Track Club; Mo Valley Road Runners Club; Mo Valley Amateur Athletic Union; Road Runners Club Amer; Toastmasters Club; Amer Frieds Serv Com. 12: Ed bd "Track Times & "Distance Runnings News. 14: Docs, ref, lib educ. 15: 1430 Fairchild, Manhattan Ks 66502.

RICHARDS, BENJAMIN BILLINGS II. b Dubuque Iowa 24 Mr 17. 4: Alice Louise Nagy. 5: Loras Col 34-36 Eng; U No Iowa 38-39 (Eng) AB; West Res 40-41 BS in LS; Claremont Grad Sch 49-50 (Amer Studies) MA; Chicago summers 53-56 (LS). 7: Jr libn State Travel Lib, Des Moines Iowa 39-40; US Navy Midshipman to Lt, NY & SW Pacific 41-45; Libn Knox Col 45-58; Libn, Prof, Chm Dept of Lib Sci Kan State Tchrs Col (Emporia) 58-63; Libn Chatham Col 63-69; Libn Tex Womans U 69-. 9: ALA-ACRL;-LD; ILLLA; KanLA; PennLA. 12: "California Gold Rush Merchant 59 Ed "The Step Ladder, poetry (52-58). 13: Yes. 14: Admin, acquis, educ. 15: Tex Womans Univ Lib, Denton Tx 76204.

RICHARDS, DENNIS LEE. b Garland Utah 7 Jl 38. 4: Judy Hess. 5: Utah State U 56-58, 60-62 (Eng) BS; Fla State U 62-63 (LS) MA. 6: Sp. 7: Asst tchg materials ibn Ind State U 63-66; Docs libn 66-67; Docs libn UMont 68-. 9: ALA; -ACRL; MontLA; PNLA. 14: Govt publ. 15: 2 Kasota ct, Missoula Mt 59801.

RICHARDS, ELINOR (ANDERSON). b Morgantown W Va. 4: Ernest Richards. 5: WVaU 37-41 (Pub welfare) BA, summers 59-63 MALS. 6: Fr. 7: Sec WVaU Med Sch 45-46; Libn Lordsburg High Sch, Lordsburg NM 59-62; Sr catlgr Amherst Col Lib 62-. 9: ALA. 14: Catlg. 15: 99 Northampton rd, Amherst Ma 01002.

RICHARDS, EMMA S(IMON). b Harr ngton Del 4 D 18. 5: UDel 36-40 (Biol) AB; Drexel 50-51 MS in LS. 7: Bkmob libn State Lib Commsn of Del, Dover Del 42-50; Asst libn Wicomico Co Lib, Salisbury Md 51-. 9: ALA; MdLA. 10: Soroptimist Clu; Wicomio Co (Md) Hist Soc; Wicomio Mental ealth Soc. 14: Ref. 15: 104 E Isabella st, Salisbury Md 21801.

RICHARDS,JAMES H JR. b Scranton Penn 4 Ag 18. 4: Adeline Gorder. 5: Wesleyan U 36-40 (Hist) BA, 40-41 (Hist) MA; Columbia 46-47 (LS) BS; UWash 68. 6: Fr. 7: Stud asst & fellow Wesleyan U lib (Middletown Conn) 36-41; (Capt) Artillery Liaison Off 63 Inf Div 41-45; Consul & libn Earlham Col 47-50; Asst libn George Washingtn U 50-52; Libn Carleton Col 52-69; Dir of libs UWyo (Laramie) 69-. 8: Bldg Consul Simpson Col 57, Centre Col 63; Collections Consul Concordia Col (Moorhead Minn) USOE 67, 68; Mem Governors Adv Com on Libs (Minn). 9: ALA (life mem, Awards Com Subscription Bks Com); -ACRL; (Dir-at-Large 65-; Com on Org 61-62; chm Col Sect 55-56, Var Coms); MinnLA (chm Intel Freedom Com 52-56 & 62-65, chm Recr Com 57-59, chm Ad HC Com on Acad Lib Coop 65-, v-chm & chm Col Sect 56-58); Midwest Acad Libns Conf. 10: AAUP; Northfield Commun Dev Com. 13: Yes. 14: Admin, acquis, bldgs. 15: Coe Lib Univ of Wyoming, Laramie Wy 82070.

RICHARDS, JOHN STEWART. b Chicago 16 F 892. 4: Irene Fry. 5: UWash 13-16 (Gen) BA; NY State Lib Sch 19-20; UCal(Berkeley) 32 (LS) MA. 7: Libn Pub Lib, Marshfield Ore 16-18; ALA War Serv, Camp Fremont Cal 18-19; LibnIda Tech (Pocatello Ida) 20-23; Libn Wash State Normal Sch (Ellensburg) 23-26; Supt of circ UCal Lib (Berkeley) 26-29, Asst libn 29-34; EXEC ASST UWash Lib 34-81, Assoc libn 41-42; Libn Seattle Pub Lib 42-57, Libn Emeritus 57-. 8: Mem, Wsh State Lib Commsn 59-64. 9: ALA (Exec Bd 45-49, pres 55-56); PNLA (pres 37-38); Wash State LA. 15: Hacienda Carmel, Carmel Ca 93921.

RICHARDS, KATHERINE MARY (ENRIGHT). b Longview Wash 31 O 41. 5: Lower Columbia Jr Col 59-60 (Eng Lit); Marylhurst Col 60-61, 62-64 (Hist) BA; IndianaU 67-68 MLS; CatholicU 68-69 (LS); Johns HopkinsU 69- (Hist of Sci). 6: Fr. 7: Stud asst LCJC Lib, Longview Wash 59-60; Stu wash 59-60; Stud asst Marylhurst Col Lib 60-61; Asst libn UOre Dental Sch Lib, Portland 65-67; Ref asst IndU Bus Lib, Bloomington 67-68; Intern hist of med Welch Med Lib, Johns HopkinsU 68-. 9: MedLA. 10: AAUW; Amer Assn for Hist of Med. 14: Rare bks, hist of med. 15: 4736 NE 32nd place, Portland Or 97211.

RICHARDS, KENNETH W. b NYC 12 N 23. 5: Simmons 49-50 (LS; Rutgers 54-60 (Hist) BA, 65-66 (Hist) MA. 7: (Sgt T-4) US Army Radio Operator 43-45; Asst libn Moodys Investors Serv, NY 46-48; Ref libn USDA Lib, Wash DC 48-53; NJ State Lib: Ref libn 53-60, Archival examiner 60-63, Head archives & hist bur 63-. 8: Spec coord on nw State (NJ) Lib bldg, 58-65; Consul Me State Lib Bldg 67-68. 9: SAA; NJLA; Amer Records Mgt Assn. 10: Civitan Club (Trenton). 13: Yes. 14: Archives. 15: 33 Forence ave, Trenton NJ 08618.

RICHARDS, MARION HERRICK LOVETT. b Grand Rapids Mich 29 Je 05. 4: Harold A Richards. 5: Wayne State U 24-25 (Langs); Denison U 25-27 (Religious Educ) PHB; UMich 56-64 MALS. 7: YWCA Sec, Detroit 27-30; YWCA Sec Girl Res Dept, Tucson Ariz 32-33; Lib asst Pub Lib, Royal OAK Mich 55-58; Head Libn Pub Lib, Madison Heights Mich58-59; Child libn Pub Lib, Southfield Mich 61-. 9: ALA. 14: Child serv, adult reading adv. 15: 617 Detroit ave, Royal Oak Mich 48708.

RICHARDS, MARY JANE (BRADY). b Fall River Mass 29 D 17. 4: Francis Asburg Richards. 5: Simmons 35-39 (Eng, Educ) BS; Hood 45-46 (Fr); UWash 66-68 MLS. 6: Fr, Ger. 7: Jr tr USA Chem Warfare In 07: Jr tr USA Chem Warfare Intelligence, Wash DC 42-44; Tchr high sch, Thurmont Md 44-45; Sch libn Sacred Heart Villa, Seattle 65-66; Asst libn Lib

Soc for the Blind & Physically Handicapped, Seattle 68-. 9: ALA; WashLA; ONLA. 10: PTA; Seattle Symphony League. 14: Serv to blind & physically handicapped. 15: 3914-48th pl NE, Seattle Wa 98105.

RICHARDS, MILDRED W. b Coehatta Miss 4 Ap 20. 4: Dr Grover C Richard. 5: Miss Col 38-40; Miss State Col for Women 40-42 (Eng) AB; UMss 62-63 MLS. 6: Ger. 7: Tchr-libn High Sch, Enterprise Miss 42-43; Tchr-libn High Sch, Ruleville Miss 43-44; Grad asst Lib Sci Lib UMiss 62-63; Libn dept of res in bus & govt UMiss 63-64; Ref libn Midwestern U 64-66; Asst libn KPL, Wichita Falls Tex 66-67; Period libn Ga So Col 67-. 9: ALA; GaLA. 10: GSC Dames Club. 14: Ref, period. 15: 209 S Edgewood dr, Statesboro Ga 30458.

RICHARDS, NETTIE ADKINS. b Opelousas La 20 Ag 34. 5: Southern U 51-55 (Math, LS) BS; Grambling Col 64. 7: Phillis Wheatley High Sch, Melville La: Tchr & libn 55-59, Libn 59-. 9: ALA; LaEA; LaLA; LaASchL; St Landry Parish EA. 10: Alpha Kappa Mu; Alpha Kappa Alpha; United Negro Col Fund. 14: Ref, sch libnship. 15: 917 Julia, Opelousas La 70570.

RICHARDS, PAUL L. b Fall River Mass 24 My 05. 4: Virginia Bartlett Greene. 5: Harvard 26-30 (Romance Lang) AB, 30-31 (Romance Philol) AM, 37-39 (Romance Philol) PhD; West Res 54-55 MS in LS. 6: Ital, Fr. 7: Instr Smith Col 30-37; Dept Head Lake Erie Col 39-55; (Lt) Army A F 42-43; Exec asst Army Exch Serv, NY 43-45; Chief circ libn Brown U 55-. 9: RILA. 10: Dante Soc of Amer; Amer Assn Tchrs of Italian. 12: Ed "Dieci novelle italiane (39). 15: 11 Belton dr, Barrington RI 02806.

RICHARDS, RUTH A. b Wilkes-Barre Penn 6 Je 24. 5: Penn State U 42-46 (Sci) BS; Drexel 63-64 (LS) MS. 7: Lab tech Anthracite Inst, Wilkes-Barre Penn 46-52; Clerk-draftsman Walter Williams Co, Wilkes-Barre Penn 52-53; Lab tech Hess Goldsmith & Co, Wilkes-Barre Penn 54-61; Asst ref Osterhout Free Lib, Wilkes-Barre Penn 61-. 14: Ref. 15: 155 W River st, Wilkes-Barre Pa 18701.

RICHARDS, STANLEY DAVID. b Toronto Can 11 F 19. 4: Grace Elizabeth Dobbin. 5: UToronto 46-50 (Hist) BA, 50-51 BLS. 7: (Cpl) Postal & Pay CORPS, Can Army 43-46; Chief Libn Kent Co Lib Cooperative 51-54; Chief Libn Wallaceburg Pub Lib 54-57; Tchr-libn Kenner Collegiate 57-60; Tchr-libn Adam Scott CVI 60-67; Tchr-libn Brampton Centennial SS 67-. 15: 22 Inglewood dr, Brampton Ont Can.

RICHARDS, VINCENT PHILIP. b Sutton Bonnington Notts Eng 1 Ag 33. 4:Ann Beardshall. 5: Royal Army Educ Corps Sch of Educ 51-52 Tchg Certif; Ealing Col(London) 54-55 (LS) ALA; UOkla 63-66 (Liberal Studies) BLS. 6: Fr. 7: Lib asst Brentford & Chiswick Pub Libs, London 49-51; Sgt Royal Army Educ Corps tchr-libn, Egypt 51-53; Lib asst Brentford & Chiswick Pub Lib, London 53-54; Catlgr Manresa Col Lib (London) 54-55; Asst ref libn Brentford & Chiswick Pub Lib, London 55-56; Asst br libn Peace River Br Pub Lib Dawson Creek BC 56-57; V&: Asst dir Fraser Valley Reg Lib, Abbotsford BC 58-67; Chief libn Red Deer Col, Red Deer Alta 67-. 8: Consul Manresa Col Lib, London Eng 55-56, St Augstines Abbey Lib, Ramsgate Kent Eng 55-56; Westminster Abbey Lib, Mission BC Can 58-; Adv Bd "School Paperback journal 64-. 9: Lib Assn (Gt Brit: Assn Asst Libns (UK); BCLA (chm Short Course Com 63); BC Reg Lib Inst (chm 60, 63, 66); PNLA (sec 59); AltaLA. 12: "Revolution in Teaching New Theory, Technology, and Curricula (64); "PNLA Golden Jubilee Proceedings 1959 (60); "The Use of Paperbacks in Public Libraries (66). 13: Yes. 14: Bk ind, paperbacks in educ, reg & co libns, rural lib serv, acad libs. 15: 48 Springfield ave, Red Deer Alberta Can.

RICHARDSON, AUGUSTA BEATTY. b Grenada Miss 14 D 09. 4: Samuel M Richardson. 5: Miss State Col for Women 27-31 (Eng) BA; UIll 37-38 BS in LS. 7: Libn Grenada Co Lib, Grenada Miss 35-37; Asst bind dept UIll Lib (Urbana) 37-38; Head bind dept UArk Lib 38-40; Dist supv WPA Lib Proj, Tupelo Miss 40-42; Asst reg libn UTenn Jr Col Reg Lib (Martin Tenn) 42-43; Libn Alcorn Co Lib, Corinth 43-51; Dir NE Reg Lib, Corinth Miss 51-. 51-. 8: Dir, Miss State Survey Com, Southeastern States Co-op Lib Survey, 46-48; 46-49; of Miss Lib Commsnrs, 47-53. 9: ALA (Coun re, MissLA; Recr Com 53-63; Jt ALA-SELA Memb Com 64-66); -PLD (Nomin Com 50); MissLA (pres 47-49, Exec BD); SELA (Exec Bd 47-49; SEast States Coun 46-49; sec Pub Lib Sect 62-64). 10: Pilot Club; Commun Fund Bd; Red Cross Bd; Delta Kappa Gamma. 11: Award of Merit, MissLA (66). 12: "Libraries in Mississippi: A Report of a Survey of Library Facilities, 1946-47 (49). 13: Yes. 14: Ref, loc hist collection, legis for devel of libs. 15: B ox 1419, Corinth Ms 38834.

RICHARDSON, DOROTHY (GRAY). b Knoxville Tenn 3 J108. 4: James H Richardson. 5: UTenn 25-29 (Lit) AB; UIll 30-31 BS in LS. 6: Fr, Sp. 7: Catlgr NC State Col Lib (Raleigh) 31-35; Lib asst Newark Pub Lib, Newark NJ 35-39; Head catlgr Elizabeth NJ 39-47; Catlg Decatur-DeKalb Reg Lib, Decatur Ga 51-61; Asst libn Oglethorpe Col 61-. 9: GaLA; SELA. 10: Delta Delta Delta. 12: Jt comp with Lois Wenman "List of Subject Headings for Information File" (4th ed 38). 14: Catlg. 15: 1352 W Nancy Creek dr NE, Atlanta Ga 30319.

RICHARDSON, ELLEN (ALLGOOD). b Easley SC 18 D 27. 4: Jacob Roy Richardson. 5: SC State Co; 45-49 (LS) AB; Atlanta summer 51 LS SC State Col summer 52 (Eng, Lit); Atlanta summer 63 LS). 6: Fr. 7: Sch libn: Finley High Sch, Chester SC 49-52, Beaufort Co Train Sch, Beaufort SC 52-53, St Helena Cons Sch, Frogmore SC 53-57, Robert Smalls Sr High Sch, Beaufort SC 57-; Robert Smalls Jr High Sch, Beaufort SC 60-. 9: ALA; Palmetto EA; Beaufort Co Sch Tchrs Assn. 14: Ref, ya. 15: 1930 Duke st, Beaufort SC 29902.

RICHARDSON, F MARIE (WYATT). b Marshall Tex 13 Jl 19. 4: Charles A Richardson. 5: LSU 38-40 (Chem) BS; Glendale Col 58-60 (Arch); USC 61 (Arch); Immaculate Heart Col (Los Angeles) 62-65 (LS) MA. 6: Sp. 7: Hd research lib Charles Luckman Assoc, Los Angeles 61-63; Econ research libn Stanford Research Inst, S Pasadena Cal 63; Econ libn Planning Research Corp, Los Angeles 63-65; Hd of lib Applied Research Dept of Northrop Nortronics, Newbury Park Cal 65-67; Lit searcher Jet Propulsion Lab, Pasadena Cal 67; Hd research lib Albert C Martin & Assoc, Los Angeles 67-. 9: SLA; ASIS; CalLA. 14: Arch ref & research. 15: 4408 Colbath ave, Sherman Oaks Cal 91403.

RICHARDSON, FRANCES CARY. b Wash DC 24 Ap 1897. 5: Lib Sch of the Los Angeles Pub Lib 18-19. 07; Lib Willows Pub Lib, Willows Cal 16-18; Child libn Fresno Pub Lib, Fresno Cal 19-21; Sr libn art & music dept Los Angeles Pub Lib 21-27; Dir of Research 20th Century Fox Film Corp, Los Angeles 28-. 9: TheatrLA; CalLA; SLA. 10: Acad of Motion Picture Arts & Scis; Art Histns; Soc of Arch Histns. 13: Yes. 14: Ref. 15: Research Dept, Box 900, Beverly Hills Cal 90213.

RICHARDSON, GAY A(THENA). b Randolph Va 24 Ap 10. 5: Longwood Col 29-33 (Eng) BS in Ed; Col of William & Mary summer 36; UNC summers 37-40 BS in LS; Radford Col summer 41. 7; Stud asst Longwood Col Lib 30-33, Act asst libn 33-34; Elem tchr Woodlawn Sch, Nokesville Va 34-35; Tchr Beaverdam Elem Sch, Beaverdam Va 35-36; Tchr Henry Clay Elem Sch, Ashland Va 36-39; High sch libn Ellerbe Ellerbe Ellebre NC 39-42; Catlgr Va State Lib: jr libn 42, lib asst V 42-45, libn i 45-49, libn A 49-. 9: ALA; SELA; Potomac Tech Proc Libns; VaLA. 14: Catlg. 15: 419 N Mulberry st, Richmond Va 23220.

RICHARDSON, GEORGIA CAROL. b Greensburg Penn 12 My 36. 5: Clarion State Col 54-58 BS in LS; Duquesne U 59-64 M Ed in LS. 6: Sp. 7: Libn Hempfield Area Sch Dist, Greensburg Penn 58-61; Libn Penn Joint High Sch, Claridge 61-. 9: NEA; PennStateEA; Sub Libns Assn. 14: Ref. 15: Rt 6, Irwin Penn 15642.

RICHARDSON, HAROLD GIPSON. b Houston Tex 31 Ja 21. 6: Sp, Fr. 7: Engineering libn columbia Gulf Transmission, Houston Tex 57-67; Gen ed "The Texas List", Houston Tex 67-. 9: SLA; TexLA. 13: Yes. 14: Ser, ref. 15: 4149 Riley, Houston Tx 77005.

RICHARDSON, HUGH ELWIN. b Eureka Kan. 4: Evelyn Ireland. 5: Kan State Tchrs Col (Emporia) 48-51 (Bus) BS Ed, 53-57 (Bus, LS) MS Ed,62-65 (LS) MS; Kan State U 68, 69. 7: (Sgt) US Army admin clerk 46-48; Tchr-libn Paradise High Sch, Paradise Kan 52-57; Tchr Russell High Sch, Russell Kan 57-61; Libn Marion High Sch, Marion Kan 61; Libn Augusta High Sch, Augusta Kan 62-; Dir of av serv, acquis libn Butler Co Commun Jr Col (El Dorado Kan) 66-. 9: Lan State Tchrs Assn; KanASchL; Kan A-V Org; NEA-DAVI. 14: Ref, acquis. 15: 1222 Helen, Augusta Ks 60710.

RICHARDSON, LOUISE M(ILLER). b Los Angeles 13 F 42: 04: Dr Thomas R Richardson. 4: Thomas R Richardson. 5: Occidental Col 58-62 (Chem) BA; ASADENA City Col 62-64 (Russian); USoCal 64-65 (LS), 67-68 MSLS. 7: Tech libn Purex Corp Ltd, Wilmington Cal 62-65; Tech libn Aerojet-General Corp, Sacramento Cal 65-66; Libn Sci Lib Wayne State U 69-. 8: Abstractor, "Chemical Abstracts 65-. 9: SLA; ACS. 10: Beta Phi Mu. 14: Ref, sers. 15: 1649 N Mayburn, Dearborn Mi 48128.

RICHARDSON, MARGUERITE (HAVILAND). b Pittsburgh 19 Mr 20.05: UPittsburgh 40-63 (Elem Educ) BS in Ed, 63-64 (LS) MS. 5: UPittsburgh 40-63 (Elem Educ) BS in Ed, 63-64 (LS) MS. 7: Sec-treas Pittsburgh Alloy Corp, Pittsburgh 47-53; Libn Hoover Sch Mt Lebanon Pub Schs, Pittsburgh 64-. 9: NEA; ALA; Penn State EA; PennLA. 10: Pi Lambda Theta; Beta Phi Mu. 14: Child serv. 15: 755 Crystal dr, Pittsburgh Pa 15228.

RICHARDSON, MARIE (SMITH). b Decaturville Tenn 2 S 24. 4: Elva Richardson. 5: UTenn 43-46 (Home Econ), UChattanooga 58-60 & 60-61 (Home Econ, Sci) BS; So Conn State Col 62 (LS). 7: Dir consumer research & testing, Chicopee Manufacturing Co, Milltown NJ 56-57; Chief libn Chattanooga div lib Combustion Engr Inc 57-60; Tchr sci & math jr high sch, Hamilton Co Tenn 60-61; Chief libn engnr research lib Combustion Engnr Inc, Windsor Conn 61-63; Dept mgr corporate lib 63-. 8: Consul: lib org for Dixie Mercerizing Co, Chattanooga Tenn 60, Lib Devel for Bowaters So Paper Corp, Calhoun Tenn, 60; John Cotton Dana Lectr LSU (Baton Rouge) 67; Mem Spec Adv Com to Conn State Lib for Lib Dev & Interlib Coop, 67. 9: SLA (Demonstr Lib Staff 63; (mem Consul Com 67-69); Conn Valley Chap; treas 63-65, pres-elect & Program Chm 65-66); pres 66-67); ConnLA (mem Com on Training Non-Prof 68-). 12: Ed SLA, Conn Valley Chap "Bulletin (62-63); Ed "Tennessee Librarian (57). 13: Yes. 14: Ref, lit searching. 15: Combusion Engnr Inc, Corpoate Lib, 1000 prospect Hill rd, Windsor Conn 06095.

RICHARDSON, MARJORIE (MARTEL). b Newport Vt 25 N 13. 4: Robert Clayton Richardson. 5: UNH 31-35 (Sci, Home econ) BS; UMd 64, 65 (LS). 7: Tchr & dietitian Newington Jr High Sch, Newington Conn 35-37; Asst period catlgr Dartmouth Col Lib 37-40; Elem tchr & libn Country Day Sch, Scranton Penn 40-42; Friends Sch, Baltimore: Chn home econ dept 43-51, Libn upper sch 51-. 8: Mem Middle Atlantic States Eval Coms 48, 49, 50, 67. 9: ALA; -AASchL; Nat Assn Independent Schs; Friends Coun Educ; MdLA; Assn Sch Libns Md (Prog Chm 63, sec 64-66); Assn Md Independent Schs; Baltimore Independent Sch Libns (chm 59). 10: Alpha Chi Omega; Md Coun Student Lib Clubs; Baltimore League for Crippled Child & Adults. 14: Sch libs. 15: 7908 Springway rd, Baltimore Md 21204.

RICHARDSON, MARY (BRESLIN). b Savannah Ga 24 Mr 30. 4: Jerrol C Richardson. 5: UWyo 47-51 (Journalism) BS; UCLA 68-69 MLS. 7: Ed asst Miller Freeman Pub Libs, San Francisco 51-52; Art asst J Walter Thompson Co, San Francisco 52-53; Advertising writer Roos Bros, San Francisco 53-57; Divisional advertising mgr The Emporium, San Francisco 58-61; Asst ed The Reporter, San Anselmo Cal 65-66. 15: 908-15th st, Santa Monica Ca 90403.

RICHARDSON, MARY T (TODD). b Pittsburgh Penn 14 F 25. 4: Fred E Richardson. 5: UPittsburgh 43-46 (Ed) BS, 64-66 MLS. 7: Tchr Harrison Twp Schs, Natrona Penn 46-48; Libn Carnegie Libm Pittsburgh Penn 66-. 9: ALA; PennLA. 10: Carnegie Lib Staff assn; Beta Phi Mu. 14: Child wk, ref. 15: 2439 Berkshire dr, Pittsburgh Pa 15241.

RICHARDSON, NANCY (McADAMS). b Wilkinsburg Penn 1 F 19. 4: Floyd T Richardson. 5: Wheaton Col, Wheaton Ill 37-41 (Eng) BA; Carnegie 41-42 BSLS. 7: Child libn Grandview Hts Pub, Columbus Ohio 42-44; Child libn Youngstown Pub, Youngstown Ohio 44-45; Child libn Multnomah Co Lib, Portland Ore 46-55; Child libn San Jose Pub, San Jose Cal 55-57; Child libn Multnomah Co Lib, Portland Ore 57-. 9: ALA. 14: Child lib, pub lib wk. 15: 6645 SE Yamhill, Portland Or 97215.

RICHARDSON, RANSOM L(LOYD). b Fillmore NY 21 Je 14. 4: Lois York. 5: Houghton Col 33-37 (Eng) AB; Syracuse 38 BS in LS. 6: Fr. 7: Br libn Hartford Pub Lib, Hartford Conn 38-43; T/3 Provost Marshal US Army ETO 43-44; Instr in Lib Sci US Army, Obermammergau Germany 45; Chief Libn Curtis Mem Lib, Meriden Conn 46-52; Ed "ALA Bulletin, Chicago 52-56; Assoc libn Flint Pub Lib, Flint Mich 56-57, Dir of Libs 57-. 8: Lib consul Conn State Bd of Educ, 49-50; Surveyed W Haven Conn Pub Lib 49. 9: ALA-PLA (pres 63-64);-LAD (Recr Com 58-); ConnLA (pres 49-50); NELA (pres 50); MichLA (pres 61-62). 10: Rotary Club; Flint Chess Club. 12: "A Plan for Library Development in the State of Connecticut (50); Ed "ALA Bulletin & Coun LA "Bulletin. 13: Yes. 14: Admin. 15: 1026 E Kearsley st, Flint Mich 48502.

RICHARDSON, RUTH (ANN). b Vinton Iowa 30 D 23. 43004 07: ;67, Secondary sch libn 68-. 5: Iowa State Tchrs Col 43-46 (Eng) BA; State U Iowa summers 49, 50; Mexico City Col summer 52; UWis 54-55 (LS) MA. 7: Tchr Taylor No 8 Rural Sch, Benton Co Iowa 42-43; Tchr Decorah High Sch, Decorah Iowa 46-52; Tchr Harlandale high Sch, San Antonio Tex 52-54; Clsf Iowa State U Lib 55-56; Prof asst Pub Lib, Cedar Rapids Iowa 56-57, Head of ref div 57-59; Visiting Asst Prof Fla State U Lib Sch 59-60; Head of adult serv Pub Lib, Cedar Rapids Iowa 60-. 9: ALA; ASCD; MichASchL. 10: Beta Phi Mu; Kappa Delta Phi. 14: Adult serv, secondary sch libs. 15: 1400 2nd ave SE, Cedar Rapids Iowa 52403.

RICHARDSON, SELMA K(ATHERINE). b McCandless Twp Penn 23 O 31. 5: Capital U 49-51; St Olaf Col 51-53 (Music Educ) BM; UMich 58- MA (Educ), MALS. 7: Elem sch tchr Berkley Sch Dist, Berkley Mich 53-60; Elem sch libn Oak Park Sch Dist, Oak Park Mich 60-67, Secondary sch libn 68-. 9: ALA; ASCD; MichASchL. 10: Pi Lambda Theta; Phi Kappa Phi; Beta Phi Mu; Alpha Delta Kappa. 14: Elem sch libs, secondary sch libs. 15: 3905 Devon rd, Royal Oak Mich 48073.

RICHARDSON, SMITH W JR. b Okmulgee Okla 21 F 34. 4: Sally Lattin. 5: Okla State U 56-60 (Hist) BS Ed; UOkla 62-63 MLS. 6: Ger. 7: CT3 US Navy, US & Germany 53-56; Eng & hist tchr Perkins High Sch, Perkins Okla 60-62; Lib asst UOkla Law Lib 62-63; Ref libn Wayne State Col 63-64; Head Libn State Satate U (Superior) 64-. 9: AL; WisLA. 10: Phi Delta Kappa; Phi Alpha Theta; Phi Gamma Mu;Lions Internat; Nat Wildlife Fed. 14: Admin, ser. 15: Wis State Univ Lib, Superior Wis 54881.

RICHARDSON, THELMA (POWELL). b Cuthbert Ga 1 Ag 23. 4: Thomas Lee Richardson. 5: WVa State Col (Sociol) AB: Atlanta 48 BS in LS; Syracuse 64 MS in LS; UIll summer 66 (Span & Lat Amer Studies); UMo 67 (Computer Based Lib Info Systems). 6: Fr.07: Ref libn Lincoln U 48-50; Asst libn Texas Col 50-54; Instr Lib Sci Southern U summer 55; Catlgr& orders libn Grambling Col 55-58; Head Libn Alcorn A&M Col 58-60; Liberal arts libn Grambling Col 60-. 9: ALA; LaLA; LaEA. 10: Zeta Phi Beta; Beta Phi Mu. 14: Reading interests of adults, catlg, computer based info systs; Latin Amer libnship. 15: Box 258, Grambling La.

RICHARDSON, VIRGINIA. b Omaha Neb 24 S 10. 5: Bryn Mawr 29-33 (Ger, Mus) AB; Columbia 47-51 summers MLS; Richmond Prof Inst 57- (Art Hist). 6: Fr. 7: Music sec Mr Henry S Drinker, Merion Penn 40-41; Circ dept Netherlands Govt Info Serv, NYC 42-45; Off mgr & sec to dir Va Mus of Fine Arts, Richmond Va 45-46; Libn Art & Music Dept Richmond Pub Lib, Va 46-. 9: MusLA; VaStateLA. 10: Adv Bd of Musicians' Club of Richmond; Placement Com of Richmond Symphony. 14: Mus catlg, ref. 15: Chesterfield 900 W Franklin st, Richmond Va 23220.

RICHARDSON, WILLIAM H. b Wooster Ohio 28 Ap 23. 4: Barbara Easter. 5: Antioch Col 41-44, 46-48 (Engnr); UNM 48-49, 50-51 (Biol) BS; UDenver 51-52 (LS) MA. 7: US Army Ordnance Lib clerk T-5 44-46; Asst circ libn UNM 49-5; Asst ref libn UDenver 52-54; Libn Engnr Col Washington U St Louis Louis0 54-56; Ref libn Sandia Albuquerque AlbuquerqueNM 56-63; Libn Allison Div Gen Motors Corp, Indianapolis 63-. 9: SLA (Prof Consul 63-, chm Resol Ref Com 62; pres Rio Grande Chap 60-61; pres Ind Cha69). 12: Ed SLA Rio Grande Chap "Bulletin (57-58). 13: Yes. 14: Admin, mechanized systems. 15: Allison Div GMC PO Box 894, Indianapolis In 46206.

RICHARDSON, WINNIFRED (STEWART). b Montreal Can 3 My 08. 4: Andrew Richardson. 5: UDenver 53-58 (Humanities) AB, 59-60 (LS) MA; Colo State Col 61-63 (Lit). 6: Fr, Sp. 7: Libn Mitchell High Sch, Neb 58-60; Asst ref Colo State Col Lib 60-64, asst catlgr 64-66, tchr lib sci 66-68, Per libn 68-. 8: Tchr, lib sci summer courses, Colo STATE Col 61-65. 9: MPLA; ColoLA; ALA. 10: AAUP; AAUW. 14: Catlg, ref. 15: 2431 25th ave, Greeley Co 80631.

RICHEL, VALETA (RAYMER). b Versailles Mo 26 D 12. 4: John Ernest Richel. 5: Kan State Tchrs Col 29-35 (LS) BS; UMd summers 60, 62; UMont summer 63. 6: Sp, Fr. 7: Tchr various schs, Kan 30-31, 36-38; Libn Sr High Sch, Fredonia Kan 39-43; Libn US Dept of Labor Lib, Wash DC 43-45; Libn NLM, Wash DC 48-59; Libn Jr High Sch, Prince Georges Co Md 60-66; Catlg libn Bd of Educ Curriculum Lib, Annapolis Md 66-. 9: ALA; NEA; MdStateEA. 14: Catlg. 15: 788 Fairview ave, Annapolis Md 21403.

RICHER, SUZANNE. b Can 25 O 3. 4: Yvon Richer. 5: College Basile-Moreau (Ville Saint-Laurent, Montreal 60-64 BA; UOttawa 64-65 BLS (summa cum laude). 6: F, Eng. 7: Tech libn Computing Devices of Can Ltd, Ottawa 65-66; Libs Forest Research Lab Dept Fisheries & Forestry, Ste Fox

Quebec 66-. 9: Association Canadienne des Bibliothecaires de Langue Francaise. 10: Assn des Anciens de LUniversite DOttawa; Prof Inst Can. 13: Yes. 14: Sci, forestry, ref, spec libs. 15: Forest Research Laboratory, PO Box 3800, Ste Fox Quebec 10 PQ Can.

RICHES, WILHELMINA (MARRS). b Denver t3 Ag 12. 4: Waldo A Riches. 5: Ore Normal 30-32 (Tchg Certif); Ore State Col 35-37 (Educ) BS in Ed; UWash summers 58-63 (LS) ML. 6: Fr, Sp. 7: Tchr Eureka City Schs, Eureka Cal 51-52; Tchr Cajon Valley Union Sch, El Cajon Cal 52-57, Libn 57-. 9: NEA; Cal Tchrs Assn. 10: AAUW; San Diego Opera Guild; San Diego Symphony Assn. 14: Sch libs. 15: 5647 Dorothy way, San Diego Ca 92115.

RICHIE, JOAN FRANCES. b Wooster Ohio 15 Mr 34. 5: Ursuline Col 52-56 (Hist) AB, Ohio High Sch Tchg Certif; KENT State U 59-64 MA in LS. 6: Sp. 7: Soc Studies tchr Hoban-Dominican High Sch, Cleveland 56-57; Soc Studies tchr Maple Heights Jr High Sch, Cleveland 57-59; Libn Jackson Mem High Sch, Massillon Ohio 59-62; Readers asst Pub Lib of Youngstown & Mahoning Co, Youngstown Ohio 62-64, Ref libn 64-66, Br libn Brownlee Woods Br 66-. 9: Ohio,la. 10: Cath Alumni Club. 14: Ref, sch libs. 15: 192 Federal st NE, Massillon Ohio 44646.

RICHISON, ROSEMARY (HOOSER). b Tuskahoma Okla 1 My 34. 4: William E Richison. 5: East Okla A&M Col 52-54; Murray State Sch of Agric (Okla) 54; East Okla State Tchrs Col 58; Middle Tenn State Col 40 (Educ) BS, 65; Admin & supv lib sci MA. 7: Tchr elem sch, Lavergne Tenn 60-63; Libn Smyrna High Sch, Smyrna Tenn 65-, Guam 67, 68, Smyrna Tenn 69 9: NEA; TennEA; TennLA; GuamLA; ALA; GuamEA. 14: Catlg. 15: 206B Cannon dr, Smyrna Tn 37167.

RICHMOND, PHYLLIS (ALLEN). b Boston 5 Ja 21. 5: West Res 38-42 (Hist) AB; Cornell U 47-48 (Hist); UPenn 45-46, 48-49 (Hist) MA, PhD; West Res 52-53, 56 MS in LS. 6: Fr, Ger. 7: Curator of Hist Rochester Mus of Arts and Sci, Rochester 43-45, 46-47; Asst to dir Inst of Hist of Med John Hopkins U 52; Asst loc hist div Rochester (NY) Pub Lib 54; Ser catlgr URochester Lib 55-60; Supv of River Campus Sci Libs URochester Lib 60-65, Info systs spec 66-68; Prof Sch of Lib Sci Syracuse U 69-. 8: Counsul, Documentation Research Proj, Amer Inst of Phys 63-, Ad Hoc Com on MARC II 67. 9: ALA-RTSD (Catlg & clsf sect; mem & chm clsf com 57-64; ser sect sec 64-65 & 66-67; Cat Policy & Research Com 66-67); ASIS (chm clsf res com 58-59); ASAZ39 (Subcom on clsf 64-; Clsf res study group chm 58-63); SLA; (Spec Clsf Com 65-. 10: Hist of Sci Soc; Amer Assn Hist Med; NY State Hist Assn; Phi Beta Kappa; Beta Phi Mu; Amer Radio Relay League; Soc for Gen Systs Research; Fellow Amer Coun of Learned Socs 47-48. 12: "Americans and the Germ Theory of Disease" PhD Diss (49); "Index to Scientific Journal Title Abbreviations from the Physical Review" (64); Ed Bd "American Documentation" (60, 65-). 13: Yes. 14: Clsf, lib automation, ser, computers in humanities, Amer sci research 19th cent, sci theory. 15: 300 Audubon pkwy apt 18, Syracuse NY 13224.

RICHMOND, SYLVIA BEATRICE. b Chelsea Mass 3 S 01. 5: Simmons 22; Boston U 24; Columbia 30. 7: Chelsea Pub Lib, Chelsea Mass; Jr asst 19-25, Sr asst 25-35, Chief asst 35-40, Ref libn 40-47, Chief libn 47-67; Libn Emeritus 67-. 8: Lit ed Chelsea Record, Chelsea Mass 40, feature writer. 9: ALA; MassLA. 10: Nat League of Amer Pen Women; NE Women's Press Assn; Red Cross; Amer Cancer Soc. 13: Yes. 14: Ref. 15: 72 Tudor st, Chelsea Mass 02150.

RICHTER, ANNE J (ONES). b Pittsburgh 10 Ap 05. 4: Eugene Richter. 5: Mary Baldwin Col 23-24; NDEA Inst 66; City Col Grad Sch of Educ 66-. 7: Sec to pres Harper & Brothers, NY 25-31; R R Bowker Co, NY: Sec to pres 37-47, Bk ed 47-, Dir 56-67, Ed-in-chief bk ed dept 68-. 9: ALA; SLA (past chm Publ Div, Spec Rep); USASI; Bksellers League, NY; NY Lib Cu21 10: Womens Nat Bk Assn. 11: Constance Lindsay Skinner Award, Womens Nat Bk Assn, 57. 12: Ed "Literary Market Place & other bktrade & lib ref bks. 13: Yes. 14: Bibliog, ref tools, indexing. 15: 1180 Ave of the Americas, New York NY 10036.

RICHTER, BELLA (TEICHER). b NY. 4: HAROLD Richter. 5: Hunter Col 32-35 (Elem Educ, Soc Studies) BA; NYU 35-36 (Secondary Educ, Soc Studies) MA; Queens Col (NY) 60-65 MLS 07: NYC Bd of Educ: Tchr elem sch in chg of lib 55-62, Reading improvement tchr in elem sch 62-64, Jr high tchr of Lib 64-, NDEA Inst 66; City Col Grad Sch of Educ 66-. 7: NYC Bd of Educ; Tchr elem sch in charge of lib 55-62, Reading improvement tchr in elem sch 62-64, Jr high tchr of lib 64-; Field libn ESEA 66-67. 9: NYC SchLA. 14: Sch libnship. 15: 162-10 72nd ave, Flushing NY 11365.

RICHTER, BERTINA. b Scottsbluff Neb 2 S 44. 5: Monterey Peninsula Jr Col 62-64 (Gen educ) AA; Sacramento State Col 64-66 (Anthrop) BA; UCal (Berkeley) 66-67 MLS. 6: Fr, Ger. 7: Catlg dept Fresno State Col Lib 67-. 9: CalLA. 14: Catlg, child lit, rare bks. 15: 1290 Hamilton st, Seaside Ca 93955.

RICHTER, REV WILLIAM L. b SI NY 10 My 27. 5: Fordham 48-49 (Educ); Maryknoll Col (Ill) 51-53 (Philos) BA; Mt St Mary Sem (Cincinnati) 54-58 (Theol); St Johns U (NY) 58 MLS; Toledo U 67-. 6: Sp, Fr. 7: Sec W R Grace & Co, NYC 44-49; Asst Pastor St Jospehs Church, Maumee Ohio 58-63; Admin Ss Peter & Paul Churc, Toledo Ohio 63-67; Spiritual dir, i Sem, Diocese of Toledo Ohio 67-. 9: Nat Assn for the Spanish-Speaking; CathLA (NW Ohio Rep); ALA; Amer Assn of Tchrs of Span & Portu. 10: Bd of Commun Rel, Toledo; Dir, Guadalupe Center for the Spanish Speaking, Diocese of Toledo; Diocesan War on Poverty Com 63-67; Toledo Area Coun of Churches Metropolitan Mission del; Toledo Diocese Ecumenical Commsn; Diocesan Secretariat for Cath-Jewish Rels. 12: "Centennial History of SS Peter and Paul Church, Toledo Ohio" (67). 14: Sem lib admin. 15: 5201 Airport hwy, Toledo Oh 43615.

RICKER, EDWARD FRANK. b Quincy Mass 26 Ap 15. 5: BostonU 46-49 (Eng) AB; HarvardU 59-60 (Slavic Langs & Lits) MA; Simmons 67-69 MSLS. 6: Russian, Bulgarian, Ger, Fr. 7: Communications tech USN 50-58; Ref & circ MIT 60-65, Exchange libn 65-66, Asst sci libn & Slavic specialist 66-; Instr in Russian BrandeisU 65-66. 14: Sci, Slavic. 15: 100 Memorial dr, Cambridge Ma 02142.

RICKER, ELEANOR LILLIAN. b Block Island RI 20 D 09. 5: Simmons 27-31 BSLS. 7: Catlgr & 1st asst Jones Lib Inc, Amherst Mass 31-42; Chief libn Lovell Gen Hosp, Ft Devens Mass 42-46; Asst chief lib div VA br off #1, Boston 46-48; Asst chief acquis lib serv VA central off, Wash DC 48-50; VA hosps: Asst chief libn, Montrose NY 50-51, Chief libn, Montrose NY 51-53, Chief libn, W Haven Conn 53, Chief libn, Boston 68-. 9: ALA; SLA; MassLA; WisLA. 14: Adult serv, patients & Med (Hosp) libs. 15: Veterans Administration Ctr, Wood Wi 53193.

RICKERBY, GREGORY (ALLEN). b Stratford Ont Can 5 N 40. 5: UWest Ont 59-62 BA; UToronto 63-64 BLS. 6: Fr. 7: Clerical asst Toronto Pub Lib 62-63, ref libn 64-67; Catlgr Douglas Lib Queen's U 67-. 9: CanLA. 10: Soc of the Cath Commonwealth. 14: Ref. 15: 45 Crooks st, Stratford Ont Can.

RICKING, MYRL. b Cincinnati 2 Ag 18. 5: UCincinnati 3640 (Eng) BA. 6: Fr. 7: Ed sec Bd of Educ, Cincinnati 40-43; Hosp wker Amer Nat Red Cross 44-46; Asst personnel off Yale U Lib 47-50; Asst field dir Amer Nat Red Cross 50-51; Ed Field Enterprises, Chicago 51-53; Chief in-serv train & personnel control Milwaukee Pub Lib 53-62; Dir Off for Recruitment ALA, Chicago 62-67; Chief Manpower Utilization Off, LC 67-. 9: ALA; Soc for Personnel Admin; DCLA. 10: Delta Kappa Gamma; Phi Beta Kappa. 13: Yes. 14: Admin, lib educ. 15: 2126 Connecticut ave NW, Wash DC 20008.

RICKS, MIRIAM GWINETTE. b Elm City NC 1 N 27. 5: Bennett Col 44-48 (Eng) BA; NC Col (Durham) 51-54 (LS) MSLS; NC State U (Raleigh) summers 59, 60 (Guidance); Agric & Tech State U 54, 58, 59; Hampton Inst summer 64; CUNY Queen's Col summer 65; UNC (Greensboro) 65. 6: Fr. 7: Stud lib asst Bennett Col (Greensboro) 45-47, Asst residence dir 47-48, Residence dir 49-51; Libn, coun, Eng instr Shepard Sch, Zebulon NC 51-60; Itinerant libn Raleigh Pub Schs, Raleigh NC 60-66, Libn 66-; Catlgr Richard Bittarrison Pub Lib, Raleigh NC summer 64; Lib Sci instr Benedict Col summer 66. 8: Planned lib prog for ITA classes (64-68); Org 4 libs 60, 61, 65; career day counsel in libnship, Henderson Inst 58-. 9: ALA; NEA; Child Study Assn Amer; NCLA; NCASchL (Standards Com 65-67); NCTA (sec Libns Dept 56-59, chm 59-61 & 69-71); sec Raleigh Unit 63-69); NC Assn Clr Tchrs (chm Prog Com Raleigh Unit 65-69). 10: Raleigh Coun Church Women United; Delta Sigma Theta. 14: Ref, admin, supv, child serv. 15: PO Box 4, Elm City NC 27822.

RIDDELL, MARGARET AITKEN. b Los Angeles Cal 1 F 14. 4: Herman I Riddell. 5: UCLA 30-34 (Philos) BA; West Res 34-35 BS in LS; USoCal 37-38 (Relig Educ) MA; Immaculate heart 62-63 (Educ) Lib Credential. 6: Ger. 7: Child libn NYC Pub Lib 35-36; Asst libn Educ Lib USoCal 36-38; Ed Talking Bks American Printing House for the Blind, Ky 38-39; Supv WPA, RI 40; Instr in . 38-39; Supv WPA, RI 40; Instr in lib sci USoCal 68-; Child libn Los Angeles Pub Lib 63-. 9: ALA; CalLA. 10: Amer Field Serv, Med Faculty Wives of USoCal. 13: Yes. 14: Child wk. 15: 5520 Red Oak dr, Hollywood Ca 90028.

RIDDICK, JOHN FREDERICK. b Kalamazoo Mich 12 O 41. 4: Joyce E Ridoutt. 5: West mich U 60-64 (Hist) AB, 64-66 (Hist) MA; UMich 68 (LS) MA. 7: Personnel off ILT US Army, RVN/CONUS 66-68; Admin asst Iowa StateU (Ames) 69-. 9: ALA; IowaStateLA. 15: RR #1 RA-17, Huxley Ia 50124.

RIDDLE, BARBARA JEAN (NORTHGRAVE). b Ottawa Ont Can. 5: Queens U 48-51 (Pol, Econ) BA; UToronto 52-53 BLS: Ont Col of Educ 64-65 Tchrs Certif; Spec's Certif in Sch Libnship. 6: Fr. 7: Bibliog UToronto Lib 53-59; Ref libn No York Pub Tib, Toronto 61-64; Sch libn Woburn Collegiate Inst, Toronto 65-66; Catlgr Ont Inst for Studies in Educ 66; Hd tech serv E York Bd of Educ 67-. 8: Tchr summer & night sch Ont Dept Educ (course for elem sch libns) 68-69. 9: CanLA; ALA; NEA-DAVI; CanASchL (mem Tech Serv Com). 10: Univ Womens Club of No York. 11: Ruby E Wallace Travel Fellowship (CanLA 69). 15: 144 Three Valleys dr, Don Mills Ontcan.

RIDDLE, FELSIE KATHLEEN. b Graham NC 28 O 14. 5: Guilford Col 31-35 (Eng, Hist) AB; UNC 40 BA in LS. 6: Lat, Fr, Ger. 7: Asst libn Guilford Col 38-39; Libn Christiansburg High Sch, Christianburg Va 40-44; Libn supv, a-v supv, Martinsville Va 44-60; Libn James Blair High Sch, Williamsburg Va 60-65; Asst Prof of Lib Sci & supv of practice Wk in Lib Sci Madison Col (Va) 65-. 9: ALA (var coms: VaEA (pres Dept of Sch Libns); NEA; VaLA. 10: AAUP; Delta Kappa Gamma. 15: Box 193 Madison College, Harrisonburg Va 22801.

RIDDLES, JAMES A. b Cleveland 2N 17. 4: Margaret Branum. 5: Ariz State U 36-40 (Music) BA; Garrett Biblical Inst 41-42; Pendle Hill 42-43; USoCal 46-47 MS in LS. 6: Sp, Ger. 7: Med tech US Army Med Corps 45-46; Asst libn Riverside City Col 47-49, Act libn 49-50; Sr libn San Diego Pub Lib 50-59; Ref libn UPacific 60-66, Dir libs 66-. 9: ALA; Cal Lib Adminrs of the North; CalLA (pres Golden Empire Dist 69). 10: AAUP; NAACP; ACLU; CORE; Fellowship of Reconciliation; Relig Soc of Friends. 14: Ref, admin. 15: 1821 Princeton, Stockton Ca 95204.

RIDENOUR, ALICE M. b Chicago 25 D 18. 5: Uminn 39 (LS) BS; Albion Col 41 (Eng, Philo) AM. 6: Fr. 7: Catlg asst UMinn Lib (Minneapolis) 40-41; Catlgr Albion Col 42-45, Libn 46-48; Asst catlgr UIda 49-50; Catlg libn Mont State U 50-58, Asst libn & head tech serv 58-. 9: ALA (Subj head com 60-62); PNLA (sec 52, chm Catlg Div 55-57, State Rep 58-60, chm Tech Serv Div 67-69); MontLA. 10: AAUP; AAUW; Phi Beta KAPPA; Soroptimists. 14: Catlg. 15: Mont State Univ Lib, Bozeman Mt 59715.

RIDEOUT, GLENNA ROWENA. b Hartland New Brunswick Can 11 My 11. 5: Acadia U 33, 34-36 (Hist) BA; Syracuse summers 51, 52, 55, 56, 57, 58 MSLS. 6: Fr. 7: Tchr New brunswick schs 29-34, 36-49; Libn St John High Sch, Saint John NC 49-66; Faculty UAlberta Dept Lib Serv summers 67 & 68; Libn Inst of Tech, St John NB 69. 8: Consul CanSchLA: Can Sch Lib Standards, Bk lists for Can schs. 9: CanLA (Exec Offr 59-61), chm YP Sect 60-61; New Brunswick TA. 10: Univ Women's Club; Can Club; Can Col of Tchrs. 13: Yes. 14: Ref, tch lib sci. 15: 85 Duke st, Saint John NB Can.

RIDER, WILLIAM J. JR. b Danbury Conn 21 O 22. 4: Ilona Krenedy. 5: Wharton Sch UPenn 40-43 BS in Econ; Rutgers 59-62 ML. 7: Dairy plant operative Rider Dairy Co, Danbury Conn 43-45, V-pres sales 45-58; Lib asst Bard Col 59-61; Asst to libn Hunter Col 62-64; Asst libn 65-; Asst Prof, Lib Lehman Col (Hunter Col) 66-. 9: ALA; NY Lib Club. 10: The Canby Singers. 14: Ref. 15: 263 West End ave, New York NY 10023.

RIDGE, ALAN DUDLEY. b Eng 2 O 26. 4: I Geraldine Ames. 5: U Col (London) 44-47 (Hist) BA (Hons); Sch of Archives Admin JLondon) 47-48 Diploma in Archives Admin. 6: Fr, Dutch. 7: Asst archivist London Co Coun, London 48-58; Head of records & registry serv Nat Coal Bd, Yorkshire Coalfield 58-62; U Archivist MCGill U 62-68; Prov Archivistof lta 68-. 8: Chm Pub Docs Com, Govt of Alta; Mem Publns Com Boreal Inst, Alt Crci (pstm of coun); SNE Se5 9: Soc of Archivists, Gt Brit (past reg chm & mem of Coun); SAA; Can Hist A"SSN (chm Archives Sect). 10: Lib bd, Roxboro Que Hist Assn of Montreal; Federation des Societes Dhistoire du Quebec. 13: Yes. 14: Train archivists, admin. 15: Provincial Museum & Archives of Alta, 12845 102 ave, Edmonton Alta Can.

RIDGE, DAVY-JO (STRIBLING). b Westminster SC 16 Ja32. 5: Queens Col (NC) 50-54 (Eng) AB: Emory 54-55 (LS) M Ln. 6: Ger, Fr. 7: Instr in catlg UGa 55-56; Head ref dept DeKalb Co Lib System, Decatur Ga 56-64; Asst ref libn USCar 65, Chief ref libn 65-. 9: ALA; SCLA. 10: Nat Auubon Soc; Carolina Bird Club; Columbia Bird Club; Amer Mus of Natural Hist; So Caroliniana Soc. 12: Comp ""Catalogue of the Treasure Room: McKissick Memorial Library,U iversity of South Carolina (65). 13: Yes. 14: Ref, rare bks, admin. 15: Ref Dept McKissick Mem Lib Univ of SC, Columbia SC 29208.

RIDGEWAY, EDITH M(ARY). b Whiting Kan 12 O 04. 5: Col of Emporia 27 (Eng) AB; Kan State Tchrs Col (Emporia)27-28 (LS); UIll summers 37-40 BS in LS; Kan State U (Manhattan) 56 (Educ) MS. 7: Libn Wyandotte High Sch, Kan City (Kan) Jr Col, Kan City 28-37; Head Libn Wyandotte High Sch, Kan City Kan 37-43; Kan State U Lib (Manhattan); Asst docum ents, circ, ref depts 43-58, Head ref dept 58-65, Educ libn 65-. 9: ALA; KanLA. 10: Delta Kappa Gamma. 14: Ref, tchr educ, sch libs. 15: 1110 Pomeroy, Manhattan Kan 66502.

RIDGWAY, HELEN A(DAMS). b Providence 16 Mr 06. 5: Pembroke 23-27 (Lit) AB; UIll 27-28 BS in LS; Columbia 29-34 MLS. 6: Fr, Ger, Lat. 7: Stud asst Pembroke Col 23-2j; Stud asst UIll 2728; Queens Borough Pub Lib, Jamaica NY: Jr asst 28-30, br ref libn 30-31, act supt m7 supt br ref-interloan dept 31-44; Lib supv ext div NY State Dept of Educ, Albany NY 44-47; Pub lib spec ALA; Chicago 47-51; Chief bur of lib serv Conn State Dept of Educ, Hartford Conn 51-64; Admin asst City Libns off San Francisco Pub Lib 65-67; lecturer U San Francisco 66-. 8: Inst, summer lib sci courses, Columbia & UIll, 39, 50; Survey, Sausalito PuxLib (Cal)summer 65. 9: ALA (Coun 54-59, 2nd v-pres 58-59, mem Sate Legis Com 54-57, Steer om on Implem of Mgt Survey 54-56); CanLA; NYLA (Coun; chm Liyb Survey Com 46); NELA (Exec Bd 52-56, pres 54-56): Conn SchLA; ConnLA (Exec Bd 51-64); Cal LA; Amer Assn Adult Educ; Conn Adult Educ Assn; LPRC; Amer Assn State Libs (v-pres 61-62, pres 62-63). 10: AAUW: LWV: UN Assn; Amer Friends Serv Com. 12: "Library Legislation and Planning in "Boof the States (49-50); "Public Libraries in "Municipal Year Book, 1948-1949. 13: Yes. 14: Pub libs, lib ext & planning, tchg & libn educ, ref, lib urveys, lib research. 15: 833 Jones st apt 15, San Francisco Ca 94109.

RIDINGS, LUCILE (DANIEL). b Waynesboo Miss 28 N 08. 5: Whitworth Col 26-28 (Art, Eng); Miss So 35, 41 (Educ, S); Sprng Hill Col 53-55 (Soc Sci); UAla (Mobile) 48 (Math, Pol Sci); Florence State 57-58 (LS); Certif in Aircraft Mechanics. 7: Tchr Adult Educ Proj, Waye Co Miss 35; Head lib asst Lib Proj, Wayne Co Miss 35-36; Lib foreman Lib Proj, Wayne Co Miss 36-41; Elem tchr pub sch, Richton Miss 41-42; Tchr, aircraft mech MOAMA, Brooklyn AFB 42-43; Supv libn Tech Lib, Brooklyn AFB 43-57;Tchr of typing Ind Educ, Mobile Ala 47-53; Supv libn ref, phys sci & Eng Tech Lib ABMA Redstone Arsenal 57-62; Libn phys sci & ed RSIC, Redstone Arsenal Ala 62-. 9: ALA (Wilson Award Jury 63-64); SLA (ALA Chap; sec-treas 58-59, Pub rel chm 63-66, pres-elect 69-70); ASIS; SELA; AlaLA (Pub rel chm 63-66). 10: AAAS; Toastmitress Club. 11: Sustained Superior Performance Award, Brookley AFB, 57. 12: Ed ""The Alabama Librarian(60-63). 13: Yes. 14: Admin. 15: 405 Randolph ave SE, Huntsville Al 35801.

RIDLEY, CHRISTY. b Murfreesboro Tenn 13 F 27. 4: Jeanne Clare. 5: Vanderbilt 44-45, 47-49 (Eng) BA; Columbia 50-51 (Law), 67-68 MLS; Vanderbilt Law Sch 57-59 LLB. 7: Pfc USA, US & Japan 45-46; Attorney-at-law, Nashville 60-62; Procedures analyst Tenn Highway Dept, Nashville 63; Claims settlement agt Penn Dept Pub Welfare, Pittsburgh 65-67; Docs libn Biddle Law Lib UPenn 68-. 9: ALA; AALL; Spec Libs Coun of Phila & Vicinity. 10: Amer Bar Assn. 14: Ref, catlg. 5 15: 250 Locust st apt 7B, Phila Pa 19106.

RIECHEL, ROSEMARIE. b Germany 29 N 37. 5: Hunter Col 55-59 (Ger) BA; Tchrs Col Columbia 61-62; Columbia 63-65 MS. 6: Ger. 7: Gen asst Columbia U libs 60-65; Libn Queens Borough Pub Lib lang & lit div 66-67; Queens Borough Pub info pub catlg div: Sr libn 67-68, Asst hd supv lib 68-. 9: ALA; NY Lib Club. 10: Queens Hist Soc. 14: Ref. 15: 151-31 25 ave, Whitestone NY 11357.

RIECHMANN, DONALD A(UGUST). b Centralia Ill 12 D 19. 4: Ruth Elizabeth Koenig. 5: Elmhrst Col 38-42 (Soc Studies) AB; Chicago 46-47 BLS. 7: US Army Signal Intelligence T/5, European Theatre 42-46; Admin asst to exec sec ALA, Chicago 47-48; Exec asst to dir Enoch Pratt Free Lib, Baltimore 48-50, Sr ref asst ref dept 50-51; Head Libn Pub Lib, Haleton Penn 51-53, Dept Head Mercantile Lib Br Free Lib, Phila 53-64, Coordinator dist lib serv 64-66; Dir Albuquerque (NM) Pub Lib 66-. 8: Part-time instr Drexel Inst Lib Sch, 60-. 66; Mem NM Lib Devel Coun 68-. 9: ALA-RSD (off & mem var cons); SA; Middle Atlantic Rg Conf (Planning Com & Exhib Chm 58, 63); PennLA (pres 59-60); NMLA. 10: . 12: Ed MdLA ""Between Librarians (49-51); Ed PennLA ""Bulletin 52-57). 13: Yes. 14: Ref, ext, admin. 15: Albuquerque Pub Lib, 423 Central ave NE, Albuquerque NM 87101.

RIEGEL, CATHERINE T(HIRZA). b Independence Kan 30 Ap 11. 5: NY State Col for Tchrs 28-32 (Lat) AB, 36 BS in LS; UVt 40; SUNY(Albany) 52 (Eng) MA. 7: Asst libn Albany Pub Lib, Albany NY 32-33; Eng tchr Roessleville Sch, Albany NY 33-34, Eng tchr-libn 34-48; High sch libn Colonie Central High Sch, Albany NY 48-54; Dir of Lib Serv Colonie Central Schs, Albany NY 54-. 8: Bibliog consul, NY State Euc Dep, several summers. 9: NEA; NYLA (com chm); NY State Tchrs Assn (DEL TO House of Del).10: Deta Kappa Gamma; Adirondack Mountain Club. 13: Yes. 14: Sch lib wk. 15: 45 Arcadia ct, Albany NY 12205.

RIEKHOF, JUNE. b Higginsville Mo 14 Ag 45. 5: Central Mo State Col 63-66 (Eng) BA; UDenver 67-68 Libnship MA. 6: Fr. 7: Ref libn Munic Lib Coop, St Louis 68-. 9: ALA (JMRT); MoLA. 14: Ref. 15: 8969 S Swan cir, Brentwood Mo 63144.

RIESTER, KATHRYN (MORRIS). b Savannah Ga 7 N 45. 4: Robert A Riester II. 5: Transylvania Col 63-67 (Rel) AB; UKy 67-69 MSLS. 6: Ger. 7: Lib asst Transylvania Col 65-67; Libn Spec Educ Instr Materials Ctr UKy 68-. 9: ALA; KyLA. 14: Tech serv. 15: 631 S Limestone, Lexington Ky 40508.

RIFE, C(HARLES) DAVID. b Bellaire Ohio 25 O 22. 4: Julia Wendt. 5: Mt Union Col 40-42, 46-48 (Eng) BA; West Res 48 MS in LS. 6: Fr. 7: Circ & ref libn Kenyon Col 49; Catlgr Union Carbide Nuclear Co, Oak Ridge Tenn 50-56; Documentalist Curtiss-Wright Corp, Quehanna Penn 56-58; Sci info coord Lockheed-Ga Co, Marietta Ga 58-. 8: Sec/Bibliogr for cobb Co (Ga) Educ Study Commsn 65-67; Tchr in Abstracting Atlanta U Sch Lib Sci 66; Chm Nat Security Indus Assn Project LEX 66. 9: SLA (So Atlantic Chap: Elect Chm, sci-Tech Div 63, Memb Chm 65-66, pres 67-68). 10: Choral Guild of Atlanta, Lockheed-Georgia Mgt Club. 13: Yes. 14: Ref, admin, music. 15: 548 Hurt rd, Smyrna Ga 30080.

RIFFEY, MADELINE SANDER. b Indiaapolis 29 Ag 13. 4: Warren S Riffey. 5: Butler U 31-33, 34 (Journalism); UIowa 43-44 (ournalism) AB; UIll 50 (LS) MS. 6: Fr. 7: Lib asst Indanapolis Pub Lib 44-49; Admin asst UIll Grad Lib Sch 50-51; Ref libn UIll Undergrad Lib 51-53; UMiami (Fla): Asst ref libn ref dept 53-54, Asst circ libn circ dept 54-62, Head Undergrad Lib 62-. 9: FlaLA; SELA. 10: Beta Phi Mu; Theta Sigma Phi; AAUP. 12: Ed "Florida Libraries (60-61). 13: Yes. 14: Pub serv, bk sel, readers adv serv, ref. 15: 5226 SW 90th ct, Miami Fla 33165.

RIFT, CLARA ANN (KUHLMAN). b Columbia Mo 15 N 24. 4: Leopold R Rift. 5: Vanderbilt 41-45 (Sociol) BA; Peabody Col 45-46 (LS) MA; UIll 51-55 (LS) MS. 7: Ref libn UTex (Austin) 46-47, Bus & Soc Sci libn 47-51; Acquis bibliogr UIll (Urbana) 51-53, Ser catlgr 53-55; Acquis bibliogr SoIllU 64-65; Acquis bibliogr Bowling Green StateU 65-67, Ref libn 67-69, Popular culture catlgr 69-. 10: Beta Phi Mu. 13: Yes. 14: Bibliog (acquis), ref, catlg. 15: 939 Carol rd, Bowling Green Oh 43402.

RIFT, LEOPOLD R. b Vinna 4 Je 17. 4: Clara Ann Kuhlman. 5: Colo StateCol 42-43; UDenver 50-51 (Latin Amer Area) BA, 51-52 (LS) MA. 6: Ger, Fr, Sp. 7: (Cpl) Tr, Interpreter US Army 43-46; Tech data Tr Wright Patterson AFB, Dayton 46-49; Asst manager Immigrant Hostels Australian Govt, Melbourne 49-50; Sci catlgr State Col of Wash 52-54; Ser catlgr UIll(Urbana) 54-55; Ser catlgr UMo 55-58; Chief ser dept So Ill U 58-65; Systs & Procedures libn Bowling Green (Ohio) State U 65-68, Asst dir for tech serv 68-. 9: ALA-LAD (CIRC Controls Com); MoLA; Mo Group of Catlgr & Clsfrs (chm 57-8). 10: Beta Phi Mu; YMCA. 12: ""A Library Plan for Jefferson Co, Colo (53). 13: Yes. 14: Systems & automation, catlg, ser. 15: 939 Carol rd, Bowling Green Ohio 43402.

RIGEL, SISTER TERESA. b Waterville Kan 5 My 23. 5: Marymount Col 49-50 (Nursing ed) BSNE; Catholic U 51-53 (Nursing) MSN; Rosary Col 59-60 MALS. 7: Asst libn & asst prof Marymount Col 60-68; High sch libn Red Cloud Indian Schs, Pine Ridge S Dak 68-. 8: Mem Com on Cath Suppl to "High School Catalog". 9: ALA; CathLA. 14: Acquis, ref, child lit. 15: Holy Rosary Indian Mission, Pine Ridge SD 57770.

RIGGENBACH, BETTY ANN. b Ravenna Ohio. 5: Kent State U 62-65 MLS; Elem Educ BS in Ed. 7: Tchr Cuyahoga Falls Schs, CUYAHOGA Falls Schs, Cuyahoga Falls Ohio; Tchr Ravenna Pub Schs, Ravenna Ohio; Libn Akron Pub Lib, Akron Ohio 65-. 9: Akron LA; OhioLA. 10: Kappa Delta Pi; Young Libns Assn. 14: Ref, catlg. 15: 445 Lincoln ave, Ravenna Oh 44266.

RIGGS, A FAYE (ANDREWS). b McKinney Tex 9 F 04. 4: John Forest Riggs. 5: N Tex State U 21-22, 26-27 (Eng) AB; Ft Hays State Col summers 52, 53; Kan State Tchrs Col summers 59-62 (LS) MS. 7: Tchr pub sch, McKinney Tex 23-26; Tchr Holcomb Cons Sch, Holcomb Kan 45-47; Tchr-libn Lakin Schs, Lakin Kan 47-58; Tchr-libn Holcomb Cons Sch, Holcomb Kan 58-65, Libn 65-. 8: Del to Kan Governors Conf, 56; N Central Assn & Kan State Dept of Pub Instr Evaluation teams Leati High Sch 68, Kinsley 69; Title II Adv Com for Kan Cons at Wkshop Media Processing 67. 9: NEA (Clr Tchrs del to 1953 Nat Conv); ALA (Memb Com, Kan, mem Nat Lib Week Com, Kan); KanLA (Bd 58); Kan State Tchrs Assn (del State Assembly 62-63); KanASchL (dist dir 54-55, treas 56, pres 58-59). 10: AAUW; Delta Kappa Gamma; Bd dirs, Finney Co Mental Health Assn; Friends of Lib. 11: Gov Safety Award 56; Kan U Tchrs Award 62. 13: Yes. 14: Sch lib serv, bk reviewing, bk exhib. 15: 1106 Pershing ave, Garden City Ks 67846.

RIGGS, DEAN EDWARD. b Hutchinson Kan 13 D 36. 5: Dodge City Col 55-57 AA; Kan State Tchrs Col (Emporia) 57-59 (Soc Sci) BS in Educ, 59-63 (Lib Educ) MS. 7: Elevator operator First Nat Bank, Dodge City Kan 55-57; Stud asst Pub Lib, Dodge City Kan 55-57; High sch libn Norton Commun High Sch libn Norton Commun High Sch, Norton Kan 59-60; High sch libn Seaman undl High Sch, Topeka Kan 60-62; Lib sst White Lib Kan State Tchrs Col (Emporia) 57-59, 62-63; sch libn US Overseas Dependents Sch System, Tripoli Libya 6365; High sch libn US Overseas Dependents Sch Syste, Wiesbaden Germany 65-68; Acquis libn UMo (Kansas City) 68-. 9: ALA; NEA (pres Col Lib Sect); KanLA; Overseas Educ Assn; Kan State TA; KanASchL (chm Legis Com); European Sch LA (treas). 10: PTA; Overseas Fed of Tchrs. 14: Col & univ acquis, ser. 15: 4724 Belleview apt 1, Kansas City Mo 64112.

RIGGS, DONALD E. b Middlebourne W Va 11 My 42. 4: Jane Vasbinder. 5: Glenville State col 60-64 (Biol sci) BA; WVaU 64-66 (Educ admin) MA; 67 Prof admin certif; UPittsburgh 67-68 (Lib admin) MLS. 6: Fr. 7: Plant pest controller US Dept of Agric, W Va Md Penn 64; Hd libn & sci tchr Warwood High Sch, WVa 64-65; Hd libn & sci tchr Wheeling High Sch, WVa 65-67; Asst prof & sci libn Cal State Col (Penn) 68-. 8: Consul Instr Materials Ctrs, Ohio Co Schs 66-67. 9: ALA; NEA; WVaLA; Tri-StateACRL. 10: AAUP; Phi Delta Kappa; Beta Phi Mu; Chi Beta Phi. 11: Outstanding Young Educator 66; Ohio Co Schs. 13: Yes. 14: Ref, admin, acquis. 15: 56 Cheryl lane, Pittsburgh Pa 15236.

RIGGS, VIRGINIA MAYFIELD. b Tchula Miss 2 F 19. 4: Marvin A Riggs. 5: a Intermont Col 36-38 AA; Millsaps Col 38-40 (Eng)BA; UDenver summers 50-53 (LS) MA. 7: Eng tchr Utica High Sch, Utica Miss 40-42; Eng tchr Sunflower Jr Col 46-48, Libn 48-54; Libn Central High Sch, Jackso Mis 54-56; Asst libn Hinds Jr Col 56-60, Libn 60-. 8: Visiting com of So Assn of Cols & Schs, 63. 9: ALA; MissLA; MissEA. 10: Delta Kappa Gamma. 15: Hinds Jr Col, aymond Miss 39154.

RIGGS, WILLIAM R. b Nampa Ida 5 Ag 42. 5: Concordia Tchrs Col 60-64 (Hist) BSed; UNeb 64 (Hist); UTex 66 & 67 (LS). 6: Ger. 7: Instr & libn St Paul's Col & High Sch, concordia Mo 64-67; Libn & media supv Concordia High Sch, Seward Neb 67-. 8: Chm Lib-Media Com Educl Serv Unit #6 68, 69. 9: ALA; -AASchL; Organ Amer Histns; NEA (Pres Lib Sect Dist #1 69); NebEA; NebLA; Neb Educl Media Assn. 10: Nat Committeeman neb Young Democrats 68-69; Alternate Democ Nat Conv 68. 13: Yes. 14: Adolesence lit, media ctrs, computer sci & libs. 15: Becker Hall Lib Concordia High School BOON, Colunbia ave, Seward Nb 68434.

RIGNEY, JANET MARY. b Yonkers NY. 5: St Johns U 40-41; Hunter Col 53-57 (Hist) BA; Colmbia 57-60 MLS. 6: Fr. 7: Coun on Foreign Rel, NY: Lib clerk 41-46, Ref asst 46-60, Ast libn 60-. 8: Bibliog on Atlantic Commun for For Policy Assn, 65; Consul UToronto Lib 69. 9: SLA (chm Soc Sci Div 62-63; NY Ch: chm Hospitality Com 0-61, chm Memb Com 65-66; chm Soc Sci Group 61-62). 14: Catlg, ref. 15: 58 E 68th st, NYC 10021.

RIGO, TIBOR. b Nagykata Hungary 15 Ja 13. 4: Martha Fraknoy. 5: Royal U (Budapest) 31-35 (Law, Pol Sci) Dr of Law 41 Bar Exam; Rutgers 61-63 MLS. 6: Hungarian, Ger. 7:

Dist Judge, Nagykata Hungary 42-45; Lawyer, com corres, legal adv, Hungary 45-56; Lib asst McGill U Law Lib 59-61; Libn Free Pub Lib, Elizabeth NJ 62-65; Libn Seton Hall U Lib 65-; Hd catlgr Southampton Col LIU 67-. 10: AAUP. 14: Catlg. 15: 85 Middle Pond rd, Southampton NY 11968.

RIGSBY, MARGUERITE LORENE (SPIEGLE). b Ensley Ala 25 Ap 09. 4: Gilbert Lynn Rigsby. 5: Birmingham So Col 27-28; Howard Col 29; Auburn 51 (Eng, Educ) BS; George Peabody Col 65 (LS). 6: Sp. 7: Cullman Co: Tchr 31-44, Prin 46-49, Lib admin 62-; Tchr cullman City 51-62. 8: Delta Kappa Gamma. 9: ALA; NEA; ClsTA; AlaEA; Ala;A (Chm Memb standards Com, sec Pub Lib Div); SELA. 10: PTA; Delta Kappa Gamma; Alpha Beta Alpha; Garden Club; Cullman Hist Soc; Ala Hist Soc; Stewardess of Church. 13: Yes. 14: Hist materials, rare bks. 15: 314 4th ave E HSA, Cullman Al 35055.

RIKE, GALEN EDWIN. b Wooster Ohio 12 O 42. 5: Ashland 60-63 (Hist, Eng) BA; UIll at Urbana 64-66 (LS) MS. 6: Sp, Fr, Ger. 7: Grad asst circ dept UIll Lib (Urbana) 64-66, bibliogr acquis dept 66-67; Research assoc Lib Research Ctr, Urbana Ill 67-. 9: ALA. 10: Beta Phi Mu; AAUP. 12: Comp "Statewide Library Surveys and Development Plans: an annotated Bibliography, 1956-1967" (68). 13: Yes. 14: Statewide lib planning & devel, interlib coop. 15: 614 W Washington, Urbana Il 61801.

RILEY, EILEEN V(ERONICA). b Hartford Conn 24 N 31. 5: Boston U 50-54 (Econ) AB; Columbia 58-59 MSLS. 6: Sp, Ital, Fr, Rumanian, Portu. 7: Clerk, trainee renewal underwriter Conn Gen Life Insurance Co, Hartford Conn 54-56; Engnr aide Canel Div Pratt & Whitney Aircraft, Maromas Conn 56-57; Engnr aide Kaman Aircraft Co, Bloomfield Conn 57-58; Lib intern NLM, Wash DC 59-60, Libn catlgr 60-61; Libn acquis NLM, Bethesda Md 61. 8: NLM Rep to Seminars on Acquis of Latin-Amer Lib Materials Salam 64, 65. 9: MedLA. 14: Bibliog, data proc, docs, sers. 15: 6304 Haviland dr, Bethesda Md 20034.

RILEY, MRS JEAN HIKLE. b LaCenter Ky 21 Mr 26. 4: Augustus Baxter Riley. 5: UKy 44-6 (LS); Murray State Col 47-49 (LS) BS; Peabody 55-57 (LS) A. 7: Tchr Gideon P ub Schs, Gideon Mo 47-49; Libn Newbern City Schs, Newbern Tenn 49-55; Libn Grand Canyon Col 55-61; Head libn Caelback High Sch, Phoenix 61-67; Elem Lib coord Ballard Co Schs, Wickliffe Ky 67-. 9: NEA; ArizLA (Exec sec 61-62); KyEA; FDLA. 10: Alpha Beta Alpha; Beta Phi M; Delta Kappa Gamma; Ariz Hist Commsn; LaCenter Womans Club. 14: Catlg, admi. 15: 2061W Ootillo rd, Phoenix 85015.

RILEY, MARY E (GRUBER). b Danville Penn 16 Jl 30. 4: James W Riley. 5: Penn State 48-52 (Eng Lit) BA; Drexel 52-53 MLS. 6: Fr. 7: Catlgr Lehigh 53-57, Ser libn 57-65, Asst ref libn 65-68, Hd ref libn 68-. 8: Adv wk & catlg Wesley Methodist Ch Lib 67-68. 10: Penn State Alum Assn. 14: Ref, ser. 15: 1533 Greenview dr, Bethlehem Pa 18018.

RILEY, MARY F (KIERNAN). b NYC 3 O 25. 5: Col of New Rochelle 45-47 (Eng Lt); Fordham U 47-49 (Eng Lit) BS in Eng; Clumbia 60-63 MLS. 7: Prof intern Columbia U Grad Sch of Bus Lib 63-64; Ref asst Scarsdale Pub Lib, Scarsdale NY 64-65; Ref asst Fordham U 65-67; Chief ref libn 67-. 9: ALA; WestchesterLA. 14: Ref. 15: 64 Sagamore rd, Bronxville NY 10708.

RILEY, PAUL WARD. b Worcester Mass 29 Je 12. 4: Marie Dickson. 5: Clark U 38 (Hist) BA; Syracuse 41 BSLS. 7: Worcester Pub Lib, Worcester Mass: Lib asst 38-40, Co-chm soc sci dept 41-42; M/Sgt spec serv USA 42-46; Libn Boston Col Bus Sch 46-64; Boston Col: Lecturer in bus research 59-63, Assoc dir libs 64-. 8: Adv Com Cary Mem Lib, Lexington Mass 56-60. 9: ALA; SLA (chm Bus Div, ed Bus Bulletin, Conv Chm 57, Fin Com, Nomin Com, Bd Dirs; pres Boston Chap). 10: AAUP. 13: Yes. 14: Library planning, spec collections. 15: 90 Concord ave, Lexington Ma 02173.

RILEY, RALPH D. B Sanford NY 30 Ap 20. 4: Elsie Ruland. 5: Pine Hill rd, Littleton NH 03561. 6: Sp. 7:Machine operator Scitilla Magneto Div Bendix Corp, Sidney NY 40-42; Machinists mate USNR 2/c 42-45; Catlgr NY State Col for Tchrs (Brockport) 49; Ref libn Lycoming Col 49-52; Ext libn NH State Li, Littleton NH 52-64; Dist consul NH State LibLittleton Dist Off 64-. 9: ALA; NELA; NHLA (treas 60-63, Memb chm 67-). 10: PTA; NH League of Craftsmen. 14: Consul wk, pub libs. 15: Pine Hill rd, Littleton NH 03561.

RILEY, SARA RUTH. b Hattiesburg Miss. 5: Miss Woman's Col 29 (Fr, Eng) BA; Peabody 48 BS in LS, 59 (LS) MA. 6: Fr. 7: Tchr pub schs, Hattiesburg Miss 27-44; Reservation clerk So RR, Hattiesburg Miss 44-46; Tchr pub schs, Hattiesburg Miss 46-48, Libn 48-51; Libn So Baptist Theol Sem Louisville Ky 51-57, Perkins Sch of Theol So Methodist U 57-59, pub schs, Hattiesburg Miss 59-. 9: NEA; ATheolLA (past mem var coms); MissEA; MissLA (Scholarship Com); Miss Clr Tchrs Assn (treas 63-65, Memb Chm 65). 10: Kappa Delta Pi; Phi Gamma Mu; Alpha Delta Kappa; Worthwhile Club; Red Cross Volunteer. 13: Yes. 14: Ref, acquis, readers adv serv, materials in spec educ & av. 15: 100 Dearborn st, Hattiesburg Ms 39401.

RILEY, STEPHEN T. b Worcester Mass 28 D 08.04 Alice Riehle. 5: Clark U 27-31 (Hist) AB magna cum laude), 31-32 (Hist) AM, 53 (Hist) PhD. UPenn 43-44 (Arabic). 6: Fr. 7: US Army, US Air Force (Sgt) 42-45; Mass Hist Soc: asst 34-47, Libn 47-63, Dir 57-. 8: Bd Trustees, Clark U 63-; Adv Com to Publ Com Winterthur Mus. 9: AHA; BSA; Soc Amer Archivists (Fellow); Amer Antige Soc;amer Acad of Arts & Scis; Inst of Early Amer Hist; Mass Hist Coc; Soc Soc; Colonia Colonial of Mass; Bay State Hist League (dir). 10: Club of Odd Volumes (Boston); Grolier Club (NY); St Botolph Club (Boston); Phi Beta Kappa; Harvard Travelers Club, Boston. 12: "The Massachusetts Historical Society, 1791-1959". 13: Yes. 14: Hist mss & rare bks. 15: 1154 Boylston st, Boston Ma 02116.

RIMSON, GOLDIE (WACHS). b Cleveland Ohio 25 Ag 04. 5: Mather Col West Res 27 (Chem) AB, 58-59 (Info sci); Columbia 30-31 (Biochem). 6: Fr, Ger, Hebrew, Sp. 7: Chem Shell Petroleum Corp, Wood River Ill 27-29; Chem NY State Psychiatric Inst, NYC 29-32; Tchr Religious schs, Cleveland Ohio 40-55; Chem clinical & pub health labs, Akron Ohio 55-56; Asst libn B F Goodrich Research Ctr, Brecksville Ohio 56-. 9: ACS (Chem Lit Div); SLA (pres Cleveland Chap). 10: Iota Sigma Pi; Mather Col Alum; Harvard Col Parents Assn; Hadassah. 14: Info proc & ret. 15: 3731 Warrensville Ctr rd, Cleveland Oh 44122.

RINALDI, ELIZABETH M. b Paterson NJ 10 Ap 16. 5: Paterson State Col 33-37 (Elem Educ) BS; Trenton State Col summers 42, 43, 47, 50 BLS; Trenton State Col summers 53-55, 57, 57 (Elem Educ) MS; Rutgers U ext 59; Seton Hall U 55, 56. 6: Fr, Ital. 7: Americaniz tchr Adult Educ Program, Paterson NJ 37-39; Asst occupat therapist Marlboro State Hosp, Marlboro NJ 3940; Asst libn Eastside High Sch, Paterson NJ 45-46; Elem sub tchr, Paterson NJ 40-41; Lib asst Pub Lib, Paterson NJ summer 46; Paterson State Col: Circl libn 46-, Educ materials libn & Asst Prof of child lit 53-, Educ materials libn & lib sci coordinator 63-, Asst Prof of Lib Sci 63-. 8: Visiting Prof, lib sci: Newark State Col, summers 57, 59 60 & UVt summer 63; Adv Com nj0 elem & Secon Educ Act; Adv Com ESEA Paterson Diocese; Lib Consul Wyckoff Pub Lib. 9: ALA; NJEA; NJLA (Charter Mem (Col & Univ Sect: sectreas 60-61; Com for Nat Lib Weec); NJSchLA; var positions Paterson State College Faculty Assn (present corrs sect). 10: AAW; Nat Womens Bk Assn; Paterson State Col Faculty ASSN; Assn of NJ State Col Faculties; Delta Kappa Gamma; Altrusa Internat; Bergen-Passaic Lib Club. 12: Ed "New Jersey School Librarian (winter 51). 14: Tchng lib sci, sch lib serv, child bks & educ materials. 15: 13 Albion ave, Paterson NJ 07502.

RINE, JOSEPH LEON. b S Bend Ind 10 F 44. 5: Hebrew Theol Col 61; Jewish U of America 61-63 AA; Nat Col of Educ 63-65 (Educ, Eng, Speech, Humanities) B Educ; Rosary Col 67-69 MALS. 6: Hebrew, Yiddish, Fr. 7: Tchr Hebry Sch Chicago Bd of Educ 66; Tchr Sanganash Sch 66-67; Guidance counselor Wicker Park Sch 67, Sub tchr 67-68, Sch libn Bridge Sch 68-. 9: NEA. 10: United Jewish Appeal; Chicago Tchrs Union. 11: Yavneh (Jewish Agency for Study in Israel) Fellowship 65-66. 14: Acquis & ref (ya materials). 15: 3727 W Leland ave, Chicago Il 60625.

RINE, PATRICIA (ANN) TAPLICK. b Madison Wis 29 My 38. 4: Peter R Rine. 5: Carleton Col 56-60 (Eng) AB; UWis summer 59, 64-66 (Ger), 66-67 (LS) MA; Mankato State Col summer 64. 6: Ger. 7: Lib asst Lib Sch Lib UWis(Madison) 66-67; Catlgr Harvard Law Sch Lib 67-. 9: Law Libns of NE. 14: Catlg (ser, govt publ, mss materials). 15: 15 Everett st apt 45, Cambridge Ma 02138.

RINEER, A HUNTER JR. b Rohrerstown Penn 24 Je 31. 5: Franklin & Marshall Col 48-52 (Hist) AB; Columbia 52-54 (LS) MS. 7: Fellow City Col (NY) 52-54; Sgt US Army 54-56; Ref libn Free Lib of Phila 56-61; Dir Lower Merion Lib Assn, Ardmore Penn 61-67; Dir gen lib bur Penn State Lib, Harrisburg 68-. 9: ALA-ACRL (SE Penn Chap); PennLA (Exec Bd; chm Col & Ref Sect; chm Explor Com on Penn Docs). 10: Hist Soc of Penn; Philobiblon of Phila; Phi Gamma Mu. 14: Ref, acquis, admin. 15: 4100 Beechwood lane, Harrisburg Pa 17112.

RINEHART, CONSTANCE OPAL. b Hutington WVa 21 J122. 5: Marshall U 39-43 (Psych) AB; UMich 43-44 ABLS, 46-48 AMS. 7: Asst catlgr Goucher Col Lib 44-45; UMich: Research asst Bur of Ind Rel 45-46, Tchg Fellow in Lib Sci 46-48, Sr catlg libn 48-55, Assoc catlg libn 55-57, Catlg libn III 57, Head European Langs unit, subj catlg sect 58-, Hd subj catlg div, 67-69, Asst Prof U Mich Sch Lib Sci,69-. 9: ALA; Mich Reg Group of Catlgrs (sec-treas 49-50). 11: Major Award in Poetry, Avery & Julie Hopwood Contest, 48. 12: "Autographed Copy, Poems (51); Comp "Subject Index to the Reference Collection on Industrial Relations (46). 13: Yes. 14: Subj catlg. 15: Box 1688, Ann Arbor Mi 48106.

RINEHART, JEANNE R. b Kendallville Ind 30 D 21 04: Robert D Rinehart. 4: Robert D Rinehart. 5: Goshen Col 40-44 (Eng) BA; So Conn State Col 60-62 (LS) MS. 7: Libn Elem Lib Dept, Milford Conn 61-63; Head Libn Staples High Sch Lib, Westport Conn 63-67; Hd libn Nepean High Sch Lib 68-. 9: ALA. 10: Ont Secondary Sch Tchrs Fed. 14: Sch lib programs, central lib systems. 15: 35 Pineglen Crescent, Ottawa 12 Ont Can.

RINEHART, MICHAEL. b Miami Fla 27 D 34. 4: Sheila Somers. 5: Harvard (Fine Arts) BA; UFla 57; Courtauld Inst (London) 58-. 6: Ital, Fr. 7: Libn Villa I Tatti (Harvard) Ctr for Ital Renaissance Studies, Florence Italy 62-64; Witt libn Courtauld Inst, London 64-66; Libn Clark Art Inst, Williamstown Mass 66-; Lectr in art Williams Col 67-. 8: Amer correspondent for the "Repertoire d'Art et d'Archeologie," 69-. 9: ALA; SLA. 10: Col Art Assn. 15: Clark Art Inst, Williamstown Ma 01267.

RING EVA L. b Mentor Tenn 4 O 16. 5: David Lipscomb Col 34-36 Diploma; Ga State Col for Women 36-38 (Lat, Eng) BA Peabody summers 41-43 BS in LS. 7: Tchr Concord High Sch, Concord Ga 38-39; Tchr Kite High Sch, Kite Ga 39-41; Libn: Tallulah Falls Sch, Tallulah Falls Ga 41-43, Dobyns Bemett High Sch, Kingsport Tenn 43-45 Fairfield High Sch, Fairfield Ill 45-46, Joliet Twp High Sch & Jr Col. Joliet Ill 46-55, Elmwood Park High Sch, Elmwood Park Ill 55-. 9: ALA-AASchL; NEA; IllLA; IllASchL; IllEA. 15: 2009 N 73rd ave, Elmwood Park Ill 60635.

RINGER, AGNES (CONANT). b Baltimore Md 5 D 14. 5: UPenn 34-38 (Eng) BA; Drexel 61-64 MS in LS. 6: Fr. 7: Sec to exec v-pres Phila Gas Co 39-40; Lib trainee Free Lib of Phila 61-64, Libn I, libn II, Fiction Dept Central Lib 64-66; Hd leisure reading dept NE Reg Lib, Phila 67-. 8: Adjunct instr Drexel Inst, Grad Sch Lib Sci 68-69. 9: ALA; PennLA. 10: Phi Beta Kappa. 13: Yes. 14: Adult serv. 15: Northeast Regional Lib, Cott man ave & Oakland st, Philadelphia Pa 19149.

RINGERING, JOYCE ELNITA. b Great Bend Kan 31 My 32. 5: Sterling Col 5054 (Humanities) BA; N Amer Baptist Sem 5557 (Relig Educ) MRE; UDenver 5758 (Libnship) MA. 7: Elem sch tchr, Ellinwood Kan 5455; Asst libn N Amer Baptist Sem 5860, Libn 60. 9: ATheolLA. 10: Soroptimist Club. 15: 1605 S Euclid ave, Sioux Falls S Dak 57105.

RINGERING, LEONA H. b E Alton Ill. 5: UIll & Chicago. 7: Libn Flagg Twp Lib, Rochelle Ill; Br libn Gary Pub Lib, Gary Ind; Reg libn Ill State Lib; Libn Park Forest Pub Lib, Park Forest Ill. 10: AAUW; Delta Kappa Gamma; Womens Club; LWV. 13: Yes. 14: Admin. 15: 81A Hemlock st, Park Forest Ill 60466.

RINGROSE, ENID MAY. b Ottawa Can.05L McMaster U Ont 36-39, 45 Classics BA UOttawa 47-51 BLS. 5: McMaster U Ont 36-39, 45 Classics BA UOttawa 47-51 BLS. 6: Fr. 7: Clerk Bank of Can Foreign Exch Control Bd Dominion Bur of Statistics, Ottawa 39-40; Clerk Tourist Sect DBS, Ottawa 40-41; Lib asst DBS Lib, Ottawa 48-50, Catlgr 51-53, Asst libn, catlgr & Lecturer U of Ottawa Lib & Lib Sch 53-58; UOttawa Lib Sch: Sec, libn & Lecturer 59-60, Admin asst & Lecturer 61-63, Asst to dir & Asst Prof 63-66, Asst to dir & Assoc Prof 66-. 9: Internat Assn of Documentalists; Association Canadienne des Bibliothecaires de Langue Francaise; CanLA; Lib Assn Ottawa; ALA; 14: Catlg, ref, research. 15: Univ of Ottawa Lib Sch, Ottawa Can.

RINK, BERNARD CARL. b Avon Ohio 22 O 26. 4: Suzane V Peplinski. 5: John Carroll U 44-48 (Eng Lit) AB; West Res 49 MS in LS. 7: Co Libn Sandusky Co Lib, Fremont Ohio49-5; Ref libn UDetroit Lib 52-55; Demonstration libn Mich State Lib 55-57; Chief Libn Northwestern Mich Col 57-. 9: ALA-ACRL (chm A-V Com 65-66; Jr Col Libs Sect: Bibliog Com); MichLA (chm Ref Sect 62-63, chm Conf Com 65, CHM Dist 6 57). 10: St Marys (Lake Leelanau) Lay Adv Sch Bd. 13: Yes. 14: Commun col libs, ref, acad libs. 15: Box 183, Lake LeeLanan Mi 49653.

RINK, EVALD. b Estonia 23 Jl 16. 4: Hildegard Romef. 5: Tartu U (Estonia) 35-41 (Hist) BA, NA; J W Geothe U (FrankfurtMain) 45-46 (Hist): Rutgers 54-56 MLS. 6: Estonian, Ger. 7: Catlgr Longwood Lib, Kennett Square Penn 56-61; Head imprints dept Eleutherian Mills Hist Lib, Greenville, Wilmington Del 61-. 9: ALA; DelLA. 14: Catlg. 15: 1428 Oak Hill dr, Wilmington Del 19805.

RIPS, RAE ELIZABETH. b Omaha 4 Je 14. 5: Chicago 32-36 (Hist) AB, 36-38 (Amer Hist) AB; UIll 39-40 (LS) BSLS. 7: Asst ref & circ dept Joseph Schaffner Lib of Com Northwestern U 40-42; US documents asst ref dept Detroit Pub Lib 42-48, Chief hist & travel dept 48-. 8: Nat Adv Com on Depository Libs to the Pub Printer; Lectr UIll Lib Sch summer 64-. 9: SLA; Geog & Map Div; ALA-RSD; Chm Hist Sect 63-64, Mem Pub Docs Com 48-68. 10: Phi Beta Kappa; Beta Phi Mu. 12: "United States Government Publicatns (rev 3rd ed 50); Ed "Detroit in its World Setting, a 250 Year Chronology, 1701-1951 (53). ; Comp of bibliog "Michigan in Books (56). 13: Yes. 14: US govt docs, ref, maps. 15: Detroit Pub Lib, Detroit Mi 48202.

RISS, JANE E. b Kansas City Mo 22 D 37. 5: MoU 55-60 (Hist, Journalism) AB, 60-61 9hist) MA; UIll 64-65 (LS) MS. 6: Sp, Ital. 7: Lib asst St Louis Pub Lib, Buder Br 62-63, Catlgr 65-66; Tech serv libn Daniel Boone Reg Lib, Columbia Mo 66-68; Curator reg hist div Spencer Research Lib KanU 68-. 9: ALA; SAA; KanLA. 10: Amer Assn for State & Local Hist; AAUP; Douglass Co Hist Soc. 13: Yes. 14: Hist mss, archival collections. 15: 2503 Alabama, Lawrence Ks 66044.

RISTOW, WALTER W. b La Crosse Wis. 4: Helen Doerr. 5: UWis 27-31 (Geog) BA; Oberlin Col 31-33 (Geog) MA; Clark U 33-35, 37 (Geog) PhD. 6: Fr, Ger, Sp. 7: Instr Berea Col summer 35; Instr E Wash Col of Educ 35-37; Head map room & chief map div NY Pub Lib 37-46; Head map sect NY Off Mil Intelligence NYC 42-44; Asst chief & act chief map div LC 46-65, Assoc chief geog & map div 65-, Chief map div 67-. 8: LC rep on US Bd on Geog Names, 47-. 9: Assn of Amer Geogrs (sec 48-50); Nat Coun for Geog Educ; Amer Cong on Surveying & Mapping; SLA. 10: AAAS. 11: SLA Geog & Map Div Honors Award, 63; Amer Congress on Surveyings & Mapping, Award 69. 12: Ed "Survey of the Roads of the US of America, 1789 by Christopher Colles (61); Auth of a number of bibliogs publ by LC. 13: Yes. 14: Geog & maps libs, rare bks, hist of cartography, bibliog. , map lib automation. 15: 1320 Ingleside ave, McLean Va 22101.

RITCHIE, BARBARA (ANN) (VERTREES). b Portland Ore 9 Ja 43. 4: Stephen B Ritchie. 5: UOre 60-64 (Span) BA; UWash 64-65 MLibr. 6: Sp. 7: Libn I Bridgeport Pub Lib, Bridgeport Conn 65-66; Libn Main St Elem Sch, Denville NJ 66-. 9: ALA; NJEA; Morris Co EA; Morris Co SchLA; Denville TA. 10: Phi Beta Kappa; Beta Phi Mu; Sigma Delta Pi. 14: Adult serv, readers guidance, ref, child & elem libs. 15: 35-50 Mt Pleasant Vil, Morris Plains NJ 07950.

RITCHIE, REBECCA SUZANNE. b Hampton Va 22 N 43. 5: Old Dominion 61-62; Christopher Newport Col 62-63; William & Mary 63-65 (Eng) AB; UNC 65-66 (LS) MS. 6: Fr, Ger. 7: Asst libn Christopher Newport Col 66-. 9: ALA; VaLA. 10: Beta Phi Mu. 14: Catlg. 15: 31 Sinclair rd, Hampton Va 23369.

RITTEL, MARY ELLEN (BRENNAN). b Rochester NY 25 Jl 42. 4: George C Rittel. 5: SUNY (Albany) 60-64 (Eng) AB, 65-66 MLS. 6: Fr. 7: Army libn Dept of Defense, Illesheim Germany 66-68; Libn (staff) State Lib of Ohio, Columbus 68-. 9: ALA; OhioLA. 10: AAUW. 14: Admin, lib educ. 15: 582 Chatham rd, Columbus Oh 43214.

RITTER, (RUSSELL) VERNON. b Valparaiso Ind 5 F 10. 4: Ruth Elisabeth Anderson. 5: Wheaton Col (Wheaton Ill) 31-35 (Eng lit) BA; No Baptist Theol Sem 35-39 (New testament) BD, 43-48 (Old Testament) ThD; USoCal 52-55 MS in LS; Brandeis U summer 58. 7: Tchg fellow No Baptist Theol Sem 43-46; Prof of Old Testament & libn Cal Baptist Theol Sem 46-54; Libn & Prof of Biblical studies Westmont Col 54-57; Libn Central Baptist Theol Sem 57-61; Tech serv libn UNM 61-62; Libn Grand Canyon Col 62-64; Libn & Prof of Biblical studies Westmonth Col 64-. 9: Amer Schs of Oriental Research; Soc of Bibl Lit; Amer Acad Relig; Evangel Theol Soc; CalLA. 10: Beta Phi Mu. 13: Yes. 14: Admin, tech proc. 15: 705 Mercer ave, Ojai Ca 93023.

RITZMAN, MARY LOUISE (CUNNINGHAM). 5: Carnegie Mellon 29-33 (Gen Studies) BS; Carnegie Lib Sch 34 BS in LS. 7: Libn Oil City High Sch, Oil City Penn 34-35; Libn Wilkinsburg High Schs, Wilkinsburg Penn 35-37; Libn Pittsburgh High Schs, Pittsburgh penn 37-44; Libn Sci & Tech Dept Carnegie Lib of Pittsburgh 67-. 9: SLA; PennLA. 15: Carnegie Lib, Pittsburgh Pa 15213.

RIVERO, A(RLINE) PUALANI. b Honolulu 17 Ag 38. 5: UHawaii 56-58 (Nursing); Ore State Col 58-60 (Biol Sci) BS; USoCal 60-61 MS in LS. 6: Fr. 7: Libn I ext div Lib of Hawaii 61-63; Libn admin Spec Serv Lib TSAC USForces Korea 63; Libn admin Spec Serv Lib 1st Cavalry Div USForces Korea 63-64; Asst libn Port Lib RUSAH Ft Brooke PR 64-65; Asst to ref supv Fairfax Pub Lib, Asst hq libn 67-. 9: ALA; VaLA. 10: Bishop Museum Assn. 14: Med lib wk, ref, pub. 15: 5000 Doyle lane, Centreville Va 22020.

RIVOIR, SARAH E (STINER). b Harrisburg Penn 18 N 18. 4: William H Rivoir jr. 5: Temple 36-40 (Hist) BS in Ed; Drexel 63 MS in LS. 7: Hd ref dept West Chester State Col 64-. 9: PennLA; Penn State EA; ALA. 10: AAUW. 14: Ref. 15: West Chester State Col, West Chester Penn 19380.

RIVOIRE, HELENA (GANNON). b Everett Wash 22 Mr 17. 5: Reed Col 33-35; UCal Berkeley 35-37 (Fr) MA, 38-39 Certif of libnship UParis 47-48; Cours de Civilisation. 6: Fr, Sp, Ital, Ger, Russian. 7: Libn Jr Grade UCal Lib (Berkeley) 39-44, Libn Sr Grade 44-45; Clerk-typist CAF-3 Naval Supply DEPOT, Balboa CZ 46-47; Asst order libn Bucknell U Lib 57-59, Catlgr 60-69, Chief tech serv 69-. 9: PennLA (sec-treas Susquehanna Valley Chap 67-); ALA. 10: PTA; Phi Beta Kappa; Pi Delta Phi; Susquehanna Valley Assn of the Arts. 14: Catlg, tech serv. 15: College Park, Lewisburg Penn 17837.

RIZZETTA, CAROLYN T PETER. b Chicago 22 Je 42. 4: Samuel C Rizzetta. 5: Rosary Col 60-64 (Art, Philos) BA, 64-65 MA in LS. 6: Fr. 7: Ref asst Dole Br Lib, Oak Park Ill 64-65; Libn I adult serv, art ref libn art dept Chicago Pub Lib 65-66; Free lance biological illustrator 66-67; Museum registrar & catlgr Kalamazoo Pub Mus 67; Asst libn Joint Atomic Info Exchange Group (JAIEG), Wash DC 68-. 8: Weekly Television Show WKZO for Kalamazoo Public Mus 67. 9: ALA: CathLA. 10: Nat Assn Col & Univ Women. 12: Jt illus "Invertebrate Zoology" (68). 14: Ref, catlg. 15: 1302 N Scott st apt 8, Arlington Va 22209.

ROACH, CLAIRE (WOHNER). b Canton Miss 24 N 27. 4: John W Roach Jr. 5: Miss State Col for Women 45-48 (LS) BS. 7: Libn Starksville High Sch, Starksville Miss 48-49; Asst libn Archbishop Chapelle High Sch, Metairie La 63-65; Libn St Edward the Confessor Elem Sch 67-. 10: La Engnr Soc Auxiliary. 15: 805 Haring rd, Metairie La 70001.

ROACH, DAVID M. b Erie Penn 16 Mr 37. 4: Margaret Anne McMennamin. 5: UNotre Dame 55-60 (Eng Lit) A: UPittsburgh 64-65 MLS. 7: Personnel clerk US Army, Ft Jackson SC 60-62; Asst ref libn Dayton & Montgomery Co Pub Lib, Dayton Ohio 65-66, Hd bkmob div 66-. 9: ALA; OhioLA. 10: Dayton & Montgomery Co Pub Lib Staff Assn. 15: Dayton & Montgomery Co Pub Lib, Dayton Ohio 45402.

ROACH, ELLA WALDRON (ALLEN). b Amelia Va 11 F 21. 4: James Caldwell Roach. 5: Richmond Prof Inst 40, 41; Col of William & Mary 42, 43 (LS, Educ) AB; UNC summer 67 (LS); Col of William & Mary Sch of Educ 68-69. 7: Sec-libn Col of William & Mary's Dept of Lib Sci 43; Libn S Norfolk Grammar Sch, S Norfolk Va 44-51; Catlgr Armed Forces Staff Col, Norfolk Va 52, 54, 55; Libn S Norfolk Mem Lib, Chesapeake Va 56-64; Libn Azalea Jr High Sch, Norfolk Va 65; Catlgr sch lib processing ctr, Norfolk Va 66-. 9: ALA; VALA; SELA; VaEA. 10: Phi Beta Kappa; Educ Assn of Norfolk. 14: Sch lib wk, catlg & processing. 15: 1124 Jackson st, Chesapeake Va 23324.

ROACH, KENNETH (JAMES). b Mt Pleasant Tex 13 F35. 4: Anita Crowson. 5: Abilene Christian Col 54-58 (Eng) BA; UTex 61-62, 65 MLS, summer 68; Multi-Media inst & other study. 7: Eng tchr Taft Ind Sch Dist, Taft Tex 58-59; Libn Howard Co Jr Col 62-. 8: Consul; creative Visuals Inc, Big Srping Tex, Big Spring Home Med Lib, Big Spring Tex. 9: Tex Jr Col Tchrs Assn (Lib Div: Program Dir & pres); Tex Jr Col Libns Coun; NEA; TexLA; SWLA; Tex State TA. 15: 1904 Eleventh pl, Big Spring Tx 79720.

ROACH, MARGARET ANNE (McMENNAMIN). b Presque Isle Me 13 O 37. 4: David M Roach. 5: Notre Dame Col of Staten Island 55-59 (Chem) BA; Duquesne 59-61 (Biochem) MS; UPittsburgh 63-65 MSLS. 6: Fr, Ger. 7: Research assoc Mellon Inst 61-62; Research tech UPittsburgh 62-64; Libn trainee West Psych Inst & Clinic, Pittsburgh Penn 65-66; Ref libn Battelle Mem Inst, Columbus Ohio 65-66; Wright State U; Ref libn 66; Act ref hd 67-68, Ref libn 68-. 9: SLA (Chm Recr Com Dayton Chap 68-69). 10: Kappa Gamma Pi; Beta Phi Mu. 14: Ref. 15: 811 Browning ave, Englewood Oh 45322.

ROAD, RACHEL E. b Peru Ind 10 Ja 12. 5: Manchester Col 30-32, 35-37 (Eng) BA; UIll 38-39 BS in LS. 7: Catlgr Ball State U 39-43; Catlgr So Ill U 43-45; Catlgr, 1st asst Purdue U 45-. 9: ALA; IndLA; Ohio Valley Group of Tech Serv Libns. 10: Nat Soc for the Preserv of Covered Bridges; Ind Covered Bridge Soc; Ind Hist Soc. 14: Catlg. 15: 2219 Carlisle rd, W Lafayette Ind 47906.

ROADEN, RALPH DONALD. b Corbin Ky 26 Ap 32. 4: Joyce Thomas. 5: UKy 59 (Commerce) BS, 69 LSMS; EasternU 63 (Educ Admin) MA; UCincinnati 63; Duquesne 65. 7: Tchr High Schs in Ohio & Ky; Instr Ark Polytech Col 63-65; Youth counselor Ky Dept of Econ Security 65-66; Admin off Ky Dept of Libs 66-68; Dir of libs Lees Col 68-. 9: ALA; KyLA. 10: Kiwanis; PTA; Bell-Whitley Citizens Coun; Coun of So Mts; Friends of Ky Libs. 14: Research. 15: Cumberland Falls Rte Box 47, Corbin Ky 40701.

ROADS, CLARICE D. b Dallas Tex 20 S 23. 4: Lester F Roads. 5: E Central State Col 39-42 (Eng); Central State Col 62-64 (Elem educ, LS) BS; UOkla 65-66 MLS. 6: Sp. 7: Lib tech Okla State Lib Capitol Bldg, Okla City 64-65; Ref libn & Edmond br libn Okla Co Libs, Okla City 66-67; Asst libn US Grant High Sch, Okla City 67-. 8: Instr okla State U Dept Lib Sci summer 69. 9: NEA; ALA; OklaEA; OklaLA; SWLA; OklahomaCityLA; OklahomaCityEA. 10: AAUW; Alphi Chi; Beta Phi Mu. 11: Scholarship, Oklahoma State Library. 14: Ref, a-v materials, lib educ. 15: 1405 S blvd, Edmond Ok 73034.

ROALFE, WILLIAM R. b Mex City Mex 22 Ag 1896. 4: Helen Snook. 7: Libn Sch of Law USOCal 27-30; Libn Sch of Law Duke U 31-42; Attorney Off of Admin, Wash DC 43-45; Libn & Prof of Law Duke U 46; Libn & Prof of Law Northwestern U Law Sch 47-64, Prof of Law Emeritus 65-; Law lib consul Cook Co, Chicago 64-67. 8: Admitted to the Bar in Cal, 21, in NC, 32. 9: ALA; AALL (pres 35-36, mem Exec Com 31-32 & 34-37); Internat ALL (pres 59-62, mem Bd Dirs 62-65); Lib of Internat Rel, Chicago (Governing Bd 51-53): Amer Bar Assn; Chicago BarAssn; Amer Soc of Internat Law. 10: AAUP; UN Assn (off var bds, coms & divs 54-64). 11: Hon LLD, Temple U, 59. 12: "The Libraries of the Legal Profession (53); Ed "How to Find the Law (57); "How to Find the Law, with Special Chapters on Legal Wrting (65). 13: Yes. 14: Admin, legal bibliog. 15: 201 E Walton st, Chicago 60611.

ROARK, VELMA E (McCOLLUM). b Clyde Tex 6 N 06. 4: William LeeRoark. 5: Abilene Christian Col 24-30 (Home Making) BA; UTex (Home Making) BS; UColo (LS); N Tex State U (LS); Tex Woman's U (LS). 6: Lat. 7: Home Making tchr, Wylie Tex 32-36; Tchr of Eng, lib & home making, Baird Tex 36-38; Libn & Eng tchr, Vernon Tex 38-44; Libn LUBBOCK Sr High Sch, Lubbock Tex 44-48; Libn USAF, Dyess AFB 57-. 9: ALA; TexLA. 15: 702 E N 13th Abilene Tex 79601.

ROBARTS, WILLIAM MOORE. b Lake City Fla 28 Ag 23. 5: Maryville Col 42-46 (Eng lit) AB; UTenn 47-48 (Eng lit); Columbia 57 MSLS. 7: Stack supv, research asst, ref asst UTenn Lib (Knoxville) 46-51; Fellow order div Lib CCNY 51-52; Prof intern Columbia Col Lib 52-53, Sr ref asst 53-56, Asst libn Union Theol Sem (NYC) 56-. 9: ATheolLA. 15: 99 Claremont ave, New York NY 10027.

ROBB, ELIZABETH G. b Leonard Mich 5 J108. 5: UMich 27-30 AB, 30-31 AB in LS. 7: Catlgr Jackson Pub Lib, Jackson Mich 31-34; Catlgr UIowa 34-39; Asst in art & music dept Enoch Pratt Free Lib, Baltimore 40-43; Army libn U S Dept of the Army, New Cumberland Penn 43-46; Dir of Lib Serv US Info Serv, New Delhi India 47-52; Program of USIA Near East Area, Wash DC 53-55, Deputy chief appraisals br bib div 56-. 9: ALA (Life mem, chm & mem Internat Round Table 55-56, 64-65); DCLA. 15: 2219 Hall pl NW, Wash DC 20007.

ROBB, ISABEL (MARY). b Los Angeles 27 N 18. 5: UCLA 36-40 (Eng) BA; Drexel 40-41 BS in LS. 7: Supv libn Ventura Co Free Lib, Ventura Cal 42-61; Supv libn Ventura Co Schs Lib, Ventura Cal 61-. 9: ALA-AASchL; CalLA; CalASchL; Sec So Sect 65-66. 10: Bus & Prof Women; Altrusa; AAUW; Delta

Kappa Gamma. 14: Sch libs. 15: 435 So Jones, Ventura Cal 93003.

ROBB, MARTHA (ELIZABETH). b Utica NY 17 Ap 34. 5: Oberlin Col 51-55 (Eng) BA; UMich 55-57 MLS. 6: Fr. 7: Lib Sci Scholar UMich Lib 55-56, Lib Sci Fellow 56-57; Asst libn Campbell Ewald Co, Detroit 57-59; Ref libn Engnr Soc Lib, NYC 59-61; Acquis libn 61-66; Libn IBM NY Scientific Ctr 67-. 8: Consul Interdok Corp 65-. 9: SLA; ASIS. 14: Acquis, indesing. 15: Apt 2B, 649 Second ave, New York NY 10016.

ROBBEN, DOROTHY D. b Richmond Va 23 O 20. 4: Rinehart A Robben. 5: Westhampton Col URichmond 38-42 (Chem & Biol) BS. 7: Chemist E I DuPont, Richmond Va 42-57; Amer Tobacco Co dept of res & dev: Records assoc 57-68, Supv lib & records 68-. 9: SLA; ASIS; VaLA; Richmond Area Spec Libs Club; Va Acad Science; ACS. 15: Amer Tobacco Co Dept of Res & Devel PO Box 799, Hopewell Va 23860.

ROBBINS, EMMA BASSINOR. b Chicago 14 Jl 16. 4: A Robbins. 5: Simmons 34-38 (LS) BS; Columbia 40-42 (Sociol) MA. 7: Positions leading to head of br Brooklyn Pub Lib 39-44; Publ: free-lance Macmillan; Dial Press, NYC 44-49; Asst ed Pub Affairs Info Serv, NYC 49-59; Supv tech serv St Paul Pub Lib 60-. 9: ALA; SLA; MinnLA; ASIS. 13: Yes. 14: Tech serv, info scis. 15: 449 Portland ave, St Paul Mn 55102.

ROBBINS, GEORGIA FAY (ELLIS). b CaldwelTex 28 Ap 13. 4: William Roland ROBBINS. 5: Southwest Texas Univ 30-39 (Soc Studies) BS; Tex U50-56 (LS) M Ed. 7: Tchr-libn Mason Jr High Sch, Mason Tex 42-46; Libn: Zavala, Austin Tex 46-53, Stephen F Austin High Sch, Austin Tex 53-65, OHenry High Sch, Austin Tex 65-. 9: ALA; TexLA. 10: Austin Lib Club; Austin Clr Tchrs Assn; Delta Kappa Gamma. 14: Sch libn. 15: 5100 Crestway dr, Austin Tex 78731.

ROBBINS, HELEN (DETWILER) (MRS). b Collegeville Penn 17 F 08. 5: Col 25-27 Col25-27 (Music); Ursinus Col 27-30 (Eng) DS; Drexel 30-31 BS in LS; Columbia 42 (LS). 6: Fr. 7: Libn Pottstown (Penn) High Sch 31-35; Child libn Phila City Inst 39-41; Child libn Lyndhurst (NJ) Pub Lib 41-43; US Army Libn, Tilton Gen Hosp 43-44, Mason Gen Hosp 44-46, Hq IX Corps, Sendai Japan 46-47; Ref libn Pub Lib, Reading Penn 47-49; Post libn, Ft Huachua Ariz 51-52; Catlgr Coalinga (Cal) Pub Lib 52-53; Coord of lib serv Tulare Co (Cal) Dept of Educ 53-68; Libn Resource Ctr Primary House Roosevelt Sch, Desert Sands Unif Sch Dist, Indio Cal 68-. 8: Instr Ariz State U Dept of Lib Sci summer 68. 9: ALA-AASchL; CalLA (pres Yosemite Dist 56); CALASchL. 10: AAUW. 14: Child bks. 15: 73-435 Shadow Mt dr apt 2, Palm Desert Ca 92260.

ROBBINS, ORTHA D. b Mitchell SD 30 O 25. 5: UMinn 47 (Ed) BS, 48 BS in LS. 7: St Paul Pub Lib; Child libn 48-50, Br libn 50-59, Supv libn circ 59-. 9: ALA (life mem); MinnLA (treas 57-60, mem-at-large 66-67). 10: AAUW. 14: Adult serv. 15: St Paul Pub Lib 90 W 4th st, St Paul Mn 55102.

ROBBINS, PEARL S (SCHWARTZ). b Brooklyn NY. 4: Arthur Robbins. 5: Brooklyn Col 51 (Educ) BA; Newark State 69 (LS) Certif. 7: Tchr Bd of Educ, NYC 51-66; Libn Bd of Educ, Montville NJ 66-. 9: NEA; ALA; NJEA; NJLA. 14: Sch libs. 15: 20 Valley View dr, Rockaway NJ 07866.

ROBBINS, RICHARD W. b Riverton NJ 21 My 27. 5: Harvard 46-50 (Eng Lit) BA; Simmons 61-62(LS) MS. 7: Sales & Ed Depts J B Lippincott Co, Phila 51-61; Dir of the Lib Pawtucket Pub Lib, Pawtucket RI 63-, Dir Pawtucket Reg Lib Ctr 67-; Lecturer URI 68-. 9: ALA; RILA (v-pres 65-67, pres 67-68). 10: . 14: Pub lib admin. 15: Pawtucket Pub Lib, Pawtucket RI 02860.

ROBBINS, RONALD EDWARD. b Connersville Ind 16 S 42. 4: Bonnie Rusterholz. 5: IndU 60-64 (Hist) AB, 64-65 (Hist) MAT, 66-68 (LS) MA. 6: Fr. 7: Tchr Detroit Pub Sch Syst MacKenzie High Sch 65-66; Asst ref libn Lafayette Col 68-69, Ref libn 69-. 14: Ref. 15: 404 McCartney st, Easton Pa 18042.

ROBERTS, AMMARETTE. b Oakalla Tex 24 Je 23. 5: Mary Hardin-Baylor Col for Women 40-43 (Chem) BA; UTex Ext (LS). 6: Ger. 7: Chem Socony Mobil, Dallas 43-47; Chem Tex Research Found, Renner Tex 47-51; Chem Wadley Research Found, Dallas 51-56; Mgr Info Serv Lone Star Gas Co, Dallas 56-59; Documentalist Mobil Research & Development Corp Field Research Lab, Dallas 69-. 9: ACS; ASIS; SLA (Tex Chap; sec 58-59, 2nd v-pres 60-61, chm Publicity Com 63-64, chm Projs Com 64-66, 1st v-pres 67-68, pres 68-69); Amer Records Mgt Assn (v-pres Reg 5 67-68); TexLA (chm Spec Libs Div 62-63). 10: Dallas Desk & Derrick Club. 13: Yes. 14: Admin. 15: Mobil Field Res Lab, PO Box 900, Dallas Tx 75221.

ROBERTS, ANNE DIXON. b Sioux City Iowa 1 Ap 16. 5: UMinn 34-38 (Math, Lat) BS in Educ; UPenn 43-44 ASTP Certif; UDenver 45-46 BS in LS. 6: Lat, Ger. 7: High Sch Tchr Regent ND 38-39, Baker Mont 39-42, Big Timber Mont 42-43; US Army Ordnance Div Aberdeen Proving Grounds Ballistics Baltistics Research Lab (Sgt) 43-45; Catlgr Detroit Pub Lib 46-47, 48-49; Partner & manager Roberts Jewelry Store, Anaconda Mont 49-61; Ser UIowa UIoza 62-. 9: ALA. 10: Soroptimist Club; AAUW; Pi Lambda Theta; Phi Beta Kappa; Lambda Alpha Psi; Sigma Epsilon Sigma. 14: Sers catlg. 15: 429 Crestview, Iowa City Iowa 52240.

ROBERTS, CAROLINE (GERLING). b Schenectady NY 3N22. 4: Donald Raymond Roberts. 5: UVt 44 (Econ, Com) BS; NYSU (Albany) 48 (Com) MS, 62 MLS. 6: Ger. 7: Chm of bus Schalmont High Sch, Schenectady NY 45-64, Libn 64-. 9: NY State Tchrs Assn; NYLA.: Phi Beta Kappa; AAUW; ENYSLA. 10: Hudson Mohawk LA; Delta Pi Epsilon. 15: 2 Knolls rd, Schenectady NY 12309.

ROBERTS, CECIL EARL. b Forestburg SD 19 O 21. 4: Elizabeth Wickham. 5: UIowa 46-48 (Pol SCI) BA; So Methodist U 49 (Religion); UIowa 50-52 t9hist) MA; UIll 57-59 MLS. 7: (Cpl) Artillery US Army, US & SW Pacific 40-45; Lib asst Pub Lib NSW, Sydney Australia 54; Head acquis dept UQueensland (Brisbane Australia) 55-57; Head Soc Sci Lib Wash State U 60-62; Head Libn Orange Coast r Col 62-63; Head ref dept Cal State Col (Fullerton) 63-67; Hd libn Imperial Valley Col, Imperial Cal 67-. 9: Lib Assn of Australia, CalLA. 10: Orange Co Hist Assn; Beta Phi Mu; Phi Delta Kappa. 14: Ref, acquis, rare bks, admin. 15: 746 Tangerine dr, El Centro Ca 92243.

ROBERTS, DONALD LOWELL. b Dodge City Kan 13 Ag38. 4: Sally Meador. 5: Wichita State U 56-57 Music); Curts Inst of Music 57-58 (Bassoon); Friends U 58-61 (Music Theory) BA; UMich 61-63 (LS, Music) AMLS. 6: Ger. 7: Fine Arts Libn UNM 63-68; Personnel mgr Albuquerque Symphony Orchestra 65-68; Visiting lecturer UAlbuquerque 66-68; Music libn Northwestern U 69-. 8: Dir NM Lib Week, 66, 67; Albuquerque Symphony Orchestra, 63-68; Lectures on Amer Indian Mus. 9: MusLA (chm Mem Com); SWLA; NMLA (sec Col Div); Col Mus Soc (Lib Holdings Com). 10: Mu Phi Epsilon; Nat Folklore Festival Assn; NM Folklore Soc; Beta Phi Mu; Soc for Ethnomusicology. 11: Woodrow Wilson Fellow. 12: Record review ed "Ethno musicology" (69-). 13: Yes. 14: Mus libnship, archiving of recorded sound, Amer Indian music. 15: Music Library, Northwestern Univ, Evanston Il 60201.

ROBERTS, DORIS E. b Goldendale Wash 23 Je 14. 5: Whitman Col 31-35 (Eng) AB; UWash 36-37 BA in LS. 6: Fr, Ger. 7: Ref & mun ref asst Lib Assn of Portland 37-42; Asst libn CWCW, Ellensburg Wash 42-43; Base libn Reno Army Base 43-45; Command libn Hqs European Air Transport Serv, Wiesbaden Germany 43-48; Field libn USAF, Wiesbaden Germany 48; Ref libn Mid-Columbia Reg Lib, Kennewick Wash 49-51; Ref libn Richland Pub Lib, Richland Wash 51; City Libn Richland Pub Lib, Richland Wash 51-. 9: ALA (Coun Rep Wash 64-67); PNLA; WashLA (Exec Bd 51-53 & 64-67); WashStateSchLA. 10: Nat Cong Parents & Tchrs; Nat Fed Bus & Prof Womens Cluds; Richland Sch-Pub Lib Coord Coun; Commun Action Com; Friends of the Richland Lib. 14: Admin, ref, personnel, commun rel bk sel. 15: Richland Pub Lib 916 Jadwin, Richland Wa 99352.

ROBERTS, ELIZABETH P. b St Louis 17 ,ja 28. 5: William Woods Col 45-47; UMo 47-49 (Bot) BA; Emory 55-56 MLS. 6: Fr. 7: Clerk, Alumnae Off Stephens Col 51-52; Analyst Seed Lab State of Ga, Atlanta 54-55; Libn A W Calhoun Med Lib, Emory U 56-57; Libn Wash State U Sci Div 57-63; Hd sers record Sci Lib 63-, Act chief Sci Lib 65-66. 9: SLA; PNLA; Amer Soc Engnr Educ (Engnr Sch Lib Div; chm Sects West 67-69). 10: AAUW; AAUP; Sierra Club. 13: Yes. 14: Ser, ref. 15: Box 2114 College Sta, Pullman Wa 99163.

ROBERTS, GLORIA A (ARONOW). b NYC 16 F 24. 4: Leonard M Roberts. 5: Vassar 41-44 (Child study & Psych) BA; Columbia 64-67 MLS. 6: Fr. 7: Asst libn NY State Psych Inst, NYC 67-. 9: ALA. 14: Ref, acquis, med libn. 15: 2711 Henry Hudson Pkwy, Riverdale NY 10463.

ROBERTS, GRAHAM (EDWARD). b DeKalb Co Ga 26 My 22. 5: U of the South 39-43 (Hist) BA; UVa 45-47 (Hist) PhD; Emory 47-48 BLS. 6: Fr. 7: Curator of mss, Dir Flowers Collection of Southern Hist Duke U Lib 48-52; Dir Drake U

Libs 52-56; Dir Southeastern Interlib Research Facilty, Atlanta 56-57; Lib consul So Reg Educ Bd, Atlanta 58-59; Ga Tech: Chief readers serv Lib 60-65, Asst Prof Sch of Info Sci 63-65, Assoc Prof 65-, Assoc dir 65-. 9: ALA; ASIS; SELA; GaLA. 10: Phi Beta Kappa; Omicron Delta Kappa. 12: Ed SE Res Lib "Newsletter 57-58 Ed "Southeastern Supplement to the "Union List of Serials (59); "Literature of Science and Engineering (66, 2nd ed 69). 13: Yes. 14: Ref serv, info org & use, sci bibliog. 15: 1639 Adela pl NE, Atlanta Ga 30329.

ROBERTS, HASSELTINE (NEAL). b Macon Ga 22 N 38. 5: Wesleyan Col 56-60 (Hist, Govt) AB; Fla State U 63-64 (LS) MS. 6 : Fr. 7: Tchr Dougherty Co Bd of Educ, Albany Ga 60-63, Camp dir Middle Ga Girl Scout Coun, Macon Ga 63; Grad asst Fla State U 64, Asst libn Wesleyan Col (Macon Ga) 64- 69, Act libn 69-. 8: Chm jr high sch soc studs dept, Dougherty Co Ga 62. 9: ALA; SELA; GaLA. 10: Pi Gamma Mu; Ga Hist Soc; Quota Internat; PEO. 14: Ref, archival materials. 15: 2712 Cherry ave, Macon Ga 31204.

ROBERTS, HELENE EMYLOU (LEEDY). b Seattle 23 Mr 31. 4: F David Roberts. 5: UWash 48-53 (Drama) BA, 56-57 (Drama) MA, summers 58-61 (LS) ML. 6: Fr. 7: Tchr Cle Elum High Sch, Cle Elum Wash 53-56; Dartmouth Col: Asst art libn 57-61, Catlgr 62-63, Art libn 63-65, Slide curator 69-. 9: ALA. 13: Yes. 14: Art. 15: RFD, Lyme NH 03768.

ROBERTS, JANET LOUISE. b New Britain Conn 20 Ja 25. 5: Otterbein 42-46 (Eng) BA; Columbia 65-66 (LS) MA. 7: Ref libn Dayton & Montgomery Co Pub Lib, Dayton Ohio 66-. 9: ALA; OhioLA. 14: Ref (lit & fine arts). 15: Dayton and Montgomery Co Pub Lib, Dayton Oh 45402.

ROBERTS, JEANNETTE EVELYN. b Sioux Falls SDak 24 N 26. 5: Cornell Col 44-46; UDenver 46-48 BA in LS; UMich 56-61 MLS. 6: Fr. 7: Child libn asst Glendale Pub Lib, Glendale Cal 48-49; Br libn Hanapepe Br Kauai Pub Lib Ltd, Kauai Hawaii 49-52; Child libn Carnarsie Br Brooklyn Pub Lib, Brooklyn NY 52-54; Hd child dept Royal Oak Pub Lib, Royal Oak Mich 54-55; Dir Lenawee Co Lib System, Adrian Mich 55-64; Br libn Wahiawa Br Hawaii State Lib, Honolulu 64-67; Hd libn US Naval Air Sta, Barbers Point Honolulu 67; Dir USA Tripler Gen Hosp Lib, Honolulu 67-. 8: Instr Mich State Lib Summer Wkshop for Non-Prof Libns 58. 9: ALA; NYLA; MichLA (chm Co & Reg Lib Sect; Pub Rel Com; sec Lib Admin Sect); HawaiiStateLA. 10: Beta Phi Mu. 14: Hosp & med libnship, blind & physically handicapped, computerization. 15: 3151 Monsarrat ave apt 502, Honolulu Hi 96815.

ROBERTS, JOSEPH GRANDON. b Flint Mich 28 O 27. 4: Lena Hallside. 5: UMich 47-52 (Eng Lit) BA; Trinity Col Dublin U 51 (Eng Lit); UMich 54-55 AMLS. 6.; fr, Lat. 7: Personnel tech (Cpl) US Army, US 44-47; Jr order libn UMich Libs 53-54; Libn & ed asst Streeter Lib, Morristown NJ 55-57; Bkmob libn Ann Arbor Pub Lib, Ann Arbor Mich 58-65, Head ext serv 65-. 8: Assisted the late Thomas W Streeter in editing "The Bibliography of Texas, 1795-1845, Parts II & III; Bkmob consul, Washtenaw Co (Mich) Lib, 62, & Ingham Co (Mich) Lib, 63. 9: ALA; MichLA (chm pro-tem Bkmob Sect). 10: Boy Scouts. 11: Hopwood Award (poetry), UMich 52. 14: Ext serv, admin, rare bks, bibliog. 15: 1320 Brooklyn ave, Ann arbor Mi 48104.

ROBERTS, JOSEPH WILLIAM. b Philadelphia Penn 4 Je 15. 7: NYC Pub Lib: Page 28-36, Stack chief 36-38, Asst rare bk & ms divs 38-42, Hd bindery recs sect 42-43; Catlgr & gen asst city bk auction, NYC 44-46; Owner St Alban's Bkshop, NYC 47-48; Yale Club of NYC: Asst libn 48-51, Libn 52-. 9: ALA. 15: 1432 Second ave, New York NY 10021.

ROBERTS, JUSTINE (TURNER). b Chicago 4 S 27. 5: UCal(Berkeley) 44-48 (Sociol) AB, 62-64 MLS. 6: Fr, Sp. 7: Libn catlgr UCal Med Center (San Francisco) 65-66, Spec project coord 67-. 9: SLA; ASIS; ALA; Med libns San Francisco Area, MedLA. 10: Beta Phi Mu; Alexander Graham Bell Assn; Marin Parents of Hearing-Handicapped Child. 14: Catlg, clsf, machine retrieval. 15: 152 Sycamore ave, Mill Valley Cal 94941.

ROBERTS, KENNETH H. b Pittsburgh 20 Ja 24. 4: Francoise C Gourier. 5: Boston U 42-47 (Eng) AB; Boston U 47-48 (Art Hist) MA; Simmons 52-54 MS in LS. 6: Fr. 7: Br lib asst, Asst chief art & music dept, admin asst, personnel dir, chief art & music div Brooklyn Pub Lib 54-64; Expert Unesco, Madagascar 63-64; Head Lib Devel Sect Div of Libs Unesco, Paris 65-. 9: ALA. 10: Phi Beta Kappa. 13: Yes. 14: Pub libs, art libs, lib devel. 15: 34 Boulevard de Grenelle, Paris 15 France.

ROBERTS, LEO B(OGAN) (MRS) (FLETCHER). b Pendleton SC 16 Je 1900. 4: Leo B Roberts. 5: USCar 17-21 (Hist) BA, 21-22 (Eng) MA; Emory 38-39 BA in LS. 6: Fr, Ger, Sp. 7: Asst Prof of Eng Millsaps Col 28-31, 35-36; Reg asst La Lib Commsn, Winnfield La 39-40; Libn Drew Co Lib, Monticello Ark 40-41, 43-45; Asst dir Ark Lib Commsn, Little Rock rk Lib Commsn, Little Rock Ark 41-43; Hdqrs libn Ala Pub Lib Serv, Montomery Ala 45-56, Asst dir 57-58; Libn Huntington Col 58-; Libn UAla (Montgomery) 51-68; Libn AuburnU (Montgomery) 68-. 9: SELA; AlaLA; chm Fed Rel 49-54, chm Bibliog Com 59-, circ mgr Alabama Librarian 49-67. 12: "Literary Map of Alabama (69). 13: Yes. 14: Ref. 15: Huntington Col, Fairview ave, Montgmomery Ala 36106.

ROBERTS, MARGARET (BAZILE). b Pass Christian Miss. 4: Bobby Roberts Sr. 5: Xavier U 42-45 (Hist) BA; LSU 62-65 (LS)MS. 6: Fr. 7: Tchr Xavier Prep, New Orleans 45-46; Tchr-libn Vernon High Sch, Mt Hermon La 46-64; Libn Lawless High Sch, New Orleans 64-. 9: LaEA; LaLA; ALA. 10: Kappa Gamma Pi; Alpha Kappa Mu. 14: Sch wk, ref. 15: 1627 N Johnson st, New Orleans 70116.

ROBERTS, MARYLYN ANTOINETTE (MALCOLM). 5: Los Angeles City Col 49-52 (Earth Sci). NM StateU Ext 62-66. 7: Libn N Amer Aviation Rocketdyne Div, Canoga Park Cal 52-60; Lib asst USAF Off Research Analysis, Holloman AFB NM 62-66; Asst libn Whittaker Corp R&D Div, San Diego 66-68; Libn McGraw Hill Inc SILC, San Diego 68; Libn Whittaker Corp R & D Div, San Diego 68-. 9: SLA; CalLA. 14: Catlg, indexing, lit searches. 15: 8563 Glenhaven st, San Diego Ca 92123.

ROBERTS, MATT TAYLOR. b New Orleans 9 My 29. 4: Elizabeth Hiza. 5: Tulane U 48-54 (Econ) BA; UPenn 56-57 (Ind Rel) MA; Rutgers 57-60 MLS. 6: Sp. 7: Radio radar tech USMC (S/Sgt), US 51-53; UPenn Lib: Shelflister ser dept 56-57, Stack supv 57, Head res bk dept 57-60; Chief circ dept Washington U Lib 60-. 9: ALA; MoLA. 10: Ethical Soc (St Louis). 13: Yes. 14: Circ, automation proc, bk binding preserv, admin, copyright, personnel. 15: 2621 Roseland ter, St Louis Mo 63143.

ROBERTS, MILDRED CAROLYN. b Chicago Ill 2 Jl 04. 5: Berea 21-26 (Ancient lang) AB; UKy summers 32-36 (Eng) MA; UMinn summer 46 (Journalism); William & Mary summer 49 (Lat); UKy summers 52-56 (LS) BS in LS. 6: Lat, Fr. 7: High sch tchr Witherspoon Col, Buckhorn Ky 26-29; High sch tchr pub schs: Scottville Ill 29-31, Olive Hill Ky 31-36, Silver Gorve Ky 36-41, Raceland Ky 41-43; Tipp City Ohio 43-53, Franklin Ohio 53-55, Order libn & Asst Prof of Lib Sci Berea Col 55-. 9: ALA; KyLA (past sec Col & Ref Sect); SELA. 10: Bus & Profess Women's Club; Berea Hosp Bd; Woman's Guild of Union Church; Phi Kappa Phi. 14: Bk sel, bks on Lincoln, ref. 15: 309 Jackson st, Berea Ky 40403.

ROBERTS, NATHAN (WARREN). b NYC 9 S 13. 4: Lilliam Pode. 5: City Col (NY) 32-38 (Soc Studies) BS; Columbia 38-39 (LS) BS, 59-60 (LS) MS. 6: Fr, Sp. 7: Libn ref City Col (NY) 38-41; Libn publ supply USA Los Angeles Port of Embarkation 42-45; Libn market research Fawcett Publ Inc, NY 46-47 Libn sch Lindenhurst (NY) Pub Schs 55-56; Libn W Islip Pub Schs, W Islip NY 56-. 8: Consul to N Babylon Pub Lib (NY) 60-. 9: NEA; ALA-AASchL; Suffolk Co LA; NY STATE Tchrs Assn; NY Lib Club. 10: Suffolk Co Civil Defense Dept. 13: Yes. 14: Bibliog, ref, reading guidance, tchg use of lib. 15: 25 Beverly rd, Oakdale LI NY 11796.

ROBERTS, OLIVE L. b Pine Grove La 26 Mr 05. 5: La Col 25-26; LSU 28-31 (Eng) BA, 43-44 BS in LS; Columbia summers 52, 57. 7: Elem tchr St Helena Parish Sch Bd, greensburg La 26-28; Tchr Pine Grove High Sch, Greensburg La 31-43; Libn catalog dept LSU 44-46; Hd catlg dept NWest State Col 46-65; Hd libn La Col 65-. 9: ALA; LaLA (mem var coms). 10: Delta Kappa Gamma; AAUW. 14: Catlg, admin. 15: 1420A Oakland, Pineville La 71360.

ROBERTS, RONALD L. b Edinburg Ill 7 F 14: 05: IlWesleyan U 32-36 B Music; UIll 40-42 (Bus) BS, 49-51 (LS) MS. 5: UIll 42 BS, 51 MSLS. 6: Fr. 7: Various positions Enoch Pratt Free Lib, Baltimore 51-57; Head Bus Lib Indianapolis Pub Lib 57-61; Asst dir Four Country Lib System, Binghamton NY 61-66; Dir North Co Lib Syst, Watertown NY 66-. 8: Lib Com, Presidents Com on Employment of the Handicapped, 58-. 9: ALA; NYLA (dir Adult Serv Sect 63-65, v-pres 68-69, pres 69-70; chm Awards Com 63-65). 10: Beta Phi Mu; Rotary. 13: Yes. 14: Rural libs, ref. 15: 1050 Arsenal st, Watertown NY 13601.

ROBERTS, SARAH ELIZABETH. b Genoa Neb 11 F 09. 5: British Inst UParis 26-28 (Fr); Sorbonne 27-28 (Fr);UCLA 28-31 (Fr) BA; UWash 31-32 (LS) BS; George Washington U 36-37 36-39 MA, 40-48 (Hist) PhD. 6: Fr, Sp, Portu. 7: Credit off wk Bullocks Dept Store, Los Angeles 28-34; Jr examiner US Civil Serv Commsn, Wash DC 34-36; Lib asst US Dept of Com, Wash DC 36-38; Jr libn US Dept of Labor, Wash DC 38-43; Internat labor economist US Dept of State, Wash DC 43-50; Intelligence research spec US Dept of State, Wash DC 50-54; Asst libn UFla 58-60; Ed wk Amer Bibliog Center, Santa Barbara Cal 65-; Assoc ed "America; History and Life" 67-. 9: ALA; Inter-Amer Bibliog & Lib Assn; CalLA. 10: AHA; AAUP. 12: "Jose Torbio Medina (41). 13: Yes. 14: Catlg, ref, acquis. 15: 7280 Hillside ave, Hollywood Cal 90046.

ROBERTS, SUSAN A. b Albany Cal 5 F 46. 5: Stanford 62-66 (Eng) AB; UCal (Berkeley) 66-67 MLS. 6: Fr. 7: Acquis libn UConn Health Ctr Lib, Hartford Conn 67-. 9: ALA; MedLA. 14: Acquis, ref. 15: UConn Health Ctr Lib 1000 Asylum, Hartford Ct 06032.

ROBERTS, WILLIAM HUGH III. b Ridley Park Penn 21 O 36. 4: Barbara Lee Howard. 5: Princeton 54-55 (Hist); Earlham Col 55-58 (Pol Sci) AB; UPenn Law Sch 58-61; Drexel 62-63 MSLS. 7: Law clerk Duane Morris & Heckscher, Phila 60-61; Ref libn Free Lib of Phila 61-63; Head spec servdept Northeast Reg Lib, Free Lib of Phila 63-65; Dir Clinton Pub, Clinton Iowa 65-67; Dir Roanoke Co Lib, Salem Va 67-. 8: Lib consul, Fulton Pub Lib, Fulton Ill 65, Comanche, Iowa Pub Lib 66; Adv, Helen Kate Furness Lib, Wallingford Penn 64-65; Instr UVa Ext 68-69. 9: ALA; PLA-RJMRT; VaLA. 10: C of C; Kiwanis; YMCA; IFIR. 12: Ed Va JSMRT "Bulletin (69-). 14: Ref, admin. 15: 3402 Overhill Trail SW, Roanoke Va 24018.

ROBERTSON, BILLY O(NEAL). b Columbia SC 27 Mr 30. 4: Helen Oglesby. 5: N Greenville Jr Col 55-56 (Eng); Furman U 56-57 (Eng, Religion); ULouisville 58-59 (Eng) BA; Nazareth Col 59-60 (LS); Ind U 60-63 (LS) MA. 6: Fr. 7: USAF, Wichita Falls Tex,Smyrna Tenn, Biloxi Miss 48-51; Tchr-libn North Central High Sch, Ramsey Ind59-60; Multi-sch libn Richmond (Ind) Community Schs 61-63; Dir of Lib Serv Greeley (Colo) Pub Schs 63-65; Lib coordinator Lincoln (Neb) Pub Schs 65-68, Dir Media Network 68-; Assoc Prof UNeb Lib Sci & Instr Media 65-; Assoc Prof Appalachian State U summer 68. 8: Exec dir, Nat Lib Neels Neb; Liaison between Neb Sch Lib Devel Coun & State Dept of Educ; Consul in lib statist for State Dept of Educ; Partic in Great Plaines Lib Dist Org Proj; Partic in N Central Assn & State Accred visits to sch systems. 9: NEA-DAVI; ALA (Reg dir Recr Prog); -AASchA; Neb State EA; NebLA; MPLA; IllSchLA (Com for Implement of Sch Lib Standards); ColoLA (see Sch Lib Div); ColoASchL (mem Bd 3 yrs); Neb Educ Media Assn (Ad hoc Com NEMA & Neb Coun for Tchr Educ to Recommend Certif and Train Requirements); LincolnEA; LinvolnLA. 10: Greeley Lib Coun; Lions Commun Theatre. 13: Yes. 14: Admin. 15: 720 S 22nd st, Box 200, Lincoln Neb 68501.

ROBERTSON, GILES BEN. b Villa Rica Ga 21 N 10. 5: Emory 32 BA, 33 BALS; UMich 40 MALS. 7: Ref libn Emory U 35-36; US Army 42-45; Lib supv VA Reg Off, Atlanta 46-47; Chief tech processes VA, Wash DC 47-54; Lecturer Catholic U 50-54; Asst treas Chicago Med Bk Co, Chicago 54-59; Ref libn UIll(Chicago) 59-63; Guest Faculty Peabody Lib Sch 64; Lecturer Chicago Tchrs Col North 64, 65; Visiting Prof Lib Sci Rosary Col 65; Head pub serv div UIll(Chicago) 65-. 9: ALA; AALS; IllLA; Chicago Lib Club (treas 62-64, Program Chm 64-66), pres 67-68). 10: AAAS; Chicago Inst of Art; Chicago Coun on For Rel. 13: Yes. 14: Ref. tchg in lib schs. 15: 1360 Lake Shore dr, Chicago Il 60605.

ROBERTSON, GRACE M (SCHOTT). b Milwaukee 4 Ag 08. 404: Percy O Robertson. 5: UWis(Milwaukee) 626-29, 26-29 (Educ, Eng) B Educ; UWis(Madison) 63-66 (LS). 6: Ger. 7: Tchr-libn Grafton High Sch, Grafton Wis 29-30; High sch libn No Div High Sch, Milwaukee 31-40; Libn Cazenovia High Sch, Cazenovia Wis 50-51; Caseworker II Child Welfare Sauk Co Dept of Pub Welfare, Baraboo Wis 56-62; Sr high sch libn Portage Pub Schs, Portage Wis 62-. 9: ALA-AASchL; NEA; WisLA (treas Sch Lib Sect 67 Nat Lib Week Coun 67); WisEA (Lib Div); PortageEA (Exec Bd 66-67). 14: Sch libs. 15: 118-12 W Franklin st, Portage Wi 53901.

ROBERTSON, JEANNE (BETTY) (ELLIOTT). b Murphy NC 16 My 34. 4: Morgan D Robertson. 5: Wesleyan Methodist Jr Col 52-54 AA; Greenville Col 54-56 (Psy, Educ) AB; UMich summers 60-64 MA in LS. 06: Fr. 7: Tchr-libn Carlyle Schs; Carlyle Ill 57-59; Tchr Oblong Schs, Oblong Ill 59-60; Tchr-libn Dye Community Schs, Flint Mich 60-61; Libn Dye Schs-Carman, Flint Mich 61-67; Libn Carmen High Sch, Flint Mich 67-. 9: NEA; MichEA; MichASchL; Mich A-V Assn. 10: CarmenEA. 14: Sch libs. 15: 1503 East dr, Flint Mich 48504.

ROBERTSON, KATHERINE F (CHASTAIN). b Klamath Falls Ore 20 F 16. 4: David E Robertson. 5: Sacramento Jr Col 33-35 (Eng) AA; StanfordU 35-37 (Eng) BA; UCal 37-38 (Libnship) Certif; Columbia 49-50 (Eng) MA. 6: Fr. 7: Libn Lincoln Jr High Sch, Sacto Cal 38-43; Libn AAFCUTC Camp Pinedale, Fresno Cal 43-46; Catlgr, asst libn libn Coalinga Dist Lib, Coalinga Cal 46-61; Prin libn San Leandro Community Lib, Sạn leandron Cal 61-. 9: ALA; CalLA. 10: Phi Beta Kappa. 14: Personnel, ref, catlg. 15: 1460 Lytelle st, Hayward Ca 94544.

ROBERTSON, LOIS (MARIE). b Huntsville Ala 20 F 30. 5: UAla 48-52 (LS) BS. 7: Libn US Army, Redstone Arsenal Ala 52-56; Libn US Army Ballistic Missile Agency, Redstone Arsenal Ala 56-60; Chief Libn US Nat Aeronautics & Space Admin, Geo C Marshall Space Flight Center, ter, Huntsville Ala 60-. 9: SLA (pres Ala Chap 66-67); AlaLA. 10: AAUW:; Bus & Prof Womens Club. 14: Ref. 15: 3304 Monarch dr SW, Huntsville Ala 35801.

ROBERTSON, MARGARET MARY. b Jacksonville Fla 15 S 21. 5: George WashingtonU 49-59 (Geog) AB; Fla StateU 68 (LS) MS. 6: Fr. 7: Admin off CWO3 USMC 43-45, 49-67; Libn I Orlando Pub Lib, Orlando Fla 69, Coord adult serv 69-. 10: Beta Phi Mu. 14: Admin, ref. 15: 3010 Northwood blvd, Orlando Fl 32803.

ROBERTSON, MARION ELIZABETH (MACKAY). b Scott Sask Can 29 My 12. 5: UAlberta 64 9eng) BEd. 6: Fr. 7: Edmonton Pub Sch Bd, Edmonton Can; Tchr 56-59; Edmonton Separate Sch Bd: Tchr 59-62, Tchr-libn 62-. 9: CanLA; Sch Lib Coun; AltaTA. 12: Former editor of Jasper Place Citizen (weekly newspaper). 15: 9840-149 st, Edmonton 51 Alberta Can.

ROBERTSON, MARY PATRICIA (PIERCE STEPHENS). b Key West Fla 10 Ja 42. 4: Richard Earl Robertson. 5: Southeastern La Col summer 59; LSU 59-63 (Speech Educ) BS (magna cum laude), 63-64 (LS) MS. 6: Fr. 7: Lib asst U High Sch LSU, Baton Rouge La 59-63; Med lib trainee VA, New Orleans La summer 62; Lib trainee La State U Lib summer 63; Grad asst in programming LSU Union Baton Rouge 63-64; Ya asst Herring Run Br Enoch Pratt Free Lib 64-65, Sr ya libn Brooklyn Br 65-66; Ref libn Baltimore Jr Col 66-67; Field libn & lib specialist St Tammany Parrish Schs 67-. 9: ALA. 10: Beta Phi Mu; Phi Kappa Phi; Mu Sigma Rho; Alpha Lambda Delta; Kappa Delta Pi; Tau Kappa Alpha. 14: Ya wk, red, admin, personnel. 15: Box 548, Covington La 70433.

ROBERTSON, MAY ROSE. b Donaldsonville La 17 My 24. 5: LSU 39-43 (Eng, Fr) BS, 43-44 BS in LS, 44-46 (Span). 6: Fr, Sp, Russian. 7: Jr circ libn LSU 44-45; Libn romance langs room 45-46; Army libn US Army Europe, Bayreuth & Coburg Germany 46-48; Asst post lib, Ft Riley Kan 49; Post libn, Mitchel AFB NY 49-51; Staff libn Hq 14th Air Force, Robins AFB Ga 51-52; Post libn Berlin Mil Post US Army, Berlin Germany 52-53; Acquis libn Hq US Army in Europe, Nurnberg Germany 53-55; Command libn No Area Command US Army, Frankfurt Germany 55-62; Prin sel off acquis Nat Agric Lib, Wash DC 62-65; Catlgr Bur of Med Food & Drug Admin, Arlington Va 65-67; Chief acquis sect Fed Aviation Admin, Wash DC 67-. 9: ALA; SLA; ASIS. 10: Beta Phi Mu; Phi Kappa Phi; Kappa Delta Pi; Alpha Lambda Delta. 14: Tech serv, acquis, catlg, ser. 15: Apt 526, 4600 S Four Mile Run dr, Arlington Va 22204.

ROBERTSON, RUSSELL CLARK. b Bingham Canyon Utah 30 D 26. 4: Yvonne Marie Drake. 5: Ore State Col 44-45 (Pre-Engnr); UCLA 45-49 (Pol Sci) BA; UUtah 53 (Pub Speaking); Brigham Young U 57-58 (Pre-Dentistry); Washington U (St Louis) 58-59 (Dentistry); UIll 59-60 (LS) MA. 6: Fr, Ger. 7: Chaplain US Army (Capt), Wiebaden Wiesbaden 55-57; Tech libn Argonne Nat Lab, Idaho Falls Ida 60-. 10: Scoutmaster; Phi Beta Kappa. 15: 223 2nd st, Idaho Falls Ida 83401.

ROBERTSON, RUTH (BURT). b Wilmington Del 27 Ap 14. 5: Los Angeles City Col 33-36; UCLA 36; UCal(Berkeley) 36-38 AB, 38-39 (LS) Certif. 7: Clerical lib aide Los Angeles Pub Lib 31-36; Co-libn Sausalito Pub Lib, Sausalito Cal 39-43; Libn Marin Dormitories Lib, Marin City Cal 43-44; Libn I Los Angeles Co Lib, Los Angeles 45-47; Coordinator adult serv Wilmington Inst Free Lib, Wilmington Del 47-63; Libn Well-Springs Found, Ben Lomond Cal 64-. 8: Lib consul: Aacad of Creative Educ, San Jacinto Cal 63 & Center ofCreative Exploration, Pasadena Cal 63-64. 9: ALA; DelLA.

10: Acad of Mental Health & Religion; Friends Conf on Relig & Psychol; Conf on Sci & Relig; YWCA. 13: Yes. 14: Readers adv, circ, pub rel. 15: 2005 Alba rd, Ben Lomond Ca 95005.

ROBERTSON, SARAH V. b St Augustine Fla 9 My 32. 5: Stratford Jr Col 50-51; Goucher Col 51-54 (Psych-Sociol) BA; American U 60-63 (Pub Rel) MA; Florida State U 66-67 MSLS; Olympic Jr Col 68- (Non destructive testing, Naval Arch, Quality Control, Int ro to Engineering). 7: Case wkr Dept of Pub Welfare, Baltimore 54-56; Ser club dir Army Spec Serv, Berlin Germany 56-59; Program dir Army Spec Serv, Ft Mead Md 59-63; Club dir Army Spec Serv, Yokohoma, Japan 63-64; Club dir Army Spec Serv, Dmz & Taegu Korea 64-65; Asst program dir Stud Union UFla 65-66; Engineering libn Puget Sound Naval Shipyard, Bremerton Wash 67-. 8: Fed woman's program adv Puget Sound Naval Shipyard, Bremerton Wash 67-. 9: SLA. 10: Beta Phi Mu. 14: Ref, admin. 15: 1104 Pacific ave, Bremerton Wa 98310.

ROBIE, BURTON ALDRICH. b Northbridge Mass 17 J3 25. 4: Barbara A Michaud. 5: Clark U 43, 46-48 (Eng Lit) BA: Brown 48-50 (Eng Lit) MA; Simmons 51-53 (LS) MS. 6: Fr. 7: Humanities libn MIT Libs 5 1-58; Head Gifts & Exchs Yale U Lib 58-63; Libn E Windham Col 63-64; Ref libn Central Mass Reg Lib Syst, Worcester Mass 64-66; Libn Norton Co 66-68; Asst libn Worcester State Col 69-. 9: ALA-ACRL; MassLA. 12: Poetry & prose publ in var journals & anthologies. 14: Acquis. 15: 6 Church st, Grafton Ma 01519.

ROBIN, FLORENCE (KESSLER). b Montreal Can 2 Je 38. 4: Ronald D Robin. 5: UCLA 56-60 (Eng) BA; USoCal 64-65 (LS) MS. 6: Fr. 7: Libn Los Angeles City Schs 68-. 9: Phi Kappa Phi. 14: Ya serv. 15: 12312 Erwin st, N Hollywood Ca 91606.

ROBINS, NORA DIANA SHEPHERD. b Scotland 17 Ag 40. 5: Mariananopolis Col (Montreal) 58-61 (Hist) BA (magna cum laude); McGill 62 BLS. 6: Fr. 7: Catlg libn Vanier Lib Loyola Col (Montreal) 62-, Hd catlg 66-. 8: Lectr in lib sci Loyola Col (Montreal) even div 68. 9: QueLA; CanLA. 14: Catlg, microfilms. 15: 5120 W Broadway, Montreal 29 Can.

ROBINSON, ADA VIOLETA (MARTINEZ). b Santurce PR 9 Ag 37. 4: Neil Robinson. 5: UPR 58 9sociol) BA; Simmons 59 (LS) MS. 6: Sp. 7: Tchr PR High Sch of Commerce, Rio Piedras 57; Asst libn PR Jr Col (Rio Piedras) 59, Libn 62, Dir Learning Resources Ctr 68-. 8: Dir & Instr Lib Tech Program PR Jr Col 67. 9: ALA (reg coord Jr Col Libs in PR); Sociedad de Bibliotecarios de PR (Bd Dir 68-; coord Nat Lib Week in San Juan Area 68). 14: Admin. 15: GPO Box AE, Rio Piedras PR 00928.

ROBINSON, ALICE LUCILE. b E Cleveland Ohio 7 My 12. 5: Baldwin-Wallace Col 30-34 (Educ, Eng) AB; West Res 40 BS in LS, 52 (Educ) MA. 7: Tchr, Medina Co Ohio 34-36; Tchr, Akron Ohio 36-38; Sch libn, Cleveland Heights Ohio 38-48; Supv of Lib Serv, Montgomery Co Md 48-57; Supv of Instr Materials Centers Bd of Educ Frederick Co, Md 57-. 8: Tchr, summer sessions, UMd & Gallaudet Col. 9: ALA (Coun 65-); -AASchL (chm Groiler Awards Com 64);-CSD (Bd);-YASD (Bd); NEA; Assn for Supv & Curr DEVEL: Assn Childhood Educ Internat; MdLA (pres 64-65); ASchL Md (pres 50); Md Assn for Supv & Curr Devel (v-pres 57); Md State Tchrs Assn. 10: Delta Kappa Gamma. 12: Co-comp "Bibliography of Books for Children (58). 13: Yes. 14: Sch lib serv. 15: Frederick Co Bd of Educ, 115 E Church st, Frederick Md 21701.

ROBINSON, ALYCE (SHEPPARD). b Seguin Tex 19 Je 23. 4: Thomas W Robinson. 5: St Philips Col 40-42 (Educ) AA; Prairie View U summers 42, 43 (Bus Educ); Fisk U summers 44-46; Geneseo State Tchrs Col 47-49 (Educ) BS; USoCal 57-59 MSLS. 6: Sp. 7: Lib clerk St Philips Jr Col 43-45, Libn 45-47 Order, circ, ref libn NJ Col for Women 49-51; USoCal: Ser libn I 51-53, Catlg libn I 53-55, Act head educ libn ii 55-57; Educ libn II Cal State Col (Los Angeles) 58-65, Educ ,libn III 65-, Ref libn III 69-. 8: Telecourse lecturer for lib orient course, Cal State Col (Los Angelee) 63-; Mem Cal State Col Speakers Bur; Mem Adv Com of Los Angeles SW Col. 9: CalLA (Coord Hospitality Com 64); Cal Tchrs Assn; Cal Col & Univ Faculty Assn (v-pres Los Angeles Chap 69-70). 10: Kappa Delta Pi; Nat Assn Col twomen; Cal Cols & Univ Faculty Assn; Assn Cal State Col Profs; Libraria Sodalitas; USoCalSch of Lib Sci Alumni Assn; Urban League; Delta Sigma Theta; Greater Crenshaw Symphony Assn; USoCal Faculty Womens Assn; USoCal LIB Staff Assn; Acad Senate Cal State Los Angeles 68-69. 11: John Cotton Dana Publicity Award, 68. 13: Yes. 14: Instr in use of lib, ref, catlg. 15: 3824 Dublin ave, Los Angeles 90008.

ROBINSON, BARRIE JOHN. b Cornwall Ont Can 30 My 26. 5: Toronto 45-47 Bio-Chem Leeds U 48-49 (Textiles); Sir George Williams U 50-51 BS; McGill 63-64 BLS. 6: Fr. 7. Tech writer RCA Victor Montreal 51-56; High sch tchr-libn No Essex Sch, Windsor Ont 58-63; Lib Dir Warren Mem Lib, Massena NY65-. 66, Ref coord Mid York Lib Syst, Utica NY 66-67; Reg libn Lake Ontario Reg Lib, Kingston Ont Can 67-. 9: ALA; CanLA; OntLA; Inst Prof Libns Ont; N Country Ref Research Resources oun; KingstonAreaLA. 10: Soc of Genealogists; 13: Yes. 14: Arch & plans. 15: 411 2nd st E, Cornwall Ont Can.

ROBINSON, CHARLES W(ELD). b Peking China 27 F 28. 4: Martha Ann Rowley. 5: Colby Col 46-50 (Hist, Govt, Econ) AB; Simmons 50-51 (LS) MS. 7: (Sgt) Personnel Mgt US Army, Korea 51-53; Libn I Free Lib of Phila 53-56; Admin asst to dir 56-59; Baltimore Co Pub Lib, Towson Md; Asst co libn 59-61, Assoc co libn 61-63, Dir 63-. 9: ALA; MdLA. 13: Yes. 14: Pub Lib admin. 15: Baltimore Co Pub Lib, 25 W Chesapeake ave, Towson Md 2204.

ROBINSON, EDNA FERGUSON (McADAM). b Custer Co SD '(S 20. 405: Harry L Robinson. 4: Harry L Robinson. 5: Ark A&M Col 38-42 (Lang, Lit) summer 40; UUtah 55-63; Black Hill State 66; Cal State (Los Angeles) 67; UCal 67-69. 6: Fr. 7: Tchr-libn Deadwood High Deadwood DDWOOD SD 44-56; Libn Sheridan High Sheridan SHSheridan Wyo 56-57; Libn Deadwood City Lib, Deadwood SD 57-59; Tchr Douglas Sch System, Ellsworth AFB SD 59-61; Libn Deadwood High Sch, Deadwood SD 61-65; Libn Bloomington High Sch, Bloomington Cal 65-. 8: Eval wk for "World Book Encyclopedia on SD & on Theodore Roosevelt, 64. 9: NEA; ALA; CalEA; SD Sch Libns (past pres West Div). 10: Delta Kappa Gamma; Beta Sigma Phi. 14: Adolescent readers. 15: 38 Denver ave, Deadwood SD 57732.

ROBINSON, ELIZABETH ANNE (KOCH). b NYC 8 Mr 29. 4: Atlee William Robinson. 5: Hope Col 46-50 (Biol, Chem) BA; Rutgers 50-52 (Bacteriology) MS, 52-53 (Zool). 7: Research asst immunohematology dept Ortho Research Found, Roriton NJ 51-55; Indexer Lib Squibb Inst Med Res, New Brunswick NJ 59; Lib asst Mem Med Lib Miami Valley Hosp, Dayton Ohio 61-66; Libn Barney Child Med Ctr, Dayton Ohio 66-. 9: SLA; MedLA. 14: Indexing, drug info, ser. 15: 3306 Harvard blvd, Dayton Ohio 45406.

ROBINSON, ETHEL L(OUISE). b Cleveland Ohio 9 F 26. 5: Cleveland State U 44-48 (Math, Chem) BS; West Res 48-49 MS in LS, 51-56 (Eng lit). 7: Cleveland Pub Lib: Asst sci & tech dept 49-54, Asst order dept ser 54-64, Asst dept hd gen ref 64-68, Dept hd gen ref 68-. 9: ALA; OhioLA. 10: Woman's Nat Bk Assn. 14: Pub lib, ref. 15: 3181 Woodlawn dr, Parma Oh 44134.

ROBINSON, EVELYN L. b Greenville NH 7 My 22. 5: Mary Washington Col UVa 41-45 (Phys Educ) BA; USoCal 45-46 (Educ) MS; UDenver 60-61 (LS) MA. 7: Asst Prof San Diego State Col 46-50; Recreation supv Dept of Army Spec Serv, Overseas 50-60; Br libn DIA, Ft Bliss Tex 60-62; Spec serv recruiter DIA; Wash DC 62-63; Asst chief reader serv The Army Lib, Wash DC 64-68, Ref asst 68-. 8: Surveyed efficiency of Army br lib 67. 9: ALA; DCLA. 14: Military ref. 15: 1201 S Courthouse rd apt 636, Arlington Va 22204.

ROBINSON, EVELYN ROSE. b Boston 15 Mr 09. 5: Columbia summers 40-44, 45 (LS); Boston U 45-50 (Eng) BS, 50-51 (Eng) Ed M, 59-62 (Eng) Ed D. 6: Fr. 7: Asst jr & sr Somerville Pub Lib, Somerville Mass 28-30; Child & sch libn Sch Lib Supv, Andover Mass 30-45; Sch libn Brockton High Sch, Brockton Mass 45-50; Lib consul sch & pub lib Mass Div of Lib Ext, Boston 51-54; Asst Prof Lib Sci State U (Albany NY) 54-56; Lecturer, Instr Lib Educ Queens Col (NY) 59-56; Lecturer in Eng Educ Boston U 59-60; Visiting Lecturer Educ & Psych Wheaton Col (Mass) 60-61; Asst Prof Lib Sci So Conn State Col 62-65, Assoc Prof 65-68, Dir Div of Lib Sci 68-. 9: NEA; ALA (Coun); -AASchL (By-Laws Com); Amer Educ Research Assn; NCTE (Com on Certif & Prep of Tchrs 62-); NELA; NESchLA (past sec, mem Recr Com); NE Sch Devel Coun; MassLA; ConnLA; ConnSchLA (Recr Chm); ConnEA. 10: LWV; Can-Amer Women's Assn; AAUW; AAUP; Engl-Speaking Union; Pi Lambda Theta. 12: "Readings About Children's Literature" (66). 13: Yes. 14: Child & yp lit, sch lib, hist of bks & printing. 15: So Conn State Col, 501 Crescent, New Haven Conn 06515.

ROBINSON, GENEVA JOAN. b Shawsville Md 14 Ap 28. 5: Maryville Col 45-49 (Eng) BA; Pratt 49-50 MLS. 7: Asst libn central circ NY Pub Lib 50-52, Asst br libn High Bridge Br 52-56; Br libn Towson Br Baltimore Co Pub Lib, Towson Md

56-61, Area br libn Towson Br & Bkmob Hdqrs 61-70; Coord of adult serv, Baltimore Co 70-. 8: Dir, Lib Aide Train Program, Baltimore Co Pub Lib, 64-65. 9: ALA (Round Table on Lib Serv to the Blind; Friends of Lib Com); -PLA;-RSD (Md Chap); MdLA (chm Constit & Bylaws Com 64-65, Intel Freedom Com: 65-, chm 68-69). 10: Baltimore Co Hist Soc; Women's Club of Towson; Pi Kappa Delta. 14: Ref. 15: 903 Dulaney Valley ct, Towson Md 21204.

ROBINSON, JANE ELIZABETH. b Pittsburgh Penn 13 Mr 15. 5: Wilson Col 33-37 (Hist) AB; Carnegie 37-38 BS in LS. 6: Fr, Ger. 7: Carnegie Lib of Pittsburgh, catlgr 38-39, continuations catlgr 39-42, tech catlgr 42-51, Sr catlgr 51-59, Libn sci & tech dept 60-66; Hd catlg dept Falk Lib of Health Prof UPittsburgh 66-. 9: ALA-ACRL (Tri-State Chap); SLA (sec-treas & dir Pittsburgh Chap); PennLA; MedLA. 14: Catlg, clsf, ref, admin. 15: 303 Fieldbrook dr, Pittsburgh Pa 15228.

ROBINSON, LAURIE (RICHMOND). b El Paso Tex 11 O 25. 05. UTex (El Paso) 42-46 (Sp) BA; UDenver 59-60 (Libnship) MA. 6: Sp, Fr, Ger. 7: San Diego State Col: Libn I 60-61, libn II 61-64, Libn III 64-68, Libn IV 68-. 9: SLA; CalLA. 14: Acquis, Latin-Amer materials. 15: 5135 Bixel dr, San Diego Ca 92115.

ROBINSON, LOUISA (SMITH). b Orangeburg SC. 4: Harold I Robinson. 5: SC State Col (Eng) AB; Atlanta BS in LS; UMich 50-51 AM in LS. 7: Libn Allen U; Libn Claflin Col 55-. 9: ALA; SCLA; SELA. 14: Admin. 15: 415 Blvd NE, Orangeburg SC 29115.

ROBINSON, LYNN H. b Morrisville NY 17S19. 5: St Johns Col (Md) 45-49 (Liberal Arts) BA; State U (Albany NY) 53-54 MSLS; State of NY Pub Lib Certif. 7: US Army 40-45; US Air Force 49-52; Adult consul Reg Lib Serv Center, Watertown NY 54-57; Ref libn Maritime Col (bronx NY) 57-62; Ref coordinator Suffolk Coop Lib System, Patchogue NY 62-67; Prin pub lib coord Providence Pub Lib, Providence RI 67-68; Assoc libn Wentworth Inst, Boston 68-69, Libn 69-. 8: Mem spec ALA Com to Select Basic Ref Bklist for Small & Medium-sized Libs. 9: ALA; NYLA; Suffolk Co LA. 14 Readers serv, ref, automated methods of info retrieval. 15: PO Box 377, Brookhaven NY 11719.

ROBINSON, MARGARET M(OREHOUSE). b Boyne City Mich 5N06. 5: East Mich U 14-28 (Hist) AB, Life certif; UMich 34 (Hist, Pol Sci) MA, 52 MLS.43179 6: Fr. 7: High sch hist tchr & libn Pub Sch, Dundee Mich 28-37; Supv of lib Practice Roosevelt Lab Sch, Ypsilanti Mich 37-52; Seattle Pub Lib summer 48; West Wash Col of Educ summers 49, 50, 52, Assoc Prof in chg Lib Sci East Mich U 52-68; Consul 68-. 9: ALA-CSD-RTSD-PLA-LED; Mem var coms -AASchL; Publs Com 6 yrs; MichEA; MichASchL; (pres 61-62); MichLA; RCR Com. 10: YWCA; Amer Contract Bridge League; Delta Sigma Theta; Pi Gamma Mu; Denver Pub Lib & Schs Jt Coun; Denver Pub Lib Staff Assn; Metro Coun Com. 12: "The School Library Budget 2nd ed 68; "Effective Use of Student Assistants in a Secondary Materials Center (64); Ed "Stars to Steer By Mich ASchL; Ed "Forward MichASchL (52-58). 14: Lib educ, recr, rare bks. 15: 944 Sheridan ave, Ypsilanti Mich 48197.

ROBINSON, MARILOU (O'CONNOR). b Klamath Falls Ore 1 Ag 28. 4: L W Robinson. 5: Mt St Mary's Col 47-52 (Eng-Educ) BA; DenverU 53-54 (LS) MA. 7: Tchr Sacred Heart Acad, Klamath Falls Ore 52-53; Asst libn Klamath Union High Sch, Klamath Falls Ore 54-60, Hd libn 60-68; Asst educ libn Portland StateU 68-. 9: NEA; OreEA. 10: AAUW; Delta Kappa Gamma; Delta Epsilon Sigma. 14: Educ, sch libs. 15: 133 Grant st, Klamath Falls Or 97601.

ROBINSON, SISTER MARY VERENA PHJC. b South Bend Ind 25 J 08. 5: DePaulU summers 32-45 (Eng) BA; Rosary Col summers 47-52 MALS; Ancilla Domini Col summer 63. 6: Ger. 7: Elem tchr: St Vincent Villa, Ft Wayne Ind 32-33, St Henry Sch, Chicago 33-39; Tchr & libn; Chicago: Angel Guardian High Sch 39-47, St Augustine High Sch 45-. 8: Adv Bd Catholic Assn of Stud Libns of Ill, Chicago 63-64, 65-66, 68-69; Catlg of Med Lib in Gary Hosp; Org child libs in other city schs. 9: ALA; CathLA; NCTE; High Sch Libns of Chicagoland. 10: Catholic Assn of Eng Tchrs; Drama Tchrs Assn of Chicago. 14: Reading guidance & ref, wl with teenagers, org child libs. 15: 5019 South Laflin st, Chicago Il 60609.

ROBINSON, NANCY DURE. b Auburntown Tenn 9 Ag 30. 5: Carson-Newman Col 49-53 (Eng) AB; Peabody 53-54 MA LS. 6: Sp. 7: Catlg libn So Baptist Theol Sem (Louisville Ky) 54-. 9: Atheolla. 14: Catlg. 15: 2825 Lexington rd, Louiville Ky 40206.

ROBINSON, NORMA M. b Crandall Ga 27 F 12. 4: Hubert Powers Robinson. 5: Berea Col 30-34 Bio AB; Peabody Col 37-38 BS in LS; UFla 49, 57 (Educ, AV); Fla StateU 57 (Lib Supv Wkshop). 6: Fr. 7: Tchr-libn The Montverde Sch, Montverde Fla 34-37, Libn 47-49; Ser libn Berea Col 42-44; Catlgr Leg & Law Lib, Frankfort Ky 45-46; Tchr Palatka High Sch, Palatka Fla 49-51; Libn Palatka Jr High Sch, Palatka Fla 51-59; Supervising libn St Johns River Jr Col, Palatka Fla 58-59, Dir of lib serv 59-. 8: Tchr of Lib Sci Berea Col 44. 9: NEA; Amer Assn Higher Educ; Fla Assn Sch Libns; FlaLA; FlaEA; CatlgrRT (Fla). 10: AAUW PutnamCoClrTA. 14: Catlg, ser, acquis. 15: 2314 Gillis st, Palatka Fl 32077.

ROBINSON, OLIVIA JUANITA. b Quincy Fla 15 Ag 32. 5: Fla A&M U 49-52 (Elem Educ) BS. Certif in Lib Sci. 54-61 (Elem Educ) M Ed; UDenver 60, 65 (LS); Trenton State Col summers of 67, 68. 6: Fr. 7: Tchr Gadsden Co, Quincy Fla 53-55, Libn 55-67; Cove Elem Sch, Panama City Fla 67-. 9: NEA; FlaLA (Planning Com 65-66; FlaASchL; Fla A-v Assn. 10: Zeta Phi Beta; Friends Club; Good Shepherds; IAARU; NAACP. 14: Ref, catlg. 15: PO Box 855, Quincy Fl 32351.

ROBINSON, PAULINE (SHORT). b Hugo Okla 31 Ja 17. 4: Howard Osborne Robinson. 5: UDenver 35-38, 41-42 (Hist, Educ) AB, 42-43, summer 44 BS in LS; Columbia summer 64. 6: Sp. 7: Denver Pub Lib: Br libn Commun Vocat Center 43-54, Head Warren Br 54-64, Coord, Child Serv 64-. 8: Libn Cal State Dept of Health, San Francisco 44-45; Chm Denver Pub Lib Vacation Reading Program & Cons for Metro Vacation Reading Program, 62-. 10: YWCA; Amer Contract Bridge League; Delta Sigma Theta; Pi Gamma Mu; Denver Pub Lib & Schs Jt Coun; Denver Pub Lib Staff Assn; Metro Coun Com. 14: Child serv, ref. 15: Denver Pub Lib, 1357 Broadway, Denver 80203.

ROBINSON, RAE F. b White Plains NY 4 Je 25. 5: Middlebury Col summer 43; Barnard 43-44, 45-48 (Amer Hist) AB; Colubia 49-50 (LS) MS.06: Sp, Fr. 7: Res desk asst Barnard Col 48-49; catlgr asst to libn Hunter Col 50-58, Asst Prof; Head catlgr 59-. 9: ALA; NY Tech Serv Libns; Lib Assn NYC. ; NY Lib Club. 10: No Broadway Assn, White Plains NY; AAUP. 14: Catlg. 15: 68 Beech st, Westmnister Ridge, White Plains NY 10604.

ROBINSON, ROBERT ARTHUR (JAMES). b Williamsport Penn 11 S 15. 5: Chicago 34-39 (Psych) BS; UPenn 45-46 (Psych) MA; Temple 50-51 (Educ); UCal 57-59 MLS. 6: Fr, Ger. 7: Lib asst circ Educ Lib UChicago 35-37; US Navy Ensign & Lt(jg) 41, 42-44; US Army 41-42; Asst in Psych Dept UPenn 45-46 Sub tchr of orthogenic-backward child Barratt Sch, Phila 51-52; Lib asst US Air Force AAG admin ref br, Wash DC 54-56 Sr lib asst UCal(Berkeley) 57-59; Libn II in chg of spec collections dept, bibliogr San Jose S Jose State Lib 59-. 9: CalLA. 10: Cal State Employees Assn; Amer Fed of Tchrs. ; Hist of Sci Soc. 12: Comp Bibliog "Writings of the School of Analytical Psychology, 1928-1958. 133: Yes. 14: Bibliog, catlg, ref, acquis. 15: P O Box 324, San Jose Cal 95116.

ROBINSON, RUTH ANN. b Bryn Mawr Penn 20 N 25. 5: Howard U 43-47 (Clasical Studies) AB; Drexel 50-51 MS in LS. 7: Asst libn St Augusting Col 51-54; Child libn toasst head libn W Oak Lane Br Free Lib of Phila 54-63, Head libn 63-. 9: ALA (Coun 67-70; mem Jaycees Good Reading Adv Com 67-); PennLA. 10: Alum Assn Drexel Inst Lib Sch. 13: Yes. 14: Child serv, admin in pub libs. 15: 673 N Franklin, apt F, Phila 19123.

ROBINSON, SHIRLEY (LEEBRICK). b Honolulu Hawaii 27 Mr 25. 4: Leslie G Robinson. 5: Stanford 43-45 (Pol sci) BA; UHawaii 65-67 MLS. 7: Med libn UHawaii Sch of Med at Leahi Hosp 67-. 9: ALA; HawaiiLA. 10: Beta Phi Mu; Phi Kappa Phi. 14: Ref, med hist. 15: 103 Kaapuni dr, Kailua Hi 96734.

ROBINSON, SHIRLEY ANNE (SPENCER). b Wash DC 24 S 34. 4: Theodore W Robinson. 5: Howard U 51-55 (Eng Lit) BA; Pratt 55-56 MLS; American U 59-60 (eng Lit), DC Tchrs Col 61 (AV Materials); Loyola U (Chicago) 68 (AV Materials). 6: Ger. 7: Ya libn Brooklyn Pub Lib 56-57; Ref libn Howard U 57-60; Libn pub schs, Wash DC 60-62; Libn pub schs, Great falls Mont 62-64; Ref libn Wilmngton Del 64-66; Ref libn Chicago Pub Lib, Chicago 66-68; Libn Pub Schs, Chicago 68-. 9: ALA-AASchL. 10: Phi Beta Kappa; Kappa Delta Pi; Alpha Kappa Alpha; AAUW. 14: Ya wk, ref. 15: 9119 S Cottage Grove ave, Chicago Il 60619.

ROBINSON, THELMA (PHEANIS). b Eaton Ohio 27 Ja 12. 5: miami U 30-34 (Soc Sci) AB; Carnegie 35-36 BS in S; 58

MedLA Certif. 7: Libn-tchr pub schs, W Carrollton Ohio 36-37; Asst loan libn Miami U (Ohio) 37-38, Loan libn 38-42; Lib asst NIH, Bethesda Md 49-51, Asst circ libn 51-58, Circ libn 58-62; Head Tech Ref Lib US Naval Med Res Inst, Nat Naval Med Center, Bethesda Md 62-. 9: MedLA; SLA. 10: AAUW; Wash Soc Hist of Med. 14: Admin, circ. 15: 7908 Sleaford pl, Bethesda Md 20014.

ROBINSON, VERNA COTTEN. b Enfield NC 6 O 27. 4: Elbert C Robinson. 5: NC Col 44-48 (Gen Sci) BS; Carnegie 48-50 MSLS. 6: Fr, Dutch. 7: Blyden Br Libn Norfolk Pub Lib, Norfolk Va 50-51; Ser libn Howard U Lib 51-52; Sch libn Spingarn High Sch, Wash DC 52-53; Sch libn Cardozo High Sch, Wash DC 55-60; Sch libn Roosevelt High Sch, Wash DC 60-67. 9: ALA; DCLA; AASL, DCASchL (Sec 60-62). 10: Delta Sigma Theta Amer Womens Club of The Hague. 14: Sch lib wk, educational technology. 15: American Embassy, APO NY 09159.

ROBINSON, WILLIAM CHANDLER. b Bakersfield Cal 25 O 39. 4: Jean Reif Robinson. 5: Claremont Mens Col 57-61 (Intenat Rel) BA; Fletcher Sch of Law & Diplomacy 61-62 (Internat Rel) MA; USoCal 63-64 (LS) MS; UIll 67- (LS). 6: Fr. 7: Admin asst USoCal Lib 64-65, Act world affairs libn 65-66, Hd World Affairs Lib 66-67; Personnel lib specialist US Army Res SPSES 62-68. 9: ALA. 10: Beta Phi Mu. 14: Educ for libnship, soc sci bibliog, publish, lib admin. 15: 1601 B2 Valley rd, Champaign Il 61820.

ROBINTON, HERMANN FREDERICK. b NYC 20 Ap 07. 4: Madeline Russell. 5: London Sch of Econ 29-30 (Hist) Certif UHeidelberg 30 JHist); LIU 31-32 (Hist) BA (cum laude); Columbia 32-39 (Hist), 52-54 MS in LS. 6: Gr. Fr, Sp. 7: Instr Hist Dept City Col (NY) even, summers 33-41; Asst reg dir & dir Survey of Fed Archives in NYC & LI, wPA 36-38; Sr analyst records mgt Off of the Compt, NYC 41-42; Deputy of the Nat Archivist NY State NYState 44-47; NY State Supv of Pub Records State Educ Dept, Albany NY 42-47; Asst sec NY State Freedom Train Commsn 48-50; Admin asst to the NY state libn & asst commsnr for libs NY State Lib State Educ Defense 47-52; Defese welfare coord, Inquiry & Inquiy Serv, Defense Welfare Serv State Dept of Soc Welfare Civil State Civl DEFENSE Commsn, NYC 52-56; Lib Dir II Seaford Pub Lib, Seaford LI NY 56-64; Curator Schs of Bus Libs, NYU 64-. 9: ALA-CRL; etc; NYLA; etc. 10: Beta Phi Mu. 11: NY State Merit Award, SAR. 13: Yes. 14: Admin, labor archives, etc. 15: 202 Columbia Hts, Brooklyn NY 11201.

ROBISON, CAROLYN LOVE. b Orlinda Tenn 9 Ag 40. 5: Dickinson Col 58-60 (Eng); Denison U 60-62 (eng) BA; Emory 64-65 MLibn. 6: Fr, Sp. 7: Tchr Dag Hammarskjold Jr High Sch, Wallingford Conn 62-64; Asst libn Sch of Arch Ga Inst of Tech 65-67; Hd circ Ga State Col Lib 67-. 9: GaLA; SELA. 14: Ref. 15: 3415 Roswell rd NE, Apt 4, Atlanta Ga 30305.

ROBISON, DENNIS EDGAR. b Ft Wayne Ind 6 D 34. 4: Louise McCaughan Robison. 5: St Petersburg Jr Col 57-58 (Soc Sci); Fla State U 58-60 (Soc Sci) BS, 60-62 (LS) MS; USFla 66-69 (Soc Sci Educ) MA. 6: Fr. 7: Fire control tech USAF (S/Sgt) 53-57; Grad asst Fla State U Lib 60-62; Asst ref libn USoFla 62-66, Ref libn 67-. 9: ALA; SELA; FlaLA (chm Ref RT 67-68; treas 67-70). 10: Phi Alpha Theta; Beta Phi Mu. 14: Ref. 15: 1548 81st ave No, St Petersburg Fla 33702.

ROBISON, JUANITA F(AYE) (FRIEND). b Columbus Ohio 25 Mr 14. 4: Thomas D Robison. 5: Ohio State U 31-35 (Eng) BA; West Res 35-36 BSLS. 6: Fr, Ger. 7: Ref libn Ohio State Lib 36-40; WPA supv Fed Govt, Cincinnati 40-41; Catlgr Cincinnati Pub Lib 41; Libn Luke Field Air Corps, Phoenix 41-43; Ref libn Ohio State Lib 54; Head catlgr Phoenix Pub Lib 55-69, Coord tech serv 69-. 9: ALA; Ariz State LA; SWLA; Salt River ValleyLA. 14: Catlg. 15: 315 W Cambridge, Phoenix Az 85003.

ROBOTHAM, JOHN STANLEY. b Concord NH 12 F 24. 4: Alice Wheeler. 5: City Col (NY) 46-49 (Foreign Trade) BA; Columbia 49-51 (LS) MS. 7: NY Pub Lib: Staff 50-52, Asst br libn 52-55, libn 55-65, Adult spec 65-. 9: NYLA. 14: Pub lib adult wk. 15: 74 Ardsley st, SI NY 10306.

ROBSON, JOHN MERRITT. b Gordon Neb 22 S 30. 4: Kathryn Baker. 5: UNeb 48-53 (Eng) BS, 55-58 (Eng); UDenver 58-59 (Libnship) MA; UMinn 63-66 (Educ). 7: Platoon leader US Army 53-55; Tchg asst UNeb 56-58; Lib asst Lincoln Pub Lib, Lincoln Neb 57-58; Lib asst UDenver Lib 58-59; Catlgr US Air Force Acad 59-61; Catlgr-acquis St Cloud State Col 61-66; Head libn SW Minn State Col 66-. 9: ALA; MinnLA (Steering Com Nat Lib eek 65); Midwest Acad Libns Conf. 10: AAUP; Minn Interfac Org. 14: Col lib admin. 15: 903 Birch st, Marshall Mn 56258.

ROBSON, LINDA (KEENAN). b Jersey City NJ 19 Mr 35. 4: John Leonard Robson. 5: UCal (Berkeley) 54-57, 60-62 (Hist) AB, MLS. 6: Fr. 7: Acquis bibliogr UCal (Berkeley) 62-63; Asst ref libn Denver Pub Lib 64; Asst ref libn Cornell U Libs 67-68; Soc sci ref libn UNC (Chapel Hill) 68-. 9: ALA. 14: Ref. 15: 204 Glenburnie st, Chapel Hill NC 27514.

ROCHE, DOROTHY (MANCINI). b NYC 22 24 D 12. 5: Marywood Col 29-33 (Eng, Ital, Soc Studies) AB; Columbia summer 37; Marywood Col 37-39 (Ital) MA; U Scranton summer 59, 61, 63 (Educ); Montclair State Col 63 (Reading, Supv). 6: Ital. 7: Libn Boys Club, Scranton Penn 33-34: Tchr Old Forge High Sch, Old Forge Penn 34-43; Tchr Shawnee High Sch, Shawnee Okla 43-44; Catlgr-lang UNC (Chapel Hill) 43; Catlgr Cornell U 44; Libn Havre de Grace High Sch, Havre de Grace Md 4647; Libn Belleville High Sch, Belleville NJ 53-. 8: Lib consul for Pub Lib in Old Forge Penn 66. 9: ALA; NEA (Life mem); NJSchLA; NJEA. 10: Civic Womens Club; Theatre Group; Essex Co Sch Libns. 12: Wilson "Bulletin April 57. 13: Yes. 14: High sch child. 15: 322 Kingsland ave, Lyndhurst NJ 07071.

ROCHELL, CARLTON (CHARLES). b Lawrenceburg Tenn 2 N 33. 4: Rebecca Ridley. 5: Peabody 57-59 (Math) BS; Fla State U 60-61 MS(LS). 7: US Navy (SO-2) 1 yr of electronics sch 53-57; Ref asst Nashville Pub Lib 57-59, Spec asst to Dir 59; Dir Hattiesburg-Forrest Co (Miss) Pub Lib 61-63; Dir Anniston-Calhoun Co (Ala); (Ala) Pub Lib 63-65; Dir Knoxville & Knox Co Pub Lib, Knoxville Tenn 65-67; Dir Atlanta Pub Lib 68-. 8: Consul, Title IVA & IVB Tenn State Lib 67, 68; Chm Spec Com to Study Lib Serv to Atlanta Metro Area, Metro Atlanta Coun on Govts. 9: ALA (Mem Award Com, Lippincott Jury Com, Interlib Coop Com); SELA (Loc Arrangts Com 70); GaLA. 10: C of C; Atlanta Model Cities Prog. 13: Yes. 14: Admin, serv to underprivileged, systems approaches to lib serv. 15: 126 Carnegie Way NW, Atlanta Ga 30303.

ROCHLIN, PHILLIP. b NYC 24 Mr 23. 4: Ruth Munt. 5: City Col (NY) 39-43 (Chem) BS; NYU 44-49(Chem) MS: Rutgers 57-60 MLS. 7: Purser, Pharm Mate (Ensign USMS) US Maritme Serv & Merchant Marine 45-47; Phys chem Pica-tinny Arsenal, Dover NJ 50-63; Sci analyst, engnr spec Nat Referral Center for Sci & Tech LC 63; Supv chem, Head Tech Lib US Naval Propellant Plant, Indian Head Md 63-. 9: SLA; Documentation & Transportation Divs); ACS; Div of Chem Lit; ASIS. 12: Ed Philatelic Literature Review (56-60); Comp "A Biblography of Recent General Books on Stamp and Coin Collecting and the Postal Seevice (58). 13: Yes. 14: Documentation, info retrieval, explosives & propellants. 15: Rte 1 Box 835, Accokeek Md 20607.

ROCKER, JANET ELAINE. b Pontiac Mich 25 Ag 37. 5: Fla So Col 56-60 (HIST) BA; West Res 60-61 MS in LS. 6: Sp. 7: Sec Bowen Heater Div, Wixom Mich 55-56; Asst libn Ferris State Col 61-64; Asst Prof of Lib Sci Central Mich U 64-. 9: MichLA. 10: Pi Gamma Mu; Kappa Pi; Phi Delta Gamma; Sigma Tau Delta; Mich Hist Soc; 4-H Club; Pere Margqette Artists & CRAFTSMEN. 14: Catlg, tchg lib sci, mus libnship. 15: Lib Central Mich Univ Lib, Mt Pleasant Mi 48858.

ROCKWELL, FORD A. b St Johnsville NY 20 O 07. 4: Barbara Hosmer. 5: Syracuse 31 (Lit, Hist) BA, 37 SLS. 7: Br libn Hartford Pub Lib, Hartford Conn 37-40; Head libn Thrall Mem Lib, Middletown NY 40-43; Asst libn Hartford Pub Lib, Hartford Conn 43-48; Head libn Wichita Pub Lib, Wichita Kan 48-. 8: Ins dept for Libnship, Kan State Tchrs Col 60-, Syracuse; SNH of Lib sci summers 60 & 65. 9: ALA; KanL (pres 60); MPLA (pres 61), 10: Rotary. 12: "Pirates & Piracy in Comptons Pictured Encyclopedia"; "Pirates & Piracy in Americana Encyclopedia; 2 different articles; Ed Mountain-Plains Library Quarterly 60-. 13: Yes. 14: Pub lib admin. , tchg. 15: Wichita Pub Lib, 220 S Main, Wichita Kan 67202.

ROCKWELL, JEANETTE (SLEDGE). b Spokane Wash. 4: David Rockwell. 5: UCal (Berkeley) 37 (Eng) AB; Columbia 38 BLS; NYU 64-65 (Syst Analysis). 7: Child libn NY Pub Lib & Lib of Hawaii 38-41; Base command libn West Pacific Base Command 42-46; Research libn Compton Advertising Co, NYC 46-49; Chief libn Nat Industrial Conf Bd, NYC 49-56; Chief libn Standard Vacuum Oil Co, White Plains NY 56-60; Lib mgr IBM Corp, Yorktown Hts NY 60-61; Mgr lib serv McKinsey & Co 62-68; Lib & lib mkting consul L-J-R Assoc, wellesley Mass 68-. 9: SLA (ed com 62-64, in charge of exhibit, Internat Mgt Cong 63); ALA; NY Lib Club. 13: Yes. 14: Lib planning & equip sel, info stor retr and automated procedures, lib admin, ref. 15: 24 Birch rd, Wellesley Ma 02181.

ROCKWOOD, RUTH (HUMISTON). b Chicago 15 O 06. 5: Wellesley Col 27 (Eng) AB; UIll 49 (LS) MS; Ind U 60 (Higher Educ) Ed D. 7: Br asst Chicago Pub Lib 28; Libn Cook Co Hosp Sub-Br, Chicago 28-29; Libn Buxton Country Day CH, Short Hills NJ 37-39; Admin asst & INTR UIll Lib Sch 49-50; Libn Union Browsing Rm, Urbana Ill 50-53; Visiting Lecturer Lib Sch Fla State tate U summer 52; Fulbright Lecturer in Lib Sci Chulalongkorn U (Bangkok Thailand) 52-53; Instr Fla State U Lib Sch 52-56, Asst Prof 56-61; Visiting Asst Prof Ind U Lib Sch 58-59; Assoc Prof Fla State U Lib Sch 61-68, Prof 68-. 8: Fulbright lecturer in lib sci, Chulalongkorn U, Bangkok, Thailand, 52-53; Consul Leon Co (Fla) Pub Lib, 55-56. 9: ALA; AALS; SELA; FlaLA (past pres). 10: AAUP; Beta Phi Mu; Pilot Club. 11: Fulbright Award. 12: Ed "ILA Record (50-52). 13: Yes. 14: Pub lib serv, catlg, adult serv. 15: Lib Sch Fla State Univ, Tallahassee Fla 32306.

ROCKWOOD, RUTH (LINDSLEY). b Orange NJ 2 S 18. 4: Robert Bruce Rockwood. 5: Vassar Col 36-40 (Eng) BA; Columbia 41-42 BS in LS; Upsala Col 53 (N Hist); Rutgers 61 (LS). 6: Fr. 7: Asst child libn NY Pub Lib 40-41; Child libn Pub Libn E Orange NJ 42-46, 50-51, 56-57; Dir Livingston Free Pub Lib, Livingston NJ 57-. 8: Essex Co (NJ) Educ & AV Aids Com, 59-; Consul, Livingston Adult Sch, 59-. 9: ALA; SLA; NJLA (chm Resol Com 64-65; corres sec 68-69). 10: Co-founder, Friends of the Livingston Lib, 59. 13: Yes. 14: Child bks, Jerseyana & loc hist. 15: 4 Essex ct, Livingston NJ 07039.

ROCOURT, M(ARY) EILEEN (CHAPPELL). b Toronto Can 18 D 22. 4: Hector Georges Rocourt. 5: Victoria Col UToronto 40-44 (Modern Langs) BA; Columbia 44-46 (PUB Law, Govt) MA. 6: FR, Sp, Ger, Ital, Portu. 7: Tr First Nat Bank of Chicago 48; Assoc libn Chicago Nat Hist Mus 48-63; Prof asst catlg Deering Lib Northwestern U 64-. 9: SLA (v-chm Museums Div 58-60); IllLA. 14: Ser, binding. 15: 734 Noyes st, Evanston Il 60201.

ROD, DONALD OLAF. b Roland Iowa 14 Jl 15. 4: Elsie Siemers. 5: Luther Col 34-38 (Lat) AB; UMich 38-40 ABLS; Chicago 40- (LS). 7: Catlg asst UMich Libs 38-40; Asst libn Luther Col 40-43; Hd libn Augustana Col (Rock Island Ill) 43-53; Dir lib serv & hd Dept Lib Sci U No Iowa 53-. 8: Spec consul, Brigham Young U Lib, 56-58; Lib bldgs consul; Sioux Falls Col 61-64, Buena Vista Col 62-65, Southeast Mo State Col 65-, Wis State U (River Falls) 65, Dordt Col 65-, & others; Surveys of libs at Wayne State Col 63 & Southeast Mo State Col 64-65. 9: ALA (Coun 61-65); IowaLA (pres 58-59). 10: AAUP; Kiwanis Internat. 11: Travelling Fellowship to Europe, ALA, 47. 13: Yes. 14: Col & univ lib admin, lib bldgs, tchg. 15: State Col of Iowa Lib, Cedar Falls Ia 50613.

RODDY, MARION (VORCE). b Detroit 25 Mr 24. 4: Arthur A Roddy. 5: Mich State U 42-46 (Fr) BA; UWis 46-47 BLS; Marylhurst Col 65. 6: Fr, Ger, Sp. 7: Circ Mich State U Lib summers 43-45, Assigned reading room summer 46; Ref libn Hardin-Simmons Col Lib 47 & 48; Sch libn for 3 schs, Grandfalls Tex 49-51; Sub Fr Marycrest High Sch, Portland Ore 66; Self employed Neighborhood Fr Class for Child 63-66; Private tutoring in Fr; Vol wk at Milwaukee Pub Lib. 10: Beta Phi Mu; Tau Sigma; Phi Kappa Phi; Episcopal Soc for Cultural Racial Unity; Milwaukie Friends of the Lib; French Club. 11: Grand Scholarship Award of Mich OES. 14: Ref, child lib wk. 15: 15088 SE Rupet dr, Milwaukie Ore 97222.

RODDY, SISTER RUTH. b Emmitsburg Md 13J110. 5: Villanova U 36-43 (Educ)BS in Ed; Catholic U 52-57 MS in LS. 7: Elem tchr St Charles Sch, Pikesville Md 30-38; Elem tchr Our Lady of Victory, Portsmouth Va 38-43; Jr high sch tchr, St Joseph Home, Phila 43-44; Jr high sch tchr St Martin Sch, Baltimore 44-51; Tch & libn St Paul High Sch, Portsmouth Va 51-59; Libn Norfolk Catholic High Sch, Norfolk Va 59-. 9: ALA; CathLA (Richmond Va) Unit; area chm 65-67, chm 67-69); VaLA; SELA. 14: High sch libn. 15: De Paul Hosp, Granby st & Kingsley ave, Norfolk Va 23505.

RODE, MARIA JANE (GABER). b Vrhnika Yugoslavia 23 Ja37. 4: France Rode. 5: U Ljubljana (Yugoslavia) 56-57 (Fr); Chicago 58 (Fr); Marywood Col 59-61 (LS) MS. 6: Fr, Slovena, Serbo-Croatian, Russian. 7: Ser catlgr John Crerar Lib, Chicago 61-62; Music catlgr Stanford U 62-68, Slavic catlgr 69-. 9: ALA. 10: . 14: Catlg, research, ref. 15: 4067 Solano dr, Palo Alto Cal 94306.

RODELL, ELIZABETH (GOODSON). b Sabine Tex 21 Ja 10. 5: Rice U 27-31 BA, 31-32 (Educ); UDenver summers 38-40 BS in LS; Chicago 46-47 (LS). 7: Libn Kinkaid Prep Sch, Houston 34-42; Catlg asst UChicago 46-47; Catlg asst Rice Inst Lib 47-53; Instr S Tex Col 55-56; Lecturer Fla State U summer 59; Hd catlg dept Rice Lib 53-61; Lecturer UDenver Sch of Libnship summer 61; Exec sec Resources & Tech Serv Div Ala, Chicago 61-68; Asst libn for tech serv Rice U Lib 68-. 9: ALA (Coun 53-57); -RTSD (Nom Com chm 69-70); TexLA. 10: Phi Beta Kappa; Beta Phi Mu. 13: Yes. 14: Catlg, tch, tech serv admin. 15: Rice University Library, PO Box 1892, Houston Tx 77001.

RODGER, ELIZABETH A. b Lanark Ont Can 29 Je 43. 5: Queen's U at Kingston 61-64 (Eng, fr, Relig) BA; UToronto 66-67 BLS. 7: Toronto Pub Lib: Clerical asst 64-66, Libn brs div 67-. 9: CanLA; OntLA. 14: Yp serv, adult serv. 15: 15 Walmer rd apt 307, Toronto 4 Ont Can.

RODGERS, CLARENCE W. b N Platte Neb 20 O 25. 4: Nancy M Pailing. 5: UNeb 55-59 (Econ) BA; Fla State U 62-63 (LS) MS. 6: Sp. 7: HA 1/c US Navy 4346; HM 2/c US Navy 50-55; Data relay manager Sperry &Hutchinson, Lincoln Neb 59-60; Toll collector NJ Trunpike, New Br Solvents, Newark NJ 61-62; Sr libn Queens Borough Pub Li, JamaicNY 63-. 9: ALA (Jr Mems Round Table); NY Tech ServLibns; NY Lib Club. 10: Econ Hist Assn; AAUP; Fla State U Alum Assn; VFW. 15: 485 Front st apt 315, Hempstead NY 11550.

RODGERS, ELMER EDWARD. b Grove City Penn 27 D 24. 4: Patricia Welsh. 5: Youngstown StateU 47-51 (Soc Sci) AB; Case West Res 51-52 MS in LS. 7: (Cpl) US Army 43-45; Mail carrier US Post Off, Farrell Pa 45-47; Laborer Sharon Steel Corp, Farrell Pa 47-51; Lib asst Youngstown StateU 47-51, Hd ref dept 52-58; Hd libn Mo So Col 68-. 9: ALA. 10: Chesterton Club; PTA; AAUP. 14: Ref. 15: 2706 Ohio ave, Joplin Mo 64801.

RODGERS, FRANK. b Darlington Eng 28 J127. 5: UDurham Kings Col 44-47 (ng) BA; ULondon U Col 50-51 (LS) Postgrad Diploma; Fellow of the Lib Assn 55. 6: Fr, Ital, Sp. 7: Sgt-Instr Royal Army Educ Corps, Great Britian 47-49; Asst Newcastle-upon-Tyne Pub Lib, Newcastle Eng 49-50; Libn Poplar Tech Col (London) 51-5; Libn St Martins Sch of Art, London 53-56; Asst libn, adult serv div Akron Pub Lib, Akron Ohio 56-58; Asst ref libn UIll(Urbana) 59-64;Ref libn Penn State U 65-, Asst dir of libs for pub serv 66-69; Dir Portland State U Lib (Portland Ore) 69-. 9: ALA-ACRL; PennLA (sec Col & Research Sect 65-66, chm Govt Docs Com & mem Exec Bd 66-68). 10: AAUP; British Film Inst; Pi Gamma Mu. 12: "Index to Directory of Japanese Learned Periodicals; Univ Microfilms" (63); Co-auth "Guide to British Parliamentary Papers" (67); "Serial Publications in the British Parliamentary Papers 1900-1968; a Bibliography" (69). 14: Ref, col & univ lib admin, lib bldgs. 15: Portland State Univ Lib, Portland Or 97207.

RODGERS, HELEN ELIZABETH. b Toronto Ohio 29 My 14. 5: UCLA 33-37 (Hist) BA; USoCal 37-38 (Hist) M; Columbia summers 45, 46; 48, 49 BLS UCLA 65, 66 Supv Credential. 7: Tchr Libn: Downey Jr High Sch, Downey Cal 43-44, Standard Sch Dist, Oildale Cal 44-47, Torrance High Sch, Torrance Call 47-48; Head Libn El Camino Col 48-. 9: ALA; CalLA (Chm Jr Col Round Table, Standards Com, Com on Coop); Cal Tchrs Assn. 10: Beta Phi Mu; Pi Lambda Theta; Soroptimist Club; Bus & Prof Womens Club. 14: Admin. 15: 1215 Date ave, Torrance Cal 90503.

RODGERS, MARGARET GRACE. b Cleveland 22 N 06. 5: Col of Wooster 28 Eng, Lat) BA; Northwestern 33 (Eng, Lat); UKy 38 (LS); Syracuse 40 (LS); Kent State U 53 (LS) MA; Col of the Immaculate Conception 60; UDenver 61. 6: Fr. 7: Tchr Plain Twp, Middlebranch Ohio 28-38; Tchr-libn Plain Twp, Middlebranch Ohio 38-57; Libn 57-66; Tchr Kent State U 40-42; Libn for Stark Co Reg Planning Commsn, Canton Ohio. 8: Sub libn & tchr various schs 66-68; Developed Lib for Calvary Presbyterian Ch; currently working on syst of clsf & arrangement. 9: NEA; OhioLA; OhioASchL. 10: Tirosis; Stark Co Stamp Club; Col Club of Canton; Canton Scholarship Found; Plain Grange; AAUW. 13: Yes. 14: Serv, to planners & staff. 15: 2201 Myrtle ave NW, Canton Ohio 44709.

RODGERS, NANCY M (PAILING). b Lincoln Neb 3 N 33. 4: Clarence Rodgers. 5: UNeb 51-56 (Eng) BA; Rutgers 60-62 MLS. 6: Fr. 7: Jr libn clerk UNeb Libs 56-60; Lib-trainee Newark Pub Lib, Newark NJ 60-62; Asst lib documents div Fla State U Lib 62-63; Documents libn Queens Borough Pub Lib, Jamaica Y 63-66; Hd docs libn Hofstra U Lib 66-. 9: ALA (Jr Mems Round Table); NY Tech Serv Libns; NY Lib Club; Nassau Co LA. 10: AAUP; Rutgers Sch of Lib erv Alumni Assn; Alpha Lambda Delta; Phi Beta KAPPA: Beta Phi Mu. 14. Govt publs, ref (soc scis, bus). 14: Govt publs, ref (soc scis), acquis. 15: 485 Front st apt 315, Hempstead NY 11550.

RODNEY, HELEN McGREGOR. b Edmonton Alta Can 4 F 24. 4: William Rodney. 5: UAlta45-49 (Eng) BA; UToronto 49-50 BLS. 6: Fr. 7: WRCNS writer (GD) Royal Can Navy 45; Stud asst UAlta Lib 45-49; Gen libn UCarleton Lib (Ottawa) 53, 57-58; Ref libn UVictoria Lib (Victoria BC) 62-63, 1st asst 63-65, Head ref dept 65-. 9: Inst of Victoria Libns (v-pres 64-65, pres 65-66); CanLA (v-pres Info Serv Sect 67-68); BCLA (chm pro tem 66, coun 66-68); UVictoria Lib Prof Staff Assn (pres 66-68). 14: Ref. 15: Res 14 Royal Rds Mil Col, Victoria BC Can.

RODRIGUEZ-BUCKINGHAM, ANTONIO. b Lima Peru 2 F 35. 4: Sue Leister Rodriguez. 5: UWash 58-64 (Romance Lang) BA, 64-66 (Libnship) MA; Harvard 67-68 (Romance Lang). 6: Sp, Fr, Ital, Portu. 7: Asst coord & lang lab supv UWadh Peace Corps Training Program, Seattle 62-66; Curator catlgs HarvardU 66-67, Catlgr special materials 67-68; Visiting prof & asst dir Inst of Libnship Training UPR (Rio Piedras) 68-. 9: ALA; NELA; PRLA. 10: ACLU; UWash Alumni Assn; Friends of Casa del Libro; Wash state Entomological Soc; Scarabs. 13: Yes. 14: Rare bks, catlg, tchg, Lat Amer bibliog, hist of printing in Lat Amer, hist of sci. 15: Harvard College Lib, Cambridge Ma 02138.

ROE, JEAN (DOROTHY) HOLMES. b E St Louis Ill 28 Mr 26. 4: Vyrle C Roe. 5: So Ill Normal 44-46 (Educ) Okla A&M 46-47 (Educ); No Tex State 55-58 (Educ) BS in Ed, 57-58 BS in LS. 7: Libn Dallas Ind Sch Dist 58-60; Libn GRAND Prairie (Tex) Ind Sch Dist 60-. 14: Teen-age bks, Texiana. 15: 514 NE 4th, Grand Prairie Tx 75050.

ROECKER, A(LAN) W(ALLACE). b Madison Wis 11 Jl 16. 4: Maxeen Spees. 5: UWis 34-38 (Biol) PhB; UOhio 40; UWis 43 (Zool) PhM, 49-50 SLS; Case West Res 63-64 (Libnship). 6: Ger. 7: Biologist Wis Conservation Commsn 38-40; Mill operator Gisholt Machine, Madison Wis 41-49; Head sci libn UOre 50-67; Libn Battelle Seattle Research Ctr, Seattle 67-. 8: Prof (part-time) UOre Dept of Lib Sci 61-67. 9: ALA; SLA; ASIS; PNLA (Phys Scis Sect Survey of Univ Libs 57). 10: Beta Phi Mu; Sigma Xi; AAUP. 14: Sci ser, admin. 15: 4000 NE 41st st, Seattle Wa 98105.

ROEDDE, WILLIAM A(DOLPH). b Vancouver BC 10 My 25. 4 Helen MARY Roedde. 5: UBC 50 BA; McGill 51 BLS. 7: Libn Ft William Pub Lib, Ft William Ont 51-5; Dir Northwestern Ont Reg Lib Co-Op, Ft William Ont 53-58; Asst dir Prov Lib Serv Ont Dep Educ, Toronto 58-60, Dir 60-. 9: CanLA; OntLA; InsProf Lis Prof Libns Ont. 11: Can Coun Fellowship to visit European libs, 59. 13: Yes. 14: Lib legis & devel. 15: Provincial Li Provincial Lib Serv, 4 New st, Toronto 5 Can.

ROEDDER, KATHLEEN REA. b Bethlehem Penn 9 O 20. 4: Edwin Roedder. 5: Douglass Col 39-42 (Eng) BA; Lehigh 43-45 (Eng) MA; Columbia 46-48 (Eng); UMd 65-67 MLS. 7: Ref libn Bethlehem Pub Lib, Bethlehem Penn 45-46; Desk asst Columbia U Lib 46-47; Child libn Wash DC Pub Lib 67-. 9: ALA; MdLA; DCLA. 10: PTA; Beta Pi Mu. 14: Child, gen ref. 15: 8405 Rayburn rd, Bethesda Md 20034.

ROEHR, ROBERT WILLIAM. b St Louis Mo 4 My 29. 5: WashU 50 (Soc sci) BS; UIll 54 MSLS. 7: USA Med Serv Corps 51-53; Asst readers' adv serv St Louis Pub Lib 51, 53; Libn Jeffersonville Twp Pub Lib, Jeffersonville Ind 54-60; Libn LaGrange Pub Lib, LaGrange Ill 60-65; Consul Mid-Hudson Libs, Poughkeepsie NY 65-68; Dir Pueblo Reg Lib, Pueblo Colo 68-. 9: ALA; MYPA; ColoLA. 14: Admin, adult serv. 15: 1625 Bonforte blvd, Pueblo Co 81001.

ROEMER, MRS LUCILE (RUNNESTRAND). b Ft Cobb Okla 16 My 10. 4: Claude F Roemer. 5: Hamline U 26-28; UWis 28-29; UMinn 29-30 (Fr BA, 32-33 BS in LS. 6: Fr. 7: Tchr & libn Watertown High Sch, Watertown SD 33-35; Catlgr UMinn(Minneapolis) 35-37; Catlg libn Lib Ext Div State Dept of Educ, St Paul 37-40; Ref libn asst UMinn Lib(Minneapolis) 44-45; Account exec KDAL radio sta, Duluth Minn 60-61, Sales manager 62-63; Dir of Libs Duluth Pub Lib, Duluth Minn 63-. 8: Exec dir, Nat Lib Week, Minn. 66. 9: ALA; MinnLA. 10: LWV; Duluth CitCoun; Trustee, Duluth Pub Lib Bd; Duluth Welfare Coun; Nat Conf Christians & Jews; Duluth Symphony Assn; Bus & Prof Womens Club; AAUW; Zonta; Delta Kappa Gamma; C of C. 14: Admin. 15: 2152 Vermilion rd, Duluth Minn 55803.

ROESCH, BROTHER RICHARD L SM. b Cleveland 14 Ag 23. 5: UDayton 41-44 (Soc Studies, Comp) BS in Ed, 45-46 (Eng, Educ); UHawaii 48-52 (Hist, Amer) MA; Inst of Marianist Studies 52-53 (Phil, Theol); West Res 53; USoCal 54-57 MSLS; City Col (San Francisco) 54-56, 59 (Photography); UDenver 65 (LS); UHawaii 63-64, 68-69; UDenver 65 (LS); State UIowa 67 (Educ Media). 6: Ger. 7: Tchr: Trinity Col (Sioux City) 44-45, St Michael, Baltimore 45, Holy Rosary, Dayton Ohio 45-46, St Mary, Hilo Hawaii 46-47, St Louis Col (Honolulu) 47-48, 49-52; Tchr-libn St Anthony, Wailuku Hawaii 48-49; Tchr-libn Riordan High Sch, San Francisco 53-60; Libn St Louis High Sch, Honolulu 60-. 8: Com Archdiocese San Francisco Eng syllabus & reading lists for secondary schs 58-59; Com Honolulu Diocese on libs 62-64; Consul Honolulu Diocese Dept of Educ 64-; Honolulu Diocese for ESEA Title II 66-68; Hawaii State Bk Eval & Processing Com, Honolulu 66-68; Hawaii's 1st Governor's Conf on Libs, Honolulu 66; Hawaii Sch Lib Standards Com, Honolulu 66-67; Com on Planning Libs for Hawaii, Honolulu 68; Co-chm 1st Jt Conf HawaiiASchL & Hawaii A-V Assn 67; ALA-CathLA Jt Com 68-71 . 9: ALA-AASchL; CathLA; HawaiiASchL (treas 64-66; v-pres 66-67; pres 67-68); Nat A-V Assn. 10: Phi Alpha Theta. 11: Schoolmen Medal Award from Freedom's Foundation 68. 13: Yes. 14: Ya lit, new lib as media ctr. 15: Bertram Lib St Louis High Sch, 3140 Waialae ave, Honolulu Hi 96816.

ROESKE, DOROTHY BRADLEY. b Brookline Mass 13 Je 20. 4: Donald M roeske. 5: Bates Col 37-41 (Hist, Govt) AB; Simmons 55-56 (LS) MS. 6: Sp, Fr. 7: Sec Com on Publ, NYC 42-45; Asst libn Principia Col 58-61, Dir of Libs 61-. 9: ALA; IllLA. 10: AAUP. 13: Yes. 14: Ref, rare bks, lib automation. 15: Principia Col, Elsah Ill 62028.

ROESS, ANNE CAROLYN. b Poughkeepsie NY 26 Ag 33. 5: Penn Col for Women 50-51 T9Liberal Arts; Penn State U 51-55 (Sci) BA Simmons 55-56 (LS) MS. 7: Ref libn John Crerar Lib, Chicago 56-59, Prin ref libn 59-62; Tech libn Inst of Gas Tech, Chicago 62-65, Supv Lib Serv 65-. 9: SLA (mem Memb Com 69-70; v-chm, program chm 69-70; chm 70-71 Pub Utilities Sect; Ill chap dir 63-64, v-pres 65-66, recr chm 64-65; ASIS (Chicago Chap; sec treas 69-70). 13: Yes. 14: Ref, info storage & retrieval. 15: Inst of Gas Tech, 3424 S State st, Chicago Il 60616.

ROETHLISBERGER, JUNE M. b Lansing Mich 26 Ja 15. 5: Hillsdale Col 32-36 (Eng, SOC Sci) BA; UMic summers 37-40 (Eng) MA: Catholic U47-48 BS in LS. 6: Lat. 7: Tchr Fenton pub schs, Fenton Mich 40-47; Seminar libn Catholic U 47-48; Asst libn U of St Thomas (Houston) 49-, Assoc libn & Asst Prof 68-. 9: CathL Cchm Galveston-Houston unit). 10: Siena Club; Houston Coun on Human Rel, AAUP. 14: Col lib, catlg, bk sel. 15: 3812 Montrose blvd, Houston Tx 77006.

ROFES, WILLIAM L. b Boston 27 S 26. 4: Paula Weinstein. 5: Harvard45-47 (Govt) AB; Columbia 47-48 (Pub Law) AM; London Sch of Econ 50-51 (Pol Sci). 6: Fr, Hebrew. 7: US Navy 43-46, 52-54 (Lt); Lecturer on American Govt Rutgers U 48; Instr of pol sci Brooklyn Col 48-52; Sr research assoc Nat Records Mgt Coun, NYC 54-56; Corp records manager Olin Mathieson Chem Corp, NYC 56-61; Supv records mgt Republic Aviation Corp, Farmingdale NY 61-64; Corp archivist IBM, Armonk NY 64-66, Mgr records creation & disposal 66-. 8: Adv Coun on Fed Reports, 60-68. 9: SAA (Microfilm OM 57-60, Records mgt Com 60-65, -, Terminology Com 67-); Tech Mss Com 67-, Bus Archives Com 65 Assn of Records Execs & Admin (dir 56-61, pres 64-65); Amer Records Mgt Assn (chm Research Com 63-64); Aerospace Industries Assn (Records Mgt Com 61-64). 12: "Case Studies in Records Retention and Control (57). 13: Yes. 14: Bus archives, bus hist, records mgt. 15: IBM Corp, Armonk NY 10504.

ROGERS, A(MOS) ROBERT. b Moncton NB Can 9 S 27. 4: Rhoda Page. 5: UNB 44-48 (Philos, Hist) BA; UToronto 48-50 (Philos) MA; ULondon (England) 50-51, 53 (Libnship) Diploma; UMich 57-64 (Libnship) PhD. 6: Fr. 7: Asst libn UNB 51-55, Libn 55-56; Adult asst Detroit Pub Lib 57-59; Asst to dir Bowling Green State U Lib 59-61, Act dir 61-64, Dir 64-; Prof lib sci Kent State U 69-. 8: Assisted with survey of Murray (Ky) State U Lib 68; Mem, Inter-Univ Lib Coun of Ohio 61-; Mem, (Ohio) State Lib Bd, Title III Adv & Com. 9: ALA; CanLA; Lib Assn (Gt Brit); Bibliog Soc Can; Lib Automation Res & Consul Assn; OhioLA (Devel Com 66-67; Bd Dirs 68-); OhioEA. 10: Bd of Trustees United Christ Fellowship; Bd Trustees, Ohio Col Lib Ctr. 12: "The White Monument" (55). 13: Yes. 14: Admin, automation, educ, bldgs, research. 15: Whitehall Ter apts, 1997 Hastings dr, Kent Oh 44240.

ROGERS, ALFRED (ELLIS). b Gorman Tex 26 Je 42. 5: UTex 62-64 (Eng) BA, 64-66 MLS. 6: Sp, Fr. 7: Shipping clk Prompt Printing Co, Ranger Tex 59-64; Off mgr Soc Sci Labs Inc, Ranger Tex 64; Ref & catlg libn Undergrad Lib UTex,

Auston 65-66, Catlg libn 66-. 9: TexLA. 10: Lib Staff Assn of UTex (Austin); Soc UTex Libns; Sierra Club. 13: Yes. 14: Catlg, rare bks. 15: Box 8330 Univ Sta, Austin Tx 78712.

ROGERS, BRIAN D. b New London Conn 26 Je 37. 4: Carol Mallett. 5: AlfredU 55-59 (Hist) BA; UDenver summer 65 (LS); Rutgers 66-67 MSLS. 6: Ger, Czech. 7: Linguist (Sp/5) US Army Security Agcy, Cal & Germany 61-64; Registrar Salem Col Clarksburg Campus 64-66; Lib asst RutgersU Music Dept (New Brunswick) 66-67; Ref libn WesleyanU (Middletown Conn) 67-. 9: ALA. 14: Ref. 15: 43 Fountain ave, Middletown Ct 06457.

ROGERS, EMMA. b New Albany Miss 29 M 22. 5: Miss State Col for Women 39-42 (Eng) BA; Peabody 42-43 (LS) BS, 57 (LS) MA. 7: Ref asst Cossitt Lib, Memphis Tenn 43; Spec serv (Cpl) WAC USAF 43-45; Teller Bank of Commerce, New Albany Miss 46-56; Libn Harris Mem Col (Manila Philippine) 57-59; Dir Wesley Foun, MSCW Columbus Miss 60-62; Circ asst UMiss 62-66, Circ libn 66-. 9: Miss LA; SELA. 15: 510 Alabama st, New Albany Ms 38652.

ROGERS, FRANK BRADWAY. b Norwood Ohio 31 D 14. 4: Barbara Pitt. 5: Yale 32-36 (Pre-Med) BA; Ohio State U 38-42 (Med) MD; Columbia 48-49 MS in LS. 6: Fr. 7: Intern Letterman Gen Hosp, San Frncisco 42-43; Med Off (Col) US Army 43-60; Dir NLM, Bethesda Md 49-63; Med Dir USPHS 60-63; Libn UColo Med Center 63-. 8: Consul (med libs): Korea 54; World Health Org, Geneva 58; Ford Foun, Nigeria 60; UN Lib 59-61; LC Automation Com 61-63. 9: MedLA (pres 62-63, chm Jt Com on Union List of Serials 59-62, chm Lib Tech Proj Adv Com 64-65); Amer Assn Hist of Med (pres 66-68). 10: Cosmos Club, Wash DC. 11 Marca Noyes Award (MedLA 61); Melvil DWEY Medal (ALA, 63); Barnard Mem Prize (Gt Brit 63) Distinguished Serv Medal (USPHS) 64. 11: Marcia Noyes Award (MedLA 61); Melvil Dewey Medal (ALA, 63); Barnard Mem Prize (Gt Brit 63); Distinguished Serv Medal (USPHS 64). 12: "Selected Papers of John Shaw Billings (65). 13: Yes. 14: Info retrieval (machine), subj bibliog, hist of med. 15: 1135 Grape st, Denver Co 80220.

ROGERS, GLENN E. b Ft Scott Kan 9 O 23. 4: Vineta Pryor. 5: John Brown U 51-53 (Soc Sci) BSSE; UArk 53-56 (Educ) M Ed; UOkla summers 57-60 MLS. 7: US Army 20th Armd Div (Cpl) Gunner on M-7 Tank 43-46; Laborer46-50; John Brown U: Dean of Men 53-57, Asst libn & dir of a-v educ 57-59, Libn 59-. 9: ArkLA. 10: Kiwanis. 14: Admin. 15: Box 1006-JBU, Siloam SPRINGS Ark 72761.

ROGERS, HELEN FRANCES). b Ottawa Ont Can. 5: Carleton U 56-60 (Eng) BA; McGill 63-64 BLS, 67-69 MLS. 6: Fr. 7: Ed asst Nat Research Coun, Ottawa 54-61, Ref libn 64-. 9: CanLA; OntLA; Lib Assn Ottawa sec; Prof Inst of Can Libns Group. 12: Asst Ed "National Library News". 13: Yes. 14: Ref, bibliog. 15: 210 Stewart st, Ottawa 2 Ont Can.

ROGERS, IRENE (MARY IRENE ANN). b Yonkers NY 12 O 32. 5: New Paltz State Tchrs Col 50-54 IEduc) BS in Ed; Columbia 58-59 (LS) MS. 6: Sp. 7: Elem tchr W Babylon Sch System, W Babylon NY 54-57; Elem tch Yonkers Sch System, Yonkers NY 57-58; Yonkers Pub Lib, Yonkers NY: Asst ref libn Main Br 59-62, Act head of ref dpt 62-64, Head of ref dept main bldg 64-67, Adult serv coord 68-. 9: ALA (Mem Basic Ref Com 65-66). 10: Yonkers Pub Lib Staff Assn; Venture Club of Yonkers. 12: Comp & ed "Consumer Education Bibliography". 14: Ref. 15: 41 Amackassin terr, Yonkers NY 10703.

ROGERS, JUDITH B. b Spencerport NY. 5: NY State Col for Tchrs Albany) 33-37 BSLS; Catholic U 58-63 MSLS. 7: Asst libn Bay Shore Pub Lib, Bay Shore NY 39-42, Libn 43; Chief central files US Army Air Tech Serv Command, Rochester NY 43-44; Chief catlg sect US Weather Bur, Wash DC 45-56 Catlgr Amer Cyanamid Co Lederle Labs, Pearl River NY 56-57; Catlgr Nat Agric Lib, Wash DC 57-62, Chief catlg sect 63-. 9: ALA; SLA; DCLA; Potomac Tech Proc Libns. 10: Beta Phi Mu. 14: Catlg. 15: 4313 Knox rd, College Park Md 20740.

ROGERS, MARIANNE PATRICIA (OBRIEN). b Los Angeles 8 F 34. 4: Delbert Clinton Rogers. 5: Orange Coast Jr Col 51-52 (sec sci) Ft Lewis Col 53-54 (Bus Admin) AA UWyo 54-56 (Bus Admin) BS, 56-57; Finance. 6: Sp. 7: Cashier US Marine Corps, Camp Pendleton Cal 51; UWyo: Sec & clerk 55-56, Grad asst 58, Lib helper 58, Lib clerk 58-59, Documents asst 61-62, Act documents libn 63; Head Libn US Bur of Mines, Laramie Wyo 63-. 10: Antque Bottle Collectors Assn. 12: "Scholarship on the Wyoming Plains, with Z M Edwards 62 ; "Bibliography of Bureau of Mines Publications on Oil Shale and Shale Oil" (68). 14: Ref tech), catlg, acquis, lit searching. 15: 1020 S 9th st, Laramie Wyo 82070.

ROGERS, MARY READ. b Uniontwon Kan 9 Ap 04. 4: Glenn K Roger. 5: Baker U 20-24 (Math) AB; UWyo summers. 6: Sp. 7: High sch tchr Kanarado (Kan) pub sch 25-26; Sub tchr High Sch, WHEATLAND Wyo 28-38, Sub tchr High Sch, Cheyenne Wyo 38-51, High sch libn 51-52; Y-teen dir YWCA, Cheyenne Wyo 52-56; Cheyenne newspapers, Cheyenne Wyo 26-59; Asst libn Wyo State Lib 59-68, Coord publ & pub rel 68-. 8: Consul for many educ orgs at local, state & nat level; Wyo State Bd of Educ. 9: ALA (Memb Com); -LAD (PR Sect serv to Pub Libs); -ALTA (Publns Com); WyoLA (Parliamentarian, chm &/or mem var coms); MPLA (Scholarship Com). 10: Nat Congress Parents & Tchrs; Nat Fed Music Clubs; Fed Womens Clubs; Nat Assn State Bds; Wyo Fed Womens Clubs; Wyo Coun Adult Educ; Wyo Coun for Econ Educ; PTA; Wyo Fed Music Clubs; Alpha Delta Kappa; Cheyenne Commun Concert Assn; Wyo Hist Soc; Wyo Press Women; Zonta Internat. 11: First Cheyenne Woman of the Year. 12: Ed "Wyoming Library Roundup (59-); Ed "The Outrider (68-). 13: Yes. 14: Pub rel. 15: 312 E Pershing blvd, Cheyenne Wyo 82001.

ROGERS, MARYJANE (JOELS). b RI 13 S 14. 4: W N Rogers. 5: Washington Square Col 5559 (Journalism) AB; St John-s U (NY) 5961 MLS. 7: Child libn Queens Pub Lib, Jamaica NYC 6164; Libn Linden Jr High Sch, St Albans NYC 6467; Tchr & libn St Andrew Sch, Orlando Fla 68. 9: ALA; CathLA; FlaLA. 15: 1515 Campbell ave, Orlando Fl 32806.

ROGERS, RUTH MAE (JONES). b Fairmont Neb 11 Jl 09. 4: Laurence L Rogers. 5: UNeb 26-30 (Math, LAT, Educ) BS in Ed, 31-32 (Lat) MA; UColo summers 29 & 38; USoCal summers 39 & 40 (LS); UDenver summers 44, 45 & 46 BS in LS. 6: Lat, Fr, Sp, Ger. 7: Tchr Lat & Math High Sch, Syracuse Neb 30-31; Tchg fellow classics dept UNeb 31-32; Prin & tchr high sch, Nehawka Neb 32-36; Tchr of Lat Eng high sch, Wymore Neb 37-42; Lat tchr Jr & Sr High Sch, Beatrice Neb 42; Prin Jr & Sr High Sch, Chadron Neb 43-44; Libn & instr Jr Col, Sterling Colo 44-48; Libn II Denver Pub Lib 48-52; Asst libn Air Force Accounting & Finance Center, Denver Colo 52-60; Histn Air Reserve Personnel Center, Denver 60-. 8; Adv bd, UDenver Sch of Libnship, 59-60. 9: ALA; SLA (pres Colo Chap 59-60); ColoLA; MPLA. 10: Internat Toastmistress Club; Bus & Prof Womens Club; lhi Beta Kappa; Pi Mu Epsilon; Delta Kappa Gamma; Air Force Hist Found. 14: Ref, documentation & retr. 15: 3250 S University blvd, Denver Co 80210.

ROGERS, RUTHERFORD DAVID. b Jesup Iowa 22 Je 15. 4: E Margaret Stoddard. 5: U No Iowa 32-36 (Eng) BA; Columbia 36-7 (Eng, Comparative Lit) MA, 37-38 (LS) BS, 38-42 (Eng, Comparative Lit). 6: Fr, Ger. 7: Asst NY Pub Lib 37, 38, Columbia Col Lib (NY); Ref asst 38-42, Act libn 42, Libn 42-46; Pvt to First Sgt AAF Air Transport Command 42-44 2nd Lt to Capt, Chief Spec Projs Sect Off of Asst Chief of Staff, Plans, AAF Air Transport Command 44-46; Research analyst Smith Barney & Co, NYC 46-48; Dir Grosvenor Lib, Buffalo NY 48-52; Dir Rochester Pub & Monroe Co Lib Systems (NY) 52-54; Chief of the Personnel Office NY Pub Lib 54-55, Chief of ref dept 55-57; Deputy libn of Congress LC 57-64; Dir of U Libs Stanford U 64-69; Libn Yale U Lib 69-. 8: Chm Adv Screening Com in Lib Sci 61-64; v-chm, Exam Com for Pub Libns Certif, NY State, 53-54; Com on the White House Lib, 63-64; chm Jt Libs Com on Copyright, 64-66; Adv Com Title II, Lib Serv & Constr Act Cal State Lib 65-; Consul to NY State Commsnr of Educ, 56; Consul, NY Pub Lib 63; Consul to UNESCO Conf on Nat Libs in Asia & the Pacific Area, Manila PI,64. 9: ALA (Coun 59-63, Exc Bd 61-66, 2nd v-pres 65-66; Chm: Com on Intel Freedom 50-51, Nomin Com 59-60, Insur Com 53-54, HQ Visiting Com62-63); BSA; NYLA (chm Memb Com 48-50); DCLA; CalLA; ARL (pres 67-68). 10: Cosmos Club, Wash DC; Founding mem US Capitol Hist Soc; AAUP; Grolier Club; Roxburghe Club. 11: Alumni Achievement Award, State Col Iowa, 58. 12: "University Library Administration (70). 13: Yes. 14: Admin, automation, bibliog contro. 15: Yale Univ Lib, New Haven Ct 06520.

ROGERS, SUSAN (HUXTABLE). b Turlock Cal 7 N 44. 4: Earl M Rogers. 5: Modesto Jr Col 62-64 (Hist) AA; UCal (Berkeley) 64-66 (Hist) BA, 66-67 MLS. 6: Sp, Ger. 7: Bibliog libn UUtah 67-. 9: ALA; UtahLA. 10: Beta Phi Mu; Phi Beta Kappa; Alpha Gamma Sigma. 14: Acquis, bibliog. 15: 220 Elizabeth st apt 21, Salt Lake City Ut 84102.

ROGERS, WILLIAM FREDERICK. b Niagara Falls NY 12 Ag 30. 4: Nancy Ann Humphrey. 5: Northwestern 51-55 (Eng) BA; UHawaii 56-58, 65 (Eng) MA; UWash 59-60 MSLS. 6:

Ger, Fr, Lat. 7: USAF Radar Repairman (Sgt) 47-50; Instr in Eng UHawaii 57-59; Stanford U Libs; Ref libn I ref div 60-62, Ref libn II ref div 62-63, Ref libn III rev div 63-65, Asst chief humanities & soc sci div 65-67; Dir Libs Beaver Col, Glenside Pa 67-69; Assoc dir Ohio U 69-. 9: ALA; CalLA. 10: Phi Eta Sigma; Eta Sigma Phi. 14: Ref. 15: RFD 3, Albany Oh 45710.

ROGERS, WILMA (HOPE) SPANGLER. b Glenn Ellyn Ill 9 My 04. 4: . 5: Westhampton Col URichmond 21-25 (Bot) BS; UFla summer 27 (Educ); USoCal 31-32 ILS); San Jose State Col 55-59 (A-V Educ) MA; Sacramento State Col 52-63 (Educ); UDenver summer 62 (LS); Chico State Col summer 62 (Programmed Learning); Nev So 65; UNev (Nev Hist); Nev Sch Law 66; Nev So U 67 (Innovations in admin of high sch). 6: Fr, Sp. 7: Pensacola Fla 26-27; Tchr-tchr train Tate Agric High Sch, Pensacols Fla 27-29; Tchr creative writing, psych Hillsborough High Sch, Tampa Fla 29-30; Prin Owensville Cons Sch, West River Md 30-31; Child libn Los Angeles Pub Lib 32-47; WAC T3 Los Alamos Atomic Lab Manhattan Dist, Los Alamos NM 44-46; Col Libn Trinity Co, Weaverville Cal 47; Ed & part owner BAYWOOD Press, Pt Reyes Sta Cal 47-51; Dist libn Tahoe-Truckee Unified Sch Dist, Hdq Truckee Cal 51-52; Dir Instr Mat Center Alpine Nev, Placer & Sierra Centers, Hdq Auburn Cal 52-63; Dist Libn Ek Grove Unified Dist High Sch, Ek Grove Cal 6364; Asst libn NCHO High Sch, Las Vegas Nev 64-65; Libn & A-v dir Ed W Clark High Sch, LAS Vegas Nev 65-. 8: Asst Prof, Lib Sci; Sacramento State Col 61-64; Part-time Even Sch, Nev So U part-time-eve 65-. 9: ALA-AASchL; YASD; NEA-DAVI; Internat Reading Assn; NCTE; Nev Tchrs Assn, NevLA. 10: Soroptimist. 12: "Guidance through Literature (61). Instr materials concept, sch libs, ya, lib sch educ. 15: 7726 W Lone Mt rd, Las Vegas Nv 89108.

ROHDE, GLADYS J(OLIDON). b Cicero Ill 12 S 15. 5: UIll 36-40 (Sociol) BA; USoCal 50-51 MS in LS. 7: Proof CHECKER Time Inc, Chicago 38-41; Field dir Girl Scouts, Evansville Ind 44-46; Lib asst Pub Lib, Berwyn Ill 46- 49; Lib asst USoCal 49-50; Los Angeles State Co: Asst order libn Order Ordr libn 52-54, Ser order lib 55-56; Ref libn San Fernando VALLEY State Col 56-59, Head circ libn 59-. 9: ALA; CalLA (State Col Libns Div pres 68); Assn Cal State Col Profs. 10: Beta Phi Mu. 14: Personnel policies for libns, lib orient & instr, lib handbks, circ systems. 15: 21500 Lassen st 98, Chatsworth Ca 91311.

ROHLF, ROBERT HENRY. b Minneapolis 14 My 28. 4: Joan Peters. 5: Col of St Thomas 45-49 (Hist) BA; UMinn 49-50 (BSLS, 50-52 LS MA, 53-54 Certif in Pub Admin. 7: Jr libn UMinn Inst of Agric (St Paul) 50, libn 51; Sr libn UMinn (Minneapolis) 52-53; Minneapolis Pub Lib; Gen asst 53, Br libn 54-55, Admin asst 56, New bldgs off 57-58; Dir Dakota-Scott Reg Lib, W St Paul 59-66; Dir Ill Lib Devel Proj, Aurora Ill 63; Coord bldg planning LC 66-68, Dir of admin 68-69; Dir Hennepin Co Lib Sys, Minneapolis 69-. 8: Visiting Instr UMinn 60; LL Consul 66; Bldg Consul to 65 libs in 12 states 58-; chm Minn State Bd of Educ Lib Adv Com. 9: ALA (Coun 63-66; Adv Com Lib Systems Study 67-68); -LAD (chm Arch Com for Pub Libs, chm Budget & Acctg Com); MinnLA (pres 59, hon life mem); DCLA. 10: Kiwanis. 11: Libn of the Year, MinnLA 66. 12: "A Plan for Public Library Development in Illinois (63); Co-auth "Interim Standards for Small Public Libraries ALA (62). 13: Yes. 14: Bldgs, admin, pub serv. 15: Hennepin Co Lib, Minneapolis Mn.

ROHMALLER, JULIANNE (ZIMMERMAN). b Chicago Ill 27 Ap 41. 4: Paul Rohmaller. 5: Albion Col 59-63 (Hist) BA; UIll 63-65 MLS. 7: Catlgr UIll Lib 65-68; Acquis libn RiceU Lib 68-. 15: 5025 Jason, Houston Tx 77035.

ROHRER, RICHARD LEE. b Hutchinson Kan 22 S 37. 4: Betty Breaux. 5: Kan State Tchrs Col 59-60 (Bio) BS in Ed, 67-68 MLS. 6: Fr. 7: Coun Kan State Employment Service, Hutchinson 65-67; Asst libn sci div Kan StateU 68-. 9: KanLA. 10: Farrell Lib Staff assn; Beta Phi Mu. 14: Ref. 15: 2449 Hobbs dr, Manhattan Ks 66502.

ROLDAN, MARIA ANTONIA. b Habana Cuba 21 F 21. 5: HavanaU 59-60 Bachelor in Lib Sci, 58-61 (Pub Admin); Escuela Cubana de Bibliotecarios 55-57 (Libn). 6: Sp. 7: Catlgr Lib of Sociedad Economica de Amigos del Pais, Havana 56-59; Catlgr State Dept Lib of dept of Intl Orgs, Habana 59-60; Catlgr Lib of Catholic UVullanova, Havana 60-61; Catlgr Columbus Mem Lib OAS, Wash DC 62-. 9: DCLA. 13: Yes. 14: Catlg. 15: 2401 Calvert st NW, Washington DC 20008.

ROLFE, RODNEY D. b Ellsworth Kan. 5: Bethany Col 58-62 (Applied Organ) BM; NorthwesternU 62-64 (Mus Hist) MM; UChicago 64-66 (LS) MA. 6: Fr, Ger. 7: Var Newberry Lib, Chicago 64-66; Mus catlgr USoCal 67-. 9: ALA; MedLA; AMS. 10: AAUP. 14: Music catlg, performing arts. 15: 101 N Normandie, Los Angeles Ca 90004.

ROLFS, CLARA E. b Milwakee 28 D 1885. 5: UWis 14-15 (LS); West Res (Cleveland Pub Lib) 15-16; Columbia summer 22; West Res 22-25 BS. 6: Ger, Sp. 7: Libn Pub Lib, W Bend Wis 10-14; Child libn Cleveland Pub Lib 15-24, 24-26; Head of child dept Pub Lib, Gary Ind 26-32; Head of child dept Tulare Col Lib, Visalia Cal 3-40; Libn Visalia High Sch, Visalia Cal 3 yrs; Head catlgr Loyola U Lib (Los Angeles) 50-56; Parish libn St Anselms Parish, Los ANGELES) 50-56; Parish libn St Anselms Parish, Los Angeles 58-. 13: Yes. 15: 6124 S Wilton pl, Los Angeles Ca 90047.

ROLLER, RACHEL (PETERSON). b Independence Mo 8 N 10. 4: George Philip Roller. 5: Brenau Col 26-30 (Hist, Eng) AB; UIll summers 57-59 (LS) MS; UWis summer 66 (LS). 6: Fr, Sp. 7: Hist tchr Bd of Pub Instr, Dade Co Fla 30-34; Eng tchr Sch Bd, Newman Ill 54-60; Libn Bd of Pub Instr, Dade Co Fla 60-62; Libn Hialeah High Sch 62-. 8: State Adv, Fla High Sch Lib Coun, 65-66. 9: ALA; NEA; Cir Tchrs Assn; FlaASchL; FlaLA; FlaEA; Dade CoLA (sec). 10: Delta Kappa Gamma; Beta Phi Mu; Pi Gamma Mu. 14: Bk binding, tchg lib sci to high sch studs. 15: 1360 NW 111 st, Miami Fla 33167.

ROLLING, GEORGE MILLER. b Pasadena Cal 20 O 26. 5: Pasadena City Col 44-46 (Soc Sci) AA; Occidental Col 46-49 (Hist) AB; USoCal 54-55 MS in LS. 6: Sp. 7: Clerical in lib & adult educ off Pasadena City Schs, Pasadena Cal 49-52 US Navy 52-54; Stud libn Los Angeles Pub Lib 54-55; Gen libn Long Beach Pub Lib, Long Beach Cal 55-59; Catlg libn Cal State Col (Los Angeles) 59-. 9: CalLA; Scal Tech Proc Group. 10: Assn Cal State Col Profs. 14: Catlg, ref. 15: 600 S Mentor ave, Pasadena Ca 91106.

ROLLINS, ARLINE (McCLARTY). b Franklin La. 5: UMinn 45-50 (English lit) BA, 50-51 BSLS; Ohio State 55; Miami U Ohio 59. 7: Asst docs libn Michigan State Lib 51-52; Asst catlgr Fisk U 52-54; Middletown City Schs, Middletown Ohio: Spec educ tchr 59-60, Elem tchr 61-62; High sch libn Franklin City Schs, Franklin Ohio 63-67; Miami U, Middletown Ohio Supv acquis catlg 67-68, Asst libn 68-. 14: Acquis, catlg, govt docs. 15: 5067 Mosiman rd, Middletown Oh 45042.

ROLLINS, LINDA K. b Wickliffe Ky 16 O 43. 5: Georgetown Col 61-62; Paducah Jr Col 62-63; West Ky State Col (65) Eng (LS) BA. 7: Lib D T Cooper Elem Sch, Paducah Ky 65-66; Libn Philippine Bapt Theol Sem, Baguio Philippines 66-68; Libn Jetton Jr High, Paducah Ky 68-69. 9: NEA; KyLA; KyEA. 14: Child bks, periods. 15: 701 Lone Oak rd, Paducah Ky 42001.

ROLLINS, OTTILIE (HIRT). b Vienna 18 N 15. 4: John P Rollins. 5: Russell Sage 42-44 (Phys Educ) BS (cum laude); West Res summers 57-60 MS in LS. 6: Ger, fr. 7: Bkeeper Apostelkeller, Vienna 33-35; Sec & Ger tchr The Putney Sch, Putney Vt 37-42; Asst in Ger Dept Russell Sage Col 42-44, Instr phys educ 45-48; Clarkson Col of Tech (sec 48-55, catlgr 56-60); Asst Prof, Asst libn & lecturer in Ger 60-66, Act libn 66-67, Hd libn & Assoc Prof 67-. 9: NYLA. 10: AAUW; Clarkson Col Faculty Womens Club; North Fold Dancers. 14: Catlg, ref. 15: 44 Bay st, Potsdam NY 13676.

ROLLINSON, DOROTHY. b Minneapolis 24 O 11. 5: Lawrence U 29-33 (Fr) BA; Northwestern summers 40-43 (Educ) MA; UWis 49-50 BLS. 6: Fr, Ger. 7: High sch tchr, Mattoon Wis 34-36; High sch tchr, Lomira Wis 36-42; Clerk Lawrence Col 43-44; High sch tchr, Mayville Wis 44-45; Hosp wker, Neenah Wiws 47-49; High sch libn, Dubuque Iowa 50-53; High sch libn, Oshkosh Wis 53-. 9: WisLA (Convention panels 64 &65); WisEA (pres Lib Sect 63-64). 10: Altrusa. 13: Yes. 15: 1238 W 9th, Oshkosh Wis 54901.

ROLLMAN, MARY EIZABETH. b Topea Kan 5 O 13. 5: Washburn Col 31-35 (Eng) AB; UMich 35-36 ABLS. 7: UMich Lib Asst period reading room 36-38, Gen serv asst 38-40, Ref libn 41-. 9: ALA. 13: . 14: Ref. 15: 332 E William st, Ann arbor Mich 48108.

ROLOFF, DAPHNE CROSS. b Simcoe Ont Can 22 Sp 31. 4: Frederick W Roloff. 5: UToronto 49-50, 53-54 (Art Hist) BA, 55-58 BLS. 7: Catlg & ref Fogg Art Museum HarvardU 55-58; Catlgr Metro Mus of Art, NYC 59; Asst libn Amer Heritage Pub Co, NYC 64; Libn Costume Inst Metro Mus of Art, NYC 65; Asst libn Sterling & Franxine Clark Art Inst, Williamstown Mass 66-. 9: SLA. 14: Catlg, ref. 15: Sterling and Francine Clark Art inst, Williamstown Ma 01267.

ROLOFF, JOYCE ELAINE (PETERSON). b Wapato Wash 13 S 26. 4: Raymond C Roloff. 5: UWash 44-48 (Sociol) BA, 64-66 M of Libnship. 7: Casewkr King Co Welfare Dept, Seattle 49; Statistician Chamber of Com Seattle 49; King Co Hosp, Seattle: Soc serv interviewer 49-50, Soc wk case aide 51-52; Libn Shoreline High Sch, Seattle 66-. 9: NEA; ALA; WashEA; ShorelineEA; WashStateASchL; WashLA. 10: Phi Beta Kappa; Beta Phi Mu. 14: Sch libnship. 15: 720 14th way SW, Edmonds Wa 98020.

ROLOFF, RONALD WILLIAM. b Madison Wis 14 Ag 22. 5: St Johns U (Minn) 40-45 (Philos) BA; Marquette U 49 (Eng); UMinn 51-53 (LS) MA. 6: Lat. 7: Instr Hist St Johns Prep Sch, Collegeville Minn 48-50; Manager Liturgical Press, Collegeville Minn 50-51; Asst libn St Johns U (Minn) 53-67, Hd libn 67-69; Staff subject catlg div LC 69-. 9: ALA. 12: Ed "Sisters Today (formerly "Sponsa Regis) (60-). 13: Yes. 15: Staff subject catlg div, Library of Congress, Wash DC.

ROMAN, RUTH STEWART. b Chicago 4 Ap 42. 4: Stanford A Roman. 5: Wheaton Col 59-61, 62-63 (Biol) BA; Chicago 61-62 (Biol); Simmons summer 63 (LS); Columbia 64-65 (LS) MS. 6: Ger. 7: Catlg asst Phillips Acad Lib, Andover Mass 63-64; Head Libn Biol Sci Lib, Columbia U 65-68; Product specialist Collier-MacMillan Lib Serv 68-. 9: . 15: 54 W 16th st, New York NY 10011.

ROMANI, DORTHY(PARBEL). b Grand Rapids Mich 12 Je 14. 4: Joseph A Romani. 5: Grand Rapids Jr Col 33-35; Maryrove Col 37; Wayne U 37-39 (Eng) BA; UWis 40-41 BLS. 7: Detroit Pub Lib: Asst libn41-51, Chief of div 51-62, Coordinator ext serv 62-. 8: Tech Adv Com, Detroit Metro Com on Aging, 63; Mich State Lib Adv Com LSCA Title IVA 67; Inst Lib Serv to Handicapped UMich 69; Inst Wayne State U; lib serv to institutions 68, to the aging 69. 9: ALA-AHIL (sec 69-70); CathLA; MichLA (v-chm Hosp & Insts Sect 67, chm 10: Nat Widlife Fed; Mich Gerontol Soc; Coord Coun on Human Rel. 14: Bkmob, hosp & other institutional libs. 15: 87 Cedarhurst pl, Detroit Mi 48203.

ROMANO, CATHERINE ROSEMARY. b Oak Park Ill 8 Mr 44. 5: UWis (Madison) 61-66 (Eng Lit) BS; UIll (Champaign) 68-69 MSLS. 6: Fr. 7: Clk Cook Co Assessor, Chicago summers 61 & 64; Sales clk Manchester's Dept Store, Madison Wis summer 65; Sec J S G Electric Co, Schiller Ill 66; Lib asst Madison Pub Lib, Madison Wis 66-68; Grad asst UIll (Urbana) 68-. 9: ALA. 14: Pub serv, personnel, ref, research. 15: 2024 N 77th ct, Elmwood Park Il 60635.

ROMANO, JOSEPH P. b Brooklyn NY. 4: Joan P King. 5: St John's U 51-58 (Eng) BA. 6: Fr, Ital. 7: Photo lib asst Assoc Press, NYC 51-67; Photo libn Newsweek Magazine, NYC 67-. 14: Photo libnship, photo research. 15: Newsweek Inc, 444 Madison ave, New York NY 10022.

ROMANS, C W. b Cumby Tex 9 O 17. 4: Rubye Doris Gandy. 5: E Tex StateU 36-39 (Math) BS, 46, 47-48, summer 56 (Math) MEd, summer 58, summer 59, 60, 62 MS in LS. 7: Prin-tchr Ireland High Sch, Ireland Tex 41-42; Sgt, aircraft mech, clk USAF, US & Overseas 42-45; Tchr Alba High Sch, Alba Tex 46-47; Tchr Brownsville Sr High Sch, brownsville Tex 48-49; Tchr Keams Canyon Pub Schs, Keams Canyon Ariz 50-51; Flight dispatcher Tex Aviation Industries Inc Hondo Air Base, Hondo Tex 51-53, Chief flight dispatcher 53-55; Prin & tchr Knippa High Sch, Knippa Tex 55-57; Tch dispatcher 53-55; Prin & tchr Knippa High Sch, Knippa Tex 55-57; Tchr Uvalde Sr High Sch, Uvalde Tex 57-60; Libn Decatur Sr High Sch, Decatur Tex 60-63; Catlgr libn McMurry Col 63-66; Asst libn & acquis libn Sul Rose State Col 66-67; Libn 67; Pub serv libn Stephen F Austin State Col 67-. 9: TexLA; SWLA. 14: Catlg. 15: 2311 S Fredonia, Nacogdoches Tx 75961.

ROMBOUGH, BEATRICE COLBY. b Stanstead Que Can. 5: Queens U 27-30 9classics) BA; Toronto 62-63 BLS. 6: Fr, Lat, Classical Gk, Russian. 7: Tchr Kingston Bus Col (Kingston Ont) 54-60; Lib asst Queens U (Kingston Ont) 60-62; Catlgr cCarleton U (Ottawa) 63-65; Catlgr Queens U (Kingston Ont) 65-. 15: 311 Westdale ave apt 3, Kingston Ont Can.

ROMIG, MADELEINE COLLINS. b Detroit 28 N03. 4: Walter Romig. 5: Wayne State U 24-37 (Eng) BA; Detroit Pub Lib Sch 24-25. 6: Fr. 7: Asst Detroit Pub Lib 23-41; Libn St Paul High Sch, Grosse Pointe Mich 61-. 9: ALA; CathLA; MichLA; Mich Cath LA. 10: Bk Sel Com, Grosse Pointe PUB Lib. 12: Collab (with husband): "American Catholic Whos Who Guide to Catholic Literature, "Book of Catholic Authors (34-61). 14: Bibliog. 15: 979 Lakepointe rd, Grosse Pointe Mich 48230.

RONGIONE, REV LOUIS A. b Aquafondata Italy 23 Ag 12. 5: Villanova Col 32-36 (Philos) AB; Catholic U 40 (Educ) MA; Villanova Col 40 (LS) BS. 6: Ital, LAT, Gk, Fr. 7: Lang Prof, libn St Rita High Sch, CHICAGO 40-41; Lang Prof, libn Augustinian Acad, SI NY 41-50; Asst Prof Villanova Cól 50-52; Libn Augustinian Int Col (Rome) 52-53; Villanova U: Prof 53-, Dean Grad Sch 56-62, Libn 62-, Chm Lib Sci Dept 68-69. 8: Bd of Governors, Gallery of Living Authors, 43-48; Auxil Chaplain, Ft Wadsworth & Halleran Vet Hosp, SI NY 41-46; St Josephs Hosp, Reading Penn, Nurs Sch Coun 59-; Adv Bd, Cabrini Col, Radnor Penn65; Bd of Trustees Amer Inst for Ital Culture; Nat Coun of Col Publ Advs. 9: ALA;-ACRL; CathLA (chm Lib Educ Div 65-67; pres NY-NJ Unit 42-45); Cath A-V Educs Assn (Exec Bd 62-, chm Eval Com 63-65, pres 65); Nat CathEA; Higher Highe Educ; PennLA; Cath Broadcasters Assn. 11: Hon Pd Steubenville Col, 57-. 12: "Conferences on the Beatitudes (59). 13: Yes. 14: Admin. 15: Villanova Univ, Villanova Penn 19085.

RONNINGEN, JOHAN. b Madison Minn 11 F 15. 5: UMinn 33-37 (Eng Composition) BA; Iowa State Col 38 (Educ) CCertif; Command & Gen Staff Col 45 Certif; UCal(Berkeley) 54 (Japanese). Certif. 7: Tchr & libn High Sch, Hampton Iowa 39-41; Intelligence off; Capt; US Army, USA, N Africa, Italy 42-45; Intelligence Instr; Capt; CMD & Gen Staff Col, Ft Leavenworth Kan 45-46; Mil Adv Grp Major, Nanking China 47-48; Chief Foreign War Material Production Research Intell Div Army Gen Staff Maj, Wash DC 49-51; Chief Intell Sect Research Asia & USSR; Lt Col; GHQ, Far East Cmd, Tokyo 52-53; Research libn H Bartholomew & Assoc, Honolulu 57-64; Ref libn Eastwest Center Lib, Honolulu 65-; Planning Opns; Div hd Oahu Transportation Study, Honolulu 64-65; Hd research div Planning dept City & Co of Honolulu 65-67; Hd planning graphics div 68-; Lib resources consul to Pacific Urban Studies & Planning Program UHawaii 67-; Hawaii Coun for Lib Serv 67-. 9: COUN OF Planning Libns; HAWAII LA (treas 59-60; chm Spec & Ref sect 60-61, Ed "Newsletter 61-62). 10: Amer Inst of Planners; Amer Soc of Planning Officials; Urban & Reg Info Systs Assn. 12: Ed "Directory of Special and Reference Libraries on Oahu" (60, 65); Ed "Pacific Progress" (58-62); Ed, All publications of Oahu Transportation Study (64-65); Ed, All Publns of Planning Dept City & Co of Honolulu 66-. 13: Yes. 14: Ref, data banks, res facilities. 15: P O Box 3521, Honolulu Hi 96811.

RONSHEIM, SALLY (BOBER). b NY Ja 20. 4: Julian Ronsheim. 5: Brooklyn Col 40 (Eng) BA; CCNY 40-42 (Educ) LIU 60-62 (LS) MS; ULondon Inst of Educ 64; NYU 67 (Higher Educ) PhD. 6: Fr, Sp. 7: Research asst Manhasset High Sch, Manhasset NY 56-58; Asst dir LIU Grad Lib Program, Greenvale NY 60-62; Libn Herricks High Sch, New Hyde Park NY 62-67; Asst Prof Eng dept LIU 67-. 9: NEA; NYLA; Nassau-Suffolk SchLA; NYSEE; NCTE (Erie Evaluation Com). 10: AAUP; Kappa Delta Phi; Bd of Trustees Nassau Co Central Ref Lib. 12: "New York Portrait, A Literary Look at the Empire State" (65). 14: Ref, Eng educ. 15: 8 Wensley dr, Great Neck NY 11021.

ROONEY, PAUL M. b Buffalo NY 16 A 18. 4: Elizabeth Dorsey. 5: State Tchrs Col (Buffalo NY) 34-38 BS in Ed; UBuffalo 38-40 BS in LS. 7: Asst in brs Buffalo Pub Lib, Buffalo NY 40-42; ARMY Air Force (1st Lt) 42-45; Ref dept Grosvenor Lib, Buffalo NY 45-59, Head of dept 46-59; Buffalo & Erie Co Pub Lib, Buffalo NY: Head Tech dept 59-61, Asst deputy dir 61-63, Deputy dir 63-. 8: Chm Pub Libns Certif Exam Com 59-60. 9: ALA; NYLA; West NY Lib Resources Coun (pres 69-). 13: Yes. 14: Ref. 15: 522 Ashland, Buffalo NY 14222.

ROONEY, REV EUGENE MATTHEW SJ. b NYC 29 N 26. 5: Woodstock Col 48-51 (Philos, Eng) AB, PhL, 54 (Educ) MA; Drexel 51-54 MSLS; Woodstock Col 54-58 (Theol) STB. 6: Fr, Lat, Sp. 7: Libn St Josephs Prep Sch, Phila 51-54; Asst libn Woodstock Col 54-58; Libn Auriesville Tertianship, Auriesville NY 58-59; Stud counselor & libn St Josephs Prep Sch, Phila 59-; Assoc ed "Best Sellers, Scranton U 61-; Libn St Josephs Col Inst of Ind Rel Phila 66-. 8: Lib exchange to Colegio San Mateo, Osorno Chile, to open new lib 67. 9: ALA; CathLA; Unit chm E Penn Unit 68-70); Nat Cath Counselors Assn; Jesuit Educ Assn; Priv Schs LA; Nat Cath Guidance Conf; PennLA. 10: NCTE; Phila Guidance Conf; Moderator for various sch clubs & teams. 12: Assoc ed for yp books "Best Sellers (62-). 13: Yes. 14: High sch guidance in reading, a-v materials. , bk sel, media standards. 15: 1730 Girard ave, Philadelphia Pa 19130.

ROONEY, SIEGLINDE E H (SCHULDT). b Hamburg-Harburg Germany 3 S 40. 5: USASK 54-62 (Ger, Hist) BA; UToronto 62-63 BLS. 6: Ger, Eng, Fr. 7: Catlgr

York U (Toronto) 63-65; Catlgr UAlta 65-67; Act asst libn educ 67; Lib analyst 68-. 9: CanLA; ALA. 10: Faculty Club; Can Assn Univ Tchrs. 14: Catlg, data proc. 15: 9915 - 115th st 202, Edmonton Alta Can.

ROOP, HELEN FREUDENBERG. b Belleville Ill 29 Ag 18. 5: UIll 36-39 (Fr) AB, 41-42 BS in LS, UCal (Berkeley) 67-68. 6: r, Ger, Sp, Fr. 7: Child libn Belleville Pub Lib, Belleville Ill 39-41; Libn Sp-4 US Nav Train Sta, Great Lakes Ill 42-43; Libn P-1 Hosp libn Marie Island Naval Hosp, Mare Island Cal 44-45; Child libn Los Angeles Pub Lib 46-47; Asst catlgr UIll Med Sch 48-49; Br libn III Chicago Pub Lib 53-62; Libn I Public Health Lib UCal Berkeley65-66; Br libn III Berkeley Pub Lib 66-. 9: Chicago Br LibnsClub pres 61). 10: Phi Beta Kappa; Phi Kappa Phi; Girl Scout Leader. 14: Pub health, pub lib wk, lib automation. 15: 577 SantaBarbara rd, Berkeley Cal 94707.

ROOS, JOSEPHINE. b Kenedy Tex 26 O 43. 5: Incarnate Word Col 61-65 (Hist) BA; UDenver 65-66 (Libnship) MA; San Jose State Col 68-69 (Hist). 6: Sp. 7: Catlgr San Jose State Col Lib 66-67, Asst acquis libn 67-. 9: CalLA; No Cal Tech Serv Group. 14: Tech serv. 15: 3282 St Ignatius pl, Santa Clara Ca 95051.

ROOSE, WALTER RANDALL. b Hartford Conn 17 D 21. 4: Virginia Giguere. 5: Rollins Col 47-51 (Hist) BA; Peabody Col 51-52 (Hist) MA; Simmons 58 (LS). 7: Sgt US Marine Corps SW Pacific 42-47; Doc libn UMass 57-60; Libn US Navy Underwater Sound Lab 60-63; Sr ref libn Sandia Labs, Albuquerque NM 63-. 9: SLA. 11: Carnegie Fellow in Tchg, Peabody Col. 12: Ed "Southwestern Union List of Serials" (65). 14: Ref. 15: 9817 Hannett pl NE, Albuquerque NM 87112.

ROOT, MIRIAM HUGHES. b Litchfield NY 24 S 05. 4: . 5: Keuka Col 23-26 (Eng) BA; Columbia 34 (LS) BS. 6: Ger, Fr. 7: Libn Keuka Col 27-44, Post, Ft Totten NY 44-46, G & C Meriam Co, Springfield Mass 46-62, West New Eng Col Lib 62-64, Holyoke Community Col Lib 64-. 9: ALA. 10: AAUW; Holyoke Bus & Prof Women. 14: Ref, bk sel. 15: 440 Appleton st, Holyke Mass 01041.

ROOT, NINA J. b NYC. 5: Hunter Col (Internat Rel) BA; 57-58 MLS. 6: Russian, Sp. 7: Jr lib asst Hunter Col 55-57; Period & ref libn Albert Einstein Col of Med 58-59; Asst Chief Med Libn Amer Cancer Soc, NYC 59-62; Chief Libn Amer Inst of Aeronautics & Astronautics Tech Info Serv, NYC 62-64; Head ref unit Sci & Tech Div LS 64-66; Mgt consul Nelson Assocs, Inc 66-. 9: SLA(Aerospace Div); ALA. 10: YWCA. 14: Sci ref, admin, info retrieval. 15: 305 E 40th st, New York NY 10016.

ROPEL, CATHERINE (QUACKENBUSH). b Canton Penn 30 N 16. 4: Edward R Ropel. 5: Penn State 36-39 (Ed) BA, summers 40-42 (LS); Syracuse summer 43 (LS). 6: Fr. 7: Tchr Greenfield Twp High Sch, Claysburg Penn 39-40; Tchr & libn Waynesboro Jr High Sch, Waynesboro Penn 40-45; Libn Morristown Jr High Sch, Morristown NJ 46-62; Libn Pitman Jr High Sch, Pitman NJ 45-46; Libn Susquehanna Twp Jr High Sch, Harrisburg Penn 63-. 9: ALA; PennLA; CapitalAreaLA. 10: Lutheran Church Women. 14: Ya lit & ref. 15: RD 1, Middletown Pa 17057.

ROPER, FRED WILBURN. b Hendersonville NC 15 My 38. 5: UNC 56-60 (Eng) AB, 60-62 MS in LS; UCLA 62-63 (Biomed Lib Train Program); Chicago 67-68 (LS); Ind U 68- (LS). 6: Fr. 7: Biomed machine methods libn UCLA Biomed Lib 63-65; Research Assoc Inst for lib research UCLA 66; Hd pub serv Chicago State Col Lib 67-68. 8: UNC Sch of Lib Sci, summers 62 & 65, 66-67, 9: MedLA; AALS; ASIS. 10: Beta Phi Mu; AAUP. 14: Tchg lib sci, ref, machines in libs; med libnship. 15: Box 1364, Bloomington In 47401.

ROPER, ROBERT JOHN. b Lowell Mass 14 N 18. 4: Dorothy Galvin. 5: Boston U 50 (Soc Studies) BS in Ed; Simmons 47 (LS) Certif. 7: Ref asst sci & tch dept Boston Pub Lib 36-51; US Navy 43-46; Tech info off Off of Naval Rsearch, Boston 51-55; Field rep ASTIA, NYC 55-57; Tech libn Tidewater Oil Co, Delaware Refinery 57-62; Tech libn TIDEWATER Oil Co Tech R&D, Valley Forge Penn 62-66; Libn CBS Labs, Stamford Conn 66-. 9: SLA. 14: Ref. 15: 163 Cynthia dr, Fairfield Ct 06430.

ROPER, THELMA (JOHNSON). b Earle Ark 16 N 09. 4: Richard Andrew Roper Sr. 5: Union U (Tenn) 33-37 (Eng) AB; LSU summers 37-40 BS in LS. 7: Tchr-libn Church Point High Sch, Church Point La 38-40; Asst libn La Lib Commsn, Baton Rouge La 40; Asst libn Bossier Parish Lib, Bentow La 41; Libn Obion Co Lib, Union City Tenn 45-46; Br libn Tangipahoa Parish Lib, Kentwood La 51-59; Tchr-libn Osyka High Sch, Osyka Miss 59-60; Br libn Tangipahoa Parish Lib, Kentwood La 60-64; Tchr-libn Chesbrough High Sch, Kentwood La 64-67, Tchr-libn Kentwood High Sch 67-. 9: La Tchrs Assn; LaLA. 10: PTA; Nat Fed of Music Clubs; Tangipahoa Parish TA; Amer Assn Tchrs of Span & Portu. 15: Box 11, Kentwood La 70444.

ROSBOROUGH, JEAN LORAINE (CLARK). b Pontiac Mich 25 Ap 08. 5: Russell Sage Col 25-26, 27-29 (Eng, Hist) AB; Mich State U 26-27; Syracuse 64-65 MLS. 6: Fr. 7: Lib Pontiac Pub Lib, Pontiac Mich 29-31; Soc ed Pontiac Daily Press, Pontiac Mich 31-33; Soc & br manager Detroit News, Pontiac Mich 32-34; Home & sub tchg Endicott pub schs, Endicott NY 57-61; S lib clerk George F Johnson Mem Lib, Endicott NY 61-64; Libn Four Co Lib System, Binghamton NY 65-. 9: NYLA; S Central Ref & Research Coun. 10: Beta Phi Mu; AAUW; Womens Nat Bk Assn. 14: Ref, interlib loan. 15: 17-C Andrea dr, Vestal NY 13850.

ROSCOW, JEAN (CUNNINGHAM). b Paterson NJ 23 D 09. 4: John FRoscow Jr. 5: Columbia 28-32 (Bus Admin) BS; UFla & Appalachian State Col 58-61. 6: Fr. 7: Priv sec W B Bradbury Co, NYC 32-41; Libn Citrus High Sch, Inverness Fla 58-. 9: NEA; ALA; FlaLA; FlaEA;FlaSchL. 10: Friends of the Lib; Inverness Womens Club; Inverness Womens Golf Assn; Womens Auxiliary of Citrus Mem Hosp, Inverness. 14: Sch libs. 15: Box 777, Inverness Fl 32650.

ROSE, BEATRICE EDNA. b Langdon ND. 5: UMinn 35-37 (Hist) BS in Ed; Col of St Catherine 40-41 BS in LS; Seattle U summer 63. 6: Ger. 7: Tchr rural schs, Langdon ND; Jr high tchr, Munich ND; Soc studies tchr, Ft Pierre SD; Dental libn Marquette U; Libn Dept of Lib Sci Catholic U; Sch libn Armed Forces, Japan 59-60; Supv of Libs Lake Forest (Ill) Pub Schs 44-59, 60-. 9: ALA-AASchL; IllLA; IllEA; IllASchL & IRS (mem Com of Basic Booklist 66). 10: AAUW. 14: Child . 15: 722 N Western, Lake Forest Ill 60045.

ROSE, GRETA LEORA. b Keswick Ridge NB 29 Jl 09. 5: AcadiaU 31 (Eng) BA; Simmons 38 (LS) SB. 7: Tchr of Eng, Sch for Blind, Halifax NS 31-34; Sec wk Halifax NS 34-37; Libn Miss Porter's Sch, Farmington Conn 37-38; Child libn pub lib, Mass; Swampscott 38-42, Quincy 42-46, Lynn 46-61; Chief libn Colchester-E Hants Reg Lib, Truro NS 61-. 9: Child RT of New England (sectreas 4143); CanLA; APLA. 10: Univ Women-s Club of Truro NS. 12: Wings Over Walls--, poetry (49); Cables and Cobwebs--, poetry (52). 13: Yes. 14: Admin, child wk. 15: 754 Prince st, Truro Nova Scotia Can.

ROSE, JEANNE. b Manhattan Kan. 5: Col of William & Mary 29-33 (Eng) BA; George Washington U 46-48 (Eng Lit) MA; American U 60-61, 63 (Comparative Lit). 6: Fr, Ger, Ital. 7: Libn Washington-Lee High Sch, Arlington Va 33-34; Clerk Nat Geographic Soc, Wash DC 34-36; Jr catlgr Folger Shakespeare Lib, Wash DC 36-48; Sr catlgr Enoch Pratt Free Lib, Baltimore 48-59; Ref supv Arlington Co Lib, Arlington Va 59-. 9: ALA (Memb Com, Chm Va 60-65; Recr Com, Chm Va 65-);-RSD (Potomac Chm Valley Chap); SLA 66-68); (chm Baltimore Chap 55-56); DCLA; SELA; Potomac Tech Proc Libns; Reg Group of Catlgrs & Clsfrs chm 56-58). 10: Arlington Hist Soc; Metro Opera Guild; Lyon Village Womens Club; Womens Com for the Arlington Symphony. 11: William & Mary Medallion, 53, for Loyalty & Service. 13: Yes. 14: Ref, catlg. 15: 4318 N Carlyn Springs rd, apt 2, Arlington Va 22203.

ROSE, MRS KATHRYN (WYNN). b Pilot Point Tex 22 Je 15. 4: John Edmund Rose. 5: Tex Womans U 32-35 (LS) BS; Columbia 53-56 (Guidance) MA. 6: Fr. 7: Libn: Sr High Sch, Burkburnett Tex 36-40, Sr High Sch, Farmersville Tex 40-42, Sr High Sch, Garland Tex 42-44; Ed Southern Aircraft Corp, Garland Tex 44-46; Ed United Bd for Christian Cols in China, NYC 46-51; Libn Sr. High Sch, Darien Conn 51-62; Libn Techrs Insurance & Annuity Assn of Amer, NYC 63-. 9: SLA (NY Chap: Insur Div). 14: Ref. 15: 205 West End Ave, apt 11-B, NYC 10023.

ROSE, SIDNEY (JEROME). b Buffalo NY 16 D 39. 5: UBuffalo 58-63 (Eng) BA; SUNY (Geneseo) 63-65 MLS. 6: Fr. 7: Libn (staff) Buffalo & Erie Co Pub Lib, Buffalo NY 64-. 9: Libn's Assn of Buffalo & Erie Co. 14: Acquis. 15: 343 Crestwood ave, Buffalo NY 14216.

ROSE, THELMA (MAY). b Cleveland 10 J3 11. 4: Harold Rose. 5: West Res 28-37 BA (Lit), BS in LS. 6: Ger, Fr. 7: From page to clerk to asst libn Cleveland Pub Lib 28-37; Asst libn NY Pub Lib 38-39; Sub libn Cleveland Pub Lib 43-45; Child wk The Temple Lib 48-58; Cleveland Pub Lib Popular

Lib: Asst libn 60-64, 1st asst 64-, Act head 65, Hd for Lit Dept 66-. 9: ALA; OhioLA. 10: LWV; PTA; Womens Nat Bk Assn. 15: 2301 Delaware dr, Cleveland Heights Ohio 44106.

ROSE, VERLINDA C. b Memphis Tenn 9 Ja 43. 5: Whitman Col 61-65 (Eng) BA; UCal (Berkeley) 67-68 MLS. 7: Asst libn Pillsbury Madison & Sutro, San Francisco 69-. 9: ALA; SLA; AALL; CalLA. 10: Beta Phi Mu. 14: Law libnship. 15: 1919 Octavia st apt 2, San Francisco Ca 94109.

ROSE, WALTER REDMOND. b Endicott NY 20 My 37. 5: Harpur Col 55-59 (Eng Lit) BA; Syracuse 60-62 MSLS. 7: Catlg dept clk Syracuse U Lib 60-62; Catlg dept libn Four Co Lib Syst, Binghamton NY 62-65; Catlg dept libn Mem Lib State U Col (Cortland NY) 66-69. 12: "A Bibliography of the Irish in the United States" (69). 14: Catlg. 15: Tristram Shanty, 145 Caswell st, Afton NY 13730.

ROSELLE, WILLIAM CHARLES. b Vandergrift Penn 30 Je36. 4: Marsha Louise Lucas. 5: Thiel Col 54-58 (Eng) BA; UPittsburgh 62-63 MLS. 7: Intelligence analyst US Army Counter Intelligence, Ft Holabird Md 58-60; Eng tchr Milton Hershey Sch, Hershey Penn 60-62; Lib trainee Penn State Lib 62-63; Asst catlg libn Penn State U 63-65; Engnr libn UIowa 65-66, Math libn 65-66; Lib admin asst UIowa 66-.14175 9: ALA; MusLA; Amer Musicological Soc; Assn for Recorded Sound Collections (chm Educ Standards Com 67-). 10: AAUP; Beta Phi Mu; Beta Beta Beta; Phi Alpha Theta; Triangle Club U Iowa. 13: Yes. 14: Catlg, bibliog. 15: 209 Tetters ct, Iowa City Ia 52240.

ROSEMAN, GLORIA (SAMUELSON). b NYC 17 Je 20. 4: Benjamin Roseman. 5: Antioch 36-41 (Art Mus Ed) BA; Villanova 60-63 (LS) MS; Temple 57-. 6: Fr. 7: Libn Wanamaker Jr High Sch, Phila 59-66; Supv instr materials & media Phila Sch Dist 66-. 9: ASCD; ALA; PennSchLA; Sch Libns Phila. 14: Sch libs. 15: 1411 Delphine rd, Philadelphia Pa 19118.

ROSEMAN, HERBERT C. b Brooklyn NY 29 Mr 32. 4: Lucy Gordon. 5: NYU 49-53 (Eng) BA, 53-60 (Educ) MA; UBuenos Aires 66-69 Certif in Lib Sci. 6: Ger, Fr, Sp, hebrew, Yiddish. 7: Film libn Assoc Artists, NYC 53-64; Curator Archive of Libertarian Lit Sch of Living for Adult Educ, Brookville Ohio & Brooklyn NY 64-. 8: Trustee & consultant Sch of Living for Adult Educ 64-69; Gen ed Sch of Living Press 64-69. 9: NCTE. 10: Yivo Inst for Jewish Research. 12: Ed "Fragments", Central Issues", "Away Out"; Authorized biographer of Harry Elmer Barnes; "An Encyclopedic History of the Film" (71). 13: Yes. 14: Archivist specializing in Amer libertarian lit & film hist. 15: 2400 Nostrand ave, Brooklyn NY 11210.

ROSEN, BETTYLOU. b Scranton Penn 9 Je 38. 5: Fla State U 56-60 (LS) BA; LSU 64-66 (LS) MS. 6: Sp. Hebrew. 7: Clerk child room Miami Pub Lib, Miami Fla 59; Libn: Tyrone Jr High Sch, St Petersburg Fla 60-61, Palm Springs Jr High Sch, Hialeah Fla 61-62, USAF Dependent Sch, Misawa Japan 62-63, USAF Dependent Sch, Tokyo Japan 63-64; Ref asst LC 66, Catlgr 67-68. 9: ALA. 10: Assn of Americans & Canadians in Israel. 15: 14050 NE 6th ave apt 308, North Miami Fla 33161.

ROSEN, IDA. b Rome NY 26N22. 5: NYState Tchrs Col(Albany) 39-44 (Eng) BA, MA; Eastman Sch of Music 45-47 (Music Educ) BM; Columbia 60 (LS) MS; Cornell U 61 (Musicology) PhD. 6: Fr, Ger, Lat. 7: Soc studies tchr Rome Jr High Sch, Rome NY 44-45; Piano tchr Bartram Sch, Jacksonville Fla 47-49; Libn Buffalo & Erie Co Pub Lib, Buffalo NY 62-64 Libn art & music div Milwaukee Pub Lib 64-65; Phonograph record libn music dept Princeton U 65-. 9: ALA; MusLA; Amer Musicological Soc. 12: The Treatment of Dissonance in the Motets of Josquin Dezpress PhD diss (61). 13: Yes. 14: Music phonograph record libnship. 15: 120 Prospect ave, apt E1, Princeton NJ 08540.

ROSENBAUM, DAVID. b Detroit 30 My 16. 4: Clare Anderson. 5: Wayne U 34-35; UMich 35-37 (Hist) BA; Chicago 37-38 (Hist); UMich 38-39 BA in LS; Harvard 41-42 (Hist). 6: Fr, Ger. 7: Jr asst Detroit Pub Lib 39-41; In bus 42-51 Libn II Detroit Pub Lib 51-64, 1st asst lang & lit dept 64-69 8: Consul (bk sel) Macomb Co, Mich Lib Syst 65-68; Instr Wayne State U Lib Sci Dept 66-; Lectr Ref Wkshops Mich State Lib 68. 9: ALA; MichLA. 10: Detroit Pub Lib Employees Union; Detroit Book Club; Phi Beta Kappa; Phi Kappa Phi. 13: Yes. 14: Ref, lib sci educ. 15: 19156 Lauder, Detroit 48235.

ROSENBERG, ANNELIE (GISELA). b Frankfurt Germany 29 S 41. 5: UIll (Chicago) 59-61 (Liberal Arts, Sci); UIll(Urbana) 61-63 (Ger) BA, 63-64 (LS) MS; UCLA 64 (Train program in Med Libnship). 6: Ger, Estonian. 7: Stud clerk UIll Off of Admissions (Chicago) 59-61; Stud asst UIll Arch Lib 61-64; Ref libn UCLA Bio-med Lib 64-66, Act hd, Hd interlib loans sect & Asst hd pub serv dept 68-. 9: MedLA; Med Lib Group So Cal (see 67-68). 10: Phi Beta Mu. 14: Ref, interlib loans. 15: Biomedical Lib Univ of Cal, Center for Heath Sci, Los Angeles Ca 90024.

ROSENBERG, DOROTHY ISABELLE (COHICK). b Williamsport Penn 6 Ap 13. 5: Lycoming Col 46-49 (Eng) BA; UDenver 49-51 (LS) MA; NM Highlands 52-53 (Educ) Educational Certif; Bucknell U 55 (Educ). 6: Fr, Ger. 7: Nurse Corps US Army (1st Lt), S Pacific Area 42-45; Elem tchr US Indian Serv, Navaho Indian Agency 52-55, Elem sch libn 55-57; Libn Willingboro elem schs, Willingboro NJ 62-. 9: NJEA; NJLA. 14: Educ & curric. 15: 44 Hawthorne lane, Willingboro NJ08046.

ROSENBERG, GERTRUDE. b New Haven Conn 11 Mr 32. 5: Arnold Col 49 (Phys Educ); Stone Bus Col 51 Bus Grad Certif. 6: Fr, Hebrew. 7: Off mgr & libn A D Steinbach, New Haven Conn 51-61; Supv & libn System Development Corp, Paramus NJ 61-65; Tech libn ITT Dta Communications, Paramus NJ 65-67; Tech libn Isotopes Inc, Westwood NJ 68; Tech libn West Union Tele Co, NYC 68-. 8: Research wk done for author gathering data for bk, NYC. 9: SLA. 10: B'nai B'rith Women. 14: Ref, research. 15: 60 Hudson st, New York NY 10013.

ROSENBERG, JOHN EDWARD. b Phila 4 F 16. 4: Esther Hirsch. 5: UPenn 33-38 (Eng) AB; Drexel 49-51 MS in LS. 6: Fr. 7: Visitor Dept ofPub Asst, Phila 41-43; Interviewer Penn State Employment Serv, Phila 43-51; Asst libn Harry Diamond Labs, Wash DC 51-58, Libn 58-. 9: SLA; DCLA. 10: Phi Kappa Phi. 14: Admin, catlg, ref, subj analysis of tech reports lit. 15: 4501 Connecitcut ave NW, apt 803, Wash DC 20008.

ROSENBERG, KENYON CHARLES. b Chicago 9 S 23. 4: Carolyn Allison. 5: Los Angeles City Col 55-57 (Lat) AA; UCLA 57-59 (LS) AB; USoCal 59-61 (LS) MS. 6: Ger, Lat. 7: Battery clerk (Cpl) US Army 91st AFA Bn, Ft Hood Tex 53-55; Catlg searcher, typist Los Angeles Co Law Lib, Los Angeles 55-58, Ref libn 59-60; Libn Los Angeles Off Cal Dept of JUSTICE 60-62; Law lib consul Alaska State Court System, Anchorage Alaska 62; Head of ref & circ Atomics Internat, Canoga Park Cal 62; Supv tech documents center Hughes Aircraft Co, Culver City Cal 62-65, Head tech lib serv 65-66; Dir tech info serv Ampex Corp, Redwood City Cal 66-68; Asst Prof Sch Lib Sci Kent State U 68-. 8: Mem, Defense Documentation Center, Industry Task Group & Info Analysis Center Task Group, Nat Security Industry Assn; Consul, Col of San Mateo, Train Prog for Lib Technicians. 9: ASIS (pres San Francisco Chap 67-68); SLA; ALA; AALA; OhioLA. 10: Chi Delta Pi; Alpha Mu Gamma; Inst Electric & Electron Engrs; AAAS; Nat Security Industrial Assn. 12: "Sedentary Critic column (music criticism) of "Bnai Brith Messenger & "The Record Whirl column, syndicated recordingsreviews. 14: Info retrieval, ref, spec libs, data proc. 15: 608 Roosevelt ave, Kent Oh 44240.

ROSENBERG, MARLENE. b Brooklyn NY 20 Ap 46. 5: Brooklyn Col 63-67 (Hist) BA; Rutgers 67-69 MLS. 6: Fr, Ger. 7: Libn (staff) Brooklyn Pub Lib, Brooklyn NY 68-. 15: 222 Lenox rd, Brooklyn NY 11226.

ROSENBERG, MELVIN HAROLD. b Detroit Mich 19 Je 25. 5: Wayne State 43-47 (Eng) BA; IndU 51 (Lit); UMinn 51-52 (Lit); Immaculate Heart Col 64-65 MALS. 7: Activities dir Grandview Sanitarium, Whittier Cal 52-64; LA Pub Lib: Y-a libn 65-68, Sr libn 68-. 9: ALA. 14: Ref, private pressbks, lit (esp poetry). 15: Memorial Branch Lib, 4623 W Olympic blvd, Los Angeles Ca 90019.

ROSENBERG, PAUL M. b Malden Mass 16N 28. 4: Ruth Sterling. 5 Boston U 48-50 (Human Ref) Rel 50-52 (Elem Educ) BS; UMass 53-57 (Educ) MS; Rutgers 61-64 MLS. 7: Bandsman US Army, US & European Command 46-48; Tchg prin Sch Dept, Westhampton Mass 53-55; Math & sci tchr Thos Jefferson Jr High Sch, Fair Lawn NJ 55-61, Libn 61-69; Libn catlgr & ref Pub Lib, Teaneck NJ 62-; Hd libn Fair Lawn High Sch 69-; Lectr in lib sci Alphonsus Col, Woodcliff Lakes NJ 69-. 9: NEA; NJEA; tnjla; BCSLA. 10: Amer Youth Hostels. 14: Censorship. 15: 2-01 17th st, Fair Lawn NJ 07411.

ROSENBERGER, MARGARET (MORTHLAND). b York Co tpenn 6 Ja 12. 4: Daniel Rosenberger. 5: Juniata Col 30-31, 32-33 (Home Econ): Phila Col of Bible 39 Diploma Bethany Biblical Sem (Chicago) 39-40 (Religious Educ) B Sacred Lit;

Pratt 44-45 BLS; Adelphi 55-57; SUNY (Geneseo) 58-61 C W Post Col LIU 63-64 (LS). 7: Nutritionist York Nursery Sch, York Penn 34-36; Stud libn Phila Col of Bible 36-38; Housemother Pub ORPHANAGE, Quincy Penn 40-43; Ref asst Martin Mem Lib, York Penn 43-44; Ref asst & circ asst Pratt Inst Lib summers 45, 47; Libn The Stony Brook Sch, Stony Brook NY 45-51; Jr high & elem libn Port Jefferson Schs (NY) 56-66; Libn E Monches Pub Sch, E Moriches NY. 9: NEA; ALA; NY State Tchrs Assn; Suffolk Co LA. 10: Three Village Garden Club; Lib Com, Emma Clark Lib, Setauket NY; Pioneer Girls Leader; Christian Womens Club; Nat Educs Fellowship. 14: Ref, reading guidance. 15: c/o Bryan College, Dayton Tn 37331.

ROSENFELD , BESSIE (SILVER). b Cleveland 1 O 16. 5: Flora Stone Mather 34-38(Eng) BA; West Res 38-39 BS in LS. 6: Yiddish. 7: Jr asst Cleveland Pub Lib40-49; Libn Fairmount Temple Lib, Cleveland 62-. 12: Co-comp "Index to Jewish Periodicals (63-64). 15: 2380 Warrensville Ctr rd, University Hts Oh 44118.

ROSENFELD, JOEL CHARLES. b Brooklyn NY 16 Je 39. 4: Susan Meerson. 5: UMich 59-61 (Eng) AB, 62-64 AMLS. 6: Fr. 7: Tchr Millington Sch Dist, Millington Mich 61-62; Libn trainee Flint Pub Lib, Flint Mich 63-64; Libn Potter Br 65-66; Admin serv libn Lincoln Trail Libs, Champaign Ill 67-68; Libn Urbana Free Lib, Urbana Ill 68-. 8: Spec instr Mott Adult Educ Program, Flint Mich 6565; Instr, Lib Sci Ext UIll 69. 9: IllLA. 10: Exchange Club. 14: Commun Lib Serv. 15: 201 S Race st, Urbana Il 61801.

ROSENGARTEN, BARBARA LYNN (CHORDOCK). b Newark NJ 26 F 43. 4: Steven B Rosengarten. 5: Marietta Col 60-61; Rutgers 61-64 (Pol Sci) BA, 64-67 MLS. 7: Circ asst RutgersU (Newark) 64-66; Ref asst NJ State Lib, Trenton 66-67; Hd ref Woodbridge Pub Lib, Woodbridge NJ 67-. 9: NJLA. 14: Ref, govt docs. 15: 131A Minebrook rd, Edison NJ 08817.

ROSENHAMER, REV JOHN HENRY. b Coalport Penn 26 Ag 38. 5: Gammon Col 5-58: St Marys Sem 58-60 (Philos) AB, 60-64 (Theol) STB; West Res summers 61-63, 65 MS in LS. 6: Lat, Ger. 7: Asst libn St Marys Sem (Baltimore) 60-64; Tchr & asst libn Bradford Central Christian High Sch, Bradford Penn 64-66; Asst libn & AV dir Verango Christian High Sch, Oil City Penn 66-. 9: ALA; NEA-DAVI; PennLA; HTA. 10: Nat Wildlife Fed; Audubon Soc; Amer Forestry Assn; Amer Mus of Natural Hist; NCCA. 14: Ref, ya, admin. 15: Fryburg Pa 16326.

ROSENSTEEL, JACK RANDALL. b Mount Union Pa 16 Ja 39. 5: Maryville Col 56-60 (Eng) BA; Drexel 60-61 MS in LS. 7: Free Lib of Phila: Libn fiction dept 61, 64-65, Asst libn bk selection 65-69; Admin asst to dir 69-; Military service 62-64. 9: ALA; PennLA. 10: Philobiblon Club. 14: Book sel, admin. 15: Free Lib of Philadelphia Logan Sq, Phila Pa 19103.

ROSENSTEIN, PHILIP. b Montreal Can 5F22. 4: Miriam Ruth Yaffe. 5: UCLA 46-48 (Anthropology) BA; Columbia 48-50 (Anthropology) MA, 52-55 MA in LS. 6: Yiddish, Ger, Fr. 7: Circ ref a st NY Acad of Med, NSC 52-55; Dir of Libs & Asst Prof of Lib Sci Brooklyn Col of Pharmacy 55-66; Libn NJ Col of Med & Dentistry 66-. 8: Staff, Lib/USA, NY Worlds Fair, 65. 9: SLA; MedLA (Adv Mgr "Bulletin 64-66, chm Pharmacy Group 59; NY Reg Group: sec 61-63, chm-elect 65-66; NY Chap: chm Biol Scis Div 56-58). 12: Ed Jt Com on Pharmacy Col Libs "Newsletter 62-66); "Know Your College Library (59). 13: Yes. 14: Ref, admin. 15: 168-30 127th ave, Jamaica NY 11434.

ROSENSTRAUCH, GERALD. b NYC 20 Ja 30. 4: Roselle Kletter. 6: Hebrew, Jewish. 7: Asst libn Choate Mitchel & Ely, NYC 45-48; Seaman US Navy 48-49: Clerk & libn Stroock, NYC 49-62;Libn Maravel Maradel Inc, NYC 62-64; Libn Kaye Scholar Fierman Hays & Handler, NYC 65-. 9: AALL; Law Libs Assn, Greater NY; SLA. 10: . 14: Catlg, ref. 15: c/o Kaye Scholer Fierman Hays & Handler, AW Lib, 425 Park ave, NYC 10022.

ROSENTHAL. ELAINE P. b Troy NY 2 Ap 21. 4: Robert J Rosenthal. 5: George Washington U 53-60 (Humanities, Art Hist) AB; Catholic U 62-63 (LS) MS. 6: Fr. 7: Circl libn American U 46-48, 52-54; Interlib loan libn US Dept of the INterior Lib, Wash DC 55-58, Asst chief ref sect 62-63, Chief ref sect 64-67, Chief info div 68-. 9: SLA; DC Chap; Direct Com (2nd v-pres 67-68, pres-elect Nat Resources Div 68-69); ALA; Recr Com; DCLA (sec 65-67). 10: AAUW; Docent Nat Gal of Art; Phi Beta Kappa; Beta Phi Mu. 13: Yes. 14: Ref. 15: 4301 Massachusetts ave NW, Wash DC 20016.

ROSENTHAL, AVRAM. b Phila 16 F 27. 4: Marilynn Warratt. 5: Wayne State U 44-48 (Music) AB, 48-51 (Music) MA; UMich 50-51 AMLS. 7: Asst in ref dept, adult serv libn Dearborn Pub Lib, Dearborn mich 51-54; Catlgr Hebrew U Lib (Jerusalem Israel) 55; Dir of Lib Wayne Co Lib, Romulus Mich 56; Dir of Lib Wayne Co Lib, River Rouge Mich 57; Instr Lib Sci UDenver summer Instr Istr Lib Sci UMich 63-; Dir Lib System Livonia Pub Lib, Livonia Mich 58-66; Div hd lib serv Henry Ford Commun Col Lib (Dearborn Mich) 66-. 8: Exec dir, Nat Lib Week, Mich 62. 9: AALS; MichLA (chm Intel Freedom Com 56-57, mem Legis Com 63-64). 10: Livonia Citizens for Better Human Rel. 14: Admin, hist of bks, lib educ. 15: 19398 Ingram, Livonia Mich 48152.

ROSENTHAL, FREDERICK JOHN. b Cologne Germany 4 S 23. 4: Carolyn Mann. 5: Columbia 48-53 (Govt, Internat Rel) BS(summa cum laude), 53-55 (internat Rel) AM, 55-56 (LS) MS. 6: Ger, Dutch, Fr. 7: Mil intelligence serv US Army (T/4) 43-46; Corp sec Pollys Exclusive Handknits, NY 48-52; LC: Lib Intern 56-57, Foreign affairs bibliog Lib Serv Div 57-62 Head Subj Spec Sect Lib Serv Div Legis Ref Serv 58-62-68, Spec in info organization & control lib serv div Legis Ref serv 68-. 10: Beta Phi Mu; Phi Beta Kappa. 14: Catlg, ref; file org, info sci. 15: 4321 Kentbury dr, Bethesda Md 20014.

ROSENTHAL, PATRICIA (GIBBONS). b Chester Mont 22 F 19. 4: Willis M Rosenthal. 5: UMont 36-40 (LS) BA; UNC Raleigh 63-64; UFla 69. 7: Asst libn Pub Lib, Kalispell Mont 40-42; Libn Jr High Sch, Logan Utah, 53-54; hild room Pub Lib, Salem Ore 56-58; Libn St Andrews Sch for Boys, St Andrews Tenn 59-60; Libn Rex Hosp & Nursing Sch, Raleigh NC 61-63; Libn Wake Co Schs, Raleigh NC 64-. 66; Libn Rockingham Pub Schs, Rockingham NC 66-67; Libn Duval Co Pub Schs, Jacksonville Fla 67-. 9: ALA; SELA; FlaLA; NCLA. 14: Child serv. 15: St Matthews Church, Stateswide rd, Salisbury NC 28144.

ROSEVEAR, MARJORIE ASHLEY (VAN ZANDT) (MRS). b Detroit. 5: UMich 43-44 AB in LS. 6: Fr. 7: Catlgr AEC, Los Alamos NM 49-51; Head libn 6th Army, Ft Huachuca Ariz 51-53; Head libn 47th Bomb Wing, Sculthorpe Eng 54-58; Coop proc center libn Nev State Lib 59-60; Reg libn Elko-Landereureka Co, Elko Nev 62-64; Curriculum libn Cal West U 64-66; Dir U San Diego Col for Mem Lib 66-68; Libn The Bishop's School 68-. 11: Dorothy Canfield Fisher Award, Elko Nb 64. 12: ""Secret Cowboy (55 & 60).13: Yes. 14: Curr lib influence on tchrs & reg wk. 15: 32 1/2 San Elijo, San Diego 92106.

ROSIER, JOSEPHINE LEHMAN. b Fairmont WVa 18 My 07. 4: Robert Rosier. 5: WVaU 24-28 (Educ) AB; Columbia 30-33 BSLS. 7: Asst libn Fairmont Sr High Sch, Fairmont WVa 28-29; Libn Fairmont Jr High Sch, Fairmont WVa 29-33; Fairmont State Col: Asst libn 33-39, Ref libn 57-58, Head Libn 58-. 9: ALA-ACRL (sec Tri-State Chap 61-62; mem Bd); NEA; WVaLA (pres 34-35). 10: AAUW; Alpha Xi Delta; Delta Kappa Gamma. 14: Catlg, ref. 15: 22 Outlook rd, Fairmont WVa 26554.

ROSINSKI, GERALDINE. b NY 21 Mr 39. 5: St Joseph's Col 57-61 (Fr) BA; Pratt Inst 68 MLS. 6: Fr. 7: Lib trainee Farmingdale Pub Lib, Farmingdale Long Is NY 61-62; Sec Emery Air Freight JFK Airport 62-68; Queen's Borough Pub Lib: Lib trainee 68, Child llibn 68-69, Asst br libn 69-. 9: ALA; NY Lib Club. 14: Ref, adult serv. 15: 143-07 Cherry ave, Flushing NY 11355.

ROSS, ANN (KLEIN). b Alden Iowa 10 Ag 23. 4: Ronald Ross. 5: Iowa State U 39-43 (Nutrition) BS, 44-45 (Sociol); Catholic U 64-67 MSLS. 7: Readers' adv DC Pub Lib 67-. 9: ALA; DCLA. 10: Beta Phi Mu. 14: Bk sel, ref. 15: 1201 N Evergreen st, Arlington Va 22205.

ROSS, CLAUDINE SKELTON (TOMMYE). b Anderson SC 26 Jl 08. 5: Claflin Col 30-34 (Eng, Fr, Math) AB; S Car Col summers 47-51 (Ed, Lib) MS; Atlanta U summers 38-39 (LS) Certif. 6: Fr. 7: Math tchr high sch, Anderson SC 34-44; Math tchr & libn high sch, St George SC 44-46, St Matthews SC 46-59; Elem tchr, Orangeburg SC 59-61; Libn elem sch, Orangeburg SC 61; Asst libn SC State, Orangeburg SC summers 54-. 8: Mem Eval Com So Assn for High Sch 59; Grantee for Proj Head Start 65. 9: ALA; NEA-DAVI; SCEA; SCLA. 10: Nat Assn Col Women; Claflin Col Alum; Reading Coun; Fed Women's Clubs; Alpha Kappa Alpha. 14: Ref. 15: 112 Wilkinson ave SE, Orangeburg SC 29115.

ROSS, ELIZABETH (CLIFFORD). b Terre Haute Ind 3 Mr 17. 5: Ind State Tchrs Col 34-38 (Eng, Fr) AB;West Res 39-40 BS in LS. 6: Fr, Ger. 7: Libn Wiley High State Tchrs Col

45-46; Libn Union Hosp Sch of Nursing, Terre Haute Ind 47-50, 57-59; Ref libn Emeline Fairbanks Mem Lib, Terre Haute Ind 59-69; Hd local hist dept Vigo Co Pub Lib, Terre Haute Ind 69-. 9: ALA; IndLA (sec-treas Ref Div 65). 10: Sesquicenten Planning Com; Ind State Hist Soc; Commun Theatre, Terre Haute; Alliance Francaise Country Club, Terre Haute; Vigo Co Hist Soc. 14: Ref, hist, geneal. 15: Butternut Hill, 4430 WABASH, Terre Haute Ind 47803.

ROSS, ELSPETH MADGE (RITCHIE). b New Brunswick NJ 19 N 19. 4: Robert Ross. 5: Rutgers U 37-39, 40-41 (Hist) BA; Glasgow U 39-40 (Hist); Toronto 62-63 BLS; NYU 41 (Law). 6: Fr, Sp. 7: Lib asst Pub Lib, Trenton NJ 42; Co Commander WAC, Kan, SC, Miss 42-44; Staff off WAC, France, Germany 44-45; Lib asst Ont Col of Educ (Toronto) 61-62; Asst research libn Ont Inst for Studies in Educ, Toronto 63-. 66; 68-69. 9: CanLA; OntLA. 10: Assn of Women Electors Toronto. 14: Ref. 15: 170 Rosedale Hts dr, Toronto 7 Ont Can.

ROSS, EULALIE (STEINMETZ). b Cincinnati Ohio 19 Ja 10. 5: UCincinnati 34-42 (Eng) AB; Pratt Inst 42-43 BLS. 6: Ger, Sp. 7: Pub Lib of Cincinnati & Hamilton Co, Cinnati: Child libn 34-42, coord child qk 55-63; NYC Pub Lib: Child libn 43-44, Supv storytelling 45-53; Lecturer UCincinnati evening col 59-62; Consul child wk State Lib, columbus Ohio 64-65; Lecturer Sch of Lib Sci Simmons Col summers 63-. 8: Vis lectr at var univs & cols on child bks and/or storytelling; Chm Storytelling Festival, Miami Beach 56. 9: ALA; FlaLA. 10: Phi Beta Kappa. 12: "The Buried Treasure" (58); The Lost Half-Hour (63); The Blue Rose (66). 13: Yes. 14: Child bks, lib serv to child, storytelling. 15: 1000 Magnolia dr, Clearwater Fl 33516.

ROSS, FRANK WILLARD. b Boise Ida 13 F 31. 4: Sally Ohling. 5: Ore Col of Educ 50-51 (Elem Educ); UOre 55-59 (Gen Soc Sci) BS, summers 59-65 MS in Libnship. 7: Supply spec A/1c USAF, US, Japan, Korea 51-55; Tchr-libn, Elmira Ore 59-60; Libn Sch Dist 19 Springfield High Sch, Springfield Ore 60-. 9: NEA-DAVI; ALA-YASD; OreEA; Ore A-V Assn; OreLA; OeASchL (v-pres 61-62). 10: Springfield (Ore) Hist Soc. 14: Sch libnship. 15: 1772 Carinal way, Eugene Ore 97401.

ROSS, GERTRUDE A(LMA). b Taylorstown Penn 2 O 13. 5: Bethany Co (Bethany WVa) (Educ, Biol) AB; Peabody 42-43 BS in LS. 7: Lib asst Carnegie Lib of McKeesport, McKeesport Penn 37-42; Stud asst Joint U Lib, Nashville 42-43; Libn ind & sci Enoch Pratt Free Lib, Baltimore 43-44; US Navy Adm Electronics Off (Lt) 44-46; Libn circ dept Lib Assn of Portland, Portland Ore 46-49; Asst ref libn San Francisco State Col 49-53, Head natural sci div 53-54; Libn sci & tech Cleveland Pub Lib 54-55; Libn sci & tech Carnegie Lib of Pittsburgh 55-57; Ref libn UCal(Davis) 57-58; Libn sci & tech Carnegie Lib of Pittsburgh 58-64, Asst head sci & tech 65-. 9: ALA-ACRL (Tri-State Chap); SLA; PennLA. 14: Sci & tech ref, admin. 15: Carnegie Lib, 4400 Forbes ave, Pittsburgh 15213.

ROSS, MARGARET (MYERS). b W Haven Conn 8 Je 14. 4: Paul Ross. 5: Conn Col for Women 32-36 (Eng) BA; Columbia 40-41 BS Lib Sci. 7: Hosp lib New Haven Free Pub Lib 37-41, Br libn 41-54; Instr lib sci So Conn State Col 60-; Libn Hamden Hall Country Day Sch 67-. 8: Consul to engring firm (Cahn), New Haven Conn 69; Org Beecher Sch Lib, New Haven Conn 59-66; Org Mishkan Israel Temple Lib, Hamden Conn 61-65. 9: ALA; ConnSchLA; SoConnLA. 14: Tchg col stud, running sch lib. 15: 970 Elm st, New Haven Ct 06511.

ROSS, RICHARD W. b Berkeley Cal 14 F 30. 5: UCal 48-52 (Drama) BA, 68 MLS; San Francisco State Col 62-66 (Fr) MA. 6: Fr, Sp, Ital. 7: Clk UCal Lib (Berkeley) 53-56; Tchr Berlitz Sch, Paris France 57-60; Designer Ray Diffen Stage Clothes, NYC 60-62; Catlgr San Francisco State Col 65-68; Libn (staff) San Francisco Pub Lib 69-. 9: ALA. 14: Catlg, ref. 15: 1456 Jones st #5, San Francisco Ca 94109.

ROSS, RYBURN McCANE. b Warrensburg NY 22 F 20. 4: Teresa Nelli. 5: City Col (NY) 9-42 (Educ) Columbia 46-49 (Educ) BS, MA, 49-50 MSLS. 7: Commsnd off (Capt) US Army Signal Corps 42-45; Ref libn Brooklyn Pub Lib 46-50; Asst libn US Naval Postgrad Sch, Monterey Cal 50-51; Libn US Naval Train Devices Center, Pt Washington NY 52-57; Assoc dir MIT Libs 57-62; Manager lib serv Aerospace Corp, Los Angeles 62-64; Asst dir tech serv CORNELL U Libs 64-. 8: Dir, Chinese Sci Proj MIT libs, 60-62. 9: Internat Fed for Documentation; SLA (Upstate NY Chap: Memb Chm 65); ALA-RTSD (chm Tech Serv); Dir of Large Res Libs Disc Group 68. 12: Ed "KWIC Index to the Science Abstracts of China (60); Ed "Current Holdings of Communist Chinese Journals in the MIT Libraries (B'). 14: Tech serv, admin. 15: 205 Winthrop dr, Ithaca NY 14850.

ROSS, VIRGINIA L(OUISE). b Covina Cal 31 Ag 15. 5: Stanford 37 (Hist) BA; Yale 39 (Anthropology) MA; UCal Berkeley 41 (LS) Certif. 7: Asst ref libn UCal(Davis) 41-42; Libn US Naval Train Sta, Farragut Ida 42-44; Hosp libn US Naval Hosp, Bethesda Md 44-46; Libn 7th Infantry Div USAFIK, Seoul Korea 46-48; Jr libn Oakland Pub Lib, Oakland Cal 48-50; San Mateo Co Lib: upv Supv Br libn, City Cal 50-52, Asst co libn, Redwood City Cal 52-54, Co Libn, Belmont Cal 54-. 8: Adv coun, State Bd of Mgrs, Cal Congress of Parents & Tchrs, 64-65; UCal Adv Coun on Educ for Libnship, 64; Adv Com, Statewide Survey of Pub Lib Serv; Lib adv comm Co Supv Assn Cal 62-. 9: ALA; (Coun Rep CalLA 67-71); CalLA (chm Intel Freedom Com 61-63, pres 65); Pub Lib Execs of Cent Cal (pres 61). 10: UCal Lib Schs Alumni Assn; Soroptimist Club; AAUW. 13: Yes. 14: Admin. 15: San Mateo Co Lib, 25 Tower rd, Belmont Cal94002.

ROSS, YVONNE (HESS). b San Antonio Tex 17 F 28. 4: Abner L Ross. 5: San Antonio Col 45-46, 54-55 (Educ); UTex 46-49 (Bus Admin) BBA, 54-58 (Educ), summers 60, 62-64 MLS & prof certif; Trinity U 56-57 (Educ) Professional elem & high sch tchrs certif; Our Lady of the Lake Col 57-58 (LS) Prov sch libns certif, 65 (Supv) Prof supv certif; Our Lady of the Lake Col 67-68 (LS, Computer). 6: Sp, Portu. 7: Libn: Jefferson Davis Jr Sch, San Antonio Ind Sch Dist, San Antonio Tx 59-61, Colonial Hills & Castle Hills Elem Schs, San Antonio Tex 61-62, Colonial Hills Elem Sch North EAST ISD, San ntonio Tex 62-65; Lib consul N East Ind Sch Dist, San Antonio Tx 65-66; Supv Lib Serv 66-. 8: Chm, elem & secon sch libns pre-sch wkshops 63-65; Summer faculty Our Lady ot the Lake Col Dept of Lib Sci 66. 9: ALA; NEA; TexLA; SWLA; Tex State Tchrs Assn (sec Lib Div Alamo Dist II 64-65); NE (Tex) Elem Libns Assn (v-chm 64-65); TexASchL (Sec 69-70). 10: Alpha Beta Alpha; Lioness Club; UTex Grad Sch of Lib Sci Alumni; Beta Gamma Sigma; Bexar Lib Assn. 14: Lib serv to child & yp, sch libs. 15: 2711 Hopeton dr, San Antonio Tx 78230.

ROSS, ZELMA (BURGET). b Francesville Ind 19 N 09. 4: F W Ross. 5: Purdue 27-31 (Eng, Soc Studies) BS; Tchrs Col 34 (Lat); Purdue 58-60 (LS) Certif as Pub or Sch Libn. 7: Libn, Francesville Ind 32-34; Tchr High Sch, Francesville Ind 34-38; Tchr High Sch, Star City Ind 40; Tchr High Sch, Dayton Ind 55; Child libn Wells Mem Pub Lib, Lafayette Ind 56-. 9: IndLA (Child & YP Round Table). 14: Child & youth libs, catlg. 15: 600 S 28th, Lafayette In 47904.

ROSSE, ROSANNA (HILDA). b The Hague Netherlands 18 Ja 20. 5: San Francisco State Col 53-58 (Prof Art) BA, 59-61 (Elem Educ) Elem Cred; UCal 64-65 MLS. 6: Dutch, Fr, Ger. 7: Sec, incl 3 yrs at Royal Lib & 1 yr for US InfoServ, The Hague Netherlands 38-46; Sec to Trade Commsnr for Netherlands Indies, NY 46-48; Sec San Francisco & Stanford Research Inst, Menlo Park 48-61; Elem tchr, Pacifica & San Francisco 61-63; Sec Edgewood, San Francisco 63-64; Libn I Contra Costa Co (Cal) Lib, El Cerrito Br 65-67; Ref libn Clarkson Col of Tech 67-. 9: ALA; NYLA; N Country Ref & Research Resources Coun. 10: AAUW; Sierra Club. 14: Ref. 15: Meadow E apts G6, 118 Leroy st, Potsdam NY 13676.

ROSSELL, GLENORA (EDWARDS). b Johnstown Penn 6 O 25. 4: James H Rossell. 5: Juniata Col 43-47 (Hist) AB; Columbia 51-52 (LS) MS; UPittsburgh 62-. 6: Sp, Fr. 7: Sch libn Harrison Twp Schs, Natrona Penn 47-48; Asst to libn Juniata Col 48-51; Trainee Brooklyn Col 51-52; Documents libn E I Dupont, Wilmington Del 52-53; Ref-educ libn Brooklyn Col 53-57; UPittsburgh: Documents libn 58-61, Libn Grad Sch Bus 61-65, Asst to dir 65-, Asst dir planning & admin serv 67-. 8: Consul Sch of Bus Atlanta U 66. 9: ALA; SLA (pres Pittburgh Chap 66-67); (Tri-State Chap); PennLA. 13: Yes. 14: Bus, docs, lib admin. 15: 1433 Beulah rd, Pittsburgh Pa 15235.

ROSSETTI, GILDA O. b Boston 11 S 11. 5: Salem State Col 30-33 (Educ) Certif; Northeastern U 40-42 (Educ) BS in Ed; Simmons 65 (LS). 6: Ital, Fr. 7: Boston Pub Lib: Asst 42-47, Prof asst 47-50, Prof asst Kirstein Bus Br 50-65; Ref libn Kirstein bus Br 65-. 9: SLA. 10: Italian Lit Club of Boston. 14: Ref. 15: 111 Perkins st, Jamaica Plain Ma 02130.

ROSSI, ALDO JOSEPH. b Stockton Cal 23 Je 30. 5: UCal(Berkeley) 48-52 (Ital) BA, 52-53 BLS, 56 (Educ) Tchr-libn Certif. 6: Ital, Sp. 7: Jr libn Stockton Pub Lib, Stockton Cal 53-54; US Army SP-3 steno, Ft Ord Cal, Ft Harrison Ind, Germany 54-56; Sr libn Stockton Pub Lib, Stockton Cal 56-58; Base libn USAF/NATO, Aviano Italy 58-62; Coordinator tech serv Stockton Pub Lib, Stockton 63-. #. 9: ALA; CalLA(pres Tech Serv Div 69). 10: Phi Beta Kappa. 11: Superior Performance Award, USAF 62. 14: Tech serv. 15: Stockton Pub Lib, 605 N El Dorado st, Stockton Ca 95202.

ROSSI, KATHERINE (PUTNAM). b Elmira NY 22 Jl 23. 4: Dominic S Rossi. 5: William Smith Col 41-45 (Biol-Chem) BA; Syracuse 65-66 MSLS. 7: Med tech St Joseph's Hosp, Elmira NY 46-47; Med tech Cornell U Infirmary 47-48; Asst libn catlg SUNY Col of Forestry (Syracuse) 66-67, Asst libn ref 67-68, Assoc libn head of tech serv 68-. 9: SLA; NYLA; SUNYLA. 15: 223 Cleveland blvd, Fayetteville NY 13066.

ROSSITER, WILLIAM A. b Worthington Penn 27 N 37. 4: Nancimay Silia. 5: Clarion State Col 56-60 (LS) BS; Jamestown Community Col 61; Canisius Col 61-66 MS. 7: Libn Panama Central Sch, Panama NY 60-61; Circ & a-v libn Canisius Col 61-63; Supv a-v & lib serv Dept of Pub Inst, Helena Mont 64-65; A-v dir Canisius Col 65-. 9: ALA; NEA-DAVI; NY State A-V Assn. 10: AAUP; Nat Rifle Assn. 14: Cross media materials. 15: 22 Russell ave, Buffalo NY 14214.

ROSSOFF, ANNIE (ROSENBLUM). b Orangeburg SC 17 Jl 16. 4: Martin Rossoff. 5: Winthrop Col 33-37 (Eng) AB; Columbia 37-38 BLS. 7: Child libn NY Pub Lib 38-41; Child libn Brooklyn Pub Lib 41-46; Sch libn NYC Bd of Educ, Midwood High Sch 51-. 9: NYC SchLA. 15: 1561 E 9 st, Brooklyn NY 11230.

ROSSOFF, MARTIN. b NYC 12 Ag 10. 4: Annie Rosenblum. 5: NYU 28-32 (Classics) AB; Columbia 32-33 (Classics) AM, 37-38 (LS) BS. 6: Fr, Ger. 7: Tchr NYC secon schs 34-41; Tech 4th grade US Army 43-45; Lib asst Lafayette High Sch, Brooklyn NY 41-47; Libn James Madison High Sch, Brooklyn NY 48-. 8: Lecturer, Queens Col, spring 56; Wkshop Dir, Col of Educ, Geneseo NY jl 56; Lecturer UToronto, Sch of Educ Jl 64. 9: NYLA; NYC SchLA. 10: Phi Beta Kappa. 12: "Using Your High Sch Library 52, 2nd ed 64); "The Library in High School Teaching(55, 2nd ed 61). 13: Yes. 14: Sch libnship. 15: 1561 E 9 st, Brooklyn NY 11230.

ROTCHFORD, LUCILLE (CAMBELL). b Chicago 13 D 01. 5: Wheaton Col (Ill) 19-23 (Math) AB; UIll 36-37 BS in LS. 7: Child libn Wheaton Pub Lib, Wheaton Ill 30-39; Libn Ga Mil Col 41-53; Hd Ref libn Naval War Col, Newport RI 53-. 9: SLA; RILA. 10: AAUW. 14: Ref. 15: Rt 1, 258 Vaucluse ave, Newport RI 02840.

ROTEN, PAUL. b Maryville Tenn 14 Ja 20. 4: Grtrude Wiebe. 5: Ottawa U (Kan) 37-41 (Eng) Ba; UMich 45-53 (Speech) MA, PhD, 64-65 MALS. 7: Tchr Levant High Sch, Levant Kan 41-42; US Army 42-45; Tchr Neodesha High Sch, Neodesha Kan 45-47; Tchg fellow UMich 48-52; Instr in speech Dartmouth Col 50; Asst Prof, Assoc Prof of speech Sioux Falls Col 53-59; Asst Prof of speech Manchester Col 59-64; Libn Mennonite Bib Sem (Elhart Ind) 65-. 9: ALA; Speech Assn Amer; Amer Educ Theatre Assn; ATheolLA. 14: Admin, catlg. 15: 2800 Benham ave, Elkhart In 46514.

ROTENBERRY, JULIA WARD. b Tuscaloosa Ala 16 D 22. 4: William Rusell Rotenberry. 5: Ala Col 41-44 (Hist) AB; UNC 44-45 BS in LS. 6: Fr, Sp. 7 Circ asst Lawson McGhee Lib, Knoxville Tenn 45-46; Arch & arts libn Auburn U 46-47; Serlibn Ala Col 54-60, Sr libn & catlgr 60-. 9: AlaLA. 14: Catlg. 15: 249 Highland st, N, Montevallo Al 35115.

ROTERS, RAMONA (MORGAN). b Port Washington LI NY 21 Mr 16. 4: Carl G Roters. 5: Syracuse 34-38 (Painting) BA, 68 MLS. 6: Fr. 7: Asst supv Norcross Greeting Card Co, NYC 39; Rate clk Atlantic Mutual Marine Ins, NYC 41-42; Info clk Penna RR, NYC 43; Tchr Syracuse Adult Educ (Everson Museum) 52-62; Tchr Syracuse Pub Schs, Syracuse NY 53; Clerical SyracuseU Lib (ser & art) 58-68; Libn SyracuseU Art Lib (slide div) 68-. 8: Prof Portrait Painter 42-. 9: Libns Assn of SyracuseU. 10: SyracuseU Women's Club; Beta Phi Mu; Col Art Assn of Amer. 11: Awards for portrait painting. 14: Art lib (slide & photographic material), art ref, catlg visual material. 15: Syracuse Univ Art Lib, Syracuse NY 13210.

ROTH, CHARITY (MACE). b Oswego NY 5 My 14. 5: NY State Col for Tchrs 31-35 (Hist) BA, 56-57 MS in LS. 6: Fr, Russian. 7: NY State Educ Dept, Albany NY: Clerk publ bur 42-47, Sr statistics clerk 47-49, Asst examinations ed 49-5; Asst ref libn U Lib SUNY(Albany) 57-. 14: Acquis, bk sel, ref, archives. 15: 3 Danker ave, Albany NY 12206.

ROTH, CLAIRE (JARETT) (MRS HAROLD). b NYC 22 F 23. 4: Harold L Roth. 5: UNC 43 (European Hist) AB; Columbia 45 BLS; NYU 50 (Voc Guidance, Personnel Admin) MA. 7: Asst yp libn Brooklyn Pub Lib 43-46; Ref asst NYU Washington Sq Lib 46-49; Supv educ reading room NYU 49-51; Asst libn Bellmore Mem Lib, Bellmore NY 53-54; Libn Sch of Nursing E Orange Gen Hosp, E Orange NJ 56-64; Author, lib & guidance consul, E Orange NJ 64-, Research asst spec projects 67-68. 9: ALA-AHIL (rep to Interagency Coun on Lib Tools for ; NJLA; NY Lib Club. 10: LWV. 13: Yes. 14: Educ. 15: 28 Edgemont ave, Summit NJ 07901.

ROTH, DANA L. b Hollywood Cal 23 O 35. 4: Eileen Koplin Roth. 5: UCLA 59-62 (Chem) BS; Cal Inst of Tech 62-64 (Chem) MS; UCLA 64-65 MLS. 6: Fr, Ger. 7: Chem libn Cal Inst of Tech 65-. 9: ACS; ASIS. 10: Sigma XI. 11: Amer Inst of Chemists Award, UCLA, 62. 14: Automation, ref, ser. 15: Millikan Lib Cal Inst of Tech, Pasadena Ca 91109.

ROTH, ERIS ESTHER (DOWNES). b Willow Lakes SD 25 F 23. 4: Kenneth E Roth. 5: Notre Dame Jr Col (SD) 40-41 (Elem Educ); Fullerton Jr Col 57-59 AA; Long Beach State Col 60-61 (Biol, Chem); CAL State Col (Fullerton) 61-63 (Biol, Chem) BA; USoCal 63-64 (LS) MS, 68-69. 6: Fr. 7: Tchr elem sch, DeGrey SD 41; Legal sec State Attorney Gen Off, Pierre SD 42-43; Cryptographer & sec US Army Womens Army Corps 43-45; Legal sec Martens & Goldsmith, Pierre SD 45-46; Lab asst sci dept Cal State Col (Fullerton) 61-63, Lib sec 61-63; Asst libn Giannini Controls, Duarte Cal 64; Head tech serv Whittier Pub Lib, Whittier Cal 67; Lib consul Xerox Prof Lib Serv, Santa Ana Cal 67; Law catlg USoCal Law Lib 68-69. 8: Fellowship Inst for Educ & Training of Info Sci Faculty (USoCal) 69. 9: ALA(Ad Hoc Com on Catlg & Clsf of Child Lit 67; Mem & Social chm of SoCal Tech Processes Group); CalLA. 10: Phi Delta Gamm; Alpha Gamma Sigma; Librarias Sodalitas. 14: Catlg, bibliog, govt docs, tech reports; automation, info sci. 15: 10346 Pounds ave, Whittier Ca 90603.

ROTH, GEOFFREY J(AY). b Willow Lakes SD 25 F 23. 4: Sharon Kirchhoff. 5: SE Mo State Col 61-65 (Eng) BS; UIll 65-67 (LS) MS. 6: Fr. 7: Lib asst SE Mo State Col, Cape Girardeau Mo 65; Aerospace analysis intern NASA MSC, Houston Tex 66; Ref libn Battelle Mem Inst, Columbus Ohio 67-. 9: SLA; ASIS. 14: Ref, automated lib syst, lib research. 15: 10346 Pounds ave, Whittier Ca 90603.

ROTH, HAROLD L(EO). b NYC 25 F 19. 4: Claire Jarett. 5: NYU 46-48 (Hist, Educ) BA; Columbia 48-50 (LS) MA; NYU 51- (Adult Educ). 6: Fr, Ger. 7: Asst advertising manager Metro Pub, NYC 38-42; Lt (jg Personnel, Operations ff US Naval Reserve, Pacific 42-46; Lib fellow Queens Col (NY)48-49; Libn grade 2 Brooklyn Pub Lib 49-50; Asst educ Ed Lib "New York TIMES, NY 50-52; 1st asst acquis br ref dept NY Pub Lib 52-54; Asst dir E Orange Pub Lib, E Orange NJ 54-57, Dir 57-; V-pres lib & instl rel The Baker & Taylor Co 67-70; Lib Dir Nassau Co Lib 70-. 8: Lib consul & surveyor (with T Hines) Internat Pipe & Ceramic Corp, 63; Index designer (with T Hines) "American Negro Reference Book. Phelps Stokes Fund, 65; Lib surveyor & 20 8 pub libs in NY, NJ, RI; Insurance adj: Bayonne Pub Lib Fire, 60, Willingboro Pub Lib Fire, 65; Tchr: Drexel Grad Sch of Lib Sci 60 & 6, Montclair State Col 63 & 64; NJ Commsnr of Educ, Adv Com for Elem & Secon Educ Act, 65-; Adj Prof St Johns U Dept of Lib Sci Bk Sel 69. 9: ALA-LAD (chm Bldg & Equip Sect 62-63); -PLA (chm Lib Devel Com 62-63, chm Com to Study Accred of Pub Libs 64-67, treas 62-64, Exec Bd Exhib Round Table 64-66); Amer Assn Adult Educ; CNLA (chm Subcom on Educ for Spec Libnship 62-67); LPRC (Exec Bd); NJLA (chm Title 40 Com, chm Adult Educ Com 58-59, chm Pub Rel Com 63-65, chm Publ Com & Ed of Newsletter 59-60, (1st v-pres & pres-elect 65, pres 66); NJ Adult Educ Assn Pub Rel chm & mem Exec Bd 62-66); Essex Co Lib Dirs Assn (sec 63-64); Middle Atlantic Reg Conf 67, Pub Rel Chm; NY Lib Club. 10: C of C; Otimist Club; Melvil Dui Chowder & Marching Assn; Phi Beta Kappa; Phi Delta Kappa; Beta Phi Mu. 12: Ed "Planning Library Buildings for Service ALA (64); Co-index designer (with T Hines) "The American Negro Reference Book (65); Ed "Education for Special Librarianship, Journal of Education for Librarianship (66-67). 13: Yes. 14: Ref, acquis, systs, tech serv, readers serv, admin, adult educ, consulting. 15: Nassau Co Lib, Garden City NY.

ROTHBERGER, FRED A. b Austin Tex 15 Je 27. 4: Betty Gene Morgan. 5: Southwest Tex State Col 48-49 (Educ); UTex 49-51 (Educ) BS in Ed, 52-53 MLS. 7: Radioman III US Navy 45-48; Libn Menard High Sch Menard Tex 51-52 Reviser Grad Sch of Lib Sci UTex 52-53; Libn Fulmore Jr High Sch, Austin Tex 53-60; Libn Educ & Psych Lib UTex 60-67, Hd of circ 67-. 9: Austin (Tex) Lib Club (past pres). 10: Phi Alpha Theta; UTex Lib Staff Assn. 14: Pub serv. 15: 2106 Peach Tree st, Austin Tx 78704.

ROTHE, ANNA (HERTHA). b Chicago. 5: Northwestern 30 (Journalism) BS; Pratt 53 MLS. 6: Danish Norwegian, Swedish, Fr. 7: H W Wilson Co, NYC: Managing ed "Vertical File Index 32-43, Tr & abstractor Scandinavian langs "Library

Literature 35-41, Compiler "Catalog of Reprints in Series 43, Ed "Current Biography 43-52; Head of circ Great Neck Lib, Great Neck NY 53-59; Seasonal ref libn Mt Vernon & New Rochelle (N) Pub Libs 60-61; Asst libn Good Counsel Col Lib 62-66; Libn adv & Tchr Fed ESEA 66-68; Asst libn Good Counsel Col Lib 68-. 9: ALA; NYLS; Com on Col Reading. 12: Asst ed "Good Reading (46-); Mngg ed (1 yr) & ed (1 yr) "Bulletin, Nassau Co (NY). 14: Readers adv, ref. 15: 41 Barker ave, White Plains NY 10601.

ROTHE, CHARLES (EDWARD). b Sherman Tex 24 F 14. 5: UTex 31-35 (Eng) BA, 35-37 (Eng) MA; Columbia 46-47 (LS) BS. 6: Fr, Sp. 7: UTex Lib: Head reserve reading room 35-37, Order asst 37-43, Head order Dept 43-46; Music libn Sarah Lawrence Col Lib 46-47; Libn Southwestern U Lib 47-48; Chief tchr educ libn Brooklyn Col 48-50, Chief acquis libn 50-. 8: Coun, "Whos Who in Library Service, 3d ed (54-55). 9: ALA-ACRL; TexLA (treas 41-43); NY Tech Serv Libns; NY Lib Club; Lib Assn City U NY. 10: AAUP; Brooklyn Col Faculty Club; Phi Beta Kappa; Beta Phi Mu; Phi Eta Sigma; Pi Gamma Mu. 14: Acquis, admin. 15: 30 Remsen st, Brooklyn NY 11201.

ROTHENBERGER, JAMES. b Logansport Ind 12 N 35. 4: Brishkai Waziri. 5: UCal (Berkeley) 54-57, 59-60 (Geog) AB; UHeidelberg (Germany) 60-61 (Geog); San Diego State Col 61-62 (Geog); USoCal 65 (LS); UOkla 66-67 MLS. 6: Ger, Fr. 7: General Dynamics Corp, San Diego Cal 57-58, 62-64; Lib asst UOkla Lib 66-67; Yale U Lib: Ref asst pub docs 67-68, Act libn pub doc rm 68, Libn pub docs room 69-. 8: Inst on Govt Publ Emory U 68. 9: ALA; -ACRL; -RSD; -RTSD. 14: Govt publs, ref. 15: 748 Elm st, New Haven Ct 06511.

ROTHLISBERG, ALLEN (PETER). b Jamaica NY 15 N 41. 4: Linde Lee Lillie Rothlisberg. 5: San Diego State Col 59-63 (Gen lib arts) AB; Ariz State U 64, 66-; No Ariz U 67-68, 69-; Our Lady of the Lake Col summer 68 (LS). 7: Dir Prescott Pub Lib, Prescott Ariz 63-68; Dir Yavapai Co Lib Syst, Prescott Ariz 68-. 8: Exec Dir Nat Lib Week, Ariz 65-67. 9: ALA; SWLA; ArizStateLA (Lib Devel Com 66-67, Awards Com 68-69; Pub Libs Div: Rep-at-Large 66, pres 66-67). 11: Arizona Libn of the Year 66. 13: Yes. 14: Co lib systems, automation in libs, servince to the blind and physically handicapped, pub rel, wk with the disadvantaged. 15: 133 Frontier dr, Prescott Az 86301.

ROTHMAN, JOHN. b Berlin Germany 21 Ap 24. 4: Gertrude P Ullmann. 5: Queens Col 41-46 (Eng) BA; NYU 46-49 (Eng) MA; Columbia 49-56 (Eng & Comparative Lit) PhD. 6: Ger, Fr. 7: (M/Sgt) Mil Intel Serv U Army, ETO 43-45; "New York Times Index, NYC: News indexer 46-50, Asst ed 50-64, Ed 64-, Dir of info serv 67-. 8: Lectur inlibnship, Pratt Inst Grad Sch of Lib Sci, 64-; Lectr Amer Mgt Assn seminars on info retrieval 67-; Consul Amer Assn of Univ Presses 69. 9: ASIS; USASI Z39 (Subcom on Indexing 57-), chm 64-). 14: Info retrieval, indexing, abstracting. 15: NY Times Inde, 229 W 43 st, NYC 10036.

ROTHMAN, MARIE (HENDERSON). b Phila 21n 31. 4: Arthur Rothman. 5: UPenn Col for Women 50-56 European 9european Hist) AB; Columbia U Russian Inst 57-58 (Hist; Columbia 61-64 (LS) MS; NYU 63- (Internat Rel). 6: Fr, Ger, Russian. 7: Semiprof & stud asst UPenn Lib 49-56; sec to Exec Dir US Coun Internat Chamber of Com, NYC 59-61; Libn & gen asst H P Kraus old & rare bks, NYC 61-63; Head UN Collection NYU Gen Lib 63-67; Govt docs libn & Asst Prof LIU Lib 67-. 9: NYLA; NY Tech Serv Libns. 10: Phi Beta Kappa; Beta Phi Mu; Phi Alpha Theta; AAUP. 14: Govt docs, ref, acquis, ser. 15: 27 E 11th st, New York NY 10003.

ROTHROCK, MARY U(TOPIA). b Trenton Tenn 19 S 1890. 5: Vanderbilt 07-11 (Eng) BS, MS; NY State Lib Sch 12-14 BLS (22). 7: Asst NY State Lib 13-14; Hd of circ, Cossitt Lib, Memphis Tenn 14-16; Libn Knoxville City Lib (Lawson McGhee), Knoxville Tenn 16-34; Supv Lib Serv TVA, Knoxville 34-38; Libn Knox Co Lib, Knoxville Tenn 49-54. 8: Adv com: on Libs, Off of Educ 41; for Pub Lib Inquiry 47-50; Consul Lib Serv, TVA Knoxville 48-51. 9: ALA (Coun 32-42, Exec Bd 38-42, 1st v-pres 45-46, pres 46-47, var com and bd chmship); SELA (chm 20-22, pres 22-24); TennLA (sec-treas 16-18, pres 19-20, 27-28). 10: Tenn Hist Soc; E Tenn Hist Soc; Tenn Hist Com. 11: Lippincott Award 38; D Litt UChattanooga 48. 12: Auth: "Discovering Tennessee" (36) "This is Tennessee" (63); Ed: "French Boad-Holston Country" (46); "Haywood's Natural and Aboriginal history of Tennessee" (59). 13: Yes. 14: Lib responsib in resource use devel, Americana. 15: 3740 Kingston Pike, Knoxville Tn 37919.

ROTHSTEIN, SAMUEL. b Moscow Russia 12 Ja 21. 4: Miriam Teitelbaum. 5: UBC 36-40 (Fr, Eng) BA, MA; UCal (Berkeley) 41-42 (Fr); UWash 42-43 (Fr); UCal (Berkeley) 46-47 BLS; UIll 51-54 (LS) PhD. 6: Fr. 7: Tchg fellow UWash 42-43; Can Army Intelligence Corps, Can & Europe 43-46; Prin lib asst UCal(Berkeley) 47; UBC; Ref libn 47-48, Head acquis div 48-51, Asst U libn 54-59, Assoc U libn 59-61, Act U Libn 61-62, Dir of libnship 61-70; Prof Sch of Libnship 61-. 8: Consul Can Govt Study of Scis Tech Info in Can 68-69; Scholar in Residence UHawaii Lib Sch Ap 69. 9: CanLA (Coun chm Lib Educ Com) ALA(Coun Com on Accredit) PNLA; (past pres) BCLA (Past pres) Inst Prof Libns Ont; AALS (past pres). 10: Bib Soc of Can. 12: "The Development of Reference Services ACRL (55); "Training Professional Librarians for Western Canada (57); Ed bd "College and Research Libraries & "Journal of Library Yes. 13: Yes. 14: Ref, univ libs, lib educ. 15: Sch of libnship, Univ of BC, Vancouver 8 BC Can.

ROTTSOLK, KATHERINE MARIE (SYRDAL). b Northwood N Dak 22 Ja 21. 5: St Olaf Col 38-42 (Eng, Hist) BA, 60-62 (LS); UWis 63, 67 (LS). 7: Tchr Ipswich High Sch, Ipswich S Dak 42; Tchr Milan High Sch, Milan Minn 43-44; Asst St Olaf Col Lib, Northfield Minn 60-62; Lib coord Burnsville Sch Dist, Burnsville Minn 62-67; Catlgr Cuttington Col Lib, Liberia W Africa 65-66; Hd libn Burnsville High Sch 62-. 9: ALA; NEA; MinnEA; MinnASchL. 14: Student serv. 15: 306 Manitou st, Northfield Mn 55057.

ROUEN, EDWARD H. b Minneapolis 26 J 109. 4: Helene Affolter. 5: Cal Polytech (San Luis Obispo) 46-47 (Aero Engnr); USoCal 47-50 (Com Aviation) BS, 57-59 MSLS. 7: LCDR Aviation Br Naval Aviation 30-57, Ret; Ref libn USoCal 58-59; Soc sci libn, act acquis libn, catlgr San Diego State Col 59-67; Catlgr Naval Amphibious Sch, Coronado Cal 67-. 8: Equipment list coord for San Diego State Col Lib. 9: ALA-RTSD; CalLA; SLA. 10: Phi Kappa Phi; Beta Gamma Sigma; Alpha Eta Rho. 14: Tech serv. 15: 6040 Adams Ave, San Diego Ca 92115.

ROUMFORT, SUSAN (BEAUREGARD). b Wash DC 2 Ag 34. 5: Marietta Col 52-56 ;hist BA; Rutgers 59-60 MLS. 7: Ser clerk Schwab Lib Bethlehem Steel Co, Bethlehem Penn 56-59; Catlgr NJ State Lib 60-62, Supv ref 62-. 9: SLA (Princeton-Trenton Chap; program chm 67-68, Projects chm 68-69); NJLA (Ref Sect; treas 66-67, v-chm 67-68, chm 68-69); NJ Hist Soc. 10: Phi Beta Kappa; Phi Alpha Theta; Beta Phi Mu. 14: Catlg, ref. 15: 34 Western ave, apt 12, Trenton NJ 08618.

ROUNDS, GERTRUDE W. b Buffalo NY. 5: Ohio Wesleyan 30-31; Syracuse 34 BS in LS; NYU 46 MA. 7: Sch libn, Camden NY 35-38; Sch libn, New Hartford NY 38-44; Sch libn, Belleville NJ 44-46; Supply libn NY Pub Lib summers 42-44; Asst libn SUNY (Oneonta) 46-49, Hd libn 49-. 8: Lib consul Walkerbilt Woodwork Inc (60-); Bd Trustees, So Cent Res Lib Coun 67-73. 9: ALA (chm Tchrs Col Sect 56-57); NYLA; Chm SUNY Libns' Conf (asst chm 68-69, chm 68-70). 10: Delta Zeta; Zonta Internat. 15: 6 Roosevelt ave, Oneonta NY 13820.

ROUNDS, JOSEPH B. b Knightstown Ind 24 My 09. 5: Earlham Col (Eng Lit) AB; UMich 31 AB in LS, 38 MA in LS; NY State Libns Prof Life Certif. 7: Libn Earlham Col 31-36, 1st order dept Oberlin Col Lib 36-37; In chg of reorg Internat Labor Off Lib, Geneva Switzerland 38-39; Manager US Off Amer Lib, Paris, NYC 40; Asst Prof Lib Sci UBuffalo 40; Assoc Prof Lib Sci UBuffalo, & libn Grosvenor Lib, Buffalo NY 41-45; (Sgt) Signal Radio Intelligence Co US Army, European Theatre 42-45; Libn Dir Grosvenor Lib, Buffalo NY 45-47; Dir Erie Co Pub Lib 47-54; Dir Buffalo & Erie Co (NY) Pub Lib 54-. 8: NY State Bd of Regents Adv Coun, 50-; NY State Educ Commsnrs Com on Ref & Res Lib Serv, 61-62; Consul, Bd of Cornell Pub Lib, Ithaca NY, on plans for new bldg, 60-65. 9: ALA(Coun 50-55 & 60-64; men Mem conf held by Com to Rev Nat Standards for Pub Libs 55, mem var coms); NYLA (Com 50-55, chm Subcom on Civil Serv of Com on Personnel Admin 64-, mem var other coms). 10: Bd of mgrs, Buffalo & Erie Co Hist Soc; Bd of mgrs, Buffalo Soc of Nat Scis. 11: Buffalo Evening News Citation 54 for outstanding pub serv. 13: Yes. 14: Admin. 15: 140 North, Buffalo NY 14201.

ROUNDTREE, ELIZABETH (SONGY). b Plaquemine La 27 Jl 25. 4: Thomas Joseph Roundtree Jr. 5: LSU 41-45 (Hist) BA, 45-46 BS in LS. 6: Fr, Ger. 7: Lafayette Parish Lib demonstration, Lafayette La Asst libn 46-47; LSU Lib: Acquis dept 47-48, Gift & exch 51-53, Ser asst 53-58, Catlgr 59-60; La State Lib: Catlgr 60-68, Coord tech serv 69-. 8: Union Catlg

Com. 9: ALA; LaLA. 14: Catlg, proc ctrs, union catlgs. 15: 1852 Pollard Parkway, Baton Rouge La 70808.

ROUNSAVILLE, STUART (BACKSTROM). b Leakesville Miss 25 S 17. 4: T C Rounsaville. 5: UMiss 36-38 (Hist); USoMiss 55-57 (LS) BS. 7: Legal sec, Leakesville Miss 38-50; High sch libn Leakesville Attendance Center, Leakesville Miss 57-68; Elem libn Leakesville Elem Sch, Leakesville Miss 68-. 9: MissLA; MissEA; Greene Co (Miss) Tchrs Assn. 10:PTA; DAR. 14: Child & yp libn 15: Leakesville Ms.

ROUNTREE, ELIZABETH (COFFEE). b Banks Co Ga 13 J137. 4: Dr George W Rountree. 5: Piedmont Col 55-58 (Eng) AB; UIll 58-59 (LS) MA. 6: Lat, Ger. 7: Libn Piedmont Col 59-65; Libn Lib Ext Serv State Dept of Educ, Atlanta summer 65; Dir Northeast Ga Reg Lib, Clarkesville Ga 65. 9: ALA; SELA; GaLA. 10: Beta Phi Mu; Demorest Womans Club; Bus & Prof Women's Club. 14: Ref, admin. 15: Box 325, Demorest Ga 30535.

ROUNTREE, SEDDON (VIBERT). b Verdum Que Can 15 Ap 22. 4: Phyllis Arlene MacDonald. 5: Dalhousie U 48-52 (Fr) BA, 53-54 Diploma in Educ; 56-57 (Fr) MA; McGill 57-58 BLS. 6: Fr, Sp. 7: Customs clerk Sherwin-Williams Co Ltd, Montreal 41-48; Circ libn Halifax Mem Lib, Halifax NC 58-60; Asst libn St Marys U Lib (Halifax 60-67, Lecturer in Fr 60-; Dalhousie U Lib, Halifax NS 68-. 9: CanLA (Budget & Fin Com 61-63); APLA; Halifax LA. 10: Halifax Musicians Assn; Club Francais DHalifax. 11: Awarded fellowship to teach Eng in Fr Lycee 52-53. 14: Ref, bibliog, catlg. 15: 2959 Winston pl, Halifax NS Can.

ROUSE, MARTHE (REMLEY). b Grain Valley Mo 5 Ja 25. 4: S I Rouse. 5: UMo 45 (Pol Sci) AB, 49-50 (Hist, LS). 6: Fr, Sp. 7: Libn Detroit News, Detroit 52-53; Libn Environmental Sci Serv Admin, Wash DC 65-. 14: Ref. 15: 4908 Aurora dr, Kensington Md 20795.

ROUSE, ROSCOE, JR. b Valdosta Ga 26 N 19. 4: Charlie Lou Miller. 5: UOkla 48 (LS) BA, 52 (Eng Lit) MA; Rutgers 56 (Groiler Soc Scholar); UMich 58 (LS) MA, 62 (LS) PhD. 6: Fr, Ger. 7: (Sgt-2nd Lt) USAAF 42-45 Lib asst UOkla, Rice U 47-48; Asst libn Northeastern State Col (Tahlequah Okla) 48-49, Act libn 49-51; Circl libn Baylor U 52-53, Prof, U Libn & Chm Dept of Lib Sci Baylor U 53-63; Tex A & M 65, etc; Visiting Prof: UOkla Sch of Liv Sci, sumer 62, No Tex State U, summer 65; Dir of lib & Hd dept of lib educ, Okla State U (Stillwater) 67-. 8: Consul; Paul Quinn Col 59-62, Tex A & M Univ 65, St Gregory's Col 68, Arthur D Little, Cambridge Mass 69; Exec Dir Nat Lib Week in Okla 69-70. 9: ALA; -ACRL (Exec Bd 69-70); -LAD (chm Com on Lib Org 69-70); SuffolkCoLA; TexLA; (chm Col & Univ Div 56-57, chm Lib Development Com 63); SWLA; (chm Col & Univ Div 60-62, chm Scholarship Com, chm Resolutions Com 62); SUNY Libns Conf (chm 65-66); NY Tech Serv Libns Assn; OklaLA (mem Exec Bd 69-70, chm Col & Univ Div 69-70). 10: Beta Phi Mu; Archons of Colophon; Melvil Dui Chowder & Marching Assn. 11: Air Medal with clusters. 12: Ed "Oklahoma Librarian (51-52); "A History of the Baylor University Library, 1845-1919 (62). 13: Yes. 14: Acad lib org & mgt, educ for libnship. 15: Rte 4 Quail Ridge, Stillwater Ok 74074.

ROUSEK, SISTER MARIE. b E Orange NJ 12 Jl 25. 5: Col of St Elizabeth 43-47 (Eng) BA; Seton HallU 51-55 (Eng) AM; St JohnsU 55-58 MLS. 6: Fr. 7: Tchr Bayley-Ellard High Sch (Madison NJ) 49-55; Tchr St Michael High Sch (Union City NJ) 55-56; Asst libn Col of St Elizabeth 56-62; Libn 63-. 9: ALA; CathLA; NJLA. 14: Ref, bk sel. 15: Santa Maria Lib Col of Saint Elizabeth, Convent Station NJ 07961.

ROUST, NORMAN LINNAEUS. b St Paul Minn 19 Mr 24. 5: UMinn 42-43 Sci 45-47 (Sci, Anthro); UCal (Berkeley) 47-51 (Anthro) BA, 54-55; Georgetown 53 For Rel. 6: Ger. 7: USA, US & Europe: 1st lt intelligence & armor, special serv admin 43-46, Capt psychological warfare specialist 51-54; Hexcel Corp, Dublin Cal: Research tech specialist 60-63, Hd research libn 63-. 8: Spec Services Admin: Psychological Warfare propaganda Analyst; Hd Spec Teams for Area Res Studies (US Mil); Archeologist 51-54; Spec Area Studies Archeol/Geol West US 50-51; Info Spec in Aerospace Construction Relating to Honeycomb and Honeycomb Structures 65-. 9: Amer Soc Metals; SLA; (Metlas/ materials & Aerospace Divs); Active in many Aerospace, Materials, and Archeol/ Anthrop Organs; Kroeber Anthropo Soc; Helibs Soc. 13: Yes. 14: Aerospace Metals/ materials/Composites; Archeol/Geol of US, Europe, & Africa. 15: Hexcel Corp 11711 Dublin blvd, Dublin Ca 94566.

ROUTT, RUTH (WARTH). b Cynthiana Ky 11 S 22. 4: Glenn Calvin Routt. 5: Transylvania 40-44 (Eng) AB; N Tex State U 63-66 MLS. 6: Fr. 7: Tchr Erlanger High Sch, Erlanger Ky 44-45; Clk Columbia U Lib Sch Lib 45-46; Clk NYC Pub Lib 46-49; Asst catlgr Tex Christian U 66-. 9: ALA; TexLA. 10: Beta Phi Mu; Alpha Lambda Sigma; YWCA; Ft Worth art Assn; TCU Fac; Womans Club; Brite Student Minister's Wives Club; Christian Women's Fellowship; Church Women United. 14: Catlg. 15: 4400 Norwich dr, Ft Worth Tx 76109.

ROUX, HELEN M. b Farrell Penn 18 Ap 18. 5: Seton Hill Col 36-40 (Math) BA; West Res summers 59-62 MSLS. 6: Fr. 7: Off manager Roux Feed Mill Inc, Sharon Penn 40-50; Libn Farrell Pub Lib, Farrell Penn 54-60; Libn New Castle Free Pub Lib, New Castle Penn 61-. 9: PennLA; ALA. 10: Beta Phi Mu; Col Club of New Castle; LWV; Coun-Commun Serg. 14: Admin. 15: 133 Northview ave, New Castle Penn 16101.

ROVELSTAD, HOWARD. b Elgin Ill 5 Mr 13. 5: UIll 32-36 (Eng, Educ) BA, 36-39 (Eng) MA; Chicago summer 38 (Eng); Columbia 39-40 BSLS. 7: Asst in Eng UIll (Urbana) 36-39; Fellow City Col Lib (NYC) 39-40; Acquis libn UMd 40-42, Ref & loan libn 42-43; (1st Lt) US Army 43-46; Dir of Libs & Prof of Lib Sci UMd 46-. 8: Consul on lib bldgs. 9: ALA (Coun 61-; chm Constit & Bylaws Com, 61-65, chm Bldgs Com 54-56, chm 2nd Lib Bldgs Plans Inst 52); -ACRL (chm Lib Bldgs Com 52, chm Jt Com on the "Union List of Serials 68); Amer Soc Engnr Educ; MusLA; SLA; Middle Atlantic Reg Lib Conf (treas 63); MdLA (2nd v-pres 47-49; Ref Serv Div); Potomac Tech Proc Libns; DCLA. 10: AAUP; Phi Kappa Phi. 12: Co-ed "Guidelines for Library Planners (60); Ed "The University and the Wise Man (59); Ed "Proceedings of the Third Library Building Plans Institute (54). 13: Yes. 14: Admin, bldg planning. 15: 8530 Adelphi rd, Hyattsville Md 20783.

ROVIRA, CARMEN. b Santiago Cuba 3 Je 19. 5: UHavana 38-41 (Art Hist) PhD, 50-51 (LS) Bibliotecario; Catholic U 62- (LS). 6: Sp, Eng, Catalan, Fr. 7: Libn art dept UHavana 42-52; Catlgr Catholic U Lib (Havana Cuba) 52-53, Head Libn 53-60; Libn spec Pan Amer Union, Wash DC 60-. 8: Sems on Acquis of Latin Amer Lib Materials (Rapporteur Gen 68). 9: ALA; DCLA; Potomac Tech Processing Libns. 12: Los Epigrafes en el Catalogo Diccionario (Havana 53, 2nd ed 66); Ed "Cuba Bibliotecologica (53 7 & 57-59); "Lista de Encabezamientos de Materia ParaBibliotecas (67). 13: Yes. 14: Catlg, educ for libnshship. 15: 3001Veazey ter NW, apt 606, Wash DC 20008.

ROVIROSA Y GONZALEZ-QUEVEDO, DOLORES (FERMINA). b Matanzas Cuba 6 D 26. 5: UHavana 45-49, 55 (Geog, Hist) PhD, 50-52, 56 MLS; UTex (Austin) 65-66 (Lat Amer Bibliog). 6: Sp, Portu, Fr, Ital. 7: Volunteer catlgr Lyceum y Lawn Tennis Club, Havana Cuba 51; Asst libn Inst de 2A Ensenanza, Havana Cuba 51-60; Asst libn Pub Lib Romon Guiteras, Matanzas Cuba 55-58; Head of catlg dept Nat Lib of Cuba, Jose Marti, Havana 59-61; Prof of catlg & clsf UHavana 61; Asst catlg libn UNev Lib 62-63; Instr lib So Ill U 63-64; Libn I UTex Lib 64-. 8: Prof of Solmization & Theory of Mus, Matanzas Cuba 45. 9: ALA; Tex Libns Assn. 10: AAUP; AAUW; Latin Amer Studs Assn; SWest Coun of Latin Amer Studs; Tex Assn of Col Tchrs; Colegio Nacional de Doctores en Filosofia y Letras, Habana Cuba. 12: ""Catalogacion y Clasificacion Simplificada Para Bibliotecas Pequenas, Habana (60); ""Las Enciclopedias Como; Instrumento de Consulta y Referencia, Matanzas (56). 13: Yes. 14: Catlg & clsf, ref, bibliog, hist, writing. 15: 3007 Duval apt 204, Austin Tx 78705.

ROWAN, RUTH McFARLANE. b Rainy River Ont Can 19 O 14. 5: UWash 31-35 (Eng) BA, 35-36 Tchrs Certif; West Res 49-50 MS in LS. 7: Tchr Maui High Sch, Hamakuapoko Maui Hawaii 36-45, Libn 45-49; Libn North High Sch, Phoenix 50-. 9: ALA; NEA; Ariz State LA; Ariz EA; ArizClrTA. 14: Sch libs. 15: 1257-A E Maryland ave, Phoenix Az 85014.

ROWDEN, DOROTHEA HARRIETT (KLEIST). b Huntington WVa 29 Je 24. 4: Eugene Lee Rowden. 5: Cedar Crest Col 42-46 (Eng, Hist) BA; Glassboro State 50 (Educ); Rutgers 58-61 MLS. 6: Fr. 7: Tchr Souderton High Sch, Souderton Penn 46-47; Dir relig educ 1st Methodist Ch, Collingswood NJ 47-48; Cost accuntant Keystone Ins Co, Phila 48-49; Tchr Bellmawr Park Sch, Bellmawr NJ 49-51; Tchr & libn Oaklyn Jr High Sch, Oaklyn NJ 51-60; Libn Sterling High Sch, Somerdale NJ 60-64; Career consul Cal Lib Assn, Berkeley Cal 66-. 8: Mem Middle States Assn Eval Com 63. 9: ALA; SLA; CalLA; CalASchL. 10: West Col Placement Assn; Rocky Mt Col Placement Assn; Internat Hospitality Ctr; World Affairs Coun No Cal; Phi Alpha Theta; Alpha Psi

Omega. 13: Yes. 14: Recr, lib educ, sch libs. 15: 1001 Pine st apt 903, San Francisco Ca 94109.

ROWE, ALICE (COLE). b Johnson City NY 12 My 23. 4: F Edward Rowe. 5: Keuka Col 41-45 (Soc Sci) BA; State U (Geneseo NY) summers 45-46 (LS) MS; Syracuse 66. 7: Tchr-libn Prattsburg Central Sch, Prattsburg NY 45-46, Port Leyden Central Sch, Port Leyden NY 46-49, Maine Central Sch, Maine NY 49-51; Sch libn Maine-Endwell Central Sch, Maine NY 51-. 9: NYLA (Sec SLS 69-); NY State Tchrs Assn. 10: Nat Campers & Hikers Club; Keuka Col Alum Club. 14: Reading guidance, ref, child work. 15: Box 229 Rte 2, Endicott NY 13760.

ROWE, EMILY L. b Greenwich NY 29 Mr 02. 5: URochester 20-24 (Eng lit) BA; West Res 30-31 BS in LS. 7: Rochester Pub Lib, Rochester NY: Br libn 32-36, Asst main libn 36-57, Main libn 57-66, Asst dir main lib adult serv 60-. 9: ALA; NYLA. 15: 115 South ave, Rochester NY 14604.

ROWE, HARRY MANUELL, JR. b Vallejo Cal 15 O 21. 4: Katherine Kasper. 5: UCal (Berkeley) 40-43; 46 (Hist) AB, 46-47 BLS, 47, Fresno State Col 49. 7: US Infantry 98th Div (S/Sgt), Pacific Theater 43-46; Ref libn Coalinga Dist Lib, Coalinga Cal 47-48; Head libn Coalinga High Sch & Jr Col Libs, Coalinga Cal 48-49; Head libn Coalinga Dist Lib, Coalinga Cal 49-52; Co libn Solano Co Lib, Fairfield Cal 52-57; City libn Fullerton Pub Lib, Fullerton Cal 57-68; Co libn Orange Co Lib, Cal 68-. 8: Adv Com: USoCal Grad Lib Sch, 62, Fullerton Jr Col Lib, 64-, Instr Jr Cols 49-, USoCal Grad Lib Sch 58-. 9: CalLA (pres 66, chm var coms & pres several dists); ALA (mem Recruitment Com, Mem Exhibits RT Exec Bd). 10: Kiwanis; Boy Scouts; C of C; Cal Hist Commsn; E Clampus Vitus (Lit & Hist Soc). 12: "California Here We Came - Orange Co in Books (64). 13: Yes. 14: Admin, lib educ, recr, ref. 15: 431 So Manchester ave, Orange Ca 92668.

ROWE, HOWARD MARSHALL. b San Francisco 22 Je 08. 4: Mary Reynolds. 5: UCal(Berkeley) 28-33 (Econ) BA, 33-34 (Hist), 34-35 (LS) Certif; UIda 36-38 (Amer Hist) MA; USoCal 61- (LS). 6: Fr, Ger. 7: Stud asst Lib UCal(Berkeley) 28-35; Law Libn Law Lib UIda 35-38; Dist libn Coalinga Union High Sch Dist, Coalinga Cal 39-44; Libn Santa Barbara al Cal Lib Dir Tacoma Pub Lib, Tacoma Wash 50-53; Libn Humboldt Co Lib, Eureka Cal 53-55; Libn San Bernardino Pub Lib, San Vernardino Cal Bernardino, 66; Inst Sch of Lib Sci USoCal 66-. 8: Lib bldg consul: San Bernardino Valley Col Lib, 61, Burbank Pub Lib, Burbank Cal, 63; Consul, Bd of Trustees, Corona Pub Lib, Corona Cal, 64. 9: ALA(Coun 48-53 & 63067, 63-67, Coun Credential Com 50); -LAD (Bd Dirs; chm Equip Com 59; chm Standards Com 61-62; chm Bldg & Equip Com 64); CalLA (pres (pres 48, pres So Dist 63); Lib Execs So Cal (pres 56); AALS. 13: Yes. 14: Pub lib admin, lib bldgs & eauip, lib research. 15: 1860 N Mariposa ave, Los Angeles Ca 90027.

ROWE, JANE (CULLER). b Lucas Ohio 17 Ja 13. 4: Richard M Rowe. 5: Wittenberg 31-33, 38-39 (Eng) AB; Carnegie 39-40 BS in LS. 7: Ref libn Wittenberg Col 41-42; Ref asst UPittsburgh 4 2-54, Circ libn 54-58; Head circ dept USoCal 58-65, Engnr libn 65-. 9: ALA (A-v Com 56-57; Copying Methods Sect; Chm Bylaws Com 56-58); SLA; Amer Soc Engnr Educ (co-chm Pacific SWest Chap Lib Div). 10: Delta Zeta; DAR. 13: Yes. 14: Ref, pub serv. 15: 7212-E So La Cienega blvd, Inglewood Ca 90302.

ROWE, MARIANNA H. b Chelmsford Mass 10 O 13. 4: Philip A Rowe. 5: Simmons 3337 BLS. 7: Gen asst Robbins Lib, Arlington Mass 37-51; Bkmob libn Greenfield Reg Lib Ctr, Greenfield Mass 51-59, Child specialist 59-64; Consul child wk West Reg Lib Syst, Springfield Mass 65-67; Hd child serv Portland Pub Lib, Portland Me 67-. 9: ALA; NELA; MeLA; New England RT Child Libns (chmelect 6971). 14: Yp, wk, child lit, storytelling. 15: 40 Richmond ter, Cape Elizabeth Me 04107.

ROWELL, EDANE F. b San Francisco 7 Ja 05. 5: UCal Berkeley 20-21, 23-25 (Eng) BA, 25-26 (LS). 6: Fr. 7: Sub libn Amlameda Med Soc Lib, Oakland Cal 26; Libn II catlgr UCal San Francisco Med mcenter Lib 26-. 9: Med Libns San Francisco Bay Area (sec 64-65) . 13: Yes. 14: Catlg. 15: 1626 Spruce st, Berkeley Cal 94709.

ROWELL, GORDON ALLEN. b Me 20 Jl 14. 4: Margaret Kenny. 5: Bowdoin Col 31-35 (Hist) BA; Columbia 45-46 (LS) BS; Tchrs Col Columbia4 6: Fr. 7: Tech Sgt US Army Coast Artillery Anti Aircraft & Combat Engnrs. European Theatre of Operations 42-45; Brooklyn Col Lib; Acquis libn 46-59, Ser acquis libn 59-61, Act chief educ div 61, Chief soc sci & educ div 62-64; Chief Libn & ssoc Porof Kingsborough Community Col Lib 64-. 9: ALA-CRLA; NY Tech Serv Libns; NY Lib Club; Lib Assn City U NY. 14: Admin, ser. 15: 67-38 108th st, Forest Hills NY 11375.

ROWELL, MARGARET (KENNY). b Fall River Mass 11 Je 06. 4: Gordon Allen Rowell. 5: pembroke 23-27 (Eng) AB: Boston 31-32 (Educ) M Ed; Columbia 36-a7 (LS) BS. 6: Fr. 7: Jr catlgr Harvard Grad Sch of Bus Admin 27-29; Tchr of Eng & Sch libn St Regis High Sch, St Regis NY 29-31; Tchr of Eng & Sch libn Central Sq High Sch, Central Sq NY 33-36; Catlgr Hunter Col Lib 37-42; Chief catlg libn Brooklyn Col 42-64; Libn Grad C Lib City U (NY) 65-. 9: SLA; NY Tech Serv Libns; Lib Assn City U NY (sec 38-43, pres 49-50); NY Lib Club; ASIS. 10: Pembroke Col Club, NY Beta Phi Mu. 12: Ed "Union List of Periodicals in the Libraries of the City University of New York" (65 -69). 13: Yes. 14: Catlg data proc of lib materials, admin. 15: 67-38 108th st, Forest Hills, NY 11375.

ROWLAND, A(RTHUR) RAY. b Hampton Ga Ja 30. 4: Jane Thomas . 5: Mercer U 46-51 (Hist) AB: Emory 51-52 (LS) ML. 7: US Navy 48-49; US Naval Res 49-53; Circ libn Ga State Col 52-53; Libn Armstrong State Col 54-56; Head circ dept Auburn U 56-57; Libn & assoc prof Jacksonville U 58-61; Libn & assoc prof Augusta Col 61-. 8: Lecturer in lib educ, UGa Ext, 63-67; Consul to United Merchants Res Center, Langley SC, 64-67; Consul Brenau Col 66-68; So Assn of Cols & Schs, mem Visiting Coms to var schs & cols, Ga, NC, Fla, Tex, Miss 62-. 9: ALA-ACRL; SELA; GaLA (v-pres 65-); Cent Savannah River Area LA (pres 64-65); GaEA. 10: Richmond Co (Ga) Hist Soc. 12: Services" SEervices (64); ""A Bibliography of the Writings on Georgia History "Historical ""Historinal Markers of Richmond County (65); "A Guide to the Study of Augusta and Richmond County, Georgia" (67). 13: Yes. 14: Catlg, admin. 15: 1339 Winter st, Augusta Ga 30904.

ROWLAND, CLARISSA MARY (LEWIS). b Cheltenham England 15 Ja 21. 4: Richard Creswell Rowland. 5: OxfordU 39-42 (Eng Lang & Lit) BA; UMd 66-68 MLS. 6: Fr, Ger. 7: Asst tchr Downe House, Newbury Berks England 42-45; Womens' League for Peace & Freedom British Consulate, Phila 45-47; Dean's off Columbia Col 45-47; Libn Macy Helen Cochran Lib Sweetbriar Col 62-66, Ref libn 68-. 14: 19th century child bks, rare bks. 15: Box AJ, Sweet Briar Va 24595.

ROWLAND, DAVID. b Summit Point WVa 10 Je 30. 4: Doris Benson. 5: WVaU 55 (Pol Sci) AB; UKy 60 (LS) MS. 6: Ger. 7: Manager Winchester Concrete Products, Winchester Va 56-59; Asst libn East Ky State Col 60-61; Libn Handley Lib, Winchester Va 61-65; Libn Lynchburg Pub Lib, Lynchburg Va 65-67; Dir Henrico Co Pub Lib, Richmond Va 67-. 8: Chm, Nat Lib Week, Va 64; Consul Va State Lib Demonstration Program 65-67; Participant ALA Manpower Dialogue Atlanta 69. 9: AL; VaLA (Recr Com 63, Lib Devel Com 64-; chm Psb Lib Sect 64); ,sela. 10: Pi Kappa Alpha; Boy Scouts (Coun). 13: Yes. 14: Admin, pub rel. 15: Box 74, Creighton rd, Richmond Va 23223.

ROWLAND, DONALD CHARLES. b Kansas City Mo 5 O 39. 4: Shirley Jean Harding. 5: Mankato State Col 63-64 (Eng) BA; UDenver 64-65 (LS) MS. 6: Ger. 7: Spec radio operator USMC, Germany 58-60; Pitkin Co libn Aspen Lib, Aspen Colo 66-67; Dir learning resources Colorado Mt Col, Glenwood Springs Colo 67-68; Dir learning resources Black Hawk Col 68-. 9: ALA; ARRL; NEA-DAVI; LAVI; IllLA. 11: Photo 1st Place USMC worldwide contest (59). 14: Ref, a-v libnship. 15: Black Hawk College 1001 16th st, Moline Il 61201.

ROWLAND, DOROTHY ESTHER. b Waterbury Conn. 5: UConn 37 (Bot, Zool) BS; Syracuse 50 MS in LS; Columbia (LS); AIC (Educ); Springfield Col (Mass) (Educ). 6: Fr, Ger. 7: Head of art & musicroom film & records Hartford Pub Lib, Hartford Conn37-50; Head Libn State Col (Westfield Mass) 5-. 8: Currently tchg child lit course; Faculty adv Col Bk Store. 99: Mem several nat & state lib & educ assns. 10: Beta Phi Mu. 13: Yes. 14:Lib sci, child lit. 15: Pine Acres Terry rd, Prospect Ct 06712.

ROWLAND, E(DITH) ALDREA (JOHNSON). b Virginia Minn 18 O 11. 5: Bradley U 29-33 (Langs & Lit) AB; UIll 39-40 BS in LS, 59-60 (LS) MS; UWis(Milwaukee) 48-. 6: Fr, Ger, Lat, Russian, Sp. 7: Stud asst Bradley U Lib 30-32; Gen asst Peoria Pub Lib, Peoria Ill 33-39; Asst libn Bradley U 40-42; Asst libn US Naval Air Sta Lib, Corpus Christi Tex 42-46; Catlgr,asst libn Del Mar Col 46-50, 53-54; Libn Robstown High Sch, Robstown Tex 50-54; Catlgr: Peoria Pub

Lib, Peoria Ill 54-56, Bradley U Lib 56-59; Stud asst UIll Lib (Urbana) 59-60; Catlgr Simpson Col Lib 60-64, Temp catlgr Tempe Pub Lib, Tempe Ariz summer 64; Asst catlgr UWis Lib (Milwaukee) 64-67; Assoc libn Ill Central ol E Peoria Ill) 67-. 9: ALA; NEA; WisLA; IllLA; Ill Valley LA; Tex State Tchrs ,assn; TexLA; Coastal Bend LA (sec-treas 51-52, Publicity 51-54). 10: Sweet Adelines Inc; AAUW; Womens League (Milwaukee); Lakeview Ctr for Allied Arts; YWCA; Bus & Prof Women's Club. 14: Catlg. 15: 1310 N Glenwood ave, Peoria Il 61606.

ROWLEY, HELEN. b Lyndonville NY 19 F 10. 5: Wells Col 27-31 (Romance langs) BA. 7: Sec Eastman Sch of Music, Rochester NY 32-38; E I duPont de Nemours; Axsst libn Textile Fibers Dept, Tech Div Lib, Buffalo NY 39-45, Libn Textile Fibers Dept, Tech Div Lib, Buffalo NY 45-50, Libn Pioneering Research Lib, Wilmington Del 50-. 9: SLA (Convention Hospitality Chm; Phila Chap: chm Sci-Tech Sect, mem var coms); ACS (chm Lit Div); DelLA. 10: AAUW; DuPont Country Club. 13: Yes. 14: Chem, info spec. 15: E I DuPont de Nemours & Co, Pioneering Res Lib Exp Sta, Wilmington De 19898.

ROWLEY, SALLY (LEIGHT). b Pittsburgh 29 Mr 26. 4: John M Rowley. 5: Carnegie 43-47 BS, 47-48 bs in LS. 7: Carnegie Inst of Tech: Ser catlgr 48-52, Head order dept 52-55, Asst ref libn 55-59, Head ref dept. 59-63; Dir of Lib Serv Robert Morris Jr Co. 64-66; Libn Mt Mery Col 66-67; Coord info serv Hillman Lib UPittsburgh 67-. 9: ALA-ACRL (Tri-State Chap); PLA. 14: Ref, admin. 15: 905 Glenshaw ave, Glenshaw Penn.

ROWSWELL, RONALD GORDON. b Edmonton Alta Can 10 F 42. 5: UAlta 60-63 (Math) BS; UBC 64-65 BLS, Banff Sch Fi rts 64; Simon Frasier U 69-. 6: Fr. 7: Jr catlgr UAlta 65-67; Catlgr Simon Fraser U 67-. 9: ALA; CanLA; Assn BC Libns. 14: Catlg. 15: Simon Fraser Univ Lib, Burnaby BC Can.

ROXAS, SAVINA AMICO. b NYC 2 N 16. 4: Richard Amico Roxas. 5: Duquesne 57 (Eng lit, psy, Phil) BA, 58-(Eng lit); Carnegie 60 MLS; UPittsburgh 66 Lib, Info sci) Adv certif, 67. 6: Fr, Ital, Portu, Sp. 7: Carnegie Inst Ref libn 60-61; Duquesne U: Catlgr 61-63, Tchr lib sci 62-65; UPittsburgh GSLIS: Tchg Fellow 65-66, Tchr lib sci 67-. 9: ALA; AALS; PennLA. 10: Women's Assn of the Pittsburgh Symphony Soc; AAUP; AAUW; Beta Phi Mu; Pittsburgh Bibliophiles. 12: Articles: "Bibliographical Societies," "London, Bibliographical Society," "Center of Libr Research, Univ Buenos Aires. 13: Yes. 14: Resource, devel, ref, catlg. 15: 265 Sleepy Hollow rd, Pittsburgh Pa 15236.

ROY, DONALD EDWARD. b Omaha 22 D 32. 5: Creighton U 49-53 (Eng, Hist) BS; Carnegie 55-56 MLS. 7: Libn Darlington Lib UPittsburgh 56-58; Catlg Falk Lib UPittsburgh 59; Libn Mercy Hosp Staff Lib, Pittsburgh 60-63; Libn Westchester Acad of Med, Purchase NY 64-. 8: Lib consul & catlgr, Hist Soc of West Penn. Pittsburgh 60-63; Lib Consul Westchester Penitentiary 68-. 9: ALA-ACRL;-AHIL (Publns Adv Com 62-63); SLA (Geog & Map Div, Biol Sci Div); MedLA (chm Pittsurgh Reg Group 63-64, Exec Com NY Reg Group 68-69); NY Tech Serv Libns; Westchester LA; NY Acad of Scis. 10: Hist Soc of Mich; Mich Archaeol Soc; NY Lib Club; Map Collectors Cir. 12: Ed "Bulletin of Mercy Hospital (Pittsburgh) (60-63). 13: Yes. 14LLib admin,tech serv, bibliog. 15: Westchester Acad of Med, Purchase st, Purchase NY 10577.

ROY, GAETAN. b Warwick Que Can 18 F 38. 4: Pierrette Farley. 5: Col de Victoriaville (Que)56-60 BA; UOttawa 60-63 B ph, 63-64 BLS. 6: Fr, Eng, Sp. 7: Libn USherbrooke (Que) 64-69, Chief libn 69-. 9: canLA; Association canadienne des bibliothecaires de langue francaise; ALA. 10: Ligue pour Integration Scolaire. 14: Govt publns, catlg, a-v, admin. 15: Biblitheque Centrale, Coll de Sherbrooke, Boul Univ, Sherbrooke Que Can.

ROY, SAKTIDAS. b Murshidabad W Bengal India 11 O 35. 5: Calcutta U 58 (Econ, Hist) BA; Simmons 64 (LS) MS. 6: Hindi, Bengali, Sanskrit, Eng. 7: Asst libn US Info Lib, Calcutta 54-60; Ser catlgr Baker Lib Harvard Bus Sch 60-65; Libn Amer Studies Research Centre, Hyderabad India 66-67; Chief libn LC New Delhi Off, India 67-68; Asst acquis libn U Lib UCal(Santa Cruz) 68-69; Sers records libn Harvard U Lib 69-. 9: Indian LA; Bengal LA. 14: Admin, catlg. 15: Harvard Univ Lib, Cambridge Ma 02138.

ROYE, JOSPEHINE (SHULTZ). b Columbia Penn 21 S 14. 4: Benjamin F Roye. 5: Millersville State Col 55-58 (LS) BS; Drexel 61-64 MSLS. 6: Fr. 7: Libn Eastern High Sch,Wrightsville Penn 58-63 Libn Columbia High Sch, Columbia Penn 63-66; Acquis libn Penn State U (Middletown) 66-68; Ref libn sfree PLancaster Penn69-. 8: Mem, Bldg Com for the Columbia (Penn) Pub Li 9: ALA; PennLA. 10: DAW; MENTAL Health & Retardation Bd of Lancaster Co (Penn); Friends of the Columbia Pub Lib; Friends of Lancaster Free Pub Lib. 14: Ref. 15: 27 S Sixth st, Columbia Pa 17512.

ROYSTON, MARY VIRGINIA. b Jamestown La 4 Ag 39. 4: Kenneth Raymond Royston. 5: Northwestern State Col 57-61 (Math) BS; LSU summers 62-65 (LS) MS. 7: Stud sec PE Dept Northwestern State Col (Natchitoches La) 58-61; Lib asst child dept Winn Parish Lib, Winnifield La summers 60, 61; Sch libn Houma Jr High Sch, Houma La 61-68; Media ctr libn Terrebonne Parish Sch Bd, Houma La 68-. 9: ALA (Recr Netwk 62-63); LaLA (Recr Com 64-66, Scholarship Com 67-); LaACHL (sec 65-66, v-pres 68, pres 69); La Tchrs Assn. 15: 111 W Park st, Houm La 70361.

ROZIEWSKI, WALTER M. b Jersey City NJ 14 Je 25. 5: NYU Washington Sq Col 47-51 (Fr) BA; Columbia 51-52 MSLS. 6: Fr. 7: US Army Infantry (99th Div & 1st Div) Hdqrs Assignment 43-46; NY Pub Lib; Ya & ref libn 52-54, Br libn Melcourt Br 54-55, Sr libn Donnell Lib Center 55-56, Br libn Riverdale Br 57-58, Supv libn Donnell Record Lib 58-60, Supv adult spec Manhattan Borough Off 60-62, Asst coordinator Manhattan Brs 63-. 9: ALA; SLA; NYLA (Memb Com); NY Lib Club (Coun; chm Memb Com). 14: Lib admin, adult serv. 15: 04 Concklin rd, New City NY 10956.

ROZKUSZKA, W DAVID. b Ludlow Mass 21 Ag 43. 5: Loyola U Chicago, Rome 61-65 (Eng lit) BS; UMass summer 65 (Educ); San Francisco State Col summer 66; Syracuse 66-67 MSLS. 6: Fr, Ital, Lat, Polish. 7: Sub tchr Chicopee Comprehensive High Sch, Mass 66; Stanford U Libs; Hist catlgr 67-68, For doc libn 68-. 9: ALA; NELA; CalLA. 10: Beta phi Mu; Pi Delta Epsilon. 14: Resources devel, ref. 15: Box 3166, Stanford Ca 94305.

RUARK, VIRGINIA (STERN). b Neb 13 F 11. 4: Doyle G Ruark. 5: LaVerne Col 29-33, 59-60 (Eng) BA; UWash summers 61-64 (LS) ML. 7: Real estate broker Ruarks Realty, Tonasket Wash 40-60; Libn Tonasket Pub Tonasket Wash 40-60; 40-6; Libn Tonasket Pub Schs, Tonasket Wash 60-. 9: ALA-AASchL; NEA-DAVI; WashEA; Wash State SchLA; WashLA. 10: Beta Phi Mu; Admin Women in Educ. 14: Sch libnship. 15: P. O. Box 7702, Tonasket Wash 98855.

RUBECK, RITA LOU. b Marion Ohio 1 F 44. 5: Kent State 62-65 (Soc studies) BS, 68-69 (LS). 7: Libn Elgin High Sch, Marion Ohio 65-68. 9: ALA; OhioLA; OhioASchL. 10: Kappa Delta Pi. 14: Catlg. 15: Rural Rte 3, Richwood Oh 43344.

RUBENIS, ARTURS TALIVALDIS. b Bergale Latvia 5 De 27. 4: Ilga Pantels. 5: Baltic U (Germany) 48-t9 (Baltic Philol); Emerson Col 51-54 (Drama) BA; Boston U 54-56 (Theatre Arts) MFA; West Res 58-59 MS in LS. 6: Latvian, Ger. Russian, Lat. 7: Catlgr West Res U Lib 59-, Sr catlgr 67-, Catlg libn slavic materials 68-. 8: Consul, Microphoto Div of Belll & Howell (Cleveland) on use of Slavic materials. 9: ALA; NE Ohio Tech Serv Gp. 14: Slavic materials, arts (esp theatre arts). 15: 1460 W Clifton blvd, Lakewood Oh 44107.

RUBENSTEIN, SADIE (RUBINSTEIN). b NYC 30 O 12. 4: Leo Rubenstein. 5: Hunter Col 28-32 (Fr) BA; Columbia 33-37 MS in LS; NYU 65. 6: Fr, Yiddish. 7: Lib asst Columbia U Lib 37-38; High sch libn NYC Bd of Educ 38-44, Elem sch tchr 57-, Tchr of lib 69-. 10: Columbia Sch of Lib Serv Alumni Assn; Beta Phi Mu. 14: Ref, child serv. 15: 245 E 178 st, NYC 10457.

RUBEY, ANN TODD. b St Louis 16 D 05. 4: Harry Rubey. 5: Agnes Scott Col 24-28 (Chem) BA; Emory 30-31 BA in LS; Chicago 48 (LS) MA. 6: Lat, Fr, Ger, Gk. 7: UMo Lib: Asst ref libn 32-40, Ref libn 40-43, Head ref dept 44-62, Head humanities dept 62-. 9: ALA (Life mem);-ACLR; MoLA (treas 46). 10: DAR; Daughters ofAmer Colonists; Daughters of Colonial WARS: US Daughters of 1812; Dames of Court of Honor; Sons & Daughters of Pilgrims; Magna Charta Dames; Colonial Daughters of 17th Century; Nat Huguenot Soc; Washington FamiyDescendants. 12: "Speaking of Families: The Tod(d)s of Caroline County, Virginia, and Their Kin (60). 13: Yes. 14: Humanities, ref, bk sel, geneal, heraldry. 15: Frederick Apts, Columbia Mo 65201.

RUBIN, AUDREY (ARNDT). b St Louis Mo. 4: Samuel H Rubin. 5: WashU 39-43 (Sociol) AB, 44-45 (Soc Wk); Columbia 64-66 (LS) MS. 7: Ref libn Parkinson Info Ctr Columbia Med Lib 66-. 8: Rep from Parkinson Info Ctr to

SUNY Biomed Communications Network; MedLA Certif. 9: MedLA. 10: Phi Beta Kappa; Beta Phi Mu. 14: Med ref. 15: 250 Glen ct, Teaneck NJ 07666.

RUBIN, HELEN M. b NYC. 5: Hunter Col 36 (Hist) BA; Columbia 44 (LS). 7: Lib asst NY Pub Lib 36-44; Libn Bd for the Netherlands Indies, NYC 44-46; Asst libn New Sch for Soc Research 46-49; Acquis libn UCLA 49-50; Ref libn US Info Agency, NYC 51-53; Ref libn Amer Heritage Found, NYC 53-54; Libn Fashion Inst of Tech, NYC 54-. 9: SLA; NY Lib Club; NY State Assn of Jr Cols; ALA. 10: Bnai Brith. 14: Ref, admin. 15: 345 - 8th ave, NYC 10001.

RUBINTON, PHYLLIS (NEWMAN). b Brooklyn NY 24 Mr 27. 4: Noel Rubinton. 5: Wellesley 45-49 (Philos) BA; Pratt Inst 64-67 MLS. 6: Fr. 7: Ser libn NY State Psych Inst 67-. 9: ALA; MedLA; SLA. 10: Beta Phi Mu; NY Wellesley Club. 14: Ser, govt docs. 15: 505 E 79 st, New York NY 10021.

RUBLE, LOUISE (PYLE). b Franklin Penn 5 O 15. 4: James Howard Ruble. 5: Monmouth Col 33-37 (Eng) BA (magna cum laude); UIll 40-42 BS in LS. 7: Asst ref libn Galesburg Pub Lib, Galesburg Ill 38-39; Libn Goode-Barren Twp High Sch, Sesser Ill 39-41; Libn Roxana Commun High Sch, Roxana Ill 41-43; Proj libn War Relocation Authority, Minidoka Ida 43-44; Libn sch dept Cleveland Pub Lib 44; Sr asst libn in chg Humanities div Wayne State U 44-. 10: Oak Park Lib Bd. 14: Ref, admin. 15: 10141 Oak Park blvd, Oak Park Mich 48237.

RUBY, ROBERT H. b Mabton Wash 23 Ap 21. 4: Lelia Jeanne Henderson. 5: Whitworth Col 39-41 (Biol) BS; Washington U Sch of Med (St Louis) 41-42 MD. 7: US Air Corps 48-49; US Pub Health 53-54; V-chm Wash Lib Trustees Assn 65-; Trustee Moses Lake Pub Lib, Moses Lake Wash 59-, chm Wash Lib Trustees Assn 67-; Mem on Title III f Lib S & C A 67-; Mem Wash Gov's Conf on Lib 67; Chm Wash Gov's Conf on Lib Week. 8: Priv practice of med. 9: AMA: Amer Col Surgeons (Fellow); Wash Lib Trustees Assn; Wash State Med Assn. 10: Moses Lake Mus; Trustee, Grant Co (Wash) Hist Assn. 11: Northwest Author of Year66; Pacific Norhwest Booksee66;GTION, Governor's Festival of Arts 67. 12: "The Oglala Sioux" (55); "Half Sun on the Columbia" (65); "Children of the Sun" (69). 13: Yes. 15: 4535 W Peninsula dr, Moses Lake Wa 98837.

RUCKER, LAURA A. b Edmond Okla 17 Ag 11. 5: Okla City U (Math) BA; Okla Med Sch 33-34; Okla 64-65 (LS) MA; Certif Med Libn. 6: Fr. 7: Clerk Sel Serv System, Bartlesville Okla 50-62; Non-prof libn Batlesville Pub Lib, Bartlesville Okla 62-64; Info & interlib loan UOkla Libs 65-67; Asst libn for pub serv U Okla Med Ctr Lib (Oklahoma City) 67-. 9: OklaLA (By-laws Com 67); SWLA; MedLA (So Reg Group Program Com 68); AA. 10: Phi Beta Mu; PEO; DAR; Amer Cancer Assn; Okla Med Auxiliary; AAUW; Cleveland Co Hosp Auxiliary. 14: Ref, med libnship. 15: 841 So Lahoma, Norman Ok 73069.

RUCKER, RONALD EUGENE. b Whittier Cal 25 My 38. 4: Nancy Turtle. 5: USoCal 56-58 (Mus); Pomona 58-60 (Mus) AB; Harvard 60-62 (Musicology) AM; UCal (Berkeley) 62-64 MLS. 6: Fr, Ger. 7: Lib asst E Whittier City Sch Dist, Whittier Cal summers 60-64; Tchg asst Harvard U 61-62; Lib trainee Richmond Pub Lib, Richmond Cal 62-64; Cornell U Lib: Asst libn 64-66, Act dept hd 66-67, Act undergrad libn 67-68, Undergrad libn 68-. 9: ALA. 14: Tech serv, admin. 15: Uris Lib Cornell Univ, Ithaca NY 14850.

RUCKMAN, STANLEY NEAL. b Scottsbluff Neb 16 Ja 36. 4: Jeanne Delano. 5: UOre 53-57 (Educ) B Ed UDenver 57-58 (LS) MA; UOre summer 68 Inst in Lib Mechanization. 7: Libn Ore City Sr High Sch, Oregon City Ore 58-51; Libn Vandenberg Jr High Sch, Vandenberg AFB, Lompoc Cal 61-63; Sr libn soc sci & sci div Lib Assn of Portland Ore 63-64; Asst libnCol of Ida 64-, Act libn 69. 9: NEA-DAVI; Assn for Higher Educ; IdaLA; ALA; PNLA. 10: AAUP. 14: Ref, circ, govt docs. 15: 1603 Beech st, Caldwell Ida 83605.

RUCKS, FRANCES BURELL. b Galva Ill 4 Mr 18. 5: Vanderbilt U 35-36; UAriz 36-37, 38-39 (Eng) AB; Peabody 39-40 BS in LS; UAla 56-58 (Eng) MA. 6: Fr, Sp, Ger. 7: Catlg asst UAriz 41; Catlg asst UIda 41-42; Circ & bibliog asst UAriz 42-43; Catlgr Bus Lib UAla 43-68; Ed Air U Lib, Maxwell AFB Ala 68-. 9: ALA; SLA (Adv Coun 62-63; pres A la Chap 62-63; chm Recr Com 66-); SELA (sec-treas SEast Reg Gp of Tech Serv Libns 68-70); AlaLA. 10: AAUP; Phi Beta Kappa; Phi Kappa Phi. 12: Ed ""Publications at the University of Alabama (54-64). 13: Yes. 14: Catlg, spec collections. 15: 3751-C Wesley dr, Montgomery Al 36111.

RUDDICK, PATSY R. b Arma Kan 16 D 32. 5: Parsons Jr Col 50-52 (Eng) AA; Kan State Col (Pittsburg) 52-54 (Lang & Lit) BS in Ed; UDenver 59-63 (LS) MA; Temple U 68. 7: Eng tchr Garden City Jr High Sch, Garden City Kan 54-63; Libn Garden City Commun Jr Col 63-. 9: NEA; Assn for Higher Educ; Kan State Tchrs Assn; Kananpuom Jr Col EA. 10: Delta Kappa Gamma. 14: Catlg, ref. 15: Garden City Commun Jr Col, Garden City Kan 67846.

RUDE, DAROLD E. b Roselawn Ind 4 O 28. 4: Elizabeth Hielema. 5: Blackburn Col 46-48 (Soc Sci) AA; Ind State U 48-51 (Bus) BS, 55-57 (Educ Admin) MS; Ind U 59-62 (LS) AMT. 7: Tchr-libn Kankakee Twp Schs, Tefft Ind 53-55; Order libn Ind State U 55-6, Asst dir of libs 65-67, 68-, Act dir 67-68. 9: ALA; IndLA (v-pres Col & Univ 6 10: Phi Delta Kappa; Theta Chi. 12: "Handbook for Student Librarians (56). 13: Yes. 14: Acquis, admin. 15: 24 Carol dr, Terre Haute In 47805.

RUDERMAN, LAURIE (PENN). b Lynn Mass 20 N 44. 4: Gerald H Ruderman. 5: SUNY (Buffalo) 62-66 (Eng) BA; Kent State 66-68 MLS. 7: Dept of Parks, Erie Penn Recreation supv 62-63; Erie Pub Lib, Erie Penn: Lib aide 63, Child room asst 64; SUNY Buffalo: Resident adv 64-66, Freshman orientation adv 65; Consul Kent State 67; Adult serv libn Akron Pub Lib, Akron Ohio 67-68; Asst med libn Metropolitan Gen Hosp, Cleveland Ohio 68-. 9: ALA; SLA. 14: Med libs. 15: 24801 Lake Shore blvd apt 401, Euclid Oh 44123.

RUDKO, TATIANA. b Kaluga Russia 13 N 14. 4: Nikita Rudko. 5: Syracuse 59-64 MSL. 6: Russian, Polish, Ukrainian, Fr. 7: Clerical asst Syracuse U Lib 58-61, Bibliogr searcher 62-64, Ser catlgr 65-. 10: Beta Phi Mu. 14: Catlg, bibliog wk. 15: 424 Westmoreland ave, Syracuse NY 13210.

RUDNICK, BARBARA KAROL. b NDak 4 Jl 07. 5: State Col (Valley City ND) 28-35 (LS) BA; Columbia MA. 7: Libn & tchr: N Dak pub sch 30-39, Wyo pub sch 39-41, Nashua High Sch, Nashua Mont 41-43; Sitka High Sch, Sitka Alaska 43-48; Libn West Sr High Sch, Anchorage Alaska 48-. 8: Dir sch lunch programs, Mont 46-48; ALA implementations of lib standards, Alaska 60; Chm lib standards, Anchorage Alaska 62. 9: Alaska EA (Standards Chm; Curr Com); ALA; NEA; Alaska Intr Media Assn; AlaskaLA. 10: Alaska Hist Assn; AnchorageLA. 13: Yes. 14: Rare bks, collection of Alaska materials. 15: Anchorage-Westward Hotel Box 520, Anchorage Ak 99501.

RUDNIK, SISTER MARY CHRYSANTHA CSSF. b Winona Minn 2 D 29. 5: LoyolaU (Chicago) 51-52; Felician Col 52-54, 58-59; Cardinal Stritch Col 54-57 (Eng); Col of St Francis (Joliet Ill) 57; DePaulU 57-58 (Eng) PhB (cum laude); Mundelein Col 59-60; Rosary Col 60-62 MA in LS; Chicago Tchrs col No 64. 7: Page clerk Hill Ref Lib (St Paul) 46-48; Tchr Holy Innocents Sch (Chicago) 48-49, 50-54; Tchr St Bruno Sch (Chicago) 54-55; Tchr Holy family Sch (Cudahy Wis) 55-57; Tchr Good Counsel High Sch (Chicago) 56-58; Instr Felican Col 63-; Libn 57-. 8: Lib consul, Chicago Archdiocesan Sch Bd 66; Mem Adv Bd, Lib Tech Prog, Wilson Jr Col (Chicago) 67-; Mem Task Force for the Study of Institutional Research, Ill Assn Commun & Jr Cols 68. 9: ALA (Recr Netwk); CathLA (No Ill Unit: v-chm 67-68, chm 68-69; Memb Chm 62-65, Pub Chm 66-67; v-chm 64-65, chm 65-66 Col & Univ Sect; Bd dirs Franciscan Libns RT 67-69); Coun Lib Tech (chm Research Com 68-); Wis Cath LA; Minn CathLA. 13: Yes. 14: Col & jr col lib admin, catlg, clsf, ref, sch libs, child lit, influence of lib serv on higher educ. 15: 3800 Peterson ave, Chicago Il 60645.

RUDNYCKYJ, JAROSLAV B. b Peremysl Poland 28 N 10. 4: Maryna Antonoych. 5: U L'vov 29-34 (Slavic Langs) MA, 34-37 (Slavic Langs) PhD; Ukrainian Tech Inst (NY) 55-56 Lib Sci Certif. 6: Eng, Fr, Ger, Ital, Russian, Ukrainian, Polish, Czech. 7: Prof U's in Prague, Munich, Heidelberg 40-48; Prof UMan 49-. 9: CanLA; Manitoba LA; Ukrainian Lib Assn in Amer (Hon mem); Bibliog Soc of Can. 10: Winnipeg Lib Bd; Deputy dir, Uvan Lib, Winnipeg. 12: 939 titles; Ed "Slavistica" & "Onomastica." 13: Yes. 14: Catlg, ref, archives, bibliog. 15: 29 Scotia st, Winnipeg 4 Man Can.

RUDOLPH, ELLEN (TODRANK). 4: L C Rudolph. 5: ULouisville 48-50, 59 (Elem Educ); DePauw 50-51 (Elem Educ) AB; IndU 67-68 MLS. 6: Ger. 7: Tchr Putnam Co Schs, Russellville Ind 51-52; Tch putnam Co Schs, Russellville Ind 51-52; Tchr Fairfield Co Schs, Fairfield Conn 52-54; Bkstore mgr Presbyterian Sem, Louisville Ky 63-67; Libn Louisville Free Pub Lib, Louisville Ky 68-69; Libn TempleU Lib 69-. 14: Acquis. 15: Acquisitions Div Temple univ Lib, Philadelphia Pa 19122.

RUDOLPH, L(aVERE) C(HRISTIAN). b Jasper Ind 24 D 21. 4: Ellen Todrank. 5: DePauwU 46-48 (Hist) AB; Louisville Presbyterian Sem 48-51 (Church Hist) BD; YaleU 52-54 (Church Hist) PhD; UZurich 60 (Church Hist); IndU 67-68 MLS. 6: Ger, Grk. 7: Capt USAF 40-46; Minister United Presbyterian Ch 50-54; Prof Louisville Presbyterian Sem 54-69; Lecturer ULouisville, Louisville Ky 65-69; Rare bks bibliogr UPenn 69-. 9: ALA. 10: AHA; Amer Soc Ch Hist; Presbyterian Hist Soc. 12: "Hoosier Zion" (63); "Story of the Church" (66); "Francis Asbury" (66). 13: Yes. 14: Ref, rare bks, bibliog, ch hist. 15: Univ of Penn Lib, Philadelphia Pa 19104.

RUDOLPH, MARY JANE (BROWN). b Chicago 5 S 31. 5: Chicago 46-53 (Eng, LS) PhB; Chicago Tchrs Col South 60-61 (LS) M Ed. 7: Asst UChicago High Sch Lib 52-53; Order libn Wilson Col 54-; Lecturer in Lib Sci Chicago State Col South 61-; Asst Prof Wilson Col 65-, Chm Wilson Col Lib Dept 68-. 9: Chicago Lib Club. 10: ACLU; Cook Co Col Tchrs Union; Hyde-Park-Kenwood Commun Conf; Ind Voters of Ill. 12: Comp "Subject Index to "Invitation to Learning Reader (57). 14: Acquis, ser, catlg, tchg. 15: 1428 E 54th st, Chicago Il 60615.

RUDY, WILFRED. b Waterloo Twp Ont Can 28 Ag 30. 5: Goshen Col 53-54 (Bible) BA; UWest Ont 54-55 (Gen Arts) BA; UToronto 57-58 BLS. 6: Fr. 7: Catlgr UAlta Lib 58-60; Child libn Hamilton Pub Lib, Hamilton Ont Can 60-61; Ref asst CBC ref lib, Toronto Ont Can 61-65; Catlgr Nat Lib of Can, Ottawa Ont 65-67; Catlg Waterloo LutheranU 67-68, Hd catlgr 68-. 8: Elem sch tchr: Waterloo Co Ont Can 50-53, McKim Twp Sudbury Ont Can 55-57. 9: OntLA. 10: Inst Prof Libns of ont. 14: Catlg, pictorial ref. 15: 19 Margaret ave, Kitchener Ont Can.

RUECKING, FREDERICK (HENRY) JR. b McAllen Tex 17 Mr 26. 4: Nadine Wilson. 5: Pan American Co 42-43; UTex 50-52 (Anthropolgy) BA, 52-55 (Anthropology) MA; UMich 62-63 (LS) MA. 6: Sp. 7: Page & searcher main lib UTex 53-55; UMich; Supv Storage Lib 55-56, Stack supv Gen Lib 56-58, Circ supv Undergrad Lib 58-62, Wk-study Scholar Lib 62-63; Head circ dept Fondren Lib Rice U 63-65, Head data processing div 65-68, Asst libn for syst development 68-. 9: ALA (Com on Lib Automation, chm 67-69);-ISAD (Bd 68-71; Ad Hoc MARC Format 67-68). 12: Ed Bd "Journal Library Automation" (68-). 13: Yes. 14: Lib automation. 15: 6919 Bellaire blvd, Houston 77036.

RUFF, JOSEPH A. b Strasbourg France 20 D 26. 4: Florence Ruef. 5: Queens Col 44, 46-48 (hist) BA Columbia 48-49 (Hist) MA, 49-50 (LS) MS; NYU 53 (Public Admin). 6: Fr. 7: (T5) Mil Police & Intelligence, US Army 45-46; Catlgr YALE U Lib 50-52; Ser catlgr Brooklyn Col Lib 2-54; Gen asst Brooklyn Pub Lib 54-57; Br libn Long Beach Pub Lib, Long Beach Cal 57-60; Asst dir Levittown Pub Lib, Levittown NY 60-65; Dir Glen Rock Pub Lib, Glen Rock NY 65-. 8: Org Bergen Co A-V Ctr & helped establish N Bergen Fed. 9: ALA; LPRC; NJLA (chm Intel Freedom Com, past chm Pub Rel Com). 13: Yes. 14: Pub lib admin, bk sel, ref, a-v. 15: 181 S Highwood ave, Glen Rock NJ 07452.

RUELKE, MARTHA (LOD). b Pittsfield Me 15 S 11. 4 E Richard Ruelke. 5: Simmons 28-32 (LS) BS; S Anselms Col 60-61 (Educ); UNH 61-62 (Educ), 65 (Sch Libs); Keene State Col 68 (AV). 7: Gen asst City Lib, Manchester NH 35-42, Circ libn 49-59; Sch libn Central High Sch, Manchestr NH 60-. 9: NHLA; NHEA; NHSchLA. 15: Rt 2 Box 73, Manchester NH 03102.

RUETH, MARION URSULA. b Wash DC 17 S 20. 5: Catholic U 43-46 (Music) M Mus; Fla State U 58-62 (LS) MA. 6: Fr, Ital. 7: Pianist & tchr Studio, Silver Spring Md 40-55; Circ dept St Petersburg (Fla) Pub Lib 55-58; Catlgr & music spec Fla State U 58-62; Asst head acquis dept UMd 62-66; Head Libn Hood Col 66-. 8: Chm Lib Coop Program of Md Independent Cols 68-70. 9: ALA; MusLA; MdLA; Potomac Tech Proc Libns Assn. 10: Beta Phi Mu; Pi Kappa Lambda; AAUP. 12: ""The Tallahassee Years of Ernst von Dohnanyi (62). 13: Yes. 14: Tech proc, admin. 15: "Willowbrook" Old Middletown rd, Jefferson Md 21755.

RUESS, LORA FRENCH (CULPEPPER). b Crowley La 9 N 14. 4: E F Ruess. 5: LSU 31-35 (Eng) BA; Columbia 35-36 BS of LS. 7: Readers adv Beaumont Pub Lib, Beaumont Tex 36-40; Libn St Marys Hall, San Antonio Tex 46-48; Libn Nassau Elem Sch & Elmwood Elem Sch, E Orange NJ 48-. 9: NEA; NJLA. 13: Yes. 14: Elem sch libs. 15: 214 Glenwood ave, East Orange NJ 07012.

RUFF, VIRGINIA FIELD. b Beford Va 19 O 07. 5: Mary Washington Col 29 (Eng) BS in Ed; Col of William & Mary (LS) AB. 7: Tchr of Eng, soc studies & sci Montvale High Sch, Montvale Va 30-39, Tchr-libn 40-45; Libn Bedford High Sch, Bedford Va 46-63; Libn Liberty High Sch, Bedford Va 64-. 8: Va State Bd of Educ: Com on "Handbook for School Libraries; High Sch Materials Com. 9: NEA; ALA; VaEA (past pres Sch Lib Dept); VaLA (past sec). 10: Bus & Prof Womens Clubs; AAUW. 14: Sch lib wk. 15: 414 Bedford ave, Bedfod Va 24523.

RUFFIER, ARTHUR (JOSEPH). b Maximo Ohio 11 Ap 30. 4: Patricia Lee. 5: Ohio U 49-52, 55-56 (Fine Arts) BFA; UWash 58-59 (LS) ML. 7: Lib asst Boeing Co, Pilotless Aircraft Div, Seattle 57; Circ libn UWash 59-60, Acquis libn 60-64; Tech serv libn Wash State Law Lib 64-66; Acquis libn UCal(Davis) Law Lib 66-67; Catlg libn Tacoma Pub Lib 67-68; Ref libn Wash State Law Lib 68-. 9: AALL. 14: Acquis, ref. 15: Temple of Justice, Olympia Wash 98502.

RUFFIN, ELIZABETH (STUART). b New Haven Conn 14 F 29. 4: Allen F Ruffin Jr. 5: UConn 46-50 (Eng) BA; Simmons 52-53 MS. 7: Enoch Pratt Free Lib, Baltimore: Asst adult serv off 53-55, Ref asst brs 55-57, Admin asst brs 57-61, Head co serv dept 61-63, Br libn Herring Run Br 63-. 8: Consul, Md Dept of Educ 63-. 9: ALA-RSD (Md Chap); MdLA (Adult Serv Div 63-64). 10: ACLU; LWV. 14: Adult serv, ref. 15: 2004 Beechfield ave, Baltimore Md 21227.

RUGELIS, RASMA. b Riga Latvia 31 D 36. 4: Imants Rugelis. 5: Toronto 56-60 (Pol Sci, Econ) BA, 62-63 BLS. 6: Latvian. 7: Ed asst Can Hosp Assn, Toronto 60-62; Catlgr, libn III York U Lib (Toronto) 63-. 14: Catlg, ref. 15: 68 Devondale ave, Willowdale Ont Can.

RUGEN, FRANCES JEAN. b Evanston Ill 12 Ja 25. 5: USoCal 42-44, 45-47 (Internat Rel) BA; USoCal 49; West Res 49-50 MS in LS. 6: Sp. 7: Jr libn Dept Fresno Co Free Lib, Fresno Cal 50-51; Libn-in-chg Main Lib US Naval Train Center, Great Lakes Ill 51-54; Asst libn Chapman col 54-55; Jr libn bnaval Air Sta, Point Mugu Cal 57-66; Catlg libn Naval Civil Engnr Lab, Port Hueneme Cal 66-. 9: ALA; CalLA; SLA. 10: AAUW. 14: Admin, ref, catlg, acquis. 15: 905-E North A st, OXnard Cal 93032.

RUGEN, PAUL R. b Schenectady NY 20 Ap 25. 5: Rutgers 42-43, 46-49 (Hist) BS in Ed; George Washington U 49-51 (Hist); Columbia 60-63 (LS). 6: Fr. 7: Aviation Radioman 3/c US Navy 43-46; Mss asst Div LC 50-51; Archivist USMC Hist Div, Wash DC 51-55, Records analyst Naremco Serv Inc, NY 56-58; Archivist Mun Archives NY Pub Lib 58-59; Mss asst Ms Div NY Pub Lib 59-. 8: Archival consul, Tamiment Lib 60-. 9: SAA. 14: Mss, archives. 15: 305 E 40th st, apt 15-K, NYC 10016.

RUGG, PATRICIA (SMITH). b Rhea Springs Tenn 22 S 32. 4: Philip J Rugg. 5: Carson-Newman Col 49-51; Peabody 51-53 (Eng) BA; UNC 53-54 MS in LS. 7: Asst gen ref dept Cleveland Pub Lib 54-55; Prof asst readers serv dept Lawson McGhee Lib, Knoxville Tenn 55-57, Prof asst ref dept 62-. 9: TennLA. 14: Ref. 15: 2315 Monterey d, Knoxville Tenn 37912.

RUGGLES, MELVILLE J. b Toledo Ohio 8 My 15. 5: Oberlin Col 32-36 (Lat, Gk) AB (summa cum laude); Columbia 39 (LS) BS, 41 (Public Law) MA. 6: Russian. 7: Semi-Clerical & ref wk NY Pub Lib 37-38; Asst libn Coun on Foreign Rel In, NYC 39-42; Naval Ensign (Sr Lt) Off of Strategic Serv, WASH DC 42-45; Cultural off & publ procurement off US Embassy, Moscow USSR 46-48; Deputy chief Div of Research for USSR & E Europe, US Dept of State, Wash DC 48-50; Coordinator Psychological Intell, US Dept of State, Wash DC 50-52; Temp dir The East European Fund of Ford Found 52; Planned & supv research on Soviet Union The RAND Corp Wash DC 52-56; Chief prod div Off of Intell & Research US Info Agency, Wash DC 56; V-pres & sec CLR Inc, Wash DC 56-67; Exec dir Nat Adv Com on Libs 67-68; Program off CLR Inc, Wash DC 68-. 8: Ed, Slavic Series, Johnson Reprint Corp, NYC. 9: ALA; ADI; Amer Assn Adv Slavic Studies. 10: Phi Beta Kappa. 12: "Russian and East European Publications in the Libraries of the US, with Vaclav Mostecky (60); "Soviet Libraries and LIBRARIANSHIP," WITH R C Swank (62). 13: Yes. 14: Slavic bibliog, automation. 15: 3355 Quesada st NW, Wash DC 20015.

RUGHEIMER, VIRGINIA (ADELAIDE). b Spartanburg SC 15 Mr 06. 5: Col of Charleston 24-28 (Eng) BS; Columbia 35-38 BS in LS. 7: Asst libn Col of Charleston 33-45; Libn Menninger High Sch 45-48; Lib Charleston (SC) Lib Soc 48-. 9: ALA; SAA; SCLA; SELA. 14: Microfilming of Charleston newspapers. 15: 164 King st, Charleston SC.

RULE, BETTY-JO. b Chicago 1 D 31. 4: Lloyd Warren Rule. 5: Allegheny Col 49-53 (Eng) BA; UCol summers 51, 52, 55. 7: Guest promotion ed ""Mademoiselle Magazine, NYC 53; Asst bridal consul Denver Dry Goods Co, Denver 53-54; Asst to dir of pub rel Denver Chamber of Com 56; Pub info rep Emily Griffith Opportunity Sch, Denver pub sch 56-58; Act pub rel off Denver PuLib 9; Free lance in pub rel, Denver 59-60; Asst exec sec Adult Educ Coun of Metro Denver 60-61; Pub info off Denver Pub Lib 61-. 9: ALA;-LAD (Friends of Libs Com 64; pvs sec 67-68; Serv to Libs Com 68-69; Mem Com - Reg Memb Chm 67-68); Pub Rel Soc Amer; ColoLA (Convention Publ Chm 65, 67, 68). 10: Coun for Educ TV; Phi Beta Kappa. ; Communications Steering Com; C of C. 12: Ed ""Denver Public Library News (61-). 13: Yes. 14: Pub rel, commun rel. 15: Denver Pub Lib, 1357 Broadway, Denver 80203.

RUMBLE, LUCY (KEPLER). b Holyoke Colo 13 Jl 09. 5: Neb Wesleyan 26-30 (Eng) AB; UIll 31-32 BS in LS, 35-39 (LS) MA. 7: Asst catlg & circ depts UNeb Lib 33-35; UIll Lib (Urbana): Asst order dept 35, Period libn 35-55, Ser libn 55-57; Asst dir tech serv Colo State U 57-. 9: ALA; ColoLA (chm Col & Univ Div 64-65); MPLA. 10: Zonta Internat; Phi Kappa Phi; Beta Phi Mu; AAUP. 14: Tech serv. 15: 1613 W Mulberry, Ft Collins Colo 80521.

RUMICS, ELIZABETH. b Steubenville Ohio 13 F 29. 5: Seton Hill Col 46-50 (Eng) BA; Columbia 54-57 MSLS; Columbia U 53-54, 59-60, 53-54 (Lit). 7: Sub-prof asst Fordham Br NY Pub Lib summer 51; Asst ref libn Duquesne U Lib 51-52; Transcriber, oral hist research off Columbia U 52-55; Asst readers serv libn Fordham U Lib 55-58; Ref libn Columbia U 58-65; Head readers serv Oberlin Col Lib 65-. 9: ALA; OhioLA. 10: Inst for Cybercultural Research; Hist Sci Soc. 14: Ref. 15: 160 S Main st, Oberlin Ohio 44074.

RUMISEK, EMIL G. b Beaver Falls Penn 2 Ag 30. 5: Geneva Col 48-50 (Math, Physics); Penn State 50-52 (Ger) BA; IndU 54-55 (Russian Area Studies) MA; UPittsburgh 67 MLS. 6: Czechm Slovak, Polish, Russian, Ger. 7: Tr (Cpl) US Army, US & Germany 52-54; Tr us govt, Wash DC 55-66; Slavic catalog libn Penn StateU Patee Lib (University Park) 68-. 10: Amer Assn for Advancement Slavic Studies. 14: Bibliog, ref, research, catlg Slavic material. 15: 1000 W Aaron dr apt H13, State College Pa 16801.

RUML, ALISON WHEELER. b Baltimore Md 31 Mr 42. 4: Beardsley Ruml II. 5: Radcliffe 59-63 (Hist) AB; Simmons 64-66 MLS. 6: Fr, Sp. 7: UChicago Lab Schs: Alumni sec 64-66, Mus libn Univ High Sch 67-. 9: ALA. 14: Sch libs, music libs. 15: 1380 E Madison park, Chicago Il 60615.

RUMSEY, CLARK H. b Seneca Falls NY 22 Ap 13. 4: Fay Bentley. 5: Syracuse 46-49 (Eng) AB, 49-50 (LS) ML. 7: Claims & serv Rumsey Pump Co Ltd, Seneca Falls NY 30-36; Claims & serv Goulds Pumps Inc, Seneca Falls NY 36-42, US Army 42-46; Army Air Force, Infantry, Engr CBN, ASTP (France Area & Lang) NYU 46-49; Page Lib Syracuse Col of Med 49-50; Circ & ref libn SUNY Col of Med 50-54, Asst libn 54-58, Assoc libn 58-68, Asst prof admin med 68-. 9: MedLA; SUNYLA. 14: Pub affairs. 15: 110 Benedict ave, Syracuse NY 13210.

RUMSEY, VIRGINIA (G). b Batavia NY. 5: State U Col (Buffalo NY) 42-45 (Educ) BS; Columbia 46-47 (Early Childhood Educ) MA in Ed; Drexel 51-52 MS in LS. 7: Prim tchr Cherry Lawn Sch, Darien Conn 45-46; Tchr, Brookville NY 46-47; Pub Sch, Nyack NY 47-49; Elem Sch, N Miami Fla 49-50; Head of br Frankford Arsenal, Phila 52-53, Head of circ 53-56; Free Lib of Phila; bus sci ind 56-60, Mercantile Lib 61-64, Art 64-66; Sch libn Phila Pub Schs; Wanamaker Jr High Sch 66-68, Drew Elem Sch 68-. 9: PennLA. 14: Ref. 15: 200 Locust st, Phila Pa 19106.

RUNDBERG, JOHN SARJENT. b St Louis 22 N 39. 4: Darlyn Myra Del Boca. 5: UMo 57-58; Ohio State U 58-61 (Journalism) BA; UWash 61-62 MLS; UMd 67-68. 7: US Army Personnel Off (Capt) 62-64; Undergrad Lib UWash 64-67, Asst bk order libn 68-. 14: . 15: 8909 27th ave NE, Seattle 98115.

RUNEY, JOSEPH BARTLEY. b Evansville Wis 9 S 14. 4: Bess Meyer. 5: UWis 36-40 (Internat Rel) BA; UMich 40-46 ABLS; UIll 50-52 (LS). 6: Fr. 7: (Maj) US Army QMC 42-46; Salesman A C McClurg, Mich 46-47; Col rep Prentice Hall, Fla, Ga, SC 47-49; Bibliog UIll Lib (Urbana) 49-51; Chief order sect Army Med Lib, Wash DC 51-53; Depot libn USAF-CAMA (Eur), Chateauroux France 53-55; Spec serv libn Fairfax Co Lib,Fairfax Va 56-. 9: ALA; VaLA (Activities Com Chm 68); DCLA; EFLA; FLIC (Bd of Dirs). 10: Kiwanis Club; Pi Kappa Alpha; Delta Phi Epsilon. 12: Ed "Virginia Librarian (60-63). 14: Films, spec serv. 15: Fairfax Co Pub Lib, 3915 Chain Bridge rd, Fairfax Va 22030.

RUNGE, DeLYLE PAUL. b Madison Wis 3 F 18. 4: Ethelyn Green. 5: UWis 35-36 (Com), 37-40 (Marketing) BA, 42-43 BLS. 7: US Army (Pvt to 1st Lt) Infantry 43-46; Ref asst bus & tech to dir pub rel & coordinator of ref serv Pub Lib, Grand Rapids Mich 46-53; US Army Res (1st Lt to Lt Col) Civil Affairs 46-; Dir Pub Lib, St Petersburg Fla 53-. 8: Bldg consul, Dunedin Fla Pub Lib, 63; Wkshop consul, Mo Libns State Meeting, Jan 65; Consul, Pub Lib Ocala Fla 67-69, Coral Gables Fla Pub Lib 68-69. 9: FlaLA (past treas, mem var coms, past sect chm, v-pres & pres-elect 67-68, pres 68-69). 10: Kiwanis; Fla West Coast Orchid Soc. 13: Yes. 14: Admin. 15: 3745 Ninth ave N, St Petersburg Fl 33713.

RUNGE, VIRGINIA F. b Springfield Mo 30 N 19. 5: Drury Col 37-41 (Eng) BA; WashU (St Louis Mo) summers 43-48 (Eng) MA; Columbia 55-56 MS in LS. 7: Instr asst prof of Eng Drury Col 42-54, 60-66; Asst ref libn Barnard Col 56-59; Govt docs libn SW Mo State Col Lib 68-. 9: MoLA. 10: AAUW. 14: Ref, govt docs. 15: SW Mo St Col, Springfield Mo 65802.

RUNGE, WILLIAM H(ARRY). b Demarest NJ 4 Ja 27. 4: Beverly Ann Hackett. 5: Stevens Inst of Tech 44-47; UVa 52-54 (Hist) BA, 54-56 (Hist). 6: Fr. 7: Draftsman Orangeburg Mfg Co, Orangeburg NY 47-48; Lab tech Great Atlantic & Pacific Tea Co, NYC 48-52; UVa Lib: Asst in mss 55-57, Act curator of rare bks 57-60, Curator of rare bks 60-. 9: ALA-ACRL (Rare Bk Sect: sec 60-61, v-chm 65-66, chm 66-67); BSA; Bibliog Soc UVa (sec 62-); Bibliog Soc, London; Cambridge Bibliog Soc; The Hakluyt Soc; Soc Hist of Discoveries; VaLA. ; SELIERa;) 10: Grolier Club (NY); Albemarle Co Hist Soc; Keswick Club of Va; Colonnade Club; Omicron Delta Kappa; Raven Soc. 11: Woodrow Wilson Felltw (54-55); Old Dominion Fello, John Carter Brown Lib (). 12: "Four Years in the Confederate Artilery: The Diary of Private Henry obinson Berkeley (61); Ed "Magazine of Albemarle County History (57-64); Ed "Jeffersonian Americana, a microcard series (57-58). 14: Rare bks, Va bibliog, So hist. 15: Univ of Va Lib, Charlottesville Va 22901.

RUNSER, ROBERT E. b Erie Penn 24 Ap 15. 4: Esther Evans. 5: West Res 39 AB, 40 BS in LS. 7: Asst Tech Dept DC Lib 40-42; Libn res & dev div Republic Steel Corp, Cleveland 42-45; Hd ref dept Youngstown Pub Lib, Youngstown Ohio 45-47; Chief tech dept Detroit Pub Lib 47-66, Special proj dir 66-68; Bibliogr Michigan State U 68-. 9: ALA; MichLA. 15: Lib Mich State Univ, E Lansing Mi 48823.

RUNTON, GLORIA CECILIA. b Tampa Fla 18 Ja 23. 5: U Tamp 40-44 (Eng & For Lang) BA (cum laude); la State U 56-59 (LS) MA. 6: Fr, Sp. 7: Br manager Robertson & Fresh Photographers, MacDill FB Fla 43-45; Statistician Dist 7 State Welfare Bd, Tampa Fla 45-53; Catlgr UTampa Lib 53-. 8: Lib consul several parochial schs & St Patrick's Parish Lib, Tampa Fla 60-; Libn consul, Cath Info Ctr Lib, Tampa Fla 63-67, Tampa Audubon Soc Libn-Histn 63-. 9: FlaLA; SELA. 10: Tampa Audubon Soc; Westown Players Theatrical Group; Pi Delta Epsilon; Sigma Tau Delta; ELTA Zeta; Tampa Audubon Soc; Sacristan St Patrick's Church, Tampa Fla 13: Yes. 14: Catlg, a-v materials, admin. 15: 3416 Ohio ave, Interbay Subdiv, Tampa Fla 33611.

RUNYON, CONSTANCE L (CROSSLEY). b Meadville Penn 31 Mr 45. 4: David M Runyon. 5: WVa Wesleyan Col 63-67 BS; CatholicU 67-68 MS in LS. 7: Searcher-ed Nat Register of Microform Masters LC 68-. 14: Ref, catlg, films. 15: Apt 220 2000 S Eads st, Arlington Va 22202.

RUNYON, ROBERT (SHERWIN). b Summit NJ 28 Je 34. 4: Sheila McCrae. 5: Wesleyan U 52-56 (Philos) BA; UParis 56-57 Rutgers 58-61 MLS; UPittsburgh 66-67. 6: Fr. 7: Tech asst NY Pub Lib 57-58; Ref asst E Orange NJ Pub Lib 58-59; Tech info group supv Mack Trucks Engnr Res Dept, Plainfield NY 59-62; Col rep John Wiley & Sons, NYC 62-63; Libn Amer Insts for Research, Pittsburgh 63-67; Spec asst to libn Johns Hopkins U Lib 67-. 8: Participant Project LEX Ed Com 66. 9: ALA; ASIS; MdLA. 13: Yes. 14: Lib mechanization, admin. 15: 3913 Keswick rd, Baltimore Md 21211.

RUONA, SARA (BURGESS). b Van Wert Ohio 25 N 41. 4: Lloyd E Ruona. 5: Ohio NoU 59-63 (Eng) BS in Ed; UMicb 63-64 AMLS. 7: Bibliogr searcher UMich acquis dept 64-66; Ref libn UMich Engring Lib 66-. 8: Libn Inst of Sci & Tech Lib. 9: SLA. 14: Sci & tech, govt docs. 15: 1837 Shirley Lane apt C1, Ann Arbor Mi 48105.

RUOSS, G MARTIN. b Steelton Penn 1 Mr 11. 4: Marilyn Miller. 5: Muhlenberg Col 29-33 (Eng, Philos) AB; Lutheran Theol Sem (Phila) 33-37 (Theol) BD, 37-41 (Theol) STM; UDenver 65-66 (LS) MA. 6: Lat, Grk, Hebrew, Ger. 7: Pastor: Christ Lutheran Ch, Lancaster Penn 36-49, Good Shepherd Lutheran Ch, Phila 49-52, St Mark's Lutheran Ch, Mechanicsburg Penn 52-60, Zion Lutheran Ch, Landisville Penn 60-65; Theol ref libn Col & Sem Lib, Naperville Ill 66-68; Circ libn UNM 68-. 9: Amer Bibliog Soc; SAA; NMLA; Greater AlbuquerqueKA. 10: Sierra Club; Luthean Soc ofr Worship; Music & the Arts; Amer Bell Assn. 12: "An Altar Guild Workbook" (53); "The Acolyte" (57); "A Church Door" (59); "Theological Libraries of the World" (68). 13: Yes. 14: Rare bks, spec collections, hist of lib sci. 15: 207 Stanford dr SE, Albuquerque NM 87106.

RUOSS, MARILYN LOUISE (MILLER). b Lebanon Penn 7 My 24. 4: G Martin Ruoss. 5: Elizabethtown 41-45 (Secondary educ) BS; UDenver 65-66 (LS) MA. 6: Sp. 7: Tchr E Hempfield Twp Sch Dist, Landisville Penn 45-52; Tchr Hempfield Union Sch Dist, Landisville Penn 62-65; Ref libn Col & Sem Lib, Naperville Ill 66-68; Ser catlgr UNM 68-. 9: ALA; NMLA; Greater Albuquerque LA. 10: AAUP; Sierra Club. 14: Catlg, ref. 15: 207 Stanford dr SE, Albuquerque NM 87106.

RUOTSALA, GEORGIANNA (CALLIES). b Oshkosh Wis 3 My 20. 4: Sulo K Ruotsala. 5: Wis State U (Oshkosh) 38-42 (Eng, Soc Sci) BS; UWis 44-45 BLS. 6: Fr, Finnish. 7: Tchr High Sch, Macmillan Mich 42-43; Tchr High Sch, Norway Iowa 43-44; Asst libn Pub Lib, Detroit 45-46; Eng tchr High Sch, Rock Mich 59-60; Base libn AirForce, K I Sawyer AFB Mich 61-. 9: ALA; MichLA. 14: Child wk, catlg, bk sel. 15: Rt 1 Box 50, Rock Mich 49880.

RUPERT, ELIZABETH ANASTASIA. b Emlenton Penn 12 Jl 18. 5: Altona Sch of Com 36 (Bus) Diploma; Clarion State Col 56-59 (Eng,LS) BS in Ed; Penn State U 60-61 (Educ); Syracuse 60-62 MS in LS; UPittsburgh 63- (LS). 6: Fr. 7: Bkkeeper Barnes Coal Co, Barnesboro Penn 37-39; Sec Sterling Oil Div QS Oil Refg Corp, Emlenton Penn 39-56; V-pres & accountant Franklin Serv & Supply nc, Franklin Penn 48-62; Tchr- libn Oil City Area Schs, Oil City Penn 59-61; Libn Venango Campus, Clarion State Col 61-62; Asst Prof Lib Sci Educ Clarion State Col (Clarion Penn) 62-65, Dir Lib Sci Educ 65-68, Assoc Prof 68-. 9: ALA; NEA; NCTE; PennLA; Penn State EA; Tri State ACRL. 10: Toledo NaturalistsAssn; Toledo Mus of Art. 14: Educ for libnship. 15: Rt 1, Emlenton Penn 16373.

RUPP, ALICE CAROLYN. b Waterville Ohio 1 O 17. 5: Bowling Green State U 36-39 (Eng) BA; West Res 40 BS in LS. 7: Asst Toledo Pub Lib, Toledo Ohio 40-58; 1 st asst art, music, drama Flint Pub Lib, Fling Mich 58-60; 1st asst soc sci Toledo Pub Lib, Toledo Ohio 60-61, Head art, music, sports 61-. 9: SLA; OhioLA. 10: Toledo Naturalists Assn; Toledo Mus of Art. 14: Art. 15: Toledo Pub Lib, 325 Michigan st, Toledo Ohio 43624.

RUPPERT, M(ARY) CLARE. b Wash DC 12 Ag 08. 5: George Washington U 39 (Hist) AB, 42 (Hist) MA Columbia 39-40 (LS) BS; George Washington U 67- (Adult Educ). 6: Fr, Ger. 7: DC Pub Lib: Asst catlg dept 26-39, Catlgr 40-43, Readers adv, hist 43-48, Chief war reading room 44-45, Chief hist div 49-50, Coordinator adult serv 50-66; Curriculum libn Trinity Col (Wash DC) Master of Arts in tchg program 67-. 8: Great Books Discussion leader, USDA Grad Sch, 47-; CHM, USDA Grad Sch Faculty Com on Acad Excellence, 64-65; Significant Books of 20th Cent Discussion Leader, USDA Grad Sch summers 57-. ALA; CathLA; DCLA (Bd 49-50 & 62-63, Prog chm 52-53, sec 60-61, Com on Continuing Prof Educ 68-); Adult Educ Assn, Adult Educ Assn of Greater Wash (Com on Nat Adult Educ Week 67-); AHA; AAUW. 9: ALA; Adult Educ Assn; AHA; DCLA (Bd 49-50 &62-63, sec 60-61, Program Chm 52-53); Adult Educ Assn of Greater Wash. 10: Pi Gamma Mu. 14: Adult educ. 15: 2924 Cortland pl NW, Wash DC 20008.

RUPPRECHT, LESLIE P. b Newark NJ 9 Je 23. 4: Diana Magill Rupprecht. 5: Seton Hall U 46-49 (Soc Studies) BS; Columbia 50-51 MLS. 6: Fr. 7: (S/Sgt) US Army, European Theater 43-46; Clerk-dispatcher Hotpoint Div Gen Electric, Newark NJ 49-50; Prin libn Bus Lib Newark Pub Lib, Newark NJ 56-. 9: ALA; SLA; CathLA. 14: Ref. 15: 49 Tremont ave, E Orange NJ 07018.

RUPPRECHT, THEODORE A. b Cleveland 22 S 23. 4: Dorothy Gengler. 5: Wright Jr Col summer 48; UIll 48-51 BSLS, 52-54 MSLS. 7: Torpedoman 2/c USNR, US & SW Pacific 42-46; IBM-EAM operator Crane Co, Chicago 46-48; Libn I Detroit Pub Conely Br 53-54; Libn II Detroit Pub Lib film div 54-56; Head dept tech info Chrysler Missile Div, Sterling Mich 56-61 Sect chief Research Lib Avco Corp, Wilmington Mass 61-62; Supv lib serv Bendix Research Labs, Southfield Mich 62-. 8: Instr Dept Lib Sci Wayne State U 67; Lib Tech Citizens Adv Com Oakland Commun COL 9: SLA (treas Aerospace Sect 64-65; Mich Chap: treas 64-65). 14: Admin, org. 15: 1011 Mohawk, Royal Oak Mich 48067.

RUSCHIN, SIEGFRIED. b Schonlanke Germany 18 My 25. 5: Washburn U 54-58 (Physics) AB; Kan State Tchrs Col (Emporia) 59-60 LS) MS. 6: Sp, Ger. 07: Readers adv Topeka Pub Lib, Topeka Kan 58-59; Lina Hall Lib, Kan City Mo: Asst ser libn 60-63, Act ser libn 63-64, Ser libn 64-. 9: ALA; KanLA. 10: Tau Delta Pi; P Gamma Mu. 14: Ser, ref. 15: 5325 Tracy, Kansas City Mo 64110.

RUSH, DARL M. b Washington NJ 6 O 29. 5: Lafayette Col 49-52 (Eng) AB; West Res 52-53 (LS) MS. 6: Fr, Sp. 7: Lib asst Enoch Pratt Free Lib, Baltimore 53-57; Libn Olin Mathieson Chem Corp, NYC 57-59; Libn Forbes Inc, NYC 60-66; Hd libn Morgan Stanley & Co, NYC 66-. 9: SLA. 10: Phi Beta Kappa; Volunteers of the Shelter. 11: MacKnight Black Poetry Award. 12: Ed "Whats New in Advertising and Marketing (63-64). 14: Bus lib admin, ref. 15: 34-35 78th st, Jackson Heights NY 11372.

RUSH, FLORENCE A (RAYMAN). b Austin Minn 9 N 22. 4: Richard Rush. 5: Austin Jr Col 40-42 AA; State U Iowa 42-44 (Eng) BA, 60-62, 64 (Educ, LS) MA. 6: Sp. 7: Columbia U Lib Sch Lib 45-47; Circ libn Austin Pub Lib, Austin Minn 47; St Agnes Br NY Pub Lib 48-49; Libn Ariz STATE Col Lib (Flagstaff) 63-65; Libn Flagstaff Ariz Sch Dist #1 66-. 9: NEA; ALA; Ariz State LA (Col & Res Lib Sect: Com on Union List of Ser for Ariz); ArizEA; Flagstaff EA. 10: Pi Lambda Theta; pta; Flagstaff Pub Lib Bd. 14: Sch libs, improvement of all Ariz libs. 15: 3307 N Patterson blvd, Flagstaff Az 86001.

RUSH, N ORWIN. b Sapulpa Okla 18 Ag 07. 4: Dorothy PAINTER. 5: Friends U 31 (Philos) AB; Columbia 32 (LS) BS, 45 (LS) MS. 6: Sp, Ger. 7: Asst Columbia U Lib 31-32; Asst in chg of main reading room NY Pub Lib 32- 36; Libn & Asst Prof of Bibliog Colby Col 36-45; Dir & Assoc Prof of Bibliog Clark U 45-47; Exec Sec ALA- ACRL, Chicago 47-49; Dir of Libs & Prof UWyo 49-57; Dir of Libs & Prof Fla State U 58-. 8: Lib bldg consul; Fla Atlantic U 60, US Ala 65-66; Estab Dept of Lib Sci, UWyo, offering MS Degree, 56-58; Lib consul, Fla Mem Col, St Augustine 66; Consul to Planning Commsn for a new Univ at Boca Raton 62. 9: ALA (Coun, mem var coms);-ACRL (treas 45-46, Exec Bd, chm several coms); BSA; MPLA (hon life mem, pres 55-56); MELA (pres 38-41); WyoLA (chm &/or mem var coms); FlaLA (chm &/or mem var coms); Rocky Mountain Bibliog Ctr (chm Bd Dirs 50-51). 10: AAUP; Kiwanis; Westerners; United Fd. 11: Fulbright Award, Eng, 52-53. 12: "History of College Libraries in Maine" (46); "Mercers Badittiof the Plains" (14: Admin, spec collections. 15: 427 Vinnedge Ride, Tallahassee Fla 32303.

RUSH, STEPHAN. b Mzhyhirya Ukraine3 Ag 20. 4: Hermina Johanna Maria Hisintveld. 5: State Tchrs Col (Rohatyn) 42-43 Redagogics Diploma; Ukrainian Catholic Great Sem 43-49 (Philos) BA; Toronto 53-57 (Bus Admin) Diploma; UOttawa 61-62 BLS, 62-66 MLS, 66-68 MA. 6: Urainian, Polish, Ger, Eng, Dutch, Russian, Lat, Ital, Fr, Gk. 7: Ref libn Nat Lib of Can, Ottawa 62-. 9: ALA; CanLA. 10: Prof Inst Pub Serv of Can (v-pres Libns Group); Lib Sch Chap, Alumni Assn UOttawa. 12: "Union List of Non-Canadian Newspapers Held by Canadian Libraries" (68). 13: Yes. 14: Ref, ser. 15: 1166 Field st, Ottawa 5 Can.

RUSHIN, BEVERLY ANN. b Herkimer NY 16 Jl 35. 4: Joseph E Rushin. 5: SUNY (Oswego) 53-57 (Educ) BS; Syracuse summers 57-67 MLS. 7: Tchr Ilion Central Sch, Ilion NY 57-60; Lib-Elem & High Sch Southwestern Central Sch, Jamestown NY 60-; Tchr SyracuseU summer 68. 8: Chautauqua-Cattragus Lib System Processing Dept summer 65; Stud tchg program Edinboro State Col. 9: NY State Tchrs Assn; Chautauqua Co Tchrs Assn; Chautauqua Co Libns; NYLA. 10: Little Theatre Civic Orchestra; AAUW; Beta Phi Mu. 14: Ref. 15: RD 4 Baker st Ext, Jamestown NY 14701.

RUSHING, NAOMI J(OHNYE). b Delhi La 12 F 01. 5: Southern U 20-22 (Elem Educ) Diploma; Columbia 25-27 (Elem Educ) BS, summers 28, 29 & 30 (LS) BS, summers 34-37, 40 MS. 7: Tchr in chg La State Sch for Colored Blind, Baton Rough La 23; Tchr Allen Parish Train Sch 23-24; Instr & asst libn Winston Salem Tchrs Col 27-30; Howard U Asst libn 30-39, Supv Moorland Found & Catlg Dept 39, Catlg libn

& supv 39-44; Asst libn Miner Tchrs Col 44-54; Libn in chg of acquis DC Tchrs Col 54-. 9: ALA; Nea; DCLA; DCEA. 10: YWCA; Urban League; Nat Assn Study of Negro Life & His; NAACP; Alpha Kappa Alpha; So Christian Leadership Conf; Wash City Drama Soc; Columbia Sch of LiSclum Assn 13: Yes. 14: Catlg, acquis, col & univ libs. 15: 3312 Holmead pl NW, Wash DC 20010.

RUSIS, ARMINS. b Bulduri Latvia 1 Jl 07. 4: Margarete Schortmann. 5: Inst of Eng (Riga Latvia) High Sch Tchr of Eng; ULatvia Sch of Law 25-29, Magister Juris, 29-37 Magister Juris Habil; Acad of Internat Law (The Hague) 31 Certif; Munich 47 Dr Jur (magna cum laude); Chicago 51-55 LLB; George Washington U Sch of Law 55 M of Comparative Law (Amer Pract). 6: Latvian, Ger, Russian, Fr, Ital, Lat. 7: LC Law Lib European Law Div: GS 7 Libn-indexer-digester 52, GS 9 Libn-legal analyst 52-60, GS 11 Libn ref, law 60-63, GS 12 Libn ref, law 63-68, Libn law, Sr legal spec 68-. 8: Mem of the Bar of Latvia, 29-44; Asst Prof Priv Internat Law & Legal Adv, UNRRA U (Munich) 46-47; Legal & admin off, US Zone Hqs (Munich) Lutheran World Fed, Serv to Refugees 49-51; Mem of the Bar; Wash DC 56, Supreme Court of the US 61. 9: AALL (For Law Indexing Com); Amer Bar Assn; Fed Bar Assn; Amer Soc of Internat Law; Wash DC Law Libns Soc; Internat Assn of Law Libs. 10: Amer-Latvian Assn. 12: "Legal Sources of Estonia, Latvia & Lithuania" (63); Co-auth "The Socialist (Soviet) Theory o international Law" (64); Co-auth 'Eastern European Law' in "Sovereignty Within the Law" (65); Co-ed "Res Baltica (Leyden)" (68); Asst comp & analyst "Guide to Laws and Regulations on Federal Libraries" (68). 13: Yes. 14: Bibliog (Law), legal dictionaries, ref, comparative & internat law. 15: European Law Div, Lsw Lib, Lib of Congress, WASH DC.

RUSIS, INITA AILA (MEDNIS). b Riga Latvia. 4: Armins. 5: City Col (NY) 5862 (Hist) BA; Pratt 62-64 MLS. 6: Latvian, Ger. 7: Libn-trainee Queensborough Pub Lib, Jamaica NY 62-64, Libn 64, Br libn sr libn 65-66; Br libn Motgomery Co Pub Lib, Md 67-. 9: MdLA; Montgomery Co Staff Assn (v-pres, pres). 10: Beta Phi Mu; Queensborough Pub Lib Staff Assn. 14 Adult serv. 15: 72-10 41st ave, Woodside NY 11377.

RUSK, ALICE (CHAMBERS). b Baltmore 28 N 15. 4: Bernard K Rusk. 5: Coppin Normal Sch 31-34 (Elem Educ) Certif; Morgan Col 34-38 (Educ) BS Ed; UPenn summers 38, 39 (Educ); Catholic U 48-58 MSLS. 7: Baltimore City Pub Sch Elem tchr 34-48, Elem tchr-libn 48-59, Spec lib serv 59-67; Act head Bur of Lib Serv 64-65; Asst Prof Lib Sci Kent State U 67-68; Dir Lib Serv Baltimore City Pub Schs 68-. 8: Visiting lecturer: UMd summer 63, Morgan State Col, summer 65. 9: NEA-DAVI; ALA (Coun);-AASchL (Bd chm Com for Improve of Sch Lib Programs); Md State Tchrs Assn; MdLA (chm Publ Com 66-67); Educ Media Assn Md. 10: Beta P hi Mu; Delta Sigma Theta; Urban League. 13: Yes. 14: Child lit, sch lib serv, admin. 15: 245 Montebello terr, Baltimore 21214.

RUSK, MARGARET SENER. b Baltimore 25 Mr 28. 5: Wellesley 44-48 (Chem) BA; Harvard 49-51 Ed M; Syracuse 58-62 LS) MS. 6: Ger, Sp, Fr, Russian, Dutch. 7: Lab tech Mass Mem Hosps, Boston 48-49; Sci tchr Brimmer-May Sch, Boston 49-51; Sci tchr George Sch, Newtown Penn 51-52; Field dir Girl Scouts, Oswego NY 53-55; Sci & Eng tchr various schs, Barranquilla Colombia 55-57; Lab tech SUNY Upstate Med Centr (Syracuse) 57-58; Circ clerk, asst circ libn, sci & Ger catlg Syracuse U Lib 58-, Hd original catlg sect Syracuse U Lib 68-. 10: Beta Phi Mu. 14: Catlg. 15: 220 Ostrom ave, Syracuse NY 13210.

RUSS, DORIS (PERSONS). b Delevan NY 2 N 10. 4: Richard L Russ. 5: Syracuse 28-32 (LS) BS; Colgate U 50-55 (Eng) MA. 7: Chld libn Thrall Pub Lib, Middletown NY 40-47; Elem libn Elem Sch, E Aurora NY 49-50; High sch libn High Sch, Mt Upton NY 50-55; High sch libn High Sch, Sidney NY 55-. 9: NEA; ALA; NY State Tchrs Assn. 14: Wk with yp. 15: Mt Upton NY 13809.

RUSSELL, ALICE (MYRTLE CADY). b Bellows Falls Vt 20 Je 11. 5: Middlebury 28-32 (Bio) AB, 32-34 (Bio) MS; West Res 65-67 MS in LS. 6: Fr. 7: Fellow in bio Middlebury Col 32-34; Neuropathology histol tech UMich Neuro Hosp 34-38; Clinical lab tech John St clinic, Bay City Mich 40-41; Co-owner & mgr Stitch-in-Time (Sewing studio), Cleveland Ohio 50-56; Cuyahoga Co Lib, N Olmsted Ohio: Adult serv asst 62-65, Lib intern 65-67, Adult serv libn 67-68, Reg ext libn, Parma Ohio 68-. 9: ALA; OhioLA. 10: Mortar Board. 15: 5859 Burns rd, North Olmsted Oh 44070.

RUSSELL, ANNA LOE. b Belleville Ark 18 D 07. 5:Ark State Tchrs Col 26-29 (Foreign Lang) AB ,northwestern summer 33 (Fr); Peabody 38 BS in LS, 42 (Eng) MA. 6: Fr. 7: High sch tchr of Eng & Fr, Ark 30-35; Asst libn Little Rck Pub Lib, Little Rock Ark 38-41; Asst libn Greensboro Col 43; Asst catlgr Womans Col of UNC(Greensboro) 44-4, Asst ref libn 46; Libn Henderson State Tchrs Col 47; Ref lbn Peabody Col 47-. 9: ALA; TennLA (treas 57-58); SELA. 10: AAUW; Women's Nat Bk Assn. 12: Annual bibliog of Faculty Publns; Indices to "Peabody Reflector. 14: Ref, archives. 15: B-6 Forrest Hills Apts, 2600 Hillsboro rd, Nashville Tn 37212.

RUSSELL, ARLENE (AGNUS). b Waverly Iowa 17 Ag 10. 5: Wartburg (Eng) BA; UMinn 43 (LS) BS. 7: Libn pub lib, Waverly Iowa 43-54; Hennepin Co Lib, Minneapolis: Bkmob libn 54-60, Chief ext serv 60-. 8: Chm Nat Lib Week Minn. 9: ALA; IowaLA (State Planning com, treas Legisl Com); MinnLA (v-pres, pres). 11: Alumni Citation from Wartburg Col. 14: Ext serv, reg planning. 15: 5521 Newton ave S, Minneapolis Mn 55419.

RUSSELL, ATHALINDA (WOODCOCK). b Lowell Mass 1 D 19. 4: William G Russell. 5: Duke U 37-39 (Eng); Simmons 39-41 SLS; San Jose State Col summer 60 (LS) Certif; Newark (NJ) State Col 56, 67; Monmouth Col (NJ) summer 68; Simmons 68-69 6: Fr. 7: Lib sec Mt Holyoke Col 41-42 Order libn URI 42-43; Libn Alfred Vail Sch, Morris Twp NJ 54-56; Libn Parsippany High Sc, Parsippany NJ 56-. 9: NEA; NJEA; NJLA; NJSchLA; ALA (mem ALA-CanLA Liaison Com 67-69); -AASL; ASIS. 10: PTA; LWV; Troy Hills Pub Lib Assn; NJ Coun for the Rightto Read; Ocean Co Hist Soc. 14: Devel of sch libs as media ctrs. 15: Apt 8-A, 3379 Route 46, Parsippany NJ 07054.

RUSSELL, BEVERLY PATRICIA. b NYC 16 F 26. 5: Queens Col 43-47 (Pol Sci) BA; UWash 63-65 (LS) ML. 7: Airline Stewardess Northwest Airlines, Minneapolis & Seattle 48-65; Libn Seattle Pub Lib 65-; Libn "Seattle Times 67-. 9: SLA. 14: Ref, newspaper libs. 15: 1095 - 7th ave W, Seattle 98119.

RUSSELL, CECELIA (DALY). b Duluth Minn 15 Je 1. 4: Thomas P Russell. 5: George Washington U 36 (Hist); UDenver 46-47 BS in LS. 7: Typist, file clerk FBI, Wash DC 39-42; Typist, sec Labor Dept, Wash DC 42-43; US Navy Secs off, Off of Procurement & Material, Wash DC 44-45; US Lt (jg) US Navy Electronics Off Pearl Harbor 45-46; Labor Dept Lib, Wash DC 46; Catlgr Harvard Bus Sch Lib 47-48; Catlgr Boston U Law Sch Lib 64-. 14: Catlg. 15: Boston Univ Law Sch Lib, Boston Ma 02108.

RUSSELL, CHARLOTTE (GRAVES). b N Hadley Mase 25 N 13. 4: Milton Russell. 5: Simmons 31-36 (LS) BS. 6: Fr, Ger. 7: Asst circ Hartford Pub Lib, Hartford Conn 36-37, Asst art & music dept 37-39; Libn Glastonbury Pub Lib, Glastonbury Conn 39-41; Va State Lib: ct head ref & circ 42-46, Asst archives div 46-51, Head order sect 51-. 9: VaLA. 14: Ref, art & music, mss, pictures, maps. 15: 200 Riverside dr apt 5B, Richmond Va 23225.

RUSSELL, CYRIL B. b Canada 11 Ag 09. 4: Pearl Davis. 5: Valley City State Col 26-32 (Eng) BA in Ed; Seabury-West Theol Sem 32-36 (Theol); Nashotah House Sem 43-44 (Theol) BD; UMich 54-57 AMLS. 6: Fr. 7: Libn Ill State Train Sch for Boys, St Charles 39-42; Libn St John's Military Acad, Delafield Wis 42-45; Parish admin Episcopal Ch, Ill & NY 45-53; Libn Godwin Hts High Sch, Grand Rapids Mich 53-54; Bkmob libn pub lib, St Clair shores Mich 54-57; Hd Dept of Lib Sci Wis StateU (Oshkosh) 57-60; Libn pub high sch, Menasha Wis 60-61; Hd libn Ill Col 61-66; Hd libn Mesa Col 66-68; Acquis libn Minot state Col 68-. 9: Amer Assn for Higher Educ; NEA; NDakLA. 14: Acquis. 15: 2005 5th st NW, Minot ND 58701.

RUSSELL, ELIZABETH. b RI 28 Mr 30. 5: Pembroke 48-52 (Hist) AB; RI Sch of Design 51-55 (Ceramics) BFA; Simons 58-60 MLS; RI Col 69 (Hist) MAT. 6: Ger, Persian. 7: Libn asst Elmwood Pub Lib, Providence 49-57; Child libn Lynn Pub Lib, Lynn Mass 58-60; Asst ref libn UMass 6061; Libn Rogers High Sch, Newport RI 61-66, 68-; Prof of Lib Sci Faculty of Educ UTehran, Iran 66-67. 8: US Peace Corps Volunteer to Iran 66-67. 9: ALA; NELA; NESchLA; RILA; RISchLA (pres 65-). 10: Appalachian Mountain Club. 11: Fulbright Grant to Germany, 55-56. 12: "A Library Manual for Peace Corps/Iran (67). 13: Yes. 14: Ya serv, lib serv to the blind, internat libnship. 15: 73 Herschel st, Providence RI 02909.

RUSSELL, J(OHN) THOMAS. b Wash DC 27 Ag 35. 4: Harriet Heit. 5: UMd 5-55 (Hist); Kenyon Col 55-57 (Hist) AB; (cum laude); UMich 58-59 MALS; UDenver 67 (Bkbinding). 6: Fr. 7: Pub serv libn Washington & Lee U

59-62; Reader serv Libn, acquis, catlgr US Naval Weapons Lab, Dahlgren Va 62-63; Spec collections libn US Mil Acad (West Point) 63-. 64, Chief spec collections div 64-68, Asst libn 68-. 8: Adv, bks & mss, Constitution Island Assn 66; Consul, mss York (Penn) Hist Soc 69. 9: SLA. 10: Newburgh (NY) Writers Club; Friends of Cornwall (NY) Pub Lib; West Point Offrs Club. 11: Outstanding Performance Award, Dept of the Army, West Point 67. 12: Ed "The West Point Thayer Papers 1808-1833 (65); "Survey of US Univ R&D Contracts in Excess of 13: Yes. 14: Rare bks, mss, archives. 15: Wilson rd, Cornwall-on-Hudson NY 12520.

RUSSELL, JOHN RICHMOND. b Manistee Mich 29 Ap 04. 4: Margaret Elizabeth Adams. 5: Chicago 27 PhB; UMich 30 AB in LS. 6: Fr, Ger. 7: Asst in ref dept UMich 28-30; Asst clsf NY Pub Lib 30-35; Chief div of catlg Nat Archives 35-40; Dir of Libs URochester 40-68; Libn Amer Col of Switzerland, Leysin 68-. 8: Libn, Rochester Acad of Sci, 40-; Mem, Regents Lib Coun for NY State; Consul Lib of Amer Studies Research Ctr, Hyderabad India 66-67. 9: ALA (chm Bks for European Libs Com, Intl Rel Bd); ARL (chm Catlg Code Rev Com; chm Coop Catlg Com; Bd); NYLA (pres 45-46); Commsnrs Com on Ref & Res Lib Resources (chm); SLA; Coun of Col Libns of 9chm); SLA; Coun of Col Libns of Rochester (chm Intermus Coun). 10: Phi Beta Kappa; Phi Kappa Phi. 12: Ed "University of Rochester Library Bulletin" (46-). 13: Yes. 14: Bibliog, lib sci, lib bldgs. 15: American College of Switzerland, 1854 Leysin Switzerland.

RUSSELL, JULIA G. b Mecosta Co Mich 4 S 17. 5: UMich 48-52 MALS; Central Mich U 34-38 (Eng) BA. 7: Tchr, Mich 38-45; Secondary tchr Flint Pub Schs, Flint Mich 46-50, Tchr libn 50-52; Br libn Flint Pub Lib, Flint Mich 52-58, Head ya dept 58-64; Ya serv consul Nassau Lib System, Garden City 64-. 9: ALA; -YASD (chm various com); MichLA (Div Sec); NYLA (CYASS Bd). 10: AAUW. 14: Ya wk. 15: Nassau Lib System, Roosevelt Field, Garden City LI NY 11530.

RUSSELL, LIBRADA BELMONTE (LALI). b Philippine Islands 20 Jl 19. 4: J B Russell. 5: Inst de Mujeres (Manila) 33-37 (Home Econ, Sci) BSHE; U St Thomas (Manila) 37-38 (Eng, Sci) BSE, 38-39 (Educ, Research) MA in Ed. 6: Sp, Tagalog, Ilocano. 7: Dept of the Army, Redstone Arsenal Ala; Asst libn, Documents catlgr & ref Guided Missile Lib 52-53, Asst libn, Chief bk sect Guided Missile Lib 53-54, Ref film libn Technical Lib 54, Chief Guided Missile Lib 54-55, Libn (Ref, Phys Sci & Engnr) Technical Lib 55; Chief Base Tech Order Lib, Dept of the Air Force, Patrick AFB Fla 55-57; Libn ref, phys sci & engnr Missile Firing Lib, Army Ballistic MSL Agency, Cape Canaveral Fla 57-60; LOD Libn Launch Operations Directorate NASA, Cape Canaveral Fla 60-62; Loc libn, Launch Operations Center, Cape Kennedy Fla 62-63; KSC Libn J F Kennedy Space Ctr NASA, Fla 63-. 8: Custodian of the Pennemunde Archives, Guided Missile Lib, Redstone Arsenal Ala 54-55; Records adminr, Missile Firing Lab, 57-62. 9: SLA. 10: Rockledge Golf & Country Club; Fla Womens Golf Assn; Rockledge Womens Golf Assn; So Women's Golf Assn. 11: Sustained Superior Performance Award, Dept of the Air Force, Patrick AFB Fla; Sustained Superior Performance Award, Missile Firing Lab, Dept of the Army, Cape Canaveral Fla. 14: Admin, docs catlg & ref, info syst. 15: NASA, J F Kennedy Space Center, Kennedy Space Center Fla 32899.

RUSSELL, LELIA FAYE. b Greenville Ala 14 Ap 43. 5: Troy State Col 61-64 (Eng) BA; Fla StateU 65-66 (LS) MS. 7: Ref & ya NYC Pub Lib 66-68; Ref libn Air Univ Lib, Ala 68-. 15: 2124B Narrow Lane rd, Montgomery Al 36106.

RUSSELL, LOCKHART M. b Forestport NY 6 O 32. 5: Syracuse 50-54 (Ch em) BS, 62-63 (LS) MS. 7: Ch em US Pub Health Serv, Cincinnati 57-59; Lit searcher Syracuse U Research Inst 59-61; Eng libn Syracuse U 63-. 9: SLA; ASIS; Amer Soc Engring Educ. 10: ACS; Beta Phi Mu. 14: Sci & tech ref. 15: Eng Lib Syracuse Univ, Syracuse NY 13210.

RUSSELL, MARGARET (ADAMS). b Pender Neb 4 Ap 07. 4: John R Russell. 5: UNeb 25-29 (Philos, Hist) AB; UMich 29-30 AB in LS. 7: Catlg: Pub Lib, Oak Park Ill 30-35, DC Pub Lib 36-38, Pub Lib, Rochester NY 56-68; Catlg Amer Studies Research Ctr, Hyderabad India 66-67; Catlg Amer Col of Switzerland, Leysin Switzerland 68-. 9: NYLA. 14: Catlg. 15: 154 Gregory Hill rd, Rochester NY 14620.

RUSSELL, MATTIE UNDERWOOD. b Randolph Miss 14 My 15. 5: UMiss 33-37 (Hist) BA, summers 37-40 (Hist) MA; Duke U 56 (Hist) PhD. 7: High sch soc studies tchr, Miss 37-43; Asst Prof of Hist Mrs Hill Col 43-46; Asst curator of mss Dke U Lib 48-52, Curator of mss 52-. 9: AHA; SAA; So Hist Assn; Hist Soc NC; NC Lit & Hist Assn; ALA. 10: AAUW; Amer Soc State & Local Hist; Mss Soc; Oral Hist Assn. 13: Yes. 14: Mss. 15: 2209 Woodrow st, Durham NC 27705.

RUSSELL, MILDRED. b Brooklyn NY 30 Mr 20. 5: Col of William & Mary 37-41 (Jurisprudence) BA; Pratt 48-49 BLS; Amer U 51-54 (Pol Sci); NYU Womens Law Class 61-62 (Law) Certif. 7: Libn Md Park High Sch, Seat Pleasant Md 49-50; Legis ref asst Army Law Lib, Pentagon 50-55; Adult serv libn Pease Mem Lib, Ridgewood NJ 57-61; Ed "Index to Legal Periodicals H W Wilson Co, Bronx NY 61-. 8: Helped to estab the Eritrean Govt Lib, Asmara Eritrea Ethiopia 55-56. 9: ALA; AALL; Internat Assn of Law Libs; NY Lib Club; Law Lib Assn, Greater NY. 10: Phi Delta Delta. 12: Ed "Index to Legal Periodicals (61-). 14: Legal ref. 15: 100 E Palisade ave, Englewood nj 07631.

RUSSELL, MILTON CHAMBERLAIN. b Raleigh NC 4 Ap 12. 4: Charlotte Graves. 5: Wake Forest Col 28-32 BA; UNC 34-35 BA in LS. 7: Stud asst, Wake Forest 29-32; Stud asst UNC 34-35; Sr asst genealogy & local hist room NY Pub Lib 35-36; 1st asst ref room Hartford Pub Lib, Hartford Conn 36-41; US Army (S/Sgt) 43-46; Head ref & circ sect Va State Lib 41-. 9: ALA-ACRL (chm Ref Sect 50-51); VALA (nd v-pres 48-49); SELA; Va Hist Soc. 14: Ref. 15: 2000 Riverside dr, Richmond Va 23221.

RUSSELL, MYRTLE L. b Carlsbad NM 31 O 10. 5: Baylor Col 28-30 (Eng). 6: Sp. 7: Reporter "Wichita Times-Record News, Electra Tex 3055; Asst libn Electra Pub Lib, Electra Tex 31-32; News Reporter Radio Station Kelt, Electra Tex 50-52; Libn Electra Pub Lib, Electra Tex 35-. 10: Internat Assn of Rebeka Assemblies; Rebekah Assembly of Tex; Bus & Prof Womens Club; PTA (Life mem). 14: Ref. 15: 213 W Garrison, Electra Tx 76360.

RUSSELL, PHYLLIS JEANNINE. b Calgary AltaCan. 5: UAlta BA; Toronto BLS; Columbia Certif of the MLA. 7: Catlg asst UAlta, Asst in Med Lib; Ref asst UBC; Catlg asst Seattle Pub Lib; Med libn UAlta. 9: CanLA; MedLA; AltaLA; ALA; ASIS. 10: EdmontonLA. 14: Med. 15: Med Scis lib, Univ of Alta, Edmonton Alta Can.

RUSSELL, RALPH ERNEST. b Bradenton Fla 25 Ja 38. 4: Linda Sherman. 5: Fla State U 57-60 (Eng) AB 60-61 (Eng) MA. 6: Fr. 7: Ref Queens Borough Pub Lib, NYC 61-62; US Navy 62-64; Circ asst USoCal 64-65, Acquis 65-66; Dir of libs Fla Jr Col (Jacksonville) 66-68; Sci libn UGa 68-. 9: ALA. 10: AAUP. 14: Ref. 15: 140 Baxter dr apt H-5, Athens Ga 30601.

RUSSELL, RICHARD A. b St Amands NY 1 Ja 28. 4: Carol Lawrie. 5: Fla State U 57-60 (Eng) AB 60-61 (LS) MS; NYU 61-62 (Eng) MA. 7: Cpl USAF 46-47; YNT 2 US Navy, Honolulu 50-51; Catlgr circ libn Buffalo & Erie Co Pub Lib, Buffalo NY 55-56; Circ libn Niagara U 56-57; Bkmob libn Buffalo & Erie Co Lib, Buffalo NY 57-59, Sci & tech dept libn 59-61, Catlgr-Sr Libn II 62-65; Sr catlgr Alanar Div of Bro-Dart Ind, Williamsport Penn 65-; Lectr in Lib Sci Williamsport Penn Area Community Col 67-. 9: ALA; SELA; FlaLA (chm-elect Tech Serv Sect 68-69). 10: AAUP. 14: Admin (acad lib). 15: 2141 Hillside ave, Williamsport Pa 17701.

RUSSELL, RUBYE S. b Fort Worth Tex 24 S 07. 5: Tex Wesleyan Col 35-39 (Soc sci) BA; Tex State Col for Women summers 41-45 BS in LS; Sul Ross State summers 49-52 (Hist) MA. 6: Fr. 7: Apprentice, staff mem pub lib, Ft Worth 26-29; Libn Cisco Jr Col 30-35; Libn jr high sch, Tex City 41-46; Hd libn H M King High Sch, Kingsville Tex 46-. 9: TexStateTA (chm Lib Div, Dist III 48-52). 10: Women's Club; Bus & Profess Women; AAUW. 14: Catlg. 15: 825 Ailsle apt 2, Kingsville Tx 78363.

RUSSELL, SUE M (MRS). b Upson Co Ga 14 D 08. 5: GA Tchrs Col 27-29; Emry 29-31 (Eng) AB, 31-32 BLS. 7: Atlanta Pub Schs: Elem tchr 32-50, High sch libn 50-52; Elem sch libn 52-; Night ref libn Ida Williams Br Atlanta Pub Lib 60-. 9: Child & yp libn (5th Dist); GaEA; (chm 52). 12: . 15: 4631 Powers Ferry rd NW, Atlanta Ga 30327.

RUSSO, MARY (TOWNSEND). b Providence RI 10 Mr 23. 4: Albert P Russo. 5: RI Col 41-45 (Educ) EdB; URI 63-66 MLS. 6: Fr. 7: Circ asst special collections John Hay Lib BrownU (RI) 63-66, Asst special collections libn 66-. 9: ALA; RILA. 14: Spec collections, catlg, ref, circ. 15: 41 Longmeadow rd, Portsmouth RI 02871.

RUSTIGIAN, JACKIE. b Hartford Conn 27 My 44. 5: Conn Col 62-66 (Eng) AB; EmoryU 66-67 MLn. 6: Fr. 7: Lib asst Trinity Col Lib, Hartford Conn 60-62; Acquis asst Yale Med Lib summer 63; Asst & preservation sect Nat Lib of med, Bethesda Md summer 64; Catalog asst Conn Col Lib 62-65; Libn Gen Serv Admin, Wash DC summer 65; Ref & circ libn OEO, Wash DC summer 66; Govt docs libn Emory U Law Lib, Atlanta 66-67; Ref libn Conn State Lib, Hartford Conn 67-69; Chief libn Martland Hosp Lib (NJ Col of Med & Dentistry), Newark NJ 69-. 9: ALA. 14: Ref, med libnship. 15: 123 S Munn ave, E Orange NJ 07018.

RUTENBERG, ALICE (LEVINE). b NYC 25 Ja 23. 4: Irving Seymour Rutenberg. 5: Brooklyn Col 39-40; Hunter Col 40-43 (Pre-Soc) AB; St Johns U 58-63 MLS; C W Post Col summer 64. 6: Fr. 7: Sch libn The Wheatley Sch, Oldwestbury LI NY 63-. 9: ALA; NYLA: Nassau-Suffolk Sch Libns Assn. 10: Roslyn Country Club Civic Assn; Hadassah; Phi Beta Kappa. 14: Bk sel, reading guidance, tchg lib skills, ref. 15: 153 Shepherd lane, Roslyn Heights NY.

RUTH, SISTER M (WHALEN) CSJ. b Wbash Ind 24 F 16. 5: St Josephs (Ind) summers 54-58; St Louis U summers 59-60; Ind State U 61-62 (Eng, Lat) BA; Rosary Col 6263 (LS) MA. 6: Lat, Fr. 7: Jr high prin & tchr St Peters Sch, Winamac Ind 49-54; Jr high prin & tchr ST Josephs Sch, Delphi Ind 56-60; Libn St Joseph Acad & Libn & Eng tchr St Joseph Jr Col, Tipton Ind 63-. 9: Nat Cath Educ Assn; ALA; CathLA; Ind CTE. 15: St Joseph Jr Col, Tipton Ind 46072.

RUTHERFORD, NANCY JANE TURNER. b Malvern Ark 28 S 02. 4: John Ferguson Rutherford. 5: Henderson-Brown Col 21-22; Sophia Newcomb 23; Ark A&M 50-52 (Eng) BA; Tex State Col for Women 55 MLS. 6: Fr. 7: Tchr Mavern Elem Sch & Jones Sch, Hot Springs Ark 23-27; WPA br libn, Pine Bluff Ark 37-41; Jefferson Co & child libn, Pine Bluff Ark 41-49; Asst libn Southeast Reg Lib, Monticello Ark 49-52; High sch libn, England Ark 52-55; Malvern & Hot Spring Co Libn, Malvern Ark 55-. 9: ALA; ArkLA. 10: Camille WATSON Serv Guild; Hot Springs Co Hist Soc. 13: Yes. 14: Rare bks, ref, child serv. 15: 341 Pine Bluff st, Malvern Ark 72104.

RUTHERFORD, RUTHE AUMAN. b LANCASTER Penn 26 Ap 18. 5: Millersville State Tchrs Col 36-40 (LS) BS in Ed; Drexel45-48 BS in LS. 6: Fr. 7: Tchr-libn Mt Union Jr-Sr High Sch, Mt Union Penn 40-42; Libn: Yeadon Jr-Sr High Sch, Yeadon Penn 42-47, Wharton Sch UPenn summer 44, Inst of Local & State Govt UPenn summer 45, 46, Ariz State Col (Flagstaff)summer 57, Haverford Twp Jr High Sch, HAVERTOWN Penn 47. 8: Recorder at Illusts wkshop Drexel. 9: NEA; ALA; Penn State E; PennLA; Del Co (Penn) SchLA (pres 45-46 & 64-65); Bksellers Assn of Phila (sec 68-69); LPRC. 14: Wk with yp. 15: Haverford Township Jr High School E Darby rd, Havertown Pa 19083.

RUTHVEN, PATRICIA E. b Doruing England 11 D 38. 4: Douglas Morris Ruthven. 5: King's col (London) 57-60 BA, 65 ALA. 6: Ger, Fr. 7: Lib asst Kensington Pub Lib 61-63; Child libn Chiswick Pub Lib 64-67; Ref libn 67-. 15: Harriet Irving Lib Univ of New Brunswick, Fredericton NB Can.

RUTKAUS, EDNA ELIZABETH (RUBIN). b Chicago 7 Ag 16. 4: Anthony C Rutkaus. 5: Central YMCA Col 34-38 (Modern Langs) AB; Catholic U 63, 64, 65 MS in LS. 6: Ger, Fr, Sp. 7: Soc wker Chicago Relief Admin 38-40; Soc wker Dept Pub Welfare, Wash DC 41-43; Finance off Fairfax Co Dept Pub Lib, Fairfax Va 64-66; Br libn Fairfax Co Lib Carter Glass Br, Reston Va 66-. 9: VaLA. 10: Sigm Delta Epsilon. 14: Child serv. 15: Fairfax County Pub Lib Carter Glass Branch 1639 Washington plaza, Reston Va 22070.

RUTKOSKI, ROSE ELIZABETH. b Wilkes-Barre Penn 14 S 09. 5: Kutztown State Col 31-37 (LS, Eng) BS in Ed. 6: Lithuanian. 7: Elem tchr Pub Sch, Wilkes-Barre Twp Penn 30-47; Typist US Army, Newark njsummers 44, 45; High sch libn Pub Sch, Wilkes-Barre Twp Penn 47-. 8: Part-time libn Georgetwon Br, Osterhout Free Lib, WILKESBarr Penn, 50-55. 9: PennLA; NE PennLA; PennStateEA; PennASchL. 10: Wilies-Barre Twp EA. 15: 668 E Northampton st, Wilkes-Barre Penn 18702.

RUTLAND, ENID ELLEN. b Flin Flon Man Can 22 Ja 35. 5: USask 53-56 (Chem) BA Type C; McGill 61-62 BLS. 6: Fr. 7: Libn Fisheries Research Bd of Can Actic Biol Sta, Montreal 62-64; Catlgr McGill Med Lib 64-65; Bodleian Lib Oxford U, (Eng) 65-66; Libn Nuffield Orthopaedic Ctr, Oxford U 66-68. 8: Adv; oxford U (67), Report on Oxford Med Libs; Consul Agnes Hunt & Robert Jones Orthopaedic Hosp Lib, Oswestry Shropshire (Eng) 69. 9: Bibliog Soc Can; SLA (Montreal Chap: Pub Rel Com 64-65). 13: Yes. 14: Med bibliog. 15: McGill Med Lib, Montreal Can.

RUTSTEIN, JOEL STEPHEN. b Burlington Vt 5 S 40. 4: Barbara Sims. 5: UVt 58-62 (Pol Sci) BA; Boston U 62-63 (Hist) AM; Simmons 66-67 MSLS. 7: Art restorer Swain's Art stores, Plainfield NJ 64-66; UNH: Asst ref libn 6-69, Catlgr 69-. 9: ALA. 10: Amer Assn Conservators & Restorers. 14: Rare bks, spec collections, hist of bks. 15: 33 Garden lane, Durham NH 03824.

RUZICKA, RUDOLPH RAYMOND. b NYC 24 S 13. 5: NYU 31-36 (Span) BS in Ed; Pratt 36-37 BLS. 7: Asst libn Cooper Union 37-38; queens Borough Pub Lib: Sub libn brs 38, Act ref libn Broadway Br 38-40, Ref asst br ref-interloan 40-41, Ref libn Steinway Br 41-42; US Army 75th Infantry Div Medics, Crp Tech 5th grade 42-45; US Army Spec Lib Serv, ETO 45; Queens Borough Pub Lib: Asst tchrs consul Teachers Room 46-50, Catlgr catlg div 5056, Libn Steinway Br 56-57, Libn Jackson Heights Br 57-58, Asst br libn Elmhrst Br 58-59, Asst br libn Ravenswood Br 59-60, Ref libn Queens Village Br 60-64, Ref libn Forest Hills Br 64-66; Ref libn Broadway Br 66-. 9: NYLA; NY Lib Club. 14: Catlg, ref. 15: 25-32 30 dr, LI NY 11102.

RYALS, JUNE H. b SANDERSVILLE Ga 9 Mr 29. 4: Leon V Ryals. 5: Middle Ga Col 46-48; Womans Col of Ga 48-50 (Elem Educ) BS; Peabody summers 61-63 MA in LS. 7: Elem tchr, McRae Ga 48-51; High sch libn, McRae Ga 51-58; Elem libn Liberty-Guinn Sch Futon Co, Atlanta 58-. 8: Staff, Lib/USA, NY Worlds Fair, 64. 9: NEA; GaLA; GaEA; SELA. 10: Nat Cong Parents & Tchrs; Beta Phi Mu. 15: Liberty-Guinn Elem Sch Lib, 4820 Long Island dr NE, Atlanta 30305.

RYAN, ANNE (REVELL). b Baltimore Md 10 S 42. 4: David M Ryan. 5: Lake Erie Col 60-64 (Eng, Ger) BA; UDenver 64-65 (Libnship) MA. 6: Fr, Ger. 7: Minneapolis Pub Lib: Asst libn 65-68, Publicity specialist 68-. 9: ALA; MinnLA (chm Publ & Pub Rel Coms). 14: Pub rel, ya wk. 15: 2532 Upton ave South, Minneapolis Mn 55405.

RYAN, SISTER BARBARA GSIC. b Los Angeles Cal 3 F 26. 5: UOttawa 44-47 (Eng) BA, 60 (Eng) MA, 61 BLS. 6: Fr. 7: Libn Immaculate High Sch, Ottawa Can 60-. 8: Lib adv Lorrain Sch of Nursing, Pembroke Ont Can 61-. 9: ALA; CathLA (Ont Unit: treas, past chm High Sch Sect, past sec); OntLA; OttawaLA. 11: Grolier Award for Ref Wk OttawaU 61. 14: High sch libs. 15: 211 Bronson ave, Ottawa 4 Ont Can.

RYAN, CLARE E. b Springfield Mass 17 Je 27. 5: Col of Our Lady of the Elms 45-49 (Eng Lit) AB; Carnegie 53-54 MLS. 7: Catlgr Enoch Pratt Free Lib, Baltimore 54-56; Head tech proc dept Racine Pub Lib, Racine Wis 57-60; Head tech proc dept Arlington Co Lib, Arlington Va 60-61; Head of catlg dept Carnegie Lib of Pittsburgh 61-68; Hd tech proc div NH State Lib 68-. 9: ALA. 14: Catlg. 15: 91 School st, Concord NH 03301.

RYAN, CONSTANCE (ANNE VAN KIRK). b Ithaca NY 27 N 31. 4: Donald Leo Ryan. 5: Nazareth Col (Rochester NY) 49-53 (Eng & Amer Lit) BA (cum laude); Columbia 53-55 MSLS. 7: Pre-prof lib Brooklyn Pub Lib, Brooklyn NY 53-55; Spec serv lib US Army Trois Fontaines France 55; Libn I UMich Undergrad Lib 58-59; Child libn, catlg libn Free Pub Lib, Glen Ridge NJ 63-66; Ref libn Montclair State Col 66-68; Catlg libn (asst hd catlg) Bloomfield Col 66-68; Libn St Patrick's Hall Sch, St John's Mfld Can 68-. 9: ALA; CanLA; NJLA. 10: League of Women Voters; Family Life Apostolate Coordinating Com (Archdiocese of Newark NJ); Kappa Gamma Pi; Nazareth College Alumnae Chap. 14: Catlg, ref. 15: 44 Newtown rd, St John's Newfoundland Can.

RYAN, DONALD L(EO). b Cambridge Mass 6 S 31. 4: Constance Van Kirk. 5: Harvard 49-53 (Eng) AB Columbia 53-54 MSLS. 6: Sp, Fr. 7: Libn NY Pub Lib 54; US Army, Verdun France 54-56; Serv libn UMich 56-59; Libn Rutgers U 59-68; Libn Memorial U of Newfoundland 68-. 8: Lectr, Rutgers Grad Sch of Lib Serv 56-58. 9: CathLA; ALA; APLA. 10: Rotary. 13: Yes. 14: Admin. 15: 44 Newtown rd, St Johns Newfoundland Can.

RYAN, DOROTHY EVELYN. b Knoxville Tenn 23 Mr 15. 5: UTenn 31-35 (Eng) AB; UIll 37-38 BS in LS; Columbia 43-48 MS in LS. 6: Fr, Ger. 7: Libn Park Lowry Elem Sch, Knoxville Tenn 35-37; Loan desk asst UIll Lib (Urbana) 37-38; Head of circ Ball State Tchrs Col Lib 38-41; 1st asst Co Dept Lawson McGhee Lib, Knoxville Tenn 41-43; 1st asst Sch of

Lib Serv Lib, Columbia U 43-44; Exec asst to dir of libs Columbia U 44-46; Head of circ UTenn Lib 46-56, Educ libn 56-58; Visiting Lecturer Div of Lib Sci Ind U 58-59; Visiting Lecturer Lib Sch USoCal summer 59; Assoc Prof & Head Dept of Lib Serv Col of Educ UTenn 59-, Prof & Hd Dept of Lib Serv 66-. 8: Commsn on a Nat Plan for Lib Educ, Div Inst on Lib Educ in SEast (61). 9: ALA (Life mem)-LED (chm Tchrs Sect 65-66); SELA (chm Nomin Com 58-59); 58-59, mem Exec Bd 68-72); (pres 64-65). 10: Delta Kappa Gamma; Pi Lambda Theta. 12: Ed "Tennessee Librarian (57-61). 13: Yes. 14: Lib educ, personnel mgt, readers serv. 15: 613 - 19th st, Knoxville Tenn 37916.

RYAN, ELIZABETH (LAWS). b Franklin CoPenn 20 F 05. 5: Longwood Col 23-26 (Educ) BS, 50-51 Sch-Libn Certif. 7: Prime tchr Norfok Pub Schs, Norfok Va 26-39; Catlg libn Hampden-Sydney Col 51-. 9: VaLA. 10: DAR; Delta Kappa Gamma. 14: Catlg. 15: 611 Buffalo st, Farmville Va 23901.

RYAN, ELOISE (J). b Virginia City Nev 25 S 13. 5: UCal(Berkeley) 29-33 (Span) AB, 33-34 Cert of Libnship; Mills Col 34-35 (Span) MA. 7: Loan desk asst Mills Col Lib 34-35; Loan desk asst Merced Co Free Lib Merced Cal 35; Jr libn order & ref sects Cal State Lib 36-40, Sr libn bks for the blind 4; Libn 2 US Naval Air Sta, Alameda Cal 41-45; Libn 2 US Naval Air Sta, San Diego 45-47; Jr libn documents sect Cal State Lib 47-48 Jr libn Cal Dept Pub Health, San Francisco 48-50; Libn Cal Div of Fish & Game, San Francisco 50-51; Med libn VA Hosp, San Francisco 51-64, Chief Libn 64-. 9: MedLA; SLA; No Cal Med Lib Group. 10: Sierra Club. 14: Med ref. 15: VA Hosp Lib, San Francisco Cal.

RYAN, FELICIA MARY. b Peoria Ill 10 D 05. 5: Bradley U 33 AB; UIll 38 BS in LS, ext 49-52 (Educ). 7: Peoria Pub Lib, Peoria Ill; Asst circ dept 26-28, Head adult dept McClure Br 28-37, Libn Lincoln br 38-40, Libn Willcox br 40-46, Head child & yp dept 46-50, Chief tech processes dept 50-54, Libn McClure br 55-62, McClure br coord libn 63-67, Prospect libn & Br coordinator 68-. 9: ALA; IllLA. 10: Beta Phi Mu; Pi Gamma Mu; Nat Fed of Bus & Prof Womens Clubs; Altursa Internat; UIll Lib Sch Alumni Assn. 13: Yes. 14: Tech serv, brs & ext serv, child & yp serv. 15: 915 N Maplewood, Peoria Ill 61606.

RYAN, FREDERICK WILLIAM. b Highland Park Mich 16 Mr 41. 4: Sally Joyce. 5: UCal 9riverside) 59-63 (Russian Lang & Lit) BA; UCLA 63-64 (Slavic Lang); UIll 64-65 9slavic Lang & Lit) MA, 65-68 (LS) MS. 6: Russian, Slavic, Ger, Sp, Fr. 7: Slavic bibliogr (hd Slavic acquis) UIll Lib (Urbana) 65-. 9: Amer Assn for Advancement Slavic Studies (chm Lib Sci Curriculum Com 69); ALA. 14: Slavic studies. 15: 1710 W Union st, Champaign Il 61820.

RYAN, JOHN FRANCIS. b Brooklyn NY 17 F 20. 4: Rita Mary Sammon. 5: Niagara U 46-49 (Hist) BS Columbia U 49-50 (LS) MS. 7: Clerk Aluminum Co of Amer, NY 40-42; US Army Infantryman & Radioman (Pfc), ETO 42-45; Ya libn Brooklyn Pub Lib 50-55, Br libn 5561; 55-61; dir New Rochelle (NY) Pub Lib 61-65; Dir N Bellmore (NY) Pub Lib 65-. 9: ALA; LPRC; (chm Packets Com); NYLA; Westchester LA (treas); NCLA; Nassau Lib Syst (chm Direct Access Com). 10: Brooklyn Pub Lib Staff Assn; Sch Bd & Finance Com, Corpus Christi Chruch, NYC. 14: Ya wk, lib admin. 15: 90 La Salle st, NYC 10027.

RYAN, L(ORETTA) DOLORES. b Cleveland 8 Jl 13. 5: Flora Stone Mather Col West Res 31-35 BS; West Res es 42-43 BS in LS. 6: Fr. 7: State rep Nat Child Labor Com 35-37; Libn asst Cleveland Pub Lib 37-43; Libn: Glenville Sr High Sch 43-46, Cleveland Trade Sch 46-59, Max Hayes Voc High Sch, Cleveland 59-62; Head Ref libn Cleveland State U 62-66; Hd Undergrad Lib & Res Bk Ctr 66-; Visiting lecturer UIll Grad Sch of Lib Sci summer 69. 8: Bd of Educ High Sch Reading List Com 61; Lib consul, Nat Radio Sch 62; Adv Com Cuyahoga Commun Col 65; Staff, Lib/USA, NY Worlds Fair 65; Instr Lib Tech Train, Cuyahoga Commu Col 65. 9: ASIS; ALA (sec Hist Sect, pres 66); -RSD; (Lib Journal List Com); SLA (Adv Com; Cleveland Cha: treas 55-56 &60-61, pres 64-65); Ohio Assn of Col Ref Libns, History Section, ALA, Secy 66 - pres. 10: Citizes League; Alumnae Hist Assn; Theta Phi Omega; AAUW. ; Womens Nat Bk Assn. 12: "Rudiments of Research (65). 13: Yes. 14: Ref, pub serv, tchg. 15: 13910 Larchmere blvd, Cleveland Oh 44120.

RYAN, MARY F. b Boston 3 Je 19. 5: Boston State Col 37-41 (Educ) BS in Educ; Simmons 41-42 (LS) BS; Boston Col 59-64 (Educ) M Ed. 7: Catlgr Boston Col 42-44; Gen asst Boston Pub Lib 44-49; Sch libn City of Boston pub schs 50-. 9: ALA-AASchL;-YSD; MassSchLA; NESchLA. 10: High Sch Womens Club; Simmons Col Grad Alumni Coun; Friends of Old Sturbridge Village; Mass Audubon Soc. 14: Catlg. 15: 26 Brahms st, Roslindale Mass 02131.

RYAN, MARY JANE. b Seattle 5 Ag 14. 5: Col of St Catherine 32-37 (LS) BS; Columbia 38-39 (LS); USoCal 54-(Guidance) MS ED, 55-67 (Ed Psych) PhD; Certif 51; Cal Libnship Credential 55-. 6: Fr, Ger. 7: Co-libn Weyerhauser Co, St Paul 37; Asst chief & act libn Gen Beadle Col 43-44; Libn US Naval Base, Lido Beach LI NY 44-46; Chief Libn VA Hosps: Ft Meade 46-47, St Cloud 47-54, Sepulveda 55; Asst Prof Lib Sci Immaculate Heart Col 59-67; Chm dept lib sci Wis State U 67-68; Liaison libn Northlands Reg Med Program, St Paul 68-. 8: Guest lecturer Lib Schs: UMinn 49-5, USoCal 53-58; Asst Dean & Act Dean, Sch of Lib Sci, Immaculate Heart Col, 60-65. 9: ALA; -AHIL (v-pres 52); SLA; Minn Assn Hosp & Med Libns (pres 53). 10: Commonweal. 12: "Librarians Perceptions of Libnship, USoCal dirs (67). 13: Yes. 14: Lib educ, hosp & med libs. 15: 23 Inner dr, St Paul Mn 55116.

RYAN, MYRNA (TRAPPEY). b New Iberia La 1 O 29. 4: William J Ryan. 5: LSU 47-50 9educ) BS; US West La 64-65 BLS. 7: Tchr, Baton Rouge La 50; Tchr, New Iberia La 65; Libn Loreauville Elem l High Sch, Loreauville La 66-. 9: ALA; NEA; LaEA; La Clr Libns Assn; IberiaTA. 10: Iberia Commun Concert Assn. 14: Sch libs. 15: PO Box 367, loreauville La 70552.

RYAN, NOEL. b Saint John NB Can 27 My 25. 4: Doreen. 5: Sir George Williams 60-64 (Psych) BA; McGill 65-67 MLS. 6: Fr. 7: V-pres Temco Electric Mfg Co, Montreal 47-57; Mgr (East) Cradle Pictures Ltd, Montreal 57-67; Chief libn Doruval Lib, Dorval 67-. 13: Yes. 14: Lib planning & bldg. 15: 11 Winchester ave, Westmont 215 PQ Can.

RYAN, RICHARD W(RIGHT). b Columbus Ohio 28 N 30. 4: Barbara M (Campbell). 5: Ohio State U 52-56 (Hist) BA, 57 (Hist); West Res 58-60 MSLS; NY State Certif 65. 7: Bkkeeper Newark Trust Co, Newark Ohio 48-50; Recruit US Navy 50; Teller Newark Trust Co, Newark Ohio 51-52; Manager merchants coun Newark C of C, Ohio 56-57; Lib asst Ohio State U Libs 57-59; LC: Spec recruit 60-61; Mss catlgr Descr CATLG Div 61, Catlg ed Ms Div 62-63, Admin asst Processing Det 63; Ser libn Denison U Lib 64-65, Acquis libn 65-66, Hd libn 66-. 9: ALA; OhioLA (Chm Col & Univ RT 69). 10: AHA; Ohio Hist Assn; Amer Assn State & Loc Hist. 13: Yes. 14: Tech proc, col & res libs, ref. 15: 954-4 Grafton rd, Newark Oh 43055.

RYAN, SHARON KAY. b Grinnell Iowa 21 Jl 38. 5: Iowa State Tchrs Col 56-59 (LS); West State Col of Colo 59-60 (Ed, sych) BA; UAriz ext 60-63; UWash 61-64 (LS) MS. 6: Sp. 7: Libn San Manuel High Sch, San Manuel Ariz 60-63; Libn San DIEGO Pub Lib 63-64; Bkmob libn 4-Co Lib System, Binghamton NY 65-66; Libn Circleville City Schs, Circleville Ohio 66-. 9: ALA; NEA; OhioEA; OhioASchL; CirclevilleTA (sec 67-68). 14: Serv to child & ya. 15: 214 1/2 E Main st, Circleville Oh 43113.

RYAN, SUSAN (MURTHA). b Columbus Ohio 22 Ja 38. 4: Owen J Ryan. 5: Ohio StateU 56-59 (Eng) BSEd; Case West ResU 61-62 MSLS; EmoryU 66 (Med Libnship) Certif. 6: Sp. 7: Libn Cleveland Pub Schs, Cleveland Ohio 62-65; Libn Natl Med A-V Ctr, Atlanta 65-67, Ref libn 68-; Ref libn EmoryU Sch Med, Atlanta 67; Coord Grad Program in Biomed Communication, New Orleans 67-68. 9: ALA; MedLA. 10: Beta Phi Mu. 13: Yes. 14: Ref. 15: 501 Montgomery Ferry rd NE, Atlanta Ga 30324.

RYAN, WILLIAM VINCENT. b Cleveland Ohio 27 Ap 25. 5: John CarrollU 46-50 (Eng Lit) AB; Case West Res 51-53 (Eng Lit) MA, 53-55 MSLS; UNotre Dame 63-68 (European Hist) MA. 6: Fr, Ital, Ger. 7: Ref circ libn Cleveland StateU 55-58; Ref libn Canisius Col 58-61; Fine arts libn OhioU 61-63; Head humanities dept Memorial Lib UNotre Dame 63-66; Head ref serv Memorial Lib MarquetteU 66-68; Dir libs Atchison Col 68-. 8: Program chm Midwest Acad Libs Conf 63; Consul "Choice" 65-; Chm Col & Unit RT IndLA 66. 9: ALA; CathLA; KanLA. 10: Atchison Art Assn. 14: Tech serv, ref, admin. 15: 503 Parallel st, Atchison Ks 66002.

RYBERG, H(ERMAN) THEODORE. b Warren Penn 13 Ja 27. 5: Gettysburg Col 48-50, 53-55 (Philos) AB; West Res 56-57 (LS) MS. 7: Radio off US Maritime Serv 44-47; US Navy 51-52; Radio off US Maritime Serv 52-53; Head catlgr Rochester Inst of Tech 57-59; Asst dir of libs UBuffalo 59-60; Asst dir of libs Syracuse U 60-63; Dir of Libs UAlaska 63-68; Dean instr serv USoFla 68-. 8: Lib 21, Seattle Worlds FAIR,

62; Tchr, lib sci, Syracuse U, 61-63, USoFla 69. 9: ALA (Coun 65-); SAA; NEA-DAVI; SELA; FlaLA; Fla A-v Inst. 10: AAUP; Forest Hist Soc; Amer-Scand Found; Assn US Army. 13: Yes. 14: Admin, catlg. 15: P O Box 16206, Temple Ter Fl 33617.

RYBIANSK, ALBERT V. b Prievidza Slovakia CSSR 15 S 16. 4: Auguste Wesner. 5: USlovakia(Commenius) (Bratislava) 34-39 (Law, Pol Sci) JD; UChicago 51-52 (LS); Rosary Col 53-54 MALS. 6: Slovak, Czech, Ger, Fr, Russian. 7: U asst USlovakia Commenius) (Bratislava) 39-42; Staff Ministry of Economy, Bratislava 42-45; Papal Mission for Refugees & UN Internat Internat Refugee Org, Austria 47-49; Asst libn UIll (Chicago) 52-54;Libn Lewis Col 54-. 9: ALA; SLA; CathLA; IllLA; Ill CathLA. 10: Fellow of Alexander Von Humboldt Found. 13: Yes. 14: Admin. 15: Lewis Col Lib Rte 53, Lockport Il 60441.

RYBICKI, STEVE A. b Detroit Mich 23 Je 41. 4: Clarice Larkins. 5: UDetroit 60-64 (Eng) AB; UMich 67-68 AMLS. 6: Fr, Lat. 7: Sales Central Steel & Wire Co, Detroit 65-66; Purchasing GM Detroit Diesel Div, Detroit 66-67; Libn Detroit Pub Lib 67-69; Hd libn UDetroit High Sch 69-. 8: Ed Detroit Pub Lib's "Staff News Bulletin", 1968-1969. 10: Detroit Pub Lib Prof Org Libns. 11: Winner Miles Poetry Contest Wayne StateU 69. 12: Comp "Abbreviations Handbook" (69). 13: Yes. 14: Ref wk with interest in mod poetry. 15: 17175 Littlefield, Detroit Mi 48235.

RYBKA, SUSAN MARIE. b Ypsilanti Mich 4 Mr 48. 5: UMich 65-68 (Hist) AB, 68-69 AMLS. 6: Fr, Polish, Russian. 7: Hd libn Markley Hall UMich (Ann Arbor) 68-69; Hd bibliog sect acquis dept Kresge Lib OaklandU (Rochester Mich) 69-. 9: ALA. 10: UMich Lib Sci Alumni Assn. 14: Acquis, ref, catlg, clsf. 15: 42106 Ford rd, Plymouth Mi 48170.

RYD, BEVERLY JEAN. b Boston 3 Ag 35. 5: Simmons Col 53-57 (LS) BS; Columbia 58-59 (LS) MS. 6: Fr, Ger. 7: Searcher, lib asst acquis dept Lib Harvard Law Sch 56-57; Law Libn Conn Gen Life Insurance Co, Hartford Conn 57-58; Ref libn Grad Sch of Bus & Pub Admin Cornell U 59-64; Asst catlgr Fed Res Bank of NY, NYC 64-65; Libn First Boston Corp, NYC 65-. 9: SLA; NY Lib Club. 10: Amer-Scand Found; Metro Mus Art. 14: Ref, admin. 15: 345 E 52nd st, New Yorm NY 10022.

RYLAARSDAM, HARRIET (WORCESTER). b Norwich Conn 20 My 16. 4: J Coert Rylaarsdam. 5: Smith 32-36 (Religion, Bib Lit) BA; Columbia 36-37 BLS. 6: Fr, Ger. 7: Catlgr & gen asst Princeton Theol Sem Lib 37-45; Libn Hyde Park Study Center, Chicago 62-. 9: ALA. 10: Nat Fed of Settlements & Neighborhood Centers; LWV; Metro Housing & Planning Coun; Citizens Schs Com; PTA; Hyde park-Kenwood Commun Conf. 14: Materials for the disadvantaged. 15: 5544 Kenwood ave, Chicago 60637.

RYS, JOHN LAWRENCE. b Minneapolis Minn 23 Ap 37. 4: Judith Erickson. 5: UMinn 55-59 (Chem) BA, 59-62 (LS) MA. 7: Pharmacy libn UMinn 59-63; Ref libn Whirlpool Corp, St Joseph Mich 63-66; Supv tech communications ctr 3M Co, St Paul 66-. 9: ASIS; ACS. 14: Indexing techniques, chem registry systems. 15: 2153 Powers ave, St Paul Mn 55119.

RYUS, JOSEPH E(MMETT, II). b Ketchikan Alaska 11 N 24. 4: Phyllis Katherine Kefalas. 5: UCal(Berkeley) 42-46 (Physics) BA, 46 (Physics), 47-49 BLS, 49- (Linguistics). 7: Page San Diego Pub Lib 41-42; Page Oakland Pub Lib 42-43, Clerical asst 43-49, Jr libn 49; UCal(Berkeley) Libn I catlgr 49-52, Libn II Head physics & chem libs 52-53, Libn II Head physical sci libs 53-55, Libn II catlgr sci & indic 55-64, Libn III admin asst catlgr sci & indic 64-67, Libn IV asst hd (act hd) 67-. 9: ALA-RTSD (Descr Catlg Com 61-65); NoCal Tech Proc Group (chm 57-8). 10: Ling Soc Amer; Math Assn of Amer; Aircraft Owners & Pilots Assn. 13: Yes. 14: Catlg, child lit, computers, wk simplification. 15: 2858 Oxford ave, Richmond Cal 94806.

RZEPECKI, ARNOLD MICHAEL. b Detroit 2 Jl 32. 4: Eleanor Chlebawski. 5: Wayne State U 49-53 (Eng) BA; UMich 53-54 AMLS; Wayne State U 57-59 (Eng) MA, 60-63 (Eng). 6: Fr, Ger, Polish. 7: Asst libn Sacred Heart Sem (Detroit) 54-63, Act libn 64-67, Libn 67-. 8: Asst Prof of Eng & Chm of Dept, Sacred Heart Sem (Detroit). 9: CathLA (chm Mich Unit 68-70); ALA; Mod Lang Assn; Nat Conf Cath Art Edurs; MichLA; Mich Col Eng Assn. 10: N Rosedale Park Civic Assn. 12: Assoc ed "Cardinal Money Lecture Series. 14: Bk sel, admin. 14: Bk sel, admin. 15: 16500 Sunderland, Detroit Mi 48219.

S

SAAL, JUNE ELAINE. b Englewood NJ 4 Je 24. 5: Col of Mt St Vincent 42-46 (Ger) BS; Pratt Inst 50-51 MLS; UMiami summer 59. 7: Child libn NYC Pub Lib 46-58; Sch libn Dade Co Sch Syst, Miami Fla 59; YA libn Hempstead Pub Lib, Hempstead NY 60-. 9: ALA; NassauCoLA. 10: LWV. 14: Ya serv. 15: 599 Front st, Hempstead Long Island NY 11550.

SAARI, MINA (EMERETT JAMES). b Seattle 19 Jl 07. 5: West Wash State Col 25-27 Tchrs elem diploma, summers 29 & 30 Tchrs life diploma. 7: Tchr Sch Dist #21, Port Angeles Wash 27-30; Child libn city lib, Port Angeles Wash 30-33, 58-. 9: ALA; PNLA; WashLA; WashStateASchL. 10: Soroptimist Club. 14: Ref, child lib. 15: 119 E Second st, Port Angeles 98362.

SAASTAMOINEN, HENRY D. b Hibbing Minn 24 Mr 21. 4: Clara Farwell. 5: No Mich U 49-54 (Chem) BA, Tchg Certif; UMex 55 (Span); UMiami(Fla) 56-57 (Chem); Fla State U 64-65 (LS) MA. 6: Sp, Fr, Finnish. 7: (S/SGT) US Army 42-45; Tchr Manistique Pub Schs, Manistique Mich 55-56; Tchr Oxford Schs, Miami Beach Fla 58-59; Tchr Brevard Co Schs, Rockledge Fla 59-63; Libn Brevard Co Schs, Rockledge Fla 63-64; Sci div libn NM State U 65-. 9: ALA; NMLA. 10: Kappa Delta Pi. 14: Ref. 15: 2110 S Solano, Las Cruces NM 88001.

SABATINI, JOSEPH DAVID. b Bronx NY 25 O 42. 5: UCLA 60-64 (Pol Sci) AB, 64-65 MLS. 7: On assignment with VISTA, doing lib & related wk for the Ala-Coushatta Indian Reservation, Livingston Tex 65-66; Volunteer, Sandoval Co Econ Opportunity Co, Bernalillo NM 66-67; US Army Res 67; Asst libn UNM Law Sch Lib 68-. 8: Ed Amer Indian Law Newsletter UNM Law Sch 68-. 9: CalLA; ALA; AALL; NMLA; Greater AlbuquerqueLA. 10: Pi Sigma Alpha. 14: Catlg, child wk. 15: 52 1/2 Garden Park cir NW, Albuquerque NM 87107.

SABIA, JAMES ANTHONY. b Stamford Conn 31 My 25. 4: Louise Gatti. 5: LIU 46-50 (Eng) BA; Tchrs Col Columbia U 50 (Eng); UConn 54; So Conn State Col 60-64 (LS) MS; UBridgeport 68 (Admin & Supv) 6th yr Diploma. 6: Fr. 7: Radioman US Navy 43-46; Sub tchr Stamford (Conn) Bd of Educ 51-54; Eng tchr J M Wright Tech Sch, Stamford Conn 55-57; Sales rep "Look Magazine 57-58; Parts lister Reflecton Inc, Stamford Conn 58-60; Sch libn Stamford (Conn) Bd of Educ 61-. 9: ALA-AASchL; StanfordEA; ConnSchLA. 10: Conn Interschol Coaches Assn; Amer Babe Ruth League Assn. 14: Ref. 15: 43 Pellom pl, Stamford Conn 06905.

SABINE, JULIA (ELIZABETH). b Chicago 4 F 05. 5: Cornell U 23-27 (Classics) AB; Inst dArt et dArch 32-34 (Ancient & Mediaeval Art) Brevet; Yale 38-39 (Hist, Art) MA equiv; Chicago 44-46 (LS) PhD. 6: Fr, Lat. 7: Lib asst Newark Pub Lib, Newark NJ 27-33, Head of NJ div 3344; Research assoc UChicago 44-46; Prin art libn Newark Pub Lib, Newark NJ 46-57, Supv art & music libn 57-. 8: Art Index Com, H W Wilson Co; Governors Commsn to Study the Arts in NJ; Visiting Instr UKy Lib Sch, summer 63; Instr, Rutgers Lib Sch 68-69. 9: ALA (chm Reading for an Age of Change Com 61-62; sec-chm Art Ref Round Table 53-54; Amer Assn of Museums; Soc of Arch Histns; Amer Assn of Arch Bibliogrs; Mediaeval Acad. 10: Sorotimist; NJ Hist Soc. 13: Yes. 14: Art ref, fine printing, lib educ. 15: Box 630, Newark NJ 07101.

SABLE, ARNOLD PAUL. b Winthrop Mass 5 D 30. 4: Aura Finkelstein. 5: Brandeis 48-52 9fr) BA Sorbonne 52 Certificat d'assiduite; Simmons 54-56 MLS. 6: Fr. 7: Ref asst Hartford Pub Lib, Hartford Conn 56-58; Asst dir Jervis Lib, Rome NY 58-59; Dir Kingston City Lib, Kingston NY 59-62; Dir Adrianie Mem Lib, Poughkeepsie NY 62-. 8: V-chm NY State Profess Libns Certification Exam Com; Trustee SEast (NY) Lib Resources Coun. 9: ALA; NYLA; DutchessCoLA. 10: Dutchess Co Hist Soc; Nat Trust Hist Preserv. 13: Yes. 14: Admin, ref, child wk. 15: 179 S Cherry st, Poughkeepsie NY 12601.

SABSAY, DAVID. b Waltham Mass 12 S 31. 4: Helen G Tolliver. 5: Harvard 49-53 (Eng lit) AB; UCal (Berkeley) 54-55 BLS, 55-56. 6: Fr. 7: Supv circ dept Richmond (Cal) Pub Lib 55-56; City libn, Santa Rosa Cal 56-65; Dir Santa Rosa-Sonoma Co Pub Lib, santa Rosa Cal 65-. 9: ALA; CalLA (chm Lib Devel & Standards Com 60, 61; chm Legisl Com 63, 64; treas 68, 69); Pub Lib Execs of central Cal (pres

65-66). 10: Beta Phi Mu; Kiwanis Internat; Harvard Club of San Francisco. 12: "Statistical Study of Public Library Systems, 1963-1968" (69). 13: Yes. 14: Admin, bldg design, reg & state lib devel. 15: 667 Montgomery rd, Sebastopol Ca 95472.

SACCONAGHI, CHARLES DAVID. b Santa Barbara Cal 14 Mr 30. 5: USanta Clara 48-52 (Pol Sci) BA; Georgetown U Lib 55-64; (Intl Law) BSFS; Catholic U 60-63 MSLS. 7: (Sgt) US Army 53-55; Georgetown U Lib 55-64; UAriz Lib 64-. 68; USoCal Lib 68-. 9: CalLA; Ariz State LA. 10: Bk Club of Cal; Cal Hist Soc. 14: West Americana, Californiana, West Outlaws. 15: 3789 Menlo ave apt 411, Los Angeles Ca 90007.

SACHASCHIK, STEVE. b Edmonton Alta Can 26 Ap 39. 5: UALTA 57-60 (Hist) BA; Toronto 61-62 BLS. 6: Russian. 7: Catlgr Edmonton Pub Lib, Edmonton Alta Can 62-. 9: CanLA; AltaLA. 14: Catlg. 15: 9519 - 107 ave, Edmonton 17 Alta Can.

SACHDEVA, DEWAN CHAND. b Fazilka India 20 Ap 39. 4: Krishna. 5: M R Col (PanjabU, India) 55-59 (Arts) BA; M S Univ (Baroda India) 61-62 (LS) Diploma; C W Post Col 68-69 (LS) MS. 6: Hindi, Urdu, Panjahi. 7: Libn, India: Govt Col of Com Patiala 60-61, Delhi Pub Lib 62-64, FAO/UN, Delhi 64-68; Grad asst C W Post Col 68-. 9: IndianLA (Pub Rel Off). 13: Yes. 14: Catlg, ref, admin. 15: Box 605 C W Post College, Greenvale NY 11548.

SACHSE, ELMA MAE. b Moscow Penn 29 D 30. 4: Arnold R Anderson. 5: Kutztown State Col 49-53 (LS, Eng) BS Ed; Syracuse summer 54-56, & 57 MS LS. 7: Sub libn Marple Newtown High Sch, Newton Square Penn 53; Libn Central Sch Dist 2, Washingtonville NY 53-58; Child libn, Head of Dept Wilmington Inst Free Lib, Wilmington Del 58; Sub libn MAIN & South Bay Schs, W Babylon NY 59; Ser libn Marywood Col Lib 59-. 9: ALA; PennLA; NYLA. 14: Child & yp, ser. 15: Marywood Col Lib, Scranton Penn.

SACHSE, GLADYS MARGETTA. b Shawnee Okla 21 Jl 18. 5: Okla Baptist U 35-36; Ark Polytech Col 36-37; Ark State Tchrs Col 37-39 (Hist) BSE; LSU summers 43-46 BS in LS; UArk summers 52-55 (Educ Admin) M Ed; UOkla summer 68. 7: Tchr High Sch, Dardnelle Ark 39-40; Tchr High Sch, Belleville Ark 40-43; Co Libn Yell Co Lib, Danville Ark 43-47; Act asst libn Ark Lib Commsn, Little Rock Ark 47-48; Asst libn & Assoc Prof of Lib Sci State Col of Ark 48-. 8: Tchr UOkla Lib Sch, summer 61. 9: ALA,-LED (Reg rep for SW); NEA; ArkLA (pres 51-52, chm Educ Com 56-57, 65-68); SWLA (Program Com 1958 Conv, Constit Com 61-62); Ark Coun on Lib Ed (chm 67-69). 10: Phi Alpha Theta; Phi Kappa Phi; Beta Phi Mu; Kappa Kappa Iota. 12: "Manual for the Elementary School Library in Arkansas with F Schader (54). 13: Yes. 14: Tchg lib sci. 15: 240 Donaghey, Conway Ark 72032.

SACHTLEBEN, CARL HENRY. b 24 Je 19. 4: Helen Rowoldt. 5: Valparaiso 3741 (Bus Admin, Geog) AB; West Res 47 BS in LS; UChicago 4850 (LS); WashU (St Louis) 53 (Educ) MA. 6: Ger. 7: US Army Transportation Corps (Maj) 41-46; Asst libn ValparaisoU 47-50, Dir libs 64-; Libn St Louis Lutheran High Sch, St Louis Mo 50-57; Asst to dir of lib St LouisU 58-64. 9: ALA-ACRL (AAC-ACRL Com on Lib Problems 66-, chm 66, v-chm Col Libs Sect 69-70); Midwest Acad Libns Conf (chm 65-67). 10: Rotary Club; Lutheran Acad for Scholarship. 12: Ed "Missouri Library Association Quarterly" (60-64). 13: Yes. 14: Admin. 15: 3501 N Campbell, Valparaiso In 46383.

SADDLER, VIRGINIA B(ERG). b Gary Ind 5 Ap 24. 4: Charles Clark Saddler Jr. 5: Cornell Col 43-45 (Eng, Philos) BA; UIll 45-46 BS in LS, 46-48 MLS S. 6: Fr. 7: UIll; Asst Union Browsing Room 45-47, Asst Journalism libn 47-51, Head journalism libn 51-53, Tchr Newspaper Ref Methods 51-53; Ser libn Hardin Simmons U 53-55; Asst libn McMurry Col 55-56; Libn Oakland City Col 57-62; Asst libn & asst prof lib sci Union Col (Barbourville Ky) 62-. 8: Publns adv, Union Col 62-, Tchg, Lib Sci 66-. 9: KyLA. 10: AAUW. 12: Pamphlet Bibliography Series in "Journalism Quarterly (51-53); "Journalism Library Handbook (53). 13: Yes. 14: Catlg, documents, tchg lib sci. 15: 122 College Park dr, Barbourville Ky 40906.

SADLER, GRAHAM HYDRICK. b Sikeston Mo 17 Ag 31. 4: Betty A Grugett. 5: Southeast Mo State Col 49-52 (Bus Admin) BS; Emory summer 55-58 (LS); So Ill U 57 (Guidance); Ind U summer 61 (Educ). 7: Mgt trainee J C Penney Co, Cape Girardeau Mo 52-54; Asst libn Inst of Lib Sci Southeast Mo State Col 54-60; Visiting Instr Ind U 60; Admin libn Kinderhook Reg Lib, Lebanon Mo 61-66; Dir Ft Lewis Col Lib 66-67; Assoc Prof Dept of Libnship Kan State Tchrs Col 67-. 8: Lib Inst Instr, UMo 64; Ref libn, Lib/USA NY Worlds Fair 65; Exec dir Nat Lib Week, Mo 64; Visiting fac IndU summer 61; Wkshop fac UMo 59. 9: ALA; MoLA (treas 65-66); Mo Assn Col & Res Libs (sec 55, chm 57); KanLA; AALS. 11: Kindrhook Reg Lib won Dorothy Canfield Fisher Award, 65. 13: Yes. 14: Admin, lib educ. 15: 1318 Rural, Emporia Ks 66801.

SADLER, HELEN (HANCOCK). b Trenton Ky 16 Ja 11. 4: John Dunn Sadler. 5: Tenn Col 29-33 (Eng Romance Langs) BA; Peabody 40-42 BS in LS. 6: Fr, Sp, Lat. 7: Tchr High Sch, Celina Tenn 35; Tchr High Sch, Montgomery Co Tenn 38-40; Libn-tchr Montogomery Central, Mongomery Co Tenn 40-43; Lib Clarksville High Sch, Clarksville Tenn 43-68; Hd libn New Clarksville High Sch, Clarksville Tenn 68-69. 8: Eval Com, So Assn of Schs & Col, 51-52. 9: ALA; NEA; TennEA (v-pres Lib Sect); TennLA; Clarksville Area LA. 10: PTA; AAUW; Monday Evening Music Club; Bus & Prof Womens Club; Commun Concert Assn. 13: Yes. 14: Ref. catlg, bk sel. 15: 174 E Glenwood, Clarksville Tenn 37040.

SADLER, KATHRYN WAGNER. b Sandusky Ohio 9 Jl 11. 4: Albert Sadler. 5: West Res 33 (Lit) AB, 34 BS in LS. 7: Lib asst Detroit Pub Lib 34-36; Br libn Wayne C Lib, Detroit 36-38, Head bk sel & order 38-49; Libn San Diego Pub Lib 62-64, Supv hist & world affairs sect 64-. 9: CalLA. 14: Hist, current affairs. 15: San Diego Pub Lib, 820 E st, San Diego Ca 92101.

SADOSKI, MICHAEL J(OHN). b Los Aneles 13 Je 27. 4: Doris Stone. 5: Long Beach City Col 47-49 (Physics) AA; Pomona Col 49-51 (Chem) BA; Claremont Grad Sch 51-52 (Chem); UCal(Berkeley) 57-58 MLS; USoCal 67-. 7: Riveter-assembler Douglas AIRCRAFT, Long Beach Cal 43; Shipfitters helper US Naval Drydocks, Long Beach Cal 44; (Pfc(US Army Signal Corps Mil Police, FT Monmouth NJ 45-47; Chief spectrographer Pacific Spectrochemical Lab, Los Angeles 52-57; Engnr libn Stanford U Libs 58-60; Ref libn Gen Dynamics/CONVAIR, San Diego 61-62; Ref libn US Navy Electronics Lab, San Diego 62-67. 9: ACM; ACS; ASIS; SLA (San Diego Chap; pres, past treas, bulletin ed); CalLA. 10: Boy Scouts; Beta Phi Mu. 11: Edna Mae Haskell Lib Prize, Pomona Col, 51. 13: Yes. 14: Ref, maps. 15: 1314 Puterbaugh st, San Diego 92103.

SADOW, ARNOLD. b Boston 12 F 18. 5: Harvard 35-39 (Biochem) AB; Chicago Inst of Design 45-47 (Photog) Certif; Pratt 53-55 MLS. 6: Fr, Ger, Lat. 7: (S/Sgt) USAF 40-45; Phtogrammetric tech USDA, Wash DC 47-49; Med photographic tech Gen Hosp, Rochester NY 49-50; Free lance photographer, NYC 50-53; Libn Queens boro Pub Lib, Jamaica NY 53-58; Tech libn Westrex Communications, Div Litton Systs, New Rochelle NY 58-66; Libn III Res lib NY Pub Lib 66-. 9: SLA; ALA; NY Lib Club; NMA. 10: Amer Soc of Photogrammetry; NY Camera Club. 11: Photographs in Museum of Modern Art Collections. 12: Ed "New Technical Books, NY Pub Lib (67-). 13: Yes. 14: Ref, patents, docs, photocopying. 15: 81-06 - 34th ave, Jackson Heights NY 11372.

SADOW, CAROLYN (LAUBHEIME). 5: Hunter Col 30-34 (Fr, Eng) BA; Columbia 63-64 (LS) MS. 6: Fr. 7: Advertising copy writer & fashion coordinator, dept stores & Advertising agencies; Libn ref info NY Pub Lib 64-. 9: SLA. 15: 140 W 57th st, NYC 10019.

SADOWSKI, FRANK E(RIC) JR. b Salisbury Md 25 S 40. 4: Alice Reade. 5: Penn State U 58-63 (Sci) BS; Rutgers 63-66 MLS. 7: Lib trainee Morristown Lib, Morristown NJ 63-65; Asst catlg libn Penn State U Libs (Univ Park) 66-67, Asst reclsf libn 67-69, Asst microform catlg libn 67-68, Sr ser catlg libn 69-. 9: ALA; -ACRL; -RTSD. 10: Beta Phi Mu; Soc Preserv and Encour of Barber Shop Quartet Singing in Amer; Antique Automo Club Amer. 14: Catlg. 15: 209 Willow ave, State College Pa 16801.

SAFFORD, HILDRED. b Highland Plantation Me 3 O 11. 5: Simmons 33-37 (LS) BS. 7: Act libn Derry Pub Lib, Derry NH 38-39; Libn Scottsville Pub Lib, Scottsville NY 41-43; Asst libn Malheur Co Lib, Ontario Ore 44-47; Libn Woodsfield Pub Lib, Woodsfield Ohio 47-51; Libn Putnam Co Dist Lib, Ottawa Ohio 51-56; Adult bkmob libn lucas Co Lib, Maummee Ohio 56-58; Libn Putnam Co Dist Lib, Ottawa Ohio 58-. 9: ALA; OhioLA. 10: Bus & Profess Women's Club; Centennial Club. 14: Hd libn of small libs. 15: Putnam Co Dist Lib, Ottawa Oh 45875.

SAGAR, VAS VIDYA. b Guntar AP India 9 S 37. 4: Mary Bharatalakshmi. 5: AndhraU (India) 52-57 (Eng) BA, 55-59

(Eng) BA (Honors), 59-60 (Eng) MA; West MichU 67-68 MSL. 6: Eng, Telugu, Hindi. 7: Lectr in Eng PR Govt Col, Kakinada India 59-67; Ref libn Kalamazoo Valley Commun Col 68-. 10: Beta Phi Mu. 14: Ref serv & media. 15: 1713 Meadow view, Kalamazoo Mi 49001.

SAGE, MARILYN JOYCE (COREY). b Detroit 31 Jl 32. 4: Richard M Sage. 5: Wayne State U 50-61 (Educ) BS in Ed; UMich 62-64 MALS. 6: Fr, Ger, Lat. 7: Preprof Detroit Pub Lib 63-64, Libn I 64-65; Br libn Warren Pub Lib, Warren Mich 65-. 9: ALA; MichLA. 10: Pi Lambda Theta. 14: Ref, child serv. 15: 32310 Coventry place, Warren Mi 48093.

SAGER, DONALD J. b Milwaukee 3 Mr 38. 4: Irene Lynn Sleeth. 5: UWis(Milwaukee) 58-63 (Eng) BS; UWIS (Madison) 63-64 MSLS; Kent State summer 67. 6: Ger. 7: Train & personnel Sgt US Army 84th Infantry Div, Milwaukee 55-56; Lab Tech Research & Dev Lab Cutler-Hammer Corp, Milwaukee 56-58; Sr documentalist A C Spark Plug Electronics Div Gen Motors, Milwaukee 58-63; Research asst UWis Lib Sch (Madison) 63-64; Dir Kingston City Lib, Kingston NY 64-66; Libn Elyria Pub Lib, Elyria Ohio 66-. 8: Bldg consul; Defiance (Ohio) Pub Lib 68, Montpelier (Ohio) Pub Lib 68. 9: ALA; OhioLA (chm A-V Serv RT 68-69; chm Staff Devel Com 67-68; v-chm Legisl Com 68-69; chm Reg Ref Wkshop Com 67); LorainCoLA (chm 67; chm Lib Careers Proj Steering Com). 10: Sigma Tau Delta; Beta Phi Mu; Pi Delta Epsilon; Lorain Co Arts Coun; Kent State U Dept of Lib Sci Adv Coun; Kiwanis; Red Cross Youth Serv. 12: "Reference, A Programmed Instruction, Ohio Lib Found (68); Ed "Cheshire Literary (63-64). 13: Yes. 14: Admin, pub rel, a-v serv. 15: 283 Washington ave apt 311C, Elyria Oh 44035.

SAGRIS, HARRY S. 4: Mary Bouzianis Sagris. 5: UNH 55-59 (Hist Educ) BA; Salem State 63-66 ME; Simmons 68-70 MLS. 6: Gr, Sp. 7: Sgt USA, Trieste 49-52; Self employed Merchandising, Portsmouth NH 52-54; Admin field, Me, Mass 60-62; Ipswich Pub Schs, Ipswich Mass: Secondary sch tchr 63-66, Sch asst libn 66, Asst libn 66-67, Libn 67-. 9: ALA; NEA; MassLA; MerrimackValleyLA; NELA. 10: Mens Club of Ipswich. 14: Adult serv, ref, libnship. 15: 13 Congress st, Ipswich Ma 01938.

SAHLI, MARILYN SUE. b Beaver Falls Penn 25 S 27. 5: Geneva Col 45-46; Denison 46-49 (Eng) AB; Columbia 49-50 (Eng); West Res 51-52 MSLS. 6: Fr, Ger. 7: Cleveland Pub Lib, Ohio: Lib aide 50-52, Ref asst gen ref dept 52-54, Ref asst hist dept 54-56, Asst hd hist dept 56-66; Cleveland State U, Ohio: Hd soc sci div 67-68, Asst dir libs for collection development 69-. 9: ALA; -ACRL; -RSD (sec Hist Sect 65-67); SLA; OhioLA (sec Ref Serv RT 68-). 10: Women's Nat Bk Assn; Great Lakes Hist Soc; Delta Omicron. 14: Bk sel, ref, admin. 15: 2580 N Moreland blvd, Shaker Hts oh 44120.

SAHLING, MARGARET (ELIZABETH). b Coshocton Ohio 28 O 05. 5: Ohio Wesleyan U 27 (Eng Lit) AB; UWis 31 Diploma. 7: Lib asst Coshocton Pub Lib, Coshocton Ohio 27-30, Libn 30-. 9: ALA; OhioLA. 10: AAUW; Bus & Prof Womens Club; New Century Club. 14: Local hist, ref, co ext. 15: 1030 E Main st, Coshocton Ohio 43812.

SAINT-HILAIRE, MARIE-THERESE. b Montreal Can 6 D 19. 5: Marie-Anne Col 54-57 (Retorique; UMontreal 57-60 (Philos, Sci) BA; UOTTAWA 61-62 BLS. 6: Fr. 7: Libn Mun Lib, Montreal 52-. 9: Association Canadienne des Bibliothecaires de Langue Francaise (v-pres Pub Lib Sect); CanLA; QueLA (sec Pub Lib Com 62-63). 14: Ref, catlg. 15: 1027 Valiquette st, Verdun 204 P Que Can.

SAINT-PIERRE JEANNE-M(ARGUERITE). b Ottawa Can 28 N 18. 5: UMontreal 36-37 Diploma in Journalism, 37-38 Diploma in Fr Lit, 41 Diploma in Lib Sci; McGill (Eng Lit). 6: Fr, Eng. 7: Libn La Bibliotheque des Enfants, Montreal 37-46 & in chg 41-46; In chg child serv Bibliotheque de la Ville de Montreal, Montreal City Lib 46-. 8: Tchr at the Univ of Montreal Lib Sch during 10 yrs (Child & Sch Libs & Child Lit); Org of Fr Publicity for "Young Canadas Bk Week 49-63, CanLA. 9: CanLA (pres French Publicity Com during Jt Conf of ALA & CanLA 60; past pres French Bk Medal Award); QueLA (past French sec; pres Child Set 60). 10: Tennis Club. 13: Yes. 14: Child libs. 15: MontrealCity Lib, 1210 E Sherbrooke st, Montreal Can.

SAIT, CHARLOTTE (SAPADIN). b NYC 25 Ag 19. 4: Edward Sait. 5: Russell Sage 49-58 (Psych); Indiana U Ext 59-60; Butler 60-62 (Psych); George Washington 66-68 (Psych). 7: Mgr file dept & lib Empire State Chamber of Com, Albany NY 54-56; Legal sec Edw M Segal Esq, Albany NY 56-58; Docs libn Adj Gen's Bd USA, Ft Benj Harrison Ind 58-63; Asst libn USA Combat Developments Command Ft McClellan Ala 63; Libn US Women's Army Corps Sch & Ctr, Ft McClellan Ala 63-65; Asst libn Naval Supply Syst Command, Wash DC 65-69; Hd libn Naval Facilities Engring Command, Wash DC 69-. 9: SLA; DCLA. 11: Awards for Sustained Superior Performance. 14: Ref, catlg, admin. 15: 3917 Rickover rd, Silver Spring Md 20902.

SAITO, SHIRO. b Pahala Hawaii 11 Mr 28. 4: Elsie Arakaki. 5: UHawaii 47-51 (Educ) B Ed, 51-52 5th yr Tchg Diploma; UMinn 55-56 (LS) MA. 7: Troop info & educ US ARMY 52-54; Tchr-libn Olaa Sch, Olaa Hawaii 54-55; Adult libn Minneapolis Pub Lib 56-58; Asst ref libn UHawaii Lib 58-66; Act hd & hd soc sci br 66-; Lecturer Grad Sch Lib Studies 68-. 8: Coord & instr, Fulbright Lib Res Course, UHawaii 65-66. 9: ALA; HawaiiLA (treas Legis Com). 10: Assn for Asian Studies; Beta Phi Mu. 11: Fulbright Research Grant, Philippines 67-68. 12: Comp "Pacific Island Bibliography," with F Cammack (62); Principal comp "Bibliography of English Language Sources on Human Ecology; Eastern Malaysia & Brunei," (56); "The Philippines; a Review of Bibliographies" (66); "Philippine Newspapers in Selected Americal Libraries; a Union List" (66); "Preliminary Bibliography of Philippine Ethnography" (68). 14: Ref. 15: Univ of Hawaii Lib 2550 The Mall, Honolulu Hi 96822.

SAKALAS, EUGENIA. b Augustavas Lithuania. 5: Prekybos Inst (Lithuania) 40 (Bus Admin) MS in BA; Georg-August U Goettingen 50 (Econ) Dr rer pol; Drexel 58 MS in LS. 6: Lithuanian, Ger, Fr. 7: Catlgr UPenn 54-. 10: Beta Phi Mu. 14: Catlg, ref, rare bks. 15: Univ of Penn Lib 3420 Walnut st, Phila 19104.

SAKAMOTO, LOUISE YUKIKO. b Los Angeles 21 Ap 40. 5: Cedar Crest Col 58-62 (Chem) BA; USoCal 62-63 MSLS. 7: Catlgr TRW Systems, Redondo Beach Cal 63-67; Libn Purex Corp Ltd, Wilmington Cal 68-. 9: SLA. 14: Catlg. 15: 15828 S Denker ave, Gardena Ca 90247.

SAKEY, JOSEPH G. b Boston 5 My 25. 4: Shirley Enman. 5: Northeastern U 46-49 (Modern Langs) AB; Simmons 49-50 (LS) MS; US Foreign Serv Inst 52; Foreign Serv Orientation, Lang Study Diploma. 6: Arabic, Fr, Ger. 7: US Army 43-46; Catlgr Boston Pub Lib 50; Head ser libn USAF Cambridge Res Lib 51-52; Dir USIS Lib US Dept of State, Trivandrum India 52-53; Asst libn in chg of Edgell Lib Framingham Town Lib, Framingham Mass 53-56; Libn Nashua Pub Lib, Nashua NH 56-. 8: Consul to 5 NH pub libs; Consul, Improved Machinery Inc Lib, Nashua NH; Citizens Adv Com for WNH-TV, 59-. 9: MassLA (Publ Com 55-56); NELA (Com on Articles of Agreement 57, Exec dir 62-63); NHLA (chm Com on Fed Aid 56-62, treas 58-60 Intel Freedom Com 64-), pres 68-. 10: Nashua Hist Soc; Nashua Symphony Assn; Arts & Sci Center of Nashua; NH Coun on World AffairsMunicipal Credit Union; Arts & Crafts League of Nashua, NH Coun for Better Schs. 11: NH Libn of the Year, 63. 14: Admin. 15: Nashua Pub Lib, 6 MAIN ST, Nashua NH 03060.

SALAM, ABDUS. b Aligarh UP India 1 Ag 37. 5: AligarhU (India) 54 BA, 57 (Geog) MA, 59 BLS; TorontoU 65 MLS. 6: Urdu, Hindusthani. 7: Catlgr & ref libn Aligarh U Central lib (India) 59-61, Lecturer Dept of Lib Sci 59-61; Act hd RajasthanU Lib bk selection & order dept, Jaipur India 62; Catlgr Sudbury Sch Bd, Sudbury Can 62-63; Libn Toronto Pub Lib catlg dept, Toronto Can 64, Libn ref dept 65-66; Libn & bibliogr Metropolitan toronto Central Lib soc sci sect 66-. 9: ALA; CanLA; Inst Profess Libns Ont; IndianLA. 11: ALA travel scholarship 65. 13: Yes. 14: Ref, bibliog, govt publ, Oriental studies. 15: 117 Walmer rd, Toronto 4 Can.

SALAS, CATHERINE (LAW). b Newark NJ 16 My 18. 4: Manuel Salas. 5: Douglass Col 34-38 (Span) BA; Smith 38-39 (Span) MA; UMex summer 40; NYU 48-49 (Span); Rutgers U 57-59 (LS). 6: Sp, Fr, Ital, Portu. 7: Tchr of Span & Fr Ashley Hall, Charleston SC 39-41; INSTR OF Span Smith Col 41-42; Span tchr Cranford High Sch, Cranford NJ 45-47; Instr of Span NYU 47-51; Instr of Span West Res U summers 45-55; Catlgr Rutgers U Lib 59-. 9: ALA; NY Tech Serv Libns. 10: Phi Beta Kappa; Sigma Delta Pi. 12: Jt auth "Fundamentos de espanol (50, 57); "Camino adelante (53, 59). 14: Catlg (Romance langs). 15: 1203 Douglas ave, N Brunswick NJ 08902.

SALB, ELAINE SYBIL. b Boston Mass 18 Mr 34. 4: Eugene Marvin. 5: BostonU 51-55 (Fr) BA; Simmons 57-58 (LS) MS. 6: Fr. 7: Ref libn Antioch Col 58-60; Circ libn Wellesley Col 60-64; Libn Microwave Assoc Inc, Burlington Mass 64-65; Tech libn Adage Inc, Boston 65-66; Lib serv supv Sylvania Electronic Systems Applied Research Lab Lib, Waltham Mass

66-. 9: ALA; SLA; MassLA. 10: Combined Jewish Philanthropies. 14: Ref, admin. 15: 4 Ross circle, West Peabody Ma 01960.

SALE, JOSEPHINE WILEY. b Victor NY 22 F 17. 5: Simmons 34-38 (LS) BS. 7: Asst Hartford Pub Lib, Hartford Conn 38-56, Head ref & gen reading dept 56-. 8: Adv Com on Ref Serv, State of Conn 65-. 9: ALA; NELA; ConnLA (Recr Chm 59-60, chm Ref Serv 60-6, chm Scholarship Com 55-58). 10: AAUW; LWV. 14: Ref. 15: 34 Knollwood rd, E Hartford Conn 06118.

SALEY, STACEY. b Brooklyn NY 24 Jl 42. 5: State U (Geneseo NY) 60-63 (LS, Biol) BS in Ed; Queens Col (NYC) 67-69 MLS. 6: Fr. 7: Med libn Hillside Hosp, Glen Oaks Queens NY 63-. 8: Lib consul Dept Psychiatry Beth Israel Hosp, NYC 69-. 9: Med & Sci Libns of LI (treas). 14: Ref, admin, lib planning. 15: 65-15 Yellowstone blvd, Forest Hills NY 11375.

SALISBURY, LUCILE VIRGINIA (MILLER). b Corning Kan 26 Ja 19. 4: Eton Eugene Salisbury. 5: Kan State Tchrs Col (Emporia) 37-41 LS) BS in Ed; uore 52; Ore Col of Educ 61, 63; UWash 63 MA in Libnship. 06 Malay. 7: Eng tchr high sch, Centralia Kan 44-46; Elem tchr Oak Grove Sch, Albany Ore 47-49; High sch libn, Dallas Ore 49-63; Asst prof UOre summer 64; Catlg & secondary resource libn Salem (Ore), Pub schs 63-65; Peace Corps trainee, Hilo Hawaii 65; Asst educ libn Portland State U 66-67; Asst prof Ore Col of Educ 68-; Asst prof UOre summer 66; Consul Salem Pub Schs 68-. 9: NEA; ALA-AASchL (pres 63); OreLA (treas 64-65); OreASchL; OreEA; ASCD. 10: Amer Friends Serv Com; Delta Kappa Gamma; AAUW. 14: Catlg, ya lit,sch lib admin. 15: 3062 Deering dr NW, Salem Or 97304.

SALMON, EUGENE NATHAN. b Sacramento Cal 2 My 17. 4: Dena. 5: Cornell U 36-37 (Animal Husbandary); UBuffalo 41-43 (Psych); UDenver 49-54 (Eng, Educ) BA, 54-55 (LS) MA; Chicago 62-63 LS); Sacramento State Col 66-. 7: ib asst circ UDenver 52-53, Stud asst 53-54; Lib asst Colo State Hist Soc, Denver 54-55; Catlgr Temple Beth Joseph, Denver 55; Head circ libn UOre 55-63; Prin libn tech serv Cal State Lib 63-64; Head humanities ref libn Sacramento State Col 64-. 8: Head info serv ALA Lib Tech Proj, Chicago 62-63. 9: CalLA (Ed Com). 10: Bk Club of Cal; Sacramento Bk Collectors Club; Phi Beta Kappa; Psi Chi; Cal Hist Found (Stockton). 12: Ed "Oregon Library News" (60-61). 13: Yes. 14: Admin, ref (esp humanities), hist of the bk, rare bks, West Americana. 15: 4924 Robertson ave, Carmichael Cal 95608.

SALMON, STEPHEN RUSH. b Brownsville Tenn 28 Ja 33. 4: Susan Humphrey. 5: Austin Col 51-53 (Eng); UCLA 55 (Eng); UCal Berkeley 55-58 AB (Eng) MLS. 6: Fr, Ger. 7: Clerk (Cpl) US Army 53-55; Orchardist UCLA 55; Telegrapher, clerk, towerman So Pacific Co, Oakland Cal 55-56; Stock helper Montgomery Ward Co, Oakland Cal 56-57; Reader UCal(Brkeley) 57; Asst merchandiser Mongomery Ward & Co, Oakland Cal 57; Asst libn Cal Col of Arts & Crafts 57-58; Ref libn St Louis Pub Lib summer 58; LC: Intern 58-59, Catlgr 59, Asst for mechanized info retrieval study 59; Libn George Mason Col UVa 59-61; Admin asst Processing Dept LC 61-62, Asst chief Photoduplication Serv 62-64; Assoc dir of Libs Washington U (St Louis) 64-66; Exec off proc dept LC 66-68, Asst dir for proc serv 68-. 9: ALA (chm Reprod of Lib Materials Sect 66-67; chm Com on Lib Automation 64-66);-ISAD (pres 66-67); Potomac Tech Proc Libns. 10: Beta Phi Mu. 11: Superior Serv Award, LC. 12: "Specification for Library of Congress Microfilming (64). 13: Yes. 14: Admin, tech serv, automation. 15: 3715 Porter st NW, Washington DC 20016.

SALMON, T G. b Glastonbury Conn. 4: Calista Banworth. 5: UNotre Dame BA; So Conn State Col MS. 6: Sp. 7: Opinion Research Corp, Princeton NJ; American Airlines, La Guardia Field NY; War relief serv, NYC; Soc wker Conn State Welfare Dept; Ref libn Curtis Mem Lib, Meriden Conn 62-. 15: Arbutus st, Middletown Ct 06457.

SALMONS, LORNA K (LONG). b Saginaw Mich 17 O 42. 4: Arthur W Salmons. 5: UMo 64-66 eng AB; Tex Woman'sU 66-68 MLS. 6: Sp. 7: Y-a libn Thomas Jefferson Lib Syst, Jefferson City Mo 68-. 9: ALA; MoLA (Jr Mems RT). 10: AAUW. 14: Ya serv, pub serv, a-v. 15: 905 St Mary's blvd, Jefferson City Mo 65101.

SALSMAN, ANNIETA (LUCHT). b Baldwin Ill 7 r 20. 5: Harris Tchrs Col 38-42 (Educ) AB; Ariz State U 57-61 (Educ, LS) MA, 61-65 (Educ, Admin) Ed LS. 7: Tchr Normandy Bd of Educ, Normandy Mo 42-43; Bkkeeper Valley Nat Bank, Mesa Ariz 43-44; Statistician Ralston Purina Co, St Louis 44-46; Personnel & bkkeeping Valley Nat Bank, Phoenix 47-49; Tchr Wilson Elem Schs, Phoenix 49-50; Tchr Cartwright Elem Schs, Phoenix 52-58, Dist libn 58-. 9: NEA; ALA-AASchL (Supv Sect); ASCD; ArizEA; Ariz State LA; Salt River Valley Libns Assn (sec); Maricopa Co Elem Libns. 10: Delta Kappa Gamma; Kappa Delta Pi; Alpha Phi Sigma. ; Nat Assn Women in Educ; Cartwright Adminrs Assn. 14: Acquis, organiz. 15: 345 W Riverside st, Phoenix Az 85041.

SALTEN, FRANCES (BROWN). 4: David G Salten. 5: Washington Sq Col 29-33 (Eng, Psych) AB; NYU 33-34, 37-38, 44 (Child Psych); Columbia 24-35 (Fr), 63-64 (LS) MS; CCNY 38 (Psych); NY Sch of Soc Wk 39 (Casewk47 (Psych); New Sch for Soc Research 65-66 (Non-Fiction Writing). 6: Fr, Yiddish. 7: Asst & reader Eng Dept, Washington Sq Col, NYC 33-34; Soc casewker Dept of Welfare, NYC 34-43, Unit supv 43-45; Pre-kindergarten tchr Green Door Day Nursery, NYC 44-45; Tchr Eng & Citizenship NYC Bd of Educ 47-48; License investigator Dept of State of NY, NYC 49-58; Libn trainee Yonkers Pub Lib, Yonkers NY 63-64; High sch libn Port Chester High Sch, Port Chester NY 64; Catlgr & asst ref libn Ryan Lib Iona Col 66-69; Acquis libn SUNY(Purchase) 69-. 9: ALA; NYLA (Memb Chm, Westchester Resources & Tech Serv Sect); Westchester LA; NY Lib Club; NY Tech Serv Libns; East Col Libns. 10: Nat Cong Parents & Tchrs; Guidance Center; Mental Health Assn of Westchester Co; AAUP; Phi Beta Kappa; Eta Sigma Phi; Beta Phi Mu. 13: Yes. 14: Catlg, ref. 15: Library, SUNY, College at Purchase, Purchase NY 10577.

SALTER, DOROTHY (COOPER). b Greenfield Ind 20 My 19. 5: DePauw U 37-41 (Amer Hist) AB; Carnegie 41-42 BS in LS. 6: Fr, Ger. 7: Child libn Brooklyn Pub Lib 42-46; Head central child room Enoch Pratt Free Lib, Baltimore 46-49; Child libn Milwaukee Pub Lib 49-53; Child libn Enoch Pratt Free Lib, BALTIMORE 61-. 9: ALA; MdLA (Memb Chm 48). 10: Alpha Chi Omega. 14: Child serv. 15: 14 W Cold Spring lane apt 716, Baltimore Md 21210.

SALTUS, ELINOR (CHAPPLE) (MRS). b Fribault Minn 13 Ja 06. 5: UND 22-26 (Pub Sch Music) BA & BS in Ed; UIll 30-31 BA in LS; UMich 50-51 AMLS. 6: Fr. 7: Tchr Eng & pub sch music pub schs, Utah, Ida, Colo 26-30; Asst libn Duluth State Tchrs Col 31-32; Libn Lincoln Jr High Sch, Duluth Minn 43-44; Catlgr & tchr Col of St Scholastica 44-50; Instr Lib Sci Butler U 51-52; Asst Prof Lib Sci & curriculum libn So Ore Col of Ed 52-56; Assoc Prof of Lib Sci Col of Ed UAriz 56-, Prof UAriz. 9: ALA (Coun, Ariz 59-63);-LED (Tchrs Sect: chm Ad Hoc Com on Undergrad Lib Educ 64); SWLA (Wk Conf on Lib Educ: chm Com on Basic Course in Catlg 62); Ariz SchL (chm Standards Implement Com 60-61). 10: Phi Beta Kappa; Beta Phi Mu. 13: Yes. 14: Catlg, child lit, sch lib materials. 15: 2130 E Helen st, Tucson Az 85719.

SALTZMAN, ALICE (BENTHALL). b Bradenton Fla 28 Je 29. 4: Joseph D Saltzman. 5: Tex christian U 47-51 (Fr) BA; LSU 53-55, 60-61 MS in LS. 6: Fr, Sp. 7: Sec to bibliogr LSU (Baton Rouge) 53-54, Romance lang libn 54-55, UN docs libn 54-55, Asst libn res reading room 55, Sec acquis dept 55; Asst ref libn Tex ChristianU 56-57; Tchr Thibodaux High Sch, Thibodaux 59-62; Asst libn Terrebonne Parish Lib, Houma La 62-63; Hd catlg dept Nicholls State Col 63-65, Hd tech processes 65-. 8: Superv tchr for langs, Nicholls State Col Oct 61 - Feb 62. 9: LaLA. 10: Alpha Beta Alpha; Mu Phi Epsilon; Phi Sigma Iota. 14: Catlg, tech proc. 15: 1030 Canal blvd, Thibodaux La 70301.

SALVATO, JACQUELINE (DANELLE). b NYC 7 Mr 27. 4: Jerome J Salvato. 5: Adelphi Col 45-48 (Hist) BA; Columbia 49-51 MS in LS. 7: Libn Brooklyn Pub Lib 49-51, Libn grade II 51-53; Bkmob libn Pierce Co Pub Lib, Tacoma Wash 53-54; Reg ya libn Brooklyn Pub Lib 54-56; Dir Garden City Pub Lib, Garden City NY 56-58; Ref & ya libn Seaford Pub Lib, Seaford NY 60-65, Asst dir 66-68, Dir 68-. 9: ALA-YASD (var coms 51-56); NYLA; Nassau Co LA. 10: Seaford Hist Soc. 13: Yes. 14: Admin, ref, ya. 15: 3991 Franklin ave, Seaford NY 11783.

SALVATORE, LUCY V. b Providence 11 Ap 22. 4: Joseph Salvatore. 5: Pembroke 39-43 (Modern Langs) AB; UIll 56-58 MS in LS. 6: Ital, Japanese, Fr, Ger. 7: Japanese Tr US Intelligence Dept, Arlington Va 43-45; Catlgr John Hay Lib Brown U 51-54; Catlgr UIll(Urbana) 56-58; Tchr asst UIll Grad Lib Sch summer 58; Libn Stoneham High Sch, Stoneham Mass 58-59; Lib coordinator Weston Pub Schs, Weston Mass 59-64; Lecturer URI Grad Lib Sch 63-64, Asst Prof 64-. 8: Lib chm, NE Schs & Cols Accred Com, 60, 63 & 64; Lib consul for several RI & Mass Communities; Exec Dir, Nat Lib Week,

RI 66-67. 9: ALA; RILA (Conf chm 65-66, Conf Com 68-69, chm Nat Lib Week 68-69); NELA (sec 66-67). 10: Beta Phi Mu. 12: Comp "Manual of Instruction for Grades 1-12"; "A Selected Bibliography of School Library Services & Functions". 14: Sch libs, reading interests, child & ya. 15: 68 Freedom dr, Cranston RI 02920.

SALVATORE, GERARD PHILIP. b Brooklyn NY 26 Ap 37. 4: Mary Louise Queen. 5: Holy Cross Col 55-59 (Hist) AB; City Col (NY) 59-62 (Soc Studies) MS; Hunter Col, Hofstra U, St Johns U, Hamilton Col 62-65 (Lang, Educ); C W Post Col 62-69 (LS) MS (NY State Certifs Lat, Gk, Fr, Soc Studies, Secondary Prin. 6: Lat, Fr, Gk. 7: Lat, Eng, Soc Studies Instr Brooklyn Prep Sch, Brooklyn NY 59-61; Lat, Eng Instr Lindenhurst Jr High Sch, Lindenhurst NY 61-62; Lat Instr Harborfields Jr-Sr High Sch, Greenlawn NY 62-65; Libn Newfield High Sch, Selden NY 65-; Smithtown Pub Lib. 8: Consul, NY State Educ Dept, 65, NYC Bd of Educ 68. 9: NYLA; Nassau-Suffolk SchLA; Suffolk Co LA (pres Sch Lib Sect 68). 10: ASIA Soc. 14: Ref, info retr. 15: 12 Stell la, E Northport NY 11731.

SALVIA, LUCY (HARRINGTON). b Scranton Penn 8 S 17. 4: Philip Salvia. 5: Marywood Col (Scranton Penn) 36-39, 60-61 (Mus) B Mus, 61-62 MLS. 6: Ital, Lat. 7: Mus therapist Rockland State Hosp, Orangeburg NY 56-57; Mus libn Tucson Pub Lib 57-58; Lib asst Queensborough Pub Lib, Jamaica NY 59-60; Lib asst Marywood Col Lib 9scranton Penn) 60-61; Libn Penn State Sch for Deaf, Scranton Penn 61-62; Libn III (Act hd tech proc div) Nev State Lib, Carson City 62-65; Catlgr Westmont Col 65; Libn II (ser bibliogr) UCal (Santa Barbara) 65-. 10: Goleta Choral Soc. 14: Catlg (esp serials), music libnship. 15: 30 San Milano dr, Goleta Ca 93017.

SALZER, ELIZABETH M. b Providence RI 5 S 44. 5: Col of St Rose 62-66 (Eng) BA; UMich 66-67 AMLS. 7: Page clk Roswell P Flower Mem Lib, Watertown NY 59-65; Cashier Food Mart Inc, Ann Arbor Mich 66-67; Asst libn SUNY (Albany) 67-. 9: ALA; NYLA; SUNYLA; Hudson-MohawkLA; Capital Dist Lib Coun. 14: Interlib loans, ref. 15: 101 Manning blvd, Albany NY 12203.

SALZER, RUTH (ARMITAGE). b Rochester NY 10 Ag 11. 5: URochester 30-34 (Fr) BA; Geneseo State U Col summer 35-37, 39-40 (LS) BS; Alfred U 36. 6: Fr. 7: Fr & lat tchr, Libn, Greenwood NY 36-38; Libn, Asst to prin Laurelton Sch, Irondequoit NY 39-40; Tchr Fr, Lat, libn Alfred-Almond Central Sch, Alfred NY 40-42; Med records off Rochester State Hosp, Rochester NY 43-44; Asst catlgr URochester 44-62, Assoc catlg 62-. 9; monroe Co (NY) LA. 10: Phi Sigma Iota. 14: Catlg. 15: 5914 W Henrietta rd, W Henrietta NY 14586.

SAMANISKY, MRS MARIE (PHILLIPS). b Minneapolis 23 F 08. 4: Gregory L Samanisky. 5: UMinn 27-32 (LS) BS. 7: Catlgr UMinn Lib (Minneapolis) 37-61; Ed asst UMinn Rural Soc Dept (St Paul) 61-62; Lecturer in catlg UMinn Lib Sch 62-. 9: AALS; MinnLA. 10: UMinn Lib Sch Alumni Assn. 14: Catlg. 15: 3500 Tyler st NE, Minneapolis Mn 55418.

SAMB, LA VERNE. b Fountain City Wis 1 O 19. 4: Walter Samb. 5: La Crosse StateU 38-41 BS. 7: Tchr-libn Galesville High Sch, Galesville Wis 41-44; Libn La Crosse Lutheran Hosp, La Crosse Wis 57-. 9: MedLA. 14: Admin, ref. 15: 2325 Winnebago st, La Crosse Wis 54601.

SAMORE, THEODORE. b Sioux City Iowa 27 Jl 24. 4: Phyllis Johnson. 5: UMo 46-49; (Philos) BA; UMich 50-53 MA (Philos), MLS. 6: Fr, Ger. 7: Stud asst Instr in lab psych UMo 48-49; Sr catlg libn UMich Law Lib 53-55; Asst libn Detroit Bar Assn Lib 55-56; asst circ libn UMich Law Lib 56-57; Period serv libn Ball State Tchrs Col Lib 57-60; Dir sch lib serv Livonia Pub Schs, Livonia Mich 60-62; Col & univ lib spec US Off of Educ, Wash DC 62-66; Prof Sch of Lib & Info Sci, UWis (Milwaukee) 66-. 8: Contrib to Nat Inventory of Lib Needs, 65. 9: ALA (chm Author Sel & Adv Com on Philos 65, chm Com on Col & Univ Lib Statistics 67-). 10: Phi Beta Kappa. 12: "Inventory of Academic Library Rsources and Services: Needs and Prospects (65); "Library Statistics of Colleges and University, Institutional Data; 1961-62 (62-63, 63-64) 4 v GPO (63-65); "Problems in Library Classification, Dewey 17 and Conversion (68); "Library Statistics of Colleges and Universities, 1963-64, Analytical Data," (68); "The Movies; a Montage of Books and Journals in the Sixties" (68). 13: Yes. 14: Ref, catlg, admin. 15: 11300 N Mulberry dr, Mequon Wi 53092.

SAMPLE, LOUISE M. b Lafayette Ind 14 Ja 38. 5: Purdue 56-60 (Eng) BS; Loughborough sch of Libnship Eng 60; UIll 61-62 (LS) MS. 6: Ger. 7: Preprof Indianapolis Pub Lib, ind summer 61; Ref asst Mont State U Lib 62-65; Ref libn IndU 65-. 9: ALA (Internat Rel RT); IndLA; Ft Wayne LA. 10: AAUP; AAUW; The Bronte Soc. 14: Bibliog, interlib loan, interlib coop. 15: 1005 Ridgewood dr apt 6, Ft Wayne In 46805.

SAMPLES, GORDON (HOWELL) JR. b Wheeler Co Ga 16 Mr 21. 5: UGa 37-41 (Eng) AB; Peabody 49-50 BS in LS. 6: Fr, Lat. 7: Tchr high sch Eng LaurensCo, Dublin Ga 41-4; USAAF 43-45; Humanities ref libn San Diego State Col 50-. 9: CalLA. 10: ACLU. 14: Ref, rare bks, films, art prints. 15: 4634 Norma dr, San Diego Ca 92115.

SAMPSON, MYRTLE (BOYKIN). b Clinton NC 30 Mr 29. 4: Robert Russell Sampson. 5: NC Col (Durham) 47-51 (Biol) BS, 51-52 MSLS; UMich summers 53-55 (Psych, Educ) MA; A&T Col (NC) 56 (Psych); UMich summers 56-57 (Psych); UNC(Greensboro 64 (Psych). 6: Fr, Sp. 7: Asst libn, Pub Health Dept NC Col (Durham) 51-52; Tchr-libn Dunbar High Sch, Mooresville NC 52-54; Libn Northwest Jr High Sch, Charlotte NC 54-60; Libn Atkins High Sch, Winston-Salem NC 61-62; Coord lib sci Bennett Col(Greensboro) 62-. 9: ALA; NCLA. 10: AAUW; Alpha Kappa Alpha; Beta Kappa Chi; YMCA; Greensboro Med Auxiliary; Nat Pharmaceut Assn Auxiliary; NC Pharmaceut Soc Auxiliary: AAUP; NC Psych Assn; Amer Personnel & Guidance Assn. 14: Lib sci ecuc. 15: Rt 10 Box 584-B, Greensboro NC 27406.

SAMPSON, RICHARD D(ODGE). b Bath Me 28 Mr 22. 4: Alice Newton. 5: Colby Col 40-43, 46-47 (Hist) AB; Columbia 51-52 (LS) MS. 6: Fr. 7: Rifleman & postal clerk US Army, USA & ETO 43-46; Hist tchr Leavitt Inst, Turner Ht Me 47-48; Clerk First Nat Stores, Augusta Me 48-49; Clerk VA, Togus Me 49-51; Asst ref libn Union Col (Schenectady NY) 52-53; Asst govt documents libn State U Iowa 53-54; Head tech serv Appleton Pub Lib, Appleton Wis 54-. 9: WisLA. 10: Appleton MacDowell Male Chorus; Elks. 14: Catlg, ref. 15: 1013 E North st, Appleton Wi 54911.

SAMS, NANCY CLAIRE. b Asheville NC 19 Mr 30. 5: Mars Hill Col 48-50; Furman U 50-51, 55-56 (Educ) BA; West Carolina U summers 60-64 (Educ) MA Ed. 7: Asheville (NC) city sch: Tchr Hall Fletcher Jr High Sch 56-57, Tchr Vance Elem Sch 57-62, Libn Aycock Elem Sch 62-. 9: ALA; NEA; Clr Tchrs Assn; SELA; NCLA; NCEA. 10: Alpha Delta Kappa. 14: Reading guidance, ref, a-v educ. 15: 141 Starnes Cove rd, Asheville NC 28806.

SAMSON, IRENE GRIFFITH. b Norwood Mo 12 N 08. 4: Roy S Samson. 5: Southwest State Col 34 (Soc Studies) BS; Peabody 42 BS in LS. 7: Tchr sch system, Neosha Mo 34-42; Lib asst St Louis Pub Lib 42-43; Libn Co Lib, Columbus Mont 43-45; Libn City LI, Anchorage Alaska 46-. 9: ALA; MonLA; AlaskaLA; PNLA. 10: Womans Club; Alaska World Affairs Coun. 14: Admin. 15: 1835 13T, Anchorage Aa 99501.

SAMSONOFF, ALICE (WEATHERLY). b Birmingham Ala 6 My 24. 4: Walter A Samsonoff. 5: Mary Baldwin Col 43-46 (ist) BA; Columbia 62-64 (LS) MS. 6: Fr. 7: Supv lending serv Columbia U Lib 62-64; Ref asst documents room Yale U 64-65; Asst libn Ford Found, NYC 65-68; Hd order dept Fordham U Lib 68. 14: Govt docs, ref (acad). 15: 14-22 Astoria Park S, Li City NY 1102.

SAMUELS, EVELYN MARIE. b Winchester Ky 28 Jl 27. 5: Ky State Col 44-48 (Eng) AB; UWis summers 58-62 (LS) MS. 6: Fr. 7: Tchr Dunbar High Sch, Somerset Ky 51-52; Tchr Oliver Sch, Winchester Ky 52-57, Tchr-libn 57-66; Libn Oliver-Hickman Schs, Winchester Ky 66-. 9: NEA; ALA; KyEA; KyASchL; KyLA; CKEA. 10: Clark Co Hosp Auxiliary. 14: Ref, child lit. 15: Oliver, Winchester Ky 40391.

SAMUELS, HERBERT STANLEY. b NYC 20 Ja 17. 5: NYU 34-34 (Psych) BA; UMich 50-51 AMLS; Emory summer 51 (Med Libnship). 6: Ger. 7: VA Hosp: Libn, Battle Creek Mich 50-51, Med libn, Battle Creek Mich 50-51, Med libn, Battle Creek Mich 51-53, Chief Libn, Chillicothe Ohio 53-54, Chief Libn, Ft Meade SD 54-61, Chief Libn, Downey Ill 61-. 9: ALA; MedLA. 10: AAAS. 14: Bibliotherapy, med libnship. 15: P O Box 103, N Chicago Ill 60064.

SAMUELS, JOEL LEE. b Newmanstown Penn 29 D 35. 4: Gilda Dawn. 5: Houghton Col 53-57, 58 (Bible) BA; Evangelical Congregational Sch of Theol 57-60 BD; E Bapt Theol Sem 63-64 (Theol) ThM; Winona Lake Sch of Theol 65; Chicago (LS) 68-. 7: Act libn Evangel Congregational Sch of Theol (Myerstown Penn) 59-60, Libn 60-65; Asst libn Trinity Evangel Divinity Sch (Deerfield Ill) 66-. 9: ATheolLA; Soc of

Bibl Lit & Exegesis; Evangel Theol Soc. 12: Ed "Library Bulletin of E C School of Theology (60-65); Assoc ed "Religious and Theological Abstracts (64-68). 13: Yes. 14: Bibliog hist, hist of biblical interpretation. 15: Trinity Evangel Divinty Sch, Bannockburn, Deerfield Ill 60015.

SAMUELS, MARTHA ELLEN. b Greesburg Ind 19 My 14. 5: John Herron Art Sch 31-35; Ind U 46-48 (LS) AB (cum laude); Chicago 51-52 (LS). 7: Asst Greensburg Pub Lib, Greensburg Ind 36-44; (Pvt) Womens Army Corps, Arligton Hall Sta, (Sgt), Ft Knox, (S/Sgt), Camp Atterbury 44-46; Libn Greensburg PubLib, Greensburg Ind 48-. 9: IndLA. 10: Bus & Prof Womens Club; Greensburg Dept Club; Phi Beta Kappa; Decatur Co (Ind) Hist Soc; Great Books Discussion Group. 15: 327 E Central ave, Greensburg Ind 47240.

SAMUELSON, KAREN. b Brooklyn NY 14 S 36. 5: Vassar 54-56 (Philos); Columbia 58-59 (Philos) BS, 59-62 (LS) MS. 7: Records manager McGraw-Hill Publ Co Lib, NYC 59; Lib asst Jacobi Lib of Mt Sinai Hosp, NYC 60-61; Catlgr Hunter Col 62-65, Ref libn 66-68; Asst libn Hunter-Bellevue Sch of Nursing 69-. 8: Staff, Lib/USA, NY Worlds Fair, 64. 9: ALA; MedLA. 10: AAUP. 15: 208 E 70th st, NYC 10021.

SAMUELSON, SISTER FRANCIS PAUL OP. b Ingallston Mich 9 Je 04. 5: MSNC (Ypsilanti) 23-24 (Eng) Life Certif; DePaul summers 32, 34 (Eng); Rosary Col 33, summers 36-39 BALS; UMich summers 46-49 MALS. 7: Libn St Joseph Acad, Adrian Mich 39-40; Libn Aquinas High Sch, Chicago 40-51; Prin St John's Sch, Unly Mich 54-56; Libn St Theresa High Sch, Detroit 56-58; Asst libn Siena Hts Col 51-54, 58-67, Hd libn 67-. 9: CathLA. 14: Ref. 15: Adrian Mi 49221.

SANBORN, EVERETT C. b Troy Me 21 Je 37. 5: UMe 55-59 (Amer Hist) BA; Columbia 59-62 (LS) MS; NY State Pub Libns (Prov Certif); State of Conn Lib-Tchrs Standard Certif; UBridgeport 69 (Educ Admin) 6th yr Certif. 6: Fr. 7: Asst libn Math Lib Columbia U 59-60; Trainee D NY Pub Lib W Farms Br 60-62; Ya libn New Canaan Pub Lib, New Canaan Conn 62-64; Libn Danbury Jr High Sch, DANBURY Conn 64-. 14: Child & ya lit. 15: 228 Catalpa rd, Wilton Ct 06897.

SANBORN, FLORENCE (McADOW). b Chicago 4 My 10. 4: William J Sanborn. 5: UMo 33 (Elem Educ) BS; USoCal 38 BS in LS. 7: Child libn Long Beach Pub Lib, Long Beach Cal 38; Los Angeles Pub Lib: Child libn 39-56, Reg child libn 56-60, Br libn 60-62, Coordinator ya serv 62-. 9: ALA-YASD (pres 67-68); CalLA-YASD (past chm var coms). 10: Pi Lambda Theta. 13: Yes. 14: Serv to ya & child. 15: 3128 Haddington dr, Los Angeles Ca 90064.

SANBORN, HERBERT J. b Worcester Mass 28 O 07. 4: Kathrine B Sanborn. 5: Nat Acad of Design 26-29 Art-Pulitzer Traveling fellowship; Columbia 32 (Educ); UChicago 35-36 9art Hist). 6: Fr. 7: Asst instr UIowa 32-33; Dir Davenport Mun Art Gallery 33-35; Dir Child Mus, Queens NY 35-36; Dir of mus Oglebay Inst, Wheeling W Va 36-43; Lt comdr USN Bur of Naval Personnel, Wash DC 43-46; Exhibits off LC 46-. 10: Amer Inst Graphic Arts; Print Club Phila; Soc Wash Printmakers. 11: Pulitzer Traveling Fellowship; Tiffany Found 29. 12: Portfolio of lithographs "Hill Towns of Spain" (Paris 30); "Modern Art Influences on Printing Design" (brochure). 13: Yes. 14: Art of the bk, fine prints. 15: 3541 Forest dr, Alexandria Va 22302.

SANCHEZ, CONSTANCE IRVING (MRS). b Poquonnock Bridge Conn. 5: Conn Col (Eng) AB; UMich AMLS. 6: Fr, Sp. 7: UMich Lib; Sec to Dir 54-56, Catlgr 56-58, Arch libn, Asst to libn 58-. 9: MichLA. 10: Phi Kappa Phi; Pi Lambda Theta. 14: Catlg slides (arch, city planning, landscape arch), art. 15: 125 Worden ave, Ann Arbor Mich 48103.

SANDER, EDNA W. b Mass 7 Ag 13. 4: Harold J Sander. 5: Pembroke 31-35 (Eng lit) AB; Columbia 40-41 (LS) BS. 7: Brown U 35-40; Amherst Col 44-45; Ind State Lib, Indianapolis 43-44, Ref asst 60-. 9: ALA; IndLA. 14: Ref. 15: 1714 E Kessler blvd, Indianapolis In 46220.

SANDER, HAROLD J. b Evansville Ind 8 Jl 13. 4: Edna Worthington. 5: Evansville Col 38 AB; Columbia 39 AB; Columbia 39 (LS) BS. 6: Ger. 7: Stud asst Evansville Pub Lib 32-38; Asst Sch of Bus Lib Columbia U 38-40; Ref libn Ind State Lib 40-48; Photointerpreter US Army (M/Sgt) 43-45; Head bus lib, Indianapolis Pub Lib 48-51; Dir pub lib, Roanoke Va 51-56; Dir Indianapolis-Marion Co Pub Lib 56-. 9: ALA; IndLA (pres 50-51 & 68-69). 10: Greater Indianapolis Info Inc; Indianapolis Lit Club; Kiwanis. 14: Pub lib admin. 15: Indianapolis Pub Lib, 40 E St Clair st, Indianapolis In 46204.

SANDERLIN, ELEANOR (BELL). b Ocala Fla 11 Ap 40. 4: John Calvin Sanderlin. 5: Orlando Jr Col 58-60 AA; Fla StateU 60-62 (Eng, LS) BA, 63-64 (LS) MS. 6: Sp. 7: Ext dept asst Leon Co Pub Lib, Tallahasse Fla 60-61; Asst ref libn Orlando Pub Lib, Orlando Fla 62-63; Grad asst F&a StateU Materials Ctr Library 63-64; Asst libn Seacrest High Sch, Delray Bch Fla 64-66; Read adv & ref libn Palm Beach Jr Col 66-68; Circ libn UKy Med Ctr Lib 68-. 9: KyLA. 10: Beta Phi Mu; Sigma Tau Delta; Nat Cong Parents & Tchrs. 14: Ref. 15: 2509 N Formosa st, Orlando Fl 32804.

SANDERLIN, JOHN CALVIN. b Flint Mich 4 F 33. 4: Eleanor Bell. 5: Orlando Jr Col 58-60 aa& fla State U 60-62 (Math) BS, 63-64 (LS) MS. 7: USMC 53-56; Inventory control Pan Amer World Airways, Patrick AFB 56-58; Asst libn Orlando Jr Col 62-63; Grad asst Fla StateU 63-64; Sci ref libn Fla AtlanticU 64-65, Catlgr 65-66, Hd tech serv 66-67; Instr UKy Sch of Lib Sci 67-. 9: KyLA. 11: H W Wilson Scholarship 63-64. 14: Systems analysis, lib automation. 15: 2509 Formosa st, Orlando Fl 32804.

SANDERS, ANDREW LAWRENCE. b St Thomas Ont Can 22 Mr 20. 4: Mary ouise Stock. 5: U West Ont 40-44 (Bus Admin) BA; Toronto 62-63 BLS; McGill 64 (Electronic Devices). 6: Fr. 7: Gen help E B Eddy Paper Factory, Hull Que 40; Can Army (Pvt), Eng 46; R Sanders Lumber Ltd, St Thomas Ont 46-60; Lumber manager Elgin Co-op Serv, St Thomas Ont 60-62; Bus spec London Pub Lib & Art Museum, London Ont 63-; Hd libn Richard Crouch Lib, London Ont 66-; Lib consul London Bd of Educ, London Ont 66-. 9: OntLA (chm Adult Serv Div 66). 10: Union Sch Bd; St Thomas Field Naturalists; St Thomas Foremans Club; Elgin Co Lumber Dealers Assn. 15: Rt 4, St Thomas Ont Can.

SANDERS, BIRDIE L (PETERSON). b Greenwood SC 1 S 11. 5: Benedict Col 28-30 (Eng); Spelman Col 30-32 (Eng) BA; Atlanta summer 36, 37 (Sch Lib) Certif, 50-51 MSLS. 7: Eng tchr Fee Mem Inst, Nicholasville Ky 32-33; Eng tchr SC pub schs 33-36, Libn 36-40; Libn Ala pub schs 46-50; Libn William Penn High Sch, High Point NC 51-68; Libn Griffin Jr High Sch 68-. 9: ALA; NEA; NC Tchrs Assn (HIGH Point Chap: chm Pub Rel Com 64-66); NCLA; Assn of NC High Sch Libns Clubs (Exec Bd, chm Scholarship & Awards Com). 10: YWCA; Ministers Wives Alliance; Les Soeurs Civic & Social Club. 14: Ref. 15: 1714 Kivett dr, High Point NC 27260.

SANDERS, BRIAN. b Kingston Surrey Eng 17 Ja 37. 5: Nottingham U 56-59 (Hist) BA Hons; ULond 59-62 (Hist) MA; Rutgers 65-67 MLS. 6: Fr. 7: Admin asst Lond U, 63-65; Libn trainee Linden Pub Lib, Linden NJ 65-66; Research asst (libn) Rutgers U 66-67; Bibliogr Mich State U 67-68; Assoc libn Lehigh U 69-. 9: ALA; AHA. 12: Co-auth "New Channels, a Report on Broadcasting" (62). 13: Yes. 14: Bldg lib collections. 15: Linderman Lib Lehigh U, Bethlehem Pa 18015.

SANDERS, EMILY C. b Beaufort SC 14 D 05. 5: Col of Charleston 23-24; Winthrop Col summer 26; Pratt 34-35 (LS); Columbia even 38-39; UNC(Chapel Hill) 40 (Sociol) AB; Chicago 53; The Citadel even 54; Berkeley Charleston Dorchester Tech Educ Ctr 69. 6: Fr. 7: Asst Timrod Lib, Summerville SC 27-30; Libn Summerville (SC) High Sch 30-36; Asst Pratt Inst Free Lib, Brooklyn NY 36-39; Dir Charleston Co (SC) Lib 40-. 9: ALA (Coun 56-60); SELA (Exec Bd 60-64); SCLA (pres 47-48). 10: LWV; UN Assn; Bus & Prof Womens Club; Country Dance Soc; Poetry Soc of SC; Garden Club of Charleston. 13: Yes. 14: Admin, bldg planning. 15: 59 Vanderhorst st, Charleston SC 29403.

SANDERS, ERHARD S. b Kaaden Austria 10 N 10. 5: Us of Kiel & Munich 30-33 LLB; Rutgers 36-37 (Econ Statistics); NYU 39-42 (Linguistics); USoCal 48-49 MSLS. 6: Ger, Fr, Portu, Sp. 7: US Army Electronics (T/5) 43-45; Bibliogr acquis USoCal 49-50; Catlgr bibliog LC 50-52; Bibliogr Biol, Vet Med USDA, Wash DC 52-53; Head acquis & catlg Naval Radiol Def Lab, San Francisco 53-57; Acquis libn Gen Electric Co, Santa Barbara Cal 57-58; Lib adv US OM ICA, Saigon Vietnam 58-60; Libn RFPB NIH, Bethesda Md 60-61; Ref Lib adv Bi-National Centers of Brazil USIS, Rio de Janeiro 61-63; Tech info specialist VA, Hines Ill 64-. 9: SLA; ASIS. 10: Chicago Art Inst. 11: Spec Recr, LC. 12: "Civil Defense 1948-52, a biblio (52); "Selected References for Civil Defense (52); "Plan de classification des ouvrages statistiques (59); "Plan de classification des ouvrages agricoles (60); Abstractor for Biol Abstracts (64-); "Notes on Info Sources in Med Research- 968). 13: Yes. 14: Ref, indexing, abstracting, ed, info retr syst. 15: P O Box 339, Hines Ill 60141.

SANDERS, GERTRUDE. b Hartwell Ga 22 S 18. 5: Ga State Col for Women Milledgeville Ga 37-39 (Eng) AB; Peabody Lib

Sch 50-51 MA in LS. 7: Libn-tchr: Acworth High Sch, Acworth Ga 39-41, Rossville High Sch, Rossville Ga 41-42; Auditor USN BuS&A, Washington DC 42-45; Libn Dobyns Bennett Sr High Sch, Kingsport Tenn 45-47; Libn Presbyterian Col (Maxton NC) 48; Libn Barton High Sch, Barton Fla 49; Libn Armed Forces Med Lib, Washington DC 51-55; Hd of circ dept McKissick Lib USC 55-65; Aquis libn St Johns River Jr Col 66-. 9: ALA; FlaLA; Fla Assn Pub Jr Cols. 14: Acquis, catlg, ref. 15: Box 147 Hart Point, Palatka Fl 32077.

SANDERS, JOAN (FLORENCE) C(OOK). b Alabama Twp NY 27 Mr 31. 4: W Thomas Sanders. 5: Keuka Col for Women 49-53 (Chem, Math) BA; Columbia 67-69 MLS. 6: Ger. 14: Wk with child & yp in sch libs. 15: 6 Jay st, Bardonis NY 10954.

SANDERS, MARCIA. b Dover NJ 30 Jl 20. 5: Middlebury Col 38-42 (Eng) BA; UWis 52-53 (Art Educ), 54-55 MS in LS. 7: Tchr Sunny Hills Sch, Hockessin Del 42-52; Tchr Madison Pub Schs, Madison Wis 53-54; Enoch Pratt Free Lib, Baltimore: Gen asst 55-56, Libn educ dept 56-57, Br libn Light st Br 58-61, Br libn Dundalk av Br 61-64, Br libn Pimlico Br 64-. 9: ALA; MdLA. 15: 2805 N Howard st, Baltimore Md 21218.

SANDERS, MARY KATHERYN. b Seattle 27 Jl 17. 5: UWash 35-39 (Sociol) BA, 46-49 LLB, 51-52 (Law Libnship) BS in LS. 7: Customers serv No Life Insurance Co, Seattle 40-42; Capt WAC US Army, Europe 43-46; Stud asst King Co Law Lib, Seattle 47-50; Priv law practice Jonson & Jonson Attys, Seattle 50-51; Asst law libn UWash Law Lib 51-53; Supv law libn Cal State Lib 53-60; Law Libn Cal Attorney Gen Off, San Francisco 60-. 9: AALL; CalLA. 10: Bus & Prof Women. 14: Ref, admin. 15: 949 Vernal ave, Mill Valley Cal 94943.

SANDERS, MELVIN. b Brooklyn NY 1 Je 26. 4: Shirley DAVIDSON. 5: City Col(NY) 44-48 (Eng) BS; Columbia 48-50 (LS) MS. 7: Ref libn Newark Pub Lib, Newark NJ 53-55; Tchr of lib sci Bd of Educ, NYC 55-; Tchr of lib Jamaica High Sch, Jamaica NY 58-. 10: United Fed Tchrs. 14: Tchg, ref. 15: 232-09 Hillside ave, Queens Village NY 11427.

SANDERS, MINDA (MORRISON) (MRS). b Pueblo Colo 19 Je 15. 5: Millersville State Col 33-37 (LS, Math, Soc Studies, Eng) BS in Ed; Penn State U 39-41; Drexel 54-59 MLS; Williams Col 63; John Hay Inst in Humanities; Columbia NDEA Inst in Sch Lib Supv; West Mich U (Educ Spec in Libnship - USOE). 6: Sp. 7: Jr-Sr High Sch libn Berlin-Brothers Valley High Sch, Berlin Penn 37-41; Asst libn Chambersburg High Sch, Chanbersburg Penn 41-42; Exec sec WAR Price & Rationing Bd Franklin Co, Chambersburg Pen 42-45; Armed forces libn & club asst Amer Red Cross, Panama 45-46; Libn & asst personnel off Jefferson Nat Life Insurance, Indianapolis 48-53; Libn Downingtown Joint Sr High Sch, Downingtown Pen 53-65; Lib Dir Monroe Woodbury Central Sch Dist, Central Valley NY 65-. 9: NEA; ALA; NYLA; Chester-Montgomery SchLA (past pres & sec); NY A-V Assn; Mid-Hudson Educ Communication Coun. 10: Beta Phi Mu; Amer Field Serv; Internat Stud Exch Program; SE Zone Sch Libns. 13: Yes. 14: Sch libs. 15: Box 493, Central Valley NY 10917.

SANDERS, NANCY P. b Lawrence Kan 24 Ap 45. 5: UKan 63-67 (Sp) BA; UDenver 67-68 MA; Fla AtlanticU 69-. 6: Sp. 7: Ref libn Fla AtlanticU 68-. 14: Ref, govt docs. 15: 201 SW 7th st, Boca Raton Fl 33432.

SANDERS, VERLYN ELIZABETH (CUTRER). b Many La 10 Ag 09. 4: Murrah A Sanders. 5: Northwestern State Col 29-33 (Eng, Soc Sci) BA; LSU summers 34-38 BS in LS. 7: Libn Many High Sch, Sabine Parish, Many La 31-36; Libn Oil City High Sch, Caddo Parish, Oil City LA 37-40; Libn Mangham High Sch, Richland Parish, Mangham La 40-42; Off manager & supv of clerical Wkers & File clerks California Oil Co, New Orleans 42-47, Libn Petroleum Tech Lib 4758; Libn Westwego Jr High Sch, Jefferson Parish La 60-62; Libn Jefferson Jr High Sch, New Orleans 62-. 9: ALA; SWLA; LaLA; La Sch Libns; New Orleans Lib Club. 10: Nat Fed of MUSIC Clubs; La Fed of Mus Clubs; PTA; AAUW; YWCA; Book Review Club; Bridge Club; La Hist Soc. 13: Yes. 14: Ref, La hist materials. 15: 4609 Utopia dr, Metairie La 70001.

SANDERS, WILLIAM. b Cedar Rapids Iowa 19 F 26. 4: Elfriede Helene Oltmanns. 5: Coe Col 46-47 (Fr); UDenver 47, 48-49 (Fr) AB; Sorbonne 47-48 (Fr) Diploma, 49-50 (Fr); Chicago 49 (Fr); UCal(Berkeley) 61-62 MLS. 6: Fr, Ger, Russian. 7: Weicker T & S Co, Denver 51; Encyclopedia Americana Wash DC 51-52; ONC Fast Freight, San Francisco 52-54; Air Express Intl Airport, SAN Francisco 54-55; Pan Amer Airways, Intl Airport, San Francisco 55-61; Ref libn Lockheed Missiles & Space, Palo Alto Cal 62-63; Asst libn US Geol Survey Lib, Menlo Park Cal 63-. 9: SLA. 10: Phi Sigma Iota. 14: Catlg, ref. 15: 1896 Lexington ave, San Mateo Ca 94402.

SANDERSON, Jessie MAE (WAGGONER). b Muncie Ind 9 My 20. 4: Charles G Sanderson. 5: Ball State Tchrs Col 37-41 (Eng, Hist, Lat) AB in Ed; UMich 41-43 BS in LS. 6: Lat, Fr, Ger. 7: Wayne Co Lib, Detroit: Asst catlgr 43, Act head catlgr 43-44, Child lin (Wayne Br) 45-46, Br libn (Lincoln Park Br) 46-51; Elem libn Livonia pub schs, Livona pub schs, Livonia Mich 61-65, Catlgr 65-. 9: ALA; MichLA (chm Memb Com 48-49); MichASchL. 10: Womens Assn. 14: Catlg, child serv. 15: Lib Serv Bd of Educ, 29530 Munger, Livonia Mi 48154.

SANDERSON, MARGARET (WATSON). b Philadelphia Penn 2 Je 16. 5: Wellesley 34-35 (Eng); Ohio StateU 35-37 (Eng); AmericanU (Cairo Egypt) 37-39 (Eng); Wooster Col 39-41 (Eng) Arts & Sci; Drexel 48-52 MS in LS. 6: Fr. 7: Sr lib asst Elizabeth Free Pub Lib, Elizabeth NJ 43-46; Libn Spec Serv 8th Army, Tokyo 46-48; Desk asst Drexel 448-52; Child libn George Mason Br Lib, Annandale Va 60-. 10: Church Libra Coun. 14: Ref, child serv. 15: 5634 - 7th rd, S Arlington Va 22204.

SANDIFER, PATRICIA ANN. b Urbana Ill 27 Ap 43. 5: So Ill U 61-65 (Hist) BS, 68- (Instr materials); UIll 65-66 (LS) MS. 6: Fr, Sp. 7: Asst libn Richwoods High Sch, Peoria Ill 66-67; SoIllU: Asst ed libn summer 67, Asst ref libn summer 68; Libn Central Jr High Sch, Belleville Ill 67-. 9: ALA; -AASchL; NEA; IllLA; IllSchL; Grade Tchrs Assn; IllEA. 10: SoIllU Alum. 14: Sch libs, adol & ya lit. 15: 201 Bellevue Pk dr apt 8, Belleville Il 62223.

SANDOR, MARGARET EVA JUDITH (FOTI). b Miskolc Hungary. 4: Peter E Sandor. 5: MAn Peter U (Budapest) 47-48; Apaczai Csere Janos U (Budapest) 53-56 (LS); Toronto 59-60 BLS. 6: Hungarian, Fr, Ger, Russian, Slovak. 7: Libn Toronto Pub Lib 57-. 14: Catlg. 15: 30 Hillsboro ave apt 1503, Toronto Can.

SANDOVAL, NELLE L (JONES). b Davenport Okla 4 F 13. 4: Fred G Sandoval. 5: Kan State Tchrs Col 35 (Soc Sci, Speech) BS in Ed; Northwestern U Sch of Speech 40 MA; UDenver 53 (LS) MA. 7: Tchr: High Sch, Plains Kan 35-37, High Sch, Cullison Kan 37-40, Jr Col, Chanute Kan 40-42; WAC Air Force (1st Lt) 42-45; Libn HIGH Sch, Aurora Colo 47-. 9: ColoLA; ColoASchL. 14: High sch libship. 15: 9220 E Lehigh, Denver Co 80237.

SANDROCK, DOROTHY M(ECHLER). b Canby Minn 17 Je 17. 4: Ashley Donald Sandrock. 5: Grove City Col 35-39 (LS, Eng, Lat, Fr) AB; Ind State Col 59-60 (A-V, Develop Reading); UGa (Athens) 66 (Sch Lib Materials & Utilization). 6: Fr, Lat. 7: Libn circ Grove City Pub Lib, Grove City Penn 37-39; Libn Bethel Twp Jr-Sr High Sc, Bethel Penn 39-41; Libn D T Wason Home for Crippled Child, Leetsdale Penn 53-59; Elem tchr Baden-Economy Jr High Sch, Freedom Penn 59, Libn 60; Libn Pine Jr High Sch, Gibsonia Penn 60-. 9: NEA; ALA-AASchL; Penn State EA; PennLA; Babcock EA (Exec Coun 65-69). 10: PTA. 14: Catlg, ref, ya reading groups. 15: Hawthorne Acres, Box 267, Sewickley Rt 4 Penn 15143.

SANDS, LU ALICE. b Clarksville Tenn 30 D 26. 4: John Earl Sands. 5: Peabody Col 44-47 (Art) BA; Austin Peay State 56-57; Fla State U 60-61 (Lib) MA; Emory U 67. 6: Fr, Sp. 7: Child libn S Ga Reg Lib, Valdosta Ga 56-59; Chm dept of lib sci N Fla Jr Col 61-. 9: ALA; SELA; FlaLA. 10: Madison Woman's Club. 12: Fla State Dept of Educ Materials Bull 22CJC-3c; bklets on philos, relig, art, music. 14: Acquis, ref (Humanities). 15: 115 Hancock st, Madison Fl 32340.

SANDS, NATHAN J. b St Louis 3 Jl 23. 4: Muriel Lee. 5: Wilson Tchrs Col 41-43 (Math); George Washington U 46-48 (Math); UCLA 48-51 (Hist) BA; USoCal 51 MS in LS. 6: Hebrew, S. 7: US Army 42-46; Head of accessioning LC 46-48; Tech ed Starnes Publ Co, Pasadena Cal 51-53; Libn sci-tech dept Los Angeles Pub Lib 53-54; Chief Libn Librascope Group Glendale Pub Lib, Glendale Cal 54-. 9: SLA (SoCal Chap: pres 60-61, chm several coms); ASIS (Memb Chm 60-65, chm Printing & Publ for 66 Convention). 10: Trade Adv Com, Los Angeles Trade-Tech Col 66-. 13: Yes. 14: Research. 15: 7902 Allott ave, Van Nuys Cal 91402.

SANDY, CATHERINE E. b Italy. 5: Rosary Col 33-34 Certif in Lib Sci; Columbia 39-53 (Langs) BS; UFlorence (Italy) summer 51 (Langs) Certif. 6: Ital, Fr. 7: Asst Port Washington

Pub Lib, Port Washington NY 26-, Ref libn 60-. 9: ALA; NYLA; Nassau Co LA. 10: Adut Educ Coun; Commun Concert Assn; Art Adv Bd, Pub Lib; Dir Alumni Assn, Sch of Gen Studies Columbia U; Trustee Cow Neck Peninsula Hist Soc. 12: Ed & publ dir "Cow Neck Peninsula Historical Societys Journal". 14: Ref, transl of for lit. 15: 35 Davis rd, Port Washington NY 11050.

SANFORD, EDWIN GILBERT. b Cambridge Mass 15 F 31. 5: Northeastern U 48-53 (Hist, Govt) AB; Boston U 53-54 (Hist) MA; Northastern U 54-56 (Educ) EdM; Simmons 58-62 MS in LS. 7: USAR armor, tank, (Pers Sgt, SFC) 51-53; Asst to libn Priv Lib, Boston 57-59; Prof lib asst Hist Dept Boston Pub Lib 59-65, Ref libn Hist Dept 65-67, Ref libn soc sci ref 67-. 9: AHA; NE Hist Geneal Soc; NE Conf Meth Hist Soc (sec, dir); Numerous loc Hist Socs. 10: Phi Alpha Theta; Men Libns Club; Gen Theol Lib (Boston). 13: Yes. 14: Hist research. 15: 53 Raleigh rd, Belmont Ma 02178.

SANFORD, ELIZABETH G(AULDING). b Tifton Ga 1 F 07. 4: Gilbert A Sanford. 5: Wesleyan Col (Macon Ga) 24-28 (Eng Lit) AB; EmoryU 31-32 AB in LS. 6: Sp. 7: Tchr Concord Pub Schs, Concord NC 28-31; Libn Atlanta Pub Schs 32-35; Libn FERA Lib Projects, Atlanta 35-36; Dist supv WPA Lib Projects, Columbus & Macon Ga 36-37; Libn Jefferson Co Sch System, Birmingham Ala 38-39; Libn tchrs ref serv Ann Arbor Pub Lib, Ann Arbor Mich 39-41; Asst libn Montgomery Pub Lib, Montgomery Ala 47-52; Doc catlg supv AirU Maxwell AFB, Ala 52-56; Asst libn & libn Nuclear Div Martin Co, Baltimore 56-63; Libn Med & Chirurgical Faculty of Md, Baltimore 63-. 9: SLA (Baltimore Chap: pres 66-67, dir 67-68; SLA-MdLA liaison rep 67-69); MedLA; Baltimore HospLA; MdLA; ALA-RSD. 15: 8803 Littlewood rd, Baltimore Md 21234.

SANFORD, FRANCES E. b Ware Mass 23 D 04. 5: Simmons 22-26 BLS. 7: Asst libn Springfield Col 26-45; Hd ref dept Providence Pub Lib, Providence RI 45-48; Ref libn Olivet Col 48-50; Ref libn Panzer Col 50-51; Ref libn Curtis Mem Lib, Meriden Conn 51-57; Libn Wallingford Pub Lib, Wallingford Conn 57-62; Libn Agawam Pub Lib, Agawam Mass 62-66; Br supv Springfield City Lib, Springfield Mass 66-. 9: ALA; MassLA; NELA; WestMassLA. 10: AAUW. 14: Admin, ref. 15: 62 Elm st, Agawam Ma 01001.

SANFORD, HELEN A (GARTLAND). b Laysburg Penn 13 Ap 07. 4: Ralph H Sanford. 5: NoIllU summers 54- (Eng); Rockford Evening Col 61 (Eng) BS in Ed; Rosary Col summer 67 (LS). 7: Libn Bethany Biblical Sem 28-29; Libn Altoona Jr High & Pub Lib 28-32; Libn Mt Morris Col 32; Dist libn Dist #271 54-58; Libn Rochelle Elem Sch 58-. 9: ALA; NEA; IllLA; IllEA. 10: 4-H wk; Home Bureau Ci Bd. 14: Sch libs, learning ctrs. 15: RR, Ashton Il 61006.

SANFORD, JANICE (PHILLIPS). b Nashville Tenn 1 F 19. 4: Granville Thurman Sanford Jr. 5: David Lipcomb Col 54-59 (Educ) BS; Middle Tenn State U 59-62 (LS, Ed) MA; Peabody 65- (Curr Inst). 7: Libn David Lipscomb Col Train Sch, Nashville 59-. 14: Child bks. 15: Nolensville Tenn 37135.

SANFORD, WILLIE MAE (DAFFRON). b Tuscaloosa Ala. 4: Julian H Sanford. 5: UAla 34 (Educ, LS) BS in Ed; Peabody 45 (LS) MA; UAla Law Sch (Law). 6: Sp, Ger. 7: Tchr Romulus Jr High Sch, Tuscaloosa Ala 28-29 Prin BROWNSVILLE Elem & Jr High Sch, Tuscaloosa Ala 29-30; Prin Greeley Elem & Jr High Sch, Tuscaloosa Ala 30-34; Tchr Buhl Elem & Jr High SCH, Tucaloosa Ala 35-36; Libn & supv lib sci Practice stud Tuscaloosa Sr High Sch, Tuscaloosa Ala 36-43; UAla: Catlg libn 43-45, Libn Sch of Law 46-54, Asst libn Sch of Law 54-. 9: NEA; AALL; ALA; AlaLA; SE Law Lib Assn; AlaEA. 10: AAUP; AAUW; Kappa Delta Pi; A;pha Beta Alpha. 14: Catlg, admin. 15: 1106 13th st, Tuscaloosa Al 35401.

SANFT, JEWEL (WEINER). b Montreal Can 21 S 42. 4: Arthur Sanft. 5: McGill 59-63 BA, 63-64 BLS. 6: Fr, Sp. 7: McGillU Redpath Lib: Catlgr 64, Ref libn 64-65, Asst hd ref dept 66, 68-69, Act hd ref dept 67, Ref libn 69-. 9: CanLA (Coun Info Serv Sect). 14: Ref. 15: 3250 Forest Hill ave, Montreal Que Can.

SANGER, CHESTER WARREN. b Waltham Mass 28 My 08. 4: Helen Sharp. 7: Clerk financial Page The Christian Science Publ Soc 29-36, Clerk to Head Libn (53) Research Lib 37-. 8: Examining Bd, The Boston Pub Lib, 56-59. 9: SLA (Newspaper Div: sec-treas, chm; Boston Chap: treas, ed Bulletin, pres); NELA(past Publicity Chm). 15: One Norway st, Boston Ma 02115.

SANGER, GLADYS VIOLA. b Oakton Va 1 Ag 09. 5: Bridgewater Col 25-27; Columbia 29-35 (Eng) BS, 36-39 (LS) BS; UMich 46-47 (LS) MA. 7: Catlgr NY Pub Lib 29-41; Head catlgr Union Col Lib (Schenectady NY) 41-43; (Cpl) Womans Army Corp Photography 43-45; Catlgr Denver Pub Lib 45-46; Head catlgr UMo Lib 47-51; Spec serv libn US Army, Japan & Korea 51-57, Catlgr Wayne State U 58-. 9: ALA. 10: LWV. 14: Catlg. 15: 19209 Riverview, Detroit Mi 48219.

SANGER, LILLIAN REBECCA. b Scotsford Va 4 Jl 01. 5: Bridgewater Col 20-24 (Eng) BA; Columbia 31-32 BLS. 7: Asst brs NY Pub Lib 24-27; Ref asst Union Theol Sem (NY) 27-31; Asst catlgr Assn of the Bar of the City of NY 33-42; Ref libn Law Dept US Army Lib, Wash DC 42-50; Indexer Legal Dept Fed Res Bank of NY, NY 51-52; Libn Royall Koegel & Rogers, NY 52-55; Catlgr Chase Manhattan Bank Lib, NY 55-59; Law libn Equitable Life Assurance Soc, NY 59-66. 9: AALL. 14: Ref. 15: 1314 Blandford st, Staunton Va 24401.

SANGSTER, JEANNE BYRD. b Austin Tex 31 Jl 45. 5: Miss State Col for Women 63-66 (LS) AB; So Conn State Col 68- (LS). 6: Fr. 7: Post Jr Col: Eng instr 66-67, Hd libn 67-. 9: ALA; ConnLA; NELA. 10: AAUW; Thomaston (Conn) Friends of the Lib. 14: Ref, acquis. 15: 19 Warner lane, Thomaston Ct 06787.

SANI, MARTHA Jo. b Versailles Mo 26 My 35. 4: Robert L Sani. 5: Mo U 53-56; SE Mo State 58-60 BS in Ed; UIll 64-66 MS in LS. 7: Clk & typist WashU Lib 56-57; Libn e jr High Sch Riverview Sch Dist, St Louis 60-64; Libn Statewater Survey Urbana Ill 65-67; Doc supv civil engring dept UIll 67-. 8: Catlgr Mallinkrod & Radiation Lab Lib 63-64; Meramec Jr Col Libn summer 64. 9: ALA; SLA. 10: AAUW; UIll Women's Club. 14: Ref (govt docs, ser, etc). 15: 1514 W Charles, Champaign Il 61820.

SANNER, MARIAN. b Baltimore 11 N 13. 5: Johns Hopkins 43-48 (Hist) BS; UNC 48-49 BSLS. 6: Fr. 7: Enoch Pratt Free Lib, Baltimore: Ref asst bus & econ dept 43-45, Catlgr 46-51, Admin asst catlg dept 51-64, Head catlg dept 64-66, Chief processing 67-. 8: Instr of catlg, UNC summer 61. 9: ALA-RTSD (chm CCS 66-67); MdLA; Potomac Tech Proc Libns (chm 51-52). 13: Yes. 14: Catlg, tech serv. 15: 400 Cathedral st, Baltimore Md 21201.

SANNWALD, WILLIAM WALTER. b Chicago Ill 12 S 40. 4: Mary G Blomberg. 5: Beloit Col 59-63 (Econ) BA; Rosary Col 65-66 MALS. 6: Sp. 7: 5 year pipe fitter apprentice program, Chicago 56-65; Dir Libertyville Twp Lib, Libertyville Ill 66-68; Dir Rochetser Pub Lib, Rochester Minn 68-. 9: ALA; MinnLA; IllLA; North Shore Lib Club 9pres). 10: Pi Kappa Alpha; Beta Phi Mu. 13: Yes. 14: Admin, bldg. 15: 3908-18th ave NW, Rochester Mn 55901.

SANTERRE, LOUIS-ANGE. b Baie-des-Sables Cte Matane Que Can 9 N 24. 4: Yvette La France. 5: Col St-Alexandre 42 Sec-4; Sem St-Victor 50 Rhetorique; UWis Ext 66 Bibliotheconomie; Ecole Universelle de Paris 68 Bibliotheconomie. 6: Fr. 7: Gerant Librairie-Imprimerie Les Agences Publicitaires 57; Journaliste Journal "Nouveau Quebec" 59; Directeur Editorialiste Journal Le Basrion 63; Directeur Bibliotheque Municipale Sept-Iles 65. 10: Chevalier de Colomb 4ieme Degre; Club Richelieu; Societe Culturelle; Societe d'Histoire; Le Festival de Musique. 12: "Sept-Iles, Terre Promise" (64). 14: Catlg. 15: 192 Cartier Sept-Iles, Cte Duplessis Que Can.

SANTO-TOMAS, MARIA (BLANCO). b Cuba 23 Ja 32. 4: Raul Santo-Tomas. 5: French Dominic Sch (Cuba) 45-51 BS, BA; UHavana (Cuba) 58-60 (LS) Degree; Kan State Tchrs Col 65-67 (Soc Sci) BSE. 6: Sp, Portu. 7: Asst libn Nat Lib, Havana Cuba 60-61; Cuban aid libn H H Filer Jr High Sch, Hialeah Fla 63-65; Sci libn & instr AuburnU Lib 67-. 10: Friends of the Lib; PTA. 14: Bibliog, catlg, ref, tchg. 15: 656 Florence dr, Auburn Al 36830.

SANTO-TOMAS, RAUL. b Cuba 1 Mr 22. 4: Maria de los A Blanco. 5: Vedado Inst (Cuba) 35-39 BS, BA; HavanaU (Cuba) 39-43 Doctor of Laws; UMiami (Fla) 61 (USA Laws); Kansas State Tchrs Col 65-67 MLS. 6: Sp, Portu. 7: Attorney at law, Havana Cuba 43-61; Soc wkr Fla State Dept Pub Welfare, Miami 62-65; Sp instr H H Filer Jr High Sch, Hialeah Fla 64-65; Gen bibliogr & instr AuburnU Lib 67-. 9: AlaLA; SELA. 10: Latin Amer Studies Assn; Hispanic Found; SEast Conf Lat Amer Studies; Friends of the Lib; Havana Bar Assn (in exile); Inst Latin Amer Studies. 12: "A Selected Checklist of works by Latin American Authors" (69). 13: Yes. 14: Bibliog & catlg (Latin Amer materials). 15: 656 Florence dr, Auburn Al 36830.

SAPIENZA, LELIA ANNA. b Everett Mass. 5: Boston U 42-46 (Applied Music) B Music; Simmons 50-52 MS in LS. 6: Fr, Ital, Ger, Sp. 7: Instr of Piano Tufts U 46-52; Catlgr Harvard Law Sch 52-60; Libn Wayland High Sch, Wayland Mass 60-. 8: Mass State Supvr Sch Libs, Coord Title II Feb 67. 9: ALA-AASchL; NELA (Tech Serv Div); NESchLA; Mass State Tchrs Assn; NEA; Wayland TA. 10: Mu Phi Epsilon. 14: Catlg, sch libs. 15: 3 Bryant rd, Framingham Ma 01701.

SAPP, LINDA (HAYES). b Lexington Ky 9 Ag 41. 4: Judson C Sapp. 5: Emory 59-63 (Eng) BA, 63-64 (Eng) MA, 65-68 (LS) MLS. 6: Fr, Ger. 7: Asst (semi prof) catlgr Emory-Chandler Lib, Atlanta 63; Elem sch libn Newark NJ Bd of Educ 64-65; Asst catlgr Emory-Chandler Lib, Atlanta 65-67, Act ser catlgr 67-68, Ser catlgr 68-. 9: ALA; SELA; Mimoe Garden Club; Phi Beta Kappa; Beta Phi Mu. 10: Metro atlanta Lib. 14: Catlg, child serv. 15: 124 Mimosa pl, Decatur Ga 30030.

SARACEVIC, TEFKO. b Zagreb Yugoslavia 24 N 30. 4: Blanche Saracevic. 5: UZagreb(Yugoslavia) 52-57 (Elec Engnr) Equiv to BS; West Res 61-62 (LS) MS. 6: Croatian, Ger, Russian. 7: Output supv Amer Soc for Metals Proj, Center for Documentation & Communication Research West Res U 62-63, Manager Med info research projs 63-, Asst Prof in lib sci West Res U 66-. 8: Org & train searching serv, documentation serv, Amer Soc Metal, Metals Park Ohio 63-64; Designed and conducted courses in Fundamentals of info retr systems, Amer Mgt Assn 67-. 9: ASIS (chm No Ohio Chap). 10: Amer Croatian Acad Club, Cleveland. 13: Yes. 14: Info retrieval systems, inf sci exper. 15: Center for Documentation, West Res Univ, Cleveland Oh 44106.

SARGENT, CHARLES WILLIAM. b Shelburn Ind 18 D 25. 4: Nanette Reed. 5: Mich State U 48-51 (Hist) BA, 48-51 (Hist) MA; UMich 52-53 MALS; UNM 56-64 (Hist) PhD. 6: Sp, Fr. 7: Curator hist collections UKan 53-54; Chief catlgr Sandia Corp, Albquerque NM 54-62; Document libn Lovelace Found, Albuquerque 62-66; Assoc Prof Sch Lib & Info Sci UMo (Columbia) 68-, Asst dir med computer program 68-; Deputy libn & Asst Prof Lib Med Scis UNM 67-68. 8: Lectr, Fed Lib Inst, USAF Acad, Feb 65, spring sem 66; Vis asst prof UNM summer 67; Adj asst prof, Grad Sch of Lib Sci, Drexel Inst; Consul UMo Sch of Med Comp Prog 67-68, Albuquerque Lib Proc Ctr, NM Lib Adv Coun. 9: SLA (Rio Grande Chap; Founding mem, Bull Ed, pres, chm var coms); ASIS; MedLA (Rep Com Z-39 USASI); NMLA (chm Exhib Com, chm Intel Freedom Com; Albuquerque LA (pres); SWLA. 10: AHA; Phi Kappa Phi; Phi Alpha Theta; Internat Cosmopolitan. 13: Yes. 14: Info sci, info system design, automated lib systems. 15: 2602 Summit rd, Columbia Mo 65201.

SARGENT, MILLARD BLAINE. b Union City Penn 20 Je 21. 4: Mary Alice Noxon. 5: Edinboro State Col 48-52 (Eng) BS in Ed; UAriz summers 53, 56, 58 (Admin) M Ed; West NMU summers 54-55 (Driver Ed, Admin); UVt summer 64 (LS); Mont State U summer 65 (LS). 7: US Navy CPO(S) ETO, PTO 42-45, Korea 50-51; Amer Brake Shoe Co expt dept, Meadville Penn 52, Tchr Bloomfield-Athens Twp High Sch, Centerville Penn 52-53; Tchr Clifton High Sch, Clifton Ariz 53-57; Libn Willcox High Sch, Willcox Ariz 57-. 9: Ariz State LA; Ariz Assn A-V Educ. 10: Phi Sigma Pi; Elks; Amer Inst for Study; Vets Foreign Wars; Nat Rifle Assn; Hunter-Safety Instr. 14: Admin, pub rel. 15: 550 N Cochise ave, Box 496, Willcox Az 85643.

SARKISSIAN, ARSHAG (OHANNES). b Sivas Armenia 7 F 05. 5: Syracuse 25-29 (Econ) BA; UIll 29-34 (Hist, Pol Sci) MA, PhD; Columbia 38-39 (LS) BS. 6: Armenian, Turkish, Fr, Ger. 7: Asst in hist UIll 30-34, Research asst in hist 35-38; Analyst in internat rel Legis Ref Serv LC 40-. 9: Amer Acad Pol Sci; Amer Oriental Soc; AHA; Hist Assn (London). 11: Research fellow in Europe, ACLS 34-35. 12: "History of the Armenian Question (38); Ed "Studies in Diplomatic History and Historiography (62). 13: Yes. 14: Ref, research in hist. 15: 3702 Woodbine st, Chevy Chase Md.

SARLE, RODNEY GRANT. b Rumford Me. 5: Brown (Econ) AB; Harvard (Bus Admin) MBA; UNC MS in LS. 6: Fr. 7: LC; Spec Recruit 58-59, Research analyst 59, Internat Org Spec Gen Ref & Bibliog Div 59-61, Sr Bibliogr Gen Ref & Bibliog Div 61, Head Gift Sect Processing Dept 61-62, Admin asst Processing Dept 62-63, Head Orders Sect Card Div 63-64; Dir PL 480 Proj Middle East LC, Cairo UAR 64-, Pakistan 67-. 9: ALA; DCLA. 10: Beta Phi Mu; Phi Beta Kappa. 13: Yes. 14: Acquis. 15: Pakistan, US Dept of State, Wash DC 20520.

SARNA, HELEN H. b London England 3 Ag 23. 4: Nahum M Sarna. 5: Jewish Theol Sem 59-64 (Judaic Studies) BHL; Columbia 59-64 (Hist) BS, 64 (LS); Simmons 65-69 MLS; Boston State Col 69 (Educ) Mass tchrs certif. 6: Hebrew, Ger. 7: Columbia U 64-65; Asst libn hebrew Tchrs Col 66-. 14: Ref. 15: 22 Russell st, Brookline Ma 02146.

SARNESE, PHYLLIS J. b Greensburg Penn 9 My 39. 5: Clarion State Col 57-60, 63-64 (LS) BS in Ed; UPittsburgh 64-69 MLS. 7: Elem tchr ST Agnes Sch, Irwin Penn 62-63; Sch libn Franklin Area Jr High Sch, Murrysville Penn 64-; Sch libn Jeannette Jr High Sch, Jeannette Penn 67-68. 9: NEA; Penn State EA. 10: Cath Daughters of Amer. 14: Sch lib wk, instr materials center. 15: 116 Main st, Hahntown, Irwin Pa 15642.

SARRAZIN, FRANCINE (BEDARD). b Hull Quebec Can 25 My 45. 4: M Pierre Sarrazin. 5: Col Bruyere (UOttawa) 66 BA; UOttawa 67 BLS. 6: Fr. 7: Bibliothecaire Bibliotheque nationale du Can, Ottawa 67-. 14: Acquis (Canadien). 15: 336 boul Riel, Hull Quebec Can.

SARTORIUS, LUCILE P. b Larned Kan 8 F 07. 4: William Sartorius. 5: Kan State U 23-27 (Journalism) BS; Rutgers 61-64 MLS. 7: Ed asst "Breeders Gazette, Chicago 27-28; Publicity writer PERCHERON Soc of Amer, Chicago 28-29; Sales letter writer Laidlaw Bros, Summit NJ 5354; Sr libn New Providence (NJ) Mem Lib 64-. 10: AAUW. 15: 6 Glen Oaks ave, Summit NJ 07901.

SASS, LOUIS DeWALD. b W Point Neb 4 S 12. 5: UNeb 33-36 (Eng Lit) AB, 36-38 (Philos) MA; Harvard 46-47 (Philos); Columbia 47-48 (LS) BS, 53 (Philos) PhD. 6: Fr. 7: Asst in philos UNeb 36-41; Instr in math High Sch, Holdrege Neb 41-42; Finance off US Army & USAR (Pvt to Lt Col) (42-65) Order catlg, & tech asst City Col Lib (NY) 47-52; Lecturer Lib Sch UCal(Berkeley) 52-53, Asst Prof Lib Sch 53-56; Dean Grad Lib Sch Pratt Inst 56-68, v-pres for acad affairs 68-. 8: Exam Asst, NYC Bd of Educ, 57-60; Consul, Div of Personnel, NYC 57-60. 9: AALS (dir 57-60); CNLA (sec-treas 59-62); ALA; SLA; Amer Philos Assn; Mind Assn; Assn for Higher Educ; NEA; ASIS; NYLA; NY Lib Club. 10: AAAS; AAUP; Archons of Colophon; Beta Phi Mu; Delta Upsilon. 14: Educ for libnship. 15: 177 Steuben st, Brooklyn NY 11205.

SASS, SAMUEL. b Russia 15 Ap 11. 4: Freda C Schaeffler. 5: UKan 31-38 (Psych, Sociol) AB; UMich 38-40 ABLS, AMLS. 6: Ger, Fr, Yiddish. 7: Asst NY Pub Lib 28-31; Asst UKan Lib 32-37, In chg Sci Lib 37-38; UMich: Asst Chem Lib 38-39, Searcher order dept 39-40, Catlgr 40-41, Sr div libn 41-45; Libn William Stanley Lib Gen Electric Co, Pittsfield Mass 45-. 9: SLA (mem & chm Prof Standards Com 57-62; Pres West NY Chap 57-58; Subcom on Prof Ethics 65, chm Admin Com 69-); ALA (Commsn on Nat Plan for Lib Educ 63-, Adv Com, Mass Lib Planning Study 69-. 10: Pittsfield (Mass) Hist Commsn, City Hall Commsn, Town Hall Arch Commsn; Berkshire Adv Coun to Mass Commsn Against Discrim. 12: "Bibliography of Electron Microscopy (50). 13: Yes. 14: Spec lib admin, lit searching. 15: General Electric Co, 100 Woodlawn ave, Pittsfield Ma 01201.

SASSCER, RUTH (PROCHOWITZ). b Winona Minn 7 Ja 39. 4: Richard Scott Sasscer. 5: Col of St Teresa 58-62 (Hist) BA; Catholic U 62-64 (LS) MS. 6: Fr. 7: Grad lib asst Catholic U 62-64; Asst libn St Joseph Col (Emmitsburg Md) 65-; Ref & ya libn Blandensburg br Prince George's Co Mem Lib, Hyattsville Md 67-. 10: Pi Gamma Mu; Beta Phi Mu. 14: Catlg, ref. 15: 8421 12th ave, Silver Spring Md 20903.

SASSE, JANE MAGUIRE (GEOGHEGAN). b NYC 20 Ag 18. 5: Smith 35-39 (Hist) AB; Rutgers 65-66 MLS. 6: Fr, Sp. 7: Asst acquis libn SUNY (Stony Brook) 66-67; Asst hd acquis dept 67-68; Hd ser dept 68; Hd acquis dept 68-. 10: Phi Beta Kappa. 14: Acquis, ser. 15: 204 Henry st, Sag Harbor NY 11963.

SASSO, LOUIS A JR. b Boston 6 Ja 36. 4: Mary Albanese. 5: Boston Col 53-57 (Hist) BS Ed; Harvard 57-58 (Hist) MA; Columbia 61-62 (LS) MS. 7: Tchr Stoneham Pub Schs, Stoneham Mass 58-60; Pre-prof libn Boston Pub Lib 60; Trainee Robert Bentley Inc, Cambridge Mass 60-61; Lib intern Harvard U 61, Libn 62-70; Asst to Dir Boston Pub Lib 70-. 9: ALA. 14: Admin, personnel. 15: Boston Pub Lib, Boston Ma.

SATEREN, ESTHER GENEVA. b Grafton ND. 5: UND 25 (Eng) BA, summers 29, 37 (Eng); UMin summers 31 (LS); UWis 53 BLS; Mont State Col summers 57 (LS). 6: Lat, Fr. 7: Elem tchr pub sch, Northwood ND 22-23; Eng, Lat tchr pub sch, Drayton ND 25-28; Eng, Lat tchr pub sch, Plentywood

Mont 28-32; Eng tchr & prin pub sch, Blooming Prairie Minn 32-41; Eng, Fr tchr Warren Twp Sch, Leavittsburg Ohio 41-45; Eng, Lat tchr, lib South Jr igh Sch, Grand Forks ND 45-51; Lat tchr, dean of girls Central High Sch, Grand Forks ND 51-54, Libn 54-. 8: Lib sci tchr UND, summer 64. 9: ALA; NEA; NDEA. 10: Delta Kappa Gamma; Pi Lambda Theta; Sigma Kappa; Zonta Club; Nat Coun of Admin Women in Educ. 15: 301 Chestnut st, Grand Forks ND 58201.

SATTERFIELD, VIRGINIA (MARY). b Mt Airy NC 6 Ap 04. 5: Peabody 23-26 BS; UNC summer 35; Columbia 27-28 BS in LS, 35-36 MS in LS. 7: Asst circ dept UNC(Greensboro) 26-27, Libn Tr Sch & Asst ref 28-30; Catlgr USoMiss summer 28; Catlgr Tex Womans U summer 29, Instr lib sci summers 30, 32, 33, 38; Sub asst NY Pub Lib 28, summer 34; Instr lib sci UIll(Urbana) summers 41-47, 67; Libn & Prof of lib sci Womans Col of Ga 30-66; Lectr Lib Sci Emory U summer 40, 45, 66-. 8: Ga State Bd for the Certif of Libns, 50-. 9: ALA (Life Mem); SLA; SELA; GaLA; Metro-Atlanta LA. 13: Yes. 14: Admin, tchg. 15: P O Box 803, Milledgeville Ga 31061.

SATTLER, BERNICE (SMITH). b Marshall Ill 3 O 09. 4: Charles Louis Sattler. 5: Ohio Wesleyan U 27-30 (Eng); Simmons 30-31 (LS) BS; Ohio State U 32; Heidelberg Col 58 (Educ). 6: Ger. 7: Libn: Donnell Jr High Sch, Findlay Ohio 31-33, Findlay Sr High Sch, Findlay Ohio 33-35, Fremont Ross High Sch, Fremont Ohio 58-60; Ref libn Heidelberg Col 60-. 9: OhioLA. 10: AAUP; Heidelberg Faculty Womens Club; Amer Field Serv; DAR; AAUW. 14: Ref, sch libs. 15: Rt 1, Tiffin Ohio 44883.

SATTLEY, HELEN R. b St Paul Minn. 5: NorthwesternU 33 (Clinical Psych) BA, 34 (Clinical Psych) MA; West Res 36 BS in LS. 7: Libn Haven Sch, Evanston Ill 36-44; Libn Civic Educ Serv, Wash DC 44-45; Tchr Dalton Sch, NYC 46-47; Asst Prof Columbia Lib Sch 47-50; Assoc Prof West Res Lib Sch 50-53; Dir sch libs Bd of Educ, NYC 53-. 8: State Adv Coms; Standards, Certification, ESEA, Title II; Asoc Soc consul on child bks, India 65; Asia Found sch lib & lit consul, Japan & Taiwan summer 66. 9: ALA (CBC Com 60-66; chm Clarence Day Award Com, Lippincott Award Com 69-70);-AASchL (Constitution Com 54-59; Sch Libs Standards Com 55-59; chm Nominating Com 58; Prof Rel Com 62-65; Intl Com 62-68; Large Urban Sch Com 68-);-CSD (Bd Dirs 60-63; v-pres & chm Newbery-Caldecott Com 63-64, pres 64-65); NEA; NYLA (Coun 54-58; Scholarship Com 58-62, chm 60-61). 10: Eng Speaking Union; WNBA; Authors Guild; NY Soc for Experimental Study of Educ; Early Eng Text Soc; Dolmetech Found; LI Hist Soc. 11: Child Study Award; Thomas Dodd for "Shadow Across the Campus" 57. 12: "Young Barbarians," (47); "Shadow Across The Campus," (57); "Day The Empire State Went Visiting," (58); "Annie," (61); Ed "Childrens Books about Foreign Countries" (49). 13: Yes. 14: Sch libs, child & ya lit. 15: 433 W 21 st, New York NY 10011.

SAUCERMAN, KATHRYN (BECHER). b Wis 13 N 14. 4: Dr Willard Hunt Saucerman. 5: Wis State Col (Stevens Point) 38 (Hist, Eng) BS; UWis 42 BLS, 44 (Hist) MA. 7: Tchr MarathonCo Schs, Wausau Wis 38-41; Revisor UWis Lib Sch 43-44; Libn: Bemidji Pub Lib, Bemidji Minn 47-49, Long Beach State Col 49-50, Costa Mesa Schs, Costa Mesa Cal 50-52, Newport-Mesa Unified, Newport Cal 55-60; Instr educ div Chapman Col (Cal) 60-. 8: Instr in educ, Even Div, Chapman Col 61-. 9: ALA-AASCHL; NEA; CalSchLA; Cal Tchrs Assn. 10: AAUW; Delta Kappa Gamma; PTA (Life mem). 14: Educ for libnship, sch libs. 15: 416 Riverside ave, Newport Beach Ca 92660.

SAUER, MARY ELEANOR. b Winona Minn 5 Ap 39. 5: Wash U 57-61 (Psych) BA; UIll 64-65 MSLS. 7: Ser catlgr LC 65-68, Asst hd ser sect 68-. 9: ALA; Potomac Tech proc Libns (Regl Coun). 14: Catlg, ser. 15: 2500 Wisconsin ave NW, Washington DC 20007.

SAUER, SERGE A. b Yugoslavia 15 D 27. 4: Alexandra Egoroff. 5: UGratz (Austria) 46-48; UWest Ont 63-66 (Geog) BA. 6: Russian, Ger, Yugoslav, Fr. 7: Interpreter US army, Austria 45-46; Civil employee 48-49; Laborer Private ranch, Winnipeg Can 50-53; Jr draftsman Dept of Highways, London Can 54-56, Draftsman 57-63; Map curator & ref libn UWest Ont 66-. 9: SLA; Assn of Can Map Libs (Com on Nat Union Catlg). 10: Boy Scouts of Canada. 14: Cartography, cartology, catlg maps. 15: 145 Wilson ave, London Ont Can.

SAUKKONEN, MIRJAM A. b Cleveland Ohio 8 Ja 25. 5: Kent State 42-46 (Elem educ) BS, 62 (LS) MA; UWis 54 (Elem educ) MS. 6: Finnish. 7: Tchr Lakewood City Schs, Lakewood Ohio 46-52; Tchr Orange Local Schs, Cleveland Ohio 52-56, Elem sch libn 56-66; Consul sch lib serv Ohio Dept of Educ, Columbus Ohio 66-. 8: Adv Coun Kent State U Sch of Lib Sci. 9: ALA; NEA; OhioASchL; Pi Lambda Theta; OhioLA; OhioEA; Educ Media Coun Ohio. 10: Beta Phi Mu; Sigma Sigma Sigma. 13: Yes. 14: Supv, child bks. 15: 22 E Gay st 444, Columbus Oh 43215.

SAUL, MARION JEAN (GRABER). b E Greenville Penn 30 Mr 27. 4: Carlton J aul. 5: State Tchrs Co (Kutztown Penn) 44-47 (Soc Studies, Eng, LS) BS in Ed. 7: Asst libn Muhlenberg Col 47-53; Libn Parkland Sr High Sch, Orefield Penn 54-. 9: ALA; NEA; PennLA; PennSchLA (Memb chm Dept of Supv & Curr Devel; Rep East Reg); Penn State EA; Penn Coun Tchrs Eng. 10: Soroptimist Internat; Citizens Adv Com to Allentown Sch Dist; Lehigh Valley Heart Assn. 14: Ref. 15: 38 S 14th st, Allentown Penn 18102.

SAUNDERS, BETTY (M) (SILVERMAN). b Boston Mass 14 Ag 25. 4: Joseph Saunders. 5: Simmons 42-46 (Eng) BS; 62-64 (LS) MS. 7: Libn Temple Sinai, Brookline Mass 63-64; Libn Central Jr High Sch, Hingham Mass 64-. 15: 3 Porter's Cove rd, Hingham Ma 02043.

SAUNDERS, ELINOR JEAN (PHILLIPS). b Elmira NY 29 N 42. 4: Harold R Saunders. 5: SUNY (Buffalo) 62-63; Muskingum Col 63-66 (Rel) BA; UMich 66-68 AMLS. 6: Sp. 7: Clk Steele Mem Pub Lib, Elmira NY 58-61; Asst in reader's serv Lockwood Lib SUNY (Buffalo) 62-63; Lib asst Muskingum Col Lib 64-66; Wk study scholar UMich Lib 66-68, Asst hd bk purchasing 68-. 10: Fac Wives. 14: Acquis, pub serv. 15: 2113 Medford #26, Ann Arbor Mi 48104.

SAUNDERS, ELMO STEWART. b Bradenton Fla 3 Ap 36. 5: DePauw U 54-59 (Pre-med Sci) BA; Ball Stat Tchrs Col 61-62 (Hist) MA; Ind U 62-64 (LS) MA. 6: Fr, Ger, Russian. 7: Intern Ohio State U Libs 64-65, Soc sci bibliogr 65-67, Ref 67-68, Govt docs 68-. 14: Hist & soc sci bibliog, acquis, ref. 15: 1494 N High st A-22, Columbus Oh 43201.

SAUNDERS, LAUREL LUCILLE (BARNES). b Ainsworth Neb 17 Ag 26. 4: Ross F Saunders. 5: USD 44-48 (Govt) AB; UMich 48-50 (LS) MA. 7: Sch libn pub schs, Howell Mich 50-51; Spec serv asst libn US Army,Ft Bliss Tex 51-53; Base libn Air Force, Biggs AFB Tex 53-62; Supv of classified documents Tech Lib US Army, Ft Bliss Tex 62-64; Chief of catlg & acquis White SANDS Millile Range Tech Lib, NM 64-. 9: ALA; SLA; Border Reg LA. 10: Eta Sigma Phi; Alpha Lambda Delta. 14: Catlg, acquis, automation. 15: 807 Gato rd, El Paso Tex 79932.

SAUNDERS, LEILA B. b Roanoke Va. 5: Roanoke Col 35-39 (Eng) BA; Columbia 39-40 BLS. 06: Fr. 7: Co Libn Dickinson Co, Clintwood Va 41-42; Circ hd Roanoke Pub Lib, Roanoke Va 42-46; Bkmob libn Lib of Hawaii, Honolulu 46-48: Army lib USA Spec Serv, Ger 48-52; Br libn Enoch Pratt Free Lib, Baltimore 52-57; Asst dir Arlington Co Pub Lib, Arlington Va 57-. 9: ALA (Coun 64-68); DCLA; VaLA (Exec Com 64-68). 10: AAUW; Altrusa; Arlington Hist Soc. 13: Yes. 14: Admin, bk sel. 15: 522 Queen st, Alexandria Va 22314.

SAUNDERS, WILLIAM B. b Smithers WVa 3 O 27. 4: Lucretia Heyward. 5: Bluefield State Col 43-47 (Soc Sci, Eng) BS in Sec Ed; WVaU 47-48 (Soc Sci, Educ)MA; Carnegie 56-57 MS in LS. 6: Fr. 7: Soc studies & Eng TCHR Locferman High Sch, Denton Md 48-51; Personnel clerkUSAF (S/Sgt) 51-56; Libn brs Free Lib of Phila 57-59; Jr lib asst Bus Lib Temple U 59-63; Head Libn Marketing Sci Inst, Phila 63-67; Libn Inst Adv Med Communications, Phila 67-68; A-v & curriculum libn Cheyney State Col 69-. 8: Consul Acad Food Marketing St Joseph's Col 65; Planning com 5th Annual Colloquium on Info Retrieval 68. 9: SLA (chm Publ Com 1965 Conv; sec Adv & Marketing Div 65-66); Spec Libs Coun Phila & Vicinity (pres 66-67); ALA; NEA-DAVI; PennLA. 10: Exec Bd Fair Housing Coun, Delaware Valley; Com for Democracy in Housing, Lansdowne Penn; Temple U Lib Staff Assn. 14: Admin, bus, educ, educ media, soc sci. 15: 337 W Mt Airy ave, Phila Pa 19119.

SAUPE, FRANCES HELEN. b Everett Wash 9 O 17. 5 UMinn 36-40 BS in LS; UIll 50-52 MLS. 6: Ger. 7: Asst Dept of Lib Sci UMinn(Minneapolis) 40-41, Asst catlg dept 41-42; Head catlgr, Instr in Lib Sci Knox Col 42-45; Asst sr catlgr Okla State U 46-48; Asst chief catlg dept Washington U (St Louis) 48-50; Asst ser div Order UIll 50-52; Head catlgr East Mich U 52-67, Bibliog searcher 68-. 9: ALA; MichLA; Ann Arbor Lib Club. 10: AAUP; AAUW. 14: Tech serv. 15: 365 Hillcrest, Ypsilanti Mich 48197.

SAUTER, HUBERT EUGENE. b Dietenheim Germany 10 Ja 23. 4: Joyce Hinsenkamp. 5: Marquette U 46-49 (Electrical

Engnr) BEE; UWis 49-50 BLS. 6: Ger. 7: Electricians Mate 1/c US Navy 42-46; Stud asst Milwaukee Pub Lib 46-49; Engnr libn Ore State Col 50-52; Libn Inst of Tech UMinn 52-56; Research info spec Lockheed Aircraft Corp, Marietta Ga 56; Sup research info Gen Electric Co, Cincinnati 57-61; Chief tech serv brNASA, Wash DC 61-65; Deputy dir Clearinghouse for Sci & Tech Info, Wash DC 65-67, Dir 67-. 8: Com on Sci & Tech Info, Panel on Operating Tech & Systems, Wash DC 65-68; USNCFID, Wash DC 65-69; USASI Z39 Com 67-. 9: SLA (chm Engnr Sect 59-60; Cincinnati Chap: Bulletin Ed 58-59, pres 60-61; Wash DC Chap: chm Sci-Tech Group 63-64); Amer Soc Engnr Educ (sec Minn Br 55-56);. 13: Yes. 14: Admin. 15: 9534 Lawnsberry terr, Silver Spring Md 20901.

SAUTER, MARY (MAGDALENE) FOSTER. b Greeley Col 27 My 26. 4: Ralph Anthony Sauter. 5: Colo State Col 43-47 (Gen Secondary Ed) BA; UAriz summer 66 (Lib inst). 7: High sch libn Adams Co Re27J, Brighton Colo 57-63; Jr-Sr High sch libn Weld Co Re3(J), Keenesburg Colo 63-69; Dis coord Title II ESEA Weld Cty Re3(J), Keenesburg Colo 66-69. 8: Consul for 3 grade sch libs for Weld Re3J 63-69. 9: ALA; ColoASchL; ColoEA (pres local gp 69-70). 10: Altar & Rosary Soc; PTA. 15: Rte 1 Box 196, Keenesburg Co 80643.

SAVAGE, DENIS J(ACQUES). b Saint Pascal Baylon Ont Can 3 Jl 41. 4: Bernadette Jubainville. 5: Petit Sem d'Ottawa 54-62 BA; OttawaU 66-67 BLS. 6: Fr. 7: Soc wkr Serv soc de Hull, Hull Que Can 63-66; Trainee Nat Lib of Can, Ottawa Ont Can 66-67, Catlgr 67-. 8: Mem, Adv Bd for "Manuel pratique de catalogage," by Guy Levesque (69); Rep Nat Lib of Can to the "Comite directeur" for transl and publ a Fr ed of the -anglo-American Cataloging Rules". 9: Assn canadienne des bibliothecaires de langue francaise; CanLA. 10: Pub Lib Bd, Twp of Gloucester; Cardinal Heights Commun Assn. 14: Catlg, geneal. 15: 843 chemin Blair, Ottawa 9 Ont Can.

SAVAGE, DOROTHY E(STHER). b Wash DC 10 F 18. 5: UMd 33-35, 36-37 (Ger) BA; UMunich 35-36, 38 (Ger, Philol); UHeidelberg 37-38 (Ger, Philol); Columbia 40-41 BS in LS. 6: Ger, Fr, Ital, Sp. 7: Lib asst DC Pub Lib 37-40, Readers adv 41-42; Ref libn US Off of Strategic Serv, Wash DC 42-43; Tec 4 Womens Army Corps, US & Overseas 43-46; The Army Lib, Wash DC; Ref asst 46-51, Asst chief Gen Ref Sect 51-55, Chief Gen Ref Sect 55-62, Chief Gen Ref Sect 67-, Chief Readers Serv Br 62-67. 8: Res analyst & visual presentation artist, Army Mil ntel Serv, Wash DC 44-45; Ger interpreter Econ Div, Off of Mil Govt, Hochst & Berlin, 45-46 Consul on Design of Nat Transp Info Ctr, GE Tempo; Consul to Santa Barbara Sch Dist. 9: ASIS; (Mil Libns); DCLA (Exec Bd 48). 10: ; Pi Lambda Theta. 11: Inst of Internat Educ grant, 35. 12: Co-comp "Egberts Law Dictionary: English-espanol-francais-Deutsch (49); Three Levels of Mechanization Within One Library System (64). 14: Ref, for langs, mil sci. 15: 2712 Wisconsin ave NW, Wash DC 20007.

SAVAGE, GRETCHEN SUSAN KORIAGIN. b Seattle 15 Ja 34. 4: Terry R Savage. 5: UCLA 51-55 (Educ) BA. 7: Head libn MSSD Douglas Aircraft Co, Santa Monica Cal 57-63; Manager Voc & Data Control Dept NASA Facility, Operated by Documentation Inc, Bethesda Md 63-64; Consul in lib systems & info retrieval, Wash DC & Santa Barbara Cal. 8: Consul on design of Pesticides Info Center, Nat Agric Lib, Wash DC 65; Nat Transp Info Ctr, GE TEMPO; Consul to Santa Barbara Sch Dist. 9: ASI S; SLA; Assn for Computing Machinery; SIGIR. 10: Phi Beta Kappa; Pi Lambda Theta. 12: ""Library Information Retrieval Program (62); ""The Education of Library Staff and Library Users for Mechanization (63); ""Experience in Man & Machinerelationships in Library Mechanization (64); Three Levels of Mechanization Within One Library System (64). 13: Yes. 14: Mechanized lib systems. 15: 6522 Camino Caseta, Goleta Ca 93017.

SAVAGE, KATRINA. b Savoy Tex 19 Ag 13. 4: James W Savage. 5: Amarillo Col 33 2-yr diploma; UTulsa 59; Tex Tech Col 64 (Eng) BA; N Tex State U 65 MLS. 7: Circ Tulsa (Okla) Pub Lib 57; REF & catlg asst UTulsa Lib 60; Govt documents asst 65-. 14: Rare bks. 15: 3315 37th st, Lubbock Tx 79413.

SAVAGE, YVLETTE (DAVIS). b Kennedy Ala 13 Ag 15. 4: Fred Savage. 5: Ala Col 33-36 (Eng); ULa 36-37 (Eng) BS, 52 (LS) Certif, 58 (LS) MA. 6: Fr. 7: Tchr elem sch, Kennedy Ala 47-58; Tchr high svh, Kennedy Ala 59-65, Libn 60-69; Bkmob libn Ala Pub Lib Serv, Winfield Ala summer 60. 9: NEA; NCTE; ALA; AlaEA (Dir of Clr Tchrs); AlaSchLA. 10: Alpha Beta Alpha; Alpha Delta Kappa; PTA; Kennedy Pub Lib Bd. 14: Ref. 15: Box 216, Kennedy Ala 35574.

SAVARO, JOSEPHINE. b Scranton Penn 14 Ja 15. 5: Marywood Col 33-37 (Fr, Eng)AB (magna cum laude) 41-42 BS in LS; Columbia 44-50 MS in LS; atholic U 63-64 (Higher Educ). 6: Fr, Ital, Sp, Ger, Lat, Russian. 7: Ref asst Penn State Lib 38-41; Asst libn Marywood Col 41-44; Head catlgr Manhattanville Col 44-47; Head Libn UScranton 47-51; Instr Marywood Col Lib Sch 51-53; Instr Catholic ULib Sch 53-54; Head Libn & org of new col lib Wheeling Col 54-63; Head soc sci div Catholic U 63-64; Head St Josephs Lib (Phila) 64-. 8: Mem Middle States Assn Accred Team 68. 9: ALA; CathLA (chm Catlg Sect, mem Exec Bd 65-71); PennLA; Pub Rel LA (Phila). 10: Kappa Gamma Pi; AAUP; Amer Inst Ital Culture. 14: Col lib admin, catlg, ref, bk sel, acquis. 15: St Josephs Col Lib, 54th & City Line, Phila 19131.

SAVERY, VIRGINIA (REMER). b Hastings Neb 13 O 10. 4: Joseph D Savery Jr. 5: Wayne State U 28-32 (Eng) BA; UMich 56-59 MALS. 7: Child ref Royal Oak Pub Lib, Royal Oak Mich 56-59; Asst catlgr, ref & br asst Dearborn Pub Lib, Dearborn Mich 59-63; Asst dir Royal Oak Pub Lib, Royal Oak Mich 63-68; Dir 68-. 8: Off-campus lib sci tchr, Wayne State U, Royal Oak 6566. 9: ALA; MichLA (Pub Rel Com), Personnel Policies Com). 10: AAUW, Soroptimists. 14: Personnel, admin, ref, catlg. 15: 2219 Linwood, Royal Oak Mich 48073.

SAVIG, NORMAN. b Boston 6 O 28. 4: Ruth Savig. 5: UDenver 48-52 (Eng) 53 (Mus), 54-55 (LS); UColo 63-67. 6: Norwegian. 7: Storekeeper 2nd class US Navy, RI 46-48; Libn III, music libn Milwaukee Pub Lib 56-62; Asst libn music lib catlg UColo 62-68, Mus bk sales 63-68; Mus libn Colo State Col 68-. 8: Org Music Lib in Musikkonservetoret, Bergen Norway 55-56; Cellist with var orchestras. 9: MusLA; MPLA; ColoLA. 14: Music libnship. 15: 1611 12th ave, Greeley Co 80631.

SAVITZKY, EVELYN (ROBBINS). b Yonkers NY 28 D 20. 5: SUNY 39-43 (Sci, Math) BA; Columbia 47; So Conn State Col 60-64 MSLS. 7: Lab asst Rockerfeller Inst, Princeton NJ 43-45; Sch libn Westport Bd of Educ, Westport Conn 60-66; Asst libn Perkin-Elmer Corp, Norwalk Conn 66-. 8: Mem Com to organ first Conn Commun Col. 10: PTA Coun. 14: Ref, lib automation. 15: 188 Perry ave, Norwalk Ct 06850.

SAVOIE, EDMOND A. b Lawrence Mass 8 Je 27. 4: Brietta D Giger. 5: MARIST Col & Sem 46-50 (Philos) AB; Simmons 54-55 (LS) MS. 6: Fr. 7: Libn, sr libn, supv libn, br libn & adult serv spec Brooklyn Pub Lib 55-66; Educ media spec ALESCO, Paramus NJ 66-. 9: ALA; NJLA. 14: Bk sel (adult & sr high sch). 15: 654 Doremus ave, Glen Rock NJ 07452.

SAVOYA, EDNA HICKS. b Hornell NY 5 My 11. 4: Charles F Savoya. 5: NY State Tchrs Col (Albany) 29-33 BS in LS; NYU 35-36; Hunter Col 36-37, 51-52. 6: Fr. 7: Pub Lib, Delmar NY 33; Law Libn NY State Supreme Court Law Lib, Elmira NY 33-34; Libn: Port Jervis High Sch, Port Jervis NY 34-36, Manhasset High Sch, Manhasset NY 36-48, NYC schs 51-52; Br libn Miami Pub Lib, Miami Fla 48-50, Head rep dept 52-. 9: ALA (Subs Bks Com 60); FlaLA; Dade Co LA. 12: Ed "Diabetes for Diabetics by G F Schmitt MD (65,68). 13: Yes. 14: Ref. 15: 97 Campina ct, Coral Gables Fla 33134.

SAWARYN, RADOMIRA MARIA. b Poland 3 S 26. 5: UCOLOGNE Med Sch 47-50 (Med); Col of Notre Dame (Md) 51-54 (Fr) BA; Drexel 55-56 MSLS. 6: Polish, Ger. 7: Libn Enoch Pratt Free Lib, Baltimore 54-55, 56-59; Ref libn West Electric Co Inc, Baltimore 59-. 9: SLA (sec-treas Baltimore Chap 61-62), 67-69). 10: Beta Phi Mu; Pi Delta Phi; Kappa Gamma Pi; Delta Epsilon Sigma. 14: Ref. 15: West Electric Co Inc, 2500 Broening hwy, Baltimore Md 21224.

SAWILOWSKY, YALE SANFORD. b Augusta Ga 26 S 27. 5: UGa 44-45 (Hist); Jr Col (Augusta Ga) 45-46 (Hist); UMiami(Fla) 46-48 (Hist) BA; UMiss 64 MLS. 7: Tchr-soc sci Valley Point High Sch, Dalton Ga 48-49; Tchr-soc sci Nahunta High Sch, Nahunta a 49-50; Analysis dept Ga RR Bank, Augusta Ga 51-52; Bkkeeper United Leather Co, Augusta Ga 52-58; Libn: LaFayette High Sch, LaFayette Ga 58-60, Pickens Co High Sch, Pickens Ga 61-63, Duluth High Sch, Duluth Ga 64-, Lawton B Evans Elem Sch, Augusta Ga 67-. 9: ALA-AASchL; GaEA; Richmond Co EA. 10: Alpha Phi Omega. 14: Ref, sch libnship. 15: 2134 McDowell st, Augusta Ga 30904.

SAWIN, PHILIP Q JR. b Hockessin Del 14 Jl 33. 4: Judith Lease. 5: Lawrence Col 53-57 (Hist) BA; UHawaii 60; UWis 61-65 MS in LS; SUNY (Albany) 69. 7: Sales rep Mid-West Phosphate Co, Madison Wis 57-60; Libn St Johns Mil Acad, Delafield Wis 60-63; Libn Taft Sch, Watertown Conn 63-67;

Libn & A-v coord Herkimer Co Commun Col 67-. 9: ALA; NYLA. 10: SUNY Hd Libns. 14: Admin. 15: 2647 Remington rd, Utica NY 13668.

SAWYER, KATHERINE H. b Cleveland 11 J 108. 5: Smith 26-30 (Eng Lit) BA; West Res 55-56 (LS) MA. 6: Fr. 7: Clerk Cleveland Pub Lib 31, Libn Hosp & Insts Dept 56-61; Med libn Med Sci Lib St Lukes Hospital, Pittsfield Mass 65-66; Curator Sophia Smith Collections Smith Col 69-. 8: Organized Natl Med Lib for Guyana, SA 66-68. 9: ALA; SLA; OhioLA. 10: Trustee, Friends of the Cleveland Pub Lib; Coun Friends of the Smith Col Lib; Archaeol Inst of Amer; Nat League of Amer Pen Wom; Cercle des Conferences Francaises. 12: Co-auth "Gardening for Blind Persons, LC Talking Book (61); Auth "Beauty, Glamour, and Style, LC Talking Bk (63). 14: Med material, ref, Eng lit. 15: 218 Elm st, Northampton Ma 01060.

SAWYER, RUTH (McMULLEN). b Dallas Tex 26 Ag 14. 4: Guy Stanley Sawyer. 5: Tex Woman's U 31-35 (LS) BS, BA. 6: Sp. 7: Libn & tchr Alvin High Sch, Alvin Tex 35-37; Libn J P Elder Jr High Sch, Ft Worth Tex 37-38; Libn Jefferson High Sch, San Antonio Tex 38-39; Lib asst Lib Sch Lib UTex 54-63; Libn Lib Sch Lib 63-. 9: ALA; TexLA; SWLA; Austin Lib Club. 10: UTex Staff Assn; Soc UTex Libns; Sponsor, Child Nurture Club. 14: Serv to the disadvantaged, ref, archives. 15: 2826 San Gabriel, Austin Tex 78705.

SAWYER, VOILA ALLEN. b Baskin La 10 D 10. 5: Delta State 28-30 (Lat); USCar 30-32 (Lat) AB, (Eng, Soc Sci, Educ, LS); Fla StateU 67-68 (LS) MS. 7: Tchr, SC: St stephens Elem, St Stephens 34-35, Edgefield High Sch, Edgefield 41-43, 51-59, Strom Thurmond High Sch, Edgefield Co SC 61-64, N Augusta Sr High Sch, N Augusta SC 64-67; Libn Edgefield High Sch, Edgefield SC 59-61; Asst Prof of lib sci & asst libn Augusta Col 68-. 8: Chm, S Car Com on Child and Youth 58-60; Chm SC Deleg to the 1960 White House Conf on Child and Youth; Deleg to the 1950 White House Conf from SC. 9: ALA; Ga;A SELA; RichmondCoLA (v-pres 69-70). 10: Phi Beta Kappa; AAUW; Bd of Women visitors, USC; Adv Bd, USC (Aiken); Soc for Crippled Child and Adults of SC; Tchr of the Year, Edgefield Co SC 62. 14: Ref, bibliog, tchg. 15: PO Box 415, Johnston SC 29832.

SAWYERS, ELIZABETH (JOAN). b San Diego 2 D 36. 5: Glendale Jr Col 54-57 AA; UCLA; 57-59 (Bacteriology) BA, 60-61 MLS. 6: Ger. 7: Lib asst Biomed Lib UCLA 58-61; NLM, Bethesda Md: Libn intern 61-62, Asst head acquis sect 62-63, Head acquis sect 63-67, Spec asst to chief tech serv div 67-69, Spec asst to assoc dir lib operations 69-. 8: Procurement Task force, Fed Lib Com; Working Group on Nat Ser Data Prog, Nat Lib Task Force; Subpanel on Transfer of Bib Info on Mag Tape COSATI. 9: MedLA; CLA. 10: UCal Lib Schs Alumni Assn; Beta Phi Mu. 14: Acquis, ser, automation, admin. 15: 9900 Georgia ave apt 411, Silver Slring Md 20902.

SAXE MINNA CLAIRE. b Providence RI 16S 38. 5: Pembroke 56-60 (Pol Sci) AB; Simmons 62-64 (LS) MS. 6: Russian, Fr, Polish, Hebrew. 7: Lib asst, Lib intern, Slavic catlgr Harvard 60-. 14: Catlg & ref (Slavic). 15: 927 Hope st, Providence RI 02906.

SAXINE, ANITA C. b Prescott Wis 31 Jl 13. 5: Va Jr Col 30-32 AS; Col of St Catherine 32-34 (Hist) BA, 34-35 BS in LS; St Mary'sU 65 (Hist) MA. 6: Fr. 7: Libn Gilbert pub Lib, Gilbert Minn 35-37; Ref libn Winona Pub Lib, Winona Minn 37-40, Hd libn 44-58; Sr high libn & 2nd dir libs Winona Pub Schs, Winona Minn 40-44; Hd adult serv San Antonio Pub Lib, San Antonio Tex 58-61; Assoc libn St Mary'sU 61-. 8: Lecturer Dept Lib Sci Our Lady of the Lake Col 67-69; State lib chm Minn State Centennial 58; Tex governor's com on aging 60. 9: ALA; CathLA (chm San Antonio Unit 69-70); MichLA (pres 51-52); BexarLA (chm San Antonio 62-63); TexLA. 10: Zonta Intl; AAUW; Phi Alpha Theta. 15: 201 Melliff dr, San Antonio Tx 78216.

SAYER, EDITH ANGIE. b Commerce Ga 3 O 21. 5: Tift Col 39-42; Furman U 42-43 (Math) BS; Peabody summers 44-47 BS in LS, summers 61-62 (LS) 7: Math & Sci Tchr Blue Ridge High Sch, Blue Ridge Ga 43-44; Libn Blackshear High Sch, Blackshear Ga 44-45; Toccoa High Sch, Toccoa Ga 45-46; Rabun Co Lib, Clayton Ga 46-47, Truett-McConnell Jr Col 47-49, N Greenville Jr Col 49-. 9: ALA; SELA; SCLA. 10: Bus & Prof Womens Club. 15: Rte 1, Travelers Rest SC 29690.

SAYRE, IRENE (EUNICE). b Haworth NJ 20Ja 09. 5: Douglass Col 27-31 AB, 30-31 (LS); Montclair State Col summer 33 (Educ & Practice Tchg); Temple U 36-37 (Educ) Tchr Certif; Rutgers 63-64 MLS. 6: Fr, Ger. 7: Asst: Morris Co Lib, Morristown NJ, Pub Lib, Montclair NJ, Pub Lib, Kearny NJ, Paterson Pub Lib, Paterson NJ 31-35; Libn Paulsboro High Sch, Paulsboro NJ 37-38; Libn Matawan High Sch, Matawan NJ 38-39; Asst NY Pub Lib ext div 39-40; Asst Olin Lib, Wesleyan U 40-41; Libn Wilmington Elem Sch, Wilmington Del 41-42; Head Libn Community Free Lib, Glenside Penn 42-63; Head of ref dept WVILMINGTON Inst Free Lib, Wilmington Del 64-66, Br libn Kirkwood br 66-67; Adult serv sr libn Franklin br E Orange Pub Lib, E Orange NJ 67-. 9: ALA; PennLA (Exec Com 61-63); Phila DistLA (pres 61-63); NJLA. 10: Soroptimist; AAUW; Every Womans Club. 14: Admin, ref, adult serv. 15: E Orange Pub Lib Franklin Branch, 192 Dodd st, E Orange NJ 07017.

SAYRE, JOHN LESLIE. b Hannibal Mo 28 Mr 24. 4: Herwanna Harrouff. 5: UOkla 43-43; Phillips U 43-46 (Bible) BA; Phillips U Grad Sem 46-47; Yale Divinity Sch 47-50 (Rel in Higher Educ) BD; UTex 61-63 MLS. 6: Gk, Lat, Fr, Sp, Ger. 7: Campus minister First Christian Church, Stillwater Okla 50-57; Campus minister UChristian Church, Austin ex 57-62; Libn Phillips Grad Sem (Enid Okla) 62-. 9: ATheolLA; (Memb Com); ALA; OklaLA (Constit Com). 10: Beta Phi Mu. 12: "History of Disciples Student Work (50); "A Study of Desegregation and Integration at the University of Texas (63); "A Manual of Form for Term Papers and Theses (66); "Basic Books for the Ministers Library (66). 14: Clsf, theol wks. 15: Box 2212 Univ Sta, Enid Okla 73701.

SAYRE, SUSAN. b Indianapolis Ind 18 Mr 26. 5: Grinnell Col 43-45; StateU of Iowa 454-7 (Sp) AB. 6: Sp. 7: Hd Amer & Brit Exch Sect LC 58-. 9: DCLA. 15: 2628 Tunlaw rd NW, Washington DC 20007.

SCALES, JOHN THOMAS. b Cambridge Mass 5 J135. 7: Lib clerk: Harvard U Law Sch 55-58, Assn of the Bar City of NY 58-60, NYU Law Sch 60-61; Libn Paul, Goldberg, Weiss, Rifkind, Wharton & Garrison (Law), NYC 61-. 9: SLA; AALL; Assn of Law Libs Upstate NY; Law Lib Assn Greater NY. 15: 145 E 15th st, New York NY 10003.

SCALLY, SISTER MARY ANTHONY RSM. b Baltimore. 5: St Mary-of-the Woods 39 (Lat) AB; Rosary Col 39-40 AB in LS; Catholic U summers 57, 59 (Educ); UPenn summer 63 (Asian Studies); West Mich U summer 64 (Asian Studies). 6: Fr. 7: Libn Mt St Agnes Col(Baltimore) 40-53; Tchr-libn Parochial Schs, Va 53-56; Tchr-libn Mt De Sales High Sch, Macon Ga 56-58; Libn Pensacola Catholic High Sch, Pensacola Fla 58-. 8: Chm, Nat Cath Bk Week 68, 69; Sec John XXIII Human Rel Coun 65-; Adv NAACP Youth Coun, Pensacola Br 68-. 9: ALA; CathLA (Mid-South Conf: sec 60-62, v-chm 64-66; Bishop Toolen Unit: sec-treas 64-66, chm 67-69); FlaLA. 12: "Negro Catholic Writers (45). 13: Yes. 14: Sch libs (ya). 15: 18 W Jackson st, Pensacola Fla 32501.

SCANLAN, ELEANOR HARRIET. b Detroit Mich 3 O 03. 5: Simmons 22-26 (Bus) BS. 6: Fr, Sp. 7: Sec Meadowbrook Sch, Weston Mass 26-30; Sec Dartmouth Col 30-32, Registrar of freshmen 32-34; Sec & admin asst UMich (Ann Arbor) 34-50, Ref libn 50-, Ed 58-68. 8: Library consul: to Mountain States Employers Coun, Denver 54; to Cone Mills, Greensboro NC 56, 57. 9: SLA (Com Univ Indus Rel Libns). 10: UMich Faculty Women's Club. 12: Mng ed "Michigan Index to Labor Union Periodicals". 14: Catlg, ref. 15: 310 Maple Ridge, Ann Arbor Mi 48103.

SCANLAN, ELLEN C. b Portland Me 11 S 15. 5: Marygrove Col 33-37 (Fr) AB; Pratt 53-54 MLS. 6: Fr. 7: Tchr Jr High & Sr High Schs Me, NJ 37-43; Admiss & employ interviewing 43-53; Ref libn Pub Lib, Newark NJ 54-56; Sr libn 68-; Med libn VA Reg Off, Newark NJ 56-68. 9: ALA. 14: Ref. 15: 55 Hobart ave, Summit NJ 07901.

SCANNELL, ELIZABETH (FITZ SIMMONS). b Boston 14 O 17. 5: Simmons 34-38 (LS) BS. 7: Asst Boston Pub Lib Mattapan Br 38-39, Ref asst Kirstein Bus Br 39-43; Lt (sg) Spec Devices Div USN, Wash DC 43-46; Boston Pub Lib: Ref asst Kirstein Bus Br 46-47, 53-60, Catlgr ref div 60-65; Admin libn Boston Sch Com 65-. 8: Mem, Mass Adv Com, Title II ESEA. 9: ALA; MassSchLA. 10: LWV. 14: Sch libs. 15: 257 Pond st, Jamaica Plain Ma 02130.

SCANNELL, FRANCIS XAVIER. b Boston 15 D 17. 4: Mary R Donovan. 5: Harvard 38-42 (Lit) AB; Columbia 42-43 (Ref) BS. 6: Fr, Lat, Gk. 7: Ref asst Boston Pub Lib 43-46; Sr ref asst Detroit Pub Lib 46-48, Asst chief ref 48-53; Mich State Lib; Hd Reader Serv 53-65, Libn Ref Lib 65-68; State Lib (Mich) 68-. 9: ALA; Amer Soc Pub Admin; MassLA; MichLA. 11: Citation from Mich Constit Conv for Lib Serv. 12: "Michigan Novelists" (64). 13: Yes. 14: Admin, ref. 15: 3627 Colchester rd, Lansing Mich 48906.

SCANNELL, KAREN (COX). b Berkeley Cal 23 Ag 38. 4: James A Scannell. 5: UCal(Davis) 56-57 (Hist); UCal(Berkeley) 57-60 (Hist) BA; UMich 60-61 AMLS. 7: Libn San Francisco Pub Lib 61-64, Libn in chg of hist & soc sci dept 64-. 9: AHA; CalLA. 14: Ref. 15: San Francisco Pub Lib Civic Center, San Francisco Ca 94102.

SCARBOROUGH, RUTH ELLEN. b Scranton Pa 31 Mr 17. 5: Marywood 35-39 (Soc studies) BS in Ed; Syracuse 39-40 BS in LS; UMich summer 50 (LS). 6: Fr, Ger. 7: Libn Monmouth Jr Col, Long Branch NJ 40-43; Ref libn post lib, Ft Monmouth NJ 43-46; Libn Centenary Col For Women, Hackettstown NJ 46-. 8: Consul on bldgs & serv to several NJ Jr Cols 59-62; Lib eval Middle States Assoc of Cols & Sec Schs Accred com, 6 two-yr cols 52-69. 9: ALA; -ACRL (Dir-at-Large 64-68; Jr Col Lib Sect: sec 49-50, chm 52-53, dir 54-57); NJLA (sec 55-56, corr sec 61-62, Exec Bd 60-63; Col & Univ Sect; sec 57-58, pres 51-52 & 62-63); NJ Sr Col Assn (sec 63-64). 13: Yes. 14: Ref, bk sel. 15: 504 E Valley View ave, Hackettstown NJ 07840.

SCARSETH, SONJA (STROM). b Decorah Iowa 1 My 32. 4: William E Scarseth. 5: Luther Col 49-53 (Hist, Langs) AB; UMich (Ann Arbor) 53-54 AMLS. 6: Ger, Sp. 7: Catlgr Ball State Tchrs Col (Ball StateU) 54-55, 57-58; Catlgr UWis (Madison) 56-57; Libn gurnee Grade Sch, Gurnee Ill 62-65; Catlgr & summer sch libn Aurora Col 65-. 9: IllLA. 10: AAUW. 14: Catlg. 15: 216 B Linn ct, No Aurora Il 60542.

SCEPANSKI, JORDAN MICHAEL. b Yonkers NY 21 N 42. 5: Manhattan Col 60-64 (Eng lit, soc sci) BS; Emory 66-67 (Libnship) MLn. 6: Turkish. 7: Eng tchr US Peace Corps, Turkey 64-66; Stud asst Emory U div of libnship 66-67; Libn Uniondale Pub Lib, Uniondale Long Is NY 67-68; Instr research analyst (Sp/4) USA QM Sch, Ft lee Va 68-. 9: ALA. 10: Beta Phi Mu. 14: Govt docs, ref, admin. 15: 78 Buena Vista ave, Yonkers NY 10701.

SCHAAF, ROBERT WARREN. b Rochester NY 6 Je26. 4: Mary Drennan Schaaf. 5: Hamilton Col 46-50 (Hist, Pol Sci) AB; Johns Hopkins 50-52 (Internat Rel) MA. 6: Fr, Ger. 7: US Army (Pfc) Infantry European & American theaters 44-46; LC: Ed asst Ser Record Div 53-54, Processing & ref asst Ser Div 54-55, Asst head Internat Org Sect 55-65; Hd 66-. 9: ALA (sec Law & Pol Sci Subsection 64-67);-ACRL Subj Spec SEect); DCLA. 12: "Documents of International Meetings (53,59) "International Scientific Organizations (62). 14: Ref, catlg. 15: 7247 Reservoir rd, Springfield Va 22150.

SCHABAS, ANN (HENRIETTA) (FAIRLEY). b Toronto Can 14 My 26. 4: Ezra Schabas. 5: Tortonto 44-48 (Physics) BA; Smith 48-49 (Physics) MA; Toronto 63-64 BLS. 6: Fr. 7: Ref libn Toronto Bd of Educ 64-66; Asst Prof UToronto Sch of Lib Sci 66-. 9: CanLA; OntLA; Inst Profess Libns Ont; ASIS; AALS; CanALS. 10: Sigma Xi. 14: Ref, documentation. 15: 78 Highbourne rd, Toronto Can.

SCHABEL, DONALD (JACOB). b Chicago Ill 20 My 37. 4: Patricia Mackey. 5: No Ill U 55-59 (Mus) BS in Ed; UChicago 60 (LS); Rosary Col 66-67 MALS. 7: Libn Blue Island Pub Sch, Blue Island Ill 59-60; Libn Thornridge High Sch, Dolton Ill 60-61; Tchr Blue Island Pub Schs, Blue Island Ill 61-66; Libn (staff) Chicago Pub Lib 67-. 9: ALA. 15: 3522 Maple lane, Hazel Crest Il 60429.

SCHABERG, MINNIE (JONES) PADGETT. b Smoaks SC 3 Je 11. 4: Henry G Schaberg. 5: Peabody 31 (LS) BS, BLS. 6: Fr, Ger, Sp. 7: Libn Tenn State U 31-33; Dist lib supv WPA, St Louis 41-42; Asst stations St Louis Pub Lib 43; Hd acquis WashU 44-51; Hd libn Mary Inst, St Louis 57-67; Hd acquis UNC (Chapel Hill) 67-. 9: ALA (Equip Com 1966 Conv); SELA (Const Com 69-71); NCLA. 10: Lib Staff Assn. 12: "Directions and Shortcuts to Book Ordering" (68). 13: Yes. 14: Acquis. 15: 1452 Smith Level rd, Chapel Hill NC 27514.

SCHACHT, DAVID (WALDRON). b Rochester Minn 23 Ap 18. 4: Evelyn Schreiber. 5: Carleton Col 36-41 (Geol) BA; UOkla 41-43, 46-47 (Petroleum geol) MS; UDenver 62-64 (LS) MA. 6:Ger. 7: Lab tech in sedimentation US Geol Survey, Norman Okla 42; Aerial photomapper US Army, US & Europe 43-46; Sedimentationist US Bur of Reclamation, Denver 47; Photogeologist Geophoto Serv Inc, Denver 47-62; Sci & tech libn UWyo 64-67; Sci tech libn Ore State U 67-. 9: Amer Assn Petrol Geolts; SLA; Rocky Mountain Assn of Geolts (chm Educ Com 59-61); PNLA. 10: Phi Beta Kappa; Sigma Xi; Sigma Gamma Epsilon; AAUP; ; Sierra Club; Citizens for Clean Environ. 12: Co-auth "Geology of the Foothills and Front Range in the Vicinity of Morrison, Colorado (62) . 14: Sci & tech ref libn. 15: William Jasper Kerr Lib, Oregon State Univ, Corvallis Or 97331.

SCHAD, JASPER GRIPPER. b Los Angeles 29 J132. 5: Occidental Col 50-54 (Hist) BA; Stanford 56-57 (Hist) MA; UCLA 60-61 MLS. 6: Sp . 7: SP3 (Records Management) US Army 54-56; Bibliog checking UCLA 61; San Fernando Valley State Col: Soc sci libn 61-63, Acquis libn 63-64, Head bibliog libn 64-66, Hd acquis libn 66-. 8: Asst Prof of Hist, San Fernando Valley State Col, 65-67. 9: ALA; Org of Amer Histns; CalLA; So Cal Tech Proc Gr; So Cal Lib Coun Cal & Loc Hist. 10: ACLU; Phi Alpha theta. 13: Yes. 14: Bk sel, acquis, lib hist. 15: 15 San Fernando Valley State Col Lib, Northridge Ca 91326.

SCHADER, FREDDY (LYMAN) (MISS). b Little Rock Ark 1 N04. 5: UArk 22-26 (Eng) BA; Peabody summer 35 (LS) 55-57(LS); LSU 55-57 (LS) MS. 7: Elem sch tchr Parker Sch, Ft Smith Ark 26-32, Elem sch libn 33-48; Ark Lib Commsn, Little Rock Ark: Head circ dept 49-59, Admin asst 59-, Elem sch lib consul 53-. 8: Chm Ark Bk Fair, 54-. 9: NEA; ALA (Memb chm Reg 3 63-);-AASchL (Newbery-Caldecott Awards Com 60, Bylaws Com 62-, Exhib Round Table Bd 63-, Rec sec 65); SWLA (sec 59-61; reg chm child & yp sect 55-57); CSD (Com for Culturally Deprived 65-68); ArkLA (treas 39, sec 40, pres 61, Exhib chm 50-; chm Sch Lib Sect 49, Rep to SWLA). 10: Phi Kappa Phi; Beta Phi Mu; AAUW; Bus & Prof Women; Womens Nat Bk Assn. 12: Ed "Arkansas Elementary School Library Bulletin. 13: Yes. 14: Bks for child & yp, lib serv for child. 15: 1103 Barber ave, Little Rock Ark 72202.

SCHAEFER, BARBARA (KIRSCH). b Buffalo NY 5 Ap 32. 4: Paul Schaefer. 5: Eastman Sch of Music 50-56 (Music) B Mus; SUNY(Albany) 56-57 MLS; UPittsburgh 64-. 6: Ger, Fr. 7: Lib asst Sibley Music Lib Eastman Sch of Music 50-56: Head Libn Jr Col of Albany & Russell Sage Even Col 57-63; Asst Prof Sch of Lib Sci SUNY(Albany) 63-67, Assoc Prof (Geneseo) 67-. 9: ALA; NYLA; ASIS; AALS. 10: AAUP. 14: Tech serv, info retrieval, catlg, lib educ. 15: State Farm rd rte 1, Guilderland NY 12084.

SCHAEFER, CAROLYN W. b McAlester Okla 7 Jl 07. 5: Young Harris Col 26-28 (Liberal arts); George Washington Law Sch, 43-44 Law; Fla State U 60-62 (Hist) AB, 63-64 (LS) MA. 7: Asst sec Dade Fed Savings & Loan Assn, Miami Fla 39-42; Lt Comdr USN 42-45, 48-57; Faculty Fla State U 63-66; Law libn (catlgr) UGa 67-. 9: AALL. 10: Phi Beta Kappa; Phi Kappa Phi; Phi Alpha Theta; Beta Phi Mu. 15: 140 Baxter dr apt H1, Athens Ga 30601.

SCHAEFER, ELIZABETH (KIENTZLE). b Chicago 10 J123. 4: Walter J Schaefer. 5: Rosary Col 40-44 (LS) BA; Chicago 47-48 (LS) MA. 6: Fr, Ger. 7: Asst catlgr in chg period & bind Schaffner Lib Northwestern U 44-45; Army libn US Army Lib Serv, ETO, Darmstadt Germany 45-46; Asst libn River Forest Pub Lib, River Forest Ill 47-48; Asst libn Liberal Arts Lib De Paul U 48-49, Libn Sci Lib 49-50; Libn Women & Child Hosp Med Lib, Chicago 52-58; Gifts & exch libn John Crerar Lib, Chicago 50-55; Instr Rosary Col Dept of Lib Sci 51-52, 58-65; Volunteer libn St Vincent Ferrer Sch 66-67; Asst libn 67-. 9: ALA; SLA(Ill Chap: mem & co-chm Educ Com 52-54); IllLA; Chicago Lib Club (treas 51-52, chm Memb Com 52-53). 10: Elmwood Park Pub Lib Bd; LWV; Suburban Lib Syst Bd; St Vincent Ferrer Guild Lib & Lit Guild; Parents Com For Better Schs. 12: Ed "Serial Slants, ALA Ser RT (52-55). 13: Yes. 14: Pub libs, ref, catlg, child wk. 15: 1722 N 74th ct, Elmwood Park Il 60635.

SCHAEFER, PATRICIA. b Ft Wayne Ind 23 Ap 30. 5: Northwestern 47-51 (Piano) BM; UIll 57-58 (Musicology) MM; UMich summers 60-63 MALS. 6: Fr. 7: Typist US Rubber Co, Ft Wayne Ind 51-52; Asst to promotion manager WOWO, Ft Wayne Ind 52-55, Sec to program manager 55; Coordinator of pub & promotion Home Telephone Co, Ft Wayne Ind 55-56; Sec Fine Arts Found, Ft Wayne Ind 56-5; Asst Columbus Pub Lib, Columbus Ohio 58-59; A-v libn Muncie Pub Lib, Muncie Ind 59-. 9: ALA; IndLA. 10: Amer Musicological Soc: Muncie Sympohony Orchestra Bd; Womens League of Muncie Symphony; Muncie Matinee Musicale; Mu Phi Epsilon. 14: A-v materials, publ. 15: 303 Tara lane, Muncie In 47304.

SCHAEFER, RENATE (SOMMERNITZ). b Czechoslovakia 2 My 24. 4: Donald A Schaefer. 5: Bryn Mawr 41-45 (Hist) BA; UCal (Berkeley) 65 MLS. 6: Ger, Fr. 7: Libn San Francisco Pub Lib 65-67; Sr libn Pearl River Pub Lib, Pearl River NY 67-68; Dir Ridgefield Pub Lib, Ridgefield NJ 68-. 9: ALA; NJLA; Beyer-Passaic Lib Gp (treas). 14: Ref. 15: 81 Grand ave, Englewood NJ 07631.

SCHAEFER, RUTH L. b Watertown Wis 1 D 20. 5: N Tex State Col 41-43 (Hist) BA; Northwestern 46-47 (Hist) MA; UIll 50-51 (LS) MS. 6: Sp, Fr. 7: Educ, phil & psych asst libn

UIll(Urbana) 51-53, Educ, phil & psych libn 53-57; Supv libn Educ Lib NY Pub Lib 57-59; Libn in chg Communications Center Lib, Mutual of NY, NYC 59-. 9: SLA. 14: Ref (bus, econ). 15: Mutual Life Ins Co of NY Lib, 1740 Broadway, New York NY 10019.

SCHAEFER, VICTOR A(NTHONY). b Hays Kan 3 My 06. 4: Agne Elaine Murphy. 5: St Benedicts Col 24-28(Philos) AB; UMich 30-31 ABLS, 31-34 AMLS; Catholic U 37-44 (Mediaeval Hist). 6: Ger, Fr, Ital. 7: Asst UMich Libs 31-35; Employee Prin A Instituto Internazionale Dagricoltura Rome 35-36; Ref libn & catlgr St Thomas Col Penn 36-37; Head Prep Dept Catholic U 37-44, Instr Dept of Lib Sci 37-39, summer 37-43; Chief acquis dept Pentagon Lib US War Dept, Wash DC 44-48; Asst Dir UMich Libs 48-52; Dir of Libs UNotre Dame Ind 52-66; on leave of absence 66-68; Dir LC off W Germany 66-68; Dir Spec Collections & Curator rare bks UNotre Dame 68-. 8: Del Federation Internationale des Techniciens Agronomes, Brussels, 35; ALA Bldgs Inst, Chicago 63, Detroit 65. 9: ALA (Coop Catlg Com 39-40; Div catlg & clsf com on admin 51-52 & 52-53, Catlg code rev com 56-65); CathLA (Exec Bd 57-65); SLA (pres DC Chap 47-48; Md, Va, DC Reg Group of Catlgrs, chm 41-42); Midwest Inter-Lib Center (Bd Dirs 52-65; Center for Res Libs; Coun 65-, Bd dirs 65-66). 10: Caxton Club (Chicago); Knight Commander Equestrian Order of the Holy Sepulchre of Jerusalem. 11: Gen Educ BD, Humanities Fellow, Rome, 35-36; Elizabeth Rockwood Oberly Mem Award, ALA, 36. 12: "Apercu des bibliographies courantes concernant lagriculture et les sciences connexes (Rome 37); (with S von Frauendorfer) "Die Schrifttumsnachweise der Landairtschaftswissenschaft (Berlin 37); Tr (with others) "Rules for the Cataloging of Printed Books ALA (48); 5 Articles in "New Catholic Encyclopedia. 13: Yes. 14: Admin, tech serv, rare bks. 15: 805 E Angela blvd, South Bend In 46617.

SCHAEFFER, ELIZAJANE (KEMMERER). b Bethlehem Penn. 5: Moravian Col 34-37 (Eng) AB; Drexel 37-38 BS in LS. 7: Asst ref libn LehighU Lib 61; Circ libn 61-65; Ref libn Bethlehem Pub Lib, Bethlehem Penn 65-69; Adult servs consul Free Pub Lib Serv of Vt, Montpelier 69-. 9: ALA. 10: AAUW; LWV. 14: Adult serv, commun coop, ya serv. 15: PO Box 612, Montpelier Vt 05602.

SCHAEFFER, MADELINE (DINGER) (MRS EUGENE). b Tuckahoe NY 20 N 12. 5: Good Counsel Col 30-34 (Educ) BA; Fordham U summer 35; NYU 39-43 (Educ) MA;St Johns U 60-63 MSLS. 6: Sp. 7: Tchr Tuckahoe Pub Schs, Tuckahoe NY 35-39; Libn Wm E Cottle Elem Sch, Eastchester NY 59-. 9: ALA; NYLA; Sch Libns SE NY; ACEI; Tchrs Assn (Memb Chm); NY State Tchrs Assn (del Prof Practices Com 54-58). 10: Bus & Prof Womens Club; Libn, Eastchester Hist Soc. 14: Elem lib wk, bk sel, story-telling. 15: 2 Manchester rd, Eastchester NY 10709.

SCHAEFFER, REX M. b Polo Mo 9N 22. 4: Margaret Sechrist. 5: William Jewell Col 40-42, 46-48 (Hist) AB; UWis 51-52 (Amer Hist) MA. 7: Admin off (1st Lt) US Army Transporation Corps, Fla & Hawaii 43-46; Admin off (civilian) Army Transport Corps, Okinawa 49-50; Libn "Indianapolis Times 52-56; Libn "Rochester Times-Union & Democrat & Chronicle, Rochester NY 56-. 9: SLA (chm Newspaper Div 64-65). 14: Indexing (both manual & automated). 15: Rochester Times-Union Dem & Chronicle, 55 Exchange st, Rochester NY 14614.

SCHAEVE, CHARLES M. b Taylor Ridge Ill. 4: Marjorie Johns. 5: Uill 46-50 (Agric) BS, 50-51 (Agric econ) MS, 65-67 (LS) MS. 7: Asst life sci libn Purdue U 67-. 9: SLA; ALA. 10: Beta Phi Mu. 14: Agric ref. 15: 2410 F4 Happy Hollow rd, west Lafayette In 47906.

SCHAEVE, MARJORIE (JOHNS). b Rochester NY. 4: Charles M Schaeve. 5: URochester (Hist) BA; NY State U Col (Geneseo) (LS) BS; Chicago (LS). 7: Eng tchr-libn Collins Center High Sch, Collins Center NY; Eng tchr-libn Angola High Sch, Angola NY; Libn: Wes High Sch, Auburn NY, Leyden Community High Sch, franklin Park Ill, Kingswood Sch Cranbrook, Bloomfield Hills Mich; Libn & Asst Prof of Lib Sci U High Sch UIll(Urbana); Libn Bradley-Bourbonnais Community High Sch, Bradley Ill; Libn Champaign Central sr High Sch, Champaign Ill 64-; Coord of libs Unit 4, Champaign Ill 68-. 8: Educ Eval Consul for Spencer Press 54-56. 9: ALA-ASchL; NEA; IllLA; IllASchL (pres 50-51, Program Chm 61-62); IllEA; High Sch Libns of Chicagoland. 10: AAUW; Phi Beta Kappa. 14: Sch libnship. 15: 2410-F4 Happy Hollow rd, West Lafayette In 47906.

SCHAFER, AILEEN S. b Rochester NY 16 Je 35. 5: Ohio U 52-56 (Eng) AB; Drexel 57-58 MS in LS. 7: Lib trainee Rochester Pub Lib, Rochester NY 56-57; Libn III Free Lib of Phila 58-. 14: Ref. 15: 4903 Woodcrest ave, Phila Pa 19131.

SCHAFER, ELIZABETH PAINE (MRS AUGUST G). b Chicago Ill 15 Mr 10. 5: Radcliffe 27-31 (Hist) AB (Magna cum laude); NorthwesternU 38 (Retailing) MBA; NYU, UMinn, UMont, LoyolaU 40-67. 6: Ger. 7: Lib & research Harvard U Grad Sch of Bus Admin 31-36; Instr & coord Northwestern U Sch of Bus (Evanston Ill) 36-40; Personnel mgr Wiebolt Stores, Chicago 39-41; Personnel mgr Sears Roebuck & Co, Chicago 41-42; Lt US Naval Res, Miami & Glenview Ill 42-45; Tchr Whitefish High Sch, Whitefish Mont 48-53; Tchr Columbia Falls High Sch, Columbia Falls Mont 58-67; Libn Whitefish Pub Lib, Whitefish Mont 67-. 9: MontLA (Publicity Chm). 10: Whitefish Women's Club. 13: Yes. 14: Ref, customer serv. 15: Whitefish Pub Lib, Whitefish Mt 59937.

SCHAFER, EMIL. b Toledo Ohio 20 Jl 23. 4: Sylvia MILDRED Axler. 5: Brooklyn Col 46-49; (Physics) BS; Columbia 49-50 MSLS; Oak Ridge Sch of Reactor Sci 52 (Nuclear Reactor Phys); UCLA 62- (Ling, DP, math, infor mgt); IBM 66-69 (Systs Analysis) Certif. 6: Ger. 7: USAF Aircraft Armorer (Cpl) 42-45; Physics div & chief ref libn Oak Ridge Nat Lab, Oak Ridge Tenn 51-53; Sci analyst "Nuclear Science Abstracts AEC, Oak Ridge Tenn 53-55; Supv tech info center atomic power dept Westinghouse Electric Co, Pittsburgh 55-59; Chief Libn gen atomic div General Dynamics, San Diego 59-60; Physicist Convair Div General Dynamics Corp, San Diego 60-61; Tech info administrator Narmco Div Telecomputing, San Diego 61-62; Head Electronic properties info centr Hughes Aircraft Co, Culver City Cal 62-67; Mgr W Coast Off Radioptics Inc, Gardena Cal 67; Lib Systs analyst USoCal 67-. 8: Developed corporate entry manual for AEC 54; Adv to Martin Corp (Denver) 66; Gp Leader, SCTPG, UCal (Irvine) Conf on Lib Automation 68. 9: SLA; (SoCal Chap, Recr chm 65-66); ALA-ISAD (Organization Com);-RSD (Info Retr Com); LACASIS (Exec Com 65-66); Assn Comp Mach; CalLA; SoCal Tech Proc Gp. 12: Ed SLA; soCal Chap Bulletin 64-65, Pittsburgh Chap Bulletin 57-58; Comp "Glossary of Electronic Properties,AD 616783 (65). 13: Yes. 14: Data proc, info analysis, automation, lib mgt, ser. 15: 17210 Haas ave, Torrance Cal90504.

SCHAFER, JAMES E. b Bremen Ind 17 F 22. 4: Pauline Meints. 5: Manchester Col 39-43 (Speech) BA; Mich State U 55-56 (Rest Mgtt0; UMich 60-61 MALS. 6: Ger. 7: Tech 4 Grade US Army Infantry Radio Operator 42-46; pres Shafers Restaurants Inc, Detroit 46-60; Libn I Wayn Co Lib, Garden City Mich 61-62, Libn II, Romulus Mich 62-63, Libn III, Lincoln Park Mich 63-69. 9: ALA; MichLA. 10: Mich H st Soc. 15: 14151 Mettetal, Detroit Mi 48227.

SCHAFER, RONALD KEITH. b Lehighton Penn 16 Ag 36. 4: Grace Elizabeth Showalter. 5: Kutztown State Col 54-58 (LS) BS; Temple 60-66 (Secondary Educ) MS in Ed. 7: Jr-sr high libn Pottsgrove Sch Dist, Pottstown Penn 58-. 8: Dir of Publns, Pottsgrove Sch Dist, 64-; Newspaper adv, Pottsgrove Sch Dist, 60-63; Sch eval visiting coms, Middle States Assn of Cols & Secon Schs. 9: NEA; Penn State EA (Dept of Supv & Curr Devel); PennLA; PennSchLA; Pottsgrove EA; Chester-Montgomery SchLA (past pres & sec). 10: Alpha Beta Alpha, Kutztown Alumni Assn. 14: Ya libs. 15: Crest View lane, Rt 3, Pottstown Penn 19464.

SCHAFFER, CARMEN (BRAVO). b Manila Philippines 31 D 43. 4: Richard Allen Schaffer. 5: Goucher 61-62; UKan 62-65 (Chem) BS; UPittsburgh 65-66 MLS. 6: Ger. 7: Lib assoc Nat Lib of Med, Bethesda Md 66-67; Exec dir Off for Lib Serv Kan Reg Med Prog, Kan City Kan 67-. 9: ACS; MedLA; SLA; KanLA. 10: Beta Phi Mu. 14: Ref, pub serv. 15: 3708 Cambridge ave, Kansas City Ks 66103.

SCHAFFER, BROTHER EAMON CSC. b Beloit Kan 12 My 16. 5: Notre Dame U 37-41 (Educ) BA, 42-47 (Hist) MSE; Santa Clara 60; San Jose State 65. 7: Libn-tchr; Chicago 41-45, Biloxi Miss 45-58, Mt View Cal 58-. 9: CathLA. 14: High sch lib. 15: 1885 Miramonte ave, Mt View Ca 94040.

SCHAFFER, N INEZ. b Lorain Ohio. 5: Jackson Jr Col AA; Mich State U 53-55 BA, 65 (Soc sci & Educ) MAT; UMich 66-67 (LS). 7: Tchr Harper Creek Pub Schs, Battle Creek Mich 55-57; Tchr Allegan Pub Schs, Allegan Mich 57-66; Libn Highline Sch Dist, Seattle 67-. 9: NEA; ALA; WashEA; WashStateASchL; HighlineEA. 14: Sch lib serv (jr high level). 15: 18225 1st ave S 218, Seattle Wa 98148.

SCHAFFSTALL, MILDRED P(AINTER). b Harrisburg Pen 14 Ag 04. 5: Penn State U 21-25 (Liberal Arts) BA; Drexel 35-36 BS in LS. 7: Ref asst Penn State Lib 27-35; Libn Camp Curtin Jr High Sch, Harrisburg Penn 37-. 9: ALA; Penn A (Dept of Supv & Curr Devel); Penn State EA. 10: Penn Fed of Tchrs; Am Fed of Tchrs (Conv del, Rome 57, NYC 63). 15: Reesers Summit Mtd Rte, New Cumberland Penn 17070.

SCHALIT, MICHAEL. b Munich Germany 10 Mr 30. 4: Myoel D Sperling. 5: UDenver 49-53 (Chem) BS, 66-68 (LS) MA. 6: Ger, Fr, Ital. 7: Chem Eastman Kodak Co color tech div, Rochester NY 53-56; Research chem Great West Sugar Co, Denver 56-68; Ref libn Sandia Corp, Livermore Cal 68-. 9: SLA; Amer Transl Assn. 14: Ref. 15: 451 Bell ave, Livermore Ca 94550.

SCHALLER, REV PASCAL J OFM CAP. b Pittsburgh 25 Ap 24. 5: Fidelis Col & Sm 43-48 (Arts, Philos) BA; Capuchin Col 48-52; Catholic U 52-53 MS in LS. 6: Lat, Ger, Fr. 7: Instr in Latin, Ger, Gk & Libn St Fidelis Sem (Herman Penn) 53-. 9: ALA; CathLA; PennLA. 12: Comp "Bibliography of the Writings of the Capuchins of the Pennsylvania Province of St Augustine, 1882-1954". 13: Yes. 15: St Fidelis Lib, Herman Penn 16039.

SCHALLER, ROSALINDE. b Norfolk Neb 15 O 42. 5: Millikin U 60-64 (Eng) BA; UIll 65-66 MSLS. 7: Ref libn UIowa 66-68, Acquis libn 68-. 9: ALA; IowaLA. 10: Phi Kappa Phi; Beta Phi Mu; AAUW; Amer Bus Women's Assn; Nat Audubon Soc. 14: Acquis. 15: 424 S Clinton, Iowa City Ia 52240.

SCHALLERT, RUTH (ANNE FORTUN). b Whitehall Wis 31 Mr 20. 4: William L Schallert. 5: Luther Col 38-42 (Eng) BA; UMich 42-43 ABLS. 6: Ger. 7: Art libn State U Iowa 43-48; Libn Pacific Salon Investig Lab US Fish & Wildlife Serv, Seattle 54-57; Ref libn US Naval Oceanographic Off, Wash DC 63-66; Libn Botany Br lib Smithsonian Inst Libs. 9: SLA; DCLA. 10: Mayaone Assn, Norwegian-Amer Soc. 14: Ref, spec libs (sci, art or music). 15: Rt 1 Box 563, Laurel dr, Accokeek Md 20607.

SCHALOW, GERTRUDE E. b Fond du Lac Wis 9 D 25. 5: Colo Womans Col 43-44; UDenver 44-46 (Chem) BS in Chem, 46-48 (Math) MS, 50-51 (LS) MA. 7: Instr Colo Womans Col 48-50; Libn, subj reviser Naval Ordnance Test Sta, China Lake Cal 51-62; Libn, Sr subj catlgr Bur of Reclamation, Denver 62-. 9: SLA (Colo Chap; pres 63-64, Recr chm 65-67, Employment chm 67-68). 10: Iota Sigma Pi. 14: Catlg reports, coord indexing info retrieval, ref. 15: 2584 S Gaylord st, Denver Co 80210.

SCHANDORFF, ESTHER (MAY DECH). b Modoc Ind 9 Ag 23. 5: Pasadena Col 41-44, 49-51 (Eng) AB; USoCal 53-54 MS in LS. 7: USNR Waves Hosp Corps Pharmacist Mate 3/C 44-46; Asst libn tech serv Pasadena Col 54-67, Act hd libn 67-68, Hd libn 68-. 9: ALA; CalLA; West Theol LA sec-treas 58-62); Christian Libns Assn (pres) 62-64). 10: Beta Phi Mu. 14: Catlg. 15: 99 N Greenwood ave, Pasadena Cal 91107.

SCHANZ, SYLVIA. b Cleveland Ohio 18 Je 42. 5: SUNY (Stony Brook) 60-64 (Hist) BA; Pratt Inst 64-65 MLS. 7: Asst libn SUNY A&T Col (Farmingdale) Lib 65-67, Assoc libn 67-. 9: SUNYLA (treas). 14: Catlg. 15: 265 Roosevelt ave, Freeport NY 11520.

SCHAPPERT, LINDA G (GROTTO). b Greenfield Mass 3 S 41. 4: Gottfried T Schappert. 5: Pembroke 59-63 (Russian Lang & Lit) AB; Harvard 63-64 (Slavic Lang & Lit) AM; Simmons 64-66 MLS. 6: Russian, Ger, Fr. 7: Intern Harvard Col Lib 64-66, Slavic catlgr 66-. 12: "Sikkim, 1800-1968: an Annotated Bibliography" (68). 14: Catlg. 15: 43 Linnaean st, Cambridge Ma 02138.

SCHARER, AGNES H. b South Pittsburg Tenn 18 O 05. 5: E Tenn State Col 2729 (Eng) BS in Ed; Peabody Col summers 3436 BS in LS. 7: Elem tchr S Pittsburg City Schs, S Pittsburg Tenn 2327; Libn Brownlow Sch, Knoxville Tenn 2936, Knoxville High Sch, Knoxville Tenn 3638, Rule High Sch, Knoxville Tenn 3860, Whittle Springs Junior High, Knoxville 6062; Tchr & libn Fulton High, Knoxville Tenn 6265; Libn Knoxville Catholic High Sch, Knoxville Tenn 65. 8: Catlgr City Schs Lib Dept, Knoxville Tenn summers; Asst br lib Knoxville Lib Syst nights 65. 9: NEA; ALA; E TennEA; TennLA; Nat Retired Tchrs Assn. 10: Coun of Catholic Women; Knoxville Catholic Bus & Prof Women-s League. 14: Ref. 15: 533 Panorama dr, Knoxville Tn 37920.

SCHARF, CHARLOTTE (HANDLER). b NYC 8 Ap 26. 4: Erich Scharf. 5: Brooklyn Col 43-47 (Chem) BS; C W Post Col 66-69 MSLS. 7: Chem Kings Co Hosp, Brooklyn NY 47-49; Chem Med Arts Ctr Hosp, NYC 49-51; Chem abstractor Amer Chem Soc UOhio 58-67; Asst libn SUNY A&T Col (Farmingdale) 68-. 9: NYLA; NassauCoLA. 14: Automation. 15: 20 Atwater pl, Massapequa NY 11758.

SCHARFENORTH, GLENN R. b Chicago Ill 15 Ag 39. 5: Waldorf Col 57-59 AA; Augustana Col 59-61 (Sppech, Drama) BA; Rosary Col 65-67 MALS. 7: Tchr Sch Dist #101, West springs Ill 61-66; Asst NEast Ill State Col Lib 66-67; Asst to dir UIll 67-. 9: NEA; ALA; IllLA; Chicago Lib Club (2nd v-pres). 14: Admin. 15: 1947 Fremont, Chicago Il 60614.

SCHATZ, NATALIE (WALLICK). b NYC 8 Je 42. 4: Arthur Schatz. 5: Hunter Col 59-63 (Hist) BA; Harvard 63-65 (Soviet area studies); Simmons 66-67 (LS) MS. 6: Fr, Russian, Ital. 7: Lib intern Harvard Col Lib 65-67; Acquis asst Harvard Law Lib 67-. 10: Phi Beta Kappa. 14: Acquis. 15: 19A Forest st, Cambridge Ma 02140.

SCHATZ, SHARON M (ONEILL). b Goshen Ind 25 Je 38. 5: Butler U 56-60 (Eng, Journalism) BA; Purdue U 60-61 (Sociol); LSU 63-65 MSLS. 6: Fr. 7: Lib asst S Bend Pub Lib, S Bend Ind 61-63; Lib trainee LSU 63-64; Lib asst La State Lib 64-65; Libn Documentaion Inc, Bethesda Md65-67; Info systems research analyst LC 67-. 9: SLA (mem Nat Recru Com; Wash DC Chap; v-chm Documentation Group, chm Publns Com); ALA. 13: Yes. 14: Ref, automation. 15: 137 Duddington pl SE, Washington DC 20003.

SCHAUB, THERESA FLORENCE. b Lake Leelaau Mich 3 Ap 23. 5: Aquinas Col 42-44, 48-50 (Hist) AB; West Mich U summer 44; UMich 50-51 AMLS; Carnegie Inst of Tech 52. 7: hild libn Carnegie Lib of Pittsburgh 51-61; Head ext dept Saginaw Pub Lib, Saginaw Mich 61-63; Child libn & dir of child serv for Grand Traverse Area Lib Fed, Traverse City Pub Lib, Traverse City Mich 63-. 9: ALA; CathLA; MichLA. 10: AAUW. 14: Child serv. 15: Rte 1 Box 200, Lake Leelanau Mi 49653.

SCHAUZ, MILDRED M. b Milwaukee 29 Jl 19. 5: UWis 37-41 (Eng) BA; UWis 46-47 BLS. 7: Milwaukee Pub Lib: Libn I to III 47-, Child libn 47-49, 63-65, Ref libn 49-54, Neighborhood lib head 54-63, 65. 9: ALA, WisLA. 10: Milwaukee Pub Lib Employee Union; LWV; Milwaukee Film Circle; UWis Alumni Club. 14: Ref, child serv. 15: 2771 S Taylor ave, Milwaukee Wi 53207.

SCHEAFNOCKER, ELEANOR (ROCK). b Milford Del 5 Jl 29. 4: William E Scheafnocker. 5: Clarion State Col 47-51 (LS, Eng) BS in Ed. 7: Med libn Torrance State Hosp, Torrance Penn 51-55; Libn Wallings Road Elem Sch, Brecksville Ohio 65-. 9: OhioEA; NE Ohio Tchrs Assn; OhioASchL; Brecksville BEA. 10: PTA; Girl Scouts. 15: 2809 Oakes rd, Brecksville Oh 44141.

SCHECHTER, DANIEL DAVID. b Cleveland 27 My 21. 4: Audrey Gould. 5: Ohio State U 40-47 (Eng) BA; Columbia 47-48 (LS) BS, 48-52 (Adult Educ) MA; Rutgers 57-62 (Ed Admin) Ed S. 7: Radio operator US Signal Corps 42-45; Br libn Newark Pub Lib, Newark NJ 48-56; Sch libn Clifton Pub Schs, Clifton NJ 56-, Reb libn Montclair State Col 58-. 8: Sch lib eval, Middle States Assn, 61. 9: NEA (Life mem); NJSchLA; NJEA. 10: Phi Delta Kappa; ACLU. 14: Sch lib admin. 15: 419 Hillside ave, Nutley NJ 07110.

SCHECHTMAN, JOAN. b NYC 26 N 33. 5: Hunter Col 50-54 (Chem) AB (cum laude); Columbia 59-64 (LS) MS. 6: Ger, Sp. 7: Chem Boyce Thompson Inst for Plant Res, Yonkers NY 54-58; Tech info clerk Shell Oil Co, NYC 58-61; Research libn Merck Sharp & Dohme Res Labs, Rahway NJ 61-63; Head libn Union Carbide Research Inst, Tarrytown NY 63-68, Hd lib & tech info serv tech ctr 68-. 9: SLA; ACS. 10: Phi Beta Kappa. 13: Yes. 14: Tech lib admin. 15: Union Carbide Corp, Tarrytown Tech Ctr, Tarrytown NY 10591.

SCHECKTER, JUNE R. b Philadelphia Penn 1 Mr 24. 4: Spencer M Scheckter. 5: Syracuse 42-45 (Lat Amer trade) BS; Drexel 65-67 MSLS. 7: Libn tech processes Burlington Co Lib, Mt Holly NJ 67-. 9: ALA; NJLA. 10: Beta Phi Mu. 15: 46 Devon rd, mount Holly NJ 08060.

SCHECKTER, STELLA J. b Phila 30 N 26. 5: Temple 44-48 (Hist) AB; Drexel 49-52 MSLS. 7: Continuations asst in acquis div Temple U Lib 49-52; Jr asst ref dept HARTFORD Conn 52-53, Asst br libn 53-54; Jr asst lit & lang dept Enoch Pratt Free Lib, Baltimore 54-56, Sr asst bus & econ dept 56-58;

Head ref & loan div NH State Lib 58-. 9: ALA (Memb Chm, NH 64-); NHLA; NELA. 10: LWV; NH Hist Soc; Strawberry Banke, Inc; Commun Players of Concord; Concord Artists; Womens College Club; Concord Music Club; League of NH Arts & Crafts. 13: Yes. 14: Ref. 15: 32 Merrimack st, Concord NH 03301.

SCHEER, GLADYS (ELIZABETH). b Somerville Mass 31 My 14. 5: Hiram Col 45-48 (Religion, Psych) BA; Col of the Bible 48-50 (Religious EDUC) MRE; UKy 51-55 MS in LS. 7: IBM key punch operator E Ohio Gas Co, Cleveland 33-45; Dir religious educ Woodland Christan Chruch, Lexington Ky 48-50; Asst libn Col of the Bible, Lexington Ky 50-65; Asst libn Lexington Theol Sem 65-. 8: Ordained to Mnistry of Christian Churches, 55. 9: ATheoLA; SELA; KyLA. 10: Nat Coun of Churches; Nat Fellowship of Disciple Dirs; Ky Assn of Christian Churches. 12: "A Manual for Writers of Theses and Term Papers at The College of The Bible (57, 65). 14: Periods, circ, stud help. 15: Lexington Theol Sem S Limestone, Lexington Ky 40508.

SCHEER, MALCOLM ELLIOT. b NYC 28 F 33. 5: City Col (NY) 51-54 (Econ) BA; Columbia 59-60 MS in LS. 6: Fr, Ger. 7: Asst libn New Sch for Social Research 61-69, Asst to the chief lib 69-. 9: SLA; ALA; NY Tech Serv Libns; NY Lib Club; Metro Col Inter-Lib Assn (sec-treas). 14: Catlg, tech serv. 15: 305 E 56th st, NYC 10022.

SCHEESSELE, SISTER MARY KENNETH OSB. b Spencer Co Ind 5 D 22. 5: Saint Benedict Col 40-45 (Educ) BS in Ed, summers 46-48 (Educ, Theol); Catholic U 49-55 MS in LS; Ind U Ext 68 (Adult Educ) Certif. 6: Lat. 7: Elem tchr: St Paul Sch, Tell City Ind 45-48, St Ferdinand Sch, Ferdinand Ind 48-49, St Anthony Sch, St Anthony Ind 49-51; Tchr-libn Mater Dei High Sch, Evansville Ind 51-52; Tchr-libn St Ferdinand High Sch, Ferdinand Ind 52-53; Libn St Benedict Col, (Ferdinand Ind) 53-58; Libn Mater Dei High Sch, Evansville Ind 61-65; Asst libn St Benedict Col (Ferdinand Ind) 65-68; Libn-tchr Acad Immaculate Concpetion, Ferdinand Ill 65-; Libn Holland, Ind & Cass Twp, Dubois Co Ind 67-. 8: Organizer of, and adv to numerous sch libs. 9: ALA; -AASchL; -YASD; -LED; CathLA (High Sch Sect; Lib Educ Sect); NEA-DAVI; Amer Benedictine Acad (chm Lib Sect 67-); IndSchLA; A-V Instr Dir of Ind. 10: . 14: Lib wk with ya, bibliotherapy, a-v media. 15: Convent Immaculate Conception, E 10th st, Ferdinand Ind 47532.

SCHEFFEL, MARIE VIRGINIA (LAVIS). b Stratford Ont Can. 4: Lewis M Scheffel. 5: McMaster U 48-52 (Eng) BA; Toronto 52-53 BLS; McMaster U 59 (Eng) MA; ULondon 60-63 (Eng) MA. 6: Fr. 7: Asst ref dept Hamilton Pub Lib, Hamilton Ont 53-56; Asst libn Sun Life Assurance Co, Montreal 56-57; Asst arts & sci dept Hamilton Pub Lib, Hamilton Ont 58-60; Ref libn York U(Toronto) 63-65, Rare bks libn & Univ archivist 65-. 9: ALA; CanLA; OntLA; Inst Prof Libns Ont. 14: Rare bks, ref. 15: Apt 1004, 225 Glenlake ave, Toronto 9 Ont Can.

SCHEFFLER, ALBERTA (ELWELL). b Rock Island Ill 17 My 08. 5: Augustana Col 29 (Eng) BA; UMich 5 AMLS. 6: Fr, Sp. 7: Ref libn Pub Lib, Richmond Ind 49-61; Asst in catlg Ball State U Lib 61-. 9: ALA; Ind State Tchrs Assn; IndLA. 10: AUW. 14: Catlg. 15: 909 Rex st, Muncie In 47303.

SCHEFTER, JOSEPH A. b Langdon ND 20 Mr 29. 4: Carol Rstom. 5: Mankato State Col 53-56 (Soc Studies) BS; Chicago 58-62 (LS) MA; Syracuse 66-67. 6: Russian. 7: Tr US Army (Sgt) 48-52; A-v dir Oak Park & River Forest Hig Sch, Oak Park Ill 58-66; Lib dir US Dependent Schs, European area 67-. 8: Bd of Educ, Dist 59 Elk Grove Ill; Guest lecturer, Tex Womans U & Rosary Col 64-65. 14: Admin, a-v. 15: Directorate USDESEA, APO NY 09164.

SCHEHL, STELLA (FISK). b Providence 31 Ja 20. 4: Francis W Schehl. 5: Goucher 39-43 (Eng) AB; Columbia 45-46 BS in LS. 6: Fr. 7: Jr catlgr John Hay Lib Brown U 43-44; Lib asst Army Med Lib, Wash DC 44-45, Catlgr 46-52; Catlg revisor Armed Forces Lib of Med, Wash DC 52-58; Unit hd catlg sect Nat Lib of Med, Bethesda Md 58-63, Catlg ed 63-66, Asst hd & catlg ed catlg sect 66-. 14: Catlg. 15: 2745 Ordway st NW, Washington DC 20008.

SCHEIBER, HAZEL ANTHENE. b Burlington Iowa 28 O 12. 5: Parsons Col 31-35 (Hist) BA; UIll summers 39-42 BS in LS. 6: Fr. 7: High sch tchr various schs, Iowa 36-42; Libn Wilson High Sch, Cedar Rapids Iowa 43-46; Head catlgr Cedar Rapids Pub Lib, Cedar Rapids Iowa 46-48; Ref asst Lansing Pub Lib, Lansing Mich 48-49; Order libn Davenport Pub Lib, Davenport Iowa 49-51; Asst libn Iowa City Pub Lib, Iowa City Iowa 51-53; Asst ref libn Lincoln Pub Lib, Lincoln Neb 53-. 9: ALA; NebLA; MPLA; Lincoln LA. 10: AAUW; Nat Audubon Soc; Lincoln Audubon Naturalists Club. 14: Ref. 15: 913 F st, apt 2, Lincoln Neb 68508.

SCHEIDE, BENTON F. b Kennard Neb 3 F 18. 4: Iris Morrell. 5: Colo A&M Col 37-38; Colo Col 38-41 UDenver 46-48 (Econ) BA, 48-49 (LS) MA; West Res summer 59, & 61-62 (LS). 6: Fr, Ger. 7: (Sgt) Tech US Army 42-45; Lib asst Bur of Bus & Soc Research UDenver 48-49; Circ libn Ore State Col 49-51; Consruction wker, Denver 51-52; Head of circ dept Ala Polytech Inst Lib 52-56; Dir of Libs NE Mo State Tchrs Col 56-62; Asst lib, head of reader serv San Diego State Col 62-68; Dir of libs Cal State Col (Bakersfield) 68-. 9: ALA; Sla (treas San Diego Chap 65-66); CalLA. 10: AAUP. 14: Admin, pub ser. 15: Cal State Col Bakersfield, 615 California ave, Bakersfield Ca 93304.

SCHEIN, BEATRICE W(EISS). b NYC 21 My 13. 4: Bernard Schein. 5: Douglass Col 32-36 (LS) AB; Rutgers & Upsala 41-42 (Educ) Tchrs Certif; Columbia 43-51 (LS) MS. 6: Fr, Ger. 7: Gen asst Howard Whittemore Mem Lib, Naugatuck Conn 31-32, Newark NJ Lib Asst 36, Lib asst High Sch Studs 37-38, Head Wk with hogh sch studs 38-44, Head Teen Div 45-53, Research asst Grad Sch of Lib Serv; Rutgers U 54 Sch Libn & Ed Asst Bd of Educ, Newark NJ 57-60, Libn Vernon L Davey Jr High Sch, E Orange NJ 60-. 8: Org, dir & partic in var insts on lib serv to teen-agers, sponsored by ALA & Rutgers, 47-58. 9: ALA (Coun 46-50 & 51-53); Intercult Action Com 52-53, Jt Com Ala-Child Bk Coun 62-68;-YSD (chm Reading Round Table 47-48, mem Adv Com Boy Scouts of Amer 65-71); NEA; NJLA; NJEA; (chm Adv Com Boy Scouts 66-67); Essex Co (NJ) SchLA; E Orange (NJ) EA. 10: Adv, Newark Youth Coun (hon mem). 12: Co-auth "Public Library Plans for the Teen Age (48); "Leisure-Time Interests and Activities of Newark Youth (51); Contrib & ed "Open the Book (62). 13: Yes. 14: Child & yp serv. 15: 405 Highland ave, Newark NJ 07104.

SCHEIN, J BERNARD. b NYC 16 N 11. 4: Beatrice Weiss. 5: Rutgers 35-39 (Hist) BA; Pratt 41-42 BLS; Columbia 44-46 (Admin of Adult Educ) MA. 6: Ger. 7: Newark Pub Lib, Newark NJ: Lib asst 35-41, Br libn 42-52, Chief Libn acquis & processing 53-54, Asst dir 54-58, Deputy dir 58-. 8: Lecturer: NJ Col for Women Lib Sch 51-52, Drexel Lib Sch, summer 64, Rutgers Lib Sch 62-; Consul; fairleigh Dickinson U 69, Chester (Penn) Pub Lib 66, Westchester Co Lib Syst 67-69. 9: ALA-LAD (chm Nomin Com 65, chm Cetif Com 57); NJLA (pres 59, treas 50; chm Certif Com 60-, chm Election Com 61-63). 10: Lions Club; Municipal Career Mens Club; Bd TRUSTEES, Family Serv Bur of Newark; Newark Civic Clubs Coun; Little Symphony of Newark. 13: Yes. 14: Admin. 15: 405 Highland ave, Newark NJ 07104.

SCHELL, ALLAN HERBERT. b Sioux City Iowa 13 Jl 31. 4: Joyce E Dillon. 5: USD 49-52, 53-54 (Chem) AB; West Res 62-63 (LS) MS. 7: Chem AEC Labs Iowa State Col 54-56; Development engnr Union Carbide Corp, Fostoria Ohio 56-68; Chem No Reg Research Labs, Peoria Ill 59-60; Mathematician Aero Chem Research Labs, Princeton NJ 60-62; Libn UNotre Dame (Ind) 63-. 9: ACS; SLA. 14: Ref. 15: 430 S 27th st, South Bend In 46615.

SCHELL, HAROLD BENTON. b E Liverpol Ohio 28 O 25. 4: Joan Bruning. 5: Kent State U 52; Wittenberg U 52-55 (Philos) AB; Ohio State U 55 (Philos); Syracuse 56-57 MS in LS. 7: Radioman 3/C US Navy 43-46; Sales agent United Airlines, Chicago 46-48; Manager Harmony House Music Store, E Liverpool Ohio 48-52; Cornell U, Ithaca NY Asst catlg libn 57-59, Admin asst to dir of lib 59-62, Coordinator of reader serv 62-63, Asst to Dir of Lib 63-64; Asst Dir of Libs Reader Serv UMd 64-66; Asst dir of libs pub serv & bldg planning UPittsburgh 66-69; Libn Fondren Lib, Assoc dir of Univ libs, Assoc Prof div of Humanities & Sci So Meth U 69-. 8: Consul; NY State Lib 66-; Wright State U, Dayton 66-; Grad Sch of Lib & Info Serv, UMd 67; UMiss 67-68; Edinboro State Col Lib 68. 9: ALA (Urban Univ Com); MDLA; DCLA. 13: Yes. 14: Bldgs & equip, admin, personnel. 15: Fondren Lib, Southern Methodist Univ, Dallas Tx 75222.

SCHELL, MARY ELEANOR. b Centerville Ind 14 N 16. 5: Ind U 35-38 (Lat) AB; UMich 41 ABLS. 7: Ref asst Ind U Lib 41-42; Catlgr Ind State Lib 42-44; Acquis libn 44-47; Cat&gr Sacramento City Lib, Sacramento Cal 47-49; Libn I-IV Govt Publ Sect Cal State Lib 49-. 9: ALA; SLA; CalLA (Documents Com 53-58 & 63-65). 14: Govt publns. 15: 3018 T st apt 4, Sacramento Ca 95816.

SCHELLENBERG, THEODORE R. b Harvey Co Kan 24 F 03. 4: Alma Groening. 5: Tabor Col 24-26; UKan 26-28 (Hist) AB, 29-30 (His) AM; UPenn 30-34 (Hist) PhD. 6: Ger, Fr, Sp, Dutch. 7: Exec sec Jt Com on Materials for Research, Amer Coun of Learned Sco & Soc Sci Rsch Coun 34-35; Hist asst Nat Park Serv, US Dept of Interior, Wash DC 35; Nat Archives: Deputy examiner 35-38, Chief agric dept archives 38-45, Program adv 48-49, Dir of archival mgt 50-56, Asst archivist of the US 57-63, Ref 63; Assoc nat dir Survey of Fed Archives WPA 36; Records OF, Off of Price Admin & War Prod Bd 45-48. 8: Fulbright lecturr, Austrailia & New Zealand, 54; Dir Insts on Archival Mgt, American Univ 59 & 61; Grad Sch of Lib Sci UTex 60; Sch of Libnship UWash 62; Sch of Lib Serv Columbia U 65; Amer Spec, State Dept, South Amer countries, 60; Div Inter-Amer Archival Seminar, 61; Grad Sch Lib Sci UIll 67; Sch Lib Sci Syracuse U 67-68; Dept Lib Sci Catholic U 68-69. 9: AHA (chm Com on Hist Source Materials 36-38); AA (chm Com on Internat Rel 55-60, chm Com on Educ & Train 64-); Internat Coun on Archives (Hon mem); Amer Assn State & Loc Hist; Sociedad mexicana de archivistas; Associacion veneolana de archiveros. 10: Phi Beta Kappa; Phi Delta Kappa; Pi Sigma Alpha. 11: Meritorious serv award Gen Serv Admin, 57; Waldo G Leland Prize, SAA, 59. 12: "Modern Archives: Principles and Techniques (56); "The Management of Archives (65); Other bks publ in Brazil & Argentina. 13: Yes. 14: Archival train, esp in lib sch, devel of archival methodology. 15: 263 Military rd, Arlington Va 23217.

SCHELLHORN, MARY (ANN) (LEIBOLD). b Decatur Ill. 4: Greuling Cope Schellhorn. 5: UIowa 61-64 (Hist), 67-68 (LS) MA; UN Dak 64-66 (Hist) BA. 6: Sp. 7: Interlib loan IN Dak Lib 66-67; Ser libn UIowa Libs 68-. 9: ALA. 14: Acquis, ref, catlg, archives. 15: 2317 Friendship st, Iowa City Ia 52240.

SCHENK, REV DEMETRIUS F TOR. b Loretto Penn 16 O 17. 5: St Francis Col & Sem 39-47 (Philos) BA; Catholic U 47-49 BS in LS. 7: Libn St Francis Prep Sch, Spring Grove Penn 48-53; Libn Col of Steubenville 53-. 9: CathLA (West Penn Unit; chm 59-60; chm Col & Univ Sect 65-67); ALA-ACRL (Tri -State Chap). 15: Col of Steubenville, Franciscan way, Steubenville Oh 43954.

SCHENKER, TILLIE (ABRAMSON) (MRS). b Baton Rouge La 12 N 10. 5: LSU 30 BS, 34 (LS) BS. 7: Field wker circ dept La State Lib 34-39; Asst libn E Baton Rouge Parish (La) Lib 39-46, Libn 47-. 9: ALA; SWLA; La Adult Educ Assn; LaLA (pres 62-63); Baton Rouge Lib Club. 10: La Conf of Soc Welfare; Baton Rouge Tuberc Assn; YWCA; Baton Rouge Guidance Ctr; Family Counseling Serv. 14: Admin, ref. 15: 220 Steele blvd, Baton Rouge La 70806.

SCHER, LEWIS (JOSEPH). b NYC 8 F 14. 4: Marion Feingold. 5: City Col (NY) 32-36 (Eng) BS in SS, 36-39 (Educ) MS in Ed; Columbia 37-40 BS in LS. 6: Fr. 7: Fellow Lib City Col (NY) 36-40, Lib asst even session 36-42; (Pvt) US Army Spec Serv Asst to 1st Corps Libn 42-43; Research libn Time Inc, NYC 40-60; Asst libn Hunter Col even session 54-65; Head Libn Jamaica High Sch, Jamaica NY 61-; Lecturer Queens Col Dept of Lib Sci (NY) 66-. 8: Bk reviewer, Bd of Educ, NYC, 60-; Lecturer lib sci Queen's Col (NY) 65-66; Lib consul ref bk sect McGraw-Hill Book Co, NYC 66-; Standing Com on Secondary Sch Lib Bks NYC Bd of Educ 65-. 9: NYC Sch Libns Assn. 14: Ref, sch admin, educ research. 15: 6700 - 192nd st, Flushing NY 11365.

SCHER, RITA (SAMET). b NYC 19 Mr 44. 4: Murray Scher. 5: CCNY 60-64 (Hist) BA; Columbia 64-66 MS in LS. 6: Fr, Sp. 7: Libn NYC Pub Lib 64-66; Asst libn SUNY(Binghamton) 66-68, Libn II UTex (Austin) 68-. 9: ALA. 14: Acquis. 15: 1202 Newning ave, Austin Tx 78704.

SCHERER, HENRY (HOWARD). b Scribner Neb 24 F 04. 4: Alice Charlotte Soker. 5: Midland Col 21-25 (Philos, Psych) AB; Central Lutheran Theol Sem 24-26, 27-28 BD; Creighton 34-39 (Educ) AM; USoCal 52-54 MS in LS, 54-60 Ed D. 7: Var parishes in Lutheran Church, Ind to Cal 28-56; Asst libn Midland Col 56-60; Libn Lutheran Theol Sem (Phila) 60-. 8: Charter mem Luth Hist Conf (Exec Com 62-63). 9: ATheolLA (chm Stat Com) 63, Exec Com 66-68). 10: Phi Delta Kappa; Boy Scouts. 13: Yes. 14: Admin. 15: 7301 Germantown ave, Phila 19119.

SCHERGER, MOZELLE (SPAINHOUR). b Stokes Co NC 17 D 16. 4: George Richard Scherger. 5: Appalachian State Tchrs Col 33-37 (Eng) BA; UNC summers 38-41 BS in LS. 7: Tchr Cramerton High Sch, Cramerton NC 37-41, Libn 41-42; Base libn Laurinburg-Maxton AFB, Maxton NC 42-43; Libn Piedmont Jr High Sch, Charlotte NC 43-44; Army libn, Camp Breckenridge Ky 45; Base libn Pope Air Field, Fayetteville NC 46; Libn Charlotte Col 57-63; Ser & docs libn UNC (Charlotte) 64-. 15: 701 St Julien st, Charlotte NC 28205.

SCHERR, JEAN W. b Columbus Ohio 28 N 14. 5: adrian Col 36 (Eng Lit); BA Ohio State U 38 (Eng Lit) MA Chicago 45 BSLS. 7: Lib asst Columbus Pub Lib, Columbus Ohio 38-42; Off of Censorship, San Antonio Tex 42-45; Asst in catlg Ball State U 45-47; Asst libn in charge of tech serv 53-; Catlgr Ohio State U 47-53. 9: ALA; RTSD Ind; Ohio Valley Group of Tech Serv Libns. 10: AAUP. 14: Catlg. 15: 2300 White River blvd apt 15, Muncie In 47303.

SCHERR, JULIAN MORRIS. b Hartford Conn 6 N 06. 4: Minnie K Nattboy. 5: City Col (NY)23-27 (Sci) BS 27-32 (Langs) AB, 32-33 (Educ) MS Ed; Columbia 33-34, 37-39 BSLS. 6: Ger, Hebrew, Lat, Gk. 7: Bacteriologist Dept of Health, NYC 27-40 Libn for Bellevue doctors dept hosps, NYC 40-62; Ref libn NY Pub Lib 45; Machine Hand Rowland Printing Corp, NYC 46; Salesman Arrow Shirt Dept Abraham & Straus, Brooklyn NY 47-57; Lib asst Bd of Educ, NYC 57-67, Tchr of Lib 62-. 8: Admin sec, Brookdale (Beth-El) Hosp, Med Ctr, Brooklyn NY 58-68. 9: NYC Sch Libns Assn; Jewish Tchrs Assn, NYC. 10: United Fed Tchrs, NYC; Amer Red Cross (LC) Braille Certif Transcriber. 13: Yes. 14: Ref bks, med bks, sch lit, bibliog. 15: 1248 E 98th st, Brooklyn NY 11236.

SCHERTZ, Morris. b NYC 3 My 29. 4: Marcia Lang. 5: NYU 48-52 (Hist) BA; Pratt 55-56 MLS. 7: Br libn Brooklyn Pub Lib 56-58; Rare bks libn Colby Col 58-62; Libn State U Col (Buffalo NY) 62-64; Assoc dir tech serv UMass 64-. 8: Mem Adv Bd NE Lib Info Netwk. 9: ALA; NELA. 10: Beta Phi Mu. 13: Yes. 14: Catlg, dta proc, acquis. 15: Univ of Mass Libs, Amherst Ma 01002.

SCHETZER, BETTY (KOFFMAN). b Detroit 4 D 23. 4: J D Schetzer. 5: UMich 42-45 (Hist) AB, 55-58 ALS. 7: Ed asst Mich Alumnus Quarterly 52-54, UMich Res Inst 58-60; Order libn Planning Res Corp, Los Angeles 64-65; Child libn Palos Verdes Lib, Palos Verdes Cal 65-66, YA libn 66-67, Br libn 67-. 9: ALA; CalLA. 15: 2623 Via Carrillo, Palos Verdes Estates Cal 90275.

SCHICK, BETH McDONALD. b Topeka Kan 29 O 10. 4: George B Schick. 5: Grand Island Col 29-31 (Langs); UNeb 31-32 (Langs) BA; Chicago 32-34 (Langs). 6: Fr,Sp, Ital, Ger, Portu, Russian. 7: Editorial Scott, Foresman Publ Co, Chicago 37-39; Purdue U; Interlib Loan Lib 52-58, Head lib documentalist Thermophysical Properties Research Center 58-65, Head lit Monitoring 65-. 12: Comp "Masters Theses in the Pure and Applied Science (ann publ). 14: Documentation of govt & sci reports, transl. 15: Purdue Ind Res Park, 2595 Yeager rd, W Lafayette Ind 47906.

SCHICK, CYNTHIA. b Xenia Ohio 17 Jl 31. 5: Northwestern 49-53 (Educ) BS; San Diego State Col currentl (LS). 6: Sp. 7: Sec in tech info & Intelligence Br Wright-Patterson AFB, Ohio 55-56; Clerk & Document Center Tech Info Serv Gen Atomic Div Gen Dynamics Corp, La Jolla Cal 56-63; Libn Mercy Col of Nursing Lib Mercy Hosp, San Diego & Med libn Mercy Hosp 64-65; Engnr libn Stromberg-Datagraphix Inc 65-. 9: SLA (Pub Rel Chm); CalLA. 10: Nat Mgt Club. 14: Ref in atomic energy field, med field & electronics. 15: 818 San Juan pl, San Diego Ca 92109.

SCHICK, FRANK L(EOPOD). b Vienna 4 F 18. 4: Renee Schick. 5: Wayne State U 40-43, 45 (Govt) BA; UChicago 46-47, 47-48 BLS, MA (Pol Sci); UMich 50-57 (LS) MLS, PhD. 6: Fr, Ger. 7: Asst to ref libn UChicago 47-48; Jr asst libn Wayne State U 48-54; Lecturer in lib sci UMich 51-54, 55-58; Assoc in lib serv & Asst to the dean Columbia U 54-55; Asst libn Wayne State U 55-58; Coord adult educ & lib stat & Asst dir lib serv br US Off of Educ, Wash DC 58-66; Dir Sch of Lib & Info Sci UWis (Milwaukee) 66-. 8: Visiting Prof (summer session) UNC 62, 6; US rep to 1964 Unesco metting on Standardization of bk publg & period stat, Paris, 64. 9: Internat Org for Standardiz TC/46 (chm Stat Com); ALA (Coun); SLA; ASA/Z39 (chm Stat Com); DCLA. 12: "The Paperbound Book in America (58); Comp "Reviews in Library Book Selection (58); Co-auth "The Cost of Library Materials; Price Trends of Publications (61); Ed "The Future of Library Service; Demographic Aspects and Implications (62); Co-auth "Statistics of Public Library Systems Serving Population of 100,000 or More, Fiscal Year 1960 (61); Co-auth "Statistics of Public Library Systems Serving Population of 50,00 to 99,999: Fiscal Year 1960 (62). 13: Yes. 14: Lib & publ stat, lib res, automation, educ for libnship, col & univ lib admin. 15: 7460 N Mohawk rd, Milwaukee Wi 53217.

SCHICKLER, CLAIRANN. b Seattle 4 Je 42. 5: UWash 60-64 (Pol Sci) BA, 64-65 M Libr. 6: Sp, Ger. 7: Libn I UCal(Irvine) 65-67; Catlgr UWash (Seattle) 67-. 9: ALA. 10: Beta Phi Mu. 14: Catlg. 15: Cat Div Univ of Washington Lib, Seattle Wa 98105.

SCHIEFERSTEIN, GRACE ANNA. b Glen Moore NJ 28 D 15. 5: Albright Col 34-38 (Ger) AB; State Tchrs Col Cal Penn 39-40 Certif; Syracuse 56-59 (LS) MS. 6: Ger. 7: Asst child libn Reading Pub Lib, Reading Penn 43-47, Br libn 48-56, Hd circ dept 57-66, Dir adult serv 67-. 9: ALA; PennLA. 10: Beta Phi Mu. 15: 1907 Bernville rd, Reading Pa 19601.

SCHIELD, SANDRA (EPPLER. b Strawberry Point Iowa 4 Ja 42. 5: Wartburg Col 59-61 (Eng); Iowa State U 61-62 (Eng); Long Beach State Col 62-63 BA in Eng; UIll 63-64 (LS) MS. 6: Ger, Fr. 7: Stud asst Wartburg Col Lib 59-61; Extramural loans libn UIll(Urbana) 64; Asst humanities & soc sci libn UHouston 65-67, Ref libn Law Lib 68, Asst sci libn 68-. 9: SLA. 10: Phi Kappa Phi; Beta Phi Mu. 11: Catherine L Sharp Fellowship. 14: Ref. 15: Box 30, 3201 Wheeler, Houston Tx 77004.

SCHILD, MARION. b Fiume Italy. 5: Munich U (Romance Lang) PhD; Columbia (LS) BS. 6: Ger, Ital, Fr. 7: Catlgr Columbia U Lib 41-45; LC: Catlgr Descr Catlg Div 46-52, Head Ger Lang Unit Descr Catlg Div 52-57, Head Post-1951 Imprints Sect Union Catlg Div 57-64, Head Eng Lang Sect Descr Catlg div 62-64, Deputy prin catlg 64-68, Field dir LC Off, Florence Italy 68-. 8: Catlgr, Rosenwald Collection, LC 47-50. 9: ALA; DCLA. 14: Catlg. 15: Via Leopavdi 4, 50121 Florence Italy.

SCHILLER, ANITA (ROSENBAUM). b NYC 16 Je 26. 4: Herbert I Schiller. 5: NYU 49 (Econ) AB; Pratt 5 MLS. 6: Fr. 7: Ref libn Amer Bankers Assn, NYC 49-51; Asst ref libn LIU 59-60; Ref libn Nat Ind Conf Bd, NYC 60-61; Instr UIll Grad Sch Bus Admin 61-62; Asst ref libn Pratt Inst 62-63; Research asst UIll Lib Research Ctr 63-64, Research assoc 64-. 8: Chief investigator, USOE, Supported study of acad lib 9: ALA; IllLA. 10: Beta Phi Mu. 12: "Library Service in the Illinois Portion of the St Louis Metropolitan Area" (66); "Characteristics of Professional Personnel in College & University Librarians" (69). 13: Yes. 14: Ref. 15: Univ Ill Lib Res Center, Urbana Il 61801.

SCHILLER, ARLINE (SLACK). b San Gabriel Cal 7 N 12. 5: UCal(Berkeley) 32-37 (Home Econ) AB; USoCal 63 MSLS. 6: Sp. 7: Prof area coord GSA, San Diego Cal 41-43; Exec dir GSA Anaheim Council Cal 45-50; Elem sch tchr, Garden Grove Cal 50-55, Jr high sch libn 55-58, Dist sch lib supv 58-65, Dir lib & textbk serv 65-66; Program specialist off lib serv Dept of Educ, Hawaii 66-. 8: Assisted in organ OrangeCoSchLA 59; Mem Adv com Textbk Div State Dept of Educ Cal 61-66; So Cal Repr State Survey pf Sch Libs 63; Maj respon for State of Hawaii Admin of Elem & Secon Educ Act (ESEA), Title II. 9: ALA; -AASchL; NEA; DAVI; CalLA; CalASchL (So Sect: chm Com to Develop "Basic Bks List" 63, treas 66. 10: Cal Congress Parents & Teachers. 13: Yes. 14: Child lit, sch libnship. 15: 2415 Ala Wai blvd apt 2006, Honolulu Hi 96815.

SCHIMMELBUSCH, JOHANNES SEVERIN. b Vienna Austria 19 Mr 35. 4: Ruth Sherwood. 5: UWash 59-64 (Ger Lit) BA, 64-65 (LS) ML. 6: Ger. 7: E-5 US Army Sig Co, Alaska Communication System, Juneau Alaska 55-57; E-5 US Army Sig Co, Seattle Wash, Alaska C Syst 57-58; Libn McNeil Island Fed Penitentiary, Wash 65-66; Engring libn Puget Sound Naval Yard, Bremerton Wash 66-67; Asst libn Bonneville Power Admin Portland Ore 67-68, Act libn 68-. 9: ALA; Wash State LA; SLA; OreLA. 10: Phi Delta Kappa; Delta Phi Alpha; Continental Club, Seattle. 14: Info retrieval, ref, rare bks, pub & univ lib admin, bibliog. 15: 3180 SW 72nd ave, Portland Or 97225.

SCHIMMELPFENG, RICHARD HAROLD. b Highland Park Ill 13 Jl 29. 5: Lake Forest Col 47-49 (Eng, Hist); UIll 49-51 (Eng, Hist, LS) BS; Columbia 54-55 MS. 6: Fr, Sp. 7: Catlgr Washington U (St Louis) 55-58, Head catlg dept 58-65; Asst dir for spec collections Conn 65-. 9: ALA; MoLA (Exec sec 63-64); ConnLA; BSA. 10: Beta Phi Mu; The Typophiles. 12: "Preliminary Subject Heading List in Adult Education (55); C&RL Indexer (55-); Ed "Proceedings of Institute on Use of the Library of Congress Classification," (68). 14: Catlg, rare bks. 15: 74 Foster dr, Willimntic Con 06226.

SCHIMMELPFENNIG, MARJORIE W. b Westboro Mo 19 Ap 12. 5: UNeb 29-34 (Fr, Ger) AB; UBonn Germany 32 (Ger); ULausanne (Switzerland) 33 (Fr); UNeb 42 (Hist) MA; Ariz State U summer 63 (LS); Tex Woman's U summer 66 (LS). 6: Ger, Fr. 7: Humphrey High Sch, Humphrey Neb: Soc studies tchr 41-57, Supt of Schs 52-57, Libn 52-. 8: NSEA-NEA Educ Travel Consul, Neb. 9: NEA (Life mem); ALA; NebLA; Neb State EA. 14m; ref. 15: Humphrey Neb 68642.

SCHINK, RONALD JOHN. b Youngstown Ohio 9 Ap 32. 4: Nancy Crofford. 5: Youngstown StateU 51-55 (Mus) BME; West Res 55-56 MLS. 7: Asst circ libn YoungstownU 51-55; Asst chem libn Case Inst of Tech 55-56; Dir Girard Free Lib, Girard Ohio 56-58; Dir State Lib Serv Ctr, Napoleon Ohio 58-68; Dir Taiwan Sem Lib, Taichung Taiwan 62; Dir Paulding Co Carnegie, Paulding Ohio 68-. 8: Bldb consul Fayette & Pemberville libs; Film juror Amer Film Festival; Pres RJ&N Finance Corp; Pres NY Henry Co Commun Concert Assn 63-; Pres Napoleon JCC 61-62. 9: ALA; OhioLA. 11: Commun Leader of Amer Award 69. 14: Admin. 15: 15 Lakeview dr, Napoleon Oh 43545.

SCHINKEL, ANNA (EVANS). b Roswell NM 4 Je 07. 5: SW Mo State Col 28 BS; SW Baptist Theol Sem 31 BRE; Fla State U 57 (LS) MS. 7: Tchr Pub Schs, Clever Mo 28-29; Sec y-p wk Furst Baptist Ch, Springfield Mo 31-33; Tchr Mather Sch, Beaufort SC 33-37; Tchr pub sch, Whigham Ga 51-54; Tchr & libn Pavo Sch, Pavo Ga 54-57; Dir Colquitt-Thomas Reg Lib, Moultrie Ga 58-. 8: Sec & mem of Ga Profess Lib Adv Com, Title II, Lib Serv & Construction Act. 9: ALA; GaLA; SELA. 10: Pilot Club; Moultrie Art Assn. 14: Ref, rare bks. 15: 1312 10th st SW, Moultrie Ga 31768.

SCHINKEL, JEAN (YEAKLEY). b New Kensington Penn 9 Ap 19. 4: Peter W Schinkel. 5: Wellesley 37-40 (Eng, Lit); Simmons 40-41 BS in LS. 6: Fr. 7: Lib asst pub lib, Knoxville Tenn 41; Asst ref libn Fla StateU Lib 44-49; Asst bklist ALA, Chicago 49-51; Libn Emory Jr Col 52; Libn Atlanta Newspapers 53; Libn USAF, Nouasseur Morocco 53, 55-56; Libn Iran-Amer Soc, Teheran Iran 59-60; Lubn USCE Gulf Dist, Teheran Iran 61; Lib asst pub lib, Tampa Fla 68-. 10: AAUW; Wellesley Club (St Petersburg Fla); West Coast Writers Guild. 14: Ref, humanities. 15: 3106 Lawn ave, Tampa Fl 33611.

SCHIPF, ROBERT GEORGE. b Mt Vernon 12 Ap 23. 4: Mary Ann Downs. 5: Brooklyn Col 47-50 (Geol) BA; UNeb 51-53 (Geol, Geog) BS, MA; UOkla 60-61 MLS. 7: US Naval Res (Lt) Aviation Ordnance 42- Ground water geologist US Geological Survey, NC & La 53-55; Asst Prof geol USouthwestern La 55-59; ASST Prof phys sci Humboldt State Col 59-60; Asst Prof & sci libn So Ill U 61-68; Assoc Prof & Sci libn UMontana 68-. 8: Chm, So Ill U Com on Automating Ref WK. 9: Geol Soc Amer; Amer Assn of Petrol Geologists. 10: Sigma Xi; Nat Rifle Assn; Nat Muzzle Loading Rifle Assn. 12: "Water Resources of the Neuse River Basin (57); "Geology and Ground Water Resources of Fayetteville Area, NC (61). 13: Yes. 14: Ref, geol, geog, anthrop. 15: PO Box 848, Missoula Mt 59801.

SCHIRMER, THOMAS EDWARD. b Cleveland Ohio 14 F 42. 5: Xavier 59-60, 61-62; Kent State 62-63 (Speech, Theatre) BA; Pratt Inst 64-66 MLS. 6: Fr, Lat. 7: Organist-choirmaster St Stephen Ch, Cleveland Ohio 60-61; Libn trainee NYC Pub Lib 64-66, Libn 67-68; Mus catlgr UMich (Ann Arbor) 66-67; Instr mus catlgr CCNY 68-. 9: MusLA; LACUNY. 13: Yes. 14: Phonorecord & mus libnship (catlg & ref) a-v materials. 15: 68 Montague st apt 4H, Brooklyn NY 11201.

SCHIWETZ, DOROTHY JANE. b Yorktown Tex 16 Mr 16. 5: Our Lady of the Lake Col 34-35; UTex 35-38 (Eng) BA; UOkla 39-40 (LS) BA. 6: Ger. 7: Asst libn Nueces Co Lib, Corpus Christi Tex 41-42; Jr libn 23rd ave br Oakland (Cal) Pub Lib 44-46; Circ asst Miami Beach (Fla) Pub Lib 49; Hd libn Bowie High Sch, El Paso Tex 50-54; Chief base lib syst USAF K-8, Korea 54-55; Hd circ dept UTulsa 56; Field consul rural lib serv tex State Lib 57-61; Libn Ludwigsberg Amer High Sch, Germany (DEG, USA) 61-62; Asst gen ref div El Paso Pub Lib 64-65; Asst basic div Tex A&M U Lib 67-. 9: ALA; TexLA. 14: Ref. 15: 600 Fairview, College Station Tx 77840.

SCHLEGEL, LAURENCE. b Was DC 4 Ag 26. 5: St Anselms Col 49 (Eng) AB; Catholic U 61 MS in LS. 6: Lat, Fr. 7: Ref libn Geisel Lib St Anselms Col 61-. 9: ALA; NCTE. 14: Ref. 15: St Anselms Col, Manchester NH 03102.

SCHLEGELMILCH, MARGARET (ROBERTS). b Montrose Minn 26 Ag 18. 4: Reuben O Schlegelmilch. 5: Cornell Col 36-40 (Eng, Lat) BA; UIll 41-42 BS in LS; Syracuse summer 67. 6: Fr. 7: Asst libn SE Mo State Col 42-43; Asst libn

Kirstein Bus Lib, Boston 44-45; Libn Endwell Jr High Sch, Endwell NY 66-. 9: ALA; NYLA; SoTierSchL. 10: Beta Phi Mu; Women's Soc Christian Serv; Endicott Woman's Club. 15: 618 Valley View dr, Endwell NY 13760.

SCHLEIFER, HAROLD BERNARD. b Bronx NY 22 O 42. 5: City Col 59-63 (Pol Sci) BA (cum laude); Columbia 63-65 MLS; Brooklyn Col & CUNY 65- (Pol Sci) PhD. 6: Sp, Russian. 7: Libn trainee NY Pub Lib Fordham Br, S George Br 63-65; Ref libn Soc Sci-Educ Div Brooklyn Col Lib 65-66; Hd acquis & Soc sci bibliogr NYU 66-68; Hd acquis div & Asst Prof Herbert H Lehman Col Lib CUNY 68-. 9: ALA; NYLA (RTSS, Organiz, Acquis Com); Lib Assn City NY. 10: Phi Beta Kappa; Beta Phi Mu; Amer Pol Sci Assn; Amer Jewish Hist Soc. 14: Acquis, govt docs, tech serv. 15: 271 Parkside ave, Brooklyn NY 11226.

SCHLENKER, KATHLEEN (INCE). b Fargo ND 16 Jl 10. 5: URI 28-32 (Bacteriology) BS; Peabody 64-65 MLS. 7: Asst child dept Memphis Pub Lib, Memphis Tenn 59-64, Proj supv reading readiness program 65-66; Hd Raleigh br Shelby Co Libs, Memphis Tenn 66-68; Asst libn URI 68-. 9: ALA. 10: Sigma Kappa; Phi Kappa Phi. 14: Ref, interlib loan. 15: 7 South rd, Kingston RI 02881.

SCHLESSINGER, BERNARD S. b Toronto Ont Can 19 Mr 30. 4: June Hirsch Schlessinger. 5: Roosevelt U 46-50 (Chem) BS; Miami U (Ohio) 50-52 (Phys Chem) MS; UWis (Madison) 52-55 (Phys Chem) PhD. 6: Ger, Fr. 7: Researcher Amer Can Co, Barrington Ill 55-56; 1st Lt (research) USAF Sch of Aviation Med 56-58; Hd gen subj indexing Chem Abstracts, Columbus Ohio 58-66; Libn Olin-Mathieson Chem Corp, New Haven Conn 66-68; Prof of lib sci So Conn State Col 68-. 8: Consult work in abstracting, indexing, and translating; Part-time tchg, chem & info sci Ohio State U 60-66. 9: ACS; ALA; SLA; ASIS; ConnLA. 13: Yes. 14: Spec libs, lib automation. 15: Southern Conn State College 501 Crescent, New Haven Ct 06515.

SCHLEY, ASBURY W. b Boston 9 S 10. 4: Eleanor W Schley. 5: Harvard 31-33, 34-37 (Fr Lit)SB, ma; UParis 37-38; Simmons 47-48 (LS) SB. 6: Fr. 7: Lt (jg) USNR 42-45; Goodspeeds Bksop Inc, Boston 45-47; Asst ref libn Boston U Col Lib Arts Lib 48-49; Circ libn, br libn Watertown Pub Lib, Watertown Mass 49-50; Asst catlgr USAF Geophysical Research Lib, Boston 50-52; Libn Lucius Beebe Mem Lib, Wakefield Mass 52-56; Libn W Hartford Pub Lib, W Hartford Conn 56-. 9: ALA; ConnLA; MassLA; NELA. 10: Harvard Club of No Conn. 14: Admin, illustrated Fr bks. 15: 31 Arundel ave, W Hartford Ct 06107.

SCHLICHTING, CATHERINE (FLETCHER) NICHOLSON. b Huntsville Ala 18 N 23. 5: UAla 41-44 (LS) BS in Educ; Chicago summers 46, 48-50 MALS. 7: Asst libn UAla Educ Lib summers 44-45; Libn Sylacauga High Sch, Sylacauga Ala 44-45; Libn Hinsdale High Sch, Hinsdale Ill 45-49; Asst libn Centre for Child Bks U Chicago 50-52; Instr ref dept Ohio Wesleyan U Lib 65-69, Asst Prof 69-. 9: ALA-ACRL; OhioLA (Col & Univ RT); Midwest Acad Libns Conf. 10: Kappa Delta Pi; AAUP; Dela Hist Soc; Ohio Wesleyan U Club. 14: Ref, wk with child & yp. 15: 414 N Liberty st, Delaware Ohio 43015.

SCHLINKERT, ROY W. b Wis. 4: Cora Lee Schlinkert. 5: UWis (Educ) BS Ed, (Hist) MA, BLS. 6: Ger, Fr. 7: Asst libn Wis State Hist Lib, Madison Wis 40-44; Research assoc legis ref lib, Madison Wis 44-47; Asst div chief LC 47-48, Div chief 48-49; Asst dir Detroit Pub Lib 49-53; Dir of personnel Free Lib of Phila 53-54; Libn Chicago Pub Lib 54-59; Hd tchr-libn Chicago Bd of Educ 59-. 9: ALA; IllLA; High Sch Libns of Chicagoland (pres 62-63). 12: Subj bibliog (Wis hist). 13: Yes. 15: 2501 W Addison, Chicago Il 60625.

SCHLIPF, FREDERICK ALLEN. b Fargo N Dak 14 S 41. 4: Diane Hillard. 5: Carleton 59-63 9hist) BA; UChicago 63-66 MA, 66-. 6: Ger. 7: Trainee Chicago Pub Lib 64-65; Research asst Nat Opinion Research Ctr, Chicago 65-66; Instr Grad Lib Sch UChicago 66-. 9: ALA. 10: Beta Phi Mu. 13: Yes. 14: Pub lib organ & admin, adult bk reading patterns, research methods in libnship. 15: 1755 E 55th st, Chicago Il 60615.

SCHLOEDER, MARY CATHERINE (HIGGINS). b Kan City Mo 25 N 18. 5: St Teresas Col (Mo) 36-38 (Eng, Soc Sci) AA; St Mary Col (Kan) 38-40 (Eng, Soc Sci) AB; Catholic U 42-44 BS in LS. 6: Fr, Ger, Lat. 7: Catlg asst Pub Lib, Kan City Mo 40-41; Asst libn St Mary Col (Kan) 41-42; Sec & libn Dept of Lib Sci Catholic U 42-44; Bibliog asst Grad Lb Sch UChicago 44-45; Asst to pres Thomas More Bk Shop, Chicago 44-45; Catlgr DC Pub Lib 51-56; Catlgr ,7 asst chief catlg sct Dept of State, Wash DC 56-61; Sr decimal clsf Dewey Decimal Clsf Off LC 61-62; Asst libn Foreign Serv Inst US Dept of State, Wash DC 62-. 9: ALA-RSD (Steering Com Potomac Valley Chap 65-68; Potomac Tech Proc Libns (Exec Bd 54-56); DCLA. 10: Beta Phi MU: Nat Coun Catholic Women; Delta Epsilon Sigma. 12: Comp Index "Books on Trial (now "The Critic) v 1-4 (45-46); Comp Index "Papal Documents on Mary, ed by Doheny (56); Ed "ATMC Monthly Memo" (65-). 13: Yes. 14: Catlg, ref, admin. 15: 3426 Gunston rd, Alexandria Va 22302.

SCHLOSSER, ISABELLA (JONES). b Pittsburgh Penn 1 O 12. 4: Galen H Schlosser. 5: Syracuse 30-33 (Lat) AB, summers 33-36 BS in LS; Penn State Col summer 37 (Eng); DenverU summer 65 (Y-A lit); Drexel 60-69 MS in LS. 6: Ger, Fr, Lat. 7: Tchr & libn truxton (NY) High Sch 33-34; Lat & Ger tchr Elizabethtown (Penn) High Sch 34-36; Eng tchr Temple U High Sch, Phila 36-38, 46; Sub tchr Phila Sch Dist 54-56; Springside Sch, Phila: Tchr 56-, Tchr & libn 62-. 9: ALA; IndependentSchTA Phila & Vic 9chm Libns Gp). 14: Sch lib wk. 15: 4101 Gypsy lane, Philadelphia Pa 19144.

SCHLUE, MILDRED L (FROMM). b Burlington Iowa 2 My 10. 5: Coe Col 30-32 (Eng, Bus) BA; UIowa 63-68 (LS) Certif. 7: Tchr Van Horne Pub Sch, Van Horne Iowa 32-35; Libn Benton commun High Sch, Van Horne Iowa 63-. 9: NEA; ALA; IowaStateEA; IowaStateLA. 10: Van Horne Pub Lib Bd. 15: Van Horne Ia 52346.

SCHLUETER, REINHOLD ARTHUR. b Milwaukee Wis 4 Ap 15. 4: Belle Selig. 5: UWis (Milwaukee) 34-37 (Chem); UWis (Madison) 38-40 (Chem, Educ) BS, 46-47 BLS. 6: Sp, Ger. 7: Libn UWis Chem Lib (Madison) 47-49; Libn Oa Ridge Inst for Nuclear Studies, Oak Ridge Tenn 49-56; Libn Inst for Defense Analysis Pentagon 56-58; Libn Intl Atomic energy Agcy, Vienna Austria 58-63, Consul, Santiago Chile 64-65; Self-employed bibliogr, Kingston Tenn 63-64; Consul UNESCO, Concepcion Chile 65; Consul Oak Ridge Assoc Libs, Oak Ridge Tenn 65-66; Lib specialist UWis (Milwaukee) 66-67, Lecturer Sch of Lib & Info sci 67-. 9: SLA. 13: Yes. 14: Spec libnship, info sci, data proc. 15: 9040 N Regent rd, Milwaukee Wi 53217.

SCHMALBERG, AARON. b Newark NJ 6 O 25. 5: NYU 45-49 (Hist) BA; NY State Col (Albany) 52-53 MSLS; UMich 57- MA (Educ), AMLS. 7: Asst libn St Clair Shores Pub Lib, Mich 55-56; Libn LAnse Creuse High Sch, Mich 56-59; Libn Oak Park High Sch, Mich 59-65; Instr Dept of Lib Sci UMich 65-. 9: ALA; MichASchL. 10: Beta Phi Mu. 14: Educ for libnship, sch libs, catlg. 15: 16516 Schaefer, apt 14, Detroit 48235.

SCHMALZ, BETTY ANN SWOGETINSKY. b Katy Tex 11 S26. 4: Jean E Schmalz. 5: Baylor U 43-47 (Eng, Hist, Educ) BA (cum laude); UHouston 51-54 (Educ) M Ed; N Tex State Col summer 57; UTex summers 60-67 MLS. 6: Sp. 7: Lang arts tchr Carr Jr High Sch, Orange Tex 47-51; Eng tchr Katy High Sch, Katy Tex 51-61, Libn 61-. 9: NEA; Tex State Tchrs Assn; TexLA; ALA; AASchL; TexASchL; Tex Assn Educ Tech. 10: PTA; Amer Field Serv; Delta Kappa Gamma; Alpha Chi; Kappa Delta Pi; SIGMA Tau Delta. 12: "A Resource Guide for English Language Arts, Secondary School, Grades Eleven and Twelve (59); "History of the First Baptist Church, Katy, Texas (63). 14: Sch libs, acquis, local, state & lib hist, a-v materials. 15: 1014 Bartlett rd, Katy Tx 77450.

SCHMAVONIAN, ARSINE ELLEN. b Constantinople Turkey 1 Ap 12. 5: Hood Col 30-34 (Eng) AB; Syracuse 65-68 (LS) MS. 7: Tchr Cazenovia Sem 36-39; Sec 1st Presbyterian Ch, Syracuse NY 42-50; Presbyterian coun Westminster Foundation of NY Hendricks Chapel SyracuseU 50-54; Off dir Ch of the Covenant, Cleveland Ohio 54-57; Ed wk Gen Coun of the United Presbyterian Ch in the USA, NYC 57-62; Ed publ & registrar Central City Bus Inst, Syracuse NY 63-66; Compiler faculty bibliog Univ Archives Syracuse U 66-68, Assoc curator of ms for publ 68-. 9: SAA. 13: Yes. 14: Archives, mss. 15: 104 Janet dr, Syracuse NY 13224.

SCHMAUS, FRANCIS THEODORE. b Paradise Penn 2 N 19. 4: Jean Barditzky. 5: UColo 48-50 (Eng) AB; UDenver 50-51 (Eng) MA, 51-53 (LS) MA; UTex 55-58 (Eng). 7: T/4 US Army 45-51; Libn (circ & res) UDenver Colorado 53-54; Ref libn UTex (Austin) 54-59, Eng libn 59-. 9: ALA; TexLA. 12: "A Library Reference Manual for Engineering students" (63). 13: Yes. 14: Ref, admin. 15: 4515 Rosedale, Austin Tx 78756.

SCHMIDT, BRUCE KENNETH. b Detroit Mich 17 N 38. 5: Wayne State 57-61 (Hist) AB, 61-62 9hist); UMich 62-63 AMLS. 6: Ger. 7: Clk Detroit Pub Lib 55-62, Libn I, II & III

63-67; Dir Southfield Pub Lib, Southfield Mich 67-; Instr in Lib Sci Wayne State 69-. 8: Tchr State Wkshop in Record Collections 65; State Exec Dir, Nat Lib Week Mich 66. 9: ALA; MichLA (Jr Mem RT). 14: Pub lib admin. 15: 3440 W Seven Mile rd, Detroit Mi 48221.

SCHMIDT, C JAMES. b Flint Mich 27 Je 39. 4: Martha Meadows. 5: Flint Jr Community Col 57-59; Catholic U 59-62 (Philos) BA; Columbia 62-63 MSLS; Ohio State U 68- (Pol Sci). 7: Asst Bus & Ind Dept Flint Pub Lib, Flint Mich 63-65; Ref libn Gen Motors Inst, Flint Mich 65; Assoc libn Southwest Tex State Col 65-67; Hd Undergrad Libs Ohio State U (Columbus) 67-. 8: Bldg consul, Genesee Co (Mich) Lib Bd 65; Staff, Lib/USA, NY Worlds Fair 64; Chm lib sch com Ohio State U. 9: ALA; OhioLA (Memb Serv Com); TexLA; MichLA (Pub Rel Com). 10: ACLU. 14: Admin, acad libs, lib bldgs. 15: 45 E Pacemont rd, Columbus Oh 43202.

SCHMIDT, DEAN A. b Webster SD 24 N 30. 5: UMinn 48-51 (Lat) BA, 51-53 (LS) MA. 7: Jr libn UMinn(Minneapolis) 53-55; US Army 55-57; UMich 57-62; Med libn UMo 62-. 9: MedLA. 14: Med libs. 15: 1204 W Rollins rd, Columbia Mo 65201.

SCHMIDT, DONALD T. b Brighton Ill 13 S 19. 4: Alice Mahany. 5: Shurtleff Col 37-39; State U Iowa 43-44, 46-47 (Hist) BA, 48-49 (Hist) MA; UDenver summers 62-64 (LS) MA. 6: Ger. 7: Coast Artillery Mil Govt (1st Lt) 41-46; Tchr Marion High Sch, Marion Iowa 47-54; Tchr Tooele High Sch, Tooele Utah 54-56; Prin Roosevelt Sem, Roosevelt Utah 56-58; Instr Brigham Young U 58-59, Instr libn 59-66, Asst Prof & Asst lib dir 66-. 8: Spec assignment, Geneal Soc Lib, Salt Lake City 64-65. 9: ALA; UtahLA; MPLA. 10: Utah Acad Scis, Arts & Letters. 14: Readers serv, ref, admin. 15: 1920 N 1500 E, Provo Ut 84601.

SCHMIDT, FRED JR (CONRAD). b Russell Kan 3 O 37. 4: Gerry Stephen Schmidt. 5: Ft Hays Kan State Col 58-62 (Hist) BA; UDenver 62-63 (LS) MA. 6: Ger. 7: (Sgt) Communications KANG, Russell Kan 55-61; Assoc libn Chadron State Col 63-65; Documents libn Ft Hays Kan State Col 65-69; Docs libn Colo State U (Ft Collins) 69-. 8: Consul; Colby Commun Col 68, Central Kan Lib Syst 68; Lectr wkshop on use sci & tech libs Kan Div Industrial Ext & UKan 68. 9: ALA; NEA; ColoLA. 10: Phi Alpha Theta. ; Sierra Club; Colo Mt Club. 13: Yes. 14: Govt docs, indexing, bibliog, ref. 15: Lib Colorado State Univ, Fort Collins Co 80521.

SCHMIDT, IRENE. b near Bonaparte Iowa 10 Ja 09. 5: Union Col (Lincoln Neb) 28, 31-33, 35-36; Pacific Union Col 38-40 (Eng) BA; USoCal 40-42 BS in LS, 59-61 MS in LS; Emory 53 MLA Grade I Certif. 7: Tchr Seventh- Day Adventist Denomination, Longmont Colo Exec housekeeper, Boulder Colo 34-35; Asst libn Col of Med Evangelists Loma Linda U 42-53, Catlgr, Hd period dept, Hd circ & ref, Assoc libn hist records 53-. 9: ALA; Christian Libns Assn, Cal; Med Lib Group, So Cal. 14: Ref. 15: Loma Linda Univ Lib, Loma Linda Cal 92354.

SCHMIDT, JOSEPH ARNOLD. b Waterloo Iowa 22 My 25. 4: Phyllis Faulkner. 5: Wash State U 46-50 (Eng BA, 50-51 (Eng) MA; UCLA 51-52 (Eng); USoCal 52-54 MS in LS. 7: Ph M 2/c USNR 43-46; Cal State Col (Los Angeles): Ref libn 54-56, Pers libn 56-57, Supv circ libn 57-59, Supv language arts libn 59-60, Chief of spec serv 60-65, Act asst col libn spec serv 65-68, Asst Col libn 68-. 10: Beta Phi Mu; Phi Kappa Phi; Sigma Delta Chi. 14: Ref, bldgs. 15: 11160 E Wildflower rd, Temple City Cal 91780.

SCHMIDT, JUDITH (GRODEN) BUSSELL. b Detroit 27 F 40. 4: Manfred Schmidt. 5: UMich 57 (Hist) AB, 64 (LS) MA. 6: Sp. 7: Libn, Wayne Mich 64-68; Libn Tappan Jr High Sch, Ann Arbor Mich 68-. 9: MichEA; MichASchL. 14: Sch libs. 15: 321 Wiliamsburg d, Ann Arbor Mich 48103.

SCHMIDT, SISTER M JOHN FRANCIS SSND. b Clayton Ill 19 Je 09. 5: Notre Dame Jr Col, Quincy Col 32-41; Loyola U (New Orleans) 34-37; Mt Mary Col 42-49 (Educ) BE; St Louis U, Xavier U 50-58; LSU 59-61 (LS) MS. 6: Fr. 7: Elem parochial sch tchr, Tex, La, Mo, Ill 31-41; Elem sch tchr pub sch, Teutopolis Ill 41-53; Libn Teutopolis Community Unit, Teutopolis Ill 50-53; Tchr of Eng & soc studies Redemptorist High Sch, Baton Rouge La 53-61; Libn Redemptorist High Sch, Baton Rouge La 53-61; Libn Rosati-Kain High Sch, St Louis 61-64; Assoc libn Notre Dame Col (St Louis) 64-. 8: Rep of the Archdiocesan Sch of St Louis on the KMOX-TV Reading Serv, 61-64. 9: ALA; CathLA. 10: Phi Kappa Phi. 13: Yes. 14: Readers serv, catlg. 15: 320 E Ripa ave, St Louis Mo 63125.

SCHMIDT, MARTHA R(OWLET). b Wash DC 10 D 07. 5: George Washington U 25-27, summer 28 (Zoo) AB in Ed, 30-35, 37 AB in LS; George Washington U 38 (LS); Adelphi Suffolk Col 60-62 (Internat Rel). 6: Ger. 7: Asst Union Catlg LC summer 28; Asst catlg dept UMich 28-31; Asst libn George Washington U 31-32; Jr clsf UMich 32-35; Libn Republican Nat Com, Wash DC 37-51; Chief libn Radio Free Europe, Munich Germany 51-58; Chief libn Adelphi Suffold Col 59-68; Chief libn Dowling Col 68-. 8: Expert consul, US Army in Vienna (Apr-Aug) to org US Info Center Libs, 47. 9: ALA; SLA (chm Soc Sci Group 40-42; DC Chap: chm Employment Com 41-44; chm Bus Group 45-47); NYLA; Suffolk Co LA (sec 60-62). 10: AAUW; Friends of Dowling Col Lib; AAUP. 13: Yes. 14: Admin, catlg. 15: 311 Vanderbit blvd, Oakdale NY 11769.

SCHMIDT, MARY (MORRIS). b Minneapolis 28 Je 26. 4: Philip F Schmidt. 5: Bennett Jr Col 44-45; UMinn 45-47 (Liberal Arts) BA, 48-50 (Art Hist) MA; UFlorence Italy 50-51 (Art Hist); UMinn 53-55 BSLS; UParis 56-57 (Art Hist); NYU 62-65 (Art Hist). 6: Fr, Ital, Sp. 7: Art libn UMinn(Minneapolis) 53-55; Catlg-ref libn Metropolitan Museum of Art, NYC 57-58; Indexer "Art Index H W Wilson Co, NYC 58-66, Ed "Art Index" 66-. 9: ALA; SLA; NY Lib Club. 11: Fulbright Scholarship, 56. 14: Catlg, art libs, illus bks, prints. 15: 155 E 96th, NYC 10028.

SCHMIDT, MERCEDES (WEED). b Evanston Ill 20 Ag 0 Ag 2. 4: Curtis John Schmidt. 5: Northwestern 48-51 (Music) BM; UIll 52-53 (LS) MA. 6: Ger, Sp. 7: Music catlgr UIll Lib (Urbana) 53-54; Libn Camp Chaffee Post Lib, Camp Chaffee Ark 54; Catlgr Monrovia Pub Lib, Monrovia Cal 57; Ref asst Alhambra Pub Lib, Alhambra Cal 57; Catlgr Covina Pub Lib, Covina Cal 58-62; Catlg libn Cal State Col (Fullerton) 62-. 9: ALA. 10: AAUW; LWV; Mu Phi Epsilon. 14: Catlg, music materials. 15: 202 W ave San Antonio, SAN Clemente Cal.

SCHMIDT, PAULINE (GUSCOTT) (MRS). b Rochester Ohio 1 Ap 15. 5: Oberlin Col 33-37 (Pre-Lib) AB; West Res 37-38 BS in LS. 6: Fr, Ger. 7: Br libn Free Pub Lib, Middletown Ohio 38-40; Br libn Dayton Pub Lib, Middletown Ohio 38-40; Br libn Dayton Pub Lib, Dayton Ohio 40-41; Libn Holmes Co Pub Lib, Millersburg Ohio 41-43; Supv of child wk Free Pub Lib, Middletown Ohio 43-49; High sch libn Middletown High Sch, Middletown Ohio 61-69; Coord of lib serv Middletown City Sch Dist, Middletown Ohio 69-. 9: NEA; OhioEA; OhioASchL. 14: Ya & child lit, ref, lib instr. 15: 7296 Carson rd, Rt 3, Middletown Ohio 45043.

SCHMIDT, THOMAS V. b Grand Rapids Mich 10 S 33. 5: Aquinas Col 52-55 (Eng) AB; UMich 55-57 (Eng) MA; Mich State U 60-63 (Eng); CatholicU 63-67 MS in LS. 6: Fr, Ger, Lat, Greek, Ital, Sp, Dutch. 7: Shop off clk US Army Ordinance, US & Germany 57-59; Instr Eng dept SDak StateU 59-60; Grad asst improvement serv Mich State U (E Lansing) 60-62, Asst instr Amer Thought & Lang 62-63; Asst hd Humanities Lib Catholic U 63-65, Asst hd ref/col lib 65-. 10: Beta Phi Mu; Lambda Iota Tau; Delta Epsilon Sigma; Heart Assn. 14: Ref. 15: 1005 Chillum rd 110, Hyattsville Md 20782.

SCHMIDT, VALENTINE LUCILLE. b NYC 21 D 19. 5: Rutgers 36-40 (Math) BS; NYU 44 (Russian); City Col (NY) 50 (Marketing Research); UNC 58-60 MSLS. 6: Russian, Ger. Fr. 7: Piano & harmony tcher, Iselin NJ 38-45; Jr high tchr Hubbard Sch, Plainfield NJ 43; Chief statistician George G Sharp NA, NYC 43-45; Asst Sect chief US Steel Export Co, NYC 45-46; Office manager Gen Moulding & Millwk Metuchen NJ 46-47; Budget dir United Merchants & Mfrs, NYC 47-51; Tech analyst US Salvage Assn, NYC 53-57; Lib asst Main Post Lib, Ft Bragg NC 57-58; Field libn admin US Army, Germany 60-62; Tech libn Babcock & Wilcox, Lynchburg Va 62-64; Libn John & Mable Ringling Museum of Art, Sarasota Fla 65-. 9: ALA; SLA; Amer nuclear Soc; Atomic Ind Forum; Amer Soc Metals (chm Spec Libs Sect 63-64); FlaLA. 10: Beta Phi Mu; Friends of the Lynchburg Lib; Altrusa Club. 14: Admin, ref, bibliog, catlg. 15: 2624 Reserve pl, Bradenton Fla 33505.

SCHMIERER, HELEN FRANCES. b Joliet Ill. 5: UNeb 59-63 (Eng) BA; IndU 63-65 (LS) MA; UChicago 67-. 6: Ger, Fr. 7: Ref asst IndU (Bloomington) 64-65; Catlgr LC 65-67. 09: ALA; ASIS. 14: Tech serv, admin, lib educ. 15: 5426 S Harper 304, Chicago Il 60615.

SCHMITT, MARTHA A (FOSTER). b Ames Iowa 10 Ag 14. 4: Martin Schmitt. 5: Drake U 32-36 (Hist) BA; Columbia 38-39 (LS) BS. 7: Br lib asst Pub Lib, Des Moines Iowa 36-38; Catlgr: Brown U Lib 41, UOre Lib 41-48, Pub Lib, Springfield Ore 56-. 8: Lib adv com, Lane Co (Ore) Commun Col. 10:

LWV; PEO; Phi Beta Kappa. 14: Catlg. 15: 45 Sunset dr, Eugene Ore 97403.

SCHMITT, MARTIN (FERDINAND). b River Forest Ill 25 Mr 17. 4: Martha Foster. 5: Concordia Col 34-37; UIll 37-38 (Journalism) BS, 38-39 BS in LS; UMo 41-42 (Journalism); American U summer 45 (Pub Admin). 6: Ger. 7: Asst circ det UIll Lib (Urbana) 39-40; Libn Eureka Col 40-41; Head bibliog & ref sect US Army War Col 42-46; Asst libn UIda 46-47; Curator spec collections UOre 47-. 9: PNLA. 10: Kappa Tau alpha; CHAOS; Round Table Eugene; West Writers of Amer. Eugen. 12: "Fighting Indians of the West, with Dee Brown (48); "Trail Driving Days, with Dee Brown (52); "Settlers West, with Dee Brown (55); Ed "General George Crook(46); Ed " "A Journal of Travel by E S McComas (54). 13: Yes. 14: Mss, rare bks. 15: 45 Sunset dr, Eugene Ore 97403.

SCHMITZ, JULIA M. b Walla Walla Wash. 5: UWash 26-31 (LS) BS; UMex (Sp) Certif; Wash State U 45-49 (Bacteriology) MS. 7: Temp catlgr Renton Pub Lib, Renton Wash 31-32; Asst libn Whitman Col 32-42; Wom en's res rep (WAVES) US Navy, Brooklyn Naval Hosp 42-45; Lecturer & asst in bacteriology Wash State U 46-53; Lecturer in chem St Mary's Sch, Walla Walla Wash 53-54; Lecturer in biol Whitman Col 54-55; Med research libn Boeing Co, Seattle 55-. 9: ALA-AHIL;-ACRL; SLA (Pac NW Chap; var com duties); MedLA; Pacific NW Reg Med Lib Group. 10: Sigma Xi; Phi Beta Kappa; Sigma Alpha Omicron. 13: Yes. 14: Ref wk in med, aerospace med, human factors, ind safety. 15: Central Med Lib, Boeing Co, 11-42, P O Box 3707, Seattle 98124.

SCHMITZ, EUGENIA EVANGELINE. b Grand Rapids Mich. 5: West Mich U (Lat, Fr, Eng) AB; Col of St Catherine BSLS; UMich AMLS. 7: Br libn Grand Rapids Pub Lib, Grand Rapids Mich; Libn Creston High Sch, Grand Rapids Mich; Libn Sr High Sch, Benton Harbor Mich; Summer Instr Dept of Libnship West Mich U Lecturer Dept of Lib Sci UMich 63-66, Asst Prof 67-68; Asst Prof Wis State U (Oshkosh) 68-. 9: ALA-AASchL (Com on Prof Growth & Devel 60-62); -LED; MichLA; MichASchL (pres 60-61; Memb Chm 56-58, chm Publns 62-63); WisLA. 10: Phi Beta Kappa; Phi Kappa Phi; Beta Phi Mu; Pi Lambda Theta. 12: "A Study of the Library Book Collections in Mathematics and the Physical Sciences in Fifty-Four Michigan High Schools Accredited by the North Central Association of Colleges and Secondary Schools," UMich PhD diss (66); Co-auth "A Survey of the Huron Valley School Libraries" (66-67). 14: Catlg, ref, lit for ya & child, lib educ. 15: Dept of Lib Sci, Wis State Univ, Oshkosh Wi 54901.

SCHMITZ, RUTH W (HANSER). b Summit NJ 16 My 20. 4: Fred W Schmitz. 5: Upsala Col 38-42 (Chem) BA; Polytech Inst of Brooklyn 46-48 (Chem); St Johns U (NY) 61-64 MLS. 6: Fr, Ger. 7: Control chem E Bilhuber Inc, Orange NJ42-46; Tchg fellow chem Polytech Int of Brooklyn 46-47; Asst Prof chem NYC Community Col 47-49, Lib asst 51, 53, 55; Libn Sugar Research Found, NYC 52-53; Control chem Torigian Labs, Queens Village NY 53-54; Libn Queensborough Pub Lib, Jamaica NY 60-. 9: ACS; SLA. 14: Sci ref, bk reviewing. 15: 91-04 216 st, Queens Village NY 11428.

SCHMOLL, DONAVON M. b Geneseo Ill 17 Jl 29. 4: Hannelore Vosberg. 5: Ill State U 47-51 (Soc sci) BSEd; NYU 55-57 (Intl rel) MA; Columbia 58-61 (Admin & Guidance); UWis 65-67 MSLS. 7: Spec wpns tech USAF SAC 51-55; Immigration serv asst Ch World Serv, NY 56-57; Hist tchr Calhoun High Sch, Merrick NY 59-61; Educ off Ministry of Educ, Kampala Uganda 61-65; Bibliogr UWis Ctr Syst Lib 66-67; Tech serv libn & hist instr st Leo Col 67-. 9: Amer Acad Pol & Soc Sci; Royal African Soc; FlaLA; SELA. 10: AAUP. 11: E African Training Fellowship 61. 15: PO Box 345, San Antonio Fl 33576.

SCHMOYER, ELIZABETH KATHRYN (FOX). b Pipersvile Pen 3 Ap 19. 4: Harold Mitchell Schmoyer. 5: Kutztown State Col 37-40 (LS, Eng); Churchmans Bus Col 40-42 (Exec Sec). 7: Planner, Sec of Ration Bd, Bethlehem Steel Co, Bethlehem Penn 42; Clerk personnel off PBNE RR, Bethlehem Penn 43-44; Elem libn E Penn Union Sch Dist, Emmaus Penn 59-61; Lib asst Allentown Pub Lib, Allentown Penn 61-65; Libn Coplay Lib, Coplay Penn 62-65; Head Libn Northampton Pub Lib, Northampton Penn 65-. 8: Lib consul, Amer Educ Coun, Phila, 63-65. 9: ALA; PennLA (chap sec 68). 10 Nat Womans Bk Assn; Girl Scouts; Womans Club; Womans Auxiliary of Muhlenberg Col; Muhlenberg Med Center Auxiliary. 15: Northampton Pub Lib, Northampton Pa 18067.

SCHMUCH, JOSEPH J. b Lynn Mass 9 Mr 28. 4: Enid L Kaler. 5: Bowdoin Col 45-48 (Classics) AB; Brown U 50-52 (Lat) MA; Harvard 55-57 (Classical Philol); Simmons 57-59 (LS) MS. 7: Master of Lat & Ger Wilbraham Acad, Wilbraham Mass 48-50; Cryptanalyst & Communications Analyst US Army Security Agency (Sgt) 52-55; Circ libn Stoneham Pub Lib, Stoneham Mass 57; Libn Reading Pub Lib, Reading Mass 58-61; Libn Belmont Mem Lib, Belmont Mass 61-. 8: Consul for bk collection devel & lib bldg planning to Ten East Mas communities. 9: ALA; NELA; MassLA; Mass Pub Lib Adminrs (pres 64-65). 10: Trustee Reading Pub Lib; Amer Philol Assn; Rotary Club. 13: Yes. 14: Admin. 15: 69 Lowell st, Reading Mass 01867.

SCHMULOWITZ, ALAN DAVID. b Brooklyn NY 16 Ap 44. 4: Regina N Atlas. 5: Brooklyn Col 61-66 (Hist) BA; Mesifla Talmudical Sem 61-67 (Talmud) Rabbinical Degree; Pratt Inst 66-67 MLS. 6: Hebrew, Yiddish, Ger. 7: Tchr of lib (secondary sch) NYC Bd of Educ 67-. 8: Lib consul Torah Vodaath High Sch Brooklyn NY Sept 67-. 10: Assn Orthodox Jewish Tchrs (NYC). 14: Sch libs. 15: 899 Montgomery st, Brooklyn NY 11213.

SCHMUTZLER, JOAN VIRGINIA. b Hamilton Ohio 16 Mr 38. 5: West Res 56-60 (Hist) BA, 60-61 MS in LS. 7: Ya & ref libn Lane Pub Lib, Hamilton Ohio 61-66; Ya libn Cuyahoga Co Pub Lib, Cleveland Ohio 66-. 9: ALA; OhioLA (sec Jr Mems Round Table 64-65; YART sec 67-68, v-chm 68-69; YASD; Nat Lib Week Com 69-71; YA Pre-Conf Chm 69). 10: AAUW. 14: Ya serv. 15: 115 S Rocky River dr, Berea Oh 44017.

SCHNAITTER, ALLENE F. b Sandusky Ohio 19 N 21. 5: UMich 45-48 (Ger) AB, 49-52 AMLS. 6: Ger, Fr. 7: Jr order libn UMich Gen Lib 48-53; Sci & music libn Antioch Col 53-54; Assoc order libn UMich Law Lib 54-61; Head order dept UMo Lib 61-67; USOE doctoral fellow Ind U Grad Lib Sch 67-. 9: ALA; MoLA; ASIS. 10: AAUW. 12: Ed "Current Publications in Legal & Related Fields, Section II" (54-61). 14: Col & univ lib admin, automation, lib educ. 15: 1700 N Walnut #306, Bloomington In 47401.

SCHNARE, ROBERT EDEY JR. b Morristown NJ 31 D 44. 5: Paterson State Col 63-67 (Soc Sci) BA; UPittsburgh 67-68 (Lib & Info Sci) MLS; UConn 69- (US Hist). 6: Fr. 07/ a-v asst Grad Sch of Lib & Info Sci UPittsburgh 67-68; Ref libn hist & geneal Conn state Lib 68-. 8: Asst instr, Inst on New Media in Lib Educ, Grad Sch of Lib and Info Sci, UPittsburgh Ag 68. 10: US East Amateur Ski Assn; Conn State Employees Assn; Corsair (soc club); Mt Laurel Ski Club, Hartford. 14: ref. 15: 132 Collins st apt 301, Hartford Ct 06105.

SCHNEIDER, ADELE (GOLDBERG). b NYC 13 My 24. 4: Noel Schneider. 5: Brooklyn Col 41-45 (Eng) BA; Columbia 51 (Human Behavior); Pratt 65 MS in LS; LIU 67 (Eng Lit). 6: Sp. 7: Contest judge Reuben Donnely Corp, NYC 44; Rep NLRB, Bloomfield NJ 45; Interviewer Gallup Poll Inc, Princeton NJ 45-49; Soc wker & admin asst NYC Dept of Welfare, Brooklyn NY 50-53; Ed Brooklyn Col Alumni Quarterly, Brooklyn NY 61-65; Even session libn Kingsborough Community Col, City Col (NY) 65-, Tech & spec serv libn 67-. 9: ALA-ACRL; LACUNY; NY Lib Club; NY State Assn Jr Cols; NY Tech Serv Libns; SLA (Publ & Mus Divs). 10: Beta Phi Mu; AAUP. 12: Free-lance writer; Ed Brooklyn Col "Alumni Quarterly" (61-65); Ed Kingsborough Commun Col "Library Quarterly" (66-); Ed "Faculty Library Handbook" (67, 2d ed 68). 14: Col lib educ, a-v. 15: 124 Oxford st, Brooklyn NY 11235.

SCHNEIDER, ANITA (L). b Panama City Panama 12 Ag 31. 4: Ronald M Schneider. 5: NorthwesternU 50-54 (Lat Amer Studies) BS; Columbia 67-69 MLS. 6: Sp, Portu. 7: Sub Sp tchr, Ridgewood NJ 65-67; Sch libn, Ridgewood NJ 69-. 9: ALA. 10: Phi Beta Kappa. 14: Sch libnship. 15: 36 E Glen ave, Ridgewood NJ 07450.

SCHNEIDER, DON WILLIAM. b Middletown Ohio 15 F 35. 4: Linda Brenneman. 5: Kalamazoo col 59-61 (Econ) BA; IndU 61-63 (Finance) MBA, 64-67 (LS) MA. 7: Personnelman USN 55-59; Statistician Eastman Kodak, Rochester NY 63-64; Lib intern IndU Lib (Bloomington) 64-67; Hd bus & soc sci div UNC Lib (Chapel Hill) 67-. 9: SELA. 10: Beta Phi Mu. 12: Mng ed "Southeastern Librarian". 14: Ref, admin. 15: BA/SS UNC Library, Chapel Hill NC 27514.

SCHNEIDER, SISTER EVELYN RUTH OP. b Chicago Ill 20 F 29. 5: Sienna Hts Col 47-49 9theol); St John Col 49-54 (Educ) BSE, 57-58 (Theol); Case West Res 66-69 MSLS. 6: Ger. 7: Athlete All Amer Girls Prof Baseball League, Chicago 45-46; Mus tchr Diocese of Cleveland Sch Syst, Cleveland Ohio 46-48, Elem sch tchr 49-59, Tchr & libn 60-66, Tchr & lib consul 66-69, Lib supv 69-. 8: Summer fac; Konstanz am Bodeusee Germ 57; Curr Rev Com: Relig 58; Soc Studies 59 & 61, Math 64. 9: NCEA; DEA; ALA; CathLA; OhioASchL. 11: Freedom Foundation Educator Award 64. 12: "The Encyclicals of Pope Pius XII: Mystical Body pf Christ and Sacred Liturgy", rewritten for child (57); Co-auth "New ways in Numbers, Book 5" (65). 13: Yes. 14: Lib educ on col level, sch libnship. 15: 1230 W Market st, Akron Oh 44313.

SCHNEIDER, GAIL (KIRN). b Louisville Ky 14 O 19. 4: Robert Schneider. 5: UKy 37-41 (LS, Art). 6: Fr. 7: Art libn UKy 39-41; Prod asst Rudolph Guttman Assoc, NYC 45-48; Prod asst art dept Viking Press Inc, NYC 48-50; Ed & libn S I Inst of Arts & Sci, SI NY 61-. 9: SLA; Amer Inst Graphic Arts; SAA. 10: SI Sci Info Com. 12: "Community of the Press on SI"; Ed "The Staten Island Walk Book". 14: Loc hist, old photographs & hist prints, early US sci publns, newspaper hists. 15: 75 Stuyvesant pl, SI NY 10301.

SCHNEIDER, HENNIE (RAND). b Baltimore 6 Jl 22. 4: Saul A Schneider. 5: Johns Hopkins 38-40; UMd 40-42 (Sociol) AB; Amer U 54-55 (Bus); Simmons 61 MS in LS. 7: Statistical clerk, statistical asst & jr econ; Ref libn & br libn Prince Georges Co Mem Lib, Hyattsville & Mt Rainer Md 57-65; Ref asst Nat Agric Lib, Wash DC 62-65; Supv ref libn Bur of the Census, Suitland Md 65-. 9: SLA (Wash DC Chap; sec biol scis group 64-65, treas Soc Scis Group 66-68); ALA; MDLA; DCLA. 12: "International Statistical Sources; a Bibliography" (68). 14: Ref, research, bibliog. 15: Apt 1414, 11200 Lockwood dr, Silver Spring Md 20901.

SCHNEIDER, JEAN (FRANCES). b Saskatchewan 20 My 19. 4: William Schneider. 5: USaskatchewan 37-40 (Hist) BA. 7: Catlgr Assoc of Univs & Cols of Can Ottawa 65-. 14: Catlg. 15: 133 Blenheim dr, Ottawa 7 Ont Can.

SCHNEIDER, LINDA (BRENNEMAN). b Springfield Ohio 21 O 39. 4: Don W Schneider. 5: Kalamazoo 57-61 (Sp) AB; IndU 61-63 (LS) MA. 6: Sp, Fr. 7: Jr catlgr IndU 61-62; Catlgr URochester 63; Catlgr IndU 65-66; Research asst USASI Committee Z39 UNC 69-. 9: ALA. 10: Beta Phi Mu. 14: Catlg. 15: 311 Severin st, Chapel Hill NC 27514.

SCHNEIDER, LOIS (ELIZABETH) (GERMECK). b Bronx NY 6 O 39. 4: Stnley Louis Schneider. 5: Queens Col (NY) 57-61 (Hist) BA, 61-65 MLS. 7: Fellow in lib Queen's Col (NY) 61-63, Ref libn 64-; Libn Central High Sch Dist #3, N Merrick NY 63-64. 9: ALA; NYLA; LACUNY; NY Lib Club. 14: Ref (educ), instr materials. 15: 110-20 71 ave, Forest Hills NY 11375.

SCHNEIDER, MONICA M(ARIE). b Menominee Mich 31 Ja 38. 5: UWis 56-60 (Hist) BS, 60-61 MSLS. 6: Lat, Ger. 7: Catlgr Catholic U 61-63; Catlgr Mich State U 63-65; Libn UWis Fox Valley Center (Menasha) 65-66; Argonne Nat Lab, Argonne Ill 66; Tinley Park Mental Health Ctr, Tinley Park Ill 68-. 10: Phi Kappa Phi; Beta Phi Mu. 14: Catlg, reclsf. 15: Tinley Park Mental Health Ctr, Tinley Park Il 60477.

SCHNEIDER, PHYLLIS JANE (LEWARS). b St Joseph Mo 27 Mr 19. 4: Lambert Gregory Schneider. 5: St Joseph Jr Col (Mo) 37-39 AA; William Jewell Col 40-43 (Span, Soc Sci) AB; USan Jose Costa Rica 40; Chicago 44; Colo State Col of Educ 53; UWyo 55; UDenver 53-55 (LS) MA; UOre 58; USoCal 66. 6: Sp. 7;: Tchr-libn: Buckeye Union High Sch, Buckeye Ariz 43-45, Eagle Co High Sch, Gypsum Colo 49-51, Windsor High Sch, Windsor Colo 52-54; Head circ dept UWyo Lib 54-55: Tchr-libn Glendo High Sch, Glendo Wyo 55-56; Head Libn Custer Co High Sch & Jr Col, Miles City Mont 56-57; Libn Jefferson Jr High Sch, Eugene Ore 57-62; Head Libn Alamogordo Pub Lib, Alamogordo NM 62-63; Head Libn Rubidoux Sr High Sch, Riverside Cal 63-. 9: NEA; ALA; Cal Tchrs Assn; Riverside Co (Cal) SchLA. 10: Silky Terrier Club Amer. 13: Yes. 14: Instr in use of lib. 15: 26604 Green ave, Hemet Ca 92343.

SCHNEIDER, REV VINCENT P. b Phila 19J113. 5: St Charles Sem 34-40 (Philos) AB; Drexel 42-45 BLS. 6: Ger, Lat. 7: Prof St James High Sch, Chester Penn 40-54, Libn Cardinal Dougherty High Sch, Penn 57-; Libn (part-time) Cath Info Center, Phila 53-. 8: Chm, High Sch Lib Adv Com, Archdiocese of Phila. 9: CathLA (Nat chm Parish Sect; East Penn Unit; Chm High Sch Sect; chm, treas, 2nd v-pres); ALA; PennLA; Synagogue LA. 12: Ed "Parish and Catholic Lending Library Manual. 13: Yes. 14: High sch libs, parish &church libs. 15: 363 E Roosevelt blvd, Phila 19120.

SCHNEIDER, STEWART P. b Orange NJ 8N24. 4: Elinor Eccles. 5: Haverford Col 42-44, 46-48 (Eng) BA; Columbia 49-50 (Eng) MA, 63-64 (LS) MS. 6: Ger. 7: Photographers Mate 3/c US Navy 44-46; Eng tchr Milford Sch, Milford Conn 50-52; Sales manager Seabury Press, Greenwich Conn 52-62; Ref libn URI 64-68, Asst Prof Grad Lib Sch 68-. 8: Adv Coun on Interlib Coop, RI Dept of State Lib Serv. 9: ALA; RILA. 10: Steamship Hist Soc of Amer; Phi Beta Kappa; Beta Phi Mu. 14: Ref, acquis, govt publ. 15: Greenwood dr, Peace Dale RI 02879.

SCHNEIDERMAN, CHARLOTTE (ROBINS). b NYC 8 Ap 26. 4: Herbert Schneiderman. 5: Norfolk Div of William & Mary 42-44; NYU 44-46 (Hist) BA; UMd 65-67 MLS. 7: Receptionist ORT-Relief Org, NYC 46-47, Welfare investigator Dept of Welfare, NYC 47-49, Attendance off Bd of Educ, Wash DC 62-64; Asst libn Spingarn High Sch, Wash DC 66; Libn Roosevelt High Sch, Wash DC 67-. 8: Mem Com to Study Standards for Lib Rooms for Jr & Sr High Schs, DC Pub Schs 67; Mem High Sch Eval Com, Middle States Assn Cols & Sec Schs 68. 9: ALA; DCASchL. 14: YA, inner city schs. 15: 3503 Northampton st NW, Washington DC 20015.

SCHNELL, ADELAIDE (McANALLY). b High Point NC 23F10. 5: Salem Col 26-29 (Music); UNC(Chapel Hill) 29-31 (Eng) AB; UNC(Greensboro) 32 (Educ) Tchrs Certif; UNC(Chapel Hill) 62 (LS). 7: Head of tech processes High Point Pub Lib, High Point NC 62-64; Catlgr Guilford Col Lib 64-67; Asst libn & lectr High Point Col 67-. 9: NCLA; SELA. 10: Pilot Club, High Point NC. 14: Catlg. 15: 918 Ferndale dr, High Point NC 27260.

SCHNURMANN, ERIKA. b Paterson NJ. 5: Pembroke 37 (Eng) AB; Simmons 38 (Journalism); Columbia 47 MLS; NJ Libns Perm Certif. 6: Ger. 7: Dir Kearny Pub Lib, Kearny NJ. 9: ALA (past chm Jr Memb Round Table; var coms); NJLA (past treas; chm Recr Com, mem other coms; pres Ext Sect); LPRC (charter mem, past Bd mem, currently treas); No Jersey Libs Round Table (charter mem, past chm). 10: Pres, Passaic Co Health Educ & Welfare Assn; PSSAIC Co Commun Coun Bd; Amer Cancer Soc; Nat Dog Week. 12: "NJLA Newsletter. 13: Yes. 14: Pub rel, acquis, admin. 15:234E 18th st, Paterson NJ 07524.

SCHOELKOPF, (RUSSELL) GERALD. b Reading Penn 6 Jl 45. 5: VillanovaU 63-67 (Eng) BA; McGill 67-69 MLS. 6: Sp. 7: Circ dept VillanovaU Lib 64-65; Res dept McGillU Lib 67-68, Circ lib Engring Lib 68-; Asst libn Tredyffrin Pub Lib, Strafford Penn 67-69 (summer). 9: ALA; SLA; PennLA. 14: Circ, computerization. 15: 139 Beidler rd, King of Prussia Pa 19087.

SCHOENFELD, MADALYNNE (GELLER). b NYC 16 O 24. 4: David Schoenfeld. 5: Brooklyn Col 40-43 (Eng) BA; Pratt Inst 43-44 (Catlg) MLS. 6: Fr. 7: Ref libn Benton & Bowles NYC 44-47; Research libn Universal Studios, Los Angeles 47-48; Y-a libn Mt Vernon Pub lib, Mt Vernon NY 59-60; Child libn Yonkers Pub Lib, Yonkers NY 60-61, Hd child dept 61-65, Child serv coord 67-; Elem sch libn, Port Chester Schs, Port Chester NY 65-67. 8: Chm, Films for Child Com, NY Lib Assn 7/67-; Mem, A-V Com, Child Servs Div, Amer Lib Assn, 68-. 9: ALA; -CSD (Audio-Visual Com 68-); NYLA (chm Films for Child Com 67-); Membership Chm, WestchesterLA (Child & YA Sect: Memb chm 67-68). 13: Yes. 14: Child wk. 15: 21 Albemarle rd, White Plains NY 10605.

SCHOENFELDER, ELIZABETH M (ERSINGER). b Amana Iowa 19S15. 4: George Schoenfelder. 5: UIowa 52-56 (Religion, Eng) BA; Rutgers 57-58 (LS) MA. 6: Ger, Hebrew. 7: Ref spec Cedar Rapids Pub Lib, Cedar Rapids Iowa 58-. 10: Alpha Lambda Delta; Phi Beta Kappa. 14: Ref, research. 15: Amana Iowa 52203.

SCHOENMANN, CATHERIN. b Worthing SD 20 Je 16. 5: Sioux Falls Col 33-35, 37-39 (Eng) BA; UDenver 45 BS in LS. 7: Tchr Colton pub schs, Colton SD 39-41; Tchr-libn Vermillion Pub Schs, Vermillion SD 41-42; Libn Watertown High Sch, Watertown SD 42-43; Tchr Sioux Falls Pub Schs, Sioux Falls SD 43-45; Sioux Falls Pub Lib, Sioux Falls SD: Ref libn 45-54, Yp libn 54-60, City Libn 60-. 9: ALA (Coun 67-); MPLA; SDLA. 10: Altrusa Internat: Sioux Falls Commun Playhouse; Sioux Falls-Augustana Symphony Concerts. 13: Yes. 15: 825 S Euclid, Sioux Falls SD 57104.

SCHOENTHALER, JEAN AUDREY. b Newark NJ 15S41. 5: Tusculum Col 59-63 (Eng, Hist, Religion, Philos) BA; Pratt 63-64 MLS. 6: Ger, Lat. 7: Clerk NJ Bell Telephone Co summers 60-62; Stud asst Tusculum Col Lib 60-61; Catlgr, head of tech serv Rocky Mountain Col 64-68; Catlgr Drew U 68-. 9:

ALA. 10: Pi Gamma Mu; Nat Organ Women. 14: Catlg, tech serv. 15: 21 Park ave, Caldwell NJ 07006.

SCHOESSOW, MATHILDA M. b Milwaukee. 5: Chicago 37-39 (Ger); Wis Conservatory Mus 37-50 (Piano & Organ) Dipl in Piano; UWis 50-51 (LS) MA. 6: Ger. 7: Tchr piano Wis Conservatory Mus 37-, Tchr organ 50-; Lib asst UWis Ext (Milwaukee) 40-51, Libn 51-56, Libn order dept & Asst Prof 56-62, Libn bibliogr & Asst Prof 62-69, Libn catlgr & Asst Prof Mus & Ger 69-. 8: Organist & choir dir Parkside Lutheran Ch, Milwaukee. 9: WisLA. 10: Civic Music Club; McDowell Club; Amer Guild of Organists; Wis Conservatory Alumni Assn; Wis Lib Sch Alumni Assn. 14: Rare bks, music, Ger. 15: 4812 W Washington blvd, Milwaukee Wi 53208.

SCHOFIELD, EDWARD TWINING. b Newtown Penn 8 Ag 12. 4: Martha Harrison Davis. 5: NJ State Col 29-33 (Eng) BS in Ed, 51 BS in LS; NYU 47-48 (Admin) AM, 51-54 (Communications) EdD. 6: Sp. 7: Tchr jr high sch, Pennsauken NJ 33-35; Libn High School, Flemington NJ 35-37; Libn var high schs, Newark NJ 37-48; US Army Med Dept 42-46; Supv Dept Libs Newark (NJ) Bd of Educ 48-60, Dir 60-68; Prof Grad Sch Lib Studies UHawaii 68-. 9: EFLA (pres 50-52); ALA-AASchL (Bd Dirs); NEA-DAVI (Ed Bd 55-60); NJSchLA (pres 48-50); NJLA (Exec Bd 53-55). 10: Kappa Delta Pi. 13: Yes. 14: A-v serv in libs, lib serv for child & yp. 15: 2640 Dole st apt E-102, Honolulu Hi 96822.

SCHOLL, JOYCE (BEATTY). b Pittsburgh 3 F 19. 4: Martin W Scholl. 5: Westminster Col 35-39 (Eng) BA; UMich 40-42 (Eng Lang, Lit) MA; Duquesne U 54-56 M Eq LS; Penn State U 54-56 (LS) PA DPI. 7: Tchr North Hills Schs, Pittsburgh 39-48, Jr high sch libn 54-62; Grad sch Lecturer UPittsburgh 63-64; Sr sch libn Sewickley Acad, Sewickley Penn 65-66; Sch lib adv W Area br div of sch libs Dept of Pub Instr, Penn 66-. 14: Lab lib, lib-based curric. 15: 122 Rose ave, Pittsburgh 15229.

SCHOLLEY, NANCY I. b Laurel Miss 23 Je 30. 4: George G Scholley. 5: Duke 48-52 (Sociol) BA; Case-West Res 62-63 (Educ) MA; UPittsburgh 64-65 MLS. 6: Sp. 7: Sch libn St Teresa Sch, Pittsburgh Penn 67-68; Elem sch libn N Allegheny Sch Dist, Pittsburgh Penn 68-. 9: ALA; PennLA; PennStateEA. 10: Pittsburgh Coun of Internat Visitors; Beta Phi Mu. 14: Sch libnship. 15: 111 Twin Oaks dr, Pittsburgh Pa 15237.

SCHOLZ, DELL (DUBOSE). b Gonzales Tex. 4: Dan R Scholz. 5: Southwest Tex State Col 42 (Music) BS; LSU 60 (LS) MS. 7: Lab Sch nstr music, San Marcos Tex 42-43; Music tchr Gonzales sch system, Gonzales Tex 45-47; Supv elem music Webster Groves ch System, St Louis 49-51; Libn Law Sch LSU (Baton Rouge) 54-59, Head films & recordings dept 60-. 9: ALA; LaLA. 10: Alpha Chi; Phi Beta Mu. 12: "Manual for the Cataloging of Recordings in Public Libraries, publ by author (64). 13: Yes. 14: Music catlg. 15: La State Lib, PO Box 131, Baton Rouge La 70821.

SCHONBRUN, RENA. b Jamaica NY 3 N 40. 5: Queens Col (NY) 58-62 (Chem) BS; West Res 62-63 MS in LS. 7: Lit chem Lederle Labs div Amer Cyanamid Co, Pearl River NY 63-66, Info chem 66-68; Libn Nat Agric Lib, Wash DC 68-. 9: ACS; ASIS; ALA; SLA. 10: AAAS. 14: Mech of lib operations, catlg. 15: 9813 Telegraph rd, Seabrook Md 20801.

SCHOOLFIELD, DUDLEY BRANCH. b Dallas Tex 27 D 30. 4: Rosemary Mizell. 5: E Tex State Tchrs Col 49-50, 52-55 (Biol) BS; N Tex State Col 55-56 BS in LS. 7: SA US Navy 50-54; Catlgr Mobil Research & Development Corp, Dallas Tex 56-. 9: ALA; SLA. 10: Mobil Mgt Assn. 12: Coed & cocomp Geologic Field Trip Guidebooks of North America, A Union List Incorporating Monographic Titles-- (68). 14: Catlg, reports, automation of lib procedures, lib serv in hosps, tchg adults to read. 15: 1619 Cedar ave, Dallas Tx 75208.

SCHOONOVER, BONNIE-BLANCHE (ROBINSON). b Ponca Neb 15N1893. 4: Lynn Irvine Schoonover. 5: Morningside 11-15 (Econ) BA; Columbia 20-21 (Dramatics) BE; Chicago summers 18-20; Radcliffe 26-27 (Eng) MA. 6: Fr, Ger. 7: Supv of reading & dramatics Sioux City (Iowa) Pub Schs 16-20; Asst in dramatics UIda 22-26; Asst in econ hist Harvard Bus Sch 27-28; Night Libn Radcliffe Col 28-42; Libn Worcester Polytech Inst 42-66; Catlgr Anna Maria Col 68-. 9: Amer Soc Engnr Educ (chm Lib Com 45-47); ALA. 10: Radcliffe Club of Worcester. 14: Bk reviewing, travel lectures. 15: 12 Monroe ave, Worcester Mass 01602.

SCHORK, FRANCIS WILLIAM. b Cleveland 12D24. 5: Oberlin Col 46-49 (Fr Lit) AB; UParis 49-50 Fr Lit it) Certif; Johns Hopkins 50-51 (Fr Lit) AM; UMich 51-52 AMLS. 6: Fr. 7: Libn Sch of Adv Internat Studies, Johns Hopkins U, Washington Center Off For Policy Res Inst of Devel Programming 52-63; Assoc dir East-West Center Lib, Honolulu 63-64; U Libn American U 64-. 8: Lib consul, The Middle East Inst, Wash DC 52-; Consul; Spec Operations Res Off, Wash DC 60-62, UHawaii Lib 63-64, UWis Lib 64, U of Wales 66, Brock U 67, U Virginia 67, Kyoto Sangyo U Japan 68. 11: Fulbright scholar, UParis 49-50. 14: Univ lib admin, lib automation. 15: 1641 Nineteenth st NW, Wash DC 20009.

SCHORMANN, MARGUERITE (TUPPER). b Clark SD. 4: Victor Schormann. 5: UILL 32 (Fr, Lat) AB, 42 (Educ, Fr, Lat) MA, 49 MS in LS; Ind U 64 (Educ) D Ed. 6: Fr. 7: Tchr-libn Illiopolis (Ill) High Sch 32-38; Tchr-libn Hebron (Ill) High Sch 40-43; Tchr Pekin (ill) High Sch 43-46; Tchr-libn Wayland Acad & Jr Col, Beaver Dam Wis 46-48; Asst Prof & Instr in Lib Sci West Ill U 49-65, Assoc Prof & Dir of Lib Sci Program 65-66; Assoc Prof of Lib Sci No Ill U 66-. 9: ALA-AASchL;-LED;-YASD; NEA; IllASchL; IllLA; IllEA; NCTE. 10: AAUP; ACLU; Amer Fed Tchrs. 14: Educ for libnship, sch libs. 15: 821 Sharon dr, DeKalb Il 60115.

SCHORMANN, VICTOR. b Staplehurst Neb 21D 18. 4: Marguerite Tupper. 5: Concordia Sem (St Louis) 39-44; UIll 47-48 (Ger) AB, 48-49, 50 MSLS. 6: Ger. 7: Tchr & asst to pastor Zion Lutheran Congregation, Pierce Neb 42-43; Statistical clerk, publ clerk, hist Res asst US War Dept Off of Chief of Chaplains, Wash DC 45-47; Order libn,Instr Lib Sci Knox Col 49-50; Circ & a-v libn Augustana Col (Rock Island Ill) 50-51; Order & a-v libn West Ill U 51-52, Period libn 52-66; Asst acquis libn No Ill U 66-. 9: ALA; NEA; IllLA; IllEA. 10: ACTU; AAUP; Amer Fed Tchrs. 14: Periods, ref. 15: 821 Sharon dr, DeKalb Il 60115.

SCHOTT, ERNEST HERMANN. b Frankfurt Germany 18 S 24. 4: Beatruce Hilderbrant. 5: UCal (Berkeley) 42-49 AB; San Francisco State 49-52 (Secondary Educ) MA; UWash 62-65 M Lib, 66-. 6: Ger, Ital, Fr. 7: Tchr & libn Modoc Union High Sch, Alturas Cal 50-52; Tchr: Oakdale J Union High Sch, Oakdale Cal 52-54, Franklin High Sch, Seattle 54-65; Libn Lincoln High Sch, Seattle 65-66; Libn Cleveland High Sch, Seattle 66-67; Research assoc UWash 67-. 8: Pres UWash Sch of Libr Alumn Assoc (67-68). 9: ALA; -ACRL; NEA; WashLA; WashEA; WashStateASchL; SeattleLA. 10: Phi Beta Mu; Phi Delta Kappa. 14: Col libs, rare bks. 15: 2028 NE 65th st, Seattle Wa 98115.

SCHOYER, GEORGE PRESTON. b Pittsburgy 11 Ag 18. 4: Anne Craig. 5: Yale U 37-41 (Hist) BA; UPittsburgh 46-48 (Hist) BA; UPenn 49-51 (Hist); Carnegie 53-54 MLS. 6: Fr. 7: US Army Infantry 41-45; Wked in bkstores, Pittsburgh 51-53; Readers Adv DC Pub Lib 54-56; Libn Hist, Pol Sci & Map Grad Lib Ohio State U 56-, Asst Prof lib admin 56-. 9: ALA; OhioLA. 10: AHA. 13: Yes. 14: Hist, soc sci, ref, bibliog. 15: 609 E Dominion blvd, Columbus Oh 43214.

SCHRADER, VIVIAN L. b Wash DC 18 Jl 21. 5: Wilson Tchrs Col 38; George WashingtonU 47. 7: Ref searcher Copyright Off LC 42-46, Catlgr 46-57, A-V catlgr descr catlg div 57-68, Asst hd a-v sect 68-. 10: Wash Film Coun. 14: Catlg. 15: 4545 Connecticut ave NW apt 519, Washington DC 20008.

SCHRAMM, HUGH. b Ft Wayne Ind 16 Ag 38. 5: UCincinnati 56-61 (Eng) BA; UKy 61-63(LS) MS. 7: Gen asst in a br Queens Borough Pub Lib, Queens NY 63-65; Asst catlgr Muskingum Col 65-68; Asst catlgr Marshall U 68-. 9: ALA. 14: Catlg, bk sel, ref. 15: Marshall Univ Lib, Huntington WVa 25701.

SCHRANK, PAUL (HARRY) JR. b Akron Ohio 21027. 5: Ohio U 46-49 (Com) BSc; UNC 54-55 (Eng); UIll 62-63 (LS) MS. 7: (Lt jg) USNR, Wash DC 52-54: Security analyst Equitable Life Assurance Soc, NYC 55-62; Asst to dir of libs Ga Inst of Tech 62-64; Asst libn admin UAkron 65, Head Libn 65-. 9: ALA: Ohio LA. 10: . . 14: Admin. 15: Univ of Akron, Akron Ohio 44304.

SCHREIBER, ELLEN (PHYLLIS). b NYC 28 S 42. 4: Fred Schreiber. 5: Queens Col (NY) 60-64 (Art Hist) BA; Simmons 66-68 (LS) MS. 6: Fr, Sp. 7: Bibliog asst HarvardU 65-66, Catlgr 66-67, Libn in charge of seaching & filing 67-. 14: Admin, personnel. 15: 34 Irving st, Cambridge Ma 02138.

SCHREIBER, PHYLLIS B(OGORAD). b NYC 18D26. 4: Murray D Schreiber. 5: Hunter Col 44-48 (Eng) AB; Pratt 57-61 MLS. 6: Fr, Sp. 7: Lib tchr Bay Ridge High Sch, Brooklyn NY 61-. 9: NYC SchLA. 10: Phi Beta Kappa Sigma Tau Delta; Beta Phi Mu. 14: Sch libs. 15: 8701 Shore rd, Brooklyn NY 11209.

SCHREIBER, ROBERT (EDWIN). b Oak Park Ill 3 My 19. 4: Patricia Gain. 5: WestIllU 37-39 (Sci); NorthwesternU 39-41 (Psych) BS; UIll 41-42 (Educ) MS; UChicago 45-47 (Educ). 7: Supv a-v aids Stephens Col 43-45; Research asst Ctr for Study of A-V Instr Materials UChicago 45-47; Supv tchg aids pub schs, Mishawaka Ind 47-49; Dir a-v serv UMe (Orona) 49-53; Asst Prof NJ State Col (Glassboro) 53-54; Libn Educ Materials Ctr No IllU 54-63, Dir 63-. 9: NEA; -DAVI; IllLA; IllEA; Ill A-V Assn. 10: Phi Delta Kappa. 12: "Building the School's Audio-Visual Program" (46); Assoc ed "Audio-Visual Guide" (49-56); Deptal ed "Educational Screen" (45-49 & 56-58), articles in Britannica Jr & New Standard Encyclopedia. 13: Yes. 14: Educ media. 15: 310 Royal dr, DeKalb Il 60115.

SCHREIBER, SARAH (INKMAN). b Minneapolis Minn 13 Ap 23. 4: Henry Allen Schreiber. 5: Los Angeles City Col 41-43 (Hist); UCal (Berkeley) 43-45 (Hist) BA, 45-46 (LS) Certif. 6: Fr, Ger. 7: Ref libn UCal (Davis) 45-51, Hd ref dept 51-56; Libn fine arts tucson Pub Lib 68-. 8: Share respons of coord a GED educl prog (evening classes), OEO, Rillito Area Coun Tucson Ariz 67-. 9: ALA; ArizStateLA. 10: Rillito Area Coun; Friends of the Library. 14: Ref. 15: 222 N Norton ave, Tucson Az 85719.

SCHREINER, LYLE RUDOLPH. b Unadilla Neb 21 My29. 4: Phyllis Ann Gobber. 5: Peru State Col 46-48 (Biol); UNeb 48-50 (Zool, Bot) BS; UOkla 56-58 MLS. 6: Ger. 7: US Army 36th Engnr Combat Group Supply & Med Areas (Cpl), Korea 51-53; Lab tech Lancaster Co-Lincoln City Health Dept, Lincoln Neb 55-56; Asst libn E Campus Lib UNeb 58-65, Asst dir for sci & tech UNeb Libs 66-. 9: ALA-ACRL;-RTSD; NebLA (Conv Com). 10: AAUP; Gamma Sigma Delta; UNeb Lib Staff Assn; AAAS. 14: Catlg & ref (agric & biol). 15: 1310 S 48th, Lincoln Neb 68510.

SCHREUR, ROBERT L. b Paterson NJ 10 D 29. 4: Joyce Schierloh. 5: Bob JonesU 47-51 (Educ) BS; Columbia 52-54 (Educ) MA; USoCal 66-67; UOre 66. 6: Sp. 7: Clk Erie RR Co, NYC 52-54; Tchr Oradell Sch, Oradell NJ 54-56; Tchr Lincoln Sch, Vista Cal 56-57; Tchr Anaheim United High Sch Dist, Anaheim Cal 57-67; Libn Kennedy High Sch, Buena Pk Cal 67-; Libn Cypress Jr Col 67-. 9: CalTA; CalASchL. 14: Catlg, period. 15: 1237 Vista del Plara, Orange Ca 92667.

SCHRIEFER, KENT K. b Higginsville Mo 21D33. 5: UMo 53-57 (Eng) AB; UCal (Berkeley) 59-60 MLS. 6: Fr, Ger. 7: Jr catlgr Tulane U Lib 60-61, Ser catlgr 61-62, Head catlg dept 62-65; Assoc libn UColo Med Center Lib 65-67; Assoc libn Health Sci Lib SUNY (Buffalo) 67-. 9: ALA; MedLA (Reprint Com); Upstate NY MedLA (sec-treas). 14: Catlg, mgt. 15: 538 Linwood ave, Buffalo NY 14209.

SCHROECK, BERNARD ANTHONY. b Erie Penn 2S17. 5: Notre Dame U 39-43 (Internat Trade) BSC; West Res 54-55 M in LS. 6: Ger. 7: Asst chief libn US VA Hosp, Roanoke Va 57-58; Bkmob libn Fairfield Co, Lancaster Ohio 59-61; Research on bibliotherapy, Harrisburg Penn 58, 61-63; Libn Divine Word Sem (Girard Penn) 63-; Ref libn Gannon Col 63-. 8: Instr in lib usage, Gannon Col 63-. 9: ALA; CathLA; PennLA. 14: Ref, rsearch, col & univ libs, bibliotherapy. 15: 2627 Chestnut st, Erie Penn 16508.

SCHROEDER, EVA I A. b Belgard Germany. 5: UGreifswald(Germany) 35-37, 38-39; UGraz(Austria) 37; UVt 37-38; UBerlin 39-42 (Eng Lit, Phil) PhD; UMich 55-56 AMLS. 6: Ger, Fr, Dutch, Ital. 7: "Die Welt (Newspaper), Hamburg Germany 47-49; Free lance tr, Hamburg Germany 45-51; Instr in Eng UVt 52-55; Intern libn NY Pub Lib 55-56, Catlgr rare bks 57-59; Prof of Lib Educ State U Col (Geneseo NY) 59-68; Assoc dir Heidelberg Col Lib (Ohio) 68-. 8: Visiting catlgr. SUNY(Buffalo) Libs summer 63; Visiting Lecturer, Grad Sch of Lib Sci, UIll summer 65; Visiting Catlgr, URochester Lib 65-66. 9: ALA-ACRL;-RTS; OLA. 10: AAUP; Beta Phi Mu. 12: Tr Barker, Ernest "Grossbritannien und das britische Volk (47). 13: Yes. 14: Catlg, admin. 15: Heidelberg Coll, Tiffin Oh 44883.

SCHROEDER, RAY (ARLO). b Tigerton Wis 26y23. 4: Melda Pockat. 5: Wis State U (Oshkosh) 54; Elem Educ BS 69; UWis 60 MSLS, UWis (Milwaukee) 68 (SS). 6: Ger. 7: Elem tchr Zion Sch, Warren Ill 49-50; Elem prin Marion pub schs, Caroline Wis 50-53; Jr high sch tchr Marion pub schs, Marion Wis 54-55; Jr high sch libn Shawano pub schs, Shawano Wis 59-62; Libn Wis State U (Oshkosh) 62-64, Asst Prof of Lib Sci 64-68; Coord of lib & a-v serv Oshkosh Area Pub Schs, Oshkosh Wis 68-. 9: ALA; NEA; WisLA; WisEA. 10: Assn of Wis State Univ Faculties; Kappa Delta Pi; Phi Beta Sigma; Beta Phi Mu. 14: Educ materials centers, ref, tchg lib sci, coord lib & a-v serv. 15: 207 N Meadow st, Oshkosh Wis 54901.

SCHROEDER, ROBERT H(ENRY). b Brooklyn NY 9 D 16. 5: Pratt Inst 33-37 (Advertising Design); Cooper Union 40-43 (Advertising Design). 6: Ger. 7: Period libn Union Theol Sem Lib 42-46, Curator rare bks 43-47, Act order libn 46, Hd acquis div 47-. 10: US Power Squadrons. 15: 3041 Broadway, New York NY 10027.

SCHROETHER, MARIAN (RUTH). b Davenport Iowa 5 A19. 5: Cornell Col 37-41 (Eng) BA; West Res 41-42 BS in LS. 7: Child libn Free Pub Lib, Winona Minn 42-44; Child libn Waukegan Pub Lib, Waukegan Ill 44-. 8: Consul, Wilsons "Childrens Catalog" 54-. 9: ALA-CSD (Newbery-Caldecott Com 57-61, Mem & chm Bk Eval Com 58-61; chm Melcher Scholarship Com 55-56); IllLA (chm child libns sect 50-51); YWCA (Child Reading RT). 10: AAUW; Phi Beta Kappa; Child Reading RT; YWCA. 13: Yes. 14: Child bks. 15: Waukegan Pub Lib, 128 N County st, Waukegan Il 60085.

SCHRYVER, (MARY) LOUISE. b Belleville Ont Can27D14. 5: Victoria Col UToronto 33-36 BA; UToronto 37-38 BLS; UMich 56-58 AMLS. 6: Fr. 7: Gen asst Corby Pub Lib, Belleville Ont 36-37; Child Libn Midland Pub Lib, Midland Ont 38-40, Chief Libn 40-43; Yp libn Calgary Pub Lib, Calgary Alta 43-44; Child libn Chatham Pub Lib, Chatham Ont 44-46, Chief Libn 46-; Dir S West Ont Reg Lib, Chatham Ont 63-65. 8: Adv Bd St Clair Col 69-. 9: ALA; CanLA (Pub Lib Div; chm Salaries & Personnel Com, mem Libns Com, Standards Com); OntLA (pres 61-62, Com Mem; Research, Legis & Grants, Provincial Lib, Pension, etc); Inst Prof Libns Ont (pres 60-61); Com Libns SWest Ont Reg System. 10: S West Ont Film Fed. 11: Ford fellowship in Adult Educ 57-58; Centennial Medal 67. 12: "Blue Print for Library Service," CanLA. 13: Yes. 14: Admin, reg devel, legis. 15: Chatham Pub Lib, Chatham Ont Can.

SCHUBERT, DONALD (FRANCIS). b Madison Wis 13 0 22. 5: Loras Col 42-44 (Eng); St Francis Col 44-48 (Philos) BA; UWis 48-49, summer 53 (Eng) BS, 54-55 (LS) MS. 6: Lat. 7: Asst libn Pockhurst Col 55-56; Tchr of Lat & Eng Liberty High Sch, Liberty Mo 60-63; Tchr of Lat & Asst libn Ward High Sch, Kan City Kan 63-, Hd libn 68-. 8: A-V dir, Ward High Sch, Kan City Kan, 65-69. 9: ALA; NEA-DAVI; KanLA; CathLA. 10: Cath Commun Club; Visitors for Christ. 14: Catlg, ref. 15: 501 W 11th st, Kansas City Mo 64152.

SCHUBERT, MARY E (WOOD). b Muncie Ind 9Ag09. 5: Ball State U 27-28 (Eng);lora Flora Mather West Res 28-31 (Eng) AB; West Res 31-32 BS in LS. 6: Fr. 7: Merchandise adjuster The May Co, leveland 33-35; Cuyahoga Co Lib, Cleveland: Sch libn 50-51, Sta libn 51-60, Bkmob libn 52-54, Adult serv libn 60-68, Br libn 68-. 9: OhioLA. 10: AAUW; Lake Shore Garden Club; Euclid Cult Coun. 14: Ref, bk sel. 15: 31 E 216th st, Euclid Ohio 44123.

SCHUCH, GRETCHEN ROSEMARY (RIESE). b Lowell Mass 15 S 24. 4: Adam F Schuch. 5: Wheaton Col (Norton Mass) 42-45 (Ger) AB; Simmons 47-50 (LS) MS. 6: Ger, Fr. 7: Ref asst Harvard Med Sch Lib 45-51; Libn QM Climatic Research Lab, Lawrence Mass 51-53; Med libn Los Alamos Sci Lab, Los Alamos Area Off, 53-57, Br libn 57-. 8: Consul, Cath Maternity Inst, Santa Fe NM 61, Los Alamos Area Off AEC 60, Espanola Hosp Lib, Espanola NM 67, Immaculate Heart of Mary Parish Lib, Los Alamos NM 68-. 9: MedLA; SLA. 10: Amer Red Cross. 12: Co-tr "Action of Radiation on Tissues" (58). 13: Yes. 14: Ref, transl, lib planning (Br libs). 15: Los Alamos Sci Libs Box 1663, Los Alamos Ca 87544.

SCHUCK, EDWIN G. b NYC 20 Jl 16. 4: Emma J Huetter. 5: CCNY 34-38 (Math) BA; Columbia 48-51 (Law) LLB, 67-69 (LS) MS; Fletcher Sch of Law & Diplomacy 55-56 (Intl Law) MA. 6: Ger. 7: Offr US Army 40-65; Asst dean Columbia Law Sch 65-67, Law libn 67-. 9: NY Bar; Supreme Court of the US; US Court of Mil Appeals. 10: Beta Phi Mu. 11: Legion of Merit 65. 13: Yes. 14: Law libnship, admin, legal bibliog. 15: 7 Fairmount rd, Ridgewood NJ 07450.

SCHUCK-KOLBEN, G(ERHARD) P(AUL). b Austria 16 Jl21. 4: Jacqueline H Lyon. 5: UIll 39-42 (Electrical Engnr); UPittsburgh even 47-50 (Ger) AB, even 52-54 (Germanics) M Litt. 6: Ger, Fr, Czech. 7: Grad trainee Westinghouse Electric Corp, E Pittsburgh Penn summers 40-42; Flight Sgt Fighter Pilot Royal Air Force, Eng 43-46; Asst Power & Fuel engr US Steel Corp, Braddock Penn summers 47, 48; Lecturer in Ger UPittsburgh 47-; Head info serv Consolidation Coal Co Res Div, Library Penn 52-. 9: Amer Assn Tchrs of Ger; ACS; Mod Lang Assn; SLA; Soc Tech Writers & Publrs; Amer Soc of Sci & Engnr Translators. 10: AAUP; Volkswagen Club of Pittsburgh. 13: Yes. 14: Communications, info sci, linguistics. 15: Consolidation Coal Co, Res Div, Library Pa 15129.

SCHUCK, EDWIN G. b NYC 20 Jl 16. 4: Emma J Auetter. 5: CCNY 34-38 (Math) BA; Columbia 48-51 (Law) LLB, 67-69 (LS) MS; Fletcher Sch of Law & Diplomacy 55-56 9intl Law) MA. 6: Ger. 7: Off US Army 40-65; Asst dean Columbia Law Sch 65-67, Law libn 67-. 9: NY Bar; Supreme Court of the US; US Court of Mil Appeals. 10: Beta Phi mu. 11: Legion of Merit 65. 13: Yes. 14: Law libnship, admin, legal bibliog. 15: 7 Fairmount rd, Ridgewood NJ 07450.

SCHUELER, FRANCES (SCHAF) (MRS). b Teaneck NJ 6 O 28. 5: Col of Notre Dame (Md) 46-50 (Hist) AB (magna cum laude); Catholic U 51-54 MS in LS. 6: Fr, Ger. 7: Catholic U Wk Fellowship in Gk & Lat Lib & Stack page Main Lib 51, Asst in educ lib 51, Head educ lib 51-53, Ref asst in Gen Ref Room 53-55, Head of Educ Lib 56-58, Head of Educ, Religious Educ, Psych Lib 58-61; Asst ref libn main lib UCincinnati Lib 63-66, Ref libn 66-68; Asst hd Soc Wk - Soc Scis Lib Catholic U 68-. 9: ALA. 10: Newman Foundation and Talbert House (Cincinnati); Delta Epsilon Sigma; Kappa Gamma Pi. 12: Co-comp "Faculty Publications, University of Cincinnati, 1963-1964" (65); "University of Cincinnati Faculty Publications and Creative Works, 1965-1966" (67). 14: Ref. 15: 1001 Varnum st NE, Washington DC 20017.

SCHULER, DONALD VERN. b Ecorse Mich 13 My 27. 4: Verna Jean Smith. 5: Mich State U 45-49 (Police Admin) BS; Cleveland-Marshall Law 57-60 Dr of Law; West Res 62-65 MLS. 7: Chief of Police, Cassopolis Mich 50-51; US Army (Major) 45-46, 51-54, 55-; Claims examiner Continental Insurance Co, Cleveland 60-65; Head catlgr Law Sch Ohio State U 65-66; Asst law libn Appellate Div Law Lib, Rochester NY 67; Dir of libs, Grove City Ohio 68-. 9: AALL; OhioALL (sec 66); ALA; OhioLA. 14: Admin. 15: 497 Mid dr, Worthington Ohio.

SCHULER, ERIC T. b Saratov Russia 9S01. 4: Melitta E Nissen. 5: Handelshochschule (Berlin Germany) 22-26 (Econ) MA; Columbia BLS. 6: Russian, Ger. 7: Lib asst NY Pub ib 35-37; Catlgr Cornell U Lib 37-43; Research analyst Off of Strategic Serv, Wash DC 43-45; Catlgr Slavic Lang LC 45-47; Research analyst Russian field Arctic Inst of N Amer, Wash DC 47-49; lc: Subj catlgr 49-52, 56-57, Head Cyrillic Union ubj Catlg Unit 52-56, Head Slavic Lang Sect Descr Catlg Div 57-. 8: Tchg Russian, Grad Sch, Dept of Agric; Assignment with Amer Tech Bk Exhib, Moscow & Leningrad, 63. 14: Slavic (espec Russian), probems of transliteration, Amer vs mod Russian catlg problems. 15: 4th & Cookman sts, Rehoboth Beach De 19971.

SCHULER, JILL LYNN. b Easton Oenn 23 N 45. 5: Gettysburg Col 63-67 (Sp) BA; UPittsburgh 68-69 MLS. 6: Sp, Fr. 7: Indexer H W Wilson Co, NYC 69-. 9: ALA. 14: Indexing, Lat Amer bibliog. 15: 511 Easton rd, Riegelsville Pa 18077.

SCHULKEN, MABEL J. b Wadesboro NC 6 Jl 14. 4: Samuel B Schulken. 7: Br libn Piedmont cts Br Pub Lib of Charlotte & Mecklenburg Co, Charloutte NC 49-55; Br lib asst Pub Lib of Charlotte & Mecklenburg Co: E Br 55-64, S Br 64-65, Sharon Br 65-. 9: ALA; NCLA; MecklenburgLA. 10: Staff Org of Pub Lib of Charlotte & Mecklenburg Co. 14: Ref, child lit. 15: 2129 Chesterfield ave, Charlotte NC 28205.

SCHULLER, MICHAEL P. b St Louis 27N18. 4: Helyne Hemstad. 5: UWash 47-52 (Journalism) BA, (LS) MA. 7: USAF (Sgt) Hq 16 Wea Squad 41-45; Libn Olympia High Sch, Olympia Wash 52-64; Libn Olympic Col 64-. 9: ALA; Wash State ASchL; WashLA. 14: Lib standards. 15: 7702 - 15th ave NE, Seattle 98115.

SCHULLIAN, DOROTHY M. b Lakewood Ohio. 5: West Res 27 AB; Chicago 31 PhD; Amer Acad in Rome 34FAAR. 7: West Res U; Albion Col; NLM; Curator hist of sci collections Cornell U Lib 61-. 8: Ryerson Fellow in Rome; Fulbright Fellow in Italy. 9: Amer Assn Hist Med; Hist Sci Soc; MedLA; BSA; Amer Philol Assn; Archaeol Inst Amer; Mediaeval Acad of Amer; Amer Classical League; Classical Assn Atlantic States. 10: AAAS. 12: Bks, articles, and reviews on the hist of med & sci; Ed 'Notes and Events' in "Journal of the History of Medicine and Allied Sciences". 14: Early bks (hist of sci & med). 15: Cornell Univ Lib, Ithaca NY 14850.

SCHULTE-ALBERT, HANS GEORG. b Gelsenkirchen Germany 26 Jl 31. 4: Dale Jackson. 5: Kent State U 51-56 (Ger Lit) AB (magna cum laude), 51-56 (Hist) BS in Ed (magna cum laude); West Res 56-57 MS in LS; U Wien 57-58 (Hist); West Res 58-65 (Hist) MA. 6: Ger, Fr, Lat. 7: Clerk Ohio Edison Co, Akron Ohio 51-56; Lib asst Case Inst of Tech 56-57; Catlgr West Res U 58-63, Sr catlgr 64-68, Supv datatext operations 68-. 9: ALA; No Ohio Tech Serv Libns (v-chm 66-67, chm 67-68). 10: Branderburgia Berlin zu Cleveland; Beta Phi Mu. 14: Catlg, col & univ lib admin, clsf, hist bks & libs. 15: 1557 Maple Grove rd, South Euclid Oh 44121.

SCHULTHEISS, LOUIS AVERY. b Cody Wyo 30 O 25. 5: UWyo 45-49 (Hist) AB; UDenver 49-50 (LS) MA. 7: UDenver: Art & arch libn 50-52, Head circ dept 52-56, Asst dir of libs 56-58; Acquis head UIll(Chicago) 58-61, Head tech serv 61-, Act dir 67-69. 8: Dir, Univ Lib Info Systems Proj, UIll 61. 9: ALA; SLA; Chicago Lib Club; Chicago Reg Group of Libns in Tech Proc (chm 65-66). 12: "Advanced Data Processing in the University Library (62). 13: Yes. 14: Tech serv, systems analysis & design, automation of tech operations. 15: 621 E 33rd pl, Chicago 60616.

SCHULTZ, BARBARA (BROWN) FISCHER. b Pittsburgh 15 Mr 40. 4: Mark P Schultz. 5: UMd 57-61 (Hist) BA; West Res 62-63 MSLS. 6: Fr. 7: Lib aide C Burr Artz Lib, Frederick Md summers 56-60; Ref libn Prince George's Co Mem Lib, Hyattsville Md 61-62; Br libn Prince George's Co Mem Lib, Bladensburg Md 64-66, Laurel Md 66-67; Asst adult coord Cuyahoga Co Lib, Cleveland Ohio 67-68, Adult coord 68-. 9: ALA; MdLA; Md Assn Adult Educ; OhioLA. 10: Prince George's Co Mem Lib Staff Assn (pres 65-66); Adult Educ Coun - Cleveland; Cleveland Young Libns Assn; Women's Nat Bk Assn. 14: Ref, adult serv, admin. 15: 2218 Murray Hill rd, Cleveland Oh 44106.

SCHULTZ, CHARLES ROY. b Giddings Tex 6 D 35. 4: Frances Harter. 5: Tex Lutheran Col 54-58 (Hist, Eng) BA; Bowling Green State U 58-59 (Amer Hist) MA; Ohio State U 60-63 (Amer Hist) PhD. 7: High sch Hist tchr Bowling Green (Ohio) Pub Schs 59-60; Mss processor Ohio Hist Soc, Columbus Ohio 60-63; Keeper of Mss Marine Hist Assn Inc, Mystic Conn 63-67, Libn 67-. 9: Manuscripts Soc; SAA; SLA (Corresp sec Conn Valley Chap 69-70). 10: Stonington (Conn) Hist Soc; Phi Alpha Theta. 13: Yes. 14: Mss. 15: GW Blunt White Lib, Marine Hist Assn Inc, Mystic Ct 06355.

SCHULTZ, CLAIRE K. b York Co Penn 17N24. 4: Wallace L Schultz. 5: Juniata Col 41-44 (Chem, Biol) BS; Womans med Col of Penn 45-46 (Med) UPenn 47-49, 58, 64 (Physiol); Drexel 49-52 (LS) MS. 6: Ger, Fr, Russian. 7: Res assoc & libn Wistar Inst, Phila 46-49; Libn Merck Sharp & Dohme, Phila 49-57; Systems analyst Remington Rand UNIVAC, Phila 58-61; Research Scientist Inst Adv Md Commun, Phila 61-. 8: Spec consul to US Govt, MEDLARS Proj 62-63: Visiting Assoc Prof, Drexel Inst Curr in Info Sci 62-; Visiting Asst Prf UWash Lib Sch, summer 63. 9: ASIS (pres 62); SLA (chm Pharmaceut Sect 54-55); Assns Comput Mach. 10: AAAS. 12: Ed "State of the Art of Documentation; a Symposium," ADI (62); Ed "H P Luhn, Pioneer in Information Science, Selected Works" Sparta (68); Auth "Thesaurus of Information Science Terminology" (68). 13: Yes. 14: Research in indexing, thesaurus constr, computer applications to info sci, tchg info sci. 15: Line Lexington Penn 18932.

SCHULTZ, ELLEN MARIE. b Buffalo NY 9 Ap 37. 4: John H Schultz. 5: State U Col (Buffalo NY) 54-58 (Educ) BS; Rutgers 59-61 MLS. 7: Tchr Tonawanda Pub Schs, Tonawanda NY 58-59; Trainee to sr libn Free Pub Lib, Linden NJ 60-62; Asst ref libn SUNY(Buffalo) 62-65; Lib asst Westminster Ref Lib, London 65; Ref asst SUNY(Buffalo) 65-67, Ref libn 68-. 8: Library/USA NY World's Fair 64. 14: Ref. 15: 114 Keil st, No Tonawanda NY 14120.

SCHULTZ, ERICH (RICHARD WILLIAM). b Rankin Ont Can 1 Je 30. 5: Waterloo Col (affil with UWest Ont) 47-51 BA; Waterloo Lutheran Sem (affil with UWest Ont) 57 BD; Knox Col of UToronto 57-58 MTh, Lib Sch UToronto 58-59 BLS. 6: Ger. Fr. 7: Pastor St Pauls Lutheran Church, Ellice Twp Ont 54-56; Libn-lecturer Waterloo Lutheran Sem (Ont) 59-. 8: Lecturer, New Testament Introduction, Waterloo Lutheran Sem 59-. 9: CanLA; Lutheran Soc for Worship, Music & the Arts; ATheolLA (Coun 64-67). 10: Can Assn UNIV Tchrs. 12: Ed "Ambulatio Fidei; Essays in Honour of Otto W Heick" (65). 13: Yes. 14: Catlg. 15: Waterloo Lutheran Univ, Waterloo Ont Can.

SCHULTZ, MARJORIE (HILL). b New Bedford Mass 11 Mr 13. 4: Arthur R Schultz. 5: Mt Holyoke Col 30-34 (Eng) BA; Wellesley 35-36 (Eng) MA; UWis 36-40 (Eng). 6: Ger, Fr. 7: Grad asst Eng UWis(Madison) 36-40; Asst catlg dept NYU Lib 41-42; Asst subj headings NY Pub Lib 42-43; Instr Eng Rensselaer Polytech Inst 43-44; Instr Eng Milwaukee-Downer Col 44-46; Acquis libn Wesleyan U Lib (Conn) 57-. 15: Wesleyan Lib, Middletown Ct 06457.

SCHULTZ, NADINE LYNN. b Maywood Cal 26 Ap 43. 5: Los Angeles Valley Col 60-61 (Hist); Cal Lutheran Col 61-64 (Hist) BA; UCLA 64-65 MLS. 6: Sp, Ger. 7: Clerk Los Angeles Valley Col Lib 60-61; Lib asst Cal Lutheran Col Lib 61-64; Clerk UCLA Research Lib 64-65; Catlgr UCal(Santa Cruz) 65-67, 69-; Clerk Otto Harrassowitz, Wiesbaden Ger 68. 9: . 14: Catlg. 15: 657 24th ave #30, Santa Cruz Ca 95060.

SCHULTZ, RUTH ANNETTE (DARLINGTON). b Racine Wis 31 O 38. 4: Gary G Schultz. 5: UWis 56-60 (Philos) BS, 60-61 (LS) MS; UIll 66 (Med Libnship) Certif. 6: Ger. 7: Ref libn Pub Lib, Winnetka Ill 61-62; Lbn Augustana Hosp Sch of Nursing, Chicago 62-65; Libn Abbott Jr High Sch, Elgin Ill 65-66; Nursing libn UWis (Madison) Med Sch Lib 66-. 8: Prog Chm, Tri-State Hosp Assembly, Conf on Lib Serv 68-69. 9: ALA. 10: Beta Phi Mu. 14: Ref. 15: 501 Elmside blvd, Madison Wi 53704.

SCHULTZ, SUSAN A. b Mountain Lake Minn 22D11. 5: John Fletcher Col 37-40 (Hist) BA; Northwestern summers 44, 45 (Guidance); UIll 45-46 BS in LS, 47-49 MS in LS. 6: Ger. 7: Dean of women John Fletcher Cel 40-45; Asst libn Bethany Col (Okla) 46-47; Libn Asbury Theol Sem 49-. 8: Org lib, Union Biblical Sem, Yeotmal, Maharashtra, India 61-62. 9: ATheolLA (Exec Sec 67-; chm Period Exch Com 57-6 chm Memb Com 64-); KyLA (2nd v-pres 57-58, chm Memb Com 57-58; chm Col & Ref Sect 57-58); chm Spec Libs Sect 66-67). 10: Beta Phi Mu; Pi Lambda Theta; Theta Phi; Withers-Jessamine Co Pub Lib Bd. 11: Outstanding Spec Libn of the year 1967, Lib Trustees Assn, Ky. 13: Yes. 14: Admin, ref. 15: Sem Post Off No 115, Wilmore Ky 40390.

SCHULZ, MILDRED (MABERRY). b Monmouth Ill. 5: Augustana Col BA; Columbia 44-45 (LS). 6:Fr, Ger. 7: Head hist dept E Moline (Ill) elem schs; Head libn Pub Lib, E Moline Ill 45-64; Ref libn Ill State Hist Lib, Springfield Ill 64-. 8: Exec dir, Nat Lib Week, Ill, 60. 9: ALA; IllLA (NLW Com 59-63, State Sel Com 61-62, Legis Com 61, Com on Coms 62-63, Lib Devel Com 60-; chm Libn Citation Com 64, sec 68-69). 10: AAUW; E Moline Womans Club; Amer Bus Womens Assn. 11: Woman of Year, 64, Capital City Chap of Amer Bus Womens Assn. 13: Yes. 14: Catlg, ref. 15: Ill State Historical Lib, Springfield Il 62706.

SCHULZ, NANCY SUE (ENGLAND). b Galesburg Ill 23 Jl 40. 4: Anson W Schulz. 5: Ill StateU 58-62 (Bus Educ) BS; UDenver (Lib Euc). 7: Asst libn West High Sch, Davenport Iowa 62-63, Hd libn 63-65; Elem sch libn Schweinfurt Amer Sch, Schweinfurt Germany 65-67; Libn Irving Crown High Sch, Carpentersville Ill 67-68; Coord ref serv El Paso Pub Lib, El Paso Tex 69-. 9: ALA; NEA; Border Reg LA; TexLA. 14: Ref, sch libs. 15: 10755 Aero Vista, El Paso Tx 79908.

SCHULZE, MARGARET. b Montclair NJ 1 My 45. 5: Rutgers (Newark) 63-67 (Ger) BA; Rutgers 9new Brunswick) 67-68 MLS. 6: Ger. 7: Adult serv libn Woodbridge Pub Lib, Woodbridge NJ 68-. 9: ALA; NJLA. 10: Phi Beta Kappa. 14: Ref. 15: 15 Coit st, Irvington NJ 07111.

SCHULZETENBERGE, ANTHONY C. b Melrose Minn 17 O 29. 4: Mary Jane Holdvogt. 5: St John'sU (Minn) 47-51 (Hist) BA; St Cloud State Col 56-63 (Educ) MS; UMinn 60-69 MALS. 7: US Army Airborne 82nd Div XVIII Corps 52-54; Instr Holdingford Pub Schs, Holdingford Minn 54-56; Instr Ely Pub Schs, Ely Minn 56-60, Hd libn 60-65; Asst Prof Media of Lib and A-V Educ St Cloud State Col 65-, Supv tech serv Keihle Lib 66-. 9: ALA; NEA-DAVI; MinnLA; MinnASchL; A-v Coord Minn. 10: Phi Delta Kappa; Interfac Assn Minn Cols; American Legion. 14: Tech serv, lib instr. 15: 1113-12th st S, St Cloud Mn 56301.

SCHUMACHER, CHARLENE LADORNA (DREHER). b Niles Mich 18 O 37. 4: Walter Anton Schumache. 5: Colo Col 55-58 (Music) BA; No Baptist Theol Sem summers 56, 62; West Mich U summers 60, 61, 65, 69 (LS); Mich State U summer 62 & 65 (Educ); No Ill U summer 65 (LS). 6: Lat, Ger. 7: Elem tchr Brandywine Pub Schs, Niles Mich 60-62; Organist First Baptist Church, Niles Mich 60-; Jr high libn Brandywine pub schs, Niles Mich 62-. 8: A-v Dir Brandywine Pub Schs 67-. 9: NEA-DAVI; Music Educrs Nat Conf; ALA; MichEA; MichLA; MichASchL; Mich A-V Assn. 10: AAUW; Amer guild of Organists. 14: Catlg, ref, child serv. 15: 1546 Clarendon ave, Niles Mi 49120.

SCHUMAN, PATRICIA ANN (GLASS). b NYC 15 Mr 43. 4: Alan B Schuman. 5: UCincinnati 60-63 (Eng) AB; Columbia 64-66 (LS) MS; NYU 68- (Human Rel). 7: Correspondent Equitable Life Assurance Soc, NYC 63-64; Libn trainee Brooklyn Pub Lib, NYC 64-66; Lib tchr Brandeis High Sch, NYC 66; Instr & acquis libn NYC Commun Col 66-69, Asst Prof & acquis libn 69-. 8: Mem Com for a more responsive ALA. 9: ALA. (RT on Soc Respon of Libs; chm Prog Com); NYStateLA; NY Lib Club; NY Tech Serv Libns; NYRT on Soc Respon of Libs; LACUNY. 10: NYCLU; Mus of Mod Art; CUNY Com on Internat Studies; Fac Coun, NYC Commun Col. 13: Yes. 14: Social respon of libs, ya serv, acquis, reviewing, materials sel, a-v. 15: 16 W 16 st, New York NY 10011.

SCHUNK, EVALINE (BECK). b Toledo Ohio 31 Mr 12. 4: Russell J Schunk. 5 Wittenberg U 28-32 (Eng) BA; West Res 32-33 BS in LS. 6: Fr. 7: Child libn: Toledo (Ohio) Pub Lib 33-36, Lakewood (Ohio) Pub Lib 36-41, Grosse Pointe (Mich) Pub Lib 41-43; Sch libn Minneapolis Pub Lib 45-55; Head child serv Orlando (Fla) Pub Lib 55-59; Prof asst ya Grosse Pointe (Mich) Pub Lib 59-63; Coord of wk with child Tucson Pub Lib 63-. 9: ALA-AASchL; Ariz State LA (Prog Chm 68 Conv). 13: Yes. 14: Child serv. 15: Tucson Pub Lib, 200 S th ave, Tucson 85701.

SCHUPBACH, HAZEL L. b Ashland Ky. 4: Lloyd C Schupbach. 5: Ky Christian Col 35-38 (Relig Hist) AB; ButlerU Sch of Relig 42-44 (Relig Hist). 6: Ger, Sp, Gr, Lat. 7: Circ libn ButlerU 44-46; Libn Ky Christian Cl 46-57; Acquis dept UCal (Riverside) 57-62, Interlib loans libn 63-. 14: Ref, bibliog. 15: 1778 N Pershing, San Bernardino Ca 92405.

SCHUPPERT, MILDRED WILHELMINA. b Waupun Wis 19Ag09. 5: Hope Col 27-31 (Hist, Music) AB; UMich 47-48 ABLS. 6: Ger. 7: Sec, Holland Mich 33-36; Hope Col: Sec to the pres 36-45, Financial sec 45-47, Instr Lib Sci 48-50; Libn Western Theol Sem Holland Mich) 50-. 9: ATheolLA. 10: Amer Guild of rganists; Hymn Soc of Amer. 12: Comp of ten-year index to "The Reformed Review, Quarterly Jour of west Theol Sem (65). 14: Catlg, ref. 15: 79 W 13th st, Holland Mich 49423.

SCHUR, BARBARA ANN (SILVER) (EISENBERG). b NYC 16 S 28. 4: Leonard P Schur. 5: UCincinnati 46-48 (Eng) AB, 48-49 (Elem Educ); Cincinnati Conservatory of Mus 49-50 (Musicology); UMinn 50-51 BS in LS; West Res 61 Certif in Med Libnship. 7: Pre-prof catlgr UCincinnati 48-50; Patents libn Armour & Co, Chicago 56-57; Mus libn Chicago Pub Lib 57-58; Med catlgr Cleveland Med Lib (Allen), Cleveland Ohio 59-61; Med libn Mt Sinai Hosp. Cleveland Ohio 61-62; Fine arts libn Cleveland Hts- univ Hts Pub Lib, Cleveland Hts Ohio 63-. 9: JewishLA (corr sec 68-69); OhioLA; No Ohio Tech Serv Libns. 10: LWV; B'nai B'rith Women. 14: Music (esp phonograph records & tapes), catlg (music). 15: 2391 Miramar blvd, University Heights Oh 44118.

SCHUSKY, MARY SUE (DILLIARD). b E St Louis Ill 7 Je 35. 4: Ernest L Schusky. 5: UWis 53-57 (Hist) BS; UIll summers 59-62 (LS) MA; So Ill U 66- (Hist). 06: Fr. 7: Eng tchr jr high Springfield Pub Schs, Springfield Ill 57-60, Sch libn 60-63; Ref libn-Educ Testing Serv, Princeton NJ 63-64; Libn Blackburn Col 64-65; Ref libn SoIll U 65-. 8: Ill State Lib Adv Com. 9: ALA-ACRL; IllLA. 10: Beta Phi Mu; Chi Omega; AAUP. 14: Ref wk, sch libs, tchg lib sci. 15: Lovejoy Lib So Ill Univ, Edwardsville Il 62025.

SCHUSTER, BONNIE (HARTWICK). b St Paul Minn 30 Mr 43. 4: ervin G Schuster. 5: UMinn 61-65 (Eng) BA, 65-68 (LS) MA. 6: Ger. 7: Soc wkr WVa Dept of Welfare, Princeton 66-67; Ref libn Iowa StateU 68-. 10: AAUW; Beta Phi Mu. 14: Ref. 15: 37 College Trailer park, Ames Ia 50010.

SCHUSTER, RICHARD LEE. b Tina Mo 24 My 33. 4: Clara Shaw Schuster. 5: East Nazarene Col 55-59 (Lit) AB, 59-60 (Secondary Educ) BS; Boston U 62-63; Simmons 63-65 (LS) MS. 7: Steno-court reporter US Army (Cpl) 5th Army Hqs, Chicgo 53-55; Legal steno Dewey, Ballantine, Bushby, Palmer & Wood, NYC 60-62; Steno Phoenix Urban Corp, Boston 62-63; Asst to libn East Nazarene Col 63-65, Asst libn 65-68; Hd libn Mt Vernon Nazarene Col (Ohio) 68-. 9: ALA; OhioLA. 14: Col lib admin. 15: 600 E High st, Mt Vernon Oh 43050.

SCHUT, GRACE W. b NYC 17O22. 5: Hunter Col 39-43 (Hist) BA; NYU 43-44 (Hist) MA; Columbia 46-47 (LS) MS, currently (Amer Hist). 6: Ger. 7: Tchr Woodstown (NJ) High Sch 44-45; Libn NY Pub Lib 45-47; Libn St Peters Col (NJ) 47-. 8: Consul, "Sign Magazine lib & Bellarmine Col (NY) lib. 9: ALA; CathLA (mem var coms); NJLA (mem &/or chm several coms, incl Bibliog & Hist Com); NY Lib Club; Metro Cath Col Libns (com duties). 10: AAUP; AAUW; Hunter Col Alumni. 14: Ref, admin, bibliog. 15: 129 Pelton ave, SI NY 10310.

SCHUTTER, MARJORIE LUCILLE McHUGH. b Tunnel Hill Ill 9 My 21. 4: Howard Schutter. 5: So Ill U 41-43 Elem Certif; West Mich U 45-47 Secondary tchg certif; UMich summers 47-52 MA in LS. 6: Fr. 7: Eng tchr & libn Romulus High Sch, Romulus Mich 47-52; Tchr & libn Milan High Sch, Milan Mich 54-59; Eng instr Huntington Col 53-54; Instr in Eng & lib sci & ref libn Central UWis 60-62; Instr in Eng & Lib Sci NWest Col 65-. 9: ALA; MichLA. 10: AAUW. 14: Ref, tchg. 15: Northwestern College, Orange City Ia 51041.

SCHUTZ, PAUL RUDOLPH. b New York NY 10 Jl 28. 5: Alfred A&T Inst 47-49 (Horticulture) Certif; Rutgers (New Brunswick) 51-54 (Horticulture); UHawaii 54-56 (Botany) BA; Columbia 61-65 MLS. 6: Ger. 7: Asst libn NY Botanical Garden Lib, Bronx 61-62; Libn trainee NYC Pub Lib 62-63; Asst libn Horticulture Soc of NY, NYC 63-64; Catlgr UHawaii Lib 65-66; Libn Hampton Ave Elem Sch, Bellport LI NY 67-68; Catlgr microfilm, ms, educ material & bks SUNY (Stony Brook) 68-. 14: Catlg (microfilm & other non-book material; hortic & botany). 15: 13 Midday dr, Centereach LI NY 11720.

SCHUTZE, GERTRUDE. b NYC 5 Je 17. 5: Hunter Col 35-39 (Chem) BS; Columbia 46-49 (LS) MS. 6: Ger, Fr. 7: Libn Virginia-Carolina Chem Corp, Carteret NJ 40-43; Tech libn Penn Salt Mfg Co, Phila 44-46; Research libn Bristol-Myers Co, Hillside NJ 46-53; Manager info dept Grace Chem R&D Co, NYC 53-59; Manager lib serv Standard & Poor's Corp, NYC 59-60; Chief libn Union Carbide Research Inst, Eastview NY 60-63; Consul on the org & utilization of info & the admin of info centers, Woodhaven NY 64-68; Mgr info serv Ayerst Labs, NYC 68-. 8: Consul, Amer Airlines Inc 58-59, Educ & World Affairs 64-65, Chas Pfizer 65, Pennie, Edmonds 66-67; Certified Profess Consul 59-. 9: ACS (Chem lit div); Amer Soc Indexers; SLA; ASIS. 12: "Documentation Source Book" (65); "Bibliography of Guides to the Scientific-Technical-Medical Literature" (58) Sup, 58-62 (63), sup 63-66 (67); Ed "Documentation Digest SLA Sci-Tech News" (48-59); "The Social Sciences, a Bibliograpby of Guides to the Literature" (68). 13: Yes. 14: Admin, ref. 15: 7620 86th ave, Woodhaven NY 11421.

SCHUTZNER, SVATO. b Bratislava Czechoslovakia 1Ap23. 4: Milada Nee Zemanova. 5: Charles U (Prague) 41-48; (Theol); UStrasbourg 51-53 (Theol) Ljcence LSU 62-63 MS in LS. 6: Czech, Fr, Ger, Lat, Slovak. 7: Catlgr LC 63-, Asst hd Ger Lang sect, descr catlgr 67-. 14: Catlg. 15: 18 Ninth st NE, apt 202, Wash DC 20002.

SCHUURMAN, GUY. b Utrecht Holland 22 Ag 31. 4: Jeannette Leni Kros. 5: UUtah 53-58 (Hist) BA; UWash 60-61 (LS) ML. 6: Dutch, Ger. 7: Libn Sonora High Sch, Sonora Cal 58-59; Chief Libn Utah State Lib Div for the Blind 59-66; Chief libn Weber Co Lib, Ogden Utah 66-. 9: Amer Assn of WKERS FOR THE Blind; UtahLA (exec sec 59-). 14: Admin, ref. 15: 2824 N 1025 E, North Ogden Ut 84404.

SCHWAB, BERNARD. b Brooklyn N 25N20. 4: Mona Fay Shapiro. 5: City Col (NY) 37-43 (Econ) BSS; Pratt 46-47 BLS. 7: US Army Med Dept, Cook, Baker, Tech 4th Grade 43-46; Sub-libn Brooklyn Pub Lib 46; DC Pub Lib; Supv Central Circ 47-50, Chief bus & econ div 50-52, Serv expediter schs div 51-52, Act chief acquis div 52, Chief ext div 53; Asst City Libn Madison Pub Lib(Madison Wis) 54-57, Dir 57-. 8: Instr, Ext Div, UWis, 60-65. 9: ALA (Coun 60-64, Sec Jt Com on Lib Serv to Labor 63-66); WisLA (v-pres 65-66, pres 66-67). 12: Jt auth "Introduction to Library Science (61). 13: Yes. 14: Pub lib admin. 15: Madison Pub Lib, 201 W Mifflin st, Madison Wi 53703.

SCHWARTZ, ADA ELZABETH. b Quincy Ill 1 S 19. 5: Culver-Stockton Col 38-42 (Fr, Ger) BA; UIll 42-43 BS IN LS.07: Hosp libn VA, Bedford Mass 45-46; Hosp libn US Army, Philippine Isands 46-47; Libn US Army, Okinawa & Korea 47-49; Asst libn circ dept UIll(Urbana) 50; Staff libn US Army, Japan, Korea, France, Germany 50-63; Asst chief libn US Army, Europe 63-64; Deputy dir Army Lib Program, Wash DC 64-68, Dir 68-. 9: ALA; SLA; ASIS. 10: Assn of the US Army. 14: Admin, adult serv, lib automation. 15: 8802 Lowell pl, Bethesda Md 20034.

SCHWARTZ, CAROLYN A (BALAS). b Glen Ridge NJ 6 Je 43. 4: Arnold Schwartz. 5: Douglass Col 61-65 (Hist) BA; Rutgers 65-68 MLS. 6: Sp. 7: Libn S Amboy Sch Syst Hoffman High Sch 65-67; Libn Middlesex Co Col 67-68; Libn Edison Sch Syst, Edison NJ 68-. 10: Girl Scout Leader; Alum Assn of Douglass Col. 14: Ref. 15: 56 Gill lane 2E, Iselin NJ 08830.

SCHWARTZ, HELEN (FRENCH). b Scranton Pa 29 N 24. 4: Harry M Schwartz. 5: Waynesburg Col 42-44, 46-48 (Eng) BA (magna cum laude); Penn State U 49-50 (Eng lit); Drexel 63-68 MSLS. 6: Sp. 7: Instr Waynesburg Col 48-49; Stipend scholar Penn State U 49-50; Bk store mgr Rutgers U 50-52; Lib asst Farrell Sch, Phila 65-67; Libn Conwell Middle Magnet Sch, Phila 67-68; Libn catlg dept Free Lib of Phila 68-. 9: ALA; -AASchL; PennLA. 10: Phi Alpha Theta; Sigma Tau Delta; Beta Phi Mu. 14: Sch libs, catlg. 15: 1458 Higbee st, Phila Pa 19149.

SCHWARTZ, JULIA L. b Hamilton Ohio 6F33. 5: Marshall U 50-54 (Span) BA; West Res 55 (LS) MS. 7: Ya libn Cleveland Pub Lib 56-58; Asst ref libn Marshall U 58-62; Documents libn USola 62-. 8: Lib/USA, NY Worlds Fair, 65; Exec dir, Nat Lib eek, Fla, 65. 9: ALA (chm Jr Mems Round Table, Coop Ref Serv Com);-RSD (Com on Common Concerns); FlaLA (Exec dir NLW; sec). 13: Yes. 14: Ref, catlg. 15: 3001 Barnhard dr, Tampa Fl 33612.

SCHWARTZ, MYRNA SHAYNE (GRUMET). b Pittsburgh 4 Ja 38. 4: Joel Joseph Schwartz. 5: UPittsburgh 55-59 (Hist) AB; Ind U 60-62 (LS) AM. 6: Russian, Hebrew. 7: Catlgr Ind U (Bloomington) 61-63; Supv printed ser listing UNC Lib (Chapel Hill) 65-68, 69-, Catlgr (Russian) 68-69. 9: ALA. 14: Catlg (Russian), automating ser recs. 15: 56 Barclay rd, Chapel Hill NC 27514.

SCHWARTZ, SHULA (LEIBSON). b Beirut Syria 24 Mr 27. 4: Ralph Schwartz. 5: Hunter Col 43 (Sci); Northwestern 43-46 (Journalism) BS; Southern Methodist 53-54 (Educ) Tchrs Certif; Tex Woman's U 62-67 MLS. 06: Ger, Fr, Hebrew, Russian. 7: Ref libn L-T-V Inc, Dallas 54-62; Head Libn sci serv div Tex Inst Inc, Dallas 62-66, Mgr central lib serv 66-. 8: Adv coun curriculum devel Lib Tech Asst's program El Centro Jr Col; Adv coun Dallas-Ft Worth Chambers of Com Educ Com; Educ Com Ind Info Serv So Methodist U. 9: SLA (chm Assn Pub Rel; Govt Info Serv Com; Adv Coun; Tex Chap: chm Pub Rel; sec, v-pres, pres, & chm Lib Tech Asst Wkshop); SWLA; TexLA (speaker at annual Spec Lib Div conf 67; speaker Automation Conf 69; chm-elect Spec Lib Div 69-70); Dallas CoLA (chm Pub Rel Com). 12: "Anti-Submarine Warfare Bibliography" (62). 13: Yes. 14: Admin, ref. 15: PO Box 5474, Dallas Tx 75222.

SCHWARTZ, VIRGINIA C. b Milwaukee Wis 27 Ap 44. 5: Knox Col 62-66 (Hist) BA; UWis (Milwaukee) 66-69 (LS) MA. 7: Jr libn Milwaukee Pub Lib 66-68, Libn I 68-69, Libn II 69-. 9: ALA. 14: Catlg. 15: 2903 E Kenwood blvd, Milwaukee Wi 53211.

SCHWARZ, PHILIP JOHN. b Mazomanie Wis 13 Je 40. 5: Wis State Col (Platteville) 58-62 (Hist) BS; UDenver 62-63 (LS) MA; Stout State U 68- (A-V Communications). 7: Pub serv libn U of Puget Sound 63-67; Circ & ser libn Stout State U 67-68, ser libn 68-. 10: ACLU; AWSUF. 12: Ed "1969 Wisconsin State Universities Union List of Periodicals". 13: Yes. 14: Ser, circ, priv presses, instr res. 15: 608 19th ave W, Menomonie Wi 54751.

SCHWARZAPEL, JOSEPHINE. b NYC 26 Jl 23. 5: Hunter Col 40-45 (Hist)BA; Columbia 45 (Speech Therapy) MA, 60-62 MLS. 6: Ger. 7: Priv speech lessons 46-50; Libn Research Inst of Amer, NYC 46-51; Libn American Druggist, NYC 51-66; Tchr of lib PS 41, NYC 66. 9: SLA; MedLA; ALA. 14: Ref. 15: 51 E Second st, NYC 10003.

SCHWARZKOPF, LeROY C. b Sebewaing Mich 9 D 20. 4: Betsy Orr. 5: Yale 40-43 (Hist) BA; UMich 49-51 (Educ) MA; Rutgers 66-67 MLS. 6: Fr. 7: Lt Col US Army, Japan, Korea, France 44-49; Logistics off (ammunition) 57-66; Soc sci ref libn UMd (Col Park) 67-. 9: ALA; SAA; MdLA; DCLA. 10: Beta Phi Mu; Reserve Offr's Assn; Retired Offc's Assn; VFW; Amer Ordn Assn; Yale Track Assn. 14: Ref, govt docs. 15: 12608 Ivystone lane, Laurel Md 20810.

SCHWEGMANN, GEORGE A JR. b New Orleans 4 S 1900. 4: Elsie Elchinger. 5: Spring Hill Col 15-18 BS; Georgetown U 25-28 LLB. 7: LC: Asst chief & Chief Union Catlg Div 26-48, Chief Photodulication Serv 40-46, Chief Div for the Blind 48-51, Chief Union Catlg iv 51-. 9: ALA; DCLA. 13: Yes. 14: Catlg, ref. 15: 3534 Porter st NW, Wash DC 20016.

SCHWEICKART, RUTH L(OUISE). b Russellville Ohio 25D 11. 5: Miami U (Ohio)29-33 (FR, Ger) BS in Ed; UIll 33-34 BS in LS, 40-44 MS in LS. 6: Fr, Ger, Sp, Russian, Lat. 7: Asst catlgr UKan 35; Asst catlgr UMo 35-36; Asst in chg of exch UKan 36-37, Period libn 37-40; Ser catlgr UIll(Ubana)

(Urbana) Active duty US Naval Reserve 44-46, 51-52; Catlgr Dayton Pub Lib, ayton Pub Lib, Dayton Ohio 46-47; Catlgr Miami U Lib 47-, Catlgr & Asst Prof 61-. 9: ALA; OhioLA; Ohio Reg Group Tech Serv Libns. 10: Beta Phi Mu; Phi Beta Kappa; Phi Kappa Phi; AAUP; Bus & Profess Women's Club. 14: Catlg (espec subj catlg), ser. 15: 111 E Walnut st, Oxford Oh 45056.

SCHWEINFURTH, EDNA. b Waldo Ohio 20 Ag 20. 5: Ohio State 38-42 (Hist) BS in Ed; Catholic U 57-60 MSLS. 7: Tchr Willard High Sch, Willard Ohio 42-43; Airline stewardess American Sirlines Inc, Cleveland Wash DC 43-60; Asst circ libn UAriz Lib 60-63; Ref libn Nat Assn of Home Builders, Wash DC 63; Libn Mt Vernon Sem & Jr Col, Wash DC 63-66; Chief processing Inst for Defense Analyses, Arlington Va 66-67; Personnel dir Prince George's Co Mem Lib, Hyattsville Md 67-. 9: ALA; MdLA. 14: Acquis, admin. 15: 2939 Van Ness st NW apt 326, Wash DC 20008.

SCHWEINFURTH, PATRICIA LYNN (KAYLOR). b Cape Girardeau Mo 13 D 39. 4: Werner Schweinfurth. 5: UChattanooga 57-61 (Art) AB; Emory 61-65 MLS. 6: Fr, Sp. 7: Stud asst Chattanooga Pub Lib, Chattanooga Tenn 58-61; Asst bk order A G Candler Lib Emory U 61-63; Child libn Atlanta Pub Lib 63-65; Gen studies libn Ga Inst of Tech 65; Libn Amer Sch, Tegucigalpa Honduras 65-. 8: Educ TV, WETV, Atlanta 65, UNESCO & Hondura Ministry of Educ Program for train sch libns. 10: Pi Beta Phi. 14: Child lit, story-telling, bus & tech ref, bk ordering. 15: American School, c/o American Embassy, Tegucigalpa Honduras Central Am.

SCHWENGELS, JACQUELINE MARY. b Sharon Wis 25 Jl 38. 5: Milton Col 56-60 (Soc Sci) BA; UWis (Madison) summers 61-67 (LS) MA. 7: Tchr Tri-Co High Sch, Plainfield Wis 60-63; Tchr & libn; Lutheran High Sch, Racine Wis 63-65, Ozaukee High Sch, Fredonia Wis 65-67; Libns Janesville Sch Bd, Janesville Wis 67-. 9: ALA; WisLA; WisEA; Janesville Assn of Libns; JanesvilleEA. 10: Delta Kappa Gamma. 14: Sch libs. 15: 916 Mineral Pt ave, Janesville Wi 53545.

SCHWENN, JANET MARILYN. b Lodi Wis 3 O 41. 5: Wis State U (Oshkosh) 59-61 (Eng); UWis 61-63 (Eng) BA, 64-65 (LS) MA. 6: Ger. 7: Lib asst UWis Mem Lib 63-64, Lib asst 64-65; Libn catlgr Wes State U Forrest R Polk Lib (Oshkosh) 65-68; Ref libn Edison Jr Col 68-. 9: ALA; FlaLA. 10: AAUW; Wis Lib Sch Alumni Assn. 14: Ref. 15: 2909 Broadway apt 110, Fort Myers Fl 33901.

SCHWERIN, GERTRUDE, D. b Ludwigshafen a Ph Germany 8 Je 10. 4: Kurt Schwerin. 5: UFreiburg, Cologne, Munich 29-33 (Eng, Fr); CCNY 38. 6: Ger, Fr. 7: Research wker & tr US AEC 43-50; Jr bibliog Portland Cement Assn 51; Libn & ed asst Amer Veterinary Med Assn 53-. 9: SLA. 14: Catlg. 15: Amer Vet Med Assn, 600 S Michigan ave, Chicago Il 60605.

SCILKEN, MARVIN H. b NYC 7D26. 4: Mary P Martin. 5: UColo 44-48 (Econ) BA; Pratt 59-60 MLS. 7 Ref libn Hicksville Pub Lib, Hicksville NY 60-61; Dir Lindenhurst Mem Lib, Lindenhurst NY 61-62; Libn Pall Corp, Glen Cove NY 62-63; Dir Harrison Pub Lib, Harrison NY 63; Dir Orange Pub Lib, Orange NJ 63-. 8: Consul, Alfred A Knopf Inc, 60; Org Garden State Film Circuit, pres 66-68; Consul Morris Co Law Lib 68; Testified on Alleged Price Fixing of Lib Bks before US Senate Subcom on Antitrust and Monopoly 66. 9: ALA (chm Jr Mems Round Table 64-65); SLA Lib Assn (Gt Brit); NJLA (chm Intel Freedom 65-66, chm Com on Coms 66-67; Personnel Com 67-, Lib Devel Com 68-, Exec Bd Mem-at-Large 68-70); 65-66); NYLA; NY Lib Club; Essex Co Lib Dirs Gp (Governor 65-66, chm Lib Attitude Survey Com 69). 10: Rotary Club; Orange C of C; Beta Phi Mu. 14: Lib admin. 15: 330 W 28th st, New York NY 10001.

SCLAR, ELAINE (GERTRUDE WALLACH). b NYC 12A24. 4: Stanley Sclar. 5: Hunter Col 42-46 (Pre-Soc) BA; Columbia 61-64 (LS) MS. 7: Clerk NY Pub Lib 43-44; Ya libn Ossining Pub Lib, Ossining NY 61-. 9: ALA; NYLA; Westchester LA. 10: LWV. 14: Ya serv. 15: 40 Twin Ridges rd, Ossining NY 10562.

SCOFIELD, BETSY LEE (AIKEN). b Brownsville Tex 16 Ag 25. 4: Louis Morris Schofield. 5: Tex Col of Arts & Ind 43-47 (Eng Lit) BA; Tex Woman'sU 65-66 (LS). 6: Sp. 7: Clk UNeb Lib (Lincoln) 47-49; Jr libn Tex Southmost Col 49-50; Clk typist Mexican Cotton Co, Brownsville Tex 51; Catlgr Midland Pub Lib, Midland Tex 58-64; Docs libn fullerton Pub Lib, Fullerton Cal 66-, Film & fine arts libn 66-. 9: CalLA; OrangeCoLA. 14: Catlg, docs, films, art reprod. 15: 2385 Daphne place, Fullerton Ca 92633.

SCOFIELD, DOROTHY. b NYC 5 O 10. 5: Ctr Col 31-33 (Eng) AB; Columbia 33-34 (Eng) MA; Pratt 36-37 BLS. 6: Fr. 7: Child libn NY Pub Lib 37-42; Child libn Dayton Pub Lib, Dayton Ohio 42-45; Br libn Atanta Pub Lib 45-62, Head child dept 62-. 8: Asst Prof, Sch of Lib Sci, Atanta U 55-57. 9: ALA; SELA; GaLA; Atlanta Lib Club (past pres). 12: "The Shining Road (57). 13; yes. 14: Child serv. 15: 608 S McDonough st, Decatur Ga 30030.

SCOFIELD, JAMES STEVE. b Cincinnati 26 S 28. 4: Jessie Axotis. 5: UIll 46,54 (Journalism) BS; Ind U 47; Northwestern 50; Syracuse 63 (Communications Libns Wkshop) Certif; Columbia 67 (Amer Press Inst) Certif. 6: Modern Gk, Sp. 7: Asst sports ed "Hammond Times," Hammond Ind 45-50, 51-55; Journalist US Navy, Great Lakes NTS 50-51; Dir Hoosier Travel Agency, Hammond Ind 55-57; Admin asst Municipal Court, Hammond Ind 56-60; Dir Fla Suncoast Publishers, St Petersburg Fla 60-62; Chief libn "St Petersburg Times & Evening Independent" St Petersburg Fla 62-. 8: Pub Rel, US Naval Reserve, 48-50; Lib consul; "Lakeland (Fla) Ledger" (67); "Congressional Quarterly"; "Editorial Research Reports" (69). 9: SLA (Newspaper Div, sec-treas); ALA; ASIS; NMA. 10: Sigma Delta Chi; Hon Citizen, Athens Greece; Titled Offr-at-Large, East Orthodox Church. 13: Yes. 14: Ref, clippings, photos, maps. 15: 6100 6th ave S, St Petersburg Fl 33707.

SCOGGIN, AUTHA JANELLE. b Dierks Ark 20 My 26. 5: Texarkana Col 51-57; E Tex State U 57-61 (LS) BS. 7: Property & stock control clerk Red River Arsenal, Texarkana Tex 47-61; Ref libn Armed Forces Staff Co, Norfok Va 61-63; Libn Post Lib Phila Air Def Site, Pedricktown NJ 63-64; Libn Main Post Lib, Ft Knox Ky 64-; Command libn US Air Force So Off Albrook AFB, CZ 67-. 9: ALA-PLA (sec Mil Libns Sect 68-69). 10: AAUW; Pilot Internat. 14: Admin, pub serv. 15: PO Box 713, APO New York 09825.

SCOLES, JOYCE (JEFFREY PIPKIN). b St Louis 27 J135. 5: UFla 52-56 (Educ) BA; Fla State U 60-61 (LS) MS. 6: Sp, Fr. 7: Asst libn Paxon Jr High Sch, Jacksonville Fla 56-60; Asst Jacksonville Pub Lib Jacksonville Fla 57-58; Grad asst Fla State Materials Center Lib, Tallahassee Fla 60-61; Jr, sr libn Queens Borough Pub Lib, Jamaica NY 61; Ser catlgr St Louis Pub Lib 62-63; Ya asst ref libn Huntington Pub Lib, Huntington NY 63-65; Catlgr Suffolk Cop Lib System, Patchogue NY 65-66; Product mgr Collier-MacMillan Lib Serv, NYC 66-68; Catlgr Santa Clara Co Lib, San Jose Cal 68-. 9: ALA; CalLA; No Cal Tech Proc Gp. 10: Beta Phi Mu. 14: Catlg. 15: 3231 Impala dr apt 3, San Jose Ca 95117.

SCOLLARD, ROBERT JOSEPH. b Toronto Can 15 Ag 08. 5: St Michael's Col UToronto 24-28 BA; UToronto 38-39 BLS; UMich summers 39, 40, 41 AM in LS; Ontario Col of Educ 29-30 Ont secondary tchrs certif. 6: Fr, Lat. 7: Libn St Basil's Sem, Toronto 30-33; Asst libn Pontifical Inst of Mediaeval Studies, Toronto 31-32, Libn 32-51; Libn St Michael's Col, Toronto 33-55; Libn St Basil's Sem, Toronto 51-58; Sec fen The Basilian Fathers, Toronto 54-68; Libn St Basil's Sem, Toronto 68-. 9: CanLA; Can Cath Hist Assn; OntLA. 10: Ordained priest 32. 12: "Dictionary of Basilian biography" (69) Found & ed "The Basilian Annals" (43-68). 13: Yes. 14: Catlg. 15: 95 St Joseph st, Toronto 5 Ont Can.

SCOON, ROBERT. b Burns Wyo 29 D 27. 4: Carole Lorraine McMillan. 5: Wittenberg U 46-49 (Hist, Eng) BA; UWyo summers 45-51 (Hist) MA; USoCal 52-54 MS LS; U West Ont 54-56 (Theol) L Th, 56-62 (Theol) BD; West Res 50-51; Bloomfield Sem 61-62; Union Theol Sem 63-64. 6: Lat, Hebrew, Ger, Sp. 7: Sub tchr W High Sch, Cleveland Ohio 49; Tchr Lyons High Sch, Lyons Ohio 49-50; Ref libn London Pub Lib, London Can 54-56; Catlgr NW Ont 54-56; Rector Anglican Church, Florence Ont 56-58, Wiarton Ont 58-61; Asst Grace Episc Church, Orange NJ 61-62; Hd libn Bloomfield Col & Sem 61-65; Rector St Mark's Episc Church, Paterson NJ 62-65; Libn Fuller Sem 65-; Asst Episc Church, Alhambra Cal 65-66; Asst rector Church of Our Savior (Episc), San Gabriel Cal 67-. 10: Lions Club; Phi Gamma Delta; Phi Alpha Theta; Phi Sigma Iota. 13: Yes. 14: Admin, catlg. 15: 2961 Emerson way, Altadena Cal 91106.

SCOTT, ALICE H(OLLY).b Jefferson Ga 8 J135. 4: Alphonso Scott. 5: Spelman Col 53-57 (Eng) AB; Atlanta 57-58 MS in LS. 6: Fr. 7: Ref libn I Brooklyn Pub Lib 58-59; Libn I Chicago Pub Lib 59-61, Libn II 61-62; Act libn Hall Br 62-67, Libn III Woodlawn br 68-. 9: ALA; IllLA; Chicago Lib Club. 10: Beta Phi Mu. 14: Adult serv. 15: 8135 S Princeton, Chicago 60620.

SCOTT, BARBARA F. b Manchester NH 4 O 16. 4: Robert Eugene Scott. 5: Smith 34-38 (Hist) AB; Drexel 63-64 (LS); Villanova 65-66 MSLS. 7: Child libn Enoch Pratt Free Lib, Baltimore 63; Asst libn Friends Lib of Swarthmore Col Lib 64; Interlib loan libn Chester Co Lib, W Chester Penn 65-66, Act asst libn 68-; Hd libn Coatesville Pub Lib, Coatesville Penn 67-68. 9: ALA; PennLA. 10: AAUW. 14: Ref, child serv, admin. 15: Jug Hollow rd, Phoenixville Pa 19460.

SCOTT, BARBARA G. b Bellingham Wash 16 Mr 42. 5: UPuget Sound 60-62 (Hist); UWash 62-64 (Hist) BA, 66-67 (Libnship) Masters. 7: Clk Seattle Credit Bureau 65-66; Acquis libn Gustavus Adolphus Col Lib 67-. 9: ALA; MinnLA. 14: Acquis, ref. 15: Box 1335 Gustauus Adolphus College, St Peter Mn 56082.

SCOTT, BILLIE JEAN (MISS). b Big Stone Gap Va 13Ag30. 5: Lincoln Mem U 47-50 (Span) AB (cum laude); Radford Col summer 55 (LS); Va Polytech Inst summers 56, 61, 62, & 63 (Educ) MS. 6: Sp, Fr, Lat. 7: Big Stone Gap High Sch, Big Stone Gap Va; Eng tchr 50-54, Span tchr 51-58, Tchr-libn 52-58, Libn 58-59; Span tchr Lincoln Mem U summer 59; Libn Powell Valley High Sch, Big Stone Gap Va 59-. 9: VaEA (Libns Sect; treas 66-68, v-pres 68-70); VaLA; Wise Co EA (sec 58-68). 10: Sigma Delta Pi; Kappa Delta Pi; Music Club; Hist Soc SW Va; Delta Kappa Gamma; PTA. 14: Pub sch libs. 15: Rte 2 Seminary, Big Stone Gap Va 24219.

SCOTT, CAROL (SEELEY). b Phila 10Ag21. 4: Harley A Scott Jr. 5: Duke 37-38, 39-41 (Sociol) AB; Conn Col 38-39; UNC 41-42 BS in LS; Winthrop Col 63-67 (MAT). 7: Libn Pittsylvania Co Lib, Chatham Va 42-43; Jr prof asst DC Pub Lib 43-44; Ed asst Off of Ordnance Research, Durham NC 52-53; Libn Winthrop Train Sch, Rock Hill SC 56- 57; Libn Rock Hill High Sch, Rock Hill SC 64-65. 9: ALA; SCLA (v-pres 66-67, pres 68-69, Nat Lib Week Com 65); SCEA. 10: AAUW; Phi Beta Kappa; Phi Kappa Phi; Federated Women's Clubs. 13: Yes. 14: Admin, ref. 15: 622 Hanover ct, Rock Hill SC 29730.

SCOTT, CATHERINE DOROTHY. b Wash DC 21 Je 27. 5: Catholic U 50 (Eng) AB, 55 (LS) MS. 6: Fr, Sp. 7: LC 45-50; Asst & clk Govt Printing Off, Wash DC 45-50; Asst & clk Export Import Bank of Wash DC 50, Lib asst 51-54; Asst catlgr Army Chief of Engrs, Wash DC 54-55; Asst libn & ref libn Nat Housing Ctr 55-63; Hd libn Bellcomm Inc(AT&T Co), Wash DC 63-. 8: Sec & Publ Chm, Nat Lib Week Com (DC) 67 & 68; Consul Republ Nat Com Lib 63. 9: SLA (Aerospace Div: Nomin Chm 67, sec 68-69; Wash Chap: Publ Chm 63-, sec 65-66; v-chm & chm Sci-Tech Gp 66). 10: V-chm DC Republ Com, del 64 Nat Conv: sec Platform Com; del 68; Conv Mem Bd Dirs League of Republ Women 56-; Y R Nat Committeewoman 56-58. 14: Ref, lib admin. 15: 700 7th st SW, Washington DC 20024.

SCOTT, DOROTHEA. b LONDON. 4: Aldo C Scott. 5: ULondon 34-35 Diploma, ALA. 6: Fr, Ger, Chinese. 7: Catlgr Victoria & Albert Mus Nat Art Lib, London 33-36; Eur intelligence sect records BBC, London 40-41; Brit Coun libn, Nanking China 47-49; Lib dir UHongkong 50-60; Asst to dir Columbia Libs 60-62; Assoc curator Wasson collection & E Asian bibliogr Cornell U Lib 63; Lecturer UWis (Madison) Lib Sch 64-. 9: ALA; Lib Assn (Gt Brit); Hongkong LA (Hon Life Mem); IFLA; WisLA. 10: Bibliog Soc, London; AAUP; Nat Bk League (London); Royal Asiatic Soc (Hongkong Br). 13: Yes. 14: Far East bibliog. 15: 3525 Topping rd, Madison Wi 53705.

SCOTT, EDITH (SMITH). b Okla City Okla 9 Mr 41. 4: Huitt L Scott Jr. 5: LincolnU 58-62 (Eng) BS; CatholicU 64-68 MSLS; AmericanU 68-. 6: Fr. 7: Ed asst LRS LC 64-65, Ref libn 65-66, Decimal classification specialist 66-. 9: ALA; ASIS. 14: Clsf. 15: 1111 Mass ave NW apt 406, Wash DC 20005.

SCOTT, EDWARD ALDERMAN. b Mobile Ala 14 My 43. 4: Monica McLean. 5: Fla State U 61-65 (Instr Materials) BS, 66 (LS) MS. 6: Sp. 7: Asst libn & instr Fla State U 66-; Libn Fla State U Study Ctr in Florence Italy 69-70. 9: ALA; NEA-DAVI; SELA; FlaLA. 13: Yes. 14: Ref, admin. 15: 1320 E Jordan st, Pensacola Fl 32503.

SCOTT, ELIZABETH (ALTSTETTER). b Wauseon Ohio 15 O 14. 4: Norman C Scott. 5: Mary Washington Col 31-34; Peabody Col 34-35 (Eng) BS, 35-36 BS in LS. 6: Fr. 7: Libn clifton Forge-Covington Div VPI 64-67; Coord lib serv Lancaster, Clifton Forge Va 67-. 15: Dabney S Lancaster Commun College, Clifton Forge Va 24422.

SCOTT, HELEN V. b NYC 22 Ag 11. 5: Randolph-Macon Woman's Col 29-33 (Hist) BA; Drexel 37-38 BS in LS. 7: Libn Moody Elem Sch, Clifton Forge Va 38-40; Libn Flagler Mem Lib, Miami Fla 40-42; Br libn Miami Pub Lib, Miami Fla 42-45; 1st asst in ref Knoxville Pub Lib, Knoxville Tenn 45-47; Ref libn Norfolk Pub Lib, Norfolk Va 47-57; Pub serv libn Abilene Pub Lib, Abilene Tex 58-62; Coordinator of adult serv Tucson Pub Lib 62-. 9: ALA; SWLA; Ariz State LA. 10: Zonta. 14: Ref. 15: 1836 E Linden st, Tucson Az 85719.

SCOTT, ISABEL AGNES. b Canaseraa NY 29 Ja 09. 5: State U Geneseo NY) 42 (LS) BS; St Bonaventures U 47-48 (ng) MA. 7: Elem tchr Canaseraga Schs, Canaseraga NY 30-45; High sch libn Salamanca NY 45-48; Sch libn Clewiston Schs, Clewiston Fla 48-50; Sch libn Fulton Schs, Fulton NY 50-54; Asst libn Oswego State Tchrs Col 51-55; Jr high libn, Penn Yan 55-63; Elem Sch libn Penn Yan NY 63-. 8: Coord, ESEA Title II, Penn Yan Central Sch, Penn Yan NY. 9: NY State Tchrs Assn; NYLA. 10: Nat Bus & Prof Women; Keuka Park Conserv Club. 15:Rt 5, Penn Yan NY 14527.

SCOTT, JACK WILLIAM. b Akron Ohio 30 J138. 4: Sarah Creager. 5: UAkron 56-57 (Philos); Heidelberg Col 57-60 (Lat, Philos) BA; West Res 60-62 MSLS; U Akron 62-63 (Law). 6: Lat. 7: Floor supv West Res U Lib 60-62; Asst libn Akron Law Lib Assn, Akron Ohio 62-64; Lib Dir Lorain Co Commun Col 64-68; Hd acquis Kent State U Lib 68-. 9: ALA; SLA; Ohio 10: AFL Musicians Union. 13: Yes. 14: Admin, catlg. 15: 1088 Lexington ave, Akron Oh 44310.

SCOTT, JANET. b Oakland Cal 9 Ja 43. 5: UIowa 61-65 (Fr) BA; UWis 65-66 (LS) MA. 6: Fr. 7: Libn Proviso E High Sch, Maywood Ill 66-67; Asst libn First Nat Bank of chicago 67-. 9: SLA. 15: 1419 N State Pkwy 501, Chicago Il 60610.

SCOTT, JANICE R (JONES). b Muskogee Okla 22 O 21. 4: William R Scott. 5: UOre 38-46 (Fine Arts) BA; Willamette U 45-46 (Fine Arts); Immaculate Heart Col 58-61 (LS) MA. 6: Fr, Sp. 7: USMC Women's Res Animation Camera, Quantico Va & Camp Pendleton 43-45; Claims clerk Soc Security Admin, Portland Ore; Child libn Reseda Canoga Park Brs, Los Angeles Pub Lib 58-, Br libn Fremont br 66-. 10: Libns; Guild (AFLCIO). 12: Art & production ed Librarians- Guild Communication--. 13: Yes. 14: Exhibits. 15: 19434 Elkwood st, Reseda Ca 91335.

SCOTT, KATHERINE K(INSMAN) (MRS). b Elmira NY 2 O 19. 5: Cornell U 36-40 (Econ) BA; NY State U (Geneseo) 58-61 MLS. 7: Hd catlg & order dept Steele Mem Lib, Elmira NY 66-. 9: ALA; NYLA. 14: Ref, catlg, ya wk, pub rel. 15: Steele Mem Lib, Lake & Church st, Elmira Ny 14901.

SCOTT, KATHLEEN (BROWN). b Tangier Ind 12 My 05. 4: Stanley LEONARD Scott. 5: Purdue U 26-30 (Home Econ) BS; Kent State 52-55 (LS) MA. 6: Lat, Sp. 7: Tchg priv tutoring 49-52; Libn Washington High Sch, Washington Court House Ohio 52-. 9: NEA; ALA; OhioASchL (Exec Bd 66-67); OhioEA. 10: Browning Lit Club; AAUW. 12: "The Library in a Vocational Guidance Plan (54); "What is Wrong with School Librarians (57). 14: Ref, rare bks. 15: 417 W Circle ave, Washington Court House Ohio 43160.

SCOTT, MARGARET BRODIE. b Dundee Scotland. 5: Toronto 38-42 (Hist) BA; Ont Col of Educ 42-43 Permanent Spec High Sch Tchg Certif; Toronto 56-57 BLS. 7: Tchr Kitchen-Waterloo Collegiate, Ketchener Ont 43-44; Libn R H King Collegiate, Scarboro Ont 45-6; Assoc Prof of Sch Libnship Col of Educ UToronto 61-. 8: Assoc of Sch of Libnship, Utoronto, 58-61; Ed of Basic Bk List for Ontario Second Sch Libs, 59-62. 9: CanLA; ALA; Inst Prof Libns Ont; OntLA (sec 58). 10: UNIV Womens Club; Beta Phi Mu. 13: Yes. 14: Sch libnship. 15: Ontario Col of Educ, 371 Bloor stW, Toronto 5 Can.

SCOTT, MARGARET CHANCELLOR. b Cape Charles Va 26 O 09. 5: Mary Baldwin Col 26-28; Mary Washington Col UVa 28-30 (Math, Lat) BS in Tchg; William & Mary summers 39-41 (LS) Certif. 7: Tchr Eastville High Sch, Northampton Co Va 30-41; Libn: Fluvanna High Sch, Carysbrook Va 41-42, Cape Charles High Sch, Cape Charles Va 42-46, Northampton High sch, Eastville Va 46-. 8: Helped write School Library Guide for Va State Bd of Educ 55; Mem High Sch Materials Com of State Bd of Educ, Va 54-. 9: ALA; VaLA; VaEA; NorthamptonEA (past sec & pres). 10: Delta Kappa Gamma; Hi-Y clubs. 11: Tchr of Year, 1962, Young Woman's Club of Northampton Co. 14: Sch lib wk. 15: Route 1, Cape Charles Va 23310.

SCOTT, MARIAN H. b NYC 19 Jl 08. 5: Mt Holyoke 27-29; Rutgers 41-46 (Educ) BS; Columbia 42-45 (LS); UCal(Berkeley) 58; Rutgers 59-61 MLS. 6: Fr, Sp. 7: Sec, Westfield NJ 29-31; Asst libn Sr High Sch, Westfield NJ 40-45, Libn 45-62; Act libn Pub Lib, S Orange NJ summers 51, 52; Instr in Lib Sci UVt summer 62; Asst Prof Rutgers Grad Sch of Lib Serv62-63, Assoc Prof & Placement Dir 63-68, Assoc Prof 68-. 8: Dir, NJ Sch Lib Devel Proj, 62-63; Survey Com NJ Lib Devel Com, 62-67; Library Journal Bk Reviewer, Adult Bks for YA, 63-65; Consul, publ of ya bks. 9: ALA (Com on Wilson Indexes 63, 64-);-YSD-ACRL-AASchL (Reg 2 rep to State Assembly; mem Awards Com); NJLA (Memb Com, Recr Com); NJSchLA (pres 50-52 & 60-62). 10: AAUP; Beta Phi Mu; Col Womens Club; Womans Club of Westfield. 12: "Evaluating Library Resources for Elementary School Libraries with Mary V Gaver (62); "Librarian and the Teacher NJ SchLA pubn; Ed "Periodicals for School Libraries," ALA (69). 13: Yes. 14: Sch libs. 15: Apt 14G, 800 Forest ave, Westfield NJ 07090.

SCOTT, MARILYNN (INEZ STEWART). b McMinnville Ore 17S22. 4: Theodore Merle Scott. 5: Linfield Col 39-43 (Eng Lit) BA (summa cum laude); Portland State Col 57-60 (Educ Secondary Certif; UPortland 60 (LS); UOre 58-64 (LS); Ore State Col 63 (Educ) Ed M; UAlaska 61-64 (Educ). 6: Fr. 7: High sch libn &tchr Vernonia Sch Dist, Veronia Ore 58-61; Anchorage Borough Sch Dist, Anchorage Alaska High sch Eng instr 61-65, High sch libn 62-65, Lib consul 65-; Dist resource libn 65-. 8: Lecturer sch libnship Alaska Methodist U 66-; Alaska Adv Coun for Interlib Coop - present. 9: NEA; ALA-ASchL; Alaska State LA; AlaskaEA; Alaska Instr Media Assn. 10: PEO; Alpha Delta Kappa; Kappa Delta Pi. 14: Sch libnship, tech proc. 15: PO Box 4-190, Spenard Alaska 99503.

SCOTT, MARY ELIZABETH. b Guymon Okla 29 O 15. 5: UOkla 31-35 (LS) AB, 35-36 (Eng) AB, 36-37 (Pre-law); Columbia summers 39-43 (LS) MA. 6:Fr, Ger. 7: Revisor & lab asst UOkla Sch of Lib Sch 35-42; 1st asst catlgr Ind U Lib 43-4; Head catlgr East Ill U Lib 48-. 9: ALA (Life Mem); IllLA (Life Mem); IllEA (Life Mem). 13: Yes. 14: Catlg, lib automation. 15: East Ill Univ Lib, Charleston Ill 61920.

SCOTT, MARY EMMA. b Walterboro SC 19 D 41. 5: Ferrum Jr Col 60-62 (Liberal arts) AA; Greensboro Col 62-64 (Soc Sci) BA; Madison Col 64-65 (LS). 7: Summer sch libn Collegiate Schs, Richmond Va 65; Asst libn Tuckahoe Jr High Sch, Richmond Va 65-67; Asst to libn in reader & tech serv Ferrum Jr Col, Ferrum Va 67-. 14: Ref, tech serv. 15: Box 194 Ferrum Junior College, Ferrum Va 24088.

SCOTT, RICHARD P. b Tokyo Japan 6 Ap 32. 5: Md State Col 52-54 (Liberal Arts) AA; UMd 54-56 (Hist) BA; Catholic U 56-58 MS in LS. 6: Fr, Sp. 07 Asst libn: period Nat War Col, Wash DC 58, bibliog 58-59, catlg NSF, Wash DC 59-62, Libn catlg 62-. 9: SLA; ALA; Potomac Tech Proc Libns; ASIS. 10: Nat Duckpin Bowling Congress; Nat Philatelic Soc. ; AAAS. 11: Sustained Superior Performance Citation, 64. 14: Catlg, acquis. 15: Lib Nat Sci Foun, 1800 G st NW, Wash DC 20550.

SCOTT, ROBERT GORDON. b Sterling Colo 23 N 16. 4: Iolanda Taddei. 5: Colo State Col of Educ 33-41 (Lit & Lang) BA; Peabody 41-42 BSLS; Columbia 50-52 MSLS. 6: Ital, Sp. 7: Ref asst CINCINNATI Pub Lib 42-44; Ambulance driver (WO 1) Amer Field Serv, Italy & Germany 44-45; Libn US Bur Reclamation, Denver 45-48; Ass engr libn Columbia U 48-52; Catlgr Battelle Mem Inst, Columbus Ohio 52-55; Catlgr Wayne State U 55-57; Libn Pub Lib, Clawson Mich 58-. 9: MichLA. 10: People-to-People; Great Bks Group. 14: Pub lib admin. 15: 240 N Webik, Clawson Mich 48017.

SCOTT, SANDRA (MARGARET). b Vancouver Can 19 Ap 41. 5: UBC 59-61 (Eng); UToronto 63-66 (Eng) BA, 66-67 BLS. 6: Fr, Ger. 7: Researcher Canadian Centennial Lib, Toronto 65; Instr Dept of Eng Ryerson Polytech Inst 65-66; Indexer "Bk Review Digest" H W Wilson Co, ny 67-68; Hd libn Carl H Pforzheimer Lib, NY 68-. 9: ALA; SLA. 14: Rare bks. 15: 16 E 94th st, New York NY 10028.

SCOTT, THOMAS L. b Council Bluffs Iowa 30 Jl 43. 4: A Carol Gilbert. 5: UOmaha 61-65 (Hist) BA; UIll 66-68 MSLS. 6: Fr. 7: Hd ref dept Omaha Pub Lib, Omaha Neb 68-. 9: ALA; NebLA. 10: Phi Alpha Theta. 14: Ref. 15: 1210 S 50th st, Omaha Nb 68106.

SCRANTON, JEANNE (TINGLE). b Arapahoe NC 15D 09. 4: George N Scranton. 5: Louisburg Col 27-29 (Prim Educ); UNC summers 27, 28, 68. 7: Toll operator So Bell Telephone & Telegraph, Charlotte NC 30; Sales & Cashier Charles Store, Charlotte NC 31-38; Relief cashier Iveys Dept STORE, Chalotte NC 49-50; Head film & sound div Pub Lib of Charlotte & Mecklenburg Co, Charlotte NC 50-. 9: ALA; SELA; NCLA (Pub Lib Sect: A-V Com 54-, chm Film Subcom 61-63; A-V Wkshop 57 & 63); MecklenburgLA. 10: Pub Lib Staff Org. 13: Yes. 14: Non-bk materials. 15: 1736 Merriman ave, Charlotte NC 28203.

SCRIBNER, HELEN (KEEBLE). b Williamsburg Va 10 Mr 10. 4: Robert Leslie Scribner. 5: Randolph-Macon Womans Col 26-30 (Lat) AB; Columbia 31-32 BS in LS. 6: Fr. 7: Asst Randolph-Macon Col Lib 30-31, Tchr- libn Whitmell Farm-Life Sch, Whitmell Va 33-34; Tch-libn Martinsville High Sch, Martinsville Va 34-35; Va State Lib: Clerk & reviser catlg 35-38, Catlgr 38-40, Head of ser sect 41-43, Head of catlg sect 43-. 9: ALA (Coun 48-50); VaLA (sec-treas 40-4, pres 51-52); SELA; Potomac Tech Proc Lbns (chm 52-53, var com & coun assignments); SE Reg Catlgrs (chm 46-48). 10: Phi Beta Kappa. 14: Catlg. 15: Va State Lib, Richmond Va 23219.

SCRIVEN, MARY LEE (SPERRY). b Cleveland Ohio 29 Ag 16. 4: Albert J Scriven. 5: West Res 34-38 (Sociol) AB, 39-41 (Pub Lib-Adult) BSLS, 62-65 (Secondary Sch Y-A) MSLS. 7: Asst Shaker Hts Pub Lib, Shaker Hts Ohio 38-42; Libn Roxboro Jr High Sch, Cleveland Hts Ohio 61-. 10: Beta Phi Mu; PTA; Girl Scouts Coun. 13: Yes. 14: YA serv. 15: 3303 Dellwood rd, Cleveland Hts Oh 44118.

SCRIVENS, CAROL VOGEL. b Greensburg Penn 24 D 35. 4: Ralph H Scrivens. 5: Chatham Col 53-57 (Eng) BA; Carnegie 58-60 MLS; UPittsburgh 68 Advanced Certif in Lib Sci. 7: Asst art div Carnegie Lib of Pittsburgh 58, Asst sci-tech dept 59; Catlgr Health Professions Lib UPittsburgh 60; Libn St Margaret Mem Hosp, Pittsburgh 60-62; Lib career consul, asst to the dean Penn State Recruiting Proj UPittsburgh Grad Sch of Lib & Info Sci 62-67; Visiting lectr Grad Sch of Lib Sci UIll summer 67; Consul Nelson Assoc Inc 67-68; Libn reg special educ instr materials ctr Hunter Col 69-. 8: Exec dir, NAT Lib Week, Penn 65. 9: ALA-LAD (Recr Admin Materials Com 65-66; sec Personnel Admin Sect 65-67); PennLA (Recr Com 62-). 10: Beta Phi Mu. 13: Yes. 14: Personnel, lib educ, lib serv to handicapped child. 15: apt 10G 200 E 36th st, New York NY 10016.

SCRUGGS, KATHLEEN (EDWARDS). b Glenville Ga 9 Mr 20. 5: Savannah State Col 44-49 (Soc Sci) BS; Fisk 52 (LS); Simmons 53 (LS); NC Col 56-60 MLS; Drexler 64 (LS); Atlanta U 66. 6: Lat, Ger. 7: Tchr-Prin Elem Sch, Sylvania Ga 37-47; Elem tchr Elem Sch, Clyo Ga 47-54; Tch-libn Sr High Sch, Springfield Ga 54-58; Itinerant libn pub schs, Savannah Ga 58-61; Libn CUYLER Jr High Sch, Savannah Ga 61-. 8: Red Cross wk during WW II, in recognition of which I received a plaque from Pres Franklin D Roosevelt. 9: NEA; ALA; Ga Tchrs & Educ Assn (Rec sec libns sect); SELA; GaLA (Reg VIII LA; Reg VIII TA). 10: Jonquil Garden Club. 14: Ref. 15: 1605 Vine st, Savannah Ga 31401.

SCUDAMORE, JOY. b Vancouver Can 6 Ap 28. 5: UBC 46-50 (Hist) BA; McGill 50-51 (LS) BLA. 7: Bkmob libn Annapolis Valley Reg Lib, NS 51-53; Indexer British Electrical Devel Assn, London Eng 54; Vancouver Pub Lib, Vancouver BC Gen libn Hist & Sociol Depts 55-59, Br head Dunbar br 59-61, Br head Hastings br 61-63, Br head Mt Pleasant 63-65, Br head Kitsilano br. 9: ALA; CanLA; BCLA. 10: Univ Womens Club of Vancouver; Eng-Speaking Union; Vancouver Opera Assn; Assn BC Libns. 14: Adult educ. 15: 3206 W 32nd ave, Vancouver 8 BC Can.

SCUDDER, MARY (CLAYTON). b Tuscaloosa Ala 29N8. 4: John Ralph Scudder Jr. 5: UAla 47-52 (LS) BS in Educ, Certif in LS. 6: Sp. 7: Libn Lithonia High Sch Lib, Lithonia Ga 52; Period libn A G Gorgas Lib UAla 52-53; Catlgr M I King Lib UKy 53-54; Asst libn Lenior Co Pub Lib, Kinston NC 54-55; Catlgr C L Hardy Lib Atlantic Christian Col 56-58; Asst libn Womans Col Lib Duke U 59-60; Asst libn C L Hardy Lib Atlantic Christian Col 62-67; Libn Elizabeth Kizer Sch, Lynchburg Va 68-69; Asst libn catlgr Knight Mem Lib Lynchburg Col 69. 9: NEA; VaEA. 10: Alpha Beta Alpha. 14: Ref, circ, catlg. 15: 3436 Landon st, Lynchburg Va 24503.

SCUDDER, ROBERT E(ARLE). b Piqua Ohio 27 N 05. 5: Northwestern 25-29 (Eng) BA, 29-30 (Eng) MA, 30-42 (Eng, Fr, Hist); UIll summers 36-39 BS in LS. 6: Fr. 7: Eng adv Jam Handy Picture Serv, Chicago 31-32; Asst bk dept Chandler's Inc, Evanston Ill 33-34; Asst document dept Northwestern U Lib 34-36, Head document dept 36-41, Asst libn 41-46; In chg USAAF Tech Libs (Maj), Wash DC 42-46; Educ consul on libs US Off of Educ Surplus Property, Wash DC 46; Head documentation & research sect div of libs & insts US Dept of State, Wash DC 46-48; Asst chief div of libs & ref US Dept of

State, Wash DC 48-53; Head soc sci & hist dept Free Lib of Phila 53-. 8: Mem, Ed Adv Bd, "International Encyclopedia of the Social Sciences" Rep ALA & its ref serv div, 62-68. 9: ALA (Coun 64-68, chm Awards Bd 55-57);-ACRL;-RSD (2nd v-pres 62-63);-RTSD; MusLA; PennLA; NY Lib Club. 10: Phi Beta Kappa; Grolier Club (NY); Philobiblon Club (Phila). 13: Yes. 14: Ref serv, bibliog, acquis, catlg, rare bks. 15: 1607 Rittenhouse, Claridge Rittenhouse sq, Phila Pa 19103.

SCULL, JUDITH ATKINSON. b NYC 20 D 26. 5: Rockford Col 44-46 (Physics); Northwestern U 46-47 (Psych); Rockford Col 47-48 (Psych) BS; USoCal 63-64 (Spec Lib) MSLS. 7: Data reduction clk Aerojet Gen, Azusa Cal 49-50; Libn Wiancko Engrg, Pasadena Cal 61; Asst libn Bell & Howell Research Ctr, Pasadena Cal 64-65; Corp libn CONRAC, Dyarte Cal 66-69; Libn Burroughs, Pasadena Cal 69-. 9: SLA; ASIS; Spec Libns in Pasadena. 14: Info communication. 15: 1365 Rexford ave, Pasadena Ca 91107.

SCULLION, DONNA G. b Highland Wis 21 D 33. 5: Wis State U (Platteville) 51-55 (Hist) BS; UWis 58-59 MS in LS; UDenver summer 63. 7: Hist tchr Cassville High Sch, Cassville Wis 55-58; Instr lib sci Wis State U(Platteville) summer 61; Libn York Commun High Sch, Elmhurst Ill 59-. 8: Gen Ref Libn, Wis State U (Platteville) summer 69. 9: IllLA; IllASchL (Spring Conf Com 68); High Sch Libns Chicagoland (pres 69-70). 10: Amer Fed of Tchrs. 14: Sch & yp serv. 15: 304 S Chase ave, Lombard Ill 60148.

SCURR, J W REGINALD. b Gilman Iowa 6 My 16. 5: St Olaf Col 36-40 (Eng) BA; State UIowa 40-47 (Comparative Ling); UChicago 47-49 (LS) MA. 6: Fr, Russian. 7: Lib aid for lang lib UIowa 44-47; Stud asst catlg & ref UChicago 48; Libn I Chicago Pub Lib 49-53, Newspaper libn 53-58, Hd shelf dept 58-64, Chief humanities 64-. 9: ALA; IllLA. 15: 3525 Seminary st, Chicago Il 60657.

SEABERG, LILLIAN M(ARIE). b Louisville Ky 8 My 11. 5: Winthrop 28-32 (Educ) AB; UNC 46 BSLS; UFla 50-54 (Anthropol) MA. 7: Tchr Clarendon Co, SC 32-43; WAC Publications Div Port of Embarkation, Charleston SC 43-46; Asst libn Longwood Col 47-49; Univ Col libn UFla Lib 49-. 9: ALA; SELA; FlaLA. 10: AAUP; Fla Hist Soc; Fla Anthrop Soc; Nat & State Audubon Soc; Amer Mus Natural Hist. 13: Yes. 14: Ref, stud orient in use of lib. 15: 1216 NW 3rd ave, Gainesville Fl 32601.

SEABROOK, MARTHA RACHEL. b ATLANTA. 5: George Washington U 42-46 (Eng) AB; Columbia 47-49 (Eng) MA; Catholic U 52-56 MS in LS. 6: Fr. 7: Instr in Eng George Washington U 46-47; Asst ref libn Georgetown U 53-54; Libn Dept of Lib Sci, Catholic U 54-58; Assoc Humanities libn UMd 58-66, Humanities libn 66-, Lect in Eng U Col 59-69. 9: ALA-RSD;-ACRL. 10: Phi Beta Kappa; Beta Phi Mu. 12: Contrib "Abstracts of English Studies" 64-. 13: Yes. 14: Ref. 15: 4313 Knox rd, College Park Md 20740.

SEABROOKS, NETTIE H. b Mt Clemens Mich 22 F 34. 4: Dr Franklyn E Seabrooks. 5: Marygrove Col 51-55 (hem) BS; UMich 55-57 AMLS. 7: Ref asst Detroit Pub Lib tech dept 56-58; Asst circ libn Tenn State U 58-62; Lib asst pub rel staff Gen Motors Corp, Detroit 62-67; Libn Pub Rel Staff 67-. 9: SLA; ALA. 14: Admin, research. 15: Pub Rel Staff Lib, room 11-235 Gen Motors Corp, 3044 W Grand blvd, Detroit 48202.

SEACORD, LAURA F. b Mt Vernon NY 8 D 25. 5: NYU 43-47 (FR) BA; Simmons 48-49 BS in LS. 6: Fr. 7: Child libn Enoch Pratt Free Lib, Baltimore 49-55; Child libn E Meadow Pub Lib, E Meadow NY 55-. 8: Lib sci instr, C W Post Lib Sch, spring 65, Hofstra U, fall 65; in-serv course East Meadow Sch Dist spring 69; Pub libns certif exam com 67-72. 9: ALA (Liaison Com on Bkstores & Bk Distributors; Child Bks in Rel to Radio & TV 64-67); NYLA (Coms on Child Bklist for Small Pub Libs, Films for Child a selected list). 10: Child theatre Conf. 13: Yes. 14: Child serv. 15: 32 Meadow lane, Levittown NY 11756.

SEAGER, DANIEL A. b Jacksonville Fla 1 Ja20. 4: Helen Medearis. 5: St Johns Col 41 AA; Okla Baptist U 48 AB; UOkla 50-53 AB, AM; Colo State Col (Educ). 7: US Army, ETO 42-45; Head libn & Eng instr Southwest Baptist Col 49-53; Head libn & chm lib sci dept, Asst Prof of Lib Sci Ouachita Col 53-56; Head libn, chm Dept of Lib Sci, Assoc Prof of Lib Sci Colo State Col 56-, Dir lib serv 66-, Consul Educl Media Program 66-. 9: ALA (Coun 65, Off for recr, dir Reg VI); -LAD; -LED; -RTSD (Com assignments); -ACRL; -AASchL; NEA-DAVI; Assn Higher Educ; MPLA (sec-treas 59-63, Exec sec 63-); Rocky Mountain Bibliog Center for Res (Bd 59-60 & 65-, sec 61-63); ColoLA (Coms, Auditor); ColoASchL (Consul); Colo Coun of Libns of State Operated Instit (sec, Com on Centralized Proc for Acad Libs); ColoEA (Com on Lib Standards for Pub Schs in Colo 64-65); Colo A-V Assn; Colo Assn Higher Educ. 10: AAUP; State Hist Soc Colo; Phi Delta Kappa; Nat Travel Club; Audubon Nature Program; Nat Geog Soc; Air Force Assn; Amer Sci Affiliation; Weld Co Soc for Mental Health; Civitan Internat; C of C; Knife & Fork Club; YMCA; Internat Platform Assn; Coun on Consumer Info, UMo; Educ for Freedom Found; Forest Hist Soc; Amer Numismatics Assn; etc. YMCA. 13: Yes. 14: Admin, lib educ. 15: Colo State Col, Greeley Colo 80631.

SEAGLE, SARA GARDNER. b Linden NC 25 Ag 12. 5: UNC(Greensboro) 29-33 (LS) BA. 7: Head of acquis dept & admin asst to libn UNC(Greensboro) 34-38; Libn Lib Sch Col of William & Mary 38-42; Base staff & command libn Dept of Army, Ft Bragg NC & EUCOM 42-48; Chief libn Va, NY 48-49; Staff libn Ninth Div Air Force, Langley AFB Va 49-50; Command libn Air Force Systems Command, Baltimore & Andrews AFB Wash DC 51-66; Libn Holding Tech Inst, Raleigh NC 68-. 9: SLA; NCLA. 14: Admin, acquis. 15: 127 E Edenton st, Raleigh NC 27601.

SEALOCK, RICHARD BURL. b Lexinton Ill 15 Je 07. 4: Mary Margaret Morrow. 5: Eureka Col 29 AB; UIll 30 BS in LS; Columbia 35 MS in LS; Eureka Col 67 LHD. 7: Queens Borough Pub Lib, NY: Order asst 30-32, Gen asst 33-34, Curator Long Island collection 34-39; Head hist travel & biog Enoch PrattFree Lib, Baltimore 39-43; Asst libn Gary Pub Lib, Gary Ind 43-44, Libn 44-49; ibn Kan City (Mo) Pub Lib 50-68; Exec dir Forest Press, Lake Placid NY. 8: Md Governors Commsn for State Lib Survey (42); Consul, Eureka Col Lib 64-67; Mo State Lib Adv Com 65-68. 9: ALA (treas 56-60, Trustee of Endowment Fund 59-, Coun 61-65, 2nd v-pres 63-64, Bd on Accred 55-56); -LED (pres 55-56); MoLA (pres 55, Devel Com 62-, chm 65-); Bibliog Center or Research (Coun 55-57); IndLA (pres 46-47). 10: Rotary Club. 12: Co-auth "Woodside Does Read (35); Co-comp "Long Isand Bibliography (40); Co-comp "Bibligraphy of Place Name Literature, US and Canada (48), (2nd ed 67). 13: Yes. 14: Admin, bldg, bibliog, rare bks, spec collections. 15: Forest Press, Lake Placid NY 12946.

SEALOR, MARGARET ANNE. b Alexandria Va 21 S 37. 5: Madison Col (Va) 55-57, 58-60 (LS) BS in Ed. 7: Tchr, coun Reading Dynamics Inst, Wash DC 61; Libn catlg US GEol Survey Lib, Wash DC 6062; Tech libn Lockheed Missiles & Space Co, Sunnyvale Cal 62-63; Libn ref Nat Agric Lib, Wash DC 63-64; Libn catlgr phys sci & engnr US Geol Survey Lib, Wash DC 64-68; Ser catlgr Smithsonian Inst Libs. 9: DCLA. 10: Ski Club of Wash DC; Geosci Info Soc. 14: Catlg (sci & tech), bibliog. 15: 601 S 22nd st, Arlington Va 22202.

SEAMAN, ANNE T(AYLOR). b Cincinnati 10 Ag 30. 4: Duncan R Seaman. 5: UColo 48-52 (Eng Lit) BA; Immaculate Heart Col 61-63 (LS) MA. 7: Libn trainee VA Sawtell Hosp, Los Angeles 62-63; Libn Honolulu Acad of Arts, Honolulu 63-. 9: ALA; HawaiiLA.14869 14: Fine art (Oriental). 15: 900 S Beretania st, Honolulu Hi 96814.

SEARCY, HERBERT. b Carrollton Ky. 5: East Ky State U 42-46 (Eng, Hist) AB; Ohio State U 47-48 (Eng) MA; UIll 52-54 (LS) MS, 54-63 (LS) PhD. 6: Fr, Ger, Russian, Sp. 7: Catlgr & Catlg Reviser UIll(Urbana) 53-62; Head tech seris Serv Wis Lib (La Crosse) 64-. 9: ALA; WisLA; Upper Miss AcadLA (co-chm). 10: Beta Phi Mu; AAUP. 14: Tech serv. 15: Wis State Univ Lib, La Crosse Wis 54601.

SEARING, CHARLES A. b Pittsburgh 28 Je 12. 4: Florence Peacock. 5: Northwestern 36-40 (Sociol) BS; Drexel 63-64 MS in LS. 6: F. 7: Field Rep, reg dir Amer Nat Red Cross,St Louis 41-44; Lt (jg) US Naval Res 44-46; Field dir Amer Nat Red Cross, Phila 46-49; Farmer, Bucks Co Penn 49-54; Insurance agent & real estate broker, Phila 54-63; Asst ref libn UConn 64-. 9: ALA; ConnLA. 14: Ref. 15: Univ of Conn Lib, Storrs Conn 06268.

SEARLS, EILEEN HAUGHEY. b Madison Wis 27 Ap 25. 5: UWis 44-48 (Hist) BA, 47-50 LLB, 50-51 (LS) MS, 67-68. 6: Sp, Portu. 7: Documents libn Law Lib UWis 50-51; Catlgr Law Lib Yale U 51-52; St Louis U; : Law Lbn & Instr 52-53, Law Libn & Asst Prof 53-56, Law Libn & Assoc Prof 56-64, Law Libn & Prof 64-. 8: Consul, Law Lib, Washburn U 65. 9: Intl Assn of Law Libs; AALL; Amer Law Sch Assn; CathLA; Nat Assn of Women Lawyers; MoLA; Wis Bar Assn. 10: AAUP; AAUW; Phi Delta Delta. 13: Yes. 14: Admin, ref, res, tchg. 15: 4946 Buckingham ct, St Louis Mo 63108.

SEARS, PHYLLIS JEAN. b Detroit 2 Ag 2. 5: Marygrove Col 40-44 (Hist) BA; Catholic U 44-46 BS in LS. 6: Fr, Ger. 7: Asst libn Dunbarton Col of the Holy Cross 45-46; Marygrove Col 46-47; Asst libn Chrysler Corp Engnr Lib, Highland Park Mich 47-65, Supv 65-. 9: SLA (sec-treas Metals Div; Mich Chap: sec-treas, bulletin ed, pres-elect 66-67, pres 67-68; chm Programs Com, & var other com posts); CathLA (Mich Unit: se-treas). 10: Cath Alumni Club of Detroit; League of Cath Women.14: Re. 14: Ref. 15: Engineering Lib Chrysler Corp P O Box 1118, Detroit Mi 48231.

SEARS, WINTHROP JR. b Arlington Mass 8 D 18. 4: Doris Davis. 5: Harvard 37-41 (Eng Lit) AB; Columbia 46-47 BS in LS; UMich 50-51 MAin LS. 7: Personnel Sgt Maj Med Dept AAF (T/St), Var air base hosps 42-45; Ref asst Enoch Pratt Free Lib, Baltimore 47-50; Archives asst Ford Motor Co Archives, Dearborn Mich 51-62; Research & info spec Ford Motor Co, Dearborn Mich 62-65; Assoc archivist, Ford Archives, Henry Ford Museum, Dearborn Mich 65-. 8: Mem, Lib Commsn, Livonia Mich. 9: ALA-ALTA; SAA; MichLA. 10: Trustee Livonia Citizens for Better Human Rel. 14: Archives (hist res & proc of collections). 15: 16845 Canterbury dr, Livonia Mi 48154.

SEARSON, MARILYN. b Walterboro SC 3 S 43. 5: Newberry Col 61-64 (Eng) AB; UNC 64-65 (LS) MA. 6: Fr. 7: Ya libn Greenville Co Lib, Greenville SC 65-66; Libn Clemson U 66-69; instr Radford Col 69-. 9: ALA; SCLA; SELA. 14: Tchg, ref. 15: Box 375, Saluda SC 29138.

SEATON, ELAINE (MAZLISH). b NY 6 My 28. 4: Robert W Seaton. 5: Chicago 45-49 (Sociol) PhB; C W Post Col LIU 63-66 MSLS. 7: Depth interviewer Market Psychology Inc, NY 54; Lib train Shelter Rock Pub Lib, Albertson NY 63-66; Hd ref lib & adult serv Shelter Rock Pub Lib 66-68; Asst dir SUNY (Old Westbury) 68-. 9: ALA; NYLA; NCLA. 10: LWV. 15: 42 Schoolhouse lane, Roslyn Heights LI NY 11577.

SEAVERS, LORETTA (BALL). b Pinsonfork Ky 5 Je 39. 4: Joseph Earl Seavers. 5: Pikeville Col 56-58, 59-60 (Educ) BS; UKy summer 67 & 68, fall 68, spring 69 (LS) MS. 6: Fr. 7: Elem sch tchr Pike Co Bd of Educ, Pikeville Ky 58-59; Claims repr Soc Security Admin, Pikeville & Covington Ky 60-66; Elem sch tchr Ludlow Bd of Educ, Ludlow Ky 67-68. 9: NEA; KyEA; LudlowEA. 14: Elem sch libnship. 15: 2517 Ann st, Ludlow Ky 41016.

SEAWELL, MARY ROBERT. b Carthage NC 20 Ap 05. 5: Meredith Col 23-27 (Math) AB; UNC 38 AB in LS. 6: Fr, Lat. 7: Tchr of Math & Hist NC High Schs 27-37; Libn Central Jr High Sch, Greensboro NC 37-45; Head order libn Womans Col UNC(Greensboro) 45-56; Bibliog & Ref libn UNC(Greensboro) 56-. 9: ALA; SELA; NCLA. 10: AAUP; Greensboro Lib Club; Friends of UNC (Greensboro) Lib. 14: Ref. 15: Univ of NC Lib, Greensboro NC 27412.

SEBASTIAN, FANNIE NICHOLSON. b Greensboro NC 25Mr20. 5: NC A&T 36-40 (Eng, Soc Sci) BS; Catholic U 44-46 BS in LS. 6: Fr. 7: US Govt: Statistical Clerk Bur of the Census 42-44, Statistician War Production Bd 44-45, Statistician Nat Housing Agency 45-47; Libn Catholic U 47-49; Libn Dept of the Army, Ft Knox Ky 50-51; Catlgr LC 52-57; Libn Dept of the Army, Ft Riley Kan 59-62; DC Libs; br libn, Commun libn 65-. 65-. 9: ALA. 10: Dupont Civic Assn; Wash DC Girl Scout Prog. 14: Ref, readers adv, catlg. 15: 3925 Ames st NE, Wash DC 20019.

SEBRING, LEILA (LOUISE). b Sebring Ohio. 5: Radcliffe Col 36 (Amer Hist) AB; Fla State U 57-59 (LS) MA. 6: Fr, Ger. 7: Tchr & libn Nat Cathedral Sch for Girls, Wash dc 40-43, 48-55; Libn US Dept of State Caribbean Commsn, Wash DC 44-45; Libn UFla citrus experiment sta 59-66; Libn S Fla Jr Col 66-. 9: ALA; FlaLA; Fla Assn Pib Jr cols. 10: Staff and Bk Club of Sebring (Fla). 14: Ref. 15: 148 S Lakeview dr, Sebring Fl 33870.

SECORD, RALPH WALLACE. b Mt Pleasant Mich 19 Mr 23. 4: Ann Gidilewich. 5: Central Mich Col 41-48 (Soc Sci, Eng) BA; West Res 49-50 MS of LS. 6:Fr. 7: (Cpl) US Army, Overseas 43-46; Gen asst Detroit Pub Lib 49; Asst adult serv Dearborn Pub Lib, Dearborn Mich 50-53; Chief libn Twin Falls Pub Lib, Twin Falls Ida 53-55; Chief libn UMatilla Co Lib, Pendleton Ore 56-57; Reg libn US Info Agency, Middle East & Africa 57-66; Dir Dickinson Co Lib & Mid-Peninsula Lib Federation, Iron Mountain Mich 66-. 8: Adv, Lebanese Lib Assn, 58-61; Treas Dickinson Co Bldg Authority, Iron Mt Mich 65-. 9: ALA; OreLA (Conv chm 57, mem Resol Com 56-57); East Ore LA (pres 56-57); IdaLA (chm Pub Lib Div 55); Adv & bus mgr "Idaho Librarian" 54-55; PNLA (Adult Educ Com 54; Title III Interlib Loan Com). 12: Ed "American Library Review UIA (beirut Lebanon 58-61) (monthly). 13: Yes. 14: Admin, pub lib. 15: 401 Iron Mountain st, Iron Mountain Mi 49801.

SECREST, VIRGINIA S. b Blackford C Ind 8 My 17. 4: Robert Madison Secrest. 5: Ball State U 36-38, 43 (Soc Sci) BS; Tex Womans U 59-60 MLS. 6: Fr, Ger, Ital. 7: Catlg libn Washington U (St Louis) 61-67; Hd catlg div 68-69. 9: ALA. 14: Catlg, soc sci bibliog. 15: 5000 Foxdale fr, St Louis 63128.

SEDELOW, WALTER A(LFRED) JR. b Ludlow Mass 17 Ap 28. 4: Sally A Yeates. 5: Amherst 44-47 (Hist) BA (summa cum laude); Harvard 50-52 (Hist) MA, 56-57 (Hist) PhD. 6: Fr. 7: Master Milton Acad, Milton Mass 47-48; Instr of hist Williams Col 48-50; Capt USAFR Officer-in-charge 28th SRW ECM Sch (53-54) 52-66; Amherst Col: Instr 54-56, Asst Prof 57-60; Chm dept of sociol Parsons Col 60-61; Chm dept of sociol Rockford Col 61-62; Human factors scientist Syst Development Corp, Santa Monica Cal 62-64; Chm dept of socol & anthrop dir health organization research program St Louis U 64-66; UNC (Chapel Hill): Dean sch of lib sci 67-, Prof sociol & computer & info sci 68-. 8: Consul Life Scis Div, Depts of Engring Psych & Aerospace Med, McDonnell Aircraft Corp, St Louis Mo 64-66; Co-dir Nat Inst of Mental Health Hosp Improv Prog, Larned State Hosp Kan summer 65; Consul Jacksonville (Ill) State Hosp 68-; Panel chm "Human Scis (Soc/Behav Sci, Human Biology and Ecology)," NSF Park City Conf on Computers in undergrad Educ, Park City Utah 68; Co-prin Investigator, NASA "Computer-aided Analysis of Interdisciplinary Discourse Barriers" Project, UNC Space Scis Prog 68-; Mem Steering Com & Sect Chm, Sect on Infl and Social Aspects of Advanced Tech 69-. 9: ACLS Com on info Tech; Amer Sociol Assn (Fellow); Assn Computing Machinery; Soc Gen Systems Research; ALA; AALS; NCLA; NC Pub Lib Certif Bd. 10: UNC (Chapel Hill) Com on Univ Govt 67-; Phi Beta Kappa; Trustee Internat Soc Sci Inst 66; Mem Admin Bd, Frank Porter Graham Child Devel Res Ctr, Chapel Hill NC 68-. 11: Henry P Field Fellow 56-57; Amherst Memorial Fellow 56-57. 12: Assoc ed "Social Forces" (66); Ser ed "The Free Press", Macmillan Co (68-); Bd Edrs "Computer Studies in the Humanities and Verbal Behavior". 13: Yes. 14: Knowledge systems, lang analysis, sociol of sci & tech. 15: Dept of Computer Science, Strong Hall, Univ of Kansas, Lawrence Kansas 66044.

SEE, RICHARD. b Hackensack NJ 3 D 23. 4: Chia Chih Yuan. 5: Harvard 43-43, 46-49 (Math) BA; UCal (Berkeley) 49-52 (Math) MA; UOslo (Norway) 49. 6: Chinese (Mandarin), Fr, Russian. 7: Sgt US Army Air Force 43-45; Prof asst doc research program NSF, Wash DC 58-60, Program dir for mech tr 60-62, Deputy dir doc research program 64-66, Dir research & studies program 66-67; Chief research & development br NLM Bethesda Md 67-. 8: Mem Panel 2, COSATI, Fed Coun for Sci & Tech 65-67. 9: ASIS; Amer Math Soc; Ling soc Amer; Assn Comput Machinery; Assn for Computl Ling. 13: Yes. 14: Info system research & deod, transl, lib systems. 15: National Lib of Medicine, Bethesda Md 20014.

SEEGRABER, FRANK JOSEPH. b Boston 8 O 16. 4: Edith Walker. 5: Holy Cross Col 34-38 (Eng, Amer Lit) AB; Columbia 41-43 (LS) BS; Harvard 52-53 (Bibliog). 6: Sp, Fr, Ger. 7: Spec lib asst Littauer Center Harvard 39; Asst gen ref dept Boston Pub Lib 39-41; Grad asst Columbia Col Lib 41-42; Asst period dept NY Pub Lib 42-43; (Pvt) US Army 43; Inventory supv Holtzer-Cabot Elec Co, Boston 44-47; Educ coun Grolier Soc, Boston Off 47; Asst Kirstein Bus Br Boston Pub Lib 48; Ref libn Boston Col 49-58; Libn Merrimach Col 58-65; Libn UMass (Boston) 65-68; Libn Col of Bus Admin, Boston Col 68-. 8: Lecturer in bibliog, Boston Col, 55-58; Lectr lib sci Northeastern U 66-. 9: ALA; BSA; Bibliog Soc UVa; SLA (chm Educ Com Boston Cha 55-56); NELA; (Bibliog Com 67-); NE Tech Serv Libns (v-chm 61-62, chm 62-63, chn 62-63, Exec Com 63-65); MassLA (Educ Com 66-68). 10: AAUP. 14: Col lib admin, bibliog, spec collections, lib bldgs & equip, interlib coop, lib educ, tech serv. 15: 6 Thwing st, Boston Ma 02119.

SEELEY, JEANE McWORKMAN. b Indianapolis 7 Je 16. 4: John C Seeley. 5: Butler U 33-35 (Chem); UMich 35-37 (Chem) BS, 52, 58-59 (LS). 6: Ger, Fr, Sp. 7: Patent license agreement res asst E I duPont de Nemours & Co, Wilmington del 38-40; Tr & owner Tech Lib Research Serv, Ann Arbor Mich 46-65; Lib asst UMich Engnr Lib 49; Tr & abstractor W L Badger Consul Chem Engnr, Ann Arbor Mich 50-53; Libn Vision Research Labs UMich 54-58; Assoc research libn Parke Davis Research Labs, Ann Arbor Mich 58-. 9: MedLA; SLA. 10: Phi Beta Kappa; Phi Kappa Phi; Kappa Kappa Gamma; ACLU; Friends of the Lib: LWV. 14: Mechanized storage &

retrieval systems, ref, transl. 15: 845 Mt Pleasant, Ann Arbor Mi 48103.

SEELIGER, RONALD A(LTON). b Lockhart Tex 3 O34. 5: UTex 52-56 (Eng) BA, 56-61 MLS. 6: Sp. 7: UTex Lib asst 57-58, Sr lib asst journalism - newspaper libn 58-60, Libn II journalism - newspaper libn 60-. 9: TexLA. 14: Ref, journalism & newspaper libn. 15: 1909 Cliff st, Austin Tex 78705.

SEELY, BETTY JANE (MALOUFF). b Trinidad Col 26 F 29. 4: George Seely. 5: Adams State Col 46-50 (Secondary Educ) BA, 62 (Elem Educ). 7: Tchr: Hooper Colo 51-52, Meeker Colo 55-57, Washington, Pueblo Colo 61, Sunset Park, Pueblo Colo 62-63; Libn Co High Sch, pueblo Colo 64; Period libn So Colo State Col 65-. 9: NEA; ColoEA; ColoLA. 10: AAUW. 14: Period, a-v materials. 15: 9 Regis, Pueblo Co 81005.

SEELY, PAULINE AUGUSTA. b Goshen NY 14 O 05. 5: Vassar 23-27 (Lat) AB; UIll 27-28 BS in LS; Columbia 41-42 (LS) MS. 7: Asst libn Eureka Col 28-29; Catlgr & reviser Queens Borough Pub Lib, Jamaica NY 29-44; 1st asst catlg div Los Angeles Co Pub Lib, Los Angeles 44-48; Head catlg dept Denver Pub Lib 48-56, Dir tech serv 56-. 8: Field Survey of Dewey Decimal Clsf Use Abroad, 64. 9: ALA (Coun 51-55 & 59-63; (chm Pub Libs Subcom of Spec Com on the DC 44-47; Dir-at-large 46-49 & 59-63, chm SpecCom on Personnel 49-51); Chm Subcom on Rules for Filing Catlg Cards 62-68; Mem Decimal Clsf Ed Policy Com 59-); ColoLA; MPLA; Mountain Plains Reg Group of Catlgrs (chm 53-54). 10: Beta Phi Mu; Amer Name Soc; Zonta Club. 11: Margaret Mann Citation, 54; Nell I Scott Mem Award 68. 12: Comp "Long Island Bibliography, with R B Sealock (40); Comp "Bibliography of Place Name Literature, with R B Sealock (48, 2d ed 67); Ed "ALA Rules for Filing Catalog Cards (2nd ed 68, 2nd ed Abridged 68). 66). 13: Yes. 14: Catlg, tech serv, ser. 15: Denver Pub Lib 1357 Broadway, Denver Co 80203.

SEFCHICK, PATRICIA (FARRELL). b Newport News Va 17 Ag 38. 4: Raymond M Sefchick. 5: UCal (Riverside) 56-60 (Eng) AB; USoCal 61-65 MLS. 6: Fr. 7: Page Riverside Pub lib, Riverside Cal 56-58; Reader Comparative Lit Dept UCal (Riverside) 58-59, Mss proofreader Geog Dept 60; Dance instr YWCA, Riverside Cal 60-61; Clk Riverside Pub Lib, Riverside Cal 60-61, Juv & y-a libn 62-. 9: ALA; ColoLA; YA Reviewers of So Cal (chm Bklist Com 68); YA Reviewers of Riverside Co. bklist Com 68); YA Reviewers of Riverside Co. 14: Child & ya wk. 15: 2327 Fairview, Riverside Ca 92506.

SEGAL, NORMA. b Pittsburgh Penn 20 Ja 25. 4: Harold L Segal. 5: Carnegie Inst 42-46 (Gen Studies) BS; SUNY (Geneseo) 65-66 MLS. 6: Fr. 7: Student asst Carnegie Inst Tech Libs 42-46; Asst art lib UMinn 48-49; Tech asst psych dept UCLA 52-53; Asst in acquis UPittsburgh Lib 54-56; Asst lib Univ City Pub Lib, University City Mo 60-64; Hd curriculum lab SUNY Col (Buffalo) 65-. 8: Vis lectr Sch of Lib and Info Studies SUNY (Buffalo) summer 68. 9: ALA; NYLA (Lib Sect); NYStateTA; LASUNY. 10: Amer Fed Tchrs; AAUP. 14: Child bks, textbks. 15: 91 Keswick rd, Amherst NY 14226.

SEGER, ROBERT M. b Detroit 16 D 26. 4: Lois A Elliott. 5: West Mich U 53-56 BA; UMich 59-60 AMLS; UWis summer 65. 7: Page Mich State Lib; Ref St Clair Co Lib, Port Huron Mich 56-59; Head Libn Presque Isle Co Lib, Rogers City Mich 60-67; Dir Clinton Pub Lib, Clinton Iowa 67-. 9: ALA; IowaLA. 10: Kiwanis. 14: Admin. 15: P O Box 401, Clinton Ia 52732.

SEGESTA, JAMES (EDWARD). b E Detroit Mich 12 N 34. 4: Elizabeth Yee. 5: UMich 52-56 9eng lit) BA; USoCal 57-59 MSLS, 66-67 (Eng lit) MA, 66- (LS). 7: Tech processes libn Cal State Col (Long Beach) 59-63, (San Bernardino) 63-66; Lib syst analyst Prof Lib Serv, Santa Ana Cal 67-68; Hd tech processes Cal Inst of Fine Aets, LA 69-. 8: Tchr summer session in catlg, Long Beach State Col 68. 9: ALA; CalLA. 10: Sierra Club. 13: Yes. 14: Tech proc. 15: 3735 Glenfeliz blvd, Los Angeles Ca 90039.

SEGUINE, VIRGINIA (MARGERY). b Chicago 20 F 32. 5: Bryan Col 50-54 (Eng) BA; West Mich U 60-65 (LS) MA. 6: Fr, Sp. 7: Tchr Greystone Christian Grade Sch, Mobile Ala 54-55; Tchr State Sch for the Deaf, Knoxville Tenn 57-58; Instr Pennfield Schs, Battle Creek Mich 59-62; Libn, Instr Appalachian Bible Inst, Bradley WVa 62-64; Libn Fellowship; ALA; TennLA. 10: Delta Kappa Gamma. 14: Admin, rare bks. 15: Bryan Col, Dayton Tenn 37321.

SEGURA, PEARL MARY. b Lafayette La 12 Je 09. 5: U Southwestern La 27-30 (Art, Fr, Eng) BA; Tulane U summer 31 (Eng); Columbia summer 39 (LS); LSU summers 36, 37, 40, 41 BS in LS; UIll summer 48 (LS); UHouston summer 54 (Educ Tour of Europe). 6: Fr, Sp, Ger. 7: Tchr-libn Indian Bayou High Sch, Indian Bayou La 30-31; Grade & high sch tchr Maurice High Sch, Maurice La 31-33; Tchr-libn Maurice High Sch, Maurice La 33-41; U Southwestern LA; Asst circ libn 41-44, Act ref libn 44-46, Ref libn 46-62, Libn Louisiana Room 62-. 9: AL-ACRL; SLA; SWLA; LaLA; La Tchrs Assn; La Hist Assn; La Geneal & Histl Assn; La Folklore Soc. 10: AAUW; Nat Trust for Hist Preserv; Mero Opera Guild; DAR; Womans Club; Lafayette Little Theater; Lafayette Commun Concerts Assn; Lafayette Art Assn; France Amerique de la Louisiane Acadienne; Phi Kappa Phi; Beta Phi Mu; Delta Kappa Gamma; Kappa Kappa Iota; LSU Alum Assn; UDC USL Alumni Assn; Mt Carmel Alumnae Assn; Cath DAU AM; Univ Womens Club; Amer Camellia Soc; La Poetry Soc; Amer Iris Soc; France-Amerique DELA Louisiane Acadienne. 12 Comp; "The Acadians in Fact and Fiction: A Classified Bibliography (55). 13: Yes. 14: Ref, La Room, rare bks. 15: 140 S Magnolia st, Lafayette La 70501.

SEHEULT, M(ARGARET) ANNE. b Ottawa Can 14 F 39. 5: UNB 56-60 BA. 6: Fr. 7: Circ-ref Lawson Mem Lib UWest Ont 64-65, Head Libn Health Sci Centre Lib 65-. 9: MelLA; Inst Prof Libns Ont; OntLA; Assn Can Med Col Standing Standing Com on Med Sch Libs (sec). 10: Canadian Assn for Advancement of Health Sci; LAssociation francaise de London. 14: Ref, admin, acquis, period. 15: Health Sci Centre Lib, Univ of West Ont, London Ont Can.

SEIBEL, ADOLF JOSEF. b Lwow Poland 31 J114. 4: 5: ULwow 32-39 (Ger, Hist, Philol) MA. 6: Ger, Polish, Ukrainian, Russian, Sp. 7: Instr Ger lang ULwow 39-41; Sch supv & tchr Ger Lang Ger Occup Govt, Lwow Warsaw 41-44; Mil serv Ger Army 44-45; Tchr of Ger & Hist with Intern Refugee Org, DP Camps Germany 46-49, Resettlement & Welfare Coun 49-51; Resettlement Coun Tolstoy Found, Munich Germany 54-57; Stockclerk Royal McBee Corp, Hartford Conn 57-59; Circ desk asst Trinity Col Conn 58-59, Ser libn 59-. 9: ConnLA. 14: Ref, ser. 15: 90 Vernon st, Hartford Ct 06106.

SEIBERT, DONALD C. b Los Angeles 3 O 29. 5: George Pepperdine Col 47-51 (Hist) BA; Columbia 58-61 LS) MS. 6: Ger. 7: Ref asst NY Pub Lib 61; Catlgr Juilliard Sch of Music 62-65, 67-68; Mus libn SUNY(Stony Brook) 65-67; Mus libn Syracuse 68-. 9: MusLA (chm Standing Com on Catlg & Clsf). 12: "Hyde Timings (64). 14: Mus libnship. 15: 382 Anderson ave, Closter NJ 07624.

SEIDEL, NANCY WARD (BIDDLE). b Anderson Ind 18 Jl 20. 4: Eugene Maurice Seidel. 5: IndU 38-42 (Fine Arts) AB; Portland StateU 59-60 (Educ) Elem Certif, 64-65 (Educ) Secondary Certif; UPortland 65-66 MLS. 7: War bond salesman Fletcher Trust Co, indianapolis 42-43; Airline hostess Trans World Airline, Kan City Mo 46-47; Recreation wkr Amer Nat Red Cross, Wash DC, Ft Eustis Va, USS Tranquility in Pacific, Germany 47-50; Kindergarten tchr Camas School Dist, Camas Wash 60-64; Libn Camas High Sch, Camas Wash 65-. 9: ALA; NEA; WashStateASchL; WashEA. 10: Kappa Alpha Theta; Camas Pub Lib Bd; Portland Art Museum; Ind U Alum Assn; Clark Co Hist Soc. 15: 2109 NW Couch, Camas Wa 98607.

SEIDEL, RICHARD REYNOLDS. b Teaneck NJ 26 Jl 37. 5: Rutgers 55-59 (Hist) AB, 63-65 mls. 6: Fr. 7: Asst order libn Rutgers U 63-66; Acquis libn UIll (Chicago Circle) 66-. 8: Consul Chicago Pub Lib Survey 68-69. 9: ALA; IllLA. 10: Caxton Club. 14: Acquis, rare bks. 15: 515 W Melrose st, Chicago Il 60657.

SEIDLER, RICHARD D. b Phila. 4: Marie M Seidler. 5: Temple 54-58 (Music Educ) BS; UTex 58-60 (Musicology) MM; Catholic U 62-64 MSLS, 60, 65- (Musicology). 7: Instr of bassoon UTex 58-60; Solo bassoon US Air Force Band, Wash DC 60-64; Instr of woodwinds Mary Washington Col 62-63; Asst Head loan dept UMd 64; Head acquis dept Arlington (Va) Dept of Libs 65-66; Asst Prof of mus No Ill U 66-. 8: Co-chm Lib Com No Ill U Mus Dept. 9: ALA; VaLA; MusLA (co-chm Documentation Com Midwest Br). 10: Amer Fed Musns; Col Mus Soc. 15: 207 Tilton Park dr, DeKalb Il 60115.

SEIDMAN, ANN (MAGINNIS). b Ithaca NY 12 Mr 23. 4: Martin Seidman. 5: Okla State U 41-46 (Chem) BS; UIll 63-65 (LS) MS. 7: Libn in chg of youth room Decatur Pub Lib, Decatur Ill 65-66; Tech libn in chg Research Lib A E Staley Mfg Co, Decatur Ill 66-. 9: SLA. 10: AAUW; Decatur Area Arts Coun; Decatur Assn for Racial Equality; Zonta. 14: Child & youth serv in pub lib, ref. 15: 346 W Maco, Decatur Ill 62522.

SEIF, BARBARA JOAN. b Cincinnati Ohio 4 Je 30. 5: Wheelock Col 48-52 (Educ) BS; UWis 64-66 (LS) MS. 6: Sp. 7: Tchr: Grand Rapids Mich 52-56, St Clair Shores Mich 55-56, Shorewood Wis 56-59, Milwaukee 61-66; Lab sch libn Wis State U (Whitewater) 66-. 9: ALA; WisLA; WisEA. 10: AAUW; Delta Kappa Gamma. 14: Child & ya wk. 15: 1036 W Shaw ct, Whitewater Wi 53190.

SEIFERT, BETTY (ROITH). b Minneapolis 19 Ag 21. 4: Donald W Seifert. 5: UMinn 43 (Soc Sci) BS in Ed, 51 BS in LS, (cum laude). 7: Tchr Glencoe High Sch, Glencoe Minn 43-47; Libn ref dept UMinn(Minneapolis) 47-51; Grosse Pointe Pub Lib, Grosse Pointe Mic: Prof asst 53-59, Park Br libn 59-63, Woods Br libn 63-. 9: ALA; NEA; MichLA (chm Publns Com 60-61, chm Adult Educ Com 64-65); MichEA; Grosse Pointe EA. 10: Phi Sigma Alpha; AAUW; Friends of the Grosse Pointe Pub Lib; Delta Kappa Gamma. 14: Ref, adult educ, admin. 15: 1616 Hampton rd, Grosse Pointe Mi 48236.

SEIFERT, BETTY LOUISE. b Cleveland Ohio 7 S 29. 5: West Res 47-51 (Eng) AB; NYU 59-64 (sociol) MA; Columbia 65-67 (LS) MS, 69- (Higher Educ). 7: Pub rel asst Republic Steel Corp, Cleveland Ohio 51-55; Pub rel asst E I duPont, NYC 55-57; Staff asst pub rel US Steel, NYC 57-66; Exec asst to Chief libn CUNY (City Col) 67-. 9: ALA; LPRC (Award Com 69); LACUNY; NY Lib Club. 10: AAUP; AAUW; Amer Sociol Assn. 14: Admin, pub rel, personnel. 15: 142 E 16th st, New York NY 10003.

SEILER, CHARLOTTE (BEDFORD). b San Antonio Tex 26 D 22. 4: Lloyd S Seiler Sr. 5: Our Lady of the Lake Col 61-64 (LS); San Antonio Col 65-66-; St Phillips Col 67-68. 7: Lib tech USAF Lib: Kelly AFB Tex 60-62, Randolph AFB Tex 62-66, Patients lib Army, Ft Sam, Houston Tex 66-. 9: ALA; TexLA; BexarCoLA. 14: Readers serv, child libs, ref. 15: 492 Turtle lane, Sequin Tx 73155.

SEIM, SISTER JULIA L IHM. b Howell Mich 9 D 16. 5: Marygrove Col (Detroit) 35-58 (Eng) BA; CatholicU (PR) 52-65; UMich summers 65-67 MALS. 6: Sp. 7: Elem sch tchr or auxiliary wks, parochial schs in Detroit area 37-49; Elem sch tchr: Colegio la Merced, Cayey PR 49-56, All Saints Sch, Detroit 56-59; Elem & high sch tchr Colegio San Joaquin, Adjuntas PR 59-65; Asst div libn Margrove Col Monroe Campus 65-. 9: ALA; CathLA; MichLA. 10: MonroeCoLC. 14: Catlg. 15: 610 W Elm ave, Monroe Mi 48161.

SEIN, OSCAR. b Estonia 27 Mr 03. 5: UTartu (Estonia) 22-27 (Law) LLB (cum laude); Rutgers 58-60 MLS. 6: Russian, Ger, Fr, Estonian. 7: Justice of a SUPERIOR Court, Estonia (Landesgericht) 38-44; Sr clerk Rutgers U Lib 56-60; Catlgr Lehigh U Lib 60-64; Sr catlgr Princeton U Lib 64-. 9: ALA. 10: Estonian Learned Soc in Amer. 14: Catlg, clsf (soc sci). 15: 120 Prospect ave, Princeton NJ 08540.

SEJOUR, LUCIENNE. b Petion-Ville Haiti. 5: Ecole Normale (PORT au Prince Haiti) 45-47 (educ) Diplome de fin d'etudes; Columbia 57-59 (LS) MS. 6: Fr, Sp. 7: High sch tchr pub sch syst, Port-au-Prince Haiti 48-52; Libn Servicio Cooperative Interamericano de la Salud Publica, Port-au-Prince Haiti 54-57; Asst libn Haitian Amer Inst, Port-au- prince Haiti 56-57; Libn Faculte de Med UHaiti (Port-au-Prince) 60-61; Catlg asst NY Acad of Med 59-60, Assoc catlgr 61-68; Catlg libn Amer Mus of Natural Hist, NYC 68-. 9: MedLA; Tech Serv Libns NY; NY Lib Club. 14: Catlg, ref. 15: Lib Amer Museum of Natural History, Central Park W at 79th st, New York NY 10024.

SEKERAK, JOHN M. b Cleveland 2 N 17. 4: Virginia Sitterle. 5: Fenn Col 36-41 (Hist) AB; UCal(Davis) 45-48 (Animal Sci) BS; UCal(Berkeley) 52-53 BLS. 6: Fr, Russian. 7: Navigator (2nd & 1st Lt) USAAF 41-45; Tchr Round Valley Union High Sch, Covelo Cal 50-51; Tchr Upper Lake Union High Sch, Upper Lake Cal 51-52; Libn I-IV UCal(Davis) 53-62; Asst libn Modesto Jr Col 62-63; Dir of lib serv Amer River Jr Col 63-66; UCal(Davis); Asst health sci libn Health Scis Lib 66-67, Subj specialist collections development sect 67-68, Hd ref dept 68-. 9: ALA-ACRL (chm- elect Biol & Agric Subsect); NEA; Assn Higher Educ; CalLA (pres Golden Empire Dist 61). 10: Rotary Intl. 11: Air Medal, Distinguished Flying Cross. 14: Ref, collection development. 15: 1122 B st, Davis Ca 95616.

SELBY, CAROL E. b Salt Lake City Utah 14 N 13. 5: UUtah 31-35 (Modern Lang) AB; UDenver 36-37 BS in LS; UUtah 51-53 (Mus) MA. 6: Sp, Fr, Ital, Ger. 7: Catlgr hd circ ref libn UUtah 37-44; Asst in main info art & arch & mus depts NYC Pub Lib ref div 44-50; Catlgr in charge of fine arts UUtah 50-57; Hd libn Detroit Inst of Arts 57-68; Hd of humanities div East Mich U Lib 68-. 9: ALA. 10: Phi Beta Kappa; Phi Kappa Phi. 14: Fine arts and music. 15: 1208 Kingwood, Ypsilanti Mi 48197.

SELDES, NORMAN M. b Brooklyn NY 21 N 30. 4: Carol Gambert. 5: Brooklyn Col 48-52 (Biol) BA; Pratt 52-5 MLS. 7: Libn trainee Brooklyn Pub Lib 53-54; Troop analyst US Army, Austria, Germany 54-56; Brooklyn Pub Lib: Libn 56, Asst to pub rel dir 56-57, Br libn 59, Dist libn 59-62, Exec asst 62-64: Lib Dir Oceanside Free Lib, Oceanside NY 64-. 8: Visiting Instr Lib Sci; utah State U summer 64, SUC (Geneseo) summer 66, St Johns U (Queens NY) summer 67 & 68. 9: ALA; LPR; NYLA; Nassau Co LA; NY Lib Club. 10: Bksellers League of NY; Rotary Intl; Oceanside Bd of Trade. 11: Outstanding Dir Award, Brooklyn Jr C of C (62). 14: Admin. 15: Oceanside Free Lib, Davison ave, Oceanside NY 11572.

SELF, HAZEL (ETTA). b Olney Tex 20 N 04. 5: N Tex U 32-33 (Elem Educ, LS) BS, summers (Secondary Educ, LS) MS; Per Elem, Per High Sch, LS Certifs. 7: Tchr Lindale Elem Sch, Lindale Tex 33-36; Libn; Brenham High Sch, Brenham Tex 36-37, Gainesville High Sch, Gainesville Tex 37-39, N Tex U 39-42; Tchr of Lib Sci Stephen F Austin State Col 42-44; Multi-sch libn Johnson Co schs, Cleburne Tex 44-49; Libn Fulton Jr High Sch, Cleburne Tex 49-. 8: Libn, Henderson State Col, summer sch; Tchr , lib sci, E Tex State Col summer sch. 9: Clr Tchrs Assn; TexLA; Tex State Tchrs Assn. 10: Delta Kappa Gamma; AAUW. 13: Yes. 15: 307 Bales st, Cleburne Tex 76031.

SELIGMAN, DAVID ISRAEL. b NYC 3A34. 5: Conservatory of Music (Cincinnati) 52-55 (Music); USoCal 55-57 (Music) BM; Los Angeles State Col 58-59 (Educ); UCLA 58-59 (Educ) Credential; Peabody 62-63 MA(LS. 7: Tchr Los Angeles City Schs 59; Tchr Nashville City Schs 60; Ref Joint U Libs Nashville 62-63; Catlgr Nashville Pub Lib 60-62; Ref Louisville Free Pub Lib Louisville Ky 63-65; Catlgr Francis A Countway Lib of Med, Boston 65-67; Asst catlgr State Col at Boston 67-68; Libn Braintree High Sch, Braintree Mass 68-69. 14: Catlg. 15: 19 Wait st, apt 2, Boston 02120.

SELLERS, FLORENCE E. b Bound Brook NJ. 5: Trenton State Tchrs Col 31-35 (Eng, Hist) BS; UPenn Ext 36-40 (Eng) MA; Drexel ext 40-44 BLS. 7: High sch libn Woodbury High Sch, Woodbury NJ 35-44; Summer positions Trenton State Col, Moorestown Free Pub Lib, Ocean Co Lib, Lib for the Blind, Phil, Gloucester Co Educ Off; Libn Glassboro State Col 44-69, Assoc Prof of Lib Sci 69-. 9: NEA; ALA; NJEA; NJLA. 10: Kappa Delta Pi; AAUW; Alpha Beta Alpha. 13: Yes. 14: Tchg in lib sch, acquis, ref. 15: 39 High st, Woodbury NJ 08096.

SELLERS, JESSE LEROY. 03Van Buren Ark 14 Ag 13. 4: Rose Zakarin. 5: Hofstra Col 47-50 (Eng) BA; Columbia 50-54 (LS) MS. 7: Boatswains mate 1/c US Navy 34-38, 39-46; Lib tchr NYC Bd of Educ 51-, Libn-inchg George Westinhouse Voc & Tech High Sch 62-. 9: SLA (YC Chap: chm Museum Group 60-62; mem Geog & Map Group); NYC SchLA (treas 63-65); NY Lib Club. 15: 4640 Bay pky, Brooklyn NY 11230.

SELLERS, PHYLLIS MARION FOX. b Des Moines Iowa 6 F 25. 4: Dan Gilbert Sellers. 5: Drake U 42-43; Iowa State Col (Ames) 43-47 (Econ His) BS; Chicago 47-48 BLS; Drake U 59-60. 6: Fr. 7: Clerical asst Des Moines Pub Lib, Des Moines Iowa 43-47; Clerical asst Educ Lib UChicago child Cild libn Winnetka Pub Lib, Winnetka Ill 48-50; Asst libn Field Enterprises Ref Lib, Chicago 50-54; Child libn Des Moines Pub Lib, Des Moines iowa 55-56, 1st asst circ dept 58-6; Libn North High Sch, Des Moines Iowa 61-. 9: ALA; IowaLA; NEA; IowaStateEA. 10: Des Moines Lib Club; Des Moines EA. 15: 3416 - 57th st, Des Moines Iowa 50310.

SELLERS, ROSE (ZAKARIN). b Brooklyn NY 25 Ja 10. 4: Jesse Leroy Sellers. 5: Hunter Col 26-30 (Lat) AB; Columbia 32-33 BS; NYU 45-50 (Higher Educ) AM. 6: Fr, Yiddish. 7: Brooklyn Col Lib: Asst to libn 34-48, Asst libn 48-56, Assoc libn 56-65; Assoc Prof 65-. 8 Chm, Confs on For Area Studies & the Col Lib, 60, 63, 64; Chm Symposia on Libnship as a Career, 57, 62, 64, 65. 9: SLA (chm-elect Museum Div 65-; NY Chap; chm Museum Group 53-54, chm Geog & Map Group 60-62); Lib Assn City Cols NY (pres 50-52); NY Lib Club (pres 54-55); CUNY LA (pres 62-64; chm Museum Div 66-67). 10: Faculty-Hillel Assocs; Phi Sigma Sigma; Pioneer Women; Amer Friends of The Hebrew Univ; Amer Mus of Nat Hist; Brooklyn Acad of Music; Brooklyn Museum; Columbia Sch of Lib Serv Alumni Assn; Country Dance Soc; Defenders of Wildlife Gem & Lapidary Soc; Hadassah; John Burroughs Mem Assn; Nat Audubon Soc; Nat Pars Assn; NY Zool Soc; Wilderness Soc; E Africa Wildlife Soc; Folk Festival

Coun; Sierra Club; Amer Prof for Peace in Middle East. 11: Guest lecturer, dedication Ceremony, Grad Lib Sch Bldg, Hebrew Univ, Jerusalem Israel, Dec 64; John Cotton Dana Publ Award (Cols & Univs), 48, 51, 58; SA Nat Lib Week Award, 64. ; H W Wilson Recruitment Award 68. 12: Ed "SLA Mus Div Bulletin (65-66). 13: Yes. 14: Admin (espec pub rel, orient of new lb publns, lib instr for col studs; pre-libnship coun, ed wk. 15: Brooklyn Col Lib, Brooklyn NY 11210.

SELLICK, EVA MAE. b Berryville Ark 20 D 41. 5: UArk 61-65 (Sociol, Soc Welfare) BA; Rutgers 65-66 MLS. 7: Asst ref libn Peoria Pub Lib, Peoria Ill 66-67, Hd bus, sci & tech 67-. 9: ALA; IllLA. 14: Ref. 15: 1527 West Moss, Peoria Il 61606.

SEMINARA, ELEANOR F. b Brooklyn NY 14 Mr 31. 5: Ala Col 52 (Chem) BS; Columbia 57 (LS, MS); Buffalo 61 (Educ); So Ill U 68-69 (Instr Mat). 7: Chem Fisher Scientific Co, NYC 52-54; Lit searcher-libn Stein Hall & Co, NYC 54-56; Head libn Olin Mathieson Chem Corp, Niagara Falls NY 57-60; Head info serv Thiokol Chem Corp, Huntsville Ala 60-61; Libn Niagara Falls Bd of Educ, Niagara Falls (NY) 61-63; Chief libn Niagara Co Community Col 63-. 8: NDEA Inst on MARC; NDEA Inst Lib/Comp Systems; ndea inst for Dirs of Media Ctrs for Jr Cols & Small Cols. 9: ALA; SLA; NEA; NYLA; NYStateTA; NY State Assn Jr Cols. 10: ACS; Col Club of Niagara Falls; Delta Kappa Gamma; Quota Club; Niagara Co Hist Assn. 13: Yes. 14: Admin, ref, catlg. 15: 5105 Dana dr, Lewiston NY 14092.

SEMLER, EVELYN (WILLIAMS). b Utica NY 7 S 21. 4: George Herbert Semler Jr. 5: Mt Holyoke 40-44 (Art) BA; Columbia 57-61 (LS) MS. 6: Fr, Ger. 7: Reading room asst Houghton Lib Harvard U 44-46; Catlgr Farnsworth Art Mus Wellesley Col 46-47; Asst dept of Egyptian art Metropolitan Mus of Aer, NYC 47-59; Catlgr Mus of Modern Art, NYC 64-68; Ref libn 68-. 9: ALA (Mus Div); Amer Musicol Soc; MusLA; NY Lib Club. 10: Columbia Sch Lib Serv Alum Assn; Mount Holyoke Clob of NY; Blue Hill Troupe. 14: Ref, rare bks, art and music. 15: 160 E 88th st, New York NY 10028.

SEMLER, GEORGE HERBERT JR. b NYC 28 O 24. 4: Evelyn Williams. 5: Bard Col 47-50 (Govt) BA; Columbia 56-58 MS in LS. 6: Fr, Ger. 7: US Navy CB Y 3/C 43-46; Clerk Irving Trust Co, NYC 50-51; Lib trainee Brooklyn Pub Lib 56-58; Jr libn Scarsdale Pub Lib, Scarsdale NY 58-64; Catlg libn Swirbul Lib Adelphi U 64-66; Sr ref libn bus lib Newark Pub Lib, Newark NJ 66-. 9: MusLA (NY Chap; sec-treas 61-62, chm 65-67); Amer Musicological Soc; NY Lib Club. 14: Catlg, ref (music). 15: 160 E 88th st, NYC 10028.

SEMONEIT, JOYCE (GWENDOLYN). b South Amboy NJ 17 Je 34. 5: Montclair State 62-63; Fairleigh Dickinson 63; Newark State Col 58-65 (Elem Educ) BA; Drexel 65-68 BS in LS. 7: Machine operator E I Du Pont Photo Products, Parlin NJ 55-58; Sr clk Newark State Col 59-64; Libn E Windsor Twp Sch Dist, Hightstown NJ 65-. 9: ALA; -AASchL; -YASD; -RSD; MLA; NEA; NJStateLA; NJEA; MCEA; HightstownEA. 10: Greater Trenton Lib Coord Coun. 13: Yes. 14: Ref. 15: PO Box 287, South Amboy NJ 08879.

SEND, BETTY ANN (STACEY). b New Brunswick NJ 15 S 18. 4: John Thomas Send. 5: Douglass Col 37-41 (LS, Pol Sci) AB. 6: Ger. 7: Asst libn League of Nations Inst for Adv Study, Princeton NJ 41-43; Spec Serv Post Lib: Lib asst, Camp Kilmer NJ 43-45, Hosp libn, Camp Kilmer NJ 45-47, Post libn, Camp Kilmer NJ 47-55, Post lib, Ft Monmouth NJ 55-. 9: ALA. 10: Monmouth Co (NJ); Lib Coord Com. 11: Sustained Superior Performance Award, Dept of the Army. 14: Admin, ref. 15: 468 Harding rd, Fair Haven NJ 07701.

SENDEK, IRENE. b Montreal Can 24 F 44. 5: Marianopolis Col 60-64 (Eng) BA; McGill 64-65 BLS. 6: Fr, Polish. 7: Catlgr Loyola Col (Montreal) 65-. 9: QueLA. 14: Catlg, ref. 15: 6679 Bordeaux st, Montreal 35 Can.

SENG, MARY (CROWE). b Appleton Wis 15 Ja 32. 4: Mark W Seng. 5: Wisconsin State Col 50-54 (Eng) BA; UMinn summer 65 (LS); UWis 65-66 (LS) MA. 7: Libn I Bus Lib UWis (Madison) 66-68; Libn II Bus Admin-Econ Lib UTex (Austin) 68-. 9: SLA. 15: 300 e riverside dr 111, Austin Tx 78704.

SENG, MINNIE A. b Muskegon Mich 30 N 09. 5: Muskegon Jr Col 27-29; UMich 29-32 BA, 33-35 BALS, 42-43 MALS. 7: Asst med libn UIowa 35-39; Catlgr Bay City Pub Lib, Bay City Mich 39-40; Order libn Mich Col of Mining & Tech 41-42; Catlgr UArk 43-44; Head catlgr Fresno State Col 44-59; Ed "Education Index" H W Wilson Co, NYC 59-66; Hd catlgr St Ambrose Col 67-. 9: NY Lib Club. 10: UMich Alumnae Club of Greater NY; AAUW; Friends of Art. 13: Yes. 14: Catlg. 15: 328 W Columbia apt 2, Davenport Ia 52803.

SENNOTT, BEATRICE (SULLIVAN). b Boston 26 Je 19. 4: ohn R Sennott Jr. 5: Harvard 57-63 (Humanities) AB; Simmons 63-64 MLS. 6: Fr. 7: Sch of Nursing Lib Cambridge City Hosp, Cambrdge Mass 65-. 15: 21 Irving st, Cambridge Mass 02138.

SENTER, REZINA ELIZABETH. b Helier Ky. 5: East Ky 38 (Hist, Geog) AB; UKy 43 BLS; Peabody 53 (LS) MA; UColo summer 60 Child Lit); UMd 64 (A-V Aids, Juvenile Delinquency). 6: Fr. 7: Tchr rural sch, Pike Co Ky 29-37; Sch libn, Elkhorn City Ky 38-43; Sch libn & prin, Elkhorn City Ky 43-46; Libn Pikeville Jr Col 46-49; Head Lib Sci Murray State Col 49-. Prof of Educ & Chm of Lib Sci Dept 53-. 9: ALA (Elem Lib Sect; Sch Lib Sect; Stud Asst Div); -ACRL; -LED; NEA; SELA; KyLA (treas 62-64; Col & Ref Sect; pres 65-66; var offs); KyASchL; KyEA. 10: Delta Kappa Gamma; Murray Womans Club; Kappa Delta Pil Alpha Gamma Delta; Alpha Beta Alpha. 14: Tchg undergrad & grad lib sci. 15: Box 1244 Col Sta, Murray Ky 42071.

SENTNER, SYLVIA (KAGAN). b W New York NJ 2 Ja 22. 4: Nathan Sentner. 5: Hunter Col 52-58 (Geol) AB; City Col 59-61 (Sci Educ); Pratt 62-64 MLS.06: Fr, Ger. 6: Fr, Ger. 7: Policewoman NYC Policewomens Bur 49-52; Tchr gen studies Beth Jacob Sch, NYC 58-59; Tchr jr high sch NYC Bd of Educ 59-61; Circ libn & Head supv even staff Cornell U Med Col Lib 62-. 9: MedLA (NY Reg Group); SLA (Documentation Gp). 10: Pratt Inst Grad Sch ofLib Sci Alumni Assn. 14: Circ, ref. 15: 329 E 5 st, New York NY 10003.

SENZIG, DONNA (KOCH). b Green Bay Wis 9 S 40. 4: Peter Senzig. 5: Uwis 58-62 (Eng) BA, 62-63 (LS) MA. 7: Chief germanic catlgr UWis Lib (Madison) 63-. 15: 6 Sherman terr, apt 3, Madison Wis 53704.

SERATA, GERTRUDE (CRYSTAL). b Pittsrove Twnship Salem Co NJ 23 Ap 07. 5: Glassboro State Normal Sch 23-25 (Elem Educ) Permanent Tchg Certif; City Col (NY) 59-61 (Hist) BA; Pratt 61-62 MLS. 6: Ger, Fr, Hebrew, Yiddish. 7: Elem tchr Minotola (NJ) pub schs 25-27; Med Bibliog Mem-Sloan Kettering Cancer Center, NY 63; Head of circ Jewish Theol Sem (NY) 64-68; Child libn Hawaii State Lib Syst 68-. 8: Pilot study of seven downtown Brooklyn Col Lbs, 62. 9: SLA; Jewish Libns Assn; NY Lib Club; HawaiiLA. 10: Hadassah; Phi Beta Kappa; Beta Phi Mu. 14: Ref, readers adv serv. 15: 1617 Keeaumoku st, Honolulu Hi 96822.

SEREIKO, GEORGE E. b Cleveand 24 Je23. 4: Maria Krins. 5: Fenn Col 45-49 (Hist) BA; Ohio State U 50 (Hist); West Res 50-51 MSLS. 7: Printer Tower Press, Cleveland 41-43; Rifleman (Pfc) US Army 43-45; Libn Ohio U 51-52; Libn Case Inst of Tech 52-59; Libn Borromeo Sem (Wickliffe Ohio) 59-61; Asst dir UNotre Dame (Ind) 62-. 9: ALA; AHA; Org Amer Histns. 10: AAUP; Chicago Hist Soc. 14: Admin. 15: 54684 Ivy rd, S Bend In 46637.

SEREMAK, JAN (JOHN). b Wnorow Poland 5 Mr 09. 4: Czeslawa Wybranski. 5: Poznan U (Poland) 34-38 (Educ); Warsaw U (Poland) 38-39 (Educ) MA; USoCal 59-60 MLS. 6: Polish, Ger, Pussian. 7: Libn Sopot Poland; Bkseller, Sopot Poland; Catlgr Atomics Int, Canoga Park Cal; Catlgr NAA Sci Center, Canoga Park Cal; Catlgr AA Sci Center, Canoga Park Cal; Lit searcher Hughes Aircraft Co, Culver City Cal, Supv of info research. 9: SLA. 10: Beta Phi Mu. 12: Ed "Mircoelectronics Bibliography (Monthly). 13: Yes. 14: Info specialist. 15: 936 Centinela ave, Santa Monica Cal 90403.

SERGEANT, MR CLARE H. b Jackson Mich 5 My 10. 5: Jackson Jr Col 32-36; UMich 36-37, 39, 46 (Sociol) AB, 46-47 AB LS. 7: Page Jackson Pub Lib, Jackson Mich 25-30, Circ 30-36; Good Year Tire & Rubber Co, Jackson Mich 38-41; USAAC (Cpl) 42-45; Libn Umatilla Co Lib, Pendleton Ore 48-53; Asst dir Jackson Pub Lib, Jackson Mich 53-62, Dir 63-. 9: ALA; Adult Educ Assn; MichLA; Mich Lib Film Circuit (pres 63). 10: Kiwanis; Mich Lib Film Circuit. 14: Admin, bus, tech, ref. 15: Jackson Pub Lib, 244 W Michigan ave, Jackson Mich 49201.

SERGOT, ALFONS PAUL. b Bydgoszcz Poland 6 Ag 04. 4: Marinette G Sophie Bresinska. 5: TechU Danzig-Langfuhr 22-23 (Gen Mech); UPoznan (Poland) 23-27 (Civil Law) Magister Juris, 29-32 (Soc Sci); George Washington U Law Sch 53-57 (Anglo-Amer Common Law) Masters of Comparative Law. 6: Polish, Ger. 7: Judge Dist Court, Poland 30-33, 45-46;

Attorney (advocate), Poland 33-39, 46-49; Legal analyst & libn LC 51-65; Law libn & asst prof CatholicU of PR 65-. 8: Legal adv of corporations & other bus & profess insts (Poland 34-39). 10: Polish- Christ Trade Unions; Internat Lions Club. 12: "Error in Civil Law" diss, Peznan 31; "Blueprint of Deception-Character and Record of the International Association of Democratic Lawyers" (57). 13: Yes. 14: For (esp civil) law, Compar law. 15: 90 Calle A Buena Vista, Ponce Puerto Rico 00731.

SERGOTT, KATHLEEN YORK. b Blue Hill Me 25 Je 17. 4: Conrad A Sergott. 5: Suffolk U 51-55 (Eng) AB; Boston U 56-57 (Eng); Simmons 58-60 (LS) MA. 6: Fr. 7: Blue Hill Pub Lib, Blue Hill Me 36-43; Mass Gen Hosp, Boston 43-60; Boston U 60; Mass Bay Community Col 61-64; Swampscott Pub Lib, Swampscott Mass 64-. 9: ALA; NELA; MassLA; Greater Boston Pub Lib Admin. 10: Bus & Prof Womens Club; Swampscott Womens Club; Swampscott Womens Republican Club; N Shore Mss Club. 13: Yes. 14: Admin. 15: 5 Oceanside terrace, Swampscott Ma 01907.

SERIS, EILEEN JANICE (BENNER). b Lyon Station Penn 27 Mr 37. 4: Michael C Seris. 5: E Stroudsburg State Col 55-59 (Eng) BS in Ed; Drexel 59-60 MS in LS; UDenver 65. 6: Fr. 7: Libn: B Franklin Jr High Sch, Ridgewood NJ 60-62, Tioga Central Sch, Tioga Center NY 62-64, Greeley West High Sch, Greeley Colo 64-. 8: Com to revise Colo Standards for Sch Libs. 9: ALA; NEA; ColoEA; MPLA; ColoASchL; CAVA (sec). 10: AAUW. 14: Sch lib wk. 15: 1163 - 25th ave, Greeley Co 80631.

SERRILL, JULIAN D JR. b Defiance Ohio 23 Je 16. 4: Margaret Jeanette Bischff. 5: UMinn 34-38 (Liberal Arts) BA (cum laude); Peabody 64-65 MLS. 7: US Navy Multi-Engine Pilot, Aviation Safety Off, Admin & Personnel Off, Naval Aviator, Commander, ret; Ref pub lib, Memphis 65-66; Ext libn 67-; Shelby Co libn, Memphis Tenn 66-67. 9: ALA; SELA; TennLA. 10: Beta Theta Pi; Delta Phi Lamdba; Beta Phi Mu; Kiwanis; Memphis Libns Com. 11: 2 Distinguished Flying Crosses; Air Medal, Presidential Unit Citation, Navy Occupation Serv Medal with Berlin Airlift Device, China Serv Medal, etc. 14: Admin, ref, ext serv. 15: 3140 E Glengarry rd, Memphis Tn 38128.

SERVICE, JANE. b Sharon Penn 22 Mr 11. 5: Allegheny Col 29-33 (Lat, Eng) BA West Res 51-53 MSLS. 7: Libn Jr High Sch, Sharon Penn 35-. 9: Penn State EA. 15: 67 Euclid ave, Sharon Pa 16146.

SERVICE, ROSE MARIE. b Youngstown Ohio 8 Je 21. 5: mich Normal Normat Col 40-44 (Eng) AB; UMinn 48-50 (Educ) MA, 54-55 (LS) MA. 7: Clerk Laidlaw Bros Educ Publ, Chicago 44-47; Tchr Benzonia High Sch, Benzonia High Sch, Benzonia Mich 47-48; Tchr Detroit Lakes High Sch, Detroit Lakes Minn 51-53; Tchr-libn Melrose High Sch, Melrose Minn 53-54; Ref libn Carleton Col 55-61; Soc sci libn UOre 61-. 9: ALA; Assn for Supv & Curr Devel; NEA-DAVI; OreLA; Ore Assn for Supv & Curr Devel; PNLA; Ore Instr Media Assn; OreASchL. 10: Bus & Prof Womens Club; AAUP; Pi Lambda Theta; Soroptimist Club. 14: Educ libn-ship, curr lib admin. 15: 889 E 29th ave, Eugene Ore 97405.

SERVIES, JAMES ALBERT. b Lafayette Ind 2 S 25. 4: Ruth Janet Oostmeyer. 5: Chicago 45-47 PhB, 47-49 (LS) MA. 7: US Army Counter-Intelligence Corps (Cpl), Baltimore 45-46; Ref asst UChicago 47-49; Asst circ Libn UMiami Fla 49-53; & circ libn Col of William & Mary 53-57, Libn 57-66; Dir of Libs U W Fla 66-. 9: SELA; FlaLA; WFlaLA. 10: Fla Hist Soc; Pensacola Hist Soc. 12: Comp "A Bibliography of John Marshall CPO (56); Ed, with C R Dolmetsch "The Poems of Charles Hansford (61); Comp "Union List of West Florida Library Periodicals (69). 13: Yes. 14: Pub serv, spec collections. 15: University of W Florida John C Pace Lib, Pensacola Fl 32504.

SERVIS, WILLIE MAE D(EARING). b Aberdeen Miss 29 Mr 23. 4: Edwin R Servis. 5: Draughon Bus Col 40-41 (Gen Bus); Miss State Col 43-44, 46-49 (Chem Engnr) BS; UWash 49-50 (LS). 6: Ger. 7: Invoice clerk I C Garber & Son Inc, Jackson Miss 41-42; Payroll bkkeeper Union Fork & Hoe Co, Jackson Miss 42-43; Aerographers Mate 1/C USNR (WAVES), Pensacola & Wash DC 44-46; Sales clerk F W Woolworth, W Point Miss 46-47; Tech libn Rohm & Haas Co Redstone Arsenal Res Div, Huntsville Ala 50-55; Tech libn Nat Bur of Standards, Boulder Colo 56-57; Libn in ref & catlg Sandia Corp, Albuquerque NM 58-66, Circ libn 66-. 9: ACS; SLA. 14: Tech ref, reports catlg. 15: Rte 3 Box 535C, Los Lunas NM 87031.

SESSA, FRANK BOWMAN. b Pittsburgh 11 Je 11. 4: Anne Johnston. 5: UPittsburgh 29-33 (Hist) AB, 33-34, (Hist) MA; Carnegie 40-42 (LS) BS; UPittsburgh summers 48-50 (Hist) PhD. 6: Fr. 7: Research Fellow Hist Soc, Western Penn 35-36; Libn & museum curator 36-40; Chief stacks & Reserve Bk room UPittsburgh Lib 40-41, Circ libn 41-43; US Navy (LCDR) 43-46; UPittsburgh Lib: Circ libn 46-47, Instr in hist 47-50, Asst Prof of hist 50-51; Dir Pub Libs City of Miami, Fla 51-66; Prof of Lib Sci UPittsburgh Grad Sch of Lib Sci 66-. 8: Active in Naval Res, 46-: Com Off, Nav Res Offs Sch, UMiami 62-65 (pres rank Capt); Critic-consul, Lib Bldg Consultants (Evanston Ill) 62-65; lib consul: 3 pub libs in Fla, 63-64; Lib serv sonsul, Dade Co & Tampa Fla, 5, 63; Bldg site consul, Gainesville Ga 65; Consul on proposed lib bldgs, Panama City & Cocoa Beach Fla & Gainesville Ga. 9: ALA (Coun 64-68, Mem-at-Large 66-69; mem &/or chm 8 coms 52-69); -LED (chm Scholarship & Awards Com 68-); -PLA (Bd Dirs 65-67); -ALTA (Nat Assembly Com 57-59); FlaLA (pres 59-60; mem &/or chm 11 coms 52-63); SELA (chm Memb Com 65-66); DadeCoLA (pres 54-55 & 65-66); PennLA. 10: Rotary; Univ Club (Pittsburgh); Phi Alpha Theta; Beta Phi Mu; AAUP; Pitt-Carnegie Alumni Assn. 12: "A Building Program for the Chattanooga Public Library (68). 13: Yes. 14: Admin, hist of libs, lib arch. 15: 346 Midway rd, Pittsburgh Pa 15216.

SESSIONS, VIVIAN S. b Ossining NY 15 D 20. 5: UMich 38-45 (Letters, Law) AB, 45-48 (Hist) MA; Columbia 58-59 (LS). 6: Fr. 7: NY Pub Lib: Trainee 57-59, Libn 59-63, Sr libn 63-65; Proj Dir Project URBANDOC City U (NYC) 65-. 9: SLA; ADI; AALL; Coun of Planning Libns (pres). 12: "URBANDOC a Report on Computerized Documentation and Information Retrieval in the Literature of Urban Planning and Renewal (64). 14: Documentation. 15: 175 W 12th st, New York NY 10011.

SETLIFF, MARGARET H. b Providence 28 My 22. 4: James A Setliff. 5: Wayne U 43 (Educ) BS in Ed, 45 (Eng) MA; Chicago 48 BLS. 07: Instr Eng Dept Wayne U (Detroit) 45-46; Asst ref & catlg libn Joint Ref Lib, Chicago 48-53; Research libn Legis Ref Bur UHawaii 53-59, Asst researcher 59-62; Deputy State libn & Dir state lib serv Hawaii State Lib 65-66; Law libn State Supreme Court, Honolulu 62-65, 67-. 8: Governor's Com on State Lib Resources 63-; UHawaii Adv Com on Lib Sch 65-69; Mem Citizen's Com on Ethics in Govt 65-66; Staff Coord First Governor's Com on Libs 66-. 9: ALA; AAStateL (Nom Com 64); -ACRL; RTSD; AALL (3 coms); HawaiiLA (pres 58-59, treas 54-55, chm &/or mem 8 sects & coms 54-); Hawaii Assn Sch Libs (co-chm Legis Com 65-66). 10: ACLU Hawaii (pres 65-66); Amer Soc Pub Admin (dir Honolulu Chap); Governor's Commsn of Status of Women (Sub-Com on Legal Rights); LWV; Hawaii Hist Assn; Friends of Lib. 13: Yes. 14: Admin, legis, intel freedom, govt research. 15: 3032 Alencastre pl, Honolulu Hi 96816.

SETTLE, ELLA (BLAKE). b Wash DC 24 O 19. 5: Mary Washington Col 35-39 (Bus Educ) BS; Madison Col 64 (LS). 6: Lat. 7: Secondary sch tchr: Caroline Co Sch Syst, Bowling Green Va 39-41, Stafford Co Sch Syst, Falmouth Va 42-43, 52-55, Fredericksburg City Sch Syst, Fredericksburg Va 66-67; Personnel clk FBI, Wash DC 41-42; Clk-stenographer Marine Corps Schs, Quantico Va 55-58, Libn Breckinridge Lib 58-66, Libn (acquis) Marine Corps Development & Educ Command 67-. 9: SLA; VaLA. 14: Acquis. 15: Rte 6 Box 220, Fredericksburg Va 22401.

SEUSS, HERBERT J. b Coburg Germany 26 D 20. 4: Ruth Abelmann. 5: Educated in Germany. 6: Ger, Fr. 7: Dept supv Korting Radio, Germany 49-52; Test supv Hevi-Duty, milwaukee 52-54, Lab tech 54-56; Engrg assoc development dept Cutler-Hammer, Milwaukee Wis 56-62, Engrg assoc tech info ctr 62-. 9: SLA (Wis Chap: Prog Com treas v-pres & pres-elect). 10: Cutler-Hammer Camera Club; Lutheran Men in Amer. 14: Indus libs, lib automation. 15: W 142 N 7416 Oakwood dr, Menomonee Falls Wi 53051.

SEVAGIAN, HELEN H. b Boston Mass 6 Je 26. 5: Boston U PAL 43-47 (Com Sci) BS; Simmons 47-49 (LS) BS. 6: Armenian, Fr. 7: Asst Mattapan br Boston Pub Lib 43-44, Asst info off 44-47, Prof asst info off 47-54, Asst-in-charge info off 54-58, Chief info off 58-. 9: ALA; -LAD Pub Rel Sect: chm PR Serv to Lib Com 67-68, past mem Bd; NELA; Pub Chm 55, 56, 57. 10: Armenian Relief Soc. 12: Ed "BPL News" (54-58). 13: Yes. 14: Pub rel, adult wk, ref, Armenian collections. 15: 104 Hilltop st, Milton Ma 02186.

SEVERANCE, ROBERT WATSON. b Florence SC 13 D 07. 4: Katharine Maddry. 5: Furman U 25-28 (Hist) AB; UVa 28-29 (Hist) AM; Peabody 32-33 BS in LS. 7: Tchr High Sch,

Greenville SC 29-30; Asst Prof hist Judson Col 30-32; Head co dept Lawson McGhee Lib, Knoxville Tenn 33-34; Head circ dept NC State Col Lib Raleigh 34-36; Libn & Prof of Lib Sci Stetson U 36-40; U Libn Baylor U 40-53; (LT) USAAC 43-45; (Maj) USAF 51-53; Deputy dir The Army Lib, The Pentagon Wash DC 53-56; Spec asst to dir NLM, Wash DC 56-57; Dir Air U Lib, Maxwell AFB Ala 57-. 8: Operations & bldg consul for several cols & federal libraries. 9: ALA (chm Com on Org 57-60, Coun 38-40, 57-60, 67-70);-ACRL (pres 52-53); FlaLA (pres 38-40); TexLA (pres 47-48); AlaLA (pres 64-65); SLA; ASIS; SELA. 10: Retired Offs Assn. 11: Life Fellow, Royal Soc of Arts, 51. 12: Ed "Texas Library Jornal (50-51). 13: Yes. 14: Admin, personnel, bldgs. 15: 3743 Berkeley dr, Montgomery Ala 36111.

SEVERANCE, ROSEMARY. b Lansing Mich 18 Ja 26. 5: Mich State U 44-48 (Eng) BA; UIll 49-51 MS in LS. 7: US Army Libn US Dept of the Army, Germany 51-55; Asst libn Boonslick Reg Lib,Sedalia Mo 56-57; Catlgr-admin Southwest Mo Lib Serv Inc, Bolivar Mo 57-63; Head materials processing Rensselaer Polytech Inst 63-64, Catlgr 64-65; Libn William H White Jr Lib Woodberry Forest Sch, Woodberry Forest Va 66-. 9: ALA; VaLA. 10: Taconic Hiking Club. 14: Catlg. 15: William H White Jr Lib Woodberry Forrest Sch, Woodberry Forrest Va 22989.

SEVERINGHAUS, ETHEL LONG. b Syracuse NY 10 D 18. 5: SUNY(Albany) 36-40 (Hist) AB; SUNY(Oneonta) 41 (Elem Educ); SUNY (Albany) 56-62 MSLS, 65 (LS), 67 (Secondary Educ Supv); UColo 68 (Media Supv, State Level Educ). 7: Libn Guilderland Central Sch Dist, Guilderland NY 57-66; Assoc Bur Sch Libs NY State Educ Dept 66-. 9: NYLA (Sch Libs Sect); NY State Tchr Assn (East Zone Lib Sect: asst chm 66); East NY SchLA (sec 59-60, pres 62-63, Bd 63-64); NYASCD. 10: Voorheesville Study Club; Bus & Prof Womens Club of Albany. 12: Ed Bur of Sch Libs "News and Notes. 14: Sch libnship. 15: 101 Patroon dr apt 12, Guilderland NY 12084.

SEVERN, THERESA (McKEE). b Chicago. 4: David J Severn. 5: Chicago 37-41 (Chem BS; Columbia 51-54 (LS) MS. 7: Research asst Lying-In Hosp, Chicago 41-43; Chem Cities Serv Oil Co, E Chicago Ind 43-44; Health physicist Manhattan Proj, NY & Chicago 44-46; Research asst Columbia U 46-47; Lit chem Texaco Inc, NYC; Ed Amer Petroleum Inst, NYC 54-56; Tech info consul self-employed, Englewood NJ 64-69; Intl Sugar Research Foundation Inc 69-. 9: ACS; SLA. 10: Nat Parks Assn; Nat Wildlife Fed; Beta Phi Mu. 13: Yes. 14: Ref, lit searching, clsf. 15: 51 Hudson ave apt 12, Englewood NJ 07631.

SEVIGNY, ALLEN. b Newton Mass 29 J126. 4: Phyllis Morre. 5: Clark U 53 (Romance Langs) AB; Simmons 59 (LS) MS. 6: Fr, Sp. 7: Ya libn Boston Pub Lib 55-58; Circ & ref libn Chicago City Jr Col 59-62; Dir Athens Co Lib, Nelsonville Ohio 62-64; Pub lib consul Lib Ext Div NY State Lib 64-68; Exec dir Central NY Ref & Resources Coun 68-. 8: Com, NY Governors Conf on Libs, 65. 9: ALA; NYLA. 14: Research libs & syst. 15: 141 Helfer lane, Minoa, NY 13116.

SEVILLE, ANN (NAULTY). b Baltimore Md 9 O 20. 4: Francis B Seville. 5: Col of Notre Dame (Md) 38-42 (Biol) AB; UNC 45-46 BS in LS. 6: Fr, Sp, Ital. 7: Enoch Pratt Free Lib, Baltimore; Asst Popular Lib 43-44, Asst Ind & Sci Dept 44-45, Admin asst Popular Lib 46-50, Br libn Hamilton Br 50-57, Admin asst ext div 57, Br libn Hamilton Br 57-. 8: Tchr bk selection courses; baltimore Co Pub Lib 65, 67, East Shore Area Lib 68, Anne Arundel Co Lib 68. 9: ALA; MdLA. 14: Br lib wk. 15: 5007 Boxhill lane, Baltimore 21210.

SEVY, BARBARA (SNETSINGER). b Montpelier Vt 4 Je 26. 4: Roger Warren Sevy. 5: UVt 44-47 (Eng) BS Sec Ed; Drexel 54-55 MSLS. 6: Fr. 7: Libn & research asst Commsn on Financing of Hosp Care, Chicago 51-54; Catlgr Amer Philos Soc Lib, Phila 55-57; Asst libn Phila Mus of Art Lib 65-67, Libn 68-. 9: ALA (sec-treas Museum Div 67-69); SL 10: Bd Dir Abington Lib Soc (Jenkintown Penn); Beta Phi Mu. 15: 242 Mather rd, Jenkintown Pa 19046.

SEWELL, JEAN (RUTHVEN). b Mt Kisco NY 7 Ap 17. 4: John R Sewell. 5: Good Counsel Col 34-38 (Math) BA; Columbia 38-39 (Eng) MA, 47-50 (LS) BS; Fordham 38-39 (Eng); NYU 45-46 (Ger). 6: Ger, Fr. 7: File clk "Readers Digest", Chappagua NY 39-40; Camp coun Westchester Recreation Camp, Croton Pt NY summers 40-42; Tchr Somers Central Sch, Somers NY 41-43; Tchr Mamaroneck Jr High Sch, Mamaroneck NY 43-44; Research asst Div War Research Columbia U 44-46; Libn; Philips Labs Inc, Irvington NY 46-56, Union Carbide Nuclear Co, NY 56-58, Bd of Educ, Seneca Falls NY 61-62, Bd of Educ, Ottawa-Glandorf Ohio 63-66; Ref libn Ohio StateU (Lima) 66-67, Hd libn 67-. 9: ALA. 10: Kappa Gamma Pi. 14: Tech libs & ref, admin. 15: 306 Green Meadows dr, Ottawa Oh 45875.

SEWELL, MARGARET (HIX). b Birmingham Ala 16 J102. 5: Randolph-Macon Womans Col 18-21 (Chem); Fla State U 46-49 (LS) BA, 50-52 (LS) MA. 6: Fr. 7: Libn Mirror Lake Jr Hig, St Petersburg Fla 64-; Libn Riviera Jr High, St Petersburgh Fla 66-69. 8: Visiting instr Fla State U summers 53-57; Ext tchr Fla State U 56-57; Visiting Prof Col of Educ UAla summers 58-66. 9: NEA; FlaASchL (Sch & Child Div); FlaEA; ClrTA FlaLA (past sec).10: Alpha Beta Alpha; Beta Phi Mu; Alpha Delta Pi. 13: Yes. 14: Sch lib wk. 15: 6919 - 7th ave N, St Petersburg Fla 33710.

SEWELL, WINIFRED (EMMA). b Newport Wash. 5: State U Wash 34-38 Eng) BA; Columbia 38-40 (LS) BS. 6: Fr, Russian, Ger,Sp. 7: Stud & Jr asst Columbia U 38-42; Asst libn Wellcome Res Labs, Tuckahoe NY 42-43, Libn 43-46; Sr libn Squibb Inst for Med Research, Brooklyn NY & New Brunswick NJ 46-61; NLM, Bethesda Md; Subj heading spec 61-62, Deputy chief Bibliogr Serv Div 62-64, Hd drug lit program 65-. 8: NAS/NRC Com on Modern Methods of Handling Chem Info, 64-; Commsn on Pharmaceut Abstracts, Int Fed Pharmacy 58-60; Ad hoc com to revise Steroid Code, US Patent Off 59; Instr Pharmaceut Lib on libnship Columbia U 59; Adjunct lectr UMd 69. 9: SLA (pres 60-61); MedLA; ASIS; ALA; ACS (Chem Lit Div); Soc Tech Writers & Publishers; Drug Info Assn. 10: Phi Beta Kappa; Phi Kappa Phi. 11: Publications Award, Sci Tech Div, SLA 66. 12: Ed "Unlisted Drugs (49-64); Ed "Medical Subject Headings, NLM (63, 64); "Drug Literature, Committee Print, Senate Committee on Government Operations (63). 13: Yes. 14: Drug info handling. 15: 6513 76th pl, Cabin John Md 20034.

SEWNY, KATHERINE WIEHE. b NYC 8 Ap 09. 4: Vahan D Sewny. 5: Wellesley 2529 (Ital) AB; Columbia 29-30 (LS) BS. 6: Fr, Ital. 7: Reviser Columbia U Sch of Lib Serv 30-31; Libn NewSch for Soc Research 31-32; Head catlr Brooklyn Col Lib 32-37; Columbia U Sch of Lib Ser chief reviser 38-39, Curator 40-48, Ed asst 48-50; Asst to libn City Col (NY) 51-55; EdColumbia U Press, NYC 56-. 8: Adv Coun, Columbia Sch of Lib Serv, 60-. 9: ALA-ACRL;-RTSD;NYLA; NY Lib Club (v-pres 57-58). 12: Jt auth (with W E Weld) "Hebert E Hawkes (58); "Directory of Social and Health Agencies of New York City, asst ed 56-57, ed 58-66, 5 v. 14: Buliography. 15: 390 Riverside dr, New York NY 10025.

SEXAUER, CAROLINE A (SCHLAGENHAUF). b Quincy Ill 21 Ag 19. 4: William E Sexauer. 5: MacMurray Col 31-33 (Educ); UIll 33-35 (Educ) BS, ummers 40, 41, 44 & 45 BS in LS. 6: Ger. 7: Free Pub Lib, Quincy Ill; Asst child dept 35-37, Asst adult dept 38-41, Catlgr 41-59, Lign 59-. 9: IllLA (past chm, sec Pub Lib Sect). , past sec; various coms). 10: Alpha Beta Phi; Altrusa; AAUW; Fed Bus & Prof Women; Hist Soc of Quincy & Adams Co; Quincy Citizens Adv Com; Quincy Welfare Coun. 14: Catlg, loc & state hist. 15: Free Pub Lib, Quincy Ill 62301.

SEXTON, IRA JOE. b Sylvester Tex 4 S 32. 5: UTex 50-53 (Art) BFA; San Jose State Col 56-58 (Art) MA; UCal(Berkeley) 63-64 MLS. 7: USAF Admin Spec 54-56; Asst libn Cal Col of Arts & Crafts 64-66; Order libn Diablo Valley Col 66-. 15: 260 Water st, Point Richmond Ca 94801.

SEYBOTH, ANN M. b Rochester Penn 18 Jl 38. 5: Pembroke 56-60 (Pol Sci) AB; UPittsburgh 66-67 MLS. 6: Sp. 7: Tchr Secondary Schs, Pennat NJ 61-66; Ref libn Ohio StateU (Columbus) 68-. 9: ALA; -RSD (Standards Com). 10: Beta Phi Mu. 14: Ref, pub serv. 15: 3005 Stadium dr, Columbus Oh 43202.

SEYFERT, CAROL ALICE. b Burlington Wis 13 O 40. 4: Daniel E Seyfert. 5: UWis(Madison) 5-62 (Eng) BA, 63 (LS) MA. 6: Sp. 7: Page Burlington Pub Lib, Burlington Wis 56-61; Libn I Milwaukee Pub Lib-Johnny Appleseed Bkmob, Milwaukee County 64-65, Libn I Finney Neighborhood Lib 65-66, Libn II 66-. 9: ALA; WisLA. 14: Child wk. 15: 4215 W Martin dr apt 15, Milwaukee Wi 53208.

SEYMOUR, CAROL ADAMS. b Phila 19 O 39. 5: Wellesley 57-61 (hist) BA; Simmons 61-63 (LS) MS. 6: Fr. 7: Catlgr Boston Pub Lib 61-67; Asst in research lib mgt research unit ULib Cambridge (Eng) 68-. 9: ALA. 14: Catlg. 15: 9 St Pauls rd, Cambridge England.

SEYMOUR, E ELIZABETH. b Seneca Hill NY 15 Mr 21. 5: Oswego State Tchrs Col 38-42 (Gen Educ) B Ed; NY State

Tchrs Col (Albany) 48-49 BS in LS. 7: Elem tchr 42-48; Libn S Kortright Central Sch, S Kortright NY 49-52; Libn Oswego City Lib, Oswego NY 52-54; Tchr-libn Guilderland Central Schs, Guilderland NY 54-57; Med libn VA Hosp, Albany NY 57-63; Catlgr NY State Veterinary Col 6365; Libn NY State Health Dept Div Labs & Research, Albany NY 65-. 9: MELA. 14: Ref. 15: 8C Old Hickory dr, Albany NY 12204.

SEYMOUR, KAY (DOROTHY). b Duluth Minn 30 Jl 36. 5: UMinn 54-58 (Speech) BA, 60-62 (LS) MA. 6: Fr. 7: Tele operator & serv repr NWest Bell Tele Co, Minneapolis 54-59; Sales sec KDWB Radio, Minneapolis 59; Child libn Minneapolis Pub Lib 60-. 9: ALA; MinnLA. 14: Pub lib, child wk. 15: 3831 Quail ave N, Minneapolis Mn 55422.

SGRO, LOREN LOUIS (LARRY). b Highland Park Mich 26 Ag 38. 4: Josephine Kolnitys. 5: Wayne State 56-61 (Soc) AB; UMich (Ann Arbor) 61-62 AMLS. 7: Asst catlgr & circ libn Oakland U, Rochester Mich 62-64; Hd circ dept UWyo 64-67; Coord collection development Wyo State Lib, Cheyenne Wyo 67-. 9: ALA; NEA-DAVI; MPLA; WyoLA. 14: Admin, collection bldg, ref. 15: 2410 Evans, Cheyenne Wy 82001.

SHA, EUNICE YUFU. b Chungking China 20 O 44. 5: SoochowU (Taipei) 62-66 (Eng Lit) BA; UWash 66-67 (Ling); Columbia 68-69 (LS) MS. 6: Chinese, Fr. 7: Stud libn NY State Psychiatric Inst Lib, NYC 67-68; Libn asst Standard Oil Co (NJ), NYC summer 68. 9: ALA; SLA. 14: Catlg. 15: 2258 Grand ave apt 5C, Bronx NY 10453.

SHABOWICH, STANLEY ANTHONY. b Byelorrusia 17 N 32. 4: Lucile Bott. 5: NortheasternU 53-54; Wayne State 57-62 (Russian) BA; West MichU 65-66 MSLS. 7: Cpl US Army, Ft bragg NC 54-56; Slavonic & Germanic langs bibliogr Mich State U Lib (E Lansing) 66-67; Hd acquis dept SW Tex State Col 67-. 14: Tech serv. 15: 203 La Vista apts, San Marcos Tx 78666.

SHACHTMAN, BELLA E(VELYN). b Malden Mass 21 My 14. 5: UNC(Greensboro)29-33 LS) BA. 7: Ref & catlg asst Carnegie Pub Lib, Winston-Salem NC 34-36; USDA Nat Agric Lib, Wash DC: Loan desk asst 36, Catlgr 37-43 Asst chief processing sect 43-44, Asst chief acquis sect, Chief sel & searching 44-50, Act chief acquis sect 46, Chief catlg & records sect 50-61, Asst dir for tech serv 61-69; Assoc U libn UCal (Berkeley) Lib 69-. 9: Internat Assn of Agric Libns & Documentalists (Program Chm for 3rd World Congress, Wash DC 65); ALA (coun-at-large 63-67); Exec Bd 68-71); SLA (Bd DIRS Wash DC Chap ASIS ADI; DCLA; Potomac Tech Proc Libns. 11: USDA Superior Serv Honor Award, 61; USDA Special Merit Award for Outstanding Cost Reduction Achievement 66. 13: Yes. 14: Admin, acquis, catlg. , syst. 15: 1200 Lakeshore apt 12H, Oakland Ca 94606.

SHAFFER, DALE EUGENE. b Salem Ohio 17 Ap 29. 5: UIll 51-52; Kent State 52-55 (Ind Mgt) BS 59-60 MALS; Ohio State 55-56 (Econ) MA. 7: T/Sgt (admin specialist) USAF, Chanute AFB Ill 48-52; Trainee (ind rel) GE Co, Chicago & Schenectady NY 57-58; Instr of econ Bethany Col (Bethany W Va) 58-59; Bus & tech libn S Bend Pub Lib, Suth Bend Ind 60-61; Train specialist Ohio State Employment Serv, Columbus 62-63; Hd libn, Hd Dept of Lib Sci Glenville State Col 63-65; Hd libn Ocean Co Col 65-67; Dir CapitalU 68-. 8: Mgt consul, Addressograph Multigraph Corp, Cleveland 67-68; Lib bldg adv, ohio Dominican Col, Columbus 69; Establ the "Peterson Library Award" at Glenville State Col 64; Establ the "William Shaffer Library Award" at Ocean County Col 66; Orig of the "Sha-Frame Pamphlet System" 64. 9: ALA; Soc Advanc of Mgt; OhioLA. 10: Delta Sigma Pi; Ohio Bus Tchrs Assn. 12: "The Maturity of Librarianship as a Profession" (68). 13: Yes. 14: Univ lib admin. 15: 437 Jennings ave, Salem Oh 44460.

SHAFFER, DALLAS YOUNG. b Spokane Wash 18 Je 40. 4: Norman J Shaffer. 5: Stanford 58-62(Hist) BA; UWash 64-65 M of Libr. 6: Ger. 7: Sr clerk St Louis Pub Lib 62-64; Child libn King Co Pub Lib, Seattle 65-66; Catlgr Off of Geog, Wash DC 66-67; Free lance indexing, bibliographic & copyright research, Wash DC 67-69. 9: ALA. 11: Frederic G Melcher Scholarship ALA 64. 13: Yes. 14: Child lit & serv, bibliog, indexing. 15: Box 384, Hooper Nb 68031.

SHAFFER, ELLEN KATE. b Leadville Colo. 5: UCLA 29 (Eng) AB; Mexico City Col 51 USoCal 54 (Sp) MA; Riverside Sch of Lib Serv Certif. 6: Sp. 7: Libn Anaheim Cal Elem Sch System 25-27; Antiquarian Bkseller Dawsons Bk Shop, Los Angeles 29-44, 46-54; WAC & AC Far East Air Serv Command, Philippines 44-45; Rare bk libn Free Lib of Phila 54-; Lectr Columbia Sch of Lib Serv 60-. 8: Lecturer in lib sci, Columbia 60-. 9 BSA; Bibliog Soc (St Brit); ALA; Manuscript Soc, (pres 66-68). 10: Friends of Bancroft Lib, Princeton Lib, UPenn Lib; Phila Art Alliance; Germantown Hist Soc; Bk Club of Cal. 12: "The Nuremberg Chronicle(50); "The Garden of Health (57); "Fray Gilberti and His Books (63). 13: Yes. 14: Rare bks. 15: Free Lib of Phila, Logan Sq, Phila 19103.

SHAFFER, HELEN HAWKINS. b Culpeper Va 31 D 19. 4: Clarence W Shaffer. 5: Longwood Col 38-42 (Eng) BA; UVa ext 51, 57; George Washington 45, 59; Fla State U ext 65-67 (LS). 7: Tchr: Woodrow Wilson Sch, Arlington Va 42-58, Lexington Park Sch, Lexington Park Md 58-60, Amer Dependents Sch, Bermuda 60-63, Warrington Elem Sch, Pensacola Fla 63-65; Libn Beulah Sch, Pensacola Fla 65-67; Libn Holland Sch, Va Beach Va 67-. 9: ALA; NEA; VaEA (Dept Sch Libns); Va Beach EA. 10: DAR; Potomac River Assn of St mary's (Md). 14: Child bks. 15: 5504 War Admiral rd, Virginia Beach Va 23462.

SHAFFER, KAY L. b Lewisburg Penn 25 Je 42. 5: Penn StateU 60-64 (Russian) BA; IndU 67-68 MLS. 6: Russian, Ger. 7: Jr catlg Penn StateU (Univ Park) 64-67; Grad asst Halls of Residence Libs IndU (Bloomington) 67-68; Slavic catlgr Ohio StateU Libs (Columbus) 68-69, Hd IULC-RAILS 69-. 9: ALA; Ohio Valley Gp Tech Serv Libns. 15: 558 Harley dr, Columbus Oh 43202.

SHAFFER, KENNETH R(AYMOND). b Indianapolis Ind 5 Je 14. 5: Butler U 31-35 (Eng) AB, 36 (Eng; UIll 40-41 BS in LS. 6: Fr, Ger, Sp. 7: Order libn Ind State Lib 35-41; Instr UIll(Urbana) 40-41; Asst dir IndU Libs 41-44; Dir Amer Bk Center for War Devastated Libs, Wash DC 45-46; Dir Sch of Lib Sci & Prof Simmons 46-, Dir of Libs 47-66. 8: Conul US Dept of State 44-45; o-chm, Princeton Conf on Lib Educ, 48; Consul, Peace Corps 62; Amer spec for US Dept of State in Denmark, Holland, Germany, Yugoslavia 62-63; Consul & Bldg programmer for more than 200 libs & states in 7 countries. 9: ALA (chm Jt Com on Lib Educ 48-49); CNLA; SLA; MassLA. 11: Silver medal, Philippine LA, 46; Fellow HebrewU. 12: "25 Short Cases in Library Personnel Administration" (59); "25 Cases in Executive Trustee Relationships" (60); "The Book Collection" (61); "Library Personnel Administration and Supervision" (63); Ed "Library Occurrent" (40-41); Ed "Indiana Quarterly for Bookmen" (44-45). 13: Yes. 14: Lib arch, admin, educ. 15: Sch of Lib Sci Simmons Col 300 The Fenway, Boston Ma 02115.

SHAFFER, MARGARET M. b New Orleans 20 S 40. 5: Col of William & Mary 58-60; F T Nicholls State Col 60-63 (Hist) BA; La State U 63-65 (LS) MA. 6: Sp. 7: Asst libn Terrebonne Parish Lib, Houma La 65-. 9: ALA; LaLA. 10: Alpha Beta Alpha; Little Theatre. 14: Pub libs, ref, child serv. 15: Rt 2 Box 733, Houma La 70360.

SHAFFER, NORMAN JOHN. b Lyons Neb 1 Mr 36. 4: Dallas Young. 5: CornellU 54-55 (Romanian) Letter of Proficiency; UNeb 58-61 (Hist, Philos) AB; Stanford 61-62 (Japanese Hist); UWash 65-66 MLib. 6: Romanian. 7: Romanian linguist & traffic analyst Airman 1st Class USAF 54-57; Casewkr: Mo Dept of Welfare, St Louis 62-64; Wash Dept of Pub Assistance, Seattle 64-65; Spec recruit LC 66-67, Preservation project libn 67-68, Preservation microfilming off 68-69; Asst dir for pub serv UNeb (Lincoln) 69-. 9: ALA. 10: Phi Beta Kappa. 11: Woodrow Wilson Fellow 61-62. 13: Yes. 14: Preserv, bibliog. 15: Love Lib Univ of Nebraska, Lincoln Nb 68508.

SHAFFER, ROBERT STANLEY. b Spencerville Ohio 16 Je 16. 4: Tulla Solberg. 5: Bowling Green State U 35-39 (Math, Phys Sci) BS; Harvard 43 (Ultra High Frequency Techniques) Certif; MIT 43 (Air-Borne Radar) Certif; Ind U 50-51 (LS) MA. 7: Electronics off & Instr Air U USAF, European Theatre & US 41-48; (Maj) 48; Spec Proj asst Bloomington Pub Lib, Bloomington Ind 49-50; Asst Dept of Lib Sci Ind U 50-51; Asst ref libn Tacoma Pub Lib, Tacoma Wash 51-52, 1st asst bus & tech dept 53-55; Ref libn pub serv div usaf acad lib 56-63, Sr ref libn 64-. 66; Phys sci & engrg libn 67-. 8: Consul, Martin Co, Denver tech report org proj, 57-58; Consul, with Reynolds Ward & Carey, Mile High Center, Dener, 60 (Automated Mfrs Catlg Proj); Advanced Math & Science Catlg Proj, Nuclear Div Kaman Sci Corp, Colo Springs Colo 66. 9: ColoLA. 10: USAF Res Instr Lt Col 63-69, Flight A, Colo Springs Squad. 13: Yes. 14: Ref, phys sci & engring. 15: 1632 N Prospect st, Colorado Springs Colo 80907.

SHAIN, CHARLES HERBERT. b Phila 6 Ag 28. 4: Helen Coutsouris. 5: UCal (Berkeley) 48-56 (Econ) BS, 62-63 MLS.07: City & reg planning libn UCal(Berkeley) 63-. 7: City & reg planning libn UCal (Berkeley) 63-. 9: ALA; SLA; Coun of Planning Libns (Exec Com; pres 67-68). 10: ACLU; Sierra

Club; Planners for Equal Opportunity. 14: Acquis, ref. 15: 1340 Grove st, Berkeley Cal 94709.

SHAMBLIN, ROSALYNE T. b Vinita Okla 8 O 08. 5: UOkla 40 BALS; UTex 55 MLS. 6: Sp, Fr. 7: Catlg asst Princeton U 30-34; Dist lib supv WPA, Amarillo Tex 38-39; Bkmob & br asst, Harris Co Tex 40-41; Co libn, Wharton Co Tex 41-43; Circ sect head US Army Med Lib 45-56; Spec bibliog asst ALA Internat Rel Off, Wash DC 46-47; Med libn Anderson Hosp, Houston 51-52, 53-55; Head libn Pub Lib, Artesia NM 57-58; Field consul Tex State Lib 58-59, 65-, Act asst libn 60-61. 8: Survey, Val Verde Co Lib, Del Rio Tex, 60. 9: ALA; SWLA; TexLA (Exed Bd 65-, Lib Devel Com 63-, chm Subcom on Tex Pub Lib Standards 63-64). 12: Ed "Texas Libraries (60-61). 13: Yes. 14: Pub lib ext. 15: 1401 Van Buren apt 209, Amarillo Tx 79101.

SHAMBROOK, SUSAN VAREY. b Hamilton Ont Can 30 Mr 44. 5: UToronto 62-65 (Fr) BA; McGill 65-67 MLS. 6: Fr. 7: Bibliogr (order dept) UAlberta summer 66; Catlgr UToronto 67-68, Hd catlg maintenance sect 68-. 9: CanLA; ALA; Inst Profess Lib Ont. 14: Catlg. 15: 320 Tweedsmuir ave #409, Toronto 349 Ont Can.

SHAMP, KATHLEEN (BETTY). b Wooster Ohio 20 Mr 28. 5: Col of Wooster 46-50 (Mus) BMusEd; West Res 52-54 MSLS. 7: Lib aide Cleveland Pub Lib, Cleveland Ohio 50-54, Mus libn 54-. 8: Mezzo soprano soloist, Plymouth Church of Shaker Heights 63-68; Asst conductor of choirs 68-. 10: Cleveland Orchestra Chorus. 13: Yes. 14: Mus ref. 15: 2790 E 130 st 7C, Cleveland Oh 44120.

SHANK, RUSSELL. b Spokane 2 S 25. 4: Doris Hempfer. 5: UWash 43-46 (Engnr BSEE) 47-49 (LS) BA; UWis(Madison) 49-52; Bus admin MBA; Columbia 55-66 (LS) DLS. 7: US Navy (Lt Cmdr) Active Duty 43-46, Inactive Duty 46-; Ref libn UWash 49; Asst engnr libn UWis(Madison) 49-51, Act engnr libn 51-52; Chief in-serv train & personnel control Milwaukee Pub Lib 52; Engnr Phys Sci libn Columbia U 53-59, Off of Instr Sch of Lib Serv 55-59; Visiting Asst Prof UWash Sch of Libnship summer 56; Asst U Libn UCal(Berkeley) 59-64, Lecturer Sch of Libnship 60-64; Sr lecturer Sch of Lib Serv Columbia U 64-66, Assoc Prof 66-67, Dir of libs Smithsonian Inst 67-. 8: Supv Sci Project NY Metropolitan Ref & Research Lib Agcy 66-68. 9: ALA (Coun 61-65, Rep to ADI 60-62; Personnel Admin Sect; Exec Com 57-58, chm 65-66; Chm in-serv train com);-ACRL (Exec Bd 61-65; chm Spec Awards Com 58; chm Research & Policy Com of Copying Methods Sect 65-67); SLA (chm Engnr Div 68-69); CNLA (chm Jt Com on Lib Educ 67-); ASIS; AAAS. 10: US Naval Research Reserve; chm Fed Lib Com Task Force on Educ. 11: Distinguished Alum Award Sch of Libnship UWash 68. 12: Comp "Bibliography of Reference Works for Engineering Research (64); "Regional Access to Scientific Information (68). 13: Yes. 14: Admin, sci lit, info syst. 15: Smithsonian Institution, Washington DC 20560.

SHANKLIN, HARRY L. b Lowell WVa 16 N 23. 4: Margaret Walker Shanklin. 5: Marshall U 46-49 (Soc Studies, Eng) AB, 49-50 (Hist) MA; UKy summers 52-57 MS in LS. 7: (Pfc) Anti-Aircraft Machine Gunner US Army, US & Europe 43-45; Prin tchr grade sch, Roseann Va 50-52; Eng tchr high sch, Buffalo WVa 52-53; Libn high sch, Hurricane WVa 53-. 9: NEA; ALA; NCTE; WVaLA; WVa SchLA; WVaEA. 10: WVa Hist Soc. 15: 207 Valley View dr, Hurricane WVa 25526.

SHANKS, BETTY M. b Ohio 29 Ja 13. 5: West Col for Women 32-34; Ohio State U summer 34; UTenn 65-66 (LS). 7: Libn St Mary's Mem Hosp med lib Knoxville Tenn 66-. 9: ALA; MedLA; TennLA. 14: Ref, catlg. 15: 319 Hermitage rd, Knoxville Tn 37920.

SHANKS, DOREEN (PATRICIA). b Pettapiece Manitoba Can 16 F 28. 4: John Edward Shanks. 5: Brandon Col 48 BA; UBC 67 BLS. 6: Fr. 7: Interlib loan libn UManitoba 67-68, Ref libn educ lib 68-. 9: CanLA. 14: Ref. 15: 929 Merriam blvd, Winnipeg 19 Manitoba Can.

SHANKS, MAUDEAN (WRIGHT). b Jamestown Tenn 21 N 25. 4: Marvin H Shanks. 5: Carson-Newman Col 43-47 (Eng) AB (cum laude); UTenn summers 49, 50 Tchr-Libn Certif. 6: Sp. 7: Tchr Fentress Co Bd of Educ, Jamestown Tenn 47-49; Libn Tenn State Dept of Educ York Agric Inst, Jamestown Tenn 49-54; Asst libn ORNL Y-12 Tech Lib, Oak Ridge Tenn 54-68, Asst libn ref & circ ORNL Central Research Lib 68-; Verifier of refs cited in bibliogs in Nuclear Safety 66-68. 9: SLA (Oak Ridge Chap: Pub Rel Chn 63-64, sec 6465). 10: Nat Cong Parents & Tchrs. 14: Catlg, ref. 15: Timbercrest dr, Clinton Tenn 37716.

SHANKS, ROBERT (EDWARD). b Sharbot Lake Ont Can 18 N24. 4: Paula Collins. 5: Queens U (Kingston Ont) 46-49 (Geol) BA; McGill 49-50 BLS. 7: Navigator RCAF Overseas Flying Officer 43-46; Asst libn Geol Survey of Can, Ottawa 50-60; Br libn Nat Research Coun, Ottawa 60-63, Asst libn tech serv 63-. 9: CanLA. 10: Prof Inst Pub Serv Can. 14: Acquis, catlg, automation. 15: National Science Lib Nat Research Coun of Can, Ottawa Can.

SHANLEY, DENNIS M(ICHAEL). b St Paul 8 ap 39. 5: UMinn 57-61 (Hist) BA (cum laude), 61-63 (LS) MA. 7: Libn II Milwaukee Pub Lib 63-67; Dir Pub Lib, Anoka Minn 67-. 9: ALA; WisLA; MinnLA. 15: 2330 Orchard pl apt 308, New Brighton Mn 55112.

SHANLEY, ELEANOR LEE. b Sioux Falls S Dak 19 F 23. 5: S Dak State Col 41-45 (Hist) BS; UDenver 46-47 BS in LS. 7: Libn Brookings Pub Schs, Brookings S Dak 47-49; Asst ref libn Iowa State Col (Ames) 49-56; Period libn Ga Inst of Tech 56-58; Catlgr augusta Col 58-67, Assoc libn 67-. 9: ALA; SDLA. 10: Altrusa. 14: Catlg, ref, a-v materials. 15: 1909 S Garfield, Sioux Falls SD 57105.

SHANLEY, SANDRA L (YOUNGDAHL). b Chicago Ill 20 S 42. 4: Dennis M Shanley. 5: UMinn 60-64 (Hist) BA (cum laude), 64-66 (LS) MA. 6: Fr. 7: Libn I pub lib, Milwaukee 66-67; Ref libn Anoka Co Lib, Blaine Minn 67-68; Info specialist Tech Info Serv UMinn (Minneapolis) 68-. 9: MinnLA. 10: Beta Phi Mu. 14: Sci & tech, ref. 15: 2330 Orchard pl apt 308, New Brighton Mn 55112.

SHANNON, BERNICE BELADEAU. b Duluth Minn 14 Ja 10. 4: Francis P Shannon. 5: UBuffalo 27-30 (Hist) BA (summa cum laude), 31-32 (Hist); UMinn 32-35 (Hist). 6: Fr, Ger. 7: Asst bursar Col of A&S UBuffalo 30-31, Tchg asst hist 31-3; Tchg asst hist UMinn(Minneapolis) 32-35; Hist tchr Lafayette High Sch, Buffalo NY 35-36; ULouisville: Instr of hist 47, Asst period libn 52, Libn Natural Sci Lib 53-. 9: ALA; SLA; KyLA; Louisville Lib Club. 10: Louisville Audio Soc; Arts Club; Ky Ornithol Soc; Ky Soc of Natural Hist; Wilson Ornithol Soc. 14: Ref, spec lib, period. 15: 3021 Eagle Pass, Louisville Ky 40217.

SHANNON, DWIGHT W. b Dayton Ohio 5 Ap 18. 4: Rosanna E Wagner. 5: UDayton 34-38 (Soc Sci, Educ) BS; Va Polytech Inst 38-39 (Agric); UIll 41-42 BSLS. 7: Ref asst Dayton Pub Lib, Dayton Ohio 40-41; (Sgt) US Army Med Dept 42-46; Payroll clerk Sheller Mfg Corp, Portland Ind 46-47; Libn Tex Engnrs Lib 47-48; Asst Col libn Tex A & M U 48-49; Sr ref asst Dayton Pub Lib, Dayton Ohio 49-51, Head ref dept & admin asst 51-56; Asst dir Dayton & Montgomery Co Pub Lib, Dayton Ohio 56-58; Sci libn Sacramento State Col 58-60; Circ libn Chico State Col 60-62, Asst col libn & tech serv libn 62-. 9: CalLA (chm Adv Coun 64; pres Mt Shasta Dist 64). 10: EXCHANGE Club; Dayton Torch Club; Chico Coun of Churches. 14: Admin. 15: 479 Redwood way, Chico Cal 95926.

SHANNON, MAMIE TENA. b W Palm Beach Fla 12 N 17. 5: Bethune-Cookman Col 35-37 (Elem Educ) Normal; Hampton Ins summers 39, 43, 44 (Elem Educ) BS,summers 48, 49, 51, 52 (Elem Educ) MA; FAMU summer 55; Hampton Inst summer 59; Syracuse summer 60. 7: Palm Beach Co: Elem tchr, Palm Beach Co Fla 38-44, Tchr Libn, W Palm Beach Fla 45-49, Elem tchr, Belle Glade Fla 49-52, Elem tchr, Riviera Beach Fla 52-59, Tchr-libn, Riviera Beach Fla 59-61, Libn, Riviera Beach Fla 61-. 9: NEA; Amer Tchrs Assn; Internat Reading Assn; ALA; Fla State Tchrs Assn; FlaASchL. 10: Lib STUDY Com of Palm Beach Co. 11: PalmBeachCoTA Honor Award. 14: Lib serv to child. 15: 638 - 5th st, W Palm Beach Fla 33401.

SHANNON, MICHAEL OWEN. b Brooklyn NY 1 Je 38. 5: Manhattan Col 57-61 BA; Fordham U Law Sch 62; Columbia U 64-65 MSLS. 7: Asst libn Engnr Lib Manhattan Col 63-64; Libn Manhattan Col Lab of Plant Morphogenesis 64-64; Municipal Ref Lib 65-66; Ref libn Herbert H Lehman Col Lib 66-. 9: ALA; ASIS; SLA (Exec Com; NY Documentation Group); Intl Assn Law Libs; Law Lib Assn of Greater NY; NYLA (Pub Docs Com) BSA; Bibliog Soc UVa. 10: Amer Acad Pol & Soc Sci; Amer Pol Sci Assn; Acad of Pol Sci; Hansard Society for Parliamentary Govt; Amer Soc Intl Law; AAUP; Amer Inst of Planners (NY Chap); Reg Plan Assn; Urban America Inc; Transit Com of Bergen Co (Exec Com); Amer Soc of Photogrammetry; Metropolitan Com on Planning; AAAS. 13: Yes. 14: Ref, govt publns, documentation. 15: 362 Durie ave, Closter NJ 07624.

SHANNON, ROSANNA E (WAGNER). b Dayton Ohio 21 S 18. 4: Dwight W Shannon. 5: UDayton 36-40 (Math) BS in Ed; UIll summer 41 (LS); Sacramento State Col 58-59 (Educ); Ind U summer 62 (LS); UDenver summers 63-65 (LS) MA. 7: Libn Dayton & Montgomery Co Pub Lib, Dayton Ohio 40-43; Tchr: Our LADY OF Assumption Sch, Carmichael Cal 58-59, Arcade Sch Dist, Sacramento 59-60, 59-63, Oroville Elem Schs, Oroville Cal 60-63, Libn 63-67; Libn Chico Jr High Sch, Chico Cal 67-. 9: CalTA; CalASchL. 10: Delta Kappa Gamma; AAUW. 14: Ref, sch lib. 15: 479 Redwood way, Chico Cal 95926.

SHAPIRO, CAROL (SCHOR). b Bronx NY 6 Jl 44. 4: George S Shapiro. 5: Queens Col 61-65 (Eng) BA; BostonU 65-67 (Eng) AM; Simmons 67-68 MLS. 6: Fr, Ger. 7: Catlg intern Harvard Divinity Sch Andover-Harvard Theological Lib 66-68, Catlgr 68-. 9: ALA-RTSD. 14: Catlg, bibliog. 15: c/o Andover-Harvard Theol Lib 45 Francis ave, Cambridge Ma 02138.

SHAPIRO, LILLIAN L(ADMAN). b NY 11 O 04: Herman Shapiro. 5: Hunter Col 28-32 (Lat) BA; Columbia 35-37 (Classics), 38-40 BLS, 68-69 MLS. 6: Russian, Fr, Ger. 7: NYC Sch System: Lat tchr 33-40, Libn Richmond Hill High Sch 40-48, Head Libn Woodrow Wilson High Sch 61-63; Act asst dir Bur of Libs, NYC 63-65; Head Libn & org New multi-media lib Springfield Gardens High Sch, NYC 65-68. 8: Free lance sch lib consul. 9: ALA (Com on Standards for Sch Libs 56-57; Com to Revise Standards 67-68; Com to Evaluate Sch Period); NYC Sch Libns Assn (pres 51-52); NY Lib Club (pres 68-69). 10: Girl Scouts; Nat Coun of JewshWomen; Queensborough Lib Coun; Beta Sigma Phi; Beta Phi Mu. 13: Yes. 14: Sch libs org & supv. 15: 82-30 210 st, Hollis Hills NY 11427.

SHAPIRO, MILTON DONALD. b Phila 8 Je 17. 4: Mildred Birstein. 5: UPenn 34-37 (Biol) BA; Drexel 64 (LS) MS. 6: Fr. 7: Admin off chem warfare serv US Army 42-46; Partner Shapiro Mfg Co, Phila 37-64; Head libn The Helen Kate Furness Free Lib, Wallingford Penn 65-. 9: ALA; PennLA. 10: H C Lea Home & Sch Assn; Lea Commun Art Center; Garden Court Commun Assn. 14: Pub lib admin. 15: 4744 Osage ave, Phila Pa 19143.

SHARBO, ESTHER (GOODMONSON). b Roland Iowa 16 N 14. 4: Arthur J Sharbo. 5: Augusta Col (Sioux Falls SD) 32-34; St Olaf Col 34-36 (Eng, Lat) AB; UMinn (Minneapolis) 36 (Lib); UIowa (Iowa City) summers 65-68 (LS). 6: Lat, Fr. 7: Eng tchr & libn Tyler High Sch, Tyler Minn 36-37; Eng tchr Washington High Sch, Cedar Rapids Iowa 64-66; Libn Linn-Mar High Sch, Marion Iowa 66-. 9: ALA; -AASchL; NEA; IowaStateEA; IowaASchL. 10: Pi Lambda Theta. 15: 1570 Country Club dr, Marion Ia 52302.

SHARE, CAROL (ROBEY). b Brooklyn NY 15 D 28. 4: Leonard Share. 5: Brooklyn Col 45-49 (Eng) AB; West Res 61-63 (LS) AM. 6: Sp. 7: Ref libn Cleveland Hts Univ Hts Pub Lib 63-, Hd br libn 67-. 9: ALA; OhioLA. 14: Ref, adult serv, readers adv. 15: 5196 Hickory dr, Lyndhurst Oh 44124.

SHARIFY, HOMAYOUN (TASLIMY). b Gazvin Iran 4 Ag 27. 4: Nasser Sharify. 5: UTeheran 49 (Hist) BA; UParis 62 (Educ); PittsburghU 65 MS in LS. 6: Persian, Fr, Arabic, Turkish. 7: Preliminary catlgr LC 55-57; Acquis libn PittsburghU Lib 63-65; Asst libn carnegie Lib catlg dept, Pittsburgh Penn 65-66; Ser rec libn C W Post Col LIU 67-. 8: Tchr of Hist & Geography, Ministry of Educ, Teheran 49-54; Prog asst, Persian Sect, voice of America, Wash DC 54-55; Staff mem, Dept of Home Economics, Ministry of Educ, Teheran 61-62; Iranian Delegate to UNESCO, General Conference 62. 10: Beta Phi Mu 65; Pahlavi Medal as the Best Student from Gazvin, Iran Normal School 45. 14: Tech serv. 15: 81 Roosevelt dr, E Norwich NY 11732.

SHARIFY, NASSER. b Teheran Iran 23 S 25. 4: Homayoun Taslimy. 05: UTeheran 44-47 (Fr Lit) Licenci s Lettres; Columbia 53-54 MS in LS, 55-58 DLS. 5: UTeheran 44-47 (Fr Lit) Licencie es Lettres; Columbia 53-54 MS in LS, 55-58 DLS. 6: Persian, Eng, Fr, Arabic. 7: Translator-Announcer All India Radio 48-49; Staff, Lib of Parliament of Iran, Teheran Iran 47-50, Deputy Dir 50-53; Staff, Descr Catlg Div LC 54-55; Program asst Libs- Devel Sect Div of Libs Documentation & Archives UNESCO, Paris 59-61; Dir-Gen Ministry of Educ in chg of Nat Pub & Sch Libs, Textbks, Publns, Transl, Reading materials, Pub info control, Statis, Teheran Iran 61-62; Act chief of serv sect, Program Spec Div of Educ Info & Materials Dept of Educ UNESCO, Paris 62-63; UPittsburgh; Asst Prof of lib sci Grad Sch of Lib & Info Sci 63-66, Dir Internat Lib Info Center Grad Sch of Lib & Info Sci 64-66, Asst Prof of Educ Sch of Educ 65-66; Dir Intl Libnship & Documentation SUNY 66-68; Dean & Prof Grad Sch of Lib & Info Sci Pratt 68-. 8: Org Com Unesco Reg Sem on Lib Devel in Arabic-Speaking States, Beirut Lebanon 59, & S E Asia, New Delhi 60; Unesco Observer IFLA Internat Catlg Conf, London 59; Lecturer on sch lib deve, TrainCourse for Dirs of Educ, Teheran Iran 60; Dir, grad lib courses, Nat Tchrs Col, Teheran 60; Chm Unesco Meeting of Educ Publrs, Geneva 61; Delegate Internat Conf on Catlg Principles, Paris 61; Chm Iranian Nat Com for Internat Conf on Catlg Principles, Teheran 60-61; Chm Unesco-sponsored Nat Sem on Distrib of Reading Materials, Teheran 61; Org Com Unesco Meeting of Educ Publrs, Paris 62; Chm, Nat Libs Group, CENTO Lib Devel Sem, Ankara Turkey 62; Chm Standing Com for the Prep of Reading Materials for New Literates, Teheran 61-62; Consul "Dsh Index 64; Adv Com, Internat Educ Program, Sch of Educ UPittsburgh 64-; Consul to Exec Dean, Internat Studies & World Affairs, NY State & 65-; Dir First Inst on Internat Compar Libnship UPittsburgh 65; Conducted advanced course on Internatl Compar Libnship Sch of Lib Sci, SUNY (Albany) summer 66; Princ invest AID Mission to Turkey & Pakistan; Survey of bk production and libs in CENTO Reg; Organ & mem, Exec Com of Consortium on Mexico on Microfilm 68-; Adv to AID/Devel Bk Proj 68-; Mem Adv Bd Encyclopedia of Library & Information Science 69-; Chm, Nomin Com IRRT 69. 9: ALA (Spec Com on Near East Material 57-58);-LED (chm Com on Equival & Reciprocity 65; mem UNESCO Panel 66-, Com on Internat Lib Sch 68-); ASIS; SLA; Association des Bibliothecaires Francais; AALS; Reg Coun for Internat Educ (Lib Resources Com; Chm of 1965 Wkshop). 10: AAUP; Alliance francaise (Pittsburgh). 12. "Library Development in Countries of Tropical Africa (61); "Cataloguing of Persian Works, Including Rules fo Transliteration, Entry and Description ALA (59);"Bibliography of Iran (58). 12: "Library Development in Countries of Tropical Africa" (61); "Cataloguing of Persian Works, Including Rules for Transliteration, Entry and Description" ALA (59); "Bibliography of Iran" (58); "CENTO; Book Production, Imporation & Distribution" in Iran, Pakistan & Turkey (66). 13: Yes. 14: Tech proc, internat compar libnship, internat educ, reading materials for new literates. 15: Grad Sch of Lib & Info Sci, Pratt Inst, Brooklyn NY 11205.

SHARMA, MONAN (LAL). b Dhanbad India 5 N 33. 4: Katherine Ziniel. 5: Lucknow U (India) 55-57 (Psych, Educ BA; Banaras U (India) 58-59 Diploma in Lib Sci; West Res 59-60 MS in LS; Johns Hopkins 60-61 (Russian Lang) Credit CertifUIll summer 66 (Computer Use in Libs). 6: Russian, Hindi, Bengali, Urdu. 7: Asst Banaras U Lib Banaras India 58-59; Prof asst Case Inst of Tech Lib 59-60; Prof asst Enoch Pratt Free Lib, Baltimore 60-61; Sr libn Educ Dept 61-63; Sci & engrg libn UWaterloo (Can) 63-65; Hd Educ Lib UAlta 65-67; Visiting Prof faculty of Educ UCalgary (Can) 68-69; Asst dir pub serv UAlta Libs (Canada) 67-. 8: Comp, NEA list of "Outstanding Books in Education 61-63; (publ in "Educational Horizons spring issue of each year; Indexer & educ consul, Can Educ Index 65-68; Consul Faculty of Educ UCalgary Materials Ctr 67. 9: CanLA; Internat Fed for Documentation; ALA; Alta LA; Inst Prof Libns Ont; ASIS. 10: Faculty Club UAlta; Assn of Acad Staff, UAlta; Univ Prof Lbns Group, Alta; Can Assn Univ Tchrs. 13: Yes. 14: Ref, info retrieval, indexing, documentation. , lib admin. 15: Univ of Alta Libs, Edmonton Alta Can.

SHARMA, OM PRAKASH. b Rawalpindi Pakistan 14 N 33. 5: Panjab U Solan India 53-54 BA, 57-60 MA; Sch of Libnship Mun Col of Com Newcastle-Upon-Tyne 60-61 ALA Chicago 63- (LS). 6: Hindi, Urdu, Panjabi, Gujarati, Prakrit, Pali, Sanskrit, Persian, Marathi, Russian. 7: Asst Panjab U (Chandigarh India)54-59; Sr asst libn Southall Pub Libs, Southall London 61-63; Catlgr LC 64-66; S Asian bibliog(r) & Hd S Asia sect UMich Lib 66-. 9: ALA; IndiaLA. 10: Assn for Asian Studies; Amer Oriental Soc. 12: Guest ed "The Indian Librarian Jullundur (India). 13: Yes. 14: Catlg, ref, org, acquis. 15: 2140 Bredefield st, Ann Arbor Mi 48105.

SHARMA, UMESH (DATTA). b Meerut City India 11 Ja 30. 4: Kanta Sharma. 5: PanjabU (India) 53-56 (Hindi Lit) BA; UDelhi (India) 60-61 (LS) Diploma, 61-63 (Hindi Lit) MA; Syracuse 64-65 MS in LS. 6: Sanskrit, Hindi, Urdu, Bengali, Panjabi, Fr, Ger. 7: Catlgr DelhiU Lib 56-60, In-charge (evening) Inst Collection 61-63; Bk selector UToronto 65-67; Acquis libn BrockU 67-68; Bibliogr Waterloo Lutheran U Lib 68-. 9: OntLA. 11: Fulbright Scholar 64-65. 12: Trans: Pustakalay Vigyan Ki Bhumika (63); Pustakalay Vargikaran Ke Mool-Tattva (68). 13: Yes. 14: Bk sel, ref. 15: Lib Waterloo Lutheran Univ, Waterloo Ont Can.

SHARP, AVERIL CAMILLA. b Jonesboro Ark 4 Ag 18. 5: Ark State U 36-40 (Eng, Bus Admin) BA; Peabody summers 42-44 BS in LS. 7: Com tchr DeWitt High Sch, DeWitt Ark 42-44; Asst libn Memphis State U 44-45; Asst libn Henderson State Col 45-49; Asst libn Ark State U 49-59; Asst libn MacMurray Col 59-63; Libn UArk tech campus lib (Little Rock) 63-. 9: ALA; ArkLA (chm Spec Lib Sect, state sec). 10: Women's Nat Bk Assn; Pi Omega Pi; Pi Gamma Mu; Phi Theta Kappa; Altrusa Club. 14: Ref. 15: 1620 N Pierce, Little Rock Ar 72207.

SHARP, CAROLYN M(ARY). b South Bend Ind 12 Je 25. 5: Maryhurst Col 43-47 (Eng) BA; Marquette U 47-49 (Eng Lit) MA; Rosary Col 51-52 MA in LS. 6: Sp. 7: Instr Marquette U 49-51; Head circ dept Oak Park Pub Lib, Oak Park Ill 52-53; Asst libn Umatilla Co Lib, Pendleton Ore 53-61; Sr Catlgr Lib Assn of Portland, Portland Ore 61-. 9: ALA-RTSD. 10: AAUW; Dachshund Club of Amer. 14: Catlg. 15: 2344 NE 59, Portland Ore 97213.

SHARP, DONALD (JAMES). b Ft William Ont Can 12 Je 37. 5: Toronto 56-60 (Eng) BA, 61-62 BLS. 6: Fr. 7: Head catlg dept Ft William (Ont) Pub Lib 62-65; Head tech processing dept Lakehead U Lib (Ont) 65-. 8: Sessional lectr lib tech LakeheadU 66-. 9: CanLA; OntLA; Inst Prof Libns Ont. 10: Port Arthur Golf & Country Club. 14: Catlg. 15: 308 N High st, Port Arthur Ont Can.

SHARP, FLORENCE R (COOK). b Lawrenceburg Ind 19 F 26. 4: William H Sharp Jr. 5: Purdue U 43-47 (Sci) BS. 7: Engnr libn Bendix Aviation Corp, S Bend Ind 48-50; Asst libn Nat Lead Co of Ohio, Cincinnati 54-61, Libn 61-. 9: SLA. 14: US AEC reports, tech lit searching. 15: Nat Lead Co P O Box 39158, Cincinnati Oh 45239.

SHARP, HAROLD S. b Alameda Cal 23 D 09. 4: Marjorie Zehr. 5: UCal 27-28 (Letters & Sci); IndU 53-54 (Bus Admin) BS; UCal 54 (Bus Admin); IndU 55-56 (Bus Admin), MALS. 06 Sp. 6: Sp. 7: Contract admin Rosenberg Bros & Co, San Francisco 28-42; Off (Capt) US Army QM Corps Supply, Transport, Comp Cmndr, Paratrooper 42-52; Partner Meat Packing Sharp-More Co, Walnut Creek Cal 54-55; Chief libn Farnsworth Electronics Co, Ft Wayne Ind 57-59; Tech libn AC Spark Plug Div General Motors Corp, Milwaukee 59-63; Engnr Info Analyst Lockheed-Georgia Co, Marietta Ga 63-64; Lib consul, writer self-employed, Berkeley Cal 64-65; Head of ref & assoc prof of Lib Studies UHawaii 65-68; Prof of Lib Sci Ind State U (Terre Haute) 68-. 8: Consul: Collins Radio Co, Cedar Rapids Iowa 62, Euclid Div General Motors Corp, Cleveland 63, etc. 9: SLA (Wis Chap; Program Chm, sec, pres-elect 61-64). 10: Beta Gamma Sigma; Beta Phi Mu. 12: "How to Use Your Library (63); "Readings in Special Librarianship (63); "Readings in Information Retrieval (64); Co-auth "Index of Characters in the Performing Arts (Part I 66, Part II 68, Part III in prep). 13: Yes. 14: Admin, ref in sci bus & tech, research in spec libnship, documentation. 15: Indiana State Univ Dept of Lib Sci, Terre Haute In 47809.

SHARP, JO GARDNER. b Ridgely Tenn 5 O 26. 4: O Harvey Sharp. 5: UTenn 44 (Socio) BA. 6: Ger. 7: Asst libn Oak Ridge Nat Lab, Oak Ridge Tenn 49-63, Lib specialist 64-. 9: SLA. 12: Ed "Radiations" (65-66). 14: Ref. 15: 514 Valparaiso rd, Oak Ridge Tn 37830.

SHARP, KATHLEEN (LUCILLE). b Lawrence Co Ark. 5: Ark Col 43-47 (Math,Langs) AB; Peabody 53-57 (LS) MA.06: Sp, Fr. 6: Sp, Fr. 7: Tchr-libn Clover Bend Pub Schs, Hoxie Ark; Tchr-libn Swifton High Sch, Swifton Ark; Sch libn Osceola Pub Schs, Osceola Ark; Co libn Greene Co Lib, Paragould Ark; Reg libn Greene-Clay Reg Lib, Paragould Ark, Northeast Ark Reg Lib, Paragould Ark. 9: ALA; ArkLA (treas 61-62; chm Sch Div 59); pres 67). 10: Beta Phi Mu; Bus & Prof Womens Club. 15: Northeast Ark Reg Lib, Paragould Ark 72450.

SHARP, OMER (JAYE). b San Antonio Tex 13 Jl 29. 4: Retta Nutter. 5: UCorpus Christi 50-53 (Relig) BA; SWest Baptist Sem 54-57 (Ethics) BD, 57-62 (Ethics); N Tex StateU 67-68 MLS; TrinityU 53 (Relig). 6: New Testament Gk. 7: Minister Amer Baptist Convention, Clarksburg W Va -64; Archivist Alderson-Broaddus Col 64-67, Asst libn 68-. 8: Tchg fellow UCorpus Christi 51-53; Departmental grader Southwestern Sem 58-61; Inst hist Alderson-Broaddus Col 64-. 9: SLA; ALA; WVaLA. 10. Optimist Club; Alpha Beta Alpha. 13: Yes. 14: Ref, admin. 15: Alderson-Broaddus College, philippi WVa 26416.

SHARP, SARAH LaVERNA (JONES). b Richmond Va 31 D 16. 4: Cifford Hendricks Sharp. 5: Va Union 35-39 (Lat, Educ) AB; Wayne State 61-63 (LS) MEd; UMich 67-68 AMLS. 6: Ger, Fr, Lat. 7: Tchr: Bd of Educ, Hanover Va 40-42, Bd of Educ, Richmond Co Va 42-44; Tchr & libn: Archdiocese of Detroit 63-64, Detroit Bd of Educ 64-68, Ministry of Educ, Conakry Guinea 68-. 9: ALA; Class Assn Amer; Classical Assn Detroit. 10: Detroit Assn Geneal Res. 14: Ref & catlg (sch libs). 15: Boite Postale 668, Conakry Guinea West Africa.

SHARPE, JAMES G. b New Westminster BC 12 Mr 35. 5: UBC 54-57 (Eng, Hist) BA, 58-59 BLS. 6: Ger. 7: Catlgr UToronto Lib 59-62; Catlgr Toronto Pub Lib, Toronto Can 62-63; Catlgr UVictoria 63-67; Catlgr UBC 67-. 9: CanLA; BCLA (treas 69-70). 14: Catlg. 15: 7288 - 11th ave, Burnaby 3 BC Can.

SHATKIN, ALLAN IRVING. b Brooklyn NY 15 N 40. 5: UCLA 60-62 (Eng) BA, 63-64 Cal gen secondary tchg credential; USoCal 67-69 MSLS. 7: Admin asst Shepherd Records Co, Hollywood Cal 62-63; Med specialist (Sp/5) US Army 64; Statistician Douglas Aircraft Co, Santa Monica Cal 65-66; Sales prod writer, Bunker-Ramo, Canoga Park Cal 66; Dir communications USoCal 66-67; Libn Los Angeles Pub Lib soc sci dept 68-. 9: ALA; SLA. 10: Beta Phi Mu. 14: Ref, lib automation. 15: 910 No Orange Grove ave, Los Angeles Ca 90046.

SHATKIN, CHARLOTTE (ARYEF). b NYC. 4: Rubin Shatkin. 5: Brooklyn Col 37 (Langs, Math) BA; NYU 37-40 (Adult Educ) MA; Columbia U 46-49 MLS. 6: Fr, Ger. 7: Asst dir Post Lib 1st ADC, Mitchell Field 46-47; Dir Post Lib, Ft Slocum 47-49; Br coordinator Elizabeth NJ Pub Lib 49-51; Hd of ref New Brunswick NJ Pub Lib 51-62; Adult serv libn E Orange NJ Pub Lib 62-63; Hdqrs admin & A-V Libn Somerset Co Lib, Somerville NJ 63-. 8: Supv libn in lib serv set up & administered 2 med libs. 9: ALA (A-V Com); NJLA (chm & founder A-V Sect; chm Memb Com); SLA; NY Lib Club. 10: Founder NJ Lib Film Circuit; NY Film Coun; Bd Film Lib Info Coun; Amer Film Festival; Amer Fed Film Socs. 12: "Films for Public Libraries ALA; "Evaluations for Educational Fim Library Association. 13: Yes. 14: Ref. 15: 59 Canterbury rd, E Brunswick NJ 08816.

SHAUGHNESSY, JEAN CULLEN, MRS HAROLD E. b oxbury NY 13 Je 09. 5: St Lawrence U (NY) 27-30 (Eng Lit) BA; State Tchrs Col (GENESEO NY) 56-61 MLS. 7: Tchr Massena Jr. High Sch, MASSENA NY 30-31; Sec Rochester Tel Co, Rochester NY 31-3; Libn Hamburg Pub Lib, Hamburg NY 57-, Dir 66-. 10: Bus & Prof Womens Club; LWV. 14: Readers adv. 15: 64 Newton rd, Hamburg NY 14075.

SHAUGHNESSY, THOMAS WILLIAM. b Pittsburgh Penn 3 My 38. 4: Marlene D Reuben. 5: St vincent Col 56-61 (Philos) BA; St Mary's U 61-62 (Theol); UPittsburgh 63-64 MLS; Rutgers 65-69 (LS). 6: Fr, Lat. 7: Lib trainee Penn State Lib, Harrisburg 63-64, Ref libn 64-65; Research assoc resurvey of Penn, Metuchen NJ summer 66; Asst instr Rutgers U (New Brunswick) 67; Research dir Chicago Lib Survey 68-. 8: Consul: John J Kane Hosp, Pittsburgh 64; Survey of New Castle (Pa) Pub Lib summer 65. 9: ALA. 10: Beta Phi Mu. 14: Admin, lib educ. 15: 33 E Cedar st apt 18H, Chicago Il 60611.

SHAULIS, DOROTHY ROBINSON (BLANCHE) . b Saltsbug Penn 1 D 08. 5: Beaver Col for Women 26-30 (Eng, Euc) AB (cum laude); Johns Hopkins 52-53, 58 (LS; West Md Col 57-60 (LS) M Ed; Rutgers summers 59-64 MLS, summer 68. 7: Kindergarten Prim tchr Edgewood Pub Schs, Edgewood Penn 30-31; Med sec & receptionist Physicians Off, Ind, Penn 32-40; Instr of Homebound Child Fed Govt, Ind, Penn 48-51; Hostess Welcome Wagon Inc, Ind, Penn 48-51; Recording & music libn Nat Music Camp UMich, Interlochen Mich summers 53-56; Libn & head libn McDonogh Sch, McDonogh Md 51-67; Assoc Prof lib educ Millersville State Col 67-68; Assoc libn Susquehanna U 68-. 8: Eval Com for Middle States Assn of Cols & Secon Schs, 59. 9: ALA; MDla; Assn Sch Libns Md (Program Com 63); Tchr Assn Independ Schs Baltimore Area (Libns Group); PennLA; PSLA. 10: PEO; Womens Aux Indiana Co (Penn) Med Soc; Womens Club; Beta Phi Mu; AAUP. 13: Yes. 14: Ref, orient to libs & lib instr, lib coop programs. 15: 408 West Pine st, Selinsgrove Pa 17870.

SHAVER, VIRGINIA H. b Oneonta NY 8 My 6. 5: Hartwick Col 34-38 (Eng) BA; State U Col (Oneonta NY) 38-40 Elem Certif; State U Col (Geneseo NY) 37-39 (Lib Educ) BSE; NYU summer 42 (Eng); Columbia 48 (Eng); State U Col (Albany NY) 50, 54 LS; UIll 56 (LS); Syracuse 65 (LS); Hofstra 68. 7: Eng tchr & libn Charlotte Valley Central Sch, Davenport NY 40-42; Eng tchr Jeffersonville Central Sch, Jeffersonville NY 42-43; Eng tchr & libn Laurens Central Sch, Laurens NY 43-46; Libn Neptune High Sch, Ocean Grove NJ

46-48; Head libn W C Mepham High Sch, Bellmore NY 48-58; Central libn CHSD No 3, Merrick NY 58-65, Dist chm for Libs 65-. 9: NEA; ALA-AASchL (East Reg Memb Chm 53-55); NY State Tchrs Assn; NYLA (Sch Lib Sect: Nomin Com, chm Sch Lib Supv Group); Nassau-Suffolk Sch Lib Assn (pres 58-59). 10: AAUW; Commun Concert Assn. 14: Supv wk with libns, central processing. 15: Chsd 3 Admin Offices 1691 Meadowbrook rd, Merrick NY 11566.

SHAVIT, DAVID. b Haifa Israel 26 Je 36. 4: Penelope Bradley. 5: HebrewU 58-60 (Middle East Affairs); HowardU 60-63 (Govt) BA; Columbia 63-65 (LS) MS. 6: Hebrew. 7: Period libn NYC Pub Lib 63-65; Hd circ dept Baker Lib HarvardU 65-66; Hd acquis dept UMass 66-69; Acquis libn No Ariz U 69-; Asst Dir Tech Serv UDenver 70-. 13: Yes. 14: Acquis, tech proc. 15: Univ Denver Lib, University Park Co 80210.

SHAW, ELEANOR (FENNER). b Gouverneur NY 2 Jl13. 4: Wilbur C Shaw. 5: Col of Wooster 30-34 (Math) BA; West Res 37-38 BS in LS; Omaha U 63, 66; San Jose State Col 67; UNeb (Omaha) 68. 7: Child libn Lorain Pub Lib, Lorain Ohio 34-37, Bkmob libn 38-41; Ind Engnr clerk Amer Steel & Wire, Cleveland 42-45; Elem sch libn: Cuyahoga Co Lib, Cleveland 56-60, Rocky River Pub Schs, Cleveland 60-62, Westside Commun SCHS, Omaha 62-. 9: NEA; NebStateEA; NebStateLA; Neb Educ Media Assn. 10: Alpha Delta Kappa. 14: Elem sch materials centers. 15: 666 J E George bvd, Omaha Neb 68132.

SHAW, HENRY KING. b Akron Ohio 22 N 04. 4: Edrie Stanton. 5: Spokane U 27-29; PhillipsU 30-32 BA; UAkron 39-42 MA Ed. 7: Minister: Riverside Church of Christ, Akron Ohio 29-30, First Church of Christ, Ada Ohio 32-35, First Church of Christ, Medina Ohio 35-42, Washington Avenue Church of Christ, Elyria Ohio 43-57; Libn Butler U Sch of Religion 57-58: Libn Dir of publs, Prof of disciple lit Christian Theol Sem (Indianapolis) 57-. 9: ATheolLA; ALA; Amer Soc Church Hist. 10: AAUP; Disciples of Christ Hist Soc; Ind Hist Soc; Theta Phi; Amer Cath Hist Assn. 11: Butler U Hon DD, 57. 12: "Saga of a Village Church (37); "The Amateur Philosopher (40); "Buckeye Disciples (52); "Hoosier Disciples (66); Managing ed "Encounter. 13. Yes. 14: Admin. 15: 557 W Westfield blvd, Indianapolis In 46208.

SHAW, IDA WINNIFRED (NOBLE). b Spooner Minn 7 D 08. 4: W Lawrence Shaw. 5: Pomona Col 26-31 (Eng, Hist, Psych) BA, Magna Cum Laude. 6: Fr. 7: Stud asst Pomona Col Lib 27-31, Lib asst in period, documents, ref, circ 31-34; Demographer US Census Bur, Oakland Cal 50; Contra Costa Cal Co Lib; Lib asst Pleasant Hill Br 56, Lib asst Martinez Cal 56, Br libn Pleasant Hill Br 56-61, Head circ & liaison Central Lib, Pleasant Hill Cal 61-64, Info desk & liaison City of Pleasant Hill 64-. 10: AAUW; Phi Beta Kappa; Friends of the Pleasant Hill Lib. 14: Ref, readers adv wk. 15: 295 Keats Circle, Pleasant Hill Cal 94523.

SHAW, INA B. b Hendricks Co Ind. 5: NWest State Col 21, 29-30, summer 24-25 (Eng, Hist); Central Normal Col 34 BS; LSU 39 BSLS. 6: Fr. 7: Libn Ponchatoula High Sch, Ponchatoula La 36-46; Libn Canterbury Col 46-51; Curriculum lab libn Ball State U 51-53; Libn Danville Pub Lib, Danville Ind 53-. 9: ALA; IndLA (Small Lib Gp). 10: Hendricks Co Hist Soc. 14: Catlg, ref. 15: 302 E Broadway, Danville In 46122.

SHAW, JOHN MACKAY. b Glasgow Scotland 15 My 1897. 4: Lillian Reamer. 7: Asst v-pres Amer Tel & Tel Co, NY 30-59; Curator childhood in poetry collection Fla State U 60-. 9: ALA; FlaLA; SELA. 10: Grolier Club (NY; Nat Coun, Boy Scouts. 12: "Childhood in Poetry, Catalog of Shaw Collection in Florida State University," (5 vols 67); "The Parodies of Lewis Carroll & Tier Originals" (60); "The Poems, Poets and Illustrators of St Nicholas Magazine 1783-1943" (65). 14: Rare bks. 15: Fla State Univ Lib, Tallahassee Fl 32306.

SHAW, JUDITH (ANNE) (HICKMAN). b Evanston Ill 27 Jl 41. 4: Kenneth Alan Shaw. 5: Purdue 59-63 (Zool) BS; UIll 63-64 (LS) MS. 6: Sp. 7: Libn I Phoenix Pub Lib 64-66; Catlg libn Ariz StateU Lib 66-68, Asst hd catlg dept 69-. 9: ArizStateLA; SWLA. 14: Catlg, spec libnship. 15: Lib Arizona State Univ, Tempe Az 85281.

SHAW, LILLIE (KING). b Indianapolis Ind. 4: Philip H Shaw. 5: Ariz State U 55-59 (Eng) BA; UDenver 60-62 (LS) MA. 7: Hd libn Glendale High Sch, Glendale Ariz 59; Assoc Prof Ariz State U 67-. 9: ALA; NEA; NCTE; Salt River Valley Libn (pres 68); Ariz State LA; ArizEA. 10: Alpha Beta Alpha; Phi Kappa Phi; Kappa Delta Pi; Sigma Alpha Iota; Phoenix Symphony Assn; Phoenix Symphony Guild. 14: Wk with ya. 15: 6802 N 37th ave, Phoenix 85019.

SHAW, MARJORIE (RUSSELL). b Brockton Mass 1 Ag 07. 5: Bridgewater State Col 25-29 (Eng, Hist) BS in Ed; BostonU 36-37 (Eng, Hist) MEd; Simmons 43-46 BS in LS. 6: Fr. 7: Tchr: Crestalban Sch, Berkshire Mass 29-34, Lesley Col 34-35; Asst & hd catlgr Brockton Pub Lib, Brockton Mass 39-49; Hd libn Milton Pub Lib, Milton Mass 49-. 9: ALA (life mem); NELA (past treas); MassLA (life mem); Old Colony Lib Club (past pres). 10: Milton Woman's Club; Milton Camera Club. 13: Yes. 14: Admin, catlg. 15: 392 Moraine st, Brockton Ma 02401.

SHAW, MARY KATHERINE. b Juneau Ak 14 Ag 44. 5: Gonzaga 61-65 (Hist) AB; CatholicU 67-68 (LS) MS. 6: Ital, Ger, Fr. 7: Mgt analyst Nat Archives, Wash DC 66-67; Descr catlgr LC 69-. 8: Spec recr LC 68-69. 9: ALA; CathLA; DCLA. 14: Catlg. 15: 633 Hamlin st NE, Washington DC 20017.

SHAW, MARY L. b Detroit 30 S 11. 5: Marygrove Col 30-34 (Philos) BA; Simmons 37-38 BSLS. 7: Jr libn Detroit Pub Lib 38-43; Casewker Amer Nat Red Cross, Wash DC 43-54; Libn Borgess Hosp Sch of Nursing, Kalamazoo 54-62; Dir Allegan Pub Lib, Allegan Mich 63-64; Dir Albion Pub Lib, Albion Mich 64-66; Libn Kellogg Bio Sta Mich State U (Hickory Corners) 66-. 9: ALA; MichLA. 10: AAUW. 15: Box 204, Richland Mich 49083.

SHAW, MINNIE LEE. b Jaksonville Tex 16 S 23. 4: Willie J Shaw. 5: Wiley Col 41-47 (Home Econ) BS; UDenver 52-57 (LS) MA; Prairie View A&M 56 (Educ); E Tex State U 65 (Guidance); Stephen F Austin Col 68 (Guidance). 7: Elem tchr Washington Sch, Stamford Tex 47-48; Asst registrar Wiley Col 48-50; Tchrlibn Fred Douglass High Sch, Jacksonville Tex 50-55; Elem tchr Dogan Elem Sch, Marshall Tex 55-62; Order libn & circ W R Banks Lib, Prairie View A&M summers 59, 60, 62; Libn Pemberton Jr High Sch, Marshall Tex 63-; Libn Rio Grande High Sch, Albuquerque 66-67; Asst libn Texas Col 69-. 9: Tex State Tchrs Assn; nea. 10: Zeta Phi Beta; Nat Assn of Negro Bus & Prof Womens Clubs; Top Ladies of Distinction, Inc; PTA. 14: Ref. 15: 1200 Barney st, Marshll Tex 75670.

SHAW, RENATA VITZTHUM. b Finland 21 Jl 26. 4: Russell R Shaw. 5: Wittenberg Col 47-48 (Art Hist); UHelsinki 45-47, 49-51 (Art Hist MA; Chicago 48-49 (Art Hist) MA; UParis 51-54 (Art Hist); Catholic U 61-62 MS in LS. 6: Finnish, Swedish, Ger, Fr, Modern Gk, Lat, Danish, Norwegian. 7: Tchr Holton Arms Sch, Wash DC 55-57; Museum aide Nat Gallery of Art, Wash DC 60; Art ref libn LC 62-. 9: SLA (Picture Div; DC Chap chm-elect 69-70); Amer Assn Museums. 10: Beta Phi Mu. 13: Yes. 14: Art, ref wk, pcture libnship, Scandinavian bk selection. 15: 4850 Langdrum lane, Chevy Chase Md 20015.

SHAW, ROBERT JAMES. b Hammond Ind 11 Ag 38. 4: Diane Branstetter. 5: Purdue 56-57; Ind U 57-59; Roosevelt U 59-61 (Bus Admin) BSBA; Chicago 61-(LS) MA. 7: Order libn Hammond Pub Lib, Hammond Ind 60-63, Head tech processing dept 63-64; Asst to the exec sec ALA-LAD, Chicago 64-66; Hd info serv ALA-LTP 66-68; Ed Lib Tech Reports ALA-LTP 68-. 8: In chg of Ford Foun proj of the main libs of the Univ of the Philippines, Haile Selassie I Univ, UAlgiers. 9: ALA. 12: "Certification of Public Librarians in the United States, ALA" (Rev ed 65); "Libraries; Building for the Future," ALA (67). 14: Admin, lib bldg planning. 15: 7945 Jackson, Munster In 46321.

SHAW, SISTER ROSE MAURICE SC. b Elizabeth NJ 19 Sp 19. 5: Col of St Elizabeth 37-50 (Eng) AB; Seton Hall U 52-58 (Eng) MA; NYU 62 (Educ); St John's U 62-64 MLS. 6: Fr. 7: Eng tchr high schs in Westfield, Newark, New Brunswick & Jersey City NJ 50-62; Circ & ref libn Col of St Elizabeth 62-66, Asst libn 62-, Ref libn 66-. 9: ALA; Nat Cath EA; CathLA; NEA; LARC; NCTE; Nat Mus Educrs Assn; NJLA; MorrisCoLA. 14: Ref, a-v. 15: College of St Elizabeth, Convent Station NJ 07961.

SHAW, W(ILFRED) LAWRENCE. b Barnesboro Penn 26 My 06. 4: Ida Noble. 5: Pomona Col 24-28 (Econ) BA (cum laude); UCal(Berkeley) 28-29 (LS) Certif; Claremont Col 33-34 (Pol Sci) MA. 6: Fr, Ger. 7: Head br & sch dept Ventura Co Lib, Ventura Cal 29-30; Prof asst in adult educ ALA, Chicago 30-32; Investigator Fed Emergency Relief Admin, Pomona Cal 34; Jr libn USDA Lib, Wash DC 35-40; Libn USDAS West Reg Research Lab, Albany Cal 40-44, Commodity-Industry

Analyst 44-61; Ind analyst Off of Admin Agric Res Serv USDA, Albany Cal 61-. 9: ALA (Life mem);-ACRL; Amer Econ Assn; Amer Agric Econ Assn; CalLA (Life mem). 14: Ref, acquis. 15: 295 Keats circle, Pleasant Hill Cal 94523.

SHAWL, JANICE (HAYS). b Spokane Wash 7 Ja 32. 4: William Frank Shawl. 5: Mont State U 49-51; East Wash State Col 51-52; Mont State U 53 (Lat) BA; UWash 55-58 (LS) MA; UCLA 66. 7: Eng tchr Highline High Sch, Seattle 55-56, Libn 56-58; Catlgr Seattle Pub Lib 58-61; Eng tchr Highline Col 61-62; Catlgr Bellevue Pub Schs, Bellevue Wash 63-67; Temp catlgr UCLA Research Lib 65-66; Lecturer UWash 67; Hd catlg dept UCal (Irvine) Lib 68-. 9: ALA; So Cal Tech Processes Group; calLA. 14: Catlg, university & col. 15: 4426 Sandburg way, Irvine Ca 92664.

SHAYNE, METTE (HANNOVER). b Copenhagen Denmark 9 O 34. 4: David Shayne. 5: Danish Royal Lib Sch 57-58 (LS). 6: Danish, Fr, Ger. 7: Study libn Gentofte Pub Lib, gentofte Denmark 55-58; Exchange libn Montclair Pub Lib, Montclair NJ 58-59; Sec Danish Lib Inspectorate, Copenhagen 60; Lib asst NorthwesternU Lib 61-63, Libn Africana Lib 64-. 9: ALA. 15: 507 Roscoe st, Chicago Il 60657.

SHEA, BROTHER PATRICK J(AMES) CFC. b Brigus Newfoundland 27 N 05. 5: St Mary's Col 34 (Chem) BS; Fordham 41 (Physics) MS; Rosary Col 50 BALS. 7: Tchg Christian Bros Schools, NY, Halifax, St John's, Victoria 28-49; Libn Leo High Sch, Chicago 49-51, 62-65; Acquis libn Iona Col 51-56; Physics tchr & libn St Patrick's Hall, St John's Nfld 56-61; Libn Brother Rice High Sch, Birmingham Mich 61-62; Libn Brother Rice High Sch, St John's Nfld 65-66; Ref libn Memorial UMfld 66-. 9: CanLA; CathLA; SchLA (St John's Nfld). 13: Yes. 14: Ref (high sch libs). 15: Brother Rice Monastery, St John's Newfoundland Can.

SHEA, JOSEPH THOMAS JR. b Boston Mass 22 Jl 42. 5: State Col at Boston 60-64 (Educ) BSEd; URI 64-68 MLS. 7: Jr high tchr Boston Pub Schs 64-68; Libn Boston Lat Sch 68-. 9: ALA; -AASchL. 10: Nat Sci Tchrs Assn; Dorchester Hist Soc; Boston State Col Alum Assn. 11: Outstanding Alumni Award, Boston State Col 68. 12: Assoc ed "Alumnus" Boston State Col. 14: Sch libs. 15: 7 Clapp st, Milton Ma 02186.

SHEARER, DAVID HR. b Buffalo NY 13 Ap 27. 4: Halcyon Burroughs. 5: Rutgers 44-45; Swarthmore 48-51 (Hist) BA; UBuffalo 54-56; UMich 56-57 MLS. 6: Fr. 7: T/3 troop info US Army, US & Italy 45-47; Chef Studio Restaurant & Four Seasons Club, Aspen Colo 51-52; Spray painter Fisher-Price Toy Co, E Aurora NY 53-54; Lib intern Free Lib of Phila 57-58, Asst to chief admin serv 58-60; Libn Fine Arts Lib CornellU 60-. 8: Consul bldg expansion, Port Jefferson Free Lib, Port Jefferson NY 64; Consul, Arch and City Planning Collection devel, Universidad del Valle, Cali Colombia 65. 9: Coun Planning Libns (pres 63-65). 10: Beta Phi Mu. 12: Film: "The Uses of The Library" (67); Film: "New Perspectives in the Study of Art" (68). 13: Yes. 14: A-v materials in the humanities. 15: 102 Turkey Hill rd, Ithaca NY 14850.

SHEARER, KENNETH DECKER JR. b Far Rockaway NY 9 Jl 37. 4: Ann Martin. 5: Amherst 55-59 (Math) AB, Rutgers 62-63 MLS, 63-69 (LS) PhD. 7: Page Peninsula Pub Lib, Lawrence LI NY 53-55, Clerk summers 55-60, Clerk-libn 60; (Pvt) Nat Guard Army 60-61; Asst dir Wachusetts Meadow Wildlife Sanctuary, Princeton Mass summer 61; Bkmob libn Peninsula Pub Lib, Lawrence LI NY 61-62; Researcher Detroit Pub Lib 64-65, Bksel libn 65-67, Asst chief br lib 67-68; Lectr UNC(Chapel Hill) 68-. 9: ALA. ; AALS; NCLA. 10: Beta Phi Mu. 14: Bk sel, reading patterns, admin, lib educ, research, systs approach to libs. 15: 607 Park pl, Chapel Hill NC 27514.

SHEARHOUSE, LYNN (JERRI). b Lakeland Fla 7 N 38. 5: Fla StateU 56-60 (Soc Sci) BS; Emory 67-68 MLibnship. 7: Research asst Foote, Cone & Belding Advertising Agcy, Chicago 60-61; Tchr Atlantic Pub Sch Syst 61-63; Tchr USAF, Lakenheath England 63-64, 65-66; Libn USAF, Beize Norton England 64-65; US Army, Lakenheath England: Libn 66-67, Hd libn 68-. 9: SchLA (England); NEA. 14: Sch libs. 15: Old School House Tuddenham Bury st, Edmunds Suffolk England.

SHEARIN, ROBERTA (BROOKS). b Wash DC 2 O 24. 4: William Gaston Shearin. 5: Spelman Col 40-42; J C Smith U 42-44 (Fr, Eng) AB; Atlanta 44-45 BSLS. 6: Fr. 7: Asst libn Talladega Col 45-47; Lib asst Army Lib, Pentagon Wash DC 51-55, Ref libn 55-67; Act chief periods 67-. 9: DCLA. 10: Delta Sigma Theta; Girl Scouts. 14: Ref. 15: 1461 Momroe st NW, Wash DC 20010.

SHEARMAN, JOHN (LEIGH STEWART). b Montreal Que Can 9 D 26. 4: (Edith) Helen (Thornton) Lamb. 5: Sir George Williams 44-47 BA; McGill 47-50 BD; UToronto 65-66 BLS. 6: Fr. 7: Minister United Ch of Can 50-61, Field sec for Christian educ, Montreal 61-64; Specialist libn for syst research Ont Inst for Studies in Educ, Toronto Can 66-. 9: ASIS. 14: Info sci, systems res. 15: 2515 Renzoni rd, Clarkson Ont Can.

SHEAROUSE, HENRY G(RADY)JR. b Sardis Ga 2 My 24. 5: Emory 45-47 BS in LS; UIll 48-49 MS in LS; Ga Tchrs Col 41-45 BS in Ed. 7: Ref asst Savannah Pub Lib, Savannah Ga 46-48; Head ref dept Atlanta Pub Lib 49-53; Dir Terrell-Calhoun Reg Lib, DAWSON Ga 53-54; Dir Tift Co Lib, Tifton Ga 54-55; Dir Watertown Reg Lib Serv Center, Watertown NY 55-56; Assoc lib supv NY State Lib 56-63; Asst libn Denver Pub Lib 63-. 9: ALA; ColoLA; MPLA. 13: Yes. 14: Ref, admin, bk sel. 15: 1285 Glencoe st, Denver 80220.

SHEDD, CAROL (JOHNSON). b NYC 24 D 29. 4: Edmund F Shedd. 5: Hunter Col 47-51 (Eng Lit) BA; OxfordU summer 56 (Eng Lit) Certif; Simmons 66-68 MLS. 7: Elem sch tchr USAF Dependent Schs, England 51-57; Libn Needham Pub Sch, Mass 67-68; Hd libn Bacon free Lib, S Natick Mass 69-. 8: Lib adv New Sch for Child, Roxbury Mass. 9: NEA; ALA; MassSchLA; MassLA; NERT child libns. 10: PTA; Nat Human Rights Coun. 14/ child serv. 15: 7 Wilson st, Natick Ma 01760.

SHEEHAN, DAVID THOMAS. b Boston 6 N 30. 4: Mary Curado. 5: Boston Col 48-52, 54-57 (Soc Sci) BS; Simmons 57-60 (LS) MS. 7: Asst Boston Pub Lib 47-52; US Army (Cpl) 52-54; Asst Boston Pub Lib 54-57, Ref asst 57-62; dir Westwood Pub Lib, Westwood Mass 62-. 9: MassLA (Exhib Chm 63-68); NELA. 15: 30 Maple st, W Roxbury Ma 02132.

SHEEHAN, FLORENCE MAUREEN. b Williston ND 24 My 09. 5: UIll 57 Fr) BA, 59 (LS) MS. 6: Fr, Sp, Ger. 7: Court reporter Self-Employed, Chicago 29-52; Catlgr UIll (Urbana) Lib 52-. 10: Phi Beta Kappa. 14: Law catlg. 15: 509 S 5th st, Champaign Il 61820.

SHEEHAN, GENEVIEVE (CALLAHAN). b Saratoga Springs NY 9 Mr 18. 4: John F Sheehan. 5: CornellU 36-40 (Home Econ) BS; Syracuse 67 MSLS. 7: Trainee Liverpool Pub Lib, Liverpool NY 65-67, Ref libn 67-. 14: Ref. 15: Liverpool Pub Library, Liverpool NY 13088.

SHEEHAN, SISTER HELEN. b Manchester NH 25 J104. 5: Trinity Col 20-24 (Eng, Math) BA; Simmons 25-26 (LS) BS. 6: Fr, Ger, Sp, Lat. 7: Reporter Manchester Mirror, Manchester NH 24-25; Br libn City Lib, Manchester NY 26-30; Libn Cathedral Lib, Manchester NH 30-31; Tchr-libn New Eng High Schs 31-34; Libn Trinity Col (Wash DC) 34-. 8: Mem several Middle States Evalteams; Consul, col & high sch libs; Chm Wkshop on Small Col Lib, Phila 65. 9: ALA-ACRL; CathLA (Exec Bd 59-65, chm Wash DC Unit 47-48, v-pres 67-69, pres 69-71). 10: Trustee, Trinity Col.11: ACRL-US Steel gran, 56. 12: Jt auth "History of the City Library, Manchester NH (29); "The Small College Library (63), Ed Bd "Choice (65-); Ed Bd "CULS (63-65); Ed Bd "Library College Journal" (67). 13. Yes. 14: Admin, bldgs. 15: Trinity Col Lib, Wash DC 20017.

SHEEHAN, KATHRYN MARY. b Chicago 26 Jl 20. 5: Clark Col 39-40; Rosary Col 40-43 (LS) BA. 6: Fr. 7: Asst libn Nat Safety Coun, Chicago 43-44; Asst libn Wright Jr Col 44-45; Libn Griffenhagen & Assocs, Chicago 45-46; Asst ref libn Field Enterprises Inc, Chicago 46-48; Asst catlgr Northwestern U 48-50; Sales Sears Real Estate Co, Winnetka Ill 50-56; Libn Rotary Internat, Evanston Ill 56-61; Libn Pure Oil Co, Palatine Ill 61-64; Bus libn Internat Minerals & Chem Corp, Skokie Ill 64-67; Hd catlg dept Evanston Pub Lib, Evanston Ill 67-69; Coord libn AT Kearney Co Inc, Chicago 69-. 9: SLA (Publ Program Com 66-68; Ill Chap: Educ Com 63-64, chm Pub Rel Com 64-65, mem Program Com 65-66). 10: Chicago Coun on For Rel. 13: Yes. 14: Catlg, ref, indexing, admin, catlg. 15: 2762 Hampton pky, Evanston Ill 60201.

SHEEHAN, MERCEDES. b McKeesport Penn 9 S 20. 5: Duquesne 38-42 (Secondary Educ) BEd; Carnegie-Mellon U 50-51 MLS; UPittsburgh 66 (LS); West Res 66 (LS). 6: Fr. 7: Tchr fayette Twp, Sturgeon Penn 42-43; Ind eng clk Nat Tube Co, McKeesport Penn 44-48; Libn McKeesport Sch Dist, McKeesport Penn 51-67; Libn Quaker Valley Sch Dist, Sewickley Penn 67-. 9: ALA; NEA; CathLA. PennLA; PennEA; Suburban Coun Libns. 14: Sch libs. 15: 237 Walnut st apt 9, Sewickley Pa 15143.

SHEEHAN, ROBERT CHARLES. b Pittsburgh. 5: Duquesne U 48-52 (Eng) BPED, Carnegie 53 MLS. 6: Sp. 7: Page Carnegie Lib of Pittsburgh 46-52, Period clerk 52, Ref trainee 52-53; Libn NY Pub Lib 53; US Army Chem (Cpl) 53-55; Army Libs libn 53-54; Sr libn NY Pub Lib, NYC 57-60, Readers adv 61-67; Prin libn soc sci & hist Mid-Manhattan Lib, NYC 67-. 9: NY Lib Club. 13: Yes. 14: Readers adv serv, adult circ, ref. 15: 400 Central Park w apt 11D, New York NY 10025.

SHEEHY, EUGENE PAUL. b Elbow Lake Minn 10 O 22. 5: St John'sU (Minn) 47-50 (Eng) BA; UMinn 50-51 (Eng) MA, 51-52 BS in LS. 6: Fr. 7: Sgt US Marine Corps 42-46; Ref libn georgetownU 52-53; Ref asst ColumbiaU 53-65, Hd ref dept 65-. 9: ALA. 12: Co-comp "Joseph Conrad at Mid-Century" (57); "The Achievement of Marianne Moore" (58); "Yvor winters; a Bibliography" (59); "Frank Norris; a Bibliography" (59); "Sherwood Anderson; a Bibliography" (60); "Index to the 'Little Review' " (61); "Index to Little Magazines, 1953-63"; Ed "Guide to Reference Books, Supplement I" (68). 13: Yes. 14: Ref. 15: 185 West End ave, New York NY 10023.

SHEETS, JANET ELIZABETH. b Winston Salem NC 25 Ja 43. 5: William & Mary 61-65 (Ancient Lang) AB; UNC 65-67 MS in LS. 7: Libn Free Lib of Phila 67-68; Ref libn DukeU 68-. 10: Phi Beta Kappa; Beta Phi Mu. 15: Apt 15 501 Dupont dr, Durham NC 27705.

SHEETS, MARIAN L. b Durango Colo. 5: UColo 27-31, 32-34 (Ger) BA, 36 MA; Heidelberg U (Germany) 34-35; Columbia 35-36; UCal (Berkeley) 42-43 (LS) Certif. 6; Ger, Fr. 7: Tchr McPherson Col 36-37; Travel agent Ask Mr Foster Travel Serv 37-40; Libn Denver Art Museum 41-42, 44-48; Libn UUtah 48-. 9: ALA; UtahLA. 10: Phi Beta Kappa. 14: Middle East collections. 15: Mid E Lib Univ of Utah Libraries, Salt Lake City Ut 84112.

SHEETS, SHIRLEY (CAROLE HOYT). b Fort Worth Tex 1 D 34. 4: John E Sheets. 5: N Texas State U 52-55 (LS) BA, 67- (LS); Tex Woman's U 57-59 (LS). 7: Asst catlgr N Tex State U 55-62; Catlgr Tex Wesleyan Col 62-63; Catlgr U Tex (Arlington) 63-67, Hd catlgr 67-. 9: ALA; TexLA. 10: Sigma Alpha Iota. 14: Catlg, lib educ, lib hist. 15: 1604 W Lovers lane, Arlington Tx 76010.

SHEFF, ALMA (ELLIS). b Lakewood Dist Denver 29 Ja 27. 4: George R Sheff. 5: Western State Col 45-49 (LS) BA; Pacific Sch of Religion summer 47; UDenver 48-49 (LS) Diploma, 66-69 MA in LS. 6: Sp. 7: Train sch libn Morehead State Col 49-50; Asst libn Friends U 51-53; Asst libn VA Hosp, Kerrville Tex 53-59; Admin asst & catlgr Colo Springs Pub Lib, Colo Springs Colo 59-61; Adult serv Pikes Peak Reg Dist Lib, Colo Springs Colo 61-; Plains & Peaks Pub Lib Syst 66-68. 9: ALA; ColoLA (Nomin Com 64, Panel mem 1962 Conv); Pikes Peak Area Libns (co-org 63). 10: AAUW; Friends of the Lib. 14: Ref. 15: 3840 Linda Vista lane, Colorado Springs Colo 80907.

SHEFFIELD, CHARLIESE (PENDARVIS) (MRS). b Orangeburg SC 30 Mr 08. 5: Claflin Col 26-30 (Educ) AB; Hampton Inst summer 32, & 33-34 BSLS; Columbia summer 47 (Educ); Drexel summer 64 (European Lib Study Tour). 6: Fr. 7: Tchr pub sch, Columbia SC 30-31; Tchr pub sch, Orangeburg SC 31-33; SC State Col: Act libn 34-35, Asst libn 35-47, Catlgr 47-53; Libn Wilkinson Jr High Sch, Orangeburg SC 53-56; Chief catlgr SC State Col 56-62, Agric libn 62-69; Asst libn 69-. 8: Sponsor SC State Dept of Educ Summer Wkshop Hampton Inst Lib Sch 32. 9: ALA-ACRL; SCLA; SELA. 10: Delta Sigma Theta; Nat Assn of Col Women; Sunlight Commun Club. 11: Criterion Club Woman of the Year, 67. 12: "A Behind the Desk of World Famous Libraries. 14: Life scis, research, spec collections, bibliog. 15: 188 Watson, Orangeburg SC 29115.

SHEFFIELD, HELEN P (PETERSON). b Cardston Alberta Can 29 S 12. 4: Wayne K Sheffield. 5: UUtah 30-32, 52-54 Libn's certif; Brigham Young 32-36 (Sociol) BS. 7: Davis Co Sch Dist: Tchr Kaysville Elem 34-36, Tchr Farmington Elem 52-53, Libn Central Davis Jr high 54-63, Libn Davis High Sch 63-65; Lib supv Davis Sch Dist Central Off 65-. 9: ALA; UtahLA. 10: AAUW; Delta Kappa Gamma. 14: Bringing people and materials together. 15: 242 W 2nd South, Kaysville Ut 84037.

SHEFTEL, . ALICE (NAISTAT). b Hdson NY 15 J111. 4: Harry B Sheftel. 5: Simmons 28-32 (LS) BS. 6: Fr, Ger. 7: Asst researcher Haskin Serv, Wash DC 36; Asst mem br Boston Pub Lib 37-39; Asst catlg dept US Nat Archives, Wash DC 39-41; Lib asst acquis George Washington U Lib 60-66, Act libn 66, Asst dir 67-. 9: ALA; DCLA. 10 LWV; Simmons Col Col Club. 14: Acquis. 15: 5813 Third pl NW. Wash DC 20011.

SHEINGOLD, SYLVIA K(RIEGEL). b NYC 30 Ap 15. 4: Abraham Sheingold. 5: Hunter Col 32-36 (Eng) BA; San Jose State Col 61-68 (LS) BA. 6: Fr. 7: Lib asst Carmel Unified Sch Dist, Carmel Col 55-64, Tchr 64-67; Libn US Naval Postgrad Sch, Monterey Cal 69-. 14: Ref. 15: Rte 3 Box 136, Carmel Ca 93921.

SHELBY, ANN AUGUSTA (ESBENSHADE). b Lebanon Penn 9 Ag 11. 4: Dwight W Shelby. 5: Lebanon Valley Col 28-32 (Fr) AB; Drexel 34-35 BS in LS; UPenn 46-48 (Clinical Psych) MA, 48-60 (Clinical Psych)PhD. 6: Fr, Ger. 7: Libn Ogontz Sch, Ogontz School Penn 35-36; Lib asst Passaic Pub Lib, Passaic NJ 36-37; Ref & circ libn Yale Divinity Sch 37-46; Ref asst UPenn Lib 46-48, Catlgr & clsfr 48-50, 52-61; Catlgr Penn State Lib 63-. 9: Phila Area Tech Serv Libns (sec58-59). 10: . 11: USPHS stipend for wk toward PhD. 14: Catlg, clsf, subj headings. 15: 138 N 33rd st, Camp Hill Penn 17011.

SHELDON, BROOKE (EARLE). b Lawrence Mass 29 Ag 31. 4: George D Sheldon. 5: Acadia 48-52 (Eng, Econ) BA; Simmons 53-54 MS in LS; Radcliffe summer 52 (Publ). 6: Fr. 7: Promotion asst Atlantic Monthly (bk club), Boston 52-53; Y-a ya libn Detroit Pub Lib 54-55; Base libn Ent AFB, Colo Springs Colo 55-56; Spec serv libn US Army, Germany 57; Br libn Albuquerque Pub Lib 59-61; Co-ord adult serv Santa Fe Pub Lib, Santa Fe NM 63-66; Child consul NM State Lib, Santa Fe 66-67, Hd pub lib development 67-. 9: ALA (chm Lib Serv to Disabled Child Com 70-72); SWLA (sec Pub Libn Div 66-68); NMLA (sec 67-68). 10: NM Adult Basic Educ Adv Bd; Santa Fe Commun Coun. 14: Pub Lib admin, sch lib ext, adult educ, child & ya serv. 15: 301 Pinos Verdes, Santa Fe NM 87501.

SHELDON, JAMES ELLIS. b Hubbard County Minn 15 S 37. 4: Maxine Helen Guida. 5: Bethel Col 54-59 (Art Educ) BA; UMinn summer 60 Lib certif; St Cloud State Col summers 61-62. 7: Stock boy Red Owl Inc, Park Rapids Minn 51-54; Stud libn Bethel Col (St Paul) 54-59; Study hall supv Minnehaha Acad, Minneapolis 58-59; Sch libn Ivanhoe Schs, Ivanhoe Minn 59-66; Camp coun Camp Arrowhead, Deerwood Minn summer 56-59; Catlg libn Bethel Col, (St Paul) 66-. 8: Curr lib consul, Bethel Col. 10: Model A Ford Club of Amer; Model A Restorers' Club; Foster Home Care of Ramsey Co Minn. 14: Tech proc. 15: Bethel Col Lib 1480 N Snelling ave, St Paul Mn 55101.

SHELDON, MARIE ANNE (GRANDE). b NYC 12 J129. 4: Edwin J Sheldon Sr. 6: Ital, Sp. 7: Steno Schuster & Davenport Attys, NYC 47-48; Sec Turner Halsey Export Co, NYC 48-49; Clerk, typist Med Lib USPHS Hosp, SI NY 56-59, Lib asst Med Lib 59-, Lib tech Med Lib. 9: ALA-AHIL. 14: Ref, bibliog. 15: 132 Guyon ave, SI NY 10306.

SHELL, ELTON EUGENE. b Woodland Cal 10 Mr 21. 4: Phyllis Hughes. 5: URedlands 39-43 (Sociol) AB; San Francisco Theol Sem 43-46 (Theo) BD; UDenver 49-51 (LS) MA; Rutgers 61-64 MLS; Claremont Grad Sch 64-65 Jr Col Tchg Credential. 7: Minister Tomales Presbyt Church, Tomales Cal 45-50; Asst libn San Francisco Theol Sem 49-53; Religion libn USoCal 53-56; Head libn SCal Sch of Theol 56-63; Head libn San Bernardino Valley Col 64-. 9: ATheolLA; CalLA. 10: Beta Phi Mu. 12: "Marins Historic Tomales and Presbyterian Church" (49); "Organize Your Library; a Manual for Home, Pastors Study, or Church" (55). 13: Yes. 14: Admin, tchg lib sci. 15: 701 S Mt Vernon ave, San Bernardion Cal 92403.

SHELLEM, JOHN J (REV). b Phila 11 Ap 26. 5: St Charles Sem 43-47 (Philos) BA; Villanova Col 47-49 BLS; St Charles charles Sem 50-52 (Sociol) MA; Villanova U 59-61 (Educ, LS) MS; UTenn 67 (LS). 6: Lat, Fr, Ger. 7: Asst Pastor Mary Queen of Peace Church, Pottsville Penn 52-53; Asst Pastor Sts Simon & Jude Church, Bethlehem Penn 52-54; Asst Paster Most Precious Blood Church, Phila 54-57; Tchr Cardinal Dougherty High Sch, Phila 57-63, Asst libn 57-63; Lecturer Villanova U 64-; Libn Cardinal Ohara High Sch, Springfield Penn 63-67; Libn St Charles Sem, Phila 67-. 8: Adv Coms; Archdiocesan High Sch Lib Co, WCAU-TV Television Reading Serv, Phila Free Lib Relig Bks List Com. 9: Amer Cath Hist Soc (chm Lib Com); CathLA (East Penn Unit: chm High Sch Sect); PennLA, ALA; Lib Pub Rel Assn (treas); Tri-State Col Lib Coop; SEast Penn SemLA. 12: Asst ed "Dimension; journal of Pastoral Concern. 13: Yes. 14: Ya bk sel, lib arch & design. , rare bks. 15: St Charles Seminary, Overbrook Philadelphia Pa 19151.

SHELLENBERGER, EUNICE MARIE (NUHNS). b Harper Kan 26 J112. 4: Wallace A Shellenberger. 5: Colo Col of Educ 33-35; Goshen Col 61-62 (Elem Educ) BS; West Mich U 64-65

(LS) MA. 6: Sp. 7: Elem tchr pub schs, Colo 30-36; Eng-lib Jefferson Sch, Goshen Ind 62-64; Elem tchr Concord Sch, Elkhart Ind 64-65; Libn Concord Jr High Sch, Elkhart Ind 65-. 9: NEA; ALA; Ind State Tchrs Assn; Ind SchLA; Ind Clr Tchrs Assn. 12: "Wings of Decision Fiction (51). 14: Sch ref serv. 15: 916 College ave, Goshen Ind 46526.

SHELLENBERGER, MARY H. b ancaster Penn 16 Je 23. 4: Charles A Shellenberger. 5: Millersville State Col 41-45 & summer 57 (LS, Eng) BS Secondary Ed. 6: Fr. 7: Libn New Brighton High Sch, New Brighton Penn 45-46; Libn & Eng tchr New Cumberland High Sch, New Cumberland Penn 46-47; Libn & Eng tchr Lancaster Twp Jr High Sch, Lancaster Penn 47-48; Head libn Penn Manor High Sch, Millersville Penn 57-. 8: Pu Lib Serv Survey Com, Lancaster Co (Penn), 63; Middle States Ass of Col & Secondary Sch Evaluation Com 68. 9: ALA; NEA; PennLA; Penn State E; Lancaster Co LA. 10: Alpha Beta Alpha; Nat Cong Parents & Tchrs; Penn Soc of Farm Women. 14: Ref, reading guidance. 15: Prospect rd, Rt 2, Columbia Penn 17512.

SHELLEY, LEO (EUGENE). b SNYDER Co Penn 26 F 42. 5: Millersville State Col 60-64 (LS) BS; San Francisco State Col 64-; UPittsburgh 68-. 7: Peace Corps Circ Libn Cottington Col Monrovia Liberia W Africa 65-67; Govt doc, period bind, Millersville SC. 9: ALA; NEA; Penn State EA; PennLA; Lancaster LA. 14: Circ, govt doc, bindery. 15: Box 192, Mifflin Penn 17058.

SHELTON, BESSIE E. b Lynchburg Va. 5: Northwestern 53-55 (Liberal Arts); Ind U 56 (Liberal Arts); WVa State Col 56-58 (Fr, Span, Music) BA; State U Col of Educ (NY) 59-60 MS in Lib Ed; Columbia 65-66 (Radio Announcing) Certif; UVa 68-. 6: Fr, Sp. 7: Personnel clerk WAVES US Naval Train Cente, Great Lakes Ill 51-55; Reader - tutor for blind WVa State Rehabilitation, Charleston WVa 57-58; Sub tchr Bd of Educ, Lynchburg Va 58-59; Young teens libn Brooklyn Pub Lib 60-62; Asst head Central ref div Queens Borough Pu Lib, Jamaica NY 62-65; Libn Bd of Educ, Lynchburg Va 66-. 8: Bd of Educ, Lynchburg Va; A-v rep 66-, Instr media specialist. 9: Mus LA; NYLA; NEA (Dept For Langs);-DAVI; VaLA (Dept Sch Libns). 10: Queens Borough Pub Lib Staff Assn; Brooklyn Philharmonic Choral Soc; Music Lovers League; YWCA; Girl SCOUTS: Volunteers of the Shelters Inc; Soc for Bus Collegiates & Professionals; Pi Delta Phi; Sigma Delta Pi; LynchburgEA; Advocates Intl Trade & Comity; World Field Research; World Tapes for Educ; Intl Entertainers Guild; Happenings Intl; Lynchburg Fine Arts Ctr. 14: Ref, fine arts, a-v, music, biog, instr media. 15: 338 Chambers st, Lynchburg Va 24501.

SHELTON, HARRIETTE W(OODWARD). b Pittsfield Mass 5 My 12. 5: Penn State U 30-35 (Langs) AB; Columbia 36-37 BS IN LS. 6: Fr, Ger. 7: Asst libn Jackson Lab E I DuPont de Nemours & Co 37-44; Libn devel div Curtiss-Wright Corp, Bloomfield NJ 44-45; Chief Foreign Documents Br Wright Field, Dayton Ohio 45-46; Ref asst Temple U Lib 46-47; Libn Wyandotte Chem Corp, Wyandotte Mich 47-48; Chem libn Cornell U Lib 48-49; Chief catlgr Health Sci Lib UMd 53-57; Libn UBaltimore 57-68; Tech serv libn Catonsville Commun Col 68-. 8: Instr Lib Tech Program Catonsville Commun Col 68-69; Mem Lib Study Com Md Coun on Higher Educ 68-. 9: ALA; MdLA; Potomac Tech Proc Libns; Md Assn Jr Col. 13: Yes. 14: Tech serv. 15: 4643 Manordene rd, Baltimore Md 21229.

SHELTON, HELEN H(IGGINS). b Roselle Park NJ 7 Mr 16. 4: William C Shelton. 5: Douglas Col 33-37 (Eng) AB; NYU 38; Fla State U 56-61 (LS) MA. 6: Fr, Ger, Sp. 7: Sec USRO, Paris 54-55; Sec Fla State U 56-58; Bkmob libn LEON Co Pub Lib, Tallahassee Fla 58-60; Montgomery Co Dept of Lib,Bethesda Md: Child libn 61, Ya libn 61-62, Asst reg libn 62-65; Asst coordinator child serv Prince Georges Co Mem Lib, Hyattsville Md 65-. 9: ALA; MdLA (Ed Bd); DCLA. 10: Beta Phi Mu. 14: Bk sel, bk reviewing. 15: 8401 Piney Branh rd, Silver Spring Md 20901.

SHELVER, ELIZABETH. b Sheldon ND 1 D 30. 5: Carleton Col 49-53 (Music Educ) BA; UMinn 58-61 (LS) MA. 7: Music tchr Pipestone Pub Schs, Pipestone Minn 53-57; Prof asst Minneapolis Pub Lib 58-, Personnel specialist 66-. 9: ALA; MinnLA. 10: Beta Phi Mu. 14: Personnel. 15: 6410 37th ave N, Minneapolis 55427.

SHEMORRY, MARY CATHERINE. b Selinsgrove Penn 28 Je 02. 5: UMinn 21-25 (Eng) BA; UWis 26-27 (LS) Certif; Columbia 38-39 Curriculum MA. 6: Norwegian. 7: Asst libn Minot State Tchrs Col 25-26; 1st asst lit dept Milwaukee Pub Lib 27-29; Libn Shorewood High Sch, Shorewood Wis 29-67; Libn UND Williston Ctr 68-69. 9: NEA; ALA; WisEA; WisLA. ; NDakLA. 10: Wis Reg Writers Assn. 14: High sch wk, catlg, admin. 15: P O Box 407, Williston ND 58801.

SHEN, CHUNG-TAI. b Republic of China 3 Mr 32. 4: Fei Chen. 5: Taiwan Normal U 51-56 (Eng) BA; Atlanta U 65-67 MSLS. 6: Chinese, Fr. 7: Lib asst Yale Departmental Lib of Pub Health 64-65; Catlgr Mead Pub Lib Sheboygan Wis 67; Chinese catlgr LC 67-. 9: ALA. 10: Beta Phi Mu. 14: Catlg, ref. 15: 319-3rd st SE apt 1, Washington DC 20003.

SHENK, ESTHER. b Annville Penn 14Je 05. 5: Lebanon Valley Col 22-26 (Hist) AB; Syracuse U summer 48-50 & 51 MSLS; U Penn 28-29 (Eng); UWis summer 39 (Eng); UColo summer 40 (Journalism). 7: Circ libn Lebanon Valley Col 44-51; Head of circ Pub Lib, Decatur Ill 51-54; Libn: Pub Lib, Hazleton Penn 54-58, S Central Reg Lib, Holdrege Neb 58-63, Pub Lib, Charles City Iowa 63-65; Asst libn Pub Lib, Hastings Neb 65-66; Bkmob libn Willa Cather Reg Lib, Hastings Neb 66-. 9: ALA. 10: AAUW; Hazleton Penn Art League. 12: Assoc ed "Encyclopedia of Pennsylvania" (32). 13: Yes. 14: Ref, publicity, pub rel. 15: 717 N Lincoln ave, Hastings Neb 68901.

SHENK, VIRGINIA ANN. b Harrisonburg Va 17 O 38. 5: East Mennonite Col 58-62 (Hist) BA; Madison Col 62-63 (LS; Peabody 63-64 (LS) MA. 7: Asst libn Atlantic Christian Col 64-68; Asst libn Bridgewater Col 68-. 14: Catlg. 15: 1013 College ave Park View, Harrisonburg Va 22801.

SHEPARD MARIETTA (DANIELS). b Kan City Mo 24 Ja 13. 4: James J Shepard Jr. 5: UKan 31-33, 34 (Span) AB; Washington U (St Louis) 39-45 (Romance Lang) MA; Columbia 39-43 BSLS. 6: Sp, Fr, Portu. 7: Order asst Kan City (Mo) Pub Lib 34-38; Chief of circ Washington U Lib (St Louis) 38-43; Dir of Lib, Prof Lib Sci Normal Sch (Santiago Panama) 43-46; Spec asst to libn LC 46-48; Consul reorg lib Sociedad Econ Amigos del Pas, Havana Cuba 48; Assoc libn Pan Amer Union, Wash DC 48-68, Chief lib development program 69-. 8: Prof of lib sci, Quito Ecuador 44; Prof of lib sci, Panama summers 49-50; Consul, Inter-Amer Inst Agric Sci, Costa Rica 50;sec-gen, Reunin Tcnica de Bibliotecarios Agrola, Costa Rica 53 Tchr Grad Sch US Dept of Agric, 50-52; Asst doc off Tenth Inter-Amer Conf, Caracas 54 & Doc off, 3rd Inter-Amer Cultural Coun 5; Consul to Univ Santo Domingo & Consul, Univ of Central Amer 65, pres, Internat Exch Coun, Inter-Amer Lib Sch, Colombia 58-; Sec, Seminars on the Acquis of Latin-Amer Lib Materials, 57-. 9: ALA (Exec Bd 68-, coun 56-57, 60-64 & 66-, mem UNESCO Panel 58-)-RTSD; Bd 63-65 -Internal Rel Round Table (chm 49-50) mem of other ALA & Div Coms 34-; DCLA (pres 57-58). 10: Chm bks for the People Fund; Beta Phi Mu; Altrusa Internat; Pan-Amer Liaison Com Womens Org. 11: ALA Letter Award (54); Sociedad Colombiana Panamericana Award 48. 12: "La biblioteca pblica en Amrica (51); "Estudios y conocimientos en accin (59); "Public and School LIBRARIES" (63). 13: Yes. 14: Internt rel, nat lib devel, admin, acquis. 15: 3025 Ontario rd NW, Wash DC 20009.

SHEPARD, ELIZABETH. b Pittsburgh 6 N 15. 5: Winthrop Col 35-39 (Eng, Hist) AB; Emory 40-41 BALS; Columbia summer 45 (LS). 6: Fr. 7: Tchr-libn Lyons High Sch, Lyons Ga 39-40; Asst catlgr Womans Col Lib Duke U 41-43, 45-46; Catlgr Randolph-Macon Womans Col 43-45; Med libn VA Hosp, Swannanda NC 46-49; Catlgr, ref asst Charlotte Pub Lib, Charlotte NC 49-52; Libn Brevard Col 52-56; Catlgr Lawson McGhee Lib, Knoxville Tenn 56-57; Ref libn Sondley Lib Li Pack Mem Pub Lib, Asheville NC ; Asst catlgr, Asst libn for readers serv, Acquis libn Julia Rogers Lib Goucher Col 61-67; Catlgr Warren Wilson Col 68-. 14: Catlg, ref. 15: 201 Hawthorn ave, Swannanoa NC 28778.

SHEPARD, MARTHA. b Toronto Can 12 D 11. 5: Queen'sU 31-35 (Eng, Hist) BA; UToronto 36 BLS. 6: Fr. 7: Ref libn Toronto Pub Lib, Toronto Can 36-50; Dir ref br Nat Lib, Ottawa Can 50-. 9: ALA; CanLA, (pres-elect 69-70, pres 70-71); OntLA; Inst Profess Libns Ont. 10: Rivermead Golf Club; Colour Photo Assn Canada. 13: Yes. 14: Ref, admin. 15: Ref Branch National Lib, Ottawa Ont Can.

SHEPARD, STANLEY A. b Elizabeth NJ 8 S 19. 4: Elisabeth Kilthau. 5: Rutgers 39-47 (Hist) BA, 47-48 (Educ) BS; Columbia 49-51 (LS) MS. 7: Radio operator (S/Sgt) Army Air Force, ETO & US 42-46; Spec collections clerk Rutgers U 49-51; Documents libn & catlgr UIda 51-54; Asst acquis libn UKan 54-56; Acquis libn Colgate U 56-61; Asst libn tech serv UIda 61-, Asst dir 68-. 9: PNLA; IndLA. 10: Friends of Music; Chorus; Boy Scout; Councilman. 14: Acquis, rare bks, loc hist materials. 15: 1301 Walenta dr, Moscow Ida 83843.

SHEPAROVYCH, ZENON. b Lviv-Ukraine 13 Ag 24. 4: Irene Hnatiw. 5: Ludwik Maximilian U (Germany) 47-49 (Natural Sci) Diploma; Kent State U 57-60 (Bus Admin) BBA; West Res 61-62 MSLS. 6: Ger,Russian, Polish, Ukrainian. 7: Cost acct DZUS Fastener Co, W Islip NY 60-61; Ref lib for bus admin URochester 62-64, Head Bus Lib 64-66; Assoc dir lib SUNY (Geneseo) 66-68; Dir of Lib Essex Co Col (NJ) 68-. 8: Asst Welfare Off for Bavaria, UN Internat Refugee Org 49-51. 9: ALA; SLA. 10: Beta Phi Mu. 12: "Quantitative Methods in Marketing(68). 14: Lib admin, mechanized data proc, av media. 15: 62 B Lakeside dr, Millburn NJ 07041.

SHEPHARD, DOROTHY (PARRISH). b Oakland Miss 20 D 12. 4: Charles P Shephard. 5: Miss State Col for Women 19-33 (Eng) BA; UIll 37-38 BS in LS, 39-41 (LS) MA. 7: Tchr Enid Consolidated Sch, Enid Mass 33-37; Asst in lib sci UIll Lib Sch (Urbana) summer 38, 39-41, Ref asst 41-45; Catlg & circ asst DePauwU Lib 38-39; Ref asst Army Lib, Wash DC 45-48, Asst chief gen ref sect 48-49, Chief gen ref sect 49-50, chief ref br 50-55; Ref libn Fairfax Co Pub Lib George Mason Br, Annandale Va 67-. 9: VaLA. 10: Beta Phi mu. 12: Ed "Chapter Notes", Wash DC Chap SLA 51-52. 14: Ref. 15: 6821 Winter lane, Annandale Va 22003.

SHEPHERD, ANTOINETTE. b Galveston Tex 19 O 43. 5: Our Lady of the Lake Col 61-65 (LS) BA. 6: Fr. 7: Lib asst Our Lady of the Lake Col 64-65; Lib asst Daughters of Republic of Tex at the Alamo Lib, San Antonio 64-65; Circ libn UTex Med Br (Galveston Tex) 65-. 9: MedLA; TexLA; TexTA. 10: Alpha Beta Alpha; Womans Club UTex. 14: Circ, ref. 15: 1912 - 54th st, Galveston Tex 77552.

SHEPHERD, BEATRICE (WILSON). b Lynn Mass 13 N 21. 4: Harry B Shepherd. 5: Bates Col 38-39; Radcliffe Col 39-42 (Psych) AB (cum laude); Simmons 64-67 MLS. 7: Ref libn Lynnfield Pub Lib, Lynnfield Mass 65-66; Ref y-a mus libn Mem Hall Lib, Andover Mass 67-. 9: ALA. 10: LWV. 14: Ref, music, y-a. 15: 14 Saunders rd, Lynnfield Ma 01940.

SHEPHERD, CLAYTON A. b Wash DC 16 My 29. 4: Louise T. 5: UMd 52 (Eng) AB, 56 (Sociol) MA; UPenn 58 (Sociol). 6: Ger. 7: Air police off USAF, Greenville SC 53; Instr UPenn Sociol Dept 56-59; Syst analyst Univac Div Sperry Rand, Wash DC 58-61, Mgr info retrieval 61-63; Asst dir info serv Amer Soc for Metals, Ohio 63-67; Assoc Prof IndU Grad Lib Sch (Bloomington) 67-. 9: Assn Comp Mach; ASIS; ALA; -ACRL. 10: AAUP. 13: Yes. 14: Info sci. 15: Graduate Lib School Indiana Univ, Bloomington In 47401.

SHEPHERD, FREEMONT (GILES) JR. b Burlington NC 21 N 12. 4: Margaret Lasley. 5: UNC 30-34 (Eng) AB; Columbia summer 35 (Spec Educ); UNC 34-36 ABLS, 39-42 (Hist; UIll summers 38, 40-42 (LS) MA. 6: Fr, Ger. 7: Asst Burlington Pub Lib, Burlington NC 28-30; Circ asst UNC Lib(Chapel Hill) 30-36; Sub NY Pub Lib summer 36; Asst to libn William & Mary Col 36-39; UNC Lib(Chapel Hill); Asst head circ dept 39, Chief documents dept 39-42, Head circ & documents 42-47; Asst dir Cornell U Libs 47-66, Assoc dir 66-. 8: Lib admin, Cornell Proj at U Liberia, 62-63; Lib consul, Four Multi-Co Systems, NY 65; Regents Adv Coun on Libs 67-; Commsners Com on Lib Development 67-; Lib consul; keuka Col 69, Concordia Cal 67. 9: ALA;-ACRLULS (chm 68-69); BSA; NYLA. 10: AAUP; Kiwanis. 13: Yes. 14: Admin, readers serv. 15: 101 Valley rd, Ithaca NY 14850.

SHEPHERD, MURRAY C. b Saskatoon Sask Can 31 Jl 38. 4: Donna Hogg. 5: USask 63 (Eng) BEd; UDenver 68 (LS) MA. 7: Tchr Walter Murray Collegiate, Saskatoon Can 63-64; Asst libn Educ Lib USask (Regina) 64-67, Hd catlg dept 67-. 9: ALA; CanLA; SaskLA; SaskASchL (past pres); ReginaLA. 12: Ed "Proceedings of the Prairie Conference on Library Standards for Canadian Schools" (68). 13: Yes. 14: Tech serv, admin. 15: 43 Richardson Cres, Regina Sask Can.

SHEPHERD, RICHARD J. b Brookline Mass 28 D 11. 4: Muriel Doyle. 5: Harvard 28-32 (Eng) AB; Columbia 49-51 (LS) MS. 7: Asst to curator of painting Cleveland Art Museum, Cleveland Ohio 32-34; A-v educ supv West Res Acad, Hudson Ohio 34-37; Investigator Dept of Welfare, Cleveland Ohio 37-39; Reporter "Cleveland Plain Dealer," Cleveland Ohio 40-42; Battalion adjutant AAA (1st Lt) US Army 42-45; Ed asst Art News, NYC 46; Ref asst NY Pub Lib, NYC 49-52; Fine arts libn UIll (Chicago) Undergrad Div 52-55; Dir info ctr Pub Rel Soc of Amer 55-63; Col libn SUC (New Paltz) 63-. 9: ALARSD (chm Publs Com); NYLA; SEast NYC Lib Resources Coun; NY Lib Club . 13: Yes. 14: Admin, ref. 15: 42 Elting ave, New Paltz NY 12561.

SHEPPARD, GENEVA T. b Hope Kan. 5: Kan State Tchrs Col (Emporia) 41 (LS) BS, 42 Lib Certif; UIll 48 (Med Lib Sci). 7: Tchr elem schs, Hope Kan 28-40; Libn High Sch, Bonner Springs Kan 42-43; Libn Army Air Base, Malden Mo 43-44 Asst chief libn VA Center, Wood Wis 44-45; Chief Libn VA Hosp, Marion Ill 45-50; Chief Lib Serv VA Center, Wichita Kan 50-. 9: ALA; SLA; MedLA; KanLA; MPLA. 10: Bus & Prof Womens Assn; Wesleyan Serv Guild. 13: Yes. 14: Med lib & wk with patients. 15: 5500 E Kellogg, Wichita Ks 65218.

SHEPPARD, GEORGE K. b Pocatello Ida 17 Jl 34. 4: Roma Baker. 5: Ida State U 52-53, 56-58 (Sociol); Utah State U 59 (Sociol) BA; UDenver 60-62 (LS) MA; Utah State U (Educ). 7: Infantry US Army US 53-56; Libn Pocatello High Sch, Pocatello Ida 60-62; Libn Highland High Sch, Pocatello Ida 62-; Instr Lib Sci Ida State U 66-. 8: Dir USOE Educ Prof Development Acts in lib sci for State of Ida summer 69. 9: ALA; IdaLA (pres-elect Sch Sect); NEA-DAVI. 13: Yes. 14: Sch libs. 15: 3B Poca Heights, Pocatello Id 83201.

SHEPPARD, RITA A . b North Bay Ont Can 21 O 13. 5: UWest Ont 48-50 (Eng) BA; McGill 50-51 BLS, 67 (LS) MLS. 6: Fr. 7: Lib asst UWest Ont 48-50; Libn Verdun High Sch, Vrdun Que 51-59; Libn S J Willis Jr High Sch, Victoria BC 59-61; Libn High Sch of Montreal, Montreal 61-66; Libn & A-v coord Macdonald High Sch, Macdonald Col 66-. 8: Lib sci tchr Victoria U, summers 60-61; Tchr of child lit, Macdonald Col Dept of Educ summers 64-65; Nat del for sch libns 1st Conf on Canadian Educ, Ottawa 59; Canadian observer Intl Fed of LA Conf 67. 9: CanLA; ALA; QueLA (pres 51-58); Lib Assn Protestant Schs, Greater Montreal. 10: Univ Womens Club; Delta Kappa Gamma; Can Inst Intl Affairs; Prof Assn Protestant Tchrs Que; St George Club. 14: Sch libs, child lit. 15: Macdonald High School Lib, P O Box 226 Macdonald College, Quebec Canada.

SHEPPARD, YVONNE. 4: William Sheppard. 5: McMaster -59 BA; UMiami 63-67 (LS) MEd. 6: Fr. 7: Tchr Burlington Bd of Educ, Burlington 57-62, Lib consul 62-69; Lib consul Bd of Educ, Hamilton Can 69-. 9: CanLA; ALA; OntLA. 10: Ont Tchrs Fed. 14: Sch libs. 15: 308 W 2nd st, Hamilton 40 Ont Can.

SHEPPERD, JANE NUTTER (SMITH). b Jonesville Va 30 Mr 23. 4: Irving J Shepperd. 7: Docs lib asst Johns Hopkins Applied Physics Lab, Silver Spring Md 53-54, Ser libn 54-63, Br libn (in charge) 54-. 9: SLA. 14: Ref. 15: 2919 Burton Hill dr, Kensington Md 20795.

SHERA, JESSE H(AUK). b Oxford Ohio 8 D 03. 4: Helen M Bickham. 5: Miami U (Ohio) 21-25 (Eng Lit & Lang) AB; Yale 25-27 (Eng Lit & Lang) AM; Chicago 38-40, 44 (LS) PhD. 6: Fr, Ger. 7: Asst catlgr Miami U Lib (Ohio) 27-28; Bibliogr Scripps Found for Research in Population Problems, Miami U (Ohio) 28-40; Chief Census Lib Proj LC 40-41; Deputy Chief Central Info Div Research & Analysis Br, US Off of Strategic Serv, Wash DC 41-44; Asst dir UChicago Lib 44-47; Asst Prof Grad Lib Sch UChicago 47-51, Assoc Prof 51-52; Dean & Prof of Lib Sci Sch of Lib Sci West Res U 52-, Dir Center for Documentation & Communication Research 59-. 8: Del (Dept of State) to Internat Conf on Bibliog Org, Unesco, Paris, 50; Del (NSF) to Internat Conf on Bibliog Clsf, Dorking Eng, 57; Guest lecturer, Brazilian Inst for Bibliog & Documentation, Rio de Janeiro, 57; President's Com on the Employment of the Handicapped; Sarada Ranganathan lectures, Bangalore India 67; Adv com, Lib research US Off Educ 66-69. 9: ALA (Coun 65-69, chm Bibliog Com 50-52, chm Interdiv Com 54-);-ACRL; SLA (chm Publns Com 57-59); CNLA (Exec Bd 64-); AALS (pres 64-65); Aslib; BSA; ASIS; OhioLA (pres 63-64). 10: Caxton Club (Chicago); Rowfant Club (Cleveland); Profess Men's Club of Cleveland; Ambassador's Club; Cliff Dweller's Club; Phi Beta Kappa; Beta Phi Mu; Phi Alpha Theta. 11: Beta Phi Mu Award for contrib to lib ed, 65; Melvil Dewey Award; Ohioana Award. 12: "Foundations of the American Public Library" (49); "Historians, Books, and Libraries" (54); "The Classified Catalog" (57); "Documentation in Action" (56); "Bibliographic Organization" (51); "Information Systems in Documentation" (57); "Information Resources: a Challenge to American Science and Industry" (58); "Libraries and the Organization of Knowledge" (65); "Classification and the Organization of Knowledge" (66) Ed "American Documentation" (53-60). 13: Yes. 14: Educ for libnship, lib hist, theory of clsf, documentation. 15: Sch of Lib Sci West Res Univ, Cleveland Oh 44106.

SHERARD, MARY. b Vicksburg Miss 16 D 20. 5: Miss State Col for Women 38-42 (Eng) AB; LSU 51-52 BS in LS. 7: Tchr

Warren Co Sch Syst, Vicksburg Miss 42-50; Libn Gulfport jr High Sch, Gulfport Miss 50-52; Hd libn Vicksburg Pub Lib, Vicksburg Miss 52-. 9: ALA; MissLA; SELA. 10: Dir Vicksburg Little Theatre Guild. 14: Admin. 15: Box 511, Vicksburg Ms 39180.

SHERARD, OLLIE (MILLER). b Prosperity SC 30 Mr 11. 5: Brewer Jr Col 31-33 (Elem Educ); AllenU 46-48 (Eng) BA; NC Col 50 (S); AtlantaU 51-54 MLS. 6: Fr. 7: Tchr: Cokesbury Elem Sch, Cokesbury SC 34-35, Calhoun Falls Jr High Sch, Calhoun Falls SC 35-41, 43-46; Tchg prin Cokesbury Elem Sch 41-43; Libn Brewer High Sch, Greenwood SC 48-. 8: Libn Developmental Reading Prog for slow learners sponsored by ESEA 66-68; Mem instr staff, Allen U Summer Inst for Elem Libns 69. 9: ALA; NEA; SCLA; SCEA; PalmettoEA (chm Dept of Libns 52-53). 10: Yellow Jessamine Garden Club; The Greenwood Museum; Commun Chest of Greenwood Co; Alpha Kappa Alpha. 14: Sec sch libn. 15: RFD 2 Box 608, Hodges SC 29653.

SHERER, ELAINE R SLIVKIN. b Cambridge Mass 8 Ap 25. 4: Robert J Sherer. 5: Boston U 42-46 (Mus Educ) Mus B, 46-53 (Musicology) MA; Simmons 53-55 (LS) MS. 6: Fr, Hebrew. 7: Tchr of piano self-employed, Boston 46-64; Asst child libn Boston Pub Lib 55-56; Asst libn Wentworth Inst, Boston 64-66; Asst libn-catlgr Mass ;bay Commun Col 66-. 8: Vol libn Maimonides Sch Brookline Mass 62-63. 14: Child wk. 15: 7 Burr rd, Newton Mass 02159.

SHERIDAN, ROBERT NEAL. b Greenwood SC 28 Mr 30. 5: USCar 48-52 (Hist) AB, 53-54 (Hist) MA; Rutgers 56-57 MLS. 7: Queens Borough Pub Lib, NYC: Libn, asst br libn 57-59, Admin asst 59-61, Dir of personnel & mgt analysis 61-63, Chief of ext serv 63-64; Dir Levittown Pub Lib, Levittown NY 64-. 9: ALA (chm Com or Org 65-69);-ASD (chm Publishers Liaison Com 65-);-LAD (Personnel Admin Sect; chm Personnel Publ Com 62-67, chm PAS Nominating Com 63, chm Com on Youth Employment Act 63, chm Com to Study Draft Standards of US Civil Serv Commsn 64); NYLA; Nassau Co LA.15 1498 Gaston st, Wantagh NY 11793. 10: Archons of Colophon; Belgium Nautical Research Assn; US Naval Inst; Navy Records Soc; Naval Records Club. 13: Yes. 14: Admin, personnel, ref. 15: 1498 Gaston st, Wantagh NY 11793.

SHERMAN, CHARLES NEIL. b Huntingdon Penn 3 D 33. 4: Aurelia Fischer. 5: Purdue U 53-55 (Psych) BS; Fla State U 62-63 (LS) MS. 7: Hd of ref Arlington Co Pub Lib, Arlington Va 63, Hd of acquis; Hd of lib Ctr for Research in Soc Systs American U 65; Chief info systs br 66; Libn-Systa analyst Wolff Research & Development Corp, Bladensburg Md 67; Sr systs analyst Syst Development Corp, Falls Church Va 68-69. 9: ALA; SLA; ASIS. 12: "The Education Information Center; an Introduction (69). 14: Admin, sys analysis, lib automation, educ info ctrs. 15: 2611 Marcey rd, Arlington Va 22207.

SHERMAN, JOHN. b Lakeside Mo 3 F 17. 4: Helen Brown. 5: UCLA 50 (Hist) BA; Columbia 55 MSLS; NYU 66 (Hist of Educ) Ed D. 6: Sp, Fr. 7: Cryptographer (Sp 2/C) USCG, Alaska & Caribbean Area 42-45; Accessions asst H E Huntington Lib, San Marino Cal 47; Ref libn Los Angeles Examiner, Ed Ref Lib 51-52; Accessions libn Folger Shakespeare Lib, Wash DC 52; Asst head circ Catholic U 52-53; Head readers serv Fordham U Lib 53-55; Asst to & asst libn Hunter Col 55-61; Chm Dept of Lib Serv Jersey City State Col 61-68; Assoc Prof dept of Lib Sci Queens Col CUNY 68-. 8: Bibliog adv, Inst for Mediterranean Affairs, 58-68; Visiting assoc prof of lib sci, Sch of Libnship, UWash summer 65, 67, 68. 9: ALA; AALS; NYLA; LACUNY; NY Lib Club. 10: AAUP; NJ Citizens Com Nat Lib Week (64); C of C; Hudson Co TB & Health League; Kappa Delta Pi; Phi Delta Kappa; Hist of Educ Soc; Amer Educ Studies Assn; United Fed Col Tchrs, AFL-CIO. 13: Yes. 14: Admin, program planning, ref & bibliog, govt docs. 15: 56 7th ave, NYC 10011.

SHERMAN, MARY CLAIRE (LESIAK). b Lincoln Neb 1 My 38. 4: Steve B Sherman. 5: Immaculate Heart Col 56-60 (Hist) BA, 65-66 (LS) MA; USan Francisco (Valencia Spain) summers 62, 64 (Sp); UAlaska US Govt Inst summer 68 (Sch Libnship). 6: Sp. 7: Elem tchr: Los Angeles City Schs 60-63, 64-65; State of Alaska, Ruby 63-64; Elem lib coord Los Angeles City Schs 66-67; Child libn City of Fairbanks Alaska 68; Dist elem libn Fairbanks N Star Borough Sch Dist 68-. 9: ALA; NEA-DAVI; AlaskaLA (treas); AlaskaEA; Alaska Instr Materials Assn. 10: AAUW. 14: Sch libnship, instr materials. 15: 4037 Iris lane, Fairbanks Ak 99701.

SHERMAN, STEVE. b Los Angeles Cal 26 Jl 38. 4: Mary Claire Lesiask. 5: Loyola U (Los Angeles) 56-60 (Philos) BA, 64-65 (Communication Arts) MA; UCLA 66-67 (LS) MA. 7: Tchr: Pater Noster High Sch 61-63, State of Alaska, Ruby 63-64; Libn UAlaska 67-. 8: Wrote, directed, filed & edited UAlaska Lib orientation film. 9: ALA; AlaskaLA. 13: Yes. 14: Ref, pub rel. 15: 4037 Iris lane, Fairbanks Ak 99701.

SHERMAN, STUART G. b Amherst Mass 30 O 16. 4: Mary E Thompson. 5: Brown 35-39 (Geol) AB; Columbia 39-40 (LS) BS. 7: Summer asst NYC Pub Lib 40; Br libn Enoch Pratt Free Lib, Baltimore 40-43; Br supv Providence Pub Lib 43-45, Asst libn 45-54, Assoc libn 54-57, Libn 57-68; John Hay libn & assoc prof of bibliogs BrownU 68-. 8: Trustee: RI Sch of Design, Citizens Savings Bank; Consul on lib bldgs; First RI chm of Nat Lib Week 57-58; Ext Lectr URI and RI Col; V-chm City of Providence Hist Dist Commsn; Old dartmouth Hist Soc Dukes Co Hist Soc. 9: ALA (life mem); BSA; MS Soc; RILA (pres 47-49); MassLA. 10: RI Hist Soc; Amer Antiq Soc; Book Club of Cal; Club of Odd Volumes (Boston); Grolier Club (NY); Melville Soc; Providence Art Club; Mem of Corp of Providence Pub Lib; Friends of John Hay Lib; Assoc of John Carter Brown Lib; Litt D Brown U; Phi Beta Kappa. 12: "The Voice of the Whaleman" (65); Preface to new ed of -history of the American Whale Fishery" by Starbuck, "The First Ninety Years of the Providence Public Library" ed "Books at Brown" (47-48). 13: Yes. 14: Rare bks, bibliog. 15: 654 Angell st, Providence RI 02906.

SHERMAN, VIRGINIA LISTER (IRWIN). b Belle Pline Iowa 5 Je 15. 4: James Herbert Sherman. 5: Westmar Col 33-37 (Eng) BA (magna cum laude); UIowa 38; UIll 41-42 BS in LS (high honors), 43-45 (LS) MS. 6: Fr, Ger, Lat. 7: Hist Tchr Otho High Sch, Otho Iowa 37-38; Libn Pub Lib, Le Mars Iowa 38-41; Libn High Sch & Jr Col Lib, Mason City Iowa 42-43; Ref Dept UIll Urbana 43-45; Libn High Sch Lib, Le Mars Iowa 48-49; Ref & Circ Dept Pub Lib, Burbank Cal 51-54; Ref libn San Fernando Valley State Col 61-. 9: ALA; CalLA. 10: Phi Kappa Phi; Beta Phi Mu; UIll Lib Sch Assn. 14: Ref. 15: 19212 Lanark, Reseda Ca 91335.

SHERMAN, WILLIAM FREDERICK JR. b Evergreen Park Ill 19 D 38. 4: Marilyn Mathis. 5: NoIllU 56-60 (Hist) BS in Ed, 60-61 (Hist); Oriel Col Oxford U (England) 59; Rosary Col 66-69 MALS. 6: Ger. 7: Grad asst NoIllU Lib 60-61; Libn Morton E High Sch, Cicero Ill 61-. 8: Lib consul Ill Visually Handicapped Inst, Chicago 65-67. 9: ALA; NEA (life mem); AFT; IllLA; IllSchLA; IllEA (State Citizenship Commsn). 10: Beta Phi Mu; Phi Alpha Theta; Alpha Beta Alpha; Commsnr Downers Grove Park Dist; Jr C of C. 14: Wk with ya. 15: 4043 Cumnor rd, Downers Grove Il 60515.

SHEROCKMAN, ANDREW ANTOLCIK. b Raccoon Penn 19 Jl 13. 4: Anna Yesko. 5: UDubuque 31-35 (Chem) BA; Columbia U Bard Col 44 (Civil Affairs Govt) Certif; UPittsburgh 45 (Sci Educ) MA; Harvard summer 49; UPittsburgh 55 (Sci Educ) PhD. 6: Slovak, Fr. 7: Head Sci Dept Union Head Sci Dept Union High Sch, Burgettstown Penn 35-42; US Army 42-46; Nuclear Research Off USAF Res (Maj) 50-; Prof of Chem Evansville Col 46-55; Dir Naval Reactor Training Westinghouse Electric Co, Bettis Lab Pittsburgh 55-59; Supv Info Res Nat Steel Corp, Weirton WVa 59-. 8: Consul in sci educ; Consul in guidance; Tech ed & writer. 9: ACS; Nat Sci Tchrs Assn; Air Force ASSN: Air Force Hist Found; SLA; Soc of Eds & Tech Writers; WVaLA; 10: AAAS; Phi Delta Kappa; Alpha Chi Sigma; Pi Kappa Delta; Phi Beta Chi; Phi Alpha Theta. 12; "Laboratory Manual for General Chemistry (53). 13: Yes. 14: Admin, ref. 15: RD 5 Box 596B McMichael rd, Pittsburgh Pa 15205.

SHERONICK, ELEANORE MARGARET (KUCK). b Cleveland 20 Ja 2904: Mike H Sheronick. 5: Wayne State U 46-51 (Hist) BA; West Res summer 52-55 MSLS. 7: Page & clerk Detroit Pub Lib 44-52; Lib aide Lib of Ft Wayne & Allen Co Ind 52-53; Child libn Toledo Pub Lib, Toledo Ohio 54-. 9: ALA; OhioLA. 14: Child & yp. 15: 3445 Fleitzdr, Oregon Ohio 43616.

SHERRARD, McCLUER. b Roanoke Va 29 S 37. 5: Richmond Prof Inst 55-56 (Interior Design); Roanoke Col 56-59 (Eng) BA; UNC 59-60 (LS) Peabody 63-64 MALS. 6: Fr. 7: Rare bk libn USCar 60-63; Temp catlgr UVa 64; Catlgr Va State Lib 65-67; Catlgr Va Commonwealth U 67-. 12: Comp "An Interim Supplement to Special Collections in the McKissik Memorial Library" (62). 15: 2121 Grove ave, Richmond Va 23220.

SHERRILL, JOSEPHINE (PRICE). b Salisbury NC 28 D 1893. 4: Richard W Sherrill. 5: Livingstone Col 12-16 (Eng) AB; Hampton Inst 28 BLS. 7: Tchr Livingstone Col 16-25,

Asst libn 25-28, Hd libn 28-. 8: Sch lib adv, State Dept of Pub Instr NC; V-pres of Salisbury Chapter of National Council of Negro Women. 9: ALA; -ACRL; NCTA; NCLA. 10: NC Soc Preserv Antiq; NY Zool Soc; NC Coun Negro Women. 13: Yes. 14: Admin, rare bks. 15: 828 W Monroe st, Salisbury NC 28144.

SHERWOOD, BETTY R (FARRIS). b Sioux Falls SD 28 D 20. 4: Stephen L Sherwood. 5: Augustana Col (SD) 39-41; Berea Col 41-43 (Biol Sci) BA; Garrett Biblical Inst 44-46; UNC 51-52 BS in LS; Columbia 52 (LS). 6: Ger, Fr. 7: Lib asst Northwestern U Lib 43-47; Lib asst Yale U Divinity Sch Lib 47-49; Ser catlgr Columbia U 49-50; Asst libn Vanderbilt U Sch of Med 52-55; Assoc libn UNeb Col of Med Lib 55-60; Libn Prof Lib Ill State Psychiatric Inst, Chicago 60-65; Libn Life Sci Lib NASA Ames Research Center, Moffett Field Cal 65-. 9: ALA; MedLA; SLA. 10: Sports Car Club of Amer. 13: Yes. 14: Med libs, catlg, ref. 15: 726 Greer rd, Palo Alto Ca 94303.

SHERWOOD, BETTY. b Ionia Co Mich 21 S 21. 5: west mich u 39-54 (educ) bs, 54-58 6: Ger. 7: Elem tchr: rural schs, Ionia Co Mich 41-48, Saranac Commun Schs, Saranac Mich 48-64; Libn Butterworth Hosp Sch of Nursing, Grand Rapids Mich 68-. 9: ALA; -AHIL; -YASD; MedLA; MichLA. 10: Beta Phi Mu. 14: Spec libs, health sci libs, admin, ref. 15: Rte 4 1928 Peck Lake rd, Ionia Mi 48846.

SHERWOOD, JANICE WINTRODE. b York Penn 15 Jl 14. 5: Smith 32-36 (Ital) AB, Magna Cum Laude; UFlorence (Italy) 36-37 (Art, Hist); Radcliffe 37-38 (Art, Hist); Drexel 49-52 MS in LS. 6: Ital, Fr, Sp, Ger. 7: Rationing panel clerk OPA, York Penn 42-45; Prin price clerk 46; Clerk War Assets Admin, Phila 48; Union Lib Catalogue, Phila; Bibiliog asst 49; Consul 49-51; Asst dir 51-. 9: ALA. 10: Phi Kappa Phi; AAUW. 13: Yes. 14: Ref. 15: 2100 Walnut st apt 13-A, Phila Pa 19003.

SHERWOOD, ROBERT LISTER. b Kalamazoo Mich. 5: West MichU 56-60 (Eng) BA; UMich 60-66 MALS. 7: A-v dir Herrick Pub Lib, Holland Mich 63-66; Asst dir 66-. 9: MichLA (chm a-V Sect). 10: Amer Numismatic Assn. 14: Admin, a-v, ref. 15: 615 Douglas ave apt D3, Holland Mi 49423.

SHETLER, CHARLES. b Tarentum Penn 15 My 18. 4: Harriet McCown. 5: UPittsburgh 46-48 (Soc Studies) BA, 48-49 (Hist) MA. 7: Newspaper wk 36-41; US Army Air Corps Weather Serv, Anti-aircraft Artillery (1st lt), ETO 44-46; Curator Reg Hist Collection WVaU 50-66; Libn State Hist Soc of Wis 66-. 9: ALA; SAA; BSA; WisLA. 10: Amer Assn State & Local Hist; Wis Hist Soc. 12: Jt Auth, "West Virginia Imprints, 1790-1863" (58); "Guide to Manuscripts and Archives in the West Virginia Collection" (59); "Guide to the Study of West Virginia History" (60); Comp; "West Virginia Civil War Literature; An Annoyated Bibliography" (63); Comp; "Catalogue of the Roy Bird Cook Collection" (64). 13: Yes. 14: Rare bks, local hist, archives & mss, bibliog. 15: 816 State st, Madison Wi 53706.

SHEVIAK, MARGARET REGINA. b Wanatah Ind 21 Jl 11. 5: IndU 51-57 (Eng Lit) AB, 57-58 (LS) MA. 7: Asst circ libn Pub Lib, LaPorte Ind 37-39; Child libn 39-55; Dir child wk Free Pub Lib, Louisville Ky 58-59; Instr Nazareth Col (Ky) 58-59; Instr lib sci IndU 59-62, Asst Prof 62-69, Assoc Prof 69-. 8: Wkshop & consul activities in-serv & materials for child & ya; Educ auth for film "The Fish That Turned Gold" (61); Lit consul auth & participant in series of TV Programs "The Legacy of the Library" (64); Lit consul for Curriculum Enrichment Series 64. 9: ALA (del to IFLA, 61); IndLA; Ind SchLA. 10: AAUP; Univ Club; Women's Faculty Club; Phi Beta Kappa; Beta Phi Mu; Pi Lambda Theta; Delta Kappa Gamma. 13: Yes. 14: Serv & materials for child & ya. 15: Div of Lib Sci Ind Univ, Bloomington Ind 47405.

SHIELDS, AGNES (MacALLISTER). b Ferndale Wash 15 My 06. 5: Radcliffe 24-28 (Fr) BA; UWash 30-31 (Fr), 34-35 (LS) BA. 6: Fr. 7: Tchr Ferndale High Sch, Ferndale Wash 29-30; Tchg Fellow UWash 30-31; Tchr-libn Prosser High Sch, Prosser Wash 31-34; Libn Mt Vernon Fr Col 35-36; Sch libn Wenatchee High Sch, Wenatchee Wash 36-38; Sch ref libn Ore State Lib 38-43, Sch lib spec 43-59, Child & yp spec 59-. 9: ALA-AASchL; OreLA;-PNLA. 12: "List of Books of School Libraries Part 1 & 2 (43, 59); "Whats New in Education (68-). 13: Yes. 14: Ref, bibliog. 15: 5241 Liberty rd S, Salem Or 97302.

SHIELDS, DOROTHY P. b OttawaCan 22 D 22. 5: Queens U (Ont) 41-44; Fr, Span BA; UDenver 60-61 (LS) MA. 6: Fr, Sp. 7: Sec Carleton U 45-46; Sec Can Embassy, Santiago Chile 47-49; Sec Atomic Energy of Can Ltd, Chalk River Ont 49-55; Temp wk, London Eng 55-57; Sec Signkraft Advertising, Vancouver BC 57-60; Libn UBC 61-. 9: CanLA; BCLA. 14: Acquis, bibliog searching . 15: 1116 W 15th ave, Vancouver 9 BC Can.

SHIELDS, GERALD ROBERT. b Waukegan Ill 24 N 25. 4: Joyce Farley. 5: Milton Col 46-48 (Liberal Arts); UWis 48-49 (Speech); UWis(Milwaukee) 59-60 (Speech) BS; UWis 60-61 (LS) MA. 6: Russian, Icelandic. 7: Linguist (S/Sgt) USAF 50-55; Personnel supv Inland Steel Prod, Milwaukee 55-59; Adult educ coordinator Central YMCA, Milwaukee 59-60; Ref libn Marquette U Lib 61-64; Head soc sci Dayton & Montgomery Co Pub Lib, Dayton Ohio 64-67; Ed ALA Bulletin, Chicago 68-. 8: Spec Assignment, USAFI Icelandic Lang Instr, 53-54; Instr Inst on Lib Pub's UKy 69. 9: ALA; OhioLA (chm Publns Com). 12: Ed Marquette University Libraries Bulletin 62-64; Ed Ohio Library Association Bulletin 64-67. 13: Yes. 14: Ref, communications, personnel. 15: 171 N Elmwood, Oak Park Il 60302.

SHIELDS, JOYCE (FARLEY). b Leland Ill 18 J130. 4: Gerald Robert Shields. 5: Lawrence Col 48-52 (Ger) BA; Columbia 52-54 (LS) MS. 6: Ger, Fr. 7: Lib tech asst NY Pub Lib 53-54; Milwaukee Pub Lib: Lib research libn 55-56, Asst coordinator ser 57-59, Selector catlgr natural sci 60-61, Catlg revisor 62-64; Chief tech serv Air Force Inst of Tech, Wright-Patterson AFB Ohio 65-66; Hd catlgr Wright State U Lib 67-68; Hd catlgr No Ill Tech Processing Ctr, Oak Park Ill 68-69; Ref coord suburban lib syst Oak Park Pub Lib, Oak Park Ill 69-. 9: IllLA. 10: Phi Beta Kappa. 12: Ed "Union List of Serials in the Libraries in the Miami Valley, Ohio" (68). 14: Tech serv, ref. 15: 171 N Elmwood, Oak Park Il 60302.

SHIELDS, SISTER MARY JEAN ELLEN BVM. b Rock Island Ill 30 Sp 12. 5: MarquetteU 45 (Hist) BA; St LouisU summers 49-54 (Hist) MA; Rosary Col summers 58-62 MA in LS. 6: Fr. 7: Elem tchr parochial schs in Wis, Ill, Iowa & Cal 33-54; Secondary tchr Holy Angels Acad, Milwaukee 54-62; Libn & secondary tchr Bellarmine-Jefferson High sch, Burbank Cal 62-. 8: Ref Libn UNotre Dame summer 68; Mem Los Angeles Archdiocesan Steering Com 67-68. 9: ALA; CathLA (SW Unit: ed "Clasp" 64-66, v-chm 66-69, chm 69-; chm Hgh Sch Sect 64-66); CalASchL. 14: Ref. 15: 520 E Orange Grove ave, Burbank Ca 91501.

SHIH, PHILIP C. b Hunan China 6 Jl 43. 5: TunghaiU 61-65 (Econ) BA; Ft Hays Kan State col 66-67 (Econ); Fla State U 67-68 (LS) MS. 6: Chinese. 7: Ref libn Wicihta State U 69-. 9: KanLA. 14: Ref. 15: Wichita State Univ Box 68, Wichita Ks 67208.

SHILCUTT, MARY (CATHERINE BRUCE). b Amarillo Tex 20 N 29. 4: Benny A Shilcutt. 5: Abilene Christian Col 47-48 (Educ); Austin Col 48-49 (Educ); N Tex State Col 49-50 (Secondary Educ) BS, 50-53 (Secondary Educ & LS) M d with lifetime tchr certif & libns certif. 7: Libn Big Spring High Sch, Big Spring Tex 50-51; Base libn Perrin AFB, Sherman Tex 51-53; Eng tchr Lake Worth High Sch, Ft Worth Tex 53-54; Libn Tex Electric Serv Co, Ft Worth Tex 57; Sub tchr Birdville Ind Sch Dist, Ft Worth Tex 59-63; Col libn Ft Worth Christian Col 63-66; Libn Richland Jr High Sch 66-69. 9: Tex State TA; Tex Ctr TA. 10: PTA; Birdsville Ctr TA. 14: School lib wk. 15: Rt 6 Box 149, Ft Worth Tex 76118.

SHILLABER, CAROLINE. b Brookline Mass 24 S 08. 5: Smith 26-30 (Eng) AB; Simmons 30-31(LS) BS. 6: Fr. 7: Asst libn Grad Sch of Design Harvard U 31-51; Libn Arch & Planning Lib MIT 51-63; Libn Grad Sch of Design Harvard U 63-. 8: Consul libn: Doxiadis Assocs, Athens Greece; Planning Serv Group, Cambridge Mass; Dept of Landscape Arch UMass; Book review ed "Landscape Architecture-, 62-64. 9: Coun of Planning Libns first pres); Amer Inst of Planners. 12: "Massachusetts Institute of Technology: School of Architectrue & Planning, 1861-1961; A Chronicle; Bk review ed for "Landscape Architecture (61-64). 13: Yes. 15: 4 McKay dr, Rockport Ma 01966.

SHILLOWITZ, LILLIAN. b Lithuania. 5: State Tchrs Col (Newark NJ) 24-26; State Tchrs col (Jersey City NJ) 53-54; Columbia 46-48, Sch libn's certif, Prof libn's certif. 6: Sp. 7: Tchr Bd of Educ, Bayonee NJ 26-53, Tchr & libn 54-. 9: ALA; -AASchL; NJEA; NJLA; NJSchLA. 14: Catlg, ref (child serv). 15: 119 W 19 st, Bayonne NJ 07002.

SHINE, CAROL ANN. b Brooklyn NY 7 Je 42. 5: HofstraU 60-64 (Fine Arts) BA; Pratt Inst 64-66 MLS. 6: Fr. 7: Clk Dalton of Amer, NYC summers 59-62; Trainee Queens Borough Pub lib, Jamaica NY 64-66, Libn (staff) 66-67; Ref libn educ resource collection AdelphiU 67-. 9: ALA. 13: Yes. 14: Ref (educ, fine arts). 15: 4 Flower rd, Valley Stream NY 11581.

SHINE, JOHN DESMOND. b Yonkers NY 25 S 19. 4: Lola Robbins. 5: St Peter's Col 50-54 (Soc Sci) BS; Columbia 54-55 MLS. 7: Ships serv operator US Navy, Africa & European Theater 42-45; Chief order clerk Western Electric, Kearny NJ 42-53; Jersey City (NJ) Pub Lib; Ref libn 55-57, Supv tech serv 57-60, Personnel dir 60-64, Chief adult serv 64-65; Asst lib dir Hackensack (NJ) Pub Lib 65-. 8: Consul Secanus Pub Lib, Secanus NJ 61-62. 9: ALA; NJLA (chm Fin Com); Hudson Co (NJ) LA (pres 62-64; Bergen-Passaic CoLA (pres 66-67). 12: Comp "Hudson County List of Periodicals" (60). 14: Ref, catlg, personnel. 15: 169 Spring Valley rd, Paramus NJ 07652.

SHINN, ANNETTE HARRIS. b Norwood NC 26 N 07. 5: Greensboro Col 24-28 AB; Emory 36-37 ABLS, 56-57 MLS. 6: Fr. 7: Tchr pub schs, Stanly Co NC 30-35; Asst libn Greensboro Col 37-39, Libn 39-43; Asst libn Concord Pub Lib, Concord NC 43-47, Libn 47-50; Libn Shelby Pub Lib, Shelby NC 50-52; Ref &circ libn Winthrop Col Lib 52-57, Ref libn 57-. 8: Planned Study of British Libs, Eng 62. 9: ALA; SCLA. 10: AAUW; Delta Kappa Gamma. 13: . 14: Ref, rare bks. 15: 813 Evergreen lane, Rock Hill SC 29733.

SHINN, EUNICE (ADELINE). b Russellville Ark 8 Ap 07. 5: Ark Polytech Col 27-29; UArk summers 44-47; Ark State Tchr Col summers 30-45 (Educ) BSE; LSU 48-54 BSLS. 7: Elem tchr Hiwasse Ark 29-30, Pottsville Ark 30-41, Des Ark Ark 41-42, Roe Ark 42, Jonesboro Ark 42-43, Luxora Ark 43-46; Libn Luxora Ark 47-50, Russellville Ark 50-57, Sylvan Hills High Sch Ark 57-62; Asst libn LSU Train Sch 53; Circ libn Ark Polytech Col summers 55-56; Ref libn Ark Lib Commsn 62-65, Lib consul 65-66, Lib consul to State Insts 66-. 8: Attended Institutional Lib Serv Inst Wayne State U April 68. 9: ArkLA (sec 62-63, sec Sch Sect 49-50); ALA; SWLA. 10: Delta Kappa Gamma; AAUW; PTA; Wesleyan Serv Guild. 14: Consul serv, bk selection for state insts. 15: 205 Country Club rd, N Little Rock Ar 72116.

SHINN, ISABELLA ELIZABETH. b Lawrence Kan 16Mr20. 5: UGa 37-41 (Hist) AB; Columbia 41-42 & 43-44, summer 47 & 50; Hist Dept UGa (Fellowship); UCal(Berkeley) summers 51, 56; UWash 58-59 LS ML. 6: Fr, Ger, Lat, Sp, Russian. 7: Instr: hist & pol sci Sullins Col 46-48, hist & pol sci Blue Mountain Col summer 49, soc sci pub schs, Ga & Cal 49-58; Libn gifts & exch UWash 59-. 9: ALA-Internat Rel Round Table; PNLA; WashLA. 10: Beta Phi Mu; AAUW; UWash Faculty Womens Club; UWash Sch of Libnship Alumni Assn; Alpha Gamma Delta. 13: Yes. 14: Acquis, gifts & exch. 15: 4337-15th ave NE No 614, Seattle Wa 98105.

SHINN, SYDNICIEL. b Nashville Tenn 28 Ja27. 5: Vanderbilt U 45-49 (Sociol) BA; Peabody 54-55 (LS) MA. 6: Fr. 7: Case wker Davidson Co Pub Welfare Dept, Nashville 51-54; Reg libn Highland Rim Reg Lib, Murfreesboro Tenn 55-62; Pub lib consul Mo State Lib, Mexico Mo 62-65; Lib career consul Mo State Lib 65-. 9: ALA;-LED; TennLA; MoLA (Fed Rel Coord 65, treas 66-68, Conv Exhib Chm 69). 10: AAUW, LWV, Indus Rel Club. 13: Yes. 14: Recr, lib ed, pub libs, ext, admin. 15: 1416 W Main, Jefferson City Mo 65101.

SHIPLEY, ERNA R. b Sulphur Springs Mo 19 N 03. 5: UWis 29 (Eng) BA, 29 (Eng) BLS; UChicago 44 (LS). 6: Ger, Fr. 7: Asst libn Winona State Tchrs Col 29-30; Libn Elmhurst Col 30-44; Staff mem Lake Forest Lib, Lake Forest Ill 68-. 10: Amer Cancer Soc. 14: Ref, adult serv. 15: 1351 N Western ave, Lake Forest Il 60045.

SHIPLEY, HELEN B(LANCHE). b Maywood Ill 16 N 14. 5: Elmhurst Col 33-37 AB; UIll 40-41 BS in LS; UMinn 53-54 (Amer Studies) MA. 6: Fr, Sp. 7: Asst br libn Pub Lib, Oak Park Ill 37-40; Libn Pub Lib, Greencastle Ind 41-44; Loan libn Beloit Col 44-46; Catlgr UKan City46-55; Catlgr Grinnell Col 55-. 9: Amer Studies Assn: Midcontinent Amer Studies Assn; IowaLA (sec, Univ & Col Sect 59-60); ALA. 10: AAUP; Nat Fed Bus & Prof Womens Clubs. 14: Catlg. 15: 1026 1/2 High st, Grinnell Iowa 50112.

SHIPLEY, MILLS. b Calgary Alberta Can 12 F 19. 5: UAlberta 42 BA, 43 LLB; McGill 48 BLS. 6: Fr. 7: Govt libn, Ottawa Can 48-50; Law libn UAlberta 50-56; Asst libn Supreme Court of Can, Ottawa 56-60, Law ed 60-. 9: AALL; CanLA; Alta Law Soc. 12: Ed "Canada Supreme Court Reports". 13: Yes. 15: Supreme Court of Canada, Ottawa Ont Can.

SHIPMAN, JOSEPH C(OLLINS). b Winnipeg Man Can 20 Ja 08. 04: Kathryn Klinger. 5: West Res 25-29 (Chem, Biol) AB, 31-32 BS in LS. 6: Ger. 7: Asst tech div Cleveland Pub Lib 33-37; Lib Coun Union Col (Schenectady NY) 37-39; Tech libn Toledo Pub Lib, Toledo Ohio 39-42; Head sci & tech Enoch Pratt Free Lib, Baltimore 42-43, Asst dir 43-45; Dir Linda Hall Lib, Kan City Mo 45-. 8: Survey of Wichita Pub Lib (with Louis Nourse) 48; Mo Governors Sci Adv Com 64-; Pres, Science Pioneers, Inc 6368; Visiting lecr UDenver Grad Lib Sch 61-63; Visiting prof UCLA Sch Lib Serv summer 66. 9: ALA-ACRL (treas 52-55); MdLA (pres 44-45); MoLA (pres 47-48). 10: Trustee, Midwest Research Inst; Rockhill Club. 11: Hon D Sc, Park Col, 56. ; Hon DHL UMo (Kansas City) 67. 12 "Milestones in the History of Science (56); "William Dampier, Seaman-Scientist (62). 13: Yes. 14: Ref, rare bks, hist of sci & tech, admin. 15: Linda Hall Lib, 5109 Cherry st, Kansas City Mo 64110.

SHIPP, RUTH E (PEERENBOOM). b Tacoma Wash 11 Ja 30. 4: Richard M Shipp. 5: Seatle U 47-51 (Eng) PhB; UWash 52-53 (LS) ML. 7: Br coordinator King Co Pub Lib, Seattle 53-55; Ref libn Seattle U 55-58; Lead catlgr Boeing Co Pilotles Aircraft Div, Seattle 58-59; Br libn Boeing Co Aerospace Group, Seattle 59-60, Tech processes supv 60-68, User serv supv 68-. 8: Consul Richard-Abel Co 67-68; Statewide Planning Com for Governor's Conf on Libs 67-68. 9: ALA; SLA (Pacific NW Cha: Awards Com of Sci-Tech Div 64-66), Aerospace Div chm-chm elect 66-68) 10: Wash State Inds Womens Auxiliary. 14: Acquis, catlg, machine applications, user serv. 15: 17210 154th ct SE, Renton Wa 98055.

SHIPPEY, ORRLINE (ELLIS). b Italy Tex 27 N 14. 4: W W Shippey. 5: Trinity U 32-36 (Eng) BA; Tex Womans U summers 35, 37, 38 BLS; Peabody summer 41. 6: Sp, Ger. 7: Libn Jefferson pub schs, Jefferson Tex 36-39; Libn White Oak pub schs, Longview Tex 39-58; Catlgr Engnr Lib Tex A&M Col summer 42; Dir Nicholson Mem Pub Lib, Longview Tex 58-. 8: Consul: Dist Wkshops of Sch Adminrs & Consul, Atlanta (Tex) Pub Sch Facultys In-Serv Train Program, 60-61. 9: ALA; SWLA; TexLA (chm Sch Div 44-45, chm Child Div 50-51, past chm Dist 6). 10: AAUW; Zonta Club; LWV; Bd & Prof Womens Club; E Tex Hist Assn; Tex State Hist Assn61-63, 69-; Bd Dir Mercantile La 69-. 13: Yes. 14: Rare bks, ref, pub rel. 15: PO Box 1311, Longview Tx 75603.

SHIPPEY, SUSAN (SAUTTER). b Detroit 17My41. 4: Frederick L Shippey. 5: UMich 59-63 (Anthropology) BA, 63-64 AMLS. 6: Fr. 7: Stud asst order dept UMich Gen Lib 63-64; Lib consul Miss Lib Commsn, Jackson Miss 64-65; Libn Annette P Edwins Elem Sch, Ft Walton Beach Fla 65-66; Bibliog searcher UMich 67, Hd bibliog searching sect 69-. 9: ALA. 14: Tech serv. 15: 1475 Kirtland dr, Ann Arbor Mich 48103.

SHIPPS, ANTHONY WIMBERLY. b Tryon NC 26Ag26. 4: Jan barnett. 5: Emory Jr Col 43-44; Mercer U 46-49 (Eng) AB; Northwestern 50-54 (Eng) MA, 59 PhD; UMich 59-60 AMLS. 6: Fr, Ger. 7: Pharmacists mate US Navy 44-46; Prin Pittsview High Sch, Pittsview Ala 49-50; Instr in Eng Wayne State U 54-59; Asst libn Utah State U 60-61; UColo Libs; Circ libn 61-62, Humanities libn 62-64, Head ref dept & Asst Prof 64-67; Libn for Eng IndU Libs 67-. 9: ALA-ACRL; Mod Lang Assn. 10: AAUP. 14: Literary quotations. 15: 2500 E 8th st, Bloomington In 47401.

SHIPPS, HARROLD SOUTHARD JR. b Macon Ga 4 O 22. 4: Mary Louise Kremp. 5: Spring Hill Col 40-43 (Hist); Bridgewater Tchrs Col 47-49 (Educ) BSEd, summers 49, 51, 60 (Educ) MEd; BostonU summer 50 (Eng); George WashingtonU 63-64 (Pub Admin) MSPA; UDenver 66-67 MALS, 67-(Libnship). 6: Fr. 7: T/Sgt US Army, US, England & France 43-46; Placement clk VA Hosp, Portland Ore 46-47; Tchr Orleans High Sch, Orleans Mass 48-52; Admin off USAF, US & Germany 52-59; Exec off USAF Acad Lib 59-62, Asst dir (Lt Col) 66-; Eng instr USAF Acad Prep Sch 62-63; Stud off Air Command & Staff Col, Maxwell AFB Ala 63-64; Dir faculty admin USAF Acad 64-66. 9: ALA; -ACRL; -RTSD; ColoLA. 10: Air Force Hist Found; Air Force Assn. 14: Lib admin. 15: 320 Mustang way (Arrowwood), Colorado Springs Co 80908.

SHIPTON, CLIFFORD KENYON. b Pittsfield Mass 5Ag02. 4: Dorothy George Boyd Mcillop. 5: Harvard 26 BS, 27 MA, 33 PhD. 6: Fr, Ger. 7: Instr of Hist Brown U 28-30; Instr & tutor Harvard U 33, 36; Custodian Harvard U Archives 38-69; Ed Sibleys Harvard Graduates Mass Hist Soc 30-; Libn Amer Antiquarian Soc, Worcester Mass 38-59, Dir 59-67. 9: Amer Acad of Arts & Scis (Fellow; SAA (pres). 10: Pres, Colonial Soc of Boston; Coun, Inst of Early Amer Hist & Culture;

Trustee, Fruitlands & the Wayside Museums, Harvard Grolier Club (NY); Club of Odd Volumes (Boston); Phi Beta Kappa; Mass Hist Commsn. 11: LittD Clark 69. 12: Ed "Sibleys Harvard Graduates v IV-XV 30-69 "Roger Conant (45; "Isaiah Thomas (48); "New England Life in the 18th Century (63); Ed "Early American Imprints (Readex Microprint Corp). 13: Yes. 15: Box 63, Shirley Center Ma 01464.

SHIRA, DONALD WHITMAN JR. b San Diego Cal 25 D 29. 5: URedlands 5054 (Educ, Eng) BA; Peabody Col 5758 MA in LS. 6: Sp. 7: Asst soc sci libn San Diego State Col 58. 9: SLA; CalLA. 14: Ref. 15: 5840 Lindo Paseo st, San Diego Ca 92115.

SHIREMAN, GRACE CATHERINE. b Melmore Ohio 16 Ag 09. 4: Edwin Shireman. 5: Heidelberg Col 27-31 (Eng) AB; Ohio State U 31 (Home Econ); UUtah correspondence 61-63 (LS). 7: Tchr Eng, Home Econ McCutchenville High Sch, McCutchenville Ohio 31-36; Tchr Home Econ Danbury High Sch, Lakeside Ohio 37-38; Tchr Eng & Home Econ, Lib New Riegel High Sch, New Riegel Ohio 41-60; Libn Hopewell-London Local High Sch, Bascom Ohio 61-. 9: NEA; ALA; OhioEA; OhioLA; Hopewell-London EA (pres). 10: Delta Kappa Gamma; PTA; 4-H Club Adv, Thespians. 14: Catlg, rare bks. 15: 11 W Perry st, Tiffin Oh 44883.

SHIRK, FRANCES (CRUVER). b Puyallup Wash 26 Ag 18. 4: Lyal D Shirk. 5: Col Puget Sound 36-40 (Eng) BA; UWash 40-41 BLS. 7: Libn summer Pub Lib, summer Wash 41-45; Catlgr Waterloo Pub Lib, Waterloo Iowa 48-52; Catlgr Pierce Co Lib, Tacoma Wash 64-66; Catlgr prof & curriculum libn Tacoma Pub Schs, Tacoma Wash 66-. 9: NEA; WashEA; Wash State ASchLA. 15: 2456 Narrows dr, Tacoma Wash 98406.

SHIRK, FRANK CHARLES. b Englewood NJ 2 Ap 17. 4: Mildred Rockwell. 5: Rutgers 35-39 (Eng) BA; Drexel 39-40 BS in LS. 7: Asst period dept Rutgers U Lib 40-41; Tech 4th grade US Army Infantry 41-45; Head documents dept Rutgers U Lib 46-48; Va Polytech Inst; Documents libn 48-50, Head Engnr Lib 50-54, Assoc libn 54-61, Act lib dir 61-62, Lib dir 62-. 8: Lib adv com State Coun of Higher Educ 63-. 9: VaLA (pres 65); ALA; SLA (pres Va Chap 68-69); SELA. 10: AAUP; Rotary Club; Montgomery-Radford (Va) Reg Lib Bd; Montgomery Co (Va) Lib Bd; Blacksburg Citizens for Better Govt; Blacksburg Dist Commun Fed; University Club. 12: Ed "Virginia Engineer" (52-59). 13: Yes. 14: Admin. 15: 111 Country Club dr, Blacksburg Va 24060.

SHIRK, MILDRED (ROCKWELL). b Inverness Md 2 Ap 18. 4: Frank C Shirk. 5: Mary Washington Col UVa 36-39 (Eng, Psych) BS; Drexel 39-40 BS in LS. 7: Lib asst Pub Lib, Morristown NJ 40-41; Libn Pub Lib, Caldwell NJ 41-43; Libn Elem Sch, Blacksburg Va 52-59; Ref libn Va Polytech Inst 59-61; Dir Montgomery-Radford Reg Lib, Radford Va 61-; Dir New River Voc Tech Sch, New River Va 67-68. 9: VaLA; SELA. 15: 111 Country Club dr, Blacksburg Va 24060.

SHIRK, VALNEY HIX JR. b Los Angeles Cal 9 S 39. 4: Linda Gettins Martin. 5: Pasadena City Col 57-59 (Humanities) AA; Cal State (Los Angeles) 59-62 (Biol) BA; USoCal 62-63, summer 67 MSLS; Humboldt State Col 67 (Biol). 6: Ger. 7: Lib page Alhambra Pub Lib, Alhambra Cal 57-60, Jr clk (ref dept) 60-62; Asst ref libn Arcadia Pub Lib, Arcadia Cal 62-64; Asst city libn Eureka City Lib, Eureka Cal 64-67; Libn I (sci & tech) Long Beach Pub Lib, Long Beach Cal 67-68, Libn II docs libn & asst hd sci & tech 69-. 9: ALA; PNLA. 10: Sierra Club. 14/ ref, bibliog serv in life scis. 15: 508 Roycroft ave, Long Beach Ca 90814.

SHIRLEY, ELIZABETH B. b Chattanooga Tenn 13 Ap 1895. 5: Smith 14-17 (Eng) AB; Syracuse 50-51 MS in LS. 6: Ger, Gr. 7: Br libn Buffalo and Erie Co Pub Lib, Buffalo NY 51-62; Med libn M J Lewi Col of Podiatry, NYC 63-69. 9: MedLA. 14: Catlg. 15: 2391 Webb ave, NYC 10468.

SHIRLEY, WAYNE (WILLIAM). b Franklin NH 12 Ja 1900. 4: Dorothy Bruce. 5: Dartmouth 18-22 (Econ)BS; Pratt 27-28 BLS. 7: Asst NY Pub Lib 28-29; Libn UNH 29-32; 1st asst NY Pub Lib 32-35; Head S & T ref room Pratt Inst 35-38, Dean & Libn 38-55; Libn Finch Col 55-62; Libn Wentworth Inst 62-. 8: Chm, Amer Lib Hist RT, 47-; SUNY Accred Com, 55-60; Consul SC State Com on tech educ 67; Rep from Durham to NH Gen Court 69-70. 9: ALA; NYLA (past pres Col & Univ Sect); AALS (pres 50). 10: Melvil Dui Chowder & Marching Assn (Founder); Rembrandt Club of Brooklyn. 12: Co-comp "Books, Libraries, Librarians. 13: Yes. 14: Lib hist. 15: Bagdad rd, Durham NH 03824.

SHISLER, SHIRLEY M. b McGregor Iowa 15 Mr 31. 5: Hamline U 48-52; Hist, Soc Studies, Educ BA Columbia 56-57 MS. 7: Tchr-libn Sleepy Eye pub schs, Sleepy Eye Minn 52-54; Libn Elbow Lake pub schs, Elbow Lake Minn 54-55; Br asst St Paul Pub Lib 55-56; Jr libn hist, travel, biog dept Enoch Pratt Free Lib, Baltimore 57-59; Pub Lib of Des Moines, Des Moines Iowa 1st asst ref dept 59-63, Act head ref dept 63-64, Head ref dept 64-. 9: ALA; IowaLA; Des Moines Lib Club. 10: LWV; AAUW; Prof Womens League; Iowa Bds of Internat Educ; Altrusa Intl. 14: Ref. 15: 3523 University ave, apt 10-A, Des Moines Iowa 50311.

SHIVELY, DANIEL (CHARLES). b Huntingdon Penn 11 S 38. 5: Princeton U 55-59 (Philos) AB; Franklin & Marshall Col 59-60 (Educ) Tchg Certif; Drexel 62-63 MS in LS; Louisville Presbyterian Theol Sem 60-61. 6: Fr. 7: Tchr Tredyffrin-Easttown Jr High Sch, Paoli Area Sch System, Berwyn Penn 61-62; Asst libn Ind State Col 63-. 9: ALA; Tri-State ACRL. 12: Ed asst "Books in Print, summers 61 & 62 "Against Fear (68). 13: Yes. 14: Catlg, data proc. 15: RD 3, Indiana Pa 15701.

SHIVELY, HELEN ELIZABETH. b Nappanee Ind 3 Mr 17. 5: Ashland Col 35-39 (Eng) BA; UIll 39-40 BS in LS. 7: Act libn Pub Lib, Nappanee Ind summers 43, 45; Ref libn Ashland Col 40-. 9: ALA; OhioLA. 10: Esoteric Club; Pi Alpha Gamma; Faculty Women's Club of Ashland Col. 14: Ref, vis aids (records, tapes, etc), govt docs, period. 15: 1003 Masters ave, Ashland Ohio 44805.

SHIVERS, GLADYS (MICKLEBORO). b Marion Ala 20 O 04. 5: Judson Col 21-26 (Eng, Piano) AB, BM; UAla LS) MA. 6: Sp. 7: Tchr Butler Co High Sch, Greenville Ala 28-29; Tchr Perry Co High Sch, Marion Ala 43-48, Libn 48-65; Libn Francis Marion High Sch, Marion Ala 65-. 9: AlaEA;-AASchL. 10: Delta Kappa Gamma; Triad Study Club; Delta Sigma Pi. 14: Teen-age & ya collections, ref. 15: 412 W DeKalb st, Marion Al 36756.

SHOAP, RUTH F. b Vaiden Miss 8 S 19. 5: La Polytech Inst 36-40 (Fr) BA; LSU 40-42 (Fr) MA. 6: Fr, Sp. 7: Tchr Brenau Acad, Gainesville Ga 42-45; Research analyst Army Security Agency, Wash DC 43-45, 48; Bibliog LC 45-47, Proj libn 55-56; Libn Central Intelligence Agency, Wash DC 56; Bus-Soc sci libn La Polytech Inst 56-. 9: LaLA; SWLA; LaTA. 10: AAUP; La Tech Fac Senate; Alpha Beta Alpha. 14: Ref, archives. 15: 209 Ragan st, Ruston La 71270.

SHOCK, ELIZABETH HUNTER. b Cleveland 8 Je 14. 5: Oberlin Col 31-35 (Fr) AB; U Poitiers (France) 35-36 (Fr for foreigners) Certif lEtudes; West Res 36-37 (Fr) MA, 45-47 BS in LS. 6: Fr. 7: Prof asst catlg dept West Res U Lib 47-55; Prof asst catlg dept Cleveland Pub Lib 55-57; Head catlgr El Paso Pub Lib, El Paso Tex 58-59; Catlgr San Diego Pub Lib 59-61; Catlgr So Methodist U 61-65; Catlgr Kan City (Mo) Pub Lib 65-66, Asst libn SW br 67-69. 9: ALA; MoLA. 14: Catlg, ref. 15: 6645 Askew, Kansas City Mo 64132.

SHOCKEY, ANNETTE (POWELL). b Milwaukee Wis 28 Mr 22. 4: Jack Shockey. 5: UWash 39-41, 43-45 (Pol Sci) BA, 45-47 (Pol Sci); West Res 60-62 MSLS. 7: Libn Parma Schs, Parma Ohio 61-67; Sch lib bk specialist Cuyahoga Co Pub Lib, Cleveland Ohio 67-. 09; ALA; OhioASchL (Legis Chm); OhioLA (Sch L Certif Com); Educ Media Coun Ohio. 10: Beta Phi Mu; LWV. 14: Elem sch libs. 15: 12520 Edgewater dr #1005, Cleveland Oh 44107.

SHOCKLEY, ANN (ALLEN). b Louisville Ky 21 Je 27. 5: Fisk U 44-48 (Hist) BA; West Res 58-59 MSLS. 7: Asst libn Delaware State Col (Dover) 59-60; Asst libn Md State Col (Princess Anne) 60-66; Assoc libn 66-69; Spec collections libn Fisk 69-. 9: MdLA. 10: AAUW. 12: Free-lance writing, magazine & newspapers "History of Library Services to Negroes in the South". 13: Yes. 14: Readers serv, spec Negro collection. 15: 25 Church st, Bridgeville Del 19933.

SHOCKLEY, CHARLOTTE LOUISE. b Cincinnati 16 Je 16. 5: UCincinnati 33-38 (Eng, LS, Educ) BA; Col of Misic of Cincinnati 39-48 (Voice, Piano, Violin, Conducting). 6: Fr, Sp, Ger, Ital. 7: Catlg & tr UCincinnati Lib 38-41; Head Libn Prof Lib Cincinnati Bd ofEduc 41-56; Head research libn Stockton West Burkhart Inc, Cincinnati 57-. 8: Dir Clifton Methodist Church Choir, Cincinnati 44-; Pres & Leading Contralto, Cincinnati Music-Drama Guild, 48-56; Contralto Soloist, Cincinnati Symphony Orchestra (14 appearances) 48-60; WLW & WLW-T Soloist & Ensemble Work 39-64; Ed "Advance" 61-63, 69-71. 9: SLA; ALA. 10: Phi Beta Kappa; Mortar Bd Elta Kappa Gamma; Chi Delta Phi: Metropolitan Opera Guild; MacDowell Soc; Matinee Musicale; Arcade Quatet;

Cincinnati Advertisers Club 61-63, 69-; Bd Dir Mercantile LA 69-. 12: "Lyneia, opera libretto(47); "The Scandal at Mulford Inn, opera libretto (49). 13: Yes. 14: Ref, adv & marketing bks, research. 15: 128 Forest ave, Wyoming, Cincinnati 45215.

SHOEMAKER, BETTY G (ELIZABETH). b Zeeland Mich 23 Ap 25. 5: Calvin Col 43-47 (Econ, Soc) AB; West Mich summers Perm Tchg Certif; UMich 57-59 AM (LS). 6: Ger. 7: Tchr Lynden Christian High Sch, Lynden Wash 47-54; Tchr Southwest Minn Christian High Sch, Edgerton Minn 54-57; Lib asst Grand Rapids Pub Lib, Grand Rapids Mich summers 55, 56, Readers adv 57-67, 1st floor serv coord 67-. 9: ALA; MichLA; Grand Rapids Libns Club. 10: Grand Rapids Program PlanningInst; Beta Phi Mu. 14: Ref. 15: 257 S Wall st, Zeeland Mich 49464.

SHOEMAKER, MARGARET (VAN CISE). b Summit NJ 8 S 16. 4: Richard L Shoemaker. 5: Ga State Col for Women 33-37 (Eng) BS in Educ; Emory 37-38 AB in LS; Columbia summer 40 (Law Lib Admin). 6: Gr, Ger, Gk. 7: Libn Handley High Sch, Roanoke la 38-40; Libn Law 38-39 Emory U 40-42; Catlgr Law Lib UVa 42-46, Ref libn 46-47; Wake Forest Col: Law Libn 51-53, Asst ref libn 57-58, Asst catlg libn 58-. 10: AAUW. 14: Catlg. 15: 1830 Meadowbrook dr, Winston-Salem NC 27104.

SHOEMAKER, RICHARD H(ESTON). b Cynwyd Penn 5 Ap 07. 4: Helen Louise Ros. 5: UPenn 25-28, 34-35 (Eng Lit) AB; Columbia 37-38 (LS) BS; Washington & Lee U 39-41 MA. 6: Fr, Ger, Gk. 7: Catlgr Temple U 38; Proj supv Mercantile Lib, Phila 38-39; Washington & Lee U; Head catlgr 39-40, Asst libn 40-44, Libn 44-47; Libn Rutgers Newark Cols 47-59; Prof of lib serv Rutger U 59-. 9: ALA-ACRL; BSA; NJLA; Bibliog Soc of UVa. 10: ACLU; AAUP; Archons of Colophon. 11: Carnegie Fellow in Lib Admin, 58. 12: Comp with R R Shaw, "American Bibliography, 1801-1819," (22 v 58-66); "Checklist of American Imprints, 1820-" (6 v 64-). 13: Yes. 15: 190 George st, New Brunswick NJ 08901.

SHOENFELD, ALICE WANDA (LATOSZYNSKA). b Tysmienica Poland 13 D 15. 4: Norbert Shoenfeld. 5: College Emulja Plater (Cracov Poland) 26-34 BA; Jagiellonian U (Cracov Poland) 34-38 (Hist) Mgr Phil; UDijon (France) 34 (Fr Lang); UVienna (Millstatt) 35 (Ger Lang). 6: Ger, Polish, Fr, Lat. 7: Research asst Guttenberg Encyclopedia, Cracov Poland 33-34; Prof hist & Ger lang Queen Wanda Col (Cracov Poland) 38-39; Resettlement off United Nat Rel Agcy, Ulm Germany 46-48; Ref lib asst & catlgr Imperial Tobacco Co, Montreal 52-64, Research libn 64-. 9: SLA; CanLA; QueLA (sec 63-65). 14: Research (hist) catlg, ref. 15: Imp Tobacco Co 3810 St Antoine st, Montreal Que Can.

SHOLD, ROSEMARY KAY. b Webster City Iowa 31 Ag 41. 5: Ellsworth Jr Col 60-62 9liberal Arts) AA; UIowa 62-64 (Fr) BA, 64-65 (Fr); Rosary Col 66-68 MALS. 6: Fr. 7: Bkkeeper Williams Savings Bank, Williams Iowa 58-60; Bkkeeper 1st Nat Bank, Ames Iowa summers 61 & 62; Ser typist Iowa StateU (Ames) Iowa 65-66; Lib asst Rosary Col Lib 66-68; Asst catlgr Washington State Lib, Olympia 68-. 9: ALA; WashLA. 14: Catlg, clsf. 15: 3800 Elizabeth A13, Lacey Wa 98501.

SHOLTZ, KATHERINE J. b Waukegan Ill 14 Jl 31. 4: Paul N Sholtz. 5: UIll 49-52 (Chem) BS, 52-53 (Chem) MS; SUNY (Albany) 64-67 MLS. 7: Research asst Nutrition Dept Sch of Pub Health Harvard U 53-55; Nutrition research Sch of Home Econ Iowa State U 55-57; Libn IBM, Rochester Minn 67; Computer applications libn Mayo Clinic, Rochester Minn 67-. 9: ALA; MedLA. 10: Sigma Xi; LWV. 14: Automation of lib procedures. 15: 2006 NE Fifth ave, Rochester Mn 55901.

SHONIKER, FINTAN R(AYMOND). b Rochester NY 13 N 14. 5: St Vincent Col 34-38 (Philos) AB; St Vincent Col (Sem) 38-40, & 40-42 (Theol) MA; Rosary Col 41-43 BSLS; UNotre Dame LS; Columbia LS. 6: Lat. 7: Libn St Vincent Prep Sch, Latrobe Penn 36-39, Instr 40-45; St Vincent Col (Latrobe Penn): Asst libn 39-44, Libn 44-49, Instr 41-48; Instr Duquesne U 45-46; St Vincent Col (Latrobe Penn): Dir of pub rel 47-54, Prof 48-, Dir of Libs 49-68, Pres 68-. 8: Mem, Amer Commsn to Survey the Montreal U Libs, 46; Visiting lecturer, Portland U, summer 49 & Rosary Col, summer 50; Mem, Visiting Coms for Middle States Assn; Ordained Roman Catholic Priest, 42. 9: ALA-ACRL (pres Tri-State Chap); CathLA (Program Chm); SLA (chm Col Sect of Pittsburgh Chap); Amer Benedictine Acad (chm Lib Sci Sect); PennLA (chm Nomin Com). 10: AAUP. 12: Assoc ed "Catholic Booklist (42-53). 13: Yes. 14: Admin, rare bk. 15: St Vincent Col Lib, Latrobe Penn 15650.

SHOOKS, DAVID M. b Grand Rapids Mich 21 Ap 34. 5: Calvin Col 51-55 (Eng) AB; UMich 61-63 MALS. 7: US Army 55-57; Audio room supv UMich Undergrad Lib 62-63; Act ref libn Ill Tchrs Col, Chicago (South) 63-64, Period libn 64-. 9: ALA; MichLA; Chicago Lib Club. 10: AAUP. 14: Music materials & listening facilities, acquis, admin. 15: Rt 1 Box 18, S Holland Il 60473.

SHOPE, GRACE ELLEN. b Monument Penn 29 O 40. 5: Lock Haven State Col 58-60 (Soc Sci); Kutztown State Col 60-62 (Soc Sci, LS) BSEd; UIll 65-67 (LS) MS. 7: High sch libn Bald Eagle-Nittany Sch Dist, Mill Hall Penn 62-65; Grad asst UIll (Urbana) 65-67, Instr of lib sci 67-68; Coord libs Abington Sch Dist, Abington Penn 68-. 8: Wkshops for the Ill State Lib's Pub Lib Devel Proj summer 67, 68. 9: NEA; ALA; -AASchL; NEA; PennLA; PennEA; Penn Learning Resources Assn; Lib Pub Rel Assn Greater Phila. 10: Beta Phi Mu. 14: Sch libnship, lib educ. 15: 1621 Old York rd, Abington Pa 19001.

SHORE, PHILIP D. b Knoxville Tenn 3 Je 32. 5: Earlham Col 50-54 (Pol Sci) AB; NC 57-58 MS in LS. 6: Sp. 7: Catlgr Cornell U 58-59; Earlham Col: Catlgr 59-60, Asst libn 60-61, Act libn 61-62, Assoc libn 62-. 8: Ford Foun Fellowship, study in Japan, 3 months 62. 9: ALA. 13: Yes. 14: Tech serv. 15: 805 College ave, Richmond In 47374.

SHORES, LOUIS. b Buffalo NY 14 S 04. 4: Geraldine. 5: UToledo 22-26 (Eng) BA; City Col (NY) 26-27 (Eng Educ) MS; Columbia 27-28, summer 29 BS in LS; Chicago 29-30 (LS); Peabody 30-34 (Educ) (Hist) PhD. 6: Fr, Sp, Ger. 7: Asst Toledo Pub Lib 18-22; Asst UToledo Lib 22-26; Ref asst NY Pub Lib 26-28; Lib, Prof Fisk U 28-33; Libn Peabody Col 33-36; Dir, Prof Peabody Lib Sch 33-46; Mil serv, Army Air Force, US & Far East theatre 42-46; Squadron Commander 43-44, Command Intel in A-2 44-46; Adv ed, Ed in Chief Colliers Encyclopedia, NY 46-59, 60-; Dean, Prof Lib Sch Fla State U 46-. 8: Fulbright Fellow, United Kingdom 51-52; Visiting lecturer Italian Seminars, Rome, Florence, Naples, spring 52; Chm, Lib Adv Bd, Air Univ Maxwell AFB Ala, 52-56; Adv ed, "Comptons Pictured Encyclopedia 34-41; Visiting instr in lib sci, 3 Univs summers 30-35. 9: ALA-RSD (chm Org Com); ALHRT (sec 47-); NEA-DAVI; SELA (pres 50-52); FlaLA (pres 51-52); SLA (La Chap pres); ASIS. 10: Chm, Tenn Citizens Com on WPA Commun Sci Projs; Lions Club; C of C; Phi Kappa Phi; Beta Phi Mu. 11: Legion of Merit (WW II); Isadore Gilbert Mudge Citation 67. 12: "Origins of the American College Library" (34); "Bibliographies and Summaries in Education, with W S Monroe" (36); "Basic Reference Books," (ALA 37, 2d ed 39); "Highways In The Sky" (47); "General Education," with W H Stickler & Paul Stoakes (50); "Challenges to Librarianship" (53); "Basic Reference Sources" ALA (54); "How to Study with Samuel Smith" (55, 58, 60); "Instructional Materials" (60); Mark Hopkins Log," Ed by J D Marshall (65); Ed "Bio-Bibliography," by J D Marshall (64); "Books, Libraries, Librarians," with J D Marshall & Wayne Shirley; "The Library College" with Robert Jordan (66); "Around The Library World" (67); "Tex-Tec," with Mayrelee Newman and others (68). 13: Yes. 14: Ref, lib educ, lib hist, compar libnship, encyclopedias, a-v educ, jr col libs. , oral hist. 15: 2013 W Randolph circle, Tallahassee Fla 32306.

SHOREY, KATHARINE ABIGAIL. b Davenport Iowa. 5: Barnard 25-29 (Hist) BA; West Res 24 (LS) certif; Edinburgh Scotland 49 (European Hist). 6: Ger, Fr. 7: Asst Davenport Pub Lib, Davenport Iowa 20-23, 24-25, 27-28; Asst ColumbiaU Lib 26-27, 28-31; Dir Greene Co Lib, Xenia Ohio 31-35; Dir Martin Mem Lib, York Penn 35-; Dir York-Adams Co dist Lib, York Penn 61-. 9: ALA; NRA; PennLA (past pres). 10: Amer Bus Womens Assn; LWV; Woman's Club of York Penn. 15: 159 E Market st, York Pa 17401.

SHORT, KATHERINE (ROY). b Alexandria Egypt 17 O 17. 4: Morris R Short. 5: Muskingum Co 35-39, summers 39. 40 (Eng, Hist) BA; NYU summer 42; Ohio State U summer 43; Columbia summers 44-47 (LS) BS. 6: Fr. 7: Tchr Jr High Sch, Newcomerstown Ohio 39-43; Sch libn Roosevelt Jr High Sch, Columbus Ohio 43-54; Sch libn East High Sch Lib, Columbus Ohio 54-58; Asst & assoc libn Muskingum Col 58-63; Readers adv Annacostia Br DC Pub Lib 63-64; Libn Ocean Twp High Sch Lib, Oakhurst NJ 65-. 9: ALA-AASchL; NJLA; NJSchLA. 10: Delta Kappa Gamma; AAUW. 13: Yes. 14: Sch libs, stud lib assts. 15: 107 Dixon ave, Elberon NJ 07740.

SHORT, MARY ALICE (SELDEN). b Le Roy NY 16 N 16. 4: Clifford H Short. 5: URochester 33-37 (Fr) AB, summers 39, 41, 43 (Fr); McGill summer 42 (Fr); Syracuse Ext 46-47, 60 (Educ), Univ Col 56, summer 65 (LS); SUNY (Oswego) Ext 50-51 (Educ); SUNY (Geneseo) summers 54-58 (Lib Educ) MS. 6: FR. 7: High sch tchr, NY: Marion 37-43, 46-54, Le Roy

43-45, Candor 45-46; Libn Central Sch, Marion NY 54-60; Libn & hd Eng dept high sch, Marion NY 60-66, Libn 66-. 8: Adv Com to Library Unit, Genesee Valley Regl Educl Ctr, Rochester NY 67-68. 9: ALA; NEA; NYLA (pres Sch Libs Sect 64); NYTA (House of Delegates 63-66). 10: Phi Sigma Iota; Delta Kappa Gamma; AAUW. 13: Yes. 14: Sch libnship (secon sch). 15: 115 N Main st, Marion NY 14505.

SHORT, MARY HELEN. b Turners Falls Mass 1 S 12. 5: Columbia 32-40 (Eng) BS in Gen Studies, 40-42 BLS, equiv MLS. 7: Libn grade 1 Brooklyn Pub Lib, Brooklyn NY 30-42, Libn grade 2 42-45, Libn grade 3 45-49, Br libn 49-64, Sr libn 64-67; Lib asst IBM, SRI, NYC 68-. 9: ALA; NY Lib Club. 14: Ref, adult serv. 15: 22 Grove st, New York NY 10014.

SHORT, VIRGINIA. b Rome 7 S 29. 5: UCal(Berkeley) 46-50 (Humanities) BA; Sacramento State Col 50-51 (Tchg Credential); West Res 51-52 MS in LS. 6: Ital. 7: Gen ref Libn Sacramento State Col 52-58; Libn USAF, Eng 58-60, Italy 60-61; Ref libn UCal(Davis) 62; Libn USAF, Italy 63-67; Ref coord Mountain-Valley Info Ctr, Sacramento Cal 68-. 9: ALA; CalLA. 14: Ref. 15: 5411 State ave, Sacramento Ca 95819.

SHOSID, NORMA J. b Dallas Tex 9 N 37. 5: Barnard 56-58 (Hist) AB; Columbia 62-64 (LS) MS; USoCal 64-68 (Pub Admin) MPA; UCLA 68- (Sociol). 6: Fr. 7: Asst Sid Pietzsch Pub Rel, Dallas 59-60; Prof asst Dallas Pub Lib 61-62; Libn Standard Oil (NJ) 63-64; Hd Crocker Lib of Bus Admin USoCal 64-68. 8: Consul: Loyola U (Los Angeles) Col of Bus Admin 68-; Whittaker Corp Marketing Research Div 69; Woodview 9psychiatric) Hosp Lib 69-. 9: ALA; SLA; Amer Sociol Assn. 13: Yes. 14: Ref, info ret, educ of libns. 15: 1918 N Grace ave, Hollywood Ca 90028.

SHOU, STEPHENS T. b China 13 Ag 20. 4: Mabel Chu. 5: Yenching U 42-46 (Pol Sci) BA; UWash 48-50 (Pol Sci) MA, 50-51 (Pol Sci & Far East Studies), 51-52 (LS) MA. 6: Chinese, Russian. 7: Ore State U: Asst circ libn 52-56, Head circ dept 56-60, ref libn 60-63; Soc sci & bus libn 63-. 9: PNLA; OreLA. 13: Yes. 14: Ref, soc scis, bus. 15: Ore State U Lib, Corvallis Ore 97331.

SHOUSE, MARGARET ELIZABETH (BETTY). b Kansas City Mo 26 F 26. 5: William Jewell Col 44-48 (Lit) AB; UDenver 49-50 MA in LS. 7: Catlgr UGa 50-51; Child libn Athens Reg Lib, Athens Ga 51-52; Circ hd UMo (Columbia) 52-53; Libn South Jr High Sch, Roswell NM 53-55; Libn Mesa Jr High Sch, Los Alamos NM 55-58; Asst libn NM Military Inst 58-60; Hd libn Roswell Pub Lib, Roswell NM 60-63; Kan City Pub Lib, Kan City Mo: Hist dept 63-64, Hd popular lib 65-67, supv reader serv 67-. 9: ALA; MoLA. 14: Pub serv. 15: 4645 Harrison, Kansas City Mo 64110.

SHOVE, RAYMOND H. b Howard S Dak 20 S 06. 4: Edna Bradbury. 5: Morningside Col 24-28 (Lang, Lit) BA; UIll 29-30 BS in LS, 30-36 MA. 7: Asst UIll Lib (Urbana) 30-37; Hd acquis dept UMinn (Minneapolis) 37-47, Assoc Prof lib sch 47-. 9: ALA; AALS (chm Archives Com 65-68); MinnLA. 10: AAUP; UMinn Campus Club. 12: "Cheap Book Production in the United States, 1870-1891" (36); Co-auth "Use of Books and Libraries" (10th ed 63). 13: Yes. 14: Bibliog, printing & publishing, lib hist. 15: 87 Orlin ave SE, Minneapolis Mn 55414.

SHOWMAN, LINDA JEAN. b Manchester Iowa 20 Ja 41. 4: Gerald L Showman. 5: State Col Iowa 59-63 (LS) BA. 7: High sch libn John K F Kennedy High Sch, Cedar Rapids Iowa 67-. 9: NEA; ALA; Iowa State EA; IowaASchL. 10: Cedar Rapids EA. 15: John F Kennedy High Sch, 4545 Wenig rd NE, Cedar Rapids Ia 52402.

SHTOHRYN, DMYTRO (MICHAEL). b Ukraine 9 N 23. 4: Eustachia Barwinska. 5: Ukrainian Free U (MUNICH) 46-48 (Slavic Studies); UOttawa 55-57 (Slavic Studies) MA, 59 BLS (Slavic Studies) PhD. 6: Ukrainian, Russian, Polish, Czech, Ger, Lat. 7: Slavic catlgr & bibliogr UOttawa Lib 59; Catlgr, libn II NRC Lib, Ottawa 59-60; Slavic catlgr UIll Lib (Urbana) 60-64, Head of Slavic catlg 64-. 8: Assoc, Center for Russian Lang & Area Studies, UIll (Urbana) 63-. 9: ALA-ACRL (Exec Com Slavic & East European Subsect 63-64); Amer Assn Adv Slavic Studies. 10: AAUP; Ukrainian LA of Amer (v-pres 64-); Shevchenko Sci Soc; Ukrainian Hist Soc. 11: Silver medal, UOttawa Award from Grolier Soc of Can Ltd. 12: Ed "Catalog of Publications of Ukrainian Academy of Sciences, 1918-1930 (66); Asst ed "Horizons: Ukrainian Students Review. 13: Yes. 14: Catlg (Slavic & East-Slavic mod lit). 15: 1102 Centennial dr, Champaign Il 61820.

SHU, AUSTIN. b China 14 My 15. 4: Hsiang-tech Fang. 5: Boone Lib Sch Boone U (China) 42 BLS; Nat Anhwei U (China) 44 (Hist) BA. 6: Chinese, Japanese, Malay. 7: Libn Nat Fu-Tan U (China) 45; Head catlgr Nat Central Lib of China 47, Taiwan Prov Lib, Taipei 49, Nan-Yang U Lib (Singapore) 58; Sr catlgr East-West Center Lib, Hawaii 63-67; Bibliogr for E Asian Studies Mich State U Lib (E Lansing) 67-. 8: Coun; Lib Assn of China, Taipei 49-58, Lib Assn of Singapore, 58-62; Lecturer, Singapore Lib Train Sch. 9: Assn of Asian Studies. 12: "Twentieth Century Chinese Works on Southeast Asia; A Bibliography" (68); "Modern Chinese Authors; A List of Pseudonyms" (69). 13: Yes. 14: China & southeastern Asia. 15: 703-208 Cherry lane, E Lansing Mi 48823.

SHUBERT, JOSEPH F(RANCIS). b Buffalo NY 17 S 8. 4: Dorothy J Whearty. 5: NY State U Col (Geneseo) 47-51 BS; UDenver summers 55-57 MA. 7: Nev State Lib; Ref & ext libn 51-57, Lib consul 57-58, State libn 59-61; Asst dir ALA Internat Rel Off, Chicago 62-66; State libn The State Lib of Ohio 66-. 8: Tchr lib sci, UNev, summers 61, 65; Wkshop consul, Colo & Wyo, Montana 63, 64, 69; Internat Confs on Lib Devel, Nigeria 62, Rhodesia 64. 9: ALA (Coun rep Nev 58-61; chm Intl Rel RT 68-69; chm Nominating Com 68-69); NevLA (pres 56, Exec sec certif com 59-); MPLA (Exec Bd 58-59. 10: Kappa Delta Pi; PTA (Life mem). 12: "Public Library Service to Englewood, Colorado, A Survey (57); "Organizing for Good Library Service (62); Ed "Nevada Library Notes (52-60). 13: Yes. 14: Adult serv, lib devel, internat aspects of libnship. 15: 2713 Cranford rd, Columbus Oh 43221.

SHUEY, ANDREA LEE. b Oakland Cal 2 N 42. 5: LSU 63-65 (Hist) BA, 65-66 MSLS. 7: Ref libn Ga Tech 66-68; Adult libn Dallas Pub Lib, Dallas Tex 68-. 9: ALA. 14: Adult guidance & ref. 15: 5839B Sandhurst, Dallas Tx 75206.

SHUFORD, WELDA (WILLIAMS). b Columbus Ga 9 S 07. 4: Norris V Shuford. 5: UNC Greensboro 23-27 (Eng) AB; Duke U summer 31 NC Life Tchrs Certif; UNC 59 NC prof libns Certif; Appalachian State Tchrs Col summer 63-65 (LS) MA. 6: Fr. 7: Tchr Gastonia City Schs, Gastonia NC 27-32, 33-39; Libn Dallas High Sch & Carr Elem Sch, Gaston Co, Dallas NC 59-65; Libn Dallas High Sch, Gaston Co, Dallas NC 69-. 9: NEA; SELA; NCLA; NCEA. 10 DAR; UDC. 14: Sch libnship, admin, ref. 15: 629 N Weldon st, Gastonia NC.

SHULENBERGER, CATHARINE TICE. b Hagerstown Md 22 D 04. 5: Sweet Briar Col 22-26 (Eng Lit, Hist) AB; UPenn 26-28 (Eng Lit) MA; UVa summer 27 (Amer Lit); Drexel 31-32 BS in LS. 6: Ger. 7: Asst Washinton Co Free Lib, Hagerstown Md 29-30; Asst 1st grade Brooklyn Pub Lib 30-31; Ref libn James V Brown Lib, Williamsport Penn 34-64, Asst dir 64-. 9: ALA; MusLA; SLA; PennLA. 13: Yes. 14: Ref, catlg, rare bks. 15: 801 Market st, Williamsport Pa 17701.

SHULER, GRACE (MADEIRA). b Manheim Penn 10 J106. 4: Chester E Shuler. 5: Juniata Col 52-56 (Eng) BA; Carnegie 56-57 MLS. 6: Fr, Ger. 7: Juniata Col Asst libn ref & circ 57-58, Act libn 58, Asst libn 59-61, Catlg libn, asst libn 61-, Assoc Prof. 9: ALA-ACRL; PennLA. 10: AAUW; Womens Fellowship, Christian Educ Commsn; Juniata Col Womens League. 15: Taylor Highlands, Huntingdon Penn 16652.

SHULTES, DOROTHEA B. b Schenectady NY 9 F 16. 5: Wellesley 32-36 (Sociol) BA; Columbia 37-38 (LS) BS. 7: Libn Crouse-Irving Hosp Sch of Nursing Lib, Syracuse NY 56-64; Asst libn DeWitt Commun Lib, DeWitt NY 62-66; Lib asst Cazenovia Col 65-66; Ref libn SyracuseU 66-. 9: ALA; NYLA. 14: Ref. 15: 31 Pickwick rd, DeWitt NY 13214.

SHULTZ, MARIE. b Texas. 4: W O Shultz II. 5: UTex -53 (Hist, Anthrop) BA, 58 (Hist, Anthrop) MA; Tex Woman's U 63 Libnship. 7: Lib researcher Governor's Staff, Austin Tex 60-63; Field consul Tex State Lib, Austin 63-64, Asst dir field serv 64-66, Dir field serv 66-69, Program Dir, Lib Syst 70-. 9: ALA; TexLA; SWLA. 10: Phi Alpha Theta. 13: Yes. 14: Pub lib devel, training consul staff. 15: 2847 Shoal Crest, Austin Tx 78705.

SHUMAKER, EDITH (ELLEN). b Lebanon Ohio 29 Ja 17. 5: Miami U 35-39 (Hist) AB; Simmons 40-41 BSLS. 6: Ger. 7: Ref dept Cincinnati Pub Lib 41-42; Post libnPalm Springs Cal 42-45; Command Libn US Forces in Austria, Vienna 45-47; Ref dept Cal State Lib 48-50; Station libn Marine Corps Air Station, El Toro Cal 50-55; Libn Southwestern Reg Lib, Silver City NM 61-64; Ed Ed libn Wis Free Lib Commsn, Madison Wis 64-66; Readers' adv El Paso Pub Lib 66-67; Tchr Azufrerd Panamericana Jaltipon, Veracruz Mexico 67-68; Libn

Assumption Sem, San Antonio Tex 69-. 9: WisA. 13: Yes. 14: Ref, readers adv, ext. 15: 315 Germania #4, San Antonio Tx 78228.

SHUMAN, BRUCE ALAN. b Chicago 16 J141. 4: Frances Aidman. 5: Chicago 59-63 (Eng) AB, 63-65 (LS) AM; Rutgers 68-. 6: Fr, Ital. 7: Libn trainee Chicago Pub Lib 63-65; Adult serv libn Ft Lauderdale Fla Pub Lib 65-67; Asst ref serv libn NC State Lib 67-68; Doctoral research fellow Grad Sch of Lib Serv Rutgers 68-. 9: ALA; FlaLA; ASIS; NCLA. 10: ADLIB. 11: HEA II Doctoral Fellowship. 13: Yes. 14: Ref (humanities). 15: Grad School of Lib Ser, Rutgers, New Brunswick NJ 08903.

SHUMAN, MARGARET COLEMAN (GAUSE). b Centerville Del 12 Ag 12. 5: Sarah Lawrence Col 31-32; Bryn Mawr 43-44; UPenn 44-46 (Sociol) BA; UMich 60-61 MLS; Johns Hopkins 64-65 (Liberal Educ) MA. 6: Fr. 7: Soc wker, case wk Wilmington Family Serv, Wilmington Del 33-36; Child case ker Soc for Prevention of Cruelty to Child, Phila 41-43; Catlgr Wayne State U 61-62; Head of catlg dept West Md Col 62-64; Dir Lib fondation des tats Unis, Cit Universitaire, UParis summers 64-65; Lib dir Amer Col in Paris 65-. 8: Lib consul Amer Ctr for Artists & Studs, Paris summers 62-64. 9: ALA. 10: AAUW; AAUP; Amer Women's Club; Assn des Femmes Diplomees d'Universitaire. 14: Catlg, ref, admin. 15: 16 rue du Petit Musc, Paris 4 France.

SHURE, AUGUSTA (COHEN). b Vergennes Vt. 4: Jack Shure. 5: UVt 30-34 (Eng, Ger) PhB; Columbia -54 (LS) MS. 6: Fr, Ger, Hebrew, Yiddish. 7: Tchr Vergennes High Sch, Vergennes Vt 36-38; Publicity sec Amer Fr of Hebrew U, NYC; Educ sec Young Judaea, NYC 43-44; Researcher & writer Amer Jewish Com, NYC 44-46; Libn Zionist Lib, NYC 46-56; Child & yp libn, Maplewood NJ 63-65; El em libn Bd of Educ, W Orange NJ 65-. 9: Essex Co Sch Libns Assn. 10: Labor Zionist Org of Amer. 14: Child. 15: 25 Garthwaite ter, Maplewood NJ 07040.

SHURTLEFF, FRANCES (GENEVIEVE). b Janesville Wis 4 Ag 17. 5: Milton Col 37-41 (Soc Sci, Psych, Educ, Eng, Gen Langs) BA; UWis 48-49 BLS. 7: WAC (Sgt) USAFI & Lib 44-48; Libn VA Hosp, American Lake Wash 58-. 9: ALA; PNLA; WashLA. 14: Child & yp, psychiatric hosp wk. 15: VA HospLi, American Lake Wash 98493.

SHUTT, THELMA MILLER. b Indianapolis 12 Ag 26. 4: James W Shutt. 5: Butler U 48-50 (Span, Lat, Eng) AB; UColo 50-53 (Educ, Guidance) M Ed; Mexico City Col 59 (Span); Ball State Tchrs Col 56 (LS); Ind U 56-63 (LS) AMT; LSU summer 67 NDEA Inst LS. 6: Sp. 7: Span detail clerk Eli Lilly & Co, Indianapolis 46-48; Censor Indianapolis Star, Indianapolis 50; Tchr Louisville High Sch, Louisville Colo 50-52; Tchr Hobbs High Sch, Hobbs NM 52-54; Tchr-libn Charlottesville High Sch, Charlottesville Ind 55-58; Libn Greenfield High Sch, Greenfield Ind 58-63; Libn Franklin Central High Sch, Acton Ind 63-. 9: NEA; Ind State Tchrs Assn; IndSchLA. 10: Beta Phi Mu. 14: Ref. 15: 91 North 16th, Beech Grove In 46107.

SHWEDER, ESTHER (MICHOWSKI). b Detroit 5 O 31. 4: Allen D Shweder. 5: Marygrove Col 49-54 (Lat, Eng) BA; UMich 54-55 MALS. 6: Fr, Lat, Sp. 7: Stud asst UMich Lib 54-55; Asst libn St Francis Col (Ft Wayne Ind) 55-61; Adult asst libn Detroit Pub Lib 61-62; Adult serv libn Cuyahoga Co Pub Lib, Cleveland 62-67; Gen serv libn Baldwin-Wallace Col 67-68, Asst ref libn 68-. 9: ALA; CathLA; Ohio LA. 14: Ref, adult educ. 15: 11833 Prospect rd, Cleveland Oh 44136.

SIBEUD, MICHELE (BROWN). b Pasadena Cal 14 Ag 35. 4: Jacques Sibeud. 5: Conn Col 53-54; Finch Col 54-57 (Art Hist) BA; Columbia 57-58 (LS) MS. 6: Fr. 7: Asst libn Dewey, Ballantine, Bushby, Palmer & Wood, NYC 58-63; Libn Chadbourne Parke, Whiteside & Wolff, NYC 67-68; Asst libn Winthrop, Stimson, Putnam & Roberts NYC 68-. 10: NY Jr League; NY Eng Speaking Union. 11: Award Finch Col 57 Ineamus Meliora. 14: Ref. 15: 314 Ridgeview rd, Princeton NJ 08540.

SIBIA, TEJINDER (SINGH). b India 20 Ag 37. 4: Doris Jean. 5: Punjab Agric U 55-60 (Genetics) BSC; Agric Kan State U (manhattan) 60-63 MSC (Hort); Kan State Tchrs Col (Emporia) 64-65 MS (LS). 6: Hindi, Punjabi, Urdu. 7: Ref libn Linda Hall Lib, Kan City Mo 65-67; Hd sci & tech div of the libs Kan State U 67-. 9: ALA; KanLA; IAALD. 14: Ref, acquis, bibliog. 15: 1510 College ave, Manhattan Ks 66502.

SIBLEY, ELIZABETH ANN. b Woodbury NJ 11 My 45. 5: East Baptist Col 63-67 (Amer Studies) BA; Rutgers (New Brunswick) 67-68 MLS. 7: Bibliog searcher East Baptist Col 64-67; Sec E I duPont de Nemours Co Chambers Wks summer 66; Ref asst RutgersU Lib (New Brunswick) 67-68; Gen ref libn NJ State Lib, Trenton 68-. 9: NJLA. 10: Phi Alpha Theta; NJ Hist Soc. 14: Ref. 15: Auburn rd, Woodstown NJ 08098.

SIBLEY, MARJORIE H. b Longview Ill 23 Ap 20. 4: Mlford Q Sibley. 5: UIll 38-40, 41-42 (Sociol) AB, 42-43 (Sociol) MA, 43-44 (Sociol); UMinn 58-59 (LS) MA. 6: Fr. 7: Elem tchr Longview (Ill) Grade Sch 40-41; Asst in sociol UIll(Urbana) 45-46; Acquis libn Macalester Col 59-61; Supv HRAF Files Cornell U Lib Circ & ref libn Augsburg Col 61-62, Act hd libn 63-64, 66-67, Ref libn 64-66, 68-; SUNY (Binghamton) 68. 9: ALA; MinnLA. 10: Phi Beta Kappa; LWV. 11: Certif of Merit MinnLA 12: Co-comp "Recent Publications of Political Interest" in American Political Science Review (44-48). 13: Yes. 14: Ref, admin, bk selection. 15: 2018 Fairmount ave, St Paul Mn 55103.

SIBULKIN, LUCILLE. b Cleveland Ohio 3 Jl 28. 4: Merwin Sibulkin. 5: UMich 43-44; West Res 44-46 (Sociol) BA; URI 64-66 MLS. 7: Asst libn Adams Lib RI Col 66-. 9: ALA; RILA. 14: Col lib, ref, catlg. 15: 287 Doyle ave, Providence RI 02906.

SICKLES, ROBERT COLIN. b Rochester NY 7 F 38. 4: Zola Blake. 5: Sterling Col 59-63 (Math) BS; Syracuse 65-66 (LS) MS. 7: Sci div libn Ida State U 66-67; Tech processing libn UCal (Irvine) 67-68; Sci bibliogr Iowa State U (Ames) 68-. 9: ALA. 10: Pi Gamma Mu. 14: Acquis, admin, systems. 15: 823 24th st #25, Ames Ia 50010.

SICKMUND, CONSTANCE (CHANDLER). b Elmwood Okla 6 S 15. 4: Gordon Sickmund. 5: UNH 33-37 (Lat) AB; UHeidelberg summer 36 (Ger); Columbia 38-41 (LS) BS. 6: Lat, Fr, Ger, Gk. 7: Lib asst UNH 35-37; Tchr Andover High Sch, NH 37-38; Lib asst Columbia U 38-41; Ref libn Conn Col for Women 41-42; Libn US Submarine Base, New London Conn 42-45; Asst libn Salisbury State Col 57-. 9: MdLA. 10: US Power Squadron; PTA; Phi Kappa Phi. 14: Ref. 15: 201 E William st, Salisbury Md 21801.

SICKREY, WILLIAM THEODORE. b Grand Rapids Mich 4 Je 32. 5: Grand Rapids Jr Col 50-51(Eng); UMich 51-54 (Eng) BA, 54-55 (Eng Lang & Lit) MA, 61-63 AMLS; Ariz State U 64 Ariz Certif; Stephens Col 67 (Educ Media Inst); UColo 68 (Writers Conf). 6: Fr, Arabic, Lat, Ger. 7: Manager Blueprint Off Kaiser-Frazer Aeronautics Div, Willow Run Mich 52-53; Promotions asst UMich Press, Ann Arbor Mich 57; Asst libn U Lib Transportation & Phoenix Mem (Nuclear Energy) Libs, Ann Arbor Mich 59-61; Sub tchr secondary schs, Ann Arbor, Saline, Whitmore Lake, Ypsilanti Mich 61-62; Hd libn Phoenix Col, Camelback Ext Lib 63-65; Dir of lib serv Glendale Commun Col Instr Materials Center, Glendale Ariz 65-. 8: Chm Planning & Development Subcom of Instr Materials Com Maricopa Co Jr Col Dist 67-69, chm adv com on Scottsdale Instr Materials Com 68-69. 9: ALA; Ariz State LA; Salt River Valley Libns Assn; NEA-DAVI; Ariz State Assn A-V Educ. 10: Phi Kappa Phi; AAUP. 11: Two UMich Hopwood Awards, 1st prize for creative writing, 54 & 63; Grand Prize Award Haiku Poetry, Station KBUZ, Phoenix 64. 12: "Witchmosis (A Satire in One Act) (63). 14: Admin, ref. 15: 1447 Margaret SE, Grand Rapids Mich.

SIDES, MARY ANN. b Altoona Penn 6 Ag 40. 5: St Francis Col 58-62 (Med Tech) BS; UPittsburgh 66-68 MLS. 6: Sp. 7: Research assoc UPittsburgh Med Sch 62-66, Research assoc Grad Sch of Pub Health 67-68; Asst tech libn Penn StateU Lib Info Syst 68-. 8: Registered Medical Technologist. 10: Amer Soc of Clin Pathol; Beta Phi Mu. 14: Ref (sci & tech). 15: Parkway Plaza apts 1002 Plaza dr, State College Pa 16801.

SIEBECKER, DOROTHY F(RANCES). b Wausau Wis 16 J103. 5: Wis State Col (Stevens Point) 20-22; Carroll Col 22-24 (Math) BA; UWis 27-28 Diploma; Chicago summer 34 (LS); UMich 40 (LS) MA. 7: Math tchr Owen (Wis) High Sch 24-26; Catlgr: Pub Lib, au Claire Wis 28-36, Bradley U 36-37, Milwaukee-Downer Col 37-46; Head of the catlg dept UAriz 46-68, Interlib loan libn 68-. 9: ALA (Coun 51-55); Ariz State LA; SWLA. 0: AAUP. 14: Catlg, interlib loan. 15: 2423 E Kleindale rd, Tucson Az 85719.

SIEBEN-MORGEN, RUTH. b Westfield NJ 11 J110. 5: Goucher Col 28-32 (Eng) AB; Columbia 37 LS) BS, 40 (LS) MA, 40 (Educ). 6: Ger, Japanese. 7: Libn depts Enoch Pratt Free Pub Lib, Baltimore 32-36; Asst ref libn Columbia U 38; High sch libn Pub Schs, Dover Del & Teaneck NJ 39-47; Chief libn 5th Air Force (Bases), Japan 48-56; Staff libn Hqa 5th Air Force, Japan 57-63; Prin libn Oakland Pub Lib, Oakland Cal

64-. 8: Mgr, biennial mil libns conf, Tokyo Japan 56-62. 9: ALA (Life mem); CalLA. 10: Sierra Club. 11: Several J C Dana Lib Publ Awards. 12: "Samuel P Avery, Engraver on Wood (40); "Library Manual, 5th Air Force (60); Co-tr "Children of the A-Bomb ed by A Osada (63). 13: Yes. 14: Tech serv. 15: 35 Eucalyptus Path, Berkeley Cal 94705.

SIEBERT, EVELYN MARIE (KANNEL). b Akron Ohio 7 Ag 16. 4: Virgil J Siebert. 5: UAkron 34-39 (Sociol) BA; West Res 39-40 BLS; Bowling Green State U summer 64. 6: Fr, Ger. 7: Clerical Akron Pu Lib, Akron Ohio 34-39; Asst child libn Cleveland Pub Lib 40-41; Asst child libn Cleveland pub schs 41-3; Child libn Cuyahoga Co Schs, Parma Heights Ohio 49-50; Child libn Lakewood pub schs, Lakewood Ohio 61-62; Elem sch libn Vermilion pub schs, Vermilion Ohio 62-. 9: ALA; OhioSchLA; NEA; OhioEA. 10: Vermilion Col Club. 14: Elem schs lib wk. 15: 5331 Portage dr Lagoons, Vermilion Oh 44089.

SIEBERT, SARA L. b Baltimore Md 7 Ap 20. 5: Goucher 38-42 (Hist) AB; McGill 46-47 BLS. 7: Y-a libn in brs Enoch Pratt Free Lib, Baltimore 43-49, Act bkmob libn 49, Br libn 50-55, Admin asst & y-a libn in brs 55-57, Asst coord wk with y-a 57-62, Coord wk with y-a 62-. 9: ALA (Coun 68(; -YASD (pres 61-62, mem var coms); MdLA (MEM VAR COMS). 10: Goucher Col Alum Assn; Walters Art Gallery; Assn Preserv of Federal Hill at Fells Point; Baltimore Mus of Art. 13: Yes. 14: Reading promotion, ya serv. 15: Enoch Pratt Free Lib 400 Cathedral st, Baltimore Md 21201.

SIEFKE, THEA W. b Buffalo NY 23 Je 27. 4: Frederick J Siefke. 5: Allegheny Col 43-47 (Psych) BS; SUNY (Geneseo) 64-66 MLS. 7: Asst child libn Cuyahoga Co (Ohio) Pub Lib, Bay Village 66, Child libn N Olmsted 67-. 9: ALA. 15: 27018 Bruce rd, Bay Village Oh 44140.

SIEFKER, DONALD L. b Seymour Ind 4 Ja 35. 4: Barbara Marshall. 5: Wabash Col 53-57 (Psych) AB; Ind U 59-61 (LS) MA. 6: Ger. 7: Clerk-typist USAR Sp4E4 57-63; Ref & catlg libn Earlham Col 61-64; Asst libn Tri-State Col 64-66, Instr in Psych 65; Hd ref libn & instr Ball State U 66-. 9: ALA; IndLA. 10: Delta Phi Alpha; Beta Phi Mu; Lamdba Chi Alpha; AAUP. 14: Ref. 15: 740 N Jefferson st, Muncie In 47305.

SIEGEL, ERNEST. b Boston 30 My 23. 4: Beatrice Berman. 5: NYU 43-47 (Psych) BA; Pratt 50-51 MS in LS. 7: Catlgr Washoe Co Lib, Reno Nev 51-53; San Diego Pub Lib: Child libn Pacific Beach Br 53-55, Br libn Pacific Beach Br 55-59, Sr libn lit & lang dept 59-60, Supv libn No Reg 60, Prin libn Central Lib 60-63; Div Libn, dir Central Lib Los Angeles Pub Lib 63-. 8: Staff, Lib/USA, NY Worlds Fair, 64; Lectr USoCal Sch of Lib Sci summer 67. 9: ALA; CalLA. 13: Yes. 14: Ref,rare bks, automation. 15: Los Angeles Pub Li, 630 W Fifth st, Los Angeles 90017.

SIEGEL, MARGOT JUDITH. b Newark NJ 26 S 32. 4: Bernard Siegel. 5: MiamiU (Ohio) 50-52 (Eng); RutgersU 52-63 (Eng) AB, 68 MLS. 7: Elem sch libn E Brunswick Pub Schs 66-67; Asst lib Princeton High Sch, Princeton NJ 68-69; Ref lib Hunterdon Co Lib, Flemington NJ 69-. 9: ALA; NEA. 14: Ref, NJ & loc hist. 15: RD 5, Flemington NJ 08822.

SIEGRIST, EDITH BARBARA. b McIntosh SD 9 My 25. 5: Huron Col 43-45, 48-50 (Eng) BA (magna cum laude); UDenver 53-54 (LS) MA. 7: Elem tchr pub sch, Mobridge SD 45-46; Rural sch tchr, Keldron SD 46-48; Elem tchr pub sch, Huron SD 50-53; Asst libn No State Col (Aberdeen SD) 54-55; Libn Everett High Sch, Lansing Mich 55-61; Asst ref libn & Asst Prof of Lib Sci USD 61-. 9: ALA (local rep; Recruitment Netwk);-ACRL; SDLA (chm Auditing Com); SDEA; MPLA. 10: AAUW; Delta Kappa Gamma. 13: Yes. 14: Ref, educ for libnship, curriculum libs. 15: 854 Eastgate dr, Vermillion SD 57069.

SIEHLER, CYNTHIA J(ANE). b Cumberland Md 11 My 44. 5: St John's Col (Annapolis Md) 62-66 (Liberal Arts) BA; UMd (Col Park) 67-68 MLS. 6: Fr. 7: Jr operations research analyst Westat Research Inc, Bethesda Md 66-68; Spec recruit LC 68-69, Research asst ser rec div 69-. 9: ASIS (Arr Chm Potomac Valley Chap). 10: Beta Phi Mu; Eng-Speaking Union. 14: Clsf, indexing, systems analysis. 15: 3020 Dent pl NW, Washington DC 20007.

SIEMENS, WILLIAM PAUL. b Los Angeles Cal 18 Ja 45. 5: Biola Col 62-67 (Eng) BA; USoCal 68 MSLS. 6: Ger. 7: Ser libn Biola Col 68-69; Tech processes libn Z J Loussac lib, Anchorage Alaska 69-. 9: CalLA. 10: Cal Col & Univ Fac Assn; Sierra Club. 14: Ser, tech proc, bibliog. 15: 14811 Ragan dr, La Mirada Ca 90638.

SIEMINSKI, VERONICA S. b Pittsburgh. 5: Pomona Col 50 (Sociol) BA; Colmbia 53-54 MLS. 7: Ser libn NM State U 55-. 9: ALA; NMLA. 10: AAUW. 14: Serv. 15: Box 1173, University Park NM 88001.

SIEMON, FREDERICK. b Bakersfield Cal 22 Mr 35. 4: Elma M Van Fossen. 5: San Jose State Col AB; UCal MLS. 6: Sp, Ger. 7: Libn Santa Clara Co Lib 63-66; Libn San Jose State Col 66-69, Sci libn 68-. 9: ALA; SLA; CalLA; CalTA. 12: Comp "Gost Story Index" (67); "Science Fiction Story Index" (69). 14: Lit of sci & tech. 15: 6517 Trinidad ct, San Jose Ca 95120.

SIEMSEN, DAVID P. b Sunbury Penn 31 O 39. 4: Lois E Sabo. 5: Pontifical Col Josephinum (Worthington Ohio) 57-61 (Scholastic Philos) BA; Syracuse 63-64 MSLS. 6: Ger, Lat. 7: Tech proc hd SyracuseU Mss Dept 64-65; Ref libn Lycoming Col 65-68; Dir lib serv Williamsport Area Commun Col 68-. 9: Mss Soc; PennLA. 14: Admin, computerization, rare bks & mss. 15: 702 Glenwood ave, Williamsport Pa 17701.

SIENITSKY, LYDIA N. b Russia 30 Mr 15. 4: Serge Sienitsky. 5: Columbia 51-54 (LS) MS. 6: Polish, Russian, Fr. 7: Asst to ed H W Wilson Co, NYC 50-53; Libn (staff) NYC Pub Lib 53-58; Hd libn Radio Liberty Committee, NYC 58-. 9: SLA. 14: Ref. 15: Research Lib Radio Liberty Committee 30 E 42nd st, New York NY 10017.

SIERECKI, JOAN JOYCE (JAKAWICH). b Chicago 15 D 42. 5: UIll(Urbana) 60-64 (Math) BS, 64 (LS) MS. 6: Fr, Sp. 7: Lib asst Newman Found Lib, Champaign Ill 63-64; Sci reflibn John Crerar Lib, Chicago 64-65; Hd tech proc Mun Ref Lib, Chicago 66-. 9: SLA; AALL. 10: AAUW. 14: Ref, catlg. 15: 121 N LaSalle st, rm 1005, Chicago Il 60602.

SIGGINS, JACK A. b Arp Tx 11 Jl 38. 4: Elizabeth Martin. 5: Princeton 56-60 (Romance lamg) BA; AmericanU 64-67 (Far East Area Studies) MA; UChicago 67- (LS) MA. 6: Japanese, Chinese, Sp, Portu. 7: Japanese interpreter/tr US Army, Hokkaido Japan 61-64; Research analyst LC 65-66; Far East Lib UChicago 68-. 9: ALA. 10: Friends of the Princeton U Lib. 14: Far East libs, censorship. 15: 5458 S Cornell, Chicago Il 60615.

SIGLER, ESTELLE (SMITH). b Vicksburg Miss 12 D 24. 7: Personnel clerk R G Letourneau, Vicksburg Miss (44-46); Waterways Expt Sta, Vicksburg Miss; Typist 47-48, Lib catlgr 55-65, libn Ref & Bibliog 65-. 9: MissLA (sec Spec Libs Sect 65-66). 11: Sustained Superior Performance Award (WATERWAYS Expt Sta). 59. 14: Ref, bibliog. 15: 1622 Martha st, Vicksburg Miss 39180.

SIGLER, RONALD F(LOYD). b Brooklyn NY 12 D 32. 4: Lorraine Smith. 5: Queens Col (NY) 51-56 (Music) BA; Long Beach State Col 58-60 (Music); USoCal 62-63 (Cinema & Music); UCLA 63-64 MLS. 7: Dept clerk art & music div Queens Borough Pub Lib, Jamica NY 53-56; Catlg asst & interlib loans Ramo-Woodridge Corp, Los Angeles 56; Libn Engnr Lib Servomechanisms Inc, Hawthorne Cal 56-57; Libn ref, interlib loans, recordings & Music Buena Park Lib Dist, Buena Park Cal 57-58, A-v lib, head a-v dept 58-64; A-v consul Mich State Lib 64-65; Coordinator of a-v serv Los Angeles Co Pub Lib, Los Angeles 65-. 8: UCal ext faculty UCLA Sch Lib Sci continuing educ program summer 68; Lectr Immaculate Heart Col Sch Lib Sci winter & summer 69. 9: ALA; NEA-DAVI; Educ Film Lib Assn; Juror Amer Film Festival NYC 65; Music Tchrs Assn of Cal; CalLA (pres A-V Div 67-68; cinema juror 69). 13: Yes. 14: A-v serv, music, adult educ, lib educ. 15: Los Angeles Co Pub Lib, 320 W Temple st, Los Angeles 90012.

SIGWORTH, ELIZABETH (WHITELEY). b Erie Penn 6 S 45. 4: Geoffrey K Sigworth. 5: Carnegie-MellonU 63-67 (Eng Lit) BA; Case West ResU 67-68 (Col & Acad Libs) MS in LS. 6: Fr. 7: Asst to coord adult serv Boston Pub Lib 68-69; Asst libn Mass Col of Pharmacy 69-. 9: ALA. 14: Acad & spec libs. 15: 93 Hampshire st, Cambridge Ma 02139.

SIHLER, EMMA (ELIZABETH). b Ft Wayne Ind 14 O 07. 5: Hillsdale Col 26-27; West Res 28-30 (Eng) AB; Cleveland Col 30-31 Lib Sci Certif. 6: Ger. 7: Lib asst Jackson Pub Lib, Jackson Mich 31-33, Head of circ 33-47; Asst libn Adrian Pub Lib, Adrian Mich 47-51, Head Libn 51-. 9: ALA; Adult Educ Assn; ALA (Memb Com); MichLA (sec 56-58, chm Nomin Com 55, chm Personnel Policies Com 63-64, chm Dist 2 51-52, chm Memb Com 67-68). 10: AAUW; Bus & Prof Womens Club; Adrian Dramatic Club; Delta Kappa Gamma. 14: Adult educ. 15: 325 N McKenzie st, Adrian Mich 49221.

SIKES, FREDONIA (WHITE. b Big Sandy Tex 20 My 18. 5: Southwestern State Col 34-35 (Eng; N Tex State U 40-43 BALS; Stephen F Austin State Col 56-58 (Educ) NEd. 6: Sp, Fr. 7: Asst libn Sul Ross State Col 41-42; Libn: Mt Pleasant High Sch, Mt Pleasant Tex 42-43, Gaston High Sch, Henderson Tex 43-47, Kilgore Col 47-. 8: Kilgore Col Eval Program, 60-6; So Assn of Sec Schs & Cols, Lib Accred Bd, 54-55; Lib Sci Inst on Jr & Commun Cols UMich summer 68. 9: ALA (Jr Bk Sel Bd); SWLA; TexLA; Tex Jr Col Assn; Tex State Tchrs Assn (pres Lib Div). 10: Bus & Prof Womens Club; Kilgore Commun Concerts; Country Club; PTA; Kilgore Col Faculty Club. 13: Yes. 14: Admin, ref. 15: 905 Crim ave, Kilgore Tex 75662.

SILBERBERG, ELSA. b Tallinn Estonia. 5: Stockholms Hgskola 48 (Ger); Mt Allison U (NB) 48-50; UToronto 50-51 (Modern Lang & Lit); UCal(Berkeley) 51-53 (Ger) AB; UDenver 53-54 (LS); UCal(Berkeley) 54-55, 59-61 MLS. 6: Finnish, Estonian, Ger, Swedish, Norwegian, Fr. 7: Libn I acquis dept UCal(Berkeley) 62-64, Libn II 64-. 10: Beta PHI Mu. 14: Bk sel, acquis, bibliog. 15: 2720 Piedmont ave, Berkeley Cal 94705.

SILIUNAS, KAZYS. b Lydavenai Lithuania 23 Ja 13. 4: Grazina Sliupas. 5: State U of Vytautas the Great (lithuania) 31-38 (Law) Dipl Jurist; Columbia 59-60 LS) MS. 6: Lithuanian, Ger, Russian, Fr, Lat. 7: Queens Borough Pub Lib: Libn-trainee Windsor Park Br 60, Asst br libn Sunnyside Br 61-62, Ref libn Glen Oaks Br 63, Asst br libn Morris Park Br 64-67, Asst br libn Richmond Hill br 68-. 14: Ref. 15: 30-11 Parsons blvd, Flushing NY 11354.

SILL, HELEN CATHERINE. b Batavia NY 19 O 06. 5: Geneseo Normal Sch 25-28 (LS) Diploma; Columbia 38 (Eng) MA, 55 (Curriculum, Tchg) Ed D, 50-51 MSLS. 6: Fr. 7: Libn: Southampton pub schs, Southampton ny 28-42, Fieldston Sch, NYC 42-47, Scarsdale Pub Schs, Scarsdale NY 47-50; Libn Sch Lib Lab Tchrs Col Columbia U 50-52, Libn Curriculum Room 52-54; Libn, Assoc Prof Willimantic State Col 54-65, Dir of Lib Serv 65-. 8: Visiting Prof East Mont Col of Ed, Billing Mont 56. 9: NEA; ConnLA (Program Chm 57-58); ConnEA. 10: Kappa Delta Pi; Delta Kappa Gamma; Bd, Eastford Pub Lib, Eastford Conn. 12: "Treasure is the Attic (child play). 13: Yes. 14: Admin. 15: Box 95, Eastford Conn.

SILLEN, ROBERT WESLEY. b Quincy Mass 11 D 21. 5: Colby Col 40-44 (Eng) AB; Simmons 45-46 (LS) BS; Boston U 63 (Eng). 7: Jr asst Williams Col Lib 46-47; Asst libn Andover Newton Theol Sch 47-48; Catlg libn Watertown Pub Lib, Watertown Mass 48-52; Act libn Andover Newton Theol Sch 52-53; 1st asst catlg dept Providence Pub Lib 53-54; Ref libn & readers consul Morrill Mem Lib, Norwood Mass 54-55; Libn Andover Newton Theol Sch 55-60; Libn Quincy Jr Col 60-63; Asst Thomas Crane Pub Lib, Quincy Mass 60-62; Catlg libn Springfield Col 63-65, Asst libn in chg of tech serv 65-. 8: Conducted radio program "Leaders Are Readers, WCRB (Waltham Mass) 49-52; Bible Inst, Saffle, Sweden 69. 9: ATheolLA (Program Com 58); Boston Reg Group of Catlgrs & Clsfrs (sec-treas 50-51); West Mass Lib Club. 10: Amer Baptist Hist Soc; Quincy (Mass) Hist Soc. 12: Ed "Bay State Librarian (55-60); Auth "Hand List of Histories of New England Baptist Churches (58); Jt ed "Union List of Periodicals in Greater Springfield" (69). 13: Yes. 14: Catlg. 15: 11 Bettswood rd, E Longmeadow Ma 01128.

SILLIMAN, ALICE (MARY. b Hoosick NY 14 Ag 06. 5: Wesleyan Col (Ga) 25-29 (Fr) AB; Chautauqua Lib Sch (Chautauqua NY) summers 31-33 Certif. 6: Fr. 7: Summer camp dir St Johnland, Kings Park NY 29, Housemother 29-30; Asst libn Pub Lib, Geneva Ohio 31-45, Head libn 45-53; Asst libn Pub Lib, Findlay Ohio 53-62; Asst libn Pub Lib, Grand Haven Mich 62-. 9: ALA; MichLA. 10: Bus & Prof Womens Club; Tuesday Musicale. 14: Catlg, ref. 15: 312 S Fifth st, Grand Haven Mi 49417.

SILLS, JEANNETTE EVANS. b Burnside Ky 4 Ap 09. 5: SoIllU 27-31 (Eng) BEd; Peabody Col 32-34 BS in LS; UHouston 51-53 (Secondary Educ) MEd. 7: Libn Carbondale Commun High Sch, Carbondale Ill 32-35; Tchr: McAllen Jr High Sch, McAllen Tex 40-43, McAllen High Sch, McAllen Tex 45-54, Edinburg High Sch, Edinburgh Tex 55-62; Gunnery instr (Spec G 3/C) Women's Res USN, Fla 43-45; Libn Nurnberg Amer High Sch, Nurnbweg germany 54-55; Libn Edinburg High Sch, Edinburg Tex 62-. 9: ALA; TexLA; TexStateTA; TexClrTA. 10: Delta Kappa Gamma. 14: Sch libs. 15: 705 Cedar ave, McAllen Tx 78501.

SILVA, HELEN L(OUISE ROHRER). b Portland Ore 23 Mr 30. 5: UCal 47-48, 54-57 (Eng) AB, 57-59 MLS. 6: Sp, Fr. 7: Tchr Mission Hill Jr High Sch, Santa Cruz Cal 57; Catlgr Berkeley Pub Lib, Berkeley Cal 59-63; Libn Cornell Sch, Albany Cal 63-. 9: ALA; NEA; Assn Childhood Educ Internat; Sch Libns Assn No Cal; Cal Tchrs Assn. 14: Child lit, sch libs. 15: 1228 Navellier st, El Cerrito Cal 94530.

SILVA, LOLITA ILEANA. b Riga Latvia 16 N 39. 5: NYU 58-62 (Russian) AB, 62-65 (Russian) MA; Columbia 65-66 (LS) MS. 6: Russian, Ger, Fr, Latvian. 7: Asst libn Inst of Pub Admin, NYC 64-66; Spec recruit LC 66-67, Ref specialist Legis Ref Serv 67-69, Asst selection off Processing Dept 69-. 9: ALA. 14: Ref, acquis. 15: 110 D st SE, Washington DC 20003.

SILVA, RITA C. b Maple Heights Ohio 24 Ja 24. 5: St John Col (Cleveland) 44-54 (Educ) BS in Ed; West Res 57-59 MS in LS. 6: Fr. 7: Elem tchr Catholic Diocese, Cleveland 44-59; Secondary sch libn Parma city schs, Parma Ohio 59-66; Ref libn Cuyahoga Commun Col (Ohio) 66-. 9: ALA; OhioASchL; OhioEA (Life mem); NE Ohio Tchrs Assn. 10: Great Bks Leader; Beta Phi Mu. 13: Yes. 14: Ref. 15: 6296 Ridge rd, Parma Oh 44129.

SILVER, BARBARA (CEIZLER). b Los Angeles Cal 4 Mr 40. 4: Martin A Silver. 5: UCLA 57-61 (Eng) BA; UCal (Berkeley) 62-63 MLS. 6: Sp. 7: NYC Pub Lib br libs 63-65; Nat Indus Conf Bd Lib, NYC 66-67; UCal (Santa Barbara) Lib 67-. 13: Yes. 14: Catlg, child bks. 15: 2860 Kenmore pl, Santa Barbara Ca 93105.

SILVER, CY H. b Berkeley Cal 5 Ag 31. 4: Carla Weiner. 5: UCal(Santa Barbara) 59-61 (Music) BA; UCLA 63-64 MLS. 6: Ger. 7: Bandsman (Sgt) US Army 54-57; Clerk UCal(Santa Barbara) Lib 61-63; dult serv libn Brooklyn Pub Lib 64-65; Br lbn Ruth Bach Br Long Beach (Cal) Pub Lib 65-67; Hd catlg libn Los Angeles Co Law Lib 67-. 13: Yes. 15: 4551 Wortser ave, N Hollywood Ca 91604.

SILVER, JOSEPH M. b Brooklyn NY 8 My 03. 4: Rhea Greenstein. 5: Hiram Col 33-37 (Chem) BS; Columbia 40-41 BS in LS. 6: Fr, Ger. 7: Ref asst Columbia Med Sch Lib 41-42; Supv libn US Corps of Engnrs, NYC 42-43; (T/Sgt) US Army, Overseas 43-46; Priv bus, Warren Ohio 46-58; Head Libn Girard Free Lib, Girard Ohio 58-; Dir Bacon Mem Pub Lib, Wyandotte Mich 67-. 9: ALA; MichLA (chm Planning Com). 10: Rotary. 14: Ref, adv serv to adults & yas, admin. 15: 2130 Oak st, Wyandotte Mi 48192.

SILVER, MARTIN A. b NYC 6 D 33. 4: Barbara Ceizler. 5: CCNY 52-56 (Mus) BA; Columbia 64 MLS. 6: Ger, Fr. 7: Libn I NYC Pub Lib br libs 63-64, Libn II Mus Circ Dept Lincoln Ctr 65-66, Libn II Music Research Div Lincoln Ctr 66-67; Assr hd Arts Lib UCal (Santa Barbara) 67-. 8: Asst dir, Sem in Music Libnship, N Tex State U 69. 9: MusLA (Exec Com So Cal Chap); Lib Assn UCal (pres Santa Barbara Gp). 10: NY Musicians Club (Bohemians). 13: Yes. 14: Music libnship. 15: 2860 Kenmore pl, santa Barbara Ca 93105.

SILVER, ROLLO G(ABRIEL). b NYC 27 Je 09. 4: Alice Gindin. 5: Brown 27-31 (Philos) PhB; Boston U 35-41 (Eng) MA; Simmons 47-48 (LS) BS. 6: Fr. 7: Asst buyer B Altman Co, NY 31-34; Managing dir Better Service Garage, Brockton Mass 34-43; US Army QM Corps (T3) 43-45; Asst dir US Army Climatic Research Lab 45-47; Ref libn Peabody Inst Lib, Baltimore 48-50; Simmons Col; Asst Prof 50-53, Assoc Prof 53-57, Prof 57-65; Consul 65-. 9: BSA (Adv Com); Amer Antiq Soc; Soc of Printers (past pres); Wynkyn de Worde Soc (London). 10: Grolier Club (NY); Essex Inst; Playboy Club; Phi Beta Kappa; Double Crown Club (London); Fellow Royal Soc of Arts. 12: Jt auth "Book in America" (51); Auth "Typefounding in America" (65); "The American Printer" (67). 13: Yes. 14: Bibliog, rare bks, hist of printing. 15: 105 Mt Vernon st, Boston Ma 02108.

SILVERA, KATHARINE MEREDITH (SCHWARTZ). b Pasadena Cal 8 D 40. 4: Ronald L Silveira de Braganza. 5: Mills Col 58-62 (Hist, Govt) BA; UCal 62-63 MLS. 6: Fr, Sp. 7: Catlgr UCal (Santa Barbara) 63-66; Catlgr Salk Inst for Biol Studies, San Diego 67, Acting sr libn 67-68; Bk catlg project Biomed Lib UCal (San Diego) 68-. 12: Comp -baja California Bibliography, 1965-66, a Supplement" (68). 14: Tech proc (computer use). 15: 221 S Nardo, Solana Beach Ca 92075.

SILVERMAN,HAROLD N. b NYC 23N28. 5: City Col (NY) 49 (Econ) BS in Soc Sci; Columbia 53 (LS) MS. 6: Sp. 7: Supv libn NY Pub Lib 52-. 14: Adult serv, ref. 15: 480 Audubon ave, NYC 10040.

SILVERMAN, JUDITH (MARKS). b Brooklyn NY 26 Ag 33. 4: Myron B Silverman. 5: Brooklyn Col 52-60 (Sociol) BA;

Pratt 61-63 MLS. 6: Fr. 7: Sec Chas Kaye Realty Co, NYC 50-54; Exec sec Fairchild Publ, NYC 54-56; Sch sec NYC Bd of Educ Jr High Sch, Brooklyn NY 56-60, Tchr of Lib Jr High Sch, Brooklyn 60-62, 68-; Child libn Brooklyn Pub Lib 64-68. 10: Beta Phi Mu. 14: Child serv. 15: 300 Ocean pky, Brooklyn NY 11218.

SILVERMAN, LUCILLE (SEGAL). b NYC 25 Je 14. 4: Robert Silverman. 5: Washington Sq Col NYU 31-35 (Geol) BA; Columbia 35-37 (Geog, Geol) MA, 61-63 (LS) MS. 6: Fr. 7: US Army Corp of Engnrs Temp war unit, NYC 43-44; Instr Queens Col (NY) 63-, Paul Klapper Lib 63-. 9: ALA; NY Tech Serv Libns; LACUNY. 14: Acquis, processing, gifts & exchange. 15: Queens College, Flushing NY 11367.

SILVERMAN, MYRON BERNARD. b Brooklyn NY 26 Ap 32. 4: Judith Marks. 5: Brooklyn Col 49-53 (Hist) BA, 54-55 (Hist); Pratt 61-63 MLS. 6: Fr. 7: NYC Bd of Educ: Hist tchr Lafayette High Sch 54-56, Hist tchr Jas Madison High Sch 57-62, Lib tchr Sheepshead Bay High Sch 62-. 9: NYC SchLA. 10: Beta Phi Mu. 14: Sch libs, catlg. 15: 300 Ocean pky, Brooklyn NY 11218.

SILVERMAN, ROBERTA E. b NYC 2 N 45. 5: Brooklyn Col 62-66 (Eng) BA; Pratt Inst 66-68 MLS. 6: Fr. 7: Trainee Brooklyn Pub Lib Kings Highway Br 66-67; Asst libn Ogilvy & Mather Advertising, NYC 68-. 9: ALA. 10: Beta Phi Mu; Brooklyn Col Alum Assn. 14: Child lit. 15: 3619 Bedford ave, Brooklyn NY 11210.

SILVERS, MARY LYNN. b Tyler Tex 21 S 37. 5: Kilgore Jr Col 56-57; Tex Woman's U 57-60 (LS) BS; E Tex State U 63-64 MS in LS. 7: Asst libn Rusk Co Lib, Henderson Tex summer 60; Jr high libn Anahuac Ind Sch Dist, Anahuac Tex 60-63; Lib asst E Tex State U 63-64; Elem libn Mesquite Ind Sch Dist, Mesquite Tex 64-65, Libn Jr High Sch 65-. 9: ALA; TexLA; TexASchL; Tex State Tchrs Assn (co-chm Dist X Lib Sect 68-69); SWLA. 10: Kappa Delta Pi; Friends of Mesquite Pub Lib; PTA; Mesquite TA. 14: Secondary schs ref, jr col lib supv. 15: 213 Highland Valley dr, Mesquite Tx 75149.

SILVERSHER, GLADYS (ROBINSON). b Philadelphia Penn 13 F 21. 4: Herman I Silversher. 5: UCLA 38-42 (Gen) AB; USoCal 43-44 (LS) BS. 6: Fr. 7: Libn Armed Forces Radio Ser, Hollywood Cal 44-45; Ref libn Los Angeles Pub Lib 49-52, 60-64; Ref libn Mountain view Pub Lib, Mountain View Cal 65-66; Hd libn Isotopes Inc Labs, Palo Alto Cal 66-. 9: SLA; CalLA. 10: Alum Assn Sch Lib Sci USoCal. 14: Ref (nuclear sci, geol, oceanography). 15: 1213 Awalt dr, Mountain View Ca 94040.

SILVERSTEEN, SOPHY. b Port Arthur Tex 22 S 31. 5: Rice 48-52 (Psych) BA; UTex 52-54 mssw, 62-64 MLS. 6: Ger, Sp. 7: Med soc wker: VA Admin Hosp, McKinney Tex 54-56, UTex Med Br (Galveston) 56-58; Catlg asst RiceU 60-65, Catlg libn 65-. 9: ALA; TexLA; SWLA. 10: Phi Beta Kappa; Delta Phi Alpha. 14: Catlg. 15: 4102 Dumbarton, Houston Tx 77025.

SILVERSTEIN, ESSIE (EPSTEIN). b NYC. 4: Edward Silverstein. 5: Smith 24-28 (Fr) BA; NY Sch of Soc Wk 32, 35, 36; Pratt 58-60 MLS. 6: Fr. 7: Soc wker Brooklyn Bur of Charities, Brooklyn NY 28-29; Soc wker Israel Orphan Asylum,NYC 29-36; Catlgr Queens Borough Pub Lib, Jamaica NY 53-60, Asst supt catlg 60-61; Catlgr Engnr Socs Lib, NYC 61-62; QueensBorough Pub Lib, Jamaica NY; Head searching sect 62-63; Head pub catlg 63-65, Asst chief tech process 65-66, Chief tech process 66-68, Hd central lib 68; Ser project engr Socs Lib, NYC 69-. 9: ALA; NYLA; NY Tech Serv Libns; NY Lib Club. 10: Beta Phi Mu. 14: Catlg. 15: 139-522 Pershing cres, Jamaica NY 11435.

SILVERSTONE, ROSE (ORLEANS). b Woonsocket RI 7 D 07. 5: CCNY (Hunter Col) 39 (Lang) BA; Pratt Inst 42 BLS; New Sch for Soc Research 44 (Sociol); Columbia 51 (LS); CCNY Sch of Educ 53, 57 (Diagnostic & Remedial Reading); Queen's Col (NY) 57 (Child Lit). 6: Fr Ger, Hebrew, Lat, Yiddish. 7: Lib asst Queens Borough Pub Lib, Jamaica NY 40-41, Ref asst 42-43; Hd ser div, govt docs & acquis Queens Col (NY) 43-44; Lib asst James Monroe High Sch, NYC 45-49; Lib asst Forest Hills High Sch, NYC 49-53, Tchr of lib 53-60, Research libn & tchr of lib 62-65, Tchr of lib in charge 65-. 8: Bd of Educ NYC: asst examiner 55-; Reading Com Bur of Libs 56-; Consul & coach in Remedial Reading, Forest hills High Sch 58-; Research Libn for the Pub Lib Pub Sch Pilot Lib Proj, Bur of Libs & Bur of Educl Research, Bd of Educ NYC 60-62. 9: ALA; Internat Reading Assn; Amer Jewish Hist Soc; YIVO Inst for Jewish Research; NYLA; NY Lib Club; NYCSchLA (treas 65-67, prof com 67-); Nassau-SuffolkSchLA (activites & positions). 10: Beta Phi Mu; Friends of the Queens Col Lib; Friends of the Floyd Mem Lib, Greenport NY; Orient Commun Activities, Orient NY; Oysterponds Hist Soc, Orient NY; East LI Hosp; Pratt Inst Grad Lib Sch Alum assn. 12: Ed "Education Abstracts" (43-44). 14: Ref & res, rare bks, lit, Govt docs. 15: PO Box 173, Orient NY 11957.

SILVESTER, ELIZABETH (VERA). b Vienna 27 N 35. 4: Peet Silvester. 5: McGill 54-58 (Hist) BA, 60-61 BLS, 67 MLS; London Sch of Econ 68 (Intl Hist) MA. 6: Fr. 7: Sec McGill U 59-60; McGill U Lib: Catlgr 61-62, Asst ref libn 62-64, Ref libn 65-67, 68-. 9: CanLA; ALA; QueLA; CACUL (Copyright Com). 13: Yes. 14: Ref, bibliog, orientation, copyright. 15: McLennan Lib McGill Univ, 3459 Mactavish, Montreal Can.

SIM, HELEN JENNIFER (MOORE). b Ontario Can 25 N 41. 4: Robert Dalton Sim. 5: UToronto 59-62 (Eng) BA; Ont Col of Educ 63 (Educ); Rutgers 67-68 MLS. 7: Tchr Central Peel High Sch Bd, Brampton Ont Can 62-63; Lib asst StanfordU Libs 64-65; Tchr & libn Los Altos Sch Bd, Los Altos Cal 65-66; Ref libn Standard Oil Co (NJ), NYC 68. 8: Volunteer, Head Start, Hartford Conn 69-. 9: SLA. 10: Pi Beta Phi. 15: W Ledge rd, Glastonbury Ct 06033.

SIMEONE, HENRIETTA (McDERMOTT). b Brooklyn NY 27 Mr 22. 4: John Simeone. 5: Col of New Rochelle 40-43 (Fr) BA; Columbia 44-45 (LS); Syracuse 52-53 (LS) MS. 6: Sp, Fr, Ital. 7: Censor US Bur of Censorship, NYC 43-45; Accessions libn Harvard Law Sch Lib 45-46; Catlgr Yale U Lib 46-48; Ser catlgr Syracuse U Lib 48-52; Libn Newman Ctr 63-; Sch libn N Syracuse High Sch, N Syracuse NY 53-68; Libn Solvay High Sch, Solvay NY 68-. 8: Libn Newman Ctr SyracuseU; Planned Cicero High Sch Instr Ctr; Sch lib consul CathLA. 9: ALA; CathLA; NYLA; NY State TA; Onondaga-Oswego ASchL. 10: Beta Phi Mu; Col of New Rochelle Alumni; Syracuse U Lib Alumni; Syracuse U Women's Club; Lib Pub Rel Coun (NYC); Newman Assn. 14: Sch libs, ya reading, relig ctrs at cols & univs. 15: 839 Cumblerand ave, Syracuse NY 13210.

SIMIS, VELTA. b Latvia 29 Ag 15. 5: Classical Gymnasium (Jelgava Latvia) 30-34; LatvianU in Riga 34-44 MPhil. 6: Latvian, Swedish, Ger, Danish, Norwegian, Lat, Fr, ancient Greek. 7: Archivist Mus of Latvian Lit & Theater, Riga 40-44; Catlgr Lib of StockholmU 47-49; Catlgr Lib University (Carolina Rediviva), Upsala Sweden 60-61; Catlgr Harvard Col Lib 61-65. 9: Akademiska organizacija Ramave (a Latvian soc for res in the humanities). 12: Co-comp "Latviesu-zviedru valodas vardnica" (52); transl -annemarija Selinko, Desire, romans" (Ger into Latvian) (55). 13: Yes. 14: Bk sel, catlg. 15: 131 Davis ave, Brookline Ma 02146.

SIMISON, BARBARA DAMON. b Northampton Mass 22 S 07. 5: Smith 25-29 (Eng) AB, 29-31 (Eng) AM; Yale 31-36 (Eng). 6: Lat, Gk, Fr, Sp, Ger, Old Eng Old Norse. 7: Asst registrars Off Smith Col 29-31; Catlgr Yale U Lib 31-43. Sr asst ref dept 43-46, Asst ref libn, research asst 46-60, Sr asst ref libn, research asst 60-62, Sr asst ref libn, assoc ed "Yale U Lib Gazette, & research asst 62-. 10: Phi Beta Kappa. 12: Ed (with S T Williams); "Washington Irving on the Prairie, by H E Ellsworth (37); "Around The Horn by E R Sill (44); Contrib, "British Authors of the 19th Century (36).13: Yes. 14: Ref, editing. 15: Cambridge Arms apt 410, 32 High st, New Haven Ct 06510.

SIMMONS, BEATRICE DOWNIN TOMEI. b Stroudsburg Penn 10 N 20. 4: John H Simmons. 5: E Stroudsburg State Col 38-42 (Health & Phys Educ) BS; Millersville State Col summers 55-57 (LS) BS; Drexel 65 MLS; Temple (Educ Media) 67-69. 6: Fr, Ital, Russian. 7: Health phys ed, soc studies, sci tchr Nicholson Pub Schs, Nicholson Penn 42-43; Health phys ed, soc studies, sci tchr Penbrook Pub Schs, Pennbrook Penn 43-44; Recreational dir Hershey Jr Col 45-53; Health & phys ed tchr Palmyra Area Schs, Palmyra Penn 53-56; Jr & sr high sch libn Lewistown Pub Schs, Lewistown Penn 56-57; Jr & sr high sch libn Steelton Pub Schs, Steelton Penn 57-61; Twp Dir of Libs Sch Dist of Abington Twp Penn 61-68; Educ specialist US Off of Educ (ESEA Title II Model Cities EPDA Coord) 68-. 8: Middle Atlantic Accred Eval Bds, Lancaster Area, 58; Temple Bur of Educ, Eval of Elem Schs, 63-65; Consul, Wilson "Childrens Catalogue Conducted Sch Libnship wkshop Drexel summer 67. 9: NEA; ALA (chm Paperback Bks for Elem Grades 67-69, Com Bldg & Equipment for Sch Libs); -AASchL; PennStateEA (Supv & Curric Com); PennLA (chm Recru Com 64, chm Exhib & Conf Site Com 65-66). 10: Bus & Prof Womens Fed of Penn; Girl Scouts. 12: "Workbook on Library Skills" (68). 13: Yes. 14: Supv of sch libns. 15: 1120 Meeting House rd, Meadowbrook Pa 19046.

SIMMONS, DOROTHY (ZUCKER). b Hartford Conn 22 N 15. 4: Irving J Simmons. 5: Hunter Col 32-36 (Biol) BA;

Columbia 40-44 (LS) BS; Tchrs Col 61. 6: Fr. 7: Lib clerk NY Pub Lib 58th st Br 36-42; Asst libn Museum of Modern Art, NYC 42-46; Elem libn Ardsley pub schs, Ardsley NY 59-. 9: NEA; ALA-AASchL; NY State Tchrs Assn. 10: . 14: Child libs. 15: 11 Glen rd, Ardsley NY 10502.

SIMMONS, ELIZABETH LEE. b Lansing Mich 1 N 14. 4: Russell E Simmons. 5: Stephens Jr col 34-36 (Eng, Pol Sci) AA; UChicago 36-38 (Hist, Soc Sci) BA; Cleveland Col (Bus); UMinn (LS). 6: Fr. 7: Educ sec Amer Unitarian Assn, Boston 39-40; Employment coun Minn Employment Serv, St Paul 45-46; Sec Phil C Justus Co (RE), St Paul 53-56; Advertising sec Minn Educ Assn, St Paul 57-61; Acquis libn Macalester Col 61-68; Libn II & pub rel & publ specialist Anoka Co Lib, Minneapolis 68-. 9: ALA; MinnLA (Legisl Com, Intel Freedom Com chm; Pub Rel for Fall 68 Conv). 10: ACLU. 14: Ref, pub rel. 15: 2503 E 19th ave, No St Paul Mn 55109.

SIMMONS, FLORENCE (LEECH) (MRS). b Nashville 15 N 08. 5: Peabody 26-30, summers 32, 38 (LS) BS; George Washington U summer 33; Chicago U Col 56. 7: Asst libn Millsaps Col 30-34; Libn & Dir of Libs Nashville city schs 36-44; Asst to ALA exec sec, Chicago 44-46; Interim exec sec AASL, Chicago 51-52; Asst to dir ALA Publ Dept, Chicago 55-59; Dir Lib Serv Chattanooga (Tenn) pub schs 59-. 9: ALA-AASchL (sec Supv Sect 65); NEA-DAVI; SELA; TennEA; Tenn LA (pres 65). 10: Phi Mu; Chattanooga Art Assn. 13: Yes. 14: Catlg, sch libs, prof educ libs. 15: 119 Crestview circle, Chattanooga Tenn 37411.

SIMMONS, GLORIA (MITCHELL). b Atlanta 7 Mr 32. 4: Henry E Simmons. 5: Bennett Col (NC) 52-55 (Eng) AB; Atlanta 55-56, summer 57 MS in LS. 6: Fr. 7: Asst circ libn Atlanta U 57-58; Asst libn Morris Brown Col 58-59; Asst libn Wilberforce U 59-60; Curriculum libn Central State Col (Wilberforce Ohio)61-64;Head Libn Kendall Col 64-67; Ref libn Chicago City Col 67-. 8: NSF Libn, Morris Brown Col, summer 59. 9: ALA; IllLA. 10: AAUW; PTA. 14: Admin, catlg, ref. 15: 7959 S Jeffery blvd, Chicago Il 60617.

SIMMONS, JAMES GEORGE. b Ann Arbor Mich 28 Mr 28. 4: Charlotte Wint Simmons. 5: Adrian Col 48-52 (Lit) BA; Oberlin 52-57 (Bible) BD; UMich 66-68 MALS. 6: Fr. 7: Aerographer USN 46-48; Minister Methodist Ch, Mich & Ohio 49-66; Libn Huron Valley Sch, Milford Mich 66-68; Catlgr Adrian Col 68-. 9: ALA; ATheolLA; MichLA; MichASchL. 14: Admin, catlg, ref. 15: Shipman Lib Adrian Col, Adrian Mi 49221.

SIMMONS, JAMES WOODROW. b Ft Worth Tex 11 D 18. 4: Lois Eileen Hodges. 5: Willamette 50-54 (Eng) BA; UCal (Berkeley) 56-59; San Francisco State Col 57-58; UWash 60-64 MLS. 6: Sp. 7: Owner-mgr Radio-Electronics Co, Paducah Tex 35-40; Head retail firm Sears & Robuck Co, Roswell NM 40-41; Communicationa off USAF & Signal Corps USA, S Amer, Africa & Europe 41-46; Hd auto accessories div McKay Chevrolet Cadillac Agcy, Salem Ore 46-50; Hd lin & a-v dir Col of the Siskiyous 60-65; Dir learning research ctr Lane Commun Col 65-66; Dir lib East Ore Col 66-. 8: Consul for high sch, col & public lib bldg and devel progs. 9: NEA-DAVI; OreLA; Ore Lib Coun. 10: AAUP; United Fund; March of Dimes; Ore-Cal Civil Defense Agencies; Soap Box Derbies. 13: Yes. 14: Lib admin. 15: 2903 North Spruce, La Grande Or 97850.

SIMMONS, JOSEPH M(ARTIN). b Fairfield Conn 6 Ap 21. 4: Mary Alice Sheridan. 5: Georgetown U 45-47 (Econ) BSFS; Columbia 51-52 MSLS. 7: Asst Foreman Alcoa, Fairfield Conn 39-42; Research asst US Dept of State, Wash DC 47-48; Lib asst LC 49-50; Head tech serv Fordham U Lib 51-53; Lib spec Remington Rand, NYC 53-60; Libn "Chicago Sun-Times 60-. 8: Instr Sch of Lib Sci, Rosary Col, 60-; Mem Adv Com Ill State Libn 67-; Lecturer on co libs Amer Mgt Assn 67-68. 9: ALA; CathLA; SLA (chm Placement Policy Com 62-64; Chap Liaison Off 67-69; pres Ill Chap 64-65); SAA; ASIS. 10: Caxton Club(Chicago); Chicago Press Club. 12: John Cotton Dana Lecturer, West Mich U, Oct (65). 13: Yes. 14: Admin, archives, planning. 15: 1456 Oak ave, Evanston Ill 60201.

SIMMONS, KATHRYN (MELTON). b Paducah Ky 8 O 08. 5: West Ky StateU 25-29 (Eng) AB, 31-32 (Eng); George Peabody Col 62-63 (Eng) MA, 68-69 MLS. 7: Tchr; Corinth High Sch, Corinth Ky 29-31, Sebree High Sch, Sebree Ky 32-33, Chamblee High Sch, Chamblee Ga 54-55; Lib asst Decatur-DeKalb Lib, Decatur Ga 57-61; Lib asst Pub Lib of Nashville & Davidson Co, Nashville Tenn 63-69, Libn 69-. 9: TennStateLA. 10: Nat League of Amer Pen Women. 14: Ref. 15: 102 32nd ave S, Nashville Tn 37212.

SIMMONS, MARION L. b Stafford NY 20 My 16. 5: Elmira Col 33-37 (Eng) AB; Columbia 37-38 BS in LS. 7: Child libn Port Washington (NY) Pub Lib 38-42; Rochester (NY) Pub Lib: Sr asst 42-43, Br libn 43-53, Pub rel dir 53-61; Chief pub rel off NY Pub Lib 61-67; Asst exec dir Metro, NYC 67-. 8: Pub rel consul; Summer A-V Wkshop Syracuse U 57-61, LSCA Pub Rel Project NY State Educ Dept 67-68, LSCA Radio-TV Project NY State Educ Dept 65-67. 9: ALA-LAD (Pub Rel Sect; sec 59-60; chm 61-63; Off of Recruitment Materials Com 64-, chm 67-; chm Local Con Publicity 66); NYLA; NY Lib Club (bulletin ed 62-65). 10: Lib Pub Rel Coun; Zonta Int; Alumnae trustee, Elmira Col. 13: Yes. 14: Pub rel, lib coop, manpower. 15: METRO, 11 W 40th st, New York NY 10018.

SIMMONS, QUEENIE C(LARA GREGG). b Rising Star Tex 1 O 11. 4: Loyed Raymind Simmons. 5: Tex State Col for Women summer 30; Howard Payne Col 36; SWest Sem 36-39; Texas Wesleyan 47-49 (Bible, Relig Educ) BA; Grand Canyon Col 56-57 Elem Tchg Credential. 7: Educ dir Evans Ave Baptist Ch, Ft Worth 49; Educ dir First So Baptist, Tucson 53-55; Tchr N Phoenix Baptist Sch 55-56; Tchr Laveen (Ariz) Sch 57-58; Cal Baptist Col Lib 60-. 14: Col archives. 15: 4406 Nellie, Riverside Ca 92503.

SIMMONS, REV WILLIAM B CSC. b Quanah Tex 14 Je 27. 5: Ntre Dame 44-48 (Classics) AB; UMich 54-55 (Linguistics) MA; Catholic U 60-65 MSLS. 6: Lat, Gk, Fr, Ger. 7: Libn Holy Cross Sem (Notre Dame Ind) 58-64, Prin & Rector 64-68; Prin Notre Dame High Sch, Niles Ill 68-. 9: ALA; CathLA. 10: Beta Phi Mu. 14: Ya serv. 15: Holy Cross Sem, Notre Dame Ind 46556.

SIMMONS, WILLIE (MAE WHITE). b Wash DC 8 D 38. 4: Chester W Simmons. 5: Howard U 56-60 (Eng) BA; Rutgers 60-61 MLS; George Washington U 65 (Educ); Catholic U 67; DC Tchrs Col 66-68. 7: Libn NY Pub Lib 61-62; Browsing libn Howard U 62-64; Libn DC Bd of Educ 64-. 8: Consul lib sci course DC Tchrs Col spring 65; Consul DCSLA wkshop fall 67; NY State pub libns certif; Wkshop in educ tech Catholic U summer 67. 9: DCLA; DCSchLA. 14: Ya & child wk. 15: 1411 Rittenhouse st NW, Wash DC 20011.

SIMMS, AURORA GARDNER. b Portsmouth Va 6 My 24. 4: Daniel M Simm. 5: William & Mary 40-42 (Pre-med); NYU 46-48 (Econ) BA; Columbia 48-49 (LS) MS. 7: Reg libn No Reg NM State Lib, Santa Fe 57-58; Libn Va Beach-Princess Anne Co Lib, Va Beach Va 58-59; Ref libn Buena Park Dist Lib, Buena Park Cal 59-60; Asst ref libn humanities dept Long Beach State Col Lib 61-65; Project libn Stockton Lib, Stockton Cal 65-66; Br supv Sacramento City-Co Lib, Sacramento Cal 66-67; Br hd Preston Royal Br Dallas Pub Lib, Dallas Tex 67-. 9: ALA; TexLA; DallasCoLA. 10: Sierra Club. 13: Yes. 14: Adult serv, circ control, admin, ref, systems organ. 15: 3525 So Polk st apt 239, Dallas Tx 75224.

SIMMS, CATHERINE A(NNE). b Peoria Ill 4 Mr 13. 5: No Ill State Tchrs Col 30-34 (Educ) B Ed& UIll 34-35, summer 36 BLS; Ill Inst of Tech 47-50 (Psych). 7: Tchr-libn Pub Sch System, Rockford Ill 35-36; Libn Scott, Foresman & Co, Chicago 36-43; Post libn Selfridge AFB, Selfridge Mich 43-46; Asst to the libn Beech Aircraft Corp, Wichita Kan 46-47; Ref libn Ill Inst of Tech 47-51; Libn Inst of Gas Tech, Chicago 51-. 8: Bibliog consul: Amer Soc Mech Engnrs 59-61, Amer Soc Tool Engnrs 57-58, Amer Power Conf 50-. 9: SLA (Sci-Tech Div: Memb Chm; chm Procedures Manual; sec-treas & chm of Pub Utilities Sect; Ill Chap: sec-treas 41-43; mem 3 coms). 10: Delta Zeta; The Cordon (Chicago); DAR. 12: Co-ed, Amer Soc Mech Engnrs, "Bibliography on Gas Turbines, 1896-1948" (62). 14: Ref, circ, acquis. 15: Inst of Gas Tech Lib, 3424 S State st, Chicago Il 60616.

SIMMS, DANIEL MASON. b Seattle 12 My 32. 5: Tex A&M Col 53-58 (Geol, Petrol Engnr); Long Beach State Col 60-62 (Marine Geol) BS; San Jose State Col 63-64 (Oceanography); UCLA 64-65 MLS. 6: Fr, Sp. 7: USMCR Rifle line co, band, underwater demolitions, machine gunner, US & Korea 49-53; Paleontology Lab Tech Standard Oil Co Cal, Los Angeles 52; Drilling rig operator Trans-Tex Exploration, Ft Worth Tex 54-56; Electric well logger Halliburton Co, Hobbs NM 56-57; Mining engnr Holly Minerals, Grants NM 57-58; Chem research tech US Borax Corp, Anaheim Cal 59-62; Assoc Oceanographic engnr Astropower, Newport Beach Cal 62-63; Engnr geol State of Cal Dept of Water Res, Los Angeles 63-65; Tech info spec Chevron Research Co, La Habra Cal 65-67; Info specialist Mobil Research & Development, Tex 67-. 8: Automation research & consulting serv; Consul to: Ft Worth Pub Lib, Amer Geol Inst. 9: SLA (Prog Chm Petrol Div 70); ASIS; Assn Comput Machinery; ASO; AMSOC; IOF. 10: Nat Geog Soc; So Cal Soc for Preserv of Dixieland Jazz; Sierra

Club; Nat Wildlife Fed; African Wil dlife Leadership Found; Wilderness Found; So Cal Hot Jazz Soc; New Orleans Jazz Club of Cal; New Orleans Jazz Club of So Cal; Jazz Inc of Cal. 13: Yes. 14: Info systems analysis & design. 15: 3525 So Polk st #239, Dallas Tx 75224.

SIMON, BRADLEY ALDEN. b Meriden Conn 9 Mr. 29. 5: Shenandoah Col 47-48 (Liberal Arts); So Conn State Col 48-51, summer 54 (Educ, LS) BS; Fla State U 54-55 MS in LS; UMiami (Fla) 56-57 (LS, Educ); Ariz State U 66-67 (Educ). 7: Ext libn Ft George G Meade Hq 2nd Army, Md 55-56; Base libn Homestead AFB, Homestead Fla 56-57; Asst dir of libs Pub Lib of Charlotte & Mecklenburg Co, Charlotte NC 57-61; Dir of libs Volusia Co Pub Libs, Daytona Beach Fla 61-64; Consul M Van Buren Lib Consuls, Charlotte NC 64-65; Lib dir Central Piedmont Col 64-65; Lib bldg consul Colo State Lib 65-66; Dir Scottsdale Pub Lib, Scottsdale Ariz 66-. 8: Consul var bldg projs. 9: ALA (mem var coms); NEA; MPLA; ColoLA; NCLA (chm Adult Serv Com); FlaLA; SELA (Nomin Com 62-64). ; SWLA; ArizStateLA (pres Pub Lib Div 68-69; mem &/or chm var coms). 10: Kappa Delta Phi; Jr C of C; Deputy Dir of Info Serv, Civil Defense; Scottsdale Fine Arts Commsn. 13: Yes. 14: Admin, lib bldg consul, pub rel, fine arts. 15: P O Box 245, Scottsdale Az 85252.

SIMON, DIANA. b Orlando Fla 30 Mr 40. 4: Karse Simon. 5: UMiami 57-61 (Span) AB; Fla State U 61-62 (LS) MA; UMiami Law Sch 63-64 (Law). 6: Sp. 7: Asst Brockway Mem Lib, Miami Shores Fla 57-61; Asst ref libn UMiami Lib (Fla) 63-64; Child libn for br Elizabeth Free Pub Lib, Elizabeth NJ 65-; Dir OEO Project Lib 67; Act coord child serv EPL 68; Tchg faculty Newark State Col 66, 67, 69. 9: NJLA. 14: Child lit, ref, tchg admin. 15: 3 Appletree lane, Morris Plains NJ 07950.

SIMON, DORIS (SELLS). b Cairo Ill. 4: Arthur G Simon. 5: UWis 60 (LS) Certif; UIll 62 (LS); UUtah ext courses 63- (LS); ULouisville 67 (Personnel Utilization) Certif. 7: Asst libn Carnegie Pub Lib, Paducah Ky 50-59, Adult serv libn 60-67; Interior libn paducah Area Pub Lib, Paducah Ky 67-68, Hd ref dept 68-. 9: ALA; KyLA (Memb Chm 69-70). 14: Ref, rare bks, bk sel. 15: Madisa apts 7th & Madison, Paducah Ky 42001.

SIMON, DOROTHY HENRIETTA (BYRON) (MRS). b NYC 14 Ja 24. 5: Hunter Col 41-45 (Music) BA; NYU 46-47 (Music Educ); Columbia 48-50 (LS) MS. 7: Pre-prof libn NY Pub Lib, Woodstock Br 45-50, Yp libn Morrisania Br 50-51; Libn-in-chg NYC Bd of Educ Boys High Annex 52-62, Tchr of lib Boys High Sch 63-. 9: NYCSchLA. 10: Natl Assn of Negro Bus and Profess Womens Clubs; Amer Guild of Organists. 14: Sch libnship, ref. 15: 220 Montgomery st. Brooklyn NY 11225.

SIMON, FANNIE. b NYC 15 Ap 1891. 5: Smith 10-14 (Hist, Ger) BA; Columbia 16 (LS); NYU 59 (Creative Writing). 6: Ger. 7: Researcher Street & Finney, NYC 19-20, 23-24; Correspondent Charles Scribners Sons, NYC 24-28; Asst libn McCann-Erickson, NYC 30-42; Libn & assoc ed "McCalls Magazine," NYC 42-58; Ref libn Amer Bible Soc, NYC 59-61; Asst to dir SLA, NYC 61-62; Libn Analytical Psychology Club of NY, NYC 63-. 9: SLA. 11: Hall of FAME, SLA. 14: Ref. 15: 201 E 35 st, New York NY 10016.

SIMON, LORRAINE (MATAE) BRISKA. b E Chicago Ind 2 Ja 11. 4: Dan Simon. 5: IndU 29-36 (Eng), 63-66 (LS) Certif. 7: Lib asst E Chicago Pub Lib, E Chicago Ind 28-37; Sec 48-50, Admin asst 55-; Sec-libn IndU NW Campus (E Chicago) 37-41. 9: ALA; IndLA; IllLA. 10: LWV. 14: Admin, pub rel, publications. 15: 4223 Fir st, East Chicago In 46312.

SIMON, LOUISE F (NYMAN). b Phila 17 N 29. 5: Temple 47-51 (Journalism) BS; Villanova U 62-65 (LS) MS. 7: Womans page ed Times Newspapers Inc, Phila 51; Asst womans page "Courier Post" Camden NJ 51-52; WAVE off US Navy 52-60; Admin asst Amer Red Coss, Coatesville Penn 60-63; Libn Ballard Spahr Andrews & Ingersoll attys, Phila 63-65; Libn Sterling High Sch, Somerdale NJ 65-67; Libn Lenape Reg High Sch, Medford NJ 67-. 9: NJSchLA; NJEA; BurlcoASch; LenapeEA. 15: 509 Lee ave, Beverly NJ 08010.

SIMON, MARILYN SANDRA MALIT. b Phila 13 N 42. 5: Temple 60-64 (Hist) AB; Drexel 64-65 MSLS. 6: Fr. 7: Lib trainee State Lib of Penn, Dre xel Inst of Tech 64-65; Libn I Free Lib of Phila 65-66; Libn II (Lib for the blind & physically handicapped) 66-68; Libn III 68-69; NE area adult coord 69-. 9: ALA; PennLA (Adult Serv Com); SLA. 14: Ref, lib serv to the blind & phys handicapped, adult serv. 15: 315 S 46th st, Phila Pa 19143.

SIMON, RENEE B (BLATT). b Brooklyn NY 25 Mr 28. 4: Harry J Simon. 5: Adelphi 44-47 (Chem) BA; Stanford 47-48 (Biochem) MS; UCLA 65-66 MLS. 6: Fr. 7: Libn Commun Hosp, Long Beach Cal 66-. 10: Beta Phi Mu; LWV; Friends of Long Beach Pub Lib; UN Assn; PTA. 14: Med libnship. 15: 545 Orlena ave, Long Beach Ca 90814.

SIMON, SAMUEL L. b Chelsea Mass 21 Mr 26. 4: Elaine Singer. 5: George Washington U 46-50 (Govt) BA; Syracuse 50-51 MLS; NYU 55- (Adult Educ). 7: (Sgt) USAF, US & ETO 44-46; Clerk: VA Wash DC 44-45, DC Pub Lib 45-50, Syracuse U Hearing & Speech Clinic 50-51; Dist libn Brooklyn Pub Lib 52-65; Dir Merrick Lib, Merrick NY 65-68; Dir Long Beach Pub Lib, Long Beach NY 68-. 9: ALA (chm Jt Com on Lib Serv to Labor Groups; chm John Cotton Dana Publicity Award); LPRC (past pres); NYLA (past chm Intel Freedom Com); NY Lib Club (Coun, chm Scholarship Com); AdultEA; Lib Pub Rel Coun; Nassau Co(NY)LA. 10: Nat Conf of Christians & Jews; West End Civic Assn; W Lynbrook Civic Assn; Lynbrooks Fine Arts Com; PTA; Dissenters. 12: "Looking Back is Forward Looking." 13: Yes. 14: Adult serv, lib mgt, adult educ in libs. 15: 21 Hawthorne st, Lynbrook NY 11563.

SIMON, WILLIAM HENRY. b New Haven Conn 26 D 28. 4: Dorothy Elaine Decket. 05: Quinnipiac Col 46-48 (Liberal Arts) AA; UBridgeport 48-50 (Experimental Psych) BA; Columbia 54-55 (LS) MS; West New England Col 62-64 (Bus Admin) MBA. 6: Sp, Ger. 7: Circ desk asst YaleU Lib 51-52, 54; Libn Civil Engring Lib US Navy C B Base, Davisville RI 52-54; Prof asst Bus & Tech Dept Bridgeport Pub Lib, Bridgeport Conn 55-56; Chief libn Olin-Mathieson Chem Corp, New Haven Conn 56-61; Tech info supv Nuclear Div Combustion Eng Inc, Windsor Conn 61, Manager, Tech & Admin Serv 61-. 8: Research mgr Miller, Starrett, West & Assocs Inc, Hartford Conn 61-62; Conn State Adv Com on Public Lib Standards 67-68; Conn State Adv Com on Interlib Coop 68; Chm Windsor Public Lib Study and Bldg Com 67-. 9: ALA; ASIS; ASTM (Com Z85); ACS (Chem Lit Div); ConnLA; Conn Assn Lib Bds (Exec Com); SLA (Conn Valley Chap; ed Bulletin, consul off). 10: Bd of Dirs Windsor Pub Lib; Justice of the Peace; Bd of Dirs Windsor Red Cross; Green Mt Club; Admin Mgt Soc. 13: Yes. 14: Lib admin, reg-state lib syst devel. 15: 17 Priscilla rd, Windsor Ct 06095.

SIMONIS, JAMES J(OSEPH). b Toledo Ohio 5 D 41. 5: Findlay Col 59-63 (Hist) AB; Pratt Inst 63-65 MLS. 6: Fr, Sp. 7: Libn trainee Brooklyn Pub Lib, Brooklyn NY 63-65, A-v libn 65-66; Hd libn Mansfield State Col 66-. 9: ALA; PennLA; APSCUF. 10: Beta Phi Mu; ACLU. 14: Admin, automation, films. 15: 24 1/2 N Academy st, Mansfield Pa 16933.

SIMONS, BARBARA ANN. b Soperton Treutlen Co Ga 13 Mr 38. 5 Womans Col of Ga 56-60 (Eng, Hist) AB; Emory 60-61 (LS) ML. 6: Fr, Lat. 7: Pub serv libn Womans Col of Ga 61-66; Asst libn Readers serv Goucher 66-. 9: ALA; GaLA; SELA; MdLA. 10: AAUW; Pi Gamma Mu. 14: Ref, readers adv, archives. 15: P O Box 102, Soperton Ga 30457.

SIMONS, BENNIE P. b Centerville Tex 16 O 13. 4: Wimmie Allen. 5: Sam Houston State Tchrs Col 36 (Sci) BS, 46 (Educ) MA; Peabody 39 BS in LS. 6: Sp. 7: Tchr Leon Co Tex pub schs 33-34; Tchr libn Huntsville (Tex)pub schs 36-41; Asst libn Sam Houston State Tchrs Col 41-42; Instr in celestial navigation USAF (S/Sgt) 42-45; Libn W Tex State Col 47-48; Dir of Lib Sam Houston State Col 48-67; Admin asst 67-. 9: TexLA. 10: AAUP; Phi Kappa Delta; Kappa Delta P; Phi Gamma Mu. 12: "How to Use Your College Library (57, 59). 15: Sam Houston State Co, Estill Lib, Huntsville Tex 77341.

SIMONS, FLORA (SIEKKINEN). b Kinsman Ohio 17 Ag 15. 4: Franklin L Simons. 5: Spencerian Col 33-34 (Bus) Diploma; Yougstown U 54-58(LS) BS Ed; West Res 58-60 MSLS; Columbia 65(LS); West Mich U 66 (LS). 6: Finnish, Fr. 7: Sec Snapout Forms, Chardon Ohio 34-36; Sec glauber Brass Mfg Co, Cleveland & Kinsman Ohio 36-41; Owner & manager Simons & Co, Farndale Ohio 42-54; Libn Kinsman Pub Lib, Kinsman Ohio 54-58; Libn & tchr Vienns Vienna High Sch, Vienna 58-60; Libn Joseph Badger Local Sch Dist, Kinsman Ohio 60-; Libn Warren Pub Lib, Warren Ohio 61-. 9: NEA; ALA; OhioEA; OhioAShL; NEOhioTA; TEA. 10: Kappa Delta Pi; Beta Phi Mu. 14: Sch libs. 15: Kinsman Ohio 44428.

SIMONS, WENDELL WAYNE. b Independence Mo 10 N 28. 4: Judith Shaw. 5: UCal (Berkeley) 45-49 (Decorative Art) AB, 53-54 BLS. 7: Radarman 3/C US Navy 50-52; Head A-v Serv UCal(Santa Barbara) 54-60, Asst libn serv 60-63; Asst U Libn UCal(Santa Cruz) 63-. 8: Consul on a-v org: Mexico City Col, Mexico DF 60, Westmont Col 63-; Consul on furniture &

furnishings Santa Cruz Pub Lib, Santa Cruz Cal 67-68. 9: ALA; CalLA. 12: "A Universal Slide Classification System with Automatic Indexing (69). 13: Yes. 14: Gen admin, a-v, bldg design & furnishing. 15: 2904 El Rancho dr, Santa Cruz Ca 95060.

SIMONTON, WESLEY (CLARK). b Cincinnati 22 Je 21. 4: Dorothy Byrne. 5: UCincinnati 37-41 (Eng) BA; Columbia 42, 46-48 BSLS, MSLS; UIll 52-53, 60 (LS) PhD. 6: Fr, Ger, Lat. 7: US Navy Lt (jg) 43-46; Sr catlgr Columbia U 47-48; Chief catlg libn UMinn(Minneapolis) 49-56; Lib Sch UMinn (Minneapolis); Asst Prof 56-60, Assoc Prof 60-65, Act dir 62-63, Prof 65-. 8: Consul, IBM Res Lib,T J Watson Res Center, Yorktown Heights NY, 63-64. 9: ASIS; ALA (chm Catlg & Clsf Sect 63-64); -RTSD (pres 65-67); AALS (sec-treas 60-64); MinnLA. 10: AAUP. 12: Ed "Information Retrieval Today (63); Ed "Information Retrieval with Special Reference to the Biomedical Sciences (66). 13: Yes. 14: Catlg, clsf, documentation, info retrieval. 15: Univ of Minn Lib Sch, Minneapolis Mn 55455.

SIMOR, GEORGE. b Bacsalmas Hungary 23 N 19. 4: Pearl Vigh. 5: Col of Philos Kassa Hungary 40-44 (Hist of Philos) PhL; Facults Philos et Thol Louvain 47-51 (Hist of Relig) STL, Columbia 62-63 (LS) MS. 6: Fr, Ger, Hungarian, Lat. 7: High sch tchr Gimnazium, Satu-Mare Rumania 44-47; Admin, Hungarian relief org, Toronto 52-58; Instr Fordham U 58-61; Asst manager Safe Way Inc, NYC, 61-62; Catlgr Columbia U 63-64; Rare bk catlgr Washington U (St Louis) 64-66; Rare bk catlgr NY Pub Lib 66-69, Hd rare bk catlg 69-. 8: Consul on immigration, Toronto Can 53-58; Stud coun Fordham U 58-61; Lib sci lectr; wash U (St Louis) 66-; Pratt Inst, St Johns U (NY). 9: ALA; Amer Bibliog Soc; Amer Lib Sch Tchrs Assn; Tech Serv Libns Assn (NY). 13: Yes. 14: Bibliog of rare bks, spec collections. 15: 1230 Woodycrest ave, New York NY 10452.

SIMPKINS, ALICE GILKESON. b Fishersville Va 5 M 16. 5: Mary Baldwin Col 33-37 (Eng) BA; Simmons 37-38 (LS) BS. 7: Libn Powhatan High Sch Lib, Powhatan Va 38-39, C H Friend High Sch Lib, S Boston Va 39-41, Staunton Pub Lib, Staunton Va 41-44, US Naval Hosp Lib, Memphis Tenn 44-45; Circ libn Wilson Mem High Sch, Fishersville Va 61-62; Asst libn Mary Baldwin Col 62-. 9: ALA; VaLA. 10: Augusta Co (Va) Hist Assn; Va Archeol Soc; DAR. 14: Ref, readers serv. 15: Box 218 Rt 1, Fishersville Va 22939.

SIMPKINS, EDGAR G(ILBERT). b Kan City Mo 11 D 22. 4: Alma Nilsen. 5: UMo(Kan City) 47-50 (Physics) BA; West Res 50-51 (LS) MS. 7: Case analyst US Fed Bur of Investigation, Wash DC 42-43; (Lt) US Army, US, Europe, Pacific 43-46; Head page Linda Hall Lib, Kan City Mo 48-50, Sr asst ser 51-53, Head ser dept 53-57; Lib supv Bell Telephone Labs, NJ, NY 57-63, Dept Head 63-. 9: ASIS. 15: Bell Telephone Labs, Holmdel NJ 07733.

SIMPKINS, IRWIN F. b NYC 18 Ap 24. 4: Marjory Davis. 5: UMo 48-51 (Eng) AB, 55-56 ABLS; UMich 57-58 AMLS; UIll 67-68 (LS). 6: Sp, Fr, Ger. 7: US Army 42-45 (Sgt), Surveyor 51-54; Catlgr Pub Lib, Columbia Mo 55; Ref asst Pub Lib, St Louis 56; Libn Police Acad, St Louis 57; Asst bus & ind Pub Lib, Flint Mich 58-61; Sci ref libn Emory U 61-67, Ref libn 68-. 10: Phi Beta Kappa; Sigma Xi; Beta Phi Mu. 13: Yes. 14: Ref, info storage & retrieval, interlib loan. 15: Emory Univ Lib, Atlanta Ga 30322.

SIMPSON, ALICE HESTER. b Oberlin Ohio 18 D 03. 05: Oberlin Col 0-24 (Fr, Eng) BA; West Res 26-27 BS in LS. 5: Oberlin 20-24 (Fr, Eng) BA; West Res 26-27 BS in LS. 6: Fr & other Romance langs. 7: Br asst Cleveland Pub Lib 24-26, Catlgr 27-29; Tech & gen ref asst Akron Pub Lib, Akron Ohio 29; Lib of Hawaii, Honolulu: Catlgr & ref asst 29-33, Calgr 33-41, Head catlg dept 41-43; Catlgr Oberlin Col Lib 43-44; Head catlg dept Lib of Hawaii, Honolulu 44-61; 1st asst catlg dept Oberlin Col Lib 61, Head catlg dept 61-65; Catlgr Ashland Col Lib 66-. 9: ALA; HawaiiLA (past treas); OhioLA; No Ohio Tech Serv Libns. 14: Catlg. 15: 617 S Broad st, Ashland Oh 44805.

SIMPSON, BETTY (PIERLOW). b St Louis Mo 13 Ap 23. 4: Alvin G Simpson. 5: WashU 40-42, 65-67 (LS, Eng) BSLS; St Louis U 62. 7: Darkroom asst, St Louis 36-40; Hostess Vanderveert's, St Louis 46; Usherette, St Louis 47-48; Sub tchr Jennings Sch Dist, Jennings Mo 57-61; Lib asst St Louis Co Lib 62-65; Elem libn Univ City Sch 65; Libn fairview High Sch, Jennings Mo 66; Libn DeSmet Jesuit High Sch, Creve Coeur Mo 67-. 9: ALA; CathLA; MoLA; MoSchLA; St Louis Suburban Sch Libns; Greater St Louis Lib Club. 10: Talking Tapes for the Blind. 14: Lib systems in schs. 15: 5614 McLaran ave, St Louis Mo 63136.

SIMPSON, DOROTHY EILEEN. b Toronto Can. 5: McMaster U 27-33 (Eng) BA; Toronto 38 BLS. 7: Lib asst McMaster U (Ont) 34-38; Ref asst Hamilton Pub Lib, Hamilton Ont 38-49, Head ref dept 50-. 9: CanLA; OntLA (chm Ref Wkshop 56-57); Inst Prof Libns (Ont), Dir 62-63; HPSLA (pres 63-64). 14: Ref. 15: 198 Sherman ave S, Hamilton Ont Can.

SIMPSON, ELAINE. b Marmaduke Ark 24 Ag 12. 4: James Y Yoneshige. 5: Ark State Col 28-34 (Eng) AB; Ark State U 36-39 (Eng) MA; Columbia 45-47 BS in LS. 7: High sch tchr, Ark & Mich 29-42, 44-45; Tchr War Relocation Camp High Sch, Rohwer Ark 42-44; Y-a libn brs NYC Pub Lib 45-48, Y-a field wker ext div 50-54, Y-a secondary schs & group wk specialist 54-61, Asst dir spec pilot project on school pub lib coop 61-62, Y-a specialist on Borough of Manhattan 62-67; Assoc Prof Rutgers Lib Sch (New Brunswick) summers 67-. 9: ALA;-YASD (Com on Selection of Bks & Other Materials 61-63, pres 69-70, mem Bd 66-68); ALA-CBC (Jt Com 59-60); NYLA (mem CYASD Bd 60-63, pres 61-62, consul for Booklist); Middlesex Co LA (pres 68-69, mem Bd 67-70). 10: Editorial Bd, Campus Bk Club, Scholastic. 11: Dutton-Macrae Award 61. 13: Yes. 14: YA serv & bks. 15: 51 University rd, East Brunswick NJ 08816.

SIMPSON, IMOGENE. b Louisville Ky 7 N 27. 5: West Ky State Col 45-47, 49-51 (Eng) BA; UFla 55; Peabody 56-60 MA in LS. 6: Lat. 7: Tchr: Franklin-Simpson Sr High Sch, Franklin Ky 50-53, Bartow Sr High Sch, Bartow Fla 53-54; Ft McCoy High Sch, Ft McCoy Fla 54-55; Libn: Ocala Jr High Sch, Ocala Fla 55-59, Hillwood High Sch, Nashville 59-60, West Ky State Col 60-62, Tchr Lib Sci 62-. 9: ALA; KyLA; KyASchL; KyEA. 10 AAUW. 10: AAUW. 14: Tchg lib sci. 15: 627 E 11th st, Bowling Green Ky 42101.

SIMPSON, J KATHLEEN. b Okla City Okla 19 F 42. 5: Central State Col 60-61; Okla StateU 61-63 (LS) BS; OklaU 64-66 MLS. 7: Jr high libn, Hobart Ind 63-65; Elem libn: Alexandria Va 66-67, Okla City 67-. 9: ALA; OklaEA. 10: Kappa Delta Pi; Phi Kappa Phi. 14: Sch lib. 15: 1227 Red Rock lane, Okla City Ok 73116.

SIMPSON, JUANITA (MILLER). b Guthrie Okla 7 J115. 4: John H Simpson. 5: UOkla 32-36 (Fr, LS) BA in LS; UOkla 63. 6: Fr. 7: Asst Okla City Pub Lib Okla City Okla 36-41; Asst libn U S Grant High Sch, Okla City Okla 58-60; Libn & dir of Materials Center Roosevelt Jr High Sch, Okla City Okla 60-. 9: ALA; NEA; OklaLA; OklaEA. 10: Okla City C of C. 14: Sch libnship, tchg materials centers. 15: 1227 Red Rock lane, Oklahoma City Ok 73116.

SIMPSON, L ANNE (PAGENSTECHER). b Austin Tex 28 Ag 40. 5: Randolph-Macon Womans Col 58-60, 61-62 (Fr) AB; Sweet Briar Jr Yr in France 60-61; Simmons 60-61 (LS) MS. 6: Fr, Sp. 7: Harvard Col Lib; Catlg dept 62-63, Intern in catlg dept 64-65, Admin off 65-66, Catlgr 65-66; Ref catlgr Morgan Guaranty Trust Co, NYC 66, Head libn 67-. 9: SLA. 10: Kappa Alpha Theta; Mass Gen Hosp Volunteer. 13: Yes. 14: Ref, catlg. 15: 67 Park ave, New York NY 10016.

SIMPSON, MILDRED JEAN (WEIERBACH). b Bethlehem Penn 15 Mr 39. 4: Richard H Simpson. 5: Bucknell U 57-59 (Fr); Lehigh U summer 58; UDel 59-60 (Fr) BA; USoCal 60-62 MS in LS. 6: Fr. 7: Clerk World Affairs Lib USoCal 60-62; Asst circ libn USoCal 62-64; Asst libn Acad of Motion Picture Arts & Sci, Los Angeles 64-68, Libn 68-. 8: Ed Adv Bd Amer Nat Film Catlg 68-. 9: ALA. 10: Beta Phi Mu; Phi Kappa Phi; UDel Lib Assocs; Alpha Chi Omega. 14: Catlg, subj spec. 15: 3122 Butler ave, Los Angeles Ca 90066.

SIMPSON, T(HOMAS) W(ILL). b Kolhapur India 7 Ja 08. 4: Britt-Marie Von Behr. 5: Col of Wooster 25-29 (Eng Lit) BA; Yale 29-30, 31-33 (Eng Lit); George Washington U 36-39 BA in LS. 7: Asst in circ & ref depts Yale U Lib 30-34; Clerk Agric Adjustment Admin, Wash DC 35-37; Catlgr & ref asst Div of Documents LC 37-42; US Army Maj) GSC 42-46; Chief Instr & Cult Materials Sect Reorient Br, CAD War Dept 46-49; Chief Libs Br ILI, Chief Center Oper Br ICS, Dept of State 50-53; Reports off & Chief Prop Mgt Br IOA/S, US Info Agency 54-63; Spec asst to chief, & Near East/So Asia Bk Off ICS, US Info Agency 63-. 9: Amer Inst of Graphic Arts. 15: 1613 Inglewood st N, Arlington Va 22205.

SIMPSON, VIRGINIA (STATLER). b Chicago 15 D 10. 4: Charles Monroe Simpson. 5: UCal (Berkeley) 30-34 (Fr) AB, 34-36 Certif in Libnship. 6: Fr. 7: Catlg Tchrs Prof Lib, Oakland Cal 36-39; Supv libn bks for blind & physically handicapped Cal State Lib 41-. 9: ALA (v-chm Round Table on Lib Serv to the blind 59); CalLA. 10: AAUW. 13: Yes. 14:

Lib serv to the blind& physically handicapped. 15: 2331 Irvin way, Sacramento Ca 95822.

SIMS, CAROL ANN (KURZEJA). b Chicago Ill 25 D 43. 4: David Arthur Sims. 5: UIll 61-65 (Amer Studies) BA; UMich 66-67 MSLS. 7: Ser catlgr UMich (Ann Arbor) 67-; Monograph catlgr Wayne StateU 69-. 14: Catlg. 15: 560 Harrison apt 51, Lincoln Park Mi 48104.

SIMS, LUCILLE (VERNITA) DAVIS. b Thomasville Ga 26 D 07. 4: Chester Arthur Sims. 5: Paine Col 25-28 (Soc Sci) AB; Atlanta summers 34-36 & 36-37 (Eng), summers 47, 49, 50 BS in LS; UWis summers 59-62 MA in LS. 6: Fr, Lat, Ger. 7: Eng tchr Lee Co Bd of Instr, Ft Myers Fla 28-29, Edward Waters Col 29-31, Polk Co Bd of Instr, Winter Haven Fla 31-38; Supv Walton Co Negro Schs, Defuniak Springs Fla 38-39; Supv Lake Co Negro Schs, Tavares Fla 39-43; Eng tchr & libn Fessenden Acad, Martin Fla 43-51; Libn Dillard High Sch Broward Co Sch Bd, Ft Lauderdale Fla 51-. 8: Ch Lib Com, So Assn of Secon Schs & Cols 57, 61; Consul, Fla State LA Wkshops 60, 61. 9: NEA; Amer Tchrs Assn; Fla State EA; FlaASchL (chm Dist 10 58-60, FlaEA (bldg rep); CTA (bldg rep); Fla A-V Assn; BCAM. 10: Entre Nous Bridge Club; Alpha Kappa Alpha; NAACP; YMCA; TB & Res Assoc Bd Trustees. 14: Ref, rare bks train lib assts. 15: 2631 NW 16th st, Ft Lauderdale Fla 33311.

SINCLAIR, CARSON FRASER. b High Point NC 19 O 06. 4: Aleen Chapman Sinclair. 5: UNC 29 (Eng) AB; UFla 32 (Law) JD; Columbia 50 BS in LS. 7: Partner Sinclair & Sinclair, Winter Haven Fla 32-35; Asst libn Supreme Court, Tallahassee Fla 35-42; (Pvt to S/Sgt) US Army 42-45; Asst libn Supreme Court, Tallahassee Fla 45-56, Libn 56-. 9: AALL; Fla Bar. 15: P O Box 172, Tallahasse Fl 32302.

SINCLAIR, DONALD ARLEIGH. b Fredonia Kan 1 J116. 4: Kathryn M Lippincott. 5: Rutgers 34-38 (Classics) BA, 38-40 (Ger Lang & Lit); Columbia 40-42 BS in LS; Cornell U (ASTP) 43-44 (Ger Lang & Area Studies); American U (Archives Admin). 6: Ger, Dutch, Fr, Lat. 7: (Cpl) Mil Intelligence US Army, ETO 42-45; Curator of New Jerseyana Rutgers U Lib 46-47; Curator of spec collections 47-. 8: Hist Adv Com, NJ Tercent Commsn, 64. 9: SAA; BSA; NJLA (Consul & mem Bibliog Com); NJ Hist Soc (Trustee 48-); Geneal Soc of NJ (Trustee, v-pres, ed). 10: AAUP. 12: Comp "The First Thirty-Five Years; The Genealogical Magazine of New Jersey; a Subject-and-Author Index" (62); "The Negro and New Jersey; a Checklist" (65); "The Civil War and New Jersey; a Bibliography" (68); Ed NJ Hist Soc "Proceedings" (52-59), "Genealogical Magazine of New Jersey" (49-66); Gen ed "New Jersey and the Negro; a Bibliography" (67). 13: Yes. 14: Spec collections, archives, bibliog, New Jerseyana & Americana. 15: Rutgers Univ Lib, New Brunswick NJ 08903.

SINCLAIR, DOROTHY (MELVILLE). b Baltimore 24 My 13. 5: Goucher Col 29-33 (Eng) AB; Columbia 39-42 BS in LS, Johns Hopkins 45-50 (Hist) MA; Case West Res 65- (LS). 6: Fr. 7: Asst ref dept Enoch Pratt Free Lib, Baltimore 34-43, Head hist dept 43-50, Asst coordinator adult serv 50-55; Prin libn Field Serv Cal State Lib 55-60; Coordinator of adult serv Enoch Pratt Free Lib, Baltimore 61-65; Lecturer in lib sci Case West Res Sch of Lib Sci 65-. 9: ALA-RSD (past pres); Adult Educ Assn. : "Administration of the Small Public Library (65); Ed Enoch Pratt Free Lib "Book Selection Policies (50). 12: "Administration of the Small Public Library (65). 13: Yes. 14: Lib educ, adult serv, ref, pub lib admin. 15: School of Lib Sci, Case West Res Univ, Cleveland Oh 44106.

SINDEL, JUDY. b King City Cal. 5: Santa Rosa Jr Col 59-61 (Hist) AA; Brigham Young 61-64 (Hist) BA; USoCal 64-65 MLS. 7: Libn Aerospace Corp, El Segundo Cal 65-. 9: SLA. 14: Catlg. 15: 848 So Oxford apt 204, Los Angeles Ca 90005.

SINEATH, TIMOTHY WAYNE. b Jacksonville Fla 21 My 40. 4: Patricia Greenwood. 5: Fla State U 58-62 (Hist) BA, 62-63 (LS) MS; UIll 66- (LS). 6: Fr. 7: Instr-libn UGa 63-66; Dir Ext Lib Sci UIll (Urbana) 66-68; HEA Title II doctoral fellow 68-. 9: ALA; SELA; IllLA; Nat Univ Ext Assn. 10: AAUP; Beta Phi Mu. 14: Lib educ, info storage & retrieval. 15: 706 South Urbana ave, Urbana Il 61801.

SINGER, ERNA (GUTTMAN). b Germany 17 Ap 30. 4: Jack Singer. 5: Hunter Col 48-52 (Eng) BA; Columbia 52-55 (Eng), 64-66 (LS) MS. 6: Ger, Fr. 7: Libn Middle Sch, Hackensack NJ 66-. 9: ALA; NEA; NJEA; HackensackEA; NJSchLA; BergenCoSchLA. 10: Phi Beta Kappa. 14: Sch libnship. 15: 71 Brookview ter, Bergenfield NJ 07621.

SINGER, SUSAN A (McMULLAN). b Phila Penn. 4: Robert E Singer. 5: URochester 47-51 (Applied Econ) AB; Rutgers 65-67 MLS. 7: Gen libn VA Hosp, Lyons NJ 66-68; Hd ref dept Morris Co Free Pub Lib, Whippany NJ 68-. 9: ALA; ASIS; NJLA. 14: Ref. 15: 145 Thackeray dr, W Millington NJ 07946.

SINGER, WILLO ISABEL. b Fergus Ont Can 7 My 09. 5: Queens U 43-45 (Eng, Hist) BA; Toronto 49-50 BLS. 6: Fr. 7: Asst libn Toronto Normal Sch 50-51; Chief Libn Tchrs Col (London Ont) 51-. 9: CanLA; OntLA; Inst Prof Libns Ont. 10: PTA. 14: Ref, child wk, schs. 15: 202-291 St George st, London Ont Can.

SINGERMAN, DONALD D(AVID). b Minneapolis Minn 19 S 07. 4: Pear Stybel. 5: UMinn 26-. 7: Acquis libn Hill Ref Lib, St Paul 25-; Libn Mt Zion Temple Lib, St Paul 29-. 8: Dramatic dir, Jewish Commun Ctr of St Paul 38-. 9: ALA. 13: Yes. 14: Acquis, ref, catlg Judaica. 15: 1226 St Paul ave, St Paul Mn 55116.

SINGERMAN, LORE (SCHWARZCHILD N). b Germany 30 Ap 32. 4: Mark Alvin. 5: SUNY (Oswego) 49-53 (Educ) BS in Ed; Penn State U 53-54 (Speech) MA; UMd (LS). 6: Ger. 7: Instr UPenn 53-54; Tchr Baltimore City 54-65; Tchr & libn S Shore Elem, Anne arundel Co Md 66-. 9: ALA; MdLA; Tchrs Assn of Anne Arundel Co. 10: Kappa Delta Pi; Nat Coun Jewish Women; Hadasah. 14: Child serv & ref. 15: 1705 Nimitz dr, Annapolis Md 21401.

SINGH, (MARJORIE) INDIRA. b Indore India 30 N 20. 5: Isabella Thoburn Col (Lucknow India) 37-39 (Hist, Eng) Intermediate Arts Certif; Indora Christian Col AgraU 39-41 (Hist, Eng, Pol Sci) BA; Govt Tchr Train Col AgraU 42-43 (Hist, Eng) BT; Jeswant Col RajasthanU 47-48, 52 (Hist) MA; UToronto 64-65 BLS. 7: Tchr Dept of Educ, Jodphur Rajasthan India 44-48; Prin Canadian Mission Girls' High Sch, Indore MP India 48-58; Tchr Regina Collegiate Bd, Regina Sask Can 58-59; Asst libn Regina Pub Lib, Regina Sask Can 59-62; Libn-in-charge 62-63; Prin St Mary's Anglican Sch, Deoghar Bihar India 63-64; Libn-in-charge Regina Grey Nuns' Sch of Nursing Lib, Regina Sask Can 64-. 8: Inspectress of rural schs in Rajasthan India 46-48; Mem Bd of Secon Educ, province of Madhya Pradesh, India 52-58. 9: CanLA; SaskLA; ReginaLA. 10: Can Fed of Univ Women; Univ Women's Club of Regina; UN Assn; United Church Women. 14: Ref (spec lib). 15: 2217 Princess st, Regina Saskatchewan Can.

SINGLEY, ELIJAH. b Bessemer Ala 29 Ja 35. 4: Sarah Harden Singley. 5: Miles Col 54-58 (Sociol) AB; Atlanta 58-63 MS in LS; UIll 67-68. 6: Fr. 7: Ref libn Va State Col 60; US rmy (Sgt), Ft Benning Ga 60-62; Ala State Col 63-. 9: ALA; AlaLA. 10: Great Books discussion group; Alpha Kappa Mu. 14: Acquis. 15: P O Box 173 Ala State Col, Montgomery Al 36101.

SINNOTT, GERTRUDE M(ANN). b Brooklyn NY 15 Mr 19. 4: Allen Sinnot. 5: Radcliffe 37-41 (Geol) AB; Rutgers 65-68 MLS. 7: Ref libn Rider Col 68-. 9: ALA. 10: Beta Phi Mu. 14: Ref. 15: 32 Merritt dr, Trenton NJ 08638.

SINSHEIMER, FLORENCE (DUBIN). b NYC 22 My 31. 4: Warren Sinsheimer. 5: Conn Col 48-50 (Eng); Barnard 55-57 (Eng) BA; Columbia 64-67 MLS. 6: Fr. 7: Clk Scarsdale Pub Lib, Scarsdale NY 63, Ref libn 67-; Clk Scarsdale High Sch Lib, Scarsdale NY 66. 9: ALA; WestchesterLA. 14: Ref, child serv. 15: 22 Murray Hill rd, Scarsdale NY 10583.

SINTZ, EDWARD F. b New Trenton Ind 6 F 24. 4: Donna Norris. 5: UKan 47-50 (Liberal Arts) BA; UDenver 53-54 (LS) MA; UMo 62-65 (Pub Admin) MS. 6: Ger. 7: Pilot Army Air Force 42-45; Asst bus & tech dept Kan City (Mo) Public Lib 54-58, Docs libn 56-60, Hd soc sci dept 60-62, Hd ref-soc sci dept 58-60, Supv readers serv 62-64, Asst libn 64-66; Asst libn St Louis Public Lib 66-67, Assoc libn 67-68; Dir Pub Libs, Miami Fla 68-. 8: Lib surveys for Mo State Lib; Instr lib sci WashU Lib (St Louis) 67-68. 9: ALA; FlaLA; Dade Co (Fla) LA; NoLA (MoLA Quarterly; bus mgr 55-56, ed 56-58). 10: Kiwanis Intl. 14; Ref. 15: Miami Pub Lib One Biscayne blvd, Miami Fl 33132.

SIPFLE, WILLIAM KARL. b Springfield Ill 23 N 41. 4: Katherine Albright. 5: MIT 59-61; Carleton Col 61-64 (Physics) BA; UWis 64-66 (Physics) MA; UMinn 68-69 (LS) MA. 6: Fr. 7: Instr in physics Ripon Col 66-68; Lib syst analyst Bell Tel Lab, Murray Hill NJ 69-. 9: Amer Phys Soc; ASIS; SLA; ALA. 14: Lib systems analysis, info retr. 15: 120 Randolph rd, Plainfield NJ 07060.

SIRKO, HLIB. b Lviv Ukraine 17 F 21. 4: Nadia Rybak. 5: Kharkiv U 37-39 (Slavic Philol) Diploma; Lviv U 39-41 (Slavic Philol) Diploma; UMontreal 57-58 BLS; UOttawa 69 (Russian Lang & Lit) MA. 6: Ukrainian, Russian, Fr, Eng. 7: Ed "LUkrainien en France, weekly, Paris 45-48; Libn UMontreal 58-61; Libn Nat Lib, Ottawa 61-; Lecturer UOttawa 65-. 9: CanLA. 14: Catlg. 15: 863 Chenier, Ottawa Can.

SIROONIAN, HAROLD ARA. b Brantfod Ont Can 13 D32. 4: Margaret Jevahirjian. 5: McMaster U (Ont) 51-55 (Geo) BS, 55-58 (Geochem) MS; Columbia 60-62 MLS. 6: Fr, Armenian. 7: Tchr Passaic (NJ) Bd of Educ 59-60; Libn Lamont Geol Observ Columbia 60-65; Libn Geol Libn 65-66; Assh hd sci & engr div Lib 65-66; Instr Sch of Lib Serv 69; Sci libn CCNY 66-. 9: SLA (NY Chap: Exec Coun Documentation 64-; LACUNY. 64-65). 14: Sci libs, documentation, admin. 15: 2879 Heath ave, Bronx NY 10463.

SISSON, HULL (SILVANUS). b Colony Kan 4 F 05. 4: Leona Jackman. 5: Baker U 24-28 (Physics, Hist) BS; UWash 30-31 (Educ, Hist) AM; Kan State Tchr Col (Emporia) 55-56 (LS) MS; UNeb 57-61 (Educ) D Ed. 6: Sp. 7: Rural grade tchr, Anderson Co Kan 22-24; High sch tchr Rural High Sch, Bucyrus Kan 28-30; Farmer Bucyrus Kan 33-35; Sch prin, Meriden Kan 35-37; High sch tcht, Roxbury Kan 37-39; Sch supt Pub Schs, Republic Kan 39-41; Merchant, Republic Kan 41-63; Head libn Neb Wesleyan U 56-60; Asst libn Central Mo State 60-. 9: ALA; MoLA; Mo State Tchrs Assn. 10: AAUP. 12: "Planning the Junior High School Library Program. 13: Yes. 14: Tchr of lib sci courses, circ procedures. 15: 303 Hillcrest, Warrensburg Mo 64093.

SISSON, JACQUELINE (DEMOREST) (MRS). b Oxford Ohio 3 Jl 25. 5: Ohio State U 42-46 (Fr Lit) BA. 6: Fr, Sp, Ital. 7: Lib asst Pub Lib, Columbus Ohio 46-47; Lib asst circ dept Ohio State U 47-48, Fine arts libn 48-61; Hd Fine Arts Lib 62-; Asst Prof 69-. 9: ALA; Franklin Co (Ohio) LA (cor sec); Col Art Assn; Internat Ctr of Med Art. 13: Yes. 14: Fine arts, ref & bibliog. 15: Fine Arts Lib Ohio State Univ, 1858 Neil ave, Columbus Ohio 43210.

SISSON, LAUREL (KLEIN). b Jamaica NY 6 Sp 31. 4: Paul Smith Sisson Jr. 5: William Smith Col 48-52 (Eng) BA; C W Post Col LIU 63-68 (LS) MS. 7: Libn Riverhead High Sch, Riverhead NY 64-66; Y-a libn Riverhead Free Lib, Riverhead NY 66-. 9: ALA; NYLA; Exec Bd Suffolk Co LA (Exec Bd). 10: Girl Scouts leader; LWV. 14: Ya wk. 15: 432 Fishel ave, Riverhead NY 11901.

SISTRUNK, JAMES DUDLEY. b Monticello Miss 13 Ag 19. 4: Helen Anna Wilson. 5: LSU 45-46; Clarke Mem 51-52; Baylor U 52-54 (Bible Gk) BA; Southwestern Baptist Theol Sem 54-57 (Religion) BD; Baylor U 54 (Philos); N Tex State U 57-59 BS in LS; UNC 60-65 (LS). 6: Fr, Gk, Ger. 7: Foreman Robinson Construction Co, Centreville Miss 40; 1st Sgt USAF 40-45; Guager Interstate Oil Pipeline Co, Natchez Miss 46-50; Circ libn Southwestern Baptist Theol Sem 57-58, Admin libn 59-64; Libn, Assoc Prof Campbell Col 64-. 9: ALA; SELA; NCLA. 10: Lions Club; Alpha Lambda Sigma; NC Hist & Lit Assn. 14: Admin. 15: P O Box 415, Buies Creek NC 27506.

SITTER, CLARA MARIE (LOEWEN). b Watonga Okla 28 Je 41. 4: Lester Dewey Sitter. 5: UOkla 59-62 (Amer Studies) BA; UTex 62-65 MLS. 6: Fr. 7: Lib asst UTex Humanities Research Center lib 62-64; Child libn Arlington Co Pub Lib, Arlington Va summer 64; Ref libn UTex Undergrad Lib 64-65; Catlgr rare bks UTex Stark Lib 65-; Act libn 66; Catlgr W Tex State U 67; Asst libn Amarillo Col Lib 68-. 9: ALA; TexLA; Tex Jr ColTA. 14: Catlg, ref. 15: 6203 Hanson rd, Amarillo Tx 79106.

SITZMAN, GLENN L(aROY). b Corn Okla 23 Ag 20. 5: Southwestern State Col (Okla) 39-42 (Eng); Okla Baptist U 42-43 (Eng) BA; Tex Tech Col 44 (Eng); Baylor U 45-47 (Eng) MA; Tulane U 47-48 (Eng); Columbia 54-56 MSLS. ; Col of Lib Wales (Aberystwyth) 67 (Intl Lib). 6: Sp. 7: Asst Prof of Eng Ouachita Col 48-49; Asst Prof of Eng Howard Col 49-53; Visiting Lecturer Grand Canyon Col summer 53; Columbia U: Searcher catlg 54-55, Catlgr trainee 55-56, Jr catlgr 56-57, Sr catlgr 57-60, Asst Sch of Lib Serv 59 & 60; Asst head catlgr UPR (Rio Piedras) 60-63; Head ref sect Nat Lib of Nigeria, Lagos Nigeria 63-65; Deputy libn Makerere U Col (Kampala Uganda) 66-; Act libn 66-67; Chief libn UGuyana, Georgetown Guyana 67-68; Assoc libn Clarion State Col 69-. 8: Ford Found Program Spec, Lagos Nigeria, 63-65; Tchg fellow TulaneU 47-48. 9: ALA; NigerianLA; NCTE: Sociedad de bibliotecarios de Puerto Rico, NY Tech Serv Libns (Memb Com 60); GuyanaLA; E AfricanLA. 14: Catlg, ref, admin. 15: 620 Wood st apt C, Clarion Pa 16214.

SIVAK, MARIE ROSE. b Chicago Ill 24 S 35. 5: West MichU 53-57 (Eng) AB, 58-62 (Eng) MA; Case West Res summer 66 (LS); Wichita StateU summer 69 (LS). 7: Tchr & libn Bloomingdale Schs, Bloomingdale Mich 57-59; Tchr & libn Three Oaks Schs, Three Oaks Mich 59-65; Lib coord River Valley Schs, Three Oaks Mich 65-. 8: Adv Bd Berrien-Cass Inst Materials Ctr 65-; River Valley Profess Study Com 68-69. 9: ALA (Memb Com 66-67); BerrienCoEA (pres 65-66); MichASchL (Supvs Sect: sec-treas 67-68). 10: Alpha Delta Kappa; Three Oaks Bk Club; Mich Congress Parent & Tchrs. 13: Yes. 14: Young adult work, storytelling, bk reviewing, sch pub rel, new prog and new bldgs devel.

SIVE, MARY (ROBINSON). 4: David Sive. 5: Conn Col BA; Rutgers MLS. 6: Ger. 7: Sch libn S Orangetown Central Sch Dist, Blauvelt NY; Sch libn Clarkstown Central Sch, New City NY; Asst catlgr Brooklyn Pub Lib. 10: AAUW; Shade Tree Commsn, Town of Orangetown; Nat Audubon Soc. 13: Yes. 14: Child serv. 15: 89 Lark st, Pearl River NY 10965.

SIVELLS, WANDA (KELLAR). b Cross Plains Tex 3O 25. 4 : Charles Graves Sivells. 5: N Tex State U 43-46 BSNIN LS; Tex Womans U 63-65 MS in LS. 6: Sp. 7: Dir of Learning Ctr Wharton Co Jr Col 46-. 8: Bldg consul 67-; consul for loc church and hospital libs. 9: ALA; -ACRL (Jr Col Sect; bibliog Com); TexLA (sec-treas Col & Univ Div, sec-treas Dist 5); Tex Jr Col Assn; Tex State Tchrs Assn; Tex Jr Col TA (chm Lib Sect); SWLA; Tex Lib Netwk. 10: Delta Kappa Gamma; AAUW; Wharton mbk Review Club; Girl Scouts; PTA. 14: Ref, admin, media prog, archives. 15: 511 Lazy lane, Wharton Tex 77488.

SIVULICH, KENNETH G. b Dixonville Pa 3 Ap 39. 5: Ind State Col 57-61 (Educ) BS; UPittsburgh 65-66 MLS. 7: Tchr S Fayette Twp Sch Dist, McDonald Penn 61-65; Asst admin & ext libn Altoona Pub Lib, Altoona Penn 66-68; Ext libn Erie Pub Lib, Erie Penn 68-. 9: ALA; PennLA (sec Co Pub Lib Div). 14: Admin. 15: Erie Pub Lib 3 So Perry sq, Erie Pa 16501.

SIZEMORE, WILLIAM CHRISTIAN. b S Boston Va 19 Je 38. 4: Anne Mills. 5: URichmond 56-60 (Eng) BA; Southeastern Baptist Theol Sem 60-63 (Church Hist) BD; UNC 63-64 MSLS. 6: Ger, Gk. 7: Lib asst URichmond Lib 59-60; Salesman Southwestern Publ Co, Nashville 62;Lib asst I UNC Lib (Chapel Hill) 63-64; Asst catlg libn Southeastern Baptist Theol Sem (Wake Forest NC) 64-65, Assoc libn 65-66; Libn & Assoc Prof S Ga Col (Douglas Ga) 66-. 8: Lecturer in res methods & bibliog, Southeastern Baptist Theol Sem grad program, 64-66; Spec lecturer comparative relig 8th Congressional Dist Honors Program, Douglas Ga 67. 9: ALA-ACRL; ATheolLA; NCLA- SELA (Ref Serv Div Nominating Com 68-69); Va Baptist Hist Soc; GaLA (Publicity Com 68-); Ga Assn Jr Cols (chm 66-67); S Ga Acad Libs (sec 66-67). 10: Beta Phi Mu; Lions Club; AAUP; Satilla Libns Coun. 12: Ed "Serial Holdings of South Georgia Academic Libraries (67-). 13: Yes. 14: Catlg, acquis, admin, automation. 15: 1302 Forrest Circle dr, Douglas Ga 31533.

SKAHILL, HELEN E. b Dubuque Iowa 8 Mr 10. 5: Clarke Col (Dubuque Iowa) 28-32 (Hist) BA; Columbia 41-42 (Lib) MA. 6: Sp, Fr. 7: Eng tchr Dubuque Sr High Sch, Dubuque Iowa 32-34; Libn asst Dubuque Pub Lib, Dubuque Iowa 34-37; Child libn Omaha Pub Lib 37-43; Child libn Seattle Pub Lib 43-65, Head Central Child Lib 64-. 8: ALA rep to NCTE Reading List Com 66-. 9: ALA-CSD (var coms; Newberry-Caldecott Com 66); PNLA (chm Child Sect, mem var coms); Wash State LA (var coms). 13: Yes. 14: Child serv. 15: 1105 Spring st, Seattle 98104.

SKALLERUP, HARRY R(OBERT). b Chicago 20 Mr 27. 4: Amy Gage. 5: UIll 48-52 (Bot) BS; Washington U (St Louis) 52-53(Bot) AM; UMinn 53-54 (LS)MA. 6: Sp, Fr. 7: Seaman 1/c US Coast Guard 45-46; Asst Mo Botanical Garden, St Louis 53; Physics libn UIll(Urbana) 54055; Head sci div So Ill U Lib 55-59; Asst Walter J Johnson Antiquarian Bks, NYC 59-62; Engnr libn UIowa 62-64; Head catlg dept 64-67; Assoc libn & Assoc Prof US Naval Acad Lib (Annapolis Md) 67-. 9: ALA-ACRL; IowaLA. ; MdLA; BSA. 10: AAUP; Sigma Xi; Beta Phi Mu; Amer Soc Engnr Educ; US Naval Inst. 13: Yes. 14: Sci bibliog, admin, catlg. 15: US Naval Academy Lib, Annapolis Md 21402.

SKARZYNSKI, STANLEY ADAM. b Przemysl Poland 17 Mr 12. 4: Millicent Bibza. 5: King John Casimir U (Lwow Poland) 30-34 (Law) Masters, State Sch of Econ & Com (Lwow Poland) 33-34 Certif; Carnegie 61-62 MLS. 6: Fr, Ger, Polish, Sp. 7: Govt Off specializing in market res & finan oper, Warsaw Poland 36-39; Artiller off prewar Polish Army 39-45;

Com attache Polish Consulates in Detroit & Pittsburgh, promoted trade, com & relief to aid in the post-war econ reconstruction of Poland 46-50; Credit manager Consolidated Home Specialties, Pittsburgh 51-55; Libn Penn State U (McKeesport) 62-66; soc studies libn Cal State Col (Penn) 66-68; Bibliogr Edinboro State Col 68-. 9: ALA; PennLA; SLA. 14: Ref, bibliog. 15: 100 Hillview dr, Elizabeth Penn 15037.

SKASKIW, BODHAN MYROSLAW. b Ukraine 24 F 15. 4: Myroslawa Luzniak. 5: Catholic Theol Acad 33-38 MST; Acad of For Trade (Cracav) 38-40. 6: Ukrainian, Polish, russian, Ger, Church Slavic. 7: Mgr Cosmos Parcels Express, Detroit 59-62; Lib asst-accessioner LC 62-63, Lib asst-searcher 63-64, Lib searcher & catlgr 64-67, Asst supv searching & preliminary catlg 68-. 10: Ukrainian Congress Com of Smer; Assn of Ukrainian Libns in Amer. 14: Catlg. 15: 1911 Dana dr, Adelphi Md 20783.

SKED, DOROTHY ANNA (DOROTHY BUSCH). b W New York NJ 6 Jl 13. 4: Harold A Sked. 5: State Tchrs Col (Newark NJ) 50 (Educ) BS; State Tchrs Col (Trenton NJ) 53 BLS; Columbia 59 (Pharmaceutical Libnship). 7: Hd libn Pennington Sch for Boys, Pennington NJ 49-51; Hd libn Thomas Jefferson Jr High Sch, Fair Lawn NJ 51-54; Hd libn Col High Sch, Montclair NJ 54-58; Hd libn Hoffman La Roche, Nutley NJ 58-62; Asst libn ITT Fed Labs, Nutley NJ 62-64; Research info scientist E R Squibb, New Brunswick NJ 64-65; Ref libn & instr lib sci State Tchrs Col (Newark NJ) 65-. 9: SLA (NJ Chap: Educ Recr Com); NEA; NJEA. 10: Newark State Col Fac Assn. 14: Ref, tchg lib serv courses. 15: 11 Hazard pl, Elizabeth NJ 07208.

SKEELE, LILLIAN (MARY). b Columbus Ohio 21 Je 06. 5: Ohio State 23-27 (Eng) BA; UIll 30-31 BS in LS. 7: Child libn Columbus Pub Lib, Columbus Ohio 27-. 9: ALA; OhioLA; FranklinCoLA. 10: Ohioana Lib. 14: Child serv. 15: 3746 Granden rd, Columbus Oh 43214.

SKEEN, LEALYS (GILLIAN). b Quanah Tex 2 D 27. 4: Douglas S Skeen. 5: Tex Woman's U 42-46 (Music Educ) BS, 61, 63-64 MLS. 6: Sp. 7: Tchr pub sch music Sweetwater Pub Schs, Sweetwater Tex 46-51; Tchr pub sch music Govalle Elem Sch, Austin Tex 53-58; Tchr libn Boyd High Sch, Boyd Tex 58-63; Libn Abernathy High Sch, Abernathy Tex 64-66; Asst libn Dallas Baptist Col 66-67; Elem libn Lubbock Pub Schs, Lubbock Tex 67-. 9: NEA; Tex State Tchrs Assn; TexLA; TexSchLA; SWLA; Assn Child Educ Intl. 14: Catlg, tech serv. 15: 1901 13th st, Lubbock Tx 79401.

SKEITH, ELIZABETH (MARY). b New Dayton Alta Can. 5: Queens U (Ont) 47-50 (Hist) BA; McGill 54-55 BLS. , 69 MLS. 6: Fr. 7: Libn "Lethbridge (Alta) Herald 50-54; Catlgr Edmonton Pub Lib, Edmonton Alta 55-56; Gen libn UWest Ont 56-58; Catlgr MCGill U 58-60; Head processing dept UAlta (Calgary) 60-66; Hd catlg div Douglas Lib Queen's U (Ont) 66-. 9: ALA-RTSD;-ACRL;-LAD; CanLA-CACUL; AltaLA (Coun 63-64); CalgaryLA (pres); Inst Prof Libns of Ont; Prof Libns Assn of Queens (chm 69-). 14: Tech serv. 15: 49-1254 Princess st, Kingston Ont Can.

SKELTON, ALAN GORDON. b Fayetteville Ark 3 Ag 12 . 4: Martha Hope Butcher. 5: UOkla 29-33 BA in LS, 33-34 (Pol Sci) BA. 6: Ger, Fr, Sp. 7: Libn: pub schs, Alice Tex 34-36, pub schs, Robstown Tex 36-38, Geol Lib UOkla 38-44; Libn & research asst Mid-Continent Oil & Gas Assn, Tulsa Okla 44-47; Head Research Center Lib US Army ngnr Waterways Expt Sta, Vicksburg Miss 47-. 8: Oil Field Nomenclature Com, Mid-Continent Oil & Gas Assn, 43-47; Corps of Engnrs rep on Engnrs Jt Coun Engnr Thesaurus Com, 62-. 9: SLA (Adv Coun 59-60; La Chap: Bulletin ed 58-59, pres 59-60, Exec Bd 60-61); MissLA (treas 58-59, pres 61; chm & v-chm Spec Libs Sect 57-58). 10: Vicksburg Beautification Commsn; Municipal Rose Garden Com; Phi Beata Kappa; Phi Delta Kappa. 13: Yes. 14: Industrial mgt. 15: P O Box 631, Vicksburg Ms 39180.

SKELTON, MARTHA HOPE (BUTCHER). b New Martinsville WVa 22 Jl 19. 4: Alan Gordon Skelton. 5: UOkla 35-39 (Geol) BS, 39-40 BA in LS; Miss Col 62-63. 6: Sp, Ger. 7: Asst Mid-Continent Oil & Gas Assn, Tulsa Okla 44; Asst Tulsa Pub Lib, Tulsa Okla 45; Libn H V Cooper High Sch, Vicksburg Miss 59-. 9: Miss LA (Scholarship Com 62, Awards Com 63-64); Recruitment Com 69); MissASchL (sec-treas 64-65); MissEA. 10: Chi Upsilon; Delta Kappa Gamma; AAUW. 13: Yes. 14: Ref, reader adv. 15: H V Cooper High School, Vicksburg Ms 39180.

SKELTON, MATTILEE (NEWMAN). b Hugo Okla. 5: UOkla 31 (Home Econ) BS, 37 (LS) BS. 7: Stud asst UOkla 28-31; Ref libn Mo State Lib 40-41; Ref & circ libn Stephens Col 42-44; Head of circ dept UKan City 44-62; Ref libnUMo(Kansas City) Lib 62-. 9: ALA; MoLA. 10: AAUP; Alpha Gamma Delta. 14: Ref, archives. 15: Univ of Mo-Kansas City 5100 Rockhill rd, Kansas City Mo 64110.

SKENE, ANN (LYN) (GROVES). b Noblesville Ind 12 S 42. 4: John H Skene. 5: Ind StateU 60-64 (Soc Sci) AB, summer 68 (Hist); UIll 64-65 MS in LS. 6: Sp. 7: Asst libn Allisonville Elem Sch, Indianapolis 65-67; Libn Grandview Elem Sch, Indianapolis 67-. 8: Asst libn Knapp Sch Libs Proj Allisonville Elem Sch 65-67. 9: ALA-AASchL; NEA; IndASchL (Recruitment Com 67-68); A-V Instr Dirs; Ind State TA; ClrTA (Legis Com 68-69). 10: Alpha Beta Alpha; Beta Phi Mu; Marion Co Lib Discussion Club. 14: Child libnship. 15: 5023 Hawthorn ter, Indianapolis In 46220.

SKENE, MELVIN, DAVID (St C). b Toronto Can 24 Mr 36. 5: Trinity Col UToronto 56-60 (Hist) BA; Toronto 60-61 BLS. 6: Fr, Russian. 7: (Lt) Infantry Can Army, Ref libn Toronto Pub Lib 61-65; Asst hd hist sect 65; Hd Met Bibliog Ctr 65-66; Hd tech serv div 66-67; Asst dir/sec-treas Lake Erie Reg Lib Syst, Ont 67-. 8: Lib consul & adv wk for var bus orgs. 9: CanLA (chm Info Serv Sect 67-70; chm Lib Mechanization Com 66-); ALA; OntLA (chm Info Serv Sect 67-68; chm Reg & Pub Libs Div 69); Inst Prof Libns Ont. 10: Arch Conservancy of Ont; Art Gallery of Toronto; Royal Ont Mus. 12: Co-ed "How to Find Out About Canada (66); Co-comp "Library Telecommunications Directory (66-). 14: Application of computer techniques to lib methods, automation of bibliog control, lib admin. 15: Lake Erie Regional Lib System 305 Queens ave, London Ont Can.

SKIDMORE, DORIS P(ACKMAN). b Detroit 16 Ja 26. 4: Ralph D skidmore. 5: Meinzinger Art Sch (Detroit) 46-50. 7: Cartographic Draftsman US Govt Corp of Engnrs, Detroit 50-52; Libn Sub trop Expt Sta Div of UFla Ext 53; Asst libn City of Homestead Fla 51-53; Child libn City of W Palm Beach Fla 55-63; Child libn City of Coral Gables Fla 63-. 8: Jt bk selection con Dade sch & lib semi-annual list primary level 66-69. 9: ALA; FlaLA; Dade Co (Fla) LA (treas 66-67). 10: Soroptimist Club; Miami Staff Org. 14: Child serv, art bks. 15: Coral Gables Pub Lib 3443 Segovia st, Coral Gables Fl 33134.

SKIDMORE, LOTTIE M. b Norborne Mo 27 N 03. 5: Ottawa U (Kan) 21-27 (Fr) AB; UIll 39-40 BS in LS, summers 44-46 (LS) MS. 6: Fr, Sp. 7: Jr high tchr, Mascoutah Ill 29-32; Tchr High Sch, Kilbourne Ill 32-37; Tchr High Sch, Ashland Ill 37-38; Libn High Sch, Rantoul Ill 40-41; Libn High Sch, Kankakee Ill 41-46 ;Libn Jr Col, Joliet Ill 46-58; Chm Libs & A-v serv Twp High Sch & Jr Col, Joliet Ill 58-64, Chm dist processing & a-v serv 64-66; Libn Jr Col Joliet Ill 66-67, chm lib & a-v serv 67-. 8: Instrin lib sci, Tex State Col for Women, summer 49; Consul to ACRL Standards Com for ALA Jr Col Lib Standards, 59. 9: NEA (Life mem); ALA-LAD;-ACRL (Jr Col Sect: reg chm 48-49, sec 49-50, chm 53-54);-AASchL;-rtsd; IllLA; Ill Tchrs Assn. 10: AAUW; Bus & Prof Womens Club; Delta Kappa Gamma. 14: Catlg, a-v serv, lib admin. 15: 1619 Avalon ave, Joliet Ill 60435.

SKIDMORE, MARY E (INGALLS). b Warren Ohio 18 O 28. 4: Edward C Skidmore. 5: Baldwin Wallace 47-49; Bowling Green State (Ohio) 51-52 (Hist) BA; West Res 52-54 MS in LS. 7: Libn NYC Pub Lib 54-58; Libn US Army, Germany 58-60; Period libn Dept of Commerce, Wash DC 60-62; Br libn Arlington Pub Lib, Arlington Va 62-. 9: ALA; VaLA. 15: 4614 34th st S, Arlington Va 22206.

SKIDMORE, WARREN L. b Akron Ohio 12 Ja 26. 4: Judith A Davis. 5: St John's Col (Annapolis Md) 43-45; Kent State U 66-67 MSLS. 6: Fr. 7: Hd adult serv div Akron Pub Lib, Akron Ohio 66-69, Hd lang lit & hist div 69-. 9: ALA (Regl Chm SORT 68-); OhioLA (chm SORT 65-66, Memb Com 65-66, Recr Com 65-66, Memb Serv Com 66-68, chm Ref Serv RT 68-69). 10: Staff Assn Akron Pub Lib; Weathervane Commun Playhouse, Akron. 12: Subed "Index to 1830 Federal Population Census of Ohio", Ohio Lib Found 2 v (64). 15: 171 Goodhue dr, Akron Oh 44313.

SKILLIN, GLENN B(ARRIE). b Worcester Mass 8 Ag 31. 4: Rebecca Jane Camp. 5: UVt 50-52, 57-59 (Eng) BA; Columbia 59-60 (LS) MS. 6: Ger. 7: Specialist-4 US Army Adjutant Gen's Corps 55-57; Ref & circ libn Bennington Col 60-61; Asst John Carter Brown Lib BrownU 62-65; Dir & libn Me Hist Soc, Portland 65-68; Assoc curator of mss SyracuseU Lib 68-. 9: Vt Hist Soc; Me Hist Soc; NH Hist Soc; RI Hist Soc; Colon Soc of Mass. 13: Yes. 14: Rare bks (Americana), hist of printing in the US, ref. 15: 111 Fordham rd apt 3B, Syracuse NY 13203.

SKINNER, A E. b Vernon Tex 19 Mr 28. 5: Kilgore Jr Col 45-47 AA; N Tex State Col 48-51 BA in LS. 6: Lat, Fr. 7: Chem libn UTex 51- . 9: TexLA. 10: Tex State Hist Assn; W Tex Hist Assn. 12: Ed "Reminiscences of a Texas Ranger (67). 13: Yes. 14: Rare bks, hist of chem, Tex local hist & memoirs. 15: Chem bldg 219 Univ of Texas, Austin Tx 78712.

SKINNER, JEAN ELLEN. b NYC 14 O 30. 5: Douglass Col 48-51 (LS); NYU 52-54 (Hist) AB; Columbia 58-59 MLS. 6: Fr. 7: Clerk NYU Lib 54-58; Catlgr Smith Col 59-62; Catlgr NYU 62-. 9: NY Lib Club. 10: Gilbert & Sullivan Soc, NY; VLOG; Soc for NYU Lib. 14: Catlg. 15: 185 West End ave, apt 8-J, NYC 10023.

SKIPPER, JAMES E. b Bartow Fla 10 D 20. 4: Margaret Emerson. 5: UNC 39-43 (Econ, Pol Sci) AB; UMich 47-48 BSLS, 48-49 MSLS, 60 PhD. 6: Ger, Fr. 7: US Army)Pfc) Field Artillery, ETO: Asst libn Washington & Jefferson Col 49-50; Acquis libn Ohio State U 53-55; Instr Dept of Lib Sci UMich 54; Asst libn for tech serv Mich State U 56-59; Dir of Libs UConn 59-62; Exec sec ARL, Wash DC 63-67; Assoc univ libn Princeton U 67-68; Univ libn UCal (Berkeley) 68-. 8: Lib bldg consul; Carnegie Fellow, Rutgers Sem on Adv Lib Admin. 9: ALA-RTSD (pres, chm CMS, mem var coms);-ACRL (com assignments); ConnLA (chm Col Sect). 10: Mich Acad Arts, Letters, & Scis; Conn cad Arts & Scis; Phi Eta Sigma, Beta Phi Mu. 13: Yes. 14: Lib resources & bibliog control, admin. 15: Univ of Cal Lib, Berkeley Ca 94720.

SKIPPER, MARIE (THORNTON). b Berry Ala. 4: Curtis R Skipper. 5: Ala Col for Women 43-46 (Sociol) AB; UAla summers 49-51 Certif in Sch Lib Serv; Peabody 56 AB in LS. 6: Sp. 7: Psychometrist Birmingham pub schs & VA Guidance Center, Birmingham Ala 46-48; Psychometrist US VA, Montgomery Ala 48; Soc studies tchr Berry High Sch, Berry Ala 48-51; Head catlg dept Mobile Pub Lib, Mobile Ala 51-62, Head tech serv dept 62-. 14: Catlg, spec collections. 15: 1557 No Birchwood dr, Mobile Al 36609.

SKIPSNA, ALVIN. b Riga Latvia 20 Ja 25. 4: Aina Abols. 5: UErlangen 46-48 (Law, Philol); City Col (NY) 52-54 (Eng) BA; Columbia 54-56 (LST) MS. 6: Ger, Lettish. 7: 1st asst microfilm sect NY Pub Lib 52-56, Catlgr 56-61; Head tech serv Skidmore Col 61-69, Acting libn 69-. 9: ALA; NYLA. 10: Phi Beta Kappa; Beta Phi Mu; AAUP. 14:Tech serv, reclsf. 15: 16 Second st, Saratoga Springs NY 12866.

SKOOG, ANNE (CATHERINE). b Rochester Penn 21 Ja 17. 5: Carnegie 35-39 BS, 39-40 BS in LS. 6: Fr, Ger. 7: Catlgr Westminster Col Lib (Penn) 40-44; Asst bus br Carnegie Lib of Pittsburgh 44-46; Soc rel br libn Carnegie Inst of Tech 46-50, Asst catlgr 50-66, Assoc catlgr 66-. 9: ALA; PennLA; Tri-State LA (Penn, Ohio, WVa); BSA. 10: Bus & Prof Womens Club; Phi Kappa Phi; Pittsburgh Bibliophiles. 12: Ed PennLA "Bulletin" (57-60). 13: Yes. 14: Catlg, rare bks. 15: 5810 Kentucky ave, Pittsburgh 15232.

SKOWRONSKA, HELEN (MARY). b Cleveland. 5: Flora Stone Mather Col 33-37 (Chem) BA; West Res 37-39 (Biochem) MS, 47-48 BS in LS. 7: Lab tech U Hops, Cleveland 40-42; Lab tech Cleveland Graphite Bronze Co, Cleveland 42-46; Indexer Chem Abstracts Serv, Columbus 46-47; Libn West Res U Pharmacy Sch 47-49; Libn Miles Labs Inc, Elkhart Ind 47-51; Research lib staff Goodyear Tire & Rubber Co, Akron Ohio51-52; Libn Sherwin-Williams Co, Cleveland 52-. 9: ACS; SLA; ASIS. 10: Cleveland Soc of Paint Tech. 15: 2364 Taylor rd, Cleveland Oh 44112.

SKUGRUD, LANA. b Oakland Cal 9 Ap 45. 5: URedlands 63-67 (Govt) AB; UCLA 67-68 MLS. 6: Ger. 7: Libn I San Jose State Col 68-. 10: Pi Gamma Mu. 14: Ref, hist of printing. 15: 1885 California #18, Mountain View Ca 94040.

SKUJA, LUCIJA (BISTRUMS, DRUVA-DRUVINA). b Prode Latvia 26 N 22. 4: V Peter Skuja. 5: URiga(Latvia) 42-44 (Baltic Langs); UKiel(Germany) 45-49 (Ger); UMich 54-58 AMLS. 6: Latvian, Lithuanian, Ger, Russian, Fr. 7: Grand Rapids (Mich) Pub Lib; Lib asst 55-57, Catlgr I 57-59, Head of Ref Dept 59-. 9: ALA; MichLA; Grand Rapids Libns Club. 10: Beta Phi Mu; Amer Latvian Assn. 14: Ref, rare bks. 15: 106 Fitzhugh ave SE, Grand Rapids Mich 49506.

SKYLES, GEORGE H. b Hill City Ida 9 Jl 35. 4: Mary Beth Anderson. 5: Brigham Young 53-55, 59-60 (Hist) BS, 60-62 (Hist) MA, 66-67 MLS; Portland State Col summer 63. 7: Tchr Lyman High Sch, Lyman Wyo 62-63; Tchr Whittier High Sch, Whittier Cal 63-66; Hd libn El Rancho High Sch, Pico Rivera Cal 67-. 9: ALA; CalTA; CalASchL; El RanchoEA (Bd Dirs). 14: Ref, ya lit. 15: 7603 Kengard, Whittier Ca 90606.

SKYNNER, HENRY JOH. b Ft William Ont Can 10 N 30. 4: Kathleen Birch Schioler. 5: UMan 46-51 BA; St Johns Col 49-52 L Th;McGill 54-58 STM; Toronto 61-62 BLS. 7: Lecturer St. Johns Col (Man) 58-, Libn & Asst Prof of Near East langs 62-68; Hd bibliog control Elizabeth Dufoe Lib UMan 68-. 9: CanLA; ManLA. 14: Catlg. 15: 540 Oakenwald ave, Winnipeg 19 Man Can.

SLACK, ERROL CARLETON. b Randolph Vt 9 D 06. 4: Ivy Hosking. 5: UVt 24-28 (Fr) PhB; Columbia summers 49-53 MS in LS. 6: Fr, Sp. 7: Instr in Fr UVt 29-40; Catlgr UVt Lib 46-68; Hist collections libn Med Lib 68-. 9: VtLA. 10: Amer Guild of Organists. 14: Catlg, rare bks. 15: 24 University terrace, Burlington Vt 05401.

SLACK, KENNETH THURSTON. b Toquerville Utah 4 Mr 20. 4: Dorothea Rasmuson. 5: UTah State Agric Col 46-49 (Pol Sci) BS; UDenver 5-52 (LS) MA; UUtah 40-41, 63-64 (Educ Admin) Ed D. 6: Sp. 7: Development man Goodyear Tire & Rubber Co, Los Angeles 41-44; US Navy Yeoman 3/c 44-46; Tchg asst Utah State U 49-50; Libn Denver pub schs 52-53; Asst libn East Ore Col 53-55; Libn The Church Col of Hawaii 55-65; Asst libn Ariz State U 65-67; Assoc Dir libs UUtah 67-. 8: Mem of var adv coms on libs of Hawaii. 9: ALA (Coun mem rep Hawaii 58); HawaiiLA (treas 57-58, pres 61-62; chm Spec & Ref Sect 56-57); ArizLA. 10: Phi Delta Kappa. 12: Ed Hawaii LA "Journal (63-64); Ed "Arizona Librarian (66-67); Ed "Hui Law Lima News (56-58). 13: Yes. 14: Admin, pub serv, ref. 15: 5542 Revere dr, Salt Lake City Ut 84117.

SLADKUS, RUTH (GUTTMAN). b N Tarrytown NY 26 Ap 3. 4: Max Sladkus. 5: Hunter Col 29-33 (Fr) BA; Columbia 33-34 (LS) MS; Good Counsel Col 64 (Educ); State U (New Paltz NY) 65 (Educ): Columbia 65-66 LS) 06: Fr, Hebrew, Ger. 6: Fr, Hebrew, Ger, Lat. 7: Lib asst Hunter Col; Lib asst & sub tchr Tarrytown Sch System; Religious Sch tchr, Tarrytown NY; Libn; Emanuel Sch, NYC, Camp Achvah, Godefroy NY, Alice E Grady Elem Sch, Elmsford NY. 9: NYStateTA; NYStateSchLA. 10: PTA; Hadassah; United Charity Fund; Sisterhood; Elmsford Sch Faculty Assn. 14: Sch libs, tchg lib skills, col libs. 15: 63 Highland ave, Tarrytown NY 10591.

SLAGLE, ALMA DOROTHY. b Madeira Ohio 11 O 04. 5: UCincinnati 32-45 (Sociol) AB; UWis 45-46 BLS; Emory summer 53 Med Libs. 7: Asst sci & ind Pub Lib of Cincinnati 27-60; Med libn Research Found Lib Child Hosp, Elland & Bethesda, Cincinnati 60-. 9: ALA; MELA; SELA. 14: Ref. 15: 6025 Miami rd, Indian Hill, Cincinnati Oh 45243.

SLAMECKA, VLADIMIR. b Brno Czechoslovakia 8 My 2 4: Elba Seoane. 5: UTech (Brno Czechoslovakia) 47-49 (Chem Engnr) ING C; USydney Australia 51-53 (Sci, Philos); UMunich Germany 54 (Sociol); Columbia 56-62 MS, DLS. 6: Ger, Czech, Russian. 7: Ind researcher, Munich & NY 54-57; Chief Chem Brookvale Breweries, NSW Australia 53-54; Chem libn Columbia U 58-60, Prin investigator 60-62; Manager Documentation Inc, Bethesda Md 62-64; Dir Sch of Info Sci Ga Inst of Tech 64-. 8: Consul; NSF, 65, Logistics Mgt Inst, 64 & 65, Scott Paper Co, 64 & 65, Computer Sci Corp 65-, Coca Cola Co 66-, HEW 66-. 9: ASIS. 10: Sigma Xi; Assn for Computing Machinery; AAAS. 12: "Science in Czechoslovakia" (63); "Science in East Germany" (63); Ed "The Coming Age of Information Technology" (65); Ed "Studies in Technical Data Management" (65); "National Information Systems in Europe" (69). 13: Yes. 14: Systems design, bibliog org. 15: Sch of Info Sci Ga Inst of Tech, Atlanta Ga 30332.

SLANKER, BARBARA OLSEN. b Springville Utah 15 Jl 34. 4: Raymond Larry Slanker. 5: Colo State U 52-56 (Eng) BA; UNM 57-59 (Eng); UIll 57-59 (LS) MS. 6: Fr, Ger. 7: Grad asst catlg dept UIll(Urbana) 58-59; Music catlgr ref dept NY Pub Lb 59-60; Lib Gen asst pub serv dept 60-62, Asst ndergrad oibn Asst undergrad libn assoc Lib Res Center 65-. 9: ALA; IllLA. 10: Beta Phi Mu; AAUP; UIll Lib Staff Assn; UIll Lib Sch Assn. 12: Co-comp "Early Geology in the Mississippi Valley, An Exhibition of Selected Work (62); "Library Resources in the North Country Area of New York State with Guy G Garrison (66); Ed "Reminiscences; Seventy-Five Years of a Library School (69). 14: Admin. 15: Lib Res Center Univ of Ill, Urbana Ill 61803.

SLATE, THEODORE. b NYC 12 Je 36. 4: Sharon Mae Pearlman. 5: Rutgers 53-57 (Hist) BA; UMich 57-60 (Hist) MA, (LS) MA. 6: Ger, Sp. 7: Filer & ref asst UMich Gen Lib 57-58, Lib serv scholar 58-59, lib serv fellow 59-60; Spec recr LC 60-61; US Army, Ft Knox Ky 61; Info system research asst LC 61-62, Bibliog Legis Ref Serv 62; Asst libn NY Times

Washington Bur, Wash DC 62-63, Libn 63-64; Asst head Arms Control & Disarmament Bibliog Sect LC 64-66; Libn Newsweek Magazine, NYC 66-. 9: SLA (NY Chap; memb chm Newspaper & News Group 66-67, chm 67-68, 1st v-pres & pres elect 68; chm Finance Com 67-68; Hdqrs Operations Com 67-68; Agenda Com Adv Coun 68); ALA. 10: Bnai Brith; Beta Phi Mu; NMA; Sierra Club. 13: Yes. 14: Ref, admin, research. 15: Newsweek Magazine, 444 Madison ave, New York NY 10022.

SLATER, JACK. b NYC 14 N 26. 4: Elizabeth Edenhoffer Slater. 5: City Col (NY) 47-50 (Econ) BSS; Wayne State U 58-59 (Educ) Tchg Certif; UMich 59-62 MLS. 7: Libn Pearson Jr High Sch, N Redford Sch Dist, Detroit 59-62; Catlgr Elizabethown Col Lib 62-64; Acquis libn Drexel Inst of Tech Lib 64-66, Asst dir of libs 66-. 9: ALA. 14: Tech serv. , admin. 15: 8 Edison lane, Willingboro NJ 08046.

SLATER, JAMES R. b Huron SD 29 My 37. 4: Nancy Nadolski. 5: Northwestern 55-60 (Hist) BA; Rutgers 61-62 MLS. 7: Stud asst Kan City (Mo) Pub Lib 61; Trainee Newark Bus Lib, Newark NJ 62; Gen asst Queens Borough Pub Lib, Jamaica NY 62-53; Head mgt Analysis 63-65; Sch liaison consul 65-66; Dir Babylon Pub Lib, Babylon NY 67-. 9: ALA; NYLA; SCLA. 14: Admin. 15: 59 Park ave apt B, Babylon NY 11702.

SLATER, JOHN G T. b London England 17 Ja 35. 5: UPenn 53-59 (Pol Sci) AB; NYU 61-63 (Finance); Wharton Sch of Finance & Com 63 (Finance); Columbia 66-67 MLS. 7: US Army, ft Knox Ky 58; Trust admin Bankers Trust Co 60-63; Free Lib of Phila 64-66; Dir info ctr White Weld & Co, NYC 67-. 9: ASIS; SLA. 10: NY C of C. 15: White Weld & Co 20 Broad st, New York NY 10005.

SLATER, LOLA (CHILDERS). b Kirksville Mo 28 Je 29. 4: Paul S Slater. 5: Hannibal laGrange Jr Col 47-49 (Liberal Arts) AA; NE Mo State Col 49-51 (Eng) BS in Ed; UIll summers 63-66 MS in LS. 6: Sp. 7: Libn Berkeley Jr High Sch, Berkeley Mo 61-. 9: NEA; ALA; MoLA; MoStateTA. 14: Ref, serv to child & yp. 15: 4222 Cameo dr, Bidgeton Mo 63042.

SLATIN, ANDREA LYNNE. b NYC 17 My 42. 5: CUNY (Hunter Col) 60-65 (Anthrop) AB; Pratt Inst 65-66 MLS; Columbia 68- (LS). 6: Fr, Sp. 7: Hd catlgr NY Inst of Tech, Old Westbury NY 66-. 9: ALA. 10: AAUP. 14: Catlg. 15: 83-30 98 st, Woodhaven NY 11421.

SLATIN, MYLES. b Brooklyn NY 3 Mr 24. 4: Diane Bluestein. 5: Queen's Col (NY) 47 (Eng) BA; Yale 49 (Eng) MA, 57 (Eng) PhD. 6: Fr, Ital. 7: SUNY (Buffalo): Instr in Eng 52-58, Asst Prof of Eng, asst dean & dir tutorial instr Col of Arts & Sci 58-61, Assoc Prof of Eng 62, Assoc dean Col of Arts & Sci, Prof of Eng 65, Act dean Col of arts & Sci, Dir univ libs & coord info & lib resources; Visiting post doctoral research fellow YaleU 64-65. 8: Mem, Adv Bd NY State Dept of Educ Col Proficiency Examin Prog; Mem Adv Bd for the coop arr between Philander Smith Col, Baldwin-Wallace col & SUNY (Buffalo); Tutor, St Augustine commun educ prog. 9: ALA; NYLA. 10: AAUP; University Club; Buffalo & Erie Co Hist Soc. 13: Yes. 15: Lockwood Memorial Lib, State Univ of NY at Buffalo, Buffalo NY 14214.

SLATTERY, WILLIAM JOSEPH. b Wash DC 25 Ag 33. 4: Marie Clare Dillon. 5: GeorgetownU 54-56 (Eng) AB; CatholicU 63-67 MSLS. 7: Personnel recs reviewer US Civil Serv Commsn, Wash DC 59-61, Refund & deposit examiner 62-63; Cook USAF, Andrews AFB Wash DC 61-62; Admeasurement reviewer Bur of Customs 63-65; Info analyst CFSTI Nat Bur of Standards, springfield Va 65-66, Chief info sect, Wash DC 66-. 9: SLA. 14: Engrg standards (ref). 15: 1723 Dublin dr, Silver Spring Md 20902.

SLAUGHTER, SARA (BARCUS). b Texas 12 D 17. 5: Tex Women's U 38 (LS) BA; AmericanU 65-67 (Tech of Mgt). 7: Chief bkmob serv Harris Co Pub Lib, Houston Tex 38-40; Libn ext div NYC Pub Lib 41-42; Chief inspection & train div Lib Depot Hqs 6th Army, San Francisco 45-48; Dir ext Ft Worth Pub Lib 48; UN docs expediter LC 57-60; Med libn DC Gen Hosp Wash DC 66-. 9: MedLA; SLA. 10: AAUW. 15: 610 A st NE, Washington DC 20002.

SLAUGHTER, VERA. b San Francisco Cal. 5: UCal (Berkeley) 24 (Econ, Pol Sci) AB; 25 (Secondary Educ) Gen Certif, 29 (Pol Sci, Econ) MA; USoCal 31 (LS) Certif. 6: Fr, Sp, Italian. 7: Sci & ind ref Los Angeles Pub Lib 31; Honig-Cooper Advertising Agcy, San Francisco 32; Standard Oil Co of Cal Geol Lib, San Francisco 33-40; Galileo High Sch San Francisco Bd of Educ 40-41; Fine arts, br admin Greene Reg Br Oakland Pub Lib, Oakland Cal 50-. 9: ALA; -ACRL (Subj Spec Sect); SLA (chm Awards Com Geog Div 55; San Francisco Chap 63); MusLA; CalLA; Ref Libn Coun Bay Area (chm Docs Com 54). 10: Oakland Museums Assn; Women's City Club of San Francisco; Oakland YWCA; AAUW; Col Women's Club of Berkeley. 14: Ref, rare bks, slides of art subject, picture sources. 15: PO Box 595, Oakland Ca 94604.

SLAUGHTER, WILLIAM JAMES. b Dallas Tex 3 Je 32. 4: Joan Mings Slaughter. 5: SouthwesternU (Georgetown Tex) 49-53 (Bus Admin) BBA. 7: Pilot (Lt jg) USN NAS, Oceana Va 53-57; Bus mgr Dallas Pub Lib, Dallas Tex 58-68, Assoc dir mgt serv 68-. 9: ALA; TexLA; SWLA (chm Perm Exh Com 68). 14: Admin, tech serv, circ. 15: 6177 Brandeis lane, Dallas Tx 75214.

SLEASMAN, KATHLEEN (STREVELL) (SHEPARD). b Albany NY 18 D 15. 4: Francis Sleasman. 5: NY State Col for Tchrs 33-37 (Eng) AB, 37-38 BS in LS. 7: Libn North Jr High Sch, Newburgh NY 38-40; Catlgr Albany Pub Lib, Albany NY 41-42; Ref asst Schenectady Pub Lib, Schenectady NY 46-47, Catlgr 47-48; Hd circ Schenectady Co Pub Lib, Schenectady NY 48-54; Libn Colonie Central High Sch, Albany NY 54-62; Lib asst SUNY (Albany) 62-64; Catlgr & asst in ref circ Miami-Dade Jr Col (N Campus) 64-65, Hd catlgr central tech processing 65-66, Ref asst (S Campus) 66-68, Dir acquis (S Campus) 68-. 9: FlaLA. 15: 11025 SW 80 ave, Miami Fl 33156.

SLETWICK, CLARENCE R. b Bemidji Minn 12 J132. 5: Bemidji State Col 50-51, 53-55 (Soc Studies) BS; Union Col (Lincoln Neb)51-52, 55-56; Peabody summers 66, 67 MLS. 7: Asst libn Bemidji High Sch, Bemidji Minn 52-53; US Army Med Corp (Sp4) 56-58; Res & period libn Bemidji State Col 58-59; Sch libn Clearbrook Pub Sch, Clearbrook Miss 59-65; Asst libn, Act libn Pacific Union Col 65-67, Hd libn 67-. 9: NEA; MinnEA; ALA; CalLA. 14: Sch libs, admin. 15: Box 183, Angwin Cal 94508.

SLETWICK, MARION ELVINA. b Bemidji Minn 10 Mr 22. 5: Bemidji State Col 40-44 (Eng) BS; UMinn 58-59 (LS) MA. 7: Tchr-libn Bird Island (Minn) pub sch 44-45; Libn Bemidji State Col 45-65; Acquis libn Pacific Union Col 65-. 9: MinnEA; CalLA; ALA. 14: Period, acquis. 15: P O Box 183, Angwin Cal 94508.

SLEVIN, ANN DAY. b Ft Lauderdale Fla 6 Ag 45. 5: Amer Col in Paris 65-66; Ohio wesleyanU 63-65, 66-67 (Pol, Govt) BA; UMich 67-68 MALS. 6: Fr. 7: Stud asst Ohio wesleyanU 66-67; Asst ref libn & Curator, Amer Negro Collection PrincetonU 68-. 9: ALA. 10: Friends of PrincetonU Lib; UMich Lib Sci Alumni Assn. 14: Ref, soc sci, Black hist. 15: 19 University pl, Princeton NJ 08540.

SLICK, MYRNA (HAYS). b Greensburg Penn 13 Ja 32. 4: Richard D Slick. 5: Hood Col 49-53 (Mus, Sociol) AB; UPittsburgh 67-69 MLS. 7: Teenage dir YWCA, Johnstown Penn 53-56; Secondary libn Conemaugh Twp Schs, Davidsville Penn 67-. 9: ALA; NEA; PennASchL; PennStateEA. 14: Secon sch libs. 15: RD 2 Box 116, Holsopple Pa 15935.

SLIEPCEVICH, NATALIE. b Anaconda Mont 10 N 15. 5: UMont summer 61 (Educ), summer 64 (Educ, Graphic Arts). 6: Serbian. 7: US Post Off, Anaconda Mont 35; Asst libn Hearst Free Lib, Anaconda Mont 37-57, Libn 57-. 9: ALA; Pacific NW Bibliog Center (Nomin Com); PNLA (ch-elect 64-66; mem 3 coms); Pub Lbs Div (com mem); MontLA (Life mem, pres 64, Conf Chm 65; mem 6 coms). 10: Phoebe Apperson Hearst Mem Assn; Mo Hist Soc; naconda C of C; Hotel Marcus Daly Corp; Deer Lodge Valley Assn for Retarded Child; World Mus of Mining; Lib Assn, UIda; Anaconda Country Club; Anaconda Ski Club; Mont Fed of Garden Clubs. 13: Yes. 14: Catlg, ref, chld serv. 15: Brentwood Apts 2, Anaconda Mont 59711.

SLIVKA, ENID (MILLER). b Buffalo NY 24 My 27. 4: Meyer Slivka. 5: UColo 44-48 (Fr) AB; UDenver 49-50 MALS; UVienna 51-52; UWash 57-58. 6: Fr, Ger. 7: Ref libn I Denver Pub Lib 49-50; Army libn US Army Spec Serv, Austria 50-53; Asst Humanities Div UNeb Libs 53-56; 1st asst br Seattle Pub Lib 56-57, Br libn 58-67; Spec libn self-employed 68-. 9: PNLA; WashLA; ALA; SLA. 10: PTA. 13: Yes. 14: Bk sel, ref, catlg, admin. 15: 2343 33nd ave So, Seattle Wa 98144.

SLOAN, ANDREW JAMES JR. b Preston Co WVa 18 J123. 4: Roberta Murphy. 5: Miami U (Oxford Ohio) 42-43, 46-48 (Eng) AB; West Res 49-50 MS in LS. 7: Page Cincinnati Pub Lib 39-41; Gear grinder Wright Aeronautical Corp, Cincinnati

41-42; (Pfc) Med Aid Man US Army, European Theatre 43-45; Reporter "Hamilton Journal News, Hamilton Ohio 48-49; Ref libn Mich State Lib 50-55; Head Libn Portland-Jay Co Pub Lib, Portland Ind 55-56; Head Libn Warsaw Commun Pub Lib, Warsaw Ind 56-. 9: ALA; IndLA. 10: Rotary; PTA; Amer Legion, Kosciusko Co Hist Assn. 13: Yes. 14: Admin. 15: 429 W Center st, Warsaw Ind 46580.

SLOAN, ELISABETH M(ONTGOMERY). b Graham NC 9 Ja 08. 5: Duke U 25-29 (Fr) AB, 29-30 (Eng); UNC 36-38 AB in LS; UCal(Berkeley) 40-41 (LS); San Francisco State Col 58 (Educ). 6: Fr. 7: Period libn Duke U Lib 28-30; Ref libn Womans Col Lib 30-40; Period dept asst UCal Lib (Berkeley) 40-41; Sub libn San Francisco Unified Sch Dist 55-65; Child libn Merced Br San Francisco Pub Lib 63-. 9: ALA. 10: AAUW; LWV; San Francisco Pub Lib Staff Assn. 14: Ref, child serv. 15: 726 - 31st ave, San Francisco Ca 94121.

SLOAN, ELIZABETH ANN. b Clarksburg WVa 10 J104. 5: Wilson Col 23-27 (Eng Lit) AB; Columbia 27-28 BLS, 40-41, 45 MLS. 7: Asst Vassar Col Lib 28-30; Queens Borough Pub Lib, Jamaica NY; Br asst, Br ref asst, Catlgr, Art & Music Div Asst, Documents & period asst, Gen ref div asst bus sci & tech div 30-46; Placement Personnel Psychiat Nurses Bur, NYC 46-48; Gen ref div head & bus sci & tech div head Queens Borough Pub Lib, Jamaica NY 48-59; Libn Salem Col Lib, Clarksburg WVa 64-68, Consul 68-; Clarksburg Pub Lib, Clarksburg WVa 68-. 9: ALA; WVaLA. 10: WVa Hist Soc; Harrison Co (WVa) Hist So. 14: Ref, lib org, admin. 15: 359 Lee ave, Clarksburg WVa 26301.

SLOAN, GEORGE WILLIAM. b Nashville 27 N 42. 4: Judith Ann Almilie. 5: City Col (San Francisco) 60-62 (Hist) AA; UCal(Berkeley) 62-64 (Hist) AB, 64-65 (Educ), 65 MLS; UMd 66-68 (Hist) MA. 6: Fr, Ger. 7: Libn trainee LC 65-66, Ref libn 66-67, Sr ref libn & Alternate recommending off in hist 67-68; Instr Dept Hist UMd (College Park) 68-69, Instr Sch Lib & Info Serv 68-. 9: ALA; AALS. 10: So Hist Assn; Beta Phi Mu; Phi Alpha Theta. 11: LC's Internship Award for Lib Sch Grads 65. 12: Editor of cumulative index to ALAs "Newsletter on Intellectual Freedom (52-65). 13: Yes. 14: Amer lib hist, clsf & info retrieval in archives. 15: 447 Old Line ave, Laurel Md 20810.

SLOAN, GWENDOLYN GARRETT. b Truro Nova Scotia Can 27 Je 29. 4: William Sloan. 5: Mt AllisonU 47-50 (Hist) BA; Columbia 53-54 BLS. 7: Catlgr NYC Pub Lib circulation Dept 54-58, Sr catlg Municipal Ref Lib 58-62; Sr catlgr McKinsey & Co Inc, NYC 62-65, Coord research materials 65-67, Mgr lib serv 67-. 9: ALA; SLA; ASIS. 14: Computerized info systems, catlg, mgt lit. 15: 235 W 76th st, New York NY 10023.

SLOAN, JAMES W. b Memphis Tenn 28 My 09. 4: Leona Grier. 5: LeMoyne Col 28-32 (Chem) BS; Hampton Inst 32-33 (LS) BS; Atlanta summer 45. 6: Fr. 7: Asst libn LeMoyne Col 33-34; Libn: Albany State Col (Ga) 34-54, Lane Col 54-59, Los Angeles Pub Lib 59-. 9: ALA. 10: Omega Psi Phi. 14: Catlg. 15: 4108 Hillcrest dr apt B, Los Angeles Ca 90008.

SLOAN, JUDITH ANN (ALMLIE). b San Francisco Calif 31 My 42. 4: George William Sloan. 5: City Col of San Francisco 60-62 AA; UCal (Berkeley) 62-63, 64-65 (Soc Welfare) AB; UMd summer 66, 67-68 MLS. 6: Sp. 7: Readers' adv DC Pub Lib 65-67, Ref libn 68-; Research asst UMd (College Park) 68; Researcher American Inst for Research, Silver Spring Md 68. 14: Lib admin, ref. 15: 447 Old Line ave, Laurel Md 20810.

SLOAN, RUTH CHANTLER. b Attleboro Mass 28 Mr 24. 4: Walter F Sloan. 5: Flora Stone Mather Col Case West Res 42-46 (Bio, Psych) AB; Rutgers 68 MLS. 7: Libn School of the Holy Child, Suffern NY 68-. 9: ALA; Amer Guild of Organists; Nat Trust Hist Preserv; Bergen Co Hist Soc; Paramus Hist Soc. 10: Friends of the Osborne and Lillian Smith Collections, Toronto; Bronte Soc, Haworth (Eng); Salvation Army. 14: Rare bks (child bks & loc hist), & ya serv. 15: 328 Graydon ter, Ridgewood NJ 07450.

SLOAN, WILLIAM JAMES. b Regina Can 11 N 27. 4: Gwendolyn Garrett. 5: Columbia 54 MS in LS. 7: Picture collection NYC Pub Lib 54-58, Film lib 58-. 8: Lectr: Pratt Inst Grad Lib Sch, NYU Grad Cinema Prog. 9: ALA (chm Motion Pic Prev Subcom); Film Lib Info Coun (Bd Chm). 10: Soc of Cinematologists. 12: Ed "Film Library Quarterly". 13: Yes. 14: Film. 15: Film Lib NY Pub Lib 20 W 53rd st, New York NY 10019.

SLOANE, MARGARET (NEWBERRY). b Dallas 5 Ja 14. 5: Southeastern State Col 31-34 (Psych) BS; UOkla 34-35 (Fine Arts, Drama) BFA, 56-57 (LS) MA. 6: Fr, Ger. 7: Post Libn Ft Ord, Monterey Cal 57-59; Manager tech info center TRW Systems, Redondo Beach Cal 59-67; Info serv mgr The Ford Foundation, NYC 67-. 8: Guest lecturer in lib sci: Immaculate Heart Col 64 & 65, UCLA 64 & 65, John Cotton Dana lectr 68-. 9: SLA (chm Sci-Tech Awards Com 64-66; chm Educ Com 67-70; sec Aerospace Div So Cal Chap Sci-Tech chm 61-62, Bulletin ed 62-63, Pub Rel Dir 63-64; ASIS; CalLA; ALA; ARMA; NMA; AMA; AREA. 10: Gamma Theta Upsilon. 13: Yes. 14: Mgt of tech info centers, data storgae & retrieval. 15: 225 E 36th st apt 21G, New York NY 10016.

SLOCUM, BETTY (FRAYSURE). b Springfield Ky 5 Ja 24. 4: Joseph T Slocum. 5: UKy 41-45 (LS) AB, 61 MSLS. 7: High sch libn Anchorage Ind Schs, Anchorage Ky 45-50; Elem libn Jefferson Co schs, Louisville Ky 51-56; Supv instr materials Manatee Co schs, Bradenton Fla 57-. 10: Delta Kappa Gamma. 14: Ref. 15: P O Box 465,Bradenton Fla 33506.

SLOCUM, GRACE (PAYSON). b Wilmington NC 7 J122. 5: Womans Col UNC 9-43 (Eng) AB; Columbia 46-47 (LS) BS. 7: Eng tchr Chestnut St Sch, Wilmington NC 43-46; Ya libn Enoch Pratt Free Lib, Baltimore 47-53; SUPT WK WITH YA Brooklyn Pub Lib 53-59; Personnel off Free Lib of Phila 59-64; Asst Enoch Pratt EnochPratt Free Lib, Baltimore 64-. 9: ALA; MdLA (pres 67-68); Adult Educ Assn Md. 13: Yes. 15: Enoch Pratt Free Lib, 400 Cathedral st, Baltimore Md 21201.

SLOCUM, MARCELLA (PARKER). b Rio Wis 9 F 20. 4: Carl M slocum. 5: UWis 44-49 (Eng) BS, 59 (LS) MA. 6: Sp. 7: Libn: Dodgeville High Sch, Dodgeville Wis 49-51, High Sch, Wisconsin Dells Wis 51-58, 67-, Dist Elem Sch, Wisconsin Dells Wis 60-67. 9: NEA; WisEA; SWEA. 10: Wis Lib Sch Alumni Assn. 14: Sch lib. 15: 300 Bowman rd, Wisconsin Dells Wi 53965.

SLOCUM, PATRICIA ANN (JONES). b Springfield Ill 7 Jl 30. 4: Paul Slocum. 5: Ill StateU 48-52 (Elem Educ) BS in ED; Springfield Jr Col summer 49; West MichU 66-67 MSLS. 6: Sp. 7: Kindergarten tchr pub shc, Bloomington Ill 52-54; Ref libn dept hd UNotre Dame (Ind) 68-. 10: AAUW. 14: Ref, catlg, admin, lib educ. 15: 112 S 4th, Niles Mi 49120.

SLOCUM, ROBERT BIGNEY. b brockton Mass 6 Ap 22. 4: Christine Stanfield. 5: Boston U 40-42, 45-46 (Hist) BA; Columbia 46-47 (Hist) MA; Simmons 48-49 (LS) BS. 6: Ger, Fr, Sp, Ital, Russian, Portu, Lat, Dutch Scandinavian, Slavic. 7: Lib asst Harvard 47-48; Lib interne LC 49-50; US Army (Pfc) 42-45; Asst to dir Simmons Col Lib 50-51; Catlgr-Instr UIll Lib(Urbana) 51-54; Assoc catlg libn Cornell U Libs 54-. 9: ALA; AHA. 10: AAUP. 12: "Sample Catalog Cards" (62); Ed "Manual of Procedures, Catalog Dept" (59); "A Bibliography of Biographical & Bio-Bibliographical Dictionaries & Related Materials"; "Sample Cataloging Forms" (68). 13: YES. 14: Catlg, biblig, clsf. 15: 92 W Main st, Dryden NY 13053.

SLON, EUGENE. b Kharkiv Ukraine 18 Mr 14. 4: Claudia Lukash. 5: Kharkiv State U (Biochem) Diploma; UOttawa 63-64 BLS. 6: Ukrainian, Russian, Ger, Polish, Serbian. 7: High sch tchr Bd of Educ, Kharkiv Ukraine: Lab Sci Research Inst, Kharkiv Ukraine; High sch tchr Dept of Educ of Ukrainian Immigrants in 45-49 (Non-Prof Wker several priv cos, Can 49-60; Can49-60; High sch tchr Dept of Educ, Can 61-63; Periods libn UOttawa 64-65; Catlgr of sci math & tech Cornell U 65-. 9: CanLA. 10: Cornell U LA. 12: "On Ruins of the Past, a novel in Ukrainian (57). 14: Catlg, subj bibliog. 15: 111 Catherine st, Ithaca NY 14850.

SLONAKER, ETHEL MAE (HOUTZ). b Andreas Penn 2 D 16. 4: Paul J Slonaker. 5: Lebanon Valley Col 34-38 (Eng) BA; United Theol Sem (Dayton Ohio) 42; West Md Col 58-59 (LS); UNC summers 60-67 (LS) MS in LS. 6: Fr. 7: Tchr of Eng & Fr High Sch, Berkeley Springs WVa 59-60; Libn Shenandoah Col & Conservatory, Winchester Va 60-69; Asst hd ref & circ sect Va State Lib 69-. 9: ALA; SELA; VaLA. 10: Womens Soc of World Serv; Phi Alpha Epsilon; AAUW; Beta Phi Mu. 14: Ref. 15: Va State Lib, 12th & Capitol sts, Richmond Va 23219.

SLOTE, STANLEY JAMES. b NYC 17 Je 17. 4: Margaret Larson. 5: Cornell U 35-39 (Eng) BA; Rutgers 63-65 MLS, 69. 6: Sp, Ger, Fr. 7: (Lt sg) US Navy Radar & Sonar Off 42-46; Chief Exec Off Crossway Construction Co Inc 50-63; Lib consul, White Plains NY 63-; Visiting lecturer Sch of Lib Sci Syracuse 68-69. 8: Cnsul to newspapers & var firms in lib org & filing; Trustee, White Plains Pub Lib, 62-63. 9: ALA; SLA; ASIS. 12: "An Approach to Weeding Criteria for Newspaper Libraries". 13: Yes. 14: Reorg of newspaper ref libs, subj headings. 15: 10 Sammis lane, Qhite Plains Ny 10605.

SLOTKIN, HELEN WILLA (SAMUELS). b NYC 22 Ap 43. 4: Edgar Morris Slotkin. 5: Queens Col (NY) 60-64 (Mus) BA; Simmons 64-65 MLS. 6: Fr. 7: Mus libn Pub Lib of Brookline, Brookline Mass 65-67; Music libn Morse Mus Lib Hilles Lib Radcliffe Col 67-. 9: MusLA (sec-treas NE Chap 68-). 14: Ref. 15: 140 Magazine st, Cambridge Ma 02139.

SMAARDYK, ELLEN LOUISE (CARLSON). b Ft Wayne Ind 8 My 20. 4: Abraham Smaardyk. 5: Hanover Col 38-42 (Eng, Soc Sci) AB; UNoIll 61-63; Rosary Col MA in LS. LS. 7: Libn Ogden ave & Goodman ave schs, La Grange Ill 64-. 8: Lib tech asst adv com Col of DuPage 68-; Chm Lyons Twp Multi Media Coop, LaGrange Ill 67. 9: NEA; IllEA; IllASchL; NAVI; ASCD; Ill A-V Assn. 14: Sch lib. 15: 257 Middaugh rd, Clarendon Hills Il 60514.

SMALL, CAROLYN A(RLENE). b Limington Me 17 D 23. 5: UMe 41-45 (Eng) BA; Simmons 45-46 BS in LS; UMich 50-51 AMLS. 6: Fr, Sp. 7: Catlgr UWash 46-50; Catlg libn Midwest Inter-Lib Center, Chicago 51-56; Lib asst Lib Assn, London 57; Catlg libn Midwest Inter-Lib Center, Chicago 58-61, Asst dir 61-64; Asst head descr catlg div Yale U 64-66, Hd descr catlg div 66-. 9: ALA (Descr Catlg Com 67-68);-RTSD (Nominating Com 69); NY Reg Group Tech Serv Libns. 14: Catlg, interlib coop. 15: 111 Park st, New Haven Ct 06511.

SMALL, FRANCIS ALOYSIUS. b Milford Mass 25 F 16. 5: Boston Col 36-40 (Philos) AB, 40-41 (Philos) MA, 41-43 (Hist) MA; Weston Col 43-47 (Theol) STL; Columbia 53-56 (LS) MS. 6: Fr, Lat. 7: Hist tchr Cheverus Classical High Sch, Portland Me 42-43; Instr Fairfield U 48-51, Asst Prof 51-53, Assoc Prof 53-63, Chm Dept of Hist & Govt 51-63, Libn 52-. 9: ALA; CathLA; NELA; ConnLA. 10: Torch Club; Beta Phi Mu. 13: Yes. 14: Admin, ref. 15: Fairfield Univ, Farifield Conn 06433.

SMALL, LILLIAN EUDORA. b Armour SD 12 F 02. 5: York Col (Neb) 25-26 Tchrs Certif; Wayne State Col (Neb) 29-30 AB; UDenver 56-57 MA in LS. 6: Sp. 7 Antelope Co rural schs, Oakdale & Tilden Neb 0-25; Bunker Hill High Sch, Tilden Neb 26-27; Miller High Sch, Miller Neb 27-29; Allen High Sch, Allen Neb 30-33; Miller High Sch, Miller Neb 33-36; Head of Normal Train Dept, Wilbur Neb 36-43; Prin High Sch, Nehawka Neb 43-56; High sch lib, Ft Collins Colo 57-59; High sch libn, Bridgeport Neb 59-, Sp instr. 9: NEA; Morrill Co (Neb) Tchrs Assn (sec 60-61). 10: Nat Toastmistress; Bridgeport TA. 15: P O Box 712, Bridgeport Neb 69336.

SMALL, SALLY (ANN) S(PANGENBURG). b Clarks Summit Penn 12 Mr 29. 4: Lewis W Small. 5: Dickinson 47-51 (Bio) BS; Drexel 53-56 MSLS. 7: Lab asst Dept Army Research & Development Phila 51-53; Instr electrical engring ICS, Scranton Pa summer 53; Research libn Merck, Sharp & Dohme Inc, W Point Penn 53-56, Indexing, abstracting & coding chem structures pharmacology div 58-67; Libn Penn stateU (Wyomissing) 67-. 9: PennLA; Spec Libs Berks Co. 10: PTA; AAUW; Repub Com Women. 14: Inter-lib coop. 15: 5 East Court blvd, West Lawn Pa 19609.

SMALL, WENDELL GREENLEAF JR. b Biddeford Me 19 Je 35. 4: Lisa Yong Cha Huh. 5: Bates Col 54-58 (Hist) BA; URI 66-67 MLS. 6: Sp. 7: Intelligence analyst & linguist US Army 59-63; Tchr Oxford Hills High Sch, S Paris Me 63-65; Libn State Mutual Life Assurance Co, Worcester Mass 65-. 9: ALA; SLA. 10: Lay minister, NE Conf United Meth Church. 14: Admin, ref. 15: 153 N Quinsigamond ave, Shrewsbury Ma 01545.

SMALLEY, ELEANOR. b Boston Mass 5 D 43. 4: Neal Smalley. 5: Pomona Col 62-66 (Philos) BA; UCLA 66-67 MLS. 6: Ger, Fr. 7: Hd libn Greenville Pub Lib, Greenville Penn 67-. 9: ALA; PennLA. 15: 33 Eagle st, Greenville Pa 16125.

SMALLWOOD, WILMA M (FRITZ). b St Clair Mich 19 O 18. 4: James G Smallwood. 5: Mich State U 36-40 (Home Econ) BS; UDenver summers 63-65 (LS) MA. 7: Interior decorator Lasalle & Kochs, Toledo Ohio 40-42; Operations agent Trans-World Airlines, Detroit 42-45; Staff asst Amer Red Cross, Far East Theater 46-47; Interior decorator Mehagians, Phoenix 48-50; Lib clerk Dept of Lib & Archives, Phoenix 61-65, Libn 65-.10: PEO. 14: Ref. 15: 335 W Willetta, Phoenix Az 85003.

SMART, CAROL (HACKETT). b N Bend Ore 20 O 27. 4: Donald C Smart. 5: UCal (Berkeley) 44-46, 49-51 (Central European Reg Studies) BA, 58-59 MLS, 68 Elem Standard Tchg Credential. 6: Ger. 7: Child & yp libn Monterey Pub Lib, Monterey Cal, Ref libn 62; Dist elem libn Pacific Grove Unified Sch Dist, Pacific Grove Cal 62-68; Libn Highland Sch, Highland Col 68-. 9: CalASchL; CalLA; ALA; NEA-DAVI. 10: LWV. 15: 1059 Cadiz ct, Seaside Cal 93955.

SMART, MARGARET. b Mauston Wis 20 F 20. 5: Col of St Benedict 37-41 (Soc Wk) BA; UDenver summers 43-45 BSLS. 7: Asst Mason City Pub Lib, Mason City Iowa 43-46; Ref & documents asst UIda Lib 46-48; Head of circ & city bkmob Mason City Pub Lib, Mason City Iowa 48-51; 1st Lt Ed asst USAF WAF Air Command Staff Sch, Maxwell AFB 52-53, Bibliogr asst Air U Lib, Maxwell AFB 53-54, Libn Air Materiel Force Pacific Area, Japan Command 54, (Capt) Air Material Force Pacific Area, Japan Adj 54-56; Ref libn UDayton 56-58; Ref libn Air Force Inst of Tech, Wright-Patterson AFB Ohio 58-60; Ref asst Dayton & Montgomery Co Pub Lib, Dayton Ohio 60-61, Head Ind & Sci Div 62-63; Documents libn Colo Sch of Mines 64-. 8: "Library Journal List Com, 62-69, Chm 66-69. 9: ALA; ColoLA (exec sec 67-); MPLA. 13: Yes. 14: Ref. 15: 4140 W 80th pl, Westminster Colo 80030.

SMARTT, HINKLEY (CHARLES). b McMinnville Tenn 11 Ag 06. 4: Vista Perryman. 5: Bethel Col 24-29 (Educ) BA; Cumberland Presbyterian Theol Sem 40-44 BD; Vanderbilt U Sch of Religion 44; Peabody 58-59 MA. ; Columbia summer 67. 6: Gk. 7: Tchr & coach Morrison High Sch, Morrison Tenn 2931; Tchr & coach Dibrell High Sch, McMinnville Tenn 31-32; Pastor First Cumberland PRESBYT Church, Detroit 32-35; Pastor Overton Cumberland Presbyt Church, Overton Tex 35-37; Pastor Cumberland Presbyt Church, Greenville Ky 37-40; Coach & tchr Bethel Col (Tenn) 40-44; Pastor Mt Pleasant Cumberland Presbyt Church, Utica Ky 44-48; Pastor Fariview Cmberland Presbyt Church, Marshall Tex 48-53; Pastor Bowling Green Cumberland Presbyt Church 53-57; Libn Memphis Theol Sem 58-. 9: ATheolLA; ALA. 10: Memphis Lib Com; Kiwanis Club; Rotary Club; Beta Phi Mu. 14: Catlg, ref. 15: 221 N Auburndale, Memphis Tn 38112.

SMEAL, RUTH (DUGAN). b Milton Penn 16 Ag 17. 4: Albert W Smeal. 5: Bloomsburg State Col 35-39 (Biol Sci, Geo Geio, Hist) BS in Ed; Penn State U summer 42 (Soc STUDIES); Marywood Col 57-60 MSLS; Temple U 66-67 (Distributive Educ). 7: Tchr High Sch, Shickshinny Penn 41-44; Libn High Sch, Millville Penn 56-64; Circ libn State Col (Bloomsburg Penn) 64-. 9: ALA; Penn State EA; PennLA; Assn Penn State Col & Univ Facs. 10: Kappa Delta Pi; Gamma Theta Upsilon; Bloomsburg State Col Faculty Assn. 15: 740 Market, Bloomsburg Penn 17815.

SMEAL, SAMUEL THEODORE. b Sykesville Penn 20 F 11. 4: Gertrude Anna Eckert. 5: Penn state Evening Courses (Engring); Penn State Lib library courses. 7: Test eng Stackpole Carbon Co, St Marys Penn 34-50, Electrical eng 50-69; Libn & admin, St Marys Penn 59-. 9: Amer Soc Tool & Manufact Engnrs (chm local chap 57-60); Inst Electric & Electron Engnrs; ALA; PennLA (Lib Devel Com 60-62). 10: Boy Scouts of Amer. 14: Ref, admin. 15: 484 Spruce, St Marys Pa 15857.

SMEDLUND, RUTH ANN. b Rhinelander Wis 6 S 29. 5: UWis (Milwaukee) 47-50 (Math) BS; UWis (Madison) 61-62 MS in LS. 6: Ger. 7: Tchr high sch, Menominee Mich 51-53; Asst ed Inst of Paper Chem, Appleton Wis 53-62; Catlg & ref Gustarus Adolphus Col 63-66; Research libn Intl Minerals & Chem Corp, Libertyville Ill 66-. 9: SLA; IllLA. 14: Ref in science areas, computer applications. 15: 425 Mill rd, Wildwood Il 60030.

SMEJA, GALINA (ROUK). b Simpheropol Russia 31 Ag 20. 4: Mieczyslaw Smeja. 5: Sir George Williams Col 48-51 BA; McGill 51-52 BLS. 6: Eng, Estonian, Ger, Russian. 7: Libn Can Marconi Co, Montreal 52-56; Asst libn Aluminium Secretariat Ltd, Montreal 56-60; Libn Malcolm Campbell High Sch, Montreal 60-64; Libn Riverdale High Sch, PIERREFONDS Que 64-. 9: CanLA; ALA. 15: 4838 Pierre Lauzon, Pierrefonds Que Can.

SMELLAGE, REBA. b Boma Tenn 17 J125. 5: Tenn Tech 45-50 (Eng) (BS) Peabody summer 52-55 MA (LS. ; UMd 60-63 (Ger, Russian, Soviet For Policy). 6: Ger, Fr. 7: High sch Eng tchr, Baxter Tenn 50-53; Jr high sch libn, Pekin Ill 53-55; Army lib serv Field libn, Hanau Germany 55-58, Main libn, Frankfurt 58-60, Area lib supv, Heidelberg 60-63, Area lib supv, Stuttgart 68, Sr staff lib spec, Munich 68-. 8: Attended Data Processing Seminar, Heidelburg Germany 64, Wkshop for Middle Mgrs, Heidelburg Germany 63, Intl Fed Lib Assns, Frankfurt Germany 68. 9: ALA (Armed Forces Libn Subsect). 11: Louis Shores Lib Award, Peabody, 55. 14: Ref, lib admin. 15: Lib Div Spec Sr Agency Europe, APO NY 09184.

SMILEY, GRACE LOIS. b Chicago. 5: Washington U (St Louis) 32 AB; Catholic U 52 MS in LS. 6: Sp, Fr, Ger, Ital, Portu, Dutch, Swedish, Norwegian, Danish, Rumanian. 7: Ed, Writing Pub Rel Wk, Translation various Prof & Civic Orgs, St Louis 32-38; Catlgr Off of the Supt of Documents Govt Printing Off 38-44; LC Catlgr Descr Catlg Div 44-52, Bibliogr US Quarterly Bk Review 52-56, Research analyst, Ref libn, Sci Internat Orgs Sect Gen Ref & Bibliog Div 56-. 9: ALA; Amer Studies Assn; CathLA; DCLA. 10: AAAS; AAUW. 14: Bibliog, internat sci meetings, ref. 15: 141 - 11th st SE, Wash DC 20003.

SMILEY, VIRGINIA E. b Union City Ind 11 N 24. 5: Ind U 44-47 (Span) AB; Peabody summer 49 (LS); Ind U 54 (LS) AM. 6: Sp. 7: Libn: Winchester High Sch, Winchester Ind 47-48, Valparaiso High Sch, Valparaiso Ind 48-50, Dana Jr High Sch, San Diego 50-55, Gen Motors Inst, Flint Mich 58-59, Spec Serv, Germany 55-57, 59-61, Pub Lib of Cincinnati 62-65; Libn Commerce Lib Ohio State U Libs 65-. 9: SLA; OhioLA. 14: Ref. 15: 1445 W Lane, Columbus Ohio.

SMILEY, WENDELL W(AYNE). b Bryson City NC 15 Ke 08. 4: Elva Parkinson. 5: Mars Hill Col 24-26 AA; UNC 27-28 (Educ) AB in Ed, 29-39 (LS, Hist) AB in LS; UIll summers 36-39 MLS. 6: Ger, Sp. 7: Tchr, NC pub schs; Marshall 26-27, Wilson 28-29; Lib staff UNC (Chapel Hill) 29-39; Libn Ga Tchrs Col 39-42; Libn MercerU 42-43; Dir lib E CarU 43-. 8: Instr lib sci UIll summer 42; Operating res US Info Agcy 59-; Licensed driver educ instr 58-; Licensed radio engr 56-. 9: ALA; SELA; NCLA; GaLA (v-pres 40-41; pres 41-43). 10: Rotarian; Pitt Coin Club; AAAS. 12: Ed ""North Carolina Libraries (47-49); ""NC Press Views The KKK (67); ""Union List of Periodicals Held by Member Institutions East Carolina Association of Colleges (67). 13: Yes. 14: Admin. 15: 249 Lochview dr, Greenville NC 27834.

SMILG, LEONA (FOX). b Cincinnati Ohio 11 Jl 21. 4: Benjamin Smilg. 5: UDayton 38-42 (Sociol) BA. 7: Clk Dayton & Montgomery Co Pub Lib, Dayton Ohio 54-55, SPC IV Lincoln Br 55-65, Lib asst IV-19C child libn E C Doren Br 65-. 9: ALA; OhioLA. 14: Child serv. 15: 3876 Dorset dr, Dayton Oh 45405.

SMITH-HUTTON (MING) JANE. b Globe Ariz 19 O 14. 4: Henri Harold Smith-Hutton. 5: Ore State Col 30-31; UPhilippines 32-33; Col of San Diego 35; Sorbonne 57; Ecole du Louvre 58. 6: Fr, Japanese. 7: Tchr, Chefoo China 32-33; Chief intelligence Off of Strategic Serv, Wash DC 42-45; Dir soc serv Amer Cathedral, Paris 60-64; Dir dept for the blind Amer Lib in Paris 65-. 8: Founder-Chm, Internat Aid to French Navy Orphans 59-62; Consul-Prof, Paris "Charm School", Flower Arranging 66-67. 9: ALA. 10: DAR; Wedgwood Soc, London; Ikebana Internat, Tokyo-Paris; Amer Women's Gp, Paris; Jr Guild, Amer Cathedral Paris. 11: Decorated by French Govt with "Merite Maritime" 13: Yes. 14: Admin, serv to handicapped. 15: 4 rue Pierre Cherest, 92 Neuilly France.

SMITH, (CONSTANCE) HOPE. b Southborough Kent England 14 My 23. 4: Sydney Howland Smith. 5: Ventura Jr Col 58-59 (Math); UCLA 59 (Math); San Jose State Col 59-62 (Soc Serv) BA; Syracuse 62-63 MSLS. 6: Fr. 7: Sec & bkkeeper Halpern & Woolf, London England 41-43; Draftswoman Telecommunications Research Establishment, Malvern England 43-46; Verbatim reporter London Sch of Stenotyping, London England 46-47; Sec A J Phillips & Co, Birmingham England 48-49; Sec & bkkeeper Krishnamurti Writings, London England & Ojai Cal 49-59; Ser catlgr UCal (Santa Barbara) 64-67, Hd order dept 68-. 9: Lib Assn (London); ALA; CalLA; Libns Assn, UCal (Santa Barbara); So Cal Tech Proc Gp. 10: Phi Kappa Phi; Beta Phi Mu; Sierra Club; Santa Barbara Braille Assn. 14: Catlg, acquis, automation.

SMITH, ADELINE (LOUISE) MERCER. b Saratoga Springs NY 28 My 15. 4: Jack Monroe Smith. 5: NY State Col for Tchrs 33-37 (LS) BS; SUNY (Albany) 64-68 (LS) MS. 6: Fr. 7: Lingerie designer & supv sampling operations Van Raalte Co, Saratoga Springs NY 39-63; High sch libn Hoosic Valley Cen Sch, Schaghticoke NY 64-. 9: ALA; NYStateTA; East NY Sch Libns; Rensselaer Co Sole Supv Dist TA; Hoosic Valley TA. 10: Beta Phi Mu; AAUW. 14: Sch libnship. 15: RD 1 Lake Lonely rd, Saratoga Springs NY 12866.

SMITH, ALICE MARGARET (GULLEN). b Farmington Mich 5 D 12. 4: Norman V Smith. 5: Wayne State 32 (Eng, Speech) BA, 59 MSLS, 66 (Tchr Educ in Lib A-V Educ(EdD; UMich (Ann Arbor) 48 (Lib) MA. 6: Fr. 7: Instr Wayne State & UMich 33-39; Tchr & libn (jr high) Kern Rd Sch Syst, Detroit 38-40; Libn Detroit Pub Sch 44-59; Instr (asst prof) Lib Sci Dept Wayne State U 59-65; Chm (assoc prof) lib & a-v educ US Fla Col of Educ 65-. 8: Dir, Wayne StateU Creative Arts Wkshop summers 62-66; Consul: Wayne StateU Creative Arts Wkshop 67-69; Polk Co (Fla) Libs 68-69; Honduras Proj for Secon Sch Libs 69-74. 9: ALA; ACEI (chm Ref Com); NCTE (Advent with Bks 64-69); FlaLA (sec col & Res Sect, 68-69); FlaASchL. 10: Pi Lambda Theta; Friends of the Lib of Hillsborough Co (Tampa Fla); Tampa Child Bk Fair. 13: Yes. 14: Ref, rare bks, child collections, lib educ. 15: Lib Educ AV dept (Bus 450), U of So Florida, Tampa Fl 33620.

SMITH, ALTA GRANGER. b Springfield Mass 31) 18. 4: Edward R Smith. 5: So Conn State Col 63 (LS) BS, 63- (LS). 7: Sch libn Wilcox Tech Sch, Meriden Conn 62-63; Catlg libn Curtis Mem Lib, Meriden Conn 63-. 9: ALA; ConnLA; NELA. 10: Meriden Womans Club; Meriden Charity Club; Cheshire Garden Club; Meriden Hosp Womans Auxiliary; Conn State & N H Co Med Auxiliary; Meriden Hist Soc; Conn Archeol Soc; Soc for Amer Archaeol. 14: Catlg. 15: 805 E Johnson ave, Cheshire Conn 06410.

SMITH, ANASTASIA (BORETOS). b Rutland Vt 23 Mr 25. 4: J Howard Smith. 5: UVt 43-47 (Eng, Fr, Sp) AB; Syracuse 50-52 MS in LS. 6: Fr, Sp. 7: Non-prof asst Syracuse U 49-52; Sch libn Crouse-Irving Hosp Sch of Nursing 52-56; Govt documents & ref UCLA Lib 57; Prof sub Santa Monica Pub Lib, Santa Monica Cal 62-63; Asst lib Educ Br UCLA 63; Elem sch libn Keeseville Central Sch, Keeseville NY 64; Ref libn SUNY(Plattsburgh) summer 64; Ref libn Daniel Boone Reg Lib, Columbia Mo 65-66; Elem sch libn Canastota NY 66-69. 9: ALA. 10: Phi Beta Kappa; Pi Lambda Sigma. 14: Ref, bk sel. 15: 44 Burton st, Cazenovia NY 13035.

SMITH, ANDREA (JOHNSON). b Tualatin Ore 14 D 21. 4: Bruce O Smith. 5: San Bernardino Jr Col 38-40 (Eng) AA; URedlands 40-42 (Eng) BA; Los Angeles State Col 56-62 (Educ Admin) MA; USoCal 61-67 MS in LS. 7: Job analyst War Dept San Bernardino Army Air Depot 42-44; Tchr Duarte School Dist, Duarte Cal 56-61; Hd libn Duarte High Sch, Duarte Cal 61-67; Dir instr materials Ontario High Sch, Ontario Cal 67-. 9: NEA; -DAVI; CalLA; CalASchL (chm Legis Com, So Sect); CalTA. 10: Duarte Tchrs Club; Associated Chaffey Tchrs. 14: Lib admin. 15: 352 E Hillcrest, Monrovia Ca 91016.

SMITH, ANITA. b Lineville Ala 10 Ag 13. 5: Ala Col 31-35 (Math) BA; UAla summer 54 (LS) MA; Auburn U summer 60 (Guidance, Coun) AA Certif. 7: Tchr Mellow Valley High Sch, Mellow Valley Ala 35-40; Tchr-libn Lineville High Sch, Lineville Ala 41-. 9: Nea; AlaEA. 10: Delta Kappa Gamma; Inter Se Club; PTA. 15: Main, Lineville Ala 36266.

SMITH, ANNIE LAURIE. b Falls City Neb 25 S 15. 5: Neb Wesleyan U 40 (Eng) AB; UIll 43 BS in LS. 7: UNeb: Asst in catlg dept 43-46, Sr asst in circ dept 46-47, Asst libn in catlg dept 47-51, Sr asst libn catlg dept 51-. 9: ALAACRL; MPLA; NebLA. 10: AAUP; AAUW; YWCA; UIll Lib Sch Alum Assn. 14: Catlg. 15: 1900 F, apt B-1, Lincoln Neb 68510.

SMITH, ANNIS E. b Horse Cave Ky 21 Jl 09. 5: Berea Col 27-31 (Math) AB; West Res summers 32-36 BS in LS. 6: Lat. 7: Libn Snead State Jr Col 32-. 9: ALA; SELA; AlaLA. 10: Delta Kappa Gamma; Twentieth Century Study Club. 14: Admin, ref. 15: Norton Lib Snead State Jr College, Boaz Al 35957.

SMITH, ANTJE (LOCKE). b Milton WVa 10 Ap 12. 5: Morris Harvey Col 29-33 (Eng, Hist) AB; Duke U summers 36, 37; Emory summers 39-41 BSLS; Ohio U summer 46; Marshall U 60. 7: Tchr & libn Cabell Co schs, Huntington WVa 33-46; Order libn Ohio U 46-47; Libn Bd of Educ, Cincinnati 56-58; Libn Bd of Pub Instr, Sarasota Fla 58-62; Br libn City of Richmond, Richmond Va 62-65, Asst city libn 65-. 9: ALA; VaLA; SELA. 15: 4016 Fauquier ave, Richmond Va 23227.

SMITH, AUDREY. b Seattle Wash 9 D 03. 5: UWash 31-35 (Fr) BA, 35-36 BA in LS. 6: Fr. 7: Catlgr pub lib: Pocatello Ida 37-41, Bellingham Wash 41-43, Seattle 43-46; Catlgr Army Med Lib, Wash DC 46-48; Admin asst catlg dept Enoch Pratt Free Lib, baltimore 48-51; Asst chief acquis UWash Lib 51-53; Reviser catlgr dept Free Lib of phila 53-. 9: ALA (Catlg Code Rev Steering Com 57-67); -CCS (chm Desc Catlg Com 57-61); PennLA; IdahoLA; WashLA; MdLA. 10: Phi Beta Kappa. 14: Catlg. 15: 48 W Tulpenhocken st, Philadelphia Pa 19144.

SMITH, AVA CLAIR. b LaFollette Tenn 1 Ja 10. 5: Mary Washington Col UVa 29-33 (Eng) BS in Ed; Emory 34-35 AB in LS. 7: Off asst Wholesale Grocery, Appalachia Va 33-34;

Sch libn Campbell Co, Jacksboro Tenn 35-37; Co libn Rabun Co, Clayton Ga 37-41; Post Libn US Army, Camp Croft SC 41-44; VA: Asst Chief libn, Dayton Ohio 44-45, Chief Libn, Ft Washington Md 45-46, Chief Libn, Martinsburg WVa 46-47, Asst chief libn, Mountain Home Tenn 47-48, Chief Libn, Mountain Home Tenn 48-. 9: ALA; TennLA; SELA. 10: AAUW; E Tenn Hist Soc; Assn for Preserv of Tenn Tuberculosis & Health Assn; Mental Health Assn of Washington Co (Tenn); Boone Tree Lib Club. 14: Educ, therapeatic & soc needs of hosp patients. 15: VA Center Lib, Mountain Home, Johnson City Tn 37684.

SMITH, BARBARA (DARRAH). b Cambridge Mass 22 O 38. 4: Mason Philip Smith. 5: Boston U 56-60 (Music Hist) BA; Simmons 64-65 (LS) MS. 6: Fr, Ger. 7: Clerktypist Yale U Sterling Mem Lib Personnel Off 60; Med sec Me Med Center, Porland Me 61; Desk asst fine arts dept Portland (Me) Pub Lib 61-64, Asst ref libn 65-66; Libn Mahoney Jr High Sch, S Portland Me 66-. 8: Mem faculty of NESLA Stud Leadership Conf UNH 68 & 69. 9: Amer Musicological Soc (NE Chap); MusLA; ALA; NE MusLA; MeSchLA (chm Research & Planning Com 68-); NEA; NESchLA. 10: Me Hist Soc; Greater Portland Landmarks Inc; Phi Beta Kappa. 13: Yes. 14: Music, ref, fine arts, sch libs. 15: 54 Eighth st, Portland Me 04103.

SMITH, BARBARA A SWART (BOULWARE). b South Bend Ind 29 Ap 29. 4: Richard Daniel Smith. 5: Winona Tchrs Col 47-48 (Music); UDenver 48-51, 52-53 BA (Humanities), UCincinnati 54; UDenver 55-61 (Educ); Chicago 65. 7: Fine arts asst Cincinnati Pub Lib 53-54; UDenver Period libn 54-59, circ libn & head of pub serv 59-61, Ref libn Hong Kong City Hall Lib 62-63; Asst Prof UDenver Lib Sch 63-64; Ref libn Chicago Tchrs Col 64-65; Circ res libn UChicago 65-68, Admin asst 68-. 9: ALA. 10: Phi Beta Kappa; Colo Mountain Club. 14: Pub serv, educ for libnship. 15: 1369 E Hyde Park blvd No. 1008, Chicago Il 60615.

SMITH, BARBARA JEAN. b Windsor Ont Can 23 Ap 29. 5: UToronto Victoria Col 48-52 (Eng) BA; Toronto 53 BLS. , 65-69 (Educ) MEd. 6: Fr. 7: Asst child libn Pub Lib, Brantford Ont 53-55; Child libn Pub Lib, Oshawa Ont 55-56; Chief libn Pub Lib, Port Credit Ont 56-58; Supv of child serv prov lib serv, Toronto 58-64; Dir elem sch libs Dept of Educ, Toronto 64-67; Prof Sch of Lib & Info Sci U West Ont (Can) 67-68; Coord of libs Peel City Bd of Educ, Mississauga Ont 68-. 9: CanLA; ALA; OntLA. 13: Yes. 14: Elem & secondary sch libs. 15: Peel County Bd of Ed, Resource Centre Windy Oaks dr, Port Credit Ont Can.

SMITH, BENJAMIN F. b Martinsville Va 13 F 17. 4: Dorothy Palmer. 4: Dorothy Palmer Smith. 5: Va Union U 40 (Math) BS; UIll 41 BS in LS, MS; NYU 48-51 (Psych) MA, PhD. 6: Fr. 7: Libn Huntington High Sch, Newport News Va 41-42; Ref libn Hampton Inst 42; US Army 42-46; NC Col (Durham): Dean Sch Lib Sci 47-49, Libn & Prof 49-51, Prof of Psy & Libn 51-65; Prof of educ psych Morgan State Col 65-. 9: ALA; NEA; Amer Psych Assn; Mental Hygiene Assn; NCLA; MdLA; MdTA. 10: Phi Delta Kappa. 13: Yes. 14: Bibliog, admin, psychological testing, research methods. 15: 3504 Sequoia ave, Baltimore Md 21215.

SMITH, BERNADINE (FRANCES). b Ransomville NY 21 S 10. 5: Alfred U 28-32 (Ceramic Art) BS; Geneseo State Col 35-36 BLS. 7: Libn Packard Com Sch, NYC 37-45; Research staff Answer Man Radio Program, NYC 45-49; Libn Bd of Educ: Hastings-on-Hudson NY 49-51, Rye NY 51-54, Poughkeepsie NY 54-. 9: NYLA. 10: Bus & Prof Womens Club. 14: Child bks. 15: 3 Pond rd, Poughkeepsie NY 12601.

SMITH, BERNICE (FERRIER). b Aberdeen Wash. 4: Cecil Haven Smith. 5: UWash 36 (Eng Lit) BA, 37 BA in LS. 6: Fr, Ger. 7: UWASH: Ref asst 37, Interlib loan lib 40-52, Educ libn Educ Br Lib 52-55, Forestry Lib libn 55-. 9: ALA; SLA;PNLA. 10: Phi Beta Kappa. 13: Yes. 14: Ref, forestry. 15: Col of Forestry Lib, Univ of Wash, Seattle Wa 98105.

SMITH, BERTHA (EDWARDS). b Woodford County Ky 20 Ja 13. 4: Arthur R Smith Jr. 5: ULouisville 30-34 (Langs) BA; UNC 34-35 BA in LS; Catherine Spalding summer 63. 7: Lib asst Louisville Free Pub Lib, Louisville Ky 35-36; Jr high libn Bd of Educ, Louisville Ky 36-43; Libn Train Intelligence Lib Air Force, St Louis 43-44, Greensboro NC 44-45; Libn Child Home, Ormsby Village KY 53-54; Jr high libn Bd of Educ, Louisville Ky 56-69. 8: Libn Deer Park Baptist Ch, Louisville Ky. 9: ALA; KyEA; KyASchL; NEA. 10: DAR; Highland Mothers Club. 14: Jr high sch libs. 15: 1960 Roanoke ave, Louisville Ky 40205.

SMITH, BESSIE (HESS). b Colon Panama 19 S 11. 4: Bernard A Smith. 5: Flint Jr Col 28-30 (Eng) AA; Baylor U 58, 60 (Eng); Eastman 60 (Mus Lib Wkshop). 7: Asst libn Jr High Sch Lib, Flint Mich 30-32; Asst libn Flint Central High Sch Lib, Flint Mich 32-34; Mus libn Baylor U Lib 55-. 9: MusLA; TexLA. 10: Soroptimists. 14: Ref, rare music, Americana, catlg. 15: 8257 Frest Ridge dr, Waco Tex 76710.

SMITH, BETTE C (WHITTAKER). b Columbia Mo 21 Mr 28. 4: James Abbuhl Smith. 5: Utica Col 63-64 (LS). 7: Lib asst AFSC, RTD, RADC, GAFB, NY Tech Data & Info Div Tech Lib Br Tech Lib Sect 56-66, Libn phys sci & engring (chief br lib) 62-. 10: Hospital Aux; Home bureau. 14: Ref. 15: RD 4 Pennystreet rd, Rome NY 13440.

SMITH, BETTY (LANE). b Belvidere Ill 16 Ag 27. 5: Milwaukee-Downer Col 45-46; UDenver 47-48; Rockford Col summer 64; Barry Col 66-68; Fla State Univ fall 67 ext course. 7: Recreational dir Spec Serv US Army, Seoul Korea 49-50; Period asst UMiami Lib 58-60, Research asst Govt Dept summer 68; Libn Ransom Sch, Coconut Grove Fla 63-. 9: ALA. 10: Miami Art Ctr. 14: Catlg, reluctant reading materials (printed and a-v). 15: 3650 Stewart ave, Coconut Grove Fl 33133.

SMITH, BYRON LAKE. b Washington Conn 8 Ap 0. 5: Wesleyan U (Conn) 39-46 (Fr) BA; Harvard 46-47 (Romance Langs) MA; UCal(Berkeley) 50-51 (Linguistics); Los Angeles State Col 57-58 (Secondary Educ); USoCal 58-59 MLS. 6: Sp, Fr, Ital, Russian, Ger. 7: US Army Signal Corps, No Africa-Italy Campaign 42-45; Instr (Span) Ripon Col, Wis 47-48; Shipping clerk Pacific Mercury TV Corp, Van Nuys Cal 51-55; Carrier US Post Off, San Fernando Cal 56-58; Tchr (Span) & libn Calipatria High Sch, Calipatria Cal 59-60; Tchr (Span & Lat) Lindsay High Sch, Lindsay Cal 60-61; Libn San Diego State Col 62-63; Libn catlgr Wash State U 64-. 9: ALA. 10: Phi Beta Kappa; Independent Order of Foresters. 14: Ref, catlg (Russian materials). 15: 1212 Maiden lane, Pullman Wa 99163.

SMITH, CAROL L. b Monterey Cal 6 N 31. 5: Monterey Peninsula Col 49-50; San Jose State Col 51-52, 66-68 (LS) MA; UCal 52-54 (Soc Welfare) BA; UNev 65. 7: Capt WAC 55-62; Recreation specialist USAF, Stead AFB Nev 62-65, Libn 65-66; Libn US Army, Ft Ord Cal 68-. 9: ALA; CalLA. 15: 404B Cedar st, Pacific Grove Ca 93950.

SMITH, CASSANDRA (CLARALENE). b Greenville SC 20 S 43. 5: Furman 61-62; USC 62-65 (Secondary Educ) AB; UNC 67-68 MS in LS. 6: Fr. 7: Catlgr USC 68-. 10: Beta Phi Mu. 14: Catlg. 15: 45 Woodbine Park apts, West Columbia SC 29169.

SMITH, CATHERINE J. b Pittsburgh Penn 22 O 25. 5: Swarthmore Col 43-47 (Eng) BA; Drexel 48-49 BS in LS. 6: Fr. 7: Acquis dept Swarthmore Col Lib 49-55; Reference libn Tech Lib E I duPont de Nemours & Co, Wilmington Del 56-60, Acquis libn 60-62; Asst libn Hahnemann Med Col Lib, Phila 62-64; Circ libn Swarthmore Col Lib 64-. 14: Circ, ref. 15: 20 Wellesley rd, Swarthmore Pa 19081.

SMITH, CHARLIE MAE (MRS). b Rosenberg Tex. 5: Prairie View A&M Col 50-54 (LS) BS Educ; UDenver 56-58 (LS); No Tex StateU 60-; Tex WomansU (LS). 6: Fr. 7: Sch libn H S Thompson Sch, Dallas 65; Asst ref libn Bishop Col 65-; Sch libn Oliver Wendell Holmes Jr High Sch. 9: NEA; ALA; TexLA; TexStateTA. 10: Delta Sigma Theta; YWCA; Dallas Bowling League; Dallas Panhellenic Coun; Alpha Phi Mu; Clr Tchrs Dallas Assn. 14: Ya & child lit, ref. 15: 1004 East Pentagon pkwy, Dallas Tx 75216.

SMITH, CHARLOTTE ANNETTE. b Greeneville Tenn 8 Mr 02. 5: Agnes Scott Col 20-25 (Fr, Eng) BA; Emory 26-27 (Eng) MA, 30-31 BA in LS. 7: High sch & jr col tchr Ga 26-30; Libn State Tchrs Col (Troy Ala) 33-38; Stetson U (Asst catlgr 39-40, Chief libn 40-58, Libn in chg of Documents 58-64, Chief libn 64-68, Libn in chg docs 68-69; Libn Howey Acad, Howey-in-the-Hills Fla 69-. 8: Org & consul Volusia Co Lib, Fla 49-. 9: FlaLA (treas 51-52, past chm Com on Res Coop; mem Col & Spec Libs Sect); SELA; ALA. 10: AAUW; Bus & Prof Women; Delta Kappa Gamma. 14: Admin, fed docs. 15: 615 N Hayden ave, De Land Fla 32720.

SMITH, CLARA (ELIZABETH). b New Brighton Penn 24 O 06. 5: Carnegie 25-30 BLS, 30-31 (LS) Diploma; UPittsburgh 31-36 (Educ). 6: Fr. 7: Summer & even sch tchr Pittsburgh pub schs 34-46; Libn Bethel High Sch, Bethel Boro Penn 46-47; Libn Elizabeth High Sch, Elizbeth Boro Penn 47-49; Tchr-libn Wilkinsburg Pub Sch, Pittsburgh 49-. 9: NEA; PennLA; Penn

State EA. 10: PTA; WEA. 14: Juv lit, remedial reading. 15: Apt 21 3265 Raleigh ave, Pittsburgh Pa 15216.

SMITH, CLARE MARIE. b Miles City Mont 14 Jl 07. 4: Kenneth Dale Smith. 5: UMont 25-29 (Sp) BA, 62 (LS); UMinn 55 (LS); East Mont Col 66 (LS). 6: Sp, Fr. 7: Tchr & libn Howard High Sch, Howard Mont 30-33; Libn Custer Co High Sch & Jr Col, Miles City Mont 42-45; Libn Miles City Pub Lib, Miles City Mont 49-; Coord Sagebrush Fed of Libs, Miles City Mont 60-. 8: Lectr East Mont Col, Billings 59-60. 9: ALA; MontStateLA; PNLA. 10: AAUW; Delta Kappa Gamma; Miles City Woman's Club. 11: Dorothy Canfield Fisher Award for Miles City Pub Lib 63. 14: Ya, loc hist. 15: 13 S Stacy ave, Miles City Mt 59301.

SMITH, COLLEEN F(ORNEY). b Kan City Mo 27 Ja 24. 4: F Janney Smith. 5: Wayne State U 49-61 (Educ) BA, 62-64 MSLS. 7: Ref libn Grosse Pointe Pub Lib, Grosse Pointe Farms Mich 64-. 9: ALA; MichLA. 10: Pi Lambda Theta;AAUW; Wayne Co Med Soc Womens Auxiliary; Henry Ford Hosp Staff Wives (Detroit); Detroit Boat Club. 14: Ref, ya. 15: 352 Moselle pl, Grosse Pointe Farms Mi 48236.

SMITH, COLLEEN S. b New Castle Ind 23 Ag 13. 4: Philip R Smith. 5: Flint Community Col 60-62 (Eng) AA; UMich 62-64 (Eng) BA, 64-66 AMLS. 6: Ger. 7: Asst libn Middletown Pub Lib, Middletown Ind 29-31; Sec State of Ind, Indianapolis 33-41; Libn Independence Twp Lib, Clarkston Mich 55-. 9: ALA; MichLA. 10: Clarkston Commun Womens Club; Mensa. 14: Small pub libs, tech serv, ref. 15: 6630 Cranberry Lake rd, Clarkston Mi 48016.

SMITH, CONSTANCE (ELIZABETH). b Humboldt Tenn 16 O 45. 5: Chestnut Hill Col 62-66 9eng) BA; UNC 66-67 MS in LS. 6: Fr. 7: Hd Child Sect, Pub Lib of Charlotte & Mecklenburg Co, Charlotte NC 67-. 9: ALA; MecklenburgLA (Recept Com). 14: Child lit. 15: 2529 Selwyn ave, Charlotte NC 28209.

SMITH, CONSTANCE DOUGLAS. b Seattle 1 Ja 25. 5: UWash 44-48 (Eng) BA, 64-65 M Libr. 7: Intern Wash State Lib 65-, Libn ref dept 67-. 9: ALA; Wash State LA; PNLA. 14: Ref. 15: 2009 Water st, Olympia Wa 98501.

SMITH, CORDELIA TITCOMB (MRS). b Bath Me 6 N 02. 5: Simmons 22-26 BLS; West Res 28-29 (LS) Certif. 6: Fr, Sp. 7: Br libn Cuyahoga Co Lib, Cleveland 26-28; Child libn Cleveland Pub Lib 28-34, Sch libn 34-36; Catlgr Fenn Col Lib 37-41; Child libn Morley Pub Lib, Painesville Ohio 47-48; Sch & pub libn Kirtland Sch Dist, Willoughby Ohio 48-55; Dir of wk with yp Lucas Co Lib, Maumee Ohio 55-. 9: ALA; OhioLA (chm ya RT). 10: Pan-Pacific & Southeast Asia Womens Assn; LWV. 12: Ed "Great Science Fiction Stories (63); "Paul Bunyan in Geauga County" (47). 13: Yes. 14: Wk with ya. 15: Lucas Co Lib, 501 River rd, Maumee Ohio 43537.

SMITH, DANIEL LEE. b Metropolis Ill 23 N 24. 4: Marjorie Goetz. 5: Wabash Col 45-50 (Hist) BA; Ball State U 53-55 (Hist); UIll 57-60 (LS) MS. 6: Sp. 7: US Army Ordnance (Cpl) 43-45; Tchr New Castle Jr High Sch, New Castle Ind 50-56; Tchr Mattoon Sr High Sch, Mattoon Ill 56-60, Libn 60-62; Circ libn West Lib DePauw U 62-. 9: ALA; IndLA. 14: Circ, ref, period. 15: DePauw U Lib, College ave, Greencastle Ind 46135.

SMITH, DANIEL LYONS. b Franklin Tenn 3 S 05. 4: Lois Lampley. 5: Peabody 54-56 (Hist) BA; Peabdy 56-57 MALS. 7: Operations Supv USAF Memphis Mun Airport (T/Sgt) 23-52; Self-employed farmer, Franklin Tenn 53-54; A-v libn Muncie Pub Lib, Muncie Ind 57-58; Ref Fresno Co Free Lib, Fresno Cal 58-. 9: ALA; CalLA. 14: Ref. 15: 5733 N Seventh, Fresno Ca 93726.

SMITH, DAVID ALAN. b Madison Wis 5 F 38. 4: Patricia Dabney. 5: Lawrence Col 55-59 (Psych) BA; UIll 60-61 (LS) MS. 6: Sp, Fr, Ger, Russian. 7: Intern & catlgr NLM, Wash DC 61-62; Descr catlgr LC 63-66; Asst hd Eng Lang sect shared catlg div 66-67, Assoc ed Nat Union Catlg Publn Project 67-68, Prin ed 69-. 9: ALA; DCLA. 10: Phi Beta Kappa; Beta Phi Mu. 14: Catlg, ser. 15: 301 G st SW, apt 417, Wash DC 20024.

SMITH, DAVID MONROE. b Montgomery Ala 25 S 44. 4: Bettye Fletcher. 5: AuburnU 62-63; Huntingdon Col 63-66 (Hist) AB; Emory 66-67 MLS. 7: Libn Gwinnett Co (Ga) Schs, Duluth (Ga) High Sch 67-68; Ala Air Nat Guard Trainee USAF, Keesler AFB Miss 68; Catlg libn & instr R B Draughon Lib AuburnU 69-. 9: GaLA; GaEA; AlaLA. 14: Catlg, lib automation. 15: Pation apts 205 420 N Dean rd, Auburn Al 36830.

SMITH, DAVID REXFORD. b amamosa Iowa 29 Jl 34. 4: Stacey C Lawson. 5: Iowa StateU 52-56 (Sociol) BS; UIowa 58-60 (Pol Sci); UMinn 61-63 (LS); Wayne State 68 (Pub Lib Bldgs) Certif. 7: Capt USMC US & Philippines 56-58; Docs asst IowaU Lib 58-60; Libn trainee pub lib, Cedar Rapids Iowa 60-61; Circ asst Macalaster Col Lib 61-63; Research fellow Anatomy Dept UMinn 62-63; Dir pub lib: Hopkins Minn 63-67, Cedar Rapids Minn 67-. 8: Loc coord, Twin Cities Metro Lib Survey 65-67; Building consul on projs in minn, Wis, Iowa. 9: MinnLA (treas, Exec Bd). 10: Rotary C of C. 14: Lib bldgs. 15: 418 Dumreath dr NE, Cedar Rapids Ia 52402.

SMITH, DAVID ROLLIN. b Pasadena Ca 13 O 40. 5: Pasadena City Col 58-60 (Hist) AA; UCal(Berkele) (Berkeley) (Hist) BA, 62-63 MLS. 6: Sp, Fr. 7: Page & asst Ms Dept H E Huntington Lib, San Marino Cal 57-62; Spec recruit LC 63-64; Asst head Amer-British EXCH Sect LC 64-65; Ref libn UCLA Research Lib 65-. 9: Manuscript Soc; CalLA. 12: "The Monitor and the Merrimac; A Bibliography" (68). 14: Ref, mss, exch. 15: 2704-C Montana ave, Santa Monica Cal 90403.

SMITH, DONALD EVANS. b Shenandoah Iowa 2 D 15. 5: Hastings Col 34-38 (Hist) BA; Ricks Col 39 (Educ); UWash 45-50 (Anthropology), 60-65 (LS) ML. 7: Chief clerk Signal Property Off, Ft Lewis Wash 40-41; US Army Signal Corps, Alaska Communication System 42-45; Libn-tchr Tenino High Sch, Tenino Wash 50-51; Off US Army Psychological Warfare 51-54; Libn-tchr Rochester High Sch, Rochester Wash 54-59; Libn N Thurston High Sch, Lacey Wash 59-67; Libn Lakes High Sch, Lakewood Ctr, Wash 67-. 8: WSASL Standards Com 68-69. 9: NEA; WashEA; Wash State LA; Wash State ASchL. 10: Phi Delta Kappa; Wash State Movie Coun; Olympia Amateur Movie Club. 14: Sch libs. 15: 4530 Redwood lane, Olympia Wash 98502.

SMITH, DONALD T(AIT). b Brooklyn NY 11 Ap 23. 4: Marjory Reed. 5: Oberlin Col 41-42; Weslyan U 42-43, 47-49 (Philos) BA, 49-50 (Philos) MA; Columbia 50-51 (LS) MS. 7: Act ref libn Colby Col 51-53; Asst libn Clarkson Col of Tech 53-55; Libn Wagner Col 55-58; Admin asst Boston U Libs 58-61, Asst dir for reader serv 61-63; Asst U lib UOre 63-. 9: ALA; Metro Col Inter-Lib Assn (pres 58); PNLA; OreLA; AEDS. 13: Yes. 14: Admin, bldgs & equip, automatiln. 15: 175 W 20th ave, Eugene Ore 97405.

SMITH, DOREEN (LORENTZEN). b Somerville Mass 23 O34. 4: William H Smith. 5: Boston U 52-56 (Music) BA; Simmons 58-60 (LS) MS. 7: Gen asst Belmont Pub Lib, Belmont Mass 51-56; Catlg asst Boston U Chenery Lib 56-57; Belmont Pub Lib, Belmont Mass: Circ asst 57-58, Catlgr 58-61, Asst libn 61-64; Child libn FAIRBANKS Pub Lib, Fairbanks Alaska 64-65, Catlgr 65-, Act libn 67-68, 69-. 8: Trustee Col Commun Lib, College Alaska 65-67. 9: ALA (Memb Com Alaska); MusLA (sec-treas NE Chap 63-64); MassLA; NE Tech Serv Libns (sec-treas 59-61, Exec Bd, Memb Chm 61-62); AlaskaLA (Program Chm Fairbanks Chap 65-66). 10: AAUW; Col Woman's Club. 14: Catlg. 15: 765 8th ave, Fairbanks Al 99701.

SMITH, DOROTHY (CAROLINE). b Shawmut Ala 3 Ja 24. 5: Randolph-Macon Womans Col 40-44 (Hist) AB; USCar 45-47 (Hist) MA; UNC 50-51 BS in LS. 7: Ref asst Pub Lib of Charlotte & Mecklenburg Co, Charlotte NC 51-52; Libn Horry Co Mem Lib, Conway SC 52-57; Field consul SC State Lib Bd, Columbia SC 57-61; Adult serv libn Richland Co Pub Lib, Columbia SC 61-63; Pub lib consul, lib ext div NY State Lib 63-67, Assoc in pub lib serv div of lib development 67-. 8: Lib 21, Seattle Worlds Fair, 62. 9: ALA; NYLA; Hudson -Mohawk LA. 10: Phi Beta Kappa. 13: Yes. 14: Personnel admin & development, pub lib admin. 15: 2135 McClellan st, Schenectady NY 12309.

SMITH, DOROTHY B FRIZZELL. b Moundrdge Kan 9 D 01. 5: Southwestern Col 20-24 (Eng, Fr) AB; Chicago 28-29 (Chaucer, Amer Lit) AM; Cambridge U 30, 36 (Eng Lit) Certif; Columbia 37-38 BSLS; UMich 49 (Classics). 6: Fr. 7: Tchr Lat & Eng Seoul Foreign Sch, Seoul Korea 26-27; Research asst Chaucer UChicago 30; Head Dept of Eng High Sch, Holland Mich 31-32; Instr Eng Dept Carroll Col (Wis) 32-37; Cryptographer P-3 US Army Signal Corps, Wash DC 43-45; Visiting libn Internat Christian U (Tokyo) 53; Visiting libn Isabella Thoburn Col (India) 65; Asst libn City Col (Long Beach Cal) 38-67; Visiting libn Colo Col 68. 9: NEA; ALA; Cal Tchrs Assn; CalLA; CalASchL. 10: Delta Kappa Gamma; UN Assn; AAUP; AAUW; LWV; Overseas Tchrs Org; Sister City Com; Los Angeles Philharmonic Assn; PEO; World Affairs Coun; NAACP; YWCA. 12; "College Handbook for Freshman English, with J Flitcroft (34); "Subject Index to Poetry for Children and Young People (57). 13: Yes. 14: Ref. 15: 82 Yacht Harbor dr, Portuguese Bend Ca 90274.

SMITH, DOROTHY FRASER. b Clarksburgh Penn. 4: Littleton K Smith. 5: Col of Wooster 37 (Sociol) BA; West Res 40 BS in LS. 6: Fr. 7: Sr asst Rochester Pub Lib, Rochester NY 40-43; Recreation wker Amer Red Cross, Overseas 43-44; Ref & info Riverside Pub Lib, Riverside Cal 63-65, Supv libn 65-68, Coord city & co ref & info 68-. 15: Riverside Pub Lib, Riverside Ca 92501.

SMITH, DOROTHY JEANNE. b Crawford Co Penn 29 Ap 32. 5: Allegheny Col 48-52 (Eng) AB; West Res 52-53 MS in LS; Yale U 54-56 (Eng) MA. 6: Fr, Ger. 7: Catlgr Yale U Lib 53-56; Circ & ref libn Allegheny Col 56-57, Asst libn 57-. 14: Catlg, ref. 15: 434 Park ave, Meadville Penn 16335.

SMITH, E MARJORIE. b Sharpsbug Iowa. 5: State Col Iowa 32 (Pub Sch Music) BA; UDenver 47-50 (LS) MA. 6: Fr, Ger, Russian. 7: Gen lib wk pub lib, Ames Iowa 46-48; Sir of Sch Libs Pub Schs, N Platte Neb 48-49; Dir of Sch Libs Pub Schs, Peoria Ill 49-53; Ser catlgr Sci & Tech, Asst Prof Iowa State U (Ames) 53-. 9: ALA; IowaLA. 10: AAUP. 14: Catlg, ser. 15: 2303 Kellogg ave, Ames Ia 50010.

SMITH, EDITH (PRINCEHORN). b Oberlin Ohio 4 F 08. 4: George H Smith. 5: Oberlin Col 25-29 (Fr) AB; West Res 30-31 BS in LS. 6: Fr, Ger, Sp. 7: Child libn Oberlin Col Lib 32-38; Gen asst Utica Pub Lib, Utica NY 40-49, Catlgr 50-60; Libn Marcy State Hosp, Marcy NY 60-. 9: MedLA (Upper NY State Reg Div); NYLA. 14: Catlg, ref (med). 15: 9562 Roberts rd, Sauquoit NY 13456.

SMITH, EDWARD FOWLER. b Toronto Ont 25 Ap 13. 4: Marion Rowley. 5: Oberlin Col 32-36 (Eng Lit) AB; West Res 36-37 BS in LS. 7: Ref libn Mo Sch of Mines & Met, Rolla Mo 37-39; Chief libn Lewis Inst of Sci & Tech, Chicago 39-42; US Army Air Corps, Inf, Antiaircraft (Art tech/5th) 42-46; Chief libn Argonne Nat Lab, Chicago & Argonne 46-52, Acquis libn 52-. 14: Acquis. 15: Rt 1 Box 218-A, Naperville Il 60540.

SMITH, ELDRED REID. b Payette Ida 30 Je 31. 4: Judith Ausubel. 5: UCal (Berkeley) 50-56 (Eng) AB, 60-66 (Eng) MA; USoCal 56-57 MSLS. 6: Fr. 7: Asst mgr Lankershim Theater, N Hollywood Cal 55-56; Ref asst Los Angeles Pub Lib 57; Acquis libn Long Beach State Col 57-59; Ref libn San Francisco State Col Lib 59-60; Bibliogr UCal (Berkeley) 60-65, Hd search div 65-. 9: ALA; CalLA; Libns Assn UCal (pres 68). 13: Yes. 14: Admin, acquis, personnel. 15: 1030 Merced st, Berkeley Ca 94709.

SMITH, ELEANOR (NOXON). b Schenectady NY 30 Mr 13. 5: Oneonta State Tchrs Col 33 (Intermediate Tchg). 7: Law libn Joseph F Egan Mem Supreme Court Law Lib, Schenectady NY 57-. 9: AALL; Nat Assn of Legal Secs; Upstate NY ALL (Dir). 15: 5 Evergreen blvd, Scotia NY 12302.

SMITH, ELEANOR TOUHEY (MRS S STEPHENSON). b Portland Ore 4 Ja 10. 5: St Marys Jr Col 26-28 (Eng) Certif; UOre 28-30 (Eng) BA; Los Angeles Lib Sch 31-32 Certif; Columbia 51-52 MSLS. 7: Gen prof Lib Assn, Portland Ore 32-36, Readers adv 36-43; Dir Vanport Pub Lib, Vanport Ore 43-45; Asst dir Santa Monica Pub Lib, Santa Monica Cal 45-49; Head of ext Ferguson Lib, Stamford Conn 49-51; Brooklyn Pub Lib: Sr libn 52-53, Personnel dir 53-55, Coordinator adult serv 55-67; Lib program off US Off of Educ Reg II, NYC 67-. 8: Instr USoCal Lib Sch, 47; Asst Prof UWash Lib Sch, summer 64. 9: ALA-ASD (pres 64-65); LPRC (pres 56-57); NY State LA (pres Adult Serv Sect 57-58);NY State LA (pres Adult Serv Sect 57-58); 57-58; v-pres 68-69; pres 69-70); Lib Club (pres 59-60). 10: Columbia Sch of Lib Serv Alumni Assn; Womens Nat Bk Assn; Phi Beta Kappa;Soroptimist; Bksellers League of NY. 11: Friends of Brooklyn Pub Lib Award, 61. 12: Ed PNLA "Quarterly (42-43); Auth of chap in "Library Reaches Out (65); Auth "Psychic People" (67). 13: Yes. 14: Pub iib adult serv, adult educ, bk sel, ref, state lib admin, lib finance, lib legis, col lib serv. 15: 201 Eastern pky, Brooklyn NY 11238.

SMITH, ELIZABETH LAWALL. b Syracuse NY. 5: Smith 33-37 (Eng) AB; WayneU 50-51 (LS). 7: Asst bus mgr Bus News Publ Co, Detroit 41-48; Ref asst Campbell-Ewald Advertising Agcy, Detroit 49-53, Asst libn 53-57, Libn 58-. 8: Consul off Mich Chap SLA 68-69. 9: SLA (sec Advertising Div 56-57; chm Exhibits Bks Proj 60-61; ref Prof Standards Com 61-62; sec 62-63; v-chm & chm-elect 63-64; Mich Chap; treas 53-54, chm Advertising Div 54-55, local rep Advertising & Publ Divs 1955 Convention, chm Nomin Com 58-59, sec 59-60, Program Com 62-63, Program chm 55-56 & 66-67, Exec Com 1970 SLA Convention). 13: Yes. 14: Lib admin. 15: 911 Henrietta st, Birmingham Mi 48009.

SMITH, ELIZABETH STRATTON. b Brooklyn NY 24 F 13. 5: Wellesley 30-34 (Eng) AB; Columbia 35-36 BS in LS. 7: Child libn Brooklyn Pub Lib 36-39; Ref & yp libn NY Pub Lib 39-41; Child libn Cyrenius H Booth Lib, Newtown Conn 44-45; Asst in chg of wk with schs Danbury Lib, Danbury Conn 46-63; Asst to the libn UBridgeport Lib 63-66; Circ asst Bridgeport Pub Lib 66-. 9: ALA; ConnLA. 10: 4-H Club, Girl Scouts. 15: 21 Cedar Hill rd, Newtown Conn 06470.

SMITH, ELIZABETH WARD. b Antelope Co Neb. 4: Charles E Smith Jr. 5: Madison Col 40-44 (Eng, LS) AB; Duke 47 (Eng); San Jose State Col 59-62 (Libnship) MA; SUNY (Buffalo) 68- (Higher Educ). 6: Sp. 7: Asst catlgr UPenn Lib 48-49; Asst supv clerical staff catlg dept UIll (Urbana) 49-54; Med libn Santa Clara Co Hosp 56-58; Instr San Jose State Col Dept of Lib 61-62, Asst Prof 65-67; Libn San Jose City Lib 62-63; Lecturer SUNY (Buffalo) Sch Info & Lib Studies 68-. 8: Consul to the Dept of Acad & Sci Res, San Jose State Col 65. 9: ALA; SLA (Upstate NY Chap: Com on Continuing Educ); NYLA. 10: Women's Club; SUNY (Buffalo). 14: Catlg, sci libnship, ref. 15: 197 Smallwood dr, Snyder NY 14226.

SMITH, ELLA SUE (DOBBINS) (MRS). b Anderson SC 26 S 11. 5: Anderson Col 29-30; Clemson Col 37-39; Emory 45-48. 7: Libn Anderson Pub Lib, Anderson SC 35-51; Head catlg dept Charleston Free Lib, Charleston SC 51-53; Libn: Charleston Air Force Base, Charleston SC 53-55, Charleston Naval Shipyard, Charleston SC 55-56, USMC Recr Depot, Parris Island SC 56-. 9: ALA; SELA; SCLA. 10: Bus & Prof Womens Club. 15: P O Box 409, Parris Island SC 29905.

SMITH, EMILLIE VARDEN. b Lexington Ky 4 F 25. 5: UKy 42-46 (LS) AB; UIll 50-53 (LS) MS. 7: UKy: Asst catlgr 46-48, Asst ser catlgr 48-55, Head mongraphu sect catlg dept 55-67, Hd catlg dept 67-. 8: Visiting lecturer UIll Grad Sch of Lib Sci, summers 55, 59, 62; Visiting instr UKy Dept of Lib Sci, summers 57, 58. 9: ALA-RTSD (Dscr Catlg Com 59-, rep to ALA Memb Com 63-); Ohio Valley Group Tech Serv Libns (sec 57-58, chm 59-60); KyLA. 14: Catlg. 15: 329 Greenbriar rd, Lexington Ky 40503.

SMITH, EMMA CAROLINE (FENSTERMACHER). b Hamburg Penn 28 Ja 16. 5: Dickinson Jr Col 4647 (Econ) Certif; Syracuse 4749 (Eng Lit) BA (cum laude), 5051 MS in LS, 5152 (Eng Lit) MA. 6: Lat, Fr, Sp. 7: Ref libn Allegheny Col 5152; Hd acquis DuquesneU 5263; Period libn SUNY (Stony Brook) 64. 9: ALA (Ser Com for Medium Sized Libs); SLA; Suffolk Co (NY) LA; NY Tech Serv Libns Assn. 10: SUNY (Stony Brook) Women-s Club. 14: Acquis, rare bks, period. 15: P O Box 574, Stony Brook NY 11790.

SMITH, ETHEL (LILLIE) KNOTT. b Granville Co NC 21 Jl 15. 4: Budd Elmon Smith. 5: Queens Col 33-34; Meredith Col 34-37 (Hist, Eng) AB; UNC 42 BSLS; Appalachian State Tchrs Col 55 (Eng) MA; Chicago 66-. 6: Fr. 7: Tchr Guilford Col High Sch, Guilford NC 37-38; Tchr Roanoke Rapids High Sch, Roanoke Rapids NC 38-42; Libn Gastonia High Sch, Gastonia NC 42-43; US Army, Camp Butner NC 43-44, Cornell Lib Assn Lib, Ithaca NY 44-45; Instr Wake Forest Col 46-51; Libn Oxford City Schs, Oxford NC 52-53; Instr Wingate Col 53-55, Libn 55-. 8: So Assn Accred Coms; Chm, Nat Lib Week, NC; Grant for world tour to study col & univ libs 69. 9: ALA; NCTE; SELA (chm Jr Col Com, chm-elect Col & Univ Sect); NCLA. 10: AAUW; Delta Kappa Gamma; Womans Club; Garden Club; Union Co (NC) Planning Bd. 11. The Wingate Col Lib has been named the Ethel K Smith Lib. 12: Assoc ed "The Junior College Library Collection". 13: Yes. 14: Admin. 15: Northwood, Wingate NC 28174.

SMITH, EVELINA L. b Warren Ohio 5 Ap 38. 4: Elliot D Smith. 5: Youngstown U 57-61 (Educ) BS in ED; West Res 61-62 MS in LS. 6: Sp. 7: Acqus & catlg libn Warren Pub Lib, Warren Ohio 62-; Dir bkmob Pub Lib of Youngstown & Mahoning Co, Youngstown Ohio 66-. 8: Consul, catlgr & adv Beth Israel Temple Lib, Warren Ohio 67-69. 9: ALA; OhioLA; JewishLA. 14: Catlg, ref, pub serv, bkmob serv. 15: 55 Princess st, Campbell Oh 44405.

SMITH, EVELYN LUCILLE. b Harrison Ohio 15 Mr 40. 5: Antioch Col 58-63 (Ger) BA; UMich 63-64 AMLS. 6: Ger, Fr, Sp. 7: Catlg libn UMich Law Lib (Ann Arbor) 64-. 9: AALL; ALA; ASIS. 11: Margaret Mann Award 64. 15: Univ of Mich Law Lib, Ann Arbor Mi 48104.

SMITH, EVELYN MANSFIELD. b Toronto Can. 4: Wendell Roy Smith. 5: UToronto 29-33 BA, 35 BLS. 6: Fr. 7: Libn Art Gallery of Toronto, Toronto Can 36-37; Asst libn "Toronto Daily Star" 38-40; Recs libn Dept of Transport Meterological Div, Toronto 41-46; Asst catlg VictoriaU Lib 46-57, Hd catlg dept 57-61, Hd tech serv 61-65, Deputy libn & hd catlg & prep dept 65-. 9: ALA; CanLA; Inst Profess Libns Ont; Bibliog Soc Com; SLA (var offs); OntLA (var offs). 10: UToronto Sch of Lib Sci Alum Assn. 13: Yes. 14: Catlg. 15: 123 Yonge blvd, Toronto 20 Ont Can.

SMITH, FAYE JOANNE. b Grove City Penn 28 J126. 5: Slippery Rock State Col 44-48 (Elem Educ) BS; Wheaton Col (Ill) summer 50 (Elem Educ); Peabody summer 62 (LS); UPittsburgh summer 63-65 MLS, 68-69 Advanced Certif. 6: Sp. 7: Elem tchr Grove City Area Sch Dist, Grove City Penn 48-59, 60-62; Elem libn Ewa Beach Elem Sch, Oahu Hawaii 59-60; Elem libn Grove City Area Sch Grove City Penn 60-66; Elem libn N Hills Sch Dist, Pittsburgh Penn 66-68; Asst prof lib sci Shippensburg State Col 69-. 8: Visiting instr WVa U summer 68. 9: NEA; ALA;-AASchL;-CSD; PennLA; PennASchL; PennEA; Pittsburgh Suburban Coun Sch Libns. 10: Delta Kappa Gamma; Beta Phi Mu; AAUW. 14: Child lit & lib serv. 15: Rt 3 Box 236, Grove City Penn 16127.

SMITH, FLORENCE (IVADEL). b Hamilton Can 12 Ja 07. 5: UToronto 28-29 (LS) Diploma. 7: Hamilton Pub Lib, Hamilton Ont, Head Fairfield & Lloyd George Brs 30-32, Head child dept Kenilworth br 32-37, Head ya sect main br 38-49, Head circ dept 49-67, Hd Kenilworth br 67-. 9: CanLA (Life mem); OntLA; Inst Prof Lbns Ont. 10: . 14: Adult serv. 15: 225 Sherman ave S, Hamilton Ont Can.

SMITH, FRANCES (SARAH). b Jackson Tenn 9 Ap 21. 5: Lambuth Col 38-42 (Hist) AB; Vanderbilt U 42-43, 45 (So Hist) MA; Peabody 55-56 LS MA. 6: Fr, Sp, Ger. 7: Elem tchr Alexander Sch, Jackson Tenn 43-44; Tchr Jackson High Sch, Jackson Tenn 44-47; Clerk All Transport Inc, NYC 47-48; Trans sales agent Eastern Air Lines, NY & Nashville 48-50; Tchr Jr high sch, Humboldt Tenn 50-55; Libn Jackson/Jackson-Madison Co Free Lib, Jackson Tenn 56-63; Readers serv libn Union U (Jackson Tenn) 63-69; Circ & ref libn Lambuth Col 69-. 9: SELA; TennLA (chm Memb Com 57-58; sec 59-61). 10: MacDowell Music Club; Joseph E Martin Shakespeare Circle; AAUP. 14: Ref, loc hist. 15: 349 Westwood, Jackson Tn 38303.

SMITH, FRANCES (SHAVER). b Nashville 9J116. 4: Edward S C Smith. 5: Vanderbilt U 32-36 (Hist) BA; Peabody 36-38 BS in LS, 36-38 (Higher Educ) MA. 6: Ger, Fr, Lat. 7: Asst libn Bethany Col (WVa) 38-41; Ref libn Ball State Tchrs Col 41-44; Asst libn Union Col (NY) 44-60, Act libn 44-45, 51; Catlg libn Penn State U Lib 60-67; Ser catlgr & Prof Lib Sci UFla 67-. 9: ALA; PennLA; ASIS. 10: Phi Beta Kappa. 13: Yes. 14: Catlg, automation. 15: PO Box 1154, Gainesville Fl 32601.

SMITH, FRANCES (SNYDER). b Niota Tenn 10 F 12. 4: Voyle V Smith. 5: Mars Hill Col 29-31 (Music); our Lady of the Lake Col 59-62 (LS) BA. 7: Tchr McMinn Co pub schs, Tenn 31-33; San Antonio Pub Lib, San Antonio Tex: Lib asst 57-59, Head circ dept 59-61, Libn bus & sci dept 61-68, Hd art mus & films dept 68-. 9: ALA; TexLA; SWLA. 10: San Antonio Pub Lib Staff Assn; Amer Guild of Organists; DAR. 14: Ref, fine arts. 15: 2358 W Gramercy, San Antonio Tx 78201.

SMITH, FRANCES V. b Howard Co Ind 9 J109. 5: Earlham Col 28-29 (Eng); UMinn 37-38 (Eng); Butler U 43-45 (Elem Educ) BS; Central Mich U 57-61 (LS) MA. 6: Fr. 7: Tchr Clay Twp Consolidated Sch, Howard Co Ind 32-36; Tchr Kokomo Sch City, Kokomo Ind 36-40; Visitor Howard Co Welfare, Kokomo In 40-43; Tchr Kokomo-Center Twp Consolidated Sch Corp, Kokomo Ind 43-62, Libn 62-. 9: NEA; ALA; Ind State Tchrs Assn, IndLA; IndSchLA. 14; Ref. 15: 5508 W Jefferson, Kokomo Ind 46901.

SMITH, GENEVA. b Altoona Ala 8 F 19. 5: Col of the Ozarks 36-40 (Sociol) BA; UIll 44-45 BSLS. 7: Asst libn US Navy, Norfolk Va 45-46; VA Asst libn, Fayetteville Ark 46-47, Chief libn, Springfield Mo 47-50, Chief libn, Poplar Bluff Mo 50-51, Chief libn, Fayetteville Ark 51-56; Supv libn US Army (Europe) 56-58; Bkmob libn US Army, Wash DC 58-60; Libn VA, Wash DC 60-62; Patient libn Nat Inst of Health, Bethesda Md 62-65; Chief libn VA, Kan City Mo 65-. 9: ALA;SLA. 14: Med ref, admin. 15: 5907 Rockhill rd, Kansas City Mo 64110.

SMITH, HANNIS SANDERS. b Charleston Miss 23 Je 10. 4: June Smeck. 5: Chicago 47-49 (LS) MA. 7: Asst libn Greenwood Pub Lib, Greenwood Miss 30-31, Libn 31-46; (T/Sgt) USAAF 42-45; Asst dir Miss Lib Survey, Jackson Miss 49; Libn Hinds Co Lib, Raymond Miss 49-52; Pub Lib consul Wis Free Lib Commsn, Madison Wis 52-56; Dir of Libs Minn State Dept of Libs Minn State Dept of Educ, St Paul 56-. 8: Consul to Tenn Legis Coun study of pub lib serv. 9: Adult Educ Assn; ALA (chm Com on Rev of Lib Serv Act 63-65; chm Com on Org 65-66; chm Com to Draft Ref of Farmers; Bulletin on Public Library Service; chm Nomin Com 63);-ASD (pres 58-59);-AAStateL (pres 66-67); SLA; MinnLA. 12: "Cooperative Approach to Library Service (62); Ed "People Without Books (49); "Informal Education Through Libraries (54); Ed "Minnesota Libraries (56-). ; Ed "Regional Public Library Systems" (65); Auth " A Seamless Web; The Systems Approach to Library Service" (67). 13: Yes. 14: Pub lib ext, lib devel, coop. 15: State Off Annex, 117 University ave, St Paul Mn 55101.

SMITH, HARDIN EVERETT. b Daisy Okla 11 F 22. 4: Margie Davis. 5: UOkla 49 BS in LS. 6: Fr. 7: (Sgt) US Army 40-45; Bkmob libn Ozark Reg Lib, Ironton Mo 49-50; Br supv Jackson Co Lib, Independence Mo 50-55; Circ libn E Chicago Pub Lib, E Chicago Ind 55-56, Dir 56-69; Dir Clark Co Lib Dist, Las Vegas Nev 69-. 9: ALA; IndLA (pres 68); ASIS. 13: Yes. 14: Admin. 15: Clark Co Lib, 1131 "J" E Tropicana, Las Vegas Ne 89109.

SMITH, HAROLD B. b Far Rockaway NY 12 Ag 39. 4: Kathryn O'Keefe. 5: C W Post Col 57-63 (Sociol) BA, 64-68 MLS. 7: Ref libn (evenings) C W Post Col 61-63; Ser libn Grumman Aircraft Engring Corp, Bethpage NY 63-66; Chief libn Fairchild Hiller Republic Aviation Div, Farmingdale NY 66-. 9: SLA; ASIS. 10: Sigma Beta Epsilon. 12: Master's report "The Development of Automation in the Library: 1936-1966" (68). 14: Info ret & automated systems in all areas of lib wk. 15: 86 Harp lane, Sayville NY 11782.

SMITH, HAROLD FREDERICK. b Kansas City Mo 9 Jl 23. 4: Carolyn Duglas. 5: Park Col 40-44 (Hist) AB; UKan 45-46 (Hist) AM; UDenver 49-50 (LS) AM; So Ill U 58-63 (Educ) PhD. 7: Time study Pratt & Whitney Aircraft Kan City Mo 44-45; Advert salesman "Kansas City Star, Kansas City Mo 46-48; Admissions coun Park Col 48-49; Asst circ libn UDenver 50-51; Sr asst libn pub serv div UNeb 51-52; Acquis libn Colo State Col 52-57; Asst soc studies libn So Ill U 57-64; Libn Park Col 64-. 9: ALA; MPLA; MoLA (legis com). 10: Soc Amer Histns; State Hist Soc of Mo; Phi Alpha Thta;Phi Delta Kappa. 12: "American Travellers Abroad; a Bibliography of Accounts Published Before 1900" (69). 13: Yes. 14: Acquis, admin. 15: Park Col, Parkville Mo 64152.

SMITH, HARRIET (EVELYN) WALLACE. b NYC 10 D 14. 5: Northwestern 32-36 (Geol) BS; UCal 36-37 (Geol); Columbia 38-39 (Tchg of Sci) MA; UIll 59-62 (LS) MS. 7: Tech asst dept Geol Sci UCal(Berkeley) 36-37; Steno Atha Wks Crucible Steel Co, Harrison NJ 40-41; Asst geol Gen Chem Div Allied Chem, NYC 41-46; Instr Dept Geol UTenn 47-48; Geol Corps of Engnrs US Army, Little Rock Ark 48-52; Tech asst Forestry Sect State Natural Hist Survey, Urbana Ill 53-54; Geol Carl A Bays & Assoc Inc, Urbana Ill 54-58; Geol libn UIll(Urbana) 62-. 9: ALA (Memb Chm Intl Rel RT); SLA; IllLA; Geosci Info Soc (org, 1st sec, 2nd pres). 10: AAUP; Sigma Delta Epsilon; AAUW. 14: Geol lit searching, ref, knowledge availability. 15: 1312 S Race st, Urbana Il 61801.

SMITH, HARRY P. b Johnson Co Iowa 18 F 1895. 5: UCal 13-16 (Liberal Arts) AB, 16-18 (Med Res) MS, 18-21 (Med) MD. 7: Asst instr, Asst prof, Prof Johns Hopkins, URochester, UIowa, Columbia U 21-60; Libn-archivist Amer Soc Clin Pathologists, Chicago 60-. 9: ALA; AMA; Amer Soc Exper Pathology; Amer Assn Path & Bact; Soc for Exper Biol & Med; Col of Amer Pathologists; Amer Soc of Clinical Pathologists. 10: Phi Beta Kappa; Alpha Omega Alpha. 13: Yes. 15: 710 S Wolcott ave, Chicago Il 60612.15489

SMITH, HAZEL (BOWKER). b Skaneateles NY 16 My 10. 4: Charles G Smith. 5: Alma Col 27-31 (Lat) AB; Syracuse U summer 37 (Fr); Pratt 39-40 BS in LS. 6: Fr, Ger. 7: Tchr Union Sch, Lysander NY 33-39; Lib asst Hunter Col 41-42; Lib asst pub lib, Stamford Conn 42-43; Queens Pub (Jamaica NY) Lib; Lib asst 43-47, Ref libn 47-54, Supv libn brs 55-. 9: NY Lib Club. 10: Queens Pub Lib Staff Assn. 14: Ref. 15: 40-18 Hampton st, Elmhurst NY 11373.

SMITH, HELEN S(PANGLER). b McDonough Co Ill 20 Ja 11. 5: West Ill U 27- (Elem Educ) BEd; UIll 47- (Educ) MEd; Rosary Col 66-67 (LS). 7: Elem tchr in rural & city schs of Ill 29-65; Child libn E Moline Pub Lib summers 56-59; Elem libn Evergreen Park Dist 124, Chicago 65-66; Jr high libn Sch Dist #105, LaGrange Ill 66-68; Sr high libn Sch Dist #172, Quincy Ill 68-. 9: ALA; -AASchL; NEA; IllLA; IllASchL (Bd mem 69-71); IllEA; CookCoTA (pres Dist #105 67-68). 10: AAUW. 14: Sch libnship, admin in sch & pub libs. 15: 1235 1/2 Kentucky, Quincy Il 62301.

SMITH, HENRY BRADFORD. b Philadelphia Penn 24 N 36. 4: Beverly Craft. 5: Hamilton Col 55-59 (Hist) AB; Cornell Law Sch 59-60 (Law); URochester 60-63 (Amer Hist) MA; Syracuse 65-69 MS in LS. 6: Fr. 07 Lib clk URochester circ dept 62-64, Chief lib clk 64-65, asst libn 65-66, Asst libn ref dept 66-; Tchr Batavia Jr High Sch, Batavia NY 64. 9: ALA; NYLA. 10: Amer Hist Assn. 13: Yes. 14: Ref, govt docs. 15: 74 Montaine park, rochester NY 14617.

SMITH (CONSTANCE) HOPE. b Southborough Kent Eng 14 My 23. 4: Sydney Howland Smith. 5: Ventura Jr Col 58-59 (Math); UCLA 59 (Math); San Jose State Col 59-62 (Soc Serv) BA; Syracuse U 62-63 MSLS. 6: Fr. 7: Sec/bkkeeper Halpern & Woolf, London England 41-43; Draftswoman Telecommunications Research Establishment, Malvern England 43-46; Verbatim reporter London Sch of Stenotyping London England 46-47; Sec A J Phillips & Co Birmingham England 48-49; Sec/bkkeeper Krishnamurti Writings London England & Ojai Cal 49-59; Ser catlgr UCal (Santa Barbara) 64-67, Hd order dept 68-. 9: Lib Assn (London); ALA; CalLA; Libns Assn, UCal (Santa Barbara); So Cal Tech Proc Gp. 10: Phi Kappa Phi; Beta Phi Mu; Sierra Club; Santa Barbara Braille Assn. 14: Catlg, acquis, automation. 15: 897 Camino Corto, Goleta Ca 93017.

SMITH, HOPE (SMALLEY). b Gladstone NJ 5 F 22. 4: James R Smith. 5: Beaver Col 39-44 9eng) BA; Columbia 45-46 (LS) BS. 6: Fr. 7: Asst libn Interchem Corp NYC 46-47; Acquis libn Naval Ordnance Test Sta, China Lake Cal 47-48, Catlg libn 48-51; Dir tech lib div Naval Civil Engring Lab, Port Hueneme Cal 51-. 8: Adv Bd, Sch of Lib Sci USoCal 66-68. 9: SLA (So Cal Chap: Sci-Tech Chm 52-53, v-pres 53-54, pres 54-55, Recr Chm 55-56, Awards Chm 64-66); CalLA (Col & Univ Libs Sect, So Div: sec 65, v-chm 66, chm 67). 10: Altrusa Club. 14: Admin. 15: 281 Mesa dr, Camarillo Ca 93010.

SMITH, HOWARD McQueen. b Charlotte NC 25 J119. 4: Elaine Wiefel. 5: UVa 37-41 (Eng) BA; UMich 41-42, 46-47 ABLS, MPA (Pub Admin). 7: USNR (Lieut) 42-46; Admin asst civics & soc dept Enoch Pratt Free Lib, Baltimore 47-49; Coordinaor of lib activities Richmond Area U Center, Richmond Va 49-50; Exec asst to dir Enoch Pratt Free Lib, Baltimore 50-53, Head films dept 53-55; Personnel off Free Lib of Phila 55-59; City Libn Richmond Pub Lib, Richmond Va 59-. 9: ALA; SELA; VaLA. 10: Rotary; Torch Club. 13: Yes. 14: Admin, personnel. 15: 4120 Hillcrest rd, Richmond Va 23225.

SMITH, HUGH (LUMMIS). b Sarnia Ont Can 29 Jl 25. 4: Barbara A Pettit. 5: UWest Ont 45-49 (Econ, Bus Admin) BA; UToronto 62-63 BLS. 7: Acquis libn UToronto Lib 63-64, Admin asst to chief libn 64-65; Libn Erindale Col UToronto (Clarkson) 66-. 9: CanLA (treas & dir 65-68; chm Budget & Fin Com 66-). 13: Yes. 14: Lib admin. 15: Glencairn ave, Toronto 12 Ont Can.

SMITH, INEZ JANE (WALLACE). b E St Louis Ill 6 O 16. 5: Sioux Falls Col 37, 41 (Educ); UMich 45 (Sp); Central Baptist Theol Sem 45 (Relig); Crozier Theol Sem 46 (Relig); Ft Valley State Col 56 (Educ) BS; AtlantaU 68 MSLS. 6: Lat, Sp, Fr. 7: Sec Hunt High Sch sci div Ft Valley State Col 57-59; Tchr & libn Bozeman Train Sch, Hawkinsville Ga 59; Libn Columbia Co Blancard Consolidated Sch 59-60, 60-61; Tchr & libn Richmond Co Jenkins Sch & Weed Sch, Augusta Ga 61-68, Libn A C Griggs Sch 67-69; Lib asst Paine Col 66-67. 9: ALA; NCTE; NEA; GaEA; GaLA; SELA. 10: NEA; YWCA; Alpha Kappa Mu. 14: Ref. 15: 1301 Steed st, Augusta Ga 30901.

SMITH, INISIOLA. b Milo Iowa 30 N 01. 5: William Penn Col 21-25 (Eng) AB; St Louis Lib Sch 26-27 Certif; UMich summers 35-37 AMLS. 7: Lib asst St Louis Pub Lib 27-28; Lib asst Grinnell Col 28-29; Libn Simpson Col 29-44; Libn William Penn Col 44-68, Consul & ref libn 68-. 9: ALA; IowaLA. 10: Delta Kappa Gamma. 14: Admin, ref. 15: 419 College, Oskaloosa Ia 52577.

SMITH, IRMA (HARRIS). b Fredericksburg Va 25 N 30. 4: Kenneth L Smith. 5: Va State Col 46-50 (LS) BS. 6: Fr, Sp. 7: Libn George Washington Carver High Sch, Fieldale Va 50-. 8: Vis com for eval of Secon sch 62. 9: NEA; ALA; VaEA; HenryCoTA. 14: Ref. 15: Route 4 Box 447, Martinsville Va 24112.

SMITH, IRVING KITCHEN. b Presque Isle Me 31 J112. 5: Aroostook State Tchrs Col 29-31; UMe 32-34 (Educ) BS(Ed), 38-41 (Agronomy) BS; Simmons 54-55 (LS) MS. 7: Tchr jr high schs, Me 34-38; Publ asst Lincoln Lab MIT 51-53; Documents asst USAF Cambridge Res Lab, Boston 53; A R Mann Lib, Cornell U; Asst circ libn 55-57, Asst acquislibn 57-60, Asst catlg-ref libn 60-64; Catlg libn Fla Atlantic U Lib 64-65, Ser libn 65-67; Ind State U sci libn 67-. 9: ALA; IndLA. 10: AAUP. 14: Data proc, biol scis, admin. 15: 200 Farrington-309, Terre Haute In 47807.

SMITH, J(ERRY) EDWARD. b Wellington Kan 20 F 36. 5: UOkla 55-58, 59-60 (Music) B Mus, 60-63 MLS. 6: Sp. 7: Lib asst UOkla 57-58; Asst ref libn Okla City Libs, Okla City Okla 60-63, 1st asst ref libn 63-64; Head of bkmob serv Okla Co Libs, Okla City Okla 64-66, Adult materials coord 66; Acquis libn & Hd tech serv New Orleans Pub Lib 67-68; Assoc dir Ingham Co Lib, Mason Mich 68-. 9: ALA; OklaLA; MichLA. 10: Phi Mu Alpha; Sinfonia. 14: Bk selection, tech serv. 15: 710 Oak st, E Lansing Mi 48823.

SMITH, JAMES HENDERSON. b Scotland 10 Ap 25. 4: Frances McGovern. 5: Champlain Col 46-48 (Liberal Arts) C 46-48 (Liberal Arts) Certif; NYU 48-50 (Eng) BSEd; UChicago 50-52 MALS. 6: Fr, Ger. 7: PhM USN 43-46; Tchr & libn Law Sch UChicago 51-52; Sch libn Ottawa Twp High Sch, Ottawa Ill 52-59; Dir instr materlak Highland Park High Sch, Highland Park Ill 59-66; Supv lib serv Dept of Educ, Pago Pago Amer Samoa 66-68; Asst Prof Dept of Lib Sci Appalachian State U 68-69; Supv lib serv Prince William Co Schs, Manassas Va 69-. 9: ALA; -AASchL; NEA-DAIV; IllASchL (Bd Dirs 57-58, treas 58-59; Asst Dir, Inst for Trng in Libnship, Appalachian State U 68-69. 10: Inst for Train in Libnship, Appalachian State U. 13: Yes. 14: Sch media spec. 15: Prince William County Schools PO Box 389, Manassas Va 22110.

SMITH, JAMES L. b Harrisonburg Va 27 Ap 37. 5: WVaU 55-60 (Recreation, LS) BS, summers 61-65 (LS) MA; UPittsburgh 68- (LS). 7: Hd libn & a-v chm Glen Burnie Sr High Sch, glen Burnie Md 60-67; Coord lib serv instr materials ctr & educ television Monongalia Co Bd of Educ, Morgantown W Va 67-; Instr lib sci WVaU 68-. 8: Bk Sel Com & In-Serv Panels & Curr Devel Com, Anne Arundel Bd of Educ, Md; Lib Curr Devel Com Chm & textbook Eval Com, Monongalis Co Bd of Educ; Adv Bd for WWVU-TV (W Va U) for Selecting Programs & Coord of WQED-TV (UPittsburgh) for Programming and In-Service Training. 9: NEA; ALA; ASCD; WVaEA; WVaASCD; WVaLA; WVaASchL; MdTA. 10: W Va U Alum Assn; Phi Delta Kappa. 13: Yes. 14: Lib supv, lib sci tchg, a-v materials. 15: 737 Ridgeway ave, Morgantown W Va 26505.

SMITH, JAMES LeROY. b Chicago 6 J128. 4: Marilyn Lea Deutsch. 5: Blackburn Col 51 (Educ) AA; Pestalozzi-Froebel 57-58 (Elem Educ) BEd; Chicago Tchrs Col 54-56 (LS) MEd; Rosary Col 57 (LS); E Ill U 65 (A-V) Mich State U 66 (Lib-Reading); No Ill U 64-67 (Curriculum). 7: RDSN-Electronics US Navy 46-48; Tchr & libn Pub Sch Dist III, Oak Lawn Ill 55-64; Lib coun Cicero Pub Schs Dist 99, Cicero Ill 64-. 8: Lib consul, Schaumburg Sch Dist #54 63-64; Consul, lib tech, Wilson Jr Col, chm Adv Com Devel of Lib Tech Prog, Morton Col, Cicero Ill 68-69. 9: ALA; NEA-DAVI; ASCD; Nat Elem Principal Assn; IllLA; IllSchL (mem Aud Com 69, Exhib chm 68); IllEA; Ill A-V Assn; CiceroEA; W Suburban Elem SchLA (pres 66-68). 10: Jr C of C; Blackburn Col Alum. 13: Yes. 14: Sch libs, lib tech. 15: 8700 S Sproat, Oak Lawn Il 60453.

SMITH, JAMES. b Toledo Ohio 27 My 28. 5: UToledo 46-50 (Bus) BBA; UIll 53-54 (LS) MS. 7: Jr libn Enoch Pratt Free Lib, Baltimore 54-56; Sr bus libn Newark Bus Lib, Newark NJ 57-59; Libn Haskins & Sells, NYC 59-68; Libn Debevoise, Plimpton, Lyons & Gates, NYC 68-. 9: SLA (NY Chap: treas & chm Bus & Fin Group 63-65); NY Lib Club. 14: Bus, ref. 15: Debevoise Plimpton Lyons & Gates, 320 Park ave, New York NY 10022.

SMITH, JANET. b Giles Co Tenn 6 N 32. 5: Martin Col 51-53 Diploma; Middle Tenn State U 53-55 (Eng) BS; Peabody 59-60 (LS) MA. 7: Bkmob libn Highland Rim Reg Lib, Murfreesboro Tenn 55-59; Asst reg libn Murfre4sboro Tenn 60-62; Reg libn Highland Rim Reg Lib, Murfreesboro Tenn 62-. 9: ALA; TennLA; SELA. 10: Beta Phi Mu; Phi Theta Kappa; Alpha Psi Omega; Tau Omicron; Delta Kappa Gamma; DAR. 14: Catlg, arch, geneal research, gen ref. 15: 2102 Mercury blvd, Murfreesboro Tn 37130.

SMITH, JEAN (ELIZABETH). b Indiana Penn 25 Ap 30. 5: Stephens Col 48-50 AA; Richmond Prof Inst of Col of William & Mary 50-52 (Art) BFA; Rutgers 59-61 MLS. 6: Ger, Fr. 7: Art consul Richmond Pub Schs, Richmond Va 52-59; Libn trainee Newark Pub Lib, Newark NJ 60; Asst art libn Smith

Col 61-64; Arts libn Penn State U Lib 64-. 9: ALA; MusLA. 10: AAUW. 14: Ref, bk sel (arts). 15: 947 Old Boalsburg rd, State College Penn 18601.

SMITH, JEAN CHANDLER. b Phila 13 Ap 18. 5: Bryn Mawr 35-39 (Span Lit) AB; Yale 49-53 (Zool) MS; Catholic U 56-59 (LS. 6: Fr, Sp, Ger. 7: Circ asst & ref libn DC Pub Lib 39-42; Tr US Off of Censorship, CZ Panama 43-44; Libn Kaneohe Naval Air Sta, Kaneohe Oahu Hawaii 44-46; Ref asst to asst ref libn & research asst Yale U Lib 47-58; Act chief acquis & ref libn Nat Inst of Health, Bethesda Md 59-63; Chief ref serv br Dept of the Interior Lib, Wash DC 63-65; Asst libn Smithsonian Inst, Wash DC 65-. 9: ALA; SLA (treas Wash DC Chap); ASIS; Conn Acad of Arts & Scis; Amer Soc of Limnology & Oceanography; DCLA (Program Chm Biol Scis Group of DC Chap). 13: Yes. 14: Ref, bibliog zool). 15: 3601 Connecticut ave NW, Wash DC 20008.

SMITH, JESSIE (CARNEY). b Greensboro NC 24 S 30. 5: NC A&T Col 46-50 (Home Econ) BS; Cornell U 50 (Textiles, Clothing); Mich State U 55-56 (Child Development) MA; Peabody 56-57 (LS) AMLS; UIll 60-64 (LS) PhD. 6: Fr, Ger. 7: Catlgr & Instr in Lib Sci A&I State U 57-60; Tchg asst UIll(Urbana) 61-63; Coordinator of Lib Serv A&I State U 64-65; U Libn & Prof Fisk U 65-. 8: Lib consul So Assn Cols & Schs 67-; Assoc dir Wkshop & Internship Program for Libns in Predominantly Negro Cols sponsored by Ford Foundation of AtlantaU 68-69. 9: ALA (Nominating Com 66-67; Ad Hoc Com on Opportunities for Negro Students in Lib Prof 66-; Spec Com on Nat Manpower Programs 67-68);-ACRL (Com on Appointments 68; Nominating Com 69; Com on Grants 68-70); SELA (Nominating Com Col & Univ Sect 65-66); TennLA (Lib Recruitment Netwk 65-; v-chm & chm-elect Col Sect 68-69). 10: Alpha Kappa Alpha; Hubbard Hosp (Nashville) Auxiiary; Beta Phi Mu; Pi Gamma Mu. 11: Fellowship from Coun on Lib Resources 69. 14: Admin, catlg. 15: 1813 - 25th ave N, Nashville Tn 37208.

SMITH, JEWELL GRACE (MINOR). b St Joseph Mo 11 Ap 22. 5: St Joseph Jr Col (Mo) 39-40; William Jewell Col 40-44 (Eng) AB; Tex Woman's U 61-62 MLS. 7: Tchr Eng, Lat Horton High Sch, Horton Kan 45-47; Tchr-libn Hiawatha High Sch, Hiawatha Kan 48-49; Sec CB&Q RR, St Joseph Mo 50-51; Sec-steno US Govt, Offutt AFB Neb 51-52; Tchr libn Weston High Sch, Weston Mo 53-54, Sabetha High 54-56, Mansfield High Sch, Mansfield Mo 56-59, Cabool High Sch, Cabool Mo 59-61; Ref libn adult serv libn Daniel Boone Reg, Columbia Mo 62-65; Ref libn Ozark Pioneer Lib System, Springfield Mo 65-67; Asst libn Springfield-Greene Co Libs, Springfield Mo 67-. 9: ALA; MoLA (pres Pub Lib Div). 10: Quota Internat; LWV. 13: Yes. 14: Ref. 15: 3162 Alphine, Springfield Mo 65804.

SMITH, JO THERESE. b Chicago 25 O 28. 5: UTex 47-50 (Chem); UWis 50-51 (Chem) BS; Mich State U 53-54 (Chem; UTex 54-56 (Chem); Rutgers 67-69 (Data Processing). 6: Ger, Ital. 7: Org chem Baxter Labs, Morton Grove Ill 52-53; Lab instr & Res asst Mich State U & UTex 53-55; Res chem Monsanto Chem Co, Texs City Tex 56-58; Org chem Alcon Labs Inc, Ft Worth Tex 58-60; Lit chem Mobil Chem Co, Metuchen NJ 60-63; Ed asst Gaylord Assoc Inc, Newark NJ 63; Res asst Nat Acad Sci, Wash DC 63-65; Self-employed tech info, Wash DC 65; Tech libn Lever Bros Co, Edgewater NJ 65-66; Tech libn Tenneco Chems Inc, Piscataway NJ 66-67; Chief tech libn Witco Chem Corp, Oakland NJ 67-. 9: SLA; ASIS; ARMA. 10: AAAS; Alpha Chi; ACS. 13: Yes. 14: Info retrieval syst design, recs mgt program design, lib org & admin. 15: 404 Palisade ave, Cliffside Park NJ 07010.

SMITH, JOHN BREWSTER. b Bryan Tex 26 Je 37. 4: Ida Hawa. 5: Tex A&M U 55-60 (Eng) BA; Columbia 60-63 (LS) MS, Law Sch 64-66 (Law). 6: Sp. 7: Columbia U Law Lib: Asst circ libn 60-62, Circ libn 62-64, Asst libn in chg of readers serv 64-65, Asst law libn 65-66; Asst dir pub serv Tex A & M Univ 66-. 9: ALA; AALL;Law Lib Assn Greater NY; Assn of Law Libs, Upstate NY; TexLA; SWLA. 12: Asst Bk Rev Ed "Law Library Journal" (63-66). 14: Admin. 15: 316 Suffolk st, College Station Tx 77840.

SMITH, JOHN EDWIN. b San Francisco 28 Ja 17. 4: Lucille Tomlin. 5: UCLA 34-39 (Pol Sci) BA; UCal(Berkeley) 39-40 Certif in Libnship. 6: Fr. 7: Ref asst Lib Assn of Portland, Ore 40-41; Jr libn USDA, Wash DC 41-42; US Army; Tech Sgt Med Dept 42-45; Head Acquis Dept UCLA 46-51; City & Co libn Santa Barbara Cal Pub Lib 52-61; Lib adv USoCal Proj, Karachi Pakistan 61-63; U Libn UCal(Irvine) 63-. 9: ALA; CalLA (chm Intel Freedom Com 50-51, chm Ed Com 64, pres So Dist 54, pres Col, Univ & Research Lib Sect 68). 10: ACLU. 13: Yes. 14: Admin, acquis. 15: 1631 Pegasus st, Santa Ana Ca 92707.

SMITH, JOHN WAYNE. b Barberton Ohio 26 S 36. 5: Tex West Col 60-64 (Bus) BBA; UDenver 64-65 (LS) MA. 6: Sp. 7: Apprentice jeweler Graves J Malone Mfg Co, El Paso Tex 51-54; Fire control tech 2/c US Navy USS Cushing, DD-797, Cal 56-60; Exec trainee Sears Roebuck & Co, El Paso Tex 60-62; Lib asst Tex West Col Lib 64, Loan libn 65-67; Asst dir El Paso Pub Lib, El Paso Tex 67. 9: ALA; TexLA; Border RegLA (pres 69). 10: E P Riding & Driving Club. 14: Ref, research, admin. 15: P O Box 12224, El Paso Tex 79912.

SMITH, BROTHER J(OSEPH) PETER FRANCIS S(EBASTIAN). b NYC 25 Ja 19. 5: Fordham 36-47 (Elem Educ) BS; Laval U 46-50 (Fr); Columbia 63- (LS) MS. 6: Fr, Sp, Ger, Lat, Gk. 7: Tchr; St Bonaventures Col (Can) 38-45, Power Mem Acad, NYC 45-51, Blessed Sacrament High Sch, New Rochelle NY 51-52; Lib asst Iona Col 52-58; Lib asst Bergen Catholc High Sch, Oradell NJ 58-. 14: All-boy high sch libs. 15: 1040 Oradell ave, Oradell NJ 07649.

SMITH, JOYCE E. b Englewood NJ 1 Ag 39. 5: HowardU 57-61 (Eng) BA; AtlantaU 65-66 MSLS. 6: Fr. 7: Sub tchr NJ Bd of Educ, Englewood 62; Compilation clk Pacific Tele Co, Los Angeles 62-63; Comptometer operator Robinson's Dept Store, Los Angeles 63-64; Lib asst Los Angeles Co Lib 64; Lib asst I W A Clark Mem Lib, Los Angeles 64-65; Supv ref libn Med-Dental Lib HowardU 66-. 9: SLA (Biol Div). 10: Beta Phi Mu. 14: Ref, admin, rare bks (med or sci), law, tech. 15: 1669 Columbia rd NW 203, Washington DC 20009.

SMITH, JUANITA J. b Muncie Ind 11 Je 23. 5: Ball StateU 40-41, 42-45 (Bus Educ, Hist) BS in Ed; UMich 50-51, 58 (LS) AMLS. 6: Fr. 7: Tchr Indianapolis Pub Schs 45-46; Sec Ball StateU 46-49; Libn asst in catlg & asst prof Ball StateU 49-. 9: ALA; IndLA; OhioValley Reg Gp Tech Serv Libns. 10: LWV; AAUW; AAUP; Delta Kappa Gamma. 14: Catlg. 15: 620 N McKinley, Muncie In 47303.

SMITH, JUDITH K(AY) (MILLER). b Olney Ill 27 O 45. 4: Jeffory L Smith. 5: Olney Commun 63-65 (Liberal Arts) AS; Murray State 65-67 (LS, Pol Sci) BS. 6: Sp. 7: Libn Mooresville Consolidated High Sch, Mooresville Ind 67-68; Libn Larue D Carter Memorial Hosp, Indianapolis 68-. 8: Conducting in-serv train for employees of state instl libs (med libs) May 69. 9: ChurchLA; IndSchLA. 14: Catlg, ref. 15: 4925 W 15th, Speedway In 46224.

SMITH, JUNE (SMECK). b Detroit 9 Je 17. 4: Hannis Smith. 5: Wayne State U 35-39 (Eng, Pol Sci) BA; UMich 39-40 ABLS; Chicago 49, 51 (LS) MA. 7: Jr lib asst Detroit Pub Lib 40-43; Ordnance planner (Lt jg) US Navy Bur of OrJnance, Wash DC 43-45; Head catlg Jg j) US Navy Bur of Ordnance Lib, Wash DC 45-46; Sr libn Detroit Pub Lib 46-48, 50; Libn State Dept StateDept of Archives & Hist, Jackson Miss 50-52; Libn Amer Fed of State Co & Mun Employees, Madison Wis 52; Head tech processes Lib Dept pub schs, Madison Wis 53-56; Col of ST Catherine Dept of Lib Instr 56-58, Instr56-58, Asst Prof & readers serv libn 59-62, Assoc Prof & Chm 62-. 8: Evaluator, 5 gen encyclopedias for Field Enterprises Educ Corp 64, Our Lady of Peace High Sch, St Paul 64, Benilde High Sch, St Louis Park Minn 65.0 9: ALA-AHIL (Exec Bd 67-69); CathLA (Adv Bd; chm Scholarship Com; sec-treas Lib Educ Sect); SLA; ASIS; MinnLA; MinnASchL. 10: AAUP; LWV. 12: "The Relationship between the Titles Circulated and Titles Held in Branches of a Metropolitan Library System (51); "The Library Staff (62); "Librarianship: A Lively Career (65). 13: Yes. 14: Lib educ, personnel. 15: Col of St Catherine, 2004 Randolph ave, St Paul Mn 55116.

SMITH, KATHARINE ELIZABETH. b Santa Ana Cal 15 Ap 43. 5: Orange Coast Jr Col 61-63 (Liberal Arts) AA; UCLA 63-65 (Eng) BA, 68-69 MLS; Cal State Co (Los Angeles) 65-66 (Eng). 7: Ser coord lib asst I & II col lib UCLA 67-68, Ref asst 68-. 9: ALA; CalLA. 14: Ref. 15: 1951 47th st, San Diego Ca 92102.

SMITH, LaMAR RALPH. b Logan Utah 12 S 23. 4: Ruth Mae Armstrong. 5: UNev 46-50 (Hist) BA; UCopenhagen summer 50 (Scandinavian Culture & Hist); USan Jose fall 50 (Art); UOkla 54-55 MLS. 6: Sp. 7: Time off supv W P McNeal Co Ltd, Hawthorne Nev 42-43; US Army Field Artillery Instrument & Survey Sect T/5 43-45; Teller Security Nat Bank, Reno Nev 51; Merchandise assoc J C Penney, Reno Nev 51-53; UNev: Asst libn res bk room 53-54, Circ libn 55-64, Educ libn 64-. 8: Chm Nat Lib Week, Nev 67; CAP-AF Adv for Aerospace Educ for Nev 68-. 9: ALA (life mem; Recr Com 58-61); NevLA (chm NW Dist 56-57, chm Recr Com 60-61, Aud Com 60-63, Authors Com 63-64). 10: Air Force Reserve. 14: Educ, ref, child bks. 15: 1201 Ralston st, Reno Nv 89503.

SMITH, LAURA DUCLOS. b Hollywood Cal 13 Jl 30. 5: UCLA 48-52 (Sociol) BA; USoCal 61-62 MS in LS; Cal State (LA) 66-68 MA in Amer Studies. 7: Readers adv Pomona Pub Lib, Pomona Cal 62-64; Asst ref libn Cal State Polytech Col 64-. 9: CalLA. 10: Beta Phi Mu; Phi Kappa Phi. 14: Col ref. 15: Cal State Polytech Col, Pomona Cal 91766.

SMITH, LAURA JEAN. b Shelbyville Ky 4 Mr 29. 5: Centre Col 46-50 (Fr) BA; UIll 53-55 (LS) MS. 7: Recruiting off USAF, Houston 51-53; Catlg asst UIll Lib (Urbana) 55-56; Ref dept Louisville Free Pub Lib, Louisville Ky 56-60; Ref dept Albuquerque Pub Lib 60-63; Hd soc sci div Dayton & Montgomery Co Pub Lib, Dayton Ohio 63-. 9: ALA; OhioLA. 10: Air Force Res; Montgomery Co Hist Soc. 14: Ref. 15: 360 Kenwood ave, Dayton Oh 45405.

SMITH, LEONARD ALLEN. b Salem Ore 13 Ag 32. 4: Mary Lonnberg. 5: Linfield Col 50-54 (Chem) BA; UCal(Berkeley) 65-66 MLS. 6: Fr. 7: Chem (Cpl) US Army Ordinance, Oppama Japan 55-56; Research chem Standard Oil Co, San Francisco 56-58; Chief chem Spreckles Sugar Co, Salinas Cal 58-65; Sci libn UCal Lib (Santa Cruz) 66-. 9: ALA. 14: Ref. 15: 121 9th ave, Santa Cruz Ca 95060.

SMITH, LESTER K. b San Diego Cal 23 Jl 25. 5: San Diego State Col 45-49 (Art) BA; USoCal 56-57 MSLS, 67- (LS). 7: Hd Humanities Div San Diego State Col Lib 57-67. 9: ALA; CalLA. 10: ACLU; Libraria Sodalitas. 14: Ref, admin, lib design & planning. 15: 2719 S Hoover st, Los Angeles Ca 90007.

SMITH, LESTER WAYLAND. b Buffalo NY 27 Ap 17. 5: UBuffalo 35-39 (Hist, Govt) AB, 39-40 (Hist, Philos); Columbia 40-41, 45 BS in LS. 6: Fr. 7: Jr archivist, Asst archivist, Assoc archivist Nat Archives, Wash DC 41-46, Libn 46-57; Chief of Res, Asst dir, Assoc dir Buffalo & Erie Co Hist Soc, Buffalo NY 58-. 9: SAA (Fellow; Ed Bd 64-; chm Com on Bibliog 47-57); ALA; Amer Assn for State & Loc Hist. 10: Phi Beta Kappa; Lit Clinic of Buffalo; Civil War Round Table; West NY Lib Resources Coun (sec 69). 12: "Preliminary List of Published & Unpublished Reports of The National Resources Planning Board" (46); Ed "Niagara Frontier," (quar journ of Buffalo & Erie Co Hist Soc); "Guide to the Microfilm Edition of the Papers of Peter B Porter" (68). 13: Yes. 14: Archives & mss, archival bibliog, Govt doc bibliog, admin. 15: 355 Bird ave, Buffalo NY 14213.

SMITH, LOIS (WILSON). b Terry Mont 21 N 18. 4: Winfield Davis Smith. 5: Guilford Col 35-39 (Fr) AB; UNC summers 39-43 BS in LS; USoCal summer 66 (LS). 6: Fr. 7: Tchr-libn Draper High Sch, Draper NC 40-43; Libn Gastonia High Sch, Gastonia NC 43-47, Weston High Sch, Weston Mass 47-48, Gibbes Jr High Sch, Columbia SC 58-62, Keenan Jr High Sch, Columbia SC 63-67; Gaffney High Sch, Gaffney SC 67-69, Columbia High Sch, Columbia SC 69-. 9: NEA; SCLA; SCEA. 10: AAUW. 14: Jr high sch libs. 15: 115 Shadow lane, Cayce SC 29033.

SMITH, LOIS MURDOUGH. b Boston 10 S 10. 4: Charles Duryea Sith III. 5: Simmons 28-30 (Eng), 31-32 BS; Tex Tech Col 30-31 (Eng). 6: Ger, Fr. 7: Asst Off of Supv of Childs Lib NY Pub Lib 32-33; Child libn NY Pub Lib 33-37; Child libn David A Howe Pub Lib, Wellsville NY 37-40; Lib asst SUNY (NY State Col of Ceramics Alfred U 49-57, Asst libn 57-66, Assoc libn 66-. 8: Org child lib David Howe Lib, Wellsville NY 37-38. 9: NYLA (chm Program Com of Child Sect 39). ; ALA. 10: Wee Playhouse, Alfred NY; Alfred Univ Womens Club. 14: Catlg, ref, art. 15: Box 1354, Alfred NY 14802.

SMITH, LOUISE (WILLIAMS). URANT Okla 22 S 09. 5: SEast State Col (Durant Okla) 25-27, summer 29 AB; So MethodistU 27-29 BM; Cincinnati Col Music 29-30; Columbia 35-36 (Educ); Tex WomansU 59-60 MLS. 7: Music tchr Murray State Sch, Tishomingo Okla 31-35, NEast State Col (Talequah Okla) 36-37; Supt music E Rutherford (NJ) Pub Schs 57-59; Circ asst Fondren Lib So MethodistU 60-63, Undergrad libn 63-. 9: TexLA; SWLA. 15: 6835 Deloache, Dallas Tx 75205.

SMITH, LOUISE. b Chicago 7 Je 05. 5: Knox Col 23-27 (Psych) BS; UIll 37-38 BS in LS. 7: Circ & ref asst pub lib, Galesburg Ill 33-37; Catlgr Colo State Col 38-40; Beloit Col Lib Tech Serv libn 40-43, Assoc libn 43-48, Act libn 48-50; Adult Serv libn Pub Lib, Okla City Okla 50-61; Asst dir Pub Lib, San Antonio Tex 61-. 9: ALA; SWLA; OklaLA; TexLA; SWLA (sec Pub Lib Sect 58-60). 12: Assoc ed "Review Index" (41); Ed "Oklahoma Librarian" (60-61). 14: Admin, pub serv. 15: 7711 Broadway apt 22C, San Antonio Tx 78209.

SMITH, LUCILE (BURFORD). b Cookville Tex 10 O 06. 5: Tex Womans Col 23-27 (Hist) BA; Tex Womans U 50-52 BS in LS; E Tex State U 63-65 MS in LS. 7: Tchr pub schs: Omaha Tex 27-30, Daingerfield Tex 30-33, Kilgore Tex 33-50; Lib asst in catl dept Ft Lewis Col summer 64; Lib asst in catlg dept Tempe Pub Lib, Tempe Ariz summer 65; Libn Kilgore Jr High Sch, Kilgore Tex 50-67; Catlgr Ft Lewis Col 67-. 9: ALA; ColLA. 10: DAR; Durango LWV; Ft Lewis Women's Club. 14: Catlg, ref, circ. 15: Box 771, Durango Co 81301.

SMITH, LYNN SUZANNE. b Honolulu Hawaii 30 S 45. 5: URedlands 63-67 (Eng) BA; UCLA 67-68 MLS. 6: Ger. 7: File clk Smith & Assoc Inc Engrs, Honolulu summers 62-66; Wardrobe mistress URedlands Drama Dept 64-67; Reader for blind studs: Dept of Voc rehabilitation, State of Cal 68-, UCLA ; Asst ser libn UCal (Riverside) 68-. 9: ALA. 10: UCal Lib Schs Alum Assn. 14: Catlg, ref, readers serv, ser. 15: 1806 Loma Vista st apt I, Riverside Ca 92507.

SMITH, MADALYN S. b Burlington Vt 28 Jl21. 5: Heidelberg Col 46-50 (Lang) AB; Rochester Inst of Tech 55-58 (Mgt) AAS; West Res summer 60, & 61-62 MS in LS. 6: Lat, Fr, Sp, Ital, Portu, Ger. 7: Gen clerical Kodak Park Eastman Kodak Co, Rochester NY 41-44, Foreign & Domestic Sales 44-61; Libn Strasenburgh Pharmaceuticals, Rochester NY 62; Acquis libn Milne Lib SUNY(Geneseo) 63-68; Catlgr reclsf Colgate/Rochester Divinity Sch (NY) 68-69; Asst libn Commun Col of the Finger Lakes 69-. 9: ALA-ACRL; SLA (Museum Div); MedLA; Upstate NY Med Libns; NYLA; MusLA West NY. 10: Rochester Civic Music Assn; Planned Parenthood. 14: Mus libnship, acquis, ref, fine arts. 15: 1028 Winton rd N, Rochester NY 14609.

SMITH, MAE B. b Hardwick Ga 26 Je 07. 4: Royce Smith. 5: Womans Col of Ga 25-27 (Home Econ) BS. 7: Eng tchr Midway Elem Sch, Midway Ga 37-4; Eng tchr Ga Mil Col 40-55; Libn May Vinson Mem Lib, Milledgeville Ga 58-. 9: ALA; GaLA. 10: Trustee, Mary Vinson Mem Lib DAR. 13: Yes. 15: 1614 Pine Valley rd, Milledgeville Ga 31061.

SMITH, MARGARET (NICHOL). b Rapid City S Dak 8 F 18. 5: Oberlin 36-40 (Sociol) BA; Bryn Mawr 43-45 Certif; Drexel 63-65 MSLS. 7: School libn Upper Perkiomen High Sch, E Greenville Penn 63-67; Catlgr LehighU 68, Acquis libn 68-. 9: ALA. 14: Acquis. 15: 202 Main st, Pennsburg Pa 18073.

SMITH, MARGARET ELLEN (BROOKS). b Portland Me 23 O 40. 4: David Hibbard Smith. 5: UMe (Orono) 63 (Psych, Ger) AB; Simmons 66 (LS) MS. 6: Lat, Fr, Ger. 7: Camp coun & swimming instr summers 55-58; Desk clk-receptionist Ontio Hotel, Ogunquit Me summers 59-61; Remotivation group therapist Amer Friends Serv Committee, Lakeland Ky summer 62; Hat saleswoman & waitress, Portland Me summer 63; Pre-prof libn Y-a Boston pub Lib 63-66; Ext libn Daniel Boone Reg Lib, Columbia Mo 66-. 8: A-V Com, Boston Pub Lib 64-65; Tchr Mo State Lib Summer Inst "The Library and the Community" 68. 9: ALA (Coun; Jr Mem RT); -ACRL (ULS Ext Lib Serv Com 68-69); NELA; MassLA (YA Bk Review Com); MoLA, (chm Adult Educ Com 67-69, Jr Memb RT, Recr Com); BooneCo (Mo) Adult Educ Assn. 10: Girl Scout Leader; Beta Sigma Phi; Boone Co Coun of Related Agencies; UMo Coop Ext Cou; LWV; Boone Co Citizens Health Com. 13: Yes. 14: Adult educ, hosp, exten, gp serv. 15: 1306 Wilson, Columbia Mo 65201.

SMITH , MARIAN (BRAINARD). b Fairbury Neb 18 Jl15. 4: Dale W Smith. 5: Cottey Jr Col 32-34 AA; UNeb 34-37 (Eng) AB; Columbia 37-38 BSLS; UWis 55-57. 6: Fr. 7: Lib asst UOmaha 38-40; Sec to ed UWis Press 40-42; Asst libn Wisconsin High Sch, UWis 56-59; Lib supv Middletown State Graded Sch System, Middleton Wis 58-. 9: NEA; WisEA; WisLA; SWEA; MEA. 10: Alpha Chi Omega; PEO. 15: 6413 Mendota ave, Middleton Wis 53562.

SMITH, MARIAN J. b Brooklyn NY 21 N 41. 5: St Bonaventure 59-63 (Hist) BA; SUNY (Albany) 63-64 MLS. 6: Fr. 7: Catlgr Siena Col 64-67; Specialist lit searching GE Co, Schenectady NY 67-. 9: SLA. 14: Catlg, ref. 15: Main Lib General Electric Co, Schenectady NY 12305.

SMITH, MARILYNN (KNOWLTON). b Indianapolis Ind 1 My 15. 5: Butler U 32-36 (Sociol, Lat) BA; UColo 49-52 (Sociol) MA; Columbia 62-64 (LS) MS. 7: Girl Scout Coun; Exec sec, Richmond Ind 37-39, Field sec, Ft Wayne Ind 39-41, Exec sec, Fond du Lac Wis 41, Field off sec, Salt Lake City 42-43; Med sec, lab asst Dr Middleton, Salt Lake City 43-44; Tec/5 med steno WAC, Denver, Heidelberg (Germany) 44-46; Clerk-steno US Armed Forces, Heidelberg Germany 46-49; Sec

Nat Coun Episcopal Church, NYC 52-54; Sec Gen Electric Co, NYC 54-55, Clerk-steno staff judge advocate, Ft Stewart Ga 56; Statistical clerk Bd of Educ, Cincinnati 57-59; Clerk-steno div Civilian Personnel 1st US Army, NYC 61-62; Libn trainee Gen Theol Sem (NYC) 62-64; Asst catlgr SUNY(Stony Brook) 64-66; Ref libn & bibliogr US Mil Acad Lib, W Point NY 66-. 9: NY Tech Serv Libns Assn; Relig Libns Group NY Area (v-chm 65-66, chm 66-67); ALA; SLA. 14: Ref. 15: Pine ter, Highland Falls NY 10928.

SMITH, MARION M(cGILL) (MRS). b St Louis 2 F 14. 5: UMont 34-37 LS, 38 (LS) BA; George Washington U 37-38 (LS); UMont 38 BA; Columbus Law Sch 40 (Legal Bibliog). 6: Fr, Ger. 7: Head libn Nat Labor Rel Bd, Wash DC 38-44; Washington Ed Research Inst of Amer, Wash DC 44; Research ed Nat Mediation Bd, Wash DC 48; Act libn Grad Sch of Bus, Stanford Cal 53-54; Chief circ libn Stanford U Libs 54-57; Dir J Hugh Jackson Lib Grad Sch of Bus Stanford U 57-. 8: Consul, Menlo Jr Col Bus Lib, Menlo Cal. 9: ALA; ASIS; SLA (sec & memb chm Bus & Finance Div 63-64; McKinsey Foundation Awards Com 63-65); CalLA (Dir San Francisco Bay Area Reg, Pub Rel 64-65, pres Bus & Tech Div 67-68). 12: Ed "Washington News Letter" Research Inst of Amer. 13: Yes. 14: Admin. 15: 819 Esplanada way, Stanford Cal 94305.

SMITH, MARVIN EUGENE. b Los Angeles 14 Ap 36. 4: Millicent Claire Levy. 5: Los Angeles City Col 54-56 (Hist); UCLA 56-58 (Geog) BA; USoCal 58-62 MS LS. 6: Fr, Ger. 7: Libn Hughes Aircraft, Culver City Cal 58-59; US Army UN Command, Seoul Korea Sp 4/c 59-61; Libn Cal State Col (Los Angeles) 61-62; Libn US Peace Corps, Kingston Jamaica 62-63; Libn Los Angeles Co Pub Lib Insts, Los Angeles 63-64; Community libn Los Angeles Co Pub Lib, Temple City Cal 64-66; Hd acquis dept Cal State Polytech Col 66-68; Asst lib dir Riverside Pub Lib/Riverside Co Free Lib, Riverside Cal 68-. 9: CalLA. 10: Sierra Club; SW Museum Assn. 14: Catlg, supv, admin. 15: 601 Windsor rd, Arcadia Cal 91006.

SMITH, MARY (HUNT). b Anderson SC 16 J123. 4: Arthur Allen Smith. 5: Lander Col 41-42 (Sci); Spartanburg Jr Col 42-43 (Sci) AA; E Tex State U 53-56 (LS, Hist) BS(LS); Fla State U 65 (LS). 6: Fr. 7: Tchr Laurel Creek Elem Sch, Greenville SC 47-48; Asst med records Doctors Hosp, Coral Gables Fla 48-49; Med records libn U Hosp, Sewanee Tenn 49-52; Med records libn Hopkins Co Hosp, Sulphur Springs Tex 54-55; Tchr Colin Eng Elem Sch, Ft Myers Fla 56-57, Tchr Dir of Lib 61-64; Dir reading clinic Cypress Lakes Jr-Sr High Sch, Ft Myers Fla summer 64; Lib serv Martin Co schs, Stuart Fla 64-67; Libn Murray 9th Grade Sch, Stuart Fla 67-68; Libn Stuart 7th-8th Grade Sch, Stuart Fla 69-. 8: Spec consul sch lib devel, Lee Co Fla 61-63. 9: Assn Childhood Educ Internat (Lib Com Lee City Chap 63-64); FlaEA; Fla Assn for Supv & Curr Devel; FlaASchL. 10: AAUW; Stuart Garden Club. 14: Libs (marine biol). 15: 512 Cortez ave, Stuart Fla 33494.

SMITH, MARY ELIZABETH (SULLIVAN). b NYC 11 My 38. 4: David N Smith. 5: St LawrenceU 56-60 (Eng) BA; Simmons 66-68 (LS) MS. 6: Sp. 7: Bibliog searcher UNC Lib (Chapel Hill) 61-63; Asst libn Attma Du BelloU, Zaria N Nigeria 63-64; Asst libn Kaduna Reg Lib, Kaduda N Nigeria 64-65; Bibliog searcher Syracuse U summer 65; Gifts & exchange asst Vassar Lib 66; Lib asst Littauer Lib Harvard U 60-61, Photographic ref asst Widener Lib 66-68, Ref libn 68-. 14: Ref, acquis. 15: 30 Fernald dr, Cambridge Ma 02138.

SMITH, MARYE JO (GREEN). b Palestine Tex 29 My 10. 5: Sam Houston State Col 37 (Music, Hist) BA; Tex Womans U 49 BS in LS, 52 MLS. 6: Fr. 7: Pub sch music tchr: Cayuga Tex 39-40, Woodhouse Sch, Palestine Tex 41-46; Libn Palestine High Sch, Palestine Tex 46-57; Consul lib serv Cass Co schs, Linden Tex 57-59; Dir of Lib Panola Col 59-61; Head Libn Hogg Jr High Sch, Houston Ind Sch 62-. 9: ALA; NEA; TexLA; SWLA (Nomin Com 64); Tex State Tchrs Assn. 10: Delta Kappa Gamma; Bus & Prof Women; Beta Sigma Phi; DAR; Magna Charta Dames. 14: Readers guidance, non-printed materials. 15: 2415 Mimosa, apt H-1, Houston Tex 77019.

SMITH, MAURICE H. b Danville Ill 16 Ag 05. 4: Cara Davis Smith. 5: Purdue 22-24 (Sci); Ind U 24-26, 29-30 (Eng) AB; Columbia 34-42 MLS. 6: Fr, Ger. 7: Asst libn Cooper Union 35-42; Libn Inst of the Aeronautical Scis, NYC 42-51: Libn Forrestal Campus Lib Princeton U 51-. 8: Consul Naval Air Devel Center, Johnsville Penn 52. 9: SLA (Conv Chm Sci-Tech Div 52); ASIS; ADI; Amer Inst of Aeronautics & Astronautics. 12: Assoc ed "Technical Literature Digest in "ARS Journal" (52-62); Assoc ed "Aeronautical Engineering Index (47-50). 13: Yes. 14: Ref (aerospace scis). 15: Forrestal Campus Lib, Princeton Univ, Princeton NJ 08540.

SMITH, MILDRED (MYRICK). b Nassau Co Fla 3 Ag 10. 4: James Franklin Smith. 5: Fla State U 29-32 (LS) BS in Ed: George Washington U 53-54, summers 61, 62; UVa 67-68. 7: Proof reader "Sanford Herald, Sanford Fla 28-29, Reporter summer 32; Tchr Nassau Co pub schs, Callahan Fla 32-35; Clerk US Gen Accounting Off, Wash DC 35-36; Clerk US Dept of Com, Wash DC 36-37; Libn mun ref serv US Dept of Com, Wash DC 37-45; Elem sch libn Arlington Co (Va) pub schs 52-. 9: ALA-AAchL; NEA; Assn Childhood Educ Internat: VaLA; VaEA. 10: Delta Kappa Gamma; PTA; ArlingtonEA. 12: "The Secret Three (63); "Ants Are Fun" (68). 13: Yes. 14: Child bks. 15: 668 S Harrison st, Arlington Va 22204.

SMITH, MILDRED LeMAI. b Grand Bay Ala 5 Mr 02. 5: UAla 40 (Elem Educ) BS, 54 (LS) MA. 7: Tchr Mobile pub schs, Mobile Ala 24-40; Supv WPA Adult Educ & Nursery Schs, Mobile Ala 40-42; Supv Train Film Lib Brookley AFB, Mobile Ala 42-47; Libn C F Vigor High Sch, Mobile Ala 47-56; Supv materials center Mobile pub schs, Mobile Ala 56-63, SUPV SCH LIB SERV 63-. 8: Tchr, lib sci class at U So Ala, 65. 9: ALA; NEA; AlaEA (past pres Sch Lib Sect); AlaLA (pres-elect Child & Sch Lib Div). 10: Delta Kappa Gamma; PEO. 13: Yes. 14: Sch lib serv. 15: 210-D DeSales ave, Mobile Al 36607.

SMITH, MORENE (DUMAS). b El Dorado Ark 6 My 05. 5: Ouachita Col 22-26 (Eng, Soc Studies) AB; UIll summers 26 & 30, spring 32 BLS; Columbia summer 27. 6: Fr. 7: Libn El Dorado High Sch, El Dorado Ark 26-29, 47-; Asst libn Ark Lib Commsn, Little Rock 30-31; Libn Union Co Lib, El Dorado Ark 40-41; Libn Ouachita Col 45-47. 8: Summer tchg undergradlib sci Southern State Col 49-50, 67-68. 9: ALA (Subscription Bk Com); ArkLA (sec). 10: Univ Women; Pilot Info; LWV. 13: Yes. 14: Bks for yp, materials for secondary sch curriculum. 15: 636 Mt Holly rd, El Dorado Ar 71730.

SMITH, MURPHY D. b Birmingham Ala 16 O 20. 5: UTenn 46-48 (Hist) BA, 49 (Hist) MA; UPenn 50-54 (Hist). 6: Fr, Sp, Ital. 7: Instr Tenn Polytech Inst 50; Miss libn Amer Philos Soc Lib, Phila 52-, Asst libn 52-. 9: AHA; SLA; SAA; Ms Soc. 10: Philobiblon Club of Phila; Phila Art Alliance. 12: "A Guide to Manuscripts Relating to the American Indian in the Library of the American Philosophical Society" (66); "Guide to the Archives and Manuscript Collections of the American Philosophical Society" (66). 13: Yes. 14: Mss (hist of sci). 15: Am Philosophical Society Lib, 105 S 5th st, Philadelphia Pa 19106.

SMITH, NANCY K. b Phila 16 N 24. 5: UPenn 57-63 (Fr) BA; Drexel 63-65 MS in LS. 6: Fr. 7: Sec Horace J Williams MD, Phila 42-43; Sec-stenog The Ballinger Co, Phila 43-51; Sec Pepper Hamilton & Scheetz, Phila 51-57; Libn Fels Inst of Local & State Govt UPenn 65-. 9: ALA-ACRL; SLA. 14: Ref, catlg. 15: 130 W Abbottsford ave, Phila Pa 19144.

SMITH, NELLENE PORTER. b Clovis New Mexico 23 My 17. 5: Southeastern State Col 36-38; NorthwesternU 40-44 (Radio, Speech, Journalism); UMich 51-53 (Eng) AB, 53-55 AMLS; USoCal 59-61 (Communications). 6: Fr, Sp. 7: Dir film & mus dept Greenwich Lib, Greenwich Conn 55-59; Tchg asstship USoCal 59-61; Dir lib Scottsdale Pub Lib, Scottsdale Ariz 62-63; Dir lib Santa Barbara Pub Lib, Santa Barbara Cal 63-66; Coord media evaluation, selection & utilization (asst prof) San Francisco State Col 66-68; Dir instr media (asst prof) Monterey Inst of For Studies 68-. 8: Consul, film and record depts; Consul to educ TV for Far Western Lab for Educ devel and Res 66-68; Free-lance writer for TV and radio 43-51; Juror, Amer Film Fest sponsored by Educ Film Lib Assn 68. 9: NEA-DAVI; Nat Assn Lang Lab Dirs; Cal A-V Educ Assn. 10: Commun Chest; San Francisco Symphony Assn; Santa Barbara Symphony Assn; World Affairs Coun; Sierra Club; Carmel Art Assn. 13: Yes. 14: Educ ledia (esp documentary and art films), art, music, arch, lit. 15: 172 Mar Vista dr, Monterey Ca 93940.

SMITH, NELLIE FORD. b Kosciusko Miss. 5: Miss State Col for Women 35-39 (Educ) BS; UWyo summer 49 LSU summers 50-54 MLS. 7: Tchr Kosciusko pub schs, Kosciusko Miss 40-45; Soc wker Amer Red Cross, US Naval Hosp, Parris Island SC 45-47; Bkkeeper Kosciusko Mercantile Co, Kosciusko Miss 47-48; Tchr Kosciusko pub schs, Kosciusko Miss 48-50; Libn Kosciusko High Sch, Kosciusko Miss 50-54; Asst Prof of Lib Sci & assoc libn Miss Col 54-. 9: ALA (State Recr Chm 60-62); SELA; MissLA (sec 57-59; Bus mgr "Mississippi Library News" 64; exec dir NLW 67). 10: Beta Phi Mu. 14: Tchg, ref, periods. 15: 802 Tanglewood dr, Clinton Ms 39056.

SMITH, NICHOLAS N. b Malden Mass 25 D 26. 4: Edyth Kummerle. 5: UMe 46-50 (Hist) BA; Columbia 57-59 MLS. 6: Ger. 7: USAAF Supply 9th Air Force 44-46; Tchr, Danforth Me 50-57; Sch libn Carmel Central Sch, Carmel NY 57-59; Dir Field Lib, Peekskill NY 59-61; A-v N Country Lib System, Watertown NY 61-63, Adult serv 63-65; Asst dir Clinton-Essen-Franklin Lib, Plattsburg, NY 65-69; Libn Ogdensburg Pub Lib, Ogdensburg NY 69-. 8: Consul; N Country Ref & Research Resources Coun, Nat Museum of Can (computerize Canadian ethnology bibliog), Champlain Valley Sch Nursing Lib; Asst prof anthrop Jefferson Commun Col. 9: ALA; NYLA (A-V Com). 13: Yes. 14: Adult serv, ref, admin. 15: Ogdensburg Pub Lib, Ogdensburg NY 13669.

SMITH, NINA MAE (TREADWAY). b Brooks Co Ga 31 My 08. 4:S Jay Smith. 5: UGa 36-39 (Educ) AB; Peabody 50-53 (LS) MS; Fla State U 64 (LS). 6: Fr. 7: State Bd of Educ (Ga) Elem tchr 30-40; High sch tchr 40-43, 49-51; High sch tchr-libn 51-53; Dir Reg Lib State Bd of Educ, Dawson Ga 53-69. 8: Participant in survey of lib serv to Negroes in Ga; Instr, lib sci, UGa(Albany), summer 65; Part time tchr UGa for ext courses in lib serv 65. 9: ALA; SELA; GaLA (sec Pub Lib Sect); GaEA; Ga Child & UP LA. 10: Bus & Prof Womens Club; Kappa Delta Pi. 14: Admin, ext serv, ref, bk sel, reading guidance. 15: 547 7th ave, Dawson Ga 31742.

SMITH, NOREEN (McDONALD). b Seattle 6 O 12. 4: Arlo Irving Smith. 5: UWash 33-37 (Bot) BS, 37-38 BA in LS. 7: Stud file clerk UWash 33-37; Circ clerk Seattle Pub Lib summers 36, 37; Seed analyst & libn Baker Seed Lab, Memphis Tenn 50-57; Circ libn Burrow Lib Southwestern, Memphis 57-. 9: TennLA. 10: AAUW; Tenn Ornithol Soc; Audubon Soc.44561 14: Circ, catlg. 15: Burrow Lib Southwestern at Memphis, Memphis Tn 38112.

SMITH, OLIVE IRENE. b Portage la Prairie Manitoba Can 26 D 06. 5: VictoriaU 32 (Eng) BA; UToronto 41 BLS. 6: Fr. 7: Hd circ Victoria U 35-41, Mgr Bk Bur 41-47; Owner bk truck mail order bus, Toronto Can 47-48; Bk selection travelling libs Govt of Ont, toronto Can 48-54; Catlgr UToronto Lib 56-57; Libn United Ch Deaconess Train Sch, Toronto Can 57-60; Owner Child Bk Shop, Toronto 59-62; Chief libn New Toronto Pub Lib, Toronto Can 62-65; Film libn Etobicoke Pub Lib 65-. 9: CanLA; OntLA; Inst Profess Libns Ont. 10: Soc Planning Coun. 14: Child, a-v. 15: Etobicoke Pub Lib, 600 Islington ave, N Etobieoke Can.

SMITH, PATRICIA (GIBSON). b Joplin Mo 14 N 42. 4: William Murray Smith. 5: UOkla 59-63 (Eng) BA, 65-66 MLS. 6: Sp. 7: High sch Eng tchr Norman Pub Schs, Norman Okla 63-65; Circ libn UOkla Med Ctr, Okla City 66-67; Coord lib serv Okla Reg Med Program, Okla City 67-. 8: Ex-off mem of Reg adv Com, For S Central Reg Med Lib prog 69. 9: MedLA (chm Nomin Co So Reg Gp 68-69); OklaLA (Recr Com 67-69). 10: Beta Phi Mu; Phi Beta Kappa; Alpha Lambda Delta; Delta Delta Delta; AAUW. 11: Grace E Herrick Award. 12: "Survey of Hospital Library Resources in Oklahoma" (67). 13: Yes. 14: Ref. 15: 2745 Meadowbrook, Norman Ok 73069.

SMITH, PATRICIA ALICE (DABNEY). b Dallas 26 N 34. 4: David Alan Smith. 5: Baylor U 52-54 (Nursing); SMU 55-57 (Eng) BA, 57-59 (Eng) MA; UIll 59-60 (LS) MS. 6: Ger. 7: Intern NLM, Wash DC & Bethesda Md 60-61, Selector 61-62; Catlgr Fed Aviation Agency Lib, Wash DC 62-63, Acquis libn 65-67, Admin libn 67-69; Asst to asst dir for pub serv Nat Agric Lib, Beltsville Md 69-. 9: MedLA; SLA (chm-elect Transportation 68-69); DCLA. 10: Phi Beta Kappa; Beta Phi Mu. 14: Acquis, admin. 15: 301 G st SW apt 417, Wash DC 20024.

SMITH, PATRICIA ANN. b Valparaiso Ind 6 Je 45. 5: Macalester Col 63-67 (Econ) BA; Rutgers 67-68 MLS. 6: Sp. 7: Ref libn Com Lib Ohio StateU (Columbus) 68-. 9: ALA; OhioLA. 14: Ref. 15: 1626 King ave, Columbus Oh 43212.

SMITH, PATRICIA EVANS. b Ft Sheridan Ill 30 Jl 27. 5: UMich 45-46 (Liberal Arts); UKy 63-64 (Educ) 67-68 MSLS; MarshallU 64-66 (Eng, Educ, LS) BA, 66-67 (Communication Arts). 6: Fr, Ger. 7: Clk-typist Govt Rec Depot, Savannah Ga 45; Sec & receptionist priv physician, Bowling Green Ky 49-50; Stud asst Ashland Commun Col Lib 63-64, Act libn 67; Elem libn Catlettsburg Sch Syst, Catlettsburg Ky 66-67; Intern-med lib admin Welch Med Lib, Baltimore 68-69; Asst libn for pub serv WashU Med Sch Lib (St Louis) 69-. 9: ALA (Memb Com 68-69; Jr Mem RT); -ACRL; MedLA; NEA; SELA; KyLA; KyASchL (Nat lib Week Chm 67); MdLA. 10: Great Bks Disc Leader; YWCA; PTA; Sigma Tau Delta; Kappa Delta Pi; Beta Phi Mu. 13: Yes. 14: Admin, computer tech. 15: Lib Washington Univ School of Med 4580 Scott ave, St Louis Mo 63110.

SMITH, PATRICIA F. b NYC 15 S 35. 5: Col of New Rochelle 53-57 (Hist) BA; Columbia 57-59 (LS) MS. 7: Lib asst ColumbiaU Lib 57-59; Jr libn New Rochelle Pub Lib, New Rochelle NY 59-61, Bkmob libn 61-63; Libn NYC Pub Lib 63-65, Sr libn 65-69, Br libn 69-. 9: ALA; NYLA; Westchester;A. 10: Woman's Club of New Rochelle. 14: Ya, br admin. 15: 2 Errol pl, New Rochelle NY 10804.

SMITH, PATRICIA L. b Otley Yorks England 10 O 31. 5: Leeds Sch of Libnship 51-52 british ALA, 54; TorontoU 56-59 (Fr) BA. 6: Fr. 7: Asst libn Ipswich Pub Lib, Suffolk England 49-50; Asst libn W Riding Co Lib, Pudsey & Wakefield, Yorks England 50-51, 52-53, Sr asst libn S Yorkshire 53-55; Interne libn Toronto Pub Lib, Toronto Can 55-59; Br libn Pub Lib Commsn, E Kootenay BC Can 59-65; Dir Pub Lib Serv, NW Territories Can 65-. 9: CanLA. 13: Yes. 14: Devel of lib serv to sparsely populated areas. 15: Box 1100, Hay River Nwt Can.

SMITH, RALPH K. b NYC 14 Ja 20. 5: Wheaton Col 41-43 (Anthrop) BS; Dallas Theol Sem 43-46 (Theol) ThM; Columbia 56-57 MLS. 06: Ger. 7: Ref libn NYC Pub Lib 57-63; Ref libn ""Newsweek, NYC 63-65, Acquis & catlgr 65-. 9: SLA; NY Lib Club. 10: Pi Gamma Mu. 14: Catlg, ref. 15: 160 West End ave, New York NY 10023.

SMITH, REBECCA LOU. b Murfreesboro Tenn 26 N 27. 5: David Lipscomb Col 45-49 (Hist) BA; Peabody Col 51-52 (Libnship) MA. 7: Tchr Franklin-Simpson Jr High, Franklin Ky 49-51; Bibliogr Ohio StateU Lib (Columbus) 52-55; Catlgr David Lipscomb Col Lib 55-56, Circ libn 56-; Circ libn Wisconsin StateU (Whitewater) Wisconsin summers 58, 59, Campus sch libn summers 60, 61, 64, Ser libn summers 68, 69; Child libn San Diego Pub Lib summer 62; Catlgr Ohio Valley Col Lib summer 63; Ref libn Seattle Pub Lib summer 67. 9: ALA; TennLA. 14: Circ, ref. 15: Lebanon rd, Murfreesboro Tn 37130.

SMITH, RICHARD DANIEL. b S Bethlehem Penn 1 My 27. 4: Barbara A Smith. 5: Penn State U 48-52 (Ceramic Engrg) BS; UDenver 63-64 (LS) MA; Chicago 64- (LS). 6: Ger, Sp. 7: US Army Mess Sgt & Cook, Germany 45-48; Asst div engnr Johns Manville, Cleveland 52-54; Cerámic engnr Ferro Corp, Cleveland 54-55; Sales engnr Ferro Corp Internat, Hong Kong 55-58; Staff tech div Ferro Corp Internat, Cleveland 58-61; Manager & dir Ferro Far East Ltd, Hong Kong 62-63. 9: ALA; SLA. 10: Amer Ceramic Soc; Nat Inst Ceramic Engrs; Intl Inst for Preservation Hist & Artistic Wks. 14: Admin, preservation & use lib materials. 15: 1369 E Hyde park 1008, Chicago Il 60615.

SMITH, RICHARD G. b Midvale Utah 6 N 18. 4: Lucille Magnon. 5: UUtah 36-40 (Speech, theatre) BA, 46-49 (Speech, theatre) MA; UIll 51-53 (LS) MS. 6: Fr. 7: Personnel NCO (Tech Sgt) US Army, US & Asiatic Pacific Theater 40-45; Asst Salt Lake Co Lib System, Midvale Utah 49-51; UIll Lib(Urbana); Circ asst 53-55, Undergrad Lib Asst 55-56, 57-62, Act Undergrad Libn 56-57, Asst Ref libn 62-, Asst Prof 63-, Assoc ref libn 68-. 9: ALA. 10: AAUP; Theta Alpha Phi; Beta Phi Mu. 14: Ref. 15: 2202 South Lynn, Urbana Il 61801.

SMITH, ROBERT C(HARLES). b Goodland Kan 13 Ja 25. 4: Mildred Phillips. 5: Kan State Tchrs Col(emporia) 47-51 (Soc Sci) BS in Ed; UDenver 59-60 (LS) MA. 7: Ref libn Kansas City (Mo) Pub Lib 60-61; Assoc libn Eisenhower Lib, Abilene Kan 60-62; Catlg libn Kan State (Manhattan) 62-64; Catlg, libn U No Iolwa 64-68; Hd of tech proc Worcester Polytech Inst 68-. 14: Catlg, reclsf. 15: 25 Dean st, Worcester Ma 01609.

SMITH, ROBERT D. b Burdett Kan 21 J120. 4: Edith Hendershot. 5: Ft Hays Kan State Col 58-61 (Eng) BA; Kan State Tchrs Col (Emporia) 62-65 (LS) MS. 7: Sch libn Sr High Sch, Junction City Kan 61-65; Instr Lib Sci Ft Hays Kan State Col 65-69; Circ libn 69-. 9: NEA; ALA; Kan State Tchrs Assn; Kan ASchL Exec Coun 61-; Dist dir elect 66-67; chm Kan Lib Assts of Sec Schs Com 61); KanLA. 10: Lambda Iota Tau. 14: Instr in lib sci. 15: 2713 Wlanut, Hays Kan 67602.

SMITH, ROBERT NEILL. b Birmingham Ala 26 D 24. 5: Duke U 45-48 (Eng) AB; UAla 49-50 (Educ); Drexel 53-54 MS in LS. 6: Sp, Ger. 7: Tchr Mobile Pub Schs, Mobile Ala 48-53; Asst UPenn Lib 53-54; Sci-tech libn Ga Inst of Tech Lib 54-56, Chief sci-tech libn 56-59; Dir Flint River Reg Lib, Griffin Ga 59-66; Hd libn Ga Col at Milledgeville 66-. 8: Consul; 3 Ga Reg Libs, 65, 66, Co Lib 68. 9: ALA (Interlib Coop Com 65-68; mem & chm Dorothy Canfield Fisher Awards Com 64-65); SELA (Exec Bd 69-71); GaLA (treas

65-67). 10: Pi Gamma Mu; AAUP. 14: Admin. 15: P O Box 522, Milledgeville Ga 31061.

SMITH, ROBERT STANLEY. b Pittsburgh Penn 4 S 43. 5: St Fidelis Col 61-65 (Philos); Duquesne 65-66 (Classics) BA; UPittsburgh 66-67 MLS. 7: Lib trainee Carnegie Lib of pittsburgh Penn 66-67; Hd libn Richland Pub Lib, Gibsonia Penn 67-. 9: CathLA (Prog Chm Penn Unit 68-); PennLA (founder & co-chm New Libns Sect 68-; Memb Chm SW Chap 68-). 10: Pittsburgh Lib Club; UPittsburgh Grad Sch of Lib & Info Scis Alum Assn. 14: Admin. 15: 2301 Los Angeles ave, Pittsburgh Pa 15216.

SMITH, ROBERTA K. b Windham Conn 14 F 21. 5: UConn 39-42 (Eng); Simmons 42-43 BS in LS. 6: Fr, Ger. 7: Circ asst Elmwood Pub Lib, Providence 43-45; Head circ dept UConn 45-48, Head ref dept 49-. 9: ALA (Memb Chm Conn 52-57); -ACRL; -RSD; ConnLA (Col & Univ Sect; chm Ref Serv Sect 64-65). 10: Mansfield (Conn) Hist Soc; Joshuas Tract Conservation & Historic Trust; Simmons Col Alumnae Assn. 14: Ref. 15: Rte 1 Box 342, Storrs Ct 06268.

SMITH, ROSEMARY. b Grayson Springs Ky 22 Ap 32. 5: Mt St Joseph Col (Cincinnati) 64-66 (Hist, Soc Sci) BA; Rosary Col 66-68 MALS; Our Lady of Lake Col HEA Inst summer 68, certif for lib wk with disadvantaged. 6: Fr. 7: Relig educ & soc wker Glenmary Sisters, Keokee Va 50-51, So Ohio 53-64; Tchr Sacred Heart Sch, Russellville Ky 51-53; Lib asst Rosary Col 66-68; Libn Chicago Job Corp 67; Libn Appalachian Study Ctr, Chicago summers 67, 68; Libn I & commun coord Chicago Pub Lib 68-. 8: Wk with Appalachians (Ky, Va, Ohio) and with migrants to cities (Cincinnati, Chicago) 52-68. 9: SLA; ALA; Chicago Lib Club; CPL Staff Assn. 10: AAUW; Beta Phi Mu; Model Cities; Chicago Pub Lib Staff Assn. 14: Adult serv, ref, lib commun, pub rel. 15: 1140 W Sunnyside ave, Chicago Il 60640.

SMITH, RUBY (JONES). b Barren Co Ky 19 S 17. 4: Kenneth C Smith. 5: West Ky State Col 38-43 (Eng) AB, summers 63, 64, 66 (Lang Arts) MA. 7: Libn Temple Hill Consol Sch, Glasgow Ky 43-47, 49-51, 53-69. 8: Trustee, Barren Co (Ky) Lib Bd. 9: NEA (Life mem); KyEA; KyLA; KyASchL(State Bk Review; chm 68-69); Ky A-V Assn. 10: Barren Co Hist Soc; 4-H Club Leader; Republican Womens Club. 14: High Sch wk. 15: Rte 1 Box 38, Summer Shade Ky 42166.

SMITH, RUTH I (RUSSELL). b Gowanda NY 9 8 11. 4: John A Smith. 5: Allgheny Col 29-33 (Eng) BA; UWis 38-39 BLS; Syracuse 56 (LS); Fredonia State Col 34 (Elem Educ). 7: Tchr rural sch, Cattaraugus Co NY 34-38; Child libn Pub Lib, Monroe Wis 39-41; Elem tchr & prin, E Otto NY 44-45; Sub tchr Pub Schs, Cattaraugus NY 45-55; Elem libn pub schs, Jamestown NY 55-. 9: NEA; ALA; NYEA; NYLA. 10: Grange; Camera Club; Cattaraugus Hist Soc; Chautauqua Co Hist Soc; Nat Hikers & Campers Club; West NY Zone Assn; ChatauquaLA. 14: Child lit & lib serv. 15: RFD, Cassadaga NY 14718.

SMITH, RUTH SCHLUCHTER. b Detroit 18 O 17. 4: T Guilford Smith. 5: Wayne U 35-39 (Eng) AB; UMich 41-42 ABLS. 7: Desk asst Parkman br Detroit Pub Lib 37-39; Clerical asst 39-41, Jr Prof 42-43 (Lt Jg) WAVES US Naval Res - Ref libn Bur of Ordnance Tech Lib, Wash DC 43-46; Research asst Moore Sch of Electrical Engnr UPenn, assigned to Wash DC 46-47; Libn Bethesda Methodist Church, Bethesda Md 56-61; Libn research & engnr support div Inst for Defense Analyses, Wash DC 61-62, Ref libn Open Lib 62-64; Chief of reader serv Open Lib Inst for Defense Analyses, Arlington Va 64-65, Chief Open Lib 65-68, Hd libn 68-. 9: SLA; ASIS; CSLA (past pres); ALA. 12: "Publicity for a Church Library (66). 13: Yes. 14: Admin, ref. 15: 5304 Glenwood rd, Bethesda Md 20014.

SMITH, SAMUEL BOYD. b Adams Tenn 23 O 29. 4: Martha Sue Fitzsimmons. 5: Milligan Col 47-48; UTenn (Knoxville) 48-49; Peabody Col 55-56 (Soc Sci) BS; Vanderbilt 56-61 (Hist) MA, PhD. 6: Russian. 7: Russian interpreter Staff Sgt USAF 51-54; Tchg fellowship (hist) VanderbiltU 59-61; Asst prof of hist USFla 61-64; Tenn state libn & archivist chm Tenn Hist Commsn State Lib & Archives, Nashville 64-; Lectr Russian hist Peabody Col 64-66; Lectr Amer & Tenn hist UTenn (Nashville) 66-. 9: AHA; So Hist Assn; SAA; SELA; Tenn Hist Soc; TLA. 10: Rotary Club. 13: Yes. 14: Pub libs. 15: Tenn State Lib and Archives Seventh ave North, Nashville Tn 37219.

SMITH, SANDRA. b Beaumont Tex 4 F 46. 5: Los Angeles Valley Jr Col 63-64; Cal West U 64-67 (Soc Sci) BA; Immaculate Heart 67-68 (LS) MA. 7: Stud libn Los Angeles Pub Lib 68; Y-a libn San Diego Pub Lib 69-. 9: ALA; CalLA. 14: Ya serv. 15: 1740 Upas st apt 10, San Diego Ca 92103.

SMITH, SARAH JEAN (WARD). b Fulmer Bucks Eng 5 Ap 41. 4: Victor Chalmers Smith. 5: St Paus Col, UMan 57-62 (Fr) BA; McGill 62-63 BLS. 6: Fr. 7: Catlgr UWest Ont 63-66; Catlgr McMaster U 66-67; Descriptive catlgr Duke U Lib 67-. 14: Catlg. 15: 2804 Erwin rd, Durham NC 27705.

SMITH, SHIRLEY (FOSTER). b Toronto 3 N 17. 5: Toronto 38-41 (Soc Sci) BA; Inst of Child Study 41-43 (Child Study, Nursery Educ); Claremeont Col Grad Sch 43-45 (Psych); Toronto 46 (Psych) MA; McGill 61-62 BLS. 7: Asst supv Scripps Col Nursery Sch, Claremeont Cal 45-46; 1 st asst War-Time Day Nurseries, Toronto 45-46; Asst dir Sunnyside Childrens Centre, Kingston Ont 46-50; Psychologist Bd of Educ, Toronto 51-54; Child development wker Hosp for Sick Children, Toronto 55-60; Child libn Scarbrough Pub Libs, Scarborough Ont 62-67; Libn St Catharines Tchrs Col (Ont) 67-. 9: CanLA; Inst Prof Libns Ont; OntLA. 10: Mary Schneider Art Club. ; Univ Womens Club (St Catharines). 14: Spec libn, educ. 15: 16 Tremont dr apt 705, St Catharines Ont Can.

SMITH, STANA L. b Longview Wash 11 N 40. 5: East Wash State Col 58-62 (Educ) BAEd; UPortland 65-66 MLS. 7: Tchr: Kennewick Pub Schs, Kennewick Wash 62-63, Fed Way Pub Schs, Fed Way Wash 63-64; Catlgr US Forest Serv Lib, Portland Ore 66-67; Catlgr Ore State Lib, Salem 68-. 9: ALA; OreLA; PNLA. 14: Catlg. 15: 570 Winter NE, Salem Or 97301.

SMITH, STEPHANIE N. b Brooklyn NY 18 Jl 42. 5: FiskU 59-63 (Eng) BA; Pratt Inst 64-66 MLS. 7: Child libn (trainee) Brooklyn Pub Lib, Brooklyn NY 63-64; Sch libn NYC Sch Syst, Brooklyn 64-. 9: ALA; NYC Sch Libns Assn; NY Lib Club. 10: Delta Sigma Theta. 14: Child, ya wk. 15: 350 McDonough st, Brooklyn NY 11233.

SMITH, STEWART P(EDEN). b Fountain Inn SC 25 N 15. 4: MAVIS Carter. 5: Presbyterian Col 33-37 (Hist, Fr) AB; Peabody 46-47 BS in LS; UIll 49-50 (LS) MS; UNC 47-49 (Hist). 6: Fr. 7: Tchr high schs, Ga 37-42; Weather observer (S/Sgt) US Air Force 42-45; Catlgr UNC(Chapel Hill) 47-49; Catlgr UIll(Urbana) 50; Asst libn Madison Col(Va) 50-51; Chief tech processes Fla State U 51-59; Libn Fla Presbyterian Col 59-61; Head ser dept UMo 61-68; Hd acquis dept 68-. 8: Lib Tech Proj Adv Com on the Conserv of Lib Materials. 9: ALA; MoLA. 10: Pi Gamma Mu; Kappa Delta Pi; Beta Phi Mu. 13: Yes. 14: Tech proc, ser. 15: 501 Bourn ave, Columbia Mo 65201.

SMITH, STEWART WORLAND. b Tomahawk Wis 8 Je 05. 4: Elna C Johnson. 5: UWis 26-29 Certif; Marquette U 34 PhB; Chicago 40 MA. 7: Gen asst Milwaukee Pub Lib 29-31, Chief hist dept 31-40; Libn Fitchburg(Mass) Pub Lib 40-43; Dir Lincoln(Neb) City Libs 44-46; Dir St Louis Co Lib, St Louis 46-68; Consul 68-. 8: Invented Booketeria (self-serv) 45; Adapted addressograph to lib proc 46; Invented audio-charge system for recording bks. 9: ALA; MoLA (pres 49-50). 12: Co-auth "Survey of Michigan State Library (39); "Survey of the Joplin, Mo Library. 13: Yes. 15: 319 Wilson, Kirkwood Mo 63122.

SMITH, SUSAN (HAMILTON). b Slate Spring Miss 17 Jl 30 . 5: Miss State Col for Women 48-52 (LS) BS; UMiss 63-66 MLS. 7: Jr libn catlg dept UMiss 52-54; Period libn Southwestern at Memphis 55; Asst catlgr Memphis Pub Lib, Memphis Tenn 63; Sr libn Catlg Dept UMiss 63-68, Catlg libn 68-. 9: MissLA; SELA. 14: Catlg. 15: Box 495, University Miss 38677.

SMITH, SWEETMAN REED. b Detroit 12 My 35. 5: UMich 55-59 (Hist) BA, 64-65 AMLS. 7: Yeoman US Coast Guard, Houston 53-55; Bkmob asst Ann Arbor Pub Lib, Ann Arbor Mich 63-65, Br libn 65-66; Libn I NY Pub Lib 66; Ref libn Fashion Inst Tech NYC 66-. 9: ALA; MichLA; United Fed Col Tchrs. 14: Ref, ext admin. 15: 11 Monroe pl, Brooklyn NY 11201.

SMITH, THEDUS GAYLE. b Muncie Ind 20 My 28. 5: Ball StateU 47-51 (Eng) BS; Peabody col 51-52 MA in LS. 7: Libn Ball Mem Hosp Sch of Nursing, Muncie Ind 52-65; Asst catlgr Ball StateU 65-. 9: ALA. 14: Catlg. 15: 840 N Mulberry, Muncie In 47305.

SMITH, THELMA ELIZABETH. b NYC 5 O 10. 5: NYU 33-42 (Hist) BAS; Pratt 43 BLS. 6: Fr. 7: Libn Brooklyn Pub

Lib 29-43; Libn ref dept NY Pub Lib 43-46; Deputy libn Mun Ref Lib, NYC 46-. 8: Spec Com on Lower Manhattan Proj 56. 9: SLA (NY Chap: chm Soc Sci Group 66-); NYLA (AdvBd). 10: Metro Opera Guild 12: "Guide to the Municipal Government of the City of New Yor (60, 2nd ed 65); Assc ed "Municipal Reference Library Notes. 13: Yes. 12: "Guide to the Municipal Government of the City of New York (60, 2nd Ed 65); Assoc Ed "Municipal Reference Library Notes. 13: Yes. 14: Ref, mun govt, NYC hist & govt. 15: 45 Parade pl, Brooklyn NY 11226.

SMITH, TOMS E(WING). b Utica NY 23 Jl 39. 4: Martha Pfahl. 5: Oberlin Col 5659 (Eng); State U Col (Geneseo NY) 60-63 (LS) BS in Ed, ext 64- (Eng). 6: Fr, Sp. 7: Asst Jervis Lib Assn, Rome NY summers 60-62; Libn trainee Rochester Pub Li, Rochester NY 63-67; Jr libn 67-69; Utica State Hosp 69-. 14: Adult serv, med. 15: 9552 Roberts rd, Sauquoit NY 13456.

SMITH, VIRGINIA CHARLOTTE. b New Cumberland WVa 8 Ja 04. 5: Oberlin Col 22-26 (Eng Lit) AB; Simmons summer 30. 7: Asst Oberlin Col Lib 28-57, Catlgr 58-. 15: 160 E College st, Oberlin Ohio.

SMITH, VIRGINIA DARE. b Nashville Tenn 26 My 30. 5: Tenn StateU 48-52 (Bus Educ) BS; UTenn summer 66 (LS); Peabody Col summers 67-69 MLS. 7: Tchr Bransford High Sch, Springfield Tenn 52-55; Sec USAF, Wright-Patton AFB Ohio 55-56; Sec Pub Sch Syst, Nashville 56-65, Libn (elemsch) 65-67, Libn (jr high) 67-. 9: NEA; ALA; Middle TennEA; TennEA; TennLA. 10: YWCA. 14: Ref. 15: 624 N Fifth st, Nashville Tn 37207.

SMITH, WALTER L. b Brookville Penn 29 Ap 42. 5: Clarion State Col 59-63 (Eng, Soc Stud) BS in Ed; UPittsburgh 67-69 MLS. 7: Libn Fla Bur of Blind Serv Talking Bk Lib, Daytona Beach Fla 69-. 9: ALA; Amer Assn Wkers for the Blind; FlaLA. 10: Nat Fed of the Blind; Beta Phi Mu. 14: Library serv to handicapped, lib educ & research. 15: 1069 North st, Daytona Beach Fl 32014.

SMITH, BROTHER WILLIAM CARL CSC. b Detroit 28 F 30. 5: St Edwards U 54 (Soc Studies) AB; Our Lady of the Lake Col 60 Certif in Lib Sci, 62 (Educ) MEd. 6: Lat, Fr. 7: Tchr Holy Trinity High Sch, Chicago 54-56; Tchr-libn Archbishop Hoban High Sch, Akron Ohio 56-57; Head libn Notre Dame High Sch, Biloxi Miss 57-62; Head libn archivist Holy Cross High Sch, New Orleans 62-. 8: Relig tchg Brother, Congregation of Holy Cross. 9: ALA; LaLA; CathLA. 14: Catlg, bk sel, archives. 15: 4950 Dauphine st, New Orleans La 70117.

SMITH, WILLIAM H(OWARD). b Catskill NY 15 Ag 33. 4: Doreen Lorentzen. 5: Eagle Grove Jr Col 52-53, 54-55 (Engnr) AA; Iowa Stae U 55-58 (Psych) BS; Simmons 58-60 (LS) MS. 7: Circ libn Northeastern U 58-60, Catlgr 60-63, Head tech serv 63-64; Head acquis dept UAlaska 64-, Act dir of libs 68-. 8: Consul for establ a lib for Andrew Alord Mfg Co, Boston. 9: ALA; AlaskaStateLA (Exec Bd 65-67); PNLA. 10: AAUP. 12: Ed asst "Bibliography of Science and Technology (64). 14: Tech proc, acquis, admin. 15: 765 - 8th ave, Fairbanks Ak 99701.

SMITH, WILLIAM KEITH. b Adrian Mich 2 F 35. 4: Elisabeth Patmos. 5: UMich 53-55; West Mich U 55-57 (LS) AB, 60-61 (LS) MA, 67-. 6: Fr. 7: Gen asst Jackson (Mich) Co Lib 57-58; Dir mob serv 60; Adv Korean Mil Acad 8th US Army Lib, Seoul Korea 58-59; Lib asst Main Post Lib, Ft Belvois Va 59-60; Coord pub serv Genesee Co Lib, Flint Mich 61-63; Dir Br Co Lib, Coldwater Mich 64-66; Dir Coldwater (Mich) Pub Lib 65-66; Instr West Mich U 67-. 8: Adv Bd, Dept of Libnship West Mich U 65; Mil adv, Korean Mil Acad Lib, Seoul Korea 58-59; Staff Mich State Bd for Libs Wkshop. 9: ALA; MichLA (chm Recr & Scholarship Com 65-66; Co & reg sect; sec-treas 64-65, chm-elect 65-66; chm 66-67; chm Dist I 66-67; Legis Com 63-64, 66-67). 10: Phi Mu Alpha Sinfonia. 12: Comp "Handbook of Scholarships for Study in Librarianship, MichLA (65). 14: Admin, educ, pub lib. 15: 3514 Edinburgh dr, Kalamazoo Mi 49007.

SMITH, WINIFRED (WALL). b Cohocton NY 21 Jl 21. 5: Elmira Col 39-41; Keuka Col 41-43 (Bus Admin) BS; High Point Col 63-64; UNC 64-66 MSLS. 6: Sp. 7: Asst libn S Ga Col 66-. 9: ALA; SELA; GaLA. 10: AAUP. 14: Ref. 15: South Georgia College, Douglas Ga 31533.

SMITH, WINIFRED JANE. b Clarksburg WVa 12 Ja 19. 5: Kent State U 37-41 (Eng) BS in Ed, 50-52 (LS) MA; UCLA 54; UAriz 55, 65; Ariz State U 64, 65, 67, 68. 6: Sp, Lat. 7: Tchr: Conventry High Sch, Akron Ohio 42-54, Palm Springs High Sch, Palm Springs Cal 54-55, Casa Grande High Sch, Casa Grande Ariz 55-56; Libn: Akron Pub Lib, Akron Ohio 59-61, Coronado High Sch, Scottsdale Ariz 61-. 9: NEA; ALA; ArizStateLA; Salt River Valley LA; ArizEA. 10: ALPHA Delta Kappa. 14: Acquis, ref,bibliog. 15: 8455 E Orange Blossom lane, Scottsdale Az 85251.

SMITH-HUTTON, (MING) JANE (See p. 1017)

SMOCK, STELLA MARIE. b San Diego 16 D 28. 5: Walla Walla Col 49-53 (Eng) BA; UWash 56-57 (LS) ML. 6: Sp. 7: Tchr of Eng & Span Newbury Park Acad, Newbury Park Cal 53-54; Tchr Elem Sch, Prescott WASH 54-56; Catlg libn U Wash 57-66; Asst hd catlg libn Jt U Libs, Nashville 66-. 9: ALA; TennLA; SELA. 14: Catlg. 15: 2108 Westwood ave, Nashville Tn 37212.

SMOLAN, GLORIA (CLAMAN). b Brooklyn NY 27 Mr 23. 4: Marvin M Smolan. 5: IndU 42 (Bus Educ); Hunter Col 46 (Bus Educ) BA; NYU 56 (Bus Educ) MA; Montclair State Col 68 (LS) Tchr-Libn Certif. 6: Sp. 7: Tchr: Brown Sch, Cal 47-48, Washington Sch, NY 48-53; Ed Mobil Travel Guide, NJ 62-66; Libn Temple Sholom, NJ 66-; Libn Irvington High Sch, NJ 67-68; Asst elem lib consul Bloomfield Elem Schs, NJ 68-. 9: ALA; Assn Jewish Libs; NJEA; NJSchLA; NJLA; EssexCoEA; EssexCoLA; EssexCoSchLA; BloomfieldEA. 10: Delta Pi Epsilon; Family Serv; Friends of Cedar Grove Lib; Montclair W Essex Guidance Ctr. 12: Ed "Mobil Travel Guide" (62-66). 15: 11 Ridge ct, Cedar Grove NJ 07009.

SMOLINSKI, REV ARCADIUS STANLEY. b Cleveland 25 My21. 5: St Francis Col (Wis) 40-44 (Philos) BA; Assumption Theologate 44-48 (Theol); Catholic U 56-57 MLS. 6: Polish, Lat. 7: Ordained minister Franciscan Order, Pulaski Wis 47-; Tchr & libn St Francis Col(Wis) 54-56 & 57-59; Libncatlgr Provincial Depository Lib, Lake Geneva Wis 60-67; Superior & libn of Convent Lib, Cedar Lake Ind 67-. 14: Catlg, Franciscan bibliog. 15: 774 S Lake Shore dr, Lake Geneva Wis 53147.

SMOLNIK, GERTRUDE R(EYNOLDS). b Brooklyn NY. 4: A William Smolnik. 5: St Josephs Col for Women 27-30 (Eng, Hist, Educ) AB; Columbia 34 am, 59 (LS). 7: Tchr of Lib NYC Bd of Educ 30 yrs. 9: NYLA; NYC SchLA. 15: 68 Montague st, Brooklyn NY 11201.

SMUTNY, ERNESTINE (SMITH). b S Norfolk Va 14 Ag 20. 4: Robert J Smutny. 5: Col of William & Mary 37-41 (Lat) BA; Columbia 46-47 (Lat) MA; UCal 51-53 BLS. 6: Lat. 7: Tchr 41-45; Ser asst Syracuse U 47-49; Prin lib asst UCal (Berkeley) 50-53; Catlgr UNM 53-55; Catlgr Stockton Pub Lib, Stockton Cal 55-57, Ref libn 57-63; Ser libn U of the Pacific 63-. 9: ALA; CalLA. 10: Phi Beta Kappa; Classical Assn Pacific States; Phi Kappa Phi. 15: 1545 W Mendocino ave, Stockton Cal 95204.

SMYTH, SHEILA ANN. b Rochester NY 25 Mr 43. 5: Nazareth Col of Roxhester 60-64 Hist AB; CatholicU 65-66 MSLS. 6: Fr, Sp, Ger. 7: Lib asst CatholicU Lib 65-66; Libn II Nazareth Col of Rochester Lib 66-. 9: Monroe Co (NY) LA. 10: Rochester Assn of Cath Laymen. 14: Tech serv. 15: 152 Lexington ave, Rochester NY 14613.

SNAPP, ELIZABETH (MITCHELL). b Lubbock Tex 31 Mr 37. 4: Harry Franklin Snapp. 5: Tex Woman'sU 54-55; So MethodistU 55-56; N Tex StateU 66-68 (LS) BA, 68-69 MLS. 6: Fr. 7: Asst to archivist Archive of New Orleans Jazz TulaneU 60-63. 9: SLA. 10: Alpha beta Alpha; Alpha Lambda Sigma; Alpha Chi; Pi Delta Phi; Woman's Shakespeare Club; N Tex State U Fac; Wives Newcomers Club; N Tex State U Fac; Wives Soc Club. 14: Ref. 15: Box 5184 N Texas Sta, Denton Tx 76203.

SNAVELY, MYRTLE (BALLINGER). b Roselle NJ 6S 16. 4: John Stauffer Snavely. 5: Kutztown State Col 60-62 (LS) BS; (Cum Magna Laude); Rutgers 62-63. Rutgers 62-63. 6: Ger, Fr. 7: Sec Union Co Park Commsn, Elizabeth NJ 36-38; Payroll clerk: Western Electric Co, Kearney NJ 38-39, Art Color Printing Co, Dunellen NJ 39-41; Curtis Publ Co, Phila 58; Elem tchr Winslow Twp Schs, Winslow Twp NJ 59-60; Elem tchr Upper Perkiomen Jt Schs, Pennsburg Penn 60-61; Secondary libn Quakertown Commun Jt Schs, Quakertown Penn 62-. 9: NEA; ALA; PennEA; PennLA; BooksCoLA. 10: Penn Nut Growers Assn; Flower Club; Bus & Prof Womens Club. 15: RD 1, Alburtis Pa 18011.

SNEAD, MARIE E. b Freedom Penn 14 Mr 21. 5: Geneva Col 39-40, 41-43 (Elem Educ) BS in Ed; Syracuse summers 44-47 BS in LS; UMich summers 57-59 AM LS; State Col (Indiana Penn) 63, 64. 6: Fr, Ger. 7: Elem tchr Pub Sch, Freedom Penn 43-45; Tchr-libn Jr High Sch, Ambridge Penn

45-48; Prof libn Main lib Syracuse U 48-51; Asst libn Geneva Col 52-63; Asst libn State Col (Indiana Penn) 63-. 9: ALA-ACRL (Tri-State Chap); PennLA; ABCUF; PennStateEA. 10: AAUP; AAUW; Beta Phi Mu. 14: Ref, govt docs, acquis, ser, catlg, bibliog. 15: 821 Oak st, Indiana Penn 15701.

SNECK, MARY HELEN. b Rochester NY 7 Jl 08. 5: URochester 32-42 (Hist) BA with distinction; SUNY Col (Geneseo) 58-64 MLS; NY State permanent certif as sch libn. 7: Off asst admin off Rochester Pub Lib, Rochester NY 28-43; Asst purchasing agent E E Fairchild Corp, Rochester NY 43-61; Sch libn Carlton Webster Jr High Sch, Rusch-Henrietta Sch Dist, Henrietta NY 61-. 9: ALA; NY State Tchrs Assn; NYLA; Pentad League of Sch Libns (sec-treas 63-64); NEA. 10: Rochester Civic Music Assn; NY State Hist Soc; Soc for the Preserv of Landmarks in Western NY; Delta Kappa Gamma; Friends Sturbridge Village; Rush-Henrietta TA; Pentad League Sch Libns. 14: Sch libs, wk yp, loc hist. 15: 72 Brooks ave, Rochester NY 14619.

SNELL, CHARLES ELIOT. b Lexington Mass 11 Fe 44. 4: Patricia Ann Poldervaart Snell. 5: UNM 62-66 (Far East Hist) BA; USoCal 66-67 (Tech Libnship) MS. 6: Ger. 7: Stud asst Zimmerman Lib UNM 63-64, Stud asst Hist Dept 64-66, Stud asst Lib of Med Sci 65-66; Lib asst USAF Spe Weapons Ctr Tech Lib, Kirtland AFB 65; Stud libn Los Angeles Pub Lib hist dept 66-67; Ser, circ, & asst ref libn Lib of Los Angeles Co Med Assn 67-; US Army Security Agcy 67-. 9: SLA; MedLA; ALA; Amer Assn Hist Med. 10: Beta Phi mu; Phi Kappa Phi; Church Libn & Histn, Grace United Meth Church, Los Angeles; Phi Alpha Theta; Libraria Sodalitas. 13: Yes. 14: Tech serv, rare bks, hist of med, lib automation. 15: 129 Shade st, Lexington Ma 02173.

SNELL, PATRICIA ANN (POLDERVAART). b Santa Fe NM 11 Ap 43. 4: Charles Eliot Snell. 5: UNM 61-65 (Hist, Educ) Tchr's Certif, BA; USoCal 65-66 MSLS. 6: Sp. 7: Stud asst ser, gifts & exchange UNM 61-65; Lib asst (circ) UCLA Law Lib 65-66; Asst educ libn USoCal 66-68; Med libn VA Hosp, Bedford Mass 68-. 9: ALA. 10: Pi Lambda Theta; Phi Alpha theta; Women's Soc of Christ Serv; Church Libn, Lexington United Meth Church 69-. 14: Spec libs (circ, gifts & exch, tech proc, and ref). 15: 129 Shade st, Lexington Ma 02173.

SNELL, RENEE (EVANS). b London England. 4: Lorne C Snell. 5: 43 British ALA. 7: Lib asst: borough lib (central), Dept Ford London England 34-39, borough lib (central & br) Finsbury London England 39-41; Sr asst Purley Coulsdon Surrey, Purley England 41-42; Br libn Central England Lib, Coulsdon 42-44; Libn town lib, Elliot lake Ont Can 58-62; Libn town lib, Labrador City Nfld 63-66; Sch libn jr & collegiate, labrador City Nfld 69-. 8: Consul sch lib and town lib, Wabosh Labrador 64-65. 14: Child yp, pub lib wk. 15: Box 2240, Labrador City Nfld Can.

SNELLING, PAULA. b Macon Ga 1 Ja 1899. 5: Wesleyan Col 16-19 AB; Columbia 24-25 (Psych) MA; Emory 61-62 (LS). 6: Lat, Fr, Sp. 7: Tchr Ga high schs: Baxley, Americus, Athens, Macon 26-35; Asst dir Laurel Falls Camp, Clayton Ga 30-48; Libn T F Sch, Tallulah Falls Ga 61-. 8: Consul UGa Libs, on papers on Lillian Smith 66-69. 9: NEA; ALA; GaEA. 11: Rosenwald Fellowship 39-41; Research Asst to Lillian Smith 45-61. 12: Co-ed "South Today" 10 yrs. 13: Yes. 14: Bk sel. 15: Box 766, Clayton Ga 30525.

SNELLINGS, GERALDINE (HUBERT). b Victoria Va 8 F 26. 4: Andrew B Snellings. 5: Fla State U 44-48 (LS) BS, 48-49 (LS) MA. 6: Sp. 7: Libn Melbourne High Sch, Melbourne Fla 49-51; Asst circ libn Fla State U 51-52; Libn Orange Co Pub Schs, Orlando Fla 52-56; Ref libn Albertson Pub Lib, Orlando Fla 56-57; Libn Orange Co Pub Schs, Orlando Fla 57-62; Dir of lib serv Lake-Sunter Jr Col 62-64; Dir of lib serv Brevard Jr Col 64-65; Spec libn Sch of Textiles NC State U Raleigh 65-66; Acquis libn Fla Tech U 67-. 9: SLA; FlaEA. 10: Beta Phi Mu; Delta Kappa Gamma. 14: Ref, tech serv. 15: Box 2525, Orlando Fl 32802.

SNESRUD, JANET E (SILVERNESS). b Eau Claire Wis 22 Mr 39. 4: Arlin D Snesrud. 5: UMinn 57-61 (Mus Educ) BS, 64-66 (LS) MA. 6: Fr, Ger. 7: Mus tchr pub schs, Bloomer Wis 62-64; Grad lib asst UMinn Mus Lib (Minneapolis) 64-66; Libn (staff) UMinn Lib (Minneapolis) 66-. 9: ALA; MusLA. 10: Pi Kappa Lambda; Sigma Alpha Iota. 14: Catlg. 15: 477 Curfew, St Paul Mn 55409.

SNEZEK, P PAUL JR. b Vermilion Ohio 4 S 36. 4: Janet E Hart. 5: Phila Col of Bible 58-61 (Christian Educ) BS; Dallas Theol Sem 61-66 (Theol) M Th; N Tex StateU 66-67 (Hist) BA; No IllU 67- (LS). 6: Fr, Greek. 7: Acquis libn Dallas Theol Sem 62-66; Hd libn Moody Bible Inst, Chicago 67-. 9: ALA; Christ Libns Fellowship; ATheolLA; Lib Automation Res & Consul Assn. 14: Lib admin, ref, theol libnship, rare Bibles. 15: 820 N LaSalle st, Chicago Il 60610.

SNIDER, FELIX EUGENE. b Fremont Mo 14 Ja 08. 4: Juanita Gertrude Smith. 5: SE Mo State Col 25-30 (Physical Sciences) BS in Ed; UIll (Urbana) 37-38 BS in LS, 39 (LS) MS, 59-60, summer 64 (LS) PhD. 7: Rural & small town tchr, Mo 23-27; Asst libn SE Mo State Col 30-41, Dir libs & prof lib sci SE Mo State Col 43-; Libn & prof lib sci E Car State Col 41-43. 8: Hist consul, feasibility study on Old Ste Genevieve Mo. 9: ALA (and its divisions); NEA; MoLA; MoASchL; MoTA. 10: Kappa Delta Pi; Nat Trust Hist Preserv; Rotary. 11: Katherine Sharpe Fellow in Lib Sci 38-39. 12: Co-auth; ""Missouri; Midland State (rev ed 61); ""Cape Girardeau, Biography of a City (56); ""Tower Rock (La Roche de la Croix). 13: Yes. 14: Col lib admin, tchg lib sci, hist of bks, printing & libraries. 15: Kent Lib SE Mo State Col, Cape Girardeau Mo 63701.

SNIDER, MARGARET (JACOBS). b Woodfords Me 19 Ap 10. 4: John L Snider. 5: Bates Col 28-30 (Eng); Simmons 30-32 BLS. 7: Asst ref libn & asst to sch libn, Portland Pub Lib, Portland Me 32-34; Ref libn Newton Free Lib, Newton Mass 58-. 9: MassLA; NELA. 14: Ref. 15: 15 Blackstone ter, Newton Ma 02158.

SNIDER, ROSE MARY (KEZELE). b Chicago Ill 20 D 24. 4: Peter F Snider. 5: Los Angeles Harbor Jr Col 63-66 (Eng) AA; Cal State Col (Long Beach) 66-68 (Eng) BA; UCLA 68-69 MLS. 7: Asst ref libn humanities Cal State Col (Long Beach) 69-. 14: Ref. 15: 1845 Valleta dr, San Pedro Ca 90732.

SNIDERMAN, FLORENCE (LAMA). b Grand Rapids Mich 21 Je 15. 4: Henry Sniderman. 5: Oberlin 32-34; Wayne State 57-59 (Eng) BA; UMich 59-60 MALS, 66 (Eng Lang & Lit) MA. 6: Fr. 7: Ref libn (soc studies) Wayne StateU 60-. 9: ALA. 10: Phi Beta Kappa. 14: Ref. 15: 17392 Pennington dr, Detroit Mi 48221.

SNODDERLY, MARY LOUISE (DAVIS). b Polk Co Ore 1 F 25. 4: CHarles Hugh Snodderly. 5: E Tenn State U 42-46 (Soc Studies) BS; UTenn 62 (Instructional Materials) MS. 7: Tchr-libn, Strawberry Plains Tenn 46-49; Sch libn Dandridge Tenn 49-52; Sch libn, Strawberry Plains Tenn 55-62; Catlgr Knoxville City schs, Knoxville Tenn 62-67; Periods & ref libn Carson Newman Col 67-. 9: NEA; TennEA; TennLA; ALA. 10: Pi Lambda Theta. 14: Period. 15: Rte 3 Box 165, Straberry Plains Tn 37871.

SNODGRASS, WILSON D. b Angleton Tex 15 Ja 32. 5: Sam Houston State Tchrs Col 49-52 (LS) BS; UTex 52-54 MLS. 7: Reviser Grad Sch of Lib Sci UTex 53-54; Documents libn Sam Houston State Tchrs Col summer 54; US Army Med Corps (Cpl) 54-56, assigned to Med Lib William Beaumont Army Hosp, El Paso Tex 55-56; Catlg libn Tex West Col 56-59; Catlgr Fondren Lib So Methodist U 59-60, Head catlg dept 60-69; Hd tech proc 69-. 9: ALA (Coun of Reg Groups rep Tex 64-65); TexLA (chm Spec Com on Round Tables 65-66); Tex Reggroup of Catlgrs & Clsfrs (sec-treas 62-63, v-chm 63-64; chm 64-65). 10: Beta Phi Mu; Alpha Chi; Kappa Delta Pi; Metro Opera Guild. 13: Yes. 14: Tech proc. 15: P O Box 505 Somethodist Univ, Dallas Tx 75222.

SNOOK, LAURENCE L JR. b Lakeland Fla 14 F 31. 5: Fla State U 49-52 (Elem Educ) BS; UFla 52-54 (Educ) MEd; Fla State U summers 55-60 MS in LS. 7: Elem tchr Auburndale Prim Sch, Auburndale Fla 52-54; Operations clerk 86th Inf Reg US Army, Kan & Germany 54-56; Libn Love Grove Elem Sch, Jacksonville Fla 57-58; Night circ libn Jacksonville U 57-58; Jacksonville Pub Lib, Jacksonville Fla: Asst br libn Willow Br 58-59, Br libn Westbrook Br 59-61, Sr asst circ dept 61-62, Asst dir of libs 62-. 9: NEA; ALA; SELA; FlaLA (Memb Chm 65-66; chm Local Arrangements; chm Memb; Citations Com; Nominating Com; NLW Com); Pub Libs Sect reporter "Florida Libraries; DuvalCoLA (past pres). 14: Admin. 15: Jacksonville Pub Lib, 122 N Ocean st, Jacksonville Fl 32202.

SNOOK, ROBERT BERNARD. b Kan City Mo 8 D 23. 5: UMo 46-48 (Journalism); Washington U (St Louis) 48-50 (LS) BS in Ed; Peabody 50-51 (LS) MA. 7: Payroll clerk Sheffield Steel Corp, Kan City Mo 41-43; US Army Voice Radio operator (Pfc) 43-45: Catlgr: Washington U(St Louis) 50, UKan 51-52, Linda Hall Lib of Sci & Tech, Kan City Mo 53-. 9: ALA; MoLA. 14: Catlg. 15: 5050 Oak st, Kansas City Mo 64112.

SNOW, HELEN MIDGETT. b Durham NC 12 Je 40. 4: Lewis F Snow Jr. 5: Duke 58-62 (Eng) AB; UNC 62-64 MS in LS. 7: Ref libn Duke U Lib 64-65, Head of ser dept 65-. 67; Ref libn Pub Lib, Summit NJ 67-. 10: Phi Beta Kappa; Beta Phi Mu. 15: 383 Morris ave, Summit NJ 07901.

SNOW, JUDITH ELLEN (BRADLEY). b Toronto Can 10 My 43. 4: David Snow. 5: YorkU 61-64 (Eng) BA; UToronto 64-65 BLS. 6: Fr. 7: Ref & circ/a-v libn Col of Educ Lib, toronto Can 65-67; Ref libn Ont Inst for Studies in Educ Lib, Toronto Can 67-. 10: Beta Phi Mu. 14: Ref. 15: 263 Islington ave N, Islington Ont Can.

SNOW, KATHLEEN MARY. b Calgary Alta Can 27 Ja 18. 4: John Harold Snow. 5: UAlta 36-40 (Eng) BA with Hon in Eng; UWash 45-46 BLS; UCalgary 67 BEd. 6: Fr. 7: Libn Calgary Pub Lib, Calgary Alta 41-, Asst libn 56-60; Admin asst Lib Serv Centre Calgary Sch Bd, Calgary Alta 60-64; Asst Prof UAlta 64-. 8: Commsn on Elem Schs, Calgary Pub Sch Bd. 9: CanLA (Coun); AltaLA (pres); Prairie Conf on Lib Standards (chm). 10: Univ Womens Club; Calgary Allied Art Center. 12: Ed "Correspondence Course for Rural Volunteer Custodians" (60); "Manual for Catlg Non-bk Materials" (67); Ed "Canadian Books for Schools" (68). 13: Yes. 14: Bk selection & evaluation, Canadian lit. 15: Ed C I Dept Faculty of Ed, Univ of Alta, Calgary Alta Can.

SNOW, KATHLYN M (STAPLETON). b El Reno Okla 18 N 20. 5: Our Lady of the Lake Col 38-40 (Bus Admin), 59-61 (LS) BA, summers 62-64 (Ed, LS), 66 (Educ) MEd, 69 (LS). 7: Sec US Govt, SanAntonio Tex 40-44; Kindergarten tchr, volunteer wk 44-61; LIbn Harlandale Ind Sch Dist High Sch, San Antonio Tex 61-65; Libn Beach Pavilion US Govt Spec Serv, Ft Sam Houston, San Antonio Tex 65-67; Supv libn Hosp brs 67-. 8: Mem state adv coun Title IV-B. 9: ALA; CathLA; NEA; TexLA; SWLA; Tex State Tchrs Assn (Lib Sect); SLA. 10: Toastmistress; BexarLA. 14: Readers serv, bibliotherapy, hosp & inst serv for patients. 15: 1231 Vanderbilt, San Antonio Tx 78210.

SNOW, LUCILE D. b Sylacauga Ala 24 My 15. 4: Dr Frank E Snow. 5: Jacksonville State Tchrs Col 32-33, summers 34, 35; UAla summers 36-39 & 39-40 (Ed, LS) BS; Peabody summers 45-47 MA LS. 7: Elem tchr Weogufka Sch, Weogufka Ala 33-39; Libn & Fr tchr Morgan Co High Sch, Hartselle Ala 40-41; Asst catlgr Miss State Col Lib 41-44; Asst libn Staunton Pub Lib, Staunton Va 44-45; Libn Stuart Hall, Staunton Va 45-46; Asst libn Roanoke Col Lib 46-49, Libn 49-. 9: ALA; SELA; VaLA. 10: AAUW. 14: Catlg. 15: Roanoke Col Lib, Salem Va 24153.

SNOWDEN, DOROTHY (PARR). b Waco Tex 27 Jl 27. 4: Claude Joseph Snowden. 5: Tex ChristianU 43-44 (Journalism); Atlantic Christian Col 51 (Educ); Flat River Jr Col 57-58 (Educ); E Tex StateU 62-64 (Eng, LS) BS, 64-65 (Educ, LS) MS. 7: Inventory libn Greenville Pub Lib, Greenville Tex 63, 65; Libn Converse Pub Lib, Converse Tex 63; Grad asst E Tex StateU 64-65; Asst ref libn SW Tex State Col 65-66, Ref libn 66-, Hd ref dept 66-. 8: Lib consul to "Upward Bound", SW Tex State Col 67, 68. 9: Internat Soc Gen Semantics; ALA; SWLA; TexLA. 10: Kappa Delta Pi; AAUP; Tex Assn Col Tchrs; ACLU; CORE; NAACP; SCLC. 13: Yes. 14: Ref. 15: Southwest Texas State College Lib, San Marcos Tx 78666.

SNOWMAN, PAUL ARTHUR III. b Ann Arbor Mich 2 Ap 36. 5: Gettysburg Col 55-59 (Amer hist) BA; UMich 60-62 AMLS. 6: Fr, Sp. 7: Stud asst, page UMich Undergrad Lib; Lib I Milwaukee Pub Lib; Br libn Free Pub Lib, Paramus NJ; Reg libn Free Pub Lib Serv, Montpelier Vt; Asst libn Sullivan Co Commun Col; Coord serv libn & title IV-A Consul Lib Commsn for State of Dela, Dover 68-. 9: ALA; DelLA; Vt Hist Soc. 10: Jr C of C (Del). 14: Acquis, consul. 15: Box 892, Dover De 19901.

SNYDER, ALLYNE TREFFRY. b Santa Ana Cal 26 S 26. 5: Santa Ana Col 44-46 (Lang, Lit) AA; UCal (Santa Barbara) 46-48 (Eng) BA; UCal (Berkeley) 48 (Eng, Educ); UOre summer 49 (Educ); Wash State Col 48-50 (Eng) MA; UWash 56, 58 MLS. 7: Tchg Fellow in Eng Wash State Col 48-50; Tchr jr high sch Eng & reading, Quincy, Plumas Co Cal 50; Clerk-typist US Army Engnrs, Tokyo 52; Tchr US Armed Forces Inst, Tokyo 52-55; Instr UCal (Seoul Korea) 53; Clerk-typist Internat Coop Admin, Seoul Korea 56-57; Libn Santa Ana Pub Lib, Santa Ana Cal 58; Libn admin Army Lib Serv, Pirmasens Germany 60-61; Catlgr Douglas Aircraft Co, Long Beach, Santa Monica Cal 61; Libn admin Douglas Aircraft Co, Charlotte NC 61-64; Catlgr Govt Printing Off, Wash DC 64-65; Catlgr Naval Weapons Bur, Wash DC 66-67; Catlgr Naval Air Systs Command, Wash DC 67-. 9: SLA. 10: Pi Lambda Theta; Alpha Gamma Sigma; Phi THETA Kappa. 14: Catlg. 15: Woodner Hotel 3636 - 16th st NW apt B561, Wash DC 20008.

SNYDER, DOROTHY HILLGARTNER. b Pittsburgh 25 Ap 21. 4: Stephen Albert Snyder. 5: CLarion State Col39-43 (LS, Eng, Soc Studies) BS in Ed; UPittsburgh 62-63 MLS. 7: Libn Norwin High Sch, Irwin Penn 45-46; Tchr Gastonville Sch, Union Twp Penn 60-61; Libn Monessen Pub Lib, Monessen Penn 63-65; Elem libn Ringold Sch Dist & supv Monongahela Pub Lib, Monongahela Penn 65-. 9: Penn LA. 10: Pi Gamma Mu, Beta Phi Mu. 14: Elem sch & child wk. 15: Box 25, Venetia Penn 15763.

SNYDER, ELLEN JO. b Racine Wis 27 Mr 42. 5: UWis 60-64 (Fr) BA, 65-66 (LS) MA. 6: Fr, Sp. 7: Asst col libn USoCal 66-67, Act world affairs libn 67-68, Asst ref libn 68-. 9: ALA. 14: Ref. 15: 2815 S Hoover st, Los Angeles Ca 90007.

SNYDER, GEORGE A. b Polk Neb 5 Je 16. 4: Esther Bauerle. 5: Olivet Nazarene Col 36-40, 41-44 (Music, Theol) BMus, ThB; Drake U 45-49 (Music Educ) M Mus Ed; Northwestern 48-49 (Educ); Kan State Tchrs Col (Emporia) 55 (LS); West Res 56-58 MSLS; URochester, Eastman Sch of Music 59 (Music Libns Seminar). 7: Manager Iowa City Mattress Co, Iowa City Iowa 40-41; American-Marietta Co, Kankakee Illl 41-43; Music faculty Olivet Nazarene Col 44-49, Dir of Radio 44-49; Music libn Pub Lib of Des Moines, Des Moines Iowa 49-59; Head music dept 59-62; Head catlg dept UDenver Libs 62-64, Head circ dept 64-. 8: Consul Arapahoe Co Lib Coun, Denver 64-65. 9: ALA; MusLA; ColoLA (Scholarship Com 65-68); Rocky Mountain LA. 10: Beta Phi Mu. 14: Rare bks, automated circ Procedures, documentation, info storage & retrieval. 15: PO Box 10052, Denver 80210.

SNYDER, GRANVILLE MEIXELL (MRS). b Atchison Kan 18 J 101. 5: Barnard 20 (Eng, Sci) AB; Columbia 21 (Eng) MA, 22 (U Scholar), 28 (LS) MS. 6: Fr, Ger, Ital, Dutch, Scandinavian. 7: Org ref file"Popular Science Monthly, NYC 18-23; Columbia U: Chem & Bus Libs 23-25, Libn Applied Sci & Engnr Libs 25-47, Lecturer Sch of Engnr 35-47; Bibliog researcher Babcock & Wilcox Co, NYC 47-58; Libn Gen Precision Lab, Pleasantville NY 58-61; Catlgr Inst of Pub Admin, NYC 62-63; Asst libn in chg NY Inst of Tech, NYC 64-68; NY libn 68-. 9: SLA (var offs); NY Lib Club. 10: Eng-Speaking Union; Croton Heights Assn; Paulist League; AAUP. 12: "Trade Catalogue Collection (34): Comp "Bibliography of Recent Literature on Metals at Elevated Temperatures (51); Ed "Technical Book Review Index (35-40); Tr "Scandinavian Banking Laws (26). 13: Yes. 14: Sci & engnr research, bibliog, catlg, documentation. 15: RD 1, Col Greene rd, Yorktown Heights NY 10598.

SNYDER, HELEN MARY. b Cleveland 30 Ap 07. 5: Park Col 29 (Eng) BA; Columbia 30 (LS) BS, 39 (LS). 7: Demonstration Sch Libn Stephen F Austin State Col 31-38;assoc libn Stephen State Col 39-46; Army Libn US Army of Occupation, Japan 46-48; Bus & ind dept S Bend Pub Lib, S Bend Ind 49-59, Br libn River Park Br 59-. 9: ALA; SLA; IndLA. 10: AAUW; Altrusa Club, YWCA; S Bend Symphony Orchestra Assn; Carlisle Mem Lib Bd, Healthwin Hosp. 15: 308 Parkovash ave, S Bend Ind 46617.

SNYDER, LILLIAN LAWYER. b Lewistown Penn 2 Ap 15. 4: William H Snyder. 5: Penn STATE U 33-37 (Eng,Hist) BA; Carnegie 37-38 BS of LS; Gettysburg Col 60-62 (Educ). 7: DC Pub Lib: Asst 38-40, Desk head 40-42, Head of ya wk 42-49; Co Libn Adams Co Free Pub Lib, Gettysburg Penn 50-52; Spec asst Hanover Pub Lib, Hanover Penn 52-60; Elem libn Hanover Boro Schs, Hanover Penn 60-63; Sr high libn 63-. 9: ALA-YASD (chm 47); NEA; PennLA; PennStateEA. 14: Yp serv. 15: Valley Grove Farm, Littlestown Penn 17340.

SNYDER, MARTHA (FLEMING). b Tarentum Penn 21 F 16. 4: Daniel J Snyder Jr. 5: Col of Wooster 33-37 (Hist, Pol Sci) AB; Carnegie 37-38 BS in LS. 7: Asst Central Lib & brs Carnegie Lib, PIttsubrgh 38-42; Asst Mt Pleasant Br DC Pub Lib 43; Libn West Moreland Hosp Nursing Sch & Med Staff Lib, Greensburg Penn 60-. 10: Trustee, Greensburg Lib. 14: Med & nurs. 15: Westmoreland Hosp, 532 W Pittsburgh st, Greensburg Penn 15601.

SNYDER, MARY FRANCES. b Newton Kan 25 S 16. 5: El Dorado Jr Col 34-36; WichitaU 38-41 (Soc Sci) AB in Ed; Kan State Tchrs Col 60-63 MS in LS; UOkla summer 67. 7: Tchr; rural schs, Butler Co Kan 36-40, high sch, Little River Kan 41-42, high sch, Mulvane Kan 42-46, jr high, El Dorado Kan 46-60; Libn sr high, El Dorado Kan 60-. 8: Chm lib curriculum com El Dorado Pub Schs, El Dorado Kan 63-; NDEA Inst

UOkla summer 67. 9: NEA; ALA-AASchL; KanStateTA; KanASchL (pres 67-68); KanLA. 10: AAUW. 14: Ref, selection, assisting tchrs & studs. 15: 524 N Denver, El Dorado Ks 67042.

SNYDER, MYRON (GEORGE). b Massillon Ohio 7 My 14. 4: Thelma Strader. 5: Capital U 36-40 (Hist) AB; West Res 45-46 BLS. 7: Inspector Tyson Bearing Co, Massillon Ohio 41-44; Tchr E Union Twp Sch, Apple Creek Ohio 44-45; Head of the Bus & Tech Dept Pub Lib of Ft Wayne & Allen Co Ind 46-. 9: IndLA. 10: Ft Wayne Railfans Club; Allen Co Hist Soc. 14: Ref (sci, tech bus). 15: 1414 Cinnamon rd, Ft Wayne Ind 46805.

SNYDER, NANCY S. b Summit NJ 11 S 31. 4: William A Snyder. 5: Douglass Col 49-53 (Eng) BA; Drexel 65-66 (LS) MS. 7: Tchr elem sch, Pittsgrove Twp NJ 63-64; Adult libn Vineland Pub Lib, Vineland NJ 64-. 8: Pres, Garden State Lib Film Circuit 69. 9: ALA; NJLA. 10: LWV. 14: A-v (esp films). 15: 1424 Nelson ave, Vineland NJ 08360.

SNYDER, PATRICIA ANNE. b Toledo Ohio 17 Mr 16. 5: Mary Manse Col 34-38 (Eng, Educ) AB; UToledo 39 (Eng). 7: Instr St Ursula Acad, Toledo Ohio 38-41; Sec to grad sch dean UDetroit 41-42; Libn Owens-Illinois Inc, Toledo Ohio 43. 9: SLA (Consul Serv Com 61-62); CathLA No Ohio Unit: chm Adult Sect); OhioLA. 10: Nat Coun Cath Women; Kappa Gamma Pi; LWV; Friends of the Toledo Mus of Art; Sci Res Soc of Amer; Zonta Club; Citizens for Educ Freedom. 14: Lib supv. 15: 1921 Firlawn dr, Toledo Ohio 43614.

SNYDER, RICHARD L(YNNE). b Toronto 18 F 27. 4: Jeanette Sutherland. 5: U Toronto 49 (Phys Sci) BA; Ind U 52 (LS) MA. 6: Fr. 7: Ind U; Libn Dept of Geol & Geological Survey 53-55, Biol libn 55-58, Sci libn 58-59, Lecturer on lit of sci & Tech 55, 58; Sci libn MIT 59-62, Assoc dir of libs 62-64; Lecturer on lit of sci & tech Simmons Col 63-65; Dir of Libs & Assoc Prof of Lib Sci Drexel Inst of Tech 65-. 8: Consul to commercial firms. 9: ASIS; ALA (past chm Subj Specialist Sect); -ACRL (chm Delaware Valley Chap); SLA (past chm Boston Chap Sci-Tech Group). 10: AAAS; Bd Dir "Information Abstracts. 12: Co-comp (with Bernadette Shih) "International Union List of Communist Chinese Serials (63). 13: Yes. 14: Sci & tech lit, use of machines in libs, admin. 15: Drexel Inst of Tech Lib 32nd & Chestnut sts, Phila Pa 19104.

SNYDER, RUTH (MIRMAN). b NYC 6 Je 16. 5: Col of William & Mary (Norfolk) 56-60 (Eng) BA; UVa summer 61, 65 (LS); Columbia 63-67 (LS) MSLS; George Washington U 67-68 (Curriculum Guidance); New Sch Soc Research 68- (Philos). 6: Ger. 7: Sec Attorney, Norfolk Va 36-38; Med sec Norfolk Va 50-53; Tchr Virginia Beach Friends Sch, Virginia Beach Va 60-61; Libn: Virginia Beach Sch System, Virginia Beach Va 61-65, Portsmouth Pub Lib, Portsmouth Va summer 65, Karen Horney Clinic, NYC 65; Libn DC Sch Syst 66-68; Libn Jersey City State Col 68-. 8: Off Naval Research Psych Serv Lib, Wash DC summer 66. 9: ALA; VaLA; So Reg LA; DCLA; Assn NJ State Col Facs. 10: AAUW; Delta Sigma Lambda; Phi Theta Kappa; Columbia Alum Assn. 14: Med ref, readers adv serv, acquis. 15: 11 Riverside dr 15S East, New York NY 10023.

SNYDER, WILLIAM E. b Johnsonburg Penn 12 N 30. 5: Penn State 48-52 (Sociol) BA, 52-53 (Sociol); UPittsburgh 67-69 MSLS. 7: Control teller Pittsburgh Nat Bank, Pittsburgh Penn 54-64; Tchr Turkeyfoot Valley Area Sch, Conflucnee Penn 64-66, Libn 66-68; Ref libn Ohio StateU (Lima Campus) 69-. 14: Ref, catlg. 15: Ohio State Univ Lima Campus Mumaugh rd on st Rte 30 S, Lima Oh 45804.

SOBEL, ESTHER (DEBORAH LEVY). b NYC 15 D 14. 4: Oscar Sobel. 5: Hunter Col 32-35 (Music) BA; NYU 35-38 (Music Educ) MA; Newark State Col 60-62 (Elem Educ); Rutgers 62-65 MLS. 6: Fr. 7: Elem tchr Franklin Sch, Westfield NJ 60-61; Libn Quibbletown Jr High Sch, Piscataway NJ 63-66; Tchr-libn Carson/DeAnza Elem Sch, Sunnyvale Cal 67-. 9: ALA; CalASchL; NEA; CalTA; STA. 10: Beta Phi Mu; Nova Vista Symphony Orchestra. 14: Yp lit, ref, child lit. 15: 28266 Christophers lane, Los Altos Hills Ca 94022.

SOBOTTKA, (M) PATRICIA (COX). b Hankinson ND 3 My 27. 4: Ronald M sobottka. 5: River Falls State Tchrs Col 45-49 (Educ, Eng) BS; UOre 50-57 (Eng) MA; Boston U 60-61 (Eng); UCal (Berkeley) 63-64 MLS. 7: Tchr Chiloquin High Sch, Chiloquin Ore 49-50; Tchr Drain High SCh, Drain Ore 50-53; Records clsf Pacific Power & Light Co, Portland Ore 54-56; Instr Portland State Col 57-60; Libn Ore State Bd of Health, Portland Ore 61-66; Asst libn, Asst Prof of Lib Sci Pacific U 66-. 9: OreLA. 14: Catlg. 15: 19430 NW Melrose dr, Portland Or 97229.

SODEMANN, ELIZABETH MARY (FRANCIS). b Madison Wis 31 Ja 20. 4: Paul Charles Dodemann. 5: UWis 38-42 (Eng) BS (Ed) 43 BLS. 6: Fr, Ger. 7: Jr libn Madison Free Lib, Madison Wis 43-45; Asst ref libn UTenn Lib 58-60; Elem tchr Our Lady of Fatima Sch, Alcoa Tenn 63-65; Libn Mun Tech Adv Serv UTenn Ext 65-. 8: Org spec lib for UTenn Bur of Pub Admin 66; Org lib for UTenn Water Resources Ctr 9: SLA; TennLA. 14: Ref. 15: RD 2, Louisville Tn 37777.

SODERBERG, ARLETTE MARCELLA. b Dresser Wis 9 O 17. 5: Gustavus Adolphus Col 35-39 (Eng, Hist) BA; UMinn 50 BS in LS. 7: Tchr-libn Pillager High Sch, Pillager Minn 39-41; Tchr-libn W Central Sch & Station UMinn, Morris Minn 41-46; Instr-libn UMinn Law Lib 46 -. 9: AALL. 14: Law ref. 15: 3124 Rankin rd NE, Minneapolis Mn 55418.

SODERHOLM, DOROTHY JOYCE. b Holdrege Neb 9 My 25. 5t; Neb State Tchrs Col (Kearney) 42-46 (Eng) BA; Evangelical Free Church Seminary (Chicago) 47-50 Diploma; Wheaton Col(Ill) 53-56 (Old TEstament) MA; UIll 58-59, sumers 59- 61 (LS) MS. 7: Tchr Logan Co Sch System, Peetz Colo 46-47; Tchr Christian Childrens Home Holdrege Neb 50-51; Attedant Bethpage Mission, Axtell Neb 51-53; Libn: Trinity Sem & Bible Col(Chicago) 56-58, 59-62, Esperanza Jr High Sch, Lexington Park Md 62-64, Takoma Park Jr High Sch, Silver Spring Md 64-66; Catlgr Kan State U Lib 66-. 9: ALA. 10: Beta PHI Mu. 14: Catlg. 15: 1615 Anderson, Manhattan Ks 66502.

SODERLAND, KENNETH W(AYNE). b Snohomish Wash 4 N 23. 4: Lorraine Atkinson. 5: UWash 40-48 (Scandinavian Lang & Lit) BA; UStockholm 48-49 (Scandinavian Lang & Lit) Certif; UWash 50-51 (Scandinavian Lang & Lit) MA, 51-52 MA in LS. 6: Swedish, Danish, Sp, Fr. 7: Pilot (1st Lt.)USAAC, SW Pacific 43-46m; Spec recr LC 52-53, Ser catlgr 53-56; Head catlg dept UChicago 56-58, Asst dir for prep 58-68; Assoc dir for prep 68-. 8: Lecturer, Grad Lib Sch UChicago 61-. 9: ALA-RTSD (chm Ser Sect 62-63); Chicago Reg Group of Libns in Tech Serv(chm60-61). 13: Yes. 14: Tech serv. 15: Thorn Creek lane, Crete Ill 60417.

SOESTER, JAMES BRUER. b Crawford Neb 15 Ag 40. 5: St Thomas Sem Col (Denver) 58-63 9philos, Theol); Chadron State Col 63-64 (Eng, For Lang) BA, 64-65 (Educ, Admin) BSEd; Kansas State Tchrs Col 67-68 MLS. 6: Fr, Lat. 7: Tchr & libn Assumption High Sch, Chadron Neb 64-67; Hd tech serv Topeka Pub Lib, Topeka Kan 68-. 8: Tech serv consul, Topeka Pub Libr 68. 9: ALA; CathLA; MPLA; KanLA. 14: Tech serv (catlg & clsfn), lib hist, rare mss & bks. 15: 819 lane No 2N, Topeka Ks 66606.

SOEY, LOUISE ELIZABETH (WRIGHT). b Hamden Junction Ohio 25 Mr 08. 5: Wooster Col 25-29 (Eng, Hist) AB; UIll 29-30 BS in LS; ButlerU 57-58 (LS); Ball State 64 (LS). 7: Libn high sch, Portsmouth Ohio 30-32; Asst libn Henderson State Col 58-. 9: ArkLA; ArkEA. 10: AAUW; DAR. 14: Period, ref. 15: RR 2, Spencer In 47460.

SOGG, JULIA (LOIS CAHN). b Cleveland 6 O 05. 4: Paul Parker Sogg. 5: Flora Stone Mather Col West Res 22-26 (Eng) BA (summa cum laude); West Res 58-60 MSLS. 6: Fr, Ger, Hebrew, Ital. 7: Ref libn Grasselli Lib John Carroll U(Cleveland) 62-. 10: Cleveland Mental Health Ass; Phi Beta Kappa, Brandeis Univ NatWomens Com; Montefiore Auxiliary; Nat Coun Jewish Women; Mt Sinai Hosp Womens Auxiliary; ACLU. 14: Ref. 15: 20305 N Park blvd, Shaker Heights Oh 44118.

SOHL, MARJORIE ANN. b Hammond Ind 27 F 19. 5: Ind U 37-44 (Eng) BA; Uill 44-46 BS of LS. 6: Ger. 7: Lib asst Hammond Pub Lib, Hammond Ind 37-46, Head of adult serv 46-. 9: ALA (life mem); IndLA (life mem). 10: Beta Phi Mu; Beta Sigma Phi; UIll Lib Sch Alumni (Life mem); Altrusa Intl. 14: Adult serv. 15: 5615 Sohl ave, Hammond Ind 46320.

SOIFER, LIBBY POTTER. b Portland Me 20 S 44. 5: UMe 62-66 (Zoology) BA; Simmons 67-68 (LS) MS. 6: Sp. 7: Acquis asst UMe (Portland) 66-67; Subj catlgr YaleU Lib 68-. 9: SLA. 14: Sci sub catlg, spec libs (espec biol). 15: 53 Victory dr, New Haven Ct 06515.

SOKOLYSZYN, ALEKSANDER. b Cerniutsi, W Ukraine 8 S 14. 4: Sophia Maria Antoniv. 5: High School Cernati-Bukovina Rumania 25-33 (Pol Sci) BA; Law Faculty U Cernati-Bukovina (Rumania) 33-38 (Law & Pol Sci) Master; Lwiw U West Ukraine 40-41 (Soviet Law); Innsbruck U Austria 45-47 (Pol Sci) PhD; Columbia 56-58 (LS) MS. 6: Ger, Fr, Ital, Rumanian, Russian, Ukrainian, Polish. 7: Foreign law catlgr Yale Law Lib 58-61; Sr libn-catlgr Brooklyn Pub Lib 61-. 9:

Amer Assn Advanc Slavic Studies; Law Libns Assn Greater NY; NY Tech Serv Libns. 10: Shevchenko Sci Soc, NY; Ukrainian Cong Com Amer; Ukrainian Hist Assn; Soc Ukrainian Libns in Amer; Ukrainian Ref & Info Ctr. 12: "Selected Bibliography on Ukraine and Other non-Russian Nations in the Soviet Union (62); Shevchenkology in English; Selected Chronological Bibliography of Taras Shevchenkos Works 964). 13: Yes. 14: East European, Soviet & Ukrainian bibliogs & ref. 15: 36-21 30th st, Astoria 6, LI NY 11106.

SOLK, ELIZABETH (EPSTEIN). b Scranton Penn 28 N 17. 5: UPittsburgh 34-36 (Pre-Educ); Wayne U 36-38 (EDUC) BS in Ed; USoCal 61-62 MS in LS. 6: Fr, Sp. 7: Elem sch tchr Bd of Edyc Detroit 38-42; Statistical clerk Bur of Labor Statistics, Detroit 42-46; Purchasing clerk War Assets Admin, Los Angeles 46-48; Lib aid Burbank Pub Lib, Burbank Cal 50-52; Recreation leader US Army Spec Serv, Korea 59-60; Libn I & II Lib of Hawaii, Honolulu 62-65; Libn III Hawaii State Lib 65-; Libn VI asst dir pub lib br. 8: Consul Lib for Blind & Physically Handicapped, Hawaii. 9: ALA; HawaiiLA. 10: Staff Assn, Lib of Hawaii (pres 64-65). 14: Pub lib serv. 15: 1630 Makiki st apt C-205, Honolulu Hi 96822.

SOLLIDAY, ETHEL MAXINE. b Chicago. 5: UWash 47-49, 50 (Eng) BA, 49-50 (LS) BA. 7: Amer Red Cross 34-46; Br libn UWash 50; Ref libn Monterey Pub Lib, Monterey Ca 50-51, City Libn 51-. 9: ALA; CalLA. 10: Phi Beta Kappa; AAUW; Monterey Hist & Art Assn; World Affairs Coun; Soroptimist Club. 14: Admin, ref. 15: 84 Wellings pl, Monterey Cal 93940.

SOLOMON, BARBARA ANN (GETSEY). b New Brunswick NJ 7 S 45. 4: Jack Solomon. 5: Mt Mercy Col (Pittsburgh) 63-67 (Eng) BA; UPittsburgh 68-69 MLS. 6: Fr. 7: Waitress Howard johnson's, NJ 62-68; Tutor aide Commun Action Program, Pittsburgh Penn 67-69; Lib supv commun Action Pittsburgh Inc 69-. 8: Consul, Commun Action, Pittsburgh 69. 9: PennLA. 10: Mt Mercy Col Alumna Club. 14: Ref. 15: 5835 Alderson st, Pittsburgh Pa 15217.

SOLOMON, LAURENCE HAROLD. b Dominica British West Indies 1 Ap 21. 4: Marion C Sharpe. 5: UNB 46-49 (Hist, Eng) BA; Toronto 50 BLS. 7: Can Army 40-46; Br libn York Twp Pub Lib, Toronto 50-52; Peoria Pub Lib, Peoria Ill 52-53; Order libn Colgate U 53-55; Head Libn: Nelsonville Pub Lib, Nelsonville Ohio 55-57; Portsmouth Pub Lib, Portsmouth Ohio 58; Parkland Reg Lib, Lacombe Alta 59-63; Tech serv libn Contra Costa Co Lib, Pleasant Hill Cal 63-65; Lib consul Oe State Lib 65-68; Dir fld serv div 68-69; Dir New Bedford (Mass) Free Pub Lib 70-. 9: ALA; OreLA (chm Lib Dev Com). 12: "Building Planning Processes (67). 13: Yes. 14: Admin, bldgs. 15: New Bedford Pub Lib, New Be dford Ma 02742.

SOLOMON, ROSALIE (VERNIER). b Phila 25 Jl 30. 5: Rosemont Col 48-52 (Eng Lit) AB; Drexel 62-65 MLS. 6: Fr. 7: Asst ref & circ libn UPenn Law Sch Lib 52-54; Asst libn Smith, Kline & French Lib, Phila 54-57; Libn Law Lib of Montgomery Co, Norristown 65; Libn Montgomery McCraken Walker & Rhoads, Phila 66-67; Consul Chester Co Law Lib,W Chester Penn 68, Sub libn 68; Sub ref libn Mem Lib Rudner Twp, Wayne Penn 69. 9: AALL (Com on New Mems, Com on Stat & Directory 61-62, Com on Chaps 65-66, Panel on Lib coop 65); SLA. 10: Phi Kappa Phi; Beta Phi Mu. 14: Ref, admin. 15: 1125 Millbrook rd, Newtown Sq Pa 19073.

SOLTESZ, KATHRYN M. b Luj Rumania 30 N 10. 5: Lyceum Domnita Ileana (Rumania) 28-32 BA; UCluj (Rumania) 32-36, 37-38 (Hist, Geog) Diplome de Licence, MA; Col of Home Econ (Rumania) 35-37 (Home Econ) Diplome de Absolvire, MA; USzeged (Hungary) 45 Diploma for Tchrs Cols, MA; Gorkiy Inst 51-53 Russian Lang Certif; West Res 58-60 MSLS. 6: Fr, Ger, Hungarian, Ital, Lat, Rumanian, Russian, Sp. 7: Prof Teachers Col & Gymnasiums, Rumania 38-44, Agric Gymnasium Hungary 44-48, State Gymnasium Hungary 54-56; Lib asst Ohio State U 57-60; Asst catlg libn Cornell U 60-62; Sr ser catlgr UCincinnati 62-63; Asst Col libn State U Col Fredonia NY 63-66; Assoc libn & hd for catlg sect intl studies & world affairs SUNY(Oyster Bay) 66-68; Instr, catlgr York Col of CUNY 68-. 10: AAUP; Faculty Assn, SUNY. 14: Catlg, acquis. 15: 3 Glen Keith rd, Glen Cove NY 11542.

SOLTOW, MARTHA JANE (STOUGH). b Shippensburg Penn 9 Jl 24. 4: James H Soltow. 5: Dickinson Col 42-46 (Psych) PhB; Pratt 52-53 MLS. 7: Libn: Hunter Col 53-55, Colonial Williamsburg Inc, Williamsburg Va 55-56, Russell Sage Col 57-59, Harvard U 59-60, Mich State U 60-. 9: MichLA; SLA. 10: Bd, Friends of the East Lansing Pub Lib. 14: Ref, labor & ind rel. 15: 620 Snyder rd, East Lansing Mi 48823.

SOLVICK, SHIRLEY (BADER). b Hartford Conn 5 Je 29. 4: Stanley D Solvick. 5: Wellesley 47-51 (Eng) AB; UMich 53-55 AMLS. 7: Lib asst Trinity Col Lib (Conn) 51-52; UMich Lib asst 53-55, Libn I & II 55-57, Libn II Bur of Govt Lib 57-60; Asst order libn Kent State U 60-61; Libn II Detroit Pub Lib Lang & Lit Dept 61-65, Libn III Fine Arts Dept 65-67, Asst chief gen info dept 67-. 8: Instr ref wkshop Mich State Lib 69. 9: ALA. 10: Citizens Dist Coun; Univ Area. 14: Ref. 15: 650 Merrick ave, D-16, Detroit 48202.

SOMERS, CARIN ALMA ELISABETH STEIN. b Frankfurt/Main Germany 18 Mr 34. 4: Frank G Somers. 5: Newton Col of the Sacred Heart 53-55 (Modern Langs) BA; Dalhousie U 55-56 (Modern Langs) MA; Toronto 60-61 BLS. 6: Ger, Fr, Sp, Ital. 7: Tr Fr & Ger, Lawyer Prov of NS, Halifax 53-; Registrar St Marys U Halifax NS 56-58, U Lecturing Fr & Ger 56-60; U Lecturing Ger Dalhousie U Halifax NS 56-57; Sr clerk Halifax Mem Lib, Halifax NS 58-60, Asst catlgr 61-64; Asst libn Halifax Co Reg Lib, Halifax NS 64-67, Chief libn 67-. 9: CanLA; CathL; APLA; HalifaxLA; APLA (v-pres NS 68-69; pres-elect 69-70). 10: Alliance Francaise. 14: Reg lib serv, catlg. 15: Box 772, Armdale PO, Halifax NS Can.

SOMERS, GERALD ALLAN. b Marshalltown Iowa 4 D 21. 4: Gloria Ann Graeszel. 5: Knox Col 45-47 (Eng); Chicago 47-48; Chicago 48-49 BLS. 6: Fr, Ger, Lat. 7: Libn dept Milwaukee Pub Lib 49-50, Br head 50-56; Dir Eau Claire Pub Lib, Eau Claire Wis 56-61; Dir Kellogg Pub Lib, Green Bay Wis 61-67; Dir Brown Co Lib, Green Bay Wis 68-. 8: Exec dir Nat Lib Week, Wis 64. 9: ALA; WisLA (treas 57-58, pres 65-66; chm Lib Development & Legis Com 66-69). 10: Rotary Club. 11: First Grolier Award for Nat Lib Week, WisLA, 64. 13: Yes. 14: Role of print in mod soc; yech dev of electronic media of communications. 15: Brown County Lib 125 S Jefferson st, Green Bay Wi 54301.

SOMERS, ROBERT B. b Meriden Conn 9 D 26. 5: Brown 47-49; Wesleyan U 49-51 (Govt) BA; Fla State U 52-53 (LS) MA. 7: US Army & US Merchant Marine Cadet Corps 44-47; Ref libn Air U Lib, Montgomery Ala 53-57; Ref libn Akron Pub Lib, Akron Ohio 57-58; Chief circ Air U Lib, Montgomery Ala 58-61; Asst dir Mobile Pub Lib, Mobile Ala 61-62; Dir Alabama Col Lib 63-. 8: Exec Dir, Nat Lib Week, Ala 65, 66. 9: AlaLA. 10: AAUP. 14: Admin, ref. 15: Ala Col Lib, Montevallo Ala 35115.

SOMERS, WAYNE FRANCIS. b Albany NY 24 S 39. 5: Union Col 57-61 (Humanities). 6: Fr, Ger. 7: Order asst Union Col Lib (Schenectady NY) 61-62, Acquis libn 62-69, Bibliogr 69-. 9: BSA. 10: ACLU. 11: Hon Master of Letters degree, Union Col, Schenectady 69. 12: Ed "Plato's Theaetetus," tr by Tayler Lewis (circa 1850) (63). 14: Bibliog, collection bldg. 15: Union College Lib, Schenectady NY 12308.

SOMERVILLE, ARLEEN NORMA (HARLIN). b Milwaukee 23 S 37. 4: James Karl Somerville. 5: UWis 55-59 (Hist, Chem) BS, 59-60 MSLS. 7: Head catlg libn Moline(Ill) Pub Lib 60-61; Tech asst Center for Documentation and Communication Research West Res U 61-62; Period ref libn Case Inst of Tech Lib 62-65; List of period ed Chem Abstracts Serv Lib, Columbus Ohio 65-67; Hd of Chem Biol & Geol Libs URochester (NY) 67-. 9: ASIS (sec-treas Central Ohio Chap 66-67; sec-treas Upstate NY Chap 69); SLA (Arrangements chm 63 fall meeting Metals/Materials Div; Ed M/M Div bulletin 68-69; memb chm Chem Div 68-69; sec Upstate NY Chap 68-69); ALA. 10: Beta Phi Mu; ACS; Geosci Info Soc. 14: Sci ref & admin, computer applications. 15: 18 Melode lane, Geneseo NY 14454.

SOMERVILLE, SALLY ANN (GEARHART). b Wash DC 19 Ap 36. 5: Col of William & Mary 54-58 (Math, Educ) BA; George Washington U summer 55; Kent State U 58-62 (LS) MA. 6: Fr. 7: Math aide NASA, Langley Field Va summer 57: Math tchr Kirtland High Sch, Kirtland Ohio 58-59; Math tchr Burton High Sch, Burton Ohio 59-61; Asst libn Euclid Sr High Sch, Euclid Ohio 61-62; Libn Southington Local Sch, Southington Ohio 62-63; Libn Mayfield Jr High Sch, Cleveland 63-. 8: Visiting Instr of Lib Sci Kent State U 67-69. 9: NEA; ALA; OhioEA; OhioLA; OhioASchL. 14: Wk with yp (Jr high age). 15: RD #2, Box 362, Wilder rd, Chardon Ohio 44024.

SOMMER, RONALD RUDOLPH. b Apple Creek Ohio 18 Ag 36. 4: Betty Neill. 5: Fla StateU 54-58 (Eng) BS, 63 (Hist, Govt) 64-65 (LS) MS; Emory summer 69 (Med Bibliog) Certif. 7: Pfc US Army Res, Ft Jackson SC 59; Instr & libn Fla Sch for Boys, Marianna Fla 59-61; Libn Hernando High Sch, Brooksville Fla 61-63; Libn trainee NYC Pub Lib 64; Asst in lib UFla 65-67, Assoc libn 67-68; Assoc libn LSU Med Sch (Shreveport) 68-. 9: SLA; MedLA; LaLA; Caddo-BossierLA. 14: Admin, ref. 15: 3713 Richmond ave, Shreveport La 71104.

SOMMERVILLE, MARY (ALICE). b Winburne Penn 7 D 09. 5: Wilson Col 26-30 (Fr) AB; Drexel 30-31 BS in LS. 7: Asst catlgr Warder Pub Lib, Springfield Ohio 31-37, Head order & catlg dept 37-43; Libn Naval Train Station, Norfolk Va 43-45; Libn Naval stations at Gulfport, Nashville, Memphis 45-46; Co Libn Joseph & Elizabeth Shaw Pub Lib, Clearfield Penn 46-59, Libn 59-. 9: ALA; PennLA. 10: Clearfield Hist Soc; Bus & Prof Womens Club. 14: Bkmob. 15: Pub Lib 6 S Front st, Clearfield Pa 16830.

SONDAG, JEANNE MARIE. b Council Bluffs Iowa 17 My 41. 5: Creighton 59-63 (Eng) BA; Rosary 63-64 MA in LS. 7: Alumni lib CreightonU 64-. 9: ALA; NebLA. 14: Catlg, ref. 15: 2614 Ave D, Council Bluffs Ia 51501.

SONDHEIMER, J PARKER. b Cleveland 22 S 04. 5: Cornell U 22-26 (Fr) AB; U Penn 26-27 (Hist, FA) AM, 27-31 (Music Composition) BMus; UParis summers 30, 32 (Fr) Brevet; NYU 28-34 (Hist, FA) PHD; Columbia even 38-41 BLS. 6: Fr, Ger. 7: Planning bd mem Fed Wks Agency, NYC 34-43; Wright Aeronautical Corp methods & procedures, Paterson NJ 43-44; Asst ed Funk & Wagnalls, NYC 44-45; Chief indexer Columbia U (SRG) 45-48; Research consul Self-employed, NYC 48-56; Ed of research Crowell-Collier, NYC 56-62; Data processing libn IBM, Armonk NY 63-67; Indexing & info retrieval 67-. 8: Lib consul to US Navy, 40-41; Consul in indexing to US Coast Guard, 41-42. 9: SLA. 10: ACM. 13: Yes. 14: Data proc methods applied to lib procedures, indexing & info retrieval. 15: 62 Park ter W, NYC 10034.

SONDROL, ROBERT O. b Wellfleet Mass 27 Ag 22. 4: Helen Leblan. 5: UMass 47-50 (Bus) BBA; St Josephs Col 56-59 (Educ); Simmons 64-65 MS in LS. 6: Fr, Ger. 7: USAF; Prof of Air Sci, Penn 55-59, Admin staff off, Mo 59-60, Personnel staff off, Germany 60-64; Asst city libn & (NH) Pub Lib 65-66; Dir Melrose Pub Lib, Melrose Mass 66-. 8: Asst Prof Mass State Col at Salem, Lectr in Lib Sci 68. 9: ALA; NELA; MassLA; NHLA (v-pres 65-66). 10: Retired Offs Assn; Societe des collectionneurs de figurines historiques; Deutsche Gesellschaft der Freunde and Sammler kulturhistorischer Figuren; Rotary Intl; Melrose Com Coun; N Shore Lib Club. 14: Admin. 15: PO Box 47, Amherst NH 03031.

SONE, CHAE S. b Korea 21 N 23. 4: Kyung Ok Kim. 5: Seoul Theol Sem (Seoul Korea) 45-48 (Theol); Hankuk Theol Sem (Seoul Korea) 48-51 (Theol) BD; Bangor Theol Sem 54-55 (Theol); UOre 55-56 (Sociol); Pacific U 56-57 (Sociol) BA; West Res 57-58 MS in LS; NYU 59-64, 67 (Human Rel) PhD. 6: Japanese, Korean. 7: Olivet Nazarene Col Lib 58-59; Stevens Inst of Tech Lib 59-65; Hicksville Pub Lib, Hicksville NY 65-. 14: Catlg, ref. 15: 29 Tudor rd, Hicksville NY 11801.

SONEVYTSKY, NATALIE A (PALIDWOR). b Roznitiw, Ukraine 27 Mr 34. 4: Ihor Sonevytsky. 5: Col of New Rochelle 52-56 (Hist) BA; Columbia 57-59 (LS) MA. 6: Ukrainian, Polish, Russian, Ger. 7: Bk buyer Mus of Nat Hist, NY 56-59; Asst ref libn Barnard Col 59-67; Hd ref 67-. 14: Ref. 15: 62 E 7th st, NYC 10003.

SONG, BYUNG KYU. b Seoul Korea 17 Ja 35. 5: Yun SeiU 54-58 (Commerce) BC; Eastern Wash State Col 60-63 (Accounting) BA; UOre 64-67 (Bus Admin) BBA; 67-69 MLS. 6: Korean. 7: Admin asst Off US Mil Adv Gp, JCS, Army, Cpl, Republic of Korea 58; Asst acquis libn, Oklahoma StateU 69-. 9: ALA. 14: Acquis, automation. 15: 217 S Ramsey st, apt 1, Stillwater Ok 74074.

SONG, CZETONG (THOMAS). b Tokyo 24 Mr 29. 4: Mary Jane Katsoris. 5: Dartmouth 49-53 (Math) BA; UMich 57-58 (Philos) MA, 59-61 MALS. 6: Fr, Japanese, Chinese, Korean, Esperanto. 7: Pers admin spec US Army (Sp-3) AGC 54-57; Ref libn & lecturer Oakland U 61-64; Deputy head info serv div Center for Application of Sci & Tech Wayne State U Libs 64-66, Libn for systs development 68-; Research assoc Yale U Lib 68-. 8: Lecturer on area studies (China) & Operations Res, Oakland U 61-64; Lecturer on docuentation Dept of Lib Sci, Wayne State U 64-68; Lecturer Info Sci Dept Lib Sci UMo 68. 9: SLA; ASIS. 10: AAUP. 12: "Bibliography of Aerospace Bibliographies (65); "Trend of Publishing in Mainland China, 1949-1958 (61). 13: Yes. 14: Documentation, info storage & retrieval, lib automation, info sci. 15: 19 Ridgewood cir, Wallingford Ct 06492.

SONGE, ALICE H. b Morgan City La 15 Je 14. 5: Southwestern U 32-36 (Liberal Arts) BA; LSU 36-37 BS in LS; Catholic U 53-56 (Educ) MA in Ed. 6: Fr. 7: Sch libn La pub schs 37-44; Head Co Lib System, Vermillion Parish, Abbeville La 44-46; Staff libn VA Hosp, Oteen NC 46-47; Head Libn St Genevieves Jr Col 47-52; Act head ref dept Catholic U Lib 52-56; Educ analyst Legis Ref Serv LC 56-63; Educ spec Dept of Health, Educ, & Welfare Lib, Wash DC 63-. 9: DCLA; NEA; AERA. 12: Comp "The Land-Grant Movement in American Higher Education; An Historical Bibliography" (62); "Vocational Education; An Annotated Bibliography of Selected References, 1917-1966" (67). 13: Yes. 14: Ref, bibliog. 15: 1619 30th st NW, Apt 103, Wash DC 20007.

SONNE, GRACE (JOLINE). b NYC 7 My 10. 4: Niels Henry Sonne. 5: Barnard 28-32 (Zool) BA; Columbia 42 (LS) BS. 6: Fr, Lat, Ger. 7: Child libn Pub Lib, Westfield NJ 3446; Child libn NY Pub Lib 47-48; Lbn St Lukes Sch, NYC 56-. 9: ALA-CSD; -AASchL. 10: Garden Club; Me Horticul Soc; Embroiderers Guild; Metro Mus of Art. 14: Child & elem sch wk. 15: 175 Ninth ave, NYC 10011.

SONNE, NIELS HENRY. b NYC 21 D 07. 4: Grace Joline. 5: Colgate U 26-27; Columbia 27-30 (Econ Hist AB; Unon Theol Sem 31-34 (Old Testament) BD; Columbia 39 (Philos) PhD, 38-42 (LS) BS. 6: Ger, Fr, Lat. 7: Ref libn & catlgr Drew U 39-42; Catlgr US Army Lib, Camp Pickett Va 42-44; Clerk 3rd ser command deml T/5 Post Publ Off, Indiantown Gap Penn 44-45; Catlgr Sperry Gyroscope Co, Garden City LI NY 45-46; Ref libn Trinity Col(Conn) 46-47; Asst libn Gen Theol Sem NYC 47-48, Libn 48-. 8: Consul, Faculte de Theologie Protestante, Yaounde Cameroun, 63. 9: ATHeolLA (Exec Com 3 yrs, var other assignments). 10: Grolier Club(NY); Archons of Colophon; Melvil Dui Marching & Chowder Assn. 12: Auth "Liberal Kentucky, 1780-1828 (39; Ed & bibliog, Wm Smallwood, "Natural History and the American Mind (41); Comp "Master List of Masters Theses in Religion (50); Issue ed "Library Trends, vol 9, no 2 (60); Auth "The Gutenberg Bible of the General Theological Seminary (2nd ed 65); Auth "John Pintard and the Early Years of the General Theological Seminary Library. 13: Yes. 14: Theological libnship, rare bks, STC & Wing items, the Gutenberg problem, exhibition wk. 15: The General Theological Seminary, 175 Ninth ave, NYC 10011.

SONNENBERG, BARBARA (H). b Cincinnati 9 D 37. 5: Col of Mt St Joseph 56-60 (LS) BA; UIll 60-61 MS in LS. 7: Cincinnati Pub Lib; Adult asst libn Hyde Park Br 61, Br libn St Bernard-Elmwood Brs 62, Br libn Price Hill Br 63-, Br libn Delhi Hills Area Brs (3) 66, Br libn Delhi Hills Br 68-. 8: Ya bk selection com 65-. 9: ALA; OhioLA. 13: Yes. 14: Bk sel. 15: 2845 E St Charles pl, Cincinnati Oh 45208.

SOO, MARGARET (S). b Hankow China 24 Ap 40. 5: Mary Manse Col 61-64 (Hist) BA; Catholic U 65-68 MSLS. 6: Chinese, Ger. 7: Lib Aide Toledo Pub Lib, Toledo Ohio 64-65; Grad lib asst Catholic U 65-66, Acting asst hd, soc sci 66-67, Acting hd 67-68; Assoc libn UMd 68-. 9: ALA; ASIS; DCLA. 10: Cath Col Alum Club (Wash DC). 14: Ref, internat libnship. 15: 4313 Knox rd 211, College Park Md 20740.

SOO, SZE. b 20 F 38. 5: Nat Taiwan U 55-60 (Physics) BS; Kan State Tchrs Col 62-63 (LS) MS; UDel 68- (Computer Sci). 6: Chinese. 7: Jr ref libn Linda Hall Lib, Kan City Mo 63-64; Tech libn Xerox Corp Res Lib, Webster NY 64-. 66; Acquis libn Worcester Polytech Inst 66-68; Evening libn Del Tech & Commun Col 68-. 9: SLA. 14: Ref, lib automation. 15: 15J Wellington Arms apts, Newark De 19711.

SOOMET, LILIAN. b Tallinn Estonia 21 Mr 40. 5: McGill 57-61 (Eng) BA; UBC 61-64 (Psych, Sociol); UWash 64-65 MLibr. 6: Estonian, Fr. 7: Lib asst Sci Div UBC Lib 62-64; Ref libn UToronto Lib 65-. 14: Ref, new devels. 15: 263 St Charles rd, Greenfield Park Que Can.

SOONG, EILEEN M. b NY 21 Ap 25. 4: James Soong. 5: UHawaii 50-54 (Elem Educ) Ed B, 54-55 (Educ) 5Yr Diploma; Rutgers 57-5 MLS. 7: Elem tchr Dept of Educ, Honolulu 54-55, Libn 55-57; Libn Bd of Educ, Dunellen NJ 58-66; Libn US Dept Interior FWPCA, NJ 68-. 8: Textbk selection com Hawaii Pub Schs 56; Middle Atlantic States Evaluation Com, NJ 63; Study individual sch lib serv, NJ 65; Consul; Establishment water resources lib for priv ind, NJ 68, Establishment Fed Water Pollution Lib, Cal 69. 9: ALA; NJEA; NJLA; NJSchLA; SLA. 14: Ref, ya. 15: 158 Clover Hill rd, Millington NJ 07946.

SOPER, MARLEY HUBER. b Leslie Mich 11 N 34. 4: Beverly Jorgensen. 5: Andrews U 53-58 (Eng) BA; UWis 65

MALS. 6: Ger. 7: Tchr-libn High Sch, Stanton Mich 58-61; Libn Wisconsin Academy, Columbus Wis 61-67; Acquis libn James White Lib Andrews U 67-. 8: Tch, col courses in lib sci. 9: ALA; MichLA. 13: (Yes. 14: Ref, acquis, circ, admin, period. 15: 352 Pam dr, Berrien Springs Mi 49103.

SOPER, MARY ELLEN. b Wichita Kan 12 Je 34. 5: UIll 51-55 (Sociol) BA, 61-63 (LS) MS, 67- (LS). 6: Sp, Ger, Fr. 7: Catlgr UIll Lib (Urbana) 61-63; Ser libn Zimmerman Lib UNM 63-67. 9: ALA. 10: Phi Beta Kappa; Beta Phi Mu. 14: Ser, tech serv. 15: 51 E Chalmers, Champaign Il 61820.

SORENSEN, EDWIN H. b Brooklyn NY 10 S 30. 4: Helen Eels. 5: Cortland State Tchrs Col 48-52 Elem Educ) BS in Ed; Columbia 55-57 MSLS. 7 Elem libn Elmont pub schs, Elmont NY 54-56; Libn Sewanhaka High Sch, Floral Park NY 56-58; Elem & jr high sch libn US Army Dependent Schs, France 58-59; Elem libn San Diego city schs 59-60; Elem libn Northport pub schs, Northport NY 60-. 9: Nassau-Suffolk Sch LA. 14: Sch libs. 15: 16 Maplewood dr Northport NY 11768.

SORGEN, HERBERT JEROME. b Brooklyn NY 29 Jl 38. 4: Nancy Lee Riffanacht. 5: Syracuse 56-60 (Eng, Educ) AB; SUC (Oswego) 61-64 (Eng, Educ) MS; UMich 68-69 (LS) AMLS. 6: Ger. 7: Teletype operator US Army Reserve, Syracuse NY 59-64; Eng tchr Paul V Moore High Sch, Central Square NY 60-64; Asst prof SUNY Col (Delhi) 65-68, Libn 68-. 8: Fac adv BradeisU rifle . team. 9: ALA; NCTE (Conf on Col Composition & Communication); NYLA; NYStateTA (co-chm Central Zone Eng Sect); Amer Fed Col Tchrs; SUNY Libns. 10: AAUP; Beta Phi Mu. 13: Yes. 14: Bk selection, ref, admin. 15: RD #2, Delhi NY 13753.

SOROKA, MARGUERITE (CULVER). b Stillwater Minn 23 Mr 18. 4: John J Soroka. 5: Bradford Jr Col 35-37 (Liberal Arts) Certif; Smith 38-40 (Hist) AB; Pratt 44-45 BS in LS. 6: Fr, Ger, Sp. 7: Supv of codes & Ciphers Air Transport Command, Wash DC 41-45; Catlgr & ref libn Lockport Pub Lib, Lockport NY 45-46; Clsf & 1st asst catlg dept Engnr Societies Lib, NYC 46-58, Head catlg dept 58-66, Hd tech serv 66-. 8: Engnrs Jt Coun Thesaurus Com. 9: ALA; SLA; NY Tech Serv Libns (sec-treas 50-51, pres 60-61, var coms); NYLA; ASIS. 10: Beta Phi Mu; Bradford, Smith & Pratt Alumnae Assns. 13: Yes. 14: Catlg, clsf. 15: 3 Fox lane, Flushing NY 11354.

SORRIER, ELIZABETH. b Statesboro Ga 24 J; 09. 5: Gulf Park Col 28-30 Diploma; Ga So Col 32-33 BS; Emory 43-45 AB in LS. 7: Swainsboro pub schs, Swainsboro Ga 33-39; Hawkinsville pub schs, Hawkinsville Ga 40-41; Statesboro Hish Sch lib, Statesboro Ga 41-. 8: Elem lib consul for Bulloch Co, Ga. 9: NEA; ALA; GaLA; SELA; GaEA (pres Lib Dept 62-63). 14: Ref. 15: 322 Savannah ave, Statesboro Ga.

SORRIER, ISABEL (LANE). b Statesboro Ga 18 Ag 17. 5: Ga So Col 34-38 (Educ, Hist, Eng) BS; Peabody 41-42 BLS. 7: Homerville High Sch, Homerville Ga 39-41; Waycross Pub Lib, Waycross Ga 42; Newnan High Sch, Newnan Ga 43; Statesboro Reg Lib, Statesboro Ga 44-. 8: Prof Lib Com, State Dept of Educ, 59; State Com, Fed Construction Act, 64-65; State NLW Com 66-67. 9: ALA; SELA; GaLA (chm Pub Lib Sect 62-63). 14: Admin, ref. 15: Statesboro Ga 30458.

SOSNOWSKY, MICHAEL. b Ternopil Ukraine 1 D 19. 4: Oksana Zawadowych. 5: Lviv U(Ukraine) 42-44; Erlangen U(Germany) 46-48; Toronto 54-57 (Pol Sci) BA; Toronto 60-61 BLS; Ukrainian Free U (Germany) 66-68 Dr rev pol. 6: Ukrainian, Polish, Russian, Ger. 7: Reporter Czas, Furth Germany 45-46; Ed Students Newsletter, Erlangen Germany 46-48; Ed Homin Ukrainy, Toronto 48-54; Bus manager Safeway Construction Co Ltd, Toronto 57-60; Catlgr & asst chief clsfr UToronto Lib 61-65; Head acquis dept Carleton U 65-67; Bibliogr Studium Research Inst, Ottawa Ont 68-. 9: CanLA; OntLA; Inst Prof Libns Ont; OttawaLA. 10: Shevchenko Sci Soc of Can; Ukrainian-Can Com; Can League for Ukraines Liberation; Studium Research Inst; Can Assn of Slavists. 12: "Ukraine in International Relations 45-65" (66). 13: Yes. 14: Tech serv, bibliog wk. 15: Studium Research Inst Inc, 1306 Normandy Cr, Ottawa 5 Ont Can.

SOTENDAHL, AUDREY (BOYUM). b Minneapolis Minn 21 S 31. 4: Henry R Sotendahl. 5: UMinn 48-52 (Bus Educ) BS, 64-68 (LS) MA. 7: Com tchr Atwater Pub Schs, Atwater Minn 52-53; Train tech Prudential Ins Co, Minneapolis 53-55; Ref libn Mohawk Valley Commun Col 68-. 14: Ref. 15: 26 Woodberry rd, New Hartford NY 13413.

SOTIRIN, PAUL GEORGE. b Milwaukee 4 Ap 25. 4: Muriel Sterland. 5: UWis (Milwaukee) 46-48; Marquette U 49-51 (Amer Hist, Lit) PhB; UWis 51-52 (LS, Amer Civil War) MSLS. 6: Gk, Fr. 7: Army of the US T/4 766 Tank Battalion 43-46; Libn IV Milwaukee Pub Lib 52-68; Libn City of New Berlin, Wis 69-. 8: Discussion leader 10 week course on urban probs & the lib. 9: WisLA. 10: Amer Assn State & Loc Hist State Hist Soc Wis; Civil War Round Table of Milwaukee; Waukesha Co Hist Soc; Sigma Tau Delta. 13: Yes. 14: Great Lakes Marine history, local hist, US Civil War. 15: 5346 N 66th st, Milwaukee 53218.

SOULE, EDMUND FOSTER. b Boston Mass 4 Mr 15. 4: Beverly Sherman. 5: UPenn 33-39 9theory Mus) BM, 39-46 (Compos Mus) MA; Yale Sch of Mus 46-48 (Theory Mus) BM; Eastman sch Mus URochester 52-56 (Theory Mus) PhD; UDenver 65-66 MLS. 7: Cpl US Army 42-45; Instr Milton Acad 48-49; Instr Wash State Col 49-51; Hd mus dept Salem Col 55-58; Asst Prof UPacific 58-61; Asst Prof Wash StateU 61-65; Asst Prof UOre Lib (Eugene) 66-. 9: MusLA. 10: Phi Mu Alph Sinfonia. 11: Kellogg Prize in Theory (Fugue-Writing) Yale 47. 12: Had published Choral Music, Piano Music, Piece for Sax & Piano, etc. 14: Music ref, catlg, sheet music collection, orientation for students. 15: Lib Univ of Oregon, Eugene Or 97403.

SOULE, HARVEY G. b Phila Pa 8 O 26. 4: Margaret F Soule. 5: UTenn 46-49 (Educ) BS; UCLA 52-53 Elem Credential; Los Angeles State Col 55-59 (Educ Admin) MA; USoCal 61-62 (LS) MS. 6: Fr. 7: Sgt US Army Artillery, USA-FECOM 50-52; Off personnel mgr Soule Const Co, Glendale Cal 53-55; Tchr Los Angeles Co Schs 56-59; Assoc libn UMd (Col Park) 62-67; Educ libn & asst prof lib admin Kent StateU 67-. 9: SLA; OhioLA. 10: Mayflower Assn; Phi Delta Kappa; Kappa Delta Pi. 14: Ref, educ. 15: 1353 Stratford dr, Kent Oh 44240.

SOULE, MARIA JOAN (GALLO). b Kenosha Wis 14 Je 44. 4: James D Soule. 5: UWis (Kenosha Ctr) 62-64; UWis (Milwaukee) 64-66 (Fr, Eng) BA, 66-68 (LS) MA. 6: Fr. 7: Libn UWis (Parkside Kenosha Campus) 68-. 9: KenoshaLA. 10: Sigma Tau Delta. 14: Sel & acquis wk. 15: 7606 - 18th ave, Kenosha Wi 53140.

SOUTAR, JOAN (URLAKIS). b Baltimore Md. 4: Bernol Soutar. 5: George WashingtonU 64 9hist) BA; UMich MALS. 7: Period libn UMich Gen Lib (Ann Arbor) 67-68; Ref libn Adrian Col 68-. 9: ALA; MichLA. 14: Ref, acquis (col libs). 15: 1155 McIntyre, Ann Arbor Mi 48105.

SOUTER, JANET (OSBURN). b Elyria Ohio 27 F 34. 4: Thomas A Souter. 5: Fla State U 51-55 (LS) AB; Syracuse 55-57 (LS) MS. 7: Asst libn Gen Educ Div Fla State U 57-60; Asst Roswell Pub Lib, Roswell NM 61-62; Asst Undergrad Lib Ind U 63-. 9: ALA. 14: Ref. 15: 309 N Hillsdale dr, Bloomington Ind 47401.

SOUTER, THOMAS A. b Adel Ga 16 My 30. 4: Janet Osborn. 5: Fla State U 47-51 (Soc Sci) BS, 54-57 (LS) MS. 7: Sgt infantry US Army, 7th Cavalry Company G 51-54; Asst libn acquis Fla State U 57-59, Asst libn soc sci 59-60; Head Libn NM Mil Inst 60-62; Dept head circ dept Ind U 62-. 10: Phi Dela Kappa. 14: Admin. 15: 309 N Hillsdale dr, Bloomington Ind 47401.

SOUTHARD, EUGENIA MAXIM. b Sangerville Me 6 M 08. 5: Bates Col 25-29 (Eng, Lat) AB; Columbia 32-36 (LS) BS. 7: Libn Grade I Brooklyn Pub Lib 32-35, Libn Grade II 35-49; Ref libn Portland Pub Lib, Portland Me 49-. 9: ALA; MeLA. 10: Bates Alumnae Club. 14: Ref. 15: Portland Pub Lib, 619 Congress st, Portland Me 04101.

SOUTHCOMBE, PATRICIA (ANN). b Kalamazoo 23 Jl 39. 5: State U Col, Geneseo NY 57-61 (LS) BS in Ed, summers 62-67 MLS. 7: Elem sch lib Union-Endicott Central Sch Dist 1, Endicott NY 61-65; High sch libn Greece Central Sch Dist 1, Rochester NY 65-68; Jr high sch libn Pittsford Central Schs, Pittsford NY 68-. 9: NYLA; NY State Tchrs Assn. 15: 68 Grecian Garden apt B, Rochester NY 14626.

SOUTHERN, W(ALTER) A. b Milwaukee 30 Ap 19. 5: UWis 37-41 BA; UMich 42-43 MALS: Chicago 46-48 (LS); Lake Forest Col (Ind Mgt Inst), 58-62 Certif. 6: Ger, Fr. 7: Stud asst UMich Engnr Lib 42-43; Libn Bur of Visual Instr UWis(Madison) 43-45; Head search dept Engnr Socs Lib, NY 45-46; Head circ ref depts UIll (Chicago) 46-48; Research libn Dearborn Chem Co, Chicago 48-49; Chief Libn Abbott Labs, N Chicago 49-61; Head sci info serv Abbott Labs, N Chicago 61-. 8: Ill State Lib Adv Bd, 49-65; John Crerar Lib Adv Bd, 64-; Exec com Midwest Reg Med Lib; Adv Bd Lib Tech Program, Kenosha (Wis) Tech Inst. 9: MedL; SLA; Aslib;

IllLA. 11: Fulbright fellowship, 48-49, affiliated with Aslib, LONDON (Study of European res libs). 13: Yes. 14: Info center admin. 15: Abbott Labs 1400 Sheridan rd, N Chicago Il 60645.

SOUTHWICK, MILDRED D. b Poughkeepsie NY 1 D 05. 5: Vassar 26 (Math) AB, 36 (Plant Sci) AM; UWis 49 (Bot) PhD; UCal(Berkeley) 54 BLS. 6: Fr. 7: Tchr Hillside Sch, Norwalk Conn 28-35; Vassar Col: Ecologist 36-39, Instr 40-48, Asst Prof 48-53; Asst in lib Purdue U summer 53; Asst catlgr E Carolina Col 54-57, Head ref libn & Assoc Prof 57-, Prof 66-, Assoc libn 67-. 9: ALA; Electron Microscope Soc of Amer; SELA; NCLA; NCEA. 10: AAAS (Fellow); AAUW; Sigma Delta Epsilon; Delta Kappa Gamma. 13: Yes. 14: Ref, catlg. 15: 1100 E Third st, Greenville NC 27834.

SOUTHWORTH, SIGRID B. b Hoolehua Molokai Hawaii 18 O 41. 4: John H Southworth. 5: UHawaii 59-61; Grinnell Col 61-63 (Lit) BA; Simmons 63-64 MLS. 7: Libn Kamehameha Sch for Girls, Honolulu 64-68; Dept chm 68-. 9: ALA; NEA; HawaiiLA; Hawaii Assn Sch Libs; OahuEA; HawaiiEA. 10: Friends of the Lib of Hawaii; Intl Stud Org (UHawaii); Hawaii Malacological Soc. 14: High sch ref. 15: Kamehameha Sch for Girls, Honolulu Hi 96817.

SOUZA, BLASE CAMACHO. b Kohala Hawaii 3 F 18. 4: Alfred Patrick Souza. 5: UHawaii 35-39 (Educ) Ed B, 39-40 (Educ) 5th Year Certif; Pratt 46-47 BLS. 6: Sp. 7: Trimmer Hawaiian Pineapple Co, Honolulu summer 37; Tutor & club leader Palama Settlement, Honolulu 38; Exhibit attendant Publ Exhibit UHawaii summer 39; Stock clerk Sears Roebuck & Co, Honolulu summer 40; Tchr Dept of Pub Instr, Honolulu spring 40; Libn: Kamehameha III Sch, Lahaina Maui 40-42, Waialua Elem Sch, Waialua Oahu 42-46, Farrington High Sch, Honolulu 47-51, Aina Haina Sch, Honolulu 56-66; Research libn Hawaii Curriculum Ctr 66-68, Hd of Libs 68-. 8: Chm, Secondary Sch Libns, Honolulu, 49; Sec, Elem Sch Libns, Honolulu, 58; Chm, Elem Sch Libns, Honolulu, 59; Intern supv in lib sci, Honolulu, 61-64; Adv Bd, Grad Sch of Lib Studies, UHawaii, 64-65. 9: NEA; ALA-AASchL (Legis Liaison Netwk); HawaiiEA; HawaiiASchl (pres; co-chm Standards Com); HawaiiLA. 10: AAUW; Mortar Board; Honolulu Acad of Arts, Theta Delta Kappa Gamma. 14: Sch libs, wk with child, curriculum research. 15: 51 Nohu st, Honolulu Hi 96821.

SOVEL, M TERRY. b Philadelphia Pa 6 My 42. 5: Penn State 59-62 (Eng) BA; UDenver 66-69 (LS) MA. 6: Fr. 7: Tchr Phoenix Jewish Commun Ctr 63; Off mgr Women in Commun Serv Inc, Denver 65; Research economist Denver Research Inst 66-. 8: Responsible for the establish, org, and maint of the Proj for the Analysis of Tech Transfer Lib 68-. 12: "Technology Transfer: a Selected Bibliography" (68); "A User's Evaluation of a NASA Regional Dissemination Center," (69). 13: Yes. 14: Research in diffusion of sci & tech info. 15: Denver Res Inst Ind Econ Div Univ of Denver, Denver Co 80210.

SOWBY, JOYCE KATHARINE (ROUS). b Toronto. 5: Toronto 46-50 BA, 50-51 BLS. 7: Libn CanLA, Ottawa 53-58; Asst libn: Nat Gallery of Canada, Ottawa 61-62, Annapolis Valley Reg Lib, Annapolis Royal NS 62-65, Scarborough Col Lib, Toronto 65-. 9: CanLA. 14: Circ, ref. 15: Apt 1, 443 Rosewell ave. Toronto 12 Can.

SPAETH, JOHN WILLIAM JR. b Phila 2 Jl 895. 4: Verna E Follett. 5: Haverford Col 13-17 (Classics) BA; Harvard 17-18 (Classics) MA; Princeton U 23-25 (Classics) PhD. 6: Lat, Fr, Gk. 7: Instr of Gk & Lat Classics Brown U 25-26 Asst Prof 26-28, Assoc Prof 28-30; Wesleyan U(Conn): Assoc Prof of classics 30-32, Prof of Classics 32-63, Dean of the Faculty 49-63, Univ Archivist 63-. 9: Amer Philol Assn; Archaeol Inst Amer; Amer Classical League; SAA: Classical Assn NE (sec-treas 37-47, pres 48-49). 10: Phi Beta Kappa; Trustee, Pasquaney Trust. 11 "A Study of the Causes of Romes Wars from 343 to 265 B.C. (26); Comp "Vergiliana: A Selected List of books for Library Exhibits (30); Comp "Index Verborum Fragmentorum Ciceronis Poeticorum (55). 13: Yes. 14: Col archives. 15: 45 Lawn ave, Middletown Conn 06457.

SPAHN, CAROLE C (KOONS). b Gettysburg Penn 22 F 34. 4: Helmut Spahn. 5: Kutztown State Col 51-55 (LS) BS in Ed; Syracuse summer 57, 58 (LS). 6: Ger. 7: Libn New Cumberland High Sch, New Cumberland Penn 55-58; Army libn Spec Serv, Mannheim & Kassel Germany 58-59; Libn No York Co Area High Sch, Dillsburg Penn 60-61; Lib asst USAREUR Spec Serv Ref Lib, Heidelberg Germany 61-64, Ar,y libn 65-. 9: ALA; (Armed Forces Libns Sect, Europ Subsect). 10: Kappa Delta Pi. 14: Catlg, ref. 15: USAREUR Spec Serv ref Lib, APO NY 09403.

SPAHN, THEODORE JURGEN. b Chicago 11 O 31. 5: Lake Forest Col 48-49; Northwestern 49-52 (Hist) BS, 52-53 (Hist) MA; Chicago 54-56 (Hist); Rosary Col 64-65 MA in LS; UMich 67- (LS). 6: Fr, Ger. 7: Asst in documents, ref & rare bks Northwestern U 57-64; Asst ref libn UIll (Chicago Circle) 65, Bibliogr 65-66, Chief bibliogr 66-67; Visiting asst prof Lib Sci Rosary Col 66-67; Lecturer in Lib Scu UMich (Ann Arbor) 67-. 9: ALA; Chicago Lib Club. 10: US Chess Fed; ACLU; Beta Phi Mu; Caxton Club; AAUP. 12: Co-ed "From Radical Left to Extreme Right (2nd ed 69). 14: Propaganda, dissident period.15 557 S 7th st, Ann Arbor Mi 48103. 15: 557 S 7th st, Ann Arbor Mi 48103.

SPAHR, JANET ELISE. b Welch W Va 15 F 34. 5: Va Polytech Inst 50-51 (Bus Admin); UTenn 52-55 (Off Admin) BS; LSU 67-69 (LS) MS. 6: Russian. 7: Sec US Govt, Wash DC 55-56; Sec Nat Acad of Sci, Wash DC 56-63; Sec RiceU 63-67; Trainee LSU (Baton Rouge) 67-69; Libn (catlgr) DukeU 69-. 9: SLA. 14: Ref. 15:, 59D Colonial apts, Durham NC 27707.

SPAIN, FRANCES LANDER. b Jacksonville Fla 15 Mr 03. 5: Winthrop Col 21-25; Fla State Col for Women summer 35 (Phys Educ); Emory 35-36 BLS; Chicago 39-41, 44 (LS) MA, PhD. 6: Fr. 7: Asst Pub Lib, Jacksonville Fla 19-21; Libn Winthrop Train Sch, Rock Hill SC 36-39; Head Lib Sci Dept Winthrop Col 36-48, Libn 45-48; Asst dir Sch Lib Sci USoCal 49-53; Coordinator child serv NY Pub Lib 53-61; Dir Lib Servs Central Fla Jr Col 61-. 8: Mem, lib group USA-USSR Cultural Exchange program, 61; Fulbright grantee to Thailand, 51-52; Rockefeller Found grantee to Thailand, 64-65; Accrediting com of ALA, So Assn of Col & Second Schs, & Fla State Dept of Educ; Visiting lecturer: Columbia U Sch of Lib Serv summers54, 56, 57, 60, Pratt Inst Lb Sch spring 56; Rutgers Grad Sch of Lib Serv fall 58; Syracuse Sch of Lib Sci summer 59. 9: ALA (pres 60-61; Commsn on a Nat Plan for Lib Educ 63-); -LED pres 59-60 Bd of Educ for Libnship 50-53, chm Dutton-Macrea Awards Com, 52-54, chm Groiler Soc Awards Com, 55-56, chm Clarence Day Awards Com 63-64); SCLA (pres 47; chm Sch Lib Sect 41-45); So Assn of Cols & Schs (Lib Com 50-58); CalLA (chm Intel Freedom Com 51 & 53); FlaLA (chm Constit Com 64). 10: Anthony Womans Club, AAUW. 11: Woman of the Year in Lib Sci, 61 citation by the Eds of "Whos Who of American Women. 12: Ed "Books for Young People", in Saturday Review (54-59); Ed "Reading Without Boundaries" (56); Ed "Contents of the Basket" (60). 13: Yes. 14: Child bks, lib educ, child serv, jr col lib serv. 15: PO Box 128, Anthony Fl 32617.

SPALDING, C(HARLES) SUMNER. b Somerville Mass 23 My 12. 5: Harvard 33 (Music) AB, 34 (Music) MA; Columbia 40 (LS) BS. 7: Music instr Belmont Hill Sch, Belmont Mass 34-35; Music arranger, NYC 36-39; Lib asst Cooper Union 37-40; Lib asst Music Div LC 40-41; US Army Bandleader WOJG 42-45; LC: Catlgr 46-49, Asst chief Catlg Maintenance Div 50, Chief 51-52, Chief Ser Rec Div 53-56, Chief Descr Catlg Div 56-62, Ed ALA Catalog Code Revision Proj 62-66; Chief descr catlg div 66-68, Asst dir processing dept for catlg 68-. 8: US Bd on Geog Names (Alternate) 60-62, 67-. 9: ALA; Coun 60-62, 68-72; Potomac Tech Proc Libns; ASIS. 13: Yes. 14: Catlg, tech serv. 15: Library of Congress, Wash DC 20540.

SPANGLER, SISTER JOSEPH DAMIEN OP. b Woodsfield Ohio 8 F 22. 5: St Mary of the Springs Col 38-42 (Classics) BA; Rosary Col 53-58 (LS) MA; Notre Dame U summer 62 (Classics). 6: Lat, Gk, Fr, Ger. 7: Tchr of classics Acad of St Mary of the Springs 46-60; Col lib Col of St Mary of the Springs 60-. 9: ALA; CathLA; OhioLA. 10: Classical Assn, Midwest & South; Amer Phil Assn; Kappa Gamma Pi. 14: Rare bks. 15: Ohio Dominican College Lib, Columbus Oh 43219.

SPANIER, LELA (MARSH). b Can 18 J 122. 4: John L Spanier. 5: Butler U (Ger, Eng) AB; UChicago 46-47 (LS) BLS. 6: Fr, Sp, Ger. 7: Catlgr Penn State U 44-45; Catlgr US Armed Forces Med Lib, Wash DC 45-49, Asst head proc sect 49-58; NLM, Wash DC Acquis area spec 58-60, Ser spec 60-61, Head ed sect 61-63, Libn US Food & Drug Admin, Wash DC 63-65; Asst ed New Ser Titles LC 66-. 9: SLA. 11: Award for outstanding service, NLM, 62. 12: Actg ed "Current List (sp 48); Ed "National Library of Medicine Catalog (62); Comp "Biomedical Serials, 1950-1960 (62); Asst ed "New Serial Titles (66). 13: Yes. 14: Bibliog, ref, catlg, admin. 15: 4201 Massachsetts ave NW, Wash DC 20016.

SPAR, BEATRICE ANNE. b Cleveland 7 My 33. 5: Malone Col 54-58 (Religion) BRE; Greenville Col 58-60 (Eng) BS in Ed; UMich summers 61-64 MALS. 7: Bkkeeper & Teller Cleveland Trust Co, Cleveland 51-54; Circ & bk ordering

Greenville Col Lib 60-64; Catlgr Malone Col Lib 64-. 9: ALA; OhioLA. 14: Catlg. 15: 820 E Maple st, N Canton Ohio 44720.

SPARE, PAULINE P. b Rochester NY 13 Jl 14. 5: URochester 31-35 (Hist) AB; Syracuse 63-64 MSLS. 7: Lib tech Rochester Pub Lib, Rochester NY; Asst dir Wayne Co Lib Syst, Newark NY 34-67, Dir 67-. 10: Phi Beta Kappa; Beta Phi Mu. 15: 3402 West Lake rd, Canandaigua NY 14424.

SPARENBLEK, MATILDA V. b Indianapolis Ind. 5: Butler U (Ger, Eng(AB; u chicago 46-47 (LS) BLS. 6: Ger, Fr, Sp, Slovene. 7: Br libn Buffalo & Erie Co Pub Lib, Buffalo NY 47-61; Ref libn Indianapolis Marion Co Pub Lib 61-. 9: ALA; IndLA. 14: Ref, govt docs. 15: 1221 N Hawthorne la, Indianapolis In 46219.

SPARKMAN, MICKEY M. b Winfield Tex 12 S 34. 5: UTex (Austin) 52-56 (Soc Sci) BS; N Tex stateU summers 60-66 (Soc Sci) MS; UTex (Austin) 65-68 MLS. 6: Sp. 7: Tchr Houston & Port Arthur Tex & Puerto Rico 56-65; Lib asst UTex (Austin) Lib 65-66, Bio libn 67-; Lib intern Brooklyn Pub Lib, Brooklyn NY 66-67. 9: ALA; SLA; TexLA; Soc UTex Libns. 10: Alumni Assn Grad Sch of Lib Sci UTex (Austin). 14: Admin, acquis, bibliog. 15: 6102 Laird dr, Austin Tx 78757.

SPARKS, DAVID E. b Phila Penn 12 Je 21. 4: Mary Reidy Sparks. 5: Swarthmore 46-50 (Romance Lang) AB; CatholicU 50-53 (Romance Lang) MA. 6: Fr, Sp. 7: Research analyst Nat Security Agency, Ft Meade 51-53; Catlg libn UVt 53-56; Asst libn General Electric Co, Lynn Mass 56-58; Libn Itek Corp, Bedford Mass 58-62; Research consul Info dynamics Co, Reading Mass 62-66; Head ref & lib serv Sci & Tech Div LC 66-67; Assoc lib for pub serv YaleU Lib 67-68. 8: Pres E B Scranton Memorial Lib Corp, Madison Conn 69-; Lib Study Com Adv Coun on Higher Educ, Md 65-67; Asst chm Bd of Trustees Lucius Beebe Memorial Lib, Wakefield Mass 60-66. 9: ALA-ALTA; ASIS (cofounder Boston Chap); SLA; NELA; NECLA; ConnLA; MLTA. 10: Lib Com; Madison Hist Soc. 12: "A Methodology for the Analysis of Information Systems" (65); "Science Information Dissemination: a Systems Study" (63). 13: Yes. 14: Pub serv, lib automation, admin. 15: 40 Cherry lane, Madison Ct 06443.

SPARKS, GLENN (CLAUD). b Commerce Tex 21 O 22. 4: J Lou Turner. 5: E Tex State Col 39-43 BS; Tex Christian U 48-49 (Eng) MA; UOkla 49-50 (Eng); UTex 50-52 MLS; UMich 61-63, 65-67 (LS) PhD. 6: Sp, Fr, Ger. 7: US Army (Sgt) US & Europe 43-45; Admin off US Va, Dallas 46-48, Tchg Fellow Tex Christian U 48-49; Tchg Fellow UOkla 49-50; Libn I UTex Lib 51; Pub serv libn Tex A & I Col 51-52; Asst ref libn UIll(Urbana) 52-53; Dir Tex Christian U Lib 53-65; Dir dept of lib serv N Tex State U 67-. 9: ALA; SWLA; TexLA. 10: Phi Beta Kappa; Phi Kappa Phi. 12: "Presidential Addresses Made to the American Library Association, 1876-1951, ACRL Microcard Series # 131 (61). 13: Yes. 14: Admin, ref, hist of bks & libs. 15: 2007 Locksley lane, Denton Tx 76201.

SPARKS, JONATHAN DAVID. b Huntington WVa 22 N 46. 5: Trevecca Nazarene Col 64-67 Music Educ AB; UNC (Chapel Hill) 67-68 (Musicology); Peabody Col summers 68-69 MLS. 7: Instr of vocal music Glen Este High Sch, Cincinnati 68-69; Libn Huntington Col 69-. 9: ALA; OhioEA. 10: Phi Delta Lambda. 14: Lib admin, ref, music libnship. 15: Librarian Huntington Col, Huntington In 46750.

SPARKS, LINDA (FRANCES). b Anniston Ala 26 O 36. 5: UAla 55-58(Educ, LS) BS; LSU 60-61 (LS) MS. 7: Asst Educ Lib UAla 58-60; Ref libn Educ Lib UFla 61-. 9: FlaLA. 10: AAUW. 14: Ref. 15: 3236 NW 30th ave, Gainesville Fla 32601.

SPARKS, MARY ELIZABETH. b London Ky 28 F 19. 5: Mary Washington Col UVa 38-42 (Eng) BA; Columbia 44-45 (LS). 6: Fr, Lat, Sp. Ger. 7: Jr catlgr Northwestern U 45-46; Libn Iowa State Hist Soc, Iowa City Iowa 46-48; Head recatlg & reclsf proj UCincinnati 48-51; Head catlg dept ULouisville 51-63; Asst libn Grand Valley State Col 63-. 9: ALA. 10: AAUW; Bus & Prof Womens Club. 14: Catlg. 15: 3740 E Omaha, Grandville Mich 49418.

SPARKS, RONALD (LEON). b Stanfordind 13 Ap 34. 5: Georgetown Col (Ky) 52-53; Ind U 53-56 (Eng) AB; Ucal (Berkeley) 57-58; Ind U 58-59 (LS) MA. 6: Fr. 7: Adult asst Indianapolis Pub Lib 56-57; Ref asst Wells Mem Lib, Lafayette Ind 59-60; Adult serv libn Rauh Br Indianapolis Pub Lib 60-62; Chief of humanities, Fine Arts dept UAriz Lib 62-66; Hd of pub serv USan Francisco Lib 66-68; Cal State Col 69-. 9: ALA; Mod Lang Assn; CalLA. 12: "Elisabeth Rethberg: a Record of Her Operatic Perfomances with the Metropolitan Opera, 1922-1942, and with the San Francico Opera, 1928-1940 (65). 13: Yes. 14: Ref, pub serv, admin. 15: 88 Crestline dr, San Francisco Ca 94131.

SPARKS, WILLIAM SHERAL. b Alden Bridge La 30 O 24. 4: Joy Eleanor Young. 5: Phillips U 43-46 (Rel, Phil) AB; Christian Theol Sem 46-49; Semitics Bd Hebrew Union Col Jewish Inst of Religion (Cincinnati) 49-52 (Bible); Iliff Sch of Theol 54-57 (Bible) THM, THD; UDenver 61-62 (LS) MA. 6: Ger, Hebrew. 7: Inst in Hebrew Lang Iliff Sch of Theol 54-60; Asst libn Kan Wesleyan U 62-66; Libn St Paul Sch of Theol Meth 66-. 9: ALA; ATheolLA. 10: AAUP. 11: Louis J & Mary E Horowitz Interfaith Fellow Hebrew Union Col-Jewish Inst of Relig, Cincinnati 49-52. 13: Yes. 14: Ref, acquis. 15: St Paul Sch of Theo Methodist 5123 Truman rd, Kansas City Mo 64127.

SPARROW, RUTH A(UGUSTA). b NYC 18 Jl 03. 5: Syracuse 23 Certif in Lib Sci. 7: Asst Syracuse U Lib 23; Asst child room Buffalo Pub Lib, Buffalo NY 23-26, Asst loan desk 26-27, Head Genessee br Lib 27-30; Buffalo Museum of Sci, Buffalo NY; Research libn 30-34, Libn in chg of Research Lib & Lib & Reading Room 34-64; Libn Research Lib 64-. 8: Org lib Allegany Sch of Nat Hist, 36. 9: SLA (chm Mus Group 47-48; dir Upstate Chap 68-69). 10: Beta Phi Mu. 12: Ed, Buffalo Soc of Nat Scis, "Bulletin (42-64). 13: Yes. 14: Research. 15: BUffalo Mus of Sci, Buffalo NY 14211.

SPAS, RUTH (HOBLER DECKER). b Johnson City NY 26 Je 07. 4: Benjamin Spas. 5: Keuka Col 25-27 (Music); Ithaca Col 27-29 (Music) MusB; Syracuse 36-38 (Educ) MS in Ed; Tex Womans U summers 59-63 MLS. 6: Fr, Ital. 7: Music supv Greene Central Sch, Greene NY 29-30; Eng tchr Dalton Union Sch, Dalton NY 31-34; Music supv & third supv dist, Broome Co NY 35-39; Music & libn Bradford Central Sch, Bradford NY 40-41; Sr clerk Your Home Pub Lib, Johnson City NY 53-58; Circ libn Harpur Col 58-64; Reg libn No Reg Lib, Espanola NM 64-66; Doc libn NM State Lib 66-67, Fine arts libn 67-. 9: MusLA; NMLA. 10: Local Action Com; San Gabriel Hist Soc; Santa Fe Gem & Mineral Club. 14: Bibliog, Southwest hist, music. 15: Box 698, Epanola NM 87532.

SPAULDING, FRANCES MURIEL. b Berkley Cal 16 Mr 08. 5: San Jose State Col 28-31 (LS, Educ) BA, Spec Secondary Certif in Lib Sci; Heald Bus Col 34-35 (Exec Sec); UCal 47-48 BLS; Middlebury Col Breadloaf Sch of Eng summer 49 (Amer Lit). 6: Fr, Sp. 7: Sch clerk & libn dept of adult educ, San Jose Cal 35-41; Typist & stenog clerk US Navy & Army Civil Serv, San Francisco & Oakland Cal 41-44; Typist & stenog clerk & US Forest Serv Civil Serv, San Francisco & Berkeley Cal 46-47; Pub rel spec WAC (Sgt), Hamilton Field Cal 44-46; Catlgr San Francisco State Col 48-49; Head catlgr, ref asst, catlgr UCal(Davis) 49-, Asst in catlg dept 61-. 9: ALA; CalLA. 10: Kappa Delta Pi. 14: Catlg (Romance langs), humanities. 15: 648 K st, Davis Cal 95616.

SPAULDING, FRANK H. b Danielson Conn 12 Jl 32. 4: Eugenia Jenewicz. 5: UConn 50-52 (Bus); Brown 54-57 (Eng) AB; West Res 60-61 MSLS. 6: Russian. 7: Disbursing & Logistics US Navy (Lt) 57-60; Supv info serv Colgate-Palmolive Co, New Brunswick NJ 61-65; Adjunct instr Drexel Inst of Tech Grad Sch of Lib Serv 64; Supv lib Tech Processes Bell Telephone Labs, Inc Holmdel NJ 65-. 9: ALA; SLA; ASIS; ASM; NYLA; NY Tech Serv Assn. 13: Yes. 14: Admin, acquis, printing, publishing. 15: 910 River rd, Piscataway NJ 08854.

SPAYDE, PEARL (AMUNDSON) (MRS). b Kalispell Mont 17 N 12. 5: USD 31-35 (Eng Lit) BA; Chicago 36; UIll 40 BS in LS. 6: Lat, Ger. 7: Tchr-libn Badger Union High Sch,Badger Minn 37-38; Tchr-libn Kansas High Sch, Kansas Ill 38-39; Asst libn Morningside Col 39-42; Libn US Army Spec Serv, Clinton Iowa 42-44; Child libn Glendale Pub Lib, Glendale Cal 45-47; Libn Visalia High Sch, Visalia Cal 47-48; Assoc col libn Sacramento State Col 48-. 8: Spec assignment, ALA Offin Wash DC, summer 42; Del to Internat Fed of Lib Assns, Rome, Sept 64; Ed SSC Lib Staff Bulletin 67-. 9:ALA; CalLA (pres Golden Empire Dist). 10: Sierra Club; Sacramento Bk Collectors; Sacramento State Col FAculty Assn; SSCCommun Affiliates. 12: Comp "Selected list of Books in English by US Authors, ALA (42). 14: Ref, lib sci educ, admin. 15: 5530 Moddison ave, Sacramento Ca 95612.

SPEAR, GRACE (BRETCH). b St Louis 27 Mr 08. 4: L Keehn Spear. 5: Washington U 26-30 (Eng) AB; St Louis Lib Sch 30-31 Certif. 6: Fr. 7: Gen asst St Louis Pub Lib 31-40; Ref asst Carnegie Lib, Okla City Okla 40-42; Gen asst St Louis Pub Lib 42-45; Head libn Maplewood Pub Lib,

Maplewood Mo 45-53; Child libn St Louis Pub Lib 53-63, Field wker with child libns 63-67, Coord child serv 67-. 8: Com on Certif, Mo State Lib, 51; Mem Mo Lib Child Serv RT Steering Com 66-68; Mem Newbery-Caldecott Com 69. 9: ALA; MoLA. 10: Alpha Xi Delta. 13: Yes. 14: Child serv. 15: 409 Summit ave, Webster Groves Mo 63119.

SPEAR, JACK B(YRON). b Ashley Ill 18 Mr 18. 5: USoIll 35-39 (Eng, Art) B of Ed; UIll 39-40 BS of LS; Columbia 47-56 MS in LS. 6: Fr, Ger. 7: Lib asst Pub Lib, Carbondale Ill 32-37, Libn 37-39; Asst Journalism Lib UIll (Urbana) 39-40; Libn Township High Sch, Herrin Ill 40-41, Lib asst Ill State Hist Lib, Springfield Ill 41-42; US Army (Capt) Chief Lib Off US Forces, Europe 42-46; Ref asst Ill State Hist Lib, Springifield Ill 46-47; Asst libn in chg of ext Pub Lib, Gary Ind 47-50; Assoc lib supv lib ext div NY State Lib 50-52 Dir Amer Heritgage Proj ALA, , Chicago 52-53; Head travel libs lib ext div NY State Lib 53-61; Assoc libn, head spec serv lib ext div 61-68; Asst Libn, Hd auxilliary serv div lib dev 68-. 8: Exec dir Nat Lib Week, NY 60 & 61; Mem, Presidents Com on Employment of the Handicapped 63-; Amer Film Festival jury chm. 9: ALA-PLD (past pres); LPRC; NYLA; Film Lib Info Coun; EFLA. 10: Sight Conservation Soc of NE NY; NY State Fed of Wkers for Blind; UIll Lib Sch Alumni; Columbia Sch of Lib Serv Alumni; Lions Intl; Melvil Dui Chowder & Marching Soc; Lake Placid Club; NY Film Soc. 13: Yes. 14: Admin, pub libs, A-V resources. 15: 397 State st, Albany NY 12210.

SPEARS, LUDI W. b Mt Morris NY 23 Je 22. 4: F Douglas Spears. 5: NYU State Tchrs Col 39-43 (LS) BA in Ed; UCLA 49-52 (Educ Admin & Supv) MA in Ed& uill 60-63 MS in LS; UFla 66-69 (African Studies). 6: Fr, Sp, Swahili. 7: Libn Columbia Prep Sch, Rochester NY 42-43; Libn Warrensburg Central Sch, Warrensburg NY 43-44; Serv Club Lib, Ft Bragg NC 45-47; Act hd lib sch NYU State Tchrs Col 49-50, Demonstration tchr Holcomb Sch 50-5; Tchr Wash Elem Sch, Champaign Ill 62-63; Libn Urbana High Sch, Urbana Ill 63-66; Asst Prof lib sci UFla 66-. 9: ALA; NEA; FlaLA; FlaASchL. 10: AAUP; Gainesville Women for Equal Rights; Human Rel Coun; Kappa Delta Pi. 14: Tchg lib sci (bk sel, adolescent lit, sch lib admin). 15: 1009 NW 7th ave, Gainesville Fl 32601.

SPEARS, NORMAN LEE. b Big Spring Tex 31 Ag 37. 4: LaNell Yielding. 5: Hardin-SimmonsU 55-60 (Hist) BA (magna cum laude); UTex 63-67 MLS. 8: Consul on self-evaluation Dallas Baptist Col 69. 9: TexLA; Tex Assn Col Tchrs; SWLA. 14: Tech serv. 15: William B Bizzell Mem Lib Univ of Okla, Norman Ok 73069.

SPECHT, DORIS SMITH. b Aberdeen SD 14 My 13. 4: Walter Albert Specht. 5: U Minn 30-35 (Hist) BA magna cum laude; USoCal 53 MS in LS. 6: Fr,Ger. 7: Engnr libn NOrthrup Aircraft, Inc, Hawthorne Cal 54-55; Catlg Douglas Aircraft, Long Beach Cal 55-56; Operations libn Jet Propulsion LAB, Pasadena Cal 56-58; Sci libn Cal State Col (Long Beach) 58-59, Head Humanities Lib 60-. 9: ALA-ACRL; SLA; CalLA (Col, Univ & Res Libns). 10: AAUP; AAUW; Cal State Employees Assn; Assn of Cal State Col Profs; Phi Beta Kappa; Phi Kappa Phi; Phi Delta Gamma; Sigma Epsilon Sigma; Service League Cal Inst of Tech. 14: Ref, admin. 15: 124 Stanford lane, Seal Beach Ca 90740.

SPECK, BEVERLY JOYCE. b Sherman Miss 13 Ap 37. 5: Memphis State U 55-57; Miss State Col for Women 57-59 (LS) BA; LSU summer 65, 66-67 (LS) MS. 6: Sp. 7: Asst ref libn ref dept Memphis Pub Lib, Memphis Tenn 59-66; Br hd Memphis & Shelby Co Libs 67-68; Asst ref libn Memphis State U 68-. 9: ALA; TennLA; SWLA. 10: Alpha Beta Alpha; Alpha Xi Delta, AAUW; Beta Phi Mu; Tenn Poetry Soc; TennEA; Tenn Ornithological Soc. 14: Ref, bk selection. 15: 3219 Cowden, Memphis Tn 38111.

SPECTOR, HERMAN K. b Phila 15 Ap 06. 4: Edna Schumacher. 5: Penn State Tchrs Col 25-29)Pedagogy); Columbia 31-32 MA in Educ Psych, 34-35 BS in LS; 35 A1-Certif life-libn NY State Dept of Educ. 7: Stud asst Tchrs Col (W Chester Penn) 25-29; Tchr pub sch, Parkesburg Penn 29-30; Lib asst Tchrs Col Columbia U 30-34; Libn Queens Borough Pub Lib, Richmond Hill NY 34-37; Libn Penitentiary, NYC 37-44; Chief libn Dept of Corrections, NYC 44-47; Libn Cal State Prison, San Quentin 47-69; Supv libn Cal State Dept of Corrections, Sacramento 48-64. 12: Asst managing ed "Prison World (39-49); Ed "Indexes to Proceedings of the Amer Prison Assn, Comp "Bibliography on Crimminology and Penology (41); Comp "Juvenile Deliquency; a Bibliography (63). 13: Yes. 14: Ref, bibliog, prison journ, correctional lib wk. 15: 10 Sonoma st, San Rafael Ca 94901.

SPEED, WM J. b Oklahoma 30 Jl 21. 4: Iris Ann. 5: USoCal 56-59 (Communications) BS. 6: Sp. 7: Film libn UCLA 45-50; A-v dir Los Angeles Pub Lib 50-. 8: Org & pd admin, SoCal Film Circuit & the Film Coun Circuit. 9: NEA-DAVI; Educ Film Lib Assn (Bd Dirs & v-pres); Film Lib Info Coun (Bd Dirs); CalLA (pres A-V Div). 13: Yes. 14: A-v materials and serv. 15: 630 W 5th st, Los Angeles Ca 90017.

SPEER, EUNICE H AZEL. b Alma Kan. 5: Kan State Tchrs Col 26-30 (LS) BED: UIll 36-37 (BS (LS), 37-39 MS (LS), 52-53 (LS). 6: Sp. 7: Asst libn Bemidjt State Tchrs Col 30-36; Asst in circ dept UIll (Urbana) 36-40, San Jose State Col: Asst ref libn 40-42; Head of circ dept 42-44, Instr of Lib Sci 40-44; Asst Prof of Lib Sci Ill State U 44-. 9: ALA (chm Jt Com on Libnship as a Career); NEA; Sch Libns Assn Cal; IllaSchL (pres); IllEA. 10: AAUP; AAUW; OES; Alpha Beta Alpha. 13: Yes. 14: Instr in lib sci, ref. 15: 208 W Ash, PO Box 129, Normal Ill 61761.

SPEER, JACK A. b Wichita Kan 3 Jl 41. 4: Judith Ann Fuller. 5: Kan State Tchrs Col 62-66 (Bus Admin) BS, 66-68 MLib; UMo (Columbia) summer 68; USoCal 69 (Info Sci). 7: Data processing libn Kan StateU 67-69. 9: ALA; -ISAD; CoLA; KanLA. 12: "Libraries and Automation: a Bibliography with Index" (67). 13: Yes. 14: Lib automation, systems design, programming, etc. 15: PO Box 3063, Torrance Ca 90510.

SPEERT, KATHRYN (HELLER). b NYC. 4: Harold Speert. 5: Vasaar (Chem) BA; Columbia 58-61 MSLS. 6: Fr. 7: Chem Reynolds Tobacco Co, Winston-Salem NC; Catlgr Westchester Reform Temple, Scarsdale NY 60-61; Libn Psych Lib Columbia U 61-64; Ref libn Med Lib Parkinson Info Center Columbia U 64-. 9: MedLA; ASIS. 10: Beta Phi Mu. 12: Ed "Columbia University Science reference Notes (61-64); Ed "Columbia University Medical Reference Notes (64-). 14: Med ref. 15: 111 Old Army rd, Scarsdale NY 10584.

SPEIK, CHARLOTTE ANN. b Los Angeles Cal 4 Mr 17. 5: Stanford 35-39 (Soc Sci) BA; USoCal 45-46 BS in LS. 6: Fr, Ger. 7: Libn (fine arts) Pasadena Pub Lib, Pasadena cal 46-51, Pub rel libn 51-52; USA Spec serv libn, Germany 53-54; Supv art & mus sect San Diego Pub Lib 54-. 9: SLA; CalLA (chm A-V RT 55). 10: San Diego Fine Arts Soc; San Diego rt Inst; San Diego Symphony Assn; San Diego Pub Lib Staff Assn. 14: Fine arts, a-v. 15: 4334 Texas st, San Diego Ca 92104.

SPEIRS, CHARLES H. b Riccarton Scotland 28 D 32. 5: Union Col 50-54 (Eng) AB; West Res 56-57 MS in LS. 7: Journalist US Navy NAF, Atsugi Japan 54-56; Sci ref libn Rochester Pub Lib, Rochester NY 57-59; Sr ref Holborn Hockorn Pub Lib, London 59-60; Art ref libn Rochester Pub Lib, Rochester NY 60-61, Head fiction div 61-63; Assoc libn Monroe Commun Col 63-. 9: ALA; NYLA. 10; Rochester Assn for the UN; UN Internat Friendship Coun; Faculty Assn SUNY. 14: Ref, admin. 15: 4 Colonial pky, Pittsford NY 14534.

SPEISER, ADEL CATHERINE (LANGENDORFF) (MRS). b San Antonio Tex 16 Je 02. 5: St Marys U 29 (Eng) BA (magna cum laude), 39 (Hist) MA; Our Lady of the Lake Col 53 (LS) MS. 6: Sp. 7: Tchr Alamo Heights Bd Educ, San Antonio Tex 24-50, High sch & elem libn 50-64; Instr Our Lady of the Lake Col64-67, Asst Prof Lib Sci 67-. 9: ALA (Memb Com); TexASchL (chm). 10: San Antonio Speech Arts Assn; Tex Hist Assn; San Antonio Hist Assn; BexarLA. 13: Yes. 14: Sch libs, child & ya lit. 15: 1045 Bailey ave, San Antonio Tx 78210.

SPELLER, BENJAMIN FRANKLIN JR. b Windsor NC 21 S 40. 5: NC Col(Durham) 58-62 (Soc Sci) AB; Ind U 64-65 (LS) MAT, summer 68. 6: Fr. 7: Period libn Livingstone Col 62-64; Grad asst U Sch Lib, Bloomington Ind 64-65; Libn pub serv & Instr Livingstone Col 65-67; Hd catlgr & instr Elizabeth City State Col 67-. 8: Adv to the Chm Visual Educ, Livingstone Col 62-64, 65-67; Dir Inst Self-Study Program Elizabeth City State Col. 9: ALA; NCLA (dir RTS Sect 67-69); NC Tchrs Assn; SELA. 10: YMCA. 14: Lib admin, tech serv. 15: 504 Roanoke ave, Elizabeth City NC 27909.

SPELLMAN, JOHN A F. b Hoquiam Wash 27 Ap 13. 4: Rosalie Nieradzik. 5: Grays Harbor Col 38-40; UWash 40-42 (Hist) BA, 45-46 BLS; UMich 50-52 MLS. 6: Fr, Ger, Swedish, Lat. 7: Asst ref dept UWash 46-48; Asst libn UWichita 48-50; Assoc UMich 51-52; Assoc libn Kan State U 52-54; Libn Grays Harbor Col 55-. 9: NEA; PNLA; WashLA; WashEA. 10: AAUP; Phi Kappa Phi; Beta Phi Mu; Phi Theta Kappa; Grays Harbor Stamp Club; Pacific Northwest Precancel Club; Wash State Hist Soc; Grays Harpur Col Fac Assn. 14: Admin, ref, catlg. 15: PO Box 73, Cosmopolis Wash 98537.

SPELLMAN, LAWRENCE EDWARD. b NYC 15 O 20. 4: Miram Bley Cox. 5: Hamilton Col 39-43 9eng Lit) BS; Rutgers 66-67 MLS. 6: Fr, Ger, Sp. 7: Off (Lt Col) USA Airborne Inf 43-66; Curator of maps PrincetonU 67-. 8: Coop partic Spec Map Proc Proj, LC 68, 69. 9: SLA. 10: Assn of the US Army; Wildlife Fed; Airborne Assn; Boy Scouts of Amer. 14: Geog, maps. 15: 98 Jefferson rd, Princeton NJ 08540.

SPELLMAN, ROSALIE (NIERADZIK). b Aberdeen Wash 13 J 1 20. 4: John A F Spellman. 5: Grays Harbor Col 38-40; UWash 40-42 (Hist) BA, 4546 BLS. 6: Fr, Ger, Swedish. 7: Libn Bur of Govt Research UWash 42-44; Asst libn Aberdeen Pub Lib, Aberdeen Wash 44-45; Child libn Seattle Pub Lib 46-48; Head tech processes Wichita City Lib, Wichita Kan 48-50; Asst curator of bks William L Clements Lib of Amer Hist UMich 50-52; Asst libn Aberdeen Pub Lib, Aberdeen Wash 54-58, Libn 58-; Area supv Timberland Reg Lib 69-. 9: PNLA; WashLA; ALA. 10: AAUW;Soroptimists; Salvation Army Bd; Monday Study Club; Phi Theta Kappa; Beta Phi Mu; Wash State Hist Soc. 14: Admin, catlg, child wk, rare bk catlg. 15: P O Box 73, Cosmopolis Wash 98537.

SPELMAN, AUDREY (YELTON). b S Bend Ind. 4: Irving Spelman. 5: Keuka Col 31 (Fr) BA; Middlebury Col summers 33, 34 (Fr); NY State Col for Tchrs (Albany) 33 BSLS. 6: Fr. 7: Tchr Jr High Sch, Patterson NY 31-32; Tchr-libn High Sch, Kinderhook NY 33-35; Catlg asst NY State Lib 37-43; Order libn Drew U 56-. 9: ALA; NJLA; Assn East Col Libns. 10: NJ Audubon Soc; Morris Nature Club; Foster Parents Plan; Masterwork Chorus. 14: Acquis. 15: 27 Speedwell pl, Morristown NJ 07960.

SPENCE, ADDIE FOREMAN. b Greenville NC 2 N 05. 5: Shaw U 25-29 (Fr) BS; NC Col (Durham) summers 42-46 BSLS; Catholic U 59-60 MSLS. 6: Fr. 7: Tchr Fr & Eng Farmville High Sch, Farmville NC 29-35; Tchr-libn Bethel High Sch, Bethel NC 36-44; Tchr-libn C M Eppes High Sch, Greenville NC 44-46; Ref libn Hampton Inst 46-62, 64-, Act libn 62-64. 8: Act libn Hampton Inst 62-64. 9: ALA; VaLA. 10: YWCA. 14: Ref. 15: 1136 - 28th st, Newport News Va 23607.

SPENCE, DENNIS (RICHARD). b Orange NJ 10 O 38. 5: Curry Col 57-60 (Fr); Upsala Col 60-61 (Fr) BA; Rutgers 61-62 MLS. 6: Fr. 7: Jr libn Bloomfield Pub Lib, Bloomfield NJ 62: US Army SP-4 Mil Police Corps, Admin clerk, & Mil Policeman 62-64; Sr libn ref Bloomfield Pub Lib, Bloomfield NJ 65-66, Hd tech serv dept 66-68, Asst dir 68-. 9: ALA; LPRC; NJLA; NYLA; NY Tech Serv Libns. 10: Rutgers Grad Sch of Lib Serv Alumi Assn; Inter Agcy Coun (Bloomfield NJ 68-). 13: Yes. 14: Catlg, ref, govt docs. 15: 35 Mountain rd, Verona NJ 07044.

SPENCE, DOROTHY VIRGINIA. b Camilla Ga 20 D 1900. 5: Shorter Col 17-19; Peabody Col 19-21 (Educ) BS; UIll 30-31 (LS) BS. 7: Act libn Bessie Tift Col 31-32; Libn Middle Ga Col 33-34; Dist lib supv WPA, Atlanta 36-39, State lib supv 39-43; Libn Mitchell Co Lib, Camilia Ga 43-44; Lib consul Ga Dept of Educ, Atlanta Ga 44-50; Dir SW Ga Reg Lib, bainbridge 50-. 9: GaLA (pres 43-44). 10. AAUW. 14: Child serv. 15: 637 Academy st, Bainbridge Ga 31717.

SPENCE, ELIZABETH (HEATON). b Tacoma Wash 26 S 20. 4: John Washburn Spence. 5: U of Puget Sound 38-42 (Eng) BA; UCal 42-44 (LS) Certif. 7: Page MCCormick Br Tacoma Pub Lib volunteer 30-35, & 37-38, Catlg, clerical catlg dept 38-42; Timekeeping clerk Todd Shipyard Timekeeping Dept summer 42; Jr asst libn Pub Lib, Berkeley Cal 43-44, Filing clerk Bendix Aviation Corp, S Bend Ind 44; Catlgr: Safeway Stores Inc Research Lib, Oakland Cal 44-45; Pub Lib, Scottsbluff Neb 59-60; Catlgr Pierce Co Pub Lib, Tacoma Wash 62-65, Coord tech serv 65-. 9: PNLA; WashLA; ALA. 14: Catlg, acquis ser. 15: 3622 N 27th st, Tacoma Wash 98407.

SPENCE, MELVILLE RAYMOND. b Hamilton Ont Can 26 Jl 19. 4: Elizabeth Henke. 5: Beloit Col 47-50 (Psych) BA; West Res 50-51 MSLS; UIll 56-58 (LS). 6: Fr, Ger. 7: Tech Sgt 108th Engr Combat Bn 33rd Inf Div US Army, SW Pacific 42-46; Accountant Grand Union Tea Co, Beloit Wis 40-47; Asst dir Beloit Col 51-58; Gen libn UIda Lib 53-56; UOkla Lib; Acquis libn 58-59, Asst Prof Sch of Lib Sci 59-, Act Dir 63-64, act dir Sch of Lib Sci 63-65, Asst dir pub serv 60-67, Assoc dir 67-. 9: ALA-LAD (Budgeting, Accounting & Costs Com 68-); AALS; SWLA (chm Tech Serv Com 59-60; Exec Bd 66-; chm Publ Com 66-); OklaLA (Bus Mgr "Oklahoma Librarian" 61-; chm Col & Univ Sect 61-62, chm Constit & By-Laws Com 60-61; rep to SWLA 66-; chm Local Arrangements Com 67-68; Exec Bd 65-). 10: AAUP; Camp Fire Girls Coun; Okla Westerners; Norman Lions Club; Beta Phi Mu. 13: Yes. 14: Admin, bk sel, copying serv, automation. 15: 2530 Beaurue dr, Norman Ok 73069.

SPENCE, PAUL HERBERT. b Geraldine Ala 25 D 23. 4: Ruth Schmidt. 5: DukeU 42-43; Emory 46-48 (Hist) AB, 48-49 (Hist), 49-50 (LS) AM; UIll 58-59 (LS). 6: Fr, Ger. 7: (Pvt) US Army, European Theatre 43-46; Asst ref libn EmoryU 50-52; Chief period ref sect Air U Lib, Montgomery Ala 53-56; Lib Dir Inst of Tech USAF, Dayton Ohio 57-58; Asst dir for soc studies UNotre Dame (Ind) 59-60; Asst dir for soc studies UNeb 60-63; Hist & phil libn UIll (Urbana) 63-66, Assoc dir pub serv UGa 66-. 8: Mem Neb Lib Devel Com 60-63. 9: ALA; SLA; GaLA; SELA. 10: AAUP; Sigma Nu; Lions. 12: Comp "Union List of Foreign Military Periodicals" with Helen Hopewell (57); Ed "Directory of Military Periodicals" (58). 14: Admin, ref. 15: 200 Hancock lane, Athens Ga 30601.

SPENCE, RUTH (SCHMIDT. b Montgomery Ala. 4: Paul H Spence. 5: Huntingdon Col 40-43, 47-48 (Eng) AB; Auburn U 44 (Arch); Simmons 49-50 MS in LS. 7: Sp(G) US Navy, San Diego 44-47 (Lt Jg) US Naval Res; Asst libn Montgomery Ala Co Lib 50-52; Air U Lib, Montgomery Ala; Bibliog asst 52-55, Ref libn 58, Air War Col libn 58-59, Circ libn 59; Libn Woodman's Life Insurance Co, Lincoln Neb 61-63; Asst humanities libn UNeb 63; Extramural libn UIll(Urbana) 63-64, Lib sci libn 64-66; Ed UGa 68-. 10: AAUW. 12: Co-ed "Bibliography of Georgia Government" (68). 14: Ref. 15: 200 Hancock lane, Athens Ga 30601.

SPENCER, ARTHUR CHAMPLIN (III). b Portland Ore 18 Je 38. 5: Lewis & Clark Col 57-60 (Hist) BA; UOre 63-65 (Hist, Art Hist) MA, 68-69 MLS. 7: Researcher Ore Hist Soc, Portland 65-66, Pub serv adv 66-68, Ref libn 69-. 8: Sec, Music Hist Resources Com, Ore Music Hist Archive, Portland Ore. 10: Phi Alpha Theta; Episcopal Laymens' Mission Soc, Portland; Old Church Preserv Soc, Portland. 14: Ref, catlg, mss, archives. 15: 743 SW Green ave, Portland Or 97205.

SPENCER, CAROLINE (ZALEWSKI). b Detroit 22 Je41. 4: William Spencer. 5: Flint Jr Col 59-62 (Eng); UMich 62-64 (Eng) AB, 64 AMLS. 6: Sp. 7: Ref bibliogr Lockwood Lib SUNY (Buffalo) 65; Hd record sect UHawaii Lib 66-. 9: ALA; HawaiiLA. 12: Co-ed" Serials in Language, Literature, Psychology, Sociology and Social Work". 14: Ref, bk sel, tech serv. 15: 47-424 Hui Nene st, Kaneohe Hi 96744.

SPENCER, EDITH (IOLA) PRUNTY. b Maybeury W Va 20 N 26. 4: J Merrill Spencer. 5: ShawU 43-46 (Eng) BA; AtlantaU 47 BSLS; Wayne StateU 60-62 (Mortuary Sci) Certif. 7: Catlgr spec proj DillardU summer 47; Circ libn Ky State Col 47-48; Asst catlgr-hd catlg dept Atlanta U Trevor Arnet Lib 48-50; Flint Pub Lib, Flint Mich; Asst catlgr hd catlg dept 51-54, 54-60; Chief tech serv 57-60; Asst in ya, ref, art, music & drama, bus & ind, brs 60-62; Libn Potler Br Lib 62; 1st asst art, music & drama dept 63-67; Hd catlg dept 67-. 9: ALA; MichLA. 10: Flint Pub Lib Staff Assn; Flint Lib Club; Genesee Co Funeral Dirs Assn; Mich Selected Morticians; Nat Assn Funeral Dirs & Embalmers; YWCA; NAACP; Urban League; ACLU; Visiting Nurses Assn; Flint Commun Planned Parenthood Assn; Mich LWV; Alpha Kappa Alpha; Alpha Kappa Mu. 14: Catlg. 15: Flint Pub Lib 1026 E Kearsley, Flint Mi 48502.

SPENCER, EUNICE ANNIE. b Waihee Maui Hawaii 16 F 1893. 5: UWash 12-16 (Hist) BA 16 Five Year Normal Diploma, 44-45 BA in Libnship. 7: Mil Sci Hist Educ Depts & Registrars off UWash 18-45; Chief catlg libn Seattle U Lib 45-66; Prof Emerit Seattle U 66-. 9: PNLA. 10: AAUW; Daughters of the Pioneers of Wash, Seattle Hist Assn; Pioneer Assn of the State of Wash; Sororia Alumnae, Guild; Phi Beta Kappa; ; Seattle Genealogical Soc Neighbor Fund. 11: Silver Jubilee Award, Cath LA Seattle Unit, 58. 14: Catlg, ref. 15: 900 Queen Anne ave N apt 102, Seattle Wa 98109.

SPENCER, HELEN ALMA. b Emporia Kan 9 D 27. 5: Kan State Tchrs Col 46-50 (Educ) BS in Educ, Lib Certif. 7: Ref circ asst Jackson Pub Lib, Jackson Mich 50-52; Child readers adv Topeka Pub Lib, Topeka Kan 52-58, Catlg dept 58-, Asst hd tech serv 68-. 9: KanLA. 14: Catlg, child bks. 15: 1018 Washburn, Topeka Ks 66604.

SPENCER, HENRY GRADY. b Kaplan La 15 Ap 11. 4: Mary (Holman) Spencer. 5: LSU 27-31 (Journalism) BA, 66-67 (LS) MS. 7: Reporter "Morning Advoate," Baton Rouge La 30-31; Enlisted man USMC, Port au Prince Haiti & Wash DC 31-35; Clk US Treasury Dept, Wash DC 35-36; Railway mail clk US PO Dept, Kan City Mo 36-40, Supv 46-66; Lt Col US Army, Europe 41-45; Ser libn Kan State Col Porter Lib 67-. 8: Dir Command & General Staff Dept US Army Reserve Sch.

Kansas City Mo 56-66. 9: ALA; KanLA; KanASchL. 10: AAUP; US Res Offrs Assn; Kiwanis Internat; Boy Scouts of Amer; Neighborhood Commissioner.\14: Admin, ref. 15: 1004 S Olive, Pittsburgh Ka 66762.

SPENCER, LEE BOWEN. b El Paso Tex 2 J 14. 4: Willa Belle Carter. 5: Okla Bapt U 30-34 (Hist) AB; UIll summers 37-40 BS in LS; UOkla 41, 46 (Hist) MA. 6: Fr. 7: Asst Carnegie Pub Lib, Shawnee Okla 31-36; Libn & instr to Prof, Okla Bapt U 36-63; Pvt to First Lt US Army Air Corps 42-46; Personnel & Intelligence Lt Col Air Force Res; Head acquis libn Air U, Maxwell AFB Ala 47; Visiting prof of lib sci, Okla State U summers 48 & 49; Head libn Prof & head Dept of Lib Sci State Col of Ark (Conway) 63-. 8: Educ Guidance Staff US Air Force Res, Okla City 50-55; Okla Baptist Gen Conv Hist Commsn, 50-63; So Baptist Hist Commsn, 62-65; Exec dir Nat Lib Week,Ark 66. 9: ALA; SWLA; OkLA (pres 50); ArkLA (pres 68). 10: Trustee Carnegie Pub Lib, Shawnee Okla; Red Cross; Faulkner Co (Okla) Hist Soc; Ark Gen Soc; Reserve Offrs Assn; SAR; Rotarian. 13: Yes. 14: Ref, admin, pub rel. 15: 2002 Prince st, Conway Ark 72032.

SPENCER, LORAINE (MARGARET INGLIS). b Halifax NS Can 16 J137. 5: McGill 55-59 (Eng) BA, 60-61 BLS, Queens U 59-60 (Eng); Toronto 67- (LS). 7: Order libn UToronto libn 61-63; Divinity libn McGill U 63-65; Research asst Royal Ont Mus, Toronto 66-67; Asst libn Centennial Col (Ont) 67-. 9: CanLA; QueLA; OntLA; IPLU. 12: "Northern Ontario, a Bibliography (68). 14: Ref. 15: Apt 507-2 Sultan st, Toronto 5 Ont Can.

SPENCER, MARION (LOUISE) DICKINSON. b Grand Rapids Mich 18 J109. 4: Ivor Debeham Spencer. 5: West Mich U 28-32 (Fine Arts) BA; Colo State Col summers 40-42 (Fine Arts) MA; USoCal 48 (Secondary Educ) State Certif; West Mich U 58-60-61 LS MA. 6: Fr, Ger, Sp. 7: Elem art tchr Kalamazoo City Schs 32-44; Dir Kalamazoo Inst of Arts 44-47; Libn Chouinard Art Inst, Los Angeles 47; Bus manager Modern Inst of Art, Beverly Hills Cal 48; Supv art Comstock Pub Sch, Comstock Mich 49-50; Instr West Mich U 50-51; Art consul Kalamazoo City Sch 52-55; Elem tchr Vicksburg Schs, Vicksburg Mich 55-58; A-v ed off West Mich U 58-60; Libn Kalamazoo Pub Lib 62-67. 9: ALA; MicLA; Mich Acad Sc Art Letters; Consult Confer on Ad Ed Literacy, Drexel Inst, Phila; UWisconsin; ALA; Detroit Natl Mtg; Mich Lib Assoc Region VII. 10: Kalamazoo Col Faculty Wives; Kalamazoo City-Co Com on Youth; AAUW; Adult Literacy Commsnr; Kalamazoo Co Delta Phi Delta; Beta Phi Mu; Mich Acad Sci, Art & Letters. 11: Mich Adult Educ Assn Annual Award, 67; Lolita D Fyan Award, 67, MichLA. 12: Ed "Bibliography of Adult Literacy Materials," Mich Dept of Educ (67). 13: Yes. 14: Fine arts, adult educ, literacy & reading improvement. 15: 804 Dobbin dr, Kalamazoo Mi 49007.

SPENCER, SHERMAN HASKELL. b Salt Lake City Utah 31 Ag 24. 4: June Hook. 5: Mont State U 46-49 (Fr) BA; Columbia 49-50 (LS) MS. 6: Fr. 7: Circ libn U of the Pacific 50-. 15: Univ of the Pacific Lib, Stockton Ca 95204.

SPENCER, VIRGINIA JUNE (RINGCHRIST). 03Springfield Mass 27 Je 18. 5: Mt Holyoke 38-40 (Eng) AB; UMich 40-41 ABLS; Mt Holyoke 55-56, 57-59 (Eng) AM; Mass U summer 58; Amer Internat Col 36-38 Mt Holyoke (Hist) 59-61; UMich summers 41, 60, 61 AMLS, 63-64, 65-66, 69-(LS); UDenver 68-69. 6: Fr, Ger. 7: Catlgr Worcester Pub Lib, Worcester Mass 41-42; Catlgr Boston Pub Lib 53-55; Sr catlgr Mt Holyoke Col 55-63; Lib wk study scholar catlgr UMich 63-64; Admin asst Mt Holyoke Col 63-65; Catlgr pt time Holyoke 67, Hd subj catlg sect 69-; Assoc Prof UDenver Grad Sch of Libnship 67-69. 9: ALA; AALS; SAA. 10: AAUP; AAUW. 14: Catlg, col & univ lib admin, archives, info retrieval. 15: 1515 South blvd, Ann Arbor Mich 48104.

SPENCER, WILLIAM G. b Upper Montclair NJ 27 Ap 19. 5: Lafayette Col 42 (Econ) BA; Columbia Bus Sch 47 (Advertising) MS; Rutgers 56 MLS. 7: Ref dept (sr ref libn) Montclair Pub Lib, Montclair NJ 56-. 14: Ref, biog, travel. 15: 24 Hillside ave, Montclair NJ 07042.

SPERL, VIRGINIA R. b Orange NJ 3 Ja 20. 5: Randolph-Macon Womans Col 39-42 (Eng) BA; UMinn 44-45 (LS) BS; Adelphi U 63- (Eng). 6: Fr, Ger. 7: Lib asst New Britain Inst, New Britain Conn 42-43; Order dept asst Harvard Law Sch 45-46; Asst Penn Sch of Soc Wk, Phila 47; Ser catlgr-asst catlg libn med Columbia 47-58; Chief catlgr Albert Einstein Col med 58-60; Catlg libn-asst libn Dowling Col 61-. 8: Tech serv consul, NY State Wkshop for Institution Libns, summers 56-58; Coord lib asst train program Dowling Col 67-. 9: ALA-AHIL; Rep to RTSD Code Rev Com 61-65; SLA; NYLA; NY Tecg Serv Libns; SuffolkCoLA; COLT; ASIS. 10: AAUP; AAUW. 14: Tech serv. 15: Dowling Col Lib, Oakdale NY 11769.

SPERLBAUM, ANDREA (LYNN). b Minneapolis Minn 30 O 42. 4: George H Sperlbaum Jr. 5: UMich 60-64 (Fr) AB, 66-67 MALS. 6: Fr, Ger. 7: Lib asst UMich Gen Lib (Ann Arbor) 64-66, Lib wk-study scholar 66-67, Bibliog searcher 67; Libn Bur of Hosp Admin 68-. 9: SLA. 14: Ref, acquis. 15: 712 W Huron, Ann Arbor Mi 48103.

SPERO, CECILE HARRIET (SCHIFFER). b Atlanta Ga 10 O 27. 4: James Sterling Spero. 5: UWis 44-48 (Eng) BA; SUNY (Albany) 64-67 MALS; NY State permanent sch libn certif. 7: Lib aide Middletown Pub Schs, Middletown NY 63-64, Libn 66-67; Libn Ithaca Sch Dist, Ithaca NY 67-. 9: ALA; -AASchL; -CSD. 10: LWV. 14: Child lit, child serv, ref, a-v materials (sel catlg & dissem). 15: 204 Salem dr, Ithaca NY 14850.

SPERRY, JOHN A Jr. b Akron Ohio 9 N 26. 4: Jean Cuff Stimson. 5: UAkron 47-49 (Hist) BA; UMich 49-50 (Hist) MA; Kent Stte U 51-53 (LS) MA. 6: Fr. 7: Tech grade V radio operator Army of the US 45-46; Grad asst UFla Libs 53-55; Resident libn Chinsegut Hill Lib UFla Lib System 55; Instr in Lib Sci UFLA 56-57; Libn & Asst prof hist Culver-Stockton Col 57-59, Libn & Assoc Prof hist 59-61, Libn & Sr Prof, hist 61-. 9: MoLA. 10: Archaeol Inst Amer; Wilson Onithol Soc; AAUP; Royal Astron Soc Can; Canton Pub Lib B; Nat Rifle Assn; Canton Table Talbe Club; Phi Alpha Theta; Beta Kappa Theta; Theta Alpha Ph; Fondation Egyptologique Reine Elisabeth; Danforth Foundation Assoc. 11: Fulbright res grant Egypt; Fulbright grant India. 13: Yes. 14: Rare bks, hist of bks & printing. 15: Culver-Stockton Col Lib, Canton Mo 63435.

SPERRY, ROBERT. b San Diego Cal 3 Ja 33. 5: UFla 50-54 (Psych) AB; Fla StateU 55-57 (Hist) MA, 60-61 (LS) MS; LSU 64-65 (Hist). 7: Airman instr, Sampson AFB NY 54-55; Tchr Chaney Jr Col 57-58; Tchr Oak Ridge Military Inst, Oak Ridge NC 58-60; Ref libn Kan StateU 61-62; Libn ValparaisoU Law Sch 62-64; Ref libn NYU Law Sch 65-67; Libn Lyndon State Col 67-. 10: Phi Eta Sigma; Phi Kappa Phi; Phi Alpha Delta. 12: "Law of Notaries Public" (67). 13: Yes. 14: Bibliog. 15: Lib Lyndon State Col, Lyndonville Vt 05851.

SPESSARD, MILTON LeRON (RONNIE). b Durant Okla 27 O 40. 5: N Tex State Col summer 58 (Bus); Cameron State Col 58-60 (Bus) AA; UOkla 60-62 (Marketing) BBA, 62-63, summer 64 MLS. 7: Asst libn & catlgr Lib Cameron State Col 64-. 8: Libn Sixth & Arlington Ch of Christ, Lawton Okla. 9: ALA; NEA; OklaLA; SWLA; OklaEA. 14: Catlg, ref. 15: 712 N 35th pl, Lawton Ok 73501.

SPICER, ELIZABETH. b Guelph Ont Can. 5: UWest Ont 34-38 (Eng, Hist) BA Honor; Toronto 42 BLS; Carleton Col (Ont) 64 Certif Archival Principles & Admin. 7: Asst in Lib Col Educ Toronto 42-43; Child libn Galt Pub Lib, Galt Ont 43-44; London Pub Lib & Art Museum, London Ont: Circ libn 44-50, Ref libn 50-55, Head gen ref dept 5566, Head humanities dept 66-68, Libn London Room humanities dept 68-. 9: OntLA (chm ref wkshop 62-64); Architectural Assn Ont (sec London Br 66-); Hist Sites Adv Com; London Pub Lib & Art Museum (sec 66-). 10: Univ Womens Club; Leader of Canadiana Gp; Mem of local, provin & nat hist socs & of local & provincial geneal socs. 12: "Descriptions of London and Its Environs, 1793-1847 (64) "A History of the London Public Library 1899-1905 (67). 13: Yes. 14: Ref, rare bks, canadiana & loc hist, archives. 15: London Pub Lib & Art Museum, London Ont Can.

SPICER, ERIK (JOHN). b Ottawa Can 9 Ap 26. 4: Helen Blair. 5: Victoria Col U Toronto 46-48 (Hist) BA; Toronto 48-49 BLS, 49-50 (Hist) ; UMich 53-54, summers 56, 59 MALS. 7: LAC CAF, (Pvt) RCIC, Can 44-45; Circ libn Ottawa Pub Lib 49, 50-51, 52-53; Lib serv fellow, UMich 53-54; Deputy libn Ottawa Pub Lib 54-60; Maj Governor-Gens Foot Guards, Ottawa 51-62; Parliamentary libn Lib of Parliament, Ottawa 60-. 8: Mem Nat Lib Adv Coun, Ottawa; chm Beta Sigma Phi Can First Novel Award Com 64-69; Canadian correspondent for Parliamentary & Admin Lib, IFLA; Canadian correspondent Intl Ctr for Parliamentary Documentation, Geneva Switzerland. 9: CanLA (Coun 64-67); ALA; Lib Assn (Gt Brit); OntLA (pres 62-63); Inst of Prof Libns Ont (pres 55-56); Ont Hist Soc (Life mem); Var com assignments in most of the above assns. 10: Pub Admin Can; Can Writers Found; Phi Kappa Phi; Beta Phi Mu; Can Club; Royal Can Mil Inst. 11: Canadian Forces Decoration (CD) 1962; Centennial Medal (67). 12: "Library co-operation in Canada (55): "Trade Unions in Libraries (59). 13: Yes. 14:

Admin, research. 15: Lib of Parliament Parliament Hill, Ottawa 4 Canada.

SPICER, ORLIN C(HALMER). b Payette Ida 3 S 10. 4: Nina Kachur. 5: Spokane U 31-33; Whitworth Col 33-35, 36 (Fr) BA; Gonzaga U 36-38 (Eng) MA; Peabody 40-42 summer 43 BS in LS; DePaul U summer 52. 6: Fr, Sp. 7: Asst in Eng Whitworth Col, Skokane Wash 35-38; Fr tchr Ellensburg Sr High Sch, Ellensburg Wash 38-39; Instr Eng Dept Ore State U 39-40; Lib asst Vanderbilt U 40-42; Asst in Ref & Circ UMo 42-43; Head Libn Monticello Col 43-45; Asst to libn & head of circ UMo 45-47; Head Libn & Assoc Prof, Ill Wesleyan U 47-51; Head of Lib Serv J Sterling Morton High Sch & Jr Col, Cicero 51. 8: Summer guest faculty Peabody Lib Sch, 60-61, 63-64. 9: ALA-AASchL; -ACLA (Jr Col Sect: sec 55, chm 56); AALS; IllLA (treas 55-56); IllEA. 10: Phi Kappa Ph; Phi Sigma Iota; Kappa Delta Pi; Pi Gamma Mu; Beta Phi Mu. 13: Yes. 14: Admin, ref, lib educ. 15: 1425 So Wayside dr, Villa Park Ill 60181.

SPICHER, MIRIAM . b Jefferson City Mo 21 Ag 10. 4: Harry E Sicher. 5: Central Mo State Col 28-35 (Home Econ) BS; Wis State Col (Eau Claire) 56-57; Colo State Col 59; UIll (Champaign) summers 60-65 (LS) MS. 7: Tchr Eau Claire (Wis) Co Sch System 54-57; Libn; Kewanee Jr & Sr High Schs, Kewanee Ill 58-64, Farmington High Sch, Farmington Ill 64-65, Glenbrook N High Sch, Northbrook Ill 65-. 10: Kappa Omicron Phi; Kappa Delta Pi; Phi Beta Mu. 14: Ref, sch libn, lib admin, lib automation. 15: Glenbrook No High Sch, Northbrook Ill 60062.

SPIECKER, RUTH E (VON BUCHHOLTZ). b Riga Latvia 7 S 09. 4: Siegfried W Spiecker. 5: Hoffbauer Stoftung (Germany) 28-30 (Bio) Abitur; Rosary Col 63-64 (LS) Masters. 6: Ger, Fr, Sp. 7: In charge of kardex NorthwesternU 61-63, Sci libn 64-. 9: ALA; SLA; IllLA. 14: Admin, bk sel, ref. 15: 407 Washington, Wilmette Il 60091.

SPIEGEL, JEANNE. b Fall River Mass. 4: Harry Spiegel. 5: Pembroke 33-37 (Philos) AB; Simmons 62-63 (LS) MS. 7: Catlgr Concord Pub Lib, Concord NH 63-66; Libn-research full chg Bus & Prof Womens Found, Wash DC 66-. 9: NHLA; ALA; SLA; Assn for Recorded Sound Collection. 10: Oral Hist Assn. 13: Yes. 14: Oral history collection & interviewing, research & ref wk in areas pertaining to women. 15: 3900 16th st NW, Washington DC 20011.

SPIELMAN, MARGARET CATHARINE (AARON). b Loysburg Penn 14 Ap 14. 4: Herbert Martin Spielman. 5: Shippinsburg State Tchrs Col 35; Penn State 44 (Elem Educ) BS; Kent state 63 (LS). 6: Fr. 7: Tchr: Sulphur Springs Penn 35-36, S Woodburg Twp, New Enterprise Penn 36-44; Libn Bedford Co Lib, Bedford Penn 44-52; Tchr Springfield Local schs, Petersburg Ohio 53-60, High sch libn 60-. 9: ALA; NEA; OhioSchLA; MahoningCoTA. 10: Cove Commun Club; DAR; Garden Club. 15: 14050 Market, Petersburg Oh 44454.

SPIER, STUART LESLIE. b New Brunswick NJ 26 J137. 5: Rutgers 56-60 (His, Psych) BA, 60-63 (Hist) MA, 63-65 MLS. 6: Fr. 7: Sr ref libn Newark Pub Lib, Newark NJ 63-. 10: Friends of the Irvington Free Pub Lib. 13: Yes. 14: Ref, catlg, exhib. 15: 93 Wilson pl, Irvington NJ 07111.

SPIESS, JOHANNA M. b Brooklyn NY. 5: Brooklyn Col 45-49 BA; Pratt 49-50 MLS. 6: Ger. 7: Libn Brooklyn Pub Lib 49-56; Exch libn Hamburger Oeffentliche Buecherhallen, Hamburg Germany 56-57; Libn to prin libn, br libn Midwood br Brooklyn Pub Lib 57-. 9: NYLA; NY Lib Club; Theatre LA. 10: . 14: Ref, admin. 15: 7520-Ridge blvd apt 4C, Brooklyn NY 11209.

SPIGAI, FRANCES (GAGE). b Salina Kan 29 S 38. 4: Joseph John Spigai. 5: City Col (NY) 56-60 (Gen Sci) BS; Catholic U 65- (LS). 6: Fr. 7: Stud asst City Col Libs (NY) 56-60; Abstractor Internat Nickel Co Lib, NYC 60; Lib asst Union Carbide Nuclear Corp, Oak Ridge Tenn 61-62; Asst libn Amer Metal Climax Inc, NYC 62-64; Libn Alfred A Yee & Assoc Inc, Honolulu 64-65; Abstractor-indexer Howard Research Corp, Wash DC 65-66; Lib asst Ore State U 66-67, Info analyst 67-; Dir consul serv Info Analysis & Mgt Assoc, Corvallis Ore 68-. 8: Bonneville Power Admin, Portland Ore 68; Consul Ore Hist Soc Lib, Portland 69. 9: SLA; ASIS; ACM SIGIR. 12: "Technical Abstract Bulletin Amer Metal Climax Inc, 3 issues (63-64). 13: Yes. 14: Info ret, indexing, data proc. 15: 1502 Dixon st, Corvallis Or 97330.

SPILLANE, ELIZABETH THERESE (MAHONEY). b St Paul 20 N 31. 4: Paul Joseph Spillane. 5: Col of St Catherine 49-53 (Fr, LS) BA; Laval (Que) 51 (Fr). 6: Fr. 7: Circ Libn U Notre Dame (Ind) 53-54, Bus dept libn 54; Minneapolis Pub Lib: Adult asst libn 54-56, Child Libn 56-58, Ref libn 58-62, Hosp libn 62-64. 9: ALA; MinnLA; CathLA. 10: Pi Delta Phi. 15: 289 Oakview rd, ST Paul 55118.

SPILLER, HARVEY ELLIOT. b Providence RI 25 O 31. 5: Harvard 49-53 (Hist) BA; BostonU 56-57 (Journalism) MS; Simmons 64-66 MLS. 6: Ger, Fr, Ital, Sp, Dutch. 7: Asst mgr irving Spiller Inc, Lynn Mass 53-63; Hd circ dept NortheasternU Libs 63-66; Acquis libn Drexel 66-67, Hd catlg dept 67-; v-pres Irving Spiller Inc, Lynn Mass 64-. 9: ALA. 14: Catlg, tech serv, lib admin. 15: 602 Washington sq apt 1015, Philadelphia Pa 19106.

SPILLERS, ROGER E. b 16 N34. 5: Alliance Col 53-57 (Slavic Studies) BA; West Mich U 57-60 MALS. 6: Sp, Fr, Ger, Portu, Polish, Russian, Czech, Serbo-Croatian. 7: Libn Nat Waterlift Co, Mich 58; Asst libn Alliance Col 58-59, Libn 59-60; Libn Helena Pub Lib, Helena Mont 60-. 8: Consul on extending serv to 3 state supported inst Mont State Lib 68-69. 9: ALA (Memb Com Mont Chm; chm Mont Intellectual Freedom Com); MontLA (past pres); PNLA (var coms). 10: Polish Nat Alliance. 14: Admin, adult educ, ext wk. 15: Helena Pub Lib, 325 North Park ave, Helena Mt 59601.

SPINKS, PAUL. b London 7 Mr 22. 4: Clarice Ada (Goode). 5: UOkla 52-53, 55-58 (Eng, Hist, Pol Sci) BA, 58-59 MLS. 6: Ger. 7: Lib asst British Museum, London 39-42, 46-52; Navigator Warrant Officer Royal Air Force 42-46; Lib asst UOkla 52-53; Proofreader UOkla Press 53-55; Stud asst tech writing UOkla 55-58, Grad asst tech writing 58-59; Tech reports libn US Naval Postgrad Sch, Monterey Cal 59-61, Assoc libn 61-. 9: SLA. 10: Beta Phi Mu. 14: Admin, documentation, machine info storage & retrieval, SDI. 15: PO Box 8685 US N Postgrad Sch, Monterey Ca 93940.

SPITZ, DONALD F. b Saint Paul Minn 7 Ja 26. 5: Sem of St Mary Garrison NY 46-50 9philos) BA; Sem of St Anthony Maratohn Wis 50-54 (Theol); Catholic U 59-62 MSLS. 7: Head libn St Lawrence Sem, Mt Calvary Wis 55-. 9: ALA; CathLA; WisLA. 12: "A Bibliography of the Writings of the Members of the Capuchin Calvary Province of St joseph in the United States" (52). 14: Admin. 15: St Lawrence Seminary, Mount Calvary Wi 53057.

SPIVACKE, HAROLD. b NYC 18 Jl 04. 4: Rose Marie Grentzer. 5: NYU 20-23 (Econ) BA, 23-24 (Philos) MA; UBerlin 29-33 (Musicology) PhD. 6: Ger. 7: Asst chief Mus Div LC 34-37, Chief 37-. 8: Chm Subcom on Music, Jt Army & Navy Com on Welfare and Recreation 41-46; Mem Adv Com on Music Dept of State 39-46; Mem Music Panel, Cult presentations, Dept of State 63-; Mem Adv Music Panel, Internat Cult Exch Serv; Amer Nat Theatre & Acad 54-63; Mem Exec Bd President's Music Com People-to-People Prog 60-; Music Adv Panel US Info Agcy 60-66; Mem Nat Com of the US on Internat Intel Coop 46; Mem Exec Com, Mem us nat Commsn for UNESCO 50-56 & 62-65; Mem Panel on Music of the US Nat Commsn for UNESCO 48-56; Chm Adv Com Mus Div Pan Smer Union 40-42 & 47-49; Mem & chm, Fulbright Adv Sel Com on Music 49-55; Chm Screening Com for Nat Endowment's audience Devel Prog for the Benefit of Chamber Music Societies 69-. 9: MusLA (pres 51-53); numerous other pertinent associations & offices herein; LC Distinguished Serv Award 65; A Ogden Butler Fellowship in Phil 23-24 (NYU); Amer-Germ Students Exch Fellow 29-30 (Berlin); Alexander von Humboldt Stiftung Fellow 30-31 (Berlin); Research asst to olin Downes NY 33-34; Cosmos Club; Phi Sigma Delta; Phi Mu Alpha Sinfonia; Pi Kappa Lambda. 10: LC Distinguished Serv Award 65; Mus D 47 (Hon, Baldwin-Wallace Col); Mus D 55 (Hon, URochester); A Ogden butler Fellowship in Phil 23-24 (NYU); Amer-Germ Students Exch Fellow 29-30 (Berlin); Alexander von Humboldt Stiftung Fellow 30-31 (Berlin); Research asst to Olin Downes NY SPIVACKE, HAROLD. b NYC 18 Jl 04. 11: Mus D 47 (Hon, Baldwin-Wallace Col); Mus D 55 (Hon, URochester). 12: "Ueber die objective und subjektive Tonintensitat" (34). 13: Yes. 14: Music ref, admin. 15: 3201 Rowland st NW, Washington DC 20008.

SPIVEY, D LORAINE. b Wichita Falls Tex 5 D 21. 5: Lon Morris Col 40-42 (Liberal Arts) AA; Texas Wesleyan Col 42-44 (Relig Educ, Eng) BA; UHouston summers 43, 44; Texas WomansU 53-54 MLS. 6: Fr, Ger. 7: Owner & mgr The Gift Shop, Houston Tex 48-51; Asst catlg libn El Paso Pub Lib, El Paso Tex 54-57; Catlgr Tyrrell Pub Lib, Beaumont Tex 57-61; Asst catlg libn Tex ChristianU 61-. 9: ALA; TexLA; SWLA. 14: Catlg. 15: 3524 Kent st, Fort Worth Tx 76109.

SPIVEY, LYDIA LUELLA. b Charlotte NC 20 F 40. 5: Mars Hill 58-60 AA; Wake Forest 60-62 (Hist) BA; Duke 62-63 (Hist) MA; UNC (Chapel Hill) 66-67 MS in LS. 7: Circ dept asst DukeU Lib 63-66; Ref asst Pub Lib of Charloote & Mecklenburg Co, Charlotte NC 67-. 9: ALA. 14: Ref. 15: 2119 Canterwood dr apt 1, Charlotte NC 28213.

SPIVEY, MARIE. b Pelican La 7 F 20. 5: Centenary Col (La) 38-40 (Eng) AB; LSU 40-41 BS in LS. 6: Fr, Ger. 7: Asst libn Sabine Parish Lib, Many La 41-43; Br libn Bossier Parish Lib, Bossier City La 43-46; Head Libn Sabine Parish Lib, Many La 46-50; Chief catlgr Research Center Lib, US Army Engnr Waterways Expt Station, Vicksburg Miss 50-54, Asst libn 54-. 8: Staff, Lib/USA, NY Worlds Fair 64. 9: SLA; (pres, La Chap 64-65); MissLA. 15: Res Center Lib US Army Engnrs Waterways Expt Station, Vicksburg Ms 39180.

SPOERRI, SIMONE VIVIANE. b Begins Switzerland 11 Je 12. 4: Paul E Spoerri. 5: NYU 51-53 (Psych) BA; New Sch for Soc Research 57-60 (Psych); Columbia MLS. 6: Fr, Ger. 7: Libn Sugar Research Foundation Inc 59-66; Research asst The Research Foundation of NY, Brooklyn 60-66; Catlgr Esso, NYC 66; Asst libn Chem Club Lib, NYC 67-. 9: SLA; ASIS. 10: Eta Tau Delta. 15: Chemists Club Lib 52 E 41st st, New York NY 10017.

SPOHRER, ANNA CECILIA. b Monroe La 10 Je 45. 5: LSU 63-67 (Eng) BA, 67-68 (LS) MS. 6: Fr. 7: Lib trainee LSU (Baton Rouge) 67-68; Asst ref libn U S Ala 68-. 9: ALA. 10: Alpha Beta Alpha. 14: Ref, interlib loan. 15: Univ of South Alabama, Mobile Al 36608.

SPOO, MARGARET (GALLAGHER). b Waseca Minn 27 My 22. 4: George Spoo. 5: Rosary Col 39-40 (Liberal Arts); UMinn 40-43 (Liberal Arts) BA, 46-47 (Romance Lang) MA, 47-48 BLS. 6: Sp, Fr. 7: Communications instructor (Lt jg) USNR USNR Midshipman's Sch Smith Col 43-44; Communications off USNR USN Yard, Wash DC 44-45; Asst catlgr Mayo Clinic Lib, Rochester Minn 48-50; Asst catlgr pub lib, Rochester Minn 62-65, Ref libn 65-67, Adult serv libn 67-. 9: MinnLA. 10: LWV; AAUW; United Fund; Art Center; Civic Theater; Charter Commsn; Pink Ladies; etc. 14: Ref. 15: 508 - 15th ave SW, Rochester Mn 55901.

SPOONER, EMILIE LOUISE (MITCHELL). b Tacoma Wash 25 J109. 4: William R Spooner. 5: Reed Col 26-30 (Hist) BA; UWash 33-36 (Fr) MA, summers 39 & 61-65 (LS) ML. 6: Fr. 7: Tchr Ecole Nouvelle, Bex Switzerland 31-33; Tchr-libn Quinault High Sch, Quinault Wash 39-42; Sch libn North Mason High Sch, Belfair Wash 61-. 9: ALA; NEA: Wash StateLA; WashtateLA; Wash StateASchL. 10: PTA; Fair Harbor Grange; AAUW; NAACP. 12: "Tales from the Elves Forest" (50. 15: PO Box 478, Grapeview Wa 98546.

SPORE, MARY KATHERINE. b Boston Mass 27 Je 43. 5: Boston Col 61-65 (Hist) BS; Peabody Col 65-66 MLS. 7: Asst to dir libs Boston Col 66-69; Libn Weston Col Sch of Theol 69-. 9: ALA; ATheolLA. 14: Admin, catlg, ref. 15: 41 Oxbow rd, Weston 93 Ma 02193.

SPOSATO, MARGARET H. b Mt Jackson Va 18 Ap 20. 4: Frank J Sposata. 7: Admin aid Johns Hopkins Applied Physics Lab, Silver Spring Md 48-68, Assoc libn 68-. 9: SLA. 12: "Glossary of Acronyms" (68). 14: Catlg, acquis, ref. 15: 19704 Meredith dr PO Box 177, Olney Md 20832.

SPRADLIN, EMILY VIRGINIA. b Louisville Ky 6 F 22. 5: ULouisville 4042 (Eng) AB; Columbia summers 44-45 (Eng) 47-48 BS in LS. 7: Eng tchr, Louisville Ky 42-44; Eng tchr, New Vienna Ohio 44-46; Louisville Free Pub Lib, Louisville Ky: Asst Iroquois Br 46-47, Asst circ dept 48-49, Asst child dept 49-50, Asst ref dept 50-55; Period libn ULouisville Lib 55-66, Hd ser dept 66-. 9: ALA; SELA; KyLA; Louisville Lib Club (sec-treas, 53-54 & 59-60). 15: 1092 Eastern Parkway, Louisville Ky 40217.

SPRADLING, MARY MACE (MRS LOUIS L). b Winchester Ky. 5: Ky State Col 29-33 (Eng) AB; ATLANTA 47-48 (LS) BA; Rutgers summers 57, 58. 6: Fr. 7: Tchr Lynch (Ky) Pub Schs 34-37; Tchr Mather Acad, SC 37-38; Asst Supt Friendship Home, Cincinnati 41-42; Tchr Eminence (Ky) schs 42-43; Tchr Lexington (Ky) pub schs 43-44; Tchr-libn Shelbyville (Ky) pub schs 44-47; Br libn Louisville (Ky) Pub Lib 48-57; Head ya dept Kalamazoo Pub Lib 57-. 8: Lecturer, West Mich U Dept of Libnship, spring 63; Consul Wkshop Ky State Col, 64, Consul Tri-Co Enrichment Ctr summer 68. 9: ALA-YASD (rep 65-); MichLA. 10: Delta Sigma Theta; NAACP; Delta Kappa Gamma; M L King Memorial Fund Bd. 13: Yes. 14: Wk with ya. 15: 307 S Dartmouth, Kalamazoo Mi 49007.

SPRAGG, EDWIN BROWNLEE. b Washinton Penn 30 S 37. 5: Washington & Jefferson Col 55-59 (Econ) BA; UPittsburgh 62-63 (Hist) MA, 64-65 MLS. 6: Ger, Sp. 7: Stock clerk-cashier Thorafare Supermarket, Washington Penn 53-59; Investigator Retail Credit Co, Washington Penn 61-65; Sgt E-5 28th Infantry Washington Penn 60-64; Asst catlg libn Cornell U Law Lib, 65-67; Order libn Mann Lib 68-. 9: Cornell Lib Staff Assn (pres 69-70). 10: Beta Phi Mu; Phi Alpha Theta. 11: Alfred Henry Sweet Prize in History; Washington & Jefferson Col 59; Pennsylvania Lib Assn Scholarship Award 65; Honor student Univ of Pittsburgh 65. 14: Ref, tech serv, admin. 15: 319 Wait ave, Ithaca NY 14850.

SPRAGUE, JULIENNE CONSUELO (SANCHEZ). b Santa Fe NM 27 Je 33. 4: Nelson Alvin Sprague. 5: UNM 50-54 (Home Econ, Sp); UTex summer 56 (LS). 6: Sp. 7: Lib asst UNM Lib 50-52; Lib asst UTex Law Lib (Austin) 56-58; Instr Amer Motels Inc, Las Vegas Nev 62-63; Asst acquis libn Tex State Lib, Austin 65, Interlib loan libn 65-. 9: ALA; TexLA; SWLA. 10: Kappa Omicron Phi. 14: Interlib loan & ref. 15: 2820 Glenview, Austin Tx 78703.

SPRAGUE, ORA ANN. b Kalamo Mich 16 F 10. 5: Spring Arbor Jr Col 30; Greenville Col 32 (Math, Greek) AB; UMich 36 (Math) AM; Syracuse 41 BS in LS; Columbia 51 MS in LS. 6: Greek, Fr, Sp. 7: Dean of women & tchr Roberts Jr Col (Roberts Wesleyan Col) 33-37, Tchr & libn 34-50, Libn 50-. 9: ALA; NYLA; Monroe Co Lib Club (pres & other offs 60-66); Rochester Regl Res Lib Coun. 10: Christian Libns Fellowship. 12: Mem Edl Com "Christian Periodical Index" (59-). 14: Acquis, admin. 15: Roberts Wesleyan College, North Chili NY 14514.

SPRAGUE, RUTH G (MILER). b Pauls Valley Okla 3 S 19. 5: Okla StateU 38-42 (Home Econ Educ) BS, summer 47; UOkla 61-64 MLS. 7: Home econ tchr pub schs: Medford Okla 42-43, Garber Okla 44-45, Monument NM 48-49; Home serv consul Okla Gas & Electric Co, Okla City & Sapulpa 45-47; Soc sci libn UOkla 64-65; Libn Sam Houston Jr High, Amarillo Tex 65-. 9: ALA; NEA; AmerClrTA; TexLA; TexStateTA; TexClrTA. 10: AAUW. 14: Sch libn. 15: 2916 Ricks, Amarillo Tx 79103.

SPRANGER, MARCIA J (ZEECK). b Cleveland Ohio 19 Mr 42. 4: Jon E Spranger. 5: St Mary of the Woods Col 60-64 (Chem) BA; Rosary Col 68-69 MALS. 7: Lit chem Universal Oil Prods, Des Plaines Ill 64-66, Asst supv research lib 66-67; Supv info ctr DeSoto Inc, Des Plaines Ill 67-. 15: De Soto Inc 1700 S Mt Prospect rd, Des Plaines Il 60018.

SPRANKLE, ANITA THOMAS. b Bellefonte Penn 10 Je 44. 4: Lynn R Sprankle. 5: Penn State 62-65 (Geog) BA, 67; Drexel 65-66 MS in LS; Penn State 67. 6: Ger, Sp. 7: Asst libn (catlgr) Penn State U Commonwealth Campuses (Univ Park) 66-67; Libn I (catlgr) Kutztown State Col 67-. 9: ALA; PennLA (sec Catlg Div). 14: Catlg, tech serv, non-bk materials. 15: RD 1, Mertztown Pa 19539.

SPRENGER, BERNICE C. b Hibbing Minn 26 S 08. 4: Daniel Robert Sprenger. 5: Hibbing Jr Col 25-27; UWis 27-29 (Hist) BA, 28-29 (LS) Certif. 7: Catlgr Burton Hist Collection Detroit Pub Lib 29-32, Ref asst circ dept 32-35, Ref asst Burton Hist collection 35-58, 1st asst hist & travel dept 58-61, Asst chief Burton Historical Collection 61-68, Chief Burton Historical Collection 68-. 14: Ref, rare bks. 15: 17350 Melrose, Southfield Mi 48075.

SPRING, JOAN (ELIZABETH). b Los Angeles Cal 18 D 33. 5: UGa 52-56 (Art) BFA; Emory 59-63 (Libnship). 7: Lib asst A W Calhoun Med Lib EmoryU 56-60, Catlgr 60-. 14: Catlg. 15: PO Box 15162 Emory Univ Branch, Atlanta Ga 30333.

SPRINGER, MARGARET ANN (WARD). b England 9 Ja 41. 4: Christopher C Springer. 5: McGillU 58-61 (Sociol, Psych) BA, 63-64 BLS. 6: Fr, Sp. 7: Soc wk Child Serv Ctr, Montreal 61-63; Libn McGillU Sch of Lib Sci Lib 64-66; Ref libn UWaterloo Arts Lib 66-68; Libn St Paul's United Col 66-. 9: CanLA. 15: 109 Greenbrier dr, Waterloo Ont Can.

SPRINGER, NELSON (PAUL). b Minier Ill 22 Ag 15. 4: Mary Elizabeth Weber. 5: Goshen Col 37-41 (Eng) BA; Goshen Col Biblical Sem 47-49; American U summer 49 Certif in archives admin; UIll 50-51, summer 53 (LS) MS. 6: Ger,Dutch. 7: Manager Goshen Col Bkstore & Snack Shop, Goshen Ind 41-47; Asst archivist Archives of the Mennonite Church, Goshen Ind 48-50; Curator Mennonite Hist Lib Goshen Col 49-; Col Archivist Goshen Col 50-. 9: ALA. 10: Mennonite Hist Soc, Goshen Col. 13: Yes. 14: Bibliog, catlg, ref, rare bks. 15: Goshen Col, Goshen Ind 46526.

SPRINKLE, MICHAEL DOSS. b Elkin NC 23 N 39. 5: UNC 58-62 (Eng) AB, 65-66 MS in LS; WashU Med Sch Lib 66-67 Pre-Doctoral Fellow in Computer Libnship. 7: Asst dir Union Catlg of Med Personnel Med Lib Ctr of NY, NYC 67-68, Act dir 69-. 9: MedLA; NY Lib Club. 10: ACLU. 13: Yes. 14: Lib automation. 15: Med Lib Center of NY 17 E 102nd st, New York NY 10029.

SPRINKLE, SYLVIA YVONNE. b Winsotn Salem NC 25 Ap 45. 5: Winston-Salem State Col 63-67 (Educ) BS; AtlantaU 67-68 (LS) MS. 6: Sp, Fr. 7: Libn I Free Lib of Phila 68-. 9: ALA. 10: Delta Sigma Theta; Exper in Internat Living. 14: Child serv, ref. 15: 330 W Johnson st apt J1, Philadelphia Pa 19144.

SPROAT, ANABEL. b Hammond Ind 22 D 16. 5: Rockford Col 34-35; Chicago 35-36; Ind U 38-40 (Soc Sci) BS in Ed; Peabody summers 41-43 BS in LS; UIll summer 50 (LS); U Copenhagen 56; UWyo 59; Peabody summer 61 MSLS; Sophia U (Tokyo) 62; USoIll 63. 6: Ger. 7: Libn Edison Sch, Hammond Ind 41-53, 55-56; Spec serv libn Europenan Command US Army 53-55; Libn Tech Voc High Sch, Hammond Ind 55-61; Consul Center for Instr Materials W Leyden High Sch, Northlake Ill 61-62, Chm 61-68; Hd libn Moraine Valley Commun Col 68-. 8: Instr NDEA Lib Inst Okla State U summer 65. 9: ALA; IllLA; IllSchLA; Ind SchLA (chm NW Sect); IndTA (sec NW Sect). 10: AAUW; Pi Gamma Mu; High Sch Libns Chicago. 14: Child libs, ref, admin. 15: 10201 S 85th ter, Palos Hills Il 60464.

SPROVIERI, CARMEN LETITIA. b Can 14 J141. 5: Gonzaga U 61-62 (Eng) BA, 62-63 (Eng) MA; UBC 63-64 BLS. 6: Fr. 7: Head Libn Notre Dame U (Nelson BC) 64-. 9: ALA; CanLA; CathLA; BCLA; ABCL (Memb Com); W Kootenay Reg Lib (Exec mem). 10: Gamma Pi Epsilon; Canadian Fed Univ Women. 12: "Basic List of Reference Books for a Small Public Library" (64). 14: Ref. 15: Notre Dame Univ Lib, Nelson BC Canada.

SPRUDZS, ADOLF. b Sakstagals Latvia 19 S 22. 4: Janina Strods. 5: URiga Sch of Law 42-44 (Law); UTUEBINGEN Sch of Law 46-47 (Law); ULovain 49-51 (Financial & Com) Licenci, 53-54 (Internat Rel) Licenci; Rosary Col 58-61 (LS) MA. 6: Latvian, Fr, ger, Russian, Flemish, Sp, Ital. 7: Lib asst Col Philos et Theol St Albert SJ (EEgenhoven-Louvain) 51-55; Head catlg & clsf dept Northwestern U Sch of Law Lib 55-60; Supv Defense Info Off, Chicago 60-63; Foreign law libn UIll Col of Law Lib (Champaign) 63-65; Foreign law libn UChicago Law Lib 65-, Lecr in legal bibliog 67-. 9: Internat Assn of Law Libs; AALL; ChicagoALL. 12: "Foreign Law Abbrvtns; french" (67); "Selected Bibliography on International Trade and Investment (67); "Max Rheinsteins Writings, a Bibliography (68); Co-ed "Res Baltica" (68). 13: Yes. 14: For law bk sel, ref. 15: Univ of Chicago Law Lib, Chicago Il 60637.

SPRUG, JOSEPH WILLIAM. b Fort Smith Ark 9 Ap 22. 4: Mary Joan Storm. 5: St Meinrad Col 46 (Philos) BA; Catholic U 47 BSLS, 49 Philos MA. 6: Lat, Ger. 7: Catlgr Catholic U 47-51, Head catlgr 51-52; Ed "Catholic Periodical Index" Catholic U 52-61; Head of tech processes Fresno Co Lib, Fresno Cal 61-62; Head of tech processes St Vincent Col (Penn) 62-64; Libn Loretto Heights Col 64-. 8: Consul, US Navy BYD (57); Consul, H W Wlson C, Indexes (64-)67. 9: CathLA (Exec Bd 59-61); ColoLA; Amer Soc Indexers. 10: Beta Phi Mu. 12: Ed "Catholic Periodical Index (52-61); Ed "Guide to Catholic Literature (60); Ed "Catholic Supplement, "Wilson Standard Catalog for High School Libraries (66-67); Comp "30-year index to Orate Fratres-Worship (57). 13: Yes. 14: Indexing, tech proc, period. 15: Loretto Heights Col Lib, Denver Co 80236.

SPRUNG, GEORGE (ALAN). b NY 3 O 26. 4: Evelyn Kass. 5: NYU 43-49 (Bus Admin) BS; LIU 65-67 MLS. 7: Cpl US Army Signal Corps, Italy 44-46; Salesman: Union Square Mus Shop, NYC 49-50, Spear & Co, NYC 50-51, Adams & Co 51-52; Jr exec Sam Goody Inc, NYC 52-64; Trainee Brooklyn Pub Lib, Grand Army Plaza 65-66; Admin asst NY Med Col 66-68; Circ coord NY Acad of Med, NYC 68-. 8: Aided a study on the Brooklyn Museum for the Director 67. 9: SLA; NYLA. 14: Ref, circ. 15: 255 W 88th st, New York NY 10024.

SPULER, ANDREW E. b Williamsport Penn 4 Ja 34. 4: Elizabeth Jane Smith. 5: Lycoming Col 52-56 (Accounting) BS; Penn StateU 56-61 (Secondary Educ) MEd; Bloomsburg State Col 58 (Bus Educ); UPittsburgh 67-69 (LS). 6: Sp. 7: Grad asst Penn StateU (Univ Park) 56-57; Accountant: Charles Krimm Lumber Co, Williamsport Penn 57-58, Gen Motors Acceptance Corp, Williamsport Penn 58-59; Tchr Williamsport Area Sch Dist, Williamsport Penn 59-61, Asst to bus mgr 61-65; Hd tech serv Williamsport Area Commun Col 65-. 9: ALA; PennLA; PennBusEA. 10: Lycoming Hist Soc; Friends of James V Brown Lib, Ind Mgt Club of W Branch Valley; Delta Pi Epsilon. 14: Tech serv. 15: 900 W 3rd st, Williamsport Pa 17701.

SPURGEON, JENNIE AKARD. b White Pine Tenn 27 Mr 14. 5: Carson & Newman Col 35-36; Appalachian State Tchrs Col 37-40 (Educ) BS (cum laude); UTenn 47-48 (Hist) MS; Columbia 56 (LS) MS. 7: Tchr-libn White Pine High Sch, White Pine Tenn 43-56; Libn West High Sch, Nashville 56-57; Asst Prof & catlg libn UTenn 57-58; Libn Bayard Jr High Sch, Wilmington Del 58-62; Libn Mt Pleasant Jr High Sch, Wilmington Del 62-64; Ref libn UDel 64-, Tchr of Lib Sci Col of Educ 65-. 9: ALA-ACRL; DelLA; ETennLA (pres 51-52); SLA. 10: AAUW; AAUP. 13: Yes. 14: Ref. 15: 1305 N Broom st, Wilmington De 19806.

SPURLOCK, LUCILLE. b Kleinwood La 28 Mr 20. 5: Northwestern State Col 39-43 (Eng, LS) BA; LSU summers 47-50 BLS. 6: Fr. 7: Lib sci supv Louisiana Col Tioga High Sch Lib 58-65; Interim libn Louisiana Col summers 60 & 62, Lib Sci Instr Louisiana Col 64-66; Libn Tioga High Sch, Tioga La 43-69. 14: Ref,catlg. 15: Rte 1 Box 262, Moreauville La 71355.

SPYERS-DURAN, PETER. b Budapest 26 Ja 32. 4: Jane F Cumber. 5: Rakoczianum 42-50 Matura; UBudapest 55 Diploma; Chicago 60 (LS) MA, 62- LS; IBM Systs Research Inst 65 (Data Processing). 6: Ger, Hungarian, Lat. 7: Asst in prep law lib UChicago 57-58; Ref libn Chicago Pub Lib 58-60; Head circ libn & instr UWichita 60-62; Asst exec sec ALA, Chicago 62-63; Admin asst & asst Prof UWis(Milwaukee) 63, Asst dir of lib & Assoc dir of libs & Assoc Prof 67; Dir of libs West Mich U 67-. 8: Bldg consul, Athens Col Lib, Athens Greece 62; Instr, Univ of Brazilia Peace Corps Proj 64; Consul to Library Movers & Consultants, Columbus, Ohio. 9: ALA; -LAD (chm Com on Ret Homes, 63-67, chm Com on Econ Status 67, Pub Rel Com 63-64; PAS Nomin Com 64); -ACRL (Com chm on Standards 65-). 10: AAUP; Kalamazoo Co Lib Bd. 12: "Moving Library Materials (64, rev ed 65). 13: Yes. 14: Tech proc, admin, data proc, pub serv, moving libs. 15: 1805 W Grand, Kalamazoo Mi 49001.

SQUILLANTE, ALPHONSE MICHAEL. b SI NY 26 My 32. 4: Diana Keilman. 5: Wagner Col 50-54 (Hist) AB; Columbia 56-57 (LS) MS; Fordham 58-62 LLB; NYU 68-. 6: Fr, Ger, Ital. 7: Pre-prof NY Pub Lib 52-54, 57; (Pfc) US Army Missile Btn, US 54-56; Head Libn SI Commun Col 57-58; Asst libn Fordham U Law Lib 58-62; Priv bus 62-63; Libn Supreme Court Law Lib of NM 64-65; Asst Prof of Law & Law Libn UDenver 65-69; Prof of Law & Dir of Legal research & info serv Drake U Law Lib 69-. 9: AALL (SW Chap). 13: Yes. 14: Admin. 15: Drake Univ Law Lib, Des Moines Ia 50311.

SRAGOW, JEANNETTE (LAPORTE). b Chicago. 4: Irving Leon Sragow. 5: Chicago 30-33 (Eng) PhB Catholic U 59-62 MSLS. 6: Fr, Yiddish. 7: Jr asst libn Chicago Pub Lib 30-35; Civil serv examiner US Civil Serv Commsn, Wash DC 35-40; Volunteer asst Arlington Co Pub Lib, Arlington Va 46-52; Catlgr & supv of recordings Prince Georges Co Mem Lib, Hyattsville Md 56-. 9: ALA; MdLA. 10: Beta Phi Mu. 14: Catlg, recordings. 15: 2512 Amherst rd, W Hyattsville Md 20783.

ST CLAIR, NORBERT. b Budapest 27 Jl 24. 4: Suzanne Forsyth. 5: Hungarian Mil Acad 42-44 (Mil Sci) BMS; U of Sci (Budapest) 47-51 (Hist, Geog BA; West Mich U 62-65 MLS. 6: Hungarian, Ger, Fr. 7: Lab supv Northwestern U 57-62; Catlgr Boston Pub Lib 63-66; Catlgr MIT 66-68; Assoc libn Fla Tech U 68-. 9: ALA; FlaLA. 14: Catlg. 15: 101 S Bumby ave, Orlando Fl 32803.

ST JULIEN, BETSY (ANDEASON). b Shawhan Ky 21 Jl 16. 4: C J St Julien. 5: East Ky Col 33-37 (Educ) BS; Peabody 38-40 BS in LS; Colo State Col 41-42 (Educ) MA. 7: Lab sch libn East KY Col 38-40; Lab sch libn Colo State Col 40-42; Lab sch libn Central Wash Col 42-43; Libn US Army Geiger Field, Spokane Wash 43-44; Lib consul Mich State Lib 44-45; Ref dept La State Lib 45-47; Head of ext E B R Parish Lib, Baton Rouge La 49-59; Libn E Baton Rouge Parish Schs, Baker High Sch, Baker La 59-66; Instr NDEA Inst Kan State Tchrs Col summer 64, 65, 66; Instr UWyo (Laramie) summer 66; Asst Prof Lib Sch LSU (Baton Rouge) 66-. 9: ALA; LaLA; La Tchrs Assn. 14: Sch libs, lib euc. 15: 2277 Edinburh ave, Baton Rouge La 70808.

STAACK, KATHERINE A. b Hebron Neb 1 N 25. 5: Augustana Col (Ill) 43-47 (Span) AB; Middlebury Col summer 48 (Span); UIll 51-52 (LS) MS. 6: Sp, Fr, Ger. 7: Sec Hartwick Col 47-48; Sec Augustana Col Lib Ill 49-50; Catlgr Lippincott Lib UPenn 52-57; Catlgr Tufts U Lib 57-. 9: ALA. 10: Beta Phi Mu. 14: Catlg. 15: 437 Medford st, Somerville Mass 02145.

STAAF, LIA (NOUKAS). b Tallinn Estonia 23 N 32. 4: Harry Johnson Staaf. 5: Bowling Green State U 51-55 (Hist) BA; West Res 56-57 (LS) MA. 6: Estonian, Ger. 7: Lib asst Toledo Pub Lib, Toledo Ohio 55; Clerk Cleveland Pub Lib 55-57; Libn George Mason Jr-Sr High Sch, Falls Church Va 57-58; Libn Horace Mann Jr High Sch, Lakewood Ohio 58-60; Child libn Lakewood Pub Lib, Lakewood Ohio 61-67; Sch libn Lakewood Bd of Educ, Lakewood Ohio 67-69. 8: Sch libn Greater Cleveland Summer Inst, 65. 9: ALA; OhioASchL. 10: Lakewood Col Club; Alpha Phi; AAUW. 14: Sch libnship. 15: 2180 Woodward ave, Lakewood Ohio 44107.

STAATS, JOAN. b Chicago 31 J121. 5: UIll 39-43 (Psych) BS, 45-47 (Physiol) MS. 7: Expt pharmacologist Wilson & Co, Chicago 43-44; Expt pharmacologist Armour & Co, Chicago 44-45; Staff sci & libn The Jackson Lab, Bar Harbor Me 49-. 9: MedLA (Life mem; chm NE Reg Group 62). 10: AAAS; AAUW. 13: Yes. 14: Ref, subj bibliog. 15: Jackson Lab, Bar Harbor Me 04609.

STABLER, PAULINE (FREDERICK). b Parkersburg WVa 7 O 09. 4: William Wilson Stabler. 5: Marietta Col 27-31 (Gk) AB; UNeb 35-37 (Classics) AM; Catholic U 56-60 MSLS. 6: Fr, Ger, Lat, Gk, Sp. 7: Instr Marietta Col 32-34; Asst libn Jr-Sr High Sch, Parkersburg WVa 34-35; Jr libn US Dept of Labor, Wash DC 36-42; Asst libn: Vitro Labs, Silver Spring Md 55-56, UMd 57-58, Assoc Libn 59-. 8: Ref libn UAlaska summer 66; Asst Nat Lending Lib for Sci & Tech, Yorkshire England summer 67. 9: ALA; SLA (Baltimore Chap: sec 61, pres 63); MdLA; DCLA. 10: Chi Omega; E Silver Spring Citizens Assn; Allied Civic Group. 14: Ref. 15: 803 Easley st, Silver Spring Md 20910.

STACHOWIAK, KATHLEEN CROFOOT. b St Paul Minn 25 Ja 45. 4: James Stachowiak. 5: Col of St Catherine 63-67 (LS) BA. 7: Libn I St Paul Pub Lib sci & ind dept 67-. 9: MinnLA. 14: Serv to bus (particularly through ref serv). 15: 2052 E Magnolia, st Paul Mn 55119.

STACK, BETTY (BUYCK). b St Matthews SC 24 O 25. 4: George William Stack. 5: Womans Col UNC 42-46 BSM; New England Conservatory of Mus 46-48 MM; Drexel 53-54 MSLS. 6: Fr, Ger, Sp, Russian. 7: Music catlgr Boston Pub Lib 48-49; Music catlgr copyright Div LC 49-54; Ref libn Detroit Pub Lib 54-57; Ed "The Music Index Info Coords Inc, Detroit 57-. 9: MusLA. 10: Phi Kappa Phi; Pi Kappa Lambda; Phi Beta Mu; Crescent Music Club. 14: Catlg. 15: 22 Primrose lane, Greenville SC 29607.

STADING, GERALD (FREDRICK). b Richardton N Dak 4 Mr 35. 5: UNDak 53-56; Valley City State Col 56-57, 59-60 (Soc Sci) BS; UDenver 63-64 (Libnship). 6: Ger. 7: Intelligence clk (specialist 4th class) US Army 57-59; Lib asst Post Lib, Ft Shafter Hawaii 58-59; Lib asst Valley City State Col 59-60; Libn sr high sch, Detroit Lakes Minn 60-61; Libn pub lib, Detroit Lakes Minn 61-63; Film tech Denver Pub Lib 63-64; Libn pub lib, Faribautt Minn 65-67; Asst curator ms Minn Hist Soc, St Paul 67-. 9: ALA; SLA; Assn State & Loc Hist; MinnLA; ColoLA. 10: Rice Co (Minn) Hist Soc; Rotary. 14: Archives, rare bks, autographs, mss. 15: 232 S Exchange st, St Paul Mn 55102.

STADLER, FRANCES (HURD). b St Louis 13 D 17. 4: Ernst A Stadler. 5: Drury Col 34-35 (Music); Washington U (St Louis) 35-38 (Ger, Eng) AB; UMunich (Germany) summer 37. 6: Ger. 7: Asst libn University City Pub Lib, University City Mo 39-40; Ref libn St Louis Post Dispatch St Louis 42-43; Soc reporter 44-45, 47-49; Staff asst Amer Red Cross, Japan & Philippines 45-47; Recreation dir spec serv US Army, Germany 49-54; Program dir YWCA, St Louis 55-56; Archivist Mo Hist Soc, St Louis 56-. 8: Free-lance writer of Hist & Loc Sketches for Radio Station KSD, St Louis 60-. 12: "St Louis from Laclede to Land Clearance" (62). 13: Yes. 14: Mss, ref. 15: Mo Hist Soc, Lindell at DeBaliviers, St Louis Mo 63112.

STADLER, BROTHER BEDE CSC. b Manawa Wis. 5: UNotre Dame 38 (Hist) BA; Rosary Col 65 MA in LS. 7: Libn Holy Cross High Sch, River Grove Ill. 15: 3000 80th ave, River Grove Ill 60171.

STAGER, JOHN R. b Latvia 27 Mr 04. 4: Biruta Kligers. 5: URiga (Latvia) 30 (Econ) MA, 33 (Law) LLM; Chicago 50-53 (LS); West Mich U 63 (LS) MA. 6: Ger, Russian, Latvian,Fr, Lat. 7: Insurance clerk Latvian Lloyd, Riga 23-33; Lawyer Riga 33-44; Instr in Russian lang & hist Valparaiso U 49-50, Asst to the libn & Instr in hist 50-53, asst Libn 53-. 8: Asst Prof in Russian Valparaiso U 63-64; Dir Educ Materials Center, Valparaiso U 65-. 9: ALA; IndLA. 10: Pi Gamma Mu. 14: Ref. 15: 155 McIntyre Court, Valparaiso Ind46383.

STAFFORD, LEVA MARIE (LASH). b Talmo Kan 21 O 16. 4: Charles M STafford. 5: Mo Valley Col 35-39 (Fr) BA; UIll 39-40 BLS. 7: Asst circ libn, order libn, ref libn UKan Lib 40-42; Army Spec serv libn Pratt Kan & Europe 42-47; Br Visitor King co Pub Lib, Seattle 48-52; Libn Albany Co Pub Lib, Laramie Wyo 52-54, Catlgr 54-68, Act hd catlg dept Coe Lib 68-. 9: ALA; MPLA; WyoLA. 14: Pub rel, catlg, ref. 15: 205 S 8th st, Laramie Wy 82070.

STAGGERS, VIRGINIA (ANN). b Bakersfield Cal 1 J 1 17. 5: San Jose State Col 41 (Educ) BA; Columbia 46 (LS) Certif, 53 (LS) MS. 7: Libn elem sch dists, Santa Maria & Riverside Cal 41-45; Army libn US Army, Korea, Guam & Japan 46-50; Command libn Far East Air Forces, Tokyo 50-52; Staff libn Central Air Defense Force, Grandview Mo 53-57; Tech asst to dir Air U Lib, Montgomery Ala 57-58; Libn OCD Research Dept of Defense, Battle Creek Mich & Wash DC 58-62; Libn Hughes Tool Co Aircraft Div, Culver City Cal 63-. 9: ALA; SLA. 11: Outstanding Performance Award DOD. 14: Docs, admin. 15: 12708 Woodgreen st, Los Angeles Ca 90066.

STAGGS, EDWIN A(LBERT). b Clevelandl1 N 29. 5: UCal(Santa Barbara) 47-51 (Chem) AB; UCLA 52-55 (Organic Chem) MS; Immaculate Heart Col 63-65 (LS) MA. 6: Ger. 7: Chemist Truesdail Labs, Los Angeles 51; Chemist Purex Corp, Ltd, South Gate Cal 51-52; Sr lab tech UCal Citrus Expt Station (Riversid55-58; Chem Calbiochem, Los Angeles 58-59; Lit searcher, Hd libn, Sr lit scientist Riker Labs div Dart Inds Inc, Northridge Cal 61-. 9: SLA; ACS; Div of Chem Lit; ASIS. 10: Drug Info Assn. 13: Yes. 14: Lit searching, ref, documentation, info retrieval. 15: 5933 Murietta ave '4, Van Nuys Ca 91401.

STAHL, ALICE M (DODGE). b Concord Mich 22 D 25. 4: Fred A Stahl. 5: Albion Col 43-47 (Hist) AB (summa cum laude); Columbia 50-52 MS in LS. 6: Ger, classical Greek. 7: Br asst Flint Pub Lib, Flint Mich 52-53; Docs libn Penn State Lib, Harrisburg 53-56; Asst catlgr Hill Ref Lib, St Paul 58-65; Catlgr UMinn Lib (Minneapolis) 66-. 9: ALA; MinnLA. 10: Phi Beta Kappa. 14: Catlg. 15: 1050 - 15th ave SE, Minneapolis Mn 55414.

STAIGER, MARGARET(BROWN). b Putnam Conn 10 Mr 22. 4: ROger P Staiger. 5: Ursinus Col 39-43 (Eng) BA. 6: Fr. 7: Asst libn, Circ libn, Ref & micro libn Ursinus Col Lib 52-. 9: ALA. 10: Pottstown Hist Soc. 14: Ref, micro media, Americana. 15: 707 Chestnut st, Collegeville Pa 19426.

STAKE, DOROTHY HARVEY. b Des Moines Iowa 22 S 18. 4: Richard J Stake. 5: UMinn 40 (LS) BS; George Washington U 56 (Educ); Cal co libn certif 67. 7: Jr asst pub lib, Hibbing Minn 36-38; Jr libn Readers Serv Pub Lib, Minneapolis 40-41; Libn State Hosp Lib, Rochester Minn 41-42; Lt jg WAVES USNR Communications US N Rep Base, Staten Island NY 42-44; Alameda Co Lib, Hayward Cal; Libn I 60-61, Libn II 62-65, Libn III 65-68, Libn IV 68-. 9: CalLA; ALA. 10: Friends of the Lib, San Lorenzo. 14: Adult serv, bk sel. 15: 15869 Corte Ulisse, San Lorenzo Cal 94580.

STALEY, VALERIA SUPEAR (HOWARD). b Georgetown SC. 4: Frank M Staley Jr. 5: Talladega Col 41-45 (Eng) BA; UChicago 45-46 BLS; Columbia summer 52 (Educ); UCLA summer 53 (Educ); Rutgers summer 64 (LS). 6: Fr. 7: Ref libn Fla A&M U 46-49; Libn Howard High Sch, Georgetown SC 49-56; Asst libn SC State Col 57-. 9: SCLA; SELA. 10: Delta Sigma Theta; Jack & Jill of Amer; NAACP; Human Rel Com; League of Church women United; VFW Aux. 14: Acquis, ref. 15: Box 1947 SC State Col, Orangeburg SC 29115.

STALKER, FRANCES. b Borden Ind 4 Ap 13. 5: Butler U 31-35 (Journalism) AB; Columbia 39-40 BS in LS; Butler U 54 (Hist) MA. 7: Indianapolis Pub Lib: Gen asst 40-44, Br libn Shelby Br 44-48, Head ref dept 48-60, Head soc sci div 60-61, Coordinator of adult serv 61-. 9: ALA (chm Jr Mem Round Table 47); ; Notable Bks Com 69-); - ACRL (chem Ref Sect 52-53); Subs Bks Com 54-56);- RSD (chm Chap Com 59-61); IndLA (Coord Ind Fed Rel COM 45-50, Loan FUND Com 47-48. Legis Com 63-, pres 64-65). 10: Indianapolis Womans Club; Womans Rotary Club; Eng-Speaking Union; Ind Hist Soc; Delta Delta Delta; Coun on World Affairs; Theta Sigma Phi. 14: Ref, adult serv. 15: Indianapolis Pub Lib 40 E St Clair St, Indianapolis 46204.

STALLARD, BRUCE E. b Norton Va 14 D 16. 4: La Verna Glass. 5: UWash 53-57 (Anthrop) BA, 59-60 (LS) Masters; Wash State U 57-58. 7: Asst ref libn King Co Lib Syst, Seattle 60-62, Spec proj libn 62-63, Hd central serv 63-. 9: ALA; WashLA; PNLA. 10: Phi Beta Kappa. 13: Yes. 14: Tech serv, admin, data proc, personnel. 15: 4727 - 37th NE, Seattle Wa 98105.

STALLING, HARRIS DEAN. b Canadian Tex 17 Mr 09. 4: Harriet Louise Pillbury. 5: Westminster Col (Utah) 29-31; Stanford U 31-33 (Pol Sci) AB; UIll 34-35 (LS) BS, 39-40 MA in LS. 6: Sp. 7: Lib asst Stanford U; Lib asst UIll; Libn SD State 35-48; US Navy (Lt) 43-46; Libn ND State U 48-, Prof Lib Sci 67-. 9: ALA; MPLA (past pres). 10: Kiwanis; Red Cross: Phi Kappa phi. 13: Yes. 14: Admin. 15: 1109 5th st North, Fargo ND 58102.

STAM, DAVID H. b Paterson NJ 11 J 135. 4: Deirdre Corcoran. 5: Wheaton Col (Ill) 51-55 (Eng Lit) BA; UEdinburgh 55-56 (Theol); Rutgers 60-62 MLS; Northwest U 68- (Hist). 6: Ger. 7: Journalist US Navy 56-58; Ed asst NY Pub Lib 59-62, Libn I 63-64; Head Libn Marlboro Col 64-67; Hd processing Newberry Lib, Chicago 67-69, Assoc libn 69-. 9: ALA; MLA. 12: "Wordsworthian Criticism (46-64). 13: Yes. 14: Ref, rare bks, bibliog, catlg, hist printing. 15: 1018 N State, Chicago Il 60610.

STAMPS, HELEN (BOXLEY). b Birmingham Ala 1 Ja 06. 5: UAla 24-27 (Eng, Langs) AB; Columbia 29-30 BS in LS. 6: Fr. 7: Typist Womans Missionary Union Birmingham Ala 27-28; Asst Birmingham Pub Lib, Birmingham Ala 28-29, 30-32, Head lit dept 32-43; Head libn Laurel (Miss) Army Air Force 43-44; Birmingham Pub Lib, Birmingham Ala; Asst catlg dept 44-45, Head fine arts dept 46-56, Head period dept 56-57, Head ref dept 57-62; Ref libn Samford U Lib 62-66, Docs libn 66-. 9: AlaLA. 10: Birmingham Lib Club (pres 65-66). 11: DAR. 14: Ref, bk selection. 15: 1614-B 29th Ct So, Birmingham Al 35209.

STANDING, DORIS (ANNABELLE). b Winnipeg Can 11 F 32. 5: UManitoba 49-52 BA; UToronto 60-61 BLS. 7: Stenog MaCleods Ltd, Winnipeg Can 53-55; Payroll clerk Govt of Can, Winnipeg 55-60; Circ libn Etobicoke Pub Lib, Toronto 61-63; Libn Pub Health Labs Ont Dept of Health, Toronto 63-69. 9: CanLA; SLA (Toronto Chap); Inst Prof Libns of Ont. 14: Med libnship. 15: 345 Dixon rd apt 202, Weston Ont Can.

STANDROD, GARLAND LEE. b Fort Smith Ark 15 Jl 40. 4: Melanie Landau. 5: Tulane 58-62 9philos) BA; LeedsU (England) 60-61 (Philos); UMd 67-68 MLS. 7: Personnelman (PN3) USN USS Charles H Roan (DD-853) 65-67; Ref libn Dept of the Interior, Wash DC 68-. 9: SLA; Law Libns Soc of Wash DC. 10: Phi Beta Kappa; South & West Lit Soc; Beta Phi Mu; Sci Fiction Research Assn. 14: Ref, bibliog. 15: Apt 2122 7615 Fontainbleau dr, New Carrollton Md 20784.

STANFORD, EDWARD BARRETT. b Moorehead Minn 31 Mr 10. 4: Maverette Ericson. 5: Dartmouth 27-32 (Biog, Comparative Lit) AB; UIll 33-34 BS in LS; Williams Col 36-39 (Eng) MA; Chicago 39-42 (LS) PhD. 6: Fr. 7: Ser asst Dartmouth Col Lib 32-33; Ed asst ALA; Chicago 34-35; Jr libn Detroit Pub Lib 35-36; Sr ref asst Williams Col Lib 36-39; Spec rep US C ivic Serv Commsn, Chicago 42-43; Asst U Libn UMinn (Minneapolis) 46-51; Prof & Dir of Libs 52-. 8: Bldg consul US Off of Educ 65. 9: ALA (Coun 64-67, chm Bd on Personnel Admin 47-49); -ACRL (chm Univ Libs Sect 58-59); Resources Com 61-63; Manuscript Soc; MinnLA (Acad Com on Coop 65); Midwest Interlib Center (Bd Dirs 52-64); ARL (Bd Dir 67-; Adv Com on Lib Lighting Study 68-); MILC (Bd Dir 52-63). 12: "Library Extension under the WPA - An Appraisal of an Experiment in Federal Aid" (44). 13: Yes. 14: Univ lib admin, lib resources, personnel admin, lib bldgs. 15: 2188 Hendon ave, Saint Paul Mn 55108.

STANGER, MARY HELEN. b Bloomington Ind 6 N 14. 5: Ind U 32-36 (Eng) AB, 48 (LS) MS. 6: Lat, Ger. 7: Asst Bloomington Pub Lib, Bloomington Ind 38-40; Libn: Orleans High Sch, Orleans Ind 40-42, Rossville High Sch, Rossville Ind 42-44, Bluffton High Sch, Bluffton Ind 44-47; Asst libn New Albany High Sch, New Albany Ind 47-50; Catlgr & sr catlgr Ind U Lib 50-57; Head catlg libn 58-. 9: ALA-ACRL; -RTSD; Ohio Valley Group Tech Serv Libns. 10: Univ Club; Women's Faculty Club; Univ Women's Club; Pi Lambda Theta. 14: Catlg, admin. 15: 606 Eastside dr, Bloomington In 47401.

STANGLE, JEAN A. b Cincinnati Ohio 4 O 36. 5: Wilmington Col 54-58 (Chem, Eng) BA; Simmons 59-60 (LS) MS. 6: Ger. 7: Bkmob libn Dayton & Montgomery Co Pub Lib, Dayton Ohio 58-59; Bkmob libn Clermont Co Pub Lib, Batavia Ohio 60-62; Asst acquis libn UCincinnati 62-68; Asst libn Lindenwood Col 68-. 9: ALA (chm Recr Com, Ohio 62-64); OhioLA (chm Jr Mem RT 65); MoLA. 10: AAUP; ACLU. 12: Asst ed OhioLA Bulletin (68). 14: Acquis. 15: 864A Thompson dr, Florissant Mo 63031.

STANKA, ELENA. b St Petersburg Russia 7 Je 10. 5: UBerlin 30 (Eng) Certif; U Kaunas (lithuania) 34 (Law) ML; Catholic U 58 MSLS. 6:Russian, Lithuanian, Ger,Fr, Polish. 7: Sec Lawyer, Kaunas Lithuania 32-38; Sec Court of Appeals, Kaunas Lithuania 38-40; Asst chief Mun Welfare Off, Kansas Lithuania 41-44; Sec British Mil Govt, Husum Germany 45-46; Lecturer Baltic U (Hamburg Pinneberg Germany) 46-49; Catlgr descr catlg div LC 49-64, Asst head descr catlg div, Slavic sect 64-67, Hd 67-. 8: Practice of law Kaunas Lithuania 42-44. 9: ALA; DCLA. 10: AAUW; Amer-Lithuanian Assn of Wash DC. 13: Yes. 14: Catlg, law. 15: 1350 You St SE, Wash DC 20020.

STANKRAUFF, JACK BOGUE. b Holly Mich 21 Jl 38. 4: Judith Elliot. 5: Monmouth Col 56-60 (Eng) BA; Syracuse 64-65 (LS) MS. 7: Advertis trainee Mann Graphic Arts, Mt Morris Ill 60; Army info spec Sp5, White Sands Missile Range NM 61-64; Asst circ libn SoIllU 65-66; Hd libn Hauner Pub Lib, Alton Ill 66-68; Coord commun rel Dayton & Montgomery Co Pub Lib, Dayton Ohio 68-. 9: ALA; IllLA; OhioLA. 10: Rotary; Jaycees; YMCA. 12: "This Month in Your Library". 14: Publ, films. 15: 215 E 3rd st, Dayton Oh 45402.

STANKRAUFF, JUDITH (ELLIOT). b Columbus Ohio 18 My 34. 4: Jack B Stankrauff. 5: Ohio Wesleyan U 52-54; Ohio State U 54-56 (Fine Arts) BA; UIll 56-57 (LS) MS. 7: Catlgr UOre Lib 57-60; Adult libn Burkhardt ave Br, Dayton and Montgomery Co Pub Lib, Dayton Ohio 60-62, Ref libn lit & fine arts dept 62-66; Br libn Hills & Dales Br 66-67; Br libn Burkhardt Ave Br 68; Br libn Kettering-Moraine Br 69-. 9: ALA; SORT (Exec Bd 66-69); OhioLA (sec Jr Mem RT 65-66). 12: Ed "Bulletin SORT (66-69). 14: Ref. 15: 215 E Third st, Dayton Ohio 45402.

STANLEY, CAROLINE H. b Wash DC 28 J 111. 5: Hollins Col 29-31; UAriz 31-33 (Psych) BA; Columbia 33-34 (LS) BS. 6: Fr. 7: Libn DC Pub Lib 34-39, 40-42; War Dept, Wash DC 42-46, USIS, Sydney Australia 46-47; Navy spec serv libn El Toro Cal 47-49, Asst libn 1Naval Dist Hq 49-51, Libn Bainbridge Naval T S 51-53; Libn adv dept of the Army, Wash DC 53-64; Personnel off DC Pub Lib 64-66; Libn BSCP George Washington U 68-. 8: Chm Ad hoc Com of Fed Libns 56-57; Recr Task Force, Fed Lib Com Wash DC 65. 9: SLA (pres MIL Libns Group, Wash DC 58-59); DCLA. 10: AAUW; Eng-Speaking Union; Phi Kappa Phi. 14: Admin, ref. 15: 2853 Ontario rd NW, Wash DC 20009.

STANLEY, NELL (NANCY). b Tex 26 N 24. 5: Southwestern Baptist Theol Sem 52-53 (Reliious Educ); Mary Hardin-Baylor Col 56 (Eng, Bible) BA; Richmond Prof Inst 64 (LS) Certif. 6: Sp. 7: Religious educ dir First Baptist Churh, Belton Tex 54-57; Religious educ dir youth First Baptist Church, Brownwood Tex 57-58; Head Libn Foreign Mission BD OF THE So Baptist Convention, Richmond Va 58-69. 9: ALA; SAA; VaLA (past Sect Mem chm). 10: Alpha Chi; Sigma Tau Delta. 13: Yes. 14: Ref, research, rare bks (Relig & Missions), archives. 15: Jenkins Lib SBC, 3806 Monument ave, Richmond Va 23230.

STANLEY, SAVANNAH (GOVERNOR). b Tallahassee Fla. 4: George A Stanley. 5: Fla A & M U 57 (LS) BS. 6: Fr. 7: Lib asst Samuel H Coleman Lib, Fla A & M U 57-. 9: FlaLA. 10: Alpha Beta Alpha. 14: Catlg, acquis. 15: 1706 Capital cir NE, Tallahassee Fla 32301.

STANLEY, WILLIAM P. b Santa Barbara Cal 16 N 27. 4: Joanne Roy. 5: URedlands 48-51 Music BM, MM; USoCal 52-54 (Music) DMA; UCal (Berkeley) 60-61 MLS. 6: Fr. 7: (Pt) US Army 46-47; Tchr Friends U 54-58; Tchr San Francisco State Col 58-60; Libn Modesto Jr Col 61-69; Hd libn Skyline Col 69-. 8: State Examiner, Cal Music Tchrs Assn 60-. 9: CalLA (pres Commun Col Div 69). 10: AAUP. 15: Skyline Col, San Bruno Ca 94066.

STANLEY, WILLIAM T. b Whiteville NC 29 N 26. 5: UCLA 47-49 (Eng) Ba; UCal (Berkeley) 49-51 (Eng) MA, 52-53 BLS. 6: Fr, Ger. 7: Pharmacist mate 3c USNR 44-46; Humanities & Soc Scis libn Caltech 53-. 9: ALA; CalLA; So Cal Tech Processes Group. 14: Ref, catlg. 15: 6511 Short Way, Los Angeles Ca 90042.

STANLIS, ALMA (NIELSEN). b Detroit 3 Ap 24. 4: Peter J Stanlis. 5: UMich 41-45 (Eng, Educ) BA & Secondary Tchrs Certif, 46-48 BALS. 6: Fr. 7: High sch Eng tchr, Trenton Mich 45-46; Libn Detroit Pub Lib, 48-50; Libn Riverview High Sch, Riverview Mich 56-60; Lib coord Riverview Schs, Riverview Mich 60-68; Hd soc scis div Rockford (Ill) Pub Lib 69, Asst coord supv of materials control 69-. 8: Faculty NDEA Inst for Sch Lib Supv West Res summer 66. 9: ALA-AASchL (Co-chm Loc Arr Com for Nat Conf 65); MichEA (sec & chm Lib Sect 61, 62);Mich Schmasters Club (sec & chm Lib Sect 64, 65). ; IllLA; IllASchL. 10: Trenton Pub Lib Adv Commsn Bus & Prof Womens Club; Phi Kappa Phi. 12: "Promotion Aids for the High School Librarian in "Better Libraries Make Better Schools (62); Co-auth "Guidelines for Supervision of School Media Programs (68). 13: Yes. 14: Sch libs, centralized acquis & processing, total sch lib program, pub lib ref, circ control, data processing, tech processing. 15: 5704 Inverness dr, Rockford Il 61107.

STANSFIELD, CYNTHIA M(ARSDEN). b Yonkers NY 7 D 40. 5: UConn 58-62 (Hist) BA; Syracuse 62-63 MSLS. 6: Fr, Sp. 7: Catlgr United Aircraft Corp Research Labs Lib, E Hartford conn 63-66; Catlgr Wilbur Cross Lib (Storrs) 66-. 9: SLA (Com Valley Chap: Corr sec 67-68, rec sec 68-69, Recr Chm 64-69); ConnLA. 10: Beta Phi Mu. 14: Catlg. 15: 91 Green Manor rd, Manchester Ct 06040.

STANTON, LEE W. b Fulton NY 3 D 44. 5: SUNY (Oswego) 62-66 (Soc Sci) BS; SUNY (Albany) 66-68 MLS. 7: Asst lib SUNY (Oswego) 68; Asst lib NY State Lib 68-. 9: ALA. 10: Pi Gamma Mu; Alpha Psi Omega. 13: Yes. 14: Ref, mss. 15: Manuscripts and History Section New York State Lib, Albany NY 12224.

STANTON, ROBERT O. b Pittsburgh 15 N 26. 4: Madalyn Pugh. 5: UPittsburgh 44-49 (Zool) BS; Carnegie 49-50 MLS. 7: Sci & engnr libn Carnegie Inst of Tech 50-54; Libn Mine Safety Appliances Co, Pittsburgh 54-56; Libn Murray Hill Lib, Bell Telephone Labs 56-63; Head publ prod dept Bell Telephone Labs NYC 63-65; Head lib operations dept I Bell Tele Labs, Murray Hill NJ 65-. 9: SLA; var offs; ASIS. 14: Tech lib admin. 15: Five Forest dr, Stirling NJ 07980.

STANTON, VIRGINIA BARBARA. b Flushing NY 7 Ja 31. 5: Douglass Col 48-52 (Hist) BA; Columbia 52-53 (LS) MS; UPenn 58-60 (Hist. 6: Sp, Fr. 7: Asst libn NJ Hist Soc, Newark NJ 52-53; Free Lib Phila: Ref libn ref Dept 53-54, Ref libn local hist 55-56, Sr ref libn gen info 57, Asst head Mercantile Lib 58-60, Asst head Bus Sci Ind Dept 60; Supv army libn US Army Europe, Germany 61-63; Head adult serv Bethpage Pub Lib, Bethpage NY 63; Asst dir Rockville Centre Pub Lib, Rockville Centre NY 64-. 9: ALA; NYLA. 15: Pub Lib, Rockville Centre NY 11570.

STANWOOD, RICHARD H. b Des Moines Iowa 24 Je 27. 4: Helen Bingham. 5: Drake U 45; Cornell Col 47-50 (Engnr) BA; West Res 50-51 (LS) MS; Va Polytech Inst 54 (Mech Engnr); UDel 53-55 (Mech Engnr) BS. 7: Shift supv E I Dupont de Nemours & Co, Aiken SC 55-59; Engnr Info Analyst Lockheed Aircraft Corp, Marietta Ga 59-60; Tech libn IBM Corp, Owego NY 60-65; Systems analyst IBM Corp, Bethesda Md 65-66, Gaithersburg Md 66-. 9: Assn for computing machinery (spec interest group on info retrieval); ASIS. 10: Exec Com, Friends f the Coburn Free Lib, Owego NY; Toastmasters Club. 12: 'MERGE; A Current-Awareness and Retrospective Searching System for Technical Documents' in "Technical Preconditions for Retrieval Center Operations" (65); Co-comp "Literature on Information Retrieval and Machine Translation" (2 vols); "Defining a Core Collection in a Technical Document Library," SLA (66). 13: Yes. 14: Bibliog, indexing, sel dissemination of info. 15: 521 Nelson st, Rockville Md 20850.

STAPLEFORD, LOIS ANN (BREAZIER). b Lincoln Kan 18 My 25. 4: Robert Stapleford. 5: Emporia State 47 (Soc Sci) BS in Ed, 49 (Eng) BA, 56 MSLS. 7: Tchr Kan 43, 47-52; Tchr-libn Sheridan Commun High Sch, Hoxie Kan 52-57; Libn Washburn High Sch, Topeka Kan 57-67; Lib coord Auburn-Washburn Unified Dist #437, Topeka Kan 68-. 8: Consul lib sci wkshop West State Col, Colo summers 65; Kan State Dept of Pub Instr Sch Lib Adv Com 62-63. 9: ALA-AASchL (State Assembly Com 57); NEA; Kan Assn of Sch LA (pres 56-57; Dist dir 54-55); William Allen White Child Bk Award Com 58-59; KanLA; Kan State Tchrs Assn. 10: Alpha Delta Kappa; AAUW. 12: Co-ed Kan ASchL "Newsletter (63-65). 14: Sch libnship. 15: 1800 Randolph, Topeka Kan 66604.

STAPLES, ROBERT H. b Toms River NJ 13 Ap 31. 5: Oberlin Col 49-53 (Hist)AB: Rutgers 57 MLS. 6: Fr. 7: Lib clerk US Army-Spec Serv, Ft Dix NJ 53-55; Prin libn NJ State Lib, Bridgeton nj 57-61; Asst dir Summit Pub Lib, Summit NJ 61-64; Dir Princeton PUB Lib, Princeton NJ 64-. 8: Coadjutant staff lecturer Rutgers Lib Sch. 9: ALA; NJLA. 10: Bd Princeton Adult Sch; Bd Princeton Jr Mus. 14: Ref. 15: 276 Nassau st, Princeton NJ 08750.

STARCZEWSKI, V WALERY. b Poland 29 Ag 1897. 4: Marie Walton. 5: Inst of Tech (Free City of Danzig) 21-26 (Reinforced Concrete & Bridge Construction) Diploma Eng; Columbia 49-50 (LS) MS. 6; Ger, Fr, Russian, Polish. 7: Civil & construction engnr-supt in the field & design & proj engnr, Poland; Electric Bond & Share Co, NY; Dir Dal, Inc, NY; Asst ref libn Army Med Lib, Wash DC; Chief Catlgr Cyrilic Sect LC. Sr research Ref Dept. 10: Polish Cavalry & Horse Artillery Assn in N Amer. 11: LC Superior Service Award. 14: Rare bks. 15: 5415 Connecticut ave NW, Wash DC 20015.

STARK, MRS ARVIL L (ELVA ACKLAM). b Racine Wis. 4: Arvil L Stark. 5: Marquette U 27-29, 30 (Eng) BS; UWis 30 (LS) Cietif. 7: Asst circ Iowa State U 30-34; Clsfr Utah State U 34-35; Asst catlgr NM State U 35-36; Asst ref UUtah 58-. 9: UtahLA; ALA. 10: PTA (Life mem); Salt Lake Safety Coun; Utah Safety Coun; Utah Assoc Garden Clubs; Holladay High Hopes Beautification Program. 14: Ref. 15: 2698 Wren rd, Salt Lake City Ut 84117.

STARK, FRANCIS D. b NYC 9 Ja 04. 5: St Francis Col 25-29 (Eng) AB; Columbia 35 (LS) Prof Certif, 50 (LS) MS, 51 (Adult Educ) Diploma in Adult Educ. 7: Lib asst The Queens Borough Pub Lib, Jamaica NY 35-42; US Army 42-46; Supv acquis div Queens Borough Pub Lib, Jamaica NY 46 9: ALA (var coms); NYLA (chm Exhib Com 51-68; var other coms); NY Lib Club. 10: Bksellers League NY. 14: Tech proc, acquis. 15: 99-11 Merrick blvd, Jamaica NY 11432.

STARK, MARIE CHARLOTTE. b Memphis Tenn 21 S 14. 5: Miss State Col for Women 30-33 (Eng) AB UArk 33-34 (Eng, Hist) MA Columbia 34-35 BS in LS. 7: Reviser Columbia U Sch of Lib Serv 35-36; Br asst Brooklyn Pub Lib 36-37; Asst archivist Nat Archives, Wash DC 36-43; Assoc archivist to asst chief, hist records sect, War Prod Bd, Wash DC 43-47; Tech asst Internat Monetary Fund, Wash DC 47-51, Archivist 51-. 8: Lecturer Record Admin American U 56-62. 9: SAA. 10: AAUW. 13: Yes. 14: Records mgt, docs indexing. 15: 3601 Wisconsin ave NW, Wash DC 20016.

STARK, RUTH K (NEESKERN). b St Johnsville NY 17 Ja 17. 4: Wesley M Stark. 5: Wm Smith Col 33-37 (Math, Biol) AB; UBuffalo 38-44 (LS, Amer Lit) MS in LS. 6: Fr. 7: Tchr of Math & Eng, High Sch, Collins Center NY 39-40; Interlib loan libn Erie Co Pub Lib, Buffalo NY 51-52; Buffalo & Erie Co Pub Lib, Buffalo NY; Jr libn br dept 52-55, Sr libn br dept 55-62, Sr libn II br dept 62-65, Sr libn II Lit dept 65-67, Sr libn II tech dept 67-. 9: ALA (Recr Netwk, Staff Org Round Table); NYLA (MEM Com). 10: Buffalo-Erie Co Pub Lib Staff Assn; Erie Co Libns Assn. 12: Ed ALA Staff Org RoundTable "Bulletin (62-63). 14: Adult serv. 15: 151 No Hampton Brk dr, Hamburg NY 14075.

STARK, SYLVANA EDMONDS. b Rigefield Wash 24 Mr 11. 4: W Hadley Stark. 5: UOre 26-29 (Drama, Eng) BA; Immaculate Heart Col 61-62 MALS. 6: Fr. 7: Eng tchr Grass Valley High Sch, Grass Valley Oe 31-33; Br libn Los Angeles Pub Lib, Los Angeles 50-56; Dist libn Westminster Sch Dist, Westminster Cal 59-. 9: ALA; CalASchL; Program Com-So Sect; OrangeCoSchLA Treas). 10: Delta Zeta. 14: Admin, bk sel. 15: 611 Bronwyn dr, Anaheim Cal 92804.

STARKE, HUGH R(ICHARDSON). b Orange NJ 6 Mr 37. 4: Mary Watson. 5: Providence-Barrington Bible Col 55-59 (Bible, Theol) BA; NYU 59-61 (Religious Educ) M; Pratt 61-65 MLS. 6: Ger. 7: Youth dir Bushwick Ave Baptst Church, Brooklyn NY 59-61; Libn Christian Freedom Found, NYC 61-65; Ya libn Huntington Pub Lib, Huntington NY 65-68; A-v libn 68-. 8: Libn Huntington Baptist Ch 69-. 9: ALA; NYLA; SuffolkCoLA. 14: Ya ref, period, a-v. 15: 81 Jackson ave, Huntington NY 11743.

STARKER, LEE NORMAN. b NYC 9 My 22. 4: Judith Starker. 5: Brooklyn Col 37-43 (Chem) AB uneb 47-49 (Chem) MS; UTenn 49-51 (Organic Chem) PhD. 6: Fr, Ger. 7: Jr-Foreman Lake Ont Ord Wks, Niagara Falls 43; Chem Cal Co Chem Div Amer Cyanamid Co, Bound Brook NJ 43; (2nd Lt) US Army Med Corps 43-46; Lab dir Borden Vitamin Co, Bloomfield NJ 46-47; Research Chem Amer Cyanamid Co, Bound Brook NJ & Pearl River NY 51-59; Chem doc group leader Amer Cyanamid Co, Pearl River NY 59-62; Manager sci info serv Warner-Lambert Res Inst, Morris Plains NJ 62-.

9: ACS; Sec Div Chem Lit, Mem Com on Documentation; Alt Councillor; ASIS; Nat Microfilm Assn. 10: AAAS; Pearl River Bd of Educ. 12: Bd of Eds "Journal of Chemical Documentation"; Bd Dir "Info Sci Abstracts". 13: Yes. 14: Info retrieval & dissemination. 15: Warner-Lambert Res Inst, Morris Plains NJ 07950.

STARKEY, RICHARD E. b Des Moines Co Iowa 17 My 32. 4: Marica Damon. 5: Drake U 50-54 (Philos) BA; Chicago 51 - BD (Ethics, Society), currently (LS). 7: Reader & tech serv Swift Lib UChicago 57-59, Gifts libn 59-60; Dir instr materials Central YMCA Community Col (Chicago) 60-64; Dir Cranbrook Central Lib Cranbrook Schs, Bloomfield Hills Mich 64-69; Dir Troy Pub Lib, Troy NY 69-. 8: Adv Com Lib Tech Program Oakland Com Col 65-69. 9: ALA-ACRL; -RTSD; -AASL; MichASL (chm Oakland Co Chap). 12: Jt ed; "Cranbrook Curriculum Conference Proceedings; "Revolution and Reaction (66); Ed "The Humanities; The Other Side of The River (68). 15: Troy Pub Lib 100 Second st, Troy NY 12180.

STARLIPER, BETTY JEANNE. b Hots Springs S Dak 30 D 22. 5: Purdue 47-51 (Sci) BS; WestNMU 55-62 (Eng) MA. 7: Med tech WAVES, St Albans & Sampson NY Hawaii 44-46, physicians Lab, Hammond Ind 42-44, summers 55-60, Ingalls Mem Hosp, Harvey Ill summers 51-54; Tchr: Glenwood Sch for Boys, Glenwood Ill 51-55, Cobre Consolidated High Sch, Bayard NM 55-63; Libn C C Snell Jr High Sch, Bayard NM 63-. 8: NDEA Inst, Our Lady of the Lake 66. 9: NEA; ALA; NMEA; NMLA; CobreEA. 10: Weslyn Serv Guild; Evergreen Garden Club. 14: Storytelling, sch libnship. 15: 809 Winefred, Bayard NM 88023.

STARR, BARBARA LOU (NOLTING). b Boston 1 O 37. 4: Robert Stephen Starr. 5: Emory 55-58 (Eng) BA, 59-60 M Lib. 6: Sp, Ger. 7: Stud asst Emory U Lib 58-59, Catlgr 59-60, Ser catlgr 60-61, Ref libn 61-62; Catlg libn Inst of Jamaica (Peace Corps Volunteer) 62-64; Typing instr (Peace Corps Volunteer) Cobbla Camp, Jamaica 64-66; Libn Peace Corps, Wash DC 66-. 13; yes. 14: Catlg. 15: 3151 Woodland lane, Alexandria Va 22309.

STARR, EDWARD CARYL. b Yonkers NY 9 Ja 11. 4: H Ruth Thomforde. 5: Colgate U 29-33 (Hist) AB cum laude; Columbia summers 36, 37, 38, 39 BS in LS; Colgate Rochester Divinity Sch 33-35, 39-40 (Church Hist) BD. 6: Fr, Ger. 7: Curator Colgate U 35-48; Curator & libn Theol Sem 48-54; Curator Amer Baptist Hist Soc, Chester Penn 48-55; Curator Amer Baptist Hist Soc, Rochester NY 55-. 10: Phi Beta Kappa. 12: Ed "A Baptist Bibliography" (v 1-13). 13: Yes. 14: Bibliog, theol & hist libs & bks. 15: 1106 S Goodman st, Rochester NY 14620.

STARR, G(AIL) L. b Great Bend Kan 4 F 43. 4: Glyndolyn Nan Warwick. 5: Abilene Christian Col 61-62; UTex (El Paso) 63-66 (Eng) BA; Case West Res 66-67 MSLS. 6: Sp. 7: Searcher UTex (El Paso) Lib 65-66; Reclassifier Sears Lib Case Inst 67; Admin consul Lib Serv Ctr Calgary Sch Bd, Calgary Alta Can 67-68; Hd tech serv Law Lib UWindsor 68-. 9: CanLA; AALL; CanALL; Profess Libns Assn, UWindsor. 10: Beta Phi Mu. 13: Yes. 14: Admin, tech serv. 15: Faculty of Law Lib, Univ of Windsor, Windsor Ont Can.

STARR, KAREN (YOUNGHANS). b St Paul 21 My 41. 4: Patrick Joseph Starr. 5: Col of St Catherine 59-63 (LS) BA. 7: St Paul Pub Lib: Bkmob libn 63, Bkmob libn & co-ordinator of child wk & displays 64, Commun rel 65-. 8: Mem Planning Com for Continued Educ, Alumnae Assn, Col St Catherine. , Exec Bd; Parents for Integrated Educ Resource Com. 9: MinnLA. 13: Yes. 15: 21 Lawton Steps, St Paul Mn 55102.

STARR, PETER M. b Nashville 28 Ap 37. 5: Colgate 63 AB; Peabody 64 MA(LS). 7: Circ libn Marquette U Mem Lib 64-67; Circ libn UWis (Milwaukee) Lib 67-68, Tech serv libn 68-. 9: ALA. 15: 2229 E Newberry blvd, Milwaukee Wi 53211.

STARR, SYDNEY (MISS). b Grand Rapids Mich 12 N 39. 5: Wellesley 57-61 (Art Hist) BA; Simmons 62-64 (LS) MS. 6: Fr, Ital, Sp. 7: Pre prof Boston Pub Lib 62-64, Ref libn Fine Arts Dept 64-66; Hd Art ref lib Pratt Inst 66-; Lectr Sch Info & Lib Sci 68-. 9: MassLA; SLA (Museums & Picture Div). 10: East Mass Bridge Assn. 13: Yes. 14: Fine arts. 15: 49 Grove st, New York NY 10014.

STARR, (BONNETT) VIVIAN. b Fond du Lac Wis 28 Mr 43. 5: Wis StateU (Oshkosh) 61-66 (LS) BS. 7: Ref libn Chicago Pub Lib 66-67; Circ libn De PaulU 67-. 14: Circ. 15: 4340 N Sawyer, Chicago Il 60618.

STARRING, ROBERT JAMES. b Detroit Mich 27 O 27. 5: Wayne State 45-49 (Speech, Theatre) BA, 54-56 (Speech, Theatre) MA; UMich 66-67 AMLS. 6: Fr. 7: Cpl USA 75th Field Artillery, Korea 52-54; Phonograph rec dept mgr Doubleday Bk Shops, Detroit 56-57, Shop mgr 57-60, Dist mgr 60-66; Lib asst UMich Pub Health Lib (Ann Arbor) 66-67; Hd bk purchasing div UMich Lib (Ann Arbor) 67-69, Asst hd circ dept Grad Lib 69-. 8: Mem, Repertory Comp, Wayne StateU, Theatre Tour of India, under auspice of US State Dept. 9: ALA. 10: Ann Arbor Civic Theatre; Fine Arts Soc of Detroit; Orpheus Club of Detroit. 14: Acquis, circ. 15: 1815 Independence, Ann Arbor Mi 48104.

STASUK, VERA SERGEI (HITOON). b Hollywood Cal 8 S 42. 4: Boris G Stasuk. 5: UCal 60-62 (Fr); Reed Col 62-65 (Russian) BA; UWash 65-66 MLS. 6: Russian, Fr. 7: Lib asst reed Col Lib 64-65; Grad asst Sch of Libnship UWash 66; Exchange & Monographs libn MIT 66-67; Slavic exchange libn UWash Libs 67-. 9: ALA. 14: Slavic & East European langs, gifts and exch. 15: 2367 Hughes SW, Seattle Wa 98116.

STEARNS, VICTORIA (BUGELSKI). b Pensacola Fla 14 O 44. 4: Gerald L Stearns. 5: SUNY (Buffalo) 61-65 (Music Hist) BA (cum laude), (Mus Performance - Piano) BFA (cum laude), 66-68 MLS. 6: Fr. 7: Trainee (mus dept) Buffalo & Erie Co Pub Lib, Buffalo NY 66-67; Grad asst Lib Sch SUNY (Buffalo) 67-68; Mus critic, "Buffalo Evening News" 67-68; Catlgr copyright div mus sect LC 68-. 8: Piano tchr 62-68; Piano accompanist (Buffalo) 65-67; Piano student SUNY (Buffalo) 63-65. 9: ALA; MuLA. 10: Phi Beta Kappa. 11: Hammerklavier Prize in Piano 65; Regents Col Tchg Fellowship 65. 13: Yes. 14: Music, catlg, ref, criticism. 15: 130 Erie st, Lockport NY 14094.

STEBEN, FLORENCE (WRIGHT). b Malta Ill 3 N 24. 4: Ralph E Steben. 5: N Central Col 42-46 (Eng) BA; UUtah 62-64; Mont State Col 63, 64; San Diego State Col 65; Chico State Col 6566. 7: Asst libn Willson Jr High Sch, Bozeman Mont 61-64; Catlgr LaMesa-Spring-Valley Sch Dist LaMesa Cal 65; Asst libn soc sci & bus Chico State Col 65-. 15: 917 Sheridan ave NE, Chico Ca 95926.

STECKL, PETER. b Brasov Rumania 7 F 23. 4: Beryl Gunstone. 5: Eidgensische Technisce Hochschule (Zrich) 45-47 UBC 48-51 BA; UMich 52-53 AM LS. 6: Hungarian, Ger, Fr. 7: Jr libn UBC 53-55; Asst catlgr Nat Research Coun Ottawa 56-57, Br libn 57-60; Asst libn USask 60-63, Act libn 61-62; Asst libn u Toronto 63-67; Chief libn Dept of Manpower & Immigration, Ottawa Can. 9: ALA-ACRL; Can Assn Col & Univ Libs; CanLA (chm Res Libs Sect 64-65); SLA. 13: Yes. 14: Sci & tech publns, lib admin. 15: Dept of Manpower & Immigration Library, Ottawa, Can.

STEED, MARIE (SIMPSON). b Arcadia La 31 My 19. 4: Gerald J Steed. 5: La Potytech Inst 35-55 (Educ) BA; NM West Col ext 55-57 (Educ); UDenver 56-58 (LS) MA. 6: Sp. 7: Elem tchr Sch System, Webster Parish La 40-41; Sch System, Roswell NM; Reading & Art tchr 55-56, Jr high sch libn 56-65, High sch libn 65-. 9: NEA: NMEA. 10: Alpha Delta Kappa. 13: Yes. 14: Elem libs. 15: 507 W 4th, Roswell NM 88201.

STEED, MARY JO. b Gilmer Tex 19 F 40. 5: E Tex State U 58-62 (Elem Educ) BS, 62-64 MS in LS. 7: Elem tchr Tyler Pub Schs, Tyler Tex 62-. 15: Box 1213, Mt Pleasant Tx 75455.

STEEGE, BARBARA RUTH (WHALEN). b Webster Mass 7 Ag 33. 4: Mark J Steege. 5: Concordia Tchrs Col 51-56 (Educ) BS;UIll 59-64 (LS) MS. 7: Tchr Trinity Lutheran Sch, Hicksville LI NY 56-57; Tchr Holy Cross Lutheran Sch, Mahwah NJ 57-58; Asst libn Concordia Theol Sem (Springfield Ill) 58-68, Dir 68-. 9: ALA; IllLA; ATheolLA. 15: Concordia Theol Sem, Springfield Ill 62702.

STEELE, CARL L. b Patoka Ill 22 Ag 34. 4: Lula Irene Saliba. 5: SoIllU 52-56 (Soc Studies) BS in Ed, 59-60 (Educ Admin) MS in Ed; Bradley 64-65; NoIllU 67-69 (LS) MA. 6: Ger. 7: Tchr: Shawneetown High Sch, Shawneetown Ill 56-57, Forrest Strawn Wing High Sch, Forrest Ill 59-61, Richwoods High Sch, Peoria Ill 61-66; US Army, Germany 57-59; Asst dir instr materials & lib serv Sauk Valley Col 66-68; Dir educ resources ctr Rock Valley Col 68-. 9: ALA; NEA-DAVI; IllLA; IllA-VA. 10: Ill Hist Soc. 13: Yes. 14: Lib admin. 15: 5758 Weymouth dr, Rockford Il 61111.

STEELE, MARGARET (SHORT). b Des Moines Iowa. 4: Wolcott L Steele. 5: Iowa StateU 30 (Home Econ) BS; NYU 31 (Retailing) MS; Drexel 65 (LS) MS. 7: Asst buyer Abraham & strauss, Brooklyn NY 31-35; Lib trainee Free Lib of Phila

62-65, Adult serv libn (Frankfort Br) 65-. 9: ALA; PennLA. 14: Ref, adult serv. 15: 4636 Pilling st, Philadelphia Pa 19124.

STEELE, MARION D. b Okla 13 F 08. 5: Park Col 27-30 (Fr) BA; Duke 32-33 (Fr) MA; Sorbonne & Institut de Phonetique (Paris) summer 36 (Fr) Certifs; UMexico summer (Span)Certif; UNC 46 BS in LS; Sophia U (Tokyo) 66-67 (Far E Hist & Civilization). 6: Fr, Sp, Portu. 7: Catlgr LC 47-51; Ref libn Naval Ordnance Lab White Oak Md 51-56; Hd catlgr US Weather Bur Lib, Suitland Md 56-57; Catlgr US Army Spec Serv Libs, Tokyo Dist 57-58, Libn-admin, Korea 58-67; Catlgr LC 67-. 13: Yes. 14: Catlg, rare bks. 15: 5649 Shadyside ave No 202, Suitland Md 20023.

STEELE, MARY BRYAN. b Louisville Ky 12 Ja14. 4: John William Steele. 5: ULouisville 32-35 (Eng); UKy 35-36 (LS) AB, 54-57 (Educ) MA, 61-64 (Educ) 7: Asst Libn Valley High Sch, Jefferson Co Bd of Educ, Louisville Ky 36-39; Libn asst Educ Lib UKy Lib 57; Libn Glendover Sch Fayette Co Bd of EDUC, Lexington Ky 59-. 9: ALA; NEA; Assn Childhood Educ Internat; Clr Tchers Assn; KyLA; KyEA. 10: Kappa Delta Pi; Alpha Delta Kappa; Pi Beta Phi; Little Garden Club of Woodford Co; Spindletop Hall; Womans Club of Cent Ky; The Lexington Cotillion Club. 14: Child bk sel. 15: Glendover Sch, Glendover rd, Lexington Ky 40502.

STEELE, MARY W. b Bele Vernon Penn 12 O 10. 4: Charles M Steele. 5: Cal State Col 30-32 (Eng) BS Sec Ed; OhioU 28-30; Penn State U summers 48-52 (LS) Eqv MS; Columbia summer 63. 6: Fr. 7: Soc Studies Tchr Belle Vernon High Sch, Belle Vernon Penn 36-40; Personnel Internat Harvester, St Paul 43-45; Libn Monongahela Pub Lib, Monongahela Penn 45-52; Belmar High Sch, Belle Vernon Penn 53-62; Baldwin High Sch, Pittsburgh 62-. 8: Chm Nat Lib Week, Penn 56. 9: NEA; ALA; Penn State EA (Dept of Supv; PennASch LA (pres 58-60); PennLA (chm Recr Com 56); Pittsburgh Lib Club; ASCD. 10: DAR; Trustee, Belle Vernon Lib Assn. 13: Yes. 14: High sch libs. 15: 104 Orchard ave, Belle Vernon Pa 15012.

STEELE, RITA EVELYN. b Boston 16 My 21. 5: Simmons 40-44 (LS) BS. 6: Fr, Ger. 7: Catlgr Millicent Lib, Fairhaven Mass 44-48; Catlgr Baker Lib Dartmouth Col 48-50; Acquis dept ser div Baker Lib Harvard Bus Sch 50-52; Asst libn Millicent Lib, Fairhaven Mass 52-53; Libn 53-. 8: Pub lib consul Survey for town of Boxford (Mass) 65; Tchr lib sci courses Mass Div of Lib Ext 60-6 1; V-chm East Mass Reg Lib Adv Coun. 9: MassLA (pres-elect 65-66); Old Dartmouth Lib Club (pres 53-54). 10: Delta Kappa Gamma; Girl Scout Mariners. 14: Ref. 15: 24 Main st, Fairhaven Mass 02719.

STEELMAN, RAYLENE (EVELYN) (MENTER). b Warren Ark 16 O 23. 4: Herman Clay Steelman. 5: Ark A & M Col 40-42 Ark State Tchrs Col 42-43; Tex Womens U 43-44 (LS) BA; UIll 50-51 (LS) MS. 6: Sp, Fr. 7: Libn Hermitage High Sch, Hermitage Ark 44-46; Asst libn Ark A & M Col 46-59; Libn Hendrix Col 59-60; Libn Ark A & M Col 60-64, Catlgr 64-. 9: ALA. 14: Catlg, ref, admin. 15: Box 434 College Heights, Ark 71633.

STEEN, JUDITH ARLENE (KIPPOLA). b Bremerton Wash 20 N 40. 4: Harold Karl Steen. 5: UWash 59-62 (Eng) BA; UPortland 63-65 MLS. 6: Fr. 7: Spec serv libn UPortland 64-65; Ref libn hist dept Seattle Pub Lib 66-. 9: ALA; WashLA. 14: Ref. 15: 812 1/2 E Gwinn pl, Seattle Wa 98102.

STEEN, NANCY GAY. b Bowling Green Ohio 4 Mr 39. 5: Bowling Green State U 57-61 9hist) BA, 61-63 (Hist) MA; UMich 65-66 AMLS. 6: Fr. 7: Stud asst Dept of Geog Bowling Green StateU 60-61, Grad asst Dept of Hist 61-62, Bibliogr 63-64, Res asst 64-66, Asst hd circ dept 66-. 9: OhioLA. 10: Beta Phi Mu; Phi Alpha Theta; Pi Sigma Alpha; Alpha Delta Pi. 14: Circ, archives. 15: 1204 Lyn rd, Bowling Green Oh 43402.

STEEVES, ALAN (HENRY) JR. b Somerville Mass 12 F 16. 4: Audrey Virginia Caesar. 5: Bowdoin Col 34-38 (Gk, Lat) AB; Columbia 41-44 (LS) BS. 7: Ref libn NY Pub Lib 40-45; Field serv consul operations res group Navy Dept Wash DC 45-46; Libn Amer Numismatic Soc, NYC 46-48; Vice pres NE Marmon Harrington Coaches Inc, Somerville Mass 48-56; Libn research Inst for Advanced Study, Baltimore 57-60; Libn Sperry Rand Research Center, Sudbury Mass 61-. 9: SLA (chm Sci-Tech Div of Boston Chap 65-66); ALA. 12: Contrib Chap "Recent Soviet Contributions to Mathematics ed by J P LaSalle &S Lefschetz (62). 13: Yes. 15: Timothy lane,Carlisle Mass 01741.

STEFANCIC, EMIL J. b Cleveland 18 S 16. 4: Jane Jevnikar. 5: Miami U 36-40 (Hist) BA; West Res 40-41 (LS) BS, 46-49 (Amer Culture). 7: Lib asst Cleveland Pub Lib 40-41; US Air Force Radio operator-gunner Tech Sgt 42-45; Asst Libn Fenn Col 41-55, Libn 55-65; Libn Cleveland State U 65-69, Assoc dir 69-. 9: ALA; OhiLA (chm Col & Unv Round Table 63-64). 10: Caterpillar Club. 11: Air Medal; Purple Heart. 14: Admin. 15: 2983 Lynn dr, Wickliffe Oh 44092.

STEFANCIC, JEAN ANN (GEISKY). b Cleveland 14 Ja 40. 4: Stanley Robert Stefancic. 5: West Res 58; Maryville Col (Tenn) 58-61 (Eng, Amer Lit) BA; Simmons 61-63 (LS) MS. 6: Fr, Ital, Serbo-Croatian. 7: Libn intern Harvard Col Lib 61-63, Ser libn 63-65; Catlgr So Methodist U Lib 65-67; Sers catlgr Oakland U Lib 67-69. 9: ALA-ACRL; -RTD. 10: LWV. 14: Ser, catlg, acquis, admin. 15: 1027 Forest st, Birmingham Mi 48008.

STEFANI, JoANN (REINER). b Eaton County Mich 11 Ag 33. 4: Andrew Stefani. 5: Mich StateU 51-55 (Eng) BA; UMiss 66-67 MLS. 7: Asst prof & libn Dept of Lib Sci UMiss 67-68; Sr libn catlg dept 68-. 9: MissLA. 15: Box 174, University Ms 38677.

STEFFEN, RUTH (ELIZABETH) S(WAN). b Marion Ohio 29 O 25. 4: W Richard Steffen. 5: Col of Wooster 43-46; UWis 46-47 (Soc Wk) BA, 65-69 (LS) MS; UMinn 62-63. 7: Bibliog searcher UMinn (Minneapolis) 62-63; Lecturer Wis StateU (Stevens Point) 63-. 9: ALA; WisLA. 14: Catlg. 15: 2009 Main st, Stevens Point Wi 54481.

STEFFER, VERNON S. b Duluth Minn 26 Ja 25. 4: Patricia Joan Thomas. 5: Macalester Col 46-52 (Hist, Eng Lit) BA, MEd; UMinn 54- (LS). 6: Sp. 7: Tchr & libn Minn Lake Pub Schs, Minn Lake Minn 51-56; Libn pub schs, Princeton Minn 56-58; Libn DOD Dependent Sch: Madrid Spain 58-62, Johnson Air Station Japan 52-64; Curriculum & lib coord DOD Dependents Schs, Japan & Korea 64-66; Lib coord Independent Sch Dist 191, Burnsville Minn 67-. 9: ALA; OverseasEA (treas; Area Chm for Spain & N Africa); MinnASchL (v-pres & pres-elect Capital Div); MinnEA; BurnsvilleEA. 10: Farmer Labor party; Boy Scouts; Hale-Ressurection Commun Sch (Minneapolis). 11: US Civil Serv outstanding Performance Award 63. 14: Sch libnship. 15: 5027 11th ave S, Minneapolis Mn 55417.

STEIGNER, MARY A. b Sandusky Ohio16 F 31. 5: Goucher Col 48-52 (Physiology & Bacteriol) BA; Howard U 60-62 (Psych) MS; Simmons 63-64 (LS) MS. 7: Research asst Johns HOPKINS U 52-53; Jr bacteriologist Bur of Sewers, Baltimore 54; Lab tech Baltimore Biol Lab, Baltimore 54-55; Bacteriologist Nat Inst of Health, Bthesda Md 56-58, Physiologist 58-60; Libn Worcester Pub Lib, Worcester Mass 64-66; Assoc libn Med Sch Lib UMass (Amherst & Worcester) 67-69. 9: MedLA. 14: Ref, tech proc, data processing, admin. 15: PO Box 718, Amherst Mass 01002.

STEIN, REV BENJAMIN JOHN OSB. b Cold Spring Minn 2 Ja 10. 5: St Johns U 26-32 (Philos) BA; UMich summer 36, & 36-37 BA S, summer 41 (LS). 6: Ger, Fr. 7: Pastoral asst St Anselms Church, NY 37-38; Ref libn St Johns U Lib (Minn) 39, Libn 36-67, Asst libn 68-; Asst libn St Bernard Col Lib (Ala) 67-68. 9: ALA; CathLA (past chm Sem Sect; past chm Minn-Dak Unit) ; MinnLA (past chm Col Sect). 13: Yes. 14: Catlg. 15: Collegeville Minn 56321.

STEIN, ELIDA B (BROMBERG). b NYC 8 O 27. 4: Jack Stein. 5: Hunter Col 44-47 (Chem) BA; Columbia 64-67 MLS. 7: Chem sec Sandoz Pharmaceuticals, NYC 47-54; Drug & chem indexer Columbia U Med Lib Parkinson Info Ctr 68-. 9: ALA; MedLA. 14: Ref. 15: 3311 Sedgwick ave, Bronx NY 10463.

STEIN, ELIZABETH ANN. b Cleveland Ohio 16 Ag 17. 5: Grove City Col 35-39 (Eng) AB; West Res 49-50 MSLS; Columbia summer 55 MedLA Certif. 7: Asst libn Euclid Pub Lib, Euclid Ohio 39-40; Libn Wickliffe Pub Lib, Wickliffe Ohio 40-47; Libn Bailey Meter Co, Cleveland Ohio 47-49; Libn Lutheran High Sch, Cleveland Ohio 49-50; Ref libn J McIntire Lib, Zanesville Ohio 50-51; Circ & ref libn US Nat Archives Lib, Wash DC 51-53; Libn Med Staff Lib St Luke's Hosp, Cleveland Ohio 53-59; Asst libn Cleveland Med Lib, Cleveland Ohio 59-63; Libn Brittingham Lib Metropolitan Gen Hosp, Cleveland Ohio 63-. 8: Guest lectr, West Res U Sch Lib Sci 57-63; Adv Com Cuyahoga Commun Col Lib Tech course 67-. 9: ALA; MedLA. 15: 171 E 216 st, Cleveland Oh 44123.

STEIN, ESTELLE F (IDELL) (MRS). b St Louis 30 My13. 5: Washington Sq Col NYU 29-34 (Eng) BA; Columbia 35-36 BLS. 6: Fr. 7: Reviser Columbia U Sch of Lib Serv 36-38; Libn NY State Tchr Train Lib, NYC 37-38; Catlgr-reviser

Brown U 38-39; Standard Catlg Series, H W Wilson Co: Asst ed 39-42, Assoc ed 43-62, Ed 62-. 9: ALA; NYLA; Tech Serv Lib Assn, NY; NY Lib Club. 12: Ed "Essay ND General Literature Index" (59-); "Fiction Catalog" (60-); "Standard Catalog for Public Libraries" (59-); "Short Story Index" (54-); Jt ed other titles of standard catalog series. 14: Catlg, indexing. 15: 790 Concourse Village W, Bronx NY 10451.

STEIN, LENORE A. b Pittsburgh 27 Je 34. 4: Herman Stein. 5: Duquesne U 52-56 (Sociol) BA; Carnegie 56-57 MSLS. 7: Carnegie Lib of Pittsburgh; Adult asst Hazelwood br 57-59, Child libn Lawrenceville br 59-65, Child libn Knoxville br 65-67; Reg libn E Africa USIA 67-68; Bus div libn DC Pub Lib 69-. 9: ALA; PennLA. 15: 4100 Cathedral ave NW, Wash DC 20016.

STEIN, ROGER R. b NYC 12 Ap 42. 5: C W Post Col 59-63 (Music, Educ) BA, 63-65 Certif as Sch Libn; Hofstra U 65-67 (Secondary Educ); MS in Ed. 6: Sp. 7: Libn Fork Lane Sch, Hicksville NY 63-64; Libn John P McKenna Jr High Sch, Massapequa NY 64-. 9: ALA-AASchL; NY State Tchrs Assn; Nassau-Suffolk Sch LA. 10: Metropolitan Opera Guild; NYC Opera Guild. 13: Yes. 14: Tech serv, a-v materials. 15: 45 Broadway, Freeport NY 11520.

STEIN, RUTH. b NY 15D 20. 4: Leo Stein. 5: Brooklyn Col 37-41 (Home Econ, Physiology) BA; Pratt 56-58 (LS) MA. 6: Fr. 7: Child libn Queens Borough (NY) Pub Lib 58-59; Tchr-libn Bd of Educ, NY 59-. 9: NYC SchLA. 10: Cunningha League for Handicapped Child; Amer Cancer Soc. 14: Sch libs. 15: 188-20C 69th ave, Fresh Meadows NY 11365.

STEINBACH, MILDRED. b Lewistown Penn 22 D 06. 5: Vassar 25-29 (Hist) AB; Columbia 41 BLS; Inst of Fine Arts 46 (Fine Arts) MA. 6: Fr. 7: Libn Inst of Fine Arts NYU 40-44; Asst libn Frick Art Ref Lib 44-. 9: ALA; SLA; Col Art Assn. 14: Ref. 15: 10 E 71st st, New York NY 10021.

STEINBERG, DAVID LEE. b Rolla Mo 22 Ag 43. 4: Grace Carolyn Fernald. 5: Central Mo State Col 59-63 (Math) BS; UNC 66-68 MSLS. 6: Fr. 7: Elem sch libn Waynrsville-Ft Leonard Wood (Mo) Schs 63-66; Jr high sch lib Louisiana (Mo) Pub Schs summer 66; Grad asst Lib UNC (Chapel Hill) 67-68; Lib UMo (Rolla) summer 67; Asst libn & instr lib sci, William Woods Col 68-; Instr UMo Sch Lib & Info Sci (Columbia) summer 69. 9: ALA; NEA; MoLA; MoStateTA. 10: Sigma Pi; Beta Phi Mu. 13: Yes. 14: Tchg, admin, a-v, genealogy. 15: Dulany Library William Woods Col, Fulton Mo 65251.

STEINBERG, ELLEN (BROWN). b Newburg Mo 31 Mr 06. 4: Roy Steinberg. 5: UMo 40 (Educ & Soc Sci) BS; Central Mo State Col 60 (LS) MS. 6: Lat, Sp. 7: Tchr: Newburg R-2 Sch Dist, Newburg Mo 23-38, Pub Sch, Carlyle Ill 38-40, Newburg R-2 Sch Dist, Newburg Mo 40-42, 47-54; Tchr Waynesville R-6, Waynesville Mo 55-61, Libn 61-. 8: Supv all lib serv in Waynesville-Fort Leonard Wood Schs; Consul La & Mo Pub Schs 66; Consul, Hillsboro Ill 69. 9: NEA; ALA; Mo State Tchrs Assn. 10: AAUW; OES. 14: Child bks, rare bks. 15: Box 176, Newburg Mo 65550.

STEINER-PRAG, ELEANOR F (EISENBERGER). b Bochum Germany 10 Ap 05. 5: Book Trade Sch Leipzig Germany) 22-23; Lib Sch (Leipzig Germany) 23-25 State Certif. 6: Ger, Fr, Swedish, Czech.07 Catlgr & Bibliog(r) Deutsche Buecherei, Leipzig Germany 25-33; Exec Sec Internat Collection of Modern Bk Art, Prague Czechoslovakia 34-38; Catlgr Yale U Lib 40-42; Catlgr & Ref libn US Off of War Info Lib, NYC 42-44; Catlgr & Ref libn Woodrow Wilson Mem Lib, NY 45-50; Ed "American Library Directory, & "American Book Trade Directory R R Bowker Co, NY 56-. 7: Catlgr & bibliogr Deutsche Buecherei, Leipzig Germany 25-33; Exec sec Internat Collection of Modern Bk Art, Prague Czechoslovakia 34-38; Catlgr Yale U Lib 40-42; Catlgr & ref libn US Off of War Info Lib, NYC 42-44; Catlgr & ref libn Woodrow Wilson Mem Lib, NY 45-50; Research asst Hist Research Gen William J Donovan, NY 50-56; Ed "American Library Directory," & "American Book Trade Directory" R R Bowker Co, NY 56-. 9: Amer Inst of Graphic Arts; SLA (chm Publ Div; NY Chap: chm Publ Group, chm Archives Com); Tech Serv Libns, NY; Amer Soc Indexers (v-pres). 10: Womens Nat Bk Assn. 12: Ed "Goethe in the Book Art of the World, Leipzig (32); Ed "50 Books of the Year (48-52); Ed "Bulletin, Publ Div SLA (57-58). 13: Yes. 14: Catlg, ref, indexing. 15: 125 Christopher st, New York NY 10014.

STEINER, REV URBAN JAMES. b Mandan ND 11 D 32. 5: St Johns U (Minn) 50-55 (Philos) BA, 55-59 (Theol); UIll 59-61 MSLS; Columba summer 64 (Theol libs); Instituto Mexicano Norteamericano de Relaciones Culturales (Mexico City) summer 68; UIll 68-69 Certif of Advanced Study (6th Yr Masters). 6: Lat, Ger, Sp. 7: Libn St Johns Prep Sch, Collegeville Minn 58-59, 61-64; Libn St Marys Col summer 63; Ref libn St Johns U (Minn) 61-. 9: Amer Benedictine Acad; CathLA (Minn- Dakota Unit: chm High Sch Sect 63-64); ATheoLA. 12: Comp "Contemporary Theology: a Reading Guide (65). 14: Ref, theol lib, catlg. 15: St Johns Abbey, Collegeville Minn 56321.

STEINER, RONALD A(LVA). b Carroll Iowa 25 Mr. 38. 4: Joanne Burkhart. 5: U Dubuque 56-60 (Hist) BA; West Res 61-62 MS in LS. 7: Lib trainee UDubuque 60-61; Ser documents libn Beloit Col 62-64; Asst ref libn No Ill U 64-68; Assoc libn Ind U (Penn) 68-. 9: ALA; PennLA. 10: AAUP; Beta Phi Mu: Phi Alpha Theta. 15: 320 S 4th st, Indiana Pa 15701.

STEINHART, HANS (ULRICH). b Hamburg Germany. 4: Margaret Koschel. 5: Friedrich-Wilhelm U 26-29 (Ger Lit); Boston U 53-55 (Social Found of Educ) Ed M; Rutgers 56-57 MLS; Boston U 58-60 (Germanic Lang & Lit). 6: Ger, Fr. 7: 15 yrs in Ger archives & libs; Ser libn Boston Col 53-55; Lib Fellow NJ Hist Soc, Newark NJ 56; Asst Prof of Lib Sci Glassboro State Col 57-. 9: NJEA: NJLA. 10: AAUP; Medieaval Acad of Aer; NJ Hist Soc; German Soc Penn; Faculty Assn NJ State Col. 13: Yes. 14: Readers adv. 15: 307 Hamilton rd, Glassboro NJ 08028.

STEINHART, SYDNAE M (ROUSE). b Harrisburg Penn 24 F 42. 4: William L Steinhart. 5: Lebanon Valley Col 60-64 (Bio) BS; UPittsburgh 65-66 MLS. 7: Lab tech Harrisburg Hosp, Harrisburg Penn summers 62-63; Research tech Johns Hopkins Sch of Pub Health 64-65, USPHS rare med bks trainee Welch Med Lib 67-68; Ref libn Health Sci Lib UMd (Baltimore) 66-67; Asst libn Frederick Co Pub Libs, Frederick Md 68-. 9: ALA; MdLA. 10: Nat Wildlife Fed; Nat Audubon Soc; Md Ornithol Soc; Arts Coun of Frederick; Amer Recorder Soc. 14: Rare bks. 15: 1824 B Willard pl, Fort Detrick Md 21701.

STEINHAUS, MARGARET WETTERAU. b Ft Plain NY 5 O 14. 4: Henry Steinhaus. 5: NY State Col for Tchrs (Albany) 31-35 (LS, Eng) BS in LS. 7: Eng tchr, Libn St Johnsville High Sch, St Johnsville NY 35-38; Libn Draper Sch, Schenectady NY 38-48; Volunteer catlgr Mercer Museum Lib, Doylestown Penn 60-64; Volunteer Ft Plain Free Lib, Ft Plain NY 65-; Media specialist Amsterdam Sch Syst, Amsterdam NY 67; Libn Canajoharie Lib & Art Gallery, Canajoharie NY 68-. 9: NYLA. 10: Friends of the Fort; Volunteer wker at Fl Plain Restoration; Cooperstown Art Assn; Dutch Settlers Soc. 14: Catlg, adult adv serv, local hist collections. 15: P O Box 342, Nelliston NY 13410.

STEINKE, CYNTHIA (ALICE). b Oak Park Ill 14 Mr 37. 5: Mich StateU 55-59 (Fr Lang & Lit) BA; UParis 57-58 (Fr Lang & Lit); UIll 64-66 (LS) MS. 6: Fr. 7: Media Young & rubicam Advertising, Chicago 59-60; Prod Sci Research Assoc, Chicago 60-61; Research asst Field Enterprises Educ Corp Research Lib, Chicago 61-64; Sci ref libn John Crerar lib, Chicago 66, Ref libn stud ref serv 67-68, Chief stud ref serv 68-. 9: SLA; ALA; IllLA. 10: Beta Phi Mu. 14: Ref. 15: John Crerar Lib 35 W 33rd st, Chicago Il 60616.

STEINKE, ELEANOR G. b Philadelphia Penn 6 D 14. 5: Wilson Col 33-37 (Eng) AB; Drexel 37-38 BS in LS; Columbia summer 39. 7: Libn City Hosp of Akron, Akron Ohio 38-41; Libn Winnebago Co Med Lib, Rockford Ill 41-45; Asst libn Vanderbilt U Sch Med 45-46, Asst libn 46-55, Libn 56-68. 8: Chm, Wkshop "Organizing the Collection"; Amer Hosp assn 67; Instr of Refresher Course, MedLA 58 & 59. 9: ALA; Assn Amer Med Cols; MedLA (chm Subcom on Curr 56-57 & 62-63, chm Com on Standards 57-58, chm Com on Bibliog Proj & Problems 63-64); TennLA (treas 65-66); Nashville Lib Club (pres 60-61). 10: Vanderbilt Soc Hist Med. 12: Revised: Cunningham, E R "Classification for Medical Literature" (5th ed 67). 13: Yes. 14: Admin, ser. 15: 4500 Shy's Hill rd, Nashville Tn 37215.

STEINMANN, BETTY EDNA. b Freeport Ill. 5: MacMurray Col 40-44 (Sociol) AB; U Wis 58-59 (LS) MA; UFla 68 (Humanities). 6: Ger, Sp. 7: Interviewer USNR, Chicago 45-46; Casewker Co Welfare Agency, Racine, Monroe Wis 46-56; Gen off Pike Co Cheese Co, Pittsfield Ill 56-58; Libn Monroe Pub Lib, Monroe Wis 59-60; Catlg ref libn Evanston Pub Lib, Evanston Ill 60-61; Catlg ref libn UDubuque 61-62; Catlgr No Ill U 62-. 9: ALA; IllLA. 10: AAUW; Alpha Beta Mu; LWV; Bus & Prof Womens Club. 14: Catlg, ref, humanities & soc sci bibliog. 15: 226 Hillcrest dr, DeKalb Ill 60115.

STEINWEG, HILDA (ESTHER). b Merrimac Wis 8 F 10. 5: State Tchrs Col (Platteville Wis) 31-35 (Eng) BEd; UWis 41-42 BLS: UChicago 48-50, 55 (LS) MA. 6: Ger. 7: Rural tchr Sauk Co Wis 28-30; Eng tchr Westboro High Sch, Westboro Wis 36-37; Clerk Wis Ind Commsn, Madison Wis 37-41; Catlgr State Hist Soc of Mo, Columbia Mo 42-43; Ref Milwaukee Pub Lib 43-44; Asst catlgr State Hist Soc of Wis, Madison Wis 44-46; Catlgr State U Iowa 46-48; Catlgr Armed Forces Med Lib, Wash DC 51-55; Catlgr Detroit Pub Lib 56-63; Head catlgr Ohio U 63-65; Head catlgr U S Ala 65-. 9: ALA-RTSD (sec Catlg & Clsf Sect 65-68); MichLA (sec-treas Tech Serv Sect 59-61). 13: Yes. 14: Catlg, clsf. 15: N Ann apt C-3, Mobile Ala.

STELLA, SISTER MARIS OS F. b BuffaloNY 27 F 20. 5: DYouville Col 37-42 (Fr) BA; UNotre Dame 47-50 (Fr) MA; Catholic U 56-60 MS in LS. 6: Fr. 7: Fr tchr St Marys High Sch, Lancaster NY 42-50; Libn: Bishop OHern High Sch, Buffalo NY 50-53, St Marys High Sch, Lancaster NY 53-56, Archbishop Carroll High Sch, Buffalo NY 56-60, St Clare Col 60-. 9: ALA; Amer Assn Tchrs French CathLA; West NY Cath Libns Conf. 14: Admin. 15: 400 Mill st, Williamsville NY 14221.

STEMPLE, RUTH M. b Hendricks WVa 10 Ag 15. 5: WVaU 24-38, 52-53, (Educ, Math, Sci) BS; Fla State U 54-55 (LS) MS. 7: Tchr: pub schs WVa 39-52, 53-54; Sr ref WVa U Lib 55-56; Documents libn Fla State U 56-6; Head Libn Radiation Inc, Melbourne Fla 60; Head Libn Agric-Engnr Lib WVaU 60-66; Oak Ridge Associated Universities, Oak Ridge Tenn 66-67; Oak Ridge Nat Lab Central Research Lib 67-. 9: SLA. 10: Beta Phi Mu. 12: "Margaret Prescott Montague, 1878-195: a chik-list, Bulletin of Bibliography, 22 (May/August 57) 62-64, "Rebecca Harding Davis, 1831-1910: a check list, Bulletin of Bibliography, 22 (September/December 57) 83-85; "Kenneth Roberts:a supplementary check-list Bulletin of Bibliography, 22 (September/December 59) 228-230; "Author-subject index to articles in Smithsonian Annual Reports, 1849-1961, by Ruth M Stemple and The Editorial and Publications Division of the Smithsonian Institution. Smithsonian Institution Publication no 4503, (63) "The Philadelphia Chromosome in Leukemia Research; A Bibliography; "Two Medical Diagnostic Isotopes, Gallium-68 and Technetium-99m; a bibliography. 14: Admin, ref, doc ser. 15: 212 N Purdue ave, Oak Ridge Tn 37830.

STENE, PEARL MARIE (KNUDSON). b Crookston Minn 19 F 35. 4: Oscar B Stene. 5: Concordia Col (Minn) 52-56 (Eng, Psych) BA; No State Tchrs Col (Aberdeen SD) (LS); UMinn 60, 61 (LS). 6: Norwegian. 7: Tchr-libn Pub Sch, Morristown Minn 56-57; Eng tchr Pub Sch, Buffalo Minn 57-58; Libn Pub Sch, Madison Minn 58-59; Asst libn Luther Theol Sem (St Paul) 59-60; Libn-tchr Pub Sch, Sacred Heart Minn 60-62; Libn-tchr Pb Sch, Boyd Minn 65-66; Libn Fulda Pub Sch, Fulda Minn 67-. 9: NEA; ALA; MinnEA. 10: PTA; Amer Horse Shows Assn; Tri-State Horsemans Assn; Lac Qui Parle Saddle Club; Commun Concert Assn. 14: Pub sch libs, teen age reading guidance. 15: Rte 2 box 34, Fulda Mn 56131.

STENNIS, RENE LEE. b Weatherford Tex 4 J102. 5: So Methodist U 22-26 (Hist) BA, 36-38 (Hist) MA; Tex Womans U 38-40 BS in LS. 6: Fr, Sp. 7: Libn: O M Roberts Sch, Dallas 29-34, J L Long Jr High Sch, Dallas 34-40, Sunset High Sch, Dallas 40-52, So Methodist U summers 52-65, N R Crozier Tech High Sch, Dallas 52-. 8: Tchr Lib sci No Tex State U summers 47, 52. 9: ALA; NEA; TeL; Tex State Tchrs Assn. 10 Delta Kappa Gamma; AAUW; Chi Omega; Phi Alpha Theta. 14: Sch lib wk, ref, circ. 15: 2804 Westminster, Dallas Tx 72505.

STEPANIAN, ELLEN MARTHA. b Elmira NY 16 Mr 37. 5: Syracuse 55-59 (Elem Educ) BS; Columbia 59-60 (Spec Educ) MA; UDenver 65; Rosary Col 66-67 MA in LS; Oklahoma StateU 67. 6: Fr. 7: Tchr: Barrington Sch Dist 4, Barrington Ill 60-64, Sch Dist 107, highland Park Ill 64-66; Asst supv libs Sch Dist 67, Lake Forest Ill 67-. 9: NEA; ALA; IllEA; IllLA. 10: PTA; Pi Lambda Theta; Delta Kappa Gamma; Kappa Delta Pi; Beta Phi Mu; Adv ch lib. 14: Sch lib serv. 15: 1970 Green Bay rd apt 2A, Highland Park Il 60035.

STEPHENS, ANN (LUPTON). b St Petersburg Fla 5 Mr 08. 5: Cottey Col 25-27; Rollins Col 27-29 (Hist) AB; Peabody 37-38 BS in LS; Fla State U summers 47-51 (LS). 7: Tchr elem schs, Fla 29-31, 34-37; Col libn, Fla & PR 38-41; Libn: high schs, Fla 42-43, Mil libs, Fla & Miss 43-44, high schs, Fla 44-50; Tchr elem schs Fla 50-56, 58-61, Libn 61-. 9: ALA; FlaLA. 10: DAR. 14: Sch lib. 15: PO Box 12203, St Petersburg Fl 33733.

STEPHENS, ARIAL AVANT. b Charlotte NC 23 J132. 4: Anne Brockmann. 5: Charlotte Col 50-52 AA: UNC 56-60 (Hist) BA, 61-62 (LS). 7: Lib asst Mecklenburg Co schs, Charlotte NC 47-52; Yeoman 2nd class US Navy, Cal 52-56; Asst libn Med Lib, Charlotte NC summer 58; Sec VI Mann Geol dept UNC (Chapel Hill) 59-60; Ref asst Pub Lib, Charlotte NC 60-61, Asst dir 62-. 9: ALA; SELA; NCLA (chm Jr Mems Round Table); chm Exhibits; exec dir NLW); Charlotte Area LA (pres);Mecklenburg LA (pres). 10: Rotary; Torch Club of Charlotte. 15: 810 Sunnyside ave, Charlott NC 28204.

STEPHENS, CLARA MAE (JANEWAY). b Ramona Cal 5 S 04. 4: Albert B Stephens. 5: Whittier Col 22-23, 24-27 (Math) AB; UCal(Berkeley) 32-33 LS Certif. 7: Libn Yorba Linda Pub Lib, Yorba Linda Cal 33-34; Asst libn Santa Maria Pub Lib, Santa Maria Cal 34-35; Off mgr & owner Stephens Ins Agency, Yorba Linda Cal 47-56; Libn Fullerton Pub Lib, Fullerton Cal 57-, Desk & bkmob libn 57-62, Br libn 62-68, Supv adult serv 68-. 9: CalLA; Orange Co LA. 10: LWV; Altrusa Internat. 15: 601 S Basque ave, Fullerton Ca 92633.

STEPHENS, DENNY. b Kilgore Tex 3 O 32. 5: Hardin-Simmon U 50-54 (Eng) BS; UDenver 57-58 (LS) MA. 6: Fr. 7: Circ Ector Co Pub Lib, Odessa Tex 49-51; Documents Div Hardin-Simmons U 51-53; Asst child libn Abilene Pub Lib, Abilene Tex 54; Roughneck Hisson Drilling Co, Midland Tex 54; Overseas radio correspondent, US Army USA Reur/Comz, Orlean France 56-57; A-v libn Denver Pub Lib 58-60; Asst libn Ector Co Pub Lib, Odessa Tex 60-61; Dir Hutchinson Pub Lib, Hutchinson Kan 61-64; Host KTVH Television, Wichita Kan 63-64; Co libn Jefferson Co Lib, Golden Colo 64-65; Admin asst & institutional consul Colo State Lib 65-67; State libn Kan State Lib 67-. 8: Dir The Hutchinson Arts & Science Found, Hutchinson Kan 63-64; dir, Nat Lib Wiik Colo 65. 9: ALA; MPLA; ColoLA; ColoEA; KanLA. 10: Amer Field Serv. 14: Admin, pub fin. 15: 2021 Lincoln, Topeka Ks 66604.

STEPHENS, DORIS (GALLIHER). b Meadow View Va 19 O 36. 4: Randall L Stephens. 5: Berea Col 53-58 (Eng) BA; LSU 59, 65-66 (LS) MS. 6: Sp. 7: Tchr Jefferson Jr High Sch, Oak Ridge Tenn 58; Trainee LSU Lib (Baton Rouge) 59, Clk (lib asst) 59-61; Libn I (catlgr) E Baton Rouge Parish Lib, Baton Rouge La 66-67; Hd libn Amos Memorial Pub Lib, Sidney Ohio 68-. 9: ALA; OhioLA. 10: AAUW. 14: Admin, ref, tech proc. 15: 414 E Court st, Sidney Oh 45365.

STEPHENS, ELEANOR (WADDELL). b Biltmore NC 14 Ag 05. 4: George Myers Stephens. 5: Bryn Mawr 23-27 (Fr) AB; UNC 53-54 BS in LS. 6: Fr. 7: Newspaper reporter "Asheville Citizen Asheville NC 27-29; Ed asst Fed Writers' Proj, Asheville NC 36; Bkstore clerk The Bookshelf Asheville NC 52-53; Elem sch libn Sand Hill Sch, Buncombe Co NC 53-63, Elem & high sch libn Asheville Country Day Sch, Asheville NC 63-. 9: ALA; NCLA. 10: Beta Phi Mu; Delta Kappa Gamma. 14: Child & yp serv. 15: PO Box 5655, Biltmore Station, Asheville NC 28803.

STEPHENS, IRLENE ROEMER. b Cottonwood Co Mn 28 Ja 28. 5: Rutgers U 45-49 BS, 49-52 MEd; Columbia 52-54 MS in LS, 60-66 (LS). 7: Asst to dir of research Schering Corp, Bloomfield NJ 49-52; Chief libn Bristol-Myers Co, Hillside NJ 52-54; Dir libs Celanese Corp of Amer, Summitt NJ 54-60; Consul Consul Amherst Consulting & Lit Serv, NYC & Maplewood NJ 60-; Lib dir S Orange Pub Lib, S Orange NJ 63-65; Tchg asst Columbia Sch of Lib Sci 65, Assoc in lib sci 65-66; Prof & libn Richmond Col SUNY (Staten Is) 66-. 8: Instr, Grad courses in Chem Lit, Brooklyn Polytech Inst evenings 57-60; Vis lectr, Scient Lit, Columbia U 56-60; Tchr lib sci; USoCal summer 66, UCal(Berkeley) summer 68; Med Lib Assist Act, Ad hoc Com, Columbia U 65-66; Spec consul, Sci Research Study METRO 66; Prog chm, East Col Libns Conf 67; Acad adv, Borough Planning Bds, Richmond Borough NYC 68-69; SUNY Senate Com on Lib Devel Subcom on New Libs 69; Numerous lib survey, many with Prof Maurice Tauber, etc. 9: ACS (chm Com on Tech Writing); ASIS; ALA;-ACRL (Com on lib surveys 66); NJ Bar Assn(Com for Making Recommendations to the US Patent Off); MedLA; Drug Info Assn; Med Writers' Assn; SLA; AFIPS (Jt Computer Conf Steering Com 66); NY Acad Scis. 12: Numerous lib surveys, scientific papers, etc, multilithed (5-page bibliog available). 13: Yes. 14: Systems design and analysis, mgt, resources devel. 15: 15 Amherst ct, Maplewood NJ 07040.

STEPHENS, LOLA W (YCKOFF). b Traverse City Mich 14 F 13. 4: Robert L Stephens. 5: UWash 32-36 (Pol Sci) BA, 36-37 (LS) BA. 7: Asst br libn Spokane Pub Lib, Spokane Wash 37; Asst co libn Wasco Co Lib, The Dalles Ore 37-41;

Ref libn Dept of Labor, Wash DC 41-46; Lib Off of Voc Rehabilitation, Wash DC 46-48; Libn Selective Serv System, Wash DC 48-49; Ref libn Bur of Ships Tech Lib, Wash DC 49-52; Chid libn Arlington Co Lib, Arlington Va 64-65; Ref asst The Army Lib, Wash DC 65-69; Chief law br 69-. 9: SLA. 10: Rock Springs Home Demonst Club; Little Falls 4-H Club leader. 12: Comp "Employment of the Physically Handicapped-Selected References with H M Steele; Comp "Union List of Serials in Naval Libraries of the Washington Area (52). 13: Yes. 14: Ref. 15: 6218 N 3rd st, Arlington Va 22207.

STEPHENS, MARGARET J (BRANDENBURG). b Elizabeth NJ 3 F 27. 5: UNC Woman's Col 44-48 (Amer Lit) BA; Rutgers 58-61 (Sch Libnship); Newark State Col 61. 6: Fr, Ger, Sp. 7: Mail clk Lidgerwood, Elizabeth NJ 44; Clk & switchbd operator McManus Bros, elizabeth NJ 48-49; Bottling line Distillers Ltd, Linden NJ 55; Clk Bd of Educ, Elizabeth NJ 56; Clk-typist Sigma Pi Fraternity 56-58; Sch libn Bd of Educ: Elizabeth NJ 58-61, Roselle Park NJ 61-. 9: ALA; NEA; NJSchLA; NJEA. 10: LWV; Civic Orchestra (Elizabeth NJ). 14: YP lit. 15: 416 Birch st, Roselle Park NJ 07204.

STEPHENS, MARIAN GLEE. b Ionia Iowa 3 F 24. 5: Wayne U 44; UIowa summer 48; Central Col (Iowa) 48-50, 51 (Hist) AB; UDenver 50; West Res 51-52, 63 MS in LS; UColo summer 54. 7: Instr & documents libn Mont State U 52-62, Asst Prof & documents libn 62-. 9: ALA; Mont State LA; PNLA. 10: AAUP; Mont Inst of the Arts; Mont Archaeol Soc; Iowa State Hist Soc; Amer Philatelic Soc. 14: Govt docs. 15: 501 S Grand, Bozeman Mont 59715.

STEPHENS, MARY (LOUISE). b Woodland Cal 25 Ap 39. 5: Occidental Col 57-62 (Hist) BA; UCal (Berkeley) 62-63 MLS. 7: Libn I UCal (Davis) 63-65; Libn II Water Resources Center Archives UCal (Berkeley) 65-69, Lectr 68-69; Co libn Yolo Co Lib, Woodland Cal 69-. 9: ALA; SLA (Recruitment chm San Francisco Bay Area Chap 68-69); CalLA (chm No Cal Col, Univ & Research Libns Div 68-69). 10: Womans Faculty Club, UCal (Berkeley); Sierra Club; Eng Speaking Union; World Affairs Coun No Cal. 14: Catlg, ref, tech proc, pub serv. 15: 535 Court st, Woodland Ca 95695.

STEPHENS, NORRIS L. b Charleroi Penn 14 D 30. 4: Donna Anderson. 5: Carnegie-MellonU 50-54, 56-57 (Mus) BFA, MFA; Union Theol Sem (NY) 54-56 (Mus) SMM; UPittsburgh 65-67 mls, 62-65, 67-68 (Musicology) PhD. 6: Ger, Fr. 7: Salesman Wagner-Bund Mus Co, Pittsburgh Penn 57-62; Libn (Mus) UPittsburgh 66-, Asst Prof (Mus) 68-. 9: ALA; ASIS; MusLA; Internat Mus LA; Amer Musicol Soc (sec-treas Allegheny Chap 69-). 10: AAUP; Amer Guild of Organists; The Hymn Soc; Amer Guild of Eng Handbell Ringers; Nat Choral Com; Phi Mu Alpha; Staff Assn UPittsburgh Libs. 12: Had published numerous arrangements and editions of chorus, handbell, and organ music. 13: Yes. 14: Rare bks (music & lit), catlg & clsf. 15: 6603 Aylesboro ave, Pittsburgh Pa 15217.

STEPHENS, PHYLLIS (S). b Chicago Ill 1 Je 39. 4: Stephen V Stephens. 5: UCLA 56-60 (Hist) BA, 60-61 (Philos) 67-68 MLS; Yale Graduate School 61-62 (Hist). 7: Supv res bk room YaleU Library 63-64, Libn Math Lib 65-66, Dir pol sci Research Lib 66-67; Asst humanities & soc sci libn Johns HopkinsU 68-. 14: Ref, catlg. 15: Phoenix rd, Phoenix Md 21131.

STEPHENS, THELMA ROWAN. b Natchez Miss 8 Ap 43. 5: FiskU 60-64 (Eng) BA; UVienna summer 63 (Liberal Arts) Certif; Peabody Sch of Lib Sci 65-66 MLS. 6: Ger, Sp. 7: Tchr Natchez-Adams Co Sch Syst, Natchez Miss 64-65; Hd catlgr Knoxville Col Lib, Knoxville Tenn 66-67; Asst libn Alcorn A&M Col Lib 67-. 9: ALA; SELA; MissLA. 10: Beta Phi Mu. 14: Catlg, data proc, info sci. 15: 906 N Union st, Natchez Ms 39120.

STEPHENSON, ANDREW DONALD. b Jopln Mo 14 F 12. 4: Betty Ann Burney. 5: US Mil Acad 29-33 BS; USoCal 63-64 (LS) MS; UCal (Riverside) summer 65 (Ger). 6: Fr, Sp Ger. 7: Off US Army 33-63; Bus & ind libn Riverside City Lib, Riverside Cal 65-. 9: ALA; CalLA. 14: Ref (sci) fields. 15: 28539 W Worcester rd, Sun City Cal 92381.

STEPHENSON, GENEVIEVE (ABEL) (KENNEDY). b Winston Salem NC 24 Ag 20. 4: Joseph L Stephenson. 5: Bennett Col (Greensboro NC) 36-40 (Hist) BA; CatholicU 65 (LS) MS. 7: Lib asst Health, Educ & Welfare Lib, Wash DC 48-51; Ref libn NLM, Bethesda Md 51-65; Nat Portrait Gallery picture libn Smithsonian Inst 65-. 9: SLA (Mus & Picture Div). 14: Rare bks, ref, portraits of famous Americans in var media. 15: 5389 Chillum pl NE, Washington DC 20011.

STEPHENSON, MARILYN (RAMEY). b Los Angeles Cal 9 S 37. 4: William E Stephenson. 5: Occidental 55-57, 58-59 (Sp) AB; UMadrid 57-58 (Hispanic Studies) Diploma; UCLA 60-61 MLS; Middlebury Col 63-64 (Sp) MA. 6: Sp. 7: Eng tchr Inst Guatemalteco-Americano, Guatemala 60; Libn: Brooklyn Pub Lib, Brooklyn NY 61-63, Westminster Pub Libs, London England 64-65, Santa Monica Pub Lib, Santa Monica Cal 66-68, Los Angeles Pub Lib 69-. 9: ALA; CalLA. 11: Smith-Mundt grantee in Guatemala 59-60. 14: Ref. 15: 1975 S Beverly Glen blvd #3, Los Angeles Ca 90025.

STEPHENSON, MILTON ERNEST. b Pontiac Mich 16 J128. 5: Wayne State U 46-52 (Eng Lit) AB; Columbia 54-55 MSLS. 6: Ger. 7: Admin spec (Sgt) US Army 52-54; Ref asst-catlgr Detroit Pub Liv 55-57; Head of tech serv Lederle Labs, Pear River NY 57-5, Head bio-med reports 59-61; Coordinator of catlg Bell Telephone Labs, NYC 61-63; Head lib tech serv Fla Alantic U 63-65; Head tech serv NYU 65-68; Chief lit serv staff sci info fac Food & Drug Admin, Wain, Wash DC 68-. 9: ALA; ASIS. 14: Tech serv, lib admin. 15: 410 "O" st SW, Washington DC 20024.

STEPHENSON, RICHARD WALTER. b Wash DC 22 N 30. 4: Sally Larrison. 5: Wilson Tchrs Col 49-51, 53-54 (Geog); George WashingtonU 55-66 (Geog) BA; CatholicU 62 (Geog). 6: Sp. 7: Map filer Geog & Map Div LC 51-53, Map titler 53-54, Ref libn 54-66, Hd acquis sect 66-. 9: Assn Amer Geogrs; SLA; (Wash DC ChapGeog & Map Gp: v-chm 67-68 & 68-69, chm 69-70). 11: LC Meritorious Serv Award (68). 12: "Selected Maps and Charts of antarctica" (59); "Civil War Maps" (61); "Land Ownership Maps" (67); Ed "Federal Government Map Collecting" (69). 13: Yes. 14: Hist of cartography, map reference wk, map acquis, map libnship. 15: 5607 Hilldale dr, Alexandria Va 22310.

STEPHENSON, ROBERT EDWARD. b Katonah NY 22 Je 23. 4: Mary Thompson. 5: Hamilton Col 41-43, 46-48 (Eng Lit) AB; Columbia 48-49, 50 (LS) MS. 7: US Army Air Force 43-46; Va Polytech Inst: Asst catlgr 49-50, Documents libn 50-62, Assoc libn tech serv 62-. 9: ALA; SELA; VaLA. 10: Blacksburg Art Assn. 14: Acquis, catlg, US docs. 15: Lib VPI, Blacksburg Va 24061.

STEPHENSON, SHIRLEY (KNOWLES). b Jackson Miss 31 O 07. 5: Millsaps Col 25-26, 28-29, 30-31 (Soc Sci); Tulane U 31-32 (Eng, Soc Sci) BA in Ed; UAla 34 (LS); LSU summers 35, 36, 39, 40 BS in LS, 43-53 (Guidance) MA, 53-57 (Educ, LS) PhD. 7: Tchr Enochs Jr High Sch, Jackson Miss 33-34; Supv Elem Libs, Jackson(Miss) pub schs 34-37; Libn Bailey Jr High Sch, Jackson Miss 37-39; Asst New Orleans Pub Lib 39-40, Asst-in-chg Alvar Br 4041; Supv Miss Lib Ext Proj WPA 41-42, State supv 42-43; La Lib Commsn 43; Instr LSU Lib Sch 43-45; Instr LSU Dept of Bks & Libs 46-51; LSU Lib Sch: Instr 51-56, Asst Prof 55-59, Assoc Prof 59-63, Prof 63-. 9: ALA (Coun 64-65); AALS; LaLA (pres 64-65; chm Trustees, Scholarship Fund); SWLA (LaLA rep 65-67); La Tchrs Assn. 10: Phi KAPPA Phi; Kappa Delta Pi; Beta Phi Mu; AAUP; Baton Womans Club; Msic Club of Baton Rouge; Baton Rouge Little Theater; Study Club of Baton Rouge. 13: Yes. 14: Reading guidance, lib promotion & pub rel, lib resources, lib systs. 15: 2664 Reymond ave, Baton Rouge La 70808.

STERLIN, ANNETTE SYLVIA. b Chicago 20 D 35. 5: UCLA 53-57 (Hist) AB; USo Cal 57-58 (LS) MS; UChicago 59-60 (Hist. 6: Sp, Ger, Hebrew. 7: Libn I Chicago Pub Lib 58-62; Libn I Hughes Aircraft C, Culver City Cal 63-. 9: SLA. 14: Ref, catlg, info retrieval. 15: 6334 1/2 W 79th st, Los Angeles Ca 90045.

STERLING, ALICE M. b Fayette Penn 28 D 1879. 5: Grove City Col 1900-03 PhB; Pratt 11-12 BS in LS. 7: Catlg & ref dept Pub Lib, Cincinnati 12-13; Catlg & ref dept Pub Lib, Newcastle Penn 13-15, Chief libn 15-58; Asst libn Township Sch, Newcastle Penn 67; Chief libn (vol) Northminster U P Church, Newcastle Penn 60-. 9: ALA; PennLA (v-pres 41-42). 10: Bus & Prof Women's Club. 11: Plaques on retirement from City Coun & Women's Clubs. 14: Catlg, ref. 15: 338 Shaw st, New Castle Pa 16101.

STERLING, JOSEPH ANDREW. b St Joseph Mo 19 Je 33. 4: Revella. 5: So Baptist Col 56-58 aa& ouachita Baptist U 58-60 BA; E Tex State U MSLS. 7: S/Sgt USAF; Tchr: Grubbs High Sch 60, Biggers High Sch 61; Libn So Baptist Col 62-65; Libn Harris Tchrs Col, St Louis 65-. 9: MoStateTA. 10: Phi Delta Kappa. 14: Materials for tchr profes. 15: Harris Teachers College, St Louis Mo 63103.

STERN, WILLIAM BERNHARD. b Wuerzburg Germany 12 Mr 10. 4: Ruth H Yarnell. 5: Julius Maximilian U 28-32, 33

(Law) Dr Jur Utr. 6: Ger, Sp, Ital, Lat, Fr. 7: Catlgr UChicago Law Sch 37-39; Foreign law libn & head catlgr Los Angeles Co Law Lib, Los Angeles 39-45, Foreign law libn 45-. 8: Consul on the devel of for law collections, Stanford U Sch of Law 55, UVa Sch ofLaw 55, UVa Sch of Law 64; Consul on the devel of law libs Universidad Nacional Autonoma de Mexico 65. 9: Internat Assn of Law Libs (pres 62-65); AALL (chm Com on Fr Law Indexing 60-); pres 69-70). 10: Mem Commsn de bibliothque; Association internationale pour lenseignement dudroit compar, Sierra Club; Intl Law Assn; Amer For Law Assn. 12: 'Mexican Marriages and Divorces' in "California Family Lawyer (v 2 63); "The Law in the United States of America - A Selective Bibliographical Guide" (65); Ed "Law Library Journal" (53-54). 13: Yes. 14: For law. 15: Los Angeles Co Law Lib, 301 W First st, Los Angeles 90012.

STERNBERG, VIRGINIA ASHWORTH. b Lawrence Mass 27 Ag 22. 4: Heinz W Sternberg. 5: UDel 40-43 (Chem BA; Drexel 49-50 MS in LS; UPittsburgh 63- (LS). 7: Chem Wilmington Chem Corp, Wilmington Del 44-46; Bio-assayist Cutter LABS, Berkeley Cal 47-49; Asst libnWestinghouse Bettis Atomic Power Lab, Pittsburgh 50-51, Libn 51-68, Supv Tech Info Ctr 69-. 8: Lect Grad Sch Lib & Info Scis UPittsburgh 67-. 9: ACS; Chem Lit Div; SLA; Sci-Tech Div; Nuclear Sic Div; Metals Div Documentation Div; ASIS; Soc Tech Writers & Publrs; PennLA. 10: AAAS. 12: "How to Locate Technical Information (64. 13: Yes. 14: Tech libs, mechanized info retrieval. 15: 130 Sylvania dr, Pittsburgh 15236.

STERNFELD, RUTH (SCHWARTZ). b Chicago 6 O 13. 4: Leon Sternfeld. 5: Mich State Col 29-30; UChicago 31-32; Northwestern U (McKintock) 32-36 (Zool) PhB; Simmons 56-58 MLS. 7: Asst cosmetic buyer Mandel Brothers, Chicago 31-40; Cosmetic buyer Martins Brooklyn NY 40-41; Libn Temple Israel, Boston 57-; Ser catlgr Harvard U 58-. 9: ALA; NELA; Assn Jewish Libs (chm Greater Boston Chap 68-69). 14: Catlg, Jewish lib, ser. 15: 360 Ward st, Newton Centre Mass 02159.

STERRITT, MARGARET (BROOKS). b Bowling Green Va. 4: George Morrison Sterritt. 5: Mary Washington Col 22-26 (Educ) BS; George Washington U 38-40 BA in LS; Southeastern U 42-45, 47 LLB. 7: Asst libn law Southeastern U Law Sch 42-45; Staff instr & supv train div US Gen Accounting Off, Wash DC 45-47, Contract examiner audit div 43-45, 47-50; Asst chief law lib sect Off of Price Stabilization, Wash DC 51-52, Chief law lib sect 52-53; Chief, tech lib USAF Aero Chart & Info Center, Wash DC 53-57; Chief of Law Lib Dept of Housing & Urban dev, Wash DC 57-. 8: Civil Serv Examiner (Certif) representing Gen Accounting Off Wash DC 42-45; Asst Prin & Head of Eng Dept, Varina High Sch Richmond Va 27-33. 9: AALL (mem var coms, incl Bylaws, mem, Fed Activities); Law Libns Soc Wash DC (Exec Bd 59-61, sec 63-65, chm Bylaws Com 61-62); DCLA. 10: Internat Toastmistress Clubs; Columbian Toastmistress Club; Commun League. 13: Yes. 14: Admin, law, ref. 15: Bowling Green Va 22427.

STEUER, PAULINE (CARLETON). b Springfield Vt 23 Jl18. 4: Robert Lauren Steuer. 5: Middlebury Col 36-40 (Amer Lit) AB; Columbia 40-41 BS in LS; Ohio State U 52-53 (Law); UIll 56-50 (Law); UMiami 61-63 JD. 7: Gen asst New Britain Inst, New Britain Conn 41-42; Lib asst Rochester Pub Lib, Rochester NY 42-46; Asst catlgr Amherst Col Lib 46-48; Catlg libn Ohio State U Law Lib 48-54; Catlg libn UOkla Law Lib 55; Asst libn UIll Law Lib 55-60; Libn Broward Co Law Lib, Ft Lauderdale Fla 62-66; Asst law libn UMiami 66-67; Libn II Miami Pub Lib, Miami Fla 68-. 9: FlaLA. 10: Kappa Beta Pi. 12: Ed AALL Publications Series no 1 & 2; Asst ed "Law Library Journal (55-56). 13: Yes. 14: Law, catlg. 15: 761 Woodcrest rd, Key Biscayne Fl 33149.

STEUERNAGEL, HARRIET LEE. b Jackson Miss 23 My 09. 5: Stephens Col 26-28 AA; WashU 28-31 BA; UIll 36-37 BSLS. 7: Ref dept St Louis Pub Lib 37-45, 1st asst applied sch 44-46; Libn WashU Sch of Dentistry 46-. 9: Amer Assn Dental Schs (chm Dental Libs Sect 67-69); SLA (Greater St Louis Chap: sec 65, chm-elect 66, pres 67-68). 13: Yes. 14: Admin. 15: Washington Univ School Of Dentistry 4559 Scott ave, St Louis Mo 63110.

STEVENS, ANNE (McLAREN). b E Orange NJ 17 My 14. 5: Barnard 32-37 (Hist) BA; Columbia 37-38 (LS) MS. 7: Libn Chicago Latin Sch 38-41; Ref asst Newark Pub Lib, Newark NJ 41-42; Engring libn Curtiss-Wright Corp, Caldwell NJ 42-44; Engring libn US Bur of Ships, Wash DC 44-46; Hd catlgr Montclair Pub Lib, Montclair NJ 53-54; Hd libn Ludington Pub Lib, Bryn Mawr Penn 61-65; Deputy dir Chester Co Lib, W Chester Penn 66-67, Dir 67-. 9: ALA; PennLA. 10: Cosmopolitan Club of Phila; World Affairs Coun of Phila. 14: Admin. 15: 222 Lansdowne ave, Wayne Pa 19087.

STEVENS, BARBARA E. b Denver Colo 1 D 28. 5: Loretto Hts Col 46-49 (Communications); UDenver 49-50 (Mus) BA, 66-67 (Libnship) MA. 7: Writer KOA Television Denver 56-63; Asst libn Denver Pub Lib 63-65; Asst libn Spec Serv Lib Dept of Army, Korea 65-67, Libn 68-. 9: ALA. 10: Royal Asiatic Soc. 14: Milit libs. 15: Special Services Lib, Camp Red Cloud Hq I Corps (Gp), APO San Francisco Ca 96358.

STEVENS, CHARLES H. b Chicago 10 D 24. 4: Patricia Peterson. 5: Principia Col 42-43, 46-49 (Eng) AB; Polytech Inst of Brooklyn 43-44 (Engnr); UNC 49-52 (LS) BS, 55 (Eng) MA. MA. 7: Pacific Theater of Operations US Army Ordinance Corps (1st Lt) 43-46; Ref asst UNC Lib 51-52; Libn US Air-Ground Operations Sch, Southern Pines NC 52-54; Aeronautical engnr libn Purdue U 54-56; Asst Prof Sch of Mech Engrg, In-charge of sci doc Thermophysical Properties Info Ctr 57-59; Dir of lib serv MIT Lincoln Lab 59-62, Dir of Lib & Publ 62-65; Staff Project Intrex MIT 65-. 8: Documentation consul: Midwest Applied Science Corp, Lafayette, Ind 57-59, Haywood Publrs Serv Corp, Lafayette Ind 58-59; Trustee Engring Index 66-69. 9: SLA (chm Sci-Tech Div 65-66; Bd Dir 66-68; chm Adv Coun); ASIS. 10: Signa XI; Sch Com, Lincoln Mass. 13: Yes. 14: Computer techniques, admin, space & bldg planning, info transfer. 15: Laurel dr, Lincoln Ma 01773.

STEVENS, CURTIS L. b Plant City Fla 6 N 33. 5: Fla A & M U 48-52 (Hist) BA, 52-53 (Hist) MS; UND 55 (Hist); UDenver 58-60 (LS) MA. 6: Sp, Ger. 7: Soc sci research asst Fla A & M U 50-53; Tchr-Hist Manatee Co Pub Schs, Palmetto La Psychological Research asst USAF (AFPTRC), Chanute AFB Ill 56-58; Research asst USAF Acad (Colo) 58-59; Sr researcher in engnr lit, Martin Marietta Corp, Denver 60-62; Engnr libn Gen Dynamics/Convair, San Diego 62-68; Chief libn Gen Dynamics/Electric Boat, Groton Conn 68-. 9: SLA (San Diego Chap: dir 65-; Mem Chm 64-65). 14: Catlg of docs, machine retrieval of ref data, mechanization of tech proc. 15: PO Box 1046, San Diego 92112.

STEVENS, DEANE (DuBOSE). b Los Angeles Cal 15 S 40. 4: Brian Lawrence Stevens. 5: Randolph Macon Woman's Col 58-62 (Econ) AB; Emory 64-65 (Educ) MAT; Peabody Col 66-67 MLS. 6: Fr. 7: Securities analyst trainee Citizens So Natl Bank, Atlanta 62-63; Tchr: T J Guire Sch, Atlanta 65, Swavesey Village Col, Cambridgeshire England 66; Ref libn Jt Univ Libs, Nashville 67-. 9: TennLA. 14: Ref. 15: 1127 Battery lane, Nashville Tn 37220.

STEVENS, DOROTHY VIRGINIA (LEAVELLE). b Hopkinsville Ky. 4: Joseph H Stevens Sr. 5: Tennessee A&I StateU 26-30 (Eng) BS; FiskU 39 (LS); UChicago 45-46 BS in LS; UIll 56-59 MS in LS; West MichU 67 (LS). 7: Asst registrar Tenn StateU 30-31; Tchr Floyd Sch, Floyd Va 31; Stenographer VA Facility, Tuskegee Ala 32-35; Teach libn & prin Clem High Sch, Greenville Tenn 35-41; Sec y-p wk Gen Bd Relig Educ CME Church, Jackson Tenn 41; Sec to pres Lane Col 41-45, Registrar 49; Instr lib sci Tenn StateU 46-48; Libn Holloway High Sch, Murfreesboro Tenn 50-64; Coord lib sci area Ala State Col 64-. 8: Visit instr Tenn State Col summers 50-54, 60-61. 9: ALA; NEA (life mem); SELA; AlaLA; Ala StateTA. 10: Beta Phi Mu; Alpha Kappa Mu; Delta Sigma Theta; Agnes J Lewis Federated Club; Criterion Federated Club; YMCA. 15: 916 Carter Hill rd, Montgomery Al 36106.

STEVENS, FLORENCE MYRTLE. b Gasport NY 15 Mr 16. 5: Muskingum Col 34-38 (Eng) BA; Drexel 44-45 BS in LS. 7: Clerical asst Haverford Col Lib 39-44; Lib asst Rochester Pub Lib, Rochester NY 45-47; Yp libn Lockport Pub Lib, Lockport NY 47-. 9: NYLA. 10: Lockport Col Womens Club; Girl Scouts. 14: Yp serv. 15: 8122 Emerson pl, Gasport NY 14067.

STEVENS, FRANK A. b Rochester NY 8 Ap 31. 4: Joanna Van Buren. 5: URochester 49-50 (Eng); SUNY 50-53 (Eng) BA; St Johns U (NY) 55-58 MLS. 6: Fr, Sp, Ital. 7: Libn Sewanhaka City High Sch Dist #2, Floral Park NY 55-61; Lib coordinator Middle Island City Sch Dist #12, Middle Island NY 61-64; Supv of sch libs, NY State Dept of Educ, Albany NY 64-68; Chief Lib Train & Resources Br US Off of Educ, Wash DC 68-. 8: Adv Com on Indexing (Coun of Nat Lib Assns 62-64); Adv Com on ESEA (US Off of Educ, 65); Consul US Dept of State Sch to Sch Program, Brazil 67. 9: ALA-AASchL (Bd Dir 68-); NYLA (Exec Bd 64-65); CathLA; NEA-DAVI. 12: ED "Added Entries (57-59). 13: Yes. 14: Sch libs, catlg, tech serv, bk sel, pub & col libs. 15: 5813 S 4th st, Arlington Va 22204.

STEVENS, HELEN (CONRAD). b Taloga Okla 30 Ap 22. 4: Robert D Stevens. 5: W Tex U 38-42 (Speech, Educ) BA; UColo 41-43 (Eng Lit) MA; Columbia 45-47 BS in LS. 7: Asst supv circ DC Pub Lib 47-49; Loan libn FAO of UN, Wash DC 50-52; Sch Libn Montgomery Co (Md) sch libs 59-64; Instr Lib Studies U Hawaii 65-68; Instr lib tech Leeward Commun Col 69-. 9: ALA; HawaiiLA. 14: Sch libnship. 15: 3265 Paty dr, Honolulu Hi 96822.

STEVENS, ICLE JEAN (SELDERS). b Lincoln Neb 25 Ag 25. 4: Jackson W Stevens. 5: UNeb 43-47 (Eng) BA; UDenver 47-48 (LS) MA. 7: Libn: Denver Pub Lib 48-51; Pueblo Pub Lib, Pueblo Colo 52; Henderson Intermediate Sch, El Paso Tex 59-67; Curriculum libn, Instr Sch of Educ UTex (El Paso) 67-. 9: NEA; Assn for Childhood Educ; Internat Tex Circ Tchrs Assn; Tex LA; Tex State Tchrs Assn; ALA. 10: OES; PTA. 14: Sch & ya serv. 15: 312 Encino dr, El Paso Tex 79905.

STEVENS, JANE (BROWNE). b Guthrie Okla 31 Ag 13. 5: Gulf Park Col 30-31; UOkla 32, 34-35 (LS) AB, 59-60 MLS. 6: Fr. 7: Libn No Okla Col 60-63; Libn Ponca City Lib, Ponca City Okla 63-. 9: ALA (Coun 67-68); Recr Nerwk Rep OklA (pres66-67, chm Recr Com) SWLA. 10: Soroptimist Internat; C of C; Kappa Alpha Theta; Amer Cancer Soc. 14: Admin, adult serv. 15: 515 E Grand, Ponca City Ok 74601.

STEVENS, JANE E. b La Salle NY 28 Ag 17. 5: URochester 3337 (Eng) AB; SUC (Geneseo) summers 3741 BS in LS; Breadloaf Sch, Middlebury Col summers 5053 (Eng) MA; Columbia 58 (LS). 6: Fr. 7: Tchrlibn; high sch, Cotton NY 3739, high sch, Oakfield NY 3942, Haverling High Sch, Bath NY 4247; Asst libn high sch, Scarsdale NY 4749; Asst libn SUC (Brockport) 4963; Ed lib lit H W Wilson Co, NYC 63. 8: Middle States Assn Accreditation Com 63; Lecturer ColumbiaU Sch Lib Serv summers 59, 61, 63. 9: ALALED (dir Tchrs Sect 6466); Amer Soc Indexers; NYLA (dir RTS Sect 6870); NY Lib Club; NY Tech Serv Libns. 10: AAUP; ACLU. 13: Yes. 14: Catlg, clsf, indexing. 15: 410 Riverside dr, New York NY 10025.

STEVENS, JANE. b New Orlens 4 Je 28. 5: Loyola U (New Orleans) 45-49 (Sociol) PhB; LSU 49-50 BS in LS. 7: Catlgr Loyola U (New Orleans) 50-55; Tulane U: Catlgr 55-58, Sr catlgr 55-65, Head catlg dept 65-. 9: ALA; LaLA; New Orleans Lib Club. 10: Sierra Club. 14: Catlg. 15: 3115 State st dr, New Orleans La 70125.

STEVENS, JEAN (BRUNDAGE). b Pelham NY 16 My 15. 4: Edward Leigh Stevens. 5: Wellesley 3236 (Chem) AB. 6: Fr. 7: Tech writer AAF Materiel Command, Dayton Ohio 4244; Libn Warner Lambert, NY 4547; Libnadmin Castle & Cooke Dol Div, Hawaii 4767, 68. 8: Tech writer duPont 4445; Auth popular sci articles published in Hawaii. 9: ALA; SLA; HawaiiLA. 10: Hawaii Chap Amer Cancer Soc; Vol Serv Bur; Hawaii Health & Commun Serv Coun; ACS; AAAS. 13: Yes. 14: Ref. 15: Dole Company Div of Castle & Cooke Inc, Hawaii.

STEVENS, JoANN SANDRA (PERKINS). b Hammond La 2 Jl 27. 4: Lawrence K Stevens. 5: Southern Col 44-46 (Elem Tchg) 2-yr Diploma; Union Col 47-49 (Secondary Educ) BS; UFla 54; Fla State U 55-58 Lib Sci MS. 7: Elem tchr S DA Elem Sch, St Petersburg Fla 46-47; Libn Forest Lake Acad, Maitland Fla 51-59; Asst libn-catlgr Andrews U 59-65; Libn Roosevelt Elem Sch, Klamath Falls Ore 65-67; Libn Mazama Secondary Sch, Klamath Falls Ore 67-. 9: ala; NEA; MichLA; OreEA;Clr Tchrs Assn; OreLA; OreASchL. 10: Nat Cong Parents & Tchrs; AAUW. 14: Catlg. 15: Rt 3 Box 387, Klamath Falls Or 97601.

STEVENS, JOCELYN E (CAIN). b Waco Tex 5 S 19. 4: James A Stevens. 5: Wiley Col 36-39; Northwestern 40-41 (Educ) BS; NC Col (Durham) 57-59 MSLS; UMich summer 63. 7: NC Col (Durham): Circ libn 61-63; Curr materials center libn 64-, Ref libn 63-. 9: ALA; SELA; NCLA. 10: Alpha Kappa Alpha; Durham Co TB Bd. 14: Ref. 15: 623 Dupree, Durham NC27701.

STEVENS, LIONA V (ODELL). b Cleveland Oh 4 F 12. 4: Marvin G Stevens. 5: Rollins Col 29-33 (Eng) AB; Kent State 58-59 MSLS. 6: Fr. 7: Br libn Cuyahoga Co Lib, N Royalton ohio 59-63; Libn VA Hosp, Brecksville Ohio 63-66, Med libn 66-. 9: ALA; MedLA. 10: Col Club of Akron. 14: Ref. 15: 11916 Glen Valley, Brecksville Oh 44141.

STEVENS, LURILLA (STOTHARD). b Hilton NY 26 Ja 06. 5: Keuka Col 23-27 (Eng, Hist, Educ) BA; SUC (Albany) 58-63 MLS. 7: Tchr: Hobart High Sch, Hobart NY 27-31, Waverly Jr High, Waverly NY 31-32; Child libn Hunting Memorial Lib, Oneonta NY 59-60; Libn Valleyview Elem Sch, Oneonta NY 60-. 9: ALA; NEA; NYStateLA; NYStateTA; Central Valley SchLA. 10: Nat Audubon Soc; NY State Hist Assn. 15: 28 Cedar st, Oneonta NY 13820.

STEVENS, MARY (NINA) (STRANGWAYS). b Toronto Can 5 O 29. 4: John E S Stevens. 5: UToronto 48-52 (Philos, Eng) BA, 65-66 BLS, 66-67 MLS. 6: Fr. 7: Tchg asst UToronto Sch of Lib Sci 67-69, Lecturer 69-. 9: CanLA; ALA; ASIS. 14: Automation, documentation, communication, systems. 15: 155 Thistledown blvd, Rexdale 613 Ont Can.

STEVENS, NICHOLAS G. b Pittsburgh 30 S 11. 4: Elizabeth (Renwick) Stevens. 5: UPittsburgh 30-33 (Hist AB, 36-40 (Lat-Amer Hist) AM; UMich 48-49 AMLS; Columbia 62 (LS); Rutgers 62 (LS). 6: Fr, Sp, Yugoslav. 7: Stud asst dept of Hist UPittsburgh 31-33, 36-40; Research asst Commonwealth of Penn, Pittsburgh 34-36; Tchr Pittsburgh pub schs 36-42; Cryptographer USAF, US, Brazil,Ascension Island 42-46; Tchr Pittsburgh pub schs 48-49; Assoc Prof of Lib Educ & Hist Kutztown State Col 49-55, Dir of Lib Educ 55-; Personnel Consul Intl Harvester Research Ctr, Ft Wayne Ind 52-53. 8: Sch lib consul, Penn Dept of Pub Instr; Middle States Assn of Col & Secon Schs accred team; Penn Dept of Pub Instr accred team; Visiting prof; tex Womens U summer 54, Marshall U summers 59-60, Villanova U Lib Sch summers 61-62, 64. 9: ALA-LED; -AASchL; PennLA (pres 63-64; ALA Councillor); Penn State EA; Penn SchLA. 10: Lions Club; Phi Alpha Theta; Phi Delta Kappa; AAUP; Alpha Beta Alpha. 11: Distinguished Educators Award, Penn Dept of Pub Instr 64. 13: Yes. 14: Educ lib admin, ref, research. 15: Kutztown State Coll, Kutztown Pa 19530.

STEVENS, NORMAN D. b Nashua NH 4 Mr 32. 4: Nora Bennett Stevens. 5: AmericanU 49-51; UNH 51-54 (Govt) BA; Rutgers 55-57 MLS, 59-61 (LS) PhD. 6: Fr. 7: Map processor, labeller, desk attendant LC 49-54; Catlgr RutgersU (New Brunswick NJ) 57-59, Instr & research assoc Grad Sch Lib Sci 59-61, Assoc libn 63-68; Act dir lib HowardU 61-63; Assoc libn UConn (Storrs) 68-. 9: ALA; NELA; ConnLA. 10: Phi Beta Kappa. 12: "Three Systems of Information Retrieval" (61); "A Dictionary of Treen" (65). 13: Yes. 14: Admin. 15: RR #1 Box 340, Storrs Ct 06268.

STEVENS, PATRICIA LEE (BARTLEY). b Champaigne Ill 25 Je 14. 4: Richard F Stevens. 5: Mont State U 34-35 (Art); Col of Great Falls 58 (Sociol) BA; East Mont Col (Spec Educ) MS. 7: Exec dir Girl Scouts, Great Falls Mont 51-52; Br libn Deposit Station, Great Falls Pub Lib, Great Falls Mont 53-56; Newspaper libn "Great Falls Tribune," Gre at Falls Mont 55-56; Sch libn Columbia Sch of Nursing 56-57 ; Sch libn Cascade Co Pub Schs, Ft Shaw, Cascade, Centerville Mont 58-65; Elem sch libn, Ft Benton Mont 65-. 9: ALA;-AASchL; NEA; NCTE; MontEA (Standing Com on Curr & Educ Devel 66-); MontLA (Sch Lib Div). 10: MENSA; AAUW; Friends of the Great Falls Lib; Postal Supv Auxiliary; Mont Psych Assn; Womens Club. 13: Yes. 14: Sch lib devel. 15: 2408 2nd ave N, Great Falls Mont.

STEVENS, PATRICIA LOIS (PETERSON). b Oak Park Ill 3 Ja 29. 4: Charles Howard Stevens. 5: The Principia 46-48; UNC 51; BostonU 61-63 (Classical Civilization) AB; Simmons 64-67 MSLS. 6: Fr, Greek. 7: Searcher BrandeisU 67-68; Libn Dept Lib Mass Dept of Educ, Boston 68-. 10: Phi Beta Kappa; LWV;Lincoln Hist Soc. 14: Spec libnship. 15: Laurel drive RFD #1, Lincoln Ma 01773.

STEVENS, ROBERT D. b Nashua NH 8 Ag 21. 4: Helen Conrad. 5: Syracuse 38-42 (Eng, Philos) AB; UColo 43-43 (Eng); Columbia 46-47 BS in LS; American U 47-65 (Pub Admin) MA, PhD. 6: Fr, Sp. 7: Stud asst Syracuse Pub Lib, Syracuse NY 38-39; Stud asst Syracuse U Lib 40-42; Interpreter Japanese (Lt) US Navy 43-46; Stud asst Columbia U Libs 46-47; LC; Admin intern head bibliogr unit, Head Amer British Exch Sect, Chief Ser Record Div, Chief Catlg Maintenance Div, Asst Chief Union Catlg Div, Asst chief Gen Ref & Bibliog Div, Asst dir ref dept, Coordinator for org & development of the collections, Coordinator of Pub Law 480 Programs 47-64; Dir East-West Center Lib, Honolulu 64-65 ; Deputy lib U Hawaii Libs 65-68, Dean Grad Sch of Lib Studies 68-. 8: Bd of Dirs, USBE, 65. 9: ALA-ACRL (Publns Com 57-58);-RSD (Catlg Use Study 63-);-RSD-RTSD (Bk Catlgs Com 60-64):-RTSD (Acquis sect Exec Com 65-); SAA (Microfilm Com 64); African Studies Assn (Libs Com 61-63); Assn for Asian Studies (Com on Amer Lib Resources for the Far East 65-66); DCLA (treas 50-60); Hawaii LA; Amer Soc Pub Admin (Honolulu Chap). 10: World Affairs Forum of Hawaii; Phi Beta Kappa; Pi Sigma Alpha. 12: "Role of the Library of Congress in the Exchange of Official Publications

(52): "Card Catalogs of the Library of Congress (53) Ed "FILING Rules for the Dictionary Catalogs of the Library of Congress (55). 13: Yes. 14: Admin, Asian materials, lib educ. 15: 3265 Paty dr, Honolulu Hawaii 98622.

STEVENS, ROLLAND E(LWELL. b St Louis 7 Ap 15. 4: Dorothy Zulauf. 5: Washington U (St Louis) 35-39 (Gk) AB; UIll 39-42 BS in LS, MA in LS, 48-51 (LS) PhD. 6: Fr, Ger, Lat, Gk. 7: Lib asst acquis dept UIll Lib 40-42; Army of the US Signal Corps Staff Sgt 43-46; Asst to the Dir URochester 46-48; Ohio State U; Acquis libn 50-53, Asst dir tech serv 53-60, Assoc dir tech serv 60-63; Prof Grad Sch of Lib Sci UIll 63-. 9: ALA-RTSD (chm Acquis Sect 57-58, chm Ser 63-64); ASIS ADI (chm Central Ohio Chap 62-63); Ohio Valley Group of Tech Serv Libns (chm 60-61). 10: Phi Beta Kappa; Beta Phi Mu. 11: Beta Phi Mu Good Tchg Award 68. 12: Co-ed "A Catalogue of the Talfourd P Linn Collection of Cervantes Materials Com by D P Ackerman" (63); Ed "University Archives; Papers Presented at the 9th Allerton Institute" (63); Ed "ACRL Monographs" (56-60); Assoc ed "Library Resources and Technical Services" (60-63); Auth "Reference Books in the Social Sciences and Humanities" (2d ed 68). 13: Yes. 14: Tchg, tech serv. 15: Univ of Ill 316 Library, Urbana Il 61801.

STEVENS, SISTER DENISE. b Hartington Neb 13 My 22. 5: Col of St Catherine 50 (LS) BS; Rosary Col 64 (LS) MA. 7: Tchr: St Anthony's Grad Sch, Hoven S Dak 47-48, indian Mission Grad Sch, Stephan S Dak 46-47; Libn Mt Marty Col 50-. 10: YanktonLA. 14: Admin, catlg. 15: Mount Marty Col, Yankton SD 57078.

STEVENSON, CHARLES A(ARCHIBALD). b Atlanta 23 Mr 27. 5: The Citadel 45-46; Birmingham-So Col 48-50 (Hist) AB; Fla State U 51-52 (LS) MA. 7: (PFC) US Army 46-48; Asst libn Jefferson Co Tchrs Lib, Birmingham Ala 50-51; Ser libn Ga Tchrs Col 52-53; Documents libn USCar 53-56, Ref libn 56-57; Asst educ libn Queens Col (NY) 57-58; Ref consul SC State Lib Bd, Columbia SC 58-60; Interlib loan libn Fla State U 60-62; Head ref dept Greenville Co Lib, Greenville SC 62-, Bk sel coord 69-. 9: ALA; SCLA; SELA. 10: Delta Sigma Phi. 14: Ref, bk selection, acquis. 15: 8-O Calhoun Towers, Greenville SC 29601.

STEVENSON, CHRIS G. b Edmonton Alta Can 15 Mr 07. 4: Irene T Stevenson. 5: UWash 30-40 (Chem) BS, 39-40 (LS) BS. 7: Dist supv WPA Statewide Lib Proj, Seattle 40-43; Libn Clark Co Lib, Vancouver Wash 43-47; Tech info manager Pacific Northwest Lab Gen Electric Co, Richland Wash 47-64; Tech info mgr Battelle Northwest, Richland Wash 65-. 8: AEC Tech Info Panel, 50-; Wash State Lib Commsn 51-59. 9: SLA (chm Com on Govt Info Serv); WashStateLA; PNLA; ASIS (Com for Sci & Tech Communication). 10: AAAS; NAS (Coun for Basic Educ). 13: Yes. 14: Org & mgt of sci & tech info. 15: 2210 Humphreys, Richland Wash 99352.

STEVENSON, JAMES WILBUR. b Mitchellville Iowa 7 Mr 28. 4: Joan Welch. 5: Iowa State U 48-50 (Agric); UTex 55-58 (Hist) BA; UDenver 59-61 (LS) MA. 6: Sp. 7: US Navy SN 46-48; Jr libn Queens Borough PubLib, NYC 61-63; Lib Dir North Castle Pub Lib, Armonk NY 63-67; Lib dir Suffern Free Lib, Suffern NY 67-69; Asst lib dir New burgh Free Lib, Newburgh NY 69-. 9: NYLA; WestchesterLA; Orange & Sullivan Pub Libns Assn. 10: Rotary Internat. 14: Ya & adult serv, admin. 15: 224 Van Wyck rd, Blauvelt NY 10913.

STEVENSON, JOAN SUZANNE (WELCH). b Rochester NY 9 O 36. 4: James W Stevenson. 5: Syracuse 54-58 (Amer Hist) AB; UDenver 59-60 MALS. 6: Fr. 7: Ya libn NY Pub Lib 60-62; Readers adv White Plains Pub Lib, White Plains NY 62-65; Head ya dept Sprain Brook Br Yonker Pub Lib, Yonkers NY 65-. 9: NYLA (Child & YA Libns Sect; v-pres, pres 66); WestchesterLA. 14: Ya serv. 15: 224 Van Wyck rd, Blauvelt NY 10913.

STEVENSON, MAXINE (MARY). b Sprta Ill 13 F 16. 5: So Ill U 36, 47 (Elem Educ) BS; UIll summer 42, 46, 48 (LS; UWis summer 50 (LS; Washington U summer 52-53 (LS); UDenver summer 61; So Ill U 62-64 (Instructional Materials) MS. 7: Elem tchr Tilden pub schs, Tilden Ill 36-43; Elem tchr Alton pub schs, Alton Ill 43-52; Bkmob libn Alton Commun Unit, Alton Commun Unit, Alton Ill 52-62; Lib Central Jr High Sch, Alton Ill 62-63; Dir of Lib serv Alton Commun; Unit Sch Dist, Alton Ill 63. 9: ALA (Ref Subscript Books Review Com); AASCJ; Mem Prof Rel Com, Recr Com, Planning Com, Conf Com 64,NEA; Del Annual Conf 51, 60, 65; IllEA; State Governing Com 59-65; IllLA; Lib Devel Com, A-V Com; IllAschL; Mem Com, Conf Com; (pres 69-70). 10: Bus & Prof Women; Delta Kappa Gamma. 13: Yes. 14: Sch libs. 15: 1211 Henry, Alton Il 62002.

STEVENSON, OCTAVE SYKES. b Wash DC 28 Ag 30. 4: Margaret Paris. 5: American U 54 (Lit) AB; Columbia 55-56 (Lit); George Washington U 56-57 (Lit); Catholic U 68 MS in LS. 7: Readers adv DC Pub Lib 57-65, Ref libn 65-68; Chief lit div 68-. 14: Bk sel, Ref. 15: 4511 Sangamore rd NW, Wash DC 20016.

STEWART, ALBERTA (GREEN). b Carnegie Penn 6 J108. 5: Cal State Col Penn 26-36 (Educ) BS; Carnegie 49-52 MLS. 7: Tchr Sewickley Twp Schs, Herminie Penn 26-45; Lib asst Main Lib UPittsburgh 49-52; Asst libn Med Sch 52-55; Asst libn Consolidation Coal Co Lib Penn 55-58; Engnr & sci libn Carnegie Inst of Tech 59-. 9: SLA; PennLA. 14: Ref (sci & tech). 15: Apt 110, 834 Washington ave, Carnegie Pa 15106.

STEWART, ALVA WARE. b Marshallville Ga 13 Je 31. 4: Barbara Johnson. 5: Auburn U 49-51; UNC 51-53 (Pol Sci) AB; Duke 53-54 (Pol Sci) MA; UNC 58-60 (LS) MS. 6: Fr. 7: Info serv off 1st Lt) USAF, Chanute AFB Ill 54-56; Newspaper reporter "Asheboro Courier-Tribune, Asheboro NC 58; Ref libn libn Pub Lib of Charlotte & Mecklenburg Co (NC) summer 5; Head Libn Methodist Col (Fayetteville NC) 60-64; Ref libn Emory U 64-65; Ref libn UNC (Charlotte) Charlotte NC 65-68; Hd libn NC Wesleyan Col 68-. 8: NC correspondent for "National Civic Review 63-. 9: ALA; Amer Freedom Assn; SELA; NCLA (chm Jr Mem Round Table 63-64; MecklenburgLA (pres 67-68). 10: Beta Phi Mu; Pi Sigma Alpha; Coun for Livable World. 12: Ed "NC Libraries (66-68). 13: Yes. 14: Ref wk with col studs & faculty, period selection & use, mun gov & admin. 15: 1316 Horne st, Rocky Mount NC 27801.

STEWART, DAVID MARSHALL. b Nashville 1 Ag 16. 4: Gladys Carroll. 5: Bethel Col (Tenn) 34-38 (Hist) AB; Peabody 38-39 BS in LS. 7: Circ asst Vanderbilt U 38-39; Co Libn Ark Lib Commsn 39-40; State Supv wpa lib Serv Proj, Tenn 40-42; Libn Memphis State Col 42-46; Lt USNR 42-46; Spec asst Card Div LC 47; Lib consul US Govt Wash DC Dir Pub Lib of Nashville & Davidson Co 60-. 60-. 9: ALA-PLA (pres 66, chm Standards Com); TennLA (pres 66); SELA. 10: Kiwanis Club; Coffee House Club; Nashville Bd Dir Travelers Aid; Friends of Chamber Music; Middle Ten Arthritis Assn; Coun of Commun Agencies. 13: Yes. 14: Admin, bldgs. 15: 222 8th ave N, Nashville Tn 37203.

STEWART, DORIS. b Oil City Penn 1 Mr 39. 5: Grove City Col 57-61 (Eng) AB; Penn state 65 (Secondary Educ) MEd; Syracuse 66 MSLS. 7: Tchr high sch: Connellsville Penn, Clinton Iowa; Libn middle sch, N Syracuse NY. 15: 415 South Main st, North Syracuse NY 13212.

STEWART, DOROTHY K. b Bristol Conn 28 S 28. 4: David B Stewart. 5: BostonU 46-50 (Romance Lang) BA; CatholicU 57-59 MS in LS. 6: Fr. 7: Child libn Brookline Pub Lib, Brookline Mass 53-55; Child libn Takoma Park Lib, Takoma Park Md 55-57; Asst libn Sligo Jr High Sch, Silver Spring Md 60; Ref libn US Geol Survey, Wash DC 61-. 9: ALA. 10: Phi Beta Kappa; Beta Phi Mu. 14: Ref. 15: 11800 Stony Creek rd, Potomac Md 20854.

STEWART, GLEN C. b Peru Ill22 Mr 16. 4: Mae Nelso. 5: UIll 36-39 (Liberal Arts) BA, 40-41 MMus; West Mich U 62-63 (LS) MA; Mich State U 57-64 (Higher Educ) Ed D. 6: Fr. 7: Dir of Music Episcopal Church, Battle Creek Mich 41-42; US Army, Eng, France, Germany 42-45; Assoc Prof Alma Col 46-48; Assoc Prof N W Mo State Col 58-61; Visiting Prof Olivet Col 62-63; Lib asst West Mich U 63-64; Head ref dept Albion Col 64-67; Dir of libs Col & Sem Lib N Central Col 67-. 9: ALA; Music Tchrs Nat Assn; Nat Soc Study of Educ; IllLA; Chicago Area Theological LA. 10: AAUP; Phi Mu Alpha; Theta Delta Chi; Kiwanis Club; Amer Guild Organists. 12: Editor of choraland keyboard music. 13: Yes. 14: Ref & readers serv, tchr of research methods, admin. 15: 13 Triton lane, Naperville Il 60540.

STEWART, HAZEL (CRANDALL). b Northloup Nev 31 Ag 1893. 5: Kearney State Tchrs Col summer 14, 16-17 Tchrs Certif, summer18 (Hist); UNeb 21-22 (Hist) AB; NY Lib Sch 25-26 Certif; Columbia summer 32 (LS). 7: Tchr Neb 14-15, 17-22; Libn Central High Sch, Omaha 26-53; Libn Curtis Pub Lib, Curtis Neb 59-. 10: Federated Womans Club; Womens Soc Christian Serv; Curtis Bk Guild. 14: Catlg, ref. 15: Curtis Neb 69025.

STEWART, HENRY R JR. b Wilmington Del 16 Ap 44. 4: Sharon Lee Schmidt. 5: Cornell Col 62-66 (Econ & Pol Sci) BA; UDel summer 65; UDenver 66-67 (LS) MA; IndU 69-. 6: Sp, Lat. 7: A-v dir & ref Cornell Col 67-69; USOE fellow IndU Grad Lib Sch (Bloomington) 69-. 9: ALA. 14: Ref, admin, lib educ. 15: Indiana University Graduate Lib School, Bloomington In 47401.

STEWART, JANICE(LAND). b Cuyahoga Falls Ohio 1 My 14. 4: Frank Howard Stewart. 5: Marietta Col 32-34; UAkron 34-36 (Lit) AB; West Res 39-40 BS in LS. 6: Fr. 7: Asst libn Stow Pub Lib, Stow Ohio 36-39; Libn High Sch, Cuyahoga Falls Ohio 40-41; Bkmob libn Pub Lib, Lorain Ohio 41-42; Womens Res USN 42-45, Lt Ret 55; Hdqrs libn Pub Lib Serv, Montgomery Ala 46; Govt ref libn Pub Lib, San Diego 46-47; Libn Pub Lib, Chula Vista Cal 51-62; Prin libn Central Lib, San Diego 62-. 9: ALA; CalLA. 10: LWV. 14: Admin, ref. 15: 526 J st, Chula Vista Ca 92010.

STEWART, JEANNETTE. b Juneau Alaska 30 Ja 14. 5: UWash 36-40 (Bot) BS, 40-41 Bot), 56-57 MLS. 7: Jr tabulator Bendix Aviation, Englewood NJ 43-46; Botanical explor self-employed Amer Arctic (Alaska) 46-47; Clerical Prelim catlgr UWash Lib 47-48; Biliogr Arctic Inst of NA, Wash DC 48-55; Chief catlgr Ore Hist Soc, Portland Ore 58-68, Bibliog 68-. 10: Arctic Inst of No Amer. 12: Ed asst "Arctic Bibliography" 53-; V1; Indexer "Oregon Historical Quarterly" 62-66. 14: Catlg, bibliog. 15: PO Box 1292, Portland Or 97207.

STEWART, JOAN (ELDSON) GUTHRIDGE. b Chicago Ill 25 Ag 16. 5: Denison 34-38 (Mod Langs) BA; Simmons 64-66 MSLS. 6: Fr, Ger. 7: Lib asst Wilmette Pub Lib, Wilmette Ill 43-44; Lib asst NorthwesternU Inst Tech Lib 44-45; Lib asst Howe Lib, Hanover NH 58-64, Hd libn 64-66; Info specialist Northwestern U Lib 66-67; Hd ref dept Evanston Pub Lib, Evanston Ill 67. 9: ALA; IllLA. 10: AAUW. 14: Ref. 15: 1866 Sherman ave, Evanston Il 60201.

STEWART, JOANNE (ROUSE) (MRS). b Chicago 27 Ja 32. 5: Stanford 49-52, 63 (Soc Sci) AB; Chicago 63-65 MALS. 6: Fr. 7: Catlgr Winnetka Pub Lib, Winnetka Ill 59-63; Hd libn East Campus Waukegan Twp High Sch, Waukegan Ill 65-. 9: ALA-AASchL; -YASD; IllEA; IllASchL. 10: Stanford Club of Chicago; Beta Phi Mu. 14: Ya, sch libs & pub libs. 15: 265 Poplar st, Winnetka Ill 60093.

STEWART, JOYCE (MAXWELL). b Bristow Okla 13 Jl 41. 4: Thomas M Stewart. 5: OklaStateU 59-63 (Eng) BS; UOkla 66-67 MLS. 6: Sp. 7: Libn Harrah High Sch, Harrah Okla 68-. 9: ALA; OklaLA. 10: Amer Assn Tchrs Spanish. 14: Spec libs, lib educ. 15: 3812 SE 26th, Okla City Ok 73115.

STEWART, KATHRYN (DONOHOE). b Springfield Ohio 10 D 42. 4: Lester I Stewart Jr. 5: Central Fla Jr Col 60-62 (Liberal Arts) AA; Fla StateU 62-64 (LS) BA; LSU 65-67 (LS) MA. 6: Fr. 7: Ref libn Central Fla Reg Lib, Ocala 64-68; Lib coord Volusia Co Pub Lib, Daytona Beach Fla 68-. 9: FlaLA. 10: YWCA. 14: Ref, child serv. 15: 521 Westmoreland rd, Daytona Beach Fl 32014.

STEWART, LOIS (DALE). b Crestwood NY 1 Je 20. 5: Middlebury Col 37-41 (Biol) AB; Catholic U 63-66 MSLS. 7: Off USN Res 43-46; Libn Parker-Gray Middle Sch, Alexandria Va 65-. 14: Sch libnship (esp integration of all media), lib serv to the disadvantaged. 15: 2917 Argyle dr, Alexandria Va 22305.

STEWART, SISTER M CHARISSA SSND. b St Louis Mo 10 Mr 11. 5: St LouisU 36-42 (Hist) BS; Our Lady of the Lake Col summers 57-62 (Educ, LS) MEd. 7: Tchr & libn, Effingham Ill 57-62; Libn Helias High Sch, Jefferson City Mo 64-68; Libn Duchesne High Sch, St Charles Mo 68-. 9: ALA; CathLA. 14: Ref. 15: 2550 Elm st, St Charles Mo 63301.

STEWART, MARGARET. b Willowemoc NY 25 Ag 11. 5: NY State Col (Albany) 28-32 (Lat) AB, summers 33-36 BS in LS; Middlebury Col 42 (Eng) MA. 6: Fr. 7: Tchr & libn High Sch, Roscoe NY 33-36; Libn High Sch, Chappaqua NY 36-. 9: ALA; NEA; NYLA (sec-treas); Westchester LA. 15: 108 Nottingham rd, Bedford Hills NY 10507.

STEWART, MARTHA (ROSS). b Salt Lake City Utah 14 Jl 15. 4: Justin C Stewart. 5: UUtah 31-35 (Art) BA. 7: Tchr Davis High Sch, Kaysville Utah 35; Sub tchr city schs, Salt Lake City 37-54; Tchg asst UUtah 38; Lib asst Salt Lake City Pub Lib 54-65; Circ libn Utah State Commsn Div for Blind & Physically Handicapped, Salt Lake City 65-. 10: Phi Kappa Phi; Chi Delta Phi; Mortar Board. 12: Ed "Pen" UUtah lit organ 34. 14: Lib serv to the disadvantaged. 15: 925 2nd ave, Salt Lake City Ut 84103.

STEWART, MARTHA LACY (MRS JOHN A). b Foochow China 3 N 09. 4: John A Stewart. 5: Ohio Wesleyan 27-31 (Sociol, Pol Sci) AB; West Res 59 MS in LS. 7: Libn Oxford Elem Sch, Cleveland Heights Ohio 52-53; Lib asst Case Inst of Tech 53-59; Head Libn Sch of Applied Soc Sci West Res U 59-. 8: Consul & mem Cleveland Planned Parenthood Assn; Phi Beta Kappa; Mortar Board; LWV. 10: Phi Beta Kappa; Mortar Board; LWV. 14: Admin, ref. 15: 896 Montford rd, Cleveland Heights Ohio 44121.

STEWART, MARY A. b Duxbury Mass 25 Je 17. 5: UMass 36-40 (Eng) AB; Simmons 42-43 BS in LS. 7: Reg libn Div of Pub Lib, Greenfield Mass 43-46; Asst libn VA Hosp, Northampton Mass 46-47; Reg libn Free Pub Lib Commsn, St Johnsbury Vt 47-55; Hd adv serv Reg Lib Serv Ctr, Watertown NY 55-59; Asst dir S Adirondack Lib Syst, Saratoga Springs NY 59-. 9: ALA; NYStateLA. 10: AAUW. 14: Ext wk. 15: Loughberry rd, Saratoga Springs NY 12866.

STEWART, ROBERT CHARLES. b Brookville Penn 20 Ap 41. 5: UPittsburgh 59-63 (Eng Lit) AB; Magna Cum Laude; Columbia 63-65 MS with Honors. 6: Fr, Ger. 7: Ref libn govt publ sect Penn State Lib 65-67; Hd govt publ sect 67-68; Ref libn UPenn 68; Hd searching sect UPenn Libs 69-. 9: ALA;-ACRL; PennLA (chm Govt Docs Com 68-). 11: Phi Beta Kappa; Beta Phi Mu. 13: Yes. 14: Ref, govt docs. 15: 2017 Locust st, Philadelphia Pa 19103.

STEWART, ROLLAND CLIFFORD. b Joplin No 4 O 07. 4: Dorothy Lemke. 5: U Tenn 25-29 (Romance Langs) AB; UMich 28-30 (Romance Langs) AM, 37-40 ABLS, AMLS. 6: Fr, Sp, Ger, Ital, Portu. 7: Instr UMich 29-30; Instr UMo 30-32; Spec lecturer Lib Sci UMich 42-53; Libn U Lib UMich 38-61, Asst dir 61-66, Assoc dir 66-. 8: Bibliog consul University Microfilms Inc 53-; Spec consul UCal (San Diego) New Campuses Program 63-64. 9: ALA. 10: ACLU; Univ Club, Ann Arbor; Barton Hills Co Club; Phi Kappa Phi. 13: Yes. 14: Bk sel, ref, admin. 15: 765 Country Club rd, Ann Arbor Mich.

STEWART, TRUDY (SMITH). b Talladega Ala 12 Ap 21. 4: John R Stewart. 5: Jacksonville State Col 38-44 (Eng) BS; UAla 59-64 (LS) MA. 6: Fr. 7: Tchr Ala Schs 41-45; Libn High Sch, Brewton Ala 58-63; Tchr of Lib Sci Jacksonville State U (Ala) 64-. 9: ALA; -ASchLA (treas 62-63); AlaEA; NEA. 10: Alpha Beta Alpha; Delta Kappa Gamma; Gen Fed Womens Club; Faculty Wives; AAUW; Alpha Xi Delta. 14: Tchg. 15: 606 8th ave N, Jacksonville Ala.

STEWART, WILBUR J. b Pittsburgh Penn 14 F 28. 4: Darlene Joanne Rodgers. 5: UPittsburgh 48-51 (Bus Admin) BS; Carnegie 58-61 MLS; UNeb 61-64 (Ger, Stat, Bus Systs). 6: Ger. 7: (Pfc) US Marine Corps Communications 46-48; Sales correspondent US Steel Corp, Pittsburgh 51-58; Lib trainee UPittsburgh Lib 58-61; Asst libn UNeb 61-64; Order libn SUNY (Buffalo) 64-66; Hd acquis dept Oakland U 67-. 9: ALA. 10: AAUP; Beta Gamma Signa. 14: Acquis, automation, admin. 15: 27690 Stephenson hwy, Madison Hgts Mi 48071.

STEWART, WILLIAM JAMES. b Annapolis Md 9 Ag 31. 4: Elisabeth Hoogland. 5: Loyola Col (Md) 54-58 (Soc Sci) BS; American U 58-59 & 60-63 MA in Hist. 7: Archivist Nat Archives, Wash DC 60-64; Archivist Franklin D Roosevelt Lib, Hyde Park NY 64-. 9: SAA; AHA. 11: Gondos Award, SAA, 63. 13: Yes. 14: Archival theory & mgt, sources for labor hist, bibliog of materials relating to Roosevelt era. 15: Franklin D Roosevelt Lib, Hyde Park NY.

STEWART, WILLIAM L(EROY) JR. b Selma Ala 17 Ja 35. 4: Faye Murray. 5: High Point Col 54-57 (Soc Studies) AB; UNC 57-63 MSLS. 7: Lib asst High Point Pub Lib, High Point NC 54-57; Head circ dept Ga State Col 59-63; Chief bibliogr USo Fla 63-67, Acquis libn 67-. 9: FlaLA; SELA. 14: Acquis. 15: 10911 N 19th st, Tampa Fl 33612.

STIBITZ, MILDRED T(HERESA). b York Pa 8 Mr 07. 5: Ursinus Col 2428 (Eng Hist) BA; Drexel 2829 BS in LS; Columbia 49 MS in LS. 7: Asst libn Ursinus Col 2930; Ref asst Dayton & Montgomery Co Pub Lib, Dayton Ohio 3043; Coord commun rel 4368; Assoc in pub lib serv NY State Div Lib Devel, Albany 68. 8: Consul ALA Adult Educ Survey 53. 9: ALALAD (chm Pub Rel Sect 5961); ASD (2nd vpres 6667; Ed Newsletter-- 68); OhioLA (pres 5051); Ohio Assn for Adult Educ (pres 5355). 10: YWCA; CLU. 13: Yes. 14: Adult serv, commun rel. 15: 352 State st, Albany NY 12210.

STICKEY, MARGARET (ADAMSON). b Tampa Fla 24 O 04. 5: Hollins Col 20-24 (Hist & Econ) BA; NYPL Training Sch 24-25 Certif. 6: Fr. 7: Catlgr to asst br libn Tampa Pub Lib, tampa Fla 26-27; WPA Lib supv, Charleston SC 40-41; VA hosp lib asst, Columbia SC 49-51; Base libn: Shaw AFBase, Sumter SC 51-54, Selfridge AFBase, Mich 54-56, Toul-Rositres AB, France 56-59, EV Reux AB (syst), France

59-66; Chief 3 base libs Kindley AB, Bermuda 66-. 9: ALA; SCLA; SELA. 10: Jr League, Kappa Delta. 11: Silver Pride Award (USAF). 14: Ref, admin, readers adv. 15: Box 133 1604 AB Gp, APO New York 09856.

STICKLER, ANN JAYLEEN. b Colon Panama 25 N 36. 5: Fla State U 54-58 (LS) BA, 60-63 (LS) MA. 7: Libn McKinley Elem Sch, Arlington Va 58. 8: Com mem for selection of children's books LC & HEW 68; Instr (part time) UVa (Arlington) 64-68. 9: ALA; NEA; VaEA; VaLA. 10: Beta Phi Mu; Arlington (Va) EA. 14: Child lit, sch lib serv. 15: 1132 N Stafford st, Arlington Va 22201.

STICKLER, WILLIAM HAROLD. b Coaldale Penn 4 Je 35. 4: Jeanne Lucretia Elder. 5: Kutztown State Col 53-57 (LS) BS in Ed; Temple 58-61, 65 (Educ). 7: Head Libn Kutztown Pub Lib, Kutztown Penn 55-5; Head Libn Whitehall High Sch, Whitehall Twp Sch Dist, Hokendauqua Penn 57-. 8: Athletic Trainer & coach 61-64; Head of Whitehall Twp Commun Lib 62-63; of lib head ofLib Serv. 9: NEA; Penn State EA (Lib Div; Br Pub Rel Com). 10: C of C; Lehigh Co Fish & Game Assn; Elem Sch Parents Club; Nat Trainers Assn; NCHA. 13: Yes. 15: Rd '3, Kutztown Pa 19530.

STICKNEY, EDITH P(IERPONT). b St Paul 7 Ja 1899. 5: Vassar 16-19 (Hist, Gk)AB; USoCal 21-22 (Hist) MA; Stanford 22-24 (Hist, Classical Lit) PhD; UDenver summers 50, 51, 54 (LS) AM; West Res summer 2 52 6: Fr. 7: Instr in hist Goucher Col 24-26; Asst Prof of hist, Pomona Col 30-31; Prof of hist Amer Womans Col (Istanbul) 31-32; Assoc ref libn LC 42; Libn Midland Col 50-60; Soc sci libn Ida State U 60-64; Asst ed "America: History and Life, Amer Bibliog Center, Santa Barbara Cal 64-67; Bibliog(r) acquis dept UCal (Santa Barbara) 67-68, Catlgr 68-. 9: ALA-RSD (Hist Sect Exec Com 62-65); NebLA (pres 58-59). 10: AAUW; UN Assn; Adv Bd Intl Soc Sci Inst. 11: G L Beer Prize, AHA, 26. 12: "Southern Albania in European International Affairs, 1912-23" (26); Ed "Readings in European International Relations Since 1879" (31). 13: Yes. 14: Bibliog, admin, ref. 15: 327 Lloyd ave, Santa Barbara Ca 93104.

STICKNEY, LORRAINE (OSBERG). b Spicer Minn 2 S 36. 4: Frederic H Stickney. 5: Augsburg Col 54-58 (Eng) BA; UMinn (Minneapolis) 57; UMe 64-67 MLS. 7: Tchr & libn Thornton Acad, Saco Me 58-59; Libn Kenyon Pub Schs, Kenyon Minn 59-60; Tchr Falmouth High Sch, Falmouth Me 60-61; Libn Gorham High Sch, Gorham Me 61-. 9: ALA; MeSchLA; MeLA; NESchLA; MeTA. 13: Yes. 15: Box 134, Standish Me 04084.

STIEG, LEWIS F(RANCIS). b North Tonawanda NY 24 O 09. 4: Mildred Graf. 5: UBuffalo 26-31 (Classics) AB, AM; Harvard 31-32 (Classics) AM; UMich 32-33 ABLS; UChicago 33-35 (LS) PhD. 6: Fr, Ger, Lat, Greek. 7: Libn StetsonU 35-36; Libn Hamilton Col 36-43; Assoc dir Prof Lib Sch UIll(Urbana) 43-47; Dir Lib Sch USoCal 47-55, Univ libn 48-. 8: Fulbright lecturer UPhilippines 5354; Consul Stanford Contract USOM UPhilippines 5455; Dir ALA Contract, Ford Foundation, Lib Inst UAnkara 5759; Visiting prof lib sci, summers; LSU 39, UCLA 63 & 64, UCal (Berkeley) 66 & 67, 69. 9: ALALED (pres 4647); SLA; BSA; CalLA. 10: Bd of Governors Otis Art Inst, Los Angeles; AAUP. 13: Yes. 14: Admin, bibliog, hist bks, bk selection. 15: 4185 Via Solano, Palos Verdes Estates Cal 90274.

STIEG, MARGARET F. b Utica NY 20 My 42. 5: Radcliffe 59-63 (Govt) AB; Columbia 63-64 (LS) MS; UCal Berkeley 64-67 (Hist) MA. 6: Fr, Sp. 7: Asst humanities libn Cal State Col (Long Beach) summers 64, 65, 67; Ref libn Harvard 68-. 9: ALA. 14: Ref. 15: Via Solano 4185, Palos Verdes Est Ca 90274.

STIFFLER, STUART ALDEN. b St Louis 6 Ja 34. 5: Hiram Col 51-55 (Hist) AB; West Res 56 (Hist) MA, 57 MSLS. 7: Ref asst dept sociol & civics, Enoch Pratt Free Lib, Baltimore 58-59; Asst libn Hiram Col 59-61, Assoc libn 62-68; Libn Findlay Col 68-. 9: OhioLA; ALA. 10: Phi Gamma Mu. 13: Yes. 14: Ref, bk sel, admin. 15: 1012 Plaza st, Findlay Oh 45840.

STILES, ANNE (KOGUT). b Conn 28 Ja 16. 5: UBridgeport 32-34(Liberal Arts) AA; Russell Sage 34-36(Bus Admin) BS; Rutgers 61-62 MLS. 7: Asst to dir Cedar Grove Pub Lib, Cedar NJ 63-66; Info specialist Nat Ind Conf Bd, NYC 66-68; Chief libn 68. 8: Bd Dirs Bloomfield (NJ) Adult Sch. 9: ALA; SLA Grove NJ 62-63; Hd circ dept Bloomfield Pub Lib, Bloomfield (chm Soc Sci 69-70); NJLA (Recruitment Com 63; Program Chm Circ Div 64). 10: AAUW. 14: Ref. 15: 70A3 Fremont st, Bloomfield NJ 07003.

STILES, PATRICIA (POLLARD). b Cincinnati 5 Mr 29. 5: Miami U 47-51 (Eng) AB; UFla 51-52 (Eng Lit) MA; Drexel 63-66 MALS. 6: Fr. 7: Instr Miami U (Ohio) 52, 56-58; Asst catlgr Lane Pub Lib Hamilton Ohio 59-64; Supv Adult Serv 65-67; Asst dir 67-. 8: Bk revewer "Library Journal" 59-67. 9: ALA (Recr Netwk); OhioLA. 14: Adult educ, ref, bk sel. 15: 630 Brookwood ave, Hamilton Ohio 45013.

STILES, WILLIAM GORDON. b London England 3 D 24. 4: Shirley Janet Love. 5: British FLA. 7: Pilot (Sgt) RAF 43-48; Asst libn Wandsworth Pub Lib, London England 49-50; Bkmob libn 3rd AF USAF, St Ruislip England 51-53; Asst catlgr British Nat Bibliog, London England 54-56; Libn Central Lib Merton Surrey Co Lib, Surrey England 56-58; Libn Pembroke Pub Lib, Ont Can 58-59; Catlgr Nat Lib of Can, Ottawa 59-63; Uplands libn Nat Sci Lib, Ottawa Can 63-65; Libn Atomic Energy of Canada Ltd Commercial prods, Ottawa Can 65-. 9: Lib Assn (London); SLA (chm-elect Nuclear Sci Div 68-69); OttawaLA. 13: Yes. 14: Subject-catlg. 15: 33 Ettrick Crescent RR3, Ottawa Can.

STILL, MARY JANE (WEAVER). b Columbus Miss 13 Ag 33. 4: William E Still. 5: Miss State Col for Women 51-55 (LS) BS; UMiss 62-66 (LS) MA. 7: Child & ref libn Fisk Pub Lib, Natchez Miss 55-56; Libn in Elem schs Independent Sch Dist, Houston Tex 57; Libn sardis High Sch, Sardis Miss 59-60; Libn ref dept UMiss Lib (Univ) 61-63, Libn circ dept 66-. 9: MissLA. 14: Ref, circ, reg lib serv. 15: 204 McLaurin dr, Oxford Ms 38655.

STILLMAN, JUNE (SMITH). 4: Donald Albert Stillman. 5: Jacksonville Jr Col 47-49 AA; Fla StateU 49-51 (LS) BA, 64-66 (LS) MA. 6: Sp. 7: Williston High Sch, Williston Fla 51-53; Naval Air Jr High, Ft Lauderdale Fla 53-55; Rogers Jr High Sch, Ft Lauderdale Fla 55-57; Ref & circ & a-v Orlando Jr Col 63-68; Ref Fla TechU 68-. 9: ALA; SELA; FlaLA. 10: Beta Phi Mu. 14: Ref. 15: 2851 Wright ave, Orlando Fl 32803.

STILLMAN, MARY ELIZABETH. b Philadelphia 31 O 29. 5: Wilson Col 46-50 (Classics) AB; Drexel 51-52 (LS) MS; UIll 63-65 (LS) PhD. 6: Lat, Fr, Ger, Gk. 7: Br libn US Naval Train Center, Bainbridge Md 52-53; Chief libn; Kimpo Air Base USAF Kimpo Korea 53-54, 5th Air Force Lib Serv Center, Pyongtaek Korea 55-56, 5th Air Force Lib Serv Center, Showa Japan 56-59; Chief educ & lib div The US Logistics Group, Ankara Turkey 60-63; Libn Export-Import Bank of the US, Wash DC 65-68; Asst Prof Grad Sch of Lib Sci Drexel 68-. 9: ALA; SLA; PennLA. 10: Beta Phi Mu. 12: Ed "Pacific Air Forces Basic Bibliographies (57-59) Ed "Drexel Library Quarterly (69). 13: Yes. 14: Spec libs, tech serv, lib hist. 15: Church rd, Collegeville Pa 19426.

STILLWELL, OLIVER (DEAN). b Kilgore Tex 28 My 45. 5: Cisco Jr Col 63-65 (Liberal Arts) AA; E Tex StateU 65-66 (LS, ENG) BS, 66-67 MS in LS; Our Lady of the Lake 68 HEA Inst. 7: Assoc libn Cisco Jr Col 67-. 10: Tex Jr Col Tchrs Assn. 14: Catlg. 15: 1202 Avenue L, Cisco Tx 76437.

STILSON, MALCOLM HARVEY. b Los Angeles 26 My 23. 4: Sue Houts. 5: USoCal 41-42, 46-49 (Soc Sci) BA; Long Beach State Col 51-53 (Educ) Cal Secondary Credential; UWash 63-64 (LS) ML. 6: Sp. 7: Admin non-commissioned off staff sgt US Army, US & India 42-46; Admin non-commissioned off sgt 1st class, US Army Los Angeles 51-52; Tchr Lakewood Jr High Sch, Long Beach Cal 53; Tchr Glenwood Sch, Glenwood Wash 53-54; Rep Internat Correspondence Schs, Seattle 54-55; Ind Engnr The Boeing Co, Renton Wash 55-63; Documents libn Law Lib UWash 64-66; Docs libn Ind U of Penn 66-. 9: ALA; WashLA. 10: Beta Phi Mu; AAUP. 14: Ref. 15: 4519 - 196th st, Bothell Wash 98011.

STINSON, KATHERINE JEAN. b Oxnard Cal 24 O 26. 5: Occidental 43-45 (Mus). 6: Sp, Fr, ger, Russian. 7: Libn Lib of Hawaii Wai alua Br 52-60, 63-64, Hd circ (main lib), Honolulu 62; Act libn Supreme Court Law Lib, Honolulu 61; Hd circ UCLA Grad Sch Bus Admin Lub 64-65, Asst libn Sch Lib Serv 65-67; Libn ITT, Los Angeles 67; Libn Signal Oil & Gas Co, Los Angeles 67-. 8: Reading consul, Wilson's "Fiction Catalog" 51-63. 9: SLA; CalLA; Los AngelesLA. 10: Internat Girl Scouts Assn. 14: Catlg, ref, sub bibliog. 15: 14519 Hart st, Van Nuys Ca 91405.

STINSON, MALONE (BALLEW). b Lenoir NC 15 Je 37. 4: Robert R Stinson. 5: Aurora Col 55-59 (Bio) BS; UNC 60-65 MS in LS. 7: Lib asst Aurora Col 59-62; Lib Fellow UNC Lib (Chapel Hill) 62-64, Asst docs libn 66-67; Libn Wilson Co Tech Inst 64-65; Ref libn greensboro Pub Lib, Greensboro NC 67-68; Docs libn UNC (Greensobor) 68-. 9: ALA; NCLA; Greensboro Lib Club. 10: Beta Phi Mu. 14: Ref, govt publ. 15: 123 1/2 McIver st, Greensboro NC 27403.

STIREWALT, CATHARINE (AMELIA). b Mulberry Ind 26 S 08. 5: Wheaton Col (Ill) 25-27; Carthage Col 27-29 (Hist) BA; NYU & Biblical Sem 36-39 (Hist of Educ) MA; Rutgers 61-62 MLS. 7: Hist tchr Lincolnton High Sch, Lincolnton NC 30-36; Missionary to China Middle Sch Tchg Tsingtao Shantung China 39-49; Bible tchr Lutheran Deaconess Sch, Baltimore 49-60; Catlgr Lutheran Theol Sem, Phila 61-. 9: ALA; ATheolLA. 10: AAUW. 14: Catlg. 15: Apt 403 Duval Manor Greene & Johnson sts, Phila Pa 19144.

STIRRUP, JUANITA (BLANCHE) MARTIN. b Clearwater Fla 1 F 21. 4: William Joseph Stirrup. 5: Bethune Cookman Col 38-40 Diploma; Hampton Inst 40-42 (Eng, LS) AB; Catholic U summers 45 & 46; NC Col 51-54 MLS. 7: Libn Booker T Washington High Sch, Miami Fla 42-64; Libn West Dunbar Elem Sch, Miami Fla 64-. 8: Chm annual cancer drive. 9: ALA; Clr Tchs Assn; Fla State Tchrs ASSN: Fla State Tchrs Assn; DCLA. 10: Delta Sigma Theta; Miami Slum Clearance Com. 14: Catlg, bk selection. 15: 3301 Charles ave, Miami Fla 33133.

STITT, LYDIA ANN B. b York Pa 3 Mr 24. 5: Wilson Col 41-45 (Eng) BA; Drexel 45-46 BLS; UPenn 49-50 (Sociol) MA. 6: Fr. 7: Child libn & admin asst brs Enoch Pratt Free Lib, Baltimore 46-49; 50-55; Libn Central High Sch, York Penn 55-61; Libn N Hills Jr High Sch, York Penn 61-. 8: Hd lib dept Central York Sch Dist 65-. 9: York Co (Penn) ASchL (past sec). 14; child lit, ref. 15: 1635 W Market st, York Pa 17404.

STJERNHOLM, KIRSTINE (JOANNE). b Fowler Col 22 Ag 31. 5: Augustana Col 49-53 (Eng) BA; Colo State Col summer 55; UDenver 61-62 MA. 7: Tchr: Baltic Consolidated Sch Dist, Baltic S Dak 53-54, Sch Dist #60, Pueblo Colo 55-61; Jr high libn Sch Dist #60, Pueblo Colo 54-55; Period libn Augustana Col 62-66; Ref libn So Colo State Col 67-. 9: ALA; ColoLA. 10: Delta Kappa Gamma; AAUW. 14: Ref. 15: 1434 Bonforte, Pueblo Co 81001.

STOAKES, CAROLYN GRACE. b Omaha Neb 13 Mr 40. 5: Oberlin Col 5862 (Eng) BA (cum laude); WesleyanU (Conn) 6263 (Educ); Columbia 6465 (LS) MS. 6: Sp, Fr, Ger. 7: Circ clerk WesleyanU Lib (Conn) 6364; Spec recruit LC 6566, Ser ref libn 66, Asst hd ref sect ser div 66. 9: ALA. 14: Ref. 15: 2008 N Adams st apt 232, Arlington Va 22201.

STOBBE, ARTHUR JOHN. b Milwaukee Wis 29 O 16. 4: Virginia Simmons Stobbe. 5: Marquette 33-37 Journalism PhB; Ore StateU 41-42; Rice Inst 44; Syracuse 46-47 mls& ucal (Berkeley) 48-49 (LS); Cal Polytech 53-59; Col of the Sequoias 64-69. 7: Radio research Sta WTMJ, Milwaukee 37; Sports reporter: "Milwaukee Sentinel" 37, "Milwaukee Journal" 37-38; Lib asst Milwaukee Pub Lib 39-41; 1st Sgt US Army 41-43; Navigator US Army AF 43-45; Art & mus libn Milwaukee Pub Lib 45-48; Acquis libn Cal Polytech (SLO) 49-64; Lib dir Visalia Pub Lib, Visalia Cal 64-. 8: Consultant, Dairy Research Wisconsin Rapids 38-39; Mgr, Baseball Team (semi-pro) Milwaukee Wis 39-40; Ref libn Grosvenor Ref Lib, Buffalo NY 47; Book Review Research Project, UCalifornia Lib Sch 48-49. 9: ALA; CalLA. 10: Optimists Internat; Rotary; Audubon Soc; US Chess Fed; Cal Chem Fed Cal Officials Assn. 14: Acquis, ref (music, sports, ornith, meterol, fine arts, Oriental hist, Latin Amer hist). 15: Box 1561, Visalia Ca 93278.

STOCK, MARGUERITE (NOSE). b Los Angeles 13 J 119. 4: John Andrew Stock. 5: UCal (Berkeley) 37-39, 41; Bryn Mawr 42-45 AB (cum laude); Columbia 47-48 (LS) BS. 6: Fr, Ger, Japanese. 7: Asst catlg dept DC Pub Lib 45-47 Catlgr Columbia U Lib 48; Catlgr Bryn Mawr Col Lib 50 Montgomery Co Pub Lib: Catlgr Gaithersburg Md 60-61, Ref libn Wheaton Md 61-65, Ref libn Silver Spring Md 65-. 9: MdLA. 14: Ref, catlg. 15: 9009 Eton rd, Silver Spring Md 20901.

STOCKERT, HELEN. b Buckhannon WVa. 5: WVa Wesleyan Col 19-23 (Eng) AB; Columbia 34-37 BSLS. 6: Fr. 7: Libn & tchr Salem High Sch, Salem Va 23 24; Libn: Buckhannon High Sch, Buckhannon WVa 24-33; Lawrence High Sch, Lawrence LI NY 34-41, So Sem & Jr Col, Buena Vista Va 42-44, Hasbrough Heights Pub Lib, Hasbrough Heights NJ 44-46, Old Trail Sch, Akron Ohio 46; Libn & Assoc Prof of Lib Sci WVa Wesleyan Col 46-. 8: Chm Dept Lib Sci WVa Wesleyan Col 50-. 9: ALA; Tri-State LA; WVaLA (chm Col & Univ Sect 65; sec 68-70). 10: AAUW; Delta Kappa Gamma; OES; Alpha Gamma Delta. 12: "Directory of Staff Members in College and University Libraries in We st Virginia, 1965-66". 14: Admin. 15: 91 Elm st, Buckhannon WVa 26201.

STOCKTON, GERALDINE ELIZABETH. b Liberty Hill Tex 25 S 09. 5: Tex State Col for Women 30-33, 36 (LS) BS. 7: Tchr Leander E Sch, Leander Tex 34-35; Child libn Austin Pub Lib Austin Tex 40-. 9: ALA-CSD(Mem Com 50-51: Tex LA(Child Div: chm 53-54, sec-treas 50-51 & 65-; Austin Lib Club. 10: Wesleyan Service Guild. 14: Child lit. 15: 2910 Cherry lane, Austin Tx 78703.

STODDARD, GRACE (LOTT). b Monetta SC 17 S 16. 4: Raymond Wickliffe Stoddard. 5: Winthrop Col 34-38 (Eng, LS) AB; Duke 44 (Educ); USCar 49, 55, 63 (Educ, LS); The citadel 66 (LS). 6: Fr. 7: Tchr & libn Ellenton High Sch, Ellenton SC 38-40; Tchr & libn Gray Ct High Sch, Gray Court SC 40-42; Tchr Cooper River Sch Dist, N Charleston SC 42-61; Libn Remount Rd Elem, N Charleston SC 61-65; Libn R B Stall High Sch, n charleston SC 65-. 9: ALA; NEA; SELA; SCEA; SC Assn Clr Tchrs; SC Dept A-v Instr 9sec-treas); CharlestonCoEA; Cooper River Dist Clrm TA (past pres). 10: Amer Legion Aux; Kappa Kappa Iota; Beta Sigma Phi; Pi Kappa Delta. 14: Admin. 15: 5054 Poole st, N Charleston SC 29406.

STODDARD, WILLIAM SANFORD JR. b Kalamazoo Mich 26 Ag 22. 4: Alice Parker. 5: Flint Jr Col 41-42; Polytech Inst (Brooklyn) 43-44 (Engring) Certif; UMich 46-48 (Bus) BBA, 48-49 (Bus) MBA, 49-51 AMLS. 7: Dock hand Associated Truck Lines Inc, Battle Creek Mich 39-41; US Army Adjutant Gen Dept (Tech Sgt) 42-46; Attendant Mobil Gas Serv Sta, Battle Creek Mich 46; Jr ref libn UMich 48-51; Lib intern Newark Pub Lib, Newark NJ 51; Asst libn Sch Bus UMich 52-55; Soc sci libn Mich StateU 56-65, Libn Grad Sch of Bus 65-. 8: Consul; Saginaw Valley Col 6768, SoIllU (Edwardsville) 68; Mich Dept of Educ, accreditation team for Northwoods Inst 6869. 9: ALA; MichLA (chm Col Sect; chm Dist 2; vchm 64 Conf; chm Exhibits 69 Conf; var coms). 10: Boy Scouts Amer; Pinecrest PTA; E Lansing Commun Coun. 12: A Selected List of Books & Periodicals in the Field of Business--(66 & 68 eds). 13: Yes. 14: Ref, soc sci & bus, admin & org. 15: 1538 Glenhaven, E Lansing Mi 48823.

STOER, MARION WEST. b Chicago 4 D 09. 4: Philip R Stoer. 5; Swarthmore Col 26-30 (Eng) BA with honors; John Hopkins, UMd, WEST Md Col 53-63 (LS) Educ Certif; UNC 64-65 MS in LS. 6: Fr. 7: Asst Doubleday Bk Shop, Phila 30-38; Libn Baltimore Co Schs, Md 53-. 8: Consul NC Advancement Sch Lib, Winston-Salem NC 65-; Asst Prof, lib sci UMd Col of Educ (night sch) 65; Consul ALA 69 edition "Bks for Elem Sch Libs. 9: ALA; NEA; Md State Tchrs Assn; MdLA. 12: Ed "Charging Out Baltimore CO (Md) libns bul (57-64), 66-). 13: Yes. 14: Sch libs, bk reviewing. 15: 1375 Wilson Point rd, Baltimore Md 21220.

STOESSER, BLANCHE. b Germany. 4: Fred Stoesser. 5: Rutgers 5460 (Eng) BA, 6063 MLS. 6: Ger. 7: Elem sch libn Chatham Twp Bd of Educ, Chatham NJ; Libn Chatham Twp High Sch 62. 15: P O Box 216, Green Village NJ 07935.

STOFFEL, LESTER L. b Lakewood Ohio 20 Ap 20. 4: Odette Felkert. 5: Wittenberg Col 38-42 (pol Sci) BA; West Res 46-47 BS in LS. 7: US Army (T5), ETO 42-46; Dir Guernsey Co Lib, Cambridge Ohio 46-49, Easton Pub Lib, Easton Penn 49-55, Oak Park Pub Lib, Oak Park Ill 55-67; Dir Suburban Lib Syst, West Springs Ill 67-. 8: Ill State Lib Development Com; State Lib Adv Coun; Consul various libs, Ill & Wis. 9: ALA-PLA (chm Legis Com 65); OhioLA; Penn LA (pres 54-55); IllLA(pres 54-55); IllLA(v-pres 65). 10: Phi Gamma Delta; Rotary Club; Bd, Family Serv of Oak Park. 11: Libn of Year Award IllLA 68. 13: Yes. 14: Admin, pub lib bldgs. 15: 325 N Grove, Oak Park Il 60302.

STOFLET, ADA M(ARGARET). bHoguestown Penn 26 N 06. 5: Coe Col 27-31 (Sociol, Econ) AB; Bryn Mawr 31-33 (Soc Econ, Ind Rel) 2-yr Certif; UWis 48-49 BLS. 6: Fr, Ger, Russian, Sp, Ital. 7: Family visitor Phila Co Relief Bd, Phila 33-34; Investigator of Handicapped Wkers Penn Dept of Labor & US Nat Recovery Admin, Phila 34-35; Field investigator & city supv Cost of Living Survey US Bur of Labor Stats, Houston 35-36; Field investigator & Jr Economist US Nat Research Project & U Penn, Phila 36-37; Legis consul US Bur of Unemployment Insurance US Soc Security Admin, Wash DC 37-48; (Cpl) Clerk Womens Army Corps, US 43-45; UIowa Lib; Catlgr 49-52, Ref libn 52-, Instr of catlg correspondence bur 56-. 9: ALA (Recr Netwk rep Iowa 63-65); Iowa LA (Iowa Author Plaque Com, State Re Recr Com). 10: UWis Lib Sch Alumni Assn; Iowa Archeol Soc; Potomac Appalachian Trail Club; LWV. 12: "The Labor Force of the Philadelphia Radio Industry in 1936 with G L Palmer (38); Comp Annual bibliogs of Civil War period articles for "Civil War History (63-). 13: Yes. 14: Ref, catlg. 15: 19 Evans st, Iowa City Iowa 52240.

STOKES, KATHARINE MARTIN. b Hoguestown Penn 26 N 06. 5: Simmons 28 (LS) BS; UMich summers 42, 44, 45 MALS, summers 51, 54 & 54-55 (Eng) MA, 59 (LS) PhD. 6: Fr, Ger, Russian, Sp, Ital. 7: Asst libn Pub Lib, Bryn Mawr Penn 28-30; Asst in circ & catlg pub lib, Harrisburg Penn 30-31; Circ libn Penn State Col 31-40; Act ref libn Swarthmore Col 39-40; Asst libn readers serv Penn State Col 40-45; Circ libn UIll(Urbana) 45-48; Libn dir of libs West Mich U 48-67; Col & U lib specialist US Off of Educ div of lib programs, Wash DC 67-. 9: ALA-LAD (pres 59-60); -ACRL (pres 62-63); MichLA; (Exec Bd 60-62); PennLA. 10: AAUP; AAUW; Beta Phi Mu. 12: Ed "Illinois Libraries (47-48); Ed "Michigan Librarian (49-50). 13: Yes. 14: Admin. 15: 1101 3rd st apt S406E, Wash DC 20024.

STOKES, MARY LOUISE. b Havana Ark 23 Je 35. 5: Ark Polytech Col 52-54 (Sci); UArk 54-56 (Sci) BS Ed; UOkla 57-58 MLS. 6: Fr, Ger. Russian. 7: UArk: Jr lib asst 56-57, Lib asst 58-63, Sr libn asst 63-. 9: ALA; ArkLA; SWLA. 10: Kappa Delta Pi. 14: Catlg, ref (univ or col). 15: 1150 N Sang, Fayetteville Ark 72701.

STOKES, PORTIA (SILVERTHORNE). b Maple Hill Kan 26 N 12. 4: James M Stokes. 5: UOkla 34 (Pub Sch Music) BFA; LSU 59 (LS) MS. 6: Sp. 7: Document libn La Polytech 57-. 9: SLA; LaLA (Ls State Doc Com). 14: Govt publins. 15: 1209 Dubach st, Rustin La 71270.

STOKES, ROY BISHOP. b Ipswich Eng 14 Ag 15. 4: Mona Jefferson. 5: Nottingham U (Eng) 64 MA; FEllow & Honours Diplomate of Lib Assn. 6: Fr. 7: Asst Pub Lib Ipswich Eng 33-38; Sr asst Pub Lib, Ilford Eng 38-46; Royal Navy (Lt Commander) 40-46; Dir Sch of Libnship, Loughborough Eng 46-. 8: Visiting lecturer in lib sci UIll 52-55, USyracuse 58, UCLA 62, Simmons 65 & 66, UPittsburgh 65-66; Koerner lecturer UBC 69. 9: Lib Assn (Gt Brit); (Can 50-); Bibliog Soc (Gt Brit); BSA; Cambridge Bibliog SOC: Bibliog Soc UVa. 10: Beta Phi Mu; Rotary Club. 11: Hon Diploma of Loughborough Col. 12: Ed Esdailes "Student Manual of Bibliography" (54 & 67); "Bibliographical Control and Service" (65); "Function of Bibliography" (69). 13: Yes. 14: Bibliog, rare bks, lib educ, hist of libs. 15: Grad Sch of Lib & Info Sci, Univ of Pittsburgh, Pittsburgh Pa 15213.

STOKES, WILLIAM HENRY. b Watertown SD 19 My 20. 5: Carleton Col 36-40 (Eng) BA; UPittsburgh 46-47 (Eng) MA; UMich 54-55 MALS. 6: Fr. 7: Medical Corps US Army, New Caledonia 43-45; Eng tchr USoMich 50-53; Libn UMich 55-64; Asst Prof of Libnship Grad Sch of Libnship UDenver 64-. 9: ColoLA. 14: Ref. 15: 2458 S Milwaukee st, Denver 80210.

STOKESBERRY, RUTH ANNA (WILLIAMS). b Novinger Mo 19 Je 22. 4: Jack E Stokesberry. 5: NEMo State Col 39-42 (Eng, Speech) BS; NorthwesternU 43-44 (Theatre Arts) MA. 7: Tchr: high sch, Green City Mo 42-43, Faribault High Sch, Faribault Minn 44-46; Instr NYU Dept of Speech 46-50; Lib asst pub lib, Des Moines Iowa 63-64, Commun serv off 64-. 9: ALA; IowaLA. 10: Des Moines Commun Playhouse; Drama Wkshop of Des Moines. 13: Yes. 14: Commun wk and pub rel, wk with organizs, publications, etc. 15: 4057 Kingman blvd, Des Moines Ia 50311.

STOKKELAND, MARGARET C. b New Westminster BC Can 6 O 25. 5: UBC 44-48 (Chem Engnr) BASC; Carnegie 49-50 MLS. 6: Fr, Ger, Ital, Russian. 7: Asst libn Eastman Kodak Co, Rochester NY 50-56; Acquis libn Nat Research Coun, Ottawa 56-63; Catlg libn Boeing Airplaine Co, Seattle Wash 63-64; Acquis libn UVictoria (BC) 64-65; Caltg libn West Wash StateCol 64-67; Libn U Calgary 67-69. 14: Catlg, ref. 15: 2306-614 5th ave SW, Calgary Alta Can.

STOKLOSSA, NICK (KLAUS). b Strelno Germany 19 Jl 40. 5: UBC 59-63 (Hist, Ger) BA, 63-64 (Educ) Tchr's Certif, 68-69 BLS. 6: Ger. 7: Tchr Surrey Sch Dist, Surrey BC Can 64-68, Libn 69-. 14: Sch libnship. 15: 823 Rondeau st, Coquitlam British Columbia Can.

STOLLER, CONSTANCE (KATZ). b NYC My 24. 4: . 5: Hunter Col 40-44 (Biol) BA; Wayne State U 56-63 (LS) MEd. 7: Libn Bd of Educ, Detroit 59-. 9: ALA; MichASchL. 10: Phi Beta Kappa. 14: Child lit. 15: 17396 Monica, Detroit Mi 48221.

STOLTZ, FLORA (LEONARD). b Yamhill Ore 30 J 121. 4: James R Stoltz. 5: Santa Monica City Col 39-40, 40-41 AA; Willamette U 41-43 (Eng) BA; Columbia 44-45 (LS) BS; UMich summer 54 (LS). 7: Documents libn Ore State Lib 45-49; Asst libn Peru State Col 50-53; Catlg libn Clackamas Co Lib, ORegon City Ore 58-. 9: ALA; OreLA; PNLA. 14: Catlg. 15: Rte 1 Box 313, Canby Or 97013.

STOLTZ, JAMES ROBERT. b Stella Neb 3 Ag 28. 4: Flora Leonard Stoltz. 5: Peru State Col 46-53 (Fr) AB, AB in Ed; UMich 52-56 (Fr); Portland StateU 57-66 (Educ); UWash 64-67 MA in Libnship. 6: Fr, Sp. 7: Tchr: Otoe Co Dist 11, Dunbar Neb 49-50, Auburn High Sch, Auburn Neb 53-54, Clackamas Grade Sch, Clackamas Ore 57-59; Libn & tchr: St Louis High Sch, St Louis Mich 54-56, Veronica Grade Sch, Veronica Ore 56-57; Libn Molalla Grade Sch, Molalla Ore 59-66; Catlg libn Maryhurst Col 66-. 9: ALA; PNLA; OreLA. 10: AAUP. 14: Catlg, ref, acquis, tchg. 15: Rte 1 Box 313, Canby Or 97013.

STOLZE, WILLIAM EDWARD. b St Louis Mo 11 F 25. 4: Patricia FitzGibbon. 5: UNotre Dame 41-43, 46-48 (Bus Admin) BS; Syracuse 66-68 MLS. 6: Ger, Ital. 7/ lt (jg) USNR, Mediterranean & Cuba 43-46; Asst mgr (wholesale) Stolze Lumber Co, Granite City Ill 48-50, Mgr (retail) 50-52; Tchr Whitfield Sch, St Louis Mo 54; Mgr (rec dept) Aeolian Co of Mo, St Louis 60-66; Searcher (acquis) SyracuseU Lib 66-67, Hd humanities div 68-. 14: Bldg res collection in the humanities, rare bks. 15: PO Box 71, New Woodstock NY 13122.

STONE, ANNE F. b Belmont Mass 4 Mr 08. 5: Radcliffe 27-31 (Hist) BA; Simmons summers 42-45 (LS) BS. 7: Union catlg Harvard U 38-45; Sr asst Malden Pub Lib, Malden Mass 45-47, Circ libn 47-. 9: ALA; NELA; MassLA. 10: Appalachian Mt Club. 14: Ref, circ. 15: 7 Alexander ave, Belmont Ma 02178.

STONE, C(LARENCE) WALTER. b Syracuse NY 25 Je 21. 4: Phyllis May Vagts. 5: Columbia 46 AB, 47 BS, 48 MA, 49 EdD. 6: Fr. 7: Naval Aviator (Lt) USNR 42-45; Libn & research asst Inst of Adult Educ Tchrs Col Columbia U 47-49; Prof of lib sci UIll 49-60; Consul on Mass Media Off of Educ, Wash DC 58-60, Dir Educ Media Br 60-62; Prof of lib sci & educ Grad Sch of Lib & Info Sci UPittsburgh 62-, Dir of U Libs UPittsburgh 65-. 8: Consul to UNESCO summer 62; Dir A-v Serv, Detroit Pub Lib 54; Dir Center for Lib & Educ Media Studies 62-;Mem survey teams to study develop mental bk activity & needs in; Republic of Korea Sept 66, Republic of Vietnam Oct 66, Philippines, Nov 66, Thailand, Aug 67; Consul USPHS Div Dental Health 69. 9: ALA; NEA-DAVI; Nat Assn Educ Broadcasters; PennLA. 10: Kappa Delta Pi; Phi Delta Kappa; Beta Theta Pi. 11: Ford Foundation Grant. 12: Ed the Professional Education of Media Service Personnel (64); Ed "Instructional Television in Western Pennsylvania (64); Co-auth "Library Development in Eight Asian Countries (69). 13: Yes. 14: Admin of communication & info serv. 15: 271 Hillman Lib, Univ of Pittsburgh, Pittsburgh Pa 15213.

STONE, CHARLOTTE (DIETRICH). b Hagerstown Md 7 Ap 10. 4: C Vernon Stone Jr. 5: Hood Col 28-32 (Eng) AB; UWis 32-33 (LS). 7: Head Engnr Lib UArk 35-36; Libn child div Pub Lib System, Wash DC 36-38; Lib asst adult dept Washington Co Free Lib, Hagerstown Md 57-60, Head of child serv 60-. 9: MdLA; Cumberland Valley LA. 10: Hood Col Club; Fountain Head Country Club. 14: Child serv. 15: 673 Oak Hill ave, Hagerstown Md 21740.

STONE, EDITH CAROLINE. b Brooklyn NY 21D06. 5: Queens Col (Indexing). 7: Ed asst Simmons-Boardman Pub Corp, NYC 25-29, Libn 30-. 8: Consul in transport, SLA. 9: SLA (chm Transport Div; Goals for 1970 Com 60-63; chm Publs Com 51-53; various positions in NY Chap). 10: Bus & Prof Womens Group. 15: Simmons-Bardman Pub Corp, 30 Church st, NYC 10007.

STONE, ELIZABETH (ANNE). b Cohuna Australia 26 My 34. 5: UMelbourne 52-55 (Hist) BA; Registration certif Lib Assn of Australia. 7: Libn Econ & Statistics Dept ANZ Bank, melbourne Australia 56-57; Libn CSIRO Research Sta, Merben Australia 57-61; Catlg asst Lond Sch of Econ & Pol Sci, Lond England 61-62; Ref off Cmmneah Parliamentary Lib, Camberra Austrlia 63-66; Soc sci libn Mills Mem Lib McMasterU 66-. 9: Lib Assn Australia; Lib Assn (Gt Brit); OntLA. 14: Ref docs, catlg. 15: Mills Memorial Lib McMaster Univ, Hamilton Ont Can.

STONE, ELIZABETH (WENGER). b Dayton Ohio 21Je18. 4: Thomas A Stone. 5: San Diego State Col 34-36 (Hist); Stanford 36-38 (Hist) AB, MA; USoCal 60 (LS); Catholic U 60-61 MS in LS; American U 61-68 (Pub Admin) PhD. 6: Fr., 7: Tchr Fontana Jr-Sr High Sch, Fontana Cal 38-39; Asst State Statistician WPA Admin Off, New Haven Conn 39-40; Asst in circ New Haven Pub Lib, New Haven Conn 40-42; Dir of pub rel UDubuque 42-46; Sub Pasadena Pub Lib, Pasadena Cal 53-60; Asst to head of dept, Assoc prof Dept of Lib Sci Catholic U 61-. 9: ALA; Asia Found Com 62-64, Memb chm, DC 67-68, Memb chm Deg VIII 68-); -LAD (Com for

Personnel Publns 64-69, chm Com on Staff Devel Sect on Personnel Admin 69); -ACRL; -LED (Tchrs Sect 69); -PLA; SLA (DC Chap; Scholarship Found Com 65-67); CathLA; DCLA (sec 63-64, pres 66-67); AALS (chm Nomin Com 68); Amer Soc Pub Admin; Spc Advanc Mgt. 10: Beta Phi Mu; Pi Sigma Alpha; Phi Lambda Theta. 12: Ed "DC Libraries" (64-66); "Clips and Quotes" (Monthly publ for DCLA, 67); "An Analysis of the Core Demonstration Course of the Library Schools Accredited by the American Library Association" (62); "Training for the Improvement of Library Administration" (67); "Historical Approach to American Library Development" (67); "Factors Related to the Professional Development of Librarians" (69). 13: Yes. 14: Admin, ref, lib hist, research. 15: Dept of Lib Sci, Catholic Univ of Amer, Wash DC 20017.

STONE, ERMINE. b Leesville La 20 O 01. 5: So Methodist U 17-21 (Lat) AB; Lib Sch of NY Pub Lib 24-25 Certif; Columbia 28-29 (LS) MS. 6: Fr, Ital. 7: Stud asst So Methodist U 19-21, Catlg & circ asst 21-24; Circ asst circ dept NY Pub Lib summer 24, Catlg asst ref dept summers 25, 26; Libn Bradford Jr Col 25-28; Faculty research libn Sarah Lawrence Col 28-30, Libn 30-64, Libn Emeritus 64-; Catlg & ref asst Scarsdale Pub Lib, Scarsdale NY 65-; Exec asst Princeton Lib in NY 66-69. 8: Vol Intl Fed for Documentation, the Hague 49; Prof staff NYU summer wkshops in educ 52-55; Mem Missile States inspection team 52-55; Cons Joseph Fels Foundation survey of lib needs 65. 9: ALA-ACRL (chm Jr Col Sect 30-31; Col Sect: chm 49-50, sec 64-65; chm Nomin Com 56-57); SWLA (sec 24); NYLA (sec Col Sect 61-63); Westchester LA (chm 44-45). 10: AAUP; Phi Beta Kappa; ACLU; NAACP; Sigma Kappa. 12: "The Junior College Librar ALA (32). 13: Yes. 14: Bk sel, catlg, ref, recr. 15: 523 W 112th st, NYC 10025.

STONE, HELEN A (HEBER). b Sacramento Cal 17 Ja 18. 4: Edmund C Stone.05: Sacrament Jr Col 36-38 AA; San Jose State Col 63 (LS) AB. 5: Sacramento Jr Col 39 AA; San Jose State Col 63 BA. 7: Child libn Hayward Pub Lib, Hayward Cal 63; Jr high sch libn Hayward Unified Sch Dist, Hayward Cal 63-66; Jr High Sch libn San Ramon Unified Sch Dist, Danville Cal 66-. 8: NDEA Inst 68, San Jose State Col Multi-Media Specialist Train. 9: ALA; CalLA; CalASchL (Jr High Sch Com 68-69; AVE AC-CalASchL Conf Com chm 69-70). 11: Encyclopedia Britanica Award 1st for San Ramon Unified Sch Dist ESEA Title II Exemplary Library 68. 14: Ref, ya lit. 15: 1359 Sandelin c, San Leandro Cal 94577.

STONE, JOYCE LAVINIA (WILSON). b Batavia NY 23 D 24. 4: Delmer Elton Stone. 5: Bethany Col (WVa) 42-44 (Biol, Fr Lit); Lake Erie Col 44-46 (Biol, Fr Lit) BA; Hartford Sem Found (Hartford Conn) 47-49; Christian Educ MA in Relig; Carnegie 55-56 MLS. 6: Fr, Sp. 7: Lib clerk East High Sch Lib, Denver 52-55; Coordinator of ya serv Topeka Pub Lib, Topeka Kan 56-58; Chief Libn NM State Lib Southwestern Region, Silver City NM 58-61; Libn admin 97th Bomb Wing (SAC), Blytheville AFB Ark 61-64; Libn admin 3960th Strategic Wing (SAC), Andersen AFB Guam 64-68; Admin libn USN, Naval Station Guam 68-. 9: ALA (Life mem)-PLA; Armed Forces Div; Guam & Trust Territory Lib Club. 10: Altrusa Internat; South Sea Searchers Scuba Club; Andersen AFB FFS Club; Chapel organist US Naval Sta, Guam. 13: Yes. 14: Mil & ya serv, publicity & pub rel, lib educ, interlib loans, acquis. 15: Naval Station Box 160, FPO San Francisco Ca 96630.

STONE, LUCIE REBECCA (HOLMAN). b Leeds Eng 10 D 07. 5: British FLA. 6: Fr, Ger. 7: Jr lib asst Pub Lib, Middlesbrough Eng 25-30; Lib asst for libn Pub Lib, Norwich Eng 30-34; Chief Libn Pub Lib, Heywood Eng 34-43; 1st chief libn Pub Lib Weymonth & Melcombe Regis Eng 43-49; Asst libn Pub Lib, Sturgis Mich 51-52; Lib asst Newberry Lib, Chicago 52; Bkmob libn Pub Lib, Elkhart Ind 53-56; Br libn Pub Lib, Norfolk Va 57-. 9: LA Gt Brit (Fellow); LA; SELA; VaLA. 13: Yes. 15: Pretlow Br Lib, 9640 Granby st, Norfolk Va 23503.

STONE , MARGARET ARNOLD. b Bath County Ky 2 Mr 31. 5: Morehead State Col 49-53 (Eng) AB; UKy summers 53-58 (LS) MS. 7: Libn Irvine High Sch, Irvine Ky 53-54; Libn Bath Co High Sch, Owingsville Ky 54-65; Ref libn Morehead StateU 65-. 9: ALA; NEA; KyEA; KyLA; SELA. 14: Ref. 15: 229 Bays ave, Morehead Ky 40351.

STONE, MARVIN (HUGH). b Marmaduke Ark 11 D 32. 5: Emory 50-54 (Romance Langs) BA; UTex 56-58 MLS. 6: Sp, Fr. 7: US Army Corps of Engnrs (Cpl) 54-56; Intern Libn Enoch Pratt Free Lib Baltimore 57-58; Dallas Pub Lib: Head lit & hist dept 59-62, Head sci & ind dept 62-65, Coordinator of adult serv 65-68, Materials coord 68-. 8: Part-time instr Lib Sch Texas Womans U 64-. 9: ALA; TexLA; Constit Com 65-66; chm 67-68; BSA; SWLA. 10: Phi Beta Kappa. 12: "Five Years Forward (The Dallas Public Libary, 1955-1960) (61). 13: Yes. 14: Ref, adult serv, rare bks, lib materials, hist printing. 15: 6341 Vanderbilt ave, Dallas 75214.

STONE, MARY. b Leesville La 19 D 05. 5: So MethodistU 22-26 (Eng) BA; Columbia 28-29 (LS) BS. 6: Fr, Sp. 7: Gen asst NYC Pub Lib circ 26-28, Ser catlgr reference 28-43; Chief catlg libn UTex Lib (Austin) 43-. 9: ALA; TexLA; SWLA; Tex Regl Catlg Gp (chm 60-61). 14: Catlg. 15: 1007 W 22nd st, Austin Tx 78705.

STONE, MICHAEL. b Boston Mass 24 Ja 36. 5: UColo (Electrical Engring) BS. 6: Ger. 7: Lib syst analyst Lib Syst Group, Boulder Colo 64-. 8: Consul: Nat Ctr for Atmospheric Res 64-68; Environmental Sci Serv Admin 66-67; Boulder Pub Lib 68-; Denver Pub Lib 68-. 9: Inst Electr & Electro Engrs. 12: Comp "Union List of Serials" (Colo). 13: Yes. 14: Analysis, design and implem of total lib systems. 15: 1320 Pearl st, Boulder Co 80302.

STONE, PHILIP JOHNSON. b Wash DC 14 Je 07. 4: Catherine Stone. 5: Cornell U 25-29 (Govt) AB; UIll 34-35 BS in LS; UCal 40-41 (LS) MA. 7: DC Pub Lib: Asst to asst libn 35-36, Info asst 36-38, Ref asst 38-39, Br ref libn 39-40, 41-43, Chief wk interests room 43-47, Chief bus div 48-49, Chief hist div 50-65, Asst coordinator of adult serv 65-. 9: ALA; Amer Soc Pub Admin; DCLA (treas 41-42). 10: Boy Scout Leader; Potomac Appalachian Trail Club; Audubon Naturalist Soc; Sycamore Island Club; Sigma Phi; Phi Beta Kappa; Phi Kappa Phi. 14: Ref, admin. 15: 3023 Macomb st NW, Wash DC 20008.

STONE, ROBERT HUGH. b Lebanon Tenn 5 F 40. 5: CumberlandU Jr Col 57-59; Peabody Col 59-61 (Math) BS, 61-62 (Math) MA, 65-67 MLS. 7: Math & physics tchr Cumberland Col of Tenn 62-65; Asst libn Baptist Hosp Lib, Nashville 65-67; Doc specialist Demonstration & Research Ctr for Early Educ Peabody Col 67-69; Catlg libn Meharry Med Col, Nashville 69-. 9: ALA; CanLA; CathLA; Amer Assn Physics Tchrs; Nat Coun Tchrs Math; SELA. 14: Ref. 15: PO Box 542, Lebanon Tn 37087.

STONE, RUTH ELAINE. b Orrum NC 15 O 11. 5: Mars Hil Col 27-29; UNC (Greensboro) 30-32 (Hist) AB; UNC (Chapel Hill) summers 48-50, 52-54 MSL. 6: Fr. 7: Tchr secondary schs NC & SC 35-40; Tchr-libn Harrisburg High Sch, Harrisburg NC 40-49; Libn Walter M Williams High Sch, Burlington NC 49-57; Act asst State Sch Lib Supv Raleigh NC summer 56; Gen serv NC State Lib summer 57; Secondary libn Charlotte-Mecklenburg System, Charlotte NC 57-63; Asst libn Rockingham Co Lib, Leaksville NC summer 58; Instr of lib sci Winthrop Col summers 59-60; Lecturer-libn Sch of Lib Sci UNC 63-. 9: ALA; AALS; SELA; NCLA. 10: Alpha Delta Kappa; Beta Phi Mu. 14: Schs, child & yp. 15: 65 Maxwell rd, Chapel Hill NC 27514.

STONE, TOBY (GAIL). b Charleston W Va 23 Ag 45. 5: Amer Col in Paris 64-65; Occidental 65-68 (Comparative Lit) BA; UCLA 68-69 MLS. 6: Fr, Ger. 7: Asst circ & acquis Occidental Col Lib 66-68; Asst ref dept UCLA Research Lib 68-. 9: ALA; CalLA. 14: Ref. 15: 1230 Clay st #104, San Francisco Ca 94108.

STONE, WILLIAM VINCENT. b Danbury Conn 1 Ja 18. 5: Yale 36-40 (Eng) BA, 40-42 (Eng) MA; Columbia 46-47 BLS. 6: Fr, Ger, Ital. 7: Br asst Tremont Br NY Pub Lib 47-48; Hosp libn BA Northport, LI NY 48-49; Asst libn UBridgeport 50-54; Asst libn St Johns U (NY) 54-56, Libn in chg 56-. 9: CathLA. 10: AAUP; Brooklyn Citizens Com; Nat Lib Week; Phi Beta Kappa; Chi Delta Theta. 12: "Phantom of False Morning (46); "Loveliest and the Best (60); "Modern Amercan Sonnet (J1 56); Ed "National Poetry Anthology (520); "A Christmas of Sonnets" (69). 13: Yes. 14: Catlg, ref. 15: 53 Cranberry st, Brooklyn NY 11201.

STONEBURG, MARY JANE. b Newburgh NY 12 Ag 34. 5: Col of William & Mary 52-55 (Govt) BA; UMich 55-57 AMLS. 7: Catlgr Gen Motors Pub Rel Lib, Detroit 57-58; Asst catlg libn East Mich U 58-61, Circ libn 61-66; Hd tech serv Chautauqua-Cattarangus Lib Syst, Jamestown NY 66-68; Hd period dept Bucknell Lib 68-. 15: RD 1, Millmont Pa 17845.

STONEHAM, FRANCES MILDRED. b Stoneham Tex 12 D 07. 5: Sam Houston State Tchs Col 24-39 (Hist) AB, MA; Our Lady of the Lake summers 40-41 (LS); N Tex State Tchrs summer 48 (LS); UTex summers 49-50; UHouston 51. 6: Lat. 7: Elem tchr Stoneham Pub Sch 26-31; Elem tchr Conroe

Independent Sch, Travis Jr 33-40, Libn 40-. 8: Consul to HUB Club, sponsor of Montgomery Co Mem Lib 46-47; Mem Montgomery Co Lib Bd 48-69. 9: ALA; TexLA (chm Sch Lib Div Legisl Com 44-46, State chm TexStateTA-TexLA Legisl Com). 10: Amer Red Cross. 12: Sch lib ed TexLA Journal (41-42). 14: Sch & co lib admin, a-v coord. 15: 901 N Fifth, Conroe Tx 77301.

STOOPS, LOUISE. b Honolulu. 5: UAriz 43-46 (Eng) BA; Simmons 51-52 (LS) MS. 6: Fr. 7: Asst libn Pop Lib Enoch Pratt Free Lib, Baltimore Md 52-53, Asst libn bus & econ 53-54; Libn advrtising info serv Eastman Kodak Co, Rochester NY 54-57; Libn Wilson Haight Welch & Grover, Hartford Conn 57-58; Asst libn US Steel Corp 58-60, Head Libn 60-68; Chief libn Bache & Co, Inc, NYC 68-. 9: SLA (treas Adv Div 64-67, NY Chap; sec 61-62; Recr Com 62-63; Program chm 65-66; chm Bus & Finance Gp 68-69); ASIS; NY Lib Club. 10: Eng- Speaking Union. 12: Monthly column "Is this a Problem in "Special Libraries. 14: Ref. 15: 7 Peter Cooper rd, New York NY 10005.

STOPPEL, WILLIAM ASHLEY. b Chicago Ill 22 F 34. 4: Helen Sue Lewis. 5: Cornell Col 51-55 (Ger) BA; UIowa 55-56, 58-64 (Ger) MA, PhD; UDenver 65-66 (Libnship) MA. 6: Ger. 7: Clk US Army 56-58; Asst Prof of Ger Cornell Col 60-65; Libn Westminster Col 66-67; Dir libs Wm Woods & Westminster Col 67-. 9: ALA. 13: Yes. 14: Ref, admin. 15: 1215 Lane st, Fulton Mo 65251.

STOPPLE, AVIS R. b Portland Ore 28 My 13. 5: UCal (Berkeley) 34 (Fr) BA, 35 Certif of Libnship. 6: Fr. 7: San Francisco Pub Lib 30-36; Hd Fire Underwriters Assn of the Pacific Lib, San Francisco 36-43; Hd libn Santa Rosa Jr Col Lib 56-63; Chief main lib San Francisco Pub Lib 63-. 9: SLA (Prog Chm); CalLA. 10: Gleason Lib Assocs USan Francisco. 12: Ed "Business Library Newsletter", San Francisco Pub Lib; Ed 1st ed -insurance Manual", Cal State Dept of Insurance. 13: Yes. 14: Admin, rare bks, pub serv. 15: San Francisco Pub Lib Main Lib Civic Center, San Francisco Ca 94123.

STORCK, JOHN N(ORMAN). b Fairbury Ill 22 F 16. 4: Elizabeth M Gabbert. 5: LIU 48-51 (Hist) BA; Pratt 51-52 MLS. 7: US Army 43; US Merchant Marine, Eur, Far E, N Amer 44-46; Correspondent Crane Co, , Chicago & NYC 36-48; Asst circ libn LIU Lib 48-52; Head Libn Upper Sandusky Pub Lib, Upper Sandusky Ohio 52-56; Head Libn Massillon Pub Lib, Massillon Ohio 56-65; Dir Lima Pub Lib, Lima Ohio 65-. 9: ALA; OhioLA (Exec Bd; chm Adult Serv RT). 10: Rotary Club; Commun Welfare Coun Lima & Allen Co; Heart Coun Bd. 12: Co-illus "Life, Land and Water in Ancient Peru" (65); Co-auth "A Survey of the Public Libraries of Mercer County, Ohio" (67). 14: Admin. 15: Lima Pub Lib 650 W Market st, Lima Ohio 45801.

STORIE, ELIZABETH (L) (SOUTH). b Boone NC 18 Ag 21. 4: James M Storie. 5: Appalachian State Tchrs Col 38-42 (Eng, Phys Educ, Soc Studies) BS, summers 60-64 (LS) MA. 7: Newspaper 42-43; Sec wk US Govt UDenver 54-57; Deputy clerk of Supreme Court Court Watauga C, Boone NC 57-60; Hist, phys educ tchr Gulfpark Jr Col 43-44; Jr high sch tchr San Lorenzo Sch, San Leandro Cal 44-45; Soc studies tchr Central Jr High Sch, Greensboro NC 48-49; Phys educ tchr Appalachian State Tchrs Col 56-57; Eng tchr Sr High Sch, Statesville NC 60-61, Libn 61-. 9: NEA; NCTE; ALA (Recr Netwk Rep NC); SELA; NCEA (Dist sec 62-64; local treas 68-69, pres Dist Lib Dept 64-65); NC High Sch LA (chm Awards & Scholarship Com 66-); NCLA; NCTE. 10: Iredell Lib Coun; Statesville Woman's Club. 15: 514 Lakeside dr, Statesville NC 28677.

STORM, DORIS (BARNARD). b Dacula Ga 14 Jl 14. 4: James H Storm. 5: Bob JonesU 36 (Speech) AB; Colo State Col 37 (Eng) MA; Peabody Lib Sch 41 BS in LS. 7: Ref libn Baptist Col (Charleston SC) 67-. 14: Ref, rare bks. 15: 441 W Carolina ave, Summerville SC 29483.

STORMO, LETITIA (HAHN). b Doland S Dak. 5: Dakota Wesleyan U 31-35 (Lat) BA; SDakU summers 42-45 (Bus Admin) MA; UDenver summers 55-57 (LS) MA. 6: Lat. 7: High sch tchr, Murdo S Dak 35-36; Registrar & bus instr Dakota WesleyanU 36-38; S Dak Benevolent Ins, Doland 31, 42; Prin, tchr & libn, Doland S Dak 42-63; Libn State Lib Commsn, pierre S Dak summers 60-63; High sch tchr, Redfield S Dak 63-64; Libn No State Col, Aberdeen S Dak 64-. 8: Adv to pub lib, Doland SD. 9: ALA; SDLA (v-pres 62); SDEA (life mem, pres Libns RT 60). 10. Shakespeare Club; Delta Kappa Gamma; AAUW. 13: Yes. 14: Curr, pub rel. 15: 1012 S Kline, Aberdeen SD 57401.

STORRS, D LEON. b Lehi Utah 24 Ap 29. 5: Brigham Young U 47-53 (Eng) BS, 55 (Eng); UWash 57 MS in LS. 6: Fr. 7: (Cpl) Mil Police Corp, US Army 53-54; Lib page UWash Lib 56-57; Catlg libn Brigham Young U 57-. 9: ALA; MPLA; Utah LA. 13: Yes. 14: Catlg, rare bks. 15: 168 S 3rd E, Provo Utah 84601.

STORRS, FLORA (REMIN). b Hartford Conn 1 N 19. 4: Richard C Storrs. 5: So Conn State Col (LS). 7: Asst libn Porter Lib Assn, N Coventry Conn 56-57; Lib asst Niantic Pub Lib, Niantic Conn 59, Libn 60-. 9: ConnLA; NLCLA (pres); ALA. 10: East Lyme Hist Soc. 14: Catlg, ref. 15: Riverbank Smith Hill Box 366, Niantic Conn 06357.

STORTZ, FRANCES MARIE. b San Antonio Tex 3 Jl 18. 5: Our Lady of the Lake Col 34-38 (Eng) BA, 51-54 MS in LS; Columbia summer 48 (LS). 6: Ger. 7: US Army, Germany: Hosp libn, Frankfurt 57, Libn Main Lib, Stuttgart 58, Acquis libn, Nurnberg & Heidelberg 58-64, Supv libn 64-65; Catlg USA Med Field Serv Sch Lib, Ft Sam Houston Tex 66, Ref libn 67-68, Libn 68-. 9: ALA; TexLA; BexarCoLA. 10: Assn of the US Army. 15: 212 Camargo st, San Antonio Tx 78210.

STOTTLE, WARD. b Scottsville NY 15 Je 07. 5: Rochester Inst of Tech 25-28, 30-31 (Art); Columbia 38 (Art Educ) BS, 49 (Art Educ) MA; State U (Geneseo NY) 62-63 MLS. 7: Art tchr pub schs, Schenectady NY 31-41, 45-47; Photogrammetrist US Army-Corps of Engnrs 41-45; Art tchr Ramapo Central Sch, Suffern NY 47-49; Dir of art pub schs, Rome NY 49-62; Ref libn City Lib, Springfield Mass 63-64; Adult serv Pub Lib, Orlando Fla 64-65, Head of fine arts dept 65-. 9: ALA; FlaLA; MassLA; NY State Tchrs Assn. 10: Phi Delta Kappa; Orlando Art Assn; Rome Art Assn. 14: Art, ref, visual aids. 15: 703 Lake Highland dr, Orlando Fla 32803.

STOUFFER, ISABELLE (MARY). b Pittsburgh 31 D 12. 5: Wilson Col 30-34 (Eng Lit) AB; Drexel 34-35 MS in LS. 6: Fr, Ger. 7: Princeton Theol Sem: Spec catlgr 35-36, Head catlgr 36-49, Asst libn 49-. 9: ALA; ATheolLA (Exec Com 68-70); NY Tech Serv Libns; Presbyterian LA. 14: Catlg. 15: Speer Lib Princeton Theol Sem, Princeton NJ 08540.

STOUGH, LUCIEN P (MRS). b Phenix City Ala 22 F 04. 5: Auburn U 41 (Eng) BS in Ed; Peabody 59 MA in LS. 6: Lat. 7: Tchr: Pittsview Elem Sch, Pittsview Ala 20-22, Autaugaville Elem Sch, Autaugaville Ala 22-23, Phenix City schs, Phenix City Ala 25-50; Libn Central Jr High Sch, Phenix City Ala 50-62; Libn Central High Sch, Phenix City Ala 62-68; Dir-Libn Phenix City-Russell Co Lib 68-. 9: AlaEA; Low-Cost Nurs Home for Tchrs Com; SELA (sec Child & Sch Div 60-62). 10: Phenix City-Russell Co Lib Bd; Delta Kappa Gamma; Beta Phi Mu. 14: Lib serv for the blind, collecting autographed bks. 15: PO Box 506, Phenix City Ala 85012.

STOUGHTON, FAITH B. b Plain City Ohio 30 My 07. 5: Otterbein Col 25-29 (Romance Lang) AB; West Res 46-47 BLS. 7: Co libn pub lib, Wooster Ohio 47-50; Hd libn pub lib, napoleon Ohio 50-53; Consul State Lib of Ohio 53-. 9: ALA; OhioLA. 10: Soroptimist internat. 15: State Lib of Ohio 65 So Front st, Columbus Oh 43215.

STOUT, CHESTER BERNARD. b Jacksonville Tex 31 My 18. 4: Shirley Mae Carradine. 5: Tulane U 51-53 (Eng); Auburn U 57-60 (Econ) BS; LSU 61-63 (LS) MS; Central Mo State Col 65-68 (Bus Admin) MA; Case West Res 68. 6: Russian, Sp, Fr. 7: Personnel admin Naval Sci Instr US Navy 37-61 ret; Asst libn Central Mo State Col 63-68; HEA Fellowship CWRU 68-. 8: Consul Operation Deepfreeze (Antarctic Expedition Libs) 55-57. 9: NEA;-DAVI; ALA; MoLA; CTA; Mo State TA. 10: AAONMS; AHE; Bd Dirs, Fleet Res Assn; ARTIS; Boy Scout Coun; AAUP; Omicron Delta Epsilon; Phi Delta Kappa. 14: Lib educ, admin, tech proc, electronics, info sci, info retrieval. 15: 318 Johnson ave, Warrensburg Mo 64093.

STOUT, ELLEN JENSEN. b Chicago 8 Ap 07. 5: UWash 24-28 (Home Econ) BS, summers 58-61 MLS. 7: Home econ tchr S Kitsap Union High Sch, Port Orchard Wash 29; Home econ tchr Shelden Jackson Sch, Sitka Alaska 30-36; Sub- prof S Puget Sound Reg Lib, Olympia Wash 58-62, Ext libn 63-69; Ref libn Timberland Reg Lib 69-. 9: WashLA. 15: Box 312, Rochester Wa 98579.

STOUT, LOIS JOYCE (SOWARDS). b Texarkana Ark 4 Ja 15. 4: Henry Neal Stout. 5: Texarkana Col 32-34 Certif; Tex Womans U 34-36 BA. 7: Libn: Del Rio High Sch, Del Rio Tex 36-37, Brownwood High Sch, Brownwood Tex 37-42, USNAS, Corpus Christi Tex 42-43,Camp Hulen Tex 43-44, Camp Hood Tex 44-45, USNATTC, Gulfport Miss 45; Asst libn Naval Air Station, Pensacola Fla 46-47; Libn Gulfport

Miss 47; Libn City-County, Hermando Miss 47-48; Libn USAF, Randolph Field Tex 48-50; Libn USAF, Chanute AFB Ill 50-51, Asst libn 56-61; Ref libn Fed Aviation Agency, Aeronautical Center, Okla City Okla 61-. 9: SLA. 13: Yes. 14: Ref. 15: 6605 NW 19th, Bethany Okla 73008.

STOVALL, MARTHA W. b Fitzgerald Ga 14 S 12. 5: Ga State Col for Women 29-32 (Eng) AB; Emory 32-33 AB in LS; Chicago 49 (Med Lib Sci). 7: Libn; Marian Co High Sch, Jasper Tenn 35-37, Gordon Lee High Sch, Chickamauga Ga 37-38, Brooks Co High Sch, Quitman Ga 38-43, US Army Hosp Thomasville Ga 43-45, US Army, European Theater of Operations 45-46; Chief libn VA Hosp; Ft Howard Md 47-51, Perry Point Md Bedford Mass 62-68, Sepulveda Cal 68-. 9: ALA- AHIL (chm Legis Com); MedLA; SLA; MassLA; NELA. 10: AAUW. 13: Yes. 14: Readers adv serv, ref. 15: 947 11th st apt 2, Santa Monica Ca 90403.

STOVER, JEAN (BORDEN). b Bayonne NJ 25 O 25. 4: William Jarden Stover. 5: Adelphi 44-48 (Eng) BA; Pratt 51-52 MLS. 6: Fr, Sp. 7: Pre-prof NYC Pub Lib 48-52, Child libn 52-55; Ref libn Millburn Pub Lib, Millburn NJ 66-. 9: NJLA. 10: AAUW. 14: Ref, child lit. 15: 128 W End ave, Summit NJ 07901.

STOVER, WEBSTER. b Nazareth Penn 4 J 1 02. 4: Marion Barbara Allen. 5: Ursinus Col 19-20, 21-24 AB; Union Theol Sem 24-27 BD; ColumbiaU 28-29 MA, 29-30 PhD. 6: Fr, Ger, Lat, Gk. 7: Asst libn Infantry Sch of Amer, Camp Benning Ga 19-25; Asst Prof Gk & Eng Col of William & Mary 27-28; Prof & Head Dept Educ & Psych Tusculum Col 30-31; Visiting Prof Educ & Psych Bates Col summer 31; Headmaster Perkiomen Sch, Pennsburg Penn 32-35; Pres Arnold Col 35-39; Proprietor Albert Tchrs Col 40-; Dir Amer Libns Agency, NYC 43-. 12: "Horace Bushnells Contributions to Religioxus Thought in America; (37); "Alumni Stimulation by the American College President; (40). 13: Yes. 14: Rare bks. 15: Rm 906, 535 5th ave, New York NY 10017.

STOW, CHARLES E(DWARD). b Greenville SC 6 Ja 14. 5: Furman U 36 (Hist) BA; Columbia 37 BS in LS. 7: Libn Hill Sch, Pottstown Penn 37-50; Ref libn Furman U 50-51; Ref libn Pub Lib, Greenville SC 51-52; Libn Co Lib, Greenville SC 52-. 9: ALA; SELA; SCLA. 13: Yes. 14: Ref. 15: Greenville Co Lib, 420 N Main st, Greenville SC 29601.

STOWE, FERN ELIZABETH. b Seymour Conn 15 D 11. 5: Berea Col 30-34 (Eng) BA; Syracuse U summers 38, 39, 42, 43 (LS) BS in LS (magna cum laude). 7: Berea Col Lib 30-34; Catlgr Fera Under Conn Dept of Educ, Conn 34-35; Sch Libn Bd of Educ, Windsor Conn 35-44; Research Pacifist Research Bur, Phila 44-45; Research Nat Coun Prev of War, Wash DC 46; Asst libn State Tchrs Col, New Paltz 46-48; Br libn Enoch Pratt Free Lib, Baltimore 48-67; Br libn Montgomery Co dept pub libs, Sandy Spring Md 67-. 9: ALA; ConnSchLA (sec 37-39); MdLA (Intel Freedom Com 49-50). 10: ACLU; Friends (Quakers) Conf on Relig & Psych; Fellowship of Reconciliation. 13: Yes. 14: Ref, adult educ serv. 15: 17401 Norwood rd, Sandy Spring Md 20860.

STOWELL, HELEN (SMITH). b Rochester NY 30 S 13. 4: Cecil B Stowell. 5: SUNY (Albany) 31-35 (Eng) AB, 35-36 BS in LS. 7: Eng & lib Savannah Hilh Sch, Savannah NY 36-38; Asst bkmob libn Delmar Pub Lib, Delmar NY 38-40; Sub libn Albany pub sch system, Albany NY 38-40; Asst libn Hackett Jr High Sch, Albany NY 40-45, Libn 45-47; Libn Schs 20 & 21 Albany Pub Sch System, Albany NY 57-62, Libn Sch 16 62-. 9: NEA; NYLA; NY State Tchrs Assn; East NY Sch LA (pres 64-66); Hudson-Mohawk LA. 10: AAUW; SUNY (Albany) Alumni Assn; Willowbrook Civic Assn; Friends of the Lib; 14: Wk with child. 15: 17 Hie ct, Schenectady NY 12303.

STRABLE, EDWARD G. b Camden NJ 12 F 22. 4: Jane Sturtevant. 5: UIll 46-48 (Journalism) BS; Chicago 49-51 (LS) MA. 7: US Army Signal Corps Infantry Med Corps (Sgt) 43-46; Advertising copywriter Scantlin & Co, Chicago 48-49; Exec asst to libn Chicago Pub Lib 52-55; Lib dir J Walter Thompson Co, Chicago 55-64, Mgr info serv 68-; Exec sec ALA-ALTA-RSD, Chicago 65-68. 8: Lecturer Grad Lib Sch UChicago 58-63. 9: ALA; SLA (Ill Chap; Dir 61-64, pres 58-59); ASIS. 12: Comp "Subject Headings in Advertising, Marketing and Communications Media with E B Christianson (64); Ed "Special Libraries: A guide for Management" (65). 13: Yes. 14: Spec libs, info retrieval. 15: Information Ctr, J Walter Thompson Co, 875 N Michigan ave, Chicago Il 60611.

STRACHAN A LURA R. b Mannhurst NB Can 29 S 09. 5: CarletonU 60 (Hist) BA; UToronto 65 Certif in Sch Libnship. 6: Fr. 7: Tchr-libn High Sch, Ottawa Can 60-69; Lib consul Ministry of Educ, Nassau bahamas 69-70. 8: Lib Coun rep on Educ TV Com & A-V Com; Wrote script & narrated "Using Your High School Library" for educ TV, Ottawa Ont Can 66. 9: CanLA; OntLA. 10: Univ Womens Club, Ottawa. 15: 61 Belmont ave, Ottawa Ont Can.

STRADER, THOMAS EDWARD. b Rittman Ohio 26 Ap 27. 5: OhioU 45-51 (Zoology) AB; Case West res 51-52 MD in LS. 6: Ger, Lat, Sp. 7: Spec/5 US Army, Korea 46-47; Chem V D Anderson, Cleveland Ohio 51; Ref libn Union Col (Schenectady NY) 52-54, Asst libn 54-56; Dir lib Rochester Inst of Tech 56-. 9: ALA; NYStateLA; MonroeCoLA. 10: Phi Kappa Tau; Sigma Phi. 14: Admin. 15: 1 Lomb Memorial dr, Rochester NY 14623.

STRAHLER, CLYTIE EVELYN. b Dayton Ohio 17 Je 07. 5: Wittenberg Col 3034 (Hist) AB (cum laude); UIll 3538 BS in LS. 6: Fr. 7: Dayton Pub Lib, Dayton Ohio; Asst child dept 2529, Asst high sch dept & sch br asst 3031, Br & sch libn 3249, Instr train class 3941, Hd train class activities & 1st asst ref dept 4956; Coord personnel serv Dayton & Montgomery Co Pub Lib, Dayton Ohio 5662; WittenbergU; Asst hd libn 6264, Chief reader serv 6466, Asst dir libs & chief readers serv 6668. Assoc dir libs & assoc prof 68. 8: Tchr lib sci (evenings & summers) WittenbergU 54; Regl Coun on Intl Educ fac seminar participant on Lat Amer Studies 6667; Adv coun on tech aid program Sinclair Col 69. 9: ALA (Coun 5860; mem & chm Notable Bks Coun 5559); OhioLA (Exec Bd 5860; chm Subprof Train Com 5960; Scholarship Com 65; Recruiting Netwk 6066); Ohio Col Assn (sec Libns Sect 6364); Dayton & Miami Valley Consortium Lib Sect (chm Personnel Com 69). 10: AAUP; Dayton Coun on World Affairs; Cincinnati Coun on World Affairs; Beta Phi Mu. 14: Univ lib personnel & admin, lib educ, research, Lat Amer area studies. 15: 5340 Brendonwood lane, Dayton Oh 45415.

STRAHLER, ELLEN L. b Dayton Ohio 1 My 09. 5: Wittenberg U 41 (Eng, Public Speaking) AB; West Res 43 BSLS. 7: Catlg dept Head Wogaman Sch Br Lib, 1st asst East Br Lib, child libn Belmont Br Lib Dayton Pub Lib, Dayton Ohio 27-42; Child libn Cleveland Pub Lib 43-60; Br libn Burkhardt Br Dayton Pub Lib, Dayton Ohio 60-; Evening Instr child lit UDayton64-67; Hd lit & fine arts div Dayton Pub Lib, Dayton Ohio 68-. 8: Libn Grace United Methodist Ch, Dayton Ohio. 9: ALA; OhioLA (past chm Serv to Schs Round TABLE); Staff Assn Dayton Pub Lib (pres 68-69). 10: Bus & Prof Womens Club. 14: Supv, ref, mus, art, lit, storytelling. 15: 19 W Siebenthaler, Dayton Ohio 45405.

STRANC, SISTER MARY CELAINE CSSF. b Buffalo NY 28 Jl 13. 5: Mt St Joseph Tchrs Col (Buffalo NY) 50 (Educ) BS in Ed; Nazareth Col (Rochester NY) 55-56 (Certif for Tchr-Libn); State U Col (Geneseo NY) 63-65 MLS. 6: Sp, Polish. 7: Tchr in schs in the Dioceses of Buffalo, Syracuse, Erie Penn 33-66; Tchr-libn Immaculate Heart of Mary Child Home & Sch (Buffalo NY) 56-58, 60-66; Libn Villa Maria Inst of Music (Buffalo NY) summer 65, 65, 66-; Instr Villa Maria Col 66-. 9: ALA; CathLA; West NY Cath Libn Conf (sec 65-66, chm Elem Sect 63-64, Cath Bk Week Chm 66, chm Memb Com 68, v-chm & Program Chm 68-69); NEA-DAVI; NYLA. 10: Girl Scout Leader; Sponsor of Sci Clubs of Amer; Girl Scout Brownie Leader; NCTE. 13: Yes. 14: Sch libnship, child lit, catlg. 15: 600 Doat st, Buffalo NY 14211.

STRASSWEG, ELSA. b Evansville Ind 30 S 08. 5: Western Col for Women 27-29; St Louis Lib Sch 29-30 Certif; Peabody 38-40 BS. 6: Sp. 7: Asst ext div Evnsville pub ldin: Vanderburgh cib,Evansville Ind 34-38; Bluffton-Wells Co Pub Lib, Bluffton Ind 40-44, New Albany-Floyd Co Pub Lib, New Albany Ind 45-. 9: ALA; IndLA (pres 44-45). 10: Ind Civil War Cent Commsn; Adv Com Ind Sesquicent Commsn; Kappa Kappa Kappa; Kappa Delta Pi; Ind Hist Soc; Floyd Co Hist Soc; New Albany Civil War Round Table; Soc Ind Pioneers. 12: "History of New Albany and Floyd Company, Indiana" (51). 13: Yes. 14: Admin, rare bks (Ind hist). 15: 207 Highland ave, New Albany In 47150.

STRATTON, FRANCES M(ARY. b Prospect Park Penn 9 Ap 24. 5: Dickinson Col 41-45 (Chem) BA; Drexel 49-50 MS in LS. 6: Fr. 7: Chem E I DuPont de Nemours Co, Phila 45-49; Asst libn Lederle Labs Div Amer Cyanamid Co, Pear River NY 50-63, Sci ref libn, lit serv dept 63-. 9: SLA (Sci-Tech Div; sec 61-63, treas 63-64, chm-elect 65-66, chm 66-67; NY Chap chm Sci-Tech Group 59-60; treas & bus mgr "Unlisted Drugs" Pharmaceutical Sect 53-56); ASIS; ACS; MedLA; NY Reg Group. 10: Soroptimist Club; Phi Beta Kappa; ACS. 13: Yes. 14: Ref. 15: 120 E Central ave, Pearl River NY 10965.

STRATTON, JOHN BROOKS. b Pioneer Ohio 9 Mr 08. 4: Betty Scovill Straton. 5: Ohio Wesleyan U 26-30 (Hist) AB; Columbia 41-42 BS in LS, 51-52 (LS) MS, 52-53 (LS). 7: Stock clerk Barnes & Noble Inc, NYC 30-32, Manager dislay dept 32-34; Rep Equitable Life Assurance Soc of US, Delaware, Ohio 34-39; Circ asst Ohio State U Lib 39-40, Stack supv 40-41; Stud asst Psych Lib, Columbia U 41-42; Asst circ libn Ohio State U Lib 46; US Army Air Force, Control Tower Operator (Cpl) 42-45; Acquis libn Okla A & M Col 46-51; Libn, Neurological Inst, NYC 51-52; Faculty asst Sch of Lib Serv Columbia U 52-53; Asst libn Okla State U 53-62; Libn Col of Agric Haile Salassie I U (Diere Dawa Ethiopia) 62-63; Asst libn Okla State U 63-. 9: ALA-ACRL; ASD;-RTSD; ISAA; SLA (pres Okla Chap 61-62); SWLA; OklaLA. 10: Phi Gamma Mu; Phi Alpha Theta. 12: "Education for Special Librarianship in "Major Problems in the Education of Librarians (54). 13: Yes. 14: Univ libs, continuing educ, bibliog org. 15: Okla State Univ Lib, Stillwater Ok 74075.

STRAUS, LESLIE SATOKO (FUJITA). b Kaslo British Columbia 2 N 44. 4: Neil Alexander Straus. 5: UWaterloo 62-65 (Eng) BA; UToronto 65-66 BLS. 6: Fr. 7: Libn II YorkU Libs 66-. 9: CanLA. 10: UToronto Sch of Lib Sci Alum Assn; York Univ Libs Staff Assn. 14: Catlg, ser. 15: 59 Carney rd, Toronto Ont Can.

STRAUSS, BERNICE (HALL) (MRS). b Tacoa Wash 16 J107. 5: Emory 25-28 (Educ) PhB in Ed; UAriz summers 50-64 (LS). 6: Fr, Sp. 7: Tchr Elem Sch, Atlanta 29-30; Tchr Priv Sch Mendham NY 30-31; Tchr of biol, hist, Eng High Sch, W Orange NJ 31-34; Sub tchr High Sch & Jr High Sch, W Orange NJ 34-44; Clerk Post Off, Tucson 45-46; Tchr Elem Sch, Marana Ariz 50-52; Tchr-libn High Sch, Marana Ariz 52-61, Libn 61; Act head libn Teen Room Tucson Pub Lib summers 62 & 63. 8: Faculty Adv Com Marana High Sch 68-69; Ch lib org summers 59 & 68. 9: ALA (Recr Com 60-62); Ariz LA (Scholarship Com 64-65). 10: Pima Co Coun. 14: Ref bks for high schs, bks on Ariz. 15: 4002 E Montecito ave, Tucson Az 85711.

STRAUSS, BEVERLY (VICTORSON). b Brooklyn NY 25 Jl 28. 4: Howard Strauss. 5: Brooklyn Col 45-49 (Eng) BA; Pratt 49-50 MLS; St Johns U 62-63; Adelphi U 63; C W Post Col 63-64. 7: Libn Grade 2 Brooklyn Pub Lib 50-52, Libn Grade 3 Lib on Wheels 53-54; Tchr of Lib Long Beach Jr High Sch, Long Beach LI NY 64-65; Tchr of Lib PS 184Q, NYC Bd of Educ 65-66; Tchr of Lib IS 145Q 66-68; Tchg programs libn - Asst Prof NYC Commun Col Lib 68-. 8: Curriculum bulletin for intermediate sch lif NYC Bd of Educ. 9: ALA; LACUNY; NYCASchL. 14: Sch libs. 15: 6814 174th st, Flushing NY 11365.

STRAUSS, ILMARS R. b Riga Lativia 28 O 25. 4: Ausma Mainieks. 5: UMan 60 (Hist, Philos, Geog) BA; Toronto 61 BLS. 6: Latvian, Ger. 7: Circ libn UMan Lib 61-65, Act head ref dept 65-. 9: CanLA; ManLA. 14: Ref, circ. 15: 684 Townsend ave, Winnipeg 19 Man Canada.

STRAUSS, L HARRY. b Spokane Wash 30 Ag 11. 4: Cora Frizell. 5: George Williams Col 35 (Group Wk Admin & Informal Ed) BS; Chicago 42 (LS) M A; UMich 48-55 (Educ). 7: Libn George Williams Col 35-45; A-v Consul Nat Coun of YMCA, Chicago 45-47; Asst to dir Educ Serv Motion Picture Assn of Amer, NY 42-48; Supt Clearwater Twp Unit Sch, Rapid City Mich 48-53; Supt Les Cheneaux Commun Schs, Cedarville Mich 53-61; Document libn & Head tech serv Cal State Polytech Col 61-65, Col Libn 65-. 8: Exec sec Commsn on Motion Pictures in Adult Educ 47-48. 9: ALA; CalLA. 12: "Look, Listen and Learn" (48). 13: Yes. 14: Admin. 15: Cal State Polytech Col Lib, San Luis Obispo Cal 93402.

STRAUSS, LUCILLE (MARY) (JACKSON). b Pittsburgh Penn 8 S 08. 4: Jerome Strauss. 5: Chatham Col 26-30 (Chem) BA; Penn State U 30-31 (Chem) MS. 6: Fr, Sp. 7: Mineral ind libn Penn State U 31-41; Libn research & development lab Vanadium Corp of Amer, Bridgeville Penn 41-48; Chem & physics libn Penn State U 48-. 8: Consul on lib & info problems to AMP, Harrisburg Penn 54; Survey of tech lib bulletins for Ind Res Inst 51; Mem US Wking Gp for Chem Tech of Universal Decimal Clsf sponsored by Intl Fed for Documentation 69-. 9: SLA (chm Non-Ser Publns Com 53-54; Pittsburgh Chap: chm Educ Com 42-44, chm Sci-Tech Gp 44-45); ACS (sec Div Chem Lit 57-58); The Chem Soc, ASIS. 10: AAUW; LWV; Iota Sigma Pi; Sigma Delta Epsilon. 11: Special Achievement Award SLA 64. 12: "Guide to Mineral Industries Literature (40); Ed "Technical Libraries; Their Organiza tion and Management" SLA (51); Co-auth "Scientific and Technical Libraries; Their Organization and Administration" (64). 13: Yes. 14: Sci & tech lib admin, lit of chem & other scis. 15: 520 W Nittany ave, State College Pa 16801.

STRAUSS, RICHARD F W. b Reading Penn 4 Ag 44. 5: Albright Col 62-66 (Eng) AB (summa cum laude); Rutgers U 66-68 MLS; UPittsburgh 68-69 (Lib & Info Scis) Advanced Certif. 6: Fr, Lat. 7: Stud asst Albright Col Eng dept 64-66; Circ ref libn Albright Col Lib summers 67, 68; Acquis libn, head Montgomery Co-Norristown Pub Lib, Norristown Penn 69-. 9: ALA; PennLA. 10: Beta Phi Mu; Phi Alpha Theta; Delta Phi Alpha. 14: Acquis, bk selection, ref. 15: Montgomery Co-Norristown Pub Lib, 542 DeKalb st, Norristown Pa 19401.

STREBEL, JANE DEAN. b Sauk Centre Minn 26 Jl 13. 5: Macalaster 31-36 (Eng) BA; UMinn 46-47 BS in LS; 56 (LS) MA. 6: Fr. 7: Secondary sch tchr, Minn 36-44; Dir of Christian Educ St Andrews Episcopal Church, Kan City Mo 44-46; Sch libn Minneapolis pub schs 47-54, Consul in lib serv 54-. 8: Consul in lib serv, Minneapolis Pub Schs; Consul UMinn Lib NDEA Inst 65. 9: ALA-AASchL (Rec Sec, Exec Bd 62-63; chm Awards & Scholarships Com; sec Supv Sect 66-67); MinnASchL (pres 57-59; chm Scholarship Com 53-; MinnEA; NEA. 10: Sierra Club. 13: Yes. 14: Sch lib admin, prof educ libs, instr materials. 15: 807 NE Broadway, Minneapolis Mn 55413.

STRECK, SISTER HELEN (TERESA). b Cherryvale Kan. 5: FriendsU 31-37 (Eng, Mus) BA, BMus; Wichita StateU 49-55 (Music Educ) M Mus; Rosary Col 64-68 MALS. 6: Ital. 7: Tchr (mus & Eng) Sacred Heart Col (Wichita Kan) 45-56, Acad dean 56-61, Hd libn 66-; Tchr & libn Holy Trinity High Sch, Okarche Okla 61-66. 8: Sec, Diocesan Unit, Music Educators. 9: ALA; KanLA. 10: Beta Phi Mu. 14: Acquis, ref, tchg. 15: Sacred Heart College 3100 McCormick, Wichita Ks 67213.

STRECKER, JOHN MARTIN. b Marietta Ohio 2 Ap29. 5: Ohio Wesleyan U 47-51 (Bus Admin) BA; UMich 55-57 MALS. 7: Lt (jg) USNR US Navy 52-55; Order libn DePauw U 57-61; Asst chief acquis Washington U (St Louis) 61-63, Chief acquis dept 63-. 9: ALA. 10: Phi Beta Kappa. 14: Tech serv, acquis, admin. 15: Washington Univ Libs St Louis 63130.

STREET, ELEANOR F(AWCETT). b St Paul 17 Jl 15. 5: Oberlin 33-35; UPenn BS in Ed; Drexel 39-40 BS in LS. 7: Asst libn Pub Lib, Bound Brook NJ 40-42; Child libn Pub Lib, Larchmont NY 42-43; Libn Jr High Sch, Mamaroneck NY 43-44; Head Libn Pub Lib, W Chester Penn 44-48; Admin asst Pub Lib, Teaneck NJ 48-49; Dir Pub Lib, Westport Conn 49-. 8: Mem of del to Swedish libs 60; H W WILSON Com on Indexes 60-63; 09: ALA (Coun 63-64, Friends of Libs Com 50); Conn LA (pres 58-59). 10: Pi Lambda Theta; Westport-Weston Arts Coun; Westport-Weston Commun Coun. 13: Yes. 14: Admin, pub rel, bldg, ref. 15: Westport Pub Lib PO Box 31, Westport Ct 06880.

STREETER, DAVID. b Los Angeles 31 D 29. 5: Colo State Col 48-50, 54-55 (Bio Sci, Eng) BA; UDenver 56-57 (LS) MA; NM State U 63-64. 7: Libn I UCal(Berkeley) 57-58; Asst libn NM Mil Inst, Roswell NM 58-59; Asst reg libn & Reg libn NM State Lib 59-60; Circ libn, Ref libn NM State U 60-64; Hd bus div, Act hd soc & bus dept Denver Pub Lib 64-68; Bus admin libn, Hd ref serv UDenver 68-. 9: SLA (vpres & preselect Colo Chap 69); ALA; RSD (Bus Ref Serv Com 6870); ColoLA (Ad Hoc Publ Com). 10: Banenji Club of Amer; Westeners. 12: Ed Columbine-SLA Colo Chap Bulletin 67-69. 14: Ref, rare bks, ephemera. 15: Rt 1 Box 568, Morrison Co 80465.

STREETER, ELIPHAL B(EARD). b Oneonta NY. 5: Keuka Col 45-49 (Eng) BA; Columbia 49-50 MLS. 7: Lib asst Colgate U Lib 43-45; Catlgr Nat Health Coun Lib, NYC 50-52; Lederle Labs Lib, Pearl River NY 52-54; Wallerstein Co Lib, NYC 55-57; Asst libn act libn Wallerstein Co Lib SI NY 57-59, Libn 59-. 9: SLA; MedLA. 14: Catlg, ref, admin. 15: 54 Orange st Apt 1-H, Brooklyn NY 11201.

STREHLE, KATHERINE (HOWE). b Oakland Cal 25 Ja 42. 4: Glenn P Strehle. 5: Wellesley 59-63 (Hist) BA; Simmons 64-65 (LS) MS. 6: Fr. 7: Catlg howardU Lib 63-65, 66-67, Catlgr in charge departmental lib catlg 67-. 14: Catlg. 15: 102 Parker rd, Wellesley Ma 02181.

STREITFIELD, SHIRLEY. b NYC 27 Jl 26. 4: Rose Leinwand Streitfield. 5: City Col (NY) 44-45 (Soc Sci); U Miami (Fla) 53-61 (Soc Sci). 6: Fr, Ger, Yiddish. 7: Lib asst II Miami Pub Lib, Miami Fla 55-. 9: ALA (Staff Org RT Memb Chm);-PLD;-ASD;-ACRL (Art Subsect); SELA; FlaLA; Dade Co LA (Hospitality chm); Amer Acad Pol Sci; Amer Jewish

Congress. 10: Staff Org of Miami Pub Lib; General Employees Assn City of Miami; The City Club of Professional Women Mimvistaamer AtSci; Amer ad Pol Sci; AmerJewish Congress. 14: Ref, reader's adv, commun rel. 15: Sea Beach Towers 1776 James ave, Miami Beach Fl 33139.

STRELNIZKI, RAISA MAMUTOVA. b Simferopol Crimea Russia 15 O 19. 4: Wladimir Strelnizki. 5: Med Inst (Simferopol Crimea) 38-41. 6: Russian, Ger, Turkish, Ukrainian, Polish. 7: Catlgr City Lib, Munich Germany 48-51; Catlgr Ind U Min Lib 59-. 14: Catlg. 15: 2632 E 5th st, Bloomington In 47401.

STREPMANIS, KATHLEEN. b Denver Col 20 F 40. 4: Pauls Strepmanis. 5: San Jose State Col 58-62 (Ger, Bus) BS; UDenver 65-67 (Libnship) MA. 6: Ger. 7: Hd libn Com City Pub Lib, Com City Colo 67; Pub serv libn Regis Col Lib 67-68, Tech serv libn 68-. 9: ALA; ColoLA. 14: Catlg. 15: 460 South Clay, Denver Co 80219.

STRICKLAND, MARIAN LOUISE. b Lockport NY. 5: SUNY (Geneseo) 54-56, 57-59 (LS) BS, Case West Res 61 MS in LS. 6: Ger. 7: Asst N Tonawanda (NY) Pub Lib (Part time); Elem sch libn Maryvale Sch System, Cheektowaga NY 59-61; Libn N Tonawanda (NY) High Sch, summer 60; Asst Cleveland Pub Lib 62; Elem sch libn Oak Park Pub Schs, Oak Park Ill 62-66; Asst prof SUNY(Geneseo) Lib Sci Sch 66-. 8: Instr lib sci, West Mich U summer 65. 9: NEA-DAVI; ALA; NYLA; NY State TA. 10: Child Reading Round Table; PTA; AAUW. 14: Child serv in sch & pub libs. 15: 125 B Main st, Mt Morris NY 14510.

STRICKLAND, NORMALIE (RICHARDS). b Efingham Ill 12 Ja 38. 4: Joseph H Strickland. 5: Marian Col 56-60 (Hist) BA; UIll 60-61 MSLS. 7: Asst sci dept Enoch Pratt Free Lib, Baltimore 61-63; Act hd sci dept Phoenix Pub Lib 63-66; Asst acquis dept UOkla 66-67; Asst libn St Anthony High Sch, Effingham Ill 67; Hd libn Helen Matthew Lib, Effingham Ill 68-. 9: ALA; IllLA. 14 Admin, catlg, ref. 15: 209 E Lawrence ave, Effingham Il 62401.

STRING, ALFRED C JR. b Marietta Ohio 6 Jl 25. 4: Gladys T Tillotson. 5: UCal 46-49 (Hist) BA; UMich 50-51 MALS. 6: Russian. 7: Catlgr Ohio State U Lib 51-53; Br libn DC Pub Lib 53-56; Hd processing unti Air Info Div LC 56-60, Curator Slavic room Slavic & Central European Div 60-64; Asst hd hdqrs lib NASA, Wash DC 64-65, Hd hdqrs lib 65-. 14: Admin, info stor & ret. 15: 7109 Ft Hund rd, Alexandria Va 22307.

STRITMAN, HARRY R. b NYC 8 My 08. 4: Henriette Remmert. 5: UMinn 27-32(Forestry) BS, 35-36 (LS) Certif; Columbia 40-41 (LS). 6: Ital. 7: Clerical & Prof grades Pub Lib, Minneapolis 25-45; (Capt) US Army Infantry, Mil Intelligence 42-45; Chief of sect US Dept of State, Wash DC 45-46; Attache in the diplomatic serv, For Serv of the US, publ procurement, sec & consul, Rome, New Delhi, Trinidad WI, Milan 46-63; Internat economist on detail to US Dept of Com 59-61; Dir LC PL 480 Proj Amer Embassy, Tel-Aviv, Israel 63-. 9: ALA (chm Jr Mems Round Table 41-42). 10: Amer for Serv Assn, Wash DC. 15: Processing Dept Lib of Congress, Wash DC 20540.

STRODACH, CATHARINE (MacDONALD). b Malden Mass. 4: George K Strodach. 5: Mt Holyoke 25-29 (Lat) AB; Simmons 30-31 BS in LS. 6: Fr. 7: Catlgr Yale Law Lib 31-38; Catlgr Lafayette Col 38-44; Libn Kirby Lib of Govt & Law Lafayette Col 63-. 10: LWV; Phi Beta Kappa. 14: Catlg. 15: 509 Mixsell st, Easton Penn 18042.

STROHECKER, EDWIN CHARLES. b LENOWN Penn 22 F 2. 4: Virginia Bell Nunn. 5: UKy 43-44 (Engnr); Penn State Col (Kutztown) 42-43, 46-49 (Hist, LS) BSEd; Peabody 49-50 MA; UMich 52-55 (Geog, LS). 6: Fr. 7: Staff Sgt Army Staff Message Control SHAEF 43-46; Asst libn circ ref Gettysburg Col 49-50; Instr in Lib Sci E Tex State Col 50-52, Act dir of lib serv summer 52; Asst math-econ Lib UMich 52-53, Libn Sch of Educ 53-55; Asst Prof of Lib Sci Kent State U 55-58; Org & catlgr of Sch Lib Northwest Sch Dist Canal Fulton Ohio 56; Storyteller Peninsula Pub Lib, Peninsula Ohio summers 56, 57; Asst libn chief catlgr LSU (New Orleans) 58-59; Chm Dept of Lib Sci, Catherine Spalding Col 59-. 8: Exec Dir, Nat Lib Week Ky 60-61. 9: OhioLA (bus mgr Bulletin 57-58); OhioASchL (chm Research Com 56-57); KyLA (chm Educ Com 64-66; chm Col & Ref Sect 61-62); Louisville Lib Club (chm var coms 59-63); ALA-LED (chm Tchrs Sect Nominating Com 66-67; chm Asia Foundation Grant com 67-71; coun 67). 10: Beta Phi Mu; Phi Delta Kappa; Kappa Delta Pi; Alpha Beta Alpha; Louisville Lib Club. 13: Yes. 14: Catlg, devel of child lit, admin, lib educ. 15: 800 Apartments #310, Louisville Ky 40203.

STROMAN, JOSH. b Ardmore Okla 11 O 38. 5: Okla State U 56-60 (Journalism) BA; UOkla 60-64 (Journalism, LS) MLS. 6: Ger. 7: Asst documents libn Okla State U Lib 64-. 9: ALA; OklaLA (chm Tech Serv Div 67-68); SWLA. 10: Sigma Delta C.i. 12: Ed "Oklahoma Librarian" (67-69). 14: Govt, docs, ref, catlg. 15: Okla State Univ Lib, Stillwater Ok 74074.

STROMER, PETER ROBERT. b Norwich Conn 16 Jl 29. 4: Martha Best. 5: UConn 48-49; UAriz 49-50; Syracuse 51-52 (LS) BA; Lincoln U 68 (Law) JD. 6: Fr. 7: US Army 46-47; Ref & circ libn David Taylor Model Basin, Wash DC 52-54; Libn Naval Powder Factory, Indian Head Md 54-56; Libn light mil electronics dept General Electric Co, Schenectady NY 56-59; Supv ref staff Hanford Labs General Electric Co, Richland Wash 59-62; Research info spec Lockheed Missiles & Space Co, Palo Alto Cal 62-68; Supv Tech Info Ctr Philco-Ford Corp, Palo Alto Cal 68-. 9: SLA; CalLA. 13: Yes. 14: Ref, admin, bibliog, legal research, info retr. 15: 2478 Alvin st, Mountain View Ca 94040.

STRONER, SANDRA JEANNE. b Berwyn Ill 8 Ap 41. 5: Marygrove Col 58-62 (Speech, Drama) BA; Rosary Col 62-63 MALS. 7: Child libn Chicago Pub Lib Norwood-Edison Br 63-66; Asst child libn Skokie Pub Lib, Skokie Ill 66-68; Dir child serv Evanston Pub Lib, Evanston Ill 68-. 9: ALA (Recr Netwk); CathLA; IllLA (Recruiting Netwk; CSD); NoIllCathLA (sec 66-68; CBW chm 66). 10: Lib Bd, sec, Grove Pub. Lib, Fox River Grove Ill. 13: Yes. 14: Child serv, story-telling. 15: 1000 Loyola, Chicago Il 60626.

STRONG, BLONDELL M. b Ft Pierce Fla 11 Ja 43. 4: Stanford Strong Sr. 5: Tenn State U 60-63 (Music Educ) BS, summer 64; Peabody summer 65, 66, 67 MLS. 07: Libn & instr Lincoln R Col 64-65; Asst libn Indian River Jr Col 65-67; Head libn Meharry Med Col 67-. 7: Libn & instr Lincoln Jr Col 64-65; Asst libn Indian River Jr Col 65-67; Head libn Meharry Med Col 67-. 9: MedLA (Dental Group sec 69); TennLA. 10: Alpha Kappa Alpha; Club Utilitas; Kappa Delta Pi. Pi; Beta Phi Mu. catlg. Catlg, commun media, admin. lpha; Club Utilitas; Kappa Delta Pi; Beta Phi Mu. 14: Catlg, commun media, admin. 15: 334 So 4th st, Nashville Tn 37206.

STRONG, DONALD RUSSELL. b Homer City Pen 2 Mr 31. 4: Mabel McKelvey. 5: UPittsburgh 49-56 (Eng) AB; Carnegie 57-58 MLS. 6: Ital, Ger. 7: Readers asst Carnegie Lib of Pittsburgh 58-60; Head bkmob serv, Head ya & Browsing div Dayton & Mongomery Co Pub Lib, Dayton Ohio 60-64; Libn W Liberty State Col 64-. 9: ALA-ACRL (Tri-State Chap); WVaLA. 13: Yes. 15: Box 187, West Liberty WVa 26074.

STRONG, GARY EUGENE. b Moscow Idaho 26 Je 44. 5: UIda 62-66 (Eng) BSEd; UMich 66-67 MALS. 6: Sp. 7: Admin asst UIda Lib 63-66; Bkmob libn Latah Co Lib, Moscow Ida 66; Hd libn Markley Residence Hall Lib, Ann Arbor Mich 66-67; Dir Lake Oswego Pub Lib, Lake Oswego Ore 67-. 8: Vis lectr Lib Sci Marylhurst Col summer 68. 9: ALA; PNLA (Exec Bd Pub Libs Div 67-68); OreLA (Mem-at-Large Exec Bd 68-69); IdahoLA. 10: Alpha Phi Omega. 13: Yes. 14: Admin, ref, catlg. 15: 706 4th st, Lake Oswego Or 97034.

STRONG, IVANA (POZAJIC). b Zagreb Yugoslavia 8 Jl 34. 4: Michael Strong. 5: UZagrer 52-57 (Eng) Diploma Philos; UToronto 63-66 (German) BA, 66-67 BLS. 6: Serbo-Croatian, Ger, Fr, Russian, Sp, Ital. 7: Tr Dubonnet, Paris 59-60; Tri-lingual sec Orema, Paris 60-61; Publ dept Berlitz, Paris 61-63; Lib asst UToronto 63-66, Catlgr rare bk dept 67-. 14: Rare bks. 15: Apt 707 33 Rosehill ave, Toronto 7 Ont Can.

STRONG, MARILYN H. b Batavia NY 10 Jl37. 5: State U Col (Brockport NY) 54-58 (Elem Educ) BS; State Univ Col (Geneseo NY) 63-64 LS. 7: Elem tchr Elba Central Sch, Elba NY 58-62; Elem tchr Jackson Sch, Batavia NY 6-63; Asst libn State U Col (Brockport NY) 64-. 9: ALA; SUNYLA. 10: Faculty Assn SUNY; Kappa Delta Phi. 13: Yes. 14: Ref, pub serv. 15: 8 Dewey ave, Batavia NY 14020.

STROTHMAN, JANET. b Orange NJ 7 O 26. 5: Smith 44-48 (Eng Lit) BA; Columbia 48-51 (Early Childhood Educ); UCal(Berkeley) 59 MLS. 6: Fr, Sp. 7: Tchr Agnes Russell Ctr Tchrs Col Columbia 48-51, USAF Dependents' Schs, London & Chester England 51-53, Woodrow Wilson Sch, Daly City Cal 54-56, E St Sch, San Rafael Cal 56-58; Libn Gen Lib UCal(Berkeley) 59-62; Libn San Jose Sch Dist, Hamilton AFB Cal 62-64; Dist libn San Anselmo Elem Schs, San Anselmo Cal 64-66; Libn San Ramon High Sch, Danville Cal 66-69. 8: Consul on ESEA applications for sch libs Cal State Dept of

Educ 66. 9: ALA; NEA (Mildred Batchelder Prize Com 70); CalLA; CalTA; Assn Child Libns No Cal; Bay Area YA Libn-s. 10: Sierra Club; Audubon Society; Wilderness Soc; ACLU; KQED (commun TV, non-commercial); KPFA (listener-sponsored radio). 13: Yes. 14: Sch libs, child lit, ref. 15: 1535 Walnut st, Berkeley Ca 93709.

STROUP, BETTY ANNE. b Pittsburgh Penn 4 Jl 23. 5: UPittsburgh 41-45 (Eng) BA, 45-48 (Eng) MA, 65-66 MS in LS. 7: Instr in Eng UPittsburgh 45-65; Asst libn Mt Lebanon Pub Lib, Pittsburgh Penn 66-68, Hd libn 68-. 9: ALA; PennLA. 14: Adult serv, ref. 15: 1238 Varner dr, Pittsburgh Pa 15227.

STROUP, ELIZABETH F. b Tulsa Okla 25 Mr 39. 5: Chicago 57-58 (Pre-Med); UWash 58-62 (Philos) BA, 63-64 (LS) ML. 6: Fr, Ger. 7: Bkseller Shield's Book Store, Richland Wash 61; Libn Boeing Co, Seattle 63-64; Grad asst UWash Sch of Libnship summer 64; Intern LC 64-65, Info Systems Research Asst 65; Asst dir N Central Reg Lib, Wenatchee Wash 66-. 8: Consul for lib automation Wash State Lib 66-67. 9: ALA; ASIS; WashLA; PNLA. 10: ACLU; Beta Phi Mu; Wilderness Soc; LWV. 13: Yes. 14: Lib automation & systems analysis, bk sel & acquis, ref. 15: 310 Douglas st, Wenatchee Wa 98801.

STROUP, RUTH M. b Pittsburgh 28 Ap26. 5: Westminster Col (Penn) 43-47 (Ger) AB; Carnegie 47-48 BSLS; UPittsburgh 52-55 (Educ) MEd. 6: Ger. 7: Asst libn Carnegie Lib of Pittsburgh 48-51; Elem sch libn West Mifflin Area Schs, Penn 51-. 9 ALA; NEA; NCTE; PennLA (Sch Libns Dept); Penn State EA; PennASchL (reg rep 64-66; sec 66-68). 10: Pittsburgh Coun of Suburban Libns (Sch). 14: Sch libs. 15: 1238 Varner dr, Pittsburgh Pa 15227.

STROUSE, DOROTHY IRENE. b Worthington Ind 2 O 01. 5: DePauw U 24-25; IndU 25-26; West Res 26-27 (LS) Certif. 7: Libn pub lib, Worthington 21-25; Catlgr Lucas Co Lib, Maumee Ohio 27-29, Libn 29-. 9: ALA (chm Co & Reg Lib Sect 4748; pres Lib Ext Sect 5455); OhioLA (pres 4546). 10: Zonta Intl; LWV. 11: Libn of year OhioLA 64. 13: Yes. 14: Ext. 15: 823 River rd, Maumee Oh 43537.

STROUSE, PAMELA M. b Punxsutawney Penn 17 AP 42. 5: Clarion State Col 60-63 (LS) BS. 7: Libn Conneaut Valley Schs, Conneautville Penn 63-65; Libn Conneaut City Schs, Conneaut Ohio 65-; Elkhart Pub Lib, Elkhart Ind. 14: Ref. 15: 7 Florence lane, Elkhart In 46514.

STROUT, DONALD E(VERETT). b Livermore Falls Me 24 Ag 09. 4: Ruth Beamer. 5: Bates 26-30 (Lat, Greek) AB; UIll 30-33 (Classics) MA, PhD; UMich 38-40 ABLS. 6: Lat, Greek, Ger, Fr. 7: Tchg asst Bates Col, Greek Dept 27-29, Latin Dept 29-30; UIll(Urbana) Univ fellow 30-33, Research asst 33-34; Prof Lat & Greek Ashland Col 34-35; Prof classics Hastings Col 35-38; Lib asst UMich Physics Lib 38-40; Gen serv libn UMo(Columbia) 40-42; Chief docs libn IndU(Bloomington) 42-43; Instr (math) US Army Spec Train Program 43; Assoc prof lib sch UMinn(Minneapolis) 44-48; Dir libs UDenver 48-53, Asst dir Sch Libnship 48-50, Dir Sch Libnship 50-53; Assoc prof Grad Sch Lib Sci UIll 53-59, Prof 59-63; Visiting prof Tex Women's U 64-65. 8: Chm, Allerton Park Insts, UIll fall 56, 61; Dir Mo Inst for Grad Libns, UMo 60, 61; Research consul, Mo State Lib, Jefferson City 61-62. 9: ALA (Coun 47-49, 61-63; Minn State Chm Fund to Establish Wash DC Off 45-47; Com on Wk with the Blind 50-52; Com on Lib Insurance 53-54; Pres & Editors' RT (pres 47-48);-LED (pres 53-54);-ACRL; BSA. 10: AAUP; Phi Beta Kappa; Beta Phi Mu. 11: Recipient, Intel Freedom Award, IllLA 61. 12: "Project Penguin" (55); Co-auth "A Study of Larger Unit Dimensions with Special Reference to Missouri Regional Libraries" (62); Ed AALS "Newsletter" 48-52; ALA-LED "Newletter" 53-54; ALA Intel Freedom "Newsletter" 57-60. 13: Yes. 14: Lib serv to adults, collection bldg, intel freedom & censorship, hist of bks, publ. 15: Box 617, Forsyth Mo 65653.

STRUFFERT, IRENE. b Orland Cal 7 F 20. 5: Fresno State Col 38-42 (Eng) AB; UCal(Berkeley) 44-45 (LS) Certif. 7: Catlgr Col of Agric UCal(Davis) 45-47; Catlgr UCLA 47-50; Army libn, Tokyo 50-53; Ref libn Sacramento State Cal 53-54; Base libn Ladd AFB, Fairbanks Alaska 54-55; Catlg sect head Engnr & Math Sci Lib UCLA 55-. 14: Catlg. 15: 11625 Kiowa ave, apt 5, Los Angeles Ca 90049.

STUARD, EVELYN (COVEY). b Federalsburg Md 1 Ja 08. 5: Sweet Briar Col 25-26: Hood Col 26-29 (Eng) AB; Cornell U summer 41; Drexel 61-62 MS in LS. 7: Tchr Bd of Educ: Milton Del 29-30, Laurel Del 31-33, Genoa NY 43-45; Libn Bd of Educ, Newport News Va 62-. 9: ALA; VaLA; VaEA; NEA; SELA. 10: Beta Phi Mu; Delta Kappa Gamma. 15: 8 Cameron dr, Newport News Va 23606.

STUART-STUBBS, BASIL FREDERICK. b Moncton NB Can 3 F 30. 4: Nancy Ballard. 5: UBC 48-52 (Philos) BA; McGill 53-54 BLS. 6: Fr, Sp. 7: Ref libn McGill U 54-56; UBC: Catlg libn 56-58, Ser libn 58-60, Spec collections libn 60-62, Supv of collections 62-63, U Libn 64-. 9: ALA; CanLA; PNLA; BCLA; ABCL; Assn Canadienne des Bibliothecaires de Langue Francaise. 13: Yes. 14: Rare bks, hist cartography, admin, collections, automation. 15: 1832 Allison rd, Vancouver BC Can.

STUART, FRANCES (CROOK). b Cameron SC 7 Je 19. 4: Thomas B Stuart. 5: USCar 36-40 (Hist) AB; Peabody 43 BS in LS. 7: Tchr-libn Calhoun Falls SC 40-41; Circ libn South Caroliniana Lib, Columbia SC 41-45; Asst & Bkmob libn Carnegie Pub Lib, Sumter SC 46-48, Act libn 49-51; Dept libn Army Lib Serv, Ft Jackson SC 51-53; Asst libn Bus &Tech Lib Atlas Powder Co, Wilmingtion Del 54; Hosp libn Army Lib Serv, Ft Jackson SC 56-57; Catlgr SC State Lib B, Columbia SC 57-66; Catlgr Richland Tech Educ Ctr, Columbia SC 66-. 8: Eval com So Assn Schs & Cols 69. 9: ALA; SELA; SCLA. 14: Catlg. 15: 3546 Greenlead rd, Columbia SC 29206.

STUART, G WILLIAM JR. b Yuba Cty Cal 28 Jl39. 5: UCal(Davis) 59-62 (Hist) AB Honors; UCal(Berkeley) 62-63 MLS. 6: Fr, Sp. 7: Rare bk libn Cornell U 64-68; Bibliogr scholarly collections Huntington Lib, Pasadena Cal 68-. 9: BSA. 10: Grolier Club (NY); Phi Beta Kappa; Phi Kappa Phi. 11: Lilly Fellowship, The Lilly Lib, Bloomington Ind. 13: Yes. 14: Rare bks. 15: 444 Ninita pkwy, Pasadena Ca 91106.

STUART, MARION MORGAN. b Beloit Wis. 5: Rockford Col 30-31; Beloit Col 32 (UWis) Madison 36-37; UCal(Berkeley) 50-51; 58-61 (Eng) BA 61-63 (LS) MA; Cal Sch Libns Credential 63-. 7: Bibliog UCal (Berkeley) 63-65, Asst to forestry libn 65-, Ms catlg papers of Emanuel Fritz 66-67. 9: CalLA. 10: Phi Beta Kappa; Phi Beta Mu; Amer Fed of Tchrs; Womens Faculty Club, Berkeley. 14: Machine techniques in libs, spec libs, ms catlg. 15: 2428 Jefferson st, Berkeley Cal 94703.

STUART, NANCY MacLAREN. b Halifax NS Can 3 Jl 5: Dalhousie U 59-63 (Eng, Hist) BA; Toronto 63-64 BLS. 7: Bkmob libn Halifax Mem Lib, Halifax NS 64-66; Sers libn Dalhousie U 66-67, Bibliog libn 68-. 8: Helped prepare bibliog for Learning Disabilities Clinic summer 67. 9: CanLA; Halifax LA (Com on Lib Serv to Handicapped); APLA. 10: Jr League University Womens Club; Alliance Francais; Ski Club; NS Heritage Trust; Halifax Film Soc; DalhousieU Alumnae. 13: Yes. 14: Circ. 15: 1576 Larch st, Halifax NS Can.

STUB, HELEN E. b Des Moines Iowa 26 My25. 5: Grand View Col 44-46; Uminn (Minneapolis) 46-48 (Eng) BS in E, summers 55-57 (LS) MA. 6: Scandinavian. 7: Tchr-libn Fairfax (Minn) schs 48-52; Tch-libn St Paul (Minn) Park schs 52-56; Libn Minneapolis pub schs Franklin Jr High Sch 56-57, Libn Edison High Sch 57-. 8: Consul instr materials Minneapolis Bd of Educ 66; Tchr, UMinn 62-65, State Col of Iowa summers 59-65; White House Conf on Educ. 9: ALA-AASchL (YP Com to select Best Adult Bks for YP); MinnASchL (treas 58). 10: Amer Fed of Tchrs; Minneapolis Fed of Tchrs. 12: Ed & comp "Orohda Va Vitabu, Bibliography of Afro-American Life". 14: Wk with yp, educ, intercultural & compensatory educ. 15: 501 E 36th st, Minneapolis 55408.

STUBBE, CECELIA ANN (DORAN). b Perry Iowa 18 D 34. 4: Jean Fred Stubbe. 5: State Col Iowa 53-57 (LS) BA; Peabody Col for Tchrs 60-63 (LS) MA. 6: Fr. 7: Tchr-libn Peetz Commun, Peetz Colo 57-59; Libn Kurtz Jr High Sch, Des Moines Iowa 59-63; Libn Berg Jr High Sch, Newton Iowa 63-66; Libn Sr High Sch, Newton Iowa 67-. 8: Chm Lib Sect Iowa State Teachers Convention in 62 (Des Moines Iowa). 9: NEA; ALA; IowaStateEA; NCEA; IowaASchL. 10: Alpha Beta Alpha; Beta Phi Mu. 14: Child & ya wk, ref. 15: 717 First ave E, Newton Ia 50208.

STUBBS, EDWARD N. b Brooklyn NY 18 Ag37. 4: Sarah Stubbs. 5: St Johns U 55-56, 58-61 (Soc Sci) BA; Rutgers 63-65 MLS. 6: Fr, Ger, Sp. 7: Employment Interviewer NY State Employment Serv, NYC 61-63; Libn trainee Brooklyn Pub Lib 63-65, Libn 65-66; Instr Queensborough Commun Col 66-68; Sr libn Brooklyn Pub Lib, Brooklyn NY 68-. 9: ALA; NYLA. 10: AAUP. 14: Pub serv, admin, tech serv. 15: 1 - 74th st, Brooklyn NY 11218.

STUBBS, GORDON T. b Manchester ENG My 18. 4: Elizabeth C Leslie. 5: Manchester U 35-40 (Music) Mus B;

UBC 63-64 BL, 64-65 (Educ) MA. 6: Fr. 7: Tchr, Eng 40-51; Exch tchr Hamilton Jr High Sch, Pittsburgh 51-52; Tchr East Calder Sch, Scotland 52-53; Tchr Jr Sec Sch, Chilliwack BC 53-54; chr Como Lake Sec Sch, Coquitlam BC 54-57, Libn 57-65; Asst Prof UBC 65-. 9: CanLA; ALA; BCSchLA; ABCL; PNLA. 10: Royal Can Col of Organists; Vancouver Art Gallery Assn; Vancouver Commun Arts Coun. 13: Yes. 14: Sch libnship, lib educ. 15: 4830 Osler st, Vancouver BC Can.

STUBBS, KENDON LEE. b Wash DC 6 Ap38. 4: Patricia Townsend. 5 St Johns Col 56-60 (Liberal Arts) BA; UVa 60-64 (Eng) MA; Columbia 64-65 (LS) MS. 6: Lat, Fr, Ger, Gk, Icelandic. 7: UVa Lib: Lib asst in ref 61-63, Sr asst in mss 63-64, 65, Act ref libn 65-66, Act acquis libn 67-68, Ref libn 66-. 9: Bibliog Soc Va (asst sec-treas); ALA; VaLA. 10: African Studies Assn. 13: Yes. 14: Ref, bibliog, Africana. 15: Reference div, Univ of Va Lib, Charlottesville Va 22901.

STUCKI, CURTIS WILLIAM. b LaCrosse Wis 24 O28. 4: Yasuko Hirabayshi. 5: Cornell Col 46-47, 48-50 (Hist) BA; UOre 7-48, 50-51, 53-54 (Hist) MA; UIll 54-56 (LS) MS. 7: Troop info & educ US Army (Cpl) 51-53; Bkstacks asst UIll (Urbana)54-56; Ref libn & bibliogr NY State Sch of Ind & Labor Rel Cornell U 56-60; Head Spec Collections dept Iowa 60-62, Head catlg dept 61-63; Chief catlg libn UWash 63-. 9: ALA (Life mem; Memb Com);-Internat Rel Round Table; PNLA. 10: Beta Phi Mu; Puget Sound Mycolog Soc. 12: Comp "American Doctoral Dissertations on Asia, 1933-1966" (68) Ed "Industrial and Labor Relations Abstracts and Annotations (57); Comp "Recent Publications in "Industrial and Labor Relations Review eview (56-60). 13: Yes. 14: Catlg, rare bks, libs in Asian countries. 15: Univ of Wash Lib, Seattle 98105.

STUCKY, MARTHA. b McPherson Kan 3 Ap19. 5: Bethel Col (Kan) 38-43 (Eng) AB; UDenver summers 49 & 50, 52 (LS) MA; Kan State U summer; UDenver summer. 6: Ger. 7: Tchr-libn Henderson High Sch, Henderson Neb 43-46; Tchr-libn Lane Co Commun High Sch, Dighton Kan46-51; Catlgr Kan State U 53-56; High sch libn Manhattan High Sch, Manhattan Kan 56-64; Coordinator of lib serv Unified Sch Dist 383, Manhattan Kan 64-. 8: Summer sch tchg Kan State Tchrs Col 60 & 65, Ft Hays Kan State Col 61, UOkla 66-67. 9:NEA; NEA; (reg chm Standards Com; Kan State Tchrs Assn (Bk Sel Com for Reading Circl); KanLA (sec; chmCatlgrs Chm Catlgrs Sect; v-pres 68-69, chm-elect; pres 69-70); (sec, pres; chm Nomin Com; dist dir); MPLA. 10: Bus & Prof Womens Club; Delta Kappa Gamma; AAUW; Phi Sigma Alpha. 14: Sch libnship. 15; 417 Fremont, Manhattan Kan 66502.

STUDHALTER, MARGARET RUTH. b Berkeley Cal 24 O 19. 5: Tex Tech Col 36-39(Span) BA; UTex 39-41 (Span) MA; UCal 46-47 BS in LS. 6: Sp, Fr, Ger, Ital, Portu, Catalan. 7: Gen asst Latin Amer Collection UTex 41-42; Censorship clerk Tr Off of Censorship, San Antonio Tex 42-45; Asst custodian W Tex Museum Tex Tech Col 45-46; Catlgr UCal Lib (Berkeley) 48-50; Catlgr Columbus Mem Lib Pan American Union, Wash DC 50; Catlgr, Libn III UCal Lib (Berkeley) 50-. 14: Catlg. 15: 2510 Bancroft way, Berkeley Cal 94704.

STUDLEY, HELEN V. b Austin Tex 9 Jl 06. 4: Hiram Orville Studley. 5: West Res -27 (Eng) BA, 62-64 MSLS. 7: Asst dir Central Volunteer Bur Welfare Fed, Cleveland 50-56; Libn Intern CUYAHOGA Co Lib, Cleveland 62-64; Adult serv libn Garfield Heights-Co Lib, Cleveland 64-, Br hd Garfield Hts 66-67, Hd Reg Lib S Euclid 67-. 9: ALA; OhioLA. 13: Yes. 14: Ref, admin. 15: 31905 Jackson rd, Chagrin Falls Ohio 44022.

STUDWELL, WILLIAM EMMETT. b Stamford Conn 18 Mr 36. 4: Ann Stroia Studwell. 5: UConn 54-58 (Hist) BA, 58-59 (Hist) MA; CatholicU 64-67 MSLS. 6: Fr, Sp, Russian. 7: Abstractor-indexer LC Aerospace Tech Div 63-66, Asst ed (tech specialist) Decimal Clsf Div 66-68; Hd libn Kirtland Commun Col 68-. 8: Mem US Study Gp to Revise the Univ Decimal Clsf under Auspices of Nat Acad of Scis, Wash DC 68-. 9: ALA. 10: Phi Beta Mu. 12: Sci & tech sects & index, 18th ed, "Dewey Decimal Classification". 14: Clsf, bk sel, admin. 15: Rte 1 Box 62, Roscommon Mi 48653.

STUEART, ROBERT D. b Monticello Ark 1 Je35. 4: Marie-Luise Hille. 5: So State Col 53-56 (Eng) BA; LSU 60-62 (LS) MS; UColo 62-65 (Anthrop, Russian); UPittsburgh 68- (Lib & Info Sci). 6: Russian, Ger. 7: UColo: Order libn 62-63, Ser catlgr 63-64, Head circ dept 64-65, Admin asst libn 65-66; Asst dir for systs & processes Penn State U 66-68; PhD Fellow UPittsburgh Grad Sch of Lib Sci 68-. 8: Russian course Army Lang Sch, Monterey Cal 57-58. 9: ALA; AALS. 10: Phi Beta Mu; Pi Delta Pi; AAUP. 14: Tech proc, admin, lib educ. 15: 6623 Ridgeville st, Pittsburgh Pa 15217.

STUFF, MARJORIE ANN. b Lincoln Neb 14 J106. 5: UNeb 23-29 (Eng Lit) BA; Bryn Mawr 29-31 (Eng Lit) MA; U Col ULondon 32-33 (Eng Lit, Ger Philol); Sorbonne summer 33 (Fr Lit & Lang): State U Iowa 33-36 (Eng Lit, Ger Philol); Columbia 37-38 (LS) BS. 6: Fr, Ger. 7: Catlgr Stetson U 38-39; Lib asst UNeb 39-40, Ser catlgr 40-43; Catlgr spec collections & Act curator rare bks Ind U 43; Asst catlg libn UNeb 44-46; Head order & catlg dept Stephens Col 46-52; Head libn Neb Wesleyan U 52-54; Head ref dept Omaha Pub Lib 54-56; Libn Hist of Med Div NLM, Bethesda Md 56-. 9: ALA (Coun 52-56)-ACRL (Rare Bk Sect); -RTSD (Catlg & Clsf Sect); MedLA; Amer Assn Hist of Med; Washington Soc Histof Med; DCLA; Potomac Tech Proc Libns. 10: Phi Beta Kappa; Alpha Chi Omega; PEO. 13: Yes. 14: Catlg, ref, rare bks. 15: 4949 Battery lane, apt 214, Bethesda Md 20014.

STUHL, ANNA NANCY (SCHWARTZMAN). b Yassy Roumania 10 Ap 24. 4: Albert Stuhl. 5: Sir George Williams Col (Montreal) 42-45 (Chem, Biol) BSc; Rutgers 57-59 MLS. 6: Fr, Roumanian, Russian. 7: Ext libn Monmoutn Co Lib, Freehold NJ 59-64, Prin libn 65-. 9: NJLA; ALA; Monmouth Co (NJ) LA (recording sec). 10: NJ Co Lib Staff Mems Assn. 14: Catlg, circ, ext. 15: 1018 Bendermere ave, Wanamassa NJ 07712.

STULIGOWA, ANNA KRYSTYNA. b St Andrews Scotland 7 F 43. 5: Barnard 60-64 (Russian Area Studies) BA; Columbia 64-66 (Russian Lit) MA, 66-68 MLS. 6: Russian, Fr, Polish. 7: Bibliog asst Coumbia U Libs 66-68; Soviet studies bibliogr Cornell U Lib 68-. 9: ALA. 14: Acquis, sel (Soviet studies). 15: 522 Dryden rd, Ithaca NY 14850.

STULL, SARAH LOUISE. b Thompsonville Ill 3 Ag 17. 5: UIll 43-57 (Eng) BA, 57-58 (LS) MS. 6: Sp. 7: Lib clerk Pub Lib, Urbana Ill 41-44; Lib asst freshman reading room UIll 44-49, Sr lib clerk Undergrad Lib 49-55; Sch libn Commun Consolidated Sch, Evanston Ill 58-59; Curriculum libn Fresno State Col 59-66; Chief soc sci lib UAriz (Tucson) 66-67; Curriculum lib & Asst Prof Fresno State Col 67-. 9: ALA-Internat Rel Round Table; -ACRL; CalLA; CalASchL; Assn Cal State Col Profs. 10: Fresno Camera Club; Photographic Soc Amer. 13: Yes. 14: Child lit & ref. 15: 1274 E Vartikian, Fresno Ca 93726.

STULTZ, GEORGE B. b Rockford Ill 4 Jl20: 04: Virginia F Holdford. 5: Morehead State Col 49-52 (Educ) BS; UIll 52-53 (LS) MS. 7: Power turret maintenance US Army Air Force 42-45; Asst engnr lib UIll (Urbana) 53; Engnr libn Goodyear Atomic Corp, Portsmouth Ohio 53-56; Libn Phillips Petroleum Co, Idaho Falls Ida 56-66; Libn Ida Nuclear Corp, Idaho Falls Ida 66-. 9: SLA; PNLA; IdaLA. 13: Yes. 14: Admin, ref, catlg. 15: 180 E Anderson st, Idaho Falls Ida 83401.

STUMM, ROBERT H. b St James Minn 17 Je 16. 4: Marion Jackson. 5: UMinn 52-54 (Hist) BA, 54-55 (LS) MA. 6: Fr. 7: Geodetic computer US Army Field Artillery (Sgt) 41-45; RR brakeman C St P M & O RR, St James Minn 45-56; Ref libn (S/Sgt) Army Transportation Sch Lib, Ft Eustis Va 46-51; UMinn Lib: Jr libn spec collections 55-56, Libn ref dept 56, Sr libn ref dept 57-63, Instr & libn ref dept 63-64, Instr & libn Map Lib 64-66, Instr & libn Law Lib 66-. 9: AALL. 10: AAUP. 14: Ref, law. 15: 1582 Fernwood, St Paul Mn 55108.

STURGIS, MARYLEE C(AROLYN) . b Collegeville Penn 9 Jl 27. 5: Ursinus Col 44-48 (Chem) BS; Columbia 48-49 (Organic Chem); UDel 49-51 (Organic Chem(MS; Carnegie 53-54 MS in LS. 6: Fr. 7: Lit chem Hercules Powder Co, Wilmington Del 51-53; Asst libn Pennsalt Chem, Wynmoor Penn 54-57; Libn Koppers Co Research Dept, Monroeville Penn 57-63; Libn FMC Corp Chem Res Center, Princeton NJ 63-. 9: ACS; SLA (Pittsburgh Chap; pres 60-61; Princeton-Trenton Chap pres 68-69; sec Chem Sect 64-65). 14: Acquis, bk sel, organic chem. 15: Apt 25, 206 Center hwy, Princeton NJ 08540.

STURSA, MARY LOU (STELTER). b Eau Claire Wis 18 Jl 29. 4: Leroy L Stursa. 5: Lawrence Col 47-49; UWis 49-51 (Bacteriology) BS; Fla StateU 66-69 (LS) MS. 6: Russian. 7: Bacteriologist Oscar Mayer Co, Madison Wis 51-53; Med tech Jackson Foundation, Madison Wis 59-61; Ser libn Fla State Lib 61-62; Research tech Fla StateU Bio Libn 62-66, Research assoc 67-69; Research libn Fla Development Commsn, Tallahassee 69-. 9: ALA; SLA; ASIS. FlaLA. 10: Beta Phi Mu; Tallahasse Women's Club; Girl Scouts Leader; Alpha Delta Pi. 14: Info sci, spec libs, indexing, etc. 15: 310 Glenview dr, Tallahassee Fl 32303.

STURTZ, REV RICHARD STEPHEN. b LOWVILLE NY 16 Ja 31. 5: Holy Cross Col 48-49 (Liberal Arts); Wadhams Hall Sem 49-52 (Philos) BA; Catholic U 52-56 (Theol), 56-57 MS in LS. 6: Lat, Fr, Koine Gk. 7: Head Libn Wadhams Hall Sem (Ogdensburg NY) 57-. 8: Diocesan priest; Master of Ceremonies to the Most Rev Bishop; Instr in Lat & Gk 57-67; Spiritual dir 67-. 9: ALA; CathLA No Country (NY) Ref Res & Resources Coun (trustee). 10: Beta Phi Mu. 14: Gk, Lat. 15: Wadhams Hall Sem, Ogdensburg NY 13669.

STUTTS, ANNIE LORRIE (MRS). b Slocomb Ala 29 My 07. 5: Judson Col 28 (magna cum laude), (Eng) BA; Auburn U 63 (LS) MEd. 6: Sp, Fr. 7: Tchr Slocomb High Sch, Slocomb Ala 38-57, Libn 57-. 8: Yp dir Southside Baptist Ch, Birmingham Ala 28-29; Libn 1st Baptist Ch, Slocomb Ala. 9: NEA; AlaASchL; AlaEA; AlaLA; SELA. 10: Delta Kappa Gamma; DAR; PTA; Judson Alumnae Assn. 11: Ala Youth Award from Birmingham News--. 14: Lib assts, catlg, av wk. 15: Box C, Slocomb Al 36375.

STUTZMAN, MARGARET (MULLEN). b Densmore Kan 20 N 10. 5: Ft Hays Kan State Col 35-38 (Bus Admin, Eng) BS; Kan State Tchrs Col (Emporia) 58 (LS) MS. 7: Tchr Wichita Co Commun High Sch, Leoti Kan 38-43; Tchr Seneca High Sch, Seneca Kan 43-47; Tchr-libn Baldwin High Sch, Baldwin Kan 47-61; Ref libn Baker U 61-65; Asst Prof of Libnship Kan State Tchrs Col (Emporia) 65-. 9: ALA; KanLA. 10: Delta Kappa Gamma; Pi Gamma Mu; AAUW; AAUP. 12: Comp & ed "The William Alfred Quayle Bible Collection: an Annotated Catalog" (62). 14: Ref, rare bks, govt docs, humanities. 15: 1233 Tomahawk rd, Emporia Ks 66801.

STUVE, WILLIAM EDWARD. b San Francisco Cal 20 D 31. 4: Kay Wright. 5: San Francisco State Col 55-56 (Sp) BA; Peabody 68-69 MLS. 6: Sp. 7: Tchr Washoe Co Schs, Reno Nev 61-68; Asst order libn Chico State Col 69-. 10: San Francisco Mycological Soc. 14: Acquis, ref. 15: Chico State Col Lib, Chico Ca 95926.

SU, TSUNG SHYUN. b Hupeh China. 5: National Wu-Han U (China) LLB; Catholic U 63-65 MS in LS. 6: Chinese, Sp, Japanese. 7: First sec Chinese Embassy, Mexico 53-56; Section chief Chinese Foreign Off, Taiwan 56-60; First sec Chinese Embassy, Australia 61-63; Catlgr John I Thompson Co, Wash DC 65-67; Indexer H W Wilson Co, NYC 67-68; Catlgr ALESCO, NJ 68-69; Libn NY Zool Soc, NYC 69-. 9: ALA; NY Lib Club. 14: Catlg, ref. 15: 1020 Grand Concourse, Bronx NY 10451.

SUBLETT, MARY (POWELL). b Mayfield Ky 23 Ja 06. 4: James L Sublett. 5: ULouisville 28 (Eng) AB; UIll 38 (LS) BS. 7: ULouisville Lib: Lib asst 28-33, Chief circ asst 34-40, Head of Circ Dept 40-51, Documents libn 51-. 9: ALA; SELA; KyLA; Louisville Lib Club. 14: Govt docs. 15: Univ of Louisville Lib, Louisville Ky 40208.

SUCHOWERSKY, CELESTIN NICHOAS. b Cherinvtsi Ukraine 8 My 13. 5: Gymnasium 25-33 Diploma de Bacaulareat; U King Karol 33-37 Diploma of Law, 37-39 Doctorate Pol Sci; UWash 59-60 MLS. 6: Ukrainian, Ger, Rumanian, Russian, Fr, Polish. 7: Barrister & soliciter Law Soc, Chernivtsi Ukraine 37-40; Manager Reichsnahrstand, Frankfurt/M 42-45; Manager legal off Undra & Iro, Aschaffenburg 46-49; Catlgr UAlta 60-64, Catlgr, Spec for Slavic Studies 64-; Asst Prof slavic bibliog 67, Bibliog slavic lit & langs & comparative lit 68. 9: Can Assn of Slaviss; Shevchenkos Sci So; Can Inst Internat Affairs; AltaLA; Edmonton LA; Assn of the Acad Staff UAlta. 10: Ukrainian-Can Com. 13: Yes. 14: Slavic & East European studies. 15: 13709 - 102 ave, Edmonton Alta Can.

SUDALL, ARTHUR D. b Yonkers NY 10 S 28. 4: Lillian Clark. 5: Hobart Col 46-50 (Sociol) BA; Columbia 54-56 (Music Educ) MA; Rutgers 64-65 MLS. 7: Clerk (Pfc) US Army Field Artillery, Ft Sill Okla 50-52; Jr soc case wker Dept of Welfare, Westchester Co NY 53; Music Instr Ft Kent State Normal Sch 57-60; Music tchr Portland & Deering High Schs, Portland Me 60-61; Music tchr Proctor High Sch, Proctor Vt 61-64; Jr libn Free Pub Lib of Woodbridge, Woodbridge NJ 65-66, Br libn Henry Inman Br 66-69; Dir Free Pub Lib, Rahway NJ 69-. 9: ALA; NJLA. 14: Ref, adult serv. 15: 17 Sand rd, Milltown NJ 08850.

SUDHEIMER, DIANE FAY (LARSON). b Spring Grove Minn 30 O 36. 5: Winona State Col 54-58 (Eng) BS; UMinn 61-64 (LS) MA. 6: Fr. 7: Libn Stewartville Pub Schs, Stewartville Minn 58-61; Libn Roseville Pub Schs, St Paul Minn 62-; Instr USask summer 65. 9: NEA; ALA; MinnEA; MinnASchl (sec Capitol Div 65-67). 14: Sch libs. 15: 705 Heinel cir, St Paul Mn 55113.

SUDOMLAK, GLADYS NADIA. b Winnipeg Man Can 22 S 38. 5: UMan 55-59 BA; McGill 61-62 BLS, 66-67 MLS. 7: Libn engnr Inst of Can (Montreal) summer 62; Libn Arch Lib UMan 62-66; Libn Air Can, Montreal summer 67; Libn Dept Nat Defence, Montreal 67-. 9: SLA. 14: Spec libs. 15: 440 Tinniswood Bay, Winnipeg 14 Man Can.

SUEMNICHT, VIRGINIA (TOLKSDORF). b Milwaukee 17 Mr 25. 4: Gilbert Suemnicht. 5: UWis(Milwaukee) 43-65 (Elem Educ) BS, 65-69 MLS. 6: Ger. 7: Tchr: Gravesville Sch, Chilton Wis 45-47, Lincoln Sch, Belgium Wis 56-58, Saukville Sch, Saukville Wis 58-59, Grafton Elem Sch, Grafton Wis 59-60; Tchr-libn Grafton Elem Schs, Grafton Wis 60-. 9: ALA; WisEA (Lib Div); Milwaukee Metro Libns; WisLA. 10: Bd, Pub Lib, Village of Grafton. 14: Sch libnship. 15: P O Box 2, Grafton Wis 53024.

SUESSMUTH, (ALBERT) CHARLES JR. b Houston 15 O 39. 4: Sharon Holm. 5: Tex A&M U 57-62 (Educ) BS; UTex 62-69 (LS) MLS. 7: Supv bus & tech room Houston Pub Lib 63-68; Chief libn Tenneco Inc, Houston 68-. 9: ALA; TexLA; Houston Lib Club; SLA. 14: Bus & tech ref. 15: 2636 Albans r, Houston 77005.

SUGARMAN, JOAN (GREEN). b Cleveland Ohio 22 S 17. 4: Norman A Sugarman. 5: Cleveland Col Case West Res 37-42 (Eng) AB; Case West Res 61-63 MS in LS. 6: Lat, Fr, Ger. 7: Libn Wash Hebrew Congregation, Wash DC 41-54; Libn Beachwood Ht (Ohio) Sch 63; Elem tchr The Temple, Cleveland Ohio 56-65; Elem libn Bryden Sch, Beachwood Ohio 64-66; Instr lib tech Cuyahoga Commun Col 67-68; Libn Dike Col 68-. 8: Tchr creative writing Jewish Commun Ctr, Univ Hts Ohio; Lecturer to; PTA (Onaway School); Writers; Wkshops; Lib Assns at Kent State; TV tape on Performing Arts series on Creative Writing for NBC 66. 9: ALA; OhioASchL; OhioLA. 11: 1st prize playwriting contest for child with The Lost Half Hour--, Wilmette Ill 68. 12: Coauth; Joel Finds Out-- (58) & wkbook (59), Inside the Synagogue-- (63) & wkbook (64). 13: Yes. 14: Wk with child, tchg lib techn & creative writing, writing for child, tchg storytelling to child & adults. 15: 2677 Green rd, Shaker Heights Oh 44122.

SUGDEN, BARBARA LEE. b Mt Clemens Mich 20 D 45. 5: West MichU 64-67 (Eng) BA; UPittsburgh 68-69 MLS. 6: Ger. 7: Tchr Charlevoix Pub Schs, Charlevoix Mich 68; Child libn N Babylon Pub Lib, N Babylon LI NY 69-. 9: ALA. 14: Child lit & serv. 15: 702 Park ave Box 33, Charlevoix Mi 49720.

SUGG, MARY JANE (NESBITT). b Columbus Ohio 16 Jl 14. 4: Harold Gray Sugg. 5: Oberlin 32-33; Denison 33-36 (Eng, Hist) AB; Carnegie Inst 36-37 BS in LS. 6: Fr, Ger. 7: Child libn Akron Pub Lib, Akron Ohio 37-40; Child libn Dist Lib, Wash DC 40-42; Sta libn Naval Air Sta, Corpus Christi Tex 42; Dist libn 7th Naval Dist, Miami Fla 43-44; Libn Norfolk Sch Syst, Norfolk Va 57-59; Tchr lib sci UVa Ext (Norfolk) 59-61; Hd processing dept Norfolk Pub Lib, Norfolk Va 61-63, Asst to city libn 64-68, Asst city libn 68-. 9: ALA; SELA; VaA. 10: AAUW; LWV; PTA; Friends of Lib; Forum Bd; De Paul Hosp Civic Bd. 14: Child lib wk, catlg, ref, ya, personnel. 15: 1300 Cloncurry rd, Norfolk Va 23505.

SUGGS, WAYNE (LUCAS). b Darlington SC 14 Jl 42. 4: Susan Goodsell. 5: Brigham Young 60-61 (Zoology); UUtah 64-67 (Zoology) BS; Immaculate Heart Col 67-69 MALS. 6: Fr. 7: Missionary Churcy of Jesus Christ of Latter Day Saints, France 61-64; Libn I Salt Lake Pub Lib, Salt Lake City 64-67; Reader's asst Pomona Pub Lib, Pomona Cal 67-. 9: ALA; CalLA. 12: "The Saunders Press" (68). 13: Yes. 14: Admin. 15: 1632 Alameda st, Pomona Ca 91767.

SUGHROE, PATRICIA. b Stockton Ill. 5: Rosary Col 42-46 (LS) BA; Loyola U 47; UColo summers 54; Rosary Col 61-65 MA (in LS). 6: Fr. 7: Asst catlgr Art Inst of Chicago 46-48; Bkmob libn Ill State Lib 48-50; Libn Fournier Inst of Tech, Lemont Ill 50-55; Arch libn UNotre Dame (nd) 55-56; Libn Argonne Nat Lab, Argonne Ill 56-66; Ref libn George Williams Col 67-. 8: Ed "Rosary Col News". 9: SLA; CathLA (Ill Unit); ALA; Libras. 14: Ref. 15: 615 W Chicago, Hinsdale Ill.

SUHLER, SAMUEL A(ARON). b Luling Tex 18 S 29. 5: UTex 46-50 (RADIO Broadcasting, Soc Sci) BFA; Southwest Tex State Col 51-54 (Hist) MEd; UTex 54-59 MLS, 66 (Hist) PhD. 6: Lat, Fr. 7: Tchr Aransas Co Ind Sch Dist, Rockport Tex 51-52; Tchr Flatonia Ind Sch Dist, Flatonia Tex 52-54; Circ asst Austin Pub Lib, Austin Tex 54-56, Ref asst 55-56, Asst ref libn 56-65; Soc sci research assoc in Tex Hist UTex 65-66; Fld consul S Tex area Tex State Lib 66-67; Libn II ref dept Fresno Co Free Lib, Fresno Cal 67-. 9: ALA; TexLA (past chm Dist 8); Tex State Hist Assn; Austin Lib Club; CalLA. 10: Phi Alpha Theta. 14: Ref, soc scis, local hist. 15: 250 N Calaveras apt 5, Fresno Ca 93701.

SULAIMAN, MOHAMMAD H KASFY. b Lebanon 12 Ja 31. 4: Huda Amin. 5: Grand Rapids Jr Col 57-59; Mich State U 59-60; West Mich U 61-63 (Eng, Soc Sci) BA; UMich 63-64 (Near East Hist) AM, 64-65 AMLS. 6: Arabic, Fr. 7: Libn II UMich Lib (Ann Arbor) 64-65, Libn III 65-66, Libn IV 66-69; Chief ref libn AmerU of Beirut Lebanon 69-. 10: Middle East Studies Assn North Amer. 13: Yes. 14: Ref, catlg. 15: Jafet Lib Amer Univ of Beirut, Beirut Lebanon.

SULJAK, NEDJELKO DINKO. b Zadar Yugoslavia 17 Ja 17. 4: Estelle Lasich. 5: UZagreb (Yugoslavia) 39 LLB; URome 46 (Law) Dr Jur; Chicago 52 (Pol Sci) MA; John Marshall Law Sch 61 LLM; Chicago 65 (LS) MA. 6: Serbo-Croatian, Russian, Ital, Fr, Lat, Gk. 7: Ref libn UCHICAGO Ind Rel Center 65-67; Ref libn UCal (Davis) 67-70, Hd Libn Inst Govt Affairs 70-. 8: Ed Amer-Croatian Newspaper, Chicago 52-54. 9: Amer Assn Internat Law; SLA; ALA. 14: Ref, rare bks, bibliogr. 15: 1005 J st, Davis Ca 95616.

SULLIVAN, ADA M. b Staten Island NY. 5: Mt Holyoke 31-35 (Eng Comp) BA; Columbia 36-39 (LS) BS. 6: Fr. 7: Ref asst DC Pub Lib 42-43; Lt (jg) Electronics US Navy WAVES, Wash DC 44-46; Catlgr DC Pub Lib 47-50; Libn US Info Serv, Hong Kong 50-52, Libn Tokyo 53-57; Catlgr Bell Telephone Labs, NYC & Holmdel NJ 58-. 9: SLA (chm-elect Engring Div 68-69). 14: Catlg, ref. 15: Bell Telephone Labs, Holmdel NJ 07733.

SULLIVAN, ANN MARY. b Columbus Ohio 24 Jl23. 5: Col of St Mary of the Springs 41-44 (Sociol) BA; Marywood COL 51-52 MA in LS. 6: Fr, Sp. 7: Br asst Columbus Pub Lib, Columbus Ohio 45-51, Asst child libn 52; Asst libn Col of St Mary of the Springs 52-53; Catlgr Ohio State U 53-. 9: ALA; OhioLA; Ohio Valley Group of Tech Serv Libs; Franklin Co LA. 14: Catlg. 15: 272 E Dunedin rd, COLUMBUS Ohio 43214.

SULLIVAN, BEN DELL. b Sanger Tex 7 Je 17. 5: Baylor 34-37 (Sp) BA; UTex (Austin) summers 38-40, 45 (Educ) MA; Tex Woman'sU 54-55 MLS. 6: Sp. 7: Tchr: Covington High Sch, Covington Tex 37-39, Somerville High Sch, Somerville Tex 39-42, Northside Jr High, Corpus Christi Tex 42-46, Stripling Jr High, Ft Worth 46-52, Meadowbrook Jr High, Ft Worth 52-54; Libn: Polytech High Sch, Ft Worth 55-56, Morningside Jr High, ft Worth 56-61, W A Meacham Middle Sch, Ft Worth 61-. 9: NEA; ALA; TexStateTA; TexLA (Memb Com Dist VII); Tex Assn Educl Tech, Ft Worth; Tarrant CoSchLA; TexClrTA. 10: Delta Kappa Gamma; Kappa Delta Pi; AAUW; Mary Elliott Lit Gp; Kappa Kappa Iota. 14: Lib serv to child & yp. 15: 2931 E Lancaster ave, Ft Worth Tx 76103.

SULLIVAN, CECIL GUINN. b Laurens SC 13 Je 08. 4: Frances Barth. 5: Presbyterian Col 26-31 (Eng) AB; Bucknell U 32, 34 (Hist) MA; COLUMBIA 38 (LS) BS. 6: Lat, Fr, Ger, Sp. 7: Tchr hist & math Gore High Sch, Gore Ga 31-32; Eng tchr Greenville High Sch, Greenville SC 36-37; Libn Wagner Col 38-43; Chief readers dept Washington Sq Lib NYU 43-49; Asst libn Com Lib NYU 49-65, Asst curator, Ref libn 65-. 9: ALA; SLA; BSA; NY Lib Club (treas 45-48). 10: France & Colonies Philatelic Soc; Soc of Philatelic Americans; Chess, NYU Faculty Club. 11: Alpha Phi Sigma. 14: Admin, ref. 15: 18 Metropolitan Oval, NYC 10462.

SULLIVAN, JEANNETTE TODD. b Concord Mass 8 F 14. 4: Max W Sullivan. 5: Mt Holyoke 31-35 (Hist of Art) AB; Columbia 38; Syracuse 65-66 MLS. 6: Lat, Fr, Ger, Sp, Ital. 7: Apprentice & designer Thomas Todd Co Printers, Boston 35-36; Sec & catlgr Fogg Mus harvard 37-39; Asst child room Concord Pub Lib, Concord Mass 41-42; Ed for survey of unemployment ins US Govt, Portland Ore 57; Sec to commsner Ore Centennial Commsn Portland 58-59; Crew leader US Govt Census, Portland Ore 59-60; Sec to pres Cazenovia Col 61-63; Sec 1st Presbyterian Ch, Cazenovia NY 63-64; Period libn SyracuseU 66, Art libn 66-. 14: Rare bks, child bks, art bks. 15: 120 Lincklaen st, Cazenovia NY 13035.

SULLIVAN, JO ANNE (STUBBLEFIELD). b Whitesburg Tenn 23 Ap 30. 4: Joe R Sullivan. 5: E Tenn State Col 47-50 (Eng, Soc Studies) BS; Peabody 51-52 MALS. 6: Sp. 7: Libn Grundy Co High Sch, Tracy City Tenn 50-51; Ref asst UTenn Lib Main Br 52-58; Oak Ridge Nat Lib, Oak Ridge Tenn: Circ, ref & period libn Y-12 Tech Lib, Circ & ref asst X-10 Lib, Bibliogr rector div 58-60; Circ & documents libn McNeese State Col 60-66; Libn Cherokee Elem Sch, Alexandria La 66-69. 9: ALA; LaLA; SWLA. 14: Ref, docs, readers serv, elem. 15: 6450 Sulgrave st, Memphis Tn 38106.

SULLIVAN, JOAN M. b Providence RI 2 Mr 39. 5: Bryant Col 56-58 (Bus Admin); US Dept of Agri Grad Sch of Lib Sci 68-69. 7: Asst humanities libn Brown U Lib 58-62; Asst libn Douglas Aircraft Co, Cal 62-63; Libn Nat Rural Elec Co-op Assn, Wash DC 63-64; Hd libn Chapman Col World Cruise (Educ Program) 64; Mgr, lib dept Communications Satellite Corp, Wash DC 65-. 9: SLA. 14: Ref. 15: 950 25th st NW, Wash DC 20037.

SULLIVAN, JOSEPH DANIEL. b NYC 28 S 10. 4: Anne Malloy. 5: Fordham 32-34, 36-38 (Soc Studies) BS; Syracuse U 48-49 BLS. 7: US Army, US, Africa, Italy 41-45; Tchr of soc studies Altmar-Parish Central Sch, Parish NY 45-47; Tchr of soc studies Christian Brothers Acad, Syracuse NY 47-48; Head of circ & ref St Michaels Col (Vt) 49-64, Libn 64-67, Asst dir 67-. 9: ALA; CathLA; NELA; NE Col LA; VTLA (sec Col & Spec Lib Sect); Vt Hist Soc; Champlain Valley LA. : Silver Star; Purple Heart. 10: Chittenden Co Hist Soc; Vt Archaeological Soc. 11: Silver Star; Purple Heart. 13: Yes. 14: Admin, ref, catlg. 15: Saint Micaels Col Lib, Winooski Vt 05404.

SULLIVAN, JOSEPHINE ELIZABETH. b Hickman Ky 28 O 14. 5: Murray State Col 35-38 (Bus Educ, Eng) BS; Peabodysummers 44-46 BS in LS. 6: Fr. 7: Tchr High Sch, Hickman Ky 38-45; Libn High Sch, Huntsville la 45-46; Catlgr UTenn Jr Col 46-47, Ref & readers adv 47-49, Instr 48-50; Catlgr Sch of Advanced Internat Studies, Wash DC 49-50; Ref libn, Ft Belvoir Va 50-52; Tchr adult educ Alexandria City Schs, Va 51-; Chief period sect US Army Lib, Pentagon 52-67; Asst chief readers serv br US Army Lib 62-67, Chief Readers Serv Br US Army Lib 68-; Lib Sci Instr UVa No Va Ctr 66-. 8: Serv rep, Inter-Agency Lib Group on For Area Studies Bibliog Proj, 64-68; Wkshop leader, 5th annual Church Lib Wkshop, Wash DC 65; Army lib rep, Mil Libns Wkshop, 58, 61-63, 66, 67. 9: SLA (Mil Libns Div: Serv rep Army 58-59, Memb Chm Wash DC Chap 64); DCLA (Memb Com 64-65). 11: Spec Serv Award, Dept of the Army, 62. 12: Co-wker "Union List of Military Periodicals (60). 13: Yes. 14: Ref. 15: 4 W Howell ave, Alexandria Va 22301.

SULLIVAN, JUDITH (EVE). b NYC 13 Ja 32. 5: Chestnut Hill Col 50-54 (Fr) AB; Laval U (Que) summer 53 (Fr); Adelphi U 55-59 (Elem Educ) NY State Certif; UDenver 63-65 (LS) MS. 6: Fr. 7: Sec Vick Chem Co, NYC 54-55; Sec Adelphi Col 55-56; Tchr: Berry Hill Sch, Syosset NY 56-59, US Dept of Defense, Mnich Germany 59-62, Village Sch, Syosset NY 62-63; Libn Belleview Sch, Englewood Colo 64-. 9: ColoASchL; ColoEA. 10: Mercy Hosp Auxiliary (Denver). 14: Elem sch libnship. 15: 1161 S Birch #406, Denver Co 80222.

SULLIVAN, JULIA A(GNES). b NYC 23 S 12. 5: NYU 39-46 (Hist) BA; UNC 46-47 BSS. ; UIll 51-52 MSS. 6: Fr. 7: Libn NY Pub Lib 42-47; Head of circ Kanawha Co Pub Lib, Charleston WVa 48-49; Br libn Peoria Pub Lib, Peoria Ill 50-51; UIll Lib (Urbana) 51-52; Libn Queensborough Pub Lib, NYC 52-56; Libn W Islip Pub Lib, W Islip NY 57-58; Libn Downtown Lib American U 59-64; Period libn Mongomery Jr Col 65-. 9: ALA; DCLA. 10: AAUP. 14: Ref, adult educ. 15: 7702 Blair rd, Takoma Park Md 20012.

SULLIVAN, KATHARINE (COLLAMORE). b Essex Conn 12 S 22. 4: Howard A Sullivan. 5: UConn 38 (Eng) BA, 48 (Eng) MA; Wayne State 67 MS in LS. 7: Acquis libn UConn (Storrs) 41-48; Acquis libn UBridgeport 48-49; Libn Furhmann Jr High Sch, Warren Mich 62-65; Libn Mott Sr High Sch, Warren Mich 65-. 9: ALA (Com YA Adult Bks for Slow Readers); NEA; MichEA; Mich a-v Assn; MichASchL. 14: Sch lib. 15: 18452 Birchcrest, Detroit Mi 48221.

SULLIVAN, LUCILLE (GUY). b Macon Miss 12 Ag 09. 5: Miss So Col 27-30 (Math) BS; UAla summer 31, 36-38 (LS) Certif; UNC 52-53 BS in LS. 7: Eng & math tchr Simpson Co Agric High Sch, Mendenhall Miss 30-34; Math tchr Newton High Sh, Newton Miss 34-36, Libn 36-39; Libn Hinds Co Jr Col 39-42; Libn Birmingham Pub Lib, Birmingham Ala 43-50; Libn Jackson Pub Lib, Jackson Miss 51-52; Bus manager Birmingham Pub Lib, Birmingham Ala 53-62; Sch lib supv State of Miss Dept of Educ, Jackson Miss 62-63; Bus manager Birmingham Pub Lib, Birmingham Ala 63-. 8: Judge Ala Favorite Tchr Contest. 9: ALA; AlaLA. 10: Altrusa Internat; AAUW. 14: Ref. 15: 2831 Highland ave, Apt 318, Birmingham Al 35205.

SULLIVAN, SISTER MADELINE CSJ. b E Orange NJ 21

Mr 31. 5: Seton Hall U 54-60 (Eng) BA; Immaculate Heart Col 61-64 (LS) MA. 6: Fr. 7: Tchg Sisters of St Joseph, NJ, WVa, Cal54-66; Libn St Genevieve High Sch, Panorama City Cal 61-65; Libn St James High Sch, Carneys Point NJ 65-69; Libn Immaculate Heart Acad, Westwood NJ 69-. 8: Eng Dept Chm, St Genevieve High Sch, 61-65; Adult Educ Salem Tech Inst 68-69. 9: NCTE; CathLA; NoCaEA. 14: High sch libs, elem libs, pub libs. 15: Immaculate Heart Convent, Van Emburgh ave, Westwood NJ 97675.

SULLIVAN, MARGARET (REYNOLDS). b Terryville Conn 20 N 02. 7: Lib asst Bristol Pub Lib, Bristol Conn 45-58, Asst libn 58-63, Libn 63-. 8: Consul Bldg Prog (Lib Addition) Plymouth Conn. 9: ALA; CathLA; NELA; ConnLA. 10: Bd of Lib Dirs, Plymouth Conn; Bristol Youth Coun; Adult Tutorial & Home Visit Prog; C of C; NAACP. 12: Ed "The Catholic Girl" (Teen-age) (29-40); "Juvenile Books" (40-50). 13: Yes. 14: Admin. 15: Pub Lib, Bristol Ct 06010.

SULLIVAN, MARJORIE (MORSE). b Emporia Kan 7 Ja 14. 4: Jay Sullivan. 5: Kan State Tchrs Col 31-35 (Soc Sci) BS, 57-61 (Educ) MS, 64-66 ML. 7: Tchr Emporia City Schs, emporia Kan 57-64; Libn Roosevelt High Sch, Emporia Kan 64-66; Asst Prof Dept of libnship Kan State Tchrs Col 66-. 8: N Central Eval Team Lib Consul 68-69; Lib Consul for Curr Study 67; Lib Wkshop Consul 65-66. 9: ALA; AASchL; NEA; KanStateTA; KanLA; KanASchL (Com on Standards). 10: AAUW. 13: Yes. 14: Sch media ctr, sel of materials. 15: 1732 Rural, Emporia Ks 66801.

SULLIVAN, MICHELE. b Butte Mont 30 Ja 41. 5: San Francisco Col for Women 59-63 (Hist, Pol Sci) BA; UCal (Berkeley) 63-64 MLS. 6: Ger, Fr. 7: Asst circ libn Sacramento State Col Lib 64-66; Sr libn Westminster Pub Libs, London England 66-67; Docs libn UKan Libs 67-. 10: Jr League. 14: For & internat docs. 15: 817 West Broadway, Butte Mt 59701.

SULLIVAN, PEGGY (MARGARET ANNE). b Kan City Mo 12 Ag 29. 5: Clarke Col 46-50 (Lang & Lit) AB; Catholic U 50-53 MS in LS; Johns Hopkins 54-56; UVa 60-62; UMd 62-63; Chicago 68-. 6: Lat, Fr. 7: Asst child libn Kan City (Mo) Pub Lib 52-53; Child libn & sch spec Enoch Pratt Free Lib, Baltimore 53-59; Instr Catholic U 58, 62-63; Child wk supv Arlington Co Lib, Arlington Va 59-61; Instr Drexel Inst 61; Instr UMd 61-62; Lib spec Montgomery Co Schs, Rockville Md 61-63; Dir Knapp Sch Lib Proj, Chicago 63-68; Instr Rutgers 67; Instr Syracuse U 68; Dir Jr Col Lib Info Ctr 68-69. 8: Survey Elmira NY sch libs 64; Consul and speaker wkshops confs, NDEA and HEA Insts. 9: ALAPLA (chm Com on Standards for Child Wk); CSD (chm Subj Lists Com, consul RTSD Com on Catlg of Child Materials, Com on Devel, Com on Wk with Except Child); MdLA (Memb Chm, Recr Day Chm); CathLA (chm DCMd Unit); NEADAVI. 10: AAUW; Beta Phi Mu; Delta Epsilon Sigma; Kappa Gamma Pi; Indep Voters of Ill. 11: Tangley Oaks Fellow 6869. 12: The Odonnels-- (56); Impact; The School Library and the Instructional Program-- (67); Realization; The Final Report of the Knapp School Libraries Project-- (68). 13: Yes. 14: Sch libs, pub libs, jr col libs, child serv, lib educ. 15: 1219 W Foster ave, apt 7, Chicago Il 60640.

SULLIVAN, RICHARD J(OSEPH). b Lawrence Mass 20 Ag 06. 4: Rachel Mary Santoliquido. 5: Dartmouth Col 24-28 (Econ) AB; Simmons 46-51 (LS) MS. 7: Asst supt street floor R H Macy Co, NYC 29; Mgt training S S Kresge Co, Paterson NJ & Lawrence Mass 30-31; Hooper-Holmes Bur, Boston 32-35, Br mgr Providence 36-38; (Cpl) USAAF statistical off 44-45; Libn Lawrence Pub Lib, Lawrence Mass 38-56; Document libn AVCO Res & Devel Corp, Lawrence Mass 57-58; Dir of Libs Suffolk U 58-. 8: Mem, sec & chm Bd of Lib Commsnrs, Mass 42-69. 9: ALA; AALL (Certif Com 64-); MassLA (pres 56-57); NELA (pres 62-63). 10: Rotary Club; Men Libns Club; Lawrence Commun Chest; Greater Lawrence United Fund. 13: Yes. 14: Lib admin. 15: 26 Tmberneck dr, Reading Mass 01867.

SULLIVAN, RICHARD V. b Wash DC 17 Ag 41. 5: GeorgetownU 59-64 (Eng) AB; CatholicU 65-68 (LS) MS. 6: Ger. 7: Decimal clsf specialist LC Decimal Clsf Div 67-. 9: ALA. 14: Clsf. 15: 5055 Seminary rd apt 1611, Alexandria Va 22311.

SULLIVAN, ROBERT COYLE. b Wash DC 29 My 27. 4: Barbara May Meehan. 5: Georgetown Col 45-49 (Hist) BS; Georgetown Law Sch 51-52 (Law); Catholic U 55-65 MLS. 6: Ger. 7: US Army 45-46; Accessioner order div LC 49, Hd mail unit order div 50-51, Hd accessioning unit order div 51-52, Asst hd & hd order sect order div 52-60, Hd orders sect card div 60, Asst chief order div 60-64, Asst chief photoduplication serv 64-. 9: ALA;-RTSD (Acquis Sect; Lib Materials Price Index Com 60-62, Bkdealer-Lib Rel Com 62-64; RLMS, sec 67-, chm &/or mem 3 coms 65-, mem Micropub Proj Subcom of P&R Com 66-); DCLA; NMA; COSATI (Micro-Media Subpanel 67-). 13: Yes. 14: Photorepro, acquis, admin, preser of collections. 15: 5415 20th pl, Washington DC 20031.

SULLIVAN, RUTH MARGARET. b Quincy Mass 25 N 13. 5: Boston U 50 (Applied Music, Violin) Mus B; URI 66 MLS. 6: Fr, Sp. 7: Sec, ed asst Dept of Chem & Dept of Physics MIT 49-50, 58 (Communications) Lt Cmndr US Naval Air Sta, Quonset Pt RI & Navy Dept, Wash DC 42-46; Line Off Navy US Naval Communication Sta, Boston 50-54; Admin asst Child Med Center, Boston 54-57; Admin asst Harper-Atlantic Sales Inc, Boston 58-62; Libn Med Lib New Eng Deaconess Hosp, Boston 63-. 9: SLA. 10: Hingham Civic Orchestra (1st Violin). 14: Admin, ref. 15: 31 Indian trail, North Scituate Ma 02060.

SULLIVAN, SARAH ELIZABETH (TURNEY). b Lubbock Tex 25 A 27. 5: N Tex State U 43-47 (LS) BS; Tex Womans U 62-69 MLS. 6: Lat, Span. 7: Libn Port Neches High Sch, Port Neches Tex 47-49; Libn Crowell High Sch, Crowell Tex 49-50; Circ libn Tex Tech Col 50; Libn Handley High Sch, Ft Worth Tex 55-57; Ref libn sci & ind Dallas Pub Lib 5769, Hd commun living dept 69-. 9: TexLA; ALA. 13: Yes. 14: Ref, ser publ. 15: 3715 Durango, Dallas Tx 75220.

SULLIVAN, SOPHIA. b Laurens SC 26 Jl 16. 5: Presbyterian Col 33-37 (Fr, Eng) AB; Peabody summers 37-39, 40, 46 BS in LS; UIll 51-52 (LS) MS. 6: Fr. 7: Tchr Fountain High Sch, Fountain Inn SC 36-37; Lib: Bennettsville High Sch, Bennettsville SC 37-38, Laurens High Sch, Laurens SC 38-40, Columbia High Sch, Columbia SC 40-46; Head Libn Ala State Col 46-51; Instr Fla State U Lib Sch 52-53; Chief of tech processes Ga Inst of Tech Lib 53-65; Head div of soc sci & humanities Clemson U Lib 65-66, Hd catlg 68-; Hd catlg UGa Law Lib 66-67. 9: ALA; SELA; SCLA. 10: Beta Ph Mu; Kappa Delta Pi. 14: Tech serv, ser. 15: Clemson Univ Lib, Clemson SC 29631.

SULLIVAN, THOMAS E(DWARD). b Worcester Mass 11 F 21. 5: Holy Cross ol 39-43 (Philos) BA; Columbia 46-47 BS in LS; Catholic U 50-52 (Philos) MA. 7: 10th Air Force, India, Burma, China 43-45; Catlgr Yale U Lib 47-49; Catlgr LC 52-59; Chief catlg dept John Crerar Lib, Chicago 59-61; Asst dir of indexing serv H W Wilson Co, NY 61-. 9: ALA; CathLA (chm Finance Com 67-69). 14: Catlg. 15: 33 E 30th st, NYC 10016.

SUMERGRADE, RUSHEL (DUHL). b NYC 24 F 24. 4: Larry Sumergrade. 5: NYU 44 (Anthropology) BA. 6: Ger, Fr. 7: Catlgr Amer Museum Natural Hist, NYC 44; Research Arthur Rosenberg Inc, NYC 44-46; Copywriter Fashion Advertising Inc, NYC 46-47; Lib clerk Willets Road Sch, E Williston NY 58-60; Chief Libn TRG Inc, Melville NY 61-68; Chief libn Computer Applications Inc, NYC 68-. 9: SLA. 10: ACM. 12: "Your Library" (61); Comp "Laser References" (65). 14: Ref, admin. 15: 60 Sutton Place S, New York NY 100 22.

SUMMERS, LURA ANN (DILLARD). b Richmond Va 5 My 39. 4: Donald Edward Summers. 5: Madison Col 58-62 (Eng, Hist) BA; CatholicU 63-65 (LS). 7: Tchr Chesterfield Co Sch Bd, Va 62; Lib asst John I Thompson & Co, Wash DC 63-64; Catlgr Bellcom Inc, Wash DC 64; Ref libn Inst for Defense Analyses, Arlington Va 65-67; Libn Planning Research corp, Wash DC 67-. 9: SLA (DC Chap Documentation Gp) (chm Publicity & Publications 68-69). 14: Ref, docs. 15: 4927 Manitoba dr 101, Alexandria Va 22312.

SUMMERS, VIRGINIA E. b Lansing Mich 22 Mr 05. 5: Taylor U 24-28 (Lit, Hist) AB; UMich 39-40 AB in LS. 6: Fr, Ger. 7: Lansing Pub Lib, Lansing Mich; Lib asst 29-39, Head of circ 40-43, Head of adult serv 43-45, Libn chief 45-59, Ref libn 59-. 8: In chg of loc hist div, Lansing Pub Lib; Tchr ref & catlg Mich State U (E Lansing) summer 59; Mich State Lib Wkshop, Mt Pleasant summer 60. 9: ALA (Coun); MichLA (chm var coms). 10: Altrusa Serv Club; Mich & Lansing Hist Soc; YWCA Bd; Women's Div Lansing Safety Coun Bd. 14: Ref, loc hist. 15: 531 Edison, Lansing Mich 48910.

SUMMERS, WILLIAM (F). b Jacksonville Fla 8 F 33. 4: Marie Marjenhoff. 5: Jacksonville Jr Col 51-53 AA; Fla State U 53-55 (LS) BA; Rutgers 58-59 (LS) MA. 7: Libn I Jacksonville Pub Lib, Jacksonville Fla 55, 57; (Lt jg) USNR US Taiwan Defense Command, Formosa 55-57; Sr libn Linden Pub Lib, Linden NJ 58-59; Dir Cocoa Pub Lib, Cocoa Fla 59-61; Assoc libn Providence Pub Lib 61-65; Lecturer URI Lib Sch 64-65; State libn Fla State Lib 65-. 8: Consul: Melrose Mass 63, Somerset Mass 64; Ohio State Lib 67, Lucas Co Ohio

68, State of Penn 58; RI Adv Bd of Lib Commsnrs, 64-65; Lecturer URI Lib Sch 64-65. 9: ALA (Coun 64; chm Code of Ethics Com; Com on Accreditation); FlaLA (chm Pub Libs Sect 61); RILA (Exec Dir Nat Lib Week, chm Com on Govt Rel, v-pres 63; pres 64). 10: Beta Phi Mu. 12: Co-auth "Library Service in Pennsylvania"; Auth "Communications, A Survey of Ohio Libraries" (67). 14: Adult readers serv, admin, lib devel. 15: Fla State Lib, Supreme Court Bldg, Tallahassee Fla 32304.

SUMMERVILLE, FRANCES LOVENIA. b Charlotte NC 3 S 42. 5: Flora Macdonald Col 60-61; St Andrews Presbyterian Col 61-64 Bible, Christian Educ) BA; Peabody 64-65 MLS. 6: Fr, Sp. 7: Asst libn Ga Southwestern Col 65-68; Catlg libn UNC (Charlotte). 9: GaLA; GaEA; ALA; SELA; Mecklenburg LA. 14: Ref, catlg. 15: 2500 Eastway dr apt 4C, Charlotte NC 28205.

SUMNER, ELLEN LOUISE. b Pearson Ga 13 N 18. 5: So Ga Col 36-38 (Eng): Ga Tchrs Col 40-49 (Eng) BS in Ed; Emory 49-50 (LS) M Ln; UGa 54-60 (Hist) MA; UMich 60-62 (LS). 6: Ger, Fr, Sp. 7: Chief bibliog Duke U Lib 50-53; Asst circ libn & inter lib loan libn UGa Lib 53-60; Chief ref libn WVa U Lib 62-65; Bibliogr UGa Lib 65-. 9: ALA; BSA; SELA; Ga Hist Soc; GaLA; WVaLA (treas 63-65). 10: Beta Phi Mu; Phi Alpha Theta; AAUP. 13: Yes. 14: Ref, bibliog. 15: 140 Baxter dr, Univ Garden apts H-10, Athens Ga 30601.

SUMNER, HAZEL JEANETTE (WHITAKER). b Wills Point Tex 2 Ag 39. 4: Bonny Louis Sumner. 5: Henderson Co Jr Col 58-60 (Elem Educ); E Tex State Col 60-62 BS in Elem Ed, 62-65 (LS) MS. 7: Tchr, Crandall Tex 61-62; Tchr, Athens Tex 62-64; Head Libn Henderson Co Jr Col 64-. 9: TexLA; Tex State Tchrs Assn; Tex Jr Col Tchrs Assn. 10: PTA; Beta Sigma Phi. 14: Catlg, acquis. 15: 710 Lakeside dr, Athens Tex 75751.

SUMNER, OWEEN. b Orlando Fla 18 Je 07. 5: Fla So Col 25-29 (Span) AB; Peabody summers 30-32 BS in LS; Duke U summer 35; Chicago summers 38, 40 (LS: Peabody summers 57, 58 MA LS. 6: Sp. 7: Libn Fla So Col 29-, Instr lib sci 34-49. 9: ALA; SELA; FlaLA. 10: Delta Kappa Gamma; AAUW; Pi Gamma Mu; Delta Zeta; Nat Fed Bus & Prof Women. 14: Admin, ref. 15: 717 Success ave, Lakeland Fla 33801.

SUMRALL, ADA MCCAA. b Scott Miss 23 Mr 14. 4: William Herbert Sumrall. 5: Hinds Jr Col 31-33; Miss State Col for Women 33-35 (Eng) AB; Peabody Col 38, 49-51 MA in LS. 6: Fr, Lat. 7: Tchr & libn, Miss: Beechstand High Sch, Wilkinson 36, Walnut High Sch, Vance 36-40, Anguilla High Sch, Anguilla 40-45; Libn Carr Central High Sch, Vicksburg Miss 45-52; Libn Peabody Demonstration Sch Lib & instr Peabody Col Lib Sch 52-59; Supv libs State Dept Educ, Jackson Miss 59-61; Tchr Miss Col 61-65; Lib consul Jackson City Schs, Jackson Miss 68; Dir spec project Millsaps Col 68-. 9: NEA; ALA (life mem); SELA; MissLA; MissEA. 10: Delta Kappa Gamma; YWCA. 14: Child & yp libs, reading guidance, lib educ. 15: PO Box 112, Clinton Ms 39056.

SUN, COSSETTE (TSUNG-HUNG WU). b Taipei Taiwan 14 Jl 37. 4: Stanley S Sun. 5: Nat taiwanU Law Sch 56 (Law) LLB; UHouston 60 (Intl Law) MA; Simmons 65 (LS) MS. 6: Chinese, Japanese, Korean. 7: Admin Church World Serv, Taipei Taiwan 63-64; Research law libn WashU Law Sch (St Louis) 65-66; Asst law libn St LouisU Law Sch 65-. 8: Amer Assn of Law Libs; W H Anderson Scholarship Winner Participant and fellowship winner; Summer Inst in Law Libnship, Berkeley Cal July 8-August 2 1968; Memb AALL Com on Catlg and Classification, Since 1966; AALL KF Wkshop on Classification and Catlg July 1968. 9: ALA; AALL (Com on Catlg & Clsf 66-); Jesuit Law Libns Gp (Chm 68-69). 14: Catlg, clsf, law lib admin, ref. 15: St Louis Univ Law Sch 3642 Lindell blvd, St Louis Mo 63108.

SUNDE, ELIZABETH (HAMILTON). b Seattle 16 N 19. 4: George William Sunde. 5: Linfield Col 38-42 (Eng Lit) BA; USoCal 42-43 BS in LS. 7: Stacks libn UWash Lib 43-44, Res libn 44-51, Bus admin libn 51-. 9: SLA; PNLA; Wash State LA. 14: Bus libs. 15: Bus Admin Lib Univ of Wash, Seattle 98105.

SUNDER-RAJ, PARANJOTHY ENOCH. b Madras India 20 S 31. 4: Sylvia Chandini. 5: UMadras(India) 49-53 (PHYSICS) BS, 54-55 Dip Lib; Syracuse U 61-63 MS(LS). 6: Tamil, Hindi. 7: Libn Leonard Theol Col (Jabalpur India) 55-60; Libn Brooklyn Pub Lib 60-61; Physics libn Syracuse U 61-63; Libn, systems analyst utoronto 63-67; Hd tech serv Dept of Manpower & Immigration Lib, Ottawa Ont 67-. 14: Lib automation, admin. 15: Library, Dept of Manpower and Immigration, Ottawa Ont Can.

SUNDERLAND, DORIS (LANGENHAN). b Lakewood Ohio. 4: Thomas E Sunderland. 5: Flora Stone Mather Col 30-34 (Biol) AB; West Res 35-36 BLS; Cleveland Col (Foreign Lit); West Res (Chem). 6: Ger. 7: Cleveland Pub Lib: Jr asst Popular Lib 36-42, yp libn Lorain Br 42, Ref libn tech dept 42-47; 1st asst Avon Lake Pub Lib, Avon Lake Ohio 58-64, Libn 65-. 9: ALA; OhioLA. 14: Readers adv, ref, exhib, catlg. 15: 220 Belmar blvd, Avon Lake Oh 44011.

SUNG, CARIN H. b China 8 My 37. 5: Tam-Kang Col 58-59 (Lit); Cheng Kung U 59-62 (Lit) BA; Kan State Tchrs Col 65-67 MLS. 6: Chinese. 7: Tchr: Chia-Chih Prof Sch, Chia-yo Taiwan 62-64, Ho-Li Prof Sch, Tainah Taiwan 63-65; Catlgr (stud asst) Kan State Tchrs Col 66-67; Libn I (catlgr) Orange Co Pub Lib, Orange Cal 67-. 9: CalLA; So Cal Tech Serv Gp; OrangeCoLA. 14: Catlg, admin. 15: 270C So Flower, Orange Ca 92668.

SUOKAITE, CHRISTINE. b Lithuania 30 O 24. 5: UHeidelberg(Germany) 46-48 (Biol); UWest Ont 49-50 (Biol) BA; Rosary Col 63-65 MLS. 6: Lithuaian, Ger. 7: Lib asst Brescia Col (Ont) 53-. 9: ALA; CanLA; OntLA. 14: Catlg, ref. 15: Bresca Col, London Ont Can.

SUPINSKI, CATHERINE (CURRAN). b NYC 27 Ag 15. 4: Edmund Supinski. 5: Hunter Col 32-36 (Fr) BA; Columbia 36-37 (Fr) MA, 40-43 (LS) BS. 6: Fr. 7: Pace Inst (NYC) 37-42; Asst libn Nat Ind Conf Bd, NYC 43-48; Libn NY Chamber of Com, NYC 48-64; Libn Dumont High Sch, Dumont NJ 64-. 8: Exec Bd Central Volunter Bur of City of NY, 54-62. 9: SLA (2nd v-pres 53-54; NY Chap: sec 49-50, pres 50-51); ALA; NEA; NJEA; NJSchLA. 15: Dumont High Sch, New Milford ave, Dumont NJ 07628.

SUPRENANT, MARGARET K(ILDUNN). b New Rochelle NY 18 Je. 5: Syracuse 21-25 (Journalism) BS; Columbia 50-54 (LS) MS. 7: Soc ed & asst city ed "New Rochelle Standard-Star, New Rochelle NY 25-26; Exec sec New Rochelle Charter League, New Rochelle NY 34-38; Asst to Adult Educ libn New Rochelle Pub Lib, New Rochelle NY 50-52; Sec to Asst Prin New Rochelle High Sch, New Rochelle NY 52-57; Libn Albert Leonard Jr High Sch, New Rochelle NY 57-. 9: SE NY SchLA. 14: Ya & gen pub lib serv. 15: 22 Otsego ave, New Rochelle NY 10804.

SUPUT, RAY RADOSLAV. b Columbus Ohio 13 My 22. 4: Mary Hansen. 5: Ohio State U 47-50 (Internat Rel) BA; Chicago 52-55 (Slavic Linguistics) MA; Case West Res (West Res) 50-51 MSLS, 67-(LS). 6: SerboCroatian, Ital, Fr, Russian. 7: Prof asst Northwestern U 51-52; Circ & ref libn, Catlgr law lib UChicago 52-57; Assoc libn & libn Garrett Theol Sem 57-64; Asst dir of U Libs, Lecturer in Slavic Linguistics & Lib Sci West Res U 64-67; Act dir & libn Freiberger Lib, Instr in Lib Sci Case West Res 67-68; Dir U Libs, Prof of Lib Sci, Ball State U 68-. 8: Mgt survey Loyola U Libs Chicago with R K Gardner; Mgt survey of Ball State U Libs. 9: ALA; ATheolLA (Microtext Bd 62-65); OhioLA; IndLA; AALS. 10: AAUP; Serb Nat Fed. 13: Yes. 14: Tech serv, acad lib admin, lib educ bibliog. 15: Ball State University Library, Muncie In 47306.

SURACE, CECILY J. b Brooklyn NY 9 Je 31. 5: Hunter Col 48-52 (Hist) BA; Columbia 52-54 (LS) MS. 7: Libn grade 2 Brooklyn Pub Lib 52-54; Libn Sam Tour & Co, NYC 54-55; Ed & ref asst McGraw-Hill, NYC 55-56; Asst libn J Walter Thompson Co, NYC 56-58; Asst supv Rocketdyne, Canoga Park Cal 58; Libn Giannini Controls Corp, 58-66; Deputy lib mgr RAND Corp, Santa Monica Cal 66-. 8: Co-chm Amer Mgt Assn Seminar on fundamentals of co lib mgt 68. 9: SLA (chm Info Com 1968 Nat Conf); ASIS. 13: Yes. 14: Syst analysis, mgt. 15: The RAND Corp, 1700 Main st, Santa Monica Ca 90406.

SURETTE, JADINE VIRGINIA (JUE). b Hollywood Cal 18 Ag 39. 4: Robert George Surette. 5: San Jose State Col 57-59 (Zool, Internat Relations); USoCal 59-61 (Slavic Studies) BA, 61-62 MLS. 6: Russian. 7: Tech document analyst Aerospace Corp, El Segundo Cal 62-64; Libn, admin asst Rand Corp, Santa Monica Cal 64-66; Govt docs libn USoCal 66-68; Interlib loan libn Antioch Col 68-. 8: Lings consul Rand Corp, Santa Monica Cal 66. 14: Ref, transl, govt docs, interlib loan. 15: R R 3, Xenia Oh 45385.

SURLES, EMILY (HEREFORD). b Dallas Tex 28 D 19. 4: Russell Surles Jr. 5: So MethodistU 36-40 (Art) BA; LSU 40-41 BS in LS; N Tex StateU 62-63 Tex Sch Lib Certif. 7: Asst libn E Dallas Br Dallas Pub Lib, Dallas Tex 43; Libn Lake Highlands Jr High Sch, Richardson Tex 63-. 9: ALA; TexLA; DallasCoLA; TexStateTA; RichardsonEA. 15: 8805 Rolling Rock lane, Dallas Tx 75238.

SURPRENANT, THOMAS TERRY. b Troy NY 3 My 42. 4: Carol Francis Vincent. 5: Siena Col 60-64 (Hist, Eng) BA; Catholic U 64-67 MSLS. 6: Fr. 7: Lib clk Siena Col 61-64; Abstractor Johns Hopkins U Applied Physics Lab, Silver Spring Md 64-65; Military publ libn ITT Research Inst Electromagnetic Compatibility Ctr, Annapolis Md 65-66, Supv tech info serv 66-69; Hd libn Northland Col 69-. 9: ALA; SLA. 10: Toastmasters internat; Siena Alum Assn; Potomac Appalachian Travel Club. 14: Computer applications, admin. 15: Lib Northland College, Ashland Wi 54806.

SURRENCY, ERWIN C. b Jesup Ga 11 My 24. 4: Ida Winn. 5: N Ga Col 41-42; UGa 45-49 (Hist, Law) AB, LLB, MA; Peabody 49-50 MALS. 6: Fr. 7: Law Libn Temple U Sch of Law 50, Prof of Law & Law Libn 60-. 8: Visiting Prof, Queen's U, Belfast No Ireland 63-64. 9: AALL (Exec Bd 63-66); Amer Soc for Legal Hist (pres 57-59). 10: PTA. 12: "Guide to Legal Research" (49); "Research in Pennsylvania Law" (2d ed 65); Ed "American Journal of Legal History" (57-). 13: Yes. 14: Catlg rare bks, admin. 15: 712 Pine Ridge rd, Media Pa 19063.

SUS, MARYANN. b E Chicago Ind 21 My 42. 5: Ball State 60-63 (Eng) BS, 63-64 (Eng) MA; West MichU 65-66 MLS. 7: Ref libn Lake Co Pub Lib, Highland Ind 67-. 9: ALA. 10: Beta Phi Mu. 14: Ref. 15: 1848 Ridge rd, Munster In 46321.

SUSMAN, BEATRICE (OSBAND). b Rochester NY 11 Jl 26. 4: Warren I Susman. 5: URochester 44-48 (Eng Lit) BA; Rutgers 60-61 MLS. 6: Fr, Sp. 7: Libn Brooke Smith French & Dorrance Inc, Detroit 49-51; Lib asst Gen Electric Co Employee Rel Lib, NYC 52-53; Libn: J Henry Helser Co, Portland Ore 54-58, Wm Hart Adler Inc, Chicago 59-60, US Trust Co of NY, NYC 61-68; Libn 1st Manhattan Co, NYC 69-. 8: Mem com & lecturer SLA NY Chap Sources of Financial Info Wkshop. 9: SLA (NY Chap: sec-treas & mem Recr Com of Bus & Fin Group 64-65). 14: Ref. 15: 100 Memorial pkwy, apt 8-S, New Brunswick NJ 08901.

SUSSMANN, NAN BRIGHT. b Des Moines Iowa 20 Mr 22. 4: Frederick Bernard Sussmann. 5: UCincinnati 4044 (Psych, Zool) BA; Pratt Inst 6062 MLS. 6: Fr. 7: Libn Queensborough Pub Lib, Jamaica NYC 6263; Chief libn Wilbour Lib of Egyptology Brooklyn Museum, Brooklyn NYC 6366; Ref libn Nat Museum of Can Ottawa 6668; Chief libn Entomology Research Inst, Ottawa Can 68. 9: SLA; OttawaLA (sec 6869). 10: Beta Phi Mu. 15: 2750A Marie st, Ottawa 14 Ont Can.

SUTCH, NANCY (SLOAN). b Altoona PENN D 10. 4: Emery H Sutch. 5: Carnegie 28-32 BS in LS. 7: Child libn Wanskuck Br Pub Lib, Providence 33-34, Child libn Tockwotton Br 34-35; Sec Carnegie Inst Tech 35-36; Pub Lib, Pittsburgh: Asst boys & girls dept E Liberty Br 36-38, Child libn W End Br 38-39, Child libn Mt Washington Br 58-59, 61-62, Asst boys & girls dept Central Div 57-58, 59-61, 62-. 9: ALA-CSD; PennLA. 14: Child serv. 15: 2974 Dwight ave, Pittsburgh 15216.

SUTCLIFFE, PRISCILLA (HEATH). b Manchester NH 8 O 15. 5: Bates Col 32-36 (Sociol, Econ) AB; Benyon Sch of Eng summers 48 & 50 (Eng & Amer Lit); UNC 67-69 MSLS. 6: Fr. 7: Dir related train NYA, Manchester NH 37, Dist coord 38, Special asst, Concord 39-40, Chief project control 41; Tchr liberal arts Bliss Bus Col, Lewiston Me 41-43; Archivist Kenyon Col 64-67; Asst ref libn (soc sci & humanities) Clemson U Lib 69, Spec collections libn 69-. 10: Phi Beta Kappa; Delta Sigma Rho; Beta Phi Mu; Friends of the Clemson Pub Lib. 14: Ref, archives, spec collections. 15: 29A Martin st, Clemson SC 29631.

SUTER, JON MICHAEL. b Holdenville Okla 30 O 41. 5: E Central State Col (Okla) 59-63 (Eng) Hist, Span) BA; UOkla 63-64 MLS; UInd summers 66, 67 (LS). 6: Sp, Ger, Fr. 7: Stud asst Linscheid Lib E Central State Col 59-63; Lib asst III UOkla Lib 63-64; Asst libn Linscheid Lib E Central State Col 64-. 9: ALA; OklaLA (Com on Intel Freedom 64; chm-elect 65); NCTE; SWLA. 10: Alpha Chi; Gideons Intl; Mod Lang Assn. 14: Catlg, tchg lib sci courses. 15: Box W-8, E Central State Col, Ada Ok 74821.

SUTHERAND, THOMAS ALLEN. b Owensboro Ky 24 O 40. 4: Gayle Moss. 5: Ky Wesleyan Col 59-64 (Hist) BA; UKy 64-65 MSLS. 6: Fr, Ger. 7: Clerk US Army, Ft Leonard Wood Mo 58-59; CHAPLAIN'S ASST US Army Sp/4, Ft Chaffee Ark 61-6; Designer Tri-State Monogram Co, Owensboro Ky 63; Asst to libn Ky Wesleyan Col summer 64; Reg dir Ky Dept of Libs, Hartford Ky 65-68; Dir Paducah Area Pub Lib, Paducah Ky 68-. 9: ALA (exec dir KY NLW); KyLA (pres-elect & 2nd v-pres; chm Pub Libs Sect); SELA (Planning & Devel Com). 10: Owensboro Art Guild; Phi Delta Theta; Rotary Intl; Toastmasters Intl; Educ TV Train & Devel Coun Ky. 14: Admin, ref, rare bks, pub rel. 15: Paducah Area Pub Lib, 707 Broadway, Paducah Ky 42001.

SUTHERLAND, GEORGIA (ELLIS THOMPSON). b Kan City Mo 18 Jl 06. 4: Harry Allen Sutherland. 5: Central Mo State Col summers 24-56 (Span, Eng) BS in Ed; UColo summer 58 Certif as a speech instr; NYU summer 59 Certif as driver educ instr; San Jose State Col summer 60 (Advanced driver educ); S E Mo State Col summer 61 Certif for lib wk; UHawaii summer 62 (S E Asian Studies). 6: Sp. 7: Elem tchr Appleton Center Rural Sch, St Clair Co Mo 23-24, Oak Grove Rural Sch, Bates Co Mo 24-25, Mingo Consol Sch, Bates Co Mo 42-49; Jr high instr Ballard Consol Sch, Bates Co Mo 49-53; High sch instr Adrian Sch Dist R 3, Bates Co Mo 53-61; Libn Butler Sch Dist R-V, Bates Co Mo 61-. 9: NEA-DAVI; ALA; Mo State TA; Mo State LA; MoASchL. 13: Yes. 14: Catlg, a-v wk. 15: 1004 N 71 Highway, Adrian Mo 64720.

SUTHERLAND, KATHLEEN MARGARET. b Sutherland Sask 16 My 11. 5: USask 28-32 (Bio) BS; McGill 54-55 BLS. 7: Libn I USask 55-57, Hd circ 57-68; Area coord Can Dept of Agric, Harrow Ont 68-. 9: CanLA. 10: Can Univ Women's Club; Bus & Profess Women's Club. 15: Apt 303 8885 Riverside dr E, Windsor Ont Can.

SUTHERLAND, LOIS S(MYSER). b Kobe Japan 31 O 06. 5: UCal 24-28 (Eng) BA, 28-29 Cal Provisional Tchrs Certif; MiamiU (Ohio) 52-53 (Educ); UMich 58-60 MALS. 6: Fr. 7: Instr bus educ: Grinnell Col 30-31, Pomona High Sch, Pomona Cal 32-34; Asst libn cambridge Lower Sch, Cambridge Mass 42-44; Tchr & libn Plymouth High Sch, Plymouth Mich 61-62; Tchr & libn Univ High Sch, UMich (Ann Arbor) 62-, Instr Sch of Educ 64-. 8: Instr Lib Sci UMich (Ann Arbor) summer 64, 65; Sch lib consul Bur of Sch Serv, UMich 67, 68. 9: ALA; -AAScjL; NEA; MichLA; MichEA; MichASchL; (chm Constit Rev Com, Parliament). 10: Beta Phi Mu; Pi Lambda Theta; Delta Kappa Gamma; Phi Kappa Phi. 11: Margaret Mann Award 60. 13: Yes. 14: Sch libnship. 15: 1614 Granger ave, Ann Arbor Mi 48104.

SUTHERLAND, ZENA BAILEY. b Winthrop Mass 17 S 15. 4: Alec Sutherland. 5: Chicago 33-37, 56-58 (Eng, LS) BA MA. 6: Fr. 7: Ed Libn Grad Lib Sch UChicago 58-; Ed Bks for Young People Saturday Review 66-. 8: Ed, contrib Britannica Jr, CTE bk com; Judson Award Com; Judge Nat Bk Award 69; Consul NBC Child Bk Show; Compton's Year Bk. 9: ALA (Newbery-Caldecott Com, Jane Adams Award Com, Notabe Bks Com, etc); Child Reading Round Table (Chicago). 10: Hyde Park Neighborhood Club; Nat Cong Parents & Tchrs; Art Inst; Babs Roberts Serv Com; UC Serv League; Quadrangle Club; Univ Colony Club; Mensa; Beta Phi Mu. 12: Ed "Bulletin of the Center for Childrens Books". 13: Yes. 14: Child bks. 15: 1418 E 57th st, Chicago Il 60637.

SUTOR, PEGGY (MARIE). b Winter Wis 3 Ap 20. 5: St Petersburg Jr Col 38-40 (Liberal Art) AA; Fla State U 40-42 (Eng) AB, 54-55 (LS) MA. 6: Sp, Fr, Ger, Russian. 7: Tchr Callahan High Sch, Callahan Fla 42-43; Biller Abbott Labs, Chicago 43-44; Tchr Orlando High Sch, Orlando Fla 44-45; Clerk, City of St Petersburg Fla 45-47; Claims clerk Phoenix of London Insurance Co, St Petersburg Fla 47-54; Libn Army spec serv, Schofield Barracks Hawaii 55-57; Libn Undergrad Lib UIll(Urbana) 57-59; Fla State U; Libn Catlg Dept 59-63, Libn Ser catlg 63-64, Libn Gen Educ Div 64-65, Libn Interlib Loans 65-68, Libn catlg Law Sch 68-. 9: ALA; SELA; FlaLA. 10: Beta Phi Mu; Staff Assn Fla State U Lib. 14: Ref, interlib loan, catlg. 15: 2111 High rd, Tallahassee Fla 32303.

SUTTERFIELD, NANCY (SCHAEFER). b 24 My 18. 5: UMich 36-39 (Speech) BA cum laude, 60-63 (LS) MALS; UWindsor Ont 62-64 (Phil). 6: Fr, Hawaiian. 7: Head Stoney Point Lib, Point-aux-Roches Ont 56-64; Pre-prof child Detroit Pub Lib 60-62; Head catlgr UWindsor Lib (Ont) 62-64; CATLG LIBN Hawaii State Lib 65-66, Libn IV 66-. 9: ALA; HawaiiLA. 14: Catlg, child serv, Hawaiiana. 15: PO Box 175, Kaaawa Ha 96730.

SUTTON, MILDRED ROBINOWITZ). b Tulsa Okla 28 Je 19. 4: Lee Sutton. 5: Los Angeles Jr Col 37-38; UCal(Berkeley) 38-42 (Psych) BA; Parsons Col 58-63 (Tchr Educ) Elem & High Sch Tchrs Certif; Columbia 63-64 MS in LS. 6: Fr. 7: Deputy probation off Alameda City Juvenile Probation Off, Oakland Cal 45-47; Circ & ref asst Wright Mem Lib Parsons Col 61-63, Ref libn 64-67; Libn John F Kennedy Col. 9: ALA. 10: Beta Phi Mu. 14: Ref. 15: 977 W 10th st, Wahoo Nb 68066.

SUTTON, OTTIE (KINTZEL). b Rockford Ill 27 O 17. 4: George M Sutton. 5: UWis 35-39 (Hist) BA, 39-40 BLS. 7: Libn Stephens Col 40-42; Ref libn USAF Acad 62-68, Sr ref libn 68-. 9: ColoLA; MPLA. 10: Alpha Chi Omega. 12: "United States Air Force Academy: a Bibliography 1954-1964"; "United States Air Force Academy: a Bibliography 1964-1967". 14: Ref, bibliog, internat affairs, internat organs (esp UN). 15: 2431 Summit dr, Colorado Springs Co 80909.

SUTTON, ROBERT F(RANKLIN). b Wash DC 25 Mr 21. 5: DC Tchrs Col 37-41, 45 (Eng, Hist) BS; UPenn 47-49 Certif in Libnship, 47-51 (Slavic & Baltic Studies) MA; Rutgers 58-60 MLS. 6: Ger, Fr, Ital, Swedish, Russian. 7: Delivery clerk The Hecht Co, Wash DC 41-42; Assignee Civilian Pub Serv Amer Friends Serv Comm, Md, Ohio, Phila 42-46; Asst Instr Temple U 46-47; In-serv trainee UPenn Lib 47-49; Curator Edgar Fahs Smith Mem Collection UPenn 49-54; Libn Ursinus Col 54-58; Assoc libn Monmouth Col 58-. 9: ALA; PennLA; NJLA; Phila Area Tech Serv Libns (pres 58-59). 10: Trustee, Wm Jeanes Mem Lib, Plymouth Meeting Penn; AAUP; SANE. 12: Ed bd "CHYMIA: Annual Studies in the History of Chemistry (48-54). 13: Yes. 14: Catlg, period, gifts & exch, rare bks. 15: Guggenheim Mem Lib Monmouth Col, W Long Branch NJ 07764.

SUZUKI, RICHARD C. b Aiea Oahu Hawaii 4 Ag 13. 4: Alice Masa Ohno. 5: UCal (Berkeley) 35-38 (Anthropology) AB; City Col (NY) 47-48 (Educ) MS; Columbia 52-54 (LS) MS. 7: Stack supv NYU, Washington Sq 52-53; Trainee NY Pub Lib 53-54, Catlgr 54-55; Libn Brooklyn Pub Lib 55-57; Libn Queens Borough Pub Lib, Queens NY 57-. 14: Ref. 15: 35-11 85 st, Jackson Heights NY 11372.

SUZUKI, SEIKO JUNE. b Pasadena Cal 1 Je 21. 4: George Suzuki. 5: UCLA 39-42; UDenver 43-44 B; UMinn 49; Catholic U 53-55 MS in LS. 7: Catlgr NLM, Wash DC 54-58; Assoc libn Mt Vernon Jr Col 63-64; Catlgr Nat Housing Center Lib, Wash DC 58-63, 65-68; Montgomery Co Pub Lib, Bethesda Md 68-. 9: ALA. 10: Beta Phi Mu; Montgomery Co Assn for Retarded Child; Red Cross. 12: Comp "Calfornia Imprints, 1833-1862: a Bibliography (61). 14: Catlg, ref. 15: 5908 Grosvenor lane, Bethesda Md 20014.

SVOBODA, FRANCES LUCILLE (SMITH). b Sandusky Ohio 14 Mr 09. 4: Clyde Kenneth Svoboda. 5: Bowling Green State U 26-30 (Soc Sci) BS in Ed; UMich 62 MLS. 6: Fr, Sp. 7: Ref dept Bryan Pub Lib, Bryan Ohio 30-32; Head Libn Greenville Pub LIB, Greenville Mich 58-. 9: ALA; MichLA: Montcalm Co (Mich) Assn of Libs (pres 64-66). 10: Current Event Lit Club; DAR; Bus & Prof Womens Club. 14: Catlg, ref, Mich bks. 15: 802 S Baldwin st, Greenville Mich 48838.

SVOBODA, PATRICIA DANIELLE. b Fairfield Cal 2 My 44. 5: Reed Col 62-66 (Pol Sci) BA; UWash 67-69 MLS. 6: Russian. 15: 5414 Soledad rd, La Jolla Ca 92037.

SWAIM, CAROL JONES. b Worcester Mass. 4: William G Swaim. 5: Maryville Col (Maryville Tenn) 44-49 (Eng Lit) BA; UHawaii 65-67 MLS. 7: 2nd Lt personnel admin USAF 50-51; Catlg libn LC 69-. 9: ALA. 10: Phi Beta Phi. 14: Catlg, a-v materials, lib admin. 15: 5936 North 4th st, Arlington Va 22203.

SWAIM, ELIZABETH ANN. b Carlisle Penn 6 D 33. 5: Dickinson Col 50-54 (Eng) BA; Carnegie 54-55 MLS; U St Andrews (Scotland) 55-56 (Eng); UPenn 60- (Eng) MA. 6: Fr, Ger. 7: Spec recr, ser catlgr LC 56-58; Catlgr Oberlin Col Lib 58-60; Rare bk catlgr Athenaeum of Phila 61-64; Catlgr, Spec collections libn Wesleyan U Lib (Conn) 64-; Antiquarian Bkseller Hamill & Barker, Chicago 69. 9: ALA; BSA; Ms Soc. 10: Bibliog Soc (London); Guild of Bk Wkers; Phi Beta Kappa. 11: Rotary Found Fellowship 55-56. 12: "Wesleyan Library Handbook (65). ; Ed "Wesleyan Library Notes" (68-). 14: Catlg, bibliog, rare bks. 15: Olin Lib Wesleyan Univ, Middletown Ct 06457.

SWAIN, HORTENSE (BOOMER). b Swan Quarter NC. 4: Grady B Swain. 5: E Carolina Col 26-30 (Eng, Hist) AB; UNC 45 BS in LS. 6: Fr, Sp. 7: Libn High Sch, Tarboro NC 43-43; Libn High Sch, Elizabeth City NC 45-47; Libn High Sch, Morehead City NC 58-60; Libn Col of the Albemarle 60-. 9: ALA; NEA; NCLA; NCEA. 10: Bus & Prof Womens Club; Commun Theater Group; AAUW. 14: Ref. 15: 203 E Church st, Elizabeth City NC 27909.

SWAN, PATRICIA A (FARR). b Honesdale Penn 26 Ap 42. 4: Barry Lee Swan. 5: Mansfield State Col 60-65 (LS) BS. 7: Elem libn Elmira City Sch Dist, Elmira NY 65-. 9: NY State Tchrs Assn; ElmiraTA; NY StateLA. 10: Kappa Omicron Phi. 14: Catlg, childs bks, filing. 15: 3532 Sing Sing rd RD 1, Horseheads NY 14845.

SWAN, PAUL DARRELL. b Dewey Okla 28 Mr 32. 5: N Tex State U 50-54 (Hist) BA, TexEA Lib Certif 59-61 (Admin, Supv) M Ed, summers 63, 67, 68 (LS); Our Lady of the Lake Col (NDEA Lib Inst) 66. 7: Libn Ector Co Ind Sch Dist, Odessa Tex 54-55; US Army Artillery clsf & assignment spec SP3 55-57; Libn Ector Co Ind Sch Dist, Travis Elem Sch Lib, Odessa Tex 57-. 9: NEA; Clr Tchrs Assn; TexLA;Tex Stae Tchrs Assn; SWLA; TexASchL; TexClrTA. 10: Phi Delta Kappa; German Shepherd Dog Club of Amer; W Tex Kennel Club. 14: Elem sch libs. 15: Rte 2 Box 715, Odessa Tx 79760.

SWANK, RAYNARD COE. b Butler Ohio 20 D12. 5: Col f Wooster 30-34 AB; West Res 36-37 BS in LS; Chicago 41-44 (LS) PhD. 7: UColo Lib; Catlgr 37-38, Documents & ser libn 38-39, Documents libn 40-41; Bibliog UChicago Lib 44; Visiting lecturer UMinn Lib Sch 44-45; Chief catlg libn & asst prof UMinn Lib (Minneapolis) 45-46; U Libn & Prof UOre 46-48; Dir of U Libs Stanford U 48-62; Visiting lecturer UCal Sch of Libnship (Berkeley) 53, 57, 62; Dir ALA Internat Rel Off 59-61; Dean & Prof UCal Sch of Libnship (Berkeley) 62-; Act dir UCal Lib Res Inst 64-66. 8: Dir ALA Internat Rel Off (extensive Foreign travel) 59-61; Mem Amer Lib Del to Soviet Union, Cultural Exch Agreement My-Je 61; Mem US Nat Commsn for UNESCO 62-68, Chm Adv Com, Cal State Sch Lib Res Proj 63-68; Consul, Ford Foun Southeast Asia rep, on univ libs & lib educ, summers 63, 64, 66; Consul to Chinese Univ of Hong Kong, Mr 64. 9: ALA (Coun 49-57 & 61-64, Exec Bd 53-57; Mem & chm A-v Bd 48-57; Dir Internat Rel Off 59-61; Mem & chm Internat Rel Com 61-64);-ACRL (Bd Dirs 55-56, Mem Steering Com 58-59; Univ Libs Sect; sec 48-49, chm 51-52);-LED; SLA; AALS; CalLA (chm A-v Com 48-50; chm Educ Com 68-; Long Range Planning Com 67-). 10: Bk Club of Cal; Roxburghe Club (San Francisco); Beta Phi Mu. 12: "Report of a Survey of the Library of Stanford University" with Louis R Wilson 47; "The Pacific Northwest Bibliographic Center, a Survey" (57); "Soviet Libraries and Librarianship with M Ruggles" (62); "The Midwest Inter-library Center with S McCarthy" (64). 13: Yes. 14: Tech proc, a-v serv, col & univ libs, internat lib rel, lib educ. 15: 700 Coventry rd, Kensington Ca 94707.

SWANKER, ESTHER (MOREY). b Syracuse NY 15 O 27. 4: Henry J Swanker. 5: Syracuse 46-50 (Eng) AB; SUNY (Albany) 58-61 MLS, 63- (Educ, Admin). 7: Field dir Albany Girl Scouts, Albany NY 50-51; Writer & Ed Gen Electric Co, Schenectady NY 51-58; Libn Burnt Hills Jr High Sch, Burnt Hills NY 58-63; Lib coord Schenectady Pub Schs, Schenectady NY 63-65; Coord Title III ESEA, NY State Educ Dept, Albany NY 65-67, Asst to deputy commsnr 67-68, Asst dir urban educ 68-. 8: Consul in sch lib wk to sch systems, NDEA Inst, Depts of Lib Sci at State Univ units in NY State. 9: ALA-AASchL (Legis Com);-CSD; NEA (Sch lib sect); NYLA; NY State Tchrs Assn. 10: AAUW. 13: Yes. 14: Info retrieval, resource centers, innovations in libnship. 15: NY State Educ Dept, Albany NY 12224.

SWANN, ARTHUR WILLIAM. b Primghar Iowa 29 D 16. 4: Mary Edna Goldsmith. 5: UMich 36-39 (Math) AB; Vanderbilt Divinity Sch 40-45 (Church Hist) BD; Peabody 45-46 BS in LS; UMich 48-49 AMLS. 6: Fr. 7: Libn Gammon Theol Sem (Atlanta) 47-48; Asst Prof Lib Sci Peabody Lib Sch 49-51; Libn Garrett Biblical Inst 51-56; Libn Cal West U 57-60; Dir of Libs U of the Pacific 60-65; Assoc Prof of Libnship UDenver 65-68; Asst dir for tech serv San Jose State Col 68-. 9: ALA; Amer Soc of Church Hist; ATheolLA. 10: Jedediah Smith Soc; Pi Gamma Mu; AAUP. 13: Yes. 14: Tech proc, lib educ. 15: 1240 Dale ave #41, Mountain View Ca 94040.

SWANSON, CLARA MAY. b Santa Ana Cal 11 Je 22. 5: San Diego State Col 40-42; UCal (Berkeley) 42-44 (Bus Admin) BS, 46-48 (Tchg, Drama); UWash summer 50 (Sch Lib); USoCal 51-52 (LS) MS. 6: Sp. 7: Accounting clerk US Navy, San Francisco 44-45; Music libn Off of War Info, San Francisco 45-46; Tchr-libn San Diego, Monroe Ore, Menlo Wash 48-51; Catlgr Dominican Col (San Rafael Cal) 52-53; Oakland Pub Lib, Oakland Cal; Ref & documents 53-62, Supv br libn 62-64, Supv catlg libn 64-66, Supv libn in-charge-of tech serv for the Lat Amer Lib 66-. 9: ALA-Internat Rel Round Table; SLA; CalLA. 10: Bd Dirs, Internat Alumni Assn. 14: Catlg, docs. 15: 1718 Addison, Berkeley Cal 94703.

SWANSON, DON R. b Los Angeles Cal 10 O 24. 5: Cal Tech 42-45 (Physics) BS; Rice 46-47 (Physics) MA; UCal 49-52 (Physics) PhD. 7: Physicist UCal Radiation Lab (Berkeley) 48-52; Research scientist Hughes Research & Development Lab, Culver City Cal 52-55; Research scientist Thompson

Ramo Woodbridge, Canoga Park Cal 55-63; Dean & Prof Grad Lib Sch UChicago 63-. 8: Vis Com, MIT Libs; SATCOM (Com on Sci & Tech Info for NAS), Trustee, Nat Opinion Res Ctr. 12: Ed "The Intellectual Function of Library Education" (65). 13: Yes. 14: Systems planning, indexing & retr, computer applications. 15: Graduate Library School Univ of Chicago, Chicago Il 60637.

SWANSON, DORIS ANN. b Akron Iowa 30 Ja 38. 5: USD 57-60 (Eng) BA; UMinn 62-63 (LS) MA. 6: Sp. 7: Jr-Sr High Sch libn, Luverne Minn 60-62; Asst ref libn soc sci & bus admin Sacramento State Col Lib 63-66, Soc studies libn 66-67; Asst dir of libs for humanities UNeb 68; Pub serv libn & Asst Prof of Lib Sci Neb Wesleyan U 68-. 9: ALA; NebLA; MPLA; LincolnLA (pres 69-70). 10: AAUW; Sierra Club; AAUP; Bus & Prof Women's Club. 12: Co-ed UNeb Lib Handbk Series #1-4 (67-68). 14: Ref, lib sci educ. 15: 5143 Cleveland apt 3, Lincoln Nb 68504.

SWANSON, DOROTHY (WICK). b Minn 8 Jl 37. 5: UMinn 55-60 (Eng Lit) BA, 60-61 (LS) MS; NYU 65-68 (Amer Civilization) MA. 6: Fr. 7: Lib trainee UMinn (Minneapolis) 60-61; Ref libn Newark Pub Lib, Newark NJ 61-64; Lib assoc NYU Tamiment Lib 64-. 9: SLA. 14: Spec collections (soc scis). 15: 471 6th ave, New York NY 10011.

SWANSON, EDWARD. b Thief River Falls Minn 10 F 41. 5: Macalester Col 60-64 (Fr) BA; UMinn 65-69 (LS) MA. 6: Fr. 7: Asst to libn Weyerhaeuser Lib Macalester Col 64-66, Asst circ libn 66-68; Hd newspaper div Minn Hist Soc Lib, St Paul 68, Hd tech serv div 69-. 8: Subst lectr, Col of Saint Catherine Dept of Lib Sci 68. 9: ALA; MinnLA (chm Reg to Reserv Com 68, chm Memb Com 68-; Tech Serv Sect: sec-treas 67-68, v-chm 68-69). 10: Minn Hist Soc; Presby Hist Soc; ACLU; Twin Cities Mss Soc; Mss Soc; Ampersand Club of the Twin Cities. 12: Ed MinnLA "Bulletin" 68-. 14: Catlg, clsf, bibliog, hist of libs. 15: 1544 Grand ave, Saint Paul Mn 55105.

SWANSON, PAUL KIMBALL. b Carlisle Mass 4 S 27. 4: Stella Drapala. 5: Defiance Col 47-48; UMass (Ft Devens) 48-49; UMass 49-51 (Eng) BA; Simmons 51-54 (LS) MS. 7: 1st F A Bn US Army (Pvt), Korea 46-47; Gen asst bkmob libn, catlgr Wellesley Free Lib, Wellesley Mass 51-54; Br libn Baltimore Co (Md) Pub Lib 54-55; Libn Brattleboro Free Lib, Brattleboro Vt 55-9; Asst catlgr Colgate U Lib 59-60; Catlgr UVt Lib 60-62; Catlg libn Forbes Lib, Northampton Mass 63-. 9: VtLA; West Mass Lib Club. 10: Mass Archeol Soc. 12: Co-ed "Revision of Cutter 2 Figure, Cutter 3 Figure, Cutter-Sanborn Author Tables" (69). 13: Yes. 14: Catlg, clsf. 15: Stage rd, Westhampton Ma 02339.

SWANSON, ROY W. b Duluth Minn 15 Ag 1899. 4: Gladys Lindberg. 5: UMinn 22 BA, 27 ma. 6: Swedish. 7: Curator newspaper div Minn Hist Lib, St Paul; Ed writer "St Paul dispatch-Pioneer" Press 30-39, Hd libn 39-. 9: SLA; Amer Newspaper Guild; Swedish Pioneer Hist Soc; Amer Swedish Inst (Minneapolis). 10: St Paul Lions Club; Svenskarnas Dag Com. 11: Recipient Swedish Pioneer Centennial medal 48. 12: "Minnesota Book of Days" (49). 14: Newspaper libs. 15: 3400 Edmund blvd, Minneapolis Mn 55406.

SWANSON, STANLEY STEWART. b Brookings SD 27 Jl 24. 4: Dora Margaret Aarness. 5: UMinn summer 41; SD State Col 42-43; Penn Mil Col 43-44; UColo 46-49 (Eng) BA, 50-53 (Educ) M Ed; UMich 53-56 MALS. 7: US Army, US & ETO 43-46; Tchr-libn Lemmon High Sch, Lemmon SD 49-52; Eng tchr Campbell Co High Sch, Gillette Wyo 52-53; Libn Sheridan High Sch, Sheridan Wyo 53-56; Libn Neb State Tchrs Col (Chadron) 56-62; Sr catlgr Ore State U 62-69, Hd bibliog sel & evaluation 69-. 9: ALA; PNLA; OreLA; NebLA (chm Col & Univ Sect 59-60, Exec Com Nat Lib Week, Neb 59-60). 10: AAUP; Beta phi Mu; Soc of Philatelic Amers; ACLU. 13: Yes. 14: Catlg, acquis, admin. 15: 819 NW 31st, Corvallis Or 97330.

SWANSON, VIOLA (SOLANDER). b Stambaugh Mich 13 Mr 12. 4: Lester T Swanson. 5: N Park Col 36-38, 61-62 (Educ) BA; No Ill U (LS) Certif. 7: Tchr Stambaugh Twp Schs, Stambaugh Mich 44-46, 52-60; Libn Dist 74, Lincolnwood Ill 62-. 9: NEA; IllEA; IllLA. 10: PTA. 13: Yes. 15: 5323 N Kimball ave, Chicago Il 60625.

SWANSON, WINIFRED L (WEATHERS). b Santa Maria Cal 11 Ja 31. 4: Thor W Swanson. 5: Allan Hancock Col 48-50 AA; UCal (Berkeley) 50-52 BA, 52-53 BLS. 6: Sp, Fr, Portu. 7: Libn US Army Spec Serv, Fairbanks Alaska 53-55, Orleans France 55-58; Ref libn Santa Rosa Pub Lib, Santa Rosa Cal 58-63; Adult serv libn Santa Rosa-Sonoma Co Pub Lib, Santa Rosa Cal 63-. 9: ALA; CalLA. 10: Sonoma Co Coun for Commun Serv. 14: Ref, catlg, adult serv. 15: 3014 Hardies lane, Santa Rosa Cal 95401.

SWANT, EVELYN LOTTIE. b Missoula Mont 7 F 10. 5: UMont 26-31 (LS) BA. 6: Fr, Ger. 7: Prof asst Missoula Pub & Co Lib, Missoula Mont 31-47, Lib Dir 47-. 9: MontLA (past sec & pres). 10: Bus & Prof Womens Club; Commun Hosp Auxiliary. 14: Catlg, ref, adult circ, admin. 15: 718 Hastings ave, Missoula Mont 59801.

SWANTON, IRENE W. b Rochester NY 4 D 11. 4: Walter F Swanton. 5: URochester 30-34 (Geol) BS, 34-36 (Geol) MS; Clark U 36-37 (Geog); State U (Geneseo NY) 60-62 (LS) MS. 6: Fr. 7: Asst dept of Geol URochester 34-36; Docent & Geologist Museum of Natural Hist, Worcester Mass 37-39; Libn Avon Free Lib, Avon NY 51-57; Lib asst Randolph-Macon 57-58; Libn Avon Free Lib, Avon NY 60-62; Asst dir Livingston-Wyoming Co Lib Systems, Avon NY 62-69. 8: Sch bd mem Avon Central Sch 60-; Mem Bd of Coop Educ, Livingston Co NY 65-. 9: ALA; NYLA. 10: Sigma Xi; PTA; Avon Sch Bd; Bd of Coop Educ; Livingston Co. 14: Pub rel, local hist. 15: 86 E Main st, Avon NY 14414.

SWARTHOUT, ARTHUR W. b Seneca Falls NY 23 My 33. 4: Elizabeth Jean Lindsay. 5: W Va Wesleyan Col 50-54 (Eng) BA; Garrett Theol Sem 54-58 (Theol) BD; UMd 66-68 MLS. 7: Minister of Christian educ various Methodist chs 58-67; Ref libn & instr in lib sci W Va Wesleyan Col 67-. 8: Ordained United Meth Church minister. 9: ALA; Church & Synagogue LA (chm Publns(; W Va LA. 12: Ed "Church and Synagogue Libraries". 13: Yes. 14: Tchg lib sci, ref, admin. 15: 121 S Florida st, Buckhannon W Va 26201.

SWARTOUT, DOUGLAS H. b Elmira NY 5 F 23. 4: Amelia Storch. 5: Syracuse 46-51 (Eng Lit) AB, 51-52 MS in LS. 7: US Army (Cpl), European Theatre 42-45; Jr libn State U Col(Cortland NY) 53-54; Asst libn Ferris State Col 54-59; Asst libn Mich Col of Mining & Tech 59-61; Asst libn State U Col (Fredonia NY) 61-63; Libn II Cal State Polytech Col (San Luis Obispo) 63-64; Head catlg Willamette U 64-65; Assoc libn, head tech serv State U Col (Fredonia NY) 65-69; Assoc Prof, order libn Mohawk Valley Commun Col 69-. 9: NYLA; SUNY Libns Assn. 10: AAUP. 14: Tech serv. 15: 9148 Hayes rd, Marcy NY 13403.

SWARTZ, RODERICK G. b Fairbury Neb 25 My 39. 4: Colleen Coatman. 5: UNeb 58-61 (Hist) BA, 61-62 (Hist) MA; Chicago 62-63 (LS) MS. 6: Ger. 7: Ref asst UNeb 58-62; Catlgr UChicago 62-63; Asst to exec sec ALA-LAD, Chicago 63-64; Pub lib consul Mo State Lib 64-66; Asst dir Tulsa City Co Lib, Tulsa Okla 66-. 8: Spec lectr lib sci UOkla 69-. 9: ALA-LAD (past chm; Statistics for Pub Libs Com);-AHIL (Bldg Com 65-); ASIS; OklaLA. 10: Rotary. 12: Ed "Problems in Planning Libary Facilities, with W Katz (64). 13: Yes. 14: Lib bldgs, lib automation. 15: 1202 E 33rd st, Tulsa Ok 74105.

SWARTZBURG, SUSAN (MARION GARRETSON). b Summit NJ 26 Ag 38. 4: Marshall Swartzburg. 5: Wells Col 56-60 (Philos) BA; NYU 60-62 (Eng) MA; Simmons 65-66 (LS) MS. 6: Fr, Ger, Ital, Lat. 7: Admin asst Walter Schwimmer Inc NYC 61-63; Sub tchr Phila Bd Educ 63; Bibliog searcher Gen Lib UMich (Ann Arbor) 63-64; Bibliog searcher NYC Pub Lib 64-65; Libn CTUW project YaleU Lib 66-. 9: ALA; ConnLA. 14: Acquis, ref. 15: 135 Florence rd, Branford Ct 06405.

SWATY, MARY (MARTIN). b Fairbanks Alaska 22 D 43. 4: Gary L Swaty. 5: UMo at Columbia 61-65 (LS, Eng) BA (honors); UTex 65-66 (LS); IndU 67-68 MLS. 7: Lib asst UMo at Columbia 65-67; Catlg libn Arizona StateU 68-. 9: ALA; ArizStateLA. 10: AAUP; Phi Beta Kappa; Sigma Epsilon Sigma. 14: Catlg, reclsf. 15: 109 1/2 W 4th st, Tempe Az 85281.

SWAYZE, MIRIAM ELIZABETH. b Wilmington Del 29 Je 13. 5: Wilson Col 31-32; UDel 32-35 (Eng) BA; Drexel 49-51 MS of LS; UDel (Eng, Educ). 6: Fr. 7: Eng tchr Del State Bd of Educ Henry C Conrad High Sch 35-49; Typist Expt Sta E I duPont de Nemours Co, Wilmington Del summers 41-44; Ref Wilmington Inst Free Lib, Wilmington Del summers 49-54; Greenwood Bk Shop, Wilmington Del summer 48; Libn Del State Bd of Educ Henry C Conrad High Sch, Wilmington Del 49-. 9: ALA; NEA; DelLA (Scholarship Chm 63-65); Del State EA. 10: Delta Kappa Gamma; AAUW. 15: 2412 Madison st, Wilmington Del 19802.

SWEAT, ANNE ELIZABETH (AREY). b Lancaster Penn 6 N 35. 4: Wesley A Sweat J 5: UPenn 53-57 (Eng) AB; Drexel 58-60 MSLS. 6: Ger, Fr. 7: Lib asst UPenn 57; Reports writer

US Govt CIA, Wash DC 57-58; Lib asst res bk dept UPenn 58-59; Research asst & reviser Drexel INST OF Tech 59-60; Br libn Prince Georges Co Mem Lib, Suitland Md 64-65; Asst libn & Eng Instr Monroe Jr Col 65-67; Asst coord adult serv Prince George Co Mem Lib, Hyattsville Md 67-. 9: ALA (RT on Social Responsibilities of Libs Program Com); FlaLA; Md Adult Educ Assn; MdLA (Com on Intellectual Freedom). 10: Prince Georges Co (Md) Literacy Coun; Beta Phi Mu; Prince George's Co Arts Forum. 14: Pub serv, readers adv serv, bk sel, adult basic educ materials. 15: 6532 Adelphi rd, Hyattsville Md 20782.

SWEENEY, URBAN JOSEPH. b St John NB Can 18 Ja 22. 4: Margaret Stretz. 5: Queens Col 49-50 (LS); NYU 51-54 (Ed Sociol) BS; Pratt 55-56 MLS. 7: Tech Supply Sgt USAAF, US, Eng 41-45; Asst archivist US Naval Records Mgt Center, Garden City NY 46-51; Ref libn Queensboro Pub Lib, St Albans NY 56-57; Asst libn Sperry Gyroscope Engnr Lib, Great Neck NY 57-58; Sr info spec Republic Aviation Engnr Lib, Farmingdale NY 58-64, Chief Libn 64-65; Prin libn Gen Dynamics electrical div 66-. 9: Suffolk Co (NY) LA (chm Spec Libs Sect). ; SLA; ASIS. 10: VFW; Nat Security Ind Assn. 12: Comp Index to Long Island Forum, 1953-1964. 13: Yes. 14: Computer info retrieval systems, lib admin. 15: General Dynamics Electronics Div, 1400 N Goodman st, Rochester NY 14601.

SWEET, EDITH. b Worcester Vt 10 Mr 18. 5: UNH 37-41 (Hist, Lit) BA; Drexel 43-44 BS in LS. 6: Fr. 7: Gen asst br libs Hartford Pub Lib, Hartford Conn 44; Temp asst acquis dept, catlgr Law Lib NYU WASHINGTON Square Lib 45-56; Asst libn Pace Col 46-50; Libn Finney Pub Lib, Clintonville Wis 50-51; Child libn Free Pub Lib, Appleton Wis 51-52; Child libn Woodside Lib Queens Borough PUB Lib, NYC 52-53; Indexer Readers Guide to Period Lit H W Wilson Co, NYC 53-55; Circ libn Leominster Pub Lib, Leominster Mass 55-56; Asst libn NY State Law Lib, Albany NY 56-63; Asst libn NY State Dept of Law Lib, NYC 63-64, Albany 64-. 9: ALA; SLA. 15: W Sand Lake rd, Box 207 Rt 1, Rensselaer NY 12144.

SWENSON, EVELYN JOYCE. b Canby Minn 24 S 21. 5: St Cloud State College 44-47 (Eng, Hist) BS; UMinn 50-51 BS in LS; UDenver summers 59-61 (LS) MA; UMinn 66-67 Fellowship Lib Sch Specialist Certif. 7: Elem sch instr Porter Pub Sch, Porter Minn 43-44; Eng instr Winnebago High Sch, Winnebago Minn 47-48; Libn Excelsior High Sch, Excelsior Minn 48-50; Asst libn Bemidji State Col 51-54; Lib supv Bemidji Pub Schs, Bemidji Minn 54-56; Ref libn UNDak 56-61; Chm dept lib sci Moorhead State Col 61-. 9: ALA; MinnEA; MinnASchL. 10: AAUP; AAUW; Delta Kappa Gamma; Pi Lambda Theta. 13: Yes. 14: Lib educ. 15: Moorhead State Col, Moorhead Mn 56560.

SWERDLOVE, DOROTHY L(OUISE). b NYC 4 Ja 28. 5: Swarthmore 44-48 (con) BA; Columbia 58-61 (LS) MS. 7: Research asst Fed Res Bank of NY, NYC 48-49; Soc sci analyst LC 49-53; Research asst Chase Manhattan Bank, NYC 54-55; Economist Cal Tex Oil Corp, NYC 55-61; Libn theatre collection NY Pub Lib 61-, 1st asst 68-. 8: Consul, Legitimate Theatre Ind Exploratory Commsn, NYC 65. 9: TheatreLA (sec-treas); Amer Nat Theatre & Acad. 10: Phi Beta Kappa; Beta Phi Mu; Amer Soc for Theatre Research; Intl Fed for Theatre Research. 12: Ed "Public Affairs Abstracts (50-51); Co-auth "Survey of United States International Finance (54); "Oxford Companion to the Theatre (3rd ed 67). 13: Yes. 14: Ref. 15: Theatre Collection, NY Pub Lib, 111 Amsterdam ave, NYC 10023.

SWIFT, LEONARD WILLIAM. b Waukesha Wis 29 Ag 27. 4: Imogene Sanders. 5: St Norberts Col 48-52 (Hist) BS; Kent State 65; UWis (Milwaukee) 60- (LS). 7: US Navy AO3 45-48; US Army Res (1st Lt) 50-63; Libn Wrightstown High Sch, Wrightstown Wis 53-56; Tchr Kewaunee Pub Sch, Kewaunee Wis 56-60; Libn Mead Pub Lib, Sheboygan Wis 60-; Libn Random Lake (Wis) Pub Schs 60-64; Libn W Bend Pub Schs, Silverbrook Sch, W Bend Wis 64-. 9: ALA; WisLA; Wis ASchL; WisEA (pres Sch Libns 65-66); WisEA. 10: Random Lake Lib Bd; W Bend EA; Toastmasters. 14: Ref, sch libnship. 15: 1168 Vern st, West Bend Wi 53095.

SWIFT, MARGARET (GREER). b Gladwin Mich 14 N 16. 4: Raymond Swift. 5: Central MichU 40 (Home Econ, Eng) BS; Mich StateU 60 (Educ) MA; West MichU 68 MLS. 7: Elem sch tchr: Gladwin & Ros Courmon Cos 36-38, Lansing Sch Syst, Lansing Mich 58-64; Home econ tchr: Reed City Schs 40-41, Mason Sch Syst 45-47; Home supv Farm Home Admin, No Mich 41-43; Control chem Wepth Lab, Mason 43-44; Elem sch libn Lansing Sch Syst, Lansing Mich 64-. 14: Educ. 15: RR 1, Eaton Rapids Mi 48827.

SWIFT, OLIVER FRANKLIN. b Buffalo NY 16 S 41. 4: Beverly Munson. 5: CornellU 58-62 (Hist) BA; URochester 62-63 (Hist); SyracuseU 64-65 MLS. 7: Gen asst Queens Borough Pub Lib, Jamaica NY 65-66, Asst br libn 66-67; Ref libn Hempstead Pub Lib, Hempstead NY 67-. 9: ALA; NYStateLA; NassauCoLA. 14: Ref, adult serv. 15: 14 Elk st, Hempstead NY 11550.

SWIFT, SAIMA. b San Francisco Cal 19 F 05. 5: UCal (Berkeley) 23-27 (Educ) AB, 27-28 Certif in libnship. 7: Deptmental asst libn Richmond Pub Lib, Richmond Cal 28-42; Sect supv Kaiser Co Inc, Richmond Cal 42-46; Libn Kaiser Serv, Oakland Cal 46-48; Supv libn oakland Pub Lib, Oakland Cal 49-. 9: ALA; SLA; CalLA; Ref Libns San Francisco Bay area. 10: Beta Sigma Phi. 15: 846 York st, Oakland Ca 94610.

SWIGART, E(DITH) BERNIECE. b Pasadena Cal 26 Je 17. 5: Walla Walla COL 35-40 (Eng) BA; UWash 43-44 BALS. 7: Assoc libn Pacific Union Col 44-45; Jr catlgr Seattle Pub Lib 45-56 Head catlg div Hawaii Co LIB, Hilo Hawaii 56-61; Asst catlg libn Wash State Lib 61-67; Bkmob libn Hawaii Pub Lib, Hilo Hawaii 67-. 9: ALA; WashLA. 14: Catlg, ref, child bks. 15: 1536 A Kilauea ave, Hilo Hi 96720.

SWIGER, LE MOYNE. b Lumberport W Va 7 F 31. 5: Lee Col 47-49 AA; UChattanooga 49-51 9sp) BA; Peabody Col 59 MALS. 6: Sp. 7: Tchr Lee Col summers 51, 56; Tchr: E Cleveland Elem Sch, Cleveland Tenn 51-53; Bradley Co Central High Sch, Cleveland Tenn 53-58; Libn Lee Col 59-. 9: ALA; NEA; TennLA; TennEA; Greater Chattanooga Area LA; E Tenn EA. 10: Delta Kappa Gamma; Beta Phi MU. 14: Catlg, tech proc. 15: 430 28th st NW, Cleveland Tn 37311.

SWINDELL, DOLORES (HOLLAND). b Indianapolis Ind 20 O 35. 4: Archie C Swindell. 5: So MethodistU 53-57 (Geol) BS; Tex Woman'sU 60-61 (LS); SUC (Cortland) 66 (Educ); UNC 67-69 MS in LS. 6: Sp. 7: Lab tech (geol) Sun Oil Co, Richardson Tex 57-60, Tech libn 61-62; Prin lib asst Olin Lib Cornell U 63-64; Lab tech Vet Virus Research Inst CornellU 64-65; Libn Dryden Central Sch, Dryden NY 65-66; Libn Cortland City Schs, Cortland NY 66-67, Libn Campus Sch SUC (Cortland) 67; Lib fellow UNC Lib (Chapel Hill) 67-68, Libn (geol & zoology) 68-. 14: Sci, sci abstracting & indexing, sch libs. 15: B9 3600 Tremont dr, Durham NC 27705.

SWINEHART, ERDINE (LONSWAY). b Tiffin Ohio 21 Jl 12. 4: Harold G Swinehart. 5: Heidelberg Col 30-34 (Educ) AB; West Mich U 61-62 (LS) MA. 6: Fr. 7: Libn Springfield High Sch, Battle Creek Mich 62-. 9: ALA; NEA; MichLA; MichEA; MichASchL; Mich A-V Assn. 10: Phi Beta Mu; AAUW. 14: Sch libs. 15: 21 Maple ter, Battle Creek Mich 49017.

SWINNEY, SARA (EMILY) CARTER. b Attala Co Miss 29 Je 36. 4: Darrell Clarence Swinney. 5: Millsaps Col summers 54-55; Miss State Col for Women 54-57 (LS) BS; Peabody Col 60-61 (LS) MA. 6: Ger. 7: Child libn: pub lib Corvallis Ore 57-59, pub lib, Salem Ore 59-60, Battle Co Lib, Droville Cal 66-; Libn US Army, Mansheim, Darmstadt, Nurnberg & Frankfurt Ger 61-66. 9: ALA; OreLA; Cal;A. 10: AAUW; Trustee Gridley Union High Sch. 14: Child wk. 15: 230 Sycamore st, Gridley Ca 95948.

SWINSON, RUTH (ETNA). b Wrightsville Ga 16 N 29. 5: Ga So Col 46-49 (Hist) BS in Ed; Peabody Col 61-62 MA in LS. 7: Readers' serv libn NWest State Col of La 63-66; Loan serv libn Ball StateU 66-67; Ref libn Armstrong State Col 67-. 9: ALA; GaLA; SELA. 10: AAUP. 14: Ref. 15: 713 Jackson blvd, Savannah Ga 31405.

SWINT, ELIZABETH (BODMER WELTER). b Wilkes-Barre Penn 10 O 12. 4: Henry Lee Swint. 5: Va Intermont 30-32 AA; King Col 32-34 (HIST) BA;Peabody 37-38 BSLS; Misericordia summer 33. 7: Asst ser catlgr Jr Univ Libs, Nashville 48-51, Res libn 53-55, Hd circ dept 55-. 9: ALA-LAD (Bd Dir 67-68; chm Circ Serv Sect 67-68; chm-elect Circ Serv Discussion Group);-ACRL (Lib Serv Com 67-); SELA; TennLA. 10: PEO. 12: Asst ed "College and Research Libraries". 14: Pub serv. 15: 2503 Kensington pl, Nashville Tn 37212.

SWINT, KATHERINE EOLINE (MOON). b Muscogee Co Ga 7 D 17. 4: Jesse Taylor Swint. 5: Tift Col 34-37; Emory summer 38; Oglethorpe Col 38-40 AB; Peabody Col summers 41-43 BS in LS. 6: Fr. 7: Tchr Seminole High, Donalsonville Ga 37-38; Tchr-libn Norcross High, Norcross Ga 38-39; Libn: Campbell High & Elem, Fairburn Ga 39-46, Russell High, E Point Ga 46-48, 51-53, Decatur High, Decatur Ga 53-55; Catlg libn Agnes Scott Col 55-60; Catlgr libn II Ga State Dept of Educ Pub Lib Serv, Atlanta 61-. 9: ALA; SELA; GaLA. 14:

Tech proc, subj hding wk. 15: 128 Parkwood lane, Decatur Ga 30030.

SWINTON, CORDELIA (WESTERVELT). b Pittsburgh Penn 9 S 39. 4: John R Swinton. 5: Lake Erie Col 58-61 (Hist of Art) BA; UPittsburgh 62-63 MLS. 6: Fr, Ital. 7: Catlgr Dickinson Col 63-64, Period libn 64-66; Libn Col of Human Devel Penn StateU (Univ Park) 66-. 9: PennLA. 14: Ref, bibliog, period, acquis. 15: Apt H 16 445 Waupelani dr, State College Pa 16802.

SWISHER, J HOWARD. b DuBois Penn 20 F 07. 5: Ind State Col (Penn) 26-30 (Eng) BS; Peabody 48-50 (LS) MA. 7: Tchr Ramey High Sch, Ramey Penn 30-34; Rec dir WPA, DuBois Penn 34-39; Tchr DuBois Area High Sh, DuBois Penn 39-41, Libn 41-42; T/5 US Army, US & Europe 42-45; Libn DuBois Area High Sch, DuBois Penn 45-. 9: ALA; PennLA. 14: Ref, supv. 15: 112 W Scribner ave, DuBois Penn 15801.

SWISHER, MARY V(IRGINIA). b McWhorter WVa 2 Mr 14. 5: WVaU 41 (Eng) AB; UIll 45 BS in LS. 7: Tchr Wood Co schs, Parkersburg WVa 37-40; Asst ref libn WVaU 41-44, 45-47; Arlington State Col: Ref libn 47-58, Head pub serv 58-65, Assoc libn 65- (now UTex at Arlington). 9: ALA; TexLA; SWLA. 10: AAUW; AAUP; Kappa Delta Pi; Phi Kappa Phi. 14: Pub serv, admin. 15: 1003 W 4th st, Arlington Tex 76010.

SWISHER, VIOLET D. b Cheshire Ohio 7 D 27. 5: Capital U 45-49 (Span) BA; Kent State U summers 52-55 (LS) MA. 6: Sp. 7: Libn & tchr of Span, Eng Logan High Sch, Logan Ohio 50-53; Libn Avon Lake pub sch, Avon Lake Ohio 53-57; Field libn: Metz QM Depot, Metz France 57-59, Berlin Command, Berlin 59-60, Orleans Area Command, Orleans France 60-61; Asst ref libn USAREUR Ref Lib, Heidelberg Germany 61-63; Staff libn So European Task Force (Army), Verona Italy 63-66; Chief libn USAREUR Spec serv ref libn, Heidelberg Germany 66-68; Catlgr USA Med Field Serv Sch, Ft Sam Houston Tex 68-. 9: ALA (European Chap Armed Forces Libns Subsect). 10: Delta Kappa Gamma; Soc for Personnel Admin. 11: Dept of Army Certif of Achievement 66. 14: Mil lit, ref, supv. 15: Stimson Lib US Army Field Ser School, Brooke Medical Center, Fort Sam Houston Tx 78234.

SWITZER, JOHN PHILLIP JR. b Erie Penn 6 Mr 44. 5: Clarion State Col 62-65 (LS) BS; UPittsburgh 66-68 (LS) MS. 6: Fr, Lat. 7: Libn greater Latrobe High Sch, Latrobe Penn 65-66; Libn E Brady High Sch, E Brady Penn 66-67; Sers libn U Notre Dame (Notre Dame Ind) 68-69. 9: NEA; Penn State EA; ALA. 10: Alpha Chi Rho. 14: Ref, admin. 15: RD 1, Knox Pa 16232.

SWODITCH, JANICE (JOHNSON). b Waterbury Conn 27 Jl 40. 4: Robert J Swoditch. 5: So Conn State Col 58-62 (LS) BS; Rutgers 62-63 MLS. 6: Fr, Ger. 7: Ref libn So Conn State Col 63-64; Ref libn & catlgr Silas Bronson Pub Lib, Waterbury Conn 66-67; Tchr & libn H C Wilcox Reg Voc Tech High Sch, Meriden Conn 67-. 9: ALA; Amer Vocat Assn; NELA; Conn Vocat Assn; ConnLA; ConnSchLA. 14: Ref, ya. 15: 58 Madison st, Waterbury Ct 06706.

SWOFFORD, LORNA L. b Ft Smith Ark 11 Jl 14. 5: Jr Col (Ft Smith Ark) 31-33 (Eng) AA; Hendrix Col 33-35 (Eng) BA; Peabody summers 39-41 BS in LS. 7: Tchr-libn pub schs, Ft Smith Ark 35-42; Libn US Army, Camp Chaffee Ark 42-44; Libn US Army, Hickam Field Honolulu 44-45; Exec libn Mid-Pac US Army, Honolulu 45-46; Chief Libn VA Hosp, Topeka Kan 46-. 8: Consul Dept Psychiatry Lib UKan 61. 9: ALA-AHIL (pres 52-53); MedLA; KanLA (chm Spec Lib Sect 55). 13: Yes. 14: Admin, bibliotherapy. 15: VA Hosp Lib, 2200 Gage blvd, Topeka Kan 66622.

SYKES, DOROTHY (KNIGHT). b Cleveland 13 F 02. 4: William E Sykes. 5: Flora Stone Mather Col West Res 20-24 (Eng) BA; Kent State U 54-57 (LS) MA. 7: Psychiatric Soc Wker Cleveland City Hosp 24-27; Nurses aide Brecsville Vet Hosp, Brecksville Ohio 43-46; Br libn Akron Pub Lib, Akron Ohio 57-67; Hd libn Peninsula Pub Lib & Hist Soc, Peninsula Ohio 67-. 9: ALA; OhioLA. 10: PTA; Civil War Round Table; Richfield Hist Soc; Women's Nat Bk Assn; Kent Lib Sch Alumni Assn. 14: Ext lib serv, ref; pub lib admin, local hist. 15: 3613 Hawthorne dr, W Richfield Ohio 44286.

SYKES, ROBERT WALTER. b Phila 11 Ap 16. 4: Martha Lake. 5: UPenn 34-38 (Marketing) BS in ECON: Syracuse 50-51 MSLS. 7: Pilot USNR LCDR 42-46; Salesman Nat Cash Register Co, Phila 46-50; Br libn supv of circ DC Pub Lib 51-60; Asst to dir Prince Georges Co Mem Lib, Hyattsville Md 60-. 9: ALA; MdLA; DCLA. 10: US Naval Reserve; Carrollton Boys Club. 14: Circ, admin. 15: 5819 Lamont dr, Hyattsville Md 20784.

SYKORA, GEORGE. b Prague Czechoslovakia 6 Mr 25. 4: Jane (Surovska). 5: Charles U Law Sch (Prague) 45-49 JUC; UMich 67-68 MALS. 6: Czech, Ger, Serbo-Croatian, Russian. 7: Sr clk Amer Embassy, Prague Czechoslovakia 59-64; Lib asst Law Sch UMich (Ann Arbor) 66-67; Sr catlgr PrincetonU Lib 68-. 14: Catlg. 15: Princeton Arms N apt 78, Cranbury NJ 08512.

SYLER, ROSA MAE. b Newton Tex. 5: Peabody 31 (Educ) BS; LSU 47 (LS) BS. 7: Tchr-libn South Park Ind Sch DIST, Beaumont Tex 26-46; Assoc libn Lamar State Col of Tech 46-. 9: ALA; TexLA; Tex Assn Col Tchrs. 10: AAUW; S Central Mod Lang Assn. 14: Catlg. 15: 777 21st st, Beaumont Tx 77706.

SYLVESTER, MARY A (WHELAN). b Rock Springs Wyo 13 Ap 06. 4: George Moore Sylvester. 5: UWyo 24-28 (Educ) BS; UColo summer 32 (Eng); UDenver summers 59-61 (LS) MA. 6: Sp. 7: Eng tchr Jr High Sch, Rock Springs Wyo 32-35; State accountant Agric Adjust Assn, Laramie Wyo 37-42; Info asst Tex State Dept of Educ, Austin Tex 42; Reg accountant War Relocation Authority, San Francisco 43; Dietician UWyo 43-46; Libn Carey Jr High Sch, Cheyenne Wyo 55-62; Sch libn Dependent Sch, Goose Bay Labrador Can 64-65; Base libn USAF, Goose Bay Labrador Can 65-67; Catlgr US Nat Archives 67; Libn (indexing & abstracting) Naval Ship Systs Co, Wash DC 67-. 9: ALA; NEA; WyoLA; MPLA; DCLA. 10: AAUW; Pi Beta Phi. 13: Yes. 14: Ref, ya libnship, lib automation, catlg & indexing. 15: 7314 Reddfield court, Falls Church Va 22043.

SYLVESTER, MELVIN ROBERT. b New Orleans La 25 Mr 39. 4: Frances Modica. 5: DillardU 57-61 (Natural Sci) BA; LIU 62-65 (LS) MS. 7: Circ & ref asst Dillard U 61-62; Hd circ dept C W Post Col 62-64, Hd ser rec dept (instr) 64-68, Hd ser rec dept (Asst prof) 68-. 9: ALA; NYLA; NassauCoLA. 10: Grad Lib Sch LIU. 13: Yes. 14: Ref. 15: 56 Glen Keith rd, Glen Cove NY 11542.

SYMON, CHARLES A. b Munising Mich 29 Jl 12. 4: Barbara Doolittle. 5: No MichU 30-32, 64-66 (Hist) BA; West MichU 66-67 (Libnship) MA. 6: Ger, Sp. 7: News reporter -marquette Mining Journal", Marquette Mich 32-40; Ed "Munising News", Munising Mich 40-43, Publisher-ed 46-66; US Army Corps of Military Police, Munising Mich 43-45; Info off Wash State Lib, Olympia 67-. 8: Feature writer: "Detroit News", "Milwaukee Journal" 37-66; Dir Mich Press Assn 55-61; Pres Upper Mich Press Assn 62. 14: Ref, pub rel. 15: 2017 N Lilly st, Olympia Wa 98501.

SYMONDS, CYNTHIA (KENDALL). b Newark NJ 25 F 18. 4: Charles Henry Symonds. 5: Simmons 36-40 (LS) BS. 7: Circ asst, catlgr Jones Lib, Amherst Mass 40-44; Catlgr Winchester Pub Lib, Winchester Mass 44-47; Circ asst, Ref libn Beverly Pub Lib, Beverly Mass 58-66; Beverly High Sch libn, Beverly Mass 66-. 9: MassLA. 14: Ref, catlg, circ. 15: 19 Pearl st Ext, Beverly Mass 01915.

SYMONS, ELEANOR. b Camborne Eng 30 Ag 25. 5: U Oxford 43-46 (Fr) BA, MA; U of London Sch of Libnship 47-48. 6: Fr. 7: Lib clerk Bodleian Lib, Oxford Eng 46-47; Asst libn U Lib, Reading Eng 48-54; Libn Homerton Col (Cambridge Eng) 54-57; Libn UKan 57-, Head prep dept 63-67, Sr bk sel off 67-. 9: Lib Assn (Gt Brit); ALA; KanLA. 10: Amer Inst of Archaeol; Amer Name Soc; Devon & Cornwall Record Soc. 11: Sir John MacAlister Medal ULondon 48. 14: Catlg, clsf, bk selection. 15: 407 W 17th, Lawrence Ks 66044.

SYNAN, A RUTH. b Taunton Mass 18 F 23. 5: Bates Col 40-44 (Econ) AB; Simmons 57-59 MLS. 7: Taunton Pub Lib, Taunton Mass: Child libn 44-46, Ref libn 46, Asst libn & catlgr 46-54, Chief Libn 54-. 9: Old Dartmouth Lib Club. 10: AAUW; Quota Club; BUS & Prof Womens Club: Girls Club; Plymouth Bay Girl Scouts. 11: Woman of Valor Award for Brotherhood Week, 62. 14: Ref. 15: 38 Ashland st, Taunton Mass 02780.

SYRING, ANNE M. b Berlin Germany 28 O 06. 4: Rudolf Syrin. 5: Miami U (Ohio) 26-30 (Ger, Eng) AB, 35 (Ger, Eng) MA. 6: Ger. 7: Catlgr Dayton Pub Lib, Dayton Ohio 30-32; Asst libn West Col for Women 36-38; Catlgr UCincinnati Lib 47-. 10: Phi Beta Kappa. 14: Catlg. 15: 510 Terrace ave, Cincinnati Oh 45220.

SYRIOPOULOS, DOROTHY A. b Milwaukee 19 Jl 21. 5: Milwaukee-Downer Col 39-43 (Eng, Speech) BA; UWis 47-48

BLS. 6: Fr, Gk. 7: High sch tchr Milwaukee pub schs 43-44; Film libn Milwaukee Pub Lib 45-47, Asst libn in brs 48-51; Med libn VA Outpatient Clinic, Milwaukee 51-66; Asst libn VA Ctr, Wood Wis 66-. 9: SLA; MedLA; WisLA. 10: YWCA. 14: Ref, research. 15: 2578 N Sherman blvd, Milwaukee Wi 53210.

SZABO, RUTH ELIZABETH (WEED). b Providence RI 28 Mr 22. 4: Joszef Szabo. 5: Pembroke 39-43 (Eng Lit) AB; URI 65-66 MLS. 6: Lat, Ger, Fr, Ital, Sp, Portuguese. 7: Cryptographer OSS, Wash DC, Ceylon & Rome 43-47; Ed CIA, Wash DC 49-51; Sec Dept of State, Cyprus 53-55; Verse writer, tr, relig ed Paramount Line Inc (greeting cards), Pawtucket RI 57-65; Med libn St Joseph's Hosp, Providence 66-. 9: MedLA; ALA; CathLA. 10: RI Civic Chorale. 11: Recipient Exceptional Civ Serv Award US Army, Ceylon 46. 14: Med ref. 15: 42 Carter st, Providence RI 02907.

SZAJBELY, ELIZABETH. b Budapest Hungary 11 Ja 46. 5: UBC 65-69 (Fr, Pol Sci) BA, BLS. 6: Fr, Hungarian. 7: Libn N York Pub Lib, N York Ont Can 69-. 9: CanLA; ALA. 14: Ref. 15: N York Pub Lib, N York Ont Can.

SZCZEPANSKI, JOHN JOSEPH. b Chicago Ill 1 Ja 17. 5: UIll (Chicago) 64-66 (Econ) BS; UIll 66-67 (LS) MS. 6: Polish, Ger, Russian. 7: Major US Army 42-62; Circ libn GeorgetownU 67-68; Ref libn Off of Chief of Engrs Lib Dept of Army, Wash DC 68-69; Libn Bd of Engrs for Rivers & Harbors Dept of Army, Wash DC 69-. 9: ALA; Acad Pol Sci; Amer Acad Pol & Soc Sci. 10: Beta Phi Mu; Chi Gamma Iota. 14: Admin. 15: 1745 No Troy apt 431, Arlington Va 22201.

SZEKELY, YORAM BEN-HAIM. 5: Columbia Col 61-65 (Oriental Studies) BA, 68-69 MLS. 6: Ger, Hebrew, Chinese. 7: Asst circ libn Intl Affairs Lib ColumbiaU 69-. 10: Phi Beta Kappa. 14: Admin, collection bldg (acquis). 15: 3123 Bailey ave, Bronx NY 10463.

SZEPLAKI, JOSEPH. b Hatvan Hungary 17 Ap 32. 4: Clara Irmai. 5: Tchrs Col Lib Sch (Apacai Cseri Janos Pedagogiai Foiskola) (Budapest) 52-54 MLS. 6: Hungarian. 7: Chief libn Union Lib, Budapest 55-56; Asst acquis libn BrandeisU Lib 63-65; Hd acquis 65-67; Sr acquis & supt tech serv Info Dynamics Corp, Reading Mass 67-68; Hd ser OhioU Lib (Athens) 63-. 9: ALA. 12: "Valahonnan . . . Valahova" (66). 13: Yes. 14: Lib automation, systems design, acquis. 15: Plaza apt 7A Rte 3/50E, Athens Oh 45701.

SZERENYI, BELA JOSEPH. b Budapest 13 N 14. 4: Irene Pornyeczy. 5: Pazmany Peter U (Budapest) 35-39 (Law) LLB; Elizabeth U (Pecs Hungary) 39-40 (Law) Dr Jur; Bus Col (Budapest) 40-41 (Bus Admin); Syracuse 60-62 (LS) MS. 6: Fr, Hungarian, Ger. 7: (Lt) Hungarian Army 43-45; Libn Pub Lib, Budapest 46-48; Lawyer, Hungary 48-56; Bkstack supv Syracuse U 60-62; Asst libn Cornell U 62-64; Dir of Lib TriState Col 64-67; Dir of lib serv East Ill U 67-. 9: ALA;-ACRL; IllLA. 10: Beta Phi Mu; Kiwanis Club; Pi Sigma Alpha. 12: Ed "Investment Laws of Hungary" (50). 14: Admin, ref, acquis. 15: 503 Coolidge ave, Charleston Il 61920.

SZETO, DORCAS (CHOW). b Canton China 16 Jl 38. 4: Paul Szeto. 5: Alliance Bible Sem (Hong Kong) 57-61 BTh; Spring Arbor Col(Mich) 63-65 (Philos, Relig) BA; Asbury Theol Sem(Ky) 65-67 (Christian Educ) MRE; UWash 67-68 (LS). 6: Chinese (Mandarin, Cantonese), Greek. 7: Tchr (music, religion) Free Methodist schs, Hong Kong 62-63; Christian Educ dir Free Methodist Ch, Seattle 67-68; Catlgr Yale Divinity Lib 68-. 9: ATheolLA. 10: Alpha Kappa Sigma. 13: Yes. 14: Catlg. 15: 409 Prospect st, New Haven Ct 06510.

SZIGETHY, MARION C. b Budapest Hungary 16 F 19. 5: Columbia 62-65 (LS) MS with honors, 65- (LS). 6: Ger, Fr, Hungarian, Russian. 7: Ser libn Hungarian Nat Szechenyi Lib, Budapest Hungary 50-52, Assoc libn 52-54, Sci asst to dir of lib 54-56; Head Libn Free Europe Inc, NYC 62-65, Chief lib & ref serv 66-. 9: SLA (Soc Scis & Newspaper Documentation Divs; Adv Coun, NY Chap Dinner Chm); ASIS; NY Lib Club; ALA. 10: Beta Phi Mu. 13: Yes. 14: Documentation in the soc cis, tech serv, info sci, foreign area studies. 15: 169 E 92nd st, New York NY 10028.

SZILAGYI, OLIVER JOHN. b Marosvasarhely Transylvania Rumania 6 Ja 08. 4: Ruth Liebmann. 5: Protestant Col 18-26 BA; UCluj(Transylvania) 26-31 Dr Jur; Rosary Col 59-61 MLS. 6: Fr, Ger, Hungarian, Rumanian. 7: Lawyer Marosvasarhely Transylvania 31-45; Evangeliches Hilfswerk, Landshut Germany 46-48; Free lance researcher & sec, Paris 49-54; Travel employee Amer Express, Paris 54-56; Travel employee Amer Express, Chicago 56-60; Bibliogr SLA Tr Center, Chicago 60-62; Catlgr John Crerar Lib, Chicago 62-. 9: ALA. 14: Rare bks, catlg. 15: 9761 S Ingleside, Chicago Il 60628.

SZOSTAK, MARY ISABELLE (PIJANOWSKI). b Buffalo NY 13 Ag 25. 4: Edward J Szostak. 5: Nazareth Col (NY) 44-45 (Med Tech); UBuffalo 52-59 (Hist, Govt) BA; Rutgers 559-60 MSL. 6: Polish. 7: Lib clerk Erie Co Pub Lib, Buffalo NY 48-49, 50; Sr lib clerk Cheektowaga Mem Lib, Cheektowaga NY 50-59; Jr libn Buffalo & Erie Co Pub Lib, Buffao NY 60-62, Sr libn I 62-69; Dir Cheektowaga Pub Lib, Cheektowaga NY 69-. 8: Supv neighborhood youth project in Hist Dept Buffalo & Erie County Pub Lib 66-; In charge Local Hist Scrapbook Collection Buffalo & Erie Co Pub Lib 65-. 9: ALA; NYLA; Buffalo & Erie Co Pub Lib Staff Assn (Exec Bd 64-66, memb chm 68-69). 10: Polish Arts Club; Buffalo Coun on World Affairs; 500 Club of WNED-TV; SPCA; UBuffalo & Rutgers Alumnae Assns. 14: Adult serv, ref, local hist. 15: Cheektowaga Pub Lib, Cheektowaga NY 14225.

SZUSZKOWSKI, SOPHIE. b Montreal Can 27 Je 39. 5: UBC 57-58; McGill 58-61 (Eng, Pol Sci) BA, 64-65 BLS. 6: Fr, Polish. 7: Sec Royal Victoria Hosp, Montreal 62-64; Period libn Loyola Col (Montreal) 65-66; Ref libn Med Lib McGill 66-. 9: CanLA; MLA. 14: Ref. 15: 4403 Ave de la Depiniere, Montreal Can.

SZYMAITIS, CAROL ANN (MAZZA). b Pittsburgh Penn 30 My 45. 4: James Adam Szymaitis. 5: Clarion State Col 63-67 (Elem Educ) BS; UPittsburgh 67-69 MLS. 6: Fr. 7: Col aid for Head Start S Fayette Schs, Pittsburgh Penn summer 65; Tchr Chartiers Valley Sch Dist 67-68, Playground leader summer 68, Elem libn 68-. 14: Child & ya. 15: 306 Elmbrook lane, Pittsburgh Pa 15243.

T

TABACHNIK, ETHEL D. b Besarabia. 5: Washington Sq Col NYU 26-31 (Ger) BA; Columbia 32-34 (LS) MS, summer 59 (Med Lit & Libnship). ; SUNY Pub Libns Prof Certif; MedLA Certif of Med Libnship. 6: Ger, Russian. 7: Lib asst brs, sr asst, spec in wk with adults NY Pub Lib 20-58; NYU Med Center Lib: Prof asst 58-60, Faculty 60-62, Asst curator, asst ref libn 62-68; Free Lance Med Bibliog - on file NY Acad of Med 68-. 9: MedLA (NY Reg Group). 14: Ref, admi. 15: 44 Gramercy Park, NYC 10010.

TABORSKY, THERESA (ELISABETH). b Budapest Hungary 12 Ja 31. 5: Nazareth Col(Ky) 50-52; Trinity Col (Wash DC) 52-54 (Span) BA; NYU 59 (Fine Arts); Columbia 60-62 MSLS. 6: Hungarian, Ger, Sp, Fr. 7: Lib asst DC Pub Lib 54-56; Refugee Welfare Off, NCWC, Austria 56-58; Spec libn Petroleum Research, Conorada NY 58-62; Foreign lang catlgr LC 62-63; Admin libn Spec Serv 7th Inf Div US Army, Korea 63-64; Ref libn US Mil Acad (W Point) 64-66; Admin libn USAF, England 66-68; Asst Prof Lib Sci - Ser & docs order libn UUtah 68-. 8: Ref libn Lib/ USA, NY Worlds Fair 65; Tchg Ger Md Univ Overseas Program, US Army, Korea 63-64. 9: ALA; Hungarian LA; Utah LA; MPLA. 14: Ref, admin (Col libs), in-serv training, lib educ. 15: 1445 Princeton ave, Salt Lake City Ut 84105.

TABORSKY, VERA. b Pardubice Czechoslovakia 2 Ap 22. 4: Milos J Taborsky. 5: Prague U (Czechoslovakia) 46-48 (Pol Sci) BA (equiv); UParis 51 (Fr Lit & Lang Certif; So Conn State Col 59-60 (LS); Catholic U 61-65 MS in LS. 6: Fr, Ger, Czech, Slovak. 7: Searching asst Yale U Lib 59-61; Catlgr George Washington U Law Lib 61-66, Asst libn 66; Libn original catlg Mich State U Lib 66-. 9: ALA-ACRL; AALL; Law Libns Wash DC (Com on Certif, chm Lib Sci Com 65-66, Com on Union List Legal Periods in DC, chm 65-66); DCLA (Memb Com 65-66); MichLA (Memb Com 66-67, chm 68-69). 10: Mich State Univ Faculty Women. 11: Law Faculty Commendation Resolution George Washington U Law Ctr 66. 14: Catlg, tech serv, admin, law libnship. 15: 307 E Point lane, East Lansing Mi 48823.

TACKETT, EVELYN (D). b Jackson Miss 25 Ag 34. 5: Belhaven Col 52-56 (Eng Lit) BA; Emory 57-59 (LS) ML. 7: Asst libn Percy Mem Lib, Greenville Miss 56-57; Circ libn Theol Lib Emory U 57-59; Field rep Miss Lib Commsn, Jackson Miss 59-64; Assoc libn Belhaven Col 65-. 8: Sr asst libn, Kensington Central Lib, London 63. 9: MissLA (Bus mgr "Mississippi Library News). 10: . 14: Ref, periods 15: Belhaven Col, Jackson Ms 39202.

TAFEL, ELEANOR M. b E Orange NJ 21 D 08. 5: Beaver Col 26-29 (Journalism) BA; Drexel 29-30 (LS) BS. 7: Catlgr Tech Lib E I duPont de Nemours Inc 30-36; Pamphlet div Free Lib of Phila 36-39; Asst libn Acad of Motion Pictures 40-41; Libn Frankford Arsenal 41-50; Libn US Naval Shipyard, Phila 50-54; Libn Curtis Publ Co 54-61; Libn Fels Inst of Local & State Govt UPenn 62-64; Libn-in-chg interlib loan serv Free Lib of Phila 64-. 9: SLA (Dir Liaison Com 62-64; Bul ed Soc Sci Div 63-64; var other div activities; (Phila Chap: Bul ed 56-57, pres 58-59, chm Soc Sci Group 61-62, chm Nomin Com 62-63, chm Exhib Com 63-64). 12: . 14: Ref. 15: 919 S St Bernard st, Phila Pa 19143.

TAFT, FREDERICK L. b Cleveland Ohio 15 Ag 06. 4: Eleanor Barnes. 5: Amherst 24-28 (Hist) AB; West Res 36-42 (Eng) PhD. 6: Fr. 7: Instr West Res U 36-38; Lt Army Air corps 43-46; Instr-to Prof Eng Case Inst 38-, Exec officer dept lang & lit 53-59, Dir lib 58-68; Act dir libs Case West Res U 67-68, Assoc dir libs 68-. 9: Internat Assn Technol Univ Libs (sec 68-); ALA; SLA; Mod Lang Assn; Renaiss Soc Amer. 10: Phi Beta Kappa. 12: Ed bd, Yale Ed of "Complete Prose Works of John Milton," vol I. 14: Admin. 15: 20849 Byron rd, Shaker Heights Oh 44122.

TAFT, PATRICIA (SPILLER). b S Dartmouth Mass 12 F 17. 4: Charles B Taft. 5: Springfield City Lib Training Class (Mass) 34-35; Springfield Jr Col (Mass) 35-36 Prof certif; Providence Pub Lib Training Class 36-37. 7: Asst child's libn Boys & Girls Rm Providence Pub Lib 37-40, Acting child's libn Sprage House Br 40-41; Child's libn Pine Point Br Springfield City Lib, Mass 41-51; Child's libn Ernie Pyle Mem Br Albuquerque Pub Lib 65-67, Child's libn San Pedro Br 67-68, Child's libn & coord of Lib Serv to Child 68-. 9: ALA; NMLA (Program Chm Child & YA Div 67-68); Greater AlbuquerqueLA (2nd v-pres). 15: 423 Central st NE, Albuquerque NM 87101.

TAGGART, DOROTHY TREKELL. b Harper Kan 20 Ap 17. 4: James H Taggart. 5: Kan 34-38 (Eng, Fr) AB; UMinn 40 (LS); Wichita State U 63; UConn 65; USoFla summer 66; UWash summer 67; Kan State Tchrs Col 69 ML. 6: Fr. 7: Tchr Eng, Speech Hope Rural High Sch, Hope Kan 38-40; Libn Wellington High Sch, Wellington Kan 40-41; Eng & Journalism Wellington Jr-Sr High Sch, Wellington Kan 59-61; Libn Wellington Sr High Sch, Wellington Kan 61-69. 8: Participant, Nat Conf on Tchr Educ & Prof Standards, 65; MARC II Conf UColo 68; Evaluation Com N Central Assn. 9: NEA-DAVI; Kan State Tchrs Assn (v-pres 65-); KanLA (Secon Prj Com 65); KanASchL (second chm); Kan A-V Org; ALA; ASCD; Kan Assn for Curriculum Dev. 10: Mortar Board; pi Lambda Theta; AAUW; Wellington TA. 13: Yes. 14: Ref, admin. 15: 315 North C st, Wellington Ks 67512.

TAGGART, JOHN COOK. b Cleveland Ohio 26 S 40. 5: Bowling Green StateU 58-62 (Geol) BA; ToledoU 64-66 MALS. 6: Ger. 7: Air Force Res Admin Spec Sgt 63-69; Catlgr UKy Agric Lib 66-. 9: ALA; KyLA. 14: Catlg. 15: 1081 Cross Keys rd, Lexington Ky 40504.

TAGGART, THOBURN JR. b Ft Worth Tex 14 O 30. 4: Elizabeth Conover. 5: U of The South 49-53 (Pol Sci) BA Optime Merens; UTex Law Sch 53-55; Peabody 57-58 (LS) MA. 6: Sp, Fr. 7: Asst circ libn Kan State U (Manhattan)58-59, Asst ref libn 59-61; Asst libn Wayne State Col (Neb) 61-62; Soc sci ref libn Wichita State U 62-66, Asst Prof, Chief ref libn 66-68, Coord pub serv 68-. 9: ALA; MPLA; KanLA (chm Intel Freedom Com 66-67). 10: AAUP; Eng-Speaking Union; Beta Theta Pi; Gold Key; Wichita LA. 14: Ref, interlib loan, admin. 15: 244 North Yale, Wichita Ks 67208.

TAGGART, WILLIAM R(EID). b Glasgow Scotland 5 My 25. 4: Helen Shaw. 5: United Col UMan 46-49 BA; McGill 50-51 BLS, 51-52 (Eng) MA. 6: Fr. 7: Leading writer Royal Can Navy, Can & UK 44-46; Ref libn UBC 52-53, LECTURER Eng Dept 53-55; Reg libn Vancouver Island Reg Lib, Nanaimo BC 56-61; Bibliogr, head of bibliog dept 61-66; Hd collections div UVictoria (BC) 66-. 1-. 9: CanLA; ALA; BCLA (past coun & v-pres); ABCL; Inst Victoria Libns. 10: Island Concert Soc (Victoria BC). 12: Ed SaskLA "Bulletin" (65-66). 14: Bibliog, bk sel, rare bks. 15: 1606 Ash rd, Victoria BC Can.

TAI, HENRY H H. b China 16 Ap 22. 4: Yvonne Chiu. 5: Nat Chengchi U (Nanking China) 45-49 (Journalism) BA; Peabody 62-63 (LS) MA. 6: Chinese, Japanese. 7: Reporter, Ed Chinese Newspapers, Taiwan China 49-60; Instr Slippery Rock State Col 63-64; Asst libn SUNY Binghamton 64-66; Oriental catlgr UCal (Santa Barbara) 66-. 9: ALA; Assn for Asian Studs. 10: Civil Serv Employees Assn. 14: Catlg. 15: 5532 Tellina way, Santa Barbara Ca 93105.

TAITANO, MAGDALENA (SANTOS). b Agana Guam 1 Ja 28. 4: Richard F Taitano. 5: Mt Mary Col 51-55 (Bus Admin) BA; Tex Womas U 58-59 MLS. 6: Sp, Chamorro. 7: Guam Pub Lib, Agana Guam: Libn III 55-58, Libn IV 59-60, Chief Libn 60-61 Ref libn Off of Tech Serv Dept of Com, Wash DC 63-64; Chief Libn Col of Guam (Agana Guam) 64-66; Territorial libn Guam Pub Lib 66-. 9: ALA; GuamLA. 10: Guam Women's Club. 14: Catlg, ref. 15: PO Box 1328, Agana Guam 96910.

TAKAHASHI, KATHERINE (YOSHIKO). b Seattle Wash 28 My 31. 5: UWash 49-54 (Pharmacy) BS in Pharmacy, 66-69 MLS. 6: Japanese. 7: Staff pharmacist Providence Hosp, Seattle 54-66; Pharmacist Valley Gen Hosp, Renton Wash 66-67; Pharmacist Hall Health ctr UWash 67-; Relief pharmacist Doctor's Hosp, Seattle 67-; Relief pharmacist Maynard Hosp, Seattle 68-; Relief pharmacist Children's Orthopedic Hosp, Seattle 68-. 10: Amer Soc Hosp Pharmacists; Amer Pharmaceutical Assn; Wash State Soc Hosp Pharmacists. 14: Med ref. 15: 2437 S Spencer st, Seattle Wa 98108.

TAKAHASHI, SUMI. b Seattle 24 F 38. 5: Seattle U 56-60 (Math) BS; UWash 61-62 LS) ML. 7: Circ libn C S Mott Lib, Flint Mich 62-63, Asst ref libn 63-65; Sci libn Oakland U 65-66; Asst ref libn Seattle U 66; Circ libn Lewis & Clark Col 67-69. 9: ALA; PNLA. 14: Ref. 15: 199 E ave 203, Lake Oswego Or 97034.

TAKESHITA, KATSUYO LILLIAN. b San Francisco Cal 24 S 05. 4: Thomas K Takeshita. 5: UUtah 21-23 (Pre-med); AmericanU 51-57 (Lit) BA; CatholicU 60-62 (LS). 6: Japanese, Sp. 7: Monitor & translator Foreign Broadcast Info Serv, Wash DC 43-45; Translator Strategic Bombing Survey, Wash DC 46; Lib asst & catlgr LC 46, Ref libn 47-50; Ref libn & Japanese ser catlgr 51-61, Ed Japanese Union catlg 61-62, Subject catlgr for Japanese materials 62-. 8: Comp & ed "The Union List of Japanese periodicals in the United States under Special Grant" 61-62. 10: Japan-Amer Soc of Wash; Japanese-Amer Citizens League. 12: Tr of "A Japanese Paper-Folding Classic" (61). 13: Yes. 14: Subj catlg of Japanese wks in hist, lit & Buddhism. 15: 201 Anacostia rd SE, Washington DC 20019.

TALAT-KIELPSZ, ERYK. b Leningrad Russia6 My 11. 4: Janina Achramowicz. 5: UWarsaw 35 (Hist) AM, 37 Tchrs Certif; UMich 52 AMLS. 6: Polish, Russian, Latvian. Ger. 7: Asst ed Nasze Zycie, Riga Latvia 39; Sec State Polish High Sch, Riga Latvia 40; Catlgr State Lib, Riga Latvia 41-42; Acountant Coal Sale Co, Riga Latvia 42-44; Tchr Polish High Sch, Germany 45-47; Lib asst, prof lib asst UMich 48-54; Catlgr Ohio State U 54-62, Catlgr & Asst Prof of Lib Admin 63-. 9: ALA; Ohio Valley Group of Tech Serv Libns. 14: Catlg. 15: 236 W Norwich ave,Columbus Ohio 43201.

TALBOT, CARL A. b Rochester NY 1N 26. 5: Bob Jones U 47-49 (Liberal Arts); URochester 49-51 (Soc Sci) BS; Syracuse 53-58 MS in LS. 7: US Army clerk-typist (T/4), Ft Dix NJ 45-46; Clerk-typist Taylor Instrument Co, Rochester NY 46-47; Tchr Myers Park High Sch, Charlotte NC 51-52; Tchr W Seneca Central Sch, Buffalo NY 53-56; Libn Tokyo Amer High Sch, Tokyo 56-57, Bd of Coop Educ Serv, Penfield NY 58-60, Monroe High Sch, Rochester NY 60-62; Head libn Monroe Commun Col 62-. 9: ALA; NYLA. 10: AAUP; Beta Phi Mu. 14: Ref, tchg function of the lib. 15: PO Box 9701, Rochester NY 14623.

TALBOT, DIXIE (BREEDING). b Marysville Kan 11 Ja 43. 4: Thomas W Talbot. 5: UKan 60-64 (Lat) BS in Ed; Kan State Tchrs Col 64-66 (Libnship) MS. 6: Lat, Sp. 7: Period asst Kan State Tchrs Col 64-66; Asst libn acquis dept UNeb Libs (Lincoln) 66-, Order libn 66-. 9: ALA (Jr Mem RT: Exec Bd Neb Chap); NebLA (Mem Com). 15: 5500 Orcutt ave s, Lincoln Nb 68504.

TALBOT, KENT DOUGLAS. b Chicago Ill 12 Ap 40. 5: Knox Col 57-62 (Sociol) AB; Loyola (Chicago) 62-66 (Law) JD; UChicago 66- (LS). 6: Ger, Fr. 7: Ref libn UChicago Law Lib 66-. 9: ALA; ABA; AALL; Ill State Bar Assn; Chicago Bar Assn; Chicago Assn Law Libns. 10: Bar Assn of the 7th Federal Circuit. 14: Law libs, readers serv. 15: 1121 E 60th st, Chicago Il 60637.

TALBOT, MARY JO (WALSH). b Minneapolis 11 Ja 28. 4: Kenneth D Talbot. 5: Col of St Catherine 45-49 (LS) BS. 6: Braille. 7: Asst libn St Mary's Col (Minn) 49-52; Libn Anoka Pub Lib, Anoka Minn 52-67; Libn Brown & Bigelow, St Paul 67-68; Br asst Hennepin Co Lib, Crystal Minn 68-. 9: MinnLA. 10: Philolectian. 14: Ref. 15: 1823 Green ave, Anoka Mn 55303.

TALBOT, RICHARD JOSEPH. b Lynn Mass 18 D 32. 4: Joanne Hines. 5: Manhattan Col 50-54 (Philos) AB; St Johns (Boston) 57-58 (Philos); Gregorian U (Rome) 58-60 (Theol); Simmons 60-61 MS in LS. 6: Fr, Ital, Lat, Russian. 7: (1st Lt) USAF 54-57; Ref libn NY Pub Lib Bronx Ref Center 61-62; Catlgr CIA Lib, Langley Va 62-63, Dep Chief acquis 63-64, Catlgr 64-65; Admin libn NASA Electronic Research Ctr Lib, Cambridge Mass 65-67; Hd catlg & systs USAF Cambridge Research Lib, Bedford Mass 67-. 9: ALA; SLA (Sci-Tech Div, Boston Chap v-pres & pres-elect 68-70). 13: Yes. 14: Catlg, lib automation. 15: 8 Joyce rd, Wayland Ma 01778.

TALBOTT, (THELMA) MAE. b Elkins W Va 24 O 33. 5: WVaU 52-56 (Secondary Educ) BS; Fla StateU 56-58, 60 (LS) MS. 6: Sp, Ger. 7: Sub-Prof in circ Washington Co Free Lib (Hagerstown Md) 57; Mus store clerk Allens Mus Store (Martinsburg West Va) 58-59; Order libn & instr Radford Col Woman's Div of Virginia Polytechnic Inst (Radford Virginia) 59-61; Asst ref libn Washington Co Free Lib (Hagerstown Md) 61-67, Ref libn 67-. 9: ALA; -RSD (Md Chap); MdLA; CumberlandValleyLA. 10: Wash Co Free Lib Staff Assn; AAUW; Suburban Music Gp. 14: Ref, catlg, a-v. 15: 930 Oak Hill ave, Hagerstown Md 21740.

TALKINGTON, DONALD EDWARD. b Detroit 19 O 36. 5: UTampa 57-59 (Bus Admin); Detroit Inst of Tech 60-61 (Bus Admin); Wayne State U 61-63 (Hist) BA; UMich 63-65 MALS. 6: Sp. 7: US Coast Guard Storekeeper Br 53-57; Accounting clerk Gen Motors Corp, Detroit 59-61; Pre-prof libn Detroit Pub Lib 63-65, Libn I 65-67; Asst ref & interlib loans Fla Atlantic U 66-67, Asst acquis libn 67, Assoc libn head sers dept 67-. 9: ALA; FlaLA; SELA. 14: Ya serv, tech serv, automation. 15: 1202 SW 1st ave apt 4, Boca Raton Fl 32670.

TALLENT, DOROTHY IRENE (DAFFER). b Wilsonville Neb 16 Ja 25. 4: R J Tallent. 5: East Wash State Col 58-62 (Elem Educ) BA Educ; UWash 65-69 MLibr. 6: Sp. 7: Tchr Auburn Sch Dist 408, Auburn Wash 60-65, Sch libn 66-. 9: NEA; WashEA; AuburnEA. 14: Child libn. 15: 502 Knickerbocker dr, Auburn Wa 98002.

TALLMAN, JOHANNA E(LEONORE) (ALLERDING). b Lubeck Germany 18 Ag 14. 4: Lloyd A Tallman. 5: Los Angeles Pacific Col 32-33; Los Angeles City Col 33-34 AA; UCal(Berkeley) 34-36 (Fr) AB, 36-37 Certif in Libnship. 6: Ger. 7: Asst libn San Marino Pub Lib, San Marino Cal 37-38; Various Los Angeles Co Pub Lib, Los Angeles 38-40, Tech ref libn 40-42; Asst libn Pacific Aeronautical Lib, Los Angeles 42-43, Libn 43-44; UCLA: Lecturer Sch of Lib Serv 61-, Coordinator Phys Sci Libs 62-, Libn Engnr & Math Sci Lib 45-. 8: Dir, Recatlg Proj, US Naval Ordnance Test Sta, Pasadena 51; Consul on Lib org & tech lit, mainly to Corporations; Fulbright lectr Brazil 66-67. 9: ALA (Coun 49-53; Subs Bks Com 54-56)-ACRL (Exec Bd 52-53; chm Engnr Sch Libs Sect 49-50)-Div Catlg & Clsf (mem va coms); SLA (co-chm Engnr Aeronautics Sect of Sci-Tech Group 47-48; So Cal Chap: pres 65-66, several offs & chm var coms); Amer Coms; chm Sci-Tech Div 69-70); Engnr Educ (Engnr Sch Libs Com: Exec Bd 49-51, chm 53-54); ADI; Soc ASIS; Tech; CalLA (mem var coms; So Dist: chm Col Univ & Res Libs Sect 54); Los ngeles Reg Angeles of Catlgrs (chm 46-47). 12: Jt comp "Subject Headings for Aeronautical Engineering Libraries SLA (49). 13: Yes. 14: Tech lit, spec lib org, ser. 15: 2253 Linda dr, Los Angeles Ca 90024.

TALMADGE, ROBERT LOUIS. b Seattle 22 My 20. 4: Phyllis Wherry. 5: Kan City (Kan) Jr Col 37-39 (Liberal Arts); UKan 39-41 (Soc Sci) AB; UIll 46 BS in LS, 46-51 MS in LS; Rutgers 56 (LS). 7: Naval Aviator (to Lt sg) US Naval Res 41-45; UIll Lib (Urbana): Catlgr 46-50, Bibliog 50-51, Admin asst to dir 51-53; Assoc dir UKan Lib 53-59, Act dir 59-60;Dir Tulane U Lib 60-66; Dir tech depts UIll (Urbana) 66-. 8: Asst dir ALA-ACRL Farmington Survey 57-58; Commsn on Higher Educ in Amer Republics Univ Lib Survey Central Amer 61; Lib Surveys; Alma Col 67, Northeast Ill State Col 67, UCincinnati 68; Dir Forest Press, Lake Placid NY 69-. 57-58. 9: ALA (Coun 62-; mem & chm Memb Com 58-62; Exec Bd 66-);-ACRL (Bd Dirs 62-, mem & chm Com on Recr 51-57; -LAD (Lib Org & Mgt Sect); State Com for Col & Univ Libs 58-64, chm 67-68);-RTSD (Tech serv adminrs of medium-sized res libs; mem 58-, chm 62-63, Tech Serv Dirs of Large Res Libs 66-); KanLA (chm Col & Univ Libs Sect 57-58); LaLA (chm State Planning Com 62-65, La Col Conf, chm Lib Sect 64-65); New Orleans Lib Club (pres 63-64; La State Bd Lib Examiners 64-66). 10: Beta Phi Mu; AAUP; Rotary; Round Table Club; Phi Kappa Phi; Boy Scouts. 12: "The Alma College Library: A Survey with R B Harwell (58); Ed "Frmington Plan Survey, Final Report with R Vosper (59). 13: Yes. 14: Univ lib admin. 15: Univ of Illinois Lib, Urbana Il 61801.

TALMAGE, REV JOHN PHILLIP. b Brooklyn NY 31 Mr 28. 4: Suzanne Kay. 5: UVa 46-50 (Music) BA; Nashotah House (Sem) 50-53, 63-65 (Theol) BD; UMinn 55 (Educ); ST Thomas Col (St Paul) 56-57 (Educ); UWis 63-65 MA(LS). 7: Vicar Church of Christ the King, E Meadow NY 53-54; Curate Gethsemane Church, Minneapolis 54-58; Exec Dir Downtown Found, Minneapolis 55-58; Vicar Holy Innocents Church, Nashotah Wis 58-63; Vicar Grace Church, Hartland Wis 62-63; Instr in Music Nashotah House Sem, Nashotah Wis 62-64; Asst ref libn UWis(Milwaukee) 65-66; Reader serv libn Marquette U 66-68, Hd of ref serv 68-. 8: Dept of Educ, Episcopal Diocese of Milwaukee 59-61; Exec Bd, Episcopal Diocese of Milwaukee 61-62; Del, Synod of the Prov of the Midwest, Episcopal Church, Peoria Ill 63. 9: ALA. 10: Milwaukee Clericus; AAUP. 14: Liturgics & liturgical music, theol libnship, bibliog, ref. 15: 610 Silver Lake st, Oconomowoc Wi 53066.

TALMAGE, SUZANNE (KAY). b Greybull Wyo 21 N 27. 4: John Philip Talmage. 5: Mary Washington Col 45-46 (Mus); UVa 46-49 BS in Ed; UWis (Milwaukee) 63-65; UWis (Madison) summers 65-67 MS in LS. 7: Tchr Meriwether Lewis Sch Ivy Va 49-50; Bus rep Wisconsin Tele Co, Waukesha Wis 50-51; Tchr: Okauchee Elem Sch, Okauchee Wis 51-53, Kenwood Sch, Minneapolis 57-58, Hartland Elem Sch, Hartland Wis 61-65; Libn Hartland Elem Sch, Hartland Wis 65-. 9: NEA; ALA; WisEA; WisLA. 14: Child bks. 15: 610 Silver Lake st, Oconomowoc Wi 53066.

TALMAN, JAMES J(OHN). b Beira Portugese E Africa 15 S 04. 4: Ruth H Davis. 5: UWest Ont 21-25 (Hist, Econ) BA, 25-27 (Hist, Econ) MA; Toronto 27-30 (Hist) PhD. 7: Asst Archives of Ont, Toronto 30-3, Archivist 34-39; Legis libn Legis Lib of Ont, Toronto 35-39; Asst libn UWest Ont 39-47; Commanding Off (Lt Col) UWO Cont COTC 47-54; Chief Libn UWest Ont 47-. 9: CanLA (treas 55-58; chm Microfilm Com); OntLA (pres 45-46). 10: Hist Sites & Monuments Bd of Can; Can Hist Assn; Ont Hist Soc; Royal Soc of Can (Fellow). 11; D Litt (Hon) Univ of Waterloo, 60. 12: "Loyalist Narratives from Upper Canada (46); "Western-1878-1953 with R Talman (5); "Basic Documents in Canadian History (59): "Hurn College, 1863-1963 (63); etc. 13: Yes. 14: Lib admin. 15: Northcrest dr, Rt 2, London Ont Can.

TAMBELLINI, DOLORES CATHERINE. b E Chicago Ind 10 N 35. 5: Ind U 57-61 (Eng) AB, 61-62 (LS) MA. 6: Fr. 7: Stud ref asst Ind U 61-62; Ref libn Pub Lib, Hammond Ind 62-64; Child libn Pub Lib San Diego, La Jolla Cl 64-67; Ref libn Cal West U 67-68; Asst circ libn San Diego State Col 69-. 9: ALA (Jr Mems Round Table); CalLA (San Diego Co Memb Chm 67-; Recruitment Chm 66-); SLA; So Cal Tech Processes Group. 10: Beta Phi Mu; Amer Nat Theatre Assn; Old Globe Theater Guild (San Diego); La Jolla Mus Art. 14: Ref, child & yp, serv to adults, col & univ libs. 15: 411 Vincente way, La Jolla Ca 92037.

TAMBLYN, ELDON WALDO. b Centralia Wash 19 N 28. 5: U Puget Sound 46-51 (Fr) BA; Syracuse 52-53 (Russian) AF Certif; UNC 61-62 MSLS. 6: Russian, Fr, Sp. 7: TV engnr WPIX-TV, NYC summer 57; Billing dept Chief Raleigh Records Inc, NYC 57-58; TV engnr WAVY-TV, Portsmouth Va 58-61; Catlgr UNC Lib (Chapel Hill) 61-62; Libn UNC Sch of Lib Sci summer 62; Catlgr Slavic materials Duke U Lib 62-64; Catlgr Slavic materals Stanford U Lib 64-67; Hd catlgr Portland State U 67-. 13: Yes. 14: Catlg. 15: Apt 501 2020 SW Main st, Portland Or 97205.

TAMS, MADGE (PENTON). b Salem NJ 19 O 06. 5: Wilson Col 24-28 (Eng) BA; UPenn 30 (Educ); LSU summer 31 (Eng); Emory 33-34 BA in LS.06: Fr. 6: Fr. 7: Eng tchr Ocean City High Sch, Ocean City NJ 28-33; Tchr-libn Temple U High Sch, Phila 34-36; Asst ref libn Temple U Lib 36-42; Libn train div US Army Signal Corps, Signal Dept Phila 42-43; Lt(jg) US Navy WAVES, Wash DC 43-46 Libn Engnr Lib Kaiser-Fleetwings, Bristol Penn 46-47; Libn Lab Div Radio Corp Amer, Pinceton Princeton 47-48; Libn Frick Chem Lib, Princeton U 48-55; Scilibn Sci libn Lib 58-60, Head bibliog room 60-67, Asst libn dept of ref & bibliog, Asst chm of dept 67-. 8: Prof Consul, Nat Lib Week, Fla 66. 9: ALA; ASIS; FlaLA (chm Ref Round Table 65-66); SELA. 10: AAUP; Philharmonic Soc of Gainesville. 13: Yes. 14: Bibliog, ref, lib application of computers. 15: Univof Fla Lib, Gainesville Fla 32603.

TANDLER, VIRGINIA CLAIRE. b Saginaw Mich 3 D 41. 5: UColo 59-63 (Elem Educ) BS; UMich 67-69 (LS) MA. 6: Fr. 7:

Elem tchr Pub Schs, Beaverton Ore 63-65; Elem tchr Pub Schs, Ann Arbor Mich 65-67; Camp dir YMCA, Penn 65-66 summer; Camp dir YMCA, NY 67- summers.

TANEJA, REMESH CHANDAR. b Dera Ismail Khan Pakistan 16 S 31. 4: Virginia A Lathers. 5: Panjab U (New Delhi India) 57 (Pre-med, Pol Sci) BA; Nagpur U (Nagpur India) 59 (LS) Diploma; Ottawa U 60-62 BLS, MLS; UCLA 65-68 (Info Analysis). 6: 32 Langs including Ger, Fr, Hindi, Sanskrit, Urdu, Persian, Arabic, Turkish, 7 African, 6 Indian. 7: Hd libn All India Radio Lib, New Delhi 55-60; Libn Canadian Lib Assn, Ottawa 61; Ref libn Kern Co Free Lib, Bakersfield Cal 62; Catlgr UCLA 63-65; Hd catlg dept Gianinni Control Corp, Duarte Cal 64-65, Hd libn 65-66; Hd catlg dept Northrop norair, Hawthorne Cal 67-. 9: SLA; CalLA. 10: Heart Assn. 13: Yes. 14: Catlg. 15: 4042 York Hill pl, Los Angeles Ca 90041.

TANG, ANGELA. b Canton China 18 Ja 38. 5: Nat Taiwan U 59 (Zool) BS; Villanova U 62 (LS) MS. 6: Chinese. 7: Ref libn St Francis Col (Loretto Penn); Mary Meuser Mem Lib, Easton Penn. 9: PennLA. 14: Admin. 15: Mary Meuser Mem Lib, Easton Penn 18042.

TANG, EUGENIA CHE-GEN (YING). b China 28 F 38. 4: Yi-Noo Tang. 5: Nat Taiwan U 57-61 (Eng Lit) BA; Peabody 62-64 MA in LS. 6: Chinese, Sp. 7: Sr descr catlgr St Louis Pub Lib 64; Catlg libn So Cal Col 65-67; Catlg maintenance libn Texas A&M U 68-. 14: Catlg. 15: 20110 Acacia st, Santa Ana Ca 92707.

TANG, WAI-FONG. b Hong Kong China 19 D 41. 5: Chung Chi Col (Hong Kong) 61-65 (Sociol) BA; UHawaii 65-67 (Sociol) MA, 67-68 MLS. 6: Chinese. 7: Grad tchg asst UHawaii 65-67; Research tr Res Pub & Tran IAP TWC UHawaii 67-68; Libn II Fresno State Col 68-. 9: CalLA. 14: Acquis. 15: 4435 S Frontenac st, Seattle Wa 98118.

TANGEN, MAY. b Menahga Minn 9 My 05. 5: Moorhead State Col 23-33 (Eng) BEd; UMinn 35-39 (LS); Chicago 41-48 (LS) MA. 6: Norwegian. 7: Tchr rural schs, Becker Co Minn 23-27; Tchr & supv Oak Mound Consolidated Sch, Moorhead Minn 28-32; Tchr & prin pub sch, Warren Mi34-38; Asst libn Moorhead State Col 39-43; Asst ref libn IndU 44-46; Ref libn UIowa Psych-Educ Lib 47-67; Circ libn Rust Col 67-. 9: ALA; IowaLA. 10: Pi Lambda Theta. 14: Ref. 15: Box 54 Rust Col, Holly Springs Ms 38635.

TANIGUCHI, MAYUMI. b Fukuoka Japan 15 My 30. 5: Tokyo Womens Christian Col 48-51 (Math) Tchrs Certif, 51-53 (Psych) BA; UMich 57-59 MALS. 6: Japanese. 7: Research asst Nagoya U Med Sch Dept of Psychiatry (Nagoya Japan) 53-56; Research asst UMich Psychological Clinic 56-57; Lib asst UMICH Lib 57-59; Sr asst libn UNeb Sch of Med Lib 59-60; Research libn Keio U Sch of Med Lib (Tokyo) 6-63; Libn & lit analyst NLM, Bethesda Md 63-65; Sr catlgr for Japanese materals LC 65-68, Supv Japanese lang unit descr catlg div 68-. 9: Potomac Tech Proc Libns; DCLA. 13: Yes. 14: Catlg. 15: Lib of Congress, Wash DC 20540.

TANIS, JAMES (ROBERT). b Phillipsburg NJ 26 Je 28. 4: Florence Borgmann. 5: Yale 46-51 (Hist) BA; Union Theol Sem 51-54 (New Testament) BD; U Utrecht 62-67 (Church Hist) D Th. 6: Ger, Dutch. 7: Co-pastor Greystone Presbyterian Church, Elizabeth NJ 54-56; Libn Harvard Divinity Sch 57-65; U Libn Yale U 65-68, Faculty Divinity Sch 68-69; Dir of libs Prof of hist Bryn Mawr 69-. 9: ATheolLA; ALA; ConnLA; ARL. 10: Presbyter of Conn Valley; Bd of Gen Theol Lib (Boston); Bd Amer Antiquarian Soc; Bd Martin Luther King Research Ctr. 13: Yes. 14: Calg, rare bks & mss, bk sel. 15: Bryn Mawr College, Bryn Mawr Pa 19010.

TANNEHILL, ROBERT S, JR. b Vicksburg Miss 3 D 40. 4: Betsy Gardner. 5: USo Miss 58-62 (Chem) BA; Drexel 66-67 (Info Sci) MS. 6: Ger. 7: Lib clk Evansville Pub Lib, Evansville Ind 62; 1st Lieut US Army Ordnance Corps 63-66; Libn Sadtler Research Labs, phila 66-67; Info scientist Med Center Lib VanderbiltU 67-69, Interim dir 69; Asst libn Chem Abstracts Serv, Columbus Ohio 69-. 9: ASIS; MedLA (So Reg Gp Program Chm 68); Mid-StateLA (Exec Coun). 10: Kappa Sigma. 14: Info syst (devel, application & mgt). 15: Chemical Abstracts Serv Ohio State Univ, Columbus Oh 43210.

TANNENBAUM, EARL. b Milwaukee 30 Jl 15. 4: Barbara E Baird. 5: UWis 34-36 (Eng) BA; Chicago 46-47 (Eng) MA; UWis 47-48 (Eng); Ind U 48-50 (Eng, 52-53 MA in LS. 6: Fr, Sp. 7: Tchg Fellow in Eng LSU 47; Instr Div of Adult Educ Ind U 50-52; Asst libn head catlgr Wis State Col (Whitewater) 53-56; Asst humanities libn So Ill U 57-61; Head Libn Regis Col (Denver) 61-68; Asst dir pub serv Ind State U 69-. 8: Visiting Lecturer; Ind u Lib Sch 58, UDenver Grad Sch of Libnship 62-. 9: ALA; CathLA; MPLA; ColoLA (v-pres 63, chm Col & Univ Sect 62-63); Bibliog Center for Research, Rocky Mountain Reg treas 63-65); IndLA. 10: Beta Phi Mu. 12: Jt auth "Introduction to Cataloging and Classification (64); Ed "D H Lawrence: an Exhibition of First Editions, Manuscripts, Paintings. (58. 13: Yes. 14: Admin, lib educ, ref, catl. 15: 2503 Dahlia st, Denver Co 80207.

TANNER, ALICE BARBIERI (NANCY). b Waterloo NY 4 Je 39. 4: Richard F Tanner. 5: SUNY (Geneseo) 57-61 (Elem Educ) BS; SUNY (Albany) 64-65 MLS; San Jose State Col 65 (LS); UCal (Berkeley) 68 (Italian). 7: Libn Waterloo Central Schs, Waterloo NY 61-64; Libn Ballston Spa Sch Dist, Ballston Spa NY 64-65; Hd libn Oakland Unified Sch Dist, Oakland Cal 66-68; Instr Chabot Jr Col, Hayward Calif 66-68; Asst educ libn San Diego State Col, San Diego Calif 69-. 8: Workshop Chm 68 Calif Assn of Sch Libns Annual Conference, San Francisco Calif (Library Technology). 9: ALA; COLT; CalASchL (Wkshop Chm 1968 Conf); CalLA. 14: Sch libnship, lib tech. 15: 3031 Kobe dr, San Diego Ca 92123.

TANNER, BRUCE A. b Des Moines Iowa 27 Ja 21. 4: Bernice Boian. 5: Drake U 41-42, 46-48, 48-54 (Bus) BCS; UWis 66-67, 68-69 (LS). 7: Radio Oper T/4 358th Sl Bn 42-46; Tchr 48-59; Asst ref libn Moines Pub Lib, Des Moines Iowa 59-60; Asst libn Drke Drake Lib 60; Libn Kirkendall Pub Lib, Ankeny Iowa 60-64; Field consul Northwest Area Coop Iowa Stae Travel Lib, Sheldon Iowa 64-. 9: IowaLA. 14: Ref, coops. 15: 305 - 10th st, Sheldon Iowa 51201.

TANNER, CLARABEL (WEIR). b Kansas City Mo 30 S 18. 4: Fred A Tanner. 5: UNM 3637; Tex Tech 3839; USoCal 3941 (Eng) AB, 6163 (LS) MA. 7: Exec asst John Robert Powers, Los Angeles 5763; Libn Santa Monica Schs, Santa Monica Cal 63. 8: Tchr of Lib Sci UOre summer 69. 9: NEA; ALA; CalASchL. 10: Santa Monica CityTA. 11: International Biography. 13: Yes. 14: Writing for child. 15: 18345 Wakecrest dr, Malibu Ca 90265.

TANTOCO, DOLORES WYTANGCOY. b Barasoain Malolos Bulacan Philippines 9 Ap 30. 5: UPhilippines 48-52 BSLS; Syracuse 55-57 MSLS. 6: Tagalog, Ger, Sp, Fr, Lat, Ital. 7: Ser gifts & exchange libn UPhilippines 52-55; Pub serv libn, SyracuseU Main Lib 55-56; Libn-in-charge, Lib Sch Lib Syracuse 56-57; Catlgr UNotre Dame Lib (Ind) 57-61; Chief catlg libn UPhilippines 61-64; Sr catlgr UNotre Dame Memorial Lib (Ind) 64, Humanities libn-catlgr 64-67, Asst libn-catlgr 67-69, Assoc libn-catlgr 69-. 8: Lib consul Cath For Mission Soc of Amer Maryknoll Fathers Lib 69-. 9: ALA; PhilippineLA; Bibliog Soc of Philippines. 10: Fac Senate UNotre Dame 68-71; AAUP; Notre Dame Lib Staff Assn; Notre DameLA. 14: Catlg, ref, ser, gifts & exchange, circ, acquis, inter-lib loans. 15: 1102 Stanfield st, South Bend In 46617.

TAPLIN, FRANKLIN P. b Wellesley Mass 28 Jl 19. 4: Nancy E Stearns. 5: Amherst 37-39 (Humanities); New Eng Conservatory of Music 39-42 (Musical Research) B Mus; Boston U 46-50 (Music Educ) M Mus Ed; Simmons 53-58 (LS) MS. 7: USAAF Adjutant Gens Dept (Cpl) 42-45; Gen & music asst Newton Free Lib, Newton Mass 52-54; Ref asst Springfild City Lib, SPRINGFIELD Mass 54-58; Asst libn Waltham Pub Lib, Waltham Mass 59; Libn Holyoke Pub Lib, Holyoke Mass 59-62; Dir West MASS Reg Lib System, Springfield Mass 62-67; Dir Westfield Athenaeum, Westfield Mass 67-. 8: Exc dir, Nat Lib Week, Mass 61; Instr Lib Sci Westfield State Col, Westfield Mass 68-. 9: ALA; NELA; MassLA (pres 63-64, chm Planning Com 67-); West Mass Lib Club (Auditor 64-67, v-pres 67-); Conn Valley Lib Club. 10: Nat Conf of Christians & Jews; Rotary; Mass Lib Trustees Assn; Coun on Arts & Humanities. 13: Yes. 14: Admin, ref, music & fine arts, INTERLIB COOP. 15: 220 State st, Springfield Mass 01103.

TAPPER, ETHEL WINIFRED. b Aurora Ill 16 Ap 15. 5: Aurora Col 31-35 (Hist, Math) BA; UIll summers 37-40 BS in ls; Chicago 47-50 (Educ) PhD. 6: Lat, Ger. 7: Tchr pub schs, Aurora Ill 35-37; Libn & Prof of Eng, chm of Eng Dept Aurora Col 37-. 9: Mod Lang Assn; NCTE; ALA. 10: AAUW; pi Lambda Theta; Bus & Prof Womens Club. 13: Yes. 14: Admin, lid bldgs. 15: Aurora Col, Aurora Ill 60507.

TARAKAN, SHELDON LEWIS. b NYC 25 Je 42. 4: Barbara Rita Chase. 5: Manhattan Sch of Mus 62-63 (Composition); Queens Col (NY) 60-65 (Mus) BA, 65-67 (Musicology), 67-68 mls. 6: Fr. 7: Asst ed Random House Inc, NYC 65-67; Children's libn Lynbrook Pub Lib, Lynbrook NY 67; Chief ref libn Bellmore Memorial Lib, Bellmore NY 67-68; Lib dir S Windsor Pub Lib, S Windsor Conn 68-. 9: ALA; NELA; ConnLA; NYLA; NassauCo (NY) LA. 10: Amer Folklore Soc; Soc for Ethnomusicology; NY Hist Soc; African Soc; Intl Folk Music Coun. 12: Music ed "Random House Dictionary of the English Language". 13: Yes. 14: Lib devel, catlg, rare bk materials, ref. 15: 115 S Main st, W Hartford Ct 06107.

TARARIN, PETER A. b Leovo Romania 18 Ag 17. 4: Maria Elsa Arancibia Bidinost. 5: Yenching U (Peking West, China) 38-42 (West Lang & Lit) BA; UCLA 52-54 (Pre-Libnship) BA; USoCal 54-56, MSLS. 6: Fr, Russian, Chinese. 7: Sec Amer Red Cross for N China WWII internees & libn Amer Red Cross Embassy Club for US Armed Forces serviceman, Peking 45-46; Instr West Lang & Lit Dept Yenching U, Peking West 46-47; Ed US Exec Hdqrs Hist Sect, Peking 46-47; Sec Off of the Rector Catholic U, Peking 47-48; Admin asst Welfare Div UN-IRD, Samar Philippines 49-50; Priv sec, San Marino Cal 51-52; Staff mem Doheny Lib USoCal 55-56, Acquis libn Sch of Med Lib 56-58; Libn Simmel-Fenichel Lib Los Angeles Psychoanalytic Soc & Inst, Beverly Hills 60-. 8: Library consul to acad med and welfare instms, and indus, private bus & private collectors in the Los Angeles area 58-. 9: ALA; Med Lib Gp So Cal. 10: Royal Asiatic soc; Assn for Asian Studies; The China Stamp Soc; The China Soc of So Cal. 12: Ed "Bulletin of The China Society of Southern California 1960". 13: Yes. 14: Ref, Orientalia bk collecting. 15: 623 North Harper ave, Los Angeles Ca 90048.

TARBOX, RUTH WADDELL. b Mellen Wis 16 O 11. 5: Northland Col 2832 (Lat) BA; UMinn 4041 BS in LS. 7: Tchr; Jr & Sr high, Drummond Wis 3233, Sr high, Shell Lake Wis 3335; Elem libn Roosevelt Sch, Wauwatosa Wis 3540, 4142; Br libn Roxboro Jr High Sch, Cleveland Hts Ohio 4243; Dir wk with child Pub Lib & Pub Schs, River Forest Ill 4346; Dir sch & lib serv Field Enterprises Educ Corp, Chicago 4665; Exec sec ALACSD & YASD, Chicago 66. 8: Consul; Sch Lib Inst Florence State Col 63; Sch Lib Wkshop USan Francisco 66; NDEA Sch Lib Inst Miss StateU 6869. 9: ALA; WNBA. 10: Beta Phi Mu. 13: Yes. 14: Child & ya wk in sch & pub libs. 15: 1360 Lake Shore dr, Chicago Il 60610.

TARLIN, HARRY NATHANIEL. b Boston 10 Mr 20. 4: Sonia Greenberg. 5: Northeastern U 45-50 (Eng Lit) BA (summa cum laude); Boston U 50-51 (Amer Lit) MA; Simmons 51-52 MSLS. 7: (T/Sgt) Air Force Communications, Greenland, Panama 41-45; Brandeis u lib: Ser libn 52-53, Acquis libn 53-55, Head tech serv 55-60, Asst dir 60-63, Assoc dir 64-67; Dir of lib Utica Col of Syracuse U 67-. 9: ALA; NYLA. 14: Acquis, admin. 15: 65 Prospect st, Utica NY 13501.

TARLTON, SHIRLEY MARIE. b Raleigh NC 8 Ag 37. 5: Peace Jr Col 55-57; Queens Cl 58-60 (Fr) AB; UNC summers 61-64 MSLS. 6: Fr, Sp. 7: Lib asst Charlotte-Mecklenburg Sch System, Charlotte NC 52-61; Head catlg dept UNC (Charlotte) 61-66, Hd tech serv div 66-68; Hd tech serv Winthrop Col 68-. 9: ALA; SELA; NCLA; SCLA. 10: AAUP. 14: Catlg, acquis, admin, ser. 15: 3122 Circles End, Matthews NC 28105.

TARNA, IMRE. b Eger Hungary 5 O 08. 4: Margaret Scherubl. 5: Ferenc Jozsef U of Sci 30 (Law) Doctor of Law. 6: Hungarian, Ger. 7: Asst ref libn UDetroit 62-. 13: Yes. 14: Ref. 15: 20099 Murray Hill, Detroit Mi 48235.

TARNAWSKY, MARTA (SENKOWSKY). b Lviv Ukraine 15 N 30. 4: Ostap E M Tarnawsky. 5: Temple 54-62 (Sociol) BA (summa cum laude); Drexel 62-64 (LS) MS. 6: Ukrainian, Polish, Ger, Fr, Russian. 7: Libn I Free Lib of Phila 64-67; For law libn Biddle Law Lib UPenn 67-. 9: AALL. 10: Phi Kappa Phi. 13: Yes. 14: Catlg, bibliog, law libnship. 15: 4626 N 13th st, Phila Pa 19140.

TARNAWSKY, OSTAP E M. b Lviv Ukrain 3 My 17. 4: Marta Senkowsky. 5: ULviv 35-39 (Langs); Polytech Inst of Lviv 39-41 Civil Engnr); Technische Hochschule Graz 46-47 (Civil Engnr); Drexel 61-62 (LS) MS. 6: Ger, Russian, Ukrainian, Polish, Lat, Gk. 7: Catlgr Newark Pub Lib, Newark NJ 62-63; Catlgr Temple U Lib 64-65; Hd catlgr Commun Col of Phila 66-. 10: Ukrainian Writers Assn. 12: Four bks of poems (in Ukrainian); Two bks of Literary Essays. 13: Yes. 14: Catlg, rare bks. 15: 4626 N 13th st, Phila Pa 19140.

TARPLEY, MARY EASLEY. b Whitmell Va 5 Ja 13. 5: Mary Washington Col 30-33 (Eng, Soc Sci) BS; UNC summers 50-51 (LS) NC & Va Sch Certif; Rutgers 60-62 MLS. 6: Fr. 7: Tchr, legal sec, cosmetician, Danville Va 33-45; Libn-tchr High schs, Pittsylvania Co Va 45-53; Tchr grade sch, Arlington Co Va 53-54; Child libn Arlington Co Lib, Arlington Co Va 54-. 9: ALA; VaLA. 10: AAUW. 14: Child bks & serv. 15: 5413 - 23rd North, Arlington Va 22205.

TARPY, JUSTINE JAEGER. b Dyersville Iowa 11 F 08. 5: Mankato State Tchr's Col 46-56 (Educ); Fla StateU 56-57 (Educ) BS, 59 (LS); UMinn 61, 62 (LS). 7: Tchr Blue Earth Co minn, Mankato Minn 46-56; Tchr Bay Co, Panama City Fla 58, Libn 59-60; Libn 59-60; Libn USAF, Tokyo 60-63; Libn US Army, Berlin 63-66; Libn Village of Arlington Heights lib, Arlington Heights Ill 66-. 14: Child. 15: 4001 Raven lane, Rolling Meadows Il 60008.

TASH, STEVEN JOEL. b Los Angeles Ca 27 N 43. 5: UCLA 63-65 (Hist) BA, 65-67 MLS. 7: Clk& typist Los Angeles Pub Lib 60-65, Libn-trainee 65-66, Libn 66-68; Libn II San Fernando Valley State Col 68-. 9: ALA; SAA; CalLA. 14: Ref. 15: 1150 N Genesee ave, Los Angeles Ca 90046.

TASHIMA, MARIE. b Monterey Park Cal 11 Ap 29. 5: Whittier Col 46-50 9chem) BA; West Res 57-58 MSLS; USoCal 50-56; UCol ULondon 61-62 (LS). 6: Ger, Fr. 7: Asst research chem Cal Res Corp, La Habra Cal 50-57; Asst libn Shell Development Corp, Emeryville Cal 58-61; Tech libn Kaiser Aluminum & Chem Corp, Permanente Cal 62-65; Sci & engnr libn UKan 66-; Mgr Tech Ctr Lib Continental Can Co, Chicago 67-. 8: Fulbright Fellow to UK (res on documentation in Gt Brit & affiliation with Aslib) 61-62. 9: ACS; ADI; SLA; Aslib;ALA. 10: AAAS; Sierra Club; AAUW; Beta Phi Mu. 12: "Alkali Metal Dispersion with I Fatt (61). 14: Info center, spec libs, sci-tech lit. 15: 70 W Burton pl #901, Chicago Il 60610.

TASHJIAN, VIRGINIA (AGABABIAN). b Brockton Mass 20 S 21. 4: James H Tashjian. 5: Simmons 39-43 (LS) BS, 69 MS in LS. 6: Armenian, FR. 7: Newton Free Lib, Newton Mass: Sr lib child asst 43-46, Br libn 46-65, Br libn, city story-teller, schs visitor 48-68, Asst libn, Storyteller 68-. 9: ALA; MassLA (Memb Com); Round Table of Child Libns (past sec, treas & chm); Charles River LA (past treas, mem Exec Com); NELA (past chm). 10: PTA; Armenian Relief Soc of Amer; Boy Scout Coun. 12: "Once There Was and Was Not, a bk of Armeian folk tales (66); "Juba This and Juba That" (69). 14: Child serv. 15: 278 Belmont st, Watertown Mass 02372.

TATA, YVONNE (ANKLEY). b St Johns Mich 3 Ag 21. 4: Joseph L Tata. 5: Marygrove Col 38-42 (Journalism) BA; UMich 64-66 MALS. 7: Women's ed Michigan Catholic, Detroit 42-43; Publicity dir Mercy Col (Detroit) 51-52; Pub rel dir Camp Fire Girls, Detroit 56-61; Press rel Detroit Inst of Arts 61-63; Press rel Detroit Pub Lib 63-68, 1st asst Commun & Group Serv 68-. 9: ALA; Program Planning Inst (Exh Chm 69, Disc Ldr 68, panelist 66); CathLA (Conv Publ Chm 63); MichLA (1967 Conf Publ Chm). 10: Theta Sigma Phi; Woman's Nat Bk Assn. 12: Mem Edl Com "Catholic Library World" (69-71). 15: Detroit Pub Lib 5201 Woodward, Detroit Mi 48202.

TATUM, GEORGE MARVIN JR. b Alexandria Va 23 O 35. 5: Lehigh U 53-57, 58 (Pol Sci) BA; UNC 58-60 MS in LS; Chicago 63-66 (LS). 6: Fr, Ger, Lat. 7: Lib aide Richmond Va 57-58; Asst catlg & acquis libn Cornell U Lib 60-63; Ref libn A G Bush Lib, Ind Rel Center UChicago 63-66; Assoc libn central ser record dept Cornell U Lib 66-. 9: ALA; Printing Hist Soc; Bibliog Soc UVa. 10: Beta Phi Mu. 12: "Translations from European Literature Published in 108 American Little Magazines, 1909-1959 microcard (60). 13: Yes. 14: Acquis, catlg, sers. 15: 138 Linden ave, Ithaca NY 14850.

TAUBER, MAURICE F(ALCOLM). b Norfolk Va 14 F 08. 5: Temple 26-30 (Eng) BS, 34-39 (Sociol) Ed M; Columbia 32-34 LS) BS; Chicago 38-41 (LS, Higher Educ) PhD. 6: Fr, Sp. 7: Temple U; Asst in Lib 27-34, Libn Tchrs Col 34-35, Head catlg dept 35-38; Research asst Grad Lib Sch UChicago 39-41; Chief catlg dept UChicago Libs 41-42, Chief prep div 42-44; Columbia U: Asst dir of libs 44-47, Asst Prof of Lib Sci 44-46, Assoc Prof of Lib Sci 46-49, Prof of Lib Sci 49-54, Melvil Dewey Prof of Lib Serv 54-. 8: Fulbright Scholar to Australia, 61; Surveyor & consul to over 100 col, univ, pub sch & spec libs in the US, Hawaii, Canada, Japan, Australia; Adv to var govt libs, incl LC, US Off of Educ, NLM, Air Univ Lib, Nat Lib of Australia, Can Dept of Agric; Mem Lib Bldg & Mgt Consuls Inc; Consul, Grolier Inc, NELSON Assocs, Documentation Inc. 9: ALA (Coun, Exec Bd);-Div Catlg & Clsf (pres, chm & mem var coms)-RTSD;-ACRL;-RSD; SLA; ADI; NYLA; NY SLA; ASIS; Libns; NY Lib Club. 10: Beta Phi Mu; AAAS; AAUP; Grolier Club (NY); Archons of Colophon. 11: Margaret Mann Award, 53; Melvil Dewey Medal, 55; Findlay Col Merit Award, 68; -ACRL Ed Award 62. 12: "The University Library with L R Wilson" (45, 56);

"The Subject Analysis of Library Materials" (53); "Technical Services in Libraries" (54); "Cataloging and Classification" (59); "Classification Systems with E Wise" (61); "Resources of Australian Libraries" (3 v 62); "Book Catalogs with R E Kingery" (63); Numerous Published Surveys; Managing ed & ed "College ND Research Libraries" (46-62); Mem Ed Bds "Library Resources and Technical Services"; "American Documentation"; "Journal of Higher Education"; "College and Research Libraries"; Issue ed "Library Trends" (4 issues); Co-auth "The Use of Printed and Audio-Visual Materials for Instructional Purposes" (66); "Papers of Louis Round Wilson"; Co-ed (67); "Louis Round Wilson" (biog 67); "Library Surveys" with I R Stephens (67); "Workshop on Teaching Dewey Decimal Classification" co-auth (68). 13: Yes. 14: Tech serv, documentation, admin, lib blgs, lib educ, research methods. 15: Sch of Lib Serv, Columbia Univ, NYC 10025.

TAVARES, VIRGINIA (COLE). b Farmingdle NJ 21 D 19. 4: Benildo Demoura Tavares. 5: Douglass Col 37-41 (Pol Sci) BA, 40-41 (LS) BA. 6: Portu, Fr, Ger. 7: Summer sub NY Pub Lib 41; Libn Princeton U Lib 41-44; Staff asst Douglass Col Alumnae Assn, New Brunswick NJ 44-45; Off histn Civilian Defense Volunteer Off, NYC 45; Research asst Advertising Executive, NYC 46; Prof staff Congressional com & Memb of Congress, Wash DC 47; Foreign affairs off Dept of State, Wash DC 48-49; Libn Dept of Agric, Wash dc 49-51; Foreign affairs off Dept of State, Wash DC 51-53; Libn Dept of State Lib, Wash DC 54-58; Libn Foreign Serv Inst Dept of State, Wash DC 58-61; Asst libn Fed Aviation Agency, Wash DC 61-62; Libn Foreign Serv Inst Dept of State, Wash DC 62-. 9: SLA; DCLA. 11: Dept of State Commendable Serv Award, 51. 14: Ref, bibliog, admin. 15: 1711 Massachusetts ave NW, Wash DC 20036.

TAYLOR, ALAN ROBERT. b London Eng 14 S 32. 4: Diana Clutton. 5: Northwestern Polytech (London) 51-52 ALA. 6: Fr. 7: Asst Ealing Pub Lib, London Eng 49-51; Asst libn London Sch of Hygiene & Tropical Med 51-53; Asst Nat Archives of Rhodesia & Nyasaland, Salisbury S Rhodsia 53-56, Libn 56-63; Hon libn Centrl African Journal of Med, Salisbury S Rhodesia 55-63; Libn for African Studies Ind U 63-, Visiting lecturer lib sch 68-69. 8: Adv to Com on fed Govt Sci Libs, Rhodesia & Nyasaland 60; Rhodesia & Nyasaland del to Internat Conf on Catlg Pinciples, Paris 61; Spec consul African Bibliog Ctr, Wash DC 68-; Mem Farmington Plan Subcom on Africa (ARL) 64-. 9: Lib Assn (Gt Brit); ALA; African Studies Assn (Fellow, chm Archives-Libs Com 65-67); Internat African Inst. 11: Fulbright Hays Ctr Faculty Fellowship, 67. 12: "Bibliographical Resources for African Studies (66). 13: Yes. 14: Ref, bibliog of Africa, prof educ. 15: 4217 Hector dr, Bloomington In 47401.

TAYLOR, ARTHUR R(OBERT). b Denver Colo 14 Jl 41. 4: Jean Boyce. 5: St LouisU 59-65 (Classics) AB, 65-66 (Eng) Lifetime Tchr's Certif; Rosary 67-68 MALS. 7: Tech serv asst Col of P&L St Louis U at Florissant & St Louis Mo 60-65; Instr Rochurst High Sch, Kansas City Mo 66-67; Libn trainee (ref) Chicago Pub Lib (Main Br) 67-68, Libn I adult serv 69; Instr lib sci Rosary Col 69-. 9: ALA-LED; -ACRL; Film Lib Info Coun. 10: Chicago Lib Club; Beta Phi Mu. 14: A-v libs, communications & multimedia. 15: 645 Madison, Oak Park Il 60302.

TAYLOR, BYRON CLYDE. b Trimble Mo 28 S 25. 4: Bettie Wright. 5: UMo(Kan City) 46-51; Kan State Tchrs Col 51-52 & summer 65 65-68 AB. 6: Ger. 7: Libn Greensburg High Sch, Greensburg Kan 52-53; Libn Olathe High Sch, Olathe Kan 53-54; Head ref libn Lib Div US Army Command & Gen Staff Col, Ft Leavenworth Kan 54-63, Asst chief 63-68; Chief libn Base Lib RAF, Lakenheath Eng 68-. 9: KanLA; SLA. 14: Ref, admin. 15: 48 CSG Box 2963, APO NY 09179.

TAYLOR, C EVERETT. b Pratt Mo 30 O 14. 4: Kathryn Mallett. 5: Ohio State U 34-37 (Educ) S in Ed; West Res 39-40 BS in LS, 55-56 MS in LS. 7: Pub sch tchr Green Rural Hig Sch, Lings Ohio 37-39; Lib asst DC Pub Lib 40-41; US Army Signal Corp 42-43, USAF (2nd Lt) 44; Catlgr: Soc Security Admin, Wash DC 41, 45-46, Armed Forces Staff Col Lib, Norfolk Va 47, US VA, Wash DC 48; Gifts & Exch libn Ohio State U Lib 49; Assoc libn & catlgr USAFIT, Wright-Patterson AFB Ohio 50-53; Libn USAF Inst of Tech, Wright-Patterson AFB Ohio 54-55; Assoc Prof & asst libn Abilene Christian Col Lib 56-. 9: ALA; TexLA; Tex Reg Group of Catlgrs & Clsfrs. 10: Beta Phi Mu. 14: Catlg. 15: 1001 Washington blvd, Abilene Tex 79601.

TAYLOR, D(ORIS) MARJORIE. b Eng 20 Ja 05. 5: The Lib Assn (Gt Brit) FLA. 7: Asst Pub Lib, Cambridge Eng 28-40; Libn: Pub Lib, Ilkley Eng 40-51, Sawyer Free Lib, Gloucester Mass 52-56, Lucius Beebe MEM Lib, Wakefield Mass 57-. 9: ALA; MassLA; GBPLA; N Shore Lib Club. 10: Kosmos Club; Womens Nat Bk Assn. 14: Admin. 15: P O Box 532, Wakefield Mass 01881.

TAYLOR, DESMOND (WILLIAM). b Detroit 27 My 30. 4: Ingeborg Krug. 5: Emory & Henry Col 49-53 (Hist, Eng) BA; Col f William & Mary 52; UIll 59-60 (LS) MS. 7: US Army Security Agency, Ga, Miss, W Germany 53-56; Ref asst Warder Pub Lib, Springfield Ohio 56-59; U of Puget Sound; Ref libn 60-63, Act libn 63-64, Dir 63-. 8: Faculty participant Semester Abroad Pogram Vienna 68-69. 9: PNLA; ALA. 10: AAUP; ACLU; Beta Phi Mu; Old Tacoma Improvement Club. 13: Yes. 14: Acquis, tech proc, ref. 15: Univ of Puget Sound Lib, Tacoma Wash 98416.

TAYLOR, DOREEN (MARY). b Ft William Ont Can 12 S 26. 5: UBC 43-44, 47-48, 48-49 (Geog, Econ) BA; McGill 50-51 BLS; UBC 65 (Geog) MA. 7: Tchr Christina Lake United Sch Bd, Cascade BC 45-56; Tchr Immaculate Conception Sch, Vancouver BC 46-47; Jr libn UBC 51-54, Sr libn 54-56; Libn B C Hydro & Power Authority, Vancouver BC 57-. 9: SLA (v-pres Pacific NWChap 64-65 & 67-68, pres 68-69); BCLA (treas 60-62). 13: Yes. 14: Ref. 15: 4214 W 14 ave, Vancouver 8 BC Can.

TAYLOR, DOROTHY K. b St Francis Kan 28 N 04. 5: UDenver Sch of Com 22-27 (Acctg) BS, (Archives, Records Mgt, Indexing). 7: Jr accountnt Myatt & Co, Monroe La 28; Head accountant Presbyterian Hosp, Denver 29-32; Accounts receivable bkkeeping Gates Rubber Co, Denver 33-34; Colo State Employment Bur, Denver 34; Supv of records Colo State SALES & Use Tax, Denver 35-41; Supv of records system Colo State Dept of Revenue, Denver 41-42, Auditor 42; Supv of records systems Denver & Rio Grande West RR, Denver 42-54; Admin asst Wyo State Archives, Cheyenne Wyo 54-55; Dir Wyo State Centralized Microfilm Dept, Cheyenne Wyo 55-60; Asst State Archivist Colo State Archives, Denver 60-. 9: SAA (Fellow); Amer Assn State & Loc Hist; Nat Microfilm Assn; Colo Hist Soc; Wyo Hist Soc. 10: Phi Chi Theta. 12: "Manual on Railroad Dewey Decimal Uniform File System. 13: Yes. 14: Records, mgt, archival microfilming. 15: 1235 Grant st, Denver Co 80203.

TAYLOR, F CHARLES. b Hartford Conn 23 My 23. 4: Jane Stevens. 5: Franklin & Marshall Cl 47 (Eng) BA; UIll 48 BSLS, 49 MSLS. 6: Fr. 7: Petty off 2/c Spec Welfare US Navy 43-46; Lib asst Hartford Pub Lib, Hartford Conn 48; Head bus tech dept Wichita City Lib, Wichita Kan 49-51; Chief libn Boeing Airplane Co, Wichita Kan 51-55; Asst libn Providence Pub Lib 55-59, Assoc libn 59-61; Assoc libn St Louis Pub Lib 61-66, Libn 66-68; Libn Providence Pub Lib 68-. 8: Lecturer in libnship, Univ Col of Washington U, St Louis 62. 9: ALA; RILA; NELA. 10: Beta Phi Mu; Trustee RI Sch of Design. 12: Ed "Missouri Library Association Quarterly (64-65). 13: Yes. 14: Admin, pub rel, rare bks. 15: 150 Empire, Providence RI 02914.

TAYLOR, FLORENCE (AYRES). b White Pine Penn 7 Ja 14. 4: Carl B Taylor. 5: Lock Haven State Col 30-35 (Eng, Hist, Elem educ) BS; Columbia 56-61 MSLS. 6: Fr. 7: Tchr Cogan House Sch Dist, Penn 35-38; Libn Liberty Joint Sch, Tioga Co Penn 50-61; Libn Morgantown Jr High, Morgantown WVa 61-65; Hd libn Morgantown Pub Lib, Morgantown WVa 65-68; Sr ref libn W Va U 68-. 9: ALA; WVaEA (Regl Chm Lib Sect 63); WVaLA (Pub Lib Chm 67). 14: Ref. 15: 773 Augusta ave, Morgantown W Va 26505.

TAYLOR, FLORENCE COMSTOCK (WHITMORE). b Lockport NY 17 N 08. 4: William Edward Taylor. 5: SUNY(Geneseo) 26-29 (LS, Eng) Certif; SUNY (Albany) 36-37 (Educ) BS; Columbia 43-45 (Personnel Admin) MA; UIll ext 56-57 (LS). 7: Lib asst Pub Lib, Lockport NY 31-36, Yp libn 37-43; Sch libn Dist 102, LaGrange Ill 58-63; Sch libn Amherst Reg JR High Sch, Amherst Mass 65-. 9: ALA; NEA; IllEA; MassEA. 10: DAR. 13; yes. 14: Org & admin sch or prof libs. 15: 104 Shays, Rt 1, Amherst Mass 01002.

TAYLOR, FRANCES CAMILLE. b Miami Fla 13 Ag 24. 5: Western Carolina 61-63 (Eng/Art) BA; UNC 63-65 MS in LS. 7: US Navy (WAVES) Intelligence S 1/C, Wash DC 44-46; Lib clerk Columbia 51-55; Lib clerk West Carolina, Cullowhee BC 62; Asst libn Edison Jr Col 65-67; Asst periods lib UMiami 67-. 14: Period ref. 15: 13902 Crooked Palm ct, Miami Lakes Fl 33014.

TAYLOR, FRANCES SHEARER. b Erie Penn 20Ja 17. 5: Pasadena City Col 50-52 (Psych) AA; UCLA 52-55 (Psych) BA, 55-60 (Psych) USoCal 59-60 MSLS, Biomed Libn Certif.

7: Libn: Catlg System Devel Corp, Santa Monica Cal 60-62, circ & ref Lockheed Aircraft Co, Burbank Cal 62, tech documents center, catlg, acquis, Culvr City Cal 63-65, Fed Aviation Agency West Reg, Los Angeles 65-. 9: SLA; ADA; ASIS. 10: Alpha Gamma Sigma; Phi Beta Mu; Psi Chi. 15: 2069 N Beverly Glen blvd, Los Angeles Ca 90024.

TAYLOR, GERRY M. b Eustis Me 7 Jl 13. 4: Myra Taylor. 5: Baylor U 48-51 (Psych) BA, 51-52 (Psych) MA; UTex 52-55 MLS. 6: Fr. 7: (Sgt) US Army, US, S Pacific 41-45; Order asst Baylor U 48-51, Circ supv 51-52; UTex: Documents asst 52-53, Sr lib asst Law Lib 53-54, Revisor Grad Sch of Lib Sci 54-55; Asst libn Tex Col of Arts & Ind 55-56; Assoc libn Sam Houston State Col 56-66; Hd libn Ark State U 66-. 8: Consul, Huntsville Tex 65. 9: TexLA (chm Dist 4 54-55); Tex Coun on Lib Educ (sec 59-62, chm 62-64); SWLA; ALA; ArkLA (chm Com on Intel Freedom); Ark Coun on Lib Educ. 10: Alpha Chi; Psi Chi; Beta Phi Mu; C of C; NE Ark Sch Masters Assn. 13: Yes. 14: Admin, automation. 15: PO Box 1017, State University Ak 72467.

TAYLOR, GLADYS M(ILLER). b Yonkers NY 29 S 23. 4: Frederick H Taylor. 5: State U (Geneseo NY) 47 (LS) BS in Ed; Cornell U 53 (Eng) MA. 7: Libn Wayland Central Sch, Wayland NY 47-57; Ref libn Rochester Inst Tech 58-. 9: ALA; NYLA; Monroe Co Lib Club (pres 69). 14: Ref, archives, gift bks. 15: 28 Midland ave, Rochester NY 14620.

TAYLOR, HUGH ALEXANDER. b CHLMSFORD Eng 22 Ja 20. 4: Daphne Mary Johnson. 5: UOxford 46-49 (Hist) MA; ULiverpool 50-51 Diploma of Archive Admin. 7: Archivist Leeds Pub Libs, Leeds Eng 51-54; Archivist Liverool Pub Libs, Liverpool Eng 54-58; Co Archivist Northumberland Co Coun, Newcastle Eng 58-65; Prov Archivist GOVT OF Alta, Edmonton 65-69; Prov archivist Govt of NB, Can 69-. 8: Tutor & examiner in archives, ULiverpool, 55-58; Archivist, Univ Lib, Newcastle-Upon-Tyne 62-65; Dir Archives Admin Course UNB (Fredericton) 69-. 12: "Northumberland History: A Brief Guide (64). 15: New Brunswick Provincial Archives, Fredericton, NB Can.

TAYLOR, INA E. b Syracuse NY 15 Je 12. 5: Syracuse 30-33, 34-35 (Fr, Lat) AB, summers 35-37; 39 BS in LS. 6: Fr, Lat. 7: Tchr Fr, Lat, Eng Gr Germantown Central Sch, Germantown NY 35-39; Libn: The Manlius Sch, Manlius NY 39-40, Bainbridge Central Sch, Bainbridge ny 40-44, Marcellus Central Sch, Marcellus NY 44-48, Onondaga Valley Acad, Syracuse NY 48-56, Wm R Boone High Sch, Orlando Fla 56-. 9: NEA; ALA; FlaEA; Cir Tchrs Assn; Orange Co (Fla) Libns (past pres); Fla A-V Assn; Orange Co EA. 10: Delta Kappa Gamma; AAUW; PTA. 14: High sch lib, acquis, ref, catlg. 15: 311 E Jersey st, Orlando Fla 32806.

TAYLOR, JEANNE (MARIE) (ANTHIS). b Wharton Tex 6 N 27. 5: Wharton Co Jr Col 46-48 (Hist); Sul Ross State Col 48-50 (Hist) BS, 53 (Educ) M Ed; Our Lady of the Lake Col 58-64 (LS) Certif. 7: Elem tchr San Antonio Ind Sch Dist, San Antonio Tex 50-52; Bkmob libn San Antonio Pub Lib, San Antonio Tex 56-61; Jr High Sch tchr NE Ind Sch Dist, San Antonio Tex 61-64; Ref libn San Antonio Jr Col 65-66; Ref libn Houston Pub Lib, Houston Tex 64-65, 66-. 9: TexLA. 10: Alpha Beta Alpha; AAUP; Alpha Chi; Phi Theta Kappa; Kappa Delta Pi. 14: Ref. 15: 3219 Rice blvd, Houston Tx 77005.

TAYLOR, KATHLEEN. b Calgary Alta Can 7 Ag 16. 5: UAlta 36-39 BS; Toronto 53-54 BLS. 7: Tech asst Inspection Bd of UK & Can, Ottawa 41-46; Asst tech Nat Researh Coun Lib, Ottawa 46-53; Tech libn Calgary Pub Lib, Calgary Alta 54-56; TECH LIBN Imperial Oil Ltd Prod Res Lab, Calgary Alta 56-60; Reg libn Imperial Oil Ltd Prod Reg Off, Calgary Alta 60-. 9: CanLA (chm Res & Spec Libs Sect 66); AltaLA (pres 58); SLA (Petroleum Div). 14: Tech libs. 15: 432 - 49 ave SW, Calgary Alta Can.

TAYLOR, KENNETH IRVIN. b Springfield Minn 28 Ap 26. 5: Hamline U 46-48 (Educ); UMinn 48-50 (Educ) BS; UIll 52-53 (LS) MS; Chicago 61-63 (Curriculum Dev). 6: Fr, Ger. 7: US Navy Stud Radio Materiel Schs, Seaman 1/c 45-46; Tchr-libn Frederic common schs, Frederic Wis 50-52; Libn U High Sch, Urbana Ill 52-53; Tchr Comfrey pub schs, Comfrey Minn 54-55; Sch dist libn pub schs, Black River Falls Wis 55-56; Libn Leyden Twp, Franklin Park Ill 56-58; Chm center for instr materials Leyden Twp, Northlake Ill 58-63; Instr East Ill U summer 59; Instr DePaul U even 59-61; Instr Fla State U summer 60; Dir media proj Leyden Twp, Northlake Ill 63-64; Asst curriculum dir for instr materials Madison pub schs, Madison Wis 64-. 8: Wkshop consul; Kent State U 61, UWis 61, 65-69, Normal (Wis) U 64, Oshkosh (Wis) U 64, Rosary Col 63, Drexel 67, St Cloud (Minn) State U 67; Mankato State U 67, Whitewater (Minn) State U 68; Adv; N Central Assn Cols & Second Schs Sch Lib Standards 67, Wis State Dept of Pub Instr Certif of Sch Libns 67. 9: ALA (Legis Liaison Com 65-68, Sch Lib Bldgs & Equipment 61-);-ASCD; NEA-DAVI (Commsn on Sch Plant Design 67-); Internat Platform Assn; Nat Soc Study Educ; Nat Assn Broadcasters; WisLA (Development & Legis Com 65-, Recruitment Com 65, Educ Com 68-, Dutton Macrae Award Com 66); Wis Div A-V Instr; Wis Assn Supv & Curriculum Development; Wis Educ Research Assn. 13: Yes. 14: Sch libs, design of materials center, col prep of media spec, data proc systs for prep of instr materials. 15: 336 Island dr, Madison Wis 53705.

TAYLOR, LILLIAN McCULLOCH. b Elizabethtown NC 29 Mr 28. 4: David W A Taylor. 5: Queens Col 45-49 (Eng, Rel) AB; Presbyterian Sch of Christian Educ 49-51 (Cristian Educ) MA; Peabody 63-64 MA(LS). 7: Tchr pub sch: Richmond Va 51-52, Harlingen NJ 52-53, Elkton Va 53-54; Libn Peabody Demonstration Sch, Nashville 64-. 9: ALA; TennLA. 10: Beta PHI Mu; Peabody Faculty Org. 14: Ref (high sch libs). 15: 4420 Milesdale ct, Nashville Tn 37204.

TAYLOR, LORINDA JEANNE. b Colo Springs Colo 20 Je 40. 5: Colo Col 57-61 (Eng) BA; Cornell U 61-62 (Eng) MA; UCLA 62-63 MLS; UTex 66-67 (Eng). 6: Fr, Ger. 7: Hd catlg libn Tutt Lib Colo Col 63-66; Libn I Stark Lib UTex (Austin) 66-67, Libn II UTex Lib (Austin) 67-68; Catlg libn Drury Col Lib 68-. 9: ALA; MoLA. 10: Phi Beta Kappa; Beta Phi Mu; Alpha Lambda Delta; AAUP. 14: Catlg. 15: Drury Coll Lib, Springfield Mo 65802.

TAYLOR, MARILYN (STUBBS). b Red Lake Ont Can 14 Ag 40. 4: Peter Thornton Taylor. 5: UBC 58-62 (Eng) B; McGill 64-65 BLS; Sir George Williams U 66 (Sci); Ariz State U 68-69 (Bus Admin). 6: Fr. 7: Lib asst McGill U 63-64, Asst libn phys sci 65-67; Ref libn Ariz State U (Tempe) 68-. 8: Chm McGill U Lib Staff Assn 65-67. 9: Ariz State LA (treas Conf 69). 14: Info retrieval, tech proc. 15: 1512 N McAllister, Tempe Az 85281.

TAYLOR, MARION RUTH. b Atlanta 9 F 22. 5: Wesleyan Col (Ga) 39-43 (Fr, Eng) AB; Emory 51-57 (LS) MA; Rutgers 66- (LS). 6: Fr, Sp. 7: Clerk-typist, prof asst Fed Bur of Investigation, Wash DC 43-49; Emory U Lib: Typist documents sect 50, Ed Union Catalog & asst in circ 51-53, Catlgr 53-54, asst ser libn 54-55; Ed Union Catalog of the Atlanta, Athens Area 55-63; Instr Div of Libnship Emory U 63-. 8: Visiting instr Div of Libnship, Emory U summer 61, 63; Visiting Prof Lib Sch LSU summer 62, 65; Visiting instr Grad Sch Lib Sci Rutgers U summer 67. 9: ALA; SLA (Ga Chap; pres 58-60, dir 60-64); AALS; SELA; GaLA (Memb Chm 59-63; Spec Libs Sect; sec-treas 61-63; Resources & Tech Serv Div; chm 66-67); ASIS. 10: AAUP; Beta Phi Mu. 11: Dogwood Award, SLA Ga Chap. 12 Ed "Bulletin Ga Chap SLA (54-56 & 57-58); Comp "GUIDE TO Latin American Reference Materials (58). 13: Yes. 14: Educ for libnship, catlg, documentation, hist of bks & libs. 15: 1223 Clifton rd NE, Atlanta Ga 30307.

TAYLOR, MARY M. b Downingtown Penn 6 F 25. 5: Skidmore 44-48 (Fine Arts) BS; Drexel 64-66 (LS) MS; Glassboro State 66-67, 69 Tchr Certif. 7: Libn Central-Jr Sch Lib, haddonfield NJ 66-. 9: ALA; NJSchLA; NJEA; CamdenCoSchLA; CamdenCoEA; HaddonfieldEA. 10: Libs Unlimited. 14: Elem & jr sch libs. 15: Central Junior School Lib, Lincoln ave, Haddonfield NJ 08033.

TAYLOR, MERRILY E. b Winchester Mass 24 My 45. 5: St Petersburg Jr Col 63-65 (Basic Studies) AA; USoFla 65-67 (Eng Educ) BA; Fla StateU 67-68 MLS. 6: Fr, Sp. 7: Asst ref libn USoFla lib 68-. 9: FlaLA. 14: Ref. 15: 6501 4th ave N, St Petersburg Fl 33710.

TAYLOR, NANCY BEUHRING. b Huntington WVa 30 Ap 15. 5: Marshall Col 33-37 (Eng) AB; UIll 37-38 BS in LS; Columbia summer 64 (Med Libnship); 65 MedLA Certif Grade I. 6: Sp. 7: Libn: Glen Ellyn Free Pub Lib, Glen Ellyn Ill 38-39, VA Hosp, Hines Ill 39-40, VA Hosp, Atlanta 40-42; Admin asst USAAF WAC (1st Lt) Lt) 42-46; Libn VA Hosp, Huntington WVa 46-47, Chief Libn 47-. 8: WVa Lib Commsn Consul LSCA-Title IV 68-69. 9: MedLA; ALA; WVaLA (Spec Libs Sect). 14: Med, adult literacy. 15: Homewood, Kennon lane, Huntington WV 25705.

TAYLOR, NETTIE (B). b Brownsville Tenn 6 Ag 14. 5: Fla State U 36 AB; UNC 42 (LS) BS; UMd 50-60 (Sociol); Johns Hopkins 67 MLA. 7: Libn Taylor Co High Sch, Perry Fla 36-40; LIBN Leon Co High Sch, Tallahassee Fla 40-42; US

Army Libn, US & Germany, US 7th Army & Constabulary 45-47; Supv Pub Libs Md Div Lib Ext, State Dept of Educ 48-60; Visiting Lecturer Fla State U summer 59; Dir Md Lib-Community Proj 55-5; Dir Div of Lib Ext Md State Dept of Educ 60-. 9: ALA (Coun 54-57 & 60-64; chm Nomin Com 65; mem Publg Com 65-67; Com on Legis 66-69, Edl Com 66-);-AAStateL (pres 69-70); MdLA (pres 60). 13: Yes. 14: Publibs, admin, adult serv. 15: 4105 Bedford rd, Baltimore 21207.

TAYLOR, RICHARD L(EE). b Quincy Ill 13 Ag 30. 4: Jo Anna Menke. 5: West Ill U 48-52 (Educ) BS; UIll 52-54 (LS) MS; Kan State U 56-58 (Educ). 7: NCO in chg of Post Libs, Ft Smith Ark 54-56; Head circ dept Kan State U (Manhattan) 56-60; A-v libn Wright Jr Col 60-61; Instr of Lib Sci East Ill U 61-64, Head circ dept & tech dir of Data Prof 64-67; Libn Chicago City Col, Wright Campus 67-. 9: ALA (Coun on Lib Tech). 10: Beta Phi Mu; Phi Delta Kappa. 14: Lib automation. a-v serv. 15: 120 E Highland, Mt Prospect Il 60056.

TAYLOR, ROBERT NOEL. b San Angelo Tex 12 Mr 40. 5: No Tex StateU 58-62 (Hist) BA; UTex 62-64 (Hist) MA, 65-67 MLS. 6: Ger. 7: Research asst N Tex StateU 61-62; Lib asst UTex (Austin) 65-67, Libn I catlg 67-. 9: TexLA. 15: 1518 Barton Springs rd Lot 79, Austin Tx 78704.

TAYLOR, RON. b Windber Penn 24 Je 32. 5: Penn StateU 55 (Eng) BA; Rutgers 66 MLS. 7: Asst br libn Ventura Co Pub Lib, Ventura Cal 64-65; Asst acquis UFla 66-67; Asst catlg Bucknell U Lib 67-68, Asst ref 68-. 15: Ikler st Thunderbird #8, Lewisburg Pa 17837.

TAYLOR, ROSAMOND (BLOSSOM). b Manassas Va 18 My 05. 4: Walter Fleming Taylor. 5: UWash 22-27 BS in LS; USan Francisco 58 (Med Lib); USoCal 61 (Med Lib). 6: Fr, Ger. 7: Pub Lib, Walla Walla Wash; Asst libn 27-30, Child libn 30-34, Asst 34-42; Asst co libn Clallam Co, Port Angeles Wash 47; Asst Pub Lib, Santa Ana Cal 49; Asst libn VA Hosp, Walla Walla Wash 50-54, Chief libn 54-57; Chief libn VA Hosp, Fresno Cal 57-. 9: CalLA (Adult Educ Com 63); MedLA; ALA; No Cal Med Libns. 10: AAUW; Daughters of Union Veterans; Phi Mu. 14: Bibliog, ref. 15: 2971 E Simpson, Fresno Cal 93703.

TAYLOR, SUE. b Grapeland Tex 14 Ag 13. 5: Sam Houston State Col 31-35, summer 36 (Eng) BA; Duke summer 37; Tex Womans U summers 42, 46-48 BS in LS; UTex summers53, 61; UWash summers 63-65 (LS) ML. 6: Sp. 7: Tchr; Grapeland Pub Schs, Grapeland Tex 35-42, Angleton Pub Schs, Angleton Tex 42-43, Alvin Pub Schs, Alvin Tex 43-45; Clerk Methodist Hosp, Houston 45-46; Libn Harlingen High Sch, Harlingen Tex 46-48; Documents & res libn E Tex State Col 48-51; Libn Nacogdoches High Sch, Nacogdoches Tex 51-55; Ref libn Stephen F Austin State Col 55-67; Veterinary med libn Tex A & M U 67-. 9: ALA; TexLA; SWLA. 10: Beta Phi Mu, 14: Ref. 15: 411-B Day st, Bryan Tx 77801.

TAYLOR, (CLARA) SYLVIA (ERICKSON). b Minneapolis Minn 4 N 06. 4: Hartley Elder Taylor. 5: UMont 23-29 (Foreign Lang) BA (cum laude); UKan 32; UChicago 60, 62, 63 Special stud. 7: Tchr Gibson Sch, Gibson Mont 24-25; Tchr Pub Sch, Wormser Mont 25-26; Tchr Barber Pub Sch, Barber Mont 30; Child's libn Cook Memorial Lib, Libertyville Ill 57-58, Bkmob libn 58-62, Ref libn 63-64, Child's libn 65-. 9: IllLA. 10: AAUW. 15: 527 W Park ave, Libertyville Il 60048.

TAYLOR, THELMA MARJORIE (VOGT). b BATTLE Creek Mich 31 Jl 02. 4: Jean Landon Taylor. 5: West Mich U 19-23, 26, 28 (Soc Studies) AB; Chicago 26, 29-30, 37-38 (Educ, LS) MA; Columbia 35-40 MLS. 6: Lat, Sp, Fr. 7: Critic tchr West Mich U 23-29; Instr Miss Spades Sch for Girls, Chicago 30-32; Libn Morgan Park Jr Col & Mil Acad (Chicago) 33-45; Lib supv Fullerton elem schs, Fullerton Cal 45-48; Asst dean in lib Los Angeles City Col 48-49; Libn Los Angeles Harbor Col 49-63, Chm Lib Div 63-68; Coord lib serv 68-. 8: Consul, Antelope Valley Col 56; Chm Lib Com, Commsn for Accred Jr Cols 61; Consul, Cal Sch Lib Proj 64; Org libs at; Morgan Park Jr Col 33, Los Angeles Harbor Col 49, Los Angeles Southwest Col 67-68. 9: NEA; Clr Tchrs Assn; ALA-ACRL (Jr Col Sect: sec 53, chm 55-56; Com on Standards & Criteria 61-67); CalASchL (Jr Col Lib Round Table: sec & pres 59-62; So Sect: Program Chm 53-54, pres 54-55); CalLA (Jr Col Lib Round Table sec & pres 59-62); Cal Jr Col (chm Table (cm Standards Com 65); SoCal Jr Col Assn (chm 51-52V. 10: Pi Lambda Theta; AAUW; YWCA; Nat Retired TA. 13: Yes. 14: Admin, standard. 15: 916 Via Nogles, Palos Verdes Estates Ca 90274.

TAYLOR, THURSTON. b Baltimore 5 Mr 05. 4: Margaret Crompton. 5: Johns Hopkins 22-26 AB; Columbia 31-32 BS. 6: Fr. 7: Research asst Johns Hopkins U 30-31; Asst Enoch Pratt Free Lib, Baltimore 32-34, 1st asst 35-36; Supv of brs Pub Lib, Hartford Conn 37-40; Asst libn Pub Lib, Worcester Mass 40-45, Head Libn 45-65. 8: Bd of dirs, Amer Foun for Continuing Educ; Lib cons, 65-. 9: ALA (past mem Ed Com & Recr Com); SLA; Adult Educ Assn; MasLA; NELA. 10: Rotary Club; Torch Club. 13: Yes. 14: Pub lib admin, adult educ. 15: 2180 Nelson ave, West Vancouver BC Can.

TAYLOR, WILLIAM HALL. b Miami Fla 16 S 37. 5: Fla State U 54-58 (Music Educ) BME, 60-64 (LS) MS. 7: Music tchr Dade Co Pub Schs, Miami Fla 58-59; Music tchr Mentor Pub Schs, Mentor Ohio 59-60; Libn Dade Co Pub Sch, Miami Fl 60-. 8: Jt Bk Sel Com, Dade Co Schs & Miami Pub Lib, 63-66. 9: ALA -AASchL; FlaASchL; FlaLA. 10: Phi Mu Alpha Sinfonia; Beta PHI Mu; Kappa Delta Pi. 14: Ref, ya. 15: 6655 SW 90th ct, Miami Fla33143.

TAYLOR, WILMA ROSEMARY (TEMPLEMAN). b Davenport Iowa 25 Jl 37. 4: John Alfred Taylor. 5: UIowa 55-59 (Dramatic Art) AB; UWis 63-67 MS in LS. 6: Fr, Ger, Russian. 7: Circ asst UNH Lib 60; Sci ref & circ asst Fondren Lib RiceU 62-64; Acquis searcher Lockwood Lib SUNY (Buffalo) 64-65, Asst acquis libn 66; Trainee music dept Buffalo & Erie Co Lib, Buffalo NY 65-66; Asst libn, ref libn Citizen's Lib, Washington Penn 66-. 9: PennLA. 10: Phi Beta Kappa; Beta Phi Mu. 14: Acquis, bibliog. 15: 134 LeMoyne ave, Washington Pa 15301.

TAYLOR, WINIFRED. b York Neb 22 S 15. 5: UNeb 33-34, 44-47 (Educ, Geog) BS in Ed; UDenver 48 (LS). 7: UNeb: Res libn 46-47, Interlib loan 48-57, Receiving libn 57-. 9: ALA; NebLA. 14: Ser, docs. 15: 1525 F st apt 7, Lincoln Nb 68508.

TEAGUE, ANNE (HARWELL). b El Paso Tex 1 Ja 24. 5: Syracuse 40-41; UTex (El Paso) 42-43 (Eng, Hist) BA; TrinityU 63-64 All-level tchg certif; UTex (Austin) 64-67 MLS. 6: Sp. 7: Caseworker Comanche Co Welfare Dept, Lawton Okla 48-49; Tchr Lawton Pub Schs, lawton Okla 49-51; Order Dept UTex (Austin) 67-68, Catlgr Lat Amer Materials 68-69. 9: TexLA. 13: Yes. 14: Catlg. 15: 2104 Stamford lane, Austin Tx 78703.

TEALL, DOROTHY ADELE (ARMSTRONG). b Nauvoo Ill 26 Je 15. 5: UMich 32-36 (Eng Lit) AB, 36-37 ABLS. 6: Fr, Ger. 7: Circ asst MacGregor Pub Lib, Highlnd Park Mich 37-38; Circ libn Ann Arbor Pub Lib, Ann Arbor Mich 38-46; Br asst Toledo Pub Lic Locke Br, Toledo Ohio 47-49; Head of circ Ann Arbor Pub Lib, Ann Arbor Mich 51-. 9: MichLA; Ann Arbor Lib Club. 10: NEA; MichEA; AnnArborEA. 14: Pub serv. 15: 1837 Alhambra dr, Ann Arbor Mich 48103.

TEASLEY, ELIZABETH (KINCAID). b Bonham Tex 10 F 19. 4: Joe HARRISON Teasley. 5: N Tex State U 41 (Mus Educ) BM, 47 (Mus educ) MM, 56 BS in LS. 6: Sp. 7: Tchr, Tex: Darst Creek Sch, Kingbury 41-42, Sam Houston Elem Sch, Conroe 42-43, Arlington High Sch, Arlington 45-46, May Hill Sch, Denton Co 46-49, Robert E Lee Elem, Denton 49-60; Grad asst (mus) N Tex State U 44, Ref & circ summer 57-60, Asst mus libn 60-63; Mus tchr & libn Woodrow Wilson Elem Sch, Denton Tex 63-65; Coord elem libs Denton Pub Schs, Denton Tex 65-. 9: ALA; SWLA; TexLA; TexASchL; TexStateTA; ClrmTA. 10: Work and Study Club; DAR. 14: Ref, mus lib, elem sch libs. 15: 421 Magnolia st, Denton Tx 76201.

TEBO, JAY DRENNER. b Morristown NJ 6 O 34. 5: Washington Col (Md) 52-54 Lycoming Lycomig Col 54-56 (Chem) BA; UIll 58-59 (LS) MS. 7: Bandsman-clerk Spec 3/c US Army 399 Band), Ft Leonard Wood Mo 56-58; Br libn AC Spark Plug Div Gen Motors Corp, Milwaukee 59-61; Libn AC Spark Plug Div, Gen Motors Corp, Wakefield Mass 61-63; Ref libn Res Labs United Aircraft Corp, E Hartford Conn 64-65; Br libn Pratt & Whitney Aircraft Div United Aircraft Corp, N Haven Conn 65-66; Mgr lib info systems div Xerox Corp, Rochester NY 66-. 9: SLA (Conn Valley Chap; treas 65-66, Recr Conn 64-65; Upstate NY Chap; chm Memb-Recr Com 67-68, treas 68-70); ALA; ASLIB; ASIS; IEEE. 10: Monroe Co Lib Club. 13: Yes. 14: Ref, bibliog, admin, indexing. 15: ISD Lib Xerox Corp 1350 Jefferson rd, Rochester NY 14623.

TECLAFF, LUDWIK A. b Poland 14 N 18. 4: Eileen Johnson. 5: Warsaw U 36-39 (Law); Oxford U (Polish Faculty of Law) 44 (Law) Mag Jur; Columbia 54-55 (LS) MS; NYU 59-65 9law) LLM, JSD. 6: Polish, Fr. 7: Ref libn Brooklyn Pub Lib, Brooklyn NY 55-59; Research libn Fordham U Sch of Law 59-61, Act law libn 61-62, Law libn 62-, Asst prof of law 62-66, Assoc prof of law 66-69, Prof of law 69-. 8: Co-dir Marine Environment Lrgal Res Proj, NYU Law Ctr 67-69; Consul UN Water Resources Survey Prog, NY 68-; Sec Wking Gp on Underground Waters, Com on Internat Water Resources Law, Internat Law Assn 68-. 9: AALL (Com for Liaison with LC, Repr to Coun of Nat Lib Assns, Com on Vis For libns); ALA (Mem-at-Large); -ACRL (Law & Pol Sci Subsect); NY Law Lib Assn (pres 69-70). 12: "The River Basin in History and Law" (67); Assoc ed "Journal of Maritime Law and Commerce". 15: 99 Joralemon st, Brooklyn NY 11201.

TEDESCO, CLAIRE (ROSATO). b Detroit 19 O 20. 4: Joseph A Tedesco. 5: UPenn 38-39; Marywood Col 39-42 BS in LS; Americn U 60-61. 6: Ital. 7: Br libn Osterhout Free Lib, Wilkes-Barre Penn 49-51; Med libn VA Hosp, Wilkes-Barre Penn 51-53, Chief Libn 53-56; Acquis libn USDA, Wash DC 56-58; Chief Law Lib US Dept Health, Educ & Welfare, Wash DC 58-61; Chief Aviation Med Lib Fed Aviation Agency, Wash DC 61-65;Chief Med & Gen Ref Lib VA, Wash DC 65-. 9: MedLA (mem Adv Com on Med Lib Problems); SLA (Hospitality Chm, Wash Chap); DCLA. 14: Info retrieval, ref, admin. 15: 6207 Cheryl dr, Falls Church Va 22044.

TEEL, ERIC (ALBERT). b Lansing Mich 26 My 24. 5: St Johns Col (Md) 45-50 BA; West Res 51-52 MS in LS. 7: Gen asst libn E Cleveland Pub Lib, E Cleveland Ohio 52-56; Head of tech serv Whittier PUB Lib, Whittier Cal 56-64; Head of adult serv Altadena Pub Lib, Altadena Cal 64-65; Ref libn Cal State Col at Fullerton 66-. 9: ALA; CalLA; SoCal TECH Proc Group (chm 62-63); OrangeCoLA. 10: Friends of Placentia Pub Lib. 14: Ref. 15: California State Col Lib 800 N State Col blvd, Fullerton Ca 92631.

TEEPLE, GLADYS B (WINDEDAHL). b Carthage S Dak 22 Ag 07. 4: Howard M Teple. 5: Augusta Col 25, 26, 29 (Educ); UOre 37 (Educ) BA; UWis 44 BLS. 6: Lat, Fr, Ger, Sp. 7: Circ libn Oregon State Lib, Salem Ore 45-46; Hd ref libn Salem Pub Lib, Salem Ore 46-47; Ser libn John Crerar Lib, Chicago 50-55; Catlgr Atlanta Pub Lib, 55-57; Hd libn Bexley Hall, Gambier Ohio 57-58; Chief catlg dept John Crerar Lib, Chicago 61-63, 65-. 9: SLA. 14: Catlg. 15: 400 Main st, Evanston Il 60202.

TEEPLE, HOWARD MERLE. b Salem Ore 29 D 11. 4: Gladys Windedahl. 5: Willamette U 33-38 (Speech) AB; Chicago 51-55 (Hist of Rel) PhD, 62-63 MA in LS. 6: Fr, Ger, Gk. 7: Farmer, Salem Ore 38-50; Research asst Emory U 55-57; Vsiting Instr Kenyon Col 57-58; Assoc Prof WVa Wesleyan Col 58-61; Prof asst order dept Northwestern U 63-65, Sr asst ref dept 65-69; Hd ref dept Chicago State Col 69-. 9: ALA; Soc of Biblical Lit. 13: Yes. 14: Ref. 15: Deering Lib Northwestern Univ, Evanston Il 60201.

TEES, MIRIAM H. b Montreal Can 24 F 23. 5: McGill 40-44 BA, 50-51 LS. 6: Fr. 7: Indexer, catlgr Internat Civil Aviation Org, Montreal 51-53; Libn The Royal Bank of Can, Montreal 53-. 9: ALA; SLA (Chap pres 57-58, chm 69 Conf Com 67-69); CanLA (Com mem); Q ueLA (treas 64-6, pres 65-66). : Girl Guides. 13: Yes. 15: Royal Bank of Can Lib P O Box 6001, Montreal 101 Can.

TEFFT, SAMUEL CURTISS. 8b Chicago 7 N 39. 5: Grinnell Col 58-62 (Sociol) AB; UIll 62-63 (LS) MS. 6: Fr. 7: Libn I Free Lib of Phila 6-64, Libn II ref libn Humanities dept, Northeast Reg Lib 65-. 10: Caxton Club (Chicago). 14: Ref, Amer decorative art. 15: Free Libof Phila, Logan Sq, Phila 19103.

TEIGLER, ELAINE E. b Chicago. 5: Northwestern U 39 (Hist, Pol Sci) BS, 44-46 (Internat Affairs, Hist) MA; Northwestern U Sch of Law 48-51. 7: Research asst, ed asst Encyclopaedia Britannica World Atlas Research libn Lib of Internat Rel 46-47; Ref libn Northwestern U Sch of Law 47-6, Asst libn head of readers serv 64-. 9: AALL; ChicagoALL. 15: Northwestern Univ Law Sch, 357 E Chicago ave, Chicago Il 60611.

TEIPE, SISTER AGATHA DC. b Baltimore 3 Je 18. 5: St Joseph Col 40 (Eng, Math) BS; Catholic U 56 MS in LS. 7: Tchr St Johns Sch, Albany NY 41-50; Tchr Seton High Sch, Baltimore 50-51; Libn Norfolk Catholic High Sch, Norfolk Va 69-; Tchr-libn Utica Catholic Acad, Utica NY 58-69. 9: NCTE;CathLA; NYLA; NY State Eng Coun. 10: Munson-Williams-Proctor Art Inst. 14: Bks for yp. 15: 6401 Gnanby st, Norfolk Va 23505.

TEISBERG, DANIEL PETER. b Fergus Falls Minn 22 My 28. 4: Grace Sperber. 5: Concordia col (Moorhead Minn) 46-50 (Eng Lit) BA; UNeb 50-51 (Eng Lit); UMinn 51-52 (Eng Lit), 53-54 (LS) MA. 6: Ger, Fr. 7: Circ page UMinn (Minneapolis) Main Lib 52-53, Grad asst Lib Sch 54; Ref & docs libn UOmaha 54-55; Libn Applied Sci & Tech Dept Chicago Pub Lib 55-58; Prof asst II tech dept Minneapolis Pub Lib 58, Prof asst II bus & mun ref 58-60, Asst hd bus & econ dept 60-65, Hd lit & lang dept 65-. 9: ALA; MinnLA. 10: Amer Fed State, Co & Munic Employees. 13: Yes. 14: Admin, ref, catlg, clsf. 15: 5241 James ave So, Minneapolis Mn 55419.

TEITELBAUM, HAROLD. b Chicago 15 S 10. 4: Tobia Frank. 5: UIll 36 (Educ) BS, 37 (Educ) MS, 39 BS in LS. 7: Ref asst Pub Lib, Chicago 37-40, Exec asst 40-51; Army of the US Corps f Mil Police (T/Sgt) 42-45; Bibliog asst Pub Lib, Chicago 52-65, Chief hist & travel dept 65-. 9: ALA. 10: Phi Delta Kappa; Kappa Delta Pi. 12: Ed "Book Bulletin of the Chicago Public Library (55-64). 14: Ref, hist. 15: 78 E Washington st, Chicago Il 60602.

TEITELBAUM, PRISCILLA. b NYC 15 F 26. 5: Brooklyn Col 42-46 (Biol) BS; Columbia 58-61 (LS) MS. 6: Ger, Fr. 7: Res asst for cancer Res Group 47-62; Lit scientist Amer Petroleum Inst, NYC 66-68; Libn NYU 62-66, 68-. 9: SLA (Exec Com Documentation Group); NY SLA (chm Documentation Group 67-68). 10: Amer Jewish Cong. 13: Yes. 14: Ref. 15: 160 E89 st, NYC 10028.

TELBAN, ETHEL. b Renton Wash 31 Mr 14. 5: Central Wash State Col 32-35, 38 (Art) BA; UWash summer 36; USoCal summer 41; UDenver 50 (LS) MA. 6: Fr. 7: Renton Sch Dist, RENTON Wash: Tchr-libn 36-50, Elem lib supv 50-60, Sch lib supv 60-. 8: Instr, UWash Sch of Libnship, summers 55 & 58-60; Instr Central Wash State Col summers 46, 51, 53, 57; West Wash Stae Col summers 65; Consul Elem Lib Wkshops: Moscow Ida 62 & Bellingham Wash 65. 9: NEA (NEA-AASchL Elem Com 63-65); ALA-AASchL (Elem Lib Com 61-6, Newbery-Caldecott Com 60); Wash State ASchL (past pres 63-64); PNLA (past pres 50-510. 10: Delta Kappa Gamma; Soroptimist Club; Municipal Arts Commsn; PEO. 13: Yes. 14: Elem sch lib serv, lib educ. 15: 508 Cedar st, Renton Wash 98055.

TEMA, WILLIAM JOHN. b Senatobia Miss 23 Je 37. 4: Janet Ruth Ross. 5: UMinn 55-59 (Soc Studies) BS, 59-61 (LS) MA. 6: Fr. 7: US Army, Ft Leonard Wood Mo 59, (Sgt) E-6 in Army Res; Ref libn Cedar Rapids Pub LIB, Cedar Rapids Iowa 61-63; Ref libn Pasadena Pub Lib, Pasadena Cal 63-65; Libn & page supv 66-67; Adult libn La Pintoresca Br 67-. 9: ALA; CalLA; IowaLA (chm Recr Com 62); Ya Bk Reviewers So Cal (treas). 10: Nat Honor Soc; Pasadena Mun Employees Assn; Area #2 Coun. 14: Ref, docs, ya, adult. 15: 2187 Cooley pl, Pasadena Ca 91104.

TEMKIN, EDWARD A. b Bronx NY 12 Mr 17. 4: Sara Schlossberg. 5: UConn 38-42 (Pol Sci) BA; Syracuse 46-47 BLS; Seton Hall U 57-61 (Secondary Educ) MA. 7: US Infantry (1st Lt), New Guinea & Philippines 43-46; Ref asst Bus Dept Enoch Pratt Free Lib, Baltimore 47-48; Supv main reading room ref div NY Pub Lib 49-50; Jr Sr prin bus libn Newark Pub Lib, Newark NJ 51-57; Libn McManus Jr High Sch, Linden NJ 57-65; Lib Dir Pub Lib, Clark NJ 61-69; Asst Prof Lib Sci NJ State Tchrs Col 69-. 9: NJLA. 10: Kiwanis Syracuse Lib Sch Alumni Assn. 14: Pub Lib admin, adult serv, pub rel. 15: 15 Lenox ave, Cranford NJ 07016.

TEMKIN, SARA ANNE (SCHLOSSBERG). b Hooken NJ 1 O 12. 4: Edward A Tenkin. 5: NJ State Tchrs Col 42-43 (LS); George Washingtn U 44-48. 6: Fr. 7: Ref libn Linden Public Lib, Linden NJ 30-43; Hosp libn Goldwater Mem Hosp, Welfare Island NYC 44; Ser libn ref Army Med Lib, Wash DC 44-48; Asst dir Cranford Pub Lib, Cranford NJ 56-. 8: Consul: Jewish Educ Center, Elizabeth NJ 62-63, Temple Emanuel, Westfield NJ 63. 9: NJLA. 10: LWV; Cranford Suburban Symphony. 12: Ed "New Jersey Bibliographer (61-63); Auth "Jinny Williams, Library Assistant. 13: Yes. 14: Ref, admin, catlg. 15: 15 Lenox ave, Cranford NJ 07016.

TEMPLE, WILLIAM (HAYES). b New Castle Penn 30 O 36. 5: Clarion State Col 56-60, 62-64 (LS) BS in Ed; Kutztown State Col summers 66, 67, 68 (Lib Ed). 7: Circ asst Westminster (Penn) (Penn0 60-62; Libn Logan Area Jr High Sch, Altoona Penn 64-66; Libn Altoona Area Sch Dist Logan Jr High Sch, Altoona Penn 66-. 9: ALA; NEA; Penn State EA. 14: Ref, circ. 15: 2012 E Brook rd, New Castle Penn 16101.

TEMPLIN, DOROTHY (ROBERTSON). b Victoria BC Can 17 F 33. 4: William G Templin. 5: UBC 50-54 (Hist) BA; Toronto 58-59 BLS, 69 MLS. 7: Clerk ser dept UBC 57-58; Catlgr UToronto 59-63, Head reclsf sect 63-64; Head catlg dept York U 64-65, Head acquis dept 65-66, Asst dir for tech serv 66-69. 8: Lecturer in catlg, Ont Col of Educ, UToronto, summers 63 & 64. 9: CanLA (sec Tech Serv Sect 67-68); ALA; Inst Prof Libns Ont (sec-treas 67-69); OntLA (sec Col & Univ Libs Div 65-66, pres Tech Serv Group 66-67, chm Educ Com 67-). 10: UToronto Sch Lib Sci Alum. 14: Tech serv, admin. 15: Apt 802, 185 Shaughnessy blvd, Willowdale Ontario Can.

TEMPLIN, VIVIAN (STOVALL). b Glen Echo Hts Md 9 Je 21. 4: Herman A Templin. 5: UIll 39-43 (Home Econ) BS; UMd 67-69 MLS. 7: Circ Trinity Col (Wash DC) 65-. 9: ALA; CathLA. 10: Amer Home Econ Assn. 15: 10912 New Hampshire ave, Silver Spring Md 20903.

TEN EYCK, ELIZABETH (MARCHANT). b Gloucester Mass 26 Ap 34. 5: Simmons 51-55 (Psych) BS, 64-66 MSLS. 7: Lib intern Harvard Col Lib 65-66, Ref libn 66-67, Admin asst 67-68, Asst libn (ref & circ) 68-. 8: Lectr Simmons Col Grad Sch of Lib Sci 67-69. 9: ALA; ASIS. 14: Admin. 15: 18 Brown st, Cambridge Ma 02138.

TEN HOOR, JOAN MARY. b Holland Mich 12 S 44. 5: Hope Col 62-66 (Humanities) AB; UMich 67-68 AMLS. 6: Ger. 7: Tchr Marysville Pub Schs, Marysville Mich 66-67; Asst ref libn MiamiU (Ohio) 68-. 14: Ref. 15: Alumni Lib Miami Univ, Oxford Oh 45056.

TEN HOUTEN, ELIZABETH S(HERIER). b Fairfax Co Va 25 Ja 13. 4: Cornelis Pieter ten Houton. 5: George WashingtonU 30-35 AB in LS, 35-36 (LS). 6: Sp, Dutch, Fr. 7: Chief field payroll files US Rural Resettlement Admin, Wash DC 35-36; Asst libn US Rural electrification Admin, Wash DC 36-40; Libn US Army Ordnance Frankford Arsenal, Phila 40-41; Asst libn in charge of ref US Army QM Gen, Wash DC 41-42; Asst libn Walter Reed Gen Hosp (gen & med), Wash DC 42-43; Lecturing libn for Hispanic Div of LC lent to Biblioteca Nata, Lima Peru 43-44; Libn Centro Ecuatoriano-Americano, Quito Ecuador 45-46; Indexer and file clerk NRA, Wash DC 34-35; Libn Iron Mines Co of Venezuela, El Pao Venez 56-63; Libn William R Ewald Jr (planning consul), Wash DC 66-67; Libn Amer Assoc of U Women, Wash DC 67-. 8: Bibliog wk in urban planning & consul; Checking hist & arch data, mss transcription for Waterman's "Mansions of Virginia" 43 & 44; Org agric lib for Agric Experimental Sta, Tingo Maria Peru 44. 9: SLA. 10: George WashingtonU Lib Sci Alumni Assn; DAR; AAUW. 12: Auth "Court Decisions on Teacher Tenure" (35). 13: Yes. 14: Ref, Lat Americana (lit, hist, etc), hist, arch, botany. 15: AAUW 2401 Virginia ave NW, Washington DC 20037.

TEPPER, ESTHER EDITH (BORTNICK) (MRS). b NYC 8 O 19. 5: Hunter Col 36-40 (Biol) BA; Columbia 50-52 MLS. 6: Ger, Fr, Yiddish. 7: Engnr aide, weather observer, tech clerk Fed Govt 40-46; NY Pub Lib: Sr libn ref 96th st Br 52-55, Sr libn Bronx Ref Center 55-59, Supv libn Bronx Ref Center 59-63, Chief bk ordering off 64-66; Chief sport fish & wildlife bibliog sect US Dept of Interior Lib, Wash DC 66-67; Asst chief sci sect Mid-Manhattan Lib NY Pub Lib 67-. 9: SLA; NYLA. 10: Phi Sigma. 14: Ref, med & sci lit. 15: 66 W 69th st, New York NY 10023.

TEPPER, HERBERT JOHN. b Detroit 10 Ja 21. 4: Betty Verone Reichard. 5: Amherst 39-43 Philos) AB; West Res 47-49 (Hist) MA; UWis 55-59 (LS) MA. 6: Fr, Ger. 7: Link trainer instr Army Air Forces, US 43-46; Self-employed 49-54; State Hist Soc of Wis, Wis: Research assoc I 54-58, Research assoc II, head newspaper sect 58-63, Libn III, head catlg sect 63-. 9: ALA; WisLA (Histn). 14: Catlg. 15: 14 Sumter ct, Madison Wi 53705.

TERESINSKI, SALLY A (SELNER). b Coleman Wis 29 My 37. 4: Dean J Teresinski. 5: Wis State U (Oshkosh) 55-59 (Eng, LS) BS; UWis 63-64 MSLS. 6: Fr. 7: Tchr-libn Coleman High Sch, Coleman Wis 59-63; Tchr Oshkosh High Sch, Oshkosh Wis 62-63; Libn Educ Materials Center Forrest R Polk IB, Wis State(Oshkosh) 64-. 9: WisLA; WDAVI. 10: Assn Wis State Univ Faculties; Wis Lib Sch Alumni Assn; Beta Phi Mu; AAUW; Wis State U (Oshkosh) Alum. 14: Ref. 15: 2912 Shorewood dr, Oshkosh Wis 54901.

TERHUNE, STANFORD (REAVES) JR. b Tulsa Ok. 5: Northwestern 59-63 (Hist) BA; UIll 63-64 (LS) MS; Tufts 68-. 6: Fr. 7: Stud searcher Northwestern U Lib 63-64; Grad asst Lib Sci Lib UIll 63-64; Acquis libn Bowdoin Col Lib 64-66; Ser catlgr; Mich State U Lib 66-68; Tufts 68-. 10: Beta Phi Mu; Brunswich Chamber Singers. 14: Tech serv in col & univ libs. 15: 108 Mystic st, Medford Ma 02155.

TERRELL, DOROTHEA. b NYC 10 N 24. 4: William L Terrell. 5: Hunter Col 41-46 (Statistics) BA; Pratt 61-63 MLS. 6: Ger, Fr. 7: Sub-prof NY Pub Lib 46-48; Lib asst Army Med Lib, Wash DC 49-51; Air Force lib asst USAF, Pacific Theater 51-53; Tchg asst Pratt Inst Lib Sch 62-63; Med nursing sch libn Hosp, SI NY 65; Nursing sch libn Willowbrook State Sch Practical Nursing Sch 65; High sch libn NYC Voc High Sch, SI & NYC 65-. 9: ALA; Eng Tchrs Assn; NY SchLA; NY Lib Club. 10: Beta Phi Mu. 14: Cat, Amer West collections. 15: 1170 Bay st, SI NY 10305.

TERRILL, PATRICIA. b Hastings Neb 3 F 11. 5: Mills Col 28-29 (Hist); UCal (Berkeley) 29-30 (Hist); UCLA 30-33 (Hist) BA; USoCal 47-48 BSLS. 7: Soc wker State Relief Admin, Los Angeles 38-41; Santa Monica Cal; Admin asst Douglas Med Plan 42-47; Ref libn Pub Lib 48-52; Chief ref libn & order libn 52-; Asst city libn 66-. 9: ALA; CalLA. 10: Beta Phi Mu; Family Serv of Santa Monica. 14: Ref, bk sel. 15: Santa Monica Pub Lib, 1343 - 6th st, Santa Monica Cal 90401.

TERRY, EDWIN W(ELLINGTON). b Brooklyn NY 4 D 18. 4; natalie Johnston. 5: Brooklyn Col 37-41 (Philos) BA; Columbia 45-46 (LS) BS, 47-49 (Educ) MA; Brooklyn Col 53-63 (Hist) MA; St Johns U 63- (Hist). 7: (Sgt) US Army Corps of Engnrs 41-45; Catlgr Columbia U 46-47; Libn Dillard U 47-48; Acquis asst Queens Col (NY) 48-59; Dir of Lib Nassau Commun Col 60-67; Chief libn Bronx Community Col 67-. 8: Mem lib adv com, Mitchel Field Planning Com, Garden City NY 64-66. 9: NYLA; NassauCoLA (1st v-pres 65-66, pres 66-67); NY State A-V Assn; NYSAJC; LACUNY; ALA; NEA-DAVI; Col Libns SUNY (chm 65-66). 10: AAUP; Beta Phi Mu. 13: Yes. 14: l, acquis. 15: 880 Thieriot ave, Bronx NY 10472.

TERRY, HELEN (HUBBS). b Kirkville NY 23 Mr 16. 4: Cyrl W Terry. 5: Syracuse -39 BA, -40 BLS. 6: Fr. 7: Lib Staff; Syracuse U 40-41, Kent State U 41-43, NY State Col of Home Econ (Ithaca) 43-51, Albert R Mann Lib, Ithaca NY 51-. 8: Survey, Binghamton Elem Schs Libs; Mem, Cornell Team Surveying Schs. 9: ALA. 14: Circ. 15: 3 Game Farm rd, Ithaca NY 14850.

TERRY, JOSEPHINE (ROEHRIG). b Chicago 3 Jl 30. 4: John A Terry. 5: Fla State U 48-53 (Geog) BS, 54-55 (LS) MS. 7: Stud catlgr Fla State Geological Survey, Tallahassee Fla 52; Asst to map curator Amer Geographical Soc, NYC 53-54; Grad asst Fla State U Curriculum Lib 54-55; Libn catlg & ref Miami Pub Lib, Miami Fla 55, Br libn 56-61; City Libn Sierra Madre PUB Lib, Sierra Madre Cal 61-65; Field serv libn Nev State Lib 65-68; Co libn Butte Co, Oroville Cal 68-. 9: ALA; CalLA; NevLA. 10: Soroptimist. 13: Yes. 14: Pub libs, admin, personnel. 15: 289 Skyline blvd, Oroville Ca 95965.

TERRY, JUAN E. b McGregor Iowa 4 Jl 27. 4: Delcie Blackwell. 5: Our Lady of the Lake Col (Tex) 62-64 (LS, Hist) BA, 64-65 MSLS; St Mary's U 63-67 (Hist). 6: Ger, Russian. 7: Ser lin AMR SW Research Inst, San Antonio Tex 66-68; Asst libn J Hillis Miller Health Ctr Lib UFla 68-. 9: MedLA; FlaLA; Fla Med Libns. 10: Phi Alpha Theta; Lutheran Laymen's League, Air Force Association. 14: Acquis, rare bks, automated systems. 15: 3613 NW 49th ave, Gainesville Fl 32601.

TERRY, JUANITA. b Acadia La 25 Jl 06. 5: LSU 25-29 (Eng & Amer Lit, Amer Hist) BA, 29-31 (Eng & Amer Lit, Amer Hist) MA; UIll 32-33 BS in LS; Columbia 38-39 MS in LS, 49-52 (LS, Amer Hist). 6: Fr, Ger, Sp, Ital. 7: LSU: Asst catlg & order depts 29-31, Sec Lib Sch 31-32, Asst in chg of gifts & exch 33-38, 39-41, Act head orer dept 42-43; Security off (1st Lt) USMC, Pacific FLEET 43-46; Ref libn Baylor U Lib 47-49; Sr ref libn Columbia Col Lib (NY) 52; Ref libn Williams Col Lib 52-. 9: ALA-ACRL. 10: AAUP; Green Mountain Club. 13: Yes. 14: Ref, govt doc, bk sel. 15: P O Box 54, Williamstown Mass 01267.

TERRY, LIZZIE McREYNOLDS. b Birmingham Ala 9 J 26. 5: Morris Brown Col 53-57 (Eng) AB; Atlanta U 63-68 (LS) MS. 7: Tchr Atlanta Pub Sch 57-65, Libn 58-68; Libn Frederick Douglass High School, Atlanta 68-. 9: ALA; NEA; SELA; GaTchrsEA. 10: Beta Phi Mu. 14: Ref. 15: 344 Taft st SW, Atlanta Ga 30315.

TERRY, MARTHA NANCY. b Chicago Ill 24 O 33. 4: Alfred Sumner Terry. 5: UMich 51-54, 65 (Eng Lit) AB, 66 (LS) MA. 6: Fr. 7: Ref libn Grand Valley State Col, Allendale Mich 66-. 9: ALA; MichLA; Mich Acad Sci, Arts & Letters.

10: Phi Kappa Phi; Beta Phi Mu; Pi Lambda Theta. 14: Ref. 15: 14323 Duneswood, Grand Haven Mi 49417.

TERRY, MONA M (LCKOVSKY). b Cleveland 10 Ag 18. 4: Thomas J Terry. 5: Kent State U 37-38; West Res 47 (Eng) BA, 47-48 BS in LS, 62-65 MS in LS. 6: Sp. 7: Libn Cleveland Pub Lib, Audubon 55-58, Cleveland Bd of Educ, A B Hart Jr High 60-62; Max S Hayes Voc High Sch 62-. 9: ALA-AASchL; Ohio ASchL. ; OhioLA. 10: Cleveland Tchrs Union. 14: Sch libs. 15: 6116 Cabrini lane, Seven Hills Oh 44131.

TERRYBERRY, ANN B(UFFINTON). b Boston Mass 1 Ap 40. 4: Richard K Terryberry. 5: Mt Holyoke Col 57-61 (Math) AB; SUNY (Albany) 65-67 MLS. 7: Tech libn Gen Electric Co, pittsfield Mass 61-68; Libn N Adams State Col 68-. 9: SLA. 10: SUNY (Albany) Lib Sch Alumni Assn. 15: West rd, Richmond Ma 01254.

TERZIAN, SHOHIG SHERRY. b Constantinople Turkey. 5: Radcliffe 33-37 (Eng Lit) AB (cum laude); Columbia 41-42 (LS) MS; UCLA Ext 57-60. 6: Armenian, Fr. 7: Ref asst Vassar Col Lib 42-43; Picture ed & research asst US Off of War Info Overseas Br US State DEPT OF Internat Info & Cultural Affairs & US War Dept Civil Affairs Div, NYC 43-46; Research libn Time Inc, NYC 47-48; Libn Prudential Insurance Co of Amer West Home ff, Los Angeles 48-61; Libn Neuropsychiatric Inst of Stae of Cal UCLA Center for Health Sci 61-. 8: 1st Training Wkshop for Libns of Cal State Dept of Hygiene. 9: MedLA; SLA (com mem: Internat Rel, Placement, Prof Activities, Pub Rel; Biol Scis Div; SoCal Chap: pres; chm Behavioral Scis Com, var other coms); CalLA (pres Hosp & Insts RT). 10: Psychiatric Libns of Los Angeles; Internat Soc of Gen Semantics; Assn of West Hosps; Mental Health Assn of Los Angeles; Radcliffe Club of SoCal; UCLA Armenian Studies Club. 13: Yes. 14: Behavioral scis. 15: Neuropsychiatric Inst, UCLA Center for the Health Scis, Los Angeles Ca 90024.

TESCH, GAIL NAOMI. b Winnipeg Can 25 F 36. 5: UMan BA; UToronto BLS. 6: Fr. 7: Circ libn Simon Frazier U Lib, Inter-lib loan libn, Bibliogr 66-69. 9: CanLA. 14: Acquis, info serv. 15: 902-1924 Barclay st, Vancouver 5 BC Can.

TESDELL, ANGELIN EMILIA. b Polk Co Iowa 31 O 06. 5: DES Moines U 24-26; UMinn 26-31 (LS) BS; UColo summer 38; Columbia summer 52; UCLA summer 53; UWash 65-66, M Lib. 6: Norwegian, Fr. 7: ND State U Circ & ref libn 31-35; Ref libn & lib methods Instr 35-39; Res libn 41-46; Acquis libn 46-47; Dir of libs Everett Commun Col 47-66; Libn periods 66-. 8: Governor;s Conf on Libs Del 68. 9: ALA (life mem); -ACRL (Jr Col Sect; sec 51-52, chm 56-57); NEA (life mem); PNLA (life mem, sec-treas Col Div 56-58); WashStateASchL (Reg 14; sec-treas 51-52, chm 53-54); WashEA (Commun Col Rep 67-68); Wash Commun Col Coop Com, Period Exch Libn 66-; Everett Commun Col EA (sec-treas 52-53). 10: AAUP; AAUW; Admin Women in Educ; Snohomish Co Museum & Hist Assn; Beta Phi Mu. 12: Ed "Library Leads Wash State ASchL (55-56). 14: Admin, ref, bibliog, acquis. 15: 710 Hoyt ave, Everett Wash 98201.

TESOVNIK, MARY E. b Milwaukee 27 Mr 08. 5: UWis 28-32 (Hist, LS) BA, Certif in Lib Sci; UMich 38-39 MALS. 7: Lib asst Milwaukee Pub Lib 32-33; Libn W Div High Sch, Milwaukee 33-36; Milwaukee Pub Lib: Catlgr 36-45, Chief of catlg Dept 45-58; Chief of processing dept 58-67; Lectr Sch of Lib & Info Sci UWis (Milwaukee) 67-. 9: ALA; SLA; WisLA. 14: Catlg. 15: Milwaukee Pub Lib, Milwaukee Wi 53233.

TEWES, SHIRLEY ANN (HILL ELLIOT). b Hicksville NY 1 Mr 33. 4: Aubrey Vincent Tewes. 5: Hunter Col 50-53 (Home Econ Educ); UIll 64-65 (Home Econ Educ) BS, 67-69 (LS) Masters. 6: Fr. 7: Home Economist Ill Power, Champaign 65-67; Special libn UIll Child Research Ctr 68-. 9: ALA; Ill Lib Serv. 10: Baha'i; PTA; Amer Home Econ Assn; AAUP; Phi Omicron Upsilon; Ill Home Econ Assn. 14: Ref, dissemination of info to scientific research commun. 15: 206 Hessel blvd, Champaign Il 61820.

TEWS, RUTH (MARIE). b Lewiston Minn 2 Ag 07. 5: UMinn 39 BS in LS (cum laude), 39 Certif of Hosp Libnship. 6: Ger. 7: St Paul Pub Lib: Lib asst 30-34, Ref libn 34-39, Chief hosp lib div 39-4; Supv Hosp Lib Mayo Clinic Lib, Rochester Minn 46-. 8: Visiting lecturer UMinn Lib Sch, 40-48; Faculty mem, Inst Hosp Libnship: UMinn 53, Amer Hosp Assn 60; Visiting lecturer, St Marys Sch of Nurs, Rochester Minn 59-; Co-dir wkshop on bibliotherapy, 64; Faculty Mem Conf St Libns UIll 67; Inst Hosp & Inst Libn Lib Sch UWis 68; Consul Soc Educ Research Develop Inc 68. 9: ALA-Hosp Lib Div (pres 54-55);-AHIL (chm Com on Org 57-59; chm Com on Bibliotherapy 60-65;-LED (chm Com on Educ of Hosp & Institutional Libns 64-67); SLA (Org &chm Hosp & Nurs Sch Libns Group 44-46; reg chm Memb Com 46-48); Minn Assn Hosp & Med Libns (pres 42-43). 10: LWV; Amer Assn Hist of Med; Olmsted Co Mental Health Chap. 12: "The Patients Library in T E Keys "Applied Medical Library Practice (58); Ed Issue on Bibliotherapy "Library Trends 11, 2 (Oct 62); Auth chap "Progress in Bibliotherapy in "Advances in Librarianship ed Melvin Voigt (69). 13: Yes. 14: Patients libs, bibliotherapy. 15: 23 - 7th ave SW, No 21, Rochester Minn 55901.

THACKERY, JOHN THOMAS JR. b Urbana Ohio 3 F 20. 4: Enid Dixon. 5: Ball State U 38-42 (Soc Sci, Math) BA; UIll 46-47 BSLS. 6: Lat, Ger. 7: (Sgt) US Army Coast Artillery, Alaska 42-45, India 45; Ref asst Ft Wayne (Ind) Pub Lib 47-50; Dayton (Ohio) Pub Lib: Ref asst 51, Br libn 52-55, Head ref dept 56-63, Coordinator personnel serv 62-63, Admin asst 63-. 8: Surveys; Mercer Co Ohio 67, Licking Co Ohio 68. 9: ALA-RSD (chm Com on Chapters); OhioLA (chm Ref Round Table). 12: "Survey of the Public Libraries of Mercer County, Ohio (67); "Survey on Library Service in Licking County, Ohio (68). 13: Yes. 14: Ref, adult serv, personnel, admin. 15: 212 College st, Urbana Ohio 43078.

THACKSTON, FRANCES(VENABLE). b Worsham Va 18 My 22. 5: Duke 41-44 (Eng, Sp, Educ) AB; UN 52-54 MSLS 59. 6: Sp, Fr, Ger, Portu. 7: Claims adjuster Liberty Mutual Ins Co, Boston & br offs 44-47; Tchr Wakelon & Charles L Coon High Schs, Zebulon & Wilson NC 47-52; Instr & libn Sch of Lib Sci UNC (Chapel Hill) 53-54; Ser catlgr DukeU 54-58, Act hd ser dept 58-61, Hd ser dept 61-65; Libn & lecturer Sch of Lib & Info Serv UMd (Col Park) 65-68; Asst catlg ed Nat Union Catlg Publ Proj LC 68-. 9: ALA. 10: Phi Beta Kappa; Bus & Profess Women's Club. 14: Catlg, ser proc. 15: Apt 1 7302 Rhode Island ave, College Park Md 20740.

THAKORE, MANHAR P. b Baroda India 11 Mr 27. 4: Niru Thakore. 5: BombayU 44-49 9chem) BS; MS UBaroda 56-57 Dip LS, 61-63 (Archaeology) MA; UIll 67-68 (LS) MS. 6: Gujarati, Hindi, Marathi, Samskrit. Pali. 7: Fine arts libn MS UBaroda India 50-56, Catlgr 56-57, Ref libn 57-62, Tech libn 62-65, Asst libn 65-67; Grad asst Lib sch UIll 67-68; Asst libn Ill StateU (Normal) 68-. 9: Ill Assn Higher Educ; McLeanCoLA. 14: Acquis, ref. 15: 306 Milner Lib, Normal Il 61761.

THALHEIMER, GERDA (STERN). b Muenchen-Gladbach Germany. 5: Us of Bonn, Berlin, Cologne 27-29 (Hist of Art); Hunter Col 53-54; Columbia 55-56 MLS. 6: Ger, Fr, Lat. 7: Ref libn Amer Mgt Assn, NYC 56-58; Catlgr Columbia U 58-. 14: Rare bks, catlg. 15: 124 - 16 84 rd, Kew Gardens NY 11415.

THARPE, JOSEPHINE M(ATHEWS). b Locust Grove Ga 30 Mr 10. 5: Fla State U 27-31 (Lat) AB; UIll 37-38 BS in LS, 42 MA. 6: Fr. 7: High sch tchr, Fla 31-37; Period asst UIll Lib (Urbana) 40-41, Asst in acquis dept 41-42; State documents libn Duke U Lib 42-4, Act head ref dept 43-45; Asst ref libn UIll Lib (Urbana) 45-57; Ref libn Cornell U Lib 47-64, U bibliogr 65-. 9: ALA (Subs Bk Com 60-62); -ACRL;-RSD (dir-at-large 63-65); NYLA. 10: AAUP; Phi Kappa Phi; Eta Sigma Phi; Beta Pi Mu; LWV. 14: Ref, bibliog. 15: 400 Triphammer rd, Ithaca NY 14850.

THATCHER, EDWARD P. b Phila 11 S 16. 4: Monette Hunkins. 5: Swarthmore Col 3539 (Biol) BA; UMinn 39-43 (Bot) MA, 51-52 BS in LS. 6: Ger. 7: Tchg asst UMinn(Minneapolis) 40-42; Agrc Agric Iowa Exp Station, Ames Iowa 43-46; Biol dept head Black Hills Tchrs Col 46-47; Instr Biol Dept Coe Col 47-50; Visiting Instr Biol Swartmore Col 50-51; Sci & map libn UOre 52-. 8: On leave as Sub-Libn (sers) Ahmadn Bello Univ, Zaria Nigeria. 9: SLA. 10: Sigma Xi; AAUP. 13: Yes. 14: Bibliog (West Amer exploration), sci & map ref, pre-Linnean natural hist bks & printing. 15: 1812 Villa rd st, Eugene Ore 97403.

THAXTER, JOHN HALL. b Roswell NM 7 O 12. 4: Esther Shoup. 5: NorthwesternU 29-30 (Engring); George WashingtonU 31-36 (Germanic Lang) BA. 6: Ger, Fr. 7: Deck attendant, binding asst, ref libn Ser Div LC 30-43, Doc expediter Exchange & Gift Div 48-49, First Lt Counter Intelligence Corps US Army 43-46, Hd govt pub sect Ser Div 50-51, Asst chief Ser Div 51-. 10: Potomac River Sailing Assn. 13: Yes. 14: US & foreign newspapers, govt publ. 15: 854 N Kensington st, Arlington Va 22205.

THAXTON, CARLTON J(AMES). b Tucson Ariz 23 My 35. 4: Donna Bradley. 5: UGa 53-57 (Journalism) ABJ; Fla State U 57-58 (LS) MS. 7: Dir Coastal Plain Reg Lib, Tifton Ga

58-68; Chief pub lib serv State Dept of Educ, Atlanta 68-. 8: Exec Dir Nat Lib Week, Ga 65-67. 9: ALA; SELA; GaLA. 15: Pub Lib Serv, 156 Trinity ave SW, Atlanta Ga 30303.

THAXTON, MARY LYNWOOD. b Detroit Mich 27 D 44. 5: Wellesley Col 62-63; Emory & Henry Col 64-66 (Eng, Philos) BA; EmoryU 66-67 MLn. 7: Asst ref libn Col of William & Mary 67-. 9: VaLA. 10: Williamsburg Players. 12: "A Guide to Historical Materials in the Swem Library" (68). 14: Ref. 15: 230 Griffin ave, Williamsburg Va 23185.

THAYER, JOHN E. 8b Asheville NC 30 N 19. 5: Duke 48 (Eng) AB; Peabody 48-49 BS in LS. 7: (S/Sgt) US Army, Ft Jackson SC 42-46; Asst catlgr Miami U (Ohio) 49-51; UAriz: Asst catlgr 51-53, Documents libn & ref 53-55, Circ libn 55-57; Ref libn Honnold Lib, Claremont Cal Supv Sup ref libn Contra Costa Co, Pleasant Hill Cal 61-64; Asst dir Tucson Pub Lib 64-65; Col Libn Prescott Col 65-67; Chief soc sci libn UArz 67-. 9: ALA; ArizStateLA (Conv Chm 55, pres Col & Univ Libs Div 68-69). 12: "Desert Padre; Eusebio Francisco Kino" (59). 14: Ref, admi. 15: 2805 E Linden st, Tucson Az 85716.

THAYER, MARLENE PARRISH. b Allegan Mich 26 My 23. 4: Melvin C Thayer. 5: Ohio Wesleyan U 41-42, 43-44 (Hist); Kent State U 42-43, 44-45 (Hist) BA, 49-50 (Soc Studies) BS in Ed, 55-56 (LS) MA. 6: Fr. 7: Asst to gen manager Goodyear Rim Div, Akron Ohio 45-47; Controller Robt J Enders Advertising, Wash DC 48-49; Corp sec Design & Prod Inc, Alexandria Va 50-53; Asst ref libn Kent State U 56-57; Head Libn Swaney Mem Lib, New Cumberland W Va 57-59; Asst libn Mary H Weir Lib, Weirton WVa 59-60; Catlgr State Lib of Mich 60-61; Libn Sr High Sch, St Joseph Mich 61-66; Hd sch catlgr State Lib of Mich 66-69; Consul 69-. 9: ALA-ACRL;-AASchL; NEA; MichEA; Mich ASchL (Legis Chm). 10: Detroit Soc for Geneal Res; NE Hist Geneal Soc; Mich Audobon Soc; Nat Audobon Soc; Nat Wildlife Fed; Amer Forestry Assn; Delta Kappa Gamma. ; African Violet Soc of Amer, Wilderness Soc. 14: Ref, ya serv. 15: 5735 Taffy pkwy, Lansing Mi 48910.

THAYER, RACHEL E (CRABB). b Jopkin Mo 15 Ag 02. 4: Lewis A Thayer. 5: Mont State U 20-24 (Hist, Pol Sci) BA; Stanford summer 25, 26-27 (Pol Sci) MA; San Jose State Col summer 28 (LS). 7: Tchr Declo (Ida) High Sch 24-2; Tchr Dinuba (Cal) High Sch 27-29; Lewis & Clark Col: Col Libn & Instr 46-57, Col Libn & Asst Prof 57-65, Act chief libn & Asst Prof 65-66; Col acquis libn & Asst Prof 66-68; Col archivist-libn 68-. 9: ALA; PNLA. 14: Acquis, admin. 15: 12504 SW Riverside dr, Portland Ore 97219.

THAYER, ROLLIN HAROLD. b St Francis Mission SD 30 D 16. 4: Ruth Marie Robinson. 5: Okla State U 40 (Poultry Sci) BS in Agric; UNeb 42 (Poultry Nutrition) MS; Wash State U 55 (Nutrition, Animal Sci). 7: Prof of Nutrition Okla State U 43-. 9: Poultry Sci Assn; Worlds Poultry Sci Assn; OklaLA Okla Acad of Sci. 10: Kiwanis Internat; AAAS (Fellow); Sigma Xi. 13: Yes. 14: Libtrustee, tchg & res in poultry nutrition. 15: 105 N Stallard, Stillwater Okla 74074.

THEALL, REV D BERNARD OSB. b Chicago 21 Ja 16. 5: St Marys Col (Minn) 33-36 (Eng) BA; DePaul U 39-40 (Educ) M Ed; Catholic U 42-46 SLS. 6: Fr, Ger, Ital, Sp, Lat. 7: Libn Priory Sch, Wash DC 42-46; Head ref dept Catholic U 47-49, Asst Prof of Lib Sci 49-67; Assoc Prof 67-. 9: ALA; CathLA (chm DC Unit 49-51); DCLA. 12: Ed Lit Sect, CathLA; "Annual Catholic Booklist (47-). 13: Yes. 14: Bk sel, ref. 15: Catholic Univ of Amer Lib, Wash DC 20017.

THEBERGE, MARJORIE (ODONNELL). b Ranger Tex 13 Ag 19. 5: UTex 42 (Anthropology) BA; Tex Womans U 57 MLS; UTex (Higher Educ Media Inst) summer 69. 6: Sp. 7: Libn Lovington High Sch, Lovington NM 55-56; Lib Sci libn Tex Womans U 56; Libn Ranger Jr Col 57-62, 66-; Asst documents libn Tex A&M U 63-66. 9: TexLA. 10: Tex Jr Col Tchrs Assn; AAUW; Columbia Study Club; Garden Club. 14: Bk sel. 15: 214 Cherry st, Ranger Tx 76470.

THERIAULT, (JOSEPH PIERRE YVES) MICHEL. b Toronto Ont Can 2 D 42. 5: UMontreal 60-62 (Philos) BPh; Pontifical USt Thomas Aquinas (Rome) 62-67 JCD; UToronto 68-69 BLS. 6: Fr, Ital. 7: Bibliogr researcher UMontreal Bkstore 67-68; Dir acquis UMontreal Gen Lib 69-. 9: ALA; CanLA; CathLA; Assn canadienne des bibliothecaires de langue francaise; QueLA. 10: Canadian Can Law Soc; Canon Law Soc of Amer; Canon Law Soc of Gt Brit; Societe pour l'etude du droit canonique. 13: Yes. 14: Selection, ordering, rare bks. 15: Apt 314 1610 W Sherbrooke, Montreal 109 Can.

THERRIEN, MARCELLA. b Windsor Ont Can 11 Ap 26. 4: Roger D Therrien. 5: UOttawa 67 BLS. 6: Fr, Ital. 7: Circ mgr No Ont Rec 62-64; Libn im charge Uudbury 67-; Asst master deputy libn Niagara Col of Applied Arts & Tech 67-. 9: Coun Lib Technology (First Can Del 68-70). 14: Lib admin. 15: 117 Margery rd, Welland Ont Can.

THIBAULT, ROBERTA L (WALBRIDGE). b Buffalo NY 8 N 40. 4: Edward A Thibault. 5: Syracuse 58-62 (Eng) AB (magna cum laude); SUNY (Buffalo) 64-65 (Eng) MA; George WashingtonU 67-68 (Eng). 6: Fr. 7: Ed asst Wm J Keller Inc, Buffalo NY 63-64; Tching fellow SUNY, Buffalo 64-65; Tchr Arlington Co Pub Sch, Arlington Va 65-66; Accessing libn Folger Shakespeare Lib, Wash DC 66-67; Tching fellow George WashingtonU 67-68; Counsellor Camp Echo Lake, Wanesburg NY 68; Asst curator Manuscripts Lib, Syracuse 68-. 10: Mod Lang Assn; Libns Assn SyracuseU; Phi Beta Kappa. 14: Mss. 15: 125 Vincent st, Syracuse NY 13210.

THIBODEAU, DORIS E. b Brooklyn NY 28 Jl 32. 5: Mt St Vincent Col (NS) 49-52 (Eng Lit) BA (cum laude), 52-53 BLS. 6: Fr. 7: Catlgr Santa Clara U 53-55; Bkmob lib Monmouth Co Lib, Freehold NJ 55; Catlgr Santa Clara U 55-56; Program dir rec Amer Red Cross, Korea & France 56-60; Ref libn Santa Clara Co Lib Hdqrs, San Jose Cal 61; Br libn Morgan Hill Br Santa Clara Co (Cal) Lib 61-63; Libn admin 1st Cav Div & 4th Missile Cmd, Korea 63-66; Asst catlgr Welch Med Lib Johns HopkinsU 66-68, Catlgr for hist materials 68-. 9: ALA; CalLA; MedLA. 10: Sierra Club; Beta Phi Mu; Amer Assn Hist Med. 14: Catlg, rare bks. 15: 914 Woodson rd, Baltimore Md 21212.

THIELKE, MARJORIE (SCHWENN). b Middleton Wis 12 S 17. 4: Dr Charles W Thielke. 5: UWis 35-39 (Eng) BS, 62-64 (LS) MS. 6: Ger. 7: Tchr High Sch, New Glarus Wis 39-41; Libn Jr High Sch, Madison Wis 64-. 9: NEA; ALA; WisEA; WisLA. 10: Garden Club. 14: Child & ya serv, sch libs. 15: 474 S Midvale blvd, Madison Wis 53711.

THIGPEN, MARY MAC (ELLINGTON). b Rome Ga 25 O 17. 4: Richard F Thigpen. 5: Shorter Col 34-38 (Hist) AB; Emory 39-40 AB in LS. 6: Fr. 7: Tchr Floyd Co schs, Rome Ga 38-39; Libn druid Hills High Sch, Atlanta 40-42; Libn Girls High Sch, Rome Ga 42-43; Libn Battey Gen Army Hosp, Rooe Rome 43-45; Catlg dept Macon Reg Lib, Macon Ga 57-58; Catlg Ga Inst of Tech Lib 59-. 9: GaLA; SELA. 14: Catlg. 15: 2700 Harrington dr, Decatur Ga 30033.

THOM, IAN W(ALTER). b Montreal Can 6 Jl 11. 4: A Nancy Forbes. 5: NYU 35-40 AB; Columbia 40-46 BS, 46-47 MS. 6: Fr. 7: Clerical asst NYU Lib 38-40; Lib asst NYU Dental Lib 40-42; US Army 42-45; Admin asst processing div Harvard U 47-51; Chief of tech serv Northwestern U 51-58; Asst libn for prep Princeton U 58-67; Assoc libn Queens Col (NYC) 67-. 9: ALA (chm Ser Sect 61-62); NY Tech Serv Libns. 10: Archons of Colophon. 13: Yes. 14: Admin. 15: 48 Valley rd, Port Washington NY 11050.

THOM, JOSEPH M. b Bronx NY 22 O 19. 4: Lillian R Rosenstein. 5: NYU 40-48 (Bus Admin) BA, 48-49 (Pol) MA; Columbia 49-50 MSLS. 7: USA Signal Corps 41-45; Night supv res reading room NYU 45-49; Lib fellow Brooklyn Col 49-50; Lecturer in libnship WashU (St Louis) 50-54, Chief ref dept 50-54, Asst to chancellor 54-55; Supv lib & recs Goodyear atomic Corp, Portsmouth Ohio 55-60; Dir libs YeshivaU 60-61; Asst to pres Gyrodyne Co of Amer, St James NY 61-62; Libn & dir educ TV Port Jefferson Pub Schs, Port Jefferson NY 62-. 9: ALA; SLA; NEA-DAVI; NYLA; SuffolkCoLA; NY A-V Assn. 12: "Reference Material in Education"; "Reference Materials in Political Science". 13: Yes. 14: Ref, info ret, instrl tv. 15: PO Box 514, Setauket NY 11733.

THOMAN, ROBERT G. b Canton Ohio 10 Jl 36. 5: Kent State U 54-58 (Hist, Eng) BS in Ed, 59 (Hist) 61-62 MA in LS. libn soc sci dept Dayton& Montgomery Co Pub Lib, Dayton Ohio 63-. 9: ALA; OhiLA. 14: Ref. 15: 1040 Cumberland ave apt 3, Dayton Oh 45406.

THOMAS, AILINE (BRIERLY). b Peculiar Mo 27 F 10. 5: Cottey Col 27-29 (Eng); Central Col (Fayette Mo) 29-30 (Eng); UMo 30-31 (Eng) BS in Ed; UDenver 53 MA in LS. 7: Eng tchr Arcadia High Sc, Arcadia Kan 31-35; Eng tchr Shawnee Mission High Sch, Shawnee Mission Kan 35-37, Libn 49-. 8: Chm, Nat Lib Week, AASL 59-61; Kan exec dir 64; Kan State Sch Lib Bk Sel Com 64-65; N Central Evaluation Com Topeka High Sch 69. 9: NEA; NEA-DAVI; ALA- AASchL (chm Loc Arrangements ALA 1957 & 68 Conf, Dist Dir 65-66); Kan State Tchrs MPLA; KanLA (Nat Lib Week Com 65); Kan ASchL (Dist 1: dir 56, v-pres 58, pres 59, Memb Chm 59;

MembChm 60, 61 & 63, Nomin Chm 64, Publicity Chm 65)Kan KAVCO. 10: Beta Phi Mu. 14: Ref, bk sel. 15: 5332 Rosewood dr, Shawnee Mission Kan 66205.

THOMAS, ALAN W. b Cleveland 28 F 26. 5: Bowling Green State U 46-48; UMich 48-50 (Eng) BA, 50 AMLS. 7: US Air Corps B29 Gunner 44-46; Catlgr San Francisco State Col 50-53; Catlgr No Ill State U 53-55; Br libn, head gen info Dept, head adult bk sel Free Lib of Phila 55-65; Assoc dir Ferguson Lib, Stamford Conn 65-67; Chief ext div Free Lib of Phila 67-. 9: ALA; ConnLA; PennLA. 13: Yes. 14: Ref, bk sel, admin. 15: 249 S Quince st, Philadelphia Pa 19107.

THOMAS, BROTHER ALEXANDER F. b NYC 22 Je 09. 5: St Marys Col 35 (Fr) AB; Fordham U 35-37 (Fr Lit); Gonzaga U 42 (Eng Lit) AM; Columbia 44 (LS) BS. 6: Fr. 7: Tchr: All Hallows High Sch, NYC 35-37, Butte Central High Sch, Butte Mont 37-41; Leo High Sch, Chicago 41-42; Instr Iona Col 42-45, Chief Libn 45-. 9: ALA; Amer Mgt Assn; CathLA (Exec Bd 64-); NYLA; WestchesterLA; NY Metro Ref & Research Lib Agency (Trustee 67-). 10: US Lawn Tennis Assn; AAUP. 13: Yes. 14: Admin. 15: Iona Col Ryan Lib, New Rochelle NY 10801.

THOMAS, BRUCE EDWIN. b Rochester NY 6 O 35. 5: Syracuse 53-57 (Hist) AB, 57-58 MS LS. 7: Gen lib asst Colgate U Lib 58-59; Humanities libn UOre Lib 59-61; Adult serv libn Albany Pub Lib, Albany NY 61-65; Libn readers serv & Asst Prof Lock Haven State Col 65-. 8: Adv consul, "Essay and General Literature Index 60-. 9: ALA; PennLA. 10: Phi Beta Kappa; Phi Kappa Phi; Pi Lambda Sigma; Beta Phi Mu. 14: Ref materials, tchg of ref, tchg of catlg a-v materials. 15: 20 Commerce st, Lock Haven Pa 17745.

THOMAS, BRUCE WALLACE. b Ravenna Ohio 25 N 18. 4: Janet Sheldon. 5; hiram Col Lang & Lit) BA; West Res 44-45 (Eng) MA, 48-49 MS in LS; Ohio State U 62-63 (Higher Educ). 7: Pilot trainee cadet USAF 42-43; Ed World Publ Co, Cleveland 45-47; Antioch Col: Ref & circ libn 49-56, Asst libn 56-61, Act libn 58-60, Assoc libn 61-65, Libn 65-. 8: Adv Coun State of Ohio LSCA Title III. 9: Midwest Acad Libns; Ohio Col Assn (chm Lib Sect 65-66). 10: AAUP. 12: Asst ed "Websters New World Dictionary (51). 13: Yes. 15: 106 Tower ct, Yellow Springs Oh 45387.

THOMAS, CAROLYN (FERGUSON). b Mansfield Ohio 30 My 10. 4: William J Thomas. 5: Western Col for Women 28-32 (Eng Lit) BA; Drexel 61-65 MSLS. 7: Ref trainee Cherry Hill Free Pub Lib, Cherry Hill NJ 61-62; Catlgr Haddon Twp Pub Lib, Westmont NJ 63-64; Ref libn Cherry Hill Free Pub Lib, Cherry Hill NJ 64-. 8: Instructor NJ Reference Workshop 67, 68; Instructor Drexel Graduate School of Library Science 68. 9: ALA (Jr Mem RT); NJLA; CamdenCoLA. 10: AAUW; LWV; Libs Unlimited. 12: Ed "Libraries Unlimited Union Catalog of Reference Books". 14: Ref, catlg. 15: 797 Park dr, Cherry Hill NJ 08034.

THOMAS, CHRISTINE (FLINT). b Alexandria Va 29 D 28. 4: Carl H Thomas. 5: LSU 45-49 (Home Econ) BS, 49-53 (LS) BS. 7: Act art libn LSU (Baton Rouge) 49-51; Asst ref libn La State Lib, Baton Roug 53-55; Exec sec La Lib Assn, Baton Rouge 67-. 9: ALA; LaLA; SWLA. 10: Baton Rouge Lib Club; Soc Sci Club. 14: Ref. 15: 4538 Arrowhead st, Baton Rouge La 70808.

THOMAS, DELLA (FARMER). b Davison Co D 27 Mr 13. 4: John E Thomas. 5: Wis State Col (Superior) 31-35 (Eng) B Ed; UWis summers 36-38 (Eng), 41-42 BLS. 7: Pub sch tchr & tchr-libn, Wis 35-41; Libn elem schs, Madison Wis 42-43; Staff Madison Pub Lib, Madison Wis 43-45; Consul & bibliogr Scott-Foresman Co 4557; Head Educ area & Asst Prof Lib Sci Okla State U Lib 57-59; Asst Prof Lib Sci & Dir Curriculum Materials Okla State U Lib 59-; Assoc Prof 65-. 8: Consul; Third Jr Bk of Authors, H W Wilson (in progress), Jr High Sch Catlg (in progress); Dir Studytours, European Backgrounds in Child Lit 67, 68, 69. 9: ALA; (Ed) Subcom on New Tools 66-; Subcom on Voc-Tech Lists 67-); -LAD; (mem & chm Subcom on Recr Materials);-YASD (Com on Sel of Bk & other Materials 64-);-CSD (Com on Eval of Lib Tools 65-); OklaLA (pres 64-65); Okla EA (rep SWLA Bd 62-64); -AASchL (Brit Award Com 68). 10; Alpha Beta lpha; Beta Phi Mu. 12: "Dime a Dozen (63). 13: Yes. 14: Bks for child (foreign, old & rare). 15: 217 N Stallard, Stillwater, Ok 74074.

THOMAS, DOROTHY (JOHNSON). b Ottumwa Iowa 10 Jl 07. 5: Grinnell Col 25-27, 29 (Eng) BA; Carleton Col 28; UWis 53-54 (LS) MS. 7 Stud asst Grinnell Col 28-29; Libn I NY Pub Lib 30-31; Asst Stewart Lib, Grinnell Iowa 48-50; Sc libn pub schs, Grinnell Iowa 51-52; Pub Lib, Cedar Rapids Iowa: Bkmob libn 54-56, Br libn 56-60, Head ext dept 60-. 9: ALA; IowaLA (chm Plaque Com; Dit Program Chm). 14: Lib ext. 15: 1824 Higley ave SE, Cedar Rapids Iowa 52403.

THOMAS, DOROTHY (McKEE). b Buffalo NY 21 Ap 05. 4: Sydney F Thomas. 5: William Smith 22-25 (Eng); UBuffalo 25-26 (Eng) BA, 25-26 BS IN LS. 6: Fr. 7: Lib asst Grosvenor Lib, Buffalo NY 26-28, 29-37; Asst in lib Amer Lib in Paris 28-2; Vick Chem Co Marketing Res Lib, NYC 40-43; Civilian libn in chg Bur of Aeronautics, Wash DC 43-45; Libn Fibreboard, Emeryville Cal 47-49; Asst libn Naval Supply Center, Oakland Cal 49-50; Head Libn Mill Valley Pub Lib, Mill Valley Cal 50-. 9: CalLA (Legis Chm 59). 10: AAUW; Audubon Soc. 14: Ref, admin. 15: 5132 Paradise dr, Corte Madera Cal 94925.

THOMAS, DUNCAN. b Hampden Sidney Va 23 D 1889. 4: Hilda Matarama. 5: Davidson Col 06-10 AB; Union Theol Sem (Richmond Va) 12-15 BD; Columbia 55-57 (LS. 6: Sp, Lat, Ital, Portu, Ger, Gk, Hebrew, Fr. 7: Minister Presbyterian Church 15-26; Lecturer Victorious Life Testimony, Phila 20-21; Clergyman Episcopal Church, NC 28-30; Tchr Colegio MEDICO DE LA Habana (Habana Cuba) 30-54; Rare bk catlgr Gen Theol Sem (NY) 56-. 9: ATheolLA. 10: Pi Kappa Alpha. 12: Confessional Verse (59). 14: Catlg, rare bks. 15: Gen Theol Sem 175 Ninth ave, New York NY 10011.

THOMAS, ELIZABETH (EUDORA). b Richmond Va 17 Ag 08. 5: Col of William & Mary 41 (Hist) AB; Va State Lib Certif. 7: Asst period & files URichmond 29-36, Circ libn 36-43; Ref & circ asst Va State Lib 43-. 9: VaLA. 10: AAUW; DAR; UDC; Va Genel Soc; Va Hist Soc; Colony Club. 14: Ref. 15: 4001 Grove ave apt 4, Richmond Va 23221.

THOMAS, ELIZABETH H. b Johnstown Penn 3 Je 19. 5: Randolph-Macon Womans Col 37-38; Smith 38-41 (Pub Health) AB; Catholic U 53-56 MS in LS. 7: Tech, bacteriologist, working on researchproblems Research Problems US Pub Health 41-47; Bacteriologist US Nat Insts of Health, Bethesda Md 47-56; Asst loan libn Libn Mount LVIBN Mont Vernon Sem & Jr Col (Wash DC) 58-63; Libn Penn State U (Mont Alto) 63-. 9: PennLA; ALA. 10: AAUW; AAUP. 14: Admin, catlg. 15: Lib Mont Alto Campus Penn State Univ, Mont Alto Pa 17237.

THOMAS, ELIZABETH. b Moncure NC 17 Ag 0. 5: UNC(Greensboro) 26-30 (LS) AB. 6: Fr, Sp. 7: Asst Charlotte PUB Lib, Charlotte NC 30-33; Sec to sch lib adv State Dept of Pub Instr, Raleigh NC 36-46; Sr asst circ dept Princeton U Lib 46-49, Supv of circ 49-. 9: NJLA (mem-at-large Exec Bd 64-67); ALA-AASL (chm Memb Com 44-46). 14: Circ. 15: Princeton Univ Lib, Princeton NJ 08540.

THOMAS, ELSIE V (von RAISON). b Libau Latvia 15 Jl 21. 4: Herbert T Thomas. 5: Posen U 40-42 (Langs, Lit); Preussische Staatsbibliothek (Berlin) 42-43 (LS) Diplom-Bibliothekarin. 6: Ger, Latvian, Lat, Russian. 7: Ref & catlgr Raczynski Lib, Posen 43-45; Sr asst libn UNeb Libs Sci & Tech Div 55-; Sr asst libn UNeb C Y Thompson Lib 66-. 9: NebLA. 12: Tr, Latvian to German: Blaumanis, Rudolfs "Rudolfs "Purva bridejs under the title "Sumpfwanderer (48). 14: Catlg, ref, for langs. 15: 5431 Francis, Lincoln Nb 68504.

THOMAS, EVALYN (MARJORIE). b Oak Hill Ohio 13 F 20. 5: Ohio U 38-42 (Fr, Lat) AB; Kent State U 60-63 (LS) MA. 6: Fr, Lat. 7: Tchr Oak Hill High Sch, Oak Hill Ohio 42-60; Tchr-libn 60-65; Ext serv libn Portsmouth Pub Lib, Portsmouth Ohio 65-66; Head libn 66-. 9: NEA; ALA; OhioEA; OhioASCHL; OhioLA; OhioValleyASchL. 10: Delta Kappa Gamma; Oak Hill Hosp Auxiliary; Portsmouth Little Theatre; Commun Concert Assn; Phi Beta Kappa; Beta Phi Mu; Bus & Prof Women. 14: Ref, publicity, admin, bk sel. 15: 1307 Bihlman dr, Portsmouth Ohio 45662.

THOMAS, GRACE HELEN. b Philadelphia Penn 24 N 43. 5: UChicago 61-65 (Sociol) BA; UCal (Berkeley) 65-66 MLS. 6: Sp. 7: Libn (staff) UCal (Santa Barbara) 66-. 14: Catlg. 15: 102 N Hope ave 15, Santa Barbara Ca 93105.

THOMAS, HELEN M (WILHELM). b Marshfield Wis 5 S 42. 4: Leslie Howard Thomas. 5: Cardinal Stritch Col 60-62; UWis 62-64 (Zoology) BS, 64-65 (LS) MS. 7: Ref libn Wis State U (Stevens Point) 65-66; Libn Sun Prairie Pub Schs, Sun Prairie Wis 66-. 9: ALA. 10: Beta Phi Mu. 14: Ref, child wk. 15: 609 Park cir, Sun Prairie Wi 53590.

THOMAS, J(AMES) LUTHER. b Quitman Ga. 4: Genevieve Wheeler. 5: Fla A&M Col 20-24 (Chem, Gen Sci) BS; Ohio State U summers 37-40 (Sci Educ) MA; Atlanta 41-42 BS in

LS. 6: Fr. 7: Instr of Eng, Fr Albany State Col (Ga) 24-25; Asst prin & sci tchr Douglass High Sch, Thomasville Ga 26-36; Fla A&M: Instr of biol & phys sci 36-42, Head Libn 42-53, Dir of Libs 53-. 8: Consul high sch sci, Fla. 9: ALA; NEA; FlaLA; SELA. 10: Fla A&M Employees Fed Credit Union; Fla Coun on Human Rel; Kappa Alpha Psi; Interinst Lib Com; Fla Inst Higher Educ. 14: Admin, ref. 15: 2825 Old St Augustine rd, Tallahassee Fla 32301.

THOMAS, J(OE) DONALD. b Norman Ark 7 Ja 24. 5: TulaneU 48 (Fr, Eng) BA; Columbia 51 MS in LS; NYU 56-57 Adult Ed. 6: Fr, Sp. 7: US Army Air Force 42-46; Gen Motors For Distributors Div, NYC 48-49; Ref asst-doc sup Columbia 51-53; Libn French Embassy Press Serv, NYC 53-56; Asst libn Hunter Col 56-57; Ref catlgr Standard Oil (NJ), NYC 57-59; Asst chief libn Montreal Star 59-60; Assoc dir for gen serv ChicagoU 60-68; Exec sec ACRL, Chicago 68-. 9: ALA-ACRL. 14: Admin, mgt. 15: 10120 So Seeley ave, Chicago Il 60643.

THOMAS, JAMES R. b St Clairsville Ohio 21 My 29. 4: Mary mkeys. 5: Ohio State U 47-51, 54 (Chem) BS. 7: Dental tech US Navy 51-53; Ref libn Battelle Mem Inst, Columbus Ohio 55-60, Assoc div chief spec projects 65-. 9: ACS; ASIS. 14: Info center mgt. 15: 505 King ave, Columbus Ohio 43201.

THOMAS, JILL CHAPMAN. b El Paso Tex 19 S 42. 5: Colo Col 61-64 Hist) BA; N Tex State U 67-69 MLS. 6: Fr. 7: Lib asst Fondren Lib So Methodist U 65-67; Soc sci ref libn Kan City (Mo) Pub Lib 69-. 9: SLA. 10: Alpha Lambda Sigma. 14: Ref, catlg. 15: 6130 Northaven rd, Dallas Tx 75230.

THOMAS, M(ILTON) HALSEY. b Troy NY 3 F 03. 5: Columbia 30 (Hist) BS, 31 (LS) BS, 42 (US Hist) AM. 6: Fr. 7: Libn Butler Lib of Philos, Columbia U 26-28; Curator Columbiana, Columbia U 28-59; U Archivist Princeton U 59-69; Consul ed The Papers of Woodrow Wilson 68-. 8: Adv Com "James Fenimore Cooper Letters, Harvard Univ Press 56-. 9: Amer Antiq Soc; Mass Hist Soc; AHA; BSA. 10: NE Hist Geneal Soc; Mass Soc of Mayflower Descendants; Nassau Club Princeton, Grolier Club (NY). 11: Carey-Thomas Award, 53; Alumni Meritorious Achievement Award, Sch of Gen Studies, Columbia U 63. 12: Comp "Bibliography of John Dewey with H W Schneider" (29, 2d ed 39); "Bibliography of the Faculty of Political Science, Columbia University, 1880-1930" (31); "Bibliography of Nicholas Murray Butler" (34); "John Dewey; A Centennial Bibliography" (62); Ed "Columbia University Officers and Alumni 1754-1857" (36); "C C Moores Early History of Columbia College" (40); "The Diary of George Templeton Strong with Allan Nevins" (4 v 52); "Elias Boudinots Journey to Boston in 1809" (55); "The Diary of Samuel Sewall 1674-1729" (2 v 69); Managing ed "Columbia University Quarterly" (30-35). 13: Yes. 14: Archives, hist editing. 15: Firestone Lib, Princeton NJ 08540.

THOMAS, MARGARET F. b Birmingham Ala 7 My 09. 5: Birmingham So Col 30 AB (cum laude); Emory 32 AB in LS; Columbia summer 36-40. 6: Fr. 7: Asst libn Ensley Birmingham, Birmingham (Ala) Pub Lib 32-33, 40-43; Asst libn Walker Co Lib, Jasper Ala 33-35; Libn Ensley High Sch, Birmingham Ala 35-40; Base Libn Birmingham Army Air Base 43-44; Command Libn, field libn WRASTC, Robins Field Ga 44-45; Howard Col: Asst libn, catlgr 4556, Act libn 56-57, Asst libn, head tech serv 57-58; Head catlg libn Jt U Libs, Nashville 58-61; Head Libn Randolph-Macon Womans Col 61-65; Head Libn Ferrum Jr Col 65-. 8: Planned & supvd; Stanley Lib Ferrum Jr Col 65-; Dana Wing to Lipscom Lib Randolph-Macon Womens Col 61-65; Consul to AAF Tech Lib Off Robins Field Ga 43-44. 9: NEA; AlaLA (treas 46-48, Program Chm 51-52); SELA; VaLA; VaEA; AlaEA (sec-treas 58). 10: Delta Kappa Gamma; AAUW; Birmingham Art Assn; Birmingham Hist Assn; Poetry Soc of Va, Womans Club, Lynchburg Va; Rocky Mount Womans Club. 12: Asst ed "Alabama Librarian (51-52); Indexer "Alabama Review (vol 4); Co-comp "Reading List for Birmingham Chapter of AAUW (58). 15: Ferrum Jr Col Lb, Ferrum Va 24088.

THOMAS, MARGIE (KLIMK). b Garrett Ind 11 N 42. 4: Michael Wright Thomas. 5: Fla StateU 61-64 (Hist) BA; Columbia 65-66 MS in LS. 6: Ger. 7: Libn James C Buckley Inc, NYC 66; Asst libn Post Lib, Ft Wainwright Ark 66-67, Post libn 67-. 9: ALA; AlaskaLA. 14: Admin, ref. 15: Box 933 N Pole Ak 99705.

THOMAS, MARGUERITE T. b Maysville Ga 19 Mr 13. 5: UGa 31-39 (Elem Educ) BS Elem Educ; Appalachian State Tchrs Col summer 56 & 57 (LS); UNC summer 58 (LS). 7: Elem sch tchr Oconee st, sch, Athens Ga 36-43; WAVE Off (Lt) US Navy, Wash DC 43-45; Owner of Dry Cleaning plant, Swansboro NC 46-53; Elem sch tchr US Dept Educ, Camp Lejeune NC 53-59; Hosp libn Med & Crews Libs US Navy, Camp Lejeune NC 59-. 9: ALA; NCLA; SELA. 10: NC Shell Club. 14: Ref. 15: US Naval Hosp Lib, Camp Lejeune NC 28542.

THOMAS, MARJORIE (ESTABROOK). b Warren Ohio 3 Ja 09. 5: Oberlin Col 26-30 (Eng Lit) BA; West Res 30-31 BS in LS; UCLA 59-62 (Eng Lit) MA. 6: Fr. 7: Child libn Rochester Pub Lib, Rochester NY 31-33; Ref libn Santa Monica Pub Lib, Santa Monica Cal 62-. 8: Consul Santa Monica Hosp Lib 58-60; Church Libn. 9: ALA; NYLA; CalLA. 10: Boy Scouts; Phi Beta Keppa; Commun Chest. 14: Ref, ya serv. 15: 260 - 21st st, Santa Monica Ca 90402.

THOMAS, MARJORIE (RAMBO). b McAllen Tex 4 J 29. 4: Alfred B Thomas. 5: UOre 46-50 (Journalism) BA, 66-68 MLS. 7: Ad writer The Oregonian, Portland 51-53; Sec State Hosp, Salem Ore 54-55; Ref consul Ore State Lib, Salem 68-. 9: ALA; PNLA; OreLA. 10: Salem City Club. 14: Ref. 15: 2360 Mountain View dr S, Salem Or 97302.

THOMAS, MARTHA LOU (MANSON). b Milwaukee Wis 5 Je 24. 4: Robert George Thomas. 5: UCLA 41-44 (Eng) BA; UCal (Berkeley) 45-46 Libnship Certif. 6: Fr, Sp. 7: Catlgr 20th-Century-Fox Film Corp, Beverly Hills Cal 46-47; Child libn Welwood Murray Mem Lib, palm Springs Cal 47-50; Rare bk catlgr Reynolds Hist Lib UAla Med Ctr Lib (Birmingham) 64-66; Asst libn Bell & Howell Research Labs Lib, Pasadena Cal 66-. 8: Res asst to Dr howard Holley in writing his book on Sir Wm Osler, "A Continual Remembrance", (68); Wrote scripts and presented child stories over weekly radio prog station KCMJ. 9: SLA; CalLA. 10: Phi Beta Kappa. 12: Comp "Rare Books and Collections of the Reynolds Historical Library" (68). 13: Yes. 14: Rare bks, catlg, child lit, pub rel, educ for libnship. 15: 635 Prospect ave apt A13, South Pasadena Ca 91030.

THOMAS, MARTIN ELLIOTT. b Merrill Ore 29 Ag 11.5. Sacramento Jr Col 29-31 (Soc Sci); Stanford 31-33 (Soc Sci) AB; UCal 33-34 (LS) Certif, 34-38 (LS) MA. 5: Sacramento Jr Col 29-31 (Soc Sci); Stanford 31-33 (Soc Sci) AB; UCal 33-34 (LS) Certif, 34-38 (LS) MA. 7: Jr libn acquis dept UCal Lib (Berkeley) 34-41; Bibliogr acquis dept UIll Lib Urbana 41-42; (Pvt) Qtrmstr Corps to (1st Lt) Trans Corps US Army Ship Transportation Off, US, Europe & Asia 42-46; Registration off US VA, San Francisco 46-47; Supv of pub distribution Cal Printing Div, Sacramento Cal 47-50; Gifts & exch libn, head Undergrad Lib UCLA 50-55; Circ libn asst govt publ libn Cal State Lib 55-. 9: ALA; CalLA (Docs Com: chm So Cal Subcom 51-52). 10: Sacramento BkCollectors Club; Sacramento Co Hist Soc. 12: Ed "California State Publications" (47-50). 13: Yes. 14: Govt publns, ref, Californiana. 15: 2801 - 37th st, Sacramento Cal 95817.

THOMAS, MARVIN. b NYC 4 Je 31. 5: Col of William & Mary Norfolk 49-51 (Govt) AA; Col of William & Mary 52-54 (Pol Sci); UMich 57-58 (LS). 6: Ger. 7: Courts & bd recorder & post commnder sec US Army, Germany 54-56; Gen asst Enoch Pratt Free Lib, Baltimore 59-60, Adult libn 60-61; Br libn Baltimore Co (Md) Pub Lib 61-63; Dir Howard Co (Md) Pub Lib 63-. 9: ALA; DCLA; MdLA (Program Com, Legis Com); Md Pub Lib Dirs Assn (pres-elect); Metro Md Pub Lib Dirs Assn. 10: Wilde Lake Vill Assn; Commun Action Assn; Howard Co Md Citizens Assn for Title III Pub Schs Program. 14: Admin, adult bk sel, ref. 15: 9421 Frederick rd, Ellicott City Md 20143.

THOMAS, MARY ELLEN. b Richmond Va 7 My 06. 5: URichmond 53-58 (Eng) BA; UVa 57; UNC 61-62, 64 MS in LS. 6: Fr. 7: Lib clerk C Med Col of Va 58-60; Tchr Henrico Co Sch Bd, Highland Springs Va 60; Lib clerk C Med Col of Va 60-61, Acquis libn 62-64; Catlg consul Alderman Lib UVa 64-69; Ref libn Va Commonwealth U, Richmond 69-. 9: VaLA. 14: Ref. 15: 1009-A Park ave, Richmond Va 23220.

THOMAS, NAOMI THELMA. b McKees Rocks Penn 10 Je 30. 5: Va State Col 48-52 (Eng) AB; UPittsburgh 53-54 (Eng); Carnegie-Mellon U 55-56 MLS. 7: Ref asst Sch Dept Carnegie Lib of Pittsburgh 56-66, Y-a & adult asst Brookline Br 66-68, Br libn Woods Run Br 68-. 9: ALA; PennLA. 10: UPittsburgh Carnegie Alum Assn; Pittsburgh Lib Club; Carnegie Lib of Pittsburgh Staff Assn. 14: Ref. 15: Woods Run Branch Lib, 1201 Woods Run ave, Pittsburgh Pa 15212.

THOMAS, PAGE A. b Leslie Ark 2 Jl 36. 4: Wenda Sue Johnson. 5: UArk 54-55; Hendrix Col 56-58 (Psych) BA; Perkins SCH OF Theol So Methodist U 58-61 BD. 6: Ger, Hebrew. 7: Stud Pastor Commerce Larger Parish, Commerce

Tex 58-59; Stud Pastor Wesley Methodist Church, Hugo Okla 59-60; Asst libn Bridwell Lib So Methodist U 61-64; Assoc libn 65-. 8: Ordained Deacon 59; Ordained Elder 62; Vol Staff Archaeol Excavations, Tell Gezer Israel 68. 9: ATheolLA. 14: Catlg. 15: 10219 Linkwood dr, Dallas Tx 75238.

THOMAS, PATRICIA DIANNE (UPHAM). b Phila Penn 1 F 44. 4: James Arthur Thomas. 5: UPenn 61-65 (Hist) BA; Drexel 65-66 MS in LS. 7: Libn (admin) Dept of the Army, Korea 66-67; Libn (admin) Dept of the Army, E Bragg NC 67-68; Acquis libn Montgomery Co-Norristown Lib, Phila 68-. 9: ALA; PennLA. 10: Drexel Lib Alumni Assn. 14: Acquis, bkmob serv, lib admin. 15: S102 Towne Court apts, Norristown Pa 19401.

THOMAS, PAULE(ROLLAND). b Montreal Can 17 My 29. 4: John Thomas. 5: UMontreal 50 (Philos) B Ph, 52 (LS) B Bibl, 57 (Philos) MA; McGill 65 MLS. 6: Fr, Ger. 7: Catlgr Catholic Sch Commsn, Montreal 52-54; atlgr UMontreal 54-57; Asst libn Nat Film Bd of Can, Montreal 57-61; Lecturer Ecole de bibliotheconomie UMontreal 61-; Assoc Prof 69-. 8: Consul for the "Manuel pratique de catalogage of the federation des Colleges classiues, Quebec 64-65; Chm Adv Com on Lib Techns Program Dept of Educ, Prov of Que 68-. 9: Internat Assn of Mus Libn; ADI; SLA; MusLA; QueLA. 12: "Bio-bibliographie de Roger Duhamel (52); Jt ed "Colloque sur les enquetes de bibliotheques et leur milieu (65); Co-auth "Vocabulaire Technique de la Bibliotheconomie et de la Bibliographie (69). 13: Yes. 14: Catlg, clsf, documentation, mus libnship. 15: 1245 Couvrette, Saint-Laurent Que Can.

THOMAS, ROBERT ELLIS. b Racine Wis 9 N 20. 4: Frances Heusdens. 5: UWis 46-50 (Econ) BA, 50-51 (LS) MS. 7: Driver-clerk Pub Lib, Racine Wis 38-40; Accounting clerk J I Case Co, Racine Wis 40-42; (Cpl) US Army 42-45; Head Libn: Pub Lib, Bismarck ND 51-56, Pub Lib, Hutchinson Kan 56-60, Pub Lib Salt Lake City 60-69; Dir Ramapo-Catskill Lib Syst, Middletown NY 69-. 9: ALA; UtahLA; MPLA. 14: Ref, admin. 15: Quickway Estates RD 3, Middletown NY 10940.

THOMAS, ROBERT JOSEPH. b Ottawa Can 21 S 13. 4: Helen Gilbank. 5: CARLETON U (Ottawa) 46-50 (Eng) BA; Toronto 52-53 BLS. 7: Clerk Can Civil Serv, Ottawa 32-40; Seaman Can Navy 40-45; Paymaster Lumber cos, Quebec 50-52; Bkmob libn Pub Lib, Saria Ont 53-54; Co Libn Lambton Co Lib, Wyoming Ont 54-56; Co Libn Middlesex Co Lib, London Ont 56-58; Ext libn NH State Lib 59-60; Dir Rutland Free Lib, Rutland Vt 60-63; Dir Holyoke Pub Lib, Holyoke Mass 63-. 9: ALA; MassL (mem Var Coms); NELA; West Mass Lib Club; West Mass Reg Lib Syst (Exec Com). 10: Family Serv Agency; Holyoke Area Kulturama Arts Coun. 14: Lib ext, admin. 15: 85 Sycamore st, Holyoke Ma 01040.

THOMAS, ROSA (ANDERS). b Blountstown Fla 23 Ag 21. 4: Shelly Dowling Thomas Jr. 5: Fla State U 39-43 (Soc Sci, Eng) AB; UNC 43-44 BS in LS; Chicago 49 (Med Lib Sci). 7: Asst NY Pub Lib summer 43; Asst libn US Naval Amphib Train Base, Solomons Md 44-45; Libn US Naval Air Station, Miami Fla 45-46; Asst libn US Naval Hosp, Bethesda Md 46; US VA Hosp; Med libn, Columbia SC 46-47, Chief libn Coral Gables Fla 47-53, Chief libn, Durham NC 53-54; Spec serv libs US Army, Europe 54-56; Chief libn spec serv libs Ft Gordon, Augusta Ga 57-60; Dist libn 6th Naval Dist Hdqrs, Charleston SC 60-61; Sub libn Dothan High Sch, Dothan Ala 62; Catlg Houston Mem Lib, Dothan Ala 65-68. 8: Licensed realtor; Operated recreation resort Kiley Springs 62-68. 9: ALA; MedLA; AlaLA. 10: Dothan Nat Lib Week Com; New Cent Study Club. 11: John Cotton Dana Publicity Award, 58 & 5. 13: Yes. 14: Armed forces libs, med libs. 15: P O Box 1811, Dothan Al 36301.

THOMAS, RUTH ANNE. b Pittsburgh Penn. 5: Col of Wooster 61-65 (Eng) BA; UDenver 65-66 (Libnship) MA; UMd 67-. 7: Assoc libn I UMd (College Park) 67-. 9: MdLA. 10: New Democratic Coalition. 15: McKeldin Lib Univ of Md, College Park Md 20742.

THOMAS, RUTH. b Baltimore 22 O 10. 5: Wellesley 29-33 (Hist) AB; Columbia 33-34 BS in LS. 7: Act 1st asst NY Pub Lib 34-41; Adult dept asst Cyrenius H Booth Lib, Newtown Conn 44-45; Asst in chg of wk with schs Danbury Lib, Danbury Conn 46-63; Catlgr UBridgeport 63-66; Catlgr Bridgeport Pub Lib, Bridgeport Conn 66-. 9: ALA; ConnLA. 14: Catlg. 15: 21 Cedar Hill rd, Newtown Conn 06470.

THOMAS, SANDRA Ione (Steffey). b Davenport Iowa 6 N 40. 4: Charles Everett Thomas. 5: Drake 59-61 (Mus); UNoIowa 61-63 BA; West Mich U 65-66 MLS. 7: Libn Des Moines Pub Schs, Des Moines Iowa 63-65; Asst libn Grand View Col 65; Asst br libn Toledo Pub Lib, Toledo Ohio 66; Libn Perrysburg Sch Syst, Perrysburg Ohio 66-. 9: ALA; OhioEA; NW Ohio EA; OhioASchL. 14: Serv to disadvantaged youth, non-print materials, displays. 15: 10521 Avenue rd, Perrysburg Oh 43551.

THOMAS, SARAH M. b Winchester Va 15 D 32. 5: Madison Col 49-52 (LS) BA; Carnegie 60-61 MLS. 7: Libn: acquis Engnr Res & Devel Labs, Ft Belvoir Va 52-53, Jeter Jr High Sch, Covington Va 53-55, J H Russell Elem Sch, Quantico Va 55-57; Asst ref libn Defense Atomic Support Agency, Wash DC 57-60; Lib asst Carnegie Lib of Pittsburgh 60-61; Libn Fairchild Stratos Corp, Hagerstwn Md 61-63; Libn Booz Allen Applied Research Inc, Bethesda Md 63-66; Head readers serv Applied Physics Lab, Silver Springs Md 66-67; Lecturer & dir continuing educ Sch Lib & Info Serv UMd 67-. 8: Lectr Ctr for Sci & Tech Info, Tel Aviv Israel D67; Various consul since 66. 9: SLA (Memb chm Documentation Div; Govt Info Serv Com, chm Subcom on Adequacy of Centralized Serv; Wash Chap; chm Documentation Group, 2nd v-pres); ASIS; DCLA. 10: Beta Phi Mu. 14: Ref, spec libnship. 15: 10427 Montrose ave apt 104, Bethesda Md 20014.

THOMAS, SYLVIA (MITCHELL). b Elizabeth City NC 26 N 39. 4: Squire D Thomas. 5: Va State Col 56-60 (LS) BS; Syracuse 60-61 MS in LS. 6: Fr. 7: Asst Elizabeth City State Tchr Col Lib summer 60; Ref asst Temple U Lib 61-68, Asst hd ref div 69-. 9: ALA-ACRL; -RSD. 10: Temple U Libs Staff Assn; Kappa Delta Pi; Delta Sigma Theta; AAUP. 14: Ref serv, bibliog. 15: 5926 Greene st, apt 202, Philadelphia Pa 19144.

THOMASON, NEVADA (ELLA) (WALLIS). b Seventy-Six Mo 9 Mr 28. 4: Paul Estes Thomason. 5: Henderson State Tchrs 46-50 (Bus) BSE; E Tex State U 56-57 MS in LS, summer 63 (Sch Admin); UDenver summer 68. 6: Fr. 7: Bus tchr Smackover High Sch, Smackover Ark 50-56; Libn: Sam Houston Jr High Sch, Borger Tex 57-58, Stephen F Austin Jr High Sch, Borger Tex 59-60, Borger High Sch, Borger Tex 60-65; Frank Phillips Col 65-. 8: Eval team So Assn Borger Pub Sch 68. 9: NEA-DAVI; ALA; Tex State Tchrs Assn (Dist 9 Lib Sect: sec 60-61, chm 63); TexLA (Reg I Publ Chm 63-64); Tex A-V Educ Assn; Tex Jr Col Assn. 10: AAUW; Delta Kappa Gamma; Red Cross; PTA; Altrusa. 13: Yes. 14: Ref, rare bks, educ media. 15: 1425 Primose, Borger Tex 79007.

THOMASON, ROBERT E. b Covina Cal 20 S 09. 5: Pomona Col 27-31 (Philos) BA; UCal (Berkeley) 38-39 (LS) Certif. 7: Jr libn Los Angeles Co Lib, Los Angeles 39-40; US Army 42-45; Libn P-2 USDA, Wash DC 45-48; Libn I UCLA 48, Ind rel libn 48-54; Supv bibliogr UNC(Chapel Hill) 54-57; Chief lib erv Serv Angeles State Col 57-63; Asst libn UCal(Irvine) 63-69; Assoc libn 69-. 9: ALA; CalLA. 14: Acquis, admin. 15: 3292 Georgia pl, Costa Mesa Cal 92626.

THOMISON, DENNIS VINCENT. b Rhinelander Wis 31 Mr 37. 5: Wis State U (Eau Claire) 55-60 (Hist, Soc Sci) BS; UDenver summers 61-63 (LS) MA; USoCal 66-68. 7: Libn Marshall Jr High Sch, Janesville Wis 60-61; Libn D C Everest High Sch, Schofied Wis 61-63; Circ libn & documents libn Wis State U (Eau Claire) 63-; Chm dept of Lib Sci 68-; Dir of lib educ Cal State Col (Long Beach) 67-68. 8: Visiting lecturer USoCal summer 68. 9: ALA; WisLA. 10: AAUP; Assn Wis State Univ Faculties. 14: Ref, admin, lib educ. 15: 2805 Stein blvd apt 203, Eau Claire Wi 54701.

THOMPSON, ALLEEN. b Waterville Me 18 S 19. 5: Colby Col 36-40 (Geol) BA; Simmons Col 40-41 (LS) BS; UCal 51-55 (LS). 6: Fr. 7: Engnr libn Penn State Col 41-43; US Navy LCDR 43-46, US Navy Res 46-; Asst libn Freeport Sulphur Co, NYC 46-47; Ref libn Safeway Stores Inc, Oakland Cal 47-48; Chief Libn Cal State Dept of Pub Health, San Francisco 49-55; Chief Libn Atomic Power Equip Dept Gen Electric, San Jose Cal 55-. 9: SLA (dir 56-60, pres 65-66; San Francisco Bay Reg Chap: sec 48-50, pres 54-55); CalLA. 10: USN Res. 14: Ref, admin. 15: Lib Atomic Power Equip Dept Gen Electric Co, 175 Curtner ave, San Jose Cal 95125.

THOMPSON, ALTA A (HODGELL). b Greeley Colo 25 F 14. 4: Paul C Thompson. 5: Colo State Col 30-34 (Bus Educ) AB, 54-56 (Bus Educ) MA; UDenver 60-62 (Libnship) MA. 6: Sp. 7: Bus Educ tchr; Del Norte High Sch, Del Norte Colo 34-35, Arriba High Sch, Arriba Colo 47-51; Bus Educ tchr, libn, hist & phys educ tchr, sec to Sch Bd Grover High Sch, Grover Colo 51-60; Bus Educ tchr & libn Lewis-Palmer High Sch, Monument Colo 60-62; Ref libn USAF Acad Lib 62-64, Spec collections libn Acad archivist 64-. 9: ColoLA (Exec sec 5861; chm No Dist); ColoEA. 10: Delta Pi Epsilon; Columbine

Circle; Little Log Church. 11: Sustained Superior Performance Award 65. 12: Comp Faculty Writings Report, USAFA--(6468). 14: Rare bks, bks on falconry, archives. 15: 3013 Drakestone dr, Colorado Springs Co 80909.

THOMPSON, BERT ALLEN. b Bloomington Ind 13 D 30. 4: Ellen Palmer. 5: Ball State Tchrs Col 49-53 (Eng) BS; Ind U summers 58-60 (LS) AM. 07: Libn Allen Mem High Sch,Bluffton Ind 53-54; Tchr-libn Alexandria Jr-Sr High Sch, Alexandria Ind 54-55; Prof libn Indianapolis Pub Lib 56-59; Head ref erv Mnkato State Col 59-61; Instr Grad Lib Sch NoIlU 61-63; Dir of Libs & Asst Prof of Lib Sci Kearney State Col 63-. 9: ALA; NEA; MPLA; NebLA (chm Col & Univ Sect 63-64). 10: AAUP. 14: Admin, lib educ. 15: 822 W 21st st, Kearney Nb 68847.

THOMPSON, BONNIE (HERRIVEN). b Lyndonville NY 14 N 41. 4: David W Thompson. 5: SUNY (Geneseo) 60-64 (Lib) BS, 68-69 (Lib) MS. 7: Libn Tonawanda Sr High Sch, tonawanda NY 64-68. 9: NYLA; NYStateTA. 10: Kappa Delta Pi. 14: Ya. 15: 61 Myrtle st, LeRoy NY 14482.

THOMPSON, CHARLOTTE ANNE. b Lansing Mich 10 N 09. 5: Hollins Col 27-30 (Lat); UMich 30-31 (Lat) AB, 31-32 AB in LS, summer 44; Columbia summers 49, 52, 53, 55 MS in LS. 6: Fr, Ger. 7: Libn UTampa 33-. 9: ALA; SELA; FlaLA (sec 36-37). 10: Zeta Tau Alpha; Delta Kappa Gamma; PEO; AAUW; Pilot Club; Tampa Womans Club. 14: Admin, ref. 15: 4015 Bayshore blvd apt 7C, Tampa Fl 33611.

THOMPSON, DIANE MARIE (KOIDAHL). b Aberdeen Wash 27 S 45. 4: Steven M Thompson. 5: UPuget Sound 63-67 (Hist) BA; UWash 67-68 MLS. 6: Fr. 7: Child libn Pierce Co lib, Wash 68-. 9: ALA; WashLA; ONLA. 14: Child serv. 15: 601 N Jackson, Tacoma Wa 98406.

THOMPSON, DON K. b Boone Co Ind 24 D 39. 5: IndU 58-62 (Hist) AB, 64-66 (LS) MA. 7: Postal off Army 1st Lieut 62-64; Ref libn IndU Northwest Campus (Gary) 66-67, acting libn 67-68; Hd Ref Div SyracuseU 68-. 10: Libns Assn SyracuseU. 14: Ref, admin. 15: 122 M Remington ave, Syracuse NY 13210.

THOMPSON, DONALD EUGENE. b McCallsburg Iowa 10 Jl 13. 4: Jean Beecher. 5: Iowa State U 30-35 (Econ) BS; UIll 36-37 BS in LS; Temple 37-42 (Econ) MA. 7: Asst bus libn Temple U 37-39, Bus libn 39-40; Bus libn UAla 40-42, Act dir of lib 42-44, Asst dir of lib 44-48; Dir of Lib State Stte U 48-55; Libn Wabash Col 55-. 8: Lib bldg consul; Consul for surveys of acad libs. 9: ALA (Coun 58-62;chm & 68-72, Subcom on Bks for Jr Cols 63-)-ACRL 63-; mem Constit & By-Laws Com 56-60); Dirs 60-61; Bldgs Com 56-58, Publns Com 64-67; chm Col Lib Sect 60-61);-LAD 60-61; chm Pure & Applied Sci Sect 53-54); Dirs 58-62, Bldg Com Col & Univ Libs 65-, Com 65-66; Org 58-62); IndLA (mem-at-large Exec Bd 59-60 & 63-65; mem & chm Planning Com 56-59, mem & chm Legis Com 60-; chm Col & Univ Sect 57-58), pres 67). 10: Pi Gamma Mu. 12: Comp "A Bibliography of the Louisiana Books and Pamphlets in the T P Thompson Collection of the University of Alabama Library (47); Auth "Exchanges & "Gifts in "State of the Library Art (61). 13: Yes. 14: Acuis. 15: 1103 W Pike st, Crawfordsville Ind 47933.

THOMPSON, DORIS CLAIRE. b Waco Tex. 5: N Tex State U (Eng, Educ) BA; Tex Womans U (Eng) MA, MLS. 7: Eng tchr High Sch, Bell Mead Tex; Eng, Lat & journalism tchr Waco Ind SCH Dist, Waco Tex; Libn Crestview Elem Sch, Waco Tex; Libn Richfield High Sch, Waco Tex 61-; Asst Prof dept of Lib Sci, Baylor (Waco) 67-. 9: ALA; NEA; TexLA (past chm Dist 7); Tex State Tchrs Assn; Tex Clr Tchrs Assn; TexASchL (past treas). 10: Delta Kappa Gamma; Wesleyn Serv Guild; AAUW. 14: Lib educ. 15: 3901 Huaco lane, Waco Tex 76710.

THOMPSON, EARLE CROSLAND. b Louisville Ky 2 Ja 17. 4: Emma Franceschi. 5: Union 34-37 (Hist) BA; Duke U 47-50 (Hist) MA; Emory 50-51 MSLS. 6: Fr, Ital. 7: Order lin Emory U 51-53, Ser libn 53-54; LSU: Acquis libn 54-5, asst dir of lib 56-62, Assoc dir of lib 62-64; Dean of Lib Serv UMONT 64-. 8: Consul Mont State Lib. 9: ALA; PNLA; MontLA. 10: Phi Kappa Phi; Rotary. 14: Admin, tech serv. 15: 426 McLeod, Missoula Mont 59801.

THOMPSON, EDNA MAY. b Stephentown NY 17 Ja 17. 5: NYS Tchrs Col(Geneseo) 38-42 (Educ) BEd; SUNY(Albany) 46-47 BSLS. 7: Elem tchr Fayette Sch, Fayette NY 42-43; USN (WAVES) 43-45; Libn NY Pub Lib 47-49; Asst lib catlgr Ft Dix Post Lib, Ft Dix NJ 49-51; Chief libn Camp Drum Post Lib, Watertown NY 51-53; Field & catlg libn Spec Serv, Germany 53-54; Area libn BASEC, ADSEC, France 54-57; High sch libn Dendent Schs Europe 57-58; Lib specialist Supt Off Dependent Schs, Germany 58-61; Acquis libn Hdq Dependents Schs, Germany 61-. 9: NEA; ALA (Armed Forces Libn Sect European Br); SLA (European Br); NYLA; NJLA; OEA; ADSA. 14: Child wk, acquis. 15: 251 Union st, Bennington Vt 05201.

THOMPSON, ELEANOR (MARGUERITE). b Baltimore 5 D 24. 5: Johns Hopkins 45-48 (Eng) BS; Rutgers 59-60 MLS; Johns Hopkins 64-69 MLA, Advanced Prof Certif. 6: Fr, Sp. 7: Sec, Baltimore 43-58; Libn, roving asst Enoch Pratt Free Lib, Baltimore 60-61; Libn Howard High Sch, Ellicott City Md 61-. 8: Middle States Evaluation Com Friends Sch Baltimore 68. 9: MdLA; Md State Tchrs Assn; Assn Sch Libns Md; NEA. 10: PTA; Pi Lambda Theta; AAUW; Walters Art Gallery; Howard Co Hist Soc; Baltimore Mus of Art; HowardCoTA. 14: Admin, ref, readers guidance. 15: Box 86, Ellicott City Md 21043.

THOMPSON, ELIZABETH (MARY). b Lafayette Ind 30 Ag 1900. 5: Purdue U 18-22 (Home Econ) BS; Presbyterian Hosp (NY) 24 Certif in Dietetics; Purdue U 38-39; Columbia 39-40 BS in LS. 6: Ger, Fr. 7: Home econ tchr Connersville High Sch, Connersville Ind 22-24; Therapeutic dietitian Mass Gen Hosp, Boston 25-27; Therapeutic dietitian Columbia Presbyterian Med Center, NYC 27-38; Asst libn in chg George Washington U 40-66; Catlgr AAUW U 40-66; Catlgr AAUW, Wash DC 67-. 9: ALA; DCLA (asst sec 61-62); Potomac Tech Proc Libns. 10: Amer Dietetic Assn: Kappa Delta Pi; Omicron Nu; Amer Cancer Soc. 14: Catlg. 15: 1633 16th st NW, Wash DC 20009.

THOMPSON, EVAN LEWIS. b Fall River Mass 26 Ag. 18. 4: Edith Swift. 5: Duke 36-40 (Eng) AB, 41-42 (Eng Lit) MA; Boston summer 46; Ohio State U 51-54 (Eng Lit); Simmons 54-55 (LS) MS. 6: Ger, Ital, Lat, Fr. 7: USAF 42-46; Instr Moses Brown Sch, Providence 46-47; Eng Instr Purdue U 47-49; Eng Instr UMe 49-51; Detroit Pub Lib: Adult asst 55-, 1st asst 58-60, Chief of div, br libn Bowen Br 60-61, Chief of dept lang & lit Main Lib 61-. 8: Consul "Essay and General Literature Index 63-64. 9: ALA; MichLA. 10: Phi Kappa Sigma; Kappa Kappa Psi; Detroit Pub Lib Staff Assn; Metro Detroit Eng Club; Friends of the Detroit Pub Lib; Founders Soc, Detroit INST OF Arts; Great Bks Leader; Bk Club of Detroit; Charles Lamb Soc. 14: Ref. 15: 4261 Bishop rd, Detroit Mi 48224.

THOMPSON, EVELYN BLANCHE (CARLSTON). b Minneapolis 22 O 08. 5: Georgetown Visitation Convent (Wash DC) 25-26; UMinn 26-27; Rosary Col 27-28 (Piano) Tchg Certif; Col of St Catherine 28-29 (Music) BA, Music diploma; UMinn 39-40 (LS) BS. 7: Libn Miss Woods Kindergarten & Tchr Train Sch, Minneapolis 40-42; Libn & Instr UMinn(Minneapolis) 42-. 9: ALA; MinnLA. 10: UMinn Faculty Womens Club; AAUP. 14: Ref, catlg, child collections. 15: 234 W 40th st, Minneapolis Mn 55409.

THOMPSON, HAROLD WILBUR JR. b Trnton NJ 6 F 23. 5: Rutgers u 47 (Educ) BS; Berlitz Lang Sch 48 (Span) Certif; NYU 49 (Educ) MA; Columbia 49 (LS) MS. 7: USAAF 42-45; Tchr Matawan (NJ) High Sch 47; Tchr-libn Central High Sch, Hopewell NJ 47-48; Libn Jr High Sch No 1, Trentn NJ 4952; Libn Trenton Jr Col 52-54; Asst lbn Newark State Tchrs Col 54; Libn Lafayette Col 55-59; Chm Dept of Lib Sch Glassboro State Col 59-. 8: Mem Eval Teams; Middle States Assn of Cols & Secondary Schs, Nat Com Accred Tchrs Educ. 9: ALA; NEA; NJEA; NJLA. 10: AAUP. 12: Asst ed "Dr Kanes Voyage to the Polar Lands (65). 13: Yes. 14: Col & univ lib admin, spec collections, catlg. 15: 408 Bellevue ave, Trenton NJ 08618.

THOMPSON, HELEN H. b Jonesboro NC 28 D 10. 5: Flora MacDonald Col 28-32 (Eng, Fr, Lat) BA; Emory 40-41 BA in LS. 7: Libn Hamlet Pub Lib, Hamlet NC 32-38; Tchr-libn High Sch, Hampton Ga 41-42; Tchr-libn High Sch, Badin NC 42-43; Post Libn, Camp Mackall NC 4/-46; 43-46; Libn, Camp Butner Durham NC 46; Libn Anson Co Lib, Wadesboro NC 46-54; Libn Scotland Co Mem Lib, Laurinburg NC 54-. 9: NCLA (Pub Lib Sect: dir 63-65, A-V Com activities). 10: Thursday afternoon Bk Club. 14: Admin, circ, ref. 15: 914 SMain st, Laurinburg NC 28352.

THOMPSON, HELEN PAULINE. b Rochester NY 28 Mr 13. 5: SUNY(Brockport) 37-40, 41-42 (Educ) BS in Ed; URochester 4549 (Educ) MEd; SUNY(Geneseo) 60-65 MLS. 7: Tchr Greece (NY) Central Dist 1, Hoover Drive Sch 41-60, Libn Autumn Lane Sch 61-. 9: NEA (Life mem); ALA; NY State Tchrs Assn. 10: AAUW. 13: Yes. 14: Sch lib wk with child & ya. 15: 102 N Union st, Rochester NY 14607.

THOMPSON, HELEN R(OBB). b Winfield Iowa 29 Ag 06. 5: George Washington U 24-28 (Eng Lit) AB; UWis 28-29 (LS) Certif. 7: DC Pub Lib: Asst to asst libn 29-32, Asst in ref dept 32-35, Ref libn 35-49, Coordinator central lib ref serv 50-. 9: ALA-Subs Bks Com (52-54 & 59-61);-RSD(New Ref Tools Com 62-64); DCLA. 10: Potomac Appalachian Trail Club; Audubon Soc. 14: Ref. 15: DC PUB Lib, 8th & K sts NW, Wash DC 20001.

THOMPSON, JAMES HOWARD. b Memphis Tenn 20 Ag 34. 4: Margareta Ortenblad. 5: Southwestern (Memphis Tenn) 52-55 (Hist) BA; UNC 55-57 (Hist) MA, 57-61 (Hist) PhD; UIll 61-62 (LS) MS. 6: Fr, Ger, Swedish. 7: Ref asst UNC Lib (Chapel Hill) 59-61; Circ asst UIll (Urbana) 61-62; Subject catlgr DukeU Lib 63-65; Asst Prof of hist USW La (Lafayette) 65-66; Asst Prof of hist UColo 66-68; Dir Undergrad Lib UNC (Chapel Hill) 68-. 9: ALA (Notable Books Program). 10: Phi Beta Kappa; Beta Phi Mu; Phi Alpha Theta; Chi Beta Phi; AHA; So Hist Assn. 13: Yes. 14: Lib admin, bibliog, ref, catlg. 15: 1911 Fountain Ridge rd, Chapel Hill NC 27514.

THOMPSON, JANET W(HITMORE). b Summit NJ 3 Jl 34. 4: Thomas L Thompson. 5: Maryville Col (Tenn) 52-56 (Fr) BA; Rutgers U 58-59 MLS. 6: FR. 7: Bkmob libn Lawson McGhee Lib, Knoxville Tenn 56-58; Child libn Morristown Lib, Morristown NJ 59-61; Libn St Genevieve-of-the-Pines Sch, Asheville NC 65-. 8: Consul libn for 4 pub elem schs & for Peck Sch (priv), Morristown NJ 59-61; Catlgr Trinity Episcopal Ch Lib 68-. 14: Child serv. 15: 68 Dillingham rd, Asheville NC 28805.

THOMPSON, JANICE L. b Rochester NY 2 F 42. 5: IndU 60-64 (Geog) AB, 64-65 (LS) MA. 6: Sp. 7: Map libn SoIllU 65-68; Asst ref libn WestIllU 68-. 9: SLA (Geog & Map Div). 14: Maps, ref. 15: 1400-4 W Calhoun, Macomb Il 61455.

THOMPSON, JOHN RICHARD. b Oil City Penn 22 O 19. 4: Helen Cousins. 5: Westminster (Penn) 39-43 (Hist) AB; West Res 46-47 BS in LS; Ind U 47-49 (Hist). 7: US Army Investigator T3 43-46; Asst circ libn Ind U 47-48; US Army MI Intelligence Off (Capt) 51-53; Asst ref libn Ind U 48-56; Info researchspec Research Spec of Defense, Wash DC 56-. 9: SLA. 10: Boy Scouts. 14: Documentation, mil. 15: 4226 Kenny st, Beltsville Md 20705.

THOMPSON, JOHNNIE C. b Jacksonville Tex 25 Je 25. 4: Wanda Sue Thompson. 5: E Tex State Col 59-61 (Hist) BA; E Tex State U 61-63 (LS) MS; 65-69 Doc-Admin Certif. 7: Railway telegrapher SVT Louis Southwestern RR, Pine Bluff Ark 43; Seamn Seaman US Coast Guard, NYC 43-46; Railway telegrapher St Louis Sothwestern RR Pine Blff Bluff 46-65; Elem lib coordinator Corsicana Ind Sch, Corsicana Tex 65-; Prin R E Lee Elem Sch 68-69. 9: NEA; Tex Tchrs Assn; TexLA. 10: Phi Theta Kappa; YMCA Health Club; Optimist Club; CorsicanaTA. 14: Ref, admin. 15: 756 W 3rd ave, Corsicana Tx 75110.

THOMPSON, JOSEPHINE (FAWCETT). b Lynchburg Va 13 Jl 11. 4: Robert A Thompson. 5: WVa State Col 28-32 (Soc Sci) AB; Atlanta 37-39 (Sociol) AM, 42-44 BLS; UIll 54 MLS. 7: Elem sch tchr Bd of Educ, Appomattox Va Girls Girs wker YWCA, Nashville 34-37; Lib asst Atlanta U 39-44; USO dir YWCA, Knoxville Tenn 44-46; Act libn Sch of Lib Serv Atlanta U 47-48, Instr 48-. 9: ALA; AALS; Ga Tctr Educ Assn (Lib Div); Atlanta Lib Club; SELA. 14: Ref, bibliog, research methods, libnship. 15: Atlanta Univ, Atlanta Ga 30314.

THOMPSON, JULIA (CATHERINE). b Lansing Mich 23 D 17. 5: Bay City Jr Col 35-37 (Eng) Assoc in Arts; NorthwesternU 37-39 (Journalism) BS in J; UMich 68-69 MALS. 6: Ger. 7: Clerical Mich State Admin Bd, Lansing 40-43; Tech writer Dow Chem Co, Midland Mich 43-66, Mktg research lib; Lib tech Sage Pub Lib, Bay City Mich 66-68; Libn Mich State Lib, Lansing 69-. 9: SLA; ALA; Soc Tech Writers & Publishers; MichLA. 10: AAUW. 13: Yes. 14: Ref, hist, sci. 15: 209 N Dean st, Bay City Mi 48706.

THOMPSON, KATHRYN (FRANCES). b Center Tex 26 N 18. 4: William Stone Thompson. 5: Rice U 34-38 (Sci, Eng) BA; Sam Houston State Tchrs Col summer 37; UColo summers 40, 41, 58, 62; 60, 67, 68; UDenver summers 59, 60, 61, 63; MA; Mich State U summer 66. 7: Tchr Houston Ind Sch Dist 39-57, Libn 57-. 8: Asst dir NDEA Media-Math Inst Houston Independent Sch Dist summer 67; Media consul Tex Gulf Coast Educ Sci Resource Ctr 67-69; Consul Prof Growth Program Spring Br Independent Sch Dist 69. 9: HoustonTA; TexStateTA; NEA-DAVI; ASCD; ALA; TexLA; HoustonASchL (pres 66-67); Tex Assn Educ Tech (Spec Publns Com 67-69, Certif Com 67-69, pres Area 4 Chap 68-70). 13: Yes. 14: Sch learning resource ctrs, in-service educ, educ tech programs. 15: 310 Bunker Hill rd, Houston Tx 77024.

THOMPSON, LAWRENCE SIDNEY. b Raleigh NC 21 D 16. 4: Ellen Hamilton Marshall. 5: UNC(Chapel Hill) 32-34 (Comparative Lit) AB, 37-38 PhD; UChicago 35 (Germanic Langs); UppsalaU 38 (Germanic Langs); Lund U 39 (Germanic Langs); UMich (Ann Arbor) 39-40 ABLS. 7: Asst to libn Iowa State Col (Ames) 40-41; Spec agt FBI, US Dept of Justice, Wash DC 42-45; Bibliogr US Dept Agric Lib, Wash DC 45-46; Libn West Mich Col 46-48; Prof of Classics UKy (Lexington) 48; Libn UKy 48-66. 8: Adv Turkish Ministry of Educ, Anakara 51-52; Surveyed Caribbean Commsn Library, Port of Spain 55; Consul & survey wk in US col & univ libs. 9: BSA (Coun); ALA (chm Rare Bks Sect 6768); ACRL (dir 5961). 10: Rotary; Filson; Mediaeval Acad Amer; Soc for Advancement Scandinavian Study; S Atlantic Mod Lang Assn. 12: Bibliography of French Plays on Microcard-- (67); Bibliography of American Doctoral Dissertations in the Classics-- (68); Bibliography of Spanish Plays on Microcard-- (68); Bibliologia Comica-- (69). 13: Yes. 14: Bk collecting, bibliog, transmission of classical texts. 15: Univ of Ky Dept of Ger and Classical Languages and Lit, Lexington Ky 40506.

THOMPSON, MARGUERITE (RAMLING). b Orangeburg SC 23 Ap 12. 5: Columbia Col (SC) 28-29; USoCar 29-32 (Eng) BA (Cum Laude); Emory summers 40-43 BS in LS. 7: Eng tchr high schs, SC 32-43; Libn: Rockingham High Sch, Rockingham NC 43-45, RANDOLPH Co Li, ASHEBORO NC 45-48, Colleton Co Lib, Walterboro SC 48-61, Florence Co Lib, Florence SC 61-. 9: ALA (Coun 69-72); SELA; SCLA (treas 57-58, v-pres 59, pres 60); chm Handbook Com & Revision 62-69; Pub Lib Sect; chm 55; chm Standards Com 63-69. 10: Delta Kappa Gamma; Florence C of C; Florence Co Coun on Aging. 14: Admin, adult serv. 15: 1012 Woodstone dr, Florence SC 29501.

THOMPSON, MARILYN (JONES). 4: Allan McMaster Thompson. 5: UNH 58-62 (Fr) BA; URI 62-65 MLS. 6: Fr. 7: Asst sci libn Brown U 62-67; Asst sci libn UDel 67-. 9: RILA. 14: Sci, ref. 15: 657 Lehigh rd Apt F12, Newark De 19711.

THOMPSON, MARILYN (TAYLOR). b Clinton Mass. 4: Roger S Thompson. 5: Larson Jr Col 41-43 AA; Simmons 49-51 (LS) BS; Rosary 67-69 MALS. 6: Fr, Ger. 7: Asst catlg dept Yale Divinity Sch Lib 43-49; Libn Harvard Sch of Dental Med Lib 49-51; Ref libn Northeastern U Lib 51-52; Head catlg dept UBridgeport 58-63; Ref libn Aurora Col Col Lib 63-64; Asst libn in chg of tech serv George Williams Col Lib 64-67; Hd libn 67-. 8: Adv Bd Lib Tech Asst Program DuPage Col. 9: ALA; IllLA. 10: Beta Phi Mu. 14: Catlg, ref. 15: 6421 Dean dr, Woodridge Il 60515.

THOMPSON, MARTHA (SCHULZ). b Omaha 18 S 20. 4: Robert E Thompson. 5: Yankton Col 37-38; UCincinnati 38-41 (Ger) AB, 41-42, 43-46 (GER) MA; Middleury Col summer 44 (Ger); Peabody 42-43 BS in LS. 6: Ger. 7: Asst in period dept UCincinnati 41-42; Asst in gen ref dept Pub Lib of Cincinnati 43-44, Readers aev readers bur 44-47; Sr asst home reading dept Detroit Pub Lib 47-50, Sr asst philos rel & educ dept 50-52; Sr asst tech dept Toledo Pub Lib, Toledo Ohio 5253, Head of filmserv bur 53-54. 8: Dir Monmouth Co (NJ) Hist Assn Lib, 62-68; Consul Brookdale Commun Col 68-; Trustee Little Silver Pub Lib 66-. 9: ALA; Amer Assn Sate & Loc Hist; NJLA. 10: AAUW; Friends of the Monmouth Co Lib; Little Silver Friends of the Lib Assn. 13: Yes. 14: Ref. 15: 44 Lippincott rd, Little Silver NJ 07739.

THOMPSON, MARTIN L. b Timblin Penn 18 Ja 21. 4: Delores J Raught. 5: Clarion State Col 51-53 (LS) BS; Penn State U 53-60 (Counseling, Psych) M Ed; Westminster 59-60 (Psych); UPittsburgh 65 (LS). 7: Salesman S-P Hardware Co, New Bethlehem Penn 37-39; Welder ARM Co, Kittanning Penn 39-44 & 46-51; Seaman 1/c (Sp. G) US Navy 44-46; Libn Redbank Valley schs, New Bethlehem Penn 53-54; Libn Philipsburg-Osceola Area Schs, Philipsburg Penn 54-59; Chm Lib Dept Slippery Rock State Col 59-65, Chm DEPT OF Lib Sci 65-. 8: Evaluator of Pub Sch, Middle States Assn, 58 & 61; Consul School Lib Development, Slippery Rock State Col. 9: NEA-ACRL (Tri-State Chap); Penn State EA (Loc Legis Chm 57); PennLA; Assn for Higher Educ. 10: Amer Legion; Nat Rifle Assn; Beta Phi Mu. 14: Lib educ. 15: 325 N Main st, Slippery Rock Penn 16057.

THOMPSON, MARY ENID THORNTON. b Idaho Falls Ida 24 D 19. 4: Donald Wesley Thompson. 5: UMont 37-41 (Eng, Econ) BA; UDenver 58-59 (LS) MA. 6: Ger, Fr. 7: Stud Train Class Ida Falls Pub Lib, Ida Falls Ida 36; Libn: Butte Free

Pub Lib, Butte Mont 39-43, Denver Pub Lib 56-62, State Hist Soc of Colo, Denver 62-. 9: SLA; West Hist Assn; ColoLA; SAA. 10: Amer Assn of Museums; Oral Hist Assn. 12: Ed "Museums Bulletin SLA (67-68). 14: Museums, rare bks, mss, oral hist, bus hist of Colo & West. 15: 3730 Allison ct, Wheatridge Colo 80033.

THOMPSON, MYRA JEAN (DEAL). b Wheeling WVa 10 Mr 36. 4: Jeffrey Koch Thompson. 5: W Liberty State Col 54-56, 58-59 (Elem Educ) AB; W Va U 67 MA in LS. 6: Ger. 7: Lib asst Ohio Co Pub Lib, Wheeling WVa 54-60; Tchr St Clairsville-Richland schs,St Clairsville Ohio 60-62, Libn k-12 62-. 9: ALA; NEA; WVaLA; OhioASchL; Clr Tchrs Assn; OHIOEA; E Ohio Tchrs; Ohio Stud Lib Assn; Belmont Co Tchrs. 10: Kappa Pi; Friends of the Lib Club; Wheeling Symphony Soc. 14: Catlg, ref, wk with high sch stud; high sch & jr col libs. 15: 17 Iona dr, St Clairsville Oh 43950.

THOMPSON, NINA R(UTH). b Tuscaora NY 20 Je 13. 5: Alfred U 31-33; Oberlin Col 33-35 (Eng Lit) BA; Columbia 35-36 BS in LS. 6: Fr. 7: Libn NY Pub Lib 38-42; H W Wilson Co, Bronx NY: Employee 42-46, Asst ed "Cumulative Book Index 47-51, Ed "Cumulative Book INDEX" 52-. 9: ALA; NY Lib Club. 10: AAUW. 14: Catlg, ref. 15: 1 Carpenter ter, Belleville NJ 07109.

THOMPSON, PAUL MADERY. b Three Rivers Mich 28 S 27. 4: Anna Beth Thompson. 5: Hope Col 46-50 (Hist) BA; West Mich U 53-54 (LS) Certif; UMich 56-58 (Hist) MA, 60-64 MALS. 7: Clerk, auditor of freight accounts Chicago Burlington & Quincy RR, Chicago 50-51; Med tech US Army (Pfc), US & Panama51-53; Panama 51-53; libn soc sci reading room UNotre Dame (Ind) 54-55; Asst libn Adrian Pub Lib, Adrian Mich 55-56; Ref libn E Chicago Pub Lib, E Chicago Ind 58-64; Ref-ser libn St Norbert Col 65-67; Ref libn UKy 67-. 9: ALA (Ref Sect); -ACRL; SELA; KyLA; WisLA (sec Ref Sect 66-67). 10: Ind Hist Soc; Hist Soc Mich; State Hist Soc Wis; Railway & Locomotive Hist Soc. 14: Ref. 15: 211 Broadway apt 11, Lexington Ky 40508.

THOMPSON, PEARLINE McREYNOLDS. b Wilcox County Ala 28 Je 40. 4: Ezekiel Thompson. 5: Ala State Col 59-62 (Eng) BS; Atlanta U summers 63, 65, 66, 67 MSLS. 6: Fr. 7: Tchr & libn Lyons Ind High, Lyons Ga 62-63; Libn Magnolia High Sch, Thomasville Ga 63-. 9: NEA; ALA; -AASchL; -YASD; GaTA (Libns Sect); GaEA (Libns Sect); ThomasCoTA; ThomasCoEA. 10: PTA; Amer Leg Aux; Magnolia Band Boosters; Washington High Touchdown Club. 14: Sch lib serv. 15: 1350 Calvary rd PO Box 294, Cairo Ga 31728.

THOMPSON, ROGER S. b New Haven Conn 4 Ap 18. 4: Marilyn Taylor. 5: Middlebury Col 35-39 (Physics) BS; Columbia 59-61 MLS. 7: Sci tchr Oakwood Sch, Poughkeepsie NY 39-41; Analyst US Civilian Pub Serv, Glendora Cal 42-46; Mechanic Connecticut Co, New Haven Conn 47-50; V pres The Thompson Shop Inc, New Haven Conn 51-56; Sci tchr Branford High Sch, Branford Conn 57-58; Libn Yale Math Lib 59-63; Physics libn Argonne Nat Lab, Argonne Ill 63-68; Libn Nat Acceleration Lab, Batavia Ill 68-. 9: SLA. 10: Woodridge Sch Bd; Woodridge Plan Commsn. 14: Sci libnship. 15: 6421 Dean dr, Woodridge Il 60515.

THOMPSON, ROSE (FRANCK). b Brooklyn NY 14 Je 27. 4: Clark Tyler Thompson. 5: UPenn 44-48 (Eng) BA; Drexel 50-51 MSLS. 6: Ger. 7: Order libn Bryn Mawr Col 51-52; Asst libn, Libn Burroughs Corp Research Center, Paoli Penn 52-61; Libn Huebner Hall Insurance Lib, Bryn Mawr Penn 61-; Libn Chester Co Law Lib Assn, W Chester Penn 68-. 9: AALL. 12: Mng ed "Insurance Literature SLA (66-68). 14: . 15: Box 31, Westtown Penn 19395.

THOMPSON, SARA VIRGINIA. b Clarendon Tex 23 O 1898. 5: Clarendon Jr Col 16-18 (Eng); W Tex State Tchrs Col 19-21 (Eng, Educ) BA; Northwestern U summer 27, 34 (Music Educ); Ft Worth Conservatory of Music 40-42 (Music Theory); N Tex State Col summers 42, 43 (Music); Tex Christian U 44-46 (Music Educ) MM Ed; N Tex State U summers 51-53; BS in LS; Columbia U & Union Theol Sem 55, 57 LS, (Hymnology) Eastman Sch of Schof Music 55, 57 (Music Libs). 6: Lat. 7: Lat tchr Canyon pub schs, Canyon Tex 21-22; Elem tchr & Pub sch music pub schs, Clarendon Tex 22-28; Pub sch music Ft Worth pub schs, Ft Worth Tex 28-45; Prof Music Theory & Music Hist Southwestern Baptist Theol Sem 45-51, Music libn 51-67; Music libn New Orleans Theol Sem 68-69. 9: MusLA; ATheolLA; TexLA. 10: AAUW; Tex Fed of Music Clubs; Music Tchrs Nat Assn; So Baptist Music Educs Conf; Altrusa Club. 14: Mus libs. 15: Southwestern Baptist Theol Sem, Ft Worth Tex 76122.

THOMPSON, SUSAN (BERGLUND). b Cornwall NY 1 O 44. 4: James B Thompson. 5: BostonU 62-66 (Hist) BS (cum laude); Simmons 66-68 MS; UAmericas summer 68 (Hist). 6: Sp, Ger. 7: Grad asst Lib Sch Lib Simmons 66-68; Ref asst Brookline Pub Lib, Brookline Mass 68-. 10: Phi Alpha Theta. 13: Yes. 14: Ref. 15: 127 Sutherland rd, Brookline Ma 02146.

THOMPSON, SUSAN (OTIS). b Nashville Tenn 9 Ag 31. 4: John Anderson Thompson. 5: Sweet Briar Col 48-52 (Fr) AB;UParis 53-54 (Modern Fr Lit); Columbia 62-63 (LS) MS, 64- (LS). 6: Fr, Sp, Ger. 7: Clerk-typist Central Intelligence agency, Wash DC 52-53; Admin asst US Army, Evreux France 54-56; Tr USAF, Paris 56-60; Sec & ref analyst US Mission to UN, NYC 61-62; Asst ref libn Columbia U 63-64; Tchg asst Columbia U Sch of Lib Serv 65-66; Tchr Hist of Bks Columbia Sch Lib Serv 66-. 9: ALA; BSA; Priv Libs Assn; NYLA. 10: Beta Phi Mu; Phi Beta Kappa. 13: Yes. 14: Rare bks. 15: 418 Central Park W, NYC 10025.

THOMPSON, THELMA VALERIE. b Greenville SC 24 S 16. 5: USCar 37-41 (Eng, Fr) AB; UNC 41-43 (Fr) MA, 43-50 (Romance Langs), 50-57 BSLS. 6: Fr, Sp, Ger. 7: Tchr of Fr, Ger, Span Davis-Elkins Col 43-44; Tchr of Fr, Span Sullins Col 47; Tchr of Fr, Span Besie Bessie Tift Col 47-49; Tchr of Fr Atlanta summer sch 49; Sub-prof catlg asst UNC Lib (Chapel Hill) 50-57, Catlgr music, music lit & Fr lit 57-64; Mus catlgr 65-. 10: Phi Beta Kappa; Pi Gamma Mu. 14: Mus catlg. 15: 7-A Williams cir, Chapel Hill NC 27514.

THOMSON, DOROTHY FRANCES (HOYT). b McAdam New Brunswick Can 15 N 24. 4: George Henry Thomson. 5: AcadiaU 43-47 (Eng Lit) BA; BostonU 51-53 (summers) (Bus Educ) EdM; Mt AllisonU 60-64 (Eng Lit) MA; UMich 66-67 AMLS. 6: Fr. 7: Legal sec Porter Ritchie et al, St John NB 47-50; Tchr Mt Allison Commercial Col 50-55; Instr Mt AllisonU 55-60; Lib clk Mt Allison Memorial Lib 64-66; Catlg libn Zion Research Lib, BostonU 67-69; Libn UOttawa 69-. 9: ALA. 10: Mod Lang Assn. 14: Bibliog, rare bks. 15: Central Lib Univ of Ottawa, Ottawa Can.

THOMSON, ELIZABETH (NELSON) W(ILLCOX). b Hendersonville NC 25 S 15. 4: Walter B Thomson. 5: Wm Smith 36 (Eng) BA; Hobart 37 (Eng) MA: Columbia 41 BS in LS. 7: Lib asst Hobart Col 37-41; Sr libn Rochester Pub Lib, Rochester NY 41-42; Libn P-1 in chg of Regimental Lib US Navy, Sampson NY 42-45; Ya libn Cleveland Pub Lib 45-46; Chief ref Dept Cuyahoga Co, Ohio 47; Lib dir Woodmere Pub Lib, Hewlett NY 47-. 8: PUBLED Childrens Record Reviews 57-65; Consul; Brandeis Sch, Lawrence Private Sch, with Architect, E Rockaway Public. 9: LPRC; Adult Educ Assn; NYLA; Nassau Co LA (sec 50-52, pres 54). 10: Five Towns Commun Coun; 5 Towns Music & Art Found; Econ Opportunity Coun of the Five Towns; Golden Age Club. 12: Auth Chancel Drama "The Fourth Wise Man. 13: Yes. 15: 1140 E Broadway, Hewlett NY 11557.

THOMSON, ISABEL (DAVANT). b Atlanta 28 Ap 30. 5: Randolph-Macon Womans Col 47-51 (Sociol) AB; Emory 64-65 MLNS. 7: Clerical Emory U Lib 51-53; Steno US Army, Atlanta Gen Depot 54-55; Elem tchr DeKalb Co Bd of Educ, Decatur Ga 57-63; Libn Emory U Lib 65; Libn Decatur-DeKalb Pub Lib, Decatur Ga 65-. 9: Atlanta Lib Club. 10: Eng-Speaking Union. 14: Ref. 15: 1779 N Decatur rd, Atlanta Ga 30307.

THOMSON, JACQUELINE (MAY SCARLETT). b Vancouver BC Can. 5: Victoria Col; UBC 59 (Eng, Creative Writing,psych) BA, 64 BLS. 6: Fr. 7: Ref libn U Victoria (BC) 64-66; Soc sic libn Vancouver BC Pub Lib 66-68; Researcher York U Inst for Behavioural Research, Vancouver BC 68-. 9: CanLA; BCLA; Inst Victoria Libns. ; ABCL. 12: "Victoria Colouring Book; (62). 13: Yes. 14: Ref, personnel, pub rel. 15: 507-2370 W 2nd ave, Vancouver 9 BC Can.

THOMSON, JOAN ALBERTA (PLACE). 4: Godfrey E Thomson. 5: Milton Col 29-33 (Eng) BA (cum laude); UWis 33-34 (Eng); Colorado Col 61-62 (Eng) MA. 6: Fr. 7: Instr in Eng So Colo State Col Lib 65-68, Acquis libn 68-. 9: ColoLA. 10: AAUP; WILPF. 15: 63 Duke, Pueblo Co 81005.

THOMSON, JUNE GWENEITH (TAYLOR). b EDMONTON Alta Can 21 Jl 28. 5: UAlta 46-50 (Fr, Ger) BA (honors); Toronto 50-51 (Fr Lit) MA; McGill 56-57 BLS. 6: Fr, Ger. 7: Research writer Nat Research Coun, Ottawa 51-56; Catlgr Lib of Parliament, 57-61; Period libn UAlta (Edmonton & Calgary) 61-64; Head catlg dept UVictoria(BC) 64-. 9: CanLA; Inst Victoria Libns; BCLA. 14: Catlg, ref, collection bldg. 15: Univ of Victoria Lib, Victoria BC Can.

THOMSON, MARGARET LUCILLE. b Wyoming Co NY 14 O 17. 5: Buffalo Deaconess Hosp 39 (Nursing) RN; UBuffalo 48 (Pub Health Nursing) BS; Case West Res 53 MLS. 7: Pub health nurse Visiting Nursing Assoc, Buffalo NY 39-44; Army nurse US Army 44-46; Univ health nurse UBuffalo 46-51; Pub health nurse Health Dept San Mateo, San Mateo Cal 51-52; Adult serv Cleveland Pub Lib, Cleveland Ohio 53-59; Reg br libn Cuyahoga Co Lib, Cleveland Ohio 59-69; Hd Napoleon Ctr State Lib of Ohio, Napoleon 69-. 9: ALA; OhioLA. 10: ESCRU. 14: Ref. 15: 2353 Belvoir blvd, Cleveland Oh 44121.

THOMSON, RALPH DANIEL. b Ephraim Utah 22 Jl 06. 4: Ruth Dame Watt. 5: Snow Col 25-27 (Soc Studies) AS; Brigham Young U 34 (LS) BS; USoCal 40 MS , 50 MS. 7: Tchr Helper Jr High Sch, Helper Utah 31-33; PRIN Kanosh Elem Sch, Kanosh Utah 34-39; Libn East High Sch, Salt Lake City 40-44; UUtah: Asst libn 44-45, Asst to pres 45-47, Assoc libn 47-64, Assoc Prof Lib Sci 47-64, Dir of Libs 63-, Hd dept of Lib Sci 63-. 8: Bd mem Ctr for Research Libs 69-. 9: ALA-ALTA;-ACRL; UtahLA (pres 48-49); Utah Lib Commsn (chm 57); Utah LTA (pres 58-60); MPLA; ARL. 10: Utah Acad Scis Arts & Letters; Utah Folklore Soc; Utah Hist Soc; Adv d, Bd, Soc Lib; Phi Kappa Phi; Phi Delta Kappa. 12: Ed "Utah Library New Letter (48-50). 14: Admin. 15: 1412 Michigan ave, Salt Lake City Ut 84105.

THOMSON, SARAH KATHARINE. b Statesville NC 25 Je 28. 5: Agnes Scott Col 47-49 (Eng) BA; Columbia 49-50 (LS) MS, 60-67 DLS, 67 (Bus). 7: Cir asst E Baton Rouge Parish Lib, Baton Rouge La summers 48, 49; Sch & ref asst Webster br NY Pub Lib 50-51; Ref asst Mun ref lib 51-55; Ref libn Barnard Col Lib 55-66; Hd of Lib Dept Bergen Commun Col 67-. 9: ALA (Interlib Loan Com 68-); NEA-DAVI; SLA; NY Lib Club; MLA; NJLA; NJEA. 10: Friends of Columbia U Libs; Columbia U Sch Lib Serv Alumni Assn; AAUP; Womens Faculty Club, Columbia U; Bergen Commun Col Faculty Assn. 12: "General Interlibrary Loan Services in Major Academic Libraries in the United States (67). 13: Yes. 14: Ref, interlib loan, admin. 15: 452 Riverside dr, NYC 10027.

THORN, SUZIE S. b San Francisco 17 Je 32. 4: Joe Wlson Thorn. 5: UCal 50-54 (Pol Sci) AB, 55-58 LLB, 60-64 MLS. 7: Libn City & Co of San Francisco 55-58; Ref libn UWash 59-60; Attorney Schapiro Thorn, San Francisco 60-. 9: AALL; State Bar of Cal. 10: Queens Bench; Girl Scout Coun; Volunteer Attny San Francisco Legal Assist Found. 13: Yes. 14: Tchg legal research. 15: 110 Sutter, San Francisco Ca 94104.

THORNE, G KATHLEEN. b San Luis Obispo Cal 21 F 42. 5: Cal State polytech Col 59-63 9eng) BS; UDenver 63-64 (Libnship) MA. 6: Sp, Irish, Ger. 7: Lib asst UDenver Mary Reed Lib 63-64; Ser acquis libn Colo State U 64-66; Ref libn San Jose State Col 66-. 9: ALA; CalLA. 10: Sierra Club. 14: Ref, music libnship. 15: 55 S 6th st apt 215, San Jose Ca 95112.

THORNE, LUCILE (MARKHAM). b Spanish Fork Utah 31 O 08. 5: Brigham Young U 25-29 (Dramatic Art) BA, 52-55 (Elem Educ) M Ed; USoCal 57-58 MS of LS. 6: Sp. 7: Libn Provo Pub Lib, Provo Utah 41-42; Tchr Provo Sch Dist, Provo Utah 42-48; Child libn Provo Pub Lib, Provo Utah 48-50; Libn: Brigham Young U 50-56; Provo Sch Dist, Provo Utah 56-57, Brigham Young U 57-; Assoc Prof Grad Dept of Lib & Info Sci 67-. 8; lib consul, Academia Juarez, Colonia Juarez, Chihuahua Mexico, summer 64. 9: ALA; MPLA; UtahLA. 10: Beta Phi Mu; Delta Kappa Gamma. 14: Ref, child bks & libs, catlg. 15: 365 N 100 E, Provo Ut 84601.

THORNE, MARCO G. b Los Angeles 13 Jl 14. 4: Dorothy Bronstein. 5: Stanford U 35-39 (Hist) BA, 40 (Hist) MA; UCal(Berkeley) 41 (Hist), 42 Certif in Libnship. 7: US Army (Pvt to Capt) 42-46; Asst co libn Washoe Co Lib, Reno Nev 46-49; Asst city libn San Diego Pub Lib 49-. 9: ALA (Coun 46-47); CalLA (treas 56-57, pres Palomar Dist 64); NevadaLA (pres 48). 10: San Diego Histl Site Bd. 12: "Ride the Ferry. (58). 13: Yes. 14: Admin, ref. 15: 4325 W Overlook dr, San Diego Ca 92115.

THORNLEY, PHYLLIS JANE (HUBBARD). b Minneapolis Minn 30 Je 25. 4: Howard R Thornley. 5: UMinn: 43-47 (Pol Sci) BA, 61-62 (Elem Educ) BS, 63-66 (LS) MA, 66-68 (Educ). 7: Tele operator AT&T, Minneapolis 43-51, Serv repr 51-53, Elem tchr Minneapolis Pub schs 62-63; Libn Univ Elem UMinn (Minneapolis) 64-65, Libn Univ High 65-68, Instr Lib sch 68-. 9: ALA; NEA-DAVI; MinnASchL; A-V Coordrs Assn Minn. 10: Pi Lambda Theta. 14: Sch libs, sch media ctrs. 15: 974 17 ave SE, Minneapolis Mn 55414.

THORNTON, EILEEN. b Wexford Ireland 12 Ag 09. 5: UMinn 27-31 (Eng & LS) BS, 36-38 (Eng); Chicago 42-45 (Educ, LS) AM. 6: Fr. 7: Sr asst libn Hibbing (Minn) Pub Lib 31-32; Asst St Louis Co Poor Commsn, Hibbing Minn 32-33; Circ asst UMinn(Minneapolis) 33-36, Asst in chg of Grad Seminars 36-38; Libn W Waterloo High Sch, Waterloo Iowa 38-39; Libn Minn State Tchrs Col (Bemidji) 39-42; Col libn UChicago 43-45, Admin asst 44-45; Libn Vassar Col 45-56; Libn Oberlin Col & Oberlin Pub Lib, Oberlin Ohio 56-. 8: Visiting lecturer in lib sci: West Res 53 & 61, Columbia 49; Col Lib consul Educ Dept, NY State 55: Survey & accred serv, Middle States Assn, Central Assn, Methodist Bd of Higher Educ, 45-; Leave to study new Eng Univ Libs, 64; Consul Col Ctr of Finger Lakes 62-63. 9: ALA (Coun 54-58 & 64-68, Exec Bd 66-70, Publ Bd 66-68); -ACRL (pres 57-58; -LAD (pres 67-68); MinnLA (pres 41-42); NYLA (v-pres 55-56); OhioLA (Exec Bd 61-62). 10: Mortar Board; Beta Phi Mu. 13: Yes. 14: Admin. 15: 164 S Prospect, Oberlin Ohio 44074.

THORNTON, EVELYN (CECILE). b Courtlnd Va 26 F 09. 5: Mary Washington Col 26-30 (Eng, Lat) BS in Educ; Col of William & Mary 40, 46, 47 (LS) AB; Fla State U 56. 6: La. 7: Tchr Surry High Sch, Surry Va 30-37; Tchr Manchester High Sch, Richmond Va 37-40, Libn 40-46; Asst supv sch libs State Bd of Educ, Richmond Va 46-47; Libn Manchester High Sch, Richmond Va 47-48; Libn Washington-Lee High Sch, Arlington Va 48-50; Supv of Libs Arlington Co Pub Schs, Arlington Va 50-. 8: Participant Golden Anniv White House Conf on Child & Youth, 60; Va State Com, Nat Lib Week 63-; Adv Com,wash Bk Fair 54-. 9: ALA (Coun 54-58; Memb Chm rep Va 53-54, mem Award Com 63);-AASchL (rec sec 59-60; mem OR CHM Chm 5, NAT & 1 reg com 55-);-LAD (mem Nomin Com of Sect on Bldgs & Equip 58); NEA; VaEA (pres Sch Libns Sect 58-60); VaLA (chm Activ Com 50-51, chm Nomin Com 55-56, chm Intel Frredom Com 63-65); SELA. 10: Arlington Hist Soc; AAUW; Child Bk Guild, Wash DC; Soroptimist Club; Delta Kappa Gamma; Alpha Phi Sigma. 12: Ed "Books for Chidren (62-65); Bd of eds "Childhood Education. 1313: Yes. 14: Admin, edu. 15: 1426 N Quincy st, Arlington Va 22207.

THORNTON, JANICE MARILYN. b Evanston Ill 25 My 37. 5: MacMurray Col 55-59 (Hist) AB; UIll 59-60 MS in LS, 68 (Sp). 6: Sp, Portu. 7: Ref libn Cincinnati Pub Lib 60-65; Libn Universidad del Norte, Antofagasta Chile 65-67; Lat Amer bibliogr UCal (Riverside) 68-. 14: Bibliog, acquis, catlg. 15: 1733 7th st apt 17, Riverside Ca 92507.

THORNTON, REV MICHAEL V CM. b NYC 10 My 33. 5: St Josephs Col 51-53; Mary Immaculate Sem & Col 55-61; BA in Philos; St Johns U 63-64; SUNY (Albany) 64-66 MLS; Fordham U 68- (Relig Educ). 6: Lat, Fr. 7: Asst libn Mary Immaculate Sem & Col (Northampton Penn 56-61; Tchr St Johns Prep Sch, Brooklyn NY 61-64; Instr & Libn Sem of Our Lady of Angels (Albany NY) 64-. 8: Asst libn, Sem of Our Lady of Angels, summers 62-64. 9: ALA; Cathla; NYLA; Hudson-Mohawk LA. 10: Cath Philos Assn; The Liturgical Conf; SUNY (Albany) Lib Sch Alum Assn. 13: Yes. 14: Catlg. 15: Box 1865 Seminary of Our Lady of Angels, Albany NY 12201.

THORNTON, SHEILA F. b Wash DC 31 Ag 35. 5: Mt St Marys Col (Los Angeles) 53-57 (Eng) BA; UCLA 64-65 MLS. 7: Libn catlgr Syst Development Corp Tech Lib, Santa Monica Cal 65; Acquis libn The Rand Corp, Santa Monica Cal 65-67; Hd catlg sect 67-. 9: SLA (So Cal Chap; mem Adv Coun 67-69; Publns Chm 68-69; chm Subcom on Monitoring, Parliamentarian 1968 Nat Conf); ASIS. 10: UCal Lib Sch Alum Assn. 12: Asst ed "Bulletin So Cal Chap SLA (67-68). 13: Yes. 14: Catlg, lib automation. 15: 11687 Montana ave apt 211, Los Angeles Ca 90049.

THORP, KATHERINE (KNOX) (MRS). b St Louis 13 My 25. 5: Maryville Col (St Louis) 43-47 (Eng) AB; Columbia 49-50 MSLS. 7: Ref-circ asst Clayton Pub Lib, Clayton Mo 47-49; Asst circ libn Ore State U 50-52; Bus lib asst Sacramento Pub Lib, Sacramento Cal 64-65; Asst catlgr Pius XII Lib St Louis U 65; Asst ref libn 66-. 9: ALA. 14: Ref, catlg. 15: 8714 Warner ave, St Louis Mo 63117.

THORP, LEONARD (WILLIAM). b Quenemo Kan 21 Ag 02. 4: Patricia Morrison. 5: Whitman Col 19-23 (Classics) AB; UWash 29-30 BLS. 6: Fr, Sp. 7: Stud asst UWash Lib 28-30; Libn Mooseheart schs, Mooseheart Ill 30-31; Act libn East Wash State Col 31-32; Act libn Central Wash State Col 32-33; Libn Wis State U (Superior) 33-39; Ref libn & act libn East Wash State Col 39-44; Asst ref libn Wash State Lib 47-49; Asst libn tech processes UIda Lib 49-54; Asst & a-v libn Renton Jr-Sr High Sch, Renton Wash 54-56; Ref & ser libn Sci Div

Wash State U 56-63; Libn Bakersfied Center Lib Fresno State Col 63-. 9: ALA; PNLA (treas 60-62); CalLA. 10: ACLU; ADA; P of H. 12: "Library Service for Idaho" (52). 13: Yes. 14: Catlg, ref. 15: 4021 Mt Vernon ave, Bakersfield Ca 93305.

THORSELL, IRENE. b Chicago Ill 2 S 28. 4: Bernard Thorsell. 5: UIll 52 (Sociol) BA; USoCal 61 (LS) MS. 7: Gen ref libn San Fernando Valley Col 61-65, Hd ser dept 65-66, Sci & tech ref libn 66-. 9: SLA; CalLA. 10: Libraria Sodalitas. 15: 20725 Ingomar st, Canoga Park Ca 91306.

THRASH, SARAH (McALLISTER). b Wash DC 23 Je 34. 4: James R Thrash. 5: Madison Col 51-55 (Eng) BA; UNC 55-57 MS in LS. 7: Bkmob libn May Mem Lib, Burlington NC 57-58; Child libn Arlington Co Pub Lib, Arlington Va 58-62; Child libn Montgomery Co Pub Lib, Wheaton Md 62-63; Child libn Jacksonville Pub Lib, Jacksonville Ill 68-69. 9: ALA (Aurienne Award Chm 63-64). 13: Yes. 14: Child bks. 15: 146 Pine st, Jacksonville Il 62650.

THRASHER, WILLIAM DEAN. b Evanston Ill 16 D 28. 5: UIll 46-50 (Journalism) BS; Rosary Col 62-64 MA in LS. 7: Info specialist US Army, Seattle 50-52; Regulations ed & sr agt United Air Lines, Denver & Chicago 53-64; Asst catlg libn & asst ref libn UIll 9chicago) 64-66, Asst ref libn 69-; Circ libn & act hd libn Wheaton Col 66-69. 9: ALA; -ACRL; TheatreLA; IllLA; Chicago Lib Club. 10: UIll Alum Assn; Tau Kappa epsilon; Nat Wildlife Fed. 14: Ref. 15: Apt A9 1047 College ave, Wheaton Il 60187.

THREATT, HELEN V (KILPATRICK). b Dover NC 31 D 29. 4: Robert Threatt. 5: St Augustines Col 47-50 (Eng) AB; NC Col (Durham) 50-51 MLS. 6: Fr. 7: Libn Ninth Ave Sch, Hendersonville NC 52-55; Ref libn H A Hunt Lib Ft Valley State Col 57-60, Asst libn Hubbrd Educ Lib 61-68, Asst libn H A Hunt Lib 68-. 9: ALA; GaTA; GaEA. 10: YWCA; Zeta Phi Beta; The Links Internat; Epis Church Woman Assn. 14: Ref. 15: PO Box 432 State College, Fort Valley Ga 31030.

THRELKELD, JEAN (EDITH). b Detroit 20 Mr 28. 4: Charles Threlkeld. 5: Wayne StateU 47-51 (Biol) BA; UWash 66-69 Master of Libnship. 6: Fr, Ger. 7: Lib aid Wayne co Lib, Detroit 52-54; Clk Detroit Pub Lib 47-50, 54-56; Libn King Co Lib, Issaquah 69-. 14: Sci ref. 15: 5303 231 ave SE Rte 3, Issaquah Wa 98027.

THROCKMORTON, EDITH H. b Denver Colo 1 My 23. 5: UDenver 40-43 (Anthropology), 59-60 (Educ) BA, 60-61 (LS) MA, 61-63 (Educ) MA; Colo Sch of Mines summer 42. 6: Sp. 7: Occupational therapy tech Ph M 1/C US Navy var Navy Hosp 43-45; Off mgr- partner Nu-Lawn Chemical Co, Redwood City Cal 46-58; Lib asst Soc Sci Found UDenver 60-63; Med libn St Anthony Hosp, Denver 63-64; Med libn UColo Med Center, Denver 64-. 9: MedLA; SLA (sec Colo Chap 63); Colo Counc Med Libns (chm 67-68); Col sla 9sec Colo Chap 63); Colo Counc Med Libns (chm 67-68); ColoLA (Denver Liaison Com). 10: Japan Soc of Colo; American Leg; Dist Hist; UDenver Alumni. 14: Ref, hist of nursing lit. 15: 2613 So Milwaukee st, Denver Co 80210.

THROGMORTON, DOROTHY J (VAN BOCKERN). b Aztec NM 14 D 04. 4: Dan Throgmorton. 5: Berea Col 25-28 (Eng) AB; West Res 52-53 MS in LS. 7: Tchr: Prestonburg Ky 29-31, Mountain Mission Sch, Frakes Ky 40-44, Tiptonville Tenn 45-51; Libn Tiptonville High Sch, Tiptonville Tenn 53-55; Asst Prof Lib Sci & asst libn Adams State Col 56-. 9: ColoEA; ColoLA. 10: AAUWV: AAUP; Kappa Kappa Iota; Faculty Dames. 14: Catlg, tchg lib sci. 15: Adams State Col, Alamosa Co 81101.

THRUSH, PAUL WILLIAM. b Homestead Penn 18 D 27. 5: UPittsburgh 48-54 (Latin Amer STUDIES) BA; Carnegie 57-61 MLS. 7: Ref asst Carnegie Lib Pittsburgh 56-59; Research libn Crucible Steel Co of Amer, Pittsburgh 59-61; Tech libn Newport News Shipbuilding & Dry Dock Co, Newport News Va 62-64; Ref libn US Bur of Mines, Pittsburgh 61-68; Hd catlg dept Cleveland (Ohio) Pub Lib 68-. 9: SLA; ALA; OhioLA. 12: Comp & ed "A Dictionary of Mining, Mineral and Related Terms" (68). 14: Catlg, ref. 15: 311 E Green st, Connellsville Pa 15425.

THUESON, JAMES DAVID (PATRICK ANDREW). b Stillwater Minn 13 Je 25. 4: Gisela Pfalzer. 5: UMinn 43-47, 60 (Pol Sci) BA, 60-62 (Pol Sci) MA, 63-64, 69 (LS) MA. 6: Ger, romansh. 7: Salesman I R Lewis Co, Chicago 52-59; Pres Callimachus Pub Co, minneapolis 63-64; Pres James D Thueson Publisher, Minneapolis 64-; Catlgr UMinn Libs 9minneapolis) 65-68, Hd catlging 68-. 8: Microfilm consul Miss Proj Square Deal Research & Development Corp, Minneapolis 68. 9: ALA; APSA. 10: Ampersand Club; Inst for No Studies; Phlogiston Soc. 14: Catlg, admin, rare bks & maps. 15: 410 Groveland ave S, Minneapolis Mn 55403.

THULIN, RUTH C. b Rochester NY 25 Jl 07. 5: URochester 26-30 (Hist) BA; Columbia 36 (LS) MA. 7: Lib asst URochester Womens Col Lib 31-36; Div libn Rochester Pub Lib, Rochester NY 37-. 9: ALA. 14: Bus & econ. 15: 129 Boardman st, Rochester NY 14607.

THUMMEL, CAROL JEANNE. b Plainville Kan 5 S 43. 5: Ft Hays Kan State Col 61-66 (Sp) AB; Kan State Tchrs Col 66-68 (LS) Masters. 6: Sp. 7: Stud asst Ft Hays Lib Ft Hays State Col 63-65; Grad asst WAW Lib Kan State Tchrs Col 67-68; Period libn Wells Lib NW Mo State Col 68-. 9: ALA; MoLA. 10: AAUW. 14: Ref. 15: College Gardens, Maryville Mo 64468.

THURBER, GERRISH. b NYC 27 Mr 07. 5: Princeton U 24-28 (Eng) AB, 28-29 (Eng) MA; Columbia 30-31 (Eng), 36-37 (LS) BS. 6: Fr. 7: Asst in Eng Horace Mann Sch, NY 30-31; Assoc ed "TRIPS Magazine, NY 36-37; Asst libn Lawrenceville Sch, Lawrencevile NJ 37-48, Libn 48-. 8: Eval Com, Middle States Assn f Cols & Scon Schs, 54, 57; Secon Educ Bd Lib Com, 51-61; Princeton Adv Com on Secon Sch Libs, 65-. ; NJ Adv Com on ESEA Title II 67-. 9: ALA; Nat Assn Indep Schs; NJLA; Princeton Area Libns; NEA-DAVI. 10: NJ Hist Soc; Princeton Hist Soc. 12: Contrib ed "3000 Books for Secondary School Libraries" (61); "The Lawrenceville School 1810-1960" (60). 13: Yes. 14: Admin, bk sel, exhibits. 15: Brook House, Lawrenceville NJ 08648.

THURBER, SUSAN M. 5: Adelphi 45-49 (Ger) BA; Columbia 52-53 (LS) MS. 6: Ger. 7: Asst ref libn & bkmob libn Levittown Pub Lib, Levittown NY 53-56; Br libn & asst br libn Queensborough Pub Lib, Jamaica NY 56-63; Asst dir Huntington Pub Lib, Huntington NY 63-65; Dir Port Jefferson Free Lib, Port Jefferson NY 65-. 9: NYLA. 10: N Shore Choral Soc; Amer Recorder Soc; Carriage House Players Inc; Country Dance & Song Soc of Amer; Hist So of Greater Port Jefferson, Inc; C of C. 14: Admin. 15: 645-42 Belle Terre rd, Port Jefferson NY 11776.

THURMAN, MARY JOHN (RODGERS). b Cordele Ga 25 N 19. 4: Kelly Thurman. 5: Georgetown Col (Ky) 37-41 (Eng & Speech) AB; Stephen F Austin 60 (Educ); Central State Col (Okla) 65 (Educ); UKy 67-69 MLS. 6: Fr. 7: Tch: pub shcs: West Point Ky 41-42, Georgetown Ky 42-43, Jackson Tenn 54-57, Nacogdoches Tex 59-62; Ref libn East KyU 66-. 9: KyLA. 14: Ref. 15: 444 Breck ave, Richmond Ky 40475.

THURMAN, PATRICIA ANN (METCALF). b Sterling Kan 21 Mr 39. 4: Michael Dale Thurman. 5: Cottey Col 57-59 (Liberal Arts); Ft Hays State Col 60-61 (Elem Educ) BS in Elem Ed; Kan State U (Manhattan) 62-63 (Educ); Kan State Tchrs Col (Emporia) 64-65 (LS) MS. 7: Elem tchr Chapman Kan 61-63; Elem tchr Amer Dependent Schs, Naha Okinawa 63-64; Grad asst Dept of Linship Kan State Tchrs Col 65; Libn Augusta Jr High Sch, Augusta Kan 65-; Readers adv William Allen White Lib Kan State Teachers Col summer 66; Acquis dept Lib Colo State U summer 67. 8: State Sel Com for Bks for Kansas Sch 69. 9: NEA; ALA; Kan State Tchrs Assn; KanLA; KanASchL; Kan A-V Communications Org; AugustaEA (sec 67-68). 10: Girl Scouts. 14: Sch libs, a-v coord. 15: 17 Augusta Mobile ct, Augusta Ks 67010.

THURMAN, S DAVID. b Salt Lake City 3 Ja 41. 5: Stanford 58-61 (Sociol) AB; Chicago 61-62 (LS); UIll 64 (Law). ; UDenver 66-67 (LS) MA. 6: Fr, Ger. 7: Asst libn ALA Hdqrs Lib, Chicago 63-64; Asst ref libn Stanford U Law Lib 64-66; Supreme Court law libn 5th Judicial Dist, Utica NY 67-69; Chief libn White & Case, NYC 69-. 9: AALL; Assn of Law Libs of Upstate NY (pres-elect 68-69). 13: Yes. 14: Legal ref wk, info retrieval, admin. 15: White & Case Lib, 14 Wall st, New York NY 10005.

THURSBY, MARY AGNES (FOUST). b Humboldt Tenn 21 Jl 20. 4: incent Victor Thursby. 5: Vanderbilt U 38-42 (Pol Sci) BA; Peabody 42-43 BS n LS. 7: Asst post libn Merced Army Air Base, Merced Cal 44-45; Circ libn Denver Pub Lib 45; Catlgr Jt U Libs, Nashville 46-47; Catlgr rare bk div Alderman Lib UVa 47-49; Instr Fla State U Lib Sch 50; Catlgr Supreme Court of Fla Lib, Tallahassee Fla 52-67, Asst law libn 68-. 9: AALL. 14: Catlg. 15: Supreme Courtof Fla, Tallahassee Fla 32304.

THURSTON, EDITH ANNE (HARRINGTON). b Kalamazoo 25 J 24. 4: John Arnold Thurston. 5: West Mich U 60-63 (Eng, Hist) BA, 64-65 (LS) MA. 7: Ref libn Los Angeles

Co Pub Lib Syst, Norwalk Val 65-67, Doc libn, Montebello 67-68; Catlgr Xerox/Prof Lib Serv, Santa Ana Cal 68-69. 9: CalLA; ALA. 15: 212 N Harrington dr, Fullerton Ca 92631.

THURSTON, EVE. b Pittsburgh 21 F 29. 5: Margaret Morrison Carnegie Col 47-50 (Eng) BS; Carnegie 50-51 (LS) MS. 6: Fr. 7: NY Pub Lib: Libn brs 51-53, Asst to tech serv libn Mun Ref Lib 53-58, Tech serv libn 58-. 8: URBANDOC info retrieval proj, 64;Ed com "Mental Health Book Review Index (63). 9: ALA; SLA (NY Tech Serv Libns; Libns RT of Soc Responsibility). 10: Pub Educ Assn; Horticul Soc of NY. 11: Skeel Foun grant, 65. 13: Yes. 14: Catlg, ref. 15: 150 E 18 st, NYC 10003.

THURSTON, JUNE TIFFANY. b Sunnyside Wash 4 Je 08. 5: Wash State Col 25-29 (Eng) BA; UWash 49-50 (LS) BA. 7: Tchr High Sch, Dayton Wash 29-31; Tchr High Sch, Longview Wash 31-32; Clerk Broads Book STORE, Yakima Wash 47-49; Adult educ libn Yakima Valley Reg Lib, Yakima Wash 50-53; Libn N E Br Seattle Pub Lib 53-60; Yakima Valey Reg Lib, Yakima Wash: Hdqrs serv libn 60-62, Asst libn 62-65, Head Libn 65-. 8: Adv Com, Lib 21, Seattle Worlds Fair, 62; Com to eval Wash state lib, 65. 9: ALA (Coun 68-); WashLA (pres 60-61); PNLA (chm Pub Libs Div 56-58). 10: UWash Sch of Libnship Alumni Assn; Altrusa Club; PEO; Kappa Alpha; Mortar Board; Phi Beta Kappa; Phi Kappa Phi. 13: Yes. 14: Reg lib devel. 15: 3205 Sharon way, Yakima Wa 98902.

THURSTON, SHIRLEY. b Muskegon Mich 10 S 26. 5: Chicago 45-47 (Liberal Arts) BA; Columbia 56-58; (Soc Studies) MA; Drexel 61-64 MS in LS. 7: Elem tchr, Mich & Penn 53-56; Secondary Eng tchr Mich 58-59; Circ dept Drexel 61-64, Ref libn -home econ 64-67; Libn Community Col of Del Co, Media Penn 67-. 9: NEA-DAVI; ALA; SLA; PennLA. 10: Womens Univ Club; LWV. 13: Yes. 14: Ref, admin. 15: 76-1 Drexelbrook dr, Drexel Hill Pa 19026.

TIBBS, CHRYSTAL GARRELL (POWELL). b Williamsport Penn 17 My 32. 5: WayneU 54-55 (Elem educ) BS, 58-62 (Elem Adm & Supv) MS; UMich 64-68 AMLS. 7: Tchr Detroit Bd of Educ 55-66, Libn 66-. 9: Amer Fed Tchrs; Mich & Detroit Fed of Tchrs. 10: Exec Bd Coord Coun on Human Rel (Detroit). 14: Sch libnship, instr materials. 15: 8163 Wetherby, Detroit Mi 48204.

TICE, LEONARD RUSSELL. b E Haven Conn 2 S 17. 5: Central Conn State Col 38-41 (Eng, Soc Sci) BS; Columbia 41-44 (Soc Sci) MA; So Conn State Col 67-68 MLS. 6: Ger. 7: Tchr Litchfield Sch for Boys, Conn 41-42; Tchr Milford High Sch, Conn 42-44; Tchr Liberty High Sch, NYC 45-46; Prof Eng Newark Col of Engring 46-47; Instr St raphael's Sch of Med Tech, New Haven Conn 49-67; Asst ref libn Yale Med Lib 69-. 8: Certif in med tech Flushing Gen Hosp, LI NY 47-49. 14: Ref, admin. 15: Yale Medical Library 333 Cedar st, New Haven Ct 06510.

TIDEMANN, VIOLA. b Valley Spring SD 12 S 18. 5: Huron Col 36-40 (Eng) BA; UDenver 52-53 (LS) MS. 7: Tchr Canning High Sch, Canning SD 40-42; Tchr Hot Springs High Sch, Hot Springs SD 43-45; Libn Rapid City Pub Lib, Rapid City SD 46-52; Libn Wichita Pub Lib, Wichita Kan 53-. 8: Tchr lib sci courses Kan State Tchrs Col 65. 9: ALA; KanLA; MPLA. 10: Bus & Prof Womens Club; Wichita Art Mus. 13: Yes. 14: Ref. 15: 704 S Broadview, Wichita Ks 67218.

TIEDT, ELIZABETH (DAVIS). b Bartlesville Okla 2 Ap 42. 5: Lake Forest Col 60-62; UKan 62-64 (Hist) BA; UGrenoble 65-66; UDenver 66-67 (LS) MA. 6: Fr. 7: Researcher of Heraldry Sanson Inst, Boston 64-65; Period asst Marathon Oil Co, Littleton Colo 66-67; Ref libn UDenver Lib 66-67; Ref libn Penrose Pub Lib, Colo Springs Colo 67-. 14: Ref, Local Hist Collections. 15: 1406 Rainier dr, Colorado Springs Co 80910.

TIEN, MARY ANNA (MITCHELL). b Flint Mich 4 Mr 20. 5: Flint Jr Col 38-40 AA; UMich 43-45 (Eng) AB, 45-47 (Oriental Civilization) MA, 45-49 BLS. 7: Clerk Credit Bur, Flint Mich 40; Sec Life Insurance Co, Flint Mich 40; Lib asst High Sch lib, Flint Mich 40-43; B libn Pub lib, Flint Mich 47; Ass documents libn Ind U 48-55; Head Libn Jacob Edwards Lib, Southbridge Mass 55-69; Tchr So Conn State Col ext 66; Dir Lib Serv Ctr, Middletown Conn 69-. 8: Chm, Hist Com Mass Sesquicentennial Observance 66. 9: ALA; MassLA (past mem Exec Bd); NELA. 10: So Worcester Co Fresh Air Program; Cath Charities Adv Bd; Southbridge Hist Soc. 11: Dorothy Canfield Fisher Award 63; Woman of Achievement Award 68 (local). 13: Yes. 14: Small pub lib admin. 15: 4 Spring, Southbridge Ma 01550.

TIETJEN, MILDRED (CAMPBELL). b Floyd Co Ga 26 My 40. 5: Berry Col 57-61 (Eng) AB; Peabody 61-62 MA in LS. 7: Libn Chickamauga Pub Schs, Chickamauga Ga 62-64; Head libn Ga Southern Col 64-. 8: Libn in State Dept if Educ (Atlanta) summers 63, 64; Instr of Lib Sci UGa summer 65. 9: ALA; NEA; SELA; GaLA (com chm 64-65, chm Col & Univ Sect 69-70). 10: AAUW; Kappa Delta Pi; Beta Phi Mu. 14: Admin. 15: PO Box 145, Americus Ga 31709.

TIGHE, ELIZABETH (BURGER). b Cuba NY 26 S 34. 4: John Lawrence Tighe. 5: SUNY (Geneseo) 52-56 (LS) BS, 63-65. 7: High sch libn Pine Bush Central Sch, Pine Bush NY 56-57; Elem libn Corning Central Schs, Corning NY 57-58; Jr high libn Pittsford Central Sch, Pittsford NY 58-62-68, Elem libn 64-; High sch libn Free Sch, Lima NY 66-67. 14: Bk sel. 15: 6371 E Avon-Lima rd, Avon NY 14414.

TIGHE, RUTH (LIEPMANN). b Wurzburg Germany 9 Jl 31. 5: Barnard 48-49; SUNY (Albany) 49-51 (Soc Studies, Eng) BA; Columbia 65-67 MLS. 6: Fr, Ger. 7: Lib asst USN Spec Serv, Hawaii 62-63; Lib asst USMA 64-65; Asst libn S Jr High Sch, Newburgh NY 65-66; Libn Thrall Pub Lib, Middletown NY 66-67; Ref libn Harvard Col Lib 67-68, Chief ref libn 68-. 9: ALA; ASIS (Arrangements Chm NE Chap). 10: Beta Phi Mu; Mensa. 13: Yes. 14: Ref, subject headings, info ret. 15: 338 Lake ave, Newton Highlands Ma 02161.

TILGER, CLARENCE A. b Hastings Neb 26Je 06. 4: Ellen R Tilger. 5: Hastings Col 31 AB; UIll 32 BLS. 7: Lib asst Neb Pub Lib Comm, Lincoln 35-37; Lib asst Lincoln Pub Lib, Lincoln Neb 37-38; Lib asst USPHS Hosp, Ft Worth 38-40; Libn USAF Brookley AFB, Mobile Ala 46-56; Libn USAF Alaskan Air Comm Ladd AF Base Eielson AF Base 56-60; Libn USAF England AF Base 60-65; Asst libn (catlgr) XavierU 68-. 9: ALA; LaLA. 14: Catlg. 15: PO Box 367, Kenner La 70062.

TILGER, ELLEN R. b Hastings Neb 8 Jl 06. 4: Clarence A Tilger. 5: Hastings Col 23-27 (Eng, Fr) AB; UIll 31-32 BLS. 7: Libn: UNeb Col of Engnr 37-39, Arlington Heights High Sch, Ft Worth Tex 40-41, Bus & tech Ft Worth Pub Lib, Ft Worth Tex 41-43, US Pub Health Serv Hosp, Ft Worth Tex 43-44; Libn asst br New Orleans Pub Lib 46-49, Libn II govt documents ref 49-. 9: ALA; LaLA. 14: Govt docs, ref (bus & sci tech). 15: PO Box 367, Kenner La 70062.

TILLER, FRANCINE (FLYNN). b Bayonne NJ 5 Mr 35. 5: Pembroke 53-57 (Eng Lit) AB; LSU 65-67 MS in LS. 6: Fr. 7: Ref libn econ div NYC Pub Lib 67; For affairs ref libn Newsweek Mag, NYC 68; Asst hd bus, tech & sci dept Orlando Pub Lib, Orlando Fla 68-. 9: SL; FlaLA. 10: AAUW. 14: Ref. 15: 318 Jamestown dr, Winter Park Fl 32789.

TILLIN, ALMA MAY (BERCOV). b Calgary Can 4 D 16. 4: Israel Tillin. 5: UAlta 34-38 (Fr) BA; Sorbonne 38-39 (Fr); UCal (Berkeley) 39-40 (Fr) MA, 40-41 Certif in Lib, Tchrs Credential. 6: Fr. 7 Libn Burlingame Sch Dist, Burlingame Cal 42-45; Catlg asst Alameda Co Tchrs Prof Lib, Oakland Cal 50-55; Libn Madison Jr High Oakland Sch Dist, Oakland Cal 59-60; Libn Lib Center Berkeley Sch Dist, Berkeley Cal 61-. 8: Cal State Wkshops on Non-Bk Materials in Lib 67-68. 9: ALA; NEA; Cal Tchrs Assn; CalLA; CalASchL (Registrar Conf 68). 12: "The Organization of Nonbook Materials in School Libraries" (67); "Operation Multi-Media Library" (69). 13: Yes. 14: Tech serv, sch lib program, child lit, a-v. 15: 1100 Woodside rd, Berkeley Cal 94708.

TILLMAN, MARY (E). b Ocala Fla 6 Jl 25. 5: Stetson U 44-48 (Fine Art) AB; U Fla 51-54 (LS); Emory 56-57 (LS) ML; UFla 61 (Educ). 6: Fr. 7: Lib asst Jackson Mem Hosp, Miami Fla 49; UFla Lib Asst Ser Dept 50, Lib asst in chg of Arch & Fine Arts Lib 51-56, Libn Arch & Fine Arts Lib 57-60, Asst catlgr Tech Process Dept 60-61; Assoc libn Head of Readers Serv Fla Presbyterian Col 61-63; Asst libn Central Fla Jr Col 63-64; Act dir of lib serv central Fla Jr Col 64-65, Asst libn in chg of ref & circ 65-66; Dir lib processing ctr Bd of Pub Instr, Ocala Fla 66-; Lib coord Marion Co Pub Schs, Ocala Fla 68-. 8: Visting asst libn Ricker Lib of Arch UIll 53. 9: SELA; FlaLA (mem com 65-66; ref Round Table chm 63-64, mem Legis Planning Bd 65-66); FlaASchL; ALA. 10: AAUW; AAUP; Nat Audobon Soc; Fla Audobon Soc; Marion Co Humane Soc; LWV; Marion Co Assn Retarded Child. 14: Ref, spec libs, jr col libs. , sch libns, catlg, acquis. 15: 1533 E Fort King ave, Ocala Fla 32670.

TILLMAN, MARY FRANCES (REID). b Henderson Co Tenn 17 Je 09. 4: Bennett Brock Tillman. 5: Lambuth Col 27-31 (Fr) AB; Peabody 40-42 BSLS. 6: Fr, Lat. 7: Tchr Fairview High Sch, Jackson, Madison Co Tenn 31-36; Elem tchr Jonetown Jonestown Sch, Jonestown Miss 36-40; Libn Tunica Co Miss, Tunica Miss 40-44; Libn Madison Co Lib, Jackson Tenn 49-50; Tchr-libn J B Young High Sch, Bemis Tenn 50-56; Libn South Side High Sch, Jackson Tenn 56-. 9: TennLA (sec-treas); TennEA (sec-teas; chm Lib Sect 2-63). 10: Delta Kappa Gamma; Sigma Kappa. 14: . 15: 243 Highview st, Jackson Tenn 38301.

TILLOTSON, MARY ELIZABETH (BARBER). b Greeley Colo 2 N 08. 4: John F Tillotson. 5: Colo State Col of Educ 29 (Eng, Educ) AB; UCincinnati 6-37 (Eng); UDenver 33 BS in LS. 7: Ref asst in circ dept Cincinnati Pub Lib 34-35; Libn Dunham Hosp Lib incinnati Ohio 35-37; Documents libn Ft Hays Kan State Col 37-39; Ref then specifications & stds Sandia Corp Lib 48-53; Catlgr libn Physical Sci & Engnr Air Force Weapons Lab Lib, Kirtland AFB, Albuquerque NM 53-. 10: Coun of Ministrias St Paul's United Methodist Ch; Albuquerque Rockhounds. 14: Catlg, ref, admin. 15: 6704 Elwood dr NW, Albuquerque NM 87107.

TILLSON, JACK EDWIN. b Boone Iowa 19 S 11. 4: Marjorie S Spring. 5: Cornell Col 33-35 (Hist) BA; West Res 40-41 BS in LS; UWis 62-66 MA in LS. 6: Fr. 7: Libn Ericson Pub Lib, Boone Iowa 41-44; Ref libn Pub Lib, Ft Wayne Ind 44-45; Libn: Boone pub schs, Boone Iowa 45-59, Ericson Pub Lib, Boone Iowa 59-62, Jr Col Lib, Boone Iowa 62-. 9: ALA; IowaLA (treas 52-; Exec sec 67-). 10: Boone Educrs Assn. 13: Yes. 14: Catlg, adult educ, pub serv. 15: Boone Jr Col Lib, 1227 1st st, Boone Ia 50036.

TIMBERLAKE, MARY ESTELLE. b Durham NC 2 D 10. 5: USCar 29-32 (Lat) AB; Peabody 42-43 (LS) MA. 6: Sp, Ger, Ital. 7: File clerk Fed Land Bank, Columbia SC 33-42; Libn Lander Col 43-45; Asst ref libn USCar 45-50; Readers serv libn Vassar Col 50-54; Libn Newberry Col 54-57; Ref libn USCar 57-59, Asst ref libn documents 60-. 9: ALA; SELA; SCLA. 10: AAUW; Adirondack Mountain Club; DAR. 14: Ref, docs, conservation. 15: Caire Towers, Columbia SC 29201.

TIMBERS, ELAINE BEATTY. b Glen Ridge NJ 6 Ag 25. 4: Harley Clark Timbers. 5: Vassar 43-46 (Eng Lit) BA; UWis 51-52 MA in LS. 6: FR. 7: Correspondent Scot Foresman & Co, NYC 46-47; Ed asst Glamour Magazine Conde Nast Publ, NYC 47-48; Lib asst Bloomfield Free Pub Lib, Bloomfield NJ 48-51; Asst libn ref World Book Encyclopedia Field Enterprises Inc, Chicago 52-53, Summit Free Pub Lib, Summit NJ 62-64, Allentown Pub Lib, Allentown Penn 64-66; Emmaus Penn; Libn Emmaus High Sch 66-67, Dir Pub Lib 67-. 8: Tchr Ref Bks Course Penn State U & Penn State Lib 65. 9: ALA; PennLA. 10: Women's Club of Emmaus. 13: Yes. 14: Ref, child serv, bk sel catlg. 15: 915 Turner st, Emmaus Penn 18049.

TIMBY, CAROL IRENE. b Batavia NY 23 N 24. 5: SUNY (Geneseo) 44-48 BS in LS. 7: Asst libn SUNY (Brockport) 48-. 8: Fac adv Canterbury Club. 9: SUNYLA; NYLA; SUNY Fac Assn. 10: Hosp Org; Parish Coun; Red Cross Commun Chest; Cobblestone Soc; Hist Soc; Kappa Delta Pi; Fac Womens Assn of SUC (Brockport). 14: Ref, vertical files, bibliog. 15: 128 Erie st, Brockport NY 14420.

TIMM, CHARLOTTE (PALMER). b NYC 26 N 18. 5: UMich 38 (Eng) BA, 45 (Educ) MA, 59 MA in ls. 6: Fr, Sp. 7: Ass bkmob libn Ann Arbor Pub Lib, Ann Arbor Mich 56-57; High sch libn Dundee Commun Schs, Dundee Mich 58-61; Asst prof & educ libn in charge curriculum lib Bowling Green State U 61-. 8: Sem at the Fundamental Educ Ctr, Patzquara Mex 57; Participant attended the Internat Literacy Conf co-sponsored by UNESCO and the Shah of Iran, Teheran 65. 9: ALA; OhioLA. 10: AAUP; AAUW; Pi Lambda Theta; Internat Reading Assn; Ohio Folklore Soc; Nat Sem in Adult Educ Res. 12: "Handbook for Student Journalists", Cleary College, Ypsilanti Mich (39). 13: Yes. 14: Ref, catlg, serv to child & ya. 15: 303 S Summit st, Bowling Green Oh 43402.

TIMMONS, ELLEN B (MRS). b Opelika Ala 14 Ja 04. 5: Huntingdon Col 21-23; Birmingham So 23-25 (Eng) AB; Peabody 40-41 BS in LS. 6: Fr. 7: Asst libn Philips High Sch, Birmingham 41-43; Libn VA Hosp, Swannanda NC 43-57; Asst libn VA Hosp, Oteen NC 57-58; Circ libn U of the South 68-. 9: ALA; SELA. : Outstanding Performance Rating, 57. 11: Outstanding Performance Rating, 57. 14: Ref. 15: Univ of the South, Sewanee Tenn 37375.

TINDALL, J(OSEPH) DOUGLAS. b Vero Beach Fla 21 Ap 40. 5: St Johns River Jr Col 59-61 AA; UFla 61-62; Fla State U 62-63 (Hist) BA, 64 (LS)MS. 6: Sp. 7: Asst acquis libn UGa 65-68; Libn grad engnr educ system UFla 68-. 9: SLA; SELA; FlaLA. 10: Amer Mus Nat Hist, Wilderness Soc. 14: Bibliog, acquis, systs analysis. 15: 4106 NW 13 pl, Gainesville Fl 32601.

TINDALL, MILDRED (D PIPES). b Ontario Cal 5 Ja 19. 4: Craig W Tindall. 5: San Jose State Col 36-41 (Educ, LS) BA. 7: Libn Dept of Adult Educ, San Jose Cal 42-43; Asst libn Placer Co (Cal) Instr Materials Center 52-63, Libn 63-65; Libn DeWitt State Hosp, Auburn Cal 65-. 9: ALA; MedLA; CalLA. 14: Child lit, bibliotherapy. 15: 5168 Westridge cir, Auburn Ca 95603.

TING, EUNICE TSE-FENG (CHEN). b Chekiang China 14 Jl 35. 4: Andrew Yuan Piao Ting. 5: Nat Taiwan U 53-57 (Foreign Langs, Lit) BA; MONTEREY Peninsula Col 58-59; UOkla 59-60 (LS) MS. 6: Chinese, Japanese. 7: Tr Ministry of Nat Defense, Liaison Bur Free China, Taipei Taiwan China 57-58; Jr catlgr Okla State U Lib 60-66; Asst docs libn Fresno State Col Lib 66-67; Asst ser & docs libn Cal State Col (Long Beach) 67-. 9: CalLA. 10: Long Beach Commun Concert Assn. 14: Catlg. 15: 229 N Knoblock apt 238, Stillwater Okl 74074.

TING, LEE-HSIA (HSU). b Yangchow China 7 F 23. 4: Nai-tung Ting. 5: Nat Central U (China) 40-46 (Eng) AB; Mt Holyoke 47-48 (Eng Lit) AM; UTex summers 59-62, 64 MLS; Chicago 67-. 6: Chinese. 7: Asst Nat Central U (Chungking & Nanking China) 44-46; Asst Prof UNanking (Nanking China) 48-51; Asst functional off Brit Co, Nanking China 49-51; Assoc ed USIS, Hongkong 53-54; Tchr CMS Heep Yunn Sch, Hongkong 54-56; Libn Edinburg (Tex) pub schs 59-61; Libn Harlingen (Tex) pub schs 61-65; Instr Wis State U (Eau Claire) summer 65; Libn Pharr-San Juan-Alamo (Tex) pub schs 65-66; Tchr Lib Sci UTex Ext Div 65-66. 10: Phi Beta Mu. 12: Tr (intoChinese); J S Wongs "Fifth Chinese Daughter, Benjamin Franklins "Autobiography, & V M Hillyers "A Childs History of the World (Hong Kong 53-56). 13: Yes. 14: Catlg, ref, hist of libs & printing. 15: 109 S Mechanic, Macomb Il 61455.

TING, ROBERT N. 4: Margaret Hsu. 5: St John's U 47 (Math) BS, 49 (Accounting) MBA; Immaculate Heart Col 61 MLS. 6: Chinese. 7: Catlgr (math) UCLA 61-63, physics libn 63-68; Faculty libn (sci & engring) SUNY (Buffalo) 68-. 8: Adv Physics Dept UWyo 65-67; Visit scientist European Organ for Nuclear Research (CERN) Geneva 67-. 9: SLA; West NY Lib Resources Coun; Five Associated Univ Libs. 14: Sci bibliog, (esp high energy physics), ref. 15: Sci & Eng Lib, State Univ of NY, Buffalo NY 14214.

TING, YING JI. b Lanchow China 15 F 27. 4: Diana Tan. 5: Fuh-Tan U 46-49 (Econ); UCLA 54-56 (Econ) AB; USoCal 57-59 MSLS. 6: Chinese. 7: Map research USoCal Engnr Center 57-63; Libn UCLA Engnr & Math Lib 60-61; Libn UCLA U Research Lib 63-; Oriental collections libn The Rand Corp 68-. 14: Catlg. 15: 5718 Coliseum st, Los Angeles Ca 90016.

TINGELSTAD, GERTRUDE BERNICE. b Maddock ND 27 O 19. 5: Pacific Lutheran U 37-39 Certif; Luther Col 39-41 (Eng) AB (magna cum laude); UMich 41-42 ABLS; UCal (Berkeley) summer 51; UMinn 58-59 (LS) MA. 6: Norwegian. 7: Catlgr Wash State U 42-43; Asst circ dept Lib Assn of Portland 48-49; Asst libn Pacific Lutheran U 43-48, 49-53; Asst libn Luther Theol Sem (St Paul) 53-64; Asst ctlg libn Ore State U 64-. 9: ALA; PNLA. 10: AAUP; AAUW; Ore State Employees Assn. 14: Catlg, ref. 15: 749 NW 11th st, Corvallis Or 97330.

TINKHAM, NATALIE ANN. b Gren Lake Co Wis 25 Ap 32. 5: UWis 49-53 (Eng) BA; UIll 53-54 MSLS. 6: Ger, Fr. 7: Bkmob libn LaPorte Co Lib, LaPorte Ind 54-58; Br libn Madison Pub Lib, Madison Wis 58-. 9: ALA; WisLA. 10: AAUW; Beta Phi Mu. 14: Readers guidance, lib ext. 15: 4218 Bagley pkw Madison Wi 53705.

TINSMAN, WILLIAM ALLEN. b Lima Ohio 28 Jl 32. 5: Kent State 48-50, 53-54 (Psych) BS; UAmericas (Mexico) 54-55 (Lat Amer Studies); Yale 57 (Chinese Lang) Diploma; UKy 9lexington) 62-64 MS in LS. 6: Sp. 7: Photographer, clk-typist US Army, Germany 50-52; Chart clk Los Angeles Gen Hosp 55-56; Intelligence researcher & tr USAF, Japan & Korea 57-61; Withdrwal clk Ohio State U Libs (Columbus) 61-62; Libn & gen asst Queens Borough Pub Lib, Jamaica NY 64-66; Asst ref libn Ind State U Lib 67-. 9: ALA;-ACRL; -RSD; IndLA. 14: Ref. 15: PO Box 661, Terre HAUTE In 47808.

TIPPETT, KENT M. b Oak Grove La 31 Jl 39. 5: Northeast La State 57-61 (Hist) BA, 6263 (Soc Studies, Euc) BA; LSU 63-65 (LS) MS. 6: Fr. 7: Instr & catlgr Ark State Col 65-66; Instr & Asst libn NE La State Col 66-. 9: LaLA. 10: Phi Alpha Theta; Beta Phi Mu; AAUP. 14: Tech serv, admin. 15: 107 Arlington dr apt A, Monroe La 71201.

TIPTON, MARY FRANCES. b Selma Ala 6 F 35. 5: Ala Col 53-57 (Eng) BA; Fla State U 60-62 (LS) MS. 6: Fr. 7: Tchr Mem Jr High Sch, Key West Fla 57-58; Tchr Melbourne High Sch, Melbourne Fla 58-59; Ser libn Ala Col 63-68, Ref libn 68-. 9: AlaLA (chm Col Univ & Spec Libs Div 68-69). 10: AAUW. 14: Publicity, pub rel, recr. 15: College View apts #2, Montevallo Al 35115.

TIPTON, MARY-LOUISE (SNYDER). b Roswell N Mex. 4: William H Tipton Jr. 5: Park Col 24-28 (Eng, Fr) AB; UNM summer 27 (Educ); USoCar 28-29 (Eng, Educ); Tex Woman'sU 64-67 MLS. 7: Tchr Washington & Albuquerque Jr High Schs, Albuquerque 29-30; Eng tchr bus col, Shreveport La 32-33; Lib asst Arlington Co Pub Libs, Arlington Va 55-59; Asst ref libn So MethodistU 67-. 10: AAUW. 14: Ref, child bks. 15: 3538 Asbury ave, Dallas Tx 75205.

TIPTON, SALLY LOU. b Oregon City Ore 16 Ag 18. 5: Marylhurst Col 37-41 (Hist) BA; UWash 41-42 (LS) BA. 7: Asst libn Oregon City Pub Lib, Oregon City Ore 43-46; CO Libn Clackamas Co Lib, Oregon City Ore 46-. 9: OreLA; ALA. 15: 406 S High st, Oregon City Ore 97045.

TIPTON, VERA HOPE (LAWRENCE). b Lorain Ohio 30 Mr 02. 4: Wilbur Hines Tipton. 5: Ohio Wesleyan U 20-24 (Math) AB; West Res 50-53 MSLS. 7: Tchr Lorain High Sch, Lorain Ohio 24-52; Sch libn Jr & Sr High Sch, Lorain Ohio 52-61; Catlgr & order libn Lorain Pub Lib, Lorain Ohio 61-69, Hd processing dept & order libn 69-. 9: NEA; OhioEA; Ohio SchLA; OhioLA; No Ohio Tech Serv Libns. 10: AAUW. 14: Catlg. 15: 1212 Seventh st, Lorain Ohio 44052.

TIPTON, VIRGIE MAE (CLEMON). b Pine Bluff Ark 3 O 34. 4: Bruce Tipton. 5: Henderson State Tchrs Col 54-59 (Elem) BSE; Tex Womans U 59-60 MLS. 6: Fr. 7: Elem tchr Pub Sch, Malvern Ark 56-59; Libn Malvern Jr High Sch, Malvern Ark 60-. 9: NEA; ArkLA; ArEA; AEAUSA; ALA. 10; aauw; PTA; CTA; Lib Com Second Baptist Ch of Malvern. 14: Yp serv. 15: 904 Edward st, Malvern Ak 72104.

TIRMENSTEIN, ADRIENNE MARTHA. b Alexandria Ind 22 My 19. 5: Evansville Col 36-40 (Elem Educ) BS; Northwestern summer 45 (Elem Educ); Peabody 46-47 BS in LS, summers 60-61 MA in LS; Evansville Col Even 45, 50-53, 61, 64, 65. 7: Prim tchr Scott Twp Sch, Evansville Ind 40-46; Asst East Br Lib, Evansville summer 46; 46; Asst in child dept Ft Wayne Pub Lib, Ft Wayne 47-48; Br libn Washington Br Lib, Evansville Ind 48-49; Br libn Dexter Br Lib, Evansville Ind 49-50; Evansville Pub Lib, Evansville Ind: 1st asst catlg dept 50-52, 1st asst tech serv dept 52-57, Chief tech serv dept 57-. 9: ALA; IndLA; Ohio Valley Reg Group TECH Serv Libns. 10: AAUW; Pi Gamma Mu. 14: Catlg, clsf. 15: 1933 Bellemeade ave, Evansville Ind 47714.

TISDALE, BARBARA. b West Roxbury Mass 24 D 13 05: Radcliffe 31-35 (Hist, Govt, Econ) AB (cum laude), summer 43; Syracuse 39-40 BS in LS; Harvard summer 39, 41; Queens Col (NY) 58-65 (LS, Ital); NYU 65- (Ital, Gr). 6: Ital, Ger, Fr, Lat. 7: Asst for docs pers catlg dept Harvard U Lib 36-39; Libn jr & sr high schs, Adams Mass 40-41; Libn Reading High Sch, Reading Mass 41-42; Asst libn & catlgr Northeastern U 42-43; Libn Bristol High Sch, Bristol Conn 43-45; Ref & circ asst Bus Div Columbia U 45-46; Ext libn Great Neck Lib, Great Neck NY 46-49, Lakeville Br libn 50-. 9: ALA; NassauCoLA. 10: Radcliffe Club NYC, of Nassau Co of LI; LWV; Women's Guild of Commun Church. 14: Readers guidance, ref, admin. 15: 70 Knightsbridge rd 1H, Great Neck NY 11021.

TISDALE, MARJORIE GARTH. b Decatur Ala. 4: William A Tisdale Jr. 5: Ill Tchrs Col 29-32 (Elem Educ); ULouisville 43-44 (Biol Sci) BS in Bio; IndU 50-52 (Educ) MS in Ed; Vassar Summer Inst 57; Catherine Spaulding Col 58-62 (LS). 6: Fr, Sp. 7: Tchr: Louisville Pub Schs: Perry Elem Sch 44-48, Virginia Ave Elem 48-50, Taylor Elem 50-55, Cotter Elem 55-63; Tchr-libn Louisville Pub Schs Kennedy Elem 63-65; Libn Louisville Pub Schs Shawnee Jr High 65-. 9: ALA; NEA; KyLA; KyASchL; KyEA. 10: Amer Fed of Tchrs; Louisville Urban League; Delta Sigma Theta. 14: Sch lib admin, child & ya lit. 15: 688 S 44 st, Louisville Ky 40211.

TISDEL, KENNETH STONE. b Mt Vernon NY 7 My 09. 4: Mary Inghram. 5: Washington U (St Louis) 27-31 (Bus Admin) BS; UWis 34-35 (LS) Certif; Chicago 46-47 (LS) MA. 7: St Louis Pub Lib: Asst 27-31, Asst catlg & order dept 31-34, 1st asst Mun Ref LIB 35-43; US Air Force Intelligence Sect Staff Sgt 43-45; Sr asst ref dept St Louis Pub Lib 45-46; Head circ dept UMo 47-50, Assoc libn 50-. 9: ALA; MoLA. 10: Delta Sigma Pi. 12: "Survey of Services and Publicity in Municipal Reference Libraries (37); Co-auth "Reviews in Library Book Selection (58). 14: Reader serv, lib equipment. 15: Univ of Mo Lib, Columbia Mo 65201.

TISH, LOIS. b Caldwell Ida 7 N 13. 5: Northwest Nazarene Col 37-39 (Eng) AB; UWash 45-46 AB in LS. 6: Fr, Ger. 7: Tchr Leadore High Sch, Leadore Ida 41-43; Tchr Homedale High Sch, Homedale Ida 43-45; Libn Cascade COL 46-. 9: ALA; PNLA; OreLA (chm Mem Com 59-60). 14: Admin, ref. 15: 705 N Kinningsworth st, Portland Ore 97217.

TISSOT, THALIA-MANON. b Detroit 12 F 30. 4: Ronald D Tissot. 5: Brooklyn Col 47-50 (Lit) BA; Columbia 50-54 MLS. 7: Lib trainee Brooklyn Pub Lib 50-51, child libn 64-. 9: ALA; NYLA. 10: PTA; Girl Scout. 15: 1625 Rockaway parkway, Brooklyn NY 11236.

TISTHAMMER, DANA JEAN (CATTERSON). b Des Moines Iowa 8 N 24. 4: Arne G Tisthammer. 5: UNeb 48 (Eng) AB; Tex Womans U 54 BS in LS. 7: Ser catlgr So Methodist U 52-53, Ser & documents libn 53-54; Catlgr UHawaii 54-55; Order libn So Methodist U 55-57; Acquis libn St Louis U Pius XII Mem Lib 57-64, Supv of tech serv 64-. 8: Lib consul Universidad Catolica Madre y Maestra, Santiago Dominican Republic 9: ALA; MoLA. 10: AAUP; Phi Beta Kappa; Beta Phi Mu. 14: Tech serv. 15: 504 E Polo dr, Clayton Mo 63105.

TITLEY, (DOROTHY) JOAN. b Chicago 20 Ja 31. 5: Maryville Col (Tenn) 49-52 (Eng) BA; UIll 52-53 (LS) MS. 7: Asst libn Chem Lib uill (Urbana) 53-55; Libn Col of Med UCincinnati 55-59; Field libn US Spec Serv, Germany 59-60; Libn & Asst Prof med bibliog ULouisville Sch of Med 60-. 8: Spec lecturer in sci lit Grad Dept, Catherine Spalding Col 63-64; Ky Gov Commsn on Libs; Ohio Valley Reg Med Prog, Chm Lib Task Force. 9: ALA; MedLA (Conv Chm 69); ASIS; Ala Hist Med. 10: AAAS; Filson Club; ULouisville Acad Senate. 11: Gottlieb Essay Prize (Med LA) 63. 12: "The David A Tucker Library of History of Medicine, Cincinnati (59); "The Library and the Community in "Handbook of Medical Lirary Practice (3d ed in press). 13: Yes. 14: Rare bks, admin, tchg. 15: Med Lib 101 W Chestnut st, Louisville Ky 40202.

TITOWSKY, BERNARD. b NY 10 F 25. 4: Rita Migliaccio. 5: Queens Col 43-47 (Hist) BA; UWis 47-48 (Amer Hist) MA; Queens COL 60-62 (LS). 7: Tchr of soc studies Bd of Educ NYC 50-63; Libn Bowne High Sch, Flushing NY 64-. 8: Owner Austin Bk Shop Kew Gardens NY; Instr of lib sci Queens Col 64-; mem Standing Com on Lib Bks for Second Schs NYC Bd of Educ 69-. 9: AHS; NYC Sch Libns Org. 10: United Fed of Tchrs; Org of Amer Histns; Amer Studs Assn. 12: "AMERICAN HISTORY: a Guide to Student Reading for Teachers & Librarians (64). 14: Bibliog. 15: 82 10 Beverly rd, Kew Gardens NY 11415.

TITUS, (CECILLA) JANE. b Jefferson Penn 15 D 15. 5: Waynesburg Col 34-38 (Eng Lit) AB; UColo 47-49 (Hist) MA; Carnegie Inst 50-51 MLS. 7: Csk USN WAVES, Phila 43-47; Instr Waynesboro Col Ctr 50-51; Sr asst hist dept Enoch Pratt Free Lib, Baltimore 51-54; Br libn Carnegie Lib of Pittsburgh 54-58, Asst hd central lending 58-62; Hd pub serv UCincinnati 63-69; Personnel libn Temple U 69-. 9: ALA (ILL Comm 66-69, Coord materials Com 66-69, chm 68-69); PennLA; OhioLA. 14: Personnel, pub serv. 15: 243 W Tulpehocken st apt 201A, Philadelphia Pa 19144.

TITUS, JANE WALLACE. b Albany NY 8 N 43. 5: Duke U 61-65 (Hist) BA; UNC 65-67 (European Hist) MA; Simmons 67-68 (LS) MS. 6: Fr, Ger, Lat. 7: Gen asst Clark Art Inst Ref Lib, Williamstown Mass 65; Act libn FTAS Lib Internal Revenue Serv, Wash DC 66 (summer); Catlgr Widener Lib HarvardU 67-69, Libn in charge Searching & Filing Sect 69-. 10: Phi Beta Kappa; Phi Kappa Delta. 14: Computer applications, rare bks, ref, catlg. 15: 83 Brattle st apt 55, Cambridge Ma 02138.

TITUS, MARGARET (HENDRIE). b Greenlawn LI NY 6 Jl 13. 4: William E Titus. 5: Goucher Col 30-34 (Internat Rel) BA; Queens Col 60-62 (Lib Educ) ME. 7: Promotion asst; Tower Magazines, NYC 34-35, G Schirmer, NYC 35-36, Life Magazine, NYC 36-45; Libn Huntington Union Free Sch Dist #5, Huntington NY 61-62; Harborfields Central Sch Dist #6, Greenlawn NY 62-. 8: Investigation for NY State Dept of Educ, of correlation of sch lib resources with Bus ed program. 9: ALA-AASchL; NEA; NYLA; NY State Tchrs Assn; Nassau-Suffolk Sch LA (pres 65-66). 10: PTA. 14: Sch libs, child lit. 15: 18 Hendrie lane, Greenlawn LI NY 11740.

TJADEN, MARGARET (KARIN) BERG. b Lynn Mass 26 O 28. 4: Norman F Tjaden. 5: Mt Holyoke 46-50 (Chem) BA; UVt 56-57; UWash 63-65 MLS. 7: Research lab tech: Harvard U 50, USPHS, Hamilton Mont 51-52, UWash Med Sch 52-56, 58-61, UVt Med Sch 56-58; Libn Seattle Pub Lib tech dept 65-67, Libn Univ Br 67-. 9: SLA; WashLA. 13: Yes. 14: Ref. 15: 8248-16th ave, Seattle Wa 98115.

TOBIAS, VERVA GRACE. b Toronto Ont Can 27 My 14. 5: Elmira Col 38-42 (Eng Lit) BA; UMich (Ann Arbor) 44-45 ABLS. 6: Fr. 7: Libn Bainbridge Naval Train Center, Bainbridge Md 45; Asst co libn Ingham Co Lib, Mason Mich 46-47; Libn VA Hosp, Butler Penn 47-51; Libn VA Hosp, Wilmington Del 51-54; USAF base libn; Toul-Rosieres AFB, Toul France 54-56, Shepherds Grove AFB, Stanton England 56-57, Plattsburgh AFB, Plattsburgh NY 57-59, Mildenhall AFB, Mildenhall England 59-64; Br libn Steele Memorial Lib, Elmira NY 65-66; Post libn Seneca Army Depot, Romulus NY 66-. 9: ALA; NYStateLA. 15: 400 Pennsylvania ave, Elmira NY 14904.

TOBIN, JAMES GOLDEN. b E Hartford Conn24 F 10. 4: Dorothy Bloosfeld Tobin. 5: Trinity Col (Conn) 32 BA; Columbia 38 BS in LS. 7: Stud asst & catlgr Trinity Col 32-37; Ref asst NY Pub Lib 39-42; Army of the US 42-47; Supv ref libn, NY Pub LIB 53-, Chief info div 66-. 15: 80 Creston ave, Tenafly NJ 07670.

TOBIN, MARGARET MARY. b Scranton Penn 11 O 28. 5: Marywood Col 46-50 (LS) BA; Duquesne U 56-58 (Educ) MEd; Penn State U 61-. 6: Fr. 7: Assoc libn St Francis Col (Penn) 50-, Dir of Lib Educ 65-, Hd libn 66-. 9: ALA-ACRL (Tri-State Chap); CathLA (Program Coord for Nat Conv 64-65); PennLA. 10: AAUP; AAUW. 12: Co-auth "Bibliographic and Library Manual (51); Co-ed "Parish Library Manual. 13: Yes. 14: Acquis, lib educ. 15: College Heights, Loretto Penn 15940.

TOBOLOWSKY, SARAH. b Dallas. 5: So Methodist U 34 (Eng, Span) BA, 38 (Eng) MA; Columbia 51 MS in LS. 7: Tchr, libn Dallas (Tex) Independent Sch Dist 35-. 8: Tchr Sch of Lib Sci N Tex State U summers 66, 67, 69. 9: NEA (Jt NEA-ALA Com 53-58); ALA-AASchL (Prof Rel Com 58-64; Dir Reg 4 65-67); Tex State Tchrs Assn (chm Lib Sect of Dist 5 59-60); Tex Clr Tchrs Assn (Legis Chm & Mem Adv Bd 52-55); Dallas Sch Libns Club (pres 47-49). 10: Delta Kappa Gamma; Dallas Tchrs Credit Union; Dallas Clr TA. 14: Sch lib serv. 15: 6838 Orchid lane, Dallas Tx 75230.

TOCKNELL, ELIZABETH (KOCHERSPERGER). b Phila 28 N 15. 4: Earl P Tocknel. 5: Queens 57-60 BA, 60-63 MS in Ed, Sch Lib Certif. 7: Elem libn Parkway Sch, Plainview LI NY 60; Libn Glen Cove High Sch, Glen Cove LI NY 60-. 9: NEA; NY State Tchrs Ass; NYLA; ALA; Nassau-Suffolk ASchL. 14: High sch & ya serv. 15: 4 Claurome pl, Freeport NY 11520.

TODD, ELIZABETH G. b Boston. 5: Boston U 44-48 (Hist, Educ) BS in Ed; Simmons 48-50 BS in LS. 6: Sp. 7: Ref libn Boston Pub Lib 48-50; Catlgr UMiami 50-58, Period libn 58-62; Head adult serv Orange Pub Lib, Orange Cal 62-64; Catlg libn Bancroft Lib UCal (Berkeley) 64-. 8: Consul Fairchild Tropical Garden, Miami Fla 59-61. 9: ALA; CalLA. 10: Zonta Internat; UCal FacultyWomens Club; Libns Assn UCal (Berkeley). 14: Catlg, ser. 15: 6876 Pinehaven rd, Oakland Cal 94611.

TODD, FRED WESTFALL. b Timpson Tex 12 S 36. 5: Stephen F AUSTIN State Col 54-58 (Gen Bus) BBA, 59-60 (Eng) MA; UTex 63-65 MLS. 7: Off clerk Westfall Gas Co, Garrison Tex 58-59; Sr admin typist (Spec 4th Class) US Army Alaska 60-63; Lib intern Stanford U Libs 64-65, Asst libn Engnr Lib 65-66, Hd libn tech info serv Stanford U Libs 66-67; Asst dir ind info serv Sci Info Ctr So Meth U 67-70; Asst libn & instr UTex Med Sch 70-. 9: ALA; SLA (2nd v-pres Tex Chap 69-70); TexLA; Dallas Co LA. 12: Ed "Bulletin" Tex chap SLA. 13: Yes. 14: Ref, sci & tech info. 15: UTex Med Sch, San Antonio Tx 78212.

TODD, HAROLD W JR. b Miami Fla 7 Je 25. 4: Mary Whinery. 5: UGa 44-46 (Forestry) BSF; Fla State U 62-63 (LS) MS. 7: Asst libn Albany Pub Lib, Albany Ga 62-66, Dir 66-. 9: ALA; SELA; GaLA. 13: Yes. 14: Mechanization & control of libs. 15: 518 Partridge lane, Albany Ga 31705.

TODOROVICH, DIVNA. b Belgrade Yugoslavia 20 Je 40. 5: AdelphiU 58-59 (Speech & drama); NYU 59-62 (Eng) BA; Rutgers 63-65 MLS. 6: Fr, Serbo-Croatian. 7: Libn trainee Elizabeth Pub Lib, Elizabeth NJ 63-65, Jr libn 65; Area child libn London borough of Newham, London England 66-68; Subject catlgr (Children's Annotated Cards) LC 68-. 10: Phi Beta Kappa. 14: Child wk, music. 15: 110 D st SE, Washington DC 20003.

TOEPFER, DONALD CARL. b Toledo Ohio 22 S 18. 5: UToledo 36-40 (Educ, Hist) BAE; UMich summers 44-47 (Lat) MA, 47-49 BALS. 6: Sp, Fr, Ger, Ital. 7: High sch tchr 41-47; Order dept clerk UMich Lib 47-48; Catlgr Tulare Co Free Lib, Visalia Cal 49-50; Ref asst Kalamazoo Pub Lib 50-. 9: ALA; MichLA; MichEA; NEA. 15: 311 Woodward, Kalamazoo Mi 49007.

TOEPPE, JOAN M. b Clyde Ohio 14 My 24. 4: Gerald E Toeppe. 5: Col of St Teresa 42-46 (Chem, Fr) BS; UMich 49-50 AMLS. 6: Fr. 7: Chem The W K Kellogg Co, Battle Creek Mich 46-49; Catlgr Los Alamos Sci Lab, Los Alamos NM 50-52; Libn Nat Lead Co of Ohio, Cincinnati 52-61; Research libn Diamond Shamrock Corp, Painesville Ohio 61-. 9: SLA (Bd Dir 62-65, chm Sci Meetings Com 62-);-Cincinnati Chap (pres 57-58);-Cleveland Chap (pres 65-66; off, chm &/or mem 4 coms & divs 57-66); -Documentation Div (chm 68-69); ACS (sec NE Ohio Sect 63). 10: Altrusa Club. 11: SLA Sci-Tech Publ Award. 12: Bus mgr "Scientific Meeting" (57-61(. 14: Sci & tech libs & info retrieval, documentation. 15: 34440 Ridge rd apt C19, Willoughby Oh 44094.

TOGASHI, WILLIAM A. b Los Angeles Cal 21 Ag 18. 4: Haruye Itagaki. 5: Aoyama Gakuin Col 39-41 (Eng); Keio Univ Japan Lib Sch 54 (LS). 6: Japanese. 7: Libn Atomic Bomb Casualty Commsn, Hiroshima Japan 54-57; Libn Nat Lib of Med, Wash DC 57-. 10: Japanese American Citizens League Wash DC Chap; Washington Peace Ctr. 14: Catlg. 15: 3959 Wendy ct, Silver Spring Md 20906.

TOLAN, EDWIN K. b Montreal Can 6 O 21. 4: H Elizabeth MacLennan. 5: McGill 4649 (Philos) BA, 5354 BLS; UGlasgow 4951 (Philos) MA; UMontreal 5153, 59 (Philos) PhD. 6: Fr, Ital. 7: Ref libn Hamilton Col 5457; Hd libn Washington & Jefferson Col 5762; Hd libn Union Col (Schenectady NY) 62. 9: ALA; NYLA; Capital District Lib Coun. 10: AAUP. 13: Yes. 15: 1443 Regent st, Schenectady NY 12309.

TOLBERT, JEAN (FURR). b Fernwood Miss 26 Ap 25. 4: Charles Madden Tolbert. 5: Miss Col 44-47 (Hist) BA; Baylor U 62-63 (LS); Tex Womans U summers 63-65 MLS. 7: High sch hist tchr Copiah-LINCOLN Jr Col, Wesson Miss 47-49; Asst libn Miss Col 50-54; Jr libn La State U 54-57; Asst ser libn Baylor U 57-64, Religion dept libn 64-. 8: Coord research project for ref serv in Tex Libs (TexLA Ref RT) 67-68. 9: ALA; TexLA; Waco Lib Club; SWLA. 10: Baylor U Round Table; AAUP. 14: Ref, ser. 15: 5206 Lake Arrowhead dr, Waco Tex 76706.

TOLES, RUTH (MIESCHER). b Winchester Tenn 22 Mr 04. 4: S E Toles. 5: UCal (Berkeley) 20-21; UAriz 21-24 (Eng) BA; JR Col (San Mateo Cal) 44; UAriz summers 51-54 Lib Certif. 7: Eng tchr-libn: Round Valley High Sch, Eager Ariz 24-25, Jr & Sr High Sch, Douglas Ariz 25-27, Santa Barbara High Sch, Santa Barbara Cal 45; Sub tchr Bisbee schs, Bisbee Ariz 46-47; Libn Copper Queen Lib, Bisbee Ariz 47-52; Libn Amphitheater Jr High Sch, Tucson 52-. 9: NEA; ALA; Ariz EA; ArizSchLA; Ariz State LA. 14: Child serv. 15: 5002 E Second st, Tucson Az 85711.

TOLL, MORRIS (MARK). b Phila. 4: Grace Toll. 5: Temple 46-49 (Bus Educ) BS in Ed; Drexel 50-51 MS in LS. 6: Fr. 7: USAAF, Pacific 43-46; Curator theatre collection Free Lib of Phila 51-53, Head acquis dept 54-. 9: ALA; PennLA. 10: Phi Kappa Phi. 14: Acquis, ser. 15: 6512 Walnut Park dr, Phila Pa 15232.

TOLMACHEV, MIRJANA (KNEZEVIC). b Trogir Yugoslavia 5 O 18. 4: Nikola Tolmachev. 5: UBelgrade (Yugoslavia) 55 (Econ); Drexel 65 MS in LS. 6: Serbo-Croatian, Russian, Fr, Ger. 7: Ref libn Penn State Lib 65-. 9: PennLA; ALA. 10: AAUW. 14: Ref. 15: 2467 Mercer st, Harrisburg Penn 17104.

TOLMAN, ARVILLA (COLBY) (MRS). b Londonderry H 28 O 04. 5: Kenne State Col 23-26 (Educ); UNH 30-31 (Educ) BS; Simmons 63-64 (LS) MS. 7: Curr libn U Miami Sch of Educ (Fla) 58-60; Interlib loans Harvard U Grad Sch of Educ 60-62; Ref libn Skidmore Col 64-66; High Sch libn, Peterborough NH 67-. 9: ALA. 10: AAUP; Sch Bd; AAUW; Womans Club. 14: Ref. 15: 15 Pine st, Peterborough NH 03458.

TOLMAN, BONNIE BRUCE (WILSON). b Detroit 10 D 42. 5: Wayne State U 60-64 (LS) BS of Ed; UMich 66-. 7: Asst

6: Fr. 7: Asst libn Blair Mem Lib, Clawson Mich 64-67; Libn I Harper Woods Pub Lib, Harper Woods Mich summers 68, 69; Libn Roseville High Sch, Roseville Mich 67-. 9: MichLA; ALA. 14: Ref, child serv. 15: 15701 Mark Twain, Detroit Mi 48227.

TOLMAN, JAMES R. b Bountiful Utah 27 My 17. 4: LaRue Barney Tolman. 5: Utah State U 46-49 (Eng) BS; UIll 49-51 (LS) MS. 7: T/Cpl US Army, Cal & Tex 42-46; Ref libn Utah State U 51-57; Asst libn Brigham Young U 57-60; Libn Weber State Col 60-. 9: ALA; UtahLA (pres 65-66). 14: Admin, bk sel. 15: Weber State Col Lib, 3750 Harrison blvd, Ogden Utah 8403.

TOLMAN, LORRAINE E. b Cambridge Mass 14 Je 20. 5: Radcliffe 39-43 (Eng) BA; USoCal 46-47 BS in LS, 46-47 (Educ) MS in Ed; Boston U 57 (Educ) DEd. 7: Libn Worcester State Tchrs Col 47-49; Libn Asst Prof Dir of program in sch libnship Sch of Educ Boston U 49-67, Dir of program in Sch Libnship. 9: NEA; ALA-AASchL (Prof Status & Growth Com 63-65, chm 65-68); NESchLA; NELA; NE Reading Assn; MassLA; MassSchLA; Mass Tchrs Assn. 10: AAUP. 12: Co-comp "High Interest - Low Vocabulary Booklist" (56, supplement 67). 13: Yes. 14: Sch libnship. 15: 5 Fife rd, Wellesley Hills Mass 02181.

TOLMAN, LUCILLE (ALM). b Chicago Ill. 4: Lucius M Tolman. 5: UMich 31-35 (Eng) BA, 35-36 ABLS. 6: Ger, Fr. 7: Classifier & subject hding wk John Crerar Lib, Chicago 36-46; Catlg libn Mich State U (E Lansing) 62-69, Asst hd catlg dept 69-. 9: ALA. 14: Catlg. 15: 511 Marshall st, E Lansing Mi 48823.

TOLMAN, MASON. b Albany NY 27 Ag 12. 4: Betsy Andrews Mullens. 5: UChicago 30-34 (Pol Sci) AB; Columbia 34-35 (LS) BS; George Washington U 35-38 (Pub Affairs) MA; Army Air Forces Statistical Sch Harvard 43; Europ Civil Affairs Div Sch of Mil Govt 45. 6: Fr. 7: Asst George Washington U 35-36, Asst libn 36-46; (Capt) US Army Air Force, European Theater of Operations 42-46; Assoc libn George Washington U 46-50; Assoc libn NY State Lib 50-63, Prin libn tech serv 63-64, Prin libn readers serv 64-65, Act dir 66-67, Dir 67-. 8: Lecturer in lib sci SUNY (Albany) 61-63; Consul Clarkson Col of Technol 61-62; Mem Visiting Com Clarkson Col of Technol 58-;Consul Penn Lib Dist Study 61; Consul on Col Libs to Div of Higher Educ N NY State Dept 50-; Consul George Washington U Lib 65; Mem NY Governos Lib Conf Adv Com 65; Lecturer in Pol Sci & Hist Russell Sage Col 51-; Cornell U Wkshop in Mgt Team Development 65; Consul Dept of Libs, Okla 67. 9: ALA;-ACRL;-RSD (chm Nomin Com 60); NYLA (2nd v-pres 62); Amer Soc Pub Admin. 10: Ecumenical Com Diocese of Albany; Hist Sites Commsn Albany; Albany Inst of Hist & Art; Pi Gamma Mu; Fort Orange Club of Albany. 13: Yes. 14: Lib admin. 15: NY State Lib Ed dept, Albany NY 12224.

TOM, CHOW LOY. b Hilo Hawaii. 5: UHawaii 37-41 (Biol sci, Soc sci, Eng) EDB, 41 (Educ) Five-yr diploma; UIll 44-45 (LS) BS, 52-53 (LS) MS; Ohio State U 65-69 (Elem Educ, Child Lit, A-v Educ, Adult Educ) PhD. 6: FR, Chinese. 7: Libn Honokaa High & Elem Sch, Honokaa Hawaii 42-43; Libn Army & Navy YMCA, Honolulu 43-44; Lib asst Allentown Free Lib, Allentown Penn 45-46; Libn Stevenson Intermediate, Honolulu 46-47; Libn Lanakila Elem Sch, Honolulu 47-48; Libn Benjamin Parker High & Elem Sch Kaneohe Kawaii 48-49; Libn Kaimuki High, Honolulu 49-52, 53-56, 57-59; Supv U High Sch Lib UIll (Urbana) 56-57; Instr of educ & Supv U High Sch Lib UHawaii 59-61; Asst Prof, Coord Lib Sci program Col of Educ UHawaii 61-65; Assoc Prof UDenver Grad Sch of Libnship 69-. 9: ALA (State Recr Com);-AASL; NEA; NCTE; HawaiiEA; HawaiiASchL (past pres); HawaiiLA (past sec); Hawaii Adult EA (v-pres); Nat Soc Stud Educ. 10: Pi Gamma Mu; Phi Kappa Phi; Beta Phi Mu. 12: "What Teachers Read to Pupils in the Middle Grades" (PhD diss). 13: Yes. 14: Sch libnship, lib educ, recr. 15: 1095 S Beretania st, Honolulu Hi 96814.

TOM, ELLEN LOUISE (WILEY). b Sudbury Ont Can 18 Mr 41. 4: Bob Tom. 5: McMaster U 60-63 (Fr, Sp) BA; UToronto 63-64 BLS. 6: Fr, Sp, Portu, Ital. 7: Catlgr UWaterloo Lib 64-66, Sr reviser 66-67; Asst hd catlg dept UGuelph Lib 67-. 9: CanLA; ALA; Inst Profess Libns Ont. 13: Yes. 14: Catg. 15: 108 Overlea dr, Kitchener Ont Can.

TOMAN, OLDRICH. b Strisov Czechoslovakia 23 F 24. 4: Vera C Toman. 5: CharlesU (Prague) 45-50 BA; Columbia 60-65 MS in LS; NYU 67-68 (Fr Lit) MA. 6: Fr, Ger, Czech. 7: Speaker of C zech programs Radio Free Europe, Munich Germany 53-60; Libn trainee Brooklyn Pub Lib, Brooklyn NY 60-62; Freelance writer & speaker of Czech programs Radio Free Europe, NYC 62-68; Assoc catlgr SUNY (Stony Brook) 68-. 15: 655-68 Belle Terre rd, Port Jefferson LI NY 11777.

TOMASSINI, CARMENINA. b Rochester NY 7 N 03. 5: URochester 21-25 (Eng, Romance Langs) BA; Columbia 38-42 BS in LS; UCal(Berkeley) 58 MLS; MedLA Certif 61. 6: Ital, Fr, Sp. 7: Eng tchr Clifton Springs High Sch, Clifton Springs NY 25-26; Asst Cincinnati Pub Lib 28-32; Libn Cincinnati Col of Med 32-50; Ref & order libn Biol Lib UCal (Berkeley) 50-51; Head ref libn Sch of Med; UCal (San Francisco) 51-55, Admin libn Med Central Lib 55-; Dir of ref lib serv Nat Ctr for Primate Biol UCal (Davis) 66-. 8: Consul on lib bldg plans Mt Zion Hosp, San Francisco 63, Cal Col of Med, Los Angeles 65, San Francisco Col of Mortuary Sci 64- 9: MedLA (Recruitment Com 67; Mem Com 59-63, Conf Chm 64); SLA; CalLA (sec Sect on Col Univ & Res Libs 59); Hist of Libs Com 65; No Cal Reg Med Lib Group. 12: "Your Library 1961". 14: Admin, ref, primatology. 15: 1804 Apple lane, Davis Ca 95616.

TOMASULO, IRIS (ROSINA). b NYC 11 F 10. 5: Barnard 26-29 (Eng) BA; Columbia 31-32 (Sch Libs) BS; American U & US Dept of Agric 35-63. 6: Ital, Fr, Sp, Portu. 7: Examining clerk US Civil Serv Commsn, Wash DC 34-37; Lib asst circ US Geological Survey, Wash DC 37-40; Lib asst US Nat Defense Adv Commsn, Wash DC 40-41; Asst NY Pub Lib Fordham Br 41-42; Asst catg sect US Geological Survey Lib, Wash DC 42-43; Libn US Beach Erosion Bd, Wash DC 43-48; Asst catlgr US Geological Survey, Wash DC 48-60, Chief catlgr 60-. 9: DCLA. 14: Catlg. 15: 1734 P st NW apt 28, Wash DC 20036.

TOMBERLIN, IRMA (RAYNE). b Baton Rouge La 23 Ag 20. 4: Robert W Tomberlin. 5: LSU 36-40 (Eng) BA, 40-41 BS in LS; UOkla 55-58 MLS. 6: Fr, Ger. 7: Asst libn Bossier Parish Lib, Bossier City La 41-43; Libn Natchitoches Parish Lib, Natchitoches La 43-44; Research libn Standard Oil Co, Baton Rouge La 44-45; Art libn UOkla 47-53; UOkla: Instr Sch of Lib Sci summers 49-53, Asst ref libn 53-56, Asst Prof Sch of Lib 56-60, Info libn 63-64, Asst Prof Sch of Lib Sci 64-. 8: Dir DHEW Inst, "The Critical Role of State Lib Agencies." 9: ALA; AALS; OklaLA (past sec, v-pres, & pres); SWLA. 10: Beta Phi Mu; Tulip Garden Club. 13: Yes. 14: Ref, bibliog, catlg. 15: 825 W Timberdell, Norman Okla 73069.

TOME, MARTHA VALENTINA. b Camaguey Cuba 14 F 33. 5: HavanaU 50-56 (Philos, Lit) PhD; GeorgetownU 57 (Eng); CatholicU 61-67 (LS) MS. 6: Sp. 7: Tchr, Cuba 56-60; Asst hd circ div Catholic U Lib 61, Hd circ div 61-66, Hd spec serv dept 66-67, Dir Proyecto leer bro-Dart Foundation/Bks for the People Fund, Wash DC 67-. 8: Compiler and Editor of the Union List of Serials of the University Libraries of the Metropolitan Washington Area-1967. 9: ALA; CathLA; DCLA; Potomac Tech Proc Libns. 10: Pan Amer Liaison Com of Women's Organs of Wash DC. 12: Comp & ed "The Union List of Serials in the Libraries of the Consortium of Universities of the Metropolitan Washington Area" (67); Ed "Proyecto LEER Bulletin" (68-). 14: Automation in libs, Spanish material for child and adults with a limited reading ability. 15: 3419 Carlyn Hill dr, Falls Church Va 22041.

TOMIYASU, EIKO. b San Francisco Cal 17 Ja 24. 4: Kiyo Tomiyasu. 5: UCal (Berkeley) 41-42 (Gen Curriculum); Hunter Col 44-47 (Chem) BA; Columbia 52-55 MS in LS. 7: Catlging libn Engring Lockheed Aircraft Corp, Palo Alto Cal 57-58; Asst catlg libn schaffer Lib Union Col (Schenectady NY) 62-. 9: ALA. 14: Catlg. 15: Schaffer Lib Union Col, Schenectady NY 12308.

TOMKINS, HELEN HAMLIN. b Boston Mass 10 Ap 25. 4: Peter B Tomkins. 5: Radcliffe 40-44 (Eng) AB (cum laude); Syracuse 66-68 MLS. 6: Fr. 7: Hd res bk room Radcliffe Col 44-47; Asst in acquis dept Dartmouth Col 54-56; Order div Syracuse Lib 68-. 10: Syracuse Lib Sch Alumni Assn; Beta Phi Mu. 14: Acquis. 15: 20 Parkwood pl, Syracuse NY 13219.

TOMKO, JEAN (ROTHERAM). b Creighton Penn 5 Jl 10. 5: Col of Wooster 27-31 (Fr) BA; Drexel 31-32 BS in LS. 6: Fr. 7: Sub Enoch Pratt Free Lib, Baltimore 39-40; Libn Dundalk Pub Lib, Dundalk Md 40-47; Educ libn Johns Hopkins U 47-61; Asst ref libn Towson State Col 61-. 9: ALA; MDLA; Md Ref Serv Div. 10: AAUP; Phi Delta Gamma; Poe Soc. 14: Ref, child bks. 15: Towson State Co, York rd, Baltimore 21204.

TOMLINSON, EDWIN WALTER McCULLOUGH. b Sioux Falls SD 10 N 15. 4: Margaret J Brown. 5: Sioux Falls Col 32-36 (Fr) BS; Columbia 49-50 MLS. 6: Fr, Ger, Sp, Russian, Old Engish, Lat, Portu, Esperant. 7: Off admin US Civil Serv, Wash DC 36-41; Engnr Supply Off US Engnr Dept, Trinidad & St Lucia BWI 41-42; Engnr field off admin Pan-American Airways, Paraguay & Brazil 42-43; (Lt) Admin US Navy, Wash DC 43-46; Registration Off US VA, Sioux Falls SD 46-49; Asst libn Amer Numismatic Soc, NYC 51-52; Catlgr UWis(Madison) 52-53; Chief catlg div Wis State Hist Soc, Madison Wis 53-63; Chief tech processes dept Santa Ana Pub Lib, Santa Ana Cal 63-64; Chief catlg dept, Hd rare bks dept, U Archivist UCal(Irvine) 64-66; Hd catlg dept Prescott Col 66-67; Independent free-lance writing, legal research, Catlg private libs 67-68; Ref libn Orange Co Free Lib, Orange Cal 68-. 9: ALA; CalLA. 10: Westerners; Orange Co (Cal) Hist Soc. 13: Yes. 14: Catlg, rare bks (Western Americana). 15: Orange County Pub Lib, 431 S Manchester, Orange Ca 92668.

TOMLINSON, ELIZABETH K (HANBY). b Brooklyn NY 19 Ap 14. 5: Maryville Col 32-35 (Chem); Birmingham-So Col 50-52 (Eng) AB; Rutgers 59-61 MLS. 7: Tech libn Houdry Process & Chem co, Marcus Hook Penn 60-66; Research libn Scott Paper Co, Philadelphia 66-68; Hd Chem Lib UMd (College Park) 68-. 9: SLA; ASIS; Spec Libs Coun Greater Phila (past Finance Chm). 10: Great Bks Prog; Nat & local Audubon Soc; AAUW; Smithsonian Associate. 14: Ref. 15: Chemistry Lib Univ of Md, College Park Md 20742.

TOMMEY, RICHARD JOSEPH (MICHEL). b Carnegie Penn 9 Je 24. 4: Marie Antonia Wiedenbauer. 5: Tarleton Col 43-44 (Engnr); Loyola Col (Md) 46-49 (Hist) PhB; Catholic U 50-51 MS in LS. 6: Ger. 7: Ya libn Enoch Pratt Free Lib, Baltimore 49-50; Interlib loan libn Catholic U 50-51; Ref libn US Govt, Wash DC 51-52, Chief loan serv 52-54, Sr ref libn 54-5; TECH LIBN & clsf Olin Mathieson-Nuclear Fuels Operation, New Haven Conn 57-60; Head libn Gulf Gen Atomic Inc, San Diego 60-. 9: SLA (San Diego Chap; Bul ed 62-63, pres 64-65, coun 68-69). 10: Friends of UCSD Libs. 14: Admin, ref. 15: 6073 Avenida Chamnez, La Jolla Cal 92037.

TOMPKINS, LOUISE. b Jersey City NJ 3 My 28. 5: Vassar 46-50 (Pol Sci) BA; U Cal (Berkeley) 62-63 MLS. 6: Fr, Russian. 7: Jr sec Princeton U 51-52, Asst in research 52-54; Research Clerk Nat Farmers Union, Denver 55; Legal sec S T Anderson, Denver 55-58; UCal (Berkeley): Sec-stenographer 58-60, Sec 60-62, Libn 63-66; Libn Pliny Fisk Lib of Educ & Finance Princeton U 66-. 9: ALA; SLA. 13: Yes. 14: Ref. 15: 140 Spruce st, Princeton NJ 08540.

TOMPKINS, MARJORIE M. 5: Phillips U 39-42 (Eng Lit) AB; West Res 42-43 BS in ls; UMich 46-48 AMLS. 7: Catlgr hist of med div Armed Forces Med LIB, Cleveland 43-46, Acquis off 48-50; Instr West Res U Sch of Lib Sci summers 49-52; Catlgr hist of med div Armed Forces Med Lib, Cleveland 50-53; Acquis libn UMich Lib 53-61, Asst to Dir for personnel & budget 61-. 10: Beta Phi Mu. 13: Yes. 15: 1807 Orchard st, Ann Arbor Mi 48103.

TOMS, EVELYN RUTH (WOODWARD). b Waycross Ga 16 F 21. 5: Valdosta State Col 37-41 (Art) AB; Ga So Col summer sch 50, 51 (Educ); Fla State U 55-58 MA in LS, summer 68; UGa summer 65; UPittsburgh (New Media in Lib Educ). 6: Sp. 7: Draftsman Southern Bell, Jacksonville Fla 42-43; Display artist Furchgotts, Jacksonville Fla 43; Elem tchr Ware Co Bd of Educ, Waycross Ga 43-44; Pre-audit clerk Army Air Forces, Wash DC 44-45; Inventory clerk Martins, Wash DC 45; Sign writer Palais Royal, Wash DC 45-46; Wired music announcer Misicale Inc, Wash DC 46; Eng tchr Ware Co Bd of Educ, Waycross Ga 47-49; Elem prin Ware Co Bd of Educ, Waycross Ga 50-51; Eng chr Brantley Co Bd of Educ, Nahunta Ga 51-52; Eng tchr Cook Co Bd of Educ, Adel Ga 52-56; High sch libn Grady Co Bd of Educ, Cairo Ga 56-; Elem lib consul Bd of Educ for Grady & Thomas Cos, Cairo & Thomasville Ga 59-; Instr in Lib Sci Berea Col 66-67; Instr in Lib Sci Wis State U (Whitewater) 67-. 9: ALA-AASchL; NEA-DAVI (Child & YP Libns); Ga A-V EA (past chm); WisLA (Sch Libns Sect, v-chm); Wis Dept of A-V Instr. 14: Adult & ya educ serv, pub rel, acquis, instr in sch libnship, sch media ctrs. 15: 416 Harmony dr, Whitewater Wi 53190.

TONEY, BERNARD J. b Nashville 16 My 28. 4: Jeanne Meakin Hasket. 5: Peabody 48-52 (Soc Sci) BA, 53-54 (Hist) MA, 55-56 MALS, 68-69 (LS). 6: Ital, Fr. 7: Naval Res 47-52; Asst Prof Dept of Lib Sci & readers adv Central Mich U 56-68; Assoc Prof Lib Sci Shippensburg State Col 69-. 8: Lib Study Tour, East Europe (Russia, Poland, etc) summer 64 (Sabbatical leave to study Indian Lib Syst). 9: ALA; MichLA; AAHE. 10: AAUP; Beta Phi Mu; Alpha Beta Alpha; Pi Gamma Mu. 13: Yes. 14: Ref, rare bks, histof bks & libs. 15: Shippensburg State Col, Shippensburg Pa 17257.

TONGATE, JOHN THOMAS. b DeKalb Ill 25 F 41. 5: NorthwesternU 59-63 (Eng Lit) BA; UPittsburgh MLS. 6: Fr. 7: Lt USN Communications 63-66; Ser libn Oberlin Col Lib 68-. 9: OhioLA. 14: Acquis, lib bldg, lib automation. 15: 54-1/2 N Prospect st, Oberlin Oh 44074.

TONSETH, PHEBE (HUNT). b Shushan NY 13 Jl 17. 4: Didrick Tonseth. 5: Simmons 34-38 (LS) BS. 7: Child libn NY Pub Lib 38-40; Child libn Akron Pub Lib, Akron Ohio 40-41; Libn & Instr in child lit Wheelock Col 41-44; Br libn Brookline Pub Lib, Brookline Mass 44-45; Child libn Lexington Pub Lib Lexington Mass 58-61; Libn Hartwell Sch, Lincoln Mass 62-; Libn Robert Pt Coffin Sch, Brunswick Me 68-. 8: New England Sch Lib Assoc. 9: Me Tchrs Assn; MassLA; MeASchL. 10: Audobon Soc. 14: Child bks. 15: Willarch rd, Lincoln Mass 01773.

TOOMBS, KENNETH ELDRIDGE. b Colonial Heights Va 25 Ag 28. 4: Ada Teresa Hornsby. 5: Tenn Wesleyan Col 50 (Soc Sci) AA; Tenn Poytech Inst (Soc Sci) BS; UVa 55 (Hist) MA; Rutgers 56 MLS. 6: Ger, Fr. 7: 1st Lt US Army 46-47, 51-53; Ref asst UVa 54-55; Research asst Rutgers Lib Sch 55-56; Chief circ libn LSU (Baton Rouge) 56-58, Hd soc sci div 58-63, Asst dir libs 62-63; Dir libs & prof lib sci U S West La 63-67; Dir libs US Car 67-. 8: Consul lib bldgs; USWestLA, Voorhees Col, Med Col of SC, USoCar; Moved & consolidated libs at LSU; Bd of Lib Examiners, 6667; Lecturer LSU Lib Sch 6163; vpres Amer Field Serv Intern Scholarships 6367; Consul Guidance Inst LSU 62. 9: ALAACRL (Legis Com; Steering Com); LaLA (parliamentarian); SCLA (Planning Com; Legis Com); SELA; SWLA (chm Col & Univ Sect). 10: Kiwanis; Wesley Foundation. 11: Danforth Assoc; Rule Essay Award. 12: Ed "Bulletin of Louisiana Library Association" (59-62); "Southwest Louisiana Journal" (63-67). 13: Yes. 14: Admin, lib bldgs & equipment. 15: 16 Garden Springs rd, Columbia SC 29209.

TOOMEY, ALICE F(INKELSTEIN). b Orangeburg SC 26 D 06. 5: Converse Col 23-27 (Math) BA; Columbia 30-32 (LS) BS, 38-45 (Educ) MA. 7: Catlgr Tchrs Col Columbia U 31-42; Asst head catlg dept UNC (Chapel Hill) 42-43; Catlgr DC Pub Lib 43-47; Catlgr Carnegie Endowment for Internat Peace, Wash DC 47-49; LC: Catlgr 49-50, Asst ed catlg publ 50-57, Ed catlg publ 57-62, Head Mss Sect Descr Catlg Div 62-63, Chief Catlg Maintenance & Catlg Publ Div 63-. 9: ALA; DCLA; Potomac Tech Proc Libns (chm 69-70); Church & Synagogue LA. 14: Catlg, catlg publns, admin, catlg maintenance. 15: 2601 Woodley pl NW, Wash DC 20003.

TOOMEY, MARY ALICE. b Los Angeles Cal 10 Ap 48. 5: Immaculate Heart Col 64-68 (Psych) BA, 68-69 MLS. 6: Fr. 7: Lib asst Hollywood Presbyterian Hosp, Los Angeles 67-68. 14: Ref, rare bks, humanities. 15: 1918 N New Hampshire ave, Los Angeles Ca 90027.

TOPFER, SUE (ACE). b Media Penn 30 Mr 25. 4: Alvin Richard Topfer. 5: Ursinus Col 42-46 (Chem-Biol) BS; Syracuse 50-51 (LS) MS. 6: Fr, Ger. 7: Research lab asst Amer viscose Corp, Marcus Hook Penn 46-50; Libn (catlg & ref) Naval Air Devel Ctr, Johnsville Penn 51-53; Libn (tech serv) Luzerne Co Commun Col 67-. 9: ALA; PennLA. 14: Catlg, ref. 15: Loop rd RD 3, Mountaintop Pa 18707.

TOPLIFFE, LORISE C. b Pittsburgh Penn 24 Ag 33. 4: Frederick W. 5: Tarkio Col 51-55 (Eng) BA; LSU 55-57 (LS) MS. 7: Sr catlg libn WVaU 57-59; Sr ref libn 59-65; Chief ref libn 65-68; Chief bibliogr 68-. 8: Lib consul E African Agric & Forestry Research Org, Muguga Kenya 66, 67. 9: ALA; WVaLA. 12: "The Southern Mountaineer in Literature, An Annotated Bibliography (64); Comp: "Appalachian Outlook (64-), "West Virginia Union list (65-), "Periodicals in East African Libraries (67-). 14: Ref, bibliog. 15: 305 Jackson ave, Morgantown W Va 26505.

TOPLIN, BARBARA L. b Pittsburgh Penn 2 My 35. 4: Irving Toplin. 5: Hood Col 53-57 9econ) BA; Rutgers 63-66 MLS. 7: Child libn Teaneck Pub Lib, Teaneck NJ 62-. 9: NJLA. 14: Child serv, a-v serv. 15: 445 E Saddle River rd, Ridgewood NJ 07450.

TOPOLCIC, IRENE (SILVER). b NY. 4: George B Topolcic. 5: Hunter Col 41-45 (Eng) BA; Columbia 63-65 (LS) MA; Hunter Col 68- (Hist). 6: Fr, Ger. 7: Ed asst Rural Electrification Mag, Wash DC 52-54; Prod asst Womans Day, NY 54-58; Prod ed Shaw Publ, NY 58-62; Prod ed Television Magazine, NY 62-63; Libn NY Pub Lib 63-65; Libn Princeton

U 66-67; Libn Hunter Col 68-. 9: LACUNY (del from Hunter Col); NY Tech Serv Libns; NY Lib Club. 14: Catlg, ref. 15: 34 E 11 st, New York NY 10003.

TORBETT, KAY (ANN). b Morilton Ark 14 O 42. 5: UArk 60-64 (Eng) BA; UOkla 64-65 MLS. 7: Bkmob libn Greene/Clay Reg, Paragould Ark 64-65; Assoc ref libn Tex Tech 65-66; Catlgr Tex State Lib 66-67; Sr libn Wolfner Lib for Blind & Physically Handicapped St Louis Pub Lib 67-68, Ser catlg 68-. 14: Ref, catlg, rare bk. 15: Box 417, Morrilton Ak 72110.

TORGRIMSON, ELLEN. b Grand Meadow Minn 9 F 03. 5: St Olaf Col 21-25 (Eng) BA; UIll summer 28 (LS); UMinn summer 29 (LS); Columbia summer 37 (LS); U Ill 55-56 (LS) MS. 7: Co libn Chouteau Co Free Lib, Ft Benton Mont 29-45; Asst libn Bus & Ind Br, S Bend Ind 45-46; Sec Mont State Lib Commsn, Missoula Mont 46-57; Ref libn Rochester Pub Lib, Rochester Minn 57-63; Asst libn Midland Col Lib 63-65; Readers Serv Div Pasadena Pub Lib, Pasadena Cal 65-66; Adult serv libn Ukiah-Mendocino Co Lib, Ukiah Cal 66-69. 9: ALA; Mont LA (Life mem; past sec & pres); CalLA. 10: Delta Kappa Gamma; AAUW; Mendocino Co Hist Soc. 12: Ed "Montana Libraries (48-56); Contrib of Articles on Mont in "Colliers Encyclopedia & "Colliers Year Book. 14: Ref. 15: 660 W Perkins st, Ukiah Ca 95482.

TORMALA, ROBERT WARREN. b Hancock Mich 28 O 44. 5: UMich 62-65 (Hist) AB, 66 AMLS. 6: Ger. 7: Asst libn No Mich U 67-68; Hd libn Lake Shore Jr-Sr High, Belle Glade Fla 68-. 9: ALA; Palm Beach Co Educl Media Assn. 14: Ref, acquis. 15: 18 Fourth st, South Range Mi 49963.

TORMES, MARY LOU (JENKINS). b Pittsburgh Penn 21 Ag 41. 4: Felix Rodriguez Tormes. 5: Ohio State U 59-63 (Eng) BA; Hunter Col 66-67 (Educ); UIll 69 (LS). 6: Lat. 7: Clk NYC Pub Lib 63-64; Market research libn Freeport Sulphur Co, NYC 64-66; Market research libn Deering Milliken Inc, NYC 66-67; Asst dir Safety Research Info Serv Nat Safety Coun, Chicago 67-. 9: SLA. 14: Systems in libs & info serv. 15: National Safety Council, 425 N Michigan, Chicago Il 60611.

TOROK, STEPHEN SR. b Budapest Hungary 2 Ag 15. 4: Claire Banyay. 5: State Tchrs Col 29-34 (Educ) BEd; Catholic Tchrs Inst 34-36 (Educ) Diploma; Sch of Journalism 39-42 Diploma; Penn State U 55-58 (Ferr Metallurgy) Certif; West Res 59-60, 63 MSLS, Med libnship Certif; UVt 65 (Data Processing); IBM(Montreal) 65 (Lib Automation); Case West Res 68 (Automated Lib Processing). 6: Ger, Hungaria. 7: Literary ed Kath Nepszovetses, Budapest 37-39; Courthouse reporter Centrum U Printers, Budapest 39-42; Literary ed Magyar Radio es Telefonhirmondo, Budapest 42-45; Tech Kramer Sharon Steel Westinghouse, Germany & US 45-57; Lib supv Youngstown U Lib 58-59, Admin asst head of circ dept 60-63; Ref libn Col of Med UVt 63-66; Doc libn SUNY(Oswego) 66-68, Assoc libn, Hd comp serv microtech 68-. 9: SLA; ALA-ACRL; SUNYLA. 10: AAUP; Amer-Hungarian Cath Soc. 14: Admin, automation, info scis, microtechn. 15: 11 West Fourth st, Oswego NY 13126.

TORRES, M BLANCA L. b Boyaca Columbia SA 19 Mr 38. 5: Universidad Pedagogica de Colombia 52-56 (Lang) BA; UMich 57-60 (Eng, For Lang) MA, 61-65 MALS. 6: Sp, Fr, Ital, Ger, Lat, Grk. 7: Lib asst UMich (Ann Arbor) 57-66; High sch libn Walled Lake Con Schs, Walled Lake Mich 66-. 10: Newman Assn (UMich); Intl Ctr (UMich). 14: Catlg, ref. 15: 320 S Div apt 1, Ann Arbor Mi 48108.

TORRES, JESSE JOSEPH. b Mex 6 Je 19. 4: Mary Bodnar. 5: Loras Col 39-43 (Eng) BA; Catholic U 45-47 BLS, 48 (Span Lit), 57- (LS); USDA (Russian Lang, Indexing) Certif. 6: Sp, Fr, Ital, Portu, Lt, Russian. 7: Catlgr Catholic U 45-49; Chief ech processes sect Pan American Sanitary Bur, Reg Off of the World Health Org, Wash DC 49-. 8: Consul to & Org of Lib Collection in Zone II Office, Mexico, Pan Amer Sanitary Bur, 59 & 64. 9: ALA; MedLA; DCLA; MLA; ParrishLA, Wash DC (chm Publicity Com 55). 14: Catlg, indexing, admin. 15: 5520-39thst W, Wash DC 20015.

TORRI, ERIKA H(ENRIETTE) L(UISE) (HOFFMANN). b Bremen Germany 22 My 42. 4: Fred torri. 5: Lib Sch (Hamburg) 63-65 (Sci) Diploma. 6: Ger, Fr. 7: Asst libn Chamberlayne Col 66; Catlgr Countway Lib, Boston 67-. 10: Verein der Bibliothekare an Offentlichen Buchereien. 14: Catlg. 15: 5 Maple st, Brookline Ma 02146.

TORRICELLI, BETTY (LOTZ). b Passaic NJ 14 Ag 18. 04 S Lawrence Torricelli. 5: State Tchrs Col (Montclair NJ) 36-40 (Eng) AB; Rutgers 58-60 MLS. 6: Fr. 7: Tchr Teaneck High Sch, Teaneck NJ 40-42; Program dir Amer Red Cross, Wash DC 42-44; Dir of wk with ya YWCA 44-46; Libn Mahwah Pub Schs, Mahwah NJ 52-. 8: Part-time faculty, Rutgers Grad Lib Sch Adv Com, Title II, Fed Educ Act, NJ, 65-; Mem NJ Lib Development Com 66-. 9: ALA (Coun 69-72); NJSchLA (pres 65-66, chm development com 67). 13: Yes. 14: Sch lbnship. 15: 257 Woodside ave, Franklin Lakes NJ 07417.

TOTH, BLANCHE IRENE. b Batva Czechoslovakia 12 D 32. 5: Hamilton Normal Sch 50-51 Elem Sch Tchrs Certif; McMaster U 52-56 BA; Toronto 60-61 BLS. 6: Fr, Hungarian. 7: Prim tchr W Flamboro Sch Bd, W Flamboro Sch Bd, W Flamboro Ont 51-53, Hamilton Bd of Educ, Hamilton Ont 54-58, E York Bd of Educ, Toronto 58-59; Asst child dept Hamilton Pub Lib, Hamilton Ont 59-60; Yp libn N York Pub Lib, Toronto 61-63; Res libn circ McMaster U (Ont) 63-67; Ref libn Burlington Pub Lib, Ont 67-. 9: OntLA. 14: Circ, ref. 15: 73 Afton ave, Hamilton Ont Canada.

TOTH, ELMA (DITTRICH). b Budapest Hungary 15 Mr 11. 4: Emerick Toth. 5: Hunter Col 29-33 (Ger) AB; Catholic U 53-57 MS in LS. 6: Hungarian. 7: Elem sch libn Montgomery Co Bd of Educ, Rockville Md 56-65, Jr high sch libn 66-; Libn Montgomery Jr Col 65-66. 9: ALA; NEA; MdState Tchrs Assn; MdSchLA. 10: PTA. 14: Sch libs. 15: 700 So elgrde rd, Silver Spring Md 20902.

TOTH, MARGARET K. b Oshkosh, Wis 6 O 07. 4: August J Toth. 5: Wis StateU (Oshkosh) Ed B; UWis 31-32 (LS) Certif. 6: Fr. 7: Circ asst & catlgr Wis StateU (Oshkosh) 32-39; Circ asst URochester 43-48, Asst subj catlgr 48-50, Ref dept & spec collections 50-53, Ed URochester Press 53-66, Hd microtext & duplications 62-66, Hd acquis dept 66-. 9: ALAACRL. 14: Acquis, rare bks, tech proc. 15: Univ of Rochester Lib River Campus Sta, Rochester NY 14627.

TOTTEN, HERMAN LAVON. b Van Alstyne Tex 10 Ap 38. 5: Wiley Col 57-61 (Music) BA; UOkla 62-64 MLS. , 64-66 PhD. 6: Fr, Sp. 7: Asst libn Wiley Col 62-63, Hd libn 66-; Asst I UOkla 63-66. 8: Media Inst Instr UOkla Sch Lib Sci (Norman) summers 68, 69. 9: ALA; NEA-DAVI; SWLA; TexLA. 10: Phi Delta Kappa; Beta Phi Mu; Alpha Phi Omega; AAUP; Alpha Phi Alpha. 13: Yes. 14: Admin, catlg, acquis. 15: 901 Barney st, Marshall Tx 75670.

TOTTEN, VIVIAN (MANNING). b Pittsburgh 12 Ja 12. 5: UMinn 28-32 (Hist) BA; UIll 32-33 BS in LS. 7: Lib asst circ & indexing, Oriental Inst UChicago 34-39, Ref asst 1st asst ref dept Mt Vernon (NY) Pub Lib 39-43; Catlgr Lib Bankers Trust Co NYC 43-44; Sr catlgr DC Pub Lib 44-47; Lib Nat War Col Wash DC; Chief Clsf Records Unit catlg sect 47-51; Chief period & documents sect 51, Chief catlg sect 51-68, Chief tech proc sect 68-69. 9: DCLA. 10: Phi Beta Kappa. 14: Catlg. 15: 4426 Ellicott st NW, Wash DC 20016.

TOURVILLE, PENE SUE. b Sparta Wis 1 O 41. 5: Manatee Jr Col 59-61 AA; Tex Womans U 61-63 (LS) AA, 65-66 MLS. 6: Fr, Sp, Ger. 7: Med libn St Francis Hosp, Honolulu 63-65; SpS Lib Flak Kas, Ludwigsburg Ger 67; SpS Lib Wm O Darby Kas, Nurnberg Ger 67-68; SpS Lib Br, Hq 7ATC Grafenwohr Ger. 9: SLA; ALA; HawaiiLA; AFLS (Europe Chap Mem Com). 14: Med libs. 15: 105 N 18th st W, Bradenton Fla 33505.

TOWER, JEAN D (DE BROSKE). b Hamilton Ont Can 4 Je 22. 4: Stephen N Tower. 5: UPittsburgh 61- (Geog) BA, (LS) MA. 7: Sec Dept Sociol & Anthrop NYU 41-44; Sec Physics Dept CornellU 46-47; Grad asst Grad Lib Sch UPittsburgh 64-65; Sch libn Churchill Area, Pittsburgh Penn 65-68; Sch libn Franklin Area Sch, Murrysville Penn 66-68. 9: ALA. 15: 4448 Old Wm Penn Hwy, Murrysville Pa 15668.

TOWERY, JAMES GASTON. b Gainesville Ga 13 Ap 06. 5: Emory 25-30 (Hist) B Ph, 44-45 (Hist) MA; Peabody 50-51 (LS) MA, 51-52 MSLS. 6: Ger. 7: Prin Hillcrest Consolidated Sch, LaGrange ga 28-29; US Army Corps of Engns Engnrs Tech 5-Spec 42-43; Ref asst Review & Herald Publ Assn, Wash DC 45-48; Asst libn Madison Col (Tenn) 49-50; Lib Dir Oakwood Col 52-55; Asst libn Simpson Col 55-60; Assoc ref libn Drake U 61-. 9: ALA (Life mem); NEA (Life mem); IowaLA; SELA. 13: Yes. 14: Ref, displays, rare bks, bibliog. 15: PO Box 1160, Des Moines Ia 50311.

TOWLES, LORRAINE (COX). b Salt Lake City Utah 10 Jl 43. 4: Charles Clifford Towles. 5: Brigham YoungU 61-67 (Eng) BA, (LS); USalzburg (Austria) 65 (Ger); Tex Woman'sU 67-68 (LS). 6: Ger. 7: Admin asst Salzburg Exchange Program, Salzburg Austria summer 65; Off relief Ford Motor Co, Dallas

Tex summers 62-64; Sec E I Du Pont Co, Dallas Tex summer 65; Stud asst lib Brigham YoungU 62-67; Research asst Mobil Oil-Field Research Lib, Dallas Tex summer 66; Libn Campbell Taggart Assoc Bakeries, Dallas Tex 67-69; Map libn So MethodistU 69-. 8: Asst to Dir of Intl Rel Program Brigham YoungU 66-67; Libn & coord a-v materials Latter Day Saint Ch, Dallas Ward Lib 68-. 9: ALA; SLA; TexLA; Dallas CoLA. 14: Maps, ref, acquis, catlg. 15: 3434 Nogales 215, Dallas Tx 75220.

TOWNER, LAWRENCE WILLIAM. b St Paul Minn 10 S 21. 4: Rachel Bauman. 5: Cornell Col (Ia) 38-42 (Eng & Hist) BA; NorthwesternU 46-55 (Hist) MA, PhD. 7: Hist master Chicago Latin Sch 46-47; Instr MIT 50-54, Asst Prof 54-55; Assoc Prof Wm & Mary 55-61; Fellow Ctr for Hust of Liberty Harvard 61-62; Libn Newberry Lib, Chicago 62-64, Dir & libn 64-. 8: Visiting Prof of Eng NorthwesternU 58-; Professorial lecturer in hist UChicago 68-; Bd Ed Journal of Amer Hist 64-67; Bd Adv Papers of George Washington 69-; Bd Ed America: Hist & Life. 9: AHA; Org Amer Histns; BSA; Amer Antiq Soc; Amer Bibliog Soc; Col Soc Mass; Mass Hist Soc. 10: Grolier; Caxton. 11: Honorary doctorates of letters from Cornell Col, Lake Forest Col, NorthwesternU. 12: Ed "William and Mary quarterly: A Magazine of Early American History" (55-62). 13: Yes. 14: Gen admin, early Amer hist. 15: 60 W Walton st, Chicago Il 60610.

TOWNESEND, GEORGE ANTHONY (FYLER). b Victoria BC Can 13 Ap 40. 5: UBC 59-63 (Hist, Eng) BA; 66-67 BLS. 6: Fr. 7: Lib asst Spec Collections UBC Lib 63-64; Plan checking asst Bldg Dept City Hall, Vancouver BC Can 65-66; Ref libn CarletonU Lib 67-68; Ref libn Burnaby Pub Lib, Burnaby BC Can 69-. 9: CanLA; ALA. 14: Ref serv. 15: 823 West 24th ave, Vancouver BC Can.

TOWNLEY, BETTY LOU (NEEL). b Pampa Tex 3 Jl 35. 4: Sam A Townley. 5: UTulsa 53-57 (Elem Educ) BA; UOkla 60-61 MLS. 6: Sp. 7: Asst dir Pioneer Multi-Co Lib, Norman Okla 61-63; Br libn Okla City Libs 63-65; Ext libn Okla Co Libs, Okla City 65-66, exec dir 66-. 9: ALA; OklaLA; SWLA. 14: Admin. 15: 131 NW Third, Oklahoma City Ok 73102.

TOWNSEND, DOLORES (DONEZ). b Torreon Coahuila Mexico 27 O 13. 4: Fred F Townsend. 6: Sp, Fr, Lat. 7: Stud lib asst Kan State Tchrs Col 33-36; Lib asst & Sp tr Kan State Hist Soc, Topeka 36-40; Sp tchr Topeka High Night Sch, Topeka Kan 37-40; Indexer Chloe Morse Inc, Santa Monica Cal 43-52; Period libn USoCal Sch of Med 53-53; Ref libn & catlgr Pepperdine Col 53-56; Card div supv USoCal 56-58; Br libn Los Angeles co Pub Lib 59-61; Sch libn Santa Monica Unified Sch Dist, Cal 61-62; Hd libn Inglewood High Sch, Cal 62-65; Hd pub serv Cal State Col (Dominguez Hills) 66-67; Sub tchr Inglewood Unified Sch Dist, cal 67-; Libn evening div Los Angeles SW Col 67-. 8: Educ libn Cal State Col (Los Angeles) to revise the Educ Pamphlet Collection Winter 68. 9: ALA; NEA; CalLA; CalASchL; CalTchrsA; InglewoodTA. 10: Kappa Delta Pi; Boy Scouts; Girl Scouts; PTA. 14: Ref, catlg. 15: 884 Victor ave, Inglewood Ca 90302.

TOWNSEND, ELEANOR (MARIE). b Sycamore Ill 9 Ap 22. 5: Stanford 39-40; Denison U 40-43 (Eng) AB; Columbia 48 (LS) BS. 7: Jr detailer Gen Motors Corp, Dayton Ohio 43-46; Jr libn Yonkers Pub Lib, Yonkers NY 48-49; Libn Gr 2 Mun Ref Lib, NYC 49-51; Asst libn Foote, Cone & Belding, NYC 51; Asst libn Cooper Union Art & Arch Lib 5267; Chief libn Sch of Visual Arts, NYC 67-. 9: SLA (Mus Div, sec-treas 62-63, Nomin Com 64, sec-treas 69-71). 10: Appalachian Mt Club; Country Dance and Song Soc; Columbia Sch Lib Sci Alum Assn. 14: Art ref. 15: 180 Park Row, New York NY 10038.

TOWNSEND, MARTHA (GRAY). b Kan City Mo. 4: Robert F Townsend. 5: Kan City Jr Col 33-35 AA; UChicago 35-39 (Eng) AB, 48-50 (LS) MA. 7: Prin film serv libn Chicago Pub LIB 50-51; Libn I Minneapolis Pub Lib 51-52; Libn for staff & patients Dept of Mental Hygiene State of Cal, Agnews State Hosp 52-53; Libn II ref & publicity Santa Monica Pub Lib, Santa Monica Cal Cal 53-66, Head ref dept 66-. 9: CalLA. 14: Ref, pub rel, displays. 15: 634 Alma Real dr, Pacific Palisades Ca 90272.

TOWNSEND, ROBERT BRUCE. b Bloomington Ill 2 Ja 33. 4: Faye Jones. 5: Ill Wesleyan U 50-51, 56-57 (Liberal Arts); UIll 57-60 (Geol) BS; UWyo 60-61 (Geol); UIll 61-62 MSLS. 7: Aerographers mate USN 52-56; Research asst Ill Geological Survey, Urbana Ill 57-60; Ref asst Dayton Pub Lib, Dayton Ohio 62-64; Sci libn Kan State U (Manhattan) 64-65, Ref libn 65-67; Chief ref & sci libn Ill State U 67-. 9: ALA. 14: Ref, sci lit. 15: 914 S Fell ave, Normal Il 61761.

TOWNSEND, RUTH R(EED). b Iowa Falls Iowa. 5: Iowa State U 37-39 (Foods & Nutrition) BS; Fla State U 39-40 (Dietetic Intern); UDenver (LS) MA. 6: Sp. 7: Dir Dining Halls Ariz State U 45-48; Gen serv libn C2 Z Lib, Balboa CZ 55-60; Ser libn Ariz State U 60-62; Post spec serv, Ft Hood Tex; Hosp libn 63, Head tech serv 63-64, chief libn 64-68; Area libn USASUPCOM Qui Nhon Spec Serv, RVN 68-69; Chief libn Spec Serv, Ft Hood Tex 69-. 9: ALA; Amer Dietetic Assn (Life Mem); TexLA (chm Dist 8 68); SWLA; Salt Water Valley LA (pres 61-62). 10: Amer Bus Women. 14: Admin, serv ctr. 15: PO Box 1013, Killeen Tx 76541.

TOY, ERNEST WILLIAM JR. b Lasadena Cal 24 Jl25. 4: Joyce Rowland. 5: Col of St Thomas 43-47 (Hist) BA; USoCal 47-48 (LS) MS; UCLA 48-50, 54 (Hist) MA. 7: Asst order libn Los Angeles State Col 52-54; Col Libn Riverside City Col 54-59; Col Libn & Assoc Prof of hist Cal State Col (Fullerton) 59-. 8: Consul Fullerton Jr Col 65. 9: CalLA. 10: Navy Records Soc; Soc Nautical Research; AAUP; Phi Alpha Theta; Delta Epsilon Sigma; Beta Phi Mu. 14: Admin, acquis. 15: 2501 E Commonwealth, Fullerton Ca.

TOZER, PEGGY M. b Shell Lake Wis. 5: Wis State Col (Eau Claire) 39-43 (Eng) BS; UWis 47-48 BLS; UMich 55, 59 MA in LS. 7: Tchr: Trempealeau High Sch, Trempealeau Wis 43, New Auburn High Sch, New AUBURN Wis 43-45, Sparta High Sch, Sparta Wis 45-47; Libn Beloit Mem High Sch, Beloit Wis 48-52; Pub serv libn East NM U 52. 9: ALA (State Recr rep 65-); NMLA (chm Univ & Spec Libs Sect 63-64, Scholarship Com 60-62, Nat Lib Week Com 65, Com on Policies, Procedures & Safeguards for Interlib Loan & Ref); SWLA; NMEA. 10: Altrusa Internat; Delta Kappa Gamma; AAUW; OES. 14: Ref. 15: 108 Oklahoma, Portales NM 88130.

TOZIER, VIRGINIA TARR. b NEWBURYPORT Mass 25 Jl 11. 5: Boston U 43-47 (Eng) AB, 47 & 54 (Educ); Simmons 51-54 MLS; Columbia 56-57 (LS). 7: Photographer & field wker Wheelan Studios, NYC 30-36; Libn: Worcester Acad, Worcester Mass 38-42, Weston High Sch, Weston NY 51-54, Edgemont High Sch, Scarsdale NY 55-57; Head libn Great Neck High Sch, Great Neck NY 57-58; Instr Sch of Lib Sci, Syracuse U 58-60; Head Libn Central Park Road Sch (Elem), Plainview NY 6-. 8: Instr Sch of Educ, UVt summer 58; Head Libn Knapp Sch Lib Project Demonst Lib 64, 65; Chm NY State Com Implement of Impleentof Sch Lib Standards 60-61. 9: ALA; NEA; NYLA (Bd Sch Lib Sect 59-61); Nassau Suffolk Sch LA. 10: AAUP; Phi Beta Kappa; AAUW; Appalachian Mountain Club. 13: Yes. 14: Child serv. 15: 127 D2 Fifteenth st, Garden City NY 11530.

TRACEWELL, MARY ANN. b Okmulgee Okla 17 Ja 44. 5: UOkla 62-66 (Math) BA; UTex (Austin) 66-67, 69 MLS. 7: Intern Tulsa City-Co Lib System, Tulsa Okla 68; Reg libn 69-. 9: ALA; SWLA; OLA. 10: Gamma Phi Beta. 14: Child & ya. 15: 1821 E Ninth st, Okmulgee Ok 74447.

TRACY, MARY ELIZABETH. b Joliet Ill 18 Ag 22. 5: Joliet JR Col 40-42 Diploma; Col of St Francis 42-44 (Eng) BA; Rosary Col 55-58 (LS) MA; Ill State U 63-65 (Educ); No Ill U 62-65 (LS). 6: Ger. 7: Tchr Fairmont Grade Sch, Lockport Ill 44-46; Tchr J M Thompson Sch, Joliet Ill 46-52; Tchr Amer Schs, Bremerhaven & Frankfort Ger 52-54; Tchr A O Marshall Sch, Joliet Ill 54-57; Libn Washington Sch, Joliet Ill 57-61; Libn Joliet Twp High Sch, Joliet Ill 61-. 9: ALA; IllLA (Elect Com 65-66); Chicagoland LA. 14: Sch libs. 15: 353 Wilson st, Joliet Ill 60433.

TRACY, WARREN FRANCIS. b Richmond Ind 26 N 14. 4: Georgia Garber. 5: Earlham Col 34-38 GGer) BA; West Res 39-40 BS in LS; Chicago 51-53 (LS) MA, 58 (LS) PhD. 7: Dir Henry Co (Ind) Lib Demonstration 40-41; US Army Quartermaster Corps & Engnrs (1st Lt) 41-46; Asst libn Knox Col 46-47; Asst libn Northwestern State Col 4751; Libn Coe Col 54-62; Libn & Chm of DEPT OF Lib Sci, U So Miss 62-. 8: Consul on Alcorn A M Col Lib 67. 9: ALA; MissLA; SELA. 10: Phi Delta Kappa; Rotary; Hattiesburg Commun Opera Assn; Phi Kappa Phi. 14: Admin, lib educ. 15: Lake Serene Rte 4, Hattiesburg Ms 39401.

TRAHAN, MARIAN L. b Berkeley Cal 22 F. 5: San Francisco City Col 46-48 (Liberal Arts) AA; San Jose Sate Col 49-51 (LS) BA. 7: Oakland Pub Lib, Oakland Cal: Jr libn 50-53, Sr libn 54-60, Supv libn Ya div 60-. 66, Dir Lat Amer Lib Project 55-56, Prin libn circ dept 67-. 9: ALA-YASD (rep to NCTE "Books for You 63-, Bk Sel Chm 59-62, Bd Dirs 62-65, pres 65-66); CalLA YA Libns Round Table (pres 58-59 & 62-63). 13: Yes. 14: Ya serv, circ. 15: Oakland Pub Lib 125 14th st, Oakland Cal 4612.

TRAINOR, JULIETTE ALICE. b Brooklyn NY 28 O 11. 5: NYU 28-31 (Fr) BA; Sorbonne 31-32; Ecole des Professeurs de Francais Diplomee, 32-33; Cours Superieur de Civilisation Francaise Diplomee (summa cum laude); Trenton NJ State Col 53 BLS; NYU 50-53 (Educ). 6: Fr, Sp. 7: Personal shopper & interpreter R H Macy & Co bk dept, NY 33-34; Bedside instr Rutherford Bd of Educ, Rutherford NJ 34-38; Lib asst Rutherford Pub Lib, Rutherford NJ 34-38; Paterson State Col: Asst Prof 38-52, Asst libn 38-50, Assoc Prof 52-, Head Libn 50-. 9: NJLA (past off & chm var coms); NJEA; Col & Univ Libns NJ (past off &chm var coms). 10: Trustee Rutherford Pub Lib, Rutherford nj; Passaic Co Educ A-V Aids Commsn. 13: Yes. 14: Admin. 15: 120 Ridge rd, Rutherford NJ 07070.

TRAMMELL, MARY PAULINE. b Alpharetta Ga 31 Mr 09. 5: Agnes Scott Col 26-30 (Hist) AB; Columbia 30-31 BS in LS; Emory summer 61, 61 Med LA Certif. 7: Catlgr Alderman Lib UVa 32-44; Libn Wesleyan Conservatory, Macon Ga 44-45; Asst libn Agnes Scott Col 45-47; Ref asst Lib UFla 47-49; Ref & catlg Air U Lib Maxwell Air Force Base Ala 49-53, Asst libn ser Mooney Mem Lib UTenn Med Units 53-. 9: MedLA (sec So Reg Group 62-63); ALA; TennLA. 10: Agnes Scott Col Alum Assn. 14: Catlg, ref, ser. 15: Mooney Mem Lib, 625 Dunlap st, Memphis Tn 38104.

TRAPANI, JOHN (GIOVANNI). b Venice Italy 23 Ag 29. 4: Marie Ferro. 5: URome 47-51 (Law) JD; St Johns U 56-59 (Law) LLB; Columbia 61- (LS). 6: Ital, Fr, Sp, Portu. 7: 2nd Lt Infantry Italian Army 51-52; Assoc Bernardini & Ungaro Law Firms, Rome 52-53; Counselor Italian Nat Research Coun (CNR) Rome 52-56; Asst libn St Johns U Law Lib (NY) 57-59; Asst libn Supreme Court Lib, Brooklyn NY 59-62; Asst foreign law libn Los Angeles Co Law Li, Los Angeles 62-65; Deputy city prosecutor, Pasadena Cal 65-68; Deputy pub defender, Los Angeles Co 68; Atty & Law libn Pasadena Legal Aid Soc, Pasadena Cal 68-. 8: For lawconsul 59-; Admitted to practice of law: NY 61, Cal 65. 9: AALL; Internat Assn Law Lib; Amer Bar Assn; For Law Assn of So Cal al; Law Lib Assn So Cal; Law Lib Assn Greater NY; NY State Bar Assn; Cal State Bar Assn; Los Angeles Bar Assn; Amer Soc Int Law; World Peace Through Law Ctr. 10: Sons of Italy; YMCA; Boy Scouts. 13: Yes. 14: Ref, rare bks (legal materials). 15: 404 S Sixth st, Alhambra Cal 91801.

TRAPNELL, FREDERICA HOLMES. b Bluefield WVa 6 Jl 09. 5: Randolph-Macon Womans Col 27-31 (Pol Sci) AB; Columbia 31-32 (LS) BS. 7: Summer asst Central Circ Br NY Pub Lib 33; Clsf & catlg spec collection Englewood (NJ) Pub Lib 33-34; Clsf & catlg & head Leg Gen File Room E I Du Pont de Nemours & Co, Wilmington Del 34-55, Law libn Leg Dept 36-. 9: AALL. 14: Catlg. 15: Legal Dept Lib, E I DuPont de Nemours & Co, Wilmington De 19898.

TRAPPAN, GRACE. b Brooklyn NY 15 D 05. 5: Conn Col 23-27 (Eng) AB; Columbia 31-33 BLS. 7: Asst Bankers Trust Co Lib, NYC 27-28; Clerk Macys NYC 28; Tchr Misses Stiles Sch, Paterson NJ 29-30; Jr & Sr asst George L Pease Mem Lib, Ridgewood NJ 30-36; Portland Pub Lib, Portland Me: Head Circ Dept 36-41; Act libn 41, Libn 41-. 9: ALA (Subsc bks bul com 54-56, mem chm, Me 42-45); MeLA (pres 49-50; Me Lib Bul Com 65-66, Com on Lin Devel in Me 64-66, Rev of Constit Com 59-62); NELA (Coun 51-53, Nomin Com 63-64, Memb Com 67-68, sec 67-68); Me Coun for Title III Interlib Coop of Lib Serv & Devel Act. 10: Portland Col Club; Me Hist Soc; Trustee, Prince Mem Lib, Cumberland; Portland Soc of Nat Hist; Portland Soc of Art. 14: Admin. 15: 199 Vaughan st, Portland Me 04102.

TRAUGH, ANTOINETTE (SPATAFORE). b Viropa WVa 12 Ap 24. 5: Salem Col 47-50 (Eng) BA; WVa U 57-60 MALS. 6: Ital, Sp. 7: Seaman 3rd class WAVES, Arlington Va 44-46; Tchr Logan Co Bd of Educ, Man WVa 50-53; Tchr Harrison Co Bd of Educ, Clarksburg WVa 55-62; Libn Salem Col 62-63; Libn Harrison Co Bd of Educ, Clarksburg WVa 63-. 8: Org Lib Gore Jr High Sch 63-64; Prepared Col Lib Salem Col for accreditation to N Central Assn of Col Libs (received citation) 63. 9: NEA; WVaEA; WVaLA. 14: Catlg. 15: 768 Locust st apt #2, Clarksburg WV 26301.

TRAVER, DOROTHY. b Highmore SD 20 S 09. 5: Pomona Col 27-31 BA; UCal 33 (LS) Certif. 6: Sp. 7: Libn Elsinore Union High Sch, Elsinore Cal 33-36; San Bernardino Co Lib, San Bernardino Cal: High sch libn 36-39, Head sch dept 40-50, Head br Dept 50-57, Co Libn 57-. 9: ALA; CalLA; Pub Lib Execs of So Cal; Cal Co LA. 10: Zonta Club; Bus & Prof Womens Club; Audubon Soc; Sierra Club. 12: "Growing ORANGES" WITH Art Millar (58); Co-auth "History of San Bernardino County Library". 13: Yes. 14: Admin. 15: 3052 Genevieve, San Bernardino Ca 92405.

TRAVILLIAN, J MAURICE. b Murray Ky 23 My 38. 4: Mary Wynn. 5: Bethel Col 56-57; Memphis State U 57-59 (Hist) BS; Peabody 61-62 (LS) MA. 6: Fr. 7: Tchr Fredericktown High Sch, Fredericktown Mo 59-61; Ext libn Daniel Boone Reg Lib, Columbia Mo 62-64; Dir Marshaltown Pub Lib, Marshaltown Iowa 64-69; Asst Dir Iowa State Trav Lib 70-. 8: Consul Iowa State Lib 67-. 9: ALA; Amer Mgt Assn; IowaLA (chm Legis Com 64-). 10: Jr C of C; Rotary Internat. 14: Admin. 15: Marshaltown Pub Lib, Marshaltown Ia 50158.

TRAVILLIAN, MARY (WYNN). b Memphis Tenn 24 Je 38. 4: J Maurice Travillian. 5: Memphis State U 56-59 (Secretarial Sci) BBS; Peabody 61-62 MA in LS. 6: Sp. 7: Libn Fredericktown Pub Lib, Fredericktown Mo 59-61; A-v & program planning libn Daniel Boone Reg Lib, Columbia Mo 62-64; A-v consul Jasper & Marshall Co Instr Materials Center, Marshalltown Iowa 65-66; A-V consul Marshall Co Instr Materials Center & Area 6 Resource Center, Marshalltown Iowa 66-. 9: ALA; A-V Educ Assn Iowa (sec 68-69); NEA-DAVI; Iowa State EA. 10: LWV; Pre-Sch Child Study Assn. 14: Catlg, a-v materials, org & admin instrl media ctrs. 15: 1101 W Main, Marshalltown Iowa 50158.

TRAVIS, MARY EILEEN (CONNOLLY). b New Glasgow NC Can 16 Mr 31. 4: Artur Joseph Travis. 5 St Francis Xavier U 49-52 (Econ) BA; McGill 52-53 LS. 7: Bkmob libn Pictou Co Reg, New Glasgow NS 53, Bkmob & child libn 55; Child libn Saint John Pub Lib, Saint John NB 60; Child libn & asst libn 62-. 9: CanLA; CanAssn Child Libns; APLA (pres 68-69); ALA. 10: Can University Womens Club; Prof Womens Club; Can Univ Press Assn; Dominion Drama Festival Assn; Cath Womens League of Canada; NS Drama League Assn. 13: Yes. 14: Child serv, pub rel. 15: PO Box 302. Rothesay, Kings Co NB Canada.

TREFZ, ROBERT OMAR. b Iowa City Iowa 8 Jl 27. 5: UColo 45-49 (Fr) AB (cum laude); UDenver 49-52 (Eng) MA, 53-54 (LS) MA. 6: Fr, Sp. 7: Ser catlgr UWyo Lib 54-55; Catlgr Denver Pub Lib 55-68; Asst catlg libn Temple Buell Col, Denver 68-. 9: ALA; ColoLA. ; MPLA. 10: Phi Beta Kappa; Colo Mountain Club; AAUP. 14: Catlg. 15: 1664 Ivey st, Denver Co 80220.

TREJO, ARNULFO DUENES. b Durango Mex 15 Ag 22. 4: Annette Marie Foster. 5: UAriz 46-49 (Educ) BA; U de las Americas 50-51 (Span) MA; Kent State U 52-53 (LS) MA; Nat U of Mex 51-52, 53-54, 58-59 (Span) PhD. 6: Sp, Fr. 7: T/4 Radioman US Army, SPacific 42-45; Ref libn U de las Americas (Mex City) 53-54; Asst libn Nat mex 54-55; Libn ref dept UCLA 55-59; Asst col libn Cal State Col (Long Beach) 59-65; Head Libn Stanford Us Escuela de Administraction de Negocios para Graduados Lima Peru 63-65; Asst Prof Sch of Lib Serv UCLA 65-66, Assoc Prof Lib Sci & bibliogr Latin Amer Collections UAriz 66-68. 8: ALA-USAID Consul, Caracas Venezuela 68-. 9: ALA; CalLA; AALS; ArizLA. 10: AAUP; Inst de Literatura Iberoamericana; Phi Delta Kappa; Phi Kappa Phi; Sigma Delta Pi; Beta Kappa Phi. 12: Comp "Bibliografia Comentada Sobre Administracion de Neocios y Disciplinas Conexas Mexico D F" (64, 2nd ed 67); "Diccionario Etimologico del Lexico de la Delincuencia" Mexico (68); Co-auth "The Hand of Zamorano; a Manuscript" (56). 13: Yes. 14: Admin, ref, tchg. 15: 624 N 7th ave, Tucson Az 85705.

TREKELL, CHARLENE (CADENHEAD). b Shamrock Tex 19 Sp 39. 4: Charles Leon Trekell. 5: W Tex State U 57-60 (Bus Educ) BBA, 61-62 Elem Tchg Certif; UIowa 62, 64-65 (LS) MA. 7: Tchr Canyon High Sch, Canyon Tex 62-64; Libn Iowa City High Sch 65-67; Period libn W Tex State U 67-. 9: ALA. 10: Pi Lambda Theta. 14: Period, ref. 15: Box 252 W Tex Station, Canyon Tx 79015.

TRELEASE, MARCIA (EWING). b Dallas Tex 23 S 41. 4: Allen William Trelease. 5: UColo 59-64 (Hist) BA; UNC 68-69 MSLS. 6: Sp. 7: Tchr Denver Pub Sch 64-66; Collegiate & local hist libn Wells Col 67; Ref asst Greensboro (NC(Pub Lib 67; Acquis asst UNC (Greensboro) 67-68, Tech processing libn 69-. 10: Phi Beta Kappa; Phi Alpha Theta; Kappa Delta Pi; Pi Lambda Theta. 14: Mss & archives, acquis. 15: 4861 Brompton dr, Greensboro NC 27407.

TRENERY, FRANK E. b Kewanee Ill 8 F 21. 4: Mary Ellen Hulshof Trenery. 5: Bradley U (US Hist); UNeb (Omaha) 64 (Gneral Educ) BGE; Rosary Col 65 msls. 6: Fr. 7: US Army, Africa & Europe 41-45; US Admin Tech Nat Guard 48-51; CWO II US Army, Japan & Korea 52-55; Lib trainee Chicago Pub Lib 64; Lib tech UIll (Chicago) 65; Docs libn UOmaha 66; Doc libn NEast Ill State Col 67-69; Lecturer Grad Sch of

Educ DePaul U 68-69; Asst to libn Divine Word Sem, Dubuque Iowa 69-; Docs libn Loras Col 69-. 8: Lect Lib Sci: Dept of Lib Sci UOmaha summer sch; State Lib River Bend System, one-month sem. 9: CathLA; IllLA. 10: AAUP; Phi Alpha Theta. 13: Yes. 14: Docs, tchg ref wk, or hist of libs, etc. 15: 2053 Key Way apt 4, Dubuque Ia 52001.

TRENHOLME, MARGERY W. b Columbia Mo 20 Ap 13. 5: McGill 31-35 (Classics) BA, 36 1st class high sch tchg diploma, 45-46 BLS. 6: Fr. 7: Tchg & bus experience 36-45; Catlgr Harvard Law Lib 46-47; Libn McGill Sch Grad Nurses 47-50; Chief libn Fraser-Hickson Lib, Montreal 50-. 9: CanLA; ALA; QueLA (past mem Exec Bd). 10: Univ Women's Club of Montreal; Can Fed of Univ Women. 14: Catlg, ref. 15: 4855 Kensington ave, Montreal 253 Que Can.

TRENT, BONITA A. b Montreal Que Can 19 Je 44. 5: Bishop's 61-65 (Eng) BA; McGill 65-67 MLS. 6: Fr. 7: Catlgr Royal Victoria Hosp, Montreal 66-67; Asst libn Montreal child Hosp 67-68; Libn McGill U Dental Lib 68-. 9: SLA; MedLA. 10: McGill Univ Lib staff Assn. 15: 1973 St Germain st, St Laurent Quebec Can.

TRENT, ROBERT MAXWELL. b Muncie Ind 4 Jl 05. 4: Sarah St John. 5: IndU 24-28 (Eng) AB; Columbia 30-31 BS in LS, 38 MS in LS. 6: Fr. 7: Libn NY Herald Tribune, NYC 31-32; Head order dept City Col (NY) 32-45; Chief of tech processes LSU 45-49; Dir of Libs So Methodist U 49-. 9: TexLA; SWLA. 10: AAUP. 15: So Methodist Univ, Dallas Tx 75222.

TRESCOTT, ELEANOR C. b Rochester NY 1 Jl 20. 4: Stanley W Trescott. 5: Houghton Col 38-42 (Soc Sci, Educ) AB; SUNY(Geneseo) summers 60-64 MLS. 7: Tchr Walworth High Sch, Walworth 42-44; Libn Avon Elem Sch, Avon Park Fla 62-64; Libn E O Douglas Sch, Sebring Fla 66-. 14: Ref, jr col lib, a-v materials. 15: Rte 1 Box 1122, Avon Park Fl 33825.

TRESSIDER, MARY (ESTHER FRENZEL). b Sentinel Okla 14 Je 19. 5: UOkla 36-40 (Eng) BA, 48 (LS) BA; UMich 50-51 AMLS; LSU 66-67 (LS). 6: Fr. 7: Libn: Carnegie Lib, Cordell okla 40-42, Garfield Co Lib, Enid Okla 43-44, Thos Branigan Mem Lib, Las Cruces NM 46-50; Dir Ingham Co Lib, Mason Mich 51-54; Dir Carnegie Lib, Grand Island Neb 54-59; Asst libn Northeastern State Col Lib (Tahlequah Okla) 60-. 9: ALA; NEA; OklaEA; OklaLA. 10: AAUW; Delta Kappa Gamma. 14: Acquis, lib sci tchg. 15: Northeastern State Col Lib, Tahlequah Ok 74464.

TRESSLER, BESSIE GWYNETH. b Emporia Kan 6 Ap 03. 5: Col of Emporia 21-24, 25-26 (Music) AB; ILL summer 28, 28 & 30 BS in LS. 7: Head of circ dept Col of Wooster 27-30; Catlgr & asst libn Neb State Tchrs Col (Chadron) 30-36; Catlgr & supv Train Sch Lib Ariz State U 36-38; Ser catlgr UIowa 38-41, Asst supt catlg dept 41-44; Asst order libn Ore State U 46-52; Order libn Ore State System of Higher Educ, Corvallis Ore 52-. 67; Hd acquis dept Ore State U Lib (Corvallis) 67-69. 9: ALA; PNLA; OreLA. 10: Beta Phi Mu. 15: 2612 Tyler st, Corvallis Ore 97330.

TRESTER, DELMER JOHN. b Winona Minn 23 Jl 21. 5: Wabash Col 39-43 (Hist) AB; Ohio state U 46-47 (Hist) MA, 47-50 (Hist) PhD. 7: Ctr histn Spec Weapons Lab, Albuquerque 55-58, Chief tech info div 58-63; Assoc program dir Off of Sci Info Serv NSF, Wash DC 63-65; Chief ref sect Nat Referral Ctr, Wash DC 65-68; Chief operations ERIC Off of Educ, Wash DC 68-. 13: Yes. 14: Sci, tech and educl info stor & ret. 15: 8350 Donnell pl A1, Forestville Md 20028.

TRESTER, DOROTHY (WEBB). b Shreveport La 1 p 23. 5: LSU 39-43 (Eng, Hist) BS, 62-63 (LS) MS. 7: Ed & histn Air Materiel Command, Dayton Ohio 51-53; Tech writer, Becker & Becker Corp, Dayton Ohio 54; Libn Albuquerque High Sch, Albuuerque Albuquerque 63-67; Ser libn Zimmerman Lib UNM 67-. 9: NMLA (Publ Chm 63-64; YP & Child Sect chm 67). 10: Beta Phi Mu; Greater Albuquerque LA; Univ Libs Staff Assn. 13: Yes. 14: Ref bks sel, acquis. 15: 1710 Princeton NE, Albuquerque NM 87106.

TREUDE, J MAI. b Tartu Estonia 2 Jl 35. 4: Arvi Treude. 5: UMinn 53-57 (Sociol) BA, 61-63 (LS) MS. 6: Estonian, Ger, Fr. 7: Hd catlgr Macalester Col 63-66; Map libn wilson Lib UMinn (Minneapolis) 66-. 9: ALA; MinnLA. 14: Maps. 15: 3304 NE 31st ave, Minneapolis Mn 55418.

TREUTER, LIRL. b New Orleans 4 O 22. 5: Tex Wesleyan Col 48 (Art) BA; UTex summer 56 (LS); Tex Christian U 64 (Art); LSU 64 MS in LS. 6: Fr. 7: Sec & greeting card designer stationery Dept Stafford-Lowden Co, Ft Worth Tex 41-43; Sec to Adjutant Gen Far East Air Forces, Leyte & Manila PI 44-45; Dir art dept Our Lady of Victory Acad & Col, Ft Worth Tex 46-48; Staff artist & 1st asst art dept Ft Worth Pub Lib, Ft Worth Tex 49-57; Head art & music dept, Ft Worth Pub Lib, Ft Worth Tex 58-65, Hd arts & recreations dept 66-. 9: SWLA; TexLA (Mem Com 65-66, sec Fine Arts Round Table 65-66, v-chm 66-67, chm 67-68). 10; phi kappa Phi; Beta Phi Mu; Amer Fed of Arts; Tex Fine Arts Assn; La Poetry Soc; Tex Poetry So; Ft Worth Art Center; Ft Worth Poetry Soc; PUO Lib Staff Assn; Recorder Quartet. 11: Tex Wesleyan Poetry Cup 48. 12: Poetry publ in anthologies. 14: Ref & research, spec collections. 15: 2212 Fifth ave, Fort Worth Tex 76110.

TREWORGY, MILDRED L. b Roslyn NY 5 Ja 11. 5: NYU 45 (Eng, Hist) BA; Pratt 39 BLS. 6: Fr. 7: Lib asst Brooklyn Pub Lib 34-39; Art ref dept Pratt Inst 40-46; Head circ dept Penn State U Lib 46-47; Head catlgr Hofstra Col 48-53; Spec reading room libn Penn State U 54-57; Head readers serv Vassar 58-62; Libn State Lib Serv Penn State U 62-. 9: ALA; PennLA. 10: AAUW; AAUP. 12: "Negroes in the United States; a Bibliography" (67). 14: Ref, publns, interlib loan. 15: Penn State Univ Lib, University Park Penn 16802.

TREYZ, JOSEPH H(ENRY). b Binghamton NY 23 N 26. 5: Oberlin Col 44-50 BA; Columbia 50-52 (LS) MS. 6: Lat, Ger. 7: T/Sgt in chg of Dept of Pub Health & Sanitation, US Army, Seoul Korea 46-47; Circ asst NY Acad of Med, NY 50-51; Catlgr Columbia U Lib 51-53; Catlgr Stevens Inst of Tech 53-54; Admin asst Yale U Lib 55, Asst head catlg dept 55-61; Head New Campuses Lib Program, UCal (San Diego) 61-65; Asst dir UMich Lib 65-. 8: Univ rep Consumer Reaction Survey Team for Catlg-in-Source 59; Consul Lib Tech Proj Catlg Card Reprod Study 61; Survey of Tech Serv Fordham Univ Libs 67, 69. 9: ALA-RTSD (chm Com on Reg Groups 66-67, chm Tech Serv Dirs of Large Research Libs 67-68, Catlg & Clsf Sect Exec Com 63-64; chm Reproduction of Lib Materials Sect 68-69);-ACRL ("Choice"; chm Com on Supps to "Books for Col Libs" 67-69, Chm Ed Bd 68-69); BSA; ASIS; NY Tech Serv Libns (pres 59-60); CalLA (Tech Processes RT; sec 63-64, v-pres 64-65; Col & Univ Res Lib Sect 63-64); MichLA (Tech Serv Sect chm 68-69). 10: Univ Club; YMCA; Clements LA; Ann Arbor Lib Club; Signature Club. 12: Co-ed "Books for College Libraries" (67). 13: Yes. 14: Tech serv, admin, automation. 15: Univ of Mich Lib, Ann Arbor Mi 48104.

TREZZA, ALPHONSE FIORE. b Phila 27 D 20. 4: Mildred Di Pietro. 5: UPenn 48 BS; Drexel 49 Lib Certif; UPenn 50 MS. 7: Page Newspaper Dept Free Lib of Phila 40-41; Navigator (1st Lt) USAAF 42-45; AGE Bkstacks & Blind Dept Free Lib of Phila 45-48, Lib asst Govt Documents 48-49; Asst ref libn & catlgr Villanova U 49-50; Lecturer Grad Sch of Lib Sci Drexel Inst of Tech 51-60; Instr Dept of Lib Sci Villanova 56-60; Head circ dept UPenn Lib 50-56; Exec sec Catholic LA & Ed "Catholic Library World" Villanova Penn 56-60; Assoc exec dir ALA & exec sec ALA-LAD, Chicago 60-67; Assoc exec dir for admin serv ALA 67-70; Ill State Librarian, 70-. 8: Nat chm Cath Bk Week 54-56; Gen chm Drexel Lib Sch Fund Raising 59-61; Lay lib consul Joliet Diocesan Sch Bd 65; Lib bldg consul; Pres Joliet Diocesan Bd of Educ 66-68. 9: CathLA (chm Phila Area Unit 50-52); ALA-ACRL (pres Phila Chap 53-5); CNLA (chm 59-61, trustee 61-65); IllLA (chm Ill Lib Devel 63-. 63-66). 10: Kappa Phi Kappa; AAUP; Drexel Lib Sch Alumni Assn. 11: Outstanding Alumnus Award 63 Drexel Grad Sch Lib Sci; Spec Lib Citation IllLA 65. 12: Ed "Catholic Library World" (56-61); "Proceedings Ann Conf CathLA" (57-60); CathLA "Membership Directory and Handbook" (57-61); Co-auth "Parish Library Manual" (56); Co-ed "Library Furniture and Equipment" ALA-LAD (62); Co-ed "Procurement of Library Furnishings" ALA-LAD (66). 13: Yes. 14: Admin, lib bldgs, data proc. 15: Ill State Lib, Springfield Il.

TRIBIT, DONALD KING. b Philadelphia Penn 19 O 34. 4: Ida Katherine Clark. 5: Shippensburg State Col 52-55 (Soc Studies) BS; Millersville State Col 61; Peabody Col 63-65 MLS, 68; Temple U 64-67; West State Col 66; Penn State U 68-69. 7: Tchr NE High Sch, North East Md 55-57; Off in charge Info & Educ Off USN, Guam & Marianas Is 58-60; Asst prof (period libn) Millersville State Col 61-. 8: Chm Steering Com, Area Col Lib Coop Proj of Central Penn. 9: ALA; PennLA; LancasterCoLA. 10: Beta Phi Mu; AAUP; Alpha Beta Alpha; Millersville State Col Fac Assn. 14: Period. 15: RD 1, Conestoga Pa 17516.

TRIBIT, KATHERINE (IDA). b Johnson City Tenn 7 D 40. 4: Donald K Tribit. 5: Tenn State Col 38-61 (Elem Educ) BS;

Peabody Col 62-63, 68 (LS) MA; Presbyterian Sch of Christian Educ 64; Temple U 66; West State Col 66; Penn State U 68. 7: Libn Lynn Ave elem Sch, Elizabethton Tenn 61-62; Libn Fall Br Sch, Fall Branch Tenn 62-63; Lib staff mem Union Theol Sem (Richmond Va) 64; Asst prof (classifier) Millersville State Col 64-. 9: ALA; PennLA; LancasterCo (Penn) LA. 10: AAUP; Millersville State Col Faculty Assn. 14: Catlg. 15: Rte 1, Conestoga Pa 17516.

TRICKETT, ANNE (ANNIE CORNELIA SANDIFER). b Leesville La 25 F 20. 4: Ed B Trickett Sr. 5: Centenary Col 36-38 (Home Econ); La Polytech Inst 65-67 (LS) BA; LSU 68-69 (LS). 6: Sp. 7: Bkkeeper to sec-treasurer Trickett's Furniture, Shreveport La 38-65; Ref asst Centenary Col Lib, Shreveport La 67-. 9: ALA; Assn for Child with Learning Disabilities; LaLA; La Assn for Child with Learning Disabilities. 10: Alpha Sigma Pi; Phi Kappa Phi; Alpha Beta Alpha; Caddo-Bossier Lib Club; Woman's Department Club. 12: Comp "Children With Learning Disabilities: a Bibliography" (66). 14: Archives, ref, tech proc. 15: PO Box 6017, Shreveport La 71106.

TRICKEY, KATHERINE WOODWORTH. b Bangor Me 15 F 1. 5: UMe 28-32 (Bus Admin) AB, 36 & 46 (Educ) MA; Columbia summer 49; Simmons 50-53 (LS) MS. 7: Tchr Brewer High Sch, Brewer Me 37-42; Filing supv Sub-DEPOT Dow Airfield, Bangor Me 42-43; S/Sgt Womens Army Corps, Camp Wheeler Ga 44-45; Libn UMe (Brunswick) 46-49; High sch libn Swampscott Schs, Swampscott Mass 49-, High Sch libn & sch lib supv 58-67, Dir Instr Materials Serv & Dir ESEA Title III Project 8: Summer instr sch lib program, Boston U 60-65; Asst dir NDEA Summer Inst for Sch Libns Boston U 65, 66, 69; Instr Sch Lib Program Boston U 60-. 9: ALA; NEA-DAVI; NESchLA (pres 56-58, chm Jt Lib Com NE Sch Devel Coun & NESchLA 54-); NELA; MassSchLA. 10: Delta Kappa Gamma; Phi Beta Kappa; Phi Kappa Phi. 12: Ed "What Does a School Librarian Do (61); "Goals for School Libraries (61). 14: Sch lib supv, lib educ for sch libns, sch media ctrs. 15: 1 Devens rd, Swampscott Mass 01907.

TRIENENS, ROGER J. b Chicago 16 Je 26. 5: Northwestern 44-51 (Eng Lit) PhD; UMich 52-53 MA in LS. 7: Asst lit dept Free Lib of Phila 53-57; Rare bk catlgr NLM, Cleveland 57-62; Ref lib & supv of reading room bk div LC 62-66, Rare bks catlgr descr catlg div 66-. 9: ALA; BSA. 10: Phi Beta Kappa. 13: Yes. 14: Rare bks. 15: 128 C st apt 65, NE Wash DC 20002.

TRIGGS, PHYLLIS McCOY. 4: William D Triggs. 5: Pensacola Jr Col 64-65; LSU 65-68 (Eng) BA, 68-69 MLS. 6: Fr. 7: Trainee LSU Lib (Baton Rouge) 68-69; Ref libn E Baton Rouge Parish Lib, Baton Rouge La 69-. 14: Ref. 15: Box 16122 LSU, Baton Rouge La 70803.

TRILLICH, MARY (HUDDLE). b Madison Wis 7 S 15. 4: BERTRAM Laurence Trillich. 5: Carleton Col 33-34; Northwestern 34-37 (Art Hist) BS; Columbia 41-42 BS in LS. 6: Sp, Fr. 7: Asst Winnetka Pub Lib, Winnetka Ill 34-39; Circ asst Ryerson Lib Chicago Art Inst 41-42; Recreation wker Amer Red Cross, Natal Brazil 42-43; Ast Winnetka Pub Lib, Winnetka Ill 43-46; Libn I catlgr Watson-Lib U Kan 61-, Libn II catlgr 69-. 8: Catlgr Kennedy Collection Univ of Costa Rica; San Jose Costa Rica, sponsored by UKansas/U Costa Rica 66. 9: KanLA. 10: Phi Beta Kappa; AAUP. 14: Catlg. 15: 621 E 15th st, Lawrence Ks 66044.

TRIMBLE, CAROL URELSA. b Westhope ND 3 Je 09. 5: Wash State Col 28-32 (Educ) BA; UDenver summers 39-41 BS in LS; Rutgers 54-55; West Res 53; U Wash 51. 7: Lib Jr-Sr High Sch, Toppenish Wash 33-43; Army Libn Walla Walla Army Air Base, Walla Walla Wash 43-44; Libn Sr High Sch, Yakima Wash 44-45; Co Libn Yakima Co Lib, Yakima Wash 45-1; Reg libn Yakima Reg Lib, Yakima Wash 51-53; Visiting Instr Sch of Libnship UDenver summer 54; Eng tchr Toppenish High Sch, Toppenish 54-55; Co Libn Douglas Co Lib, Roseburg Ore 55-. 9: ALA (sec Lib Ext Div 52-53); WashLA (Exec Bd 46-47); OreLA (pres 59-60); PNLA (chm Pub Libs Div 62-64). 10: AAUW; Douglas Co Inter-Agency Coun; Mental Health Assn of Douglas Co. 13: Yes. 14: Admin. 15: 1387 SE Lane ave, Roseburg Or 97470.

TRIMBLE, ELEANOR (CRARY). b Brooklyn NY 21 Jl 09. 4: Glen Walker Trimble. 5: Mt Holyoke 26-30 (Eng) AB; Columbia summer 30 (Ger); UFlorence Italy) summer 31 (Ital); Tufts 30-32 (Eng Lit, Drama) MA; San Francisco Col 38-39 (Hygiene, Psych); Boston U Sch of Educ 55-56; Rutgers 58-61 MLS. 6: Fr, Ital. 7: Tchr Fellow Tufts U 30-32; Instr Eng dept Wheaton Col (Mass) 32-34; Soc case wker SRA Infant Shelter & Co Welfare, San Francisco 37-42; Area correspondent & feature writer "Old COLONY Memorial, Plymouth Mass 52-53; Tchr Marshfield Schs Mass 53-55, Elem libn 55-56; Aide Westwood Pub Lib, Westwood NJ 57; Elem sch libn Tenafly schs, Tenafly NJ 57-. 8: Chm BergenCom for Lib Serv Educ 61-; Instr in Lib Minro Prog, Paterson State 64-. 64. 9: ALA (& several divs); NEA; NJSchLA; NJEA; Bergen Co EA. 10: Fair Housing Com of Tenafly; Delta Kappa Gamma; Bergen Co SchLA; Tenafly TA. 13: Yes. 14: Tchg child use libs. 15: 32 Hillside ave, Tenafly NJ 07670.

TRIMBLE, LEE S JR. b Griffin Ga 14 Mr 23. 4: Mary M Cobb. 5: UFla 41-43; Duke 43-44; UGa (Journalism, Sp) ABJ; Tulane (Sp, Eng); Emory 51-52 MLibnship. 6: Sp. 7: USMC 43-46; Br libn Jacksonville Lib Syst, Jacksonville Fla 52-54; Reg dir BHM Reg Lib, Washington NC 54-59; Reg dir Dalton Reg Lib, Dalton Ga 59-. 9: CalLA (past treas). 14: Admin. 15: Box 1567, Dalton Ga 30720.

TRIMBLE, MARY MARGARET. b Wash DC 12 N 17. 5: Okla Col for Women 35-39 (Fr) BA; LIU 36-38; George Washington U 43-47 Sp-Amer Lit) MA; Columbia 53-54 MS in LS. 6: Fr, Sp. 7: Libn (catlg) US Dept of Agric, Wash DC 54-58; Libn Med Info & Intelligence Agcy 58-63; Libn (catlg supv) Defense Intelligence Agcy, Arlington Va 63-68, Libn 69-. 9: SLA; DCLA. 14: Catlg, info sci. 15: 423 N Park dr, Arlington Va 22203.

TRIMBY, MADELINE JEAN. b Ann Arbor Mich 15 Ag 43. 5: UMich 61-65 (Eng) BA; Rutgers 65-67 MLS. 7: Storyteller & child room asst Lansing Pib Lib, Lansing Mich summer 66; Ref asst Rutgers U Lib (New Brunswick) 66-67; Asst prof Ferris State Col 67-. 8: Panel member 1st general session of Michigan Library Assoc annual convention Grand Rapids mich Oct 30, 31, Nov 1, 1968; Panel member Council on Library Technology winter meeting, Detroit Michigan Dec 12-14, 1968. 9: ALA; Coun Lib Technology; MichLA; Mich Occup EA. 10: AAUP; Beta Phi Mu. 14: Ref, lib sci educ. 15: 313 Division, Big Rapids Mi 49307.

TRIMINGHAM, ROBERT. b San Francisco 4 N 23. 4: Joyce D Harris. 5: UCal (Berkeley) 41-43, 46-48 (Internat Rel) BA; Ind U 43 (Military ASTP, Turkish Lang); UCal (Berkeley) 50-51 BLS, 52-54 (Internat Rel) MA. 6: Ger. 7: Master Sgt US Army (Europe) Mil Intelligence Serv 44-46; Soc sci ref libn UCal Lib (Berkeley) 51-54; Pub affairs trainee US Info Serv, Teheran Iran 55-56; Asst order libn Sacramento State Col Lib 56-59; Order libn 59-. 9: CalLA (past mem Fin Com). 10: Phi Beta Kappa. 14: Acquis, sers. 15: 4927 Eye Parkway, Sacramento Cal 95823.

TRIMMINGHAM, HARRIET BERNARDINE (LAWSON). b Frakfort Ky 3 D 06. 4: Rupert Stanley Trimmingham. 5: UChicago 23-27 (Lat, Gk) AB; Hampton Inst 29-30 (LS) BS; UChicago summer 32 (LS); UCal 38 (LS). 6: Fr, Ger, Sp, Ital, Lat, Russian. 7: Libn NC Agric & Tech Col 3031; Libn SC State Col 31-32; Catlg libn Atlanta U 33-38; Catlg libn Lincoln U (Mo) 40-43; Libn Serv Club No. 1 Ft HUACHUCA Ariz 43; Catlgr Roosevelt U 47-50; Asst chief catlgr John Crerar Lib, Chicago 50-56; Catlg libn UMich Libs 56-. 9: ALA; MichLA. 13: Yes. 14: Catlg, ser. 15: 621 W Summit st, Ann Arbor Mich 48103.

TRINDELL, DANICE JEAN (LIVENSPIRE). b Pennsylvania 19 Je 36. 4: Roger Thomas Trindell. 5: Montclair State Col 54-58 (Hist) BA; LSU 60-62 MSLS. 7: Browsing room libn LSU (Baton Rouge) 62; Circ & ref Millersville State Col 63-64; Acquis & ref Plattsburgh State Col 65-66; Ref libn E Lansing Pub Lib, E Lansing Mich 67-. 8: Lib/21 NY World's Fair 65. 9: ALA; MichLA. 10: AAUW. 14: Ref serv. 15: 547 Charles st, East Lansing Mi 48823.

TRINKNER, CHARLES L. b Green Bay Wis 25 My 20. 4: Marian R Trinkner. 5: Purdue U 43; UFla 50 BAE, 51 (Admin) MEd, 52 APG (Rank I); LSU 54 MSLS; U Fla 56 EdS. 6: Sp. 7: Instr Platoon Leader Co Commander US Marine Corps 40-46; Instr Mil Train Unit Infantry US Marine Corps Res 46-55; Resarch asst research bur Col of Educ UFla 49-50; Libn a-v spec tchr State of Fla Pub Sch System 49-55; Instr Dept of Lib Sci Educ Bibliogr N Tex State U 55-56; Ref & assoc libn Arlington State Col 56-57; Lib Dir Asst Prof of Lib Sci Ark State Col 57-58; Dir of Lib Serv Lib Sci Instr Ficus Lib Admin Pensacola Jr Col 58-68; Libn & Ed publns Gull Point Press 68-. 8: Visiting Prof Lib Sci, Tex Womans U summer 55; Fla Schs Evaluative Studies 59-; Consul Res Libn Appalachian State Tchrs Col summer 60; Pensacola Jr Col Self-Study & Evaluation 61 & 62; Surveys of 6 Southern Col Libs 61-65; Visiting Prof Dept of Libnship UOre summer 63; Visiting lecturer lib sci UIll summer 64; Dir Instr materials wkshop, Utah State U summer 64; Dir lib wkshop (Sch-Pub

Libns) UMont summer 65. 9: NEA (Life mem); -Assn Higher Educ; ALA-ACRL; BSA; FlaEA (Life mem); SELA; FlaLA (Jr Col Sect 64-65); FlaSchLA; SWLA; LaState LA. 10: Amer Assn State & Loc Hist; AAUP; Pensacola Hist Soc; Fla Hist Soc; AHA; SHA; Lions Club; West Fla Reg Lib Bd; Escambia Co Lib Bd; Kappa Delta Pi; Psi Chi; Phi Delta Kappa; Alpha Phi Omega; Beta Phi Mu; Beta Alpha Beta;Alpha Kappa Delta; Gamma Iota Xi. 11: Commsn on Hon Ky Colonel, Staff of the Governor of Ky 64. 12: Ed "Better Libraries Make Better Schools (62); "Library Services for Junior Colleges (64); "Book Selection for Better Book Collections (70); "Trends in Junior College Libraries (65); "Teaching for Better Use of Libraries" (70); Comp: "Basic Books for Junior College Librarie: 20,000 Vital Titles (63); "Florida Lives, The Sunshine State Whos Who (66). 13: Yes. 14: Lib educ, ref, jr col libs, sch libs, publns. 15: 2026 Peacock dr, Pensacola Fl 32504.

TRIPICCHIO, ANGELO. b NYC 12 Jl 37. 4: Emily Ann Guido. 5: Brooklyn Col 55-59 (Eng) BA; Columbia 62 (LS); Queens Col 62-66 MLS; Pratt Inst 68 (LS). 6: Ital, Fr. 7: Personnel Sp/4 US Army A G Corps 59-61; Lib clk Cornell U Med Col Lib, NYC 61; Lib trainee NYC Pub Lib 61-62; Libn Island Trees Mem Sch, Long Is NY 62-63; Libn Polytech Prep Country Day Sch, Brooklyn NY 64-67; Libn (instr) Kingsborough Commun Col 67-. 9: ALA; LACUNY. 10: AAUP. 14: Readers serv, ref, automation. 15: 1436 83rd st, Brooklyn NY 11228.

TRIPLEHORN, JULIA (HARDESTY). b Clarksburg W Va 5 D 35. 4: Don M Triplehorn. 5: Ohio Wesleyan 53-57 (Geog) BA; UIll 58-59 MSLS. 7: Asst UIll ref desk (Urbana) 60; Ref libn Wooster Pub Lib, Wooster Ohio 60-61; Asst libn Sinclair Research, Tulsa Okla 62-64; Med libn St Francis Hosp, Tulsa Okla 64-65; Ref libn Oral Roberts U 66-. 9: SLA; OklaLA. 10: Tulsa Audubon Soc; AAUW. 14: Ref. 15: 5215 S Oswego, Tulsa Ok 74135.

TRIPPLETT, M GLENN. b Charlotte NC 6 Mr 39. 5: Fla StateU 58-62 (Govt) BA, 63-65 (Libnship) MS. 7: Lib trainee Yonkers Pub Lib, Yonkers NY 62-63; Grad asst Fla StateU, Tallahasse Fla 63-65; Lib asst Miami-Dade Jr Col (S) 65-66, Acquis libn 66-68, Dir central tech proc 68-. 9: NMA; FlaLA (Exhibits co-chm); DadeCoLA; SELA. 14: Acquis, rare bks, ref, automation, microforms. 15: Central Tech Processing 11380 NW 27th ave, Miami Fl 33167.

TROITSKY, NIKOLAI. b Russia 20 Ap 03. 4: Vera Troitsky. 5: Institute of Tech 22-26 (Engnr); Inst of Arch (Moscow) 30-32 (Arch); Sch of Lib Serv (NY) 58-59 (LS) MS. 6: Russan, Ger. 7: Libn Russian Pub Lib, Munich Germany 49-50; Dir & Libn Inst for the Study of the USSR, Munich Germany 51-6; Documents libn Syracuse U 59-62; Slavic bibliog Cornell U 62-68, Adv in bk sel 69-. 8: Adv Harvard Proj on the Soviet Social System, Munich. 12: Asst Ed "Thirteen Who Fled; "The Concentration Camps of the USSR (in Russian) Munich (55); "Soviet Munich" Munih (56); Ed "Literarurnyi Svremennik; (pen-name: Boris Iakovlev); Bibliog of work Boris Pasternak & Literature About Him printed in Russian (69). 14: Slavic collections. 15: 311 Roat st, Ithaca NY 14850.

TROITSKY, VERA. b Russia 13 Ja 24. 5: SyracuseU 59-63 BA, 63-64 (LS) MS. 6: Russian, Ukrainian, Ger, Polish, Ch Slovak. 7: Catlgr Inst for the Study of the USSR, Munich Germany 52-56; Sr lib asst ColumbiaU Lib 57-59; Asst lib (Slavic catlgr) CornellU 63-. 14: Slavic collections. 15: 311 Roat st, Ithaca NY 14150.

TROJE, PATRICE (HARPER). b St Paul Minn 13 Ap 47. 5: Col of St Catherine 65-69 (LS, Hist) BA. 6: Fr. 7: Libn I St Paul Pub Lib 69-. 9: ALA; MinnLA. 13: Yes. 14: Commun & pub rel, inner city serv. 15: 1184 Mackubin apt 107, St Paul Mn 55117.

TROKE, MARGARET KLAUSNER. b Omaha 21 N 11. 4: Frank J Troke. 5: UDenver 39 (LS) AB. 7: Sacramento City Free Lib, Sacramento Cal: Lib asst 29-35, Ref asst 35-37, Br libn 37-41, Supv ref libn 41-44, Asst city libn 43-44; Libn Napa Co Lib, Napa Cal 44-46; Dir of Lib Serv Stockton-San Joaquin Co Pub Lib, Stockton Cal 46-; Admin 49-99 Coop Lib Syst 67-. 8: Dir 5th Ann Inst Wkshop on Planning Pub Lib Bldgs, Sacramento 57; Mem Nat Com on Rev of Pub Lib Stats, Dept of Health, Educ & Welfare 60; Dir 3 Lib Serv Act Projs 57-59 & 65; Consul on 7 pub lib bldgs n Cal 58-65; Adv Com Cal State-wide Pub Lib Serv Survey Sacramento 64; Cal PubLib Devel Bd 63-67; UCal Coun for Sch Libnship 55-56; Lib Adv Com to Co Supv of Cal 68, 69. 9: ALA (Mem Com to develop revis costs of Lib Serv 59; Coun 60; Jt ALA-CathLA Com 65-66; pres Pub Lib Admin Div 59-60; mem Com Reg 2 57-58);-LAD (pres 59-60, Com on Costs of Pub Lib Serv 59); -LAD (Com on Org 65); CalLA (pres 53; pres Pub Lib Sect 59, v-chm Liaison Com for Cal Pub Lib Commsn). 10: Commun Youth & Welfare Coun Stockton; United Crusade; Cath Soc Serv; Calaveras Grove Assn; AAUW; BUS & Prof Women; LWV; Sierra Club of Cal; Amer Soc of Pub Admin. 11: Citizen of the Month Civitan Club Stockton 57; Woman of the Year 63, Stockton Bus & Prof Womens Club. 12: "Routine Library Operations in Punched CARD" (51). 13: Yes. 14: Admin, ref. 15: 605 N El Dorado st, Stockton Cal 95202.

TROMBETTA, CHRISTINE. b Pittsburgh Penn 7 D 41. 5: UPittsburgh 59-63 (Pol Sci) BA, 64-65 MLS. 6: Sp. 7: Lib asst UPittsburgh 64; Libn Robert Morris Jr Col 65-. 8: Catlg consul, Cath Info Ctr Pittsburgh 67-68. 9: ALA; Tri-StateACRL. 10: UPittsburgh Grad Sch Lib & Info Scis Alum. 14: Catlg, ref, acquis. 15: 104 High st, McMurray Pa 15317.

TROST, KEITH R Sr. b Concordia Kan 20 F #). 4: Sharon Joan Eyres. 5: Westmar Col 49-51, summers 54-56 (Hist) BA; Kan State Tchrs Col 60-61 (LS) (MLS). 7: Rural tchr Prairie Gem, Jamestown Kan 51-53; Tchr Elem Sch, Mahaska Kan 53-54, Prin 54-56; Co Supt Cloud Co, Concordia Kan 56-58; Elem tchr Army, Germany 58-59, Tchr-prin 59-61; Curriculum lin Libn (Grad Fellowship); State Tchrs Col (Emporia) Kan 61-62; Pub serv libn Kan State Col (Pittsburg) 62-67; Consul Kan Lib Syst 67-68; Dir of Lib Serv Barton Co Commun Jr Col 68-. 9: KanLA; ALA; MPLA (rep from Acad Libs of Kan); Kan Jr Col Libs, chm Ks Lib Jr Col Div. 10: Lions Club; Barton Co Commun Jr Col Admin Coun. 14: Pub serv, admin. 15: 2806 24th, Great Bend Ks 67530.

TROST, THEODORE LOUIS. b Freeport Ill 30 O 05. 4: Mary Ann McRoberts. 5: UMich 23-26 (Ger) AB, 26-27 (Semitics) AM, 28-30 AMLS; Eden Theol Sem 30-31 (Ch Hist) BD; Union Theol Sem & Columbia 47, 59 (Theol Educ) EdD. 6: Ger. 7: Searcher order dept Gen Lib umich (Ann Arbor) 28-30; Libn & Prof bibliog Colgate Rochester Divinity Sch 31-. 9: ALA; ATheolLA; NYLA. 10: Evangelical & Reformed Hist Soc; Rochester Torch Club; City Club of Rochester; Kappa Delta Rho; Amer Soc Ch Hist. 13: Yes. 14: Bibliog, admin, rare bks. 15: 91 Commonwealth rd, Rochester NY 14618.

TROTIER, ARNOLD HERMAN. b Henkhausen Westphalia Ger 25 D 1899. 4: Eva Marie Wisely. 5: Neb State Tchr Col Kearney 18-20, summer 22-25 (Educ) AB; UIll 25-26, 30-33 (LS) AM. 6: Ger. 7: Tchr High Sch, Merna Neb 21-23; Supt OFallons Commun Sch, Hershey Neb 23-25; Asst libn Neb State Tchr Col (Kearney) 26-30; UIll (Urbana): Ser catlgr 30-33, Catlg lib 33-41, Asst U libn for catlg 41-47, Assoc dir for tech depts & Prof of Lib Admin 47-65, Dir tech depts, & Prof of Lib Admin 65-. 8: Fulbright lecturer in lib sci, Chulalongkorn U Bangkok U Bangok Thailand 54-55. 9: ALA (chm Catlg & Clsf Sect 35-36, chm Com on Catlg Clsf 35-40, chm Univ & Ref Libns 35-36, chm Ed Com 48-51, chm Bk-binding Com 52-54 &59-63, chm Adv Com, Lib Binding Perf Standards Proj 59-66, mem Adv Bd & Ed Subcom "A.L.A. Cataloging Rules for Author and Title Entries 2nd ed, mem Steering Com Catlg Code Rev Com 54-66); IllLA (pres 41-42; chm Lib Planning Bd 35-37, 38-41 & 44-54). 10: AAUP; Beta Phi Mu; ACLU; Nat Exch Club; Urban League. 12: Ed "Doctoral Diesertations Accepted by Amerian Univerities (45-56); "Cataloging and Classification in G R Lyles "The Administration of the College Library B44, 49, 61). 13: Yes. 14: Univ lib admin, tech serv, catlg. 15: 2405 Hibiscus st, Sarasota Fl 33579.

TROTTER, LAVINA E. b Cimmaron Kan 29 Ap 04. 5: Ft Hays Kan State Col summers 23-27 (Educ) BS; UDenver summers 48-52 (LS) MA. 7: Elem tchr Kinsley City Schs, Kinsley Kan 23-40; Libn Kinsley High Sch, Kinsley Kan 40-. 9: NEA; KanASchL (pres 64-65); Kan State Tchrs Assn. 10: Delta Kappa Gamma; kansas Dinner Club; C of C. 14: Ref, circ. 15: PO Box 192 Kinsley Kan 67547.

TROTTI, (MARY) LOUISE. b Decatur Ga 17 Je 16. 5: Brenau Col 38 (Hist) AB; Emory 49 (LS) BS. 6: Fr, Sp. 7: Alumnae sec Brenau Col 38-45; Bkmob asst Decatur-DeKalb Lib, decatur Ga 46-48, Bkmob libn 49-51, Ext libn 52-59, Asst dir 60-61; Dir DeKalb Lib Syst, Decatur Ga 62-. 8: Mem Ga Lib Bldg Adv Com 64-; Lib consul for Hancock Co Ga 68. 9: ALA; SELA; GaLA (v-pres; chm Pub Lib Sect). 10: DeKalb Co Commun Coun; Delta Kappa Gamma; Bus & Profess Women's Club; Brenau Col Trustee. 14: Ext serv, admin. 15: 230 Wilton dr, Decatur Ga 30030.

TROTTIER, DONALD H. b Salt Lake City Utah 11 Ap 42. 4: Julia Stephenson. 5: Brigham Young 60-65 (Eng Lit) BA; UWash 65-66 MSLS. 7: Child libn Enoch Pratt Free Lib,

Baltimore 66-67; City libn Provo Pub Lib, Provo Utah 67-69; Exec sec Amer Lib Trustee Assn, Chicago 69-. 8: V-chm Utah Nat Lib Week. 9: ALA; UtahLA; MPLA. 10: Beta Phi Mu; Rotary. 14: Pub lib admin. 15: 50 E Huron st, Chicago Il 60611.

TROUT, SYLVIA MARION (FESSLER). b Heidelberg Twp Penn 11 N 31. 4: Robert D Trout. 5: Kutztown State Col 49-53 (L, Soc Studies) BS in Ed. 7: Libn Palisades Jr & Sr High Sch, Ferndale Penn 53-55; DC Pub Lib: Adv schs div 55-61, Asst child libn 61, Asst chief schs div 61-64, Child libn bkmob 64-65, Chief schs div 65-. 68; Libn St Croix Country Day Sch 68-. 9: DCLA. 14: Child serv. 15: Box 1136 Christiansted, St Croix US Virgin Islands 00820.

TROWBRIDGE, ELEANOR R. b Somerville Mass 23 O 11. 5: Tufts Col 28-32 (Romance Langs) BS; Simmons 48 (LS) BS. 6: Fr. 7: Sub Lexington High Sch, Lexington Mass 33-47; Sub Lexington Jr High Sch, Lexington Mass 33-40; Br libn Cary Mem Lib, Lexington Mass 40-54, Yp libn & ref libn 54-60; Libn Newton S High Sch, Newton Mass 60-68; Hd libn 68-. 9: NEA; ALA; MassLA; Mass Tchrs Assn; NELA. 10: Lexington Choral Soc. 14: Sch libnship. 15: 31 Lincoln st, Lexington Mass 02173.

TROXEL, FLORA IMOGENE. b Tecumseh Okla 20 S 18. 5: Central State Col 37-41 (Math) BA; UOkla summers 45-49 (Educ) EdM, summers 50-54 BALS. 7: Eng & math tchr: Weathers (Okla) pub schs 42-43, Greenfield (Okla) pub schs 43-44, Bridge Creek pub schs, Blanchard Okla 44-45; Math tchr Blanchard (Okla) pub schs 45-47; Elem tchr Bray (Okla) pub schs 47-49; High sch libn & math & Eng tchr Rush Springs (Okla) pub schs 49-52; Jr high sch libn & Eng tchr Blackwell (Okla) pub schs 52-54; High sch libn libn & Math tchr Moore (Okla) pub schs 54-60; Asst libn Southwestern State Edmond (Weatherford Okla) 60-62, Curriculum libn Central State Col (Edmnd Okla) 62-. 9: OklaEA; OklaLA. 10: AAUW. 13: Yes. 14: Catlg, curr materials. 15: 311 E Lincoln, Edmond Okla 73034.

TROXEL, WILMA (ALLENE). b DeLand Ill 29 S 05. 5: ill Wesleyan U 22-26 (Math) BS; UIll 26-27 BS in LS, 30-32 (LS) AM. 7: Asst libn Ill Wesleyan U 27-30; Catlgr U Ill (Urbana) 30-34; Dir uill Lib of Med Sci (Chicago) 34-. 8: Instr USVA Spec courses for Train Med Libns 49-50; Consul USVA Chicago Area Libs 59; Co-dir Inst on mdevel in Med Lib Admin Chicago 63; Consul Faculty of Med Lib, Chiengmai, Thailand 64-65. 9: MedLA (pres 54-55, Exec Bd: chm Com on Standards for Med Libnship); SLA (pres Ill Chap 45-46); ALA; IllLA. 10: Phi Kappa Phi; Beta Phi Mu. 13: Yes. 14: Admin, tech proc. 15: 5965 W Huron st, Chicago Il 60644.

TROY, MARGARET H. b Somerville Mass 30 Ag 21. 4: John G Troy. 5: Radcliffe 43 (Biochem Sci) AB; ULondon 50. 6: Fr. 7: Res asst Sch of Med Harvard U 43-48; Res asst Sch of Med at Child Hosp, Boston 48-51; Res libn Nat Research Corp, Cambridge Mass 51-53; Res libn United Fruit Co, Boston 53-55; Exec asst Chem Documentation Sloan Kettering Inst, NY 55-59; Chief tech libn Bolt Beranek & Newman Inc, Cambridge Mass 59-. 9: SLA (Educ Com; chm Hospitality Com 63-64 & 65-66, Wkshop Com on Automation), chm Employment Com (68-70). 10: Sigma Xi; Cath Guild for the Blind, Marine Tech Soc. 13: Yes. 14: Adminof tech lib. 15: Bolt Beranek & Newman Inc, 50 Moulton st, Cambridge Mass 02138.

TROY, SHANNON MARY. b Rochester NY 19 F 41. 5: Nazareth Col of Rochester 58-62 (Eng) BA; URochester 62-64 (Eng) MA; Rutgers 65-66 MLS. 7: Lib trainee (supv gen circulation) Nazareth Col of Rochester 63-65; Asst Rutgers Prep Sch, New Brunswick NJ 65-66; Acquis libn W Chester State Col 66-. 9: SLA. 14: Acquis, ref. 15: 888 Chili ave, Rochester NY 14611.

TRUDELL, ROBERT JAMES. b Buffalo NY 6 S 3. 4: Arlene Holzka. 5: UBuffalo 56-60 (Eng Lit) AB; Columbia 60-61 (LS) MS. 7: Radio operator USAF 51-55; Stud asst UBufalo Lib 57-59; Buffalo & Erie Co (NY) Pub Lib: Lib trainee 59, Jr libn sci & tech 61-63, Sr libn lit 63-66; Fld consul Chautauqua-Cattaraugus Lib Syst, Jamestown NY 66-; Dir Olean Pub Lib, Olean NY 69-. 8: Dir Ref Wkshop Bowling Green L I 68. 9: NYLA (chm Adult Serv, Wkshop Com, Reg Rep Memb Com); WYY Lib Resources Coun (Interlib Com 67-); Analysts Book Catlg Com 69. 14: Ref. 15: Pub Lib Olean NY.

TRUELSON, STANLEY DUNHAM JR. b Cambridge Mass 19 Mr 29. 4: Elsie Sousa. 5: Harvard 47-51 (Eng Lit) AB CUM LAUDE, 54-55 (Secondary Sch Tchg of Eng) MAT; Simmons 55-56 (LS) MS. 7: (Cpl) US Army, US 51-54; Subprof asst Harvard Col Lib 55-56; Libn John Jay High Sch, Cross River NY 56-57; Circ libn & Instr in Lib Sci Tufts U Lib 57-58; Libn & Asst Prof of Lib Sci Tufts U Schs of Med & Dent 58-60; Libn & Asst Prof of Med Bibliog SUNY Upstate Med Cent (Syracuse) 60-63; Med Libn & Assoc Prof of Med Bibliog URochester 63-66; Libn Yale Med Lib 66-. 8: Ad hoc Panel on Sel of Jours for "Index Medicus NLM 65-66; v-chm Lib Task Force Conn Reg Med Prog 67-68; Adv Com NE Reg Med Lib Serv 67-; Consul Div Reg Med Prog USPHS 69. 9: MedLA (chm Upstate NY Reg Group 65), chm Publ Com 66-, Eliot Prize Essay Com 67-68; Spec Jt Com on Libs in Int Educ 67-. 12: Assoc ed "Bulletin of the Medical Library Asociation (62-). 13: Yes. 14: Med lib admin. 15: 51 Haverford st, Hamden Ct 06517.

TRUESDELL, EUGENIA R (Van BUSKIRK). b Elmira NY 4 Ag 21. 4: Douglas L Truesdell. 5: Elmira Col 39-43 (Eng, Fr) AB; Syracuse 46-47 (LS) BS, 48-49 (Lat); NM State U 5 (Eng). 6: Fr. 7: Jr libn Syracuse U 4850; Lib asst Niagara Falls Pub Lib, Niagara Falls NY 50-52; Asst col libn State U Col (Buffalo NY) 52-61; Libn Tibbetts Jr High Sch, Farmington NM 65-68; Curriculum Lab libn W Chester State Col (Penn) 69-. 9: ALA-AASchL. 10: AAUP; Phi Beta Kappa. 14: Catlg. 15: 1135 Westtown rd, W Chester Pa 19380.

TRUESDELL, WALTER GEORGE. b NYC 22 O 19. 4: Mary Schurok. 5: Columbia 41 AB; Theol Sem of the Reformed Episcopal Church 44 BD; Pratt 50 BLS. 7: Asst minister First Ref Episc Church, NYC 44-54; Rector Church of the Redemption, Brooklyn NY 56-; Libn Shelton Col 51; Libn Theol Sem of the Reformed Episc Church, Phila 64-. 9: ALA (Life mem); NJLA. 14: Catlg. 15: 306 E 90 st, NYC 10028.

TRUETT, ERLENE (ANNA). b Lanett Ala 2 Mr 31. 5: LaGrange Col 49-53 (Home Econ) AB; Emory 54-56 MLibn. 7: Asst to libn LaGrange Col 53-54; Catlgr-indexer Amer Enka Corp Ashville NC 56-60; Libn Amcel Propulsion Inc, Asheville NC 60-61; Libn Oak Ridge Inst of Nuclear Studies, Oak Ridge Tenn 61-63; Ref libn Ga State Col 63-67; Ref libn La Grange Col 67-. 9: ALA; SELA; GaLA; Atlanta Lib Club. 14: Ref, catlg. 15: 1509 Vernon rd, La Grange Ga 30240.

TRUHER, MARY GERTRUDE. b Tacoma Wash 23 N 09. 5: Immaculate Heart Col (Sociol, Educ) BA & gen elem educ credential; Mont State Col 62-63 Mont secondary educ credential; catherine Spalding Col 63-64 MSLS; Cal State credential for tchg & libnship. 6: Sp. 7: Asst archivist USanta Clara 65-66; Ref libn pub lib, Santa Clara Cal 65; Admin lib & docs vault Amer Standard Tech Lib 66-67; Organizer curriculum lib Holy Family Col summer sch, San Francisco 67; Main libn Applied Tech Inc, Palo Alto Ind Park Cal 67; Hd libn Woodside Priory Col Prep Sch, Portola Valley Cal 68-. 8: Re-org Amer Standard Adv Tech Lib and Applied Technology Inc. 9: ALA; -ACRL; SAA; SLA; CalLA. 10: AAUW. 14: Admin. 15: 1060 Noel dr, Menlo Park Ca 94025.

TRULOCK, JOY B. b Donalsonville Ga 8 Ag 25. 5: Wesleyan Col (Ga) 42-46 (Psych) BA; Emory 53-54 (Hist) MA; Peabody summers 56-58 (LS) MA; Emory 59-60 Med Libn Certif. 7: Psychometrist Mercer U 46-48; Tchr; r e lee High Sch, Thomaston Ga 49-52, Tifton High Sch, Tifton Ga 52-53; Moultrie High Sch, Moultrie Ga 54-55; Asst circ libn & ref libn Savannah Pub Lib, Savannah Ga 55-59; Pub serv libn A W Calhoun Med Lib Emory 59-60; Supv adult work Chatham Co Chatham-Effingham-Liberty Reg Lib, Savannah Ga 60-64; Ref libn Richard H Powell Lib Valdosta State Col 64-. 9: ALA; GaLA; SELA. 10: AAUP; Beta Phi Mu. 14: Ref. 15: Box 2233, Valdosta Ga 31603.

TRUMBULL, ZAIDEE B(EATRICE). b Keene Valley NY 12 F 24. 5: St Lawrence U 41-44 (Eng) BA; Syracuse 45 BLS. 7: Syracuse Univ Lib 45-46; Trumbull's Hardware 46-66; Keene valley Lib, (Keene Valley NY) 66-. 9: ALA. 10: Adirondac Mt Club; AAUW. 15: Keene Valley NY 12943.

TRUMP, ALFRED G(EORGE). b Kahoka Mo 23 Ap 07. 4: Anne Arnold. 5: Oberlin Col 25-26; UChicago 26-30, 33-34 (Germanics, LS) PhB; UMich 32-33 ABLS, 34-35, 38 AMLS. 6: Ger, Fr. 7: Page Chicago Pub Lib 27-30; Stud asst UCHICAGO 30-32, 33-34; asst UMich 34-35; Mich State Lib: Law Libn 35-38, Ref asst 38-44, Genealogy libn 46; Libn Va JR Col (Minn) 47-48; Libn Dir SD State U 48-. 9: ALA (Coun 59-67); SDLA (pres 57-58); MPLA (sec 52). 10: Pi Gamma Mu; Phi Kappa Phi. 13: Yes. 14: Ref, admin, bk sel. 15: 638 Faculty dr, Brookins, SD 57006.

TRUMPETER, MARGO J. b Akron Ohio 21 O 43. 4: Paul William Trumpeter. 5: Muskingum Col 61-65 (Fr) BA;

UIll(Urbana) 65-67 (LS) MS. 6: Fr. 7: Research assoc Lib Research Ctr UIll (Urbana) 67-. 13: Yes. 14: Research. 15: 906 So Maple st, Urbana Il 61801.

TRUNT, CLAUDIA (KUZMICK). b Clifton NJ 11 N 10. 4: Francis J Trunt. 6: Polish. 7: Exec sec Crucible Steel, Harrison NJ 38-45; Asst to div manager A B DuMont Labs, Clifton NJ 45-55; Confidential sec Wright Aero, Woodridge NJ 55-57; Asst libn Lehn & Fink PROD, Bloomfield NJ 57-58, Research libn 58-66; Research libn consumer prod div Tech Lib Amer Cyanamid, E Paterson NJ 66-. 9: SLA; ALA; NJLA. 10: YMCA. 14: Research (cosmetics). 15: 218 Lanza ave, Garfield NJ 07026.

TRYON, IOLA B. b Ansonia Conn 23 Jl 08. 5: UConn 28-32 Dietetics BS; So Conn State Col 60-62 (LS) MS. 7: Dietitian Cedarcrest Sanitorium, Hartford Conn 32-35; Home economist Landres, Frary & Clark, New Britain Conn 35-36; Asstlibn Buck Lib, Portland Conn 44-47; Dir film dept Russell Lib, Middletown Conn 47-. 8: Consul on film care & repair Conn Film Circuit 60-61 & 63-64; 67-69; on new Conn film; Lectr on films UConn Ext Course 67, 68. 9: Educ Film Lib Assn (Bd Dirs 59-61, 62-65, sec of Bd & Chm of Nomin Com 61 & 64); ALA; ConnLA, (chm Film Sect & Exec Bd 68-69); Amer Film Festival (Festival Com 62, 64, chm Jury 58-65, chm Pre-Screening Com 58-); NELA (Bd Dirs Film Sect 66-67). 10: AAUW; Middlesex Co Hist Soc; Soroptimist Internat; Friends Davison Art Ctr. 12: Comp "Educational Film Liary Association Evaluation Cards for Films (49-); Ed "Evaluation (film) Film News. 13: Yes. 14: Films. 15: 54 Gleeson rd, Middletown Conn 06457.

TRZEPACZ, MARTHA JOHNSTON. b New Milford Conn 12 Je 44. 4: Mathew Edmond Trzepacz. 5: Russell Sage Col 62-66 (Amer Hist & Govt) BA; SUNY (Albany) 66-68 MLS. 7: Acquis dept Union Col (Schenectady NY) summer 67; Act exec dir Capital Dist Lib Coun 68; Asst dir Capital Dist Lib Coun 68-. 14: Child, ya & adult ref. 15: 12 103rd st, Troy NY 12180.

TSAI, BETTY L. b Taipei Taiwan Republic of China 22 Ap 39. 4: Kuo-Yuan Tsai. 5: Nat Taiwan U 58-62 (Foreign Langs & Lit) BA; Rutgers 63-65 MSLS; SUNY (Stony Brook) 65-67. 06: Chinese, Fr, Ger. 7: Eng sec Eng Joo Hung Ltd, Taipei Taiwan China 62-63; Trainee asst catlgr Rutgers U Lib 64-65; Sr catlgr SUNY (Stony Brook) 67-68; Catlgr Trenton State Col 69-. 14: Catlg, ref, ser. 15: Lib Trenton State Col, Trenton NJ 08625.

TSAI, RACHEL JO-CHAO (CHEN). b Peiking China 4 Ja 38. 4: Chi-tsung Tsai. 5: Nat taiwanU 56-60 (Psych) BS; WesleyanU 62-64 (Psych) MA; Peabody Col 64-65 MLS. 6: Chinese. 7: Tchg asst Nat TaiwanU (Taipei) 60-62; Catlgr UAlta Lib 65-. 9: Can Assn Univ Tchrs. 10: Assn of Acad Staff UAlta. 14: Catlg. 15: 5711-112 st #206, Edmonton 70 Alberta Can.

TSAI, SHEH-GNI. b Sinchuk Formosa 1 S 33. 5: Nat Taiwan U 54 (Eng) BA, 58 (Cultural Anthropology) MA; Columbia 63 (LS) MS. 6: Hakkas, Mandarin, Japanese. 7: Taipei Taiwan; asst Academia Sinica 60-63; Instr in linguistics Nat Chengchi U 62-63; Gen asst Columbia Libs 63-65; Catlgr Brigham Young U Lib 65-69. 9: ALA; SLA; ASIS; ADI; Amer Acad Pol & oc Sci; UtahEA. 10: AAUP; ACLU; Amer Sociol Assn; Utah Acad of Sci & Letters. 14: Catlg, info serv, fields - Asian studies & soc scis. 15: Box 195 Univ Sta, Provo Ut 84601.

TSANG, WAI-MAU. b Hong Kong 12 My 36. 4: Irene Seto. 5: Nat Chengchi U (Taipei Taiwan) 6-60 (Arts) BA; McGill 61-62 BLS. 6: Fr, Chinese. 7: Asst head ya dept Ottawa Pub Lib 62-65; Catlgr Can Deptof Agric Lib, Ottawa 65-67, Ref 67-. 15: PO Box 1161 Station B Ottawa 4 Canada.

TSCHANZ, KAREN (SCHMIDT). b Schenectady NY 19 S 40. 4: Erwin A Tschanz. 5: Cornell U 58-62 (Ger Ling) BA; Syracuse summers 63-64, 65 MLS. 6: Ger, Fr. 7: Operator Bell Tele, Syracuse NY 58-59; Engring libn URochester Lib 62-63, Prof asst Dept of Sci Libs 63-6, Asst supv 66-67, Act supv 66, Ser catlgr ser sect catlg dept 67-68, Ger monographs catlg catlg dept 69-. 9: ALA. 14: Lib admin. 15: 17 Kent pk, Rochester NY 14610.

TSCHAPPAT, MARY A. b Kingston Ont Can. 5: Queens U 34-38 (Ger, Eng) Honors BA; Ont Col of Educ 39-40 High Sch Spec Tchr; Toronto 57-58 BLS. 6: Fr, Gr. 7: Libn Nat Defense Col, Kingston Ont 58-60; Ref libn Kingston Pub Lib, Kingston Ont 60-64; Tchr-libn Loyalist Collegiate & Voc Inst, KINGSTON Ont 64-; Catlgr Lake Ont Reg Lib, Kingston Ont 68-. 9: CanLA; OntLA. 14: Catlg, ref. 15: 109 Livingston ave, Kingston Ont Canada.

TSEOU, JOSEPH. b Suchow China 22 N 25. 5: MontrealU 49-53 (Educ) BA; Fordham 53-55 (Educ) MS; Columbia 56-58 (LS) MS. 6: Chinese, Fr, Lat. 7: Marketing analyst Pulse inc, NYC 55-56; Libn Brooklyn Pub Lib, Brooklyn NY 57-63; Catlg libn Xerox Corp, Rochester NY 63-. 9: SLA; Monroe Co Lib Club. 14: Catlg. 15: 205 Culver rd, Rochester NY 14607.

TSIEN, TSUEN-HSUIN. b Kiangsu China 1 D 09. 4: Wen-ching Hsu. 5: UNanking 28-32 BA; Chicago 47-52 (LS) MA, 52-57 (LS) PhD. PhD. 6: Chinese, Japanese. 7: Libn Ginling Col (Nanking China) 31-32; Asst libn Nat Chiao-tung U (Shanghai China) 32-37; Head Shanghai Off Nat Lib of Peiping 37-47; Curator Far East Lib Chicago 49-, Prof Lecturer 49-57, Assoc Prof 57-64, Prof of Chinese Lit 64-, Dir Inst For Far East Libnship 69. 8: Ed Adv, Tsing Hua Journal of Chinese Studies 59-; Visiting Prof of Asian Studies UHawaii Honolulu summer 59. 9: ALA; Intl Assn Oriental Libs; Amer Oriental Soc; Assn for Asian Studies (chm Com on E Asian Libs 66-68). 10: Chinese Stud & Alumni Serv Inc. 11: ACLS-SSRC Award 68-69. 12: "Written on Bamboo and Silk: Beginnings of Chinese Books and Inscriptions (62); Co-ed "Area Studies andthe Library (66); Ed "Library Resources on East Asia (68). 13: Yes. 14: Hist of bks, paper, ink, ptg, bibliog, Chinese-Western lit rel. 15: Far Eastern Lib Univ of Chicago, Chicago Il 60637.

TSUFFIS, MARY LEE (TOOMES). b Keokuk Iowa 10 Ap 27. 4: James Tsuffis. 5: Iowa Wesleyan Col 45-48 (Chem) BS; Drexel 49-50 MSLS. 7: Ref libn: Brooklyn Pub Lib 50-53, State U Iowa Lib 54-57; United Aircraft Corp, E Hartford Conn 57-65; Supv lib serv Xerox Corp, Webster NY 65-; Mgr Tech Info Ctr Xerox Corp, Webster NY 65-. 8: Mem Adv Com Rochester Inst Tech State Tech Serv Proj 67-; Mem Adv Com Libns Rochester Regl Research Coun and Interlib Loan Com 67-. 9: SLA (Recr Chm 65-67; Jt CNLA-SLA Com on Lib Wk as a Career; Conn Valley Chap Pres 62-63; UNY Chap Pres 69-70; Chm Nat Chap Rel Com 69-70); ASIS; NYLA; Soc Tech Writers & Pub. 14: Mgt, admin, ref. 15: 122 Country manor, Webster NY 14580.

TSUI, SUSAN L. b China 11 Ja 38. 4: James B Y Tsui. 5: Nat TaiwanU 57-61 (Liberal Arts) BA; UIll 62-64 (LS) MS. 6: Chinese. 7: Bibliogr MiamiU (Oxford Ohio) 64; Catlgr UDayton 65-. 14: Catlg. 15: 5324 Bliss pl, Kettering Oh 45440.

TSUNEISHI, WARREN M. b Monrovia Cal 4 Jl 21. 4: Betty T Tsuneishi. 5: Syracuse 43 (Pol Sci) BA; Columbia 48 (Chinese, Japanese) MA, 50 (LS) MS; Yale 60 (Pol Sci) PhD. 6: Japanese, Chinese. 7: NCO in charge of 306th Hqrs Intelligence Detachment XXIVth Corps US Army 43-46; Catlgr & research assoc Yale U Lib 50-52, Curator far East collections 53-57, Curator E Asian coll 61-66; Hd f East lang sect LC 58-61, Chief Orientalia div 66-. 8: Lectr: Dept of Pol Sci, Yale U: Japanese Govt & Politcs spring 63; Japanese For Policy spring 64; Asst Prof Dept of Govt Quinnipiac Col Hamden Conn US Govt & Politics; Lectr Grad Sch of Lib Studies UHawaii Technical Proc in Asian Collctions summer 67, 68. 9: Assn f Asian Studies; ALA; ARL (chm Far East Subcom of Farmington Plan Com). 10: Japan-Amer Soc. 12: "Japanese Political Style: an Introduction to Institutoons and Processes" (66). 13: Yes. 14: Catlg, ref, lib educ. 15: Orientalia Div Lib of Congress, Washington DC 20540.

TSUSAKI, EDNA K OGATA. b Honolulu 7 D 31. 4: Jun Tsusaki. 5: UHawaii 49-53 (Span) BA; Syracuse 53-55 (LS) MS. 6: Sp, Fr. 7: Bind asst Syracuse U Lib 53-55; Libn I ref Hild Reg Br Chicago Pub Lib 55-57; Libn II bkmob Lib of Hawaii, Honolulu 58-60, Head bkmob 60-62, Head Libn Kaimuki Br 63-68; Hd ref Hawaii State Lib 68-. 9: ALA; Hawaii LA. 10: Beta Phi Mu; Nat Cong Parents & Tchrs; Cub Scouts Parents; Lib of Hawaii Staff Assn. 13: Yes. 14: Ref, Hawaiiana. 15: 1916 Hoolehua st, Pearl City Hi 96782.

TUBB, ELEANOR (RUTH). b Amory Miss 11 Ag 32. 5: Miss State Col for Women 50-54 (Home Econ) BS; Fla State U 57-59 (LS) MS. 7: Asst child libn Pub Lib, Lima Ohio 59-61; Libn S Hills Br Jackson Mun Lib, Jackson Miss 61-. 9: ALA; MissLA; SELA. 10: . 14: Child serv. 15: 515 McDowell rd, Jackson Miss 39204.

TUBBS, SIBYL OPDYKE. b Council Bluffs Iowa 18 Ap 07. 5: UIowa 29 BA; UIll33 BS in LS. 7: Asst libn South High Sch, Omaha 29-32; Catlgr & ref libn UOmaha 33-36; Gen asst Omaha Pub Lib 36-40; Chief Libn 7th Serv Command Hdqrs, Omaha 40-46; Asst command libn Fifth Army Area, Chicago 46; Command Libn Fourth Army Area, Ft Sam Houston 46; Act Chief placement off ALA 47; ; Br libn Enoch Pratt Free Lib, Baltimore 47-48; Libn McKeesport Penn 48-52; Br libn Omaha Pub Lib 52-. 9: ALA; NebLA. 10: DAR. 14: Ref, assistance. 15: 601 S 51st st, Omaha Nb 68106.

TUBBS, WILLIAM JOHNSTON. b Philadelphia Penn 21 My 38. 4: Gail Lewis. 5: Potomac State Col 56-58 (Engring); Davis & Elkins Col 58-60 (Math) BA; Princeton Theol Sem 60-63 BD; WesleyanU 63-64 Spec grad stud; Columbia 65-66 MS. 6: Lat, Grk. 7: Catlgr olin Lib WesleyanU (Middletown Conn) 66-67, Reclsf supv 67-68, Hd catlgr 68-. 14: Tech serv. 15: 273 Pine st, Middletown Ct 06457.

TUCCI, VALERIE ANN (KARVEY). b Pittsburgh Penn 25 Ag 38. 4: Edmond R Tucci. 5: Mt Mercy Col 56-60 (Chem) BA; UPittsburgh 65-68 MLS. 6: Ger. 7: Lit chem Koppers Co Inc, Monroeville Penn 60-. 9: ACS; SLA; ASIS. 10: Beta Phi Mu; Delta epison Sigma. 13: Yes. 15: 4269 Old William Penn Highway, Murrysville Pa 15668.

TUCKER, ANNIE-BELLE (WESLEY). b Crozet Va 2 Ja 12. 5: Va Union U 28-32 (Humanities) AB; Hampton Inst 35-36 BS in LS; U of the Americas 68; Va Commonwealth U 69. 6: Fr, Sp. 7: Tchr Albemarle Pub Schs, Charlottesville Va 32-35; Br libn Okla City Pub Lib, Okla City Okla 36-43; Documents libn Ohio State Lib 47-53; Child libn Dayton Pub Lib, Dayton Ohio 53-55; Asst br libn Cleveland Pub Lib 56-61; High sch libn Baltimore City Schs 61-. 9: ALA; NEA; ASchLMd. 10: ACLU; Alpha Kappa Alpha. 15: 4046 Hilton rd, Baltimore Md 21225.

TUCKER, BEATRICE (C). b NJ. 5: UCLA 51-55 (Eng) BA, 55-58 (Eng) MA, 58-59 Jr Col Tchg Cred, 60-62 (LS) MA. 6: Fr, Sp. 7: Legal sec; Research asst UCLA; Libn Los Angeles Co Lib 62-. 9: ALA; CalLA. 14: Ref. 15: 10547 Valparaiso st, Los Angeles Ca 90034.

TUCKER, BENNY R. b Clanton Ala 8 S 35. 5: Birmingham-So Col 52-56 (Lat) AB; WashU 56-57 (Classics); UNC 58-59 MS in LS. 6: Ital. 7: Bkmob libn pub lib, Birmingham Ala 57-58, Spec recruot LC 59-60, Catlgr for lang sect descr catlg 60-62, catlgr S Asian lang sect 62-66, Asst hd 66, Deputy prin catlgr 67-. 9: ALA. 14: Catlg. 15: 122 10th st SE, Washington DC 20003.

TUCKER, ELLIS (EUGENE). b booneville Miss 15 S 31. 5: UMiss 50-52 (Eng) BAE; Emory 55-58 (Old Testanment) BD; LSU 64- (LS). 6: Hebrew. 7: Youth wk Methodist Church, N Miss 52-55, 58-63; Libn Lepanto pub schs, Lepanto Ark 63-64; Asst libn & catlgr McLemore Lib, Frederick Col 64-65, Act libn 65-67; A-v & asst libn Allegany Commun Col 67; Proj dir Ala Lib Learning Ctr, Jacksonville Ala 68-. 8: Adv to filmstrip series "The High School Media Center". 9: ALA; SLA; SELA; AlaLA; AlaEA; AlaASchL. 10: Alpha Phi Omega; ClrTA; Commun Concert. 11: Commun leader of Amer 68. 13: Yes. 14: Catlg, admin. 15: Box 142, Jacksonville Al 36265.

TUCKER, FERRELLINE (VIVIENNE). b Lindale Tex 8 F 19. 5: Tex Tech Col 36-40 (Eng) BA; UCal (Berkeley) 48-49 BS in LS. 6: Lat, Sp, Ger. 7: Eng tchr Shallowater High Sch, Shallowater Tex 40-4; Tchr of Eng & hist Paducah High Sch, Paducah Tex 41-42; Sec to libn Tex Tech Col Lib 42-47; Sec to supv Lubbock pub schs, Lubbock Tex 47-48; Documents lbn Tex Tech Col Lib 49-. 9: TexAssn of Col Tchrs, (Tex Tech Chap sec 66-67). 10: AAUW; Wesleyan Ser Guild; AAUP. 13: Yes. 14: US govt publns. 15: 1506 Avne R, Lubbock Tex 79401.

TUCKER, FLORENCE RAY. b Henderson Ky 11 Jl 21. 5: Flint Jr Col 38-40; UMich 42-44 (Hist) AB, 44-45 ABLS. 7: Clerical asst Flint Pub Lib, Flint Mich 40-42; Ref asst tech dept Detroit Pub Lib 45-59; Asst hd tech & sci dept 59-66; Act hd tech & sci dept 66; Coord catlg dept 66-. 8: Instr Wayne State U Dept of Lib Sci 65. 9: ALA; MichLA; SLA. 10: Phi Beta Kappa; Phi Kappa Phi. 14: Ref (tech & sci), info sci, tech serv. 15: Detroit Pub Lib, 5201 Woodward a Detroit Mi 48202.

TUCKER, HAROLD W. b Waco Tex 24 Mr 15. 4: Madlyn hayward. 5: Rice U 36 AB; UIll 38 BSLS; Chicago 41 (LS) MA. 6: Fr, Ital. 7: Ref asst Enoch Pratt Free Lib, Baltimore 38-40; Tech serv & sci ref asst Dayton (Ohio) Lib 41-42; (Capt) Med Serv Corps AUS 42-46; Spec Asst to dir Army Med Lib 51-52; Asst libn Pub Lib, Gary Ind 46-47; Assoc dir Pub Lib, St Louis Co Mo 47-50; City Libn Gary Ind 50-54; Chief Dir Borough Pub Lib, Jamaica NY 54-. 8: Nat Lib Wk Steering Com 63-64. 9: ALA (chm NY Worlds Fair Adv Com 63-66, chm Adv Com Access to Libs Study 62-64, Mem Com on Legis 68); ALA-ABPC Reading Devel Com 63); NYLA (pres 64-65, chm Fed State Lib Rel Com & Standards & Leg Com 62-64, chm Personnel Adm Com 56-59, rep & chm NY State DeputyCommsnr of Educs Com to Eval ExperLib Tech Program (63); LPRC; NYLibClub (pres 58-59); Nat Bk Com Adv Group (Exec Coun); NY Lib Tech Serv; Metro Ref & Research agency (sec Bd Dirs); NY Metro Reg Libn Recruitment Project (pres Bd Trustees). 10: Rotary Club; Queens Central YMCA; Queensboro Cun for Soc Welfare; Jamaica (NY) Hosp Bd of Trustees; C of C; Human Resources Coun; Adv Com St Johns U Ann Cong Libns; Queensboro Tuberculosis & Health Assn. 12: Res asst-Wheeler & Githens "American Pubic Library Building (41); Res asst, Wilson & Tauber "The University Library (56); Co-auth (with S W Smith) "Survey of the Joplin (Mo.) Public Library. 13: Yes. 14: Admin. 15: Queensborough Pub Lib, 89-11 Merrick blvd, Jamaica NY 11432.

TUCKER, JENNIE STREETER. b Oberlin Ohio 10 Je 06. 5: Oberlin Col 22-26 (Eng Lit) AB, 32-51 (Eng Lit) AM; West Res 50-53 MS in LS. 6: Fr. 7: Stenographer The Burrows Brothers Co, Cleveland 27-29, Advertising manager 29-47; Asst Oberlin Col Lib 49-62, Acquis libn 62-. 9: ALA; OhioLA; No Ohio Tech Serv Libns. 10: AAUW; Phi Beta Kappa; Oberlin Stamp Club; Oberlin Lib Staff Assn. 12: "Oberlin College Library, 1833-1885 (microcard 53). 14: Acquis, catlg, bibliog searching. 15: 82 South Cedar st, Oberlin Ohio 44074.

TUCKER, JOSEPH. b Columbus Ga 5 Mr 20. 4: Vivian Hampton. 5: FiskU 64-50 (Relig) BA; Union Theol Sem (NY) 50-53 (Ethics) BD. 7: Tech 5th grade 1888 Engr Avn Bn CBI 42-46; Headmaster & asst dean of men FiskU 53-54; Pastor Bethlehem Presbyterian Ch, Chicago 55-56; Minister Garden Valley Neighborhood House, Cleveland Ohio 57-58; Ser asst Law lib ColumbiaU 58-59; Period libn The Library Union Theol Sem (NY) 59-. 8: Pastoral coun Harlem Interfaith Counseling Serv 67-68. 10: Fisk Alumni Assn; NAACP; Minister's interfaith Assn. 13: Yes. 14: Period, ser. 15: 76 E Marshall st, Hempstead Long Island NY 11550.

TUCKER, MAE S. b Mount Holly NC 5 O 22. 5: Appalachian State Tchrs Col 40-43 (Educ) BS; UNC 44-45 (BS in LS. 6: Fr, Sp. 7: Ref asst Pub Lib of Charlotte & Mecklenburg Co, Charlotte NC 45-56, Head Main Lib pub serv 56-. 9: ALA-RSD (chm SE Chap 60-62); SELA; NCLA (chm Jr Mem Round Tablechm 48-49, Corr sec 55-57, Pub Libs Sect: chm 57-59, rec sec 63-65), chm Lib Resources Com 65-67); MecklenburgLA (pres 62-63). 10: Staff Org Pub Lib of Charlotte & Mecklenburg Co; AAUW; Bus & Prof Womens Club; Beta Phi Mu. 12: Comp "Textiles, A Bibliography; (52). 13: Yes. 14: Ref, adult educ. 15: Pub Lib 310 N Tryon st, Charlotte NC 28202.

TUCKER, ROBERT C(INNAMOND). b Senatobia Miss 16 O 15. 4: Mary Kent Seagle. 5: LSU 36 (Hist) AB, 37 BS in LS, 41 (Hist) MA; UNC 58 (Hist) PhD. 7: LSU (Baton Rouge): Asst ref libn 37-40, Asst order libn 40-41, Gift & exch libn 42; US Army Air Force 42-45; Exec libn XXIV Corps (Korea) US Army 46-47; Libn Furman U 47-. 9: ALA (Coun 61-64); SCLA (pres 56); SELA; So Hist Assn; SC Hist Assn (sec-treas 63-69); So Baptist Hist Soc; SC Baptist Hist Soc. 10: AAUP; Phi Kappa PHI: Beta Phi Mu. 12: "James Henry Hammond, South Carolinian PhD diss, microfilm (58). 13: Yes. 14: Acquis. 15: 117 Broughton dr, Greenville SC 29609.

TUCKER, ROSALIE (GETMAN). b Watertown NY 25 F 08. 5: Vassar 25-29 (Music) AB; Oberlin Col 29-32 (Organ) MusB; UBuffalo 40-41 BLS. 7: Sec to Gen exec YMCA, Buffalo NY 35; Sec Mac Jannet Schs & Camps, St Cloud & Talloires France 36; Organist priv tchg, Buffalo NY 37-40; Catlgr UBuffalo Law Lib 40-41; Vassar Col: Sec to libn 41-43, Admin asst43-64, Readers serv & spec collections libn 64-. 66; Readers serv libn 66-. 9: ALA; NYLA; SENYLRC. 10: Amer Guild Organists. 14: Ref, interlib loan. 15: Vassar Col, Poughkeepsie NY 12601.

TUCKER, SHIRLEY CLAIRE (SLICHTER). b Wenatchee Wash 25 D 34. 4: Trueman Dale Tucker. 5: Wenatchee Vally Col 53-54 (Pol Sci); U of Puget Sound 54-57 Pol Sci) BA; UWash 57-58 MLS. 7: Child libn King Co Lib System, Seattle 58-59, Asst to dir child wk 59-60; Asst to ref libn Mid-Columbia Reg Lib, Kennewick Wash 62-3, Child libn 63-64; Adult serv libn King Co Lib System, Seattle 64-65; Child libn Mid-Columbia Reg Lib, Kennewick Wash 65-68; Adult serv libn 69-. 9: ALA; PNLA; WashLA (Recr Com) 64-67; mem of an ad hoc Com)on certif 65, sec 68-69); Tri-Cities LA. 10: Beta Phi Mu; Seattle Weavers Guild. 14: Child & adult serv, ref, br ext. 15: 1523 W Pearl st, Pasco Wash 99301.

TUCKWOOD, DWIGHT ORLAN. b Fennimore Wis 25 Mr 24. 4: Jo Ann Wiles. 5: U Wis 46-49 (Music) BA, 49-50 BSLS; UIll 55-58 MS. (LS). 7: T5 US Army Quartermaster Corps 43-46; Asst order libn Ore State Col 50-53; Asst order libn Purdue U 53-55; UIll Lib (Urbana): Bibliogr 55-57, Asst ref libn 57-58, Bkstacks libn 58-61, Research asst Lib Research

Center 61-62, Undergrad libn 62-65; Dir of tech serv UMo Lib 65-. 9: ALA-ACRL. 10: AAUP; Beta Phi Mu. 14: Data proc, ref, educ for libnship, tech serv. 15: 807 N Valley View dr, Columbia Mo 65201.

TUCKWOOD, JO ANN (WILES). b Ardmore Okla 1 D 27. 4: Dwight Tuckwood. 5: Okla State U 45-49 (Hist) BA; UIll 50-52 (LS) MS. 7: Reviser UIll Lib Sch 50-52; UIll (Urbana): Asst catlg dept 52-53, Asst Undergrad Lib 53-54, Libn Lib Sci Lib 54-64, Visiting Asst Prof Grad Lib Sch 64-65; Lectr in Lib Sci UMo (Columbia) 68-. 9: ALA-ACRL. 10: LWV; Beta Phi Mu; Phi Kappa Phi. 14: Lib lit, educ for libnship, catlg. 15: 807 No Valley View dr, Columbia Mo 65201.

TUDIVER, LILLIAN. b NYC 3 O 27. 5: Brooklyn Col 45-48 (Eng) BA; Columbia 51-52 MS in LS. 7: Libn br Brooklyn Pub Lib 52-53, Libn Central telephone ref 53-54; Br libn Tottenham Pub Lib, Eng 54-55; Brooklyn Pub Lib centrl soc sci div: Libn 55-57, Asst Chief 57-60, Chief 60-. 8: Disussion eader, ALA Conf Within a Conf 63. 9: ALA; -ASD (mem D L Nat Lib Week Com 67-69); NY Lib Club. 14: Ref, bk sel, training prof libns. 15: 61 Eastern Parkway, Brooklyn NY 11238.

TUDOR, DEAN (FREDERICK). b Toronto Ont Can 26 My 43. 4: Nancy Rice. 5: UToronto 9york Col) 62-65 (Hist, Pol Sci) BA; McGill 65-67 MLS. 7: Ref libn York U Libs 67-68; Hd libn Ont Dept of Revenue, Toronto Can 68-. 8: Study of Lib Resources in Toronto on Urban Studies 69-. 9: CanLA; ALA; -ACRL; SLA; ASIS; Coun Planning Libns; Inst Profess Libns Ont. 10: World Future Soc; Can Hist Assn. 13: Yes. 14: Mgt, urban studies. 15: Ont Dept of Rev Library, Frost Bldg, Queen's Park Toronto Can.

TUDOR, NANCY PATRICIA (RICE). b Ottawa Can 13 D 43. 4: Dean Tudor. 5: CarletonU 62-65 (Geog) BA; McGill 65-67 MLS. 7: Catlgr UToronto Lib 67-68; Catlgr Metro Toronto Pub Lib Toronto Can 68-. 9: OntLA. 14: Music catlg. 15: 45 Oakmount rd apt 802, Toronto Ont Can.

TUFTS, GLADYS (COWSILL). b Wash DC 20 S 12. 4: Arthur J Tufts. 5: American U 30-34 (Math) AB; Queens Col (NY) 58-63 (Lib Educ) MS. 7: Sec "Washington Post, Wash DC 34-35; Sec US Govt, Wash DC 35-39; Clerk great Neck Lib, Great Neck NY 53-59; Libn Hicksville pub schs, Hicksville NY 59-61; Libn Bethpage pub schs, Bethpage NY 61-. 9: ALA; NYLA; Nassau-Suffolk Sch LA; NEA; NY State TA. 10: Bethpage TA; Womans Club; Mill River Club. 14: Child & yp. 15: 233 Sugar Toms lane, East Norwich NY 11732.

TULL, WILLIS C(LAYTON) JR. b Crisfield Md 22 F 31. 4: Taeko Itoi. 5: Towson State Col 54-57 (Educ) BS; Rutgers 61-62 MLS. 7: Admin NCO US Army US & Japan 49-52; Ed clerk (GS-4) US Mil Intelligence, Japan 52-53; Soc studies tchr Hereford Jr-Sr High Sch, Parkton Md 57-59; Educ philos & religion asst (LPS-I) Enoch Pratt Free Lib, Baltimore 59-61, Sr ref asst (LPS-2) 62-64; Head adult serv Washington Co Free Lib, Hagerstown Md 64-67; Asst area libn East Shore Area Lib, Salisbury Md 67; Br libn Baltimore Co Pub Lib, Pikesville Md 67-. 9: ALA; Md Assn Adult Educ (Reg Coord for West Md 65-66); MdLA (Publicity Com 64-66). 10: Friends Hist Assn; Unitarian Hist Soc; Universalist Hist Soc; Kappa Delta Pi; Md Hist Soc. 14: Adut bk sel, pub rel, adult educ. 15: Baltimore Co Pub Lib 1111 Reisterstown rd, Pikesville Md 21208.

TULLIS, ISABEL (BOEHM). b Defiance Ohio 24 N 08. 4: Roy Tullis. 5: Defiance Col 25-27; Whittenberg Col 27-29 (Educ) BA; UMich summers 37-39 (Eng) MA; West Res 40-41 BS in LS. 7: Tchr Payne High Sch, Payne Ohio 29-34; Tchr Defiance High Sch, Defiance Ohio 34-40; Catlgr Central Wash Col of Educ 41-45; Catlgr Ohio StateU 45-46; Catlgr UIda 46-47; Ref libn Central Wash Col of Educ 47-49; Catlgr UPortland 49-51; Portland Pub Schs, Portland Ore Catlgr 51-55; Asst supv of libs 55-57; Supv of libs 57-59; Catlgr Portland State Col 59-. 9: ALA; OreLA. 14: Catlg. 15: 1909 NE 24th, Portland Or 97212.

TULLOS, THOMAS W. b Trumann Ark 6 Ja 22. 5: Ark State Col 39-43 (Hist) BA; Peabody 52-53 (LS) MA. 7: Acquis libn UMiss Lib 53-64; Acquis libn Memphis State U Lib, Memphis Tenn 64-65; Bibliogr & asst dir of libs UMiss 65-. 9: Miss LA. 14: Acquis. 15: Box 221, University Miss 38677.

TULLY, SHARON (ISABEL). b Winnipeg Manitoba 2 O 43. 5: UMan 61-64 BA; UBC 66-67 BLS. 7: Lib asst Winnipeg Pub Lib, Winnipeg Man Can 64-66; Ref libn Elizabeth Dafoe Lib uman 67-. 9: CanLA; ManLA. 14: Ref and map sect of ref info serv. 15: Ref Info Serv, Elizabeth Dafoe Lib, Univ of Manitoba, Winnipeg 19 Manitoba Can.

TUNG, TIMOTHY T S. b China 7 S 22. 4: Birgit Holst. 5: St John'sU (Shanghai) 45 (Eng) BA; UMo 47-52 (Eng, Journalism); New Sch for Soc Research 54-55 (Creative Writing); Columbia 63-64 MLS. 6: Chinese, Japanese, Fr, Swedish. 7: Reporter "Shun Pao", Shanghai 45-46; Asst city ed SEast Daily, Shanghai 46-47, Spec correspondent 47-49; Managing ed "The United Journal" (Chinese daily), NYC 52-53; Circ & humanities ref libn CCNY 64-. 9: ALA; NY Lib Club. 12: Member Edl Bd: "World Forum" (Chinese monthly), (58-62); "Editorial Anthology" (57-59). 13: Yes. 14: Ref. 15: 242 E 19th st, New York NY 10003.

TUNIS, MILDRED (CROCKETT). b New London NH 11 N 1900. 4: Alford B Tunis. 5: Oberlin Col 20-24 (Eng Lit) AB; SUNY Col (Albany) 60 MLS. 7: Ser catlgr, NY State Lib 52-60; Ref libn Fernald Lib, Colby Jr Col 60-66; Libn Lucy Scribner Lib Skidmore 66-68; Manuscript libn Dartmouth Archives Baker Lib, Dartmouth 68-. 14: Ref. 15: Trussell House, New London NH 03257.

TUNNELL, MOLENA (WILLAMS). b Farmersville Tex 1 O 04. 4: Thurman C Tunnell. 5: Tex Womans U 21-25 (Eng) BA; N Tex State U summer 25; UMex summer 26; Tex Womans U summers 49-51 BSLS; UWash summer 62 (LS). 6: Sp. 7: Tchr Span Lat Grandview High Sch, Grandview Tex 25-27; Tchr Span Eng Nacogdoches High Sch, Nacogdoches Tex 27-29; Elem tchr Maverick Sch, Maverick Tex 35-42; Tchr Span Eng Lake View High Sch, San Angelo Tex 42-49; Tchr Span Lat Lee Jr High Sch, San Angelo Tex 49-51; Libn Central High Sch, San Angelo Tex 51-66; VISTA volunteer 66-67; Lib supv Lawn Green Co Schs 68; Catlgr Angelo State Col 68-. 9: NEA; TexState Tchrs Assn; Clr Tchrs Assn; Tex LA (dist chm); Tex Assn Col Tchrs. 10: Delta Kappa Gamma; AAUW. 15: 69 E 37th st, San Angelo Tx 76901.

TURCHYN, ANDREW. b Chernytsia Ukraine 17 Jl 12. 4: Late Olga Salamacha. 5: Theol Acad (Lviv) 33-38 (Philos, Theol) BD; Munich U 46-49 (Philos, Psych, Journ) PhD; UMich 52-53 MALS; Ind U 55-60 (Slavic Studies) MA. 6: All Slavic Langs, Ger, Lat. 7: Tchr, Poland & Ukraine 39-44; Ed Christian Voice, Munich 49-50; Wker, US 50-52; Catlgr & sr catlgr Ind U Lib 53-59; Asst catlg libn 59-66; Libn Slavic & E Asian collections 66-69; Libn for Slavic studies 69-. 9: ALA-ACRL (Subj Spec Sect chm Nomin Com 65-66; Slavic & E European Subsect Exec Com mem 63-66; chm 64-65; Nomin Com mem 67-68. 10: Amer Assn Tchrs Slavic & E European Langs; Amer Assn Adv Slavic Studies; Shevchenko Sci Soc; Ukrainian Hist Soc. 13: Yes. 14: Slavic bibliog & ref. 15 Ind Univ Lib, Bloomington Ind 47405.

TURCOTTE, MILDRED (MULLANE). b Cincinnati Ohio 15 Jl 24. 5: UCincinnati 61-64 (Early European Hist) AB; UIll 64-66 MSLS. 6: Fr. 7: Registered nurse US Navy Nurse Corps - Ensign 47-49; Registered nurse 50-61; Pharmacy-chem libn UPacific 66-68; Ser libn UCincinnati 68-. 9: OhioLA. 10: ACLU; United World Federalists; Phi Beta Kappa; Phi Alpha Theta; Beta Phi Mu. 15: Apt 1102 2930 Scioto, Cincinnati Oh 45219.

TURGEON, RAYMOND H. b Fall River Mass 1 Jl 28. 5: USoCar 49-52 Fr AB, 52-53 Fr MA; Rutgers 65-67 MLS. 6: Fr, Ital. 7: Admin asst State Commercial Ptg Co, Columbia SC 54-57; Reading coord-tchr Collegiate Sch, NYC 57-65; Sch libn Wisdom Lane Jr High Sch, Levittown NY 65-68; Dir Info Retr & Dissemination Ctr, Levittown NY 68-. 9: ALA; NYLA; NassauCoLA; Phi Beta Kappa. 14: Ref, sch libs. 15: 1498 Gaston st, Wantagh NY 11793.

TURIEL, DAVID. b NYC 5 O 22. 4: Judith Berenblatt. 5: Brooklyn Col 39-50 (Eng) BA; ULondon (England) 49 Certif in 20th Century Eng Lit; Columbia 50-51 MSLS. 6: Sp, Fr. 7: Mgr Turiel Bros Inc (Exporters) NYC 40-43, 46-49; Sgt US Army 38th Field Hosp 43-46; New bk asst Brooklyn Pub Lib bk order off 50-52, Libn Williamsburgh Br 52, Supv binding 52-53, Asst coord bk order off 54-58, Asst br libn East Parkway Br 58-59; Adult serv consul Westchester Lib Syst, Mt Vernon NY 59-67; Chief bk ordering off NYC Pub Lib 67-. 8: Lectr in libnship Pratt Inst Grad Sch Lib and Info Sci 67; Mem com on Wilson Indexes 67-. 9: ALA (Com on Bkbinding 54-55 & 57-59; Exh RT treas 54-56; Advert Mgr Lib Resources and Tech Serv 58-67; ABPC-ALA Publishers Liaison Com Chm 63-66; Ala Notable Bk Coun 67-70); NYLA (Exh Com co-chm 56); NY Lib Club. 12: "Reference Service in the Nassau Library System, Nassau County, New York" (67). 13: Yes. 14: Collection devel, acquis, lib educ. 15: 2547 West 2nd st, Brooklyn NY 11223.

TURIEL, JUDITH (BERENBLATT). b Bronx NY 2 D 27. 4: David Turiel. 5: Brooklyn Col 45-50 (Eng) BA; Columbia

50-52 MSLS. 6: Ger. 7: Pre-prof libn Brooklyn Pub Lib 50-52, Prof libn 52-54; Per-diem sub tchr NYC schs 65; Sub libn tech serv div Bur of Libs NYC Bd of Educ 66, Libn in ESEA Title I program 66, Lib consul for ESEA Title II 66-. 14: Child & ya wk, catlg. 15: 2547 W 2 st, Brooklyn NY 11223.

TURK, BEATRICE E (NORDENGREN). b La Crosse Wis 28 Ag 23. 4: Joseph Turk. 5: La Crosse State Col 41-43; UMinn 43 (Sp); Col of St Catherine 43-45 (LS, Hist) BS; Cleveland Col 48; Case West Res 62-64, 64-65 MS in LS. 6: Sp. 7: Child & sch libn Lakewood Pub Lib, lakewood Ohio 45-48; Sch lib organization vol Bd of Catholic Educ, Cleveland Ohio 48-66, Coord sch libs 66-. 8: Adv to: PACE Assn in the establishment of sch libs 64-66; Bd of Cath Educ Diocese of Cleveland 64-66; NDEA Inst 66; Case West Res U; Adv Bd, Sch of Lib sci Kent State U 66-69. 9: CathLA (sec Supvr's Sect; No Ohio Unit: past chm Child Sect); ALA-AASchL; NEA-DAVI; OhioASchL. 12: "Elementary School Libraries: Staff Manual" (66); "Audio Visual Manual for Educational Media Centers" (69). 13: Yes. 14: Sch lib admin. 15: 16719 Claire ave, Cleveland Oh 44111.

TURK, ELIZABETH (SCHELIN). b New Orleans La 27 S 18. 4: William Brooke Turk. 5: Tulane U 34-38 (Ger) BA; Auburn U 68 (Educ, LS). 6: Ger, Sp. 7: Sec Pathol Dept LSU Med Sch (New Orleans) 38-41, Med Lib (German tr & research) 41-42; Geol Dept 42; Ser libn AuburnU 66-. 9: AAUW. 14: Ser libnship. 15: 426 Sehoy, Auburn Al 36830.

TURLEY, MARY OLIVIA (KUEBLEAR). b Livingston Co Ky. 5: Murray State U 34-56 (LS) BS; Peabody Col 56-58 MA in LS. 7: Tchr Livingston Co Bd of Educ, Livingston Co Ky 35-48, high sch libn 48-58; Med libn Mid-State Baptist Hosp, Nashville 58-63; Hd libn Paducah Jr Col 65-67; Libn Nursing Dept Murray State U 68-. 9: ALA; KyLA; First Dist (Ky) LA. 14: Ref, catlg. 15: 905 Olive st, Murray Ky 42071.

TURMAN, NORA MILLER. b Minden La 27 S 01. 5: Peabody Col 22-26 (Home Econ, Eng) BS; Cornell U 30-31 (Sociol) BA; Longwood Col summers 57-59 (LS); Endorsement Study Abroad NCTE & Smith Col summers 65, 67. 7: Home econ ext NC Ext, Burgaw 26-30; Home econ ext Va Polytech Inst, Accomack Co 31-38; Vol chm civilian mobilization for Accomack Co during World War II; Libn Atlantic High Sch, Accomack Co Va 56-65; Libn Parksley Combined Sch, Accomack Co Va 65-67; Ccord lib serv Accomack Co Va 67-. 8: Screening Com for high sch lib bks for State Dept of Educ (Va). 9: ALA; NEA; VaEA (Reporter); Accomack Co EA (sec-treas); VaLA. 10: Va Hist Soc; Accomack Co Hist Soc; Va Fed of Women's Clubs; Parksley Three Arts Club; Va Museum of Fine Arts. 12: "The Girl in the Rural Family" (35); "George Yeardley Governor of Virginia and Organizer of the General Assembly in 1619" (59); "The Episcopal Church in Accomack County from 1652" (54); "The Eastern Shore of Virginia -603-1964" (64). 13: Yes. 14: Ref (17th cent hist). 15: PO Box 276, Parksley Va 23421.

TURNBULL, BARBARA A. b Philadelphia Penn 15 O 36. 5: Goucher 54-58 (Hist) BA; Drexel 61-65 MSLS. 7: Lib asst City Planning Collection Fine Arts Lib UPenn 58-65; Catlgr Lib Fed Reserve Bank of Phila 65-. 9: SLA; Spec Libs Coun of Phila. 14: Catlg, ref. 15: 117 Gilmore rd, Havertown Pa 19083.

TURNBULL, WILLIAM ROBERT JR. b Providence 11 Je 28. 4: Anne Iafrate. 5: URI 54-57 (Biol) BS; Rutgers 57-59 MLS. 6: Ger. 7: Libn Newark Pub Sch, Newark NJ 58-59; Head circ dept URI 59-60; Head Libn US Naval UnderwaterOrd Lab, Newport RI 60-62; Head Libn Aerospace Corp, San Bernardino Cal 62-64; Bibliog US Naval Weapons Ctr, Corona Cal 64-. 12: "Scientific and Technical Dictionaries, Volume 1, Physical Science and Engineering (67). 14: Admin, bibliog. 15: 634 Sonora, San Bernardino Ca 92404.

TURNER, ANNE L(EACH). b Greensboro NC. 5: UNC (Chapel Hill) 32-33 (Eng) BA; Columbia 35-36 BSLS; UMich summers 45, 47-48, 49 MLS. 6: Fr, Ger, Lat, Russian. 7: Lib asst in circ & ref Hunter Col 36-37; Head order dept NC State Col 37-63; Chief bibliog & head of dept of bibliog NC State U 63-. 9: ALA; NCLA. 10: NC State Art Soc; NC State Lit & Hist Soc; AAUW; Womans Club; NC State U; Sesame Club. 14: Bibliog, rare bks, ref. 15: 903 W Johnson st Cameron Park, Raleigh NC 27605.

TURNER, BERTHA B. b Franklin Va 6 N 26. 5: Va State Col 43-47 (LS) BS; Hampton Inst 59-62 (Secondary Educ, Admin) MA. 6: Fr. 7:Fr.tchr-libn Fr Sch, Charlotte Co Va 47-48; Eng & Fr tchr-libn High Sch, Dendron Va 49-63; Libn High Sch, Franklin Va 63-. 9: NEA; Va Tchrs Assn (sec-treas Dept of Libns); VaEA (Dept of Libns; Exec Bd); Franklin Co TA (past v-pres). 10: Cosmonette Civic & Social Club; Nat Assn Col Women. 14: Ref, org of materials, catlg. 15: 215 Maple st, Suffolk Va 23434.

TURNER, ERRETT S. b Richmond Cal 8 S 19. 4: Irka Eitingon. 5: Modesto Jr Col 37-40 AA; UCal (Berkeley) 40-42 (Chem) BS; UArk 47-49 (Phys Chem) MS; Purdue 49-58 (Biochem) hD. 6: Sp, Fr, Ger. 7/ research asst APF Project Cal Tech (Pasadena) 42-44, Project leader rocket program (China Lake) 44-46; Research chem Naval Ordinance Test Sta, China Lake Cal 46-47; Research fellow Ordark Project UArk 47-49; Analytical chem State Chem Lab Purdue (Lafayette) 49-51, Electron microscopist Biochem Dept 51-54; Lit analyst Central Research Dept 3M Co, St Paul 55-57, Hd tech info sect 57-64; Info scientist Bell Tele Labs Inc, Murray Hill NJ 64-. 9: ACS (Div Chem Lit); Amer Inst Chemists; ASIS; Inst of Info Scientists (UK); SLA. 12: Article on Patnet Literature in Kirk-Othmer Encyclopedia of Chemical Technology. 13: Yes. 14: Tech info problems (recording, dissem, ret). 15: Bell Telephone Labs Inc, Murray Hill NJ 07974.

TURNER, GEORGE GODFREY. b New Westminster BC 10 F 28. 4: Marjorie Alldritt. 5: McGill 45-49 BA; UBC 50-53 LLB; Toronto 55-56 BLS. 6: Fr. 7: Royal Canadian Air Force Res Educ BR Flight Lt 51-64; Barrister & solicitor Collins, Green,Eades & Collins, Vancouver BC 53-55; UBC: Catlgr 56-59, Acquis libn 59-60, Head catlg div 60-62, Supv of tech serv 62-64; Asst libn UAlta 64-67; Assoc libn 67-. 9:CanLA (chm (coun 66-69, Libns Com 60-63); ALA; Constit Com 65-69); Inst Prof Lbns Ont; Alta mla 9sec 65-66). 10: Law Soc fbc; Beta Phi Mu; Can Assn Univ Tchrs; Alta Lib Bd. 11: Awarded Canadian Forces Decoration 63. 12: Assoc ed & ed "British Columbia Library Quarterly (57-61). 13: Ye. 14: Collection dev, admin. 15: 11807 - 91 ave, Edmonton 61 Alta Can.

TURNER, GLADYS W. b New Orleans. 4: Edwin Turner. 5: Hampton Inst 38-39 BLS; Northwestern 53-55 (Counseling) MA. 6: Fr. 7: Libn Tex Col 39-42; Ref & circ Southern U 42-44; Catlgr VA Union U 44-45; Sr catlgr Roosevelt U 47-50, Chief circ libn 50-. 9: ALA; IllLA (past Publicity Chm); Chicago Lib Club. 10: LWV; AAUP. 14: Readers adv, circ. 15: 514 Clavey lane, Highland Park Ill 60035.

TURNER, GURLEY. b NYC 4 Je 21. 4: Howard Brenner. 5: Hunter Col 38-42 (Sociol) BA; Columbia 45-47 MLS, 65 (LS). 7: Lib asst NY Pub Lib 42-47; Supv libns Queens Borough Pub Lib, NY 49-64; Head Libn Inst of Internat Educ, NY 64-68; Hd info & ref div 69-. 9: SLA; NYLib Club; ALA. 10: Commun Coun. 14: Bk sel, admin, ref. 15: 114 E 72 st, New York NY 10021.

TURNER, HAROLD McLEOD. b NYC 9 Ag 14. 4: Virginia Binford. 5: Yale 33-37 (Classics) AB; Columbia 58-59 (LS) MS. 6: Fr, Ger. 7: Gen libn NY Pub Lib 59-60; Asst Sarah Laurence Col Lib 60-62; Lecturer Sch of Lib Serv Columbia U 62-. 9: ALA. 10: Beta Phi Mu. 13: Yes. 14: Pub lib wk. 15: 35 Valley rd, Bronxville NY 10708.

TURNER, HELEN. b LaGrange Ark 4 Mr 16. 5: Ark State Col 33-34, 37 (Educ); Blue Mountain Col 34-35 (Educ); Ark State Tchrs Col 41-44 (Educ) BSE; Memphis State U 59-60 (LS); Peabody 52-55 MA (Ed), 60-63 MA(LS). 6: Fr. 7: Tchr Aubrey Elem Sch, Aubrey Ark 37-41; Tchr Barton Elem Sch, Barton Ark 41-44; Postal clerk USX Post Office Dept, Wash DC 44-46; Searcher LC 46; Church sec Columbia Heights Christian Church, Wash DC 47-51; Tchr Hughes Elem Sch, Hughes Ark 52-57; Tchr Memphis Pub Schs, Memphis Tenn 57-59; Libn Memphis Pub Lib, Memphis Tenn 59-66; Memphis State U Lib 66-. 9: ALA; SELA; TennLA. 10: Tenn Ornithol Soc; TennEA. 14: Ref. 15: 2985 Walnut Grove rd apt 3, Memphis Tenn 38111.

TURNER, HOWARD (BOOTH). b Vale Tenn 18 O 08. 5: UTenn 26-30 BS in Ed; UNC 36-37 BA in LS. 7: Tchr-libn Copperhill High Sch, Copperhill Tenn 30-31; Tchr Carroll Co pub schs, Huntingdon Tenn 33-35; Jr lib asst Tenn Valley Authority, Decatur Ala 35-36; Libn Darlington Co Lib, Darlington SC 37-38; Lib asst US Dept of Agric Lib, Wash DC 38-41; Libn Lincoln Br USDA Lib, Lincoln Neb 42; (Sgt) US Army Air Force, China, Burma, India 43-45; Bibliog US Dept of Agric Lib, Wash DC 46-47; Chief period & documents sect Nat War Col Lib, Wash DC 47-48, Chief bibliog & search sect 48-61; Chief Lib Br Off of the Chief of Engnrs Dept of the Army, Wash DC 61-67; Chief catlg dept lib scis group John I Thompson & Co, Wash DC 67-. 9: SLA (sec-treas Mil Libns Dv 63-64; Wash Chap: bus mgr, "Chapter Notes 58-59; sec-treas Mil Libns Group 59-60); DCLA (treas52-54). 10: Wash Athletic Club. 12: Jt auth "Bibliography on Cooperation in Agricuture (48). 14: Catlg. 15: 1801 - 16th st NW apt 310, Wash DC 20009.

TURNER, JOAN (BRAILEY). b Boston Mass 2 My 26. 4: U Victor Turner. 5: Wellesley 43-47 (Pol Sci) BA; Columbia 62-66 (LS) MS. 7: Dir tech serv S Huntington Pub Lib, S Huntington NY 63-66; Docs libn Huntington Pub Lib, Huntington NY 66-69, Asst dir 68-69. 15: 14 Mulberry dr, Huntington NY 11743.

TURNER, MABEL ALEXANDRA. b Sault Ste Marie Mich 6 Ap 03. 5: UOre 22-26 (Eng) AB; Columbia 30-31 (LS) BS,57-58 (LS) MS. 6: Fr, Sp. 7: Circ asst Spokane Pub Lib, Spokane Wash 21-22, 24-25; Libn The Dalles High Sch, The Dalles Ore 26-28; Asst libn Lewis & Clark High Sch, Spokane Wash 28-30, 31-37; Asst libn N Central High Sch, Spokane Wash 37-39; Libn Lewis & Clark High Sch, Spokane Wash 39-41; Instr UWash 41-47, Asst prof 47-53, 55-59; Visiting instr Keio U Japan Lib Sch (Tokyo) 54-55; Assoc prof UWash 49-68; Libn East Wash State Hist Soc, Spokane Wash 68-. 9: ALA; Wash State ASchL (pres 61-62) PNLA; WashLA. 13: Yes. 14: Sch libnship, research, ref, bk sel, hist spec libs. 15: W 2223 Ohio ave, Spokane Wa 99201.

TURNER, MARGARET ANNE (OLWEN). b Sarnia Ont 21 Ja 39. 5: Stephens Col 55-57 (Music) AA; UToronto 57-61 (Musicology) Honour BA; McGill 62-63 BLS. 7: Lib asst Sarnia Pub Lib, Sarnia Ont 61-62; Libn UToronto 63-64; Libn Catlgr UWest Ont 64-66; Libn in charge of Mus Lib 66-67; Libn in charge of Lambton Col (Sarnia Ont) 67-. 9: CanLA; Coun of Commun Col Libns Ont (mem Exec Coun 67-68). 10: Womens Club Sarnia U. 14: Music, catlg, admin. 15: Univ of West Ont Lib, London Ont Canada.

TURNER, MARGARET K. b Carona Ala 17 My 07. 5: UAla 25-32 (Eng) AB in Ed, summers 44, 46 (LS) Lib Certif; UMiss summer 45 (LS); UIll summer 50 (LS); Fla State U summr 59 (LS). 6: Sp. 7: Libn Neville High Sch, Monroe La 46-47; Asst libn NE Jr Col (Monroe La) summer 46; Libn High sch, Gadsden Ala 47-53; Catlgr & asst libn Jr-Sr high sch, shalimar Fla 53-63; Hd libn High sch, Brooksville Fla 63-64; Lib supv Marshallton Sch Dist, Wilmington Del 64-67; Libn 3 elem schs, S Plainfield NJ 67-. 9: NAEB; NEA; -DAVI; ALA; -AASchL; NJEA; NJ Sch Libns; MiddlesexCoEA; S PlainfieldEA. 14: Child bks, catlg. 15: 20 Lamar ave, Edison NJ 08817.

TURNER, MARY LOUISE. b Quincy Ill 13 O 25. 5: Gem City Bus Col 43 (Bus); UMo 62-67 9psych, LS) AB, 67-68 (LS) MA. 6: Ger, Lat. 7: Lib asst Little Dixie Reg Lib, Moberly Mo 59-62; Lib asst UMo Lib (Columbia) 62-67; Consul for inst serv Mo State Lib Jefferson City 68-. 9: ALA; MoLA. 10: Staff Assn Mo State Lib; Art Club of Jefferson City; Missouri Alum of UMo. 13: Yes. 14: Bibliotherapy. 15: 2107 St Mary's blvd apt E, Jefferson City Mo 65101.

TURNER, PATRICIA. b Indianapolis 17 Je 28. 5: Butler U 46-50 (Hist, Pol Sci) AB; Ind U 56-60 (LS) MA. 6: Fr. 7: Claims examiner US Army, Indianapolis 52-56; Child libn Indianapolis Pub Lib 56-60; Child libn NY Pub Lib 60-63; Humanities libn Lib UAriz 63-66; Instr Lib Sch UMinn 67-. 9: ALA; Ariz StateLA. 10: Beta Phi Mu. 14: Ref, wk with child. 15: 727 University ave SE, Minneapolis Mn 55414.

TURNER, PATRICIA. b Lawrence Kan 25 Mr 31. 5: Kan State Tchrs Col (Emporia) 52-53 (LS) BA; UMich 57-58 MALS. 7: Ser acquis UKan 53-56; Child ya libn brs Dallas Pub Lib 56-57; Scholarship-govt publs UMich 57-58; Ref libn US Army Co Command & Gen Staff Col Ft Leaveworth Kan 59-64; Base libn Kindley Air Force Base, Bermuda 64-66; Base libn Athens AFB, Greece 66-69; Base libn Shaw AFB, SC 69-. 9: ALA. 14: Docs, ref. 15: Apt 123 Hurstwood, Sumter SC 29150.

TURNER, PEGGY. b Abilene Tex 24 F 31. 5: Tex Wesleyan Col 48-51 (Eng) BA; No Tex State U summers 52-54 (Eng) MA; Tex Womans U summers 59-62 MLS. 6: Sp. 7: Eng & Speech tchr Everman High Sch, Everman Tex 51-52; Eng tchr Handly Jr High Sch, Ft Worth Tex 52-60; Libn Meadowbrook Jr High Sch, Ft Worth Tex 60-68; Libn Leonard Middle Sch, Ft Worth Tex 68-. 8: Instr Sch of Lib Sci Texas Womans U summer 65, 66, 67. 9: ALA; NEA; TexLA (sec-treas Dist 7); Tex State Tchrs Assn; (Dist II Lib Sect Chm); Tex Cir Tchrs Assn; Tex Assn of Reading; Tarrant Co ASchL. 10: Delta Kappa Gamma; AAUW; Altrusa. 14: Ref, sch libs. 15: 8408 Leo ct, Fort Worth Tex 76116.

TURNER, RUTH (THOMASON). b Bainbridge Ga 26 Ag 13. 4: Hamish Turner. 5: Winthrop Col 29-33 (Hist) BA; UNC 33-34 ABLS; USCar 55; UHawaii 62. 7: Elem libn Spartanburg City schs, Spartanburg SC 34-35, 51-. 9: NEA; ALA; SCLA (past treas); SELA; SCEA; Clr Tchrs. 10: AAUW. 14: Ref, child. 15: 576 Otis blvd, Spartanburg SC 29302.

TURNER, RUTH NEWHALL. b Dayton Ohio. 5: UCal 22-26 (Eng) BA, 27 Certif of Libnship. 6: Fr. 7: Asst libn "San Francisco Chronicle 27-29; In chg filing dept Shell Oil Co, San Francisco 29-30; Contra Costa Co Lib, Martinez Cal: Asst br dept 31-34, Ref libn 34-44, Supv br libn 44-58, Prin libn readers serv 58-64, Prin libn coordinator info programs Pleasant Hill 64-. 9: ALA; CalLA. 10: AAUW; Theta Sigma Phi. 12: Ed CalLA "Newsletter 62-63). 14: Pub rel, ref, readers serv, ed, adult educ. 15: 162 Hemme av, Alamo Cal 94507.

TURNER, SYLVIE JUNE (ERIKSSON). b NYC 2 Jl 36. 5: Clark U 53-57 (Hist) AB; Cornell U 57-58 (Amer Hist) MA; Simmons 66-69 (LS). 6: Fr, Swedish. 7: Catlgr Cornell U Archives 58; Libn Amalgamated Clothing Workers, NYC 58-61; Research histn Od Sturbridge Villge, Sturbridge Mass 61-63; Archivist Conn State Lib 63-. 9: SAA; ConnLA (Archivist 68-69). 10: Phi Beta Kappa. 13: Yes. 14: Mss. 15: 1310 Berlin tpk, Wethersfield Ct 06109.

TURNER, TREVA IRENE. b Houston Ky 6 D 38. 5: Berea Col 57-61 (Eng) BA. 6: Sp, Fr. 7: Accounting asst Robert Acomb Advertising Inc (Cincinnati Ohio) 62; Lib asst Pub Relations Pub Lib of Cincinnati 62-63, Lib asst Map Div 63-64, Libn Hist & Lib Dept 64-65; Asst to the Hd Pub Ref Sect LC 65-66, Libn Subject catlging annotated card program 66-. 14: Ref, catlg. 15: 110 D st SE apt 303, Washington DC 20003.

TURNER, VIRGINIA (KELLEY). b Riverside Cal 22 Ap 19. 4: Richard Turner. 5: Riverside (Cal) Jr Col 36-38 (Phys Educ) AA; UCal (Santa Barbara) 38-40 (Phys Educ); Lake Forest U 50-54 (Psych) BA; No Ill U 61-67 (LS) MA. 7: Tchr Elem Dist #75, Mundelein Ill 48-59, Tchr & libn 59-. 9: ALA; NEA; IllLA; IllASchL; IllEA. 14: Sch libs. 15: 17 E Park, Mindelein Il 60060.

TURPIN, CALVIN COOLIDGE. b Granite City Ill 8 N 24. 4: Josie Eudell Coody. 5: UArk 45-47 (Law, Pre-law); Baylor U 49 (Religion) BA, 52 (Religion) MA; Tex Tech Col 50 (Hist); So Baptist Theol Sem 55 BD; Vanderbilt U Divinity Sch 55-56 (Theol); So Baptist Theol Sem 58 MRE; Peabody 62 MA (LS); Golden Gate Baptist Theol Sem 67 (Theol) STD. 6: Ger, Lat, Hebrew, Gk. 7: US Army 43-45; Minister: Calvary Baptist Church, ODonnell Tex 49-50, First Baptist Church, palmer Tex 50-52, Little West Fork Baptist Church, Clarksvile Tenn 55-57; Minister of Educ Baptist Tabernacle, Louisville Ky 58; Minister of Educ Immanuel Bptist CHURCH, Nashville 58-61; Assoc libn Golden Gate Baptist Theol Sem 61-66; Libn Minot State Col 66-67; Dir of the Lib Judson Col 67-. 8: Tchr; jacksonville Col 50-52, Belmont Col 55-. Austin-Peay State Col 57, Golden Gate Baptist Theol Sem 62-66; Minot State Col 66-67, Judson Col 67-. 9: ATheolLA; West Theol LA; NDLA; AlaLA. 10: BETA Phi Mu. ; Lions Club; Amer Soc of Ch Hist; AAUP. 14: Admin, catlg, ref. 15: Judson College, Marion Al 36756.

TURPIN, EMMA POSTON. b Memphis Tenn. 5: Southwestern Col 31 (Gk) BA; Memphis State U 32 (Hist) BS; Drexel 33 BS LS. 7: Libn: Miss Hutchisons Sch, Memphis Tenn 33-36, Alma High Sch, Alma Ga 37, Ville Platte High Sch, Ville Platte La 37-38, Homer High Sch, Homer La 38-40, Southern Col of Optometry 40-. 15: Kimbrough Towers apt 211, Memphis Tn 38104.

TURPIN, EVELYN WAINWRIGHT. b Wash DC 24 Jl 05. 5: Radcliff 26 (Hist) AB; Pratt 30 BS. 7: NY Pub Lib 26-29; Los Angeles City Sch Lib 30-33; Wash DC Pub Lib child dept 33, Br libn 58-. 13: Yes. 15: 4520 Fessenden st NW, Wash DC 20016.

TURPIN, LOUISE W. b Richmond Ky. 5: Ohio U 32-35 AB; UIll 38-40, BS in LS; UCal summer 44 (Hist & Internat Rel). 7: Dayton Pub Lib 35-45; Lib asst USVA Kingsbridge rd Hosp, Bronx NY 45; Brooklyn Pub Lib: Asst then ref libn Williamsburgh Br, 45-49 Br libn Brownsville Br 49-50, Chief hist div 50-65, Br libn Brooklyn Heights Br 65-. 9: ALA; NYLA. 10; civil War Round Table of NY; LI Hist Soc; Brooklyn Heights Assn; Friends of Prospect Park. 13: Yes. 14: Ref, loc hist, Civil War hist. 15: 50 Plaza st, Brooklyn NY 11238.

TURRENTINE, VIRGINIA. b Bell Buck E Tenn 21 F 14. 5: Maryville Col 35-36 (Lat); UVa summer 39; UTenn summers 38, 40-43 & 41-42 (Lat) BA; Peebdy 52-53 MA in LS. 7: Libn

Webb Sch, Bell Buckle Tenn 31-41, 42-43; Asst catlgr Fla State U 44-52; Head Libn Maryville Col (Tenn) 53-. 9: ALA; SELA; TennLA (ch Col & Univ Sect 58-59). 10: AAUW. 14: Acquis, admin, periods, catlg. 15: 118 Miller ave, Maryville Tenn 37801.

TUSLER, ADELAIDE (GEST). b NY 24 F 23. 5: UCLA 47 (Music & Hist) BA, 47-48 (Music), 61 MLS. 6: Fr. 7: Libn & off supv - UCLA Oral Hist Program 62-. 9: Oral Hist Assn; CalLA; UCLA Libns Assn. 12: Co-auth "A Bibliography of Oral History" (Oral history Association, 67, Rev ed 68). 13: Yes. 14: Oral hist interviewing, mss processing. 15: 807C Princeton, Santa Monica Ca 90403.

TUTTLE, HELEN WELCH. b Larned Kan 13 Ap 14. 4: Preston H Tuttle. 5: UKan 31-35 (Math) AB, 35-36 (Math) MA; UIll 41-42 BS in LS. 7: Math tchr Atlanta High Sch Atlanta Kan 36-39; Math Tchr Burlington High Sch, Burlington Kan 40-41; UIll Lib (Urbana): Bibliog 42-47, Asst acquis libn 47-52, Acquis libn 52-, Acquis libn & Prof Lib Admin 62-68; Asst U libn for preparations & prof Princeton U Lib 68-. 9: ALA-RTSD (pres 61-62); IllLA (treas 48-52). 10: AAUP; Beta Phi Mu; Phi Beta Kappa; Phi Kappa Phi; Pi Mu Epsilon; Phi Lambda THETA. 12: Asst ed for acquis "Library Resources and Technical Services (57-60). 13: Yes. 14: Acquis, tech serv, automation. 15: 75 S Stanworth dr, Princeton NJ 08540.

TUTTLE, JANICE (TURKLE). b Youngstown Ohio 18 My 43. 4: Jon Franklin Tuttle. 5: YoungstownU 61-62; OhioU 62-65 (Speech Pathology & Audiology) BSEd; UPittsburgh 66-69 MLS. 6: Sp. 7: Concessionaire summers 57-61; Playground dir City of Youngstown Ohio summers 62-64; Speech asst OhioU 65; Speech therapist Mt Lebanon Sch Dist, Mt Lebanon Penn 65-68; Grad asst UPittsburgh 68-69. 9: NEA; PennStateEA. 10: Mt LebanonEA. 15: 692 F Robinwood dr, Pittsburgh Pa 15216.

TUTTLE, LEAH JANE. b Lansing Mich 18 N 21. 5: Mich State U 39-45 (Speech, Radio) BA; UMich 53-55 (Speech, Televisoon) MA, 57-58 AMLS. 7: Asst program dir Radio Station WOOD, Grand Rapids Mich 45-46; Dir radio advertising Herpolsheimer's, Grand Rapids Mich 46; Women's ed Radio Sta WILS, Lansing Mich 47-52; Part-time writer UMich TV Off (Ann Arbor) 53-54; Writer Radio & TV Sta WJIM, Lansing Mich 54-55; Communications skills instr Heidelberg Col 55-56; Communications skills instr Mich State U (E Lansing) 56-57; Ref, publicity, group serv & gen asst, Baldwin Pub Lib, Birmingham mich 58-62, Ref dept, Hd publicity 62-. 9: ALA; MichLA. 10: Beta Phi Mu; Alpha epsilon Rho; Phi Kappa Phi; Alpha Xi Delta. 14: Ref, pub rel. 15: 525 Watkins st, Birmingham Mi 48009.

TUTTLE, MARCIA (LEE). b Charlotte NC 11 Ap 37. 5: Duke 55-59 (Religion) AB; Emory 59-61 MLn; UVt 67-68; UNC 69-. 7: Res libn Theol LVIB Emory U 59-61; Catlgr Princeton Theol Sem 61-64; Asst ref libn Princeton U 64-66; Hd ref libn UVt 66-68; Hd Interlib Ctr UNC 68-69; Hd ser 69-. 9: ALA; NCLA; SELA. 10: Assn of Amer Geogrs; Alpha Chi Omega. 14: Ref, interlib loan, lib coop. 15: 2B Towne House, Chapel Hill NC 27514.

TUTTLE, RODMILLA. b Gary Ind 2 O 36. 5: DrakeU 54-58 (Hist) BA; IndU 64-65 (LS) MA. 7: Br chil libn Gary Pub Lib, Gary Ind 62-63, Y-a libn 64-67; Y-a consul Onondaga Lib System, Syracuse NY 67-. 10: Phi Beta Kappa; Beta Phi Mu. 14: ya serv. 15: 1310 Park st, Syracuse NY 13208.

TWEIT, JOAN (CANNON). b Berkeley Calif 3 Ap 31. 4: Robert Tweit. 5: UCal (Berkeley) 49-53 (US Hist) BA; Rosary Col 66-69 MALS. 7: Libn Harper Elem Sch (Wilmette Ill) 67-. 9: ALA; IllLA; IllEA. 10: Sigma Kappa Alpha; Phi Beta Kappa; Bd Dirs Onward Neighborhood House; Village wide PTA; Bd Dirs Wilmette Human Rel Com; Wilmette Girl Scouts Coun. 14: Child serv, a-v materials. 15: 2104 Birchwood ave, Wilmette Il 60091.

TWELVES, JUNE D. ALT Lake City Utah 20 Je 14. 4: Robert D Twelves. 5: UUtah 32-36 (Eng) AB; Drexel 36-37 BS in LS. 6: Ger, Sp. 7: Sub pub serv libn New Haven Pub Lib, New Haven Conn 39-40; Clk Bd of Educ, North Haven Conn 59-60; Asst br libn Hamden Pub Lib, Whitneyville Conn 60-62; Libn Browns Mills Lib & Pemberton Lib, Pemberton NJ 63-64; Circ libn l readers advisor Burlington Co Lib, Mt Holly NJ 64-. 9: ALA&ASD; -RSD; YASD; NJLA (Adult Serv Sect). 10: LWV. 14: Readers adv serv, adult & ya, ref, circ serv. 15: Burlington County Lib Court House Sq, Mt Holly NJ 08060.

TWISS, WALTER HAZZARD. b Chehalis Wash 19 Je 10. 5: Centralia Jr Col 29-31 (Engnr) Diploma; UWash 31-32, 33-35, 36-37 (Eng Lit) BA, MA; UDenver 54-55 MA in LS. 7: Tchr Jr High Sch, Shelton Wash 35-36; Tooling dept Boeing Airplane Co, Seattle 42-43, Purchasing det 43-50; Washington Title Insurance Co, Seattle 52-54; Sci libn Denver Pub Lib 55-58; Sci libn Seattle Pub Lib 58-. 9: ALA; PNLA; WashLA. 14: Ref, loc hist, geneol, sci, engnr. 15: 1110-8th ave, Seattle Wa 98101.

TWITCHELL, ELIZABETH (CLO). b Chicago 15 Jl 09. 5: UKy 31 (Eng) BA; Columbia 32 BS in LS;UIll 40-41 (LS) MA. 6: Fr. 7: Gen asst Freeport (LI NY) Mem Lib 32-33; Sub circ dept Queens Borough Pub Lib summer 33; Libn Baldwin (LI NY) Pub Lib 33-40; Asst-in-chg Illini Union Browsing Room UIll 40-41; 1st asst bus & tech dept Trenton(NJ) Free Pub Lib 42-44; Sub bk info desk Kan City (Mo) Pub Lib 46-47; Sub Hockaday Sch Lib Dallas 48; Head ref dept, Fondren Lib So Methodist U ;8-53; Asst LibnLAW Lib 53-60; Bus libn Deering Lib Northwestern U 60-61; Asst libn Bridwell Lib, Perkins Sch of Theol So Methodist U 61-64; Ser libn Sci Lib So Methodist U 64-68; Ref libn Sci Lib 68-. 9: ALA; SLA; TexLA (Exec Bd 58-60); DallasCoLA. 10: Beta Phi Mu. 14: Ref, docs. 15: 3322 Daniels ave, Dallas Tx 75205.

TYDEMAN, JAMES EDWARD. b Minneapolis 2 N 20. 4: Betty Swanson. 5: UMinn 46-49 (Pol Sci) BA, 49-50 BS in LS; Chicago 52-55 (LS) MA. 7: Period libn UKan 50-52; Lib Sch libn UChicago 53-55; Ser libn So Ill U 55-58; Bus libn West Mich U 58-. 9: ALA; SLA; MichLA (chm Tech Serv Sect 65-66). 14: Spec libs, us, tech serv. 15: 731 Edgemoor, Kalamazoo 49001.

TYER, TRAVIS E(ARL). b Lorenzo Tex 23 O 30. 4: Alma Lois Davis. 5: Abilene Christian Col 48-49 (Pre-Pharmacy); Midwestern U 49-50 (Pharmacy); Abilene Christian CVOL 50-52 (Secondary Educ) BS; Tex Tech Col 52-54 (Educ); No Tex State U summers 53, 54, 55, 59 BS in LS; Tex Tech Col 54, summers 57, 58 (Span); Odessa Col 56 (Span). 6: Sp. 7: Tchr-libn av coordinator Borden Co pub schs, GAIL Tex 52-54; Lib Thompson Jr High Lubbock pub schs, Lubbock Tex 54-55; Lib SrHigh Sch Seminole pub schs, Seminole Tex 55-61; Vacation relief libn Lubbock Pub Lib, Lubbock Tex summer 58; Wkshop dir Sch of Lib Sci Tex Womans U summers 60 & 61; Dallas Pub Lib: Head ya dept 61-62, Head Oak Lawn Br 62, Coordinator ya serv 62-64; Dir Lubbock Pub Lib, Lubbock Tex 64-68; Doctoral candidate Fla State U 68-. 8: Selected by Tex Educ Agency to coop with So States Wkshop Conf on the status of sch libs in 4 so states 57-60; Consul "School Library Journal6-66; Consul "Standard Catalog for High Sch Libraries 6-; Adv Com for the sel of bks for blind ya, Selection Sect Div for the Blind LC; Mem Award Jury for 1965 Grolier Award. 9: ALA-AASchL (SchhLib Standards Implement Com 59-6, Rep for the Prof Re -YASD (Magazine Eval Com 61-63, Chm Sel of Bks & Other Materials Com 63-66); -ASD (Nomin tcom 66); TexA-V Educ Assn (Program Com 61); Tex State Tchrs Assn; TexLA (mem-at-large Exec Com 61-62, mem &/or chm Program Coms63 & 65; chm YA Round Table 65-66; mem &/or chm 3 other coms); Teen-Age Lib Assn Tex(state sponsor 60-61); TexASchL (TREAS, VCHM & chm 58-61). 10: Friends of the Dallas Pub Lib. 12: Ed Bd "Educational Resources and Techniques (60-62) (Texaved); Ed "TALAActivity Book Teen-Age Lib Assn Tex (60). 13: Yes. 14: Wk with yp, sch libs, lib educ. 15: 1814 Sunset lane, Tallahassee Fl 32303.

TYLER, CAROLYN (SMITH). b Culverton Ga 30 Ja 23. 4: Josie Lee Tyler Jr. 5: Ga State Col for Women 40-44 (Eng) AB; Emory 44-45 AB in LS. 6: Sp, Fr. 7: Libn Emory U Div of Libnship 45-56; Ser catlgr Ser Dept, Duke U 56-57; Catlgr Colleton Co Lib, Walterboro SC 57-58; Libn USCar Educ Lib 60-. 9: ALA; SCLA. 10: AAUW. 14: Catlg, lib educ. 15: 1100 Eastminster dr, Columbia SC 29204.

TYLER, ESTHER (VIRGINIA). b Lansing Mich 19 Jl 38. 5: So Missionary Col 56-60 (Home Econ) BS; Peabody 63-64 MA (LS). 7: Asst dietition Fla San & Hosp, Orlando Fla 60-61; Catlgr Andrews U 64-. 9: ALA. 14: Catlg. 15: Box 156 Andrews Station, Berrien Springs Mich 49104.

TYLER, GLADYS ELLEN (BROCKWELL). b London England 20 N 20. 4: R Anthony Tyler. 5: LondonU (England) 39-42 (Bio) BS; OttawaU 65-68 BLS. 7: Tchr Gloucester Pub Sch bd, Ottawa Can 60-67; Libn March Twp Sch Bd, Ottawa Can 67-68; Libn Ottawa Collegaite Bd, Ottawa Can 68-. 9: CanLA; OttawaLA. 14: Sch libs. 15: 728 Lonsdale rd, Ottawa 7 Ont Can.

TYLER, JACK MAURICE. b Salt Lake City Utah 11 N 38. 4: Linda Terry Tyler. 5: UUtah 56-58 (Geol); Brigham

YoungU 61-63 (Applied Sociol) BS; UPittsburgh 63-64 MLS. 6: Sp. 7: Ref asst Brigham YoungU (Provo Utah) 62; Bkmob libn Salt Lake Co Lib (Salt Lake City Ut) 63; Grad research asst UPittsburgh GSLIS (Pittsburgh Pa) 63-64; Dir Campus Info Res Ctr Jr Col Dist of St Louis, Mo 64-65; Ref libn KASC (UPittsburgh) (Pittsburgh Pa) 65; Dir ext Utah Stste Lib (Salt Lake City Ut) 65-68; State libn Wyo State Lib (Cheyenne Wyo) 68-69; State libn Del State Lib 69-. 8: NY World's Fair ALA Exhibit, Library/USA; Ref libn NYC 64. 9: ALA; MPLA; UtahLA; WyoLA. 12: Ed "Horsefeathers" (Utah State Library publication). 13: Yes. 14: Admin, ref, consul. 15: 508 Princeton lane, Cheyenne Wy 82001.

TYLER, RUTH VINE. b Salt Lake City Utah. 4: Wilfrid M Tyler. 5: UUtah 19; Brigham Young 35; UCLA 54-55. 7: Elem tchr, Salt Lake City: Jordan Dist 20-21, Granite Dist 21-22; Lib asst Salt Lake City 23-38; Hd libn Salt Lake Co Lib 39-. 9: ALA (Coun); UtahLA (past pres, 2 terms). 10: PTA. 11: State Bk of the Month Award 63. 14: Pub rel, adult educ. 15: 80 E Center st, Midvale Ut 84047.

TYLER, SARA ELIZABETH. b Bowling Green Ky 31 D 10. 5: West Ky State Col; Jr lib asst 33-37, Head period dept 37-56, Head libn 56-65, Dir of lib serv 65-. 9: ALA; SELA (Dir 54-58); KyLA (Dir 46-48, pres 50-51; sec 65-67). 10: AAUW; Ky Hist Assn; Twentieth Cent Club; Beta Phi Mu; Pi Gamma Mu; Kappa Delta Pi; Phi Alpha Theta. 11: KyLA Outstanding Col Lib Award 68. 14: Admin, ref. 15: 1349 State st, Bowling Green Ky 42101.

TZARNAS, MANOLATOS ANNE. b Camden NJ. 4: Chris Tzarnas. 5: Temple 42; George WashingtonU 44 (Pol Sci, Hist) BA. 6: Gr, Fr, Sp. 7: Catlgr & reviser US Army Map Serv, Wash DC 54-62; Supv & catlgr David Taylor Model Basin, Wash DC 62-65; Libn & supv 9phys sci & engring) Bur of Ships, Wash DC 65-66; Libn (med) Bethesda Naval Hosp 66-68; Ref libn Atmospheric Sci Lib (ESSA) 68-. 9: SLA. 10: AAUW; Women's Sux of Suburban Hosp. 14: Catlg, ref. 15: 9732 Byeforde rd, Kensington Md 20795.

U

UBEL, JAMES ANDREW. b St Paul 14 N 37. 4: Hiltrud M Masuch. 5: Col of St Thomas (St Paul) 55-56 (Music Educ); UMinn 56-59 BA, 60 (LS) MA. 7: Clerical & sub prof St Paul Pub Lib 53-59; Grad Lib asst UMinn 59-60; City Libn Scottsbluff Pub Lib, Scottsbluff Neb 60-62 Hdqrs libn Dakota Scott Reg Lib, W St Paul Minn 62-66; Dir Shawnee Lib Syst, Carterville Ill 66-. 9: ALA; MinnLA (pres 5-66; numerous chmships of coms & sects); IllLA. 10: Beta Phi Mu. 13: Yes. 14: Bk sel, eval of lit, lib admin. 15: 710 Ridge ave, Carterville Il 62918.

UDINSKY, J CALVIN. b New Orleans 26 N 24. 5: Loyola U (New Orleans) (Educ) BS, (Educ) M Ed; LSU MS in LS. 6: Fr, Lat. 7: Libn Brother Martin High Sch, New Orleans. 8: Lib serv consul for SE USA. 9: ALA; NCTE; CattLA; Ala High Sch Libns. 14: Ref. 15: 5940 Franklin ave, New Orleans La 70122.

UEBELACKER, SUSAN C. b Milwaukee 29 Je 39. 5: Mt Mary Col 57-61 (Hist, Eng) BA; Catholic U 61-63 MS in LS. 7: Interlib loan libn catholc U Libs 62-63; Ya libn Prince Georges Co Mem Lib, Hyattsville Md 63-; Vision sect libn 64-67; Hd ya dept Oxon Hill br 67-. 9: ALA; MdLA; DCLA. 10: AAUW. 13: Yes. 14: Ya wk, wk with the blind. 15: 3900 Hamilton st, A301, Hyattsville Md.

UHL, EDNA (GOODARD). b YC 15 Ap 20. 4: William Edward Uhl. 5: U Bridgeport 61-62 So Conn State Col 62-(LS). 7: Libn (volunteer) Nicholas MEM Lib, Trumbull Conn 57-59, Libn 59-60; Catlgr (volunteer) Trumbull Bd of Educ, Trumbull Conn 60-61; Lib asst Trumbull High Sch Lib, Trumbull Conn 61-62; Catlgr (olunteer) Trumbull Bd of Educ, Trumbull Conn 62-64; Catlgr Trumbull (Conn) Bd of Educ Daniels Farm Sch summer 63; Catlgr Sratford Pub Lib, Stratford Conn 64-. 9: ALA; ConnLA (Lib Adminrs Group, Catlg Div). ; Nichols MemorialLA (v-pres). 10: Trumbull (Conn) Hist Soc; Cub Scouts; Girl Scouts; Friends of Levittown LIB: Nat Soc of Prof Engnrs Auxiliary. 14: Catlg. 15: 100 Daniels Farm rd, Trumbull Conn 06611.

UHLE, KATHARINE (BUTSON). b Hampton Iowa 29 S 27. 4: Alvan F Uhle. 5: Drake U 45-49 (Eng) BS in Ed; West Res 51-52 MS in LS. 7: Child libn Detroit Pub Lib 52-59; Elem sch libn Coldwater Schs, Coldwater Mich 65-. 9: ALA; MichLA. 10: AAUW. 14: Child lib and/or sch libs (Elem). 15: 24 Park pl, Coldwater Mi 49036.

UHLENDORF, B(ERNHARD) A(LEXANDER). b Kisselbach Germany 6Mr 1893. 4: Evelyn Ruth Hill. 5: Washington U (St Louis) 12-15 (German Lit), 15-16 (German Lit & Psych) AM; UWis summers 14-16; UIll(Urbana) 16-18, 20 (German Lit & Philol) PhD; UMich 30-32 ABLS, 32-33 AMLS. 6: Ger, Fr, Sp, Ital. 7: Asst in German Washington U (St Louis) 15-16; Instr UIll 16-18, 20-22; Psych examiner US Army, Camp Funston(Kan) & Ft Oglethorpe(Ga) 18-19; Assoc UIll 22-25; Assoc Prof Northwestern U summer 25; Asst Prof UCLA 25-30 (chm of German Dept 28-30); Acquis bibliogr UMich Lib 31-38; Dir Mich Imprints & Mss Inventories (WPA) 38-42; Dir publs Edwards Bros & J W Edwards, Ann Arbor Mich 42-50; Ed publs (Sci & Tech) UMich Off of Research Admin 50-63; Ed Emeritus 63-. 8: Org & first pres UMich Lib Sci Alumni Assn 33-34; in chg of Edwards Bros program f reprinting by license of Off of Alien Property Custodian) war-important German sci & tech bks & journals & the wks of Bach, Beethoven, & Brahms, 42-50. 10: Zamorano Club, Los Angeles (Hon life mem); Eta Phi; Pi Delta Phi (Hon); YM-YWCA Signature Club, Ann Arbor; Amer Rhododendron Soc. 12: "Charles Sealsfiedl; ethnic Elements & National PROBLEMS IN His Works (21); "German-American Poetry: A Contribution to Colonial Literature (24); Ed Charles Sealsfields "Nathan, der Squatter-Regulator (26); "Mitten im Leben-Short Stories from Contemorary German Literature, with W Diamond (28); Ed & tr "Letters from Major Baurmeister to Colonel von Jungkenn Phila campaign 177-78, with E Vosper (37); "The Siege of Charleston, in 1780 (38); Comp (Analytic Index of Michigan History Magazine, v 1-25 (44); Amer ed & contrib "Deutsches Literatur-Lexikon (27-30); Ed "Books in Print (48-52); Ed & tr "Revolution in America (57); Assoc ed "Whos Who in Library Service (66, 70). 13: Yes. 14: Hist of printing, fine printing, rare bks. 15: 1309 Gardner, Ann Arbor Mi 48104.

UHLER, EDWARD HENRY. b Lebanon Penn 21 Ja 31. 4: Edna Wehr. 5: Houghton Col 48-52 (Chem, Math) BS. 6: Ger. 7: Research chem Callery Chem Co, Callery Penn 52-55; Lit chem 56-59; Tech abstractor & libn Hercules Powder/ABL, Cumberland Md 59-65; Tech libn SKF Ind Inc, King of Prussia Penn 65-. 9: SLA. 14: Mgt of small libs. 15: 106 Cinnamon Hill rd, King of Prussia Pa 19406.

UHRICH, HELEN BORDNER. b Myerstown Penn 13 Ja 08. 5: Albright Col 25-29 (Soc Sci) AB; Drexel 29-30 (LS) BS; Biblical Sem (NY Theol Sem) 31-36; Columbia 35-36 (LS); Yale Divinity 37-46. 6: Ger, Fr, Dutch. 7: Catlgr Queens Borough Pub Lib, Queens Borough ny 30-31; Catlgr Biblical Sem (NY) 31-32, Libn 32-36; Hd catlgr Hartford Sem Foundation, Hartford Conn 36-37; Catlgr Yale Divinity Lib 37-39, Hd catlgr 39-46, asst libn in charge catlg & clsf 46-67, Asst libn 67-. 8: Bd Dirs "Index to Religious periodical Literature 60-; Staff Columbia Sch of Lib Serv summer 68. 9: ALA (Catlg code Rev Com, Sub-Com on Relig Hdings 61-65); ATheolLA (pres 56-57; Exec Bd 57-58; Catlg & Clsf Sect 52-55); NY Tech Serv Libns. 10: Quota Club. 11: Albright Col Alumni Citation 53. 12: Co-ed "Index to Religious Periodical Literature" v 3, 55-56 (64); v 5, 60-62 (63). 13: Yes. 14: Catlg, clsf, ref, admin. 15: 216 Bishop st, New Haven Ct 06511.

UIBEL, BARBARA (STEWART). b Salt Lake City Utah 3 Mr 36. 4: Howard F Uibel. 5: Brigham Young 54-58 (Elem Educ) BS, 66-67 MLS. 6: Ger. 7: Elem tchr Nrookside Sch, Springville Utah 58-61; Instr media libn Poston Road Sch, Martinsville Ind 67-68; A-v libn East Wash State Col 68-. 9: ALA. 14: Instr media materials. 15: 1028 2nd st, Cheney Wa 99004.

UKNALIS, IRENA SUSAN. b Philadelphia Penn 23 S 42. 5: Holy Family Col 60-64 (Art) BA; Drexel 64-65 MSLS. 6: Fr. 7: Libn (child specialist) Free Lib of Phila 66-. 9: ALA; PennLA. 14: Child serv. 15: 2738 Lardner st, Philadelphia Pa 19149.

ULM, RUBY (McCULLOUGH). b Madison Co Fla 4 Jl 20. 4: Anderson C Ulm. 5: Fla State U summers 38-50 (Elem Educ) BS, summers 54-57 (LS) MS, 60, 65, 66 (Educ Admin). 7; tchr elem schs, Madison Co Fla 37-54; LIBN Madison High Sch, Madison Fla 54-; Libn N Fla Jr Col 59-, 8: State sponsor Fla High Sch LibCoun, 61-62 & 63-64; Mem Eval Team So Assn Sec Schs & Col 64. 9: ALA; NEA; SELA; FlaEA; FlaLA; FlaASchL (MEM Exec Bd 64, chm-elect 66-67, chm 67-68); Fla High Sch Lib Coun (Exec Bd 61-65). 10: Maison Co (Fla) Clr Tchrs Assn; Bus Womas Club; Beta Phi Mu; Madison Co (Fla) EA. 13: Yes. 14: Admin of lib serv, sch libs. 15: Rt 1 Box 129, Lee Fla 32059.

ULMER, MARY ELLEN (HAMROCK). b Pittsburgh Penn 12 Je 40. 5: Clarion State Col 58-62 (LS, Eng) BS in Educ. 7: Libn Neshannock Twp Sch Dist, New Castle Penn 62-64; Libn Ringgold Sch Dist, Monongahela Penn 64-65; Libn Wasatch Acad, Mt Pleasant Utah 65-67; Asst tchr Wilmington Area Schools, New Wilmington Penn 67-68; Libn Neshannock Twp Sch Dist, New Castle Penn 68-69. 8: Hd coord com for 10 year Plan at Ringgold Sch Dist. 15: RD 1, Mercer Pa 16137.

ULRICH, B(ARBARA)ELIZABETH. b Enders Penn 18 My 10. 5: Lebanon Valley Col 28-32 (Eng Lit, Fr, Educ) AB; Carnegie 33-34 BS in LS; Penn State U 37-44 (Eng Lit) MA; 15th Inst of Geneal Res American U 65 Certif. , Temple U 67. 6: Fr, Sp. 7: Eng tchr Swatara Twp High Sch, Oberlin Penn 32-33; Sub temp catlgr Hershey Free Lib, Hershey Penn 34-35; Asst Allentown Free Lib, Allentown Penn 35; Br, schs asst Harrisburg Pub Lib, Harrisburg Penn 35-37; Penn State U: Ser asst 37-40, Asst ref libn 40-44, Circ lib 44-45; Advacnced ref asst, ext div Penn State Lib 45, Advanced ref asst, documents libn 45-47; Libn Penn Economy League State Div, Harrisburg Penn 48-55; Asst bibliog US Army War Col Lib, Carlisle BARRACKS Penn 55-57; Ref Libn, chief Penn State Lib 57-.09: ALA; PennLA. 12: Co-ed "Years Works in Pennsylvania Studies" (67). 14: Ref. 15: 643 S 29th st, Harrisburg Penn 17111.

ULRICH, ELIZABETH (TEALL BENDER). b Pittsburgh Penn 4 My 16. 4: Paul Theodore Ulrich. 5: Lebanon Valley Col 34-38 (Eng) AB; Columbia U 38-39 BS in LS; UMd (overseas br) 60-61; San Jacinto Col 62; UHouston 68. 7: Tchr-libn high sch, New Cumberland Penn 39-41; Yp libn NYC Pub Lib 39-42; Child libn pub lib, Port Wash NY 42-43; Lib asst pub lib, Wash DC 59; Sch libn Benjamin Stoddard Jr High, Prince George Co Md 59-60; Sch libn Amer Dependent High Sch, Madrid 61-62; Founder & libn Freeman Memorial Lib (pub), Clear Lake City Houston Tex 63-67; School libn Westwood Elem Sch, Friendswood Houston Tex 63-67. 8: Vol serv; Reorg elem sch lib, Dover Del 58,; Reorg elem school lib Amer Dependents Sch, Madrid Spain 60-61. 9: ALA; NEA; TexLA; TexStateTA. 11: Distinguished Serv Award Clear Lake Jaycees 65. 13: Yes. 14: Sch libs. 15: 1702 Silverpines, Houston Tx 77058.

ULVELING, RALPH A(DRIAN). b Adrian Minn 9 My 02. 4: Elizabeth Baer. 5: DePaul U 18-22 PhB; Columbia 27-28 (LS) BS; Wayne State U 56 LHD (Honorary). 7: Multi Electrical Mfg Co, Chicago 22; Hart Schaffner & Marx, Chicago 23-24; Newberry Lib, Chicago 24-26; Libn Pub Lib, Amarillo Tex 26-27; Detroit Pub Lib: Chiefof brs 28-34, Assoc dir 34-41, Dir 41-67; Prof Dept Lib Sci Wayne State U 68-. 8: Adv to Jt Army-Navy Com on welfare & recreation 44-46; Adv to USVA, 48-54; Adv com on educl projs W K Kellogg Foun, 44-48; Adv com Acad Freedom Study, 51-53; Ed adv bd, World Book Encyclopedia, 52-; Surveyed US Army libs in Europe, 46; Surveyed pub libs of Tulsa Okla, 0; Oak Park Ill, 51; Madison Wis, 52 (with Ruth Rutzen); Lib bldg consul for 26 pub libs & 1 state lib, 53-. 9: ALA (pres 45-46); Amer Assn Adult Educ (v-pres 44-45); US Nat Commsn for Unesco 46-49; Amer Lib Inst (Fellow); MichLA (pres 37-38); Mich State Bd for Libs 38-39. 10: Engnr Soc of Detroit; Econ Club of Detroit; Acanthus; Detroit Club; Prismatic; Torch Club of Detroit; Bd of trustees Crabrook Cranbrook of Sci 55-; Bd Dirs Detroit Educl TV Foun 5-; Bd of Dirs Family Serv of Metro Detroit 38-63 (pres 43-44); Cath Commsn on Intell & Cultural Affairs 46-; Bd Dirs Great Books Foun 47-49. 11: Joseph W Lippincott award, 56; Citation, Merrill-Palmer Inst, 4; 64 degree, Doctor of Humane Letters, Wayne State U 56. 12: Chaps in bks: "Administration of Branch Systems in C B Joeckels "Current Isues in Library Administration (39); "The Public Library in the Lare COMMUNITY" IN "The Library in the Community ed by Carnovsky 7 martin (44). 13: Yes. 14: Admin, adut educ, lib bldg planning. 15: 20434 Lichfield rd, Detroit Mi 48221.

UMBACH, STEPHANIE EDNA. b Valparaiso Ind 19 Je 38. 5: Valparaiso U 55-59 (Eng) BA; Ind U 59-60 (LS) MA. 7: Asst libn Valparaiso So U 60-. 9: ALA; IndLA. 14: Catlg.46127 15: 2302 Linden dr, Valparaiso Ind 46383.

UMLAND, EVELYN LOUISE (WALDO). b Brooklyn NY 20 Ap 21. 4: Lewis Orville. 5: AdelphiU 39-43 (Math) AB; Syracuse 62-65 MSLS; SUNY (Cortland) 65-66. 7: Chem G W Loper Lab, NYC 43-44; Statistician Marsh McLennan, NYC 45-46; K-12 Libn BOCES Cortland Co, cortland NY 62-66; Elem libn Cortland Bd of Educ, Cortland NY 66-67; Elem libn Cincinnatus Central Sch, Cincinnatus NY 67-68; Dir lib serv St Joseph Col 68-. 8: Consul IMC for Cortland Co NY Bd Coop Educ Serv summer 67. 9: ALA; CathLA; FlaLA; Sch Libns So Tier (sec-treas 66-67). 10: Beta Phi Mu; Girl Scout Leader; Red Cross; Commun Chest. 14: Ref, wk with yp. 15: 329 North Fork rd. Stuart Fl 33494.

UNDERHILL, CHARLES STERLING. b Buffalo NY 3 My 3. 4: Margaret Mary Riley. 5: Williams Col 30-34 (Ger) AB; SUNY(Buffalo) 44 BLS; SUNY(Buffalo) & arvard 35-38 (Eng, Comparative Lit). 6: Ger, Fr. 7: Asst order dept Buffalo Pub Lib, Buffalo NY 44-49; Br libn Buffalo & Erie Co Pub Lib, Buffalo NY 49-55; Lib dir Pub Lib, Corning NY 55-58; Lib dir Pub Lib, Newark NY 58-65; Asst libn catlg dept NY State University Col (Buffalo) 65-69, Hd periods dept 69-. 9: NYLA. 12: Ed "Your Soldier Boy Samuel: Civil War Letters of Samuel Edmund Nichols" (29); Auth "Sketch for a Picture Collection (56); Comp "Handy Key to Your National Geographics" (55, 7th ed 66); (8th ed 68). 14: Catlg, ref, pub rel. 15: 128 Pine st, E Aurora NY 14052.

UNDERWOOD, ELLEN (MYERS). b Racine Wis 17 My 08. 5: Milwaukee-Downer Col 27-29; UWis 29-31 (Eng) BA, 31-32 BSLS; UCLA Lib Admin Clinic summer 56; Kenyon Col summer 61 (LS). 7: Br asst Racine Pub Lib, Racine Wis 33-36 Adult serv S Bend Pub Lib, S Bend Ind 36-41; Hosp libn Army Lib Serv, Hawaii 42-47; Catlgr Air U Lib, Maxwell AFB, Montgomery Ala 47-49; Ref libn Houston Pub Lib 49-53; Br libn Kern Co Lib, Taft-Bakersfld Cal 53-64; Ext libn Maui Co Lib, State Stae Lib 64-. 9: Adult Educ Assn; ALA; HawaiiLA. 10: AAUW; Bus & Prof Womens Club; Girl Scouts; Maui Toastmistress Club; Sierra Club. 14: Adult educ. 15: P O Box 943, Wailuku Hawaii 96793.

UNDERWOOD, MARGARET (HANSELMAN). b Manistee Mich 1 N 02. 5: UMich 21-25 (Eng). 6: Fr. 7: Ref libn Ann Arbor Pub Lib, Ann Arbor Mich 25-29; Asst Chem Lib UMich (Ann Arbor) 25 summer, Asst East Engring Lib 25 summer, Asst museum libn 29-39, Libn arch Lib summer 57, Ed sci bibliog 55-56, Asst libn Phoenix Lib 58-60, Libn Phoenix Lib (nuclear engring) 61-. 10: Fac Women's Club UMich. 12: "Bibliography of North American Minor Natural History Serials in the University of Michigan Libraries" (54). 14: Ref, bibliog. 15: 3175 Glazier Way, Ann Arbor Mi 48105.

UNGER, DOROTHY (KALBUS). b Neenah Wis 28 N 20. 4: James W Unger. 5: Wis State U (Oshkosh) 38-42 (Nat Sci, Biol) BS; UWis 52-53 MSLS. 6: Ger. 7: Tchr pub schs, Oshkosh Wis 42-48; Tchr & libn schs, Holland Mich 48-52; Faculty asst UWis Lib Sch (Madison) 53; Libn Wis State u Oshkosh 53-54; Libn & Instr of Lib Sci Wis State U (Oshkosh) 63-64; Libn Oshkosh Area Pub Schs, Oshkosh Wis 64-. 9: ALA; WisLA; WisEA; NE WisEA; NEA. 10: AAUW; PEO; Womans Reading Club; Wis State U Faculty Dames; Club; Phi Beta Sigma; Kappa Delta Pi. 14: Sch libs, ref serv, govt docs, educ for libnship, media ctrs. 15: 1212 E New York ave, Oshkosh Wis 54901.

UNGER, MARY E WALKER. b Des Moines Iowa 2 My 14. 4: Steven Unger. 5: Columbia 38 (Art) BS; Pratt 44 BLS. 7: Sch libn Lindenhurst Pub Schs, Lindenhurst LI NY 54-62; 54-62; Sch libn Middle Co Sch Dist, Centerreach LI NY 63-. 9: NEA; NY State Tchrs Assn. 10: Nat Congress of Parents & Tchrs. 14: Wk with yp, ref. 15: 245 S 5th st, Lindenhrst LI NY 11757.

UNGER, SUSAN (LEIGH). b Atchison Kan 28 N 35. 4: Donald B Unger. 5: Mount St Scholastica Col 53-57 (Eng) BA; UOkla 64-65 MLS. 7: Eng asst AT&T Long Lines, Kan City 58-64; Libn (staff) UKan Libs 65-. 14: Acquis, ref. 15: 2605 Ridge ct, Lawrence Ks 66044.

UNTERBURGER, GEORGE W(ILLIAM). b Dayton Ohio 29 Ap 20. 4: Mary L Wilkerson. 5,; otterbein Col 37-41 (Eng, Soc) AB; UMich 47-48 ABLS. 7: Ref libn Dayton Pub Lib, Dayton Ohio 41-42, 46-47; US Army 42-45; Detroit Pub Lib: Ref serv 48-53, Home reading serv 53-56, Ref serv 56-, Tech lit spec 61-. 09: ALA; MichLA. 11: Detroit Pub Lib Staff Memorial & Fellowship Award, 68. 15: 15326 Mansfield ave, Detroit Mi 48227.

UPCHURCH, GRACE. b Hackett Ark 10 N 02. 5: Ark State Tchrs Col 23-24; UArk 22-23, 27-29 (Educ) BSE; UIll 30-33 BSLS. 7: Loan asst UArk 29-40, Head of circ 41-. 9: ALA-ACRL; ArkLA; SWLA. 13: Yes. 14: Circ, mss & archives. 15: 606 Storer ave, Fayetteville Ark 72701.

UPCHURCH, MARY ANN (COMER). b Nashville Tenn 9 O 41. 4: Sam Bayliss Upchurch. 5: Vanderbilt U 59-62 (Psych) BA; Peabody 63 (LS) MA. 7: Catlgr Nashvile Pub Lib 63-64; Catlgr Northwestern U 65-68; Catlgr Media Ctr Warren Cons Sch, Warren Mich 68-. 9: ALA; SLA; TennLA. 10: Beta Phi Mu. 14: Catlg. 15: 32662 Mound rd apt 6, Warren Mi 48092.

UPDEGROVE, PAT (ETHEL) (FORD). b Jacksonville Fla 12 D 25. 4: Robert C Upgrove. 5: William & Mary 36-40 (LS)

BA; UHouston 54-55 (Educ) MA. 7: Tchr-libn High Sch, Lawrenceville Va 40-41; Libn Blair Jr High Sch, Norfolk Va 41-45; Libn Armed Force Staff Col, Norfolk Va 45-49; Catlgr UTex (Austin) 49-51; Tchr Fry Jr High Sch, Tex city Tex 51-58, Libn 59-66; Lib coord Tex City Independent Sch Dist 67-. 8: Eval Team; So Assn Schs & Cols. 9: ALA; NEA; DAVI; TexLA; Tex Assn Educ Tech; TexStateTA. 10: Tex Cong Parents & Tchrs; Delta Kappa Gamma; Tex State Hist Assn; Galveston Co Hist Survey Com; Tex City Hist Coms; LWV. 14: Supv of sch lib as media cts. 15: 111 Seaside lane, Texas City Tx 77590.

UPHAM, MARGARET E (CLEMENT). b Java NY 6 Mr 18. 4: Earl T Upham. 5: Houghton Col 34-38 (Eng) BA; State U Col (Geneseo NY) 61-64 MLS. 6: Lat. 7: High sch Eng, lib Antwerp Sch, Antwerp NY 43-45; High sch Eng Cattaraugus Sch, Cattaraugus NY 45-46; Elem lib Iroquois central Sch, Elma NY 60-. 10: PTA (Life mem). 14: Ref, child bks, research. 15: 12377 Big Tree r, Wales Cente, NY 14169.

UPSON, THEDA SPICER. b Hastings Neb 6 Ag 14. 4: U L Upson. 5: UOre 33-37 (Eng) BA; UCal (Berkeley) 39-40 (Lib training) Certif. 6: Fr. 7: Asst libn Safeway Stores Lib, Oakland Cal 40-42; Jr libn Cal Sect Cal State Lib, Sacramento 42-44; Ref libn Richland Pub Lib, Richland Wash 56-. 10: Phi Beta Kappa; AAUW; ACLU. 14: Ref, ordering. 15: Richland Pub Lib, Richland Wa 99352.

UPTON, JOY (WHITSON). b Peery Co Ill 11 Ag 41. 4: K Edward Upton. 5: So Ill U 59-63 (Eng) BS in Ed summer 64 (reading guidance); UIll summers 66-69 MS in LS. 6: Fr. 7: Ser searcher Morris Lib SoIllU 59-63; Libn Georgetown High Sch, Georgetown Ill 63-64; Libn Triad High Sch, St Jacob Ill 64-66; Libn Webster Jr High Sch, Collinsville Ill 66-68; Lib & materials coord L&M Ctr, Collinsville Ill 68-69. 9: NEA; ALA; IllEA; CollinsvilleEA; IllLA; IllASchL. 10: Troy Womens Club. 13: Yes. 14: Admin & org of dist unit lib serv K-12. 15: 501 Lanahan dr, Troy Il 62294.

URBAN, ANNA MARY. b Lancaster Penn 18 Ja 06. 5: Cornell U 26-29 (Hist, Pol Sci) AB; Emory 37-38 ABLS; UMd 51 (Pol Sci) AM. 6: Fr, Lat. 7: Asst libn Armstrong Cork Co, Lancaster Penn 29-30; Tchr-libn Chesapeake CITY High Sch, Chesapeake City Md 30-36; Tchr Lancaster Twp Jr High Sch, Lancaster Penn 36-37; Asst ref libn &instr, lib use Womans Col UNC(Greensboro) 38-42; Documents catlgr Emory U 42-44; UMd: Asst ref & loan libn 44-45, Head ref dept 45-58, Coordinator of ref serv 58-. 8: Fulbright lecturer in lib sci, UDacca, Dacca East Pakistan, 61-62. 9: MdLA. 10: AAUP; Phi Kappa Phi; Pi Sigma Alpha; Pi Beta Phi; Tau Beta Sigma. 12: Ed "Student Library Handbook, UMd Lib (58 & 64); Co-ed "Faculty Library Handbook, Womans Col Lib (40). 13: Yes. 14: Ref, admin, bk sel, govt docs. 15: 7017 Fordham ct, College Park Md 20740.

URBAN, EUGENE A. b Podolie Slovakia 2 Ja 14. 5: Komensky U (Bratislava Slovakia 32-36 (Fr, Slovak) MA in Educ; Slovenian U (Ljubljana Yugoslavia) 35 (Slavistics); UCatholique(Lille France) 35 (Fr Lit); Rosary Col 57-60 MALS; Loyola U (Chicago) 66- (Sp). 6: Fr, Ital, Sp, Slovak, Croatian, Slovenian, Czech, Polish. 7: Prof Fr, Slovak Gymnasium (Malacky, Levoca, Slovakia) 36-40; Press attache Legation of Slovak Republic, Vatican City 43-45 Accountant Compania Compania Argentina de Electricidad, Aires Argentina 48-55; Ed "Osadne Hlasy (Slovak weekly), Chicago 57-59; Bibliog John Crerar Lib, Chicago 59-60; Libn Inland Steel Co Research Lib, Hammond Ind 60-. 8: Adv, Off of Comparative Sch Legis, Ministry of Pub Instr, Rome Italy 45-47. 9: SLA. 12: "Novelle Slovacche transl, Rome (45); "Censorship Policies in Czecho-Slovakia, 1918-1938, With Special Emphasis on Slovakia, "Slovakia (65). 13: Yes. 14: Ref, transl. 15: 6904 Olcott ave Apt 10, Hammond In 46323.

URBAN, RUTH H(ALL). b Phila. 4: William Urban. 5: Col of Wooster 32-36 (Eng) AB; Drexel 38-39 BS in LS. 7: 1st asst catlgr Lehigh U 39-45; Bibliog UPenn 45-47; Newark Pub Lib, Newark NJ: Jr libn catlgr 47-48, Sr libn 48-53, Prin libn ya 53-. 9: ALA-YASD Mem var coms); NJLA (sec Sect for Wk with Child & YP 63-65, mem var coms). 13: Yes. 14: Ya. 15: 583 Mt Prospect ave, Newark NJ 07104.

URBAN, SARA JANE. b Richland Wash 17 D 44. 5: Queens Col (Charlotte NC) 62-66 (Bible, Relig) BA; UWash 66-67 MLib. 6: Fr. 7: Intern Aiken-Bamburg-Barnwell-Edgefield Reg Lib, Aiken SC 65; Ext libn Abbeville-Greenwood Reg Lib, Greenwood SC 67-. 8: Reg supv to Abbeville Co Lib, Abbeville SC 69. 9: ALA; SCLA. 10: AAUW; Human Rel Coun of Greenwood. 14: Child, yp, ext wk. 15: 3423 Summit dr, Aiken SC 29801.

URBAN, WILLIAM. b Trenton NJ 15 O 13. 4: Ruth Hall. 5: Trinity Col (Conn) 33-37 (Psych) BS; Drexel 38-39 BS in LS. 7: Libn I Brooklyn Pub Lib 39-41; Army of the US 41-46; Libn SCH OF Educ UPenn 46-47; Newark PUB Lib, Newark NJ: Sr libn 47-51, Prin Lending & ref libn 51-62, Chief lending & ref libn 62-. 9: ALA; NJLA (treas 63-66). 14: Ref, sci & tech. 15: 583 Mt Prospect ave, Newark NJ 07104.

URIDGE, MARGARET D (WHITNEY). b Berkeley Cal 7 N 05. 4: Francis C Uridge. 5: Mills Col 22-26 (Pre-med) AB; Yale 31-33 (Sci of Society); Vassar 36-38 (Econ, Sociol); UCal(Berkeley) 39-40 Certf in Libnship. 6: Fr, Ger, Sp, Russian. 7: Jr lib asst Carmel Cal 28; Catlgr, sr libn, act libn Dorsch Mem Lib, Monroe Mich 29-30; Yale U Lib:Asst & asst head loan dept 30-3, 30-31, chg interlib loans, ref dept 32-33, Catlgr & asst in rare bk room 33-36; Sr libn Vassar Col Lib 36-39; UCal Lib (Berkeley): Sr libn ref dept 41-45, Act head loan dept 45-46, Head interlib borrowing serv 46-Hd gen ref serv 66-. 8: Lecturer, Sch of Libnship, UCal spring 49 & 50; Guest lecturer 56-; Lecturer Lib Sch Program USan Francisco 59-62; Consul to the program, 62-; Consul on Application of wk simplification to lib problems, 51-56; Lecturer UCal Ext Div, summer 65; Lecturer lib confs & assns 53-; Cal Governors Conf on Educ TV, 52; Del United Womens Conf, UN Internat Org Conf 45; Del Pacific Coast Cone UNESCO, 48. 9: ALA (Convention Com 47 & 58; org Interlib Loan Libns group 58, co-designer Interlib Loan Form 51-52; Bd of Resources: SUBComon Bibliog Centers 48-52);-ACRL (Interlib Loan Com 51-56);-RTSD (Com Co-auth Interlib Loan Code 52 & Revised 56); on Interlib Coop 56-61); SLA (Adv Coun 47-48,Nomin Com 48-49; San FRANCISCO Bay Reg Chap: pres 47-48, Exec Bd 47-49; chm&/or mem 4 coms 48-); CalLA (Adv Coun 43-44, pres Div Reg Resources Coord Com 46-55); WEST Theol LA; NoCal Tech Proc Group; Ref Libns Coun of Bay Area. 10: World Affairs Coun of No Cal; United World Federalists; ACLU; Save the San Francisco Bay Assn; AAUW; Womens Faculty Club of UCal; Cal State Employees Assn; Nat League for Womens Serv; UCal Lib Schs Alumni Assn. 13: Yes. 14; Ref,interlib loans, lib coop, catlg, automation, tchg. 15: 1110 Keith ave, Berkeley Cal 94708.

URLING, ELIZABETH JAYNE. b E Orange NJ 7 O 42. 4: C John Urling Jr. 5: Bethany Col (Bethany W Va) 60-64 (Hist, Pol Sci) BA; UMd summer 62; UPittsburgh 65-66 MLS. 6: Fr. 7: Playground asst Montgomery Co Recreation Dept, Silver Spring Md summer 61; Stud asst acquis dept UPittsburgh 65, Stud asst grad lib sch lib 65; Sub-prof libn Monroeville Pub Lib, Monroeville Penn 65-66; Libn Penn State U (McKeesport) 66-. 9: ALA; PennLA. 10: Beta Phi Mu. 14: Ref, planning libs. 15: 228 Clover dr, monroeville Pa 15146.

URLING, MARGARET ANNE. b Pittsburgh Penn 15 Mr 43. 5: Wilson Col 61-62; UPittsburgh 62-66 (Mus) BA, 66-68 MLS. 6: Fr, Ital. 7: Res bk supv UPittsburgh 66-68; Mus catlgr StanfordU 68-. 9: MusicLA. 14: Catlg, ref. 15: Music Lib The Knoll Stanford Univ, Stanford Ca 94305.

URMSTON, DOROTHY McKNIGHT. b San Francisco 3 Ja 18. 4: David T Urmston. 5: Radcliffe 34-38 (Econ) BA; Columbia 61-63 (LS) MS; NY State Certif 65. 6: Fr. 7: Yonkers Pub Lib, Yonkers NY: Clerk 60, Lib trinee 61-63, Asst ref 63, Ya 64, Asst ref libn 65-66; Hd ref Sprain Brook br 66-. 9: ALA; NYLA; Westchester (NY) LA. 14: Ref. 15: 150 Pennsylvania ave, Yonkers NY 10707.

URQUIDI, JOHN (de BELFORT). b El Paso Tex 1 Ja 27. 5: Los Angeles State Col 49-51 (Educ) BA; USoCal 57-59 MSLS; UParis 59-60 (Fr Lit) Licencie es lettres; Ecole de Perfectionnement des professeurs de Francaisa letranger a la Sorbonne 60-61, 62 9fr Lang) Certif Superieur. 6: Fr, Sp, Ital, PORTU. 7: US Air Force 45-47; Tchr Los Angeles City Sch Dist51-59; Asst ref libn UCal(Riverside) 63-65; Gift libn UCLA 65-. 8: UAlgiers (Algeria) Lib 67-69; Consul UTunis Bibliotheque Faculte de Droit 68-69; On loan to Agcy for Intl Development Tunis 69. 9: NEA; CalLA. 10: Alliance Francaise; Anciens de lUniversite de Paris; Alpha Mu Gamma. 11: Summer scholarship Univ of the Americas, Mexico, 65. 14: Ref, rare bks, catlg. 15: 1820 S Orange ave, Monterey Park Ca 91754.

USES, ANNE KATHERINE (JOSEPHA). b Shenandoah Penn 14 Ja 22. 5: Kutztown State Col 39-43 (LS, Soc Studies) BS in Ed; Drexel 43-44 BS in LS; Bucknell U summers 59-63 (Hist) MA. 6: Polish, Fr, Sp. 7: Libn Lewes Spec Sch Dist, Lewes Del 44-46; Libn Holmes Jr High Sch, Phila 46-50; Libn Sayre Jr High Sch, Phila 50-54; Libn John High SR Hgh Sch, Phila 54-, Libn Adult Evening Sch. 9: NEA; CathLA; Penn State EA; Phila Tchrs Assn; Sch LA Phila (pres 52-54); PennLA; Penn Stud Lib Asst Assn (sponsor). 14; Sch libnshi. 15: 229 S Jardin st, Shenanandoah Pa 17976.

USHER, ESTHER. b Lynn Mass 10 O 17. 5: Simmons 34-38 (LS) SB. 7: Catlgr to assoc libn Essex Inst, Salem Mass 38-56; Libn Jackson & Moreland Div United Engnrs & Constructors Inc, Boston 56-. 9: ALA; SLA; MassLA. 10: Photographic Soc of Amer; Mass 4-H All Stars. 12: Asst ed Essex Inst Hist Collections (43-55). 14: Catlg, ref. 15: 22 Centre st, Danvers Mass 01923.

USSERY, MRS IVA BERNICE (EDWARDS). b Hamilton Ohio 5 Mr 08. 5: Ohio No U 25-28 (Eng, Hist, Pol Sci) AB;Miami U (Ohio) summers 56, 57; UKy summers 58, 59, 61-63 MS in LS; UWis summer 65 (LS). 6: Fr. 7: Eng tchr Taggart Jr High Sch, E Palestine Ohio 28; Eng & libn Seven Mile High Sch, Seven Mile Ohio 55-60; Eng & Greenhills High Sch, Greenhills Ohio 60; Eng & libn Trenton High Sch, Trenton Ohio 61-65, Libn 65-. 9: ALA; NEA; OhioASchL; SWOhioEA; OhioEA (del to State Convention 67); ButlerCoTA (past pres); Edgewood Local TA. 10: Hamilton Civic Theatre; Bus & Prof Womens Club; Alpha Phi Gamma; Butler Co Hist Soc. 14: High sch lib wk, rare bks. 15: 121 Vista dr, Hamilton Ohio45011.

UTHMAN, VIRGINIA ANN GREER. b Danville Ky 10 O 42. 4: Dilawar Faisal Uthman. 5: TuftsU 60-61 (Govt); Mich StateU 61-64 (Hist) BA; Johns HopkinsU 64-65 (S Asia & Middle East); UMich summer 65 (Arabic); UKy 67 MSLS. 7: Asst libn Ctr for Applied Ling, Wash DC 64; Tchr of Eng Smer Inst of Lang (USIS), Baghdad Iraq 65-66; Catlg-asst order libn San Francisco State Col 68-. 8: Amer Red Cross vol 67. 14: Catlg, automation. 15: 484 Reina del Mar, Pacifica Ca 94044.

UTTERBACK, ROBERT T. b Delta Iowa 1 Ag 22. 4: Lois Boucher. 5: William Penn Col 40-43, 47 (Eng) AB; UIowa 48-49 (Music); URedlands 49-51 (Music); UCal 55-56 MLS. 7: (Lt jg) US Naval Res, Pacific 43-46; Bus, Sigourney Iowa 46-48; Instr Corcoran High Sch, Corcoran Cal 51-53; Instr Pacific High Sch, San Bernardino Cal 53-55; Jr ser libn Fresno State Col 56-57, Head div of processes 57-65; Asst libn Ariz State U 65-67; Col libn Southwestern Col (Chula Vista Cal) 67-. 9: CalLA (chm CURLS No Cal 59); CalASchL. 10: Beta Phi Mu. 14: Ser, mechanization. 15: 2222 Debco dr, Lemon Grove Ca 92045.

UYEHARA, HARRY YOSHIMI. b honolulu 6 Ja 34. 5: UHawaii 54-58 (Educ) B Ed; UMich 64-65 MALS. 7: US Army Infantry (Spec 4) 58-60; Tchr-libn Waiakea-kai Sch, Hilo Hawaii 60-61; Libn Wahiawa Intermediate Sch, Wahiawa Hawaii 61-66; Program specialist Sch Lib Serv Hawaii State Dept of Educ, Honolulu 66-. 9: NEA-DAVI; ALA; HawaiEA; HawaiiLA; (treas 67-69); HawaiiASchL; Hawaii A-v Assn; ASCD; Hawaii ASCD. 14: Sch libs. 15: 834-1 Bannister st, Honolulu Hi 96819.

UZELAC, CONSTANCE PORTER. b Wash DC 22 Ag 39. 4: Milan Uzelac. 5: Howard U 56-60 (Zool) BS, 60 (Parasitology); Catholic U 60-61 MSLS. 6: Fr, Serbo-Croatin, Russian. 7: Admin asst Seton Hall Col of Med & Dentistry Lib 61-64; Consul Lagos U Med Sch Lib Nigeria summer 64; Research Analyst Gen Ref & Bibliog LC 65; Train Coordinator Biomed Lib UCLA 65-68; Acquis libn USoCal 68-. 8: Consul Lagos Univ Med Sch Lib. 9: MedLA; SLA. 10: Sigma Xi. 14: Catlg, ref, tech serv. 15: 1129 Iliff st, Pacific Palisades Ca 90272.

V

VAETH, HELEN LOUISE (GALLAHER). b Wauwatosa Wis 29 My 17. 4: Charles E Vaeth. 5: Oberlin Col 34-36;hUWis 36-39 (Hist) BA, 31-38 Certif of LS. 6: Fr. 7: Child libn Antigo Pub Lib, Antigo Wis 39-40; Milwaukee Pub Lib; Ref asst 2, 44-46, Bk sel asst 42-44; Acquis libn 50-; Asst chief of processing 55-. 9: ALA; WisLA. 14: Tech proc, acquis, bk sel, data proc. 15: 5051 W Washington blvd, Milwaukee 53208.

VAGIANOS, LOUIS GEORGE. b Weirton WVa 8 My 35. 4: Marilyn Quartier Vagianos. 5: Hiram Col 52-56 (Philos) BA; West Res 58-60 MSLS; Suffolk U 60-62 (Educ) MA; Boston U 65- (Philos). 6: Fr, Gk. 7: Personnel admin US Army, Europe 56-58; Asst to asst dir of libs West Res U 59; Asst to libn Brown U 60, Asst libn 64; Libn Southeastern Mass Tech Inst 64; Asst libn Brown U 65-66; Libn Dalhousie U 66; Dir of Libs 67-; Dir Sch of Lib Serv & Prof 68-. 8: Lib 21 Seattle Worlds Fair 62; Lecturer URI Grad Sch Lib Serv 62-65; Consul to insts in W Indies 66; Mem Sci Secretariat Study Group on Sci & Tech Info in Can, chm lib subgroup 67-68. 9: ALA; RILA (pres-elect, chm sev coms); CanLA; APLA; HLA. 10: Beta Phi Mu. 12: Ed "APLA Bulletin (67-). 13: Yes. 14: Admin, automation, tech serv, lib educ. 15: Head of St Margarets Bay, Halifax County Nova Scotia Can.

VAGT, PAUL (JOHN). b Jackson Minn 28 N 23. 4: Mary Evelyn Hooker. 5:N N Tex State U 47-49 (LS) BA; UTex 51-53 MLS. 7: US Army Quartermaster Corps (Sgt) 45-47; Asst libn Tarleton State Col 49-51; Ref asst UTex 51-53; Libn Howard Co Jr Col (Tex) 53-61; Libn Odessa Col 61-64; Dir of Libs Midwestern U 64-67; Dir of Lib Serv Tarrant Co Jr Col Dist 67-. 9: ALA; NEA; SWLA; TexLA (2nd v-pres & chm Dist 2 & 3, chm Dist Planning Com); chm Col & Univ Div). 10: Phi Delta Kappa; Gideons. 13: Yes. 14: Admin, jr col libs. 15: 3313 Jamestown dr, Ft Worth Tx 76119.

VAIL, NORWOOD BLAIR. b Plainfild NJ 5 F 21. 4: Jane Waite. 5: Earlham Col 39-44 (Eng) AB; Chicago 45-46 BLS. 6: Sp, Fr. 7: NY Pub Lib: Clerk prints div summer 44, Clerk main reading room 44-45, Ref asst prints div summer 46, Ref asst art div 46-62, Ref asst map div 62-68; 1st asst map div 68-. 9: ALA. 10: Soc of Friends Recs Com (NYC). 14: Ref, (maps, art, Amer or local hist). 15: 2278 Palmer ave, New Rochelle NY 10801.

VAILLANCOURT, PAULINE M(ARIETTE). b Fall River Mass. 5: St Johns U Col (NY) (Biol) BS; Columbia 53 MSLS, 68 PhD. 6: Fr. 7: Period libn Nat Health Lib, NYC 49-51; Visiting Assoc Prof SUNY(Albany) summer 62; Libn Mary Immaculate Hosp Schof Nursing, Jamaica NY 51-58; Chief Libn Kings Park State Hosp, KINGS Park NY 58-60; Chief libn Sloan-Kettering Cancer Ctr, NYC 60-68; Lectr SUNY (Albany) Grad Lib Sch; Adjunct Assoc Prof LIU Grad Sch 69-. 8: Consul, United Hosp Fund (NY), 55; Consul, Queensboro Tuberculosis & Health Assn, 52-54; Catholic Med Ctr of Bklyn & Queens 68, Countway Lib of Med 68-, Cancer Research Inst of New England, Deaconess Hosp, etc. 9: SLA (chm Scholarship & Stud Loan Fund Com 53-54; sec NY Chap 56-57, chm Biol Scis Div 51-52); MedLA (chm Hosp Sect 56-57); ALA (rep to Interagency Coun on Lib Tools for Nursing 65-67); & 67-70); LIB Club (Coun 64-68); ASIS. 10: AAAS; NY Acad of Scis; Soroptimists. 12: "Bibliographic Control of the Literature of Oncology, 1800-1960 (69); Ed "Scientific Information Notes (69-). 13: Yes. 14: Med & sci libs, in-serv educ, lib planning. 15: P O Box 624 Lenox Hill Sta, New York NY 10021.

VAINSTEIN, ROSE. b Edmonton Alta Can 7 Ja 20. 5: MiamiU (Oxford Ohio) 37-41 (Eng) AB; West Res 41-42 BLS; UIll (Urbana) 51-52 (Libnship) MS. 7: Jr libn Cuyahoga Co Lib, Cleveland Ohio 41-42; Yp libn Brooklyn Pub Lib, Brooklyn NY 42-44; Army libn, US, Hawaii, Japan 44-47; Br libn Contra Costa Co Lib, Martinez Cal 47-51; Research asst UIll Lib Sci Grad Sch(Urbana) 51-52; Lib consul Cal State Lib, Sacramento 53-55; Hd ext Gary Pub & Lake Co Lib, Gary Ind 55-57; Pub lib specialist US Off Educ, Wash DC 57-61; Assoc prof UBC Sch Libnship 61-64; Lib dir Bloomfield Twp Pub Lib, Bloomfield Hills Mich 64-68; Prof UMich Sch Lib Sci Ann Arbor 68-. 8: Dir, Pub Lib Res Study (for Pub Lib Commsn of BC, Can0 62-64; Consul for pub libs, to the Stat Coord Com LAD-ALA, on its "Nat Plan for Lib Stat" 68-69. 9: AEAUSA (sec Sect on Aging 58-60); ALA (Friends of Libs 54-58; Coun 56-60); -ASD (Bd Dirs 61-64; chm ASDIRSD Com on Orientation of Adult Readers, Lib Serv to an Aging Population Com 58-61); -LED (Pub Rel Com 62-65, Bd Dors 68-71); -LAD (O&M Sect: Nomin Com 58-59, Exec Com 63-65); -PLA (Bd Dirs 58-60, chm Subcom, Rev of Pub Lib Standard, 66-67, Nomin Com 67-68); -AHIL (Research Com 69-71); BCLA (spec consul to libs for Hosp Com 61-63); CalLA (mem & co-chm Intel Freedom Com 54-56); CanLA (govt assistance to Pub Libs Com 62-64, Pub Lib standards Com 62-63, Stat Com 62-63); Inst Profess Libns (Can); Lib Assn (Gt Brit); Mich Adult EA; MichLA (Intel Freedom Co 66-68; Dist III: sec-treas 66-67, pres 68-69); PNLA (Pub Lib Div: Nomin Com 62-63; Adult Educ Com 62-63); SLA. 10: LWV; Altrusa internat; Women's Res Club, UMich; Beta Phi Mu. 11: Fulbright Award 52-53. 12: "Public Libraries in British Columbia, A Survey with Recommendations" (66); "Service to the Aging," (59); (ASD Guide to the Literature, No 5); Co-auth "State Standards for Public Libraries," GPO (60). 13: Yes. 14: Pub libs, admin, adult educ, lib educ. 15: 2013 Medford rd apt #261, Ann Arbor Mi 48104.

VAJDA, ELIZABETH. b Budapest 15 N 28. 5: Pazmany Peter U 46-51 (Law) JD; Columbia 64-65 (LS) MS. 6: Ger, Fr, Hungarian. 7: Asst catlgr NYU summer 65; Asst ref libn LIU 65-; Assoc dir United Commun Funds & Couns of Amer 67-. 9: ALA; SLA. 14: Ref, lib admin & supvn. 15: 420 E 72 st apt 2-C, New York NY 10021.

VALE, MICHELLE ROBYN. b Los Angeles 28 N 35. 5: UCLA 53-56 (Pol Sci) BA; USoCal 60-61 MS in LS. 7: Jr soc sci Syst Development Corp, Santa Monica Cal 56-58; Libn Los Angeles Pub Lib 61-65; Research libn div of lib programs Off of Educ, Dept of Health Educ & Welfare, Wash DC 65-67; Evaluation specialist div of lib programs 67-. 9: ALA-YASD (Nomin Com 67, chm Exhibit Booth #67); DCLA (Publicity Chm 66-67); CalLA (past chm YA Libns, RT Com 64). 10: Beta Phi Mu; LWV; ACLU. 14: Ref, ya serv, research, evaluation. 15: 800 - 4th st SW apt S724, Wash DC 20024.

VALENCIK, MAY VIRGINIA KUNZ. b Newark NJ 25 Mr 09. 5: Douglass Col 31 (LS) AB; Cornell U summer; NY Sch of Social Research; Columbia (L; (LS). 6: Sp. 7: Lib asst Pub Lib, Passaic NJ 31-36; Sr ref asst PUB Lib, Utica NY 36-41; StateSupv Ky Statewide Lib Proj 41-42; Head Libn Free Lib, Allentown Penn 42-63; Dir Pub Lib, White Plains NY 63-. 8: Consul, small libs in Penn; Pres Eienhowers Com on Traffic Safety 55-57; Nat Womens Adv Com to Federal Civil Defense Admin 55-57; Freedoms Found at Valley Forge 1952 Jury Awards. 9: ALA (chm Coun 49-55), (Jury Citations for Trustees 60; mem var coms);-PLA (By-laws Com 61, & var other coms); Middle Atlantic States Lib Conf (chm 53-58); PennLA (Exec Com 46-55 & 58-63, pres 50-51; chm &/or em var coms 44-63; Lobbyist 51); NYLA; Westchester LA, (Bull Circ Mgr 63, chm Lib Adminrs 66-68); Lehigh Valley DistLA (chm 49); METRO (chm Personnel Com 67-); ANLYTS (Com on Acquis Procedures 69). 10: Quota Club Internat Delta Kappa Gamma;LWV; AAUW; Col Club of White Plains NY; White Plains C of C; YWCA; Freedom Found (Valley Forge); Coun of Serv Clubs (Allentown Penn); Mental Health Assn; Lehigh Valley Kennel Club; Pub Rel Coun. 11; hon LLD, Cedar Crest Col, 52. 13: Yes. 14: Admin. 15: Briarview Manor apts 6F 10 Nosband ave, White Plains NY 10605.

VALENTINE, JONETT (SANFORD). b Lambert Miss 24 F 36. 4: John White Valentine. 5: Delta state Col 54-57 (Soc Sci) BS in Ed; Fla State U 57-58 MS in LS. 7: Asst circ libn Delta State Col 58-64; Ref & circ libn 64-. 9: SELA; MissEA; MissLA (chm Col Sect); reporter Sr Col Sect). 10: AAUW; Kappa Delta; Cleveland (Miss) Little Theatre; Miss Little Theatre Assn; Ephfie Womans Club. 14: Ref, circ. 15: 1215 Farmer st, Cleveland Ms 38732.

VALIQUETTE, SISTER MARJORIE. b Rock Island Ill 6 F 32. 5: St Ambrose Col 58 (Educ) BA; Rosary Col 64 (LS) MA. 7: Hd libn Immaculate Conception Tchr Train Inst, Peoria Ill 65-; Hd libn Bergan High Sch, Peoria Ill 67-. 14: ya serv. 15: 2408 W Heading ave, Peoria Il 61604.

VALK, GENE (ELIZABETH). b GloversvilleNY 18 Ag 24. 5: NY State Col for Tchrs (Oneonta) 42-45 (Educ) B Ed; NY State Tchrs Col (Albany) 46-47 BSin LS. 7: Tchr Scotia Jr High Sch, Scotia NY 45-46; Asst libn NY State Col for Tchrs (Oneonta) summer 46-47; Acquis libn Triple Cities Col of Syracuse U (Endicott NY) 48-50; Head catlgr RENSSELAER Polytech 50-62; Libn Gloversville High Sch, Gloversville NY 62-. 8: hurch Lib Consul for var churches in area. 9: NY State Tchrs Assn; Huson-Mohawk LA; EastASchL. 10: Fulton Co (NY) Hist Assn. 13: Yes. 14: Catlg, high sch lib, ref, local hist. 15: 402 N Main st, Gloversville NY 12078.

VALLEE, DOROTHY (MONAGHAN). b NYC. 4: William L Vallee. 5: Manhattanville Col of the Sacred Heart (Eng) AB; Columbia 59-61 (Child Dev); Pratt 65-68 MLS. 6: Fr. 7: Ed UWash 53-57; Ed Amer Inst Electrical Engineers, NYC 57-59; Remedial reading tchr Rockland Co Pub Schs, Rockland Co NY 59-63; Libn Finkelstein Mem Lib, Spring Valley NY 64-. 9: NYLA; NY Lib Club; Rockland Co (NY) Pub Libns Assn. 14: Adult serv. 15: 278 N Main st, Spring Valley NY 10977.

VALORE, EVELYN GRACE HUNT. b Benson La 8 F 37. 4: Abram Valore Jr. 5: Southern U 53-57 (Eng) BA; UWis summers 58, 60-62 (LS) MS; Northwestern State Col 68; LSU (HEA Inst) summer 68. 6: Fr. 7: Libn Geo W Carver High Sch, Shreveport La 57-64; Libn Valencia High Sch, Shreveport La 64-67; Libn educ div Grambling Col summer 66; Libn Capt Shreve High Sch, Shreveport La 67-. 9: ALA; NEA; LaEA (chm 4th Dist Lib Div -64); Caddo Parish Tchrs Assn; Caddo Parish Libns Assn; LaLA. 10: Kappa Delta Pi; Alpha Kappa Alpha. 13: Yes. 14: Ref, circ, pub rel. 15: 5812 Dowdel st, Shreveport La 71108.

VALVO, FRANCINE. b Buffalo NY 26 O 37. 5: Jamestown Commun Col 55-57 (Humanities) AA; NY State Col for Tchrs (Albany) 57-59 (Eng, LS) BA; Syracuse 59-60 MLS. 6: Fr, Ital. 7: Br libn Buffalo & Erie Co Pub Lib, Buffalo NY 60-. 8: Child libn at Lib/USA, NY Worlds Fair, 64. 9: ALA; NYLA. 10: W Side Businessmans Assn. 13: Yes. 14: Child wk, storytelling. 15: 415 Lafayette ave, Buffalo NY 14213.

VAMBERY, JOSEPH THOMAS. b Sarajevo Austria-Hunary 9 Je 08. 4: Dr Rose Veronica Deri. 5: U of Sciences (Budapest Hungary) 26-30 (Law, Pol Sci) Dr JUR: Catholic U 58-60 MSin LS. 6: Hungarian, Ger, Lat. 7: Candidate attorney at law Law Dept of Hofherr-Schrantz, Clayton, Shottleworth Ltd, Budapest Hungary 31-35; Practicing attorney at law, Budapest Hungary 35-56; Chief attorney at law Electrotrust, Buapest Hungary 50-56; Sr law catlgr Columbia U 60-67; Intl law libn Columbia 67-. 9: AALL; NY Tech Serv Libns; ASIS. 10: Phi Mu; AAUP; Mens Faculy Club of Columbia Univ. 13: Yes. 14: For & internat law, catlg, ref docs of intl orgs. 15: 167 Chestnut, Demarest NJ07627.

VAN ALLEN, NEIL KENNEDY. b Little Falls NY 17 Jl 25. 4: Mary Louise Alstein. 5: Union Col (Schenectady NY) 43, 46-49 (Humanities) AB; Cornell U 49-50 (Amer Lit) MA; Simmons Col 62-64 (LS) MS; Worcester State Col (Educ); Drew Theol Sem (Religion), Drew Theol Sem 52-53 (Theol). 06: Fr, Sp. 7: US Navy Aviation Electronics Tech 1/c 43-46; Pastor United Church, Luneburg Vt 51-52; Circ manager "Sanford Tribune," Sanford Me 53; Off manager "Daily News," Milford Mass 53; Advert manager Botwinik Bros of Mass Inc, Worcester Mass 53-58; Off manager R&H Machinery Inc, Worcester Mass 58-60; Sci ed & lib Wyman-Gordon Co, Worcester Mass 60-64; Tech libn Gen Electric Co M&AD, Burlington Vt 64-66; Safety ref libn Gen Motors Corp Research Lab, Warren Mich 66-. 9: SLA; ASIS. 10: Appalachian Mountain Club; Sierra Club; Boy Scouts. 12: Asst ed SLA "Metals/Materials Division News." 13: Yes. 14: Indexing, info retrieval syst. 15: 259 Nesbit lane, Rochester Mi 48063.

VAN ANTWERP, MARGARET CARRINGTON (STEBBINS). b Halifax Va 25 S 10. 4: John Franklin Van Antwerp. 5: Randolph-Macon WomansCol 27-31 9eng) BA. 7: Child asst NY Pub Lib 31-36; Child asst Cuyahoga Co Pub Lib, Chagrin Falls Ohio 55-61, Child libn 61-67; Sub gen asst 67-. 15: 112 Meadow lane, Solon Oh 44139.

VAN AUKEN, NANCY (ELIZABETH ORTON). b Dublin Tex. 4: Thomas Vincent Van Auken. 5: N Tex State U 57-61 (Mus) BA; UTex 62-63 MLS. 7: Lib intern Enoch Pratt Free Lib, Baltimore 64-65; Lib asst (rec libn) Kanawha Pub Lib, Charlestown WVa 65-66; Catlg libn WVa Lib Commsn, Charleston WVa 66-67; Ed WVa Libs WVa Lib Assn 68-. 9: ALA; WVaLA (Exec Bd). 12: Ed "West Virginia Libraries" (68-). 14: Catlg, music libnship. 15: 1136 Mulberry cir, Charleston W Va 25314.

VAN BENTEN, SISTER M LUCIA. b Beech Grove Ind 23 My 28. 5: Marian Col 46-48, summers 48-58 (Educ, Psych) AB; Xavier U 61-62; Rosary Col summers 58-63 MALS. 6: Fr, Lat. 7: Libn Scecina Mem High Sch, Indianapolis 63-. 9: CathLA; IndStateLA; Hoosier Libn Assn; ALA. 14: Tchg lib sci. 15: 5000 Nowland ave, Indianapolis In 46201.

VAN BENTHUYSEN, ROBERT F. b NYC 11 Mr 24. 4: Thelma Chirico. 5: Seton Hall U 46-50 (Eng) BS; Drexel 50-51 MS in LS. 7: Libn II NY Pub Lib 51-52, Senior Libn 52-56; Sch libn Pascack Valley Reg High Sch 56-57; Assoc libn Monmouth Col 57-69, Libn 70-. 9: ALA; NJLA (pres Ref Sect 65-66, pres Col & Univ Sect 67-68). 10: Friends of the West Long Br Lib. 13: Yes. 14: Ref. 15: 147 Wall st, W Long Branch NJ 07764.

VAN BRANDEGHEN, RITA ELLEN (LINDEMANN). b Ottawa Ill 3 Jl 40. 4: John Thomas Van brandeghen. 5: UIll 58-62 (Hist) BA, 62-63 (LS) MS. 7: Libn I Detroit Pub Lib 63-64, Libn II 64-66, Libn III 66-. 14: YA serv. 15: 2412 Beverly blvd, Berkley Mi 48072.

VAN BRUNT, JANE. b Chicago Ill 31 Ja 45. 5: UCal (Berkeley) 67 (Hist) BA, 68 MLS. 6: Fr, Ital. 7: Libn World Affairs Coun Lib, San Francisco 68-. 14: Ref, subj bibliog, rare bks. 15: 406 Sutter st, San Francisco Ca 94108.

VAN CAMP, ANN J. b Indianapolis Ind 3 D 31. 5: Hanover Col 50-54 (Chem) AB; IndU 65-67 MLS. 7: Assoc physical chem Eli Lilly & Co, Indianapolis 54-61; Staff asst tech Sandia Corp, Albuquerque 61-64; Research chem H I Thompson Fiber Glass, Gardena Calif 64; Research asst IndU Inst of Psychiatric Research 64-66; Asst ref libn IndU Sch Med Lib 67-. 9: ASIS; SLA. 10: Alpha Delta Pi; Sports Car Club of Amer; Beta Phi Mu; Theta Alpha Phi. 13: Yes. 14: Lit searching, ref, info sci. 15: 420 N Union Box 311, Westfield In 46074.

VAN CAMP, GEORGE. b Battle Creek Mich 30 N 22. 4: Mary Louise Rice. 5: U Toledo 48 (Philos) BA; UMich 50

(Philos) MA, 61 MALS. 7: Asst libn Detroit Inst of Tech, Detroit 59-61; Libn Niles Pub Lb, Niles Mich 61-65; Head Libn Grand Junction Pub Lib, Grand Junction Colo 65-67; Mess Co Pub Lib 67-. 8: Mem Colo Coun for Lib Dev 66-. 9: ALA; MichLA (chm of Dist 1); MPLA; ColoLA (v-chm Pub Lib Div). 10: Rotary. 15: 327 Mesa Grande dr, Grand Junction Co 81501.

VAN DE BRAAK, PHYLLIS ELAINE (RANDALL). b Brockton Mass 3 Jl 17. 4: Florens Van de Braak. 5: Occidental Col 32-33 (Hist); UCLA 33-37 (Hist, Gen Secondary) BA; USCal 63-64, 65 (LS) MS. 7: Tchr Sch Dist, Vista Cal 37-38; Tchr Sch Dist, Artesia Cal 38-42; Tchr Sch Dist. Los Angeles 42-43; Tchr & libn Sch Dist, Inglewood Cal 65-. 8: Adv Cal Sch Fed; Los Angeles Co Careers Com (schs) 65-67. 9: NEA; ALA; CalASchL; Cal Tchrs Assn; CalLA. 10: PTA (Hon life mem): Girl Scout Leader; Delta Zeta; Phi Kappa Phi; Beta Phi Mu; Centinela Valley Hist Assn. 14: Sch lib, educ. 15: 1406 Diamond st, Redondo Beach Ca 90277.

VAN DE VOORDE, PHILIP (EVERETT). b Moline Ill 11 Mr 36. 4: Sharon Swanson. 5: Kalamazoo Col 54-55; Augustana Col (Rock Island) 55-56 (Sociol); Bethel Col (St Paul) 56-58 (Sociol) BA; Central Baptist Theol Sem 58-61 (Rel Educ) BD; UMinn 63-66 (LS) MA. 6: Ger. 7: Minister First Baptist Ch, Phillipsburg Kan 61-62; Lib asst Northwestern Col 63-65; Asst libn Bethel Col (St Paul) 65-66; Docs libn Iowa StateU (Ames) 66-. 9: ALA. 13: Yes. 14: Govt docs. 15: 1122 Scott, Ames Ia 50010.

VAN DE VOORDE, RONALD ANDRE. b Fairfield Iowa 3 N 29. 4: Janet Steele. 5: Parsons Col 47-51 (Eng) BA (magna cum laude); UWash 53-54 (Eng), 55-56 MLS. 7: (Cpl) US Army Signal Corps 51-53; Eng tchr Raymond High Sch, Raymond Wash 54-55; Libn Sunnyside Sch Dist, Sunnyside Wash 56-58; Libn & chm Mercer Island Schs, Mercer Island Wash 58-64; Ref libn Santa Rosa Jr Col 64-65; Asst Prof of Lib Sci Bemidji State Col 65-66; Asst Prof UAriz (Tucson) 66-. 9: ALA-AASchL; Ariz State LA. 10: Beta Phi Mu; Phi Kappa Phi; AAUP. 13: Yes. 14: Sch libs, lib educ, child bks. 15: 432 N Plumer ave, Tucson Az 85719.

VAN DEN BERG, ROBERT WILLIAM F. b Paree Indonesia 8 Ja 27. 4: Barbara Anita Newman. 5: Sir George Williams U 57-60 (Psych) BA; McGill U 60-61 BLS. 6: Dutch, Fr, Ger. 7: Catlgr Sir George Williams U Lib (Montreal) 61-64, Head acquis dept 64-; Hd acquis dept McGill 67-. 15: Sir George Williams Univ Lib, Montreal Can.

VAN DER BELLEN, LIANA. b Tartu Estonia 20 O 25. 5: McGill 48-52 (Modern Langs) BA, 52-53 BLS, 66 MLS. 6: FR, Ger, Estonian. 7: Catlgr McGill U Lib 53-61; Libn & lecturer U de Montreal Ecole de bibliotheconomie 61-65, Lecturer 65-; Asst Prof 67-. 9: ALA-ACRL; CanLA; Assn canadienne des bibliothecaires de langue francaise; Bibliog Soc Can; QueLA. 13: Yes. 14: Rare bk, bibliog. 15: 3500 Atwater, Montreal Can.

VAN DER POLL, ADA. b Brooklyn NY 12 Mr 23. 5: Amer Inst of Banking 51-53 (Foreign Banking) Womens Certif, 51-55 (Foreign Banking) Standard Certif; Hunter Col 51-57 (Fr, Span) BA; Pratt 61-64 MLS; Pace Col 58-61 (Accounting), 65- (Taxation); Seton Hall U 68- (Law). 6: Dutch, Ger, Fr, Sp. 7: Sec Jobs in Holland 40-48; Supv Lutheran Resettlement Serv, NY 49-51; Sec Grace Nat Bank, NY 51-53; Asst bkkeeper City Bank Farmers Trust Co, NY 53-54; Legal sec Lord Day & Lord, NY 54-56; Legal sec Chadbourne Oneill & Thomson, NY 56-58; Legal sec Winthrop Stimson Putnam & Roberts, NY 58-60; Law libn The Internat Nickel Co Inc, NY 60-68; Ref & circ libn Fordham U Sch of Law 68-. 9: Internat Assn Law Libs; AALL; Assn Law Libs, Upstate NY; Law Lib Assn Greater NY. 14: Comp of union list of for legal materials in downtown NY law libs, research in for law. 15: 8700 Blvd East, N Bergen NJ 07047.

VAN DEVANTER, WILLIS. b Wash DC 27 D 30. 4: Ann Cutler. 5: Yale 48-52 (Amer Studies) BA; Columbia 53-54 (LS) MS. 6: Fr, Ger, Sp. 7: Catlgr LC summer 52; Catlgr Histl Mss Yale U Lib summer 53; (Sgt) US Army Pub Info Off, Wiesbaden Germany 54-56; Asst curator Graphic Arts Div Princeton U Lib 56-57; Libn to Paul Mellon The Brick House, Upperville Va 57-. 9: ALA; Ms Soc. 10: Grolier Club; Baltimore Bibliophiles; Trustee, Yale Univ Lib Assocs; Colonial Soc of Mass; Va Hist Soc; Fanquier Co (Va) Hist Foundation. 14: Rare bks. 15: The Brick House, Upperville Va 22176.

VAN DOREN, RUTH M(AE). b Cleveland Ohio 1 Ag 15. 5: West ResU 33-36 (Eng) AB, 37, 45 (Amer Civilization); Rutgers 65-68 MLS. 7: Sec Cleveland Col 38-39; Sec Citizens Tax League of Ohio Inc, Columbus 39-41; Writer ed bkkeeper Heights Press, Cleveland Hts Ohio 42-43; Assoc dir pub info West ResU; Dir pub rel Cleveland YWCA 45-47; Asst dir pub rel Col of Wooster 48-51; Adult activities program dir Jackson YWCA, Jackson Mich 51-52; Dir pub info Wilson Col (Chambersburg Penn) 52-61; Info off Woodrow Wilson Nat Fellowship Foundation, Princeton NJ 61-68; Hd libn Coyle Free Lib, Chambersburg Penn 69-. 9: Educ Writers Assn; Amer Col Pub Rel Assn. 10: Women's City Club, Cleveland Ohio; Women's Advertising Club of Cleveland; YWCA; Sorotimist International. 12: Ed Wilson College bulletin (53-61); Ed Fellowship Newsletter, Woodrow Wilson Nat Fellowship Foundation (62-68). 14: Ref. 15: Coyle Free Lib 102 N Main st, Chambersburg Pa 17201.

VAN DYKE, BELLA ADRIANA. b Middleburg Netherlands. 5: Central Col (Pella Iowa(24-26; Jamestown Col 27-29 (Fr, Eng) BA; Columbia 43-44 BSLS. 6: Dutch, Fr. 7: Eng tchr High Sch, Wolford ND 29-32; Head of Eng Dept High Sch, Kerhonkson NY 32-39; Supv of tech serv Free Pub Lib, Paterson NJ 39-. 8: Consul in org spec libs. 9: ALA-RTSD; NJLA (past sec-treas Catlgrs Sect & Personnel Com); Bergen-Passaic Lib Club. 10: AAUW; (Bd) YWCA; Philharmonic Soc of No NJ; Cathedral Oratorio Chorus; Glen Rock Commun Church Choir. 14: Catlg, tech proc. 15: 238 E 18th st, Paterson NJ 07524.

VAN DYKE, FLORA ZOE. b Pittsburgh 25 s 27. 5: Westminster Col (Penn) 45-49 (Elem Educ) BS in Ed; UIll 64-65 MS in LS. 7: Tchr pub schs, Dayton Ohio 49-55; Child libn Dayton & Montgomery Co Pub Lib, Ohio 55-64; Adult asst Enoch Pratt Free Lib, Baltimore 65-69; Asst Prof Dept Lib Sci Mankato State Col 69-. 9: NEA; AL; OhioEA; OhioLA: IllLA; MdLA. 10: Dayton Coun on World Affairs; Dayton Film So; Baltimore Mus of Art. 14: Sch & pub libs, adult & child wk. 15: Dept Lib Sci, Mankato State College, Mankato Minn 56001.

VAN DYKE, HEDVIG ANN (LUNDBERG). b Chicago 28 D 01. 4: Edward Van Dyke. 5: Chicago Music Col 23-25 (Violin, Orchestra Harmony); Chicago Pub Lib Train Sch 24-32; Lewis Inst 28-29 (Home Econ); Northwestern 30-31 (Amer & Eng Lit); Chicago 33 (Lib Admin). 6: Ger, Swedish. 7: Child libn Chicago Pub Lib 24-29, Head Libn 29-37; Child libn Chicago Heights Pub Lib 54-59; Sch of Nursing Libn Roseland Community Hosp, Chicago 60-. 8: Vounteer libn for large Chicago church, 43-49. 9: ALA; IllLA (Child Reading Round Table); Women's Nat Bk Assn; MedLA. 13: Yes. 14: Ref, child wk. 15: 12021 S Yale ave, Chicago Il 60628.

VAN DYKE, MARILYN (CAROL). b Rochester Penn 16 Ag 33. 5: Geneva Col 51-54 (Eng) BA; Carnegie Lib Sch 54-55 MLS. 7: Lib asst Carnegie Free Lib, Beaver Falls Penn 54; Asst libn Geneva Col 55-. 9: ALA; PennLA (Four Co Lib Chap: sec-treas 62-63, Exec Bd 68-69). 10: Beaver Falls Area Civic League. 14: Catlg, ref. 15: 821 Ninth st, Beaver Falls Pa 15010.

VAN GOETHEM, GERALDINE (BLEVINS). b No Wilkesboro NC 2 Je36. 4: John Lawrence Van Goethem. 5: UNC(Greensboro) 54-58 (Eng) AB; UNC(Chapel Hill) 59-60 MSLS. 6: Fr. 7: Sch libn Little Creek Elem Sch, Norfolk Va 58-59; Sch libn Sunset Park Jr High Sch, Wilmington NC 60-61; Army libn US Army Spec Serv, Germany 61-65; Ser catlgr Duke U 65-; Instr Sch of Lib Sci NC Col 69-. 9: ALA. 14: Catlg, admin, educ. 15: 829 Tinkerbell rd, Chapel Hill NC.

VAN HAITSMA, SYLVIA JOAN. b Landis Saskatchewan Can 13 Mr 42. 5: UAlta 60-63 9pharmacy) BS; UBC 68-69 BLS. 6: Ger. 7: Pharmacist Edmonton Gen Hosp, Edmonton alta 63-66; Pharmacist Staurt Bailey Drug Co, Camrose Alta 66-68; Libn Okanagan Reg Lib, Kelowna BC 69-. 15: 7 Montclare ave, Camrose 4 Alta Can.

VAN HANDEL, RALPH A. b Appleton Wis 17 Ja 19. 4: Alice C Hogan. 5m; uwis 38-41, 45-46 (Econ) BA; UMich 46-47 ABLS. 7: Libn Lawrence Pub Lib, Lawrence Kan 47-51; Head Libn Hibbing Pub Lib, Hibbing Minn 51-5; Dir Gary Pub Lib, Gary Ind 54-. 8: Consul, Kokomo (Ind) Pub Lib, 63; Survey of, Glenview (Ill) Pub Lib, 65; Pub lib consul, Ind; Anderson 68, Crown Point 68, Kokomo 69; Adv Richmond Pub Lib, Richmond Ind 69. 9: ALA; KanLA (v-pres 51); MinnLA; IndLA (pres 64). 10: Rotary Internat; Anselm Forum; Boy Scouts; Serra Intl. 12: Contrib "Focus on Indiana Libraries" (68). 13: Yes. 14: Lib planning & bldg. 15: 5801 Taft pl, Gary Ind 46408.

VAN HORN, MARTHA PRIMM (KARSCH). b Farmington Mo 22 D 15. 5: UMo 34-40 (Fr, Ital) AB; USoCal 56-58

MSLS. 6: Fr. 7: Catlg dept asst UMo 35-47; Kern Co Lib, Bakersfield Cal: Sr libn 47-59, Libn II 59-62, Libn III 62-. 9: ALA; CalLA (chm Staff Orgs Round Table 59, coun-at-large 69-; sec Black Gold Dist 67). 10: AAUW; Kern Co Employees Assn; Zonta Club. 14: Catlg, acquis. 15: 3905 Stockdale, Bakersfield Cal 93309.

VAN JACKSON, WALLACE (M). b Richmond Va 6 My 1900. 4m; ruth Taylor. 5: Va Union U 24, 27-34 (Sociol) BA; Hampton Inst 29-30, 34 BLS; UMich 34-35 AMLS; Chicago 39-41 (LS. 7: Prin Scottsville Graded Sch, Scottsville Va 26-27; Libn Va Union U 27-39; Prof Sch of Lib Serv Atlanta U 41-42; Libn Atlanta U 42-47; Pub affairs off Amer Embessy, Monrovia Liberia 47-49; U Libn Tex mso U 49-54; Acquis libn Nat Lib of Nigeria, Lagos Nigeria 62-63; Lib Dir Va State Col 54-62, 63-68; Libn Mary Holmes Col 68-. 8: Consul: Acquis Proj, Ala State Col & Ala A&M Col, 52-55; Claflin Col 56; Fayetteville State Tchrs Col 57-58. Ad: Elizabeth City Tchrs Col, 58; Morristown Jr Col, Morristown Tenn 59. 9: ALA (Coun mem 56-60; Com on Intel Freedom 52-54, Common Econ Opportunity Programs 65-67); TexLA (chm Dist 5 Col Div 52-53); Va Tchrs Assn (chm Dept of Libns 56-58); Libns Club of Atlanta (pres 41-43). 10: US mem Unesco Lib Sc, London & Manchester, 48; Citizens Com on Pub Educ, Atlanta, 45-47; Alpha Phi Alpha; Assn for Study of Negro Life & Hist. 11: Decorated, Star of Africa, Liberia, 49. 12: Ed Richmond Va "Voice (25-26); Ed bd, "Phylon, Atlanta U Publ (42-47). 13: Yes. 14: Admin, acuis. 15: 22 Boisseau st, Ettrick Va 23802.

VAN NICE, DOROTHY E. b Evanston Ill 14 Ja 21. 5: Iowa State Tchrs Col 40-41 (Kindergarten, Prim) 2 yr degree; San Diego State Col 43-50 (Hist, Eng, Geog) AB; UWash 56-58 (LS) ML. 7: San Diego Pub Lib: Lib clerk 50-55, Lib trainee sci sect 56-58, Libn sci sect 58-61, Sr libn & documents libn sci sect 61-. 9: CalLA. 10: Beta Phi Mu. 14: Govt docs. 15: 3552 Mississippi st, San Diego Ca 92104.

VAN NORD, JOAN ELAINE (HAMILTON). b Charlotte Mich 17 Ag 35. 4: Wayne Van Nord. 5: West Mich U 53-57 (Eng) BA; UIll 61-62 MS in LS. 6: Fr. 7: Asst libn Kalamazoo Central High Sch, Kalamazoo Mich 57-58; Patients' libn Kalamazoo Pub Lib 56-58; Elem & high sch libn USAF, Tokyo 59-61; High sch libn UIll(Urbana) 62-. 9: IllLA; IllASchL; IllEA. 10: Toastmistress Intl. 13: Yes. 14: Wk with ya. 15: 202 Univ High Sch, Urbana Ill 61801.

VAN NORDEN, FRED R. b Plainfield NJ 10 N 26. 5: BostonU 46-50 (Econ) AB; URI 68 MLS. 7: Mgt trainee J C Penney Co Inc, Waltham Mass 50, 52-53; Sgt (E-5) (admin specialist) US Army Signal Corps (ASA) 50-52; Asst buyer Parke Snow Inc (Dept Stores), Waltham Mass 54-56; Pre-prof asst Boston Pub Lib 59-63; Supv of Bk Processing Belmont Mem Lib, belmont Mass 63-. 9: MassLA. 14: Catlg, tech serv, lib admin. 15: PO Box 254, Belmont Ma 02178.

VAN NORT, MARY CROMWELL. b Scranton Penn 27 Mr 16. 5: Keystone Jr Col 34-36 AA; Bucknell 36-38 (Sociol) BA; Marywood Col summer 51-59 (LS) MS. 7: Asst dean of women Keystone Jr Col 42-50, Libns 51-. 9: ALA (Penn State chm; Spec Projects Com; Jr Col Libs Sect);-ACRL; PennLA. 14: Catlg, ref. 15: 101 N Turnpike rd, Dalton Penn 18414.

VAN NOTE, ROY NELSON. b Mattoon Ill. 5: East Ill U 35-39 (Eng) B Ed; UParis summer 45 (Fr) Certif; UMich 45-46 ABLS; UIll 48-49 (LS)MS, 51-61 (LS) PhD. 6: Fr. 7: US Army First Spec Serv Force 41-45; Acquis libn Franklin & Marshall Col 46-48; Gift & exch libn LSU 49-51; Bibliog UIll Lb (Urbana) 41-61; Libn Mansfield State Col Lib 62-64; Dir Wis State U Lib (La Crosse) 64-. 8: Dir, Dist Lib Center, Mansfield Penn 62-64; Lib Com Col Center of the Finger Lakes, 62-64; Field consul for sch libs, Penn 62-64. 9: ALA (Sch Lib Proc Com 62-0; WisLA (chm Col & Univ Sect); Upper Miss Acad LA (chm). 10: Beta Phi Mu; AAUP. 12: "Brush and Pencil PhD diss (61). 13: Yes. 14; admin. 15: Wis State U Lib, La Cross Wis 54601.

VAN ORDEN, PHYLLIS JEANNE. b Adrian Mich 7 Jl 32. 5: East Mich U 50-54 (Elem Educ) BS; UMich 57-58 AMLS; Wayne St U 67- (Curriculum Devel). 7: Elem sch libn E Detroit Pub Schs, E Detroit Mich 54-57; Bkmob libn, child libn San Diego Pub Lib 58-60; Instr materials consul Royal Oak (Mich) Pub Schs 60-64; Head Instrl Materials Center Oakland U (Mich) 64-66; Visiting Asst Prof UOkla 66; Instr Dept Lib Sci Wayne State U 66-. 9: Assn Supv & Curr Devel; NEA-DAVI; ALA-AASchL;-CSD; Mich A-V Assn; MichASchL (Mich Week Resources Chm); MichEA; MAHE. 10: Pi Lambda Theta; AAUP. 13: Yes. 14: Instrl materials centers. 15: apt 407 630 Merrick, Detroit Mi 48202.

VAN ORSDALE, MARION F(RANCES). b Buffalo NY 2 D 40. 5: Syracuse 58-62 (Hist, LS) BA, 62-63 MSLS. 6: Ger. 7: Sr libn I Buffalo & Erie Co Pub Lib, Lafayette Sq, Buffalo NY 63-. 8: Ref Lib, Lib/USA NY Worlds Fair, 65; CSD Dev Com 69-71. 9: ALA; NYLA. 10: Beta Phi Mu. 14: Adult serv, ref, info retrieval. 15: 51 Darlich ave, Hamburg NY 14075.

VAN SLYKE, DOROTHY GENEVRA. b Perth Ont Can 8 F 28. 5: McMaster U 46-49 (Hist) BA; Toronto 50-51 BLS. 6: Fr. 7: Catlgr & ref libn Pub Lib, Niagara Falls Ont 51-. 9: Inst Prof Libns Ont (past dir & treas); OntLA (past chm Ref Sect). 12: Adv bd & contrib "Niagara Falls, Canada; a History of the City" (67). 14: Catlg, ref. 15: Niagara Falls Pub Lib, 1017 Victoria ave, Niagara Falls On Can.

VAN STAAVEREN, ELIZABETH (KELLY). b Adel Ga 13 N 23. 4: Jacob Van Staaveren. 5: George WashingtonU 40-44 (Eng) AB in Ed, 47 (Econ); American U 45-47 (Econ, Statistics); UCal (Berkeley) 53-54 BLS. 6: Fr. 7: Labor economist US Dept of Labor, Wash DC 45-53; Libn US Army Spec Serv, Germany & France 54-56; Libn (catlgr) US Dept of Labor Lib, Wash DC 58-61, 67-. 9: ALA; SLA; DCLA. 14: Catlg. 15: 1611 Francis Hammond Pkwy, Alexandria Va 22302.

VAN SYOC, EDNA E. b Ackworth Iowa 26 Ag 13. 5: Simpson Col 30-34 (Math) BA; UIll 38-39 BS in LS; UMich 53-54 MALS. 6: Sp, Fr. 7: Libn Mapleton Pub Sch Lib, Mapleton Iowa 33-38; Asst catlgr Ore State U 42-45; Head catlgr Fla State U 46-63; Decimal clsf spec Decimal clsf Off LC 64-68, Asst chief decimal clsf div 69-. 9: ALA; SELA (chm Catlg Sect); DCLA; Potomac Tech Proc Libns. 10: AAUW; Beta Phi Mu; Pi Lambda Theta. 14: Catlg, clsf, acquis. 15: 220 C st SE, Wash DC 20003.

VAN TIJN, BEATRIX J. b Leipzig 21 Jl 10. 5: UGrenoble(France) 29-30 (Fr Lit); Lib Sch ULeipzig (Germany) 31-33 Libns Certif; Columbia 53-54 (Amer Hist & Lit), 54-55 (LS) MS. 6: Fr, Ger, Dutch, Sp, Lat. 7: Stud libn Deutsche Buecherei & Deutsches Buchmuseum, Leipzig 31-33; Employee Centens Bkshop, Amsterdam Netherlands 33-35; Asst libn Nt Bur of Econ Research, NYC 46-47; Med Lib research for Miss Virginia Henderso NYC 52-53; Asst libn The Wool Bur, NYC 53; Sr catlgr Columbia U 55-. 9: SLA (Mus Group); NY Lib Club. 14: Catlg. 15: 600 W 111th st, New York NY 10025.

VAN TILURG, CONSTANCE V. b Mansfield Ohio 17 S 35. 5: Capital U 53-57 (Eng) AB; UPittsurgh 63-64 MLS. 6: Sp. 7: Libn I circ dept Columbus Pub Lib, Columbus Ohio 57-58; Lib aide circ dept Canton Pub Lib Assn, Canton Ohio 59-60; Lib aide group serv dept Akron Pub Lib, Akron Ohio 60-63, Libn II Adult serv div 64-67; Sr asst br libn NY Pub Lib 67-. 9: ALA. 10: Beta Phi Mu. 14: Ref humanities & soc sci), biliog. 15: 382 Central Pk W apt 8-G, New York NY 10025.

VAN VALKENBURGH, FRANCES B. b Salida Col 1 Mr 1900. 5: Colorado State Col 18-27 9hist, Pol Sci) BA; USC 32 (Hist) MA, 28 (Hist); San Diego State Col 24 (Hist). 6: Fr. 7: Tchr Red Cliff High Sch, Red Cliff Colo 20-22; Tchr Salida High Sch, salida Colo 22-26; Tchr & libn Logan Co High Sch System, Sterling Colo 27-35, 53-58; Libn Sterling High Sch, Sterling Colo 58-. 9: NEA; ALA; -AASchL; ColoLA; ColoASchL (past pres); NEColoSchL (past pres). 10: Kappa Delta Pi; Phi Alpha Theta; Pi Delta theta; OES; WSJ; PEO; Bus & prof orgs. 14: Ref. 15: 428 Elwood st, Sterling Co 80751.

VAN VELZER, VERNA (JEAN). b State Col Penn 22 Ja 29. 5: UIll 46-50 BS in LS; Syracuse 54-57 MLS. 7: Ref asst Dayton Pub Lib, Dayton Ohio 50; Geol libn Ohio State U 51-54; Ser asst SYRACUSE U Lib 54-57; Chief catlgr Stanford Research Inst, Menlo Park Cal 57-58; Head Libn Gen Electric Tube Operation, Palo Alto Cal 58-64; Head Libn Fairchild Semiconductor R&D Lab, Palo Alto Cal 64-65; Head Libn Sylvania Collateral Intelligence Acivities, Mt View Cal 65-66; Hd libn ESL Inc Research Lib, Sunnyvale Cal 66-. 8: Comp of set of botanical keys for the flora of NY State, 57; Org & catlg of bk collection for child health coun of Stanford Cal, 60. 9: SLA (chm Elect com 63); CalLA. 10: Beta PHI Mu; Pi Lambda Sigma; Soc Tech Writers & Publrs; Inst Electrical & Electron Engnrs; Alpha Theta Upsilon. ; Amer Inst Aero Astro Engring; Amer Ordnance Assn; Marquis Biog Lib Soc. 14:Ref, Ref, info retrieval. 15: 4048 Laguna way, Palo Alto Cal 94306.

VAN VLACK, LAURA RUTH. b Lansing Mich 29 D 45. 5: UMich 63-67 (Microbiol) BS, 67-68 AMLS. 6: Fr. 7: Libn Upjohn Co, Kalamazoo Mich 68-. 9: SLA. 10: Phi Beta Kappa; Beta Phi Mu. 14: Lit searching. 15: Upjohn Co, Kalamazoo Mi 49001.

VAN WAGTENDONK, ROELINA JANTINA (LOTTERING). b Groningen Netherlands 3 N 09. 4: Willem J van Wagtendonk. 5: Rijksuniversiteit (Groningen) 29-35 (Fr) BA; Ind U 59, 62-63 (LS) AM. 6: Fr, Dutch, Ger. 7: Interlib loan libn Ind U 59-60; Clerk UMiami (Coral Gables Fla) 60-62, Catlgr 63-. 9: DadeCoLA. 10: Beta Phi Mu. 14: Catlg (sci, Slavic). 15: 9720 SW 114th st, Miami Fla 33156.

VAN WECHEL, HELEN C. b Maurice Iowa 15 Je 04. 5: Northwestern JR Col 28-30; UIowa 30-32 (Zool) BA; UDenver 57-59 (LS) MA. 7: Rural schs, Sioux Co Iowa 22-24; Pub sch, Maurice Iowa 22-28; Pub sch, Monroe Iowa 32-43; PUB SCH, Hartley Iowa 34-38; W Jr High Sch, Waterloo Iowa 38-43; Northwestern Classical Acad, Orange City Iowa 46-49; Admissions coun & asst registrar Northwestern Col (Iowa) 49-52, Libn 56-. 9: ALA, IowaLA. 10: Delta Kappa Gamm; Womens Club. 14: Ref, catlg. 15: 615 Arizona ave SW, Orange City Iowa 51041.

VAN WEZEL, LILLIAN S. b NYC 10 Ag 37. 4: John Van Wezel. 5: Marymount Manhattan 55-59 (Eng Lit) BA; Fla State U 59-61 MLS. 6: Sp, Fr. 7: Libn trainee Miami Pub Lib, Miami Fla 59-61, Child libn 62-66, Supv Co lib serv 66-. 9: ALA; FlaLA; SELA. 10: Beta Phi Mu. 14: Pub libs, child wk, ext, bkmob. 15: Miami Pub Lib, 1 Biscayne blvd, Miami Fl 33132.

VAN WEZEL, PATRICIA. b Montgomery Ala 9 S 42. 5: Randolph-Macon Woman's Col 60-62; NorthwesternU 62-64 (Eng) BA; UIll 64-65 (LS) MS; EmoryU 65 Med Lib Assoc Certif. 7: Ref libn M D Anderson Hosp & Tumor Inst, Houston Texas 65-66, Catlgr 66-67; Ref libn Ga Inst of Tech 67-. 9: MedLA. 15: 28 Cantey pl NW, Atlanta Ga 30327.

VAN WINKLE, ELVA YOUNG. b Silverton Col 10 O 06. 5: Radcliffe 24-28 (Classics, phil) BA (cum laude); Simmons 31-32 BS in LS; IndU 54-59 (Folklore) MA. 7: Page & asst Salt Lake City Pub Lib 19-24, summers 25-28; Child bk buyer Pilgrim Press Bkstore, Boston 28-31; Asst & child libn Utica Pub Lib, Utica NY 32-38; Child libn: SE Br DC Pub Lib 39-40, SW Br 41-44, Petworth Br 44-46; Chief central child room DC Pub Lib 46-. 8: Cond, In-serv Train in Storytelling, Pub Lib, DC 50-; Consul & cond, travelling Fablers, Urban Serv Corps, Wash DC 65-. 9: ALA; -CSD (Storytelling Handbk Com 60-61; Storytelling Survey Com 65-68); Amer Folklore Soc; DCLA. 12: "Storytelling Time", brochure (56). 14: Child libnship, storytelling. 15: 2127 California st NW, Washington DC 20008.

VAN ZANTEN, FRANK (VELDHUYZEN). b The Netherlands 21 O 32. 4: Lois Holkeboer. 5: (Horticultural Sch (Netherlands) 50-52 (Horticulture) Diploma; Calvin Col 55-59 (Hist, Eng) AB; UMich 60-61 (LS) MA. 6: Dutch, Ger. 7: US Army, US & Europe 53-55; Tchr Lynden Christian Sch, Lynden Wash 59-60; Processing libn Mich Sate Lib, White Cloud Mich 61-62; Head Libn Dickinson Co Lib, Iron Mountain Mich 62-65; Dir St Clair Co Lib System, Pt Huron Mich 65-68; Dir Tucson Pub Lib 68-. 9: ALA; MichLA (Memb Com, Legis Com, Planning Com); Mich Lib Film Circuit (chm 64). ; Ariz State LA (Jr Ariz Mem; Lib Dev Com; Subcom on Standards for Statewide Lib Serv); SWLA. 14: Pub admin. 15: City Hall PO Box 5077, Tucson Az 85703.

VAN ZEE, GERTRUDE MAUDE. b Kalaazoo 19 O 12. 5: Hope Col 30-34 (Modern Langs) AB; West Mich U summers 34, 35; UCal summer 36; UMich 39-41 & summers 43-45 ABLS, MALS. 6: Fr, Ger. 7: Jr catlgr Mich State U 41-42; Catlgr & asst libn Kalamazoo COL 42-52 Tchr of catlg Penn State U summer 50; West Mich U: Head catlgr 52-61, Head catlgr 61-68, Sr catlgr 68-. 9: ALA; MichLA. 10: AAUW. 14: Catlg. 15: 328 W Michigan ave, Kalamazoo Mi 49007.

VANCE, KENNETH E. b Pewamo Mich 20 My 17. 5: Central Mich U 38-43 (Eng) BS; UMich 46-48 (Eng) MA, 56-62 (LS) Ed D. 7: Elem tchr rural schs, Clinton Co Mich 35-42; (S/Sgt) US Army Med Detachment 350th Inf 88th Div 43-46; Assoc ext libn UMich 50-55; Sch lib consul Bur of Sch Serv UMich 50-65; Assoc Prof of Lib Sci Dept of Lib Sci UMich 63-. 9: ALA (Count);-AASchL (treas); -LAD (Bd); MichLA (2nd v-pres); MichASchL (exec sec). 14: Sch libs. 15: 415 Manor dr, Ann Arbor Mich 48105.

VANCE MARIE (SPERLA). b Cincinnati Ohio 15 Ag 15. 5: UAriz 61 (Sp) BA, 63 (LS, Educ) MEd. 6: Sp, Fr. 7: US Army 44-46; Sp tchr Globe High Sch, Globe Ariz 61-62; Libn tombstone High Sch, Tombstone Ariz 63-64; Libn Arizona Sch, Riverside Cal 64-65; Libn 9staff) Dept of Defense, overseas 65-. 9: OverseasEA. 15: Star Rte 1 Box 355, Morongo Valley Ca 92256.

VANCE, MARY-LOUISE (HINTON). b Lumberton Miss 29 Je 09. 4: Harvey Clifton Vance. 5: Miss State Col for Women 27-31 (Fr) BA, & Voice Diploma; UColo summer 41 (Hist); LSU 42-3 BS in LS; UIll 47-49 (Hist, LS). 7: High sch tchr & priv tutor, Miss & NYC 31-42; Ref asst econ div NY Pub Lib 43-46; Asst ref libn UAla 46-47; Bibliog UIll(Urbana) 47-49; Asst libn Valley Forge Army Hosp, Phoenixville Penn 50-51; Catlgr Redstone Arsenal Tech Lib, Huntsville Ala 53-54; Acquis libn UHouston 51-53, 54-. 9: ALA; SWLA (Exec Coun); TexLA (chm Acquis Round Table); Houston Lib Club. 10: AAUP; Univ Huston Faculty Club; Univ Houston Womens Assn; Univ Oaks Civic Club; Beta Phi Mu. 14: Acquis. 15: 4360 Harvest ln, Houston Tx 77004.

VANDALE, ELSIE H. b Phila Penn. 5: Westminster Col (New Wilmington Penn) 38-42 (Eng) BA. 7: USNR Lt (jg) 42-45; A-v dir Azusa Pub Lib, Azusa Cal 64-. 9: Cal (pres A-V Div 69). 15: 428 N Westridge ave, Glendora Ca 91740.

VANDENBERG, GRACE (O'BRIEN). b Durango Colo 25 Ja 13. 4: Steven G Vandenberg. 5: Mich StateU 31-36 (Hist & Pol Sci) AB; UMich 38-45 ABLS. 6: Fr. 7: Soc studies tchr Bd of Educ, Belding Mich 36-37; Tchr & radio coord Bd of Educ, Lansing Mich 37-50; Critic tchr Eastern MichU 50-54, Libn (critic tchr) 58-60; Libn Bd of Educ, Willow Run Mich 54-58; Libn Jefferson Co Bd of Educ, Louisville Ky 60-67; Libn Bd of Educ, Boulder Colo 67-. 9: NEA; ColoEA. 10: Delta Kappa Gamma. 15: 501 13th st, Boulder Co 80302.

VANDENBERGE, PETER N(ICHOLAS). b Kalamazoo 16 D 15. 4: Julia Van Genderen. 5: Hope Col 33-37 (Hist) AB; UNeb 38 (Hist) MA; Brown U 38-40; New Brunswick Theol Sem 40-43 BD; Rutgers 57-59 MLS. 6: Ger, Fr, Dutch, Gk. 7: Pastor First Refomed Church, Walden NY 43-48; Pastor Lincoln Park Commun Church, Yonkers NY 48-56; Lecturr in Christian Educ New Brunswick Theol Sem 56-57, Libn Gardner A Sage Lib 57-67; Assoc libn Colgate Rochester Div Sch 67-. 8: Chm, HIST & Research Com Reformed Church in Amer, 59-67. 9: ATheolLA (treas; Exec Com; chm Com on Finan Assistance from Founs, past mem Com on Stat), chm Com on Appraisal). 12: Ed "Historical Directory of Reformed Church in America (66). 13: Yes. 14: Admin, acquis. 15: Colgate Rochester Div Sch/Bexley Hall 1100 S Goodman st, Rochester NY 14620.

VANDER VELDE, ESTHER R(UTH). b Emporia Kan 20 O 17. 5: Col of Emporia 35-39 (Hist) AB; Kan State Tchrs Col (Emporia) 39-40 Lib Certif, 42-. 6: Ger. 7: Asst catlgr UWichita 40-42; Head catlgr Kan State Tchrs Col (Emporia) 44-. 9: ALA; KanLA; MPLA. 10: AAUW; LWV. 14: Catlg, tech proc. 15: W A White Lib, Emporia Ks 66801.

VANDER VELDE, JOHN JACOB. b Emporia Kan 12 Ag 36. 5: Yale 59-60 (Mandarin Chinese, lang Specialist) (Honors); Kansas State Tchrs Col 54-58, 65-67 (Mus) BA, 67-68 (Libnship) ML. 6: Chinese (Mandarin). 7: Clk Vander Velde Bros Groc, Emporia Kan 58-59; Linguistic & admin specialist USAF, Lackland & Goodfellow AFB Tex, Okinawa Taiwan 59-65; Catlgr W A White Mem Lib, Emporia Kan 66-68; Catlgr-bibliogr Kan State U Lib 68-69, Supv acquis div 69-. 9: ALA-ACRL; MusicLA; KanLA. 10: Kan StateU Lib Staff Assn; Alumni Assn Kan State Tchrs Col. 12: Co-ed "Farrell Footnotes" (bulletin of Kan StateU Lib Staff Assn). 14: Tech serv (electronic info storage & retrieval). 15: 1837 College Hts rd apt 11, Manhattan Ks 66502.

VANDERBURG, MARY ALICE. b Bloomington Ind 31 Jl 22. 5: Ind U 40-49 (Govt) AB, 49-50 (LS) MA. 6: Fr. 7: (Sgt) USMC Women Res 43-45; City Libn Franklin Pub Lib, Franklin Ind 50-51; Br libn Peoria Pub Lib, Peoria Ill 52; Sr libn Indianapolis Pub Lib 52-54; Patients libn VA Hosp, Indianapolis 54-58; Chief Libn VA Center, Cheyenne Wyo 58-59; Chief Libn VA Hosp, Marion Ind 59-66; Chief lib serv VA Hosp, Palo Alto Cal 66-. 9: ALA-AHIL. 10: Ladies Auxiliary of Brotherhood of Local Trainmen; Zonta Intl. 14: Admin. 15: 1903 Bayshore #31, Redwood City Ca 94063.

VANDERLIP, MYRTLE (ELIZABETH). b Traverse City Mich. 4: Eldad C Vanderlip. 5: Marion Col 35-37; Houghton Col 46-48 (Hist, Soc Sci) AB; UMich 52-54 MA in LS. 7: Registrar Detroit Bible Inst 48-50; Recorder Houghton Col 50-52; Ref libn Long Beach Pub Lib, Long Beach Cal 54-56; Catlg libn Westmont Col 56-57, 59-63, Act lib 57-59, 63-64, Pub serv libn 65-. 9: ALA. 14: Catlg, ref. 15: 654 Circle dr, Santa Barbara Ca 93103.

VANDERMOLEN, JOHN FREDERICK. b Fond du Lac Wis 2 Ja 29. 5: UWis 49; LSU 49-52 (Liberal Arts) BA; UWis 54-55 (LS) MA; UIll 64- (LS). 6: Sp. 7: US Army (Cpl)

Infantry, Ft Riley Kan 52-54; Libn I Free Lib of Phila 55-57; Asst catlg libn Purdue U 57-59; Catlg libn Main Lib G E Co, Schenectady NY 59-61; Asst order libn So Ill U 61-63; Documents libn Wis State U (Platteville) 63-;67; Sci libn USoCal 67-. 9: ALA; SLA; ASIS. 10: Assn Wis State Univ Faculties. 14: Tech serv, tchg, sci, engnrg. 15: 1434 Tenth st, Santa Monica Ca 90404.

VANDERVEEN, EUNICE ELIZABETH (IRISH). b Fillmore NY 22 Ja 18. 4: Hugh Calvin Vanderveen. 5: Mich State U 35-39 (Soc Wk) AB; UMich 60-65 MLS. 7: Bkmob libn Kent Co Lib, Grand Rapids Mich 56-59; Asst sch lib consul 59-63; Br libn E Grand Rapids Br, E Grand Rapids Mich 63-65; Br Supv Kent Co Lib, Grand Rapids Mich 65-. 9: Grand Rapids Chap Womans Nat Bk Assn (2nd v-pres). 15: Kent Co Lib 726 Fuller NE, Grand Rapids Mich 49503.

VANDERWEG, JUDITH (GREVILLE). b Montclair NJ 9 Je 43. 4: Phillip D VanderWeg. 5: Skidmore 61-63 (Liberal Arts); UMich 63-65 (Sociol) BA; Peabody 68-69 MLS. 7: Personnel clk Rand McNally & Co, Skokie Ill 65-66; Sec to dir purchasing UMich 66-68; Libn Webb Sch, Bell Buckle Tn 69-. 9: ALA. 15: Apt B-6 1315 E Castle st, Murfreesboro Tn 37130.

VANDIVER, LA NELLE. b Jefferson Ga 29 My 16. 5: Ga State Tchrs Col 31-33; Womans Col of Ga 33-35 (Eng) AB; Fla State U summers 48-52 MALS. 6: Fr. 7: Tchr-libn Ray City High Sch, Ray City Ga 35-36; Tchr-libn Manchester High Sch, Manchester Ga 36-41; Tchr-libn Mt Dora High Sch, Mt Dora Fla 41-52; Documents libn UTenn 52-53, Head processing dept 53-. 9; ala; TennLA; SELA. 10: Beta Phi Mu. 13: Yes. 14: Catlg. 15: 1631 Laurel av, Knoxvile Tenn 37916.

VANEK, EDNA V. b Cleveland 4 Jl 08. 5: Ohio Wesleyan U 25-27; West Res Flora Stone Mather 27-29 (Fr) BA; West Res 30-31 BLS. 7: Apprentice Pub Lib, Cleveland 29-31; Catlgr Pub Lib, Davenport Iowa 31-42; Asst "The Booklist ALA, Chicago 42-52, Ed 52-. 9: ALA; SLA; IllLA. 10: AAUW. 14: Bk sel, catlg. 15: 50 E Huron st, Chicago Il 60611.

VANN, J(OHN) DANIEL III. b Raliegh NC 14 Je 35. 4: Ellen Jane Rogers. 5: UNC (Chapel Hill) 53-57 (European Hist) BA; Yale 57-65 (Medieval Hist) MA, PhD; Columbia 62-63 (Higher Educ Admin); Emory 69- (Libnship). 6: Fr, Lat. 7: Resident freshman coun Yale U 59-60; Assoc Prof of hist Campbell Col 61-63; Bibliogr of European hist & lit, asst ref libn Newberry Lib Chicago 63-65; Prof of hist Cal Baptist Col 65-66; Dir lib & Prof of hist, Baptist Col (Charleston SC) 66-69; Libn Keuka Col, Keuka Park NY 69-. 9: ALA; AHA; Med Acad Amer; BSA; SELA. 10: Phi Alpha Theta. 13: Yes. 14: Admin, bk sel, rare bks. 15: Keuka College, Keuka Park NY 14478.

VANN, SARAH KATHERINE. b Macon Ga 15 My 16. 5: Womans Col of Ga 33-36 (Eng, Fr) AB; UNC summer 37-39 ABLS; UMich 40-44 AMLS; Chicago 49-58 (LS) PhD. 6: Fr. 7: Catlgr UGa 40-42; Catlgr rare bks UMich 42-45; Catlgr "Standard Catalog H W Wilson C summers 46-48; Assoc Prof Carnegie Lib Sch 45-60; Visit Assoc Prof Sch of Lib Serv Columbia 60-61; Visit Assoc Prof Grad Sh of Lib Sci UTex 62-64; Prof Sch Info & Lib Sci SUNY (Buffalo) 66-69; Prof Grad Sch Lib Studies UHawaii 69-. 8: Tchr Emory, George Peabody Col, Syracuse U, UCal, West Res summers 45-60; Consul ALA/Rockefeller Grant, Inst of Lib Sci U of the Philippines, 61-62; Dir Field Survey of DDC Ise Abroad, 64-65; Surveyor, SE Penn Proc Center Feasibility Study, Penn State Lib, 65-. 9: ASIS; BSA; SLA; ALA (chm Jt Com on Lib Wk as a Career 54-55; mem Adv Com on U Philippines 61-65, Panel on Unesco 62-, Internat Rel Round Table);-RTSD (Program Com; chm Ctlg & Clsf Sect 60-61);-Div Catlg ;chm Nomin Com 59-60; chm Internat Rel Com 68-; Margaret Mann Award Com mem 63-64 & Clsf (Exec Bd 52-56, Clsf Com, Recr Subcom);-LED (Tchrs Sect: Exec Bd 60-62, chm 64-65); AALS (Exec Bd Internat Lib Sch Com 67-);-ISAD (mem Nom Com 63-66);-ACRL;-Rare Bks Sect; 52-5, Program Chm 57-58). 10: AAUP; Archaeol Inst Amer; Amer Acad of Pol & Soc Sci. 11: Scarecrow Press Award for Lib Lit, 62. 12: "Training for Librarianship Before 1923 ALA (61); "Field Survey of Dewey Decimal Classification Use Abroad" (65); "Southeastern Pennsylvania Processing Center Feasibility Study" (67). 13: Yes. 14: Catlg, rare bks, educ for libnship. 15: Grad School of Lib Studies, Univ of Hawaii, 2425 Campus rd, Honolulu Ha 96822.

VANNORSDALL, MILDRED MAY. b Madison Co Ohio 10 My 18. 5: Miami U (Ohio) 36-39 (Eng) AB; UWis 39-40 BLS; Ohio State U 46; UCincinnati 53-54; Xavier U 53; UMich 63-64 AMLS, 64- (LS). 6: Fr. 7: Catlgr Waukegan Pub Lib, Waukegan Ill 40-45; Head catlgr State Lib, Columbus Ohio 45-47; Head ref dept Cuyahoga Co Pub Lib, Cleveland 47-53; 1st asst Educ Dept, Positions in other depts, Pub Lib of Cincinnati & Hamilton Co, Cincinnati Ohio 53-56; Subj spec Tottenham Pub Libs, Tottenham London Eng 56-57; Ref libn Lane Pub Lib, Hamilton Ohio 57-58, Adult serv supv 58-63; Lecturer Dept of Lib Sci UMich 64-65, Pre-Doctoral Instr 65-67. 9: ALA (chm Ref Sect Survey Com 53-54; Subs Bks Com 57-63);-RSD (Pub Lib Ref Survey Com 54-60); AALS; British Lib Assn (cor mem); OhioLA (sec-treas 61-63). 10: Pi LAMBDA Theta; phi Beta Kappa; Ohio Hist Soc; United Nations Assn. 11: University Fellowship, 64-65, UMich. 13: Yes. 14: Bk sel, ref, bibliog, serv to adults, lib hist. 15: 801 E Hurson st apt 7, Ann Arbor Mi 48104.

VANSETH, DONNA KAY (SEILER). b Green Bay Wis 1 Ja 40. 4: Richard Arlington Vanseth. 5: UWis 58-62 (Chem) BS, 62-63 MS in LS. 7: Asst libn Shell Development Co, Emeryville Cal 62; Lit chem Chevron Research Co, Richmond Cal 63-65; Tech libn Kimberly-Clark Corp, Neenah Wis 65-. 9: SLA. 10: Phi Beta Kappa. 14: Ref. 15: Tech Libn Res & Eng Div, Kimberly-Clark Corp, Neenah Wi 54956.

VANSTON, JOHN. b Scranton Penn 18 Ja 10. 4: Grace G. 5: U Scranton (even) 47-53 BA. 7: Insurance Agent Gen Insurance, Scranton Penn 29-39; Law Libn Lackawanna Bar Assn, Scranton Penn 39-43; (Sgt) US Army, Burma, US 43-45;Law Libn Lacakwanna Bar Assn, Scranton Penn 46-. 8: Ed "The Lackawanna Jurist". 9: AALL. 12: "Tropical Index of Law Reviews, 6 Penn Law Schs. 14: Research, admin. 15: Law Lib Court House, Scranton Penn 18503.

VanWINKLE, JEANETTE (MABEL ALEX). b Chicago Ill 25 My 41. 4: Ronald David VanWinkle. 5: Ill State Normal U 59-63 (Elem Educ, LS) BS; UArk 63; NoIllU 64-69. 6: Sp. 7: Sec, Wauconda Ill 58-59; Coun Camp Chickagami, Winter Wis 59-63; Hd libn School dist #47, Crystal Lake Ill 63-. 9: ALA (Resol Com); IllLA (Memb Com). 10: Alpha Beta alpha; Girl Scout Leader. 14: Sch libs. 15: PO Box 323, Crystal Lake Il 60014.

VARADIAN, ROXIE. b San Francisco Cal 12 Jl 16. 5: Fresno State Col 34-38 (Math) AB, summers 39-; UCal (Berkeley) 38-39 (Math); Cal Libnship Certif. 6: Fr, Ger. 7: Tchr & libn Clovis Unified Sch Dist, Clovis Cal 40-66, Dir compensatory educ 66-68, Dist libn 67-. 9: ALA; NEA; CalASchL; CalTA. 10: AAUW; Alpha Delta Kappa. 15: 620 De Witt ave, Clovis Ca 93612.

VARELA-VALENTIN, IRIS. b Santurce PR 5 Ja 29. 5: UPR 47-51 (Soc Sci, Educ) BAED; Drexel 55-56 MS in LS. 6: Sp. 7: Tchr Dept of Educ, San Juan PR 51-55, Libn 56-58; Libn Ant Command S Army Caribbean, Ft Buchanan PR 58-62; Libn admin Ant Command US Army Caribbean, Ft Brooke PR 62-66; Libn admin 10th Air Force Lib Serv Ctr, Richards-Gebaur AFB Mo 66-. 9: ALA; Sociedad de Bibliotecarios de Puerto Rico; Asociacion de Maestros de PR. 14: Child wk, admin. 15: 708 Walnut, Belton Mo 64012.

VARENAIS, HERTA S. b Latvia. 5: ULatvia(Riga) (Law) Mag Iur. 6: Latvian, Ger, Russian. 7: Tchg jurisprudence at a pub col (Bauska Latvia) 34-35; Law practice, Latvia 35-40; Asst Northeastern U 51-55; Asst libn Boston Col 55-. 9: AALL. 10: Latvian Acad Women's Org "Gundega". 14: Admin, ref. 15: 4 Hagar st, Jamaica Plain Mass 0130.

VARIEUR, NORMAND L. b RI 15 Mr 27. 5: UOttawa 45-50 (Philos, Theol) BA, BPh, STL; Catholic U 56-57 MS in LS; Amer U 58-59 (Archives). 6: Fr. 7: Head pub catlg div Queens Borough Pub Lib, Jamaica NY 64-66; Hd catlg dept Eng Soc Lib, NYC 66-68; Chief tech proc sect Picatinny Arsenal, Dover NJ 68-. 9: ALA (Life mem); SAA (Life mem); NJLA; NY Lib Club; CLA; SLA (chm Bylaws Com Sci-Tech Group NY Chap). 14: Catlg. 15: PO Box AR, Denville NJ 07834.

VARNER, MRS JEANNETTE (JOHNSON). b Selma Ala 12 Ag 09. 4: John Grier Varner. 5: UAla27-31 (Romance Langs) AB, MA; UVa 34-38 (Romance Langs) PhD. 6: Sp, Fr, Ital. 7: Fr tchr Blue Mountain Col 37-39; Span tchr UVa Ext Div 41-43; Span tchr Fairfax Hall Jr Col 41-43; Libn & Eng tchr Centro Venezolano-Americano, Caracas Venezuela 43-47; Head of ref Austin Pub Lib, Austin Tex 48-. 9: ALA; TexLA; SWLA. 10: Alpha Delta Pi. 11: Real Academia de Ciencias, Bellas Letras y Nobles Artes de Cordoba (Espana). 12: Co-ed & co-tr (with husband)Garcilaso de la Vegas "The Florida of the Inca (51); Co-auth of "Encyclopedia Americana; article on Garcilaso de la Vega, el Inca. 14: Ref. 15: P O Box 2287, Austin Tex 78767.

VARNUM, VIRGINIA (SCALES). b Providence RI 13 F 15. 4: Myron W Varnum. 5: Bates Col 32-36 (Psy, Lang) AB; Harvard summer 38 (Fr); Institut Brittanique Sorbonne 38-39 (Fr civilization); Northeastern U 42-43 (Wage Admin) ESMWT Certif. 6: Fr. 7: High sch tchr Me 36-38, 39-40; Labor rel research asst West Electric, NYC 44-49; Info ed Nat foreman's Inst, NYC 58-62; Labor rels research & reference libn Nat Assn of Mfrs, NYC 62-64; Communications researcher United Hosp Fund, NYC 65; Libn Amer Mgt Assn, NYC 66-. 9: SLA. 13: Yes. 15: 55 Austin pl, Staten Island NY 10304.

VASCO, GERHARD M. b Berlin Germany 11 Jl 15. 4: Erna B. 5: NYU 54 (Fr) BA, 61 MA, 69 PhD; Rutgers 57 MLS. 6: Ger, Sp, Fr. 7: Catlg libn NY Pub Lib 57-61; Instr Fr & Ger Rutgers 61-65; Asst hd Descriptive catlg 66-67; Subject specialist SUNY (Stony Brook) 68-. 10: Mod Lang Assn. 14: Bibliog. 15: 35-11 85 st, Jackson Heights NY 11372.

VASH, LUCY T. b Baltimore 6 O 30. 5: Col of Notre Dame (Md) 48-52 (Hist) AB; Middlebury Col Summer Lang Schs 52, 53, 56 (Ital) MA; UNC 55-56 BSLS. 6: Ital, Sp, Fr. 7: Tchr soc studies Montrose Sch, Reisterstown Md 52-54; Libn Enoch Pratt Free Lib, Baltimore 54; Libn UNC Lib 55; Libn Baltimore Co Bd of Educ, Catonsville Md 56-58; Libn US Army Spec Serv, Europe 58-60; Libn DC Pub Lib 61; Libn Dept of Defense (DIA), Wash DC 62-63; Libn Navy Dept, Wash DC 63-66; Libn US Air Force, Ramstein Germany 66-. 9: ALA (Armed Forces Libns Sect, sec-treas European Subsect); DCLA. 10: Beta Phi Mu. 14: Ref, admin. 15: 4315 Sidehill rd, Baltimore Md 21229.

VASILAKIS, MARY. 5: UPittsburgh 44-47 (Biol, Chem) BS; Duquesne U 63 ME in LS. 7: Research asst Mellon Inst, ittsburgh 49-57; Asst libn Bettis Atomic Power Lab, Pittsburgh 57-63; Libn Westinghouse Atomic Power Div, Pittsburgh 63-67; Lib mgr, Westinghouse Nuclear Energy Systs 67-. 9: SLA; PennLA; ASIS. 15: 1106 Woodward ave, McKees Rocks Penn 15136.

VASLEF, MRS IRENE. b Budapest Hungary 23 Mr 34. 4: Nicholas P Vaslef. 5: San Jose State Col 60 (Fr) BA; Simmons 63 (LS) MS; Columbia summer 67-; UMunich (Ger) 67-68. 6: Hungarian, Fr, Ger. 7: Lib asst Widener Lib Harvard U 61-62; Libn Peabody Sch, Cambridge Mass 62-64; Libn Horace Mann Jr High SCH, Colo Springs Colo 64-67; Asst catlg libn Colo Col 68-. 9: ALA; ColoLA. 14: Catlg. 15: Quarters 4311-F, USAF Acad, Co 80840.

VASSALLO, PAUL. b Marsa Malta 3 Ag 37. 5: Wayne State U 54-61 (Pol Sci) BA; UMich 61-62 MALS. 6: Maltese, Ital, Sp, Fr. 7: Asst Wayne State U Law Lib 59-61; LC: Spec recruit 62-63, Asst head Hispanic Exch Sect 63, Subj catlgr Soc Sci Subj Catlg Div 63-64, Head Newspaper & Period Sect Ser Div 64-65, Asst head Ref Sect Ser Div 65-66, Asst chief ser record div 66-67; Asst to dean Sch Lib & Info Serv UMd 67-68; Chief congressional ref div LC 68-. 9: ALA; SLA (mem Jt Com to Revise List of Internat Subscription Agents). 10: LC Welfare & Recreation Assn. 11: LC Meritorious Service Award 66. 14: Ref, acquis, subj catlg, sers, file & records mgt, automation. 15: 8150 Lakecrest dr, Greenbelt Md 20770.

VAUGHAN, DAVID LANE. b Belle Haven Va 19 N 34. 4: Gene Sellers. 5; Roanoke Col 53-57 (Eng) AB; UNC 58-59 MSLS. 7: Reporter "The Roanoke Times, Roanoke Va 57-58; ASST LIBN Roanoke Co Pub Lib, Salem Va 59-61; Co Libn Davidson Co Pub Lib, Lexington NC 61-65; Asst dir Toledo Pub Lib, Toledo Ohio 65-68; Dir Greensboro Pub Lib, Greensboro NC 68-. 8: Exec dir, Nat Lib Week, NC, 65. 9: ALA; NCLA; SELA; OLA. 10: Greensboro Chamber of Com; Sierra Club; NAACP. 14: Admin. 15: 4809 Susan ter, Greensboro NC 27410.

VAUGHAN, DELORES K. b Austin Minn 8 O 34. 5: Macalester Col 52-56 (Eng) BA; Col of St Catherine summers 57-62 BS in LS; UChicago 64-69 (Lib) MA, (doctoral study LS). 7: Tchr, libn LeRoy-Ostrander Pub Sch, LeRoy Minn 56-60; Libn Moose Lake Pub Schs, Moose Lake Minn 60-64; Research asst G L S UChicago 66-68; Summer fac Dept Lib Sci Ind StateU (Terre Haute) 66, 67; Summer fac Sch Lib Sci UIowa 68; Summer fac Grad Sch of Lib Sci UTexas (Austin) 69; Asst exec sec lib educ div ALA, Chicago 69-. 9: ALA; NCTE. 10: Beta Phi Mu; Pi Lambda Theta. 13: Yes. 14: Sch libs, child & adolescent lit. 15: 5442 S Harper ave, Chicago Il 60615.

VAUGHN, BETTY JANE (BITTNER). b Rochester NY 10 Ja 26. 4: Harold A Vaughn. 5: SUNY(Albany) 43-48 (Soc Sci) BA; Chicago 55-56 (LS); SUNY(Albany) 56-57 (Soc Sci) MA, 59-60 (LS) MS. 7: Hist tchr Coxsackie-Athens High Sch, Coxsackie NY 48-50; Catlgr NY State Lib 51-53; Hist tchr Saratoga Springs High Sch, SARATOGA Springs NY 54-55; Circ libn UChicago 55-57; His tchr Ft Edward High Sch, FT Edward NY 59-60; Libn of a spec adult educ collection Syracuse U 61-. 9: AEAUSA; ALA; Coun of Nat Adult Educ Assns; NY Adult Educ Assn. 10: PTA; Girl Scouts; Boy Scouts; Experiment in Internat Living. ; AAUW; Nat Congress of Parents & Tchrs. 14: Adult educ, acquis. 15: 351 Bruce st, Syracuse NY 13224.

VAUGHN, MRS FLORENCE E(RCELL) (FOWLER). b Greenville Tex 30 O 07. 5: Tex Col 25 -27, 33-35 (Educ) BA; Prairie View Col summers 40-43 (Eng) MS; UDenver summers 45-47 BS in LS; UWis summers 50-52, 54 MS in LS. 7: Tchr of prim grades pub schs of Tex 27-37; Tchr of high sch Eng & libn Pub Schs, Greenville Tex 37-44; Tchr of high sch Eng & libn Longview Col High Sch, Longview Tex 44-46; Libn pub schs, Wichita Falls Tex 46-47; Assoc state supv of libs Hdqrs, Prairie View Col 47-50; Supv of Libs & Instr Smith Co Schs, Tex 50-56; Libn Tyler Pub Schs, Tyler Tex 56-. 8: State Bd of Examiners for Tchr Educ (Tex), 58-63; Adv Com to wk with Staff of Tex Educ Agency in Devel Guide for Sch Lib Programs, 62-65. 9: ALA-AASchL (Mag Com); NEA; Tex State TA; Tex Assn Educ Tech. 10: YMCA. 14: Sch lib serv. 15: 1620 N Moore ave, Tyler Tex 75703.

VAUGHN, ROBERT VERNON. b Carey Ohio 21 N 24. 5: Ohio State 47-50 (Bus Admin, Geog) BS, BA; UMich 54-55 (LS). 6: Fr, Sp. 7: Sales asst: Marion Power Shovel Co, Marion Ohio 52-53, Hydraulic Press Mfg Co, Mt Gilead Ohio 53-54; Asst to v-pres mkg Fenestra inc, Detroit 55-62; Statistician analyst Gen Motors Corp, Detroit 62-65; Libn St Dunstan's Sch, St Croix USVI 66-. 9: ALA. 14: Ref. 15: Box 1122 Christiansted, St Croix USVI 00820.

VAUGHN, SUSAN (SIMON). b Detroit 13 Je 41. 4: Edward Jeffrey Vaughn. 5: Marygrove Col 59-63 (Hist, Pol Sci) AB; UMich 63-64 MALS. 7: Ref libn Detroit Pub Lib 64-68; Ref libn UMich Sch Bus Admin 69-. 9: ALA. 12: "Statistical Supplement" to "Modern Society," by John Biesanz (68). 14: Ref. 15: 5264 St Clair, Detroit Mi 48213.

VAUGHN, WILLIAM ANDREW. b Russellville Ark 13 F 34. 4: Marian Sacrey Vaughn. 5: Ark Polytech Col 52-55 (Hist) BS; UArk 55-56 (Educ) M Ed; Peabody 56-57 MA in LS. 7: Asst libn Ark Polytech Col 57-63, Libn 63-. 8: Commsn on Coord Higher Educl Finance in Ark, Lib Com 66-; Exec Dir Nat Lib Week in Ark 68. 9: ArkLA (chm Col Sect 2, chm Recr & Scholarship Com 64); ALA; SWLA. 10: Lions Club, C of C; Pi Gamma Mu; Ark Consistory. 14: Catlg, admin. 15: Ark Polytech Col Lib, Russellville Ar 72801.

VAUGHT, EDWIN F. b Sheridan Ark 23 N 17. 4: Kathryn Johnson. 5: UTex 48-50 (Eng) BA, 50-51 (LS). 7: US Army 41-45; Letter carrier US PO Dept, Pine Bluff Ark 45-48; Ref asst UTex (Austin) Educ Lib 51, Ref asst (humanities) 51-52, Ref asst Law Lib 52-54; Libn SW Research Inst, San Antonio Tex 54-; Libn Applied Mechanics Reviews, San Antonio Tex 67-. 9: SLA (pres Tex Chap 63-64); Amer Soc Testing & Materials; Amer Soc Metals; TexLA; BexarCoLA. 14: Ref, acquis. 15: 8500 Culebra rd, San Antonio Tx 78228.

VAUGHT, MARION (NEWBURY) McDERMOTT). b Mobile Ala 18 Ja 16. 4: Raymond Vaught. 5: LSU 33-37 (Mus Educ) BM, 37-39 (Eng Lit) BA, 39-41 BS in LS. 7: Lib asst NYC Pub Lib summer 41; Lib asst Eastman Sch of Mus, Rochester NY 41-42; Libn (vol) Holy Name Hosp Lib, Teaneck NJ 44-46; Lib asst Teaneck Pub Lib, Teaneck NJ 46-47; Libn State St Jr high Lib, Hackensack NJ 47-51; Lib asst Lib of Hawaii, Honolulu 51-54; Asst libn Camp Zama Lib, Camp Zama Japan 54-56; Fine arts libn Hawaii State Lib, 56-. 8: Music consul: to Maui Co Lib 61; to Kauai Co Lib 68; to Honolulu Theater for Youth; HawaiiLA rep to Citizens Adv Com of Oahu Transpr Study 65-; Adv Bd UHawaii Lib Sch. 9: ALA; MusLA; TheatreLA; HawaiiLA (pres 64-65, Prog chm, Publ Chm 65-; chm Ref Sect). 10: Sigma Alpha; Honolulu Acad of Arts; Honolulu Theater for Youth Bd Dirs; Hawaii Govt Employees Assn; Honolulu Chamber Music Soc; Bishop Museum; Hawaiian Hist soc; Friends of the Lib. 13: Yes. 14: Art, music, recreation. 15: 2629 Haili rd, Honolulu Hi 96813.

VDOVIN, GEORGE. b Shanghai China 12 MY . 4: Alice Williams. 5: UCal 39-41, 48-53 (Zool) AB, 54-55 MLS. 7: Army Air Forces Weather Observer (Sgt) 41-46; Stanford U Libs: Asst biol sci libn 55-58, Head tech info serv 58-60, Chief sci div 60-61; Head pub serv dept ULib UCal(San Diego) 61-65, Head Sci & Engnr Lib 65-. 12: Co-auth "Final Report, Serials Computer Project (64). 13: Yes. 14: Automation systs, info systs. 15: PO Box 109, La Jolla Ca 92037.

VEATH, MARIAN S. b Des Moines Iowa 4 Je 24. 4: Byron M Veath. 5: Iowa State U 42-45 (Gen Engnr) BS. 7: Libn Iowa State U 47-51; Libn Reynolds Metal Co, Louisville Ky 52-55; Libn UKy Col of Pharmacy 56-57; Libn Sylvania Electronics, Buffalo NY 58-61; Tech libn Gen Electric Co, Louisville Ky 62-. 8: Prof Lib Consul, SLA. 9: SLA; KyLA; Louisville Lib Club. 10: PEO; Square dance & round dance clubs; Camp Fire Girls. 14: Ref, mgt. 15: 3701 Foxglove lane, Louisville Ky 40222.

VEBLEN, MARTHANNA E. b Seattle 3 O 20. 4: John Veblen. 5: Mills Col 38-40; UWash 40-42 (Sociol) BA, 59 M Libr. 7: Gen reading libn UWash59; Seattle Pacific Col: Asst libn 60-65, Asst libn & Instr in Lib Sci 65, Libn & Assoc Prof 65-66; King Co Lib Syst area libn 69-. 8: Research Consul Wash State Governors Coun on Aging, 59-60; v-chm Metropolitan Area 67-71; Bd mem Seattle & King Co Coun on Aging 68-69. 9: ALA; PNLA (sec Lib Educ Div); NW Col LA (chm 64); Puget Sound Lib Club. 10: Jr League of Seattle; Womens Univ Club; UWash Sch of Libnship Alumni Assn; Beta Phi Mu; Alpha Kappa Delta; Carkeek Memorial Fund Com on Selection. 12: "Aging in the State of Washington (61). 14: Ref. 15: 5228 Sand Pt way NE, Seattle Wa 98105.

VEDDER, MARION H. b Fayetteville NY 11 Ap 05. 5: SUNY(Albany) 23-27 (Eng) AB; Syracuse 28-30 BS in LS. 7: Asst libn Fayetteville Free Lib, Fayetteville NY 28-30; Br libn Rochester Pub Lib, Rochester NY 30-32; Libn Fayetteville High Sch, Fayetteville NY 32-35; Head ext dept Rochester Pub Lib, Rochester NY 35-45; Lib Ext Div NY State Lib; Jr libn 45-49, Asst educ supv 49-53, Sr libn & supv 53-59, Assoc libn & supv 59-67, Assoc in Inst Lib Serv 67-. 9: ALA (Coun-at-Large 60-65);-AHIL -AHIL Survey Com 64-66; Bd mem 64-67; pres 66); Correctional Assn (Bd Dirs 57-59, chm Com on Institution Libs 54-); Correctional Educators Assn; NYLA (chm Com on Institution Libs51-53; Adv Liaison 53-); LPRC. 10: AAUW; Phi Kappa Phi; Pi Lambda Sigma. 11: AHIL Exceptional Serv Award 66; Edward R Cass Corr Achievement Award 66. 13: Yes. 14: Pub lib org & serv, lib serv for state institutions &disadvantaged people, lib adv or consul wk. 15: 1075 Park ave, Shenectady NY 12308.

VEENSTRA, JOHN G. b Muskegon Mich 24 Ja 28. 4: Joyce Dusendorf. 5: Muskegon Jr Col 44-46; UMich 49-50, 53-55 (Span) BA, 55-57 AMLS. 6: Sp, Fr, Ger, russian. 7: Jr bibliog UMich 57, Sr bibliog 57-58; Order libn Purdue U Libs 58-63; Dir of Libs Universidad Del Valle (Cali Colombia SA) 63-66; Asst dir UFla Libs 66-. 8: Rockefeller Stasf, 65-; Dir of Libs, Univ Del Valle, Colombia 63-65; Ford Foundation consul Universidad Nacional (Lib), Bogota Colombia 66-. 9: ALA (Jt Com on Internat List of Subs Agents); Asociacion de Bibliotecarios en Colombia; FlaLA; Assn SEast Libns; Asociacion Interamericana de Bibliotecarios y Documentalistas Agricolas. 10: AAUP; Civitan Int. 12: Co-auth "International List of Subscrption Agencie (63). 13: Yes. 14: Admin, lib bldgs, acquis, Lat Amer. 15: Univ of Fla Libs, Gainesville Fl 32601.

VEGELER, ROBERT H. b Ft Wayne Ind 2 Mr 17. 4: Eldon Baker. 5: Manchester Col 38-41 (Hist) AB; UIll 42-44 BSLS. 7: Ft Wayne Pub Lib, Ft Wayne Ind: Clerical wker 37-41, Ref asst 41-48, Phonograph record room libn 48-52, Record room & ya libn 52-56, Co-ordinator Adult serv 56-65, Asst libn 65-. 9: IndLA (past chm publicity, memb, & recr coms); ALA. 10: Kiwanis; PTA; C of C. 14: Operational procedures. 15: 1720 Florida dr, Ft Wayne In 46805.

VEIT, FRITZ. b Emmendingen Germany 17 S 07. 4: Lucille Stearns. 5: Us of Freiburg, Berlin, Heidelberg 26-32 (Law) Dr JUR: Peabody 35-36 BS in ls; Chicago 36-41 (LS) PhD. 6: Ger, Fr. 7: Libn of Grad Lib Sch Soc Sci Reading Room, Act Law UChicago 37-43; Law libn US RR Retirement Bd, Chicago 43-49; Libn Chicago City Jr Col Englewood Eve br 41-48; Supv John Marshall Law Sch Lib (Chicago) 49-57 Dir of Libs Chicago State Col & Chicago City Col (Wilson Campus) 49-. 8: Visiting faculty: West Mich U summer 59, Ariz State U summers 64-65, 67-68; Visiting Prof Rosary Col 50-. 9: ALA-ACRL (Bd Dirs 60; chm Tchr Educ Libs Sect 60-61, Loc chm Chicago Conf 63); IllLA; Chicago Lib Club (pres 64-65). 10: Pi Gamma Mu. 12: Assoc ed "ACRL Monographs (53-60). 13: Yes. 14: Admin, lib educ. 15: 6800 S Stewart ave, Chicago Il 60621.

VEITCH, CAROL J. b Irwin Penn 27 O 42. 5: Clarion State Col 60-64 (LS, Soc Studies) BS in Ed; UPittsburgh 65-66 MSLS; Cal State Col 67-68; Edinboro State Col NDEA Inst 68. 7: Elem libn Norwin Sch Dist, Irwin Penn 64-. 9: NEA; ALA; Penn State EA; PennSchLA. 10: Confraternity of Christian Doctrine; Pi Gamma Mu; Westmoreland CoSchLA. 14: Elem libs. 15: Box 18 Hempfield Highlands, 93 Lincoln highway W, Jeannette Pa 15644.

VELICS, LASZLO. b Szombathely Hungary 23 Jl 19. 4: Maria Grandjean. 5: Pazmany U (Budapest) 38-44 (Pol Sci) PhD; West Res 61-62 MSLS. 6: Fr, Ger, Hungarian, Dutch. 7: Researcher Free Europe Inc, NYC 50-61; Ref libn UCincinnati Lib 62-66; Acquis libn Mich Tech U 66-. 9: ALA. 14: Ref, acquis. 15: 506 Garnet st, Houghton Mi 49931.

VELLEMAN, RUTH (SALTMAN). b NYC 12 Ap 21. 4: Moritz Velleman. 5: Smith 38-42 (Soc Studies) BA; C W Post Col 61-64 (LS) MS, 64-65 NY State Sch Libn Certif. 7: Ed Spec Events Off of War Info, Wash DC 43-45; Libn Kindergarten thru 12th grade program for Physically Handicapped Child Human Resources Sch, Albertson NY 63-; Libn Human Resources Center Research Lib for Rehabilitation of The handicapped, Albertson NY 63-. 9: ALA (Coun on Exceptional Child); NYLA; Nassau SchLA. 10: LWV; Child Guidance Assn. 13: Yes. 14: Lib serv to exceptional child, rehabilitation of disabled. 15: 15 Cliffway, Port Washington NY 11050.

VELLUCCI, MATTHEW JOHN. b White Plains NY 19 D 35. 5: St Pius X Sem 54-58 (Philos) BA; Columbia 60-62 MSLS. 7: Grad lib asst Catholic U Libs 60; Lib trainee Westchester Lib System, Mt Vernon NY 60-62, Jr libn 62-63; Sub asst to libn Queens Col (NY) 63-64; Asst libn Esso Standard Eastern Inc, NYC 64-66, Libn 66-68; Spec asst to the dean Sch of Lib & Info Serv UMd (College Park) 68-. 8: Lectr; Queens Col (NY) Lib Sci Program, fall 66; UNC (Chapel Hill) SchLib Sci summer 68. 9: SLA; NYLA (pres Resources & Tech Serv Sect 67-68); AALS. 12: Ed "Reources & Technical services Sect in NYLA "Bulletin (65-). 13: Yes. 14: Catlg, clsf, educ for libnship, special libraries. 15: 7212 13th ave, Takoma Park Md 20012.

VELTEN, ERIKA. b Chicago 25 S 31. 5: UMiami(Fla) 49-50; Marquette U 50-54 (Ger) BS; UIll(Champaign) MLS. 6: Ger. 7: Milwaukee Pub Lib 56. 9: ALA; WisLA. 14: Child wk. 15: 1646 N Prospect ave, Milwaukee Wi 53202.

VENABLE, LEUCIA BUTLER. b Suffolk Va 14 Jl 24. 5: West Md Col 41-45 (Eng, Soc Studies) AB; Drexel 57-58 MS in LS. 6: Fr. 7: Libn US Naval Train Center, Bainbridge Md 51-57; Libn Mt Pleasant Sr High Sch, Wilmington Del 58-. 8: NDEA Summer Inst for Libns UDenver 65. 9: ALA; NEA; DelLA; Del State EA. 10: Alpha Delta Kappa; Beta Phi Mu. 15: 508 Marsh rd, Wilmington Del 19809.

VENDEMIA, JOHN ANTHONY. b Capitol Hts Md 3 D 18. 5: St Fidelis Col 42-44 (Relig) Diploma. 6: Ital, Fr, Sp, Ger. 7: Preliminary catlgr & searcher LC 57-67, Sr catlgr 67-. 14: Catlg. 15: 403 60th ave, Capitol Hts Md 20027.

VENETT, ANTHONY JOHN. b Farrell Penn 3 Je 31. 4: Gloria Jane Durbin. 5: Penn State U 51-55 (Sci) BA; Carnegie 61-62 MSLS. 6: Sp. 7: US Navy Submarine electronics ETSN(SS) 49-51; US Navy Communications, Electronics, Registered publs (Lt jg) 55-58; Prod supv Amer Cyanimid, Bridgeville Penn 58-61; Research libn Youngstown Sheet & Tube Co, Youngstown Ohio 62-66; Project div Lib Info System Penn State U 66-. 9: SLA (Metals Div, Finance Chm 64-65). 10: Beta Phi Mu. 14: Admin & supv. , tech searching, spec libs. 15: Penn State Univ Pattee Lib, University Park Pa 16802.

VENNE, LOUISE. b St-Jean P UVE 30 Ja 44. 5: UMontreal 66 (Botany) BS, 67 MS, 68 BLS. 6: Fr, Ger. 7: Libn (Ref) ULaval 68-. 9: Societe de Biologie de Montreal; Assn du Personnel Admin & Profess de ULaval. 14: Ref. 15: Bibliotheque des Sciences, Universite Laval Quebec Can.

VENNIX, ARTHUR J. b Chinook Mont 29 Ag 14. 05Jordan Col 32-36 (Eng) BA; UDenver 48-49 MA in LS; UNeb 50- (Amer Hist). 5: Jordan Col (Mich) 32-36 BA; UDenver 48-49 MALS; UNeb 50- (Amer Hist). 6: Fr, Norwegian, Turkish. 7: Interviewer, coun, job analyst US Employment Serv, Appleton WIS 36-43, 45-48; Clerk typist us army, European Theater 43-45; Assoc dir of libs UNeb 49-62, Law Libn 64-. 8: Lib consul, Ataturk U, Erzurum Turkey 62-64; Prof of Legal Bibliog, uneb Col of Law, 57-. 9: ALA; AALL; MPLA; NebLA. 10: AAUP. 12: "American Troops in Normandy" (48); "Look to Your Library" (54). 13: Yes. 14: Law lib admin. 15: Univ of Neb Law Lib, Lincoln Neb 68508.

VERBOUT, MARIE ELIZABETH (GORMAN). b Litchfield Ill 3 S 21. 4: Edward J Verbout. 5: Ill State U 39-43 (Eng) B Ed; UIll 48-51 MS in LS. 7: Asst libn Waukegan High Sch, Waukegan Ill 46-49; Libn Barrington igh Sch & Elem Sch, Barrington Ill 49-55; Libn N Chicago High Sch, N Chicago Il 55-56; Libn Kewanee High Sch, Kewanee Ill 59-62; Libn

Pueblo Hgh Sch, Tucson 62-63; Head ya secttucson Pub Lib 63-64; Libn Palo Verde High Sch, Tucson 64-66; Tech serv libn Tucson Pub Sch 66-. 9: NEA; ArizEA; TucsonEA; Ariz StateLA. 14: Bk reviewing, tech serv. 15: 342 S Stratford dr, Tucson Az 85716.

VERHAAREN, JOHN EDWARD. b Phila 14 Je 39. 5: La Salle Col 57-61 (Ger) BA; Drexel 61-62 (LS) MS. 7: Prof asst I Baltimore Co PUB Lib, Towson Md 62-63; US Army chaplains asst spec 4/c, Verona Italy 63-65; Libn I Free Lib of Phila 65-67, Libn II 67-68, Libn III 68-. 9: ALA (Jr Mem RT);-PLA;-ASD;-RSD; PennLA (New Mems Sect). 10: Amer Topical Assn; Fine Arts Philatelists; Philatelic Lit Assn; Germantown Stamp Club. 14: Ref, adult serv, admin. 15: 440 W Annsbury st, Phila Pa 19140.

VERHOEF, ADELIA MEYER. b Cleghorn Iowa 16 Ja 13. 4: John M Verhoef. 5:UIowa summer 36 (LS). 7: Lib asst Cherokee PUB Lib, Cherokee Iowa 31-36, Child libn 36-39; Med & nursing sch libn Iowa Lutheran Hosp, Des Moines Iowa 58-61; Med libn Iowa Methodist Hosp, Des Moines Iowa 61-. 9: ALA. 10: PTA; Mother Singers; Wa-Tan-Ye; Civic Music Assn; Des Moines Commun Playhouse. 14: Ref, bibliog. 15: 1423 Merle Hay rd, Des Moines Iowa 50311.

VERITY, JOHN BURRITT. b Los Angeles 17 O 28. 4: Carol Holmstrom. 5: Maryville Col (Tenn) (46-47); UCal(Berkeley) 47-48; UCLA 48-51 (Eng) BA; USoCal 54-55 MS in LS. 7: (Cpl) Finance Corps US Army 51-53; Head Libn Curtiss Wright Corp, SantaBarbara Cal 55-59; Ref asst UCal(Santa Barbara) 59; Head tech processes Ampex Corp, Redwood City Cal 60-63; Head info planning Lawrence Radiation Lab, Livermore Cal 63-. 9: SLA; ASIS. 10: Beta Phi Mu. 14: Ser, acquis, catlg, machine systems, br admin, mgt. 15: 1387 4th st, Livermore Cal 94550.

VERNEI, BARBARA RoJEAN (WALKER). b Caldwell Ida 7 Ja 31. 4: Emil L Vernei. 5: UWash 48-52 (Mus) BA; Kan StateU 61-62 (Mus) MA; UWash 65-67 M Libr. 6: Ger, Fr. 7: Clk UWash Mus Lib, Seattle 50-52; Clarinetist Seattle Symphony Orchestrea 51-61; Instrumental instr Seattle Pub Sch 54-61; Instr Kan StateU Mus Dept (Manhattan) 62-65; Pre-prof Seattle Pub Lib Mus Div 65-66; Asst Prof ref libn Central Wash State Col 67-69; Catlgr mus specialist Cal Inst of the Arts 69-. 8: Clarinetist, Aspen Festival Orchestra, Aspen Colo summers 51-57. 9: PNLA. 10: AAUP; Mu Phi Epsilon. 13: Yes. 14: Ref, lib orient, spec libs. 15: Lib Cal Inst of the Arts, Valencia Ca 91355.

VERNEI, EMIL L. b Youngstown Ohio 5 N 14. 4: Barbara R J Walker. 5: Royal Hungarian P Pazmany U (Budapest) 34-39 (Hit of Art, Early Christian Archaeol) PhD (summa cum laude); Columbia 53-54 MSLS; NY State Pub Libn.s Prof Certif. 6: Ger, Fr, Hungarian, Ital, Lat, Sp, Gk. 7: Research libn Wenner-Gren Found for Anthrop Research, NYC 48-53; Ref libn sci & tech div Brooklyn Pub Lib 54-56; Monogreph catlgr NY Pub Lib 56-59; Monograph catlgr City Col (NY) 59-62; Asst dir of libs Fairleigh Dickinson U (Teaneck) 62-65; Asst Prof of Libnship & head ref libn Central Wash State Col 65-69; Hd acquis libn Cal Inst of the Arts 69-. 9: ALA. 10: AAUP. 12: "Medieval Tombstones of Hungary Magyar kozepkori siremlekek, PhD diss Budapest 39). 13: Yes. 14: Ref, lib orientation classes, tchg lib serv classes, exhibits & promotion, bibliog. 15: California Inst of the Arts, 2404 W 7th st, Los Angeles Ca 90057.

VERNER, MATHILDE MARIA. b Kempten Germany 12 Ag 20. 5: Us of Tuebingen & munich (Germany) 46-50, 53 (Romance Lang & LS) PhD; Catholic U 59-60 MSLS. 6: Ger, Fr, Ital, Sp. 7: Catlgr Mt St Marys Col (Los Angeles) 53; Sch libn Yoyogi Elem Sch, Tokyo 54-56; Assoc Prof of Lib Sci Catholic U 60-. 8: Visiting prof UMontreal spring 69; Consul Planning Research Corp, Wash summer 68; Grant from German Acad Exchange Serv to study German libs summer 69. 9: ALA; CathLA; Compar Educ Soc; AALS; Potomac Tech Processing Libns. 10: AAUP; Beta Phi Mu. 13: Yes. 14: Comp libnship, tech serv, ref. 15: 4206 Longfellow st, Hyattsville Md 20781.

VERNON-WILLIAMS, ELEANOR (DUNHAM). b New Bedford Mass 11 Ag 23. 4: Frederick R Vernon-Williams Jr. 5: Flora Stone Mather Col 41-45 (Soc Sci) BA; West Res 45-46 BS in LS. 7: Y-a libn, adult serv, & br libn Enoch Pratt Free Lib, Baltimore 46-. 9: ALA; MdLA. 14: Adult serv. 15: 849 W Univ Parkway, Baltimore Md 21210.

VERNON, ELIZABETH V. b Augusta Ga 6 Ap 12. 5: Wesleyan Col (Macon Ga) 29-33 (Biol) AB; Columbia summers 57-61 (LS) MS; Pikeville Col 56, 60 (LS); Morehead Col 61-63 (LS); UFla Ext 61 & 63. 6: Fr. 7: X ray tech U Hosp, Augusta Ga 33-35; Libn Pikeville High Sch, Pikeville Ky 56-61; Libn Oak Ridge High Sch, Orlando Fla 51-62; Libn Evans High Sch, Orlando Fla 62-65; Libn Oak Ridge High Sch, morlando Fla 65-67; Curriculum specialist lib serv Bd of Pub Instr Co of Orange, Orlando Fla 67-. 9: NEA; ALA; Clr Tchrs Assn; FlaLA; FlaASchL; SELA; Fla A-v Assn; Orange Co Libns Assn. 10: PTA; AAUW; Delta Kappa Gamma; Execs Club; Pilot Club. 14: Ref, catlg, proc ctr. 15: 2508 Hastings st, Orlando Fla 32802.

VERNON, HARRIET (ANNE VanSTONE). b Bridgeport Conn 30 N 15. 4: Thomas S Vernon. 5: Bates Col 32-36 (Sociol) BA; UMich 61 MALS. 7: Loan dept Bay City Pub Lib, Bay city Mich 56-57, Ref libn 57-59; Libn Pinckney High Sch, Pinckney Mich 59-62; Lib asst (loan dept) UArk Lib (Fayetteville) 62-67, Lib asst Engring Lib 67-68, Lib asst ref dept 68-. 9: ALA. 14: Ref. 15: 1308 Crestwood dr, Fayetteville Ar 71701.

VERSCHOOR, HELEN (LYON). b White Plains NY 23 O 14. 4: Irving Alton Verschoor. 5: Vassar 32-35 (Plant Sci) AB; Columbia 42-48 (LS) BS. 6: Fr, Ger. 7: Licensed real estate saleswoman, Small House Designer, Landscaper Edward I Margolin & Gilchrest Realty Corp, Great Neck NY 36-40; Lib asst Great Neck Lib, Great Neck NY 40-46; Ref libn Educ NY State Lib 47; Asst dir, Act dir Great Neck Lib, Great Neck NY 48-51; Catlgr sch of lib sci SUNY(Albany) 60-61; Catlgr Jr Col of Albany & Albany Even Col (Russell Sage Col) 60-65, Hd libn Jr Col of Albany 65-. 8: Trustee, Ravena Free Lib, 57-. 10: CommunCultural Coun; No NY Vassar Club; Albany Inst of Hist & Art. 14: Catlg, ref, admin. 15: Star Rt, Ravena NY 12143.

VERTANES, CHARLES AZNAKIAN (YEZNIQUE CARAPET). b Alexandria Egypt 14 Mr 05. 4: Lillian Hines. 5: Nat Bible Inst (Shelton Col) 26-28 (Theol) Diploma; NYU 28-29 (Secondary Educ) BS; Columbia 30-31, 37-40 (Hist & Philos of Educ) MA; Union Theol Sem 30-33, 39-40 (Rel Educ & Ethics) BD (magna cum laude), STM; LIU 61 MSLS. 6: Armenian, Turkish, Fr, Arabic, Hebrew, Ger, Gk. 7: Clsf & head of stud lib staff Union Theol Sem (NY) 37-41; Exec Dir Armenian Nat Coun of Amer 45-56; Libn, Det Head Audits & Surveys Co Inc, NYC 57-58; Libn LI Lighting Co, Hicksville NY 58-61; Libn Hauppage Col of LIU 61-63; Lib consul & Assoc Prof of Educ Mitchell Col of LIU 63-64; Libn Brentwood Pub Schs, Brentwood NY 61-; Lib consul & Dir of Lib development Friends World Col 66-69. 8: Active in pastoral ministry for 15 yrs at intervals between 28 and 57 in NY, NJ & Wash DC; Soc wker Dept of Welfare, NYC 36-37; Instr of Turkish & Arabic, Gorge Washington U (Ext) & Berlitz Sch of Langs, Wash DC; Tr-analyst & consul, US Dept of Justice, Wash DC 43-44; Lib consul, Suffolk Co NY State Bd of Coop Serv, 64-. 9: ASIS; ALA-ACRL;-RTSD (Catlg & Clsf Sect 66-69; Subj Anal & Organ of Lib Materials Com 69-71); AASL; SLA; NY State Tchrs Assn; NYLA; Suffolk Co LA; SLA (NY Chap; Program Com Sci-Tech Group); NEA-DAVI. 10: NY State Hist Soc; LI Hist Soc; Nassau Co Hist Soc; Kappa Delta Pi; Phi Delta Kappa. 12: "The Armenian Question in Its Historical Perspective (46); "Armenia Reborn (47); "Quakerism nd the Armenian Language (52); Co-auth "Armenia: the Cradle of Gothic Architecture (53); two Thousand Years of the Armenian Language (54); Ed "Armenian Affairs, A Quarterly Journal (49-50); "Teghekatoo, Bulletin of the Armenian Nat Coun of Amer (4851); Comp "Directory of Public, School an Special Libraries on Long Island (60); "The Capitalistic Orientation of Moral and Religious Instruction in Early Modern Times (40); LILCO Lib Printed Catalog (61), ESEA Title III School Libraries Automation Project (67). 13: Yes. 14: Lib automation, bibliog, catlg, clsf, organ of learning resources ctrs in secon schs. 15: 14 Riviera dr, Smithtown NY 11787.

VERYHA, WASYL. b Kolodribka Ukraine 3 Ja 22. 4: Oksana Albota. 5: Toronto 55-59 (Hist) BA, 59-60 (Hist), 60-61 BLS; UOttawa 62-64 (Hist). 6: Ukrainian, Polish, Ital, Ger, Russian. 7: Metal sprayer The Casewin Co, Mimico Ont 51-57; Postal clerk Toronto Post Of 57-61; Libn UToronto Lib 61-64, Libn III catlg dept 68-. 8: Tchg Ukrainian Hist in Weekend Ukrainian Sch, Toronto. 9: CanLA; ALA. 10: Ukrainian Nat Fed of Can; Ukrainian Hist Assn; Assn Adv Slavic Studies; Can Assn Slavists. 12: "Ukraine; A Syopsis (64); Ed "Veterans News" in Ukrainian (66-). 13: Yes. 14: Catlg. 15: 215 Grenadier rd, Toronto 3 Can.

VESCELIUS, DIANA (LLOYD). b Alliance Ohio 18 N 41. 4: Lee E Vescelius. 5: Malone Col 59-61; Kent State 61-63 (Hist) BS in Ed, 64-65 MS in LS. 6: Fr. 7: Div asst Kent State U Lib 63; Libn II Akron Pub Lib, Akron Ohio 65-67, Info div 69-;

Catlgr Evanston Pub Lib, Evanston Ill 67-68. 9: ALA; OhioLA; Young Libns Assn (sec 69-). 10: Phi Alpha Theta. 14: Ref, readers guidance. 15: 232 F Northwest ave, Tallmadge Oh 44278.

VESENYI, PAUL (EUGEN). b Budapest Hungary 16 Ag 11. 4: Catherine Farago. 5: P Pazmany U (Budapest) 29-34 (Pol Sci) PhD; Columbia 60-61 (LS) MS. 06 Fr, Ger, Hungarian, Lat. 7: City of Budapest Dept of Culture 36-49; Belgian-Amer Bank NY 57-60; Hunter Col Lib 61-. 12: "Handbook to the European Periodical Literature in Social Sciences and Humanities" (69). 13: Yes. 14: Periods. 15: 177 E Hartsdale ave, Hartsdale NY 10530.

VESPER, COLEETA KAY (NORRIS). b Yale Mich 13 N 42. 4: Larry Ralph Vesper. 5: Port huron Jr Col 60-62 AA; Central MichU 62-65 (LS) BA; UMich 65-66 (LS) MA. 6: Fr. 7: Act dir St Clair Co Lib, Port Huron Mich 68, Hd child serv 66-. 9: MichLA; MichASchL. 10: St Clair Co 4-H Coun. 14: Child lib wk. 15: 9209 Beard rd, Avoca Mi 48006.

VESSELOWSKY, CONSTANTIN (THEODORE). b Poltava Russia 13 N 1891. 5: U Petrograd Law Sch 14 LLB; UMich 31 AB in LS. 7: Ref asst Pub Lib, Detroit 28-30; Catlgr UMich Lib 30-31; Subj catlgr & clsf NY Pub Lib 31-56; Catlgr & ref asst Middlebury Col 56-57; Asst head catlg dept UNotre Dame Lib (Notre Dame Ind) 57-. 12: Tr (with others) "Vatican Library Rules for the Catalog of Printed Books (48). 13: Yes. 14: Catlg. 15: Univ of Notre Dame Lib, Notre Dame Ind 46556.

VESTLING, CHRISTINA (MEREDITH). b Narbeth Penn 23 N 13. 4: Carl S Vestling. 5: Dickinson Col 30-34 (Gk) AB; Johns Hopkins 34-38 (Archaeol) AM; UIll 60-62 (LS) MS. 6: Fr. 7: Tchg asst UIll(Urbana) 60-61; Admin asst UIll Lib Sch 61-63; Instr Lib E UIowa summer 65; Libn catlgr UIowa Law Lib 65-. 9: ALA. 10: Phi Beta Kappa; Beta Phi Mu. 14: Catlgr, ref. 15: Fairview Knoll Rt 1, Iowa City Iowa 52240.

VETTESE, RICHARD (JR). b Detroit 30 O 41. 5: Wayne State U 59-64 (Span) AB; UMich 64-65 MALS; UIll 66. 6: Sp, Fr. 7: Libn Detroit Pub Lib 65-; (Sgt), Admin, Lib Serv US Air Force 66-69. 9: ALA. 14: Ref, fine arts, hosp & instit lib serv. 15: 5313 Farm Brook, Detroit Mi 48224.

VIACAVA, LILLIAN D. b Brooklyn NY. 5: Col of New Rochelle 47-51 (Hist) BA; Columbia 53-54 (LS) MS, summer 68 (Inst on For Area Studies for Col libns), spring 69 (LS). 6: Fr, Ital. 7: Summer asst Glen Rock Pub Lib, Glen Rock NJ 53, 54; Ref libn Ryan Lib Iona Col 54-59, asst libn 60-. 8: Adult Bk Com, Nat Conf of Christians & Jews, 59-. 9: ALA; CathLA; WestchesterLA(NY); Metropol Cath Col Libns Unit (sec-treas 55-58). 10: AAUP; Museum of Mod Art. 14: Ref, admin. 15: 43 Calton rd apt 4B, New Rochelle NY 10804.

VICK, NANCY JANE (HARPER). b NC 10 Ja 35. 4: Joseph Clinton Vick. 5: E Car U 57 (LS) BS; William & Mary 67 (Educ) MEd. 6: Sp. 7: Tchr Chesapeake Schs, Chesapeake Va 52-56, 59-60, 63-65; Libn pub lib, Farmville NC 57-59; Jr high libn: Chesapeake Schs, Chesapeake Va 60-62, Norfolk Schs, Norfolk Va 65-67; Ref libn pub lib, Rocky Mt NC 62-63, summer 64-65; Libn Norfolk Schs, Norfolk Va 67-. 9: ALA; NEA-DAVI; SELA; VaEA; VaLA. 10: Sigma Pi Alpha. 14: Sch libnship. 15: 3912 Providence rd, Chesapeake Va 23325.

VICTOR, LINDA GERTRUDE (BARTH). b Englewood NJ 20 Ag 41. 4: Jesse R Victor. 5: ClarkU 59-61 (Romance Lang); Harvard 67-69; Simmons 69 (Eng). 7: Interlib loans asst Harvard Med Lib 63-65; Mgr copy serv Countway Lib of Med, Boston 65-67; Sr admin asst NE Reg Med Lib Serv Countway Lib of Med 67-. 14: Interlib loans, reg lib serv. 15: 1 Crawford st, Cambridge Ma 02139.

VICTOR, LINDA MAE (MAU). b Keokea Maui 24 Ja 40. 4: Lincoln L Victor. 5: UHawaii 58-61, 62-63 (Elem Educ) BEd, 63-64 (Elem Educ, LS) Fifth Yr. 6: Fr. 7: Sch libn Dept of Educ, Honolulu 64-. 8: Act v-prin Makaha Elem Sch 67-69. 9: ALA; HawaiiASchL. ; HawaiiLA; Amer Fed Tchrs; Hawaii Fed Tchrs Assn. 10: Waianae Jaycees Auxiliary. 14: Child wk, sch lib. 15: 87-232 Mikana st, Waanae Hawaii 96792.

VICTOR, SARAH FRANCES (HARDEN). b Fairmont WVa 9 N 20. 4: John T Victor. 5: Fairmont State Col 38-42 (Eng) AB in Educ; Carnegie 46-47 BS in LS. 7: Eng tchr Monongah High Sch, Monongah WVa 42-43; Libn Fairmont Jr High Sch, Fairmont WVa 43-46, 47-51; Libn Barackville High Sch, Barrackville WVa 64-. 9: NEA; WVaEA; WVaLA; WVaASchL. 14: Second sch libs. 15: Box 67, Barrackville WV 26559.

VIETS, LOLA M. b Aurora Kan 19 N 27.7 5: Kan State Tchrs Col (Emporia) 45-49 (Soc Sci) BS in Ed, summers 50-55 MS in LS; UMinn(Minneapolis) summer 59; UColo summers 62, 63, 65. 7: High sch tchr-libn Hanover High Sch, Hanover Kan 49-54; Libn Winfield Jr-Sr High Sch, Winfield Kan 54-. 8: Bk Review Com for "Books for Kansas Schools" (68, 69). 9: NEA; ALA; Kan State Tchrs Assn; KanASchL. 14: Sch libs. 15: 1615 Ames, Winfield Kan 67156.

VIGEANT, JEANETTE M (HEYVAERT). b Mishawaka Ind 4 S 29. 4: Robert J Vigeant. 5: St Mary's Col (Holy Cross) 47-49 (ng); IndU 49-52 (Elem Educ) BS; Carnegie 55-56 (Child wk) MLS. 7: Child's libn pub lib, S Bend Ind 53-55; Child's libn pub lib, Detroit 56-58; Elem sch tchr pub schs, Sault Ste Marie Mich 59-60; Elem sch libn sch syst, Haverhill Mas 69-. 8: Libn N Essex Co Assn for Retarded Child. 10: PTA. 14: Sch & child wk. 15: 9 Academy ave, Haverhill Ma 01830.

VIGEANT, ROBERT JOSEPH. b Worcester Mass 26 Ap 28. 4: Jeanette M Heyvaert. 5: Assumption Col 46-50 (Educ) AB; Simmons 55-57 (LS) MS. 6: Fr. 7: Lib asst Assumption Col 54-56; Ref libn Free Pub Lib, Worcester Mass56; Li asst Simmons Col 56-57; Ya libn Detroit Pub Lib 57-59; Head Libn CARNEGIE Pub Lib, Sault Ste Marie Mich 59-61; Consul Mich State Lib 61-62; Head tech serv Finger Lakes Lib System, Ithaca NY 62-66; Libn Haverhill Pub Lib, Haverhill Mass 66-. 8: Study feasibility of centralized processing for libs in Upper Peninsula of Mich, Base Br of State Lib at Escanaba Mich 61-62; 09: ALA; NYLA; Mass Bd Lib Commsner's Adv Com on Statewide Lib Serv 69. 9: ALA; MassLA; Merrimack ValleyLA (v-pres 68-70). 14: Admin, tech serv. 15: 9 Academy ave, Haverhill Ma 01830.

VIGELIS, ADELINE (RAMOND). b Cleveland 13 D 20. 5: Chicago 38-39; Colo Col 39-42 (Art) BA; Yale 44-45 (Drama); UCal(Berkeley) 59-62 MLS. 6: Fr, Ger, Sp, Russian. 7: Libn San Diego Soc of Natural Hist, Sen Diego 62-63; Libn San Diego Museum of Man, San Diego 63-. 9: ALA; SLA; CalLA. 14: Ref. 15: Scientific Lib Museum of Man, Balboa Park, San Diego Ca 92101.

VIGLE, JOHN BARRY. b Chattanooga Tenn 11 S 25. 4: Marjorie Britton. 5: UKy 46-49 (Psych) AB, 49-50 (Philos), 55-56 MS in LS. 7: US Naval Res Pharm Mate 3/c 43-45; US Army Res Mil Police (Capt) 48-64; Commercial artist self employed, Lexington Ky 51; Fire insurance inspector Ky Inspection Bur, Louisville Ky 52-54; 1st asst br libn Brooklyn Pub Lib 56-58; Head of period acquis UDayton 59-64, Asst dir of libs 65-. 8: Part-time Instr in Philos UDayton, Dayton Ohio 61-65. 10: AAUP. 12: "Periodical Holdings of the Libraries of the University of Dayton (2nd ed 60, 3rd ed 61, 4th ed 65); Assoc ed "Union List of Serials in the Libraries in the Miami Valley" (68, 2nd revised ed 69). 13: Yes. 14: Admin, period acquis, ref. 15: 824 Buckingham rd, Dayton Oh 45419.

VIGUERS, RUTH (ALFARATA) HILL. b Oakland Cal 24 Jl 03. 4: Richard Thomson Viguers. 5: Willamette U 20-24 (Eng) AB; UWash 25-26 BS in LS. 6: Sp, Fr. 7: Child libn Seattle Pub Lib 26-27; Child libn NY Pub Lib 27-29; Libn Internat Inst for Girls in Spain, Madrid 29-31; Libn Amer Lib in Paris 31-32; Child libn NY Pub Lib 32-36; Instr Boone Lib Sch, Wuchang China 36-37; Asst supt of wk with child NY Pub Lib 37-43; Lecturer Simmons 58, Tchr child bks Sch of Publ 50-; Ed "The Horn Bk Mag", Boston 58-67; Tchr child lit Dept of Educ UHawaii (Honolulu) 58. 8: Instr Writers Conf UNH; Memorial lectureships; CM Hewkins NELA 5555, AC Moore NY Pub Lib 62, MA Wessel Detroit Pub Lib; Amer Juror Biennale of Illus Bratislavia 67; Instr Dept Educ UHawaii 68. 9: ALA (Coun, past mem var coms);-CSD (Bd); NELA; MassLA; New England RT Child Libns. 10: Bd Friends of Wellesley Free Lib; Women's Nat Bk Assn; Quota Club Intl; Nat League Amer Penwomen. 11: Honorary D Ed Portia Law Sch 66; Constance Lindsay Skinner Award 68; Alumni Citation WillametteU 67. 12: "Margin for Surprise" (64); Co-auth "Illustrators of Childrens Books, 1946-1956" (58); "A Critical History of Childrens Literature " (53); Ed "The Horn Book Magazine" (58-67); Co-auth "Children's Books from Foreign Languages" (37). 13: Yes. 14: Wk with child. 15: 110 Cliff rd, Wellesley Ma 02181.

VIKSE, ALETA (JOSEPHINE). b Donalda Alta Can 8 S 17. 5: UAlta 35-38 BA; UWash 38-39 BS in LS. 7: Bk sales clerk C Woodwards, Edmonton Alta 40-42; Child libn Winnipeg Pub Lib, Winnipeg Man 42-43; Edmonton Pub Lib, Edmonton Alta: Child br lbn 43-44, 1st ass child dept 44-52, Pub rel off 52-54, Head circ dept 54-55, Act chief libn 55-56, Assoc dir 56-. 9: CanLA (chm Elections 56); AltaLA (sec 44 & 52, pres 56); ALA; EdmontonLA. 10: Univ Womens Club. 14: Child wk. 15: 903-9927 114th st, Edmonton 10 Alta Can.

VILLA, ROBIN (BRACKEN). b Seattle Wash 25 My 43. 4: Roy W A Villa. 5: Smith 61-65 9philos) BA (magna cum laude); Columbia 67-68 MS. 7: Sec Dean Witter & Co, Seattle 65-67; Catlgr CCNY 68-. 9: LACUNY; NY Tech Serv Libns. 10: Phi Beta Kappa. 15: 440 Riverside dr, New York NY 10027.

VILLENEUVE, JOCELYNE. b Val DOr Que Can 9 F 41. 5: Laurentian U (Sudbury Ont) 62 (Econ) BA; UOttawa 64 BLS. 6: Fr. 7: Acquis libn Laurentian U (Sudbury Ont) 62-63, 64-. 9: CanLA; Association Canadienne des Bibliothecaires de Langue Franaise. 14: Acui, bk sem catlg. 15: 1184 Diane st, Sudbury Ont Can.

VILUMS, ROLAND. b Riga Latvia 2 Ag 06. 4: Valida Stark. 5: ULatvia 25-30 (Law) ML; UMich 56-58 MA in LS. 6: Latvian, Ger, Russian, Fr, Lat. 7: Judge Dist Court, Riga Latvia 34-44; Lat tchr High Sch for Latvian Refugees, Oldenburg Germany 46-49; Catlgr & Asst Prof of Lib Admin Ohio State U 58-. 8: Faculty adv to Latvian studs club at Ohio State U. 9: ALA; Ohio Valley Reg Group of Tech Libns; FRANKLIN Co Lib Assn. 13: Yes. 14: Catlg publs in for langs (spec Ger & Slavic). 15: 2355 Neil ave, Columbus Ohio 43202.

VINCE, THOMAS L. b Cleveland Ohio 13 Mr 40. 5: John CarrollU 58-62 (Eng) BS; Ohio StateU 62-64 (Eng) MA; Case West Res 64-66 MS in LS. 7: Tchg asst Ohio StateU Dept of Eng (Columbus) 62-64; Lib trainee Cleveland Pub Lib, Cleveland Ohio 64-66, Hd popular lib. 9: ALA (Jr Mem RT: Prog Com); OhioLA (chm Jr Mems 68-69). 10: Beta Phi Mu; Case West Res Lib Sch Alum Assn. 13: Yes. 14: Adult serv, hist of bks. 15: 1338 E 187th st, Cleveland Oh 44110.

VINCENT, DONALD EDWARD. b Martins Ferry Ohio 26 D 22. 4: Nancy Elizabeth Suliburk. 5: UBuffalo 40-43, 48-49 (Math) BA; UMich 51-52 AMLS, 53-57 (Pol Sci) MA, 57-(LS). 6: Fr, Ger. 7: (Lt jg) US Naval Res, Pacific Theater 43-47; Catlgr Wayne State U 52-58, Lecturer in Lib Sci 57-5, Bibliog 58-59; Dir of Lib Serv UMich(Dearborn) 59-62; U Libn UNH 62-. 8: (NH) Governors Com for Better Libs, 62-63. 9: ALA; NLA, NECLA, NHLA (treas 63, 1st v-pres 63-65; chm Intel Freedom Com 64-). 10: Phi Kappa Phi; AAUP; Durham Hist Assn (Trustee). 13: Yes. 14: Admin, tech proc, ref. 15: Univ of NH Lib, Durham NH 03824.

VINCENT, ROSE (STRONG). b Mitchell SD 18 Ja 01. 5: Dakota Wesleyan 18-22 (Biol) BS; UIll 23 (Eng); Wayne State U 51-52 (Eng); UMich 50-52 MALS, 53-55 (Eng) MA, 56, 64-(LS). 7: Tchr Edgerton Consol Schs, Farmer SD 22-25; Staff Detroit Pub Lib 26-30; Libn Van Buren Consol Schs, Belleville Mich 50-64; Visiting lecturer East Mich U 64-68; Instr Wis State U(Oshkosh) 68-. 8: Summer tchg; East Mich U, West Wash State Col, 56-68. 9: NEA; ALA-AASchL; MichEA; MichASchL (Publns Coord). 10: Bd of Human Rel. 12: Ed "SLAAM Handbook" (59); Ed "Recommended Materials for a Professional Library (62). 13: Yes. 14: Tchg child & ya lit. 15: 41985 Expressway, Belleville Mich 48111.

VINCZE, MARY (GATHY). b Szeged Hungary 20 F 12. 4: Tibor Vincze. 5: Hungarian Royal Bus Acad 32 BA; IndU 56 (LS). 6: Hungarian, Ger. 7: Bibliogr Notre DameU (Ind) 52-54; Bibliogr IndU (Bloomington) 55-56; Curriculum libn UDayton 62-65, Asst ref libn 65-. 9: OhioLA. 14: Ref. 15: 2801 Pinegrove dr, Dayton Oh 45449.

VINCZE, TIBOR. b Szolnok Hungary 10 My 12. 4: Mary Gaty. 5: St Elizabeth U 33-37 (Law, Pol) PhD; Ind U 55-56 (LS) MA. 6: Hugarian, Ger, Fr. 7: Lawyer, Budapest Hungary 39-45; Ref libn Tech Lib Wright-Patterson AFB, Ohio 56-58; Ref libn AF Inst of Tech Lib Wright-Patterson AFB 59-62, Chief reader serv 62-67; Act dir 67, Dir Libs 67-. 14: Ref, lib mgt. 15: 2801 Pinegrove dr, Dayton Oh 45449.

VINDAL, GLADYS (MEEKS). b Lakeland Ga 28 My 11. 4: Harold M Vindal. 5: Wesleyan Col (Ga) 29-32 (Hist) AB; Emory 32-33 AB in LS. 6: Fr, Sp. 7: Libn Whitmell Farm Life Sch, Whitmell Va 35-36; Jr lib asst US Bur of Pub Rds, Wash DC 36-38; Lib asst US Weather Bur, Wash DC 38-42; Catlgr US Dept of Agric, Wash DC 42-43; Catlgr La Crosse Pub Lib, La Crosse Wis 56-60; Child libn Fairfax Co Lib, Fairfax Va 60-61; Catlgr Arlington Co Lib, Arlington Va 61-64; Hd catlg dept George Washington U Lib 65-. 9: ALA; Potomac Tech Proc Libns; DCLA. 14: Catlg. 15: 5901 N 27th st, Arlington Va 22207.

VINING, CORA M. b S Weymouth Mass 15 S 07. 5: State Col (Bridgewater Mass) 24-28 (Eng) BS in Ed; Boston U 41 (Eng) AM; Simmons 44 (LS) BS. 6: Fr, Lat. 7: Lib asst State Col (Bridgewater Mass) 28-40; Libn State Col (N Adams Mass) 40-48; Libn South Jr High Sch, Quincy Mass 48-58; Assoc Prof & head catlgr State Col (Bridgewater Mass) 58-67, Acquis libn 67-. 9: ALA; MassLA; Mass Tchrs Assn; Plymouth Co Tchrs Assn; Coun Mass State Col Libns. 10: Mass State Col Faculty Assn; Bridgewater Improvement Assn; Bridgewater Alumni Assn; Old Bridgewater Hist Soc; Alden Kindred of Amer. 12: Ed "Alumni News". 14: Catlg, acquis. 15: 65 Grove st, Bridgewater Ma 02324.

VINNES, NORMAN VINNES. b St Paul Minn 20 Mr 38. 4: Eileen Winther. 5: St Olaf Col 56-58; UMinn 59-61 (Phil) BA, 61-62 (Elem Educ) BS, 67 (LS) MA. 7: Tchr St Paul Pub Schs, St Paul 62-66, Lib consul 66-69; Libn N St Paul-Maplewood Pub Schs, N St Paul minn 69-. 9: NEA-DAVI; ALA-AASchL; MinnEA; A-v Coord Assn Minn; MinnASchL. 10: Phi delta Kappa; Beta Phi Mu. 13: Yes. 14: Sch lib & a-v prog. 15: 2163 Mohawk rd, N St Paul Mn 55109.

VINSON, CHARLES G. b Milledgeville Ga 27 Ja 45. 5: UGa 62-66 (Classics) BA; EmoryU 66-68 MLibnship. 6: Ger, Latin. 7: Lib asst Atlanta Pub Lib 67; Catlgr Lib Ga Col 68-. 9: ALA; SELA. 14: Catlg, docs. 15: McIntyre Ga 31054.

VINSON, JOYCE EILEEN (DANIELS). b Jersey City NJ 18 Ja 44. 4: Thomas J Vinson. 5: UCal (Berkeley) 63-65 (Hist) BA, 65-66 MLS. 7: Supv child serv (libn II) Los Altos Pub & Santa Clara Co Lib Syst, Los Altos Cal 68-. 9: Assn Child Libns Cal. 10: ACLU. 14: Ref. 15: 584 Menker ave apt F, San Jose Ca 95128.

VINSON, LU OUIDA. b Falls Co Tex 30 Jl 24. 5: Mary Hardin-BAYLOR Col 41-42, 47-49 (Biol, Educ) BA; UConn summer 57; UTex summers 58-59, 63 (Educ Admin) MEd; UTex summer 59 (LS); Tex Womans U summer 65 (LS), 67 MS in LS. 6: Sp. 7: Elem tchr Floyd Co Pub Schs, Irick Sch 42-43; Tchr, Coun, State of Tex State Orphans Home, Corsicana Tex 43-46; Elem tchr Los Frenos Tex 46-47; Waco Pub Schs, Waco Tex; Elem tchr 49-59, Multilibn 59-62, Libn 62-63, Intern prin 62-63, Intern prin 62-63; Sch & lib consul Field Enterprises Educ Corp, Chicago 62-66; Exec sec Amer Assoc of Sch Libns, Chicago 67-. 9: ALA; NEA; ACEI; Assn Supv & Curr Devel; DESP; Nat Coun Soc Studies; NCTE; Internat Reading Assn; Tex State Tchrs Assn; SWLA. 10: Delta Kappa Gamm; Pi Gamma Mu. 12: Adv Bd "New Explorer". 13: Yes. 14: Ref, child serv. 15: 50 E Huron, Chicago Il 60611.

VINT, JEAN PERRY. b NYC 30 My 12. 4: Kenneth C Vint. 5: Antioch Col 30-36 (Eng) AB; Simmons 60-61 (LS) MS. 6: Fr. 7: Production, retail advert Montgomery Ward, Chicago 35-36; Publicity Amer Bk Co, Cincinnati 37-38; Correspondent Book of the Month Club, NYC 39-43, 48-50; Lib asst Richland Pub Lib, Richland Wash 50-52; Ya libn Boston Pub Lib 62-63; Assoc libn Brooks Sch, N Andover Mass 63-64; Asst libn Memorial Hall Lib, Andover Mass 64-68. 9: ALA; NELA; Mass Round Table of Libns for YA (Exec Com). 14: Lib serv to ya. 15: Box 34, Boxford Mass 01921.

VIRDEN, ALICE MAYES. b Cynthia Miss 5 Ja 02. 5: Agnes Scott Col 19-23 (Eng) BA; LSU summers 34, 36-38 BS in LS. 6: Fr. 7: Tchr pub schs, Jackson Miss 24-36; Asst child dept Memphis Pub Lib, Memphis Tenn 36-55, Asst catlg dept 55-. 9: ALA-RTSD; SELA; TennLA. 10: Friends of Memphis Pub Lib. 12: Ed "Singing Mississippi, anthology of the Miss Poetry Soc" (35); Ed "Library Horzons, Memphis Pub Lib Staff Bul (59-). 14: Catlg. 15: Apt 712, 6 S McLean, Memphis Tenn 38104.

VIRGO, JULIE ANNE (NOOLAN). b Adelaide South Australia 14 Je 44. 4: David Virgo. 5: Lib Assn of Australia 62-65 (LS) ALAA; UChicago 66-68 (LS) AM, 68-. 6: Fr. 7: Lib asst Child Lib Pub Lib of S Australia Adelaide 61-62; Libn Pub Health Dept, Adelaide S Australia 62-63; Libn Repatriation Gen Hosp, Adelaide S Australia 63-66; Research asst Grad Lib Sch UChicago 66-67, Tchg asst 68-69, Lecturer 69-. 8: Ed consul, Educational Methods Inc (Chicago) 68-. 9: ALA; -ACRL; SLA; ASIS; Lib Assn Australia (pres Spec Libs 65-66). 10: Beta Phi Mu. 14: Biomed communication, theories of indexing & clsf, info stor & ret, sociol of sci. 15: Grad Lib School Univ of Chicago E 59th st, Chicago Il 60637.

VIROSTEK, FRANK EDWARD. b Homestead Penn 18 Je 38. 4: Geraldine Indovina. 5: St Columban's Col & Maj Sem 56-60 (Philos); Duquesne 61-62 (Philos) BA; UPittsburgh 68 MLS, 69 (Inter Affairs). 6: Fr. 7: Admin asst US Army, Ft Sam Houston Texas & USARC, Pittsburgh 62-67; Dept Mgr & Exec Trainee Sears Roebuck & Co, Pittsburgh Penn 65-68; Ext serv hd B F Jones Mem Lib, Aliquippa Penn 69-. 9: ASIS;

PennLA. 10: UN Assn of Pittsburgh; Hi-Fi Investment Club of Beaver Co. 14: Ref, ext serv (Interlib loan & coop), pub rel & promotion. 15: 338 Frederick ave, Sewickley Pa 15143.

VISCARRA, JOSEPH R. b Las Cruces NM. 5: Tex West Col 51-55 (Music Educ) B Mus; USoCal 57-59 MSLS. 6: Sp. 7: (Sp3) US Army, Ft Riley Kan 55-57; Acquis asst USoCal 58-59; Asst head fine arts Queens Pub Lib, Queens NY 59-66; Admin asst NYC Commun Col Lib 66-67, Chief catlgr 67-. 9: MusLA; NY State LA; NY Tech Serv Lib; UFCT; NY State A-V Assn; LACUNY. 10: UFWOC W Side Organizer. 14: Mus & fine arts ref, catlg. 15: 219 W 81st st, New York NY 10024.

VISKOCHIL, LARRY A. b Traverse City Mich 3 Jl 39. 5: NWest Mich Col 57-59 (Liberal Arts) AA; Central MichU 59-61 (Hist) BA, 61-63 (Hist) MA; UMich 66-67 MALS. 7: Hist tchr Ubly High Sch, Ubly Mich 63-65; Hist tchr Highland Pk High Sch, Highland Park Mich 65-66; Hd ref libn Chicago Hist Soc 67-. 9: ALA. 14: Ref, rare bks (Americana). 15: Chicago Hist Soc Clark st at North ave, Chicago Il 60614.

VITAI, JEAN (GEORGINA TREGLOAN). b Bristol England 4 Jl 33. 4: Andras Vitai. 5: Brighton Tech Col 54, NWest Polytech (London Eng) 62-63 British ALA, FLA. 6: Fr. 7: Jr asst pub lib, Bristol England 51-55, Sr asst 55-58; Sr ref asst pub lib, Ipswich England 58-62; Sci libn UWest Ont 63-66, Gifts & exchange libn 66-68, Sci libn 68-. 9: Lib Assn (Gt Brit); Aslib; ALA. 13: Yes. 14: Ref, Admin. 15: 571 Adelaide st apt 20, London Ont Can.

VITEK, CLEMENT GERARD. b Baltimore 6 Mr 20. 4: Grace Carolyn Easter. 5: Baltimore Bus Col 38-39; Loyola Col (Baltimore) 66-67. 7: Copyboy "Baltimore Sun, 39-41; Tool crib clerk Glenn L Martin Co, Baltomore 41-42, Template layout 42-44; Navy Air Force S1/C 44-46; Asst libn "Baltimore Sun, 46-50, Chief Libn 50-. 9: ALA-RSD (Baltimore Unit); SLA (chm Newspaper Div 63; pres Baltimore Chap 65; mem Pub Rel Com 62 & 63, 66-67, dir 66 & 67); Md Hist Soc; MdLA; NMA. 12: Ed SLA Baltimore Chap "Newsletter". 14: Adult ref, newspapers. 15: Sunpapers Lib, 501 Calvert st, Baltimore Md 21203.

VITINS, VERNERS JANIS. b Latvia 13 Ja 03. 4: Irma E Mednis Vitins. 5: ULatvia (Riga Latvia) 23-28 (Law) Magister Iuris; UMich 53-55 AMLS. 6: Ger, Russian, Latvian. 7: Ref libn Pub Lib, Royal Oak Mich 54-57; Various prof libns positions UMinn(Minneapolis) 57-63; Asst Prof & Head Libn of St Paul Campus Lib UMinn (St Paul) 63-. 9: ALA; SLA; Internat Assn of Agric Libns & Documentalists. 15: 2349 Summer st, St Paul Mn 55113.

VITOLINS, ILGA. b Riga Latvia 22 Je 37. 5: Chicago 56-63 BA, MA. 6: Latvian, Ger. 7: Catlgr UChicago Lib 60-. 14: Catlg. 15: 2633 N Dayton st, Chicago Il 60614.

VITROGAN, BLANCE (PEARL). b Newark NJ 23 My 10. 4: David Vitrogan. 5: Hunter Col 31 (Pol Sci) BA; Columbia 33 (Psych) MA; Pratt 59 MLS. 7: Ed asst Literary Agency, NYC 31-45; Libn Brooklyn Pub Lib, Brooklyn NY 59-61; Libn Brooklyn Col Lib 63-. 9: ALA; NY Lib Club. 14: Ref. 15: 130 St Edwards st 10D, Brooklyn NY 11201.

VITTANDS, ALEXANDER T. b New Pebalg Latvia 17 O 06. 4: Elza Ozolitis. 5: ULatvia (Riga) 37 (Law) Magister Iuris; UMich 58 MALS. 6: Latvian, Ger, Russian. 7: City Dist judge, Riga Latvia until 40, & 42-44; Libn catlgr Clarke Hist Lib, Mt Pleasant Mich 58-. 8: Leader in Displaced Persons camp, Germany 47-48; Hd bkkeeper Brit Armed Forces Clubs, Germany 46-50. 9: Mich Assn Higher Educ; MichLA; ALA. 10: Alpha Beta Alpha; Mich Hist Soc; Amer Assn Latvian Lawyers. 14: Rare bks & mss, hist of Great Lakes area. 15: 814 S Franklin st, Mt Pleasant Mi 48858.

VITZ, CARL (PETER PAUL). b St Paul Minn 3 Je 1883. 4: Alda Clayton. 5: Adelbert Col West Res 1900-04 (Classics) AB; Lib Sch West Res 04-05 Certif; NY State Lib Sch 06-07 BLS. 6: Ger, Lat, Grk, Fr. 7: Page, clk, asst Cleveland Pub Lib 1898-1905; Asst Adelbert Col Lib West ResU 03-05; Asst libn & hd useful arts dept NY State Pub Lib, Wash DC 07-09; Dir's asst & hd order dept NY State Lib 09-12; Instr NY State Lib Sch 09-13; 2nd v-libn Cleveland Pub Lib 12-19, V-libn 19-22; Instr Lib Sch West Res 22-23; Libn Pub Lib, Toledo Oh 22-37; Libn Minneapolis Pub Lib 37-45; Instr UMinn Lib Sch 37-44; Libn Cincinnati Pub Lib 45-55, Libn-Emeritus 55-. 8: Consul lib building plans, sites, remodeling for approx 60 libs: including Baltimore, Denver & Seattle Pub Libs, Marietta Col. 9: ALA (pres 44-45; Exec Bd 37-41; Coun 24-29, 37-41, 44-; mem &/or chm many bds & coms); OhioLA (pres 20-21, 32-33; chm Legis Com 21-36); DCLA (sec 08-09); Ohio and LA (trustee 47-). 10: Ohio Hist Soc; Cincinnati Hist Soc; Cincinnati Nature Ctr Assn; Nat Trust for Hist Preservation; Lit Club (Cincinnati). 11: LittD WestResU 54; Dr Humanities Marietta Col 62; Citation US Navy & Army Depts; Citation US Off Educ; Citation Merit ALA-PLA 54; Lippincott Award 52. 13: Yes. 15: 323 Waverly ave, Cincinnati Oh 45215.

VLANTIKAS, CONSTANTINE ANDREW. b Athens 23 Mr 34. 4: Mary Philippides. 5: American UBeirut 58-63 (Philos) BA; CornellU 64-65 (Philos); UChicago 65-68 (LS) MA. 6: Classical Grk, Mod Grk, Latin, Fr. 7: Libn I Chicago Pub Lib 66-68; Catlgr Harvard Col Lib 68-. 9: ALA. 14: Catlg. 15: 20 Prescott, Cambridge Ma 02138.

VLASIC, IVAN. b Zagreb Yugoslavia 23 N 33. 5: UZagreb (Yugoslavia) 54-56 (Arch); West ResU 61-66 (Slavic Lang) BA; Case West ResU 66-67 (Slavic Langs) MA, 67-68 MLS. 6: Russian, Serbocroatian, Ger, Czech, Bulgarian. 7: Draftsman: Zagreb Yugoslavia 51-54, Hamburg Germany 57-58; Drill inspector Cleveland Twist-Drill Co, Cleveland Ohio 59-65; Libn (catlgr) Ohio StateU Libs (Columbus) 68-. 9: ALA; ASIS. 10: American Croatian Academic Club; Nat Slavic Honor Soc. 14: Catlg, automation (Marc pilot proj). 15: 1800 Lafayette place A4, Columbus Oh 43212.

VLEMINCKX, GERARD. b Montreal Can 21 Jl 20. 4: Tellier Huguette. 5: UMontreal 38 9lib) Dipl, 0 (Soc Sci) Dipl. 6: Fr. 7: Prof, Montreal 40-56; Libn, Montreal 56-66; Libn USherbrooke 66-. 9: Assn canadienne des bibliothecaires de lange francaise. 14: Acquis. 15: 730 Buck App 9, Sherbrooke Que Can.

VOCELLE, MARY D. b Kalamazoo 1 S 13. 5: Nazareth Col (Mich) 30-34 (Eng Lit) BA; UWis 37-38 (LS) BS; Columbia 49 (Med Libs); UDetroit 50-51 (Psych). 7: Catlgr Lewis Inst, Chicago 38-39; Catlgr S Ill Normal U 39-40; Libn Pub Lib, Glen Ellyn Ill 40; Libn US Naval Train Center, Great Lakes Ill 40-46; Bibliogr declsf & tech serv Com Dept, Wash DC 46; Chief lib div Br Off 4 VA, Richmond Va 46-47; Chief lib div Br Off 7 VA, Chicago 47-49; Com libn USAF in Europe, Wiesbaden Germany 52-. 8: Adv Hq Allied AF Central Europe (SHAPE), Fontainebleau France 54-. 9: ALA (past mem &/or chm var sects & coms; Armed Forces Libns Sect, European Subsect chm-elect). 10: Kappa Gamma Pi. 11: Civilian awards from US Navy & USAF for outstanding performance. 13: Yes. 14: Mgt & admin, personnel, sel of materials, ref. 15: HQ USAFE (DPSRL), Library branch, APO NY 09633.

VODRA, CAROL JEAN (KOENIG). b Cincinnati Ohio 1 Ag 41. 4: William W Vodra. 5: Col of wooster 59-63 (Econ & Pol Sci) BA; UMich 64-65 MALS. 6: Fr, Ger. 7: Searcher & filer Catlg T UMc (Ann Arbor) 64; Ref libn T J Watson Lib of Bus & Econ (Columbia) 65-68; Ref ast Herbert Lehman Col 68; Asst ref libn UCincinnati 68-. 14: Ref. 15: Apt 407 310 Oak st, Cincinnati Oh 45219.

VOELKER, MARGIE L. b Hastings Minn 23 Je 25. 4: Karl B Voelker. 5: Col of St Benedict 43-47 (Math' BA; UMinn 67-68 (LS) MA. 7: Tchr Zumbrota High Sch, Zumbrota Minn 47-48; Libn Math-Physics Lib UMinn 69-. 9: ALA; MedLA; MinnLA. 15: 905 W 4th st, Hastings Mn 55033.

VOGEL, DOROTHY (HOFFMAN). b Elmira NY 14 My 35. 4: Herbert Vogel. 5: UBuffalo 53-55; Syracuse 55-57 (Eng Lit, LS) BA; UDenver 57-58 (LS) MA. 7: Libn Brooklyn Pub Lib 58-61; Libn Brooklyn Pub Lib 58-61, Sr libn 62-65, Asst bus libn 66-. 9: SLA; NY Lib Club; Bksellers League of NY; NYLA. 14: Bus lib ref. 15: 305 E 86th st, New York NY 10028.

VOGEL, ELIZABETH FRY. b Pittsburgh 20 Ap 17. 4: Lawrence H Vogel. 5: SUSQUEHANNA U 34-38 BA; Carnegie 38-39 BS in LS. 7: Asst libn State Tchrs Col (Slippery Rock Penn) 39-40; Libn US Steel Corp, Pittsburgh 40-57; Chm Avalon Pub Lib, Avalon Penn 63-. 9: SLA (dir 55-57; pres Pittsburgh Chap 53-55). 10: Avalon Womans Club; Sr Womens Auxiliary Suburban Gen Hosp; Highland Country Club. 14: Admin. 15: 918 California ave, Avalon Pa 15202.

VOGEL, HELEN (ELDRIDGE). b Newark NJ 24 J 19. 4: Harvey O Vogel. 5: Douglass Col 37-41 (Journalism) Litt B; Catholic U 65-66 MSLS. 6: Fr. 7: Admin asst Alfred Wagg Pictures, Wash DC 56-58; Lib asst Falls Church Pub Lib, Falls Church Va 59-63, Child libn 63-65, Asst libn 66-. 9: ALA; VaLA; DCLA. 10: Lib Guild; Kappa Tau Alpha; Beta Phi Mu; Douglass Alumnae Club. 12: Ed "Near the Falls" (69). 13: Yes. 14: Ref, child & ya wk, pub rel, admin. 15: 2234 Highland ave, Falls Church Va 22046.

VOGEL, SOPHIE B(ARONOWSKY). b NYC 19 Ja 18. 4: Arthur Charles Vogel. 5: Hunter Col 35-39 (Music, Fr) BA; Columbia 40 MSLS; UVa 58, 65. 6: Russian, Ger, Ital, Fr. 7: Boat Statistics & Pub Co, NYC 39; Asst Music Lib Columbia U 40-43; Music libn Queens Col (NY) 43-46; Libn Walter Reed Elem Sch, Arlington Va 57-. 9: VaLA; Arlington Educ Assn. 10: PTA. 13: Yes. 14: Music, child lit, a-v. 15: 1917 N Nottingham st, Arlington Va 22205.

VOGEL, VERNON WILLIAM. b Akron Ohio 20 Ag 38. 4: Ruth Anne Gaugh. 5: UAkron summers 56-60, 62-63; Otterbein Col 56-60 (Eng, Hist, Educ) BA, BS in Ed; Kent State U summer 59; West Res summer 62, 63-64 MS in LS; Notre Dame U 64-66 (Eng); Emory summer 67; UPittsburgh 68-69. 6: Ger. 7: Tchr Copley Bd of Educ, Copley Ohio 60-61; Tchr Lorain Bd of Educ, Lorain Ohio 61-63; Libn UNotre Dame humanities dept 64; Libn UNotre Dame Math & Computing Sci Research Lib 64-68; Edinboro State Col, Ser libn 68-. 8: Coord Penn Union List Periodicals 68-69. 9: ALA; American Soc of Indexers; PennLA. 10: Beta Phi Mu; AAUP. 13: Yes. 14: Res, admin, serials, syst. 15: Box 24, Ednboro Pa 16412.

VOGELBACK, JUDITH (CLAIBORNE) FEILD. b West Point Va 29 Ja 21. 4: Arthur Lawrence Vogelback. 5: Hood Col 38-39; Mary Washington Col 39-40, 47-50, 52; (Hist) BA; NYU summer 48; Rutgers 60-66 MLS. 7: Ensign US Coast Guard Res 44-45; Ed & bkkeeper Alumnae Off Sweet Briar Col 56-60; Clk Mary Helen Cochran Lib Sweet Briar Col 61-62; Libn Amherst Co Pub Lib, Amherst Va 64-66; Ref libn Lynchburg Pub Lib, Lynchburg Va 66-67; Libn East Shore Bk Processing Ctr, Salisbury Md 67-. 9: ALA; VaLA; MdLA. 10: LWV. 12: Co-ed "Sweet Briar Alumnae Magazine" (56-60). 14: Catlg. 15: 524E Alabama ave, Salisbury Md 21801.

VOGT, EARL C. b Spokane Wash 2 D 41. 4: Sharyn (Masters) Vogt. 5: Whitman Col 62-63 9biol); UIda 64-66 (Zool) BS; UWash 68-69 ML. 6: Sp, Ger. 7: Sales rep Nat Cylinder Gas, Seattle Wash 67-68; Research libn Chevron Research, Richmond Cal 69-. 9: ALA; SLA. 14: Sci ref, info syst. 15: Chevron Res Co 576 Standary ave, Richmond Ca 94802.

VOGT, HOWARD (SHEPPARD). b Orange NJ 10 O 24. 5: Eastman Sch of Music URochester 47-51 (Voice) B Mus, 51-52 (Music Lit) M Mus; Rutgers 55-59 MLS. 6: Fr, Ger, Ital. 7: US Army CAC Tech 4th grade (Act Sgt Maj), European Theater 43-45; Lib asst Sibley Music Lib Eastman Sch of Music 50-52; Libn trainee Newark Pub Lib, Newark NJ 53-56; Asst Prof & music libn No Ill U 56-61; Asst Dir & music libn Bloofield Pub Lib, Bloomfield NJ 61-67, Dir 68-. 8: Lib consul, Turtle Bay Mus Sch, NYC 62; Prof singer (baritone); numerous recital & concert appearances in the East & Midwest. 9: MusLA; NJLA. 10: Delta Phi lpha. 13: Yes. 14: Adult serv. 15: 11 Park pl, Bloomfeld NJ 07003.

VOGT, NORMAN E. b Chicago 20 Ag 35. 4: Lorna Patton. 5: NoIllU 53-57 (Music) BS in Ed; Colo State Col summer 59; UWis 60-61 MSLS; UIll summer 65, fall 67. 7: Music dir Richmond Community Schs, Richmond Ill 57-60; Music libn No Ill U 61-68, Asst acquis libn 68-. 9: MusLA; IllLA. 10: Phi Mu Alpha Sinfonia; Beta Phi Mu. 14: Tech serv, mus libnship. 15: Swen Parson Lib, DeKalb Ill 60115.

VOGT, WILMA LUCILLE (SMUTZLER). b Los Angeles 16 S 10. 4: Stanley Byron Vogt. 5: USoCal 28-32 (Socio) BA; UCal(BERKELEY) 32-33 (LS) BS; UCLA 58-62 (Guidance); 66 (Educ Media), 68 (Lib Personnel). 6: Ger, Sp. 7: Jr libn Los Angeles Pub Lib 27-28; Jr catlgr Los Angeles City Schs 34; Bkkeeper Hollywood Linen Serv, Hollywood Cal 34-36; Catlgr Paramount Pictures Inc, Hollywood Cal 36-42; Dist Libn Tenple City Unified Sch Dist, Temple City Cal 54-. 9: CalLA; Cal Tchrs Assn. 10: Camp Fire Girls Leader; Delta Kappa Gamma; Alpha Ka;a Delta; UCal Lib Schs Alumni Assn; Caravaners Club of Temple City; Phi Kappa Phi; Temple City EA. 14: Catlg, sch libnship. 15: 5737 GOLDEN West ave, Temple City Cal 91780.

VOIGT, ANNELENE (JENSCH). b Magdeburg Germany 4 Ja 23. 4: Hellmut R Voigt. 5: Oberlyzeum (Hamburg-Harburg Germany) 38-41 (Sci, Humanities) BA; Inst of Lib Sci (Berlin Germany) 41-43 (LS) BS. 6: Ger, Fr. 7: Dipl libn Pub Lib, Berlin-Friedrichshain 43-45; Chief catlgr Museum Lib Altonaer Museum, Hamburg Germany 45-47; Chief catlgr Central Adv Off for Pub Libs Ministry of Educ, Hannover Germany 50-55; Catlgr libn Lockheed Missile & Space C, Van Nuys Cal 60-61; Catlgr libn Lockheed Cal Co, Burbank Cal 61-. 68, Info research analyst 68-. 9: SLA; NMA; LOCKHEED Mgt Club. 10: United European Amer Club. 14: Catlg, ref, transl, info research. 15: 11821 Redbank st, Sun Valley Cal 91352.

VOIGT, EDNA ELISABETH. b Oyster Bay LI NY 4 My 01. 5: Pratt 19-21 (Arch Design) Diploma, 24-26 (Interior Decoration) Certif. 7: Drafting, surveying Title Guarantee & Trust Co, NYC 21-23; Lib Planning Lib Bur, NYC 23-66; Free lance lib planning consul 66-. 8: Library Planning grew into consul wk on scores of pub & univ libs. 9: ALA; NY Lib Club. 10: Horticul Soc of NY; NY Botanical Garden; Pratt Arch Club. 14: Planning lib bldgs & equipment (color & design). 15: 2207 Beech st, Wantagh NY 11793.

VOIGT, HARRY RAYMOND. b Houstonia Mo 7 F 09. 4: Esther Yaeger. 5: Concordia Tchrs Col (Ill) 41 (Educ) BS; Appalachian State Col 51 (Educ) MA; UDenver 58 MALS. 6: Ger. 7: Elem sch prin, St Louis 31-39; Elem sch prin, Chicago 39-46; Elem sch prin, Conover NC 46-54; Libn & Assoc Prof St Paul's Col (Concordia Mo) 55-58, Assoc Prof & libn 58-. 8: Tchr Placement Com 56-61. 9: ALA; Mo Assn Col & Res Libs (past pres). 10: Lafayette Co (Mo) Hist Soc; Concordia Commun Betterment Assn. 12: "Concordia MISSOURI: A Centennial History (60). 13: Yes. 14: Admin, catlg. 15: P O Box 364, Concordia Mo 64020.

VOIGT, MELVIN J(OHN). b Upland Cal 12 Mr 11. 4: Susie Warkentin. 5: Bluffton Col 31-33 (Math) AB; UMich 33-38 ABLS, AMLS. 6: Ger. 7: Libn Bluffton Dist Lib, Bluffton Ohio 33-35; Physics libn & asst clsf UMich 35-42; Head Lib & Publ Research Dept Gen Mills, Minneapolis 42-46; Libn & Prof of Lib Sci Carnegie Inst of Tech 46-52; Asst libn & lecturer UCal(Berkeley) 52-59; Dir & Prof Kan State U (Manhattan) 59-60; U Libn UCal (San Diego) 0-. Unesco consu, Documentation Centre, Cairo UAR 63. 9: ALA-RTSD (pres 60-61);-LED (pres 63-64); ADI; SLA; CalLA; PennLA (pres 51-52). 10: AAUP; AAAS (Fellow). 11: Fulbright res scholar, UCopenhagen, 58-59. 12: "Subject Headings in Physics (44); "Scientists Approaches to Information (62); "Books for College Libraries" (67). 13: Yes. 14: Admin, data processing. 15: Lib Univ of Cal, San Diego, La Jolla Ca 92037.

VOISINE, SISTER MARY EMMA, RSM. b Linwood Mich 13 Je 14. 5: Mt Mercy Col (Mich) summer 33-38 (Educ); Ferris State Col summer 39 (Bus Educ); UNotre Dame summer 41, 54, 55; Mercy Col (Detroit) summer 42-49 (Eng) BA; W MichU summer 50 (LS); UMich summer 59-63 mals. 6: Fr, Latin, Polish. 7: Tchr Parochial Elem Schs of Mich 34-38, Prin-tchr 48-53; Libn Parochial Secondary Schs of Mich 53-69, Tchr 53-60; Hd libn Our Lady of mercy High Sch Lib, Farmington Mich 67-69; Media center dir Rel Educ Coord St Clare Parish, Farmington Mich 68-69. 8: Chm bldg plans Our Lady of Mercy High Sch Lib 63-64; Chm Catholic Bk Week, Saginaw Area 57-60; Nat Catholic Bk Fair Com 58-65; Chm Sisters of Mercy Lib Com, Mich, Ind, Iowa; Mich Dept Educ; Jt School Lib Devel Com 68, curriculum Planning Com 64-67; Taught lib sci. 9: ALA; CathLA (Mich Unit: sec 60-62; Memb Chm 62-63); Nat Assn Eng Tchrs; MichASchL. 11: Nat Catholic Bk Fair Trophy 57. 13: Yes. 14: Lib planning, design & org. 15: 29300 Eleven Mile rd, Farmington Mi 48024.

VOLCKER, RUTH P(AULINE). b Lebanon Penn 25 Jl 16. 5: Simmons 34-38 (LS) MS. 7: Asst research libn Eastman Kodak Co, Rochester NY 38-43; Tech libn Tenn Eastman Co, Oak Ridge Tenn 43-44; Research libn Tenn Eastman Co, Kingsport Tenn 44-. 9: SLA (pres Appalachian Chap 69-70); TennLA. 10: AAUW; Altrusa Internat; Kingsport Girls Club Bd; Kingsport Citizens Adv Com; Boone Free Lib Club. 15: Tenn Eastman Co, Kingsport Tenn 37662.

VOLKERSZ, EVERT (JAN). b Amsterdam Netherlands 18 O 36. 4: Linda DeBardeleben. 5: UWash 54-58 (FAR Eastern) BA, 58-59 (Hist), 62-63 MLS. 6: Dutch, Ger. 7: Spec 4th class (E-4) Bandsman US Army 59-62; Libn II spec collection UCLA Lib 63-69; Spec collections libn SUNY(Stony Brook) 69-. 9: ALA; CalLA (chm Com on Acad Status 69-). 14: Spec collections. 15: Special Collections Librarian, SUNY, Stony Brook NY.

VOLKMANN, HELEN (REBECCA) (HULL). b Gasport NY 6 S 16. 4: Max Volkmann. 5: Muskingum Col 34-36 (Eng); Hartford Sem Foundation (onn) 36-38 (Relig Educ) BRE; Iowa Wesleyan Col 62-64 (Eng) BA; UIowa 66-68 MA in LS. 6: Fr, Ger. 7: Tchr Danville High Sch, Danville Iowa 64-65; Ser & catlg asst Iowa Wesleyan Col Lib 65-67, Hd catlgr 68-. 9: ALA. 10: LWV. 14: Catlg. 15: 703 North White, Mt Pleasant Ia 52641.

VOLLAND, MARY (BENNETT). b Lakeland Fla 19 Ja 42. 4: Lawrence Karl Volland. 5: Fla StateU 59-63 (Eng, Sp) BA; IndU 63-65 (Slavic Lang & Lit) MA; UMich 66-67 MLS. 6: Russian. 7: Lib research asst IndianaU Lib 64-65; Sub serv UMich Grad lib 65-66sst libn (ref, acquis, bibliogr, interlib oan) Corning Community Col 67-, Instr in Russian 68-. 9: NYLA. 10: Friends of Corning Pub Lib; AAUW; AAUP; Phi Beta Kappa; Phi Kappa Phi. 14: Ref, Russian area studies. 15: Hickok rd RD 3, Corning NY 14830.

VOLLMAR, EDWARD ROBERT S J. b Platteville Colo 23 Jl 11. 5: Regis Col (Denver) 29-33, 36 (Hist) AB; St Louis U 36-39 (Hist) MA; Catholic U 47-48 BS in LS; ST Louis U 53-55 (Hist) PhD; American U summer 60 Certif in Archival Admin. 7: Instr Marquette High Sch, Milwaukee 39-41; Instr Regis High Sch, Denver 41-42; St Louis U: Assoc dir 48-51, 55-, Instr in hist 50-55, Asst Prof of hist 55-60, Assoc Prof of hist 60-67, Prof of Hist 67-. 8: Ordained Priest, 45; Bibliog Vatican Lib 58. 9: ALA-ACRL; CathLA; AHA; Amer Cath Hist Assn; SAA. 12: "The Catholic Church in America (56, 2d rev ed 63); Asst ed "Manuscripta (52). 13: Yes. 14: Admin, bibliog. 15: 3655 W Pine, St Louis Mo 63108.

VOLLMAYER, KARL A. b Toledo Ohio 17 F 16. 4: Catherine A Vollmayer. 5: U San Francisco 48-50 (Eng) BA; UWash 51 (LS) BA. 7: US Army Air Corps (Maj) 41-48; Ref libn Washoe Co Lib, Reno Nev 51-53; Asst libn Richmond (Cal) Pub Lib 53-60; City Libn Redwood City (Cal) Pub Lib 60-. 8: Legis advocate CalLA (59). 9: ALA; CalLA (pres Pub Lib Sect 67); Pub Lib Execs of Central Cal (pres 68); Peninsula Lib Assn. 10: Kiwanis Club. 14: Bldgs, ref, admin. 15: Redwood City Pub Lib, 881 Jefferson, Redwood City Ca 94063.

VOLM, DOROTHY (BISCHOFF). b Johnston Penn 29 Mr 08. 4: M H Volm. 5: McPherson Col 43-46 (Sociol) AB; Elgin Community Col 52, 53; UPittsburgh 64-67 MSLS. 6: Ger. 7: Admin asst General Brotherhood Bd Church of th 07: Admin asst General Brotherhood Bd Church of the Brethren, Elgin Ill 46-53; Admin asst Nat Council of Churches, NYC 53-57; President's sec Indiana UPenn 59-65, Libn (catlgr) Stabley Lib 65-. 8: Libn at off-campus centers Indiana UPenn. 10: AAUW; Beta Sigma Phi; Bus & Prof Woman's Club. 14: Catlg, circ, ref. 15: 822 Grant st, Indiana Pa 15701.

VOLNY, JAMES GEORGE. b Columbus Ohio 10 Ag 31. 4: Doris Karabek. 5: Kent State 49-53 (Chem) BS; Northwestern U 53-54 (Chem); West Res 62-63 MSLS. 6: Ger. 7: Asst hd Gen sci dept UNotre Dame Memorial Lib (Ind) 63-64, Act asst hd acquis 64-65, Libn Chem-Physics Research Lib 65-66; Univ libn Loyola U (New Orleans) 66-. 9: SLA; CathLA; (Col & Univ Sect Bd Mem); LaLA; La Conf Cols & Univs (Lib Sect: chm 69-70). 10: Beta Phi Mu. 15: 4800 Tartan dr, Metairie La 70003.

VOLZ, DONNA AGNES. b Silverton Ore 23 My 39. 5: Mt Angel Col 57-61 (Educ) BA; UDenver 64-65 (LS) MA. 7: Elem tchr St Marys Pub Sch, Mt Angel Ore 61-64; Sch libn Ft Collins High Sch, Ft Collins Colo 65-68; Sch libn Tachikawa Elem Sch, Tachikawa AFB Japan 68-. 9: NEA; ALA; Far East EA. 14: Sch libs. 15: Box 55, 6100 Support Wing, APO San Francisco 96323.

von BARFUSS, MICHAEL (PETER). b Copenhagen Denmark 18 O 23. 5: UHawaii 56-59 (Geog) AB; UDenver 64 (LS) MA. 6: Ger, Danish, Japanese. 7: US Army, Danish tchr at Army Lang Sch, Monterey 49-51; US Army (Sgt) Mil Intelligence, Germany 52-54; Asst manager Queens Surf, Honolulu 60-62; Asst manager MS Ranch House, Honolulu 62-64; Libn Lib Assn of Portland, Portland Ore 64-66; Reclass libn UHawaii 66-67; Base libn 6917 Sec Gr APO NY 68-. 14: Acquis, admin. 15: 50 Nohes st, Hilo Hi 96720.

VON BODUNGEN, (BETTY) SUE (BARHAM). b Mena Ark 22 S 36. 4: Joseph P Von Bodungen. 5: UArk 54-58 (Eng) BA; LSU 62-64 (LS) MS. 6: Fr. 7: Tchr Indian Hill Jr High Sch, Prairie Village Kan 58-62; Lib trainee LSU Lib (Baton Rouge) 62-64, Info desk libn (humanities) 64-65, Asst to dir 65-. 8: Child libn Lib/USA NYC 64. 9: ALA; SWLA; LaLA. 10: Beta Phi Mu; Lambda Iota Tau; Delta Delta Delta. 12: Ed "Library Lectures" (series) (67-); Ed "SWLA Newsletter" (66-68). 14: Lib admin, ref. 15: La State Univ Lib, Baton Rouge La 70803.

von BROCKDORFF, ERIC. b Kongsberg Germany 15 Mr 32. 4: Marie Lorraine Cormier. 5: Hamilton Col 51-55 (Hist) AB;NYU 55-58 (Finance); Columbia 59-60 MSLS. 6: Ger. 7: Trainee & credit analyst The Marine Midland Trust Co of NY, NYC 55-59; Asst ref libn Colgate U Lib 60-63, Ref libn 63-67; Dir of Libs Hartwick Col 67-. 9: ALA; NYLA. 10: AAUP. 13: Yes. 14: Ref, admin. 15: PO Box 59, W Oneonta NY 13820.

von BROCKDORFF, HANS. b Hambrug Germany 3 O 38. 4: Sigrid B M Meyering. 5: Hobart Col 58-62 (Ger, Fr) BA; Syracuse 65-66 MSLS. 6: Ger, Fr. 7: Radio- teletype operator US Army Sp/4, Mannheim Germany 62-64; Asst libn St University Col, Potsdam NY 66-68; Ref libn Elmira Col 68-69; Hd libn Belknap Col 69-. 9: ALA. 10: AAUP. 14: Ref, admin. 15: RFD, Center Harbor NH 03226.

von ENDE, EUNICE A. b Iowa City Iowa 9 O 06. 5: UIda 24-29 (Hist) BA; Drexel 30-31 BS in LS. 7: Lib asst DC Pub Lib 31-37; Head Libn Pub Lib, Boise Ida 37-45; Libn asst lib sect Bur of Naval Personnel NAVY Dept, Wash DC 45-47, Asst head lib ser br 47-67; Bibliogr BSCP George Washington U 68-69. 9: ALA (Notable Bks Coun 63-66);-PLA (pres Armed Forces Libns Sect 59-60); DCLA. 10: Phi Beta Kappa. 14: Ref, bk sel, admin. 15: 2430 Pennsylvania ave No 823, Wash DC 20037.

VON GLAN, MARY LOUISE. b Breda Iowa 26 Mr 10. 5: Iowa State Tchrs Col 36 (Eng) BA; UWis 38-39 BLS. 7: High sch libn Ft Morgan Col 39-43; Asst order libn UInd (Bloomington) 43-45; Asst ref libn pub lib, Wichita Kan 45-46; Asst ref libn pub lib, Grand Rapids Mich 46-47; Ref libn pub lib, Waterloo Iowa 47-50; Soc welfare case-wker, Carroll Iowa 51-52; High sch libn, Carroll Iowa 52-55; Ref libn pub lib, Waterloo Iowa 55-. 9: ALA; IowaLA. 10: AAUW; Altrusa Internat; Cedar Valley Hist Soc. 14: Ref. 15: 1230 Rainbow dr, Waterloo Ia 50701.

von HAKE, MARGARET JOAN. b Santa Monica Cal 27 O 33. 5: La Sierra Col 51-55 (Eng) BA; USoCal 60-62 MSLS, Spec Secondary Credential in Lib Sci. 6: Fr. 7: Tchr Newbury Park Acad, Newbury Park Cal 55-57 Tchr-libn 57-60; Clerk-typist Los Angeles Pub Lib 60-62; Asst l bn Columbia Union Col 62-67, Libn 67-. 9: ALA; MdLA. 14: Child & ya bks, sch libnship, educ for libnship. 15: Columbia Union Col, Takoma Park Md 20012.

VON HAUSEN, (ILSE GEORGINE) INGRID. b Austria 18 Ag 33. 4: Alexander Von Hausen. 5: UToronto 51-56 (Eng, Ger) BA; Ont Col of Educ summer 57, 58 (Eng, Fr) Type B Certif, summers 59, 60 (Libnship) Specialist. 6: Ger. 7: Clk Unemployment Ins Commsn, Oshawa Can 56-57; Tchr Port Perry High Sch, Port Perry Can 57-59; Tchr & libn Scarborough Bd of Educ, Scarborough Can 59-61; Libn Preston High Sch, Preston Can 66-. 15: 7 Melrose ave, Galt Ont Can.

von KHRUM, PAUL. b Brockton Iowa 31 O 09. 5: UUtah 35 (Classics, Eng) AB; Columbia 41 (LS) BS; Sorbonne 49-50 (Compar Lit). 6: Lat, Fr. 7: Various positions NYU 50-, Asst dir 61-. 13: Yes. 15: 333 E 43rd st, New York NY 10017.

VON LANG, FREDERICK WILLIAM. b Scranton Penn 6 My 49. 4: Ilsabe von Wackerbarth. 5: Kutztown State Col 47-51 (LS, Soc Studies) B; Syracuse 52-55 MSLS; Lehigh U 53-54 (Hist). 6: Ger, Fr. 7: Libn Broughal Jr High Sch, Bethlehem Penn 51-66; Asst circ libn Bethlehem Pub Lib, Bethlehem Penn 52-55; Asst libn Enoch Pratt Free Lib, Baltimore summer 56; Asst libn Manhassett PUB Lib Manhassett NY summer 62; Lib dir Lehigh Co Commun Col 66-. 9: ALA; PennLA (treas & Exec Bd Lehigh Valley Chap 67-68; v-chm Jr & Commun Col Sect 69-). 10: Friends of the Bethlehem Pub Lib; Jr C of C; SAR; Penn Soc of Mayflower Descendants; Bradford Family Compact; Moravian Hist Soc; Beta Phi Mu. 12: Assoc ed "Genealogiches Handbuck des in Bayern Immatrikuliertn Adels" v IV (53). 13: Yes. 14: Ref, geneal, loc hist, admin. 15: 3057 Cornwall rd, Bethlehem Penn 18017.

von NELL, CARL CONRAD. b Phila 13 My 32. 5:La Salle Col 49-53 (Lat, Gk) BA;Drexel 53-54 (LS) MS; Middlebury Col 58-62 (Ger) MA. 6: Ger. 7: Libn La Salle High Sch (Prep), Phila 54-63; Ref libn Free Lib of Phila 63-. 9: ALA; CathLA. 14: Ref. 15: 339 Unruh st, Phila Pa 19111.

VON OESEN, ELAINE (ANNA). b Wilmington NC 6 S 13. 5: Lenoir Rhyne Col 38 AB; UNC 40 BA in LS, 51 (Hist) MA. 7: Asst libn Rockingham Co Lib, Leaksville NC 40-42; Dir of Libs Walker Co, LaFayette Ga 42-43; Army libn, Camp Davis NC 43-44; Instr & Asst Prof Sch of Lib Sci UNC 47-52; Field lin NC Lib Comsn, Raleigh NC 52-56; Ext serv libn NC State Lib 56-65, Asst state libn 65-. 9: Adult Educ Assn; ALA (treas lib periods round table 55-56, chm adv com Small Libs Proj 61-63);-AAStateL (sec 61-62); SELA (Exec Bd 54-58, Chm Nomin Com 58-60; pres 68-70); NCLA (Exec Bd 55-57, chm Com on Org 61-65); NC Adult Educ Assn (Exec Bd 58; treas 64-65; sec 68). 10: Beta Phi Mu; Alpha Psi Omega. 12: Ed "North Carolina Libraries (53-57). 13: Yes. 14: Ext, coop, bldgs. 15: P O Box 2889, Raleigh NC 27602.

von SCHON, (CATHERINE) VIRGINIA. b Wash DC 2 O 20. 5: Hillsdale Col 38-42 (Lat) AB; UMich 49-50 (Eng) MA, 60-61 AMLS. 6: Ger, Fr. 7: Tr & monitor For Broadcast Intel Serv, Wash DC 42-45; Tr & interpreter War Crimes Trials, Nuremberg 45-48; Soc reporter & ed "Daily Tribune, Royal Oak Mich 50-54; Copy writer J L Hudson Co, Detroit 54-60; Work-study scholar Lib Sci Lib UMich 60-61, Asst libn 61-62; Catlgr UMich 62-68; Subj specialist SUNY (Stony Brook) 68-. 9: ALA; MichLA; Ann Arbor Lib Club. 14: Acquis. 15: 200A Jefferson apt 2D, St James NY 11780.

von STRALENDORFF, VICCO (HELMUTH). b Rostock Germany 6 My 29. 4: Lilo Schulli. 5: Franklin Col 55-59 (Econ) BA; Ind U 59-61 (LS) MA. 6: Ger, Fr, Sp. 7: Cost accountant Gutermann Sewing Silk, Gutach Germany 49-55; Lib asst pre-prof Indianapolis Pub Lib 59; Asst libn Franklin Col 59-, Assoc libn & asst Prof of Ger 69-. 9: Mod Lang Assn; IndLA. 14: Catlg, ref, bk sel. 15: 901 E Monroe, Franklin Ind 46131.

von SUCK, MARJORIE. b Winchestr Mass 4 Mr 16. 5: Simmons Col 33-38 (LS) BS. 6: Fr, Ger. 7: Soc wker Town of Ipswich, Mass 55-60; Libn Ipswich High Sch, Ipswich Mass 60-63; Libn Marlboro High Sch, Marlboro Mass 63-64; Libn Manchester High Sch, Manche ter Mass 64-; Libn Free Pub Lib, Rowley Mass 67-. 8: NESDEC Sch Lib Com, 62, 63. 9: NEA; ALA; ass Tchrs Assn; NELA; MasschLA. 10: Ipswich Hist Assn; LWV. 13: Yes. 14: Sch libs, pub lib. 15: 109 High st, Ipswich Ma 01938.

von WAHLDE, BARBARA (KETTERMAN). b Pasadena Cal 6 O 37. 4: Peter H C von Wahlde. 5: IndU 55-61 (Hist) BS, 64-66 (LS) MA. 6: Ger. 7: Ref libn Monroe Co Pub Lib, Bloomington Ind 65; Asst docs libn IndU Lib (loomington) 65-66; Catlgr UMaine Lib (Orono) 66-69; Catlgr USoMiss Lib 69-. 8: Consul Manpower Resources Proj UMe 68; Tchr beginning & advanced catlg UMe spring & summer 69. 9: MeLA. 14: Catlg, docs. 15: RR 6 Box 500, Anderson In 46011.

VON WICKLEN, JANE (HOGAN). b Atkins Ark 29 S 15. 4: Frederick C Von Wicklen. 5: Col of Ozarks 34-39 (Bio) BS; UNeb 44-46 (Parasitology) BS; UOkla 65 MLS. 7: Circ libn, mt Vernon Ohio 52-54; Pub sch tchr, NM 57-58; Instr SWest State Col (Okla) 62-63, 64-65, Circ & gen ref libn 65-68, Sci ref & ser libn 68-. 9: ALA; MedLA; OklaLA; Okla Ornith Soc; Okla Acad Sci; SWLA. 14: Sci ref. 15: 607 E Oklahoma, Weatherford Ok 73096.

VONDER LINDT, ALICE M. b Phila. 5: UKy 58 (Liberal Arts) BA, 60 MSLS. 7: Libn Va Hosp, Lebanon Penn 59-62; Chief libn Va Hosp, Beckley WVa 62-63;Chief libn Va Ctr, Martinsburg WVa 64-67; Chief libn VA Hosp, Coatesville Penn 67-. 9: ALA; WVaLA; PennLA; Phila Reg Med Lib Com. 10: AAUW; Soroptimist. 14: Hosp & med libnship, biol. 15: Black Hawk apt, E Lancaster ave, Downington Pa 19335.

VOORHEES, EDWARD H. b Winona Minn 23 O 18. 4: Helen Bennett. 5: State Tchrs Col 9dul 9duluth Minn) 36 & 40 (Educ); UMaryland (College Park) 52-53 (Military Sci) BS; UMich (Ann Arbor) 37-39 (Econ), 68-69 AMLS. 7: Off (Colonel) US Marine Corps 40-68; Dept hd Sci & Industry Dallas Pub Lib (Texas) 69-. 9: ALA; SLA. 10: Soc Logistic Engrs; Armed forces Mgt Assn; Delta Sigma Pi; Marine Corps Assn. 15: Sci & Ind dept Dallas Pub Lib 1954 Commerce, Dallas Tx 75201.

VOOS, HENRY. b Homburg Germany 10 A 28. 4: Jane Rhein. 5: NYU 46-48 (Ger) BA, 48-53 (GER) MA; Columbia 51-53 MSLS; Rutgers 62-65 (LS) PhD. 6: Ger. 7: Lib asst NY Pub Lib 48-53; Libn Internat Ladies Garment Wkers Union, NYC 53-56; Supv libn Picatinny Arsenal Tech Info br, Dover NJ 56-68; Assoc Prof Grad Sch Lib Serv Rutgers 68-. 8: Consul; US Army Corps of Engrs, US Army Picatinny Arsenal, Farmingdale Pub Schs, Fed Lib Com. 9: ALA; SLA (chm Clearinghouse Consul); NJLA (chm Educ Com 61). 12: "Organizational Communication" (67); "Information Needs in Urban Areas (69). 13: Yes. 14: Tech proc, automation, lib mgt, wk measurement. 15: 28 Wenonah ave, Rockaway NJ 7866.

VORE, ROBERTA B(ELCHER). b Las Vegas NM 16 Je 44. 5: Colo State Col 62-66 (Hist) AB; UKy (Lexington) 66-67 (LS) MS. 6: Fr, Ger. 7: Ref libn N M Highlands U 68-. 9: ALA; NMLA. 14: Acquis, ref, rare bks, lib hist. 15: 1034 Fifth st, Las Vegas NM 87701.

VORMELKER, ROSE L. b Cleveland 11 Je 1895. 5: Oberlin Col summers 16, 21; West Res 18-19 (LS) Certif; UMich ext 20-2; Cleveland Col ext 25-26. 6: Ger, Fr. 7: Ref asst tech dept Detroit Pub Lib 19-22; Ref asst Tech Div Cleveland Pub Lib 23-24; Research libn White Motor Co, Cleveland 25-28; Org & head bus info bur Cleveland Pub Lib 28-55; Asst dir Cleveland Pub Lib 55-56; Lib dir Forest City Publ Co, Cleveland 56-62; Asst Prof Kent State U 63-; Consul in org of bus & newspaper libs 63-, Organizer lib ctr Urban Regionalism 67-68. 8: Head publicity & exhibits, USIS, 42; Instr: bus info sources, Cleveland Col 33-54, spec libs West Res 43-, UMich summers 56-58; Chap consul Spec Libs, SLA Cleveland Chap 58-; Exec dir Kent State U Lib 66. 9: ALA (chm Bus & Tech Sect 47-48);-LED (pres 67-68); SLA (sec-treas 26-28, pres 48-49); Amer Stat Assn (pres Cleveland Chap 44-45); OhioLA (var com assignments); Lib Club of Cleveland & Vic (pres 51-52); AALS. 10: AAUP; Womens Nat Bk Assn; Womens City Club of Cleveland; Womens Advert Club; Zonta Club; Inter-club Coun of Cleveland. 11: SLA Prof Award, 53; SLA, Hallof Fame 63. 12: "Special Library Resources" 2 v (41, 46);"The Company Library - What It Is and Does" (47); "Community Research Resources"(64);Jt auth "Careers in Todays Libraries" (40). 13: Yes. 14: Ref & research bus, org of spec libs, bus & newspapers, govt publns. 15: 12700 Shaker blvd, Cleveland Oh 44120.

VORWERK, RICHARD JAMES. b Akron Ohio 1 Ag 34. 4: Susan Jane Richard. 5: UNotre Dame 52-56 BA; Loyola U 59-61 (Philos) MA; IndU 65-66 (LS) MA, 68- (LS). 6: Lat, Fr. 7: Instr: UDetroit High Sch 61-63, Springfield High Sch, Akron Ohio 63-64; Lecturer in lib sci IndU (S Bend) 66-68; Hd philos & theol Memorial Lib UNotre Dame (S Bend) 66-68. 8: Visiting lecturer in LS Ind UNW Bloomington Ind summer 68, 69. 9: ALA; ASIS; IndLA. 14: Admin. 15: 703 W Gourley Pike #88, Bloomington In 47401.

VOSS, HILDA (HACKER). b Portland Me 13 Je 10. 5: Syracuse U 28-32 BS in LS. 7: Jr asst Pub Lib, Detroit 34-44; Asst Spokane Pub Lib, Spokane Wash 44-45; Head of child serv Pub Lib, W Allis Wis 49-65; Child libn Maui Co Lib, Wailuku Hawaii 65-67; Br libn Maui Pub Lib, Kahului Hawaii 67-68, Child coord 68-. 9: ALA; WisLA (chm Child Sect 55); HawaiiLA. 10: AAUW; Toastmistress; Maui Co Com on Child & Youth. 14: Child wk. 15: PO Box 1136, Wailuku Ha 96793.

VOSS, RUTH (SWEET). b Claverack NY 7 Ja 12. 4: Lawrence S Voss. 5: Simmons 29-33 (LS) BS; Worcester State Tchrs Col summer 59. 7: Libn Lasell Jr Col 34-37; Libn-tchr Uxbridge High Sch, Uxbridge Mass 58-60; Libn Nipnuc Reg High Sch, Mendon Mass 60-. 9: NESchLA; MassSchLA; Mass Lib Trustees Assn. 10: Trustee, Uxbridge Pub Lib. 14: Reading guidance, ref, sch lib & curr coord. 15: 107 Oak st, Uxbridge Mass 01596.

VOTH, ANNETTE. b Topeka Kan 31 D 39. 5: UKansas 57-61 (Mus Hist) BMu; UCal (Berkeley) 63-64 MLS. 6: Norwegian, Danish. 7: Lib asst UKan Lib 61-62; Lib asst Deichmanske Bibliotek, Oslo Norway 62-63; Bibliogr UCal (Berkeley) 64-68; Ref libn UKan 69-. 14: Bibliog, ref. 15: 2505 Burnett rd, Topeka Ks 66614.

VOYLES, JUDSON. b Picher Okla 2 Mr 18. 4: Louise Larned. 5: Long Beach City Col 36-37 (Eng); UCal (Berkeley) 39-42, 50 (Eng) BA, 50-51 (LS) BS. 6: Fr. 7: (T/Sgt) US Army Infantry, Pacific 42-45; Libn fiction dept Los Angeles Pub Lib 51-53; Long Beach Pub Lib, Long Beach Cal: Libn art dept 53-54, Br libn 54-63, Head tech processing div 63-. 9: ALA; CalLA; So Cal Tech Proc Group (Memb & Soc Chm; Program Com Chm 68-69). 14: Bk processing (catlg, acquis, binding); adult serv, lib automation. 15: Long Beach Public Library, Ocean & Pacific ave, Long Beach Ca 90803.

VREELAND, ELEANOR P. b NYC 21 Mr 30. 5: NYU & Queens Col. 6: Ital. 7: Asst advertising promotion dir Peck & Peck NYC 47-58; Dir pub rel Brooklyn Pub Lib 60-65; Dir Pub Rel Queens Borough Pub Lib, Queens NY 65-; V-pres Francis R St John Lib Consuls Inc, NYC 65-68; Educ serv consul Collier-Macmillan Lib Serv, NYC 68-. 8: Spec proj for Peck & Peck in exec offs, NYC 59 7 60. 9: ALA (Reg chm memb com);-LED; Nat Lib Week Com;-LPRC (pres); NYLA; NY Lib club. 10: PUB Rel Offrs Soc, NY; Bus & Prof Womens Assn. NY. 15: St John Lib Consultants Inc, 21 E 40 st, New York NY 10016.

VROMAN, LAURA E(LIZABETH). b Middleburgh NY 22 D 12. 5: SUNY(Albany) 30-34 BS in LS, 48 (Eng) AB; UIll 53-54 (LS) MS. 6: Fr. 7: Libn & Eng tchr High Sch, Warners NY 34-35; Libn & Eng tchr High Sch, Fayetteville NY 35-39; Head Libn Chautauqua Int, Chautauqua NY summers 36, 37; Libn High Sch, Middletown NY 39-43; Libn High Sch, Glens Falls NY 43-53; Asst Prof Lib Sci Trenton State Tchrs Col 54-55; Libn High Sch, Great Neck NY 55-57; Libn Niskayuna High Sch, Schenectady NY 57-. 8: Lib consul, NY State Educ

Dept, summers 48-51, 53, 54; Wkshop dir SUNY(Geneseo) summer 52; Visiting Prof SUNY(Albany) sumers 54, summers & SUNY(Geneseo) summer 58. 9: ALA; NEA; NYLA (pres Sch Lib Sect 59); NY State Tchrs Assn; East Sch Libns Assn; Hudson-Mohawk LA. 10: Zonta; AAUW; Beta Phi Mu. 13: Yes. 14: High sch libs. 15: 8 Van Kortrijk Bldg, Netherlands Village, Schnectady NY 12308.

VROOMAN, GEORGE KENDALL. b Mars Hill Ind 1 S 18. 4: Charlina M Nicol. 5: UIll 39-40 (Bus Admin); Siena Col 46-49 (Econ) BS; State U Col (Albany NY) 61-64 MSLS; NY State Prof Cert 67. 7: Alco Prod, Schenectady NY: Supv Est dept, Value analysis engnr, Proj engnr new prod dep, Supv lib serv Nuclear Engr dept, Adm supv engnr dept, Sr estimating engr; Chief tech info serv Watervliet Arsenal, Watervliet NY 63-. 8: US Army rep, Lib/USA, NY Worlds Fair, 64-. 9: ADI; Hudson-Mohawk LA (Dir 68-69). 14: Tech reports, phys scis ref, admin. 15: Ashdown rd, Rt 3, Ballston Lake NY 12019.

VRUWINK, RUTH ELIZABETH. b El Reno Okla 1 Ap 14. 5: Bollins Col 31-35 (Eng) AB; Pratt 36-37 BLS; Columbia 40-41 (Eng). 6: Fr, Ger, Russian. 7: Catlgr Albany Pub Lib, albany NY 37-39; Libn, lang & lit sect Brooklyn Pub Lib, Brooklyn NY 41-48; Ser catlgr PrincetonU 5o. 9: ALA; NJLA. 14: Catlg. 15: 120 Prospect ave, Princeton NJ 08540.

VUJICA, NADA (KESTERCANEK). b Sarajevo Yugoslavia. 4: Stanko M Vujica. 5: UZagreb 35-41 (Slavic Studies) MA; Marywood Col 51-52 MA in LS. 6: Croatian, Polish, Ger, fr, Ital. 7: Libn Wilkes Col 47-. 9: ALA; PennLA. 10: AAUP; Croatian Acad of Amer. 12: Several publications in Croatian. 15: Eugene Shedden Farley Lib, Wilkes College, Wilkes Barre Pa 18703.

VUKADINOV, RUTH LAKE. b Windsor Ont Can 30 My 34. 4: Milan Vukadinov. 5: UWindsor 52-55, 56-64 (Eng) BA, MA; Toronto 55-56 BLS. 07: Windsor (Ont) Pub Lib: Ref asst 56-59; 1st Asst to head of ref dept 59-63, Act head ref dept 63-65, Head ref dept 65-. 9: OntLA (past chm Ref Wkshop); CanLA; Inst Prof Libns Ont. 13: Yes. 14: Ref. 15: 416 Victoria ave, Windsor Ont Can.

W

WABY, MARIAN L. b Hetland SD 22 Jl 13. 5: Pasadena Jr Col 30-32; UCLA 32-34 (Eng) AB; UIll 34-35 BS in LS. 7: Order asst Ore State Col 35-44; UCal(Berkeley) libn I 44-47, Libn II 47-52, Libn III 52-65, Libn IV 65-. 14: Acquis. 15: 2324 Dwight way, Berkeley Ca 94704.

WACHTL, CARL. b Vienna Austria 3 O 10. 5: St Mary'sU (San Antonio Tex) 41-43 (Chem); UTex (Austin) 46-48 (Chem) BS; NorthwesternU 49-53 (Biochem) PhD; Ohio Dominican Col 63- (LS). 6: Ger, Fr. 7: Research chem Lithographic Tech Foundation, Chicago 48-49; Research assoc Kresge Eye Inst, Detroit 53-60; Asst ed Chem Abstracts Serv, Columbus Ohio 60-61, Asst dept hd 61-62, Hd phys & inorganic chem ed dept 62-. 8: Asst prof of ophthalmic Chem, Wayne StateU; Detroit 55-60; Fellowship Nat Gas Assn of Amer UTex 47-48. 9: ACS; SLA; Tissue Culture Assn; ALA; OhioLA. 10: YMCA; AAAS Fellow; Phi Lambda Upsilon; Sigma Xi. 13: Yes. 14: Ed, info sci, ref. 15: Apt 31 4050 N High st, Columbus Oh 43214.

WADDEL, DEAN ALLEN. b N Loup Neb 14 Je 37. 4: Barbara Ellen Eloe. 5: Kearney State col 55-61 (Eng, Soc Sci) BA in Ed; UWis summers 66, 67, 68 (LS) MA. 6: Fr. 7: Eng-Fr tchr High Sch, Emmett Ida 59-60; Prin-libn High Sch, Madrid Neb 61-64; Tchr-libn High Sch, Grant Neb 65; Ref & doc asst Kearney State Col 66-67, Hd tech serv 68-. 9: NebLA. 14: Tech serv, archives. 15: 3609 Ave D, Kearney Nb 68847.

WADDELL, JOHN NEAL. b Cape Charles Va 23 Jl 12. 5: UVa 29-32 (Eng) BA, 32-33 (Eng) MA; Columbia 46-47 (LS) BS, 64- (LS). 6: Fr, Ger. 7: High sch tchr, Va pub schs 33-36; Col exec Hollins Col 36-42; (Lt) USNR 42-46; Ref asst NY Pub Lib 47-54; Ref asst Unesco, Paris 51; Columbia U: Asst ref libn 54-61, Head ref dept 62-65, Lecturer in Lib Serv 53-. 9: ALA; AALS. 12: Asst ed, 3 & 4 sups to Winchells "Guide. 14: Lib educ, ref. 15: 21 Claremont ave, New York NY 10027.

WADDELL, MINA JEAN (GILLESPIE). b Kan 15 D 6. 4: Stanford C Waddell. 5: UWichita 34-38 (Zool) BA; Kan State Tchrs Col (Emporia) 63-65 (LS) MS. 7: Case wker Sedgwich Co Welfare Bd, Wichita Kan 39-43; Interviewer Kan State Employment Serv, Wichita Kan 43; lib clerk Wichita Pub Lib, Wichita Kan 55-58; Ref libn Wichita State U Lib 58-68; Chief ref libn 68-. 9: ALA-AASchL (State Assembly Del 61-); NEA; WVaLA (chm Sch Lib Standards Com 61-64; pres 68-69); WVaEA. 10: AAUP; Wichita Lib Club; Sweet Adelines; Alpha Chi Omega. 14: Soc sci ref, Kan hist collections, archives.17245 15: 1444 Salina, Wichita Ks 67203.

WADDELL, MRS LUCILLE (McLEMORE). b Tolr Tex 3 Je 05. 5: UTex 34, 39 (Eng); Abilene Christian Col 35 (Educ) BS; N Tex State U 34, 49-51 BS in LS; UDenver 62, summer 63 (LS). 7: Tchr Tex Pub Schs: Glen Rose Tex 33-36, Millsap Tex 36-42, Baytown Tex 42-45; Libn Horace Mann Jr High Sch, Baytown Tex 45-52; Libn Robert E Lee High Sch, Baytown Tex 52-. 9: NEA; Tex State Tchrs Assn; TexLA; Tex CTE. 10: Delta Kappa Gamma; Civic Concert Assn. 14: Ref, catlg. 15: 1601 Adams st, Baytown Tex 77521.

WADDINGTON, ELAINE (ROBINSON SOLKIN). b Montreal Can 28 O 24. 4: Patrick Waddington. 5: McGill 42-46 (Biochem) BS; Toronto 46-48 (Biochem) MA; McGill 56-57 BLS. 6: Fr. 7: Lab tech Royal Victoria Hosp, Montreal 48-49; Lab tech McGill U 50-53; Libn dept of obstetrics & gynaecology Royal Victoria Hosp, Montreal 57-. 8: Volunteer libn & catlgr, lib of the Can Assn of Amateur Musicians, 63-. 9: MedLA; QueLA. 10: McGill U Lib Staff Assn; Amer Recorder Soc; Can Assn Amateur Musicians. 14: Ref, indexing. 15: 7631 Ostell Crescent, Montreal 9 Can.

WADDLE, LINDA LOU (VAN DOREN). b Webster City Iowa 24 N 36. 4: William Waddle. 5: Webster City Jr Col 54-56 (Liberal Arts) AA; State Col Iowa 58-61 (LS) BA. 6: Fr, Ger. 7: Circ asst Kendall Young Lib, Webster City Iowa 56-58; Sch libn Hudson Community Schs, Hudson Iowa 61-63; Sch libn Cedar Falls Community Schs, CEDAR Falls Iowa 63-. 9: ALA; NEA; IowaASchL (Recr Chm 64-65); Iowa State EA. 14: Sch libs. 15: 2130 Valley Park dr, Cedar Falls Iowa 50613.

WADDLE, RICHARD L. b Sterling Colo 7 N 27. 4: Helen Carlsen. 5: Lower Columbia Jr Col 49-51 (Hist) AA; Marietta Col 51-53 (Hist) BA; UWash 53-55 (Hist) MALS; Wash State U 64-67 (Educ) PhD. 7: US Army Signal Corps Spec, US & Germany 46-49; Ref libn Marietta Col 55-58; Soc sci libn Ida State Col 58-60; Head Libn Yakima Valley Col 60-64; Summer staff Wash State U 64-66; Hd acquis libn Central Wash State Col 67-. 9: ALA. 10: Phi Beta Kappa. 14; col lib admin, new educ media. 15: 800 E Capitol ave, Ellensburg Wa 98926.

WADE, B GERTRUDE. b Beverly Mass. 5: Boston U 41-45 Eng Lit) BA, 45-47 (Eng Lit)MA; Simmons 63 (LS) MS. 7: Boston Pub Lib: Gen prof asst 47-53, Bk sel libn 53-56, Adults libn Codman Sq Br 57-62, Br libn Fanueil Br 62-64, Br libn Mem-Mt Pleasant Brs 64-65; Lib consul NH State Lib 65-67; Supv wk with adults Concord Pub Lib, Concord NH 67-. 9: ALA-SORT (Steering Com); Massla; Charles River Lib Club (v-pres 64-); NHLA (chm Intel Freedom Com); NELA. 10: Appalachian Mountain Club; dorchester United Neighborhood Assn; Brighton Commun Coun; Orchard Park (Roxbury0 inter-Agency Coun; NAACP; Urban League; Citizens for Pub Schs (Boston). 14: Pub lib admin, lib-comun rel, personnel, adult serv. 15: 11 Beacon st, Concord NH 03301.

WADE, BETTY JANE. b Morgantown WVa 13 Ja 22. 5: Salem Col 3941; UWVa 41-43 (Eng) AB; UIll summers 50-53 MSLS. 6: Fr, Ger. 7: Instr Marshall U summer 62; Instr UTenn summer 56; Libn Shinnston High Sch, Shinnston WVa 43-. 8: Dir WVa Sch Lib Devel Proj, 61-62; Chm WVa "School Lirary Manual Rev Com, 64-. ; Dir WVaU Stud Lib Assts Wkshop 65-67; Instr WVaU summers 66, 68-69. 9: ALA-AASchL (State Assembly Del 61-); NEA; WVaLA (chm Sch Lib Standards 61-64; pres 68-69); 61-64); WVaEA. 10: AAUW; Womans Club of Shinnston; WVa Fed of Womens Clubs; Delta Kappa Gamma. 14: Sch libs. 15: 61 W High st, Salem WVa 26426.

WADE, GORDON STANFIELD. b Minneapolis 13 D 36. 5: UMinn 54-58 (Sociol) BA, 59-60, 62-63 (LS) MA. 6: Fr. 7: Bkmob libn Hennepin Co Lib, Minneapolis 60-62; US Army Med Serv (Pfc) 61; Documents libn Hennepin Co Lib, Minneapolis 62-63; Head Libn Carroll Pub Lib, Carroll Iowa 63-. 9: ALA; MinnLA; IowaLA; Iowa Lib Admins RT. 10: Amer Field Serv. 14 Admin, catlg, ref, admin. 15: 1326 N Adams st, Carroll Ia 51401.

WADE, HAZEL ELLEN. b Russell Springs Ky 24 Ag 14. 4: Cephas G Wade. 5: Valdosta State Col 50-54 (Elem Educ) BS; Peabody summers 60-63 MALS. 7: Tchr elem & jr high sch, Russell Springs Ky 34-38; Elem tchr Brooks Co, Dixie Ga 48-56; Elem prin Brooks Co, Paro Ga 56-59; Asst dir Colquitt-Thomas Reg Lib, Moultrie Ga 59-. 66; Dir of Lib Serv & Materials Ctr Thomas Co Schs, Thomasville Ga 66-. 8:

Consul to sch libns; served on eval com for schs; Part-time instr lib sci UGa (Thomasville Center) 67-; Guest ed Random House Enrichment Aid Program of juvenile bks published 67. 9: ALA; NEA; GaEA (Lib Dept); GaLA (Child & YP Sect, past sec Pub Lib Div); SELA. 10: PTA; Delta Kappa Gamma. 14: Serv to schs, br lib supv, ref. 15: 206 W MacDonald st, Pavo Ga 31778.

WADE, JAMES C. b Schenectady NY 5 Ja 19. 4: Evelyn Amuedo. 5: Union Col 35-39 (Eng) AB; NY State Col 39-40 (Educ); CatholicU 48-53 MS in LS. 7: GE Co, Schenectady NY 40-41; Sgt USA 42-46; US Govt 47-48; Libn Dept of State, Wash DC 48-53; Chief libn engr Research & Development Labs, Ft Belvoir Va 53-58; Liaison off Defense Documentation Ctr, Alexandria Va 58-; Ref libn Fairfax Co Pub Lib, Springfield Va 65-. 8: Mem Lib Adv Coun, George WashU 68-69. 9: Soc Amer Mili Eng; SLA; DCLA. 10: Lions club. 14: Documentation, mech retr systems. 15: 6418 Fairland st, Alexandria Va 22312.

WADE, PEARL MAY (MORGAN). b Okla 17 O 06. 5: Mary Hardin Baylor 50-52; Temple Jr Col 52-55 AA; Tex State Col for Women 55-57 BA in LS; Baylor U 61 (Educ). 6: Sp, Fr. 7: Legal sec Justice of Peace, Boyer & McConnell Perryton Tex 43-48; Sec & accountant VA Center, Temple Tex 48-55; Asst catlgr City Lib, Lubbock Tex 57; Chief Libn Mather AFB Cal 57-58; Med libn & gen libn VAC, Temple Tex 58-62; Med libn Darnall Army Hosp, Ft Hood Tex. 9: MedLA; Tex LA (Spec Libs Sect). 10: DAR; Temple Municipal Concert Assn; Phi Sigma Alpha. 14: Med, ref, bibliog, catlg. 15: 102 W Walker, Temple Tex 76501.

WADHAM, NORMAN (HARVEY). b Tenafly NJ 26 My 18. 4: Mary Wilson. 5: Hampden-Sydney Col 37-38 (Gen Arts); Columbia Col 39-40 (Liberal Arts) BA; Columbia 47-49 (Eng) MA, 49-52 (LS) MS. 6: Fr, Sp, Ger. 7: Advertis asst NJ Soc Hygiene Assn, Newark NJ 39-40; Pub rel asst Assn for Aid to European Children, NYC 40-41; Advertis asst Clco Chem Co, NYC 41; Advertis & pu rel asst Crouse-Hinds C, Syracuse NY 41-42; US Army (Cpl) tr Mil Govt, Europe 42-45; Circ libn Columbia U Burgess Lib 47-48; Asst coordinator ref serv Tchrs Col Columbia U 49-67, Asst to libn 67-. 8: Recorder at Paperbacks in Educ Conf, Oct 65; Asst coord Design for Paperbacks Conf June 66. 9: ALA. 10: PTA. 13: Yes. 14: Ref, readers serv, admin, bibliog. 15: Columbia Univ, Tchrs Col Lib, New York NY 10027.

WADLEY, CAPITOLA JOY (ANDERSON). b Stonewall Okla 26 Jl 16. 4: Dean M Wadley. 5: E Central State Col 33-37 (Eng, Elem Educ) BS; Columbia summer 40; LSU summer 41; Northeastern State Col 54-55 (Elem Educ) MAT; UOkla 63-65 MLS. 6: Sp. 7: Elem tchr Seminole Co Schs, Seminole Okla 36-40; Elem tchr Kit Carson Sch, San Diego 43-45; Elem tchr city & co schs, Tahlequah Okla 49-62; Asst libn Northeastern State Col (Tahlequah Okla) 63-. 9: NEA; OklaEA; OklaLA; SWLA; ALA. 10: Friends in Coun Study Club; PTA; Kiwanis; Chamber of Com; Faculty Wives Aux. 14: Govt docs, catl, ref, instr lib sci, info sci. 15: 110 Garrison, Tahlequah Okla 74464.

WADSWORTH, CAROL (ECKBERG). b Rochestr NY 28 D 27. 4: James W Wadsworth. 5: Wellesley 45-49 (Pol Sci) BA; Geneseo State Tchrs Col 49-50 BS in Lib Ed; Columbia 55-57 MLS.06: Fr. 7: Bkmob libn Berkshire Athenaeum, Pittsfield Mass 50-52; Libn Queens Borough Pub Lib, Jamaica NY 52-55, Sr libn 55-58, Supv libn 58-60; Asst dir Mid-York Lib System, Rome NY 61-63; Ref & readers adv Farmingdale Pub Lib, Farmingdale LI NY 63-65; Adult serv spec Brooklyn Pub Lib 65-. 9: NYLA; ALA; NY Lib Club. 10: ACLU. 13: Yes. 14: Ref. lib ext, adult serv. 15: 102 W 85th st, New York NY 10024.

WADSWORTH, CHARLOTTE (RILEY). b Paterson NJ 19 Ja 18. 4: Philip A Wadsworth. 5: Mt Holyoke 35-39 (Fr) BA; Columbia 39-40 (LS) BS; Mt Holyoke 41-43 (Fr) MA. 6: Fr, GER. 7: Res bk libn Mt Holyoke Col 40-42; Asst period room NY Pub Lib 43-44; Teen room libn Urbana Free Lib, Urbana Ill 60-62; Acquis asst UIll Lib (Urbana) 62-64; Acquis asst Rice U Lib 64-. 13: Yes. 15: 2114 McClendon st, Houston Tex 77025.

WADSWORTH, MARILYN (JENSEN). b Wellsville NY 25 Mr 43. 4: John A Wadsworth. 5: Harpur Col 61-63; Syracuse 63-65 (Geog) BA (Cum Laude), 65-66 MLS. 6: Fr, Ger. 7: Elem sch libn Cazenovia Central Schs, Cazenovia NY 66-67; Sci-tech ref libn Tech Info Ctr URochester 67-. 9: ALA; SLA; NYStateLA. 10: Rochester Mem Art Gallery; Beta Phi Mu. 14: Ref, circ, pub serv, lib educ. 15: 288 Yarmouth rd, Rochester NY 14610.

WADSWORTH, ROBERT WOODMAN. b Chicago 3 My 13. 5: Chicago 30-34 (Eng) PhB; Columbia 34-35 (Eng) AM; Chicago 39-43 (LS) AM. 6: Fr, Ger. 7: Research asst & assoc eng UChicago 37-43; Ref asst LC 43-44; UChicago Lib; Asst Prep Div 44-45, Chief Searcher Order Dept 45-46, Hd Ser Dept 46-47, Asst hd acquis dept 48-51, Hd acquis dept 52-66, Bibliogr for spec projects 67-; Lecturer grad Lib Sch UChicago 56-. 9: ALA (Chm DCC Com on Pub Rel & Recr 52-53; Bd on acquis of lib materials 54-56);-RTSD (Exec Bd 57-59, Coun-at-large 57-59; Tech serv coord routines survey com 63-66); Chicago Reg Group of Catlgrs & Clsfrs (pres 48-49); Chicago Lib Club (treas 53-54). 10: Phi Beta Kappa; Beta Phi Mu. 12: "Some Lacunae in Foreign Bibliography in "International Aspects of Librarianship (53). 13: Yes. 14: Bibliog, univ libnship, Govt publs. 15: 5451 Woodlawn ave, Chicago Il 60615.

WAGAR, ELSA (ANDERSON). b Arlington Mass 1 O 15. 4: Robert L J Wagar Jr. 5: Simmons 33-37 (LS) BS; Columbia 38; Heidelberg Col 63, 64, (Educ) Prov Spec; Ohio U 64-65 (Educ). 6: Swedish, Fr, Sp, Ger. 7: Child libn NY Pub Lib 37-41; Head Youth dept Parlin Lib, Everett Mass 41-42; Libn Bellevue High Sch, Bellevue Ohio 42-46; Head Libn Carnegie-Stahl Free Pub Lib, Bellevue Ohio 46-49; Head catlg dept Birchard Lib, Fremont Ohio 52-56; Libn Bellevue High Sch, Bellevue Ohio 63-. 9: ALA; NEA; OhioEA; OhioLA; OhioASchL. 10: Trustee, Carnegie-Stahl Free Pub Lib, Bellevue Ohio, 63-; Delta Kappa Gamma; Bus & Prof Women's Club. 14: Serv to ya, ctlg, ref. 15: 140 Huffman st, Bellevue Ohio 44811.

WAGBO, OLGA MARIE. b E Jordan Mich 29 Ap 07. 5: St Olaf Col 23-24; UChicago 25-29, 29-50 (Philos, Psych) PhB; ; UBesancon (France) summer 36 (Fr) UMich 58-59 BALS. ; UOslo (Norway) summer 61 (Norwegian). 6: Norwegian, Danish, Swedish, Fr, Ger, Sp, Lat. 7: Exec sec Chicago Sect Amer Chem Soc 29-52; Biller E Jordan Iron Wks, E Jordan Mich 53-55; Asst in research UMich 55-58; Order libn Herrick Pub Lib, Holland Mich 59-61; Readers adv Grand RRapids Pub Lib, Grand Rapids Mich 61-62, Catlg libn 62-. 9: ALA; MichLA; Grand Rapids Libns Club. 10: Grand Rapids Pub Lib Staff Assn; French So; ACLU. 14: Catlg, ref, rare bks. 15: 1510 Burke ave NE, Grand Rapids Mi 49505.

WAGEMAN, LYNETTE M. b Trinidad W Indies 18 Ag 34. 5: Park Col 55-59 (Mod For Lang) BA; UHawaii 65-66 MLS. 6: Fr, Sp, Hindi, Ger. 7: Ser libn EW Ctr Lib, Honolulu 62-65, Catlg libn 66-. 8: Lectr to Fulbright Orientation Gp in lib res in the humanities, summer 68. 9: HawaiiLA. 14: Catlg, ref. 15: 3655 Woodlawn ter pl, Honolulu Hi 96822.

WAGENKNECHT, ROBERT E(DWARD). b Seattle 8 D 35. 4: Therese Mueller. 5: Harvard 54-58 (Eng Lit) AB; Simmons 58-59 (LS) MS. 6: Fr. 7: Ref asst Detroit Pub Lib 59-61; Head Libn Stoneham PUB Lib, Stoneham Mass 61-63; Head Libn Winchester Pub Lib, Winchester Mass 63-67; Dir Lincoln Lib, Springfield Ill 67-. 8: Mem Mass State Commsn for Nat Lib Week (64, 65). 9: ALA; MusLA; NELA; Mass LA (Exec Bd 64-); Charles River Lib Club (pres 64-66); Greater Boston Pub Lib Admins (v-pres 66-67). 10: Rotary; Admin Mgt Soc; Sangamon Co Hist Soc. 12: Ed "Bay State Librarian (64-)66). 13: Yes. 14: Admin, educ, bldgs, comparative libnship. 15: 326 S 7th st, Springfield Il 62701.

WAGENKNECHT, THERESE (MUELLER). b Chicago 4 Mr 36. 4: Robert Edward Wagenknecht. 5: UMich 54-58 (Music) BMus, 58-60 (LS) MA. 6: Ger. 7: Research sec UMich Dept of Physiology 58-60; Music libn Wellesley Col 60-67; Lecturer in Lib Sci Northeastern U 65-67; Lecturer in Lib Sci Div So IllU 68-. 9: ALA; MusLA (Bd Dirs 65-67; chm Memb Com 64-68 chm NE Chap 63-65); , (chm Nominating Com 69-70). 10: Mu Phi Epsilon. 14: Admin, music ref. 15: 721 Woodland ave, Springfield Il 62704.

WAGENKNIGHT, MARGARET G (GASTON). b Chicago Ill 18 Jl 17. 4: Frank W Wagenknight. 5: Rutgers 61-66 (Hist) BA, 67-69 MLS. 6: Fr. 7: Clk Rutgers Lib (Camden) 66; Lib trainee Pennsauken Free Pub Lib, Pennsauken NJ 67, Act dir 67, Dir 68-. 9: ALA; NJLA. 14: Ref, tech serv. 15: 29 Evergreen dr, Willingboro NJ 08046.

WAGENVOORD, ELIZABETH V (GILLEY). b Cheyenne Wyo 29 Ja 15. 4: Cornelius Wagenvoord. 5: UNeb 32-36 (Eng, Hist) AB; Columbia 40 (LS) MS. 7: Asst libn pub lib, Cheyenne Wyo 38-44; Br libn Lib Assn of Portland Ore 44-52; Libn pub lib, Bethesda Md 52-55; Ref dept pub lib, Lansing Mich 60-65, Supv central serv 65-. 9: ALA (State chm Memb Com Mich); NEA; AEAUSA; MichLA; MichEA. 10: Altrusa; AAUW; Commun Serv Coun; Conserv Club; YWCA. 14: Adult serv, ref, a-v. 15: 401 S Capitol ave, Lansing Mi 48914.

WAGES, ORLAND. b Canton Tex 2 Ag 14. 4: Alice Humphreys Wages. 5: Tex Tech 36-39 (Educ); Stephen F Austin State Col ; BS in LS; E Tex State Col 57-58 MS in LS. 6: Ger. 7: Armed Serv Cavalry 40-42; Air Force (Capt) 42-48; Salesman Ralph Johnson Appliances, Salem Ore 48-51; Libn Jacksonville Col (Tex) 51-59; Documents libn & Instr in Lib Sci E Tex State Col 59-63; Libn Bridgewater Col (Va) 63-. 8: Ordained Minister of Missionary Baptist Church. 9: ALA; Amer Educl Research Assn; VaLA; SELA; Christian Lib Fellowship. 10: Ministerial Alliance; Kiwanis Internat; Rotary Intl; Nat Geneol Soc; Phi Delta Kappa; AETA; Shenandoah Valley Folklore Soc; Rockingham Hist Soc. 12: "The Church Librarians Handbook (61); Ed "Virginia Librarian. 1: Yes. 13: Yes. 14: Admin, catlg, rare bks. 15: Bridgewater Col Lib, Bridgewater Va 22813.

WAGG, MARILYNN. b Uxbridge Ont Can 28 Je 33. 5: Macdonald Inst 51-55 (Clothing & Textiles) BHS; Toronto 56-57 BLS. 6: Fr, Ger. 7: Br libn Dept of Labour, Ottawa 57, Ser libn 58-59; Asst catlgr Dept of Nat Health & Welfare, Ottawa 59-60, Tech serv libn 61-. 9: CanLA. 10: Prof Inst (Libns Sect) of The Govt of Can. 14: Catlg, acquis, ref. 15: Apt 1020, 1071 Ambleside dr, Ottawa 4 Can.

WAGGONER, JOHN PHILIP JR. b Roanoke Va 15 My 13. 4: Kathryn Byrne Ware. 5: Duke 31-35 (Religion) AB; Duke U Sch of Religion 35-38 (Comparative Religion) BD; UNC 46-47 BS in LS. 7: Bibliog LC 40-42; Mil Intelligence US Army (Capt) 43-46; Duke U Lib: Bibliog 46-47, Ref libn 47-48, Head circ dept 48-54, Asst libn 54-. 9: ALA; SELA; NCLA. 14: Readers serv. 15: 2812 Devon rd, Durham NC 27707.

WAGGONER, MIRIAM. b Dupont Ind 26 O 08. 5: Hanover Col 27-30 (Phys Educ, Lat, Soc Studies) BA; State U Iowa 30-34 (Phys Educ) MA; Ind U 51-54 (LS) MA. 6: Lat, Sp. 7: Phys educ tchr Winchester Pub Schs, Winchester Ind 30-32; Dir of Phys Educ Iowa Wesleyan Col 34-35; Dir of Phys Educ Northwest Mo State Tchrs Col 35-42; Interviewer in personnel Eli Lily Pharmaceuical Co, Indianapolis 42-45; Head Libn Baptist Bible Sem (Johnson City NY) 50-. 9: ALA; Christian Libns Fellowship (Pub Rel off, mem ed com); PennLA. 10: Pi LAMBDA Theta. 15: Baptist Bible Seminary 538 Venard rd, Clarks Summit Pa 18411.

WAGGONER, PHYLLIS (ANDERSON). b Kirkland Wash 20 Je 21. 4: Kenneth L Waggoner. 5: UCal(Berkeley) 43 (Hist) AB, 44 Sch of Libnship Certif. 7: Pan Amer World Airways, Pacific-Alaska Div, San Francisco Asst libn 44-45, Libn 46-57, Research analyst 58-59; Libn & research analyst First Western Bank which merged into United california Bank, San Francisco 60-61; Libn Fed Reserve Bank of San Francisco 62-. 9: SLA (Chap pres, & var other offs); CalLA (var com duties). 10: San Francisco Symphony; San Francisco Mus of Art. 15: Fed Res Bank of San Francisco 400 Sansome st, San Francisco Ca 94120.

WAGMAN, FREDERICK H(ERBERT). b Springfield Mass 12 O 12. 4: Ruth Jeannette Wagman. 5: Amherst 33 AB; Columbia 34 AM, 42 PhD; Amherst 58 LHD; Alderson-Broaddus 67 LLD. 6: Ger, Fr. 7: Instr in Ger in Ext Columbia U 33-35; Tchg Fellow Amherst Col 36-37; Instr in Ger UMinn 37-42; Head Planning UNIT & Regulations & Train Sect, & Regulations Off US Off of Censorship, Postal Div 42-45; Act dir of personnel & admin serv, Asst dir Ref Dept, Dir of Processing Dept, Deputy chief asst libn & Dir of Admin LC 45-53; Dir UMich Lib 53-. 8: V-chm Commsn on Obscenity & Pornography 68-; Nat Lib Med Bd Regents 67-. 9: Coun on Lib Resources Inc (Bd Dirs 58-); ALA (pres 63-64, Coun 57-61); ARL (Exec Bd 65-68); Nat Union Catlg Subcom; Nat Lib Week (v-chm 64, Steering Com 62-64); Nat Bk Com (Nat Bd 61-); MichLA (pres 59). 10: Rotary Club; Univ Club; Mich Acad of Sci, Arts& Letter; Phi Beta Kappa; Phi Kappa Phi. 12: "Magic and Natural Science in German Baroque Literature (42). 13: Yes. 15: Univ of Mich Lib, Ann Arbor Mich 48104.

WAGNER, ALICE LOUISE. b Hamilton Ohio 20 F 28. 5: Millersville State Col 46-50 (LS) BS in Ed; Columbia 53-57 MS in LS; Penn State U, Temple U, West Mich U ; UColo 50-. 7: Reserve bk asst Sullivan Lib Temple U 46; Summer sub libn Free Lib of Phila 44-52; Libn Council Rock Jr-Sr High Sch, Newton Penn 50-60; Lab Sch Libn Millersville State Col 60-68; Asst Prof Lib Educ 60-. 9: ALA; NEA; PennLA; PennStateEA (Dept of Supv & Curr); PennSchLA (memb chm, pres 68-70); ASCD. 10: Girl Scouts; Commun Coun Lancaster Co; AAUP. 14: Ch libs, child & yp wk, lib educ. 15: 207 E Orange st, Lancaster Penn 17602.

WAGNER, BARBARA LOU. b Youngstown Oho 28 Mr 40. 5: Heidelberg Col 58-60, 61-62 (Biol) AB; UHeidelberg (Germany) 60-61 (Ger); ohio State U summer 62 (Bot); Ore State U 62-63 (Microbiology); West Res 63-64 MS in LS. 6: Ger, Fr. 7: Tchg asst Microbiol Dept Ore State U 62-63; Grad asst Mather Col West Res U 63-64; Gen prof asst Winchester (Mass) Pub Lib 64-66; Libn Tiffin U 66-69; Circ libn Colo State U (Ft Collins) 69-. 9: ALA; SLA; OhioLA. 10: AAUW; Town & Country Garden Club. 14: Ref, info storage & retrieval, admin. 15: The Libraries Colo State Univ, Ft Collins Co 80521.

WAGNER, BETTY LOU. b Miles City Mont 20 My 28. 4: Ronald Wagner. 5: Wash State U 46-50 (Eng, Journalism) BA; UWash 50-51 (LS) BA; Seattle U 52-54. 7: Libn Arch & Urban Planning Br UWash 51-. 9: SLA; Coun f Planning Libns; SLA (Pacific NW Chap: Program Chm 62-63, Memb Chm 64-65); pres 65-66; dir 66-67; Nominating chm 67-68; ALA. 14: Spec libs. 15: Arch & Urban Planning Lib Univ of Wash, Seattle 98105.

WAGNER, CAROLYN ANN. b Elgin Neb 5 N 42. 5: Neb WesleyanU 60-61; Kearney State Col 61-64 (Home Econ) BS in Ed; UDenver 64-65 (Libnship) MA. 7: Asst libn sci & tech div uneb (Lincoln) 65-67, Asst pub serv libn asst prof 67-68; Army libn Spec Serv Lib us army Hosp, Wurzburg Germany 68-. 9: ALA (European Subsect Armed Forces Sect); NebLA (chm Col & Univ Sect). 10: AAUP. 14: Ref, sci libs. 15: Special Serv Lib US Army Hosp Wurzburg, APO NY 09801.

WAGNER, ELSIE BARBARA LOUISE. b Central Butte Sask Can 2 N 17. 5: Victoria Normal Sch 49-50 BC Tchrs Certif; UBC 62 (Hist, Sch Libnship) BEd, 66 (Sch Libnship) MAEd. 6: Ger. 7: Sch Dist #11, BC Can: Tchr Central Sch 50-51 Tchr & libn Laura J Morrish sch 51-56, Tchr Jr Secondary Sch 57-59, Libn Jr Secondary Sch 59-64, 65-67, Libn Rossland High Sch summers 64 & 65, Libn J Lloyd Crowe Sr Secondary Sch 67-; Exchange tchr Morgan Sch, Cincinnati 56-57; Libn N Vancouver Secondary Sch 65. 9: CanLA; BCLA; BCSchLA (pres). 10: Luth Acad for Scholarship; Trail and Dist Assn of Univ Women; Assn of BC Libns; Rossland-Trail Soroptimists. 13: Yes. 14: Sch libnship. 15: 313 Sylvia Crescent trail, BC Can.

WAGNER, ERNEST CHRISTOPHER. b Crockett Tex 25 D 18. 4: Johnice Sutton. 5: Morehous Col 48 (Hist) BA; Atlanta 49 BS in LS; UIll 56 MS in LS. 7: Head Libn Butler Col 50-51; Head lIbn Shaw U 51-52; Acquis libn Tex So U 52-53; Head Libn Dillard U 5363; Head Libn Col of the Virgin Islands (St Thomas) 63-. 9: ALA; SWLA (chm Const & By-Laws Com 52-53). 14: Col lib admin. 15: P O Box 2463, St Thomas VI 00802.

WAGNER, FRANCIS STEPHEN. b Korpona Hungary 28 F 11. 4: Irene Trefny. 5: USzeged (Hungary) 31-35 (Hist, Ling, Philos) Tchrs Diploma, 35-37 (Hist, Philos) Tchrs Diploma, 40 (Hist, Lit, Philos) PhD. 6: Hungarian, Slovak, Czech, Russian, Ger, Polish, Fr, Lat. 7: Instr & libn USzeged Hist Dept (Hungary) 35-38; Prof State Tchrs Col, Budapest 38-45; Hd Ministry of For Affairs Czech Div, Budapest 45-46; Hd Hungarian Consulate Gen, bratislavia Czechoslovakia 46-48; Asst ed E European Accessions Index LC 53-61, Subj catlgr-tr Cyrillic Bibliog Project 62-65, Subj catlgr subj catlg div 65-. 9: AHA; Amer Studies Assn; Civil War RT DC; Washington Phil Club. 10: Helicon Soc of Toronto. 12: "Citanka" (39); "First Period of Slovak Nationalism" (40); "Cultural Revolution in east Europe" (55); "The Hungarian Revolution in Perspective" (67). 13: Yes. 14: Subj catlg, rare bks, bibliog, hist of the bk. 15: 4610 Franklin st, Kensington Md 20795.

WAGNER, FRANK (STEVENS) JR. b Temple Tex 26 Ag 25. 4: Marian Johnson. 5: Southwest Tex State Col 47 (Chem) MA. 6: Ger, Fr, Ital, Sp. 7: Prof of chem Schreiner Inst, Kerrville Tex 48-50; Chem Celanese Corp of Amer, Bishop Tex 50-54; Tech libn Celanese Chem Co, Corpus Christi Tex 54-65, Hd info ctr 65-. 8: Decipherment of Middle & Old Egyptian hieroglyphics; Author articles on acetals, ketals, crotonaldehyde, cyclic alcohols in encyclopedias. 9: SLA (pres Tex Chap); ACS (So Tex Sect; past sec, pres). 13: Yes. 14: Chem info center. 15: P O Box 2768, Corpus Christi Tex 78403.

WAGNER, JANE (ELIZABETH). b Elba Ohio 1 O 27. 5: Ohio State U 44-48 (Hist) BA; West Res 48-49 MSLS. 7: Asst ref dept Lima Pub Lib, Lima Ohio 49-2; Cincinnati Pub Lib: Asst circ dept 52-53, Asst govt & bus dept 53-56, 1st asst educ & religion dept 56-. 9: ALA; OhioLA; -ASD (Coord Com on Materials 68-69). 10: Pilot Club Phi Beta Kappa. 14: Ref. 15: 3424 Brookline ave, Cincinnati Oh 45220.

WAGNER, LLOYD FELIX. b Dubuque Iowa 29 Je 18. 4: Martina App. 5: Lafayette Col 46-49 (Pol Sci) AB; Catholic U 49-50 (LS) MS. 7: US Army Field Artillery (T/4 Sgt) 41-45; Order libn Iona Col 50; Ref libn US Army Lib Pentagon Wash DC 51; Libn Central Intelligence Agency, Wash DC 52; Libn Combat Surveillance Group, Alexandria Va 58; Supv Whippany Lib Bell Telephone Labs Inc, Whippany NJ 58-65; Chief lib serv div Fed Aviation Agency, Wash DC 66; Dir libs Catholic U 67-. 9: SLA (dir NY Chap 64-). ; ALA; CathLA (various offs); ASIS. 14: Lib admin. 15: 9220 Manchester rd, Silver Spring Md 20901.

WAGNER, MARIE KATHARINE. b Wiliamsport Penn 28 My 11. 5: W Chester State Tchrs Col 28-30 Tchg Certif, 30-40 BS Ed. 7: Tchr Williamsport Pub Sch System, Williamsport Penn 32-43 Off WAC, US Army 43-46; Asst circ libn UOre Med Sch Lib 47-65, Circ libn 65-. 9: MedLA; OreLA; Portland area Spec Libns. 10: Geol Soc of the Ore Country; Portland Art Assn; YWCA. 15: Univ of Ore Med Sch Lib, Portland Ore 97201.

WAGNER,PAUL R. b Springfield Vt 3 S 38. 5: Clark U 56-60 (Eng) AB; Yale (Hist of Theater) 60-61; Simmons 62-63 (LS) MS. 6: Fr. 7: Research asst UConn summer 59; Instr Eng N Plainfield (NJ) High Sch 61-62; Subj spec Pub Lib, Worcester Mas 63-64, Head humanities div 64-66; Curator spec collections Princeton U Lib 66-. 10: Phi Beta Kappa. 12: Mem ed bd "The Princeton University Library Chronicle. 13: Yes. 14: Ref, rare bks & spec collections. 15: Princeton Univ Lib, Princeton NJ 08540.

WAHL, KATHRYN JANE. b Portland Ore 27 Je 25. 5: Clark Col 58-60 (Liberal Arts); Portland State Col summer 59; UPortland 60-62 (Liberal Arts) BA, 62-63 MLS66- (Hist). 7: UPortland: Spec serv libn 63-64, Circ ref 64, Circ libn 64-65, Spec serv libn 65-66; Circ libn 66-68; Asst libn 68-. 9: ALA; PNLA; Pacific NW Bibliog Center (UPortland rep 64-); OreLA; CathLA. 10: Portland Area Spec Libns. 12: Circ ed "University of Portland Review. 14: Ref, circ, periods. 15: 2307 NE 49th st, Vancouver Wash 98663.

WAHLS, FREDERICA (BUNTON). b Marion Ind 19 Je 15. 5: UDayton 44-46 (Eng) BA; UMich 47-49 ABLS; UWis 54-59 (Eng); De Paul U 64 (Eng). 6: Fr. 7: Circ asst Dayton Pub Lib, Dayton Ohio 46-47; Lib serv scholar UMich 47-49; Head of ref Tex So U 50-52; Ref libn & Consul on mus Madison Pub Lib, Madison Wis 52-60; Ref libn Roosevelt U 60-61; Head libn Camp McCoy, Camp McCoy Wis 62; Head libn De La Salle Inst, Chicago 62-. 8: Chicago Mayors Commsn on Human Rights. 9: ALA; CathLA; IllLA. 10: YWCA. 12: "Poems in Ebony Rhythm, B M Murhy ed (48). 13: Yes. 14: Ref. 15: 3420 Cottage Grove ave, Chicago Il 60616.

WAHOSKI, HELEN (ISABEL). b Ripon Wis 7 Jl 10. 5: Ripon Col 32 (Eng) BA; UFribourg Switzerland summer 49 (LS); UMich 52 (LS) AM. 7: Ref libn State Hist Soc of Wis, Madison Wis 37-46; Catlgr Wis State U (Oshkosh) 46-50 Head Libn 50-, Assoc Prof Lib Sci 50-; chm Lib Sci 50-68. 8: Chm lib sci dept Wis StateU (Oshkosh) 65-68; Assoc Prof 65-; Seminar in changes in upper secondary & higher educ in Europe, March 69. 9: ALA (v-chm & chm Tchr Educ Sect 58-62; chm State Recr Lib Educ Div 57-); WisLA (pres 63-64; chm Awards & Honors Com 61-62; chm Personnel & Prof Problems Com 57-58; chm Org & By-Laws Com 66-67; mem 67-69; chm Lib Educ Com 67-68; Exec Bd Col & Univ Lib Sect 67-68); WisEA. 10: Beta Phi Mu; Oshkosh Catholic Womens Club; AAUW; LWV; Oshkosh C of C Womens Div); Delta Kappa Gamma; Bus & Prof Womens Club. Clu; Amer Assn for State & Local Hist; Wis State Hist Soc; Intl Platform Assn; Intl Reading Assn; Delta Kappa Gamma; Coord Coun on Higher Educ Adv Com on Libs. 11: WisLA Libn of the Year, 58. 13: Yes. 14: Univ lib admin, lib educ, recr for libnship. 15: 1005 E New York ave, Oshkosh Wi 54901.

WAIDELICH, ANN ELIZABETH (RYAN). b Baltimore 1 D 41. 5: Miami U 59-63 (Speech Theraph) BS; Rosary Col summer 63 (LS); UDenver 63-64 (LS) MA. 7: Libn trainee Chicago Pub Lib 63; Lib asst UColo Med Lib 64; Libn II Madison Wis 64-. 9: WisLA; ALA. 14: Ref. 15: 317 Norris court, Madison Wi 53703.

WAINIO, BETTY DENT. b Quincy Mass 15 Mr 18. 4: Walter W Wainio. 5: Conn Col 36-40 (Econ) BA; Rutgers 60-63 MLS. 6: Fr, Sp. 7: Research libn Chicopee Mfg Corp, Milltown NJ 57-62; Ref libn Princeton Pub Lib, Princeton NJ 63-64; Ref libn Free Pub Lib, Somerville NJ 65-69, Dir 69. 9: ALA; NJLA. 14: Ref. 15: 477 Walnut lane, Princeton NJ 08540.

WAINWRIGHT, ALEXANDER D. b Ventnor NJ 26 Je 17. 5: Princeton U 35-39 (Eng) AB; Columbia 40-41 (LS) BS. 6: Fr. 7: Asst Libn Cooper Union, NYC 41-42; 1st Lt Ord US Army 42-46; Princeton U Lib: Asst prep dept 46-48, Curator Morris L Parrish Collection 48-, Asst libn for acquis 62-. 9: Association Internationale de Bibliophilie; ALA; BSA; Bibliog Soc UVa; Bibliog Soc (England); Mss Soc. 10: Grolier Club; Hist Soc of Penn. 12: Ed "The Princeton University Library Chronicle (49-62). 13: Yes. 14: Acquis, rare bks. 15: 46 N Stanworth dr, Princeton NJ 08540.

WAINWRIGHT, JUDITH. b NYC 10 Ap 23. 5: UIowa 44-48 (Speech, Drama) BFA; UCal (Berkeley) 65-66 MLS. 6: Fr, Ger. 7: Asst in costume UWash 48-50; Warehouse supv camp Roberts Cal 50-52; Asst acquis libn USan Francisco 66-68, Asst ref libn 68, Act hd ref 68, Hd ref 69-. 14: Ref, rare bks, acquis. 15: 2674 McAllister st, San Francisco Ca 94117.

WAITERS, DOROTHY. b Charlotte NC 8 F 43. 5: Johnson C Smith 62-63, 65-68 (Soc Sci) BA; AtlantU 68-69 MS in LS. 6: Fr. 7: Lib page Pub Lib of Charlotte & Mecklenberg Co, Charlotte 65, Adult commun serv libn 66-68. 9: ALA; NC Adult EA; MecklenburgLA. 14: Commun serv. 15: 1833 Irma st, Charlotte NC 28208.

WAITY, GLORIA (ANDERSON). b Wausau Wis 27 F 33. 4: Charles Nelson Waity. 5: UWis 51-55 (Recreational Leadership) BS (Ed), summers 56, 57, 59 MLS, 67-69. 7: Libn Monona Grove High Sch, Madison Wis 55-60; Bkmob libn Wis Free Lib Commsn Hdqrs, Madison Wis summer 60; Ya libn Madison Pub Lib, Madison Wis 60-63; Libn La Follette High Sch, Madison Wis 63-67; Lib career specialist WisLA 69-. 9: ALA (Coun 65-69);-YASD (Magazine Eval Com 62-68); WisLA (co-chm Memb Com 63-64); WisEA (v-pres Lib Sect 59-60). 10: Mortar Board. 13: Yes. 14: Ya, sch libs, lib educ, recruitment. 15: 530 E Lakeview ave, Madison Wis 53716.

WAJENBERG, ARNOLD S(HERMAN). b Indianapolis Ind 11 Ap 29. 4: Joyce Elaine Dunham. 5: Butler U 47-51 (Gk) BA, 51-53 (Hebrew, Aramic) MA; Chicago 53-55 (LS) MA, 55-59 (Ancient Near East Hist). 6: Sp, Ger, Fr, Hebrew, Aramaic, Gk, Ugaritic. 7: Br floater Indianapolis Pub Lib 51-53; Catlgr UChicago Lib 53-61, Asst head catlgr 61-. 9: ALA; Chicago Reg Group of Libns for Tech Serv. 14: Catlg. 15: Univ of Chicago Lib, Chicago Il 60637.

WAKEFIELD, GRACE (SMITH). b Glen Allen Ala 12 My 1900. 5: Florence State summers 24-28 (Eng); Howard Col summers 30-34 (Eng) BS Ed; UGa summers 54 (Educ); Peabody summers 57-60 MALS. 6: Fr. 7: Eng tchr Jr High Sch, Glen Allen Ala 20-26; Eng tchr-libn Sr High Sch, Addison Ala 26-35; Eng tchr-libn Ala Boys Ind Sch, Birmingham Ala 35-46; Eng tchr-libn & asst prin Sr High Sch, Addison Ala 46-48; Prin elem & sr high sch, Addison Ala 48; Eng tchr Sr High Sch Marion Co, Guin Ala 48-50; Libn sr high sch, Rossville Ga 50-58; Head libn Mt Berry Acad 58-. 8: Catlgr Mt Berry Col Mem Lib summer 65. 9: ALA; SELA; GaEA; GaLA. 10: Alpha Delta Kappa; Bus & Prof Womens Club; Intl Quto Club; Berry Womans Club; AAUW. 13: Yes. 14: Admin, catlg, ref. 15: Barstow Mem Lib, Mt Berry Ga 30149.

WAKEFIELD, JACQUELINE M (HANSEN). b Pasadena Cal 10 Je 29. 4: Ralph E Wakefield Jr. 5: Pasadena City Col 46-48 (Arch) AA; USoCal 48 (Arch); Cal State Col (Los Angeles) 63-67 (Amer Studies) BA; Immaculate Heart Col 67-68 MLS. 6: Ger. 7: Proctor Arcadia Unified Sch Dist, Arcadia Col 63-66; Child libn Los Angeles Pub Lib, Canoga Park Br 68-69; Coord child serv Ventura Co & City Lib, Ventura Cal 69-. 9: ALA; CalLA; So Cal coun on Lit for Child & yp. 14: Child bks and serv. 15: 4341 No Hartfield ct, W Lake Village Ca 91360.

WAKEFIELD, SUSAN POLK. b Shelbyville Tenn 28 D 40. 5: Middle Tenn State Col 59-63 (ENG) AB; Peabody 63-64 MA(LS). 6: Ger, Sp. 7: Ser libn; Vanderbilt Med Ctr Lib, Nashville 64-67, UVa Sch of Med Lib fall 67; Ref libn A W Calhoun Med Lib Emory 68-. 9: MedLA; TennLA. 10: Beta Phi Mu; Mended Hearts Inc. 14: Ser, ref. 15: AW Calhoun Mem Lib, Woodruff Res bldg, Emory Univ, Atlanta Ga 30322.

WAKELAND, KAY. b Oklahoma City Okla 29 Mr 38. 4: Edward W Wakeland. 5: UOkla 56-59, 61-62 (Journalism) BA, 62-63 MLS. 7: Trust dept clk, Denver 59-60; Acquis clk UOkla 60-61, Page 61-62; Okla State Lib Pub Libs Div summer 64; Asst adult serv Okla City Pub Libs 64-66; Hd libn Ardmore Pub Libs, Ardmore Okla 67-. 9: ALA; OklaLA. 10: AAUW; Commun Concert Assn. 14: Admin. 15: Grand & E NW, Ardmore Ok 73401.

WAKEVAINEN, ALDEN W. b Ramsay Mich 23 S 23. 5: UMich 41-46 BA, 48-49 AMLS. 6: Finnish. 7: Libn Armed Forces Med Lib, Wash DC 49-51; Dir US Info Ctr, helsinki, Finland 51-53; Libn Bessemer Twp Pub Lib, Ramsay Mich 53-57; Dir Upper Peninsula Br Mich State Lib, Escanaba 57-60; Ref libn Pub Lib Development Mich State Lib, Lansing 60-62; Dir Mich State Lib for the Blind, Lansing 62-63; Hd standards & evaluation Penn State Lib, Harrisburg 63-. 9: ALA; -AHIL; Amer Correct Assn; PennLA. 14: Pub lib devel, inst libs. 15: 936 N Second st, Harrisburg Pa 17102.

WALBRIDGE, SHARON LEE. b Kalamazoo Mich 8 Ja 42. 5: West MichU 59-63 (Eng) BA, 63-64 (LS) MA. 6: Sp, Ger. 7: Asst catlgr West MichU 64-66; Asst catlgr Penn StateU (University Park) 66-67, Hd bibliog control div 67-68; Reclsf dir Antioch Col 68-69, Libn for tech processes 69-. 9: ALA. 10: US Twirling Assn. 14: Catlg, acquis. 15: 325 W Center College apt 129, Yellow Springs Oh 45387.

WALCH, DAVID BEAN. b LaGrande Ore 19 My 36. 4: Phyllis Collins. 5: East Ore Col 54-56, 58-60 (Hist) BA, M Ed; UIll 61-62 MS, MLS; UIll 68-69 Certif of Advanced Study. 7: Tchr LaGrande Pub Schs, LaGrande Ore 60-61; Asst libn The Church Col of Hawaii, Laie Hawaii 62-65, Dir of Lib Serv 65-67; Asst Prof of Lib Sci UUtah 67-. 8: Libn, Hawaii Br GENEAL Lib, 65-. 9: NEA; ALA; UtahLA. 13: Yes. 14: Admin, ref, tchg, instr media. 15: 39 East 1400 S, Bountiful Ut 84010.

WALCOTT, M ALENA. b Lachine Que Can 25 Je 15. 5: McGill 33-37 (Lat, Gk, Eng) BA, 37-38 BLS; UIll 52-53 (LS) MS, 54-56 (LS). 6: Lat, Fr, Sp, Gk. 7: Libn Kings Col (NJ) 38-41; Asst Engnr Lib Columbia U 41-44; Sr catlgr act supv ser div catlg dept Columbia U 44-48; Head catlgr Law Lib UVa 48-52; Ser reviser catlg dept UIll(Urbana) 52-56; Asst Prof Lib Sch Pratt Inst 56-58; Head catlgr Brandels U Lib 58-. 9: ALA; SLA; Bibliog Soc UVa; NELA. 10: Inter-Varsity Christian Fellowship. 14: Catlg. 15: 29-9 Garden Circle, Waltham Mass 02154.

WALDECK, FRED. b b Muenster Germany 4 My 03. 5: UFreiburg(German) 22-23 (Chem); Upsala Col 48-49 (Modern Langs) BA; Columbia 50 MS(LS). 6: Ger, Fr, Sp, Russian, Dano-Norwegian, Dutch. 7: D A Censor analyst US War Dept US Mil Govt (OMGB) Munich 45-48; Ref asst UIda 50-52; Asst ref libn Oakland (Cal) Pub Lib 53-57; Asst hd ref A R Mann Lib Cornell U 57-. 9: ALA. 13: Yes. 14: Ref, rare bks (HIST OF SCI). 15: 522 E State st, Ithaca NY 14850.

WALDEMAR, DAVID L. b Rochester Minn 30 My 34. 4: Carla Bryce. 5: Rochester Jr Col 52-55 AA; UMinn 55-56 (Art Hist) BA, 56-57 (LS) MA. 6: Fr. 7: Jr libn Milwaukee Pub Lib 57-60; Prof asst Minneapolis Pub Lib 60-65; Libn Hennepin Co Pub Lib, Excelsior Minn 65-69, St Louis Park 69-. 9: MinnLA. 10: Walker Art Center; Center Opera Co; CLU. 14: Ref. 15: 2632 Humboldt S, Minneapolis Mn 55408.

WALDEN, CAROL MARGARET. b Uncasville Conn 26 F 07. 5: Radcliffe 24-28 (Eng) BA; Simmons 42-44 BSLS. 6: Fr. 7: Lib asst Harvard Med Sch 28-31; Head catlgr Brookline Pub Lib, Brookline Mass 31-47; Music libn Radcliffe Col 47-49; Head Libn New Eng Conservatory of Music 49-68; Ref libn Wellesley Free Lib, Wellesley Mass 68-. 9: MusLA; MassLA. 10: The Cecilia Soc; Nat Travel Club. 14: Admin, catlg. 15: 146 Great Plain ave, Needham Mass 00192.

WALDEN, ELIZABETH H. b New Haven Conn. 5: Columbia 44 (Educ) BS; West Res 48 BS in LS, 53 MS in LS. 6: Fr. 7: Br libn New Haven Pub Lib, New Haven Conn 32-45; Circ chief Central Conn State Col 45-64 Asst Prof spec serv libn 64-. 9: ConnLA; East States Assn for Tchr Educ (past treas, pres). 10: AAUW; AAUP; Charter Oak Color Slide Assn; Bus & Prof Womans Club. 13: Yes. 14: Tchg lib sci, wk with yp, ref. 15: 119 Marlin rd, New Britain Conn 06053.

WALDHORN, KATHARINE (WOHL). b Tampa Fla 13 O 23. 5: UTampa 40-44 (Eng, Hist) BS in Ed; UWis 48-49 BLS; UMich 61-63 Advanced MLS. 6: Anglo-Saxon. 7: Libn UWis Lib (Madison) 48-49; Libn Med Research Mun Tuberculosis Sanitorium, Chicago 49-50; Libn Dearborn Pub Lib, Dearborn Mich 50-57, Dir of publicity & publns 57-64; City libn Ypsilanti Pub Lib, Ypsilanti Mich 64-. 9: MichLA (Recr Com, chm Adult Educ Sect, sec Ref Sect). 14: Admin, rare bks. 15: 4792 Washtenaw rd, Ann Arbor Mi 48104.

WALDNER, CLAIRE (R). b Ashland Penn 18 O 23. 5: Allegheny Col 41-45 (Langs) BA; Drexel 62-63 MLS. 7: Clerk Foreign Serv of US Dept of State, Wash DC, Prague, Berlin, Panama City 45-51; Records consul Remington Rand Div of Sperry Rand, Phila & Denver 51-61; Bus libn Merck Sharp & Dohme, W Point Penn 63-65; Supv of research info Towers Perrin Forster & Crosby Inc, Phila 65-67; Hd reader serv UPenn Med Sch Lib 68-. 9: SLA; Spec Libs Coun, Phila (Recr Chm); Memb Chm. 10: AAUW; Pilot Club; Phi Beta Kappa; Rittenhouse Swim Club. 14: Admin, info retrieval, ref. 15: 2100 Walnut, Phila Pa 19103.

WALDRON, ESTHER C. b Pittsburgh. 5: UPittsburgh 47-51 (Chem) BS; Carnegie 51-55 (Chem) MS, 57-61 MS in LS. 7: Libn Carnegie Lib of Pittsburgh 57-66; US Bur of Mines 66-67; UPittsburgh 68-. 9: SLA; ACS. 10: Beta Phi Mu. 14: Sci-tech ref, catlg. 15: 7316 Woodlawn ave, Pittsburgh Pa 15218.

WALDRON, HELEN J. b Nampa Ida 15 Ag 16. 5: UWash 35-38 (Fr) BA, 38 Sch Lib Certif; UGrenoble 48-49 (Fr); UCal 50-51 (Fr) MA. 6: Fr. 7: Secondary sch tchr & sch libn pub high schs, Wash 39-44; Womens Air Corps (T/Sgt) 44-48; Catlgr & ref libn Nat War Col, Wash DC 51-55; Head of tech documents sect Naval Proving Ground, Dahlgren Va 55-58; Asst libn The Rand Corp, Santa Monica Cal 58-62, Libn 62-. 8: Adv Bd; usoCal Sch Lib Sci 64-68; Cal State Lib 68-71; Occasional lectr; usoCal Sch Lib Sci, UCLA Sch Lib Serv, Immaculate Heart Col Sch Lib Sci. 9: SLA (Program Conv Chm 68, pres So Cal Chap 63-64); Program Chm Internat Conf 68, chm Assoc Adv Coun 69-70); ASIS; Nat Microfilm Assn; CalLA. 10: AAAS. 13: Yes. 14: Admin, ref, automation. 15: RAND Corp, 1700 Main st, Santa Monica Cal 90406.

WALDRON, RODNEY KING. b Newberg Ore 15 F 19. 4: Virginia Lay. 5: UDenver 48-50 (Hist) BA, 50 (LS) MA. 7: (M/Sgt) 77th Infantry Div, Pacific Theatre 42-45; Asst state archivist Colo State Archives, Denver 50; Catlgr Mo Hist Soc, Columbia Mo 51; Admin asst UIda 51-52, Asst libn 52-54; Ore State U: Admin asst 54-65, Asst libn 65, Libn 65-. 8: Lib consl (bldg planning) Pacific Luth U, 64-65; Chm Ore State U Archives Com; Chm Ore State U Centennial Com 64-; Tchr, Lib Admin, UOre Grad Sch of Libnship summer 69. 9: PNLA (treas, pres 65-66, chm numerous coms). 10: Rotary Internat; Cub Scouts; Phi Theta Kappa; Pi Gamma Mu; PTA. 12: Comp "Theses & Dissertations, 1943-1959" (60); Co-auth "Instructions for Ore State U Preparation of the Thesis" (57, rev 62, 64, 66); Auth "Use of a Technical Library," Engrg Exper Stat Circ 6 (64). 13: Yes. 14: Admin, catlg, automation. 15: 445 N 31st, Corvallis Ore 97330.

WALDROP, RUTH WIGGINS. b May Tex 30 Mr 11. 4: James Curtis Waldrop. 5: Livingston State Tchrs Col 29-34 BS; UAla 43-46 (LS), 59-60 (Educ) MA; UDenver summer 62 (LS)SUNY (Albany) 62 (Media). 7: Libn: Hewitt-Trussville High Sch, Trussville Ala, Shades Valley High Sch, Birmingham Ala, Howard Col; Staff UAla Lib; Lib consul Jefferson Co Bd of Educ, Birmingham currently60-68; Staff NDEA Insts; usoCal 66, UTenn 67, Auburn U 68; Instr UAla 60-67; Lib consul State Dept Educ, Montgomery Ala 68-69; Chm Dept of Sch Libnship UAla 69-. 8: Chm, Summer wkshop, Ala Sch Libns 65. 9: NEA; ALA-AASchL; Dist Dir Reg V 68-70); SELA (chm Child & Sch Libns Div 65-67); AlaLA; pres 67-68, chm Lib Educ Com 68); AlaASchL (pres 65); AlaEA. 10:Alpha Alpha Alpha; Delta Kappa Gamma. 12; evaluating the Elementary School Library Program (64). 13: Yes. 14: Consul serv for sch libs. , instr media. 15: 3638 E Fernway dr, Montgomery Al 36104.

WALENSKY, LUCILE C. b Sioux City Iowa 3 Mr 21. 5: Morningside Col 39-40, 42-43 (Eng, Hist) BA; Grinnell Col 40-42; Tex Woman'sU 63-64, 65 MSLS. 6: Fr. 7: Reader's adv Sioux City Pub Lib, Sioux City Iowa 64-66; Adult serv libn Marshalltown Pub Lib, Marshalltown Iowa 66-67; Dir Yankton Carnegie Lib, Yankton SDak 67-. 8: Asst dir Nat Lib Week SD 69. 9: ALA; SDLA (chm Pub Lib Div 68-69); YanktonLA (v-pres 68-69, pres 69-70). 10: Sioux City Jr League; Yankton Civic Coun; Yankton Woman's Club. 14: Readers adv, adult educ. 15: Yankton Carnegie Lib 401 Capitol, Yankton SD 57078.

WALES, (INA) KATHERINE. b Bracebridge Ont Can 28 Mr 07. 5: Toronto 24-28 BA; Columbia 61-62, 63 MS. 7: UToronto Lib 31-, Head of ref dept 62-. 9: CanLA; ALA; OntLA Inst Prof Libns Ont. 10: Beta Phi Mu; Stratford Festival Shakespeare Found Can; Can Opera Guild. 14: Ref. 15: 52 Elm ave, Toronto 5 Ont Can.

WALFORD, BESS PATERSON. b Richmond Va. 5: Westhampton Col 35-39 (Hist) BA; Drexel 39-40 BS in LS. 7: Libn Mathews Co High Sch, Mathews Va 40-41; Supv of Libs Va Dept of Mental Hygiene & Hosps 41-44; Libn Ft George G Meade Md Post Lib 3 44-46; Libn VA Reg Off Med & Tech Lib, Richmond Va 46-48; RESEARCH LIBN Fed Res Bank of Richmond, Richmond Va 49-59; Tech libn Philip Morris Inc Research Center, Richmond Va 59-. 8: Instr, Spec Lib Serv, Richmond Prof Inst, 64-; First Supv of Mental Hosp Libs in Va; Org first Lib Inst at Richmond Prof Inst, 65. 9: SLA (Govt Rel Com 64-67, co-chm Bus & Fin Div 58-59, v-chm Fin Sect 57-58); VaLA (pres 61-62, 2d v-pres & Memb Chm 60-61; chm Spec Lib Div 55-57); Richmond-Hopewell Area Spec Libs Club chm 56-57; chm Constit Com 60-61, chm Educ Com 63-65). 10: Friends of the Richmond Pub Lib; Ginter Park Citizens Assn; AAUW; ACS; AAAS; Mental Hygience Soc of Va; Amer Inst Banking; Va Mus of Fine Arts; Westhampton Col Alumnae Assn 39-; Drexel Alumni Assn 40-. 12: Ed SLA Fin Div "Bulletin (57-58). 14: Spec libs. 15: 3908 Chamberlayne ave, Richmond Va 23206.

WALKER, ALICE E (MORRIS RASPA). b Shanghai China 23 D 11. 5: Simmons 31-34 (LS) BS; UHawaii 65-69 MLS. 6: Fr, Ital, Sp, Ger. 7: Libn St Mary's Hall, Shanghai China 34-36; Libn Ginling Col, Nanking China 36-37; Catlg for West langs United Christian cols in E China, Shanghai 38-40; Catlg asst lib ext Phila Free Lib 40-41; Libn Penn hosp, Phila 42-43; Exec sec protem United China Relief, Phila 44-46; Co-ed "Asia Calling", Santa Monica Cal 46-47; Br libn Prince George's Co Memorial Lib, Md 51-52; Libn Harcum Jr Col 58; Libn Westtown Sch, Westtown Penn 55-57; Asst catlgr East West Ctr Lib, Honolulu 66-69. 8: Honorary Libn, North China Branch, Royal Asiatic Soc, Shanghai, China during most of 1941. 10: Simmons Col Alumnae Assn. 15: East-West Center Lib, Honolulu Hi.

WALKER, BILLY J. b Graham Ky 21 Mr 39. 5: UKy 57-61 (Hist) AB, summers 62-67 (LS) MS. 7: Tchr: Rockport Elem, Rockport Ky 61-65, Ohio Co High Sch, Beaver Dam Ky 65-66; Libn Beaver Dam Elem, Beaver Dam Ky 66-. 8: ETV Consul Team, Ohio Co 68-69. 9: ALA; KyEA; KyASchL. 10: Kappa Delta Pi; Nat Wildlife Fed; Phi Alpha Theta. 14: Child & yp lit. 15: 507 Kentucky st, Beaver Dam Ky 42320.

WALKER, CLARA (MOSLEY). b Selma Ala 22 N 33. 4: Charles Allen Walker. 5: Ala State Col 50-54 (Eng, Secondary Educ) BS in Secondary Educ; Atlanta 54-56 MS in LS. 6: Fr. 7: Asst libn Fla Normal & Mem Col 56-57; Circ libn Prairie View A&M Col 57-61; Asst libn WVa State Col 61-62; Asst libn Selma U 62-63; Asst circ libn Fla A&M U 63-68, Catlg libn 68-. 9: ALA; FlaLA. 15: Box 93, Fla A&M Univ, Tallahassee Fla 32307.

WALKER, CONSTANCE MAE (TAYLOR). b Providence 22 Jl 28. 4: Billy Jack Walker. 5: UTex 52-54 (Eng) BA, 54-56 MLS. 6: Fr. 7: Libn undergrad reading room UTex 55-56; Ref libn Houston Pub LIB 56-60; Asst libn S Tex Jr Col 60-67, Libn 67-. 9: TexLA (chm Scholarship Sels Com 65-66; chm Conf Info Com 69). 10: Phi Beta Kappa; Beta Phi Mu. 14: Ref. 15: 8117 Albacore dr, Houston Tx 77036.

WALKER, DEAN E. b Columbus Ohio 7 Ag 21. 4: Mary A Euphrat. 5: Butler 40-49 (Eng, Lat) AB; Bowling Green State 52-55 (LS); UToledo 69 MALS. 6: Lat. 7: Tchr & libn high sch: Hicksville 49-56, Wauseon 56-63; Libn Ottawa Halls High, Toledo Ohio 63-68; Libn UC & TC ToledoU 65-66; Libn Fremont Ross High, Fremont Ohio 68-. 8: Consul libn-tchr UC & TC ToledoU designing the new lib in the commun col. 9: ALA; OhioLA; OhioASchL. 10: Kiwanis. 14: Tchg students to use the lib. 15: 1100 North st, Fremont Oh 43420.

WALKER, ELINOR. b Enderlin ND 16 Mr 11. 5: Macalester Col 29-33 (Lat) AB; UMinn 36-44 (LS) BS. 7: Tchr-libn pub sch, Grasston Minn 35-36; Tchr-libn pub sch, Cottonwood Minn 37-41; Libn-tchr pub sch, Plainview Minn 41-43; Yp libn Pub Lib, St Paul 43-46; Ya ed ALA "ALA Booklist 46-48; Coord, wk with yp Carnegie Lib, Pittsburgh 48-; Instr Carnegie Lib Sch 48-62. 9: ALA-YASD (pres 49-50, chm Publns Com 64); -PLA (pres 59-60; rep White House Conf 60); 10: AAUW; YWCA; GAR. 12: Ed "Top of the News (53-54); Ed "Book Bait (57); Ed "Doors to More Mature Reading (64); Ed "Book Bait (2nd ed 69). 13: Yes. 14: Wk with teen-age readers. 15: 5624 Fifth ave, Pittsburgh 15232.

WALKER, ESTELLENE PAXTON. b Bristol Va 13 S 11. 5: UTenn 30-33 (Eng) BA; Emory 34-35 BA in LS. 6: Fr. 7: Lib asst Lawson McGhee Lib, Knoxville Tenn 33-34, Head co Dept 35-41; Post libn Ft Jackson, Columbia SC 41-45; Libn army Spec serv USFET, Paris 45, Materials-supply libn, Frankfurt Germany 46; Dir SC State Lib Bd, Columbia SC 46-. 8: Adv com Lib Serv Act, US Off of Educ, 57; Del to White House Conf on Child & Youth, 60. 9: ALA; -AAStateL; SELA; SCLA (Legis Com 66-68). 10: SC Com on Welfare to Child & Youth; Coun for Common Good; State Adv Comon Adult Educ; So Caroliniana Soc; Phi Kappa Phi; Amer Humane Assn. 12: Woman of the Year from "Progressive Farmer Magazine (68). 13: Yes. 14: Lib ext, personnel. 15: SC State Lib Bd, 1001 Main st, COLUMBIA SC 29201.

WALKER, GRACE (WYCKOFF). b Brooklyn NY 28 Ag 07. 4: Bryan Lawrence Walker. 5: Maxwell Train Sch for Tchrs 27. 7: Asst to child libn Norristown Lib, Norristown Penn 53-60, Hd circ 60-65; Hd a-v Montgomery Co Norristown Pub Lib, Norristown Penn 65-. 9: PennLA (sec a-v com). 14: A-v materials & serv. 15: 1209 W Oak st, Norristown Pa 19401.

WALKER, HELEN E. b Pascagoula Miss 19 Mr 21. 5: Fla State U 45-47 (Physiology) BS; UVa 47-48 (Sociol) MA; Catholic U 60-61 MSLS; AmericanU 56-57 (Sociol, Anthrop). 6: Fr. 7: Soc wker City of Alexandria Va 48-50; Instr UMd 50-51; Asst dir & Instr UVa Ext Center (Arlington) 52-60; Br libn Fairfax Co Pub Lib, Fairfax Va 61-66, Supv adult serv 66-68; Coord adult serv Anne Arundel Co Pub Lib (Annapolis Md 68-69; Personnel off Fairfax Co Pub Lib, Fairfax Va 69-. 8: Consul for Ramal Inc, Mannasas Va; Comparative study of bk collections of Wash Urban Libs. 9: ALA; VaLA; MdLA. 10: Beta Phi Mu; Fairfax Hist Soc. 11: Phelps-Stokes Fellowship, UVa. 12: "The Negro in the Medical Profession" (48). 13: Yes. 14: Loc hist, bk selection, acquis. 15: 5421 Back Lick rd, Springfield Va 22151.

WALKER, JANE ELEANOR (HOBSON). b Phila 24 Ja 18. 4: John Allison Walker. 5: Drexel 60-63 (LS). 7: Sec H A Smith Advertising, Phila 35-36; Billing clerk Presbyterian Bd Educ, Phila 36-38; Teller Germantown Trust Col, Phila 38-44; Lib asst Abington Lib, Jenkintown Penn 61-64; Libn Roslyn Lib, Roslyn Penn 64-66; Asst libn Abington Lib Soc, Jenkintown Penn 66-. 8: Ch libn Grace Presbyterian Ch, Jenkintown Penn 61-66. 9: ALA; PennLA. 10: PTA. 14: Child serv, catlg. 15: 511 Runnymede ave, Jenkintown Penn 19046.

WALKER, JEAN MARIE (GRINDLE). b Hammond Ind 23 Je 28. 4: Robert L R Walker. 5: Ind U 50 (Eng) BA; Chicago 56; Ind U 62 (LS) MA. 6: Fr. 7: Accounting dept R R Donnelly Co, Chicago 46; Asst Whiting Pub Lib, Whiting Ind 46-48; Hd ya serv Gary Pub Lib, Gary Ind 50-54, Br libn 54-64, Hd popular lib dept 64-, Adult educ coord 68-. 9: ALA; IndLA, (chm Scholarship Com 68-69). 10: Gary Womans Club; Beta Phi Mu; Greater Gary Arts Coun Bd; Lake City Adult Educ Coord; Lake City Pub Rel Com. 13: Yes. 14: Adult educ, a-v serv. 15: 145 N Grnd blvd, Gary Ind 46403.

WALKER, JOE L. b Kenton Ohio 19 Mr 38. 5: Baldwin Wallace Col 56-60 (Hist) AB; West Res 63-65 MSLS, 67-68 (Hist). 6: Sp, Russian. 7: Lib asst Baldwin-Wallace Col 60-61; Interlib loan asst West Res U 61, Govt docs asst 64-65, Catlg 65-68; Radio operator (Pfc) USA 61-63; Catlg & ref St Clair Shores Pub Lib, St Clair Shores Mich 69-. 9: ALA. 14: Catlg, ref. 15: 22712 Worthington, St Clair Shores Mi 48081.

WALKER, JOHN ROBERT JR. b Mecca Cal 19 S 37. 4: Nancy Karen Brown. 5: UCal 9riverside) 55-59 (Classics) BA; Immaculate Heart Col 67-69 (LS) MA. 6: Ger. 7: Playground leader Recreation Dept, Riverside Cal summer 58; Tchr Episcopal Day Sch, Ontario Cal 59-60; Admin asst Christ Episcopal Ch, Ontario Cal 60; Tchr Ontario Sch dist, Ontario Cal 61; Lib clk Ontario City Lib, Ontario Cal 62-67, Lib asst (period, a-v, ref) 67-68, Hd y-a serv 68-. 14: Ya serv, a-v serv. 15: Ontario City Lib 215 E C st, Ontario Ca 91761.

WALKER, KATHERINE. b Byron Mich 28 O 09. 5: Millikin U 28-33 (Hist) BA; UIll summers 38-41 BSLS; UMich 49-50 (LS) MA. 7: Lib asst Elgin High Sch, Elgin Ill 27-28; Lib asst Gail Borden Pub Lib, Elgin Ill summers 27-32; Asst libn & catlgr Millikin U 33-42; No Ill U: Circ libn 42-45, Ref libn 45-48; Act libn 48-49, summer 57, Asst dir 59-. 8: Com on Reclsf of Civil Serv positions for the state univs of Ill, 58; Consul to Lib Bldgs Consuls, Inc, Evanston Ill 64. 9: ALA-ACRL (sec & chm Tchr Educ Libs Sect 55-57, B Dirs 57-61, Nomin Com 59-61, Nat Lib Wk Chm 61-62); NEA; IllLA (Planning Sch Libs Quarters Com 48-50, chm Memb Com 53-55; Col & Ref Sect: sec 59-60, chm 60-61, Com 63-64, Memb Com 64-65); Ill Adv Com on Educ, rep IllLA 57-59; Midwest Acad Libs Confs 56-. 10: AAUW; AAUP; Delta Kappa Gamma; Pi Mu Theta of the Lib, DeKalb; PEO; Univ Faculty Club; Univ Dames Club; Commun Concert Assn; Family Serv Agency; YMCA; Nat Travel Club; Theatre Guild; Nat Wildlife Assn; UIll Lib Sch Alumni Assn (Life mem); UMich Lib SciAlumni Assn (Life mem); Ellwood House; Millikin U Alumni Assn; DeKalb Co Assn for Mental Health; Univ Homecoming Com 71; Grace & Nix Scholarship Com. 12: "Planning School Library Quarters ALA (50). 14: Admin, personnel problems, ref. 15: No Ill Univ Lib, DeKalb Ill 60115.

WALKER, LILLIE (SUMMERS). b Millen Ga 3 Ap 27. 4: Daniel Wilber. 5: SC State Col 44-48 (LS) AB; NC Col (Durham) summers 50, 52 MSLS, 55. 6: Fr. 7: Sch libn, Lancaster SC 48-51; Sch libn, Columbia SC 51-56; SC State Col: Period libn summer 53, Asst Prof Lib Sci 56, Asst libn circ 58-60, Head reders serv 60-62, Catlgr 63-. 8: Ford Foundation Scholarship Wkshop-Internship Program Atlanta U & Goucher Col 68. 9: ALA; SELA; SCLA, (Recruitment Com). 10: Alpha Kappa Alpha; Emanon Bridge. 14: Catlg. 15: Box 1681 SC State Col, Orangeburg SC 29115.

WALKER, LLOANNE GAYLE (PURKIS). b Pincher Creek Alberta Can 17 Ag 42. 4: John Anthony walker. 5: UAlta 60-63 (Hist) BA; UBC 63-64 BLS. 7: Catlgr (libn I) UAlta 64-. 9: CanLA. 14: Catlg. 15: 305 10835-86 ave, Edmonton 60 Alta Can.

WALKER, LOIS JANET. b Valley City ND 24 My 04. 5: Canadian Jr Col 24-26 Certif; Emmanuel Missionary Col 33-35 (Eng) AB; UNeb summers 39-44 (Eng) MA; UDenver summers 45-47 BS in LS; Columbia summer 55. 6: Ger. 7: Sec Sask Con of SDAs, Saskatoon Sask 23-24; Elem sch tchr SDA church schs, Carolina & Fla 26-33; Supv tchr So Jr Col (Collegedale Tenn) 35-38; Secondary sch tchr-libn Plainview Acad, Redfield SD 38-42; Secondary sch tchr-libn Maplewood Acad, Hutchinson Minn 42-45; Asst libn Pacific Union Col 45-47, HeadLibn 47-64; Assoc libn La Sierra Col 64- 67; Assoc libn Kettering Col of Med Arts 67-. 8: Consul several second schs; Consul Kettering Col of Med Arts. 9: ALA. 10: Nat Audubon Soc;Soroptimist. 12: "A Guide for the Librarian in Seventh-day Adventist Secondary Schools (63). 13: Yes. 14: Ref, catlg, lib educ. 15: 3737 Southern blvd, Kettering Oh 45429.

WALKER, LUISE E(LISABETH). b Ferndale Mich 14 N 27. 5: UWash 49-51 (Sociol) AB; UMich 45-46, 53-55, 58 (LS, Forestry) AMLS; UNotre Dame 55-58 (Bot); SUNY Col of Forestry 58 (Bot) MS. 6: Fr. 7: US Naval Res HMC (Hosp Corps) 49-; Biol libn UNotre Dame (Notre Dame Ind) 55-58; Math libn Syracuse U 58-60; Grad asst SUNY Col Forestry (Syracuse NY) 60-61; Research aide Bundesforschunsanstalt fur Forst- und Holzwirtschaft, Schmalenbeck Germany 61; Readers serv libn SUNY Col Forestry (Syracuse NY) 61-67; Hd sci libn UOre (Eugene) 67-. 9: SLA (archiv West NY Chap); ALA (Com on Costs of Publns 60). 10: Nat RifleAssn; Sigma Xi; Amer Soc of Ichthyol & Herpetol; Ore State Rifle & Pistol Assn; AAUP. 12: Abs "Bilogical Abstracts. 13: Yes. 14: Biol sci ref, forestry ref, tchg freshman bot & gen forestry. 15: Science Lib Univ of Oregon, Eugene Or 97403.

WALKER, LYNN WESLEY. b Okeechobee Fla 30 Sg 28. 4: Joyce Orr. 5: UFla 46-49 (Hist) BA; Fla StateU 49-50 (LS) MA. 7: Catlgr UTenn Lib (Knoxville) 50-53; Catlgr UFla Lib 52-53; Sci libn 53-54, Libn eng & physics lib 54-66; Dir instr resources Fla TechU 66-. 9: ALA (State Memb Chm 67-); SELA (State Memb Chm 67-); FlaLA (treas 64-67, chm Col & spec Libs Div 59-60, chm; Memb Com 67-68). 10: Beta Phi Mu; Kiwanis Internat; Fla State U Lib Sch Alum Assn. 13: Yes. 14: Lib admin, lib automation. 15: 640 Berwick dr, Winter Park Fl 32789.

WALKER, MARGARET LOUISE. b Columbus Ga 12 Ap 17. 5: Paine Col 35-39 (Eng) AB; Atlanta 50-51 MSLS; UChicago 59-60. 7: Eng tchr Spencer High Sch, Columbus Ga 40-50; Child libn West Hunter Br Pub Lib, Atlanta 50-52; State lib consul Ga State Dept of Educ, Atlanta 52-. 8: Consul for wkshops sponsored by the So Educ Foun; Participated in the Golden Anniv of The White House Conf on Child & Youth; Admin to the Ministry of Educ on Sch Libs, Malaya 64. 9: ALA; Ga Tchrs & Educ Assn (Libns Sect); SELA. 10: Beta Phi Mu; Alpha Kappa Alpha. 11: Fulbright Lectureship to Malaya, 63. 12: "School Library Development in Perspective" Kuala Lumpur, (64); "School Library Manual," Kuala Lumpur Min of Educ (64). 14: Child libn. 15: 247 Willis Mill rd SW, Atlanta Ga 30311.

WALKER, MARILYN (EILEEN). b Redlands Cal 4 Jl 41. 5: Los Angeles Pacific Col 59-63 (Soc Sci) BA; USoCal 63-65 MS in LS. 6: Ger, Sp. 7: Stud asst Lib Los Angeles Pacific Col 59-65; Clerk child dept A K Smiley Pub Lib, Redlands Cal 63-64; Lib asst Los Angeles Pacific Col 63-65; Catlgr Asbury Theol Sem 65-. 9: ALA; ATLA; KyLA. 14: Ref, catlg. 15: ASBURY Theol Sem, Wilmore Ky 40390.

WALKER, MARJORIE. b Lewisville Ark 24 S 12. 5: URedlands 30-34 (Fr) BA; UArk 48; E Tex State 54-55 MS in LS, 57, 60, 63 (LS); 67. 6: Fr. 7: Fr & Eng tchr Lewisville High Sch, Lewisville Ark 34-54; LibnLewisville High Sch, Lewisville Ark 54-; Lib coord Lewisville Pub Schs, Lewisville Ark 67-. 8: Ark Adv Coun on Secon Educ, State Dept of Educ, 57-; State Dept of Educ Com to Implement Lib Standards, 60-; Summer instr in lib sci, E Tex State U, 58-; State Adv Coun on Title II, ESEA 65-. 9: ALA (Loc Recr Chm); NEA; NCTE; ArkLA (Recr Com); ArkEA (sec Coord Com 60-61); Lafayette Co TA (sec 64). 10: Lafayette Co Hist Soc; Lafayette Co Devel Coun; PTA; C of C. 13: Yes. 14: Sch lib serv. 15: 104 W 8th st, Lewisville Ar 71845.

WALKER, NANCY (CHILDS). b Columba SC 24 Ap 20. 4: H Thomas Walker. 5: USCar 36-40 (Fr) AB; Emory 40-41 BLS; Johns Hopkins 63-67 (Master of Liberal Arts. 7: Libn Hand Jr High Sch, Columbia SC 41-42; Co dept libn Richland Co Pub Lib, Columbia SC 42-43; Bkmob libn NY Pub Lib 44; Catlgr Caroliniana Lib USCar 47-50; Elem sch libn pub schs, Columbia SC 51-53; Elem sch libn pub schs, Baltimore Co Md 54-61; Supv sch libs Bd of Educ, Anne Arundel Co Md 61-. 9: ALA; NEA; -DAVI; MdLA; Md State Tchrs Assn; Assn Sch Libns Md. 11: Encyclopedia Britannica Sch Lib Award, 63. 13: Yes. 14: Sch libs. 15: 3725 Patterson ave, Baltimore Md 21207.

WALKER, OLGA EMILY (FORTENBERRY). b Edinburg Miss 10 Ja 05. 5: Miss State Col for Women 26-29 (Home Econ); Peabody 29-30 (Home Econ) BS; UMiss 58-59 MLS. 6: Lat. 7: Home Econ & Eng, Henrietta-Caroleen NC 30-31; Home econ & chem Rosman NC 31-33; Home econ Alcorn Agric High Sch, Kossuth Miss 34-38, 44-45, libn 46-48; Eng libn & sci Rienzi High Sch, Rienzi Miss 48-54; Home econ & Eng Marietta High Sch, Marietta Miss 54-56; Libn Kossuth High Sch, Kossuth Miss 56-. 9: MissEA; MissLA. 10: Kappa Kappa Iota; Pilot Club; UTO. 13: Yes. 14: Ref, rare bks. 15: 504 Cass st, Corinth Ms 38834.

WALKER, RICHARD D(EAN). b Hammond Ind 17 Ap 30. 4: Margaret (Margy) Zwickel. 5: Ind U 48-55 (Chem) AB, 55-57 (LS) AM; UIll 58-63 (LS) PhD. 6: Fr, Ger. 7: Army (Pfc) 52-54; Geol libn Ind U (Bloomington) 55-58; Physics libn UIll (Urbana) 58-61; Research assoc & Hd Lib Research Ctr Grad Sch of Lib Sci 61-63; Asst Prof SoIllU (Carbondale) 63-64; Asst Prof UWis Lib Sch 65-67; Assoc Prof 67-. 9: ALA; SLA; Nat Soc Programmed Instr; NEA-DAVI; AALS; WisLA; IllLA; Aslib, LA (Brit); ASIS. 10: AAUP; ACLU; Urban League; NAACP; CORE; Beta Phi Mu; Geosci Info Soc. 12: "Anntated Bibliography of Indiana Geology through 1955 (62); "The Availability of Library Science and Academic Achievement (63). 13: Yes. 14: Lib educ, a-v, mass communications, sci bibliog. 15: 4113 Paunack ave, Madison Wis 53711.

WALKER, SUE ELLEN (ALBERTSON). b Bloomsburg Penn 1 My 43. 4: Robert Smith Walker. 5: Millersville State Col 61-64 (Lib Educ) BS; Syracuse 64-67 MSLS. 7: Libn Benton Area High Sch, Benton Penn 64-68; Libn Falls Ch High Sch, Falls Ch Va 68-. 8: Consul Amer Vocat Assn Wash DC summer 68. 9: ALA; NEA; VaLA; VaEA; FairfaxCoEA. 14: Admin (high sch), col tchg. 15: 6129 Leesburg pike A204, Falls Church Va 22041.

WALKER, VIRGINIA (STELLA) CHAMBLISS. b Xenia Ohio 5 N 08. 5: UCincinnati 26-28 (Educ); Berea Col 57-59; UKy 59-61 (LS) BA. 6: Fr. 7: Asst libn Procter & Gamble Co, Cincinnati 30-33; Asst circ UKy 61-64, Asst ref libn 64-. 9: ALA; KyLA; SELA. 14: Ref. 15: 497 Lamont dr, Lexington Ky 40503.

WALKER, W LORETTA. b Ala 9 D 22. 4: James L Walker. 5: HowardU 46-49 (Math) BS; SUNY (Albany) summer 62, 66-68 MLS. 7: Bkkeeper Henry Fuel Co Inc, Wash DC 49-52; Asst ref libn Schenectady Co Pub Lib, Schenectady NY 68; Asst ref libn Union Col (Schenectady NY) 68-. 9: ALA; Capital Dist Lib Coun. 10: ACLU. 14: Ref. 15: 713 Pearse rd, Schenectady NY 12309.

WALKER, WENDELL K(IRSHMAN). b Battle Creek Mich 9 Ja08. 4: Marjorie Knappbalch. 5: West Mich U 26-30 (Hist) BA; UExeter (Eng) 30-31 (Hist) Certif; Columbia 32, 47 (LS) BS. 7: Lib asst Grand Lodge F & AM, NY 32-42; (Lt & Capt) US Army 42-46; Libn Grand Lodge F & AM,NY 46-51; (Capt & Maj) US Army Res, Korean Emergency 51-53; Dir Lib & Museum Grand Lodge F & AM, NY 53-63, GRAND Sec 63-. 9: ALA; SLA (NY Chap; pres, chm Museum Group); Amer Mgt Assn; NY Lib Club. 10: Metro Mus of Art; Mus of Mod Art; Mus of the City of NY; Goethe House; Res Officers Assn Grand Jury Assn, NY; Soc Arch Histns. 13: Yes. 14: Ref, rare bks, circ. 15: 71 W 3rd st, NYC 10010.

WALKER, WILLIAM BOND. b Brownsville Tenn 15 Ap 30. 5: State U Iowa 49-53 (Fine Arts) AB; Rutgers 56-58 MSLS. 6: Fr, Ger, Sp. 7: Bibliog searcher UPenn Lib 54-55; Libn trainee NY Pub Lib Donnell Br 55-57; Catlgr, ref libn Lib of

Metropolitan Museum of Art, NY 57-59; Chief Libn Art Ref Lib Brooklyn Museum, Brooklyn NY 59-64; Libn Nat Collection of Fine Arts & Nat Portrait Gallery Smithsonian Inst, Wash DC 64-. 8: Wk with LC Subj Catlg Div on revision lib clsf schedule "N Fine Arts 65-; chm Exhibit Task Force DC Com for NLW 68. 9: SLA (Museum & Picture Divs; chm Museum Div 61-62; chm DC Chap Picture Group 67-68); ALA-ACRL; DCLA; NY Lib Club. 10: Phi Beta Kappa. 12: Ed "Bulletin of Museum Division, SLA (60-61). 13: Yes. 14: Ref & bibliog of fine arts, fine arts lib clsf syst. 15: 1072 Thomas Jefferson st NW, Washington DC 20007.

WALKEY, ELIZABETH MEDILL. b Lancaster Ohio 10 S 15. 5: Western Col 34-38 (Chem) BA; Ohio State U 40 (Chem); USoCal 57 (LS); Immaculate Heart Col 60-61 (LS). 6: Sp, Fr. 7: Chem Ohio Fuel Gas, Columbus Ohio 42-44; Lt (jg) Radar USNR WAVES, Wash DC 44-46; Libn Mkt Researcher Dan B Miner (Advert), Los Angeles 47; Chem libn Motion Picture Research Coun, Hollywood Cal 48-51; Chem Film-Effects, Hollywood Cal 51; Tech writer, Ed US Naval Ordnance Test Station, Pasadena Cal 51; Chief ed Jet Propulsion Lab, Pasadena Cal 52; Chief libn Consolidated Electrodynamics Corp, Pasadena Cal 53-59; Manager lib serv Bell & Howell Research Labs, Pasadena Cal 60-. 8: West Coast Sales Mgr, Info for Ind, 56-57; Guest lecturer, Lib Sch, Immaculate Heart Col, 62 & 64; Amer Mgt Assn 68; Lib Sch UWash; Lib Sch Adv Bd USoCal 68-71. 9: SLA (chm Tr Activ Com 61-64, mem Publns Com 61-64, Motion Pict Com 65-; Los Angeles CHAP: Memb Chm, Pub Rel Dir, adv, sec0; ACS (cm Wom Serv Com 58); ASIS Nat Microfilm Assn; CalLA. 10: Soroptimist Internat; aaas; Nat Honor Soc; Los Angeles Tech Socs Coun; Los Angeles Trade Col, Lib Adv Bd. 11: SLA del to Unesco Meeting on Sci Trs & Term, Rome, 64. 12: Ed "SCALACS, loc ACS j (56-58); Author of a US patent. 13: Yes. 14: Ref, reader serv, icrofilm systems. info storage & retrieval, mgt communicatio, tech tr, euc for spec libnship, stud recr. 15: Bell & Howell Res Labs 360 Sierra Madre Villa, Pasadena Ca 91109.

WALKONEN, HELVI E. b Sundell Mich 16 D 25. 5: N Mich U 43-46 (Eng, Hist) AB; UMich 46-51 (Eng) MA, 53-55 MALS. 7: Tchr high sch, Manistique Mich 46-47, 49-52; Tchr high sch, Ishpeming Mich 47-49; Tchr-libn High Sch, Munich Germany 53-54; Libn St Josephs Sch of Nursing, Ann Arbor Mich 54-55; Head libn High Sch, Grosse Pointe Mich 55-63; Asst libn No Mich U 63-64, Head libn 64-. 9: NEA; ALA; MichEA; MichSchLA; MichLA. 10: Kappa Delta Pi; Delta Kappa Gamma; AAUP. 15: 1519 Lincoln, Marquette Mi 49855.

WALL, C EDWARD. b Cherokee Iowa 3 Mr 42. 4: Mary Ellen Stratton. 5: State UIowa 60-64 (Hist, Pol Sci, Chinese Lang & Civilization) BA; UMich 64-66 (Hist, LS) MALS. 6: Chinese Mandarin. 7: Ref libn UMich Lib (Dearborn) 66-67, Hd libn 67-. 8: Publisher, The Pierian Press, Ann Arbor Mich; Bldg consul, Lewis Col; Consul compu Print Corp, St Louis Mo. 9: ALA (New Ref Tools Com 68-70). 10: Phi Beta Kappa; Beta Phi Mu; Assn for Asian Studies. 12: "Subject Index to New Serial Titles 1950-1965" (68); "Periodical Title Abbreviations" (69); Co-ed "Words and Phrases Index (69-). 13: Yes. 14: Admin, ref, lib constr, publishing. 15: 420 Fair lane, Dearborn Mi 48128.

WALL, CAROL. b NYC 5 Jl 41. 5: E Stroudsburg State Col 59-63 (Soc Sci) BS; SUNY (Albany) 64-65 MLS; SUNY Col (Oneonta) 68 (Soc Sci) MEd. 7: Asst libn Auburn Commun Col 65-66; Ref libn Shippensburg State Col 67-. 9: ALA; Area Col Lib Coop Prog of S Central Penn (chm Ref Com); Cumberland Valley LA. 10: AAUP; Bus & Profess Women. 13: Yes. 14: Ref, interlib loan. 15: 221 E King st, Shippensburg Pa 17257.

WALL, DUNCAN (HERMON) JR. b Tulsa Okla 6 Ag 33. 4: Carol Carter. 5: Wesleyan U (Middletown Conn) 51-57 (Eng) BA; Columbia 57-60 MS. 6: Fr. 7: Loan ref asst LC 56-57; Sec, Receptionist Columbia Lib 57-60; Hd catlg dept Curtis Mem Lib, Meriden Conn 60-63; Tech libn United Aircraft Corp, Farmington Conn 63-65; Systs engr 66-67; Systs consul Ont Coun of U Libns, Toronto Ont 68-69; Assoc libn for planning & development Kent State U Libs 69-. 9: ConnLA (chm Res & Tech Serv Sect 64-65); ALA-ACRL; SLA; ASIS. 14: Lib planning, tech serv, info retrieval, lib automation, info syst design, requirement & performance analysis, bibliolinguistics; info econ & netwks. 15: Kent State Univ Libs, Kent Oh 44240.

WALL, MINNIE (ELNORA). b Rayle Ga 13 Ag 07. 5: Tift Col 24-27 (Fr) AB; Peabody 40-42 BS in LS; Auburn U 54-56 (Educ) M Ed. 6: Fr. 7: Prim tchr Hogue Sch, Wilkes Co Ga 28-29; Tchr Oak Park High Sch, Oak Park Ga 30-31; Prim tchr Rayle High Sch, Rayle Ga 31-33; Elem grade tchr Coosa High Sch, Coosa Ga 34-37; Tchr Lyerly High Sch, Lyerly Ga 37-39; Tchr-libn Warwick High Sch, Warwick Ga 39-42; Libn Benton High Sch, Benton Tenn 42-43; Libn Thomasville High Sch, Thomasville Ga 43-47; Auburn U Lib; Catlg libn 47-56, Head of catlg div & asst prof 56-65, Head of catlg div & assoc prof 65-. 9: ALA; SELA; AlaLA. 10: AAUW; Delta Kappa Gamma; Kappa Delta Pi; Auburn Univ Faculty Club. 14: Catlg. 15: 739 Mercer cir, Auburn Ala 36830.

WALLACE, BARBARA DAN. b Arlington Mass 1 Ja 45. 5: Northwestern State College (La) 63-67 (Primary Educ) BA; LSU (Baton Rouge) 67-68 (LS) MS. 7: Lib page pub lib, Shreveport La summers 61-64; Lib asst Russell Lib, Natchitoches La 63-67; Child libn, Barksdale AFB La summers 66-67; Elem sch libn, Rock Springs Wyo 68-69. 9: ALA; WyoLA; WyoSchLA (Proj Chm). 10: Phi Kappa Phi; Sigma Kappa; PTA; AAUW. 14: Storytelling, filing, proc, tchg lib skills. 15: 261 E Fairview, Shreveport La 71104.

WALLACE, BURMA (MORGAN). b Eva Ala. 4: James Bob Wallace. 5: UAla 48-50 (LS) BS, 64-65 (Sch Libnship) MA. 7: Libn: Misses Howards Sch for Girls, Birmingham Ala 52-54, Central Park Sch, Birmingham Ala 54-57, Hewitt-Trussville High Sch, Trussville Ala 58-65, Jefferson State Jr Col 65-, Dir of Lib Serv. 9: AlaSchLA (Dist Org Chm); AlaEA; AlaJrColAssn; AlaJrColLA; AlaLA. 15: 1516 2nd pl NW, Birmingham Ala.

WALLACE, CAROLYN (MARY) (ANDREWS). b Hillsborough NC 30 S 19. 4: Wesley Herndon Wallace. 5: Meredith Col 36-40 (Hist, Eng) AB; UNC (Chapel Hill) 44-47 (Amer Hist) MA, 48-50, 53-54 (Amer Hist) PhD. 7: Instr hist dept Woman's Col UNC (Greensboro) 47-48; Curator mss dept UNC Lib (Chapel Hill) 49-50, 53-. 9: SAA; Hist Soc NC (Coun mem); NC Lit & Hist Soc (v-pres); So Hist Assn. 13: Yes. 14: NC & so hist and mss. 15: PO Box 875, Chapel Hill NC 27514.

WALLACE, DOROTHY LOUISE. b Kan City Mo 31 Ja 10. 5: Col of St Catherine 27-31 (Eng) BA, 32-33 Art Certif, 54-56 (LS) MA. 6: Fr. 7: Elem tchr St Thomas Sch, Minneapolis 31-32; Tchr Art, Eng, Hist St Josephs Acad, St Paul 32-34; Tchr of Blind Handicaps & Supv of Sheltered wkshop Minneapolis Soc for Blind 43-49; Sec-bkkeeper Church, Minneapolis 49-54; Art & ref libn Art Dept Minneapolis Pub Lib 54-63; Catlgr Prince Georges Co Mem Lib, Hyattsville Md 63-64, Coordinator of tech serv 64-. 8: Lib Consul; services Devel, Inc, Raleigh NC 68, PGCML to data processing dept at Marlboro, Prince George Co, Md; Dir conversion serv in Techn Serv, Prince Georges Co Lib. 9: ALA-RTSC (Memb Com 64-67); MdLA; DCLA. 12: "Book Catalog for Basic Adult Collection, Prince Georges Co Lib," 3 v (2nd ed 66). 14: Art, caltg, ref, computerization of pub libs. 15: Prince George's Co Lib, 6532 Adelphi rd, Hyattsville Md 20782.

WALLACE, GRACE (BURNILL). b Toronto Can 20 Ja 10. 5: Toronto 26-29 (Arts) BA, 63-64 BLS. 6: Fr. 7: Surveyor "Los Angeles Times 29-30; Owner The Reading Lamp, Hollywood Cal 30-34; Owner Burnills Bk Shop, Toronto 39-63; Libn Etobicoke Pub Lib, Toronto 64-65, Br libn 65-. 8: Bk reviewer, KTM Radio, Los Angeles, 33-34. 9: CanLA; OntLA; Inst Prof Libns Ont. 10: Univ Womens Club, Toronto. 14: Adult serv, ref, child serv. 15: 1607-22 Oakmount rd, Toronto 9 Can.

WALLACE, JAMES OLDHAM. b San Antonio Tex 22S 17. 4: Lillie Ruth Franklin. 5: San Antonio Col 34-36 St Marys U 36-40 (Hist) BA, MA; Our Lady of the Lake Col 46-50 BS in LS. 6: Sp. 7: Tchr Natalia Ind Sch Dist, Natalia Tex 40-41; Tchr Ls Angeles Hights Ind Sch Dist, San Antonio Tex 41-42; Clerk Kelly AFB, San Antonio Tex 42-43; Payroll chief Randolph AFB, Tex 43-49; Libn First Baptist Church, San Antonio Tex 39-64; Tchr-libn Lanier High Sch, San Antonio Tex 49-50; San Antonio Col: Asst libn 50-51, Act libn 51-52, Libn 52-. 8: Instr Dept of Libnship, OUR Lady of the Lake Col 54-55; Consul US Off of Educ 67-68. 9: ALA (Coun 67-71; -ACRL (Exec Bd 60-63, 68-71; Com on Standards 62-65, 67-70; chm Sub-com on Revision Jr Col Standards 68-; Nominating Com 63; Jr Col Lib Sect; chm 61-62, Nominating Com 57, 62, 64, chm Spec Projects Com 60-61, Instr Materials Ctr chm 67-69, Pre-conf Com 67-69; Lib Research Sect; com on Stat for Col & Univ Libs 62-65); Jt Com ALA & Amer Assn Jr Cols 65-; NMA; TexLA (2nd v-pres 55-56; Legis chm 56-58; Conv chm 59; Program chm 65; chm Spec Libs Div 53-54; chm Col & Univ Libs Div 65-66, 69-70; sec Dist 8 52-53, 55-56, v-chm 69-70, chm 70; Aud Com 61-62; Loc Arrangements Com 62; Formula Com 69); Tex Coun Jr Col Libns; Tex Coord Bd Lib (chm); Coun Research & Acad Libs 9pres 66-68); ALA-RTSD

(Duplications Exchange Com 67-69). 10: AAUP; Tex Jr Col TA; San Antonio Hist Assn; Nat Soc Study of Educ; Phi Theta Kappa; Trustee Baptist Memorial Hosp (65-67). 11: Tex Libn of the Year (69). 12: "In the Shadow of His Hand (61). 13: Yes. 14: Catlg, admin, lib bldg. 15: P O Box13041, SAN Antonio Tex 78213.

WALLACE, M MAURINE (OVERFIELD). b Poplar Bluff Mo 24 Jl 16. 4: Charles E Wallace. 5: UEvansville 34-38 (Sci) BA; UUtah 56-58 (LS); UIll 62-66 MS in LS. 6: Fr. 7: Libn Rossville High Sch, Rossville Ill 56-61; Coord libs Fisher Commun Unit Schs, Fisher Ill 61-. 8: Bk reviewer for Ill Reading Serv. 9: ALA; -AASchL; NEA; IllLA; IllASchL; IllEA. 10: Beta Phi Mu; Phi Beta Chi; DAR; Rossville Women's Club. 14: Child libn, child bks. 15: 2418 Maplewood dr, Champaign Il 61820.

WALLACE, M RUTH. b Toronto Can 23 F 18. 5: Toronto 36-40 (Eng Lang & Lit) BA, 40-41 BLS. 6: FR, Ger. 7: Libn: London Pub Lib, London Ont 41-43, Toronto Pub Libs 44-51, UWash52-59, Phoenix Pub Lib 59-, Head art & philos sect 62-. 8: Chm, Nat Lib Week, Arix 63, 65. 9: ArizStateLA (mem var coms); SWLA. 10: Altrusa; Colour Photography Assn of Can; Imperial Order Daughters of the Empire; Recreation Adv Conf (Phoenix); SaltRiverAdultEA; AAUW. 13: Yes. 14: Ref, readers adv serv. 15: 330 W Medlock dr, apt 107, Phoenix 85013.

WALLACE, MARY (WALLBRIDGE). b Louisville Ky 9 Je 35. 5: Wellesley 53-57 (Mus Theory) AB; Simmons 59-62 (LS) MS. 6: Fr, Ger. 7: Pre-prof ref asst pub lib (mus dept), Boston 59-62; Hd art & mus pub lib, Brookline Mass 62-64; Mus libn Radcliffe Col 64-67; Mus libn Wellesley Col 67-. 9: ALA; MusLA (chm Lib Bldgs & Equip Com 68-; NE Chap: v-pres 66-67, sec-treas 67-68, pres 69-70; NELA. 14: Mus lib. 15: 265 Putnam ave, Cambridge Ma 02139.

WALLACE, MARY LOUISE. b Lexington Ky 28 F 13. 5: UKy 29-33 (LS) AB, 34 (LS). 7: Special catlg Project Ky Dept of Mines, Lexington 34-35; Sch libn Louisville & Jefferson Co Child Home, Ky 35-37; Asst Child Dept Louisville Free Pub Lib, Ky 37-38; Project union list of ser UKy (Lexington) 33, Lib-sec Lib Sci Dept 43-46; Sec VA, Lexington Ky 46-47; Sch libn Dixie Hts High Sch, Covington Ky 38-43, 47-51; Chief libn US Army Armor Sch, Ft Knox Ky 51-. 9: SLA; KyLA (Legis Com). 14: Ref, bk selection. 15: US Army Armor School Lib, Fort Knox Ky 40121.

WALLACE, RICHARD EDMUND. b Schenectady NY 9 F 41. 4: Mary Lynne Schafer. 5: Arlington State Col 59-61 (Math); Mich State U 61-63 (Math) BS; West Res 63-65 MS in LS. 7: Lib asst Pub Lib, Arlingto Tex 58-61; Page Mich State U 62-63; Page West Res LibSch Lib 63-64; Adult serv libn Cuyahoga Co Pub Lib, Cleveland 64-65; Engnr research libn Deere & Co, Moline Ill 65-66; US Army Info spec (SP/4) 66-68; Asst supv Lib Systs Deere & Co, Moline Ill 68-. 9: SLA; ASIS; ALA. 10: Beta Phi Mu. 14: Catl, lib hist, info storage & retrieval, tech serv, automation. 15: 2934 1/2 - 5th ave, Rock Island Il 61201.

WALLACE, ROBERT JACKSON. b River Ky 7 Ja 13. 4: Nancy Jane Stephens. 5: Berea Col 32-36 (Eng, Fr) AB. 6: Fr. 7: Tchr Martin High Sch, Martin Ky 51-52; Tool & die form block maker N Amer Aviation Columbus Ohio 52-54; Libn Floyd Co Lib, Prestonsburg Ky 54-57; Dir E Ky Reg Lib SYSTEM, Prestonsburg Ky 57-64; Libn Prestonsburg Commun Col 64-. 9: KyLA; KyEA. 10: Kiwanis Internat Floyd Co (Ky) Hist Soc. 11: Man of the Year Award, Floyd Co Hall of Fame. 12; Books to Grow By (61). 14: Bibliog. 15: 331 Riverside dr, Prestonsburg Ky 41653.

WALLACE, RUTH W(AGNER). b Scranton Penn 29 N 09. 4: Jack Wallace. 5: Elmia Col 27-32 (Eng) AB; Pratt 60-63 MS in LS. 6: Ger, Lat, Fr. 7: Asst Scranton (Penn) Pub Lib 30-31; Asst libn Brooklyn Pub Lib 33-41; Head circ dept Utica Col of Syracue U 48-50; Pratt Inst Lib: Ref asst 52-5, Head circ dept 57-59, Asst head ref dept 59-, Asst head ref dept & archives lbn 64-67; Asst to libn Del Valley Col 67-. 9: NY Lib Club. 10: Pratt Inst Grad Lib Sch Alumni Assn; Elmira Col Club of NYC. 14: Ref, archives. 15: RR #1, Furlong Pa 18925.

WALLACE, MRS VICTORIA (ZAVATSKY). b Wilkes-Barre Penn 26 S 33. 4: Dana Wallac. 5: Wilkes Col 52-56 (Educ) BS; Pratt 57-58 MSLS. 7: Brooklyn Pub Lib: Libn trainee 57-58, Ref libn 58-59, 1st asst libn 59-60; Ref acquis libn Long Beach Pub Lib, Long Beach NY 61-62; Br libn Northport Pub Lib E Northport Br, Northpoyt NY 62-64; Asst dir Northport Pub Lib, Northport NY 64-69, Dir Northport Pub Lib 69-. 8: Ref libn, Lib/USA, NY Worlds Fair, 64; Chm Nat Lib Week, Suffolk Co (NY), 64. 9: ALA (Subcom for Materials for Sp Speaking 67-; East Div chm Nominating Com for Exhibits RT); NYLA; Suffolk Co (NY) LA (Exec Bd; chm Publicity Com 64-65; chm Exhibits Com 66-; Scholarship chm). 10: Northport Commun Band. 12: Ed "Data (SuffolkCoLA 65-67). 14: Admin, ref. 15: Ocean Beach, Fire Island NY 11770.

WALLACE, SARAH LESLIE. b Kan City Mo. 5: Col of St Catherine 32-35 (Eng) BA, 35-36 BS in LS. 6: Fr, Ger. 7: Minneapolis Pub Lib; Ref asst 36-42, Publicity 42-45, Admin asst 45-54, Admin asst in chg of pub rel 54-58, Pub Rel Off 58-63; Publ Off LC 63-; Instr Lib pub rel & admin Col St Catherine 44-60. 8: Instr, lib sci, Col of St Catherine, 44-60; Instr or consul on pub rel or related subjects, 58-62; Consul, Com to study ALA docs structure. 9: ALA (Coun 58-61, chm Memb Com 62, Loc Publ Conf 5, Lib Period Round Table 60-61, GALA Com 60);-LAD (Friends of Libs Com 59, Exec Com of Pub Rel Sect 60-62, Chm Pub Rel Sect 64-65, var other coms);-ASD (chm Spec Promo Com 61-, Adv Com to 2 Ala Coms 61-62, Miami Beach Program Com 61-62, SORT Constit Rev Chm 62-65, SORT Steering Com 62; Amer Inst of Graph Arts; Fed Editors Assn; DCLA; MinnLA. 10: Delta Phi Lambda; Kappa Gamma Pi; Franklin Tech Soc; Potomac Tech Processing Libns; Internat Fed of Cath Alumnae. 11: St Joan of Arc Award for Civic Contributions. 12: "Patrons Are People"; "Promotion Ideas for Small Public Libraries"; Ed "The Quarterly Journal of the Library of Congress"; Ed "Friends of the Library" (62); Ed "Definition: Library" (61); Auth "So You Want to Be a Librarian" (63). 13: Yes. 14: Pub rel, admin, writing, publ. 15: 8705 Jones Mill rd, Wash DC 20015.

WALLACE, WILLIAM TEARLE. b York Penn 11 D 24. 4: Elizabeth Ways. 5: Penn State 42-43, 48-49 (Labor Mgt Rel) AB; George WashingtonU 46-47, 50-51 (Ind Psych); Columbia 67-68 MLS. 6: Fr, Sp. 7: Statistician US Dept of Labor, Wash DC 49-50; Aviator (Major) USMC, US & For East 42-46, 51-66; Registered rep Hornblower & Weeks Hemphill Noyes, York Penn 66-67; Ref libn StanfordU 68-. 8: Squadron Command Offr US Marine corps, Brigade G-1, US Marine Corps 62, Far-East. 9: Marine Corps Assn; ASIS; Helibs of No Cal. 10: US Marine Corps, Ret. 11: Navy Letter of Commendation, Korea 53. 14: Automated bibliog control, admin. 15: 26850 St Francis rd, Los Altos Hills Ca 94022.

WALLACE, WILLIAM S (WILLING). b Springfield Ill 18 Jl 22. 4: Almina Wiggins. 5: West State Col of Colo 41-45 (Hist) BA; UMont 49 (Hist) MA; UDenver 52-53 MALS. 6: Sp. 7: Pub sch tchr Hot Springs NM 45-48; Hist instr UMont 49; Consul archivist, Yakima Wash 50-52; Libn & archivist Highlands U 53-. 9: ALA (Life mem); AHA (Life mem); SAA (Life mem); NMLA. 10: Rouce & Coffin Club (Los Angeles); Phi Alpha Theta. 12: "Antoine Robidoux, 1794-1860" (53); "A Journey Through New Mexicos First Judicial District in 1864" (56); "The Land Between" (57). 13: Yes. 14: West Americana, lib hist. 15: 2916 San Rafael SE, Albuquerque NM 87106.

WALLACH, EILEEN (LOVETT). b Arlington Mass. 4: John M Wallach. 5: Simmons 31-35 (LS) BS; Columbia 38-43 MS in LS. 6: Ger, Fr. 7: Sch & ref libn NY Pub Lib 35-37; St Johns U (NY): Asst libn 37-42, Instr 39-42, Asst Prof 45-46; Head catlgr Pease Mem Lib, Ridgewood NJ 49-50; Head catlgr Perrot Mem Lib, Old Greenwich Conn 59-61, Head Libn 61-. 9: ALA; NELA; ConnLA; Lib Admin Group Fairfield Co. 10: Rocky Point Club, Old Greenwich; Simmons Club of So Fairfield Co; Jr League. 14: Admin, catlg. 15: Perrot Mem Lib, Old Greenwich Ct 06870.

WALLACH, JOHN SIDNEY. b Toronto Ohio 6 Ja 39. 4: Jane Springett. 5: Kent State 57-63 (Educ) BS in Ed; URI 66-68 MLS. 7: Dir Mercer Co Lib, Celina Ohio 68-. 9: ALA; OhoLA. 10: US Naval Res. 14: Admin. 15: 923 Hemlock st, Celina Oh 45822.

WALLACH, KATE. b Krefeld Germany 17 My 05. 5: UCologne31 JD; UWis 40 LLB; UMich 42 ABLS. 6: Ger, Fr, Ital, Sp, Lat. 7: Asst to Prof Harry Shulman Yale 62-68 Law Sch 36-38; Catlgr UMich Law Lib 40-42; Attorney US Nat Labor Rel Bd, Wash DC 43-46; Asst law libn unc 47-49; Law Libn LSU 49-,Law Libn & Prof of Law 64-. 9: Internat Lib Assn; AALL (Exec Bd 62-68, pres 66-67, pres SE Chap 58-59); ALA; SLA; LaLA (pres 60-61). 10: Phi Delta Delta; Amer Bar Assn; Wis Bar Assn; Order of the Coif. 12: "Research in Louisiana Law (58). 13: Yes. 14: Bibliog, legal hist. 15: Law Lib La State Univ, Baton Rouge La 70803.

WALLAD, RUTH (BERKOWITZ). b Trenton NJ 3 Ag 10. 4: Harry E Wallad. 5: NJ State Col (TRENTON) 27-31 BS; Pratt 34-35 BLS; Columbia 37-50 (LS). 6: Fr, Ger. 7: Asst Lib NJ

State Col Trenton 31-34; Sub tchr pub schs, Trenton NJ 31-34; Indexer State Tax Commsn, Newark NJ 35-36; Ed asst H W Wilson Co, Bronx NY 36-40; Ed "Industrial Arts Index H W Wilson Co, Bronx NY 40-44; Lib asst Straubenmuller Textile High Sch, NYC 44-49; Lib asst Washington Irving High Sch, NYC49-54; Libn Thomas Jefferson High Sch, Brooklyn NY 54-. 9: NYSchLA; NYLA; NY Lib Club. 12: Co-comp "Industrial Arts Index (40-49). 14: High sc libs. 15: 35-31 - 85th st, Jackson Heights NY 11372.

WALLER, CAROLYN (ADAMS). b E Providence RI 16 Jl 25. 4: Rowell L Waller Jr. 5: Pembroke 42-46 (Sociol) AB; Columbia 51-52 MS in LS. 7: Asst libn Pembroke Col 46-49, Libn in chg 49-54; Libn Nursing Lib Roger Williams Gen Hosp 59-60, Libn Med Lib 61-62; Consul libn Providence Lying-In Hosp Med Lib 62-; Consul libn Providence Chld Guidance Clinic Lib 63-67; Libn Levy Lib Emma Pendleton Bradley Hosp, Riverside RI 67-. 8: Lib trustee Seekonk Pub Lib, Seekonk Mass 62-68, chm 63-67. 9: RI Med Libn Assn. 10: Seekonk Bldg Com for No Lib; Seekonk Bd of Lib Trustees. 14: Estab small spec libs. 15: 17 Bradley st, Seekonk Mass 02771.

WALLER, ROWELL LUCIAN. b Memphis Tenn 2 Je 28. 4: Carolyn Adams. 5: Southwestern at Memphis 46-48; Vanderbilt 48-50 (Hist, Pol Sci) BA; Columbia 52 MS in LS. 7: Gen asst Walter Harvey Jr Col 50-51; Gen prof asst Washington Heights & Bloomingdale Brs & Bronx Ref Center NY Pub Lib 51-53; 1st asst in info & ref dept Providence Pub Lib 53-56; Head Libn Attleboro Pub Lib, Attleboro Mass 57-. 8: Consul in lib sci NortheasternU, lectr -65-. 9: ALA; MassLA (treas 62-66; Old Dartmouth Lib Club, (pres 59-60). 10: C of C of the Attleboros. 14: Ref. 15: Attleboro PUB Lib, Attleboro Mass 02703.

WALLING, HELEN (PICKRELL). b Colfax Wash 20 S 10. 4: Dow Overbaugh Walling. 5: UWash 28-32 (Fr) BA; Columbia 49-50 (Eng) MA, 52-55 MLS. 6: Fr, Sp, Ger. 7: Secondary tchr Bd of Educ, Bellingham Wash 32-37 Secondary tchr Bd f Educ, New Rochelle NY 45-48, Secondary sch libn 52-. 9: SE SchLA NY State. 10: Beta Phi Mu; Manor Clubof Pelham Manor NY. 14: Sch lib wk. 15: 4784 Boston Post rd, Pelham Manor NY 10803.

WALLING, RUTH. b Hutto Tex 16 Jl 11. 5: So Methodist U 29-31 (Eng) BA; Tex Womans U 34-35 BA in LS; Chicago 40-41 (LS) MA. 6: Fr, Sp, Lat. 7: Ref libn E Tex State Col 35-44; Act chief circ libn LSU 44-46, Chief ref libn 47-54; Chief ref libn Emory U 54-, Assoc U libn 63-. 9: ALA (chm Subsc Bks Com 59-61); -ACRL (Com on Standards 54-59); GaLA; SELA. 11: Isadore Gilbert Mudge Citation, 64. 13: Yes. 14: Ref. 15: 139 E Hill st apt 51, Decatur Ga 30030.

WALLIS, CARLTON LAMAR. b Blue Springs Miss 15 O 15. 4: Mary Elizabeth Cooper. 5: Miss Col 32-36 (Eng) AB; Tulane 41-42 (Eng) MA; Chicago 46-47 LS. 6: Fr. 7: Tchr Miss Pub Schs, Saltillo & Oelzoni 36-41; Instr Tulane U 41-42; Chief Warrant Off US Army, European Theatre 42-45; Chief libn Rosenberg Lib, Galveston Tex 47-55; Chief libn Richmond Pub Lib, Richmond Va 55-58; Dir Memphis Pub Lib, Memphis Tenn 58-. 8: Lib bldg consul, Mid South, 59-; Ark Lib Com, 65-; Bd mem, Great Bks Found 64-68, Fed Rel Coord, Tenn 64-66. 9: ALA (mem Greater ALA and var other coms 47-);-PLA (chm ILCC Com 66-67); TennLA (pres 68-69; chm Legis Com 59-60); SELA (chm Pub Lib Div 62-64; chm Nomin Com 60-61). 10: Rotary Club; Memphis RT NCCJ; Travelers' Aid; Memphis Opera Theater; Richmond Symphony; Va Educ TV. 12: "Libraries in The Golden Triangle" (66). 13: Yes. 14: Admin, lib bldgs. 15: Memphis Public Library, 258 S McLean blvd, Memphis Tn 38104.

WALLIS, (MARY) WILMA. b Denton Tex 16 Mr 43. 5: Tex Woman'sU 61-65 (Fr) BA, 65-66 MLS. 7: Army libn USA Spec Serv Agcy: Wiley Bks, Neu-Ulm Germany 66-67, Hawkins Bks, Oberammergau Germany 67-. 9: ALA (Armed Forces Libns Sect, Europ Subsect). 14: Ref. 15: Spec Serv Lib Hawkins Barracks, APO New York 09172.

WALLIS, MARIE POPE. b Des Moines Iowa 18 Jl 01. 5: UCLA 23-25 (Eng) BA; USoCal 28, 34-35 (Speech, Drama, Soc Wk) MA, MS in SW; UNM 39-42, 46-47, summers 53, 57, 60 (Span, Portu, Elem Educ) PhD, MA; UOkla 57-58, summers 58, 59 MLS. 6: Sp, Portu. 7: Actress & dir, Cal, NY NJ 26-31; Soc wker, Cal & NM 33-38, 38-39, 42-44, 51-52; Coun Womens Army Corps, Ft Sam Houston Tex 44-45; Asst Prof Span UNM 39-42, 45-50; Pub sch tchr, Cal & NM 25-26, 28-29, 31-32, 53-6; Sch libn Albuquerque & Taos (NM) Schs 60-64; Ref libn Principia Col 64-65; Dir instr materials center Bur INDIAN Affairs Wingate High Sch, Ft Wingate NM 65-66; State of Hawaii travel libn 66, 68; Ext libn Dept of the Army, Okinawa 66-67; Army libn, Ft Huachuca Ariz 69-. 8: State commun serv consul, NM, 51-52; CONSUL NM Comsn on Child & Yoth, 51-52; NM Wing, Civil Air Patrol, Womens Activ & Aviation EducProjs adv 52-56. 9: Internat Platform Assn; NEA; ALA; NASW; AATSP; NMEA; NMLA. 10: AAUP; Phi Kappa Phi; Mortar Board; Alpha Kappa Delta; Theta Alpha Phi; Tau Kappa Alpha; Phi Sigma Iota; Sigma Delta Pi; Sigma Alpha Iota; Phi Alpha Theta; Phi Delta Gamma; Pi Lambda Theta; Delta Kappa Gamma; Alpha Eta Rho; Albuquerque Hist Soc; Amer Legion. 11: Recogniton by Brazilian Acad of Letters, Rio de Janeiro, 50. 12: "Intersection (50). 13: Yes. 14: Materials centers, lib ctred media, child theater operations. 15: Box 1024, Grants NM 87020.

WALLMANN, MARY (WATKINSON). b Albany Cal 21 Ap 27. 5: UCal (Berkeley) 45-49 (Fr) BA, 49-50 BLS, 65-66 (Educ) Tchg Credential. 6: Fr. 7: Child libn La Grange Pub, LaGrange Ill 50-51; Sch libn Albany High Sch, Albany Cal 66-. 10: Phi Beta Kappa. 15: 1675 Marin ave, Berkeley Ca 94707.

WALLOWER, LUCILLE. b Waynesboro Penn. 5: Penn Mus Sch of Art; Traphagan Sch of Fashion (NY); Penn State Lib Assn Certif 61. 7: Sch libn Harrisburg Pub Lib, Harrisburg Penn 43-44, Asst child libn 44-46; Dir Harrisburg Art Assoc Studio, Harrisburg Penn 43-48; Fashion artist, Harrisburg Penn: Pomeroy's Inc 46-49, Bowman's Inc 49-52; Freelance writer-illustrator 52-59; Child libn Abington Lib Soc, jenkintown Penn 59-. 8: Author-in-residence, Springfield Twp Sch Dist, Delaware Co, Penn, fall 68, spring 69. 9: PennLA. 10: Child Reading RT; Hist Soc Penn; Old York Rd hist Soc. 12: Author-illustrator of numerous children's bks (40-69). 14: Child bks. 15: Abington Lib York and Vista rds, Jenkintown Pa 19046.

WALLS, ANNA A. b McComb Okla 4 O 37. 5: Okla CityU 58-60. 7: Clk pub docs div Okla Dept of Libs 55-56, Libn asst law div 56-63, Libn asst legisl ref div 63-68, Hd legisl ref div 68-. 12: Ed "Directory and Manual of the State of Oklahoma, 1961"; "Oklahoma State Agencies, Boards, Commissions, Courts, Institutions, Legislature and Officers" (61); "Who's Who in the Oklahoma Legislature" 32nd (69-). 13: Yes. 14: Ref. 15: 814 East dr, Oklahoma City Ok 73105.

WALLS, ESTHER JEAN. b Mason City Iowa 1 My 26. 5: Mason City Jr Col 46-48 (Liberal Arts); State UIowa 46-48 (Romance Lang) BA; Columbia 49-50 (LS) MS. 6: Fr. 7: NYC Pub Lib: Voc schs specialist, Spec projects libn Central Research Lib, Supv Clasons Point Br, Supv Countee Cullen Reg Br 49-65, Dir N Manhattan Lib Project 64-65, Dir adult new libs project 65-66, Asst dir for Africa Franklin Bk Programs 66-68, Dir bk & lib serv Franklin Bk Programs 68-. 8: Extensive travels in Africa as consl on bks, libs, women's activities; Participant in radio & educ TV progs. 9: ALA; -AASchL; -YASD; -Internat Rel RT; African Studies Assn; African-Amer Inst (Coun); NY Lib Club. 10: Harlem Cult Coun. 12: "Some Observations on Nigerian Libraries" (64); Co-comp "African Encounter, A Selected Bibliography of Books, Films and Other Materials" (ALA 63); Co-auth "A Basic Development Project in Nigeria 1964-1968" (68). 13: Yes. 14: Internat libnship. 15: 160 W End ave, New York NY 10023.

WALLS, JOE THOMAS. b Naples Tex 14 Jl 35. 5: Baylor U 53-57; Music theory & Lit) BM; UDenver 64-65 (LS) MA; UColo summers 62-65 (Music Educ) MMus Ed. 7: Tchr Ft Worth Pub Schs, Ft Worth Tex 59-64; Documents libn Tex A&M U Lib 65-. 9: TexLA; SWLA. 14: Govt docs, admin. 15: 406 Madeleine dr, Bryan Tx 77801.

WALLS, MADELYN E. b Mason City Iowa 5 My 24. 5: Mason City Jr Col 42-44; State U Iowa 44-46 (Eng) BA; Columbia summer 51. 6: Fr. 7: Tchr, Keysville Ga 47-48; Circ libn Mason City (Iowa) Pub Lib 49-. 9: IowaLA. 14: Adult serv, ref. 15: 626 S Adams, Mason City Iowa 50421.

WALPER, LUCILLE (MILLS). b Webb City Mo 6 D 08. 4: Robert G Walper. 5: Wichita U 51-52. 7: Glenn L Martin Co, Baltimore: Clerk engnr planning 42-45, Clerk Engnr Lib 45-48, Libn 48-50; Clerk production lanning Piaseki Helicopter Corp, Morton Penn 50-51; Libn Beech Aircraft Corp, Wichita Kan 51-52; Libn Boeing Airplane Co, Wichita Kan 53; Catlg libn Solar Aircraft Co, San Diego 59-6, Libn 61-65; Salk Inst, San Diego Lib asst 66-67. 9: SLA. 15: 4824 1/2 Old Cliffs rd, San Diego Ca 92120.

WALSDORF, JOHN J. b Sheboygan Wis 19 Je 41. 4: Karen Wendt. 5: Wis State U (Oshkosh) 59-63 (LS, Eng) BS; UWis

(Madison) 63-64 MLS. 6: Ger. 7: Cheese maker Lake-to-Lake, Kiel Wis 58-62; Lib aide Wis State U (Oshkosh) 61-62; Clothing salesman Oregon Clothing House, Oshkosh Mich 63; Govt docs & ref libn Milwaukee Pub Lib 64-66; Sr lending libn Oxford Pub Lib, Oxford England 66-67; Lib serv adv B H Blackwell, Oxford England 67-. 9: ALA; CanLA; WisLA. 10: Private Libs Assn (London); William Morris Soc (London). 12: 1969 AB Yearbook, "The Antiquarian Book Trade in Great Britain". 13: Yes. 14: Rare bks, acquis. 15: PO Box 4932, Milwaukee Wi 53215.

WALSH, BERTRAND M. b Montreal Can 21 Mr 5. 4: Dorothy J Seesholtz. 5: McGill 33-37 BA; Sir George Williams U 38-42 (Gen Sci) BSc; McGill 46-47 BS in LS; Columbia 47-51 MS in LS. 6: Fr. 7: Jr chem Can Copper Refiners Ltd, Montreal 38-42; Can Army Lt Artillery, Capt Sel Personnel, Europe 42-46; Ref asst NY Pub Lib S&T div 47-50; Libn orgnic chem dept Jackson Lab Lib Du Pont, Wilmington Del 51-. 9: SLA; ACS. 10: Du Pont Country Club. 14: Ref (sci, chem). 15: Wedgewood dr RD 1, Chadds Ford Pa 19317.

WALSH, CARMEN (WILSON). b Detroit 3 Je 16. 4: Daniel James Walsh. 5: Beloit Col 35-37 (Chem); Northwestern 37-39 (Chem, Eng) BS; UIll 40-41 BSLS. 6: Fr, Ger. 7: Northwestern U; Clerical asst 39-40, Circ asst 41-42, Libn Tech Inst 42-46; Ref libn UIll (Navy Pier) Chicago 46-47; John Crerar Lib, Chicago; Ref asst 47-48, Asst chief ref dept 49-51, Chief ref dept 51-56; Libn Internat Minerals & Chem Corp, Skokie and Libertyville Ill 56-. 9: SLA; ALA; IllLA. 10: PHI Beta Kappa. 13: Yes. 14: Admin, ref. 15: Internat Min & Chm Corp, Old Orchard rd, Skokie Ill 60078.

WALSH, EDWARD JOHN. b E Orange NJ 2 S 41. 4: Katherine L Tamminen. 5: SUNY (Albany) 58-63 (Teahcer Educ, Soc Studies) BA, 64-65 MLS. 6: Fr. 7: Catlgr asst libn James A Milne Mem Lib SUNY (Oneonta) 65-. 9: ALA; SUNYLA (Coun). 14: Catlg. 15: 101 Center st, Oneonta NY 13820.

WALSH, ELLEN LUCILLE. b Huron SD 2 S 04. 5: UMont 22-24; UWash 24-26 bs in LS. 7: 1st asst Everett Pub Lib, Everett Wash 26-28; Ref libn SD Free Lib Commsn, Pierre SD 35-39; Ref asst Tacoma Pub Lib, Tacoma Wash 40-42; 1st asst circ dept Seattle Pub Lib 42-51, Head adult educ dept 51-. 9: Adult Educ Assn; ALA (Coun rep Wash 59-63); PNLA (2d v-pres 54-55); WashLA (2d v-pres 63-65; chm General Wkshops Proj 64-65); Exec Com 47-49; chm By-Laws Com 67-68). 10: Seattle King Co Com for Adult Educ; Seattle King Co Coun on Aging; Seattle-KOBE Affiliation Com; The Mountaineers; Bus & Prof Womens Club; Seattle UN Assn; Sundowners Bus & Prof Women's Club; NW Adult EA. 11: Fund for Adult Educ Study Grant, 54. 13: Yes. 14: Adult educ. 15: 6033 - 6th NE, Seattle Wa 98115.

WALSH, REV JOSEPH PSJ. b Portland Me 10 Mr 27. 5: Boston Col 47-51 (Philos) AB, 51-52 (Philos) MA; Weston Col 55-59 (Theol) STL; Simmons 61-65 MSLS. 6: Lat, Fr, Ger, Sp. 7: Tchr Cranwell Sch, Lenox Mass 52-54; Assoc libn Weston Col 60-; Libn Bishop Connolly High Sch. 9: ALA. 12: Assoc ed "New Testament Abstracts (56-58). 15: Bishop Connolly High School 373 Elsbree st, Fall River Ma 02720.

WALSH, SISTER M NAOMI SC. b Lackawanna NY 2 D 09. 5: Seton Hill Col 28-32 (Hist) BA; Carnegie 35-36 BSLS. 7: Tchr St Luke Sch, Carnegie Penn 33-35; Asst libn Seton Hill Col 36-42; Libn-tchr St Joseph Acad, Greensburg Penn 36-39, 42-45; Libn-tchr Pittsburgh parochia schs 45-51; Libn Sacred Heart High Sch, Pittsburgh 51-67; Asst libn Seton Hill Col 67-; Sch lib consul Diocese of Greensburg 67-. 8: Com on Cath Supplement to "Standard Catalog for High School Libraries. 9: ALA; CathLA (Exec Bd 62-69; High Sch libs Sect: sec-treas 55-63, sec 63-65); PennLA; Coun of SchLibns Sub Pittsburgh; SWest PennLA. 12: Ed Basic Reference Books for Catholic High School Libraries (59, 2d ed 63); Ed CathLA High Sch Lib Sect "Newsletter (55-57). 13: Yes. 14: Bk sel for ya, catlg, tchg use lib & bks. 15: Seton Hill Col, Greensburg Pa 15601.

WALSH, SISTER MARIAN TIMOTHY SND. b Brookline Mass5 F 02. 5: Trinity Col (Wash DC) 21-25 (Eng, Chem) AB; Boston U 25-26 (Fr); Catholic U summers 31-41 BS in LS, summers 56, 58 (Braille). 6: Fr, Ger. 7: Lib asst Trinity Col (Wash DC) 31, Catlgr sci libn 32-45; High sch libn Maryvale, Towson Md 45-47; Libn Notre Dame Acad, Wash DC 47-61; Sci & art libn Trinity Col (Wash DC) 61-. 8: Braille transcribing tchg, Notre Dame Acad & Trinity Col. 9: CathLA. 15: Trinity Col Lib, Wash DC 20017.

WALSH, MARY (ROSE ANN). b Belleville Ont Can 24 Jl 22. 5: UToronto 41-45 BA; McGill 47-48 BLS. 6: Fr. 7: Asst libn Bank of Montreal Lib 48-50; Asst libn Sir George Williams U 50-59; Libn Johnson & Johnson Research Lib, Montreal 59-61; Libn Sun Life of Can, Montreal 61-67, Chief libn 67-. 9: SLA; CanLA; QueLA. 14: Ref. 15: Sun Life Assurance Co of Can PO Box 6075, Montreal 110 Can.

WALSH, MAURICE DAVID. b NYC 24 D 24. 4: Alice Louise Flynn. 5: UMo 46-49 (Advertising, Pub Rel) BJ; LSU 62-63 MS in LS. 6: Sp. 7: US Army; Asst Rifle Sqd Leader (Sgt), Europe 43-45, Rifle Platoon Leader (2d Lt), Korea 50-52; Asst acquis libn Jefferson Parish Lib, Gretna La 59-61, Ref libn 61-63, Admin 63-. 8: Maj US Army Reserve. 9: ALA; LaLA. 10: BPOE; Assn of US Army; Alpha Delta Sigma Eleventh Armored Div Assn; First Cavalry Div Assn; Press Club of New Orleans. 11: Bronze Star with "V device (2nd Award); Purple Heart with Cluster, Combat Infantrymans Badge (2nd Award), ETO Ribbon with3 Battle Stars, Korea Ribbon with 1 battle Star. 13: Yes. 14: Admin, personnel. 15: P O Box 7608 N Causeway blvd at Melvil Dewey dr, Metaire La 70002.

WALSH, S PADRAIG. b Llanelly S Wales 18 Ja 22. 4: Violet OShea. 5: Assoc mem Lib Assn (Gt Brit) 50. 6: Sp. 7: Deputy libn Pub Lib, Llawelly S Wales 39-59; 1st asst ref div Akron Pub Lib, Akron Ohio 62-63; Head catlgr UDEL 64-65 Spec proj ed R R Bowker Co, NY 65-. 9: ALA; -ACRL; Lib Assn, Gt Brit; CathLA. 12: "General World Atlases in Print (66); "General Encyclopedias in Print (63-); "English Language Dictionaries in Print (65); "Anglo-American General Encyclopedias 1703-1967 (68); "Home Reference Books in Print (69). 13: Yes. 14: Clsf, catlg, ref. 15: R R Bowker Co, 1180 Ave of the Americas, NYC 10036.

WALSWORTH, MARGARET W. b Roanoke La 7 O 08. 5: Ind Central Col 26-29 (Eng); UIll 29-31 BA, BLS. 7: Copy reader Law Bk Div Bobbs-Merrill Publ Co, Indianapolis 32-35; Asst Ext Div Indianapolis Pub Lib 35-39; Asst libn Tri-Parish Demonstration Lib La State Lib, Winnfield La 39-41; Libn Winnfield (La) High Sch Lib 43, Catahoula Parish Lib, Harrisonburg La 52-55, Natchitoches Parish Lib, Natchitoches La 55-56, Vermilion Parish Lib, Abbeville La 56-. 9: ALA; LaLA. 10: Delta Kappa Gamma. 14: Ref, loc hist & materials. 15: Box 640, Abbeville La 70510.

WALTEMADE, HENRY J(OHN). b Ohiowa Neb 27 O 10. 4: Joan Halloran. 5: Neb State Col 29-33 (Hist) BA; UIll 34-35 BS in LS, 35-38 (LS) MA; Washington & Jefferson 43 (Army Class Sch). 7: Prof asst order dept UIll Lib (Urbana) 35-38; Assoc dir UColo Libs 38-63; US Army (S/Sgt) 42-45; Act dir UColo Libs 54-55, 57, Assoc dir for spec collections 63-. 9: Bibl Soc Amer; Bibl Soc (London); ColoLA. 10: AAUP. 14: Rare bks, mss, printers ornaments. 15: 2443 - 6th st, Boulder Co 80302.

WALTER, GARY D. b Fergus Falls Minn 1 N 39. 4: Chonghui Lee. 5: UMd (Overseas) 60-62 (Korean Lang); UWash 62-64 (Chinese Lang & Lit) BA, 64-65 (Korean Hist) MA, 66-67 MLS. 6: Korean, Chinese. 7: Research fellow (Asian libs) For Area Fellow, Seoul Korea 67-68; Libn (ROK Forces Vietnam) 8 US Army, Seoul Korea 68-. 9: KoreanLA; ALA; Assn Asian Studies. 10: Korean Studies Soc (Seattle). 11: Fulbright Fellow (Korea). 13: Yes. 14: Admin (Asian area). 15: 3538 S Hudson st, Seattle Wa 98118.

WALTER, HUGO ALPHONSE. b Fredericksburg Tex 21 Ap 32. 4: Jennie Elisabeth Walter. 5: UTex (Austin) 49-54 BS in Ed; E Tex StateU 66-68 MS in LS. 6: Ger. 7: Asst in E Tex hist Stephen F Austin StateU 68-. 9: ALA; TexLA; SWLA; TexStateTA. 10: E Tex Hist Assn. 14: Loc hist, archives. 15: SFA Sta Box 6134, Nacogdoches Tx 75961.

WALTER, KENNETH GAINES. b Emory Univ Ga 14 Mr 32. 4: Eva Lou McClelland. 5: Emory 50-54 (Geol) AB; UGa(Atlanta) summer 51, 52; Emory 54-55 (Geol) MS; UNC 58-61, 62-63 (Ger, LS) MSLS; UWien(Vienna) 61-62. 6: Ger, Fr. 7: US Army Qm Corps Petrol Prod Lab, Sr Lab NCO (Cpl), Ariz & France 56-57, USAR Sch Unit NCO in chg of S-1 Sect (S/Sgt) 58-63; Asst card order clerk UNC (Chapel Hill) 59-61 & 62-63; Asst catlg libn Ohio U Lib 63-65, Head catlg dept 65-68; Asst dir of libs USoCar 68-. 9: ALA; Ohio Valley Assn Tech Serv Libns; SELA. 10: AAUP; Delta Tau Delta; Sigma Gamma Epsilon; Beta Phi Mu; Ga Acad of Sci. 11: Fulbright & Austrian Govt grants for study at U Wien, Vienna, 61-62. 12: "Library Guide of Ohio University (64). 13: Yes. 14: Catlg, admin, tchg lb sci, research. 15: 8 Lakecrest dr, Columbia SC 29206.

WALTER, PAT (LEBENSART). b Vienna 19 D 27. 4: Donald O Walter. 5: Pomona Col 46-50 (Eng) BA; USoCal

50-51 MLS. 6: Ger. 7: Intern LC 51-52; UCLA: Circ libn I 52-53, Atomic energy proj libn 53-54, Bibliog Physiol Dept 60, Catlgr Biomed Lib 61, Train Coordinator Biomed Lib 61-64, Head bibliog unit Brain Info Serv 64-. 9: MedLA (chm Subcom on Internship). 10: Phi Beta Kappa. 14: Info storage & retrieval. 15: Biomed Lib UCLA, Los Angeles Cal 90024.

WALTER, VIOLA IDA. b Madison SD 28 Mr 29. 5: Gen Beadle State Tchrs Col 47-51 (Educ, Eng, Journalism) BS; UColo summer 54; UDenver summers 55-58 (LS) MA. 7: Eng tchr Henry High Sch, Henry SD 51-52; Eng tchr & libn Redfield High Sch, Redfield SD 52-58; Jr high libn Sch Dist 318, Grand Rapids Minn 58-. 9: NEA; ALA-AASchL; MinnEA; MinnASchL. 10: Beta Sigma Phi; AAUW. 13: Yes. 14: Sch lib serv. 15: 214 3rd ave NE, Grand Rapids Minn 55744.

WALTERS, BEVERLEY ANN (STOTTS). b Malta Mont 18 Ag 37. 4: Edward F Walters. 5: Olympic Col 55-58 (Eng) AA; UWash 58-59 (Eng) BA, 59-60 MLibnship. 6: Fr, Sp. 7: Receptionist, sec Soc Security Admin, Bremerton Wash55-57; Supply clerk UWash Lib 58, Clerk typist 58-59; Asst libn Olympic Col 62-63, 64-; Adak Sch (K-12) libn, Alaska 69-. 9: ALA; -CSD; SLA. 10: Beta Phi Mu. 14: Acquis, catlg, bibliog, sch. 15: US Naval Sta Box 2, FPO Seattle Wa 98791.

WALTERS, CLARENCE R(ONALD). b Detroit 11 Je 32. 5: Wayne State U 50-54 (Hist) AB; UMich 57-60 MALS. 6: Ger. 7: Stock clerk A&P Tea Co, Detroit 48-54, 56-57; PLT Ldr, CO Exo, Tk Bn US Army, Hanau Germany 54-56; Detroit Pub Lib: Pre-prof asst 57-60, Ref asst tech dept 61-62, Br asst 62-64; Lib bldg consul Mch State Lib 64-66; Asst co libn Wayne Co Fed Lib Syst, Wayne Mich 66-. 9: ALA; MichLA, (chm Pub Lib Div). 10: Mich Soc of Planning Officials. 13: Yes. 14: Bldgs & equip, admin. 15: 31493 Capri ter, Westland Mi 48185.

WALTERS, HEATHER MARY. b Perth Australia 30 Ap 34. 5: UWest Australia (Fr) BA, Honours deg, (Dental Sci); Registration Certif of the Lib Assn of Australia. 6: Fr, Ger. 7: Catlgr Nat Lib of Australia, Canberra 59-61; Indexer "Applied Science & Technology Index H W Wilson Co, NY 62-63; Catlgr Polytech Inst of Brooklyn 64-. 9: Lib Assn Australia; ALA; NY Lib Club; NY Tech Serv Libns. 14: Catlg, indexing. 15: 142 Henry st, Apt 8, Brooklyn NY 11201.

WALTERS, HELEN J. b Mt Holly NJ 22 O 19. 5: Duke U 37-41 (Fr) BA; Rutgers 54-58 MLS. 7: Clerk actuarial Prudential Insurance Co, Newark NJ 42-44; Lib asst duke U 45-47; Libn Grier Sch, Tyrone Penn 47-49; Lib aset UOre 49-51; Asst hosp libn US Army, Ft Dix NJ 51-53, Acquis & dispositions libn 53-54; Base libn USAF, McGuire AFB NJ 54-68; Sr libn Burlington Co Lib, Mount Holly NJ 68-. 9: ALA; NJLA. 10: DAR. 14: Catlg, ref. 15: Marne Highway, Mt Holly NJ 08060.

WALTERS, MARGARET. b Canton Ohio 12 Je 23. 5: Wilson Col 41-45 (Eng) BA; Columbia 46-47 (LS) BS. 7: Asst West Side Br Ryerson Lib, Grand Rapids Mich 47-51; Libn Kamehamehe Sch for Girls, Honolulu 51-53; Ya libn 2 brs Akron Pub Lib, Akron Ohio 53-56; Libn Morley Lb, Pinesville Ohio 56-64; Spec proj for Kamehameha Sch for Boys, Honolulu 64-65; Libn Waterford Pub Lib, Waterford Conn 65-. 9: ALA. 14: Pub lib admin, ref, arts. 15: 49 Rope Ferry rd, Waterford Ct 06385.

WALTHALL, HARRY RONALD. b Kan City Kan 9 Ap 31. 5: Ottawa U (Kan) 49-53 (Hist) BA; Kan State Tchrs Col (Emporia) 55-56 (LS) MS. 7: (Pfc) Army of the US 53-55; Asst libn West State Col (Gunnison Colo) 56-57; Libn Ottawa U (Kan) 57-60; Libn II Fresno State Col 60-62; Asst libn Col of the Desert 62-. 9: CalLA. 14: Pub serv. 15: 43-500 Monterey, Palm Desert Ca 92260.

WALTHER, CONSTANCE JOYCE. b Ft Dodge Iowa 8 Mr 43. 4: Richard A Walther. 5: Iowa State U 60-64 (Hist) BS; UMinn 64-65 (LS) ma. 6: Sp. 7: Instr & catlgr Iowa State U Lib 65-67; Ref libn Cedar Rapids Pub Lib, Cedar Rapids Iowa 67-. 9: ALA; IowaLA. 10: AAUW: Alpha Lambda Delta; Phi Kappa Phi, Beta Phi Mu. 14: Catlg, ref. 15: Rte 2, Marion Ia 52302.

WALTHER, LaVERN (SIEGGREEN). b Sacramento Cal 15 Mr 16. 4: John Walther. 5: San Francisco State Col 34-38 (Hist) AB; UWash 38-39 AB in LS; Columbia 43-44MS in LS; Ind U 57 (LS) Ed D. 7: Act libn AUBURN Pub Lib, Auburn Cal 39-40; Asst libn US Research Org, Wash DC 40-42; Head Libn Oroville Pub Lib, Oroville Cal 42-43; Head catlg & order depts Osterhout Pub Lib, Wilkes-Barre Penn 44-46; Catlgr Cal State Lib 46-47; Instr in Lib Sci Ind U 47-50, Asst Prof of Lib Sci 50-59; Assoc Prof Lib Sci No Ill U 59-60, Head Dept of Lib Sci 60-. 9: ALA; IndLA; IllLA. 10: AAUP; Pi Lambda Theta; Delta Kappa Gamma; Altrusa Internat. 13: Yes. 14: Lib sci educ. 15: No Ill Univ, Dept of Lib Sci, DeKalb Ill 60115.

WALTNER, NELLIE (LAIRD). b Harper Kan 6 S 18. 4: Arthur W Waltner. 5: BethelU 36-41 (Mus) AB; Morehead State fall 42 (Liberal Arts); UNC (Chapel Hill) 43-44, 66-69 MS in LS; NC StateU 62-66. 6: Fr. 7: Bkkeeper, Newton Kan 37-41; Sec to Mus Dept & supv pub serv UNC Mus Lib (Chapel Hill) 44-48; Circ asst D H Hill Lib NC StateU 56-62, Searcher summer 66, Catlgr summer 68; Supv project to prodyce catlg in machine readable form Coop Raleigh Cols, Raleigh NC 68-. 10: Beta Phi Mu. 14: Catlg. 15: 1204 Westmoreland dr, Raleigh NC 27609.

WALTON, BARBARA (KING). b Spokane Wash. 5: Mills Col 36-37 (Child Psych); UWash 38-40 (Gen Studies, Mus) BA, 59-60 (LS) MA. 7: Olympia Wash; ext serv libn S Puget Sound Reg Lib 60-64, Ref 64-67, Red Hdqrs Timberland Reg Lib 68-. 14: Ref, child adult readers serv. 15: 404 S 16th, Shelton Wash 98584.

WALTON, CLYDE C. b Chicago 8 Mr 25. 4: Anne Hoover. 5: Cornell Col 46-48 (Eng) BA; Chicago 49-50 (LS) MA. 7: State U Iowa Lib; Ser res 50-51, Curator of rare bks & univ archivist 51-55, Head ref dept & asst prof 55-56; State histn & Head Ill State Hist Lib, Springfield Ill 56-67; Exec dir Ill State Hist Soc, Springfield Ill 56-67; Exec dir Ill State Hist Soc, Springfield Ill 56-67; Assoc Prof & Dir of libs No Ill U 67-. 8: Sec Civil War Centennial Commsn of Ill, 59-65; Ill Higher Bd Master Plan Lib Com; chm Lincoln Home Adv Commsn 61-67. 9: ALA (Life mem); AHS; Miss Valley Hist Soc; Amer Assn State & Loc Hist; IllLA (2nd v-pres 65-66). 10: Sangamo Club; Rotary; Abraham Lincoln Assn; U S Grant Assn; Springfield Central Area Devel Assn; Chicago Civil War RT. 11: LLD, LINCOLN Col, Lincoln Ill, 56. 12: Found & ed Civil War History (55-59); Ed "Journal of the Illinois State Historical Society (56-); Ed "Indian War of 1864 (60); Ed "Private Smiths Journal (63); Ed "Behind the Guns (65). 13: Yes. 14: Spec collections, rare bks, mss, admin. 15: Ill State Hist Lib Centennial Bldg, Springfield Il 60115.

WALTON, JAMES B. b Wilmington NC 26 My 22. 4: June Stewart. 5: Harvard 46-48 (Soc Rel) AB; Columbia 49-50 MSLS. 6: Fr. 7: Period ref Ohio U 50-52; Asst libn Franklin & Marshall 52-55; Assoc libn George Washington U 55-59; Asst libn readers serv Johns Hopkins U (Homewood Campus) 60-. 15: 140 W Lanvale st, Baltimore Md 21217.

WALTON, LADY VIRGINIA BOGGS. b Scottsville Va 5 D 09. 4: Leslie Hughes Walton. 5: Longwood Col 31-35 (Soc Sci) BS; Col of William & Mary 39 (LS) UVa 53, 60, 64; Okla State U For study tour 68. 7: Tchr Buckingham Co Schs, Buckingham Co Va 27-28, 29-32; TCHR Gilmer Co Schs, Gilmer Co WVa 28-29; Albermarle Co Schs: Tchr, Warren Va 32-33, Tchr, Greenwood Va 33-35, Tchr & libn, Scottsvile Va 35-47, Tchr, Greenwood Va 51-53, Libn Albermarle High Sch, Charlottesville Va 53-63; Libn Charlottesville City Schs, Greenbrier, Charlottesville Va 63-. 9; nea; ALA chm Recr Com, Va); NCTE; Nat Coun of the Soc Studies; VaEA; VaLA (pres 65-). 10: Delta Kappa Gamma. 11: Rotary award for foreign travel. 13: Yes. 14: Sch libnship. 15: Rt l Box 2, Crozet Va 22932.

WALTON, MARGARET A (MacDONALD). b Orillia Ont Can 2 D 13. 4: William M Walton. 5: Toronto 35-39 (Eng) BA; So Conn State Col 55-59 (LS) MS. 6: Fr. 7: Sch libn Sara J Rawson Sch, Hartford Conn 56-59; Sch libn Talcott Jr High Sch, W Hartford Conn 59-. 9: NEA; ALA; ConnEA; ConnLA. 10: Eng-Speaking Union; Wampanoag Golf & Country Club. 14: Ref. 15: 14 Linnard rd, W Hartford Conn 06107.

WALTON, VIRGINIA (EDITH). b Indianola Iowa 6 Ja 08. 5: Simpson Col 25-29 (Eng) BA; Iowa State U summer; UDenver 38-39 BSLS; UKan 62-63; San Jose State Col summer 64. 6: Fr. 7: Dist lib supv WPA Dist 2, Kan City Mo 39-43; Br libn Kan City (Kan) Pub Lib 45-46; Co Libn Stillwater Co Lib, Columbus Mont 46-51; Co Libn Cass Co Lib, Harrisonville Mo 51-53; Libn Hist Soc of Mont, Helena Mont 53-59; Publib consul Mo State Lib 59-62; Libn Haskell Inst, Lawrence Kan 62-66; Adult serv spec Mid-continent Pub Lib, Independence Mo 66-. 9: ALA; Mont State LA (pres 55-56); PNLA (2nd v-pres 56-57); MoLA; KanLA; KanASchL; Amer Assn State & Loc Hist; Adult EA of US. 10: Delta Kappa Gamma; Bus & Prof Womens Club; Soroptimist Club; LWV. 14: Adult euc, pub lib serv, west hist. 15: 1717 Sterling, Independence Mo 64052.

WALZ, JAMES F(REDERICK). b Saugatuck Mich 5 Ap 31. 4: Grace Burgess. 5: West Mich U 54-56 (Pre-journalism); UMich 56-58 (Journalism) BA; West Mich U 61-62 (LS) MA; Hope Col 61, 62 Tchg Certif. 7: US Army field wireman (Cpl), Korea 51-53; Freelance writer 58-60; Libn Fennville High Sch, Fennville Mich 63-. 9: ALA-AASchL;-YASD; MichASchL. 10: Beta Phi Mu; Kappa Tau Alpha; ACLU. 14: Sch libnship, ref. 15: Rt 2, Fennville Mi 49408.

WALZ, RICHARD (JAMES) OSB. b Poplar Bluff Mo 15 My 41. 5: Sublaco Col & Sem 59-62, 63-67 (Theol) Ordained Minister; St Bernard's Col 62-63 (Philos) AB; LoyolaU (New Orlenas) summers 66-67 (Mus); Peabody Col 67-68 MLS. 6: Lat, Sp. 7: Stud libn Abbey Lib, Subiaco Ark 59-65, Libn 65-67; Hd libn Subiaco Abbey & Acad Libs 68-. 8: Ordained Roman Catholic priest 67. 9: ALA; NEA; ArkLA; ArkEA. 13: Yes. 14: Ref, reading interests on the High Sch level. 15: New Subiaco Abbey, Subiaco Ar 72865.

WAMSLEY, DOLLIE M (GOFF). b Fort Cobb Okla 27 D 11. 4: Charles Dwight Wamsley Sr. 5: Okla Col for Women 30-32 Elem Educ Life Certif; SWest State Tchrs Col summer 39; St Mary Col 53-56 (Elem Educ) BS, 58-68 LS correspondence courses. 7: Elem sch tchr, Carnegie Okla: Pleasant View 33-37, Fairview 37-38, Spring Valley 38-40; Clk typist US Govt, Ft Leavenworth Kan 43-45; Ref libn St Mary Col (Xavier Kan) 67-. 9: ALA; Cath;A: 10: Leavenworth (Kan) Hist Soc; Saint Mary Col Alumnae; Leavenworth Co Organ Soc; Buffalo Bill Cody Parks Com. 14: Rare bks, Americana, loc hist. 15: 535 Ohio, Leavenworth Ks 66048.

WAN, ELIZA SHOW JANG (HSU). b Fukien China 24 My 43. 4: Peter Chung-chu Wan. 5: Taiwan NormalU 60-65 (Adult Educ) BEd; Peabody Col 66-68 MLS. 6: Chinese. 7: Tchr Keelung Municipal Jr High, Keelung Taiwan China 64-66; Asst libn docs dept ufla Libs 68-. 9: ALA. 14: Docs, catlg. 15: PO Box 13178, Gainesville Fl 32601.

WAN, WEN-PING. b Hankow China 3 Ap 20. 5: Nat TaiwanU 50-54 (Hist) BA; UGa 62 (Hist) MA; UPenn 65 (Hist); West MichU 66 MSLS. 6: Chinese, Japanese, Fr. 7: Catlgr USoCar Libs 67-. 15: 928 Maple st, Columbia SC 29201.

WANCURA, ELDON N. b Garden City Kan 5 Mr 35. 4: Glenda Robertson. 5: Kan StateU 53-57 (Bio Sci) BS; UDenver 59-60 (LS) BA. 7: 1st Lt US Army Med Serv Corps, 57-59; Asst circ libn Ore StateU 61-62; Asst acquis libn Kan StateU 62-63, Ser libn 63-65, Supv acquis div 65-68, Syst analyst 69-. 14: Acquis, catlg, data proc. 15: 1737 Winne dr, Manhattan Ks 66502.

WANG, AH BI (TAN). b Amoy Fukien China 22 F 37. 4: Shu-Teh Wang. 5: Far EastU (Philippines) 55-59 (LS) BSEd; Philippine Chinese Jr Normal Col 59-61 Diploma; UOttawa 62-63 BLS; Sir George Williams 63-65. 6: Chinese, Tagalos, Russian. 7: Tchr: Philippine Chinese Confucius Sch, Manila 56-58, Quiapo Anglo Chinese Sch, Manila 60-62; Asst libn Philippine Chinese Jr Normal Col, Manila 58-61; Asst libn Aluminum Ltd Group Lib, Montreal 63-66; Asst libn Research Sta Can Dept of Agric, Winnipeg 66-67; Libn Forest Research Lab Dept of Forestry & Rural Development, Winnipeg Can 67-. 9: SLA. 14: Catlg, ref. 15: 55 University Crescent, Winnipeg 19 Manitoba Can.

WANG, ANDREW HSING-JEN. b Taiwan Rep of China 12 Je 39. 4: Chrsity Li-man Ho Wang. 5: National Cheng-chiU 58-62 (Journalism) BA; AtlantaU 66-67 MS in LS; St Mary's Col of Md 67-69 (Ger). 6: Chinese, Ger, Japanese, Taiwanese. 7: News reporter "China Times", Taipei Taiwan 64-66; Period libn AtlantaU 67; Catlg libn St Mary's Col, St MaryS City Md 67-. 10: Beta Phi Mu. 14: Catlg. 15: St Mary's Col of Md, St Mary's City Md 20686.

WANG, ANN CHIH-CHING. b Chekiang China 23 Mr 23. 5: UManila(Philippines) 59-62 (Hist) AB (magna cum laude); Peabody 63-64 (LS) MA. 6: Fr, Sp, Chinese, Japanese. 7: Tchr Sun Yat-Sen High Sch, Manila Philippines 52-53; Tchr Chiang Kai-Shek High Sch, Manila Philippines 53-58; Assoc ed "Fookien Times," Manila Philippines 53-54; Libn Philippine Chinese Pub Lib, Manila Philippines 55-63; Catlgr West Mich U Lib 64-66; Libn-descr catlgr LC 66-. 8: Consul "Choice; Books for College Libs 64-; Bk Review Com Embassy of the REPUBLIC OF China, Manila Philippines54-58. 9: ALA. 10: Beta Phi Mu; Sigma Kappa Lambda (Manila, Philippines). 13: Yes. 14: Catlg, bibliog. 15: Library of Congress, Washington DC 20540.

WANG, BOB (PENG-SHENG). b China 25 My 28. 5: NatU of Pol Sci 45-49 (Journalism) BA; IndU 65-68 MLS. 6: Chinese. 7: Instr & tr (Major) Chinese Army, China 50-54; Liaison off (Col) Chinese Guerrilla, China 54-55; Specialist USN, Formosa 55-65; Grad asst IndU Educ Lib (Bloomington) 66-68; Asst libn pub lib, Peru Ind 68; Inst lib consul Ind State lib, Indianapolis 68-. 10: Internatl Y's Men's Club. 12: "Survey of Institutional Library Service Programs in USA" (69). 14: Pub serv, ref, internatl serv. 15: Ext Div Ind State Lib, Indianapolis In 46204.

WANG, HERBERT (YAO). b Hopei China 1 Jl 21. 4: Louisa Wang. 5: Nat North-western U (China) 43-47 (Econ) BL; State U Col (Geneseo NY) 59-60 (LS) MS. 6: Chinese, Japanse, Ger. 7: Accountant Ministry of Transportation, Shen-Ying China 47-48; Tchr Pub High Schs, Taiwan China 48-56; Instr Taiwan Normal U (Taiwan China) 56-58; Asst libn Westmar Col 60-62; Libn Mt St Marys Col Downtown Campus (Los Angeles) 62-68. 14: Catlg, admin. 15: 162 N Kenmore ave, Los Angeles Ca 90004.

WANG, HUNG I. b Yangchow China 9 D 14. 4: Hwei Ming Chang. 5: Nat Central U 36-40 (Educ) BA; Columbia 47-48 (Educ) MA, 56-58 (LS) MS. 6: chinese. 7: Catlgr Law Lib Columbia U 58-60; Catlgr Asian Lib Colubmia U 60-62, Chief catlgr 62-. 9: ALA; NY Reg Tech Serv Libns; NY Lib Club. 14: Catlg. 15: East Asian Lib Columbia Univ, New York NY 10027.

WANG, JOYCE ERH-LI. b Ho-Pei China 9 F 42. 5: SoochowU (Taipei Taiwan) 59-64 (Law) LLB; Catherine Spalding Col 67-69 MLS. 6: Chinese, Japanese. 7: Catlgr CapitalU 69-. 14: Catlg. 15: 2122 E Main st, Columbus Oh 43209.

WANG, PETER S. b Taiku Shansi China 6 Ap 31. 5: SoochowU (Taipei) 54-58 (Law) LLB; UWis (Madison) 63-65 MS in LS. 6: Chinese. 7: Interpreter (2nd Lt) Liaison Sect 2nd Field Army, Kaohsiung Taiwan 59-6; Purchasing off Central Trust of China, Taipei Taiwan 60-62; Ser catlgr John Crerar Lib, Chicago 65-. 10: UWis Lib Sch Alum Assn; Chinese cath Students Assn. 14: Catlg. 15: 856 W Fullerton, Chicago Il 60614.

WANG, PHYLLIS C. 5: UIll 48-50 MSLS, summer 56 (Med Lit) Certif Med Libnship. 6: Japanese, Fr, Ger. 7: Act libn Lingnan U (Canton China) 45-48; Govt document libn Occidentlcol Lib 50-51; Catlgr USoCal 51-52; Ser libn Falk Lib of Health Professions UPittsburgh 52-64; Catlgr (GS-9) US Army Command & Gen Staff Col, Ft Leavenworth Kan 64-65; Ser libn Agric Lib, Penn State U 65-67; Ser catlgr, Libn II Penn State Lib 67-. 9: MedLA (Nomin Com Pittsburgh Reg Group 64-65); ALA; PennLA. 10: Chinese Univ Club of Pittsburgh. 11: Fellowship from US Board for Christian Coll in China 48 Scholarship from MEDLA 56. 12: "Index to Chinese Periodical Literature (42); Asst ed "List of the Foreign Journals of the Library, Lingnan University (43); "Reading Interest of High School Students (50). 14: Catlg, ser, ref. 15: Penn State Lib Tech Serv Bureau Box 1601, Harrisburg Pa 17126.

WANG, PHYLLIS T (LIU). b Peking China 9 Ja 35. 4: Ting-I Wang. 5: Taiwan U (China) 52-55 (Eng); Rockford Col 55-56 (Eng) BA; UArk 56-58 (Eng) MA; Simmons 61-62 (LS) MS. 6: Chinese, Russan. 7: Ref asst USan Francisco 62-64; Ref libn Cal State Col (Fullerton) 64-65. 9: Orange Co (Cal) LA. 14: Ref, docs, catlg. 15: 1009 Boxwood ave, Fullerton Cl 92631.

WANG, SZE-TSENG. b Tsinan China 18 Mr 13. 5: Nankai U (Tientsin) 33-37 (Eng Lit) BA; Columbia 52-53 (LS) MS. 6: Fr, Sp, Portu, Chinese. 7: Lecturer Nat Acad of Dramatic Arts, Nanking China 37-39; Comp & tr Nat Inst of Compilation & Trans, Chungking China 43-46; Spec asst Ministry of For Affairs 46-48; 3rd sec Chinese Embassy in Rio de Janeiro 48-50; Research assoc UChic 50-51; Prof asst NY Pub Lib 53-54; Catlgr Youngstown Pub Lib, Youngstown Ohio 54-57; Catlgr Penn State U Libs 57-62; Asst libn State U Col Lib (New Paltz NY) 62-63; E Asian catlgr Ohio State U Libs 63-. 9: ALA; Franklin CoLA. 10: Phi Tau Phi. 14: Catlg. 15: 306 W Lane ave, apt 29, Columb us Oh 43201.

WANG, TERESA C (LEE). b China 28 F 44. 4: John Ching-Yee Wang. 5: Nat TaiwanU 61-65 (Hist) BA; No IllU 65-67 (LS) MA. 6: Chinese. 7: Catlgr San Francisco Col for Women 67-68; Catlgr Wichita StateU Lib 69-. 9: IllLA. 14: Catlg. 15: 3643 W 13th st apt 8Q, Wichita Ks 67203.

WANG, YEN-NING. b China 25 Ag 40. 5: Nat TaiwanU 60-64 (Eng Lang) BA; USoCal 65-67 MLS. 6: Chinese. 7: Libn Orange Co Pub Lib, Costa Mesa Col 67-. 9: CalLA. 14: Ref. 15: 625 Shalimar dr apt 1, Costa Mesa Ca 92627.

WANKMILLER, MADELYN (CLISH). b Norwich Conn 17 Je 07. 4: Max Wankmiller. 5: Conn Col 23-27 (Romance Langs) AB; West Res 29-30 BS in LS. 6: Fr, Sp, Ger. 7: Lib asst NY Pub Lib 27-29; Lib asst Cleveland PUB Lib 29-30; Head Child dept New Britain (Conn) Pub Lib 30-51; Supv wk with child Worcester (Mass) Pub Lib 52-58, Assoc libn 58-. 9: ALA; ConnLA (pres 40-41, sec 49-50); MassLA; NELA (pres 58, Round Table of Child Libns). 10: Child Guidance Assn; Youth Guidance; Delta Kappa Gamma; Quota Club. 12: Spec ed "Horn Book Magazine (55-58). 13: Yes. 14: Child serv. 15: Worcester Pub Lib Salem sq, Worcester Ma 01608.

WANNARKA, MARJORIE BERNICE. b Fairmont Minn 12 S 29. 5: Col of St Teresa 47-49; Mankato State Col 50-51; Col of St Catherine 51-52 (LS) BS; Catholic U 57; UMinn summers 61-64, 67 MA. 6: Lat, Fr. 7: Libn Creighton U Schs of Med & Pharmacy 52-. 9: MedLA; CathLA; NebLA; Omaha-Council Bluffs Libns Club. 10: Neb Acad of Sci; Amer Med Writers Assn. 11: Murray Gottlieb Award MedLA (67). 12: Ed "The Hospitaller, newsletter of the CathLA Hosp Sect (59-64); Auth "Medical Collections in Public Libraries of the United States; a historical Study (Thesis 67); News ed "Bulletin of the Medical Library Association (69-). 13: Yes. 14: Ref, rare bks, hist med libs. 15: 657 N 27th st, Omaha Nb 68131.

WARANIUS, FRANCES B (BERGOLD). b Chicago Ill 29 Mr 31. 4: William A Waranius. 5: Col of St Francis 49-53 (Chem) BS. 7: Libn Libby McNeill & Libby, Blue Is Ill 53-55; Asst libn Intl Minerals & Chem, Skokie Ill 55-57; Libn Ill Farm Supply, Chicago 57-60; Libn Meissner Engrs, Chicago 60-62; Library processing group leader ITT/FEC NASA-MSC, Houston Tex 66-. 9: SLA. 10: AAUW; Kappa Gamma Pi. 14: Catlg, info ret. 15: 927 22nd ave N, Texas City Tx 77590.

WARBURTON, SISTER MARGARET ROSE CDP. b Victoria Tex 20 S 12. 5: Our Lady of the Lake Col 28-31 (Span) BA, 3-32 BS in LS; Catholic U summers 34-39 (Hist) MA; Chicago summers 40-45 (LS) MA. 6: Sp, Fr. 7: Tchr of Span, hist Our Lady of the Lake High Sch, San Antonio Tex 33-40; Our Lady of the Lake Col: Instr Dept of Lib Sci 40-42, Asst Prof Dept of Lib Sci 42-55, Libn 55-. 8: Bd Dirs, Our Lady of the Lake Col, 63-6. 9: ALA; CathLA; TexLA. 10: Alpha Chi; Mirasol Homes Residents Assn. 13: Yes. 14: Admin, catlg. 15: Our Lady of the Lake Col, 411 SW 24th st, San Antonio Tex 78207.

WARD, ANN (MARY). b Newport News Va 14 Ja 36. 5: Woman's Col UNC 54-58 (Chem) AB. 6: Fr, Ger. 7: Asst tech Dow Chemical Co, Williamsburg Va 58-61, Lib clk 61-62, Asst libn 62-63; Libn Dow Badische Co, Williamsburg Va 64-. 9: SLA (offr Textile & Paper Sect); VaLA. 10: Hampton Roads Spec Lib Club. 14: Info sci. 15: Dow Badische Co, Williamsburg Va 23185.

WARD, ANN (RHINEHART). b Chicago Ill 5 D45. 5: Vanderbilt 63-67 (Hist) BA; UMich 67-68 MALS. 6: Fr. 7: Aurora Pub Lib, Aurora Ill summers 66 & 67; Catlgr Alderman Lib UVa (Charlottesville) 68-69; Libn Bell Tele Labs, Naperville Ill 69-. 9: SLA; VaLA. 10: Beta Phi Mu; Chi Omega. 13: Yes. 15: 483 N Lake st, Aurora Il 60506.

WARD, ANNA (LOUISE) RICHARDS. b Princeton W Va 16 Ag 19. 4: Robert L Ward. 5: Concord Col 36-40 (Eng, Home Econ) AB, summer 65; W VaU summers 41-42, 44-46 (Home econ & Educ) MS; UWash fall 46; Ga State Col summer 64 Ga tchr certif; UGa fall 67. 7: Tchr: Bramwell High Sch, Bramwell W Va 40-43, Iaeger High Sch, Iaeger W Va 43-46, 50-51, Matoka High Sch, Matoka W Va 56-57; Tchr & libn W Clayton Elem, College Park Ca 64-. 9: NEA; ALA; GaLA; SELA; ClaytonCoLA; GaEA. 10: AAUW; Alpha Sigma Tau. 15: 2354 Country Club lane SW, Atlanta Ga 30311.

WARD, BARBARA A. b Lewiston Ida 4 Mr 30. 5: UWash 53-56 (Eng) BA (cum laude), Tchg Certif, summers 56-60 (LS) ML. 6: Fr. 7: Typist-clerk Gen Insurance Co of Amer, Portland Ore 51-52; Jr high sch libn Moses Lake Schs, Moses Lake Wash 56-57; Asst libn high sch Seattle Pub Schs 57-59, Elem tchr & elem libn 59-61; Elem libn Santa Monica Unified Schs, Santa Monica Cal 61-64; Asst prof of sch libnship in chg of lib educ program Central Wash State Col 64-65; Supv of elem libs Wenatchee Pub Schs, Wenatchee Wash 65-67; Asst prof & coord lib educ Cal State Col at Long Beach 68-. 8: Chm Elem Lib Bldg Planning Com, Santa Monica Unified Schs, 64; chm Bldg Com for Elem Libs Santa Monica Unified Sch Dist 63-64; Mem Evaluation Com ESEA Title III Reg Project Central Wash State Col 65-66; Planning Com for Lib Techns Program wenatchee Valley Jr Col 65-67. 9: ALA-AASchL; NEA-DAVIS; WashStateSchLA (Bk Review Com 59-60, 67-68, chm Recr 67-68); WashLA; CalASchL (mem Elem Com); A-V Educ Assn Cal; CalTA; CCUFA. 10: Delta Kappa Gamma; AAUW. 12: "Elementary Library Handbook, a Curriculum Guide, Santa Monica Unified Schs (63). 13: Yes. 14: Sch libs, instr med ctrs. 15: 5900 Fairbrook, Long Beach Ca 90815.

WARD, BETTY CAROLYN. b Monroe Co Tenn 8 Ja 36. 5: Tenn Wesleyan Col 54-56 (Liberal Arts); UTenn 56-58 (Eng, Educ) BS in Ed; Peabody 63, 64, 65 MLS. 6: Fr. 7: Libn Sweetwater High Sch, Sweetwater Tenn 58-61; Bkmob libn Ft Loudoun Reg Lib, Athens Tenn summers 59, 60; Libn Rhea Central High Sch, Dayton Tenn 61-62; Period libn Merner-Pfeiffer Lib Tenn Wesleyan Col (Athens Tenn) 62-65, Ast lbn 65-66; Hd adult serv High Point Pub Lib, High Point NC 67-. 9: ALA-RSD (sec-treas Tenn Chap 65-66); SELA; TennLA; TennEA; NCLA. 10: AAUP; Alpha Beta Alpha; Pilot Club. 14: Catlg, ref, periods, govt docs, circ. , admin, acquis, interlib loan, ya serv, adult serv, bk sel. 15: 511 Westwood ave apt #4, High Point NC 27262.

WARD, CAROL (JEFFERS). b New Haven Conn 15 Ap 40. 5: Douglass Col 57-59 (Mus); So Conn State 60-62 BS in LS; SUNY (Albany) MS in LS. 6: Fr, Ger. 7: Asst libn Columbia High Sch, E Greenbush NY 62-63; Stud libn SUNY (Albany) 63-64; Research libn State Dept of Motor Vehicles, Albany NY 65, Research asst 66; Libn I Free Lib of Phila 66-. 14: Ref. 15: 2222 Green st, Philadelphia Pa 19130.

WARD, DEDERICK C. b Baltimore 22 Je 34. 4: Ruth Megenhardt. 5: Washington & Lee U 52-56 (Geol) BA; UColo 56-58 (Geol) MA; UDenver 60-61 (LS) MA. 7: US Army Reserves (Capt) Corps of Engns Active 58, Res 56-65; Enoch Pratt Free Lib, Baltimore 59-60; Earth ci libn UColo 61-; Hd Sci Lib 67-. 9: SLA; Geosci Info Soc; (pres 68); Nat Assn of Geol Tchrs; ColoLA. 10: Sigma Xi; Geol Soc of Amer; AAAS. 12: "Geologic Reference Sources 67. 13: Yes. 14: Ref (geol). 15: Earth Sci Lib Univ of Colo, Boulder Co 80302.

WARD, DOROTHY MARIE (POOL). b Houston Tex 26 O 35. 4: Jack Cooper Ward. 5: UTex 53-57 (Sociol) BS in Ed; Tex Woman's U 58-59 MLS. 7: 1st asst Dallas Pub Lib Jefferson Br 58, Ya libn 59-60; Jr high sch libn Irving Ind Schs, Irving Tex 60-61; Eng tchr Mineral Wells Ind Schs, Mineral Wells Tex 62; Head libn Ranger Jr Col 62-63; Soc sci area libn UOkla 63-64; Asst libn Vernon Parish Lib, Leesville La 64-65, Parish libn 65-67; Elem libn El Paso Pub Schs, El Paso Tex 67-69; Asst chief libn Med & Tech Lib, El Paso Tex 69; Instr lib serv UTex(El Paso) 69-. 8: Exec sec NLW, Vernon Parish La 65-67. 9: ALA; LaLA; TexLA; OklaLA; Border Reg LA (Hospitality Com) 68-69; SWLA; 8th Dist Lib Trustees (Exec sec 65-66). 10: PTA; Pilot Club. 14: Ref, soc sci, home econ. 15: 8713 Moye dr, El Paso Tx 79925.

WARD, EDITH (HALPERN). b NYC 17 Jl 28. 4: Benjamin Ward. 5: Hunter Col 44-48 (Eng Lit) BA; Columbia 65-67 (LS) MS. 6: Fr, Yiddish. 7: Lit analyst project Urbandoc CUNY 67-68; Catlgr McKinsey & Co Inc, NYC 68-. 9: ALA; SLA; ASIS. 14: Catlg, lib applications of electronic data proc. 15: Rte 340, Palisades NJ 10964.

WARD, FRANK J. b Blackburn England 29 Mr 30. 4: Mary Flores. 5: UManchester (England) 50-51 (LS) British ALA; UToledo 65-68 (Pol Sci) AB; UMich 68-69 AMLS. 6: Sp. 7: Hd catlgr Blackburn (UK) Pub Lib 51-55; Asst dir Accrington (UK) Pub Lib 55-56; Bkmob libn Sarnia (Ont) Pub Lib 56-57; Br libn Toledo (Ohio) Pub Lib 57-65; Ref asst UToledo Lib 67-69, Chief processing libn & instr in lib admin 69-. 9: ALA (SORT: pres-elect 64); OhioLA (SORT: pres 63). 10: Pi Gamma Mu; Beta Phi Mu. 15: 1030 Oakdale ave, Toledo Oh 43605.

WARD, GLADYS (SIRMON). b Perry La 13 Ja 16. 4: William Whitman Ward. 5: La State normal Col 32-35 (Eng, Fr) AB; LSU summers 38, 39, 47 BS in LS, LSU Inst 68-69. 6: Fr. 7: Tchr & libn: E Broussard High Sch, Abbeville La 35-40, Okaloosa High Sch, Eros La 40-43, Transylvanoa Junior High, Transylvania La 46-49; Tchr Lake Providence high Sch, Lake Providence La 49-51; Libn NE La State Col 52-54; Libn Ouachita Parish High Sch, Monroe La 54-64; Libn Glen Oaks High Sch, Baton Rouge La 64-66; Dir Central Processing E Baton Rouge Parish Schs, Baton Rouge La 66-. 8: "art-time vis prof lib sci: NE La State Col 61, 63, La StateU 65, 67; Wkshop consul U So Miss 66. 9: NEA; ALA; SWLA; LaLA (treas 61-62, 2nd v-pres 69-70); LaASchL (chm Stud Rel Com 58, treas 59, chm Proj Com 67); OuachitaASchL (pres 57). 10: Baton Rouge Lib Club; Delta Kappa Gamma. 11: Modisette Award 63. 13: Yes. 14: Catlg. 15: 615 Cora dr, Baton Rouge La 70815.

WARD, JACK COOPER. b Obannon Ky 25 N 22. 4: Dorothy Pool Ward. 5: John Brown U 39-42 (Printing) BS; N Tex State U 59-61 (LS) BA; UOkla 63-64 MLS. 6: Sp. 7: USAF 42-56; Post libn Dept of Army, Ft Wolters Tex 61-63; Chief libn Dept of Army, Ft Polk La 64-67; Chief libn Ft Bliss 67-68; Chief Tech Lib White Sands Missile Range NM 68-. 9: ALA (mem Sect Devel Com); PLA (Armed Forces Libns Sect); TexLA; Border Reg LA (Exec Bd 68). 11: Supv 2nd place entry in 4th US Army Lib Serv Award competition, Ft Polk 65, 67, Ft Bliss 68. 14: Admin, tech processes. 15: 8713 Moye dr, El Paso Tx 79925.

WARD, JAMES EVERETT. b Dardanelle Ark 10 Ap 34. 4: Betty Jo Wells. 5: Hendrix Col 51-54 (Phys Educ) BA; UArk 54-55 (Phys Educ) MEd, 59-62 (Phys Educ) EdD; Peabody Col 66-68 MLS. 7: Tchr: Carlisle High Sch, Carlisle Ark 55-57, Rogers High Sch, Rogers Ark 59-60; Chm dept of HPER & dir athletics Central Methodist Col 61-63; Assoc Prof Dept of HPE David Lipscomb Col 63-66, Dir lib 66-. 9: ALA; Amer Assn Health, Phys Educ & Recreat; Nat Col Phys Educ Assn Men; TennLA; SELA; Tenn Col Phys Educ Assn; Tenn Assn Health, Phys Educ & Recreat. 10: Phi Delta Kappa; Kappa Delta Pi; Beta Phi Mu. 14: Admin (Col or Univ). 15: 3710 Rosemont ave, Nashville Tn 37215.

WARD, MARIETTA (McMANIGAL). b St Charles SD. 4: John R Ward. 5: UOre 41-46 (Psych) BS; UWash 50-52 (LS) MS. 7: Music libn UWash 52-64, Art libn 65-. 9: SLA; PNLA; ALA. 10: Phi Beta Kappa. 15: 8403 31 NE, Seattle 98115.

WARD, MARGARET JEAN. b Castle Rock Colo 26 Ja12. 5: UColo 29-34 (Eng Lang) BA; UDenver 36-37 BS in LS; UColo 48-52 (Personnel Serv) MPS. 7: Sr asst circ Denver Pub Lib 37-39; Jr high sch libn Denver Pub Sch 39; Denver Pub Lib: Sr asst circ 39-40, Yp libn 40-48, Lib personnel off 48-61; Lib consul Cal State Lib 61-. 9: ALA (Nomin Com 47-48);-LAD (Exec Bd of Personnel Sect 60-62, Recr Com 60, Adv Com of Off of Recr 65-);-Div of Libs for Child & YP (YP Reading Round Table: chm Bk Sel Com & Ed of Bks for YP in "Booklist 44-45); CalLA (chm Personnel Admin Com 65); ColoLA. 10: Denver Personnel Club; Pub Personnel Assn; Amer Soc of Train Dirs; Adult Educ Coun of Denver; Phi Beta Kappa; Kappa Delta Pi; YWCA; AAUW; Sacramento Bk Collectors Club. 12: Assoc ed "Top of the News (47). 13: Yes. 14: Personnel admin, adult educ, reg pub lb systems, metro lib problems. 15: 1801 T st, Sacramento Cal 95814.

WARD, MARTHA (EADS). b Quincy Ill 21 Jl 21. 5: Knox Col 38-40; USoCal 40-42 (Advertising) BS; Pratt 46-47 BLS; Quincy Col 62-63 (Educ) Ill Secon Tchrs Certif. 6: Fr. 7: Civilian instr Army Air Force) Lincoln Neb 43-44; Child libn Free PUB Lib, Quincy Ill 47-. 8: Tchr child lit, Quincy Co. 63. 9: ALA (Area Recr); IllLA (Child Libns Sect: chm 59 & 65, sec 61). 10: Quincy Commu Little Theatre; Phi Beta Phi; Deaconess First Union Congregational Ch; USoCal Alum. 12: "Authors of Books for Young People," with D Marquardt (64); Auth "Adlai Stevenson; Young Ambassador" (67). 13: Yes. 14: Child lit. 15: 2300 Hampshire st, Quincy Il 62301.

WARD, MARY (MIX). b Troy Kan 24 Jl 13. 4: Clarence E Ward. 5: Highland Jr Col 30-32 (Eng); Park Col 32-34 (Eng Lit) BA; Kan State Tchrs Col summers 60-64 (LS) MS; ITESM (Monterrey, NL, Mex) summers 65-66 (Sp lang). 6: Sp. 7: Tchr elem rural sch, doniphan Co Kan: #20 35-36, #33 52-53; Tchr & libn, Kan high sch: White Cloud 53-58, Elwood 58-59, Troy 59-64; Libn & instr Highland Jr Col 64-. 9: NEA; ALA; KanStateTA; KanASchL; KanPCJCEA. 10: Delta Kappa Gamma. 14: Catlg, ref. 15: PO Box 59, Troy Ks 66087.

WARD, MARY JANE. b Reading Penn 25 F 21. 5: ALbright Col 38-42 (Eng, pan, Lat) AB (cum laude); Middlebury Col summer 50 (Span); Drexel 51-54 MS in LS. 6: Sp, Lat. 7: Tchr of Eng & Spn Borough High Sch, Wernersville Penn 42-46; Instr in Span Albrght Col 46-52; Head of circ dept Albright Col Lib 52-53; Asst circ libn Reading Pub Lib, Reading Penn 53-57, Head br libn 57-58; Libn Southern Jr High Sch, Reading Penn 58-. 9: ALA-AASchL; NEA; PennLA; Penn State EA (Dept of Supv & Curr); PennSchLA; Reading Educ Assn. 10: Beta Phi MU; Phi Kappa Phi; Pi Gamma Mu; Sigma Tu Delta; YWCA; Fellowship House, Readig Penn; Drexel Grad Lb Sch Alumni Assn; Phi Delta Sigma. ; ReadingEA. 14: Ref, bks for Jr high reading level. 15: 337 Miller st, Reading Penn 19602.

WARD, MARY O(RPAH). b Jacksonville NC 26 Ag 15. 05 Columbia Col 32-36 (Hist) BA;USCar summer 37 (LS); UNC summers 40-42 (LS) BS. 5: Columbia Col 32-36 (Hist) BA; USoCar summer 37 (LS); UNC summers 40-42 BSLS. 7: Libn High Sch, Myrtle Beach SC 37-43; Libn High Sch, Wilson NC 43-44; Lib asst NY Pub Lib summers 43, 44; Asst fiction div DC Pub Lib 44-45; Base libn Myrtle Beach AFB, Myrtle Beach SC 45-47; Base libn Turner AFB, Albany Ga 47-49; Post libn Ft McPherson, Atlanta 49-51; Base libn Mitchel AFB, LI NY 51; Staff libn Hq 18th AF Donaldson AFB, Greenville SC 51-57; Base libn Homestead AFB, Homestead Fla 57-58; Staff libn Hq 2d AF, Barksdale AFB La 58-59; Bibliog Air U Lib, Maxwell AFB Ala 59-. 9: SLA. 14: Ref, bibliog. 15: 7 Clayton st, Montgomery Al 36104.

WARD, PEARL L. b Greeley Colo 30 N 20. 4: Ralph E Ward. 5: UDenver 39-41; Pepperdine Col 49-51 (Hist) BA; USoCal 51-52 MS in LS, 69 PhD. 7: Head Libn Pepperdine Col 53-58; Instr child lit Los Angeles State Col 59-60; Catlgr Aero Space Corp, Los Angeles 61-62; Libn Los Angeles city schs 62-64; Ref libn El Camino Col 64-66; Instr Sch of Lib Sci USoCar 66-. 9: ALA; CalLA; CalASchL; NEA-DAVI. 10: AAUW. 13: Yes. 14: Ref, bibliog, sch libs. 15: 3211 W 78 pl, Los Angeles Ca 90043.

WARD, VICTORIA MILLER. b Phila 1 F 40. 4: Peter C Ward. 5: Ursinus Col 58-61 (Pol Sci) BA; Drexel 61-62 MS in LS. 7: Libn I Free Lib of Phila 62; Asst law libn Morgan Lewis & Bockius, Phila 63-64, Head libn 65-. 9: AALL. 10: Beta Phi Mu. 14: Legal ref. 15: 2106 Locust st, Phila Pa 19103.

WARD REV WILLIAM P. b Hazleton Penn 30 Ap 31. 5: Mt St Marys Col (Md) 49-53 Philos) AB; Mt St Marys Sem (Md) 53-57 (Theol); CathU 63-64 MSLS; UScranton 65-69 (Coun Educ). 6: Lat, Fr. 7: Asst Pastor St Mary of Mt Carmel R C Church, Dunmore Penn 57-63; Lectr in Theol Marywood COL 61-63; Spiritual Dir St Pius X Sem (Penn) 64-, Libn 64-. 8: Asst pastor; st Patrick Ch, Milford Penn, St Agnes Ch, Forest City Penn, St Matthew Ch; E Stroudsburg Penn; Chaplain St Francis Assisi Chapel, Eagles Mere Penn. 9: ALA; CathLA; PennLA. 14: Admin. 15: St Pius X Seminary, Dalton Pa 18414.

WARD, WILLIAM S. b Mill Creek WVa 18 O 30. 5: Morris Harvey Col 49; Northwestern 49-52 (Hist); Marshall U summer 53, 61-64 (Hist) AB; Rutgers 64-65 MLS. 6: Fr. 7: Field repr Childcraft-Field Enterprises Inc, Chicago summer 51; File clerk Merchants Nat Bank, Montgomery WVa 54-55, Bkkeeper 55-58; Hotel clerk Sterling Hotel, Atlantic City NJ summer 62; Hotel clerk Broadbent Hotel, Atlantic City NJ summer 63; File clerk WVa Lib Commsn, Charleston WVa 64; Asst libn Morehead State Col 65-66; ; Ref libn Va Polytech Inst 66-. 10: Alpha Theta Chi. 14: Ref. 15: Terrace View Apts - 800C, Blacksburg Va 24060.

WARDE, WILLIAM D. b Boston 10 Ag 35. 5: Haverford Col 53-57 (Lat) AB; Simmons 59-60 MSLS. 7: Lib asst LaMont Lib Harvard 57-59; Ref asst Hist Dept Enoch Pratt Free Lib, Baltimore 60-62; Ref asst Ref Dept Boston Pub Lib 62-65; Asst dir Framingham (Mass) Pub Lib 65-68; Dir Emerson Col Lib 68-. 9: Charles River Lib Club (pres); MassLA (Exec Bd). 14: Ref, admin. 15: 9 Norris rd, Hyde Park Ma 02136.

WARDELL, MARGARET (LUCY). b Tracy Minn 27 Je 05. 5: Carleton Col 23-27 (Eng) BA; UIll 31-32 BS in LS, 35-37 MA. 7: Tchr & libn High Sch, New York Mills Minn 27-29; Tchr & libn High Sch, Plainview Minn 29-30; Gen asst Carleton Col Lib 30-31; Order asst & catlgr UIowa Lib 33-35; Feculty asst UIll Lib Sch 35-37; Ref libn West Ill U 37-. 9: ALA; IllLA; 10: Phi Beta KAPPA: Beta Phi Mu; AAUW; AAUP; Bus & Prof Womens Club. 14: Ref. 15: 518 N Albert, Macomb Ill 61455.

WARDEM JOSEPHINE P(AULINE) (JAWORSKE). b Berea Ohio 17 F 37. 4: Paul G Warden. 5: Baldwin-Wallace Col 61-63; Kent State 63-66 (Sp) BS in Ed, 67-68 MLS. 6: Sp, Fr. 7: Clk Deputy Registrar State of Ohio Bur of Motor Vehicles 54-55; Clk Cleveland Pub Lib Film Bur Ohio 56-59; Off mgr Deputy Registrar State of Ohio Bur of Motor Vehicles 59-63; Libn Akron Pub Schs, Akron Ohio 66-67; Libn Field Local Schs, Mogadore Ohio 68-. 9: ALA; -AASchL; NEA; OhioLA; OhioEA; OhioASchL; NE Ohio TA; Young Libns Assn. 10: Commun House, Inc; AAUW. 14: Sch libnship. 15: 228 E Erie st, Kent Oh 44240.

WARDLAW, BARBARA RUTH (McCULLEY). b Del Rio Tex 4 Je 30. 5: Our Lady of the Lake Col 63-67 (LS) BA, 67-68 MS in LS. 6: Sp. 7: Tech serv libn Bee Co Col 68-. 9: TexLA. 10: Alpha Chi. 14: Ref, wk with child & ya. 15: 1017 E Randall, Beeville Tx 78102.

WARDROP, ELAINE (LaPOINTE). b Ramsey Co Minn 30 Mr 20. 4: Donald J Wardrop. 5/ col of St Catherine 37-41 (LS) BS; UMinn 41. 6: Fr. 7: Libn 3M Co Central Research

Lib, st Paul 41-47, Libn Tech Lib 66-. 9: SLA. 15: 3294 Owasso Hts dr, St Paul Mn 55112.

WARE, GLADYS COLE. b Orchid Va 24 N 15. 5: Fla State Col for Women 34-38 (Lat, Eng) AB, summers 38-40 (Lat, Eng); UMexico Summer Sch 41 (Sp); UMiami summer 58 (Hist); Fla StateU 60-61 (LS) MS. 7: High sch tchr Pub Schs, Fla 38-44; Civilian clerk US Navy, Hawaii 44-46; Clerk UNRRA, Wash DC 46; Recreation aide Amer Red Cross, Japan 46-47; Recreation dir US Army; Japan 47-48, Germany 49-51, PR 51; Recreation dir USAF; La 52, Okinawa 52-53, Libya 53-57; High sch tchr pub schs, Fla 58-60, Sch libn 61-62; Base/depot libn US Army, Okinawa 62-64; Base libn USAF; Pakistan 64-65, Turkey 65-67, Taiwan 67-. 9: ALA; FlaLA. 10: Beta Phi Mu. 14: Catlg, ref. 15: 1600 SW 32nd st, Ft Lauderdale Fl 33315.

WARE, MALCOLM STEWART. b Verona Miss 20 F 33. 4: Betty Jane Hocks. 5: Miss State U 51-53 (Ind Arts, Educ); USoMiss 58-61 (LS) BS. 7: Communication Center Op (Sgt)US Army Signal Corps, Austria & Italy 55-57; Tchr-libn Gulf Coast Mil Acad, Miss CITY Miss 60-61; Br libn USoMiss resident Center, Biloxi Miss 62-63; Spec libn Gulf Coast Research Lab, Ocean Springs Miss 64-. 9: MissLA. 14: Org of spec collections. 15: Gulf Coast Res Lab P O Box AG, Ocean Springs Ms 39564.

WARE, WILLIAM B. b Los Angeles 17 N 18. 4: Stella Pietrowski. 5: UCal 37-40 (Animal Sci); Harvard 42 (Radar Engnr); Newark State Col 65 LS; Amer U 68 (Records Mgt). 6: Portu, Sp. 7: US Army Ret Lt Col 42-62; Grad of Comm Gen Staff Col, Signal & Chem Corps Adv Courses & Sch Libn, Radiol Engnr Course, Adv Mgt Cours 53-59; Operations Ed Gaylord Tech Info Serv, Newark NJ 63-64; Mgr Lib & Off Serv Electronic Assocs Inc, W Long Branch NJ 64-. 8: Mil adv Brazilian Army 60-62; Mem Monmouth Co (NJ) Lib Commsn 6. 9: SLA; ASIS; Amer Stat Assn; Assn for Computing Machinery; Assn Recs Execs & Admins. 10: AAAS. 11: Military (BSM, ACM, 10 battle stars campaigns. 13: Yes, US & Brazilian Military Pubs. 14: Machine indexing & retrieval. 15: 1216 Turf dr, Oceanport NJ 07757.

WARHEIT, ELIZABETH (LIMBERG). b Saginaw Mich 20 F 11. 4: I Albert Warheit. 5: East Mich U 29-33 (Fr, Math) AB; UMich 34-35 ABLS. 6: Fr, Ger. 7: Catlgr Hoyt Pub Lib, Saginaw Mich 35-36; Catlgr Research Labs Gen Motors, Detroit 36-41; Catlgr Elmhurst Ill 53-56; Asst catlgr Montgomery Co Dept of Pub Libs, Gaithersburg Md 57-61; Catlgr Research Div IBM, San Jose Cal 62-65; Assoc libn 66-. 9: SLA; Potomac Valley Tech Proc Libns. 14: Catlg, sci-tech ref. 15: 1204 Chateau dr, San Jose Ca 95120.

WARHEIT, I(SRAEL) ALBERT. b Toronto Can 12 D 12. 4: Elizabeth Limberg. 5: East Mich U 29-33 (Mod Langs) AB; UMich 33-34 (Mod Langs) MA; UZurich (Switzerland) 35-36 (Germanics); UMich 34-35, 36-40 PhD (Germanics), ABLS. 6: Ger, Fr. 7: Libn Allison Div Gen Motors, Indianapolis 41-46; Chief lib serv US AEC, Oak Ridge Tenn 46-52; Head lib dept Argonne Nat Lab, Chicago 52-56; Chief Libn US AEC, Wah DC 56-59; Sr systems analyst IBM, San Jose Cal 59-. 8: NY Commsnrs Com on ref & res libs 60-61; UCal Statewide Adv Coun on Educ for Libnship 62-65. 9: SLA (chm Documentation Div); ASIS; (res San Francisco Bay Area Chap); Internat Fed for Documentation (US Nat Com 60-61). 13: Yes. 14: Catlg, systems design for proc, computer applications. 15: c/o IBM Monterey & Cottle rds, San Jose Ca 95114.

WARING, PAULINE (GALLERY). b Rochester NY 8 D 04. 5: NY State Tchrs Col (Geneseo) 50 BLS; NY State Tchrs Col (Geneseo & Brockport) 50-62 (LS). 6: Fr. 7: Elem tchr, Greece NY 25-38; Attendant Rochester Pub Lib, Rochester NY -50; Sch libn K-12 Kendall Central Sch, Kendall NY 50-65; Hd libn High Sch, Kendall NY 66-69. 9: NY State Tchrs Assn; NY LA. ; Niagara OrleansASchL. 15: 16753 Roosevelt hwy, Kendall NY 14476.

WARKENTIN, MARY CLARKE. b Montreal 16 Ja 35. 5: UWest Ont 55-58 (Psych) BA; Ont Col of Educ 59-60 Interim High Sch & Elem Sch Certifs; McGill 64-65 BLS. 7: Soc wker Sarnia Child Aid Soc, Sarnia Ont 58-59, 63; Clerk Sarnia Pub Lib, Sarnia Ont 63-64; Libn-calgr York 65-; Ref libn 65-. 9: CanLA. 10:Univ. Womens Club. 14: Catlg, ref. 15: 210 Essex st, Sarnia Ont Can.

WARMBRUNN, PATRICIA (DUNLAVY). b New London Wis 14 O 37. 4: Frank Warmbrun. 5: Oshkosh State Col 55-59 (LS, Eng) BS; UMilwaukee summer 65 (Reading); UWis (Fox Valley) 66 (A-V Instr). 7: Jr high sch libn & tchr Eng & Math Wilson Jr High Sch, Appleton Wis 59-62, Libn 65-69. 10: Christian Mothers Club. 15: Rte 4 Box 326, Appleton Wi 54911.

WARMINGTON, ANNE A(MELIA). b NYC 12 Ja 12. 5: Hunter Col 39 (Geol) BA; UMich 59 MALS. 6: Fr, Ger, Sp. 7: Jr geologist Hunter Col 42-48; Geologist US AEC, NYC 48-54; Libn US AEC, Grand Junction Colo 54-58; Head Child Hosp Lib Ohio Sate U Libs 59-. 9: MedLA; ASIS. 10: Beta Phi Mu. 13: Yes. 14: Med libnship, ref. 15: Child Hosp Lib 17th at Livingston park, Columbus Ohio 43205.

WARNCKE, RUTH (ELIZABETH). b Chicago 20 Je 10. 5: Crane Jr Col 27-29 AA; UIll 29-31 (Educ) BS; UChicago 32 (Eng Lit) MA; Northwestern 33-36 (Educ); Columbia 41-42 BS in LS. 7: Casewker Ill Unemployment Relief Serv, Chicago 31-32; Tchr-libn Glenview Pub Schs, Glnview Ill 32-40; Ya libn Schenectady Pub Lib, Schenectady NY 42-44; Readers adv Grand Rapids Pub Lib, Grand Rapids Mich 44-45; Dir Kent Co Adult Educ Cound, Grand Rapids Mich 45-47; Dir Kent Co Lib, Gand Rapids Mich 47-55; Dir Amer Heritage Proj-ALA, Chicago 55-56; Dir Lb Commun Proj-ALA, Chicago 56-60; Asst Prof Sch of Lib Sci West Res U60-63, Assoc Prof 63-65; Deputy exec Dir ALA, Chicago 65-. 8: Research assoc, Rural adult educ study Mich State U 53; Guest lecturer Dept of Libnship West Mich U summer 60. 9: ALA (chm Adult Educ Bd 53-54;-LED (sec 61-62);-ASD (pres-elect 64-65); Adult Educ Assn (co-chm Conf Program Com 58-59; sec 57; v-pres 65-66); MichLA (pres 53-54); IllLA. 10: ADA; CLU. 12: "Studying the Community: A Basis for Planning Library Adult Education Activities, ALA (60); Public Library Services in Missouri: Adult Services, in "Public Library Service in Missouri: A Survey (62); "Survey of ASHEVILLE AND Buncombe County (North Carolina) Libraries, with W Chatt ALA (65); "Plan for Development of Library Service in Montana (65). 13: Yes. 14: Coord of lib serv within a commun, lib educ, adult serv. 15: 50 E Huron st, Chicago 60611.

WARNE, KEITH WARNELL. b Hetland SD 3 N 19. 5: Yankton Col 39-43 (Eng) BA; USD 49 (Eng) MA; UMinn 54 (LS) MA. 6: Sp. 7: US Army 43-45; High sch tchr, SD 46-53; Doc-ref UNeb Lib 55-56; Ref Rochester (Minn) Pub Lib 57; Doc ND State U Lib 58-63; Doc-ref No State Col Lib (Aberdeen SD) 63-. 9: ALA; SDLA (sec 68-69); MPLA. 10: Phi Delta Kappa; Shaw Soc; Blue Key; NY Shavians; Elks. 14: US docs, ref, State pubs, catlg. 15: No State Col Lib, Aberdeen SD 54701.

WARNER, BETTY J (ZEHENDER). b Findlay Ohio 12 S 29. 4: Donald P Warner. 5: Findlay Col 47-51 (Soc Sci) BS; Drexel 63-64 MS in LS. 7: Ref libn Biddle Law Lib UPenn 64-66, Docs libn 66-68, Acquis libn 68-. 9: AALL. 13: Yes. 14: 15: Biddle Law Lib, Law School, Unv of Penn, Phila 19104.

WARNER, EDWARD S. b Toledo Ohio 29 F 36. 4: Sandra Easton. 5: Miami U (Ohio) 54-58 (Bus) BS; UToledo 60-61 (Pol Sci) AM; Mich 62-63 AMLS; American U 67- (Pol Sci). 7: Lecturer UToledo 60-61; Instr Columbus Acad, Columbs Ohio 61-62; Asst (Bur Govt Lib umich 63; Asst ref libn Miami U 63-64; Instr Dept Libnship West Mich U 64-67; Asst Prof UMd (College Park) Sch Lib & Info Sci 68-; Temp ref libn; UNotre Dame, Kalamazoo Pub Lib, DC Pub Lib, 66-68. 8: Consul Md Interlib Loan Network, 69. 9: ALA; AALS; MichLA. 10: Great Lakes Hist Soc; Nautical Research Guild. 13: Yes. 14: Soc sci bibliog, Govt PUBLS, ACAD LIBS. 15: 2414 Seminary rd, Silver Spring Md 20910.

WARNER, F(AYLENE) ELEANOR (PAUL). b Belfast Me 6 S 21. 5: Jackson Col (TuftsU) 40-44 (Eng) BA; Eliot-Pearson (TuftsU) 54 & 57 (Early Childhood Educ); Simmons 62-67 (LS) MS. 7: Jr eng Gen Radio Co, Cambridge Mass 44-45; Ed (newsletter) Follen Commun Ch, lexington Mass 66-68; Asst libn Amer Sci & Engring Inc, Cambridge Mass 67-68, Libn 68-. 8: Lectr Wkshops on Church Libs, Cary Mem Lib, Lexington Mas 63, Vis lectr NDEA Wkshop, simmons Col Sch of Lib Sci, Boston 66. 9: ALA; SLA. 15: 21 Normandy rd, Lexington Ma 02173.

WARNER, HELEN L. b Kalamazoo 23 Mr 09. 5: Kalamazoo Col 27-31 (Lit) AB; UMich 31-32 AB in LS. 7: Asst ref dept Mich State Lib 34-35, Org ext dept 36-37; Dir Pub Lib, Mt Pleasant Mich 38-43; Dir Willard Lib, Battle Creek Mich 43-. 8: Mem Mich State Bd Libs 41-51; Mem Lib Sci Adv Com U West Mich. 9: ALA; MichLA (chm Jt Com on Lib Standards 58-59; chm Com on IntellectualFreedom; chm Com for Study of Constitution & By Laws 56; chm Lib Laws Com 60). 10: Altrusa Club. 15: 112 Frelinghuysen, Battle Creek Mi 49017.

WARNER, JOYCE E(STHER). b Ingham Co Mich 1 My 30. 5: Asbury Col 48-52 (Music Theory) AB; East Mich U 54; UHawaii 59-62; UCal Berkeley 64-65 MLS. 7: Elem tchr: Tecumseh Pub Schs, Tecumseh Mich 52-54, Lakeview Schs, Battle Creek Mich 54-58, Barbers Point Elem Sch, Barbers Point, Oahu 58-59; Libn: Barbers Point Elem Sch, Barbers Point Oahu 59-61, Pauoa Elem Sch, Honolulu 61-62, Kalihi Elem Sch, Honolulu 2-64, College Elem Sch, Humboldt State Col 65-66, Linapuni Elem Sch, Honolulu 66-. 9: ALA; HawaiiASchL (Nene Award Chairman 68; "The Golden Key" 68-69); NEA (convention del 63); HawaiiEA (convention del 67-68). 10: AAUW. 14: Elem sch lib wk, child serv. 15: 1519 Nehoa st apt 306, Honolulu Hi 96822.

WARNER, MADELINE (LOUISE ESTABROOK). b Gobles Mich 1 Ap 17. 4: Hollis K Warner. 5: West Mich Col 35-37, 53-59 (Libnship) BS, 62-66 (Libnship) MS. 7: Libn Parchment Pub Schs, Parchment Mich 48-59; Asst libn Loy Norrix High Sch, Kalamazoo 59-66; Hd libn Central High Sch, Kalamazoo 66-. 8: Bus & production mgr "School libraries", AASchL (66, 67), assoc ed (68); Bus & Prod Mgr: Sch Libs (Pub AASL) 66, 67; Assoc ed: Sch Libs 68. 9: ALA; -AASchL; NEA; MichLA; MichEA; MichASchL. 10: Beta Phi Mu; Delta Kappa Gamma; Quota International. 14: Sch libs, yp. 15: 117 S Orient st, Parchment Mi 49004.

WARNER, PATRICIA A. b Somerset Penn 11 D 6. 5: Clarion State Col 55-59 (LS) BS in Ed; UPittsburgh summer 61; Ind U (Penn) summer 62; Seton Hill Col 63; Peabody summers 64, 65 (LS. 6: Sp. 7: Asst Mary S Biesecker Pub Lib Somerset Co Lib, Somerset Penn summers 59, 60; Libn Chestnut Ridge Sch Dist, Fishertown Penn 59-61; Libn Hempfield Area Sch Dist, Greensburg Penn 61-, W Hempstead Jr High Sch 66-. 9: NEA; ALA-AASchL; PennLA (Intel Freedom Com 64 & 65); Penn State EA; Pittsburgh Suburban Libns; Westmoreland Co Libns; Hempfield Area Libn (Dept of Supv & Curriculum). 10: Greensburg Col Club. 14: Sr High Sch libs. 15: Uhl Street Ext, Somerset Pa 15501.

WARNOW, JOAN (NELSON). b Buffalo NY 1p D 31. 5: UBuffalo 50-52 (Hist); Simmons 49-50, 52-53 BLS; Columbia 53-55; 65 (LS); Hunter Col 60-62 (Educ). 7: Libn: NY Pub Lib 53-55; Queensboro Pub Lib, Queens NY 60-62; Amer Inst of Physics, NY 65-. 9: SLA; ALA. 14: Ref in hist physics, ms collections, displays. 15: Amer Inst of Physics 335 E 45th st, NYC 10017.

WARREN, CAROL H (MOSHER). b Motley Monn 5 S 19. 4: Robert Harold Warren. 5: East Nazarene Col 59-63 (Hist) BA (magna cum laude); BostonU 63-65 (Hist) AM; Simmons 65-67 (LS) MS. 6: Fr. 7: Aircraft repair Civil Serv US Naval Air Sta, Pearl Harbor 42-43; Tchr Woodward Sch for Girls, Quincy Mass 63-64; Asst dir Mass Assn for Adult Blind, Egpyt Mass summer 64; Lib asst BostonU Educ Lib 64-65; Lib intern Boston Pub Lib Hist Dept 65-66; Asst ref libn Bentley Col Lib 66-67; Asst libn Colby Jr Col 67-. 9: NHLA. 10: AHA; Phi Alpha Theta; AAUP; African Studies Assn. 14: Ref, bibliog. 15: RFD 1, New London NH 03257.

WARREN, CHARLES DAVID. b Martin Tenn 12 Je 44. 5: UTenn (Martin) 62-67 (Eng, Hist) BS in Liberal Arts; UIll (Urbana) 67-69 (LS) MS. 6: Sp. 7: Grad asst Math Lib UIll 68; Lib asst Reelfoot Reg Lib, Martin Tenn 63-67, Libn 69-. 9: ALA; SELA; TennLA; W Tenn Reg LA. 10: Beta Phi Mu; Alpha Tau Omega; Sigma Tau Delta. 15: 111 S McComb st, Martin Tn 38237.

WARREN, EMMA (ANDREWS). b Plainfield NJ 6 Ag 27. 4: Reginald L Warren. 5: Douglass col 45-49 (Chem) BS; Columbia 50-51 (Catlg); Rutgers 54-57 MLS. 7: Libn US AEC New Brunswick Lab, New Brunswick NJ 49-56; Libn RCA Semiconductor Div, Somerville NJ 56-58; Med research libn Esso Research & Engring Co Med Resew 56-58; Med research libn Esso Research & Engring Co Med Research Div, Linden NJ 59-64, Research libn Tech Info Sect 67-; Indexer Amer Smelting & Refining Co, S Plainfield NJ 65-67. 9: SLA (NJ Chap: dir 56-58, Memb Chm 63-64, Mem Com 67-69). 10: Nat Assn col Women; Delta Sigma Theta; Visiting Nurse Assn. 12: Ed SLA NJ Chap Bulletin (61-62). 14: Spec libs. 15: 277 Chelsea blvd, Plainfield NJ 07062.

WARREN, HUGH P(ARKER). b Huron SD 3 D 22. 4: Lois Bowers. 5: SD State Col 40-42 (Gen Sci): USD 46-48 (Hist) AB; UCal 50-52 BLS. 7: US Army Signal Corps Teletype operator (Sgt) ETO 43-46; Asst supv Traffic Sect Highway Planning Survery, Pierre SD 48-50; Adult libn deposits dept Chicago Pub Lib 52-57; Supv of ext wk Grace A Dow Mem Lib, Midland Mich 57-63; Admin asst S Bend (Ind) Pub Lib 63-. 9: ALA; IndLA (Lib Planning Com 68-70). 10: UNA/USA; South Bend Art Assn; Audubon Society. 14: Data proc, a-v, ext, admin. 15: Pub Lib 122 W Wayne, South Bend Ind 46601.

WARREN, KATHERINE (FLEISCHMANN). b Chicago 22 Ja 15. 4: Dr Harris G Warren. 5: Northwestern 32-36 (Geol) BS, 36-38 (Hist) MA; UMiss 48-50, 52-53 (Educ); Miami U 58; UDenver summers 61, 63, 64 (LS) MA. 6: Ger. 7: Libn Geological Survey, State of Miss, University Miss 50-57; Libn Talawanda High Sch, Oxford Ohio 59-61; Catlg Western Col for Women 61-65; Ref libn Miami U (Ohio) 65-. 10: Kappa Delta Pi; Ohio Acad of Hist. 13: Yes. 14: Ref. 15: 1022 S Locust st, Oxford Ohio.

WARREN, LOIS (BOWERS). b Pocahontas Iowa 27 Mr 26. 4: Hugh P Warren. 5: Aurora Col 43-45; UIll 45-47 (Chem) BS; Far East & Russian Lang Sch UCal Ext 49-50 (Russian); UCal (Berkeley) 50-52 BLS. 6: Fr, Russian. 7: Asst libn Shell Development Co, Emeryville Cal 47-49; Asst small br libs UCal (Berkeley) 52; Hd libn Victor Chem Wks, Chicago Hts Ill 52-57; Ref libn Dow Chem Co, Midland Mich 60; Freelance scientific tr 58-69; Asst libn UNotre Dame 68-. 10: Alliance Francaise; AAUW. 14: Catlg. 15: 1610 Sunnymede ave, South Bend In 46615.

WARREN, MARGARET J. b Sioux Falls S Dak 25 Ja 22. 5: Augusta Col 40-41; UMinn 41-44 (Journalism) BA; UNC 58-59 MS in LS. 6: Fr, Ger. 7: Off asst US Senator Karl E Mundt, Wash DC 53-58; Catlgr Cornell U Lib 59-62, Asst hd central ser rec 62-63; Descr catlgr LC 63-65, Decimal clsf specialist 65-69, Asst ed Dewey decimal clsf 69-. 9: ALA; AALL. 10: Phi Beta Kappa; Beta Phi Mu. 14: Clsf, law. 15: 423 West Building Hunting Towers, Alexandria Va 22314.

WARREN, PAMELA. b Rock Port Mo 31 D 40. 5: Neb Wesleyan U 60-62 (Hist) BA; UIll 62-63 (LS) MS. 6: Sp. 7: Admin asst Trails Reg Lib, Warrensburg Mo 63-66; Ref libn Rolling Hills Reg Lib, St Joseph Mo 66-. 9: ALA (Com Orient Adult to Pub Lib 68-; Recruiting Network; Jr Mem RT); MoLA (Recruiting Com; Pub Lib Div; treas 65-66, sec 69-70, chm-elect 69-70). 10: AAUW; LWV; Alpha Mu Gamma; Alpha Psi Omega; Alpha Gamma Delta; Altrusa; Bus & Prof Women; Beta Sigma Phi. 14: Ext, a-v, ref, admin. 15: 102 W South, Warrensburg Mo 64093.

WARREN, THOMAS D. b Franklin Tenn 30 Ja 31. 4: June Halliday. 5: Peabody Col 49-53 (Music Theory) BM, 56-57 (Music Theory) MM, 62 (Music) Ed S, 68-69 MS in LS; Brantridge Forest Sch 67 (Music) PhD. 6: Fr, Ger, Ital. 7: US Army Band Dir Vocal Mus 97th Army Band, Ft Sill Okla 53-55; Music supv, Richland Co Ohio 55-56; Hd Music Dept Reinhardt Col 58-62; Asst Prof music Jacksonville StateU 62-68; Dir lib Country Music Foundation, Nashville 68-. 9: Nat Assn Tchrs of Singing; ALA; MusicLA; MTNA. 10: Phi Mu Alpha. 14: Archival procedures, catlg. 15: 307 Third ave S, Franklin Tn 37064.

WARRINGTON, CAROL SUE. b Canton Ill 15 Jl 43. 5: MacMurray Col 64-66 (Hist) BA; No IllU 66-67 (LS) MA; UMinn summer 68 (LS). 7: Asst libn Parlin Ingersoll Lib, Canton Ill 62-64; Tech asst MacMurray Col Lib, Jacksonville Ill 64-66; Instr dept of Lib Sci No IllU DeKALB Ill 67-. 9: ALA; IllLA. 14: Child lit, catlg. 15: Dept of Lib Sci Northern Ill Univ, DeKalb Il 60115.

WARTLUFT, DAVID J(ONATHAN). b Stouchsburg Penn 22 S 38. 4: Joyce C Dittmer. 5: Muhlenberg Col 56-60 (Eng & Amer Lit) AB; Lutheran Theol Sem 60-64 BD; UPenn 62-64 (Eng & Amer Lit) AM; Drexel 66-68 MSLS. 6: Ger, Lat, Gr, Hebrew (Biblical). 7: Asst chaplain Springfield Col 62-63; Pastor Jerusalem Lutheran Ch, Sllentown Penn 64-66; Catlgr & ref asst Lutheran Theol Sem 66-69, Asst libn 69-. 8: Com on archives, East Penn Synod 67, archist 69-. 9: ALA; ATheolLA; Luth Hist Conf. 10: Beta Phi Mu; Eta Sigma Phi; Phi Sigma Tau; Luth Soc for Worship, Music & the Arts. 13: Yes. 14: Ser, archives, rare bks. 15: 7328 Rural lane, Philadelphia Pa 19119.

WASBY, ELLEN GAIL (CHARTRAND). b Kan City Mo 14 Je39. 5: Antioch Col 57-59 (Sociol); UOre 59-63 (Sociol) BS; UIll 63-65 (LS) MS. 6: Fr. 7: Clerk-acquis UOre Lib 61-63; Grad asst-acquis UIll Lib (Urbana) 63-64, Grad asst-SE Asian div 64-65; Catlgr LC 65-66, Info systs research analyst 66-. 9: ALA. 10 AAUP; Beta Phi Mu. 12: Management of Program and Training Information in the Peace Corps" (68). 14: Tech serv, data proc, catlg, programming. 15: 406 Wolfe, Alexandria Va 22314.

WASCHER, CORINNE (JACKSON). b Vermillion SD 15 N 13. 5: USD 29-33 (Fr) BA; UIll 45-46 BSLS. 6: Fr, Sp. 7: Catlg-ref Free Lib Commsn, Pierre SD 41-45; Catlgr Willard Lib, Battle Creek Mich 45-46, Head ref dept 46-. 9: ALA; MichLA. 10: Bus & Prof Women's Club. 14: Catlg, ref. 15: Willard Lib, Battle Creek Mi 49016.

WASELKOV, ELIZABETH (JAMES). b Wooster Ohio 8 N 23. 4: Alexander Waselkov. 5: Col of Wooster 48 (Psych) BA; West Res 56 MS in LS. 6: Ger, Fr. 7: High sch libn, New Philadelphia Ohio 48-51; Libn Euclid Pub Lib, Euclid Ohio 51052; Jr high sch libn Willoughby-Eastlake Schs, Willowick Ohio 61-65; High sch libn Euclid Schs, Euclid Ohio 65-. 15: 33850 Willowick dr, Eastlake Ohio 44095.

WASH, MELBA EURYDICE WILSON. b Benton Tenn 6 Ag 18. 5: Berea Col 35-39 (Eng) AB; Peabody summers 40-42 BS in LS. 7: Tchr Old Fort Elem Sch, Old Fort Tenn 39-41; Tchr-libn Oneida High Sch, Oneida Tenn 41-42; Asst libn Mc Donogh Sch for Boys, McDongh Md 42-43; libn 43-46; US Army Libn US Spec Serv, Germany 46-48; Reg libn W Tenn Reg Lib, Jackson Tenn 49-50; Reg libn Reelfoot Reg Lib, Martin Tenn 50-. 9: ALA (Coun 50-53); TennLA(treas 54, chm Pub Libs Sect 65-66); SELA. 10: AAUW. 13. Yes. 13: Yes. 14: Reg libs, rural lib serv. 15: 126 Fonville ave, Martin Tn 38237.

WASHBURN, DONALD A. b Brimley Mich 13 Ap 16. 4: Ruth V Tupper. 5: Albion Col 38 (Biol) BA; Northwestern U Dental Sch 41 DDS; UChicago 46 BLS. 6: Fr, Ger, Sp, Portu. 7: Act libn Coldwater (Mich) Pub Lib 46; Bibliogr US Quartermaster Depot, Chicago 46-48; Research consul & asst research libn John Crerar Lib, Chicago 48-49; Libn & dir bur of lib & indexing serv Amer Dental Assn, Chicago 49-. 9: Amer Dental Assn; Amer Col of Dentists; Amer Acad Hist Dentistry; MedLA (past bus mgr & treas); SLA; ASIS; Ill State Dental Soc. 12: Part Ed "Bulletin of the History of DEntistry. 13: Yes. 15: Amer Dental Assn 211 E Chicago ave, Chicago 60611.

WASHBURN, GWENYTH E. b Kitchener Ont Can 6 Ap 23. 5: UToronto 46-49 BA; McGillU 58-59 BLS; Ont Col of Educ 66-67 HSA Certif, Specialist Certif in Sch Libnship. 7: Ref & film libn Kitchener Pub Lib; Br hd Edmonton Pub Lib; Br hd Eccles Pub Lib (England); Asst libn Toronto Tchrs Col; Libn (asst hd) Oakwood Collegiate Inst. 15: 52 Leacrest rd apt 7, Toronto 17 Ont Can.

WASHBURN, HOWARD D(eMOTT). b Great Falls Mont 20 Ag 12. 5: Albion Col 35 (Eng) AB; Columbis 39 (LS) BS. 7: Act ctlgr & asst libn Albion Col 35-36; Stack chief, stack supv, ref asst econ div NY Pub Lib 36-42; Libn New Sch for Social Research 42; US Army Signal Corps 42-45; Bus ref libn C ity Col Baruch Sch (NY) 47-63, Gen ref libn 63-65; Libn Col of Police Sci (NY) 65-. 09. 9a; SLA; NY Lib Club. 10: Nat Arts Club. 14: Ref, acquis. 15: 40 E 10th st, NYC 10003.

WASHINGTON, CHANEY P. b Tuscaloosa Ala. 4: Solomon Wesley Washington Jr. 5: Stillman Col 42-44; Ala State Col 44-46 (Soc Studies) BS; Atlanta U 53-54 MLS; Simmons summer 66; West Mich U 67. 6: Sp. 7: Tchr Central Elem Sch, Tuscaloosa Ala; Tchr Castle Hill Sch, Tuscaloosa Ala; Libn Druid High Sch, Tuscaloosa Ala 55-. 8: Ala State Rep forthe Implementation of Standards; Mem, Reviewing Com, So Assn of Cols & Second Schs 63-65; Co-dir of three 5-week lib wkshops Ala State Col 63-65; Reviewing com So Assn Cols & Schs 69, Juror 69; State chm Stud Lib Asst of Ala. 9: ALA (State Assembly rep 61, State Standards rep 62); NEA; SELA; Alatla; AlaASchL (Pres 62, dist chm 65-); Ala State Tchrs Assn. 10: Delta Sigma Theta; Thursday Study Club; Trustee, Stillman Col. 14: Catlg, ref. 15: 118 Tenth st, East Tuscaloosa Ala 35403.

WASHINGTON, LEONARD S. b New Orleans La 8 Jl 24. 4: Earlena Williams. 5: SouthernU 47 (Eng) BA; UMich 49 (Eng) BA, 57 MALS. 7: Assoc Prof LangstonU 49-54; Hd libn SouthernU 59-. 9: ALA; LaLA. 14: Automation sci, ref. 15: 6400 Press dr, New Orleans La 70126.

WASHINGTON, PANSEY HOOEY. b Tex 17 Je 18. 5: Samuel Houston Col 33-40 (Home Econ) BS (magna cum laude); Wiley Col 42; UAriz 47; USoCal 46-52 MS in LS, summer 62; NYU summer 56. 6: Sp, Ger. 7: Tchr high school biol, lit & Eng 40-42, 42-43, 46-48; Tchr-libn 43-46; High sch libn Charlton-Pollard High Sch, Beaumont Tex 49-54; Circ libn Educ Lib, San Francisco State Col summer 53; Asst Prof of Lib Sci Atlanta U Grad Lib Sch 54-57; Admin libn US Army Spec Serv, Far East 57-59; Asst catlgr, lecturer Idaho State U 60-64; Catlgr, asst head catlgr, sers Kan State U (Manhattan) 64-67; Catlgr Ill State U at Normal 67-. 9: ALA; IllLA. 10: AAUP; AAUW; Beta Phi Mu. 13: Yes. 14: Ref, educ. 15: 602 Dry Grove apt 2, Normal Il 61761.

WASSENICH, RUTH (SIEGFRIED). b Brunswick Ohio 26 F 15. 4: Paul G Wassenich. 5: Oberlin Col 32-36 (Fine Arts) AB; Chicago Theol Sem 37-39 (Relgion, The Arts) MA; UTexas 49, 57 (LS). 6: Fr, Ger. 7: Tex Christian U; Asst order libn 57-59, Asst catlg libn 57-65, 67, Act head catlg dept 65-66, 68-. 9: ALA; TexLA. 14: Catlg. 15: 2501 W Lowden st, Fort Worth Tex 76109.

WASSERMAN, CORINNE (SEBOLD). b Newark NJ 16 Ag 28. 4: Lee Wasserman. 5: Upsala 46-50 (Eng) AB: Newark State 64-65 (LS). 7: Sch libn Morris twp (NJ) Schs. 9: ALA. 14: Sch libs. 15: 25 Tremont ter, Livingston NJ 07039.

WASSERMAN, MORTON N. b Newark NJ 24 Ja25. 4: M Dell Hamilton. 5: Rutgers 47-55 (Biol) BA, 56-59 MLS. 6: Sp, Ger. 7: Staff Sgt USAAF 42-45; Sr lib asst Newark Pub Lib, Newark NJ 50-56, Jr libn 56-60; Asst libn Naval Supply Research & Development Facility, Bayonne NJ 60-62; Libn Communication Systems Inc, Paramus NJ 62-68; Mgr Lib & Exec serv Curtiss Wright Corp, Woodbridge NJ 68-. 9: ASIS; SLA)NJ Chap; Educ & Recr Com). 11: Navys Outsatanding Achievement Award, 61. 13: Yes. 14: Catlg computer-pfepared bk catlgs. 15: 175 S Highwood ave, Glen Rock NJ 07452.

WASSERMAN, PAUL. b Newark NJ 8 Ja 24. 5: City Col (NY) 41-48 (Bus) BBA; Columbia 48-49 (LS) MS, 49-50 (Econ) MS; UMich 59-60 (LS) PhD; West Res 63-64 (Data Proc). 6: Fr, Ger. 7:(Pfc) US Army, Infantry 43-46; Adverstising manager laundry supply manufacturer 46-48; Asst to bus libn Brooklyn Pub Lib 49-51, Chief sci & ind div 51-53; GradSch Bus & Pub Admin, Cornell U: Lbn & Asst Prof 53-56, Libn & Assoc Prof 56-62, Libn & Prof 62-65; Dean SCh of Lib & Info Serv, UDd 65-70. 8: Mem Mayors Industrial Devel Com, Ithaca NY 54-55; Market res consult Laux Advertising Inc, Ithaca NY 55-59; Mem Tech Adv Com Cornell U Soc Sci Res Center 55-56; Lecture Amer Mgt Assn Seminars, NYC 56-58; Res & edl consultant Gale Res Co, Detroit 59-60, 63-64; Research Planning consult Ind U Sch of Bus 61-63; Prof consult sla 61-63; Directed the development of a lib in admin for Middle Eastern Tech U, Ankara Turkey, under terms of a Cornell-USAID contract; Consul to PHS, NLM Manpower Train Rev Com 66-; Co-dir Lib Adminrs Devel Prog, UMd Sch of Lib & Info Serv 67-. 9: SLA (Com on Promotion & Devel of Spec Libs 57-59; ed & chm Sources of Commodity Prices Proj 56-60; Com on Standards 60-62; Fin Com, mem & chm 60-63, chm Com on Res Prog Planning 63; West NY Chap; chm Com on Spec Libs/State Lib Rels 55-58); LPRC (treas 51); ALA (rep to the Nat Health Coun 52-53); RSD (chm Bus & Tech Com 52-53, New Ref Tools Com 64);-LAD (Lib Org & Mgt Sec; dir 60-61, v-chm & chm 61-64); LAD (Research Com, 65); -ISAD (Bd 67-68); Internat Assn of Documentalists (US rep com for the Study of Technico-Econ Documentation 64-66. 10: AAUP. 12: "Toward a Methodology for Objective Formulation in Public Libraries" (60); "Information for Administrators" (56); "Basic Library in Public Administration" (57); "Decision-Making; An Annotated Bibliography" with Silander (58, sup 64); Comp "Measurement and Evaluation of Organizational Performance; An Annotated Bibliography" (59); "Sources for Hospital Administrators" (61); "Librarian and the Machine" (65); Ed "Service to Business" (51-53); Bk review ed, "Administrative Science Quarterly" (56-59, 60-61); Ed "Sources of Commodity Prices" SLA (60); Ed "Directory of University Research Bureaus and Institutes" (60); Co-ed "Directory of Health Organizations" (61, 2nd ed 65); Co-ed "Statistics Sources" (62, 2nd ed 65); Managing ed "Management Information Guide Series" (63-). 13: Yes. 14: Admin, bus & econ bibliog, internat libnship, lib educ, automation of lib activities, ref, bibliog. 15: McKeldin Lib Univ of Md, College Park, Md.

WASSERMAN, SHERRY T. b Cincinnati Ohio 11 D 45. 5: URochester 63-67 (Hist) BA; UMich 67-68 MLS. 7: Adult libn Oak Park Pub Lib, Oak Park Mich 68-. 9: ALA. 15: 15312 Northgate blvd, Oak Park Mi 48237.

WASSOM, CYNTHIA (ELIZABETH) BETTY (JOHNSON). b Fullerton Cal 9 Ag 26. 4: Earl E Wassom. 5: Bethany Nazarene Col 44-50 (Home Econ) BS; E Tenn State U 60-62 (LS). 7: Elem tchr pub schs: Okla 50-52, Ark 52-54, Tenn 56-60; High sch libn pub schs: Tenn 61-62, Md 62-63; Documents libn Okla STATE U 63-67; Instr Dept of Lib Sci West Ky U 68-. 9: NEA; ALA; SELA. 14: Docs, ref, lib educ. 15: 548 Brentmoor dr, Bowling Green Ky 42101.

WASSOM, EARL EUGENE. b Blackwell Okla 20 S 23. 4: Cynthia Elizabeth (Betty) Johnson. 5: Bethany Nazarene Col

47-50 (Philos) BA; E Tenn State U 60-62 (LS) MA; Okla State U 64-67 (Educ Admin) EdD. 7: 1st Lt Pilot USAF 2nd AF, US 42-44; 1st Lt Aircraft Comm USAF 8th AF, European Theatre 44-46; Secondary sch tchr pub schs, Ark & Tenn 53-56; Minister Church of Nazarene, Tex, Okla, Tenn 50-62; Secondary libn Montgomery Co (Md) Schs 62-63; Educ doc libn Okla State U 63-67; Assoc dir Lib Serv & Hd Dept of Lib Sci West Ky U 67-. 9: ALA;-AASchL; NEA; SELA; KyLA; KyEA. 10: AAUP; Phi Delta Kappa; Friends of Ky Libs; Ky Hist Assn. 14: Admin, educ, docs, ref. 15: 548 Brentmoor dr, Bowling Green Ky 42101.

WASSON, BETTY. b Newport Ark 29 J 121. 5: Ark Col 38-42 (Combined Langs) AB; Washington U 43-44 (Hist) MA; Carnegie 57-58 MLS. 6: Fr. 7: Tchr Jr HIgh Sch, Jonesboro Ark 42-43; Tchr Jr High Sch, Chattanooga Tenn 45-48; Asst in Lib Sch of Fine Arts Washington U (St Louis) 48-49; Asst libn Cleburne-Independence Reg Lib, Batesville Ark 51-55; Accountant clerk Batesville White Lime Co, Batesville Ark 51-57; Admin asst Mt Holyoke Col Lib 58-60, Head of readers serv 60-66; Libn West Col for Women 66-. 9: ALA; Ohio Col Assn (sec Col Libns Sect); OhioLA; Ohio Valley Group Tech Libns. 10: Beta Phi Mu. 14: Readers serv, circ, ref. 15: 4775 Booth rd, Oxford Oh 45056.

WASSON, DONALD. b Ashtabula ohio 23 D 13. 5: David Lipscomb Col 35-37 Diploma; Vanderbilt U 37-39 (Sociol) AB, 39-40 (Sociol) AM; Chicago 40-42 (Ch Hist) DB, 42-47 (Hist & Sociol) PhD; Oxford U (Eng) 55 (Hist & Sociol); Amer U 64 Certif in Archival Admin; Peabody 67 MLS. 6: Fr, Ital, Ger, Sp. 7: Gen asst NY Pub Lib 37-38; Period asst Okla A & M 38-39; Stack supv Ohio State U 39-41; US Army (Capt) CML Corps, Intelligence 41-46, 51-52; Asst libn Coun on For Rel, NYC 46-50, 52-60, Libn 60-. 8: Consul, Carnegie Endowment for Internat Peace. 9: SLA (treas, 2nd v-pres, dir; chm Fin Com, etc, var dates); NYLib Club (treas, sec, coun, var dates). 10: Coun on For Rel. 12: Comp "American Agencies Interested in International Religion and (64) 13: Yes. 14: Ref. 15: Coun on For Rel, 58 E 68th st, NYC 10021.

WASSON, WOODROW W(ILSON). b Cottontown Tenn 6 Je 16. 4: Frances Marie Tallman. 5: David Lipscomb Col 35-37 Diploma; Vanderbilt U 37-39 (Sociol) AB, 39-40 (Sociol) AM; Chicago 40-42 (Ch Hist) DB, 42-47 (Hist & Sociol) PhD; Oxford U (Eng) 55 (Hist, Sociol); Amer U 64 Certif in Archival Admin; Peabody 67 MLS. 6: Fr, Ger. 7: Prof of US Hist Okla State Col; Prof of hist of religious UHouston; Prof of ch hist & Dean of Christian Col UGa; Archivist & Dir of research Disciples of Christ Hist Soc; Curator of spec collections dept Joint U Libs; U Archvist & Assoc Prof of Bibliog Vanderbilt U. 10: Vanderbilt Univ Club. 12: "James A Garfield; a Study in Religionand Politics (52); Co-ed Christian-EvangelistIndex, 3 v (64). 13: Yes. 14: Archives, mss, rare bks, lib admin. 15: 1900 Randolph pl, Nashville 37215.

WATANABE, STELLA K. b Kahului Maui Hawaii 15 O 30. 5: UHawaii 48-52 (Psych) ba; West Res 53-54 MS in LS. 6: Japanese. 7: Libn aide Hawaii Co Lib, Hilo Hawaii 52-53; Child libn Cuyahoga Co Lib, Cleveland 54-55; Child libn Lib of Hawaii, Honolulu 55-57, Br libn 57-61; Army Libn Hq USARYIS, Okinawa 61-63; Air Force Libn 439th Combat Support Gp, Misawa Japan 63-65, Air Force Libn, Pacific AF Base Com, Hickam Honolulu 65-. 9: Hawaii LA; ALA. 10: Bus & Prof Womens Club. 14: Ref, catlg, admin, child serv. 15: 45-570Awanene pl, Kaneohe Hi 96744.

WATERMAN, KATHLEEN (WALLACE). b Canaan Conn 6 Ja 07. 4: Marshall N Waterman. 5: MacMurray Col 25-29 (Eng) AB; Drexel 29-30 BS in LS. 6: Ger. 7: Passaic Pub Lib, Passaic NJ: Jr asst 30-34, Br libn 34-41, Head Child libn 41-43; Lib in chg br child room Newark Pub Lib, Newark NJ 43-45; Dir Chatham Pub Lib, Chatham NJ 45-65, Volunteer storytelling 67-. 9: ALA; NJLA (treas 48-50). 10: Chatham Hist Soc; Chatham Commun Players; Womans Club of Chatham; Friends of the Chatham Lib; Overpook Hosp Womans Aux. 13: Yes. 14: Admin, child ref. 15: 67 Linden lane, Chatham NJ 07928.

WATERS, EDWARD NEIGHBOR. b Leavenworth Kan 23 Jl 06. 4: Lilly Lesin. 5: URochester Eastman School of Music 23-28 (Music) B Mus, M Mus. 6: Fr, Ger. 7: Priv tchr & organist, Palmyra NY 28-30; Tchr Juniata Col 30-31; LC Music Div: Asst 31-34; Ref libn 34-37, Asst chief 37-. 9: Mus LA (pres 41-46): Amer Musicological Soc (sec 2 yrs); CNLA 9chm 2 yrs); Music Tchrs Nat Assn; Amer Studies Assn (founder); USBE (past pres & chm of Bd); DCLA (Bd of Dir 65-67). 11: Fulbright Sr Research Fellow 62-63; Ford Foundation Fellow 62-63; Chapelbrook Foundation Fellow 68. 12: "Victor Herbert" (55); "Frederic Chopin by Franz Liszt" (tr with intro 63). 13: Yes. 14: Ref. 15: Music Division Library of Congress WashingtonDC 20540.

WATERS, ELEANOR LOIS (YOUMANS). b Waycross Ga 25 Ag 28. 4: Thomas Edward Waters. 5: Perry Bus Col 44; UWis correspondence 64-65 (LS). 7: Sec to supt Shipbuilding Brunswick Marine Corp, Brunswick Ga 44-45; Chief bkkeeper Western Union, Brunswick Ga 45-47; Br manager Western Union, Sea Island Ga 47-48; Libn Biol Lab Bur of Com Fisheries, Brunswick Ga 59-69, Libn Explor Fishing & Gear Research 69-. 9: GaLA; SLA; Soc Bibl Nat Hist (London). 10: Glynn Co Lib Coun. 11: Bur of Commerical Fisheries Superior Performance Award (65). 14: Catlg, ref, rare bks in ichtyology, bibliog. 15: 2606 Starling st, Brunswick Ga 31520.

WATERS, FRANCES R. b Providence 18 Jl 14. 4: Gene Waters. 5: New Haven State Teachers Col 50-53 (Educ) BS; So Conn State Col 62 MS in LS. 7: Lib asst Stratford Pub Lib, Stratford Conn 52-53; Child Libn Milford Pub Lib, Milford Conn, 53-56 Lib tchr Stratford High Sch, Stratford Conn 56-60; Lib tchr Bunnell High Sch, Stratford Conn 60-67; Lib tchr Franklin & Stony Brook Elem Schs, Stratford Conn 67-. 8: Title II State Consul 67-68. 9: ALA-AASchL; NEA; N ENG Sch LA; Conn Sch LA. (pres 64-); Conn LA (Standard Chm 60-62); Scholarship chm 67-69); SEA (sec 69-); ConnEA. 10: AAUW. 11: Alumni Award for Outstanding Leadership and Distinguished Serv (lib sci). 14: Wk with child, ya. 15: 402 Patterson ave, Stratford Conn 06497.

WATERS, JOHN J(OSEPH). b Rome NY 8 Mr 16. 5: Syracuse 38-47 (Pol Sci), 47-48 (LS) BS. 6: Fr. 7: Cpl US AAF 43-46; Ref libn Enoch Pratt Free Lib, Baltimore 48-50; Catlg libn QM Tech Lib, Ft Lee Va 50-56; Research & development libn Rome Air Development Ctr, Griffiss AFB NY 56-59; Tech reports libn EIMAC, San Carlos Cal 59-61; Ref libn Contra Costa Co Lib, Pleasant Hill Cal 61-; Catlg libn San Jose State Col Lib 62-. 9: ALA; SLA; CalLA. 14: Catlg, info systems. 15: 2310 Cornell st, Palo Alto Ca 94306.

WATERS, JUDY GAYLE. b Ft Smith Ark 16 Mr 45. 5: UArk 63-65 (Elem Educ); UOkla 65-67 (LS) BS, 67-68 MLS. 7: Br libn Tulsa City Co Lib, Tulsa Okla summer 66, Child libn summer 67; Hd y-a dept Lincoln Lib, Springfield Ill 68-. 9: ALA; IllLA. 10: UOkla Alum Assn; Springfield Theatre Guild; AAUW; Springfield Lib Club. 14: Child & ya wk. 15: 1836 S First apt B, Springfield Il 62704.

WATERS, MARJORIE JUNE (BROWN). b Satanta Kan 10 F 24. 4: J W Waters. 5: UArk 47-49 (Soc Welfare) BSSW, summers 50-52 (Educ Admin) MS, summer 62 (LS) 3 hrs Ark Tech summer 61, 64 (LS); UOkla summers 67, 68 (LS). 7: Com tchr Deer High Sch, Deer Ark 49-60; Libn Deer Consolidated Schs, Deer Ark 61-. 8: Proj dir title ESEA PL 89-10 "Model Saturated School Library" summer 66. 9: Newton Co EA (pres 58-67). 15: Jasper Ark.

WATERS, MARY LOU (TUGGLE). b Cadiz Ky 30 Jl 37. 5: Stetson U 55-56 (Elem Educ); Murray State Col 56-59 (Elem Educ) BS; Peabody summers 60, 61, 65 MLS. 7: Elem tchr Ft Campbell Dependent Schs, Ft Campbell Ky 59-60; Elem libn Jefferson Co Schs, Louisville Ky 60-62, 63-64; Libn Trigg Co Schs, Cadiz Ky 65-. 9: NEA; KyEA; KyLA; Ky ASchL. 10: Girl Scout Leader; Cadiz Womans Club; PTA. 14: Ref, child serv. 15: Box 232, Cadiz Ky 42211.

WATERS, RICHARD J. b Boston Mass 23 Ag 22. 5: Boston Col 47-50 (Hist) BS, 50-52 (Hist) MA; URI 63-66 MLS. 6: ger, Fr. 7: Libn P-1 Boston Pub Lib 50-59; Supv libn US Naval underwater Ordinance Sta, Newport RI 59-60; Tech libn Raytheon Co, Portsmouth RI 60-68; Chief tech processes US Naval War Col, Newpo 60-68; Chief tech processes US Naval War Col, Newport RI 68; Dir lib syst, E Providence RI 68-. 9: SLA; RILA. 10: Amer Red Cross& Bd of Trustees Jamestown Pub Lib; Medieval Acad Amer; Company of Mil Histns. 13: Yes. 14: Admin. 15: 43 Longfellow rd, Jamestown RI 02835.

WATERS, RICHARD L. b Golden City Mo 7 O 37. 4: Judith K (Van Hoesen). 5: Drury Col 55-56; Friends U 56-57; Southwest Mo State Col 57-60 (Bus Admin) BS; UWash 64-66 MLibr. 6: Sp. 7: Clerk-typist US Army (Pfc) Ft Chaffee Ark 56; Bkkeeper Springfield (Mo) Pub Lib 59, Ref asst 59-60, Head bus & tech dept 60-61; Admin asst Pub Lib, Wichita Kan 62-64; Pre-prof Pub Lib, Seattle 64-66; Hd sci & ind dept Pub Lib, Dallas Tex 66-67, Chief of br serv 67-. 9: ALA;-RSD (Div Affiliates Com 68-70; Centennial Anniversary Com); KanLA (Exhib chm 64); TexLA (chm Pub Lib Div 68-69; chm Jr Mem RT 69-70); SWLA. 10: Beta Phi Mu. 13: Yes. 14: Pub lib admin. 15: 4509 Oleander tr, Mesquite Tx 75149.

WATERS, SAMUEL T. b Boston 29 Jl 25. 4: Mary Lizer. 5: URochester 46-47; U Colo 47-50 BA; BA summa cum laude; Catholic U 53-59 MSLS, Law Sch 64-66 (Law). 6: Fr, Ger. 7: Infantry Rifle Squad Leader (S/Sgt) US Army, Europe 43-46; Prelim catlgr LC 51-55; Head catlgr Georgetown U 55-59; Assoc libn George Washington U 59-60; Asst libn Georgetown U 60-66; Chief ref serv div Nat Lib of Med, Wash DC 66-68, Deputy assoc dir lib operations 68-. 9: ALA (Com Mem); DCLA (past off); Potomac Tech Proc Libns. 10: Phi Beta Kappa; Beta Phi Mu. 13: Yes. 14: Admin. 15: 713 Fletcher pl, Rockville Md 20851.

WATERSON, MARY (ZIMMERMAN). b Mishawaka Ind 19 Ag 37. 4: Willard Wade Waterson. 5: Ind U 55-59 (Hist) AB; Denver U summer 60; Catholic U 61-62 MS in LS. 7: Lib asst S Bend Pub Lib, S Bend Ind 59-61; Libn Ind U (S Bend 62-66; Hd Hist & Travel Dept S Bend Pub Lib, S Bend Ind 66-. 9: ALA; IllLA. 10: Zonta Club; AAUW; Faculty Womens Club. 14: Ref, catlg. 15: So Bend Pub Lib 122 W Wayne, S Bend In 46601.

WATKINS, DAVID ROY. b Rock Island Ill 23 Ap 15. 5: St Ambrose Col 3437 (Soc Sci) AB; UIll 4041 BS in LS; UMinn 60 (LS) MA. 6: Ger. 7: Instr St Ambrose Col 37-40; Instr & libn Spalding Inst, Peoria Ill 42-44; Instr & assoc libn St Bede Col 42-44; Libn & assoc prof Col of St Thomas (St Paul Minn) 44-53; Prin libn Ref Dept & instr in lib sch UMinn 53-56; Head of the ref dept Yale U Lib 56-65; Dir of libs Fordham 66-70; Dir Lib Brandeis U 70-. 8: Ed Bd, Yale Ed of the complete works of St Thomas More 58; Inst for Study & Tchg of Medieval Canon Law (sectreas); Consul; New Haven Col, Catholic U (PR) Central NY Ref & Resources Coun. 9: ALA;-RSD (sec-treas, chm Interlib Loan Com, chm Ad Hoc Com on Catlg Code Rev, pres 67-68); BSA; MinnLA (pres 52-53); ConnLA (pres 65-66; Chm Metro Com on Lib Use & Resources). 10: Conf on British Srudies Assn; Amici Thomae Mori Archons. 11: St Ambrose Col Alum Achievement Award. 13: Yes. 14: Ref, admin of acad libs, catlg. 15: 129 Wilmot circle, Scarsdale NY 10583.

WATKINS, DOROTHY J. b Granville Ill 28 Ja 05. 5: Ind State Tchrs Col 23-26 (Eng); Ind U 29-31 (Eng, Ger) AB; Simmons 31-32 BS in LS. 6: Ger, Fr. 7: Libn Central High Sch, Kalamazoo 26-29, Ref asst Kalamazoo Pub Lib 26-29; DC Pub Lib: Readers adv & circ asst 32-34; 1st asst fine arts dept 34-35; Readers adv hist, travel 35-37, Asst curator Washingtoniana div 37-39, Asst br libn 39-45; Denver Pub Lib: Head pub affairs div 45-52, Asst coordinator Off of Group Serv 52-54, 1st asst documents dept 54-55; Field consul NM State Lib 55-59, State Libn 59-. 9: ALA; NMLA; SWLA (2nd v-pres 58-60); SLA. 10: Altrusa Internat; AAUW; Old Santa Fe Assn; Commun Concert Assn; Santa Fe Opera Guild; Phi Mu; Santa Fe LA. 12: Ed "New Mexico Library Bulletin" (59-68); Ed "The Columbine" (52-53); Ed "The New Mexico State Library Reports" (68-). 13: Yes. 14: Southwest rare bks, govt docs, ref, admin. 15: PO Box 134L, Santa Fe NM 87501.

WATKINS, ELEANOR JOSEPHINE (CARROLL). b Oakland Cal 6 Ag 12. 4: John R Watkins. 5: UCal 28-32 (Eng) AB, 32-33 Certif of Libnship. 7: Jr libn Oakland Pub Lib, Oakland Cal 35-43, Asst ref libn 43-50; Br libn Concord Br Contra Costa Pub Lib, Pleasant Hilll Cal 50-51, Ref libn 51-61, Supv libn ext serv 61-. 9: ALA; CalLA; Bay Area Ref Libns Coun. 14: Ref. 15: 1362 Homestead ave, Walnut Creek, Cal 94598.

WATKINS, EVA (WILLIAMS). b Bogata Tex 25 Ja 11. 4: Tom Payne Watkins. 5: E Tex U 30-38 (Eng) BS, 52-54 MS in LS. 7: Prin Rosalie Sch, Bogata Tex 31-41; Tchr Red River Co 41-50; Tchr-libn Bogata Sch, Bogata Tex 54-. 9: Tex State Tchrs Assn; Red River Co TA. 10: PTA; Rivercrest Band Club. 14: Child serv. 15: RFD 1, Bogata Tex 75417.

WATKINS, MARION ESTHER (NEVILLE). b Sudbury Ont 9 Ap 42. 4: John Dawson Watkins. 5: Laurentian U (Sudbury Ont) 60-63 (Lat) BA (magna cum laude); UToronto 63-64 BLS. 6: Fr. 7: Libn Huntington Col 64; Catlgr NS Prov Lib, Halifax NS 64-65; Catlgr Loyalist Col Lib, Belleville Ont 68-. 9: CanLA. 10: Belleville Univ Womens Club. 14: Catlg; Child serv. 15: RR 3, Belleville Ont Can.

WATKINS, THOMAS T. b Hazleton Penn 21 S 18. 5: New Eng Conservatory of Music 36-38 (Piano); State Tchrs Col (West Chester Penn) 38-41 (music Educ) BS; Columbia 49-51 (LS) MS. 7: Instrumental dir E Mauch Chunk Sch Dist, Penn 41-42; Chaplains asst US Army 43-45; Organist-choir dir Methodist Church, Nesquehoning Penn 46-49; Ref asst Columbia U Music Lib 50-51, Libn 51-. 8: Instr, music bibliog, Columbia Grad Music Dept 54-56 & 65, Guest lecturer on music topics, Columbia Sch of Lib Serv. 9: MusLA (Exec Coun 54-56, rep to Nat Music Coun 55-61); NY Mus LA; NY Lib Club. 13: Yes. 14: Admin. 15: 61 Jane st, New York NY 10014.

WATROUS, LYLE (CAROLYN) C(ROCK). b East Haddam Conn 19 J 1 19. 5: Womans Col UNC 36-40 (Eng) BA; Carnegie 40-41 BS in LS; So Conn State Col 57-59 (Educ) School Lib Certif; Ariz State 63-68 (Educ) MA. 6: Fr. 7: Asst child libn Osterhout Pub Lb, Wilkes Barre Penn 41-42; Libn E Haddam Pub Lib, Moodus Conn 44-45; Libn Charles McKew Parr Lib, Chester Conn 55-56; Sub tchr Elem Sec Sch System, Chester Conn, 56-57; Jr & sr high sch libn, Old Saybrook Conn 57-62; EDuc ref Ariz State U 62-64, Hd educ ref serv 64-. 8: Consul Evaluating Com State Bd Educ (Conn) 62; Exec Bd Conn State Sch Lib Assts 61-62. 9: NEA; ArizEA; Ariz State Lib Assoc (Conv Program chm of Univ & Col Div 65, pres-elect Col & Univ Div 68-69, pres 69-); Ariz Assn Col & Univs; AEA; ASU Higher Educ. 10: PTA; Ariz State U Faculty Women's Club; Kappa Delta Pi; Salt River Libns. 14: Ref, child lit, instr materials. 15: 7239 E Vernon ave, Scottsdale Ariz 85257.

WATSON, ALICE GAYLE (HUDGENS). b Artesia NM 20 Ap 41. 4: Hal Watson Jr. 5: UNM 59-63 (Inter-Amer Affairs) BA; UTex 64-66 (LS). 6: Sp, Port, Fr. 7: Libn I Latin Amer Col, UTex 65-; Archivist DeGolyer Foundation Lib, Dallas Tex. 8: Lib consul for Dept of Hist, So Methodist U 69-. 9: ALA. 10: Phi Kappa Phi; Phi Sigma Iota; Kappa Kappa Gamma; AAUW; Univ Woman's Club, SMU. 12: "A Guide to Reference Materials of Colombia, Ecuador and Venezuela Useful in the Social Sciences and Humanities" (67). 14: Latin Amer materials. 15: 3541 Rosedale, Dallas Tx 75205.

WATSON, ALTHEA (LOUISE ORTIQUE). b New Orleans 26 Jl 22. 4: Hunter B Watson. 5: Dillard U 38-42 (Eng) AB; Atlanta U 45-46 BSLS. 7: Catlg libn Ala State Tchrs Col 46-48; Libn Dudley High Sch, Greensboro NC 48-49; Patients libn VA Hosp, Montrose NY 59-. 9: Westchester LA. 10: Trustee, Field Lib, Peekskill NY. 15: 1412 Lincoln terrace, Peekskill NY 10566.

WATSON, DOROTHY (LANIER). b Bartow Ga 17 Mr 09. 4: Dixon Watson. 5: Tift Col 25-29 (Fr) AB; UGa summer 32 (LS); Emory summers 43-49 AB in LS. 6: Fr, Lat. 7: Tchr: Twiggs Co High Sch, Jeffersonville Ga 29-32; Tchr Cass High Sch, Cassville Ga 42-45; Tchr & libn: Hawkinsville High Sch, Hawkinsville Ga 32-33, Georgetown High Sch, Georgetown Ga 33-37, Eufaula High Sch, Eufaula Ala 37-41, Cartersville High Sch, Cartersville Ga 42-45; Libn: Wesleyan Conservatory, Macon Ga 45-46, Miller Sr High sch, Macon Ga 46-65, Lasseter High Sch, Macon Ga 65-. 8: Memb eval team, So Accred Assn 52. 9: ALA; NEA; GaLA; GaEA; BibbCoEA. 10: Garden Club. 14: Ref, catlg. 15: 515 Pinecrest rd, Macon Ga 31204.

WATSON, ELBERT L. b Birmingham Ala 10 My 30. 4: Ramona Jo Bennett. 5: Bethany nazarene Col 48-52 (Hist) AB; UOkla 52-54 (Hist) MA; Peabody Col 65-66 MLS. 6: Gr. 7: Minister Ch of the Nazarene, Gadsden Ala 54-62; Sr archivist Tenn State Lib, Nashville 62-66; Dir Anniston-Calhoun Co Pub Lib, Anniston Ala 66-69; Dir Huntsville-Madison Co Pub Lib, Ala 69-. 9: ALA; SELA; AlaLA; Ala Hist Assn. 10: Anniston Civitan Club; Calhoun Co Hist Soc; Calhoun Co Sesqui-Centennial Com. 13: Yes. 14: Ref. 15: Huntsville-Madison Co Lib, Huntsville Al 35801.

WATSON, GEORGE FRANKLIN. b Luning Nev 20 F 18. 4: Mary Virginia Gooch. 5: Peabody 57-60 (BUS Educ) BS, 61-62 MSLS. 6: Sp, Russian. 7: Chief Petty Off US Navy 35-57; Tchr, High Sch, Hampton Va 60-61; Sr libn Tenn State Lib 62-65; Head libn Jr Col Lib, Rainsville Ala 65-66; Dir of the Lib Columbia State Commun Col (Tenn) 66-. 8: Research asst Pub Schs Survey in Beauregard Parish La. 9: ALA; SELA; TennLA; Nashville Lib Club. 10: BPOElks; Assn for Preservation of Tenn Antiquities-Carter House Chap; Williamson Co Hist Soc. 14: Automation in libs. 15: Executive House - B-17, Franklin Tn 37064.

WATSON, HATTIE RUTHERFORD. b Rome Ga 23 N 1886. 4: John Brown Watson. 5: Spelman Col 1894-1907 (Foreign Lang) BS; Atlanta U 54-55, 56 (LS) MS. 6: Ger. 7: Instr Piano Spelman Col 07-09; Instr Bible Morehouse Col 15-20; Dir Neighborhood House Community Proj, Atlanta 10-14; Bkkeeper Leland Col 24-27, Instr & Dean of Women 27-28; Act libn AM & N Col (Pine Bluff Ark) 30-32, Asst libn & catlgr 43-. 9: NEA; Ark Tchrs Assn, ArkLA. 10: Pine Bluff Br of Col Women; Social & Art Club; NAACP. 13: Yes. 14: Catlg, rare bks, spec collection of bks by & about Negroes. 15: Box 86 AM & N Col, Pine Bluff Ark71604.

WATSON, LINA HAYES. b Fayetteville Ark 15 My13. 4: Edmond Penn Watson. 5: UArk 29-33, 33-34 (Eng) BA; Columbia U summer 39 (Law Lib Admin). 7: Law Libn UArk 37-42; Libn Fayetteville Pub Lib, Fayetteville Ark 46-48; Lib asst UArk 46, 52-53, Law Libn 54-66, Sr lib asst 66-. 9: AALL; ArkLA. 14: Ref. 15: Univ of Ark Lib, Fayetteville Ar 72701.

WATSON, LOUISE M. b Ellensburg Wash 27 S 36. 5: Central Wash State Col 54-57 (Educ) BA in Ed; UWash 61-62 MLS. 7: Elem tchr, Stockton Cal 57-60; Elem tchr Amer Dependent Schs, Okinawa 60-61; Elem lib, Ephrata Wash 62-68; Child libn Pub Lib, Renton Wash 68-. 8: Wash State Reading Com; Vol reviewer Wash State Child Bk Evaluating Com. 9: NEA; ALA; WashEA; Wash State ASchL; Wash State LA; PNLA. 14: Child serv. 15: 903 E 8th, Ellensburg Wash 98926.

WATSON, MARGARET (ROSE) (DIMMOCK). b Ottawa Ont Can. 5: Bishop's U 49-52 (Eng) BA; McGill 52-53 BLS; Royal Conservatory of Mus of Toronto 47-53 (Violin) ARCT. 6: Fr. 7: Asst libn & catlgr Dept of Finance (Can), Ottawa 53-55; Asst libn & chief catlgr Dept of Nat Defence, Ottawa Can 55-58; Asst libn & catlgr Pub Archives of Can, Ottawa 60-62; Libn-in-chg Defence Research Bd Hdqtrs, Ottawa Can 62-68; Chief libn Dept Indian Affairs & No Development, Ottawa Can 68-. 9: SLA; OntLA. 10: Profess Inst Pub Serv of Canada Libns Group. 14: Admin, catlg, automation in the lib. 15: 225 Lisgar st apt 1101, Ottawa 4 Ont Can.

WATSON, MARY CALDWELL. b Paducah Ky 29 Ap 10. 5: UKy 27-31 (Eng) AB; UIll 39-40 BS in LS. 7: Asst circ & ref ULouisville 40-44; Lib Recreational Lib USAF Wright Field, Daytn Ohio 44-46; Asst br libn Pub Lib of Cincinnati & Hamilton Co, Norwood Ohio 46-48; Libn Ginling Col (anking China) 48-51; Head circ dept ULouisvile 52-60; Soc sci ref libn UFla 60-. 9: ALA; SELA; FlaLA. 10: AAUP. 14: Ref. 15: 1141 SW 9th rd, Gainesville Fl 32601.

WATSON, ROBERT JAMES. b Buffalo NY 8 Mr 22. 4: Ruth L Youngwirth. 5: SUNY Col (Buffalo) 41-43, 46-47 (Educ) SUNY Col (Albany) summers 50-56 (Pol Sci, Hist) MS; SUNY Col (Geneseo) summers 59-63 MLS. 7: (Pfc) 101st Infantry 26th Div Army, US & Europe 43-46; Jr high soc studies tchr Alexander Central Sch, Alexander NY 47-54; Jr high soc studies tchr Williamsville Central Sch, Williamsville NY 54-57; Sr high soc studies tchr Newfane Central Sch, Newfane NY 58-62; Sr asst readers serv ref SUNY(Buffalo) 62-64, Asst circ libn 64-66, Hd verification, acquis 66-67, Asst acquis libn 67-. 8: Tchr subj bibliog SUNY Col (Geneseo) 66. 9: ALA; NYLA. 10: Phi Delta Kappa. 14: Acquis, ref. 15: 320 N Ellicott st, Williamsville NY 14221.

WATSON, SUSAN M. b Wash DC 13 Mr 41. 5: UMich 59-63 (Physics) BS; Columbia 63-64 (LS) MS. 6: Russian. 7: Systems engnr lib automation & info retrieval IBM Corp, NYC 64-. 8: IBN Lib spec for cols, univs & prof orgs. 9: SLA; ASIS. 10: Beta Phi Mu. 14: Lib automation & info retrieval. 15: IBM Corp, 220 Church st, NYC 10013.

WATSON, WILLIAM (JOHN). b Walkerville Ont Can 12 A 28. 4: Flora Price. 5: Carleton Col 47-50 (Journalism) BJ; McGill U 52-55 MA (Islamic Studies) BLS. 6: Fr. 7: Libn Inst of Islamic Studies, McGill U 55-65; Asst libn UBC 65-69; Libn UWaterloo (Ont) 69-. 12: Ed "Persia in Islamic Times," Comp by G M Wickens & R Savory (64). 15: Univ of Waterloo, Waterloo Ont Can.

WATT, CLIFFORD R. b Winnipeg Man Can 13 F 27. 5: UMan 47-51 (Eng, Philos) BA; McGill 52-53 BLS. 6: Fr. 7: Circ asst UMan Lib 51-52; Newspaper & period libn Pub Archives of Can, Ottawa 53-54; Massey Lib, Royal Mil Colof Can, Kingston Ont: Asst libn & Chief of prof serv 63-. 8: Kingston Arts; Honorary Governor of the Dominion Draa Festival, 64; Patron Kingston Symphony Assn; UManitoba Alum Assn; Bd Dirs Gallery Assn Queens U. 10: Kingston Arts Coun; Kingstn Film Soc; Off of var Royal Mil Col Athletic Coms; RMC Curling Club; RMC Art Club. 14: Ref, circ, catlg, admin. 15: Massey Lib Royal Mil Col of Can, KINGSTON Ont Can.

WATT, DONALD A(NDERSON). b Ottawa Ont Can 25 Ja 19. 5:UToronto 35-39 (Fr, Ger) BA; Ont Col of Educ 39-40, 42-43 (Fr, Ger) HSA, Spec Certs; UToronto 46-47 BLS, 48-52 (Educ Theory) MA. 6: Fr, Ger. 7: Clerk admin RCAF Toronto & Eng 41-45; Toronto Pub Lib: Libn ref div 47-48, Libn bus & tech sect 48-57, Head bus & tech sect 57-63, Deputy head central lib div 63-65, Head tech serv div 65-66, Hd Hist Sect 66-68, Gen Info Ctr 68-. 9: CanLA Ref sect ; OntLA; Inst Prof Libns (Ont). 10: Metropolitan Toronto Pub Lib Staff Assn. 13: Yes. 14: Ref, catlg. 15: 50 Pinewood ave, Toronto 10 Can.

WATT, JOHN RILEY. b Tilden Ill 26 My 29. 5: UIll 47-49; McKendree Col 49-51 (Eng) BA; UIll 52-54 MSLS. 6: Fr. 7: Inst of high sch Eng & hist, Martinsburg Mo 51-52; Consul Ill State Lib 54-56; Libn Botetourt-Rockbridge Reg Lib, Lexington Va 56-60; Tracy Br libn Stockton-San Joaquin Co Pub Lib, Stockton Cal 60-. 9: CalLA (chm Personnel Admin Com 67); ALA. 14: Adult serv. 15: Tracy Br Lib 1340 Holly dr, Tracy Cal 95376.

WATT, LOIS (BELFIELD). b Wash DC 2 Mr 14. 4: Ralph W Watt. 5: UMd 30-34 (Educ, Eng) BA; Harvard Grad Sch of Educ summer 38; UMd 40 (Eng) MA; Catholic U 61 MSLS. 6: Fr. 7: Tchr pub schs, Wash DC 36-40; Asst libn Sidwell Friends Sch, Wash DC 46-58; Curriculum materials asst Educ Matls Lab US Off of Educ, Wash DC 58-60, Chief 60-. 8: Lecturer, Dept of Lib Sci Cathol U, 65-. 9: NEA; ALA-CSD (Pubns Planning Com 63-65; Newbery-Caldecott Com 65); -AASchL (chm Instr Materials Com 65-; Assn for Childhood Educ Internat (Ed Bd 57-59); DCLA. 10: DC Coun of Admin Women in Educ; Child Bk Guild of Wash; Beta Phi MU: Delta Kappa Gamma. 12: Auth "Textbook Classification Scheme (4th ed 67); Co-comp "Childrens Books 1964 (also 1965-1968)". 13: Yes. 14: Child lit, clsf, educ for libnship. 15: 1206 Parker ave, Hyattsville Md 20782.

WATT, MARY C (Di CINTIO). b Toronto Can 5 O 38. 4: Gordon C Watt. 5: UToronto 56-60 (Philos) BA, 66-67 BLS. 6: Fr. 7: Tchr St Joseph's Col Sch (Toronto) 60-63; Lib asst Defence Research Establishment, Downsview (Toronto) Can 64-66; Lib asst UToronto Lib 63-64, Libn sci & med div 67, Sunnybrook Hosp 67-. 14: Spec libs. 15: 304 Kennedy rd, Scarborough Ont Can.

WATTERSON, RONALD MILTON. b Butler Penn 21 Mr 33. 5: UPittsburgh 55-59 BS; Rutgers 59-60 MLS; UPittsburgh. 6: FR, Ger. 7: Armed Forces Spec Serv 53-55; Asst circ UPittsburgh Main Lib 55-58, Lib asst Med ib 50; Libn Pittsburgh PlateGlass Co Glass Research Center, Pittsburgh Penn 60-62; Asst libn UPittsburgh Med Lib 62-65; Deputy dir Johns Hopkins U Welch Med Lib 65-67; Libn Med Col of Ohio (Toledo) 67-. 9: MedLA. 14: Admin, catlg. 15: Johns Hopkins Univ, Welch Med Lib, 1900 E Monument st, Baltimore 21205.

WATTS, DORIS RYDER. b Stamford Conn. 4: Wayman S Watts. 5: Oberlin Col 26-27 (Eng); Conn Col 27-30 (Eng) BA; USoCal 44-45 BS in LS. 6: Fr. 7: Br libn Long Beach Pub Lib, Long Beach Cal 45-52, Coord of ya serv 52-59; Pub lib ya consul NY State Lib Ext Div, Albany NY 59-61; Ya serv consul Nassau Lib System, Hempstead NY 61-62; Coord programs & serv Queensborough Pub Lib, Jamaica NY 62-64; Asst co libn Contra Costa County Lib, Pleasant Hill Cal 64-. 8: Lecturer in child lt, UCLA, summer 57; Instr in child lit & ya lit UCal Ext 57-59; Instr ya serv CW Post COL 63-64; Coun on Educ for Libnship UCal 67-. 9: ALA (Coun 52-56);-YASD (v-pres, assoc ed "TON," mem var com); NYLA (Coun 62-63, pres child & ya sect 63-64, mem bd 60-64); CalLA (v-pres ya libns round table 58-59; mem var coms; pres Golden Gate Dist 68); Nassau Co LA (Bd); NY Lib Club (Coun 64; Pub lib exec Central Cal; Bd dirs 65). 12: Bi-monthly column Library and te Teen-Age in "Wilson Libary Bulletin (60-64); Ed Naseau Co LA "Odds and Book Ends (63); Auth When Teens Reach for Books in "The childrens Bookshelf, (rev ed 65). 13: Yes. 14: Lib educ, bk sel, coop system devel, ya serv. 15: 1841 Laguna apt 16A, Concord Ca 94520.

WATTS, HENRIETTA (DOUGLAS). b McAfee Ky 28 Ja 21. 5: UKy 42-46 (LS) AB. 7: Libn Denver Bible Col 46-47; Libn catlgr Moody Bible Inst 48-. 14: Catlg. 15: Lib, Moody Bible Inst, 820 N LaSalle st, Chicago 60610.

WATTS, JAMES BAKER. b Chipley Fla 2 F 18. 5: Birmingham-So Col 40-44 (Speech) BA; Peabody 50 (LS)MA; UIll 55-61 (Mass Communicatons). 6: Fr, Ger. 7: Asst to bursar Birmingham-So Col 41-44, Manager Col Bk Store 44-46; Special Agent Counter Intel Corps US Air Force (Sgt) 47-49; Dir Carnegie Pub Lib, Sumter SC 51; Special Agent Off of Spec Investigation US Air Force (Maj), Offutt Air Force Base Neb 51-53; Dir Carnegie Pub Lib, Sumter SC 53-54; Sec UIll(Urbana) 55-56; Asst catlg dept UIll Lib(Urbana) 56-57, Bibliog acquis dept 57-61; Chief tech processing div Long Beach Pub Lib, Long Beach Cal 61-63; Dir lib serv & instr materials Clearwater Campus, St Petersburg Jr Col 63-66; Dir lib serv Harvey A Andruss Lib Bloomsburg State Col 66-. 9: NEA; PennLA; PennStateEA; ALA. 10: Beta Phi Mu; Phi Sigma Iota; Kappa Phi Kappa; Eta Sigma Phi; Lions Club. 13: Yes. 14: Admin, acquis, automation. 15: Hotel Magee 20 W Main, Bloomsburg Pa 17815.

WATTS, JUDITH (GEISLER). b Morenci Mich 6 Mr 41. 4: John M Watts Jr. 5: Alma Col 59-63 (Psych) BA; UVienna 62 (Psych); CatholicU 64-66 (LS); Pratt Inst 66-68 MLS. 6: Ger. 7: Libn MFOD Lib Goddard Space Flight Ctr, Greenbelt Md 64-66; Libn NY Pub Lib 66-68; Asst libn Hampshire Col 68-. 9: ALA. 14: Tech serv, lib systems, ref. 15: Hampshire College, Amherst Ma 01002.

WATTS, MARIAN (REED) (MRS). b Fredericksburg Va 08. 4: . 5: Goucher Col 25-29 (Hist) AB; Drexel 38-39 BS in LS; Columbia 39, 40 (Educ). 6: Fr, Sp. 7: High sch tchr Stafford Co Va & Fredericksburg va 29-38; Soc sci reading room Tchrs Col Lib, Columbia U 39-41; Head circ Northeastern Br DC Pub Lib 41, Head sociol dept Main Bldg 42; Naval res-WAVES (Lt) Naval Torpedo Station Alex Va 42-43; Naval res-WAVES (Lt) Bur of Naval Personnel Tech Lib, Wah DC 43-46, Civilian Head 46-51; Head catlgr Mary Washington Col Lib 52-. 9: ALA; VaLA; Potomac Tech Proc Libns. 14: Catlg. 15: 1215 Buckner st, Fredericksburg Va 22401.

WAUGH, ARTHUR B. b Sacramento Cal 14 N 22. 5: Sacramento Jr Col 41-42 AA; UCal(Berkeley) 41-42, 46-48 AB(Eng), BLS. 6: Ger, Fr, Sp, Ital. 7: Armed forces Infantry 43-46; Page Sacramento Pub Lib, Sacramento Cal 40-41; Clerk period div Cal State Lib 47; UCal(Berkeley): Circ upv res bk dept 48-49, Asst in-admin 50-51, Head Arch Lib 51-54, Head Environmental Design Lib 55-. 9: Soc of Arch Histns. 10: ACLU. 14: Admin. 15: 686 Euclid ave, Berkeley Cal 94708.

WAUGH, DORIS (HANNER). b Greensboro NC 4 Je 28. 5: Appalachian State Tchrs Col 46-50 (LS) BS; UNC summers 52-55 ms. 6: Sp. 7: Libn: Black Mountain High Sch, Black Mountain NC 50-51, Burlington city schs, Burlington NC 51-53, Chas D McIver Sch, Greensboro NC 53-68; Calvin Wiley Elem Sch, Greensboro NC 68-. 9: ALA; NEA; SELA; NCLA; NCEA. 10: Greensboro Lib Club. 14: Wk with child. 15: Rte 1, Climax NC 27233.

WAUGH, SHIRLEY (STEWART). b Johnson Wash 1 Jl 5. 4: Robert Burton Waugh. 5: Wash State U 33-37 (Home Econ) BS; UWis 60-61 (LS) MS. 6: Sp. 7: Lt (jg) US NR (W), Seattle & Boston 43-45; Ref libn Yakimo Valley Col 61-63; Period libn Central Wash State Col 63-. 9: ALA. 10: AAUW. 14: Sers, ref, NW hist. 15: 3 Radio rd, Ellensburg Wash 98926.

WAWRZYSZKO, ALEKSANDRA (KRYSTYNA). b Gdynia Poland 10 N 34. 5: UWarsaw 53-57 MA; UToronto 61-62 BLS; Mt ST Vincent Col (Halifax Can) 58-59, 60-61 (Eng Lit); Dalhousie U (Halifax Can) 64-65 (Russian). 6: Polish, Russian, Ital. 7: Tchr of lit & hist, Warsaw Poland 57-58; Lib asst Mt St Vincent Col (Halifax Can) 58-59, 60-61; Med sec, Windsor Ont 59-60; Bkmob libn Halifax Co Reg Lib, Halifax Can 62-65; Bibliog serv libn dept hd Simon Fraser U Lib (BC) 65-68, Humanities libn 68-. 9: CanLA; BCLA; ALA. 10: Amer Assn for Advancement Slavic Studies; Canadian Assn Slavists. 13: Yes. 14: Ref, lib research (bibliog wk), info, pub rel, circ. 15: 599 Sperling, Burnaby 2 BC Can.

WAX, IRENE (MILLER). b Boston 12 Ap 19. 4: Bernard M Wax. 5: Cambridge Sch of Liberal Arts 36-37; UNH 37-38; Simmons 38-40 (S) BS. 6: Fr. 7: Libn Ursuline Acad, Dedham Mass 62-66; House in the Pines Sch 66-. 9: ALA. 14: Catlg, bk sel, ya. 15: 45 Pine Grove ave, Sharon Ma 02067.

WAY, SARAH (SIMS) (MRS). b Charleston SC 28 S 05. 5: Womens Col of Ga 20-22; UGa 53-59 (Eng) AB MA; Emory 59-60 (LS) ML. 7: Asst libn UGA 61-. 9: ALA; SELA; GaLA (chm Col & Univ Sect). 10: Beta Phi Mu; Delta Kappa Gamma; Phi Beta Kappa, Phi Kappa Phi. 14: Acquis (gifts & exchange). 15: 423 Milledge Heights, Athens Ga 30601.

WAY, WILLIAM (PAUL). b Hollywood Cal. 4: Nancy Waers. 5: Los Angeles City Col (Mus, Liberal Arts) AA; Los Angeles State Col (B us, Econ) BA; UCLA (Math, Engring). 6: Ger, Fr. 7: Statistician & research libn Gilfillan Bros Inc, Los Angeles 54-56; Sr engring asst & libn Tasker Inds, Van Nuys Cal 56-62; Engring writer Litton Inds Data Syst Div Van Nuys Cal 62-64; Lib staff asst & programmer RAND Corp, Santa Monica Cal 64-. 9: ASIS; SLA. 13: Yes. 14: Lib data proc systems. 15: 21615 Bryant st, Canoga Park Ca 91304.

WAYNE, MARY HELEN (COLLIER). b S Pasadena Cal 9 My 13. 4: Robert D Wayne. 5: Occidental 31-35 (Philos, Rel) AB; Columbia 38-39 (Stud Personnel Sdmin) MA; USoCal 62-66 (LS) MS. 7: Sec First Congregational Ch, Los Angeles 35-36; Sec Occidental Col 36-38, 43-45; Dir of stud personnel Woman's Col Furman U 39-42; Clk S Pasadena Pub Lib, S Pasadena Cal 55-62, Ref libn 62-67, Asst city libn 67-. 9: ALA; CalLA. 10: Friends of the Lib (Hintington Lib); Mem of Bd, Friends of the Lib (Occidental Col). 14: Ref. 15: 909 Lyndon st, S Pasadena Ca 91030.

WEACHTER, EVELYN. b Akron Ohio 12 Ap 08. 5: Col of Wooster 28-32 (Lat) AB; Columbia 38-40 BS in LS. ; State Col at Fitchburg 61-63. 7: Lib asst Akron Pub Lib, Akron Ohio 33-45; Ref lib & asst libn Fitchburg Pub Lib, Fitchburg Mass 45-60; Libn State Col (Fitchburg Mass) 60-66; Libn Cocoa Beach Pub Lib, Cocoa Beach Fla 69-. 8: Wrote Correspondence Course for Ext Div, Comm of Mass 59; Tchr ref courses Harvard, Clark U & at Fitchburg Pub Lib all for Ext Div Comm of Mass 55-60; Consul Leominster Hosp Sch of Nurs Lib 63-. 9: MassLA (past mem & chm Planning Com). 13: Yes. 14: Ref wk, admin. 15: Twin Towers apt 510S, 2020 N Atlantic ave, Cocoa Beach Fl 32931.

WEADICK, MARILYNNE (LUNZ). b Hamilton Can 8 O 21. 4: William James Weadick. 5: UToronto 40-43 (Arts) BA, 62-63 BLS. 7: Clk West Life Assurance Co Hamilton Ont Can 43-44; Sec Maple Leaf Broadcasting Co (CHML), Hamilton Ont Can 44-46; Libn's asst hamilton Pub Lib, Hamilton Ont Can 61-62, Child libn 63-. 9: ALA; CanLA; OntLA. 10: Cath Women's League. 14: Child serv. 15: 51 Wentworth st S, Hamilton 20 Ont Can.

WEANT, REBECCA ELLIS. b Salisbury NC 28 Jl 18. 5 Guilford Col 34-38 (Hist) AB; UNC summers 39-42 BS in LS; UMich 53-54 AMLS. 7: Eng tchr Rockwell High Sch, Rockwell NC 38-39; Libn Tarboro High Sch, Tarboro NC 39-42; Asst libn New Hanover High Sch, Wilmington NC 42-45; Asst hosp libn US Army Hosp, Camp BUTNER NC 45-46; Army libn US Army, PI Okinawa Japan Austria Germany 46-5; Air Force libn Donaldson AFB, Greenville SC 52-53; Ref libn Enoch Pratt Free Lib, Baltimore 54-65; Asst head ref dept Greensboro Pub Lib, Greensboro NC 65-67; Asst dir Rowan Co Pub Lib, Salisbury NC 67-. 9: ALA; MdLA (treas 57-59); NCLA-(Pub Lib Sect sec); SELA. 14: Ref. 15: 618 S Fulton st, Salisbury NC 28144.

WEAR, NEDRA V. b Earlington Ky 10 N 19. 4: Pat Waterfield Wear. 5: Murray State Col 27-41 (Home Econ) BS; Berea 52-55 (LS); East State Col currently. 7: Tchr Lone Oak High Sch, McCracken Co Sch, Paducah Ky 41-42; Child welfare wker Ky Dept of Child Welfare, Madisonville Ky 44-46; Tchr Earlington High Sch, Earlington Ky 46-47; Berea Found libn Berea Col 54-56; Ser libn Berea Col 56-. 9: KyLA. 10: Kappa Delta Pi. 14: Ser, ref. 15: 101 Van Winkle dr, Berea Ky 40403.

WEATHERBE, GRACE ANNE (COUPAL). b Regina Sask Can. 5: UOttawa 37-40 (Philos) BA; UToronto 61-62 BLS, 66-69 MLS. 7: Libn St Catharines Pub Lib, St Catharine's Ont Can 62-66, Hd tech serv 65-67; Libn St Jerome's Col 64-65; Chief libn Mohawk Col 67-. 9: COLT; OntLA (chm Com on Standards for Commun Col Libns); Inst Prof Libns Ont (dir); HamiltonRegionLA (Stud Serv Com). 14: Tech services, train of lib tech. 15: 609-157 Pearl st S, Hamilton 12 Ont Can.

WEATHERFORD, JOHN W. b Decatur Ill 5 Ja 24. 4: Louise Fristoe. 5: MillikinU 41-47 (hist) BA; UNM 47-48 (Hist) MA; UMich 49-54 (Hist, LS) MSLS. 6: Fr, Sp. 7: Message ctr chief US Army Engrs 43-46; Mss catlg asst Clements Lib UMich 52-54; Mss libn Ohio Hist Soc, Columbus 54-57; Asst to dir MiamiU (Ohio) 57-65, Asst dir 65-67, Assoc dir & univ libn 67-69; Dir of Libs, Central Mich U Mt Pleasant 70-. 9: ALA. 10: AAUP. 13: Yes. 14: Admin. 15: Central Mich Univ Lib, Mt Pleasant Mi 48858.

WEATHERLY, LORENA P. b Fremont Neb 10 Mr 09. 4: John F Weatherly. 5: UNeb 26-30 (Eng) BA; UIll BS in LS. 7: Asst Pub lib, Lincoln Neb 30-33; Circ head PUB Lib, Lincoln Neb 38-45; Ref libn Waltham Pub Lib, Waltham Mass 45-. 15: 735 Main st, Waltham Mass 02154.

WEATHERS MARQUA (ELIZABETH). b Springfield Mo 28 Ap 24. 5: Southwest Mo State Col 41-44 (Pre-Med) AB; Washington U 50-52 (Biochem); UIll 57-59 MSLS; UOkla (LS) 65. 6: Fr, Ger. 7: X-ray Tech Jewish Hosp, St Louis 44-47; Research libn Anheuser-Busch Inc, St Louis 47-50; Chem libn Washington U (St Louis) 50-52; Chemist St Louis 52-54; Biochemist Fifth Army Lab, St Louis 54-56; Med libn Washington U Med Sch (St Louis) 59-62; Med libn UWis Med Sch 62-63; Head Libn Carthage Pub Lib, Carthage Mo 64-66; Dir of pub serv Drury Col 66-69; Chief med libn Mennepin Co Med Soc, Minneapolis 69-. 8: Mem planning com for org of Border Lib Syst, Sec-treas Admin Bd 64-66; Sch lib consul Fair Play R-II Sch Dist Fiair Play Mi 68-69. 9: MedLA; SLA; MoLA; St Louis MedLA (pres 60-62). 10: AAUP; Soroptimist Club; Bus & Prof Womens Assn; Carthage Coun of Soc

Agencies; Carthage Arts & Crafts Assn; Beta Phi Mu. 14: Admin, ref, ser. 15: Hennepin Co Med Soc, 2000 Med Arts Bldg, Minneapolis Mn 55402.

WEAVER, ALICE (OHLINGER). b Toledo Ohio 8 Mr 25. 4: Ernest W Weaver. 5: Swarthmore 42-44; UToledo 44-46 (Hist) AB, 61-65 MALS. 6: Fr. 7: Elem sch libn Toledo Pub Schs, Toledo Ohio 66-67; Asst ref libn UToledo 68-. 14: Ref, col libs. 15: 3638 Brunswick dr, Toledo Oh 43606.

WEAVER, ALMA (SNYDER). b Spartanburg SC 22 S 19. 5: US Dept of Agric Grad Sch 59-67 lib Techniques Certif; George WashingtonU 67-. 7: Clk-typist (lib) DA Off of the QM Gen, Wash DC 51-55, Lib supv clk 55-56, Ed research clk (lib) 56-57; Lib asst (lib-intelligence) QM Intelligence Agcy, Wash DC 57-61; Libn (catlg) Ind Col of the Armed Forces, Wash DC 61-63, Libn (pub serv sect) 63-64, Libn (chief classified ref sect) 64-. 8: ICAF Course, Econ of Nat Security, Wash DC 64-65; Hqs, USAF Reading Improvement Course, Wash DC 66; DA Supvr Devel Course, Wash DC 67; Introd to Computers (Study Gp) US Mil Acad, West Point 68. 9: SLA (Mil Libns Div); DCLA; Soc Lib Info Spec & Technicians. 10: Federally Employed Women; Nat Fed of Federal Employees; DC (Woodridge Area) Civic Assn. 11: Two Outstanding Performance Awards; two Sustained Superior Performance Awards; and one Spec Serv Award. 14: Ref, research. 15: 2612 Hamlin st NE, Washington DC 20018.

WEAVER, ANNIE BELLE. b Tupelo Miss 6 F 04. 5: Miss State Col for Women 22-26 (Eng) BA; Emory 27-28 ABLS; UChicago summer 40 (LS); NYU Sch of Educ summer 46. 6: Fr, Lat. 7: High sch Eng tchr Smith Co Consolidated Sch, Miss 26-27; Libn Emory Jr Col 28-31; Catlgr Southwestern Col (Memphis Tenn) 31-33; Libn W Ga Col 33-68; Dir of libs 68-. 8: Lib consul, San Juan Jr Col 56. 9: ALA; GaEA; GaLA (sec 29-3); SELA. 10: Lit-Mu Club, Carrollton Ga; Arts Study Club; Mutual Concert Assn. 11: Founders Day Award, W Ga Col 52. 14 Catlg, ref. 15: 705 Rome st, Carrollton Ga.

WEAVER, BARBARA FRANCES (WEISSE). b Boston 29 Ag 27. 4: George Briggs Weaver Jr. 5: Radcliffe 45-49 (Math) BA; URI 63-67 MLS. 6: Fr. 7: Exec sec Electronics Corp of Amer, Cambridge Mass 49-51; Tech report writer, then head tech Reports dept Edgerton, Germeshausen & Grier Inc, Boston 51-59; Libn Thompson Lib Inc, Thompson Conn 61-69; Asst dir Lib Serv Ctr Conn State Lib 69-. 9: ALA; ConnLA; (rep-at-large 68-69). 10: Sports Car Club of Amer. 14: Ref, small pub libs. 15: PO Box 99, Thompson Conn 06277.

WEAVER, BARLOW ALLEN. b Dallas 1 My 30. 5: UTex 47-51 (Econ) BA, 51-52 (Econ); Columbia 57-59 MS in LS; UCal Ext 66; U San Francisco 65, 67. 6: Sp. 7: Stud asst UTex Lib 48-49; Clerk Tex Employment Commsn, Austin Tex 49-53; Spec 4 US Army Guided Missile Gp, Ft Bliss Tex 53-56; Manager Weavers Variety Store, Bridgeport Tex 56-57; Asst to libn Queens Col Lib (NY) 57-59; Libn II in chg Downtown Center Lib San Francisco State 59-67; Tech serv libn Chabot Col 68; Audio libn Col of San Mateo 68-. 9: ALA; CalASchL; CalLA; CalTA; NY Lib Club. 14: Ref, catlg, a-v. 15: 1740 Lexington ave, San Mateo Ca 94402.

WEAVER, CLARENCE L(AHR). b Delaware Ohio 5 N 04. 4: Gertrude Pratt. 5: Ohio Wesleyan U 22-23, 25-26 BA; West Rs 33-34 BS in LS; UMich 59 MA in LS. 6: Lat, Fr. 7: Off clerk Order of Bkfellows, Chicago 26; Proofreader Lakeside Press, Chicago 26-30; Landscaping John Mahl, S Euclid Ohio 31-32; Dairying Chester Bolton, S Euclid Ohio 32-34; Head catlgr & asst ed Ohio Hist Soc, Columbus Ohio 34-46; Chief catlg & order dept Grand Rapids Pub Lib, Grand Rapids Mich 46-69. 9: ALA; MichLA; Mich Reg Group of Catlgr (past chm); GRAND Rapids Lib Club. 10: Verse Writers Guild; ohio Poery Day Assn; Bards of Grand Rapids (Mich); Poetry Soc of Mich; Kent Philatelic Soc; Theo Soc Amer; World Poetry Soc; United Amateur Press. 12: Ed & publ "Quickening Seed, Poetry" (32-46); Ed "Bardic Echoes, Poetry" (60-); Asst ed Ohio State Archaeol & Hist Soc "Publications" (34-46); Auth "With All My Love" poems (36); " Bard's Prayers" (67). 13: Yes. 14: Tech proc. 15: 1036 Emerald ave NE, Grand Rapids Mich 49503.

WEAVER, ESTHER MARIE (RICHTER) (MRS). b Marble Falls Tex 9 N 14. 5: SW Tex State Col 33-38 (Eng) BA; Tex Womans U summers 39-41 BS in LS, NDEA Lib Inst summer 66; UTex summer 62 (A-V Arts). 6: Ger, Sp. 7: Prin & tchr Spring Creek Sch, Sandy Tex 35-37; Tchr Catarina High Sch, Catarina Tex 38-40; Libn La Feria High Sch, La Feria Tex 40-41; Libn Pharr-San Juan Alamo High, Pharr Tex 41-44; Asst order dept UTex Lib (Austin) summer 43; Libn Galveston Army Air Field, Galveston Tex 44-45; Libn & tchr Marble Falls High Sch, Marble Falls Tex 48-53; Libn Lampass High Sch, Lampasas Tex 53-54; Libn Burnet Co Free Lib, Burnet Tex 54-56; Libn Fredericksburg High Sch, Fredericksburg Tex 59-. 08: Correspondent for Austin American, 1950-1955, in Marble Falls, Tex; Mem of staff of The College Star, SWTSC newspaper, 1937-38. 9: ALA; NEA; TexLA; TexStateTA. 10: Delta Kappa Gamma; Zonta Club; First Methodist Ch; Commsn on Missions; Gillespie Co Hist Soc; Alpha Chi. 13: Yes. 14: Ref. 15: 701 N Washington st, Fredericksburg Tx 78624.

WEAVER, JAMES E(DWIN). b Marion Ohio 14 O 42. 4: Sara Fox. 5: McPherson Col 60-64 (Philos, Relig) AB; Bethany Theol Sem 64-68 (Theol) M Div; No IllU 68; IndU 69-. 6: Hebrew, Greek (Koine). 7: Page Marion Pub Lib, Marion Ohio 59-60; Study asst McPherson Col Lib 60-64; Stud asst Bethany Theol Sem Lib 64-66, 68; Catlgr Armour Food Research Div, Oak Brook Ill 66-67; Stud asst No Baptist Theol Sem Lib 67-68; Lib asst McPherson Col 68-. 9: SLA. 10: Brethren Hist Assn; Penn Poetry Soc. 14: Catlg (tech serv). 15: 110 Olivette, McPherson Ks 67460.

WEAVER, JOHN M. b Kan City Mo 20 My 22. 4: Irma Krompasky. 5: Bucknell U 39-43 (Hist) BA; Cornell U 44-45 (Ger Area Studies); UAriz 46-48 (Hist) MA; Columbia U 49-54 MSLS. 6: Fr, Ger. 7: Army Air Corps Radio Operator (Cpl) 43-45; Ref libn Coun on Foreign Rel, NYC 50-54; Libn Rand Corp, Wash DC 54-55; Head circ sect NLM, Wash DC 56-59; Asst libn Army Off Chief of Engnrs, Wash DC 59-60; Libn NASA Goddard Space Flight Center, Greenbelt Md 60-68; Deputy dir of lib Dept of Housing & Urban Development, Wash DC 68-. 8: Fed Lib Survey; Com on Weeding & Storage, 61; Fed Lib Com Task Force on Automation, Wash DC 68-; chm Silver Spring Lib Adv Bd 66-. 9: ALA (Recr Netwk rep 63-64); SLA (Chem Div: chm Nomin Com 63; Wash DC Ch: rec sec 62-64, chm Mem Com 65-66; treas Sci-Tech Group 61-62, Mem Com Mil Libns Group 60-61); DCLA(treas 62-63, Exec Bd 63-64, chm Publ Com 5-66); v-chm & chm Sci-Tech Group 68-70). 13: Yes. 14: Admin, automation. 15: 10313 Pierce dr, Silver Spring Md 20901.

WEAVER, JOSEPHINE ELIZABETH. b McSherrystown Penn 28 S 23. 5: State Tchrs Col (Millersville Penn) 46-49 (LS) BS in Ed; Rutgers U 57-58 MLS. 7: Post Libn Dept of the Army; Army Chem Center, Md 49-54, Ft Lee Va 54, Ft Greely, Alaska 54-56, Ft Hancock NJ 56-58, Chief Libn Ft Devens Mass 58-. 9: ALA (chm Mem Comm Armed Forces Libns Sect). 14: Admin. 15: 17 Nashua, Ayer Ma 01433.

WEAVER, LILY ROUSE (CARR). b La Grange NC 15 My 19. 4: Harroll David Weaver. 5: E Carolina Col 35-38 (Fr Hist) AB, 51-52 (LS, Educ) MA; UNC 41-42 (LS) Libn Certif; NorthwestU summer 46 (LS). 6: Fr. 7: Child libn Marshall Field, Chicago 44-45; Libn New Hope Sch, Goldsboro NC 49-51; Libn Wahl-Coates Lab Sch & asst prof e cardinaU 51-. 9: ALA; Alpha Beta Alpha; Alpha Delta Kappa; NCLA; NCEA, Clr Tchrs. 10: Alpha Beta Alpha; Alpha Delta Kappa; Charter memb Oakmont Baptist Church; Greenville Woman's Club; Garden Club. 13: Yes. 14: Child wk. 15: 1710 Rosewood dr, Greenville NC 27834.

WEAVER, MARGARET (TEMMA). B Parsonsburg Md 22 Ag 28. 5: Maryville Col (Tenn) 45-49 (Eng) BA; Peabody 49-50 MALS. 7: Jr catlgr Mary Washington Col 50-52, Act head catlgr 52-53; Catlgr Furman U 53-61; Catlg libn UTenn Martin 61-. 9: ALA; SELA; SCLA; TennLA. 10: AAUP; AAUW; YWCA; LWV; Alpha Delta Kappa; Martin Arts Comm, Rep from Martin to Reelfoot Reg Lib Bd; Fortnightly Club; Commn on Christian Soc Concerns. 14: Catlg. 15: 248 Oakland, Martin Tn 38237.

WEAVER, WILLIAM BANCROFT. b Buffalo NY 5 Ap 18. 4: (Clara) Frances Tuttle. 5: UMiami (Coral Gables Fla) 37-41 (Mod Lang) AB; Fla State U 63-64 MS in LS. 7: 1st Lt USA 41-44; Traffic rep Pan Amer World Airways, Miami Fla 44-59; Lay brother Ourder of St Francis (Episcopal), Mt Sinai LI NY 59-62; Clk UMiami Lib (Coral Gables Fla) 64-67; Ref & circ libn Hume Lib Inst Food & Agric Sci UFla 67-. 9: SLA; FlaLA. 14: Ref. 15: 1214 NW 8th st, Gainesville Fl 32601.

WEBB, ALLIE BAYNE (WINDHAM). b Blanchard La 19 F 16. 4: John W Webb Jr. 5: LSU 35-38 (Hist) BA, 44-45 (Educ) BS, 47-48 (Hist) MA, 54-55, 63 (Hist) PhD. 6: Lat, Ger, fr. 7: Tchr: Caddo Parish Sch Bd, La 45-47, E Baton Rouge Sch Bd, Baton Rouge La 58-59, 62-63; Asst Prof LSU (Baton Rouge) 48-58, Ref archivist 60-61, 63-64, 69-, Curator rare bks 64-69. 9: ALA; Internatl Trust Hist Preserv; La Found Hist Preserv; La Hist Assn; N La Hist Assn; LaLA. 10: Delta Kappa Gamma; LSU Lib Staff Assn. 13: Yes. 14: Rare bks, archives, spec collections. 15: 5174 Houston dr, Baton Rouge La 70809.

WEBB, ANN ELIZABETH. b Jefferson City Mo 3 Ag 44. 5: UMo (Columbia) 52-66 AB; USoCal 66-67 MLS. 6: Fr, Ger. 7: Reader serv libn St Charles (Mo) Co Lib 67-. 9: ALA (Jr Mem RT); MoLA. 14: Adult serv, a-v serv. 15: St Charles County Lib 1900 Merrill dr, St Charles Mo 63301.

WEBB, DOROTHY (MARGARET). b Montreal 3 Je 41. 4: James Antony Webb. 5: McGill 57-61 (Hist) BA, 2-63 BLS. 6: Fr. 7: Ser libn Can Nat RR, Montreal 63-65; Libn Can Nat RR Telecommunications, Great Lakes Reg Lib, Toronto Ont 65-67; Ed research supv Can Nat RR pub rel dept, Montreal 67-. 9: SLA; (Newspaper & Transportation Div). 14: Catlg, indexing. 15: 3078 Marcel st, St Laurent Que Can.

WEBB, EVA (LAURA). b Sumter Co Ga 1 O 10. 5: Womans Col of Ga 27-28, summers 59 (Educ) BS; Peabody summers 60-62 MA in LS. 7: Typist sec adm clerk US Govt Dept of Agric & Employment Serv, Macon, Atlanta, Americus Ga 40-45; Sec Ga Dept of Educ Voc Rehabilitation, Macon Ga 4559; Libn catlgr Middle Ga Reg Lib, Macon Ga 59-. 9: GaLA; SELA. 10: Bus & Prof Womens Club. 15: 233 Corbin ave Apt B1, Macon Ga 31204.

WEBB, EVA. b Vancouver BC Can 23 S 20. 5: UBC 38-42 BA; UToronto 43-44 BLS. 7: Libn Royal Can Naval Lib Serv 44-46; Boys & girls libn Toronto Pub Lib 46-49; Child libn Reading (Eng) Pub Lib 50-51; Child libn Okanagan (BC) Reg Lib 52-57; Supv of child wk Regina (Sask) Pub Lib 57-. 9: Can Assn Child Libn; SasLA; ReginaLA. 14: Child serv. 15: Regina Pub Lib 2311 - 12th ave, Regina Sask Can.

WEBB, HELEN (STEPHENSON). b Harbor Beach Mich 18 Ap 1898. 4: William Webb. 5: East Mich U BA (Eng), MA (Admin); UMich MALS. 6: Ger. 7: Libn McKinley Sch, Flint Mich 29-35; Libn Flint Jr Col 3558; Lib Dir UOrlando 58-. 8: Visiting Prof lib sci Summer courses UNev 62, San Jose State 63, UGa 65, 68; Fla State U 61. 9: ALA; FlaLA; SELA. 10: AAUP; AAUW; Sorosis; American Friends; Kiwanis Ladies. 11: Silver Book Award 63. 14: Recr & training studs. 15: 160 Minnehaha cir, Maitland Fl 32751.

WEBB, ILSE B(LOCH). b Nurnberg Germany 7 O 32. 4: Kenneth L Webb. 5: Antioch 49-52 (Sociol) AB; Columbia 65-66 MSLS. 6: Ger, Fr. 7: Research asst Human Engring Lab Antioch Col 51-52; Research asst Aviation Psych Lab Ohio State U (Columbus) 52-60; Libn UGa Marine Inst (Sapelo Is) 60-65; Eng asst N Amer Aviation Inc Advanced Syst Sect, Columbus Ohio summer 65; Asst catlgr Swem Lib Col of William & Mary 66-68, Catlg libn 68-. 9: ALA; SLA; SELA; VaLA; Va Jr Memb RT (prov chm). 10: Beta Phi Mu. 12: Asst ed "Virginia Librarian". 13: Yes. 14: Tech serv, sci ref. 15: Swem Lib Col of William and Mary, Williamsburg Va 23185.

WEBB, JANE (MARY) WARE. b Sparta Tenn 27 Je 15. 4: John H Webb. 5: Tenn Polytech Inst 33-35 (Eng); Vanderbilt U 35-37 (Eng) BA; Peabody summers 59-63 (LS) MA. 6: Fr, Sp. 7: Eng tchr White Co High Sch, Sparta Tenn 37-40, 52-53; Eng tchr Pompano Beach High Sch, Pompano Beach Fla 55-56; Bkkeeper Juanita Sweet Interiors, Ft Lauderdale Fla 57-59; Asst libn Crisman Mem Lib David Lipscomb Col 60- 67, Assoc libn 67-. 9: TennLA; Nashville Lib Club; SELA. 14: Acquis. 15: 336 Blackman rd, Nashville 37211.

WEBB, LORRAYNE BETH. b Fargo Okla 25 A 25. 5: Tex Womans U 43-47 (Eng) BA, 47-48 BS in LS. 7: Libn San Marcos (Tex) High Sch 48-49; Libn Houston Ind Sch Dist 49-52; libn UTex Dental Br (Houston) 52-. 9: MedLA; TexLA. 14: Rare bks, dental collections. 15: 3214 Avalon pl, Houston 77019.

WEBB, MARGARET JANE. b Edmonton Alberta Can 29 S 45. 5: UAlta 63-66 (Eng) BA; UNC 67-68 BLS. 6: Fr. 7: Act hd of info dept Edmonton Pub Lib 68-. 9: CanLA; AltaLA; EdmontonLA. 14: Ref. 15: 21 Wellington Crescent, Edmonton Alberta Can.

WEBB, MARGARET LEA. b Phila 14 Je 7. 5: Chestnut Hill Col 53-57 (Hist) AB, Tchr Certif in Hist, F, Eng; St Johns U (NY) 58-60 (Amer Hist) MA; Rutgers 61-63 MLS. 6: Fr. 7: Eng tchr Wildwood High Sch, Wildwood NJ 57-58; Grad asst St Johns U (NY) 58-60; Clerk-typist Phoenix Title & Trust Co, Phoenix 60-61; Trainee Pub Lib, Plaifield NJ 61-63; Ref libn Pub & Sch Lib Serv BUR OF NJ State Lib 3-64, Asst lending serv libn 64-67; Libn NJ Dept of Transportation Lib 67-. 9: ALA; CathLA; NJLA; SLA. 10: Beta Phi Mu; NJ Hist Soc; AAUW; Rutgers Grad Sch & Lib Serv Alumni Assn; Mercer Co Chorus. 14: Ref, acquis, history sci-tech, bus & admin. 15: 104 Washington ct, Trenton NJ 08629.

WEBB, MARY ALICE. b New Castle Penn 6 S 20. 4: James H Webb. 5: JacksonvilleU 60-65 (Educ) BS; Fla StateU 65-66 (LS) MS. 7: Lib clk Jacksonville Pub Lib, Jacksonville fla 38-43; Sec Gen Electric Co, Jacksonville Fla 45-48; Sec Bd of Pub Instr, Jacksonville Fla 60-63; Catlgr State Bd of Health Lib, Jacksonville Fla 65; Asst hd libn Fla Jr Col (Jacksonville) 66-68, Hd libn 68-. 9: SELA; FlaLA (sec-treas Col & Spec Libs Div); Duval Co LA (Hospitality chm). 10: Fla Pub Jr Col Assn; AAUW; Fla State U Lib Sch Alum. 14: Lib admin, ref, tech serv. 15: 4335 Lakeside dr, Jakcsonville Fl 32210.

WEBB, MARY ELIZABETH (ROBERTS). b Porter Okla. 4: S Frank Webb. 5: Northeastern State 47 (Educ) BS; OklaU 52 AB in LS, 68 MLS. 7: High sch tchr & libn Moore Pub Schs 47-50; Elem tchr Norman Pub Schs 50-52; Circ libn OklaU 52-61; Libn Ponca City Sch Syst: West Jr High 61-67, high sch 67-. 9: NEA; ALA; OklaLA; OklaEA; ClrTA; Ponca CityEA. 14: Pub rel. 15: 1516 Cookson dr, Ponca City Ok 74601.

WEBB, MARY JOSEPHINE. b Meadville Penn 6 Ag 06. 5: Allegheny COL 23-27 (Fr) AB; Columbia 29-32 BLS. 7: Libn Chaney High Sch, Youngstown Ohio 27-32; Asst 7 libn Horace Mann Sch, NYC 32-56; Libn, Campbell, Strthers & Belmont Brs, Youngstown Ohio 56-64, Dir Pub Lib, Meadville ,penn 65-. 9: ALA; PennLA. 15: 628 Highland, Meadville Penn 16335.

WEBB, PRISCILLA ANNE (PECK). b Battle Creek Mich 8 My 18. 4: Clifford D Webb. 5: Kalamazoo Col 38-41 (Eng) AB; Carnegie 43-44 BS in LS. 7: Asst Kalamazoo Pub Lib 38-41, 42-43; Asst Carnegie Lib of Pittsburgh 43-44; Child libn Wilkinsburg Pub Lib, Wilkinsburg Penn 44-47; Elkhart PUB Lib, Elkhart Ind: Child libn 47-53, Asst adult dept 55-58, Asst ref dept 59-66; Hd child dept 67-. 9: ALA; ndLA. 10: BUS & Prof Womens Club; Elkhart Civic Theatre. 14: Ref. 15: Elkhart Pub Lib 300 S Second st, Elkhart Ind 46514.

WEBB, THELMA ELIZABETH (HOOPER). b Bethlehem Penn 24 Mr 14. 4: Harold W Webb. 5: Baldwin-Wallace Col 32-36 BA; Rosary Col 69 MLS. 6: Sp. 7: Tchr: Jr High Sch, Wellington Ohio 36-40, Dist 89, Ill 62-64; Tchr & libn Dist 89, Ill 64-68, 69-. 9: NEA; IllEA. 10: Bus & Prof Women; Pi Gamma Mu; Alpha Pi Gamma. 14: Elem sch libnship. 15: 913 N 9th ave, Maywood Il 60153.

WEBBER, EBBERT T. b Edgewood Md 22 O 21. 4: Marjorie Renfroe. 5: UNev summer 44 (Aeronautcis) Certif; Whitworth Col 60-65 (Journalism) BA; Portland StateU 67-68 (LS); UPortland 65-68 MLS. 7: Photo journalist (Cpl) USA Signal Corps 40-45; Photo journalist, Wash 45-55; Resident mgr Sperry Rand Corp, Seattle, Lewiston & Spokane Wash 55-61; Chief photo serv Whitworth Co 62-65; Libn hd media serv Waluga Sch, Lake Oswego ore 65-. 8: Curr consul Dept of Lib Sci, Portland StateU. 9: OreASchL (chm Conf Exh & adv mgr for Journal). 10: Clackamas Co Hist Soc; Boy Scouts; Ruling Elder, Presby Church USA. 12: "The Pacific Northwest in Books" (67), 2nd ed (69); Ed "The Clackamas County Historical Annual" (69). 13: Yes. 14: Tchg lib sci (bibliog, ref, catlg, sel of media, a-v). 15: 1540 Worthington st, Lake Oswego Or 97034.

WEBBER, JOHN P(UTNAM). b Newton Mass 26 Mr 17. 4: Ingrid Hahner. 5: Amherst Col 35-39 (Hist) BA, MIT 39-41 MS in Meteorology; Catholic U 57-61 (LS). 6: Portu, Sp, Fr, Ger. 7: Research asst to Instr Dept of Meteorol MIT 41-43; Meteorol Pan Amer-Grace Airways, Lima Peru, Santa Cruz, Bolivia & Buenos Aires Argentina 43-47; Meteorol US Weather Bur, Manila Philippines 47-48; Assoc Prof of Meteorol & Chief of the Lib Inst Tech de Aeronautica, Rio de Janeiro, Patu Sao Jose dos Campos Brazil 48-53; Res Assoc Blue Hill Observatory, Milton Mass 53-54; Meteorol US Weather Bur, Wash DC 54-55, Head of the Lib 55-67; Chief libs br US Environmental Sci Serv Admin, Rockville Md 67-. 8: Adv to Philippine dele, North Pacific Reg Conf, Internat Civil Aviation Org, Seattle 48. 9: SLA (past chm Wash DC Chap Sci-Tech Group); Amer Meteorol Soc; Amer Geophys Union; DCLA; ASIS. 10: PTA. 14: Admin, info netwks. 15: 2621 Sigmona st, Falls Church Va 22046.

WEBBERT, CHARLES A. b Kearney Neb 18 Je 16. 5: Kearney State Tchrs Col 33-35; UWash 35-37 (Lit) BA; KSTC 37-38; Peabody 39-40 (LS) BS; UIll 46-47 (LS) MS. 7: Proof reader Neb Legslatur, Lincoln Neb 39; Catlgr SD State Col 40-42; Clerk US Army Air Force (Sgt) 42-45; Asst libn SD State Col 47-48; Ref libn UIda Lib 48-57, Soc sci libn 57-69, Hd dept of spec collections & archives 69-. 9: ALA (Life mem); PNLA (Life mem, Bd 54-57, 61-63); IdaLA (Life mem, v-pres 64-65, pres 65-66); SAA. 10: Beta Phi Mu. 12: "Bibliography of Master Theses, University of Idaho,

1898-1958" (58); "Evaluation of the Holdings in Social Science in the University of Idaho Library" (62); "Jerome J Day Collection; a Bibliography" (63); "Idaho; a Bibliography" (63); "Checklist of Theses and Dissertations Accepted for Higher Degrees at the University of Idaho through May 30, 1966" (66); "The Earl Larrison Collection of Sir Walter Scott" (68). 13: Yes. 14: Ref, rare bks, archives. 15: Univ of Idaho Lib, Moscow Ida 83843.

WEBBY, ERNEST JOSEPH JR. b Brockton Mass 8 Je 39. 4: Roberta Rubin. 5: FairfieldU 59-62 (Hist) BS; State Col at Boston 63-66 (Educ) MEd; Simmons 65-66 MSLS; C W Post Col 68-69; NYU 68-69. 7: Clk-typist (Sp/4) US Army, Ft Dix NJ 62-63; Soc studies tchr dawnwood Jr High Sch, Centereach NY 64-65; Libn & tchr Bay Shore Sr High Sch, Bay shore NY 66-69; Ref libn Smithtown Pub Lib, Smithtown NY 67; Libn & tchr Sayville summer High Sch, Sayville NY 68; Chm learning resource ctrs Brockton High Sch, Brockton Mass 69-. 9: ALA; -AASchL; Nassau-Suffolk (NY) SchLA; Bay Shore Clr TA. 13: Yes. 14: Ref, lib admin. 15: 35 Provost st, Brockton Ma 02401.

WEBER, DAVID C(ARTER). b Waterville Me 25 Jl 24. 4: Natalie McLeod. 5: Colby Col 42-43, 46-47 (Hist) AB; Bowdoin Col 46 (Hist); Columbia U 47-48 (LS) BS; Harvard 49-53 (Hist) AM; Rutgers 56 (LS). 7: Harvard U Libs: Catlgr 48-50; Asst to the dir 50-57, Asst dir & asst libn of Harvard Col 57-61; Asst dir of Libs Stanford U 61-65, Assoc dir of libs 65-; Dir Stanford 69-. 8: Bldg consul, Bradford Col 59, UHawaii, 62, Peralta Col 66, Col of Notre Dame 66, St Patricks Sem 67, Santa Rosa Col 67, Pacific Union Col 68. 9: ALA-LAD (chm, Stat Coord Com 57-61);-RTSD (pres 67-68; chm, Copying Methods Sect 64-65);-RSD (chm Bk Catlgs Com 59-63);-ACRL (dir 68-). 10: AAUP; Bk Club of Cal; Roxburghe Club (San Francisco). 12: Comp "Index to the Minutes of the Association of Research Libraries for 1932-1954; Asst ed "Library Resources and Technical Services (57-60); Co-auth "Colleges and University Accreditation Standards (57); ed "Studies in Library Administrative Problems (60). 13: Yes. 14: Col & res libs. 15: Stanford Univ, Stanford Ca 94305.

WEBER, DONALD JOHN. b Queens NY 30 Ag 43. 4: Diane Irene Looms. 5: State U Col (Geneseo NY) 60-64 (Secondary Educ) BS Ed, 64-65 MLS. 6: Sp. 7: High sch libn Patchogue-Medford Sch System, Patchogue NY 65-67; Proj libn Peace Corps Middle East Tech U, Ankara Turkey 67-68; Admin libn TUSLOG Lib Sys, Izmir Turkey 68-. 13: Yes. 14: Sch lib admin. 15: Box 2926, APO NY 09224.

WEBER, SISTER MARGARET MARY SSJ. b Detroit. 5: Marygrove Col 27-31 (Lat) AB; Wayne State U 33; Educ UDetroit 32-39 (Lat) MA; Nazareth Col (Nazareth Mich) 38-66; Cath U 43-48 BS in LS; West Mich U 61-66 MSL; Wayne State U 65-66 (Educ). 6: Lat, Fr, Ger. 7: Tchr, Mich; detroit Schs 31-35, Nazareth Acad, Nazareth 36-38, St Bernard High Sch, Detroit 38-41; Tchr-Libn St Augustine High Sch, Kalamazoo 41-44; Libn Nazareth Col & Acad, Nazareth Mich 44-57; Tchr-Libn, Mich; st James High Sch, Ferdale 64-66, St Francis Xavier High Sch, Ecorse 66-68; Libn St Agnes High Sch, Flint Mich 57-64, 68-. 9: ALA-AASchL; CathLA; (Mich memb chm); Amer Classical Leaue; Cath Assnof For Lang Tchrs; MichLA; MichASchL; Detroit Classical Assn; Mich A-V Assn; NEA-DAVI. 13: Yes. 14: Instrl materials centers; centralized proc, in-serv train of libns & tchrs, sch system org, a-v centers. 15: St Agnes High Sch, 530 W Pierson rd, Flint Mi 48505.

WEBER, MILADA (PAUKOVA). b Brno Czechoslovakia 2 Mr 11. 4: Josef Weber. 5: Konsularakademie (Vienna) 31-33 (Econ, Pol) Dipl Kons; Masaryk U (Brno Czechoslovakia) 34-39 Dr of LAW: UParana (Curitiba Brazil) 49 (Eng, Fr) Tchrs Certif; CW Post Col LIU 62-64 (LS) MS. 6: Fr, Sp, Portu, Ger, Cech, Russian, Lat. 7: Diplomatic off Czechoslovakian Govt, Prague CSR 45-46; Attache Czechoslovakian Legation, Rio de Janeiro 46-48; Tchr Colegio Jose Bonifacio, Paranagua Brazil 49-52; Sec consulate Gen of Venezuela, Houston 55-58; Lib asst Poly Prep Country Day Sch, Brooklyn NY 62-63; Catlgr Elmont Pub Lib, Elmont Pub Lib, Elmont LI NY 63-65; Catlgr Hofstra U 65-68; Catlgr Northwestern U Law Sch Lib (Chicago) 68-. 9: Chicago Assn Law Libs; ALA. 14: Catlg, intl for law. 15: 8842 Lavergne, Skokie Il 60076.

WEBER, NOLA (STAMBAUGH). b Bay City Mich 1 Ag 42. 4: John L Weber. 5: West MichU 60-64 (Educ) AB; UMich 67 MALS. 7: Elem tchr, Mich: Livonia Pub Schs 64-65, Wayne Commun Schs 65-66; Elem libn, Mich: Monroe Pub Schs 67-68, Riverview Pub Schs 68-. 9: ALA; NEA; MichEA. 14: Child lit. 15: 7599 South Stony Creek rd, Monroe Mi 48161.

WEBER, ROSEMARY. b Lancaster Penn 25 Ag 26. 5: UPenn 44-48 (Eng) BS in Ed, 48-51 (Eng) MS in Ed; Drexel 55-57 MS in LS; UPenn 60- (Tchr Educ). 7: Tchr Trainer Borough Sch dist, Chester Penn 48-56; Elem libn Upper Merion Twp Sch Dist, King of Prussia Penn 56-60; Elem libn Radnor Twp Sch Dist, Wayne Penn 60-67; Assoc Prof West Chester State Col 67-68; Asst Prof Grad Sch Lib Sci Drexel Inst 68-. 9: ALA-AASchL (Prof Rel Com 60); NEA; NCTE; Penn State EA; PennLA (sec Dept of Work with Child, Schs & Yp 63-64); Delaware Co Sch LA (pres 65-66); PennASchL. 10: Beta Phi Mu; Pi Lambda Theta; Mens; Phila Child Reading RT; Lib Pub Rel (Phila); Phila Bksellers; AAUP. 13: Yes. 14 Child lit, sch libs (elem). 15: 209 Hiawatha rd, Drexel Hill Pa 19027.

WEBER, RUTH ALMA. b Baltimore 29 Jl 24. 5: Randolph-Macon Womans Col 41-45 (Eng) BA; Drexel 45-46 BS in LS. 7: Enoch Pratt Free Lib, Baltimore; Ya libn brs 46-52, Br libn, Hampden br 52-56, Admin asst Pimlico br 56-57; Coord of brs, Schenectady Co Pub Lib, Schenectady NY 57-60; Deputy dir Mohawk Valley Lib Assn, Schenectady NY 60-64; Asst dir Suffolk Cooperative Lib System, Bellport NY 64-. 9: ALA; ASD (chm Materials Selection, Policies, Practices & Procedures Com 67-); NYLA (92nd v-pres 69); Suffolk Co (NY) LA. 10: AAUW; Nat Audubon Soc. 14: Admin adult & ya serv, a-v serv, consul. 15: 313 Robinson ave, E Patchogue NY 11774.

WEBER, SHEILA K. b NYC 7 S 35. 4: Irwin J Weber. 5: NYC Community Col 52-54 (Sci) AAS; NYU 54-55 (Educ) BS; Yeshiva U 59-60 (Educ); Pratt 59-61 MLS; UCal 63-65 (LS). 6: Ger. 7: Lib asst Brooklyn Pub Lib 49-54; Tchr Bethpage Sch System, Bethpage NY 54-57; Tchr E Meadow Sch System, E Meadow NY 57-61; Libn Queens Col (NY) 61-62; Supv child serv Menlo Park Pub Lib, Menlo Park Cal 62-64; Dir of Libs Los Altos Schs, Los Altos Cal 64-65; Instr USanta Clara 64-67; Instr Glendale City Col 68-. 8: Child Libn Lib/USA NY World's Fair 64; Instr Santa Clara Univ, Santa Clara cal 64-; Consul child serv Redondo Beach Pub Lib, Redondo Beach Cal. 9: NEA; CalLA (Child Libns Sect: Nomin Com, Bk Sel Com, Newbery-Caldecott Com); CalASchL; Cal Tchrs Assn; ALA. 10: AAUW. 14: Child & ya serv. 15: 1609 Via Montemar, Palos Verdes Estates, Palos Verdes Peninsula Ca 90274.

WEBKES, LILLIAN (SISTER). b Ft Madison Iowa 6 Je 1896. 5: DePaul 34-39 Phil BA, 39-44 (Educ) MA, 60-61 A-v certif; Cardinal Stritch Col 54-59 LS Certif; Hadely Sch of the Blind 69-. 6: Ger. 7: Tchr: Sacred Heart Sch, Peoria Ill 16-24, St Rose Sch, Monroeville Ill 24-29, St Maurice Sch, Chicago 29-34, St Nicolas, Chicago 40-45, creaton Grade Sch, Creaton Neb 45-50, St Rose Sch, Randolp Neb 50-54, Frankenstein high Sch, Frankenstein Mo 54-56; Prin & tchr St John Sch, Allentown Wis 34-40; Prin St John High Sch, Petersburg Neb 56-60; Libn St Bendict High Sch, Chicago 60-. 8: Braille tchr. 9: ALA; CathLA; High Sch Libns Chicagoland; IllLA. 10: Nat Cath Student Lib Assn; Moderator of Lib Assistants; Moderator of Projectionists; Agent for Hunduras poverty stricken; Dir Freedom for Democracy Essays. 13: Yes. 15: 2222 W Byron st, Chicago Il 60618.

WEBSTER, ALMA AILLEEN. b Sask. 5: USask 40 BA, 41 (Educ) Certif; UToronto 46-47 BLS , summers 67-69; UAlta 51-52 BEd; U West Mich summers 65-66. 6: Fr. 7: Catlgr Saskatoon Pub Lib, Saskatoon Sask 47-49; Sch libn Pub Sch Bd Edmonton Alta 49-54; Asst libn Pub Lib Moose Jaw Sask 54-56; Chief Libn Pub Lib, Port Arthur Ont 56-62; Asst spec Pub Sch Bd, Edmonton Alta 62-64, Lib spec 64-66, Lib supv 66-. 9: CanLA (chm Adult Serv Sect 60-61); CanASchL (chm 65-66); Encyclopedia Britannica Sch Lib Awards Com 67-; SaskatoonLA (sec 48-49); EdmontonLA (sec 51-52; coun 63-64); AltaLA (pres 52-53); Alta Sch Lib Coun (pres 68-69). 10: Delta Kappa Gamma; Univ Women's Club; Soroptimist Club; Canadian Col of Tchrs. 12: Ed "Adult Services Newsletter"; Ed "Mocassin Telegraph". 14: Yp schs, ref. 15: 10010 107A ave, Edmonton 17 Alta Can.

WEBSTER, DONALD F. b NYC 1 O 32. 4: Margaret F Webster. 5: Hofstra U 55-59 (Eng) BA; Queens Col (NY) 60-63 MLS, 60-63 Diploma in Lib Educ. 7: US Army Artillery (Cpl), Alaska 53-55; Tchr of Eng Island Trees High Sch, Island Trees NY 59-61; Libn Island Trees Jr High Sch, Island Trees NY 61-62; Head libn Commack High Sch, Commack NY 62-66; Readers adv Farmingdale Pub Lib, Farmingdale NY 62-66; Ext libn Hofstra U Ext Center (Commack NY) 63-66; Dir of lib serv Cazenovia Col 66-; Visiting faculty Sch of Lib Sci Syracuse 67-. 9: ALA;-ACRL (Adhoc Com for the Study of Two-Yr Priv Col Libs); NYLA; NY State Ass Jr Cols; Cent NY Ref on Resources Coun; Col Ctr of the Finger Lakes. 10: Kappa Delta Pi; AAUP. 13: Yes. 14: Admin. 15: 4480 Lincklaen rd, Cazenovia NY 13035.

WEBSTER, ELLEN PAGE. b Yarmouth NS Can. 5: Dalhousie U BA; West Res 48-49 MS in LS. 7: Libn Pub Archives of NS, Halifax NS; Libn Can Legion Lib, Halifax NS; Intern libn Rochester Pub Lib, Rochestr NY 47-48; Libn Detroit Pub Lib 49-51; Chief ref libn & deputy chief libn Halifax Mem Lib, Halifax NS 51-. 9: CanLA (chm Ref Sect 63-64); APLA; Halifax LA (pres 62-63). 10: Univ Womens Club. 14: Ref. 15: Halifax Mem Lib 5381 Spring Garden rd, Halifax NS Can.

WEBSTER, HELEN EMILY. b E Weymouth Mass 30 Ag 07. 5: UCLA 25-29 (Eng) BA; UCal(Berkeley) 29-30 (LS) Certif. 6: Fr. 7: Sr libn Long Beach Pub Lib, Long Beach Cal 30-42; Libn VA Hosps, Camp White Ore, Ft Harrison Mont, Ft Meade SD, Fayetteville Ark 42-50; Womens ed Radio Station KMED, Medford Ore 5153; Asst libn Vet Hosp, American Lake Wash 54; Dir Grays Harbor Co Lib, Monte ano Wash 54-55; Dir Pub Lib of MVEDFORD AND Jackson Co, Meford Ore 55-59; Sr libn Ventura City & Co Lib, Ventsra Cal 59-. 9: ALA; CalLA; MontLA; PNLA (chm Hosp & Institutional Libs Com 49-50); OreLA (Lib Deelop Com 55-57). 10: LWV; Humane Soc; Amer Kennel Club; Amer Friends Serv Com; Sierra Club. 12: "Shower Parties forAll Occasions (48). 13: Yes. 14: Admin, publs, develop ext. 15: 1444 Buena Vista st, Ventura Cal 93001.

WEBSTER, JAMES KELSEY. b Buffalo NY 13 My 33. 4: Carol J Mast. 5: UBuffalo 52-56 (Math) BA; SUNY (Geneseo) 63-66 MLS. 7: Indexer-abstractor Cornell Aeronautical Lab (Buffalo) 57-66, Sr libn 66-. 8: Creator & chm Akron Jaycees' "Books for Nigeria" Proj, Akron NY 61 (collected, catlgd, and shipped 20,000-volume lib to the Merchants of Light School, Oba Nigeria). 9: SLA; Highway Res Bd (Highway Safety Info Rev Com). 10: Village of Akron Bd of Trustees; C of C; Foothills Trail Club; Lions Club; ACLU; Erie Co Republican Com; Akron-Newstead Recreation Com. 14: Ref, indexing, selective dissem of info. 15: 8 Cedar st, Akron NY 14001.

WEBSTER, KATHRYN AMENT. b Holden Mo 5 S 15. 5: Central Tchrs Col (Warrensburg Mo) 34-37 (Hist), Com BS in Ed; UIll 63-65 (LS) MA. 7: Stud libn Central Tchrs Col (Warrensburg Mo) 34-37, Asst lib summers 38-40; Tchr High Sch, Meadville Mo 37-41; Tchr High Sch, Bone Terre Mo 41-42; Jr train spec OPA, Wash DC 42-43; Lib clerk II UIll(Urbana) 62-63, Bibliogr 65-. 15: 705 S Race, Urbana Ill 61801.

WEBSTER, MARY (POE). b Owen County Ky 21 Ap 02. 4: Franklin Webster. 5: East Ky State Col 29-33 (Hist, Eng) BA; UKy 55 MSLS. 7: Tchr libn: Grant Co schs, Mason Ky 42-50, Grant Co schs, Dry Ridge Ky 50-53, Pendleton Co schs, Butler Ky 53-56; Libn Lloyd High Sch, Erlanger Ky 56-61; Libn Dupont Manual High Sch, Louisville Ky 61-62; Libn Turkey Foot Jr High Sch, S Ft Mitchell Ky 62-67; Libn Dixie Hts High Sch, Ft Mitchell Ky 67-69. 9: NEA; ALA; KyEA; KyLA KyASchL (treas 51, pres 61-62); Pres NLASLA 67-68; NoKYASchL (pres 67-68). 10: Grant Co Womans Club; N Ky High Sch Women Tchrs Club; Faculty Club of Kenton Co. 14: Ref, wk with child & yp. 15: Ridgelea dr, Williamstown Ky 41097.

WEBSTER, MARY RUTH (SCOTT). b Durham NC 29 Mr 40. 4: Deleron Lafayette Webster Jr. 5: Appalachian State Tchrs Col 58-60 (Soc Studies); E Carolina Col 60-62 (Soc Studies, LS) BS; E Carolina U Lib Inst summer 68. 6: Fr. 7: Libn Winston-Salem (NC) City schs, Philo Jr High Sch 62-63; Libn Durham (NC) high schs 63-. 9: NEA; NCEA (sec Sch Libs Div); NCLA; NC High SchLA (co-advis to State Conv). 10: Bus & Prof Womens Club; Epsilon Sigma Alpha. 11: NC Woman of Epsilon Sigma Alpha for 1968. 14: Catlg, bk sel, proc. 15: 3141 Rose of Sharon Rd, Durham NC 27705.

WEBSTER, NORMAN. b Benton Harbor Mich 10 D 28. 5: UMich 48-51 AB; UCal(Berkeley) 61-62 MLS. 6: Fr, Sp, Ital, Lat. 7: LC 57-61; Hd govt publ dept Fresno State Col 62-64; Asst to Univ libn UCal(San Diego) 64-66; Libn Newton Col of Sacred Heart 66-. 14: Admin. 15: Newton Col of Sacred Heart, 885 Centre st, Newton Ma 02159.

WEBSTER, VIOLA E. b Hamilton Ont Can 7 Mr 21. 5: McMasterU 39-43 (Eng, Fr) BA; UMich 55 AMLS. 6: Fr. 7: Tchr: Milverton Continuation 43-44, Sutton Continuation 44-45, Elmira High Sch 45-47, Scarborough Collegiate 47-54; Tchr & libn West Hill Collegiate, Scarborough Ont Can 55161; Libn, Scarborough Can: R H King Collegiate 61-65, Laurier Collegiate 65-. 8: Mem, Dept of Educ's Basic Bklist Com. 9: OntLA (sec-treas Sch & Intermed Sect); Metro Toronto Studies in Educ Facilities (Adv Com). 10: Ont Tchrs Fed. 14: Sch libs. 15: Sir Wilfrid Laurier Collegiate Lib 145 Guildwood Parkway, Scarborough Ont Can.

WEBSTER, WILLENE. b Talbot County Ga 12 Ap 03. 5: Tift Col 20-24 (Eng, Hist) AB; Peabody summers 47-49 BSLS; UGa summers 28, 32, 36. 7: Tchr-libn; Barwik High Sch, Palmetto Ga 28-29, Conyers High Sch, Conyers Ga 25-28, Meriwether High Sch, Loodbury Ga 32-36, Ft Gaines High Sch, Ft Gaines Ga 36-37, Adrain High Sch, Adrain Ga 37-38, Shiloh High Sch, Shiloh Ga 39-41; Libn Campbell High Sch, Fulton Co Ga 46-62; Libn Manchester High Sch, Manchester Ga 62-. 9: ALA-AASchL; NEA; GaLA (sec 57-59, chm Stud Assts Com 61-63, Libns Sect; sec 51, treas 63-65, Dist chm 52; Sec A-V Sect 65); SELA; GaEA. 10: Delta Kappa Gamma; PTA. 11: Lib won John Cotton Dana Publicity Award 57, 65. 13: Yes. 14: Ref. 15: Woodland Ga 31836.

WEBSTER, WILLIAM GILBERT. b Northbridge Mass 8 N 23. 4: Alice Kawamura. 5: Amherst 41-43, 46-48 (Eng) AB; Syracuse 48-49 BS in LS. 6: . 7: Ref libn Enoch Pratt Free Li, Baltimore 49-51; Catlgr & head of processing US Civil Admin of the Ryukyus Islands Okinawa 51-53; Adutl serv libn Hayward Pub Lib, Hayward Cal 54, Lib Dir 55-. 9: ALA; CalLA; Pub Lib Exec Cent Cal. 10: . 13: Yes. 14: Admin. 15: 26340 Ventura ave, Hayward Ca 94544.

WECHSLER, LILLY (IOSIPOVICI). b Rumania 22 S 24. 4: John Wechsler. 5: Univ of Educ (Rumania) 44-48 (Rumanian, Ger) BS; Lib Sch (Rumania) 49. 6: Rumanian, Ger, Fr. 7: Libn Nicolae Balcescu Lib, Bucharest 48-50; Research wkr: Inst of Ling, Bucharest 50-54, Inst of Hist, Bucharest 54-57; Sec Publ House, Bucharest 57-65; Asst libn treadwell Lib, Boston 67-. 12: Com "Dictionary of Rumanian Language" (54). 14: Catlg, ref. 15: 461 Washington st, Brookline Ma 02146.

WECKER, JOHN C(LEMENT). b Bismarck ND 14 Ap 22. 5: St Marys Col (Cal) 39-40; Pasadena Jr Col 40-41 AA; Loyola U (Los Angeles) 41-42 (Eng); USoCal 46-47 (Eng) AB, 47-48 (Eng, Educt0 ma, 50-51 MSin LS. 6: Fr, Lat. 7: Stud fingerprint clsfr Fed Bur of Investigation, Wash DC 42; (Sgt) cryptog tech USAAF, US & S Pacific 43-46; Tchr Cathedral High Sch Los Angeles 48-50; Stud lib as t Doheny Mem Lib USoCal 50-51; Libn circ dept Pasadena Pub Lib, Pasadena Cal 51-55; John F Kennedy Mem Lib Cal State Col (Los Angelest0: Ref libn 56-57, Supv ref libn 57-58, Head Libn Educ Dept 58-; Hd educ libn 58-. 8: Lecturer in Pilot Project for Lib Orientation through Educ TV, Cal State Col (Los Angeles) 63-64. 9: ALA (Recr Netwk); CalLA (chm Com on Recr & Prof Educ 59-60) 10: Assn of Cal State Col Profs; Cal State Employees Assn; Phi Kappa Phi. 14: Ref, admin, prof educ. 15: 131 S Electric ave, Alhambra Cal 91801.

WEDDLE, ETHEL (HARSHBARGER). b Girard Il 6 S 1897. 4: Lemon Talmadge Weddle. 5: La Verne Col 12-13 (Dramatics). 7: Libn Girard Twp Lib, Girard Ill 47-. 10: Girard Woman's Club; Amer Legion Aux. 12: "Leasant Hill" (56); "Walter Chrysler, boy Machinist" (60); "Joel Chandler Harris, Young Storyteller" (64); "Alvin C York, Young Marksman" (67). 13: Yes. 15: RFD 1, Girard Il 62640.

WEDGE, LAURA L. b Lebanon NY 12 My 19. 5: Elmira Col 40 AB; SUNY (Geneseo) 41 (LS) BS in Ed; Syracuse 60 MLS; SUNY (Albany) NDEA Inst. 7: Libn & tchr: Bloomfield Central Sch, E Bloomfield NY 41-42, Peru Central Sch, Peru NY 42-44; Libn: Bolivar Central Sch, Bolivar NY 44-45, Herkimer High Sch, Herkimer NY 45-58; Sch lib supv Norwich City Schs, Norwich NY 58-. 8: Consul, Sch Libs, State Educ Dept summer 48. 9: NEA-DAVI; ALA; NYStateTA; NY Educ Communication Assn; NYLA (Sch Libs Sect: treas 51, 59, pres 69, Com on Sch Lib Standards); Chepapoo Co Sch Libns (pres 66-67). 10: AAUW; Zonta Club; Bus & profess Women; PTA; Pi Gamma Mer; Beta Phi Mer. 12: Ed "Newsletter", Sch Libs Sect, NYLA. 13: Yes. 14: Elem and second sch instr materials ctrs. 15: 20 Hayes st, Norwich NY 13815.

WEDGEWORTH, PEGGY (FLORENCE). b Carthage Tex 18 D 41. 5: Tex Womans U 62-64 (LS) BS, 64-65 MLS. 7: Catlg libn Stephen F Austin State Col 65-. 14: Catlg. 15: 214 Carolyn apt D, Nocogdoches Tx 75961.

WEDGEWORTH, ROBERT JR. b Ennis Tex 31 Jl 37. 5: Wabash Col 55-59 (Eng Lit) AB; UIll 59-61 (LS) MS; Washington U (St Louis) 65- (Span Lit); Rutgers (New Brunswick) 69- (Lib Serv). 6: Sp, Fr. 7: Catlgr Kan City (Mo) Pub Lib 61-62; Asst libn Park Col Lib 62-64, Act head libn 63-64; Head Libn Meramec Commun Col 64-66; Asst chief order libn Brown U (RI) 66-. 8: Staff, Lib 21 Seattle Worlds Fair, 62, Consul Roger Williams Col 69-70. 9: ALA; ASIS;

RILA. 11: Coun of Lib Resources Fellow 69. 13: Yes. 14: Tech proc, info sci. 15: 175 Benefit st, Providence RI 02903.

WEDNER, MOLLIE (HECKER). b NYC 4 Ag 10. 4: Nathan Wedner. 5: Wayne Law Sch 27-30 LLB; UMich60-63 MALS. 6: Fr, Ger. 7: Detroit Pub Lib 64; Harper Hosp Dept of Libs 64-65; Wayne State U Law Lib 65-68. 9: MedLA; AALL. 10: State Bar of Mich. 14: Catlg, journals, ref. 15: 100 Oceano ave apt 21, Santa Barbara Ca 93105.

WEECH, TERRY L. b Galesbury Ill 8 Jl 37. 4: Euce Hovis. 5: Knox Col 55-59 (Philos) AB; Emory 59-60 (Philos); UIll 60-61 (Philos), 64-65 (LS) MS. 6: Fr, Ger. 7: Aircraft engine mech US Army, Va & NC 61-63; Docs libn Ill State Lib, Springfield 65-67; Research assoc UIll Lib Research Ctr (Urbana) 67-68. 9: ALA; IllLA. 13: Yes. 14: Govt publns, lib educ, lib admin. 15: 107 N Coler, Urbana Il 61801.

WEED, MAE (COUNSELMAN). b Wellsburg WVa 27 Jl 09. 4: onald W Weed. 5: Transylvania Col 26-30 (Biol) AB; Johns Hopkins Hosp, Baltimore 30-32 (Nursing) RN; Pratt 58-60 MLS. 7: Faculty Scarritt Col 32-33; Pub health nurse; Bk trailer libn Massapequa Pub Lib, Massapequa NY 61-65, Ref libn 58-61, 65;Head of ref Smithtown NY 65-. 9: NYLA; Suffolk Co LA; ALA. 10: Beta Phi Mu; Trustee Amityville Free Lib; Trustee Amityville Sch Bd; Amityville Commun Chest. 14: Ref. 15: 94 Bennett pl, Amityville NY 11701.

WEEKS, ALICE (WALTER). b Syracuse NY 25 N 32. 4: David H Weeks Jr. 5: Geneseo State Tchrs Col 51-55 BS in LS; Syracuse 64-65 (LS), 67-69. 7: Head of circ dept Union Theol Sem Lib (NYC) 55-58; Br libn Berkshire Athenaeum, Pittsfield Mass 58-59; Bd of Educ, Niagara Falls NY: Sub tchr 60, Elem libn 60-63; Elem libn Bd of Educ Minoa Central Sch, E Syracuse NY 63-64; Elem libn Bdof Educ, Schenectady, NY 64-67; Elem libn N Syracuse Central Schs, N Syracuse NY 67-. 9: ALA; ATheol LA; NYLA. 10: Kappa Delta Pi. 14: Child serv. 15: 1433 Lancaster ave, Syracuse NY 13210.

WEEKS, ELIZABETH H(ARRIET). b Haverhill Mass. 5: Colby Col 30-34 (Biol) BS; Andover Newton Theol Sch 34-36 (Religious Educ) MRE Simmons 37-38 BS IN LS. 7: Libn State Normal Sch Farmington Me 38-41; Libn Williams Mem Inst, New London Conn 41-43; Ref libn Union Theol Sem, NYC 43-47; Ref libn NY Pub Lib Ref Dept 47-54; Catlgr Brookhaven Nat Lab, Upton NY Lib; Asst libn Bradford Jr CL 55"5; Libn Raytheon Co Res Div, Waltham Mass 57-62; Sci libn Brandeis U 62-63; Catlgr Esso Res & Engnr Co, Linden NJ 63-64; Sr catlgr Avco Corp RAD Div, Wilmington Mass 64-66; Libn Smithsonian Astrophy OBS 66-69; Hd Monographs Dept UCal(Riverside) 70-. 9: ALA; SLA. 10: Phi Mu. 13: Yes. 14: Ref, catlg. 15: UCal Lib, Riverside Ca 92507.

WEEKS, HARRY SANDFORD. b Middletown NY 10 Jl 24. 5: Cty Col (NY) 42-48 (Lit) BS in SS; Columbia 49-50 MS in LS. 6: Fr. 7: NY Pub Lib: Asst br libn 51-52, Readers adv 52-55, Prin libn Donnell Lib Center 55-58; Chief Libn Insurance Soc of NY Inc, NYC 58-63; Gen servlibn Bucks Co Free Lib, Doylestown Penn 63-67, Asst dir 67, Dir 67-. 9: ALA; SLA; PennLA; NY Lib Club; PennLA (v-chm Lib Development Com). 13: Yes. 14: Admin, bldgs, pub rel. 15: Box 116, Point Pleasant Penn 18950.

WEEKS, JOSEPH R JR. b Winnfield La 29 Ap 35. 4: Karen M Loesch. 5: La Polytech Inst 53-54; LSU 57-59 (Sociol) BA, 60-62 (LS) MS. 6: Fr. 7: USMC 54-56; Stud asst LSU (Baton Rouge) 57-59, Grad trainee 60-62; Hd ref, hd pub serv & act dir F T Nicholls State Col 62-66; Hd ref, asst dir pub serv Cleveland State U 67-. 9: ALA; OhioLA. 14: Pub serv. 15: 12000 Edgewater dr #804, Lakewood Oh 44107.

WEEKS, MARY CATHERINE. b Hampton Iowa 23 S 25. 5: State Col Iowa 43-46, 56 (Soc Sci) BA; UWis 50, 51-52 MA in LS; State U Iowa 59-68; Iowa State U 63. 7: Secon tchr Britt Pub Schs, Britt Iowa 46-48; Secon tchr Colfax Pub Schs, Colfax Iowa 48-50; Lib asst Mason City Pub Lib, Mason City Iowa 50-51; Elem libn Long Beach Ind Schs, Long Beach Cal 52-53; Jr ref libn Kan State U (Manhattan) 53-56; Lib coordinator Iowa Falls Community Schs & Ellsworth Col, Iowa Falls Iowa 56-68; Hd libn Ellsworth Col 68-. 9: NEA; ALA; Iowa State EA; IowaLA; IowaASchL; Iowa Jr Col Lib Assn. 10: Kappa Delta Pi; Pi Gamma Mu; Delta Kappa Gamma. 14: Sch & jr col libnship. 15: 116 Meadow lane, Iowa Falls Ia 50126.

WEERS, ROSALIND MARIE (VAN DORN). b Boulder Colo 14 Ag 26. 4: Elmer B Weers. 5: State Col Iowa 43-45 (Eng); State U Iowa 47-48 (Eng) BA. 6: Fr. 7: Stud asst in lib State Col Iowa 43-45; High sch Eng tchr Mallard Consolidated Schs, Mallard Iowa 48-49; Ya libn Pub Lib, Mason City Iowa 57-58, 60-. 9: IowaLA. 14: Ya bks. 15: RFD #3, Mason City Iowa.

WEGG, MARY (FREEMAN). b Menomonie Wis 16 Jl 11. 5: Carleton Col 28-32 (Eng) BA; UWis 33 (LS) Certif; UDenver 51 (LS) MA. 6: Fr. 7: 1st asst Pub Lib, Marshalltown Iowa 33-37; Libn Pub Lib, Rice Lake Wis 37-47; Catlgr Weld Co Lib, Greeley Colo 47; Catlgr Denver Pub Lib 47-. 9: ALA; MPLA; ColoLA. 10: DenverLA. 14: Catlg ser & west hist collection. 15: 732 Cherry st, Denver Co 80220.

WEHBRING, OLIVE (MINUSE). b Wash DC 26 Ag 05. 4: Leon A Wehbring. 5: Smith 27 (Hist) AB; Columbia 59 (LS) MA. 7: Libn Pub Lib, Mt Vernon NY 46-58; Hd ref dept Pub Lib, White Plains NY 59-67; Libn Hudons River Valley Commsn, Tarrytown NY 67-. 9: Coun Planning Libns. 14: Catlg, ref. 15: 29 Wayne ave, White Plains NY 10606.

WEHNCKE, JANE (BARUS). b Orange NJ 18 O 23. 4: John Wehncke. 5: Swarthmore 41-45 (Psych) BA; Rutgers 62-63 MLS. 6: Fr, Ger. 7: Sec, NYC: Scholastic Mags 47-48, ACLU 48-49, RJ Metz Ins Co 49-50; Ref libn Montclair State Col 67-69; Libn Montclair State Col & associated high sch 69-. 9: NJLA; ALA; Essex Co Sch Libns Assn. 10: LWV; PTA; AAUW; Montclair Fair Housing Com; Beta Phi Mu; UN Assn; Montclair Adult Sch Curriculum Com. 14: Ref (col & univ). 15: 525 Park st, Upper Montclair NJ 07043.

WEIBEL, GLADYS. b Minneapolis Minn 14 Ap 05. 5: UMinn 31-34 (Eng Lit) BA (magna cum laude), 34-35 (Eng Lit) MA, 35-37. 6: Ger, Fr. 7: Acquis libn UColo 61-64, Ref libn 64-. 9: ALA; ColoLA. 10: Phi Beta Kappa. 13: Yes. 14: Ref, bk sel. 15: 1700 Columbine ave, Boulder Co 80302.

WEICK, ROBERT J. b Ft Wayne Ind 15 Jl 25. 4: Lois Kuhlmann. 5: IndU (Ft Wayne) 45-48; Manchester Col 48-50 (Hist) BA; West Mich U 52-58 (LS) MA; Washington U 60; UMo 56; IndU (Ft Wayne) 68. 7: Lbn-Eng tchr Chinook High Sch, Chinook Mont 50-51; Libn-a-v Flat River Jr High Sch, Flat River Mo 51-62; Libn Portage Jr High Sch, Ft Wayne Ind 62-65; Asst lib consul Ft Wayne Commun Schs, Ft Wayne Ind 65-68; Libn S Side High Sch, Ft Wayne Ind 68-. 8: Libn Ind Inst of Tech summers & part- time. 9: NEA; ALA; Ind State Tchrs Assn; IndSchLA. 14: Sch libnship, ref, col libs. 15: 1251 Maxine dr, Ft Wayne Ind 46807.

WEIDLE, CATHERINE E. b St Louis. 5: Fontbonne Col 46 (Hist) AB; ST Louis U 49 (Amer Hist) MA; UIll 54 MS in LS; UDenver 62 (Archival admin) Certif. 7: Instr: Acad of the Visitation, St Louis 47-48, Notre Dame Acad, St Louis 48-49, Acad of the Sacred Heart, St Louis 50; St Louis U Lib: Clerical asst 50-53, Catlgr 54-57, Rare bks libn 57-. 8: Mem of MoLA Com on Special Collections in Mo Libs 56-57. 9: ALA; CathLA (Nomin Com Greater St Louis Unit 60) SAA; Manuscript Soc; MoLA (Com on Spec Collections in Mo Libs 56-57). 10: State Hist Soc Mo; Mo Hist Soc; Amer Assn for State & Loc Hist; Delta Epsilon Sigma. 13: Yes. 14: Rare bks. 15: 1201 Fargo dr, Ferguson Mo 63135.

WEIDNER, RUTH IRWIN. b Philadelphia Penn 20 My 34. 5: Hood Col 52-56 (Hist of Art) AB; Drexel 66 MSLS. 6: Sp, Ger. 7: Bibliog asst Lib College of Phys, Phila 67; Music libn w chester State Col 67-. 9: MusLA; ALA. 10: Beta Phi Mu. 14: Music libnship, lib educ. 15: 27 S High st, W Chester Penn 19380.

WEIGAND, EVA MAE (BRUNER). b Near Alva Okla 20 Jl 18. 4: Palmer H Weigand. 5: NWest State Col 35-42 (Elem Educ) BS; USoCal 65-66 MSLS. 6: Fr. 7: Tchr: Alva Pub Schs, Alva Okla 48-49, Whittier City Elem Schs, Whittier Cal 59-65; Dist libn Buena Pk Elem Sch Dist, Buena Pk Cal 66-. 9: NEA; ALA; CalTA; CalASchL. 10: Pi lambda Theta; Soroptomist Fed. 14: Child serv. 15: 13964 La Forge st, Whittier Ca 90605.

WEIGH, SAMUEL. b China 14 My 40. 4: Peace Chen. 5: Hon Kong Baptist Col 57-61 (Eng Lit) BA; Baylor 61-62 (Eng Lit); Columbia 62-64 (LS) MS. 6: Chinese. 7: Libn Queens Borough Pub Lib, Jamaica NY 62-66, Asst br libn 66-68, Br libn 68-69; Inst serv libn nj state libn NJ State Lib, Trenton 69-. 9: ALA; NJLA. 10: Full Gospel Bus Men Fellowship Internatl. 14: Bk sel, ref and adv serv, admin, supv. 15: 118 Elderberry dr, Levittown Pa 19054.

WEIHER, RONALD LEE. b Kan City Mo 16 Mr 38. 4: Nancy Jo Ricketson. 5: UMo (Kan City) 56-60 (Hist) BA; West Res 60-61 (LS) MS; UMo (Kan City) 65-68 (Bus Admin) MBA. 07: Asst libn Jr Col of Kan City 61-62; Gen ref libn UMo (Kan City) 62-65, Bus & pub admin ref libn 65-68 Asst libn Harvard Bus Sch 68-. 9: ALA; SLA (Program chm Heart of Amer Chap); MoLA; ASIS. 10: Torch & Scroll Honor Soc. 14: Ref, lib mgt. 15: 35 Eliot, Boston Ma 02130.

WEIHERER, PATRICIA DEE. b Reading Penn 17 S 33. 5: Albright Col 51-55 (Eng) BA; Rutgers 59-61 MLS. 6: Sp, Fr. 7: Eng tchr Manheim Central High Sch, Manheim Penn 55-56; Reading Pub Lib, Reading Penn: Asst br libn 56-58, 2nd asst catlgr 58, Br libn 59, Asst ref libn 61-66, Ref libn 66-. 9: ALA; PennLA (Lehigh Valley publicity chm). 10: YWCA. 14: Ref, catlg. 15: 917 N 10th st, Reading Penn 19604.

WEIL, BEN H. b St Joseph Mo 8 Jl 16. 4: Carolyn Loeb. 5: St Joseph (Mo) Jr Col 35-37 (Chem Engnr) AS; UMo 37-39 (Chem Engnr) BS in CHE; UWis 39-40 (Chem Engnr) MS in CHE. 7: Head info sect chem div Gulf Research & Devel Co, Pittsburgh 40-45; Head tech info div Ga Tech Engnr Expt Station, Atlanta 45-50; Head tech info div Ethyl Corp Res Labs, Detroit 50-57; Head tech info sect Esso Research & Engnr Co, Linden NJ 57-. 8: Free-lance tech writing, 44-60; Adjunct prof tech abstracting Rutgers Grad Sch of Lib Sci, 61-63; V-pres (65-67) & mem bd dirs, Engineering Index Inc 65-69; Sec (68-69) & mem Bd Dirs, Nat Fed of Sci & Abstracting Indexing Serv 68-; Chm Subcom USASI Com Z39 69-. 9: Inst of Info Sci (Fellow); SLA; ; ASIS (chm NYC Chap 68); ACS (chm Div of Chem Lit 58, coun or alternate coun 60-65); Soc Tech Writers & Publishers (dir 56); Amer Petroleum Inst (chm Abstr Adv Subcom 59-61). 10: AAAS. 11: Certif of Merit, ACS Div of Chem Lit, 56. 12: Jt ed "Chemical Literature" (49-57); "Research Engineer" (46-50); "Filter Press 1949"; Books; Sr auth, Sole auth, or ed "Plastic Horizons" (44), "Synthetic Petroleum from the Synthine Process" (48); "The Technical Report" (54); "Technical Editing" (58); Bd of Ed "Journal of Chemical Documentation" (65-68). 13: Yes. 14: Admin, abstr, tech writing & ed. 15: Esso Res & Engnr Co, PO Box 121, Linden NJ 07036.

WEIL, CHERIE (BURESH). b Evanston Ill 13 O 41. 4: Roman L Weil Jr. 5: Wellesley 59-63 (Biblical hist, lit & interpretation) BA; UChicago 66-67 (LS) MA. 6: Fr. 7: Sec Reed, Smith, Shaw & McClay, Pittsburgh Penn 64-65; Libn Inst for Computer research UChicago 67-. 9: ALA. 10: Beta Phi Mu; Wellesley Club. 13: Yes. 14: Automation of lib serv, systems analysis, computer lit. 15: 5115 S Cornell ave, Chicago Il 60615.

WEILER, DOROTHY (ESSER). b Hartford Wis 21 F 14. 4: Henry Carl Weiner. 5: UPuget Sound 31-34; Wash StateU 34-35 (For Lang) BA; UWash 35-36 BALS. 6: Ger. 7: Libn Valley View Elem Sch, Phoenix 53-59; Ext libn Ariz State Dept of Lib & Archives Ext div, Phoenix 59-67; Dir Tempe Pub Lib, Tempe Ariz 67-. 8: Assoc prof Lib Sci Dept Col of Educ Ariz StateU 68. 9: ALA; ArizStateLA. 10: Soroptimist, Internat; Maricopa Co-City of Phoenix Civil Defense and Disaster Organiz; Radio Amateur Civil Emerg Serv; Amateur Radio Operator (K7BLV). 12: Ed "Roadrunner", quarterly Ariz State Lib Ext Serv (59-67); "Tumbling Tumbleweed", newsletter (59-67). 14: Admin, ref. 15: 226 West Siesta way, Phoenix Az 85041.

WEILERSTEIN, DEBORAH (EVE). b NYC 13 Jl 29. 5: URochester 47-51 (Soc) BA; Drexel 53-54 MLS. 7: Clerk NY Pub Lib 51-53; LIBN: Enoch Pratt Free Lib, Baltimore 54-56; Cleveland Pub Lib 56-62; Arlington Co Lib, Arlington Va 62-, Child wk supv 66-. 9: ALA; DCLA; VaLA. 14: Child wk. 15: 5055 Seminary rd, Alexandria Va 22311.

WEILL, MARIANNE (COOPER). b Boston 14 Ja 43. 4: David PAUL Weill. 5: Jackson Col 60-64 (Sociol, music) AB; Columbia 64-65 MLS. 6: Fr. 7: Libn Brooklyn Pub Lib 65-66; Adult serv hd Uniondale Pub Lib, Uniondale NY 66-. 9: ALA; NYLA; 14: Adult serv, ref, admin. 15: 214 West End ave apt 6D, Freeport NY 11520.

WEIMER, WANDA GREEN. b Youngstown Ohio 29 Ag 16. 4: Wilfred Weimer. 5: Westminster Col (Penn) 4-35; Col of Wooster 35-38 (Eng) BA; West Res U summers 40, 41 (LS): Kent State U 61-64 MLS. 6: Fr. 7: Tchr Milan High Sch, Milan Ohio 38-40; Tchr & libn Bardman High Sch, Youngstown Ohio 40-43; Tchr & libn Canfield High Sch, Canfield Ohio 51-52, 56-60; Libn Canfield High Sch, Canfield Ohio 60-. 9: NEA; ALA; OhioASchL. 10: AAUW; Delta Kappa gamma; Fed of Womens Clubs; Great Books Discussion Group. 14: Ya reading guidance. 15: 114 Skyline ave, Canfield Ohio 44406.

WEIMERSKIRCH, PHILIP JOHN. b Tiffin Ohio 11 Ag 29. 5: UDetroit 47-49; St Charles Col 49-50 (Lat); St Marys Sem & Univ 50-54 (Philos) AB; UDetroit 54-58 (Philos) MA; Columbia 59-61 (LS) MS, 62-69 (LS). 7: Clerical wk Columbia U 58-59; Lib asst Mem Centr for Cancer, NYC 59; Ref libn NY Acad of Med, NYC 59-62; Ref libn Columbia U Med Lib 62-64 Tchg asst Columbia U Sch of Lib Serv 64-65; Ref libn Columbia U Med Lib 65, Libn Webster Lib of Plastic surgery 65-66. 9: BSA; Bibliog Soc; Oxford Bibliog Soc; Cambridge Bibliog Soc. 10: Printing Hist Soc; Renaissance Soc of Amer. 11: Murray Gottlieb Prize of MLA 65. 13: Yes. 14: Rare bks. 15: 552 W 114th st, New York NY 10025.

WEINBERG, FLEUR (HALPERN). b Phila 9 Ap 26. 5: Temple 44-48 (Sociol) AB; Rutgers 57-59; Drexel 61 (LS), 68 MLS. 7: Research asst Dept of Pub Assistance, Penn 48-49; Lab tech Thiokol Chem Corp, Trenton NJ 51-52, Ms asst 52-53, Libn 53-59; Libn Insurance Co of N Amer, Phila 59-61; Catlgr-indexer Auerbach Corp, Phila 61-62; Tech info spec UPenn Proj Summit, Phila 62-67; Libn Research for Better Schs 67-. 9: SLA; Spec Libs Coun, Phila (Soc Div: treas 60, Recr Chm 61, Program Chm 62); ASIS. 10: Dir, Thiokol Employees Fed Credit Union. 12: "An Annotated Bibliography of Benefits and Costs in the Public Sector" (68). 14: Admin, designing, new systems, ref. 15: 1724 Spruce st, Phila 19103.

WEINBRECHT, RUBY YORK. b Spartanburg SC 19 Mr 27. 4: Standau E Weinbrecht. 5:Mary Washington Col 44-48 (Hist) BA; Peabody Col 49-50 (LS) MA; UChicago 54-55 (LS). 6: Sp, Fr, Russian. 7: Ref libn Ball StateU 55-56; Chief readers serv Ind StateU (Terre Haute) 56-58; Catlg ed Union List of Ser LC 59-60, Sr decimal classifier decimal clsf off 60-63; Libn Dept of Commerce Marketing Lib, Wash DC 63-65, Ed "Marketing Info Guide" 65-67; Chief tech info div Equal Employment Opportunity Commsn, wash DC 68-. 8: Lib survey, Foxcraft Sch, Middleburg Va. 9: Educ Press Assn Amer; Amer Marketing Assn; DCLA. 10: Mary Washington Col Alumnae; Corcoran Art Gallery. 12: Ed "DC Libraries" (67). 13: Yes. 14: Ref. 15: 8107 Touchstone ter, McLean Va 22101.

WEINER, SEYMOUR S(IDNEY). b NYC 4 S 17. 4: Bobbie West. 5: UPoitiers (France) 37 (Fr) Diplome UDijon(France) 37-38 (Fr) Diplome; Cty Col (NY) 34-40 (Fr) BA; UCal(Berkeley) 40-42 (Fr) MA; Columbia 42-50 (Fr) PhD, 51-52 MS in LS. 6: Fr, Sp, Ital, Ger, Lat. 7: Instr in Romance Lang Brooklyn Col 46-47; Lecturer, Instr in Fr Columbia U 46-50; Acquis asst, head photographic div UIll Lib (Urbana) 52-53; Visiting Lecturer in romance lang & libnship UWash 53-54, Ast & Assoc Prof of romance lang & lit 54-62; Assoc Prof of Fr SUNY (Stony Brook) 62-63; Prof of romance lang UMass 63-. 8: Chm, Master Planning Com for the Univ Lib, UMass 64-; Consul, survey of lib facilities for res in the humanities, PNLA 57; Consul, "Test of Developed Activities, Educ Testing Serv 55; Chm Dept Lib Com UWash 54-63; chm Fac Lib Com UMass 64-68. 9: Mod Lang Assn; Amer Assn Tchrs Fr; ALA; ACLA; MHRA; Societe dEtude du XVII-Siecle; Renaiss Soc of Amer; Amer Soc for Aesthetics; PAPC (sec & chm Romance Sect). 10: AAUP; Phi Sigma Iota; Pi Delta Phi; ACLU. 11: Chevalier, Order of Academie Palms (France). 12: "Francis Carco the Career of a Literary Bohemian (52); Gen ed"A Critical Bibligraphy of French Literatur; Managing ed "The French Review. 13: Yes. 14: Bibliog, methodology of research. 15: Dept of Romance Langs, Univ of Mass, Amherst Ma 01002.

WEINRAUCH, JUDITH ANN. b Wilkes-Barre Penn 29 Je 38. 4: John R Weinrauch. 5: De Paul U 59-64 (Eng) AB; Rosary Col 64-65 (LS). 6: Sp, Fr. 7: Lib asst Penn State Law Lib 57-59; Asst law libn De Paul U Law Lib 59-65; Libn St Vincent Ferrer Grade Sch 68-. 9: AALL. 14: Law libnship (ref), sch libn. 15: 217 S Oak Park ave, Oak Park Il 60302.

WEINSTEIN, EDWARD ALLEN. b Portland Ore 8 Ag 28. 4: Martha Haaga. 5: Portland U 47-49 (Bus Admin); UWash 49-51 (Eng Lit) BA, 56-57 (LS) ML. 6: Fr. 7: Chem libn UWash 57-60; Catlg libn Boeing Sci Research Labs, Seattle 60-63; Lib supv 63-. 8: . 9: SLA; ASIS (corp rep). 13: Yes. 14: Lib automation. 15: 712 36th ave, Seattle Wa 98122.

WEINSTEIN, FREDERIC D. b NYC 22 My 25. 4: Suzanne Reitz. 5: NYU 44-48 (Eng Lit) AB; UChicago 48-50 (LS) AM; Columbia 57- (LS). 6: Fr. 7: Priv ASTP US Army, NJ & Tex 43; Circ asst NYC Pub Lib 46; Ref asst NYU 47-48; Research asst Carnegie Corp UChicago 49-50, Admin asst educ lib 52; Ref libn Chicago Pub Lib Art Dept 50-52; Instr & asst libn New Haven State Tchrs Col 52-56; Libn SoConn State Col 56-59, Dean lib sch 56-61; Lecturer Columbia U Sch of Lib Serv 62-65; Assoc prof & dir of admissions Sch of Lib Sci SUNY (Albany) 65-68, Prof 68-. 8: NY State Civil Serv Bd of Examrs 66-68. 9: ALA; -LED (Regl rep NY & Middle Atlantic Reg); NYLA. 10: AAUP; mem of several national conservation societies. 13: Yes. 14: Lib educ. 15: School of Lib Sci SUNY 1400 Washington ave, Albany NY 12203.

WEINSTEIN, LOIS. b Phila 29 N 42. 5: Penn State 60-64 (Elem Educ) BS; Drexel 65-68 (LS) MS. 7: Tchr Phila Bd of Educ 64-65; Interlib loan serv Drexel Inst Lib 65-68; Libn I Phila Free Lib 69; Pub serv Villanova Law Lib 69-. 9: SLA; ALA. 14: Ref serv. 15: 3701 Conshohocken ave, Phila Pa 19131.

WEINSTEIN, SAUL. b New Kensington Penn 28 N 27. 4: Bonnie McCoy. 5: Millersville state Col 57-60 (LS) BS; UPittsburgh 64-66 MLS, 66-67 Advanced Certif in LS. 6: Ger, Hebrew, Yiddish. 7: Instrument flying instr USAF 46-49; Aircraft tech Ozark Air Lines, Chicago 50-52; Time-study Alcoa, New Kensington Penn 53-57; Libn Susquehanna Twp Schs, harrisburg Penn 60-02; Libn Broward Co Schs, Ft Lauderdale Fla 62-64; Libn Jeannette City Schs, Jeannette Penn 64-66; Hd acquis Edinboro State Col 66-67, Hd tech serv 67-68, Act chief libn 68-69, Dir libs 69-. 9: ALA; PennLA (chm Bldg & Equip Sect). 10: AAUP; Assn Penn State Col Facs. 14: Bldgs, equip, admin, acquis. 15: 26 Valley View dr, Edinboro Pa 16412.

WEINSTEIN, SEYMOUR. b Chicago Ill 22 F 29. 4: Laura Bordes. 5: RooseveltU 50-53 (Hist) AB; UMd 65-66 MLS. 6: Fr. 7: Co clk US Army, US & Germany 53-54; High sch tchr chicago Bd of Educ 55-57; Dist mgr Great Bks, Wash DC 57-66; Hd circ dept UIowa Libs 66-. 9: ALA. 14: Admin, circ. 15: 1414 Keokuk st, Iowa City Ia 52240.

WEINSTEIN, SHIRLEY (SACHER). b Brooklyn NY 1 F 42. 4: Bernard Weinstein. 5: Newark State Col 59-63 (Eng) BA; Rutgers 65-66 MLS. 6: Sp. 7: Tchr, Newark NJ: Madison Jr high Sch 63-64, West Side High Sch 64-65; Asst Prof lib serv Newark State Col 66-. 8: Trained lib assts 68. 10: Phi Beta Mu; Kappa Delta Pi. 14: Tchg, ref. 15: 12 Tudor ct, Elizabeth NJ 07208.

WEINTRAUB, BENJAMIN. b Presov Czechoslovakia 9 My 16. 5: Roosevelt U 46-49 (Hist) BA; UChicago 49-51 (Hist) MA, 51-53 (LS) MA. 7: Libn III Detroit Pub Lib 53-62; Lib development adv Penn State Lib 62-65; Asst Prof Graduate Sch of Lib Serv Rutgers U 65-. 9: ALA; NJLA. 14: Ref, bk sel, trustee wkshops, bibliog. 15: Rutgers Grad Sch of Lib Serv, New Brunswick NJ 0893.

WEINTRAUB, D KATHRYN. b Cincinnati 29 Jl 32. 4: Karl Joachim Weintraub. 5: UChicago 47-51 AB; Columbia 53-54 (Pol Sci; UChicago 55-60 (LS) AM; UChicago 64-69 LS. 6: Fr, Sanskrit, Ger. 7: Head searcher acquis dept UChicago Lib 55-59, Instr Grad Lib Sch 61-67. 9: ALA; AALS; Linguistic Soc Amer; ASIS. 10: Quadrangle Club (Chicago); Assn Computational Linguistics. 13: Yes. 14: Bibliog, classification,linguistics, lib syst. 15: 5557 S Kimbark, Chicago Il 60637.

WEIR, DENNIS J. b Oneonta NY 14 Ja 41. 4: Ruthanne Zitek. 5: Syracuse 59-64 (Hist) BA, 64-66 (LS) MA. 7: Lib stack supv Syracuse U Lib 65-66; Jr lib ref Yonkers Pub Lib, Yonkers NY 66-67, Sr libn I Bkmob 67-69, Sr Libn I in charge of order dept 69; Sr libn i in charge of Hudson River Mus Br 69-. 9: ALA; NYStateLA; WestchesterLA. 10: YMCA; Yonkers Hist Assn. 14: Ref, child, ya, pub rel. 15: Yonkers Public Lib, Yonkers NY 10701.

WEIR, GERTRUDE (BURGESS). b Portland Me 20 Ja 17. 5: Radcliffe 33-37 (Hist) BA; Simmons 61-64 (LS) SM. 6: Fr. 7: Saleswoman; hathaway House Bkshop, Wellesley Mass 48-50, Dartmouth Bkstall, Boston 49, Personal Bkshop, Newtonville Mass 48; Exec sec Wellesley Community Chest & Coun Inc, Wellesley Mass 49-54; Amherst Col Lib: Circ asst 55-59, Asst in chg of reserves 59-64, Readers serv ref irc 64-65, Cir head 65-. 9: ALA-ACRL; West Mass Lib Club. 10: LWV; Amherst Human Rel Coun; Commun orchestras; Audubon Socs. 14: Ref, circ. 15: 1310 South East st, Amherst Mass 01002.

WEIR, MARY JEAN. b Wash DC 15 Ja 21. 5: Bethany Col (WVa) 38-42 (Psych) AB; Mt Union Col summer 39; Drexel 57-58 MS in LS; USoCal summer; San Jose State Col (NDEA Inst) summer 66; UILL (HEA Inst) 68-69. 7: Interviewer Navy Labor Bd, San Diego 43-44; Interviewer US Employment Serv, San Diego 44-45; Claims examiner State of Cal Dept of Employment, San Diego 45-56; Readers serv libn Colby Col 58-59; Catlgr asst libn Millikin U 59-60; Catlgr San Digo State Col 60-61; Libn Spring Valley Jr High Sch, Spring Valley Cal 61-. 8: Lib sci lecturer (asst prof) San Diego State Col 67-68, summer 69. 9: ALA; NEA; Cal Tchrs Assn; CalASchL; CalLA. 10: Beta Phi Mu. 14: Catlg, ref, tchg lib sci. 15: 7374 Princeton st, La Mesa Cal 92041.

WEIS, AIMEE (LeVITA). b Philadelphia Penn 11 Ja 25. 4: Henry Weis. 5: TempleU 42-46 (Psych) AB; Drexel 65-67 MSLS. 7: Libn Elkins Pk Free Lib, Elkins Pk Penn 65-67; Libn laMott Free Lib, Cheltenham Twp Penn 66-67; Libn Commun Col of Phila 68-. 9: ALA; PennLA. 14: Ref, acquis. 15: 412 S Sterling rd, Elkins Park Pa 19117.

WEIS, INA JEANNETTE (HELLSTERN). b Toledo Ohio 12 Mr 21. 4: Edgar Weis. 5: UToledo 39-43 (Hist) AB; West Res U summers 46-49 BS in LS, 61 MS in LS. 6: Ger. 7: Chief circ libn & Asst Prof of Lib Sci UToledo Lib 43-. 9: ALA; Ohio LA. 10: AAUP; AAUW; Univ Women Beta Sigma Phi; PEO; Wesleyan Serv Guild. 14: Circ, catlg. 15: Rte 1 Box 311A, Elmore Oh 43416.

WEIS, THEOFIELD G. b Lehigh Kan 28 D 01. 4: Janet Louise Hess. 5: Columbia Union Cl 26 (Amer Lit) AB; UMd 38 (Amer Lit) AM; Catholic U 41 BS in LS. 6: Ger. 7: Prin Resthaven Elem Sc, Sidney BC 26-27, Kelowna Jr Acad, Kelowna BC 27-28, Winnieg Jr Acad, Winnipeg Man 28-29; Eng dept head Battleford Acad Battleford Sask 29-30; Prin Edgecombe Jr Acad, Baltimore 30-31; Libn olumbia Union Col 31, Prof of Lib Sci 54-, 54-68, Libn emeritus 69-. 9: ALA-ACRL; MDLA. 13: Yes. 14: Admin, ref. 15: 900 Prospect ave, Takoma Park Md 20012.

WEISBERG, RUTH (DYSKEN). b Dayton Ohio 21 Ap 11. 4: 5: UCincinnati 29-30 (Liberal Arts); Antioch Col 30-35, 36 (Lit) BA; Columbia 37 BLS. 7: Placement dir Bus Train Col, Pittsburgh 40-43; Staff asst Personnel & Train, Carnegie Ill Steel Corp 43-44; Ed asst to v-pres Ind Rels Carnegie Ill 44-45; Ed McKinsey & Co NYC (mgt consuls) 45-46; UPittsburgh; Gen asst to the libn 61, Res bk rooms libn 61-62, Gift & Exch libn 62-67, Admin asst Soc Sci Info Ctr 68-. 15: 6448 Nicholson st, Pittsburgh 15217.

WEISENBERGER, ELSIE JANET. b Mission Tex 11 Mr 17. 5: UArk 49 (Math, Sci) BSE; uokla 40-42 (LS); Peabody 52 MALS. 7: Tchr Liberty Elem Sch, Hope Ark 37-39; Co Libn Hempstead Co, Hope Ark 40-47; Libn & Math tchr Hope Jr-Sr High Sch, Hope Ark 49-50; Head Libn Pub Lib, N Little Rock Ark 50-56; Elem libn Houston Ind Schs 57-59; Libn McReynolds Jr High Sch, Houston 59-61; Libn Furr Sr-Jr High Sch, Houston 61-. 9: ALA; ArkLA (past treas; past pres Pub Libns); TexLA; SWLA; Tex Sc la past sec). 10 AAUW; Delta Kappa Gamma; Bus & Prof Womans Club; Weslyan Serv Guild; PTA; Houston Country Club; Civic Club. 13: Yes. 14: Ya serv, catlg. 15: 6527 Pinehurst, Houston Tx 77023.

WEISER, DAVID REUBEN. b Shawnee Ohio 7 D 22. 4: Ann L. 5: Ohio Wesleyan U 40-43, 46-47 (Chem) BS; Miami U (Oxford) 42 (Organic Chem); UCincinnati 43 (Biochem); Shrivenham U (Eng) 45 (Advanced Inorganic Chem); UDayton 57 (Pat Law). 6: Fr, Ger. 7: Libn Champion Papers Inc, Hamilton Ohio 47-61; Head Libn Tektronix Inc, Beaverton Ore 61-63; Manager tech info Phillips Petroleu Co, Bartlesville Okla 63-. 8: Prof consul for SLA 69. 9: SLA (chm Tr Ctr Com 60-61; chm Paper & Textile Sect 55-57; Cincinatti Chap; v-pres 51-52 & 53-54, pres 52-53; pres Okla Chap 67-68); ASIS. 10: ACS; Hamilton Toastmasters Club; Seven Mile Chamber of Com; Seven Mile (Ohio) Bd of Educ. 12: "Directory of Libraries of Paper and Allied Industries in the United States and Canada (55). 13: Yes. 14: Admin, mgt, info syst, syst design, documentation. 15: 265A Chem Labs Phillips Petroleum Co, Bartlesville Ok 74003.

WEISER, SYLVIA. b NYC 9 Jl 17. 4: Manuel Weiser. 5: George WashingtonU 34-38 (Sociol) BS; CatholicU 57-59 MS in LS. 7: Libn Johns HopkinsU Applied Physics Lab, Silver Spring Md 57-. 9: SLA; ASIS. 12: "Guide to the Literature of Engineering, Mathematics and the Physical Sciences" (59, 2nd ed 64); "Index and Abstracts of APL Reprints" 62-63, 64-65. 13: Yes. 14: Lib admin, ref. 15: 1001 Devere dr, Silver Spring Md 20903.

WEISER, VIRGINIA R. b Fairbanks Ak 31 Ag 26. 5: CUNY (Hunter Col) 43-47 (Home Econ) BA (cum laude); Mich StateU 47-49 (Foods & Nutrition) MS; UIll 65-67 (LS) MS. 7: Tchg grad asst Foods & Nutrition Dept Mich StateU (E Lansing) 47-49; Women's ed & broadcaster WKAR Radio 54-61; Instr Foods & Nutrition Dept Ore StateU (Corvallis) 49-51, Deschutes Co ex agt (home econ asst prof) Ore Coop Ext Serv (Bend) 51-54, Ext nutrition specialist (assoc prof) Ore Coop Ext Serv (Corvallis) 61-65; Asst to libn Math Lib UIll (Urbana) 65-67; Area specialist (Neuroendocrinology) UCLA Biomed Lib Brain Info Serv bibliog unit 67-. 9: MedLA; Amer Home Econ Assn (life mem). 10: Beta Phi Mu; Sigma Delta Pi. 12: Comp & ed "Neuroendocrine Control Mechanism; The Hypothalmic-Pituitary-Gonadal System" (68); "Neuroendocrine

Control Mechanism; The CNS-Pituitary-Adrenocortical System'' (69); As Ext Nutrit Spec, prepared several bulletins for pub distrib. 14: Ref, manual and automated. 15: Brain Info Serv Biomed Lib Univ of Cal, Los Angeles Ca 90024.

WEISJOHN, RHYLLIS IRENE. b Los Angeles 16 S 23. 5: Los Angeles City Col 52-55 (Pre-libnship) AA; UCLA 55-57 (Pre-libnship) AB; USoCal 57-58 MS in LS. 7: Los Angeles Pub Lib; messenger clerk 48-53, Clerk typist 53-57, Libn trainee 57-58, Child libn 58-62, Sr libn 62-69, Prin libn 69-. 9: ALA; CalLA. 10: Beta Phi Mu. 13: Yes. 14: Ref, Commun br serv. 15: 1169 N Berendo st, Los Angeles 90029.

WEISS, AARON. b Brooklyn NY 29 D 06. 4: Evelyn Meyers. 5: Brooklyn Law Sch St Lawrence U 28-31; 32 Admitted to Bar of State of NY; admitted to Fed Courts, East & So Dists, & Treasury Dept & Tax Court of US. 7: (Sgt) Army of the US 43-45; Practice of law, NYC 32-36; Prin Law Libn City Court of the City of NY 46-63; Prin Law Libn & Chief Law Asst Civil Curt of the City of NY 63-. 9: Law Lib Assn Greater NY; NY Co Lawyers Assn; Assn Law Libns Upper NY State. 15: c/o Civil Court Cit of NY, 111 Centre st, NYC 10017.

WEISS, ABRAHAM AARON. b Bronx NY 2 Ag 17. 5: Yeshiva Col 33-35; City Col (NY) 35-37 (Eng) BSS; Columbia U 49-52 MLS. 6: Hebrew. 7: Ed Off of Civilian Defense, Wash DC 43-44, Chem Warfare Serv, Edgewood Md 44-45, Army Transportation Corps, NYC 45-46; Hebrew tchr Temple Beth Sholem, Miami Beach Fla 46-47; Libn Boro Hall Acad, Brooklyn NY 48-50; Libn Ramaz Sch, NYC 51-56; Libn in chg Samuel Gompers High Sch, Bronx NY 68-. 9: NYC High Sch Libns Assn; NYC Sch Libns. 10: United Fed of Tchrs; Kingsbridge Hts Jewish Ctr; Assn Orthodox Jewish Tchrs; Hebrew Lang & Culture Assn. 13: Yes. 14: Wk with yp. 15: 2545 Sedgwick ave, New York NY 10468.

WEISS, EGON ARTHUR. b Vienna 7 Je 19. 4: Renee H Weiss. 5: Berea Col 38-40 (Philos, Math); Harvard 46-47 (Econ) AB; Boston U 48-49 (Ger Lang & Lit) MA; Simmons 49-51 (LS) MS. 6: Ger, Fr. 7: Air Corps Mil Intelligence Mil Govt, EUROPEAN Theater 42-46; Lt Col CA-USAR Civil Affairs, US Army Res 48-; Prof asst Pub Lib, Brookline Mass 9-51, 49-51 dir 51-58; US Mil Acad (W Point): Asst libn 58-62, Act libn 62-63, Lib Dir, Archivist & Histn 63-. 8: Program Adv Com Off of Chief of Military Hist 63; Com for Army Lib Career Program Off of Adjutant Gen 64-65; Program Com & host 9th Military Libns Wkshop; Long Range Planning Com for Military LibnsWkshops 69; Fed Lib Com (Task Force on Pub Rel) 69. 9: ALA (pres Armed Forces Libns Sect 67-68); SLA (v-chm & chm-elect Military Libns Div 69-70); SE NY Lib Resources Coun (Trustee 63-; chm For Area Resources Com 68). 10: Res Offs Assn; Mil Govt Assn; Harvard Club of the Mid-Hudson Valley; Archons of Colophon; Consititution Island Assn; Museum of Hudson Highlands; Assn of US Army. 13: Yes. 14: Admin, lib facilities (bldgs & equip), lib resources, communications, automation. 15: 33 Spruce st, Cornwall-on-Hudson NY 12520.

WEISS, GLENNA (MANNING). b Worcester Mass 24 Ap 07. 5: Lesley Col 28-30 (Elem Educ) Diploma; Columbia 43-45 (Early Childhood) BS; Queens Col 62-64 (Lib Educ) MS. 6: Sp. 7: Propriet nursery sch, Worcester Mass 30-33; Santiago Col Kdg & First Grade, Santiago Chile 33-36; Kdg & First Grade St Johnland Sch, King Park NY 37-43; Elem tchr Brooklyn Friends, Brooklyn NY 43-45; Kdg & High Sch Libn Kew Forest Sch, Forest Hills NY 46-60; Elem Sch Libn Barnum Woods Sch, E Meadow NY 60-. 9: NEA; ny state Tchrs Assn; Nassau (NY) LA. 10: Nat Cong Parents & Tchrs; AAUW; Eng-Speaking Union. 14: Tchg lib tech & skills to child. 15: 70-20 108th st, Forest Hills NY 11375.

WEISS, JACQUILIN R. b Pittsburgh Penn 10 Je 25. 5: UPittsburgh 43-46 (Bio) BS, 62-63 mls, 64 (Computers & Info Retrieval). 6: Fr. 7: Ref & circ libn Falk Lib Health Prof UPittsburgh 63-66; Biomed & forensic researcher 66-; Catlgr admin collection St Francis Gen Hosp, Pittsburgh Penn 67-68. 9: SLA; MedLA. 13: Yes. 14: Biomed, ref. 15: 5309 Pembroke pl, Pittsburgh Pa 15232.

WEISS, LAURA (OAKS). b Anglica NY 25 D 18. 4: Irvin M Weiss. 5: AlfredU 36-40 (Eng) BA; Geneseo State 40-41 Prof Libn Life Certif. 7: Stud asst Syracuse U Lib 41-42; Circ clk Dayton Pub Lib, Dayton Ohio 45; Ref asst Detroit News Lib 47-48; Hd bus & tech/Mich Room Grand Rapids Pub Lib 56-59; Ref asst Detroit Pub Lib Edison Br 60-61; Assoc dir N Oakland Lib Coop, Pontiac Mich 61-66; Spec serv Bloomfield Twp Lib, bloomfield Hills Mich 66-67; Asst dir Macomb Co Lib Syst, Mt Clemens Mich 67-. 9: ALA; MichLA (Com for Nat Lib Week 68, Legis Com 68-69); Lib Systems RT. 10: DAR; Macomb Co Interagency Coun. 14: Counsul wk, lib systems admin. 15: 4871 Malibu dr, Bloomfield Hills Mi 48013.

WEISS, MIRIAM (RATNER). b Newark NJ 13 1 19. 4: Martin Weiss. 5: Temple 36-40 (Hist, Soc Studies) BSin Ed; Drexel 61-64 MSLS. 6: Yiddish, Ger. 7: Yeoman 3c WAVES, NY, Okla, Phila 44-46; Catlgr , Asst libn, Act hd libn Beaver Col Lib 64-. 9: ALA; PennLA (Recr Cim, Nat Lib Wk Com). 10: United World Federalist. 14: Catlg, ref, biblio g, pub rel, admin. 15: 1102 Orleans rd, Cheltenham Pa 19012.

WEISS, RUDI. b Mannheim Germany 12 Ap 1 5: Realgymnasium Mannheim 22-31; Columbia 49-50 (Econ) BS, 50-51 (LS) MS, 51-56 (LS). 6: Ger, Fr. 7: Army Off of Strategic Serv 43-46; Chief libn Off of US Chief of Coun for War Crimes, Nuremberg Germany 46-48; Brooklyn Pub Lb, Brooklyn NY 51-59; Chief tech Serv Westchester Lib System, Yonkers NY 59-68, Asst dir tech serv 68-. 9: ALA; SLA (Reg Proc Com) NYLA (pres Resources & Tech Serv Sect 64-65); NY Lib Club. 13: Yes. 14: Tech serv, admin. 15: 80 La Salle st, NYC 10027.

WEITZEL, JULIET LOUISE. b Wash DC 29 Ap 12. 5: Wilson Tchrs Col 33-36 (Primary Educ) BS in Ed; George Washington U 39, 43-44 (Educ); Carnegie 46 BS in LS. 7: Elem sch tchr DC Pub Schs 36-44; DC Pub Lib; Jr lib asst 44-46, Child libn 46-58, Supv wk with ya 58-. 9: ALA; Adult Educ Assn; DCLA (Publicity Chm 65). 10: AAUW; Amer Univ Park Citizens Assn; Neighborhood Youth Coun Area 10. 12: Ed AAUW Newsletter Wash Br (59-60). 13: Yes. 14: YA SERV. 15: 4640 Brandywine st NW, WASH DC 20016.

WEITZEL, WILLIAM I. b Pasadena Cal 18 N 21. 4: Janice Cole. 5: Pasadena Col Co 39-41 (Liberal Arts) AA; Stanford 46-47 (Soc Sc) BA, 47-48 (Educ) MA; Immaculate Heart Col 60 (LS) MA. 7: Tchr Kern Co Union High Sch, Bakersfield Cal 48-52; Tchr Pasadena City Schs, Pasadena Cal 53-58; Libn & assoc prof Pasadena City Col 58-. 9: NEA; Cal Tchrs Assn CalLA; CalASchL. 10: Sierra Club. 14: Ref. 15: 1570 E Colorado blv, Pasadena Cal 91106.

WEITZENKORN, LILLIAN (UDMAN). b Pittsburgh 7 Je 22. 4: William W Weitzenkorn. 5: Carnegie 39-43 (Soc Wk) BS, 61 (LS); Pittsburgh 62-64 MLS. 7: Sub tchr Pittsburgh Bd of Educ 61-63; Asst libn Carnegie Lib of Pittsburgh 64-67; Educ libn Pt Pk Col 67-. 9: ALA;PennLA. 10: PTA; Bnai Brith Women; Beta Phi Mu. 14: Child serv. 15: 1111 Sheridan ave, Pittsburgh 15206.

WELCH, DALE (THOMPSON). b York Ala 3 Ja 25. 4: Henry Welch. 5: Belhaven Col 42-44; UAla 44-46 (Art) AB, summers 66-68 (LS) MA. 7: Asst libn W Ga Col 48-50; Libn Core Elem Sch, Panama City Fla 56-59; Libn Monroe Co High Sch, Monroeville Ala 59-65; Libn Patrick Henry State Jr Col 65-. 9: NEA; AlaEA. 10: Twentieth Century Study Club. 14: Acquis, reader serv. 15: 511 Fore ave, Monroeville Ok 36460.

WELCH, DARRELL P. b Gloversville NY 1 Ag 37. 4: Yvonne Krause. 5: SUNY (Albany) 54-59, 61-62 (Soc Studies) BA, 62-63 (Soc Studies) MA, 63-64 MLS. 7: Pfc US Army 59-61; Asst libn Auburn Commun Col 64-65; Acquis libn DenisonU 65-68; Rare bks libn State of NY. 9: ALA. 14: Rare bks. 15: Box 265, West Sand Lake NY 12196.

WELCH, JANET M (MARTIN). b Chicago Ill 12 Ja 45. 4: Harry William Welch. 5: Bucknell 63-67 (Sociol, Geog) AB; Rutgers 67-68 MLS. 7: Research asst Penn Lib Survey, Metuchen NJ 66; Comptroller Chicago Pub Lib Survey 68-69; Dir tech info ctr Nat Lead co Research Lab, Hightstown NJ 68-. 9: ASIS. 10: Phi Beta Kappa; Beta Phi Mu; Rutgers Grad Sch of Lib Serv Alum Assn. 14: Info systems. 15: 89 Rose st, Metuchen NJ 08840.

WELCH, MARGERY (MARY) (MILLER). b Celina Ohio. 4: Charle Edgar Welch. 5: Ohio Wesleyan U 23-27 (Sociol, Fr) AB; orbonne summer 30 certi; Columbia 35 BSLS. 6: Fr, Sp. 7: igh sch tchr Rockford (Ohio) ub sch 27-28; Soc wker Christamore House, Indianapolis 28-30; Libn Celina Pub LIB, Celina Ohio 30-55; Elem libn pub sch, Westfild NY 56-60; Asst libn SUNY Lib (Fredonia) 60-. 10: AAUW. 14: Catlg. 15: 54 Crandall st, Westfield NY 14787.

WELCH, TERESE M. b Rock Isl Ill 21 Je 42. 5: Col of St Francis 60-64 (Hist) AB; Rosary Col 64-66 (LS) MA. 7: Tchr & libn Commun High Sch, W Chicago Ill 64-66; Ref (soc sci) UNotre Dame (Ind) 66-67, Catlgr 66-67, Catlgr 67-68, Act hd ser sect 68-69, Hd ser sect 69-. 10: Cath Alumnae Club. 14: Catlg, ser. 15: 421 S 25th st, South Bend In 46615.

WELCH, THEODORE FRANKLYN. b Los Angeles Cal 10 O 33. 4: Letha Riter. 5: USoCal 51-54, 62-63 (Music, Asian Studies) BA; UCal (Berkeley) 63-65 MLS. 6: Japanese. 7: Flutist USAF NYC & Tokyo 58-62; Flutist San Francisco Ballet US Tour for two seasons 63, 65; Ref libn Fairfax Co Pub Lib, Fairfax Va 65; Catlgr Independent LC 65-67; USIS Reg libn E Asia-Pacific Area, Tokyo 67-69; Asst U libn pub serv Northwestern U (Evanston) 69-. 8: Del First Japan-US Conf on Lib & Info Sci in Higher Educ Tokyo 69. 9: ALA. 14: admin, intl rel. 15: Deering Lib, Northwestern Univ, Evanston Il 60201.

WELCH, THOMAS LARRY. b Merced Cal 26 Je 42. 5: Sacramento State Col 58-62 (Soc Sci) BA; UIll62-63 (LS) MS. 6: Sp, Portu. 7: Asst circ libn UIll (Urbana) 62-63; Circ libn UNM 64-66; Ref dept Pub Lib of New S Wales, Sydney Australia Summer 66; Pub serv libn Fresno State Col 66-. 9: ALA; SWLA; NMLA; CalLA (chm Memb Com); Yosemite Dist LA; Beta Phi Mu. 10: Beta Phi Mu; Org Amer Histns; Amer Assn Tchrs Spans Portu; Inst for For Study; Mod Lang Assn. 11: Freedom Found Medal. 14: Ref, admin, pub serv, Latin Amer materials. 15: 24391 Roberston blv, Chowchilla Ca 93610.

WELCH, WALTER L. b Syracuse NY 4 Ja 01. 4: Dolores Baxter. 5: Syracuse 40-46 (Landscape Arch) BA. 7: Assoc Prof SyracuseU 50-64, Curator & dir Lib Audio Archives & thomas Alva Edsion Foundation Re-Recording Lab 64-. 9: Assn Recorded Sound Collections (chm Fin Com); SAA (Prog Com). 10: Trustee, Empire State Theater and Musical Instrument Museum; Active in conserv wk. 12: Co-auth "From Tin Foil to Stereo" (59). 13: Yes. 14: Techniques of re-recording. 15: Syracuse Univ Audio Archives lib Annex 1009A E Water st, Syracuse NY 13210.

WELCOME, JENNIE DARLING. b Douglas Ariz 9 S 10. 5: Ariz State U 38 Educ, Com) BA in Ed; West Res 62 MS in LS; UAriz ext 49-64. 7: Tchr Sch Dist #50 Douglas Ariz 33; Circ asst Cleveland Pub Lib 42-43; Libn Mus Natural Hist, Cleveland 61-62; Sub libn Seattle Pub Lib summers 58, 60, 62, 63, Catlg Calg libn Matthews Lib Ariz State U summer 57; Catlg libn State Dept Lib & Archives, Phoenix summer 61; Sch libn Sch Dist #27, Douglas Ariz 33-. 8: Pub libn, Shelton Wash 66; Libn I Ore State Lib, Salem summer 67; Libn santa Ana Pub Lib, Santa Ana Cal summer 68. 9: NEA; ALA; ArizEA; ArizStateLA (pres 48-49; "Arizona Librarian"; ed 46-48, bus mgr 49-50; chm Nominations Com 60; Fed Rel Coord 57-58). 10: Delta Kappa Gamma; Kappa Delta Pi; Beta Phi Mu. 12: Ed Ariz Sch Lib Div; Ed "See Also Your Professional Library. 13: Yes. 14: Secondary sch libs, jr col libs. 15: 1504 San Antonio dr, Douglas Ariz 85607.

WELD, ELEANOR VIRGINIA. b NYC 11 Ag 16. 5: Park Col 35-39 (Fr) BA; U Denver 39-40 BS in LS. 6: Fr. 7: Summer asst 2 brs NY Pub Lib 40; Ref asst PRINCETON Theol Sem Lib 40-43; US Navy (WAVES Lt (jg) Armed Guard Sch, Shelton Va 43-46; Ref asst Princeton Theol Sem Lib 46-47; Princeton U Lib: Ref asst 47-59, Asst ref libn 59-64, 1st asst ref libn 64-. 9: ALA. 10: Princeton Soc of Musical Amateurs. 14: Ref. 15: 187 Ewing st, Princeton NJ 08540.

WELKER, DORIS M. b Cleveland 22 F 19. 5: Allegheny Col 37-39 (Eng); Youngstown U 39-43 (Eng, Music) BA, BMus; UMich summer 45 (Musi) UDenver summers 58-61 (LS) MA. 6: Ger, Lat. 7: Mus supv Fairfield Local Sch, Columbiana Ohio 43-45; Mus supv vocal Minerva pub schs, Minerva Ohio 45-46; Mus tchr & libn Jr High Sch, E Palestine Ohio 46-57; Mus & Eng tchr Woodrow Wilson High Sch, Youngstown Ohio 57-59; Libn Hillman Jr High Sch, Youngstown Ohio 59-63; Asst catlg libn Kent State U 63-66; Catlg libn Shaker Hts pub schs, Shaker Hts Ohio 66-. 9: ALA; No Ohio tech serv libns; NEA; OhioEA.; SHTA. 10: Sigma Alpha Iota; Delta Kappa Gamma. 13: Yes. 14: Catlg. 15: 20763 Ellacott pkwy apt 725, Warrensville Hts Oh 44128.

WELKER, MARY (BURT). b Moore County 20 S 42. 4: J Franklin Welker Jr. 5: Guilford Col 60-64 (Eng) BA; UNC (Chapel Hill) 64-65 MLS. 7: Y-a libn Greensboro Pub Lib, greensboro NC 65-67, Group serv libn 67-. 9: NCLA. 14: A-v materials, ref. 15: PO Box 37, Julian NC 27283.

WELLE, REV JACOB MSC. b Allentown Penn 22 My 25. 5: Sacred Heart Mission Sem 43-44; Sacred Heart Sem 45-47 (Philos), 47-51 (Theol); Rosary Col 58-61 MA in LS; Loyola U 60-61. 6: Lat, Ger. 7: Asst Pastor Holy Family Church, Nazareth Penn 51-53; Sacred Heart Mission Sem (Geneva Ill): Tchr 53-, Libn 56-, Rector 61-67; Asst libn Allentown Col 69-. 8: Provincial consul, US Province, Missionaries of the Sacred Heart 61-67. 9: ALA; CathLA. 14: Catlg, clsf. 15: MSC Seminary, Ctr Valley Pa 18034.

WELLER, ELIZABETH ANNA. b Dale Ind 13 Je20. 5: Ind State Tchrs Col 38-42 (Eng) BS; Peabody 43-47 (LS) MS; Ind State U 60, 65; Ind U 66-69. 6: Ger, Fr. 7: Libn Rockport High Sch, Rockport Ind 42-48; Lib asst Ind State Tchrs Col Lib 48-49, Libn Lab Sch 49-60; Head Tchg Materials Ctr Ind State U 60-61, Asst Prof of Lib Sci 61-. 8: State consul Hoosier Stud Libns Assn 62-66. 9: ALA; IndSchLA; Ind State Tchrs Assn; ASIS; IndASchL. 10: Altrusa Club; Delta Kappa Gamma; Zeta Tau Alpha; Alpha Beta Alpha; Pi Lambda Theta. 13: Yes. 14 Elem sch libs, child lit. 15: 203 S 26th st dr, Terre Haute Ind 47803.

WELLER, IDA (COOKSEY). b Henderson Ky 3 D 11. 5: West Ky State Col 29-31, 63; Ind State U 63; UIll(Chicago) 67. 7: Elem tchr Shepherdsville Ky 31-32; Elem tchr, Ft Knox Ky 34-40; Libn Deaconess Nurs Sch, Evansville Ind 63-. 15: 600 Edgar st Evansville Ind 47710.

WELLER, JOHN MARVIN. b Columbia Mo 28 D 40. 5: Knox Col 58-60, 61-62 (Pol Sci) BA; Syracuse (Florence Italy) 60-61; UIll 62-63 (LS) MS. 6: . 7: Clerk UIll Bkstore (Champaign) summer 59; Asst soc sci libn Okla State U 63-66; Coding clerk med record dept UOkLA Med Ctr 66-68; Catlgr Winnipeg Pub Lib, Winnipeg Man 68-. 9: ALA; CanLA. 10: Pi Sigma Alpha. 13: Yes. 14: Catlg. 15: 23 Frederick ave, St Vital 8 Man Can.

WELLINGER, KITTY (PEARL B). b Pittsville Md 24 S 09. 4: Karl E Wellinger. 5: West Md Col 27-31 (Music, Fr) BA; UMich 39; George Washington U 48; Madison Col 50-51 BLS. 6: Fr. 7: Tchr Pittsville High Sch, Pittsville Md 32-33; Tchr Margaret Brent High Sch, Helen Md 33-39, Tchr-libn 39-41; Personal sec Mgr Naval Powder Factory Hotel, Indian Head Md 41-44; Recreation & soc hostess 4th Serv Command War Dept, Camp Wheeler Ga 44-45; TCHR Alexandria pub schs Alexandria Va 47-50; Libn Carles Barrett Sch, Alexandria Va 50-. 9: NEA; ALA; VaLA; NoVaLA (treas 64-65); VaEA; Intl Assn Child Educ. 10: Zonta Club; Bus & Prof Womans Club; PTA; Alexandria EA; Alexandria Hosp Corp. 14: Catlg, ref. 15: 7925 Ft Hunt rd, Alexandria Va 22308.

WELLINGTON, FLORA H (ERMAN) MRS. b St Louis 13 Ap 20. 5: Col of William & Mary 36-41 (Math) BS; UNC 49-50 BS in LS. 7: Libn US Naval Med Center, Guam MI 47-49; Intern Rudolph Mats Med Lib, Tulane U 50-51; Asst libn in chg of catlg Mooney Mem Lib UTenn 51-53; Libn Fla State Bd of Health, Jacksonville Fla 54-55; umiami Sch of Med Lib: Asst libn 56-61, Act libn 61-62, Assoc libn 63-. 8: Consul, St Vincents Hosp Med Lib, Jacksonville Fla 55. 9: MedLA (chm Subcom on Internship 56-57); SLA; FlaLA; S Reg MedLA (sec-treas 64-65); Dade Co LA (pres 61-62). 14: Admin, ref, catlg. 15: 3120 SW 27th st, Miami Fl 33133.

WELLOCK, ELOISE GRACE. b Harbor Beach Mich 26 Ja 17. 5: East Mich U 35-39 (Eng, Hist) AB & Tchrs Certif; West Res 47-48 BSLS; UMich 53 AMLS. 7: Tchr Pub Sch, Harbor Beach Mich 41-43; USNR Wave Y(T), 1/c, US 43-45; Libn Flint Northern High Sch, Flint Mich 48-. 8: Planning com for Northwest High Sch Lib (Flint Mich) 63-64; City & bldg curr com 61; Prof Day CONF Com 64, 65, Planning Com for a new Northern High Sch 67-68. 9: ALA; NEA; MichEA; MichASchL: MichLA; Flint Lib Club. 10: Sorosis Club, Alpha Gamma Delta, Epsilon Sigma Omicron. 12: Co-auth "Library Methods Course Outline (65). 14: High sch, ya. 15: 412 W Second ave apt J3, Flint Mi 48503.

WELLS, ALICE (BEEBE). b NYC 1 N 17. 5: St Johns U 40-46 BA. 6: Fr. 7: Stat analyst Home Insur Co, NYC 36-44; Libn Amer Airlines, NYC 44-47, Libn 48-. 9: SLA (NY Chap: chm Constit & By-Laws Com; Asst chm Spring Dist; Directory of Greater NY Com; Recr & Train Com). 13: Yes. 14: Ref. 15: Amer Airlines Inc 633 Third ave, NYC 10017.

WELLS, DOROTHY V(IOLA). b Boulder Colo 6 F 16. 5: UWyo 34-38 (Hist, Eng) BA; UIll 38-39 BSLS. 6: Sp, Fr. 7: Stud asst UWyo 34-38 & summer 39; Asst libn documents Ft Hays Kan State Col 39-42; Act head libn loan dept UWyo 42; UCLA: Libn Bur of Govt Res 42-52, Libn Bur of Govt Research and the John Randolph Haynes and Dora Haynes Found Collection 52-62, Libn Govt & Pub Affairs Reading Room & John Randolph Haynes and Dora Haynes Found Collection 62-. 8: Guest seaker UCLA Sch of Lib Serv 61-. 9: SLA (So Cal Chap: chm Soc Sci Group 46-47, v-pres 48-49); Coun of Planning Lins; West Governmental Res Assn (chm Exhib Com 49 & 51) 10: Cal State Employees Assn; Pi Gamma Mu. 13: Yes. 14: Ref wk (local govt & pub affairs). 15: Govt & Pub Affairs Reading Room UCLA, Los Angeles 90024.

WELLS, ELGIN ARTHUR. b Saskatoon Sak Can 24 Ap 41. 4: Susan Margaret Johnston. 5: UAlta 62-65 (Eng) BA; McGill 65-67 MLS. 7: Research asst Canadian Experimental Farm, Lethbridge 60-62; Lt Royal Can Armoured Corps, Edmonton 62-65; Ref libn Lond pub Lib, London Can 67-68; Co libn Elgin Co, St Thomas Can 68-. 9: CanLA (treas info Serv Sect 69). 14: Pub serv. 15: 9 Gladstone ave, St Thomas Ont Can.

WELLS, ELLEN B. b Berlin Ger 23 Jl 34. 5: Cornell U 52-56 (Art Hist); Okla State U of Agric & Applied Sci 56-57 (Art Hist) AB; UCal (Berkeley) 61-63 MLS; UCLA 63-64 (Med Lib Internship). 6: Fr, Ital. 7: Lib asst Cornell U 52-56; Med libn Mountain View Gen Hosp, Tacoma Wash 58-60; Clerk III Tacoma Pub Lib, Tacoma Wash 59-60; Lib asst Med Lib UCal (San Francisco) 60-61; Lib asst acquis dept Gen Lib UCal (Berkeley) 61-63; Intern-trainee Biomed Lib UCLA 63-64; Catlgr of 17th Cent materials His of Med Div NLM Bethesda Md 64-65, Curator of prints & photographs collection 65-68; Assoc Osler Lib McGill 68-. 8: Staff, Lib/USA NY Worlds Fair, 65. 9: MedLA(Hist Med Luncheon CTEE 66-68). 12t; exhibit catlg: "Animal Experimentation in Medicine through the 18th Century (65). 13: Yes. 14: Rar bks catlg, acquis. 15: Osler Lib McGill Univ, Montreal 109 PQ Can.

WELLS, FRANCES DEHNERT. b Lewistown Mont 1 Ja 26. 5: All Saints Col 43-44 (Eng); Col of William & Mary summer 44 (LS); UMont 44-46 (Eng, LS); Rocky Mountain Col 46-47 (Eng) BA; UDenver 48-49 (LS); Mont State U summer 59, 67, 68 (LS); East Mont Col 62-63 (Educ) MS. 7: Tchr Colstrip High Sch, Colstrip Mont 47-48; Libn Albuquerque High Sch, Albuquerque NM 49-51; Libn Cheyenne High Sch, Cheyenne Wyo 51-52; Tchr-libn Belgrade High Sch, Belgrade Mont 54-56; Libn Helena Sr High Sch, Helena Mont 56-61; Grad asst Lib Sci East Mont Col summer 62; Libn Billings West High Sch, Billings Mont 61-. 8: Mem of Sch Lib A-V Com Mont State Dept of Pub Instruction 58-; Consul "Standard Catalgo for High School Liraries, 8th ed & supv; "Standard Catalog for Junior High School Libraies; ALA-AASchL Lib Devel Proj 61; Instr in lib sci Mont State U, summer 65-66-67-68. 9: ALA (Recr Netwk rep Mont);-AASchL; NEA; MontLA; Mont ASchL; MontE A (chm 1960-61). 10: AAUW; Delta Kappa Gamma; Alpha Chi Omega; DAR. 13: Yes. 14: Ref, high sch libs, col inst. 15: 2112 Fairview pl, Billings Mont 59102.

WELLS, FRANK BENJAMIN. b Barre Mass 4 My 10. 5: NYU 49-56 (Eng, Classics); Clark U 56-60, 61 (Hist) BS, 61-63 (Classics) BA. 6: Lat, Fr, Gk. 7: (Pvt-Sgt) US Army, Hawaii 28-31; Pvt-Sgt US Army DEML-OR, US 33-41; (2nd to 1st Lt) Adjutant Gens Dept Res; Orders & ser Clark U Lib 56-64; Order Prep Sect LC 64-66, Photoreproduction specialist 67-. 9: ALA; Capitol Hill Commun Coun. 14: Acquis. 15: 11 Second st NE, Wash DC 20002.

WELLS, JAMES M. b Charleston W Va 4 N 17. 5: NorthwesternU 34-38 (Eng) BS; Columbia 38-39 (Eng) MA, 40-41, 46-49 (Eng). 6: Fr. 7: Eng instr WVaU 39-41; Lt USNR, Paciic 42-46; Eng instr Columbia 46-49; Cu 42-46; Eng instr Columbia 46-49; Custodian Wing Foundation Newberry Lib, Chicago 51-, Assoc dir 65-. 8: Tchr: UChicago Sch of Lib Sci 62, UIll (Ext), Rare Bk Libnship 68. 9: BSA (chm Mid-West Reg). 10: Caxton Club; Grolier Club; Soc of Typographic Arts; Societe Typographique de France (hon mem); Rounce and Coffin (hon mem); Mod Lang Assn; Renaissance Eng Text Soc; Renaissance Soc Amer. 11: Fellow, ACLS 41, 49-51. 12: Ed -opera di.Tagliente" (52); Auth "The Scholar Printers" (64); "The Circle of knowledge" (68); Ed "Newberry Library Bulletin". 13: Yes. 14: Rare bks, printing hist, eng lit. 15: Newberry Lib 60 W Walton st, Chicago Il 60610.

WELLS, LOIS ELIZABETH. b Quincy Ill 3 Jl 24. 5: Swarthmore 41-43; Bryn Mawr 43-45 (Sociol) BA; UParis 47-48 (Fr) Certif; Bryn Mawr 51-52 (Pol Sci); Drexel 55-56 MSLS. 6: Fr, Ger. 7: Admin asst Intergovtl Com on Refugees, Wash DC 45-46; Admin asst Coun of Relief Agencies, Berlin 46-47; Field Wker Amer Nriends Serv Com Darmstadt Germany & Phila 48-51; Ref asst UPenn Lib 56-57, Jr prof lib asst Sch of Soc Wk 57-59; Soc wk libn Bryn Mawr Col 59-63; Asst MacMurray Col Lib 63-64; Nursing sch libn Jacksonville State Hsp, Jacksonville Itl 64-68, Act chief lib dept 68, Chief Learning Media Ctr 68-. 9: ALA; IllLA. 10: AAUW; Beta Sigma Phi; Bus & Prof Womens Club. 14: Spec libs. , (Hosp libs). 15: 1207 W Walnut st, Jacksonville Il 62650.

WELLS, MARION J (PIERCE). b SWANTON Vt 15 Je 10. 5: Wheaton Col (Mass) 31 (Eng Lit) AB; Syracuse 60 MS in LS; Ind U 66. 6: Fr, Lat. 7: Asst libn SUNY Brockport 60-63 Assoc libn 63-65, Act dir 65, 68-69, Assoc libn 65-68. 9: ALA NEA; NYLA; NY State Tchrs Assn; Faculty Assn SUNY; Rochester Reg Research Lib Coun Hd Libns SUNY. 10: AAUP; Beta Phi Mu. 13: Bk review ed "The Library-College Journal". 14: Pub serv, ref. 15: 57 College st, Brockport NY 14420.

WELLS, MERLE (WILLIAM). b Lethbridge Alta Can 1 D 18. 5: Boise Col 37-39; Col Ida 39-41 (Hist) AB; UCal (Berkeley) 41-42 (Hist) MA, 46-50 (Hist) PhD. 7: Instr in hist Col Ida 42-46; Assoc prof of hist Alliance Col 50-58; Assoc prof of hist Boise Col 65-; Histn & archvist Ida State Archives, Ida State Histl Soc, Boise Ida 59-68, Dir 68-. 8: Consul histn Ida State Histl Soc Boise 56-59, Barton, Stoddard, Smith & Milholli, Boise 57-58. 9: AHA; SAA; Amer Assn State & Loc Hist; West Hist Assn; IdaLA; PNLA; Coun on Reg Res in Progress; chm 68-69). 10: AAUP; Ida Coun tf Churches; Nat Coun of Churches; Ida Farm wkers Serv Inc; Bd Dir Ida State Employees Credit Union. 12: "History of Idaho with M D Beal (59); "Rush to Idaho (61) "Gold Camps and Silver Cities (64); Ed "Idaho Yesterdays. 13: Yes. 14: Archives. 15: 1325 Longmont, Boise Ida 83706.

WELLS, MURIEL MARGARET (HOLMES). b Aberdeen Sask Can 23 F 14. 5: USask 32-35 (Math) BA, 35-36 (Educ) Certif & Tchg Certif, 39-40 (Educ) BEd; McGill 48-49 BLS. 7: Tchr Sch Bd, Waldheim Sask 36-39; Tchr Collegiate Bd, Saskatoon Sask 39-41, 46-48; Tchr Govt Correspondenc Sch, Regina Sask 41-42; WRCNS Operations Merchant Shipping Liaison & recriting 42-45; Catlgr Tchrs Col (NY) 49-50; Catlgr Fraser-Hickson Inst, Monteal 50-53; Libn Shell Oil Co of Can, Montreal 53-55; CWAC asst adjutant with RCEME Militia in chg of CWACS 57-58; Libn MacDonald Nol McGill U 59-. 9: CanLA; SLA; QueLA. 10: McGill Univ Lib Staff Assn; McGill Ass Univ Tchrs. 14: Admin. 15: Box 256 MacDonald Col PO, Quebec Can.

WELLS, NANCY ELIZABETH. b Winnipeg Can 3 My 37. 5: UManitoba -61 (Eng) BA; UBC 65-66 BLS. 7: Libn UManitoba Libs 66-. 9: CanLA; ALA. 13: Yes. 14: Col libs, ref. 15: 6B-220 Hugo st, Winnipeg 9 Manitoba Can.

WELSH, DORIS V. b Avalon Penn 3 O 07. 5: Fla State Col for Women 26-30 (ECON) AB; Peabody 32-33 BS in LS; UIll 45-46 MS in LS. 6: Ger, Fr, Sp, Portu. 7: High Sch libn: Frostproof Fla 31-34, Key West Fla 34-36, FRANKLIN La 36-37, Dania Fla 37-39, Easley SC 39-43; Catlgr UFla 43-47; Catlgr Newberry Lib Chicago 47-57, Head catlg dept 57-65, Catlgr 65-. 9: ALA; BSA. 10: Beta Phi Mu. 12: Comp "Checklist of Philippine Linguistics in Newberry Library" (50), "Checklist of French Political Pamphlets in Newberry Library" (50), ALOG OF THE William MB Greenlee Collection and Other Portuguese Materials in the Newberry Library" (53), "A Second Checklist of French Political Pamphlets in the Newberry Library" (55), "A Catalog of Printed Materials Relating to the Philippine Islands in the Newberry Library" (59). 14: Catlg, rare bks. 15: 8 W Oak apt B2, Chicago Il 60610.

WELSH, HELEN C. b Albany NY 20Je 07. 5: Col of St Rose 27-31 (Eng) AB cum laude; Columbia summers 31-34 (LS) BS; NY State Col for Tchrs 41-42 (Eng) AM; Columbia 46-47 (LS) MS. 6: Fr. 7: Lib asst NY State Lib 25-32; Asst libn Albany High Sch, Albany NY 32-35; Libn Schuyler High Sch, Albany NY 34-55; Instr Lib Sci Marywood Col 45; Assoc Prof Lib Sci SUNY (Albany) NY summers 45-63; Instr Lib Sci Col of St Rose ext 54; Libn North High Sch, Valley Stream NY 55-59; Head Libn Seaford High Sch, Seaford NY 59-66; Libn Prof Lib Seaford Sch Dist, Seaford Ny 66-69; Dir of sch lib, Seaford NY 69-. 8: Consul & Writerof mfilmstrip on Bus Ed for State Ed Dept, Albany 54; Asstship Columbia U Sch Lib Serv 46-47; Producer 16mm film for Voc Homemaking for Schuyler HS 55; Producer 16mm film for Valley Stream Bd of Educ 59. 9: ALA; NYLA (pres Sch Libs Sect 55); CathLA (pres Albany Unit 48-49); NY State Tchrs Assn; Nassau-Suffolk Sch LA. 10: Delta Epsilon Sigma; Metro Motion Picture Club of NY; Intl Fed of Cath Alumnae; Inst of Amateur Cinematographers; Photographic Soc of Amer; Soc of Amer Cinematographers. 13: Yes. 14: Sch lib admin, Hist of bks & printing, org media ctrs. 15: 44 Parkwood st, Albany NY 12208.

WELSH, JAMES ANTHONY. b DeGraff Minn 21 Ja 28. 5: Minn 51-55 (Internat Rel) BA; UWash 60-62 (LS) ML. 6: Japanese. 7: Br libn Seattle Pub Lib 62-. 9: ALA; Wash State LA. 10: Jackson Street Commun Coun; Garfield Commun Coun. 14: Pub serv, Black bibliog. 15: 484 Lake Washington blvd, East Seattle Wa 98102.

WELSH, WILLIAM JOSEPH. b Weatherly Penn 15 N 19. 4: Winifred Hatfield. 5:UNotre Dame 37-40 (Philos) AB, 40-41

(Law). 7: (Maj) US Air Force 41-47; LC: Lib asst Cooperative Acquis Proj 47-48, Head Order Unit Order Div 48-49, Head Order Sect Order Div 49-52, Head EEAI Proj Exch & Gift Div 52-58, Exec Off Prod Dept 58-60, Assoc dir of admin 60-64, Assoc dir Processing Dept 64-66, Dir processing dept 68-. 8: Chm Fed Lib Com Task Force on Acquis of Lib Materials & Correl of Fed Lib Resources 65-; V-chm LCs Acquis Com 64-; LC rep ASAZ39 64-; Mem 6 other LC coms 59-; LC rep Jt Com on Union Lists of Sers 67-; Mem Decimal Clsf Edl Policy Com; consul NY Pub Lib. 9: ALA; DCLA (Bus Mgr 57-59). 11: Several LC commendations & Outstanding Performance ratings 49-57. 13: Yes. 14: Acquis, admin, catlg. 15: 4805 Edgefield rd, Bethesda Md 20014.

WELT, ISAAC D. b Montreal Can 13 My 22. 4: Rhoda Gloria Litwin. 5: McGill 40-44 (Biochem) BS, 44-45 (Anatomy) MS; Yale 46-49 (Biochem) PhD. 6: Fr, Ger, Hebrew, Yiddish, Ital. 7: Research assoc Pub Health Research Inst, NYC 49-51; Asst Prof of Biochem Baylor U Col of Med 51-53; Research assoc Chem-Biol Coordination Center NAS-NRC, Wash DC 53-55; Dir Cardiovascular Lit Proj, Wash DC 55-; Staff Div of Med Sci Nat Acad of Sci, Wash DC 55-61; Assoc dir Inst for Advancement of Med Communication, Wash DC 61-64; Deputy dir Center for Tech & Admin & Prof info sci American U 64-. 8: Consultant for US Govt 65-. 9: ASIS (chm Potomac Valley Chap 60-61); Sci & Tech Writers & Publishers (pres DC Chap 67); SLA; MedLA; ACS (Div Chem Lit); Drug Info Assn Found; Bd of Trustees 66-68). 10: AAUP; AAAS; Sigma XI; Amer Med Writers Assn. 12: Assoc ed "Am. Documentation (64-); Ed bd "Methods of Information in medicine (61-); Ed "Index-Handbook of Cardiovascular Agents v 1-3 (60-). 13: Yes. 14: Indexing of sci lit, tchg documentation & info sci. 15: Center for Tech & Admin, The American Univ, Mass & Neb aves NW, Wash DC 20016.

WELTER, GLORIA JEAN. b S Bend Ind 9 S 39. 5: Ball State U 57-61 (Lang Arts) BA in ED; West Mich U summer 63, 64-65 (LS) MA, summer 68; State Col at Framingham spring 66; Boston U summer 67. 7: Libn Manchester Jr High Sch, Middletown Ohio 61-64; Libn UNotre Dame (Ind) summer 65; Libn Pollard Jr High Sch, Needham Mass 65-67; Libn Needham High Sch, Needham Mass 67-69; Libn Devotion Sch, Brookline Mass 69-. 9: ALA; NEA-DAVI; NESLA; MassSchLA (sec; co-chm Standards Com); MassTA; Mass A-V Assn. 10: Kappa Delta Pi; Beta Phi Mu. 14: Ref. 15: 52 Jacqueline rd apt 16, Waltham Ma 02154.

WELTSCH, RUBEN ERNEST. b Berlin Germany 10 F 21. 4: Patricia Jacobs. 5: Amherst 38-42 (Pol Sci) BA; Columbia 41-45 (Libnship) BS; UColo 54-56 (Hist) MA, 56-61 (Hist) PhD. 6: Ger, Fr, Ital, Czech. 7: Ser libn Amherst Col 43-46; Ref libn Kenyon Col 46-49; Ref libn RiceU 49-52; Ref libn UCincinnati 52-54; Libn SUNY (Stony Brook) 58-63, Asst dir collections 63-67, Act dir libs 67-68, Dir libs & assoc prof of hist 68-. 8: Libn UNESCO Tchrs' Sem, Garden City NY summer 48; Part-time instr of German, UColo & SUNY 56-60; Adj assoc prof of Hist SUNY (Stony Brook) 65-68. 9: ALA; AHA; NYLA; SuffolkCoLA; NY Tech Serv Libns. 10: Phi Alpha Theta; Suffolk Museum; Civic assn of the Setaukets; NAACP. 12: "Archbishop John of Jenstein (1348-1400)"; "Papalism, Humanism and Reform in Pre-Hussite Prague" (68). 13: Yes. 14: Admin, lib res, tech serv. 15: 8 Yorktown rd, Setauket NY 11733.

WELTY, GLADYS MARIE (WEAVER) (MRS). b Shipshewana Ind 27 Ag 05. 5: Internat Bus Col (Ft Wayne Ind) 30 (Gen Bus); West Mich U 44 (Eng, Sci) BS, 55 (LS) MS. 7: Clerk Gen Store, Shipshewana Ind 23-24; Elem tchr, Sturgis Mich 25-43; Elem libn, Sturgis pub schs, Sturgis Mich 55-. 8: Coun High Sch Lib Wkshop, West Mich U summers 60-64; Hd libn Federally sponsored enrichment program for elem sch studs, Sturgis Mich summers 66-69. 9: NEA; MichEA; MichASchL MichLA. 10: PEO; Bus & Prof Org; Beta Phi Mu. 14: Ref, chg lib sci. 15: 201 N Lakeview, Sturgis Mich 49091.

WELWOOD, RONALD (JOSEPH). b Penticton BC Can 14 F 40. 4: Frances Josephine Clay. 5: UBC 63-66 (Geog) BA, 66, 67 (Sociol) BLS. 7: Ref libn Nat Lib of Can, Ottawa 67-68, Hd newspaper sect 68-. 9: CanLA. 10: Profess Inst Pub Serv Canada, Libns Gp. 11: Librarian-in-training prog Govt of Can 66-67. 12: Ed "Centennial issues of Canadian newspapers" (8 microfilm reels). 14: Ref, newspapers. 15: 122 Stewart st, Ottawa Ont Can.

WEMBER, BERTHA (CLAIRE KORNBERG). b NYC 6 Mr 22. 4: Lawrence Wember. 5: Brooklyn Col 39-43 (Eng) BA; Pratt 46-47 BLS; Brooklyn Col 47-48 (Eng). 7: Eng thr NYC high schs 43-44; Desk asst chid libn DC Pub Lib 44-46; Asst circ dept Brooklyn Col 41-48; Child libn DC Pub Lib 48-49, 1st asst lang & lit dept 49-51; Catlgr Br 1st ast, head of foreign lang collection, asst in educ film dept Detroit Pub Lib 51-8, 59-60; Libn Temple Israel, Deroit 62-; Catlgr Oak Park Sch Dist, Oak Park Mich 68-. 9: Jewish LA (rec sec 64-). 10: Jewish Commun Center; Jewish Commun Coun; LWV. 14: Ref, catlg, bk sel, child serv. 15: 17300 Prairie, Detroit Mi 48221.

WEMBER, LAWRENCE. b W New York NJ 1 My 21. 4: Bertha Kornberg. 5: Brooklyn Col 38-42 (Eng) BA; Columbia 47-48 BS in LS. 7: Asst econ dept NY Pub Lib summer 48; Readers adv DC Pub Lib 48-51; Detroit Pub Lib: Asst chief tech dept 51-55, Br libn 55-56, Chief Mun Ref Lib 56-68; Hd libn Oak Park (Mich) Pub Lib 68-. 9: ALA; MichLA. 14: Ref, admin. , tech serv. 15: 17300 Prairie, Detroit 48221.

WENDEL, CLARA ELIZABETH. b Harvey Ill 1 Je 04. 5: Rollins Col 21-22; Fla State Col for Women 22-25 (Mod Langs) AB; UMich 36-38 ABLS; UChicago 45-46 AMLS. 7: Tchr pub schs, Winter Garden Fla 25-28; Tchr Mem Jr High Sch, Orlando Fla 29-30; Supv of art pub schs, Winter GARDEN Fla 30-37; Libn Orlando Sr High Sch, Orlando Fla 38-41; Instr Fla State Col for Women 41-43; Dir Orlando Pub tlib, Orlando Fla 43-. 8: Instr Lib Sch Fla State U summer 50. 9: ALA (chm Friends of the Lib Com 61); Adult Educ Assn; FlaLA (pres 49-50); SELA (Exec Bd 57-60); Treas 69-70). 10: AAUW; LWV; Mental Health Assn; Orlando Art Assn; Coun of Arts & Sci of Central Fla; Country Club of Orlando; Rosalind Club; Fla Hist Soc. 13: Yes. 14: Admin. 15: 328 Colombo circle, Orlando Fla 32804.

WENDER, RUTH (WISENBERG). b Laurel Miss 27 My 19. 4: Simon H Wender. 5: Rice 35-39 (Eng, Fr); UOkla 66-68 MLS; Med libn certif class 1 from Med Lib Assn. 7: Tchr Houston Independent Sch Dist Houston Tex 39-41; Off Wisenberg Ins Agcy Houston Tex 41-42; Interlib loan libn UOkla Med Ctr Lib 68-. 9: MedLA; OklaEA; OklaLA. 10: Phi Beta Kappa; Pi Delta Phi; Beta Phi Mu. 14: Interlib loan, ref. 15: 2614 Meadowbrook dr, Norman Ok 73069.

WENGER, LILLIAN GERTRUDE (SUTTON). b Hamilton Ontario Can 3 S 18. 4: Larry Wenger. 5: McMaster U 38-40 (Pol Econ); UToronto ext 53-58 (Art, Archeol) BA; Osgood Hall Law Sch 58-59; UToronto 64-65 BLS. 6: Fr. 7: Sub-prof bkmob NY Pub Lib 60-64, Libn child room 65-66; Adult libn Forest Hill (Ont) Pub Lib 66; Wellesley Hosp Med Lib, Toronto Ont 67; Sub staff tchr-libn N York (Ont) secondary schs 67-. 9: CanLA; OntLA. 15: 101 Old Forest Hill rd, Toronto 10 Can.

WENGER, MILTON BARRY. b Brooklyn NY 8 S 18. 4: Sara Krimmer. 5: Miami U (Ohio)39-41 (Eng, Biol) BS; High Point Col 37-39; Peabody 41-44 BSLS, 41-44 (Chem, Biol) MS. 6: Fr, Ger. 7: Med abstractor E R Squibb & Sons, Brooklyn NY 44; Tchr-libn Lake Grove Sch, Lake Grove NY 45-46; Supv sci libs NYU Washington Square Lib 46-50; Tech libn NY QM Procurement Agency, NYC 50-55; Tech libn & Lit Chem Picatinny Arsenal US Ord, Dover NJ 55-56; Tech libn & Ed Vitro Eng Co, NYC 56-60; Mgr Info Ctr Halcon Intl Inc, NYC 60-. 8: Abstractor, "Chemical Abstracts 55-; Bk reviewer "Library Journal" 57-; Lib consul 68-. 9: ACS; SLA (NY Chap; chm Biol Sect 45-46; Exec Bd Sci-Tech Group 63-64); ASIS; Nat Microfilm Assn. 10: Brooklyn Philharmonia Choral Soc; Phi Delta Kappa. 14: Ref, lit searches, info retrieval, indexing, patent searching, clsf, bibliog. 15: 1411 E 34th st, Brooklyn NY 11210.

WENMAN, LOIS M. b New Vernon NJ. 5: NYPub Lib Sch 23 Certif. 6: Fr. 7: Assoc Morristown Pub Lib 21-22; Newark Pub Lib: Ref libn 23-30, Head pamphlet & Info files 30-44, Period libn 44-57; Libn Fairleigh Dickinson 59-61; Morris (NJ) Free Lib 61-, Col of St Elizabth 62-. 10: Nt Audobon Soc; NJ Audobon Soc; NJ Hist Soc; Morris Co (NJ) Hist Soc; Torrey Botanical Club; Summit (NJ) Nature Club; Morris (NJ) Nature Club; Watnong Garden Club. 12 Ed "List of SUBJECT Headings for the Information File (46). 12: Ed "List of Subject Headings for Information Files" (3rd, 4th, 5th eds). 14: Subj hdings for vertical files, govt docs. 15: Morris Co Free Lib, Morristown NJ 07960.

WENSLEY, DOROTHY (DEVLIN). b White Plains NY 15 S 24. 5: Col of New Rochelle 42-46 (Eng) BA; C W Post Col LIU 63-65 MLS. 7: Asst child libn E Meadow Pub Lib, E Meadow NY 64-. 15: 125 E Hempstead Gardens dr, West Hempstead NY 11552.

WENSRICH, CARL J. b Calgary Alta Can. 4: Jeanne Patrecia Clairmore. 5: UCal (Berkeley) 45-49 (Liberal Arts) BA, 49-50 BLS. 6: Ger. 7: Stud Stack Supv UCal(Berkely) 46-50; Head circ dept UCal(Santa Barbara) 50-55; Soc sci libn

Pub Lib, Portland Ore 55-56; Engnr research libn UCal(Richmond EFS) 56-59; Head prof serv Lawrence Radiation Lab, Livermore Cal 59-64; Head reader serv UCal(Santa Cruz) 64-. 13: Yes. 14: Ref, rare bks, lc hist. 15: 1980 Newport, Santa Cruz Ca 95060.

WENTEN, RUTH P. b Brooklyn NY 28 Ap 17. 4: Wolfgang C Wenten. 5: Central Conn State Col 33-37 (Educ) BE; So Conn State Col 59-64 (LS) MS. 7: Lib asst Bridgeport Pub Lib, Bridgeport Conn 38-42; Tchr Bidgeport Bd of Educ, Bridgeport Conn 42-43; Tchr Fairfield Bd of Educ, Fairfild Conn 55-61, Lib tchr 61-. 8: Supv tchr for lib studs So Conn State Col; Reviewer "Scholastic Teacher Magazine. 9: ALA; NEA; Conn Sch LA; (Exec Bd 68-69) 10: Fairfield EA; Fairfield Hist Soc; Park Ave, Temple Lib Com. 13: Yes. 14: Child & ya bks, multi-media. 15: 210 Barry Scott dr, Fairfield Conn 06432.

WENTROTH, MARY ANN. b Jasper Co Mo 31 O 14. 5: UOkla 32-36 BA in LS. 7: Lib asst Okla City Lib 36; Libn Mangham High Sch, Mangham La 36-37; Harding Br Okla City Pub Lib 37-42; Libn Classen Br Okla City Pub Lib 42-43, Asst in child dept 43-48, Head child dept main lib 49-56; Coord child serv Oklahoma Co Libs 56-66, Child materials specialist 66-67; Child serv specialist Okla Dept of Libs, Okla City 67-. 9: ALA; -CLA (Coun 56-57, mem &/or chm 4 coms 53-61); -CSD (mem &/or chm 3 coms 60-); SWLA (chm child and YP sect 51-52 & 69-70); OklaLA (pres 62-63; Exec Bd 52-53 & 63-64, sec 51-52, treas 66-68; chm child & YP Div 60-61, mem 2 coms 68-). 13: Yes. 14: Child serv in pub libs. 15: 3216 NW 44, Oklahoma City Ok 73112.

WENTWORTH, CHARLOTTE BROWN. b Everett Mass 23 Ja 05. 4: Carl Merrick Wentworth. 5: Smith 24-27 (Bot) AB. 7: Lib asst Ramsey Pub Lib, Ramsey NJ 56-58; Lib asst Paramus Pub Lib, Paramus NJ 58-59, Catlgr 59-60, Child libn 60-62; Libn Cornwall Lib, Cornwall Conn 62-64; Libn Kent Sch, Kent Conn 64-. 8: Coord planning com Paramus Pub Lib & Paramus Sch Libs, Paramus NJ. 9: ALA; N ELA; ConnLA. 10: High Sch Curriculum Lay Com to Fairlawn (NJ) Bd of Educ; Educ Com, Fairlawn LWV; Trustee Fairlawn Bd of Educ. 14: Admin. 15: Great Hollow rd, West Cornwall Ct 06796.

WENZEL, DIANE RAE. b Jersey City NJ 22 N 44. 5: URochester 62-66 (Hist) AB; Drexel 67-69 MSLS. 7: Lib trainee Free Lib of Phila 66-68, Tech 68-69, Child libn I 69-. 9: ALA; PennLA. 14: Child serv. 15: 200 Locust st apt 15A, Philadelphia Pa 19106.

WERES, ROMAN. b Paryshche Ukraine 27 N 07. 4: Eugenia Sokolovsky. 5: Law School ulviv (Ukraine) 26-30 ML; Ukrainian Free U (Munich) 46-57 Dr Jur; West Mich U 57-58 MALS. 6: Ukrainian, Polish, Ger, Russian. 7: Attorney at Law, Ukraine 31-44; Catlgr Pub Lib, Adrian Mich 58-59; Catlgr NorthwesternU Law Lib 59-60; Asst libn Presbyterian-St Lukes Sch of Nurs 60-66, Libn 66-68; Asst libn Rush Med College Lib 68-. 8: Libn Ukrainian Museum of Chicago. 9: MedLA; Assn of Ukrainian Libns in US (pres). 12: Comp "The Ukraine; Selected References in the English Langauge" (61); Comp "Index of the Ukrainian Essays in Collections Published outside the Iron Curtain"; Issues for yrs 51-62, 63-64, 65, 66, 67 Microfilm; Univ Microfilms Inc. 14: Catlg, bibliog. 15: 3306 W Crystal, Chicago Il 60651.

WERLE, GERTRUDE MARILYN. b Saskatoon Sask Can 17 O 39. 5: USask 57-58, 59-60 (Eng) BA; Toronto 61-62 BLS. 7: Lib asst Prov Lib, egina Sask 60-61; Libn Med Lib USask 62-63; Catlgr Pub Lib, Calgary Alta 63-65; Catlgr lib serv centre Calgary Sch Bd, Calgary Alta 65-66; Catlgr, Ft William Ont; Pub Lib 66-68, centralized processing Northwestern Reg Lib 68-. 9: CanLA; AltaLA (Coun 65-66); CalgaryLA; OntLA; IPLO. 14: Catlg. 15: Northwestern Regional Lib System, 910 Victoria ave, Fort William Ont Can.

WERNER, EDWARD COOPER. b Piqua Ohio 8 Je 15. 4: Neva Jo Mills. 5: Ind U 34-39 (Bus) BS; UIll 39-40 (LS) BS, 50-54 (LS) MS; NM West Col 46-59; Winona Sch of Photography 63, 65 (Port Photog). 7: Asst law libn Ind U 34-39; Asst libn Pub Lib, Bloomington Ind 40-41; Libn Wabash Col 41-43; Dept libn Ind U 43-44; Accountant E I DuPont, Hanford Wash 44-45; Reporter "Daily Dispatch, Douglas Ariz 45-46; Libn & Dir of a-v West NM U 46-. 8: A-v consul USOE, Wash DC 61-62; A-v consul, UPittsburgh, 64; Lib bdg consul, Educ Facilities Lab, 63; Furniture design consul, Fleetwood Mfg Co, Zeeland Mich, 60; Lib bldg consul, Odell & MacConnell Assocs, Stanford U 65. 9: ALA; NEA-DAVI; NMLA (past pres). 10: Prof Photographers of Amer; Amer Radio Relay League; NM Photographes Assn. 13: Yes. 14: Admin, a-v, bldg & furniture design. 15: P O Box 246, Silver City NM 88061.

WERNER, GLORIA (STOLZOFF). b Seattle Wash 12 D 40. 4: Newton Davis Werner. 5: Oberlin 58-61 (Fr) BA; UWash 61-62 MSLS; UCLA 62-63 Grad Train Program in Med libnship. 6: Fr. 7: Ref libn UCLA Biomed Lib 63-64, Asst hd pub serv dept 64-66, hd ref div 66-67, Hd pub serv dept 68-; Asst libn Wellcome Hist Med Lib, London England 67-68. 9: MedLA (Med Lib Gp So Cal: chm Contin Educ Com 66-67, chm Nomin Com 68-69). 14: Ref. 15: UCLA Biomedical Lib Ctr for Health Sci, Los Angeles Ca 90024.

WERNER, JOYCE COLLINS. b Baton Rouge La. 5: LSU 51 (Eng) BA, 53 (LS) MA. 6: Fr, Sp. 7: Asst ref libn Okla State U 53-55; Asst ref libn UIll(Urbana) 55-62; Ref libn Emory U 62-. 9: SELA; Atlanta Lib Club; GaLA. 10: Beta Phi Mu. 14: Ref. 15: 1410 E Rock Springs rd NE, Atlanta 30306.

WERNER, SISTER MARY DIONETTE CSSF. b Cuman Poland 20 S 29. 5: Loyola of Chicago 49-62 9educ) BS; St Francis Col (Joliet) summer 62, UMinn summer 63; Villanova 64-69 MSL. 6: Polish. 7: v-chm NoIll Unit Catholic Lib Assn, Chicago 67-68, Chm 68-69; Supv-consul Felician Lib Serv, Chicago 65-; Tchr & libn St Wenceslaus Sch, Chicago 65-. 8: Consul, Felician Lib Serv 65-. 9: CathLA (No Ill Unit: past v-chm & chm). 10: Chicago Jr High Tchrs Assn. 14: Catlg, clsf, ref. 15: 3435 N Lawndale ave, Chicago Il 60618.

WERNER, MONA MAY. b Pittsburgh Penn 5 Ap 28. 5: Chatham 46-50 (Speech, Drama) BA; UPittsburgh 51-52 (Law), 63-65 MLS. 6: Sp. 7: Clk US Bur Internal Revenue, Pittsburgh Penn 52; Clk Main, Lafreutz & Co, Pittsburgh Penn 52-55; Bkkeeper Planned Parenthood Committee & Clinic, Pittsburgh Penn 55-63; Acquis clk & trainee UPittsburgh Lib 63-65; Asst art div Carnegie Lib of Pittsburgh Penn 65-67, Br libn 67-68, Hd pittsburgh reg libn for the Blind & Physically Handicapped 68-. 8: Part-time libn, Profess Lib, Dixmont State Hosp, Glenfield Penn 67. 9: ALA; NEA-DAVI; SLA (Pittsburgh Chap: chm Archives Com 67, chm H W Wilson Award Com 68); PennLA (mem Com Union List Penn Newspapers 64-67, chm Resol Com 67-68, mem A-V Com 68-69). 10: Bus & Profess Women's Club. 14: A-v, ref, acquis, talking bk serv, admin. 15: 450 Perrysville rd, Pittsburgh Pa 15229.

WERNER, OLIVER (JOHN) JAMES JR. b St Louis Mo 14 Je 24. 4: Nora Campbell. 5: UChicago 46-48 (Liberal Arts) PhB, 49-51 (Philos) Certif Advanced Studies, 53-56 (Law) JD; UWash 68-69 M Law Libnship. 6: Fr, Sp. 7: Bkkeeper City Nat Bank & Trust, Kan City Mo 41-42; Radioman 3/c US Coast Guard, US, Atlantic, Caribbean 42-46; Admin Continental Assurance Co, Chicago 51-53; Trust off Seattle-First Nat Bank 56-68. 9: ALA. 14: Admin, acquis, ref. 15: 2335 Yale E, Seattle Wa 98102.

WERNER, WENDY MARIE (HOLT). b Reading Penn 7 F 44. 4: Frank Werner Jr. 5: Albright col 62-66 (Ger) AB; Drexel 67-68 MS in LS. 6: Ger, Fr. 7: Sales clk Boscov's West, Sinking Spring Penn 62-66; Single needle operator Letisse Inc, Reading Penn summers 63-66; Br asst Reading Pub Lib, Reading Penn 66-67, 3rd asst ref libn 67-68, 2nd asst ref libn 68-. 9: ALA; PennLA. 14: Ref. 15: Reading Pub Lib 5th & Franklin st, Reading Pa 19602.

WERT, ALICE L HECK. b MONROE Co Mich 29 Mr 22. 4: William G Wert. 5: East Mich U 39-43 (Elem Educ) BS; LSU summer 44 (LS); UMich 48-49 MALS; Ind State U 62-65 Supv Certif. 7: Elem tchr Van Buren Twp Sch, Belleville Mich 43-44; Elem tchr E Baton Rouge Parish, Baton Rouge La 44; Army libn Avenger Field Lib, Sweetwater Tex 45; Libn Willow Run pub schs, Willow Run Mich 45-48, 52-53; Libn Bellaire City Lib, Bellaire Tex 55-58; Elem libn: Huston Ind Sch Dist, Bellaire Tex 60, Vigo Co Sch Corp, Terre Haute Ind 61-63, Ind U div of univ schs 63-64, Vigo Co Sch Corp, Terre Haute Ind 64-66; Supv lib Vigo Co Sch Corp, Terre Haute Ind 66-67, Act coord MC 67-68, 69-; Admin assts Asst Prof HEA Inst Purdue U 68-69. 8: Instr, NDEA Inst for ibns, Ind U summer 65; Admin asst Inst IndU summer 65-, Elem lib consul. 9: ALA; NEA-DAVI Ind State Tchrs Assn; IndSchLA (Memb Chm 64-65, 2nd v-pres 65-66), 1st v-pres, pres-elect 6971); Assn Childhood Educ; Ind A-V Dir Assn. 10 Delta Kappa Gamma. 13: Yes. 14: Child & yp libs. 15: 406 S Brown ave, Terre Haute Ind 47803.

WERT, LUCILLE (VIVIAN) MATHENA. b sioux City Iowa 24 My 19. 4: Dr Charles Allen Wert. 5: Morningside Col 38-42 (Gen Sci) BA; Simmons 44-45 BS in LS; UIll 61-63 (LS) MA, 63- (LS). 6: Fr, Ger. 7: Clerical asst ser dept Widener Lib Harvard U 43-44; Asst libn Electrical Engnr Lib MIT 44-45; Libn Math Physics Lib UIowa 45-47; Libn Math Physics Lib UChicago 48-50; Visiting Lecturer Grad Sch of Lib Sci UIll (Champaign) summer 65, Research asst 68-. 8: Visiting

Lecturer Grad Sch of Lib Sci Uill summer 65; Ill Governors Conf on Devel the Talents of Ill Youth, 62; US Off of Educ grant to study relationship between reader serv offered in high sch libs & formal lib educ of libn. 9: ALA-AASchL; IllLA; IllSchLA. 10: Beta Phi Mu; Citizens Educ Coun, Champaign Commun Schs. 14: Wk with ya, lib research, reader serv, lib educ. 15: 1708 W Green st, Champaign Il 61822.

WERTHEIMER, LEONARD. b Berlin 7 Ag 14. 4: Ruth Jacobs. 5: Berlin U 32-33 (Law); UCape Town 49 certif in Libnship; USouth Africa 50-53 (Fr, GER) BA. 6: Fr, Ger, Afrikaans. 7: S African Defence Force, Royal Natal Carbineers Infantry 43-44; Lib asst prof Lib Serv, Cape Town S Africa 50; Lib asst U Cape Town Lib 50-63; Head Langs & Lit Centre Met Toronto Pub Lib, Toronto Ont 63-. 9: CanLA; ALA; S African LA; OntLA; Assn Canadienne des Bibliothecaires de Langue Francaise. 10: . 13: Yes. 14: Ref, for lit, adult educ. 15: 99 Tyndall ave, apt 807, Toronto 3 Can.

WERTSMAN, FILIP VLADIMIR. b Secureni USSR 6 Ap 29. 5: UAI Cuza Iasi-Romania Law Sch 49-53 (Law) Diploma of Merit; Columbia 68-69 MLS. 6: Russian, Ukranian, Fr, romanian, Sp, Ital, Ger. 7: Lawyer Ministry of Justice, Iasi Badav Romania 53-67; Examiner stock certif 1st Nat City Bank, NYC 67-68. 9: ALA; AALL. 13: Yes. 14: Bibliog, acquis, internatl & for law. 15: 3444 Knox pl, Bronx NY 10467.

WESCOTT, ELIZABETH CARROLL. b Bluehill Me 2 Ag 18. 5: Colby Col 36-40 (Hist) AB; Miami U 46; Simmons 48-50 MS. 7: Asst circ dept Hartford Pub Lib, Hartford Conn 47-48; Asst instr Simmons Col Sch of Lib Sci 49-50; Ref asst Penn State U 50-52, asst ref libn 52-60; Ref libn Brown U 60-. 9: ALA (Subscr Bks Com 55-61);-ACRL;-RSD;-LED; RILA. 10: AAUP; AAUW; AAAS; Pi Gamma Mu. 13: Yes. 14: Ref, docs, lib educ. 15: 67 Medway st, apt 7, Providence 02906.

WESLEY, MARY VERNIS. b Johnson Co Ga 15 Je 37. 5: Paine Col 56-61 (Natural Sci) BS; Ft Valley State Col summer 62-64 (LS) Certif. 6: Ger. 7: Dock Kemp Sch, Wrightsville Ga; Elem tchr 61-63, Tchr-libn 63-64, Libn 65-. 8: Pres loc GTEA 67-69. 9: ALA; NEA; Amer Tchrs Assn; Ga Tchrs Assn (LIBNS Sect); GaEA (Libns Sect). 14: Ref, proc. 15: Rt 2 Box 207, Wrightsville Ga 31096.

WESLEY,PHILLIP. b Los Angeles 3 Je 30. 5: UCLA 50-56 (Music) BA; USoCal 56-59 MSLS. 7: Order libn Los Angeles Co Law Lib, Los Angeles 57-59; Asst circ & ser libn los Angeles State Col 59-60; Order libn Los Angeles Co Law Lb, Los Angeles 60-61, Head catlg libn 61-66; Hd catlg libn San Fernando Valley State Col 66-67, Chief tech serv 67-69, Act Col libn 69-; Libn Cal State Col, Dominguez Hills 69-. 9: SLA (SoCal Chap; Chm Com on Archives 65-66); AALL (chm Com on Chaps 64-65, Mem com on catlg & clsf 64-66; SoCal ALL (v-pres 63-64, pres 64-65). 13: Yes. 14: Admin. 15: Cal State Col, Dominguez Hills Ca 90247.

WESSEL, JANET (ELIZABETH) ALTER. b Beloit Kan 2 Ap 28. 5: UHawaii 45-47; Whitman col 47-49 (Hist) AB; UWash 49-50 (Libnship) BA. 7: Bkmob libn Richmond Pub Lib, richmond Cal 50-51; Bkmob libn Hawaii Co Lib, Hilo Hawaii 51-52, Catlg libn 62-64, ya libn 64-66, 53-62; Ref & processing libn Hawaii Pub Lib, Hilo 66-67, Adult serv 67-68; Hd Hawaii & Pacific unit Hawaii State Lib, Honolulu 68-. 9: ALA; HawaiiLA (Bd mem 65-66). 10: Hawaiian Hist Soc; Bishop Museum Assn. 14: Hawaiiana, ref. 15: 478 S King st, Honolulu Hi 96813.

WESSELLS, HELEN E(LIZABETH PIERSON). b Morristown NJ 3 Je 03. 4: Herman S Herringer. 5: Newark State Normal Sch 20-21; NY Pub Lib Sch 25-26 Certif. 7: Asst libn Morristown Lib, Morristown NJ 22-25; Asst Olivia Raney Lib, Raleigh NC 25; Br libn NY Pub Lib 26-42; Dir Victory Bk Campaign NYC 42-43; Cultural Off US For Serv, Melbourne Australia 43-47; Act assoc dir ALA Intl Rel Off, Wash DC 48; Chief Lib Br USIS Dept of state, Wash DC 49-50; Ed "Library Journal" 51-57; Lib consul 57-. 8: Consul: US Off of Educ; Rockefeller & Carnegie Founds; Conn State Dept of Educ; Tasmanian & New South Wales govts, Australia; New Bks Preview Coord 67-69; Consul & dir Wing Associates Inc & Wing Productions Inc 65-. 9: LPRC; ALA (Coun 57-61; chm Memb & Awards Coms); chm intl Rel RT & ed "LEADS"; LAD chm Pub Rel Sect; Wilson Indexes Com; SLA (chm Publ Div); CNLA (chm Com for Vis For Libns); DCLA (pres 49-51); NY Lib Club (pres 52-54); NYLA. 10: Amer Inst Graphic Arts; Women's Nat Bk Assn; NGO observer to UN US Mission, una-USA Conf Gp 58-; Nat chm "Eng-Speaking Union Bks-Across-the-Sea Com; Chm Bk Sel panel 58-. 12: Ed: "Library Journal" 51-57; "LEADS" 57-; auth: "The Public Library for Lifelong Learning"; "The Public Library: a Tool for Modern Living". No 1 Small Libs Proj. 13: Yes. 14: Intl pub rel, graphic arts, ref, rare bks. 15: 433 W 21st st, New York NY10011.

WESSELLS, ROBERT STEPHEN. b Portchester NY 27 F 36. 5: Union Col (NY) 54-58 (Hist) BA; UPenn 58-59 (Hist) MA; Columbia 62-64 MS in LS. 6: Ger. 7: Battalion clerk US Army (SP4), Munich 59-61; Libn I NY Pub Lib 61-66; Asst libn Carnegie Endowment for Intl Peace, NYC 66; Circ libn NYU Grad Sch of Bus Admin 66-67; Acquis libn Trenton State Col 67-69. 9: ALA; SLA; United Tchg Prof. 10: Internat Assn Jazz Record Collectors; NY Hot Jazz Soc; Amer Soc Pencil Collectors; Amer Feline Soc; AHA; AAUP; OAH. 14: Circ, educ ref, acquis. 15: 67 Florence ave apt 4, Trenton NJ 08618.

WESSLER, CAROL (RUTH). b Sheboygan Wis 30 Mr 33. 5: Wis State Col (Milwaukee) 51-55 (Elem Educ) BS; UIll 61-62 LS MS. 7: Tchr Long Beach Unified Sch Dist, Long Beach Cal 55-58; Tchr Sheboygan Co Sch Dist 1, Sheboygan Wis 58-61; Ref libn Wis Valley Lib Ref Serv, Wausau Wis 61-. 9: ALA; WisLA (chm Ref Sect 66-67). 10: Wausau (Wis) Civic Music Assn. 14: Ref. 15: 500 Strollers lane, Wausau Wi 54401.

WEST, ALMA (BROGWELL). b Pittsburgh Penn 1 S 10. 4: F Montell West. 5: UPittsburgh 24-28 (Hist) AB; Hampton Lib Sch 33-36 ABLS. 6: Sp, Fr. 7: Libn W Ky State Col, paducah Ky 36-38; Libn Grambling Col 40-44; Libn Carnegie Branch Lib, Pittsburgh Penn 45; Libn (staff) Dept of Com, Wash DC 46-. 14: Acquis, catlg. 15: 11512 Old Fort rd SE, Washington DC 20022.

WEST, CARLTON PRINCE. b Kingston Mass 21 Jl 05. 5; boston U 22-26(Hist) BA; Yale 26-28 (Hist) MA; UNC 45-46 ,bs in LS. 6: Fr. 7: Wake Forest Col: Instr 28-33, Asst Prof 33-45, Libn Z Smith Reynolds Lib 46-. 9: ALA; SELA; NCLA (pres 63-64). 14: Admin. 15: Box 7777 Reynolda Sta, Winton-Salem NC 27109.

WEST, CARRIE LYNNE. b Athens Ala 10 N 35. 5: Tex ChristianU 52-54 (Intl Affairs); Inst Tecnologico de Monterrey summer 53 (Sp); UNeb 54-56 (Intl Affairs, Sp) BS; Columbia 60-62 MS in LS. 6: Sp, Fr. 7: Lib asst W Hartford Pub Lib, W Hartford Conn 57-58; Co-hd child dept Englewood Pub Lib, Englewood NJ 58-62; Bibliog searcher UN Lib, NYC 62; Asst head acquis libn Joint Univ Libs, Nashville 62-65; Hd libn Lambuth Col 65; Asst to dir Marquette U Libs 66-69; Asst dir libs Marquette U 69-. 9: ALA. 10: AAUP; AAUW; Phi Beta Kappa; Phi sigma Iota. 14: Admin, acquis, ref. 15: Marquette Univ Lib 1415 W Wisconsin ave, Milwaukee Wi 53233.

WEST, DOROTHY H. b Mt Vernon NY 2 Mr 09. 4: Everett West. 5: Barnard 27-31 (Econ) BA; Drexel 59-62 MS in LS. 7: Ref libn Haddonfield Pub Lib, Haddonfield NJ 63; Libn Los Angeles Pub Lib 63-64; Pub lib consul Penn State Lib (Phila) 64-67; Asst dir framingham Pub Lib, Framingham Mass 68-. 8: Consul on In-Serv Train for NJ State Lib, Trenton NJ 66, 67; Wkshop Instr Penn & NJ Oub Libs. 9: ALA; NELA; MassLA. 10: Beta Phi Mu; Phi Kappa Phi. 13: Yes. 14: Ref, in-serv train, admin. 15: 14 Temple st apt 6E, Framingham Ma 01701.

WEST, INA (BAIRD). b Cleburne, Tex 2 O 01. 5: Texas Woman's U (Tex State Col for Women) 18-22 (Eng) BA, summers 54-57 MLS. 7: Tchr: Cleburne High Sch, Cleburne Tex 22-26, Houston Independent Sch, Houston Tex 27-30, Beeville Jr High, Beeville Tex 44-54; Libn A C Jones High Sch, Beeville Tex 54-. 9: ALA (Recr & Memb Coms); NEA; TexLA (v-chm & chm YART 65-67, chm Didt IVm); TexStateTA (chm Lib Sect Dist XII 61); TexASchL (sec 66-67); Coastal Bend LA (chm 60). 10: Bee Co Lib Bd; Rosetta Club. 14: YA serv. 15: 1107 E Bowie st, Beeville Tx 78102.

WEST, LAURA (McGARITY). b Chester SC 2 O 1895. 4: James Richard West. 5: Chicora Col 12-13; Winthrop Col 13-14, summers 42-47 (Eng) BA, summers 48-51 (Eng) MA, summers 55-60 (Lib Sci) Certif. 6: Sp. 7: Tchr elem sch: Chester Co 14-17, Kershaw Co 17-20, 41-44, Floyd Dale 44-46, Dillon City 46-61; Libn elem sch, Latta (Dillon Co) 61-. 8: Act supv or adv to libns, Latta Area Schs 64-. 9: NEA; ALA; SCEA; SCLA; DillonCoEA. 10: Dillon Co Hist Soc. 13: Yes. 14: Catlg. 15: Box 303, Dillon SC 29536.

WEST, MARCIA LANE. b Alexandria La 31 Ag 44. 5: LSU (Alexandria) 62-64 (Eng); USoWest 64-66 (Eng) BA; LSU (Baton Rouge) 66-67 MLS. 7: Page LSU (Alexandria) 64; Page USoWestLa 64-66; Trainee LSU (Baton Rouge) 66-67; Gen adult libn NYC Pub Lib 67-69, sr libn (Asst br libn) 69-. 9: ALA; -ACRL; -PLA. 14: Adult wk. 15: Box 306B 123 W 13th st, New York NY 10011.

WEST, MARTHA WOODHAM. b Greenville SC 28 Ap 31. 4: Jack Kutil West. 5:Dunbarton Col 47-51 (Eng) BA; USCar 51-53 (Eng) MA; Emory 53-54 (LS) MA; USoCal 59 MedLA Grade I Certif; UCal (Berkeley) 66-67 (LS). 6: Fr, Ger. 7: Asst child libn Richland Co Pub Lib, Columbia SC 52-53; Supv libn US Army, Germany 54-56; Med libn VA Hosp, Palo Alto Cal 57-59, Head Libn 59-60; Tech libn United Tech, Sunnyvale Cal 60-61; Head info sect Syntex;Research, Palo Alto Cal 61-64; Lib consul self-employed, ,ext, spring 65; Dir info serv EDEX Corp, Mt View Cal 65-66; Sr lib systs analyst Info Gen Corp, Palo Alto Cal 67-; Asst Prof San Jose State Col 69-. 9: SLA (71 Conf treas; (San Francisco Bay Reg: Pubns Chm 65-66, mem Union List Com) 68-; treas 67-69); ASIS (68 Conf Com); MedLA. 12: Co-ed "The Library SLA (67); Co-ed "Union List of Periodicals; science, Technology, Economics SLA (65); Co-auth "Libraries and Industry (67). 14: Lit searching, admin, acquis, ref, lib educ, sci lit. 15: 994 Van Auken cir, Palo Alto Cal 94303.

WEST, RUSSELL JAMES. b York Penn 3 Ap 18. 4: Margaret West. 5: OhioU 47-49 (Eng) BSEd; West Res 51-54 MSLS. 6: Sp. 7: US Air Corps 41-45; Libn Clyde High Sch, Clyde Ohio 51-56; High sch libn, Toledo Ohio 56-61; High sch libn Riverside Pub Sch, Riverside Cal 61-63; Dir tech serv Riverside Pub Lib, Riverside Cal 63-67; City libn Torrance Pub Lib, Torrance Cal 67-. 9: ALA; SLA; NEA; CalLA. 10: Kiwanis; Toastmasters. 13: Yes. 14: Catlg, rare bks. 15: Torrance Pub Lib 3031 Torrance blvd, Torrance Ca 90503.

WEST, RUTH (FRANCES). b Muncie Ind. 5: DePauw 17-21 (Germ Romance Lang); Stanford 24-26 (Germ Sp) AM; UMich 36-37 ABLS; Ball State 30-35 (Lat). 6: Ger, Sp. 7: Tchr Central High Sch, Muncie Ind 22-24; Asst prof Okla Col for Women 28-29; Asst in circ Cal State Lib, Sacramento 45; Libn Mather AFB, Cal 47-48; Libn Lincoln Col 65-. 9: SLA; MedLA; ALA. 10: DAR; DAC. 14: Ref, rare bks. 15: 3148 N Pennsylvania st, Indianapolis In 46205.

WEST, STANLEY LeROY. b Los Angeles 15 Ja 12. 4: Caroline Cockrell. 5: UCal(Berkeley) 29-30, 31-33; Internat Rel of the Far East AB 33-34 (Pub Admin); UFla 36-38 LLB; Columbia summers 37-42 BS in LS; UFla 68 JD. 7: Asst law libn UFla 38-40; Law Libn & Instr in Law UPittsburgh 40-42; Asstto Dir of libs Columba U 42-43; Lt (jg) - Lt (USNR) U S Navy 43-46; Assoc law libn Columbia U 46; Dir of Libs & Head Dept Lib Sci UFla 46-67; Prof lib sci UHawaii 67-68, Univ libn 68-. 8: Adj Prof Rutgers Grad Sch of Lib Sci, spring 61; Fulbright Lectureship in Rome, spring 57; Consul to Hispanic Found LC, 64-65. 9: ALA(chm Bd Resources Subcom on Resources of So Libs 50 & 56) -ACRL (chm Com on Constit & By-laws 56, chm Nomin Com 58-59, chm Adv Com on Coop with Euc & Prof Orgs 63-66); SELA; FlaLA (pres 50); Assn SE Res Libs (chm 59-60); Hawaii LA. 10: Rotary Internat; Phi Sigma Kappa; Phi Alpha Delta. 13: Yes. 14: Admin, Latin-Amer acquis, rare bks. 15: 3279C Beaumont Woods pl, Honolulu Ha 96822.

WEST, WILFRED LaVERNE. b Keokuk Iowa 21 My 38. 4: Diane Tenglin. 5: Keokuk Commun Col 56-58 (Liberal Arts) AA; State U Iowa 58-60 (Hist); Carthage Col 60-64 (Bus Admin) BS; UDenver 64-65 (LS) MA. 7: Clerk Keokuk Commun Col Lib 55-56; Clerk Keokuk Pub Lib, Keokuk Iowa 56-60, Act asst 60-64; Field consul Iowa State Travel Lib, Des Moines Iowa 65-; Ottumwa Iowa; dir Pub Lib 66-, Admin Prairie Hills Lib Syst 67-. 8: Estab hqrs lib for thoerner Boxes Inc, Keokuk Iowa 63-64; Consul Iowa Statewide Automated catlg project 66-, Iowa Statewide union list of ser 69-, Video tape project for handicapped 68-. 9: ALA; IowaLA. 10: Alpha Psi Omega; Jaycees; Kiwanis; Optimists; Big Brothers. 13: Yes. 14: Publibs, ext wk, reg lib systems, automation. 15: Ottumwa Pub Lib 129 N Court, Ottumwa Ia 52501.

WEST, WILLIAM ROYSTER. b Detroit 4 Jl 23. 5: Va Polytech Inst 41-43; UBern (Switzerland) 46-47; George Washington U 47-50 (Hist) BA; Columbia 50-51 (LS) MS. 6: Fr, Ger. 7: US Army 43-46; Catlgr Cornell U 51-52; Ref libn Pratt Lib, Baltimore 52-56; Ref libn tech div Detroit Pub Lib 57-59; Ref libn Bus Lib, Cleveland Pub Lib 59-60; Head bus tech & soc sci dept Norfolk Pub Lib, Norolk Va 60-66; Dir Lockport Twp Pub Lib, Ill 66-68; Hd processing dept Med Col of SC 68-. 9: SLA; ALA; VaLA; SELA; MedLA. 14: Bk sel, ref, catlg. 15: Apt 10A Ashley House, Lockwood dr, Charleston SC 29401.

WESTALL, JOHN CAREY. b Lawrenceville Ill 6 O 34. 4: Carol Joan Hannie. 5: UIll 52-56 (Eng Lit) BA; UWis 59-60 (LS) MS. 6: Fr, Sp. 7: US Army 49th Army Band (Pfc) musician 57-59; Ref asst Chicago Pub Lib 60-62; Ser libn, catlg asst Ill Wesleyan U Lib 62-65; Catlgr 65-68, Dir tech serv 68-. 9: ALA; IllLA; McLean CoLA. 14: Catlg, tech serv. 15: 604 N School st, Normal Il 61761.

WESTBROOKS, ALLEGRA MAREA. b Cumberland Md 13 Mr 21. 5: Fayetteville State Col 36-40 9elem Educ) BLS; AtlantaU 45-46 BLS. 7: Elem sch tchr Onslow Co Pub Sch Syst, Jacksonville NC 40-42; Sec & program aide Person St USO, Fayetteville NC 42-45; Child libn Louisville Free Pub Lib, Louisville Ky 46-47; Br libn Pub Lib of Charlotte & mecklenburg Co, Charlotte NC 47-56, Acquis libn 57-. 9: ALA; NCLA (Exec Bd 59-61); SELA (pres Staff Org 58-59); MecklenburgLA. 10: YWCA; Girl Scouts; United Commun Serv; Bethlehem Ctr. 11: Charlotte's Outstanding Career Woman, 1968. 14: Acquis. 15: 1509 LaSalle st, Charlotte NC 28208.

WESTBY, BARBARA MARIETTA. b Luverne Minn 20 Ag 19. 5: Augustana Col (SD) 37-41 (Eng) BA; UDenver 44-45 BS in LS. 6: Norwegian, Swedish, Danish, Fr, Ger. 7: Catlgr SD Free Lib Commsn, Pierre SD 41-42; Asst libn Augustana Col (SD) 42-43; Libn HURON High Sch, Huron SD 43-44; Catlgr Detroit Pub Lib 44-48; Catlgr & reviser Army Med Lib, Wash DC 48-51; Asst & act libn US Info Lib, Stockholm Sweden 51-53; Detroit Pub Lib: Supv ref serv catlg 53-54, Ast chief 55-56, Chief 56-63, Coordinator 63-66; Field dir LC Off, Oslo Norway 66-69, Asst chief Descr catlg sect LC 69-. 8: Mem Faculty Wayne State U 66. 9: ALA-RTSD (chm Nomin Com 57-58, Exec Com Catlg & Clsf Sect 58-61, chm Descr Catlg Com 66-67, chm Coun Reg Goups 61-63);-Internat Rel Round Table (Memb Chm); MichLA (sec 60-63; sec-treas Catlg Sect 46-47, pres Tech Serv Sect 58-59); Detroit Jr Libns (treas 46-47, pres 47-48); IFLA (American mem Org Com 69); Mtg Catlg Experts 69. 12: Ed "Sears List of Subject Headings" 9th ed 65; Ed 'Advanced Planning' in "Libraries; Building for the Future" ALA (67); "Shared Cataloguing" (Dublin 69). 13: Yes. 14: Catlg, tech serv, automation, internat libnship. 15. Asst chief Descr Catlg Sect, Library of Congress, Wash DC.

WESTENDORF, GERDA (OCKERMUELLER). b Shanghai China 3 Mr 25. 4: Kurt Westendorf. 5: Kaiser Wilhelm Schule 31-42 Gen Sr Matriculation; German-Chinese Med Acad 42-44 (Pre-med) Physicum; UTuebingen (Germany) 53-54 (Languages) Diploma Interpret; German pub Lib Sch 55-56 Pub Libn. 6: Ger, Fr. 7: Asst libn US Info Ctr, Tuebingen Germany 53-56; Asst libn Calgary Pub Lib, Calgary Alta Can 56-57; Libn Memorex Corp, Santa Clara Cal 63-67; Libn Inter Video Corp, Sunnyvale Cal 67-. 9: SLA; Amer Transl Assn. 14: Tech transl. 15: 675 Almanor ave, Sunnyvale Ca 94086.

WESTER, MARILYN DELOISE. b Dunsmuir Cal 5 N 17. 5: St Helens Hall Jr Col 35-37 Diploma; UWash 37-39 (Eng Lit) BA; UCLA summer 41 (LS); UWash 45-46 BALS. 7: Jr libn Ser UWash Lib 46-47, Jr libn catlgr 47-52; Jr libn catlgr Cal State Polytech Col 52-53; Sr libn catlgr San Francisco State Col 53-54; Sr libn catlgr Lib Assn of Portland Ore 54-61; Instr catlgr Portland State Col Lib 61-66; Sr libn catlgr Lib Assn of Portland Ore 66-. 9: ALA-ACRL; -RTSD; OreLA; PNLA. 10: AAUp; LWV; AAUW; Ore Hist Soc; Portland Art Assn. 14: Catlg. 15: 1717 SW Park ave apt 504, Portland Or 97201.

WESTERMAN, ROBERT CECIL. b O'Donnell Tex 7 Ja 24. 4: Van Jones. 5: UNM 46-49 (Anthrop) BA; LSU 66-68 (LS) MA. 6: Fr. 7: Libn USN 43-46; Libn NY Pub Lib; Libn UCal (San Diego) 68-. 9: ALA; SLA; CalLA; UCal (San Diego) LA. 14: Ref, bibliog. 15: 7623 Eads, La Jolla Ca 92037.

WESTERN, DOROTHEA. b Webster City Iowa 20 Mr 08. 5: State U Iowa 31-33 (Eng) BA; UDenver summers 37-39 BS in LS. 6: Sp. 7: Libn; State U Iowa 31-35, W Waterloo High Sch, Waterloo Iowa 35-38, Thomas Jefferson High Sch 38-39, Proviso Twp High Sch, Maywood Ill 39-45, US Spec Serv, Germany 45-46, Proviso Twp High Sch, Maywood Ill 46-50, Libn US Info Agency (Djakarta) 51-55, Wash DC 55-58, Mexico City 59-67; For info distribution spec USIA, Wash DC 67-. 15: 7325 Maple terr, Wauatosa Wis 53213.

WESTGAARD, MARGARET (WALLIS). b Calgary Alberta Can 29 O 16. 5: UAlberta 33-38 (Classics) BA; UCal 38-39 (Archeology), 39-40 (Libnship) Certif. 7: Asst co libn malheur Co Lib, Ont Or 40-42; Asst order libn Ore State Syst of Higher Educ, Corvallis 43-44; Acco unt clk Shell Chem, San Francisco 44-45; Libn Safeway Stores inc, Oakland Cal 45-46; Order libn San Francisco State Col 46-54, Asst libn tech serv 56-. 8: Memb Daly City Lib Commsn 54-60; Instr Lib Tech Prog, Col of San Mateo 69. 9: CalLA (Col, Univ & Res Libs Div: sec 50-51, v-pres 66, pres 67); No Cal Tech Proc Gp (chm 68-69). 14: Tech serv. 15: 233 Wilshire, Daly City Ca 94105.

WESTLING, OLIVER KIP. b NJ 9 Jl 10. 4: F Dorothy Habighorst. 5: Rutgers 29-33 (Floriculture) BS. 6: Lat, Sp. 7: Nurseryman, Foreman at Julius Roehrs, Wallington NJ 33; Crew supv USDA, E Orange NJ 34; Lab tech USDA, Morristown NJ 35; Res desk libn Rutgers U 35-42; Priorities allocator E I DuPont, New Brunswick NJ 42-45; Dept head Photoduplication Rutgers U Lib 45-. 14: Photoduplication. 15: 20 Cypress ave, N Brunswick NJ 08902.

WESTMAN, DIANE CECILE. b San Francisco Cal 22 D 42. 5: City Col of San Francisco 60-62 (Liberal Arts) AA; UCal (Berkeley) 62-64 (Comparative Lit) BA; UWash 66-67 MLS. 6: Ger. 7: Serv rep Pacific Tele & Telegraph, San Rafael Cal 64-65; Clk Seattle Pub Lib 65-66, Pre-prof 66-67, Libn I (jr grade) 67-. 9: ALA; PNLA. 10: Sierra Club; Seattle Mountaineers. 14: Ref, map libnship. 15: 6217 1/2 5th ave NW, Seattle Wa 98107.

WESTMORELAND, N JEAN (CHAPPELL). b Wichita Kan 6 Ag 17. 5: SW Mo State Col 63 (Elem Educ) BS Elem Ed; UIll 65 MALS. 7: Kindergarten tchr Grace Methodist Church, Springfield Mo; Springfield & Greene Co Libs, Springfield Mo 63-66; Libn Greenwood Lab Sch SW Mo State Col 66-69. 9: MoLA (Child Serv RT; Recruitment Netwk); MoASchL (Reorg Com). 10: SpringfieldLA. 14: Ref, child serv. 15: 826 State st, Springfield Mo 65806.

WESTON, FRANKLIN ATWATER. b Bangor Me 25 O 34. 5: UMe 53-57 (Philos) BA, 57-58 (Educ) Tchg Certif Columbia 59-62 (LS) MS; Fordham 63 (Law). 6: Fr. 7: Asst catlgr NY Pub Lib 58-59; Asst catlgr Columbia Law Lib 59-60, Asst acquis libn 60-62; Acquis libn Fordham U Law Lib 62, Ref libn 62-64; Libn Simpson Thacher & Bartlett, NYC 64-66; Marketing libn Ronson Corp, Woodbridge NJ 67-. 8: Bus mgr, "Law Library Journal (62-). 9: AALL; SLA; Law Lib Assn Greater NY; (dir 64-65, 66-67); Law Lib Assn Upstate NY. 14: Ref, law libs; marketing. 15: One Beach 105th st, Rockaway Park NY 11694.

WESTPHAL, JEAN (MARCH). b New Brunswick NJ 10 F 10. 4: Albert C F Westphal. 5: Wellesley 27-31 (Hist, Eng Lit) BA; Columbia 31-32 (LS) BS; Rutgers summers 31-32 (Amer Hist); Columbia 34-39 (LS); Drexel summers 64, 67 (LS). 6: Fr, Sp. 7: Catlgr & head of Card Rev Princeton U Lib 32-34; Head Columbia Col Browsing Room (NY) 34-39; Head libn Buchanan Lib Landon Sch, Bethesda Md 56-. 9: DCSchLA; AIMS; WashAreaIndependentASchL. 10: Beta Phi Mu; Wash Drama Soc; LWV; Daughters Amer Colonists; United Ch Women. 14: Catlg, ya bk sel, ref. 15: 4010 Warren st NW, Wash DC 20016.

WETHERBEE, KATE BELK (ALICE). b Kenilworth NJ 10 Mr 20. 4: Robert Thomas Wetherbee. 5: UMass 38-42 (Hist) BA; UVt 61-62 (Hist); Syracuse 66-69 MSLS. 7: Elem tchr Burlington Pub Schs, Burlington Vt 58-61, Jr high tchr 62-63, Jr high libn 63-. 8: Consul, H W Wilson "Junior High School Library Catalog" 65-. 9: VtASchL (pres 65-67; State Sch Lib Standards Com: mem 65-67, chm 68-). 10: Mortar Board; Phi Kappa Phi. 14: Sch libs. 15: 1 Ivy lane, Burlington Vt 05401.

WETHERSTINE, PHEBE (ROMIG). b Moorestown NJ 14 Mr 1900. 4: William C Wetherstine. 5: Simmons 18-22 (LS) BS. 7: Asst Dayton Pub Lib, Dayton Ohio 23; Asst libn Harrison Pub Lib, Harrison NJ 24; Dept head Reformed Church Bk Store, Phila 25-28; Owner Gift & Yarn Shop, Germantown Penn 33-37; Head Libn Upper Darby Pub Lib, Upper Darby Penn 57-. 9: PennLA. 10: AAUW; Upper Darby Forum Bd; Upper Darby Hist Soc. 15: 873 Windermere ave, Drexel Hill Pa 19026.

WETMORE, ROSAMOND (BAYNE). b Middlesboro Ky 1 N 14. 4: Thomas H Wetmore. 5: Lincoln Mem U 32-34; Earlham Col 34-36 (Eng, Hist) AB; Columbia 36-40 BS in LS; Ball State U 57 (Hist) MA. 6: Fr. 7: Asst in lib Earlham Col 36-37; Libn Lloyd High Sch, Erlanger Ky 37-40; Libn Beechwood Sch, Ft Mitchell Ky 40-41; Asst in catlg & asst prof Ball State U 46-. 9: ALA; Ind State Tchrs Assn; Ohio Valley Tech Serv Libns (sec 60, chm 62). 10: AAUW. 12: "Guide to the Organization of Library Materials (66, rev 67, 69). 14: Catlg, tchg, govt publns, lib educ. 15: 1501 Riverside, Muncie Ind 47303.

WETTERLING, MRS CATHERINE W (HISTER). b Bordentown NJ 7 S 17. 4: Edmund Parmentier Wetterling. 5: Lebanon Valley 39 BA; Drexel 40 BS in LS. 7: High sch libn Upper Freehold Twp, NJ 40-41; Libn Wm MacFarland High Sch, Bordentown NJ 41-43; Documents sect asst Princeton U 43-44; Acquis dept asst Harvard U 45-47; Child room asst Trenton Pub Lib, Trenton NJ 47-48; Tech serv libn Lib Serv Bur Div State Lib, Trenton NJ 48-57; Dir Burlington Co Lib, Mt Holly NJ 57-. 8: Chm, Nat Lib Week, NJ 63. 9: ALA (Notable Bks Coun 60-64); NJLA (2nd v-pres 63). 14: Admin, tech serv. 15: 41 Elizabeth st, Bordentown NJ 08505.

WETZEL, FRANK J. b Trenton NJ 1 N 17. 4: Jean Wetzel. 5: Yale 35-39 BA; Drexel 64; Catholic U 64-65 MLS. 6: Fr, Sp, Ital. 7: Catlgr Milton S Eisenhower Lib Johns Hopkins U 65-66; Admin, Act libn US Naval Acad Libs, Annapolis Md 66-68. 15: Box 159 Rt 3, Centreville Md 21617.

WETZEL, GERTRUDE R (DILBA). b Emerson NJ 26 Ag 22. 4: George A Wetzel. 5: Fairleigh Dickinson U 57-62 (Eng) BA; Rutgers 63-65 MLS. 7: Libn Indian Hills High Sch, Ramapo Reg High Sch, Oakland NJ 64-. 9: ALA; NJLA; NJSchLA. 14: Ya serv. 15: 96 Eleventh st, Cresskill NJ 07626.

WETZEL, MARJORIE D (TAYLOR). b Peabody Mass 6 F 02. 5: Simmons 20-24 BLS; NYU Sch of Com 26-28. 7: Circ libn LehighU 24-26; Circ libn NYU Sch of Com 26-28; Circ libn Westerly Pub Lib, Westerly RI 50; Circ libn Elmwood Pub Lib, Providence 51; Ref asst Martin Memorial Lib, York Penn 57; Catlgr NY State Hist Assn, Cooperstown 58-. 14: Catlg. 15: Hartwick NY 13348.

WETZEL, NORMAN P. b Chicago Ill 15 Ag 23. 4: Miriam G Warburton. 5: UChicago 42; Mt Union Col 46-49 (Bus Admin) BA; William McKinley Law Sch 49-50; Kent State 63-69 MLS. 7: Signal aircraft warning S/Sgt USA 43-46; Accounting clk Republic Steel Corp, Canton Ohio 49-62; Adult serv libn Canton Pub Lib, Canton Ohio 63-68; Hd libn Dover Pub Lib, Dover Ohio 68-. 9: ALA; OhioLA. 10: Rotary Club. 14: Adult serv. 15: 1615 - 35th st NE, Canton Oh 44714.

WEYHRAUCH, ERNEST E. b NYC 20 Jl 26. 4: Mary Ekris. 5: NYU 45-51 (Eng) BA; City Col (NY) 55-57 (Educ, Eng); Columbia 57-59 MS in LS. 6: Fr. 7: Lib asst NYU 48-52; Lib tech asst NY Pub Lib 52-55; Tchr NYC Bd of Educ 55-57; Brooklyn Col Lib: Catlgr 57-59, Asst educ libn 59-61, Chief circ libn 61-64; Educ libn Ind U Sch of Educ 64-66; Dir of libs East Ky U 66-. 9: ALA; KyLA; SELA. 10: Ky Hist Soc; Madison Co Hist Soc. 13: Yes. 14: Admin. 15: Director of Libs East Kentucky Univ, Richmond Ky 40475.

WEYMULLER, MARGARET A. b Omaha Neb 31 O 07. 5: Barnard 29 (Eng) AB; Columbia 36 (LS) MS. 6: Fr. 7: Asst libn Barnard Col 29-37; Head Libn & a-v coordinator Central High Sch, Omaha 37-. 9: ALA; NEA; NebSchLA; Neb State Tchrs Assn; Omaha-Council Bluffs LA. 10: AAUW; Chi Omega; Alliance francaise; Omaha Athletic Club; OmahaEA. 13: Yes. 14: Catlg. 15: 4415 Franklin st, Omaha Neb 68111.

WEZEMAN, FREDERICK (HARTOG). b Oak Park Ill 1 My 15. 4: Marjorie Vaughn. 5: Lewis Inst 33-37 (Sci) BS; Chicago Tchrs Col 39-40 (Educ) ME; Chicago 47 BLS. 6: Dutch. 7: Sp 2/c USNR 42-45; Head Libn Pub Lib, Racine Wis 47-53; Head Libn Pub Lib, Oak Park Ill 53-55; Assoc Prof Lib Sch UMinn 55-66; Dir UIowa Lib Sci Sch 66-. 8: Lib surveys of 17 pub libs, 55-65. 9: ALA; SLA; CanLA; AALS; MinnLA. 10: AAUP; Minneapolis Pub Lib Friends; Mayor's Com on the Minneapolis Pub Lib; ACLU. 12: Co-auth "The Use of Books and Libraries" (10th ed 63); "A Study of Branch Libraries, Lincoln Nebraska" (67). 13: Yes. 14: Ref, govt publns, pub lib serv. 15: 114 Mt Vernon dr, Iowa City Ia 52240.

WHALEN, JEAN MARIE. b San Diego Cal 17 O 42. 5: San Diego State Col 60-64 (Eng) 65-67 (Eng); Universite d'Aiz (Marseille) 64-65 (Fr Lit); UMich 67-68 AMLS. 6: Fr. 7: Intern Ohio StateU Libs (Columbus) 68-. 9: ALA. 14: Ref, acquis, period. 15: 2711 Nutmeg pl, San Diego Ca 92104.

WHALEN, LUCILLE. b Los Angeles 26 Jl 25. 5: Immaculate Heart Col 43-49 (Eng) BA; Catholic U 53-54 MSLS; Columbia 61-65 DLS. 6: Fr. 7: Tchr Immaculate Heart Sisters var elem & secondary schs, Los Angeles & Long Beach Cal 45-52; Libn-tchr Los Angeles Catholic Girls High Sch 52-53; Ref libn-tchr Immaculate Heart Col 54-58, Dean Sch of Lib Sci 58-61, 65-. 9: ALA; CathLA; SLA; ATheolLA; ASIS; Lib Assn (Gt Brit); CalLA; CalASchL; ASLIB. 13: Yes. 14: Lib educ, ref. 15: 2021 N Western ave, Los Angeles Ca 90027.

WHALEN, MRS PAULINE K (MALZAHN). b Boulder Colo 11 My 21. 5: UColo 39-42 (Eng Lit) BA, 45-46 (Eng Lit) MA; UDenver 49-50 (LS) MA. 6: Lat, Ger. 7: Sp(T)3/c Link trainer Inst Naval Res WAVES 42-44; Ed Stechert-Hafner Bk News, NYC 46-47; Tchr Lafayette High Sch, Lafayette Colo 48-49; Asst documents libn UColo 50-51; Base libn Ent AFB, Colorado Springs Colo 51-53; Documents catlg libn Colo Sch of Mines 53-55; Order libn UColo 55-64; Ref libn Santa Rosa-Son Co Lib, Santa Rosa Cal 65-66; Humanities bibliog(r) UCal(San Diego) 66-67; Libn Salk Inst, La Jolla Cal 68-. 9: ALA; SLA; MedLA. 10: Nat Wildlife Fed; Pet Pride; 14: Acquis. 15: Rte 1 Box 29B, Del Mar Ca 92014.

WHALON, MRS MARION K. b Barnegat NJ 24 My 13. 5: NJ Col for Women 30-34 (Ger) BA; Bread Loaf Sch of Eng summer 36; Harvard summers 37 & 38; UCal (Berkeley) 56-58 (Eng Lit) MA, 58-59 MLS; UNev summer 56. 6: Ger, Fr. 7: Asst humanities ref lib Sacramento State Col 59-62; Art asst Lib Assn of Portland 62-63, Head music dept 63-65; umanities div libn Ida State U 65-66; Ref libn UCal (Davis) Lib 66-. 9: ALA; CalLA; OreLA; Libns Assn UCal. 10: Phi Beta Kappa; Portland Art Assn. 14: Ref, humanities, fine arts, theater arts, bibliog. 15: 120 C st apt 6, Davis Ca 95616.

WHARTON, BETTY (MARY MASON). b Pasadena Cal 26 Je 11. 4: John F Wharton. 5: Pasadena Playhouse Col of Theatre Arts 29-31 (Drama) Diploma; Columbia 62-63 (LS). 7: Actress motion pictures, Hollywood Cal 31-34; Featured player theatre & Radio, NYC 34-49; Asst casting dir George Abbott, NYC 51-55; Volunteer libn Dalton Sch, NYC 55-60; Theatre collection NY Pub Lib 63-. 9: TheatreLA (Com for Revising Constit); Amer Soc for Theatre Research; Internat Fed Theatre Research (sec 69 Cong). 14: Theatre ref & acquis. 15: 141 E 72nd st, NYC 10021.

WHATLEY, MRS EVELYN (SKINNER). b Eastland Tex 11 D 08. 5: N Tex State U 47 (Eng) BA, 51 BS in LS. 6: Lat. 7: Eng tchr High Sch, Eastand Tex 44-48; Libn & tchr of Eng & Lat, Eastland Tex 48-66; Libn; rylie Jr High Sch, Dallas Tex 66-67, Marsh Jr High Sch, Ft Worth 67-. 9: Tex State Tchrs Assn; NEA. 10: Delta Kappa Gamma; Alpha Lambda Sigma. 15: 5437 Santa Barbara, Fort Worth Tx 76114.

WHEAT, MRS HELEN (FITCH). b Pilot Point Tex 12 N 20. 5: N Tex U 38-42 (LS) BA; Peabody 48-49, 58 (LS) MA. 6: Fr. 7: High sch libn Perryton pub schs, Perryton Tex 42-43; Control tower operator Nat Airport, Wash DC 43-46; High sch libn Farmsville pub schs, Farmsville Tex 47-48; Acquis libn Rice U 48-49, Catlgr 49-52; Acquis libn Sam Houston State Col 57-61, Head tech process & Asst Prof Lib Sci 62-. 9: TexLA (Acquis Round Table). 10: Governing Bd of Huntsville Pib Lib; AAUP; PTA; Huntsville tudy Club; Huntsville Bk Discussion Group; Beta Sigma Phi. 12: Ed "Directory of Faculty Achievements Sam Houston State College (64-). 14: Catlg, acquis, recr. 15: 2125 Ave P, Huntsville Tx 77340.

WHEATLEY, ERMA JOSEPHINE. b Kingsport Tenn 7 Ja 45. 5: Immaculate Heart Col 63-66 (Eng) BA, 66-67 MALS. 6: Fr. 7: Researcher & asst libn Paramount Pictures (Research Dept), Hollywood Cal 67-68; Soc sci bibliogr Cal Inst Tech Humanities Lib 68-. 9: SLA; CalLA. 14: Ref. 15: 156 St Albans ave, Pasadena Ca 91030.

WHEATLEY, LOUISE E. b York Penn 5 My 05. 5: Goucher Cl 25-29 (Eng) AB; Columbia 33-34 BS in ls; UMich 45-47 (LS) AM. 6: Fr, Ger, Ital. 7: Documents clerk Columbia U summer 42; Sch libn Sch Dist of City of York, York Penn 34-. 14: Jr high sh wk. 15: 1411 Third ave, York Penn 17403.

WHEELER, AUGUSTA MARIE. b Louisville Ky 11 Jl 04. 4: James Edward Wheeler. 5: Catherine Spalding Col 53 (Psych, Biol) BS, 60 (LS) MS. 6: Sp. 7: Catherine Spalding Col: Acquis & circ 57-59, Acquis libn 60, Ref & a-v libn 61-. 9: ALA; CathLA (past chm Louisville Unit); KyLA (Col & Ref Sec: past sec-treas; mem Nomin Com 65); Louisville Lib Club; SELA; NEA-DAVI. 10: AAUP; Ky Hist Soc. 14: Ref, a-v. 15: 4217 Southern pky, Louisville Ky 40214.

WHEELER, EULA (VIRGINIA KRUEGER). b Nampa Ida 3 Ja 23. 4: Walter Hall Wheeler. 5: UCLA 41-43 (Econ); UWis 43-44 (Econ) BA; UNC 63-65 MSLS. 6: Fr. 7: Libn Highland sch of Nursing, Highland Hosp Oakland Cal 66-67; Acquis libn & asst catlgr DukeU Med ctr Lib 67-. 9: MedLA; SLA. 10: Phi Beta Kappa; Beta Phi Mu. 14: Ref (psychiatry- psychol collection). 15: 28 Mt Bolus rd, Chapel Hill NC 27514.

WHEELER, EVANNE. b Chicago 20 Mr 16. 5: Long Beach Jr Col 39-41 (Hist); Long Beach State Col 49-51 (Soc Sci) BA; UCal(Berkeley) 51-52 BLS. 7: Br libn Contra Costa Co Lib, Martinez Calif 52-57; Proj libn Amador-Stockton Fed Proj, Jackson Cal 57-58; Co libn Amador Co Lib, Jackson Cal 58-64; Co libn Humboldt Co Lib, Eureka Cal 64-. 8: Dir Humboldt Co Employees Fed Credit Union. 9: ALA; CalLA (pres Golden Empire Dist; pres Redwood Dist 67; Coun-at-large & Exec Bd 69-70). 10: Humboldt Genealogical Soc. 14: Admin, genealogy. 15: 2260 Crest dr, Fortuna Ca 95540.

WHEELER, GERALDINE (DESSAU). b Macon Ga 2 Ja 08. 5: Wesleyan Col (Ga) 25-29 (Math) AB; Mercer U 44-50 (Educ) M Ed; UDenver 59-63 (LS) MA. 7 Elem & jr high tchr, Porterdale Ga 29-32; Elem & jr high tchr Bibb Co, Macon Ga 32-34; High sch tchr Jefferson Co, Fern Creek Ky 34-35; Operator Naval Ordnance Plant, Macon Ga 43-44; Tchr & libn Dudley M Hughes Voc Sch, Macon Ga 37-43, 44-. 8: Instr in libnship UGa 65-68. 9: NEA; ALA; GaEA; GaLA. 10: Delta Kappa Gamma. 14: Sch libs. 15: 307 HINES TERR, Macon Ga 31204.

WHEELER, HELEN RIPPIER. b NYC 19 F 26. 5: Jr Col of Packer Collegiate Inst 44-46 (Span) AA; Barnard 47-50 (Foreign Areas, Latin Amer) BA; USan Carlos (Guatemala) summer 49 (Span) Certif; Columbia 50-51 (LS) MS; Chicago 53-54 (Educ) MA; Columbia 64 (Educ) EdD. 6: Sp. 7: Asst libn UChicago Upper Lab Sch 53-55; Head tchr-libn Waller High Sch, Chicago 55-56; Libn Agnes Russel Center Tchrs Col Columbia U 56-58; Br head libn & av coordinator Chicago City Jr Col 58-61; Latin Amer Spec Columbia U Libs 62-64; Adjunct Asst Prof Grad Lib Sch Drexel 64-65; Assoc Prof; Grad Sch of Lib Studies UHawaii 65-66, Ind State U (Terre Haute) 66-68, St Johns U (Jamaica NY) 68-. 9: NEA; Amer Assn Jr Cols; ALA-ACRL (Bibliog Com Jr Cols Sect); NYLA; SLA. 10: Internat House Assn; Pi Lambda Theta; Mensa; AAUP; Nat Organ Women; Barnard Alumnae. 12: "The Community College Library; a Plan for Action (65); "A Basic Book Collection for the Community College Library (68). 13: Yes. 14: Commun jr col lib prgramming, lib educ, admin, ref, bibliog (tchg). 15: 206-15 86 rd apt 2E, Queens Village NY 11427.

WHEELER, HUBERT. b Elkland Mo 14 O 05. 4: Georgia Hutchinson. 5: SW Mo State Col BS; UMo MA. 7: Tchr, Webster Co 24-28; Dist circ mgr Springfield News-Press, Springfield Mo 28-30; Elem prin, Aurora Mo 30-35; Co supt of schs, Lawrence Co 35-37; City supt of schs, Butler Mo 37-41; City sput of schs, Marshall Mo 41-47; State commissioner of educ 47-. 8: Memb Mo Lib Commsn: Bd Dirs Central Midwest Reg Educ Lab Inc & Mid-ontinent Reg Educ Lab; Bds of Regents of the five Mo State Cols; Bd Trustees, Pub Sch Retirement System; Chm, Mo Educ Conf, Mo White House Conf Com on Child & Youth. 9: Nat Coun of Chief State Sch Officers (pres-elect); Nat Commsn on Safety Educ (past pres); NEA; Nat Assn State Bds Educ; MoStateTA (Legisl Com); Mo Assn Sch Adminrs (Adv Com). 10: Rotary Internat; Men's Club; First Meth Church; Governor's Offic Coord Com on Traffic Safety; Mo Interagency Coun on Smoking and Health; Phi Delta Kappa. 11: Cited by UMo for Distinguished Serv to Educ; Recipient of First Outstanding Alum award, SW Mo State Col; Hon DLL Degree from Culver-Stockton Col. 15: State Department of Educ, Jefferson City Mo 65101.

WHEELER, JANE (MURSCHEL). b Sandusky Ohio 7 Mr 16. 4: onald R Wheeler. 5: Col of Wooster 34-36; Ohio State U 36-38 (Bus Admin) BS; Columbia 46-47 BS IN LS. 6: Fr. 7: Asst libn Sandusky Pub Lib, Sandusky Ohio 39-46; Catlgr NYU Grad Sch of Bus Admin 47-48; Wright-Patterson Tech Lib, WP AFB Ohio; Head Documents Unit 48-50, Head Tech Serv 50-60, Head libn 61-. 9: SLA; OhioLA. 10: Col Womens Club of Dayton Ohio; Dayton Womans Club. 14: Admi, catlg. 15: 2377 Rustic rd, Dayton Ohio 45406.

WHEELER, JOSEPH L. b Dorchester Mass 16 Mr 1884. 5: Brown 06 (Pol Sci) AB, 07 (Pol Sci) MA; NY State Lib Sch 09 BLS. 7: Stud asst BrownU Lib 02-06, 2d asst libn 06-07; Evening & Sunday asst Providence Pub Lib 04-06; Asst libn DC Pub Lib 09-11; Libn Jacksonville (Fla) Pub Lib 11-12; Asst libn Los Angeles Pub Lib 12-15; Libn Youngstown (Ohio) Pub Lib 15-26; Libn Enoch Pratt Lib, Baltimore 26-45; Act libn Castleton State Col 69. 8: Vt Lib Commsn 21-22; Md Lib Commsn 26-45; Surveyor or consul 175 admin or bldg projs 24-; Initiated; Wilson Co "Indust Arts Index" 10, AAAS series of 27 pop sci reading lists 29-34, Lib Literature 31, ALA Small Libs proj & Drexel Small Libs Method Study 61-64; Lectr NY State, West Res, Columbia, Drexel Lib Schs 21-63; In chg ALA exhibs San Francisco 15 & Phila Worlds Fair 26. 9: ALA (chm Bkbind Com 12-19; chm Legis Com 17-18; Coun 18-23; 1st v-pres 26-27, Exec Bd 29-33; Bd of Educ for Libnship 31-36, hon life mem 65-); NEA; SLA (chm Tech Lib Com 08-10); OhioLA (pres 19-20); Hon mem Md & Vt Lib Assns. 10: Md Hist Assn; Vt Hist Assn; AHA; Amer Soc Pub Admin; NAACP; Rotary internat (hon); Crown Pt Rd Assn. 11: Hon MLS, NY State Lib Sch 24; LittD UMd 34 & Brown U 36; Class of 73 Award (Hist) 06; Baltimore Civic Award, 33; VtEA Award 61; Lippincott Award 61; Pratt Lib Auditorium designation 63; Scarecrow Award (with H Goldhor) 63; Drexel Lib Sci Alumni Award 66. 12: "The Library and the Community" (24); Jt auth "My Maryland" (34); "American

Public Library Building," with A M Githens (41 repr by ALA 47); "Progress & Problems in Education for Librarianship" (46); "Effective Location for Public Library Buildings" (58); "Practical Administration of Public Libraries," with H Goldhor (63); "Small Public Library Buildings" (63); "Reconsideration of Public Library Location" (67); "The Mt Independence-Hubbardton 1176 Military Road" (68). 13: Yes. 14: Promoting reading & lib use, ref, admin, bk sel, bldgs. 15: Benson Vt 05731.

WHEELER, LORA JEANNE. b Rockland Ida 28 Je 23. 5: UUtah 40-44 (Educ) BA; Columbia 44-45 (LS) BS; UCal 52-53 (LS). 6: Sp. 7: Circ libn UUtah 45-48, Ref libn 48-53; Libn Amer Inst for Foreign Trade (PHOENIX) 53-. 9: ALA; Ariz State LA (sec 60-61). 10: Soroptimist Club; Alpha Kappa Delta. 12: "International Business and Foreign Trade; a guide to Information Souces, Mgt Info Guide 14 (69). 14: Ref. 15: P O Box 191, Phoenix 85001.

WHEELER, MARGARET (LEONORA). b Newberry SC 23 F 42. 5: Newberry Col 60-64 (Hist, Pol Sci) AB; UNC 65-66 MS in LS. 7: Ref trainee Pub Lib of Charlotte & Mecklenburg Co, Charlotte NC 64-65, Ref libn 66-. 9: ALA; NCLA; Charlotte Area LA (sec-treas); Mecklenburg LA. 10: Pub Lib of Charlotte & Mecklenburg Co Staff Org. 15: 310 N Tryon st, Charlotte NC 28202.

WHEELER, MARGARET W. b Paducah Ky. 5: Conn Col 23-27 (Eng Lit) BA; UIll 36-37 BS in LS; UMinn 40-41 (Econ, Sociol). 6: Fr, Sp. 7: Jr libn circ dept, soc sci dept, Sr libn, Hd Info Ctr Detroit Pub Lib 37-48; Jr libn, Ref specialist, 1st asst govt doc sect, Sr libn, Hd admin ref serv, Libn II catlg dept Cal State Lib 48-55; Libn II catlg reviser Free Lib, Phila 55-60; Libn III catlg dept UPenn Lib 60-. 9: ALA; PennLA; 10: Beta Phi Mu. 14: Catlg, ref. 15: 2201 Benjamin Franklin pky apt 1011, Phila Pa 19130.

WHEELER, MARJORIE (WOODBERRY). b Boston 26 Mr 16. 4: Robert Reid Wheeler. 5: Smith 33-37 (Geol) BA; Tex Womans U 62-63 (LS); Johns Hopkins U (Geol) MA 37-39. 6: Fr. 7: Boston Museum of Natural Hist 39-40; Sec Gemological Inst of Amer, Boston 40-41; Bibliogr, Dallas 61-63; Ref libn UTex (Arlington) 63-64; Libn SW Ctr for Adv Studies, Dallas 64-68. 9: ALA; SLA; TexLA; Geosci Info Soc (sec 68-69). 10: Sigma Xi. 13: Yes. 14: Ref, sci research problems. 15: 5775 Viking dr, Beaumont Tx 77706.

WHEELER, SARA (HUTCHINGS). b Falls City Neb 13 Ja 15. 5; uneb 32-36 (Eng, Psych) BA; Columbia 38-40 BS in LS; Chicago 52-54 (Anthropology) MA. 6: Fr. 7: Child libn NY Pub Lib 39-40, 44-45; Head wk with child Oak Park PUB Lib, Oak Park Ill 46-51; Asst Prof Sch of Libnship UWash 55-60, Assoc Prof 60-65; Child coord Ventura Co & City Lib, Ventura Cal 65-. 8: Tchr, adult educ (child lit), Santa Barbara City Col. 9: ALA (Coun 62-65; chm 2 awards coms);-CSD (pres 65-66; mem & chm Newbery-Caldecott Com); Assn Childhood Educ Internat; PNLA (sec Young Readers Choice Award 55-65); CalLA. 10: YWCA; Seattle Anthropol Soc; Archaeol Inst Amer; Psi Chi. 12: Storytelling in "World Book Encyclopedia (59-); "Literature for Children in "World Book Encyclopedia (58-); "Childrens Books in "Book of the Year (56-58). 13: Yes. 14: Child lit, story-telling. 15: Ventura Co & City Lib, 651 E Main st, Ventura Ca 93001.

WHEELER, THELMA (BLACKBURN). b Eldorado Ill 14 N 21. 4: Robert Wheeler. 5: Wayne State U 45-51 (Biol) BA; UMich 60-63 AMLS; Wayne State U 64 (Educ) Tchr Certif. 6: Ger. 7: Libn: Wayne Co Lib, Wayne Mich -61, Huron High Sch, New Boston Mich 61-64, Trenton High Sch, Trenton Mich 64-. 9: ALA; NEA; MichEA; MichLA; MichASchL. 14: Pub & high sch libs. 15: 18551 Valade, Riverview Mi 48192.

WHEELER, VELMA (BANE). b West Ripley Me 11 O 12. 5: NorthwesternU 55 (Eng Lit) PhB; Rosary Col 65 MLS. 6: Fr. 7: Supv R R Donnelley Printing Co, Chicago 42-65; Libn (catlgr) Garrett Theol Sem Lib 65-. 9: ALA; ATheolLA. 10: Swedish Choral Club; Christian Choral Club. 14: Catlg, theol materials. 15: 719 Forest ave, Evanston Il 60202.

WHEELOCK, GENEVIEVE LOUISE. b Cooperstown Penn 25 D 02. 5: Ohio Wesleyan U 26 (Eng Lit) AB; West Res 40 BSLS. 6: Fr. 7: Tchr of high sch Eng, Bucyrus Ohio 26-28; Tchr of high sch Eng, N Canton Ohio 28-39; High sch libn, Cuyahoga Falls Ohio 40-45; Circ libn Kent State U 45-49; Head Libn Ohio No U 49-58; Asst law libn Ohio No U Col of Law 60-. 9: ALA; OhioALL. 10: Womans Federated Club; Twice-Ten Art Club. 15: OHIO No UNIV OF Law, Ada Ohio 45810.

WHEELWRIGHT, JESSIE CALDWELL. b Gary Ind 19 S 11. 4: George Milton Wheelwright. 5: UCal (Berkeley) 34 (Pol Sci) AB; Post Grad Univ of Hawaii 34, 61; Simmons 49-50 (LS) MS. 7: Lib asst Maui Co Lib, Wailuku Mau Hawaii 41-43; Libn "Hilo Tribune Herald, Hilo Hawaii 44-45, 46-49; Libn Hawaiian Telephone Co, Honolulu 50-; Lecturer UHawaii Grad Sch Lib Sci 68, 69-. 8: Two Hawaii Governors Exec Coms on Employment of the Handicapped, 64-, 68-. 9: ALA; SLA (chm Pre-Planning Com Mid-Pacific Tour 61); HawaiiLA (pres 60-61, chm Legis Com 56-58, chm Nomin Com 55, 62, 64, 69; chm Lib Devel Com 59-60. 10: Aeta Tau Alpha; Altrusa. 13: Yes. 14: Radio, telev, electron, pub utility wk. 15: 745 Ulumaika, Honolulu 96816.

WHELAN, JOHN FRANCIS. b St Paul 4 Jl 29. 5: Col of St Thomas 47-51 (Eng) BA; UMinn 53-54 (Law); Catholic U 55-56 (LS). 6: Fr, Lat. 7: US Army (Pfc) Signal Corps, Ga & Frankfurt Germany 51-53; Ref libn: US Weather Bur Lib, Wash DC 55-56, Army Lib Law Br, The Pentagon, Wash DC 56-57, AEC Law Lib, Wash DC 57-58; Ref libn Army Lib Law Br, The Pentagon, Wash DC 58-60, Act chief 60-61; Chief Fed Aviation Agency Law Lib, Wash DC 61-62; Assoc libn Nat Geographic Soc Illustrations Lib, Wash DC 62064; Chief Fed Aviation Agency Law Lib, Wash DC 64-68; Libn Arnold & Porter, Wash DC 68-. 9: AALL (chm Fed Activ Com 61-62); chm Statist Com 67-; Law Libns Soc of Wash DC (treas 65-66). 10: Aviation Club. 12: Co-auth "The Military Law Dictionary" (60); Ed "Union List of Legislative Histories" (59); Ed "Union List of Legal Periodicals" (63); Comp "Bibliography on the Philosophical and Historical Developments of the Regulatory Agencies" (62). 14: Ref, admin, legal research, bibliog, automation. 15: 2121 P st NW, Washington DC 20037.

WHELAN, MARY HARRIET. 5: UWis (Madison) 61-65 (Eng) BA, 65-66 MA in LS. 6: Fr, Ital. 7: Sr libn NY Pub Lib 66-68; Sr catlgr Wheaton Col Lib 68-. 9: NELA. 10: Beta Phi Mu. 14: Ref, catlg. 15: 124 S Worcester st Box 962, Norton Ma 02766.

WHICHER, SCOTT (FRANKLIN). b Chicago 2 F 33. 4: Waltraut Hinz Whicher. 5: UIll 51-55 (Hist) BA, 60-61 (LS) MS. 6: Ger, Fr. 7: US Army ordnance (SP2) 55-57; Mail order clerk Morehouse-Gorham Co, Chicago 58-59; Casewker, voc coun Cook Co Dept of Welfare, Chicago 59-60; Documents libn Humboldt State Col Lib 61-66; Catlg libn UOre (Eugene) 66-. 8: Tchr, ext course (Intro to Catlg & Clsf), Humboldt State Col 64-65. 9: ALA; OreLA. 10: Assn Cal State Col Profs; Cal State Employees Assn. 14: Govt docs, catlg, info retrieval. 15: 4745 Brookwood, Eugene Or 97405.

WHICKER, GENE ALLEN. b Loyall Ky 1 N 26. 4: Gloria Cree. 5: UKy 43-47 (Music) AB; Columbia 47-50 (Music, Music Educ) MA; UWis 52-55 (Music); UKy 58-60 (LS) MS. 6: Fr, Ger. 7: Musician NC Symphony Assn, Chapel Hill NC 48-50; Bandsman US Army 50-52; Tchr: Bourbon Co Schs, Paris Ky 54-56, Knoxville Unit schs, Knoxville Ill 56-57, Wyanet Sch systems, Wyanet Ill 57-59; Libn Oberlin Col Conservatory 60-64; Libn East Ky U 64-. 9: ALA; KyLA. 10: Amer Fed Musicians. 14: Docs, ref. 15: 112 Buckwood dr, Richmond Ky 40475.

WHICKER, GLORIA MARIE (CREE). b Frederic Wis 15 Mr 27. 4: Gene Allen Whicker. 5: Wis StateU (River Falls) 45-49 (Eng, Hist, Educ) BS; UWis 54-55 MLS. 6: Fr. 7: Tchr & libn; Goodhue Schs, Goodhue Minn 50-52, St Charles Schs, St Charles Minn 52-54; Stud asst UWis Lib (Madison) 54-55; Tchr Bourbon Co High Sch, Paris Ky 55-56; Libn Lexington City Schs, Lexington Ky 59-60; Catlg libn East Ky StateU 68-. 9: KyLA. 14: Sch lib, child room, ref. 15: 112 Buckwood dr, Richmond Ky 40475.

WHIFFIN, JEAN IRIS. b London Eng 15 N 28. 5: Birkbeck Col ULondon 46-50 (Fr) Certif; Toronto 58-61 (Eng) BA, 61-63 BLS. 6: Fr, Sp, Ital. 7: Sec & libn Mod Langs Dept London Sch of Econ ULondon 46-57; Lib asst UToronto Lib 57-62, Head of ser sect, Acquis dept 62-65; Spec acquis libn UVictoria Lib 65-66; Hd ser div 66-. 9: CanLA; ALA; BCLA (dir & Conf Chm 67-68); ABCL; Inst Victoria Libns (treas 66-67). 10: Beta Phi Mu; CAUT. 14: Ser, docs, maps, rare bks. 15: No 308, 1527 Cedar Hill Cross Rd, Victoria BC Can.

WHISENTON, VERA N(ORMAN). b Galveston Tex 13 Jl 43. 4: Andre Carl Whisenton. 5: Spelman Col 60-64 (Bio, Chem) BS; AtlantaU 64-65 MS in LS. 6: Ger, Sp. 7: Hd tech serv Ft Valley State Col 65-66; Descr catlgr LC 66-68; Hd catlg dept Fed City Col 69-. 8: Consul for setting up a United Planning Org lib in inner-city commun (Wash DC) 68-. 9: ALA. 14: Catlg, automation. 15: 7600 Maple ave, Takoma Park Md 20012.

WHITAKER, DOUGLAS ALBERT. b Litchfield Minn 1 My 32. 4: Karel Nordgaard. 5: UMinn 53-58 (Asian Area Studies) BA, 58-59 (LS) MA. 6: Chinese (Mandarin). 7: Interpreter (1st Lt) USA Army Security Agcy USAR; Jr libn UMinn (Minneapolis) 59-60; Dir Chippewa Co Lib, Montevideo Minn 61-62; Asst dir N Central Reg Lib, Wenatchee Wash 62-65; Asst co libn Wayne Co Fed Lib Syst, Wayne Mich 65-. 8: Wash Rep, Pacific NW Bibliog Ctr Bd 64-65; Bkmob consul Wash State Lib 64; Tech Proc consul: Flint Mich Pub Lib 67, Niles Mich Pub Lib 67. 9: PNLA; WashLA (v-chm Legisl Com 64-65); MichLA. 13: Yes. 14: Tech proc, data proc, lib mgt. 15: 33030 Van Born rd, Wayne Mi 48184.

WHITAKER, GERALDINE (McCORMACK). b Corinth Miss 10 My 24. 4: Mirl W Whitaker. 5: Millsaps Col 42-43; Lambuth Col 43-45 (Hist) BA; SUNY (Geneseo) 65-67 MLS; Rosary Col 67. 7: Tchr: Deering High Sch, Deering Mo 45-46, Corinth Jr High Sch, Corinth Miss 46-48; Remedial tchr Lake Bluff Child Home, Lake Bluff Ill 48-51; Child libn Morton grove Pub Lib, Morton Grove Ill 67-68; Ref libn Lincoln Lib, Springfield Ill 68-. 15: 224 Kenyon dr, Springfield Il 62704.

WHITAKER, LESLEY (G). b New Orleans La 17 D 21. 5: Sacramento Jr Col 38-40 (Eng) AA; URedlands 40-42 (Eng) BA; UCal 42-43 Certif. 7: US Signal Corps, Arlington Va 43-45; Ref libn Berkeley Pub Lib, Berkeley Cal 44; Ref libn (sci & soc sci) Lib Assn of portland Ore 49-57;R ef libn (sci & tech div) Cleveland Pub Lib 57-66; Hd acquis & catlg serv NASA Lib Ames Research Ctr, Moffett Field Cal 66-. 9: SLA; ALA. 14: Sci & tech ref, tech proc. 15: NASA Lib 202-3 Ames Res Center, Moffett Field Ca 94035.

WHITAKER, WALTER LEE. b Los Angeles 20 F 25. 5: UGeneva(Switzerland) 45 (Hist); UCLA 46-50 (Hist) BA, 51-56 (Educ) M Ed; USoCal 64 (LS). 7: (Cpl) US Army 75th Infantry 42-45; Tchr Monterey City Schs, Monterey Cal 50-52; Culver City Unified Schs, Culver City Cal; Tchr 52-59, Elem libn 59-60, Jr high libn 59-64, Coord Secondary Sch IMC 68-. 8: Instr, UCLA Educ Ext on New Math Curr & Sch Lib Serv. 9: NEA-DAVI; ALA; Cal Tchrs Assn; Cal SchLA. 10: Phi Delta Kappa; YMCA. 13: Yes. 14: Sch lib serv, tech proc. 15: Culver City Sec Schools 4601 Elenda ave, Culver City Ca 90230.

WHITBECK, GEORGE W. b Lewiston Me 17 F 32. 4: Ruth Myers. 5 Bates Col 50-52 (Liberal Arts); Columbia Col 55-57 (Hist, Oriental Studies) AB; Columbia U 57-62 (Hist) AM, 58-59 (LS) MS; Rutgers U 68-. 6: Fr. 7: Med corpsman US Army (Cpl), Korea, Hawaii 52-55; Reservations agent United Air Lines, NYC 57-58; Asst to libn City Col (NY) 59-61; Ref asst Levittown Pub Lib, Levittown LI NY 62-63; Assoc libn State U Col (New Paltz NY 63-67. 9: ALA; AHA; Org Amer Histns; NYLA; SENY; Lib Resources Coun; ASIS. 10: Adirondack Mountain Club; AAUP; Catskill 3500 Club. 13: Yes. 14: Reader serv, admin, research, tchg. 15: 222 Dennison st, Highland Park NJ 08904.

WHITBY, THOMAS J(OSEPH). b Chicago Ill 12 Ja 19. 4: Mary Elizabeth Darrow. 5: UChicago 38-47 Geology PhB, 47-52 (LS) MA; UMontreal 47 (Fr) Certif; GeorgetownU 51 (Russian). 6: Russian, Fr. 7: Steel wkr Carnegie-Illinois Steel Co, Chicago 37-42; Surveyor US Coast & Geodetic Survey, Tex 42-43; Rifleman (sgt) USA (Inf), European Theatre 43-46; Sr subj catlgr LC 52-61; Info scientist Olin Mathieson Chem Corp, New Haven Conn 61-63; Chief libn Martin Marietta Corp, Denver 63-68; Assoc prof Grad Sch of Libnship UDenver 68-. 8: Visited Soviet Union in 1967 to survey libraries. 9: Amer Mgt Assn; SLA; ColoLA. 10: AAAS; Coun for ETV; Little Britches Youth Assn; Southglenn Civic Assn. 13: Yes. 14: Catlg, tech serv, documentation, lit of the scis. 15: Graduate School of Librarianship Univ of Denver, Denver Co 80210.

WHITCOMB, DOROTHY (E). b Cedar Point Kan 25 O 16. 5: Long Beach City Col 56-59 AA; Kansas State Tchrs Col 60-62 (Phys Sci) BA, 65-66 (LS) MA. 7: Catlgr Kan City (Kan) Pub Lib 66-. 9: ALA; KanLA; MPLA. 14: Catlg. 15: 1601 Washington blvd, Kansas City Ks 66102.

WHITE, ALMA LOIS (FOSTER). b East Baton Rouge Parish La 30 Je 13. 4: Horace Greely white. 5: Baton Rouge La, SouthernU 29-33 (Eng) BA, summers: 38, 48, 60- Certificate 9ls0, 3 summers between 62-67 (Admin & Supv) MEd; Louisiana StateU Baton Rouge La, Ext courses (Educ) 55 & 56. 6: Fr. 7: High Sch Eng Tchr & Libn F P T Sch Winnsobro La 32-60; Asst prin also parih libn, Franklin Parish Training Sch, Winnsboro 60-64, Libn (Grs 1-12) 64-66; Libn: Nicholson Lib & S Blvd Lib, Baton Rouge La 66-. 9: Nat Tchrs Assn; LaStateTA; LaCTE; ALA; LaLA; Franklin Parish LA. 10: Fine Arts Club; Entre Nous club; Mem of several organizs, soc clubs. 13: Yes. 14: Catlg. 15: 2045-78th ave, Baton Riuge La 70807.

WHITE, BERTHA MARGARETHE ROTHE. b Syracuse NY 26 Mr 15. 4: Kermit D White. 5: Syracuse 30-34 (Ger, Lat) AB (cum laude), 35 (Ger) AM, 40 BS in LS; George Washington U Sch of Law 48 JD, 56 (Law) LLM. 6: Ger, Fr, Sp, Lat. 7: Instr Auburn Collegiate Center, Auburn NY 36-37; Sub Tchg Syracuse Pub Schs, Syracuse NY 37-38; Eng tchr & Libn Central Sch, Richmondville NY 38-40; Libn Central Sch, Ovid NY 40-41; Lib asst Syracuse Pub Lib, Syracuse NY 41-43; Catlgr US Dept of State Lib, Wash DC 43-45; Catlgr & reviser LC 45-48; Catlgr US Army Map Serv, Wash DC 48; Ref libn US Dept of Justice, Wash DC 48-50; Law Libn: US Housing & Home Finance Agency, Wash DC 50-53, George Washington U Sch of Law 53-60, Bur of Old-Age & Survivors Ins, Baltimore 60-62; Asst ref libn Los Angeles Co Law Lib, Los Angeles62-64, Asst head ref libn 64-. 9: AALL; SoCal Law Lib Assn (sec-treas 64-65, v-pres 65-66); pres 66-68, var other offs; Law Libns Soc of Wash DC (pres 56-58,var other offs). 10: Phi Beta Kappa; Phi Kappa Phi; Pi Lambda Theta; Phi Gamma Phi. 12: "Daniel Webster Reader (56); "Biographical Directory of Law Librarians in the US & Canada (64); "The Law of Buying and Selling (68). 13: Yes. 14: Ref, bk reviewing, indexing, legal writing. 15: Los Angeles Co Law Lib, 301 W First st, Los Angeles 90012.

WHITE, BON-JEAN (NETTE). b Lampasas Tex 23 N 08. 5: Baylor Col 28 (Eng, Fr) BA; UIll 39 BS in LS. 7: Asst acquis dept UMo 29-36, Act head acquis dept 36-39, Head acquis dept 39-50; Order libn, Asst Prof Lib Sci Tex Christian U 50-55; Order Libn, Asst Prof Lib Sci Baylor U 55-64, Asst libn in chg of pub serv 64-. 9: ALA; TexLA; SWLA. 10: AAUP. 14: Bibliog. 15: Fairmount 210, 1600 S 5th st, Waco Tex 76706.

WHITE, BRENDA HAMILTON. b Latrobe Penn 17 My 40. 4: Gary Hamlin White. 5: Thiel Col 58-61 (Eng) BA; Duquesne 63 (Eng); UPittsburgh 64-66 MLS. 6: Fr. 7: Tchr Penn Hills Sch Dist, Sena Jr High Sch 61-66, Libn Penn Jr High Sch 66-68, Libn John H Linton intermed High Sch 68-. 9: NEA; PennLA; PennStateEA; Coun of Sch Libns Suburban Pittsburgh; Coun of PennHillsEA (chm Legis Com). 10: Beta Phi Mu. 14: Materials sel & acquis, ref. 15: Oakmont ave Ext, Oakmont Pa 15139.

WHITE, CARL M(ILTON). b Burnet Okla 12 Ag 03. 4: Ruth Bennett. 5: Okla Baptist U 21-25 (Sociol) AB; Mercer U 27-28 (Philos) MA; State U Iowa 29-30; Cornell U 30-33 (Philos) PhD; Columbia 33-34 BS in LS. 6: Fr, Ger. 7: Prin Bacone Col 25-26, Act pres 26-27; Instr in Eng Mercer U 27-28; Instr in Eng Burleson Col 28-9; Libn Fisk U 34-38; Libn & Chm of Div of the Lib & Sch of Lib Sci UNC 38-40; Dir of Lib & Lib Sch UIll 40-43; Columbia U: Dir of Libs 43-53, Dean of Sch of Lib Serv 43-54, Prof of Lib Serv 43-62; Program specialist in lib admin The Ford Foundation 62-67; Specialist UCal (San Diego) 65-. 8: Asst Prof of Lib Sci, UMich, summer 38; Adv, Dept of State on or & program of Unesco, 44-45; Coun, Amer Geog Soc 50-53; Chm, Coun on "Whos Who in Library Service 3d ed, 54-55; Dir, Inst of Libnship, UAnkara 59-61, & "Chair Prof of Lib Sci 60-61;in Africa, Asia, Latin Amer, & Carribean 62-66; Lib Adv to Fed Govt of Nigeria62-64; Lab staff, UCal (San Diego) 65-66. 9: ALA (Exec Bd 41-45); ACRL (chm Policy Com 38-40); ARL (Adv Com 43-47); NYLA; TennLA (Lib Legisl Com 36-38); CalLA. 11: Awarded Grad Prize in Philosophy for best essay embodying results of research, Cornell U 32. 12: Origins of the American Library School 61 "Sources of Information in the Social Sciences (64); "Bases of Modern Librarianship (64); Ed "College and Researh Libraries (41-48). 13: Yes. 14: Lib educ & admin, bibliog. 15: 5811 Beaumont ave, La Jolla Cal 92038.

WHITE, CLOTEA (COLLINS). b Meridian Miss 8 O 1900. 5: Rust Col 17-21 (Eng) AB; Atlanta summers 47, 49, 50 BSLS; UWis(Madison) summers 53-56 MSLS. 6: Lat, Fr, Ger. 7: Tchr & Libn Okolona Col 21-46; Head Libn St Pauls Col 46-. 9: ALA; NCTE; VaLA; Va Tchrs Assn. 10: Nat Assn Col Women NAACP; Delta Sigma Theta; SPCA; Garden Club; Bridge Club. 14: Admin of col libs, catlg. 15: P O Box396, Lawrencevile Va 23868.

WHITE, DALE EDWIN. b Grand Junction Col 6 Jl 34. 5: UNotre Dame 53-57 (Sociol) BA, 59-61 (Sociol) MA; UVienna 57; UDenver 57-58 (LS) MA; UMexico 62. 6: Sp, Fr. 7: Soc sci libn UNotre Dame (Ind) 58-59, 60-61, Latin Amer bibliogr 68-; Libn St Thomas Sem, denver 63-64. 9: ALA. 10: Phi Delta Kappa. 11. NDEA fellow UNotre Dame 64-67. 12: Span to Eng transls for private press. 14: Latin Amer subject collections. 15: Box 24, Grand Junction Co 81501.

WHITE, DIANE INNIS (CRIPPEN). b Tacoma Wash 24 O 39. 4: Jerry Lee White. 5: UPuget Sound 57-61 (Eng, Educ) BA; UWash 66-69 (LS) MA. 7: Tchr: Clover Park Schs, Park lodge 61, Auburn High Sch 62, Tacoma (Wash) Sch Dist Mt Tahoma High Sch 65-67; Peace Corps vol tchr, Iringa Tanzania 63-65; Libn Tacoma Sch Dist Mt Tahoma High Sch 68. 9: NCTE; NEA; Wash Tchrs Eng; Tacoma Area Eng Coun (sec). 14: Sch libnship. 15: 6066 Wapato Lake dr, Tacoma Wa 98408.

WHITE, DIANE. b Cape Girardeau Mo 20 Ag 43. 5: SE Mo State Col 60-64 (Eng) BS in High sch Educ; Peabody Col 66-67 MLS. 6: Sp, Portu. 7: Peace Corps vol Venezuela 64-66; Latin-Amer catlgr StanfordU 67-. 14: Latin-Amer catlg. 15: Dorena Mo 63844.

WHITE, DONALD J. b Peoria Ill 26 My 43. 4: Adelina Escamilla. 5: Elmhurst Col 61-63; San Jose State Col 63-65 (Soc Sci) BA; Rutgers 67-68 MLS. 7: Tchr Peace Corps, Liberia 65-67; Libn Mem UNewfoundland 68-. 14: Ref, Africana. 15: Lib Memorial Univ of Newfoundland, St John's Newfoundland.

WHITE, E LEONORE. b Baltimore Md 7 D 11. 5: Goucher Col 34 BA; Columbia 41 (LS) BS; UMd Lib Admins Devel Program 68 Certif. 6: Fr, Ger. 7: Lib asst Enoch Pratt Free Lib, Baltimore 39-40; Kanawha Co Pub Lib, Charleston WVa: Readers adv 41-42, Head of adult dept 42-43, Asst libn 43-45; Regimental libn 21st Inf Reg 24th Div, Kumamoto Japan 46-48; Lib asst Enoch Pratt Free Lib, Baltimore summer 47; Head of ref lib for European Command US Army, Heidelberg Germany 47-49; Post Libn, head of 3 libs Munich Mil Post, US Army, Munich Germany 49-52; Lib Dir Schenectady Co Pub Lib, Schenectady NY 53-; Lib Dir Mohawk Valley Lib Assn, Schenectady NY 59-. 9: ALA (chm Interlib Coop Com 67-69); NYLA (1st v-pres 61-62); Hudson-MohawkLA (pres 55). 10: C of C; Commun Welfare Coun; Mus of Mod Art; Alliance francaise; Schenectady Mus Assn; Schenectady Hist Assn; Freedom Forum; Munson-Williams Proctor Inst. 13: Yes. 14: Pub lib admin, ref. 15: Schenectady Co Pub Lib, Union st & Seward pl, Schenectady NY 12305.

WHITE, EDITH R. b Passaic NJ 4 N 23. 4: Forrest P White. 5: Vassar 40-44 (Drama) BA; UVa Ext 62; Old Dominion 62-66 Lib Sci Certif. 6: Fr. 7: Lt (jg) USN, Wash DC & sampson NY 44-46; Libn Norfolk Acad, Norfolk Va 61-. 9: ALA; VaLA. 10: AAUW; LWV; Norfolk Symphony Bd; Little Theatre Bd; Tidewater Choral; Human Rels Coun; YWCA; Norfolk Museum. 14: Tchg lib skills. 15: 1079 Algonquin rd, Norfolk Va 23505.

WHITE, ERNEST MILLER. b Robinson Ill 8 My 17. 4: Jessie Allen. 5: Vanderbilt U 39 BA; Peabody 41 BS in LS, 59 MA. 6: Ger. 7: Libn Dalton High Sch, Dalton Ga 40-41; Asst libn Union Theol Sem (Richmond Va) 41-44; Libn Louisville Presbyterian Sem 45-. 9: ALA; ATheolLA (past treas); KyLA (past sec-treas); Louisville Lib Club (past pres). 15: Louisville Presbyt Sem 1044 Alta Vista rd, Louisville Ky 40205.

WHITE, EULA (TOAL). b Albuquerque NM 24 Jl 17. 4: LeRoy J White. 5: Geneseo State Tchrs Col 35-39 (S) BS in Ed; UColo summer 41; URochester 51; UMich 52 AMLS; Lib U/S/A 65 (Data Processing). 7: Libn State Tchrs Col (Fredonia NY) summer 39; Libn Central Sch, Phelps NY 39-43; (1st Lt) WAC Personnel US Army, La & Australia 43-47; Resort store owner, Conesus Lake NY 47-61; Assoc dir NDEA Lib Inst, GENESEO NY summer 65; Assoc Prof of Lib Educ State U Col (Geneseo NY) 61-. 8: Consul Webster Central Sch Dist Media Wkshop 67. 9: ALA;NYLA; Faculty Assn State of NY; NEA-DAVI. 10: AAUW; Mem, Geneseo Bd of Educ; Girl Scouts. 13: Yes. 14: Catlg, ref, data proc, central proc, child lit. 15: 108 Center st, Geneseo NY 14454.

WHITE, FREDERICK S(TERLING). b Bandera Tex 20 N 19. 4: Edith Gott. 5: Trinity U 51 (Fr) BA; Our Lady of the Lake Col 52 MSLS. 6: Sp, Fr, Portu. 7: US Army (S/Sgt) 41-46; Libn USAF, Kelly AFB Tex 50-53; Bibliog Tex Engnr Expt Station, College Station Tex 53-59; Libn Tex Engnrs Libn, College Station Tex 59-61; Assoc libn Ariz State U 61; Assoc col libn Tex A&M U 61-63; Staff Sandia Corp, Albuquerque NM 63; research libn Tex Transportation Inst 63-. 8: Consul, Nat Bituminous Concrete Assn, 61-. 9: SLA. 10: Little League Baseball; Brazos Valley Youth Assn; Tex Collectors Inst. 14: Ref, bibliog, rare Texana. 15: 305 Laurel, Bryan Tex 77803.

WHITE, FREDERICK THOMAS HERBERT. b Calgary Alberta Can 24 F 23. 4: Valerie J Fay. 5: Mt Royal Vol 46-47; UAlberta 47-49 (Hist) BA; UToronto 49-50 BLS. 7: Catlgr Tacoma Pub Lib 50-51, Hd order dept 52-54; Hd circ dept Victoria Pub Lib 55-62; Dir Vancouver Is Reg Lib 62-. 9: CanLA; BCLA; PNLA. 13: Yes. 14: Automation, acquis. 15: 350 Eberts st, Nanaimo BC Can.

WHITE, GLORIA B. b Commerce Hunt Co Tex 2 O 35. 5: Tex WomansU 53-56 BA; E Tex StateU 62 MS in LS. 7: Circ & ref libn Waco Pub Lib, Waco Tex 56; Libn Sam Houston Elem sch, Port Arthur Tex 56-60; Asst catlgr Ft Worth Pub Lib 60-61; Libn Mineola High Sch, Moneola Tex 61-62; Libn Austin Pub Schs, Austin Tex 62-66; Ser libn Stephen F Austin State Col 66-. 9: TexLA; SWLA. 15: Box 4642 SFA Sta, Nacogdoches Tx 75961.

WHITE, HENRY FREDRICK. b Stockton Cal 31 Mr 37. 5: Modesto Jr Col 55-57 (Journalism) AA; UCal(Berkeley) 57-60 (Hist) AB, 62-64 MLS. 7: Stud asst interlib borrowing serv UCal Lib (Berkeley) 57-60, 61-64; Lib asst Bus Lib Columbia U Lib 60-61; Admin asst UCal Sch of Libnship (Berkeley) 64-. 9: ALA. 10: UCal Lib Schs Alumni Assn. 14: Ref, admin. 15: 2329A Dwight way, Berkeley Ca 94704.

WHITE, HERBERT S. b Vienna Austria 5 S 27. 4: Mary Virginia Dyer. 5: City Col (NY) 44-46, 47-49 (Chem) BS; Syracuse 49-50 (LS) MS. 6: GER, Sp. 7: (Pfc) US Army Air Corps 46-47; Lib trainee Queensborough Pub Lib, Jamaica NY 49; Spec recruit internship program LC 50; Catlgr,bibliogr, ed Sci-Tech Div LC 50-53; Tech libn Y-12 Plant Union Carbide AEC, Oak Ridge Tenn 53-54; Chief Libn Chance Vought Aircraft, Dallas 54-59; Proj manager IBM Engnr Lib, Kingston NY 59-62; Proj manager IBM Tech Info Center, Poughkeepsie NY 62-64; Exec Dir NASASci & Tech Info Facility, College Park Md 64-68; V-pres Leasco Systs & Research Corp, Bethesda Md 65-. 8: NY State Commsnr of Educ Lib Technician Eval Program, 60-61; John Cotton Dana lecturer in spec libnship, Syracuse U 62, UMinn 66; Mem, Adv Bd, Manpower Research Proj, UMd Sch of Lib & Info Serv 67-; Presidents Adv Coun on Col Lib Resources 66-. 9: SLA (chm Adv Coun 65-66, Mem Bd Dirs 64-66, mem Adv Coun 58-66; Pres 68-69; Tex Chap: pres 58-59; chm Sci-Tech Div 60-61, Chm Aerospace Div 66-67, Nat Recr Chm 61-65); ASIS. 10: Boy Scouts; Beta Phi Mu. 11: Spec recr, LC Intern Prog. 12: "Bibliogaphy of OSRD Reports, LC; "Prior Art Sources and the Use of Engineering Libraries ASME; "What Is a Special Librarian SLA; "Special Librarianship - Information at Work, SLA. 13: Yes. 14: Lib & info center mgt, info retrieval, lib mechanization. 15: Leasco Systems & Research Corp 4833 Rugby ave, Bethesda Md 20852.

WHITE, JAMES WILLIAM. b Cedar Rapids Iowa 5 My 35. 4: Dorothy Jean Henderson. 5: Iowa StateU 53-55 (Electrical Engring); State UIowa 60-63 (Hist, Educ) BA, 67-68 (LS) MA. 6: Ger. 7: Tool engring Allis-Chalmers, Cedar Rapids Iowa 55-56; Draftsman collins Radio, Cedar Rapids Iowa 56-58; Electronic instrument repair (Sgt 1st class) US Army 57; Quality control tech Square D, Cedar Rapids Iowa 58-60; Lib asst Cedar Rapids Pub Lib, Cedar Rapids Iowa 60-63; Tchr Linn-Mar Commun Schs Cedar Rapids Iowa 63-68; Lib dir P M Musser Pub Lib, Muscatine Iowa 68-. 9: ALA; IowaLA (Dist VII: Chm Legisl Com). 10: Muscatine Co Mus Assn; Central States SPEBSQSA; Muscatine Commun Theatre. 14: Ref, adult serv. 15: 304 Iowa, Muscatine Ia 52761.

WHITE, JANE (NEAL). b Portland Me 4 My 18. 4: Winston W White. 5: Ky Wesleyan Col 38-39; UKy 61-64 (Elem Educ) AB, 64-65 MS in LS. 6: Fr. 7: Clk-typist US Signal Corps Lexington Signal Depot 42-43; Libn Col of Educ UKy (Lexington) 65-. 14: Ref, pub serv. 15: 405 Greenbriar rd, Lexington Ky 40503.

WHITE, JANET CARTWRIGHT. b Waynesville Ohio 17 Mr 08. 4: David W White. 5: West Col for Women 26-30 (Eng) AB; West Res 30-31 BS in LS. 6: Fr. 7: Sci & tech, bus bur Cleveland Pub Lib, Fed Res Bank Lib, Cleveland 31-34; Spec wk with Co offs, 1st asst ref dept Cincinnati Pub Lib 34-37; Med Lib St Johns Hosp, Santa Monica Cal & Kennedy Child Study Center 52-. 9: Med Lib Group of So Cal (v-pres & Program Chm, pres). ; Assn West Hosps (Hosp Libns Sect; v-pres, Adv Bd); MedLA (Adv Com Med Lib Probs); CathLA (Health Scis Sect; mem Com). 15: Med Lib St Johns Hosp, 1328 22nd st, Santa Monica Ca 90405.

WHITE, JANETTE HUNTER. b Toronto Can 6 Ag 21. 5: Toronto38-42 (Modern Langs) BA; Ont Col of Educ UToronto 42-43 (Educ) High Sch Spec Certif; Columbia 56-57 MSLS. 6: Fr, Ger, Russian. 7: Censorship asst Dept of Nat War Serv Censorship Br, Ottawa 43-45; Deputy-asst censor Control Commsn for Germany (BE), Hamburg W Germany 45-47; Research asst Nat Research Coun, Communications Br, Ottawa 49-55; Ref libn gen ref div Toronto Pub Lib 57-59;

Gen libn Lib Meteorological Serv of Can, Toronto 59-61; Head ref & circ div Toronto Bdof Educ 61-67; Assoc Prof Sch of Lib & Info Sci U West Ont 67-. 9: CanLA; SLA (Toronto Chap: sec 62-63, v-pres 65-66); OntLA. 14: Ref. 15: School of Lib & Info Sci Univ of West Ont, London Ont Can.

WHITE, JANET FALCONER. b Bloomingdale NJ 6 S 15. 5: Elmira Col 32-36 (Eng, Hist) AB; Drexel 36-37 BS in LS; UMich 44-48 (Hist) AM. 7: Child libn Lucas Co Lib, Maumee Ohio 37-38, Br libn 38-41; Yp libn various brs NYC Pub Lib 41-44; Libn UMich Math-Econ Lib (Ann Arbor) 44-46; Ref libn UMich (Ann Arbor) 46-. 8: Lecturer lib sci UMich 69. 9: ALA. 10: Mich Acad of Sci Arts & Letters; AAUW; Phi Kappa Phi. 14: Ref, govt docs. 15: 332 E William st, Ann Arbor Mi 48108.

WHITE, JEANETTE (BOWEN). b Providence 12 Ag 04. 4: George Preston White. 5: Simmons 23-27 (LS) BS. 6: Fr, Sp. 7: Ind U Lib 27-29; NYU Lib 29-30; Wilbur Cross Lib UConn 30-41; Spaaf Post Lib, Spokane Wash 44-45; Hillyer COL Lib 47-50; Wilbur Cross Lib UConn 55-. 14: Catlg. 15: Rt 1, N Windham Conn 06256.

WHITE, JOHN B(ROWNING). b Monument Colo 7 My 14. 4: Lucille Margaret McVey. 5: West State Col of Colo summer 31; UColo 31-35 (Pol Sci) AB (cum laude); UDenver summers 38, 40, 41 BS in LS; UNM summer 39; UNeb 41-42, 48-53 (Hist) MA, PhD. 7: Tchr rural sch dist 23, Yuma Co Colo 35-36; Tchr jr-sr high sch, Weldona Colo 36-38; Libn-tchr jr-sr high sch, Artesia NM 38-41; Asst ref libn City Lib, Lincoln Neb 42-43; USNR Mailman 2/c 43-46; Ser libn UNb 46-50; Dir of Lib & Archives Neb State Hist Soc, Lincoln Neb 50-63; Assoc Prof of Lib Sci No Ill U 64-. 9: ALA-LED;-ARCL; SAA; IllLA (Life mem); MPLA(life mem). 10: AHA; Org Amer Histns; AAUP; Amer Inter-prof Inst; ACLU; SANE; United World Federalists; UN Assn; ASIS; NAACP; Amer Humanist Assn; ADA. 12: "Published Sources on Territorial Nebraska (56); "Index-Guide to the Contents of the Publications and the Magazine of the Nebraska State Historical Society (58). 13: Yes. 14: Lib hist, lib & soc, bibliog of hist & soc scis. 15: Dept of Lib Sci No Ill Univ, DeKalb Ill 60115.

WHITE, JOHN WESLEY. b Jackson Miss 25 D 31. 5: Wayne State 51-56 (Elem Educ) BS 58-61 9admin, Supv) MA; UMich 65-66 MALS. 6: Sp. 7: Tchr Detroit Pub Schs 56-58, Staff coord 68-; Soldier US Army, Ariz 56-58; Adult ref libn Detroit Pub Lib 66-. 10: NAACP; Boy Scouts of Amer; UMich Detroit Club; Detroit Metro Schoolmen's Club; Mich Lib Alum Assn. 14: Adult ref. 15: 2110 E Wald cir apt 34, Detroit Mi 48238.

WHITE, JOYCE LOUISE. b Phila 27. 5: UPenn 45-49 (LS) BA; Drexel 61-64 MS LS. 6: Fr. 7: Ser dept UPenn Main Lib 49-53; Period & ref ULondon (Eng) 53-54; Acquis dept UPenn Main Lib 54-57; Libn UPenn Sch of Educ 57-. 8: Dir, Drexel Inst of Lib Sch Ann Conf for Church Libns, 63-67; Consul, Van Guard Sch, Haverford Penn 67-68. 9: ATheolLA; PennLA; Church & SynagogueLA (Ann Conf Chm 67, v-pres 68, pres 69). 10: LWV; Episcopal Soc for Cultural & Racial Unity. 12: "Proceedings of the Annual Church Library Conference (63, 64); Ed Bd "Current Contents in Education (69). 13: Yes. 14: Ref (educ & religion). 15: Penniman Lib Univ of Penn 36th & Walnut sts, Phila Pa 19104.

WHITE, KENTON STOWELL. b Long Beach Cal 9 Jl 33. 4: Elizabeth Laurenson. 5: UCal(Berkeley) 51-55 (Eng) BA, 3-64 MLS. 7: Clerk typist Oakland Army Terminal, Oakland Cal 57-58; Eng tchr Alameda High Sch, Aameda Cal 58-60; Eng tchr San Lorenzo High Sch, San Lorenzo Cal 60-61; Asst br libn Alameda CoLib, Fremont, Newark Cal 62-63; A-v & ref libn San Bernardino Pub Lib, San Bernarino Cal 64-68; Libn & coord Inland Lib Syst A-V Ctr, San Bernardino Cal 68-69; Asst libn Huntington Beach Pub Lib 69-. 8: Ed "Arrowhead Allied Arts Council Bulletin, San Bernardino 68-69. 14: Info retrieval, a-v, ref. 15: 878 Edgehill, San Bernardino Ca 92405.

WHITE, LESLIE ESAU. b Boston 9 S 11. 4: Samuel S White. 5: Mt Holyoke 29-33 (Lat) AB (cum laude); Simmons 33-34 BS in LS; Mt Holyoke 6-38 (Span). 6: Lat, Sp, Fr, Ital, Ger. 7: Catlgr Mt Holyoke 34-38; Ser catlgr Temple U 38-41; Asst libn Radio Corp of Amer, Moorestown NJ 56-57; Libn II Free Lib of Phila 57-58; Catlgr Fed Res Bank of Phila 58-61; Catlgr-Dir Cherry Hill (NJ) Pub Lib 61-63; Libn III Free Lib of Phila 63-. 9: ALA. 14: Catlg. 15: 619 Linwood ave, Collingswood NJ 08108.

WHITE, LUCIEN. b Hillsdale Ill 16 N 14. 4: Lois Sanuelson. 5: Augustana Col 31-35 (Fr) AB; UIll 41, 43-44 (Fr) MA, 46-47 (Fr) PhD; UGrenoble 49-50 (Fr); UIll 53-54 (LS) MS. 6: Fr, Sp. 7: Prof of modern langs Augustana Col (Ill) 39-53, Libn 54-58; Assoc dir of pub serv depts UIll(Urbana) 58-65, Dir of pub serv depts 65-68; Assoc Dean of Lib Admin 68-. 8: Ill State Lib Adv Coun 65-. 9: ALA (chm Interlib Loan Com 63-64); IllLA (pres 64-65), Chm Budget Com 64-65, chm Nomin Com 66-67, Lib Devel & Legis Com 63-). 10: Champaign Pub Lib. Bd; Phi Beta Kappa; Beta Phi Mu; AAUP. 11 Ed "Augustana Library Publications (54-58); Pub Bd "Library Trends (58-). 13; yes. 14: Acquis, pub serv, resources, bldgs. 15: 514 Willis, Champaign Ill 61822.

WHITE, LUELLA EVELYN. b San Francisco Cal 14 My 29. 5: San Francisco State Col 47-49 (Sociol); SeattleU 51-64 (Soc Sci) BEd; UWash 64-65 M Lib; Central Wash State Col 67-69; West Wash State Col 69. 6: Sp. 7: Religious tchr Dominican Sisters, Edmonds Wash 49-66; Asst libn Auburn Sch Dist (high sch), Auburn Wash 66-67; A-v coord Auburn High Sch, Auburn Wash 67-68; Pub libn Seattle City Lib summers 66, 68; Elem libn (Lake Youngs & Fairwood) Kent Sch Dist (Wash) 68-. 8: Young Adult Consul to Renton Pub Lib Winter 68. 9: NEA-DAVI; ALA; WashEA; WashStateASchL. 10: PTA; Cath Alumni Club: UWash Lib Alum Club. 13: Yes. 14: Res on learning, media, ref. 15: 10406 SE 174th #21, Renton Wa 98055.

WHITE, MARGUERITE (BARKER). b Coldwater Ohio 17 Je 19. 4: George A White. 5: Bowling Green U 37-41 (Lat, Fr) BE in Ed; West Res 42-43 BS in LS. 6: Fr, Sp. 7: Ross High Sch Lib, Fremont Ohio 43-46; Shaker Heights Elem Libs, Shaker Heights Ohio 47-51; Tchr & libn Thompson High Sch 52-54; Tchr & libn Clyde High Sch 54-57; Orange High Sch & Middle Sch Libn 57-. 9: NEA; OhioEA; Ohio SchLA. 14: High sch & jr high sch wk. 15: 3889 Ellendale rd, Chagrin Falls Oh 44022.

WHITE, MARILYN (WARKOW). b Aurora Il 6 N 31. 4: Herbert L White Jr. 5: Oberlin Col 49-53 (Fr) BA; Ind U 54-55 MA in LS. 7: Asst Thailand Proj Ind U 55-56; Asst libn Ellensburg Pub Lib, Ellensburg Wash 56-57; Readers adv Indianapolis Pub Lib 57-58; Circ asst De Pauw U Lib 58; Ser libn Iowa State Tchrs Col 58-59; Ref asst Oak Park Pub Lib, Oak Park Ill 60, Head of ref 60-69. 9: ALA; IllLA; Lib Admins Conf of NoIll (chm Ref Sect 68-69). 10: Beta Phi Mu. 14: Ref. 15: 622 Belleforte ave, Oak Park Ill 60302.

WHITE, MARY HARRIET. b Rock Hll SC 6 D 26. 5: Salem Col 44-48 BMus; Emory 59-62 (LS) ML. 6: Fr. 7: Priv & pub music tchr, Rock Hill SC 48-54; Accompanist Winthrop Col 55-56; Lib asst Emory U 59-62; Catlgr Wake Forest Col 62-63; Catlgr Ga Tech 63-68; Acquis libn SC State Lib Bd, Columbia SC 68-. 9: ALA; GaLA; SCLA. 10: USC Soc. 13: Yes. 14: Tech serv. 15: SC State Lib Board 1001 Main st, Columbia SC 29201.

WHITE, MILDRED K(ENNEDY). b Wash DC 21 Ja 20. 4: William Sidney White. 5: Talladega Col 37-41 (Eng Lit) BA; Catholic U 42-44 BS in LS; Jacksonville U summer 61; UMinn(Minneapolis) summer 62. 6: Fr. 7: Libn Fla Mem Col 50-51; Catlg libn Fla A&M U 51-57; Catlg libn Edward Waters Col 57-; Lib asst br Jacksonville Pub Lib, Jacksonville Fla 57-62; Libn Duval Co High Schs, Jacksonville Fla 58-62; Night libn in charge of catlg Edward Waters Col 62-. 9: ALA; NEA; FlaLA. 10: Alpha Kappa Alpha. 14: Caltg, ref. 15: 934 Scriven st, Jacksonville Fla 2209.

WHITE, MYRA NAOMI (GOLLOM). b Toronto Can 27 N 40. 4: Lawrence W White. 5: Toronto 58-61 (Anthropology) BA, 61-62 BLS; West Res 65 (Anthropology). 7: Catlgr UToronto Lib 62-63; Ya libn Cleveland Heights Pub Lib, Cleveland 63-64. 9: Inst Prof Libns Ont. 10: ADA. 15: 3711 Rawnsdale rd, Cleveland Oh 44122.

WHITE, MYRA. b NYC 17 Je 26. 4: Alvin M White. 5: Brooklyn Col 45-49 (Fr) AB; Far East & Russian Lang Sch UC ext summer 50 (Russian) Certif; USoCal 63-65 MSLS. 6: Fr, Russian. 7: Asst to head of process dept Hoover Lib, Stanford Cal 52-53; Libn For Chem dept Stanford U 55-56; Russian Instr Col f Notre Dame (Cal) 59; Russian catlgr UCal(Riverside) 64-65; Libn Rancho Santa Ana Botanic Garden, Claremont Cal 65-68; Catlgr Stanford U 68. 9: ALA; CalLA. 10: Beta Phi Mu. 15: 934 Harvard, Claremont Ca 91711.

WHITE, NEVA LOIS. b Newton Kan 14 D 15. 5: Goshen Col 41-44 (Eng) BA; UMich 44-46 ABLS. 6: Ger, Persian. 7: Libn Goshen Col 43-50; Relief wker Mann Cent Comm, Hong Kong 50-51; Libn St Marys Hosp Libs, Wausau Wis 52-53; Chief tech proc Marquette U Lib 53-59; Lib adv Kabul U Lib USAID Wyo Team (Kabul Afghanistan) 59-66; Chief catlgr

Kan State U 66-. 8: Lib adv Kabul U, Afghanistan 59-66. 9: ALA; MedLA. 13: Yes. 14: Catlg. 15: 2465 Vaughn dr, Manhattan Ks 66502.

WHITE, PEGGY (SUZANNE). b Atlanta Ga 6 Ap 44. 5: SamfordU 62-65 (Eng) AB; UNC 65-66 MSLS. 7: Ref asst Mobile Pub Lib, Mobile Ala 66-68, Supv adult serv 68-. 9: ALA; SELA; AlaLA. 14: Ref, adult serv. 15: 1008 Marine st, Mobile Al 36605.

WHITE, REX ALBERT. b Tulsa Okla 24 Ag 23. 4: Elizabeth Kloosterboer. 5: UTulsa 46-51 (Eng) BA; Catholic U 61-64 MSLS. 7: (Maj) artillery & supply off USMC 42-64; Soc sci libn Ida State U 64-66; Assoc libn for readers serv 66-69; Assoc libn 69-. 8: Mem, Adv coun LSCA Title II 68-. 9: ALA; IdaLA (chm Lib Devel Com 67-69); PNLA. 10: Marine Corps Assn; Beta Phi Mu. 13: Yes. 14: Ref, docs, ser, admin. 15: 37 Dartmouth, Pocatello Ida 83201.

WHITE, RHEA (AMELIA). b Utica NY 6 My 31. 5: Utica Col Syracuse U 49-51 (Eng); Penn State U 51-53 (Eng) AB; Pratt 63-65 MLS. 6: Fr. 7: Research fellow Parapsychology Lab Duke U 54-58; Research & ed assoc Amer Soc Psychical Research, NYC 59-62; Research Fellow Menninger Found, Topeka Kan 62-65; Libn Dept of Psychiatry Maimonides Hosp, Brooklyn NY 65-67; Info off Amer Soc Psychical Research, NYC 65-Asst ref libn E Meadow (NY) Pub Lib 66-. 9: ALA; SLA; Parapsychol Assn (Coun 58, 60-63, sec 58, 62). 10: AAAS; Soc for Psych Res (England); Amer Soc for Psych Res; Beta Phi Mu. 11: Hans Peter Luhn Award, NY Chap of ADI, (ASIS) 65. 12: Ed "Journal of the Amer Soc Psychical Research (60-62). 13: Yes. 14: Ref, devel of improved subj headings, bibliotherapy. 15: 2 Plane Tree lane, Dix Hills NY 11746.

WHITE, ROBERT CURTIS. b Buffalo NY 20 F 05. 4: Jane Boren. 5: USMA 23-27 BS; UMich 57-58 MALS. 6: Fr. 7: Col US Army Artillery 27-57; Map & geog libn UIll (Urbana) 58-. 9: SLA (Geog & Map Div: sec-treas 61-63, chm 63-65). 13: Yes. 14: Maps, gazetteers. 15: 1007 Devonshire dr, Champaign Il 81820.

WHITE, ROBERT LOUIS. b Herrin Ill 8 Ja 38. 4: Nancy Hostetler. 5: State U Iowa 56-57 (Zoo) BA, 60-62 Instr Materials) MS; UMinn 63-64 (Curriculum Instr), 65-68 (Instr Materials). 6: Fr. 7: Research asst SoIllU 60-61, Instr nstr 62; Instr & Libn St Cloud State Col 62-65; Supv & a-v serv SoIllU 65-67; Media coord 67-. 8: Educ consul Nepal 67. 9: Ill A-V Assn; IllEA; NEA-DAVI. 10: Phi Delta Kappa; AAUP. 13: Yes. 14: Instr materials. 15: Learning Resources Service So Ill Univ, Carbondale Il 62903.

WHITE, RUTH M(ARGARET). b Ludlow Ky 7 S 14. 5: Ohio State U 32-35 (Eng, Soc Studies) BS in Ed; West Res 37-38 BS in LS; Chicago 58-63 (LS) AM. 7: Tchr Clark High Sch, Carnegie Penn 35-37; Libn Gilbert Stuart Jr High Sch, Providence 38-40; Asst libn U High Sch, Ohio State U, Columbus Ohio 40-41; Libn Ottawa Hills High Sch, Ottawa Hills Ohio 41-42; Libn Nathan Hale Jr High Sch, Cleveland 42-43; Commander US Coast Guard 43-46; Asst buyer T A Chapman Co, Milwaukee 46-47; Libn Chula Vista Pub Lib, Chula Vista Cal 47-51; Libn US Army Spec Serv Libs, Tokyo 51-53; Libn Chippewa Falls Pub Lib, Chippewa Falls Wis 54-55; Libn I Detroit Pub Lib 55-58; Asst to exec sec PLA & AAStateL of ALA, Chicago 58-62; Libn Hdqrs Lib ALA, Chicago 63-67; Exec sec adult & ref serv div 68-. 9: ALA; SLA; IllLA. 10: US Coast Guard Res; Res Offs Assn; Pi Lambda Theta Beta Phi Mu. 13: Yes. 14: Adult serv, ref. 15: 5518 Cornell ave, Chicago 60637.

WHITE, RUTH WILLIAMS. b Jericho Vt My 20. 5: UVt 36-40 (lat) AB; Simmons 55-56 MSLS; UFla ext 6-162 (Curriculum); USoMiss 62-63 (Curriculum) PhD. 6: Fr, Lat. 7: Lang tchr Vt high schs 40-44; Acquis, ref, interlib loan UVt Lib 45-47, 53-55; Libn W Springfield High Sch, W Springfield Mass 56-59; Libn Graham-Eckes Sch, Palm Beach Fla 59-60; Head Libn Brevard Jr Col 60-62; Ref libn USoMiss 62-63, Assoc Prof of Lib Sci 63-64; Dir Dept of Lib EDuc UGa 64-, Prof 69-. 8: Staff of Learning Resources Center, Lib 21, Seattle summer62; Dir, NDEA Inst for Sch Lib Personnel, UGa summer 65, 66, 67; Dir HEA Insts 68-70. 9: ALA (Subscr Bks Com 65-69); -RSD (mem Standards Com 69-); NEA; Assn for Supv & Curr Develop; SELA; GaLA (mem Sch Lib Standards Com); FlaLA; GaEA. 10: AAUP; AAUW; Delta Delta Delta; Phi Deta Kappa; Kappa Delta Pi; Athens Womens Club. 11: Woman of Yr in Educ (Athens Bus & Prof Womens Club) 68. 12: Sch Lib Ed "Film News (67-); Dir Lib Series I-IV (Colonial Film Co 67). 13: Yes. 14: Lib educ, sch libs, ref, advanced lib techniques. 15: 520 Venita dr, Athens Ga 30601.

WHITE, SUMNER. b Boston 12 D 22. 4: Marilyn Richardson White. 5: BostonU 4852 (Sociol) BA; Simmons 5253 MSLS. 7: Staff Sgt US Army Inf 4346; Libn Detroit Pub Lib 5357; Supv libn E Orange pub Lib, E Orange NJ 5763; Consul Ramapo Catskill Lib Syst, Middletown NY 6365; Asst dir 65. 9: ALA; NYLA (Pub Rel Coun); NY State Educ Communications Assn. 14: Admin, bldgs, circ control. 15: 68 Spring st, Goshen NY 10924.

WHITE, SHARON (LAPHAM). b Rochester NY 18 N 43. 4: David Robert White. 5: Syracuse 61-64 (Eng Lit) BA; Rutgers 64-65 MLS; Syracuse (Educ) NY State Tchg Certif. 6: Sp. 7: Libn Minoa Middle Sch, Minoa NY 65-66; Ser libn Syracuse 66; Admin USAF Hancock Field, Syracuse NY 67-; Catlgr Colgate-Rochester Divinity Sch 69-. 9: ALA; NEA; NY State Tchrs Assn. NYLA; SLA. 10: PTA; Dames; Lib Club; Literary Club; Wives Club. 14: Univ & spec libs. 15: Norway rd, Kendall NY 14476.

WHITE, MRS WILLIE GLENN. b Waxahachie Tex 25 O 08. 4: Roberts Sidney White. 5: Trinity U 26-28; Tex Womans U 28-31 (LS) BS; St Marys U 45. 7: Libn Clarendon High Sch & Jr Col, Clarendon Tex 33-52; Catlg libn Tex Christian U 52-. 9: TexLA. 10: Delta Kappa Gamma. 15: 3504 Rogers, Ft Worth Tx 76109.

WHITEHEAD, SISTER ALICE. b Chicago 3 Ap 13. 5: DePaul 40-44 (Classical Lang) BA; Rosary Col 46-53 MALS; UNotre Dame 59-63 (Eng) MA; St Bonaventure 67 (Theol). 6: Fr. 7: Tchr & libn elem schs, Chicago & Sault Ste Marie Mich 37-53; Libn Loretto Acad, Chicago 53-57, Libn-media specialist 61-65; Libn St Francis High Sch, Wheaton Ill 57-61; Libn & media specialist Loretto Central High Sch, Sault Ste Marie Mich 65-; Research Title III Pub Schs of Sault Ste Marie, Mich 67-68; Lib consul elem & secondary schs of Inst of the Blessed Virgin Mary 69-. 8: Off-campus libn St Procopius Col, Lisle Ill 57-64. 9: ALA; NCTE; MichLA; Tri-Coun Libns Assn. 10: Trustee, Carnegie Pub Lib, Sault Ste Marie Mich 67-; Trustee, Systems Pub Libs, Eastern Upper Peninsula Mich 68-. 11: 3-M Award for creative use of overhead proj 64. 15: 377 Maple st, Saulte Ste Marie Mi 49783.

WHITEHEAD, IDELLE (ROBERSON). b Roger Mills Co Okla 19 F 12. 4: Shelby A Whitehead. 5: E Tex Baptist Col 57-60 (Elem Educ) BS; E Tex State U 60-63 MSLS. 7: Elem tchr 51-55 High Sch 55-57; Asst libn E Tex Baptist Col 57-62; Libn Ark A&M Col 64-. 9: ArkLA; ArkEA. 10: AAUW; Alpha Chi. 14: Org, admin. 15: Box 563, College Heights Ar 71655.

WHITEHEAD, OLIVE F(RANCES). b Washington Conn 18 N 16. 5: Westminister Col (Penn) 35,36-39 (Math) BS; Drexel 40-41 bs in LS. 7: Lib asst UPenn 39-40; Asst libn Hercules Powder Co, Wilmington Del 41-47; Libn Amer Sugar Refining Co R & D Div, Phila 47-58; Asst libn Radio Corp of Amer, Camden NJ 58-69, Libn 69. 9: SLA; ALA; Spec Libs Coun of Phila & Vicinity; (treas 55-57; chm Directory Com 62-; chm Nominating Com, chm Sci-Tech Gp); 62-); Phila Area Tech Serv Libns; DelLA (sec 46-47). 14: Reports catlg & ref. 15: 204 S 42nd st, Phila Pa 19104.

WHITEHEAD, THOMAS MAYNARD. b Williamsport Penn 26 Ag 41. 4: Dianne Miller. 5: Bucknell U 59-63 (Hist) BA; Syracuse 64-65 (LS) ms. 6: Fr. 7: libn trainee Rochester (NY) Pub Lib 63-64; Catlgr rare bk room Syracuse U Lib 65-, Bibliog(r) rare bk room 66-67; Curator rare bks & mss Temple U Lib 67-. 9: BSA. 10: Philobiblon Club, Phila. 11: Amy Loveman Nat Bk Award, 63. 14: Rare bks & spec collections. 15: Temple Univ Lib Berks & 13th sts, Philadelphia Pa 19122.

WHITEHILL, MARGARET (EMILY). b Lander Wyo 3 F 35. 5: UMinn 53-57 (Hist) BA, 57-58 (LS) MALS, 58-59 (Eng, Secondary Educ) BS. 6: Sp, Ger. 7: Sch libn UMinn Elem Sch, Minneapolis 58-59; Army libn US Army lib serv Europe, Germany 59-61; Asst sch libn Hampton Twp schs, Allison Park Penn 62; Asst ref libn UPittsburgh 62-63; Ya libn Tucson Pub Lib 63-64; Ref libn Juniata Col Lib 65-66; Spec serv libn USMC Camp S D Butler, Okinawa 66-68; Base libn Personal serv USAF, Udorn Thailand 69-. 9: ALA; PennLA. 10: LWV; DAR; Commun Little Theatre Assn; Amer Forestry Assn. 14: Ref, readers guidance. 15: 432 Cmbt Spt Gp Box 10 Base Lib, APO San Francisco Ca 96237.

WHITEHILL, MARY EVELYN (PERROTT). b Newburgh NY 9 Mr 20. 4: W Hugh Whitehill. 5: Wells Col 41 (Fine Arts) BA; SUNY (Albany) 65 (LS) MS. 7: Br libn Newburgh Free Lib, Newburgh NY 65-. 9: Orange Sullivan Pub Lib Assn (sec). 10: Girl Scout Coun. 14: Phono-record catlg, ref. 15: Grand ave MD #16, Newburgh NY 12550.

WHITEHORN, CATHERINE LOIS. b Columbus Neb 5 My 11. 5: Rockford Col 27-31 (Eng, Span) BA; URochester 31-32, 33-34 (Eng) MA; NY State Col (Albany) 32-33 BS in LS; Chicago 41-45 (LS). 6: Fr, Sp, Ital. 7: Libn Gen Beadle State Col 38-41; US Off of Censorship, Chicago 42-43; Libn Hinsdale (Ill) Twp High Sch 43-45; Ref asst ref dept Carnegie Lib, Pittsburgh 45-46; Libn Kingswood Sch Cranbrook, Bloomfield Hills Mich 46-52; Catlgr Stephen F Austin State Col 52-55; Catlgr Baltimore pub schs, lib processing & catlg center 55-09: ALA-AASchL;-RTSD (chm Central Catlg Com 62-64);-CSD; MdLA; Assn Sch Libns Md. 10: AAUW; College Club; Walters Art Gallery. 13: Yes. 14: Sch libs, centralized catlg. 15: 2407 E Cold Spring lane, Baltimore 21214.

WHITEHOUSE, ELEANOR (FRENTZEL). b Brooklyn NY 4 My 13. 4: Frederick A Whitehouse. 5: St Joseph's Col for Women 30-33 (Hist) BA; LIU 66-68 (LS) MS. 7: Clk SE&M Vernon Inc, Elizabeth NJ 33-36; Stenographer Liggett & Myers Tobacco Co, NYC 37; Sec Boyd, Weir & Sewell Inc, NYC 37-42; Asst ref libn Garden City Pub Lib, Garden City NY 67-. 9: ALA; NYLA; NassauCoLA. 10: AAUP; LWV; Fac Women's Club of HofstraU. 14: Ref. 15: 68 Transverse rd, Garden City NY 11530.

WHITELEY, WILLIAM HENRY. b Vancouver BC Can 6S29. 5: UBC 47-51 (Hist) BA; Queens U (Ont) 51-52 (Canadian Hist) MA; Cornell U 52-56 (Eng Hist) PhD; McGill 61-62 BLS. 6: Fr. 7: Sessional Lecturer in Hist UBC 56-57; Archivist-Histn Mem U (Newfoundland) 58-60; Histn historic sites div Govt of Canada, Ottawa 60-61; Order libn Queens U (Ont) 62-63; Period libn UAlta 63-65; Asst libn Simon Fraser U (BC) 65-. 9: CanLA. 10: Can Hist Assn; Can Inst of Internat Affairs. 11: Can coun grant for hist research 69. 13: Yes. 14: Univ lib bk collections. 15: 2105 W 32nd ave apt 218, Vancouver 8 BC Can.

WHITELOCK, MARGARET (MOOSE). b Covington Tenn 19 S 35. 4: Wayne R Whitelock. 5: Maryville Col 53-57 (Fr) BA; CatholicU 66-67 MS in LS. 6: Fr, Ger. 7: Gen asst Maryville Col Lib 57-61; Typist & descr catlgr Princeton Theol Sem 61-65, Catlgr 67-. 9: ALA; ATheolLA. 14: Catlg. 15: 36 Hibben rd, Princeton NJ 08540.

WHITELY, ESTHER R(ISSER). b Lancaster Penn 19 Mr 06. 4: Paul L Whitely. 5: UPittsburgh 31 (Eng) BA; Temple summer 26, 27 (LS); Ind U 60, 62 (Lib Educ) MA. 7: Tchr-libn Jr High Sch, Bethlehem Penn 28-29; Libn Stevens High Sch, Lancaster Penn 29-34; Libn Manheim Twp High Sch, Neffsville Penn 44-46; Asst libn State Tchrs Col (Millersville Penn) 50-57, Ref libn 57-60; Ref libn Earlham Col 61-62; Ref libn & Asst Prof Millersville State Col 62-. 9: ALA; NEA; PennStateEA; PennLA. 10: AAUW; LWV; Delta Kappa Gamma; YWCA; Beta Phi Mu; Franklin & Marshall Faculty Wives; Bd of Mgrs of Church Women United; Cliosophic Soc. 14: Ref. 15: 425 N President ave, Lancaster Penn 17603.

WHITENACK, CAROLYN IRENE. b Mercer Co Ky 20 Ap 16. 5: Georgetown Col 32-34 (Eng); UKy 45-48 (Hist); UIll 50-56 (LS) MA. 7: Elem tchr Mercer Co (Ky) Schs 34-47; Instr & libn dept of Lib Sci UKy 47-50; Sch lib serv Louisville Pub Schs, Louisville Ky 50-53; Dir Tchg Materials Ind Dept of Pub Instr, Indianapolis 53-56; Asst Prof Dept of Educ, Purdue U 56-60, Assoc Prof Dept of Educ 60-69; Prof Chm Educ Media Curriculum. 8: ALA del to IFLA, Berne Switzerland 62; NEA del to World Confederation of Orgs of the Tchg Prof, Stockholm 62; Vancouver 67, Dublin 68; Consul, Ind State Dept of Pub Instr & pub schs in area. 9: ALA (Coun 55-60; mem NEA-ALA Jt Com 55-60, chm Com on Apportionment 59; chm Coun Nomin Com 62-63);-LED;-LAD;-RTSD;-YASD; NEA-DAVI; Assn Higher Educ; Assn for Supv & Curr Devel; Ind Assn for Supv & Curr Devel; A-V Instr Dirs of Ind; Ind State Tchrs Assn. ; IndSchLA. 10: PTA; Ind Hist Soc; AAUP; Kappa Delta Pi; Beta Phi Mu. 13: Yes. 14: Educ media, sch libs, tchr educ, educ for libnship. 15: Dept of Educ Purdue Univ, Lafayette In 47907.

WHITESIDES, WILLIAM LEE. b Gaston Co NC 12 J131. 4: Mary Janet Patat. 5: Appalachian State Tchrs Col 49-53 (LS) BS; Fla State U 53-54 (LS) MA. 6: Fr. 7: Asst libn Co div Atlanta Pub Lib 54-55; US Army, Ft Jackson SC 55-57; Br libn Atlanta Pub Lib 57-58; Dir Cobb Co-Marietta Pub Lib, Marietta Pub Lib, Marietta Ga 58-61; Dir Roanoke Pub Lib, Roanoke Va 61-65; Asst dir Fairfax Co Pub Lib, Fairfax Va 66-. 8: Personnel report spec US Army (assigned to Ft Bragg NC) 57; Consul, Kennestone Hosp, Marietta Ga 60-61; Exec dir, Na Lib Week, Va, 63; Staff, Lib/USA NY Worlds Fair, 64. 9: ALA; SELA; VaLA (Exhib Chm 61 & 65, treas 64, Nat Lib Wk chm 63); DCLA (chm Admin RT Com). 10: Kiwanis Internat; Phi Kappa Phi; Beta Phi Mu; Fairfax Presbyterian Bd Deacons. 13: Yes. 14: Admin, pub rel, personnel. 15: 12111 Wayland st, Oakton Va 22124.

WHITFORD, HAROLD C. b Leonardsville NY 5 J102. 4: Josephine Culver. 5: Amherst 19-23 (Eng Econ) BA; Harvard Law Sch 23-24; NYU (Eng Lit) MA; Columbia BS in LS. 6: Fr. 7: Ed asst Nat Occupational Conf 35-38; Libn circ lib Juilliard Sch of Music 39-42; Cooper Union Lib: asst libn 42-47, Assoc libn 48-52, Act chief libn 50-51; Ref libn spec in advertising & marketing econ div NY Pub Lib 52-67; Libn in chg UN Collection NYU Lib 67-. 8: Spec consul, Time Inc 63-; Lecturer in Eng Sch of Gen Studies, Columbia U 46-61; Instr in Eng, Manhattan Sch of Music 48-, & sometime lib consul. 9: ALA. 10: Andiron Club, NYC; Columbia U Mens Faculty Club; Bd Dirs, La Touraine Apts Inc. 12: Contrib to Lib Journal, Modern Language Notes, Studies in philology; Auth (with R S Dixson) "A Handbook of American Idioms (53). 12: Contrib to Lib Journal, Modern Language Notes, Studies in Philology, auth with R S Dixson; "A Handbook of American Idioms" (53); "A Dictionary of American Homophones and Homographs" (66). 14: Ref (bus & econ), govt doc, Eng lang & lit. 15: 50 Morningside dr, New York NY 10025.

WHITFORD, MERRY VIRGINIA. b Rogers Ark 25 D 36. 5: Milligan Col 54-58 (Eng) BA; Peabody Col 58-59 (LS) MA. 7: Libn II Brooklyn Pub Lib, Brooklyn NY 59-61; Sch libn Orange City Sch Bd, Orlando Fla 61-64; Base libn GS 9 Civil Serv: Chasn Naval Sta SC 64-68, Mildenhall AFB England 68-. 15: Box 1284, APO NY 09127.

WHITFORD, ROBERT H(ENRY). b NYC 9 S 07. 4: Lilian L Stevens. 5: City Col (NYC) 24-30 (Sci) BS, 30-31 (Engnr) ME; Columbia 32-36 BS in LS, 36-39 MS in LS, 39-52 (Educ) EdD. 6: Fr, Sp. 7: City Col (NYC): Stud asst 25-28, Lib asst order div 28-38, Jt charge tech div 39-52, Physics tchr 43-44, Head a-v div 49-52, Head tech div 52-, Asst libn 53-65, Asst Prof 65-66, Assoc Prof 67-. 9: Amer Phys Soc; Amer Soc Mech Engnrs; Amer Soc Engnr Educ; ALA-ACRL; NYLA; NY Lib Club. 10: AAUP; Phi Beta Kappa; Tau Beta Pi; Kappa Delta Pi; tbeta Phi Mu. 11: City Col (NYC) Alumni Serv Medal, 55; Forty Years Serv Award 66, Engnr Alumni Serv Award 67. 12: Auth "Physics Literature; A Referenc Manual (54), 2nd ed 68). 13: Yes. 14: Ref (engnr, sci). 15: 680 Riverside dr, New York NY 10031.

WHITING, ELEANOR M(ARJORIE). b Virginia Minn. 5: UMinn 38-39 BLS; State Tchrs Col (St Cloud Minn) 28-30, 31-33 (Eng) BE. 6: Fr. 7: Sch libn, Cokato & Wadena Minn 39-41; Lib asst US Govt Printing Off Documents Lib, Wash DC 42-44; Catlgr Nat Bur of Standards Lib, Wash DC 44-46; Sr catlgr Dept of Health Educ & Welfare Lib, Wash DC 46-67, Hd tech proc sect 67-. 9: ALA; DCLA (treas 66-68); Potomac Tech Proc Libns. 14: Catlg. 15: Apt 216, 1725 17th st NW, Wash DC 20009.

WHITING, F BROOKE II. b Md 5 D 18. 5: UVa 37-41 (Hist) AB; UAriz 47-49 (Hist); Columbia 56-57 (LS) MA. 7: Literary mss libn UCLA Lib 57-. 9: ALA. 10: Rounce & Coffin Club (Los Angeles); Western Bks Exhib Com. 12: Comp "Lawrence Durrell: A Checklist with R A Potter (61). 14: Mss, rare bks. 15: UCLA Lib, Los Angeles Ca 90024.

WHITINGER, ELAINE HELMS. b Hamilton Co Ind 2 O 14. 4: Harold Whitinger. 5: Butler U 34-39 (Eng) BA; Ind U 54-59 (LS) MA. 7: Reserve libn Butler U 49-53; Asst loan libn Ind State Lib 53-58; Sch of Nursing Libn Ind U 58-. 9: MedLA. 10: Ind Univ Womens Club; Beta Phi Mu. 14: Catlg, ref. 15: 3967 N New Jersey st, Indianapolis In 46205.

WHITLEDGE, FRANCES (MELTON). b Poole Ky 8 My 10. 4: Mason Allen Whitledge. 5: West Ky Tchrs Col 29-33 (LS, Eng) AB; Peabody 40 (LS; Ind U 64-65 (LS) MA. 6: Fr. 7: Tchr-libn Poole High Sch, Poole Ky 34-38; Libn: Bowling Green Bus U 38-40, WA, Glasgow & Louisville Ky 40-42, high schs, Evansville Ind 61-64, Evansville-Vanderburgh Sch Corp, Evansville Ind 64-. 9: ALA; NEA; IndLA; IndSchLA; Ind Tchrs Assn. 10: Delta Kappa Gamma. 14: Sch libs, centralized proc. 15: 700 E Powell ave, Evansville Ind 47713.

WHITLER, HELEN (CLARK). b Emmetsburg Iowa 26 Ja 01. 4: Tallman A Whitler. 5: James Millikin U 20-24 (Biol, Lat) AB; UIll summers 45-48 MLS. 6: Lat. 7: Latin instr Township High Sch, Arcola Ill 24-27; Latin instr Community High Sch, Hillsboro Ill 27-42; Latin instr & Libn Community High Sch, Litchfield Ill 42-53; Libn Township High Sch, Streator Ill 53-66; Hd libn Winston Churchill Col (Ill) 66-68; Assoc libn, Hd tech serv Lincoln Col (Ill) 68-. 9: NEA; ALA; IllEA (del); IllLA (Elect Com, chm Co Lib Dept). 10: Delta Kappa

Gamma; Bus & Prof Womens Club; Callere Study Club. 14: Ref, catlg. 15: 514 Pine st, Lincoln Il 62656.

WHITLEY, REV JOHN RAYMOND. b Rochester NY 28 Je 27. 5: UWest Ont 45-49 (Hist) BA; UToronto 49-50 BLS; St Basils Sem 51-54; URochester 57-58 (Educ) M Ed; Wayne State U 54 (LS; Catholic U 58 (LS); URochester 69- (Educ). 6: Sp. 7: Libn St Michaels Col Sch, Toronto 50-51; Libn Aquinas Inst, Rochester NY 54-. 9: CathLA (past chm High Sch Sect); ALA(Standards Com);AASchL; DAVI; NYLA; West NY Cath Libns Conf; Diocesan Lib Com (chm). 10: West NY Drum Corps & Band Assn; All-Amer Assn of Contest Judges ; Diocesan Liturgy Com. 11: Cert of Merit, CathLA 68. 12: Ed "Best in Catholic Reading" (63); "Guide to Scholarship Planning" (64). 13: Yes. 14: Admin. 15: 1127 Dewey ave, Rochester NY 14613.

WHITLOW, HUBERT H JR. b Atlanta Ga 16 F 30. 5: Emory 47-51 (Hist) BA, 55-56 (LS) MLn; UFla 60-61 (Pol Sci) MA. 7: Pub info spec, Ground safety spec USAF (S/Sgt) 51-55; Asst catlg, humanities libn UGa Libs 56-57, Soc sci libn 57-59; Emory U Lib: Res libn 61-62, Chief ser & bind dept 62-64, Chief circ libn 64-67, Docs libn 67-68, Chief circ libn 68-. 9: ALA; SELA; GaLA. 15: Emory Univ Lib, Atlanta Ga 30322.

WHITMAN, AINSLEY ABBOTT. b Pomona Cal 22 S 12. 5: Chaffey Jr Col 30-32 (Soc Sci); San Jose State Col 32-35 (Soc Sci) AB; LSU 35-36 BS in LS. 7: Libn Rayne (La) High Sch 36-38; Libn Poinsett Co Lib, Harrisburg Ark 38-39; Lib asst La Lib Commsn, Baton Rouge La 39-40; Lib asst San Jose State Col 40-42; (S/Sgt) US Army Med Corps, European Theatre 42-46; Libn: Cal State Polytech Col (San Luis Obispo) 46-49, Col of Agric UGa 49-50, Willamette U 50-55, Central State Col (Edmond Okla) 55-57; Asst libn Jacksonville State Col 57-62; Libn UNC (Asheville) 62-. 9: ALA; SELA; NCLA; ArkLA (past v-pres); OreLA (past pres); PNLA (Exec Bd). 10: Men's Garden Club of Amer. 14: Lib bldg planning, admin. 15: Univ of North Carolina, Asheville NC 28801.

WHITMAN, JANICE (MARGARET) (ELKINTON). b Kan City Mo 31 D 31. 4: Donald E Whitman. 5: Sterling Col 49-53 (Chem) BS; Kan State U summers 54, 60, 61; Kan State Tchrs Col (Emporia) 63-65 (LS) MS. 6: GER. 7: Tchr Auburn High Sch, Auburn Kan 54-57; Instr Washburn U 57-59; Readers adv Topeka Pub Lib, Topeka Kan 58-59; Tchr-lib Berryton High Sch, Berryton Kan 59-62; Libn Shawnee Heights High Sch, Tecumseh Kan 62-67; Lib coord Shawnee Heights Unified Sch Dist 450, Tecumseh Kan 67-. 9: NEA-DAVI; ALA; Kan State Tchrs Assn; KanASchL; Shawnee Heights EA (Salary chm 65-68). 10: Alpha Delta Kappa. 14: Sch libnship. 15: 5530 W 15th, Topeka Kan 66604.

WHITMIRE, MAVIS J. b Marshalltown Iowa 27 N 22. 5: State Col Iowa 40-42, 50-51 (Soc Sci & Second Educ) BA; UDenver summers 62-65 MALS; West Mich U 66. 7: Rural sch tchr Grundy & Tama Co Iowa 42-45; Prim Grades tchr Holfa Iowa 46-49; High sch tchr Kensett, Chelsea & Dunkerton Iowa 51-56; High sch tchr-libn Klemme & Williamsburg Iowa 56-64; High sch libn Sr High Sch, Ft Madison Iowa 64-. 8: NDEA Inst West Mich U summer 66; Lib consul summer reading program Ft Madison Sch Dist 68. 9: NEA; ALA; Iowa State EA; IowaASchL. 10: AAUW; Delta Kappa Gamma; Bus & Prof Women. 14: Sch libs. 15: Rte 3, Waterloo Ia 52627.

WHITMORE, DOROTHY E (McCULLOUGH). b Hagerstown Md 19 S 15. 4: John William Whitmore. 7: Lib asst adult dept Wash Co Free Lib, Hagerstown Md 34-40, Co ext libn 40-43, Catlg & lib asst adult dept 46-51, 59-60, Asst to hd adult circ serv & interlib loan libn 61-63, Hd circ serv 64-. 9: MdLA; Cumberland Valley LA. 10: Suburban Music Group; Beaver Creek Country Club, Internatl Oceanog Found. 14: Adult pub lib serv. 15: 1760 Harwood ave, Hagerstown Md 21740.

WHITMORE, ELLIE NELSON. b DENTON Tex 14 Mr 20. 5: Tex Womans U 38-41 (Journalism) BA; UWis 47-48 (Journalism) MA; Tex Womans U 55-56 MLS. 7: Reporter "The Alvin Sun, Alvin Tex 41-42; Copywriter Robt I Cohen Dept Store, Galveston Tex 42-43; Reporter pub rel off WAC with USAF, Stockton (Cal) Air Base 43-45; Copywriter Leonards Dept Store, Ft Worth Tex 46-47; Tchr Mem High Sch, Ely Minn 48-49; Tchr & dir publicity Amarillo High Sch, Amarillo Tex 49-52; Tchr Polytech High Sch, Ft Worth Tex 52-55; extramural Loans UTex 56-63; Biol libn 63-67; Asst ref libn N Tex State U 67-. 9: ALA (Memb Com for Tex); TexLA; Austin Lib Club (pres 62). 10: AAUW; Zonta Club; DELTA Kappa Gamma; UTex Lib Staff Assn; Austin Br AAUW. 12: Ed "Directory of Austin Libraries 2nd ed, mimeo (63). 14: PUB SERV, BIOLOG SCI, ref. 15: 418 Texas st, Denton Tx 76201.

WHITMORE, HARRY EARL. b Sharon Conn 24 S 30. 5: UMe 53-57 (Romance Lang) BA; Rutgers 59-61 MLS. 6: Fr, Sp, Ger. 7: Bkmob libn Me State Lib 58-59; Period asst RutgersU (Newark) 59-61; Asst br libn Queens Borough Pub Lib, Jamaica NY 61-63; Ref libn UMe (Orono) 63-67; Instr Sch of Lib Sci Simmons Col 67-. 9: ALA. 10: Phi Beta Kappa; AAUP; ACLU. 13: Yes. 14: Lib educ, ref. 15: 121 St Stephen st, Boston Ma 02115.

WHITMORE, MARILYN P. b Grand Forks ND 25 Jl 32. 4: George D Whitmore. 5: Jamestown Col 50-51; UND 51-54 (Marketing) BA; Rutgers summers59-64 MLS; Cal State Col (Penn) summer 65 (Educ). 6: Fr, Sp. 7: Desk asst Pub Lib, Grand Forks ND 54-56; Sr catlgr Penn State U Lib 56-60; Catlgr UPittsburgh Lib 61-66, Hd catlg dept 66-. 9: ALA. 10: Beta Phi Mu;Sem Acquis Latin Amer Lib Materials. 14: Catlg, Latin Amer. 15: 125 Johnston rd, Upper St Clair, Pittsburgh Pa 15241.

WHITMORE, VIRGINIA ANNE. b Cambridge Mass 7 Je 34. 5 Smith 52-53 (Fr); So Methodist U 53-57 (Fr, Educ) BA Elem Educ Certif; USoCal 62-64 (LS) MS. 6: Fr. 7: Libn Los Angeles City Pub Lib 62-68; Libn Los Angeles Co Pub Lib 68-. 9: SLA; ALA. 10: UN Assn of Los Angeles; Los Angeles Co Employees Assn; Pi Delta Phi. 14: Ref, acquis, readers adv, child wk. 15: 2929 Saint George st #8, Los Angeles Ca 90027.

WHITNEY, DUANE. b Jackson Mich 14 Sp 15. 4: Rose Marie Hinkel. 5: West MichU 62-65 (Geog) BA, 66-67 (Libnship) MS. 6: Sp. 7: USN CQM 42-45; Ind sales mgr, Vibradamp Corp, Jackson Mich 46-55; Sales McArthur Dairy, Ft Lauderdale Fla 55-61; Sales kuehmann Foods, Jackson Mich 61-62; Bus libn Willard Lib, Battle Creek Mich 65-. 9: ALA; MichLA. 14: Map libs, ref, res. 15: 319 N 27th st, Battle Creek Mi 48914.

WHITNEY, ELMA A. b Columbus Ohio 9 Mr 09. 5: Ohio State U 30 (Eng) BSEd; West Res 32 BSLS. 7: Asst Columbus Pub Lib, Columbus Ohio 27-31; Asst & act libn USch Ohio State U 32-37; Head Libn Euclid Pub Lib, Euclid Ohio 37-40; Co-ordinator of adult bk serv for brs Enoch Pratt Free Lib 40-42; Instr of Lib Tch Denison U Lib 42-43; Head Libn Worthington Pub Lib, Worthington Ohio 43-67; Asst libn Capital U Lib 67-. 9: OhioLA (past pres); Franklin Co LA (past pres). 10: Ohio Pub Employees Ret System; Columbus Altrusa; Columbus Area Info Center; Franklin Co Commun Serv Coun. 14: Admin, ref. 15: 146 E Dunedin rd, Columbus Oh 43214.

WHITNEY, JEANNETTE (ANDERSON). b Dover NJ 10 Ag 18. 4: Benjamin C Whitney. 5: Mansfield State Col 36-39 (Sci) BS in Ed; Syracuse 39-40 BS in LS. 7: Libn: Housatonic Valley Reg High Sch, Falls Village Con 40-45, Warsaw Central Sch, Warsaw NY 52-63, Housatonic Valley Reg High Sch, Falls Village Conn 63-64, Emma Willard Sch, Troy NY 64-67, Warsaw NY 67-68, Greece Central Schs, Rochester NY 68-. 8: Adv Wyoming Co Commun Hosp Sch of Nurs Lib 67-. 9: ALA; NEA-DAVI; NYLA; NYStateTA. 14: Ya ser. 15: 28 Wyoming st, Warsaw NY 14569.

WHITNEY, JOSEPHINE JERRY (EDWARDS). b Chicago Ill 27 F 25. 4: Joseph G Whitney. 5: Phoenix Col 43-45 (Gen Sci, Math); Ariz StateU 45-50 (Psych, Educ) BA, MA; San Jose State Col 60-61 (LS). 6: Sp. 7: Operations agt Amer Airlines, Phoenix 43-51; Aircraft dispatcher USAF WAF, Biloxi Miss 50-51; Asst aircraft dispatcher Alaska Airlines, Anchorage Alaska 53-54; Tchr Scottsdale (Ariz) elem sch dist 55-56, 59-60; Asst traffic mgr Ampex Corp, Redwood City Cal 56-57; Tchr Sunnyvale Elem Sch Dist, Cal 58-59; Libn Philco WDL, Palo Alto Cal 61-63; Libn Vidya Div Itek, Palo Alto Cal 63-65; Tech libn United Air Lines, San Francisco 65-. 9: SLA. 10: Mgt Club, United Airlines. 14: Tech manuals, catlg. 15: United Air Lines Engineering Dept Lib SF Intnl Airport, San Francisco Ca 94128.

WHITNEY, KAREN (WESTBERG). b Norwalk Conn 2 S 41. 4: Jerome W Whitney. 5: So Conn State Col 59-65 BSLS; Columbia 68-. 7: Catlgr-desk asst Fairfield Pub Lib, Fairfield Conn 57-61, Child libn 66-; Asst libn Whitneyville Br Lib, Hamden Conn 62; Desk-ref- asst Westport Pub Lib, Westport Conn 62-65; Child libn Plumb Mem Lib, Shelton Conn 65-66. 9: ConnLA (chm Child Sect 69-70). 10: Urban Ministry of Coun of Churches of Greater Bridgeport; Free Sch of New Haven. 13: Yes. 14: Child lit, rare child bks, fine arts. 15: Children's Lib 1333 Post rd, Fairfield Ct 06430.

WHITNEY, PATRICIA (ROOS). b Wilkes-Barre Penn 18 N 25. 4: Paul W Whitney. 5: Bucknell 44-48 (Bio) BS; Drexel 65-67 MS in LS. 7: Histology tech: Hahnemann Hosp Phila 48-50, UChicago Med Sch 51-52; Adult serv libn Moorestown Free Lib, Moorestown NJ 67-. 9: NJLA. 14: Ref. 15: 126 E Oak ave, Moorestown NJ 08057.

WHITNEY, STEPHEN LOUIS. b Chicago Ill 18 Jl 43. 4: Jean Lujan. 5: Rockhurst Col 61-65 (Eng) AB; Case West Res 65-66 MSLS. 6: Fr. 7: Adult serv libn Crunden Br St Louis Pub Lib 66-67; Coord Mun Lib Coop, Kirkwood Mo 67-; Instr UMo Ext Div (lib sci), St Louis Co 68-. 9: ALA (Jr Mem RT: chm Guidelines Com 68-); MoLA (chm Jr Mem RT 68-). 14: Adult serv, admin. 15: 140 E Jefferson, Kirkwood Mo 63122.

WHITNEY, VIRGINIA (EVELYN) P. b Medford Mass 1 D 14. 4: Raymond L Whitney. 5: Middlebury Col 32-36 (Pol Sci) BS; Rutgers 61-62 MLS. 6: Fr. 7: Sec Socony-Vacuum Oil Co Foreign Prod, NYC 37-40; Lib asst E Orange Pub Lib Franklin Br, E Orange NJ 55-62; Libn Urban Studies Center-Ruters U 62-67, Assoc libn for pub serv 68-; Libn Douglass Col 67-68. 8: Asst dir & dir, Volunteer Urban Agents, Rutgers U 64-67; Lectr, Grad Sch of Lib Serv, Rutgers U 65 (Jt appointment). 9: ALA; NJLA. 10: AAUP. 15: Rutgers Univ Lib, State Univ of NJ, New Brunswick NJ 08901.

WHITNEY, VIRGINIA (KOOGLER). b Hillsboro NM 6 F 27. 4: Cliff W Whitney. 5: NMU 44-46; Adams State Col -59 (Sci) BA, 66 (Lib) MEd; Mich StateU (A-v). 7: Tchr Aztec Pub Sch, Aztec NM 59-61; Libn C V Koogler Jr High, Aztec NM 61-. 08. Geneal res consul, San Juan Co Records 67-; Lib trustee Altrurian Pub Lib 54-68, Chm Lib Bd 68-. 9: ALA; NEA (deleg 62 & 68); NMLA; NMSchL (v-pres 68-69); NMEA (NW Dist: treas, chm Lib Div); NM A-V Assn (Memb Com 67-69). 10· Kappa Kappa Iota; Altrurian Club; Amer Legion Aux; Delta Kappa Gamma; DAR. 12: "Koogler Family of Virginia" (68). 13: Yes. 14: Child & yp, SE lit, geneal. 15: 200 Willow lane, Aztec NM 87410.

WHITSON, HELENE (HOWARD). b San Francisco Cal 24 O 41. 4: William Lester Whitson. 5: City Col of San Francisco 60-62 (Eng) AA; UCal (Berkeley) 62-64 (Eng) BA, 64-65 mls. 7: Jr clk Fed Res Bank of San Francisco 59-60; Clk Retail Credit Bur of San Francisco summer 63; Libn Fireman's Fund Ins Co, San Francisco summer 65; Asst educ/ interlib loan libn San Francisco State Col 66-. 9: CalLA. 10: San Francisco Civic Chorale; Berkeley Commun; Chorus; Nat Parks Assn; Save the Redwoods League; Beta Phi Mu; Sierra Club. 14: Ref, educ & psych materials, interlib loans, archives, rare bks. 15: 1824 Arch st, Berkeley Ca 94709.

WHITTAKER, EDWARD L. b Highland Park Mich 3 S 37. 4: Darlene Kay Bostick. 5: Olivet col 55-58 (Liberal Arts); Murray State 58-59 (Eng, Speech) BS; UMich 60-63 MALS. 7: Adult serv libn Detroit Pub Lib 60-63; Br libn Tucson Pub Lib 63-66; Ref libn pacific LutheranU 66-68; Hd libn & chm lib sci dept Whitworth Col 69-. 9: ALA. 10: AAUP. 14: Ref, instr, admin. 15: N 10212 Ivanhoe rd, Spokane Wa 99218.

WHITTEMORE, ELMA EVANS. b Greenfield Tp Twp 9 Ag 1. 4: John A Whittemore. 5: UPittsburgh 30-34 (Hist) AB; Columbia U 34-35 (LS) BS (MS equiv). 6: Fr, Ger. 7: Asst libn Sch of Nursing NY Hosp, NY summer 35; Asst libn NY State Col for Tchrs (Albany) 35-38; Libn: Atlas Powder Co, Wilmington Del 39-42, CURTISSWright Research Lab, Buffalo NY 42-45, Cornell Aeronautical Lab, Buffalo NY 46-57; Asst libn Buffalo & Eire Co Pub Lib, Buffalo NY 57-58; Libn A C Spark Plub Div Gen Motors, Flint Mich 58-. 9: SLA (several com assignments, sci-tech div; chm 43-46, dir 46-49). 13: Yes. 14: Ref. 15: 5317 Seymour rd, Swartz Creek Mi 48473.

WHITTEN, BENJAMIN GOODMAN. b Kan City Mo 8 Ap 07. 4: Laura Hodges. 5: UCLA 27-31 (Fr) AB; USoCal 35-38 (Fr) AM, 38-47 (Fr) PhD; UCal (Berkeley) 32-33 Certif in Libnship. 6: Fr, Ger, Sp. 7: US Army Signal Intelligence Staff Sgt 43-45; Asst libn Whittier Col 33-40, Libn 40-. 9: ALA; CalLA (So Br: pres Col, Univ & Ref Sect). 14: Admin. 15: 11341 E Whitley st, Whittier Ca 90601.

WHITTEN, JOSEPH N. b Jackson Miss 30 N 17. 5: Miss Col 35-39 (Hist) BA; Peabody 41, 46 BS in LS; Columbia 46-47 (LS) MS; NYU 48-58 (Higher Educ) EdD. 6: Fr. 7: Hist tchr & libn, Miss 39-41; US Navy 41-45; Asst libn Bethany Col (WVa) 45-46; Libn & a-v educ Lycoming Col 47-49; Instr UKy 50-53; Libn & Prof Cooper Union 53-60; Libn & Prof SUNY Maritime Col (Bronx) 60-. 8: Lib sch tchg: Ga Tchrs Col summer 46, UTex summer 50, UNC summer 53, Columbia U spring 54, Fla State U summer 56 & 57; Grad Lib Sch LIU 60-; Lib consul, Instr SLA Wkshop 69. 9: ALA; NYLA (Bd, pres-elect Col & Univ Sect); Metro Col Inter-lib Assn (Bd 55-60, pres 59); NY Lib Club (Bd 64-69, pres 67-68, chm SUNY Lib Conf 67-68). 10: AAUP; Phi Delta Kappa; Beta Phi Mu; Kappa Delta Pi; Archons of Colophon; Columbia U Sch of Lib Serv Alumni Assn. 13: Yes. 14: Admin, catlg. 15: Apt 11-H 3131 Grand Concourse, Bronx NY 10468.

WHITTEN, SAM GERALD. b Talco Tex 23 O 24. 4: Virginia White. 5: UTex 46-49(Journalism) BJ, 49-50 (Econ) BA, 50-52 MLS. 7: Ensign Supply Corps US Naval Res 43-46; Ref asst bus & soc sci reading room UTex 51; Pub rel asst asst head br libs San Antonio (Tex) Pub Lib 52-53; Physics libn & lecturer Grad Sch of Lib Sci UTex 53-55; Head sci & ind dept Dallas Pub Lib 55-58, Coordinator of br libs 58-60; Libn Sci Lib So Methodist U 60-67; Assoc Prof Grad Sch of Lib Sci UTex (Austin) 67-. 9: ALA (Coun 63-66); SLA; TexLA (treas 54-56, v-pres 67-68, pres 68-69); SWLA (treas 65-66). 13: Yes. 14: Lib bldgs, lib serv to indus, pub libs. 15: 1601 Rio Grande, Austin Tx 78701.

WHITTEN, TERESA AGNES. b Gary Ind 22 Je 30. 5: Loyola U (Chicago) 58-61 (Hist) BS (Hum); Rosary Col 63-64 MALS; Loyola U Chicago 61-62, 64-67 (Hist) MA. 6: Fr. 7: Clerical wk Loyola U Lib (Chicago) 61-62; Hist tchr Andrean High Sch, Gary Ind 62-63; Trailer libn Gary Pub Lib, Gary Ind 64-65, Chid libn John F Kennedy Br 65-68; Ref libn Loyola U (Chicago) 68-. 8: Lib consul St Marys Mercy Hosp Gary Ind 64-65. 9: ALA; CathLA; IndLA. 10: Phi Sigma Tau; Pi Gamma Mu; Beta Phi Mu; Cath Hist Assn. 14: Child serv, ref.5 15: 4373 Monroe, Gary Ind 46408.

WHITTINGTON, ERMA (ELIZABETH) P(ADEN). b Lawrence Co Penn 14 F 17. 4: Tolbert M Whittington Jr. 5: Westminster Col (Penn) 35-39 (Fr) AB; Slippery Rock State Tchrs Col 40-41 Elem Certif; UNC 48-49 BS in LS; Duke U 45-51 (Amer Lit) MA. 6: Fr. 7: Tchr: S New Castle Boro, New Castle Penn 41-42, Union Twp High Sch, New Castle Penn 42-47, Sharpsville High Sch, SHARPSVILLE Penn 47-48; 1st asst subj catlg dept Duke U Lib 49-62, Head Subj catlg dept 62-. 9: ALA; NCLA (sec-treas Resources & Tech Serv Sect 60-61). 10: Duke U Faculty Club. 14: Catlg. 15: Box 4472 Duke Station, Durham NC 27706.

WHYTE, FREDRICA (ALVA) HARRIMAN. b Hampton Iowa 9 Ag 05. 4: Robert Whyte. 5: UMich 24-26, 27-28 (Fr) AB, 31-37 (Fr) AM; UParis 26-27 (Hist, Art) 2 Medailles; USoCal 55, 58 MS in LS. 6: Fr. 7: Tchr: S Haven High Sch, S Haven Mich 29-30, Univ High Sch, ann Arbor Mich 30-36; Libn in pub sch, Long Beach Cal 55-58; Libn pub lib, Long Beach Cal 60-, Curator & libn Rancho Los Cerritos Mus & Lib 65-. 9: So Cal Coun on Local Hist; CalLA. 10: West Museum League; Cal Conf Hist Socs; So Cal Coun Local Hist. 12: "Whyte's Atlas Guide" (61). 13: Yes. 14: Research (gathering, compiling, indexing loc hist materials). 15: 4600 Virginia rd, Long Beach Ca 90807.

WICHELMAN, RUTHANN. b NYC 27 N 27. 5: Adelphi 45-49 (Hist) BA; NYU 50-53 (Educ Psych) MA; Rutgers 64-67 MLS. 7: Tchr: W Hempstead Pub Schs NY 52-54, US Army, Tokyo 54-55, Valley Stream (NY) Pub Scgs 55-57, Chatham Pub Schs, Chatham NJ 57-60, Berkeley Hts, berkeley NJ 60-65; Libn Berkeley Elem Sch, Berkeley Hts NJ 65-. 8: Tchr SyracuseU Reading Comp, Raeguette Lake NY. 9: ALA; NJLA (Hospitality Com); NJEA; UnionCoSchLA. 14: Child libn, ref. 15: Berkeley School Snyder ave, Berkeley Heights NJ 07922.

WICK, DONALD E. b Enfield Middlesan England 15 F 28. 4: Wendy Mallard. 5: Cambrdige 49-52 (Hist) BA, MA; Loushborough Col 52-53 (Libnship) British ALA, FLA. 7: Asst Middlesex Co Libs, London England 53-54; Br libn Worthins Pub Libs, Sussex England 54-55; Intern libn Toronto Pub Libs, Toronto Can 55-56; Bkmob libn Etobicoke Pub Libs, Toronto Can 56-59, Hd ref dept 59-65; Col libn Selkirk Col 65-67; Univ libn ULethbridge 67-. 8: Chm Com for the Survey of Ont Ref Serv 65. 9: CanLA; Lib Assn (Gt Brit); ALA; AltaLA; BCLA; OntLA. 12: "A Finding List of Manuscripts and Printed Materials associated with the History of Krobicoke Township" (65); "A Survey of Reference Services in Ontario Public Libraries" (65). 14: Ref, admin, bibliog of Hi Can for trade. 15: 1117 18th st South, Lethbridge Alberta Can.

WICK, HILDA (M). b Rier Rouge Mich 3 My 23. 4: Lawrence B Wick. 5: UMich 40-43 (Eng) AB, 43-44 ABLS, 45-47 MLS. 6: Fr. 7: Asst libn Shaw High Sch, E Cleveland Pub Lib 44-45; Serv Fellow UMich Gen Lib Ext Dept 45-47; Circ libn Cedar Rapids Pub Lib Cedar Rapids Iowa 50; Ref asst Hild Br Chicago Pub Lib 53, Head Norwood Park Sub-Br Chicago Pub Lib 54; Sub libn Maine Twp High Sch Des Plaines Ill 58; Instr of Eng Drury Col 58-60; Bkmob libn Delawae Co Dist Lb, Delaware Ohio 60-62; Asst Prof ref asst Slocum Lib Ohio Wesleyan U 62-, Ref libn Beeghly Lib 68-. 8: Bd Dirs Des Plaines Pub Lib, Illinois 55-58. 9: ALA;-ACRL; OhioLA (sec Subcom to study Functions & Programs Col & Univ RT); Midwest Acad Libns Conf. 10: Ohio Wesleyan U Faculty Club; Univ Womens Club; AAUP. 14: Ref, Methodist hist materials, govt docs. 15: 119 Troy rd, Delaware Ohio 43015.

WICKERSHAM, ANNE M. b Minneapolis Minn 4 My 30. 5: West Res 54 (Fr) BA; Columbia 66 MLS. 6: Fr. 7: Asst libn McCann-Erickson, NYC 66-68; Libn Cyrus J Lawrence & Sons, NYC 68-. 9: ALA; SLA. 14: Bus & finance. 15: 333 E 79th st, New York NY 10021.

WICKERSHAM, LUCILLE (HELEN). b St Louis 9 F 04. 5: Drury Col 21-25 (Eng) AB; UMich 31-32 AB in LS, 40-42 MA in LS. 7: Tchr: Sr High Sch, Bolivar Mo 25-26, Sr High Sch, W Plains Mo 26-29, Jarrett Jr High Sch, Springfied Mo 29-31; Asst libn Tchrs Col, (California Penn) 32-35; Libn Sr High Sch, Pontiac Mich 35-37; Asst libn DePauw U 37-42; Chief ref libn asst dir City Lib, Springfield Mass 42-64; Libn Bay Path Jr Col 64-. 8: Instr & coord, pub lib techniques (Mass) 62; Spec consul, ri dept of State lib serv 64. 9: ALA; MassLA; NELA. 10: College Club of Springfiel; Quota Club; Springfield Womens Club. 12: Jt auth (with J A Humphry) "Library Cooperation: The Brown University Study of Univesity-Schol-Community Library Coordination in the State of Rhode Island. 14: Ref, admin. 15: 250 Union st, Springfield Ma 01105.

WICKHAM, MYRTICE (MORRIS). b Denison Tex 19 Ap 01. 4: George Dorrance Wickham. 5: Baylor U 19-23 (Eng, Educ) AB; Columbia 26-27 (LS) BS; UDel 53-55; Rutgers summer 59; Drexel summers 63, 64; UIll 66; Columbia (NDEA) 67. 7: Libn Carnegie Pub Lib, Sherman Tex 23-26; ref libn Carnegie Pub Lib, Boise Ida 27-29; Libn Mt Pleasant Spec Sch Dist, Wilmington Del 52-58, Supv & coordinator of libs 58-. 9: ALA (State Mem Chm): CLA (Newbery Caldecott Com); NEA; DelLA (pres); Del State EA (pres Lib Sect); DelASchL; NC Co EA; DAVI; BrandywineLA. 10: Delta Kappa Gamma; Del Hist Soc. 15: 1100 Brandywine blvd, Wilmington De 19809.

WICKLIFFE, WARREN BRADFORD. b Louisville Ky 12 Ag 13. 5: Olivet Col 37-41 (Eng) AB; UTenn 41-42 (Eng); Chicago 46 (Eng) AM, 49-51 (LS). 6: Fr. 7: Stud instr of Eng Olivet Col 39-41; Grad Fellow Eng UTenn 41-42; Communications Off & C2 USAF, US & ETO 42-45; Instr in Eng Boston U 46-47; Instr in Eng UTenn 47-48; Jr ref libn Chicago Pub Lib 49-51; Head Lower Div Lib UOkla 52-54; Acquis libn UOkla 54-55; Sr libn ref readers adv interlib loan bk sel music & recordings Burlingame Pub Lib, BURLINGAME Cal 55-. 8: Lectr, Sch of Lib Sci, UOkla 52-55. 9: ALA; CalLA. 10: ACLU. 14: Ref, bk sel, interlib loan, readers adv. 15: 770 2nd ave, Redwood City Ca 94063.

WICKLINE, MARIAN E. b St Louis 18 F 15. 5: Mills Col 31-35 (Chem) BA; UCal (Berkeley) 35-37 (Chem). 6: Fr, Ger. 7: Tech files asst Shell Development Co, Sn Francisco 38-45; Asst libn Dow Chem Co, Pittsburg Cal 45-47, Head Libn 47-62; Head Libn Dow Chem Co, Walnut Creek Cal 62-. 9: SLA; ASIS; ACS. 15: 232 Rutherford dr, Danville Ca 94526.

WICKMAN, ALMA. b Bloomington Ill 3 N 07. 5: Neb Wesleyan U 27-28, 29-32 (Bus Admin) BS; UDe ver summers 39-41 BS in LS. 7: Libn Morrill Pub Lib, Morrill Neb 33-39; Libn Scottsbluff Pub Lib, Scottsbluff Neb 39-45; Asst libn Grand Island Pub Lib, Grand Island Neb 45-46; Libn Norfolk PUB Lib, Norfolk Neb 46-. 8: Consul Neb Pub Lib Commsn in northeast Neb 62-. 9: ALA; MPLE; NebLA (Hon Life mem; sec 48-50, pres 59-60; chm Nomin Com 61, chm Constit Com 62-64; 10: Bus & Prf Womens Club; Delta Kappa Gamma; Wesleyan Serv Guild. 14; admin. 15: 109 N 9th st, Norfolk Neb 68701.

WIDDICOMBE, RICHARD P. b Paterson NJ 12 Ap 41. 5: Alfred 59-63 (Eng) BA; Syracuse 63-64 MSLS. 7: Jr libn Yonkers Pub Lib, Yonkers NY 64-65; Asst libn Cooper Union 65-66; Asst libn Stevens Inst 66-. 8: Lib Systems Analyst, Stevens Inst of Tech; Exec secy, Presvyterian Church of White Plains 67-. 14: Admin, automation, tech serv. 15: 120A Greenacres ave, White Plains NY 10606.

WIDIGER, CAROLE JEAN. b Chicago 27 S 42. 5: J Sterling Morton Jr Col 60-61 (Eng); West Mich U 61-64 (Eng) BA; UWs 64-65 (LS) MS. 6: Sp. 7: Asst libn Triton Col 65-67; Ref libn Mich State U 67-. 9: ALA; IllLA; MichLA. 10: AAUW. 14: Ref. 15: 5947 Bois Ile dr, Haslett Mi 48840.

WIEDEL, ANN (ELIZABETH). b Los Angeles Cal 14 Mr 44. 5: Immaculate Heart College 62-66 (Hist) AB; USoCal 66-67 MS in LS. 6: Sp. 7: Catlgr Walt E Disney Enterprises Inc, Glendale Cal 67-. 9: SLA; ALA; CalLA. 10: Hist Soc of Centinela Valley. 14: Catlg, resea resea research. 15: 10702-8th pl, Inglewood Ca 90303.

WIEMAN, CHARLES DAVID. b Woodford Wis 18 Mr 35. 4: Caroline Kohlhaas. 5: St Olaf Col 53-57 (Eng, Econ) BA; State U Iowa 58-59 Tchrs Certif; UWis 62-63 (LS) MS, 68-69 (LS) Spec. 6: Fr. 7: Cost accountant Milprint Inc, Milwaukee 57-58; Eng & soc studies tchr N Fond du Lac (Wis) High Sch 59-60; Eng tchr Brodhead Jr High Sch, Wis 60-62; Ref libn Bowling Green State U 3-65; Asst circ & res libn Wis Stat U (Whitewater) 65-. 9: ALA; WisLA. 10: AAUP; Assn of Wis Univ Faculties. 14: Pub serv, ref. 15: R3 Box 466, Whitewater Wi 53190.

WIEMAN, JEAN MARGARET (RONKEN). b Eau Claire Wis 26 Je 32. 4: Thomas Edward Wieman. 5: Pacific Lutheran Col 52-53 (Educ); Seattle Pacific Col 51, 54 (Educ) BA (cum laude); UWash 58-62 (LS) ML; SUNY (Albany) 65 (Instructional Materials). 7: Elem sch tchr S Central Schs, King Co Wash 54-58; Jr high sch libn Highline Schs, King Co Wash 58-62; Coordinator lib servs Fed Way Sch Dist, Federal Way Wash 62-65; Supv of learning resources serv State Dept of Pub Instruction, Olympia Wash 66-. 9: NEA-DAVI; WashStateASchL (sec, chm Recr); Wash EA-DAVI. 10: Alpha Delta Kappa; AAUW. 13: Yes. 14: Supv of learning resources serv. 15: 3800 Elizabeth ave #205, Lacey Wa 98501.

WIENER, HELEN (McNEEL). b spokane Wash 1 N 15. 4: Bernard Andre Wiener. 5: Monmouth Col 34-38 (Ger) BA; UMich 40-41 ABLS. 6: Ger, Fr, Sp. 7: Waitress Davenport Hotel, Spokane Wash 38-40; Lib asst UMich 41; Catgr Med Sci ,dept Detroit Pub Lib 41-45; Army Lib, Wash DC: Catlgr 45-47, Chief order sect 47-49, Period libn 49-50, Chief procurement sect 50-66, Chief tech serv br 66-. 9: SLA. 10: UMich Assn of Lib Sci Alumni. 14: Tech serv. 15: 2428 39th pl NW, Wash DC 20007.

WIENER, THEODORE. b Stettin Germany 28 S 18. 5: Syracuse 35-36; UCincinnati 36-40 (Hist) BA; Hebrew Union Col 36-43 (Hebrew & Jewish Studies) BHL, MHL, Rabbi. 6: Ger, Fr, Hebrew, Yiddish. 7: Rabbi: Mount Sinai Temple, Sioux City Iowa 43-44, Rodef Shalom temple, Port Arthur Tex 44-47, Beth El Temple, Corsicana Tex 47-48; Catlgr of Hebrew bks Hebrew Union Col Lib 50-59, Hebraica libn 59-63, Hd catlgr 63-64; Supv Hebraic lang unit descr catlg div LC 64-, Catlgr of Judaica subj catlg div 67-. 8: Chaplain, home for the Jewish Aged, Cincinnati 58-64. 9: Cent Conf Smer Rabbis; Assn Jewish Libs (Coun 66-68; v-pres Res & Spec Lib Div 68-); ALA (Coun rep Assn Jewish Libs 68-). 10: United Jewish Appeal of Greater Wash. 12: Ed "The Writings of Nelson Glueck, a Bibliography", by William J Gordon (62). 13: Yes. 14: Catlg, Jewish bibliog. 15: 1701 N Kent st, Arlington Va 22209.

WIENPAHL, ROBERT W. b Rock Springs Wyo 22 D 17. 4: Miltona Moore. 5: UCLA 35-38, 46-53 (Pol Sci, Music) BA, MA, PhD; USoCal Law Sch 38-40 (Law) USoCal 54-55 MSLS. 6: Fr, Ger, Sp, Ital, Lat. 7: (Lt) US Army, US & Asiatic Pacific 41-43; Asst catlgr Los ANGELES Co Law Lib, Los Angeles 55-56; San Fernando Valley State Col: Asst ref & catlg libn 56-57, Head of acquis & ser 57-60, Chief of pub serv & Assoc Prof Music 60-63, Humanities bibliog 63-65, Assoc Prof Music Dept & Head Music Lib 65-. 9: Amer Musicological Soc; MusLA. 10: Beta Phi Mu; Phi Mu Alpha Sinfonia. 11: Hnry E Huntington Lib Grant 64-65. 12: "The Emergence of Tonality (59). 13: Yes. 14: Ref, music. 15: 264 Conway ave, Los Angeles Ca 90024.

WIENS, LUELLA. b Neb. 5: Reedley Jr Col 33-36 AA; UCal (Berkeley) 36-39 (Ger) AB, 39-40 (LS) Certif; USoCal 53 (Educ) MS; Columbia 56-57 (LS). 6: Ger. 7: Libn Coalinga High Sch & Jr Col, Coalinga Cal 40-43, Fremont Union High Sch, Sunnyvale Cal 43-46, Hartnell Col 46-. 9: CalLA; SLA Cal; NEA; CalTA; A-V Educ Assn Cal. 10: Bus& Prof Womens Club; Soroptimist Club; Delta Kappa Gamma; Phi Beta Kappa. 15: 56 Homestead ave, Salinas Ca 93901.

WIER, GWEN(DOLEN) (JANE). b Austin Tex 14 Ja 39. 5: UTex 56-62 (Elem Educ); S W Tex State summer 59; San Antonio Jr Col 61; Tex Womans U 62-63 (LS) BS; UTex 68- (LS). 7: Elem sch tchr Edgewood Ind Sch Dist, San Antonio

Tex 60-61; High sch libn El Campo Cons IND Sch Dist, El Campo Tex 63-68; Libn Robert E Lee Sch Austin Ind Sch Dist, Austin Tex 68-. 9: ALA; Tex State TCHRS Assn; TexLA. ; AustinEA; Austin Lib Club. 0: Jr Girl Scout Leader; Alpha Beta Alpha. 14: Ref, catlg. 15: 4603 B Lyons rd, Austin Tx 78702.

WIERER, OTTO. b Prague/c52SR 8 Ja 12. 4: Maria Magdalena Rohrer. 5: Realgymnasium (Prague) 24-32 (Sci, Linguistics); Free Sc of Pol Sci (Prague) 32-34 (Pol, Journal, Law) Dipl Sci Pol;Charles U (Prague) 32-38-39 (Law, Philos) Dr jur; Maxmilian U (Munich) 46-47 (Philos, Linguistics) Absolut; Columbia 57-58 MS in LS, 58-60 (Philos, Near & MIDDLE E Langs). 6: Czech, Ger, Sp, Fr, Portu, Slavic, Pers. 7: Legal adv, Prosecutor US High Commsn Courts for Germany, Munich 46-51; External researcher RFE, Munich 51-55; Export-Import RMT, Rio de Janeiro 55; Legal collab, Tr libn Internat Commsn of Jurists, Munich 56; Libn catlg dept NY Pub Lib 56-60; Asst head lang div Queensborough Pub Lib, Queens NY 60-65; Subj catlg Widener Lib Harvard U 65-66; Assoc libn IV, Hd Internat Info Ctr SUNY(Oyster Bay) 66-68; Hd libn Elliott Campus US Internat U 68-, Lectr communications, Grad Sch Leadership & Human Behavior 68. 9: ALA; SLA; NYLA; NY Lib Club. 10: Amer Oriental Soc; Oriental Inst, Prague; USIV Doc Soc. 12: "Mitsui Oriental Inst, Prague (38). 13: Yes. 14: Catlg, rare bks, bk sel (linguistics). 15: 5945 Gullstrand, San Diego Ca 92122.

WIERSCHIN, HANNELORE (HASELHORST). b Berlin Germany 3 D 41. 4: Martin Werner Wierschin. 5: Winthir-Oberrealschule (Munich) 58-61 (Langs) Abitur; Bibliotheksschule 9bayer Staats bibl) 61-63 (LS) Diploma; Inst Francais (Munich) 62-63 (Fr Lang); UMunich 64-66 (Danish Lang & Lit). 6: Ger, Fr, Danish, Lat, Norwegian, Swedish. 7: Bibliogr & ref libn Bayer Staats bibliothek, Munich 63-66; Libn I (catlgr) StanfordU 66-67; Libn II (catlgr) UCal (San Diego) 67-. 10: La Jolla Civic orchestra and Chorus. 14: Catlg, bibliog, ref. 15: 6658 Draper ave, La Jolla Ca 92037.

WIESE, BERNICE (MARION). b San Francisco 18 Ap 05. 5: Goucher Col 22-26 (Hist) AB; Col of William & Mary summer 27 (Hist); Duke 28-29 (Hist) MA; UVa summer 36 (LS); Columbia 31 summers 42, 43, 47, 48 MSLS. 7: Eng tchr Clifton Park Jr High Sch, Baltimore City Pub Schs 26-28; Hist tchr Tubman High Sch, Augusta Ga 29-35; Baltimore City Pub Schs libn Gwynns Falls Jr High Lib Serv 46-59, Dir of lib serv 59-68. 8: Tchr lib sci summer courses: Johns Hopkins 50, SUNY (Geneseo) 57, Drexel 60, etc; Sch lib adv to Ministry of Educ Malaysia (Fulbright-Hays Grant) 64-65; Fulbright-Hays Grant Tchrs Training Col, Singapore (Lectr in Lib Sci) 68-69. 9: ALA (Coun; sec Bldgs & Equip Sect 56-60); -AASchL (2nd v-pres 62-63, chm Com on Planning Sch Lib Quarters 55-59, chm NEA Adv Com); NEA; Assn of Supv & Curr Devel; Nat Assn Secon Sh Principals; Nat Sch Pub Rel Assn; MALAYANLA; MdLA (sec 46-48);Assn of Sch Libns, Md (treas 42, pres 44-46); Singapore LA (Coun 68-69).' 10: Quota Club. 13: Yes. 14: Central proc bldgs & equip for sch libs, lib staffing & personnel, for sch lib devel. 15: c/o Mrs E A Anderson, 245 Rodgers Forge, Baltimore Md 21212.

WIESE, HELEN G. b NYC 17 Ag 14. 5: Brooklyn Col 57-62 (Eng) BA; Columbia 62-64 (Eng) MA; Rutgers 64-66 MLS. 6: Fr. 7: Tchr C E Hughes High Sch, NYC 62-66, Libn 68-; Libn Veteran's Hosp, Plainfield NJ 67-68. 9: SLA. 10: Kappa Delta Pi; Alpha Sigma Lambda. 14: Ref, drama. 15: 433 W 21 st, New York NY 10011.

WIESE, IRIS J(EAN). b Centralia Ill 27 My 36. 5: Concordia Tchrs Col (Ill) 54-59 (Elem Educ) BS in Ed; Wayne State U summer 56, 60-63 (LS) MEd; Rosary Col 65 (LS). 6: Turkish. 7: Tchr-libn Trinity Lutheran Sch, Hicksville LI NY 59-61; Tchr-libn Lutheran High Sch E, Harer Woods Mich 61-63; Tchr DOD Dependent Sch, Eng 63-64; Asst libn curr libn Instr in child lit Concordia Tchrs Col (Ill) 64-65; Elem libn Dept f Defence Overseas Dependent Schs, Okinawa 65-67; Elem libn DOD, Turkey 67-68, High sch libn 68-. 8: Libn wkshop revise USDESEA Lib Curr; Karlsruhe Ger summer 68, 69. 9: ALA; NEA; Overseas EA; MchASchL. 10: Wayne State U Lib Sci Alumni Assn; Woman of Wayne. 13: Yes. 14: Child lit, ref, Instr media ctr concept. 15: 18010 Rutherford, Detroit Mi 48235.

WIEST, REX (MERRIT). b Oswego NY 20 Ja 12. 4: Temperance R Wiest. 5: Buffalo State Tchrs Col 37 (Educ) BS in Ed; CornellU 41 (Eng Lit) MA; Syracuse 52 MS in LS. 6: Ger, fr. 7: Sgt US Army 41-45; Tchr Rochester NY 37-40, 46-51; Prof asst Pub Lib of Charlotte & Mecklenburg Co, Charlotte NC 52-53, Hd ext div 53-. 9: ALA; NCLA; MecklenburgLA. 14: Bus collections, lang. 15: 3510 Rogers st, Charlotte NC 28208.

WIEST, RUTH PAULINE. b Scranton Penn 3 Mr 10. 5: Union Col 28-33 (Langs) BA; UMinn 37-39 (Eng) MA; UDenver 58-60 (LS) MA. 6: Sp, Fr. 7: Tchr of Span & Fr Indiana Acad, Cicero Ind 34-36; Eng tchr-libn Mountain View Acad, Mt View Cal 39-42; Eng tchr San Diego Union Acad, San Diego 42-43; Eng tchr Broadview ACAD, LA Grange Ill 43-53; Tchr-libn Mt Vernon Aca, Mt Vernon Ohio 53-58; Tchr-libn Sandia View Acad, Albuquerque NM 59-60; Head Libn Southwestern Union Col 60-67, Assoc libn 67-. 9: ALA; TexLA. 10: Writers Club. 14: Ref, catlg. 15: Southwestern Union Col, Keene Tex 76059.

WIETHORN, MARION E(VELYN). 5: Syracuse 33-37 (Fine Arts) BFA; Simmons sumers 48-51 (LS) BS. 7: Asst artist & photographer Dept of Genetics Carnegie Inst of Wash DC, Cold SPRING Harbor LI NY 37-38; Lib asst Huntington Pub Lib, Huntington NY 39-45; Picture Collection NY Pub Lib: Lbn 45-, Sr libn 56-, Supv lbn 58-. 9: SLA (Picture Div). 10: Huntington Hist Soc; Huntington Twp Art League; Camera Club; The Heckshen Museum. 14: Picture research & info. 15: Picture Collection, NY Pub Lib, Fifth ave & 42nd st, New York NY 10018.

WIGENT, EVELYN STODDART (MIRIAM). b East Orange NJ 13 S 20. 5: Douglass Col 37-41 (LS, Soc Studies) AB; Rutgers summers 38-40; Ind U Ext 44, 45; Purdue U 48-50 (Sociol); Ind State Tchrs Col (Logansport) 62; Purdue U 60-63 MS in Ed; UPittsburgh (LS) MS. 7: Ser unit asst, head child room in br lib Newark Pub Lib, Newark NJ 41-43; Libn Barrlington (RI) High Sch 43-44; Sales Comptons Encyclopeia, Lafayette Ind 50-54; Sub-prof period dept Purdue U Lib 54-55; Head of child room act head of lib W Lafayette Pub Lib, W Lafyette Ind 55-59; Chief of research div for television tchrs Midwest Program on Airborne Television Instr Purdue U summer 61; Tchr-libn Battle Ground Sch 59-64; Instr of Lib Sci Educ Dept Purdue U 64-66; Head Riley High Sch, S Bend Ind 67-. 8: Instr, admin of sch libs, NDEA Educ Media Inst, Purdue U summer 65. 9: ALA; NEA; NCTE; Ind Sch LA (chm Prof Rel Com 65-66). 10: ACLU; Amer Humane Assn. 11: John Cotton Dana Publicity Award for Sch Libs 60. 13: Yes. 14: Sch libs, pub rel. 15: 2819 Beechwood lane, South Bend In 46615.

WIGGIN, CYNTHIA BISHOP (SHERMAN). b New Bedford Mass 14 O 10. 4: Richard Le Favor Wiggin. 5: State Col (Framingham Mass) 29-30; Certif as Prof Libn by Commonwealth of Mass 57. 7: Asst libn Hamilton Pub Lib, Hamilton Mass 44-58; Child libn Lynn Pub Lib, Lynn Mass 58-60; Libn Salem Althenaeum, Salem Mass 60-. 9: ALA-ACRL (Rare Bks Com); MassLA (Exec Com & Nomin Com 63-65); No Shore Lib Club (pres 63-65, Exec Com 65-). 10: Salem Garden Club; Womans Friend Soc Ind; House of Seven Gables Settl Assn; Hist Salem Inc; LWV; Conserv Commsn Salem; Essex Inst; N Shore Framingham State Col Club. 12: "A Short History of the Salem Athenaeum (64); "The Kirwan Collection at the Salem Atenaeum (66); "The History of the Salem Book Club" (67). 13: Yes. 14: Admin, rare bks, research. 15: 7 Pickering st, Salem Mass 01970.

WIGGINS, EMILIE V(ERNE). b Richmond Ky 29 Jl 17. 5: East Ky State Col 34-38 (Fr, Lat) AB; UCincinnati 40-44 (Fr); UMich 45-47 BS in LS. 6: Fr, Sp, Ger. 7: Tchr Lynch High Sch, Lynch Ky 38-40; Tchr Rushville Twp High Sch, Rushville Ohio 41; Subprof catlgr UCincinnati 41-45; Catlgr Army Med Lib, Wash DC 47-50; Catlg rev NLM, Wash DC 60-62, Head catlg sect TSD, 62-. 9: ALA; MedLA; SLA; (past chm several coms); DCLA. 10: United World Federalists; ADA; CLU; US Com for UN; Unitarian-Univers Serv Com. 11: UMich Margaret Mann Award. 14: Catlg (automated). 15: 2950 Newark st NW, Wash DC 20008.

WIGGINS, JAMES WALLACE. b Butler Penn 5 Je 24. 5: Westminster Col (Penn) 42-43, 46-48 (Bus Admin) BA; UPittsburgh 63-64 MLS. 7: T-5 Med Corps US Army 43-46; Salesman W I Berman, Pittsburgh 48-51; Saleman J A Thoson, Westview Pittsburgh 51-54; Asst manager Coxs Inc, Mckeesport Penn 54-61; Post Libn US Army Sup Det Pittsburgh Air Defense Command, Oakdale Penn 64-. 10: McKeesport Leadership Train Sch. 14: Ref, period. 15: 2000 Monongahela blvd, Park Forest McKeesport Pa 15132.

WIGGINS, KATHLEEN MARIE. b Detroit Mich 24 D 45. 5: UMich 64-67 (Eng) BA, 67-68 (LS) MA. 6: Sp, Fr. 7: Interloan libn Ingham Co Lib, Mason Mich 68-. 8: Write weekly column for local paper called "Library Nook"; Mem Mich State Lib Scholarship Com 69-. 9: MichLA. 10: Phi Beta Kappa; Beta Phi Mu; UMich Assn of Lib Sci Alumni. 14: Ref, interlib loan. 15: 2176 Meadowlawn dr, Holt Mi 48842.

WIGGINS, LORNA A. b Birmingham Ala 17 D 30. 5: Agnes Scott Col 48-52 (Hist) BA; Emory 55-56 (LS) MLibn. 7: Asst re libn Biomed Lib UCLA 57-60; Asst catlgr & acquis libn Med Center Lib UAla 60-61; Sci-tech libn Ga Inst of Tech 61-63, Data processing libn 63-65; Dir M Paul Phillips Lib Birmingham-So Col 65-68; Asst Prof & Hd acquis div Auburn U Lib 68-. 9: ALA; MedLA; SELA; AlaLA. 14: Ref, bk sel, data proc. 15: Auburn Univ Lib, Auburn Al 36830.

WIGGINS, MARGUERITE (MINNIE). b Mount Olive NC 6 Ap 25. 5: E Carolina Col 44-47 (Hist, Sci) AB A Tchrs Certif; UNC 61-63 (LS, Hist) MSLS. 6: Fr. 7: Farm Operator, Mt Olive NC 47-54; Chapel Hill Chapter Amer Red Cross, Chapel Hill NC 55-56; NC Heart Assn, Chapel Hill NC 56-57; Lib asst NC Collections, UNC Lib(Chapel Hill) 57-62; Circ ref libn USCar Undergrad Lib 64; Asst acquis libn E Carolina U 64-67; Asst bibliogr 67-68, N Carolina Libn 68-. 9: ALA; NCLA; SELA. 10: AAUW; NCMusic Soc; NC Art Soc; Wesleyan Serv Guild; Nat Trust Hist Preserv; NC Lit & Hist Assn; Bus & Profess Women's Club; Carolina Art Soc. 14: Ref, bibliog, research. 15: E Carolina Col Lib, Greenville NC 27834.

WIGGINS, MARVIN E. b Ogden Utah 25 Mr 41. 4: Annette Christensen. 5: Weber State 60-61 (Sociol) AS; Brigham Young 63-66 (Sociol) BS; Rutgers 66-67 MLS. 6: Fr. 7: Asst gen ref libn Brigham Young 67, Gen ref libn 67-. 14: Ref (soc scis & educ). 15: Lib Brigham Young Univ, Provo Ut 84601.

WIGGINS, PATRICIA N. b Marion Ind 8 Je 31. 5: Marion Col 49-54 (Eng Lit) BA; UIll 54-57 (LS) MS. 6: Ger. 7: Asst in sci & tech Indianapolis Pub Lib 57-64; Asst in readers' serv Miami-Dade Jr Col 64-. 9: ALA; SLA (treas Ind Chap 61-63); FlaLA; DadeCoLA (sec 68-69). 14: Ref. 15: Miami-Dade Jr College 11380 NW 27th ave, Miami Fl 33167.

WIGHT, BARBARA L. b Oakland Cal 30 D 23. 5: USoCal 42-46 (Letters) BA, 46-47 (LS) BS. 6: Fr. 7: Los Angeles Co Lib: Hosp libn Harbor Hosp, Torrance Cal 47-57, Reg institutions libn, Los Angeles 57-61; Reg libn E San Gabriel Valley Reg, W Covina Cal 61-67, Reg libn Rosemead Cal 67-68, Reg libn Huntington Park Cal 68-. 8: Ref libn, Lib/USA NY Worlds Fair 64. 9: ALA (loc recr rep); SLA; CalLA (Legis Com, Exhib Com). 10: Phi Beta Kappa; Libraria Sodalitas; Bus & Prof Womens Club; USoCal ; Sch Lib Sci Alum Assn. 13: Yes. 14: Admin, recr. 15: 4223 Don Mariano dr, Los Angeles Ca 90008.

WIGHT, GUDRUN PAULINE (PALMESEN). b Aadal Norway 27 Ap 26. 4: Frank L Wight. 5: UAlberta 60-63 (Eng) BEd; UBC 67-68 BLS. 6: Norwegian. 7: Stenographer Stanley Brock Ltd, Calgary Can 54-59; Stenographer Da Silva World Travel, Calgary Can 59-60; Tchr Carstairs High Sch, Carstairs Alta Can 63-64; Tchr & libn R T Alderman Jr High, Calgary Can 68-. 14: Ref. 15: 430 - 12 st NW, Calgary Alta 41 Can.

WIGHTMAN, CLIFFORD B. b Chicago 18 S 06. 4: Bertha Woodhurst. 5: Central Mich U 24-26 (Eng) Life Certif; UMich 28-29 (Educ) AB in Ed; 29-30 AB in LS, 30-34 MA in LS; Chicago summer 41. 6: Fr, Ger. 7: Tchr Croswell Pub Sch, Croswell Mich 26-28; In chg Engnr Lib UMich 30-34; Ref libn Colo State Col of Educ, Greeley Colo 34-38; ssoc libn Pub Lib, Grand Rapids Mich 38-41; Libn Pub Lib, Lancaster Penn 41-48; Dir Hackley Pub Lib, Muskegon Mich 48-. 9: ALA; MichLA (pres 58; chm Ann Conf 56). 10: Kiwanis; Torch Club; Adult Educ Assn of Greater Muskegon; Muskegon Tchrs Club. 12: "The Bay City Public Library and School Libraries with R J Hurley mimeo (49). 13: Yes. 14: Admin. 15: 2460 Wickham dr, Muskegon Mich 49441.

WIGHTMAN, MARIE R. b Norfolk NY. 5: St Lawrence U 16-20 (Math) BS; Syracuse 46-48 BLS. 6: Sp, Fr. 7: Math tchr Parish High Sch, Parish NY 20-23; High sch libn Reading pub schs, Reading Penn 24-36; Asst libn Med Sch Syracuse U 47-48; Med libn Mary Imogene Bassett Hosp, Cooperstown NY 48-. 9: MedLA. 10: Criterion Club. 14: Ref. 15: 52 Beaver st, Cooperstown NY 13326.

WIGHTMAN, MARY FRANCES (THOMPSON). b Baton Rouge La 7 O 24. 4: Frederick C Wightman Jr. 5: Mary Baldwin Col 42-43; Vanderbilt 44-45 (Sociol, Psych) BA; Columbia 46-47 (LS) BS. 7: Ref asst Dartmouth Col Lib 47-48; Libn Water Sci Lib PrincetonU 59-63, 67-. 10: Univ League; Women's Col Club of Princeton; Present Day Club. 14: Lib admin, ref, catlg. 15: 66 Bertrand dr, Princeton NJ 08540.

WIGIM, JANET (COLLINS). b Iowa City Iowa 16 Ag 31. 4: Tom Walter Wigim. 5: Marycrest Col 49-53 (Eng) BA; State UIowa 53-57; Rosary Col 57-58 (LS) MA; Fresno State Col 68-69. 7: Newspaper soc ed "Press-Citizen", Iowa City Iowa 53-57; Libn Oak Park, Pub Lib, Oak Park Ill 58; Grad asst Fresno State Col curriculum lib 68-69. 10: YWCA. 14: Child serv, ref in pub lib wk, sch libnship (elem level). 15: 4614 N 2nd st, Fresno Ca 93726.

WIGMORE, SHIRLEY KATHLEEN. b Gowganda Ont Can 14 S 28. 5: Mt Allison U 7-48; UToronto 48-52 (Eng Lang & Lit) BA, 52-53 BLS, 66 (LS) MLS. 6: Fr. 7: Asst libn Ont Co of Educ 53-58, Research libn Dept of Educ Research 58-65; Lecturer & Libn Ont Inst for Studies in Educ, Toronto 65-. 9: CanLA; ALA; SLA (Toronto Chap: treas 56-57, Recr chm 57-58, Bull ed 60-62, Employment Chm 62-63, pres 64-65); OntLA; Inst Prof Libns Ont. 10: Canadian Amateur Musicians. 12: "An Annotated Guide to Publications Related to Educational Research (60). 14: Admin, ref, personnel, arch. 15: 102 Bloor st W, Toronto 5 Can.

WIIRET, MARGARET. b Cloquet Minn 29 Ja 19. 5: UMinn 37-41 (LS) BS. 6: Finnish. 7: Asst Pub Lib, Eau Claire Wis 42; Jr asst Pub Lib, Duluth Minn 43-44; Asst libn Pub Lib, Cloquet Minn 44-64; Manager & co-owner Bk Shop, Cloquet Minn 65-. 9: ALA; MinnLA (past sec Child Div). 14: Proc bks & a-v materials. 15: Red Rover Bk Shop, 24 S Tenth st, Cloquet Mn 55720.

WIKANDER, ETHEL MARIE (WHITLOW). b Wash DC 20 F 17. 4: Lawrence E Wikander. 5: American U 33-37 (Pol Sci) AB; Columbia 38-39 BS in LS. 7: DC Pub Lib: 1st asst adult dept NE Br 39-40, Asst br libn Takoma Park Br 40-42, Asst libn 42-45, Music libn 45-46; Smith Col Lib: Catlgr 53-63, Asst head catlgdpt 63-64, Head circ dept 64-68; Catlgr Clark Art Inst Lib, Williamstown Mass 68-. 9: MusLA; NELA; MassLA. 10: LWV; Hampshire Chorus. 14: Music libnship, catlg, circ, art. 15: Clark Art Inst Lib, Williamstown Ma 01267.

WIKANDER, LAWRENCE EINAR. b Pittsburgh 16 D 15. 4: Ethel Marie Whitlow. 5: Williams 33-37 (Pol Sci) AB; Columbia 38-39 BS in LS; UPenn 46-49 (Hist) MA. 6: Fr, Ital. 7: Circ & ref asst, Carnegie Lib Pittsburgh 39-40, Supv of circ DC Pub Lib 40-42; Capt Mil Intelligence US Army 42-46; Supv tech processes Temple U 46-48, Asst libn 48-50; Libn Forbes libn, Northampton Mass 50-68; Libn Williams 68-. 8: Bd dirs, Hampshire Inter-lib Center 56-68; Chm West Mass Reg Pub Lib System Adv Coun 64-68. 9: ALA (Coun 62-69, Bk Acquis Com 52-54, Amer Bk Publrs-ALA Com on Reading Devel 65-69);-PLA (Legis Com 63-65, Pubns Com 55-56); NELA (treas 63-65, pres 67-68); MassLA (pres 60-61); West Mass Lib Club (pres 53-55). 10: Rotary Club; ACLU; Northampton Hist Soc; C of C; Amer Motorcycle Assn; Several loc hist socs. 12: "Name It Northampton (54); "Completing a Century (62); Ed "The Northampton Book (54);"The Hampshire History (64). 13: Yes. 14: Acquis, tech proc. 15: Williams Col Lib, Williamstown Ma 01267.

WIKOFF, RUTH (SLATER). b Atwood Ill 3 Ja 05. 4: Russell L Wikoff. 5: Millikin U 23-27 (LS) BA; Houston 33-36 (Eng) BS, 40-45 (Admin Educ) MA; UTex summer 30. 6: Fr, Ger. 7: Libn: Chilocco Indian Sch, Okla 27-30, Washington Jr High Sch, Houston 30-33, Houston Jr Col 33-34; UHouston: Libn 34-50, Gen libn 50-63, Assoc dir of lib 63-67, Emerita 67-. 8: Consul Tex Dental Col, 36. 9: ALA; SWLA; TexLA; Tex Assn Col Tchrs. 10: AAUP; AAUW; LWU; Faculty Club; Willowisp Country Club. 12: Comp "Bibliography of Theses and dissertions. . 40-58 & sup 58-63. 13: Yes. 14: Ref, admin. 15: 3319 Plumb, Houston Tx 77005.

WIKTOR, CHRISTIAN L. b Voillecomte France 23 Je 33. 4: Bodil Stig Madsen. 5: UWroclaw (Poland) 57 (Law) ML; UParis 58-60 (Internat law); Columbia 62-64 MS in LS. 6: Fr, Polish, Russian. 7: NY Pub Lib: Lib tech asst I 61-63, Lib tech asst II 63-64, Libn I 64-65;Asst libn catlgr SUNY Sch of Law (Buffalo) 65-67, Assoc libn III internat & for law 68-. 9: AALL; Amer Soc Internat Law. 14: Internat & for law, tech serv. 15: 42 Monica rd, Grand Island NY 14072.

WILBANKS, MARY ELIZABETH. b Eastaboga Ala 15 Ap 20. 5: Ala Col 38-42 (Hist) AB; Emory 46-48 (Eng) MA; UNC 51-52 (Eng), 57-59 MSLS. 6: Sp. 7: Tchr Lanett City schs, Lanett Ala 42-44; WAVES Spec (S) 3/c 44-46; Instr in Eng: Fla State U 48-53, Murphy High Sch, Atlanta 54-55, Young Harris Col 55-56; Gifts & exch libn & Instr Auburn U 59-63, Spec collections libn & Instr 63-, Asst Prof 69-. 9: ALA; SELA; AlaLA (Bibliog Com). 10: Beta Phi Mu; AAUW; Pilot Internat. 14: Ref, rare bks, tchg lib sci. 15: 46 Woodland ter, Auburn Al 36830.

WILBER, (BILEY) KAYLENE. b Union City Penn 16 Je 45. 4: Wesley K Wilber. 5: Clarion state Col 63-67 (Libnship) BS; West MichU 67-69 MLS. 6: Sp, Fr. 7: Libn Corry Area high

Sch, Corry Penn 67; Grad asst Educ Resources Ctr West MichU 67-69; Jr libn USoCar Reg Campus (Spartanburg) 69-. 8: Consul to Fisher Pub Co 67-69; SEast rep Denver Off 69-. 9: ALA. 14: Ref, wk with fac. 15: Carriage House Garden apts #46, Spartanburg SC 29301.

WILBUR, LOWELL ROGER. b Cherokee Iowa 19 D 28. 4: Maxine J Watson. 5: Buena Vista Col 47-51 (Eng, Sociol) BA; UMinn 57-58 (LS) MA. 7: Jr asst Pub Lib, Des Moines Iowa 56-57; Tchg asst Lib Sch, UMinn 57-58; Ext libn Pub Lib, Mason City Iowa 58-59; Dir Pub Lib, Belleville Ill 59-62; Dir Pub & Co Libs, La Porte Ind 62-66; Dir Pub Lib, Mason City Iowa 66-. 9: ALA; IowaLA. 10: Sigma Tau Delta; Rotary. 15: 225 Second st SE, Mason City Ia 50401.

WILBUR, SHARON FAYE. b Fort Worth Tex 16 My 41. 5: UTex (Arlington) 59-61; Tex woman'sU 61-63 (LS) BA, 65-66 MLS. 7: Libn Ft Stockton Pub Lib, Ft Stockton Tex 63-65; Libn Spec Serv Lib I, Ft Sill Okla 66-68, Libn (supv) 68-. 9: ALA; SLA. 14: Ref. 15: 2309 N 38th st apt 4C, Lawton Ok 73501.

WILBURN, DOROTHEA (BAXTER). b Philadelphia 16 N 06. 4: Louis Oakey Wilburn. 5: Goucher Col 23-27 (Hist) AB; UPenn 27-28 (Hist, Eng Lit); Drexel 28-29, 30 BS in LS. 7: Asst in circ Free Lib of Phila 29-30, Asst in spec catlg 30; Libn Candler Sch of Theol, Emory U 30-32; Libn E C Glass High Sch, Lynchburg Va 59-60; Yp libn Roanoke Pub Lib, Roanoke Va 65; Asst libn Ferrum Jr Col 65-68, Assoc libn 68-. 9: ALA; SELA; VaLA; NEA; VaEA. 10: AAUW; Federated Womens Club. ; AAUP. 14: Catlg, ref, spec libs. 15: Lib Ferrum Jr Col, Ferrum Va 24088.

WILCKEN, BARBARA ANN. b Minneapolis 18 F 39. 5: UMinn 57-61 (Eng) BS, 63-65 (LS) MA. 6: Fr. 7: High sch Eng tchr E Grand Rapids Pub Schs, Grand Rapids Mich 61-62; Libn San Francisco Pub Lib 62-63; Tchg asst Lib Sch UMinn 63; Asst supv of sch libs State Dept of Educ, St Paul 63-68; Inst for Devel of Lib Serv for Minn Indians 69-. 9: ALA-AASchL; NEA; Amer Educ Res Assn; MinnEA; MinnASchL. 10: ACLU; Pi Lambda Theta; Sigma Epsilon Sigma. 13: Yes. 14: Sch libnship. 15: 5132 Park ave, Minneapolis 55417.

WILCOX, ALYCE JOY (JACOBS). b Auburn NY 4 N 41. 4: Robert E Wilcox. 5: State U Col (Geneseo NY) 59-63 (Elem Educ, LS) BS; State U Col (Cortland NY) summers 63-65 (Elem Educ) MS. 7: Elem sch libn Moravia Central Sch, Moravia NY 63-. 8: A-V consul 63-. 9: NY State Tchrs Assn; Cayuga Co TA; Educ Communications Coun of Cayuga Co (sec). 10: 20th Century Culture Club; Delta Kappa Gamma. 14: Child libs. 15: RD 4 Long Hill rd, Moravia NY 13118.

WILCOX, BETTY JANE. b Alexandria Bay NY 9 O 44. 5: NorthwesternU 62-63 (Speech, theatre); SUNY (Albany) 63-67 (Eng Lit) BA, 67-68 MLS. 6: Fr, Ger. 7: Catlgr (sub-prof) SUNY (Oneonta) 67; Asst acquis libn Union Col 68-69, Acquis libn 69-. 10: ACLU; Soc of Bibliophiles (Albany NY). 14: Acquis, catlg. 15: PO Box 149, Schenectady NY 12301.

WILCOX, GRANT S JR. b Yakima Wash 13 N 09. 4: Mary Monks. 5: Antioch Col 28-31 (Sci); UMich 31-33 (Engnr) BS Mech Engnr; West Mich U 60-61 (LS) MA. 7: Spec assignment to pres product & program development Chrysler Corp Plymouth Div 36-53; Tech asst to ge manager Ford Motor Co Dearborn GEN Manufacturing Div, & Supt in assembly operations Lincoln Mercury-Wayne Plant 53-56; Product manager Cleveland Pneumatic Ind Nat Waterlift div & Sales rep & supv serv repirs Ind Sales Div 57-60; Lib asst Bus Lib West Mich U 60-61; Head A-V Dept & Community goup coun Kalamazoo Lib System 61-. 9: SLA; Amer Soc Tool & Mfg Engnrs; MichLA; Engnr Soc Detroit; Mich Soc Prof Engnrs. 10: Aero Club of Mich. 13: Yes. 14: A-v, radio & TV, ub rel, electronic storage & retrieval of info. 15: 5130 Greenhill rd, Kalamazoo 49001.

WILCOX, JUNE. b Los Angeles Cal 4 Jl 25. 5: Occidental 47 (Eng & Amer Lit) AB; UMich 50 MALS. 6: Ger. 7: H E Huntington Lib, San Marino Cal: Asst in order dept 47-49, catlgr 50-55, 58-67, Asst hd preparations dept 67-; US Army Spec Serv; Field libn, Nurnberg Germany 56, Field libn, Grafenwohr Germany 56-57, Post libn Verdun France 57-58. 9: CalLA. 14: Proc of ref & rare bk material, supv rare bk catlg. 15: 1715 E Oakwood st, Pasadena Ca 91104.

WILCOX, MARY (MONKS). b Boston 26 N 09. 4: Grant S Wilcox Jr. 5: Antioch Col 28-31; UMich 31-34 (Fr, Sci) AB; West Mich U 57-59 (LS) MA. 6: Fr, Ital, Ger, Sp. 7: Catlg libn West Mich U 59-. 9: ALA; MichLA. 10: AAUW; Faculty Womens Club. 14: Catlg. 15: 5130 Greenhill rd, Kalamazoo 49001.

WILCOX, ROSA S. b Griswold Conn 11 Ag 1896. 5: Conn Col 15-19 (Classical Phil) BA; UVa summer 40; BostonU summers 41-43; UMich summers 44-46 ABLS; UVt summer 47; UConn summer 48; Mystic Seaport summer 54; Radcliffe summer 55; URI summer 57-58. 6: Fr. 7: Tchr: Farmington High Sch, Unionville Conn 19-20, Norwich Free Acad, Norwich Conn 20-57; Libn Wickford High Sch, North Kingstown RI 57-58; Libn Curry Col 58-62; Libn Faulkner Hosp Sch of Nursing, Jamaica Plain Mass 62; Libn Catherine Laboure Sch of Nursing, Dorchester Mass 62; Libn Vernon Court Jr Col 63-66. 10: Norwich Col Club. 14: Catlg, ref. 15: 1 Lathrop lane, Norwich Ct 06360.

WILCOX, VIRGINIA LEE. b Portsmouth Ohio 28 N 11. 5: Averett Col 30-31, 33-34 (Liberal Arts) Diploma; UDenver 35-37 (LS) AB & Diploma in LS, t2 (Eng) MA. 7: Libn Colo Fuel & Iron Corp, Pueblo Colo 37-40; Asst libn Colo Sch of Mines 40-42; Base libn US Air Force, La Junta Colo 43-45; Army Libn US Army ETO, Hq Reims France 45-46; Colo Sch of Mines: Asst libn 46-55, Act libn 55-56, Hd libn 56-. 9: ALA; SLA (chm Petrol Div 65-66; pres Colo Chap 56-57); ColoLA (sec 48-49; chm No Dist 61-62); MPLA; Amer Soc Engnr Educ (sec Engnr Sch Lib Div 67-69; co-chm Rocky Mtn Sect 66-67); Coun of Libns of State Insts of Higher Educ in Colo (chm 64-66); Bibliog Center for Res (Rocky Mt Reg; Exec Com 55-56, chm 59-60). 10: Colo Hist Soc; The Westerners; PEO. 12: "Colorado; a Selected Bibliography of its Literature 1858-1952" (54); "Index to the Westerners Brand Books, All Posses, 1954" (55); "Comprehensive Index to Westerners' Brand Books, 1944-1961" (2nd ed 62). 13: Yes. 14: Admin. 15: Colo Sch of Mines Lib, Golden Colo 80401.

WILCZYNSKI, MIMI INES. b Urbana Ill 30 Jl 09. 5: UChicago 37 (Romance Langs & Lits) MA, 40 (Romance Langs & Lits) PhD. 6: Lat, Fr, Ital, Sp, PORTU, Ger. 7: Asst in romance langs UChicago 40-51; Catlgr UChicago Lib 46-58, Sr catlgr. 59-. 9: ALA-ACRL; Amer Assn Tchrs Italian; Dante Soc; Societa filologica friulana; Chicago Reg Catlgrs (Resources & Tech Serv). 10: Quadrangle Club, Chicago. 12: "Sources and Analogues of Chretiens Yvain (43). 13: Yes. 14: Rare bks. 15: 5709 Kimbark ave, Chicago 60637.

WILDEN-HART, MARION. b London England 15 Mr 31. 5: NWest Polytech Sch of Libnship 50-53 British ALA; ULondon 55-58 Diploma in Hist of Art. 6: Fr, Ital. 7: Lib asst Holborn Pub Libs, London England 47-49; Ref libn Reform Club Lib, London England 49-50; Sr asst Buckingdhamshire Co Libs, England 53; Catlgr Kensington Pub Libs, London Englabd 54-55; Dist libn Middlesex Co Libs, England 55-58; Stock ed Lambett Pub Libs, London England 59-66; Co-ord acquis SyracuseU Libs 68-. 8: Lectr Northwest Polytech Sch of Libnship 54-64; Lectr UMalaya Dept of Educ 66-68; Lib adv Malaysia 66-68. 9: Lib Assn, UK (Univ & Res Br, Lib Hist Gp, Spec Libs Gp). 10: Fellow, Royal Geogr Soc; Assoc, Archaeol Inst. 11: Lib Assn Essay Prize 56; Eng-Speaking Union scholarship 64. 12: "The Librarian-Technician or Bookman" (56); Reviewer Times Library Supplement 59-64. 13: Yes. 14: Bibliog and readers adv wk. 15: Syracuse Univ Lib, Syracuse NY 13210.

WILDER, ANNETTE BEDFORD. b Natchez Miss. 4: Eugene Wilder. 5: Miss Womans Col 29 (Fr, Eng) BA; Tulane 32 (Fr, Eng); Peabody 48 MLS. 6: Fr, Sp. 7: Instr USo Miss 28-33; Tchr Hattiesburg (Miss) High Sch 37-40; USo Miss: Libn Demonstation Sch 40-55; Acquis libn & Asst Prof of Lib Sci 55-60, Ref libn 60-64, Ref libn & Assoc Prof of Lib Sci 64-. 9: NEA; ALA; SELA; MissLA; Miss EA. 10: Delta Kappa Gamma; AAUW; AAUP; Hattiesburg Womans Club; Magna Charta Dames; DAR; DAC; Hattiesburg (Miss) Pub Lib Bd; Miss Hist Assn; Kappa Delta Pi. 14: Ref. 15: 902 W Pine st, Hattiesburg Miss 39401.

WILDER, DAVID (THOMPSON). b Rochester NY 26 N 17. 4: Olga Mary Hitchcock. 5: Union Col (Schenectady NY) 36-40 (Soc Studies) AB; URochester 40-41 (Hist) MA; Columbia 41-42 (LS) BS. 7: S/Sgt Weather Serv USAAF 42-45; Fellow in intern lib rel ALA, Wash DC 46; Col libn Hamilton Col 46-51; Univ libn AmericanU (Beirut Lebanon) 51-54; Asst dir libs (pub serv) Ohio StateU (Columbus) Ohio 54-60; Univ libn OaklandU 60-64; Program specialist in univ libraries Ford Foundation, Middle East Reg, Baghdad Iraq 64-66; Dir libs UMan 66-. 8: Soc Sci Res Coun; Consul to Comm on Near & Middle East 57, Rep on Subcom on Lib Prob, Jt Comm on Near & Middle East 59-62. 9: ALA (Coun 48-51); Internat Rel RT (chm Middle East Area 61-64, 67-68);-ACRL (Col Sect; sec 49-50; Com on Non-West

Materials 67-); NYLA (Coun 48-51). 10: AAUP; Amer Commun Sch (Beirut Lebanon) Sch Bd; PTA; Rochester(Mich) Sch Study Com; All Saints Anglican Church(Winnipeg) Vestry Mem 69-. 12: "The Acquisition and Control of Publications from the Near and Middle East," in ARL "Farmington Plan Survey" (59). 13: Yes. 14: Lib org & admin, rel of lib to univ acad and res progs, collection develop, lib bldgs. 15: 211-1 Snow st, Winnipeg 19 Can.

WILDER, ULAH. b Winslow Ind 18 F 16. 5: Oakland City Col 53-56 (Soc Studies) BA; Ind State U 56-59 (LS) MA. 7: Oakland City Col: Dormitory housemother 54-61, Asst libn 56-61, Head Libn 61-. 9: ALA; IndLA (v-pres Dist V 68). 10: College Womens Club; Alpha Beta Alpha; Oakland City Col Alum Assn; Md State U Alum Assn. 14: Circ, catlg, ref. 15: 218 N Clay st, Oakland City Ind 47560.

WILDER, VERNIE BERT. b Franklinton NC 14 F 32. 5: E Carolina Col 50-54 (Eng) BS, 54-57 (Educ) MA. 7: Libn W Edgecombe Sch, Rocky Mount NC 54-57; Libn E Carolina Col 51-, Dir catlg 67-. 9: ALA; NCLA; SELA. 10: AAUP; NC Lib & Hist Assn; Amer Wildlife Assn; Amer Forestry Assn. 14: Catlg. 15: 1204 E Third st, Greenville NC 27834.

WILDIN, NANCY (YAHN). b Portland Ore 2 Je 43. 4: Howard W Wildin II. 5: Pacific lutheranU 61-63; UWash 63-65 (Eng) BA, 66-67 MLib. 7: Lib asst UWash Lib 65-66; Libn I Seattle Pub Lib 68-. 9: PNLA. 15: 203 W Comstock #6, Seattle Wa 98117.

WILDMAN, IRIS J. b Chicago 10 My 30. 5: Northwestern 48-52 (Pol Sci, Eng) BS; West Res 53-54 MS in LS. 6: Sp. 7: Catlgr Copyright Off LC 54; Law catlgr Army Lib Pentagon, Wash DC 54-56; Catlgr, Dept of Justice Lib, Wash DC 56-57; Head tech serv Ohio State U Law Lib 57-59; Head tech serv Skokie Pub Lib, Skokie Ill 59-60; Head catlg & clsf dept Northwestern U Law Lib 61-64; Head acquis dept Yale U Law Lib 65-. 8: Consul Corp Coun Govt of DC, Wash DC 57; AALL Inst on Law Catlg, UCLA summer 66; Consul UPR Law Lib 68. 9: ALA; AALL (chm 3 coms 56-68); Law Lib Assn Greater NY; Law Libns NE; ConnLA. 10: Beta Phi Mu; Ctr for Dem Insts. 12: "A Study of Law Library Classification nd Its Problems ACRL Microcard series no. 30 (54); Ed "Law Libraries in the United States and Canada (58); "Directory of Law Libraries (64 & 66). ; Jt comp "Current Publications in Legal and Related Fields, Section II; Supplements and Continuations" (67-). 13: Yes. 14: Catlg, law clsf, acquis. 15: 92 W Walk, West Haven Ct 06516.

WILDNER, GERTRUDE (PHILLIPS) (MRS). b Madison Fla 18 F 22. 5: Rollins Col 43 (Speech) AB; Fla State U 55 (LS) MA. 6: Fr, GER. 7: Head Libn Leon High Sch, Tallahassee Fla 55-57; Libn Fla Geological Survey, Tallahassee Fla 57-59; Gifts & exch libn Fla State U 59-. 9: FlaLA. 10: Tallahassee Hist Soc; Alpha Phi; DAR. 15: 405 Hillcrest, Tallahassee Fl 3303.

WILDS, DEBORAH BARRINGTON. b Los Angeles Cal 15 Jl 07. 5: UCLA 26-30, 51-52 (Eng) BA; USoCal 52-54 MLS. 6: Fr. 7: Br supv & bk selector Los Angeles Pub Lib 54-56, Reg libn Hawthorne 56-. 10: USoCal Lib Sch Alumni Assn; Kappa Kappa Gamma; Friends of the Culver City Lib; UCLA Art Coun; Museum Alliance Los Angeles Co Museum. 14: Reg lib admin, bk sel. 15: 120 - 20th st, Manhattan Beach Ca 90266.

WILDS, THOMAS. b Detroit 19 S 25. 4: Tatiana C Pytkovsky. 5: UMich 43-44, 47-49 (Oriental Langs) BA, 48-50 (Far East Area Studies) MA, 49-50 (Hist) MA; American U 55-56 (Archival Sci); NYU 58-64 (Bus Admin). 6: Japanese. 7: Tr Off (Capt) US Army, US, Japan, Korea 44-47; Histn US Army, Wash DC 50-54; Sr archivist State of Md, Annapolis Md 54-56; Consul Union Carbide Corp, NYC 56-68; Exec v-pres Doc Systs Inc, NYC 68-. 8: Asst prof of mgt, Mgt Inst NYU. 9: SAA (Coun 63-66); Assn Reords Execs & Admins (pres 63); SLA; ASIS. 13: Yes. 14: Mgt info systems, info retrieval. 15: 91 Putnam Park, Greenwich Conn 06830.

WILER, LINDA LOU. b Chicago Ill 31 Jl 40. 5: Pasadena City Col 58-60 (Liberal arts) AA; Immaculate Heart Col 60-61 (Hist); UCLA 61-62 (Hist) BA, 62-63 MLS. 6: Fr. 7: Sci libn John Crerar Lib, Chicago 63-65; Catlgr UChicago Lib 65-66; Ref libn Chicago Pub Lib 66-. 9: ALA; Organiz Amer Histns; Acad Polit Sci. 12: Ed Chicago Pub lib "Staff News". 14: Ref. 15: 2901 King dr, Chicago Il 60616.

WILEY, BETH I (RIGGS). b Ames Iowa 12 Je 13. 4: John A Wiley. 5: York Col 31-33 (Educ); DrakeU 36-38 (Educ) BS. 7: Tchr pub sch: Runnells Iowa 38-40, Perry Iowa 40-41; Libn Judson Baptist Col 62-. 9: ALA; Willamette Christ Col Libs. 15: Judson Baptist College Lib 9201 NE Fremont, Portland Or 97220.

WILEY, RONALD ROSS. b Flushing LI NY 19 J136. 5: UPittsburgh 55-59 (Pol Sci) BA, 62-63 MLS. 7: Stud asst libn Lib Sch UPittsburgh 63: Vol libn Amer Civil Liberties Union, NYC 65; Libn Brooklyn Pub Lib 63-65; Asst libn W Va State Col 66-. 9: ALA-PLA; -ACRL;-RTSD;-AS;-LAD; SLA (Docs Div; Sci-Tech Div: Chem Sect). ; W Va LA. 10: AAAS; ACLU. 14: Ref, catlg, adult serv. 15: P O Box 183, Institute W Va 25112.

WILHELM, ERICA. b Bonn Germany 16 Ap 26. 4: Hellmut Wilhelm. 5: URochester 44-49; Manhattan Sch of Mus 49-51 (Musicology) MM; UWash 64-66 MLS. 6: Ger, Fr. 7: Asst libn Art Dept Seattle Pub Lib 66-67, Asst libn Muni Ref Lib 67-. 9: WashLA. 15: 2448 Delmar dr E, Seattle Wa 98102.

WILHELM, RUTH I(MELDA MARY). b Pittsburgh 20 My 19. 5: Col Misericordia 37-41 (LS) AB; Duquesne U 46-48 (Guidance) MEd; Syracuse 50-51 (LS) MS. 7: Tchr-libn Lilly Boro Sch Dist, Lilly Penn 42-44; Libn Monaca Sr High Sch, Monaca Penn 44-48; Asst libn St Vincent Col, Latrobe Penn 48-50, Assoc libn 51-54; Instr ext courses Marywood Col 55-56; Instr ext course Penn State Col, Beaver Co Ext 65-66; Libn B F Jones Mem Lib, Aliquippa Penn 54-68; Asst Prof Dept of Lib Sci Slippery Rock State Col 68-. 8: Adv Dist Lib Ctr Dir Pub Libs Beaver Co Penn 62-68. 9: ALA; CathLA (chm Col & Univ Sect W Penn Unit 52-53); Tri-State ACRL; PennSchLA; PennLA (chm Pub Lib Div 60-61, chm (ad hoc) Student Use of Libs 62-63, sec 64-65, chm Org & Bylaws 66-68, chm Nomin 68-69; Four Co Chap; sec 55-57, chm Bylaws Com 55-56, 64-65, 66-67, pres 63-64); Butler Co Learn Res Assn (chm Org & Bylaws 69-). 10: C of C. 14: Admin, tchg lib sci. 15: 433 Hallett pl, Bellevue Pittsburgh 15202.

WILHELMI, ILSE (EMMA). b Lawrence Kan 20 O 1894. 5: UKan 13-17 (Ger) BA; UWis summers 14-16; Columbia 28-29 BSLS. 6: Ger. 7: Ser libn UKan 29-31,Accessions libn, med libn, sci libn 21-28; Asst Prof Lib Admin & Supv of Dept Libs Ohio State U 31-65, Faculty Emeritus 65-. 9: ALA; SLA; OhioLA; Ohio Col Assn; Ohioana Fr Co LA (pres 49-50, Nomin Com Chm 61-62). 10: AAUP; AAUW; PEO; Faculty Club; Univ Womens Club; Faculty Womens Club. 14: Admin. 15; 1608 Grandview ave, Columbus Ohio 43212.

WILHITE, BOBBYE (CROSS). b Ky 21 My 40. 4: Carlos Wilhite. 5: Ky State Col 57-58; UKy 58-61 (LS) BA, 61-63 MSLS; Wayne State U 63. 6: Fr. 7: Detroit Bd of Educ: Campau Elem Sch 61, Dwyer Sch 62-64, Central High Sch 64-68; Denby High Sch 68; Chadsey High Sch 69-. 9: MichASchL. 10: Delta Sigma Theta. 14: Ya serv, ref. 15: 17596 Santa Rosa, Detroit 48221.

WILHITE, CAROLYN ANN (HAUGHTON). b Bessemer Ala 21 My 37. 4: Billy Joe Wilhite. 5: Memphis State U 58. 7: Typist Fairfield Abstract Off, Faifield Tex 54-56; Typist Nat Burial Ins Co, Memphis Tenn 56; Sec Builders Serv Inc, Memphis Tenn 56; Sec-libn W R Grace & Co, Memphis 57-62, Libn 62-. 9: ALA; SLA; TennLA (sec Spec Lib Sect 61-62, Lib Resources Com 63, Steering Com 64; Oak Ridge Chap). 10: Bus & Prof Womens Club. 12: Co-comp "A Directory to 49 Memphis Libraries (64). 14: Ref. 15: 6640 Old Tipton rd Rte 1 Box 75, Millington Tn 38053.

WILKENS, LAURA H(ACKETT). b Cleveland 27F20. 4: Frederick A Wilkens. 5: Flora tone Mather Col West Res 39-42 (Eng) AB; Kent State U 60-65 MLS. 6: Fr. 7: Child libn Chagrin Falls Br Cuyahoga Co Pub Lib, Chagrin Falls Ohio 60-67; Libn Gurney Elem Sch, Chagrin Falls Ohio 67-. 9: ALA; OhioASchL. 14: Child lit. 15: 266 E Washington st, Chagrin Falls Ohio 44022.

WILKERSON, M ELIZABETH. b Tenn 27 Jl 22. 5: IndU 60-66 (Hist) BS, 67-68 (LS) MAT. 7: Catlgr (sch), Libn Wirt High Sch, Libn Lew Wallace High Sch, Gary Ind 66-. 9: ALA; IndSchLA. 15: 5101 Virginia, Gary In 46409.

WILKINS, ALICE LINA (ANDREWS). b Fillmore NY 4My39. 4: David B Wilkins. 5: Houghton Col 56-60 (Eng) BA; Columbia 60-62 MS in LS. 7: Stud asst Willard Houghton Mem Lib, Houghton Col 54-60; Lib asst US Steel Corp Lib, NYC 60-62; Catlgr Friendship Lib, Fairleigh Dickinson U 63-65; Catlg libn Joint U Libs, Nashville 65-67; Tech ser libn Kings Col (Briarcliff Manor) 67-. 8: Consul in Tech Serv, Tead Lib Briarcliff Col, Briarcliff Manor NY 67-. 9: ALA; WestchesterLA. 10: PTA. 13: Yes. 14: Tech serv. 15: 48 McKeel ave, Tarrytown NY 10591.

WILKINS, KATHRYN S. b Sayville NY 16 Mr 13. 5: SUNY (Albany) 30-34 BLS, 34-38 (Eng) BA; Columbia 49 (Curriculum) MA. 6: Fr. 7: Libn; ellenburg High Sch, Ellenburg NY 34-36, Ellenville High Sch, Ellenville NY 36-42; US Navy, Bethesda Md 45-47, S Jr Hifg Sch, Great Neck NY 47-69; Asst Prof Grad Lib Sch C W Post Col LIU 60-. 8: Ed consul, Atheneum Press, NYC 65. 9: ALA; NEA; NYLA; Nassau-Suffolk SchLA. 12: "To Bridge the Gap, "Young Teens Like These Give Me A Gimmick. 13: Yes. 14: Sch libnship. 15: 18 West End ave, Great Neck NY 11023.

WILKINS, MADELEINE J (SZEMEREI). b Budapest Hungary 7 Mr 14. 4: Otto Wilkins. 5: U f Science (Budapest Hungary) 32-36 (Linguistics) BA, 36-37 (Comparative Linguistics) MA, 38 (Linguistics) PhD; Catholic U 53-54 MS in LS. 6: Hungarian, Ger, Fr, Ital. 7: Subj Header Current List Div Army Med Lib, Wash DC 51-52; Subj Header, Cyrillic Catlg Div LC 52-53, Bibliogr Sci & Tech Div 54-58; Chief Foreign Documentation Dept of the Interior Lib, Wash DC 58-64; Asst chief acquis sect Com Clearinghouse, Wash DC 64-66; Chief info acquis Nat Inst of Mental Health, Chevy Chase Md 66-68; Asst hd spec bibliog sect sci & tech div LC 68-. 9: SLA; Assn for Computing Machinery; DCLA; ASIS. 10: Beta Phi Mu. 12: "Aviation Medicine; an Annotated Bibliogaphy 2v (56, 58); "Evaporation Suppression: Review of Foreign Literature (61); "Subject Specialties in the Department of the Interior (62). 14: Bibliog standards, tr activities in the govt, info retrieval, documentation. 15: 7223 Delfield st, Chevy Chase Md 20015.

WILKINS, MAGNOLIA LEOLA (ECHOLS). b Stone Mountain Ga 25 Ja 15. 5: Butler U 33-36, 37-39 (Fr) AB; Atlanta 39-40, 41 (Fr) MA; West Res summes 44, 45, 50, 51 (LS) MS; Miami U summer 57 (Fam Fin Wkshop). 6: Fr. 7: Instr of Fr Fla A & M Col 41-42; Libn Champion Jr High Sch, Columbus Ohio 42-. 9: NEA; OhioEA; OhioASchL; ColumbusEA; ColumbusTA. 10: YWCA; NAACP; Phi Kappa Phi; Kappa Delta Pi. 14: Yp lit. 15: 1487 Atcheson st, Columbus Ohio 43203.

WILKINS, OTTO. b Sarajevo Yugoslavia 7 Ja 14. 4: Madeleine J Szemerei. 5: U of Science (Budapest Hungary) 37 (Law) BA, 38 (Law) LLM; Georgetown U 44 (Foreign Area Study); Catholic U 58 MS in LS. 6: Hungarian, Ger, Ital. 7: Tech 4th Grade US Army, Overseas, CBI 40-45; Bibliog Nat Agric Lib, Wash DC 59-. 9: SLA; DCLA. 10: Beta PHI Mu. 14: Info retrieval, documentation. 15: 7223 Delfield st, Chevy Chase Md 20015.

WILKINS, WALTER ROLAND. b Chicago Il 25 D 42. 4: Marilyn Dahlquist. 5: Ill Wesleyan 60-64 (Hist) BA; UIll 64-65 (LS) MS; Ill StateU 63- (Russian, Hist); UHawaii 68. 6: Fr, Ger, Russian. 7: Tchg asst UIll Lib Sch (Urbana) 64-65; Period & a-v libn Ill wesleyanU 65-68, Soc sci div libn 68-. 8: Bd Dirs, Ill Coun on Educl Telecommunications 67-68; Com on Church Publs, Central Ill Conf United Meth Church 69-. 9: ALA; IllLA. 10: AAUP; Beta Phi Mu; Phi Kappa Phi; Phi Alpha Theta; Commsn on Archives and Hist, central Ill Conf, United Meth Church. 14: Ref, bk sel, subj catlg, a-v. 15: 1508 N Linden st, Bloomington Il 61701.

WILKINSON, ANN M (MATTHEWS). b Pottsville Penn 8 Mr 40. 4: Billy R Wilkinson. 5: Wilson Col 58-62 (Econ) AB; West Res 62-63 MSLS. 6: Fr, Sp. 7: Asst ref libn Bus Lib CornellU 63-64, Asst ref libn Ind & Labor Rel Lib 64-65, Assoc libn Bus Lib 65-67; Libn Columbia Col, ColumbiaU 67-. 9: SLA. 10: Friends of Columbia Libs; Sierra Club. 12: "Administration of Long-Term Care Institutions: Guide to Information Sources" (67). 13: Yes. 14: Bus libs, res bk systems. 15: 392 Central Park W apt 5P, New York NY 10025.

WILKINSON, BILLY R. b Newton NC 8 S 33. 4: Ann Louise Matthews. 5: UNC (Chapel Hill) 51-55 (Eng) BA, 55-56, 58-59 MSLS; Columbia 67- (LS). 6: Sp, Fr, Ger. 7: UNC (Chapel Hill) Lib 54-56; Libn Catawba Co Pub Lib, Newton NC 56; Specialist 4 US Army, Ft Belvoir Va 57-58; Goldwin Smith libn Cornell U 59-60, Asst ef libn 60-61, Libn Uris Undergrad Lib 61-67. 8: Lib Admin Devel Prog UMd 68. 9: ALA; ASIS; NYLA. 10: Phi Beta Kappa; Phi Eta Sigma; Beta Phi Mu; Friends of Columbia Libs; Sierra Club. 13: Yes. 14: Organiz l admin of univ libs, ref, undergrad libs. 15: 392 Central Park W apt 5P, New York NY 10025.

WILKINSON, ELLEN (ESTERLY). b Reading Penn 4 O 41. 5: Millersville State Col 59-63 (LS) BS in Ed; UKy summer 68 (LS); TempleU 68- (Educ Media). 7: Elrm libn: Conestoga Valley Schs, Lancaster Penn 63-64M Centennial Schs, Warminster Penn 64-. 8: Memb Filmstrip Review Com, The Phila Regl Exam Ctr, Div of Sch Libs, Harrisburg Penn. 9: ALA (Jr Memb RT); PennStateEA; BuckCoSchLA (v-pres); Centennial Educ Assn. 13: Yes. 14: Sch libs, child libs. 15: McDonald Elementary Lib st rd and Reeves la, Warminster Pa 18974.

WILKINSON, FLORENCE B. b Goldsboro NC. 5: Hampton Inst 42 (Educ) BS; Columbia 53 (LS) MS, 60 (Philos of Educ) MA. 6: Fr. 7: Elem tchr Pub Sch, Elm City NC 39-40; Elem tchr Pub Sch, Kingsport Tenn 42-44; Asst libn ref dept Tchrs Col Columbia U 53-69, Supt libn ref dept 70-. 14: Ref. 15: 119-18 190th st, St Albans NY.

WILKINSON, HELEN (WOOLARD). b Greenville NC 7 Jl 45. 4: Kenneth William Wilkinson. 5: Queens Col (Charlotte) 63-65; Fla StateU 65-67 (LS) BA. 7: Libn Savannah-Chatham Pub Sch Syst, Savannah Ga 67-68; Asst child libn Charlotte-Mecklenberg Pub Lib, Charlotte NC 68-69, W Br libn 69-. 9: ALA. 14: Child bks. 15: 912A McAlway rd, Charlotte NC 28211.

WILKINSON, JOHN PROVOST. b Exeter Eng 12 S 27. 4: Isobel Ellen Althouse. 5: UToronto 45-49 (Hist) BA, 49-50 BLS, 51-54 MLS; Chicago 55-66 PhD. 7: Ref libn Toronto Pub Lib 50-51; Asst libn Ont Col of Educ 51-57; Asst dir UNeb Lib 57-60; Chief Libn Dalhousie Lib (NS) 60-65; Prof of Lib Sci UToronto Sch of Lib Sci 65-. 9: ALA; CanLA (Bd Dirs Col & Univ Libs 62); APLA; OntLA. 13: Yes. 14: Acad lib admin. 15: 14 Whittaker cres. Willowdale No York Ont Canada.

WILKINSON, MARTHA ALLAN. b Birmingham Ala 8 D 19. 5: Judson Col 39 (Hist, Eng) BA; UAla 40 (Hist) MA; UNC 48 BS in LS. 6: Fr. 7: Asst libn Birmingham Pub Lib, Birmingham Ala 40-41; Libn Fairfield Jr High Sch, Fairfield Ala 42; USNR W(A)T (Lt) 43-46; Instr St Marys Jr Col 46-47; Ref libn Air U Lib, Maxwell Air Force Base 49-52, Bibliog for Warfare Systems Sch 5368; Bibliog Inst for Prof Devel 68-. 9: SLA; AlaLA (sec). 10: Altrusa Internat; AAUW. 14: Ref, res & devel, weapons employment & astronautics. 15: 39 The Prado, Montgomery Ala 36105.

WILKINSON, RONALD STERNE. b Chicago Ill 16 F 34. 5: ,ich State (Hist) PhD. 6: Fr, Lat. 7: Rare bk libn Mich StateU E Lansing 66-. 9: Brit Soc Hist Sci; Soc Study Alchemy and Early Chem; Soc Bibliogr Nat Hist. 10: Fellow, Linneau Soc London; Fellow, Roy Entomol Soc London; Lepidopterists' Soc; AAAS. 11: Woodrow Wilson Fellow, HarvardU 60-61; Fulbright Scholar, Univ Col (London) 65-66. 12: Ed "The Michigan Entomologist" 66-. 13: Yes. 14: Rare bks, bibliog (hist of sci). 15: Lib Mich State Univ, E Lansing Mi 48823.

WILKINSON, SUSAN (GAIL). b Montreal Can 16 Ag 43. 5: McGill 60-64 (Pol Sci) BA; UOttawa 65-66 BLS. 6: Fr. 7: Trainee for personnel Bank of Montreal 64-65; Asst libn USIS ULondon & Amer Embassy, London England 66-67; Libn Sun Life Assurance Co, montreal 68-. 9: SLA (Prog Chm Montreal Chap 68-69). 14: Ref. 15: Sun Life Assurance Co PO Box 6075, Montreal 101 Quebec Can.

WILKINSON, TOM. b Mt Vernon Tex 11 My 32. 5: So MethodistU 49-53 (Eng) BA; UTex 54-56 (Eng) MA, 60-62 MLS. 6: Sp, Fr. 7: Instr of Eng So MethodistU 56-60; Mss catlgr Acad Ctr UTex (Austin) 62-64; Ref libn S Tex Jr Col 65-66; Dir LTA Program El Centro Col 66-69, Dir lib serv 69-. 9: ALA; TexLA; Tex Assn Col Tchrs. 12: "The Tex-Tec Syllabi" (68). 15: El Centro College Main & Lamar, Dallas Tx 75202.

WILKINSON, VIRGINIA (FRANCES). b Cornersville Tenn 17 Je 15. 5: Middle Tenn State Col 34-38 (Eng, Soc Sci) BS; Peabody summers 49-52 MA in LS. 7: High sch Eng tchr 38-47; Libn Anniston High Sch, Anniston Ala 49-52; Acquis libn Middle Tenn State U 52-. 9: TennLA; SELA. 10: Little Gardens Club; Colonial Dames of 17th Cent; Dames Club. 14: Acquis. 15: 1118 E Clark blvd, Murfreesboro Tn 37130.

WILKINSON, WILLIAM A. b Petrolia Ont Can 16 D 26. 4: Jessie Yellowley. 5: UWest Ont 48-52 (Chem) BA; Carnegie 52-53 MLS. 6: Fr, Ger. 7: Asst tech libn Imperial Oil Ltd, Sarnia Ont 53-56; Monsanto Co, St Louis: Research libn 56-61, Tech libn 61-62, Mgr info center 62-. 9: SLA (past pres St Louis Chap; chm Non-Ser Publ Com 67-68); ASIS. 10: AAAS; Phi Kappa Phi. 12: Ed "The Slate, St Louis Chap SLA (58-60). 13: Yes. 14: Lib automation, catlg, searching. 15: Monsanto Co, 800 N Lindergh blvd, St Louis 63166.

WILL, GRINTON I. b Mamaroneck NY 15 Ap 03. 4: Clarissa Lord. 5: Columbia 20-22, summers 27-30 Prof Certif in Lib Serv, 46-47; Wesleyan U 30-32 (Fr) BA with Gen Honors;

Columbia 46-47 (LS). 6: Fr, Ger. 7: Clerk First Nat Bank, Mamaroneck NY 20; Head Libn Free Lib, Mamaroneck NY 23-30; Prof Lecturer Pratt Inst 50-52; Lib Dir Pub Lib, Yonkers NY 33-; Deputy dir Westchester Lib Syst, NY 59-62. 8: Consul State Dept on Bkmobiles 46; Surveys: Free Pub Lib Borough of Ridgefield NJ 52 & Levittown NJ 63; Lib consul, Englehardt Englehardt & Leggett, Educ consul; Adv,Mamaroneck Free Lib 30-; Hastings-on-Hudson Pub Lib 59 & othersMayors Commun Rel Com 62-. 9: ALA (chm Com for NY State on Reorg of ALA 41-42, chm Com on Rel with The H W Wilson Co 45; Bd of Salaries Staff & Tenure; Subcoms on Exch of Prof Libns, Civil Serv, Lib Revenues 43-48); NYLA (Coun 42-43; Founding chm Civil Serv Com, chm Com on Bldgs & Equip 62-65, Com on Br Lib Standards 67-68, etc); Westchester LA (Charter mem, chm var coms). 10: Adv Coun NYA; Archons of Colophon; Rotary Club; C of C; Yonkers Off of Civil Defense; Yonkers Hist Soc. 11: Award of Merit for excellence of planning & design of the Sprain Brook Br of Yonkers Pub Lib Amer Inst of Archs, ALA, & Nat Bk Com 64; Family Serv Soc Yonkers Award For "Outstanding Service to Strengthen Wholesome Family Life (67); Citations, Bd Trustees Yonkers Pub Lib 63, 68. 12: Edgar Allen "Poe in Westchester (29); "The Story of the Printing House of Wm. Edwin Rudge (30); Jt auth "Civil Service and Libraries ALA (47); "Choral Music (23-); Ed "Consumer Education Bibliography USGPO (69). 13: Yes. 14: Pub lib admin, bldgs & equip, civil serv, trusteeship. 15: 70 S Broadway, Yonkers NY 10701.

WILLAR, ARLINE. b Worcester Mass 23 Jl 32. 5: UChicago 48-51 Liberal Arts) BA; Simmons 54-55 (LS) MS; UGrenoble summer 58 French Certif DAssiduite. 6: Fr. 7: Readers adv Northwestern U 55-56; Ref asst Brown U 56-59; Asst libn Sch of Educ, Harvard U 60-61; Libn Garland Jr Col 61-68; Asst libn for pub serv Northeastern U 68-. 8: Act libn, Pierce Col Athens Greece 65; Ser catlg & spec UN docs projs, Technion Lib, Haifa Israel 68. 9: ALA; NELA (sec Col & Univ Sect 68-69). 10: AAUW; Boston Ski Club. 14: Admin, calg, ref. 15: 62 Fayerweather st, Cambridge Mass 02138.

WILLARD, D(ERALD) DEAN. b Marble Hill Mo 22 N 30. 4: Helen Park. 5: UMo 49-53 (Pol Sci) AB, 57-59 (LS) BS; UIll 59-60 MS in LS. 7: Air Police Off (Capt) USAF, Crete Greece 54-56; Asst law lbn Law Lib UIll (Urbana) 60-. 9: AALL. 10: UIll Lib Staff Assn; Beta Phi Mu. 13: Yes. 14: Admin, ref. 15: 2311 Rainbow view, Urbana Il 61801.

WILLARD, HELEN D. b Chicago 1 N 05. 5: Oberlin Col (Eng Lit); UWis 27 AB; Columbia 31-32. 6: Fr, Ital. 7: Tchr, Waukesha Wis 2 yrs; Ed & publ, Newton Mass 7 yrs; Journalism & archival wk; Sec, curatorial wk Harvard U Fogg Art Museum 13 yrs; Boston Museum of Fine Arts 2 yrs; Curator Harvard Theatre Collection Houghton Lib Harvard Col 60-. 9: TheatreLA (Com Mem, Exec Bd). 14: Rare bks, theatre. 15: Harvard Theatre Collection, Cambridge Mass 02138.

WILLBANKS, FEROL (LEE). b Pollock La 20 S 19. 5: Northeast La State Col 37-39; N Tex State U 54-55 (LS) BA; La State U 64-65 (LS) MS. 6: Fr. 7: Libn USAF, Japan & Korea 55-57; Med libn VA, Okla City Okla 57-63; Libn Stine Lab, Newark Del 63-64; Hd serv to pub UMiss Med Lib (Jackson) 66-68; Asst libn Mem Lib Tex Med Assn, Austin Tex 68-. 9: MedLA. SLA. 12: Ed "The Reminder, Biol Group SLA (63-64). 14: Ref, admin, instr in use of lib & lib tools. 15: 1218 Baylor apt 104, Austin Tx 78703.

WILLERFORD, FREDERICK PAYNE. b New Haven Conn 22 Mr 30. 5: UWash 49-52 (Russian Studies) BA; Middlebiry Col summer 52 (Russian Lang); Columbia 52-54 (Pub Law & Govt) MA; Pratt Inst 58-60 MLS. 6: Russian, Fr. 7: 1st Lt USAF Air Intelligence 54-56; Lib trainee Brooklyn Pub Lib, NY 57-59; Guide to Amer Exhibition in Moscow 59; Ref libn Coun on For Rel, NY 59-60; Ref libn NYC Pub Lib Research Div 60-67; Readers serv libn Richmond Col CUNY 67-68; Chief libn Manhattan Commun Col CUNY 68-. 8: Acad consul to commun liberation schs, NYC. 9: ALA; SLA; NY Lib Club. 10: Soc Educ & Ethn Xul; NAACP; Assn Study Bus Econ. 11: John Hay Whitney Fellow 52. 14: Ref, admin. 15: 410 Central Park W, New York NY 10025.

WILLERS, ALFRED CARL. b Davenport Iowa 22 Jl 33. 5: Columbia 55-59 (Eng) BS, 60-62 (Eng) MA, 66-68 MLS. 6: Fr. 7: A/1C USAF, US, Japan & Korea 50-53; Sec NYC Pub Lib picture collection 53-55; Ed asst "New Yorker" Mag, NYC 61-62; Eng instr Carnegie Inst 62-65; Eng instr Hunter Col 65-66; Asst libn Walter Hampden Memorial Lib, NYC 67-. 9: TheatreLA. 13: Yes. 14: Ref & res (spec collections and res libs). 15: Walter Hampden Mem Lib 16 Gramercy park, New York NY 10003.

WILLIAM, EDWIN E(VERITT). b Los Angeles 13 Jl 13. 4: Harriette Louise Greene. 5: Stanfor 28-32 (Letters) AB; UCal (Berkeley) 34-37 (LS)AM; Harvard 40-42 (Eng). 6: Fr, Sp. 7: Libn Jr Grade UCal (Berkeley) 35-37; Asst to the exec sec ALA, Chicago 37-40; Harvard Col Lib: Asst to the libn 40-50, Chief of Acquis dept 50-56, Asst libn for bk sel 56-59; Harvard U Lib coun to dir on the collections 59-64; Asst U libn 64-66; Assoc U libn 66-; Mem Faculty of Arts & Sci 64-. 8: Prepared "Preliminary Memoranda for Conf on Internat Cultural Educ & Sci Exchs (assisted by RUTH V Noble) 46; In chg of sel original bk collection for Lamont Lib, Harvard 47-48; In chg of ARL Farmington Plan Off 51-63; Sec Mass Governors Admin Lib Commsn 55-56; Surveyed USBE 58-59; Surveyed resources of Can Univ libs for res in the humanities & soc scis 62; Surveyed Bibliotheque de lUniversite Laval, Quebec (asstd by Rev P E Filion) 62 & 65; Sec Com on Lib Needs of the Commsn on the Humanities 63-64; Surveyed Boston Theol Inst 68-69. 9: CanLA; ALA (Coun rep ACRL 48-52; mem & chm Bd on Acquis of Lib Materials 53-56, chm Com on ALA Publ 59-61; Program Eval & Budget Com 56-57 & 63-66); -ACRL (chm Com on Lib Surveys 67-); -RTSD (v-chm Org Assn 56-57); ARL (sec Com on the Preserv of Res Lib Materials 61-. 12: Auth "Trgedy of Destiny (40); "Racine depuis 1885: Bibliographie raisonee . . . (40); "Farmington Plan Handbook (53); "A Serviceble Reservoir (59); "Farmington Plan Handbook Revised to 1961 and Abridge (61); "Resources of Canadian University Libraries for Research in the Humaities and Social Sciences (62); Ed: "Conference on International Cultural, Educatonal, and Scientific Exchanges (47); "Farmington Plan Letter (49-62); "Problems nd Prospects of Research Library (55); "Libraries & Universities, (P Buck) (64); Ed "Harvard Lib Bulletin 68-. 13: Yes. 14: Bk sel. 15: 3 Craigie cir, Cambridge Mass 02138.

WILLIAMS, ALBERT LOUIS. b Redfield NY 13 Jl 37. 5: State U Col(Geneseo NY) 57-61 (LS) BS in Ed provsional certif Sch Libn; Ind U 61-62 (A-V) MS in Ed, Perm Certif Sch Libn. 7: Head libn Pulaski Acad & Central Sch, Pulaski NY 62-65; Lib consul dept of educ, Govt of Guam, Agana Guam 65-67; Ref libn UGuam 67-. 9: NEA; ALA; NY State Tchrs Assn; NYLA; GuamEA; GuamLA (Exec v-pres). 10: Orer of Prometheus. 14: Readig serv, catlg. 15: P O Box 2649, Agana Guam 96910.

WILLIAMS, ALEXANDER. b Boston 6 Je 22. 4: Eleanor S Williams. 5: Harvard 40-4 (Physics) AB; Boston U 46-48 (Bus Math); Ohio State U 52-53 (Econ, Bus) MA; Syracuse 49-50 MS in LS. 6: Fr, Ger. 7: BUS LIBN Northwestern U 55-58; Tech libn Gen Electric Co Aircraft Nucear Propulsion Dept, Cincinnati 58-61; Tech libn Reactor Catlg Concept Proj/John Martens Argonne Nat Lab, Argonne Ill 61-62; Tech libn Chrysler Corp Space Div, New Orleans La 62-65; Sci ibn So Ill U 65-68; Tech ref libn NASA Goddard Space Flight Ctr, Greenbelt Md 68-. 9: SLA. 15: 3 Stow rd, Harvard Ma 01451.

WILLIAMS, AVERY (WHITE). b Rio Miss 23 F 25. 4: Bismarck S Williams. 5: Jackson Col 44-48 (Educ) BS; Atlanta 49-50 MS in LS. 6: Fr, Ger. 7: Libn Harris High Sch, Meridian Miss 50-53; Tchr Lib Wkshop Ark AM& N Col summers 53, 54; Catlg asst UCHICAGO 54-55; Roosevclt U: Jr ref catlg 55-57, Sr catlgr 57-64; Chief ref libn 64-. 9: ALA; IllLA (Memb Com 62-63); Chicago Reg Libns in Resources & Tech Serv (sec-treas 62-63). 14: Ref. 15: 5704 So Kenwood ave, Chicago Il 60637.

WILLIAMS, SISTER BARBARA ANNE. b Camden NJ 14 O 38. 5: Georgian Ct Col 57-63 (Eng) AB (cum laude); Rutgers 63-65 MLS. 6: Sp. 7: Registrar Georgian Ct Col, Lakewood NJ 60-66, Libn Farley Mem Lib 66-. 9: ALA; CathLA; NJLA; OceanCoLA. 10: Ocean Co Lib Adv coun. 14: Admin, ref. 15: Georgian Ct Col, Lakewood NJ 08701.

WILLIAMS, BARBARA (CHAPMAN). b New Kensington Penn 8 O 23. 4: L G Williams. 5: Bethany Col (WVa) 41-44 (Hist) BA; Fla State U 59-61 (LS) MA. 7: Jr lib asst Hunter Col Lib 46-48; Cairo Pub Lib, Cairo Ga: Catlgr 49-53, Circ libn 57-58, Asst libn 59-. 9: ALA; SELA; GaLA. 10: PTA; Girl Scouts; Beta Phi Mu; Delta Kappa Gamma. 14: Catlg, ref. 15: Roddenbery Mem Lib, Cairo Ga 31728.

WILLIAMS, BARBARA (INNIS). b Deckerville Mich 6 Ag 21. 4: Arthur H Williams. 5: UDenver 39-43 (LS) BA; UNM 62-63 & 63-69 (Educ); Col of Santa Fe 69 (Educ). 6: Sp, Ger. 7: Child libn Amarillo Pub Lib, Amarillo Tex 43-44; Asst br libn Denver Pub Lib 44-46; Asst purchasing libn UDenver 47-50; Sub sch libn Los Alamos schs, Los Alamos NM 64-67; Libn Pajarito Elem Sch, Los Alamos NM 67-. 9: NMEA; NMLA. 10: Los Alamos Hop Axiliary. 14: Wk with child. 15: 2382 - 33rd st, Los Alamos NM 87544.

WILLIAMS, BARBARA (JEAN MAY). b Prestonsburg Ky 5 Je 27. 4: James Lewis Williams. 5: Centre Col 45-49 (Span) AB; Columbia 57 (LS); UKy 57-58, 61-62 MS in LS. 6: Sp, Fr. 7: Music tchr Ky Sch Systems 59-60; Catlgr Midway Jr Col 60-63; Catlgr tech serv div Ky Dept of Libs, Berry Hill, Frankfort Ky 65-68; Planning libn Ky Program Devel Off, Frankfort Ky 68-. 9: ALA-PLA; -RTSD; Ky LA; SELA. 10: Ky Hist Soc; Ky FED OF Womans Clubs; Friends of Ky Libs. 13: Yes. 14: Planning libn. 15: Ky Program Development Off The Capitol, Frankfort Ky 40601.

WILLIAMS, BARBARA CAROLYN. b Springfield Mo 27 S 44. 5: SW Mo State Col 62-66 (Hist) BA; UIll 66-67 (LS) MS. 6: Fr, Sp. 7: Stud asst SW Mo State Col Lib 64-66; Asst ref libn Ozark Pioneer Lib Syst, Springfield Mo 67-. 9: ALA; MoLA. 10: Beta Phi Mu; Springfield Libns Assn; Springfield Lit Coun. 14: Ref. 15: 1340 E Cozy, Springfield Mo 65804.

WILLIAMS, BARBARA JEAN. b Union SC 17 Ag 34. 5: Bennett Col (NC) 51-55 (Eng) BA; UIll 55-56 MSLS, summer 58; UNC (Chapel Hill)summer 61; Atlanta summer 65. 6: Fr, Sp. 7: SC State Col Lib: Res & circ asst 56-58, Ref & documents libn 58-63, Head Libn 62-. 8: Career consul Nat Lib Week, Savannah State Col, 64; Mem Eval Team Commsn on Cols, So Assn of Cols & Secon Schs 69. 9: ALA (Jr Mem Round Table); SELA; SCLA (chm elect Col Sect). 10: Nat Assn of Col Women; Delta Sigma Theta; Thirteen Hearts; Alpha Kappa Mu; NAACP. 13: Yes. 14: Ref, admin. 15: Box 1565 SC State College, Orangeburg SC 29115.

WILLIAMS, BERTIE MAY. b Sulphur Springs Tex. 5: W Tex State Tchrs Col 22-25(Eng) BA; UColo 28 (Eng Lit) MA; UTex 29; UDenver 39 BS in ls. 7: Bkkeeper Star Lumber Co, Albuquerque NM 30; Bkkeeper Melody CHEVROLET Co, Las Vegas NM 30-32; Asst to libn W Tex State Tchrs Col 34-37, Asst libn 37-54; Ref libn W Tex State Col 54-65; Head ref & documents serv W Tex State U 65-. 9: ALA; Tex LA; SWLA; Tex Assn Col Tchrs. 10: AAUP; Panhandle-Plains Hist Soc. 14: Ref, docs. 15: PO Box 121, Canyon Tex 79015.

WILLIAMS, BETSEY ELIZABETH (LIBBEY). b Detroit Me 4 Ap 19. 4: G Dean Williams. 5: Colby Col 37-38, 39-42 (Eng) AB; Northeastern U 43 (Engnr); Boston U 58-60 (Educ); Simmons 63-65 (LS) MS. 6: Fr, Lat. 7: Asst engnr Gen Electric Co, Lynn Mass 43-45; Tchr-libn Lynnfield Jr Sr High Sch, Lynnfield Mass 58-63; Libn Winchester High Sch, Winchester Mass 65-. 9: NESchLA; MiddlesexTA; MassTA; MassLA. 10: Lynnfield Hist Soc. 14: Sch libnship. 15: 500 Lowell st, Lynnfield Mass 01940.

WILLIAMS, BETTY (HIPP). b Jackson Miss 28 Je 43. 4: Michael Clark Williams. 5: Lander Col 61-64 (Hist) AB; UNC 64-65 MSLS. 7: Asst libn Lander Col Lib 65-. 9: ALA; SCLA. 14: Ref, ya wk. 15: Rte 5 Box 115, Greenwood SC 29646.

WILLIAMS, BEVERLY (CHAN). b Ancon CZ 5 D 27. 4:Charles J Williams. 5: CZ Jr Col 45-47 (Liberal Arts) AA;Syracuse 47-49 (Home Econ) BS, 49-51 (Home Econ) MA; Columbia 53-58 MLS. 6: Sp. 7: CZ Lib-Museum, Balboa Heights CZ: Lib asst 51-52, Museum aid 52-53, Lib asst 53-54, Libn 54-55, Ref libn 55-63, chief readers serv 63-. 9: Associacion de Bibliotecarios Graduados del Istmo de Panama (past sec); SLA. 10: Pacific Area offs Club; Confraternity of Christian Doctrine. 14: Ref. 15: PO Box 113, Balboa CZ.

WILLIAMS, BONNIE E. b Chicago 10 Ap 35. 5: Sherwood Music Sch (Chicago) 52-55 (Voice) BMus; UPITTSBURGH 63-65 MLS. 7: Sec Pub rel dept Amer Col of Surgeons (Chicago) 55-60; Sec UPittsburgh Sch of Med 60-63; Trainee UPittsburgh Lib 63-64; Gen libn NY Pub Lib 65-; Group wk spec Off Adult Serv 68-. 9: ALA; NY Lib Guild (Dist Coun). 10: Sigma Alpha Iota; Beta Phi Mu; ACLU; NY Civil Liberties Union; AFL-CIO. 14: Adult serv, reader adv serv. 15: 273 Bemmett ave apt 1a, New York NY 10040.

WILLIAMS, BRYAN M. b St Louis 13 Ag24. 4: Joan Williams. 5: Southeast Mo State Col 48-51 (Eng, Educ) BS; Peabody 51-54 (LS) MA. 6: Fr, Ger. 7: S Navy 43-46; Tchr Elvins High Sch, Elvins Mo 51; Libn Bollinger Co Lib, Marble Hill Mo 51-56; Asst libn UMo (Rolla) 56-. 9: ALA; MoLA. 0: Amer Heritage Discussion Group Leader; Bollinger Co Welfare Bd. 14: Col lib admin, automated lib techniques. 15: Rte 3 Box 48, Newburg Mo 65550.

WILLIAMS, CATHERINE OPAL. b Frisco Tex 18 O 03. 5: Tex Woman'sU 21-25 (Hist, Bio) BA; UIll 30-31 BS in LS; Columbia 47-48 MS in LS. 7: Libn Randolph Jr Col, Cisco Tex 25-28; Asst libn & circ libn Tex Woman's Col summer 26; Asst libn hd libn E Tex StateU 28-. 8: Lib consul, Sulphur Springs Pub Lib (remodeling of post off bldg to lib use) 66-67; Exec v-pres Commerce Pub Lib. 9: ALA (Reg Memb Chm 2 yrs); TexLA (sec dist VI: chm several times). 10: Delta Kappa Gamma; AAUW; Friends of Commerce Pub Lib. 14: Supv. 15: 1410 Bois d'Arc, Commerce Tx 75428.

WILLIAMS, CHARLOTTE (MARY) (ANDREWS). b Fountain City Tenn 21 S 15. 4: Dr Edwin Lea. 5: UTenn 34-38 (Eng) AB; UNC 39-40 BA in LS. 6: Fr, Ger, Sp. 7: Circ asst Lawson McGhee Lib, Knoxville Tenn 33-34; Clerical asst UTenn Lib 34-38; Circ asst Lawson McGhee Lib, Knoxville Tenn 38-39; Circ 1st asst UTenn Lib 40-41, Engnr libn 40-42; Med lib asst Vanderbilt U 44-45; Catlg asst Joint U Lib, Nashville Tenn 45-47, Acquis asst 65-67, Asst data processing 69-. 10: Assn Preserv Tenn Antiq; Ladies Hermitage Assn; Vanderbilt Aid; Vanderbilt Hosp Sewing Club; Planned Parenthood Assn; Baldwin Organ Club; Nashville Symphony Assn; Tenn Bot Gardens & Fine Arts enter; Davidson Co Med Auxiliary; Centennial Club; Bk Club; Hist Landmarks Assn; Repub Womans Club; Tenn Hist Soc; YWCA. Clu. 14: Ser, bibliog. 15: 3424 Valley Brook rd, Nashville Tn 37215.

WILLIAMS, CLARICA. b Meta Ky. 5: Pikeville Jr Col 31-33 Certf; East Ky State Col 35-36 (Eng) AB; UKy summer 46 bs in LS; Peabody summer 57 (LS) MA, summers 64, 65 (LS). 7: Tchr Pike Co schs, Pike Co Ky 36-42; Libn Belfry High Sch, Belfry Ky 42-50; Asst libn ref dept Louisville Pub Lib, Luisville Ky summers 47-49; Libn Train Sch, Morehead State Col 50-58; Asst Prof Lib Sci, Morehead State Col 58-67; Assoc Prof Lib Sci 67-; Hd Lib Sci Program 68-. 9: ALA (chm Ky State Com on Legis); NEA; KyLA (pres & chm Educ Com): KyEA (chm Sch Libns); SELA. 10: Kappa Delta P; Alpha Beta Alpha; Beta Phi Mu; Delta Kappa Gamma; AAUP; AAUW; Morehead Womans Club; Morehead Book Club; Ky Hist Soc; LWV. 14: Lit for child & yp. 15: Box 875 Morehead State Univ, Morehead Ky 40351.

WILLIAMS, DANIEL ALBERT. b wichita Kan 30 D 14. 4: Edna Goble. 5: Chiago 35-44 (Hist) BA, 44-45 BLS, 48 (LS). 7: Stud asst UChicago Lib 35-39, Sub-prof asst 39-43; Ref libn Gary Pub Lib, Gary Ind 44-45; Chief Libn Muncie Pub Lib, Muncie Ind 45-51; Assoc libn Des Moines Pub Li, Des Moines Iowa 51-52, Dir 52-. 8: Visiting lecturer UMinn Lb Sch summer 57 & 65; Survey of the Evergreen Park (Ill) Pub Lib 63. 9: ALA (mem var coms); -LAD (past sect chm & mem of Bd); IowaLA (pres 57); Iowa Adult Educ Assn (pres 64). 10: Kiwanis Club; Torch Internat; Des Moines Assn for the UN; Governors Com for the UN; Des Moines Bd for Internat Educ. 13: Yes. 14: Ref, admin. 15: 100 Locust st, Des Moines Iowa 50309.

WILLIAMS, DARLEEN DOROTHY (FRITZ). b Bay City Mich 8 My 38. 4: Joe Williams. 5: Central MichU 56-59 (Eng) BA; UMich 60-63 MALS; CatholicU 65 (LS). 6: Fr. 7: Asst libn T L Handy High Sch, Bay City Mich 59-63; Libn R O Gibson Jr High Sch, Las Vegas 63-66; Asst ref libn UNev (Reno) 66-. 9: NevLA. 14: Ref, interlib loan. 15: 2600 Gellert dr, Reno Nv 89503.

WILLIAMS, DONALD CHARLES. b Faith SDak 2 D 24. 4: Hedy Kraft. 5: No State Col (Aberdeen SDak) 53-56 (Bus Educ) BSEd; UMinn (Minneapolis) 64-66 (Educ Admin) MA, 66- (LS). 6: Ger. 7: EM, M/Sgt, Sgt Major US Army QM Corps, US & Europe 43-53; Tchr minneapolis Bd of Educ Sanford Jr High 56-66, Libn 66-. 9: ALA; MinnASchL. 10: Amer Fed Tchrs. 14: Ref, Americana. 15: 2500 W 91st st, Minneapolis Mn 55431.

WILLIAMS, DOROTHA V(ILETTA). b Conneaut Ohio 30 Jl 09. 5: Penn State U 28-30 (Eng) BA; UMich 30-31 BA in LS; UMinn 50-53 (LS) MA; UIll 63- (LS. 6: Fr. 7: Libn Mt Clemens High Sch, Mt Clemens Mich 31-32; Asst libn: Grinnell Col Lib 3536; Wheaton Col Lib (Ill) 36-43, James Millikin U 43-47; Libn Northwestern Col (Minn) 47-66; Dir Lib Trinity Col (Deerfield) 66-. 9: ALA; NCTE; MinnLA (chm Col Sect 52-53 & 64-65); IllLA. 14: Catg, ref. 15: NorthwesternCol Lib 50 Willow st, Minneapolis 55403.

WILLIAMS, DOROTHY (ANDREWS). b San Francisco Cal 23 Ag 11. 4: Arthur P Williams. 5: UCal (Berkeley) 30-33 (Hist, Speech) AB, MLS. 6: Fr. 7: Asst libn Standard Oil Co of Cal; Libn & org N Amer Investment Corp, San Francisco; Libn & org Pan Amer Airways, San Francisco Airport; Libn & org Crocker Citizen's Nat Bank, San Francisco; Libn & org Bank of Cal, San Francisco 67-68; Lib consul Org of New Libs, San francisco 69-. 8: Lib consul & adv wk for org of new libs (church, botan park libs, bank libs, aviation, etc). 9: SLA (San Francisco Bay Reg Chap: pres, numerous coms). 10: Mayor's Com to Study Freeways; Ciic chm, Forest Hills Assn

& Forest Hill Garden Club. 13: Yes. 14: Ref. 15: 175 Dorantes ave, San Francisco Ca 94116.

WILLIAMS, DOROTHY (PAYNE). b Tallahasse Fla 24 N 38. 5: Fla A&MU 56-60 (LS) BS; Syracuse summers 64-67 (LS) MS. 6: Sp. 7: Libn Lincoln High Sch, Palmetto Fla 60-61; Hd libn Johnson Jr High Sch, Jacksonville Fla 62-68; Hd libn Raines High Sch, Jacksonville Fla 68-. 8: Guest instr, Fla A&MU summer 68. 9: NEA; FlaLA; DuvalCoLA. 10: Amer Fed Tchrs; YWCA; Young Women of Allen; Alpha Beta Alpha. 14: Ref, acquis. 15: 1324 Prince st apt 20, Jacksonville Fl 32209.

WILLIAMS, DOROTHY. b Orange NJ 13 Ap 05. 5: Wellesley Col 23-27 (Hist) BA; USoCal 29-31 LS Certif. 7: Sr libn Los Angeles Pub Lib Var depts & brs 31-37; Libn Gr III NY Pub Lib Book Order Off 37-42; Sr libn E Orange Pub Lib, E Orange NJ 42-56, Asst lib dir 56-66; Lib Dir 67-. 9: ALA; NJLA (past chm Scholarship Com), (2nd v-pres 68-69). 10: Bus & Prof Womens Club; LWV; Red Cross & Adv Bd; C of C; Mayors Sr Citizens Coun; CAC Lib & Educ Com. 14: Adult serv, admin. 15: East Orange Pub Lib 291 Main st, East Orange NJ 07018.

WILLIAMS, E LOUISE. b Collins Miss 7 Ag 08. 5: MedLA Certif 53. 7: Libn Miss State Bd of Health Lib, Jackson Miss 36-52; Chief catlgr & ref asst Tulane U Sch of Med Lib 52-53; Libn Miss State Bd of Health Lib, Jackson Miss 53-. 9: MedLA (chm Memb Com 41-46, chm Subcom on Train & Recr 48-49, v-chm Com on Standards for Med Libnship 49-50, chm 4 other coms 48-62; chm So Reg Gp 58); MissLA (sec-treas 46-48), CHM Spec Libs Sect57). 10: Miss Pub Health Assn. 13: Yes. 14: Catlg, ref. 15: 611 Seneca ave, Jackson Miss 39216.

WILLIAMS, EARLON. b Cushing Tex 11 Ja 28. 4: Sarah Fowler. 5: Stephen F Austin State Col 47-51 (LS) BA, 58-63 (Educ) MEd; UHouston 61-62 (Educ). 7: Libn Livingston High sch, Livingston Tex 53-55; Libn West Columbia High Sch, West Columbia Tex 55-68; Dir lib div Angelina Col 68-. 9: ALA; Tex Jr Col Tchrs Assn; TexStateTA; TexLA. 10: PTA; Commun Concert Assn. 14: Jr col libs. 15: 1502 Wildbriar, Lufkin Tx 75901.

WILLIAMS, EDNA (LOCKHART). b Blackshear Ga 1 D 30. 4: Lucius A Williams. 5: Clark Col 46-48; Bennet Col (NC) 48-50 (Hist, Soc Sci) AB; Atlanta 50-51 MS LS. 7: Catlg libn DILLARD U 51-52; Catlgr James W Johnson Collection Yale U 52-53; Circ libn Dillard U 53-55; Lbn Sch of Nursing Lib Tuskegee Inst 56-59; Catlg libn Tuskegee Inst 64-. 9: ALA. 10: Beta Phi Mu. 14: Catlg. 15: 101 Bulls ave, Tuskegee Institute Ala 36088.

WILLIAMS, ELISABETH (MARY). b Atlanta 3 O 06. 5: Vanderbilt U 23-27 (Hist) BA; UIll 28-29 BS in LS. 7: Circ asst Cossitt Lib, Memphis Tenn 29-39; Bienville Parish Demonstration La State Lib, Arcadia La 39-40, Bossier Parish Demonstration, Benton La 40-41; Parish libn Bossier Parish Lib, Benton La 40-63; Demonstration libn Red River Parish Lib, Coushatta La 62-63; Parish libn Bossier-Red River Parish Libs, Benton La 63-67; Hd catlg dept Pub Lib of Nashville & Davidson Co, Nashville 67-. 9: ALA; LaLA (chm Pub Libs Sect 41, sec Trustees Sect 65-66, Bus mgr "Bulletin" 65-67); TennLA. 10: Kappa Alpha Theta. 14: Admin, catlg. 15: 3000 Hillsboro rd #7, Nashville Tn 37215.

WILLIAMS, ELIZABETH RAY (LACKEY). b Shelby NC 1 Mr 38. 4: Edwin W Williams Jr. 5: Wake Forest Col 56-60 (Eng) AB; UNC 61-63 MS in LS. 7: Tchr Cool Springs High Sch, Forest City NC 61; Hd libn Averett Col 63-65; Asst libn Brevard Col 65-67; Asst docs libn UNC(Chapel Hill) 67-. 9: ALA; Mod Lang Assn; VaLA; NCLA. 10: AAUW. 14: Ref. 15: 104 Kay st, Carrboro NC 27510.

WILLIAMS, EMILY (VANDER LINDEN). b Henderonville NC 19 Je 23. 5: Lenoir Rhyne Col 40-44 (Eng) AB; UNC 44-45 (LS) BS. 7: Libn civil serv US Marine Corps Air Force, Cherry Point NC 45; Asst libn T H Braswell Lib, Rocky Mount NC 46-49; Winston-Salem Pub Lib, Winston-Salem NC: Libn I 49-54, Libn II 54-58, Libn IV Head of tech processing dept 58-. 9: NCLA. 14: Catlg, North Caroliniana. 15: 910 Gales ave, Winston-Salem NC 27103.

WILLIAMS, EMMA (ROSSBACHER). b Corry Penn 8 F 36. 4: Dr Jack Williams. 5: Clarion State Col 54-58 (LS) BS in Ed; West Res summers 62-65 MS in LS. 7: Edinboro State Col; circ libn 58-65; Hd readers serv & ref libn 65-68; Asst to chief libn 68-. 9: NEA-Assn of Higher Educ; ALA-ACRL (Tri-State Chap; PennLA; Penn State EA. 10: AAUP; Alpha Beta Alpha; Delta Zeta; Penn Assn of State Col & Univ Facs. 14: Readers serv, ref, chil lit, admin. 15: Box 177, Garden Terrace dr, Edinboro Penn 16412.

WILLIAMS, EVAN W(ILLIAM). b St Louis 10 Je 30. 5: Washington U 55 (Sociol) AB; UIll 56 MSLS. 6: Fr, Ger, Russian. 7: Asst catlg & ref libn DePauw U Lib 56-58; Docs & asst ref libn 59; Circ libn Ind U Lib (Bloomington) 61; Asst ref libn 60, 62, 63; Ref asst Kan State U Lib (Manhattan) 64-65; Asst soc sci libn 66; Asst libn prep div 67; Libn spec collections div 68-. 9: ALA; SAA. 10: AAUP. 12: Co-auth "Author & Subject Indices to Kan State University Doctoral Dissertations, Masters Theses and Masters Reports, 1886-1968 (69). 13: Yes. 14: Rare bks, archives, microforms. 15: 2305 Anderson, Manhattan Kan 66502.

WILLIAMS, FLORENCE (MAE). b Keokuk Iowa 25 O 11. 5: Blackburn Col 30-32; Quincy Col 40-41 (Fr) AB; USoCal 46-47 BS in LS; Colo State Col 49-53 (Eng) MA; UGuadalajara summer 60 (Span); UChicago summer 62 (LS). 6: Fr, Sp. 7: Elem tchr co schs, Adams Co Ill 32-40; Asst child libn Quincy Pub Lib, Quincy Ill 42-43; Sch libn Gonzales Elem Sch, Gonzales Cal 44-46; Chief ofbrs Merced Co Lib, Merced Cal 47-49; Asst catlg libn Colo State Col 49-55; Catlg libn So Ore Col 55-59; Asst libn Hartnell Col 59-. 9: ALA; CathLA; CalASchL; CalLA; Cal Tchrs Assn. 10: AUUP; Pi Lambda Theta; Cath Daughters of Amer. 14: Catlg, child bks, ser. 15: Hartnell Col 156 HOMESTEAD AVE, Salinas Cal 93901.

WILLIAMS, FRANCES (CLOPTON). b Norman Okla 25 Ap 20. 4: Harold L Williams. 5: UOkla 37-40 (Fr) BA, 41-42 (Fr) MA, 66 MLS. 6: Fr. 7: Child libn Midland Co Lib, Midland Tex 61-64, Asst libn 64-66, Co libn 67-. 9: ALA; TexLA (chm Dist II 64; chm Pub Libs Div 69-70). 14: Pub lib admin. 15: 3307 Neely, Midland Tx 79701.

WILLIAMS, FRANCES MARION. b Elkton Ky. 5: Agnes Scott Col 37-40 (Ger); Transylvania Col 40-42 (Sociol, Psych) AB; West State U 49-50 (LS, Educ); Asutin Peay State Col (LS); Peabody Col (LS). 7: Clk USAF Wright Field, Dayton Ohio 43-49; Libn-tchr Todd Co High Sch, Elkton Ky 50-63; Libn Todd Co Consolidated High Sch, Elkton Ky 63-. 9: ALA; NEA; KyASchL; KyEA. 10: Nat Soc Magna Charta Dames; DAR; WKy Press Assn. 14: Ref. 15: Elkton Ky 42220.

WILLIAMS, FRED E. b Jamieson Fla 22 Mr 27. 4: Catherine Vaughn. 5: Emory 44-48 (Pre-med); Fla StateU 48-49 (Zoology) BS, 49-52 (LS) MA; IndU 56-61 (A-V Educ) Ed D. 7: Tchr Wakulla Co Schs, Crawfordville Fla 49-51; Film libn Ball StateU 52-54; Line off (Lt) USN 54-56; Lecturer in educ IndU (Bloomington) 56-59; Dir a-v serv Bowling green StateU 59-65, Educ fac 59-. 8: Area Coord Midwest Prog on Airborne TV Instr 60-63. 9: ALA; -AASchL; NEA-DAVI; AERA; EMCO; OhioASchL; Educl Media Coun Ohio (Exec Sec). 12: Ed Educ Media Coun Ohio "Newsletter" (68; Ed Bd "Audio Visual instruction". 13: Yes. 14: Sch instr media ctrs, profess media courses. 15: 212 Williams st, Bowling Green Oh 43402.

WILLIAMS, GENEVA M. b Pocasset Okla 27 Mr 23. 5: Okla Col for Women 59-62 (Elem Ed, Span) BS; UOkla 62-65 MLS. 6: Sp. 7: Span tchr Chickasha High Sch, Chickasha Okla 62-64; Child libn Okla ity Pub Libs, Okla City Okla 64; Ref libn West State Col f Colo 65-; Tchr child lit summers. 9: ALA; OklaLA; ColoLA. 10: AAUW; AAUP. 14 Ref, child serv, tchg. 15: West State Col of Colo Lib, Gunnison Co 81230.

WILLIAMS, GLADYS (GRAY). b Marietta Ohio 10 Ap 06. 5: Marietta Col 24-28 (Math, Lat) BA; Miami U Summer 53; Kent State U 54-60 (LS) MA 06: Lat. 7: Lat math, home econ tchr Newport High Sch, Newport Ohio 43-45; Math home Econ tchr Cardington High Sch, Cardington Ohio 45-46; Math, Eng tchr McConnelsville High Sch, McConnelsville Ohio 46,47; Lat, home econ, Eng tchr Adelphi High Sch, Adelphi Ohio 47-48; Lat, home econ, Eng tchr Bartlett High Sch, Bartlett Ohio 48-50; Lat, math, Eng tchr Cadiz High Sch, Cadiz Ohio 50-56; Lat tchr Wadsworth Sr High Sch, Wadsworth Ohio 56-57, Libn 57-. 9: NEA; OhioASchL; OhioEA. 10: Delta Kappa Gamma; Bus & Prof Women; Wadsworth Club. 14: Sr high sch lib wk. 15: 199 N Lyman st, Wadsworth Ohio 44281.

WILLIAMS, GORDON R(OLAND). b Ontario Ore 26 Jl 14. 4: Jane Smith. 5: Stanford 32-36 (Psych) AB; Chicago 49-52 (LS) MA. 6: Fr, Ger. 7: Asst force control off US Naval Res (Lt) 42-45; Vice-pres Brentanos Inc of Cal 45-49; Exec asst to libn John Crerar Lib, Chicago 50-52; Asst libn UCLA 52-9; Dir Center for Research Libs, Ch cago 59-. 8: Bldg consul; unev 51, UCLA 52. 9: ALA (chm Com on Resources, 60-66; chm Nat Union Catlg Subcom 60-; chm Copying Methods Sect

62-63; chm Com on Nat Lib Info Systems 66-); -ARL (chm Automation Com 64-67; Preserv Com 61-; Bd Dirs 65-68; For Acquis Com 68-); Mss Soc (Bd Dirs 69-). 10: Rounce and Coffin Club (Los Angeles); Soc Typographic Arts; Caxton Club (Chicago). 12: "Ravens and Crows (67); "Bewick to Dovaston, Letters, 1824-1828 (68). 13: Yes. 14: Admin. 15: 5721 Cottage Grove ave, Chicago 60637.

WILLIAMS, GRETA A. b Headland Ala. 5: Carson-Newman Col 53-55 (Home Econ); Peabody Col 55-57 (Elem Educ) BS, 65-66 MLS. 7: Clk Nat Life & Accident Ins Co, Nashville 52-53; Tchr Davidson Co Sch Syst, Nashville 57-58; Lt USN, Kingsville Tex & London England 59-64; Libn Radford Col 66-. 9: VaLA. 14: Circ wk. 15: Belle Heth Gardens apt 111, Radford Va 24141.

WILLIAMS, HARRIETTE L(OUISE) (GREENE). b Evansville Wis 23 O 03. 4: Edwin Everitt Williams. 5: UWis 20-24 (Econ) BA, 29-30 (LS) Diploma. 7: Tchr Soc Sci High Sch, Antigo Wis 24-27; Tchr soc sci High Sch, S Milwaukee Wis 27-29; Ref asst Newark Pub Lib, Newark NJ 30-34; Libn High Sch, Janesville Wis 34-36; Hdqrs libn ALA, Chicago 36-44; Ref libn div lib ext Mass Dept of Educ 44-46; Baker Lib Harvard Grad Sch of Bus Admin; Ref libn 46-48, Head ref dept 49-, Asst libn for Pub Serv 63-. 9: SLA (v-pres 58-59, chm Constit & Bylaws Com 59-61; pres Boston Chap 56-57); ALA. 10: Phi Kappa Phi. 14: Ref, personnel. 15: 3 Craigie ci, Cambridge Mass 02138.

WILLIAMS, HELEN (TOMBLIN). b Peoria Ill 15 S 20. 5; rockford Col 52 (Sociol) BA, 61 (Tchg) MA; No Ill U 65 (L) MA. 6: Fr. 7: Clerk-typist US Govt, Camp Grant Ill 42-44; WAVES Storekeeper S2 44-45; Receptionist, Thayer Action Co, Rockford Ill 46-47; Compliance negotiator US Govt Off of Housing Expediter RFD 47-49; Soc wker, Amer Cancer Soc, Rockford Ill 50; Registrar Keith Country Day Sch, Rockford Ill 52-59; Br libn Rockford Pub Lib, Rockford Ill 61-66; Sch libn Auburn High Rockford Pub Sch, Rockford Ill 66-. 9: ALA; IllLA; NEA; IllEA; RockfordEA. 10: AAUW; Nat Writers Club. 14: Sch libn. 15: 1903 Bell ave, Rockford Il 61103.

WILLIAMS, HELEN FLORINE (LITTLE). b Eastport Md 21 Jl 15. 4: Norman Harris Williams. 5: Morgan State Col 30-34 & summers 41, 48 (Lat) BA; Columbia summer 49 (LS); UWash 58-59 (LS) ML; Johns Hopkins 62-66 MLA. 7: Lib asst Annapolis & Anne Arundel Co Pub Lib, Annapolis Md 41-46; Morgan State Col: Lib asst 46-58, Ref libn 59-62; Assoc libn, Readers serv 62-65; Act libn 65-66; Assoc dir readers serv 66-. 9: ALA; MdLA (corr sec 61-63). 10: Md Classified Employees Assn. 14: Ref, indexing, rare bks. 15: 5-E Cross Keys rd, Baltimore Md 21210.

WILLIAMS, HELEN MARIE (SNELL). b McArthur Cal 29 Ag 15. 4: Richard Gordon Williams. 5: UHawaii 64-68 (Sociol) BA, 68-69 MLA. 7: Asst base libn USAF, Hickam Hawaii 69-. 10: Phi Beta Kappa. 14: Serv to mil. 15: 99-1701 Aiea Hts dr, Aiea Hi 96701.

WILLIAMS, HENRY L. b Pueblo Colo 23 Ap 23. 5: UNM 41-42; Moravian Col 46-48 (Eng) BA; Moravian Theol Sem48-49, 50-51 BD; UManchester (England) 49-50; Rutgers 58-62 MLS. 7: US Army Amphibian Engrs, New Guinea, Philippines & Japan 42-45; Moravian Ch Development Fund, Bethlehem Penn 51-52; Moravian pastor, Phila 58; Moravian Col Development off 58; Moravian Col Lib 58-. 8: Sec Moravian Hymnal Revision Com 55-69. 9: ATheolLA. 10: Moravian Hist Soc; Hymn Soc Amer. 12: "The Development of the moravian Hymanl"; "Bibliography of Moravian Books for Theological Libraries" (65); Ed "Newsletter of Moravian Studies". 13: Yes. 15: Reeves Lib Moravian Col, Bethlehem Pa 18018.

WILLIAMS, HOWARD H(ENRY). b Milwaukee Wis 14 S 11. 5: Lake Forest Col 28-32 (Eng, hist) AB; Milwaukee State Tchrs Col 32-33 (Educ); Columbia 36-37 (Eng) AM, 37-39 (Eng), 47-48 BS in LS. 6: Ger. 7: A F Gallun & Sons, Milwaukee 33-36; Maintenance supv Columbia U Residence Halls 39-43, 46-47; ,/Sgt ETO & 5th Army Hq, Italy 43-45; Asst libn (ref & order) Tchrs Col ColumbisU 48-49; Circ libn Swarthmore Col 49-50, ref & spec serv 50-. 9: ALA; PennLA (Com on Docs, 2 terms); ACRL, Phila Area (past pres & Dir). 10: Trustee Swarthmore Pub Lib 57-67; Mem Phila Reg Adv Com, Free Lib of phila 64-69. 14: Ref, interlib loan, govt publ, lib admin. 15: 144 Park ave, Swarthmore Pa 19081.

WILLIAMS, JAMES FRANKLIN II. b Montgomery Ala 22 Ja 44. 4: Madeline McClellan. 5: Morehouse Col 62-66 (Sociol) BA; AtlantaU 66-67 (Ref, Catlg) MSLS. 6: Fr, Sp. 7: Off asst Morehouse Col, Atlanta 64-67; Research asst Wayne StateU, Detroit 67-68; Libn I (Ref Libn) 68-. 8: Recr for the Internship in Med Libnship, Wayne StateU Sch of Med Lib 68. 9: MedLA. 14: Ref, catlg. 15: 615 W Hancock st apt 208, detroit Mi 48201.

WILLIAMS, JAMES WELDON. b Morrisville Mo 10 My 43. 5: Sch of Ozarks 61-63 (Eng) AA; SW Mo State Col 63-65 (Educ) BS in Ed; Fla StateU 65-66 (LS) MS. 7: Descriptive catlgr St Louis Pub Lib 66-68; Ser catlgr UIll Lib (Urbana) 68-. 9: ALA. 14: Catlg. 15: 909 S First st #20, Champaign Il 61820.

WILLIAMS, JANE (MILDRED). b Charlotte NC 9 N 44. 5: Pfeiffer Col 62-66 (Eng) BA; UNC 66-67 MS in LS. 7: Summer asst Pub Lib of Charlotte & Mecklenburg Co 63-66, Ref asst 67-. 9: ALA. 10: N Carolinians for better Libs. 14: Ref. 15: Canterwood dr apt 1, Charlotte NC 28213.

WILLIAMS, JANE L (LOONEY). b Raymond Wash 29 D 17. 4: John Howard Williams. 5: Occidental 36-38 (Phys Educ, Hygiene); UCal (Berkeley) 39-41 (Phys Educ, Hygiene) AB; San Jose State Col 63-65 (Libnship); Cal Stat Polytech Col 63-66 (Educ) MA; San Francisco State Col 67-69 (Counseling). 7: Soc wkr Madera Co Dept of Pub Welfare, Madera Cal 41-43, 51; Asst supv Home Serv Amer Red Cross, San Jose Cal 43-44; Soc wkr Mendocino Dept of Pub Welfare, Ukiah Cal 48-49; Tchr & phys educ dir Ashview Sch, Chowchilla Cal 51-53; Supv Hosp Soc Serv Merced Co Dept of Pub Welfare, Merced Cal 54-62; Dist libn Pismo Sch Dist, Pismo Beach Cal 62-66; Libn Colmo Intermediate & Jefferson Elem Schs, Daly City Cal 66-. 8: Registered Soc Wkr 46-. 9: ALA; NEA; APGA; CalASchL; CalLA; CalTA; ACL. 10: Chowchilla Women's Clubs; Camp Fire Girls Councils; Epsilon Sigma Omicron. 14: Jr high sch libs. 15: 2490 Eucalyptus way, San Bruno Ca 94066.

WILLIAMS, JANET D. b NYC 27 O 42. 4: Roy E Williams. 5: Oberlin Col 59-63 (Math) BA; Columbia 63-65 (LS) MS; Leigh U 65-67. 6: Ger. 7: Trainee Libn I NY Pub Lib 64-65; Sci catlgr Lehigh U Lib 65-67; Catlg-ref libn Mann Lib Cornell U 67-. 15: 527 E State st, Ithaca NY 14850.

WILLIAMS, JEAN E (ASTMAN). b Watertown NY 13 Jl 38. 4: Frederic Malcolm Williams. 5: SUC of Educ (Geneseo) 56-60 (Educ, LS) BS; Syracuse 60-61 (LS) MS. 7: Post libn US Army, Camp Kilmer NY 61; Ref libn Syracuse U summer 63; Elem sch libn Onondaga Central sch, Rockwell Elem Sch, Nedrow NY 61-66; Ref libn Cazenovia Col 67-. 8 Onondaga-Oswego Co (NY) LA (sc 64-65); Sch lib consul Cazenovia Central Schs, Cazenovia NY 67-68. 9: ALA; NYLA; Onondaga-Oswego Co (NY) LA (sec 64-65). 12: Kappa Delta Pi; Beta Phi Mu. 14: Sch libs, ref. 15: 11 Lincklaen ter, Cazenovia NY 13035.

WILLIAMS, JEAN LOUISE. b Wilkes Barre Penn 3 Mr 11. 5: Wellesley 29-33 (Botany) BA, 35-37 (Botany) MA; Harvard 50-51 (Educ); Columbia 66-67 MLS. 6: Fr. 7: Tchr & sec to prin Mary A Burnham Sch 34-35; Botany dept asst Wellesley Col 35-38; Hd sci dept Dana Hall Sch, Wellesley Mass 38-43; Liason off (Lt) USN Res Educ Serv 44-45; Asst to dir admissions Vassar Col 46-48; Dir admissions Cedar Crest Col 48-50; Asst dean Sweet Briar Col 51-57, Dir admissions 57-66; Asst libn Bio-Geol Lib PrincetonU 67-. 9: ALA. 10: AAUW. 14: Ref, acquis, bibliog. 15: 39 Green ave, Lawrenceville NJ 08648.

WILLIAMS, JIMMIE NELL (MISS). b Hamilton Ala 30 My 36. 5: Florence State Col 54-58 (Soc Sci) BS; Peabody 61 (LS) MA. 7: Libn Fairview High Sch, Cullman Ala 58-62; Libn Alabama Col62-68; Catlgr Jacksonville State U 68-. 9: AlaLA; AlaEA. 14: Ref, circ, catlg. 15: Jacksonville State Univ Lit, Jacksonville Al 36265.

WILLIAMS, JOHN CLEMENS. b Detroit 14 N 25. 4; barbara Coder. 5: UMich 46-51 (Hist, Soc Sci) AB, 64-65 AMLS. 6: Russian. 7: Sr asst sci & tech div Toedo Pub Lib, Toledo Ohio 65-67; Ref libn Colgate U 67-. 9: ALA. 12: "Bibliography of Educational Long Range Planning (69). 14: Bibliog, ref. 15: 25 Madison st, Hamilton NY 13346.

WILLIAMS, JOHN T. b Oak Park Ill 11 Mr 24. 5: Central Mich U 46-49 (Soc Sci) AB; UMich 49-50 (Hist) AM, 50-51 AMLS; Mich State U 60- (Soc Sci). 7: US Army 43-46; Head period reading room UMich 55-57, Ref libn 57-59; Ref libn Bowling Green U 59-60; Ref libn Mich State U 61-62; 1st asst ref dept Flint Pub Lib, Flint Mich 62-65; Head ref serv Purdue U 65-. 9: ALA; IndLA (chm Ref Serv Div 66-67). 10: AAUP; Alpha Kappa Delta. 12: Abstractor for "Historical Abstracts &

"America: History and LIFE". 14: Ref. 15: 115 Connolly st, West Lafayette In 47906.

WILLIAMS, JOSEPHINE (CARPENTER). b Detroit Mich 13 Je 20. 5: Connecticut Col 38-40 (Eng); UMichigan 40-42 (Educ) BA; USoCal 65-67 MSLS. 7: Tchr Detroit Pub Sch 42-43; Communication Off USNR VR-7, Miami Fla 43-45; Libn Palos Verdes Lib Dist, Palos Verdes Cal 67-. 9: ALA; Oral Hist Assn; CalLA. 14: Ref. 15: Palos Verdes Lib Dist 650 Deep Valley dr, Palos Verdes Peninsula Ca 90274.

WILLIAMS, JUDY RAE SLICK. b Colorado Springs Colo 22 O42. 4: Richard Gordon Williams Jr. 5: Albion Col 60-61; Ind U 60-63 (Biol Sci) BS; UMich 63-64 (LS) AM; Boston U 66. 6: Fr. 7: Biol Sci libn Columbia U 64-6 ; Elem libn pub schs, Lexington Mass 65-66; Sch libn Lincoln-Sudbury Reg High Sch, Sudbury Mass 66-67; Hd acquis UWis (Parkside) 67-. 8: Mem ESEA Evaluating team State of Maine 67; Instr-coun Stud Assts summer wkshop; ind U 65, UWis (Madison) 68. 9: ALA-ACRL; -RTSD; -JMRT; WisLA (mem Memb Com); KenoshaLA (sec-treas 68-69); MassASchLA (sec 65-67). 10: Phi Kappa Phi; Pi Lambda Theta; AAUW; LWV; UMich & IndU Alum Assns; YWCA. 13: Yes. 14: Yp serv, ref, biol sci, acquis, tech serv. 15: 4046 N Main st A-5, Racine Wi 53402.

WILLIAMS, LEE GERALD. b Dover NC 20 Je03. 4: Alva Sawyer Williams. 5: UNC 25-29 (Hist) AB; Columbia 30-31 (LS) BS; Richmond Prof Inst 47-48 (Soc Wk). 7: Circ asst UNC Lib, Chapel Hill 28-30; Stud asst Sch of Lib Sci Columbia U 30-31; Libn US Penitentiary (Atlanta) 32-33, Lewisburg Penn 33-34, Atlanta 34-36; Supv libn US Bur of Prisons, Wash DC 36-39; Adv asst Fed Correctional Inst, Sandstone Minn 39-42; Photographer 1st class, US Navy Construction Battalion 42-45; Supv clsf & Parole Fed Reformatory, Petersburg Va 45-54; Correctional Inst Administrator US Bur of Prisons, Wash DC 54-57; Circ libn & Dir tech serv E Carolina U 57-. 14: Circ & tech serv. 15: 1403 N Overlook dr, Greenville NC 27834.

WILLIAMS, LEE H JR. b Madison Co Ga 18 Mr21. 5: UWash 41-46 (Span) BA; Columbia 53-54 (LS) MS. 6: Sp. 7: Tech 4, Hqs Co 88th Inf Div N Africa & Italy 42-45; Consular clerk Amer Embassy, Madrid Spain 48-52; Catlgr Columbia U Lib 54-55; Catlgr, rare bks catlgr, order libn, head catlgr lib Wesleyan U (Conn) 55-60; Dir tech serv lib UPR (Rio Piedras) 60-64; Asst dir for tech serv lib SUNY(Stony Brook) 64-67; Curator Latin Amer Collection Yale U Lib 67-. 9: ALA; NY Tech Serv Libns(sec-treas). 14: Tech serv. 15: 496 Fountain st apt A-1, New Haven Ct 06515.

WILLIAMS, LELIA (ERNESTINE) (MRS). b Mathews Va. 5: Hampton Inst 40 (En) BS; Simmons 49 BSLS; Columbia 60 MSLS. 6: Fr, Ger. 7: Eng tchr Thomas Hunter High Sch, Mathews Va 35-37, Tchr-libn 37-48; Norfolk Div Va State Col; Head Libn 49-62, Instr in Lib Sci 62, Ref libn 62-. 9: ALA; NEA; SELA; VaLA; Va Tchrs Assn. 10: AAUP. 14: Admin, bk sel. 15: 2835 E Princess Anne rd, Norfolk Va 23504.

WILLIAMS, LINDA EILEEN. b Jackson Mich 2 Mr 44. 5: Jackson Jr Col 62-64 (Liberal Arts) AA; West MichiganU 64-66 (Hist) BA, 68- (LS). 6: Sp. 7: Libn Bad Axe High Sch, bad Axe Mich 66-67; Libn Napoleon Sch Dist, Napoleno Mich 67-. 9: NEA; ALA; MichEA; MichASchL. 10: Ella Sharp Museum. 14: Ref. 15: Napoleon High School, Napoleon Mi 49261.

WILLIAMS, LUCRETIA (ALDEN). b Mason County Ky 6 Ag 05. 5: Union Col (Ky) 25-28 (Math) AB; Peabody 36-37 BS in LS, ummers 60-62 (LS) MA. 7: Catlgr U Cincinnati 37-42; Circ & ref US Weather Bur, Wash dc 42-43; Sr catlgr UCincinnati 43-. 9: ALA; Ohio Valley Reg Group Tech Serv Lins. 15: 471 Ward ave, Bellevue Ky 41073.

WILLIAMS, LYNDA L. b Fort Morgan Col 7 D 37. 5: Johnson Bible Col 55-59 (Bible) BA; ButlerU 66-67 (Relig) BA; IndU 66-68 MLS. 7: Bible tchr pub sch, Corinth Miss 59-65; Circ asst IndU Sch of Dentistry Lib (Indianapolis) 65-67; Circ libn Shippensburg State Col 68-. 14: Circ, ref. 15: 200 N Prince st, Shippensburg Pa 17257.

WILLIAMS, MARGARET (POINDEXTER). b Clay Co Ga 18 N 12. 5: Ala Col 29-33 (Eng) AB; Florence State Col summers 58-60 (LS) MA; Peabody Col summer 66. 7: Social wkr WPA, Tuscumbia Ala 37-43; Elem tchr Russellville Elem Sch, Russellville Ala 45-47; Tchr Russellville High Sch, Russellville Ala 49-54, Libn 54-63; Libn for wkshop Alabama Col summers 62 & 63; Instr Jacksonville StateU 63-68, Libn 68-. 9: AlaLA. 15: 312 N Gayle st, Jacksonville Al 36265.

WILLIAMS, MARGARET NELL (LAWTON). b Austin Tex 12 N 17. 5: Guadalupe Jr Col 33-35; Wiley Col 37-39 (Educ, Sociol) AB; UDenver summers 49-52 MA inLS; Mexino City Col 59 (Guidance, Psych). 6: Fr, Sp, Lat. 7: Tchr Wilson-White High Sch, Rosebud Tex 40-42; Tchr Dunbar High Sch, Temple Tex 42-47; Tchr- libn Dunbar High Sch, Temple Tex 47-53; Libn DunbarJr-Sr High Sch, Temple Tex 53-57; Jr libn Mt Vernon Pub Lib, Mt Vernon NY 57; Libn Dunbar Jr-Sr High Sch, Temple Tex 57-63; Ref & circ libn Mexico City Col summer 59; Libn Moore Jr-Sr High Sch, Waco Tex 63-. 8: Del Little White House Conf, Hawaii (69). 9: ALA (mem Mem Com Tex 66-); -AASchL (Adult Group Leader Nat Convs; penn 67, Tex 68, Md 69); NEA-DAVI; Amer Tchr Assn; SWLA; Tex State Tchrs Assn (Lib Sect, chm 58-61, v-chm 61-64); Waco Lib Club; TexLA. 10: PTA; YWCA; YMCO; Conner Study Club; Delta Sigma Theta. 11: Grad Libn Fellowship Mexico City Col, summer 59. 14: Secon sch & ya serv, bk sel, reading guidance, ref, circ. 15: 1702-D Dallas cir, Waco Tex 76704.

WILLIAMS, MARGARET (TERESA). b St Johns Newfoundland Can 11D31. 5: Mem U (Newfoundland) 49-53 (Classics) BA; Toronto 60-61 BLS. 7: Memorial U (Newfoundland): Ser libn 53-55 Catlgr 55-60, Asst libn 61. 9: CanLA; APLA; ALA. 14: Catlg. 15: 119 Freshwater, St Johns Newfoundland Can.

WILLIAMS, MARGERY M. b Painesville Ohio 6 D 14. 4: Robert R Williams. 5: Oberlin Col 32-36 (Art Hist) BA, 36-38 (Art Hist) MA; West Res 57-60 (LS) MS. 6: Fr, Ger, Ital. 7: Lib asst Occidental Col 56-57 Bkmob libn Morley Lib, Painesville Ohio 57-60; Art libn Oberlin Col 60-. 10: LWV. 14: Art bks. 15: 302 N Prospect st, Oberlin Oh 44074.

WILLIAMS, MARIE HELENE (STUMBERG). b New Haven Conn 17D23. 4: Roger John Williams Jr. 5: Lindenwood Col 40-41 (Eng); UTex 41-44 (Eng) BA; Columbia 47-48 MLS. 6: Fr. 7: Child libn Rochester NY Pub Lib 48-50; Falls Chruch Va 50-53; Sch libn Strongsville Ohio 54-57 Mountainside (NJ) Pub Lib 65-; Libn washington Elem Sch, Westfield NJ 69-. 10: PTA; Alphs Phi; Col Club; YWCA. 14: Child lit. 15: 425 Topping Hill rd, Westfield NJ 07090.

WILLIAMS, MARILYN (SIMPSON). b Nashville 14 F 28. 4: Benjamin Buford Williams. 5: Mary Baldwin Col 46-50 (Speech, Drama) BA; Peabody 50-51 MA in LS. 7: Asst ref & circ libn Baylor U 52; Head libn Martin Col 52-53; Air U Lib, Maxwell AFB Ala; Asst period libn 53-54, Chief authority sect 54-58, Bibliog 58-60, Bibliogr CED & Chaplain's Writers Bd 60-62, Bibliogr Command & Staff Col 62-. 9: SLA; AlaLA. 10: PTA; Res Offrs Assn ; LADIES; Air Force Assn. 14: Ref, bibliog. 15: 3813 Marie Cook dr, Montgomery Ala 36109.

WILLIAMS, MARJORIE (GILSON). b Winfield Kan 5 JI07. 4: Ralph L Williams. 5: Kan State Tchrs Col (Emporia) 23-30 (Speech), 58-59 (LS) MS. 7: Kan State Tchrs Col (Emporia), Circ libn William Allen White Lib 59-62; Lib Sch libn 62-64; Instr in libnship 64-66; Admin asst to chm Dept of Libnship 66-. 9: ALA (Memb Chm, Kan); -LED (Staff Org Round Table, chm Steering Com 64-65); MPLA; KanLA; (Coun); KanASchL; Kan State Tchrs Assn. 10: AAUW; Coun of Faculty Women; Emporia Friends of Art. 13: Yes. 14: Lib educ, child lit. 15: Dept of Libnship Kan State Tchrs Col, Emporia Ks 66801.

WILLIAMS, MARTHA MAI (WILLIAMS). b Madison Fla 2 S 33. 4: Willie Howard Williams. 5: Fla A&M U 53-54 (Home Econ); 55-58 (LS) BS. 6: Fr. 7: Libn; Fla A&M U summer 58, Hampton Jr Col 58-60, Holden Street Sch, Orlando Fla 60-67, Richmond Hts Sch, Orlando Fla 67-. 9: ALA; FlaEA; FlaASchL. 10: Nat Coun Negro Women; Jack & Jill of Amer. 14: Sch lib wk. 15: 404 Lionel ave, Orlando Fl 32805.

WILLIAMS, MARVIN DALE JR. b Indianapolis 27 O35. 5: Butler U 53-58 (Religion) BA; Christian Theol Sem (Indianapolis) 57-62 (New Testment) BD; Butler U 60-63 (New Testament MA; Peabody 62-63 MA(LS); Amer U 66. 7: Pastor Olive Christian Church, Paragon Ind 59-60; Period libn Christian Theol Sem, Indianapolis 60-62, Head period libn 62; Catlgr Disciples of Christ Hist Soc, Nashville 63-65, Head of tech serv 65-66, Dir of the Lib 66-67, Dir of the Lib & Archivist 67-. 8: Indexer, Chr Evangelist Indixing Proj, Disciples of Christ Hist Soc, Nashville 62; Consul, Carolina Discipliana Lib, Atlantic Christian Col Lib, Wilson NC 68. 9: ALA; ATheolLA; SELA; TennLA; SAA. 10: Bta Phi Mu; Theta Phi. 11: ATheolLA Lilly Endowment scholarship for grad wk in theol Libnship. 12: Co-ed ed "Discipliana (65-). 13: Yes. 14: atlg, bibliog, theol libnship. 15: 1101 Nineteenth ave S, Nashville Tn 37212.

WILLIAMS, MARY E BUCHANAN. b Oxford Miss 26 Ja23. 4: Robert W Williams. 5: Millsaps Col 40-43 (Eng) BA; E Carolia Col 61-62 (LS) MA. 7: Libn Co Consolidated Sch, Shaw Miss 43-44; Libn head Browsing Room Newspaper Depts Howard-Tilton Lib, Tulane U 50-56; Asst libn ref dept Joyner Lib E Carolina Col 60-61, 67, Chief ref libn 67-. 9: NCLA. 14: Ref. 15: 103 Dalebrook cir, Greenville NC 27835.

WILLIAMS, MARY ELIZABETH. b Milwaukee 30S 02. 5: Fairmount Col21-25 (Hist) AB; UMich 28, 30 ABLS; Ft Hays Kan State Col 34-37(Econ) MS. 7: Tchr RADIUM High Sch, Radium Kan 26-28; Libn Peckham Jr High Sch, Milwaukee 28-30; Circ libn Ft Hays Kan State Col 30-37; Libn Worthington Jr Col 37-39; Asst libn Neo State Tchrs Col Kearney 39-48; Circ libn Ill Inst Tech 48-62, Ref libn 62-. 9: ALA. 10: Ill Tech Faculty Womens Club; Kappa Phi Delta. 14: Ref. 15: Ill Inst of Tech 3300 S Federa, Chicago 60616.

WILLIAMS, MARY ELIZABETH. b Clarion Penn 29 Mr34. 4: Arthur R Williams. 5: Clarion State Col 52-56 (LS) BS; Penn State U summer 58 (LS); UPittsburgh summer 64-67 MLS. 6: Sp. 7: Libn Albion Area High Sch, Albion Penn 56-57; Libn S Side Jr High Sch, Oil City Penn 57-58; Asst libn Sr High Sch, Oil City Penn 58-61; Temp Oil City Pub Lib, Oil City Penn summer 61;head Libn Sr High Sch, Oil City Penn 61-62; Libn Venango Campus Clarion State Col 62-. 9: ALA; PennLA; Tri-State ACRL. 10: AAUP; Delta Kappa Gamma; YWCA; Assn Penn State Col Fac. 14: Ref. 15: 9 Smedley st, Oil City Pa 16301.

WILLIAMS, SISTER MARY SHEILA. b Yonkers NY 24 Jl 28. 5: Mt St Mary Col 48-49; VillanovaU 50-54 (Educ) BS; CatholicU 58-61 MLS. 7: Libn Mt St Mary Acad Lib 65-; Instr child lit Mt St Mary Col 68-69. 8: Commun sch lib consul 68-; Coord of sch libs for NY Archdiocese 68-. 9: ALA; CathLA (Exec Bd NY Unit 66-69); NYStateLA; SELA; Orange CoLA. 14: Child lit (wkshops, tchg). 15: Mt St Mary Academy, Newburgh NY 12550.

WILLIAMS, MAUDE ROBERTSON. b Bay Minette Ala. 4: Ferdinand Williams. 5: Alabama State Col 52-54 (Elem Educ) 2 yr Certif, 54-56 (Elem Educ) BS; Atlanta summers 60-64 MLS. 6: Fr. 7: Asst libn Hogan Pub Lib, Prichard Ala summer 58-59; Libn Blount High Sch, Prichard Ala 56-. 9: NEA; Ala Tchrs Assn. 10: Hogan Pub Lib Bd. 14: Sch libn. 15: 136 North st, Prichard Ala 36610.

WILLIAMS, MURIEL. b Montclair NJ 17 My 09. 5: Randolph-Macon Womans Col 27-29; Conn Col for Women 29-31 (Psych) BS; Columbia 31-32 (LS) BS; Life Off Mgt Assn Inst Certif. 6: Fr. 7: Lib asst Great Neck Lib, Great Neck NY 34-37; Br libn Hartford Pub Lib, Hartford Conn 37-46; Libn Phoenix Mutual Life Insurance Co, Hartford Conn 46-61; Circ & asst libn Wethersfield Pub Lib, Wethersfield Conn 61-62; Libn Conn Pub Expenditure Coun, Hartford Conn 63-64; Temp consul Kinnelon Pub Lib, Kinnelon NJ 65; Catlgr Montclair Pub Lib, Montclair NJ 65- 9: SLA (past chm Insur Div; past pres Conn Valley Chap); ALA. 10: AAUW. 14: Ref, bus, bk sel, catlg. 15: 5 Roosevelt pl, Montclair NJ 07042.

WILLIAMS, NANCY KATHERINE. b Little Rock Ark 26 Jl 31. 5: Tex Christian U 49-53 (Eng) BA; Inst Tecnologico y de Estudios Superiores Monterey Mex) summer 52; LSU 60-63 (LS) MS, 62-63 (Hist). 6: Sp. 7: Soc wker City of Chicago Dept of Welfare 54-55; Welfare visitor Jefferson Parish, Gretna La 55-60; Catlgr Duke U Lib 63; Ref libn NC State Lib 63-64; Ref libn New Orleans Pub Lib 64-65; Libn Mather Sch of Nurs So Baptist Hosp, New Orleans 65-68; Asst libn Miami U (Hamilton Ohio) 68-. 9: ALA. 10: LWV; Internat Club. 14: Ref, docs. 15: 1195 Colonial dr, Hamilton Oh 45013.

WILLIAMS, NAOMI (SAUNDERS). b Texarkana Tex 18 My 08. 04: Vernon B Williams Jr. 5: Crane Jr Col 26-29 (Eng) Diploma; Chicago summers 38, 39 (LS). 6: Sp, Fr. 7: Asst med soc wker Chicago Relief Admin 35-37; Chicago Pub Lib: Jr lib asst 36-46, 2nd asst Hiram Kelly Br 46-52, Ref asst Woodlawn Reg Lib 52-60, Head asst Chathan Br 60-61, Act libn Chatham Br 61-62, In chg Altgeld Gardens Sub-Br 62-63, Head asst S Chicago Br 63-64, Head asst Pullman Br 64-67, Act libn Dr Martin Luther King Jr Br 68, Libn (CP L) Chatham Br 69-. 8: Asst org in Chicago Baptist Inst. 9: ALA; IllLA; Chicago Lib Club. 10: Great Bks Group; YWCA; YMCA; NAACP; Nat Honor Soc; Chicago Lib Club; Woman's Aux Chicago Lib Club. 14: Ref wk (adults & ya). 15: 7026 S St Lawrence ave, Chicago Il 60637.

WILLIAMS, PAMELA ANN. b Atlanta Ga 5 D 29. 5: Antioch Col 46-51 (Lit) BA; UMich 54-55 MALS; Ecole Francaise dEte McGill U summer 59. 6: Fr, Ger, Sp. 7: X-ray Therapy Tech Grady Mem Hosp, Atlanta 51-54; Libn (GS-6) Kingsbridge Vet Hosp, Bronx NY 55-56; Ref libn Nat Ind Conf Bd, NYC 56-59; Soc sci libn Brooklyn Col Lib 59-62; Research asst Laurence Witten Rare Bks, New Haven Conn 62-65; Head libn Westover Sch, Middlebury Conn 65-. 9: ALA; SLA. 10: Inst of Gen Semantics;Amer Youth Hostels. 14: Ref, stud lib orientation. 15: Westover Sch, Middlebury Conn 06762.

WILLIAMS, PARKER. b Fruitvale Tex 26Jl29. 5: N Tex State U 46-49 (LS) BA; 53 (Elem sch Admin) ME; E Tex State U summers 62, 65 (Supv, Curriculum, Instr), 69 PhD. 6: Sp, Fr, Ger. 7: System-wide libn Grand Saline Pub Schs, Grand Saline Pub Schs, Grand Saline Tex 49-55; Pub libn Pasadena Pub Lib, Pasadena Tex 55-61; Col libn San Jacinto Col 61-. 8: Adv Memb, Marquis Biog Soc. 9: Amer Assn Jr Cols (Lib Div); TexLA (past chm Dist 5); Tex Jr Col Assn. 10: Delta Kappa Gamma; San Jacinto Col Faculty Womens Club; Soroptimist Club; Epsilon Sigma Alpha; YWCA; Pasadena Fine Arts Coun; Alpha Beta Alpha; Harris Co Reading Coun; Bd of Neighborhood Centers for Harris Co; Kappa Delta Phi; Pasadena Pub Lib Bd. 11: Community Leader of Amer (68). 13: Yes. 14: Col lib admin. 15: 1603 Ave M apt 2, S Houston Tx 77587.

WILLIAMS, PATRICIA ANN (CROSS). b Detroit 26 Ag 37. 4: Eugene P Williams. 5: E Mich State Col 55-56 (Eng); Wayne State U 56-59 BS in LS; UMich 60-64 (LS) AMLS. 7: Libn I Detroit Pub Lib 63-65, Libn II 65-66; Libn III 66-68; Hd libn Saints Jr Col 68-69. 8: Internat Afro-Amer Mem Mus Lib Com (adv), Memphis Tenn 69-. 9: NEA; ALA; MissEA. 14: Ya wk, instr materials. 15: 17568 Sorrento, Detroit Mi 48235.

WILLIAMS, PATRICIA ANNE. b Syracuse NY 27 O 39. 5: Armstrong State 57-59 (Liberal Arts); USCar 59-60 (Sociol); UGa 60-61 (Psych) AB; UMich 66-67 MALS. 6: Sp. 7: Hd br libn Tampa Pub Lib, Tampa Fla 65-68; Asst libn educ resources, USoFla 68-. 14: Child lit. 15: 5409 Park pl, Tampa Fl 33617.

WILLIAMS, RAYMOND E. b LaGrange Ill 37 Ap 1 6. 4: M Alexia Fichter. 5: Lehigh U 33-38 (Hist) AB; Syracuse 39-40 BS in LS, 51-54 MS in LS. 06: Fr. 6: Fr. 7: Sr asst Rochester Pub Lib, Rochester NY 39-40; Asst to libn Hartford Pub Lib, Hartford Conn 40-41; Ensign USNR, USS Hornet 42; Lt (jg) USNR engnr, USS Iowa 43; (Lt) USNR, USS Tambor 44-45; Dir Steele Mem Lib, Elmira NY 46-48; Reg libn Reg Lib Serv Center, Watertown NY 48-51; Asst dir Enoch Pratt Free Lib, Baltimore 51-57; Libn Minneapolis Pub Lib 57-63; Dir McIntire Pub Lib, Charlottesville Va 63-. 8: Consul; Dover (Del) Pub Lib 57; Schenectady Pub Lib 61-62; Lake County (Ind) Pub Lib 64; Handley Lib, Winchester Va 65. 9: ALA (Coun 69-72, Treas Lib Ext Div 48); -PLA (Bd 60-64); -ALTA (Wkshop Com 63-65); LED (Com on Federal Funds 64-65. Coun 60 & 64); NYLA (Legis Com 46-48, pres 48); MdLA (Legis Com 51-57); MinnLA (pres-elect 63-64); VaLA (Activities chm 65). 10: Rotary Internat; Phi Kappa Phi; Torch Club; United Givers Fund. 13: Yes. 14: Admin, bldgs. 15: 717 Park st, Charlottesville Va 22901.

WILLIAMS, RICHMOND DEAN. b Reading Mass 10 D 25. 4: Lynn Washbourne. 5: Williams 47-50 (Amer Hist & Lit) AB; UPenn 50-53 (European Hist) MA, 69 (European Hist) PhD. 6: Fr. 7: Instr & asst dean Williams Col 54-56; Dir Wyoming Hist & Geol Soc, Wilkes-Barre Pa 56-60; Asst dir Amer Assn for State & Local Hist, Madison Wis 60-61; Assoc dir Longwood Lib, Kennett Sq Penn 61; Dir Eleutherian Mills Hist Lib, Greenville Del 62-. 8: Consul Md Hist Soc 67; Appraiser Ford Motor Co Archives 64. 9: Amer Assn State & Local Hist; Philobiblion Club of Phila; Museum Coun of Phila; Hist Soc Del. 10: DelLA; Del Educ TV Assn; MidAtlantic Reg Lib Fed; Coun Hist Libs in Del; Phi Beta Kappa. 11: Pennfield Fellow. 12: Coauth A Look at Our Selves-- (62); They Also Served-- (65). 13: Yes. 14: Research in Amer tech, lib mgt. 15: 202 Brecks lane, Wilmington De 19807.

WILLIAMS, ROBERT VIRGIL. b Brooksville Fl 10 O 38. 5: Fla Christian Col 56-58 AA; Harding Col 59-61 (Elem Educ, Soc Sci) BA; UColo fall 62 (LS); Fla State U 63-64 (LS) MS; Ga State Col 67-68 (Hist). 6: Sp. 7: Elem tchr Jefferson Co schs, Lakewood Colo 61-63; Grad asst Fla State U 63-64; Ref libn Atlanta Pub Lib 65; Head Microfilm Lib Ga Dept of Archives & Hist, Atlanta 65-68; Hd Mss Div 68-. 9: ALA; SLA; (So Atlantic Chap, 2nd v-pres, Program Chm); SAA; GaLA; Atlanta Lib Club. 11: Ga State Col Prize for Writings in Colonial Hist (68). 12: Mem ed bd "Journal of Library History (68-); Auth Document Sources for the History of Federal Government Libraries in "Approaches to Library History (66). 13: Yes. 14: Archives, hist libs, ref, records mgt, mss. 15: 1136 Lullwater rd NE, Atlanta 30306.

WILLIAMS, ROSEMARY (McDONALD). b Hamilton Co Ind 12 Je 20. 4: Thomas Adrian Williams. 5: Ball StateU 37-42 (Soc Sci) AB, 51-62 (LS) MA in Ed. 6: Fr. 7: Tchr Noblesville High Sch, Noblesville Ind 42-44; Clerk-typist Finance Off US Army, Ft Monroe Va 44-45; Tchg materials serv asst Ball State U 47-48, Catlgr 60-; Tchr-libn Middletown High Sch, Middletown Ind 48-55; Tchr-libn Highland High Sch, Anderson Ind 55-60. 9: ALA; Ohio Valley Gp Tech Serv Libns; IndLA; IndASchL; A-V Instr Dirs of Ind. 10: Pi Lambda Theta. 14: Catlg. 15: RR 8 Box 524, Muncie In 47302.

WILLIAMS, RUTH LUCILLE. b Port Washington Wis 23Jl43. 5: Sioux Falls Col 61-62; Iowa Wesleyan Col 62-64 (Hist) BA; UDenver 64-65 (LS) MA. 7: Ref libn Midland Col 65-. 9: ALA; NebLA. 10: AAUP. 14: Ref, archives. 15: 752 W 11, Fremont Nb 68025.

WILLIAMS, SAM P(EMBERTON). b Sedalia Mo 23 O 22. 5: UKan City 38-39; UMo 40-41 (Eng) BA, 57-58 (Eng) MA; Pratt 60-61 BS in LS. 6: Fr, Sp. 7: (Sgt) USAAF, US Guam 43-46; Standard-Vacuum Oil Co, China & India 46-55; NY Pub Lib 60-. 8: Camp reprints in printser. 9: ALA. 12: Ed "Reprint Expediting Service Bulletin" (61-65). 13: Yes. 14: Bibliog, illus bks. 15: RD 1 Box 315, Salisbury Hills NY 12577.

WILLIAMS, SARAH ELIZABETH (FOWLER). b Nacogdoches Tex 22 Jl 33. 4: Earlon Williams. 5: Stephen F Austin State Col 50-53 (LS) BS; N Tex StateU BDEA Inst Lib Serv 66; SW Tex State Col 60 (Elem Math). 7: Libn Jefferson High Sch, Jefferson Tex 53-54, Aldine Jr High Sch, Aldine Tex 54-55, W Columbia Elem, Brazoria Elem, Charlie Brown Jr High-Elem, Columbia Intermediate, W Columbia Tex 56-68; Libn & Eng tchr: Westminister Jr Col & Bible Inst, Tehacana Tex 55-56, Temple Jr High, Diboll Tex 68-. 9: ALA; TexStateTA; TexLA; AngelinaCoTA. 10: PTA; Commun Concert Assn; Beta Sigma Phi. 14: Elem sch libs. 15: 1502 Wildbriar dr, Lufkin Tx 75901.

WILLIAMS, SHARON (MITCHELL). b Denver Col 29 D 37. 4: J F Williams. 5: UDenver 55-58 (Hist) BA; UHawaii 65-66 MLS; UNeb 67-69. 6: Fr. 7: Libn Pearl Harbor Kai Elem Sch, Honolulu 66-67; Elem media specialist Bellevue Pub Schs, Bellevue Neb 67-68; Media specialist Ligan Fontanelle Jr High Sch, Bellevue Neb 68-. 9: ALA; -AASchL; NEA-DAVI; NebStateLA; NebASchL; NebStateEA; Neb Educ Media Assn. 14: Child serv. 15: 12210 So 26th st, Omaha nb 68123.

WILLIAMS, TERRENCE. San Francisco Cal 16 Ja 29. 4: Nancy McCammon. 5: Iowa State Col 46-47; UIowa 47-49 (Eng); UKan 50, 53 (Eng) AB, 53-56 (Eng) MA; UDenver 58-60 (LS) MA. 6: Ger, Fr, Sp, Lat. 7: Asst instr in Eng UKansas 53-54, Instr in Eng 54-55; Instr in Eng Colo Sch of Mines 56-60; Apprentice & catlgr Wm P Wreden Rare Bks Palo Alto Cal summers 55, 56; UKan Lib; Libn I catlgr 60-63, Libn II asst head of spec collections 63-65, Libn II asst to the Dir of Libs 65-66, Libn III, Chief ref libn 66-67, Libn III, Asst dir 67-. 9: ALA; BSA; KanLA. 10: AAUP; ACLU; Diaconate; Lay Reader, Episcopal Chur. 12: Comp "A Checklist of Linneana, 1735-1835 (64). ; Ed "Books and Libraries. 14: Rare bks, ref, univ interlib serv. 15: 3 Westwood, Lawrence Ks 66044.

WILLIAMS, THOMAS P. b Wauwatosa Wis 25 S 38. 4: Jennifer Ann Devonshire. 5: UWis 56-60 (Geog) BS; DePaulU 63-65; LSU 67-69 MSLS. 6: Sp. 7: Instr West Allis Pks, west Allis Wis 57-59; Petty Off 3/C Personnelman (US Navy Res) 60-62; Intl Banking Continental Bank, Chicago 62-67; Hd soc sci & humanities ref dept, (Asst Prof), Miss StateU 69-. 9: SELA; MissLA. 14: Ref, photo archives. 15: PO Box 4571, State College Ms 39762.

WILLIAMS, VIRGINIA (MARGARET) J(ONES). b Gurley Ala 13 D 03. 4/ ernest F(rancis) Williams. 5: George WashingtonU 23-28 (Bio Sci) AB & Diploma in Educ. 6: Lat, Sp, Ger. 7: Asst Card Div 23-26, Catlgr-proofreader Catlg Div 26-40, Asst hd Copyright sect catlg div 41-42, Hd new bks unit eng lang sect descriptive catlg div 42-46, Sr catlg reviewer 47-67, Supv libn (asst hd & problems unit supv) 67-68, Asst hd 68-. 8: Assisted in the establishment of the Book Section of the Cataloging Division of the Copyright Office of the Library of Congress, 1946-47. 9: Potomac Tech Proc Libns; DCLA. 10: Delta Theta Chi; Delta Phi Sigma. 12: Ed "Cataloging Rules of the American library Association and the Library of Congress, Additions and Changes, 1949-1958" (59); "Cataloging Service", Bull 27-64 (52-64); "Rules for Descriptive Cataloging in the Library of Congress: "Books in Raised Characters" (53), "Phonorecords" (52 & 64), "Pictures, designs, and Other Two-Dimensional Representations" (59). 14: Catlg, ref, rare bks. 15: 4451 Albemarle st NW, Washington DC 20016.

WILLIAMS, WILEY (JULIAN). b Headland Ala 3 Mr 24. 5: UNC 45-49 (Marketing) BS; Peabody 51-52 MLS; UMich 59-60 (Pub Admin) MPA, 57-58, 59-64 (LS) PhD. 7: Sheetmetal wker 558th Air Force Base Unit, Nashville 42-45; Store mgr trainee W T Grant Co, Chattanooga Tenn 49; Personnel clerk Spur Distributing Co, Nashville 50-51; Ref libn Bus Lib UAla 52-59; Instr-libn Bowling Green State U 61-63; Visiting Instr & Bibliog(r) 64; Visiting instr UNC (Chapel Hill) summer 63; Asst prof Sch of Lib UWash 65; Asst prof Peabody Lib Sch 65-68; Assoc Prof 68-. 9: ALA; SLA; AALS; SELA; TennLA. 10: Alpha Kappa Psi; AAAS; AAUP. 13: Yes. 14: Tchg, ref, govt docs, spec libs, principles of research. 15: 3401 Benham ave, Nashville Tn 37215.

WILLIAMS, WILLIAM H. b Seattle Wash 18 Ap 24. 4: Helem Sims. 5: Brigham Young 64-68 (Hist) BS, 68-69 MLS. 6: Fr. 7: Pilot USAF 43-64; Tchg asst Brigham Young U Lib 68-69; Dir Provo Pub Lib, Provo Utah 69-70; Wyo State Libn 70-. 9: ALA; UtahLA; MPLA. 10: Phi Alpha Theta. 14: Admin. 15: Wyo State Lib, Cheyenne Wyo.

WILLIAMSEN, SISTER AUDREY MARY OP. b Little Chute Wis 20 Je 26. 5: Dominican Col (Racine Wis) 44-51; St Norbert Col 52-58 (Educ) BS; Col of St Catherine 59-63 (LS) BS; UMinn summer 65 (NDEA Inst); West Mich U 69 MS in Libnship. 7: Libn; St Clement High Sch, Center Line Mich 64-68, Dominican Col (Racine) 68-. 9: CathLA; NEA-DAVI; LARC. 14: Ref. 15: 5915 Erie st, Racine Wi 53402.

WILLIAMSON, ANN (GARRETT). b Clarksville Ark 3 N 19. 4: John W Williamson. 5: Col of the Ozarks 39-40; Okla CityU 64-65 (Hist) BA; UOkla 65-67 MLS. 7: Tchr Clarksville Pub Schs, Clarksville Ark 39-42; Clk Off of Price Admin, Clarksville Ark 42-44; Sec Fox-Vliet Wholesale Drug Co, Okla City 45-47; Sec Okla CityU 52-62, Admin asst 57-, Acquis asst 62-63, Catlg asst 63-64, Asst catlgr & ser libn 67-68, Asst catlg & gift & exchange libn 68-. 9: ALA; SWLA; OklaLA. 15: 7406 NW 36th, Bethany Ok 73008.

WILLIAMSON, ELIZABETH A. b West Chester Penn 10 F 02. 5: W Chester State Col (Eng) BS in Ed; Drexel 39 BS in LS. 7: Libn: Bus Lib Atlantic Refining Co, Phila 25-27, Sr High Sch, Lansdale Penn 27-53, Rosemary Hall, Greenwich Conn 53-57, Agnes Irwin Sch, Rosemont Penn 59-63; Dir of Libs Harcum Jr Col 63-. 15: 630 Ardmore ave, Ardmore Penn 19003.

WILLIAMSON, HAROLD W. b Winfield Kan 16 F 11. 4: Marna B Lindsay. 5: Okla State U 34 BS; UOkla 57 LS. 7: Tchr-libn Marietta High Sch, Marietta Okla 54-58; Circ libn Southwestern State Col, Weatherford Okla 58-61; Asst order libn Central State Col, Edmond Okla 61-62; Assoc libn pub serv Mankato State Col 62-. 9: ALA; MinnLA. 14: Pub serv. 15: 1303 Noretta dr, No Mankato Minn 56001.

WILLIAMSON, JEANETTE (GORSKI). b Houston 8 N 08. 4: Pierce MacDonald Williamson. 5: Rice U 25-29 (Hist) BA; USoCal summer 30; LSU 44-47 BS in LS. 6: Polish, Sp. 7: High sch tchr Houston Ind Sch System 29-34; Catlg libn UTex 39-43; Order libn, libn Lib Sch Lib LSU 44-47; Ref libnSampson Col ACUNY 47-49; Libn Grade II-III circ dept NY Pub Lib 49-52; Ref libn USAF Inst of Tech, WPAFB Ohio 53-59; Ref libn, chief of catlg & index br Foreign Tech Div, WPAFB Ohio 59-. 9: ALA-ACRL; SLA. 10: Nat Fed Bus & Prof Womens Clubs; Phi Beta Kappa; Phi Kappa Phi; Beta Phi Mu. 14: Catlg, ref. 15: 3285 Tralee trail, Dayton Ohio 45430.

WILLIAMSON, MARGARET JEAN (MADISON). b Wash DC 26 Je 35. 4: Nathaniel Howard Williamson. 5: UMd 53-57 (Eng) BA; Columbia 64-65 MSLS. 6: Ger, Fr. 7: Sr clsf record asst LC 57-64; Asst catlg libn UHouston 65-67; Catlg libn 67-. 9: ALA; TexLA. 10: Mensa.14: Catlg. 15: 1617 Fannin apt 2003, Houston Tx 77002.

WILLIAMSON, MARNA L. b Jones Okla. 4: Harold W Williamson. 5: Southeastern State Col (Okla) (Bus) BS; UOkla 64 MLS. 7: Land-title clerk Gulf Oil Corp, Ardmore Okla 48-58; Tchr Thomas pub schs, Thomas Okla 58-60; Contract interpreter Sohio Petroleum Co, Okla City Okla 60-62; Catlg libn Mankato State Col 62-. 9: MinnLA. 14: Catlg, ref. 15: 1303 Noretta dr, No Mankato Minn 56001.

WILLIAMSON, NANCY JOYCE. b St Stephen NB Can 4 Jl28. 5: Mt Allison U 45-49 (Hist, Eng) BA; Toronto 49-50 BLS, 64 MLS. 7: Hamilton Pub Lib, Hamilton Ont: Gen libn arts & sci dept 50-56, 1st asst catlg dept 56-64, Head catlgr 65; Asst Prof of Lib Sci Sch of Lib Sci UToronto 65-. 9: ALA; CanLA (sec-treas Tech Serv Sect 64-65); OntLA (chm Ont

Resources & Tech Serv Group 64-65); Inst Prof Libns Ont. 12: Ed OntLA "News (65-66). 14: Catlg. 15: 77 St Clair ave E apt 1001, Toronto Can.

WILLIAMSON, ROSALIE. b Columbus Ga 12 O 43. 5: St John's Col 61-62; Lake Forest Col 63-64; RooseveltU 64-67 (Hist) BA; Rosary Col 67-68 MLS. 6: Fr. 7: Trainee Chicago pub Lib 68; Libn Harper & Row Publisher, Evanston Ill 69-. 14: Ref. 15: 2727 Central st, Evanston Il 60201.

WILLIAMSON, WILLIAM LANDRAM. b Lexington Ky 13 Ag20. 4: Daisy Levy. 5: UKy 37-38; UWis 38-41 (Amer Hist) BA (Honors); Emory 41-42 BA in LS; Columbia 48-49 (LS) MS; Chicago 51-54, 59 (LS) PhD. 6: Fr, Indonesian. 7: Ref asst Atlanta Pub Lib 42, 46; (Pvt to 1st Lt) US Army 42-46; Asst libn, assoc libn Baylor U 47-48, 49-51; Lib consul Ford Found SUNY Indonesia Proj, Indonesia 60-62; Butler libn Columbia U 54-60, 62-64; Head Libn Montclair State Col 64-66; Visiting lectr Chicago summer 66; Prof Lib Sci UWis (Madison) 66-. 8: Lib consul, Bd of Md State Col 65. 9: ALA;-LAD (chm Circ Serv Sect 68-69); WisLA. 10: AAUP; Archons of Colophon. 12: "William Frederick Poole and the Modern Library Movement (63). 13: Yes. 14: Acad libs, lib hist, internat libnship. 15: 5105 Tomahawk trail, Madison Wi 53705.

WILLIFORD, DOXIE KENT. b Water Valley Miss 13 J138. 5: UMiss 56-60 (Eng) BA, 64-68 (LS) MLS. 7: Ensign USNR, USS Canberra (CAG-2) 60-61; Tchr R-IV High Sch, Alton Mo 61-62; Eng tchr Tchula High Sch, Tchula Miss 62-64; Jr libn The Library, University Miss 64-; Sr libn 68-. 9: MissLA. 14: Acquis, ref, spec collections. 15: Box 965, University Miss 38677.

WILLIFORD, JUDITH ANN HARWOOD. b Montreal Can 9 O 38. 4: Harry F Williford. 5: UND 56-60 (Eng, Sci) BA; UVt summer 58; UMinn summer 61 (LS); UIll 64-65 (LS) MS. 7: Tchr Sch Dist No 318, Grand Rapids Minn 60-64; Asst libn UIll(Urbana) 65-67; Asst libn Parkalnd Col 67-. 9: ALA. 10: Delta Zeta; PEO; Beta Phi Mu. 14: Ref. 15: 1523 Lincolnshire apt 7, Champaign Il 61820.

WILLIS, DAWN E. b Howard NY. 5: Geneseo State Normal Sch 31-34, 38-39 (LS); George Washington U 43-44 (Educ) BA; Catholic U MSLS. 7: Circ asst usda, wash DC 43-44; Br libn USDA, Asheville 45-46; Ref libn Bur of Pub Roads, Wash DC 46-56, Chief research & bibliog 56-. 9: SLA (chm Transp Group 58-59); DCLA (Publicity Chm 53-54). 14: Ref, bibliog. 15: 532 20th st NW, Wash DC 20006.

WILLIS, DOROTHY (OCTAVIA HUNGERFORD). b Athens Ga 19D35. 4: Robert Calvin Willis. 5: Shorter Col 53-55; UGa 56-57 (Journalism) ABJ; Emory summers 60-64 (LS) ML. 6: Sp. 7: Ed clerk Ga Dept of Educ, Atlanta 57; High sch Tchr Muscogee Co, Columbus Ga 58; High sch tchr Sumter Co, Plains Ga 58-61; Jr high sch libn Muscogee Co, Columbus Ga 61-62; High sch libn DeKalb Co, Lithonia Ga 62-64; Catlgr Ga State Col 65; High sch libn DeKalb Co, Clarkston Ga 65-66; Libn Div of Libnship Emory 67-68; Ed Union Catlg of the U Ctr, Ga 69-. 9: ALA; GaLA; SELA. 10: Phi Beta Kappa; Phi Kappa Phi; Kappa Tau Alpha. 14: Catlg. 15: 4095 Blackhawk dr, Stone Mountain Ga 30083.

WILLIS, EILEEN (BROOKHART). b Kittanning Penn 14 My 25. 4: Richard P Willis. 5: Tenn Wesleyan Col 43-44 (Music); UTenn 44-47 (Hist) BA; 47-48 4748 BS in LS. 7: Libn Cumberland Co High Sch, Crossville Tenn 48-49; Bkmob libn Lepper Lib, Lisbon Ohio 49-50; Asst reg libn W Tenn Reg Lib, Martin Tenn 50-52; Bkmob libn Albertson Pub Lib, Orlando Fla 52-59, Ya libn 59-61; Adult serv, ref Orlando Pub Lib, Orlando Fla 61-67; Hd local hist & genealogy dept 67-. 9: ALA; FlaLA. 14: Loc hist (Fla), geneal. 15: 2041 Dundee dr, Winter Park Fla 32789.

WILLIS, KATHERINE (TAPPERT). b Fairfield Iowa 29 S 1883. 4: Grinnell Willis. 5: Parsons Col 05 (Hist, Eng) BA; Pratt 10 BLS; Oxford 22-23. 6: Fr, Ital, Sp. 7: Libn New Rochelle Pub Lib, New Rochelle NY 10-13; V-libn Washington Co Free Lib, Hagerstown Md 14-18; Org Hosp Lib, Camp Upton & Camp Lib Navy Yard, Charleston SC; Libn "Evening Post, NY 18-22; Libn Morristown Lib, Morristown NJ 24-27; Spec asst Ferguson Lib, Stamford Conn 52-60; Bk sel info serv Greenwich Lib, Greenwich Conn 60-. 9: ALA (Life mem); ConnLA; FlaLA. 10: Trustee, Morristown (NJ) Lib; Cosmopolitan Club. 13: Yes. 14: Rare bks, ref, reading for pleasure. 15: Ituri Towers, Greenwich Ct 06830.

WILLIS, MARILYN. b Magnolia Ark 10 Mr 33. 5: La Polytech Inst 51-54 (Piano); LSU 54-55 (Piano) BMus, 65-66 (LS) NS. 6: Fr. 7: Sec WBRZ-TV, Baton Rouge La 55-56, Continuity 56-57; Sec Wyandotte Chemicals Corp, Geismar La 57-65; Acquis libn LUSU, Shreveport 67-68, Ser libn 68-. 9: LaLA. 14: Ser, catlg. 15: 2524 Sheri lane, Shreveport La 71109.

WILLIS,SHARON OZELL (FARMER). b W Frankfort Ill 11 Je 38. 4: Carl G Willis. 5: So Ill U 56-60 (Kindergarten, Prim) BS; UIll 61-63 MS in LS. 7: Kindergarten tchr & high sch libn Columbia Unit Dist, Columbia Ill 60-61; Elem tchr Mahomet Unit Dist, Mahomet Ill 61-62; Instr & libn of the Ames Lab Sch Wis State U (River Falls) 62-64; Catlgr & instr Okla State U 64-66; Info libn & instr Sch of Lib & Info Sci UMo (Columbia) 67-. 9: ALA; -AASchL; -CSD; NEA; OklaLA; MoLA; MoASchL. 10: Alpha Beta Alpha; Epsilon Beta; Bibliophiles. 12: Co-auth "The Elementary School Library; Theory and Practice". 14: Lib sci instr, child & yp lit. 15: 606 Westridge dr, Columbia Mo 65201.

WILLMERING, WILLIAM J. b St Louis Mo 7 Ja 44. 5: Marian Col 62-66 (Eng) BA; UIll (Urbana) 66-67 MSLS. 6: Fr. 7: Asst ref libn UMont 67-. 14: Ref. 15: Univ of Montana Lib, Missoula Mt 59801.

WILLOCKS, ROBERT MAX. b Maryville Tenn 1 O 24. 4: Neysa Ferguson. 5: Maryville Col 42-43, 46-49 (Philos) BA; Golden Gate Baptist THEOL Sem 49-52 (Missions) BD, 62 (Missions) ThM; Peabody 61-62 (LS) MA. 6: Korean, Hebrew, Sp, Gk. 7: Clerk Kenney Shoe Co, Knoxville Tenn 39-42; 2nd class petty off US Navy Radioman 43-46; Pastor So Baptist Churches, Cal 50-56; Missionary So Baptist for Mission Bd, Korea 56-65; Korea Baptist Sem, Korea; Prof of Church Hist 57-65, Act pres 58-59, Libn 59-65; Assoc dir of the lib Heidelberg Col 65-67; Dir of Lib Columbia Col (SC) 67-. 8: Consul, Chung Nam Province LA, Korea 62-65; Adv, Korea Christian Acad Lib, 62-65. , Dir Union List of Serials Proj, SC Found of Independent Cols 69-. 9: ALA; KoreaLA; SCLA; SELA. 10: AAUP; LARC. 12: Dir-Ed "Korea Baptist Press"; Ed Korean ed of "Thus It Is Written" by H C Goerner (63); "The Progress of Worldwide Missions" by Robert H Glover (65). 13: Yes. 14: Admin, catlg. 15: 703 Kingsbridge rd, Columbia SC 29210.

WILLS, FLOREID. b Tyler Tex 15 S 09. 5: Tyler Jr Col 37-39 Diploma; Tex Woman'sU 39-40 (LS) BA, 44, 47, 48 BS in LS; BaylorU 47-50, 52-54, 56 (Eng) MA. 7: Bindery wk hixson-Ellis Printing Co, Tyler Tex 28-35; Sec Calvary Bapt Ch, Tyler Tex 35-37; Libn Srguin High Sch, Seguin Tex 41-44; Tchr-libn Union Grove High Sch (Gladewater Tex) 44-45; Hd catlg BaylorU 45-54; Catlg libn SWest Bapt Theol Sem 54-. 8: Mem, Adv Com on Lib Wk, Baptist Con Tex 58-59. 9: ATheolLA; TexLA; Tex Reg Gp of Catlgrs & Clsfrs. 10: AAUW; Phi Theta Kappa. 14: Catlg. 15: 1313 W Boyce, Fort Worth Tx 76115.

WILLS, JO (DAVIES). b Mt Pleasant Iowa 20 N 42. 4: David A Willis. 5: UMinn 60-64 9amer Studies) BA; UMich 65 MLS. 7: Ref Detroit Pub Lib 66; Br libn Kent Co Lib, grand Rapids Mich 67, Asst child serv coord 68-. 9: MichLA (Recr Com; Mat Lib Week Com). 10: Puppeteers of Amer. 11: Loleta D Fyan Award 68. 14: Child wk. 15: 530 Morris SE, Grand Rapids Mi 49503.

WILLS, KEITH CAMERON. b McCleary Wash 11 Ag 17. 4: Olin Taylor. 5: UWash 36-41 (Govt Serv) AB; Southwestern Baptist Theol Sem 47-50 9christian Ethics) BD, 51-58 (Christian Ethics) ThD; N Tex State Col 58 (LS); UDenver 65-66 (LS) MA. 6: Ger, Fr, Gk. 7: Housing economist Nat Housing Agency, Wash DC 41-47; Chief of circ SWest Baptist Sem Lib 50-51, 53-57, Ref libn 57-58, Dir of Lib 66-; Libn Midwestern Baptist Sem Lib 58-66. 9: ALA; ATheolLA (chm Memb Coms); TexLA. 10: So Baptist Hist Soc; Civitan Club. 14: Admin, acquis, ref. 15: 6133 Wrigley way, Ft Worth Tx 76133.

WILLS, ROBERTA JUNE. b Lebanon Ind 14 Je 13. 5: Ball State Tchrs Col 43 (Eng, LS) BA, 51 (LS) MA; Syracuse 68 MSLS. 6: Fr, Ger. 7: Tchr-libn Fairmount High Sch, Fairmount Ind 44-48; Libn Sr High Sch, Connersville Ind 48-52; Circ libn Bradley U 52-54; Circ libn UWichita 54-57; Asst libn & Eng Instr Alma Col 57-62; Assoc Prof Lib Educ Mansfield State Col 62-, Head of Dept 65-66. 9: ALA-AASchL; PennLA; NEA-DAVI; Penn State LA; Penn State EA; Penn Assn Higher Educ. 10: Kappa Delta Pi; Sigma Tau Delta; Delta Kappa Gmma; Quill & Scroll; Nat Poetry Assn; AAUP; AAUW; Alpha Beta Alpha; Assn Penn State Col & Univ Facs. 13: Yes. 14: Lib educ. 15: 40 N Hill ter, Mansfield Penn 16933.

WILLSON, ELLA JEAN. b Cana 3 Ja 12. 5: Wayne State 30-34 (Eng, Ger) BA, 36-40 BSLS, 40-44 (Eng) MA, 61-65 (Curriculum Development, LS) EdD; UMich 41-42 (LS). 7: Libn Wayne StateU Detroit 38-40; Libn elem schs, Detroit 40-63; Libn Nolan Jr High Sch, detroit 60-62; Libn SE High Sch, Detroit 62-63; Instr lib sci Wayne StateU 66-; Instr lib sci UMich 68; Supv sch libs, Detroit 63-. 9: ALA; -AASchL; MichLA; MichASchL. 13: Yes. 14: Child & ya lit. 15: 11611 Morang apt 32, Detroit Mi 48224.

WILLSON, JIMMIE DORIS. b Moro Ark 2 S 28. 5: UKy 46-50 (LS) BA; ULouisville 62 (Secondary Educ) M Ed. 7: Asst libn Valley High Sch, Valley Station Ky 50-52, Asst libn Eastern High Sch, Middletown Ky 52-54, Head Libn 54-. 9: ALA; NEA; KyLA; KyEA; KyASchL; Ky Assn Cols, Secon & Elem Schs (mem Secon Sch Commsn 63-65). 10: Kappa Delta Pi. 14: Sch libnship. 15: 207 N Madison, Middletown Ky 40243.

WILMANN, ALDIS (LOUISE). b Washington DC 6 Mr 08. 5: Mt Holyoke Col 26-30 (Zool) BA; Columbia 32-38 (LS) BS. 7: Mt Vernon Pub Lib, Mt Vernon NY: Lib asst circ 30-32, Lib asst catlg 32-42, Jr & sr libn I, ref 42-57, Head ref dept 57-. 9: NYLA; Westchester LA (sec 48-50, chm Ann Mtg 52); NY Lib Club. 10: Bus & Prof Womens Club; Mount Holyoke Club of Westchester. 14: Ref, art, hist. 15: 590 E 3rd st, Mt Vernon NY 10553.

WILMER, FLORENCE CONRATH. b Mahaffey Penn 2 Je 1898. 4: William B Wilmer. 5: Washington Col 33-37 (Fr, Ger) AB (magna cum laude; Columbia 37-38 BLS; Johns Hopkins 58-60; UMd 59. 6: Fr, Ger. 7: Br libn Enoch Pratt Free Lib, Baltimore 38-43; Dir US Libs in S Africa Owi, Johannesburg S Africa 43-46; Chm Dept of Hist UBaltimore 46-53, Dir of Lib 53-57; Dir of lib serv Catonsville Commun Col 57-68; Consul to jr col libs 68-. 9: ALA: NEA; Md State Tchrs Assn; MdLA (pres 43-44); Md Assn Jr Cols (pres 51-52). 10: Baltimore Civic Opera Co; Beta Sigma Phi. 13: Yes. 14: Admin, lib arch. 15: 1506 Lochwood rd, Baltimore 21218.

WILSON, ALDEN P. b Oberlin Ohio 28 Ag 24. 4: Bernice Franz. 5: Fenn Col 42-43, 46-47 (Hist) AB; West Res 48-49 MS in LS. 7: US Army Corps of Engnrs T/5 grade 43-46; Lib aide Cleveland Pub Lib 48-49; Asst ref libn Dearborn (Mich) Pub Lib 49-51; Head Libn Berkley (Mich) Pub Lib 51-57; Head Libn St Joseph (Mo) Pub Lib 57-62; Head Libn Park Ridge (Ill) Pub Lib 62-. 9: ALA; IllLA; Lib Adminrs Conf No Ill (v-chm 68-69). 10: Lions Club. 14: Admin. 15: 2800 Habberton ave, Park Ridge Ill 60068.

WILSON, ALENE (PETERSON). b Madison Wis 14 Jl 37. 4: Kline R Wilson. 5: UWis 55-59 (Eng) BS; UWash 60-63 (LS) ML, summer 65 (NDEA Inst). 7: Jr high tchr Eng, math Seattle pub sch 59-61; High sch tchr Bloomington pub schs, Bloomington Minn 61-62; Jr high libn Bellevue pub schs, Bellevue Wash 63-66, Acquis libn 67-. 9: NEA; ALA; Wash State EA; Wash State SchLA (Scholarship Com 65-66); Bellevue EA. 10: Phi Beta Kappa; Phi Kappa Phi; Pi Lambda Theta; Seattle Mountaineers; Friends he Pub Lib. 14: Sch libnship, acquis, ref. 15: 2539 82nd ave NE, Bellevue Wa 98004.

WILSON, ALLIE CAROL. b Atkins Ark 24 Ap 06. 5: Central Col (Conway Ark) 24-26 (Speech, Eng) AA; UArk 31-33 (Eng, Soc Sci) BSE, 36-37 (Eng, Hist) MA; Peabody Col summers 43-46 BS in LS; UChicago 52 LS; Emory summers 57, 59 LS; UMinn summer 63. 7: Tchr: Ark pub schs 26-28, Hector (Ark) High Sch 28-32, Smackover (Ark) High Sch 34-37, Hartshorne (Okla) High Sch 37-41, High sch, Haskell Okla 41-43; Instr Eng & libn Ark State U 43-44; Hd high sch Eng dept, Huntsville Srk 44-46; Instr Eng & asst libn Little Rock Jr Col 46-48; Hd libn & assoc prof Henderson State Col 48-. 9: ALA; NEA; ArkLA (life mem, pres 63); ArkEA. 10: Delta Kappa Gamma; Woman's Library Assn of Arkadelphia. 14: Admin, lib educ, catlg. 15: Henderson State College, Arkadelphia Ar 71923.

WILSON, ANTHONY MARK. b Ellensburg Wash 24 D 40. 4: Mary Laura Goud. 5: Central Wash State Col 60-65 (Eng, Philos) BA; UWash 65-66 MLib. 7: Self employed in trucking bus, Ellensburg Wash -66; Tech serv libn Highline Col Lib, Midway Wash 66-. 8: Mem Adv Com to State Bd for commun col educ 68. 9: ALA; Commun Col LBNS Oraniz. 10: Puget Sound Mycological Soc; Commun Col Profess Assn of Wash; AAUP. 13: Yes. 14: Tech serv, systems analysis, info retr. 15: 11826 Holmes Pt dr NE, Kirkland Wa 98033.

WILSON, BARBARA LOUISE. b Cincinnati Iowa 15 D 21. 5: So MethodistU 50 (Educ) BS; Tex Women'sU 51 BSLS; UMich 65 AMLS. 6: Fr. 7: Tchr Acad of Sacred Heart, St Louis 44-47; Tchr Acad of Sacred Heart, New Orleans 47-48; Libn Jesuit High Sch, Dallas Tex 48-51; Libn Reinhardt Elem, Dallas Tex 51-54; Libn W H Gaston Jr High Sch, Dallas Tex 54-64; Libn UMich Undergrad (Ann Arbor) 65-68; Dir Muskegon Commun Col 68-. 9: ALA; MichLA. 10: Delta Kappa Gamma; Zonta Internatl. 14: Ref, circ. 15: 435 Mitzi apt 12, n muskegon Mi 49445.

WILSON, BERNARD E(UGENE). b Detroit 26 Je 15. 5: UToledo 32-37 (Chem, Math) BS; UMich 38-39 (Math) MS, 53-54 AMLS. 6: Fr, Ger, Ital. 7: Statistical clerk Amer Mutual Alliance, NYC 40-42; US Army, USAF, statistician (S/Sgt) 42-45; Placement off, civilian US Army, Vienna Austria 45-48; Intelligence off, civilian USAF, Vienna Salzburg Austra 48-52; Music catlgr UMich 54-59; Msic catlgr Newberry Lib, Chicago 59-65, Head processing dept 65-67, Rare bk catlgr 68-. 8: Saw through the press 36 vs (of 40) of The Edwards Brothers Reprint of the Breitkopf & Haertel; Ed of the complete works of Mozart (Ann Arbor Mich 55-56). 10: Phi Kappa Phi. 13: Yes. 14: Catlg, music research, tr. 15: 1002 N State st, Chicago Il 60610.

WILSON, BERNICE F. b Cleveland 15 Ap 25. 4: Alden P Wilson. 5: Fenn Col 43-47 (Hist) AB; Rosary Col 64-68 MA in LS. 7: Lib aide Cleveland Pub Lib (Ohio) 48-49; Tech asst libn Wayne State U 50-54; Tchr Bd of Educ, St Joseph Mo 60-62; Sch libn Bd of Educ Dist 64, Park Ridge Ill 64-. 9: ALA; NEA; IllLA; IllEA; Ill Assn Clr Tchrs; IllASchL. 10: LWV. 14: Sch libs. 15: 2800 Habberton ave, Park Ridge Il 60068.

WILSON, CELIANNA (ISLEY). b Youngstown Ohio 8 Ag 17. 5: Denison U 35-39 (Philos) AB; West Res 41-42 BS in LS; Ohio State U 54-55 (Bus Org, Personnel Mgt). 6: Fr. 7: Circ desk asst E Cleveland Pub Lib, Cleveland Ohio 39-42; Ya libn Wellsville (NY) Pub Lib 42; Asst libn Macon (Ga) Pub Lib 43; Head Union Catalog West Res U 44; Asst catlgr West Res U Lib 47-48; Head catlgr Battelle Mem Inst, Columbus Ohio 51-53; Personnel libn & Asst Prof in Lib Admin Ohio State U 54-65, Coord info serv & Assoc Prof Lib Admin Ctr for Voc & Tech Educ 66-. 9: ALA;-LAD (Personnel Admin Sect, Lib Org & Mgt Sect);-LED;-RTSD-ACRL; OhioLA; Amer Vocat Assn; ASIS. 13: Yes. 14: Info sci, admin, pub serv, tech serv, vocat educ. 15: 2985 Northwest blvd, Columbus Oh 43221.

WILSON, CORINNE (GREEN). b Muskogee Okla 21 Jl 24. 5: Rockford Col 39-43 (Lat, Gk) AB; UNC 43-47 (Lat, Gk) PhD, 50-51 BS in LS. 6: Fr, Ger, Lat, Sp, Gk. 7: Tchg fellow UNC 43-47, instr 47-48; Assoc Prof of Classics Queens Col (NC) 48-50; Ref libn LSU (Baton Rouge) 51-52; Chm Dept of Classics Hollins Col 59-60; Programmer Lat text Center for Programmed Instr, NYC 60-62; Libn & Asst Prof of Classics New Col 62-68, Libn & Assoc Prof of Classics 68-. 9: Amer Philol Assn; ALA; Classical Assn of the Middle West & So; FlaLA. 10: AAUW; Jr League; LWV. 13: Yes. 14: Admin. 15: New Col Lib, Box 1898, Sarasota Fla 33578.

WILSON, MRS CREOLA DANIEL. b Galax Va 17 D 01. 5: George Washington U 35 AB in LS. 6: Fr, Ger. 7: Catlgr US Supt of Documents Lib, Wash DC 37-42; Libn: US Fish & Wildlife Serv, Wash DC 42-44, US Bur of Mines, Wash DC 44-45, Catlg Div US Armed Forces Med Lib, Wash DC 45-55; Subj catlgr LC Tech Inf Div 55-56; Asst libn St Elizabeths Hosp Med Lib, Wash DC 56-58; Libn Defense Documentation Center, Cameron Stn, Alexandria Va 58-. 9: MedLA (Memb Com); LA (Wash DC Chap: Memb Com, sec, & chm Bio Scis Group). 11: Sustained Superior Performance Award, Defense Documentation Center. 14: Admin, catlg. 15: Rt 2 Box 103 A, Leesburg Va 22075.

WILSON, DONALD G. b Culver CITY Cal 7 Je 31. 4: Mary Keogh. 5: URedlands 48-52 (Govt) BA; UCLA 52-58 (Hist) MA; USoCal 59-60 MS LS; SUNY (Albany) 64-. 6: Sp, Ger. 7: UCLA Lib asst stack supv 54-56, Supv stack serv 56-59, Asst Geology Lib 59-60; Asst libn Tech Proc Cal State Col (Hayward) 60-61; Head libn UHawaii (Hilo) 61-64; Head tech serv SUNY(Albany) 64-67; Tchg fellow hist 66-67; UCal(Riverside); Acquis libn 67, Asst U libn res & tech serv 68, Act U libn 68-. 8: Proj chief, Data Processing Controlled Rclsf Implementation of DP Controlled Circ System, SUNY(Albany) 65. 9: ALA (Hawaii State Chm);-LAD (Recr Com 63-64); CalLA. 10: Beta Phi Mu; AAUP; AHA; Org Amer Histns; Amer Acad Pol & Soc Sci; Nat Wildlife Fed. 12: Co-ed "UCLA Library Staff Manual (58); Ed "Fantasy Annual (48). 13: Yes. 14: Resources & tech serv, univ lib admin. 15: 291 Hillandale ct, Riverside Ca 92507.

WILSON, EMILY (CALHOUN). b Atlanta. 4: W Janney Wilson. 5: Mercer U 42-44, 45-46 (Psych) AB; Vanderbilt U

44-45; UGa 49-50 (Pol Sci) MA; Drexel 61 (LS); Emory 61-62 (LS) MA. 6: Sp. 7: Libn Loudoun Valley High Sch, Purcellville Va 62-63; Elem sch libn Loudoun Co Sch Bd, Leesburg Va 65; Med libn Phila State Hosp, Phila 65-67; Ref libn Pub Lib Serv Ga Dept of Educ, Atlanta 68-. 10: LWV. 14: Psychiatry bks, child bks, catlg, ref. 15: 1106 Briar Vista ter NE, Atlanta Ga 30324.

WILSON, ENID. b Boston 3 My 21. 5: Brown 39-43 (Eng) AB; Simmons 52-53 (LS) MS. 7: Asst in lib Grad Sch of Pub Admin Harvard U 43-44, Seminar sec & in chg seminar lib Grad Sch of Pub Admin 44-52; Documents libn URI Lib 53-54; Catlgr Sch of Educ Lib Boston U 54-55; Catlg libn catlg div Boston U Libs 55-. 9: ALA-ACRL;-RTSD; SLA; MassLA; NELA; NE Tech Serv Libns (pres 64-65). 10: AAUW; Mass Soc for the Univ Educ of Women; Brookline Hist Soc. 14: Catlg. 15: 42 Brington rd, Brookline Mass 02146.

WILSON, EUGENE HOLT. b Harrison Ark 13 My 09. 4: Jane Stoddard. 5: UArk 26-28; Ark State Tchrs 28-30 (Eng) BA; UIll 31-33 (LS) BS, MA, 33-37 (Educ) PhD; Yale 40-41. 6: Fr, Sp, Ger. 7: Dir news serv Ark State Tchrs Col 30-31; Catlgr UIll Lib (Urbana) 33-37; Libn Ohio Wesleyan U 37-38; Asst libn Iowa State 38-42; Chief div tech processes USDA Lib, Wash DC 43; UColo: Dir of Libs 43-57, Dean of the Faculties 57-60, V-pres 59-. 8: Visiting lecturer, Columbia U Sch of Lib Serv, 46; Com on Sch Lib Study, No Central Assn, 53-55; Dir Human Rel Area Files, Yale 53-57; Lib Serv to Blind (nat survey) 56-57; Chm Air Force Acad Lib Adv Com, 56-58. 9: ALA (Life mem; Exec Bd, Coun, chm Com on Accred; serv on many coms);-ACRL (dir, Sect Offs, many coms); SLA; BSA; ColoLA (Life mem, pres); MPLA; Bibliog Center, Denver (pres). 10: AAUP; Beta Phi Mu; Newcomen Soc of Amer; Boulder Pub Lib Commsn; Rotary; Williams Found. 12: "A Survey of the Library of Montana State University, with M F Tauber, ALA (51). 13: Yes. 14: Admin. 15: 485 College ave, Boulder Colo 80302.

WILSON, FLORABELLE (WILLIAMS). b Indianapolis Ind 12 Ja 27. 4: John A Wilson. 5: Ind Central Col 49 (Educ) BS in Ed; IndU 61 MA in LS. 6: Ger. 7: Elem tchr Indianapolis pub schs 49-57; Asst libn Ind Central Col 57-. 9: ALA; IndLA. 10: Beta Phi Mu; AAUW; NAACP; Presbyt Interracial Coun. 14: Catlg, ref, a-v. 15: 5344 N Kenwood ave, Indianapolis In 46208.

WILSON, FLORENCE N. b Denver Colo 10 Je 17. 5: UDenver 35-39 (LS) AB. 6: Swedish. 7: catlgr WASH State Col 39-41; Catlgr Lincoln Pub Lib, Lincoln Neb 41-45; Instr UDenver Grad Sch of Libnship 46-54; Catlgr Denver Pub Lib 54-60, Head catlg dept 60-. 9: ALA; MPLA; ColoLA. 14: Catlg. 15: 2936 Stuart st, Denver Co 80212.

WILSON, FRANCES LOUISE (EGGEMAN). b Carthage Mo 21 O 34. 4: Doss Randell Wilson. 5: Tex State Col for Women 53-54 (LS); Tex Christian U 58-59; Tex Womans U 59-61 BS in LS, 61-62 MLS. 7: Asst catlgr UMo(Kan Cit) 62-. 9: ALA. 14: Catlg. 15: 5601 Charlotte, Kansas City Mo 64110.

WILSON, FRANCIS ROBERT. b Ithaca NY 12 Ja 22. 4: Ilse Rochelsohn. 5: Pasadena City Col 40-41 (Sp); Fresno State Col 41-43 (Sp) AB; Occidental 53-55 (Hist) MA; USoCal 55-57 MLS. 6: Sp, Fr, Portug, Ital. 7: Tr FBI, Wash DC summer 42; Lt (jg) USN 43-47, Lt (sg) 50-52; Catlgr USoCal 56-57; Catlgr Pasadena Pub Lib, Pasadena Cal 57-58; Asst city libn Monrovia Pub Lib, Monrovia Cal 58-59; Chief ref libn Cal Tech 59-62; Abstraxtor & indexer Aerojet-Gen Corp, Azusa Cal 63-64; Asst libn Electro-Optical Syst Xerox Corp, Pasadena Cal 64-68; Chief libn Stuart Div Atlas Chem Ind, Pasadena Cal 68-. 9: ASIS; SLA; MedLA; Med Lib Gp So Cal. 13: Yes. 14: Catlg, abstracting & indexing, info ret, lit searching, translating. 15: 1777 Las Lunas st, Pasadena Ca 91106.

WILSON, REV GENE REGINALD. b Charleston WVa 18 My 28. 5: St Joseph Col 51-53 (Liberal Arts); UDayton 54-56 (Liberal Arts) AB; UDetroit 60-61 (Educ, Psych, Sociol); Catholic U 63-64 MS in LS; Loyola U summers 65 & 66 (Rel Educ); Purdue summer 67 (A-v Educ). 6: Lat, Fr, Ital, Gk. 7: Asst Pastor St Adalbert Roman Catholic hurch, Cleveand 61-63; Libn, Eng tchr, Coun, Rel tchr Brunnerdale Sem (Canton Ohio) 64-. 9: ALA; CathLA; OhioLA; Stark Co LA. 10: Cath Interracial Coun; Urban League; Black Priests' Caucus; Human Rel Coun. 14: Ref. 15: Brunnerdale Sem, 4001 Brunnerdale ave, Canton Ohi 44718.

WILSON, GEOFFREY. b Ticonderoga NY 31 Jl 25. 4: Elizabeth DeCamp. 5: Yale 46-49 (Hist) BA; Columbia 51-53 (Hist) MA, 53-54 (LS) MS. 7: (Cpl) USMC 43-46; Free Lib of Phila: Libn I ya 54-57, Libn II br head 57-59, Libn III br head 59-61, Libn IV acad bk sel unit 62-65, Libn V head adult bk sel 66-. 9: ALA; PennLA. 14: Bk sel, lib serv to the culturally disadvantaged, pub rel. 15: 375 Gowen ave, Phila Pa 19119.

WILSON, GORDON G. b Mt Vernon NY 12 F 19. 4: Lenore Bryson. 5: DenisonU 36-40 (Art, ger) BA; UMich 63-66 AMLS. 6: Ger. 7: Illustrator (Advertising) Sears, Roebuck & Co, detroit 40-47; 1st Lieut (German interrogator) US Army, France, Germany 41-46; Mfrs Agent W R Wilson & Assoc, Detroit Mich 47-58; Mfrs Agent Plastic Sales Assoc, Grosse Pte Mich 58-63; Libn II Detroit Pub Lib 63-68; Ref & tech serv libn Detroit Inst of Tech 68-. 9: MichLA (Acad Libs Div). 10: YMCA. 11: Josenhans Award 65. 14: Ref, Ger lit, catlg. 15: 4320 Devonshire rd, Detroit Mi 48224.

WILSON, GREGORY C. b Wilmington Del 4 N 38. 5: UDel 56-61 BA; UPittsburgh 62-63 MLS; Harvard U Sch of Design 65-67 (Planning); Kennedy Inst (Govt). 6: Fr. 7: Photographic Sch USAF (A1/c), Denver 61-62; Child serv New Castle Co, Del 65; Resarch asst Grad Lib Sch UPittsburgh 62-63; Spec serv State Lib Commsn, Del 63-65; Asst dir Lamont Lib, Harvard U 65-68; Curator Theodore Roosevelt Collection Houghton Lib 68-. 8: Exec dir, Nat Lib Week, Del, 64; Consul for Cambridge Paper Box Co, to develop ms containers 67-68. 9: ALA; DelLA (Pub Rel Chm 64). 10: Harvard Lib Club; NE Wild Flower Assn; Del Wildlife Assn; Protectors of Wildlife; Sierra Club. 12: Ed "Journal of the State Library Commission, Delaware" (63-65).# 13: Yes. 14: Undergrad serv & spec tech collections, rare bks. 15: 58 Kirkland st, Cambridge Ma 02138.

WILSON, HAROLD DUNCAN. b Tacoma Wash 24 Ag 25. 4: Marguerite Bennetton. 5: SeattleU 46-49 (Eng) BA; UWash 49-51 BALS. 7: Seattle Pub Lib: Sr ref asst 51-55, Mun ref libn 66-; Libn Engring Lab Puget Sound Naval Shipyard, Bremerton Wash 55-66. 9: ALA; SLA; PNLA; WashLA. 14: Ref. 15: 2307 Shoreland dr So, Seattle Wa 98144.

WILSON, HELEN (GRAY). b Gainesville Tex 19 F 27. 4: Michael O Wilson Jr. 5: Gainesville Jr Col 44-45; N Tex State U 45-48, 50 (LS) BA. 7: Tchr McMurray Elem Sch, Gainesville Tex 48-49; Libn itinerant Krum Sch, Sanger Sch, Denton Co Tex 49-51; Libn Pampa Sr High Sch, Pampa Tex 65-. 15: 2214 Aspen dr, Pampa Tex 79065.

WILSON, HELEN W. b W Haben Conn 27 Mr 18. 5: Ill Wesleyan 46-47; UColo 47-50 (Eng, Hist, Psych) BA, 50-52 (Educ) Certif; UDenver 61-63 (Libnship) MA; Ft Lewis Col 69-(Anthrop). 7: AMM 2/c (Aviation) WAVES (US Navy), Tex, Hawaii 42-45; Var positions in bus, Denver 50-55; Asst personnel AF Res Records Ctr, Denver 55-62; Dir Anchorage Commun Col (UAlaska) 63-65; Ref libn ed psych div Humboldt State Col 65-67; Asst dir hd pub serv Ft Lewis Col 67-. 9: ColoLA; Hummoldt State Col LA (pres). 14: Ref. 15: Rte 1 Box 146, Durango Co 81301.

WILSON, JANE (MARY). b Chicago Ill 1 S 25. 5: Knox Col 42-44; UIll 44-46 (Hist) BA; UCal(Berkeley) 46-47 BLS. 7: Libn Cal Hist Soc, San Francisco 47-48; Air Force libn European Command 48-51; Asst libn Asia Foundation, San Francisco 51-54, 54-67; Act hd, Dept Spec Collections UCal(Davis) 67-68. 8: Travel in S Amer studying lib devel 69. 9: ALA(IRC Panel on UNESCO 58-59; chm Reception for For Libns 67);-ACRL (chm Law & Pol Sci Subsect Subj Specialists Sect 66-67); SLA (Intl Rel Com 64-66; dir San Francisco Bay Reg Chap 56-60); CalLA (Reg Research Coord Com 58; State chm 60-64; chm No Div 59-66; Long Range Planning Com 67-). 10: Bk Club of Cal. 13: Yes. 14: Lib devel abroad, spec libs, rare bks especially fine printing, ref, admin. 15: c/o E B Stofft, 2315 W Cherry st, Park Ridge Il 60068.

WILSON, JANE B(LISS). b Durham NC 24 F 14. 5: Duke 31-34 (Amer Lit) BA; UNC 36-37 BA in LS; Duke 46-47 (Amer Lit) MA. 6: Fr. 7: Med sec Duke Hosp, Durham NC 34-36; Child libn Detroit Pub Lib 37-40; Child & yp wk Durham Pub Lib, Durham NC 40-41; Child libn Olivia Raney Lib, Raleigh NC 41-43; Head Libn Reynolds High Sch, Winston-Salem (NC0 Pub Schs 44-46; Dir of Libs Durham City Schs, Durham NC 46-68; Pub lib consul on child serv NC State Lib 68-. 8: NC Governors Commsn on Lib Resources; Prof Consul on Sch Libs NC 63-64; Tchr, Lib Sci summer courses; UMd, UKy, UNC; Educ courses Duke U; Consul, H W Wilson Co; "Childrens Catalog". 9: ALA; NCLA (pres 52-54); SELA. 10: Alpha Delta Kappa. 12: Assoc ed "North Carolina Writers. 13: Yes. 14: Child lit, story-telling. 15: Rt 2 Farrington rd, Chapel Hill NC 27514.

WILSON, JESSIE ELIZABETH. b Keysville Va 20 Je 26. 5: Va State Col 43-44; Va UnionU 44-47 (Eng) BA; AtlantaU 47-48 BS in LS; UMd (College Park) 59, 60, 61; Johns

Hopkins 65-68 (Liberal Arts) MLA. 7: Libn Hoffman-Boston High Sch, Arlington Va 48-49; Adult serv libn R B Harrison Pub Lib, Raleigh NC 49-51; Lib asst Army Lib Pentagon Bldg 51-52; Hosp br libn post lib Army Spec Serv, Ft Devens Mass 52-54; Asst ref libn Va State Col 54-58; Libn: Bates High Sch, Annapolis Md 58-62, Corkran Jr High Sch, Glen burnie Md 62-63, Bates Jr High Sch, Annapolis Md 63-65; Libn & mgr Library Processing Ctr Bd of Educ of Anne Arundel Co, Annapolis Md 63-. 9: ALA; NEA; MdLA; ASch Libns Md; MdStateTA; Tchrs Assn Annr Arundel Co. 10: Delta Sigma Theta. 14: Tech proc, automation, acquis. 15: 7901 - 13th st NW, Washington DC 20012.

WILSON, JOHANNA (HANSEN). b Bridgeport Conn 15 Jl 37. 4: Ormon Lee Wilson. 5: Lebanon Valley Col 55-59 (Elem Educ) BS Educ; SUNY (Albany) MLS; UHawaii (Inst in Asian Studies) summer 68. 7: Tchr Pettibone Sch, New Milford Conn 59-60; Tchr Tinmouth sch, Tinmouth Vt 60-61; Tchr Middle Granville, Middle Granville NY 61-64; Libn Millbrook Elem Sch, Millbrook NY 64-66; Circ libn ColgateU 66-67; Libn Torrington High Sch, Torring sch, Torrington High Sch, Torrington Con 67-. 9: ALA; ConnLA; NELA; ConnTA; TorringtonEA. 10: Litchfield Hill Reg Planning Com. 14: Sch libnship. 15: RD 1 Belden rd, Burlington Ct 06085.

WILSON, JOHN H JR. b Toledo Ohio 2 S 22. 4: Dolphine Berkant. 5: Bowling Green State U 43-44 (Math, Physics) BS, 47-48 (Eng, Writing) MA. 7: Head ed br Naval Ordnance Test Station, China Lake Cal 51-57; Head tech infoAtlantic Research Corp, Alexandria Va 57-63; Head systems identif & anal Nat Referal Center, Wash DC 63-; Tech info div Lawrence Radiation Lab UCal (Berkeley). 9: ACS; ASIS. 12: "A A Michelson, biography. 13: Yes. 14: Info systems. 15: Univ of Cal (Berkeley), Lawrence Radiation Lab, Berkeley Ca 94707.

WILSON, LEWIS KENNETH. b Lamar Colo 15 Mr 25. 4: Wilma Flederman. 5: Colo Col 42-43, 46-47 (Liberal Arts) AA; UCLA 47-49 (Eng) BA; USoCal 5152 MS in LS. 6: Sp, Fr. 7: UCLA Lib: Stack supv 49-51, Temp asst Wm Andrews Clark Mem Lib 52, Geology Lib br libn 52-54, Asst head circ dept 54-56, Geology libn & coordinator of dept libs 56-57; Bus & tech libn, libn II Santa Barbara (Cal) Pub Lib 57-58; Act libn, III City & Co of Santa Barbara (Cal) Pub Lib 58-59; City Libn City of Palo Alto (Cal) Pub Lib 59-68; Managing dir Dept Commun Serv, Palo Alto Cal 68-. 8: UCal Adv Coun Lib Educ 60-64; Ed "California Librarian" 68. 9: CalLA (Docs Com 59, Adult Educ Com 61); Pub Lib Execs Central Cal pres 64). 10: Bd Dir Peninsula Kiwanis Club of Palo Alto; YMCA; United Fund. 14: Admin. 15: 1430 Parkinson ave, Palo Alto Ca 94301.

WILSON, LILLIAN M. b Minot ND 24 N 09. 5: Minot State Col 28-30, 35-36 (Hist, Soc Sci) BA; UDenver summers 47, 48, 51-53 (LS) MA; UPittsburgh 66. 7: Tchr Pub Sch, Towner ND 44-47; Libn Sr High Sch, Minot ND 47-58; Asst libn Minot State Col 58-67; Libn elem schs, Valley City ND 67-. 9: NEA; ALA; NDEA; NDLA. 10: Bus & Prof Womens Club; Delta Kappa Gamma; AAUW. 14: Ref, tchg. 15: 365 Third ave NW, Valley City ND 58072.

WILSON, LINDA (LOU). b Rochester Minn 17 N 45. 5: UMinnesota (Morris) 63-67 (Sp & Math) BA, 67-68 (LS) MA. 6: Sp, Norwegian, Fr. 7: Clk Lib UMinnesota (Morris) 63-67; Husker libby's Canning Factory, Rochester Minn summer 64; Bkkeeper Vernon Co-op Creamery Assn, Hayfield Minn summer 65 & 66; Libn UCal (Riverside) 68-. 9: So Cal Tech Proc Gp. 14: Ref, catlg & govt docs. 15: 6567 Harley st, Riverside Ca 92506.

WILSON, LOUIS ROUND. b Lenoir NC 27 D 1876. 5: Haverford Col 1895-98 (Classics); UNC 1898-99 (Classics) AB, 01-02 (Eng) AM, 02-05 (Eng) PhD. 6: Fr. 7: UNC(Chapel Hill); Libn 01-32, Dir Div of Ext 12-20, Dir U Press 22-32, Dir Sch of Lib Sci 31-32; Dean Grad Lib Sch UChicago 32-42; Prof Sch of Lib Sci UNC 42-47, 51-59. 8: Chm NC Lib Commsn 09-16; Exec Com Amer Coun on Educ 36-39; Org Friends of the Lib UNC, chm 45-55; Chm, Exec Com Tenn Valley Lib Coun 46-49; Consul on devel UNC 51-54; Consul on consol UNC 59-; Consul on lib admin UNC 59-; Del to Brit Lib Assn & Com of the IFLA, Cheltenham Eng, 31; ALA del to Internat Conf of Libs & Bibliog, Madrid Spain, 35. 9: ALA (Life mem, pres 35-36; mem & chm Bd of Educ for Libnship 25-32, Chm Spec Com on Fed Aid 35-36, mem & chm Lib Ext Bd 36-41); AALS (pres 38-39); NCLA (sec 04-09, pres 10-11, 21-22, & 30-31); SELA (pres 24-26); NC Lib Commsn Chm 09-16. 10: Phi Beta Kappa. 11: Carnegie Corp Medallion, 32; LLD Haverford Col, 32; D Litt UDenver, 32; LLD UNC, 34; White Medal, 39; DHL Catawba Col, 49; Herbert Putnam Hon Award ALA, 54; UNC (Chapel Hill) Lib named Louis Round Wilson Lib, 56; Beta Phi Mu Award for Distinguished Serv, 60. 12: Auth "Chaucers Relative Constructions (06),"County Library Services in the South with E A Wright Wight "The Geography of Reading (38), "The University Library with M F Tauber (45, "The Library in College Instruction with others (51), "The History of the University of North Carolina, 1900-1930 (57), "Harry Woodburn Chase (60), "The Library of the First State University (60), "The University of North Carolina Under Consolidatiom, 1931-1963(64); Ed: "Library Trends (37), "The Role of the Library in Adult Education (37), "The Practice of Book Selection (40), "The Library in General Educaton (43), "Librares of the Southeast (49), "The Selected PAPERS OF Cornelia Philips Spencer (53); Gen ed: UNC "Alumni Review (12-24), UChicago "tudies in Library Science 25 v (33-43), UN "Sesquicentennial Publications 18 v (43-53); Ed Bds: "Studies in Philology (10-14), "Social Forces (22-32), "Journal of American Association of Adult Education (31-41), "Library Quarterly (32-). 13: Yes. 14: Admin, ext, federal aid to lib, lib educ, lib surveys. 15: 607 E Rosemary st, Chapel Hill NC 27514.

WILSON, LOUISE L (LOEFFLER). b Pittsburgh Penn 15 My 31. 4: Robert K Wilson. 5: Chatham Col 49-52 (Eng) BA. 6: Fr, Ital, Ger. 7: Pension planner, actuary Marsh & McLennan, Boston & Pittsburgh 52-53, 57-58; Act dir pub rel Chatham Col 55-57; Budget analyst Allstate Ins, Pittsburgh Penn 61; Libn research assoc writer Foundation for Study of Cycles, Pittsburgh Penn 61-66; Lit searchr analyst KAS Ctr UPittsburgh 67; Info coord Alcoa, Pittsburgh Penn 67-. 12: "Catalogue of Cycles: Part I-Economics (64). 13: Yes. 14: Catlg, ref, res, info retr. 15: Aluminum Co of Amer 1501 Alcoa bldg, Pittsburgh Pa 15219.

WILSON, LUCY (COLE). b Winthrop Mass 2 D 20. 4: Charles George Wilson. 5: Fla State Col for Women 38-42 (Lat) BA; Columbia 46-47 (LS) BS. 6: Sp, Fr. 7: Libn Ft Meade High Sch, Ft Meade Fla 42-43; Supv libn elem schs, Gainesville Fla 43-44; Yeoman 2/c WAVES US Navy Educ Off 44-46; Hosp libn Pub Lib Flint Mich 47-49; Med libn VA Hosp, Indianapolis 49-52, Chief Libn 52-54; Sondley ref libn Pack Mem Lib, Asheville NC 62-63; Libn Tobacco Lit Serv D H Hill Lib, Raleigh NC 64-. 9: ALA; SLA (Ind Chap:chm Med & Hosp Lib Sect 53); NCLA; SELA. 10: PTA; Girl Scouts; Womans Club, NC State U. 15: 1101 Lakeside dr, Garner NC 27529.

WILSON, MARILYN J (FIELD). b San Francisco Cal 5 Je 28. 4: Darrell L Wilson. 5: StanfordU 47-51 (Intl Rel) BA; ULund (Sweden) 48-49; UMinn 52-53 (Scandinavian Area Studies); UCal (Berkeley) 59-60 MLS. 6: Swedish, Ger, Fr, Sp, Ital. 7: Libn 9jr) NY Pub Lib 61-63; Asst libn Carnegie Endowment for Intl Peace, NYC 63-64; Sr libn Sunnyvale Pub libn Sunnyvale Pub Lib, Sunnyvale Calif 65-66; Libn III UCal (San Diego) 66-. 9: CalLA. 10: UCal Lib Schs Alum Assn; Beta Phi Mu. 14: Ser, ref. 15: 5736 Ferber st, San Diego Ca 92122.

WILSON, MARION CATHERINE (CONROY). b Edmonton Alta Can 28 Ja 16. 4: William Arthur Wilson. 5: UALTA 33-36 (Eng Lit) BA; UWash 41-42 BA in Libnship. 6: Fr. 7: Lib asst UAlta 36-41; Jr catlgr UWash 42-43; Royal Canadian Air Force Lib clerk (Cpl), Vancouver BC 43-45; Catlgr British Bk Centre, London Eng 45-46; Catlgr Westmount Pub Lib, Westmount Que 60-62; Assoc ed Canadian Periodical Index, Ottawa 63-67; Field off & Exec sec CanLA 67-70; Hd period sect, ref br Natl Lib Ottawa Can 70-. 8: Trustee, Notre Dame de Grace Lib for Boys & Gils, Montreal 53-62, Chm of Bd 58-60. 9: CanLA; ALA; Inst of Profess Libns Ont; Lib Assn Ottawa. 13: Yes. 14: Indexing. 15: Natl Lib, Ottawa Can.

WILSON, MARTIN PAUL. b Malden Mass 19 O 39. 4: Rebecca Mastry. 5: UBuffalo 60-61; Brevard Jr Col 61-65 AA; Florida StateU 66-67 (Eng) BA; UOre 68-69 MLS. 6: Fr. 7: Catlgr USoFla 69-. 13: Yes. 14: Catlg. 15: 4705 Citrus cir 11, Tampa Fl 33617.

WILSON, MELBA (MAE MORRISON). b Calgary Alta Can 14 Jl 28. 4: Douglas M Wilson. 5: UBC 47-50 (Eng, Hist) BA; Toronto 50-51 BLS; McGill 68- (LS). 6: Fr. 7: Ref libn UAlta 51-56; Sci libn Loyola Col (Montreal) 62-64; Lecturer YWCA Adult Educ Centre, Montreal 65-; Lecturer evening div Loyola of Montreal 63-. 8: AltaLA List of Can bks for small libs 57-59; Loyola Col Vander Lib Bldg Adv Com, 63-64. 9: CanLA; QueLA (Eng sec). 10: Jr League of Montreal; YWCA; Bd Montreal Oral Sch for Blind. 13: Yes. 14: Ref, sci adult educ. 15: 129 Percival ave, Montreal 263 Can.

WILSON, MYRA JO (WALKER). b Mendenhall Miss 20 Ap 34. 4: William Ray Wilson. 5: Miss Col 53-56 (Eng) BA; UMiss 61 MLS. 6: Fr. Lat. 7: High sch libn: Belzoni Miss 56-58, Port Gibson Miss 58-60, Shaw Miss 56-58, Port Gibson Miss 58-60, Shaw Miss 60,; Libn Delta State Col 68-. 9: ALA; MissLA. 10: AAUW; Delta State Col Faculty Wives Club. 14: Catlg. 15: PO Box 1843, Delta State Col, Cleveland Ms 38732.

WILSON, NINA M(ARIE). b Gravelly Ark 9 Ap 19. 5: UCLA 47-50 (Pre-Lib Sci) BA; USoCal 50 (LS); Tex Woman's U (LS) MA. 7: (M/Sgt) US Army, US, France & Germany 42-46; Los Angeles Pub Lib: Clerk-typist 46-50, Child libn 51-56, Sr libn 56-60, Prin libn 60-. 9: ALA; CalLA. 10: Coord Coun No Hollywood; San Fernando Valley Welfare Planing Coun. 14: Ref, admin. 15: 6652 Belmar ave, Reseda Ca 91135.

WILSON, PATRICIA ANN. b Dustin Okla 28 S 35. 5: Okla BaptistU 52-56 (Hist) BA; USoCal 62-63 MLS. 6: Sp. 7: Trade bill clk Union Bank, Los Angeles 57-59; Sales correspondent Interchem Corp, Los Angeles 60-62; Ref libn Los Angeles Pub Lib 63-67, Sr libn 67-. 9: ALA; CalLA. 10: Museum Alliance. 14: Ref. 15: 4855 Lexington ave, Los Angeles Ca 90029.

WILSON, PATRICK (G). b Santa Cruz Cal 29 D 27. 5: UCal (Berkeley) 45-49 (Philos) BA, 52-53 BLS, 57-60 (Philos) PhD. 6: Fr. 7: Lib asst UCal (Berkeley) 50-53, Ref libn 53-54, Libn for South Asia Studies 54-59; Instr Philosophy Dept UCLA 60-61, Asst Prof 61-65; Asst Prof Sch of Libnship UCal (Berkeley) 65-68, Assoc Prof 68-. 12: "Two Kinds of Power: an Essay on Bibliographical Control" (68). 13: Yes. 14: Theory of bibliog org, content analysis. 15: School of Librarianship Univ of Cal, Berkeley Ca 94720.

WILSON, PAULINE. b Cleveland Ohio 26 My 19. 5: Kent StateU 37-40; Baldwin Wallace Col 59-60 (Hist) BA; West Res 60-61 MLS; UIll 68-69 (Soc Sci). 7: Hd y-a dept Lakewood Pub Lib, Lakewood Ohio 61-67; Asst libn & instr lib sci Ill StateU 67-. 9: ALA. 12: Ed "Top of the News" (65-66). 14: Ref, subj collection, soc scis. 15: 104 Eisenhower dr apt C10, Bloomington Il 61701.

WILSON, REBECCA (MASTRY). b St Petersburg Fla 18 Je 44. 4: Martin P Wilson. 5: St Petersburg Jr Col 62-64 AA; Fla StateU 64-67 (Libnship, Eng) BA, MSLS. 6: Sp. 7: Map room libn UOre (Eugene) 68-. 9: ALA; West Assn Map Libns. 10: Beta Phi Mu. 14: Map libnship, ref. 15: 4705 Citrus cir #11, Tampa Fl 33617.

WILSON, SALLY MAY (ALEXANDER). b Providence 17 D 25. 4: William Charles Wilson. 5: Hood Col 44-48 (Hist) AB; Simmons 51-52 (LS) MS. 7: Asst to ref libn NS Reg Libs, Halifax NS 52-54; Catlgr Emerson Col Lib 64-65; Asst libn in catlg RI Col Lib 65-66, Asst libn in charge of tech serv 66-. 14: Catlg. 15: 61 Arlington, Providence RI 02906.

WILSON, THOMAS B. b Detroit 1 Ag 32. 5: UFla 53-57 (Hist) BA; Columbia 62-64 MSLS. 6: Fr. 7: Head of circ Washington hington Sq Lib NYU 61-65; Dir Friendship Lib Fairleight Dickinson U 65-. 9: NJLA. 10: NY Hist Soc; NJ Hist Soc; Geneal Soc NJ. 12: Ed "The Ontario Register". 14: Americana. 15: Box 217, Madison NJ 07940.

WILSON, VIRGINIA (MURPHEY). b Augusta Ga 29 Ap 07. 5: Converse Col 25-29 (Piano) B Mus; UGa 36-38 (Eng) AB; Emory 38-39 AB in LS. 7: Jr catlgr UGa 39-42, Ser catlgr 44-46; Libn clsf documents Air U Lib, Maxwell AFB Ala 46-49, Chief bks catlg 49-52, Chief bks-separates 52-58, Chief bks-ser catlg 58-67, Chief bks systs 67-. 9: SLA; AlaLA. 14: Catlg. 15: 29 The Prado, Montgomery Al 36105.

WILSON, VIRGINIA L (CAVE). b Seattle Wash 14 N 30. 5: UWash 48-52 (Hist) BA, 52-53, 65-69 (child Serv) MLS. 6: Sp, Portu. 7: Br libn Kitsap Reg Lib, Bremerton Wash 69-. 14: Child serv. 15: Rte 6 Box 6320, Bainbridge Island Wa 98110.

WILSON, VIVIAN (LUNSFORD). b Hamilton Ohio 6 My 16. 4: Joseph Paul Wilson. 5: Mars Hill Col 38-40 AA; Coker Col 40-42 (Soc Studies) AB; Peabody 42 & 43 BS in LS; Wake Forest Col 52. 6: Fr, Ger. 7: Asst libn Mars Hill Col 42-48; Catlgr Wake Forest Col Lib 48-52; Tchr AurelianSprings High Sch, Littleton NC 54-58; Libn Roanoke Rapids High Sch, Roanoke Rapids NC 58-60, Law Libn Wake ForestCol Law Lib 60-. 9: AALL; SE ALL. 10: Delta Kappa Gamma. 14: Law. 15: 1971 Faculty dr, Winston-Salem NC 27106.

WILSON, WILLIAM G(ERRISH). b Shreveport La. 3 O 36. 5: MIT 54-55 (Arch); LSU 55-58 (Econ) BA; UMich 58-60 AMLS; Emory summer 67. 7: Lib Scholar/Fellow Undergrad Lib UMich 58-60; Asst catlgr Beloit Col Lib 60-62, Ref libn 62-64; Sr libn gen ref dept Enoch Pratt Free Lib, Baltimore 64-65, Admin asst gen ref dept 65-67; Libn & Assoc Prof Catawba Col 67-. 8: Ref staff, Lib/USA, NY Worlds Fair, 65. 9: ALA; NCLA (chm Lib Affairs Com of Piedmont Univ Ctr 69-70). 10: Beta Phi Mu; ACLU; Mu Sigma Rho; Tau Kappa Alpha; Omicron Delta Kappa; Phi Kappa Phi; AAUP. 13: Yes. 14: Acquis, admin. 15: Catawba Col, Salisbury NC 28144.

WILT, H DAVID. b Millersburg Penn 16 D 39. 5: Lycoming col 57-1 (Psych, Eng) BA; Drexel 62-64 MS in LS. 7: Asst in ref dept J V Brown Lib, Williamsport Penn 61; Child libn Free Lib of Phila 62-65; Reg child libn Los Angeles Co Pub Lib, Los Angeles 65-67; Child & ya specialist Bro-Dart, Williamsport Penn 67-. 9: ALA (Jr Mem RT); PennLA. 10: Lambda Chi Alpha; Williamsport Players. 12: Co-comp "Colonial American Round-Up, Bro-Dart" (69). 14: Child serv, story-telling. 15: 413 Rural ave, Williamsport Pa 17701.

WILT, M(ATTHEW) RICHARD. b Hollidaysburg Penn 14 Al 24. 5: San Luis Rey Sem 42-46 (Philos) BA; Catholic U 48-49 (Hist) MA; Columbia 54-55 MSLS. 6: Fr, Sp, Lat. 7: Tchr-libn Highland Hall Prep, Hollidaysburg Penn 49-55; Acquis libn Dept of Defense, Wash DC 55-56; Foreign order libn Sidney Kramer Bks, Wash DC 56-57; Acquis libn Georgetown U 57-60; Exec Dir Catholic Lib Assn, Haverford Penn 60-. 8: Bk-buying consul Georgetown U Bkstore, 57-60; Part-time faculty; Drexel Sch of Lib Sci, 65, Villanova U Sch Lib Sci 68. 9: ALA; CNLA (Exec Bd 65-67); PennLA (Conf Planning Com 65, Chm Eval Com 65, Exec Com 68, Exec Bd 68-69, Nat Lib Wk chm 69); Pub Rel Assn Phila (chm 69). 10: Nat Assn of Exhib Mgrs; Cath Press Assn. 12: Ed "Catholic Library World (62-63). 13: Yes. 14: Acquis, admin, pub rel. 15: 1530 Locust st, Phila Pa 19102.

WIMAN, WILLIAM J. b Rock Island Ill 16 F 33. 5: Loras Col 54-59 (Philos) BA; UIll 63-64 (LS) MS. 7: US Army Radio Operator (Cpl) 52-54; Tchr Ottumwa High Sch, Ottumwa Iowa 60-63; Libn Freeport Pub Lib, Freeport Ill 64-. 9: ALA; IllLA (chm Memb Com). 10: Kiwanis. 14: Admin. 15: 1531 W Lincoln, Freeport Il 61032.

WIMBISH, EMERY (JR). b Atlanta. 5: Clark Col (Eng) AB; Atlanta 49 BLS; Columbia 62-63. 6: Fr. 7: Asst libn Vail Mem Lib Lincoln U (Penn) 50-65, Act head libn 65-67, Hd libn 67-. 8: Danforth Found rep 67-; New Lib Bldg Com 68-. 9: ALA-ACRL (Bd Dirs Phila Chap 61-64; v-pres, pres-elect Dela Valley Chap 68-); PennLA. 10: YMCA; NAACP; Commun Players, Lincoln U; AAUP. 14: Acquis. 15: Box 132, Lincoln University Pa 19352.

WIMMER, THEODORE R. b Ophir Ore 10 Ag 30. 5: Pacific U 47-48 (Eng); Humboldt State Col 48-51 (Eng) BA; UCal (Berkeley) 54-55 MLS. 6: Fr, Sp. 7: R A Gleeson Lib USan Francisco: ASST catlgr 55-56, Head catlgr 57-60, Acquis libn 60-65, Head of tech Processes 65-68; Catlgr Humboldt State Col 69-. 14: Acquis, rare bks, catlg. 15: Humboldt State Col Lib, Arcata Ca 95521.

WINANS, BARBARA ANN. b Moderly Mo 15 O 39. 5: Christian Col 57-59 (Soc Studies) AA; UMo 59-61 (Soc Studies) BEd, 64- (Curriculum, LS) MEd. 7: Soc studies tchr Fulton high Sch, Fulton Mo 61-63; Libn & instr UMo (Columbia) 65-67; Libn West Jr High, Columbia Mo 67-68; Libn Hickman High Sch, Columbia Mo 68-. 9: ALA; NEA; MoASchL (v-pres); MoStateTA. 10: AAUW; Pi Lambda Theta; Zeta Tau Alpha. 13: Yes. 14: Sch libs. 15: 105 W Broadway, Columbia Mo 65201.

WINANS, NANCY (ALLISON). b Franklin Penn 19 Mr 31. 4: Ralph J Winans. 5: Clarion State Col 49-53 (Phys Sci, Math) BS in Ed; Carnegie 56-58, MLS. 6: Ger. 7: Tchr chem phy, math Mars High Sch, Mars Penn 53-54; CHEM LIT SEARCHER Callery Chem Co, Callery Penn 54-56, Head Libn 56-59; Head Libn PITTSBURGH PLate Glass Co, Harmerville Penn 59-60; Research libn Youngstown Sheet & Tube Co, Youngstown Ohio 60-62; Asst libn Goodyear Tire & Rubber Co,Akron Ohio 62-64, Tech patent libn 64-; Ref libn Akron Pub Lib, Akron Ohio 67. 8: Asst tech ed, Callery Chem Co, 56-57, Consul on Machine Retrieval Systems, 55-59. 9: SLA; ACS. 13: Yes. 14: Computer retrieval methods, catlg spec materials. 15: Rt 1 Box 367, Berlin Center Oh 44401.

WINBURY, BLANCHE. b New York NY 27 S 21. 4: Martin M Winbury. 5: LIU 39-42 (Bio) BS; Caldwell Col 63-65 (LS); Newark State Col 64-66 (Educ). 6: Fr. 7: Bio tech: USDA, Bettsville Md 42-44, NOPCO, Harrison NJ 45-46, Reed & Cornrick, Jersey City NJ 46-47; Pediatric research Dr H Jacobs, Chicago 48-49; Sub libn Jr & Sr High Schs, W Orange & Livingston NJ 64-66; Libn David Brearley Reg High Sch,

Kenilworth NJ 66-. 9: ALA; NJStateLA. 10: LWV; Americans Abroad. 15: 27 Baker rd, Livingston NJ 07039.

WINCH, BARBARA (SCHEELE). b NY 24 Mr 42. 4: Kevin Winch. 5: Hunter Col 59-63 (Eng Lit) BA; Simmons 65-66 MS in LS. 7: Tchr Commack Pub Schs, Commack NY 63-65; Ref libn columbia 66-68; Acquis libn Brooklyn Col 68-. 9: NY State Tech Serv Libns; LACUNY. 14: Acquis, ref. 15: 188 Sixth ave, Brooklyn NY 11217.

WINCHELL, CAROL (FRENCH). Columbus Ohio 16 Jl 36. 4: James F Winchell. 5: Ohio State U 54-58 (Music) BM, 58-60 (Music) MA; West Res 62-64 MSLS. 7: Med aid Ohio State U Hosp, Columbus 58-60; (Music) Lib Ohio State U Libs 60-62, Various positions 64-, Ref libn & main lib 64-. 9: ALA. 14: Readers adv, ref. 15: 3840 Schirtzinger, Columbus Oh 43220.

WINCHELL, CONSTANCE M(ABEL). b Northampton Mass 2 N 1896. 5: UMich 14-18 (Humanities) AB; Lib Sch of the NY Pub Lib 19-20 Certif; Columbia 28-30 (LS) MS. 7: Libn Central High Sch, Duluth Minn 18-19; Asst lighthouse div US Merchant Marine Serv, NY 20: Reviser catlg dept UMich 20-21, Ref asst 21-23; Head catlgr Amer Lib in Paris 24-25; Columbia U Lib: Ref asst 25-33, Asst ref libn 33-41, Chief ref libn 41-62. 8: Ed wk, 62-67. 9: ALA-ACRL. 11: Isadore Gilbert Mudge Citation, 60. 12: "Locating Books for Interlibrary Loan (30); "Guide to Reference Books 7th ed (51) & sups; "Guide to Reference Books 8th ed (67) 13: Yes. 14: Ref. 15: Box 642 Rte 2, New Paltz NY 12561.

WINCKLER, PAUL ALBERT. b Brooklyn NY 17 My 26. 4: Anne O'Regan. 5: St John's U 44-48 (Eng) BA; Pratt 49-50 MLS; NYU 48-49, 53 (Eng) MA. 6: Fr. 7: Libn Brooklyn Pub Lib, Brooklyn NY 50-51; Libn St John's U 51-56; Lib dir Bryant Lib, Roslyn NY 56-60; Libn Suffolk Co Commun Col 60-62; Assoc Prof lib sci Grad Lib Sch LIU 62-68, Prof lib sci 68-. 8: Mem, Res Com, CW Post Col 64-65; Chm, Curr Com, Grad Lib Sch, LIU 67-, Mem Acad Coun. 9: LPRC (treâs 59-60); ALA;-ACRL (Univ Sect, Rare Bks Sect);-LED (Spec Com on Illust Materials for Hist of Bks & Libs, Tchrs Sect);-LAD (Lib org & Mgt sect; Pub Rel Sect);-RSD (Hist Sect); NYLA (Col & Univ Libs Sect); Nassau Co LA (Exec Bd 57-61, 1st v-pres 59-61; Com duties 57-60); Suffolk Co LA; NY Lib Club; Amer Assn Higher Educ; NEA; Printing Hist Soc (England). 10: AAUP; Glen Cove United Civic Assn; D'Oyly Carte Opera Trust Ltd; Phi Delta Kappa; Kappa Delta Pi; LI Arts Coun. 12: "Bibliography of Source Materials for Library Research" (65); "Charles Clarence Williamson (1877-1965); His Professional Life and Work in Librarianship and Library Education in the United States," PhD diss NYU (68); "History of Books and Printing" (58); "Library Periodicals Directory" (67). 13: Yes. 14: Hist of bks & printing, ref servs, hist of libs, lib educ. 15: 49 Hammond rd, Glen Cove LI NY 11542.

WINDHAM, EULA HEARD. b Tifton Ga 3 F 19. 5: Womans Col of Ga 36-40 (Hist) AB; So Baptist Theol SEm 47-50 (Religious EDUC) MRE; Emory 56 MLS. 7: Tchr Tifton pub schs, Tifton Ga 40-46; Bkkepper State Nat Bank, Sheffield Ala 46; Case wker Dept of Pub Welfare, Tifton Ga 46-47; dept leader Ga Baptist SS Dept, Atlanta 49-55; Asst libn Hardin-Simmons U 57-61; Libn Middle Ga Col 61-. 9: NEA; ALA-RTSD (Loc Area Chm); SELA; GaLA (chm RTSD0; Jr Col Assn Ga (chm Lib Div); GaEA (loc pres). 12: "Sanford Library Handbook" (62); "Roberts Memorial Library Handbook" (65). 14: Admin. 15: Middle Georgia Col, Cochran Ga 31014.

WINDSOR, ELIZABETH (ARNOLD). b Austin Tex 20 Je 09. 5: Uill 31 (Hist) BA, 32 BS in LS, 38 MS. 6: Fr. 7: Libn Pub Lib, Charleston Ill 32-35; Libn Flagg Twp Pub Lib, Rochelle Ill 35-37; Asst ref libn Hackley Pub Lib, Musekgon Mich 38-40; Ref libn Stewart Mem Lib Coe Col 40-42, Libn 42-54; Head ref dept Iowa State U of Sci & Tech 54-. 9: ALA (Coun 59-62, Subscription Bks Com 55-59);-ACRL; RSD (Bd Dirs 59-62, Catlg Use Com 63-67); IowaLA (chm Col Sect 55, mem Auditing Com & Nomin Com, Bd Dirs 66-67, mem Johnson Brigham Plaque 66-69). 10: AAUP; AAUW; PEO; Phi Beta Kappa; Phi Kappa Phi; Beta Phi Mu. 14: Ref, col & univ libs, maps. 15: 2004 McCarthy rd, Ames Ia 50010.

WINDSOR, MARYLEE B(LACKMAN). b Cottonwood Ala 24 D 06. 4: Arthur B Windsor. 5: Col of Charleston 24-26; Howard Col 26-28 (Eng) AB; UAla summers 42, 59-62 (LS) MA; UGa summer 65 (LS). 7: Elem tchr, Springville Ala 28; Eng tchr, Ragland Ala 29; Hist, Fr tchr, Miss 31-34; Elem tchr, ALA 41-43, Eng, hist tchr 43-44; Tchr Cottonwood High Sch, Cottonwood Ala 44-53, tchr-libn 53-67, libn 67-. 8: Libn Cottonwood Baptist Church. 9: NEA; AlaEA; AlaLA; AlaASchL; Houston Co TA (v-pres). 10: Alpha Delta Kappa. 11: Civic Club Outstanding Serv Award. 14: Lib serv to grades 1-12. 15: P O Box 126, Cottonwood Ala 36320.

WINDSOR, RUTH J (MILLER). b Toronto Can 12 O 22. 4: David Windsor. 5: UToronto 39-43 BA, 45-46 BLS. 6: Fr. 7: Child libn Lethridge Pub Lib, Alta Can 46-49; Libn, Baie Comeau Que Can 50-52; Child libn Islington Borough Lib, London England 53; Catlgr St John Pub Lib, St John NB Can 54-55, Chief libn 56-59; Reader's adv Ottawa Pub Lib, ottawa Can 60-62; Lib asst NYC Pub Lib 63; Sch libn PSBGM, Montreal 64-. 15: 33 Staynor st, Montreal 215 PQ Can.

WINDUS, CREE MARGUERITE. b NYC 21 Je 37. 5: Adelphi 55-57 (Elem Educ); NY State Col of Educ 57-60 (Elem Educ) BS; Columbia 63-64 (LS) MS. 7: Lib trainee Queens Borough Pub Lib, Queens NY 63-64; Libn Camp Henry Lib 64-65; Libn Camp Carroll Depot 65-66; Libn RC #4 Lib 66-67; Area lib dir RC #1 67-. 9: ALA. 11: Outstanding Performance Award, Dept of the Army 67. 14: Pub lib wk. 15: 26-14 96th st, E Elmhurst NY 11369.

WINE, H EUGENE. b Dayton Ohio 29 Jl 28. 4: Marilyn P Wine. 5: Miami U 50 AB; Ohio State U 55 B Ed; West Res 58 MS in LS. 6: Fr, Sp. 7: Asst ref libn Union Col 58-61, ref libn 61-64; Libn Ind U Northwest Campus 64-65: Libn Miami-Dade Jr Col Palmetto Center 65-66, Libn S Campus 66-68, Dir pub serv Learning Resources Ctr 68-. 9: ALA; FlaLA. 10: PHi Beta Kappa. 14: Admin, ref. 15: 17860 SW 113 ave, Miami Fl 33157.

WINEARLS, DAPHNE JOAN. b Toronto 4 N 37. 5: Toronto 55-59 (Hist) BA, 59-60 BLS. 6: Fr. 7: Libn Toronto Pub Lib Bibliog Center 60-62; Libn India Off Lib, London Eng 62-64; Map libn UToronto 64-. 9: SLA; Assn of Canadian Map Libs; chm, Natl Union Catalogue com 68-. 12: Co-comp "Directory of Canadian Map Collections" (Toronto) 69. 14: Map libnship. 15: Univ of Toronto Lib, Toronto 5 Can.

WINFREY, DORMAN HAYWARD. b Henderson Tex 4 S 24. 4: Ruth Carolyn Byrd. 5: UTex 50 (Hist) BA, 51 (Hist) MA, 62 (Hist) PhD. 7: US Army Artillery (Sgt Maj) Tech 4th Grade 43-46; Soc sci research assoc; Research in Tex Hist, Tex State Hist Assn UTex 46-58; State archivist, Austin Tex 58-60; Archivist UTex 60-61; Dir-libn Tex State Lib 62-; Chm of State Bd of Lib Examiners, Austin Tex 62-; Chm of State Records Preservation Adv Com, Austin 65-. 8: Chm, Tex State Bd of Lib Examiners, 62-; Chm, State Records Preserv Ad Com 65-; Adv Com on Lib Research & Training Projs, HEW 66-. 9: ALA-AAStateL (chm Jt Com on Loc & State Hist); SAA; Amer Assn State & Loc Hist; AHA; TexLA; SWLA; Tex State Hist Assn (v-pres, (Fellow & Exec Coun mem); Tex Inst of Letters; Austin Lib Club (past pres). 10: Austin Com For REl; West Hist Assn; Org Amer Histns; So Hist Assn; Phi Alpha Theta; Pi Sigma Alpha. 12: Ed "Texas Indian Papers, 1825-1859 3 v (59-60); "A History of Rusk County, Texas (61); "Julien Sidney Devereux and his Monte Verdi Plantation (64); "Arturo Toscanini in Texas" (67); Staff writer,"The Hndbook of Texas (52). 13: Yes. 14: Rare bks, ref. 15: Tex State Lib Drawer DD - Capitol sta. Austin Tex 78711.

WING, DONALD GODDARD. b Athol Mass 18 Ag 04. 4: Charlotte Farquhar. 5: Yale 22-26 (Eng) BA; Harvard 26-27 (Eng) AM; Trinity(Cambridge) 27-28 (Eng); Yale 29-32 (Eng) PhD. 6: Fr. 7: Yale U Lib; Order dept 28-, Asst ref libn 32-35, Libn Linonia & Brothers Lib 35-, Head accessions 35-39, Assoc libn 39-, Assoc libn in chg of collections 66-. 8: Libn Silliman Col, Yale 41-60; Consul Syracuse U Lib, 61. 12: "Short-Title Catalogue, 1641-1700" 3 v (45-51). 13: Yes. 14: Acquis. 15: Rimmon rd, Woodbridge Ct 06525.

WINGATE, ROBERT BRAY. b Harrisburg Penn 21 S 25. 5: Lebanon Valley Col 44-48 (Biol) AB; Penn Acad of Fine Arts summer 48 (Fine Art); Johns Hopkins 48-51 (Med Illustration) Certif; Drexel 59-60 (LS) MS. 6: Ger. Fr. 7: Med illustrator researchm; walter Reed Army Med Center, Wash DC 54-56, Opthalmol Found Inc, NYC 56-60, Wash Med CEnter Georgetown U Mitchell Found 56-60p Ref libn Harrisburg Pub Lib, Harrisburg, Penn 60; Ref libn Penn State Lib 61-64; Libn Penn Dept of Agric, Harrisburg Penn 64-65; Head rare bks sect Penn State Lib 65-. 8: Free-lance med illus. 9: Royal Soc of Arts, London (Life Fellow); Royal Soc of Med, LONDON; BSA.12 VNEN"MUMEN"Atlas of Strabsmus967). 10: AAAS; Beta Beta Beta; Beta Phi Mu. 12: Illus: Berens King "Atlas of Ophthalmic Surgery (61); Fasanella "Modern Advances in Cataract Surgery (63); "Complications of Eye Surgery (2d ed 65). 13: Yes 14: Rare bks, sci, fine arts, med illus. 15: 136 Shell st, Harrisburg Penn 17109.

WINGER, ANNA K. b Waynesboro Penn 13 O 30. 5: Juniata Col 49-53 (Eng) AB; Drexel 53-54 (LS) MS. 6: Fr, Ger. 7: Libn James Buchanan High Sch, Mercersburg Penn 54-56; Asst libn Juniata Col 56-61; Catlgr UDel 61-63; Libn Franklin Co Lib, Chambersberg Penn 63-66; Libn Defense Logistics Serv Ctr, Battle Creek Mich 66-. 9: ALA; PennLA; SLA; MichLA. 10: AAUW; AmrBuswte c ea Libns. 14: Catlg. 15: 39 1/2 James st, Battle Creek Mi 49017.

WINGER, FAITH L. b Niagara Falls NY 21 Mr 24. 5: Houghton Col 41-45 (Fr) BA; Biblical Sem 47-49 (Relig Educ) MRE; Columbia 61, 63 MS in LS; Near East Sch of Theol 62-. 6: Fr, Arabic. 7: Tchr Montrose Sch for Girls, Essex Falls NJ 45-47; Tchr Aleppo Col for Girls, Aloppo Syria 50-60; Libn Near East Sch of Theol, Beirut Lebanon 61-. 9: ALA; LebaneseLA; ATheolLA. 14: Catlg, rare theol bks (incl Arabic). 15: Box 235, Beirut Lebanon.

WINGER, HOWARD WOODROW. b Marion Ind 29 O 14. 4: Helen Gray. 5: Manchester Col 32-36 (Hist) AB; Peabody 41-45 BS in LS; Washington U 43-44 (German Lang); UIll 45-53 (LS) MS, PhD. 6: Ger, Fr. 7: Eng tchr Swayzee HIGH Sch, Swayzee Ind 36-37; Copy writer Crowell Publ Co, Springfield Ohio 37-38; Tchr-libn Jefferson Twp High Sch, Warren Ind 40-42; Tchr Stud Army of US (Cpl), Camp Crowder Mo, St Louis 42-44; Lib asst, tchg asst UIll(Urbana) 45-50; Asst Prof UWis(Madison) 50-53; Asst Prof, Dean of Studs, Prof UChicago 53-. 8: Bd Dirs, Park Forest (Ill) Pub Lib, 55-61; Ed consul for libs & bibliog, "Encyclopedia Americana" 59-62. 9: ALA (Coun 56-60);-ACRL (Ed Bd Monograph ser 67-69); AALS (sec-treas 53-56); Bibliog Soc (London); Bibliog Soc UVa; IllLA. 10: Beta Phi Mu. 12: "Iron Curtains and Scholarship" (59); "Seven Questions About the Profession of Librarianship" (61); "The Medium Sized Public Library" (62); "Area Studies and the Library" (65); Ed "Library Quarterly" (61-). 13: Yes. 14: Hist of bks & libs, hist of scholarships. 15: 121 Walnut st, Park Forest Il 60466.

WINGERT, DENISE (CANDACE). b Kirksville Mo 30 S 44. 4: Everett Arvin Wingert. 5: UMich 62-64 (Hist); UWash 64-66 (Hist) BA, 66-67 MLS. 6: Ger, Sp. 7: Stud asst Suzzallo Lib UWash 64-66; Asst catlg libn SeattleU Lib 67-. 9: ALA. 10: Phi Alpha Theta. 14: Catlg, computer & automation applictions. 15: Seattle Univ Lib - Tech Processes, Seattle Wa 98122.

WINGERTER, CAROL J (MINDOCK). b LaSalle Ill 5 S 42. 4: Curtis A Wingerter. 5: MacMurray Col 60-64 (Eng) BA; URI 66-67 MLS. 7: Preprof libn Indianapolis Pub lib 64-65; Child libn Newport Pub Lib, Newport RI 67-. 9: ALA; RILA. 10: AAUW; Newport Players Guild; Friends of Newport Pub Lib. 14: Child serv. 15: 19 Reardon dr, Middletown RI 02840.

WINIFRED, SISTER MARY (THOMAS) RSM. b Phillipsburg NJ 05 Ja 18. 5: Georgian Court Col 45-52 (Eng) AB; Drexel 53-55 MSLS; Syracuse summer 62 (LS); UWis summer 65 (LS); USoCal 69. 6: Ger, Sp. 7: Libn Camden Catholic High Sch,Camden NJ 50-60; Libn Mt St Marys Acad, North Plainfield NJ 61-62; Asst St Francis Col (Penn) summer 62; Libn Camden Catholic High Sch, Cherry Hill NJ 63-. 8: NJ Lib Devel Sch Libs Survey Com; NJ Adv Com on Title II, Elem & Secon Educ Act. 9: ALA; CathLA (Phila Chap); NJSchLA; Camden Co SchLA (v-pres). 10: Beta Phi Mu. 14: Wk with yp, secon sch libs, ref. 15: Rte 38 & Cuthbert rd, Cherry Hill NJ 08034.

WINKELMAN, JOHN HERMAN. b NYC 12 Ag 34. 4: Marion Jacqueline Vece. 5: Los Angeles City Col 55-57 (Hist); Mexico City Col 57-58 (Hist) BA; UColo 58-60, 60-62 (Hist) MA; So Conn State Col 60-61 (LS) MS; UChicago 62-68 (LS) PhD. 6: Chinese, Japanese, Fr. 7: Aviation machinist (3rd class) USN 52-55. 11: Ford Foundation For Area Fellowship 68-70. 13: Yes. 14: East Asian bibliog. 15: 34 Eld st, New Haven Ct 06515.

WINKLER, PAUL W(ALTER). b Buda Il 15 Jl 12. 5: Ill State Normal U 39 (Soc Sci) BEd; Uill 41 BS in LS, 49 (LS) MS. 6: Fr, Ger. 7: Tchr Rural Schs, Ill 31-35, 36-38, 39-40: libn McPherson Col 41-42; Catlgr: UIll Lib (Urbana) 42-44, Yale U Lib 44-46, Bk sect, copyright catlg div LC 46-47, Asst Head 47; Catlgr Yale U 48-51, Head subj catlg div 52-54; Instr UKy Lib Sch summer 53; ASST ASSOC Prof UDenver Sch of Libnship 54-59; Assoc Prof USoCal Sch of Lib Sci 59-62; Dir catlg dept Prof Lib Serv, Santa Ana Cal 62-64; Head Eng LANG Sect Desc Catlg Div LC 64-66, Asst chief Shared Catlg Div 66-68, Prin catlgr Descr Catlg Div 68-. 9: ALA-ACRL; BSA. 10: Kappa Delta Pi; Pi Gamma Mu. 13: Yes. 14: Catlg, govtl publns, hist of the bk. 15: 955 So Columbus st apt 515, Arlington VA 22204.

WINN, (J) KARYL (LEIX). b Bay City Mich 2 Ap 42. 4: Norman L Winn. 5: UMich 60-64 (Eng) BA, 64-65 MALS, 06. Fr. 7: Libn I Milwaukee Pub Lib 65-67; Catlgr UWash 67-. 9: ALA; PNLA; WashLA. 10: Seattle Mountaineers; Sierra Club. 14: Catlg, ref. 15: 466 N 44, Seattle Wa 98103.

WINN, HELEN (HARTMANN). b Houghton Ny 21 Ag 16. 4: Burkhard Daniel Winn. 5: Barnard 33-37 (Eng) BA; Columbia 52-54 (En0 ma,56-57 ls0 ms. 6: Fr. 7: Tchr-libn Oradell Jr High Sch, Oradell NJ 54-56; Libn River Dell Jr High Sch Oradell NJ 56-58; Libn River Dell Sr High Sch, Oradell NJ 58-. 8: Chm Lib Com Middle Atlantic States Assn Eval Team, Elmont NY 59; Title III dir River Dell Humanities Ctr, Oradell NJ. 9: ALA-AASchL; NJEA. 10: PTA; River Dell Music Parents Assn; Music & Arts Assn. 11: John Hay Fellowship in Humanities to Williams Col 65. 15: 248 Country Club dr, Oradell Nj 07649.

WINN, RUTH ELLEN. b Somersworth NH 18 O 24. 5: UNH 42-46 (Eng lit) BA, 46-49 (Eng lit) MA; Pratt 54-55 MSLS; Mus Sch of Fine Arts (Boston) 62-64 (Art). 7: Child asst winchester Pub Lib, Winchester Mass 55-56; Prof asst adult wk Boston Pub Lib 56-59; Asst enginring libn MIT 59-61; Order libn Boston U Libs 61-62; Ref asst Brookline Pub Lib, Brookline Mass 64-67; Asst catlgr Andover Newton Theol Sch 68-. 9: NE Theol Libns. 10: Beta Phi Mu; Lib rep, Brookline Lib Soc of Srtists. 11: Fulbright Scholarship to study Eng lit at DurhamU, Newcastle upon Tyne, England 49-50. 14: Catlg, ref. 15: 83 Ivey st, Brookline Ma 02146.

WINNABERG, MARIE JOSEPHINE. b Kendallville Iowa 7 Jl 27. 5: Luther Col 46-50 (Soc Sci) BA; State Col Iowa summer 57; UIll 58-59, summer 60 MSLS. 6: Sp, Norwegian. 7: Tchr rural elem schs, Cresco Iowa 50-52; Elem tchr, Calmar Iowa 53-55; Elem tchr-libn, Mason City Iowa 55-58; Elem & Jr high libn, Winona Minn 59-61; Instr & catlgr Luther Col 61-63, Head catlg 63-65; Ref libn Rochester (Minn) Pub Lib 65-66; Materials Ctr & Jr High Sch libn, Cresco Iowa 66-. 9: NEA; ALA;-AASchL; IowaLA; Iowa State EA; Iowa ASchL; Howard-Winneshiek EA. 10: Amer Philatelic Soc. 14: Ref, child serv. 15: Rte #1, Cresco Iowa 52136.

WINNICK, PAULINE. b Boston 21 N 15. 5: Simmons 32-36 (LS) BS. 6: Fr, sp, Ger. 7; Boston Pub Lib: Child libn 36-52, Readers adv for ya 52-57, Coordinatorof ya serv 57-63; Pub Lib spec, serv to child & ya US Off of Educ, Wash DC 63-. 8: Tchr, lib sci courses, Simmons 60-62 & Northeast U (Womans Nat Bk Assn); Rep ALA-YASD at White House Conf on Child & Youth, 60; Mass Com on Child & Youth 62-63; Consul "School Library Journal 64; Consul ALA-AAStateL Discussion Gp of State Lib Consuls on Pub Lib Serv o Cild 68-. 9: ALA-YASD (pres 58-59, chm Publrs Rel Com 59-60, chm By-laws Com 57-58, chm Com on Lib Serv to Disadvantaged YP 65); NE Round Table of Childs Libns (chm 51-53). 10: BNAi Brith: Anti-Defamation League; BNai Brith Youth Org; Nat Conf of Christians & Jews; ACLU; LWV. 12: Guest ed "School Library Journal (Je 15, 66). 13: Yes. 14: Pub lib serv to child & ya. 15: 2800 Quebec NW, Wash DC 20008.

WINNIKE, MARY ELIZABETH. b Carroll Iowa 19 N 38. 5: Iowa StateU 56-60 BS; UIll 65-67 MSLS; UTenn Med Units Program for Sci Libns 67-68 Certif. 7: Ref catlg libn Rush Med lib Presbyt St Lukes Hosp, Chicago 68-. 9: MedLA. 13: Yes. 14: Catlg, ref. 15: 1743 West Harrison, Chicago Il 60612.

WINOWICH, NICHOLAS. b Pittsburgh 6 O 23. 4: Ruth Ellen Flemming. 5: Bethany Col 46-49 (Hist, Pol Sci AB; UPittsburgh summers 47, 48 (Hist, Pol Sci); Carnegie 49-50 MSLS. 6: Serbian. 7: (Cpl) US Army, US & OVerseas 42-45; Br lib asst Carnegie Lib of Pittsburgh 50-52; Head Libn Carnegie Free Lib, McKeesport Penn 52-56 ; Lib Dir Kanawha Co Pub Lib, Charleston WVa 56-. 8: SPec Adv COM, WVa Lib, Commsn 64-; Instr WVa U Ext Div, Lib Sci 62, 64; Lib bldgs consul, St Albans WVa & S Charleston WVa. 9: ALA (Coun 57-59; Penn mem chm 53-56); PennLA (sec 55-56); Middle Atlantic Reg Lib Conf (Publicity chm 63); WVaLA (pres 59-60); Middle Atlantic Reg Lib Conf (Exh chm 67). 10: Child mus & planetarium Charleston WVa; Sunrise Found Inc; Bd Dirs, Creative Arts Festival of WVa 64-; C of C (Bd Dirs); UPittsburgh Carnegie Lib Sch Assn; Bd Dirs Charleston WVa YMCA. 13: Yes. 14: Admin, rare bks, bldgs. 15: 123 Capitol st, Charleston WV 25301.

WINSHIP, ROBERT BRADLEY. b St Johnsbury Vt 8 S 21. 5: UVt 40-42, 46-48 (Hist) AB; Drexel 49 BS in LS; UMich 52-53 AMLS. 6: Fr. 7: Infantry (Cpl) US Army, tcamp Butner NC 42-46; Asst ref libn Miami U (Ohio) 49-52; Ser catlgr Temple U 53-. 8: Libn Jefferson Med Col Sch of Nursing 55-. 9: ALA; 14: Ser, govt docs. 15: 112 W Tulpehocken st, Phila Pa 19144.

WINSHIP, SHEILA (GAIL). b Austin Tex 6 Ja 39. 5: UTex 57-60 (Fr) BA, 61-62 MLS. 6: Fr, Sp. 7: Claims rep Soc Security Admin, Corpus Christi Tex 60-61; Ref libn La retama Pub Lib, Corpus Christi Tex 62-68; Ref libn Undergrad Lub UTex (Austin) 68-. 9: ALA; TexLA. 14: Ref. 15: 5601 Exeter, Austin Tx 78723.

WINSLOW, FLORENCE F (HENNIG). b Los Angeles Cal 9 Je 20. 4: Roger C Winslow. 5: Adelphi 37-41 (Eng) BA; So Conn State Col 63-69 (LS). 7: Lib asst & child libn floral Pk Pub Lib, Floral Pk NY 37-41; Lib asst Fox Lane High Sch, Bedford Central District #1 NY 63-64, Libn Bedford Hills Elem Sch 64-65; Libn Oak Hill Sch for the Blind, Hartford Conn 66-. 9: ALA; Assn Educ Visually Handicapped (co-chm Lib Wkshop 68-70). 10: Simsbury Chorale. 14: Lib serv and facilities for the handicapped. 15: 28 Wright dr, Avon Ct 06001.

WINSLOW, LUCY PRESCOTT. b Boston Mass 3 D 14. 4: Richard Sears Winslow. 5: Radcliffe col 31-35 (Govt) BA; OxfordU (England) 35-36 (Politics, Philos); UChicago 37-39 (Soc serv) MA; Columbia 60-62 MLS. 7: Jr libn (ya) Yonkers Pub Lib, Yonkers NY 62-63, Act hd, Adult Dept 63-67, Hd Adult Dept (Sprainbrook Br) 67-. 9: NYLA; WestchesterLA. 10: Phi Beta Kappa; Beta Phi Mu; LWV. 14: Adult libnship. 15: 51 Barry rd, Scarsdale NY 10583.

WINSOR, KATHLEEN R(OSE) (KRAFT). b London England 28 F 27. 5: Cornell 44-48 (Chem) BA; Columbia 53-56 MLS. 7: Research asst Sterling Winthrop Research Inst, Rensselaer ny 49-52; Catlgr Stevens Inst 55; Tech ed Colgate-Palmolive, Jersey City NJ 56-57; Sci libn Queens Col (NY) 64-66; Catlgr UCal (San Diego) 68-. 8: Archivist, Leo Szilard Collection, La Jolla Cal 65-. 9: ALA; SLA. 13: Yes. 15: 8115 El Paseo Grande, La Jolla Ca 92037.

WINSOR, VIRGINIA (RUTH) (GONNASON). b Hillsboro Ore 2 Ap 17. 5: UWash 36-41 (Chem) BS in Chem, 61-65 M of Lib. 6: Fr. Sp. 7: Tchg fellow Dept of Chem UWash 39-41; Lab asst State Health Dept, Seattle 50-51; Abstractor Gen Electric Co Hanford Labs, Richland Wash 51-63, Info spec 63; Libn order & catlg Los Alamos Sci Lab UCal, Los Alamos NM 63-. 9: ACS; SLA (Bulletin Ed 65-67); NMLA; ASIS. 10: AAAS; AAUW; Los Alamos Outdoor Assn; Los Alamos Swimmers Club. 13: Yes. 14: Info retrieval, catlg. 15: 2003-D 23rd st, Los Alamos NM 87544.

WINSTANDLEY, (GRACE) VIRGINIA. b New Albany Ind 24 Je 01. 5: ULouisville 19-23 (Eng) BA; Columbia summers 26 & 28, summers 30, 32-34 (LS) BS, summers 38-41 (LS) MS. 7: Jr high sch tchr: New Albany Ind Pub Schs 23-26, Louisville Ky Pub Schs 27-29; Gen lib asst ULouisville Lib 29-34, Asst libn & hd acquis dept 34-66, Asst libn in charge spec collections & assoc prof lib sci 66-. 9: ALA; SELA; KyLA; Louisville Lib Club. 10: AAUP; Louisville Lib Staff Assn; ULouisville Women's Club; ULouisville Lib Assocs; Beckham Bird Club; Ky Ornithol Assn; Woodcock Honor Soc. 14: Rare bks, spec collections. 15: Univ of Louisville Lib Belknap Campus, Louisville Ky 40208.

WINSTON, FRANK C(URRY). b Hampden-Sydney Va 14 Je 05. 4: Alice Sitterly. 5: Hampden-Sydney Col 23-27 (Lat) BA; Col of William & Mary 31-32 (LS); Peabody summers 49-51 BS in LS. 7: Catlg Hampden-Sydney Col Lib 33-43; Ref & circ libn No Sch of Mines 45-48; Catlgr Va Poly Inst 48; Dir of Lib So Ga Col 48-55; Dir of Lib Athens Col 55-56; Catlgr Free Pub Lib, Paterson NJ 56-. 9: NJLA. 10: SAR. 14: Catlg. 15: 281 19th ave, Paterson NJ 07504.

WINSTON, MARIAN (EDITH) PRINCE. b NYC 2 F 24. 5: Hunter Col 39-43 (Journalism) BA; UCLA 64-65 MLS. 7: Staff writer Current Biography H W Wilson Co, NYC 43-47; Staff writer PIX Inc, NY 47-49; Free lance ref wk for authors & inquirers, NYC 49-50; Ed instr materials lab dept of voc educ, Oakland Cal 51-52; Asst ed "Edison News" SoCal Edison Co, Los Angeles 52-53; Ed Prosthetics Educ Program Engnr Dept & Med Sch UCLA 53-57; Ed II UCLA Forum in the Med Sci 65-67; Rand Corp, Santa Monica Cal; Resident consul spec indexing project 67-68, Editor reports dept 68-. 9: Soc Tech Writers (Bd 57). 10: LWV; ConsumersCo-op of Santa Monica (Cal); Mensa. 12: Co-auth ""The Distelfink in Pennsylvania Dutch Folk Art. 13: Yes. 14: Repackaging of info, annotation, abstracting, indexing. 15: 16018 Junaluska way, Pacific Palisades Ca 90272.

WINSTON, MARY LEE. b Rural Retreat Va 18 Mr 06. 5: Va Polytech Inst 24-28 (Bus Educ) BS; Fla State U 49-50 (LS) MS. 6: Fr. 7: Va Poly Inst Lib: Clerical wker 33-39, Agric libn 40-49, Ser libn 50-. 9: SELA; VaLA. 14: Ser. 15: 202 Rose ave, Blacksburg Va 24060.

WINTER, BEVERLY. b Mendota Ill 13 F 2. 5: Bradley U 45-49 (Art) BFA, 57-58, summers 59 & 60 (Educ) MA; UDenver summer 62, 63-64 (LS) MA. 7: Sec dept store, Radio Station & Insurance Cos, Peoria Ill 49-57; Tchr Dist 44, Lombard Ill 58-62; Tchr Aurora Pub Schs, East Side, Aurora Ill 62-63; Libn sch dist #6, Euclid Jr High Sch, Littleton Colo 64-67; Starved Rock Lib Syst, Mendotta Ill 68; Libn Sch dist #44, Lombard Ill 68-. 9: NEA; IllEA; Lombard EA. 14: Ya & jr high bks. 15: 1107 Monroe st, Mendotta Il 61342.

WINTER, HELEN L (FAULKNER). b Kokomo Ind 10 Ag 21. 4: Henry M Winter. 5: Hanover Col 39-43 (Eng, Hist, Educ) AB; UHouston 52 (Creative Writing); UWash 63-64 (LS) ML. 6: Lat, Fr. 7: Proof girl "Kokomo Tribune," Kokomo Ind 43-44; Copywriter window display Jacobson's, Ann Arbor Mich 44-45; Display advertising space sales woman "Ann Arbor News," Ann Arbor Mich 45-51; Copywriter Foley's Dept Store, Houston Tex 51-53; Free-lance copywriter & reporter, Houston, Seattle 53-62; Lib asst III UWash 62-63; Documents libn UChicago Law Lib 64-65; Asst libn Scott Forman Co, Chicago 65-66; Libn Mich State U Sci Lib (E Lansing) 66-. 9: ALA-ACRL; -LAD (Rare Bks Sect); ChicagoALL. 10: Beta Phi Mu; Alpha Phi Gamma; Phi Mu. 14: Docs, admin, govt publs. 15: 4930 Dawn ave, E Lansing Mi 48823.

WINTER, HELEN VAN DYKE. b Worthington Ohio 11 Ag 08. 5: NY State Col (Albany) 27-31 BS in LS; Columbia 45-51 MS in LS. 6: Fr, Sp. 7: Libn Chatham Pub Lib, Chatham NY 31-43; Jr libn Newark NJ 43-44, Sr libn 44-45; Maplewood Mem Lib, Maplewood NJ; Ref libn 45-48, Act dir 48-49, Dir 49-. 9: ALA; LPRC (Bd 54); NJLA (chm Personnel Com 52-54, Bd 61-64, Parliam 64-); NY Lib Club. 10: LWV; Forest Hill Lit Soc; Maplewood Serv League; AAUW; Amer Assn for the UN; Nat Women's Bk Assn; NJ Hist Soc; Newark Museum; NY Zool Soc. 14: Admin. 15: 618 Ridgewood rd, Maplewood NJ 04070.

WINTERS, JEANNETTE ETHEL. b Council Bluffs Iowa 13 F 09. 5: UIowa 31 (Eng, Relig Educ) BA, 32 (LS). 7: Asst libn UOmaha 31-37; Libn Red Oak Pub Lib, Red Oak Iowa 38-. 9: ALA; IowaLA. 10: Delta Kappa Gamma; Altrusa Internat. 14: Pub libs, wk with child. 15: Red Oak Pub Lib, Red Oak Ia 51566.

WINTERS, LINDA (SMITH). b Kan City Mo 13 F 44. 4: Robert Bruce Winters Jr. 5: UKan 62-66 Eng BA; EmoryU 66-67 MLn. 6: Ger. 7: Asst spec collections libn UGa (Athens) 67-. 9: SELA; GaLA. 14: Spec collections. 15: PO Box 16, Loganville Ga 30249.

WINTERS, MICHELE (MANN). b Wash DC 25 Jl 43. 4: Lewis Winters. 5: Wilson Col 61-64 (Hist); Beaver Col 64-65 (Hist) AB; Drexel 65-66 MS in LS. 6: Ger. 7: Page Wilson Col Lib 62-64; Subprof Temple U Lib 65; Hd libn Glenside Free Lib, Glenside Penn 66-. 10: Beta Phi Mu. 14: Ref, admin. 15: 1000 Walnut st apt 202, Philadelphia Pa 19107.

WINTERS, NELLE K (HALL). b Dunlap Iowa 7 My 05. 4: Herbert Winters. 5: IowaU 21-25 (Eng) BA; Iowa StateU 29-31 (Educ) MS; UChicago 36, 62-63 (LS); UNoIll 65- (LS). 7: Jr high tchr, Iowa: Mo Valley 25-27, Dunlap 27-29; Hd Eng dept Marinette Jr & Sr High, Marinette Wis 31-36; Libn Alan B Shepard Jr High, Deerfield Ill 62-. 15: 938 Rosemary, Deerfield Il 60015.

WINTERS, WILMA E(LLSWORTH). b Woonsocket RI 27 Mr 18. 5: Larson Jr Col 36-38 (LS) AA; Boston U 40-43 (Secondary Educ) BS in Ed, 45-50 (Hist) MA; Simmons 58-60 (LS) MA. 7: Lib asst Franklin Pub Lib, Franklin Mass 38-42; Libn Dean Jr Col 40-42; Asst Boston U Sch Med 42-43; Asst libn 43-54; Med libn VA Hosp, Brockton Mass 54-57; Asst libn BostonMed Lib 57-62, libn Retina Foun Dept Clin Eye Research, Boston, 62-65; Libn Harvard Center for Population Studies, Boston 65-. 9: MedLA; Amer Med Writers Assn; NE Reg MedLA; Mass Hosp Libs Group; AAAS; Population Assn Amer. 15: 665 Huntington ave, Boston Ma 02115.

WINTLE, MARY JACK. b Pittsburgh Kan 25 Je 34. 5: LSU 52-56 (Eng Lit) BA, 61-62 (LS) MS; Yale 56-57 (Tchg Eng) MA. 7: Tchr Abington Sr High Sch, Abington Penn 57-58; Legal sec Goode, Shea & Dietz, Shreveport La 58-61; Libn trainee LSU Lib (Baton Rouge) 61-62; Spec recruit LC 62-63; Reg libn LC Div for the Blind & Physically Handicapped 63, Asst selection & publ off 64-66, Selection & publ off 67-69, Asst chief acquis 69-. 9: ALA; Coun Except Child; AEAUSA; LPRC; DCLA. 10: Beta Phi Mu; Jr League of Wash DC; Smithsonian Associates; Yale Club of Wash DC; LSU Alum Assn. 13: Yes. 14: Bk sel, publ, ref, admin. 15: 117 E st SE apt 303, Washington DC 20003.

WINTON, ALMA. b Townville Penn 7 D 05. 5: Allegheny Col 23-27 (Philos, Educ) AB; Columbia 32-33 BS in LS; Penn State (Educ) M Ed. 7: Lat tchr Mercer High Sch, Mercer Penn 27-28, E Bethlehem Twp High Sch, Fredericktown Penn 28-32; Libn Morrisville Jr-Sr High Sch, Morrisville Penn 33-35; Asst libn Shippensburg State Col 35-41, Head libn 41-. 8: Pres Fac Assn Shippensburg State Col 64-65. 12: "Library Instruction for Freshmen," Shippensburg State Col Bulletin (56). 14: Admin. 15: 16-1/2 S Prince st, Shippensburg Pa 17257.

WINTSCH, ENID (STEIG). b Churches Ferry ND 18 Jl 09. 4: Harry Wintsch. 5: UWis 26-30 (Eng, LS) BA in LS. 6: Ger, Norwegian. 7: Asst libn Whittemore Mem Lib, Naugatuck Conn 30-32; Yale U Lib; Catlg asst 55-59, Asst head desc catlg div 59-62, Head desc catlg div 62-66; Tech serv coord Waterloo Co Lib, Preston Ont 66-. 9: ALA; NY Tech Serv Libns. 10: Woodbridge Club; Can Fed of Univ Women. 14: Catlg, child lib wk. 15: 249 Central ave, New Haven Ct 06515.

WIREN, HAROLD NELSON. b Teaneck NJ 31 Ja 24. 4: Alice Pariminter Wiren. 5: UIll 47-48, 49-51 (Marketing, Mgt) BS; UStockholm 48-49; UIll 54-56 (LS) MS. 7: Engring lib asst UIll(Urbana) 56-57; Asst libn (sci-tech) Rochester Pub Lib, Rochester NY 57-62; Sr asst libn (sci-tech) UNeb 62-63, Asst dir sci-tech libs 63-65; Hd Engring Libs Ohio State U 65-69; Engring libn UWash Libs 69-. 9: ALA; ASIS; ASEE (Engring Sch Libs Div; chm Bylaws Com, ed Newsletter); NebLA (chm Col & Univ Sect 64-65). 10: AAUP. 14: Collection bldg, automation. 15: UWashington Libraries, Seattle Wa 98105.

WIRTH, JOAN MARIA. b NYC 21 Je 44. 5: Douglass Col 62-66 (Hist) AB; UOkla 66-67 (LS); Rutgers 67-68 MLS. 6: Sp. 7: Asst libn MY State Off of Planning Coord, Albany NY 67; Ref libn NY State Lib Hist and Manuscripts 68; Asst libn Grad Sch of Bus and Pub Admin 68-. 14: Research, ref. 15: Apt 1-2C Lansing E, Ithaca NY 14850.

WISE, EDITH (CROFT). b Muncie Ind 6 Mr 07. 5: Ball State U 24-25 (Lat); Lake Forest Col 27-28 (Theatre, Speech) Hartford Sem Found 31-32 (Lat, Amer Hist & Culture);UChicago 36-37 (Span, Lat Amer Hist & Lit); George Washington U 40-41 (Span & Lat Amer Hist & Lit); Rutgers 54-57 MA in LS. 6: Sp, Portu, Fr. 7: Lib asst MUNCIE Ind 24, 28-31, Instr & Libn Colegio AMericano (Bogota Col) 31-36, 37-39; LC: Libn in chg of Hispanic Found Reading room 40-42, Lat Amer spec Dept of Acquis 42-48,Spec asst to the dir of the Hispanic Found 48-49; Ref libn UN Dag Hammarskjold Lib, NY 54-56; info off Educ sect UN, NY 57-58; Spec research proj Rutgers U 58-59; Head, UN collection GEn U Lib NYU 61-62, REF LIBN & supv of UN Collection 62-. 8: Mission of the Pan American Union, Wash DC of direct tech asst to the Instituto Caro y Cuervo, Bogota Colombia 59-60; Unesco mission to the CENTRO DE Documentacion Internacional, Bueonos Aires 61; Lib consul cCtr for Inter-Amer Rel NY 66; Lib spec The Educ and Cult Exch prog, US Dept of State; Mexico 67 Biblioteca Central Univ Nacional de Tucuman Argentina 67. ALA. 9: ALA. 12: "Classificaton System with Maurice F Tauber (61)V. 14: Internat exch, internat rel (lat America). 15: 20 Fifth ave apt 17, New York NY 10011.

WISDOM, DONALD FARRELL. b St Louis Co Mo 24 Ag 28. 4: Margaret King. 5:Georgetown U 48-52 (Pol Sci, Hist, Econ) BS in Foreign Serv, 54 (Govt). 6: Sp. 7: (Sgt) US Army 52-54; LC; Ref libn Govt Publ Sect 55-56, Ref libn Sci Div 56-58, Asst head Govt Pub Sect 58-63, Head Govt Publ Sect 63-66; Asst dir Hispanic Foundation 66-. 8: Spec survey for the Farmington Plan Com of the ARL, Oct 60- Jan 61, on holdings of for govt publs in Amer libs. 9: ALA; DCLA; Ser Acquis Lat Amer Lib Materials. 11: Bronze Star, US Army, 54. 12: "Foreign Government Publications in American Research Libraries" (61). 13: Yes. 14: Ref, bibliog. 15: 5812 Massachusetts ave, Bethesda Md 20016.

WISE, ELAINE MAY (LIU). b Peking China 19 N 43. 4: Matthew Norton Wise. 5: Wash StateU 61-65 (Philos) BA, 65-67 (Eng) MA. 6: Fr, Ger. 7: Humanities libn AuburnU 67-. 10: Phi Kappa Phi; Phi Beta Kappa. 14: Humanities ref & bibliog. 15: 416-C E Magnolia, Auburn Al 36830.

WISE, KENDA CAROLYN. b Warren Ark 19 Jl 29. 5: UAla 47-51 (LS) BS; Fla State U 54-55 MSLS. 6: Sp. 7: Bus Lib UAla; Res libn 51-54, Asst ref libn 55-59, Ref libn 59-69; Ref libn Air U Lib (Maxwell AFB) 69-. 9: SLA; AlaLA; SELA. 10: AAUP; Altrusa. 14: Ref, circ. 15: 32D The Prado, Montgomery Al 36105.

WISE, LEONA LEILANI. b Sacramento Cal. 5: U of the Pacific 50-53 (Eng) AB; UHawaii 53 (Eng); USoCal 53-55 (Eng) MA, 58-59 MS in LS, Jr Col Tchg Credential. 6: Sp . 7: Eng tchr Monrovia High Sch, Monrovia Cal 55-56; Eng tchr; Rosemead High Sch, Rosemead Cal 56-57; Libn II Ser Hancock Lib of Biol & Oceanography USoCal 60-67, Docs libn 67-68, Ser libn 68-. 9: ALA. 10: Phi Delta Gamma; AAUW; USoCal Lib Alum Assn. 13: Yes. 14: Exch ser. 15: 3445 Monterey rd, San Marino Cal 91108.

WISE, MARY KATHERINE. b Pittsburgh Penn 12 N 45. 5: Mt Mercy Col 63-67 (Hist) BA; UPittsburgh 67-68 MLS. 6: Fr. 7: Tech Mine Safety Appliances Co Lib, Pittsburgh 62-67; Intern boys & girls dept Carnegie Lib, Pittsburgh Pa 67-68; Asst bus-industry sci dept Providence Pub Lib 68-. 9: SLA; NELA. 10: Beta Phi Mu; Soc Advanc Mgt. 14: Ref. 15: 281 Benefit st, Providence RI 02903.

WISE, MARY PORTER. b Baltimore 24 Jl 22. 5: WVaU 39-43 (Eng) BS; UMiami 50-51 (Eng) MA; Fla State U 55-58 (LS) MS. 6: Fr. 7: Jr engnr Western ELEC Co, Baltimore 43-50; Lib clerk UMiami (Fla) Coral Gables Fla 51056, Documents libn 56-. 10: Beta Phi Mu; Kappa Delta Pi. 14: Govt publns. 15: 5880 SW 32 st, Miami Fl 33155.

WISE, ZILPHA (FITTS). b Reading Kan 12 O 1897. 4: William R Wise. 5: Kan State Tchrs Col summers 20-50 (Elem Educ) BS, 51-58 (LS) MS; IndU (Bloomington) (Elem Educ). 7: Tchr: Lyon Co Kan 19-50, Cimarron Kan 50-54, Herington Kan 54-55, Newton Kan 55-58; Libn Chisholm Jr High, Newton Kan 58-67; Elem libn Remington Unified Dist, Whitewater Kan 67-. 8: Lib asst William Allen White Lib, Emporia Kan summers 56-58; Instr in Lib courses Bethel Col, North Newton Kan 67-68 summers. 9: ALA; KanStateTA; KanLA; KanASchL (past Dist Chm). 10: YMCA; Delta Kappa Gamma; AAUW. 13: Yes. 14: Tchg, ref. 15: Box 162, Walton Ks 67151.

WISEMAN, DEIRDRE (GUNNISON). b St Louis Mo 6 Jl 29. 4: Melvin M Wiseman. 5: Skidmore Col 47-49 (Philos); Boston 58-63 (Philos) AB; Simmons 63-65 (LS) MS. 7: Asst ser libn Harvard Col Lib 65-68, Asst libn Peabody Mus Lib 68-. 15: 93 Perry st, Brookline Ma 02146.

WISEMAN, HARVEY BRUCE. b Klamath Falls Ore 22 N 25. 5: Yakima Valley Col 43-45 (Eng) LD Certif; UWash 46-48 (Eng) BA, Tchg Certif; 53-54 MLib; Denver U 57. 6: Fr, Ger. 7: Catlgr Engnr Societies Lib, NYC 54-56; High sch & col libn Ketchikan Pub Schs, Ketchikan Alaska 56-59; Catlg libn UOre Lib 59-62; Ed & Libn Wadsworth Publ Co., Belmont Cal 63-65; Ref libn Alameda Co Lib, Hayward Cal 9: ALA; CalLA. 14: Catlg, ref in pub lib. 15: 24547 Amador st, Hayward Ca 94544.

WISHARD, ELIZABETH MARY. b Marion Co Ind 31 D 09. 5: Western Col 28-32 (Eng Lit) AB; ButlerU 48-49, 50-51 (Educ) MA; IndU 52-53 (LS). 6: Fr. 7: Tchr Hancock Co Schs, Fortville Ind 44-45; Tchr (Hd div for physically handicapped) LaPorte Co Schs, Hanna Ind 45-49; Libn Indiana State Lib 49-. 9: ALA (RT for the Blind); IndLA. 10: Wesleyan serv Guild; Ind Assn for the Blind. 13: Yes. 14: Lib serv to the physically handicapped. 15: 6036 E 43rd, Indianapolis In 46226.

WISSLER, MARY VIOLA. b Hagerstown Ind 29 Jl 07. 5: Earlham Col 26-30 (Eng) AB; Columbia 30-31 (LS) BS, 32-33. 7: Compiled bibliog & helped organized lib Lab of Anthrop, Santa Fe NM 31-32; Vol in lib of Amer Geog Soc, NYC 34-35; Columbia U E Asiatic Collections 35, Arch 35; Amer Mus of Natural Hist 35-. 9: ALA. 14: Ref. 15: 423 W 120th st, New York NY 10027.

WITHERELL, JULIAN (WOOD). b Wash DC 29 Ag 35. 5: Bowdon 52-56 (Hist) BA; UWis 56-58 (Hist) MA, 58-62 (Hist) PhD. 6: Fr. 7: Ref libn LX 62-64; Area specialist (Africa) 64-66; Hd African sect 66-. 8: Publ survey trips to Africa for LC 63-64, 64-65, 66, 67-68. 9: African Studies Assn; ALA; AHA. 12: "Official Publications of French Equatorial Africa, French Cameroons, and Togo, 1946-1958" (64); "Madagascar and Adjacent Islands: A Guide to Official Publications" (65); "French-speaking West Africa: A Guide to Official Publications" (67). 13: Yes/ 14: Ref & bibliog wk in Africana. 15: 7109 Braddock rd, Springfield Va 22151.

WITHROW, BETTY (ANN). b Clifton Forge Va 24 Ja 27. 5: Mary Washington Col (UVa) 44-47 (Eng) BA; Peabody Col 47-48 BS in LS. 7: Intern VanderbiltU Sch Med Lib 48-49; Asst libn Cincinnati Gen Hosp Lib 49-53; Ref libn UAla Med Ctr Lib 53-55; Ref libn UMiami Sch Med Lib 55-57; Libn UVt Col Med Lib 57-61; Libn SUNY (Buffalo) Health Sci Lib 61-63; Libn Wake ForestU Bowman Gray Sch Med 63-67; Libn Cal Col Med UCal (Irvine) 67-. 8: Consul MedLA adv coun on educ needs in med libnship 67-. 9: MedLA (sec 64-66); SLA; ASIS; CalLA; Med Lib Gp So Cal. 10: Town and Gown, UCal (Irvine); AAAS; Amer Assn for Hist Med. 13: Yes. 14: Admin, ref. 15: Cal Col of Med Lib Univ Cal Irvine, Irvine Ca 92664.

WITMER, JOHN ALBERT. b Lancaster Penn 29 N 20. 4: Doris Ferry Witmer. 5: Wheaton Col 38-42 (Eng Lit) AB, 42-44 (Theol) AM; Dallas Theol Sem 44-46 (Systematic Theol) ThM, 46-48 (Systematic Theol) ThD; E Tex State U 64-65 MSLS. 6: Hebrew, Lat, Fr, Gk.18265 7: Tchr Fellow Wheaton Col Ill 42-44; Ed "Child Evangelism Magazine, Dallas 44-46; Dallas Theol Sem: Instr in systematic theol 47-54; Asst Prof of systematic theol 54-, Act libn 63-64, Libn 64-. 9: ALA; ConnLA (sec, rep-at-large; mem Com to Draft Constit for Col & Univ Sect; Exec Bd Ref Sect, Exec Bd Col & Univ Sect). 13: Yes. 14: Catlg. 15: 3909 Swiss ave, Dallas Tx 75204.

WITTE, LOUISE W. b LaSalle Ill 17 O 15. 4: Michael Witte. 5: Uill 40 (Educ) MS Ed; Rutgers 65 MLS. 7: Tchr Eng & Polish S Milwaukee High Sch, S Milwaukee Wis; Libn Maxson Jr High Sch, Plainfield NJ 65-. 8: Tchr ENG & Polish S Milwaukee High Sch, S Milwaukee Wis; Libn Maxson Jr High Sch, Plainfield NJ 65-; Asst libn Westfield Sr High Sch, Westfield NJ. 9: ALA; NJLA. 13: Yes. 14: Readers serv. 15: 85 Emerson lane, Berkeley Heights NJ 07922.

WITTEN, KATHLEEN RUBICAM. b Philadelpha 22 S 17. 5: Vassar 35-39 (Modern European Hist) AB; Columbia 54-55 (LS) MS; Wesleyan U 57-64. 6: Fr. 7: Reearch asst Audience Research Inst, Princeton NJ 40-41; Circ asst Hartford Pub Lib, Hartford Conn 53-54; Ref libn Wesleyan U (Conn) 55-64; Acquis libn Sarah Lawrence Col 64-68; Assoc libn SUNY (Purchase) 68-. 9: ALA; ConnLA (sec, rep-at-large, mem Com to Draft Constit fol 10: AAUP; LWV; PTA; Jr League (Bronxville); Portland Congreg Church Bd Trustees. 14: Bk sel, ref. 15: 4 Merestone terrace, Bronxville NY 10708.

WITTENBERG, ELEANOR EULALA (MARSH) b Falls City Neb 24 J 120. 4: David Franklin Wittenberg. 5: Arkansas ity Jr Col 38-40 (Educ) 2 yr Tchrs. Certif; Kan State Tchrs Col (Emporia) 45-47 (LS) BS in Ed, Lib Certif; Colo State Col of Educ summer 46. 7: Tchr Cowley Co rural sch Vinton Kan 40-42; Sheet metal assembler G & H Tool Mfg Co. Wichita Kan 43-45; Child libn, catlgr Whiting Pub Lib, Whiting Ind 47-51; Army libn Spec Serv US Army, Bad Nauheim Germany 51053; Catlgr Whiting Pub Lib, Whiting Ind 60-. 10: Property Owners Assn, Highland Ind; Highland Consol Charities Coun; PTA: Pincohle Club. 14: Catlg. 15: 3215 Glenwood ave, Highland Ind 46322.

WITTENMYER, (MARY) OLETA (HAMILTON). b Bowie Tex 20 Jl 20. 5: N Tex State U 50-54 (LS) BA; Tex Woman's U 60 MLS. 7: Asst mus libn N Tex State U 54-60, Asst ref libn 60-63; Asst libn Northeast La State Col 63-65; Ser libn Tex Christian U 65-. 9: ALA; TexLA. 10: AAUW. 14: Ser, catlg. 15: Box 11563, Ft Worth Tx 76109.

WITTGRUBER, PATRICIA (WOODALL). b Cleveland 6 Ag 19. 4: William C Wittgruber. 5: WIttenberg Col 37-41 (Eng) BSin Ed; Miami U 57- (LS). 7: Bibliog Armed Serv Tech Info Agency, Dayton Ohio 51054, Catlgr 55-57; Libn Aerospace Research Labs, Wright-Patterson AFB, Ohio 57-. 9m;sla. 14: Admin (small lab lib), catlg, documentation. 15: 1030 Wenbrook dr, Kettering Oh 45429.

WITTIG, ALICE J. b Lincoln Neb 2 F 29. 4: Donald R Wittig. 5: UNeb 47-51 BS in Ed; UNC 52; UDenver 59-60 (Libnship) MA. 7: Tchr Raleigh Pub Schs, Raleigh NC 51-53, World Coun of Churches, Europe 53-56; Docs asst Texas Tchr 58-59; Docs libn UDenver 60-62; Asst ref libn Law Lib StanfordU 66-68, Circ libn 68-. 9: ALA. 14: Law, govt docs. 15: 25391 O'Keefe ave, Los Altos Hills Ca 94022.

WITTIG, DONALD R. b New Haven Conn 16 S 19. 4: Alice Josephine Smith. 5: Pratt Inst 41-44 (Electrical Engring) BEE; Iliff Sch of Theol 50-51 (Theol); Syracuse 51-54 (Voice, Music Hist); UDenver 59-61 (Voice) MA, 61-62 (Libnship) MA. 6: Ger. 7: Engr & train foreman Tenn Eastman Corp, Oak Ridge Tenn 44-45; Recording engr & instr in electroacoustics Jordan Conservatory, Indianapolis 45-46; Instr in physics & electronics ButlerU 46-49; Engr GE Co, Syracuse NY 51-53; Singer & instrumentalist NY Concert Choir, commun concerts, NYC 53-57; Instr in physics, electrical engring & math Westminster Col (Salt Lake City) 57-58; Instr in voice UDenver 59-61, Instr in mus hist 61-62; Circ libn Foothill Col 62-64; Catlg libn StanfordU 64-66; Sci ref libn San Jose State Col 66-67, Sci libn 67-68, Asst Prof libnship 68-. 9: SLA; ASIS; CalLA; CalTA. 10: Amer Fed of Musicians; Mendocino Art Ctr; Los Altos Hills Assn; NAACP. 11: Developed and copyrighted catlg filing aid; Copyrighted a setting of 23rd Psalm to Music of Handel. 14: Educ for libnship, intel freedom, civil liberties, verbal & non-verbal communication. 15: 25391 O'Keefe ave, Los Altos Hills Ca 94022.

WITTKOPF (von SCHLICHTER) BARBARA HEAN. b Yonkers NY 28 Jl 43. 4: Eugene Robert wittkopf. 5: ValparaisoU 61-65 (Elem Educ) BSEd; Syracuse summers 66-67, 67-68 MSLS. 7: Tchr Nassau Lutheran Sch, Mineola NY 65-66, 66-67; Libn asst main dept readers serv Syracuse Pub Lib, NY 68-. 10: Phi Beta Mu. 14: Readers serv, ref, govt publs. 15: 315 Comstock ave apt 12, Syracuse NY 13210.

WITTROCK SISTER JEANNE MARIE. b St Louis 7 Ap 09. 5: St Louis U 33 (Eng) AB; Fordham 40 (Fr) MA. 7: Libn: St Louis Pub Lib 31-34, AQUINAS High Sch. Bronx NY 36-50, St Mark High Sch, St Louis 50-. 15: 1327 Academy ave, St Louis Mo 63113.

WITTY, FRANCIS JOSEPH. b Hampton Va 26 Mr 28. 4: Barbara Ann Braun. 5: St Charles Borromeo (Baltimore) 44-46 (Lang); CatholicU 46-48 (Philos) BA, 48-50, 53-55 (Lat, Gk) MA, 55-56 MS in LS, 57-67 (Lat, Gk) PhD. 6: Latin, Gk, Ger, Fr, Sp, Ital, Hebrew. 7: Curator Gk & Lat Lib CatholicU 48-50; Instr in radio & Morse code Stuttgart Signal Sch, Stuttgart Germany 52; Catlgr CatholicU 53-55, Hd catlg div 56-58, Instr Dept Lib Sci 58-61, Asst Prof Dept Lib Sci 62-67, Assoc Prof Dept Lib Sci 67-. 8: Organist St Anthony's Roman Catholic Ch, Wash DC. 9: ALA; AALS; Potomac Tech Processing Libns 10: Amer Philological Assn; Amer Schs Oriental Research. 13: Yes. 14: Hist bks & libs, catlg, indexing & abstracting, clsf. 15: 16220 Oxford ct, Mitchellville Md 20716.

WODEHOUSE, MARGARET E (ROSE). b Tampa Fla 13 O 23. 4: Robert F Wodehouse. 5: UTampa 40-44 (Eng, Hist) BS in Ed; UWis 48-49 BLS; UMich 61-63 Advanced MLS. 6: Fr. 7: Libn & period indexer in circ dept UToronto Lib 36-42; Can Womens Army Corps (Lt) 42-45; Canadian Index to Period & Documentary Films, Indexer 48-49, Ed 48-59 Cumulation 59-62, Ed 62-. 9: CanLA. 10: May Court Club of Ottawa. 14: Admin, rare bks. 15: 97 Stanley ave, Ottawa Can.

WOELFL, NANCY PATRICIA (NEWMAN). b Cleveland Ohio 8 Jl 45. 4: John N Woelfl. 5: Notre Dame Col (Ohio) 63-67 (Eng) BA; Case West ResU 67-68 MSLS. 6: Ger. 7: Asst libn Case West Res Sch of Med Lib 68; Ref libn Ohio State U Health Ctr Lib (Columbus) 68-. 9: MedLA; ASIS. 14: Ref, automated bibliog searching. 15: Health Ctr Lib Ohio State Univ 1645 Neil ave, Columbus Oh 43210.

WOELFLEIN, ANN (BUCKLEY). b Boston Mass 2 Jl 33. 4: Kevin G Woelflein. 5: Regis Col 51-55 (Chem) AB; Drexel 59-63 MS in LS. 7: Lit chem Arthur D Little, Cambridge Mass 55-57; Tech libn Allied Chem Corp, Glenolden Penn 57-59; Ref libn Wharton Sch UPenn 61-63; Indexer & abstractor Catholic Period Index Catholic Lib Assn, Haverford Penn 65-67; Ref wk Mundeline Col Learning Resources Ctr 69-. 9: SLA; CathLA. 10: Beta Phi Mu; Chicago Lyric Opera Guild; var commun renewal organizations. 14: Ref, admin. 15: 1001 Greenleaf st, Wilmette Il 60091.

WOELLER, RICHARD WILLIAM. b Kitchener Ont Can 22 Ap 39. 5: Waterloo LutheranU 59-62 (Econ) BA; UOttawa 66-67 BLS. 7: Tchr Eganville Dist High Sch, Eganville Ont Can 62-64; Circ asst Waterloo LutheranU 65-66, Period libn 68-. 14: Ref. 15: 111 Filbert st, Kitchener Ont Can.

WOERNER, W(ILLIAM) ROBERT. b Louisville Ky 29 Ja 41. 5: ULouisville 59-63 (Hist) BA, 65-65 (Hist) MA; Columbia 65-66 MS; NYU 66. 6: Ger. 7: Ref libn NY Hist Soc, NYC 66-67; Soc sci libn Rutgers 67-69; Libn Behrend Campus Penn StateU 69-. 9: AHA; ALA; Org Amer Histns BSA; PennLA; NY Tech Serv Libns (Prog Chm 66-67). 10: Filson Club. 14: Lib hist, ref, admin. 15: Behrend Campus Penn State Univ, Erie Pa 16510.

WOHLSEN, THEODORE (OELRICH) JR. b Lancaster Penn 9 Mr 37. 4: Grace Zahn. 5: Franklin & Marhsall 54-58 (Ind Mgt) BS in Ec, 59-60 Temp certif to teach pub schs; Drexel 62-63 MSLS. 7: Tchr Lampeter-Strasburg Jr High Sch, Lampeter Penn 60; Lib asst Millersville State Col 60-62; Lib asst Congregation Keneseth Israel, Elkins Park Penn 62-63; Ser catlgr URochester Lib 63-64; Child libn & br hd Free Lib of Phila 64-66; Asst in ref dept & asst to hd ref dept Penna State U Lib (Univ Park) 66-68; Hd gen ref & govt docs unit Conn State Lib, Hartford 69-. 9: ALA; TheatreLA. 14: Ref, theater bibliog. 15: 21 Natick st, Hartford Ct 06106.

WOINOWSK, ORRINE LILIAN. b San Antonio Tex 11 Ag 20. 5: Our Lady of the Lake Col 40-44 (Hist) BA, 45-46 BS in LS; UTex summers 48, 50, 52 (Hist) . 7: Tchr Barkley Elem Sch, San Antonio Tex 44-45; Assoc libn Tarleton State Col 46-53; Libn US Civil Serv; Japan 53-55, Okinawa 55-56, Brooke Gen Hosp, Ft Sam Houston Tex 56-57; Div libn USMC US Civil Serv, Okinawa 57-59; Admin asst Pub Lib of Stockton & San Joaquin Co Cal 60; Engnr libn Gen Dynamics/Convair, San Diego 60-62; Admin libn NARMCO Research & Development, San Diego 62; Med libn US Civil Serv Brooke Gen Hosp, Ft Sam Houston Tex 62-64; Tech info spec head systems, Lawrence Radiation Lab, Livermore Cal 64-66; Admin libn Human Resources Lab, Lackland AFB Tex 66-. 14: Admin, systems, catlg. 15: 10614 Burr Oak dr, San Antonio Tx 78230.

WOJTOWICZ, SIGMUND WALTER. b Bayonne NJ 12 D 32. 5: Seton Hall U 52-56 (Eng) AB (cum laude) 56-58 (Eng) Am; Rutgers 57-61 MLS; NYU 63-64 (Literary criticism). 6: Anglo-Saxon, Fr, Ger, Lat, Polish. 7: Free Pub Lib, Bayonne NJ; Libn trainee 57-61, Jr libn 61-64, Sr libn 64-65, Libn Sr & Hd circ dept 65-. 9: ALA-RTSD;-ACRL; NJLA. 10: Mod Lang Assn; Nat Wildlife Fed; Amer Assn for UN; NAACP. 13: Yes. 14: Catlg, bibliog, educ for libnship, translation. 15: 123 W 19th st, Bayonne NJ 07002.

WOLCOFF, PHILIP. b Bronx NY 17 N 32. 4: Sandra Sontz Wolcoff. 5: CCNY 50-53 (Eng) BA; Pratt 53-54 MLS. 7: Pub info specialist Sp/4 USA 2nd Army Hdqtrs, Ft Beorge Mead 55-56; Sr br libn Gun Hill Br NY Pub Lib 57-58, Sr asst br libn Wakefield Br 59-61, Sr asst br libn Castle Hill Br 61-63, Supv br libn Castle Hill Br 64-; Libn, Instr Paul Klapper Lib Queen's Col 68-. 8: Co-Coordinator of Bibliographical Research Project for cultural History Research Inc (Rye NY) Involving the Central Research Library of the ny public Library 67-68. 13: Yes. 14: Adult serv. 15: 43-44 Kissena blvd, Flushing NY 11355.

WOLCOTT, CHRISTINA. b Akron Ohio 23 Je 40. 5: Ohio Wesleyan U 58-62 (Fr, Eng) BA; West Res summer 62 (LS); Catholic U 64-65 MS in LS. 6: Fr, Ger, Russian. 7: Clerk Purdue U Libs 62-63; Catlgr analyst LC Gen Ref & Bibliog Div Internat Org Sect, Wash DC 65; Bibliogr Spec langs dept, slavic div, ser sect, UIll Lib (Urbana) 65-68, Catlgr 68-, Asst Prof 69-. 9: ALA. 10: Phi Beta Kappa; Beta Phi Mu. 14: Ser, catlg. 15: 2303 S First st apt 202, Champaign Il 61820.

WOLCOTT, MERLIN DEWEY. b Sandusky Ohio 22 O 20. 5: Bowling Green State U 50(Educ) BS; Kent State U 53 (LS) MA; West Res 53-54. 7: (Cpl) US Army 42-45; Tchr Marion Ohio 50-52; Asst sci & tech div Cleveland Pub Lib 52-53; Head Libn Avon Lake Pub Lib, Avon Lake Ohio 55-56; Head Libn Elyria Lib, Elyria mohio 55-62; Head Libn Canton Pub Lib, anton Ohio 62-. 9: ALA; SLA; OhioLA. 10: Mayflower SOC; SAR; NE Hist & Geneal Soc; West RES Hist Soc; Lorain Co Hist Soc; Soc of Descendants of Henry Wolcott; Lib CLUB (Cleveland); Welfare Coun, Coun of Churches. 13: Yes. 14: Geneal. 15:506 Aultman ave NW, Canton Oh 44708.

WOLD, LAURANE EVELYN. b Pequot Lakes Minn 13 My 15. 5: UMinn 3338 (LS) BS; Columbia 4954 (LS) MS, summers 5760 (LS). 7: Libn Giles Co Sch Dist, Pearisburg Va 3943; Sch & pub libn, Hastings Minn 4448; Libn Sch Dist #206, Alexandria Minn 48. 9: ALA; NEA; MinnASchL; MinnEA. 10: Bus & Prof Woman-s Club. 14: Sch libs. 15: Box 403, Alexandria Mn 56308.

WOLF, CAROL JANE. b Tulsa Okla 2 S 39. 5: UColo (Denver) 57-59; UOkla 60-63 (Hist) BA, 63-65 MLS. 7: Catlgr Sheppard AFB, Wichita Falls Tex 65-66; Hd child dept Ontario City Lib, Ontario Cal 66-. 9: ALA; CalLA. 15: 1145 WI apt 16, Ontario Ca 91762.

WOLF, EDWARD GEORGE. b Greensburg Penn 6 Je 30. 4: Nancy Snider. 5: Duquesne U 49-53 (Hist) B Ed; UPittsburgh 54-58 (Hist) M Letters; Harvard 56 (Hist): Drexel 59-62 MSLS; UPittsburgh (LS). 7: Program dir Jeanette Recreation Assn, Jeanneatte Penn 51-56; Tchr soc studies Shaler Twp High Sch, Glenshaw Penn 53-58; Tchr soc studies Abington Twp Sr High Sch, Abington Penn 58-61; Libn Huntington Jr High Sch, Abington Penn 61-62; Asst libn Ind State col (Penn) 62-, TchrI Learning Resources and Mass Media summer 68. 8: Lib asst Penn Room Carnegie Lib Pittsburgh summer 58. 10: AAUP; Pi Gamma Mu; Beta Phi Mu; Phi Delta Kappa. 13: Yes. 14: Ref, tchg, admin. 15: 162 Lantern lane, Indiana Pa 15701.

WOLF, EDWIN II. b Phila Penn 6 D 11. 4: Mary Paxton. 7: Catlgr & bibliogr Rosenbach Co, Phila 30-43, Mgr 46-52; S/Sgt Military Intelligence, ETO 43-45; Curator Library Co of Phila 53-55, Libn 55-. 8: Lectr in Bibliog, BrynMawr Col 41-42; Res Assoc Winterthur Museum 63-; Rosenbach Fellow in Bibliog 63-64. 9: BSA (pres 67-68); ALA-ACRL (Rare Bk sect 64); Jewish Publ Soc (pres 53-59); Nat Found for Jewish Cult (pres 60-65); Inst early Amer Hist (Coun 66-68); Amer Antiq Soc; Mass Hist Soc: Penn Hist Assn; Hist Soc of Penn. 10: Philobiblon Club (Phila); Franklin Inn Club (Phila); Grolier Club (NY); Friends of UPenn Lib. 11: Guggenheim Fellow 61; Athenaeum of Phila Lit Award 61; DHL Col of Jewish Studies, Chicago 65. 13: Yes. 14: Rare bks. 15: 1314 Locust st, Philadelphia Pa 19107.

WOLF, REV EUGENE. b Allenton Wis 18 O 27. 5: Mary Immaculate Sem 47-51 (Philos) BA; Catholic U 56-61 (Catholic Soc Thought) MA, 61-64 MS in LS. 6: Ger, Lat, Sp. 7: Tchr Capuchin Sem of St Felix (Huntington Ind) 54-59; Tchr Capuchin Sem of St Mary (Crown Point Ind) 61-, Libn 64-. 9: ALA; CathLA. 10: Nat Cath Soc Action Conf; Nat Cath Rural Life Conf. 15: Capuchin Sem of St Mary Lib, 8400 Burr st, Crown Point In 46307.

WOLF, GEORGE. b NYC 21 D 25. 4: Fay Lieberman. 5: Yeshiva Col 44-49 (Sociol) BA; Hunter Col 58-59 (Hist) MA; Columbia 61-62 MS in LS. 6: Hebrew, Yiddish. 7: Libn Brooklyn Pub Lib 62-. 13: Yes. 14: Adult serv. 15: 2122 78th st, Brooklyn NY 11214.

WOLF, MORRIS. b NYC 3 Ap 27. 4: Regina M Markowitz. 5: Yeshiva U 44-49 (Sociol) BA; Hunter Col 58-60 (Hist) MA; Columbia 60-62 (LS) MS; SUNY 64 Pub Libns Prof Certif. 6: Yiddish, Hebrew. 7: Tchr priv schs, NJ 55-57; Libn adult serv Brooklyn Pub Lib 62-67; Sr catlg libn descr catlg div Sterling Lib Yale 67-68; Libn III ref & reader serv dept New Haven (Conn) Free Pub Lib 68-. 13: Yes. 14: Ref. 15: 33-E Liberty st, New Haven Ct 06519.

WOLF, MURIEL (G). b NYC 19 Mr 20. 4: Sidney Wolf. 5: HUNTER Col 37-41 (Pre-Joalism) BA; Broolyn Col 56-60 (Eng) MA; Pratt 61-64 MLS. 7: Tchr of lib Franklin K Lane High Sch, brooklyn NY 60-. 9: NYC SchLA; NY Lib Club. 10: United Fed of Tchrs. 15: 29 DeKoven ct, BROOKLYN NY 11230.

WOLFE, CHARLOTTE ANN. b Cedar Falls Iowa 22 D 36. 5: Peabody 54-58 (Soc Studies) BA; Umich 59-60 AMLS. 7: Catlg libn UMich60-. 9: ALA; MusLA. 10: Sigma Alpha Iota. 14: Catlg (music). 15: 505 Packard apt 1, Ann Arbor Mich 48104.

WOLFE, EUNICE (LUCILE). b Ellsworth Kan 14 F 13. 5: Kan State Tchrs Col 31-36 (LS) BS, 45 (Sociol) AB. 7: Lib Jr Col, Dodge City Kan 36-38; Ext libn Kansas Travel Libs, Topeka Kan 38-40; Ext libn Kan State Tchrs Col (Emporia) 40-43; Asst memb Dept ALA, Chicago 43-44; Libn Paseo br Lib, Pub Lib, Kan City Mo 45-47; Asst libn Pub Lib, Decatur Ill 47-50; Br libn & head of brs Pub Lib, Tacoma Wash 50-53; 1st asst Gen Reading Lib Assn, Portland Ore 53-55, Head Popular Lib 55-62; Head circ dept Kan State Tchrs Col (Emporia) 62-63; Spec asst Pub Lib, Kansas City Mo 63-64; Libn Rockwood Br Lib Assn, Portland Ore 64-65, Libn Gregory Heights Br 65-66; Hd Bks for the Blind 67-. 9: ALA; PNLA; OreLA. 15: Lib Assn of Portland, 801 SW 10th ave, Portland Or 97205.

WOLFE, ITHMER (COFFMAN). b Coldwater Mich 1 Ag 05. 4: Hugh C Wolfe. 5: U Mich 24-28 (LS) BA, Mich Tchrs Certif; Rutgers 56-61 (LS). 6: Fr, Ger, 07: Asst Coldwater PVUB Lib, Coldwater Mich 22-24; Asst kindergarten tchr pub schs, Coldwater Mich 23-24; Asst: child dept Pub Lib, Ann Arbor Mich 25-28, High Sch Lib, Fordson Sch System, Fordson Mich 28-29, City Sch Lib Los Angeles Sch System 29-30; Libn Mackay & Stillman Schs, Tenafly Sch System, Tenafly NJ 58-65; Libn Stillman Sch System, Tenafly NJ 65-. 9: NEA; ALA; NJEA; NJSchLA (Memb Chm 60-62). 10: LWV; UN Assn. 12: Co-auth "How to Organize and Maintain a Library Picture/Pamphlet File" (68). 13: Yes. 14: Child serv. 15: 30 Lawrence pky, Tenafly NJ 07670.

WOLFE, RICHARD JAMES. b Pittsburgh 7 My 28. 4: Elin L Wolfe. 5: UPittsburgh 49 (Classical & Modern Langs) AB; Carnegie 54 MLS. 7: Intel lang off USAF, US & Abroad 50-53; Research lbn si-tech libn UPittsburgh 54-56; Asst ref dept NY Pub Lib 56-64; Ref libn Lilly Lib Ind U 64-65; Rare bks libn Francis A Countway Lib of Med of Harvard U 65-; Lectr on the bk arts & rare bks Sch of Lib Sci Simmons 66-. 9: BSA; Bibliog Soc UVa; Bibliog Soc, London; Private Libs Assn; Printing Hist Soc. 10: Amer Antiq Soc; Colonial Soc Mass. 11: Grants: NY Pub Lib 58-64, Amer Philos Soc 64, ACLS 65. 12: Comp "Secular Music in America; a

Bibliography of Ship Passenger Lists, 1538-1825 (63); Assoc ed "A Concordance to the Complete Writings of William Blake (65). 13: Yes. 14: Bibliog, rare bks, ref. 15: 10 Shattuck st, Boston Ma 02115.

WOLFE, ROBERT J. b Dunkirk NY 30 Ap 34. 5: SUNY (Fredonia) 52-56 (Elem Educ) BS; Syracuse 59-62 (LS) MS. 7: Grad asst catlg dept Syracuse U 59; Pfc Glockenspiel player - Tanker US Army 56-58; Libn Niagara St Sch, Niagara Falls NY 60-63; Libn Craven Crawford Elem Sch, Liverpool NY 63-64; Child libn Lib/USA World's Fair 64; Head central child room Free Pub Lib, Woodbridge NJ 65-66; Chief tech serv West NY Reg Lib, Medina NY 66. 9: ALA; Niagara Orleans Area Assn of Sch Libns (pres 68-70); NYLA; NJLA; NJStateTA. 10: Orleans Theatre of Performing Arts. 14: Tech serv, wk with child & sch libs. 15: 1014 W Center st, Medina NY 14103.

WOLFE, WILLIAM JEROME. b Chicago 24 F 27. 5: UChicago 47-48, 49-51 (Eng) AB; Roosevelt U 51-53 (Eng, Music) BA; UIll 55-58 (LS); Chicago Tchrs Col 59-63 (LS) MEd. 6: Fr. 7: Clerk-typist US Army Camp Pickt Va, Stuttgart Germany 45-46; Biller-typist sales E I duPont de Nemours & Co, Chicago 48-49;. En tchr: Crescent City Community High Sc, Chicao 56-60; Tchr of Eng & Amer Hist S Mountain High Sch, Phonix 60-61; Libn Safford Jr High Sch, Tucson 61-. 9: ALA; NEA; Ariz State LA (Sch libs div, Exec Bd, Jr High Sch Libs Com 65-66); ArizEA; TucsonEA. 10: Tucson Gilbert & Sullivan Theatre; Classic Guitar Soc; Jr Great Bks Discussion Leader. 14: Sch libnship, story-telling, ref. 15: 8460 E Rosewood, Tucson Az 85710.

WOLFENBERGER, CHAS M. b Chicago 10 Jl 03. 4: Ann E Leary. 5: UIll 21-25 (Chem.07: Acme Steel Co, River- dale Ill: Chem 25-38, Chief clerk 38-47, Tech libn 47-53, Dir Tech Lib 53-62; Libn Chicago Police Acad 62-64;Libn Penn State U Grad Center (King of Prussia) 64-. 9: SLA (chm 2 tr coms; tresas Metals Div; Ill Chap: past dir & chm var coms). 15: Rt 23 & Henderson rd, King of Prussia Penn 19406.

WOLFERT, RICHARD JEROME. b Chicago 18 O 29. 4: Ann Zaslavsky. 5: Chicago City Jr Col Wright B 51-52; Chicago 52-55, 59 (LS) AM. 7: Tech processes libn Municipal Ref Lib, Chicago 57-60; Head tech processes dept Racine Pub Lib, Racine Wis 60-64; Dir ref & loan lib div for lib serv, Dept of Pub Instr, State of Wis, Madison Wis 65-68; Dir Bismarck ND Pub Lib 68-. 9: MusLA; WisLA. 12: "The Government of the City of Chicago (60. 13: Yes. 14: Adult serv, tech serv, admin. 15: 1322 N 4th st, Bismarck ND 58501.

WOLFF, EMILY DOAK. b Grand Forks ND 24 Jl 17. 4: Nathan Wolff. 5: Bryn Mawr 35-39 (Gk, Lat) BA; UMich 42-44 ABLS; Columbia 50-57 (Gk) MA PhD. 6: Lat, Fr, Ger, Gk. 7: Asst in lib UMich 42-44; Catlgr Brooklyn Col Lib 46-50; Instr in Classics Barnard Col 56-57; Catlgr Pace Col 59-67; Catlgr Borough of Manhattan Commun Col Lib 67-68, Circ libn 68-. 9: LACUNY; Amer Classical League. 14: Circ, ref, catlg. 15: 82-24 135th st, Jamaica NY 11435.

WOLFF, WALTER J. b Hamburg Germany 13 S 23. 4: Rachael Fischman Wolff. 5: CCNY 50-56 (Bus Admin) BBA; Columbia 56-58 (LS) MS. 6: Ger, Danish, Swedish. 7: Libn grade 2 Brooklyn Pub Lib, Brooklyn NY 58-60, Libn grade 3 60-62, Libn grade 4 62-, Chief sci & ind div, Grand Army Plaza 62-. 9: ALA; SLA; Ms Soc; NY Lib Club. 10: Soc Philatelic Americans. 14: Ref. 15: 2153 E 14 st, Brooklyn NY 11229.

WOLFORD, JANET. b McKinney Tex 19 Jl 39. 5: Tex ChristianU 56-60 (Mus) BME; N Tex StateU 65-66 MLS. 7: Tchr: Weatherford Pub Schs, Weatherford Tex 60-62, 63-64, Amarillo Pub Schs, Amarillo Tex 62-63; Catlgr N Tex StateU 65-66; Acquis libn Mobil Research & Development Corp Field Research Lab, Dallas Tex 66-. 9: SLA (Memb Chm Tex chap 68-70); TexLA; Dallas Co (Tex) LA. 14: Tech processes, automation. 15: Apt 234 3631 Folklore trail, Dallas Tx 75224.

WOLLTER, PATRICIA M. b San Francisco Calif 30 Mr 41. 4: Terry D Wollter. 5: San Francisco State Col 62-66 BA; UCal (Berkeley) 67 MLS. 6: Fr, Ger. 7: Sec San Francisco State Col; Asst ref libn San Francisco Pub Lib 68; Asst ref libn LIU 69-. 9: ALA. 10: ACLU; AFSC; Sierra Club; AAUP. 14: Ref. 15: 6 Winnebago rd, Yonkers NY 10710.

WOLOHAN, JULIET FRANCES. b Albany NY. 5: Siena Col 41-45 (Hist) BA; SUNY 44-45, 49-50 MS in LS, ext 47-49 (Pol Sci; American U 58 (Preservation & Admin of Archives) Certif. 6: Fr. 7: NY State Lib: Lib asst 32-45; Jr libn 45-54, Asst libn 54-58, Sr libn 58-66, Assoc libn 66-. 9: ALA; CathLA; SAA; Amer Assn State & Loc Hist; Amer Soc Pub Admin; NYLA; NY State Hist Assn; Rensselaer Co Hist Soc. 10: NY State Civil Serv Employees Assn; Coun of Women, NY State Educ Dept; Delta Epsilon Sigma. 14: Ref & research in NY State & loc hist, mss, archives, maps. 15: 210 Lindbergh ave, Rensselaer NY 12144.

WOLSKI, EDWARD D. b Holyoke Mass 18 S 13. 4: Ruth Bigger. 5: Poznan (Poland) 32-39 (Chem, Agric) BS; Catholic U 50-51 (LS); Middlebury Col 58-63 (Soviet Area Studies) MA. 6: Russian, Polish, Ger, Fr, Sp. 7: LC: Prelim catlgr 50-51, Catlgr indexer 52, Tr indexer 53-54, Research spec 55-. 8: Reviewer, Quality Control Br, European Abstracting Proj, Wiesbaden Germany; Conf reporter, Internat confs, Europe 62; Escort-interpreter on spec assignments for the State Dept (US-USSR sci Exch dels) 61-. 9: SLA; ACS; Soc of Fed Linguists. 13: Yes. 14: Ref, sci & tech info proc. 15: 4000 Tunlaw rd NW, Wash DC 20007.

WOLSTENCROFT, ALAN LAMBERT. b Denton Lancs England 31 D 29. 5: Leeds Sch of Libnship 51-52 (LS) ALA; UOre 59-62 (Gen Arts & Letters) BA. 7: Lib asst Hyde Pub Lib, Hyde England 50-51; Mobile libn Warwickshire Co Lib, Alcester England 53-55; Hd catlgr Fraser Valley Reg Lib, Abbotsford BC Can 55-56; Traveling libs & reg libn Pub Lib commsn, Victoria BC Can 57-59; Ref libn UOre 59-62; Pub lib consul Ore State Lib 62-65; Doc specialist San Francisco State Col 65-. 9: CalLA. 10: Phi Beta Kappa. 14: Govt docs. 15: San Francisco State Col Lib 1630 Holloway ave, San Francisco Ca 94132.

WOMACK, (SHARON) KAY. b Hominy Okla 23 Jl 43. 5: UOkla 62-66 (Fr) BA, 66-67 MLS. 6: Fr. 7: Ref libn I UWash Suzzallo Lib 67-. 9: ALA; Wash StateLA; PNLA; Pac NW Assn Church Libns. 10: UWash Fac Women's Club; UWash Lib Staff Assn. 14: Ref, orientation. 15: 1620 E McGraw, Seattle Wa 98102.

WOMACK, J PRINTISE. b Auburn Ky 25 N 15. 4: Rhoda Hill. 5: U Redlands 32-35 (Chem); UCal (Berkeley) 37-38; San Francisco State Col 54-56 (Lang Arts) AB; Fresno State Col 56-57; UCal (Berkeley) 57-58 MLS. 7: (Pvt) US Army Coast Artillery W Pt Prep Sch, W Pt NY 36-37; Hd catlg dept Fresno State Col Lib 58-. 9: CalLA. 10: Amer Fed of Tchrs; Cal State Employees Assn; Assn Cal State Col Profs; ACLU. 14: Catlg. 15: 3575 Circe Court E, Fresno Cal 93703.

WOMACK, NELLEEN RUTH (STROUD). b Honey Grove Tex 13 Ja 26. 4: Aaron Monroe Womack Jr. 5: N Tex StateU 43-44 (Home Econ); E Tex StateU 54-57 (Elem Educ) BS, 58-60 (LS) MEd, 66-67 MS in LS. 6: Fr. 7: Elem tchr Mesquite Pub Schs, Mesquite Tex 57-60; Libn Garland High Sch, Garland Tex 60-63; City libn Mesquite Pub Lib, Mesquite Tex 63-. 8: Consul for four Tex libs 66-69. 9: Dallas Metro LA (v-pres 65, pres 66); Tex Munic LA (pres 66-67); TexasStateTA (chm Lib Sect 62-63). 10: Bus & Profess Women's Club; Women's Coun of Clubs, Mesquite Tex; Delta Kappa Gamma; C of C; AAUW. 14: Admin. 15: 520 Kathy dr, Mesquite Tx 75149.

WOMELDORF, JOHN HUBERT. b Richmond Va 1 Jl 39. 5: Davidson Col 57-61 (Pre-med) BS; UNC (Chapel Hill) 66-68 MS in LS. 7: Antisubmarine warfare off USN (Lt), Atlantic 62-65; Lib fellow UNC (Chapel Hill) 66-68; Spec recruit LC 68-69, Descr catlgr 69-. 9: ALA. 10: Beta Phi Mu. 14: Proc, admin, rare bks, ref. 15: 510 2nd st SE, Washington DC 20003.

WONG, CHUCK (CHAK-CHUNG). b Hong Kong 19 Ag 34. 4: Margaret Lee. 5: Nat Taiwan U (Taipei) 54-58 (Eng) BA; Toronto 58-61 (Sociol) BA; UOttawa 63-64 BLS. 6: Chinese, Fr. 7: Catlgr Laurentian U (Sudbury Ont) 64-. 14: Catlg, ref. 15: Laurentian Univ Lib, Sudbury Ont Can.

WONG, CLARK C Y. b Canton China 9 O 37. 4: Rosalyn Darrah. 5: Nat Chengchi U (Taiwan) 56-60 (Eng Lit) BA; UNev 61-64 (Secondary Educ) MA; UMich 64-65 (LS) MA; USoCal (NDEA Inst) summer 66 (LS); UNev 68-69 (Sch Admin, Supv). 6: Chinese, Fr. 7: Eng tchr Oriental Col (Hong Kong) 60-61; Asst libn high sch, Reno Nev 65-69; Asst dir Learning Materials Ctr Commun Col of Denver (Colo) 69-. 8: Tech Planning Com, Nev Ctr for Coop Lib Serv 67; Curr Lib Steering Com, Washoe Co Sch Dist, Reno Nev 67-. 9: ALA; NEA-DAVI; Nev State EA; NevLA; Washoe Co ASchL. 10: Nat Cong Parents & Tchrs Assn; UMich Alum Assn; UNev Alum Assn. 14: Sch libn. 15: Commun Col of Denver, No Campus - 1001 E 62nd ave, Denver Co 80216.

WONG, DOROTHY (HUIE). b NYC 30 N 02. 5: Hunter Col 20-24 (Biol Sci) BA; Columbia 24-5 (Bacteriology) MA;

Simmons 54-55 MLA. 6: Chinese, Fr, Ger. 7: Asst Dept of Bacteriology Peiping Union Med Col (Peiping China) 25-29, Assoc Dept of Bacteriology 30-34; Asst Prof Dept of Bacteriology Nat Med Col (Shanghai China) 34-38; Asst Prof Dept of Bacteriology St Joyns Med Sch (Shanghai China) 45-47; Research asst Pub Health Research, NYC 49-51; Jr mycologist Harvard Med Sch 52-53; Ref libn Yale Med Lib 55-57; Med libn VA Hosp, West Haven Conn 57-61, ChiefLibn 62-. 9: MedLA. 13: Yes. 14: Readers serv. 15: 308 Great Oak rd, Orange Ct 06477.

WONG, EVELYN (EKARD). b Iowa Falls Iowa 20 Ag 25. 5: Rockford Col 43-45; UIll 45-47 (Fr) AB; UCLA 66-67 MLS. 6: Fr, Sp, Portu. 7: Lib asst Dayton & Montgomery Co Pub Lib Vandalia Br, Vandalia Ohio 54-58, 63-66; Gift & exchange libn Zimmerman Lib UNM 68-. 9: ALA; NMLA. 14: Acquis. 15: 7007 Edwina ave NE, Albuquerque NM 87110.

WONG, HELEN. b Canton China 12 S 19. 5: Nat Sun Yat-senU (Canton China) (Educ) BA; UMich (Ann Arbor) MALS. 6: Chinese. 7: Hr libn USIS Lib, Hong Kong 50-56; Lib asst Grand Rapids Pub Lib, Grand Rapids Mich 56-58, Asst catlgr 59-62; Chinese catlgr Asia Lib UMich (Ann Arbor) 62-63; Spec materials libn Grand Valley State Col 63-. 14: Catlg. 15: 1428 Burke NE, Grand Rapids Mi 49505.

WONG, ISAAC (SING HON). b Hong Kong 27 F 34. 4: Emily Cheng. 5: Chung Chi Col 52-56 (Eng) Diploma; bBaylor U 58-61 (Eng) BA; UOkla 61-63 MLS. 6: Chinese, Ger. 7: Asst to registrar Hong Kong Baptist Col 56-57, Asst Eng dept 57-58; Stud asst Science Lib UOkla 62-63; Asst libn catlgr Lake Forest Col Lib 63-65, Asst libn for acquis 66-. 10: AAUP. 14: Tech proc. 15: Lake Forest Col Lib, Le Forest Ill 60045.

WONG, MARGARET C(HENG). b Canton China 25 My 38. 4: Leon Wong. 5: Nat Taiwan U 54-58 (Lang & Lit) BA; USoCal 59-60 MS in LS. 6: Chinese. 7: Libn & sr libn Brooklyn Pub Lib 60-64; Ref libn Ft Wayne Pub Lib, Ft Wayne Ind 64-67; Ref libn Los Angeles Co Pub Lib, Los Angeles 67-. 9: IndLA; CalLA. 14: Ya & ref serv. 15: 18602 Rhine pl, Cerritos Ca 90701.

WONG, SMAY LI. b China 20 Je 42. 4: Kea Ling Wong. 5: MacMurray Col 63-65 (Psych) BA; UIll 66-67 (LS) MA. 6: Chinese, Fr. 7: Catlgr Tech Inst Lib NorthwesternU 67-. 9: ALA; ASIS. 14: Catlg, info stor & retr. 15: 2016 1/2 Sherman ave, Evanston Il 60201.

WOO, WINNIE (HSIAO). b Hupei China 6 O 43. 4: Wallace D Woo. 5: Nat TaiwanU 60-64 (Eng) BA; UOre 65 (LS); UPittsbirgh 66 MLS. 6: Chinese, Fr, Japanese, Ital. 7: Stud asst UOregon 65; Stud asst UPittsburgh 66; Catlgr UMass 67-. 14: Catlg. 15: 435 N Pleasant st apt 113, Amherst Ma 01002.

WOOD, ANN (RAYNER). b London England 13 Ag 18. 4: Charles E Wood. 5: UColo 36-40 (Psych) BA; UDenver 40-41 BS in LS. 7: Circ libn pub lib, Lake Forest Ill 41-43; Vol libn: Newport Hosp, Newport RI 48-49, Ascension Sch, Sierra Madre Cal 50-53, Grace Hosp Med Lib, Hutchinson Kan 59-61; Libn W Deptford High Sch, Woodbury NJ 62; Sci libn NorthwesternU 62-65; Ext coord Spokane Co Lib, Spokane Wash 69-. 10: Girl Scouts (var official duties). 12: Weekly Radio program on libs: KCVL Colville Wash 66-68, KZUN Spokane Wash 69-. 15: E 1003 Indiana ave, Spokane Wa 99207.

WOOD, BARBARA JANE. b Brooklyn NY 23 D 39. 5: Queens Col (NY) 57-60 (Eng) BA; Hunter Col 61-63 (Eng) MA; Columbia 63-64 MS in LS. 6: Fr. 7: Instr Lib Dept CCNY 64-. 9: BSA; NYLC; William Morris Soc. 10: Phi beta Kappa. 14: Rare bks. 15: 35-15 78th st, Jackson Heights NY 11372.

WOOD, BARBARA WANETTE (HOLLEMAN). b Normangee Tex 18 F 40. 4: Clinton Ray Wood. 5: Texas A&M U summer 58; Sam Hoyston State Col 58-62 (Eng) BA; LSU 66-67 (LS) MS. 6: Fr. 7: Lib clk UHouston 64-66; Libn catlgr LC 67-. 9: ALA. 10: Phi Kappa Phi. 14: Catlg of ser. 15: 15128 Concord dr, Woodbridge Va 22191.

WOOD, DANIEL (ALFRED). b Titusville Penn 27 Je 23. 5: Columbia 46-50 (Comparative Lit) BS, 59-60 MSLS. 6: Ger, Fr. 7: Libn NY Pub Lib circ dept 59-62; Ref libn Engring Socs Lib, NYC 62-65; Chief libn Ctr for Urban Educ, NYC 65-. 9: ALA; ASIS; SLA; NY Lib Club. 10: Archons of Colophon. 14: Admin, catlg, bibliog, documentation. 15: 16 Sidney pl, Brooklyn NY 11201.

WOOD, DARROW (CRAIG). b Rochester NY 28 Ag 40. 4: Judith Goldberg. 5: MIT 58-61 (Math & Econ) URochester 62-64 (Eng) AB; UMich 65-66 AMLS; CUNY 67- (Eng). 6: Fr. 7: Math libn ColumbiaU 66-69; Asst acquis libn NYC Community Col 69-. 10: Phi Kappa Phi; Beta phi Mu. 14: Acquis, ser, admin. 15: 890 West End ave, New York NY 10025.

WOOD, EVELYN L (ERICKSON). b Tustin Mich 24 Ag 09. 5 Mich State Normal Col 7-31 (Eng) AB; UMich summers 56-57, 62,63,64 (LS) MA. 6: Fr. 7: Tchr Mecosta Pub Sch, Mecosta Mich 36-39; Tchr-libn Barryton Rural Agric Schs, Barryton Mich 51-62; Supv libn & instr Lincoln Consol Lab Schs, Ypsilanti Mich 62-63; Libn Reedley High Sch, Reedley Cal 63-66; Head period sect Cal State Polytech Col 66-. 10: Kappa Delta Pi; Alpha Sigma Tau. 14: Ref. 15: 510 Foothill blvd apt A4, San Luis Obispo Ca 93401.

WOOD, JAMES LESLIE. b Kan City Mo 6 Ag 26. 4: Mary E Overslaw Wood. 5: U Mo (Kan City) 48-50 (Geol) BA; West Res 50-51 MSLS. 7: Page Linda Hall Lib, Kan City 48-50; Lib asst Case Inst 51; Jr libn State Col of Wash 51-52; Head bus & tech dept Wichita City Lib 52-54; Head libn Chem Abstracts Serv, Columbus Ohio 54-. 8: Consul, Battelle Mem Inst Lib 58-, ISTIM, SATCOM, UNISIST, 150. 9: SLA; ASIS; ACS; USASI Z39 (v-chm); NFSAIS. 12: "List of Periodicals in "Chemical Abstracts (56,61); "Access-Key to Source Lit for Chem Sci" (69). 13: Yes. 14: Admin, standards. 15: 5395 Harvest st Rt 1, Dublin Ohio 43017.

WOOD, JEANNE. b Kan City Mo 18 N 23. 5: Ward-Belmont Col 41-42 (Art, Hist); UMo 43-45, 48. 7: Asst libn Employers Reinsurance Corp, Kan City Mo 45-48, Libn 48-. 9: SLA (chm Insur Div 63-64); MoLA. 10: Amer Philatelic Soc. 14: Ref. 15: 1251 W 72nd ter, Kansas City Mo 64114.

WOOD, JEREMY SPRAGUE. b NYC 2 N 23. 4: Bonnie Jean Trotter. 5: Cornell U 41-43, 46-47 (Eng) BA; Stanford 48-52 (Music); UCal (Berkeley) 52-53 BLS. 7: Asst ref libn Santa Clara U 64-. 14: Ref, rare bks. 15: 12963 Nash rd, Los Altos Ca 94022.

WOOD, JOHN BRENT. b Montgomery Co Tex 21 D 31. 5: UTex 50-55 (Liberal Arts) BA; UDenver 55-56 (Libnship) MA. 7: Ref libn San Diego State Col 56-58, Period libn 58-59, Hd circ dept 59-62; Supv period libn Cal State Col (Los Angeles) 62-64, Prin period libn 64-68, Hd period acquis sect 68-. 9: ALA; CalLA. 10: Assn Cal State Col Profs; AAUP. 13: Yes. 14: Personnel, recr, automation. 15: 5388 Poplar blvd apt 7, Los Angeles Ca 90032.

WOOD, JOHN ROBERT. b Brooklyn NY 20 My 33. 5: City Col (NY) 54-57 (Econ) BA; Fordham 57-59 (Econ) MA; Rutgers 60-62 MLS. 7: A/3c USAF, Tex 51-53; Prod control Palizzio Shoe Co, NYC 58-60; Lib trainee, libn, asst hd sci & tech, hd sci & tech, asst supt acquis Queens Borough Pub Lib, Queens NY 60-68; Acquis libn Essex Co Col 68-. 9: ALA; NYLA; NY Tech Serv Libns. 10: SANE; League for Ind Democracy; Brooklyn Inst Arts & Sci. 14: Acquis, collection bldg. 15: 175 Willoughby st, Brooklyn NY 11201.

WOOD, JUDY (GOLDBERG). b NY 7 Ag 42. 4: Darrow C Wood. 5: CCNY 61-64 (Hist) BA; UMich 64-65 MLS. 7: Catlgr Gen Motors Corp, NYC 66; Asst libn Bor of Manhattan Commun Col 66-67; Acquis libn Fashion Inst of Tech 67-. 9: SUNYAL. 10: UFCT; FDR-Woodrow Wilson Demo Club. 14: Tech serv, ref. 15: 890 W End ave, New York NY 10025.

WOOD, LINDA KAY. b Kenton Ohio 27 O 45. 5: Ohio StateU 63-67 (Hist) BA; UPittsburgh 67-68 MLS. 6: Fr. 7: Lib asst UPittsburgh 68; Vista vol, Fauquier Co Va 69-. 9: ALA. 14: Ref. 15: 3152 Parsons, Columbus Oh 43207.

WOOD, LINDA MAY (WILEY). b Ames Iowa 6 N 42. 4: C James Wood. 5: Portland State Col 60-64 (Eng) BA; UWash 64-65 MLibr. 6: Fr. 7: Jr libn Lib Assn of Portland, Portland Ore 65-67, Albina br libn 8 Gregory Heights br libn 69-. 9: ALA-PLA; OreLA; PNLA. 14: Ref, adult serv. 15: 8249 NE Beech st apt 1, Portland Or 97220.

WOOD, LISSIE CHARLOTTE (MILLER). b San Diego Cal 16 Ap 20. 4: Robert Beard Wood. 5: Mo So Col 38-40 (Hist); UIll 40-41 (Hist); San Jose State Col 57-63 (Libnship) BA, 64-68 (Libnship) MA; USanta Clara 67-68 (Eng & Hist). 7: Chief lib clk UIll (Urbana) 51-56; Lib clk San Jose State Col 57-58; Libn Sylvania Elec Prods, Mt View Cal 58-63; Libn Leigh High Sch, San Jose Cal 63-; Instr San Jose City Col 68-. 9: CalTA; CalASchL; CalLA (Legis Com 65-67); Santa Clara

Co Assn Secon Sch Libns (pres 69-70). 14: Catlg, reading guidance, admin. 15: 5210 Leigh ave, San Jose Ca 95124.

WOOD, SISTER MARY JOHN. b Appleton Wis 5 Mr 24. 5: Holy Family Col 42-58 (Educ, Eng) AB; Edgewood Col summer; CatholicU summers 62- (LS). 7: Tchr: St Andrew Sch, Potosi Wis 44-47, St Anthony Sch, Oconto Falls Wis 47-51; Tchr-libn: St Mary Sch, Algoma Wis 51-56, St Mary Sch, Hilbert Wis 56-57, St Mary Sch, Waukesha Wis 57-64; Tchr-prin-libn St Mary Sch, Algoma Wis 64-. 9: ALA; CathLA; WisLA. 10: Green Bay Diocesan Principals Assn. 15: 230 Church st, Algoma Wi 54201.

WOOD, NORMA W(ODE). b Borger Tex 26 My 27. 4: Robert D Wood. 5: UOkla 44-48 (LS) BA, 50-51 (Ger) BA. ; UIll summer 67 (LS, Catlg), summer 68 (ComptLibysems). 7: Asst libn Doane COL 48-50; Night supv of the Loan desk UOkla 50-51; Br libn Lents Br Lib Assn of Portland, Ore 51-52, Catlgr 52-53; Base libn Vance AFB, Enid Okla 53-54; Head tech processes Miss Lib Commsn, Jackson Miss 55-57; Head catlg & order dept E Chicago Pub Lib, E Chicago Ind 57-. 8: Tchr (educ, clsf, catlg) Purdue U 68; Tchg (lib sci) Ind U (Gary) 69. 9: ALA; IndLA (sec 64-65); CHICAGO Reg Group of Libns in Tech Serv. 14: Catlg. 15: 5504 Wegg ave, E Chicago In 46312.

WOOD, RAYMOND F(RANCIS). b London Eng 9 N 11. 4: Margaret Pee. 5: St Marys U (Baltimore) 27-31 (Philos) AB; Gonzaga U 3639 (Philos) MA; UCLA 46-49 (Hist) PhD; USoCal 49-50 MS in LS. 6: Lat, Fr, Sp. 7: Instr Eng DeptU Santa Clara 39-41; Tchg asst Hist Dept UCLA 41-42; Warrant off AUS Supreme Hdqrs personnel div,ETO 42-46; Registration off VA Rehabil Program, Los Angeles 6-48; PRIN REF LIBN Fresno State Col 50-66; Assoc Prof Sch Lib Sci UCLA 66-, Asst Dean 67-. 8: Dir Inst on Map Libnship UCLA summer 68. 9: ALA; CalLA (mem var coms). 10: Woodmen of the World; Fresno Co Hist Soc; Alliance fracaise de Fresno; Oral Hist Assn; Assn Col Hist Socs; Boy Scouts; E Clampus Vitus; Armenian Cultural Assn. 12: "Californias Agua Fria: the Early History of Mariposa County (52); "The Life and Death of Peter Lebec 54); Ed "Fresno Past and Present v 1 (59-); "Brief History of Mission San Jose" (58). 13: Yes. 14: Ref, spec collections (Cal hist), bibliog soc sci, tchg humanities. 15: 18052 Rosita st, Encino Ca 91316.

WOOD, ROBERT D(ILLON). b Chicago 29 My 19. 4: Norma Wode. 5: Doane Col 46-50 (Psych) BA; UOkla 50-51 (LS) BA. 7: Clerk Jays Rental Lib, Chicago 38-41; Operations NCO (814) Qtrmstr Corps (M/Sgt), AUS 41-45; Bkmob libn Lib Assn of Portland, Ore 51-52, Request asst 52-53; City Libn Enid Pub Lib, Enid Okla 53-55; Field rep Miss Lib Commsn, Jackson Miss 55-57; Asst dir & br libn E Chicago Pub Lib, E Chicago Ind 57-69, Dir 69-. 9: ALA (State Memb Chm 65-66); IndLA; Chicago Reg Group f Libns in Tech Serv. 10: Rd Cross; Rotarian; Phi Eta Sigma; Apha Psi Omega. 13: Yes. 14: Adult serv, admin. 15: 5504 Wegg ave, E Chicago Ind 46314.

WOOD, SAMUEL DEES. b Ada Okla 31 Ja 26. 4: Ruth Whitford. 5: UOkla 44-49 (Eng) BS Ed, 50-51 BALS. 7: Documents catlgr Okla State U 51-55; Asst libn NE State Col (Tahlequah Okla) 55-57; Catlgr Mo State Hist Soc, Columbia Mo 57-61; Asst catlgr UNev 61-. 14: Catlg. 15: 1570 Auburn way, Reno Nev 89502.

WOOD, THOR E. b Wash DC 3 N 32. 4: Ann Curtis. 5: Pomona Col 50-54 (Music) BA; UCal(Berkeley) 56-57 ML; Princeton U 57-60 (Music) MFA. 6: Ger, Fr. 7: (1st Lt) Comm Instr US Army, Ft Sill Okla 54-56; Sub Music Div NY Pub Lib summers 58-60; Music libn UIll (Urbana) 60-65; Chief of Research Lib of the Performing Arts at Lincoln Center NY Pub Lib 65-. 9: MusLA (Exec Bd 62-64, Placement Sec 60-67); Amer Musicological Soc; Theatre LA; Internat Assn Mus Libs (v-pres Bd 69-, chm US Br 68-); Archons of Colophon; Amer Soc Theatre Research. 10: Amer Mus Ctr Bd; Assn Recorded Sound Collections. 14: Performing arts, admin. 15: 394 Pacific st, Brooklyn NY 11217.

WOOD, VEVA (BOEKE). b Kan City Kan 11 O 1899. 4: L E Wood. 5: Baker 17-21 (Eng) BA; Okla CityU 36-38 (Educ) MEd; UKan summer 37-38 (Eng); UOkla summer 41 (Eng; UColo summer 44 (En; Tex Womans U 50-53 MLS. 7: Eng tchr: Waverly High Sch, Waverly Kan 21-25, Burns Consolidated High Sch, Burns Kan 25-27, El Dorado High Sch, El Dorado Kan 27-33; Okla City U: Instr of Eng 38, Asst Prof 41, Assoc Prof 43-49; Instr of Eng Baylor U 49-51; Assoc libn Armstrong Browning Lib Baylor U 52-60, Libn 60-. 9: ALA-ACRL; TexLA (sec 5758);WLA. 10: AAUW; Zeta Tau Alpha; Beta Phi Mu; Cardinal Key; AAUP; YWCA. 15: 1812 Seneca, Waco Tex 76707.

WOODALL, NANCY (CARBOY). b Englewood NJ 9 D 34. 5: Middlebury Col 52-54 (Eng); UMd 54-56 (Eng) AB; Catholic U 59-60 MS in LS. 7: Asst br libn Baltimore Co Pub Lib, Pikesville Md 58-59; Pre-prof asst Arlingtn Co Pub Lib, Arlington Va 59-60; Br libn Fairfax Co Pub Lib, Fairfax Va 60-65; Dir Prince William Co Pub Lib, Manassas Va 65-66; Dir Irvington Pub Lib, Irvington-on-Hudson NY 66-68; Br coord Anne Arundel Co Pub Lib, Annapolis Md 68-. 8: Staff, Lib/USA, NY Worlds Fair, 65. 9: ALA (Memb Chm Va 65-); VaLA (chm Pub Libs Sect 62-63); MdLA; NYLA; LPRC (sec). 10: Beta Phi Mu; Pi Beta Phi. 14: Lib admin. 15: 710 Americana dr #45, Annapolis Md 21403.

WOODARD, HELEN (BOTKA). b Scranton Penn 28 Jl 12. 4: Howard A Woodard. 5: Hillsdale Col 31-35 (Eng) BA; Rutgers 56-58 MLS. 6: Hungarian, Fr, Ger. 7: Elem sch tchr Hillsdale Co, Bankers Mich 35-36; Lab tech United Aircraft, Stratford Conn 41-47; Newark Free Pub Lib, Newark NJ; Trainee-libn 56-58, Libn jr & sr 58-64, libn Prin Br 65-. 9: ALA; NJLA. 10: Weequahic Adult Sch Bd; Roseville YM-YWCA Bd; Roseville Commun Coun. 14: Ref, adult serv, ya serv. 15: 94 West Cedar Lake rd, Denville NJ 07834.

WOODARD, MARION (BOYAJIAN). b New Britain Conn 15 F 27. 4: Paul Esty Woodard. 5: Central Conn State Col 44-45; Houghton Col 45-48 (Hist, Soc Sci) BA; Columbia 55-58 MS in LS. 6: Armenian. 7: Ref libn Moody Bible Inst, Chicago 49-52; Lib asst Hartford Pub Lib, Hartford Conn 52-55; Asst libn Kings Col 55-58; Libn Greenwich High Sch, Greenwich Conn 58-62; Libn Mass Col of Art 62-64; Lib consul Ruggles St Baptist Church, Boston 68-. 9: NEA; ALA; MassLA; MassEA; NELA. 10: Boston Christian Womens Club; NE Baptist Hosp (Boston) Womens Auxiliary; Nat Hon Soc. 14: Ref, secon sch lib wk. 15: 46 Hickory Cliff rd, Newton Mass 02164.

WOODARD, PAUL ESTY. b Chico Cal 24 O 21. 4: Marion Boyajian. 5: Pasadena City Col 38-41 Diploma; FriendsU 46-47, 50-52 (Nursing, Educ) BA, RN; Harvard 52 (Sci Educ) Certif; WesternU (Cal) 52-55 (Educ) PhD. 6: Sp. 7: Libn asst Alhambra Pub Lib, alhambra Cal 40-41; Production control expeditor Douglas Aircraft Corp, Long Beach cal 41-42; Stud health counselor FriendsU 50-52; Special nurse central directory dist V Mass Nu dist V Mass Nurses Assn, Boston 52-62; Med libn Doctors Lib NE Bapt Hosp, Boston 64-. 8: Consul Phys Fitness Coun, Cambridge Mass YMCA 61-63. 9: MedLA; Amer Nurses Assn; Amer Sci Affiliation; Amer Soc Train & Devel; Mass Nurses Assn. 10: Amer Nat Red Cross Nurs Serv; Fellow, Royal Numismatic Soc; Med Acad Amer (life mem); Geog Soc; NE Hist Geneal Soc. 13: Yes. 14: Ref, period. 15: 46 Hickory Cliff rd, Newton Upper Falls Ma 02164.

WOODBRIDGE, HENSLEY CHARLES. b Champaign Ill 6 F 23. 4: Annie Emma Smith. 5: Col of William & Mary 39-43 (Fr) AB; Harvard 46 (Romance Langs) MA; UIll 47-50 (Span) PhD, 50-51 MS in LS. 7: Instr for langs URichmond 46-47; Ref libn Auburn U 51-53; Libn Murray State Col 53-65; Lat Amer bibliog(r) SoIllU 65-, Assoc Prof for Langs. 9: BSA; Amer Assn Tchrs Sp & Portu. 10: Ky Hist Soc; Ky Folklore Soc; Instituto de Estudios Madrilenos. 12: Ed "Kentucky Folklore Records" (63-64); Ed KYLA "Bulletin"; Comp "Jesse Stuart; a Bibliography" (60); Ed & publ "Jack London Newsletter" (67-); Co-comp "Jack London; a Bibliography" (66). 13: Yes. 14: Latin Amer bibliog, Jack London. 15: 1804 W Freeman, Carbondale Il 62901.

WOODBURN, JUDY. b Raleigh NC 18 O 43. 5: DukeU 61-64 (Hist) BA; UNC 64-65 MSLS. 7: Ser libn Guilford Col 65-67; Ser libn DukeU Med Ctr 67-. 9: MedLA. 14: Ser. 15: 3600 Tremont dr apt D5, Durham NC 27705.

WOODFORD, ARTHUR MacKINNON. b Detroit 23 N 40. 4: Margaret Holmes. 5: UWis 58-60 (Civil Engr); Wayne State U 61-63 (Hist) BA; UMich 63-64 MALS. 7: US Naval Res 58-64; Ref tech & sci dept Detroit Pub Lib 64-66, Adult asst Sherwood Forest Br 66-67, First asst Campbell Br 67, Asst chief Downtown Br 67-68, Asst to personnel dir 68-. 9: ALA; SLA; MichLA. 10: US Naval Inst; Gt Lakes Maritime Inst; Prismatic Club; Algonquin Club. 12: "All Our Yesterdays; A Brief History of Detroit" (69). 13: Yes. 14: Ref, sci & tech. , personnel admin. 15: 1603 Edgewood dr, Royal Oak Mi 48067.

WOODFORD, JEANN (APPLEGATE). b Willoughby Ohio 19 Mr 26. 4: William H Woodford. 5: Ohio StateU 44-48 (Educ) BSc in Ed; West ResU 49-50 MS in LS; State Tchrs Col of NY summer 54; UMd (Japan) 57-58, (Korea) 59-60; Fla StarkU (Canal Zone) 63; AmericanU 67. 7: Asst libn Shaw High Sch, E Cleveland Ohio 50-53, Libn 53-54; Ya libn

Lakewood pub Lib, Lakewood Ohio 54-55, Asst adult dept 55-56; Army Spec Serv: Asst libn, Camp zama Japan 56-58, Field libn, Korea 59-61, Hosp libn, Ft Meade 61-62, Post libn, Ft Kobbe Canal Zone 62-63; Tech libn DOD Tropical Test Ctr, Ft Clayton Canal Zone 63-64; Post libn Army Spec Serv, Ft Amador Canal Zone 64-65; Catlgr Defense Atomic Support Agcy, Wash DC 65-68; Asst depot libn Army Spec Serv, Korea 59, 61, Catlgr, asst libn 68-. 10: National Genealogical Society; Ohio Geneal Soc; Friends of the Caleb Pusey House; Fairfield Heritage Assn. 14: Ref, geneal. 15: 3310 Kauffman ave, Vancouver Wa 98660.

WOODFORD, SUSAN ESTHER. b Muskegon Mich 3 Jl 41. 5: Hood Col 59-64 (Chem) AB; West MichU 65-66 MSL. 6: Fr. 7: Catlgr Lib of Med Sci UIll (Chicago) 66-69; Lit search specialist Francis A Countway Lib of Med, Boston 69-. 9: ALA; SLA. 10: Beta Phi Mu. 14: Catlg, Medlars search special. 15: 3600 N Lake Shore dr, Chicago Il 60613.

WOODLING, ANN (MORGAN). b Kansas City Mo 27 Je 43. 4: Robert Alan Woodling. 5: Lake Forest Col 61-63; UKan 63-65 (Eng) BA; UDenver 65-66 (LS) MA. 6: Lat, Fr. 7: Libn I Seattle Pub Lib 66-. 14: Ref. 15: 18146 NE 30th st, Redmond Wa 98052:

WOODRING, NELLIE MAE. b Cecilia Ky 13 Jl 22. 5: Campbellsville Jr Col 41-43 (Educ); West Ky State Col 53 (Elem Educ) BS, 62 (Educ) MA, 62 Certified for Libnship Gr 1-12. 7: Tchr Hardin Co (Ky) Bd of Educ, Howevalley Sch 44-61; Elem libn Elizabethtown (Ky) Bd of Educ Valley View Sch & Helmwood Heights Sch 61-. 9: NEA; KyEA; KyASchL. ; KyLA. 10: Dir of lib serv for Severn's Valley Baptist Assn. 15: Rt 1, Cecilia Ky 42724.

WOODRUFF, ELAINE (LINDHOLM). b Cloquet Minn 08 O 14. 4: Willard H Woodruff. 5: UMinn 35-37 (Soc Sci, Eng) BS, 39-40 (LS) Certif American U 44-46 (Public Admin) MA. 66: Ger, Fr, Finnish. 7: Libn Columbia Heights Schs, Minneapolis 40-43; Asst libn, catlgr US Civil Serv Commsn, Wash DC 43-53, Libn 54-. 9: SLA(Exec Bd DC Chap); DCLA (Exec Bd); Law Libns Assn, DC; Fed Lib Com (chm Task Force on Recr). 13: Yes. 14: Mgt, personnel admin. 15: US Civil Serv Commsn, 1900 E st NW, Wash DC 20415.

WOODRUM, FRANCES LUCILLE. b Springfield Ill 03 N 34. 5: UIll 52-56 (Eng) BA, 56-57 (LS) MS. 07: Circ asst Lincoln Lib, Springfield Ill 57-58, Asst ref dept 58-. 7: Circ asst Lincoln Lib, Springfield Ill 57-58, Asst ref dept 58-68, Hd circ dept 68-. 9: ALA; IllLA. 14: Ref, circ. 15: 2 Alberta lane, Springfield Ill 62704.

WOODRUM, PATRICIA ANN (HOFFMAN). b Hutchinson Kan 11 O 41. 4: Clayton Eugene Woodrum. 5: Kan State Col of Pittsburg 61-63 (Lit) BA; UOkla 63-64 (LS) MS. 7: Page Parson Pub Lib, Parsons 59-61; Stud asst ref dept Porter Lib Kan State Col of Pittsbirg 61-63; Libn Woodland View Br Tulsa City-Co Lib Syst 63-64, Asst chief brs 64-66, Hd ref 66-67, chief ext 67-. 9: ALA; SWLA; OklaLA (chm Sequoyah Com). 14: Pub serv. 15: 10221 South 76th E ave, Tulsa Ok 74145.

WOODS, BILL M(ILTON). Pottawattamie Co Iowa 26 My 24. 4: Janice Thumm. 5: Peru State Col 41-45 (Geog, Eng) AB; UNeb 45-46, 47-48 (Geog); UIll 46-47 BS in LS, 49-53 (LS, Pol Sci) MS. 7: UNeb Lib; Circ asst 45-46, Asst libn in soc studies & map curator 47-49; UIll(Urbana); Act map libn 46-47, Map libn 49-56, Instr in lib sci 55-58, Map & geog libn 56-58; Hd proc sect LC Map Div 58-59; SLA, NYC; Exec sec 59-63, Exec dir 63-67; Exec dir Engring Index Inc, NYC 68-. 8: Visit lecturer Grad Sch Lib Sci Drexel Inst 62, 66, 67, 68; Nat Adv Com on Lib summer 67; Mgt planner Engring Index Inc, NYC 67-68; Other consultantships for map collection. 9: CNLA (chm 64-66; sec-treas 62-64, Trustee 60-62); SLA (chm Geog & Map Div 55-57; sec Adv Coun 56-57); NY Lib Club (trustee 62-66); ASIS (sec-treas Spec Interest Gp for Educ); NY Metropolitan Ref & Research Lib Agcy, Inc (chm, sec, dir). 10: Beta Phi Mu; Amer Assn Geogrs; Sigma Tau Delta; Kappa Delta Pi; Nat Assn of Exhib Mgrs; NY Soc of Assn Execs; Amer Soc of Assn Execs; NY Metro Ref & Res Lib Agency Inc. 11: Louise W Meers Geog Award, 45; SLA Geog & Map Div Honors Award, 59 13: Yes. 14: Spec libs, maps, educ. 15: 345 E 47th st, New York NY 10017.

WOODS, DONALD A. b Jacksonville Ill 19 F 09. 4: Phyllis Marie Mathers. 5: Ill Col 32 (Eng) AB; UIll 33 BLS, 45 MLS. 6: Ger, Fr. 7: Asst libn Knox Col 35-38; Salesman Lib Bureau, Chicago 38-39; Head Libn State Tchrs Col (Superior Wis) 39-45; Head Libn Wis State Col (Milwaukee) 45-62; Archivist UWis (Milwaukee) 63-. 9: ALA (chm Tchrs Col 50-51); SLA (pres Wis Chap 55-57); WisLA (chm Col Lib Sect 62-63, dir 63-); SAA. 10: Civil War Cent Commsn of Wis; Whitefish Bay (Wis) Lib Bd; Milwaukee Civil War Round Table. 14: Archives (col & univ). 15: 6031 N Lydell ave, Milwaukee Wi 53217.

WOODS, ELMER B. b Phila 29 Mr 22. 4: Esther J Harris. 5: Bucknell U 40-43, 46-47 (Soc Sci) BA; UAriz 47-48; Rutgers 49-50 BS in LS; Drexel 59-62 MS in LS. 7: Semi-skilled musician US Army Serv Forces 306th ASF Band, Springfield Mo 43-46; Ref asst Free Pub Lib, Trenton NJ 50-52; Bus exp insurance div & real estate, Camden NJ & Phila 52-58; Ref asst Wilmington Inst Free Lib, Wilmington Del 58-59; Head libn Glassboro Pub Lib, Glassboro NJ 59-60; Head libn Clayton High Sch, Clayton NJ 60-61; Circ libn Glassboro State Col 62-64; Ref asst Gen Ref Dept UMd 64-65; Head libn W Deptford Twp, Westville NJ 65-66; Ref libn Rider Col 66-. 9: ALA-RSD;-ACRL (Col Sect); NJ. 10: ACLU; Beta Phi Mu; AAUP. 14: Ref. 15: Apt 8A 1501 Parkside ave, Trenton NJ 08638.

WOODS, FRANCES BABCOCK. b Hartford Conn 20 N 26. 5: Smith Col 44-48 (Hist) BA; Columbia 49-51 (LS) MS. 7: Catlgr Brooklyn Pub Lib 48-53; Yale Law Lib: Sr catlgr 53-59, Reviser 59-64, Chief catlg dept 65-. 9: ALA; AALL; NELA; NY Reg Tech Serv Libns; Law Libns Greater NY; Law Libns NE (pres 64-65). 14: Catlg, law libnship. 15: 572 Whitney ave apt 3-F, New Haven Ct 06511.

WOODS, JANICE LOVAINE (THUMM). b Malden WVa 28 Ag 24. 4: Bill M Woods. 5: Morris Harvey Col 41-45 (Eng) AB; UIll 46-47 B in LS. 7: Ref libn Baldwin Wallace Col 47-48; Humanities asst UNeb Lib 48-49; Revising a-v printed catlog Bd of Educ Montgomery Co, Rockville Md 59; Revising Pamphlet file Levittown Pub Lib, Levittown NY 60; Child libn Huntington Pub Lib, Huntington NY 61, Ref asst 62-66; Ref asst Half Hollow Hills Commun Lib, Dix Hills NY 66-. 14: Ref. 15: 6 Frontier lane, E Northport NY 11731.

WOODS, LINDA ANN. b Reading Penn 24 Ap 43. 5: Kutztown State Col 61-64 Lib (Educ) BS in Ed; Drexel summers 65-67 MS in LS. 6: Sp. 7: Libn Pottsgrove Sch Dist, Pottstown Stowe 64-66; Libn Reading Sch Dist Tyson-Schoener in Reading 66-68; Ref & circ libn Kutztown State Col 68-. 9: ALA. 10: Kutztown State Col Fac Assn. 14: Ref. 15: 237 E Main st, Fleetwood Pa 19522.

WOODS, WILLIAM EDWARD. b Chicago 21 Ja 28. 4: Margaret BYRNES. 5: Clemson A & M fall 45 (Liberal Arts); Wilson Jr Col 47 (Liberal Arts); Chicago Tchrs Col 47-51 (Educ) B Ed, 53-58 (Educ) M Ed in LS; Chicago 60-65 MA in LS. 7: US Army (Cpl) 45-47; US Naval Reserve Ensign 48-61; Tchr & Tchr libn Chicago pub schs 51-60; Circ libn, ref libn Chicago Tchrs Col 60-65; Materials center libn & Asst Prof of Lib Sci Ill Tchrs Col, Chicago 65-67; Br libn Wilson Campus Chicago City Col 67-. 8: Fellowship Chicago City Col Innovations Ctr (to devel program in lib tech) 68; Owns Woods Library Publ Co. 9: IllLA; Chicago Lib Club; COLT (trustee central US); ALA. 10: AAUP; Amer Fed of Tchrs; Kappa Mu Epsilon; AMER Math Soc. 12: "Woods Cross Reference System and Manual" (68). 13: Yes. 14: Ref, materials centers, indexing, info retrieval. 15: 12131 S Elizabeth st, Chicago Il 60643.

WOODWARD, ANNE MONTGOMERY. b Staunton Va 15 Ap 17. 5: Mary Baldwin Col 35-39 (Fr) AB; Columbia 39-40 (LS) BS, 49-50 (LS) MS. 6: Fr, Sp. 7: Child libn Brooklyn Pub Lib 40-41, Circ asst 41-42; Asst libn Staunton Pub Lib, Staunton Va 43; Asst libn Mary Baldwin Col 46-49; Asst to libn Wellesley Col 50-54; Readers adv White Plains Pub Lib, White Plains NY 54-55; Libn Staunton Pub Lib aunton Va 55-. 9: ALA; VaLA; SELA. 14: Admin, ref. 15: 229 E Beverly st, Staunton Va 24401.

WOODWARD, BETTY M(OULTON). b Middleboro Mass 16 O 32. 5: UMass 50-54 (Eng) BA; Drexel 54-55 MS in LS; UMass 64-68 (Educ) MEd. 7: Hosp libn US Army Lib, Ft Devens Mass 55-56; Tchr-libn Jr-Sr High Sch, Norton Mass 56-57; Lib asst Talcott Lib Northfield Sch, E Northfield Mass 57-58; Libn High Sch, Marshfield Mass 59-63; Asst libn Mason Lib Keene State Col 63-64; Libn High Sch, Keene NH 64-68; Lib asst Taunton Pub Lib, Taunton Mass 68-. 8: Catlgr & adv for recatlg bk collection Pierce Memorial Lib, N Scituak Mass 61-63. 9: ALA-AASchL (Memb Com NH); NELA; NESchLA (chm Educ Com; NESchLA-NESch Devel Coun Jt Publns Com 61-); NHSchLA; NHEA; MassSchLa; MassLA. 10: Middleboro Hist Assn; Appalachian Mountain Club; Beta Phi Mu; NH Audubon Soc; Green Mt Club. 13: Yes. 14: Catlg, ref, music. 15: 6 Reland st, Middleboro Ma 02346.

WOODWARD, DANIEL HOLT. b Ft Worth Tex 17 O 31. 4: Mary Jane Gerra. 5: UColo 48-51 (Philos) BA, 54-55 (Eng) MA; Yale 55-57 (Eng) PhD; CatholicU 68-69 (LS) MS. 7: Cpl us army, Ft Leonard Wood Missouri 52-54; Asst Prof Eng Mary Washington Col UVa 57-61, Associate Prof 61-66, Prof 66-69, Libn & Prof of Eng 69-. 8: Research leave in England, 64-65. 9: Mod Lang Assn; ALA; Renaiss Eng Text Soc. 10: ACLU; Grolier Club; Phi Beta Kappa. 12: Ed "The Poems and Translations of Robert Fletcher" (69). 13: Yes. 14: Col lib admin, rare bks. 15: 1439 College Sta, Fredericksburg Va 22401.

WOODWARD, DAVID ALFRED. b Leamington Spa England 29 Ag 42. 4: Rosalind Bailey. 5: UWales 61-64 (Geog) BA; UWis (Madison) 61-64 (Geog) MA, 67-69 (Geog). 6: Fr. 7: Instr in geog UWis (Madison) 69; Fellow in hist of cartography & consul Newberry Lib, Chicago 69-. 9: Amer Geog Soc; Brit Cartographic Soc; Printing Hist Soc (London). 11: Fulbright travel grant 64. 13: Yes. 14: Hist of cartographic tech, rare maps. 15: Newberry Lib 60 W Walton st, Chicago Il 60610.

WOODWARD, EDITH (STEPHENS). b Kiowa Kan 4 Je 17. 4: Ernest B Woodward. 5: George Washington U 42-46; (Span-Amer Lit) BA; UMich summers 55-58 MALS. 6: Sp. 7: Tchr Rural sch, Lake City Kan 36-39; Clsf records sect Fed Bur of Investigation, Wash DC 41-45; Asst libn Columbus Pub Lib, Columbus Ohio 47-57; Head documents div Ohio State Lib 57-69; Res libn Ohio Legis Serv Commsn 69-. 9: SLA; ALA; OhioLA; Ohio Reg Law Libn Assn. 10: Pi ambda Theta;Beta Phi Mu. 14: Docs & ref. 15: 4160 Lyon dr, Columbus Ohio 43221.

WOODWARD, FRANCES MARY. b Golden BC Can 13 D 38. 5: Queens U (Ont) 57-59 (Eng, Hist); UBC 59-60 (Eng, hist) BA; McGill 60-61 BLS. 7: Archivist Provincial Archives, Victoria BC 61-66; Ref libn UBC 66-. 9: BCLA; Inst Victoria Libns; ABCL; ACML; WAML; SAA. 10: BC Govt Employees Assn; BC Hist Soc; Vancouver Hist Soc; Can Hist Soc. 14: Map catlg, hist & geog res, archives. 15: Special Collections Div Univ of Brit Columbia Lib, Vancouver 8 BC Can.

WOODWARD, MARY MARGARET (CARROLL). b Westernport Md 29 N 22. 4: Reginald Vaughn Woodward. 5: Davis & Elkins Col 40-44 (Com) BA; WVaU 55-61 (LS) MA. 6: Fr. 7: Sec to financial sec Randolph Co Bd of Educ, Elkins WVa 44-45; Tchr Parsons High Sch, Parsons WVa 45-47; Libn Tygarts Valley High Sch, Mill Creek WVa 55-62; Period libn Davis & Elkins Col 62-, Asst prof lib sci 64-. 9: ALA; WVaLA. 10: Chi Omega; Elkins Women's Club; Amer Legion Aux. 14: Period, microfilm, phonodiscs. 15: 167 Guy st, Elkins W Va 26241.

WOODWARD, ROBERT CROZIER. b Lancaster NH 26 My 24. 4: Eliane Cornellier. 5: Bates Col 42-43, 46-48 Hist) AB; Boston U 48-49 (Hist) AM. 6: Ger, Fr. 7: US Army Infantry & Calvary T-Sgt 43-46; Tchg Fellowship Boston U 49-51; Asst ref dept Boston Pub Lib 51-53, Ref libn hist dept 53-56; Dir Dedham Pub Lib, Dedham Mass 56-62; Dir Bangor Pub Lib, Bangor Me 62-. 8: Chm, East Mass Reg Lib Adv Coun, 59-60. 9: ALA; NELA (pres 64-65); MeLA (treas 63-66); MassLA. 13: Yes. 14: Admin, ref. 15: Bangor Pub Lib, Bangor Me 04401.

WOODWARD, RUPERT C. b Bulloch Co Ga 4 Mr 18. 4: Angela Mora. 5: Armstrong Jr Col 37-38; Peabody 38-40 (Soc Studies) BS, 46-47 BS in LS; LSU 56-61 (Hist) MA. 6: Sp. 7: Asst catlgr UAla Lib 47-48, Order libn 48-49; Lib: Inst Guatemalteco Americano, Guatemala City 50-51, Inst Brasileiro-Americano, Rio de Janeiro 51-52, Centro Cultural Costarricense Amer, San Jose Costa Rica 52-54; Chief acquis libn LSU Lib (Baton Rouge) 54-63; Assoc lib dir Tex A&M U Lib 63-66; Dir of libs George Wash U 67-. 8: US del, Unesco Conf on Pub Lib Devel in Latin AMER, Sao Paulo Brazil, 51; Asst investigator "A Survey of Library Automation in Texas" (66); Consul (Ford Found) Nat Engnr Univ Libs, Lima Peru 66. 9: ALA; Asociacion Costarricense de Bibliozkrios (Hon); SWLA; TexLA; Tx Assn Clr Tchrs; DCLA (mem Intel Freedom Com 67-69); SLA. 10: USBE Corp. 14: Admin, Latin Amer bibliog, lib bldgs. 15: Univ Lib Geo Washington Univ, Washington DC 20006.

WOODWARD, WAYNE WILLIAM. b Greensburg Ind 4 My 30. 4: H Corinne Vaughn. 5: TaylorU 50-52 (Relig) AB; Asbury Theol Sem 52-55 BD; Appalachian State Tchrs Col 58-60 (Educ) MA; UKy 65-67 MS in LS. 6: Fr. 7: Minister West NC Conf of Methodist Ch 55-59, 61-65; Tchr Mt Pleasant NC High Sch 59-61; Admin Asst to libn Asbury Theol Sem 65-67; Libn Asbury Col 67-. 9: SELA; KyLA. 10: Christ Libns Fellowship. 15: 112 E College st, Wilmore Ky 40390.

WOODWORTH, BONNIE JEAN. b Oswego NY 30 Mr 41. 5: SYCG (Geneseo) 59-63 BLS. 7: Libn bechtel Corp NYC 63-65; Assr libn Gen Motors Pub Rel Lib NYC 65-67; Libn Diebold Group NYC 67-68; Libn Hartford Ins Group, Hartford Conn 68-. 9: SLA; ConnLA. 15: 31 Gillett st, Hartford Ct 06105.

WOODWORTH, HOWARD CLINTON. b Chicago Ill 17 Jl 23. 4: Phyllis Bannan. 5: UCal (Berkeley) 47-50 (Fr) AB; USoCal 55-56 MSLS. 6: Fr. 7: Catlgr Long Beach State Col 56-57; Catlgr Los Angeles City Schs 57-58; Libn E Los Angeles Col 58-65; Libn Los angeles City Col 65-. 8: Delegate to IFLA 68. 9: ALA; CalLA. 10: Amer Fed Tchrs. 14: Ref. 15: 1709 N Lucile ave, Los Angeles Ca 90026.

WOODWORTH, MARY LORRAINE. b Richland Center Wis. 5: UWis 48 (Educ) BS Ed, 56 MS LS, 68 LS, Educ PhD. 6: Sp. 7: Tchr Voc Sch, Green Bay Wis 48-51; Libn West High Sch, Green Bay Wis 56-58; Libn Wis High Sch UWis (Madison) 58-64; Instr in Lib Sci, UWis (Madison) 64-67; Asst Prof 67-. 9: ALA-AASchl (Bd); -YASD (Bd, pres 68, Magazine Eval Com, Period List Subcom); WisEA; WisLA. 10: Pi Lambda Theta. 12: "Survey of Secondary School Libraries in Wisconsin (60); "Survey of Elementary School Libraries in Wisconsin (62); "Identification & examination of Areas of Needed Research in School Librarianship (68). 13: Yes. 14: Sch libs, ya lit, lib educ. 15: 3637 Cross st, Madison Wi 53711.

WOODYARD, NANCY (INGMIRE). b Columbus Ohio 11 D 35. 4: Donald H Woodyard. 5: Ohio StateU 53-57 (Eng Lit) BA; UHawaii 56; Columbia 57-58 MS in LS. 7: Child libn Cincinnati Pub Lib 58-60; Army libn Spec Serv Kitzingen Germany 60-61; Asst catlgr El Paso Pub Lib, El Paso Tex 65-66, Y-p libn 66-67, Coord y-p & boxs & girls serv 67-. 8: Lib consul, Jesus & Mary High Sch, El Paso Rex. 9: ALA; TexLA; BorderRegLA (corr sec). 10: Alpha Gamma Delta. 14: Child & y-a wk. 15: 4940 Ajax ct, El Paso Tx 79924.

WOOLEY, HELEN McCLELLAND. b Fowler Ind 11 Mr 07. 4: Wesley T Wooley. 5: UIll 24-28 (Eng) AB, 54-57 MS in LS. 7: Instr UIll Undergrad Div Galesburg 45-48; Asst in rare bk room UIll Urbana 57-60; Catlgr Illinois Col 61-62; Calgr Baldwin-Wallace Col 62-. 9: ALA; OhioLA. 10: Phi Beta Kappa; Beta Phi Mu. 14: Rare bks, catlg. 15: 337 Beech st, Berea Ohio.

WOOLFE, MARIANNE. b Berea Ky 3 Ja 28. 4: George Woolfe. 5: SUNY (Albany) 45-49 (Eng) BA; Tex State Col for Women 49-50; Pratt 60-61 MLS. 7: Jr libn Queens Borough Pub Lib, Queens NY 61-62; Dir Lindenhurst Mem Lib, Lindenhurst NY 63-65; Dir Deer Park Pub Lib, Deer Park NY 65-68; Dir Danbury Pub Lib, Danbury Conn 68-. 9: ALA; NYLA; ConnLA; SWest Com Adminrs Gp. 10: Beta Phi Mu. 15: 37 Hi Vu dr RD #4, New Milford Ct 06776.

WOOLLEY, DAVIS C. b Tuscaloosa Ala 22 S 08. 4: Kate Fristoe Wilkins. 5: Howard Col 26-30 (Hist) AB; Auburn U 37-38 (Hist). 7: Dir ext div Howard Col 53-59; Dir Dargan-Carver Lib Historical Commsn So Baptist Conv, Nashville 59-. 8: Lib & arch consul So Baptist Agencies, Nashville 59-. 9: SAA (Church Archives Com); Amer Assn State & Local Hist; So Baptist Hist Soc; Ala Hist Assn; Tenn Assn of Museums; Inter Coun of Museums of Nashville. 12: Ed "Baptist Advance" (64); Auth "Champion of Religious Freedom," Ed "Baptist History and Heritage" (Jour); Assoc ed "Quarterly Review"; Auth "Guide for Writing History of a Church" (69). 13: Yes. 14: Rare bks, archives, indexing. 15: 127 Ninth ave N, Nashville 37203.

WOOLLS, BLANCHE (ESTHER) (SUTTON). bLouisville Ky 30 Mr 35. 4: Donald Paul Woolls. 5: Ind U 52-58 (Fine Arts) AB, summers 60-62 (LS) MA. 6: Fr. 7: Libn Calumet City Pub Lib, Calumet City Ill summer 58, 59; Sch libn Hammond CITY Schs, Hammond Ind 58-65, Coordinator of sch lib serv 65-67; Coord sch libs Roswell City Schs, Roswell NM 67-68, Coord materials ctr 68-. 9: Ind SchLA; Ind State Tchrs Assn; ALA-AASchL; NMLA. 10: Pi Lambda Teta; AAUW. 14: Sch libs. 15: 503 W Lewis, Roswell NM 88201.

WOOLLUMS, MARTHA FAYE (FOUTS). b Denver Mo 21 Ja 16. 4: Orville Woollums. 5: Northwest Mo State 48 (Mus, Eng, Bus) BS, 57 (Elrm Supv) Masters, Certif for life for tchg. 6: Fr. 7: Tchr: Gentry Co Elem, Denver Mo 34-47, Maitland High Sch, Maitland Mo 47-48, Mercer High Sch, Mercer Mo 48-49, Martinsville High Sch, Martinsville Mo 49-66; Libn Eagleville Sch, Eagleville Mo 66-. 8: Tchr of bus & psych NW Mo State Col Ext. 9: NEA. 10: Beta Sigma Phi; Musician for Goldn Age Club; DAR; AAUW. 14: Sch libnship. 15: Denver Mo 64441.

WOOSTER, HAROLD ABBOTT. b Hartford Conn 3 Ja 19. 4: Alice Hammond. 5: Syracuse 35-39 (Chem) AB (magna cum laude); UWis 39-43 (Physiological Chem) MS, PhD. 6; fr. 7: Research asst UChicago Toxicity Lab 43-43; Research assoc Pepper Lab of Clinical Md UPenn 46-47; Sr Fellow Mellon Inst, Pittsburgh 47-56; Dir of Info Sci Air Force Off of Sci Research, Wash DC 56-. 8: Exec sec, Panel on Info Scis Tech, Com on Sci & Tech Info, Fed Coun of Sci, 65-66. 9: ASIS (chm Potomac Valley Chap 65-66); RESA (pres Aerospace Tech Chap 65-66); ACS; Assn for Computing Machinery; Assn for Mechanical Tr & Computat Linguistics. 10: AAAS; Phi Beta Kappa; Sigma Xi. 12: "Nutritional Data (49,54,56); (with M Taube) "Information Storage & Retrieval (58); Coauth "Vistas in Astronautics (58); "Nutritional Observatory (47-52); "Basic Research Resumes (69). 13: Yes. 14: Info storage & retrieval, mgt info systems, research in info scis. 15: 2108 Seminary rd, Silver Spring Md 20910.

WOOTEN, MILDRED CROZIER. b Winnfield La 3 O 10. 4: Dan J Wooten. 5: Northwestern State 26-29 (Eng, Soc Sci) BA; LSU 39-40 BS in LS. 7: Tchr Eunice High Sch, Eunice La 33-38, Libn 41-49; Period libn LoyolaU (New Orleans) 40-. 9: LaASchL (chm Student Rel 66, pres 68-69, chm Standards Com 68-69). 10: Delta Kappa Gamma; Friends of La State U. 14: High sch libn. 15: 601 W Oak ave, Eunice La 70535.

WOOTTON, THELMA (McCARTY) (SKOMP). b Bringhurst Ind 24 My 05. 5: Ind U 27 (Eng) AB, 59 (LS) MA. 6: Sp. 7: Sch libn Jefferson High Sch, Lafayette Ind 27-36; Lib asst Pub Lib, Lafayette Ind 38-43, 45-55, Head Libn 55-. 9: IndLA (chm Dist 3 58-66). 10: Altrusa Club; Phi Mu; Delta Kappa Gamma. 14: Admin, bk sel, publicity. 15: 2605 S 9th st, Lafayette In 47905.

WORDEN, HELEN MORISON. b Oakland Cal 6 O 15. 4: John B Worden. 5: UCal (Berkeley) 33-37 (Hist)AB, 37-38 (LS) Certif, 42 (LS) MA. 6: Fr. 7: Jr libn Oakland Pub Lib, Oakland Cal 38; Ref asst UCal(Berkeley) 38-43; Archivist USAAF Intelligence, Wash DC 43-44; UCal(Berkeley): Ref asst 44-48, Head ser dept 48-53, Asst U libn 53-65, Assoc U libn 65-. 9: ALA-ACRL. 14: Lib admin. 15: Univ of Cal Lib, Berkeley Cal 94720.

WORLEY, PARKER (EVANS). b Muskogee Okla 25 F 20. 4: Lillian H Worley 05: UOkla 39-41, 46-47 (Letters) BA, 47-48 BA in LS; Rutgers 57-58 MLS, 58-61 (Hist) MA. 5: UOkla 39-41, 46-47 (Letters) BA, 47-48 BA in LS; Rutgers 57-58 MLS, 58-61 (Hist) MA. 6: Sp, Fr. 7: Intern LC 48-49; Asst libn Ursinus Col 49-52; Libn Thiel Col 52-57; Readers adv Trenton State Col 58-61; Libn Rutgers Lib in S Jersey (Camden NJ) 61-. 9: ALA; NJLA. 10: Amer Studies Assn. 14: Col libs. 15: 310 Jess ave, Haddonfield NJ 08033.

WORSLEY, DORCAS. b Tucson Ariz 25 D 07. 5: UCal 25-27 (Eng); UAriz 27-30 (Eng) BA; UCal (Berkeley) 34-35 Certif in libnship. 6: Sp, Fr. 7: Libn I Berkeley Pub Lib, berkeley Cal summer 35; Catlgr San Mateo Co Lib, Redwood City Cal 35-36, 37-39; Chief circ San Mateo Pub Lib, San Mateo Cal 36-37; Libn doc div DukeU 40; Field wkr & chief asst to State libn NC State Lib 41-42; Libn Bancroft Lib UCal (Berkeley) 44-45; Research & ref libn Columbus Memorial Lib, Pan Am Union, Wash DC 48-50; Hd catlgr Redlands U Lib 51-53; Libn II Ventura Co Free Lib, Ventura Cal 55-57, libn 61-64; Libn fiction & order depts Los Angeles Pub Lib 57-58, sr libn Hollywood Reg Br 58-60, sr libn & asst hd catlg dept 60-61, libn 64, libn 65-66; Libn III UCLA Agency for Intl Devel Fed Advanced Tchrs col, Lagos, Nigeria 65; Asst dir Tucson Pub Lib 66-. 8: Organized and taught (with M D Sheaprd) first profess course for libns in Ecuador (Spons by Rockefeller Found, US State Dept and ALA) 44; Secretariat, First Assembly of Libns of the Americas (LC and US State Dept) & guide-interpreter for cross-country tour summer 47; Bibliogr, LC, to prepare bibliog on slavery for UN 50; Consul LC, to survey ref serv, Hispanic Found 50. 9: ALA (chm Internat Rel RT 52-53); ArizStateLA; (chm Recr & Scholarship Coms 67-68); SWLA. 10: Sierra Club; AAUW; LWV; Tucson Art Center; S Ariz Hiking Club; Ariz Pioneers Hist Soc; Tucson Coun of the Arts. 12: Ed "LEA," Columbus Mem Lib, Organ Amer States, Nos 1-12 49-50. 13: Yes. 14: Mgt, tech serv, ref. 15: 5464 E Willard ave, Tucsin Az 85716.

WORSLEY, KATHLEEN (GLEASON). b San Jose Cal 2 N 39. 4: Stephen Worsley. 5: San Jose State Col 58-62 (Hist) BA, 65-66 (Libnship) MA. 7: Lib clk Santa Clara Pub Lib, Santa Clara Cal 63-64; Libn I St Thomas Pub Lib, Virgin Islands 64-65; Libn I Seattle Pub Lib 66-68; City libn Sausalito Pub Lib, Sausalito Cal 69-. 9: AL; CalLA; Pub Lib Execs Central Cal. 10: Cal Hist Soc; DeYoung Museum Soc. 14: Priv press bks, local hist collections, lib applications of data proc. 15: 89 Lupine ave, San Francisco Ca 94118.

WORTH, ELIZABETH L. b Oakmont Penn 3 F 10. 4: Warren J Worth. 5: UMich 26-30 (Fr, Eng) BA, 54-58 MA in LS. 6: Fr. 7: Wayne Co Lib: Lib page, Plymouth Mich 54, Lib aid, Plymouth Mich 55, Libn 1, Plymouth Mich 59, Libn 2, Belleville Mich 60, Libn 3, Garden City Mich 61, Libn 3, Plymouth Mich 63-. 9m; ala; MichLA. 10: AAUW. 15: 51000 N Territorial rd, Plymouth Mi 48170.

WORTH, KATY. b Chicago Ill 6 D 11. 4: John Finley Worth. 5: Stanford 28-31 Eng; Ariz StateU 65-67 Eng BA; UOkla 68-69 MLS. 6: Fr, Sp. 7: Reporter-photographer -grants Pass Daily Courier", Grants Pass Ore 46-58; News Dir KIVA-TV, Yuma Ariz 58-59; Ed "Phoenix Sun", Phoenix Ariz 61-63; Copywriter John S Turner & Assoc, Phoenix Ariz 63; Reporter photographer "Tempe Daily News", Tempe Ariz 63-65; Libn I "Tempe Pub Lib, Tempe Ariz 65-68; Libn I Santa Ana Pub Lib, Santa Ana Cal 69-. 9: ALA; SWLA; ArizLA. 14: Ref. 15: Apt 113 511 E Washington st, Santa Ana Ca 92701.

WORTHY, EDYTHE MARIE CARNES. b Boaz Ala 10 Ap 18. 4: Charles Donald Worthy Sr. 5: Snead Jr Col 37-39 Diploma; Auburn U 39-40 (Soc Studies, Eng) BS; Peabody 59-61 MA in LS. 6: Fr, Ger. 7: Lib asst Tech Lib, Redstone Arsenal Ala 52-53; Br libn Spec Serv Lib, Ft Benning Ga; Libn Irving High Sch Lib, El Paso Tex; Libn Pub Lib, Kan City Mo; Libn Belton High Sch Lib, Belton Mo. 9: ALA (Recr Netwk); MoLA; Mo State Tchrs Asn. 10: AAUW. 14: Sch libs, catlg, ref. 15: 306 Main st, Arab Al 35016.

WORTIS, IRVING (EDWARD). b NYC 23 D 37. 4: Joan Gainer. 5: Antioch Col 55-57; UWis 57-59 Hist) BA, 59-60 Theatre MA; Columbia62-64 (LS) MS. 7: Libn II Theatre Collection NY Pub Lib 62-64, Libn 64-. 12: Free-lance writer. 13: Yes. 14: Adult serv. 15: NY Pub Lib, 5th ave & 42 st, NYC 10018.

WORTMAN, WINIFRED. b Salida Colo 1 Mr 13. 5: UDenver 39-42 BS in LS. 6: Ital, Ger, Lat. 7: Denver Pub Lib; Bkmob Trailer Lib 38-43, Libn Byers br 43-56, Libn in chg of Decker br 56-. 9: ALA. 14: Pub serv. 15: Decker Lib 1501 S Logan, Denver Co 80210.

WOY, JAMES BAYLY. b Moorefield WVa 19 My 27. 4: Sara Elln Germon. 5: WVa U 45-49 (Sociol) AB; UIll 50 MS in LS. 7: Ref asst Brooklyn Pub Lib 50-53; Head circ dpt UDel 53; 1st asst bus sci & ind dept Free Libof Phila 54-61; Free Lib of Phila: Head Lehigh Ave Br 62, Had stations dept 63, Head Mercantile Lib 64-. 8: Ref asst, Lib/USA, NY Worlds Fair, 65. 9: ALA-RSD (chm Bus Ref Serv Com 68-69); SLA; PennLA. 12: Ed "Business Trends and Forecasting (65); Co-ed "Encyclopedia of Business Information Sources" (70). 13: Yes. 14: Bus ref. 15: 405 W Stafford st, Phila Pa 19144.

WOY, SARA ELLEN (GERMON). b Wellsburg W Va 25 D 25. 4: James B Woy. 5: Bethany Col 43-47 (Eng Lit) AB; Carnegie 50-51 MLS. 7: Tchr-libn Cross Creek Pub Sch, Steubenville Ohio 47-50; Yp libn Brooklyn Pub Lib 52; Catlgr UDel 53; Asst to ya coord Free Lib of Phila 54-61; Asst coord Off of Wk with Adults & Ya Community Serv, Free Lib of Phila 61-65; Libn Germantown Friends Sch, Phila 65-; Hd Friends Free Lib of Germantown Phila 69-. 8: Adjt instr Drexel Lib Sch 65. 9: ALA (Coun 61-64);-YASD (chm "Richer by Asia" Com 58-59, "Richer by Asia" Rev Com 64-69); PennLA. 12: Ed Richer By Asia--, ALA (59). 13: Yes. 14: Wk with ya. 15: 405 W Stafford st, Phila Pa 19144.

WOZNIAK, GRACE I. b NYC. 4: John F Wozniak. 5: Mary Wash Col UVa 56-57 (Art); Wilkes Col 57-60 (Art) BA; Drexel 63-66 MSLS. 6: Fr. 7: Ref asst Reading Pub Lib, Reading Pa 62-64; Ref circ asst Col of Phys of Phila Lib 64-65; Lib dev asst Bur of Lib Dev Penn State Lib 67-. 9: ALA; PennLA. 14: Ref, lib dev, med libnship. 15: Bureau of Lib Dev Penn State Lib Box 1601, Harrisburg Pa 17126.

WRANOVSKY, MERLE DEAN. b Cudahy Wis 20 S 25. 5: GeorgetownU 47-50 (Diplomatic & Consular) BSFS; CatholicU 54-59 MSLS. 7: T/5 Army Japanese Intelligence Lang Sch, ann Arbor Mich 44-46; Asst catlgr Enoch Pratt Free Lib, Baltimore 59-60; Catlgr St Francis Sem, Milwaukee 61-. 9: ALA; CathLA. WisLA. 14: Catlg. 15: 826 N Cass st apt 105, Milwaukee Wi 53202.

WRAY, CAROLYN (LAMAR). b Gastonia NC 18 O 10. 5: Meredith Col 30-34 (Eng, Lat) AB; UNC 37-38 ABLS; Pe abody summers 45, 47, 48 MS in LS. 6: Sp, Fr. 7: Tchr 34-38; Temp lib positions 38-42; Libn Campbell Col 42-43; Libn Gardner-Webb Col 43-53; Libn Judson Col 53-58; Libn Berry Col 58-62; Asst libn Middle Ga Co l 62-64; Head tech serv Gaston Co Lib, Gastonia NC 64-. 9: ALA; NCLA; SELA. 10:

Delta Kappa Gamma; Pilot Internat; Kappa Nu Sigma; Pi Gamma Mu; Beta Phi Mu; Great Bks Discussion Group. 14: Catlg. 15: 1420 McArver st, Gastonia NC 28052.

WRAY, WENDELL L. b Pittsburgh Penn 30 Ja 26. 5: Bates Col 46-50 (Psych) AB; Carnegie inst 51-52 MS in LS. 6: Sp. 7: Army Engrs 44-46; Libn Carnegie Lib, Pittsburgh Penn 52-59; Adult gp specialist NY Pub Lib 59-65, Dir N Manhattan Proj 65-. 9: ALA. 10: Phi Beta Kappa; Delta Sogma Iota. 14: Adult gp wk. 15: 307 W 107 st, New York NY 10025.

WRIGHT, AILEEN (HARTWIG). b Edmonton Alberta Can 18 N 35. 4: Robert E Wright. 5: UAlta 53-56 (Mus) BA; UWash 56-57 M Lib. 6: Fr. 7: Libn Multnomah Co Lib, Portland Ore 57-58; Libn Presbyterian Ch, Coeur d'Alene Ida 62-66; Instr UIda, Moscow Ida summer 66; Field consul Ida State Lib 67-68; Asst to Dir UWash Sch of Libnship 68-. 9: ALA; IdaLA; PNLA (va pnla 9var com assignments). 10: AAUW. 13: Yes. 14: Admin, lib educ. 15: 20217 - 8th ave NE, Seattle Wa 98155.

WRIGHT, ALICE E (MRS). b New Lebanon Ohio 27 Mr 05. 5: Ohio U 23-27 (Lit, Lang) BA; Kent State U 50-52 (LS) MA. 6: Ger. 7: Br asst Akron Pub Lib, Akron Ohio 27-28, 30, 33, Br libn 51-59; Chief clk OPA, Akron Ohio 43-44; Exec sec Cancer Soc, Akron Ohio; Br libn Burbank Pub Lib, Burbank Cal 59-60, Ya libn Main Lib 60-64; Hd libn Morley Lib, Painesville Ohio 64-. 9: ALA; OhioLA (Legis Com); CalLA. 10: Quota Club; AAUW; LWV; Daughters of Amer Colonists; Phi Mu. 13: Yes. 14: Ref, ya. 15: 7 N Park Place, apt 31, Painesville Oh 44077.

WRIGHT, CAROL CARTER (MRS). b Fillmore Co Minn 1 D 21. 5: UArk 38-41 (Home Econ) BS UOkla 63-64 MSLS. 7: Lib asst pub lib, Fayetteville Ark 60-63; Ref libn pub lib, Sioux City Iowa 64-68; Ref libn Ozarks Reg Lib, Fayetteville Ark 68-. 9: ALA; IowaLA; ArkLA. 10: Altrusa. 14: Ref. 15: Ozarks Regional Lib, 217 E Dickson st, Fayetteville Ar 72701.

WRIGHT, DAISY ORR. b Rockey Mount NC 21 N 22. 5: Fayetteville Tchrs Col 39-42 (Elem Educ); Broklyn Col 47 (Elem Educ); NYU 67 (Info Retrieval Systs & Devices, Microfilm Syst). 6: Fr. 7: Records clerk THE Great A&P Tea Co, NYC 46-47; Records clerk Amer Can Co, NYC 47; Subj clsf Girl Scouts of the USA, NYC 51-53; Records admin United Cerebral Palsy Assn Inc, NYC 53-54; Libn records dept head Alfred Politz Research Inc, NYC 54-66; Libn Foundation Lib Ctr, NYC 66; Corp records admin Amer Broadcasting Cos Inc, NYC 66-. 8: Summarized in monthly report Form, trade publns chem, cosmetics& toiletries for J H Breck Inc, Marketing Execs, 57-59. 9: Amer Records Mgt Ass; SLA Records Mgt Assn, NY. 12: Ed "Selected Bibliography of Books and Pamphlets Concerning Philanthropic Foundations (66). 14: Ref. 15: 75 Henry st, Brooklyn NY 11201.

WRIGHT, DONALD EUGENE. b Boulder Colo 25 Jl 30. 4: Verna Vorpahl. 5: UColo 48-52 (Eng) BA; UDenver 52-53 (LS) AM. 6: Fr. 7: Lib asst Pub Lib, Denver 52-53; Ref asst Pub Lib, Ft Wayne Ind 53; Ref asst Pub Lib, Detroit 53-56; Lib N Platte Pub Lib, N Neb 56-58; Consul Conul Neb Pub Lib Commsn, Lincoln Neb 58-60; Dir di Lincoln City Libs, Lincoln Neb 60-61; Dir Small Libs Proj ALA, Chicago 61-63; Exec sec ALA-RSD, & ALA-ALTA, Chcago 63-64;Chief bur of lib serv Conn State Dept of Educ, Hartford Conn 64-65; Assoc state libn Ill State Lib, Springfield Ill 65-67; Libn Evanston Pub Lib, Evanston Ill 67-. 8: Exec dir, Nat LIB Week, Neb 59; Survey (with Peter Bury) Council Bluffs Pub Lib 68; (with John Thackery) Libs in Licking Co Ohio 68; Survey, SW Ohio Rural Libs 69. 9: ALA (Life mem; Jury on Citation of Lib Trustees 60); Nat Lib Week Com 67; Ed Com 67-69, chm 69); -LAD (chm Small Lib Publns Com 64-); -RSD (chm Nomin Com 65-66, mem ASD/RSD Com on Orientation 65-); -AAStateL -AASchL (mem Nomin Com Bd Dirs); 66-67); -ALTA (mem Wkshop Com 2nd v-pres); 65-66); Conn Sch LA (Hon Bd mem 64-65); NELA (Com for a Reg Office of Recr 65t0; IllLA. 10: Rotary Club, Univ Club. 12: CONTRIB "The Library Trustee: A Practical Guide (64. 13: Yes. 14: Admin, ref, bk sel, adult ser. 15: Evanston Pub Lib 1703 Orrington ave, Evanston Il 60201.

WRIGHT, DOROTHY (HOFFMAN). b Roswell NM 18 S 22. 4: John Webb Wright. 5: East NM Col 39-41; NM A&M 41-42; UDenver 42-43 (LS) BA; Tex Womans U summer 65-68. 7: Child libn Enoch Pratt Free Lib, Baltimore 44; Child libn Midland Co Lib, Midland Tex 45; Ast libn Austin High Lib, Austin Tex 45-46; Libn: Hobbs High Sch, Hobbs NM 54, Hays Elem Sch, Odessa Tex 5759, Burnet Elem Sch, Odessa Tex 59-. 9: Tex State Tchrs Assn; TexLA; TexClrTA. 10: PEO. 14: Child reader adv. 15: 3600 Springdale dr, Odessa Tex 70762.

WRIGHT, DOROTHY ROSE PRIMM. b Indianola Miss 11 Jl 35. 4: Frederick Williston wright III. 5: Miss State Col for Women 53-57 (LS) BS. 7: Libn Brownsville Jr High, pensacola Fla 57-59; Libn Blount Jr High, Pensacola Fla 64-65; Dist libn Central Union Elem Sch Dist, Lemoore Cal 67-. 9: ALA; CalASchL. 14: Ref. 15: 125 Corsair ave NAS, Lemoore Ca 93245.

WRIGHT, EDITH (BARKER). b Indian Gap Tex 28 Ja 19. 4: Glover C Wright. 5: Daniel Baker 41 (Eng) BS; Tex Woman'sU 59 MLS. 7: Tchr Hamilton Co, Hamilton Tex 37-41; Tchr Merkel Independent Sch Dist, Merkel Tex 48-51; Asst libn Abilene Independent Sch Dist, abilene Tex 53-54; Libn Whiteface Independent Sch Dist, Whiteface Tex 54-58; Libn Lakeview Independent Sch Dist, San Angelo Tex 58-59; Libn Ector Co Independent Sch Dost, odessa Tex 59-. 9: TexStateTA; ClrTA. 14: Catlg. 15: 3645 Bonham, Odessa Tx 78760.

WRIGHT, ELIZABETH (JANE) HILGENDORFF. b Elizabeth NJ 11 Mr 25. 4: C Conrad Wright. 5: Vassar 43-46 (Psych) AB; Columbia 46-47 (LS) BS; Simmons 64-65 LS). 7: Catlgr: Baker Lib Dartmouth Col 47, Peabody Museum Lib Harvard U 48-49, Gordon McKay Lib Harvard U 65-. 14: Catlg, ref. 15: 9 Lowell st, Cambridge Mass 02138.

WRIGHT, ELIZABETH KEHLER. b Chicago 21 Jl 10. 4: Robert LL Wright. 5: UWis 27-31 (Econ) BA; Catholic U 53-56 MS in LS. 6: Fr. 7: Readers adv sci & tech div DC Pub Lib 56-65; Consul in adult educ 66-. 9: ALA; AEAUSA; AEA Greater Wash; DCLA. 10: Phi Beta Kappa; Beta Phi Mu. 15: 7927 Deepwell dr, Bethesda Md 20034.

WRIGHT, ELIZABETH REID. b Fayettevile NC 23 N 18. 4: Manly Emerson Wright. 5: Randolph Macon Womans Col 35-39 (Phlos, Hist) AB; Emory 39-40 BS in LS. 6: Fr. 7: Asst in circ dept DePauw U 40-41; Libn Asheville Biltmore Col 47-55; Lib consul Highland Hosp, Asheville NC 56-. 10: Tuberc Assn; Beta Phi M; Phi Beta Kappa; Pi Gamma Mu; Phi Theta Kappa; AAUW; Amer Contract Bridge League. 15: 300 Griffing blvd, Asheville NC 28804.

WRIGHT, ELIZABETH. b Baltimore Md 12 Ag 40. 5: Swarthmore 58-62 (Fine Arts) BA; Drexel 64-65 (LS). 7: Asst-in-charge Tyler Sch of Fine Art TempleU 62-64; Catlgr Johns HopkinsU 65-68; Catlgr UMd (Catonsville) 68-. 9: ALA (Jr Mem RT). 15: 118 Oak dr, Baltimore Md 21228.

WRIGHT, (MARVIN) EUGENE JR. b Alexandria La 4 S 36. 4: Diana Smith. 5: Northwestern State 54-58 (Pol Sci) BA; LSU 60-61 (LS) MS. 6: Fr. 7: Tchr Port Sulphur (La) High Sch 59-61; Libn Queens Borough Pub Lib, Jamaica NY 61-62; Parish libn Jackson Parish Lib, Jonesboro La 62-63; Lib dir Scottsdale (Ariz) Pub Lib 64-66; Asst city libn New orleans Pub Lib 66, City libn 67-. 9: ALA; LaLA (parliamentarian); SWLA; New Orleans Lib C&ub. 10: Young Men's Bus Club. 13: Yes. 14: Admin, lib construct. 15: 2124 Gibson, Gretna La 70053.

WRIGHT, FRANCES VALENTINE (DALEY). b Choteau Mont 3 D 16. 4: Reginald H Wright. 5: West Wash Col 36-40; UWash 40-41 (Lit) BA, 41-42 (LS) BA. 6: Fr, Ger. 7: Asst bk order libn Seattle Pub Lib 42; Asst br libn Evansville Pub Lib, Evansville Ind 43; Asst k order, asst br & bind processes libn UWash Lib 47-54; Br supv Marin Co Li, Marin Co Cal 56-60; Asst br libn Seattle Pub Lib 60-62; Reserve lib, catlgr UWash Lib 62-. 9: PNLA (sec Circ Div 62-64). (chm Ref Div Subcomon NW Authors 67-). 10: Univ of Wash Faculty Womens Clu. 12: Ed "Whos Who Among Pacific Northwest Authors (69). 14: Catlg, ref. 15: Univ of Wash Lib, Seattle Wa 98105.

WRIGHT, FRANCES. b Baltimore Md 14 Ja 1900. 5: Wilson Col 20-24 (Lat, Sp) AB; Drexel Inst 26-27 BS in LS; Columbia summers 40, 41 (LS). 7: Ref libn Drexel Inst 27-63, Asst dir 63-65, Spec collections libn 63-66; Chief humanities libn UAriz Lib 66-. 9: ArizStateLA. 14: Bibliog, ref. 15: 2475 N Haskell dr #462N, Tucson Az 85716.

WRIGHT, GEORGE E(DWARD). b Northampton Mass 15 Mr 27. 4: Hope Gilson. 5: UMass 44-45, 46-49 (Pol Sci) BA; UNH 49-50 (Govt); Syracuse 55-56 MSLS. 6: Fr, Russian. 7: (Sgt) US Army, US & Germany 45-46; Asst br libn Citizenship br Syracuse U Lib 56-58; Rare bks catlgr Syracuse U Lib 58-59; Catlgr UMass Lib 59-63, Asst libn, Head Monographic Catlg 63-. 9: ALA. 10: Beta Phi Mu. 14: Catlg, tech proc. 15: RD 2, Amherst Ma 01002.

WRIGHT, GRACE (EVANS). b Bath Co Ky 12 F 12. 4: Alonzo Wayne Wright. 5: Morehead StateU 32-33, 60-61 (Elem Educ, LS) AB; Memphis StateU 34-35; MarshallU 58-59, 59-60. 7: Tchr: Rowan Co Schs, Farmers Ky 33-34, Bath Co Schs, Midland Ky 34-35, 35-36, Wayne Co Schs, Ft Gay W Va 61-62, Lawrence Co Schs, Louisa Ky 62-65; Elem sch libn Lawrence Co Schs, Louisa Grade Sch, Louisa Ky 65-. 9: ALA; NEA; KyASchL; KyLA; KyEA. 10: Louisa Womans Club; PTA; Red Cross. 14: Child serv. 15: 418 Lock ave, Louisa Ky 41230.

WRIGHT, GWENDOLYN (FLORENCE) (TITUS). b Sydney Nova Scotia Can 25 O 21. 5: USask 38-41 BA; UToronto 56-57 BLS. 7: Ref asst Regina Pub Lib, Regina Sask Can 55-56; Ref & govt docs Legis Lib, Regina Sask Can 57-64; Canadiana & govt docs McGillU 64-66; Chief educ libn Queen'sU 66-. 9: CanLA. 15: 131 Notch Hill rd apt 410, Kingston Ont Can.

WRIGHT, I MARLENE PHILLIPS. b Manhattan Kan 8 Jl 40. 4: John Richard Wright. 5: Maryville Col 58-59; UFlorence (Italy) 60 (Lang); UMd (Wiesbaden Germany) 61; Kan state Tchrs Col 61-63 (Soc Sci) BSEd, 63-64 BSLS; Old Dominion 65-66. 7: Grad asst Waw Lib Kan State Tchrs Col 63-64; Hd libn Pottawatomie Wabaunsee Reg Lib, St Mary's Kan 64-65; Sub tchr City of Norfolk Va 65-66, Elem sch libn 65-66; Libn Sch of Nu 64-65; Sub tchr City of Norfolk Va 65-66, Elem sch libn 65-66; Libn Sch of Nursing & Doctor's Lib DePaul Hosp, Norfolk Va 66-67; Instr UVa Sch Gen Studies (Falls Church) 68-. 9: ALA; MPLA. 10: Alumni Assn Kan State Tchrs Col; DAR; Trustee John C Wright Foundation. 14: Lib educ. 15: 1 Orr cir, Leesburg Va 22075.

WRIGHT, JANE (ELIZABETH). b Anderson SC 21 D 18. 5: Winthrop Col 36-40 (Math) BA; UNC summers 48-50 BS in LS; Columbia summers 57-59 MS. 7: Elem tchr Anderson City Schs, Anderson SC 40-44; Clerk Shell Oil Co, NY 44-45; Transit clerk Carolina Nat Bank, Anderson SC 45-46; Libn Boys High Sch, Anderson SC 46-50; Asst libn Polytech High Sch, Long Beach Cal 50-51; Instr Winthrop Col 51-59; Grad asst Columbia U 58-59; Asst Prof Winthrop Col 59-67; Visit asst prof Sch of Libnship UWash summer 61; Child libn Lib/USA, NY Worlds Fair summer 65; Visit asst prof Sch of Lib Sch UNC summers 61-65; Visit asst prof Sch of Lib Sci UNC 64-66; Chm Lib Sci sect Educ Dept Furman U 67-. 8: Consul Insts for Sch Libns, UNC summer 67; Vis Prof Sch of Lib Serv, Columbia U summer 68; Ed Bd, Cadmus Books, Eau Claire Wis 69-. 9: ALA-AASchL; -LED (Tchrs Sect, Publ Com 69-71); -YASD; SCEA (Sec Libns Sect 49-50); SCLA (chm Planning Co 68-69, treas 61-62); NCLA; SELA. 10: Beta Phi Mu; Delta Kappa Gamma; Altrusa. 13: Yes. 14: Sch libs, wk with child & yp, lib educ. 15: Box 28541 Furman Univ, Greenville SC 29613.

WRIGHT, JANE E. b Fulton NY 20 Ap 27. 5: Oswego State Tchrs Col 44-48 (Educ) BE, 51-55 9educ) MS; Syracuse 54-55 MS in LS. 7: Tchr: Lowville Acad, Lowville NY 48-49, City Sch Dist, Oswego NY 49-54; Child libn Rochester Pub Lib, Rochester NY 55-61; Assoc libn SUNY Col (Oswego) 61-. 9: ALA; NYStateLA. 10: Beta Phi Mu. 14: Period. 15: 79 E Mohawk st, Oswego NY 13126.

WRIGHT, JANE ELLEN. b Sidney Ohio 9 Mr 44. 5: Col of Wooster 62-66 (Eng, Hist) BA; UMich 66-67 MALS. 6: Fr, Ger. 7: Asst libn Toledo Mus of Art, Toledo Ohio 67-. 9: SLA. 10: Beta Phi Mu. 14: Ref, ser. 15: Box 1013, Toledo Oh 43601.

WRIGHT, JANIE M(UCKLEROY) (MRS). b Nacogdoches Tex 13 N 20 04 Dr Floyd K Wright. 5: Stephen F Austin State Col 37-40 (Eng) BA, 50-51 (Educ) MA; UDenver 55-57 (LS) MA; Ind U summer 66. Sp. 6: Sp. 7: Math tchr Cushing High Sch, Cushing Tex 40-42; Math tchr Pittsburg High Sch, Pittsburg Tex 42-43; Elem tchr Buna Ind Sch Dist, Buna Tex 48-50, Libn 50-52; Libn Little Cypress Ind Sch Dist, Orange Tex 52-62; 7th gr supv SE Mo State Col 62-66, Libn 66-. 9: Mo State Tchrs Assn; MoLA. 10: AAUW; Commun Tchrs Assn; Facultyettes; Faculty Dames; Nat Honor Soc; Alpha Chi. 14: Ref, fiction. 15: 1432 Price dr, Cape Girardeau Mo 63701.

WRIGHT, JASPER HENRY. b Clintonville Wis 28 Ja 19. 4: Arletta Garbutt. 5: UWis 47 (Span) BA, 49 BLS. 6: Sp. 7: Stud asst period ref dept UWis Lib (Madison) 39-41; Jr clerk Pub Lib, Madison Wis 48-49; Jr libn music dept Pub Lib, Oakland Cal 49-51; Br Libn Fair Oaks Br Pub Lib, Stockton Cal 51-53; Asst dir Pub Lib, S Bend Ind 53-. 9: ALA (Life mem);-LAD (Mem & chm Arch & Equip Com 63-69); IndLA (chm Intel Freedom Com 56, 59; chm Publs Com 66, chm Pub Rel Com 61). 10: Wis Lib Sch Alumni Assn; Kiwanis Club; Toastmasters Internat; Amer Soc for Personnel Admin; N Ind Hist Soc; YMCA; S Bend Civic Planning Assn; S Bend Symphony Orchester Assn. 12: Ed "Focus on Indiana Libraries (63-64). 13: Yes. 14: Admin, personnel. 15: 122 W Wayne st, South Bend Ind 46601.

WRIGHT, JEAN (ACKER) WIESNER. b Springfield Mo 24 F 28. 4: William Fred Wright. 5: Vanderbilt U 45-49 (Span) BA; Peabody 49-51 (MA) LS. 6: Sp, Portu, Fr. 7: Admin asst Nashville Pub Lib 51-52; Catlgr Tenn State Lib 52-56; Ser catlgr Joint U Libs, Nashville 61-. 14: Catlg (ser). 15: 2709 Wortham ave, Nashville Tn 37215.

WRIGHT, JIMMY DEAN. b Clinton SC 16 Ja 34. 5: Spartburg Jr Col 56-57, 59-60 AA; Wofford Col 60-62 (Educ, Psych) AB; Peabody Col 65-66 MLS. 6: Sp. 7: USAF Personnel S/Sgt 52-56; Page Spartanburg Co Lib, Spartanburg SC 60-62; Libn Edmunds High Sch, Sumter SC 62-63; Catlgr Wofford Col 63-64; Ya libn Spartanburg Co Lib 64-65; Asst libn Converse Col 66-67, Libn 67-. 8: Consul (Book Collection) Spartanburg Jr Col summer 67, Adv (Circulation) summer 68. 9: ALA; SELA; SCLA. 10: AAUP; Spartanburg Kennel Club. 14: Admin, ref. 15: Box 216, Mayo SC 29368.

WRIGHT, JOHN COTTON. b Sharon Mass 27 Jl28. 4: Mary Massey. 5: UHawaii 50-55 (Philos); American U 63 (Archives Inst). 7: Archivist-histn OR&L Honolulu 58-60; Manager off serv (records archives, lib) Dillingham Corp, Honolulu 61-65; Histn Bishop Mus, Honolulu 66-. 9: SAA; Amer Assn of Museums; Amer Assn State & Loc Hist; HawaiiLA; Hawaiian Hist Soc; Bishop Mus Assn (Charter mem). ; Soc Hist Tech. 10: Friends of the Lib; Internat Counc on Archves; Nat Maritime Hist Soc; Trustee Palama Settlement Bd of Trustees. C. 12: Ed "Journal of Oriental Literature (53-55). 14: Private papers, rare bks, mss. 15: Bishop Museum, Honolulu Hi 96819.

WRIGHT, JOHN GARRICK. b Star City Sask Can 24 O 28. 5: Saskatoon Normal Sch summers 47-49 Tchg Certif; USask 49-52 (Eng, Hist) B Ed; Columbia 56-57 MLS. 6: Fr. 7: Tchr Orchard Sch Dist Melfort Sch Unit, Star City Sask 47-48; Tchr Star City Pub Sch, Melfort Sch Unit, Star City Sask 48-49; Tchr Tisdale Composite High Sch, Tisdale Sch Unit, Tisdale Sask 52-56; Libn, supv of sch libs Wadena Sch Unit, Wadena Sask 57-58; Sch libn Aden Bowman Col, Saskatoon Collegiate Bd, Saskatoon Sask 58-62; Supv sch libs Sask Dept Educ, Regina ask 62-68; Assoc Prof Sch Lib Sci U Alberta 68-. 9: CanSchLA (Coun Exec Com, pres 67-68); CalLA (Coun 68-71); SaskASchL (Co-chm Standards Com, pres 60); SaskLA. 10: Lib Proj Com, Sask Fed of Home & Sch Adv Com, Sask Sch Lib Demonstration Coun; Instr Materials Com, Sask Tchrs Fed; Beta Phi Mu. 12: Ed Newsletter Sch Lib Div, Sask Dept Educ. 13: Yes. 14: Sch libs. 15: 902 Varscona Tower, 11007 83 ave, Edmonton 61 Alberta Can.

WRIGHT, JOYCE M. b Canada. 5: UWash 34-38 (Fr) BA, 38-39 (LS) BA; UHawaii (Pol Sci). 6: Fr, Ger. 7: Jr ref libn UWash 39-40, Asst libn Parrington Br Lib 40-43; Asst ref dept Seattle Pub Lib 43-46; Asst circ ref UHawaii Lib 46-52; Head Reed Col Lib 52-54; Head ref dept UHawaii Lib 54-64; Assoc dir East West Center Lib, Honolulu 65-66, Assoc dir 66-68, Dir 68-. 8: Instr Grad Sch Lib Sci (Lib Sci - ref sources) summer 68. 9: ALA; HawaiiLA (pres 68-69). 10: Assn for Asian Studies; Bishop Mus Assocs; Honolulu Acad of Arts; Phi Beta Kappa; Delta Phi Alpha. 14: Ref (Asian-Pacific area). 15: East-West Center Lib, Honolulu Hi 96822.

WRIGHT, LOTTIE M (THOMAS). b Jonesboro Ark 10 O 20. 4: Alvin Wright. 5: AM&N Col 38-41 (Home Econ); American U 56-57 (Psych) BS; Catholic U 57-60 MSLS. 7: Statistical clerk Bur of Immigration & Naturalization, Wash DC 53; Storekeeping clerk DC Pub Sch 60-62, Readers Adv DC Pub Lib 63-. 10: PTA. 14: Ref. 15: 1228 E Capitol st, Wash DC 20002.

WRIGHT, MARCUS A. b Moravia NY 27 My 16. 4: Helen M Eaton. 5: Cazenovia Sem Jr Col 34-35; Houghton Col 35-38 (Eng, Soc Studies) AB; Syracuse U 38-39 BS in LS. 7: Asst libn Your Home Pub Lib Johnson City NY 39-41; Libn Chemung Co Lib, Elmira NY 41-43; US Army (Maj) US & Pacific 43-46; Libn Dunkirk Free Lib, Dunkirk NY 46-48; Head order dept Erie Co Lib Buffalo NY 48-52; Dir Bing Binghamton Pub Lib, Binghamton NY 52-65; Dir Four Co Lib System, Binghamton NY 61-. 8: NY Commsnr of Educ Com on Lib Serv 56-58 & Certif & Exam Com 65-, Trustee S Central Research Lib Counc. 9: NYLA (pres 57-58, past Coun mem, v-pres, & chm var coms). 10: Rotary Club; Civic Music Assn, Binghamton. 13: Yes. 14: Admin & serv in reg lib. 15: 117 Court st, Binghamton NY 13901.

WRIGHT, MARGARET ALICE. b Danville Penn 16 My 27. 5: UConn 44-48 (Hist) BA; Columbia 52-54 MS in LS. 7: Ref libn Gen Theol Sem (NYC) 54-57; Catlg libn Trinity Col Lib ib (Conn) 57-. 9: . 14: Catlg. 15: 1580 road st, Apt D-6, Hartford Ct 06106.

WRIGHT, MARJORIE (PHILYAW). b Perry Fla 15 My 23. 4: Edmund A Wright Jr. 5: Fla State 41-45 (Chem) BS, 46-49 (LS) MA; Fla Inst of Continuing Studies 63 Certif from State of Fla; Fla State U summer 63; Ohio State Certif; UFla 67, 68 (A-V Wkshop); Fla State U 69. 7: Chemist Tenn Eastman Co, Oak Ridge Tenn 45; Tchr-libn Port St Joe High Sch, Port St Joe Fla 45-47; Dir of Lib Sch Lib & Curriculum Lib Fla State U Lib Sch 47-48; Tchr Nagoya American High Sch, Nagoya Japan 51 Instr Okla State U Lib 54-56; Libn Oakland Heights Elem Sch, Ft Walton Beach Fla 61, 62-64; Libn Ortona Elem Sch Daytona Fla 67-. 9: ALA; FlaLA (chm Sch & Child Sect 47-48); FlaEA. ; Okaloosa CoSchL (chm 63-64); VolusiaCoLA. 10: PTA; Red Cross;Beta Phi Mu; Off Wives Club; Delta Delta Delta Alumni; Wesleyan Serv Guild. 14: Sch & child, tchg lib serv. 15: 128 Windward lane, Ormond Beach Fl 32074.

WRIGHT, MARY ELEANOR. b St Louis 9 Je 08. 5: Washington U 25-29 (Eng) AB; St Louis Lib Sch 29-30 Certif. 6: Fr, Sp. 7: Asst St Louis Pub Lib 30-39; Libn Lafayette Co Lib (WPA), Higginsville Mo 39-41; Ref libn Tenn Reg Lib System, Lenoir City, Morristown, Kingsport, Clarksville Tenn 41-57; Consul Pub Libs Div Tenn State Lib & Archives, Nashville 57-67; Libn W Knoxville Br Pub Lib of Knoxville & Knox Co, Knoxville Tenn 67-. 9: ALA; SELA; TennLA (pres 57-58). 10: Womens Nat Bk Assn; So-Mountain Wkers Coun. 13: Yes. 14: Pub lib serv. 15: Pub Lib of Knoxville, 217 Market st, Knoxville Tn 37902.

WRIGHT, MARY JANE. b Lima Ohio 18 Ag 40. 4: Byron B Wright. 5: Col of Wooster 58-62 (Hist) BA; UMich 63-64 (LS) MA. 7: Asst child room Lima Pub Lib, Lima Ohio 62-63; Elem libn Willow Run Pub Schs, Ypsilanti Mich 64-65; Libn NY Pub Lib 65-67; Rep Lincoln Ctr, NYC 68-. 9: ALA. 10: Pi Lambda Theta; Phi Alpha Theta. 14: Child serv. 15: 160 West End ave apt 30M, New York NY 10023.

WRIGHT, MEREDITH (SMITH). b Cleveland 15 Ag 20. 5: Columbia 37-41 (Geol) BA; West Res 44-45 BS in LS, 51-54 (Eng) MA. 6: Fr, Ger. 7: Manager tech info serv Union Carbide Corp, Cleveland 45; Petrographer Republic Steel Corp, Cleveland 42-45; nstr West Res U Sch of Lib Sci 58-. 9: SLA (chm Pub Rel Com, chm Clsf Com; pres Cleveland Chap); ASIS. 11: Alpers Memorial Award. 12: "Subject Index "ASM Review of Metal Literature 46-50. 13: Yes. 14: Indexing, info mgt. 15: Union Carbide Corp, PO Box 6116, Cleveland Oh 44101.

WRIGHT, NANCY M (KEMP). b Pittsburgh Penn. 4: James A Wright. 5: Carnegie Inst 43-47 (Chem Engring); Carnegie Lib Sch; UPittsburgh 65 (Computer Courses). 7: Carnegie Free Lib of Allegheny, Pittsburgh Penn; Apprentice libn 43-47, Asst libn 47-54; Libn H J Heinz Co, Pittsburgh Penn 54-. 9: ALA-ACRL; PennLA; SLA (pres Pittsburgh Chap 65-66). 13: Yes. 15: H J Heinz Co Lib P O Box 57, Pittsburgh Pa 15230.

WRIGHT, NAOMI (OTT). b Pleasantville NJ 1 S 07. 5: Rutgers 33 (Eng, Educ) BS, 34 9curriculum in Educ) Ed M; Trenton State Col 50 BLS. 6: Fr, Ital, Ger. 7: Libn Glassboro High Sch, Glassboro NJ 46-50; Libn Alexis DuPont High Sch, Wilmington Del 50-52; Libn Tower Hill Sch, Wilmington Del 52-60; Ref libn UDel 60-64; Asst dir Cecil Co Lib, Elkton Md 64-65; Libn The Pingry Sch, Elizabeth NJ 65-. 8: Instr in lib sci UDel 62-65. 9: ALA (Memb Com, Del 62-65); DelLA; MdLA; NJLA; NAIS. 10; So Jersey Chamber Orchestra; Garden Club. 12: "Fertile Fields Bibliography (50). 13: Yes. 14: Ref, tchg lib courses, child lit, rare bks. 15: One De Witt rd, Elizabeth NJ 07208.

WRIGHT, PATRICIA CLARE. b Chicago Ill 21 S 41. 5: USt Thomas 59-63 (Eng Lit) BA; UTex 64-67 MLS. 6: Fr. 7: Sec Tex Med Ctr Lib, Houaton 63-64; Senior libn asst mss catlgr utex (Austin) 64-67; Lib I ref libn San Diego Co Lib 67-68, Lib II ref consul 68-. 9: ALA; CalLA. 14: Pub rel, commun involment, bk catlg develop, ref. 15: 4113 Winona, San Diego Ca 92105.

WRIGHT, PATRICIA L. b Thayer Mo 22 My 35. 4: Kenneth I Wright Jr. 5: UMo 53-57 (Soc wk) BA; VillanovaU 65-67 MSLS. 7: Lib asst UPenn Sch of Soc Wk (Phila) 57-58; Lib asst Lib-Bryn Mayn Col summer 67; Circ libn Lib Sweet Briar Col 67-. 14: Circ, interlib loans. 15: 8 Faculty row, Sweet Briar Va 24595.

WRIGHT, PAUL FRANKLIN. b Albion Penn 19 Je 07. 4: Virginia Ross. 5: Mt Union Col 28-32; (Eng, Educ, Hist) AB; UPittsburgh 39-40 (Hist, Eng) Litt Masters; West Res 40-41 BS in LS. 7: Asst libn Adelbert Col West Res 41-42; US Army Signal Corps (S/Sgt), Australia, New Guinea 42-45; Head Libn Carnegie Public Lib, Conneaut Ohio 45-47; Catlgr & ref libn James Prendergast Lib, Jamestown NY 47-53; Head acquis & catlg Gary Pub Lib, Gary Ind 53-. 8: Lib consul & chief catlgr, Northwest Campus, Ind U 54-64. 9: ALA; IndLA (Recr Com, Catlgrs Round Table). 14: Catlg (art & music). 15: 127 S Sullivan, Gary Ind 46403.

WRIGHT, SYLVIA (HART). b NYC 14 F 33. 5: Cornell U 49-53 (Eng) BA; Columbia 56-58 (LS) MS. 6: Fr. 7: Lib asst Cornell U 53-54; Sr ya libn NY Pub Lib 55-60; Sec to assoc dir Cornell Med Col Sloan-Kettering Div (NYC) 60-61; Ya libn Brooklyn Pub Lib 61; Spec libn CATRALA of Cal, Oakland Cal61-64; Sr child libn Oakland Pub Lib, Oakland Cal 64-66; Ser libn Franklin Sq Agency, Teaneck NJ 67-68; Libn U Ctr SEEK Program CUNY 68-. 8: Consul, Peace Info Lib, NYC 63; Consul NY State Governors Commission on Crime 67-68. 9: ALA; NYLA; LACUNY. 10: Beta Phi Mu. 13: Yes. 14: Service to disadvantaged yas, period. 15: 870 W 181 st, New York NY 10033.

WRIGHT, VIRGINIA (LINCOLN). b Fayetteville Tenn 12 D 26. 4: Andrew Wright. 5: UTenn 45-48 (Eng) BA; Peabody Col 48-49 BS in LS; Peabody Col 63-65 MLS. 7: Base libn AF Lib, Furstenfeldbruck Germany 49-50; Circ libn BostonU Lib 52-53; Base libn AF Lib, Anchorage Alaska 54-57; Med libn 5005th Hosp Lib, Anchorage Alaska 57-58; Ref libn los Angeles Pub Lib sci & tech 58-60; Tech libn Hughes Tool Co Lib, Culver City Cal 60-62; Asst libn & aerospace libn, Patrick AFB Fla 62-63; Sch libn Meadowlane Elem sch, Melbourne Fla 63-. 9: ALA; FlaLA; FlaASchL. 10: AAUW. 14: Ref (child & y-a lit). 15: 86 Highland dr, Indialantic Fl 32901.

WRIGHT, WALTER W(OODMAN). b Cambridge Mass 15 My 15. 4: Aagot C Horn. 5: Harvard 33-37 (Eng) SB; Columbia 37-38 (LS) BS. 6: Fr. 7: In chg Exch Harvard Col Lib 38-40, Asst cir & ref 40-41; Ref asst NY Pub Lib 41-42, In chg Exch 42; Libn Harvard Club of NYC 42-44; Gen asst Johns Hopkins U Lib 44-45, Coordinator tech proc 45-47; Head circ dept UPenn Lib 47-49, Asst libn serv div 49-57; Libn & asst prof Ohio U 57-61, Dir of libs & asst prof lib sci 61-68; Curator Rare Bks & Chief Spec Collections Dartmouth Col Libs 68-. 8: Trustee Narberth (Penn) Pub Lib 56-57. 9: "Have served var prof assns in var off capacities. 12: "The Fifth and Sixth Library Building Plans Institutes ACRL Monographs No 15 (56). 13: Yes. 14: Spec collections. 15: 30 Bank st, Lebanon NH 03766.

WRIGHT, WYLLIS E(ATON). b Jacksonville Fla 13 D 03. 4: Helena Lawrence Kellogg. 5: Williams Col 21-25 (Philos) BA 25-26 (Philos) MA; Columbia 27-28 (LS) BS. 7: Page Lowell (Mass) Pub Lib 16-20; Stud asst Williams Col Lib 21-25, Lib asst 25-27; Catlgr NY Pub Lib 27-30; Libn Amer Acad in Rome 30-33; Chief clsf NY Pub Lib 33-36, Chief catlgr 36-45; Libn Army Med Lib, Wash DC 45-46; Libn Williams Col Lib 47-68. 8: SSTC, Columbia Sch of Lib Serv, 39-45; Sec Amer Bk Center for War-Devastated Libs, 44-48; Chm Jt Com on Union List of Serials 47-54; Chm DC EDR Policy Com 60-66; US Deleg to Internat Conf on Catlg Principles, Paris, 61. 9: ALA (Exec Bd 63-67, chm Aid to Libs in War Areas Com 44-47, chm Union List of Ser Com 39-45);-ACRL (pres 49-50);-DCC (pres 42-43);-RTSD (chm Catlg Code Rev Com 54-67); BSA; CNLA (chm 49-50); NELA; NY Lib Club (pres 42-43). 10: Trustee, Williamstown Pub Lib 50-56. 11: Dewey Medal, 57; Margaret Mann Citation, 62. 12: Tr (with others) "Vatican Library Rules for the Catalog of Printed Books (48); Ed (with others) "Journl of Peter Irving (43); Ed (with others) "Catalogers and Classifiers Yearbook (37-39); Ed (with others) "Bowker Annual (56-). 13: Yes. 14: Catlg. 15: 1736 Oak Creek dr, Apt 303, Palo Alto Ca 94304.

WRIGLEY, ELIZABETH (SPRINGER). b Pittsburgh 4 O 15. 4: O Kenneth Wrigley. 5 UPittsburgh 31-35 (Eng Lit) AB; Carnegie 35-36 (LS) BS. 6: Fr. 7: Sec Cooper-Bessemer Corp, Grove City Penn 39-41; Procedure analyst US Steel Corp, Carnegie Ill, Pittsburgh 41-43; Francis Bacon Found Inc, Los Angeles: Research asst lit 44-45, Curator or rare bks 45-50, Curator of rare bks & dir of research 50-54, Pres of Corp & dir of research 54-60; Pres of Corp & Dir-Libn of Francis Bacon Lib, Claremont Cal 60-. 9: ALA; CalLA; SLA; San Antonio Lib Club. 10: Renaiss Soc of Amer; Mod Humanities Res Assn; Amer Cryptogram Assn; Alpha Delta Pi. 12: "STC Numbers in the Library of The Francis Bacon Foundation(58); "Wing Numbers in the Francis Bacon Library (59); Ed "The Skeleton Text of Shakespeare Foio by W C Arensberg (52);

Suppl To Francis Bacon Library Holdings in the STC of English Books (67). 13: Yes. 14: Rare bk bibliog. 15: The Francis Bacon Lib, 655 N Dartmouth ave, Claremont Cal 91711.

WRINKLE, BARBARA DEANE. b Carlsbad NM 14F 36. 5: Pasadena Col 54-58 (Home Econ) BA; USoCal 58-59 MSLS. 7: Ref & circ libn Pasadena Col 59-64, Ref & acquis libn 64-66; Admin libn US Army Village Lib, Kamsruhe Germany 66-68; Admin libn US Army Robinson Barracks Lib, Stuttgart Germany 68-. 9: ALA; -PLA (Armed Forces Libns, European sub-sect); CalLA; Cal Tchrs Assn. 14: Ref, acquis. 15: Spec Ser Lib Robinson Barracks, APO New York 09154.

WRINKLE, MARY L(EWIS). b Burley Ida 10 Je 13. 4: Raymond Laurence Wrinkle. 5: UCal 30-31; San Francisco State Col 31-32. 6: Fr. 7: Asst libn Daly City Pub Lib, Daly city Cal 34-42; Page Oakland Pub Lib, Oakland Cal 42-43, Jr libn 43-45, Sr libn 45-60, Supv libn 60-. 10: Cal Scholarship Fed. 14: Lib ext, br lib admin. 15: 1373 El Centro ave, Oakland Ca 94602.

WRISLEY, LOIS E. b Burlington Penn 25 O 29. 5: Millersville State Tchrs Col 47-51 (LS) BS Ed; Syracuse 53-57 MLS; Johns Hopkins 59. 7: Libn Athens High Sch, Athens Penn 51-57; Libn Annapolis Sr High Sch, Annapolis Md 57-60; Head Libn Stranahan Sr High Sch, Ft Lauderdale Fla 60-. 8: So Assn Eval Team, 63; Fla Assoc Sch Lib, Program Consultant on Library Standards, 68; Hd of a Fla Demonstration School Library 68. 9: ALA; NEA; FlaASchL; FlaEA. 10: Friends of the Libs. 11: Fullbright Scholarship Tchr Exch Program, Winnipeg Man Can, 54-55. 13: Yes. 14: Sch libs. 15: 5261 SW 3rd st, Plantation Fl 33314.

WROBEL, SUSAN ANN (COLIANNI). b Oak Park Ill 23 Ag 45. 4: Lester Wrobel. 5: Rosary Col 63-67 (Fr) BA, 67-68 (LS) MA. 6: Fr, Sp. 7: Ref libn Mem Lib, Arlington Heights Ill 68-. 14: Ref. 15: 415 W Miner, Arlington Heights Il 60005.

WROBLEWSKI, STEPHAN. b Glendale Penn 16 D 15. 5: UHawaii 40-45 (Eng) BA, 45-46 (Eng); Ohio State U; summer 46 (Russian); Columbia 46-47 (Russian); LSU 47-48 BS in LS; NYU 57-61 (Eng) MA. 6: Polish, Russian, Slovak. 7: (Pvt) Hawaii Territorial Guard 41-42; Tr US Off of Censorship, Honolulu 42-44; Proofreader Honolulu 44-46; Libn order div City Col Lib NYC 48-50; Libn Christian Brothers Acad, Syracuse NY 50; Catlgr, ref libn Linden Free Pub Lib, Linden NJ 51-52; Ref libn Bus Sci & Tech Div, Catlgr of Foreign Bks, Br libn, Lit Spec Queens Borough Pub Lib 52-. 8: Indxer, Grolier Soc, NYC 58-62. 14: Ref, catlg. 15: 355 - 8th ave, New York NY 10001.

WROTENBERY, CARL R. b Mt Pleasant Tex 14 D 29. 4: Julia Winn. 5: Baylor U 49-51 (Religion) BA; Southwestern Baptist Theol Sem 51p64 (Theol) BD, ThD; No Tex State U 62 (LS); UTex summers 64, 65, 66, 67 (LS). 6: Gk, Hebrew. 7: Minister Prairie Creek Baptist Church, Lindale Tex 54-58; Minister First Baptist Church, Big Sandy Tex 58-60; Minister N Hillside Baptist Church, Wichita Kan 60-61 Asst circ Fleming Li Lib Baptist Theol Sem 61-62; UCorpus Christi: Libn 62, Dir 63-, Prof of Religion 62-. 9: ALA; Amer Acad of Relig; Amer Assn Higher Educ; TexLA (v-chm & chm-elect Acquis RT 69-71). 10: Phi Delta Kappa. 13: Yes. 14: Admin. 15: PO Box 6010, Corpus Christi Tex 78411.

WU, AGNES CHING (CHANG). b Peiping Rep of China 20 O 39. 4: Jonathan Ke-chiang Wu. 5: Chung HsingU (Taiwan) 57-61 (Accounting & Statistics) BS; Peabody Col 64-65 MLS. 6: Chinese. 7: Catlgr Duluth (Minn) Pub Lib 66; Catlgr Col of St Scholastica 66-. 14: Catlg. 15: 1908 E 3rd st apt 6, Duluth Mn 55812.

WU, AI-HWA, YOUNG. b Soerabaya Java Indonesia 18 O 39. 4: Pei-Hsien Wu. 5: Nat Taiwan U 58-62 (Eng Lit) BA; UWash 62-64 (LS) MS. 6: Chinese, Fr. 7: Tutor, Taipei Taiwan 58-62; Dental asst, Seattle 63-64; Stud asst UWash Lib 64; Catlg libn Ariz State U Lib 64-. 9: Ariz State LA. 10: Staff Assn, Ariz State U Lib; Womens Club, Ariz State U; UWash Lib Sch Alumni Assn. 14: Catlg. 15: 1252 E Campus dr, Tempe Az 85281.

WU, DOROTHEA WAN LIEN. b Peking China 19 Jl 27.05: Fu Jen U (Catholic) 44-46 (Eng Lit); Yenching U 46-48 (EngLit) BA; UCal summer 49 (Fr); UAla 49-50 (LS); Simmons 50-51 MS in LS. 5: Fu Jen U (Catholic U) 44-46 (Eng Lit); Yenching U 46-48 (Eng Lit) BA; UCal summer 49 (Fr); UAla 49-50 (LS); Simmons 50-51 MS in LS. 6: Chinese, Fr, Japanese. 7: Chinese catlgr Harvard-Yenching Lib Harvard U 51-58; Gen asst Music Dept Chicago Pub Lib 58-60; Asst head art & music div Queens Borough Pub Lib, Jamaica NY 60-65, Head picture div 65-66; Asst Head Art & Music Div 66-68, Head 68-. 9: ALA; Internt Assn of Mus Libs; MusLA; NY Lib Club. 10: Metro Mus of Art; Friends of Metro Opera; Mus of Modern Art; NY City Center ofMusic & Drama. 14: Catlg, ref. 15: 88-15 168 st, Apt 7W, Jamaica NY 11432.

WU, HARRY PAO-TUNG. b Shantung China 1 My 33. 4: Irene I-Len Sun. 5: Nat Taiwan U 59 BA; KENT State U 60-61, 63-64; Ohio State U 62; Kent State U 65 MALS. 6: Chinese, Fr, Japanese, Sp. 7: Archive & lib asst Promotion Ctr, Taipei Taiwan 59-60; Stud asst Kent State U Lib 60-61; Ref libn Massillon Pub Lib, Massillon Ohio 64-65; Act asst libn 65-66; Asst libn & head adult serv 66; Head libn Flesh Pub Lib, Piqua Ohio 66-68; Dir St Clair Co Lib System, Port Huron Mich 68-. 9: OhioLA; ALA; MichLA. 10: Port Huron Internat Club; Lions; Rotary. 14: A-V, admin, ref. 15: 2008 White st, Port Huron Mi 48060.

WU, JONATHAN KE-CHIANG. b Szechwan Rep of China 13 Je 40. 4: Agnes Ching Chang. 5: Tamkang Col (Taiwan) 58-62 (Eng) BA; Peabody Col 64-65 MLS; MinnU 67-69 (Chem) BA, 69-. 6: Fr. 7: Asst catlgr Wis StateU (Superior) 65-67. 14: Catlg, ref. 15: 1908 E 3rd st apt 6, Duluth Mn 55812.

WU, TSAI-EN. b Enshih Hupei China 21 O 40. 5: SoochowU 60-64 (Foreign Langs & Lits) BA; EmoryU 65-67 M Ln. 6: Chinese, Fr. 7: Stud asst Emory U Div of Libn Lib 66-67, Act sec 67; Asst catlgr Wilmington Col Lib 67-. 9: ALA; NCLA. 14: Catlg, ref. 15: 2802 Lyndon ave, Wilmington NC 28401.

WUERDEMAN, LOIS M. b Wauwatosa Wis 10 D 19. 5: UWis 39-44 (Amer Inst) BS. 7: Asst libn Allis-Chalmers Mfg Co, W Allis Wis 51-54, Libn 54-56; Asst libn A O Smith Corp, Milwaukee 56-62; Libn A O Smith Harvestore Corp, Arlington Hts Ill 62-64; Libn Sieber & McIntyre Inc, Chicago 65-66; Libn McManus, John & Adams Inc, Chicago 66-. 9: SLA (sec, Advert & Marketing Div; Chicago Chap: ed chap bulletin). 10: Women's Advertising Club, Chicago; Women's Overseas Serv League. 13: Yes. 14: Ref, marketing. 15: MacManus John & Adams Inc 430 N Michigan, Chicago Il 60611.

WUEST, FRANCES (CAMPBELL). b Kansas City Mo 30 Jl 1899. 5: Randolph Macon Woman's Col 17-21 (Eng) AB. 7: Child libn Paseo Br Kan City (Mo) Pub Lib 24-29; Libn Platte Co (Mo) Co Lib 41-44; Libn N Kan City (Mo) Pub Lib 45-66; N area admin libn Mid-Continent Pub Lib, Independence Mo 66-. 14: Child & adult serv. 15: 502 E 26th ave, N Kansas City Mo 64116.

WULFF, YVONNE (LOIS). b Seatlle 23 N 40. 5: Wash State U 58-62 (Psych) BS; UWash 62-63 (LS) ML. 6: Ger. 7: Prof intern Ohio State U 63-64; Hd docs div 64-66; Prin investigator Terrestrial Hypoxia Project 66-67; Search analyst UWash Health Sci Lib 68-69. 9: ALA. 12: Co-auth "Physiological Factors Relating to High Terrestrial Altitudes; A Bibliography" (68). 14: Info control & dissemination, ref. 15: 4919 Phinney ave N #206, Seattle Wa 98103.

WURFEL, CLIFFORD RANDALL. b Oakland Cal 24 Mr 27. 5: San Jose State Col 47-50 (Fr) AB; UCal (Berkeley) 51-52 BLS. 6: Fr, Rumanian, Ger, Sp, Ital. 7: Catlgr UUtah 52-54; Catlgr Biomed Lib UCLA 54-57; Catlgr UCal (Riverside) 57-63, Hd catlgr 63-68, hd dept of special collections 68-. 9: ALA; Assoc Internatl de Bibliophilie, Paris; CalLA (CURLS); So Cal Tech Proc Gp. 14: Rare bks, catlg. 15: 8272 Briarwood dr, Riverside Ca 92504.

WURSTER, MARGUERITE RAY SMITH BATEY. b Ocala Fla 7 S 16. 4: Robert Frederick Wurster. 5: UFla 49-63 (Hist) BA; Fla State U 65 (LS); USoFla 65- (Lib A-V Educ). 7: Lib asst UFla Libs 52-58; Libn Fla State Dept of Agric, Gainsville Fla 58-63; Asst to the dir of lib serv Fla Inst for Continuing U Studies, St Petersburg Fla 63-65; Asst dir Ext Lib USoFla (St Petersburg) 65-. 9: SLA; SELA; FlaLA(chm Col & Spec Libs Div 68-69). 10: Univ of So Fla Womens Club; YWCA; DAR. 13: Yes. 14: Admin, ref. 15: 6514 - 27th ave N, St Petersburg Fl 33710.

WUTZKE, GERTRUDE C (GRINGER). b Jubbulpore Madhya Pradesh India. 4: Clyde R Wutzke. 5: Butler 25-28 (Bot) BA; UIll 28-29 BS in LS; No Ill summer 62. 7: Catlgr UIll(Urbana) 29-35; Libn Sandwich High Sch, Sandwich Ill 57-. 9: ALA; NEA; IllLA; IllEA. 14: Ser, catlg, ya serv. 15: Rt 1, Plano Ill 60545.

WYATT, JAMES (FRANKLIN). b WVa 4 Jl 34. 4: Mary Walters Wyatt. 5: URichmond 53-56 (Eng) BA, Colgate

Rochester Divinity Sch 56-57, 63-65; UNC(Chapel Hill) 65-66 MS in LS. 6: Fr. 7: Aviator (Lt) US Coast Guard 58-63; Hd libn Mars Hill Col 66-. 8: Memb Vis Com on Accred So Assn of Cols 68, 69. 9: ALA; NCLA (chm Intel Freedom Com). 10: Bd Dirs, Z Smith Reynolds Commun Devel Organ. 14: Admin. 15: Box 224, Mars Hill NC 28754.

WYATT, MILDRED VIVIAN. b Gainesville Tex 27 O 1900. 5: Randolph Macon Womans Col 18-22 (Eng) AB; UTex 24-25 (LS: Columbia 35-36 MS in LS. 7: Priv tutor, Clearwater Fla 22-23; Priv sec First Nat Bank, Haley Realty Clearwater Fla 25-27; Circ asst UTex 28-30; Stephen F Austin State Col; Asst libn catlgr 30-38, Head lib serv dept 42-53, Libn 38-66, Dir E Tex collections & Research asst E Tex hist 66-. 9: ALA (Coun 51-53); -ACRL (Tex rep 57-60); SWLA (Exec Bd 42-43); TexLA (Exec B 41-45 & 51-53, Coun 64-65, pres 42-43; off Dist 6 59-60; v-chm Col & Univ Libs Div 63-4, pres 64-65); Tex State Tchrs Assn. 10: Tex As of Col Tchrs; E Tex Hist Assn; Delta Kapa Gamma; Alpha Phi; Tex State Hist Assn; Tex Old Missions Restoration Assn. 13: Yes. 14: Loc hist, archives. 15: 320 E Austin, Nacogdoches Tx 75961.

WYGNANSKI, MRS YADWIGA. b Warsaw Poland 18 My 23. 4: Adam Wygnanski. 5: UMontreal 62 BA, 6 (Slavistics) MA; McGill 65 BLS; 67 MLS. 6: Polish, Russian, Fr. 7: Asst libn McGill RVC (MONTREAL) 62-64; Libn McGill U Fac of Dentistry 65-68; Ser libn McGill McLennan 68-. 9: CaLA; ALA; QueLA. 14: Catlg, ref, sers. 15: 1550 McGregor ave, Montreal Can.

WYLIE, MARGERY (BABIN). b Lutcher La 10 D 20. 5: Northwestern State Col (La) 37-41 (Eng) BA LSU 41-42 BS in LS. 6: Fr. 7: Circ Carnegie Pub Lib, Clarksdale Miss 42-43; Circ US Naval Air Station Lib, Pensacola Fla 43-44; Asst circ libn E Baton Rouge Parish Lib, Baton Rouge La 59-60; Catlgr Tulane U Lib 60-62, Ref libn 62-68; Hd humanities fine arts div 68-. 9: ALA; New Orleans Lib Club; LaLA (sec-treas 68-69). 10: Tulane Univ Womens Assn; PTA; Delta Zeta; Tulane U Lib Staff Assn. 12: "Bibliography of Tulane University Theses Relating to Louisiana 1897-1963 (65). 14: Ref. 15: 16 Karen ct, New Orleans La 70121.

WYLLIE, STANLEY CLARKE JR. b Clearwater Fla 19 N 35. 4: Martha Ann Thomason. 5: Fla So Col 54-58 (Soc Sci) BS; Fla State U 61-63 (LS) MS. 7: Stud lib asst E T Roux Lib Fla So Col 54-57; Seaman recruit US Navy, San Diego 58; Spec libn Park Trammell Pub Lib, Lakeland Fla 58-60; Civics & Eng tchr Lakeland Jr High Sch Lakeland Fla 60-61; Grad asst Strozier Lib Fla State U 61-62; Libn I Tampa Pub Lib, Tampa Fla 62; Dir Chestatee Reg Pub Lib System & libn Hall Co Pub Lib, Gainesville Ga 63-64; Ref libn Ind & Sci Div Dayton & Montgomery Co Pub Lib, Dayton Ohio 64-66; Libn Dayton collection & soc sci div 67-; Sub tchr Dayton Pub Schs, Dayton Ohio 68-. 9: ALA; OhioLA (Jr Mems RT, chm Memb Com 67); Ch & Synagogue LA. 10: Amer Topical Assn; Dayton Philatelic Soc; Sons of Confederate Veterans; SAR; Tau Kappa Epsilon; Omicron Delta Kappa; Fairbanks Family in Amer; F & AM; Fla State U & Fla So Col Alum Assns. 11: Jr C of C, Gainesville Ga, Presidents Award. 12: "Education in Americanism (67). 13: Yes. 14: Ref, geneal, local hist, bk reviewing. 15: 1715 Riviera ct, Dayton Oh 45406.

WYLY, MARY GAE (PORTER). b Sheridan Wyo 11 Je 40. 4: James Wyly. 5: Grinnell Col 58-62 (Mus) BA; UChicago 62-64 (Mus) MA, 66-68 (LS) MA. 6: Fr, Ital, Lat, Sp. 7: Proj asst Papers of James Madison 63-65; Sec Coop Bur for Tchrs (NY) 65-66; Tech asst NYC Pub Lib Lib & Mus of the Performing Arts summer 66; Lib asst UChicago Mus Dept Record Collection 66-67; Special collection libn Elmhurst Col 67-68; Ref libn Grinnell Col 68-. 9: MusicLA. 10: ACLU; Beta Phi Mu; Pi Kappa Lambda. 14: Ref, mus, art. 15: 1130 East st, Grinnell Ia 50112.

WYNAR, BOHDAN STEPHAN. b Lviv Ukraine 7 S 26. 4: Christina Gehrt. 5: U Munich 45-49 (Econ) Diplomvoklswirt, 49-50 (Econ) PhD (magna cum laude); UDenver 57-58 (LS) MA. 6: Ukrainian, Ger, Russian, Polish, Czech, Lat, Gk. 7: Grad asst in Dept of Econ, UMunich 49-50; Methods analyst Tramco Corp, Cleveland 51-55; Free lance journalist & recipient of research grants, Cleveland 55-58; Admin asst to dir UDenver Libs 58-59, Head tech serv div 59-62; Assoc Prof Grad Sch of Libnship UDenver 62-66; Dean SUNY (Geneseo) Lib Sci Sch 66-. 8: Mem Grad Coun, UDenver, 64-. 9: ALA (chm-elect 66);-ACRL (Subj Spec Sect, Slavic & East European Subsect); NYLA; ColoLA (Denver Chap; Exec Bd 63-64). 10: Amer-Ukrainian Assn of Univ Profs; Amer Assn Adv Slavic Studies; AAUP; Ukrainian Congress Com; Internat Club, UDenver (Hon mem); Shevchenko Sci Soc; Ukrainian Acad of Arts & Scis. 12: "Technical Processes in Libraries" (61); "Research Methods in Librarianship" (62); "Introduction to Bibliography and Reference Work" (3d ed 65); "Introduction to Cataloging and Classification" (65); "Reference Work in Social Sciences" (66); Ed Studies in Librarianship, Grad Sch of Libnship, UDenver, 63-; Comp "Colorado Bibliography; A Classified List of 10,000 Books and Government Documents Pertaining to Co lorado History"; Also auth & ed of Ukrainian publns; "Library Acquisitions (68); Ed "Library Science Text Series." 13: Yes. 14: Ref, catlg, research methods, admin. 15: Sch of Library Science SUNY at Geneseo, Geneseo NY 14454.

WYNAR, LUBOMYR R. b Lviv Ukraine 2 Ja 32. 4: Anna Kuzmycz. 5: Ludwig-Maxmillian U 49-51 (Soc Sci); Ukrainian Free U 50-57 (Hist) MA, PhD; West Res U 59 MS in LS. 6: Ger, Ukrainian, Polish, Russian, Czech, Lat. 7: Instr, ser libn Case Inst of Tech 59-62; Asst prof, head of soc sci lib UColo 62-65; Asst prof & head of ref dept Bowling Green State U 66, Hd info & ref serv 66-68, Asst dir & Assoc prof 68-. 8: Tchr UDenver Grad Sch of Libnship, summers 61, 63-65; Consul, Educ Res Coun Greater Cleveland Res Grants, Coun on Res & Creative Wk, UColo, 63-65; Bowling Green U Faculty Research Grant, NS & Canada 67, 68; Consul Harvard U in Ukrainian Area Study, 68. 9: Amer Assn Adv Slavic Studies; Ukrainian Free Acad of Arts & Sci; OhioLA; ColoLA; ALA-ACRL (chm Slavic Holdings Com Libs 67-69). 10: AAUP; Ukrainian Hist Soc. 12: Comp "History; a Bibliographical Guide" (63); "History of Early Ukrainian Printing" (62); Auth "Political Science" (guide to ref materials 67, 68); "Prince Dmytro Vyshnevetsky" (64); Ed "The Ukrainian Historian" (65-68); Ed "Bio-Bibliographical Series" (62-65). 13: Yes. 14: Ref, res, hist of the bk, admin, Slavic hist. 15: Bowling Green State Univ Lib, Bowling Green Oh 43402.

WYNKOOP, ANNE. b Glendale Cal 1 N 43. 5: Whittier Col 61-65 (Hist) BA; UCLA 65-66 (LS) Masters. 6: Fr. 7: Child libn Los Angeles Co Pub Lib, Norwalk 66-69; Libn & resource tchr Bellflower Unified Sch Dist May Thompson Sch Will Roger Sch 69-. 9: ALA; NEA; CalLA; CalASchL; CalTA; BellflowerEA. 14: Child libn, subject areas. 15: 13204 E Hadley, Whittier Ca 90601.

WYNKOOP, NORMA. b Vancouver Can 13 D 13. 5: Cal State (Fullerton) 65 (Eng) BA; UCal (Berkeley) 66 (LS) Master. 7: Libn Los Angeles Co Pub Isabel Henderson 66-67, Libn Villa Carson Lib 67-. 9: ALA; CalLA. 10: Bus& Profess Women's Club. 14: Ref, admin. 15: 315 W Third apt 912, Long Beach Ca 90812.

WYNKOOP, SALLY (BOHNER). b Utica NY 27 Ap 44. 4: Steven Neil Wynkoop. 5: SUNY (Geneseo) 62-66 (Eng) BA; UDenver 66-67 (LS) MA. 7: Clk-lib Capital Newspapers Inc, albany NY (summer) 66; Clerk-lib "Denver Post" 66-67; Grad asst UDenver 67, Ref & period libn 67-69; Research libn King Resources Co, Denver 69-. 8: Consul to King Resources Comp Publ Dept (Denver) to start picture lib 68-69. 9: SLA. 10: Partners of the Alliance (Colo). 12: "Bibliography of US Government Directories" (69). 14: Research, ref. 15: 1422 E 8th ave #8, Denver Co 80218.

WYNNE, ALLEN DEAN. b Great Falls Mont 25 D 35. 5: UNeb 53-58 (Geol) BS; UDenver 65 (LS) MA. 7: Div off (Lt) US Navy, San Diego 58-63; Asst acquis libn Colo State U 65-67; Math-Physics libn UColo 67-. 9: SLA; ColoLA (chm Scholarship Com). 10: Fac Club, UColo; Denver Quarterback Club; Denver Blueliners. 14: Ref, math, physics, earth sci lit. 15: 2750 Heidelberg dr, Boulder Co 80302.

WYNNE, MARJORIE GRAY. b Petersburg Va 7 Mr 17. 5: Duke 34-38 (Eng) BA; UCal (Berkeley) 40-41 (LS) Certif; Yale 44-48 (E G) MA. 6: Fr. 7: Libn Penn Military Col, Chester Penn 41-42; Ser catlgr Yale U 42-43, Asst in rare bk room 43-46, Libn rare bk room 47-63, Edwin J Beinecke Research libn, Beinecke Rare Bk & Ms Lib 63-. 9: ALA; BSA. 10: Conn Acad of Arts & Scis. 13: Yes. 14: Rare bks, mss. 15: 2065 Yale Sta, New Haven Ct 06520.

WYNNE, NANCY (GRAVES). b Fort Worth Tex. 5: Tex Woman'sU 41-42, 64-67 MLS; UTex (Austin) 42-44 (Eng) BA. 6: Sp. 7: Libn Amon Carter Mus, Ft Worth Tex 67-. 9: SLA; Tex. 10: West Hist Assn. 14: Amer art, West Americana (Spec lib). 15: PO Box 2365, Fort Worth Tx 76101.

WYNNE, VIRGIL JOSEPH. b Princeton W Va 5 Fe 21. 4: Rosa Marie Hogan. 5: Concord Col 47 (LS) BS; George Peabody Col 49 (LS) MA. 6: Fr, Ger. 7: Libn & mus instr Shenandoah Col & Conservatory of Mus, Dayton Va 47-50; Circ ref libn Madison Col summer 50; Libn W Va Inst of Tech 50-52; Acquis libn & lib sci instr Mankato Col 52-59; Dir lib serv & assoc prof lib sci Morningside Col, Sioux City Iowa

59-. 9: ALA; IowaLA. 10: Kappa Sigma Kappa; Kappa Delta Pi; Blue Key. 14: Catlg, admin. 15: 3738 - 5th ave, Sioux City Ia 51106.

Y

YABROFF, ARTHUR. b Horicon Wis 17 O 10. 4: Ethel Walker. 5: UWis 28-32 (Accounting) BA; West Res 36-37 BLS. 7: Accountant Cook Coffee Co, Cleveland 32-37; Mathematician Jam Handy Org, Detroit 42-43; US Navy 43-45; Gen lib asst Detroit Pub Lib 45-46, Bus dir 46-64; Chief of Fiscal Serv LC 64-68; Asst dir for mgt serv 68-. 8: Consul for numerous pub libs on serv & bldgs; Mich State Bd for lib, 51-61. 9: ALA (treas 60-64, mem Program Evaluation & Budget Com 60-67, Pub Bd 66-). 13: Yes. 14: Admin. 15: 2121 Columbia pike, Arlington Va 22204.

YABROFF, LEAH. b Russia 6 S 01. 5: UWis 19-23 (Hist) BA; West Res 30-31 BSin LS, 57-58 MS in LS. 7: Tchr of Hist & Amer Govt Wausau High Sch, Wausau Wis 23-30; Libn South High Sch, Akron Ohio 31-33, Shawnee High Sch, Louisville Ky 33-35, High Schs Pittsburgh 35-47, John Carrol U 47-67; Ser libn Cleveland State U 67-. 9: ALA; NOhioLA. 10: Phi Beta Mu; Hadassah; ACLU; LWV; Phi Beta Kappa; West Res Sch of Lib Sci Alumni. 13: Yes. 14: Col lib admin. 15: 3474 Tullamore rd, Cleveland Oh 44118.

YACOBELLIS, RUTH CLEVELAND. b Marshfield Mass 21 Ap 10. 4: Charles Yacobellis. 5: BostonU 27-33 (Fr Lang & Lit) AB; Middlebury summers 48, 49, 58 (Fr); Yale 51-53 MAT; Pratt 66-67 MLS. 6: Fr, Lat, Ital. 7: Hd lang dept & tchr Hamden Hall, Hamden conn 45-53; Tchr Berkeley Inst, Brooklyn NY 53-54; Tchr Collegiate Sch, NYC 54-68, Libn lower sch 62-67, A-v coord & asst libn 67-. 8: Mem of com for Middle States assn eval Dec 65; Deleg to AASchL Preconf & ALA Conf Jl 66; Deleg to Amer Film Festival 67 & 68. 9: Member of AATF; NAIS; ALA; -ACRL; -RTSD (Internatl Rel RT); USSN Tchrs of Indep Schs; NYLA; Film Lib Info Coun. 10: Amer Assn Tchrs French; Alpha Phi; Beta Phi Mu; Yale Grad Sch Assn; Pratt Alumni Assn. 14: A-v serv, admin (sch or col lib). 15: 45 Sutton Place S, New York, NY 10022.

YAKURA, THELMA (PAULINE). b Wilmington Del 26 Ag 24. 4: James N Yakura. 5: UDel 42-45 (Fr) BA with distinction in Fr; Drexel 46 (LS). 6: Fr, Sp. 7: Ref asst UPittsburgh 46; Libn Engnr Br Lib Carnegie Inst of Tech 47-50 Child libn Cuyahoga Co Pub Lib, Cleveland 50-54, Supv adult bkmob 55; Asst head bkmob Dayton Pub Lib, Dayton Ohio 60, Br libn 61-65; HeadLibn Wright Lib, Oakwood Ohio 65-. 9: ALA (Recr Netwk Ohio); OhioLA (sec Lib Admins RT). 10: PTA; Zonta Internat; Dayton Literary Coun; Oakwood Hist Commsn; Dayton Urban League; NAACP; Phi Kappa Phi. 14: Pub Lib Admin. 15: 1327 Carlwood dr, Miamisburg Oh 45342.

YAMAMOTO, M(ITSUKO) CATHERINE. b Enumclaw Wash 22 D 25. 5: Col ofthe Ozarks 46-50 (Biol) BS; West Res 53-54 (LS) MS. 7: Clerk circ, gen asst Decatur Pub Lib, Decatur Ill 50-51, 51-53; Stud asst Cleveland Pub Lib 53-54; Asst br child libn Enoch Pratt Free Lib, Baltimore 54-55, Br child libn 55; Decatur Pub Lib, Decatur Ill; Child libn, Head of Magic Carpet Room 56-58, Coordinator of child serv 58-63, Chief child serv 63-66; Child serv consul Mid-Hudson Libs, Poughkeepsie NY 66-. 9: ALA-CSD (Newbery-Caldecott Awards Com 66-67; Internat Rel Com UBCM 61-63); IllLA (Exec Bd 61-62; Child sect; Publicity chm 57-58 & 61-62, v-chm 60-61, Exec Bd 60-63); NYLA. 10: Decatur Pub Lib Staff Assn; Amer Bus Womens Assn; AAUW; Zonta Internat; Coun of Commun Serv. 13: Yes. 14: Child serv. 15: Colonial Gardens apt B-4, Poughkeepsie NY 12601.

YAMASHITA, HISAKO. b Hawaii 6 N 23. 5: UHawaii 42-44, 46-48 (Eng) BA;Columbia 49-50 (LS) BS. 7: (T/Sgt) WAC US Army, Wash DC 44-46; Tchr Dept of Educ, Honolulu 48-49; Supv libn NY Pub Lib 50-. 9: NY Lib Club. 14: Ref. 15: 37 W 84 st, NYC 10024.

YANARELLA, MARIE (THERESE). b Yonkers NY 28 N 18. 5: Col of New Rochelle 35-39 BA (cum laude); Columbia 40 (Eng Lit) MA, 53 (LS) MS. 6: Fr. 7: Jr lib clerk Yonkers Pub Lib, Yonkers NY 43, Jr libn bkmob 43-45; Tchr Central Valley High Sch, Central Valley NY 45-48; Tchr W C Mepham High Sch, Bellemore LI NY 48-59; Jr libn ref & ya Yonkers Pub Lib, Yonkers NY 49-53; Asst libn Burroughs Wellcome Inc, Tuckahoe NY 53-59; Asst libn Nat Indust Conf Bd, NYC 59-60; Catlg libn Gen Foods Research Center, Tarrytown NY 60-62; Fine arts libn Yonkers Pub Lib, Yonkers NY 62-64, Br admin 64-; Lecturer NYU Sch of Continuing Educ 67-. 9: ALA; SLA; NYLA; WestchesterLA. 14: Catlg, admin, data proc. 15: 279 N Broadway, Yonkers NY 10701.

YANG, JANE C (HWANG). b Amoy China 9 Jl 32. 4: W Tseng Yang. 5: Taiwan Normal U 55 (Educ) B Ed Chen-Chi U 57-58 (Educ Psych); So Ill U 61 (Guidance) MS Ed; Pratt 63 MSLS. 6: Chinese, Russian, Ger. 7: Math tchr Fu Shing High Sch, Taipei Taiwan 54-57; Libn Chatham Hall, Chatham Va 61-62; Asst libn ref Amer Insurance Asn Lib, NYC 62-63; Asst libn II catlgr SUNY(Cortland) 63-65; Catlgr UNH 65-. 15: 18 Oyster River rd, Durham NH 03824.

YANG, LOUISE (CHANG). b Kuling China 23 Je 16. 4: Daniel Teh-en Yang. 5: Yenching U (Peiping China) 34-35; Vassar 35-38 (Euthenics) AB; UMich 38-40 (Sociol) MA; UKy 57-59 (LS) MS. 6: Chinese, Fr, Burmese. 7: Asst prof of Eng Ginling Col (Nanking China) 48-49; Tchr of Sr high sch Eng, Taipei Taiwan 49-50; Catlgr Yale U Lib 51-56, Sr catlgr & research asst 57; Instr in lib sci Berea Col 59-61, Catlg libn & asst prof of lib sci 61-65; Head catlg & asst prof of lib sci 65-67; Head tech serv & asst prof of lib sci 67-. 9: ALA; Ohio Valley Group Tech Serv Libns (treas); KyLA. 10: Beta Phi Mu; AAUW. 14: Catlg. 15: Col Post Off, Box 2276, Berea Ky 40403.

YANG, MYRTLE LOWE. b San Francisco Cal 9 Jl 16. 4: Richard F S Yang. 5: YenchingU (Peiping) 35-40 (Mus) BA; UWash 55-57 (LS) MA. 6: Chinese. 7: Asst city libn R enton Pub Lib, Renton Wash 57-60; Child libn Los Angeles Pub Lib 60-63, Br libn 63-67; Child libn Carnegie Lib of Pittsburgh, Penn 67-. 9: ALA; PennLA. 10: Phi Tau Phi. 14: Ref, child wk. 15: 1150 Bower Hill rd apt 1105A, Pittsburgh Pa 15243.

YANG, TERESA S. b Nanking China 26 Ag 37. 4: Winston Yang. 5: Taiwan Normal U 54-59 (Hist, Geog) BA; Peabody 62-63 MALS; Columbia summer 65 (LS); Chicago 69 (Far East Libnship) Certif. 6: Chinese. 7: Catlg libn Queens Col (NC) 63-68; Sr libn Hoover Inst Stanford 68-69; Asst Prof & Hd docs dept Winthrop Col 69-. 9: ALA; NCLA; SELA; AAS; CalLA. 12: Co-ed "Asian Resources in American Libraries (68); Co-comp "Bibliography of the Chinese Language (66). 13: Yes. 14: Catlg, Asian materials, govt docs. 15: Winthrop College Lib, Rock Hill SC 29730.

YANG, YUNG-SHI. b Rep of China 9 F 35. 5: Nat TaiwanU 52-56 (Law) BA in Law; UOkla 66-68 MLS. 6: Chinese, Japanese. 7: Catlgr Bloomfield Col Lib 68-. 14: Catlg. 15: 78 Thomas st, Bloomfield NJ 07003.

YANICK, BARBARA N(AUMES). b Chicago 1 O 13. 4: Nicholas S Yanick. 5: De Paul U -44 (Chem) BS. 7: Libn Nalco Chem Co, Chicago 41-. 9: ASIS (sec-treas Chicago Area Chap 65-66). 13: Yes. 15: Nalco Chem Co, 6216 W 66th pl, Chicago 60638.

YARBROUGH, HATTYE MAE (THOMAS). b Grand Junction Tenn. 4: Ordrell W Yarbrough. 5: Lane Col 41-45 (Soc Sci) AB; FiskU summers 48, 49, 50, 52 (LS) Certif; Peabody Col summers 64-66 MLS. 6: Fr. 7: Elem tchr Frazier Elem Sch, Covington Tenn 45-63; Libn frazier High Sch, Covington Tenn 63-. 9: NEA; ALA; TennEA; TennLA; TiptonCoTA; WTennLA; WTennEA. 10: Alpha Kappa Alpha; Aids Club. 14: Acquis, ref. 15: 902 Hatchie ave, Covington Tn 38019.

YAST, HELEN T. b Sturgis Mich 19 Ja 17. 5: Ind U 33-37 (Lat) AB; Rosary Col 51-67 (LS) MA. 6: Fr. 7: Tchr-libn Rolling Prairie High Sch, Rolling Prairie Ind 38-41; Lib clerk US Pub Health Serv, Wash DC 42; Libn Rocky Mountain Lab, Hamilton Mont 43; Libn US Naval Hosp, New Orleans 43-45; Patients libn Hines Hosp, Hines Ill 45-46; Libn VA Hosp, Ft Benjamin Harrison Ind 46-47; Asst libn Amer Hosp Assn, Chicago 47-54, Libn 54-. 8: Coord, Amer Hosp Assn Insts on Lib Serv in Hosps. 9: ALA-AHIL (chm 59-60); CathLA (chm Hosp Sect 63-64); MedLA ((chm Midwest Reg Group 57). 10: Phi Beta Kappa; Beta Phi Mu. 11: Exceptional Serv Award -AHIL. 13: Yes. 14: Health sci libs. 15: Amer Hosp Assn 840 N Lake Shore dr, Chicago Il 60611.

YATES, DUDLEY. b Henleyfield Miss 31 O 32. 4: Darlene Humphreys. 5: NE La State Col 55-61 (Eng) BA; LSU 61-63 (LS) MS, 64-67 (Anthrop) MA. 7: Dir Madison-Tensas Reg Lib, Tallulah La 63; Pub serv libn Parsons Col, Fairfield Iowa 63-64; Asst ref libn USWest la 64-65, Hd circ dept 65-66, Hd ref dept 65-66, Asst dir 66-68; Dir duPont-Ball Lib stetsonU 68-. 9: ALA; ACRL; SELA. 13: Yes. 14: Admin, lib automation, ref. 15: duPont Ball Lib Stetson Univ, DeLand Fl 32720.

YATES, ELLA (MAE) GAINES. b Atlanta Ga 14 Je 27. 4: Clayton R Yates II. 5: Spelman Col 44-47, 48-49 (Eng) BA; AtlantaU 50-51 MSLS; Rutgers 59. 7: Stud ref asst AtlantaU 47-48; Br asst libn Brooklyn (NY) Pub Lib 51-54; Child libn Orange (NJ) Pub Lib 56-59; Libn (med) Orange Mem Hosp, Orange NJ 63-64; Br libn E Orange (NJ) Pub Lib 60-, Coord Bookwagon serv summers 67 & 68. 9: ALA; NJLA (chm Human Rel Com 57-60, corr sec Exec Bd 65-66; v-pres Child & YP Sect 60-63). 10: E Orange Pub Lib Staff Assn; NJ State Women's Coun on Human Rel. 11: Profess Woman of the Year 61. 12: "Annotated Cumulative index of the Journal of Negro History for the First 25 Years" (51). 14: Adult serv admin, ext. 15: 21 Willowmere ave, Montclair NJ 07042.

YATES, HELEN (MARIE) KING. b West Liberty Ohio 3 Jl 18. 4: James Franklin Ohio. 5: East Mennonite Col 42-44, 48-50 (Eng) BA; UNC 50-51 BS in LS. 6: Ger. 7: Asst libn (Cat) Eastern Mennonite Col 51-53, 55-57; Overseas serv (relief) Mennonite central Com, Akron Penn 53-55, Central files supv 57-63; Catlgr Va Polytech Inst 63-64; Catlgr Radford Col 66-. 9: VaLA. 14: Catlg. 15: 200 Marlington st, Blacksburg Va 24060.

YATES, JEANNETTE B. b Dunbrooke Va 22 Ag 04. 4: Joseph Ashton Yates. 5: Col of William & Mary 21-22; summers 22-24, 38, 39, 48, 49 BA in LS; UVa 34, 38, 56, 57; Richmond Prof Inst 34, 38. 6: Sp, Lat. 7: Tchr-libn Charles City High Sch, Charles City Va 22-57; Asst libn Transportation Research & Devel Lib, Ft Eustis Va 56; Tchr-libn Charles City High Sch, Charles City Va 56-57; Tech libn Naval Mine Engnr Facility, Yorktown Va 57-61; Tech & gen libn US Naval Weapons Station, Yorktown Va 61-. 9: SLA; (chm Recruitment Com Va Chap); ALA (Constit & Rules Com of Mil Libns Group); tvaEA (Legis Com, del to NEA Conv 51 & 55); Tri-CountyTA (pres 48-50). 10: Hampton Roads Spec Libs Assn. 13: Yes. 14: Admin, catlg, ref. 15: Rt 1, Charles City Va 23030.

YATES, MARIANNE. b Griggsville Ill 14 O 14. 5: UChicago 33-40 (Pol Sci) BA; Rosary Col 40-41 ABLS. 6: Fr. 7: Catlg & ref asst Joint Ref Lib, Chicago 41-45, Asst libn 45-57; Head of readers serv Transportation Center Traffic Inst, Evanston Ill 57-59, Libn 59-64; Brookings Inst ed assoc, Wash DC 65; Lit analyst URBANDOC, NYC 65-67; Libn Davee Koehnlein & Keating Co, Chicago 67-. 8: Consul lib reorg Welfare Coun of Metro Chicago, 66; Bibliog consul, training personnel, Ind Rel Coun-Amer Hosp Assn, Chicago, 66. 9: ALA (var coms); SLA (chm Soc Scis Div 50-51, chm Transport Div 62-63); ASIS. 12: "Administrative Reorganization of State Government (48, 51); "Civil Rights Legislation at the STATE AND Local Level (48); Ed supv "Sources of Information in Transportation (64); Ed supv "A Reference Guide to Metropolitan Transportation (64); Comp "Current Literature in Traffic and Transportation (59-); Indexer of var bks. 13: Yes. 14: Ref, catlg, clsf for computer retrieval. 15: 1528 E 59th st, Chicago Il 60637.

YAX, LAWRENCE D. b Cleveland 12 Jl 37. 4: Una Giroux. 5: Case West Res 56-60 (Chem, Eng) BA, 69 (Eng Lit) PhD. 6: Fr. 7: Abstracter Amer Soc Metals, Cleveland 60-63; Even supv Case Lib Case Inst Tech 63-64; Head research libn The Brush Beryllium Co, Cleveland 63-. 9: SLA (Engnr Br Cleveland Chap). 14: Doc ref spec. 15: Tech lib Brush Beryllium Co, 17876 St Clair ave, Cleveland Oh 44110.

YEAGER, B EILEEN (McCARTY). b Sheldon Iowa 03 My 17. 4: Francis Scott Yeager. 5: Sheldon Jr Col 35-37; Col of St Catheri e 40-42 (LS) BS. 7: Lbn Mandan pub schs, Mandan ND 42-44; Asst libn Kan City (Mo) Pub Lib 44-45; Libn Anoka pub schs, Anoka Minn 46-47; Asst libn Reagan High Sch, Houston Tex 60-64; Libn Duchesne Acad, Houston 64-. 9: ALA; CathLA (Houston Br, pres 67-69); TexLA; TexEA; Tex A-V Assn. 10: Mus of Fine Arts Assn, Houston; Fine Arts Assn, U St Thomas. 14: Sch libnship. 15: 5095 Fieldwood, Houston Tx 77027.

YEAMANS, GEORGE THOMAS. b Richmond Va 7 N 29. 4: Mary Ann Seng. 5: URichmond 47-48; UVa 48-50 (Econ) BA; UKy 53-55 MSLS; IndU 55-57 (A-v educ) EdD. 6: Ger, Lat. 7: Sgt US Marine Corps 50-52; Sales rep XXX US Marine Corps 50-52; Sales rep Crown Oil Co, Richmond Va 52-53; Graduate asst IndU (Bloomington) 55-57; Admin asst to a-v dir Ind StateU (Terre Haute) 57-58; Film libn & Assoc Prof Ball StateU 58-. 8: Consul to: Pendleton (Ind) Sch Systems, Van Buren (Ind) Sch System, Shelbyville (Ind) Sch System, Muncie (Ind) Sch System 67; Consul to: Ind Soldiers and Sailors Child Home 66, Captioned Films for the Deaf Wkshop 63. 9: -ALA; -ACRL; -AASchL; -LAD; -LED; -ISAD; NEA-DAVI; A-V Instr Dirs Ind (pres 66-67, convention Chm 64 & 66); IndSchLA; IndLA. 10: AAUP; Phi Delta Kappa; Educ Com, First univers Ch, Muncie Ind; Westview Commun Assn. 12: "An Experimenta& Comparison of Equated Verbal and Pictorial-Verbal Teaching Machine Programs in Promoting the Acquisition, Retention, and Transfer of Information by College Students", IndU diss, Univ Microfilms (65). 13: Yes. 14: Film lib and a-v serv, tchg lib sci. 15: 4007 Burton dr, Muncie In 47304.

YEATES, ELIZABETH J. b Greensburg Penn 6 D 30. 5: UPenn 49-53 (Chem) BA, 56-58 9microbiol) MS, 61-62 (Fr); St Joseph's Col 62 (Russian); Case West Res U 62-63 (Info Retrieval) MSLS; Ohio State U 65 (Computer programing and systems analysis); UMd 68 (Automation & Math). 6: Fr, Ger. 7: Research asst YaleU 55-56; Research asst UPenn 57-59; Research asst VA Hosp, Phila 59-60; Supv ed Med Lit, Phila 60-62; Research asst ctr for Doc and Communication Research Case West Res U 62-63; Research asst Chem Abstracts Serv, Columbus Ohio 63-65; Assoc dir tech serv Spec assignment Ohio State U Libs (Columbus) 65-66; Chief bibliogr serv sect Nat Inst of Health Lib, Bethesda Md 66-69, Sci & tech info specialist Off of the Libn 69-. 8: Consul to Ohio StateU Libs spring 65. 9: ASIS (Spec Interest Gp on Libs & Automation: past chm Publ Com; Spec interest Gp on Biomed & Biochem Communications); ACS; (Div of Chem Lit); SLA; Drug Info Assn (Wkshop on Biomed Vocab Control 64, Resol Com). 10: Beta Phi Mu. 12: Ed "Cancer Chemotherapy Abstracts" (61-62); Res ed "Chemical-Biol Activities" (64). 13: Yes. 14: Admin, info retr & related lib automation. 15: 10201 Grosvenor pl 619, Rockville Md 20852.

YEATON, EDMUND PHILIP JR. b Newburyport Mass 4 N 27. 5: UConn 45-52 (Bus Admin) BS; So Conn State Col 61-66 (LS) MSLS. 7: US Army (Pvt) Signal Corps 46-47; Buyer Colt Mfg Co, Hartford Conn 52-55; Asst sales manager Scovill Mfg Co, Waterbury Conn 56-60; Buyer Olin Matheson Chem Corp, New Haven Conn 61-63; Libn Portland High Sch, Portland Conn 63-. 8: Lib Adv to Conn Dept of Ed (Basic Adult Educ) 67. 9: ConnSchLA; ConnEA. 10: Charter Oak Confed. 15: Box 422-A, Middlefield Ct 06455.

YEATS, WENDELL A JR. b Richmond Va 15 O 36. 5: Harvard 54-58 WEng, Psych) BA; Simmons 62-64 (LS) MS. 6: Russian. 7: Asstmarket ed "Richmond Times-Dispatch, Richmond Va 58-59; Russian linguist US Army, Army Security Agency 59-63; Asst manager circ dept Widener Lib Harvard Col 62-63; Ser libn Harvard Bus Sch Lib 63-65; Head data proc dept UMo Lib 65-67; Proj libn Univ Research Lib Syst Staff UCLA 67-69; Syst libn Olin Lib Wash U (St Louis) 69-. 9: SLA. 14: Tech serv, utomation. 15: Olin Library Washington U, St Louis Mo 63130.

YEE, KENNETH M. b NYC 14 F 27. 5,: City U 46-50 (Foreign Trade) BBA (cum laude); Columbia 55-59 MLS. 6: Sp. 7: Catlg trainee Brooklyn Pub Lib 56-59; Asst catlgr - Asst Prof LIU 59-. 9: ALA; NYLA (Mem Com on Preservation of Lib Materials Resources & Tech Serv Sect). 10: AAUP; UFCT. 14: Catlg, acquis, adult educ, automation. 15: 11 Mott , NYC 10013.

YEE, WAI CHEE (CHUN). b Honolulu 27 Je 17. 4: Jewett C Y Yee. 5: UHawaii 34-38 (Eng) BA; Columbia 38-39 BS in LS. 6: Fr, Ger. 7: Minor lib asst Stations Dept Lib of Hawaii, Honolulu 39-40; Lib UHawaii; Lib asst in catlg dept 40-42, 1st asst catlgr 42-43, Catlgr 48-49, Head ser & exch 49; Catlg libn 62-. 65, Jr lib specialist 66-. 9: HawaiiLA (sec 41). 10: Mortar Bd; Assoc Chinese Univ Women. 14: Catlg. 15: 2209 McKinley st, Honolulu Hi 96822.

YEH, THOMAS YEN-RAN. b Nanking China 27 S 36. 4: May Yun-Mei Whang. 5: Soochow U 54-58 (Pol Sci) BA; UMinn 60-62 (Internat Rel) MA , 62-65 (LS) MA. 6: Chinese. 7: Catlg libn Central Wash State Col 65-. 68, Asst Prof & catlg libn 68-. 9: ALA; PNLA. 10: AAUP. 14: Catlg, automation. 15: 1316 Brook lane, Ellensburg Wa 98926.

YELTON, DONALD CHARLES. b Pasadena Cal 7 Jl 15. 4: Sarah Elizabeth Sheerar. 5: Hamilton Col 31-35 (Eng) AB; Georgetown U 46-47, 50 (Hist) MA; Columbia 49-50 (LS) MS, 50-52,62 PhD. 6: Fr, Ital, Sp, Ger. 7: Info asst NYA of NY State, Albany NY; Priv-Maj Army Med Admin Serv Hosp Adjutant, Exec Off, N Africa, Italy, PI 41-46; Instr of Eng UVt 47-49; Lib Fellow City Col (NYC) 50-52; Libn Lincoln U (Penn) 52-65, Act pres 60-61; Head Libn State U Col (Buffalo NY) 65-67, Prof & Dir of Libs 67-. 8: Mem visiting teams of Middle States Assn 62-65; Lib consul, Del State Col 55, Mt St Joseph Col 64; Mater Dei Col 67-68. 9: ALA-ACRL; NYLA; West NY Lib Resources Coun (trustee 66-67); N Country Ref & Research Resources Coun (v-pres 69-). 10: AAUP; Bd Dirs, Chester Co (Penn) Lib; Phi Beta Kappa. 12: "Mimesis and

Metaphor; An Inquiry into the Genesis and Scope of Conradia Symbolic Metaphors" The Hague (67). 13: Yes. 14: Admin. 15: 30 Hillcrest dr, Potsdam NY 13676.

YEN, CHARLES CHIH-HUNG. b Peiping China 20 Ap 37. 4: Huo-Mei Ling. 5: Tunghai U (Taiwan China) 56-60 (Foreign Langs & Lit) BA; Peabody 62-63 (LS) MA. 6: Chinese. 7: Jr catlgr LSU Lib (New Orleans) 63-65, Gifts & exch libn 65-67; Catlgr Ohio State U Lib (Columbus) 67; Ref libn Seton Hall U Lib 67-. 14: Ref, catlg. 15: 6037 Pasteur blvd, New Orleans La 70122.

YEN, WEN-YU. b Hanchuan Hupeh China ı S 06. 4: Hsien-hua Ko. 5: Boone Lib Sch 25 Certif; Central China U 27 (Liberal Arts) BA; Columbia 32 MLS. 6: Fr, Ger, Japanese. 7: Chief catlgr Metropolitan Lib, Peiping 28-30; Head catlg dept & ref dept Nat Lib of Peiping 33-35; Libn & Assoc Prof of bibliog Nat Peking U 35-43; Prof of Lib Sci Nat Col of Soc Educ (Pishan) 43-46; Dir Nat Roosevelt Lib, Chungking 47-49; Chief catl sect UN Lib 52-54; Libn of Asian studies Assoc Prof of Lib Admin studies Ohio State U 64-. 8: Exch libn to Prussian State Lib, 32-33; Spec rep Ministry of Educ for Distrib b of Bks donated by Amer libs to Chinese Univs, 46-47; Consul to Nanyang U, Singapore, for org of its lib; Guest of ALA & US Dept of State to study lib admin in the US, 47-48. 9: ChineseLA (Standing Com, Exec Com); Chungking LA (chm). 10: Rotary Internat, Chungking Chap. 11: Fellowship, Humbolt Stiftung, Berlin. 12: Ed "Book Review, Chungking (47-49). 13: Yes. 14: Pub & col lib admin, catlg, ref. 15: 1841 Hove rd, Columbus Ohio 43221.

YENISH, JOSEPH. b Russia 9 My 08. 4: Pearl Slot. 5: TempleU 34-37 BS in Ed, 42 (Hist) MA; Columbia 47-48 BS 6: Yiddish, Hebrew. 7: Home visitor Penn Dept Pub Assistance, Phila 38-43; Arbitrator US Dept Labor, Phila 43-48; Libn YeshivaU Grad Lib 48-49; Libn TempleU 49-65; Hd libn Gratz Col 65-. 9: Assn Jewish Libs (v-pres Synagogue Div); Jewish Lib assn Greater Phila (v-pres).10: Poaue Zion Labor Zionist Org. 12: Comp "Collateral Reading Workbook in Social Science" (62). 13: Yes. 14: Lib admin. 15: 8403 Williams ave, Phila Pa 19150.

YEOUNG, KAP LEE KIM. b Seoul Korea 25 S 41. 5: Ewha Woman'sU 59-63 (Sociol) BA; San jose State Col 64-66 (Sociol) BA; UOre 66-69 MLS. 6: Korean. 7: Child libn Plattsburgh (NY) Pub Lib 69-. 14: Child lit. 15: 142 Broad st, Plattsburgh NY 12901.

YERKE, THEODOR B(RUCE). b Great Falls Mont 17 Ap 23. 4: Roberta Shearer. 5: UCLA 47-49 (Ger) BA, 49-51 (Ger); UCal(Berkeley) 51-52 BLS. 6: Ger. 7: Head libn Cal Col of Arts & Crafts 52-58; Degolyer libn So Methodist U 58-59; Asst libn The Asia Found, San Francisco 59-60; Chief libn US Forest Serv, Berkeley Cal 60-. 8: US Forest Serv rep, Nat Agric Lib Task Force, info retrieval 62-63; US Forest Serv Rep, Nat Agric Lib Agric/Biol, Vocab Project 66-67; US Forest Serv , Dir "Famulus" Project (Info Retrieval) 67; Chas Bullard Fellow in Forest Research, Harvard U 67-68. 9: SLA (pres San Francisco Bay Area Chap 65-66); CalLA; ASIS (Publicity chm, Natl Meeting 69). 10: AAUP. 12: "Organizing Collections by the Oxford System" (66). 13: Yes. 14: Clsf, catlg, computer applications. 15: US Forest Serv Lib, Box 245, Berkeley Cal 94701.

YERKEY, A NEIL. b Akron Ohio 04 F 38. 4: Nancy Anna Puffenbarger. 5: UAkron 55-59 (Speech) BA, 66- (Data Processing); West Res 61-62 MSLS. 7: Film Inspector Group Serv Dept Akron Pub Lib, Akron Ohio 55-59, Film clerkgroup serv dept 59-60; US Army Res Infantry 61; US Army Armor (Capt), Ft Knox Ky 60-61; Asst Group Serv Dept Akron Pub Lib, Akron Ohio 62-65, 1st asst Group Serv Dept 65-66; Libn Goodyear Aerospace Corp, Akron Ohio 66-. 8: Asst admin, Ohio Valley Film Circuit, 62-66; Great Bks Leadership 62-66. 9: ALA; OhioLA; SLA (treas Cleveland Chap 67-68). 14: Films, info scis. 15: 2448 Kermit st, Akron Ohio 44305.

YESNER, BERNICE L. b Boston 10 Ja 24. 4: Raymond Yesner. 5: UVt 41-45 (Eng) BA; So Conn State Col 57 (LS) MS. 6: Lat, Fr, Sp, Yiddish. 7: Child libn Woodbridge Town Lib, Woodbridge Conn 57-59; Libn Amity Reg Jr High Sch, Orange Conn 59-62. 8: Free-lance sch lib consul 62-; Proj dir for Demonstration Elem Sch Lib Proj of Conn, 63-65; Instr UConn 66-. 9: ALA-AASchL (reg chm Legis Com 65); -ASCD; ConnSchLA (Exec Bd; Legis Chm); NESchLA (Exec Bd); NEA-DAVI; Conn A-V EA; NY State Educ Communication Assn. 10: PTA; LWV; Amity Players Inc; Yale Wive Org. 12: "Administering a Filmstrip Collection" (67); "Use of Filmstrips for Educational Purposes" (68); "Administering Filmstrip & Record Collections" (68). 13: Yes. 14: Sch lib devel, serv to child & youth, continuing educ, recruitment. 15: Sunbrook rd, Woodbridge Conn.

YETT, DANIEL J. b Barre Vt 09 S 36. 4: Beverly Roth. 5: Colby Col 54-58 (Eng Lit) Columbia 60-61 0-61 MS in LS; Brooklyn Col 63-64 (Russian). 6: Fr. 7: Bk sales Brentanos Inc, NYC 60, 61; US Army Active serv Spec serv 60, active res (Cpl E-4) 60-65; Libn I NY Pub Lib 61-62; Sci libn Brooklyn Col Lib 62-64; Research libn Va Assoc Research Center, Newport News Va 65-68; Lectr Eng lit Christopher Newport Col 67-68; Bibliogr sci/engr George Washington U 68-. 9: SLA. 12: Comp (with A Ciolli) "Basic Reference Books in the Sciences (62 . 12: Comp (with A Ciolli) "Basic Reference Books in the Sciences" (62). 14: Admin, ref, bk sel, automation techniques. 15: George Washington U Lib, 2023 G st NW, Wash DC 20006.

YEUELL, EUGENIA OSBURN. b Tuscaloosa Ala 12 O 32. 5: Averett Jr Col 49-51 (Speech) Literary Diploma; UAla 51-54 (LS) MA, 58 (LS). 7: Asst libn Westover Sch, Middlebury Conn 54-56; Army libn Spec Serv, Germany 56-57; Med nursing libn Druid City Hosp, Tuscaloosa Ala 57-58; Head catlgr Nashua Pub Lib, Nashua NH 58-60; Asst catlgr Amherst Col 60-61; Med nursing libn Norfolk Gen Hosp, Norfolk Va 61-62; Head tech processing Portsmouth Pub Lib, Portsmouth Va 62-. 8: Instr in bk sel UVa (Tidewater Ext Div), spring 62. 9: VaLA; SELA. 10: Alpha Beta Alpha; Delta Psi Omega; Alpha Psi Omega; Bus & Prof Womens Club. 14: Catlg, acquis. 15: 1 Crawford pkwy, Apt 703, Portsmouth Va 23704.

YEUNG, PEGGY SIU PING (HA). b Canton China 14 Je 42. 4: Kin-Sang Yeung. 5: St Patrick's Col (Ottawa Ont) 62-66 (Sociol and Psych) BSc in Soc Sci; TorontoU 66-67 (catlg) BLSc. 6: Chinese. 7: Private sec Rediffusion (H K) Ltd (Hongkong) 60-62; Catlgr CarletonU 67-68; Catlgr IllU Med Ctr 69-. 11: Governor-General's medal for acad excellence 66. 14: Catlg. 15: 1434 W Jarvis ave apt 2B, Chicago Il 60626.

YIEN, TAN-JU (LU). b Shanghai CHINA. 4: Chen Hwa Yien. 5: UNeb 48-49 (Pol Sci) MA; Rutgers 59-60 MALS. 6: Fr, Chinese. 7: Research asst Rutgers 59-60; Bibliog UKan 60-61; Asst acquis libn UNeb 61-63, Acquis libn 63-. 9: ALA; NebLA; MPLA. 10: AAUP; AAUW. 14: Acquis, ref. 15: Rte 2, Lincoln Nb 68506.

YIH, PAULINE. b Shanghai China 05 O 36. 5: UCal 59-61 (Bus Admin) BS; UPittsburgh 63-64 (LS) MS. 6: Chinese. 7: Bkkeeper W T Grant Co, Pittsburgh 61-63; Catlgr Tri-State Col 64-67; Catlgr Prince William Co Lib, Manassas Va 67-. 9: ALA. 14: Catlg. 15: 340 N West st, Manassas Va 22110.

YIM, SISTER MARY ANCILLA. b Honolulu 17 F 27. 5: UDayton 57 (Eng) BS in Ed; Catholic U 62 MS in LS. 7: Libn St Joseph High Sch, Hilo Hawaii 52-; Prin St Joseph High &Elem Sch, Hilo Hawaii 66-69. 9: ALA; ASCD; CathLA; HawaiiLA; Hawaii Co Com; Hawaii High Sch LA; NEA; NCTE; Hawaii Island Eng Tchrs Assn (treas 67-69). 10: AAUW. 14: High sch libs. 15: St Joseph High Sch, Ululani & Hualalai sts, Hilo Hi 96720.

YINGLING, ANN. b Harrisburg Penn 20 Jl 37. 5: UCal 55-58 (Eng); USoCal 59-61 (Eng) BA, 61-62 (LS) MS. 7: Ref, circ asst City of Bellingham Lib, Bellingham Wash 62-63; Libn Atascadero State Hosp, Atascadero Cal 63-64; Jr libn Sunnyvale City Lib, Sunnyvale Cal 64-66, Sr libn & Hd tech serv 66-. 9: ALA; CalLA. 14: Ref, catlg, admin. 15: 1202 W McKinley ave, apt 3. Sunnyvale Ca 94086.

YLVISAKER, MARIE (SLETVOLD). b Clay Co SD 21 N 05. 5: Augustana Col (SD) 28-30 (Elem Educ) DIPLOMA: Moorhead State Col summer 47 (LS, Hist) BA; Concordia Col (Minn) 47-49; UMinn summer 50, 63-64 (LS). 6: Norwegian, Danish. 7: Elem tchr: pub sch, Bryan SD 26-28, Astoria SD 30-32, Fargo ND 32-34; Asst libn Concordia Col (Minn) 49-63, Ref libn 64-. 8: Tchr bk repair Ch Lib Wkshops. 9: ALA; MinnLA. 10: Pi Kappa Delta; Concordia Col Womens League. 14: Ref, bk preserv. 15: 1106 8th st S, Moorhead Mn 56560.

YOAS, JEAN (SPRATT). b Sanger Tex 28 F 25. 5: N Tex State U 42-45 (LS) BA, 69 MLS. 7: Libn; Weslaco High Sch, Weslaco Tex 45-47, Iraan High Sch, Iraan Tex 47-52, Hobbs High Sch, Hobbs NM 52-54, Travis Elem Sch, Odessa Tex 54-55, Highland Park Jr High Sch, Dallas 61-62; 1st asst Walnut Hill Br Dallas Pub Lib 62-63; Asst acquis Tex State U 63-. 9: TexLA. 14: Ya serv, acquis. 15: 912 Sierra dr, Denton Tex 76201.

YOAST, REGINA MARIA (HYATT). b Wichita Kan 10 Jl 13. 4: Charles Yoast. 5: Tex Christian U 39-43 (Eng, Geol)

BA; Columbia 43-44 BLS; UGlasgow 60-62 (Educ). 6: Fr, Ger, Russian. 7: Lib asst & dept head Ft Worth Pub Lib, Ft Worth Tex 32-43; Geologist-research analyst Mil Geol Br US Geol Survey, Wash DC 44-45; Head Libn Ill State Geol Survey, Urbana Ill 45-47; Head Libn Frances Shimer Col 47-48; Chief catlgr Central Intelligence Agency, Wash DC 48-49; Chief bibliog Mil Geol Br US Geol Survey, Wash DC 49-51; Dist libn Sixth Naval Dist US Dept of the Navy, Charleston SC 55-60; Tchr Newton-on-Ayr Acad, Ayr Scotland 62-63; Head Libn Armstrong State Col 63-. 8: Consul on estab lib: Berkeley Inst, Hamilton Bermuda 54, Newton-on-Ayr Acad, Ayr Scotland 63. 9: ALA; SELA; GaLA. 10: AAUP. 14: Admin, ref. 15: 4 Canterbury ct, Savannah Ga 31406.

YOCHIM, CHARMAINE STANDER. b Saginaw Mich 23 S 40. 4: David A Yochim. 5: NorthwesternU 58-60; UMich (Ann Arbor) 60-62 (Hist) BA, 65-66 MALS. 7: Ref libn Arlington Co Pub Libs, Arlington Co Va 66-67; Libn Prince George's Commun Col 67-. 9: ALA; MdLA; DCLA; Md Assn Jr Cols (Learning Resources Div; chm Com on Coop; ed Newsletter). 10: UMich Alumni Club; Phi Kappa Phi; Beta Phi Mu. 14: Ref, catlg of non-bk materials. 15: 209 Eighth st SE, Washington DC 20003.

YOCOM, MARGARET. b Oberlin Ohio 9 Je 03. 5: Oberlin Col 21-25 (Ecology BA; West Res 28-29 BS in LS. 6: Fr, Sp. 7: Asst in catlg dept Oberlin Col Lib 26-28; Head of catlg dept & Prof of Lib Sci Bowling Green State U 29-. 9: ALA; OhioLA; No Ohio Tech Serv Libns. 14: Catlg. 15: 225 Wolfley, Bowling Green Ohio 43402.

YODER, FLORENCE B. b Lynchburg Va 12 O 12. 5: Washington Co Train Class 30 Certif; Trenton (NJ) Summer Lib Sch 38 Certif. 7: Libn New Canaan (Conn) Pub Lib 30-31; Gen asst Hartford (Conn) Pub Lib 31-36, Asst child libn 36-43; Libn Rockingham Pub Lib, Harrisonburg Va 43-56; Head ext div Va State Lib 56-. 9: ALA; SELA; VaLA (pres 53-54). 10: Quota Club. 13: Yes. 14: Ext wk. 15: 16 N Laurel, Richmond Va 23220.

YOELL, FLORENCE M(OORE). b Brooklyn NY 3 Je 17. 4: William A Yoell. 5: Brooklyn Col 35-38 (Govt) BA; Queens Col 62-65 (LS) MS. 7: Libn Brookside Elem Sch, Yorktown Heights NY 62-. 14: Child lit. 15: 2880 Hickory st, Yorktown Heights NY 10598.

YOGMOUR, OLGA. b Akron Ohio 11 Je 36. 5: UAkron 55-59 (Educ) BA in Ed; West Res 60-62 MS in LS. 6: Gk. 7: Tchr Cuyahoga Falls Bd of Educ, Cuyahoga Falls Ohio 58-60; Lib aid Akron Pub Lib, Akron Ohio 59-61; Sci & tech libn & Instr in Bibliog UAkron 61-; Ref libn sci & tech Akron Pub Lib, Akron Ohio. 9: OhioLA. 10: AAUP. 14: Sci & tech. 15: 1464 Brydan dr, Akron Oh 44313.

YOLTON, JEAN (SEBASTIAN). b Norwood Ohio 22 Mr 24. 4: John W Yolton. 5: UCincinnati 42-46 (Romance Langs) BA; UCal (Berkeley) 46-47 BALS. 6: Fr, Lat, Ger, Sp, Gk. 7: Libn I Oakland Pub Lib, Oakland Cal 47-50; Asst libn II UMd 61-63; Catlgr Cooperative Bk Center of Can 64; Ser catlgr UToronto Lib 64-; Libn I, Libn II, Libn III 64-. 9: ALA; CanLA; OntLA; Ont Resources & Tech Serv Group. 14: Catlg (ser). 15: 18 Paulson rd, Toronto 15 Can.

YOO, YOUNG H. b Hongsong Korea 15 Jl 27. 4: Sun G Im Yoo. 5: USoK Univ (Seoul) 57 (Law) LLB; Peabody Col 58 MALS; Seoul Nat U 60 (Law) LLM. 6: Korean, Japanese, Chinese, Ger. 7: Chief of west bks sect TonggukU (Korea) 55-59; Lectr YonseiU, Seoul Nat U, USOK U, Nat Communications Col 58-63; Mem Tr Com of Dewey Decimal Syst, Rep of korea 58-62; Libn Col of Law Seoul NatU 59-63; Ed & councelor Korean LA 62-63; Ref libn Orientalia div LC 63-68, Japanese catlgr shared catlg div 68-. 8: Consul, Automated Korean Bibliog Proj, Human Rel Area Files, YaleU (sponsored by NSF) 68-69. 9: ALA; KoreanLA (Coun); Korean Legal Ctr; Criminal Law Soc of Korea. 11: Grant, Internat& Coop Admin 57-58. 12: P Butler's "An Introduction to Library Science" (Korean tr 62); "English-Korean Dictionary Romanized" (62); "An Analysis of the Criminal Law and Procedure of Yi Dynasty of Korea, 1392-1910" (60); "Source Materials on Korean Economy (66); etc. 13: Yes. 14: Lib automation (catlg & ref), lib admin, lib educ. 15: 7404 Rose ct, Camp Springs Md 20022.

YORK, GERTRUDE J. b Waco Tex 30 Jl 15. 4: Christopher L York. 5: Baylor U 32-36 (Educ) AB; Emory 38-39 AB in LS. 7: Tchr Jr High Sch, Clarendon Tex 36-38; Lbn Jr High Sch, Gladewater Tex 39-4; Libn Waco Pub Lib, Waco Tex 43-46; Catlgr UTex 46-50; Libn Belton High Sch, Belton Tex 54-. 9: NEA; Tex LA; Tex State Tchrs Assn. 14: Catlg. 15: 409 W 9th st, Belton Tex 76513.

YOSHIDA, SADAO. b Shiga Japan 29 Je 24. 4: Mitsue Yoshida. 5: DoshishaU 47-50 (Eng lit) BA; AtlantaU 53-55 (LS) MS; UCLA 69- (LS). 6: Japanese. 7: Libn USIS Amer Cultural Ctr, Osaka Japan 55-58; Instr DoshishaU 59-63; Assoc Prof 63-. 8: Mem, Exec Com on the Lib Wkshop for the Libns of All-Japan Private University Union, Tokyo 66-68. 9: JapanLA; Japan Documentation Assn. 13: Yes. 14: Info sci, documentation. 15: 5-2 Morokicho Kamitakano Sakyo, Kyoto Japan 606.

YOSHIMOTO, PAMELA CHIKAKO (MATSUDA). b Honolulu Hawaii 21 Je 42. 4: Kenneth Tadayoshi Yoshimoto. 5: UHawaii 60-64 (Secondary Educ) EdB, 67 (Secondary Educ) 5 yr Diploma, 68 MLS. 6: Japanese. 7: Tchr Radford High Sch, Honolulu 65; Asst libn Farrington High Sch, Honolulu 66-. 8: Bk reviewer Hawaii State Lib Syst 66-67, 68-69. 9: NEA; ALA; HawaiiASchL; Hawaii Coun Tchrs Eng. 10: Beta Phi Mu; Pi Lambda Theta; Mortar Bd Alumni. 14: Sch lib wk. 15: 45-411 Kulauli st, Kaneohe Hi 96744.

YOSHINAGA, TSUGIO. b Sacramento Cal 5 S 20. 5: UGrenoble 50-52 (Fr) Certif; CCNY 52-56 (Art) BA; Pratt 56-58 MLS. 6: Fr, Japanese. 7: T/Sgt GHQ 44-46; Sr libn Brooklyn Pub Lib, Brooklyn NY 56-. 9: SLA; ALA; NY Lib Club. 10: Pratt Inst Lib Sch Grad Alumni Assn. 14: Ref. 15: 75 Wadsworth terr, New York NY 10040.

YOST, REV CHARLES EDWARD SCJ. b Pittsburgh 4 My 32. 5: Sacred Heart Monastery Col 51-55; (Liberal Arts) BA; Sacred Heart Monastery Sch of Theol 55-59 (Theol) STB; Cardinal Stritch Col summer 57, 58; Catholic U 59-60 (Theol) STL, 60-61 MS in LS. 6: Ger, Lat, Indonesian. 7: Asst libn Sacred Heart Monastery, Hales Corners Wis 55-59; Libn St John Col (Gisting Sumatra Indonesia) 62-63; Libn & prof of Liturgy & Patristic Theol Sacred Heart Monastery Sch of Theol, Hales Corners Wis 63-. 8: Prof of ecclesiology, Marygrove Col, Monroe Campus, Monroe Mich summers 64, 65; Retreat Master. 9: CathLA; Cath Capitol Hist Assn; The Liturgical Conf; WisLA (v-pres 66); ALA. 12: Assoc ed "Reign of the Sacred Heart" (63-67). 13: Yes. 14: Catlg, ref. 15: Sacred Heart Monastery, Hales Corners Wis 53130.

YOST, RUTH K(UDER) (MRS). b Alburtis Penn 29 D 06. 5: Ursinus Col 23-27 (Eng, Hist) AB; Drexel 30-31 BS in LS; Lehigh U 56-58 (Educ) MA; Drexel 61, 62(LS). 7: Tchr So Whitehall Twp High Sch, Allentown Penn 27-30; Libn Boys High Sch, Lancaster Penn 30-38; Libn J P McCaskey High Sch, Lancaster Penn 38-39; Asst libn Kutztown State Col 52-58, Head libn 58-. 8: Com on Standards for Penn State Col Libs. 9: NEA; ALA; Penn State EA; PenLA. 10: AAUW; Alpha Beta Alpha; Penn-German Folklore Soc; Ursinus Women's Club; Kutztown Women's Club. 14: Ref, first eds. 15: 439 E Walnut st, Kutztown Pa 19530.

YOUMANS, ALICE I. b Detroit Mich 15 Ja 46. 5: UMich 63-67 (Hist) BA; Columbia 67-68 ms. 6: Fr. 7: State doc libn Govt Doc Div, StanfordU Libs 68-. 10: Beta Phi Mu. Kappa Phi; Phi Beta Kappa. 14: Ref. 15: 555 Forest 3, Palo Alto Ca 94301.

YOUNG, BONNIE RENISON. b Albany NY 6 J140. 4: Deo R Young. 5: State U Col (Geneseo NY) 58-62 (Elem Educ, LS) BS; SUNY (Albany) 66 (European Area Studs). 6: Fr, Sp, Ger. 7: Elem & jr high libn Central Sch, Canajoharie NY 62-. 8: Child libn, Lib/USA, NY Worlds Fair, 65. 9: NEA; Central NYLA; Montgomery Co (NY) Tchrs Assn (Legis Chm). 10: Mohawk Valley Chorus; PTA; Bowling League. 15: 12 Goodrich ave, Ft Plain NY 13339.

YOUNG, CHARLES F J. b Nassau Co NY 1 Ja 36. 5: City Col (NY) 53-57 (Hist) BA; Columbia 58-60 MLS. 6: Ger. 7: Operations supv photo serv div NY Pub Lib 57-60; Ref libn Queens Borough Pub Lib, Jamaica NY 60-63, Chief period div 63-66, Chief tel ref div 66-67, Admin asst to dir 67-. 8: Libn, Linnaean Soc of NY, 58-60. 9: ALA; New York Lib Club. 10: Amer Ornithol Union; Brit Trust for Ornithol; Wilson Ornithol Club; Brit Ornithol Union; Linnaean Soc of NY. 14: Ref, photoduplication, admin. 15: 205-11 36th ave, Bayside NY 11361.

YOUNG, CHESLAH (LAKE). b Albany Ore 2 My 07. 5: Ore Col of Educ 25-28, 50-54-58 (Educ); Ore Ext 45-54 BS; UOre 62-63 (LS) 5th year. 7: Tchr Sch Dist, Lebanon area Ore 30-33, 36-53; Tchr-libn Sch Dist 16-c, Lebanon Ore 53-57, Lib coord 57-. 9: ALA; NEA-DAVI; OreLA; OreEA; OreASchL; Ore Instr Materials Assn. 10: Alpha Delta Kappa; Amer Legion aux; AAUW. 11: Lib award LEA. 14: Child wk. 15: 265 Hiatt, Lebanon Or 97355.

YOUNG, DOROTHY B(EATRICE). b Fond du Lac Wis 29 Mr 22. 5: St Marys Col 39-43 (Eng) AB; UMich 46-47 BS in LS; Tex Tech Col 48; UToledo 49-50. 7: Cryptanalyst Mil Intelligence, Arlington Va 43-45; Order clerk LC 45-46; Ref libn Tex Tech Col 47-49; Libn & 1st asst tech dept Toledo Pub Lib, Toledo Ohio 49-57; Tech libn Servo Corp of Amer, Hicksville NY 57-61; Tech libn Amer Chicle Co, Long Island City NY 61-68; Sr libn Bus Lib, Brooklyn Pub Lib 68-. 9: SLA. 10: AAUW. 14: Ref (sci & tech). 15: 2311 Coney Island ave, Brooklyn NY 11223.

YOUNG, EDDIE MAE (WILSON). b New Orleans 10 S 35. 4: James E Young Jr. 5: Souhern U 56 (Soc Studies) BS (cum laude); Atlanta 62 MSLS. 6: Fr. 7: Sub tchr Orleans Parish Pub Sch, New Orleans 57-58; Libn St. Tammany Parish Pub Sch, Slidell La 58-59; Asst libn Southern U Law Sch (Baton Rouge) 59-60; Asst libn Southern U (New Orleans) 60-. 8; lecturer, Southern U (New Orleans) 63-. 9: LaEA. 10: AAUP; Delta Sigma Theta. 14: Ref. 15: 4624 Lafon dr, New Orleans La 47646.

YOUNG, FERN E. b Clarinda Iowa 30 N 02. 5: Tarkio Col 20-25 (Math) BS; Colo A&M Col summer 28 (LS) Certif; West Res summers 31-36 BS in LS; Iowa State U 37-45 (Modern Langs). 6: Lat, Fr, Ger, Sp, Gk. 7: Libn Community High Sch, Crystal Lake Ill 29-37; Circ & ref libn State U Iowa 37-47; Ya dept Albuquerque Pub Lib, Albuquerque NM 47-54, Head ref dept 54-67; Libn Iran Bethel Col of Girls 68-. 8: Adv, Amer Heritage Proj, Albuquerque Pub Lib, 52; Consul; Essay and General Literature Index 60-63; Mem, NM Governors Com for White House Conf on Aging, 59; Governor's Commsn on White House Conf on Child & Youth, NM 60. 9: ALA (Memb Com NM 58 & 64-65, Hammond Map Award Com 65);-YASD (treas 54); SWLA (Reg News Chm 52); NMLA (chm Wkshop on Sch & Pub Lib Coop with Youth Wk 63; Recr Com 56; chm Wkshop on Mending 61; Com on Grants 68). 10: Bus & Prof Womens Club; AAUW; Albuquerque LA. 12: Reg SWest News Ed "Top of the News". 13: Yes. 14: Ref, ya serv. 15: 2922 Terrace dr, Des Moines Ia 50312.

YOUNG, FRANK DWIGHT. b Greenwood NY 7 F 09. 4: E Caroline Young. 5: Alfred U 27-31 (Eng) BA; NY State Col for Tchrs 31-37 (LS) BS; NYU 36-40 (Eng) MA. 7: Eng tchr & libn Greenwood Union Sch, Greenwood NY 31-35; Eng tchr Valley Stream Central High Sch, Valley Stream NY 35-52; Libn Valley Stream Summer & High Sch, Valley Stream NY 40-; Libn Valley Stream Central High Sch, Valley Stream NY 52-. 9: NEA; NY State Tchrs Assn; Nassau-Suffolk SchLA. 15: 235 Fletcher ave, Valley Stream NY 11580.

YOUNG, HEARTSILL H(ENRY). b San Augustne Tex 2 Mr 17. 4: Fay Grote. 5: UTex 34-38 (Journalism) BJ, 50-53 MLS; UIll 52-53, 55-56 (LS).06: Sp. 7: Tex & fed govt agencies 38-41; Business, Ft Worth & Austin Tex 41-44, 46-50; US Navy 44-46; Revisor Grad Sch of Lib Sci UTex 50-52; Ser acquis libn UTex Lib 53-55; Lecturer Grad Sch of Lib Sci UTex 53-54, summers 55-57, 61, & 64; Lecturer Grad Sch of Lib Sci UIll summer 64; Asst libn UTex Lib 57-66, Assoc libn 67-. 9: ALA; SWLA; TexLA (pres 65-66); Tex Assn Col Tchrs. 12: Ed "Texas Library Journa (54-55, 57-58 & 64-65). 13: Yes. 14: Acquis, catlg. 15: 1706 San Gabriel st, Austin Tx 78701.

YOUNG, HELEN A. b Cokeville Penn 16 F 09. 5: UMinn 27-32 (LS) BS. 7: Lib asst Minneapolis Pub Lib 34-38; Bkmob & ext libn Hennepin Co Lib, Minneapolis 38-47, Dir 47-. 9: ALA (Life mem; Memb chm Minn 61-65, Memb Chm Reg 5 65-67; sec Bldg & equip Sect 65-67, mem Budget, Acctg & Costs Com 64-66, chm 68-70); MinnLA (Legis Com 49-59, chm Co & Reg Sect 59-60, Fed Rel Coord 63-65, 1st v-pres & pres-elect 68-70). 10: Zonta Internat; Citizens League of Minneapolis & Hennepin Co. 14: Pub lib serv, Co & reg lib devel, metro area pub lib problems. , admin. 15: 300 Nicollet Mall, Minneapolis Mn 55401.

YOUNG, JEAN (KERR). b Titusville Penn 20 D 21. 4: W Rollin Young. 5: Clarion State Col 39-43 (LS, Eng) BS in Ed. 7: Asst libn Washington Irving High Sch, Clarksburg WVa 64-67; Asst libn Salem Col Clarksburg Campus Lib (WVa) 68-. 9: NEA; WVaLA. 10: Union Protestant Hosp Auxiliary. 14: Catlg, ref. 15: 125 Euclid ave, Clarksburg WVa 26301.

YOUNG, JERRY F. b Springfield Mo 3 S 37. 4: Judith Kay Fort. 5: Southwest Mo State Col 55-60 (Eng) AB; UDenver 60-61 (LS) MA. 7: Reg libn Rolling Hills Reg Lib, St Joseph Mo 61-66; Pub lib consul Wis Dept of Pub Instr, Madison 66-69; Dir Anoka Co Lib, Minneapolis Minn 69-. 9: ALA (LAD/PRS Com on Pub Rel Sev to Libs); MoLA (Legis Com); WisLA; MinnLA. 10: Rotary Club. 13: Yes. 14: Pub lib admin. 15: Anoka Co Library, 707 Highway #10, Minneapolis Mn.

YOUNG, JOHN PAUL. b Cranberry Creek NY 31 Jl 42. 4: E Patricia O'Bryan. 5: William Jewell Col 60-64 (Philos) BA; UDenver 66-67 (LS) MA. 7: Circ libn William Jewell Col 64-65, Period libn 65-66, Ref libn 67-68, Act dir lib 68-69, Dir lib 69-. 9: ALA; MoLA. 10: AAUP. 14: Ref, admin. 15: 194 Jackson, Liberty Mo 64068.

YOUNG, MARGARET (ELIZABETH KOBER). b Wash DC. 4: Raymond A Young. 5: American U 31-36 (Fr) AB; Strayer Bus Col (Wash DC) 32; URI 64-66 MSLS. 6: Fr. 7: Lib asst catlg dept Smithsonian Inst 36-37; Lib asst catlg dept Enoch Pratt Free Lib, Baltimore 37-38; Asst libn Sch of Dentistry Lib UMd 38-40; Lib asst tech processes div US Dept of Agric Lib, Wash DC 43; Asst to head of acquis div Smithsonian Inst. Wash DC 43-52; Asst supv acquis & period sect Lib US Bur of Pub Roads, Wash DC 52-53; Ed writer Sci Press, Lancaster Penn 54-55; Ser libn Tufts U Med & Dental Lib 55-60, Asst libn 60-. 9: MedLA (chm Dental Libns Group 66); SLA; NELA; MassLA. 10: Bus & Prof Womens Club; AAUW 14: Med libnship. 15: 30 Alma ave, Belmont Ma 02178.

YOUNG, MARIAN C. b Cincinnati 15 Jl 08. 5: UCincinnati 25-29 (Eng) AB, 29-30 (Educ) BE; Columbia summers 35-37, 41, 42, 44-45 (LS) BS. 6: Fr. 7: Child libn Cincinnati Pub Lib 30-38; Instr child lit Drake U summer 44-45; Supv wk with child Des Moines Pub Lib, Des Moines Iowa 38-46; Instr of lib sci Marygrove Col 52, 55; Lecturer in lib sci UMich 60-; Coordinator child serv Detroit Pub Lib 46-. 9: ALA (Coun; Com on rg); DLCYP (pres 53-54); -CLA (pres 56-57); NCTE; MichLA (pres 50-51). 10: Camp Fire Girls Detroit Area Coun; PTA; Pi Lambda Theta; Woman's Nat Bk Assn. 12: Ed "Top of the News (49-50); Ed v 5 "In Your Own Back Yard. 13: Yes. 14: Child serv. 15: 1057 Yorkshire rd, Grosse Pointe Park Mich 48230.

YOUNG, MARIANNE (FEELEY). b Scranton Penn 30 N 41. 4: Paul D Young. 5: Marywood Col 59-63 (lat) AB; Villanova U 63-64 MS in LS. 7: Grad asst Dept of Lib Sci Villanova U 63-64; Jr high libn Irvington Bd of Educ, Irvington NJ 64-65; Elem sch libn Piscataway Twp Bd of Educ, Piscataway NJ 65-66; Child libn Lincoln Trail Lib Syst, Champaign Ill 66-68; Pub serv libn St Andrews Presb Col 69-. 8: Adv wk in Child Areas Pub Libs in Lincoln Trail Libs. 9: NEA; CathLA; NJEA; IllLA. 14: Catlg, interlib loan, circ, ref, pub serv. 15: Blue's Farm rd, Laurinburg NC 28352.

YOUNG, MARY LORAINE. b Whites Creek Tenn 6 O 10. 5: Austin Peay State Col 30-40 Two-Year Certif; Peabody 36-39, 50-51 (Elem Educ) BS, Tenn Permanent Prof Elem Certif 51-52 (LS) MA, Tenn Permanent Prof High Sch Certif; 67 Mich Libns Permanent Prof Certif. 6: Lat, Fr. 7: Elem tchr Hickman Co Bd of Educ, Centreville Tenn 30-43; Clerk Detroit Pub Lib 46-50, Child asst 52-53; High sch libn Davidson Co Bd of Educ, Nashville 53-54; Catlgr Carson Newman Col 54-57; Child libn Detroit Pub Lib 57-59, Adult asst 59-. 8: Evaluated Lib in Jefferson City High Sch, Jefferson City Tenn 54-57. 10: Kappa Delta Pi; Pi Gamma Mu. 14: Ref. 15: 9140 Whittier, apt 7, Detroit Mi 48224.

YOUNG, MICKI JO (TATMAN). b Kansas City Kan 16 N 39. 4: James D Young. 5: Tex ChristianU 58-61 (Elem Educ) BS; CatholicU 68-69 (LS) MS. 7: Tchr DEG (Army) Karlsruhe Germany 62, 64; Research asst Dept of Lib Sci CatholicU 69-. 9: DCLA. 10: Congressional Preparatory Sch Booster Club Lib Com; Beta Sigma Phi. 12: Ed "Clips and Quotes" (DCLA Newsletter). 14: Pub rel. 15: 35 S Aberdeen st, Arlington Va 22204.

YOUNG, OLIVIA (KNOWLES). b Benton Arkansas 3 S 22. 4: Calvin B Young. 5: Tenn Polytech Inst 38-42 (Fr) BS; Peabody Col 45-46 BS in LS. 7: Period & docs libn Peabody Col Lib 46-49; Area libn US Army Spec Serv, Linz Austria 49-51; Asst libn Cairo Pub Lib, Cairo Ga 55-58; Bkmob libn Caney Fork Reg Lib Syst, Sparta Tenn 58-59; Chief libn US Army spec Serv, Ft Stewart Ga 60-63; Dir Watauga Reg Lib Syst, Johnson City Tenn 63-. 9: ALA; TennLA (treas 69-70); SELA. 15: 1206 Welbourne st, Johnson City Tn 37601.

YOUNG, RITA (KUNG). b Chungkin China 27 My 39. 4: Victor Young. 5: TunghaiU 57-61 (Econ) BA; Peabody Col 62-64 MALS. 6: Chinese. 7: Catlgr Bartholomew Co Lib, Columbus Ind 64-66; Catlgr Staunton Pub Lib, Staunton Va 67; Catlgr Kanahwa Co Lib, Charleston W Va 68-. 9: WVaLA. 14: Catlg. 15: 509 1/2 6th ave, Montgomery W Va 25136.

YOUNG, ROBERT N. b Brooklyn NY 9 S 18. 4: Patricia Saum. 5: Columbia 48-49 (Math) BS, 49-50 (Tchg of Math) MA, 51-52 (LS) MS; UIll 57-58 (LS). 7: Clerk acct dept

Mutual Life Insurance Co of NY 36-41; US Army Infantry Platoon Leader (1st Lt) 41-46; Math tchr Union Sch, E Islip NY 50-51; Libn DC Pub Lib 52; Stack supt Columbia U Lib 52-54; Asst acquis libn Albert R Mann Lib, Ithaca NY 54-57; Circ asst UIll Lib (Urbana) 57-58; Head order dept UMo 58-61; Chief photoduplication serv John Crerar Lib, Chicago 61-64, Chief acquis dept 64-65; Head Libn Maine Twp High Sch, Park Ridge Ill 65-. 9: ALA; NEA; IllLA; IllEA; Chicago Lib Club. 14: Secon sch libs. 15: 120 Park ave, Wilmette Ill 60091.

YOUNG, ROBERT W. b Pittsburgh Penn 23 D 39. 4: Karen Peterson. 5: Carnegie Inst 58-60 (Chem, Eng); Kent StateU 60-63 (Chem, Eng) BS in Ed; UDenver 65-67 MALS; UAkron 68- (Law). 6: Sp. 7: Tchr Stanton Local High Sch, Irondale Ohio 64-65; Grad asst UDenver Lib 65-66; Research libn The Martin Co, Denver 66-67; Hd S&T Lib UAkron 67-. 9: SLA; Akron-Area LA. 10: AAUW. 14: Sci-engrg lit in univ or spec libs. 15: 303 South ave #17, Tallmadge Oh 44278.

YOUNG, ROBERTA E. b Walsenburg Colo 4 F 30. 5: UColo 48-51 (Educ); Adams State Col 52-53 BA; USoCal 54; UDenver 55-56 (LS) MA. 7: Tchr Huerfano Co schs, Walsenburg Colo 51-52; Tchr Florence pub schs, Florence Colo 52-53; Tchr-libn Corcoran pub schs, Corcoran Cal 53-54; Tchr-libn Santa Maria Pub Schs, Santa Maria Cal 54-55; Grad asst UDenver 55-56; Sch Lib Supt Colo State Dept of Educ 56-. 9: ALA-AASchL; NEA-DAVI; MPLA; ,coloLA; ColoASchL; ColoEA (many com assignments in all assns). 13: Yes. 14: Sch libs. 15: 1353 Elm, Denver Co 80220.

YOUNG, ROGER DAVID. b Vancouver BC Can 26 Ag 40. 5: UBC (Zool) BA, 67-68 BLS. 7: Docs libn ULethbridge 68-. 14: Govt docs. 15: Lib Univ of Lethbridge, Lethbridge Alberta Can.

YOUNG, MRS RUTH H. b Fitzgerald Ga 25 Ap 1898. 4: William E YOUNG. 5: Womans Col of Ga 34-38 (Educ) BS; Fla State U 55 (LS) MA. 6: Fr. 7: Libn Carnegie Lib, Moultrie Ga 29-38; Libn Flint River Reg Lib, Griffin Ga 56-58; Libn Wesleyan Col (Macon) 58-63; Libn Satilla Reg Lib, Douglas Ga 63-. 8: Consul on bk collection, Tallahassee Pub Lib, Tallahassee Fla; Buyer Rare Bks for Wesleyan Col in Eng, Scotland. 9: ALA; NEA; SELA; GaLA; GaEA. 10: AAUP. 14: Admin, ref, adult educ. 15: 617 E Ward st, Douglas Ga 31533.

YOUNG, TOMMIE LERLINE MORTON. b Nashville Tenn. 4: James Johnson Young. 5: Tenn StateU 48-51 (Eng, Speech, Drama) BA; CatholicU 53-54 (LS); Peabody 54-55 MALS. 6: Fr. 7: Eng & libn Prentiss Inst, Prentiss Miss 51-52; Asst catlgr US Navy Tech Lib, Wash DC 52-53; Ser asst LC 53; instr Tenn StateU 56-59; Instr Prairie View Col 59-61; Asst Prof AtlantaU 64-66; Dir Instr materials ctr, Assoc Prof Eng AM&N Col 66-. 8: Dir, Sch Lib Inst, So U for So Educ Found, 63; Consul, Individualized Conf, So U, 62; Consul, A-V Conf Grambling Col, summer 62; Mem Eval Teams for Accred Sch Libs, Consul So Cetnral Reg Educ Lab. 9: AALS (Personnel & Recr Com); ALA; NEA; Ga Tchrs Assn; Atlanta Lib Club. 10: AAUP; aauw; Zeta Phi Beta; Univ Women''s Club; Beta Phi Mu; YM-YWCA Bd. 13: Yes. 14: Lib educ, acad & sch libs, catlg. 15: 40 Watson blvd AM & N Col, Pine Bluff Ak 71601.

YOUNG, VERNA H F. b Honolulu 12 Je 39. 5: Chaminade Col (Honolulu) 58-62 (Hist) BA; UHawaii summer 62; UCal(Berkele) 62-63 MLS. 6: Fr, Ger. 7: Libn I G M Sinclair Lib UHawaii 63-65, Catlg libn I 65-. 66; Jr lib specialist II T H Hamilton Lib UHawaii 66-. 9: ALA; HawaiiLA. 10: Schs of Lib Sci Alumni Assn. 14: Catlg, sers. 15: 1612 Houghtailing st, Honolulu 96817.

YOUNG, VICTOR C. b Shanghai China 27 Jl 31. 4: Rita Kung. 5: Nat TaiwanU 51-55 (Law) BA in Law; Sch for Judge Advocate 55-56 (Military law) Certif; Peabody Col 63-65 MLS. 6: Chinese, Japanese. 7: Mgr Today's Mainland Magazine, Taiwan China 56-58; Tchr Oversea's Chinese High Sch, Seoul Korea 58-61; Asst dir Bartholomew Co Lib, Columbus Ind 65-66; Asst dir West Va Tech Lib, Montgomery W Va 67-. 9: WVaLA. 14: Ref, a-v materials, admin. 15: 509 1/2 6th ave, Montgomery W Va 25136.

YOUNG, VIRGINIA G(ARTON). b Mountain View Mo 16 Ja 19. 4: Raymond A Young. 5: UMo 36-37, summer 38 (Journalism); SW Mo State Col 37-39 (Eng) AB; UOkla 39-40 (LS). 6: Fr, Ger. 7: UMo; Catlgr 40-41, Act ref libn 43; Dir Williams Woods Col Lib 41; Lecturer Columbia U 66; Commsner & past pres Mo Lib Commsn, Jefferson City 65-66. 8: Trustee Columbia (Mo) Pub Lib Bd 51-54, 56-59, 62-65, Pres 57-58, 62-64; Trustee Amer Lib in Paris, France 68-. 9: ALA (Coun 62-66; Fed Rel Com 60-61; Com on Org 62-66; Awards Com 68-70, chm Trustee Jury Citation 66; NLW Steering Com 61-63); -ALTA (pres 59-61; Bd 59-65 & 68-69); Nat Bk Com (66-); MoLA (pres 67-68; pres Trustee Div 55-57; co-chm Legis Com 56-57; Mo Lib Planning Com 53; Mo Lib Survey Com 61-62). 10: LWV; AAUW; YWCA Bd; Bd Friends of UMo Lib. 12: "Trustee of the Small Public Library," (62); "The Library Trustee; A Practical Guidebook" (69). 13: Yes. 14: Lib development, trustee educ, rare bks. 15: 10 E Parkway dr, Columbia Mo 65201.

YOUNG, WILLIAM. b NYC 29 D 29. 4: Nancy HACKLEMAN. 5: City Col (NY) 46-50 (Pol Sci) BSS; NYU 50-51 (Internat Affairs); Pratt 59-60 MLS. 6: Fr. 7: Soc sci research asst (cpl) US Army, Tokyo 51-53; Asst col libn Columbia U Libs 60-62, Col Libn Columbia U Libs 62-65, Asst to dir internat collections 65-. 8: Amy Loveman Award Com Mem, 65, 66, 67, 68. 9: AIL. 10: Beta Phi Mu. 14: Admin, acquis. 15: 21 Claremont ave, NYC 10027.

YOUNGBLOOD, IRMA RUTH. b Reserve NM 13 N 16. 4: Thomas J Youngblood. 5: UNM summer 45, 46; State of NM Libn's Certif 68. 6: Sp. 7: Tchr-Elem Sch 45-46; Bus mgrs off NM Sch of Mines 45-46, Asst libn 50-; Lib supv & ref libn 69-. 8: Commercial hereford rancher 39-. 9: NMLA. 10: Bus & Prof Womens Club; Socorro Co Ext Club; Amer Legion Aux; NM Cattlegrowers Assn; NM Farm & Livestock Bur. 13: Yes. 14: Ref, SWest bks, tech serv. 15: 506 School of Mines rd, Socorro NM 87801.

YOUNGER, MILDRED (LEASE). b Long ranch NJ 7 Jl 24. 4: Roy R Younger. 5: Monmouth Col 41-42, 44-45 AA; Simmons 45-47 (LS) BS; Columbia 50-53 (LS) MS. 7: SP 4 battery test operator US Signal Corps, Ft Monmouth NJ 42-44; Asst libn MT Hermon Sch for Boys, Mt Hermon Mass 47-48; Child libn Monmouth Co Lib, Freehold NJ 48-58; Libn Freehold Reg High Sch, Freehold NJ 58-64; Libn Howell High Sch, Farmingdale NJ 64-. 9: ALA-AASchL; NEA; NJLA; NJSchLA; NJEA. 10: AAUW; Trustee, Friends of Monmouth Co (NJ) Lib, 65; Monmouth County Area Lib Coord Coun, 65. 14: Sch libs. 15: Manaqua rd, Rt 2, Freehold NJ 07728.

YOUNGS, MARIAN A. b Charlotte Mich 17 Ap 08. 5: Fla StateU 25-26, 28-30 (Educ) AB in Ed; Rollins Col 26-27; West Res 32-33 BS in LS; UMich 37-38 MALS. 6: Lat, Fr, Ger. 7: Pub sch tchr, Miami Fla 30-32; Libn UMiami 33-34; Asst catlg & ref depts UFla Lib 34-38, Catlgr & asst prof lib sci 49-; Catlg libn Kan State Tchrs Col 38-40; Chief catlg dept UPittsburgh Lib 40-45; Sr asst II (catlgr) Detroit Pub Lib 45-49. 9: ALA (var catlg coms); PennLA (past chm Catlg Sect); FlaLA (chm Catlgrs RT 57-58); SELA. 10: Phi Kappa Phi; Kappa Delta Pi; Phi Mu; LWV. 13: Yes. 14: Catlg, tchg catlg. 15: 2041 NW 12th rd, Gainesville Fl 32601.

YOUNKIN, C GEORGE. b Great Bend Kan 13 O 10. 4: Ruth Ward. 5: Washburn Col 32-35 (Econ); Southeastern U 37-38 (Law). 6: Sp. 7: Admin Off USDA Soil Conserv Serv, Wash DC 35-42; (Sgt Maj) Armed Serv 43-45; Records off USDA Soil Conserv Serv, WashDC 45-51; Chief records mgt div Nat Archives & Records Serv GSA, Dallas 51-58; Supv archivist Fed Records Center, Ft Worth Tex 58-68, Reg Archives Off 68-. 8: Consul restor of pub records from fire, flood, or other natural disasters. 9: SAA (Com Preservation of Records). 10: Boy Scouts; Tex State Geneal Soc; Arlington Betterment Assn; Dallas Inter-Tribal Assn; West Hist Assn; Org Amer Histns; Amer Assn State & Local Hist. 11: Spec Serv Award Ft Worth Bus Assn 67; GSA Pub Serv Award 66. 14: Locating & catlg Indian records. , promote use of reg archives in scholastic commun of Ark, Okla, La & Tex. 15: Rte 2 Box 236, Quail dr lane, Arlington Tx 76010.

YOURMAN, MADELINE (CORD). b Raceland La 28 Ag 12. 5: UIll 35 (Liberal Arts, Ger) AB, 37 BS in LS, 42 (LS) MS. 6: Fr, Ger. 7: Stud-sec UIll Lib Sch 30-35; Loan asst UIll Lib(Urbana) 36; Reviser UIll Lib Sch 37; Ref asst UIll Lib (Urbana) 37-41; Admin asst to Dir of Processing Dept LC 42-48; Staff asst club serv Overseas Amer Red Cross (MTO) 45-46; Act chief ref libn Brooklyn Col Lib 48-49; Employment & Train Off LC 49-50; Brooklyn Col Lib; Supv of even & weekend lib serv 50-53, 54-, Chief ref div 53-59, Chief Humanities Div 59-65, Coordinator of reader serv 65-, Dep libn & dept chm lib dept 66-, Act chief libn & act chm lib dept 67-68, AssoC Prof 68-. 9: ALA-ACRL; NY Lib Club (Exec Coun 67-73); Lib Assn City Us NY (pres 59-60, treas 56-59). 10: Beta Phi Mu; AAUP; Phi Beta Kappa; Phi Kappa Phi. 12: Ed NY Lib Club "Bulletin (54-55). 14: Admin, ref. 15: 160 Columbia Height, Brooklyn NY 11201.

YU, KYUNG-SOOK. b Seoul Korea 5 O 39. 5: Ewha Woman'sU (Seoul Korea) 61 (Fr) BA; GeorgetownU 67 (Fr) MS; Columbia 68 MLS. 6: Korean, Fr. 7: Catlgr Drexel 68-. 14: Bk sel. 15: 4230 Regent st, Philadelphia Pa 19104.

YU, PRISCILLA (CHANG). b NYC 24 O 33. 4: George Tzuchiao Yu. 5: UCal (Berkeley) 51-55 (Gen Curriculum) AB; Columbia 55-57 MLS. 6: Fr, Sp, Chinese. 7: Asst ref libn UCal Lib (Berkeley)57-61; Chem libn UNC(Chapel Hill) 62-63. 14: Ref. 15: 6 Shuman cir, Urbana Il 61801.

YUAN, BARBARA (YEN). b Chungking China 5 Ag 45. 4: John S C Yuan. 5: Queens Col 62-64 (Fr); Ohio StateU 64-66 (Fr) BA; Columbia 66-67 MS. 6: Fr, Chinese. 7: Catlgr CCNY 67-. 9: ALA; LACUNY; NY Tech Serv Libns. 10: AAUP. 15: 2451 Webb ave apt 6F, Bronx NY 10468.

YUCHT, DONALD (JULIAN). b Brooklyn NY 30 D 39. 4: Alice Heymont. 5: Brooklyn Col 57-61 (Eng) AB; Pratt Inst 62-65 MLS. 6: Fr. 7: Libn Brooklyn Pub Lib Ingersoll Bldg 62-65 & Hd circ dept asst curator NYU Gen Lib 65-. 9: ALA. 10: Phi Beta Kappa; Beta Phi Mu. 14: Admin. 15: 130-07 229th st, Laurelton NY 11413.

YUEH, NORMA N (YU). b Peking China 21 Ja 28. 5: St Joseph Col 50 (Eng) BS; Stanford 51 (Eng); USoCal 55 MSLS; Columbia U 66-. 6: Chinese.07: Admin asst USoCal Lib 55-57; Adu,t serv libn NY Pub Lib 58-60; Sch libn Yonkers High Sch, Yonkers NY 60-61, 62-63; Acquis libn Paterson State Col 64-. 9: NJLA; ALA. 10: Beta Phi Mu. 14: Bk sel, admin. 15: Paterson State Col, Wayne NJ 07470.

YUNKER, J OLIVIA. b Hudson NY 19 S 29. 5: NY State Col for Tchrs 45-49 (Sp, Eng) BA, 50 (Eng) MA; SUNY 66 MLS. 6: Ger, Sp. 7: Tchr: Maine Central Sch, Maine NY 50-51, Ravena-Coeymans' Central Sch, Ravena NY 51-52; Accounting Gen Electric Co, Schenectady NY 52-62, Ref 62-65, Specialist catlg 65-. 8: Consul serv extended to dept libns in Gen Electric Co. 9: SLA (Upstate NY Chap Bulletin co-ed, ed 66-68); NYLA; Hudson-MohawkLA. 10: Schenectady Light Opera Co; Adult Educ Div, Schenectady Sch Syst; SUNY Alumni Assn. 13: Yes. 14: Ref, catlg. 15: 2414 Albany st, Schenectady NY 12304.

YUSK, FRANCES (SOBIESKI). b Brooklyn NY. 4: Stanley Alexander Yusk. 5: AdelphiU 27-31 (Econ) BA; Peabody Col 51 (LS) MA. 6: Fr. 7: Ed Amer Bk Co, NYC 31-33; Libn: high sch, Cookeville Tenn 42, high sch, Smithville Tenn 43, Van Buren High Sch, Spencer Tenn 43-45; Cheatham Co High Sch, Ashland City Tenn 45-47, Dickinson High Sch, Dickinson Tenn 57-58, William James High Sch, White Bluff Tenn 58-. 9: NEA; ALA; TennEA (Lib Sect: sec-treas, v-pres, pres); Middle TennLA (sec-treas, v-pres, pres); tennLA (sec-treas, v-pres, pres). 10: ChathamCoTA; DicksonCoTA; Delta Zeta; Delta Kappa Gamma. 14: Ref, sch lib. 15: 111 W Lake dr, Dickson Tn 37055.

Z

ZABLOCKI, AUDREY (BAUGUESS). b Traphill NC 19 Je 29. 4: Frank Stefan Zablocki. 5: Appalachian State Tchrs Col 46-50 (Eng) BS; UNC(Chapel Hill) 57 (LS); UNC(Greensboro) 65 (Eng, LS). 6: Sp. 7: Sch libn Draper High Sch, Draper NC 50-52; Army Libn Spec Serv, Germany 52-53; Catlgr AT&T Co, NYC 54; Tech ed West Electric Co, Winston-Salem NC 54-55; Bibiliogr UNC Lib (Chapel Hill) 55-59; Asst libn Salem Col Lib 59-62; Libn Forsyth Tech Inst, Winston-Salem NC 64-. 10: Beta Phi Mu. 14: Catlg, tech libs. 15: Forsyth Tech Inst, 2100 Silas Creek pkwy, Winston-Salem NC 27104.

ZABOR, BARBARA LYNNE. b Evanston Ill 3 N 42. 5: Col of Wooster 60-62; UMich 62-63 (Eng) AB, 64-65 AMLS. 6: Ger. 7: Organist Grosse Ile (Mich) Naval Air Staton 58-60; Gen asst Wyandotte (Mich) Pub Lib 63; Asst UMich Dept of Lib Sci 64-65; Acquis libn Lehigh U Lib 65-68; Libn in charge bus reading room Northwestern U 69-. 9: ALA. 14: Acquis, readers adv, bus. 15: PO Box 65, Evanston Il 60204.

ZABRISKIE, MARY ELIZABETH. b NYC 28 Je 14. 5: NY State Col for Tchrs (Albany) 31-35 (Fr, Hist) BA; Columbia 37-38, 39 (LS) BS. 6: Fr. 7: Catlgr Columbia U Lib 38; Sch & ref asst NY Pub Lib 38-42; Sr asst, then head soc sci div Rochester (NY) Pub Lib 42-46; Libn Radio Corp of Amer, Lancaster Penn 46-. 9: ALA; SLA; PennLA. 10: AAUW; LWV. 13: Yes. 14: Ref, tech libs. 15: Radio Corp of Amer, Lancaster Penn 17604.

ZACHERT, MARTHA JANE (KOONTZ). b York Penn 7 F 20. 4: Edward G Zachert. 5: Lebanon Valley Col 37-41 (Eng) AB; Emory 50-54 (LS) ML; Columbia 58-68 DLS. 6: Fr, Ger. 7: Jr libn Enoch Pratt Free Lib, Baltimore 41-46; Libn Wood Research Inst, Atlanta 47; Sch libn DeKalb Co Schs, DeKalb Co Ga 50-51; Asst prof Emory U Div of Libnship 58-59, 59-61; Libn & Prof Hist of Pharmacy So Col of Pharmacy Mercer U 53-62; Instr Fla State U Lib Sch summer 61, Asst Prof 63-68; Assoc Prof 68-. 8: Consul, So Col of Pharmacy, Mercer U 58-60; Consul St Josephs Sch of Nursing. 9: SLA (var coms); MedLA; ALA-LED (var coms); Coun of Planning Libs; FlaLA; SELA. 10: Beta Phi Mu; Delta Kappa Gamma; Amer Inst Hist of Pharmacy. 12: Ed SLA Ga Chap "News"; Ed Bd "Journal of Library History". 13: Yes. 14: Spec libs, admin, ref, lib hist, med. 15: Box 2293, Tallahassee Fla 32304.

ZACK, PHYLLIS (GOODRICH). b Pittsfield Mass 28 S 25. 4: Daniel Zack. 5: UMass 44-48 (Chem) BS; SUNY (Albany) 65-69 MLS. 7: Chemist Gen Electric Co, Pittsfield Mass 48-51; Ref lib Berkshire Athenaeum, Pittsfield Mass 59-. 8: Tchr, ref course, West Reg Pub Lib System, Pittsfield Mass 65; Ref & Interlib Loan Libn, West Reg Pub Lib System, for the Berkshire Co area. 9: West Mass Lib Club; Berkshire LA. 10: Phi Kappa Phi; Pittsfield Col Club; Friends of the Berkshire Athenaeum. 13: Yes. 14: Ref. 15: 40 Maryland ave, Pittsfield Ma 01201.

ZADNER, PATRICIA A (GARBACK). b Upper Darby Penn 4 N 41. 4: Paul A Zadner. 5: DYouville Col 59-63 (Fr) BA; Syracuse 63-64 MSS. 6: Fr, Sp. 7: Asst libn, catlgr Lockwood Mem Lib SUNY (Buffalo) 64-. 9: Beta Phi MU. 14: Catlg, readers adv. 15: 2402 Kensington ave, Snyder NY 14226.

ZADNER, PAUL A. b Buffalo NY 9 S 40. 4: Patricia Garback. 5: SUNY (Buffalo) 5862 (Educ) BS; SUNY (Geneseo) 6364 MSLS. 7: Libn trainee Buffalo & Erie Co Pub Lib, Buffalo NY 62-63; Jr libn 64-65; Act hd N Jefferson Br Lib 65; Asst circ libn SUNY(Buffalo) SUNY(Buffalo) Ridge Lea Lib 67-68; Circ libn SUNY(Buffalo) Lockwood Lib 68-. 9: ALA; NYLA; AFT. 10: Assn Univ Libns SUNY (Buffalo); AAUP. 14: Readers adv, circ. 15: 2402 Kensington ave, Snyder NY 14226.

ZAEHRINGER, DAVID JOHN. b Clinton Iowa 11 Ag31. 5: Loras Col 49-53 (Eng Lit) BA; Columbia 54-55 (Directing), 56-59 (LS) MS. 6: Ger, Lat. 7: Circ dept Lib Columbia U 55-59, Ref libn Bus Lib 59-62; Bus libn UIowa 62-67; Head readers serv Stanford U Bus Lib 67-. 9: SLA (treas Bus & Fin Div 65-67). 10: Beta Gamma Sigma; Delta Epsilon Sigma. 13: Yes. 14: Ref. 15: 1777 Woodland ave apt 4, Palo Alto Ca 94303.

ZAFREN, HERBERT C. b Baltimore 25 Ag25. 4: Miriam Koenigsberg. 5: Johns Hopkins 41-44 (Lat) BA; Baltimore Hebrew Col 41-44 Diploma; Johns Hopkins 46-49 (Medieval Hist); UMich 49-50 AMLS. 6: Ger, Fr, Lat, Hebrew, Yiddish. 7: Electronics techs mate 3/c US Navy 44-46; Jr Instr Johns Hopkins U 47-49; Bibliog searcher Law Lib UMich 49-50; Exec Dir Amer Jewish Period Center, Cincinnati 58-; Libn Hebrew Union Col Jewish Inst Relig (Cincinnati) 50-; Prof of Jewish bibliog 68-; Dir of libs Hebrew Union Col, Jewish Inst of Relig (Cincinnati, Jerusalem, Los Angeles, NYC) 66-. 50-. 9: ALA; JewishLA (pres 65-66); AHA; Amer Jewish Hist Soc; Amer Acad for Jewish Res; Med Acad of Amer; OhioLA; Assn Jewish Libns (pres 66-67). 10: AAUP; Soc of Jewish Bibliophiles; Phi Beta Kappa; Grolier Club. 11: Litt H D Baltimore Hebrew Col (69). 12: Ed "Studies in Bibliography and Booklore; (53-); "Bibliographica Judaica (69-); Auth "A Gathering of Broadsides (67). 13: Yes. 14: Rare bks, automation, lib arch. 15: 7320 Eastlawn dr, Cincinnati Oh 45237.

ZAHN, GERALDINE (DILLER). b Washington Co Kan 9 Ap17. 4: Joseph B Zahn. 5: Kan State U (Manhattan) 35-40 BS; UIll 41-42 BS in LS. 7: Head class res Kan State U (Manhattan) 38-42; Catlgr UColo 42-43; Catlgr Sioux Falls Pub Lib, Sioux Falls SD 43-46; Asst Command & Staff Col Lib, Leavenworth Kan 45-46; Chief tech proc Topeka Pub Lib, Topeka Kan 46-50; Libn Prof Lib Topeka State Hosp, Topeka Kan 50-54; Libn Tecumseh Grade Schs, Tecumseh Kan 63-. 9: ALA; KanLA; KanSchLA; KAVCO. 10: Girl Scouts; Boy Scouts; PTA. 15: Rt 4, Topeka Ks 66605.

ZAHRT, GENEVIEVE ROSALIE (KOTTLER). b Canby Minn 4 Mr 13. 5: UArk 43-44, 46-48 (Art); Ft Hays Kan State Col 49-50 (Art); Ithaca Col 50-52 (Eng) BS; San Jose State Col 63-64 (Libnship) MA. 7: Lib circ asst CornellU 58-63; Period libn USanta Clara 64-65; Child libn Queens Borough Pub Lib, Jamaica NY 65-. 9: ALA; NYLA; NY Lib Club. 10: Ithaca commun Players; Ithaca Artists Club. 13: Yes. 14: Period, ref, story hours, puppet shows. 15: 28-04 44th st apt 22, Long Island City NY 11103.

ZAICHICK, NORMAN P. b Berlin Wis 24 O29. 5: UWis 51 (Gen Sci) BA, 52 (Anthropology) MA, 56 (LS) MS. 7: Ref libn Argonne Nat Lab, Argonne Ill 57-. 9: SLA (Nuclear Sci Bylaws Com). 10: Sci Research Soc Amer. 14: Bibliog. 15: Lib Serv Dept 203- D144, Argonne Nat LAB, Argonne Ill 60440.

ZAIDEL, JOHN N. b Buffalo NY 21 N35. 4: Mary Louise Shinskey. 5: Canisius Col 53-57 (Lat) AB; Syracuse 58-59 (LS)MS. 7: Buffalo & Erie Co Pub Lib, Buffalo NY: Br asst 59-62, Ya libn 62-63; Ref asst 62-63; Baltimore Co Pub Lib, Baltimore Md; Adult serv specialist 63-67; Area br libn 68-. 9: ALA-PLA; -RSD (chm 69-71); MdLA. 10: Beta Phi Mu. 14: Ref, readers serv. 15: 818 Glen Allen dr, Baltimore Md 21229.

ZAKRZEWSKI, CARL EDWARD. b Buffalo NY 18S36. 5: Canisius Col 54-58 (Eng) AB; Catholic U 58-60 MS in LS. 6: Fr. 7: Stud asst Catholic U 58-59: Libn Catholic U 58-59; Libn Cranwell Sch, Lenox Mass 59-60; Asst catlgr Iona Col 60; Catlg libn Canisius Col 60-67; Assoc libn catlg dept SUNY (Buffalo) 68-. 9: CathLA; ALA; LA at SUNY (Albany). 10: Beta Phi Mu; Alsph Sigma Nu. 13: Yes. 14: Catlg, col libs. 15: 2996 Bailey ave, Buffalo NY 14215.

ZALE, PHYLLIS J(UNE) (KELLERMANN). b Brooklyn NY 25 Je 30. 4: Irving Zale. 5: Brooklyn Col 48-52 (Eng) BA; Columbia 52-55 MLS. 7: NY Pub Lib: Page 47, Clerk 48-52, Trainee 52-55, Libn 55-57, Sr libn 57-59, Per Diem sr libn 60-66; Per diem libn 67-. 8: Lib Consul Yeshiva R M Soloveichik, NYC. 14: Ref & ya wk in pub libs. 15: 11 Fort George Hill, NYC 10040.

ZAMBUSI, WILLIAM (JOSEPH). b Matachewan Ont Can 11 Je 41. 5: UOttawa 61-65 (Fr, Hist) BA; UToronto 67-68 BLS. 6: Fr, Ital. 7: Tchr secondary sch, Canadian Univ Serv Overseas, Biafra 65-67; Libn Hamilton Pub Lib, Hamilton Ont Can 68-. 9: CanLA; Inst prof Libns Ont; OntLA. 14: Pub serv. 15: Apt 205 116 Charlton ave W, Hamilton 10 Ont Can.

ZARECHNAK, GALINA V (DRONOV). b Novocherkassk Russia 27 S 16. 4: Michael Zarechnak. 5: KomenskyU (Bratislava Czechoslovakia) 36-41 (Slavic Lang) PhD; CatholicU 52-58 (LS) MS. 6: Russian, Czech, Slovak, Ger. 7: Lectr SlovakU, Bratislava Czechoslavakia 41-45; Researcher-linguist Acad of Sci, Bratislava, Czechoslovakia 44-45; Tr & ed Med Lib, wash DC 52-55, Supv publ ed 55-57; Libn (acquis) Armed Forces, Bethesda Md 57-65; Hd selection & search sect Nat Lib of Med, Bethesda Md 65-67, Exchange coord 67-. 9: SLA (sec DC Chap Bio Sci Div); MedLA. 10: Soc Fed Linguists. 12: Asst ed "INSPEL". 13: Yes. 14: Intl exchange of publs. 15: 1308 Farragut st NW, Washington DC 20011.

ZATEZALO, MARY (ADAMS). b Cusseta Ala 07 My 17. 4: Mike Zatezalo. 7: Lib asst Air Univ Lib, Maxwell AFB Ala 47-52, Doc circ libn 53-57, Asst rd 58-59, Doc asst 60-62, asst ed 63-64, Doc catlgr 65-. 9: SLA; AlaLA. 14: Catlg. 15: 2560 Churchill, Montgomery Al 36111.

ZAWADZKI, DANUTA MARIA (SIENKIEWICZ). b Warsaw Poland. 4: Michael I Zawadzki. 5: URI 56-59 (Fr) BA; Immaculate Heart Col 64 MLS. 6: Polish, Fr, Russian. 7: WAAF, Great Britain 40-42; Sr lib clerk UIll(Urbana) 52-54; Lib asst UChicago 55; Lib asst Brown U 56; Libn Pacific Semicond Inc, Lawndale Cal 60-62; Catlgr Space Tech Labs, Redondo Beach Cal 62-63; Asst supv Tech Doc Ctr Hughes Aircraft Co, Culver City Cal 64-. 9: SLA; ALA. 14: Catlg, tech libnship docs indexin. 15: 8036 Gonzaga ave, Los Angeles Ca 90045.

ZBIERANSKA, KRYSTYNA (PAULLY de LELIWA). b Krakow Poland. 4: Czeslaw M Zbieranski. 5: Jagellonian U (Krakow Poland) 33 (Modern Langs) MA; Royal U (Rome) 33 (Ital Lit) PhD; UClermont Ferrand (France) Diplome dEtudes Francaises; McGill 43 BL; S. 6: Polish, Fr, Ital, Sp. 7: Ital tchr Dante Alighieri Soc Krakow U (Poland) 34-35; Writer Polish Ministry of Info in France, Paris; Guest Scholar Queens U Ont) 41-42; Ref libn & co-ed of Can Bibliog, Toronto Pub Libs 43-46; Exec dir & admin of real estate org, NY 46-58; Research wk Free lance, Libs in Europe - 59; Libn in chg Cathedral Col Lib, NYC 60-. 9: ALA; SLA (NY Chap Documentation Group, Exec Coun 67-68); CathLA (Greater NY Unit, Exec Coun 68-69); Metro Cath Univ & ColLA (Exec Coun 67-68). 10: Polish Inst Arts & Scis; Kosciuscko Found; Pidulski Inst for research in mod hist. 12: Comp "The Canadian Catalogue of Books Published in Canado . . . 1944-1947 (yearly publn). 13: Yes. 14: Org of lib serv. 15: 1540 York ave, Apt 10N, New York NY 10028.

ZEALBERG, CATHERINE L. b Mahanoy City Penn 9 F 20. 5: Kutztown State Col 39-43 (LS) BS in Ed; Peabody 47 (LS) MA. 7: Libn Wellsboro Jr Sr High Sch, Wellsboro Penn 43-46; Instr Lib Sci West Ill State Col 47-48; Head Libn Bloomsburg State Col 48-51; US Army War Col, Carlisle Barracks Penn: Ref libn 51-53, Chief acquis sect 53-55, Chief processing br 55-. 9: ALA; SLA; PennLA. 10: AAUW; LWV; Nat Coun Cath Women. 14: Tech proc. 15: 300 "E st, Carlisle Pa 17013.

ZEBROWSKI, MARTHA (MAY KADERLY). b Charlotte NC 26 Ap 22. 4: Edward Zebrowski. 5: MercerU 39-42 (Hist) AB; Adiran Col 58-59 (Educ); Siena Heights Col 59-63 (LS); UMich 65 (LS) Permanent Tchg Certif State of Mich. 7: US Civil Serv Clk Soc Sec Bd, Macon Ga 43; US War Dept Clk War Dept, Deming NM 44-45, Wendover Utah 45; Sec Pub Schs, Willow Run Mich 55-56; Libn clk Adrian Elem Schs, Adrian Mich 58-59; Libn tchr Adrian Jr High Sch, Adrian Mich 60-65; Libn I Edinboro State Col 66-. 9: PennLA. 10: Phi Mu. 14: Acquis in col lib. 15: PO Box 152 31 High st, Edinboro Pa 16412.

ZEIDES, SOLOMON. b Jersey City NJ 15 Ja24. 4: Rita Freedman. 5: Yeshiva Col 41-45 (Eng) AB; Columbia 46-48 (Psych) AM, 50-52 MLS. 6: Hebrew, Yiddish, Fr, Ger. 7: Asst libn Yeshiva Col Lib 45-48; Asst libn Pollack Lib Yeshiva U 48-52, Libn in chg of main acad lib & central acquis-tech processing 52-, Instr Lib Sci 53-66, Assoc Prof Lib Sci 67-. 8: Lib consul: Jewish Educ Center, Elizabeth NJ 59, Shulamith Sch for Girls, Brooklyn NY 60, Hebrew Inst of LI, Far Rockaway NY 62-. 9: ALA; SLA; NY Lib Club; NY Tech Serv Libns. 10: Rabbi in NJ & NY 55-61; Rabbi, Shaarey Tfiloh Cong, Spring Valley NY 62-; Chaplain Spring Valley Fire Dept. 12: Contrib ed "Annual Magazine Subject Index (48). 13: Yes. 14: Admin, catlg, ref. 15: 14 Brian ter, Spring Valley NY 10977.

ZEIMET, MARY IRENE. b Pringle SD 26 Ap10. 5: Black Hills State Col 25-30 (Educ) BS; UDenver summers 40, 42, 43 (LS) BS, summers 51-53 (Educ) MA; summers 59, 63, 66; UMont 57. 7: Tchr Rapid City High Sch, Rapid City SD 30-36, Libn 36-. 8: Instr Ext Classes Black Hills State Col in ref bks & sch lib mgt 66-68. 9: ALA; NEA; SDEA (chm Sch Libns Round Table 57-58); Sec 67-68). 10: Delta Kappa Gamma; Kappa Delta Pi; Bus & Prof Womens Club; Annie D Tallent Club SD. 14: High sch libnship. 15: 316 Franklin, Rapid City SD 57701.

ZEISS, CAROLINE (WEISS). b Copperas Cove Tex 17 F 15. 4: George H Zeiss. 5: Blinn Jr Col 33-35 AA; UTex 38-41 (Math) BA; Tex Woman'sU 60-62 MLS. 6: Ger. 7: Tchr Austin co, Bellville Tex 36-39; Typist-clerical LSU (Baton Rouge) 41-43; Ref asst So MethodistU 62-68, Catlgr 68-. 9: SLA; TexLA; DallasCoLA. 14: Catlg, ref. 15: 3240 Rankin ave, Dallas Tx 75205.

ZELINSKY, SHERMAN BENNETT. b Manchester NH 14 Jl24. 5: UNH 41-42; Boston U 42-47 B Mus, 50-51 M Mus; Colo State Col summer 54; UNeb 54; UDenver 58-59 (LS)MA. 7: Tchr-lib: Maxwell High Sch, Maxwell NM 52-53, Summit Co High Sch, Breckenridge Colo 53-54, Maywood High Sch, Maywood Neb 54-56; Tchr Montrose High Sch, Montrose Colo 56-57; Tchr-libn Platte Canon High Sch, Bailey Colo 57-58; Libn: Englewood High Sch, Englewood Colo 59-61, UDenver summer 61, Brooklyn Pub Lib 61; Tchr Concord High Sch, Concord NH 61-62; Head Libn Danville Jr Col (Ill) 62-. 14: Ref. 15: 227 E Woodlawn, Danville Ill 61832.

ZEMAN, ANNE JOSEPHINE. b Charlotte NC 12 D 09. 5: UNC (Chapel Hill) 48-51 (Pol Sci) AB; UDenver 52 (LS) MA. 06: Ger. 6: Ger. 7: Sec, Examiner of Accts VA, Charlotte NC 28-44; WAC, Wash DC & Germany 44-48; Pub Lib Charlotte & Mecklenburg Co, Charlotte NC 52-55; VA Hosp, Salisbury NC 55-58; Glenndale Hosp, Glenndale Md 58-62; Mercy Sch of Nursing, Charlotte NC 63-65; Libn; Ashley High Sch, Gastonia NC 67, VA Hosp, Danville Ill 69-. 8: Del to Md Conf on Aging, 60; ALA del to White House Conf on Aging, 61. 9: ALA; NCLA; SELA; MecklenburgCoLA. 10: Bus & Prof Womens Club; AAUW; Charloote & Danville Toastmistress Club; LWV; Great Bks Discussion Group. 14: Bibliotherapy. 15: VA Hospital Lib, Danville Il 61832.

ZENICH, MARGRETT BARTON. b Mead Okla 4 D 15. 5: SEast State (Durant Okla) 34-38 (Eng, hist) BA; Okla StateU (Stillwater) 43 (Aircraft Engring); San Jose State 47 (LS); UOkla 51 (LS, Fr) BALS; Tex West 64-65. 7: Tchr Big Cabin Pub Lib, Big Cabin Okla 38-39; Libn Carnegie Br Okla City

Pub Lib 46-48; Libn Okla City Pub Sch 48-51; Post libn Army Missile Test Ctr, White Sands NM 51-55, Tech libn 55-68; Chief sci & tech info off US Army Corps of Engrs, Wash DC 68-. 8: Consul Detroit Arsenal Lib 62; Dir Army Tech Info Support Activities Proj Army Research Off, Wash DC 68-. 9: SLA (Rio Grande Chap: sec-treas, pres; sec-treas Docs Div); Border RegLA. 10: El Paso Co humane Soc. 14: Admin, lib & tech info resea5 humane Soc. 15: 4712 Popular dr, Alexandria Va 22310.

ZENK, MARGARET L(OUISE). b Youngstown Ohio 8 Je 10. 5: Capital U 27-29; Carnegie 29-31 BS in LS; UPittsburgh 57-61 (Bus) MA. 7: Lib asst Hampton Inst 31-32; Pub Lib of Youngstown & Mahoning Co, Youngstown Ohio: Lib asst 33-35, Lib Poland Br 35-37, Libn Struthers Br 37-45, Head circ dept 45-47, Dir order & catlg dept 51-55; UPittsburgh Dir tech serv 55-57, Admin asst 57-59, Assoc catlgr 59-60, Head circ dept 60-65, Supv of collections control 66-; Act dir tech ser & Chm catlg dept 67; Asst to dir pub serv & bldg planning 67-. 9: ALA-ACRL (Tri-State Chap); SLA; PennLA; Pittsburgh Lib club; PennLA (chm Col & Research Sect 59-60, sec 62-63, archivist 63-68, 2nd v-pres 68-69). 10: UPittsburgh Carnegie Lib Sch Alumni Assn. 13: Yes. 14: Catlg, circ, acquis, bldgs & equipment. 15: 101 Lloyd ave, Apt 4, Pittsburgh Pa 15218.

ZENNER, HANS O. b Mulheim/ Ruhr Germany 1 Mr18. 4: Marianne Scherner. 5: UCologne (Germany) 46-52 (Hist) PhD; Kent State U 55-58 (LS) MA. 6: Ger, Fr, Lat. 7: Prof of foreign langs Sioux Falls Col 55-58, Libn 58-66; Libn Thiel Col 66-. 9: ALA; SDLA (Com on State ocs). 10: Delta Phi Alpha; Greenville Symphony Orchestra; Thiel Col Chamber Orchestra. 13: Yes. 14: Rare bks. 15: Thiel Col, Greenville Pa 16125.

ZENS, MILDRED IREME (LARSON). b Racine Wis 14S17. 4: Clarence M Zens. 5: Marquette U 36-38 (Journalism); Milwaukee-Downer Col 38-40 (Eng, Hist) BA; UWis (Milwaukee) summer 40 (Drama); Catholic U 62-63 MLS. 6: Fr, Danish, Sp. 7: Tchr sub libn Washington Park & Horlick High Sch, Racine Wis 40-41; Tchr, libn Lake Linden-Hubbell High Sch, Lake Linden Mich 41-42; Tchr, chm Eng Dept Frank McKee High Sch, N Muskegon Mich 43-44; Reporter, writer Racine Journal-Times, Racine Wis 44 & 45; Libn Fairfax Co Pub Lib, Fairfax Va 58, 59; Libn Gonzaga Prep, Wash DC 65-. 9: SLA; CathLA; DCLA. 10: AAUW; Friends of the Lib Fairfax Va;Boy Scouts. 14: Ya, publ rel. 15: 406 A st SE, Wash DC 20003.

ZEYDEL, JEANNE. b NJ25. 5: George Washington U 46-49 (Eng Lit) AB; Columbia 49-51 (LS) MS. 6: Fr. 7: Seamens Church Inst, NYC 50-51;NY Hist Soc, NYC 51: US Army Spec Serv Libs Europe, Germany & France 51-53; US Patent Off Sci Lib, Wash DC 53-60; US Info Agency, Wash DC 60-. 9: SLA. 14: Ref, admin. 15: US Info Agency 1750 Pennsylvania ave NW, Wash DC 20547.

ZIBILICH, BERNICE (GOODMAN). b San Antonio Tex. 4: Robert J Zibilich. 5: Our Lady of the Lake Col 41-45 (Eng, Educ) BA (cum laude), 46-47 BS in LS. 6: Fr. 7: Libn I info Order Ref New Orleans Pub Lib 47-60; Child libn 61-. 8: Coord US State Dept "Open Door program entertaining off for guests to US. 9: ALA-CSD; SWLA; LaLA (Hospitality Com 61); New Orleans Lib Club (sec 60-61); CathLA (Official ALA rep to CLA conv 69). 10: LWV; Delgado Mus of Art; Nat Coun of Christians & Jews; Womens Auxiliary, C of C; Vista Shores Country Club; Friends of the Cabildo. 13: Yes. 14: Wk with child & yp, pub rel. 15: 1350 Fillmore ave, New Orleans La 70122.

ZIEBOLD, EDNA B. b Columbus Ohio 3 Jl 09. 5: Ohio State U 26-30 (Fr) BA; UWash 41-42 BA in LS. 6: Fr. 7: Lib asst Columbus Pub Lib, Columbus Ohio 31-39; Head libn Linden Br Lib, Columbus Ohio 39-41; Asst ref libn Seattle Pub Lib 42-43; Asst libn Worthington Pub Lib, Worthington Ohio 44; Act ref & circ libn Central Wash Col of Educ 45; Lib in chg of schs San Diego Co Lib, San Diego 46-47; Dir of lib serv San Diego Co Dept of Educ, San Diego 47-. 8: Tchr of child lit: USoCal Ext 60, Cal West U summer 63; Adv Com Gaver Elem Sch Lib List; ESEA mem Ad Hoc Com Cal State Dept Educ. 9: ALA-AASchL (Bd 57-58); NEA; SLA; Assn for Supv & Curr Devel; CalLA; CalASchL; Cal Assn for Supv & Curr Devel. 10: AAUW; Phi Beta Kappa. 12: Consul "New Book of Knowledge" (64); Ed Consul "Sagas of the West" series; Guest ed "School Librarian" (Mr 60). 13: Yes. 14: Child lit, admin. 15: 5176 Foothill blvd, San Diego Ca 92109.

ZIEGAUS, WARREN. b Tacoma Wash 1 Ap10. 4: Virginia Ziegaus. 5: U of Puget Sound 29-33 (Chem) BS; UWash 35-37 (LS) BA. 6: Ger. 7: Asst Sci & tech NY Pub Lib 37; Order libn UMd 37-40; Head accessions Kan City (Mo) Pub Lib 40-46; USAF, Eng 42-45; Fed Pub Housing Authority, Seattle 46-48; Bibliog Center Denver Pub Lib 47-49; Head acquis dept Enoch Pratt Free Lib, Baltimore 49-. 15: Enoch Pratt Free Lib, Baltimore 21201.

ZIEGLER, JANET M. b Rhinelander Wis 10 My40. 5: San Fernando Valley State Col 58-60; UCLA 61-63 (Hist) BA, 63-64 MLS. 6: Fr, Sp, Ger. 7: Temp Clerk-typist Grolier Soc, Los Angeles 60-61; Stud clerk circ UCLA Lib 62-64; Catlg libn UCLA Research Lib 64-69; Ref libn Research Lib 69-. 8: Lectr bibliog, UCLA Sch of Lib Serv, summers 68, 69. 9: AHA; ALA; CalLA; SoCal Tech Prog Group. 12: "World War II; Books in English, 1945-1965 (69). 14: Catlg, bibliog, ref. 15: 5633 Topanga Canyon blvd #317, Woodland Hills Ca 91364.

ZIEGLER, MAZIE (IRENE LUCY). b Lehighton Penn 15 Ap 13. 5: Kutztown State Col 30-34 (Lib, Eng, Math, Fr) BS, 35 (Elem Curriculum) Certif; Columbia 43-46 (Lib) Certif, 47-49 (Stud Personnel Adm) MAL Rheinische Friefrich WilhelmsU (Bonn Germany) 54-55 9german); UIll summer 67 (LS). 6: Ger. 7: Elem tchr Parryville (Penn) Pub Sch 37-42; High Sch Libns Lehighton Area Sch Dist, Lehighton Penn 42-. 8: Fulbright Exch tchr, English, Clara-Schumann-Schule, Bonn Ger 54-55. 9: NEA; PennLA (Child, YP & Sch Libns: v-chm 56, chm 57); PennASchL (v-pres 56, pres 57); PennStateEA; Lehigh Valley Dir LA; LehighEA (sec 42-48, pres 53-54). 10: Bd Trustees, Lehighton Pub Lib. 13: Yes. 14: Ya lib serv. 15: 134 North Fourth st, Lehighton Pa 18235.

ZIEGLER, RONALD MELVIN. b Cuyahoga Falls Ohio 10 Ag 35. 4: Elli Resch. 5: UMiami (Fla) 60-66 (Eng) AB; Fla StateU 67-68 (LS) MS. 6: Ger. 7: Reporter Alameda Star, Alameda Cal 66; Cafeteria mgr Army-Air Force Exchange Serv, San Francisco 67; Ref libn Florida AtlanticU 68-. 9: FlaLA. 14: Ref. 15: 621 NW 36th st, Pompano Beach Fl 33064.

ZIELINSKA, MARIE F (NALECZ-ODRZYWOLSKA). b Cracow Poland 26 Je27. 4: John Andre Zielinska. 5: Jagiellonian U (Cracow) 44-47 (Agronomy) Eng Agr & M SC; Sch of Soc Sci (Cracow) 46-48 (Journalism) Certif; UMontreal 62 BLS; McGill 69 MLS. 6: Fr, Ger, Russian, Polish. 7: Research asst & libn dept of Microbiol Jagiellonian U (Cracow) 47-49; Bacteriologist Health Dept City Hall, Cracow Poland 51-53; Libn Manufac Comp SIEW, Cracow Poland 53-56; Research tech in biochem Allan Mem Inst, McGill U 58-61; UMontreal; Loan & ref libn Central Lib 62-63, Catlgr Central Lib 63-64, Head libn Biol Lib 64-. 8: Lecturer in ref course, Ecole de Bibliotheconomie UMontreal. 9: CanLA; ALA; Association Canadienne des Bibliothecaires de la Langue Francaise (pres Montreal Chap 65-66); QueLA (Coun 65-67; sec Univ & Col Sect 64-65; ABQ pres 68-69). 10: Assn of Polish Engnrs. 13: Yes. 14: Admin, ref. 15: 3250 Ellendale ave apt 201. Montreal 26 Can.

ZIEMER, OPAL (EVELYN). b New London Wis 18 Je 17. 5: N Central Col 35-39 (Eng, Soc Sci) BA; UWis 39-40 BLS. 7: Child asst Green Bay (Wis) Pub Lib 40-41, Clinton (Iowa) Pub Lib 41-42, Antigo (Wis) Pub Lib 42-44, Dearborn Pub Lib 44-47, Br libn 47-68, Supv child wk 68-. 9: ALA; Women's Nat Bk Assn; MichLA (sec-treas Sch & Child Sect 62-64). 14: Child wk. 15: 6442 Schaefer rd, Dearborn Mi 48126.

ZIENOWICZ, NINA (KROLOKOWSKA). b Warsaw Poland 11 Jl 24. 5: Ctr for Training of Libns (Jaracin Poland) 50 (LS). 6: Polish, Russian. 7: Chief libn Co Pub Lib, Szczecinek Poland 46-52; Sr catlgr US Bk Exchange, Wash DC 66-. 9: Polish Union of Libns & Archivists. 14: Catlg. 15: 1567 N Colonial ter, Arlington Va 22209.

ZIESSMAN, YOLAN (AUERBACH). b Cleveland 23 O 14. 4: Alex Ziessman. 5: Flora Stone Mather Col West Res 31-36 (Lit) AB; West Res 37-38 BS in LS. 7: Stud asst Flora Stone Mather Col Lib 32-36; Desk asst Cleveland Heights Pub Lib, Cleveland Heights Ohio 36-38; 2nd asst & catlgr Shaker Heights Pub Lib, Shaker Heights Ohio 38-41, 1st asst ref libn 41-43; Ref & readers adv asst Evansville Pub Lib, Evansville Ind 58-65; Asst head of main lib Euclid Pub Lib, Euclid Ohio 65-67, Br libn 68-. 9: OhioLA; ALA. 14: Ref, adult serv. 15: 631 E 222 st, Euclid Oh 44123.

ZIETZ, ROBERT J. b Menominee Mich 7 S 22. 4: Norma Corners. 5: Spring Hill Col 40, 46-49 (Eng) BS; Emory 49-50 M Lib. 6: Ger, Sp. 7: (Sgt) US AAF 43-46; Asst libn Spring Hill Col 50-61, Libn 61-. 9: ALA; CathLA (Adv Bd; chm Mid-South Conf 65-67); chm Col & Univ Sect 68-); SELA; AlaLA (v-pres 65-66, pres 66-67). 10: Exec Coun, Mobile Mus Bd; Alpha Sigma Nu; Col Club. 12: Co-auth "Writing and Research; A Style Manual"; Ed CathLA Mid-South Conf

"Newsletter". 13: Yes. 14: Admin. 15: Spring Hill Col Lib, Mobile Al 36608.

ZIFFER, SHIRLEY (MISHLER). b Brooklyn NY 17 S 19. 4: Jack Ziffer. 5: Brooklyn Col 36-40 (Chem) BA; UWis (Milwaukee) 63-67 (LS) MA. 7: Jr chem Col Phys & Surgeons columbiaU 40-41; Chem Schenley Research Inst, Lawrenceburg Ind 41-43; Pol surveyor Louis Harris Assoc, NYC 60-61; Instr-libn UWis (Milwaukee) Sch Lib & Info Sci 67-. 8: Citizens Urban Renewal & Planning Com, Milwaukee 56-66. 9: ALA; WisLA. 10: LWV. 14: Catlg, lib educ. 15: 3156 N 54 st, Milwaukee Wi 53216.

ZIMMER, GAIL ENID. b Jersey City NJ 10 JI42. 5: Trenton State Col 59-63 (Sci) BA; Rutgers 63-64 MLS. 6: Fr. 7: Catlg asst Rutgers U 64; Libn NY Pub Lib Hamilton Grange Br 64-65, Ref libn Donnell Lib Center 65-; Asst ref libn & Film coord Free Pub Lib, Fair Lawn NJ 67-. 9: Bergen-Passaic Lib Club. 10: Internat Club; Seamens Church Inst. 14: Ref, film libnship. 15: 25-26 Southern dr, Fair Lawn NJ 07410.

ZIMMER, NAOMI. b Gallupville NY 29 S 37. 5: SUNY Col of Educ (Oneonta) 55-59 (Elem Educ) BS in Ed; SUNY Col of Educ (Albany) 59-60 MSLS. 7: Elem sch libn Burnt Hills-Ballston Lake Sch System, Burnt Hills NY 60-61; Child libn Schenectady Co Pub Lib, Schenectady NY 61-65; Ref libn Mohawk Valley Lib Assn, Schenectady NY 65-. 9: NYLA. 14: Ref. 15: Gallupville NY 12073.

ZIMMER, SZCZEPAN KAROL. b Zborow Poland 26D03. 4: Halina Cieszewska. 5: U of King Jan Casimir (Lwow) 21-28 (Polish Lit) MA, PhD; Immaculate Heart Col 61-62 MALS. 6: Polish, Russian, Ukrainian, Ger. 7: Tchr & libn Trade Gymnasium & Lyceum, Przemysl Poland 34-39; Res Lt Polish Army Infantry 39-45; Supt of chs for Polish displaced persons, Germany 45-50; Lab tech Chicago Rawhide Mfg Co, Chicago 51-60; Research libn Los Angeles Co Gen Hosp Med Lib, Los Angeles 62-66; Med libn in charge of Unit II 66-68; Act hd libn Los Angeles Co, USoCal Med Ctr 68-. 9: Med Lib Group So Cal(treas 68-70). 10: Polish-Amer Congress; Polish Univ Club, Los Angeles; Polish Millenium Lib Com, Los Angeles. 12: "Dalton System," Lwow Poland (30); "Stanislaw Wyspianski, Biog Sketch in Polish & Eng, W Germany" (57-59); "The Jagellonian University Library in Cracow" (63); "From Hut to Parnassus" (London 68). 13: Yes. 14: Ref, research, rare bks (incunabula). 15: 8008 W Blackburn ave, apt 1, Los Angeles Ca 90048.

ZIMMERMAN, GLEN ANDREW. b Chicago Ill 13 Je 41. 4: Bonnie Talley. 5: Iowa StateU 59-63 (Hist) BS; UMich 66-67 MALS. 6: Ger, Fr. 7: Capt Artillery off USA Field artillery 64-66; Bibliogr LRS LC 67, Special recriot 67-68, Subj catlgr 68, Exec asst proc dept 68-. 9: ALA; DCLA. 10: Phi Kappa Phi; Beta Phi Mu. 11: Margaret Mann scholarship, UMich 66-67. 14: Tech proc, lib admin. 15: 9612 Taylor ave, Oxon Hill Md 20022.

ZIMMERMAN, GRADY (MORTON). b Little Rock Ark 27N37. 4: Patricia Ann Dutzi. 5: UCLA 55-60 (Philos) BA, 60-62 MLS. 6: Ger, Sp, Lat. 7: Tech writer Chas Martin Electronics, Beverly Hills Cal 56-57; Free lance writer 58; Bibliogr searcher Pacific Aeronautical Lib, Los Angeles 60-62; Clerk, stud asst circ dept UCLA Lib 58-60, Sr lib asst catlg dept 60-62; Ref libn Fresno State Col Lib 62-63; Dist libn Coalinga Dist Lib, Coalinga Cal 63-. 8: UCLA Grad Lib Coun, 61-2. 9: CalLA (Yosemite Dist: sec-treas 63-64; pres Pub Rel 64-65); Intel Freedom Com 66-68). 10: Coalinga Dist Lib Puppet Club; E Vitus Clampus (San Francisco); Chess Club; UCLA Bruin Alumni Fencing Club; Salle DNorde; NRA; PTA. 13: Yes. 14: Admin, lib systems devel & design, child serv, ref. 15: 324 Walnut ave, Coalinga Cal 93210.

ZIMMERMAN, IRENE. b Idana Kan 23 F 07. 5: Col of Emporia 24-27 (Eng, Span) BA; UMex summer 30; UHawaii summer 32; Chicago summers 34-37 (Span) MA; Columbia 37-38, summers 38-39 (Tchg of Hist) MA; Cornell U summer 42 (Latin Amer); iddlebury Col summer 44; UHavana summer 46; UMich summers 4849, 50-51 AMLS, summer 51 & 56 (LS) PhD. 6: Sp, Fr, Portu. 7: Tchr of Span & hist & Libn Ray High Sch, Ray Ariz 27-37; Span tchr Columbia High Sch, S Orange NJ 38-39; Hist tchr Lewis & Clark High Sch, Spokane Wash 39-41; Instr Span, Hist of Americas Colby Jr Col 43-48; Asst Prof of Span Bucknell U 48-50; Asst libn Latin Amer spec Dept Ref & Bibliog UFla 51-62, Assoc libn, LatinAmer spec 62-67; Libn Lat Amer Collection 67-. 8: Exch with asst dir ref dept UPR, Spring 62; Consul Micro-Photo Inc (Latin Amer Periods) 63; Lectr Lat Amer bibliog UMich summer 66. 9: ALA (Life mem); - ACRL (Bd 61-63; chm Subject Spec Sect 61-62, Sem on the Acquis of Lat Amer Lib Materials 56-, chm Com on Bibliog 62-); Amer Assn of Tchrs of Span & Portu (Life mem); FlaLA; SELA; SE Conf on Latin Amer Studies. 10: AAUP; AAUW; US Assn for the UN; Beta Phi Mu; Phi Alpha Theta; Gainesville Coun on Human Rel; Sigma Delta Pi. 12: "Guide to Current Latin American Periodicals: Humanities and Social Sciences (61). 13: Yes. 14: Ref, bibliog, Caribbean materials, Latin Amer studies, Latin Amer libs. 15: P O Box 13655, Gainesville Fl 32603.

ZIMMERMAN, JOHN JACOB. b Penn 4 N 18. 4: Mary Vooz. 5: Muhlenberg Col 37-41 (Eng) PhB; Lehigh U 46 (Educ); UFla 48-49 (Eng) MA; Emory 49-50 (LS) MA. 7: Clerk Bethlehem Steel Corp, Bethlehem Penn 42-43; Tchr Apollo High Sch, Apollo Penn 43-45; Instr Admiral Farragut Acad, St Petersburg Fla 45-48; Acquis UGa Lib 50-57; Dir Frostburg State Col Lib 57-. 8: Citizens Conf on Libs, 65; Lib Study Com, Md Coun Higher Educ 64-; Md Adv Coun on Interlib Coop 67-; Pres Bd of Dirs, Middle Atlantic Reg Lib Fed 69-. 9: ALA; MdLA (Memb Chm 59-60, pres-elect 65-66); (pres 66-67, Nomin Chm 67-68). 10: AAUP; Alpha Psi Omega; Tau Kappa Epsilon. 12: "In the Poet's Hand" (65); Ed Bd "Maryland Libraries" (63-65). 13: Yes. 14: Admin. 15: 169 Ormand st, Frostburg Md 21532.

ZIMMERMANN, DORIS F. b North Hempstead NY 6 Jl 14. 5: Mt Holyoke 36 (Hist) AB; Columbia 38 (Educ) MA; UPenn 46 (Finance). 6: Fr, Sp, Ger. 7: Tchr NY Inst Ed Blind, Bronx NY 36-37; File clerk Cravath Swaine & Moore, NYC 38-43; Research libn Fed Res Bank, Phila 43-58, Libn 58-. 9: SLA. 10: Eng-Speaking Union; Phi Beta Kapa. 12: "Federal Reserve Bank Monthly Reviews: Selected Subjects 50-68. 14: Ref. 15: Fed Res Bank, Phila Pa 19101.

ZIMPFER, WILLIAM EDWARD. b Columbus Ohio 3 Je 26. 5: Capital U 43-46 (Hist) AB; Evangelical Lutheran Sem 46, 47, 48-50 (Theol) BD; UMich 47-48 (Classical Lang) MA; Columbia 63 MSLS. 6: Ger, Fr, Lat, Gk, Heb. 7: Instr Capital U 47, 49; Pastor First St John Lutheran Church, Pittsburgh 50-60; Assoc Pastor Zion Lutheran Church, Pittsburgh 60-62; Catlg asst Columbia U 62-64; Libn Boston U Sch of Theol 64-. 9: ATheolLA. 13: Yes. 14: Admin, ref. 15: 745 Commonwealth ave, Boston Ma 02215.

ZINCEAU, JOSEPHINE CLAIRE. b Chipman Alta Can 8 Ag 11. 5: St Marys Hosp (Madison Wis) 27-30 (Nursing) RN; UMinn 36 (Pub Health Serv) Certif for Wis; ULouisville (Ky) 49-53 (Eng) AB; Fla State U 53-54 & 56-57 (LS) MA. 6: Russian, Fr, Polish. 77: Gen nursing Local registry, Madison Wis 30-34; Pub health nursing wis State Bd of Health 34-43; Army Nursing 117th Evac Hos, US & ETO 43-46; Pub health nursing Wis State Bd of Health 46-49; Staff libn Atlanta Pub Lib 57: Libn Spec Serv, Ft Benning Ga 57-67; Ext supv libn 68-. 9: Amer Dialect Soc. 10: Amer Legion; Nat Travel Club. 14: Ref, bk sel, art. 15: 4325 Old Cusseta rd, Columbus Ga 31903.

ZINGALES, PHILIP. b NYC 16 Mr 33. 5: City Col (NY) 51-55 (Eng) BA; Pratt 58-60 MLS. 6: Ital, Fr. 7: Clerk typist (Sp4) US Army, Loring AFB Me 56-58; Head catlg dept Adelphi U 60-. 9: ALA. 14: Catlg. 15: 251 Winthrop st, Brooklyn NY 11225.

ZINGLER, GILBERTA M (HEID). b Ind 24 F 11. 4: ERVIN Kenneth Zingler. 5: Butler U 28-32 (Eng, Lang) AB; UIll 34-35 BS in LS. 6: Sp, Fr, Ger. 7: Asst loan libn Butler U 3234; Asst libn George Washington High Sch, Indianapolis 35-36; Asst loan libn UIll(Urban) 36-39; Asst ref libn La State Lib Commsn, Baton Rouge La 39-43; Order libn So Methodist U 43-53; Rice U Lib: Catlg libn 53-54, Order libn 54-57, ead acquis dept 58-. 9: ALA; LaLA; TexLA; SWLA. 10: Phi Mu. 14: Acquis, ref. 15: 5701 Jackson No 609, Houston Tx 77004.

ZINK, IRVE WM. b Cudahy Wis 12 S08. 4: Anne Heinen. 5: Milwaukee State Tchrs Col 31-35 (Hist, Soc Sci, Eng) BE; UWis 35-36 (LS) Certif; Marquette U 39-41 (Hist, Pol Sci) MA. 6: Ger. 7: Asst hist & soc sci Pub Lib, Milwaukee 36-42, Chief hist & soc sci 42-. 10: Milwaukee Co Hist Soc; Milwaukee Com for the Observance of UN Day; Mitchell Park Fourth of July Assn. 13: Yes. 14: Ref. 15: 7300 W Honey Creek dr, Milwaukee Wi 53219.

ZINN, NANCY W. b Chicago Ill 28 Je 35. 4: William M Zinn. 5; udel 53-57 (Hist) BA; Bryn Mawr 5759 (Hist) MA; Drexel 61-62 MSLS; Emory 62-63 (Med Libnship) Certif. 6: Sp, Ger, Fr. 7: Jr ref libn Free Pub Lib, New Haven Conn 59-60; Lib trainee Free Pub Lib, Phila 60-61; Head ref circ Col of Physicians (Phila) 63-65; Admin head hist collection Med Center Lib UCal (San Francisco) 66-. 9: MedLA (Memb Com, Internship Com); Amer Assn Hist Med. 10: Phi Kappa Phi;

Beta Phi Mu. 13: Yes. 14: Rare bks, ref. 15: Univ of Cal Med Lib Center, Parnassus ave, San Francisco Ca 94117.

ZIPLANS, EMILIJA EMILIE (KARKLINS). b Latvia 17 Je 17. 4: Erwin M Ziplans. 5: Inst of Eng Lang (Riga) 37-40; ULatvia(Riga) 41-44 (Baltic Philol); Toronto 56-60 (Psych) BA, 60-61 BLS. 6: Latvian, Ger. 7: Accountant Nickam Instrum & Supply Ltd, Toronto 56-59; UToronto: Lib asst 59-60, Libn 61-64, Libn in chg New Col 64-67; Undergrad bk sel 67-. 9: CanLA; ALA; (Ont Rep Memb Com); OntLA; Inst ROF Libns Ont. 10: Latvian Sororities Assn, Toronto; Stratford Shakespearean Festival Found Can; Art Gallery Toronto. 14: Circ, ref, bk sel. 15: Univ of Toronto, Toronto 5 Can.

ZIPSER, MARJORIE (CONVERY). b Oak Bluffs Mass 14 N 42. 4: Richard Alfred Zipser. 5: Colby 60-64 (Amer Lit) BA; UMd 66-67 MLS. 6: Fr, Ger. 7: Asst libn & catlgr UMd Law Sch Lib (Baltimore) 67-. 9: ALA; AALL. 14: Catlg, clsf. 15: 65 Bay rd, Barrington RI 02806.

ZIPSIE, ALVIN L. b Winslow Ill 28 Jl29. 4: Josephine Harvey. 5: Blackburn Col 48-52 (Hist) BA; UWis summers 58-62 (LS) MS. 7: Med libn US Army Hosp, Ft Belvoir Va 56-57; Prof trainee Pub Lib, Cedar Rapids Iowa 57-60; Libn Pub Lib, Reedsburg Wis 60-62; Dir Pub Lib, Portage Wis 62-64; Sauk Co Libn-Consul Sauk Co, Baraboo Wis 64-. 9: ALA; WisLA(Lib Legis & Devel Com). 10: Kiwanis Club; Jr C of C; Wis Sheriffs Assn; Boy Scouts; Sauk Co Art Assn; Sauk Co Pistol League; UWis Alum Club; Baraboo-Sauk Co Univ Ctr. 14: Admin. 15: 227 Martin, Baraboo Wi 53913.

ZIRKLE, AILENE (ANNE). b Wash DC 9 S35. 5: Madison Col (Va) 53-57 (LS) BA in Ed; Peabody summers 60-63 MA in LS. 6: Sp. 7: Libn Madison Heights High Sch, Madison Heights Va 57-61; Tchr libn Dahlgren Sch US Naval Weapons Lab, Dahlgren Va 61-63; Asst catlg libn Col of William & Mary 63-64, Acquis libn 64-. 14: Acquis. 15: 1411 B Spring rd apts, Williamsburg Va 23185.

ZIRKLE, SARA O. b Asheville NC 21 Ag 11. 4: George A Zirkle. 5: Duke U 28-32 (Psych) AB, 32-33 (Psych) MA; Ind U 61-62 (LS) MA. 6: Fr. 7: Hanover Col: Instr in psych 40-53, Lib asst 53-61, Asst libn 62-. 10: Phi Beta Kappa. 14: Periods, docs, ref, tech serv. 15: Box 92, Hanover In 47243.

ZISKIND, SYLIA (GOLDBERG). b Phila 12 Ja 06. 4: David Ziskind. 5: Cumnock Sch of Expression 25-27 (Speech Arts); UCal 29-30 (Pub SpeakingT) BA; USoCal 30-31, 37 (Speech) MA; Immaculate Heart Col 53, 62 MA in LS. 7: Tchr Cumnock Sch, Los Angeles 33-35; Tchr, Wash DC 36-40; High sch libn Bellflower Sch Dist, Cal 49-62; Asst Prof Immaculate Heart Col 62-67; Assoc Prof 67-. 9: CaASchL (pres So Sect 60-61); CalLA Pres So Dist)67); So Cal Coun on Lit (v-pres 67); ALA. 10: Zeta Phi Eta; AAUP. 13: Yes. 14: Child lit, drama & poetry,ref. 15: 2339 Silver Ridge ave, Los Angeles Ca 90039.

ZITKOVICH, ANNE THERESE. b Hinsdale Ill 20 Je26. 5: Col of St Francis 45-48 (Sociol); Loyola U 48-51 (Sociol) BS: Rosary Col 63-65 MALS. 6: Sp. 7: Casewker Catholic Charities of Chicago 51; Casewker Cook Co Dept of Pub Welfare, Chicago 52; Libn USAF, Park Ridge Ill 53-56; Libn Nat Safety Coun, Chicago 57-63; Research libn Assn of Sch Bus Officials, Chicago 65-69; Med libn Swed Covenant Hosp, Chicago 69-. 9: SLA (chm Educ Com Ill Chap 67-68, chm Memb Com Ill Chap 66-67); MedLA. 10: Phi Beta Mu. 14: Admin, indexing. 15: 807 Asbury, Evanston Il 60202.

ZITTRAUER, GLORIA ESTHER. b Charleston SC 5 O 44. 5: Winthrop Col 62-66 (LS) BS. 7: Sch libn US Govt Robins AFB, Warner Robins Ga 66-68; Libn grade I Haydon Burns Lib, Jacksonville Fla 68-. 9: StudNEA; ALA. 14: Art, music. 15: 5606C Auburn rd, Jacksonville Fl 32207.

ZOLLER, CHARLES EDWARD. b Danvers Ill 7 N17. 4: Mary Bremer. 5: Ill State U 38-41 (Educ Psych, LS) B Ed; Washington U 48-54 (Bus Admin) MA, 56 Libnship Certif. 7: US Army Adjutant Gen Dept (S/Sgt) 45-46; Ref asst Withers Pub Lib, Bloomington Ill 40-41; McDonnell Aircraft Engnr Lib, St Louis: Catlgr 47-49, Asst supv 50-55, Supv 55-67; Lib supv McDonnell Douglas Corp, St Louis 67-. 9: SLA; ALA. 14: Ref, org, admin. 15: 309 Louisa, Ferguson Mo 63135.

ZONLIGT, MARTIN JULIUS. b Ixelles Belgium 14 N 34. 4: Margaret Cooper. 5: UUtah 51-53 (Liberal Arts); UCal(Berkeley) 53-58 (Sociol) AB, Gen sec tchg cred; USan Francisco 60-62 (LS) Sch lib cred; UCal(Berkeley) 63-64 MLS. 6: Dutch, Fr, Sp. 7: Tchr Mt Diablo Sch Dist, Concord Cal 58-60; Tchr Burbank Sch Dist, Burbank Cal 61-62; Libn I Alameda Co Pub Lib, Hayward Cal 62-63; Libn I Santa Rosa-Sonoma Co Pub Lib Santa Rosa Cal 64-68; Libn Nassau Lib System, Garden City NY 68; Libn adult serv & ref Bethpage Pub Lib, Bethpage NY 68-. 8: Orgr mini-mobile project for Nassau Lib Syst summer 68. 9: ALA; YASD (Com on Lib Serv to Disadvantaged Youth, Subcom on Rural Youth); -RSD; -RTSD (Com on Pub Docs); CalLA. 10: Books Unlimited Cooperative; Sierra Club; Boy Scout Leader. 12: Co-auth "Rural Library Services to Disadvantaged Youth (69). 14: Ref, docs, community action. 15: 32-34 - 77th st, Jackson Heights NY 11372.

ZORNMAN, DOROTHY (JOAN). b Houston 28 Je 39. 5: Portland State Col 57-62 (Hist) BS; UWash 64-65 (LS) ML. 6: Fr. 7: Shaker Oregon Laundry Cleaners, Portland Ore 58-62; Feeder Portland Laundry Dry Cleaners, Portland Ore 62-64; Libn I asst child libn Pierce Co Pub Lib, Tacoma Wash 65-68; Jr libn in lit & hist dept LA of Portland, Portland Ore 68-. 9: ALA. 15: 422 S Tacoma ave apt 307, Tacoma Wa 98402.

ZOUCK, BETTY GRAY (LONG). b Roanoke Rapids NC 15 S 12. 5: St Marys Sch 29-31; UNC 31-33 (Eng) AB, 33-34 ABLS. 6: Fr, Lat, Sp, Ger. 7: Libn Gastonia High Sch, Gastonia NC 34-35; Lib asst circ: Charlotte Pub Lib, Charlotte NC 35-38, DC Pub Lib 39-41, Enoch Pratt Free Lib, Baltimore 41; Lib asst order UNC Lib (Chapel Hill) 49-57, Libn bot & zool 57-63; Bot libn 63-. 10: Pi Beta Phi; N Car Art Soc; N Car Soc Preservation Antiquities. 14: Bot ref, acquis. 15: D1 Graham ct, Chapel Hill NC 27514.

ZSCHOCK, SUSANNE A (JUNKERS). b Krefeld Germany 1 Jl 10. 4: Bernhard W Zschock. 6: Ger. 7: Aid Cleveland Pub Lib, Cleveland Ohio 56-61; Clk Schroeders Bkstore, Cleveland Ohio 61-62; Lib asst Hall Memorial Lib, Ellington Conn 62-66; Libn Stafford Lib Assn, Stafford Springs Conn 66-. 9: ALA; ConnLA (chm Small Lib Sect 68-70). 14: Wk with ya, gen pub readers serv. 15: Boyer rd RFD 2, Rockville Ct 06066.

ZSUFFA, MARY MARGARET. b Copaigue LI NY 25 My43. 5: State U Col (Geneseo NY) 61-65 (LS) BS in Ed; Penn State U summer 68. 7: Elem sch libn Pub Sch, Island Trees Levittown NY 65-66; Elem sch libn Patchogue-Medford Pub Sch, NY 66-69. 9: NEA; ALA; NYLA; NYStateTA. 10: Kappa Delta Pi. 14: Sch libnship. 15: 4 Sutton pl, Massapequa NY 11758.

ZUBATSKY, DAVID SAMUEL. b Milwaukee Wis 17 S 39. 5: UWis 57-62 (Sp) BA, 62-66 (Hist) MA; UIll 66-67 MSLS. 6: Portu, Sp. 7: Grad asst UWis 62-64; Jr libn Milwaukee Pub Lib 64-66; Grad asst UIll Grad Sch of Lib Sci 66-67; Bibliogr for LA & Iberian Peninsula WashU Lib 67-. 9: ALA; Latin Amer Studies Assn; Sem Acquis of Latin Amer Lib Materials; Midwest Assn Latin Amer Studies. 10: Amer Assn Tchrs Span & Portug. 13: Yes. 14: Bibliog, ref, acquis. 15: Washington Univ Libs, St Louis Mo 63130.

ZUCKER, PHYLLIS. b Jamaica NY 11 F 44. 5: Queens Col 62-66 (Eng Educ) BA; UMich 66-67 AMLS; UCLA summer 68 (Cinema, Ital); NYU 68- (Cinema) MA. 6: Fr. 7: Mineola mem Lib, Mineola NY 59-64; Queens Col Lib 62-63; Temple Judea of Manhasset Synagogue Lib, Manhasset NY 64-66; UMich Bus Lib 66-67; Brooklyn Pub Lib, Brooklyn NY 67-68; Elmont Pub Lib, Elmont NY 68-. 9: ALA. 11: B'nai B'rith Human Rel Award. 13: Yes. 14: Ref, theatre arts, ya serv. 15: 367 Andrews rd, Mineola NY 11501.

ZUCKERBERG, NATHAN b Austria 28 Jl 1900. 4: Josephine Schachter. 5: Upsala Col 23-27 BA; Hebrew Union Col 35-37 (Hebrew) Tchrs Certif; Pratt 45-46 BLS; Columbia 47-49 (Educ) MA. 6: Yiddish, Hebrew, Ger. 7: Tchr NYC Bd of Educ 28-42; (Pfc) US Army Engnr Corps 42-44; Tchr NYC Bd of Educ 45-57; Asst Libn NYS Dept of Labor Div of Employment 46-62; Libn Yeshiva U High Sch 62-63; Tchr of lib & Libn St Stephen High Sch, Brooklyn NY 64-. 9: ALA-AASchL; SLA; NY Lib Club; CathLA (Brooklyn-LI Unit). 10: Bnai Zion. 13: Yes. 14: Catlg. 15: 549 W 123 st, New York NY 10027.

ZUCKERMAN, ARLINE (ROSENBERG) . b NYC 11 Je40. 4: Gordon Shea Zuckerman. 5: Cal State Col (Long Beach) 58-61 (Eng) AB; UCLA 61-62 MLS. 7: Libn UCLA 62-. 9: ALA; CalLA. 14: Catlg. 15: 4027 McLaughlin ave apt 4, Los Angeles Ca 90066.

ZUCKERMAN, MARIE-LOUISE (MILLER). b Mobile Ala 6 Jl 43. 4: Ira S Zuckerman. 5: Coe Col 61-65 (Eng) BA; Rutgers 65-66 MLS. 6: Fr, Ger. 7: Ref libn Bergenfield Pub Lib, Bergenfield NJ 66-67, Hd Child Dept 67-68; Asst to dir Urbana Col 68-. 9: ALA; NJLA (Pub Rel & Press Com);

Mid-Bergen Fed of Libs. 14: Ref, pub rel. 15: 75 Westside ave, Bergenfield NJ 07621.

ZUGBY, LILLIAN (COURY). b Lowell Mass 11S11. 4: Emile Zugby. 5: Woods Bus Col (Lowell Mass) (Secretarial) Certif; State Tchrs Col (Lowell Mass) 33 (Educ) BS in Ed; Catholic U 56-64 MS in LS; UMd 66-67 (Amer Studies). 6: Arabic, Fr, Lat. 7: Clerk-typst Assessors Off, Lowell Mass 34-35; Clerk-typist State House, Boston 35; Sr clerk Dept of Agric AAA, Wash DC 35-41, Jr rof asst 41-44; Elem tchr Prince Georges Co, Md 54-58; Catlg asst Map Div LC 58; Ref libn Montgomery Jr Col 59-68; Libn (voluntary) Prince Georges Co Elem Sch, Md 56-58; Asst Prof & head ref Montgomery Jr Col 68-. 8: Guest lectr, Eng, Montgomery Jr Col 67-. 9: NEA; ALA; Md State Tchrs Assn; MdLA; NFA; MontgomeryCoEA (del 66-). 10: Philosophy Club; AAUP. 12: "Bibliography of Juvenile Literature in the Library of Congress (64). 13: Yes. 14: Ref, research, col libnship. 15: 6914 New Hampshire ave, Takoma Park Md 20012.

ZUIDEMA, PATRICIA (MARCUS). b Rochester NY 21 N 42. 4: Robert John Zuidema. 5: SUNY (Geneseo) 60-64 (Lib) BS. 7: Libn Eastman Kodak Co, Rochester NY 64-67; Libn Spencerport Central Sch, Spencerport NY 67-. 14: Ref, childs collections. 15: 2589 Spencerport rd, Spencerport NY 14559.

ZULICK, MARGUERITE A. b Philadelphia Penn 20 O 11. 5: UPenn 30-32 (Educ) BS in Ed; CatholicU 40-41; Drexel 65-67 MS in LS. 7: Lib helper UPenn summer 32; Soc wker Co bd Assistance, Phila 33-38; Proofreader Haddon Craftsmen, Camden NJ 38-40; Libn Volta Bur Lib, Wash DC 40-43; Gen off wker Air Assocs Inc, Dallas Tex 44; Proofreader Allen, Lane & Scott, Phila 44-45; Libn Farm Journal Inc, Phila 45-. 9: SLA; Spec Libs Coun of Phila & Vicinity. 10: Phi Kappa Phi. 15: 609 S Bambrey st, Philadelphia Pa 19146.

ZUMSTEIN, MARJORIE ANNE. b Wakefield Mich 30 S 25. 5: Purdue 42-46 (Hist, Eng) BS; UChicago 46-47 BLS. 7: Asst ref libn UChicago Lib 47-49; Hd educ psych lib UIowa Libs 49-61; Educ libn PurdueU Libs (Lafayette) 62-66, Hd educ & psych libs 66-. 9: ALA. 14: Ref, supv of dept libs. 15: 912 Teal rd, Lafayette In 47905.

ZUWIYYA YAMAK, LABIB. b Lebanon 12 Ja26. 4: Lois Harder. 5: American U (Beirut Lebanon) 43-47 (Philos) BA, 47-49 (Pol Sci) MA; Columbia 53-54 (LS) MS; UMich 59-64 (Pol Sci) PhD. 6: Arabic, Fr. 7: Instr in pol sci American U (Beirut Lebanon) 49-50 ; Instr in hist Maqasid Col (Sidon Lebanon) 50-52; American U (Beirut Lebanon): Lecturer in pol sci 54-56, Arabic catlgr 54-56, of tech oftech processes 56-58; Middle East spec Harvard Col Lib 59-62, Asst libn for the Middle East Collections 62-; Lectr on Middle East bibliog 66-. 8: Adv, Maqasid Col Lib, Sidon Lebanon, 51; Chm, Farmington Pan Subcom on the Middle East, 65-; Consul UPenn Lib on Mid-East Resources (67). 10: Amer Pol Sci Assn. 11: Ford Found Fellow, 61-62. 12: Ed "Harvard College Library Catalogue of Persian Book, prel ed (64); "The Syrian Social Nationalist Party; An Idological Analysis (66). 13: Yes. 14: Middle East bibliog (Arabic & Islamica). 15: Middle East Div Harvard Col Lib, Cambridge Mass 02138.

ZUWIYYA, JALAL Z. b Sidon Lebanon 12 O 32. 4: Nancy Bennett. 5: Amer UBeirut 50-54 (Bus) BBA; SUNY (Geneseo) 62-63 MLS. 6: Arabic, Fr. 7: Ref libn USIA, Beirut 55-62; Jr libn Queen's Borough Pub Lib, NY 63-64; Assoc libn SUNY (Binghamton) 64-. 9: ALA. 10: Middle East Assn of Amer; Amer Friends of Middle East; Amer Oriental Soc. 14: Middle East libnship. 15: 4632 Salem dr, Binghamton NY 13903.

ZVIGAITIS, SISTER MARIE DE BREBEUF IHM. b Philadelphia Penn 21 S 15. 5: Immaculata Col 34-38 (Eng) AB; TempleU 46 (LS); VillanovaU 50-51 (Educ); MarywoodU 59-65 MSLS. 6: Fr, Lithuanian, Lat. 7: Tchr Archdiocese of Phila 40-44; Tchr-libn Immaculate Heart High Sch, Fountain Springs 44-46; Tchr-libn St John the Baptist High Sch, Phila 46-48; Tchr-libn Immaculate Conception High Sch, Jim Thorpe Penn 48-49; Tchr-libn Archbishop Prendergast High Sch, Drexel Hill Penn 59-62; Libn Catholic High Sch, Lancaster Penn 65-. 8: Tchr, Lib Wkshops for elem sch volunteers in Phila & Lancaster cos 66-67; Mem Adv Lib Com, Harrisburg Diocese 66-; CathLA consul on sch libs 44-; Mem eval coms of second schs, Middle States Assn. 9: ALA; -AASchL; CathLA (mem &/or chm bk Fair Com 67-71; East Penn Unit: sec 59-60, chm Cath Bk Week 59); PennLA (Nat Lib Bk Week Com 68); Lancaster Co LA. 14: Org of elem & second sch libs, col libn (summers). 15: 565 W Walnut st, Lancaster Pa 17603.

ZWEIFEL, LeROY G. b Milwaukee 2 F 24. 4: Joan M Hinsenkamp. 5: Marquette U 45-48 Electrical engnr BEE; UWis 49-50 BLS. 7: Ref libn Milwaukee Pub Lib 49-50; (Capt) USAF electronics div Electronics Lib Air Command & Staff Sch, Montgomery Ala 50-52; Engnr Libn-Prof Col of Engnr UWis (Madison) 52-; Dir info serv div U Ind Research Program UWis 65-. 9: Amer Soc Engnr (Engnr Libs Com; SLA; ADI; ASIS; FID. 14: Ind-univ rel, info sci. 15: 121 N Prospect ave, Madison Wis 53705.

ZWEIZIG, DOUGLAS LOUGH. b York Penn 3 Ap38. 4: Lynne Clewell Zweizig. 5: Lafayette Col 56-60 (Eng) BA; Harvard 60-61 (Eng) MA; Rutgers 64-65 MLS. ; Syracuse 67-. 7: Instr in Eng UNH 61-64; Asst libn Middlesex Pub Lib, Middlesex NY 64-65; Libn Eng & speech grad reading room Ohio State U Libs 65-67; Lectr Sch of Lib Sci Syracuse 67-68; Asst Prof & Asst to dean 68-. 14: Ref, admin, lib educ. 15: 125 Clarendon st, Syracuse NY 13210.

Appendix

This list contains the names of persons for whom entries appeared in the fourth edition of *Who's Who,* but who did not return updated or new questionnaires for the fifth. In these instances users are referred to the earlier edition. The editors have attempted to delete the names of persons who have died.

Aaskov, Olga A(strid)
Abbott, Elizabeth M(arie)
Abbott, Lysla I.
Abbott, Mrs Susan B.
Abell, Millicent D(emmin)
Abernethy, (Charlotte) Isabel
Ablard, Eleanore (Stuve)
Abramov, Peter III
Abramowicz, Dina
Abramson, Mrs Betty (Friedson)
Abramson, Mark Leo
Accola, Ferol (Ann)
Acker, Elizabeth (Schmidt)
Adams, Audrey J.
Adams, Ida (Girvin)
Adams, Marion (Sheffield)
Adams, Ruth (Lauren)
Adamson, Katherine Virginia (Anthony)
Addison, Florence (Phillips)
Adelman, George
Adrian, Sister Mary (Kettler)
Adsit, Hope I(sabel)
Aeschbach, William Driver
Agnew, Eloise
Aiken, Mary (Johnson)
Aiken, Richard Sumner
Ainsworth, Katherine (Lake)
Aitken, Mrs Barbara (Boyd)
Akers, Sara Kathryn
Akery, Peggy (Collins)
Alaire, Maurice
Alberico, Mrs Patricia (McCormick)
Albert, Donald D
Alberta, Sister M OP.
Albertini, Delores Ann (Drenon)
Albrecht, Edgar (George John)
Albright, Thomas Edward
Alden, Paul D(unham)
Alexander, Dorothy Jane
Alexander, Frances L.
Alexander, Helen (Stovall)
Alexander, Jeanette Y.
Alexander, Merle Imogene (Smith)
Alexander, Odessa K.
Alexander, Virginia (Alice)
Alfred, Brother D (Gruenwald)
Algermissen, Virginia (Rae) (Lantz) (Lutterbie)
Allan, Ann (Gould)
Allbritton, Sylvia Dawn
Allen, Beverly E.
Allen, Daphne Theresia
Allen, Donna-Mai (Dillard)
Allen, Dorothy K.
Allen, Fern (Litchard)
Allen, Jessie S.
Allen, Rosemary Von Storch
Alley, Cornelia Margaret (Egan)
Allison, Laurie (Mac Callum)
Al-Musawi, Mustafa M.
Alper, Celia (Palant)
Alston, Ethel Clarice (Jones)
Altman, Barbara
Altmann, Berthold
Amandes, Joanne (Vivien Beran)
Amaral, Loretta Anne (Richey)
Ambriano, John Dolph
Ambrose, Ethel N.
Amen, Dora (Beck)
Ammons, Shirley Marie
Amrhein, John K.
Anama, Mrs Shirley (Ho)
Anders, Ora Elizabeth
Anderson, Bernice E.
Anderson, Biverous (Pretty)
Anderson, Mrs Carolee (Q)
Anderson, Clara (Ritchey)
Anderson, Dorothy (Bandy)
Anderson, Dorothy Lee (Ingebretsen)
Anderson, Ella (Ingeborg)
Anderson, Ella B
Anderson, Ella Trew (Simpers)
Anderson, Hazelle M.
Anderson, Jerome W.
Anderson, Margaret K(elly)
Anderson, Nancy Jean
Anderson, Nancy Steele
Anderson, Nedra Bushong
Anderson, Polly G.
Anderson, Roger Charles
Anderson, Sandra C.
Andree, (Paul) Howard
Andrekovich, Donald J.
Andrews, Anne Elizabeth
Andrews, Helen Louise
Andrews, Kenton B.
Andrews, Mary M(cChesney)
Andrews, Phyllis (Cole)
Angela, Sister Mary (Santor) SSJ, TOSF
Angele, Sister Mary (Beausoleil)
Angelotti, Marie Evelyn
Ankrum, Wilma Elizabeth (Mooney)
Annette, Sister Mary (Kutaj) SSJ
Anthes, Harriet (Dunham)
Anthony, Louise
Apetz, Frances (Clapp)
Appelman, Carolyn Diana

Arnold, Joyce Marie
Arnold, Sister Miriam Claire
Arnold, Richard C O.
Arnold, Winnie Ann
Aronoff, Leah (Steinberg)
Aronsson, Dolores (Oppenheim)
Arthur, Sister Mary (Hoagland) IHM.
Artman, Agnesjean (Neeley)
Aseo, Astrid Karla Erika (Diemert)
Ashley, Edwin M.
Ashley, Katherine Elizabeth
Ashton, Jon Richard
Asseln, Barbara B (Watkins)
Aston, Mrs Marcia (Harmon)
Atallah, Shakeeb
Atchison, Margaret K(atherine)
Aten, Mrs Jean (Chiseyo Kawatachi)
Atkinson, Elizabeth Lee
Atkinson, Gloria Lewis
Aubry, Claude B.
Auchenbach, Ruth M.
Audet, Claire (Michele)
Auringer, Alberta Gjertine
Ausherman, Marian R.
Austin, Marian
Auxier, Margaret
Avery, Theodore M Jr.
Avizonis, Mrs Angele (Asevicius)
Ayer, Charles Joseph

Babbit, Thea (Elizabeth Branstead)
Babcock, Gladys (Vatnsdal)
Babcock, Judith Ann
Babcock, Lucy Ann
Babusis, Grazina Ada (Lauzikas)
Bachmann, Eleanor (Atherton)
Backus, Kathleen L.
Bacon, Grace W(illiams)
Bacon, James Howard
Bader, Barbara (Brenner)
Badger, Elizabeth
Baehr, Margaret (Zeigler)
Baer, Eberhard Alex
Baer, Nadine Lucille
Bagnato, Jean (Grimm)
Bahr, Jacquelin Marie (Woehrle)
Bailey, C Hamilton
Bailey, Catherine Ann
Bailey, Florence (Hooten)
Bailey, Julie
Bailey, Mary Ellen (Whitefield)
Baird, Karen (Harriman)
Baker, Anna (Henckel)
Baker, Elmer Earl
Baker, James Gerard
Baker, Joy (Seabourn)
Baker, (Jerry) Wayne
Bakewell, Dennis charles
Ball, Gerald Lawrence (Peter)
Ball, John Leslie
Ball, Laurel Lea
Ball, Mary Ellen
Ballentine, Mollie Douglas
Ballou, Elmа Marie (St John)

Balsam, Norma A.
Bander, Edward J.
Bandes, Joan (Korach)
Barbash, Walter Vladimir
Barbour, Sabra Walker
Barbuto, Carmela M.
Bard, Catherine R (Roberts)
Bard, Catherine R (Roberts)
Barden, Joan Marie
Bardeen, Janice Elaine
Barker, Fletcher Jr.
Barker, June Elaine
Barlow, Harriet K.
Barnes, Betty Dolores (Bennett)
Barker, June Elaine
Barker, Ray Stannard Jr.
Barnes, Ellis D.
Barnes, Jeannette L.
Barnes, Muriel de Beixedon
Barnett, Ellen (Wescott)
Barone, Mrs Helen L (Good)
Barnhart, Janet Hooven
Barr, Margaret (Georgia) Jackson
Barra, Marguerite Katherine
Barringer, Edity (Preston)
Barrow, Hallie Logan (Trout)
Barra, Marguerite Katherine
Barron Kathleen M(cCroan)
Barron, Robert Edward
Barsky, Cecile
Barth, Octavia Stephanie (Ritz)
Bartholow, Gladys S(tine)
Bartle, Elizabeth F.
Bartlett, Merle C.
Bartow, James C.
Basinski, Cornelia (Johnson)
Bass, Corinne
Bassett, Miss Terry (Louise)
Batch, Opal (Marie Cripe)
Batra, Baldev Raj.
Battistini, Midori (Yamanouchi)
Bauer, Ann Elizabeth (Small)
Baughman, Dorothy
Batch, Opal (Marie Cripe)
Bates, Bruce
Baumbach, Jane
Baumert, Sister M Ursula Ann, OSF.
Bayne, Rev Thomas Barry
Bays, Billy E
Beach, Eleanor Margaret
Beagan, Catherine Elizabeth (McSoley)
Bean, Gladys (Hyde)
Beard, Frances Reding
Beatrice, Sister Maria (Colla) RSM.
Beattie, Margaret Ellen
Bebee, Charles Nelson
Bechanan, H Gordon
Bechard, Rev Bernard J SSE.
Bechkowiak, Mary Anne
Beck, Frances L.
Bec, George Floyd
Beck, Louise (Fager)
Beck, Rose M.
Becker, Barbara Ruth (Pepper)

Becker, Orabel (Mohn)
Bedwell, Mary Elizabeth
Beebe, Lois W.
Beelick, Susan Amelia (Williams)
Begg, Barbara A(nne)
Behnke, Bebe Ann
Beihold, Enid (Imogene)
Belch, Caroline Jean (Ahrens)
Belcher Yvonne (Baker)
Bell, Anne (Wright)
Bell, Barbara Joanne
Bell, Edythe A(dcock)
Bell, George William
Bell, Mrs Laura (Russell)
Bell, Linda Ruth
Bell, Sarah
Benbow, Evelyn (Patricia) Jones
Bendigeri, Krishna H.
Benham, Sarah (Virginia Canan)
Benjamin, Hazel C.
Benner, Carol Lee
Bennett, Mrs L Tifton (Betsy Harrell)
Bennett, (William) Regis
Bennett, Victoria Muriel
Benson, Marjorie (Cleese)
Benton, Mary Jane
Benton, Mildred Catherine
Benwitz, Constance B(uckman)
Benz, Anthony
Benz, Marcia (Sue)
Beretta, Kathleen (Catherina Maria)
Berg, Marilyn Georgina
Bergen, Marilyn (Kratt)
Berger, Abraham
Berger, Abraham
Bergeuin, Gilles Morin
Bergman, Ruth (Elizabeth)
Bergstrom, Doris Marion
Berk, Robert (Ashby)
Berkihiser, Frances Friend
Berman, Mrs Reva (Katz)
Bernadette, Sister Marie (McCarthy)
Berndt, Mrs H C (Helen Hale)
Berner, Rita Consuela
Bernhardi, Robert C.
Bernstein, Norbert
Bernstein, Rosa M.
Berry, Ada DeVohn (Ainsworth)
Berry, (Mary) Elizabeth (Wright)
Bersie, Helen L.
Bertrand, Heléne
Bestul, Valborg E.
Betancourt, José A.
Betts, Robert E(dward)
Beville, Katherine Hay
Beyer, Mrs Ann (Hatch)
Beyer, Mrs Ann (Hatch)
Beyer, Ellen (Rose)
Biddle, Edith Carolyn (Ford)
Bidwell, Robert Gordon
Bigelow, Leonard
Bigelow, Marilyn (Kay, Seeger)
Bignell, Polley Ann
Billings, Eleanor M.

Billings, Robert Keeler
Biloskurska, Oresta
Bingham, Lloyd Combs
Binkowski, Mary J.
Bird, Mrs Thelma C(alfee)
Birkhimer, Robert Eugene
Birmingham, Sister Catherine David GNSH
Bisaccia, Guiseppe Elia
Bisbee, Prudence H.
Bishop, Lucie Mae (McMullan) (Mrs James Morgan Bishop)
Black, Rev (James) Bernard
Black, Carl Monroe
Black, Donald V.
Black, Rev Frederick Arthur
Black, Theresa Ann
Black, Thomas Shepherd
Blackmon, Myrtle Claire
Blackwell, Jaqueline Poff
Blair, Freda (Vodovosoff)
Blair, Mary A (Novotny)
Blake, Viola Caesara
Blake, Violet (Smith)
Blakeley, Mamie (Leonie Ready)
Blanchard, Alan Johnston
Blanchard, Bertha Brundage
Blánco De Sanchis Brígida
Blankenship, Iva Leader
Blasick, Henry John
Blatterman, Nancy (Irene Calfee)
Blazer, Linda Gayle (Hugg)
Blevins, Donald L.
Blizzard, Catherine
Bloch, Eileen M (Brophy)
Bloch, Eileen M (Brophy)
Bloch, Thomas
Bloomfield, Edith Stone
Bloxom, Ann (Martin) Dow
Blumberg, Ruth W C.
Blumenthal, Evan E.
Blustein, Anna Frances
Bobbie, Constance Helen
Boblett, Mary (Welsh)
Bobrow, Susan Gail
Bodge, Richard Albert
Boehm, Magda (Roder)
Boehm, (Lena) Maye Horton
Boersma, Kathrine Ann
Boettger, Judith Anne
Bogart, Christine E (Murphy)
Bogen, Mitchell Arthur
Bogle, Edra C.
Bohlen, Jeanne Louise
Bohn, Dorothy Carolyn,
Bohlen, Jeanne Louise (Alexander)
Boisen, Harold L(ouis)
Bolden, Ethel (Evangeline) Martin
Bole, Kathryn C.
Bolinger, Shirley (Goodwin)
Bolman, Helen P(atricia)
Bomberger, Harry Fred
Bond, Elizabeth M.
Bond, Guyla Ann
Bond, Mrs Margaret Jackson
Bonk, John
Bonnar, Mary
Bonner, Ida Munro
Bonthron, Bonnie B.
Boodis, Maxine (Snyder)
Booher, Thelma (Watson)
Booker, Zenos Francis
Boone, Jon Adrian
Boone, Shirley (Walker)
Borden, Barbara
Bormann, Senta Antonia
Borth, Hallie (Thompson)
Borys, Irene (Bakowska)
Boski, Marina (Maria)
Boss, Richard Woodruff
Boude, Katherine Shaw
Bower, Mrs Charlotte M (Tropman)
Bower, Linda (Strander)
Bowermaster, Mrs Izora W.
Bowler, Roberta
Bowman, Albert Hall
Bowman, Dorothy (Jane) (Davis)
Bowman, Mrs Harold J (Edna Goodwin)
Boyce, Dorothy A.
Boyce, Richard (Dempster)
Boyd, Mrs Julia (Greer)
Boyd, Mary Guy
Boyd, Mildred (Felten)
Boyd, Muriel (Isabel) Belton
Boyd, Sandra (Hughes)
Boyd, Virgie Lou (Smith)
Braasch, Gladys (Gamble)
Braden, Irene Andrea
Braden, Lillian (Foote)
Bradford, Beverly Ann
Bradford, Elizabeth Lebby
Bradford, Mrs Madalyn (McVey)
Bradley, Louise (Brooks)
Bradley, Mrs Ruth (Margaret) Beaton
Bradner, Amy Lee (Hatcher)
Bradshaw, Gloria Charliese (Johnson)
Bradshaw, Marcia
Bradshaw, Sherry Diane (Calvert)
Brady, Vera (Miller)
Brait, Marsha S.
Brake, Elizabeth Jean (McKee)
Bramlette, Selma G(eorgia) (Mitchell)
Brandolino, Richard R.
Brandt, Patricia Elizabeth
Brandwein, Lawrence
Brann, Harrison Allen
Brastins, Dagmar I (Dadzis)
Braun, Sister M Jane FSPA.
Brav, Elizabeth (Sturdevant)
Bravmann, Meir M.
Breitbart, Rhoda (Klein)
Bremer, Rev Nolan Richard
Brender, Elizabeth Una
Breninger, Julia (Rowland)
Brennan, Ellen
Breslaw, Elaine G(ellis)
Bretz, (Alma) Linda (Mazza)
Brewer, Frances Joan (Werner)
Brewer, Sarah Elizabeth
Brewster, Barbara M
Brichta, Mary-Ann (Georgia) (Andler)
Brick, Myrtle Anna
Bridgham, Miriam Louise
Bridgman, Alicemae
Bridwell, Eugene Edgar Jr.
Briggin, Samuel M.
Briggs, Donald (Robert)
Briggs, Michael J.
Bright, Lavinia (Shepardson)
Brin, Ernest Josephy
Brinkley, Charles (Edward)
Briston, Anne Gwen
Brkic, Beverly (Thomas)
Brock, James Patrick
Broderick, (J) Earl
Broderick, John Anthony
Bronston, Marion (Hitch)
Brooking, Ruth Patricia
Brooks, Mrs Claude M.
Brooks, Mrs Dorothea (Grizzard)
Brooks, Dorothy May (Estep)
Brooks, Jean Eileen (Dumler)
Brooks, Roger D.
Brooks, William A.
Brooksbank, Eleanor (Hodkinson)
Bross, Mary Louise
Brown, Barbara Anne
Brown, Caren Eber
Brown, Edna Earle
Brown, Emma Lee
Brown, Eula (Armitage)
Brown, Gwendolyn (Virgel)
Brown, Hope Buxton
Brown, Isabelle Lena
Brown, Jack E(rnest)
Brown, James V(incent)
Brown, Jane (Fisher)
Brown, Karl
Brown, Mary Louise
Brown, Mary Sue
Brown, Muriel (Stewart)
Brown, Oral William
Brown, Redahlia Riggins
Brown, Ruth Ann (Runkles)
Brown, (Anna) Sue
Brown, Timothy A(lbert)
Browne, Mrs Russell A (Margaret Woodall)
Browner, Louise M.
Brumberg, Elaine
Brunat, Alice Louise
Brunn, Alice (Lefler)
Brunswick, Sheldon Roy
Bruseau, Joan Eileen (Hassing)
Brush, Alvira Irene
Brush, Jeannette M.
Brush, Maryanne
Bruya, Mrs Ethel Lucille (MacInerney)
Bryant, Agnes (Rennie)
Bryant, Charles R(oss)
Bryant, Jean (Bacon)
Bryant, Mary Nell (Ingram)

Brynildsen, Palmer A.
Buchanan, Jean B.
Buchanan, Joanne Russell
Buchanan, Mrs Lillian (Barker)
Buchanan, Orpha (Roberts)
Buck, John W(alter)
Buckler, Leah (Herrup)
Bucy, Frances (Anne)
Buddle, Jean Renee (Aichele)
Buell, Elizabeth K(nowles)
Buell, Ruth C.
Bullard, Beulah L.
Buller, Nora Grace
Bulmer, Michael Thomas
Bunn, Sarah A.
Bunting, (Helen) Margaret
Burch, C(arolyn) Cecilia
Burch, James Rossiter
Burch, Vella Jane
Burck, Karen Ruth (Taylor)
Burdick, Charles Albert
Burford, Bonnie Carol
Burg, Corinne (Evangelyn)
Burg, Karl O.
Burgarella, Jean Frances
Burge, Alice Juanita (Ring)
Burgess, Sara Jean
Burke, Adrienne Joan
Burke, (Mary) Nancy (Fahey)
Burnette, Paul Jean
Burns, Alice Elizabeth
Burns, Freddye (Mayes)
Burnes, Inez
Burnes, Mrs William T (Virginia Colley)
Burt, Opal (Brown)
Burtnett, Isabel (K)
Burton, Arlynn Ruth (Schmidt)
Busch, Katharine Cornelie
Busemeyer, Rosella F.
Bush, Douglas P.
Bushelman, Herbert
Busovne, Bernard Joseph
Butler, George E.
Butler, Kenneth William
Butler, Patricia Mary
Butler, Ruth C(andee)
Butterworth, Beverly N (Foss)
Butz, Helen (Schwartz)
Buwalda, Philippina J.
Buzzard, Henry (Lewis)
Byergo, Margaret (Jones)
Byerly, (Edna) Mary
Bystram, Agatha (Maria) (Petho)

Cahill, Alice Marie
Cain, Ruth (Jane)
Calbick, Ian MacKinnon
Caldwell, Georgia (Thomas)
Calhoun, Linda (Reynolds)
Call, Mrs Norma Ann (Comstock)
Callahan, Sister Mary Gerard SND.
Callanan, Isabella M (Porter Zimmerman)
Callanan, Rev Richard James CSP.
Callaway, Evelyn Margaret (Grow)
Cameron, K Elizabeth
Cammack, Floyd M.
Camp, (Mary) Suzanne
Campbell, (Avis) Arline (Butler)
Campbell, Carolyn Janice (Moore)
Campbell, Celia Pope
Campbell, Freda
Campbell, Kathleen (Roseanne)
Campbell, Lola (Henrietta)
Campbell, Sister M Immaculata OSB.
Campbell, Myra (Kershaw)
Cannel, Phoebe Ann
Canning, Joan Meredith (Hill)
Canty, Linda Elaine (Helms)
Capen, Elizabeth (Dew)
Capon, Edity (Swanton)
Capps, Nancy Ellen
Carey, Anne Marie (DeMasi)
Carey, Elizabeth
Carey, Mrs Marion (Sterenberg)
Carlock, Irene Martha (Paul)
Carlson, Albert Paul
Carlson, Elsa
Carlson, Ruth A.
Carlton, Helen (Young)
Carman, Stanley Beck
Carnall, Kathleen A.
Carnie, Janet Margaret
Carpenter, June
Carpenter, Lucile Fell
Carpenter, Olie Atkins
Carr, Anna Groover
Carr, Sharon (Tully)
Carrick, Yvonne Iris (West)
Carrigan, Mary Louise
Carroll, John M.
Carson, Hallie Houston
Carstens, Jane Ellen
Carter, Margaret (Anne)
Carter, Mary Alice (Bateman)
Carter, Verna June
Caruso, Maryelsie
Carver, Jane Anne (Warren)
Carver, Mary Beatrice
Cary, Maxine M (Runnels)
Cash, Annabeth
Cash, Mary Casemer(Daly)
Caso, Gasper Jr.
Cassidy, Raymond C.
Castell, Linda Jean
Causby, Margaret N.
Cawthorne, Edythe O (Mayberry)
Caya, Louis-Marie (Joseph Guy)
Cecile, Sister Marie (Mazurowski)
Cermaks, Janis Otto
Cesvet, Helen E (Keller)
Chadwick, Barbara
Chaffe, Alberta (Lapham)
Chaloupka, Marge
Chamberlain, (M) Lucile
Chamberlin, Mildred Clapp
Champness, Grace L.
Chan, Lois (Mai)
Chance, Homer R.
Chandler, Sister M Clare Louise CSJ.
Chandler, Mrs Marion N.
Chang, Maria Chia-Wei (Yang)
Chang, Nancy Nai-Hsueh (Wang)
Chapman, Harry W(ilbur)
Chapman, Ione M.
Chapman, Marcia (Scarborough)
Chapman, Margaret L(ouise)
Chappell, Yvonne (Worrell)
Charles-Court, Phyllis
Chase, George
Chase, Linda (Smith)
Chavis, (Pauline) Patricia
Cheatham, Bertha M.
Chechak, Dolores (Smith)
Chen, Betty Chong-Chu (Chen)
Chen, Catarina Kuan Ling
Chen, Diana W S (Liou)
Chen, Fei Chien
Chen, Johanna Else (Hartung)
Chen, Lawrence Hsing-Hsia
Chen, Min-Sun
Chen, Sally Shiu-Jen
Cheney, Roberta (Spotser)
Cheng, Catherine (Ning-Ann) Beh
Cheng, Jennie Cecilia Shun-Ling
Cheng, Wai Kin
Chenoweth Evelyn (Frohock)
Cherlow, Eleanor (Pollack)
Cherry, Flora B
Chesson, Reva (Jones)
Cheves, Vera L (Cederstrom)
Chiang, Charlotte C.
Chiang, I-Min
Chiarito, Americo
Chien, Jenn
Childers, Beulah R.
Chilelli, Elizabeth (Hezlett)
Chin, Tieh-Peng
Chisholm, D(avid) Hugh
Chitty, Murela Elizabeth (Sandioge)
Chobanian, Peter
Chona, Harbans Singh
Chou, Belinda Sheau-Ping
Christensen, Jane (Tucker)
Christensen, John A.
Christie, Mrs Georgeina G (Turnbull)
Chu, Tao-Shu
Chuang, Elizabeth (Tsai)
Chung, Yong Sun
Church, Clarice Emily
Church, Frances (Ellen Thomas)
Church Virginia K (Balun)
Cianciulli, Jeanne (Seh)
Cisinski, Joan (Rucker)
Clapp, Jane Leslie (Halliley)
Clare, Mary Catherine (Nichols)
Clare, Sister Regina OP.
Clark, Alson
Clark, Azelie De Lendrecie (Campbell)
Clark, Cynthia Luise
Clark, Gertrude (Gomber)
Clark, Jimmy Ed.

Clark, Joan E (Merriss)
Clark, John E Jr.
Clark, Laron Jefferson Jr.
Clark, (Mary) Margaret
Clark, Margaret B.
Clark, Marilyn (Slawson)
Clark, Marilyn R (Chickowsky)
Clarke, Berta Lou
Clarke, Leslie (shaw)
Clemen, Pauline Edna
Clement, Wenda Ruth (Heater)
Cleveland, Donald Bruce
Clifton, Sharon Gayle (Cryer)
Cline, Fred Albert Jr.
Clinton, Edity (King)
Clopper, Elizabeth Summers
Coates, Genevieve E.
Code, Mary Ann
Cofer, (Elizabeth) Diane
Cohen, Judith Suzanne
Cohen, Lucille (F)
Colby, Edward Eugene
Colchin, Helen
Cole, Eva Lee
Cole, Mrs Juanita (Tucker)
Coleman, Anne White
Coleman Jacqueline A.
Coleman, Virginia L.
Coley, Mrs Mildred S(piller)
Collier, Juanita (Augustono)
Collier, Robert Gordon
Colliflower, Charles Ernest
Collin, Mrs Bernadine (Titlow)
Collins, Christine Ann
Collins, Donald Edward
Collins, Edward Milton
Collins, Elizabeth Gail (Mullins)
Collins, Jeanne Dale
Collins, Thomasine D(ulaney)
Collins, Tressa Mae (Dietz)
Collis, Florence
Colman, Elizabeth
Clovig, Richard M.
Compton, Charles H.
Compton, Miles Stuart
Condon, William J.
Conley, Mrs Joan E (Carroll)
Connell, (Nancy) Ruth (Samis)
Connelly, Dorothy (Van Graafeiland)
Conner, Mrs (Nancy) Annice (Broughton)
Conner, Mary (Adeline)
Connolly, (G) Florence
Connolly, Mary E.
Connor, Dorcas (Worsley)
Connor, Evelyn I (Bring)
Conrad, Dorothea
Conradt, Brother Joseph SM
Constatine, Brother J(ulian)
Consuelo, Sister Mary (Schumann) SSND
Contant, André
Cook, Carol Ann
Cook, Elizabeth (Maurice)
Cook, Frances Atwood
Cook, Gail Winnefred (Fleming)
Cook, Lillian (Collins)
Cook, Merribeth
Cooke, Addie Mae
Cooke, Enid (Graysun)
Cooke, Lucy (Finkel)
Cooke, Nannabell Woodward
Cooks, Constance Jane
Cooley, David Sears
Cooley, Marcia W(illard)
Cooper, Eleanor
Cooper, Florabel (Hazelman)
Cooper, James Anna (Rutledge)
Cooper, Mrs Mary Ella (Lewis)
Cooper, May Elizabeth
Cooper, Suzanne T.
Cooper, Sylvia (Rauch)
Cope, Helga (Molzer)
Copeland, Marian (Dixon)
Copeland, Marie (Turpen)
Copeland, Robert M(ilton)
Copoulos, Pauline
Copp, Madeline (Erbach)
Copps, N(ellie) Imogene
Corbacho, Henry Francis
Corbin, Nancy Ann
Corcoran, Sister Febronia CSJ.
Corin, Judith (Levenson)
Corlies, Frances Jean (Sugden Specht)
Corlies, Robert Peter (Paul)
Corner, Ruth W.
Cornish, (Gwennie) Evelyn
Corrigan, Marie C.
Corrigan, Ruth Ann (Robertshaw)
Corson, Cornelia (Metz)
Corson, Richard Hays
Cory, Mrs Patricia Blair (O'Connell)
Cottrell, Edith W (Van Sickle)
Coughlin, Margaret Morgan
Coulbourn, Jane (Higgins)
Coulthard, Xavier Gregory SDS.
Coumbe, Robert E.
Councill, Elisabeth Agnes
Cousins, Paul M Jr.
Covino, Joseph
Cox, Charles Garland
Cox, Donna (Pearle)
Cox, Estaline
Cox, James C(harles)
Coxe, (Eugenia) Carol
Coyte, Dona (Evelyn)
Crabb, Margaret Stuart
Crabill, Lois (Conway)
Craft, Nancy Mae (Runyan)
Craig, Margaret (Macaulay)
Craig, Mr Vivian Ezra
Cramer, Rose (Fulton)
Crane, Marie Caroline (Suydam)
Crane, Sylvia Doris
Crater, Betty Jane
Craven, Barbara Jean (Cope)
Cravey, Wilma (Sowell)
Crawford, John Carlisle
Crawford, Julia Loomis
Crawford, Kay (Frances)
Crawford, Lucille V.
Crawford, Virginia (Esmond)
Cress, Alice (Moore)
Crippen, Alice (Crawford)
Cripps, Mary Ley
Cromwell, Frederick (Nathaniel)
Crooks, Nancy Jean
Cropp, Gladys (Garesché)
Crosby, Aaron
Crossland, Dorothy (Mary)
Crouch, (Richard) Keith (Chamberlain)
Crouse, Eleanor (Mae)
Crow, Mrs Mattie Lou Teague
Crow, Richard V(aljean)
Crowell, Evelyn Idell
Crowley, (Mary) Inez (Hare)
Crumpacker, Celia Frances
Cryer, Elisabeth Huldah (McCoy)
Culbertson, Marjorie Grace
Cullen, Dorothy Thomas
Culley, Mrs Betty G.
Cullins, June (Dwellingham)
Cummings, Dorothy E.
Cunetto, Ida (Loving)
Cunningham, Sister M Anselm OP.
Cupit, Beverly Jane (Smith)
Curley, Marie (Sullivan)
Curran, Ann T.
Currie, Martha (Colcord)
Curtis, Eugene T.
Cusac, Imogene
Cuthell, M(argaret) Agnes (Nancy)
Cutlip, Mary E(lizabeth)
Cutter, Margaret (Simpson)
Cutting, Helen Frances
Czanyo, Monica Joy (Kellman)
Czarlinsky, Marlene Joan
Czarnecki, Jan Augustyn

Dabbs, Charlotte (Harper)
da Costa, Patricia (Farrell)
Dahl, Marguerite (Walter)
Dailey, James F.
Dailey, Mrs Kazuko (Miyazaki)
Dallap, Chester J.
Dalton, Mrs Elie Hunter (Pauline)
Daly, Mary F.
Dana, Dorothy (Grant)
Daniel, Frances (Veronica) (Ephlin)
Daniels, Leona (Jacobs)
Daniels, Velma (Seawell)
Dannefelser, Ruth
Dansby, Willene A Ragin
Dare, Ruby Elaine
Darrow, Dorothy
Darst, Mary Ellen
Datesman, Beatrice Urban
Daugherty, Jack E.
Davenport, Mrs Vivien (Ardalia Harmon)
Davidson, Carol June (Darling)
Davidson, Helen L (Lahman)
Davidson, Hester (Wolgamott)

Davies, Charlotte Genevieve
Davies, Geraldine (Smith)
Davis, Agnes (Moses)
Davis, Anne (Crosby)
Davis, Anne W.
Davis, Beatrice (Farr)
Davis, Betty (Faye) (McDowell)
Davis, Beulah Myrtle
Davis, Carol Jarvis
Davis, Celina J(osephine)
Davis, Dora (Martin)
Davis, Mrs Douglas J (Ruth Johnston)
Davis, (Dorothy) Geraldine
Davis, Hubert E.
Davis, Lora-Frances
Davis, Mabel Beatrice (Hess)
Davis, Mary Roberts
Davis, Mildred (Parker)
Davis, Sara Bond
Davis, Vinita (Bond)
Davison, Robert (Leitch)
Dawe, Audrey Elaine
Dawn, Mildred (Faulkner)
Dawson, Barbara Lilian
Dawson, Mary H(owland)
Day, Ashley T.
Days, Everett A.
D'Costa, Anita Cynara
Deal, Mrs Hazel H.
Dean, Marsha (Rosier)
De Angelis, Ralph F.
Dearnaley, Carolyn
deBenkö, Eugene
de Cambre, Iris Ribera-Mendez
DeCaria, Mary Ester
Dee, Rev Jerome (Francis)
Degnan, Gwendolyn Bert
Deitch, Donald Gerald
De Jardin, Rev Joseph Raymond SJ.
De Jonge, Judie (Pike Miller)
Dejonge, Helen Elizabeth (Moffitt)
de Kalman, Csiszar
De Los Santos, Alfredo G Jr.
Deluca, Christine Anne
DeLucia, Mrs Mary (Biagiarelli)
deMilan, Sister St Charles FSE
Dempster, Shirley Ann Elizabeth
(Potter)
Denis, Sister M (Donegan)
Denise, Sister M (Monahan) IHM.
Dennis, Rodney Gove III
Denny, Anne (Hood)
Denny, Sue M.
Denton, Francis D.
Denton, Jean (Brumfield)
Denues, Elizabeth H(ay)
Depew, Sara Margaret (Coulter)
Depuy, (Charles) Rolfe
Deronde, Virginia
Derrenbacher, Merle C(atherine)
Derrick, Anya (Berezina)
Deschamps, Rev Aimé (Alphonse)
Desmarais, Marjorie (Crosby)
DeTreville, Virginia (Evans)
Develbiss, Elizabeth (Muenscher)
DeVette, Juanita
Devine, Marie Eileen
Devolder, Arthur Leon
Devolder, Jean (Davis)
DeVoy, Ruth V.
deVries, Florence (J)
Devrnja, Milutin
De Waal, Ronald Burt
Dewhirst, Joyanne
DeWind, Helen Susan (Rogers)
DeWolfe, Helen
De Young, Julia M.
De Young, Mrs Margaret (Wilson)
DeYoung, Robert Allen
Dickenson, Emily (Highes)
Dickey, Pennie Ruth (Williams)
Dickinson, Julia (Frances) Terry
Dickinson, Lucinda
Dickson, Diane (Waggoner)
Diehl, Katherine Smith
Dietrich, Marilyn Marie (Shaver)
Dietz, Dorothy Whitehill
Diffley, Edward J.
Digby, Helen Noren Rose
Dillon, A. Kay
Dillon, Joan (Stuart)
Dillon, Mary Unity
Dillon, Ruth Marie (Sherwood)
Di Mauro, Paul
Disney, Eunice Maude
Dixon, Elizabeth I(sabel) (Creviston)
Dixon, Madeline (H)
Dmyterko, Roman Jaroslaw
Doares, Wade Albert
Dobb, (Theodore Cameron) Ted
Dobler, Lavinia G(race)
Dobrovolny, Mary Ann (McDermott)
Doctoroff, Shayla (Mindell)
Dodd, Mary Ann
Dodendorf, Mary (Louise Seely)
Dodge, Nima M
Dodman, Sister M St Angela CSJ.
Dogil, Phillip John
Doherty, Teresa Jane
Dohm, Janice H.
Doig, (Anne) Judith
Dole, Elizabeth Anne
Doleschal, Eugene
Dolores, Sister Francis (Marie
Dolores Donnelly)
Domas, Marilyn Cecile
Dombra, (Bilovska) Irena
Dommerstern, Carl Alexander
Donahue, Mary Kaye
Donaldson, Jane Stuart (Bankier)
Donaldson, LaNelle (Love)
Donaldson, Mildred (Nicholson)
Dondero, (S) Alice
Donghia, Anthony J.
Donnelly, Barbara Carver
Donnelly, Eleanore Catherine
Donnelly, Joan A.
Donnelly, Sister M Immaculata OSB.
Donze, Sara Lee (Hathaway)
Dooley, Kathleen
Doran, Joan Forster
Dorfman, Mrs Margaret (Cameron)
Dorigan, Margaret Mary
Dorio, Joseph Paul
Dorman, David
Dorman, Ruth (Gammage)
Dornbluth, Verna Helen (Goppert)
Dorothy, Sister Marian (Byrnes) SC.
Dorsey, Clarene Hargrove
Doss, Chriss H.
Doty, Carol L.
Doty, Roland W Jr.
Douglass, Louise (Virlinda)
Dover, Leta (Sowder)
Dow, Orrin B.
Downey, Brother Berchmans
Downey, Margaret A(bigal)
Downing, Hilda Anne (Guenther)
Doyle, Judith Ann (Clark)
Doyle, Mary V(eronica)
Dozier, Lois G.
Draisin, Phebe (Hayes)
Drake, Jean (Marcia)
Draper, Hal
Draper, Walter Dillaway Jr.
Drellich, Barbara Jean (Bates)
Dressler, Margaret
Driggs, Margaret (Brazier)
(Mrs Howard R Driggs)
Driver, Lottie Elizabeth
Drolsum, Alton Raymond
Droppers, Elizabeth
Drumm, Sister Robert Mary OP.
Drvota, Mojmir
Dry, Lloyd Crichton
Duane, Patricia E.
Duarte, (Maria) Guizelda
Dubay, Martha
Dubon, Roger (Jacques)
Duckles, Vincent Harris
Duckworth, Avis (McCrillis)
Duckworth, Peggy (Jane)
Duffy, Jane L (Brownlow)
Dugan, Mary E (Elizabeth)
Dugas, Mildred Elizabeth (Stohlgren)
Duggleby, Esther Irene
Duhrsen, Kathryn Nova (Brown)
Duhrsen, Lowell R II
Duino, Russell (Alfred)
Duke, Sister Mary Fidelis SCN.
Duke, Patricia Gail (Mayers)
Dulany, Mary A(nderson)
Dumantt, Mary de Fitzpatrick
Duncan, Anne (McKay)
Duncan, Florence (Wright)
Dungey, Allyn (K Gibson)
Dunham, Betty Jean
Dunham, Lisbeth (Brookfield Klein)
Dunkley, Kathleen Naomi
Dunlap, Mollie E(rnestine)
Dunlap, Sherry Lynn
Dunn, Eileen Sheriden

Dunn, Josephine Joy
Dunne, Doris (Pianski)
Dunnetski, Stanley F.
Dunnington, Doris (Bennett)
Dunton, Chester
Dupree, Paralee (Garrick)
Durance, Patricia Ruth
Durant, (Homer) Lawrence
Durbin, Hugh A.
Durbin, Ramona J.
Durocher, Rev George E.
Durr, Irma Sue (Pate)
Duso, Bernardine (I)
Du Vall, Frances
Duvall, Mary Ellen L.
Dwyer, Francis Xavier
Dwyer, Melva Jean
Dyck, Kaete J.
Dyer, George John (Rev)
Dyer, Mrs Lucile (Harwick)
Dyer, Marcia Virginia
Dyke, James (Parvin)
Dyrud, John Oliver Jr.
Dyson, James Wynne

Eads, D(orothy) Kathleen
Eagleson, Melva Mary Edna
Eakin, Mary K.
Eames, Marjorie Benson
Earles, Marion (Blair)
Eastman, James Alfred
Easton, David Karl
Eastwood, Edna Mae
Eaton, Conrad Paul
Eaton, Mabel
Echols, Claudia (Lee)
Eckert, Leone (Wooden)
Eddy, Lucy (Reynolds)
Edmonds, Anne C(arey)
Edney, Frances (Gertrued)
Edwards, Fern L(ouise)
Edwards, Leslie W Jr.
Edwards, Margaret Henderson (Mitchell)
Eitingon, Thomas Lee
Elberfield, Catherine (Kyes)
Eldred, Mary Wilson
Eldridge, Muriel E.
Elkhorne, Barbara Gail
Ellington, Elizabeth (Roark)
Elliott, Clark Albert
Elliott, Gwendolyn (Warren)
Elliott, Robert A.
Ellis, Carol Charlene (Eudailey)
Ellis, Edward F.
Ellis, Ethel Mae (Vaughan)
Ellis, Hanni Levi
Ellison, Bettye Holmes
Elsenburg, Elizabeth M.
Elvidge, Mary Ann
Emmaline, Sister Mary CSJ (Comeau)
Emmerich, Liberata
Emrick, Mrs Hamilton R(uth Gilbert)
Eng, Henry K.

Engen, Richard Bruce
English, Kathleen S.
Ennen, Roberg Campion
Eno, Isabel Verena
Enslow, Rev Kenneth Francis SJ.
Ephraim, Gail (Frances)
Eppenberger, Katherine Cordell
Eppink, Alice Jeanette
Epstein, Mrs Dena J(ulia Polacheck)
Ebert, Sister M Dorissa (Rose)
Erickson, Betty (G Kitchens)
Erickson, Donald Robert
Erwin, Vergie Evans
Erwin, William R Jr.
Esch, Vivian (Currin)
Eschenbacher, Herman Francis
Eshelman, Larry (LeRoy) (Benedict)
Esposito, Mrs Olive (Chace)
Estep, Bea (Mantooth)
Estes, Glenn E.
Estes, Sally Catherine (Ackerman)
Etchison, Josephine Pearre
Etter, Freddie L.
Eubank, Margaret A.
Evans, Anne Gliddens
Evans, Barbara (Florence)
Evans, David L.
Evans, Sally (Romer)
Everett, David Graham
Ewing, Jerry Lynn
Eyth, Mary Jo
Ezell, Francis Hays

Fabian, George N.
Fabian, Miriam (Heestand)
Fader, Herbert Louis
Fagan, Joseph Anthony
Fagerstrom Dalphy Irving
Fairchild, Virginia D.
Fall, James Edward
Fallowfield, Jack Alan
Fantini, Jean (McNierney)
Faragoh, Elizabeth Merrell
Faries, Elizabeth
Farley, Ruth L(avern Swanson)
Farmann, Kathleen (Godfrey)
Farmann, Stanley
Farmer, Thelma S.
Farnsworth, Edna Parker
Farrar, Blanche R.
Farrell, Mary E.
Faruquee, Atauar R.
Faulkner, (Florence) Olivia
Fauré, Doreen (B)
Fausett, Carol Jean
Favero, Anita (Marie)
Fedders, Cynthia (Fobes) Smith
Feely, Eleanor Ruth
Fehner, Cornelia Maria
Feldman, Betty Toba
Feldman, Horace Joseph
Feldman, Irma Marie (Tomassetti)
Feng, Margaret Shu-Chun (Yang)
Fenner, Donna Eleanor

Fenner, Sarah G(illespie)
Ferguson, Betty-Jane R (Dugger)
Ferguson, Lawrence J.
Ferguson, Paul F.
Ferguson, Rodney J.
Ferguson, Virginia K.
Ferkett, Mary-Helen (Corbett)
Fern, Wallace E. J.
Ferrari, Angelina Polsinelli
Ferstl, Kenneth Leon
Fesler, Virginia Frances
Field, Marilyn J.
Field, Rochelle J.
Field, Ruth (Rutledge)
Field, Rev William Noe
Fielden, Marjorie (Mason)
Fields, Gale
Filgo, Sarah Joyce
Finch, Catherine Elizabeth (Stentz)
Findlay, Judith Gail (Black)
Finger, Mary Joan
Finkin, Michael C.
Finlay, Billie (Ruth) Nixon
Firestone, Sharon (Marush)
Fischer, Marion (Knoll)
Fishbein, Meyer H(arry)
Fisher, Dixie Lou (Lyons)
Fisher, Elmer H.
Fisher, (Mary) Frances
Fisher, Frances Arlene (Sands)
Fisher, Hazel
Fishman, Naomi Regina (Wald)
Fitts, Miriam
Fitz, Caroline Moul
Fitz, Judith Ann (Schwendener)
Fitzgerald, Lucy Ellen
Fitzsimons, W(illiam) Glenn
Flahiff, Sister Therese Carmel
Flanagan, Lynn Lane
Flandorf, Vera (Sangernebo)
Flannery (Peggy) Anne
Fleck, Charlot Williard
Fleischner, Charles Maurice
Fleming, Thomas P(aul)
Fletcher, Phoebe
Flinchum, Marian (Burkert)
Flintermann, Peter C.
Flora, Betty (Ogden)
Florence, Agnes Louisa
Florentine, Sister Mary (Wathen) SCN.
Flott, Nancy Lee (Fate)
Floyd, Helen S (Josephine) (Sutherin)
Floyd, Louise (McKnight)
Flueckiger, Jane (Lipson)
Fluker, Martha Moon
Flynn, Frances
Foerstel, Herbert Neil
Feldman, Irma Marie (Tomassetti)
Felts, Margaret D(avis)
Foley, David (William)
Foley, M(ark) Jerome
Fontaine, Henry A Jr.
Ford, Martha Jane
Ford, Mawdelle (Scarlett)

Forget, Guy
Forgione, Barbara Catherine (Jones)
Forrest, Carol J G(reer)
Forrest, Earl Arwin Jr.
Forsythe, David N.
Forsythe, Joann
Foster, Donald Leroy
Foster, Florence T(opolski)
Foster, Jeannette H.
Foster, Martha Jane R(obison)
Fountain, Frances (Harris)
Fountaine, Jean L.
Fox, Elizabeth Ann
Fox, M Allyn
Fox, Roberta (Kisloff)
Fox, Sherry (gail) (Isbell)
Foyle, James Kenneth
Fracchia, Doris L.
Francesca, Sister Mary (Kelly) PBVM.
Francis, Mrs Bernice (Kelley)
Francis, Rosemary
Francis, Virginia Gladys
Franco, Diane Marion
Francois, Lillian P(earl)
Frankel, Joan
Franklin, Elizabeth (Clare)
Franklin, Freeda B(ear)
Franklin, Hardy R.
Franko, Joan Ann (Pritchett)
Franosch, Maimu V(abasalu)
Franz, Eleanor (Waterbury)
Frappier, J C Gilles
Fraser, Joan (Audrey)
Fraser, Lorna Dawn
Fraser, Margaret Ashby
Fraser, Sam(uel) E(dward)
Frazer, Elizabeth (Warner)
Frazer, Georgia A(nn)
Frazier, Catherine Audrey (Bell)
Frazier, Jean D(ouglas)
Frazier, Mildred C(arroll)
Fredin, Lillian E.
Freeman, Patricia Harper
Freeman, Ruth T.
Freese, H Mildred
Freitag, Rosalie (Virginia)
Fremd, Edward George
French, Barton Coleman
French, Martha A.
Fretz, Evelyn Claire (Wertley)
Freudenberg, Anne E H.
Frew, Martha Gale
Fried, Shelah (Smith)
Friedman, Charlotte A.
Friend, Llerena
Frisbie, Mary Lee
Frisby, (Prihoda) Sylvia (Hejna)
Frone, Peggy Marie
Fry, Ray MacNairn
Fulforth, Charles J.
Fullenwider, Nancy Dee
Fuller, Dorothy (Edsall)
Fuller, Helen R(ussell)
Fuller, Nell (Benton)
Fuller, Rebecca (Phillips)
Fulton, (Margaret) Jane
Fung, Margaret (Ding-Chong Chang)
Funckhouser, Myrtle
Furbish, Barbara Ann
Furbush, Mrs Eleanor (Saunders)
Furmanek, Florence M (Kelczka)
Fuss, Felicia
Fyan, Loleta D(awson)
Fye Iris Anne

Gable, June (Roberts)
Gaffney, Marion
Gakovich, Robert Predrag
Gale, Violet (Haugwitz)
Gaker, Mary Jane (Perkins)
Galer, Robert Fulton
Gallagher, Nancy (Alison)
Galli, Louis J.
Gallivan, Barbara Ann
Galloway, Jean A.
Gallup, William A Jr.
Gamage, Gay (Kimball)
Gamble, Bernadette Edith
Gambrill, Georgia
Gandt, Karl O.
Ganley, Linda V.
Gans, Marion (Reinstein)
Gardin, Martha Louise
Gardner, Frances M(arie)
Garelick, Alexander L
Garn, Almeda
Garner, Ralph
Garrison, Barbara (Shepherd)
Garrison, Joanne Ruth (Sergeant)
Garvey, Mary Louise
Gaskill, Gordon A.
Gately, Charles Francis
Gates, Earl William
Gates, Geraldine Manson
Gates, Sandra F (Stanley)
Gath, Mildred (Myers)
Gatter, E Susanne
Gatz, Joan
Gauer, (Catherine) Joan
Gawur, MR Marian
Gay, Ebenezer
Gay, Karen (Anders)
Gaylord, Mrs Catherine Scott
Gazdik, Olga S.
Gee, Fauntleroy
Geenen, George J.
Geimer, Rev Alfred F.
Geist, Mrs Olga (Henriette)
Geitzler, Frances Ella
Gelperin, S(onia N) Michèle
Gemlich, Kathryn (Anne)
Genest, Paulette M.
Gens Lafrance, Suzanne
Genus, Arnold Silvester
Georgas, Margaret (Tenold)
George, Nadine (Felton)
George, Rachel
Gerhardt, Robert William
Germaine, Shirley Anna Margaret
German, Marian E (Singley)
Gersitz, Brother Athanasius
Gerstner, Clara (Greenberg)
Getchell, Sylvia (Fitts)
Getman, Mrs Lola (Woodcock)
Getz, Richard Edward
Ghazisaid, Rosetta (Palmer)
Giambrone, Eunice E (Houghten)
Gibian, Germaine L.
Gibson, Arrell Morgan
Gibson, Elisabeth Ann (Coulthard)
Gibson, Judith Mae
Gibson, (Mary) Louise
Gibson, Mary Jane
Gibson, Sibylia A(ndrews)
Giemza, Mrs Florence Frances (Micek)
Gilbert, Mary Frances
Gilbo, Edna Genevieve
Giles, Margaret Ellen
Gill, Gale (Alnette) Scribner
Gilliam, Mrs Mary (Meacham)
Gilman, Grace (Wilson)
Gilmary, Sister M (Spiers) IHM.
Gilstrap, Helen Isabel (Routledge)
Gindlesberger, Erma (Logsdon)
Ginoza, Kathryn K.
Ginsberg, Harry
Giordano, Julie (De Louise)
Gipprich, Mrs Joan Mary (Krausmann)
Girard, John Andrew
Girard, Roland SJ.
Girton, Gladys Marie (Schemahorn)
Githens, Harold Lewis
Gittleman, Lenore Sandra
Gittlen, Betty (Golden)
Glad, Beverly Joyce (Smithson)
Glatzer, Daniel (F)
Glenn, Delitha E.
Glick, Nada Beth (Ellend)
Glozer, Liselotte Erlanger
Goddard, Ruth
Godefroy, Isabel (Maud)
Godley, Margaret (Walton)
Goff, (Mary) Elizabeth
Goff, Jennifer Dixwell
Gohlke, Dorothy Annette (Phillips)
Gohmert, Janice
Goldberg, Barbara
Goldberg, Harry
Goldberg, June (Lewin)
Goldfine, George
Goldstein, Helen J(ohnston)
Goldstein, Marilyn (Simon)
Goldstein, Marilyn Susan
Goldstein, Sidney
Goldzweig, Arthur
Gondrella, Pearl J.
Gonthier, Rev Denys Armand AA.
Gonthier, Dorothy G.
Gonzales, Anne Louise (Schilbe)
Gooch, Hope (Leonard)
Gooch, William D.
Good, Mrs Eliza Caroline (Ross)

Good, Margaret W.
Goodman, Eleanor (Humphries)
Goodno, Carol (Marks)
Goodrich, Charlotte G(elzer)
Goodrich, Robert C(arlyle)
Goold, Martha (Lane)
Gordon, Mrs Elizabeth J(anney)
Gordon, Ina (Ella)
Gordon, Laurel
Gordon, Lawrence
Gordon, Mary Frances
Gorena, Amelia Adriana (Alamia)
Gotham, Cassandra (Gentile)
Gott, (Mary) Jane
Gottneid, Carolyn Marie
Gottry, Lucille
Gottschalk, Helen
Goudeau, John Milfred
Gough, Chester R.
Gove, Esther C.
Graber, Normand T.
Gracille, Sister Mary CSFN.
Grady, Marion B(ehethlan)
Graham, Aubry Lee (Hill)
Graham, Irene (Ellen)
Graham, Joy M.
Graham, Maura Heloisa (Napoleão)
Graham, Rosemond Eve (Toner)
Grahek, Joan Josephine (Hoffman)
Grainger, Mary (Green)
Grainger, Shirley Jeannette
Granger, Diana Kathryn (Ladd)
Grant, Henrietta Arnold
Grant, Penelope Anne (Tucker)
Grant, Ruth (Hitchcock)
Grant, Shirley (Conant)
Grasty, Susan Hatchett
Graves, (Anna) Catharine
Graves, Jane S(teele)
Graves, Ruth Constable
Gray, Lucile Merriwether
Gray, Nancy (Bynum)
Gray, Mrs Phyllis S(herman)
Gray, Ruth
Gray, Virginia H.
Grayson, Bessie Rivers (Leola)
Greaves, E Leslye (Platt)
Greco, Gloria Theresa
Green, Ada (Lucille)
Green, Anne M.
Green, Mrs Elizabeth (Henderson) Baren
Green, Elizabeth Haynes
Green, Evalane Roberta
Green, Frank Lester
Green, Miss Jamye A.
Green, Joan Marie
Green, Larry Grant
Green, Sister Mary Zita OSF.
Green, Ronald Robert
Greenall, Elizabeth Constance Ellen
Greenberg, Emil
Greenberg, Phoebe
Greene, Mrs Charity H
Greene, Ellin (Peterson)
Greene, Elwin J.
Greene, James Thomas
Greene, Jane
Greene, Linda (Butler)
Greene, Mary Alyce (Carter)
Greene, Virginia Lee
Greenfield, Kathleen Elizabeth
Greenhill, virginia (Lee)
Greenlee, Joanne (Emidy)
Greenwood, Audrey Gates
Greer, Mrs W H (Mary Myrtle Jones)
Greer, William L C
Gregar, Willis A.
Gregory, Viola (Bonner)
Gresham, William Dew
Gresser, Marylyn (Evans)
Grieder, Theodore
Griffin, Al David
Griffin, Hazel
Griffin, Richard G(eorge)
Griffis, Faye (Campbell)
Griffith, Alice B(ailey)
Griffith, David W.
Griffith, Mrs Jean (Green)
Griffith, Martha (Pace)
Griffith, William Jenkins
Griffiths, Evelyn (Peffley)
Griffiths, Lillian (G)
Griggs, John Bradford
Grim, Frances M.
Grimes, Virginia
Grainger, Carol A.
Griner, Elaine (Smith)
Grinsfelder, Marion (Kahnweiler)
Gripton, Judith Ahlborn
Griswold, Enid (Karsten)
Grogan, James C.
Gross, Elizabeth Henry
Gross, Lucy Mary
Gross, Miriam (Teitelbaum)
Gross, Nancy (Hayward)
Grouchy, Mother M Margaret OP.
Grove, Lynn Albert
Gruenwoldt, Barbara
Grygo, Alice M (Bjorkman)
Grygotis, Gerard D.
Gscheidle, Gertrued E(lizabeth)
Guerra, Debe'n ana L.
Guggenheim, Selma Katherine (Sims)
Gugielmo, Sister M Francine Mzsh
Guillaume, Sandra A(rlene)
Guinn, Gene A.
Guinn, James Melvin
Guinn, Mary Evelyn
Gulko, Christina, Marie
Gullett, Sara Davis
Gulley, Mary Beth (Owen)
Gunn, Margaret (Holt)
Gunther, Sister Mary Virginia OP.
Gurner, Betty (Jo) Evans
Guthrie, Margaret Adeline
Gutierrez, Ida Mae (Corbett)
Gutteridge, Mary (Stevenson)
Gutzman, Stanley Dean
Guy, Wendell Arthur
Gwinn, Hettie Belle
Gygax, Alice (White)

Haar, Mrs Jeanette (Hill)
Haar, Vivian Joya (Cori)
Haas, Herbert Peter
Habrowych, Lubomyra
Hack, Leo Milton
Hackman, Martha L.
Hackney (West) Bernice
Hadidian, Dikran Y(enovk)
Hagar, Alice
Hagen, Mrs Daniel J (Charlotte-Kelley)
Haglund, Doris (Erlene Ellis)
Hagstrom Mary (Fallon)
Hagy, Miriam Lois
Hahn, Felice R.
Haid, Terri (Grammer)
Haigh, Alice Lilian
Haigis, Joanne
Hairgrove, Dorothy (Grace)
Hake, June Horton
Hale, Hazel Beaty (Elizabeth)
Haley, Mrs Elizabeth Ann (Potts)
Halferty, Joanne Marie (Bullock)
Hall, David
Hall, Joan Ann (Glenck)
Hall, Margaret Esther
Hall, Mary A.
Hall, Morton
Hall, Sadie Elizabeth
Hallenburg, Marie (Hill)
Haller, Blanche (Wohl)
Hallett, Julia (Herrick)
Halloran, Vera A.
Halmos, Mrs Dorothy M(oyer)
Halverson, Mrs Susan (Schwartz)
Hamby, Luclare (Robinson)
Hamer, Jean
Hamilton, Anna Belle
Hamilton, Benjamin Arthur
Hamilton, Janet D (Sheard)
Hamilton, Joan E(lizabeth)
Hamilton, Mrs Mabel (Crawford)
Hamilton, Mary (McDonald)
Hamilton, Violet Emily (McCredie)
Hamlen, Dorothy (Alice)
Hamlyn, (Mary) Grace
Hammer, Leonard
Hammer, Olive (Ober)
Hammersley, Martha Faye
Hammerstein, Mrs Isabelle M (Robbe)
Hammett, Leila Mae
Hammond, Mildred A(llerton)
Hampden, Betty Brill
Hampshire, John A.
Hamrell, Larry George
Hamrock, Mary Ellen
Han, Wan Chun (Wanda)
Hanaway, William Lippincott Jr.
Hancock, Dan Smith Jr.
Hancock, Katharine Adele

Hand, Karen (Hampe)
Handel, Dorothy Maria (Menczel)
Haney, Sue Marie (Watson)
Hanke, Maxine (Kennedy)
Hanks, Janice Lorraine (Wood)
Hanks, Judith (Paschke)
Hanlon, Peter Francis MacLean
Hann, Barbara Jean
Hanna, (Dorothy) Gay Fortner
Hansbery, Joseph E(dward John)
Hansen, Mrs Catherine Z(ottoli)n
Hansen, Marilee Ann
Hansen, Marion M
Hansen, Natalie (Elizabeth)
Hansen, Ralph John Jr.
Hanson, Ann Marie
Harbin, Dorothy Mary
Hard, (Norma) Jean (Somers)
Hardendorff, Mrs Jeanne B
(deGraffenreid)
Harding, Bruce Charles
Hardy, Rev Anselm F OFM.
Hardy, Elizabeth (Lloyd)
Hardy, Jacqueline (Lee)
Harkins, (Vernita) Nadine
Harkins, William Gregory
Harlan, Robert D.
Harmer, Wallace E(dward)
Harmes, Douglas Lee
Harmon, Elmer Glynn Jr.
Harper, Patricia Bernice
Harper, Susan (Hagelberger)
Harper, Violet Balfour (Cairns)
Harrar, H(elen) Joanne
Harrill, Rosalie
Harris, Aaron
Harris, Eleanor C.
Harris, George
Harris, Harriet Jane
Harris, Helen W(adsworth)
Harris, Jane Innes
Harris, Jane (Elizabeth) Reynolds
Harris, Marinelle (Marie)
Harris, Mary Beth
Harris, Ruth Dittmar
Harris (M) Sylvia
Harris, Thomas C.
Harrison, Annie (Willis)
Harrison, Barbara Joan
Harrison, Eleanor Farnsworth
Harrison, Helen (Dortch)
Harrison, Maude
Hart, Margaret Gibson
Hart, (Mary L) Sue
Hartbank, Betty Ruth
Harter, Mrs Mary (Reese)
Hartman, Anne-Marie
Hartman, Elizabeth (Davis)
Hartman, Elizabeth R.
Hartmann, Marlene Käthe Christel
Harty, Marcia (Cottis)
Hartzell, Mary Elizabeth)
Hartzler, Homer W.
Harvey, Dorothy Aileen
Harvey, Lois Marie
Haslett, Frances E.
Hastings, Eleanor R.
Hastings, Alice Turner
Hatch, Orin Walker
Hathaway, Mrs Edith (Hart)
Hatten, Freda (Westensee)
Hatton, Frances Arnold
Haubold, Ella
Haugh, Gunnar E.
Hauser, Vesta Margaret (Moore)
Hausrath, (Mrs) Sydney (Clark)
Haver-Droeze, Frederik (Jan)
Havig, Christian Moïnichen
(Lt Col Ret)
Hawkins, Cornelia Frances
(Keuzenkamp)
Hawkins, Edity (McRae)
Hawley, Betty (Bull)
Hawthorne, Maude
Hay, Sara Elizabeth
Hayden, Arline Lucille (Hall)
Hayes, Catherine D.
Hayes, Margaret Leslie
Hayes, Ruth Marie
Hayland, Theresa Elizabeth
Haywood, Dorothy C (Flynn)
Heacock, Loretta Ellen
Head, (Lucy) Cary
Head, Dorothy (Womack)
Headings, Bernice E.
Heald, Jesse Heston
Healy, Charles Joseph
Healy, Sister Mary Visitation SSMN.
Heaps, Margaret (Quigley)
Heaps, Williard Allison
Hearne, Miriam Lindley
Heath, Graham Leonard Jr.
Heath, Maxine Shoemaker
Hecker, Margaret A.
Heckert, Frances Eleanor
Heckman, Marlin L.
Hedblom, Eleanor
Hedenbergh, Ethel Agnes
Hedstrand, Lillian
Heery, Sister Mary Gabriel SSJ.
Hegardt, F Irene
Hegstad, Patsy Ann (Adams)
Heidler, Louise (Wall)
Heimanson, Rudolf H(ermann)
Heitmann, Helen Elizabeth
Helburn, Jeanette (Kahnweiler)
Helfeld, Dorothy (Gordon)
Helgerson, Douglas M.
Helgeson, Duane M.
Heller, Elizabeth Carolyn
Heller, Judith Ruth
Helt, Frances (Edwards)
Helvey, Mary Sewell
Hemink, Marian J(ean) (Partridge)
Henckel, Jane (Cadwallader)
Henderson, Helen (Huntoon)
Henderson, (Ruby) Marie
Hendricks, Mrs Barbara (Elaine) Parks
Hendrickson, Mildred Claire
(Richardson)
Harvey, Lois Marie
Harwell, Richard Barksdale
Henefer, Ina (Davis)
Heneghan, Sophie (Cameron)
Henke, Mrs Frances (Sawyer)
Henricks, Duane Edward
Henriques (D) Elaine
Henry, Betty (McShane)
Henry, Sara Elizabeth
Herbage, Helen Louise (Bishop)
Herber, Katharine Harriet
Herbert, Brother Luke A.
Herod, Jane Lee
Herrick, Mildred Eloise
Herriott, Mrs Gaylord M
(Margaret Hecei)
Herschcopf, Richard Donald
Hershey, Fred(erick) E(arnshaw)
Hertz, Faith Barbara
Hertz, George W.
Hertzman, Gay (Mahaffy)
Herzing, Louise (Brown)
Heslop, Norma Mary (MacFarlane)
Hespen, Celeste F.
Hess, Robert Walter
Hetrick, John Murray
Hettinger, Mrs Herman S, see
Wessells, Helen E.
Heurtley, Jasna
Heutte, Frederic Alford
Hewit, Gertrude E(dna)
Hewitt, Clara D(enwiddie)
Heyart, (Ella) Fredene Foster
Heywood, Carmen (Couvillion)
Hiatt, Peter
Hickman, Marcia Stuart
Hicks, Paul R.
Hieronymus, Nancye (Eastin)
Higgins, Mary H.
Higgins, Ruth (Elizabeth) Rowell
Higginson, Isabella (Lukens)
Higgs, E Lucille
High, Doris (Marion)
Highum, Clayton Douglas
Higley, Verna C (Freemore)
Hilb, Horace
Hilber, Sister M Leocadia OSB.
Hildebrandt, Florence Marion
Hilberbrand, Elizabeth (Curry)
Hill, Ann (Elnora) Bolin
Hill, Barbara (Welch)
Hill, J Evelyn
Hill, Ruth (Ina) E(dmonds)
Hill, Shirley (Daphene)
Hille, Michael John
Hillyard, Ethel Maud
Hilton, Margaret (Lewis)
Hilton, Mary L.
Hilyard, Stevens Woods
Himeno, Emma Lee
Himoe, Charlotte L.
Himsel, Robert Christian

Hinds, Charles Franklin
Hinrichs, Pauline E(sther)
Hinson, Anna Jane
Hinton, Frances
Hintz, Carl W(illiam Edmund)
Hirata, Lucie (Cheng)
Hirsch, Leda (Treskunoff)
Ho, Philip W J.
Ho, Stephen Y C.
Hoag, Marjorie
Hobbs, Barbara Houston
Hobbs, Brian (Eric)
Hock, Corrine Hutchins (Antoinette)
Hodges, Elizabeth De Salles
Hodges, M Eugene
Hodgson, Thekla (Roese)
Hodock, Irene H.
Hoefler, Barbara Burton (Elizabeth)
Hoffman, Carlton E.
Hoffman, Dorothy (Collins)
Hoffman, Ida Rheba (Palmer)
Hoffmann, Fredrick Karl
Holbrook, Frances Karr
Holden, Mary Lou (Johnston)
Holder, Sharon Rogene (Hubbard)
Holgate, Mary Brown
Hollander, Janet
Hollar, Marion (Werey)
Hollar, Rosita (Holdsworth)
Holliday, Shirley James
Hollis, Mrs Beulah (Inez)
Holloman, Elizabeth Spindler
Holloway, Lelia Frances
Holm, Grace (Prentice)
Holman, LeRoy Glover
Holmgren, Eric Joseph
Holsinger, Gerald E(lliott)
Holt, Marjorie Louise
Holtman, Eugene A.
Holtzman, Anita Constance
Honeycutt, Bonnie (Green)
Hong, Mrs Byung Hee (Min)
Hood, Lottie Estelle
Hood, Lottie Howlett Curlin
Hoodless, Jean (Hazen)
Hooker, Lloyd W.
Hoon, Barbara
Hooper, Jacqueline (Jones)
Hooser, Mrs C G (Anna Mae Graves)
Hoover, Ferne R Hoover
Hoover, Grace V(ivian)
Hoover, John (Douglas)
Hoover, Mildred E.
Hope, Josephine Alice
Hopkins, Dorothy Agnes (O'Hara)
Hopkins, Florence Martin
Hopkins, John Feely
Hopper, Hazel W(hiteleather)
Hoppes, Muriel Ann
Horn, Margaret
Horner, Kent Chambers
Hort, Margaret Janvier
Horton, Barbara Ruth
Horvis, Martin

Houle Rev André (Laurent) OMI.
Houle, Jacqueline (Marie)
House, Jan(E Robbins)
Houser, Mrs Mabel Hines
Houston, Mary Elizabeth
Howard, Elizabeth (Hicks)
Howard, Esther Margaret (Rae)
Howard, (Sara) Margaret
Howard, Martha S(wearengen)
Howard, Mary Anna
Howard, Nell Elizabeth
Howell, Ellenor (Hardeman)
Howell, Freda (Lovrien)
Howell, Isabel (Rupp)
Howell, Lilith
Howell, Opal (Margaret) (Pemberton)
Howell, William Franklin
Howes, Elizabeth (Harkins)
Howie, June (Attig)
Hoy, Eileen Monica
Hoyle, Ruth (Gordon)
Hoynes, Emmet (Edwin)
Hoyt, C Eugene
Hrdlicka, Rev Adolph Edward
Hsia, Shu-Fang (Miss)
Hsia, Stella Te-Chen
Hsu, Grace (Shen)
Hsu, Mercedes Y(Un-Yun Tai)
Hsu, Mona R.
Hsu, Mrs Oon-Bee (Khoo)
Hu, Shih-Sheng
Huang, Dora (Liu Nee)
Huang, Wenhong
Hubbard, Frances (Elizabeth) Cressey
Hubbard, Hazel (Carter)
Hubbard, Mary (Backer)
Hubbell, Ruth (Louwerse)
Hubble, Faunice
Hubli, Mrs Joseph (Judith A Cleveland)
Huculak, Wasyl
Hudson, Barton
Hudson, Geneva M (Hall)
Hudson, Marian Edythe
Hudson, Rebecca Alberta (Mitchell)
Huebner, Joseph Herbert
Huff, Robert W.
Huffman, Marian (Porter)
Hugghins, Patricia Ann
Hull, Harvey R.
Hull, Thomas V.
Hulsey, Elizabeth (Ann Benbrook)
Hulsker, William F.
Humble, Marion
Humby, Marjorie I.
Humenuk, Stanley
Humphries, Beverly (Nell Harris)
Hung, Lilian (Chang)
Hunt, Mary B.
Hunt, Nancy Ann
Hunter, Gladys B.
Hunter, Jacqueline (Ethel Burnett)
Hunter, Jean B.
Hunter, Lois (Corey)

Huntley, June (Francis) Leath
Hurley, Barbara Brooke
Hurst, Billie Katherine
Hurst, Simone Camillia
Husted, Carol Henderson
Husted, Caroline Elizabeth
Hutcherson, (Ethel) Madge
Hutchings, Marion (Connors)
Hutchins, Mrs Mary (Janssen)
Hutchinson, Martha (Lawrence)
Hwang, Aileen (Chang)

Iddings, Mary (Elvina)
Ignatieff, Anatoly
Igoe, James Gerard
Ilic, Ursula D (Van Bebber)
Inch, Fredrick James
Ingles, Mrs C L (Ballard)
Inks, Cordelia (Catherine Rugeley)
Ireland, Mary (Elizabeth) N(eely)
Ireland, Patricia
Irons, Lillian (Coutts)
Irving, Hubh (Lansfield Caven)
Irwin, Mrs Margaret (Strong)
Isaac, Oliver Burns
Isabella, Sister Mary (Stokes) OP.
Isabelle, Sister Mary (Jones) SSC.
Isbell, Mary Charlotte
Isely, Mrs Mildred L(oshbough)
Isner, Edith (Mildred)
Israel, Fred Carl
Israel, Kathleen (James)
Iverson, Helen (Mudry)

Jaadan, Ruth N.Jablonowski, (Wladyslau) Feliks
Jacks, Gerald
Jackson, Mrs Arnold Osborne
Jackson, Eleanor (Brown, Walz)
Jackson, Ellen (Pauline)
Jackson, Grace Melva (Mahin)
Jackson, H Kenneth
Jackson, Herbert Cross
Jackson, John F.
Jackson, Marianne (Perdue)
Jackson, Marie Hull
Jackson, Nola
Jackson, Robert Blake
Jacob, Albertha M.
Jacobs, Clara Mae (Kizer)
Jacobs, John Hall
Jacobs, Judi (Jones)
Jacobs, Nina Frances
Jacobson, Beverly Jean
Jadlos, Katherine (Kittle)
Jadot, Mrs Evelyn (Ferry)
James, Diane Elise
Jan, May (Young)
Janisse, John B(aptist Joseph)
Janowski, Mary Ellen (Tilley)
Janzer, Barbara Anne
Jarred, Ada (Delony)
Jarrell, Howard R.
Javelin, Muriel C(ann)
Jeansonne, Henrietta W.

Jedlicka, Elizabeth (Lang)
Jefferson, Elizabeth W.
Jeffrey, Laura M.
Jeffs, Joseph E.
Jenkins, Florence M (Doyle)
Jenkins, Leora R.
Jenks, Carolyn K(olbe)
Jenks, Lynn (Moore)
Jenney, Claire Elaine (Watt)
Jennings, Dorothea (Pearson)
Jennings, Willie Virginia
Jensen, Marilyn Anne
Jerkovich, George C.
Jerng, Wan-Wan
Jeschke, Walter Jon
Jessen, Nancy Elizabeth
Jetton, Marcia Lou (Marks)
Jewett, Madge McGrew
Jilka, Wanda (Zirkle)
Johannes, Fannie D(ubofsky)
Johnson, Anne (Douglass)
Johnson, Betty Jo (Drees)
Johnson, Carolyn (Edwina)
Johnson, Clifford R(obert)
Johnson, Mrs Corinne (Harrison)
Johnson, Dina G.
Johnson, Eleanor
Johnson, Eleanor L (Carlson)
Johnson, Elizabeth Ann
Johnson, Elmer Douglas
Johnson, Florence (Kribs)
Johnson, (Mary) Frances Kennon
Johnson, Frances R.
Johnson, Gladys
Johnson, (Martha) Gladys
Johnson, Goldye (Kent)
Johnson, Jacqueline K(nowles)
Johnson, Jo Ann
Johnson, Marjorie A (Burnham)
Johnson, N Elizabeth (Taylor)
Johnson, Robert Dale
Johnson, Robert Kellogg
Johnson, Ronald D.
Johnson, Ruth B(oynton)
Johnson, Mrs Sara
Johnson, Sue (Gay) Lane
Johnston, Robin (Patrick)
Jolicoeur, Louis-Philippe
Jones, A(lice) Kathleen
Jones, Agnes B(roddus)
Jones, Alice Ratcliffe Gurnett
Jones, (Harriett) Allyne P(adgett)
Jones, Audrey V.
Jones, Catherine E.
Jones, Dora Ann
Jones, Eleanor
Jones, Helen Jane
Jones, James Victor
Jones, Jeannette (Maiden)
Jones, John B.
Jones, Katherine (Derr)
Jones, Leon I.
Jones, Leone Fay (Andrews)
Jones, Lillie (Chambers)
Jones, Mable Ruth (White)
Jones, Margaret (Palcich)
Jones, Marianna (Chandler)
Jones, (Amy) Marjean Wright
Jones, Marjorie B(ang)
Jones, Mary C (Ternes)
Jones, Myra (Eittreim)
Jones, (Jesse) Ray Jr.
Jones, Robert E.
Jones, Rubye Jean
Jones, Sarah L(ewis)
Jones, U V.
Jones, Zola
Jonikas, Peter
Jordahl, Anna J.
Jordan, Helen Louise
Jordan, Judith Simonds
Jorgensen, Joan M (Fergen)
Jorve, Ronald M.
Josel, Clair (Solomon)
Joseph, Miss K jouree
Jost, Lillian (Mohr)
Joyce, Donald Franklin
Judd, Mrs Etta (Westenhouse)
Julian, Lawrence (Clark)
Junier, Artemisia J(ones)
Jurich, Mary (Piliponis)
Jury, Florence N(iles)
Jussim, Estelle

Kagan, Ilse Echt
Kalichevsky, Kira
Kalnins, Milda (Mezulis)
Kaltenbach, Margaret
Kammerlohr, Barbara (Jean)
Kanders, Herman
Kane, Barbara J(ane)
Kane, Mrs Leona (Torke)
Kane, Mrs Ruth (Hamilton)
Kanka, A Gerald
Kannitzer, Columban (Rev Father Dom)
Kao, Anita S(han-Shan, Liu)
Kao, Anna
Kao, Irving K Y.
Karges, Joann
Karic, Seid
Karier, Rev Raymond
Karlowich, Robert Anthony
Karr, Jeannette (Lawrence)
Kassis, Shukrieh Ruth (Jabbour)
Katz, Gail J(acobs)
Kaufmann, Robert (Carl)
Kaye, Rhona Carol
Keathley, Mary Katharine (Fergeson)
Keebler, Elaine M.
Keefer, Mary
Keehan, Anne L.
Keenan, Elizabeth L.
Keene, Shelagh (Elizabeth)
Keener, Donald Spring
Kees, Stephen John
Keevil, Susan (Deane)
Kehaya, (Alexander) Dimitri (Carl Constantine)
Kehl, M Margaret
Kehm, Gladys J.
Keim, Eileen
Keith, Frances (Peele)
Kellaway, Marjorie A (Braunz)
Kelleher, Joseph Cornelius
Kelleher, Loretta E.
Keller, Kenneth E.
Keller, Nancy Clara
Keller, Thelma Pollock (Betty)
Kelley, Linda Lou (Franklin)
Kelley, Mary Elizabeth
Kelly, Anne M.
Kelly, Elinor Claire (Dawes)
Kelly, Mary Ruth
Kelly, Paul William
Kelman, Rosalind (Schribman)
Kemp, (Ernest) Ann
Kemp, Barbara Elaine
Kemper, Sister Agathena
Kemper, Joyce Joanne (Poe)
Kemper, Robert E.
Kendall, John Dickson
Kendall, Priscilla (Ainsworth)
Kenn, Barbara Kay (Hagle)
Kennedy, Billie Beatrice
Kennedy, Florence (Baker)
Kennedy, Janice Elizabeth
Kennedy, Ted (Theodore)
Kennington, Frances Rogers
Kenny, Margaret El zabeth
Kent, Carl Albert
Kent, Mary Ann
Kerbaugh, Mary Campbell
Kerby, Mary (Ellen) Ward
Kerner, Norma (Jean Evans)
Kerr, Albert S(antee)
Kerr, Jean (Asher)
Kerr, Laura
Kerr, Mildred Annette
Kerr, Virginia Lee (Pilstl)
Kerstetter, Oscar E.
Kerstetter, Virginia (McGill)
Kessinger, Rev David Robert
Kessler, David Robert
Kessler, Myer Michael
Ketchum, Carol (Joyce Weed)
Ketchum, Mrs Milo S (Gretchen Allenbach)
Kettering, Marguerite (Snodgrass)
Khanna, Tilak Raj.
Kibrick, Jane (Mittau)
Kidder, Eleanor
Kidwell, Mary (Elizabeth)
Kiefer, William Joseph SM.
Kieler, Mary C.
Kilfoil, Thomas Francis
Kilgour, Raymond L(incoln)
Killian, Julia Helen
Killingsworth, Amy Ruth (Byers) (Reed)
Kilpatrick, Clayton E.
Kim, Han Kyung
Kim, Mrs Soowon (Yoon)
Kim, Stephen

Kimball, Jane (Allison)
Kimmel, Margaret Mary
Kimmel, Minna (Gross)
Kinchloe, Martha Estelle
Kinder, Celesta V.
Kindsvater, Ellen Marie (Palmer)
King, Catharine (Bradner)
King, Charles Henry Jr.
King, Elizabeth L.
King, Glennie Beanland
King, Jessie Yai Ping
King, Mary
King, Richard Eugene
King, Rita Sue
King, Sally Ray
Kingery, Alice C.
Kingsbury, Norma E (Ford)
Kingsley, James Morse Jr.
Kinney, Anne (Markley)
Kinzly, Mrs Ethel (Kinsey)
Kirk, Ennid J.
Kirk, James Henry
Kirkendall, Hugh (Richmond)
Kirkland, Mary Newberry (Louelle)
Kirkpatrick, Judith Entrican
Kirschner, Gertrude (Georgianna)
Kirshenbaum, Sandra (De Nola)
Kisling, Frances Rita
Kisner, Arlene H.
Kite, Grace Elizabeth
Kite, Lena Evelyn
Kittner, Sandra Marleen
Kittrell, Mrs. H. Tom (Gene Chaffin)
Klaus, Ruth Gayle
Klauser, Laurie C.
Klein, Jean (Stein)
Kleinjan, Hendrine (Rozendal)
Klemm, Virginia Adrienne
Kline, Rev Lawrence Oliver
Kling, Fleurette (Stock)
Kingler, Mrs Isabella O (Young)
Klingmeyer, Faye (Michener)
Klontz, Mary (Ross) Paysinger
Klueg, Rev Frederick Eugene OP.
Klundt, Waldemar Jerome
Kneebone, Sydney A.
Knego, John Michael
Knight, Margaret L.
Knisely, Barbara B(ernice)
Knoetgen, Theresa A.
Knollmeyer, Isabelle Alice
Knowlton, Audrey
Knox, Virginia Alma
Kocher, Mabel C.
Koenigsberg, Audrey Kay
Kohl, Elizabeth (Thierfelder)
Kohler, Daniel Edward
Kohut, Louise Conrad (Holt)
Kõiv, Mrs Ira
Kolody, Anne (Olga)
Korf, Harold E.
Korowytsky, Ivan
Korver, John Randolph
Korzelius, Paul H.
Kostka, Frances V.
Kovacs, Evelyn M.
Kovacs, Helen
Kraemer, Mary Frances (James)
Kraig, Alfred R.
Kramer, Gaetana (M)
Kramer, Joseph R Jr.
Kramer, Lloyd Allan
Kramer, William F.
Kratz, Eva (Loarca)
Kraus, Irwin
Krebs, Raymond
Krehbiel, Leona G.
restini, Mrs Marie (Dlussky)
Krettingen, Tamara Nina (Stepanov)
Kreyenbuhl, (Helen) Jeannie
Kridl, Mrs Katherine W.
Krieger, Vivien (Greenberg)
Kritzman, Ellen Baird
Krizman, Geraine (Strong)
Krober, Alfred Clarence
Kroeger, Karl Douglas
Krohn, Mildred Louise
Krolicki, Lucille Marie
Kron, Irvin Wayne
Krueger, Ruth Caroline
Krupp, Mary (Foster)
Ku,Shih Lun (Peter)
Kugelman, Mary M (Peg)
Kuhn, Margaret Lou (Klee)
Kuhns, Helen (Faustine)
Kuhns, Jolene (Hoppe)
Kulys, Alfred V.
Kummermann, Nell I.
Kummings, Estella (Snyder)
Kuncaitis, Yadwiga (Cerniauskas)
Kunkel, A William
Kunkle, (Hannah) Josephine (McCann)
Kunz, Alice I(rene)
Kurlents, Alfred Karl
Kuvshinoff, Boris William

Labunka, Miroslav
Lacey, Maybelle (Ely)
Lacey, Mrs William F (Mae Hessler)
Ladewig, Eleanor J.
Ladwig, Charles Thomas
Lahman, Donald E(dward)
Lakshmanan, Teresa (Romanowska)
Lally, Helen R(ose)
LaMar, Georgia (Criswell)
Lamb, Nathalie A.
Lampson, Virginia E.
Lancaster, Edith E(arle)
Lancaster, Serena (Weggenmann)
Landgrabe, Mary Bonnie
Landon, Barbara (Anna Barrett)
Landrum, Frank W.
Lane, Catherine (Richardson)
Lane, Gretchen (Augustine)
Lane, Laura (Alice)
Lane, Patricia Anne
Langer, Lillian (Myers)
Langhammer, (Else) Birgit
Langhans, Rufus B(urford)
Langs, Helen Ruth
Langsam, Devra Michele
Lantz, Priscilla
Larsen, Inga (Margaret Schultz)
Larson, Carolyn Jo (Sherman)
Larson, (Ellen) Johanna
Larson, (William L) Larry
Lasher, Beatrice (Hamman)
Lasley, Mrs Ellen (Greve)
Lasley, Norma Jean
Lassiter, Dorothy (Tate)
Lastrapes, Blanca Judith (Quiñones)
Lathe, Mary (Hosford)
Lathrop, May (Belle Bodey)
Lathrope, Mary (Frost)
Latimer, Grace F.
Latimer, Mrs William Oliver (Catherine Parker)
Laubenthal, Charles J. Jr.
Laurimore, Judith M.
Lautner, Ione (LaVerne)
Lavellée, Marie
Lavine, Frank
Lawrence, Ann P (Duoba)
Lawson, Alberta Louise (Tarver)
Lawson, Glenda Kathleen
Lay, June (Peters)
Layton, Patricia (Ann Carr)
Lazare, Susan (Krayna)
Lazorick, Gerald J.
Leach, R Virginia (Beaty)
Leaf, Lawrence Arthur
Lean, Alice (Chiang)
Leanhard, Margaret Lillian (Bilkey)
Leavitt, Priscilla (Edwards)
Lebensohn, Waltea (Chaim)
Lechay, Rose
Lee, Carolyn Thorpe
Lee, Rev Chung Young
Lee, Fang Jen (Fang-Jen Li)
Lee, Heo-Peh
Lee, Mrs Hyun Kee (Kim)
Lee, Kanghee
Lee, Katherine (Gunther)
Lee, Marlyce Irene (Asp)
Lee, Michael Min-Song
Lee, Olive
Lee, Pauline (Willis)
Lee, Peggy Marguerite
Lee, Pier Ming-Wei (Hsu, Ming-Wei)
Lee, Ruby H J.
Lees, Gladys L.
Leeseberg, Barbara (Ann)
Leet, Mary H.
Lefond, Anne May (Newman)
Legaré, Roland (Joseph-Charles-Emile) FMS.
Legendre, Georges F I C.
Lehman, Carol Lee
Leiber, Gerald (Gerry)
Leif, Mary (Denny)
Leigh, Dawson M.
Leighton, Barbara J.

Leipold, Lance Jerome
Leith, Marian (Pollensky)
LeJeune, Ena Kay (Hudson)
Leland, Emily Whitney
Lénárt, Adrienne (Ching)
Lengyel, Suzanna
Lennon, Suzanne (Lucheta)
Lentz, Marjorie (Kirby)
Leonard, Faye Elaine
Leonard, Harriet Virginia
Leslie, Gena Kester (Elizabeth)
L'Esperance, Jean Lawrence (Mills)
Lessel, Alan J.
Leung, Beverly (Eng)
Leveille, Rev Roland Edmund
Leventer, Harriet Robbin
Leventer, Marshall David
Levering, Philip Clark
Leversedge, Lilian E M.
Levin, Pauline G (Horwitz)
Levine, Esther (Sarah)
Levine, Marion (Holena)
Levine, Robert Ivan
Levinton, Phyllis
Levy, Mrs Nancy Wilson
Lewicky, George I.
Lewin, Kate E.
Lewis, Elaine (Rosemary) (Wagner)
Lewis, Elizabeth M(arckworth)
Lewis, Ella (Marvin)
Lewis, Janis Mary (Thomson)
Lewis, William Gary
Lhotka, Jana M (Kristofova)
Liao, Yuan-Heng
Liberman, Eva
Lichtenberg, Virgil William
Lichtenstein, Aniela (Lerner)
Liddle, Carol Jean
Lieberman, Judith
Liebler, Jean Marie
Liebold, Kathryn (Jane)
Light, Eleanor Bird (McElrath)
Lightfood, Eloise A.
Lillis, Patricia Ann
Lin, Chin-Juang
Lin, Ivy (Li)
Lin, Nancy Ru-woei
Lin, Ivy (Li)
Lin, Miss Jui Yao
Lindenstruth, Mary Ellen
Lindler, Gloria (Jean)
Lindner, Ann I.
Lindquist, Raymond C.
Lindsay, (Mary-)Edythe (Shelley)
Lindsey, Rosalie V.
Lindt, Heinz W.
Linn, Dorotha Catherine
Linquist, Winifred
Lipkind, Jacob
Lipkind, Rochelle Anita (Zaglin)
Lippe, Larissa (Zdanko)
Lipscomb, (Marion) Ernestine (Anthony)
List, Barbara (Turner)
Liszewski, Edward Henry

Litchfield, Lucile (VanVoris)
Little, Susan (Jane)
Little, William Henry
Lifflefield, Karen Alden
Littlejohn, Ann W.
Littlepage, John Marshall
Littleton, Sue (Foscue)
Liu, Kai Hsien
Livingstone, John Hurst Jr.
Lloyd, Helen (Ditson)
Lloyd, Jeanne B.
Lloyd, Julia Margaret (Noel)
Lloyd, Mrs Sarah (Hathcock)
Lo, Chung Yen
Lo, Mary (shih)
Lobaugh, Gertrude E.
Lochhead, Douglas Grant
Lockard, Robert Rogers
Lockett, James D.
Lockhart, Elizabeth (Humphrey)
Lockhart, Mary Southall (Bridges)
Lodewick, Robin (Brant)
Loewy, Kathleen K.
Loftus, Joan
Logan, George King
Lombard, Frances
Londo, Leonard
Long, Mrs Carol (Naguin)
Long, Marie Ann
Long, Mary Belle
Longstaff, Marian (Jaehning)
Longworth, Mrs Ruth (Olander)
Loomis, Frances
LoPresti, Maryellen
Lord, Hazel Doreen
Lord, Milton Edward
Lorenz, Sister Marialein OP.
Lorey, Mrs Evaleen (Parks)
Lortscher, Hester (Hill)
Loskouski, Peter
Lostegaard, Esther Otelia
Lothian, Frances Louise (Tilley)
Lotko, Stanley A.
Lott, Barbara Ann
Loudermilk, Charles A.
Lougheed, Richard Lewis
Louis, Helen
Louise, Sister Mary (Zurawski) CSSF.
Love, Mary C.
Lowe, Cornelia
Lowe, Mary Louise
Lowe, Velma (Singleton)
Lowenberg, Patricia (Carter)
Lowery, Mrs Phyllis D (Clark)
Lowrey, Anna Mary (Smith)
Lowry, Aline
Lowry, William Houston
Lowther, Barbara Joan
Lloyd, DeLap
Lu, Robert Bang Ping (Chu)
Lucas, Marjorie (Seckel)
Lucas, Rita L (Thomson)
Luce, Gordon R(aymond) Jr.
Luce, Mary Eleanor (Cameron)

Luchsinger, Dale Frederick
Luciw, Wasyl Orest
Luck, Donald
Ludington, Margaret (Dow)
Ludlow, Helen M.
Ludwig, Genevieve Anne
Ludwig, Sister Virginia Marie
(Gladys Elizabeth)
Lukens, Catherine
Lum, Frances
Lum, Wanza Sue (Brooks)
Lund, Edith (Schultz)
Lundeen, Rev Joel W.
Lunin, Lois F.
Luttrell, Squire G.
Lutz, Bethel C.
Lyle, Linda Kay
Lyles, Louise Carolyn (Moore)
Lynch, Sister Cecilia OP.
Lynch, Mother Mary Dennis SHC J.
Lynden, Deborah (Oehler)
Lyndon, Thomas J.
Lyon, Alice (Masland)
Lyon, Cathryn C.
Lyons, Mrs Bernard P (Agnes Doyle)

Ma, Laurence J C.
McAfee, Robert Jr.
McAlee, Rev Eugene (Allen) CSSR.
Macalinao, Mirla Francisco
McAllister, Thomas Wayne
McAlpin, Mary Margaret
McArdle, James J.
McAuliffe, Sister Mary Mercy
McBride, Mrs Betty Anne (Smith)
McBride, Carroll Raymond Jr.
McBride, Dwight Leigh
McBride, R Pamela (Dewdney)
McCall, Frances D.
McCall, John Dean
McCallie, Judy Fern
McCallister, Carlyne L (Naber)
McCallum, Dorothy (Thompson)
McCart, Mrs Kenneth A (Margaret E
Mills)
McCart, Walter Harold
McChesney, Anne
McCloskey, Patrick John
McClung, Doris (Wilson)
McClure, Mary (Dunham)
McClure, (Margaret) Sharon
McCombs, (Veronica) Anne Conway
McConnell, Mary Grace (Sheridan)
McConnell, Ruth M.
McCord, Myrtis (Moore)
McCoy, William F.
McCraw, John B Jr.
McCray, Evelina (Williams)
McCulloch, Mary Linn
McCurdy, Anna May
MacCurdy, Helen Christine
McDaniel, Miss Davis Cecile
McDavid, Edna (Louise)
McDiarmid, Marjorie Louise

McDonald, (Marie) Blanche
MacDonald, Esther C(ravens)
McDonald, Timothea F (Allen)
McDonough, Delia P.
McDougall, Mrs Maria Sophie (Laddy)
McDowell, Mary Anna (Pennington)
McDuffie, (Betty) Jean Stovall
Mace, Mary (Martinez)
McFadden, Mrs (Mary) Inez Cogdell
McFadden, Marilyn
McFarland, Jane E(lizabeth)
McGee, Elaine P.
McGeever, Emmett Bernard
McGeever, Nancy (Boothe)
McGlynn, Patricia C.
McGowan, Isabel A.
McGrath, Sister Marian
McGrattan, Margaret Ann
McGreger, Louise (Warden)
McGregor, Helen Ames
McGrew, Mrs Mary Lou (Dempsey)
McGuire, Robert Eugene
McGuirk, Kathleen (Oliver)
Machmer, Gretchen Bonine
McIlvaine, Eileen (Roy)
McInnis, Carolyn (Arnold)
McIntosh, Edward Roy
MacIntosh, Helen Anne (McCauley)
McIntyre, Helen (Lucille)
Mack, Theodore (Durham)
McKellen, Teresa (Flanders)
McKelvie, Alice (Bryan)
McKenney, Ora Herbert Jr.
McKinney, Abigail Beshers
McKinney, Alex (Marcellus) Jr.
McKinnie, Lorraine Ella (Lashley)
McKinnon, Katherine Donalda
McKnight, Margaret (Curtis)
McLachlan, Sylvia (Adkins)
McLain, Thelma (Louise)
McLaughlin, O Lucille (Landis)
MacLaurin, (Evelyn) Margaret
McLean, Frederick F(remont) ("Rick")
McLean, Isabel Kathleen
McLean, Joan (Pitcher)
McLean, Mary (Pierson)
MacLean, Mary E. (Parker)
McLeod, Dwight (Leon)
McLeod, Margaret
McLoone, Harriet V.
McMahon, Ann (Griffin)
McManus, Beulah Lee (Reitzammer)
McManus, Evelyn (Cooke)
McMennamin, Margaret Anne
McMillan, Sherrill (Elizabeth)
McMullen, Marilee Jane
McNairy, Alice Hall
McNatt, Susanne (Leasure)
McNinch, Joseph Hamilton
MacPherson, Lillian (Vilborg Biarnason)
MacPherson, (May) Philippa
McQuade, Kathryn (Kellerhals)
McQuaid, Gena (Gavin)
McVicker, Mary Louise
McWilliams, Gail M.
Maddox, Lucy Jane
Maddox, Naoma Estelle (Hollis)
Mader, Marion (Constance)
Maestri, Helen Louise
Magavero, Filomena (Martemucci)
Magdalena, Sr Marie OSF.
Magee, Carol (Anne) (Kitchen)
Magner, Eugene (Joseph)
Magraw, Katherine L(ouise)
Magrish, Mary Corinne
Maher, Waler Gerald
Mahon, Mrs Clare Reardon
Maier, Nancy Ann
Maith, G Vivian Haddon
Maitland, Ellen (Hybarger)
Major, Margaret C.
Maki, Helen Miriam
Malcolm, Ethel Lorine
Malmont, Valerie (Skuse)
Malval, Fritz (Joseph)
Mandell, Richard Donald
Manheimer, Martha (Jane Lose)
Maniece, Olivia (Susetta)
Manley, Gloria Royster
Mann, Joyce (Turner)
Mann, Ruth Gore
Manni, Florence (Drafts)
Manning, Dorothy Marie
Manning, Josephine (Asaro)
Manning, Mildred (Williams)
Manning, Rosalie
Manning, Sharon Frances
Maquiso, Juanito (Granada)
Marengo, Mary Patricia (O'Day)
Margaret, Sister Mary (Kelley) OP.
Marie, Sister Joseph CSJ.
Marie, Sister Paschal (Anna Cantone)
Marie, Sister Perpetua (Sullivan) OP.
Marie, Sister Theresa RSM.
Marinovic, Lydia (Petromila)
Markey, Anne
Markey, Sister Mary Richard MHS.
Markson, Linda M.
Marley, (Martha) Laverne
Maroscia, Marie Filomena
Marquard, Catherine
Marr, Antony (Frank)
Marrero, Betty-Ruth (Wilson)
Marrero, Carlos Enrique
Marriott, Lois I.
Marshall, Clyde Vernon
Marshall, Grace
Marshall, Ruben
Marshall, Thomas H(enry) P(aton)
Marshburn, (Albert) Lawrence
Marston, Robert (Dewey)
Marteena, Constance Hill
Marthinson, Normakay
Martin, Barbara A.
Martin, Charlotte (Smith)
Martin, Elaine (Sharon)
Martin, Emily (Dunstan)
Martin, Eva M.
Martin, (Mason) Gene
Martin, George M.
Martin, Helen A(ndrews)
Martin, Mrs Mary (Morgan)
Martin, Sister Mercedes Maria
Martin, Patricia Jane
Martin, Rosemary (Scarborough)
Martin, Roxanne Marie
Martin, Vernon E.
Martna, Maret H(elga)
Marton, Mary (Facci)
Marton, Tibor William
Marvin, Patricia (Harmon)
Mascioni, Antoinette A.
Mason, Bernice P.
Mason, David Bruce
Mason, Diana (Lockhart)
Mason, (Helen) Louise (Lawrence)
Mason, Marion Evelyn
Mason, Mary Elizabeth
Mason, Norma Lucille (Springston)
Mason, Zula Adelaide Hamilton-Herring
Massee, William M.
Massengale (Rosalie MacNeill)
Massey, Sue (Mae)
Master, Sevaklal M.
Mathies, (Mary) Lorraine
Matley, Rev Marcel Bernard
Matlon, Sister M St Anne OSF
Matonti, Emily Johanna
Matsushige, Hatsue (Kadota)
Matt, Sister John Gregory CSJ.
Matta, Seoud akram
Matthews, Mrs Beverley (Smith)
Matthews, Edith (Satterlee)
Matthews, Jessie Louise
Mattingly, Sister Jane Agnes
Mauerhoff, Elisabeth R.
Maulding, Marjorie A (Stone)
Maxson, Mary Elizabeth (Beckley)
Maxwell, Dolores Melvin
Maxwell, Lois S.
Maybury, Catherine (Marie)
Mayer, Clara
Mayer, Hans
Mayes, Milton Cooper
Maynard, Grace E (Bailey)
Mayol, Josefina (Gonzalez)
Mead, Dorothy (Cummings)
Meador, Mary Judith (Martin)
Meadows, Marion Elspeth (Cook)
Mealey, Catherin E (Crum)
Meals, Frances Loretto
Medcraft, John Wallace
Mederos, Amelia (Ferregur)
Mehoke, Barbara (Boyle)
Meier, Marilyn C.
Meikle, Allison (Whyte)
Meinersmann, Rosali (Bronenkant)
Meinzer, Lorraine Ann Lois
Mellor, Roberta White
Melnyk, Peter

Melton, Vera (Bolick)
Meng, Lorrain Cheng-Hsien
Menihane, Rev Daniel Joseph OSA.
Merala, Marjan
Mercer, Patricia
Merrett, Cecilia (Magdalen)
Merritt, C Allen
Merritt, Neutrice (Wilson)
Mersman, Patricia Sue
Messner, Mrs Sara (Robinson)
Metz, Ritz Lenore
Metzler, Agnes (Margery)
Meuter, Robert Gerald
Meyer, Floyd Raymond
Meyer, Grace (Walsh)
Meyer, Margaret (Alexander)
Meyer, Margery Claire
Meyerend, Maude (Hitze)
Meynen, Constance Ann
Michael, Louise E (Shenaut)
Michel, Julian G(erard)
Mickelbury, Mexico (Hembree)
Milde, Mrs Marjorie (Haeberlin)
Miles, Jane W(ilkinson)
Milheim, Carolyn I.
Millard, Bradley Furrs
Millen, Irene
Miller, Alice J.
Miller, Bernice Love
Miller, Byron B.
Miller, Carole (Bissinger)
Miller, Brother Cassian CSC.
Miller, Dick (Dale)
Miller, Edith (Duckstad)
Miller, Evelyn Rose
Miller, G Lynette
Miller, George Bertram Jr.
Miller, Glenn E.
Miller, Mrs Helen (Rochester)
Miller, Mrs Ina Mae (Nail)
Miller, James S.
Miller, Jean Corson
Miller, John Albert
Miller, Julia Cecil (Rutledge)
Miller, Mrs Laura (Bennett)
Miller, Marilyn (Ann)
Miller, Sister Mary Carlina (Marian) CPPS.
Miller, Maurine (Boucher)
Miller, Merna (Eileen) Brooks
Miller, Mildred F.
Miller, Olive Lione (Robinson)
Miller, Pauline Allan
Miller, Roger Miles
Miller, Ruby Irene (Porter)
Miller, Ruth (Custance)
Miller, Ruth Elizabeth
Miller, Shelby Marie
Miller, Virginia (Brewster)
Miller, Virginia (Johnson Harris)
Miller, Wharton H(oward)
Millican, Alta Lucille
Milligan, Marian (Dinsmore)
Mills, Annie B(elle)
Mills, Frances B(erry)
Mills, Jesse Cobb
Mills, Mrs Josephine MacConnell
Mills, (Aline) Lambert
Mills, Rolland Wayne
Minder, Thomas Leo
Mine, Eileen (Arnold)
Mink, William Robert
Miska, Mrs Eloise (Tabor)
Misner, Dorothy (Martin)
Missar, Charles (Donald)
Mitchel, Nonie Jean (Lilliard)
Mitchell, Ann (Mathilda) (Levich)
Mitchell, Ann Therese (Drinan)
Mitchell, Frances (Pauline) (Gardner)
Mitchell, George Dampier III
Mitchell, Janice Alma
Mitchell, June M.
Mitchell, Martha Maude (Wilson)
Mitchell, Mary Moore
Mitchell, Patricia Lynne
Mitchell, Ruth (Ferguson)
Mitchem, Avis Dean
Miyazaki, Arthur M.
Moe, Melba M.
Mokede, Ernestine (Virginia Kinkler)
Monaghan, Mary Bridget
Moncure, Scott
Monihan, William J SJ.
Monroe, Elizabeth Jean (Carter)
Monsell, Thomas (Oliver)
Montag, Hermina Raff
Monteith, Barbara Gail
Montgomery, Annie Sue
Montgomery, James W.
Montgomery, John McVey
Montgomery, John Warwick
Moore, Arlene (McDaniel)
Moore, Carey Moffett
Moore, Esther Louise (Smith)
Moore, Gertrude Edith (Wright)
Moore, Grace Alice
Moore, Lou Ann (Schmidt)
Moore, Lucy (Bailey)
Moore, Marece Elizabeth (Gibbs)
Moore, Mary Ann
Moore, Robert Andrew
Moorhouse, Miss Vi
Morash, Eileen (Belton)
Morehead, Joseph H Jr.
Moretz, Olive Virginia
Morgan, Charles Lewis Jr.
Morgan, Elizabeth Harriett (Huntsman)
Morgan, Majorie (Bailey)
Morgan, Melvin Babcock
Morgan, Mendell D Jr.
Morgan, Rosalie (McNeely) Avery (Dowdy)
Morison, Edith (Rayner)
Moritz, Ralph
Morley, Elizabeth Graves
Morrell, John Dorrance
Morris, Carole (Lawrence)
Morris, Ella Lucille (Glenn)
Morris, Evalyn F.
Morris, Gerald Edward
Morris, Mary (Powers)
Morris, Warren
Morrison, Mrs Carol Jean (Smith)
Morrison, Julia Maria
Morrison, Louise E (Beck)
Morrison, Margaret (Cotant)
Morrison, Stephen Gerald
Morrow, Helen (Marie Therese) Thomas
Morrow, (Olive) Irene
Morrow, John J(oseph)
Morrow, Judith Wynn
Morsch, Lucile M.
Morse, Margaret J.
Morton, June Elizabeth
Moseley, Elizabeth G.
Moser, Margaret (Broderick)
Moses, Ruth Elizabeth
Mosher, Ailene Elizabeth (Lager)
Mosimann, (Elise) Madeleine
Mosimann, Margaret Delia
Mostecky, Vaclav
Motylewski, Jo
Mounce, Virginia Ann (Newton)
Mounts, Hester (Gribben)
Mountz, Louise Smith
Mowen, Keith Leland
Muhl, Marcella Catherine
Mulholland, Frederick Fletcher
Mulholland, Marie (Marton)
Mullendore, (Jessie) Marian
Muller, Mrs Dorothy A (Thompson)
Mullins, LeNona
Mulloney, Paul Francis
Multhauf, Lettie (Stibbe)
Mumper, Mary Jane (Snyder)
Munday, Bessie (Sue)
Munger, Nancy Terry
Munroe, Maimie Tapley
Munson, Beverly M.
Murphy, Dennis D.
Murphy, Michael Francis
Murphy, S Burchell
Murra, Mrs Katherine O(liver)
Murray, Helen (Ryan)
Musgrave, John Knox
Musgrove, Louis (Kelley)
Mutch, Donald (George)
Mutchler, Peter Knox
Myers, Eileen (Smythe)
Myers, Elizabeth B.
Myers, Nancy Jane (Woolley)
Myers, Robert J(oseph)
Mylod, Sandra R (Larkin)

Nabor, Madelene Louise (Barnard, Hirth, Marshall)
Nadeau, Leonard
Nadelman, Florence (Guterman)
Nag, Mrs Preeti Sudha (Sircar)
Nagle, Sister M Ferdinand
Naik, Panna Nikul
Nakatani, Kay (Keiko)

Nalley, Maurice Edward
Nantier, Alyce (Beachler)
Nantier, Stéphane
Naomi, Sister M (Walsh) SC
Napier, Sara (Ashcraft)
Napper, Marjorie
Naragon, Nancy (Douglas (Aitken)
Narbut, Keltah Tam
Nardi, Helen (Cooper)
Natanson, Leo
Nation, Margaret Ann (Harris)
Naughton, Dorothy M(ae)
Naughton, Louise
Naumann, Virginia Elisabeth
Neal, Loraine
Neal, (Margaret) Marnie I.
Nearhood, Reva
Neely, Nancy B.
Neff, Jesse Eugene
Neff, Wilma
Negherbon, Rev Vincent Robert
Neilson, Francine
Neiswender, Rosemary
Nelson, Adeline Elizabeth (Ritschel)
Nelson, Dorothea (Harriet) D(udley)
Nelson, Harry Arthur
Nelson, Helen Martha
Nelson, Jerold Arthur
Nelson, Katherine (Morton)
Nemeck, Dorothy (Ewan)
Neprash, Dorothy (Ready)
Ness, Charles Henry
Nessler, Minerva (Kraft)
Nettleton, Jane (Cornwell)
Neubauer, Edythmaree
Neubauer, Susan (Sheriff)
Neugebauer, Carolyn Joan
Neuman, Mary Agnes
Neumeyer, Marian (Youngs)
Nevels, O'Celia Ragland
Neille, Margaret W.
Nevin, Mary Kathleen
Newbolt, Mrs William E (Nona Barlow)
Newcomb, Janet (Enid)
Newcomb, Wilburn (Wendell)
Newhall, Margaret Elizabeth
Newland, Anna Ray
Newman, Jane Katherine (Mashburn)
Newman, Jennie Patricia
Newman, Vivian (Dowling)
Newnham, Mrs June Inabell (McCaig)
Newton, Katherine (Ann Paulson)
Ng, Hwei Wen
Nicefaro, Julia (Velleca)
Nichols, Beatrice (Olmstead)
Nichols, Pencelia Dakan (Elizabeth)
Nichols, Susan (Jane)
Nicholson, Lillian Geraldine
Nicholson, Natalie Neill
Nicholson, Valeska (Lambertus)
Nickens, Cleo S.
Nickerson, Elathier A(melia)
Nickle, Elizabeth Anne
Nicole, Roger (Robert)
Nicolosi, Anthony Scalvatores
Nielsen, Andre S.
Nielsen, Roy James Maurice
Nelson, Eve
Neinstedt, Joyce Elizabeth
Nigels, Vanda Marie
Nikkel, Tillie M(arie Markham)
Nile, Russell Abbott
Nimmons, Helen (Hentschel)
Nimms, Donald Farwell
Niven, Georgianna (Hayes)
Nixdorf, Mrs Adelaide Armstrong
Nixon, Edgar Burkhart
Njoku, Scholastica Ibari
Noble, Ruth S (Epstein)
Noblin, Evelyn (Blanchard)
Noel, Charmaine (Wava) (Grinnell)
Noel, Evelyn (Frances)
Nolan, Martha Dasha
Noreen, Sister Mary (Graney) RSM
Norman, Nelle (Marie Strouse)
Norris, Sarah (Louise) (Ryder)
North, B Jean
Northrop, Everett H(ollister)
Northway, Philip Edward
Norton, Mrs Jimmie (Smith)
Norton, Mary Elizabeth
Norton, (Betty) Sue (Brantley)
Noyes, Mary Hall
Noyes, Nancy Eleanor
Nuessle, Barbara Ann (Slatcher)
Nuhfer, Frances Ann
Nunn, Frances (Elizabeth)
Nunnally, Josephine
Nylund, Anne
Nysewander, Patricia Jane

O'Bar, Jack W.
Obear, Elizabeth G(aillard)
O'Brien, Ann M(urashko)
O'Brien, (Marietta) Cade
(Brockelbank)
O'Brien, James Michael
O'Brien, John Richard
O'Brien, Rev Roger Gerard SS.
O'Connell, Catherine
O'Connell, Rev Edward George
Oddy, Joyce (Loraine)
Oderman, Martha Pearl
Odile, Sister Marie (St Germain ML)
Odom, Murvise Ruth (Hearon)
O'Donnell, Michael M(artin)
O'Donnell, Moira (Frances)
O'Dowd, Sister Ann Charles CDP
O'Dowd Sister Joseph Ann CDP
Oellrich, Gertrude L(ouise)
Oeschger, Helen C.
O'Hara, Frederic James
O'Harra, Do ning (Palmer)
Ohmes, Frances Hall
O'Keefe, Lois (Hill)
Olien, Neil Arnold
Oliver, Katherine M (O'Neill)
Oliver, Margaret W.
Olmstead, Almeda L(eake)
Olmstead, Dorothy Alice
Olsen, Constance Balcom
Olsen, Mrs Grace (Elizabeth) Elliott
Olsen, Humphrey A.
Olsen, Robert A Jr
Olsen, Sarah Elizabeth (Griffiths)
Olson, Bess
Olson, Richard DeForrest
O'Malley, Ruth
Omdahl, Ingjerd O(lga)
O'Neil, Rev Charles Hugh
Ooton, Inez E.
Opgrand, Harold J.
Oppenheimer, Mildred (Karnofsky)
Orcutt, Annabel (Jones)
Orfanos, Minnie
Ormsby, Lois Fae
O'Rourke James Ralph
O'Rourke, (Margaret Norah)
Orsagh, Polly (Fisher)
Orser, Mrs A O (Dorothy Potter)
Oritz, Alma
Oritz, Barbara H(ornbeck)
Orton, Gerhard (Hirsekorn)
Ory, Mary (Butler)
Osborn, Laura K.
Osborne, Anne (Rogers)
Osborne, Margaret B(aker)
Osburn, Edwin C(alhoun)
Osgood, Rufus F(reeman)
Osmond, Mrs Alverna (Wright)
Osowski, Joan Marie
Ostrem Walter Martin
Oswalt, Minnie (Laura)
Ottemiller, John H(enry)
Ottenbacher, Viia (Vali)
Ottey, Grace D.
Otto, Gladys (Roach)
Otto, Margaret Mattern
Ouellette, Helen (Credle)
Overend, (William) Howard
Overfield, Peggy Ann ((O'Hare)
Overmyer, Muriel (Champ)
Owen, Carol Ann
Owen, Mrs Eleanor E(lizabeth Stevens)
Owen, Estelle B(ain)
Owen, Mary Jeanne (LaFrance)
Owens, James Kevin
Owens, Judith Eloise (Minick)
Owens, Linda Elin (Nittel)
Owens, Mrs Olin Jackson (Loulie
Latimer)
Owrid, Edwin Weaver
Owsley, Lucile Clark
Oxee, Hazel Ruth (Yater)
Oxley, Philip C(arle)

Pace, Eula Raye (Simmons)
Packard, Charles B
Packer, Ruth (Mildred Johnson)
Paddock, Rita L(udwig Caroline)
Paden, Oleta T(hompson)
Page, Mrs Effie (Millican)

Page, Elsie P(earson)
Pageau, Henrietta Cecelia
Pall, Emily Ann
Palmer, Helen H(anssen)
Palmer, Jessie H(yde)
Palmer, Marie (Gain)
Panek, Robert
Pang, Kai Ian
Pankovich, Helen N(ikachevich))
Pappas, Aristides (Xenophon)
Parch, Grace Dolores
Pardee, Josephine H
Pardo, Anne W(adstorth)
Parise, William C Jr.
Parish, Margaret H(olt)
Park, Gemma Rhee (Gum-Btn)
Parker, Delcie Hobson
Parker, Edna Gertrude
Parker, Edward Kinne
Parker, Ladye Huntington
(Longsine Van Matre)
Parker, Lois S.
Parker, Patricia R(oberts)
Parker, Verna (Rowe)
Parkhill, John Taylor
Parkhurst, Muriel Taylor
Parks, M(ary) Lethene (Dennis)
Parks, Thomas E(dwin)
Parmelee, Margaret F(rances)
Parnell, Annie D(avis)
Parrish, James H
Parrish, Lu(Pearl)
Parsley, Revice B(rumley) Kegler
Parsons, Carolyn Rush (Kay)
Parsons, Frances E.
Parsons, Marcia A(nne) Moss
Partridge, Allen B. Jr.
Pasmik, Eleonor E.
Passenger, Anita Louise
Patterson, Ruth
Paton, Mary-Elizabeth
Patrick, Violetta F.
Pattee, Edwin John
Pattela, Rao (R)
Patten, Carmita S(iaba)
Patterson, Flora E(laine)
Patterson, Joan E(vans)
Patterson, Robert D.
Patton, Edna M.
Patton, Jane V(andike)
Patton, Jessie Bernice L(ee)
Patton, Virginia Taylor
Paulson, Sylvia B(ertha)
Payne, Dorothy B Shingles
Payton, Annette Deloris
Payton, Laura M(artin)
Pchelkin, Hildegard (Elisabeth Wolf)
Pearce, Lucy
Pearce, Nancy Anne
Pearcy, Maureen A(nita)
Pearson, Dorothy Wiley
Pearson, Edith R B(eatty)
Pease, Mary K.
Pecht, Beverly Elaine
Peck, Dorothy H(ouston)
Pedley, Katharine G(reenleaf)
Peitsch, Margaret Rose
Pelkey, Don S.
Pelletier, Claire G(enevieve)
Pelton, Doris L.
Pelton, Emily J(ackson)
Pemberton, Margaret Dorothy W(ilson)
Pemberton, Willie Mae
Pendleton, Ruth Jane
Pennell, Evadne D (King)
Pennington, B Blaine
Penyak, Barbara
Peppers, Ray
Perkins, Dale Warren
Perkins, Mrs Flossie (Leighton)
Perrine, Mrs Maxine (Lewis)
Perry, Patricia J.
Perry, Pennie Ellene
Perry, Rosemary Therese (Harbrecht)
Persanyi, John F.
Persky, Phyllis (Charick)
Pertzoff, Peter A.
Peters, Jane A.
Peters, Sister Mary Dennis OSB
Peters, Nancy Katherine (Arnold)
Peters, Ruth (Evelyn) (Wheelock)
Peters, Ruth Esther
Peters, Wilk S(mith)
Peterson, Betty Alice
Peterson, Carolyn Sue
Peterson, Dona Bell
Peterson, Gordon Charles
Peterson, Mrs (Florence) Lois (Ott)
Peterson, Marion Elizabeth
Peterson, Mildred Othmer
Peterson, Patricia Sue (Walters)
Peterson, Powena Beryl
Petri, Maria (Hlatky)
Petrie, Patricia (Repass)
Petty, Frank Albert Jr
Petty, Martha Jeannette
Petty, Ruth A.
Pfeil, Dorothea Sanderson
Pfiester, Ralph Gerald
Phelan, Mildred (Treman)
Phelps, Doris (Reynolds)
Phelps, Ralph H(uyett)
Phillippsen, John Joseph
Phillips, Rosemary (Brewer)
Phillips, Brian Frederick
Phillips, Camille (Johnson)
Phillips, Delores Joan (Lavoie)
Phillips, Elsie Anne
Phillips, (Virginia) Estelle
Phillips, Floramae Davies
Phillips, Getty (Davis)
Phillips, Juanita
Phillips, Verna Marie
Picca, David
Pichler, Mrs Christina Maria
(de F Czeydner)
Pickett, Leo William
Piel, Mark
Pieper, Ann (Gerstley)
Pieratt, Asa Bradford
Pierce, Anna Edith
Pierce, Norman Albert
Piggford, Carole Meanor
Pimentel, Irene (Kidd)
Pinkerton, Ruth (Weaver)
Pinkett, Maude Moore (Louise)
Pinkston, Alfreda (Jones)
Pinkwas, David
Pinzelik, John
Pipes, Charles Duane
Pipes, Wanda Lucille (Hammel)
Pirrotta, Nino
Pita, Lorene S.
Pitzer, John Dillworth
Pius, Sister Mary (O'Donnell)
Pizzini, Mrs Frica G.
Platt, Suzy
Plavny, Stanley S.
Ploch, Richard A(llen)
Ploom, Aili (Aarend)
Plummer, Callie (Daniels)
Plummber, Julia W.
Poe, Jackie (Jacqueline Deleta)
Pogue, Christine (Brown)
Pohl, Rev Zachary M (Robert)
Pohle, Ruth (Hayes)
Poit, Katherine (Ingersoll)
Polacheck Dem (Demarest Lloyd)
Pollard, William Robert
Pollmann, Mary Ann
Pollock, Esther (Goldfield)
Polonsky, Aaron
Pomranka, Edwin Carl
Pont, Paul T.
Poole, Barbara Hunt
Poole, Frazer Glendon
Poole, Harold A.
Poole, Janice (Irene)
Poole, Mrs Mary F.
Poole, William R.
Pope, Frances
Poray-Wybranowski
Porten, Helen Anna
Porteous, Constance Mildred
(MacFarlane, Harris)
Porter, Hilda (Baulk)
Porter, Kathryn F.
Porter, Robert Bernard
Portuondo, Georgia (Álvarez)
Posell, Elsa (Z)
Posey, Merne (Hines)
Possner, Susan Frances (Robinson)
Poth, Mrs (Marion) Lynn (Eileen)
Pothier, Patricia E.
Potter, Emily (Bain)
Potterfield, Joseph (Ralph Edward)
Poucher, Lucy Anne
Powell, Martha (Gallion)
Powell, Mildred
Powell, Rosemary Maxine (Mullins)
Powell, Ruth (Laney)
Powell, Whiton

Powers, Dorothy L.
Powers, Katherine (McCamy)
Powers, Mary Carol
Pozezanac, Bessie (Basto)
Pratt, Mrs Marian (Urband)
Pratt, Richard L.
Preisman, Sophia
Prendergast, Virginia (Hyatt)
Press, (Mary Elizabeth) Deanne
Press, Helen D.
Preston, Margaret M.
Preston, Mildred Ella (Stanyon)
Prete, M Lazzavi (Gioconda)
Price, Anna Louise
Price, Mrs Carol Ann (Josephy)
Price, Eugene Hanley
Price, Genevieve
Price, Madeline (Dilworth)
Price, Ramona (Dungan)
Price, Sara M.
Primmer, Esther Carol
Primrose, Robert A.
Prince, Barbara Alden
Prince, Helen Kennedy (Jean)
Pringle, Miss Callan M.
Pringle, Eugene A.
Pringle, Wanda C(laire)
Probstein, Irène (Weindling)
Prochovnick, Ammiel
Proescholdt, Laura Lee (Sabin)
Proschek, Ervin (Charles)
Proto, Emma (Romano)
Proudfoot, Harriet
Pruett, James Worrell
Pruyne, Margaret (Doughton)
Przepasniak, James Raymond
Przybylski, Edmund Stanley
Puckett, Richard L.
Pullam, Marimae
Pusifer, Josephine (Sturdivant
Punke, Alma (Davis)
Purdie, Eileen (Kelley)
Purdy, G Flint
Purkis, Lloanne Gayle
Pursel, Luella (Oberg)
Purucker, Mary (Irene Mahoney)
Putnam, Alethea Nadine (Hoff)
Putney, Virginia Bertha
Pyle, Lois (Walls)
Pyrch, Jeannette (Anne) (Taschuk)

Quier, (Charlotte) Elizabeth (Metzger)
Quigley, Elizabeth-Anne
Quimby, Lois (Duffy)
Quinlan, Dorothy (Jeanne)
Quinn, Frances M.
Quinsey, Joyce (McLoed)
Quint, Mary D(orothea)

Rabinowitz, Pearl Baskin
Raker, Mary Ann (Steinmann)
Raley, Ann (Jones)
Ralston, Anne (Coleman)
Ralston, Mrs Bettie Louise
Ralston, Jolinda (Burney)
Ramm, Dorothy (Victoria)
Ramsey, Helen Lowery
Rancier, Esther May
Rand, Duncan Dawson
Randall, Elaine (Bonfield) Coddington
Randel, Myrtle Avis (Clements)
Rankin, Lynne
Raphael, Martin
Rappaport, Gersten
Rappaport, Philip
Rappelt, John F.
Rappelt, Madeline Marie (McDermott)
Rasmussen, Stuart Ricard
Ratcliffe, Charlotte (West)
Rather, Lucia (Johnson)
Rathgeb, Eileen (Sweeney)
Raunig, Diane (Baker)
Rausch, Naomi Gretchen
Rausen, Ruth (Greiner)
Rawlins, Nancy Jo (Cotton)
Rawlinson, Alfred (Harris)
Ray, Dorothy Laura (Jackson, Edwards)
Razek, Cordelia (Lindsey)
Rea, Jeannette Anna
Reading, Sister M Carmelina CSC
Reagan, Evelyn (Densmore)
Reamer, Phyllis (Kerel Folk)
Reaves, LaRose Pine
Rector, Gladys Louise
Redding, Bobbie (Newman)
Reece, Dorothy Anne (Weaver)
Reed, Charles N.
Reed, Lola (Nicholson)
Reed, Marjorie E (Warner)
Reedy, Lucie (Starr)
Reents, Carol-Lou
Reeling, Patricia Ann (Glueck)
Rees, Virginia Frances
Reese, Anna Lucille (Anderson)
Reeves, Dorthea D.
Regina, Sister Mary (Mix, Martha)
Regli, Esther La Zetta
Reichard, Edwin Walter
Reid, Eileen M(ary)
Reid, Miss Marion Hall
Reidy, Genevieve L.
Reiff, Julie (Webster)
Reilley, Jeanne M.
Reinbold, Dorothy Anne
Reinburg, Jesse Taaffe
Reiner, Leona Mary (Hudak)
Reisner, Phyllis
Reister, John F.
Remmel, Stanley William
Renshaw, Jane (Parker)
Rescoe, A(ntoine) Stan(ley)
Rettig, E Reade (Washington)
Rettig, John R.
Revell, Peter
Revesz, Gabrielle S(tern)
Reynarowych, Roman
Reynolds, Frances (Haley)
Reynolds, Karen (Ann) (Moore)
Reynolds, Mrs Margaret Norene (Allen)
REynolds, Mary B.
Reynolds, Mary Edna
Reynolds, R Yvonne
Reynolds, Richard Champlin
Rhen, Ruth (Phillips)
Rhew, David Thompson
Rhine, Audrey
Rhoads, Mrs Mary-Elizabeth (Hawke)
Rhudy, Mary Agnes
Rianhard, Alice Ruffin (Mebane)
Ricci, Frances E (Lawler)
Riccio, Dorothy (Manfredi)
Rice, L Estelle
Rich, Louise (Truitt)
Richard, Ethel (Pruitt)
Richards, Frances Helen (Hess)
Richards, Gayle Anne
Richards, Melva (Croisant)
Richards, Mildred Ware
Richardson, Gail
Richardson, Margaret (Milhous)
Richardson, Mildred (Copelin)
Richardson, (Mary) Virginia (Jones)
Richey, Naomi Alice (Monette)
Richmond, Joy (Stokes)
Richter, Edward Anthony
Ricketts, Arthur S.
Rider, Mary E.
Ridgway, Helen A(dams)
Riebel, Ellis Fred
Riesenfeld, Barbara (Lindsay)
Riess, Marion
Riggs, Dean Edward
Riggs, John Alan
Riggs, Letetia A (Pifer)
Rilee, Virginia Paige
Riley, Annadele
Riley, Dorothy Pauline (Bale)
Riley, Gloria (Marcelette)
Riley, Louise E.
Riley, Marjorie Madsen
Riley, Sister Mary Gabriel GNSH.
Ringo, Ruth Cheaney
Rinker, Catherine C.
Riordan, Pauline Ellen
Rios, Mrs Joan Elizabeth (Gable)
Rippley, Beatrice Mary (Dwiggins)
Rissone, Joyce (Adele)
Rivera-Davis, Vilma L.
Roach, Mrs Elizabeth (Schenken)
Robb, John M.
Robbins, Irene Lenore (Davis)
Robbins, Katherine L.
Robbins, Mrs Ruth K.
Robbins, Stella M.
Roberson, Mrs (Frances) Jean (Adamson)
Robert, Frank Wall
Roberts, Elizabeth E.
Roberts, Marion P Taylor
Roberts, (Edna) Pearl (Wilson)
Roberts, Samuel Washburn
Robertson, Ann Estelle

Robertson, Katherine E (Chastain)
Robie, Caroline (B)
Robillard, Marie-Thérèse A.
Robinson, Dana Lynn
Robinson, Mrs Dorothy (Richards)
Robinson, Eleanore M.
Robinson, Mrs Eloise (McCarthy)
Robinson, Fay
Robinson, Helen M(artin)
Robinson, Irene Hall
Robinson, Mary Lee
Robinson, Mollye Lacretelle (Alford)
Robinson, Olivia Juanita
Robinson, Mrs R Wayne (Lois C)
Roblee, Mildred M.
Robnett, Valta Scott
Robson, Betty Jane (Sampson)
Rockman, Doris A (Weigel)
Rockmuller, Rebecca (Nitchun)
Rode, Werner
Roers, Gertrude J (Dorn)
Rogalski, Leonore
Rogers, Barbara (Orkin)
Rogers, Dorothy Helen (Stitely)
Rogers, Patricia L (Davis)
Rogers, Peggy (Wade)
Rogofsky, Murray
Roland, Edith (Blissett)
Rolich, Alexander
Roller, Ernestine (Burton)
Rollins, Jane Gray
Rollins, Mrs Winston E (Doris Wiley)
Rolls, Erlinda (Hill)
Rongione, Rev. Louis A.
Ronnquist, Helen Christina
Rooney, Francis James
Rooney, Mary
Rooney, Sean Leo
Rope, Irene Justine (King)
Roppolo, Maria Elena
Rosasco, Barbara (Holmes)
Rose, Dorothy (Hyde)
Rose, Mrs Estelle (Bruckner)
Rosenbecker, Arlene (Schmidt)
Rosenberg, Betty
Rosenberg, Lucille (Lieberman)
Rosenberg, Patricia Noel
Rosenstock, H(ans) Michael L(udwig)
Rosenstock, Morton
Rosenthal, Irving
Rosenthal, Lewis T
Roser, Margaret
Roskoz, Ruth (Warrell)
Ross, Annie V.
Ross, Barbara (Tracy)
Ross, Leola (Myrick)
Ross, Sister M Collette
Ross, Margaret (Miller)
Ross, Noël Louise (Davis)
Rossi, Gerald R.
Rossi, Peter C.
Rossing, Marlene A (Barrett)
Rossiter, William A.
Roth, Mrs Elizabeth (Boutelle)
Roth, Gerald
Roth, Marlayne
Rothacker, J(ohn) Michael
Rothfuss, Mrs Elizabeth Long
Rourke, Harriet L.
Roush, Mrs L M (Myla T)
Rowan, James F.
Rowatt, Robert James
Rowe, Emily Lyon
Rowell, Jo Ann (Ayers)
Rowland, Lois (Parker)
Rowley, Geraldine (Elizabeth)
Rowley, M(ary) Catherine
Royal, Norma M.
Royce, Robert H.
Roze, Astra
Rozeboom, Frank Sylvester
Rubacher, Patricia (Pole)
Rubendall, Elizabeth
Ruby, Carmela M.
Ruch, Pauline G(ruber)
Rucker, James Bernard
Rucker, Mildred G(reene)
Rumberger, Christine (Valinda)
Rumps, Andrea Jean
Runge, Elisabeth (Dorthea)
Runzo, Frankie Gene (Castelletto)
Rupert, Sister Mary (Lyvers) SSND.
Ruppé, Mrs Carol (Varley)
Rushing, Reba J.
Ruskin, Eugene D.
Ruskin, Mary
Russell, Dorothy E.
Russell, Mrs Edith (Moore)
Russo, Erna (Serebrenik)
Russo, Mrs Mary Ann (Bryant)
Rust, Jane Esther
Rust, Margaret E.
Rutauskas, Mrs Dona
Rutkovskis, Gunars
Ryan, David Michael
Ryan, Richard John
Ryder, Kathryn P (McGuire)
Rye, Helen (Nervis)
Ryll, Francis

Saab, Jacqueline
Sadek, Mrs Nancy Caroline (Powell)
Sadlier, Mrs Mary Ann (Danaher)
Sager, Lorna Jane (Barker)
Sagers, Jeanetta Kathleen
St Anthony, Sister (Teafee, Lillian Anthony) CND.
Saint-Clair, Guy L.
St John, Francis R.
St John, Mrs Vernon L (Virginia Thomas)
St Leger, John B.
Saisslin, Mary K.
Salik, Felicia
Salisbury, Ruth
Saller, Marceil G.
Salley, Mrs VonEtta M.
Salmon, Elaine (Earhart)
Salvatore, Jane (Phillips)
Salzman, Louise Starr
Sammis, Marian (Elizabeth)
Samsel, Sister M Ancillia FSSJ.
Samuel, Harold Eugene
Samuelson, Richard Thurston
Sanadi, Mary Jane (McElhinney)
Sanborn, Dorothy (Choppell)
Sanborn, Rachel (Bourne)
Sander, Ann Kathleen
Sanders, Patricia J.
Sanford, Jaspyr (Bookman)
Sangster, Collette Mary
Sargent, Anita M.
Sauer, Dora (Kelley)
Sauer, Jean
Saunders, Lucy Bates
Savage, John Addison
Savage, Vandolyn Joyce (Browning)
Savidge, Mrs Alice (H)
Sawyer, Donald Frank
Sawyer, Joan E.
Sayward, Mildred (Fenton)
Scannell, Francis Xaviercarlott, Mary (Tice)
Scatterty, Edna (Elizabeth) Morrison
Schalau, Robert Duane
Schanz, Virginia Lee
Scheele, Marianne (Male)
Scheie, (Ingeborg) Marie
Scheinholtz, Joan (Freeman)
Schellings, Mary Elizabeth
Schenk, Rachel Katherine
Schenkman, Deanna (Owen)
Scherr, Elizabeth (Babcock)
Schetina, Miriam (Shapiro)
Scheu, James William
Scheuerman, Luanne (Lebsack)
Schick, Wendy Mary E (Warner)
Schiel, Martha (Prudence Church)
Schiele, Mildred (Tschop)
Schiff, Judith Ann
Schieffer, Rita Elinore
Schilling, Sally (Brown)
Schlaff, Sylvia (Dunn)
Schlenk, Margaret Karin
Schlosser, Ann (Griffin)
Schlosser, Mary Jacqueline
Schlundt, Carolyn L.
Schmidt, Alice Anne
Schmidt, Philip Arthur
Schneider, Donna Jean (Allen)
Schneider, Josephine A.
Schoengold, Morris D.
Scholberg, Henry
Scholz, William Howard
Schommer, Rev Lambert Jerome
Schorr, Norma
Schott, Ernest
Schreiber, Israel Reuben
Schroeder, Melinda (Lucy)
Schroth, Margaret (Boal)
Schubach, Bernice (Woodbury)
Schuetz, Elizabeth J (Roper)

Schuhle, Jacob Harris
Schultz, Carole Lynn (Holt)
Schultz, Gwendolyn A.
Schumacher, Mrs Le
Schutz, Vivian (Vickers)
Schuyler, Jane (Almert)
Schweitzer, Alina (Rayman)
Schwingel, Ruth (Barber)
Sciacca, Mary Ruth (Goodman)
Scoles, Maribel
Scollon, Marthena
Scors, Taisa (Novicki)
Scott, Carolyne Elizabeth
Scott, Mrs Dixie (Emma)
Scott, Edith
Scott, Jerry M.
Scott, Mrs Mary Martha (Wheeler)
Scott, Priscilla Rhoda
Scott, Robert Edward
Scott, Roland Francis
Scott, William H(enry) Oliver
Scott, Mrs Willodene (Alexander)
Scougall, Jean (Jephcote)
Scrogin, Margaret A.
Scura, Rose M(artina)
Seabern, Clifford
Sears, Marvin Wayne
Seaton, Claire (Millikin)
Sebastian, Fannie Nicholson
Sebesta, Mary (Cecil Mumberson)
Secundilla, Sister Mary CSFN.
Sedgwick, Frederica M.
See, Elizabeth W.
Seebeck, Nancy (Heath)
Seelery, Patricia Louise
Segreto, Josephine (Esposito)
Seim, Charles Jr.
Seitz, Carol Rita
Selby, Doris A.
Sellen, Betty-Carol
Selsam, Mrs J Paul (Georgia Kauffman)
Sen, Gouri (Dasgupta)
Sendall, George Thomas
Serex, S(ophie) Emily
Sessa, Frank Bowman
Severns, Hannah
Sexton, Anne Mary
Shaffer, Frank Kenneth
Shaffer, Mrs Mary Elizabeth (Mayo)
Shafia, Georgia (Cohen)
Shair, Sandra
Shaklee, Alice (Clegg)
Shandrick, Maureen (Fugate)
Shank, Ernest C(harles)
Shank, William
Shannon, Mrs Winifred J.
Shannonhouse, Mrs Anne Donald
Shanoski, Stephany (Rajca)
Shappy, Raymond Arthur
Sharp, Eunice E.
Sharp, John Darrell
Shaver, Dorothy M.
Shaver, Terry Nanette (Peters)
Shaw, Betty Belle
Shaw, Laura (Klein)
Shaw, Lillie (King)
Shaw, Mrs Lucile (Byrd)
Shaw, Mabel Watson
Shawl, Janice (Hays)
Shay, Sister Anne Maureen
Shea, Frances (Margaret)
Shea, Margaret Elizabeth (Reed)
Sheats, Viola (Underwood)
Sheehan, Jelka (Pogacnik)
Sheel, Frieda (Elizabeth)
Sheffield, Duncan R B
Sheible, Doris Ann (Covic)
Sheldon, Paul C Jr.
Shelton, J Walter
Shelton, Jaynie M
Shen, Betty Pei-Te
Shen, Ming-Ming
Shen, Shirley Si-Fon
Shen, Shirley Tan
Shephard, Josephine (Leach)
Sheppard, Croinne
Shera, Eizenija (Bergman)
Sherbrooke, Rosalie (Castin)
Sheridan, Philip James
Sherlock, Sister Therese CSJ.
Sherwood, Barbara (Ann)
Sherwood, Richard Allan
Shih, Walter Dyson
Shilling, Sandra Rae (Strong)
Shimko, Florence (Gasper)
Shimla, Mary Elizabeth
Shinagel, Ann (Mitchell)
Shine, Frances (Lathrop Smith)
Shober, Joyce Lee
Shoemaker, Sally Lee
Shoffner, Ralph Merl
Sholar, Thomas Patterson
Shook, Zeb V.
Shooter, Elizabeth (Gillen)
Short, Eleanor Bedford
Shoughro, Elizabeth Anne
Shouse, Richard (Gibran)
Shoyinka, Patricia (Hopkins)
Shreve, Doris L(ingenfelder)
Shreve, Jean (Malcolm)
Shreve, Margaret L(ee) D(ick)
Shrimpton, Eleanor (Jane)
Shtasel, Dorothy Marguerite (Drawz)
Shull, Lois (Davis)
Schumaker, Edith (Ellen)
Shumsky, Ellen Ruth
Shupe, Marjorie E.
Shymansky, Russell W.
Sibley, Florence Weldon
Sickler, Nancy Gibbs
Siderakis, Mrs Basiliane (Antonatos)
Sidhu, Karamjit S(ingh)
Siebert, Roger David
Siefkes, Ruth Winifred (Long)
Siegeltuch, Marian
Siemsen, Walter H
Sierocki, Muriel A (Kreig)
Sigerson, Ruth Carolyn (Webb)
Silley, Laura W.
Silver, Myra (Weiss)
Silverman, Osca A
Silvers, Joan M
Silverstein, Louis Henry
Simkins, Elizabeth
Simmons, Dorcus Rose (Phoenix)
Simmons, Jessie Lee
Simms, Genevieve Ballard
Simon, Barbara Louise
Simon, Ralph Charles
Simon, Susan Jane
Simonds, Mrs Margaret Elizabeth
Simonsen, Frances Ann
Simpson, Beth (Atkinson)
Simpson, Eileen A.
Simpson, Jerome Dean
Sims, Mary E(va)
Singleton, Geneva
Sinnette, Elinor (Des Verney)
Sipes, Georgia (Alberta) ERB
Sipkov, Ivan
Siren, Ilona Signe
Sisson, Elizabeth (Brigtsen)
Sisson, Mrs Jacqueline (DeMorest)
Sisson, Miss Marion Anita
Sittner, Mollie (Lay)
Sivells, Mrs Wanda (Kellar)
Skau, Mrs Dorothy Beckemeyer
Skehan, Sister James Marie RSM
Skerritt, Linda (Elaine)
Skinner, (Mary) Elizabeth (Danner)
Skolnick, Irene Ruth (Rinde)
Skoog-Smith, Mrs Marion (Kask)
Slade, Louise (Laybourn)
Slagowski, Maxine (Hammond)
Slanker, Barbara Olsen
Slate, Corrine
Slatoff, Saul H.
Slattery, James J(oseph)
Slattery, James J.
Slavens, Cora (Hart)
Sledge, Jeanette
Sliekers, Hendrik
Sloman, Alberta (Law)
Sluiter, Barbara Betty
Slyfield, Donna (Christensen)
Small, Louise Armitage
Smallwood, Ann Carter (Hays)
Smart, Roselind Jane (Knoll)
Smishkewych, Roxanne A.
Smith, Adelieu Irene (Cook)
Smith, Andrenette (Fournier)
Smith, Anita
Smith, Barbara Crocker
Smith, Barbara Merrill
Smith, Betty Anne (Elizabeth Anne)
Smith, Bryant (Chelsey) Jr
Smith, Carol Ann (Manteufel)
Smith, Cecil Haven
Smith, Charlotte P.
Smith, Miss Clyde
Smith, Dana Raymond
Smith, Darleen Florence

Smith, Donna Kay (Pantzer)
Smith, Elizabeth
Smith, Elizabeth (Moody)
Smith, Elizabeth (Thurman)
Smith, Elizabeth Ann (Sawatsky)
Smith, Eurydice (Williams)
Smith, Flossie (Snyder)
Smith, Mrs Frances (Nelson)
Smith, Mrs Frances S.
Smith, Frederick Edward
Smith, G Donald
Smith, Gloria L.
Smith, Hal Haynes
Smith, Helen (Alexander)
Smith, Josephine Alice
Smith, Josephine Metcalfe
Smith, Katherine M(arks)
Smith, L(eonora) Blanche
Smith, Leland Rooy
Smith, Lora E(lizabeth)
Smith, Lucy Lee
Smith, Martha (Marion Cameron)
Smith, Martha Frances
Smith, Mrs Meredith (Rice)
Smith, Neil Gregor
Smith, Nina L.
Smith, Norma (Lucille) McAfee
Smith, Ray (W)
Smith, Raymond W.
Smith, Reginald Weldon
Smith, Rosalee (Moore)
Smith, Solomon Charles
Smith, Susan Seabury
Smits, Sister Alexine OSU
Smits, Lia (Dagmara)
Smock, Mildred K(atherine)
Smogard, Elaine Carol
Smoot, Lila French
Snelgrove, Clarence P
Snider, Helen Frances (Griffith)
Snider, Sylvia W.
Snowden, Dorothy (Parr)
Snowfield, Barbara
Snyder, Constance (Kossoff)
Synder, Esther (Bauerle)
Snyder, Joan Marie
Snyder, Leona B (Prosser)
Snyder, Loretta Marie (Kidd)
Synder, Nancy Louise (Wenrich)
Snyder, Samuel S.
Sobel, Richard Allan
Soderholm, Dorothy Joyce
Sone, Charles Forrest
Sonnenberg, Joanne Ruth
Sorensen, Marian (Bennett)
Sowell, (Marian) Joyce
Spafford, Mary W.
Spalding, Ronald Alexander Spark
Spangler, Kathleen G.
Spangler, William John
Spann, Patricia Ann (Spurlock)
Spaulding, Genevieve P.
Spaulding, Sylvia (Gardner)
Spector, Florence
Spence, Jacquelyn
Spencer, Frances Elizabeth
Spencer, Louise (Johnson)
Spencer, Michael J.
Spencer, Muriel Matilda (Blome)
Spera, Verna (Ethel)
Spidell, Carolyn (Hendrix)
Spiegel, Alice H (Blach)
Spinelli, William Basil Jr.
Spitz, Dorothy (Henssgen)
Spitzer, Ernest F.
Spottiswoode, Harriet F.
Sprague, M(orteza) D(rexel)
Spreitzer, Francis F.
Sproule, Phyllis (Eileen Turner)
Spurr, Barbara Roxana (Price)
Squire, Ina
Srygley, Mrs Sara (Krentzman)
Srygley, Ted F.
Stacy, Mrs George H Jr (Bernice Krout)
Staehlin, Robert H.
Stafford, Sister M Incarnata (Rosalind Stafford)
Stager, Lynada Louise
Stahl, Mila D(aniel)
Stahle, Marilyn (Bilzi)
Stamm, Betty Mae
Standring, Eleanor (Perlee Bartindale)
Stanka, Sister Mary Marguerite OP
Stanley, Margaret Eleanor
Stanton, Marie Jane
Stanworth, Helen (Marilyn)
Stapleton, Rev John Francis
Stark, Lewis M(orgrage)
Starnes, Reba Cleo
Startzman, Madeline (Sellman Summer)
Stearnes, Mrs Jo Ann (Thornbrough)
Steele, Jean (Riden)
Steele, Mary L(eigh McAliley)
Steele, Rita Evelyn
Steffen, Adeline E.
Steffen, Nancy E.
Steffy, Clarence Donald
Steider, Alma Tool
Stein, Rose (von Janosi-Engel)
Steinbarger, Marion DeFontes
Steinke, Eleanor G.
Steinmann, Mrs Lois S.
Stenstrom, Ralph H(ubert)
Stephen, Fred M.
Stephen, Islay (McLarty)
Stephens, Elizabeth (Meadows)
Stephens, Jean K.
Stephens, Jerome K(enneth)
Stephens, Jon Kent
Stephens, Mary Patricia (Pierce)
Stephens, Rebecca Ann (Cook)
Stephens, Rosa (Lee)
Stephenson, Betty Jean
Stephenson, John Dudley
Stephenson, Marjorie B.
Sternecker, Carol (Greb)
Stevens, Alice Katherine
Stevens, Elizabeth L (Bodwell)
Stevens, Florence Myrtle
Stevens, Helen (Taylor)
Stevens (P) Jill
Stevens, Richard C.
Stevenson, Gordon
Stevenson, M(ary) Virginia
Stevenson, Mary E (Loucks)
Stewart, Barbara (Jean) Johnson
Stewart, Catherine (Prassell)
Stewart, Jean
Stewart, Sister Mary Ian SSND
Stewart, Mildred Estelle (Spencer)
Stewart, Sharon Joy
Stewart, Theresa Romona
Steyer, Alma Josephine (Adkisson)
Stibolt, Marcie H.
Stierwalt, Ralph Edward
Stiffler, Bernice Ilene
Stigall, Phyllis (Graham)
Stiles, H(ubert) Edmond
Stiles, Helen Jean
Stiles, Lauren (Albert)
Stiles, Sandra Lynn
Stillwell, Ray
Stinson, (Helen) Arnette
Stinson, Mrs Duffy Marie
Stobba, Rev Joseph George OSA
Stockwell, Dorothy (Smith)
Stoehr, Brother Frederick R FSCH
Stolper, Gertrude
Stoltenberg, Marianne (Pirrie)
Stone, Hal (Harry)
Stone, John Paul
Stone, Katherine (Moss)
Stone, May N(orma)
Stoner, Clara E(llen)
Storms, Barbara (Overholser)
Stos, Angela Louise
Stostad, Janice Carol
Stout, Juanita (Margaret)
Stout, Virginia Louise
Stout, Vivian D.
Stowe, Shirley (Ann)
Stowell, Fern Elizabeth (Moore)
Stowers, Marianne (Williams)
Straessle, Patricia Mary
Straka, Leora E.
Straka, Rev William John OSC
Stratton, Doris (Virginia)
Strauss, Ruth Nora
Streiff, Ann Weir
Strickland, Albert C(arson)
Strickland, Elizabeth May (Hurst)
Strickler, Margaret (Heatwole)
Striemer, Pauline Marie
Stringer, Norma Jean
Stroehlein, Iola R (Glock)
Stromsvold, Lucy E (Lawatsch)
Stroud, Beulah Benton
Stroud, Lois Clifford
Stroup, (Gayle) Yvonne
Strowd, Elvin Emerson
Struble, Billie Marie (Batten)
Struglia, Erasmus J(oseph)

Strunk, Sister Mary Dolores
Stuart, (Ryland) Chase
Stuber, Mrs (Mary) Helene (Griffin)
Stuckey, Evelyn S(etre)
Stucki, Loretta (Herzins)
Stude, Alice Marie (Johnson)
Stumpe, Ruth Ann
Sturgis, Gladys Marie
Sturm, Mrs Charlotte (Mason)
Suber, Catharine E.
Sublett, Barbara (Overby)
Suchenski, Nancy (Ann)
Sudar, Dan (Dushan)
Suddarth, Emma Elizabeth
Suelflow, August Robert
Suess, Fania (Gitlin)
Sullivan, Beverly M.
Sullivan, Frances Anna
Sullivan, Mrs Glen (Norene Janelle)
Sullivan, Howard A(ugustine)
Sullivan, Margaret M.
Sullivan, Mrs Marian (Millard)
Sullivan, Martha J(oanna)
Sullivan, Mary Jo
Sullivan, Peggy (Margaret Anne)
Summers, Arwilda Wilson
Summers, George V.
Summers, Virginia E.
Sun, Chun–Lan
Sund, Ingeborg
Sundberg, Burton
Sung, Ming Yang
Sunshine, Fradene M.
Superka, Patricia Mary (Newnard)
Sussman, Elisabeth (Sacks)
Sutherland, Alvern Hunt
Sutherland, Doris Bradley (Francis)
Sutherland, Elizabeth
Sutherland, Eugene W.
Sutherland, Karen Elaine (Sandine)
Sutton, Evelyn (McCracken)
Sutton, Inez (Shepherd)
Sutton, Lee
Sutton, Suzanne (Davis)
Suzuki, Yukihisa
Sved, Ignacio
Svuksts, Erika (Bergmanis)
Swackhamer, Louise (Weiersbach)
Swaffin, Charlotte (Anne Whittaker)
Swander, Judith Ann
Swank, Eunice M.
Swanson, Adelaide (Berr)
Sweeney, Ruth (DeLong)
Swensen, Jean (Fairgrieve)
Swenson, Evelyn (Totzke)
Swenson, Sally
Swinburne, Ralph E Jr.
Swistock, Phyllis (McGarry)
Sydnor, Mrs Ella (Gaines)
Sypert, Mrs Haydon (Bryant)
Szabo, Mrs Eve (Parsons)
Szegedi, Laszlo
Silassy, Sandor
Szücs, Margaret (Fitch)

Tabler, Grayson B.
Tachok, Cecelia (Florence)
Taggart, Mary Ellen (Hogan)
Taine, Seymour Irving
Tait, Mary (Gocher)
Talbert, Edward James
Talley, Clara (Frances)
Talley, Mabel Theresa (Apple)
Tallmadge, Diane (Sperberg)
Tallman, Helen Jane (Van Ostrand)
Tan, Ah Bi
T'ang, Shu-Min (Sherman)
Tanner, Mary Catherine
Tanner, Opal Florence
Tanner, Stanley J.
Tao, Clinton W.
Taormina, Karen H(osack)
Tárczy, Stephen István
Tarencz, Clarice Lee
Tarlin, Harry Nathaniel
Tarver, Elizabeth
Taschuk, Diana Reddick (Eager)
Taub, Barbara (Cohen)
Tavrytzky, Sarah Carmen (Diaz)
Taylor, Beatrice
Taylor, Beth (Winona)
Taylor, Carolyn (Cole)
Taylor, Donna (Dowling)
Taylor, Dorothy (Mooter)
Taylor, Ellyn M (Kramper Black)
Taylor, Harriet L.
Taylor, Miss Harrison
Taylor, Tucker (Neel)
Teale, Janet Claire
Teders, Mrs Elizabeth G.
Teel, Gloria F(ritchley)
Teeple, (Fiona) Diane
Teeter, Mrs Lulu (Woodruff)
Teggman, Karen (Ann)
Teitge, Virginia
Temple, Gail
Templin, Mrs Ruth Elizabeth
(Heffelfinger, Linder)
Tenenbaum, Susan (Brown)
Terhune, Dorothy Ann (Sheriden)
Ternes, Sister M Bernadine
Ternes, Patricia (Gaven)
Terpo, Mary A.
Terra, Phyllis (Cecilia)
Terry, Ellen Martha
Terry, Grace (Myrtle)
Tessen, Leonard Lewis
Thaxter, Pamela J(oyce)
Thayer, Shirley M.
Theis, Anna Virginia (Locke)
Theodore, Sister M RSHM
Theorell, Viola (Franklin)
Thexton, June (Wilson)
Thieda, Robert W.
Thom, Ruppert, Crisman Jr.
Thomas, Brother Aurelian FSC
(John Francis Lavery)
Thomas, Barbara Ann
Thomas, Brenda

Thomas, (Wanda) Carol
Thomas, Diana Margaret
Thomas, Dorothea (Mae) (Barcus)
Thomas, Dorothy M(ay)
Thomas, Mrs Lois (Brown)
Thomas, Lucille (Cole)
Thome, Helen E.
Thommasson, Alan A(ugustus)
Thompson, Arlene (Vruwink)
Thompson, Eleanor Neville (McDowell)
Thompson, (Mary) Elizabeth
Thompson, Elsa Smith
Thompson, Jean (Beecher)
Thompson, Louise Ogilvie (Stuart)
Thompson, Margaret W.
Thompson, Mary Ragland
Thompson, Pauline (Conduff)
Thompson, Ruth Mildred
Thompson, William R.
Thomson, (Barbara) Gillian (Michell)
Thomson, Mrs (Ja) Gloria (Lauriston)
Thomson, Julia (Clemens Landon)
Thomson, Mrs V Leslie (McCammon)
Thornburg, Mrs Ruth Galvin
Thorne, Bonnie (Baker)
Thorne, Herbert Wm.
Thornton, Dorothy G.
Thornton, Patricia Anne
Throckmorton, Mary
Thurlow, Martha
Tierna, Constance Alicia (Carrier)
Tierney, Clifford Leo
Tietjen, Marian (Frances)
Tiff, Georgiana (Morse)
Tillman, Jeanne
Tillman, Ola Belle
Tillman, Rosebud (Harris)
Tilly, Frances (Finch)
Tilson, (Alice) Faye (Smith)
Timmons, Gwendolyn (Patrice)
Tincovich, Mary Elizabeth
Tindell, Frances (Waters)
Tinyanoff, Irving
Tippitt, Audrey (Baines)
Tipton, Anna Marie (Aickin)
Titman, Gisela (Miller)
Tittle, Kathryn (Jo) Nickell
Tobias, H Patricia
Tochner, Joan M (Schwartz)
Todd, Helen (Moore)
Todd, Katherine
Todd, Margaret (Garman)
Toelle, Rev Gervase R.
Toensing, Waldermar Frank
Tolerico, Carol Ann
Tolford, Janice (Jelbart)
Tollafield, Ronald C.
Tollette, Sammie Nell (Irving)
Tomczak, Thomas (Albert)
Tompkins, Edgar
Tompkins, Josephine (Lynch)
Tondro, Helle Stueland
Toner, Paul David
Toohey, Barbara Ann (McAfoos)

Tooker, William Stebbin
Torrence, Rosa L(illian)
Toth, Georgina Gy
Toth, Mary Jo (Bleich)
Tower, Catherine
Tracy, Elizabeth R(oberta)
Tracy, Janet R.
Trammell, Georgia R.
Trammell, Nannie B.
Transue, Constance Elizabeth (Parson)
Trautman, Ray L.
Traven, Lee Winston
Travis, Marguerite W(alsh)
Traylor, Margaret (Henrietta)
Trebbi, Jean (Driber)
Treffinger, Elizabeth
Tremblay, Mother Mary Rose OSU
Trent, Sarah (St John)
Trimble, Jacquelyn (Whitney)
Trombitas, Ildiko (Duffek)
Trout, Joan (Gwendolyn)
Truber, Helen Sande
True, Beverly Gail
Tsai, Julie (Chou)
Tse, Kitty (Toa Kit Ng)
Tsien, Lily C.
Ts'o, Petrina (Chan)
Tsonev, Natalie (Bondar)
Tsukamoto, Jack Toru
Tubby, Ruth (Peckham)
Tucker, Cynthia Furneaux
Tucker, Dolores (Williams)
Tucker, Jane (Comin)
Tuffley, Anna Frances
Tumbleson, Ira A.
Tung, Mrs Yueh–Chiung (Pu)
Tunstall, Valance Townsend
Turgeon, Lawrence Joseph
Turk, Margaret L.
Turner, Audrey Jean (Wendlandt)
Turner, David Edwin
Turner, Gary
Turner, H David
Turner, Lucile
Turner, Winifred (Thraves)
Turney, Martha (Kendrick)
Turrentine, Virginia
Turyn, Andrew S G.
Tweedale, Dellene Marie (Moreland)
Tyler, Travis E(arl)
Tyler, Addie Lee (Ferguson)
Tyler, Worth Wilshire
Tyson, Edwin L.
Tyson, Willie Kate
Tysse, Agnes Nelle

Uehlin, Katherine
Ulman, Ruth D(orman)
Ulmer, Beverly Riley
Underbrink, Robert L.
Upans, Skaidrite (Ella) (Spalvainis)
Upham, Joyce (Elaine Harris)
Upton, Jane Ellen
Upton, Ruth (Nordberg)
Urbaniak, Maria (Puzynowska)
Urdang, Laurence
Urness, Carol Louise
Urschel, Lilian Tressel
Usher, Mrs Elizabeth (Reuter)

Vair, Phyllis, Lyon
Valentekovic, Ljubica (Superina)
Valukas, Mrs Salomeja (Laima Nasvytyté
Van Beynum, William J.
Van Bronkhorst, Margaret E.
Vance, Bessie Mary
Vanden Engel, Helen
Van der Boom Yvonne (Novak)
Vandergrift, Kay E.
Vander Ven, Mary (Alice)
Vander Zee, Andrew
Vander Ziel, Bernard Charles
Van Horn, Dorothy (Adelaide)
Van Horn, Myrna Eileen (Sherman)
Van Hulsteyn, Yildiz (Phillips)
Van Luik, James
Van Meter (Lina) Louise (Wright)
Van Ravensway, Leila (Edwards)
Varner, Sister Christina
Vautrian, Alice (Walsh)
Vavrek, Bernard
Veigel, Katharine E.
Venables, Mrs Florence (Seldon)
Vermes, Chayah (Rosenberg)
Verschoor, Irving Alton
Vespry, (Horace) Arthur
Viets, Ellen (Campbell)
Vigo–Cepeda, Luisa C.
Vincent, Henrietta Jane (Gamble)
Vinson, Eugenia
Visser, Audrae Eugenie
Vivian, Frances L(ouise)
Voigt, Louis
Vollmer, Sister M Anita OSF
Volz, Mrs J B (Elizabeth Duff)
von Dorster, Nellie (Shue)
von Kries, Beverley Ann (Smith)
Vorwald, Doris Lauretta
Voss, Charles S.
Vradenburgh, Evelyn (Marston)
Vrooman, Hugh T.

Waaser, Sonja Elisabeth
Waddington, Charles C.
Waddington, Richard C.
Waddington, Susan (Royal)
Wade, Joy (Lambert)
Wade, Pattie (Cole)
Wadlow, Laura Wilson
Wagner, Edward F.
Wagner, M Lynn
Wagner, Margaret
Wagner, Mary (Eleanor)
Wagner, Mildred Estelle (Robie)
Wagner, Robert G.
Wagstaff, (Ruby) Mildred
Wai, Lily (Chang)
Wakefield, George (Washington)
Waldhart, Thomas J.
Waldman, Betty (Klusner)
Walker, Annetta (Ross)
Walker, Celine (Foster)
Walker, Dora Fogarty
Walker, Dorothy (Bushell)
Walker, Fawn
Walker, Frances Rebecca
Walker, H Thomas
Walker, T MacCallum
Wall, Patricia Ann
Wallace, Mrs Alice (Alberta Malcolm)
Wallace, Katharine (Ritter)
Wallace, Mary Elizabeth
Wallin, Lorene Lou
Wallis, Rev Francis Bernard
Walls, Russell R Jr.
Walmsley, Grace Hope
Walsh, Barbara (Ammon)
Walter, Otto Wallace
Walter, Ruth (Pewterbaugh)
Walters, Mary (Dawson)
Walters, Mrs Opal (Headstream)
Walters, Patsy (McElroy)
Walters, Ruby Nell (Lewis)
Walton, Mrs Artence Vivian (Johnson)
Wan, Weiying
Wang, Josephine (Sun)
Wang, Mary
Ward, Byrl Manelvia (Warrick)
Ward, Louise
Ward, Lucy A.
Ward, Mary Stella
Ward, Myrtle Loh
Ward, Richard Walter
Ward, Suzanne M (Whaley)
Warner, Joanne Elizabeth
Warner, John Ellsworth
Warner, Marjorie F.
Warren, John William
Warren, Suzanne
Wash, Mrs Eleanor E (Moran)
Washburn, Phyllis B(arbara)
Washington, Caroline Minerva
Waterman, Nancy Mayo
Waters, Marie Bell
Waters, Polly Thomas
Waters, Ruth (Cramer)
Watkins, Jessie (Beach)
Watkins, Ruth Louise
Watson, Aine Elizabeth
Watson, Anita Nickels (Bartholy)
Watson, Constance Margaret (Hollis)
Watson, Jack Mitchell Jr.
Watson, Joyce Norine
Watson, Justine Patricia
Watson, Susan M.
Watt, Ann Marguerite (Stewart)
Watt, Louis (Belfield)
Watts, (Mabel) Camille
Waymer, Barbara (Moye)
Waymire, Virginia (Long)
Weatherwax, Philip E.

Weaver, Lola (Osborn)
Weaver, (Frances) Nadine Grayson
Weaver, Ruby
Webb, Blanche (Doolittle)
Webb, David Aiken
Webb, Helmer Lewis
Webb, Margaret A.
Weber, Diane Irene (Looms)
Weber, Hans H.
Weber, Joan M.
Weber, Marie Elizabeth
Weber, Pau. M(artin)
Weglarz, Lorraine Denise
Weide, Constance (Karfunkel)
Weigand, H(erbert) William
Weigel, John Wesley II
Weikert, Barbara (Ruth)
Weill, David Paul
Weinberger, Lester
Weine, Mae
Weinrich, Gloria (Beilin)
Weinstock, Melvin J.
Weinstock, Nancy L(ora)
Weinthal, Edward
Weir, Adelaide
Weir, Sister Mary Rose OP.
Weiss, Marcia
Welge, Anita E.
Welken, Marion Lucile
Wellborn, Cecil W.
Wells, Grace (Pearl)
Wells, Susan (Margaret)
Welsch, Erwin Kurt
Welshinger, Shirley B(lanche)
Weltmer, L Grace (Mueller)
Weniger, Virginia Helma
Wentz, Charlotte
Wentz, Frances (Decker)
Werk, William Robert
Wernham, Evelyn I.
Wescott, Lou Carol
Wescott, Ruth Audrey
West, Dorothy Herbert
West, Suzanne
Westbrook, Betty Sue
Western, Dorothea
Westhuis, Judith Anne (Loveys)
Weston, Muriel (Audrey)
Wetherbee, Mrs Miriam (Curry)
Wetherell, Pauline (Ward)
Wettengel, Ledelle
Wetterstrom, Betty Barbara (Chase)
Whalen, Barbara (Anne)
Whalin, Mrs Esther (Phares)
Wheatley, (Victoria) Bernice (Croft)
Wheaton, Marjorie E.
Wheel, Robert James
Whelan, Alice (Tedford)
Whelchel, (Laura) Kate
Wherry, Juanita M.
Whitaker, Elaine (Croshier)
White, Aris H.
White, Barbara A (Waller)
White, Catharine (Johnson)
White, Eva Margie
White, Helen
White, Juanita (Boyer)
White, Mary Daugherty
White, Rev Richard Felix MM.
White, Sophia (Polovina)
White, Sylvia (Moon) Young
Whitelaw, John Leonard
Whiteman, Amram
Whiteman, Margaret Beverley
Whitledge, Mrs Lois (Richards)
Whitman, Nancy Reid
Whitmire, Georgia E.
Whouley, Mary (Hall)
Whyte, Helen (Mary Gale)
Whyte, Irene (Schiller)
Wicker, William Walter
Widman, Nancy Pauline (Barbus)
Wiebe, Phyllis Walrafen (Kusmaul)
Wiederecht, Marion (Jean)
Wierwill, Wilma (Mitchell)
Wight, Edward Allen
Wikle, Mrs Adelaide (Dutcher)
Wikoff, Susan Finley
Wilcock, Marilyn E (Rumball)
Wilcox, Benton H.
Wilcox, Cynda (Buxton)
Wilcox, Harold E.
Wilcox, Mrs Jerome K (Grace Giffin)
Wilder, Ruby Catherine
Wiley, Don Del Marr
Wiley, Lockwood E.
Wilford, Valerie Jane
Wilhite, Flora Richardson
Wilkes, Rachel Caldwell
Wilkins, Eleanore Elizabeth
Wilkins, Thomas Ambler
Wilkinson, J Marilyn
Wilkinson, Richard Thomas III
Wilkoc, Meta (Neuburg)
Willemson, Vaino
Williams, Ann Elizabeth
Williams, Barbara (Chapman)
Williams, Charles Reise
Williams, Daniel Thomas
Williams, Dorothy E.
Williams, Edmond Alonzo
Williams, Elizabeth
Williams, Ethel (Langley)
Williams, Helen Elizabeth
Williams, Lois Anne (Taylor)
Williams, Mabel (Downer)
Williams, Margaret (Starks)
Williams, Marsha Gayle (Terry)
Williams, Mary Isabelle
Williams, Mary Lois
Williams, (Catherine) Opal
Williams, Richard Clarence
Williams, Virginia (Irwin)
Williamson, Estelle (Buxton)
Willis, Alliene (Horne)
Williston, Alfreda (Walker)
Willits, Robert Dean
Willoughby, Mabel (Elizabeth)
Wilson, Celia Ann
Wilson, Donald K.
Wilson, Doris Bernice
Wilson, Gene B.
Wilson, Hulda A.
Wilson, (Bertha) Inez
Wilson, Kirke C.
Wilson, Margaret (Kelley)
Wilson, Mary (Margaret) Burnett
Wilson, Mrs May Pearl (Pye)
Wilson, Sarah Elizabeth
Wilts, Joan (Johannesen)
Wiman, Laura Alice (Christopher)
Wimble, Barton L.
Wimersberger, Evelyn
Winchel, Beulah Rhea
Windsor, Margaret
Winearls, Daphne Joan
Winfree, Waverly Keith
Winiecki, Mary Alice
Winkelman, Janie M (Scarlett)
Winkler, Mae Reynolds (Peacock)
Winn, Herbert Eugene
Winslow, Dorothy S(hampo)
Winstead, Verna S(tover)
Winter, Anna Belle
Wise, Mary Adelaide (Pearson)
Wiseman, Frances Mayme
Wiser, Martha (Mary)
Witcher, Carolyn (Matthews)
Wittenberger, Marian Esther
Wittkopf, Paul Pierre
Wittmann, Mona (Keitt)
Woehr, Gladys T (MacDowell)
Wohlsen, Grace (Zahn)
Wolf, Carolyn J.
Wolf, Keith Alan
Wolf, Marian Elizabeth
Wolf, (William) Vere
Wolfe, Marion (Christine)
Wolfe, Theodore
Wolff, Ernst
Wolford, Betty (Kelley)
Wolford, Joanne (Morton)
Wong, William Sheh
Woo, Lan Hing (Fong)
Woo, Linda (Chi Hsiao)
Wood, Arlin (Lacy)
Wood, Barbara
Wood, David Allan
Wood, Elizabeth B(olding, Ingerman)
Wood, Frances (Grace) (McCarthy)
Wood, J B.
Wood, Jeanette (Poor)
Wood, Kathleen (Bethune)
Wood, Muriel Beatrice
Wood, R(ulon) Kent
Wood, Richard G.
Wood, William Bliss
Woodard, John (Raymor) Jr.
Woodard, Joseph Lamar
Woodard (Mrs) Patsy P(restridge)
Woodard, (John) Russell
Woodfork, Suewilla (Wright)

Woodman, Edwin R Jr.
Woods, Caroline Dunnington
Woods, Hortense Elizabeth (Johnson)
Woods, Susan Dean
Woods, William Robert
Woodward, Edith Mills
Woody, Helen L.
Woosley, Constance Coburn
Wooster, Ruth (Delancy) S(cudder)
Wooten, Elizabeth (Boykin)
Work, Mabel A(ustin)
Worrell, Elizabeth D(ecker)
Worthy, John
Wostel, June H.
Wright, Elizabeth L(ewis)
Wright, Gertrude Sydney (Munro)
Wright, Lillian (Taylor)
Wright, Lottie M (Thomas)
Wright, Marjory H(awley)
Wright, (Inabelle) Marlene (Phillips)
Wright, Raymond Clifford
Wright, Thomas W.
Wright, Verna Vorpahl
Wrigley, Nancy (Pendlebury)
Wu, Elsa Liang–Chen (Chen)
Wu, Pei–Ling
Wu, Shirley (Su–Ling Lin)
Wuertley, Ruth C.
Wurgler, Dorothy Jeanne
Wurtz, Rayma (Rita)
Wurzburger, Marilyn J (Menchhoff)
Wyatt, (Edith) Lillian
Wyckoff, Marjorie (Walker)
Wylie, Dorothy
Wylie, Mary
Wynn, Elizabeth
Wynn, Virgil Joseph
Wyppich, Margaret (Witte)
Wysocki, Bernard Benjamin

Yagello, Virginia Elizabeth
Yagendorf, Sanford
Yang, Dolores Wen–Hsueh (Sun)
Yang, Winston L.
Yanke, Olga Beatha (Harem)
Yanosko, Alice Margaret
Yao, Celia Yen-Chu (Chen)
Yao, Joseph Yung–Tsin
Yao, Margaret (Lee)
Yarborough, (Miriam) Maxine
Yarbro, Virginia Claire
Yardum, Barbara Zita
Yates, Annie Lee
Yates, Stanley (Martin)
Yates, Virginia H.
Yeamans, Sandra Kay
Yee, Siew-Pun
Yee, Siu-Ling Irene (Sham)
Yeh, Rita (Ron-Hwa Yang)
Yen, Lucy (Wong)
Yenawine, Wayne Stewart
Yngve, Victor H.
Yoshimura, Yoshiko
Yost, Karen Lou
Young, Mrs Elizabeth (Harris)
Young, Elizabeth Bleakley
Young, Mrs (Gladys) Fay Grote
Young, Frances (Bristow)
Young, George G.
Young, Harold Chester
Young, Ida (Jean)
Young, Mrs Mary (Hassman)
Young, Mary E(velyn) F(leming)
Young, Patricia M E.
Young, Seville (Shagrin)
Young, Verna D.
Young, Mrs Virginia (Staub)
Youngman, Charles L.
Youngman, Clifton
Youssef, Farida (Iskander)
Youtz, Arthur R.
Yu, Kuang Hua (Kao)
Yu, Stephen (Cho)
Yucht, Alice (Heymont)
Yukawa, Manae
Yutani, Elji

Zabrosky, Frank A.
Zachman, Helen
Zackheim, Michael R.
Zacks, Sanora (Faye)
Zadkovich, Mrs Simon (Elsie)
Zahler, Lionel (Judah)
Zaic, Carmen Marin
Zamacona, JoAnn Carol (Hawley)
Zandstra, Daisy Antonia
Zaragoza, Lois
Zatopa, Valerie Ann
Zdanowski, Adelia P.
Zebker, Avis (Gregory)
Zehner, Sylvia Kay (Ruble)
Zein, Diane Mary (Darling)
Zeldis, Muriel (Gladys)
Zermuehlen, Donald D.
Zeuthen, Fritz Jonason
Zeydel, Walter H.
Ziaukas, Francis J.
Zich, Joanne (Amundson)
Zich, Robert G.
Zike, Ruth Deborah (Swift)
Zimbalist, Mrs Dorothy (Hirsch)
Zimmerman, Carolyn L (Guernsey)
Zimmerman, Lee Franklin
Zimmerman, Lois Mary
Zimmerman, Marguerite L.
Zimmermann, Mildred Lafon
Znayenko, Myroslava (Tomorug)
Zolnay, Vera J (La'Nyi)
Zongor, Endre
Zorach, Margaret B(ritton Harris)
Zucchero, Frankie (Hardman)
Zuwiyya Yamak, Labib